עץ חיים

ETZ HAYIM

Senior Editor: DAVID L. LIEBER

Editor of the P'shat Commentary: CHAIM POTOK
based on the JPS Torah Commentary by Nahum M. Sarna, Baruch A. Levine, Jacob Milgrom, and Jeffrey H. Tigay

Editor of the D'rash Commentary: HAROLD KUSHNER

Literary Editor: JULES HARLOW

Editors of Halakhah l'Ma·aseh: ELLIOT DORFF *and* SUSAN GROSSMAN

Author of the Haftarah Commentary: MICHAEL FISHBANE

עץ חיים

ETZ HAYIM

TORAH AND COMMENTARY

THE RABBINICAL ASSEMBLY
THE UNITED SYNAGOGUE OF CONSERVATIVE JUDAISM

Produced by THE JEWISH PUBLICATION SOCIETY

The Rabbinical Assembly
3080 Broadway
New York, NY 10027

Blessings for the Torah and haftarot have been adapted from
Siddur Sim Shalom for Shabbat and Festivals, *© 2000 by The Rabbinical Assembly.*
Maps © by Oxford University Press, supplied by Oxford Cartographers. Used by permission of Oxford University Press.
Illustrations of the tabernacle and its furnishings by Joe Sikora.

Composition by VARDA Graphics, Skokie, Illinois
Design by Adrianne Onderdonk Dudden
Manufactured in the United States of America

01 02 03 04 05 06 07 08 09 10 10 9 8 7 6 5 4 3 2 1

Library of Congress Cataloging-in-Publication Data
Bible. O.T. Pentateuch. Hebrew. 2001.
Etz Hayim: Torah and commentary / senior editor, David L. Lieber; literary editor, Jules Harlow; sponsored by the Rabbinical Assembly and the United Synagogue of Conservative Judaism.
p. cm.
Text of the Pentateuch in Hebrew and English; commentary in English.
Includes the haftarot and commentary on them, p'shat and d'rash commentaries, comments on Conservative halakhic practice, topical essays, and other material.
Includes bibliographical references and index.
ISBN 0-8276-0712-1
1. Bible. O.T. Pentateuch—Commentaries. 2. Haftarot—Commentaries. 3. Bible. O.T. Pentateuch—Theology. 4. Conservative Judaism—Customs and practices. I. Lieber, David L. II. Harlow, Jules. III. United Synagogue of Conservative Judaism. IV. Rabbinical Assembly. V. Bible. O.T. Pentateuch. English. Jewish Publication Society. 2001. VI. Title.

BS1222 .L54 2001
222'.1077—dc21

2001029757

ETZ HAYIM

TORAH AND COMMENTARY

THE RABBINICAL ASSEMBLY
THE UNITED SYNAGOGUE OF CONSERVATIVE JUDAISM

Produced by THE JEWISH PUBLICATION SOCIETY

The Rabbinical Assembly
3080 Broadway
New York, NY 10027

Illustrations of the tabernacle and its furnishings by Joe Sikora.

Composition by VARDA Graphics, Skokie, Illinois
Design by Adrianne Onderdonk Dudden
Manufactured in the United States of America

01 02 03 04 05 06 07 08 09 10 10 9 8 7 6 5 4 3 2 1

Library of Congress Cataloging-in-Publication Data
Bible. O.T. Pentateuch. Hebrew. 2001.
Etz Hayim: Torah and commentary / senior editor, David L. Lieber; literary editor, Jules Harlow; sponsored by the Rabbinical Assembly and the United Synagogue of Conservative Judaism.
p. cm.
Text of the Pentateuch in Hebrew and English; commentary in English.
Includes the haftarot and commentary on them, p'shat and d'rash commentaries, comments on Conservative halakhic practice, topical essays, and other material.
Includes bibliographical references and index.
ISBN 0-8276-0712-1
1. Bible. O.T. Pentateuch—Commentaries. 2. Haftarot—Commentaries. 3. Bible. O.T. Pentateuch—Theology. 4. Conservative Judaism—Customs and practices. I. Lieber, David L. II. Harlow, Jules. III. United Synagogue of Conservative Judaism. IV. Rabbinical Assembly. V. Bible. O.T. Pentateuch. English. Jewish Publication Society. 2001. VI. Title.

BS1222 .L54 2001
222'.1077—dc21

2001029757

This commentary is offered in loving tribute to the memory of

Sarah and Ralph *Davidson*

. . . תורה צוה־לנו משה
מורשה קהלת יעקב

. . . *Moses charged us with the Teaching*

As the heritage of the congregation of Jacob. Deuteronomy 33:4

and in appreciation to

Dorothy and Byron Gerson

Karen Davidson

Ethan *and* Marla Davidson

by William Davidson

This commentary is offered as a loving tribute to our parents

Sylvia Freider Estrada — Dave Estrada

Sarah Hartman Kushner — Julius Kushner

Who were our first teachers of Torah.

. . . למען יארכון ימיך . . .

. . . that you may long endure . . . Exodus 20:12

Rabbi Harold and Suzette E. Kushner

This commentary is offered in loving memory of

Alexander Rapaport

עץ חיים היא למחזיקים בה . . .

Torah is a tree of life for those who take hold of it . . . *Proverbs 3:18*

from his niece and nephews

Herbert M. Marton

Myron S. Rapaport

Robert D. Rapaport

Michael S. Rapaport

Martin S. Rapaport

Peter A. Rapaport

Lois Rapaport Shugar

David A. H. Rapaport

Richard A. Rapaport

To honor his lifelong support for the

United Synagogue of Conservative Judaism

In loving memory of our parents

Shirley Whizin שרח בת שמואל והאשע

a gentle and beautiful woman, who transmitted to us her love of the Synagogue and of Judaism and taught us the joy of dedicating oneself to the service of the community

and

Arthur Whizin אברהם נתן בן חיים ומינה

an energetic and extraordinarily generous man, who set an example for community leadership and demonstrated what one person can do to affect the life of many generations

To them and their parents who raised them to be devoted Jews, we owe a great debt of gratitude for making it possible for us to experience the happiness that flows from Jewish living and to realize some of their dreams for enhancing Jewish life.

. . . ותפארת בנים אבותם

. . . the glory of children is their parents Proverbs 17:6

Shelley and Bruce Whizin

CONTENTS

Foreword xvi

Introduction xvii

בראשית GENESIS B'REISHIT

בראשית	3	B'reishit
נח	41	No·aḥ
לך לך	69	Lekh L'kha
וירא	99	Va-yera
חיי שרה	127	Ḥayyei Sarah
תולדות	146	Tol'dot
ויצא	166	Va-yetzei
וישלח	198	Va-yishlaḥ
וישב	226	Va-yeishev
מקץ	250	Mi-ketz
ויגש	274	Va-yiggash
ויחי	293	Va-y'ḥi

שמות EXODUS SH'MOT

שמות	317	Sh'mot
וארא	351	Va-era
בא	374	Bo
בשלח	399	B'shallaḥ
יתרו	432	Yitro
משפטים	456	Mishpatim
תרומה	485	T'rumah
תצוה	503	T'tzavveh
כי תשא	523	Ki Tissa
ויקהל	552	Va-yak·hel
פקודי	564	P'kudei

ויקרא LEVITICUS VA-YIKRA

ויקרא	585	Va-yikra
צו	613	Tzav
שמיני	630	Sh'mini
תזריע	649	Tazri·a
מצרע	660	M'tzora
אחרי מות	679	Aḥarei Mot
קדשים	693	K'doshim
אמר	717	Emor
בהר	738	B'har
בחקתי	747	B'ḥukkotai

במדבר NUMBERS B'MIDBAR

במדבר	769	B'midbar
נשא	791	Naso
בהעלתך	816	B'ha·alot'kha
שלח לך	840	Sh'laḥ L'kha
קרח	860	Koraḥ
חקת	880	Ḥukkat
בלק	894	Balak
פינחס	918	Pinḥas
מטות	941	Mattot
מסעי	954	Mas'ei

דברים DEUTERONOMY D'VARIM

דברים	981	D'varim
ואתחנן	1005	Va-etḥannan
עקב	1037	Eikev
ראה	1061	R'eih
שפטים	1088	Shof'tim
כי תצא	1112	Ki Tetzei
כי תבוא	1140	Ki Tavo
נצבים	1165	Nitzavim
וילך	1173	Va-yeilekh
האזינו	1185	Ha·azinu
וזאת הברכה	1202	V'zot ha-B'rakhah

HAFTAROT FOR HOLIDAYS AND SPECIAL OCCASIONS

הפטרה למחר חודש	1215	Shabbat and Erev Rosh Ḥodesh
הפטרה לשבת וראש חודש	1219	Shabbat and Rosh Ḥodesh
הפטרה לראש השנה (יום ראשון)	1224	Rosh ha-Shanah, First Day
הפטרה לראש השנה (יום שני)	1230	Rosh ha-Shanah, Second Day
הפטרה לשבת שובה	1234	Shabbat Shuvah
הפטרה ליום כפור (שחרית)	1240	Yom Kippur Morning
הפטרה ליום כפור (מנחה)	1245	Yom Kippur Afternoon
הפטרה לסוכות (יום ראשון)	1252	Sukkot, First Day
הפטרה לסוכות (יום שני)	1256	Sukkot, Second Day
הפטרה לשבת חול המועד סוכות	1259	Sukkot, Intermediate Shabbat
הפטרה לשמיני עצרת	1263	Sh'mini Atzeret
הפטרה לשמחת תורה	1266	Simḥat Torah
הפטרה לשבת חנוכה (א׳)	1269	First Shabbat of Ḥanukkah
הפטרה לשבת חנוכה (ב׳)	1273	Second Shabbat of Ḥanukkah
הפטרת פרשת שקלים	1276	Parashat Sh'kalim
הפטרת פרשת זכור	1280	Parashat Zakhor
הפטרת פרשת פרה	1286	Parashat Parah
הפטרת פרשת החודש	1290	Parashat ha-Ḥodesh
הפטרה לשבת הגדול	1295	Shabbat ha-Gadol
הפטרה לפסח (יום ראשון)	1299	Pesaḥ, First Day
הפטרה לפסח (יום שני)	1303	Pesaḥ, Second Day
הפטרה לשבת חול המועד פסח	1307	Pesaḥ, Intermediate Shabbat
הפטרה לפסח (יום שביעי)	1310	Pesaḥ, Seventh Day
הפטרה לפסח (יום שמיני)	1315	Pesaḥ, Eighth Day
הפטרה ליום העצמאות	1315	Israel Independence Day
הפטרה לשבועות (יום ראשון)	1320	Shavu·ot, First Day
הפטרה לשבועות (יום שני)	1325	Shavu·ot, Second Day
הפטרה לתשעה באב (שחרית)	1329	Tish·ah b'Av Morning
הפטרה לתענית צבור (מנחה)	1335	Fast Day Afternoons

ESSAYS

Biblical Life and Perspectives

Biblical Archaeology 1339
Ancient Near Eastern Mythology 1344
Israelite Society in Transition 1348
Marriage and Family 1353
Women 1356
Matriarchs and Patriarchs 1359
Education 1365
Ecology 1369
Land of Israel 1372
Dealing with Strangers: Relations with Gentiles at Home and Abroad 1377
War and Peace 1382

Biblical Religion and Law

The God of Israel 1390
Revelation: Biblical and Rabbinic Perspectives 1394
Medieval and Modern Theories of Revelation 1399
The Nature of Revelation and Mosaic Origins 1405
Prophecy and the Prophets 1407
Moses: Man of Israel, Man of God 1412
The Covenant and the Election of Israel 1416
Biblical and Ancient Near Eastern Law 1420
Civil and Criminal Law 1423
Justice 1427
Reward and Punishment 1430
Eschatology 1434

Worship, Ritual, and Halakhah

Biblical Concepts of Holiness 1440
Priests and Levites in the Bible and Jewish Life 1441
Sacrifices 1446
Biblical Prayer 1450
Shabbat and the Holidays 1455
Dietary Laws 1460

T'fillin and *M'zuzot* 1464
Tzitzit (Tassels) 1468
Midrash and the Legal Process 1470
Medieval and Modern *Halakhah* 1474

Text and Context

Torah Reading 1479
The Torah Scroll 1484
Haftarah 1486
Midrash 1490
Traditional Methods of Bible Study 1494
Modern Methods of Bible Study 1499
A Note on the Spirituality of Texts 1503
Ḥazak Ḥazak v'Nitḥazzek 1504

Blessings for Torah and Haftarah 1506
Names of the Trope and Their Notations 1508
Decalogue with "Upper" Accents 1509
Abbreviations 1511
Maps of Biblical Lands After 1512
Glossary 1513
Transliteration of Hebrew 1518
Artist's Rendition of the Tabernacle and Its Furnishings 1520
Time Line for the Hebrew Bible 1522
Etz Hayim Committees 1523
Contributors 1524
Index of Names and Subjects 1526

FOREWORD

Judaism is above all a life of dialogue. Ever since Sinai, God and Israel have conversed and interacted through the medium of Torah. Revelation destined Israel to become a nation of readers and interpreters. Yet as the incarnation of the divine word, Scripture bore an infinite range of meanings. Jews learned to read deeply rather than quickly, disjunctively as well as contextually. Each generation and every Jew was bidden to pore over the text afresh to internalize its normative force and to garner another layer of undetected meaning. Endlessly malleable because it was supremely venerated, Scripture functioned as a canon without closure.

Ben Bag-Bag, an early rabbi and possible convert to Judaism, caught the spirit of this reciprocal bond to Scripture when he counseled: "Study it and review it—you will find everything in it. Scrutinize it, grow old and gray in it, do not depart from it. There is no better portion of life than this." For Jews, Scripture serves as a fount and refuge. To the extent that we strive to illuminate its inexhaustible contents, it rewards us with insight into the meaning of our own lives. Commentary is the quintessential genre of Jewish expression, an unending series of encounters with the divine that refract the history and mind-set of each age and author.

To this awesome library of commentaries, *Etz Hayim* adds a distinctively new Conservative voice, both scholarly and religious, theoretical and applied. Like many Jewish classics, it is the work of many hands, a tapestry of kaleidoscopic power. I salute the editors and contributors who joined their talents and sensibilities to bring it to fruition. My prayer is that it will soon become not only the standard commentary for every Conservative synagogue but also the home study companion for every serious student of Torah.

Ismar Schorsch
May 2000 / Nisan 5760

INTRODUCTION

The Torah is the foundational sacred text of Judaism; the study of its words and their meaning is at the core of Jewish religious experience. Also known as the Five Books of Moses, or the Pentateuch (*Ḥumash*), the word *torah* literally means "instruction." Jews view the Torah as the teaching par excellence about God's relationship to the world and to the Jewish people, about God's covenant with the people Israel, and about the laws by which they are to live that they might be a "holy people" (Deut. 26:19).

As early as the 5th century B.C.E., the Book of Nehemiah (8:1–8) records, Ezra gathered the people outside the Temple area and read aloud to them from "the scroll of the Teaching of Moses" (*seifer torat Mosheh*). This was accompanied by the explanation of the text by the Levites, who served as teachers among the people. In the century that followed, it became customary for Jews to read from the Torah on holy days and other times of public gathering. In succeeding centuries, the four special Sabbaths preceding *Purim* and *Pesaḥ* also provided for such occasions, including the exposition of the laws relating to the festivals. Not long thereafter, the practice of reading selections from the Torah at every *Shabbat* service developed. This may have been the reason that the Torah was translated into Greek (the Septuagint) in the 3rd century B.C.E., when the Jews of Alexandria, according to Philo, read the Torah in their synagogues every *Shabbat*. But a fixed cycle of consecutive readings, such as the one we have today, is not documented until the Rabbinic period.

The teaching of the Torah gave rise to a rich tradition of interpretation, later subsumed under the title of the "Oral Torah" (*torah she-b'al peh*), which, the Rabbis taught, Moses had also "received at Sinai" (M Avot 1:1). With the passage of time, the Oral Torah expanded greatly and was redacted (edited) in the classic volumes of Rabbinic literature, including the Mishnah, both Talmuds (the Babylonian and the Jerusalem, or "Yerushalmi"), and a number of midrashic collections. Biblical commentaries arose in the Middle Ages and have proliferated ever since. Each commentary reflected the age in which it was written, as well as the interests and concerns of its author. Some commentators, like Rashi, presented the Rabbinic worldview. Others, like Ibn Ezra, were more philologically and philosophically oriented. Some were polemical, responding to views of the Karaites (Saadiah) or Christians (Radak). Others, like the 19th-century commentators Samson Raphael Hirsch and Malbim, sought to demonstrate the eternal validity of the teachings of the Torah in the face of the rise of Reform Judaism. Jews have produced hundreds of commentaries on the Torah; Christian scholars and religious leaders have written many as well. None, however, can exhaust the Torah's riches; there is always room for more plumbing of its depths. Moreover, as the Sages observed, *"dor dor v'dorshav"* (BT Sanh. 38b), "each generation needs to bring forth its own interpreters," and ours is no exception.

Key Features of This Book

Etz Hayim: Torah and Commentary is a product of the Conservative (*Masorti*) Movement. As such, it incorporates the very best of modern Bible scholarship derived from the works of internationally renowned scholars who are or have been associated with the Conservative Movement.

The first commentary on the page under the

Bible text is the *p'shat,* the contextual meaning of the text. It is illuminated by the finest contemporary scientific scholarship on the Torah.

The second commentary on the page is the midrashic commentary (*d'rash*). It presents an eclectic range of insights, from the classical *midrashim* to the medieval commentators, from Hasidic masters to contemporary religious leaders and secular thinkers.

Also included at the bottom of many of the pages is a section on Conservative halakhic practice (*halakhah l'ma·aseh*), indicating how contemporary Conservative *halakhah* is linked to the biblical text.

This book includes a liturgically complete set of haftarah selections, as approved by the Committee on Jewish Law and Standards. It presents some of the characteristic variance between the traditions of *Ashk'nazim* and *S'fardim,* selecting its passages from among the much larger variety of haftarot selections among traditional Jews, for the sake of simplicity and of promoting uniformity in Conservative synagogues. The commentary on each *haftarah* is unparalleled in clarity and erudition. Generally, the *haftarah* for each Shabbat has been placed after the *parashah* with which it is associated. However, in the case of a *parashah* that in some years is read together with the following *parashah*, its associated *haftarah* has been placed after the combined *parashiyyot,* so that the position of a *haftarah* never interrupts the flow of Torah reading. The *haftarot* for holy days, special Sabbaths, and weekdays are grouped together at the end of the Torah.

In addition, we have included 41 topical essays, each written by a rabbi or scholar affiliated with the Conservative Movement. Taken as a whole, these essays provide a comprehensive introduction to the central themes of the Torah and their context in Judaism. The topics are organized into four sections: "Biblical Life and Perspectives," "Biblical Religion and Law," "Worship, Ritual, and Halakhah," and "Text and Context." The book concludes with a large number of essential reference tools for the worshiper and for the student of Torah.

We are proud to note that this work is also influenced by perspectives of the first generation of female scholars and rabbis contributing to a Torah commentary. This is not a feminist commentary per se, but *Etz Hayim* is sensitive to the roles of women in the biblical world. Although this sensitivity is perhaps most apparent in our examination of the family narratives of Genesis, laws of ritual purity, and the treatment of women, it has added a depth of insight to the entire commentary.

Hebrew Text and English Translation

The Hebrew text is based on the Leningrad Manuscript B19A (L), the oldest complete manuscript of the Hebrew Bible, dating from approximately 1009 C.E. It was copied directly from manuscripts of the renowned Masoretes of Tiberias. The Jewish Publication Society (JPS) has made available its carefully prepared edition of that text. (See the Preface to the *JPS Hebrew-English Tanakh,* published in 1999.)

The original manuscript contains four errors in the accentuation marks (trope) of the Torah text; we have changed them to conform with other extant Masoretic manuscripts. (The trope in those manuscripts—and this volume—does not match all the existing printed editions of the Hebrew Bible, which differ from one another in about 70 places in the Torah. This accounts for the differences among the *tikkunim* from which Torah readers prepare their cantillation for the synagogue.)

Furthermore, as the reader may know, the Hebrew text's *k'tiv* (written tradition) and *k'rei* (reading tradition) differ from each other for occasional words; where this occurs, our edition first prints that word's *k'tiv* letters in small type, followed by the pointed *k'rei* letters in normal text type.

The English rendering, meanwhile, is that of the most recent JPS translation, as corrected in the 2000 edition of its *Hebrew-English Tanakh,* based on a thorough 1967 revision. This

English translation is considered by scholars to be the standard in the Jewish world and we have abided by its language, though it has become customary in the Conservative Movement to favor gender-neutral translation wherever possible in liturgical publications.

In keeping with suggestions of the authors of the five-volume *JPS Torah Commentary,* published by JPS (1989–1996), we have retranslated a few of the terms related to sacrifices. Thus for "sin offering" we have substituted "purification offering," and for "unclean" we use the word "impure" when referring to ritual impurity.

P'shat Commentary

The reader will recognize that, while reverential, the commentary is not apologetic. It does not attempt to justify all of the statements in the Torah or demonstrate that they conform to our view of scientific truth. Nor does it seek to rationalize institutions such as slavery or commands like the one to kill all of the Canaanites. Such passages are viewed as a reflection of the age in which they were composed, in need of being reinterpreted by later generations in light of the principles of equity, justice, and compassion that are central to the Torah.

The *p'shat* to this work is based on the *JPS Torah Commentary.* The scholars who created that five-volume commentary brought to their task not only a dedication to the sophisticated discipline of modern scholarship and a keen awareness of its demands for objectivity but also a profound love of the text and its sanctity. Truth and reverence suffuse their words. In editing the *p'shat,* Chaim Potok, the original literary editor of the five volumes, brought unity to the series. The erudite scholarly arguments were reduced to basic conclusions; the different styles of writing were given a coherent single voice.

Archaeology, philology, anthropology, a new awareness of ancient cultures—all of these have added to our knowledge of the biblical world. We see our people in the flow of time, in history, participating with the civilizations around them, yet with their very own perspectives. What they gave to the ancient world and what they took from it—these are embedded in the *p'shat,* the plain basic meaning of the text. We try to understand the Torah as it was once understood by Israelites—before the rabbis of the Talmud began to use the text for the fashioning of the great civilization known as Rabbinic Judaism. We use the tools of modern-day *p'shat* to recover ancient Scripture. Were Rashi and Ibn Ezra, those two great medieval proponents of *p'shat,* alive today, they would likely be using the same tools.

The hallmark of the *p'shat* is lucidity; its goal is to see the text in a time and a place and to have it speak to us. Much of the Torah is glorious; some of it is deeply problematic; some of it is still not understandable. But this work represents the best efforts of the finest scholars of our generation to unpack its meaning. Future generations will no doubt find understandings reflective of their own time.

D'rash Commentary

D'rash (or *midrash*) is a traditional nonliteral way of reading sacred texts. The term comes from a Hebrew verb meaning "to inquire, to investigate," and it refers to a process of close reading of the text to find insights that go beyond the plain meaning of the words. In Jakob J. Petuchowski's felicitous simile, Jews read Torah as one reads a love letter, eager to squeeze the last drop of meaning from every word: Why was that word used rather than another? What is the significance of the repetition of certain words? What does the choice of a word reveal about the speaker's innermost thoughts?

D'rash is at its most subtle and insightful when it elucidates elements in the text that the casual reader might overlook. Thus in Gen. 4:3–5, *d'rash* might ask, does the Torah give any hints as to why God might have favored Abel's offerings over Cain's? Or in Exod. 2:5, why does Pharaoh's daughter go down to bathe

in the Nile when she has servants to draw her bath in the palace?

The *d'rash* commentary in this volume contains selected insights from more than 2000 years of Torah study. There are passages from the Talmud and Midrash, the teachings of the Sages in the first five centuries of the Common Era. There are insights of Rashi, the great French commentator of the 11th century. And there are homiletic and psychological insights by 19th-century Hasidic teachers and by contemporary rabbis and thinkers. Readers will note that in the *d'rash* commentary, renderings of biblical passages do not always precisely match the JPS translation; *midrash* by nature plays on the multivalent nature of the Hebrew text, which no one translation can capture.

In keeping with our commitment to Conservative Judaism, we have sought to learn from the Torah rather than to judge it. There are passages that challenge our moral conscience, a conscience informed by Torah values. Among them, for example, are verses about the treatment of non-Israelite nations and the legal and social standing of women in ancient Israel; and the commentary reflects our discomfort. The *d'rash* commentary has approached the text with reverence, asking not "Do we approve of this passage?" but "Because this was sacred to our ancestors, what can it teach us?"

Halakhah l'Ma·aseh

Etz Hayim contains an additional layer of commentary, *halakhah l'ma·aseh,* that addresses the question of how the Jewish community has responded to the words we read in the Torah. The Hebrew word *"halakhah"* refers to the Jewish legal tradition. *Halakhah l'ma·aseh* refers to the practice and observance of Jewish law as applied to every aspect of daily life, including personal relations, business practices, religious observances, social policy, and acts of social conscience. Our observance of *halakhah* is our effort as Jews to walk in God's ways and to fulfill God's will.

As Conservative Jews, while we affirm the holiness of the Torah we recognize that Jewish law developed over time and has been shaped by historical influences. Although Jewish law is strongly rooted in the Torah, Jewish practice in our day cannot be identified exclusively with what we read in the Torah. One goal of the *halakhah l'ma·aseh* section, then, is to indicate how we act in response to the words we read in the Torah, through Jewish law as it is lived in our time. Many comments will articulate the ways in which modern Jewish practice closely follows the Torah. Other comments will show where Jewish practice follows the interpretation and application of the Torah by rabbis from the time of the Mishnah (ca. 100 B.C.E.–200 C.E.) to our own day, including Rabbinic customs and traditions. There are some instances, though, where modern Jewish practice differs from what was, or appears to have been, biblical or Rabbinic practice. This will be especially true in such areas as medical ethics, the role of women in Jewish life and in society at large, and our interactions with non-Jews.

The *halakhah l'ma·aseh* section is not a code of Jewish law. Rather, it describes Jewish practice and demonstrates the role of Jewish practice in our quest for God. As Conservative Jews, we believe that the historical development of Jewish law was not only the product of the interactions of our ancestors with the historical, social, moral, and economic contexts in which they found themselves but also the fruit of their response to God's call to be a holy people. We hope that its comments will inspire an interest in applying the Torah text to how we "walk with God" in our lives. (For more on *halakhah* in the Conservative Movement, see Elliot Dorff's essay "Medieval and Modern *Halakhah*.")

Haftarah Commentary

Finally, *Etz Hayim* features commentary on each *haftarah* written by Michael Fishbane, with the exception of the *haftarah* for *Yom*

Kippur afternoon. (The latter is presented with a brief introduction.) This *haftarah* commentary was composed with the intention of serving the liturgical, intellectual, and religious interests of the contemporary Jewish community. In the words of Dr. Fishbane, the purpose of this commentary is "to foster and develop a mode of biblical literacy that might transform the words of the prophets and the ancient prophetic literature, read on Sabbaths and other sacred occasions, into words of living instruction."

Conservative Judaism is based on Rabbinic Judaism. It differs, however, in the recognition that all texts were composed in given historical contexts. The Conservative Movement, in short, applies historical, critical methods to the study of the biblical text. It views the Torah as the product of generations of inspired prophets, priests, and teachers, beginning with the time of Moses but not reaching its present form until the postexilic age, in the 6th or 5th century B.C.E. The Torah is viewed by us, in the words of Harold Kushner, as "God's first word, not God's last." Like the ancient Rabbis we do not limit Torah to the Five Books of Moses. Torah represents the spiritual and intellectual entirety of the Jewish religious tradition that continues to grow and develop. And the foundation for this tradition is in the sacred text of the *ḥumash.* In the words of the late Gerson Cohen, its call to us is "timeless and universal." It provides an endless source of religious insight and inspiration and its enduring vitality transcends generations.

In Grateful Acknowledgment

As the reader will recognize, this volume is the result of a team effort, and it owes much to many people, first and foremost to my fellow editors, whose names are listed on the title page—Elliot Dorff, Susan Grossman, Jules Harlow, Harold Kushner, and Chaim Potok—as well as Michael Fishbane, the author of the commentary on the *haftarot,* with whom it was a joy to work. I thank them not only for their contributions to the commentaries, but also to this introduction. For these scholars, working on this edition of the *ḥumash* was more than a labor of love; it was *m'lekhet kodesh,* a sacred undertaking to help the Torah speak to our time. Each one of us owes a great debt to the Jewish Theological Seminary, for more than a century one of the foremost institutions of higher Jewish learning in the world, where most of us were ordained. At the seminary, we were privileged to sit at the feet of some of the great Judaic scholars of the 20th century, learning how to interpret biblical and rabbinical texts and make them address the issues of our time.

This work would not have been possible without the learned, profound commentaries of the scholars who produced the five-volume *JPS Torah Commentary,* under the general editorship of Nahum Sarna and the literary editorship of Chaim Potok. The volumes include commentaries on Genesis and Exodus by Nahum Sarna, on Leviticus by Baruch Levine, on Numbers by Jacob Milgrom, and on Deuteronomy by Jeffrey H. Tigay. *The JPS Commentary on the Haftarot,* by Michael Fishbane (2001), serves as the basis for his commentary on the *haftarot* in this volume. Each scholar has graciously contributed a brief introduction to the book(s) on which he has written his commentaries. The reader is urged to refer to their original works for a study of the texts in greater detail and depth.

I am also grateful to two other highly regarded Bible scholars, Stephen Geller of the Jewish Theological Seminary and Shalom Paul of the Hebrew University in Jerusalem, for reviewing the entire *p'shat* and making suggestions for its supplementation. At the same time, I would like to acknowledge, together with *D'rash* Committee Chair Harold Kushner and Associate Chair Susan Grossman, the contributions of the following colleagues: Pamela Barmash, Nina Beth Cardin, Diane Cohen, Daniel Pressman, Jack Riemer, Benjamin

Edidin Scolnic, David Wolpe, and Shoshana Brown. I would like to join Elliot Dorff and Susan Grossman, editors of the *halakhah l'ma·aseh* section, in thanking the Committee on Jewish Law and Standards of the Conservative Movement and its chair, Kassel Abelson, for their suggestions for revision of earlier drafts of that material. Special thanks also to Nina Beth Cardin, Diane Cohen, Avram Reisner, and Joel Roth. I would also like to thank members of the Reading Committee and especially those who faithfully read the entire commentary, Ivan Caine and Daniel Pressman, as well as Jonathan Ginsburg and Susan Safyan, who made suggestions throughout for its improvement.

Each of the supplementary essays in this volume was composed by a rabbi or scholar associated with the Conservative Movement as a labor of love. I appreciate the patience with which they carefully revised their work at the prompting of our literary editor. Every effort was made to avoid gender-specific terms, with the help of Leonard Gordon and members of his special advisory committee. This was not always possible, for as the reader recognizes, our ancient sacred texts are the product of a world in which women generally did not play a prominent public role, as reflected both in the laws and narratives of Scripture.

The two sponsoring organizations of the commentary, the Rabbinical Assembly and the United Synagogue of Conservative Judaism, are owed a debt of appreciation, as is The Jewish Publication Society. The Ḥumash Publication Committee was chaired by Irwin Groner, whose skillful management and commitment to this work and unflagging enthusiasm were instrumental in its success. JPS Trustees Martin Cohn and Jerome Shestack offered valuable guidance in the early stages of this project. The United Synagogue's effective participation was led by its president, Stephen S. Wolnek. In addition to handling the myriad details involved in the publication of the volume, JPS made available its Hebrew text and translation, as well as the volumes of commentary referred to above. Thanks, then, are due to Ellen Frankel, CEO and editor-in-chief of JPS and to the members of the production team: Carol Hupping, managing editor; Robin Norman, production director; Adrianne Onderdonk Dudden, designer; David E. S. Stein, project manager; Alex Gendler and his crew of compositors; Candace B. Levy, copy-editor; Janet Finegar, proofreader and editorial assistant, and proofreaders Emily Law, Helaine Denenberg, Carole Martin, Robin Damsky, and Moshe Halfon. Michael Monson, Dr. Frankel's predecessor, was instrumental in establishing the partnership with the Conservative Movement to produce the volume and guided JPS in initiating the venture. Serious discussions were begun with Albert Lewis, then president of the Rabbinical Assembly, who was succeeded by Irwin Groner. Thanks also are due to Jerome Epstein, the executive vice-president of the United Synagogue for Conservative Judaism, for his significant advice and active contributions to the project.

I would like to offer special acknowledgment to Jules Harlow and Joel Meyers. Rabbi Harlow, the former director of publications for the Rabbinical Assembly, came out of retirement to help ensure the high quality of the literary editing of the entire commentary. Rabbi Meyers, the executive vice president of the Rabbinical Assembly, contributed to every facet of the production of this work, coordinating the efforts of the three organizations represented on the editorial board, looking after the finances, and providing a steadying hand when one was required. He was largely responsible for securing the initial funding to help make the project possible, and we are grateful to the generous donors whose names are listed at the beginning of the book. Thanks also to members of the Rabbinical Assembly staff: Amy Gottlieb, who made numerous editorial contributions to the introductions and essays; David J. Fine, who checked the references and prepared the glossary; and Hoa

Browne and Jennifer Meyers Klor, who typed portions of the manuscript and undertook a variety of administrative details.

I would also like to thank Robert Wexler, president of the University of Judaism, for his personal encouragement and for providing a warm, supportive environment in which I could carry out my work these past eight years, as well as Eileen Bernstein, my able assistant, and Larisa Zadoyen, who provided technical assistance. My appreciation is also extended to Ismar Schorsch, chancellor of the Jewish Theological Seminary, who has taken a keen interest in our work and who wrote the foreword. I would like to acknowledge the help of my wife, Esther, without whose encouragement and active support I could not have undertaken this effort and seen it through to a successful conclusion. Finally, on behalf of all the editors, we want to thank God for enabling us, in the words of the morning liturgy, "to understand, to discern, to heed, to learn, and to teach, to observe and to do and to fulfill all the words of the teachings of Your Torah in love."

In the liturgy of the Torah service, the Torah is referred to as *etz ḥayyim* (a tree of life, Prov. 3:18). This phrase—simplified as *etz hayim*—was selected as the title of our commentary in the hope that readers may indeed experience the Torah as a tree of life. May we, like our ancestors, derive from it the inspiration to live in the presence of God as members of a *k'hillah k'doshah,* a sacred community, ever growing in wisdom and moral sensitivity, rooted in our ancestral faith, and open to the new insights and revelations the Almighty grants us.

Ḥazak ḥazak v'nitḥazzek!

David L. Lieber
March 2001 / Adar 5761

Words cannot adequately express our deeply felt gratitude and appreciation for the leadership and wisdom of David Lieber, senior editor of *Etz Hayim*. From the very outset of this project, which began several years ago, Rabbi Lieber provided vision and guidance to a stellar and diverse group of rabbis, teachers, and editors, who labored on the humash commentary and essays. His firm but gentle hand is discernable everywhere in this magnificent volume. More than all else, Rabbi Lieber has, throughout his rabbinate, been a teacher of Torah, beloved by his students, respected by his colleagues, and admired by all who continue to gain from his imparting of our sacred tradition.

Irwin Groner
Chairman, Humash Committee

בראשית

GENESIS

בראשית

נח

לך לך

וירא

חיי שרה

תולדות

ויצא

וישלח

וישב

מקץ

ויגש

ויחי

GENESIS

NAHUM M. SARNA

The opening book of the Bible is generally known as *Genesis* in English or by its first Hebrew word, *B'reishit.* In the Middle Ages it was also termed among Jews *Seifer Ha-Yashar* (The Book of the Upright), referring to the patriarchs.

Genesis is the book about origins: the origin of the world of humankind, of the people of Israel, and of the unique relationship of God with that people. In its entirety, the book claims to cover a time span of 2,309 years. It offers a rapid sketch of 1,948 years of universal human history from Adam to the birth of Abraham, with the remaining 361 years to the death of Joseph making up the bulk of the work. This imbalance is there by design. The theme of Creation serves merely as an introduction to the central motif: God's role in history. The opening chapters serve as a prologue to the historical drama that commences in chapter 12. They serve to set forth the worldviews and values of the civilization of the Bible, the pillars on which the religion of Israel rests.

The God of Genesis is the wholly self-sufficient one, absolutely independent of nature. He is the unchallenged sovereign of the world, who is providentially involved in human affairs, the God of history. The human being in Genesis is the pinnacle of Creation, a creature of infinite preciousness who enjoys a unique relationship with God. Humankind is endowed with free will and, consequently, is also charged with moral responsibility and inescapable accountability. Moreover, the entire human race constitutes a single family, which becomes fractured after the perverse exercise of freedom of will. God singles out one people as His chosen instrument, destined to fill a central role in the unfolding of His plan of history. Through a generational process of moral selection in which Noah and Abraham signify fixed points, this people evolves into a nation.

The narratives about the patriarchs of Israel are framed by two historic migrations: into the Promised Land, and out of it. Between these migrations we are not given a continuous history, but cycles of individual episodes about Abraham, Isaac, and Jacob. Of these generally disconnected stories, some serve as guides in formulating principles of behavior, whereas others demonstrate the moral degeneration of the inhabitants of Canaan, thereby implicitly providing the explanation for the future displacement of these peoples by the Israelites.

A major theme of the patriarchal narratives is the divine promise of nationhood and of national territory, both of which constitute the essential introduction to the second book of the Bible, Exodus. The Book of Genesis closes with the divine promise of redemption.

When God began to create heaven and

בְּרֵאשִׁית* בָּרָא אֱלֹהִים אֵת הַשָּׁמַיִם

v. 1. ב׳ רבתי לפי נוסחים מקובלים

CREATION (1:1–2:3)

The Creation narrative in the Bible is a document of faith. In its quest for meaning it gives expression to the fundamental premise of the religion of the people Israel: The universe is entirely the purposeful product of the one God, a transcendent being, beyond nature, and sovereign over space and time.

INTRODUCTION (1:1)

1. When God began to create The conventional English translation reads: "In the beginning God created the heaven and the earth." The translation presented here looks to verse 3 for the completion of the sentence and takes

---

Time has not diminished the power or the majesty of the familiar biblical account of the creation of the world, nor has familiarity dulled its impact. It still moves us, conveying so much in so few words. What kind of world does the Torah envision God creating? The opening chapters of Genesis are not a scientific account of the origins of the universe. The Torah is a book of morality, not cosmology. Its overriding concern, from the first verse to the last, is our relationship to God, truth about life rather than scientific truths. It describes the world God fashioned as "good," a statement no scientific account can make.

God's world is an orderly world, in which land and water each has its own domain, in which each species of plant and animal reproduces itself "after its own kind." But it is also an unpredictable world, a world capable of growth and change and surprise, of love and pain, of glory and tragedy, not simply replication of what is, because it includes human beings who have the freedom to choose how they will act. And it is an unfinished world, waiting for human beings to complete God's work of creating.

CHAPTER 1

The Torah assumes the existence and overwhelming power of God. We find here no myth of God's birth, as we find in other cultures' accounts of creation, only a description of God's actions. It seems that the Torah is saying, "This is the premise on which the rest stands. Only if you accept it is everything that follows intelligible." God created the world, blessed it with the capacity to renew and reproduce itself, and deemed it "good." This is the answer to the basic and inevitable questions: Why is there something instead of nothing? Why is there life instead of inert matter?

The first letter of the first word in the Torah, "*b'reishit*," is the Hebrew letter *bet*. This prompted the Midrash to suggest that, just as the letter *bet* is enclosed on three sides but open to the front, we are not to speculate on the origins of God or what may have existed before Creation (Gen. R. 1:10). The purpose of such a comment is not to limit scientific inquiry into the origins of the universe but to discourage efforts to prove the unprovable. It urges us to ask ourselves, "How are we to live in this world?" And it urges us to live facing forward rather than looking backward. Jewish theology generally has been concerned with discerning the will of God rather than proving the existence or probing the nature of God. Ultimate origins ("Who made God?") are hidden from view, but all the rest of the world is open to inquiry. The Torah begins with *bet*, second letter of the Hebrew alphabet, to summon us to begin even if we cannot begin at the very beginning.

The Midrash takes the word for "beginning" (*reishit*) as a synonym for "Torah" (as in Prov. 8:22), interpreting the first verse as declaring: "With *reishit* did God create the heaven and the earth." God created the world by consulting the Torah, fashioning a world based on Torah values, or for the sake of the Torah, so that there would be somewhere in the universe where the values of the Torah could be put into practice (Gen. R. 1:1,6).

1. When God began The beginning of all knowledge and morality lies in the recognition that God created the world. Akiva taught: "Just

earth—2the earth being unformed and void,
with darkness over the surface of the deep and
a wind from God sweeping over the water—
3God said, "Let there be light"; and there was

וְאֵ֥ת הָאָֽרֶץ׃ 2 וְהָאָ֗רֶץ הָיְתָ֥ה תֹ֙הוּ֙ וָבֹ֔הוּ
וְחֹ֖שֶׁךְ עַל־פְּנֵ֣י תְה֑וֹם וְר֣וּחַ אֱלֹהִ֔ים
מְרַחֶ֖פֶת עַל־פְּנֵ֥י הַמָּֽיִם׃ 3 וַיֹּ֥אמֶר אֱלֹהִ֖ים

verse 2 to be parenthetical, describing the state of things at the time when God first spoke. Support for understanding the text in this way comes from the second half of 2:4 and of 5:1, both of which refer to Creation and begin with the word "when."

God The Hebrew term for God used throughout this account of Creation is not the unique sacred divine name *YHVH* but *elohim,* a general Hebrew word for "deity," which can also refer to pagan gods. Although plural in form, it almost always appears with a singular verb or adjective. The name, connoting universalism and abstraction, is most appropriate for the God of Creation.

create The Hebrew stem of the word translated as "create" (ברא) is used in the Bible only for divine creativity. It signifies that the created object is unique, depends solely on God for its coming into existence, and is beyond the ability of humans to reproduce. The verb never means "to create out of nothing."

heaven and earth The observable universe is here specified by the use of the definite article in Hebrew (literally, "the heaven and the earth"). The combination of opposites ("heaven and earth") expresses the totality of cosmic phenomena, for which there is no single word in biblical Hebrew.

THE PRIMORDIAL WORLD
(v. 2)

2. unformed and void The Hebrew for this phrase (*tohu va-vohu*) means "desert waste." The point of the narrative is the idea of order that results from divine intent. There is no suggestion here that God made the world out of nothing, which is a much later conception.

darkness In the Bible, darkness is often a symbol of evil, misfortune, death, or oblivion. Here it seems to be not just the absence of light but a distinct entity, the origin of which is left unclear.

the deep The Hebrew word for "the deep" (*t'hom*) refers to the subterranean waters that ancient humans believed were beneath the earth. The text says nothing about how or when this body of water came into existence. In Proverbs (8:22–24) it is one of God's creations. The word is related etymologically to Tiamat, the maritime goddess in the Babylonian creation story. In all of the ancient Near Eastern creation stories, the primal element is water. To the ancients, the formless nature of water seemed to represent the state of affairs before chaos was transformed to order.

a wind from God Or, as others suggest, "a mighty wind." The Hebrew word *ru·aḥ* means "wind, breath, spirit." "Wind" is the prevalent understanding of the word here in ancient and medieval Jewish sources. As a physical phenomenon, wind conforms to the picture of primal chaos evoked by this verse.

sweeping Movement is the basic idea underlying this Hebrew verb (רחף). Motion, the essential element in change, originates with God's dynamic presence.

water This is either the cosmic ocean believed by the ancients to surround the earth or the water referred to in verses 6, 7, 9, and 10, namely, that which covered the solid mass of earth. These two bodies of water were probably not clearly differentiated in the ancient Hebrew mind.

THE FIRST GROUP OF CREATED OBJECTS (vv. 3–13)

DAY ONE

3. God said The divine word shatters the cosmic silence and signals the beginning of a

---

as the existence of a house testifies to the builder and the existence of a garment testifies to the weaver, so the existence of the world testifies to God who fashioned it" (Mid. Tem. 3). "Whoever teaches a child the Torah's account of Creation is to be considered as having created the world personally." To shape the moral imagination of a child is to create a new world.

3. God creates the world with words. This is the first invocation of the Torah's belief in the reality of words, their power to create and to destroy.

Let there be light Light, the first thing God created, can be seen as symbolizing Judaism's commitment to clarity rather than mystery, to openness rather than concealment, to study

light. 4God saw that the light was good, and
God separated the light from the darkness.
5God called the light Day, and the darkness
He called Night. And there was evening and
there was morning, a first day.

יְהִי אוֹר וַיְהִי־אוֹר׃ 4וַיַּרְא אֱלֹהִים אֶת־
הָאוֹר כִּי־טוֹב וַיַּבְדֵּל אֱלֹהִים בֵּין הָאוֹר
וּבֵין הַחֹשֶׁךְ׃ 5וַיִּקְרָא אֱלֹהִים ׀ לָאוֹר יוֹם
וְלַחֹשֶׁךְ קָרָא לָיְלָה וַיְהִי־עֶרֶב וַיְהִי־בֹקֶר
יוֹם אֶחָד׃ פ

new order. "God said" means that God created the world with His words. This signifies that the Creator is wholly independent of Creation. It implies effortlessness and absolute sovereignty over nature.

Let there be This instruction (*y'hi*), found again in verses 6 and 14, is reserved for the creation of celestial phenomena.

light The first creation by God's utterance. Light in the Bible serves as a symbol of life, joy, justice, and deliverance. The notion of light independent of the sun (which appears again in Isa. 30:26 and Job 38:19–20) derives from the observations that the sky is illumined on days when the sun is obscured and that brightness precedes the sun's rising. As in the ancient world generally, light itself is a feature of divinity.

4. God saw God perceived.

was good This affirms the flawlessness of God's creation. Reality is imbued with God's goodness.

God separated Separation, or differentiation, is another aspect of creation. Light, like darkness, is viewed here as a separate entity.

5. God called Not to possess a name is tantamount to nonexistence in the worldview of the ancient Near East, including Egypt and Babylonia. Name giving was thus associated with creation and domination, for the one who gives a name has power over the object named. In this narrative, God names day and night, the sky, the earth, and the sea. This is another way of expressing God's absolute sovereignty over time and space.

evening . . . morning The Hebrew words *erev* and *boker* literally mean "sunset" and "break of dawn," terms inappropriate before the creation of the sun on the fourth day. Here the two words signify, respectively, the end of the period of light (when divine creativity was suspended) and the renewal of light (when the creative process was resumed).

a first day Better: "the first day." The Hebrew word *"eḥad"* functions as both a cardinal

---

rather than blind faith. Light, God's first creation, becomes a symbol of God's Presence, in the fire of the Burning Bush and the revelation at Sinai, in the perpetual light (*ner tamid*) and the *m'norah* of the tabernacle. For some theologians, light functions as a symbol for God because light itself is not visible but makes everything else visible. "By Your light do we see light" (Ps. 36:10).

4. God separated The process of Creation is a process of making distinctions and separating—light from darkness, sea from dry land, one species from another—imposing order where there had been chaos and randomness. Throughout the Torah, we find this emphasis on distinction and separation: sacred and ordinary time, permitted and forbidden foods, ritually pure and impure persons, no mixing of diverse seeds or cross-breeding animal species. Aviva Zornberg suggests that separation, specialization, is almost always achieved with pain and sacrifice, even as there is a sense of sadness in the *havdalah* service that marks the separation of *Shabbat* and weekday, even as there is pain when an infant is born out of its mother's body, even as there is a sense of painful separation when a child outgrows its dependence on parents. The Midrash (Gen. R. 5:3) pictures the lower waters weeping at being separated from the upper waters, suggesting that there is something poignant in the creative process when things once united are separated.

5. a first day Literally, "one day," taken by the Midrash to mean "the day of the One," the

HALAKHAH L'MA·ASEH

1:5 there was evening and there was morning According to Jewish law, the 24-hour cycle begins at sunset. *Shabbat* and holy days, therefore, begin in the evening, with candles lit 18 minutes before sunset, and continue until the following night when three stars can be clearly seen or 25 minutes after sunset if no stars are visible. (On determining the beginning of *Shabbat*, see S.A. O.Ḥ. 261:1–4.)

6 God said, "Let there be an expanse in the
midst of the water, that it may separate water
from water." 7 God made the expanse, and it
separated the water which was below the expanse from the water which was above the expanse. And it was so. 8 God called the expanse
Sky. And there was evening and there was
morning, a second day.

9 God said, "Let the water below the sky be
gathered into one area, that the dry land may
appear." And it was so. 10 God called the dry
land Earth, and the gathering of waters He
called Seas. And God saw that this was good.

6 וַיֹּ֣אמֶר אֱלֹהִ֔ים יְהִ֥י רָקִ֖יעַ בְּת֣וֹךְ הַמָּ֑יִם
וִיהִ֣י מַבְדִּ֔יל בֵּ֥ין מַ֖יִם לָמָֽיִם׃ 7 וַיַּ֣עַשׂ
אֱלֹהִים֮ אֶת־הָרָקִיעַ֒ וַיַּבְדֵּ֗ל בֵּ֤ין הַמַּ֙יִם֙
אֲשֶׁר֙ מִתַּ֣חַת לָרָקִ֔יעַ וּבֵ֣ין הַמַּ֔יִם אֲשֶׁ֖ר
מֵעַ֣ל לָרָקִ֑יעַ וַֽיְהִי־כֵֽן׃ 8 וַיִּקְרָ֧א אֱלֹהִ֛ים
לָֽרָקִ֖יעַ שָׁמָ֑יִם וַֽיְהִי־עֶ֥רֶב וַֽיְהִי־בֹ֖קֶר י֥וֹם
שֵׁנִֽי׃ פ
9 וַיֹּ֣אמֶר אֱלֹהִ֗ים יִקָּו֨וּ הַמַּ֜יִם מִתַּ֤חַת
הַשָּׁמַ֙יִם֙ אֶל־מָק֣וֹם אֶחָ֔ד וְתֵרָאֶ֖ה הַיַּבָּשָׁ֑ה
וַֽיְהִי־כֵֽן׃ 10 וַיִּקְרָ֨א אֱלֹהִ֤ים ׀ לַיַּבָּשָׁה֙ אֶ֔רֶץ
וּלְמִקְוֵ֥ה הַמַּ֖יִם קָרָ֣א יַמִּ֑ים וַיַּ֥רְא אֱלֹהִ֖ים

number (one) and an ordinal number (first) in many texts.

DAY TWO

6. an expanse The verbal form of the noun translated as "an expanse" (*raki-a*) is often used for hammering out metal or flattening out earth, which suggests a basic meaning of "extending." The vault of heaven is here viewed either as a vast sheet of metal or as a layer of solid ice.

water from water The expanse was to serve as a separation between the celestial source of rain and the water on earth.

7. And it was so Henceforth this is the standard formula for expressing the fulfillment of God's command.

DAY THREE

9. water below the sky That is, the terrestrial waters.

the dry land The terrain that now has become visible.

---

day on which God, whose name and essence are one, established a world suitable for the divine Presence (Gen. R. 3:1).

6. expanse The word traditionally has been translated "firmament," a shell holding up the heavens. Once science understood that no physical barrier separates heaven from earth and that references to "opening the heavens" to cause rain to fall are poetic and metaphorical, medieval (Ibn Ezra) and modern commentaries (Malbim and this translation) came to understand the word as referring to the atmosphere that encircles our planet.

8. Sky In Hebrew: *shamayim*. The Midrash (Gen. R. 4:7) understands the word as a combination of *esh* (fire) and *mayim* (water), that is, the sun and the rain clouds. Were the rain clouds to extinguish the sun or were the sun to evaporate the rain clouds, the world would perish. Therefore, God works a daily miracle. Fire and water agree to co-exist peacefully so that the world can endure. Another midrash (Deut. R. 1:12) links this idea to a passage in our prayers: "May You who established peace in the heavens [teaching fire and water to get along] grant that kind of peace to us and to all the people Israel." In other words, we pray for the miracle that both individuals and nations with the power to harm each other will learn to get along in peace—even as fire and water do in the heavens.

On the second day we miss the formula "and God saw that it was good." The Sages explain this as due to the act of separation on that day, which may be necessary but is never wholly good, or because the process of separating the waters would not be concluded until the third day and one does not recite a blessing over an incomplete project (Rashi). The formula occurs twice on the third day (vv. 10 and 12). This is the source of the tradition that Tuesday (the third day) is a propitious day for weddings and other important occasions.

11And God said, "Let the earth sprout vegetation: seed-bearing plants, fruit trees of every kind on earth that bear fruit with the seed in it." And it was so. 12The earth brought forth vegetation: seed-bearing plants of every kind, and trees of every kind bearing fruit with the seed in it. And God saw that this was good. 13And there was evening and there was morning, a third day.

14God said, "Let there be lights in the expanse of the sky to separate day from night; they shall serve as signs for the set times—the days and the years; 15and they shall serve as lights in the expanse of the sky to shine upon the earth." And it was so. 16God made the two great lights, the greater light to dominate the day and the lesser light to dominate the night, and the stars. 17And God set them in the ex-

כִּי־טֽוֹב׃ 11וַיֹּ֣אמֶר אֱלֹהִ֗ים תַּֽדְשֵׁ֤א הָאָ֨רֶץ֙ דֶּ֗שֶׁא עֵ֚שֶׂב מַזְרִ֣יעַ זֶ֔רַע עֵ֣ץ פְּרִ֞י עֹ֤שֶׂה פְּרִי֙ לְמִינ֔וֹ אֲשֶׁ֥ר זַרְעוֹ־ב֖וֹ עַל־הָאָ֑רֶץ וַֽיְהִי־כֵֽן׃ 12וַתּוֹצֵ֨א הָאָ֜רֶץ דֶּ֠שֶׁא עֵ֣שֶׂב מַזְרִ֤יעַ זֶ֨רַע֙ לְמִינֵ֔הוּ וְעֵ֧ץ עֹֽשֶׂה־פְּרִ֛י אֲשֶׁ֥ר זַרְעוֹ־ב֖וֹ לְמִינֵ֑הוּ וַיַּ֥רְא אֱלֹהִ֖ים כִּי־טֽוֹב׃ 13וַֽיְהִי־עֶ֥רֶב וַֽיְהִי־בֹ֖קֶר י֥וֹם שְׁלִישִֽׁי׃ פ

14וַיֹּ֣אמֶר אֱלֹהִ֗ים יְהִ֤י מְאֹרֹת֙ בִּרְקִ֣יעַ הַשָּׁמַ֔יִם לְהַבְדִּ֕יל בֵּ֥ין הַיּ֖וֹם וּבֵ֣ין הַלָּ֑יְלָה וְהָי֤וּ לְאֹתֹת֙ וּלְמ֣וֹעֲדִ֔ים וּלְיָמִ֖ים וְשָׁנִֽים׃ 15וְהָי֤וּ לִמְאוֹרֹת֙ בִּרְקִ֣יעַ הַשָּׁמַ֔יִם לְהָאִ֖יר עַל־הָאָ֑רֶץ וַֽיְהִי־כֵֽן׃ 16וַיַּ֣עַשׂ אֱלֹהִ֔ים אֶת־שְׁנֵ֥י הַמְּאֹרֹ֖ת הַגְּדֹלִ֑ים אֶת־הַמָּא֤וֹר הַגָּדֹל֙ לְמֶמְשֶׁ֣לֶת הַיּ֔וֹם וְאֶת־הַמָּא֤וֹר הַקָּטֹן֙ לְמֶמְשֶׁ֣לֶת הַלַּ֔יְלָה וְאֵ֖ת הַכּֽוֹכָבִֽים׃ 17וַיִּתֵּ֥ן אֹתָ֛ם אֱלֹהִ֖ים בִּרְקִ֣יעַ הַשָּׁמָ֑יִם

---

11. Let the earth sprout According to the biblical worldview, it is God who endows the earth with generative powers. The forces of nature are not independent spiritual entities.

seed-bearing Endowed with the capacity for self-replication.

of every kind The various species.

THE SECOND GROUP OF CREATED OBJECTS (vv. 14–31)

The creations of days four to six are parallel to those of days one to three. The difference is that the former creations were endowed with motion and the latter were not.

DAY FOUR

14. Let there be lights This corresponds to

"Let there be light" in Gen. 1:3. The emergence of vegetation (v. 12) before the existence of the sun, the anonymity of the luminaries, and the detailed description serve to emphasize that the sun, moon, and stars are not divinities, as they were universally thought to be in other creation narratives. Rather, they are the creations of God, who assigned them the function of regulating the life rhythms of the universe.

signs for the set times The Hebrew terms for "signs" (*otot*) and for "set times" (*mo·adim*) are here a single thought expressed by two words. The "set times" are then specified as "the days and the years."

16. two great lights The general term "luminaries" is more precisely defined. No special role is assigned to the stars.

---

12. In every living thing, plant and animal alike, God has implanted the irrepressible urge to reproduce, to create life out of its own life.

14. God creates the sun and the moon on the fourth day. But light was created on the first day! The primordial light created then was so intense that humans would have been able to see everything happening in the world. God realized that humans could not endure seeing reality that clearly. To make the world tolerable

for human beings, God hid the primordial light until such time as humans would be able to stand it, replacing it with the light of the sun (BT Hag. 12a).

16. the two great lights, the greater . . . and the lesser The two luminaries originally were equal in size, prompting the moon to ask God, "Can two kings share a single crown?" God responded, "Make yourself smaller!" The moon cried, "Because I presented a proper claim, must

panse of the sky to shine upon the earth, 18to
dominate the day and the night, and to separate light from darkness. And God saw that this
was good. 19And there was evening and there
was morning, a fourth day.

20God said, "Let the waters bring forth
swarms of living creatures, and birds that fly
above the earth across the expanse of the sky."
21God created the great sea monsters, and all
the living creatures of every kind that creep,
which the waters brought forth in swarms,
and all the winged birds of every kind. And
God saw that this was good. 22God blessed
them, saying, "Be fertile and increase, fill the
waters in the seas, and let the birds increase on
the earth." 23And there was evening and there
was morning, a fifth day.

לְהָאִיר עַל־הָאָרֶץ׃ 18 וְלִמְשֹׁל בַּיּוֹם
וּבַלַּיְלָה וּֽלֲהַבְדִּיל בֵּין הָאוֹר וּבֵין הַחֹשֶׁךְ
וַיַּרְא אֱלֹהִים כִּי־טוֹב׃ 19 וַֽיְהִי־עֶרֶב וַֽיְהִי־
בֹקֶר יוֹם רְבִיעִי׃ פ
20 וַיֹּאמֶר אֱלֹהִים יִשְׁרְצוּ הַמַּיִם שֶׁרֶץ
נֶפֶשׁ חַיָּה וְעוֹף יְעוֹפֵף עַל־הָאָרֶץ עַל־פְּנֵי
רְקִיעַ הַשָּׁמָיִם׃ 21 וַיִּבְרָא אֱלֹהִים אֶת־
הַתַּנִּינִם* הַגְּדֹלִים וְאֵת כָּל־נֶפֶשׁ הַֽחַיָּה ׀
הָֽרֹמֶשֶׂת אֲשֶׁר שָׁרְצוּ הַמַּיִם לְמִֽינֵהֶם
וְאֵת כָּל־עוֹף כָּנָף לְמִינֵהוּ וַיַּרְא אֱלֹהִים
כִּי־טוֹב׃ 22 וַיְבָרֶךְ אֹתָם אֱלֹהִים לֵאמֹר
פְּרוּ וּרְבוּ וּמִלְאוּ אֶת־הַמַּיִם בַּיַּמִּים
וְהָעוֹף יִרֶב בָּאָרֶץ׃ 23 וַֽיְהִי־עֶרֶב וַֽיְהִי־
בֹקֶר יוֹם חֲמִישִׁי׃ פ

v. 21. חסר י׳ בתראה

DAY FIVE

20. Let the waters bring forth swarms In the Torah, water does not possess autonomous powers of procreation, as it does in ancient Near Eastern pagan mythologies. The waters generate marine life only in response to the divine command.

living creatures This term in Hebrew (*nefesh ḥayyah*) means, literally, "animate life," that which contains the breath of life. It is distinct from plant life, which was not considered to be living.

across the expanse of the sky Literally, "over the face of." The viewpoint is that of an observer on earth looking upward.

21. God created This is the first use of the verb *"bara"* since verse 1, signifying that these monsters, too, were creatures of God—rather than mythologic divine beings, as the Canaanites believed.

the great sea monsters Both the Hebrew word for these creatures (*tannin*) and the word "Leviathan" appear in Canaanite myths from the ancient city of Ugarit, as the name of a dragon god from earliest times who assisted Yam (god of the sea) in a battle against Baal (Canaanite god of fertility). Fragments of an Israelite version of this myth are present in several biblical poetic texts in which the forces of evil in this world are figuratively identified with "Tannin," the embodiment of the chaos that God had vanquished in earliest time. By stating that they were part of God's creation, the narrative deprives them of divinity.

22. God blessed them Animate creation receives the gift of fertility through the divine blessing of sexual reproduction. Plant life was not so blessed, because it was thought to have been equipped with the capacity for self-reproduction by nonsexual means.

I be diminished?" God recognized the justice of the moon's plea and compensated for its diminution by promising that only the moon would be seen by both day and night. It also would be accompanied by an honor guard of stars, and the Jewish people would calculate months and years according to its phases (BT Ḥul. 60b).

20. God adds a new dimension to the world of plants and streams by creating life.

22. God blesses the animals, giving them the power to produce new life even as God creates new life. The birth of any living creature is an instance of God's continuing creative power.

[24]God said, "Let the earth bring forth every kind of living creature: cattle, creeping things, and wild beasts of every kind." And it was so. [25]God made wild beasts of every kind and cattle of every kind, and all kinds of creeping things of the earth. And God saw that this was good. [26]And God said, "Let us make man in our image, after our likeness. They shall rule the fish of the sea, the birds of the sky, the cattle, the whole earth, and all the creeping things

24 וַיֹּאמֶר אֱלֹהִים תּוֹצֵא הָאָרֶץ נֶפֶשׁ חַיָּה
לְמִינָהּ בְּהֵמָה וָרֶמֶשׂ וְחַיְתוֹ־אֶרֶץ לְמִינָהּ
וַיְהִי־כֵן׃ 25 וַיַּעַשׂ אֱלֹהִים אֶת־חַיַּת הָאָרֶץ
לְמִינָהּ וְאֶת־הַבְּהֵמָה לְמִינָהּ וְאֵת כָּל־
רֶמֶשׂ הָאֲדָמָה לְמִינֵהוּ וַיַּרְא אֱלֹהִים כִּי־
טוֹב׃ 26 וַיֹּאמֶר אֱלֹהִים נַעֲשֶׂה אָדָם
בְּצַלְמֵנוּ כִּדְמוּתֵנוּ וְיִרְדּוּ בִדְגַת הַיָּם
וּבְעוֹף הַשָּׁמַיִם וּבַבְּהֵמָה וּבְכָל־הָאָרֶץ
וּבְכָל־הָרֶמֶשׂ הָרֹמֵשׂ עַל־הָאָרֶץ׃ 27 וַיִּבְרָא

DAY SIX

24. Let the earth bring forth This image of the earth producing animals may be related to the ancient concept of "Mother Earth," or it may simply be a figurative way of expressing the normal habitat of these creatures.

25. creeping things A general term for creatures whose bodies move close to the ground. Here it seems to encompass reptiles, creeping insects, and very small animals.

26. Let us make The extraordinary use of the first person plural here evokes the image of a heavenly court in which God is surrounded by an angelic multitude. This is the Israelite version of the assemblies of pagan deities prevalent in the mythologies of the ancient world.

man The Hebrew word *adam* is a general term for humankind. It encompasses both man and woman (as shown in vv. 27–28 and in 5:1–2). It never appears in the feminine or in the plural. In the first five chapters of Genesis, it also serves as the proper name Adam.

in our image, after our likeness In the ancient Near East, the ruling king was often described as the "image" or the "likeness" of a god, which served to elevate the monarch above ordinary mortals. In the Bible, this idea became democratized. Every human being is created "in the image of God"; each bears the stamp of royalty. Further, the symbols by which the gods are generally depicted in ancient Assyrian royal steles (Asshur by the winged disk, Shamash by the sun disk) are called "the image (*tzalamu*) of the great gods." Thus the description of mortals as "in the image of God" makes humankind the symbol of God's presence on earth.

They shall rule In the prevailing beliefs of the ancient world, the forces of nature are gods with the power to enslave humankind. The

---

26. So far, the account of Creation has alternated between activities on high (the heavens, the sun and moon, the birds) one day and activities on earth (the waters, the plants) the next. The Torah now turns to the creation of human beings, who will be a combination of the heavens and the earth, the sublime and the physical (Vilna Gaon).

Let us make man in our image Commentators in every generation have puzzled over the plural language in this verse. The Midrash envisions God consulting with the angels, perhaps hinting at a measure of divine ambivalence. Truth and Peace oppose creating humans on the grounds that such creatures would surely be deceitful and contentious. Love and Righteousness favor their creation, for without humanity, how can there be love and righteousness in the world? God sides with those favoring creation (Gen. R. 8:5).

Or perhaps God was speaking to the animals: Together let us fashion a unique creature in our image (yours and Mine), a creature like an animal in some ways—needing to eat, to sleep, to mate—and like God in some ways—capable of compassion, creativity, morality, and self-consciousness. Let the divine qualities manifest themselves in this culmination of the evolutionary process. Albo sees each animal species contributing its choicest quality to this new creature (*Ikkarim*, pt. 3, ch. 1).

They shall rule Animals and insects expand horizontally—to "fill" the earth. Humans grow vertically—to "master" the earth and serve as its custodians, by changing, controlling, and improving their environment (Zornberg).

אֱלֹהִים ׀ אֶת־הָאָדָם בְּצַלְמוֹ בְּצֶלֶם
אֱלֹהִים בָּרָא אֹתוֹ זָכָר וּנְקֵבָה בָּרָא אֹתָם׃
28 וַיְבָרֶךְ אֹתָם אֱלֹהִים וַיֹּאמֶר לָהֶם
אֱלֹהִים פְּרוּ וּרְבוּ וּמִלְאוּ אֶת־הָאָרֶץ
וְכִבְשֻׁהָ וּרְדוּ בִּדְגַת הַיָּם וּבְעוֹף הַשָּׁמַיִם
וּבְכָל־חַיָּה הָרֹמֶשֶׂת עַל־הָאָרֶץ׃
29 וַיֹּאמֶר אֱלֹהִים הִנֵּה נָתַתִּי לָכֶם אֶת־
כָּל־עֵשֶׂב ׀ זֹרֵעַ זֶרַע אֲשֶׁר עַל־פְּנֵי כָל־
הָאָרֶץ וְאֶת־כָּל־הָעֵץ אֲשֶׁר־בּוֹ פְרִי־עֵץ
זֹרֵעַ זָרַע לָכֶם יִהְיֶה לְאָכְלָה׃ 30 וּלְכָל־
חַיַּת הָאָרֶץ וּלְכָל־עוֹף הַשָּׁמַיִם וּלְכֹל ׀
רוֹמֵשׂ עַל־הָאָרֶץ אֲשֶׁר־בּוֹ נֶפֶשׁ חַיָּה

that creep on earth." 27 And God created man in His image, in the image of God He created him; male and female He created them. 28 God blessed them and God said to them, "Be fertile and increase, fill the earth and master it; and rule the fish of the sea, the birds of the sky, and all the living things that creep on earth."

29 God said, "See, I give you every seed-bearing plant that is upon all the earth, and every tree that has seed-bearing fruit; they shall be yours for food. 30 And to all the animals on land, to all the birds of the sky, and to everything that creeps on earth, in which there is the breath of life, [I give] all the green plants for food." And

words of this verse, in contrast, declare mortals to be free agents with the God-given power to control nature.

27. male and female Sexual difference is not noted regarding beasts in the Creation narrative. Human sexuality is a gift of God woven into the fabric of life.

28. God blessed them and God said to them God addresses the man and the woman directly. The transcendent God of Creation becomes the immanent God, the personal God who enters into communion with human beings.

Be fertile and increase These words are uttered as a blessing, not a command. Only when repeated in 9:7, after the depopulation of the earth by the Flood, are they a command.

30. for food God now makes provision for sustaining human and animal life. It is a reminder that the man and the woman are entirely dependent on God's benevolence.

---

27. Every human has irreducible worth and dignity, because every human is fashioned in the image of God. The Second Commandment (Exod. 20) forbids fashioning an image of God. We do not need one because every person represents the divine. "A human king strikes coins in his image, and every one of them is identical. God creates every person with the die of the first human being [i.e., in the divine image], and each one is unique" (BT Sanh. 38a).

male and female The Midrash (Gen. R. 8:1) alludes to a legend, also found in Plato's *Symposium* and in other ancient traditions, that the first human being was actually a pair of twins attached to each other, one male and one female. God divided them and commanded them to reunite, to find the other person who will make each of them complete again, in order to reproduce and attain wholeness. (The Midrash takes the words "and God blessed them" to mean "God presided over their wedding ceremony" [Gen. R. 8:13].) This would imply that Eve was not fashioned out of Adam's rib as an afterthought but was created at the same time as Adam, as half of the first human creature. (The word translated "rib," *tzela,* in 2:21–2, means "side" in Exod. 26:20 and elsewhere in biblical Hebrew.)

29. According to the Torah, humans were meant to be vegetarians. Eating meat would be

HALAKHAH L'MA·ASEH

1:28 Be fertile and increase According to the Mishnah, each married couple must have at least one son and one daughter to fulfill this commandment (M Yev. 6:6). However, Jewish law and historical practice urge Jews to have as many children as possible (BT Yev. 62b). Couples who cannot have children through their own sexual intercourse are, of course, exempt from this commandment. They may pursue fertility treatments, but they are not obligated to do so.

it was so. 31 And God saw all that He had made,
and found it very good. And there was evening
and there was morning, the sixth day.

אֶת־כָּל־יֶרֶק עֵשֶׂב לְאָכְלָה וַיְהִי־כֵן׃
31 וַיַּרְא אֱלֹהִים אֶת־כָּל־אֲשֶׁר עָשָׂה
וְהִנֵּה־טוֹב מְאֹד וַיְהִי־עֶרֶב וַיְהִי־בֹקֶר יוֹם
הַשִּׁשִּׁי׃ פ

2 The heaven and the earth were finished,
and all their array. 2 On the seventh day God
finished the work that He had been doing, and
He ceased on the seventh day from all the work

ב וַיְכֻלּוּ הַשָּׁמַיִם וְהָאָרֶץ וְכָל־צְבָאָם׃
2 וַיְכַל אֱלֹהִים בַּיּוֹם הַשְּׁבִיעִי מְלַאכְתּוֹ
אֲשֶׁר עָשָׂה וַיִּשְׁבֹּת בַּיּוֹם הַשְּׁבִיעִי מִכָּל־

31. very good A judgment on the totality of Creation, now completed.

the sixth day The definite article in Hebrew, used here and with the seventh day, points to the special character of these days within the scheme of Creation.

THE SEVENTH DAY (2:1–3)

The account of Creation opened with a statement about God; it now closes with a statement about God. The seventh day is the LORD's day, through which all the creativity of the preceding days achieves fulfillment.

1. all their array The word translated as "array" (*tzava*) usually applies only to heaven. In this phrase, it is extended to apply to the earth as well.

2. On the seventh day That is, Creation was completed with the act of cessation from work.

God finished See Exod. 40:33, which suggests a parallel between the completion of the tabernacle in the wilderness and the completion of the creation of the world.

He ceased This is the primary meaning of the Hebrew verb שבת. The idea of resting is secondary. The use of the verb anticipates the later establishment of *Shabbat.*

---

a later concession to their willful appetites (cf. Gen. 9:3).

31. very good According to the Midrash, this includes the egocentric drive, the *yeitzer ha-ra,* sometimes described as the "evil impulse." Without it, no one would build a house, establish a business, marry, or raise a family (Gen. R. 9:7). According to Meir, "very good" (*tov m'od*) even includes the inevitability of death: *tov mot,* "death is good" (Gen. R. 9:5). Knowing that our days are numbered invests our deeds and choices with greater significance. Although the death of someone we love is searingly painful, we can recognize that a world in which people die and new souls are born offers the promise of renewal and improvement more than a world in which the original people live forever.

As the chapter concludes, God surveys with satisfaction the newly fashioned world, teeming with life in all its variety, culminating in the creation of that unpredictable creature, the human being.

CHAPTER 2

The opening verses of chapter 2 belong thematically to chapter 1. The division of the Torah into chapters is a late development, by non-Jewish authorities. Jewish tradition divides the Torah into *parashiyyot.*

1. were finished A talmudic passage reads, "They (that is, people) finished the heavens and the earth." God left the world a bit incomplete so that we might become God's partners in the work of Creation. We complete God's work

HALAKHAH L'MA·ASEH

2:1–3 The heaven and the earth The Rabbis include these verses in the Friday evening service and in the Friday evening *kiddush* recited over wine. In refraining from creative or constructive work on *Shabbat,* we emulate our Creator, who ceased from all the work of creation.

that He had done. [3]And God blessed the seventh day and declared it holy, because on it God
ceased from all the work of creation that He
had done. [4]Such is the story of heaven and
earth when they were created.

מְלַאכְתּוֹ אֲשֶׁר עָשָׂה׃ 3 וַיְבָרֶךְ אֱלֹהִים
אֶת־יוֹם הַשְּׁבִיעִי וַיְקַדֵּשׁ אֹתוֹ כִּי בוֹ
שָׁבַת מִכָּל־מְלַאכְתּוֹ אֲשֶׁר־בָּרָא אֱלֹהִים
שני לַעֲשׂוֹת׃ פ 4 אֵלֶּה תוֹלְדוֹת הַשָּׁמַיִם
וְהָאָרֶץ בְּהִבָּרְאָם*

v. 4. ה' זעירא לפי נוסחים מקובלים

3. God blessed . . . declared it holy Unlike the blessings in Gen. 1:22,28, which are specific and relate to living creatures, this blessing is undefined and pertains to time itself. God has already established sovereignty over space; here God is perceived as sovereign over time as well.

holy This first use of the biblical concept of holiness relates to time. This is a striking contrast to the view of the Babylonians, whose creation epic concludes with the erection of a temple, thereby asserting the sanctification of space.

all the work of creation that He had done The Hebrew words read, literally, "all His work that God created to do." Ibn Ezra and Radak took the final verb (*la·asot*) as connoting "[for man] to [continue to] do [thenceforth]."

EDEN AND THE EXPULSION: THE HUMAN CONDITION (2:4–3:24)

The narrative turns from the God of Creation to the wretched condition of humankind. What disrupted the harmony between God, man, and nature? How are we to explain the harsh, hostile workings of nature, the recalcitrance of the soil to arduous human labor, and the existence of evil?

4. Such is . . . when they were created This first half of the verse completes the first story of Creation. Note in this verse the inversion of the phrases "heaven and earth" (*ha-shamayim v'ha-aretz*) and "earth and heaven" (*eretz v'sha-mayim*). It signals a shift in focus between the two creation stories.

---

of imposing order on chaos when we process wheat into bread, find cures for disease, sustain the poor, strengthen families. "One who recites these verses (1–3) on Friday night (*leil Shabbat*), acknowledging God as the Creator, helps God complete the work of Creation" (BT Shab. 119b).

3. The true conclusion of the work of Creation was not the fashioning of the first human, but the institution of *Shabbat*, imposing on the world a rhythm of work and leisure, changing and leaving alone. There could not have been *Shabbat* before there were human beings, for animals are controlled by time; but humans have the ability to order time, to impose their purposes on time, to choose to set days aside for special purposes, to celebrate holy days and anniversaries.

"To set apart one day a week for freedom, a day on which we would not use the instruments which have been so easily turned into weapons of destruction, a day for being with ourselves, a day of detachment from the vulgar, a day on which we stop worshiping the idols of technical civilization, a day of armistice in the economic struggle with our fellow men—is there any institution that holds out a greater hope for human progress than the Sabbath?" (A. J. Heschel).

In verse 3, God is described as "blessing" *Shabbat*. "To bless," or to sanctify, is to set something apart as special. It means partaking of a higher level of spiritual worth. This concept could be invoked only when there were human beings in the world.

The Vilna Gaon suggests that God ceased work on the seventh day, even though the world was still somewhat incomplete, as an example to us to put aside our unfinished business on Friday afternoon and leave the world as it is on *Shabbat*.

Legend has it that God created other worlds before this one, but was not pleased with any of them. One world was based on the principle of strict justice; anyone who did wrong was punished. Every righteous person who gave in to temptation was struck down. Rejecting that world, God fashioned a world based on the

When the LORD God made earth and
heaven—5when no shrub of the field was yet
on earth and no grasses of the field had yet
sprouted, because the LORD God had not sent
rain upon the earth and there was no man
to till the soil, 6but a flow would well up from
the ground and water the whole surface of
the earth—7the LORD God formed man from
the dust of the earth. He blew into his nostrils
the breath of life, and man became a living
being.
8The LORD God planted a garden in Eden, in

בְּיוֹם עֲשׂוֹת יְהֹוָה אֱלֹהִים אֶרֶץ וְשָׁמָיִם׃
5 וְכֹל ׀ שִׂיחַ הַשָּׂדֶה טֶרֶם יִהְיֶה בָאָרֶץ
וְכָל־עֵשֶׂב הַשָּׂדֶה טֶרֶם יִצְמָח כִּי לֹא
הִמְטִיר יְהֹוָה אֱלֹהִים עַל־הָאָרֶץ וְאָדָם
אַיִן לַעֲבֹד אֶת־הָאֲדָמָה׃ 6 וְאֵד יַעֲלֶה מִן־
הָאָרֶץ וְהִשְׁקָה אֶת־כָּל־פְּנֵי־הָאֲדָמָה׃
7 וַיִּיצֶר יְהֹוָה אֱלֹהִים אֶת־הָאָדָם עָפָר
מִן־הָאֲדָמָה וַיִּפַּח בְּאַפָּיו נִשְׁמַת חַיִּים
וַיְהִי הָאָדָם לְנֶפֶשׁ חַיָּה׃
8 וַיִּטַּע יְהֹוָה אֱלֹהִים גַּן־בְּעֵדֶן מִקֶּדֶם וַיָּשֶׂם

THE CREATION OF MAN (vv. 4b–7)

The second Creation story begins with the second half of verse 4.

4. the LORD God This combination of the unique, personal divine name *YHVH* with the general term *elohim* appears 20 times in this narrative but only once again in the Torah (in Exod. 9:30). *YHVH* signifies compassion (as well as protection and personal relationship). Its combination here with *elohim* (signifying justice) is to indicate that these are two aspects of the one God.

5. no shrub in the field This passage simply describes the initial, barren state of the earth after the formation of the dry land, which was briefly recorded in Gen. 1:9–10. The earth itself is still a desert, lacking rain, greenery, and humankind.

rain Rain is a blessing from God, not solely a natural phenomenon.

no man to till the soil Agriculture is regarded as the original vocation of human beings; the earth is integral to their being.

6. a flow The subterranean waters, whose existence is presupposed here, are moistening the arid earth. This makes it receptive to the growth of vegetation, enabling it to provide the raw material proper for the molding of the first mortal.

7. the dust of the earth In 1:27, nothing was said about the substance from which man was created. Here it is given as "dust," a word that can be used synonymously with "clay."

formed man The verb "formed" (*va-yitzer*) is often used in the Bible to describe the activity of a potter (*yotzer*). The creation of the first human being is here portrayed with God first shaping and then animating the clay soil, an image widespread in the ancient world.

man . . . earth In Hebrew they are *adam* and *adamah,* a wordplay that expresses humankind's earthly origin.

the breath of life The Hebrew phrase *"nishmat ḥayyim"* appears only in this verse. It matches the unique nature of the human body which, unlike the bodies of creatures in the animal world, is given life directly by God.

THE GARDEN OF EDEN (vv. 8–17)

The first home of mortals is a garden planted by God. An ancient Sumerian myth tells of an idyllic island, a "pure, clean, bright" land where all nature is at peace, where beasts of prey and tame cattle live together in tranquility. Sickness and old age are unknown on this island called Dilmun, now identified with the modern island of Bahrain in the Persian Gulf. The *Gilgamesh* epic likewise knows of a mythic garden of jewels. The

---

principles of compassion and forgiveness; God understood why some people were driven to do wrong and forgave them for it. As a result, people who saw their neighbors getting away with criminal activity did likewise. Finally, God fashioned this world based on both law and compassion, which is why Scripture (in v. 4) uses both divine names: *"YHVH"* represents the principle of compassion and *"Elohim"* represents the principle of justice.

7. "Thus the human being is a combination of the earthly and the divine" (Rashi). After death, the body returns to the earth, its source, and the soul to God, its source.

שָׁ֔ם אֶת־הָֽאָדָ֖ם אֲשֶׁ֥ר יָצָֽר׃ 9 וַיַּצְמַ֞ח
יְהוָ֤ה אֱלֹהִים֙ מִן־הָ֣אֲדָמָ֔ה כָּל־עֵ֛ץ נֶחְמָ֥ד
לְמַרְאֶ֖ה וְט֣וֹב לְמַאֲכָ֑ל וְעֵ֤ץ הַֽחַיִּים֙ בְּת֣וֹךְ
הַגָּ֔ן וְעֵ֕ץ הַדַּ֖עַת ט֥וֹב וָרָֽע׃
10 וְנָהָר֙ יֹצֵ֣א מֵעֵ֔דֶן לְהַשְׁק֖וֹת אֶת־הַגָּ֑ן
וּמִשָּׁם֙ יִפָּרֵ֔ד וְהָיָ֖ה לְאַרְבָּעָ֥ה רָאשִֽׁים׃
11 שֵׁ֥ם הָֽאֶחָ֖ד פִּישׁ֑וֹן ה֣וּא הַסֹּבֵ֗ב אֵ֚ת
כָּל־אֶ֣רֶץ הַֽחֲוִילָ֔ה אֲשֶׁר־שָׁ֖ם הַזָּהָֽב׃
12 וּזֲהַ֛ב הָאָ֥רֶץ הַהִ֖וא ט֑וֹב שָׁ֥ם הַבְּדֹ֖לַח
וְאֶ֥בֶן הַשֹּֽׁהַם׃ 13 וְשֵֽׁם־הַנָּהָ֥ר הַשֵּׁנִ֖י גִּ֑יחוֹן
ה֣וּא הַסּוֹבֵ֔ב אֵ֖ת כָּל־אֶ֥רֶץ כּֽוּשׁ׃ 14 וְשֵׁ֨ם
הַנָּהָ֤ר הַשְּׁלִישִׁי֙ חִדֶּ֔קֶל ה֥וּא הַהֹלֵ֖ךְ

the east, and placed there the man whom He
had formed. 9 And from the ground the LORD
God caused to grow every tree that was pleasing to the sight and good for food, with the tree
of life in the middle of the garden, and the tree
of knowledge of good and bad.
10 A river issues from Eden to water the garden, and it then divides and becomes four
branches. 11 The name of the first is Pishon,
the one that winds through the whole land of
Havilah, where the gold is. (12 The gold of that
land is good; bdellium is there, and lapis lazuli.) 13 The name of the second river is Gihon,
the one that winds through the whole land of
Cush. 14 The name of the third river is Tigris,

Genesis account omits all mythological details, is very sparing in its account of the garden's nature and function, and places gold and jewels in a natural setting.

8. a garden in Eden The Hebrew word for "garden" is *gan.* The ancient Greek version of the Bible (Septuagint) translates this word as *paradeisos,* from the Old Persian *pairi-daeza,* meaning "an enclosed park." This translation was adopted by the Latin version (Vulgate) and went from there into other European languages; witness "paradise" in English. Eden is the geographic location of the garden. The name means "luxuriance." Because *eiden* was interpreted to mean "pleasure," the word "paradise" took on an exclusively religious connotation as the place of reward for the righteous after death.

9. caused to grow every tree The verse tells nothing about the garden except that it is a tree park where food, nutritious and delectable, is always at hand.

the tree of life We know from 3:22 that the fruit of this tree—either through a single bite or through frequent eating—could grant immortality to the eater. Man, created from perishable matter, was mortal from the outset, although the possibility of immortality lay within his grasp. The "tree of life" is not included in the prohibition of verse 17.

the tree of knowledge of good and bad Ibn Ezra, followed by many modern scholars, explained "knowledge of good and bad" as referring to carnal knowledge, because the first human experience after eating the forbidden fruit is the consciousness of nudity accompanied by shame. Most likely, "good and bad" is a phrase that means "everything," implying a mature perception of reality. Thus "knowledge of good and bad" is to be understood as the capacity to make independent judgments concerning human welfare.

THE RIVERS OF PARADISE (vv. 10–14)

The story is unaccountably interrupted by a description of the garden's geographic setting. The reader is left wondering about the role of the two trees.

10. A river issues from Eden Eden was on a mountain (see Ezek. 28:14). The garden does not depend on the caprice of seasonal rainfall. Its source of life-nourishing water is a river somewhere in Eden outside the garden, which it irrigates as it passes through.

12. Bdellium This is mentioned again only in Num. 11:7, where it is assumed to be a well-known substance, either a precious stone or a valued aromatic resin called *bdellion* by the Greeks.

lapis lazuli The Hebrew word *shoham* is an oft-mentioned precious stone, now of uncertain identity.

13. Gihon The name of a spring in a valley in Jerusalem.

Cush In the Bible, Cush often refers to Nubia. Here, however, it refers to Babylonia and designates one of the many rivers found there.

the one that flows east of Asshur. And the fourth river is the Euphrates.

[15]The LORD God took the man and placed him in the garden of Eden, to till it and tend it. [16]And the LORD God commanded the man, saying, "Of every tree of the garden you are free to eat; [17]but as for the tree of knowledge of good and bad, you must not eat of it; for as soon as you eat of it, you shall die."

קִדְמַ֣ת אַשּׁ֑וּר וְהַנָּהָ֥ר הָרְבִיעִ֖י ה֥וּא פְרָֽת׃
15 וַיִּקַּ֛ח יְהֹוָ֥ה אֱלֹהִ֖ים אֶת־הָֽאָדָ֑ם וַיַּנִּחֵ֣הוּ
בְגַן־עֵ֔דֶן לְעָבְדָ֖הּ וּלְשָׁמְרָֽהּ׃ 16 וַיְצַו֙ יְהֹוָ֣ה
אֱלֹהִ֔ים עַל־הָֽאָדָ֖ם לֵאמֹ֑ר מִכֹּ֥ל עֵֽץ־הַגָּ֖ן
אָכֹ֥ל תֹּאכֵֽל׃ 17 וּמֵעֵ֗ץ הַדַּ֙עַת֙ ט֣וֹב וָרָ֔ע
לֹ֥א תֹאכַ֖ל מִמֶּ֑נּוּ כִּ֗י בְּי֛וֹם אֲכׇלְךָ֥ מִמֶּ֖נּוּ
מ֥וֹת תָּמֽוּת׃

14. east of Asshur The Hebrew word translated here as "east of" (*kidmat*) literally means "in front of," which is eastward from the vantage point of one who faces the rising sun, the standard orientation in the Bible. Asshur may be either the city of Asshur, west of the Tigris, or the larger region of Assyria, to which the city gave its name.

Euphrates To an Israelite, this great river needed no further description.

THE PROHIBITION (vv. 15–17)

15. took the man The opening line of this section repeats the contents of Gen. 2:8. It resumes the narrative interrupted by the digression of verses 10–14.

to till it and tend it It is the responsibility of the man to nurture and conserve the garden, by the labor of his hands. No strenuous exertion is required of him, for nature responds readily to his efforts.

16. you are free to eat As in chapter 1, the assumption here is that humankind originally was vegetarian.

THE CREATION OF WOMAN (vv. 18–24)

The ancient Near East has preserved no other

---

15. to till it and tend it From the outset, God intended humans to be farmers, to work the soil. Thus they might learn that success depends both on their efforts and on the blessings of Heaven—that is, favorable weather (Levi Yitzḥak of Berdichev). Presumably, God could have created a maintenance-free world but decided that it would be better for us to take responsibility for the world we live in. We tend to value something more when we have invested our own labor in it.

16. From this verse the Sages derived "the Noahide laws" (*mitzvot b'nei No·aḥ*) to explain why Adam and Cain should be held responsible for their acts. These are laws incumbent on all of humankind (literally, incumbent on all the descendants of Noah). They include the prohibitions of blasphemy, idolatry, adultery, murder, and robbery. They also enjoin the establishment of a just system of laws and courts. After the Flood, eating the limb of a living animal was added to the list of prohibitions. Gentiles are not expected to obey all the laws of the Torah. They are required, however, to obey the Noahide laws if they are to live in a land governed by Jews.

17. you must not eat Why did God create the tree if eating from it was forbidden? The usual interpretation teaches that having a commandment would give the human being an opportunity to choose morality and obedience. A modern commentator (see 3:16) takes it not as a prohibition but as a warning: If you acquire a knowledge of good and evil, life will become infinitely more complicated and painful for you than it is for any other creature.

as soon as you eat of it, you shall die Perhaps this should be understood as, "you shall realize that you are mortal. You will have to live with the knowledge that one day you will die, a burden of awareness that no other creature bears" (Ramban).

HALAKHAH L'MA·ASEH

2:15 to till it and to tend it This requirement that we preserve nature even while we use it underlies classical and contemporary concern for ecology in Jewish law and thought.

18 The LORD God said, "It is not good for man
to be alone; I will make a fitting helper for him."
19 And the LORD God formed out of the earth all
the wild beasts and all the birds of the sky, and
brought them to the man to see what he would
call them; and whatever the man called each
living creature, that would be its name. 20 And
the man gave names to all the cattle and to the
birds of the sky and to all the wild beasts; but for
Adam no fitting helper was found. 21 So the
LORD God cast a deep sleep upon the man;
and, while he slept, He took one of his ribs
and closed up the flesh at that spot. 22 And the
LORD God fashioned the rib that He had taken

18 וַיֹּאמֶר יְהוָה אֱלֹהִים לֹא־טוֹב הֱיוֹת
הָאָדָם לְבַדּוֹ אֶעֱשֶׂה־לּוֹ עֵזֶר כְּנֶגְדּוֹ׃
19 וַיִּצֶר יְהוָה אֱלֹהִים מִן־הָאֲדָמָה כָּל־
חַיַּת הַשָּׂדֶה וְאֵת כָּל־עוֹף הַשָּׁמַיִם וַיָּבֵא
אֶל־הָאָדָם לִרְאוֹת מַה־יִּקְרָא־לוֹ וְכֹל
אֲשֶׁר יִקְרָא־לוֹ הָאָדָם נֶפֶשׁ חַיָּה הוּא
שלישי שְׁמוֹ׃ 20 וַיִּקְרָא הָאָדָם שֵׁמוֹת לְכָל־
הַבְּהֵמָה וּלְעוֹף הַשָּׁמַיִם וּלְכֹל חַיַּת
הַשָּׂדֶה וּלְאָדָם לֹא־מָצָא עֵזֶר כְּנֶגְדּוֹ׃
21 וַיַּפֵּל יְהוָה אֱלֹהִים ׀ תַּרְדֵּמָה עַל־
הָאָדָם וַיִּישָׁן וַיִּקַּח אַחַת מִצַּלְעֹתָיו וַיִּסְגֹּר
בָּשָׂר תַּחְתֶּנָּה׃ 22 וַיִּבֶן יְהוָה אֱלֹהִים ׀ אֶת־

independent narrative of the creation of primordial woman. Now, with her appearance, the biblical account of Creation is complete.

18. I will make This declaration of intent balances that which precedes the creation of the man in 1:26. It is God who takes the initiative to provide a wife for Adam.

a fitting helper The Hebrew is, literally, "a helper corresponding to him." The Hebrew word *"eizer"* (helper), used here to describe the intended role of the woman, is often applied to God in relation to mortals.

19. The LORD God formed The narrative now focuses on human mastery over the animals, whose creation is mentioned here incidentally, without any intent to indicate their place in the order of Creation.

20. And the man gave names Clearly, the first man is assumed to have been endowed with a level of intellect capable of differentiating between one creature and another, and with the linguistic ability to coin an appropriate name for each. By assigning to man the role of naming terrestrial creatures, God bestows human authority and dominion over them. See Comment to 1:5.

Adam The vocalization *l'adam* (to Adam) rather than *la-adam* (to the man) makes the word a proper name for the first time, probably because the narrative now speaks of the man as a personality rather than an archetypal human.

no fitting helper was found Man, in his review of the subhuman creation during the naming process, becomes aware of his uniqueness, of his inability to feel direct kinship with the other animate beings.

21. a deep sleep The Hebrew word *tardemah* is used for a divinely induced heavy sleep. Here it has the function of rendering the man insensible to the pain of the surgical procedure and oblivious to God at work.

one of his ribs The rib here connotes a physical link and signifies the partnership and companionship of male and female.

22. The LORD God fashioned Literally, "built"; the only use of this verb in the Creation narratives. It echoes ancient Near Eastern poetic traditions, in which it is widely used for the action of the deity in creating humankind.

---

18. Until now, everything God made was seen as good. For the first time, something is seen as "not good"—human loneliness in the absence of a human association. The Hebrew for "a fitting helper" (*eizer k'negdo*) can be understood to mean "a helpmate equivalent to him." It need not imply that the female is to be subordinate or that her role would be only as a facilitator.

21. took one of his ribs Or separated one side (Rashi). See Comment to 1:27.

22. This is alluded to in one of the seven blessings of the traditional Jewish wedding ceremony (*sheva b'rakhot*).

from the man into a woman; and He brought
her to the man. [23]Then the man said,
"This one at last
Is bone of my bones
And flesh of my flesh.
This one shall be called Woman,
For from man was she taken."
[24]Hence a man leaves his father and mother
and clings to his wife, so that they become one
flesh.

[25]The two of them were naked, the man and
his wife, yet they felt no shame. [1]Now the ser-
3 pent was the shrewdest of all the wild
beasts that the LORD God had made. He

הַצֵּלָע אֲשֶׁר־לָקַח מִן־הָאָדָם לְאִשָּׁה
וַיְבִאֶהָ אֶל־הָאָדָם׃ 23 וַיֹּאמֶר הָאָדָם
זֹאת הַפַּעַם
עֶצֶם מֵעֲצָמַי
וּבָשָׂר מִבְּשָׂרִי
לְזֹאת יִקָּרֵא אִשָּׁה
כִּי מֵאִישׁ לֻקְחָה־זֹּאת׃
24 עַל־כֵּן יַעֲזָב־אִישׁ אֶת־אָבִיו וְאֶת־אִמּוֹ
וְדָבַק בְּאִשְׁתּוֹ וְהָיוּ לְבָשָׂר אֶחָד׃

25 וַיִּהְיוּ שְׁנֵיהֶם עֲרוּמִּים הָאָדָם וְאִשְׁתּוֹ
ג וְלֹא יִתְבֹּשָׁשׁוּ׃ 1 וְהַנָּחָשׁ הָיָה עָרוּם
מִכֹּל חַיַּת הַשָּׂדֶה אֲשֶׁר עָשָׂה יְהוָה

He brought her to the man This verse conveys the idea that God established the institution of marriage.

23. Then the man said Man's first recorded speech is a cry of elation at seeing the woman.

This one at last And not any of the animals.

shall be called Woman The power of naming implies authority, and the text here reflects the social reality of the ancient Near East. Yet the man gives her not a personal name, but a generic name (*ishah*), one that sounds like his own (*ish*), although derived from a different root. This implies that he acknowledges woman to be his equal.

24. Hence The Hebrew term translated "hence" (*al ken*) is not part of the narration, but introduces an observation on the part of the narrator, who attributes the institution of marriage to this specific event in the past.

25. they felt no shame The Hebrew word for "shame" here expresses mutuality; that is, "they felt no shame for each other."

THE TRANSGRESSION (3:1–7)

God's Creation was termed "very good"; the life of man and woman in the Garden of Eden has been described as idyllic. How, then, did evil come into existence?

1. ***the serpent*** A creature of enduring mystery. Throughout the ancient world, it was endowed with divine or semidivine qualities, venerated (as a symbol of fertility, immortality, health, occult wisdom, and chaotic evil), and often worshiped. The serpent in this narrative, however, is reduced to one of the creatures "that the LORD God had made." It possesses no occult powers. Its role is to place before the woman the enticing nature of evil and to fan her desire for it.

the shrewdest The serpent's cunning reveals itself in the way it frames the question, in its

---

23. This one shall be called Woman The first female has two names, symbolizing her double function in life. She is Ishah, "woman," the complement/companion of Ish, "man." And she is Eve, "mother," in her procreative role (*Arama*).

24. they became one flesh When two animals mate, it is simply a matter of biology, perpetuation of the species. When a man and a woman join in love, they are seeking more than reproduction. They are seeking wholeness, striving to recapture that sense of total union with another person that we are told existed at the very beginning.

25. they felt no shame They were capable of sexual activity ("be fertile and increase," 1:28) but had not come to associate their sexual organs with misuse, lust, or shame.

said to the woman, "Did God really say: You
shall not eat of any tree of the garden?" 2The
woman replied to the serpent, "We may eat of
the fruit of the other trees of the garden. 3It is
only about fruit of the tree in the middle of the
garden that God said: 'You shall not eat of it or
touch it, lest you die.'" 4And the serpent said to

אֱלֹהִים וַיֹּאמֶר אֶל־הָאִשָּׁה אַף כִּי־אָמַר
אֱלֹהִים לֹא תֹאכְלוּ מִכֹּל עֵץ הַגָּן׃
2 וַתֹּאמֶר הָאִשָּׁה אֶל־הַנָּחָשׁ מִפְּרִי עֵץ־
הַגָּן נֹאכֵל׃ 3 וּמִפְּרִי הָעֵץ אֲשֶׁר בְּתוֹךְ־הַגָּן
אָמַר אֱלֹהִים לֹא תֹאכְלוּ מִמֶּנּוּ וְלֹא תִגְּעוּ
בּוֹ פֶּן־תְּמֻתוּן׃ 4 וַיֹּאמֶר הַנָּחָשׁ אֶל־הָאִשָּׁה

knowledge of the divine prohibition, and in its claim to be able to probe God's mind and intent. Note the link of *arum* (shrewd) here, with *arumim* (naked) in 2:25.

to the woman She, rather than her husband, is approached because she has not received the prohibition directly from God. She is, therefore, the more vulnerable of the two, the more susceptible to the serpent's manipulation.

say The serpent subtly softens the severity of the prohibition by using this word in place of the original "command." Then it deliberately misquotes God so that the woman cannot give a one-word reply but is drawn into a conversation that forces her to focus on the forbidden tree that God had not mentioned.

3. or touch it In correcting the serpent, she either unconsciously exaggerates the severity of the divine prohibition or is quoting what her husband told her.

4. You are not going to die By emphatically contradicting the very words God used in 2:17, the serpent allays her fears.

CHAPTER 3

The account of Adam and Eve disobeying God's command in the Garden of Eden is a strange and elusive story. If they gained a knowledge of good and evil by eating the forbidden fruit, does that mean that they did not know good from evil before that? If so, how could they be held accountable for doing wrong? Moreover, we note that neither here nor anywhere else in the Hebrew Bible is their act characterized as a sin, let alone the Original Sin. There is no indication that this represents a permanent rupture of the divine–human relationship. God expels Adam and Eve from Eden, which can be seen as a punishment. But it can also be seen as a painful but necessary "graduation" from the innocence of childhood to the problem-laden world of living as morally responsible adults. And because God fashions clothing for them to protect them against the rigors of the world outside the Garden, it seems clear that God is not unalterably angry at our first ancestors.

Hirsch sees the story as representing the eternal encounter between animal nature (driven by instinct and physical attractiveness) and human nature (capable of saying no to temptation).

1. Who is the serpent and what is its role in the story? Many commentators see it as jealous of the special gifts and status of human beings and determined to cause a breach between them and God. Others see it as the embodiment of temptation, particularly sexual temptation. The serpent may be a phallic image, and the tree of knowledge may refer to the sexual awareness that accompanies coming of age. Still others see the serpent as the spirit of rebelliousness that arrives when a person moves from the innocence of childhood to adolescence, resenting the imposition of rules. If the serpent represents something within the human soul rather than outside of it, that would explain why it alone of all the animals has the power of speech. Some commentators see the serpent as God's agent: God wants Adam and Eve to grow up and become fully human, acquiring a knowledge of good and evil, rather than remaining at the level of obedient animals.

3. nor touch it God, however, did not prohibit touching the tree (cf. 2:17). This is an example of the dangerous tendency of religion to multiply prohibitions to safeguard the essence of the law. When the prohibitions become too onerous, people may disregard them and come to disregard the basic intent of the law itself. "Make a fence too high and it may fall and destroy what it was meant to protect" (Gen. R. 19:3).

the woman, "You are not going to die, [5]but
God knows that as soon as you eat of it your
eyes will be opened and you will be like divine
beings who know good and bad." [6]When the
woman saw that the tree was good for eating
and a delight to the eyes, and that the tree was
desirable as a source of wisdom, she took of its
fruit and ate. She also gave some to her husband, and he ate. [7]Then the eyes of both of
them were opened and they perceived that
they were naked; and they sewed together fig
leaves and made themselves loincloths.

[8]They heard the sound of the LORD God
moving about in the garden at the breezy time

לֹא־מ֖וֹת תְּמֻתֽוּן׃ 5 כִּ֚י יֹדֵ֣עַ אֱלֹהִ֔ים כִּ֗י
בְּיוֹם֙ אֲכָלְכֶ֣ם מִמֶּ֔נּוּ וְנִפְקְח֖וּ עֵֽינֵיכֶ֑ם
וִהְיִיתֶם֙ כֵּֽאלֹהִ֔ים יֹדְעֵ֖י ט֥וֹב וָרָֽע׃ 6 וַתֵּ֣רֶא
הָֽאִשָּׁ֡ה כִּ֣י טוֹב֩ הָעֵ֨ץ לְמַאֲכָ֜ל וְכִ֧י תַֽאֲוָה־
ה֣וּא לָעֵינַ֗יִם וְנֶחְמָ֤ד הָעֵץ֙ לְהַשְׂכִּ֔יל וַתִּקַּ֥ח
מִפִּרְי֖וֹ וַתֹּאכַ֑ל וַתִּתֵּ֧ן גַּם־לְאִישָׁ֛הּ עִמָּ֖הּ
וַיֹּאכַֽל׃ 7 וַתִּפָּקַ֙חְנָה֙ עֵינֵ֣י שְׁנֵיהֶ֔ם וַיֵּ֣דְע֔וּ
כִּ֥י עֵֽירֻמִּ֖ם הֵ֑ם וַֽיִּתְפְּרוּ֙ עֲלֵ֣ה תְאֵנָ֔ה
וַיַּעֲשׂ֥וּ לָהֶ֖ם חֲגֹֽרֹת׃
8 וַֽיִּשְׁמְע֞וּ אֶת־ק֨וֹל יְהוָ֧ה אֱלֹהִ֛ים מִתְהַלֵּ֥ךְ
בַּגָּ֖ן לְר֣וּחַ הַיּ֑וֹם וַיִּתְחַבֵּ֨א הָֽאָדָ֜ם וְאִשְׁתּ֗וֹ
מִפְּנֵי֙ יְהוָ֣ה אֱלֹהִ֔ים בְּת֖וֹךְ עֵ֥ץ הַגָּֽן׃

5. but God knows The serpent ascribes self-serving motives to God in its attempt to undermine the Creator's credibility.

your eyes will be opened Finally, the serpent appeals to an attractive standard of common sense: eating of the tree's fruit elevates one to a higher level of existence and endows one with unique mental powers and the capacity for reflection, which allows for the making of decisions independently of God.

like divine beings The Hebrew word understood here as "divine beings" (*elohim*) is a general term referring to supernatural beings and is often used for angels.

who know good and bad See Comment to 2:9. The serpent is saying that the woman and the man will have the capacity to make independent judgments regarding their own welfare, with no concern for the word of God. Defiance of God's law is presented as the necessary precondition for human freedom.

6. good for eating The beguiling word of the serpent triumphs over the constraining word of God.

as a source of wisdom Better: "beautiful in form."

and he ate The woman does not say a word but simply hands her husband the fruit, which he accepts and eats, without resistance or hesitation. Contrary to the popular assumption that it was an apple, the Sages state that the fruit probably was a date or a fig.

7. ***the eyes . . . were opened*** Just as the serpent had predicted! Ironically, however, the new insight they gain is only the consciousness of their nakedness, and shame is the consequence.

fig leaves The fig tree has unusually large and strong leaves.

loincloths Their innocence is gone. In a sense, this action has already taken them outside Eden, for the act of putting on clothing is a clear mark of civilization.

THE INTERROGATION (vv. 8–13)

The scene between the serpent and the woman had taken place as though God were not nearby. Now Adam and Eve are suddenly aware of the divine presence.

---

6. good for eating and a delight to the eyes This is the classic argument of the evil impulse: "If it is so enjoyable, how can it be wrong?"

7. the eyes of both of them Only after eating the forbidden fruit did they begin to think of themselves as separate individuals with separate needs and interests (Simḥah Bunem).

they perceived that they were naked There was no one else in the world to see them in their nakedness. Perhaps it was not physical nakedness but the sense of being subject to judgment and evaluation that caused them to feel self-conscious. (The Midrash [Gen. R. 19:6] takes the words to mean "naked of mitzvot," conscious of their lack of moral uprightness.) If they were as innocent as children before, they are now as self-conscious as adolescents, new to the world of knowing good and bad.

of day; and the man and his wife hid from the Lord God among the trees of the garden. 9The Lord God called out to the man and said to him, "Where are you?" 10He replied, "I heard the sound of You in the garden, and I was afraid because I was naked, so I hid." 11Then He asked, "Who told you that you were naked? Did you eat of the tree from which I had forbidden you to eat?" 12The man said, "The woman You put at my side—she gave me of the tree, and I ate." 13And the Lord God said to the woman, "What is this you have done!" The woman replied, "The serpent duped me, and I ate." 14Then the Lord God said to the serpent,

"Because you did this,
More cursed shall you be
Than all cattle
And all the wild beasts:

9וַיִּקְרָ֛א יְהוָֹ֥ה אֱלֹהִ֖ים אֶל־הָֽאָדָ֑ם וַיֹּ֥אמֶר לֹ֖ו אַיֶּֽכָּה: 10וַיֹּ֕אמֶר אֶת־קֹלְךָ֥ שָׁמַ֖עְתִּי בַּגָּ֑ן וָֽאִירָ֛א כִּֽי־עֵירֹ֥ם אָנֹ֖כִי וָאֵֽחָבֵֽא: 11וַיֹּ֕אמֶר מִ֚י הִגִּ֣יד לְךָ֔ כִּ֥י עֵירֹ֖ם אָ֑תָּה הֲמִן־הָעֵ֗ץ אֲשֶׁ֧ר צִוִּיתִ֛יךָ לְבִלְתִּ֥י אֲכָל־מִמֶּ֖נּוּ אָכָֽלְתָּ: 12וַיֹּ֖אמֶר הָֽאָדָ֑ם הָֽאִשָּׁה֙ אֲשֶׁ֣ר נָתַ֣תָּה עִמָּדִ֔י הִ֛וא נָֽתְנָה־לִּ֥י מִן־הָעֵ֖ץ וָֽאֹכֵֽל: 13וַיֹּ֨אמֶר יְהוָֹ֧ה אֱלֹהִ֛ים לָֽאִשָּׁ֖ה מַה־זֹּ֣את עָשִׂ֑ית וַתֹּ֨אמֶר֙ הָֽאִשָּׁ֔ה הַנָּחָ֥שׁ הִשִּׁיאַ֖נִי וָֽאֹכֵֽל: 14וַיֹּאמֶר֩ יְהוָֹ֨ה אֱלֹהִ֥ים | אֶל־הַנָּחָשׁ֮

כִּ֣י עָשִׂ֣יתָ זֹּאת֒
אָר֤וּר אַתָּה֙
מִכָּל־הַבְּהֵמָ֔ה
וּמִכֹּ֖ל חַיַּ֣ת הַשָּׂדֶ֑ה

8. hid from the Lord The attempt to evade God is a clear sign of guilt.

9. God called out to the man Because only he had heard the prohibition directly from God.

Where are you? The question, a formal civility, is used to begin a conversation.

10. I heard the sound of You There is a hint of irony in the man's reply, for the Hebrew words here rendered "I heard the sound of You" can also be translated "I obeyed You," the opposite of the truth.

I was afraid because I was naked This is another evasion of the truth. The statement reflects the sense of all Semites that it was improper to appear naked in public.

11. that you were naked Self-awareness results from the radical change in the human condition that has taken place.

forbidden Literally, "commanded not to," in contrast to the milder verb used by the serpent in verses 1 and 3.

12. The man said He stands self-condemned; he obeyed his wife and not God.

THE PUNISHMENT   (vv. 14–19)

The man and the woman have taken the right to make their own decisions, choosing to be independent of God and to defy God's norms. Having lost their innocence, they must assume full responsibility for their actions. The three transgressors are now punished, in reverse order of their original appearance on the scene.

9. God asks Adam, "Where are you?" so that Adam might ask himself, "Where am I in relation to God?" God's question means, "Have you changed, have you regretted what you did?"

12. Uncomfortable with their guilt and uncertain as to what will happen if they accept responsibility for what they did, Adam and Eve seek to blame everyone but themselves for what happened. Adam blames Eve and even blames God for giving him Eve; Eve blames the serpent. If Eve did wrong by eating the forbidden fruit, Adam does wrong by refusing to take responsibility for his act of eating. Milton, in *Paradise Lost*, blames Eve for her disobedience but perversely admires Adam for his loyalty to Eve, not wanting to survive while she perishes. A modern reader can as easily see Eve as the heroine of the story, bravely crossing the boundary from animal to human and willingly sharing her newfound wisdom with her mate.

On your belly shall you crawl
And dirt shall you eat
All the days of your life.
15 I will put enmity
Between you and the woman,
And between your offspring and hers;
They shall strike at your head,
And you shall strike at their heel."
16 And to the woman He said,
"I will make most severe
Your pangs in childbearing;
In pain shall you bear children.
Yet your urge shall be for your husband,
And he shall rule over you."

עַל־גְּחֹנְךָ תֵלֵךְ
וְעָפָר תֹּאכַל
כָּל־יְמֵי חַיֶּיךָ׃
15 וְאֵיבָה ׀ אָשִׁית
בֵּינְךָ וּבֵין הָאִשָּׁה
וּבֵין זַרְעֲךָ וּבֵין זַרְעָהּ
הוּא יְשׁוּפְךָ רֹאשׁ
וְאַתָּה תְּשׁוּפֶנּוּ עָקֵב׃ ס
16 אֶל־הָאִשָּׁה אָמַר
הַרְבָּה אַרְבֶּה
עִצְּבוֹנֵךְ וְהֵרֹנֵךְ
בְּעֶצֶב תֵּלְדִי בָנִים
וְאֶל־אִישֵׁךְ תְּשׁוּקָתֵךְ
וְהוּא יִמְשָׁל־בָּךְ׃ ס

14. On your belly This reflects a popular notion, found in the art of the ancient Near East, that the serpent once walked erect. Having flagrantly exalted itself in a challenge to God, it is now doomed to a posture of humiliation.

dirt shall you eat The transgression involved eating and so does the punishment. The flicking tongue of a slithering serpent appears to be licking the dust.

15. enmity The curse seeks to explain the natural revulsion humans now feel toward the serpent. Clearly, when it entered into conversation with the woman, it was not so regarded; indeed, it posed as her friend and she responded with ease.

the woman She is singled out because she conducted the dialogue with it. But here she represents the entire human race, as the reference to her "offspring" shows.

16. Your pangs in childbearing Intense pain in childbearing is unique to the human species.

your urge Rashi understood this and the next clause to reflect that the satisfaction of female sexuality traditionally depends on the husband's initiative. Ramban understood "your urge" to mean that, discomfort and pain of childbearing notwithstanding, the woman still longs for the sexual act that brings about this condition.

he shall rule over you From the description of woman in 2:18,23, the ideal situation was equality of the sexes. Male dominance is viewed

---

16. We can see God's pronouncements to Adam and Eve as punishments for disobeying the divine command. Or we can see them instead as the consequences of acquiring a knowledge of good and evil, which makes a human life infinitely more complicated than the life of a beast. Food and mating are relatively straightforward for animals, but work and sexuality can be terribly painful—and profoundly gratifying—for humans.

in pain shall you bear children The Talmud suggests that the verse refers to both the physical pain of childbirth and the emotional pain of trying to raise children (BT Er. 100a). The Hebrew word *etzev* is not the usual biblical word for "pain." It recurs in 6:6, referring to God's regret at the way humanity turned out in the days of Noah. Could the recurrence of the word imply that God, contemplating how human beings sometimes turn out, can sympathize with the pain Eve and her descendants will feel when they cannot be assured that their children will grow up as they hoped?

your urge shall be for your husband, And he shall rule over you Nevertheless, Exod. 21:10 indicates that a husband may not withhold his wife's conjugal rights. This requirement is amplified by the Mishnah (Ket. 5:6).

17To Adam He said, "Because you did as your
wife said and ate of the tree about which I
commanded you, 'You shall not eat of it,'
Cursed be the ground because of you;
By toil shall you eat of it
All the days of your life:
18Thorns and thistles shall it sprout for you.
But your food shall be the grasses of the field;
19By the sweat of your brow
Shall you get bread to eat,
Until you return to the ground—
For from it you were taken.
For dust you are,
And to dust you shall return."

20The man named his wife Eve, because she

17 וּלְאָדָם אָמַר כִּי־שָׁמַעְתָּ לְקוֹל אִשְׁתֶּךָ
וַתֹּאכַל מִן־הָעֵץ אֲשֶׁר צִוִּיתִיךָ לֵאמֹר לֹא
תֹאכַל מִמֶּנּוּ
אֲרוּרָה הָאֲדָמָה בַּעֲבוּרֶךָ
בְּעִצָּבוֹן תֹּאכֲלֶנָּה
כֹּל יְמֵי חַיֶּיךָ׃
18 וְקוֹץ וְדַרְדַּר תַּצְמִיחַ לָךְ
וְאָכַלְתָּ אֶת־עֵשֶׂב הַשָּׂדֶה׃
19 בְּזֵעַת אַפֶּיךָ
תֹּאכַל לֶחֶם
עַד שׁוּבְךָ אֶל־הָאֲדָמָה
כִּי מִמֶּנָּה לֻקָּחְתָּ
כִּי־עָפָר אַתָּה
וְאֶל־עָפָר תָּשׁוּב׃

20 וַיִּקְרָא הָאָדָם שֵׁם אִשְׁתּוֹ חַוָּה כִּי

as a deterioration in the human condition, resulting from the defiance of God's will.

17. To Adam He said Adam bears the greatest share of the blame, for he received the prohibition directly from God.

Cursed be the ground The matter from which the man sprang is turned against him. His transgression disturbs his harmony with nature. Human immorality corrupts moral ecology.

By toil The word translated as "toil" (*itzavon*) is also used in verse 16 to describe the childbearing pain of the woman. Backbreaking physical labor is the male equivalent of the labor of giving birth. Work is not the curse; work was decreed for man even in Eden (2:15). The curse is the new uncooperative nature of the soil, so that henceforth the wresting of crops from it demands ceaseless toil.

All the days of your life This same phrase is used of the serpent in verse 14. Man and beast were created mortal from the beginning. The phrase is absent from verse 16 because childbearing does not occur throughout a woman's life.

18. Thorns and thistles In the face of humankind's need to subsist on the grasses of the field, weeds rob cultivated plants of light and water, drain the soil of its nutrients, and require vast effort to control.

19. By the sweat of your brow The man and the woman had attempted to raise themselves to the level of God. All they achieved was condemnation to a ceaseless struggle for subsistence, with the awareness of life's fragility forever hanging over them.

A MEASURE OF RECONCILIATION
(vv. 20–21)

20. The man named his wife In an act that reflects a social ideal based on male domination, the man gives the woman a personal name that expresses her essential nature and destiny.

Eve The word *ḥavvah* could mean "living thing" or "propagator of life." It also has been derived in rabbinic sources and by modern scholars from the Aramaic and Arabic word for "snake."

mother of all the living A similar phrase is used to describe the mother goddess in ancient

19. Originally, God decreed that Adam would eat plants (Gen. 3:18). Adam pleaded, "Having acquired a knowledge of good and evil, shall I eat grass like a donkey?" God relents. "You will eat bread," that is, you will use your unique human attributes to turn plants into bread, adapting the natural world to your needs as no other creature can (BT Pes. 118a).

הִ֖וא הָיְתָ֥ה אֵ֥ם כָּל־חָֽי׃ 21 וַיַּ֩עַשׂ֩ יְהוָ֨ה
אֱלֹהִ֜ים לְאָדָ֧ם וּלְאִשְׁתּ֛וֹ כָּתְנ֥וֹת ע֖וֹר
וַיַּלְבִּשֵֽׁם׃ פ
רביעי 22 וַיֹּ֣אמֶר ׀ יְהוָ֣ה אֱלֹהִ֗ים הֵ֤ן הָֽאָדָם֙ הָיָה֙
כְּאַחַ֣ד מִמֶּ֔נּוּ לָדַ֖עַת ט֣וֹב וָרָ֑ע וְעַתָּ֣ה ׀ פֶּן־
יִשְׁלַ֣ח יָד֗וֹ וְלָקַח֙ גַּ֚ם מֵעֵ֣ץ הַֽחַיִּ֔ים וְאָכַ֖ל
וָחַ֥י לְעֹלָֽם׃ 23 וַֽיְשַׁלְּחֵ֛הוּ יְהוָ֥ה אֱלֹהִ֖ים
מִגַּן־עֵ֑דֶן לַֽעֲבֹד֙ אֶת־הָ֣אֲדָמָ֔ה אֲשֶׁ֥ר לֻקַּ֖ח
מִשָּֽׁם׃ 24 וַיְגָ֖רֶשׁ אֶת־הָֽאָדָ֑ם וַיַּשְׁכֵּן֩
מִקֶּ֨דֶם לְגַן־עֵ֜דֶן אֶת־הַכְּרֻבִ֗ים וְאֵ֨ת לַ֤הַט
הַחֶ֙רֶב֙ הַמִּתְהַפֶּ֔כֶת לִשְׁמֹ֕ר אֶת־דֶּ֖רֶךְ עֵ֥ץ
הַֽחַיִּֽים׃ ס

was the mother of all the living. 21 And the LORD God made garments of skins for Adam and his wife, and clothed them.

22 And the LORD God said, "Now that the man has become like one of us, knowing good and bad, what if he should stretch out his hand and take also from the tree of life and eat, and live forever!" 23 So the LORD God banished him from the garden of Eden, to till the soil from which he was taken. 24 He drove the man out, and stationed east of the garden of Eden the cherubim and the fiery ever-turning sword, to guard the way to the tree of life.

Near Eastern mythology. Here the image has been demythologized. It simply expresses the biblical concepts of one human race and of woman's primary role—motherhood.

21. The LORD God made Because their nakedness causes them shame, God provides them with clothing, thereby displaying concern for their welfare and restoring their dignity. Thus, despite their transgression, Adam and Eve are not totally alienated from God.

garments The Hebrew word *kutonet* refers to a long-or short-sleeved shirt that is made of linen or wool and reaches down to the knees or the ankles.

of skins This assumes that humankind's earliest clothing was made of animal skins.

THE EXPULSION FROM EDEN (vv. 22–24)

The transgression of the man and the woman distanced them spiritually from Eden. God's punishment now separates them physically from its environs. By exceeding the limits of creaturehood, humankind has altered the perspective of its existence. It will live henceforth with full awareness of its mortality.

22. the tree of life See Comment to 2:9.

23. from which he was taken This refers back to 2:7–8. Man, created from earth outside of Eden, is now returned to his place of origin.

24. east of the garden The entrance was considered to be on the east, facing the rising sun. Thus Adam and Eve could walk back into the garden anytime they desired unless something was done to keep them from doing so. See Comment to 2:8

the cherubim The Hebrew word *k'ruvim* is derived from the Akkadian word *kuribu,* referring to guardian demons. They are described in detail in the first chapter of Ezekiel, as composite beings with lion's bodies, eagle's wings, and human heads.

and the fiery ever-turning sword This is not held by the cherubim, but is a separate guardian blade. Because it too carries the definite article, it must have been an object well known to the Israelite imagination.

---

21. God set an example here for all human beings. Just as God clothed Adam and Eve, so must we look after the needy among us (BT Sot. 31a).

22. the man has become like one of us By gaining the capacity for moral awareness, the human being has become one, unique, on earth, as God is one, unique, in heaven (Rashi).

It has been suggested that the tree of life represents the force of instinct, whereas the tree of knowledge of good and evil represents the force of conscience. Once our ancestors acquired a conscience, they could no longer eat of the tree of life, that is, live instinctively, doing whatever felt good to them. People ever since have sought to re-enter the Garden of Eden, to return to the days of childhood before they knew that certain things were wrong; but the way is barred. Other commentators see the wish to return to Eden as a yearning for a world where harmony will once again reign between humans and nature, between humans and ani-

4 Now the man knew his wife Eve, and
she conceived and bore Cain, saying, "I have
gained a male child with the help of the LORD."
2She then bore his brother Abel. Abel became a
keeper of sheep, and Cain became a tiller of the
soil. 3In the course of time, Cain brought an

ד וְהָאָדָם יָדַע אֶת־חַוָּה אִשְׁתּוֹ וַתַּהַר
וַתֵּלֶד אֶת־קַיִן וַתֹּאמֶר קָנִיתִי אִישׁ אֶת־
יְהוָה׃ 2 וַתֹּסֶף לָלֶדֶת אֶת־אָחִיו אֶת־הָבֶל
וַיְהִי־הֶבֶל רֹעֵה צֹאן וְקַיִן הָיָה עֹבֵד
אֲדָמָה׃ 3 וַיְהִי מִקֵּץ יָמִים וַיָּבֵא קַיִן מִפְּרִי

REALITY OUTSIDE EDEN (4:1–26)

The narrative now turns to the fortunes of humankind in the harsh world outside Eden. The focus of the narrative is not history but the human condition, the place of the irrational in human conduct, and the reality of death.

CAIN AND ABEL (vv. 1–16)

1. the man knew The Hebrew stem translated here as "knew" (ידע) encompasses a range of meanings: involvement, interaction, loyalty, and obligation. It also can be used of the most intimate and hallowed relationships between husband and wife and between humans and God. Here the Hebrew may be understood as meaning "the man had known," that is, Adam and Eve had been sexually active inside the garden.

I have gained The stem translated here as "gained" (קנה) means "to produce" in Hebrew, Ugaritic, and Phoenician.

a male child The Hebrew translated as "a male child" (*ish*) means "man." Nowhere else does the word *ish* refer to a newborn babe. Eve says, in effect: "I, woman (*ishah*), was produced from man (*ish*); now I, woman, have in turn produced a man."

the LORD For the first time, the most sacred divine name *YHVH*, the personal name of God, is uttered by a human being, a woman.

2. his brother The absence of the formula "she conceived and bore" (as in Gen. 4:1) led to the tradition that Cain and Abel were twins.

Abel No explanation for this choice of name is given. The Hebrew for Abel (*hevel*) means "breath, nothingness."

keeper of sheep . . . tiller of the soil Cain, the first-born, follows his father's occupation, agriculture, whereas Abel branches out to stock breeding. The two parts of the economy supplement each other. In the biblical view, human-

---

mals, a world without blame or quarrel, without sickness, and without pain and death.

CHAPTER 4

1. Deprived of eternal life, Adam and Eve gain vicarious immortality by having children. The Vilna Gaon saw this as a gesture of grace on God's part. Rather than have Adam and Eve live forever with the knowledge of what they had done wrong, God arranged for them to give way to a new generation born in innocence.

with the help of the LORD Just as God is a presence in every marriage, God is a presence in the birth of every child (Mid. Tad.). Eve's gratitude to God is a corrective to the danger, implicit in her first words, of thinking that she "owns" her child.

Or we can understand Eve's words to mean: "I have brought a new life into being, just as God did."

2. Though Abel is the younger, the Torah describes him as a shepherd and his older brother as a farmer. Anthropologists believe that ancient humans were breeders of animals first and only later became tillers of the soil, claiming a portion of earth as permanently theirs. (The Bible regularly portrays younger siblings as more virtuous and has a special fondness for shepherds, including Abraham, Moses, and David.)

It is possible that Cain became a farmer to make up to his parents for the garden, the agricultural wonderland they had lost, as children often strive to fulfill or replace the unfulfilled or lost dreams of their parents.

3ff. Cain and Abel each bring an offering to God. It would seem that the urge to thank God for our blessings and to return to God a small portion of that with which God has blessed us is innate and requires no religious code or formal clergy to compel us (Hirsch). God's favoring Abel seems arbitrary, with no reason given.

הָאֲדָמָה מִנְחָה לַיהוָה׃ 4וְהֶבֶל הֵבִיא
גַם־הוּא מִבְּכֹרוֹת צֹאנוֹ וּמֵחֶלְבֵהֶן* וַיִּשַׁע
יְהוָה אֶל־הֶבֶל וְאֶל־מִנְחָתוֹ׃ 5וְאֶל־קַיִן
וְאֶל־מִנְחָתוֹ לֹא שָׁעָה וַיִּחַר לְקַיִן מְאֹד
וַיִּפְּלוּ פָּנָיו׃ 6וַיֹּאמֶר יְהוָה אֶל־קָיִן
לָמָּה חָרָה לָךְ
וְלָמָּה נָפְלוּ פָנֶיךָ׃
7הֲלוֹא אִם־תֵּיטִיב
שְׂאֵת
וְאִם לֹא תֵיטִיב
לַפֶּתַח חַטָּאת רֹבֵץ

v. 4. ב׳ רפה

offering to the LORD from the fruit of the soil;
4and Abel, for his part, brought the choicest of
the firstlings of his flock. The LORD paid heed
to Abel and his offering, 5but to Cain and his
offering He paid no heed. Cain was much distressed and his face fell. 6And the LORD said to
Cain,

"Why are you distressed,
And why is your face fallen?
7Surely, if you do right,
There is uplift.
But if you do not do right
Sin couches at the door;

kind was vegetarian until after the Flood. Thus the function of animal husbandry at this time was to supply milk, hides, and wool.

3. from the fruit of the soil A terse account, with no further explanation or detail, an indication perhaps of a grudging heart behind the offering.

the choicest of the firstlings Abel's offering, fully described, appears to have been brought with a full heart and mind.

4. paid heed Ancient and medieval commentators imagined fire descending from heaven to consume Abel's offering, leaving Cain's untouched.

5. his face fell The Hebrew describes sadness and depression. The same image appears in other ancient Near Eastern texts.

7. if you do right Humankind is endowed with moral autonomy, with freedom of choice. We can subdue our anger and even our sense of unfairness by an act of will, or we can be controlled by them.

The Sages, however, search the text for clues. Some commentators fasten on the Torah's mentioning that Abel brought "the choicest of the firstlings," whereas Cain merely brought "an offering . . . from the fruit of the soil," not necessarily the best. The words translated as "for his part" (*gam hu*) can be understood literally as "he too," implying that Abel brought "himself" to God along with his offering (*S'fat Emet*). The words for "in the course of time" (*mi-ketz yamim*), literally "at the end of [a certain number of] days," are taken by Simḥah Bunem to suggest that Cain brought an offering only because he was afraid that he was dying, that he was approaching the end of his life and was bargaining with God for more time.

6–7. God seeks to comfort Cain in an important but enigmatic utterance, over the meaning of which scholars differ. Shneur Zalman of Lyady understands the first half to mean "if you have lived an upright life, you will be able to bear any misfortune or undeserved affliction." *Midrash Psalms* (119) understands "sin couches at the door" to mean "if you take yourself to the House of Study you will be safe, for sin has no power to enter there." Another *midrash* sees the impulse to sin as waiting outside one's door, waiting to be invited in. Once admitted, it makes itself master of the house (Gen. R. 22:6). The primary punishment for sin is that it makes another sin more likely. We acquire the habit of behaving in a certain way. John Steinbeck, in his novel *East of Eden* based on the story of Cain and Abel, describes philosophers debating the various translations of *timshol.* Is it a command, "You are to master it"? Is it a promise, "You will master it"? Or does it tell us, as the translation here would have it, that our fate is in our own hands, "You *can* be its master"?

Because the Torah does not quote any conversation between Cain and Abel preceding Cain's murder of his brother, the Sages seek to fill the vacuum. They imagine Cain and Abel arguing over which of them would marry Eve after Adam's death or over which half of the

Its urge is toward you,

Yet you can be its master."

⁸Cain said to his brother Abel . . . and when they were in the field, Cain set upon his brother Abel and killed him. ⁹The LORD said to Cain, "Where is your brother Abel?" And he said, "I do not know. Am I my brother's keeper?" ¹⁰Then He said, "What have you done? Hark, your brother's blood cries out to Me from the ground! ¹¹Therefore, you shall be more cursed

וְאֵלֶ֙יךָ֙ תְּשׁ֣וּקָת֔וֹ
וְאַתָּ֖ה תִּמְשָׁל־בּֽוֹ:
⁸וַיֹּ֥אמֶר קַ֖יִן אֶל־הֶ֣בֶל אָחִ֑יו וַֽיְהִי֙ בִּהְיוֹתָ֣ם
בַּשָּׂדֶ֔ה וַיָּ֥קׇם קַ֛יִן אֶל־הֶ֥בֶל אָחִ֖יו וַיַּהַרְגֵֽהוּ:
⁹וַיֹּ֤אמֶר יְהֹוָה֙ אֶל־קַ֔יִן אֵ֖י הֶ֣בֶל אָחִ֑יךָ
וַיֹּ֙אמֶר֙ לֹ֣א יָדַ֔עְתִּי הֲשֹׁמֵ֥ר אָחִ֖י אָנֹֽכִי:
¹⁰וַיֹּ֖אמֶר מֶ֣ה עָשִׂ֑יתָ ק֚וֹל דְּמֵ֣י אָחִ֔יךָ
צֹעֲקִ֥ים אֵלַ֖י מִן־הָאֲדָמָֽה: ¹¹וְעַתָּ֖ה אָר֣וּר

8. Cain said to his brother Abel The Hebrew does not tell us what was said. The ancient Greek translation (Septuagint) adds here: "Come, let us go into the field."

in the field The Hebrew word *sadeh* refers to the open, uninhabited countryside, often the scene of crime.

killed him Cain's depression gives way to an act of murder. The first recorded death is not from natural causes but by human hands.

9. the LORD God immediately intervenes.

Where Cain either has fled the scene of his crime or buried his brother immediately. As in 3:9, the question is a means of opening the conversation.

I do not know Cain defiantly lies, expressing no remorse.

Am I my brother's keeper? "Brother" is mentioned seven times in this chapter, to emphasize the relationship of Cain and Abel and to teach that man is indeed his brother's keeper and that all homicide is fratricide.

10. What have you done Not a question, but a cry of horror.

Hark The Hebrew translated as "hark" (*kol*), a noun in the singular meaning "voice," is here used as an exclamation. It cannot be the subject of the following plural verb (*tzo·akim*).

cries out The Hebrew stem צעק connotes a plea for help or redress on the part of the victim of great injustice.

11. more cursed than the ground Better: "cursed from the ground." Cain, tiller of the soil, stained the earth with his brother's blood. It

world each of them would inherit or over the question of in whose territory the future Temple would be built (Gen. R. 22:7). Ever since, sexual rivalry, economic conflict, and religious quarrels have been the source of violence among human beings.

9. The Vilna Gaon faults Cain for calling Abel "brother" and then not treating him like a brother, prompting God to challenge Cain: "Where is your brother Abel?" Where is the brotherly affection you claimed to have for him?

For Judaism, the answer to Cain's question "Am I my brother's keeper?" is an unequivocal yes! Survivors of the *Sho·ah* painfully remember not only the cruelty of the Nazis but the cold indifference of their neighbors who looked on and did nothing; or they recall the exceptional courage of the righteous gentiles who sought to help them.

10. your brother's blood The Hebrew word for "blood" here is plural, the form that the word

usually takes when it appears in contexts of violence. Cain killed not only Abel; he deprived all of Abel's potential descendants of their lives (BT Sanh. 37a). We might add further that, when a person is murdered, the murderer kills something in the survivors' souls as well. Their lives will never be as they were before. In the same way, when we save or sustain one life, we sustain all the human beings who will be descendants of that person.

In a bold interpretation, the Midrash takes God's words—"your brother's blood cries out to Me"—to mean "your brother's blood cries out 'against' Me, accusing Me of letting this injustice happen!" (Gen. R. 22:9). However, it was Cain, not God, who chose to lash out and cause this tragedy. In the same way, the challenge of the *Sho·ah* is not, "Where was God? How could God have let this happen?" The challenge is, "Where was Man? How could people have been so cruel to other human beings?"

אַתָּה מִן־הָאֲדָמָה אֲשֶׁר פָּצְתָה אֶת־פִּיהָ
לָקַחַת אֶת־דְּמֵי אָחִיךָ מִיָּדֶךָ׃ 12 כִּי תַעֲבֹד
אֶת־הָאֲדָמָה לֹא־תֹסֵף תֵּת־כֹּחָהּ לָךְ נָע
וָנָד תִּהְיֶה בָאָרֶץ׃
13 וַיֹּאמֶר קַיִן אֶל־יְהוָה גָּדוֹל עֲוֺנִי מִנְּשֹׂא׃
14 הֵן גֵּרַשְׁתָּ אֹתִי הַיּוֹם מֵעַל פְּנֵי הָאֲדָמָה
וּמִפָּנֶיךָ אֶסָּתֵר וְהָיִיתִי נָע וָנָד בָּאָרֶץ וְהָיָה
כָל־מֹצְאִי יַהַרְגֵנִי׃ 15 וַיֹּאמֶר לוֹ יְהוָה לָכֵן
כָּל־הֹרֵג קַיִן שִׁבְעָתַיִם יֻקָּם וַיָּשֶׂם יְהוָה
לְקַיִן אוֹת לְבִלְתִּי הַכּוֹת־אֹתוֹ כָּל־מֹצְאוֹ׃
16 וַיֵּצֵא קַיִן מִלִּפְנֵי יְהוָה וַיֵּשֶׁב בְּאֶרֶץ־נוֹד
קִדְמַת־עֵדֶן׃

than the ground, which opened its mouth to
receive your brother's blood from your hand.
12 If you till the soil, it shall no longer yield its
strength to you. You shall become a ceaseless
wanderer on earth."

13 Cain said to the LORD, "My punishment is
too great to bear! 14 Since You have banished me
this day from the soil, and I must avoid Your
presence and become a restless wanderer on
earth—anyone who meets me may kill me!"
15 The LORD said to him, "I promise, if anyone
kills Cain, sevenfold vengeance shall be taken
on him." And the LORD put a mark on Cain, lest
anyone who met him should kill him. 16 Cain
left the presence of the LORD and settled in the
land of Nod, east of Eden.

is fitting that the earth be the instrument of his punishment.

13. My punishment The text can also be translated "My sin is too great to be forgiven" or "Is my sin too great to be forgiven?" The Hebrew word *avon* means both "sin" and its penalty. In the biblical worldview, the two are inseparable; that is, the penalty that follows is inherent in the sin.

14. I must avoid Your presence A crime against a human being is simultaneously a sin against God. Cain fears that he will no longer be the recipient of God's providence.

15. The LORD said to him The words are directed first to Cain, to allay his mortal fear, and then to the world at large, as a kind of royal proclamation to the effect that Cain, despite his crime, still remains under God's care.

sevenfold Some commentators understand this as a figure of speech meaning "abundantly" or "severely." Others take it to mean, literally, that seven of the assailant's family would be killed or that vengeance would continue to the seventh generation.

vengeance The biblical Hebrew stem נקם, which usually has the sense of remedying the imbalance of justice, here has its primitive meaning of exacting revenge.

a mark This is not a stigma of infamy but a mark signifying that the bearer is under divine protection. Perhaps some mark on the body or forehead served the same function as the blood of the paschal lamb smeared on the lintels and doorposts of each Israelite house in Egypt.

16. left the presence of the LORD The audience with God is now concluded.

the land of Nod A symbolic name. The Hebrew word *nod* means "wandering," as in verses 12 and 14.

THE GENEALOGY OF CAIN (vv. 17–22)

Cain and his descendants are now listed, seven generations in all. There appears to be some link between the family of Cain and the later wan-

---

12. Cain, who used the earth to hide the evidence of his crime, is forever alienated from the earth. Cut off from nature, he becomes the builder of the first city (Gen. 4:17).

14. When Cain repents, God diminishes the punishment. This causes Adam to reproach himself, saying "If only I had known the power of repentance, I could have had my punishment reduced as well." We think we cannot change the past, but repentance is so powerful that it enables us to change our sense of who we are and reduce the power of the past to determine our future.

17. his wife According to a tradition in the Book of Jubilees (4:9) and in the Talmud (BT Sanh. 58b), Cain married his sister.

17 וַיֵּדַע קַיִן אֶת־אִשְׁתּוֹ וַתַּהַר וַתֵּלֶד אֶת־
חֲנוֹךְ וַיְהִי בֹּנֶה עִיר וַיִּקְרָא שֵׁם הָעִיר
כְּשֵׁם בְּנוֹ חֲנוֹךְ׃ 18 וַיִּוָּלֵד לַחֲנוֹךְ אֶת־
עִירָד וְעִירָד יָלַד אֶת־מְחוּיָאֵל וּמְחִיָּיאֵל
יָלַד אֶת־מְתוּשָׁאֵל וּמְתוּשָׁאֵל יָלַד אֶת־
לָמֶךְ׃ 19 וַיִּקַּח־לוֹ לֶמֶךְ שְׁתֵּי נָשִׁים שֵׁם חמישי
הָאַחַת עָדָה וְשֵׁם הַשֵּׁנִית צִלָּה׃ 20 וַתֵּלֶד
עָדָה אֶת־יָבָל הוּא הָיָה אֲבִי יֹשֵׁב אֹהֶל
וּמִקְנֶה׃ 21 וְשֵׁם אָחִיו יוּבָל הוּא הָיָה
אֲבִי כָּל־תֹּפֵשׂ כִּנּוֹר וְעוּגָב׃ 22 וְצִלָּה גַם־
הִוא יָלְדָה אֶת־תּוּבַל קַיִן לֹטֵשׁ כָּל־חֹרֵשׁ
נְחֹשֶׁת וּבַרְזֶל וַאֲחוֹת תּוּבַל־קַיִן נַעֲמָה׃

[17]Cain knew his wife, and she conceived and bore Enoch. And he then founded a city, and named the city after his son Enoch. [18]To Enoch was born Irad, and Irad begot Mehujael, and Mehujael begot Methusael, and Methusael begot Lamech. [19]Lamech took to himself two wives: the name of the one was Adah, and the name of the other was Zillah. [20]Adah bore Jabal; he was the ancestor of those who dwell in tents and amidst herds. [21]And the name of his brother was Jubal; he was the ancestor of all who play the lyre and the pipe. [22]As for Zillah, she bore Tubal-cain, who forged all implements of copper and iron. And the sister of Tubal-cain was Naamah.

dering Kenites–Midianites. No details are given of Cain's span of life, and his death goes unrecorded. The same is true of his descendants.

17. Enoch The basic meaning of the stem חנך in this verse has to do with initiation, dedication, and education. Thus the name may be symbolic, signifying the inauguration of urban life.

he then founded a city The soil, being accursed and unproductive for Cain, is put to use by him for wholly new purposes. He becomes the founder of urban culture.

Enoch In 25:4, one of the sons of Midian is also named Enoch, and the Midianites are closely connected with the Kenites in several biblical texts.

18. Irad The name is related to the oldest city in Mesopotamia, Eridu.

Lamech A similar word in Arabic means "a strong young man," and in Akkadian, a class of priests.

19. two wives Lamech is apparently the first polygamist.

20. ancestor He is the archetypal pastoral nomad. Abel, a shepherd, was not nomadic.

herds The Hebrew word *mikneh* (property) includes all types of livestock. This statement indicates an awareness that the rise of animal husbandry was a major development in human history.

21. who play The Hebrew translated as "play" (*tofes*), literally, "hold," also came to mean "to be skilled in." It would thus suggest specialization and professionalism.

lyre *Kinnor* is the only stringed instrument mentioned in the Torah and is one of the earliest documented musical instruments in the Near East, with a history traceable to ca. 3000 B.C.E.

pipe In Hebrew: *ugav;* apparently a general term for wind instruments of various kinds.

22. Tubal-cain The name Tubal means "metalworker," derived from Akkadian and Sumerian. And in several Semitic languages, *kayin* means a "smith."

copper The Hebrew word *n'ḥoshet* actually refers to bronze—an alloy of copper and tin—which was worked extensively in southern Mesopotamia and in Sinai as early as the 3rd millennium B.C.E.

iron This metal, worked even by preliterate peoples, was used sporadically in the region during the Bronze Age.

Naamah This statement, with no further remarks about her, implies that she once was a well-known personage. The Hebrew stem of her name (נעם) means "good, lovely," which

---

21ff. By attributing urbanization, music, and tool and weapon making to Cain and his descendants, the Torah may be signaling its ambivalence about human efforts to detach from, and improve on, the world of nature. (See the story of the Tower of Babel in Gen. 11.)

23 And Lamech said to his wives,
"Adah and Zillah, hear my voice;
O wives of Lamech, give ear to my speech.
I have slain a man for wounding me,
And a lad for bruising me.
24 If Cain is avenged sevenfold,
Then Lamech seventy-sevenfold."
25 Adam knew his wife again, and she bore a
son and named him Seth, meaning, "God has
provided me with another offspring in place of
Abel," for Cain had killed him. 26 And to Seth, in
turn, a son was born, and he named him Enosh.
It was then that men began to invoke the LORD
by name.

23 וַיֹּאמֶר לֶמֶךְ לְנָשָׁיו
עָדָה וְצִלָּה שְׁמַעַן קוֹלִי
נְשֵׁי לֶמֶךְ הַאְזֵנָּה אִמְרָתִי
כִּי אִישׁ הָרַגְתִּי לְפִצְעִי
וְיֶלֶד לְחַבֻּרָתִי׃
24 כִּי שִׁבְעָתַיִם יֻקַּם־קָיִן
וְלֶמֶךְ שִׁבְעִים וְשִׁבְעָה׃
25 וַיֵּדַע אָדָם עוֹד אֶת־אִשְׁתּוֹ וַתֵּלֶד בֵּן
וַתִּקְרָא אֶת־שְׁמוֹ שֵׁת כִּי שָׁת־לִי אֱלֹהִים
זֶרַע אַחֵר תַּחַת הֶבֶל כִּי הֲרָגוֹ קָיִן׃
26 וּלְשֵׁת גַּם־הוּא יֻלַּד־בֵּן וַיִּקְרָא אֶת־שְׁמוֹ
ששי אֱנוֹשׁ אָז הוּחַל לִקְרֹא בְּשֵׁם יְהוָה׃ פ

may reflect either her beauty or her character. The same stem in Arabic, Syriac, and rabbinic Hebrew also means "to sing."

THE SONG OF LAMECH (vv. 23–24)

This is a representative example of biblical Hebrew poetic style. Although it displays neither meter nor rhyme in the present sense of these terms, it does have a notable rhythm. Its formal structure is known as "parallelism," a feature of biblical and Canaanite poetry. The second line of a couplet restates the thought of the first line in different words, as here. The second line could also supplement the first, be antithetical to it, or be the climax of the poem.

The poem itself perhaps explains the origin of the nomadic institution of blood vengeance.

23. I have slain a man Lamech's taunts, threats, and boasts are of the kind customarily uttered in ancient times by those about to engage in combat. He is bragging that he does not need divine protection because he can defend himself with the new iron weapons of war. He places his faith in the power of technology.

a lad As if to say: "This man, my antagonist, is but a mere child in combat!"

for wounding me Another possible translation is: "My mere wounding/bruising of my combatant is fatal."

SETH AND ENOSH (vv. 25–26)

Humankind is regenerated through another son of Adam and Eve.

25. Seth The name is here connected with the stem meaning "to place, put, set" (שית). The birth of Seth compensates for the loss of Abel. Seth, in turn, named his son Enosh, which, like Adam, means "man."

meaning The Hebrew word translated here as "meaning" (*ki*) means, literally, "because." The necessary phrase "she said" is understood in the Hebrew.

26. men began to invoke the LORD by name This expression refers to the worship of God.

---

26. began to invoke the LORD by name Once people became numerous, they began to form communities to share their hopes, joys, and fears. Hirsch is one of the few commentators to agree with the positive interpretation of this ambiguous verse. Most others take the word translated as "began" (*huḥal*) in its other sense, meaning "to desecrate, blaspheme." Thus the Midrash understands the text to mean that people began to call the work of their own hands "God." The further the generations were from God's intimate encounter with Adam and Eve, the more remote God seemed to them. They were lacking ways to recognize God's presence in their lives. Maimonides traces the origin of idol worship to this stage of human development. As people came to depend on nature to sustain them with food, they were inclined to honor nature (MT Idol Worship 1:1). Another *midrash*, understanding the text

5 This is the record of Adam's line.—When
God created man, He made him in the likeness of God; 2male and female He created
them. And when they were created, He blessed
them and called them Man.—3When Adam
had lived 130 years, he begot a son in his likeness after his image, and he named him Seth.
4After the birth of Seth, Adam lived 800 years
and begot sons and daughters. 5All the days
that Adam lived came to 930 years; then he
died.

ששי ה זֶה סֵפֶר תּוֹלְדֹת אָדָם בְּיוֹם בְּרֹא
אֱלֹהִים אָדָם בִּדְמוּת אֱלֹהִים עָשָׂה אֹתוֹ׃
2 זָכָר וּנְקֵבָה בְּרָאָם וַיְבָרֶךְ אֹתָם וַיִּקְרָא
אֶת־שְׁמָם אָדָם בְּיוֹם הִבָּרְאָם׃ ס
3 וַיְחִי אָדָם שְׁלֹשִׁים וּמְאַת שָׁנָה וַיּוֹלֶד
בִּדְמוּתוֹ כְּצַלְמוֹ וַיִּקְרָא אֶת־שְׁמוֹ שֵׁת׃
4 וַיִּהְיוּ יְמֵי־אָדָם אַחֲרֵי הוֹלִידוֹ אֶת־שֵׁת
שְׁמֹנֶה מֵאֹת שָׁנָה וַיּוֹלֶד בָּנִים וּבָנוֹת׃
5 וַיִּהְיוּ כָּל־יְמֵי אָדָם אֲשֶׁר־חַי תְּשַׁע
מֵאוֹת שָׁנָה וּשְׁלֹשִׁים שָׁנָה וַיָּמֹת׃ ס

THE BOOK OF GENEALOGIES (5:1–6:8)

The narrative now presents a 10-generation genealogy that spans the period between the creation of the world and the advent of Noah, who witnessed its destruction. Such 10-generation genealogies are also found in some ancient Near Eastern historical records. The remarkably long lives enjoyed by those who lived before the Flood accord with the ancient widespread folkloristic notion that associates heroes before the Flood with extraordinary longevity. Compared to the Mesopotamian worldview, however (the Sumerian King List adds up to 241,200 years), the biblical figures represent restraint.

Note the general parallelism between the 7-generation Cainite genealogy and the 10-generation genealogy of Seth, both ending with Lamech.

1. This is the record of Adam's line The Hebrew translated here as "record" (*seifer*) refers to a written document, not an oral composition. Thus these words most likely constitute the title of an ancient genealogical work that served as the source for the data provided in this chapter.

in the likeness of God This refers to 1:26.

2. He blessed them A knowledge of 1:27–28 is assumed here. Because the theme of the chapter is the replication of humankind, the reader is reminded that sexuality is a divine blessing and procreation a God-given duty.

ADAM (vv. 3–5)

3. a son in his likeness after his image Via procreation, the first two human beings transmitted "the image of God" in themselves to all future generations.

he named him In 4:25, the woman named Seth. The masculine is used here because only the fathers are featured in the genealogy.

Seth Cain and Abel are ignored because the sole concern of this document is to trace a linear genealogical chain from Adam to Noah.

4. After the birth of Seth The continuity of the line is in jeopardy until the birth of the first son, who becomes, for that reason, a child of destiny. Hence, this event marks a major point of demarcation in the measurement of a human lifetime.

---

as referring to God's name, suggests that, in the age of Enosh, people worshiped idols but God tolerated their sin (because there is no mention of punishment). In the days of Noah, however, people were cruel to each other, which God would not forgive.

CHAPTER 5

1. This is the record of Adam's line Ben Azzai called this the all-inclusive principle of the Torah, teaching us that we are all descended from a single ancestor. No one can claim a more illustrious lineage than anyone else (JT Ned. 9).

2. male and female Although the Torah is largely an account of men's exploits, with women playing a crucial but secondary role, and although the births of male offspring are recorded here and elsewhere to the almost total exclusion of female children, we are reminded here at the outset that the human race consists of both men and women, fashioned equally in God's image.

6When Seth had lived 105 years, he begot Enosh. 7After the birth of Enosh, Seth lived 807 years and begot sons and daughters. 8All the days of Seth came to 912 years; then he died.

9When Enosh had lived 90 years, he begot Kenan. 10After the birth of Kenan, Enosh lived 815 years and begot sons and daughters. 11All the days of Enosh came to 905 years; then he died.

12When Kenan had lived 70 years, he begot Mahalalel. 13After the birth of Mahalalel, Kenan lived 840 years and begot sons and daughters. 14All the days of Kenan came to 910 years; then he died.

15When Mahalalel had lived 65 years, he begot Jared. 16After the birth of Jared, Mahalalel lived 830 years and begot sons and daughters. 17All the days of Mahalalel came to 895 years; then he died.

18When Jared had lived 162 years, he begot Enoch. 19After the birth of Enoch, Jared lived 800 years and begot sons and daughters. 20All the days of Jared came to 962 years; then he died.

21When Enoch had lived 65 years, he begot Methuselah. 22After the birth of Methuselah, Enoch walked with God 300 years; and he be-

6וַיְחִי־שֵׁת חָמֵשׁ שָׁנִים וּמְאַת שָׁנָה וַיּוֹלֶד
אֶת־אֱנוֹשׁ׃ 7וַיְחִי־שֵׁת אַחֲרֵי הוֹלִידוֹ אֶת־
אֱנוֹשׁ שֶׁבַע שָׁנִים וּשְׁמֹנֶה מֵאוֹת שָׁנָה
וַיּוֹלֶד בָּנִים וּבָנוֹת׃ 8וַיִּהְיוּ כָּל־יְמֵי־שֵׁת
שְׁתֵּים עֶשְׂרֵה שָׁנָה וּתְשַׁע מֵאוֹת שָׁנָה
וַיָּמֹת׃ ס 9וַיְחִי אֱנוֹשׁ תִּשְׁעִים שָׁנָה
וַיּוֹלֶד אֶת־קֵינָן׃ 10וַיְחִי אֱנוֹשׁ אַחֲרֵי
הוֹלִידוֹ אֶת־קֵינָן חֲמֵשׁ עֶשְׂרֵה שָׁנָה
וּשְׁמֹנֶה מֵאוֹת שָׁנָה וַיּוֹלֶד בָּנִים וּבָנוֹת׃
11וַיִּהְיוּ כָּל־יְמֵי אֱנוֹשׁ חָמֵשׁ שָׁנִים וּתְשַׁע
מֵאוֹת שָׁנָה וַיָּמֹת׃ ס 12וַיְחִי קֵינָן
שִׁבְעִים שָׁנָה וַיּוֹלֶד אֶת־מַהֲלַלְאֵל׃
13וַיְחִי קֵינָן אַחֲרֵי הוֹלִידוֹ אֶת־מַהֲלַלְאֵל
אַרְבָּעִים שָׁנָה וּשְׁמֹנֶה מֵאוֹת שָׁנָה וַיּוֹלֶד
בָּנִים וּבָנוֹת׃ 14וַיִּהְיוּ כָּל־יְמֵי קֵינָן עֶשֶׂר
שָׁנִים וּתְשַׁע מֵאוֹת שָׁנָה וַיָּמֹת׃ ס
15וַיְחִי מַהֲלַלְאֵל חָמֵשׁ שָׁנִים וְשִׁשִּׁים
שָׁנָה וַיּוֹלֶד אֶת־יָרֶד׃ 16וַיְחִי מַהֲלַלְאֵל
אַחֲרֵי הוֹלִידוֹ אֶת־יֶרֶד שְׁלֹשִׁים שָׁנָה
וּשְׁמֹנֶה מֵאוֹת שָׁנָה וַיּוֹלֶד בָּנִים וּבָנוֹת׃
17וַיִּהְיוּ כָּל־יְמֵי מַהֲלַלְאֵל חָמֵשׁ וְתִשְׁעִים
שָׁנָה וּשְׁמֹנֶה מֵאוֹת שָׁנָה וַיָּמֹת׃ ס
18וַיְחִי־יֶרֶד שְׁתַּיִם וְשִׁשִּׁים שָׁנָה וּמְאַת
שָׁנָה וַיּוֹלֶד אֶת־חֲנוֹךְ׃ 19וַיְחִי־יֶרֶד אַחֲרֵי
הוֹלִידוֹ אֶת־חֲנוֹךְ שְׁמֹנֶה מֵאוֹת שָׁנָה
וַיּוֹלֶד בָּנִים וּבָנוֹת׃ 20וַיִּהְיוּ כָּל־יְמֵי־יֶרֶד
שְׁתַּיִם וְשִׁשִּׁים שָׁנָה וּתְשַׁע מֵאוֹת שָׁנָה
וַיָּמֹת׃ פ 21וַיְחִי חֲנוֹךְ חָמֵשׁ וְשִׁשִּׁים
שָׁנָה וַיּוֹלֶד אֶת־מְתוּשָׁלַח׃ 22וַיִּתְהַלֵּךְ
חֲנוֹךְ אֶת־הָאֱלֹהִים אַחֲרֵי הוֹלִידוֹ אֶת־

ENOCH (vv. 21–24)

Enoch, the seventh on the list, is singled out for special mention. The brevity of this biographic note suggests the one-time existence of some well-known story connected with his life and death. In postbiblical Jewish literature, Enoch was the focus of legends connecting him with a knowledge of the secrets of heaven, with the invention of mathematics and astronomy, and especially with the devising of a solar-based calendar.

22. walked with God The regular formula, "he lived," is replaced by a description of how he lived. The idiom, used again only of Noah in

מְתוּשֶׁלַח שְׁלֹשׁ מֵאוֹת שָׁנָה וַיּוֹלֶד בָּנִים
וּבָנוֹת׃ 23 וַיְהִי כָּל־יְמֵי חֲנוֹךְ חָמֵשׁ
וְשִׁשִּׁים שָׁנָה וּשְׁלֹשׁ מֵאוֹת שָׁנָה׃
24 וַיִּתְהַלֵּךְ חֲנוֹךְ אֶת־הָאֱלֹהִים וְאֵינֶנּוּ כִּי־
שביעי לָקַח אֹתוֹ אֱלֹהִים׃ פ 25 וַיְחִי מְתוּשֶׁלַח
שֶׁבַע וּשְׁמֹנִים שָׁנָה וּמְאַת שָׁנָה וַיּוֹלֶד
אֶת־לָמֶךְ׃ 26 וַיְחִי מְתוּשֶׁלַח אַחֲרֵי
הוֹלִידוֹ אֶת־לֶמֶךְ שְׁתַּיִם וּשְׁמוֹנִים שָׁנָה
וּשְׁבַע מֵאוֹת שָׁנָה וַיּוֹלֶד בָּנִים וּבָנוֹת׃
27 וַיִּהְיוּ כָּל־יְמֵי מְתוּשֶׁלַח תֵּשַׁע וְשִׁשִּׁים
שָׁנָה וּתְשַׁע מֵאוֹת שָׁנָה וַיָּמֹת׃ פ
28 וַיְחִי־לֶמֶךְ שְׁתַּיִם וּשְׁמֹנִים שָׁנָה וּמְאַת
שָׁנָה וַיּוֹלֶד בֵּן׃ 29 וַיִּקְרָא אֶת־שְׁמוֹ נֹחַ
לֵאמֹר זֶה* יְנַחֲמֵנוּ מִמַּעֲשֵׂנוּ וּמֵעִצְּבוֹן
יָדֵינוּ מִן־הָאֲדָמָה אֲשֶׁר אֵרְרָהּ יְהוָה׃
30 וַיְחִי־לֶמֶךְ אַחֲרֵי הוֹלִידוֹ אֶת־נֹחַ חָמֵשׁ
וְתִשְׁעִים שָׁנָה וַחֲמֵשׁ מֵאֹת שָׁנָה וַיּוֹלֶד
בָּנִים וּבָנוֹת׃ 31 וַיְהִי כָּל־יְמֵי־לֶמֶךְ שֶׁבַע
וְשִׁבְעִים שָׁנָה וּשְׁבַע מֵאוֹת שָׁנָה וַיָּמֹת׃

v. 29. שני טעמים

got sons and daughters. 23 All the days of Enoch came to 365 years. 24 Enoch walked with God; then he was no more, for God took him.

25 When Methuselah had lived 187 years, he begot Lamech. 26 After the birth of Lamech, Methuselah lived 782 years and begot sons and daughters. 27 All the days of Methuselah came to 969 years; then he died.

28 When Lamech had lived 182 years, he begot a son. 29 And he named him Noah, saying, "This one will provide us relief from our work and from the toil of our hands, out of the very soil which the LORD placed under a curse." 30 After the birth of Noah, Lamech lived 595 years and begot sons and daughters. 31 All the days of Lamech came to 777 years; then he died.

6:9, describes a life spent in closest intimacy with God.

24. Enoch walked with God The unusual idiom is repeated here, as Bekhor Shor noted, so that the brevity of Enoch's life would not be seen as a punishment for sin.

then he was no more A term used for an unexpected and unexplained disappearance.

for God took him The text is deliberately obscure, suggesting that Enoch did not die but rather ascended alive to heaven (see the nonbiblical yet ancient Book of Enoch).

METHUSELAH (vv. 25–27)

25. Methuselah . . . lived The man with the longest life span was fathered by the one with the shortest. Methuselah died at the onset of the Flood.

LAMECH (vv. 28–31)

28. Lamech See Gen. 4:18.

he begot a son The 10th generation is a critical turning point in human history and brings the list to an end.

29. Noah The name derives from the stem meaning "to rest" (נוח). The explanation given in the narrative is based on similarity of sound, not on etymology, because Noah cannot originate from the stem meaning "to comfort, give relief" (נחם).

relief This probably refers to a tradition about Noah as a culture hero. He was said to have invented the plow, initiating true agriculture, as opposed to hoe agriculture or horticulture. According to another tradition, he initiated a revolution in food production, effect-

24. Some commentators see Enoch as a saint. God "took" him to keep him from being corrupted by his wicked counterparts. Others see him as morally deficient. He "walked with God" but would not deign to be involved in the concerns of less pious neighbors (Ḥatam Sofer).

[32]When Noah had lived 500 years, Noah begot Shem, Ham, and Japheth.

6

When men began to increase on earth and daughters were born to them, [2]the divine beings saw how beautiful the daughters of men were and took wives from among those that pleased them.—[3]The LORD said, "My breath shall not abide in man forever, since he too is flesh; let the days allowed him be

ס 32 וַיְהִי־נֹחַ בֶּן־חֲמֵשׁ מֵאוֹת שָׁנָה וַיּוֹלֶד
נֹחַ אֶת־שֵׁם אֶת־חָם וְאֶת־יָפֶת׃

ו וַיְהִי כִּי־הֵחֵל הָאָדָם לָרֹב עַל־פְּנֵי
הָאֲדָמָה וּבָנוֹת יֻלְּדוּ לָהֶם׃ 2 וַיִּרְאוּ בְנֵי־
הָאֱלֹהִים אֶת־בְּנוֹת הָאָדָם כִּי טֹבֹת הֵנָּה
וַיִּקְחוּ לָהֶם נָשִׁים מִכֹּל אֲשֶׁר בָּחָרוּ׃
3 וַיֹּאמֶר יְהוָה לֹא־יָדוֹן רוּחִי בָאָדָם
לְעֹלָם בְּשַׁגַּם הוּא בָשָׂר וְהָיוּ יָמָיו מֵאָה

ing an enormous saving of time and energy. Another tradition views him as the initiator of viticulture: the first to discover the soothing and enlivening effects of wine (see 9:20).

NOAH (v. 32)

32. Noah had lived 500 years The extraordinarily advanced age at which he begets a child, compared to his forebears, is required by the statement that he was 600 years old at the time of the Flood (according to 7:11), and there were no grandchildren in the ark.

Shem Meaning "name, fame, renown."

Ham Possibly derived from the Hebrew word *ḥam,* "a wife's father"; the Hebrew *ḥam,* "hot, dark skinned"; or the Egyptian *ḥm,* "servant."

Japheth It is possibly the same name as Iapetus, found in Greek mythology, but with no known etymology.

CELESTIAL–TERRESTRIAL INTERMARRIAGE (6:1–4)

Legends about relationships among gods and mortal women and among goddesses and men, resulting in the propagation of demigods, are widespread and familiar subjects of pagan mythology. The version presented here, highly condensed from what was once a well-known and fuller story, adds to the ancient myths the Israelite notion that the offspring of such unnatural unions may possess heroic stature but are devoid of divine qualities. They are flesh and blood like all humans, and their life span is severely limited compared to the individuals listed in chapter 5.

1. men The Hebrew word *ha-adam,* literally, "the man," is here a collective: humankind.

2. the divine beings The definite article points to a familiar term. The context in Job 1:6, 2:1, and 38:7 indicates that the reference is to the angelic host, the celestial entourage of God, an image drawn from human kings surrounded by their courtiers.

The Hebrew for "divine beings" here is *b'nei* (which also can mean "sons of" or "children of") *elohim* (which usually is translated as "God"). The word *b'nei* often means "members of a category," so that the Hebrew phrase here means "members of the category of divine beings" (*elohim*). Similarly, *b'nei yisra·el* does not mean "the children of Israel," but Israelites.

saw how beautiful Driven by lust, their only criterion in the selection of mates was external beauty, not character.

took wives The Hebrew phrase לקח אשה is the regular term for the beginning of the marriage relationship. There is no hint of violent possession, nor is there any condemnation of the women involved.

3. My breath The "breath of life" (Gen. 2:7) that issues from God. Its presence or absence determines life and death.

in man The reference here is not only to the offspring of these unnatural unions but also to all humankind, because disorder has been introduced into God's creation.

flesh They are not divine, despite their nonhuman paternity. "Flesh" connotes human frailty.

CHAPTER 6

2. the divine beings . . . took wives Traditional commentators (Onkelos, Rashi, Hirsch) strive to avoid the mythologic implications of this account. They understand the "divine beings" to be the noble descendants of Seth, intermarrying with the descendants of Cain

one hundred and twenty years."—4 It was then, and later too, that the Nephilim appeared on earth—when the divine beings cohabited with the daughters of men, who bore them offspring. They were the heroes of old, the men of renown.

5 The LORD saw how great was man's wickedness on earth, and how every plan devised by his mind was nothing but evil all the time. 6 And the LORD regretted that He had made man on earth, and His heart was saddened. 7 The LORD said, "I will blot out from the earth the men whom I created—men together with beasts, creeping things, and birds of the sky; for I regret that I made them." 8 But Noah found favor with the LORD.

וְעֶשְׂרִים שָׁנָה׃ 4 הַנְּפִלִים הָיוּ בָאָרֶץ
בַּיָּמִים הָהֵם וְגַם אַחֲרֵי־כֵן אֲשֶׁר יָבֹאוּ
בְּנֵי הָאֱלֹהִים אֶל־בְּנוֹת הָאָדָם וְיָלְדוּ
לָהֶם הֵמָּה הַגִּבֹּרִים אֲשֶׁר מֵעוֹלָם אַנְשֵׁי
הַשֵּׁם׃ פ
מפטיר 5 וַיַּרְא יְהוָה כִּי רַבָּה רָעַת הָאָדָם בָּאָרֶץ
וְכָל־יֵצֶר מַחְשְׁבֹת לִבּוֹ רַק רַע כָּל־
הַיּוֹם׃ 6 וַיִּנָּחֶם יְהוָה כִּי־עָשָׂה אֶת־הָאָדָם
בָּאָרֶץ וַיִּתְעַצֵּב אֶל־לִבּוֹ׃ 7 וַיֹּאמֶר יְהוָה
אֶמְחֶה אֶת־הָאָדָם אֲשֶׁר־בָּרָאתִי מֵעַל
פְּנֵי הָאֲדָמָה מֵאָדָם עַד־בְּהֵמָה עַד־רֶמֶשׂ
וְעַד־עוֹף הַשָּׁמָיִם כִּי נִחַמְתִּי כִּי עֲשִׂיתִם׃
8 וְנֹחַ מָצָא חֵן בְּעֵינֵי יְהוָה׃ פ

one hundred and twenty years The duration of human life is reduced, a mark of moral and spiritual degeneration.

4. *the Nephilim appeared on earth* The offspring of the divine beings. These Nephilim—the etymology of the word is unknown—generated other Nephilim in the course of their married lives. Some suggest that the term means "fallen ones," a reference to the later myth of "the fallen angels."

heroes of old Their heroic exploits were the subject of many popular tales.

PROLOGUE TO THE FLOOD (vv. 5–8)

Humankind has abused God's gift of life and is now deep in moral decadence. The narrator asserts that the universal cataclysm into which the world is about to be plunged is not the result of blind fate or divine caprice but of God's judgment made inevitable by human evil.

5. ***every plan devised by his mind*** Literally, "every product of the thoughts of his heart." In the Bible, the heart is not only the organ of feeling but also of thought, understanding, and volition.

6. *regretted* The ascription of human emotions to God is a feature of biblical narrative.

saddened God's decision is made in sorrow, not in anger.

8. *Noah* Mention of him without further detail presupposes the reader's knowledge of 5:28–29.

found favor The reason for this is given in verse 9 and in 7:1.

---

who offered physical attractiveness but no moral standards. Whatever the ancient roots of this story, no Jewish commentator accepts the notion of a sexual union between divine beings and mortals, giving rise to a semidivine race.

3. *one hundred and twenty years* The purpose of this verse may be to anticipate the question "Why don't people here live as long as people did in earlier chapters?" The ideal, ultimate lifespan remains 120, exemplified by Moses (Deut. 34:7) and retained in the blessing "May you live a full life, to 120."

In the opening verses of this *parashah,* God created a pristine, orderly world and declared it "very good." By the end of the *parashah,* 10 generations later, that world has been so defiled by human depravity that God sees no alternative but to wash it clean and begin the human race anew with Noah.

הפטרת בראשית

HAFTARAH FOR B'REISHIT

ISAIAH 42:5–43:10 (*Ashk'nazim*)
ISAIAH 42:5–21 (*S'fardim*)

This *haftarah* is part of a collection of prophecies addressed to the Judean community in Babylonian exile in mid-6th century B.C.E. The prophet particularly emphasizes God's universal dominion and power as Creator but also notes His special concern for the people Israel, whose future liberation is presented as a light that will radiate to all nations.

The tradition of *S'fardim* concludes the *haftarah* with 42:21. The prophetic message is thus framed by an assertion about God's grace (*tzedek;* v. 6) and God's concern for His servant's vindication (*tzidko;* v. 21). The decision to end the *haftarah* at this point was apparently influenced by a reinterpretation of the word *"torah"* (v. 21, translated here as "teaching"). In its original context, the word *torah* refers strictly to a divine instruction (as in Isa. 2:3, "for instruction [*torah*] shall come forth from Zion"). The meaning of the word changed later, however, indicating the Torah of Moses as a whole.

In the tradition of *Ashk'nazim*, a longer selection from Isaiah is read. As a result, this reading presents a certain theological counterpoint. After declaring that the people neither see nor hear the prophecies of hope addressed to them (42:18–20), the prophet announces that God will nevertheless restore the people Israel to its homeland (43:3–6). At the climax of this prediction, the theme of Israel's blindness is repeated (43:8). God's deliverance of Israel from this state provides a triumphal echo to Israel's role as servant mentioned at the outset of the *haftarah,* a servant whose specific task is to lead the blind and the burdened into the light of freedom (42:6–7). The opening oracle is referred to again in the concluding challenge to all the nations. God's power to predict events before they occur (as in 42:9) is stressed as the reason to believe the new call of hope (43:9).

What is the precise identity of the "servant" in this *haftarah?* At the outset, the servant appears to be an individual, because words are directed in the second person singular to an unnamed "you" whom God has summoned to open "eyes deprived of light" (42:7). On the basis of 42:1–4 (verses that precede the *haftarah*), this individual is called to be a light of hope and consolation for the nation in exile. However, in the context of the *haftarah* (which begins at 42:5), the nation as a whole is addressed. Rabbinic editing thus gives the opening task a universalistic tone. It is the people Israel who are to be a light to all nations, calling them forth from servitude and darkness.

This was not necessarily the original intent of the oracle. Indeed, later verses focus on God's attempts to deliver blind Israel from its own darkness (42:16, 43:8), with no mention of liberation for all nations. Nevertheless, a universalistic reading of this passage is a recurrent feature of Jewish thought. In modern times, the challenge to Jews to be a beacon of light for all the downtrodden has been regarded as the moral imperative of the passage.

Declaring that Israel is God's witness to His power and uniqueness (43:10), the prophet states that the very history of this nation testifies to the truth of divine predictions (43:10; cf. 44:8). He thus derived theology from historical events, considering the truth of prophecy to be an argument for God's incomparable existence and majesty. Such declarations, however, fell on the deaf ears of a people in exile who had experienced history as a dark and hopeless sphere. In this state, they remained spiritually blind to the theological challenge to their condition.

RELATION OF THE *HAFTARAH*
TO THE *PARASHAH*

The theme of creation links the readings, showing us something of the range and purposes of the theologies of Creation in the Bible. Compared to the exalted and impersonal narrative style in Gen. 1:1–2:4, references to the creation in the *haftarah* (Isa. 42:5–6) are part of a divine proclamation though His prophet. The prophet expresses the continuity of divine action or its effects by using verbs in ongoing present time. This stands in marked contrast to the verbs in Gen. 1, which indicate past, completed action. Thus in the *haftarah*, the theme of creation serves as the basis for theological reflection on God's ongoing concern for the world.

In the prophet's theology, the images of light and darkness undergo a significant shift. In the *parashah,* darkness makes up the original state of the world, which is transformed by the reality of light on the first day of Creation. Light (*or*) marks difference, clarity, and order. In the *haftarah,* the images of darkness and light express other realities. The darkness of exile is both the oppression of servitude, to be transformed by divine liberation, and the inner void of despair that is redeemed by God's promise of renewal. Recreated anew by God, Israel will be the light (*or*) of hope in the eyes of all (42:6–7).

42 5Thus said God the LORD,
Who created the heavens and stretched them out,
Who spread out the earth and what it brings forth,
Who gave breath to the people upon it
And life to those who walk thereon:
6I the LORD, in My grace, have summoned you,
And I have grasped you by the hand.

מב 5 כֹּה־אָמַ֞ר הָאֵ֣ל ׀ יְהוָ֗ה
בּוֹרֵ֤א הַשָּׁמַ֙יִם֙ וְנ֣וֹטֵיהֶ֔ם
רֹקַ֥ע הָאָ֖רֶץ וְצֶאֱצָאֶ֑יהָ
נֹתֵ֤ן נְשָׁמָה֙ לָעָ֣ם עָלֶ֔יהָ
וְר֖וּחַ לַהֹלְכִ֥ים בָּֽהּ׃
6 אֲנִ֧י יְהוָ֛ה קְרָאתִ֥יךָֽ בְצֶ֖דֶק
וְאַחְזֵ֣ק בְּיָדֶ֑ךָ

Isaiah 42:5. The Creation account in Gen. 1–2 relates how God created (*bara*) the heavens (*ha-shamayim*) and the earth (*ha-aretz*), a wind (*ruaḥ*) from God sweeping over the water, an expanse (*rakia*) in the midst of the water, and the breath of life (*nishmat ḥayyim*) that enlivens the first creature. Correspondingly, the prophet (Isa. 42:5) speaks of God "who created (*borei*) the heavens (*ha-shamayim*) . . . (and) spread out (*roka*) the earth (*ha-aretz*)"; and "Who gave breath (*n'shamah*) to the people upon it / And life (*ruaḥ*) to those who walk thereon." Clearly, Isaiah's theology of creation is aware of the earlier tradition and its vocabulary.

6–7. The passage is a personal exhortation by God ("I the LORD . . . have summoned you"). It presumably refers to the servant mentioned in 42:1. Rashi understood the addressee in verse 5 to be the prophet himself, called on to restore the nations to God's covenant, the nations here being the tribes of Israel. It is also possible to interpret the messenger as an individual with the task of re-establishing the people Israel so that they may serve as a beacon of light for all peoples (Ibn Ezra). If, however, the messenger is Israel, then the phrase would mean that God has established the entire people for a universal mission (Radak).

6. I the LORD This emphasis on the name *YHVH* occurs first in God's unique disclosure to Moses (Exod. 6:2). The strong emphasis of this name in Isaiah goes together with the prophet's emphasis on an absolute and uncompromising monotheism. Israel's particular and personal God is the universal, transcendent God of all creation.

in My grace The Hebrew here (*b'tzedek*) literally means "with grace." The word *tzedek* has many meanings in the Bible, depending on context.

I created you, and appointed you
A covenant people, a light of nations—

7Opening eyes deprived of light,
Rescuing prisoners from confinement,
From the dungeon those who sit in darkness.

8I am the Lord, that is My name;
I will not yield My glory to another,
Nor My renown to idols.

9See, the things once predicted have come,
And now I foretell new things,
Announce to you ere they sprout up.

10Sing to the Lord a new song,
His praise from the ends of the earth—
You who sail the sea and you creatures in
    it,
You coastlands and their inhabitants!

11Let the desert and its towns cry aloud,
The villages where Kedar dwells;
Let Sela's inhabitants shout,
Call out from the peaks of the mountains.

12Let them do honor to the Lord,
And tell His glory in the coastlands.

13The Lord goes forth like a warrior,
Like a fighter He whips up His rage.
He yells, He roars aloud,
He charges upon His enemies.

14"I have kept silent far too long,
Kept still and restrained Myself;
Now I will scream like a woman in labor,
I will pant and I will gasp.

וְאֶצׇּרְךָ֥ וְאֶתֶּנְךָ֖
לִבְרִ֣ית עָ֔ם לְא֖וֹר גּוֹיִֽם׃
7 לִפְקֹ֖חַ עֵינַ֣יִם עִוְר֑וֹת
לְהוֹצִ֤יא מִמַּסְגֵּר֙ אַסִּ֔יר
מִבֵּ֥ית כֶּ֖לֶא יֹ֥שְׁבֵי חֹֽשֶׁךְ׃
8 אֲנִ֥י יְהֹוָ֖ה ה֣וּא שְׁמִ֑י
וּכְבוֹדִי֙ לְאַחֵ֣ר לֹֽא־אֶתֵּ֔ן
וּתְהִלָּתִ֖י לַפְּסִילִֽים׃
9 הָרִֽאשֹׁנ֖וֹת הִנֵּה־בָ֑אוּ
וַֽחֲדָשׁוֹת֙ אֲנִ֣י מַגִּ֔יד
בְּטֶ֥רֶם תִּצְמַ֖חְנָה אַשְׁמִ֥יעַ אֶתְכֶֽם׃ ס
10 שִׁ֤ירוּ לַֽיהֹוָה֙ שִׁ֣יר חָדָ֔שׁ
תְּהִלָּת֖וֹ מִקְצֵ֣ה הָאָ֑רֶץ
יֽוֹרְדֵ֤י הַיָּם֙ וּמְלֹא֔וֹ
אִיִּ֖ים וְיֹֽשְׁבֵיהֶֽם׃
11 יִשְׂא֤וּ מִדְבָּר֙ וְעָרָ֔יו
חֲצֵרִ֖ים תֵּשֵׁ֣ב קֵדָ֑ר
יָרֹ֨נּוּ֙ יֹ֣שְׁבֵי סֶ֔לַע
מֵרֹ֥אשׁ הָרִ֖ים יִצְוָֽחוּ׃
12 יָשִׂ֥ימוּ לַֽיהֹוָ֖ה כָּב֑וֹד
וּתְהִלָּת֖וֹ בָּֽאִיִּ֥ים יַגִּֽידוּ׃
13 יְהֹוָה֙ כַּגִּבּ֣וֹר יֵצֵ֔א
כְּאִ֥ישׁ מִלְחָמ֖וֹת יָעִ֣יר קִנְאָ֑ה
יָרִ֨יעַ֙ אַף־יַצְרִ֔יחַ
עַל־אֹֽיְבָ֖יו יִתְגַּבָּֽר׃ ס
14 הֶֽחֱשֵׁ֣יתִי מֵֽעוֹלָ֔ם
אַחֲרִ֖ישׁ אֶתְאַפָּ֑ק
כַּיּֽוֹלֵדָ֣ה אֶפְעֶ֔ה
אֶשֹּׁ֥ם וְאֶשְׁאַ֖ף יָֽחַד׃

---

9. The things once predicted Because these prophecies of Isaiah postdate the fall of Babylon (539 B.C.E.), they probably refer to that event. Reference to earlier prophecies is a major motif of the prophet (see Isa. 41:22, 44:7, 45:21, 46:10, 48:3), used to motivate the people to trust this new prophecies of restoration.

10. Sing to the Lord The exhortation to "sing to the Lord a new song" in verses 10–12 echoes the liturgical formulations in passages such as Ps. 33:3 and 149:1. Clearly, there is a complex cultural interaction between this prophet and communal liturgy, although the precise direction of influence is difficult to determine.

14. I have kept silent Traditionally, this is understood as God's silence since the destruction of the Temple and during the exilic sorrows of the nations (Rashi, Radak).

15Hills and heights will I scorch,
Cause all their green to wither;
I will turn rivers into isles,
And dry the marshes up.
16I will lead the blind
By a road they did not know,
And I will make them walk
By paths they never knew.
I will turn darkness before them to light,
Rough places into level ground.
These are the promises—
I will keep them without fail.
17Driven back and utterly shamed
Shall be those who trust in an image,
Those who say to idols,
'You are our gods!'"

18Listen, you who are deaf;
You blind ones, look up and see!
19Who is so blind as My servant,
So deaf as the messenger I send?
Who is so blind as the chosen one,
So blind as the servant of the LORD?
20Seeing many things, he gives no heed;
With ears open, he hears nothing.
21The LORD desires His [servant's] vindication,
That he may magnify and glorify [His] Teaching.

22Yet it is a people plundered and despoiled:
All of them are trapped in holes,
Imprisoned in dungeons.
They are given over to plunder, with none to rescue them;

15 אַחֲרִיב הָרִים וּגְבָעוֹת
וְכָל־עֶשְׂבָּם אוֹבִישׁ
וְשַׂמְתִּי נְהָרוֹת לָאִיִּים
וַאֲגַמִּים אוֹבִישׁ׃
16 וְהוֹלַכְתִּי עִוְרִים
בְּדֶרֶךְ לֹא יָדָעוּ
בִּנְתִיבוֹת לֹא־יָדְעוּ
אַדְרִיכֵם
אָשִׂים מַחְשָׁךְ לִפְנֵיהֶם לָאוֹר
וּמַעֲקַשִּׁים לְמִישׁוֹר
אֵלֶּה הַדְּבָרִים
עֲשִׂיתִם וְלֹא עֲזַבְתִּים׃
17 נָסֹגוּ אָחוֹר יֵבֹשׁוּ בֹשֶׁת
הַבֹּטְחִים בַּפָּסֶל
הָאֹמְרִים לְמַסֵּכָה
אַתֶּם אֱלֹהֵינוּ׃ ס

18 הַחֵרְשִׁים שְׁמָעוּ
וְהַעִוְרִים הַבִּיטוּ לִרְאוֹת׃
19 מִי עִוֵּר כִּי אִם־עַבְדִּי
וְחֵרֵשׁ כְּמַלְאָכִי אֶשְׁלָח
מִי עִוֵּר כִּמְשֻׁלָּם
וְעִוֵּר כְּעֶבֶד יְהוָה׃
20 ראית רָאוֹת רַבּוֹת וְלֹא תִשְׁמֹר
פָּקוֹחַ אָזְנַיִם וְלֹא יִשְׁמָע׃
21 יְהוָה חָפֵץ לְמַעַן צִדְקוֹ
יַגְדִּיל תּוֹרָה וְיַאְדִּיר׃

22 וְהוּא עַם־בָּזוּז וְשָׁסוּי
הָפֵחַ בַּחוּרִים כֻּלָּם
וּבְבָתֵּי כְלָאִים הָחְבָּאוּ
הָיוּ לָבַז וְאֵין מַצִּיל

21. The LORD desires His [servant's] vindication The Sages used this passage to support their view that the Jews are vindicated before God through their magnification of the written Torah and its oral expansions, the commandments (see M *Avot* 6.11; BT *Mak.* 23b). This phrase forms the liturgical climax to the daily morning service and concludes the future-oriented prayer that begins, "A redeemer will come for Zion" (*U-va l'tziyyon go·el*).

To despoilment, with none to say "Give back!"
23 If only you would listen to this,
Attend and give heed from now on!
24 Who was it gave Jacob over to despoilment
And Israel to plunderers?
Surely, the LORD against whom they sinned
In whose ways they would not walk
And whose Teaching they would not obey.
25 So He poured out wrath upon them,
His anger and the fury of war.
It blazed upon them all about, but they heeded not;
It burned among them, but they gave it no thought.

מְשִׁסָּ֖ה וְאֵין־אֹמֵ֥ר הָשַֽׁב׃
23 מִ֥י בָכֶ֖ם יַאֲזִ֣ין זֹ֑את
יַקְשִׁ֥ב וְיִשְׁמַ֖ע לְאָחֽוֹר׃
24 מִֽי־נָתַ֨ן למשוסה לִמְשִׁסָּ֧ה יַעֲקֹ֛ב
וְיִשְׂרָאֵ֥ל לְבֹזְזִ֖ים
הֲל֣וֹא יְהוָ֗ה ז֚וּ חָטָ֣אנוּ ל֔וֹ
וְלֹֽא־אָב֤וּ בִדְרָכָיו֙ הָל֔וֹךְ
וְלֹ֥א שָׁמְע֖וּ בְּתוֹרָתֽוֹ׃
25 וַיִּשְׁפֹּ֤ךְ עָלָיו֙ חֵמָ֣ה אַפּ֔וֹ
וֶעֱז֖וּז מִלְחָמָ֑ה
וַתְּלַהֲטֵ֤הוּ מִסָּבִיב֙ וְלֹ֣א יָדָ֔ע
וַתִּבְעַר־בּ֖וֹ וְלֹא־יָשִׂ֥ים עַל־לֵֽב׃ פ

43 But now thus said the LORD—
Who created you, O Jacob,
Who formed you, O Israel:
Fear not, for I will redeem you;
I have singled you out by name,
You are Mine.
2 When you pass through water,
I will be with you;
Through streams,
They shall not overwhelm you.
When you walk through fire,
You shall not be scorched;
Through flame,
It shall not burn you.
3 For I the LORD am your God,
The Holy One of Israel, your Savior.
I give Egypt as a ransom for you,
Ethiopia and Saba in exchange for you.
4 Because you are precious to Me,
And honored, and I love you,

מג וְעַתָּ֞ה כֹּֽה־אָמַ֤ר יְהוָה֙
בֹּרַאֲךָ֣ יַעֲקֹ֔ב
וְיֹצֶרְךָ֖ יִשְׂרָאֵ֑ל
אַל־תִּירָא֙ כִּ֣י גְאַלְתִּ֔יךָ
קָרָ֥אתִי בְשִׁמְךָ֖
לִי־אָֽתָּה׃
2 כִּֽי־תַעֲבֹ֤ר בַּמַּ֙יִם֙
אִתְּךָ־אָ֔נִי
וּבַנְּהָר֖וֹת
לֹ֣א יִשְׁטְפ֑וּךָ
כִּֽי־תֵלֵ֤ךְ בְּמוֹ־אֵשׁ֙
לֹ֣א תִכָּוֶ֔ה
וְלֶהָבָ֖ה
לֹ֥א תִבְעַר־בָּֽךְ׃
3 כִּ֗י אֲנִי֙ יְהוָ֣ה אֱלֹהֶ֔יךָ
קְד֥וֹשׁ יִשְׂרָאֵ֖ל מוֹשִׁיעֶ֑ךָ
נָתַ֤תִּי כָפְרְךָ֙ מִצְרַ֔יִם
כּ֥וּשׁ וּסְבָ֖א תַּחְתֶּֽיךָ׃
4 מֵאֲשֶׁ֨ר יָקַ֧רְתָּ בְעֵינַ֛י
נִכְבַּ֖דְתָּ וַאֲנִ֣י אֲהַבְתִּ֑יךָ

I give men in exchange for you
And peoples in your stead.

5 Fear not, for I am with you:
I will bring your folk from the East,
Will gather you out of the West;
6 I will say to the North, "Give back!"
And to the South, "Do not withhold!
Bring My sons from afar,
And My daughters from the end of the earth—
7 All who are linked to My name,
Whom I have created,
Formed, and made for My glory—
8 Setting free that people,
Blind though it has eyes
And deaf though it has ears."

9 All the nations assemble as one,
The peoples gather.
Who among them declared this,
Foretold to us the things that have happened?
Let them produce their witnesses and be vindicated,
That men, hearing them, may say, "It is true!"
10 My witnesses are *you*
—declares the LORD—
My servant, whom I have chosen.
To the end that you may take thought,
And believe in Me,
And understand that I am He:
Before Me no god was formed,
And after Me none shall exist!

וְאֶתֵּ֤ן אָדָם֙ תַּחְתֶּ֔יךָ
וּלְאֻמִּ֖ים תַּ֥חַת נַפְשֶֽׁךָ׃

5 אַל־תִּירָ֖א כִּ֣י אִתְּךָ־אָ֑נִי
מִמִּזְרָח֙ אָבִ֣יא זַרְעֶ֔ךָ
וּמִמַּעֲרָ֖ב אֲקַבְּצֶֽךָּ׃
6 אֹמַ֤ר לַצָּפוֹן֙ תֵּ֔נִי
וּלְתֵימָ֖ן אַל־תִּכְלָ֑אִי
הָבִ֤יאִי בָנַי֙ מֵֽרָח֔וֹק
וּבְנוֹתַ֖י מִקְצֵ֥ה הָאָֽרֶץ׃
7 כֹּ֚ל הַנִּקְרָ֣א בִשְׁמִ֔י
וְלִכְבוֹדִ֖י בְּרָאתִ֑יו
יְצַרְתִּ֖יו אַף־עֲשִׂיתִֽיו׃
8 הוֹצִ֛יא עַם־עִוֵּ֖ר
וְעֵינַ֣יִם יֵ֑שׁ
וְחֵרְשִׁ֖ים וְאָזְנַ֥יִם לָֽמוֹ׃

9 כָּֽל־הַגּוֹיִ֞ם נִקְבְּצ֣וּ יַחְדָּ֗ו
וְיֵאָֽסְפוּ֙ לְאֻמִּ֔ים
מִ֤י בָהֶם֙ יַגִּ֣יד זֹ֔את
וְרִאשֹׁנ֖וֹת יַשְׁמִיעֻ֑נוּ
יִתְּנ֤וּ עֵֽדֵיהֶם֙ וְיִצְדָּ֔קוּ
וְיִשְׁמְע֖וּ וְיֹאמְר֥וּ אֱמֶֽת׃
10 אַתֶּ֤ם עֵדַי֙
נְאֻם־יְהוָ֔ה
וְעַבְדִּ֖י אֲשֶׁ֣ר בָּחָ֑רְתִּי
לְמַ֣עַן תֵּ֠דְעוּ
וְתַאֲמִ֨ינוּ לִ֤י
וְתָבִ֙ינוּ֙ כִּֽי־אֲנִ֣י ה֔וּא
לְפָנַי֙ לֹא־נ֣וֹצַר אֵ֔ל
וְאַחֲרַ֖י לֹ֥א יִהְיֶֽה׃ ס

Isaiah 43:10. My witnesses are you Israel's historical existence is proof of God's incomparable existence, by virtue of the fulfillment of divine prophecies made about them. In Rabbinic times, the Sages extended Isaiah's insight, formulating it with more paradoxical and daring rhetoric. Commenting on the formulation in Isa. 43:12, they say: "When 'you are My witnesses—declares the LORD'—then I am God, but when you are not My witnesses then I, so to speak, am not God" (Sifrei Deut. 346).

[9]This is the line of Noah.—Noah was a righteous man; he was blameless in his age; Noah
walked with God.—[10]Noah begot three sons:
Shem, Ham, and Japheth.
[11]The earth became corrupt before God; the
earth was filled with lawlessness. [12]When God

9 אֵלֶּה תּוֹלְדֹת נֹחַ נֹחַ אִישׁ צַדִּיק תָּמִים
הָיָה בְּדֹרֹתָיו אֶת־הָאֱלֹהִים הִתְהַלֶּךְ־נֹחַ׃
10 וַיּוֹלֶד נֹחַ שְׁלֹשָׁה בָנִים אֶת־שֵׁם אֶת־
חָם וְאֶת־יָפֶת׃
11 וַתִּשָּׁחֵת הָאָרֶץ לִפְנֵי הָאֱלֹהִים וַתִּמָּלֵא

NOAH AND THE FLOOD (6:9–9:17)

By the 10th generation after Adam, the moral corruption of humankind is so great that the world must be cleansed. There are numerous parallels between the biblical account of the Flood and the many ancient Near Eastern flood stories. Yet the biblical account differs significantly from all the other versions, which the Commentary will show.

THE INDICTMENT (6:9–13)

9. This is the line of Noah Because this is the caption for the entire narrative in which Noah plays a central role, it is preferable to translate: "This is the story of Noah."

righteous . . . blameless A righteous person (*tzaddik*) is one whose conduct God finds to be irreproachable. A blameless person (*tamim*) is one whose unimpeachable integrity makes the enjoyment of God's fellowship possible. See Pss. 15 and 101:6.

in his age In the face of universal corruption, he maintained civilized standards of behavior.

walked with God See Comment to Gen. 5:22.

11. The earth The use of such all-embracing terms as "the earth," "man's wickedness" (v. 5), and "all flesh" (v. 12) in the indictment of humanity serves to justify God's actions. The totality of the evil makes inevitable the totality of the punishment.

corrupt The Hebrew stem for "corrupt" (שחת) occurs seven times in the narrative in various forms.

lawlessness The universal corruption is further defined as *ḥamas,* a term that elsewhere is

---

In the first *parashah* of Genesis, the world deteriorated over the course of 10 generations, from the pristine perfection of its beginning to corruption in the days of Noah. God chooses not to destroy the world totally (a *midrash* suggests God did destroy previous disappointing worlds). Instead, God continues with the same creatures, human beings, blessed with free will and cursed with the tendency to misuse that free will, who have brought matters to this point. Noah's capacity for righteousness gives God cause for hope.

9. This is the line of Noah.—Noah The first person Noah "gave birth" to was himself. Confronting the moral corruption of his time, Noah had to decide what kind of person he really was.

in his age The Sages debate whether this is a true compliment or qualified praise. Yoḥanan sees Noah as righteous only relatively, in contrast to the wicked people around him. In a more respectable age, he would have been no better than average. Resh Lakish, on the other hand, says that anyone who had the moral backbone to be a good person in an immoral society would have been an even better person in a generation that encouraged goodness (BT Sanh. 108a). One emphasizes the power of society to shape the behavior of its members; the other champions the power of the individual to withstand the pressures of society.

11. corrupt before God God deemed their behavior corrupt, but they themselves saw nothing wrong with it.

the earth was filled with lawlessness The Jerusalem Talmud understands the word translated as "lawlessness" (*ḥamas*) to mean that people cheated each other for such small sums that the courts could not prosecute them (JT BM 4:2). This caused people to lose faith in the power of government to provide them with a fair and livable world, and society began to slip into anarchy.

הָאָ֖רֶץ חָמָֽס׃ 12 וַיַּ֧רְא אֱלֹהִ֛ים אֶת־הָאָ֖רֶץ
וְהִנֵּ֣ה נִשְׁחָ֑תָה כִּֽי־הִשְׁחִ֧ית כָּל־בָּשָׂ֛ר אֶת־
דַּרְכּ֖וֹ עַל־הָאָֽרֶץ׃ ס 13 וַיֹּ֨אמֶר אֱלֹהִ֜ים
לְנֹ֗חַ קֵ֤ץ כָּל־בָּשָׂר֙ בָּ֣א לְפָנַ֔י כִּֽי־מָלְאָ֥ה
הָאָ֛רֶץ חָמָ֖ס מִפְּנֵיהֶ֑ם וְהִנְנִ֥י מַשְׁחִיתָ֖ם
אֶת־הָאָֽרֶץ׃ 14 עֲשֵׂ֤ה לְךָ֙ תֵּבַ֣ת עֲצֵי־גֹ֔פֶר
קִנִּ֖ים תַּעֲשֶׂ֣ה אֶת־הַתֵּבָ֑ה וְכָֽפַרְתָּ֥ אֹתָ֛הּ
מִבַּ֥יִת וּמִח֖וּץ בַּכֹּֽפֶר׃ 15 וְזֶ֕ה אֲשֶׁ֥ר תַּעֲשֶׂ֖ה
אֹתָ֑הּ שְׁלֹ֧שׁ מֵא֣וֹת אַמָּ֗ה אֹ֚רֶךְ הַתֵּבָ֔ה
חֲמִשִּׁ֤ים אַמָּה֙ רָחְבָּ֔הּ וּשְׁלֹשִׁ֥ים אַמָּ֖ה

saw how corrupt the earth was, for all flesh had corrupted its ways on earth, 13God said to Noah, "I have decided to put an end to all flesh, for the earth is filled with lawlessness because of them: I am about to destroy them with the earth. 14Make yourself an ark of *gopher* wood; make it an ark with compartments, and cover it inside and out with pitch. 15This is how you shall make it: the length of the ark shall be three hundred cubits, its width fifty

the synonym of "bloodshed," "falsehood," or "deceit." It parallels "no justice" in Job 19:7.

12. all flesh The corruption extended to the animal kingdom as well, through the intermating of species (BT Sanh. 108a). In this way, the Sages confronted the disturbing question of why *all* life had to perish when only human beings were corrupt.

13. God said to Noah God speaks to him directly seven times in this narrative. In the Mesopotamian tales, the decision of the gods to destroy the world, intended to be kept secret from humankind, was revealed by one of the gods to a specific individual.

because of them They brought it on themselves. The impending catastrophe is not the result of God's caprice or nature's blind fury.

with the earth Underlying this is the fundamental biblical idea that moral corruption physically contaminates the earth, which must then be cleansed of its pollution.

INSTRUCTIONS FOR BUILDING THE ARK
(vv. 14–16)

14. Make The stem meaning "make" (עשה) appears here seven times, to stress the point that Noah himself must shape the agency of his own salvation.

ark The Hebrew translated here as "ark" (*tevah*) appears in the Torah again only in connection with the rescue of the baby Moses (Exod. 2:3–5). It refers to a boxlike vessel made to float on water. It has no rudder, sail, navigational device, or crew. In the Mesopotamian flood stories, the hero builds a regular ship and employs boatmen to navigate it.

gopher wood The term appears only here. Some scholars link it to the cypress, which was used widely in shipbuilding in ancient times because of its resistance to rot.

compartments The plural *kinnim* traditionally has been interpreted to mean "cubicles" (from the singular *ken,* "nest"). Most likely, it is related to the same word in Akkadian, meaning "reeds," from which the boat in one of the Mesopotamian flood stories was constructed.

pitch The Hebrew word for "pitch," borrowed from the Akkadian *kupru,* is the same one found in the Mesopotamian flood stories for the substance used to caulk the boats.

15. cubits The Hebrew word *ammah* literally means "forearm," the distance between the elbow and the tip of the middle finger of an average-size man. The standard biblical cubit is about 18 inches (45 cm), yielding dimensions here of about 450 feet (157 m) in length, 75 feet (23 m) in width, and 45 feet (14 m) in height and a displacement of about 43,000 tons. In a Mesopotamian flood story, the vessel has a tonnage three or four times that of Noah's.

---

14. Why did God command Noah to build an ark? Surely God could have saved Noah and his family by supernatural intervention. Perhaps God hoped that the project would serve as a warning, moving onlookers to contemplate the threat of destruction and mend their ways (Tanḥ. 5). Or perhaps God wanted Noah to participate in some way in his own salvation, as the Israelites would—many centuries later—at the time of the Exodus.

קוֹמָתָֽהּ׃ 16 צֹ֣הַר ׀ תַּעֲשֶׂ֣ה לַתֵּבָ֗ה וְאֶל־
אַמָּה֙ תְּכַלֶּ֣נָּה מִלְמַ֔עְלָה וּפֶ֥תַח הַתֵּבָ֖ה
בְּצִדָּ֣הּ תָּשִׂ֑ים תַּחְתִּיִּ֛ם שְׁנִיִּ֥ם וּשְׁלִשִׁ֖ים
תַּעֲשֶֽׂהָ׃
17 וַאֲנִ֗י הִנְנִי֩ מֵבִ֨יא אֶת־הַמַּבּ֥וּל מַ֙יִם֙ עַל־
הָאָ֔רֶץ לְשַׁחֵ֣ת כָּל־בָּשָׂ֗ר אֲשֶׁר־בּוֹ֙ ר֣וּחַ
חַיִּ֔ים מִתַּ֖חַת הַשָּׁמָ֑יִם כֹּ֥ל אֲשֶׁר־בָּאָ֖רֶץ
יִגְוָֽע׃ 18 וַהֲקִמֹתִ֥י אֶת־בְּרִיתִ֖י אִתָּ֑ךְ וּבָאתָ֙
אֶל־הַתֵּבָ֔ה אַתָּ֕ה וּבָנֶ֛יךָ וְאִשְׁתְּךָ֥ וּנְשֵֽׁי־
בָנֶ֖יךָ אִתָּֽךְ׃ 19 וּמִכָּל־הָ֠חַי מִֽכָּל־בָּשָׂ֞ר
שְׁנַ֧יִם מִכֹּ֛ל תָּבִ֥יא אֶל־הַתֵּבָ֖ה לְהַחֲיֹ֣ת
אִתָּ֑ךְ זָכָ֥ר וּנְקֵבָ֖ה יִהְיֽוּ׃ 20 מֵהָע֣וֹף לְמִינֵ֗הוּ
וּמִן־הַבְּהֵמָה֙ לְמִינָ֔הּ מִכֹּ֛ל רֶ֥מֶשׂ הָֽאֲדָמָ֖ה
לְמִינֵ֑הוּ שְׁנַ֧יִם מִכֹּ֛ל יָבֹ֥אוּ אֵלֶ֖יךָ לְהַחֲיֽוֹת׃
21 וְאַתָּ֣ה קַח־לְךָ֗ מִכָּל־מַאֲכָל֙ אֲשֶׁ֣ר יֵֽאָכֵ֔ל
וְאָסַפְתָּ֖ אֵלֶ֑יךָ וְהָיָ֥ה לְךָ֛ וְלָהֶ֖ם לְאָכְלָֽה׃
22 וַיַּ֖עַשׂ נֹ֑חַ כְּ֠כֹל אֲשֶׁ֨ר צִוָּ֥ה אֹת֛וֹ אֱלֹהִ֖ים
שני כֵּ֥ן עָשָֽׂה׃ ס

cubits, and its height thirty cubits. 16Make an opening for daylight in the ark, and terminate it within a cubit of the top. Put the entrance to the ark in its side; make it with bottom, second, and third decks.

17"For My part, I am about to bring the Flood—waters upon the earth—to destroy all flesh under the sky in which there is breath of life; everything on earth shall perish. 18But I will establish My covenant with you, and you shall enter the ark, with your sons, your wife, and your sons' wives. 19And of all that lives, of all flesh, you shall take two of each into the ark to keep alive with you; they shall be male and female. 20From birds of every kind, cattle of every kind, every kind of creeping thing on earth, two of each shall come to you to stay alive. 21For your part, take of everything that is eaten and store it away, to serve as food for you and for them." 22Noah did so; just as God commanded him, so he did.

16. an opening for daylight The Hebrew word *tzohar* refers here to a "roof," as it does also in Akkadian, Ugaritic, and Arabic. The directive to "terminate it within a cubit of the top" (literally, "from above") could mean that the slanting roof should project one cubit beyond the side of the ark.

THE PURPOSE OF THE ARK (vv. 17–22)

17. For My part The sense is, "When you, Noah, have built the ark, I, God, will act."

the Flood The definite article before the Hebrew term *"mabbul"* implies some well-known entity. The phrase that follows, "waters upon the earth," serves to indicate a celestial origin. It suggests that "Flood" (*mabbul*) probably refers to the upper part of the original cosmic ocean that is about to fall upon the earth.

18. My covenant This is the first use in the Bible of the Hebrew term *"b'rit"* ("covenant"), one of the core concepts of biblical theology regarding the relationship between God and mortals. In this passage it can mean either that the divine blessing made to Adam in Gen. 1:28 will be fulfilled through Noah and his line (who would all survive and regenerate the world) or that a new, unconditional guarantee of salvation is now being given to Noah.

you shall enter the ark Eight persons in all, a single family, from which a renewed humankind will emerge.

your sons The males are listed first, then the females.

21. of everything that is eaten The vegetarian diet prescribed in 1:29–30.

22. Noah did so The text emphasizes Noah's trust in God. According to Rashi, this verse refers to the actual construction of the ark.

---

17. to destroy all flesh A corrupt, lawless society brings destruction on all of its citizens, innocent and guilty alike, and on the environment around it.

7 Then the LORD said to Noah, "Go into the ark, with all your household, for you alone have I found righteous before Me in this generation. 2Of every pure animal you shall take seven pairs, males and their mates, and of every animal that is not pure, two, a male and its mate; 3of the birds of the sky also, seven pairs, male and female, to keep seed alive upon all the earth. 4For in seven days' time I will make it rain upon the earth, forty days and forty nights, and I will blot out from the earth all existence that I created." 5And Noah did just as the LORD commanded him.

6Noah was six hundred years old when the Flood came, waters upon the earth. 7Noah,

שני **ז** וַיֹּאמֶר יְהוָה לְנֹחַ בֹּא־אַתָּה וְכָל־בֵּיתְךָ
אֶל־הַתֵּבָה כִּי־אֹתְךָ רָאִיתִי צַדִּיק לְפָנַי
בַּדּוֹר הַזֶּה: 2מִכֹּל | הַבְּהֵמָה הַטְּהוֹרָה
תִּקַּח־לְךָ שִׁבְעָה שִׁבְעָה אִישׁ וְאִשְׁתּוֹ
וּמִן־הַבְּהֵמָה אֲשֶׁר לֹא טְהֹרָה הִוא שְׁנַיִם
אִישׁ וְאִשְׁתּוֹ: 3גַּם מֵעוֹף הַשָּׁמַיִם שִׁבְעָה
שִׁבְעָה זָכָר וּנְקֵבָה לְחַיּוֹת זֶרַע עַל־
פְּנֵי כָל־הָאָרֶץ: 4כִּי לְיָמִים עוֹד שִׁבְעָה
אָנֹכִי מַמְטִיר עַל־הָאָרֶץ אַרְבָּעִים יוֹם
וְאַרְבָּעִים לָיְלָה וּמָחִיתִי אֶת־כָּל־הַיְקוּם
אֲשֶׁר עָשִׂיתִי מֵעַל פְּנֵי הָאֲדָמָה: 5וַיַּעַשׂ
נֹחַ כְּכֹל אֲשֶׁר־צִוָּהוּ יְהוָה:
6וְנֹחַ בֶּן־שֵׁשׁ מֵאוֹת שָׁנָה וְהַמַּבּוּל הָיָה
מַיִם עַל־הָאָרֶץ: 7וַיָּבֹא נֹחַ וּבָנָיו וְאִשְׁתּוֹ

THE EMBARKATION (7:1–9)

1. Your household In the Mesopotamian stories, by contrast, the hero's relations, craftsmen, and boatmen, enter the vessel along with him and his immediate family.

for you alone The Torah does not tell us whether Noah's family is saved solely through his merit or whether they were individually righteous as well.

2. pure . . . impure These categories refer only to suitability for sacrifice, not for human consumption. The criteria for that were issued only after the Flood, when people were first permitted to eat the flesh of animals. See 9:2–3. Although only animals are mentioned here, 8:20 shows that the birds were similarly classified.

seven pairs There is a discrepancy between this verse and the instructions of 6:19–20, which mention one pair of each species. This has prompted modern scholars to assert that the two passages originate from diverse strands of ancient Israelite tradition. Traditional commentators explain that 6:19–20 refer to the minimum number needed for the regeneration of the species, whereas 7:2–3 include the additional pure animals needed for the sacrifices after the Flood.

4. in seven days' time Presumably, this is the period of time needed for the future occupants of the ark to get aboard and be properly accommodated. Seven-day periods are characteristic of this story.

I will make it rain The phrase resonates with the awesome power and transcendence of the one God who alone will determine the dimensions and the duration of the Flood.

forty days The number 40, a symbolic number in the Bible, is often connected with purification and the cleansing of sin and has that significance here (see Exod. 24:18, 34:28, Num. 13:25, Ezek. 4:6).

5. Noah did This refers to boarding the ark.

6. six hundred years old For Mesopotamians, the basic unit of time is 60. Their mathematics did not employ the decimal system but a system (sexagesimal) based on 60. That system

---

CHAPTER 7

7. The word order—which lists all the husbands first, then the wives—implies that Noah and his sons enter the ark separately from their wives. It would have been unseemly for them to enjoy marital intimacy while the rest of humanity was drowning. Only after the Flood would they again live as husbands and wives (see Gen. 8:16; Gen. R. 31:12).

with his sons, his wife, and his sons' wives,
went into the ark because of the waters of the
Flood. 8Of the pure animals, of the animals
that are not pure, of the birds, and of everything that creeps on the ground, 9two of each,
male and female, came to Noah into the ark, as
God had commanded Noah. 10And on the seventh day the waters of the Flood came upon
the earth.

11In the six hundredth year of Noah's life, in
the second month, on the seventeenth day of
the month, on that day

All the fountains of the great deep burst
apart,
And the floodgates of the sky broke open.

(12The rain fell on the earth forty days and
forty nights.) 13That same day Noah and
Noah's sons, Shem, Ham, and Japheth, went
into the ark, with Noah's wife and the three
wives of his sons—14they and all beasts of every kind, all cattle of every kind, all creatures
of every kind that creep on the earth, and all
birds of every kind, every bird, every winged

וּנְשֵׁי־בָנָיו אִתּוֹ אֶל־הַתֵּבָה מִפְּנֵי מֵי
הַמַּבּוּל׃ 8 מִן־הַבְּהֵמָה הַטְּהוֹרָה וּמִן־
הַבְּהֵמָה אֲשֶׁר אֵינֶנָּה טְהֹרָה וּמִן־הָעוֹף
וְכֹל אֲשֶׁר־רֹמֵשׂ עַל־הָאֲדָמָה׃ 9 שְׁנַיִם
שְׁנַיִם בָּאוּ אֶל־נֹחַ אֶל־הַתֵּבָה זָכָר וּנְקֵבָה
כַּאֲשֶׁר צִוָּה אֱלֹהִים אֶת־נֹחַ׃ 10 וַיְהִי
לְשִׁבְעַת הַיָּמִים וּמֵי הַמַּבּוּל הָיוּ עַל־
הָאָרֶץ׃
11 בִּשְׁנַת שֵׁשׁ־מֵאוֹת שָׁנָה לְחַיֵּי־נֹחַ
בַּחֹדֶשׁ הַשֵּׁנִי בְּשִׁבְעָה־עָשָׂר יוֹם לַחֹדֶשׁ
בַּיּוֹם הַזֶּה
נִבְקְעוּ כָּל־מַעְיְנֹת תְּהוֹם רַבָּה
וַאֲרֻבֹּת הַשָּׁמַיִם נִפְתָּחוּ׃
12 וַיְהִי הַגֶּשֶׁם עַל־הָאָרֶץ אַרְבָּעִים יוֹם
וְאַרְבָּעִים לָיְלָה׃ 13 בְּעֶצֶם הַיּוֹם הַזֶּה בָּא
נֹחַ וְשֵׁם־וְחָם וָיֶפֶת בְּנֵי־נֹחַ וְאֵשֶׁת נֹחַ
וּשְׁלֹשֶׁת נְשֵׁי־בָנָיו אִתָּם אֶל־הַתֵּבָה׃
14 הֵמָּה וְכָל־הַחַיָּה לְמִינָהּ וְכָל־הַבְּהֵמָה
לְמִינָהּ וְכָל־הָרֶמֶשׂ הָרֹמֵשׂ עַל־הָאָרֶץ
לְמִינֵהוּ וְכָל־הָעוֹף לְמִינֵהוּ כֹּל צִפּוֹר כָּל־

still survives in some of our reckoning, such as 60 seconds in a minute and 60 minutes in an hour. Note that 600 is a multiple of 60, just as 120 is. See Comment to Gen. 5:32.

9. two of each See Comment to 7:2.

THE CATACLYSM (vv. 10–24)

10. The seventh day The end of the period mentioned in verse 4. Rabbinic traditions differ as to whether the Flood took place in the fall or in the spring.

11. All the fountains This line of poetry and the next ("And the floodgates . . .") are a striking example of the ancient poetic form known as parallelism.

great deep The cosmic waters in the ocean depths. See Comment to 1:2.

floodgates of the sky The openings in the expanse of the heavens through which water from the celestial part of the cosmic ocean can escape onto the earth. The world is being returned to the condition that preceded Creation (1:2).

---

because of the waters of the Flood Rashi cites the tradition that Noah did not enter the ark until the water reached his ankles. Did he not really believe God's threat? Or was he hoping to the very end that the people would see the rain and repent, making the punishment unnecessary?

14. Lions and lambs, predators and prey, set aside their natural enmity and lived together peacefully in the ark. Only when the danger was over did they revert to their old habits. It will be a mark of the Messianic Age (Isa. 11) when traditional enemies learn to live cooperatively without facing an external threat.

thing. [15]They came to Noah into the ark, two each of all flesh in which there was breath of life. [16]Thus they that entered comprised male and female of all flesh, as God had commanded him. And the LORD shut him in.

[17]The Flood continued forty days on the earth, and the waters increased and raised the ark so that it rose above the earth. [18]The waters swelled and increased greatly upon the earth, and the ark drifted upon the waters. [19]When the waters had swelled much more upon the earth, all the highest mountains everywhere under the sky were covered. [20]Fifteen cubits higher did the waters swell, as the mountains were covered. [21]And all flesh that stirred on earth perished—birds, cattle, beasts, and all the things that swarmed upon the earth, and all mankind. [22]All in whose nostrils was the merest breath of life, all that was on dry land, died. [23]All existence on earth was blotted out—man, cattle, creeping things, and birds of the sky; they were blotted out from the earth. Only Noah was left, and those with him in the ark.

[24]And when the waters had swelled on the

8 earth one hundred and fifty days, [1]God remembered Noah and all the beasts and all the cattle that were with him in the ark, and

כָּנָף׃ 15 וַיָּבֹאוּ אֶל־נֹחַ אֶל־הַתֵּבָה שְׁנַיִם
שְׁנַיִם מִכָּל־הַבָּשָׂר אֲשֶׁר־בּוֹ רוּחַ חַיִּים׃
16 וְהַבָּאִים זָכָר וּנְקֵבָה מִכָּל־בָּשָׂר בָּאוּ
כַּאֲשֶׁר צִוָּה אֹתוֹ אֱלֹהִים וַיִּסְגֹּר יְהוָה
בַּעֲדוֹ׃
שלישי 17 וַיְהִי הַמַּבּוּל אַרְבָּעִים יוֹם עַל־הָאָרֶץ
וַיִּרְבּוּ הַמַּיִם וַיִּשְׂאוּ אֶת־הַתֵּבָה וַתָּרָם
מֵעַל הָאָרֶץ׃ 18 וַיִּגְבְּרוּ הַמַּיִם וַיִּרְבּוּ מְאֹד
עַל־הָאָרֶץ וַתֵּלֶךְ הַתֵּבָה עַל־פְּנֵי הַמָּיִם׃
19 וְהַמַּיִם גָּבְרוּ מְאֹד מְאֹד עַל־הָאָרֶץ
וַיְכֻסּוּ כָּל־הֶהָרִים הַגְּבֹהִים אֲשֶׁר־תַּחַת
כָּל־הַשָּׁמָיִם׃ 20 חֲמֵשׁ עֶשְׂרֵה אַמָּה
מִלְמַעְלָה גָּבְרוּ הַמָּיִם וַיְכֻסּוּ הֶהָרִים׃
21 וַיִּגְוַע כָּל־בָּשָׂר ׀ הָרֹמֵשׂ עַל־הָאָרֶץ
בָּעוֹף וּבַבְּהֵמָה וּבַחַיָּה וּבְכָל־הַשֶּׁרֶץ
הַשֹּׁרֵץ עַל־הָאָרֶץ וְכֹל הָאָדָם׃ 22 כֹּל
אֲשֶׁר נִשְׁמַת־רוּחַ חַיִּים בְּאַפָּיו מִכֹּל אֲשֶׁר
בֶּחָרָבָה מֵתוּ׃ 23 וַיִּמַח אֶת־כָּל־הַיְקוּם ׀
אֲשֶׁר ׀ עַל־פְּנֵי הָאֲדָמָה מֵאָדָם עַד־בְּהֵמָה
עַד־רֶמֶשׂ וְעַד־עוֹף הַשָּׁמַיִם וַיִּמָּחוּ מִן־
הָאָרֶץ וַיִּשָּׁאֶר אַךְ־נֹחַ וַאֲשֶׁר אִתּוֹ בַּתֵּבָה׃
24 וַיִּגְבְּרוּ הַמַּיִם עַל־הָאָרֶץ חֲמִשִּׁים
ח וּמְאַת יוֹם׃ 1 וַיִּזְכֹּר אֱלֹהִים אֶת־
נֹחַ וְאֵת כָּל־הַחַיָּה וְאֶת־כָּל־הַבְּהֵמָה

15. two each See Comment to 7:2.

16. the LORD shut him in Unlike the story of the two survivors in the Mesopotamian flood tales, who shut the hatch themselves, the text here is careful to note that the salvation of Noah is due entirely to the will of God.

18. drifted The rudderless vessel floated about helplessly on the floodwaters.

20. higher The waters crested at a little less than 23 feet (nearly 15 cubits) above the highest peak. The ark was half-submerged in water just above the highest mountain.

21. all . . . all . . . all Here and in the following verse, this word emphasizes the total nature of the catastrophe.

22. dry land Marine life did not perish.

23. blotted out God's intention, proclaimed in verse 4, has been fulfilled.

24. one hundred and fifty days That is, five months of 30 days each. The waters drained away so gradually that they appeared to remain at their maximum height for that length of time.

THE FLOOD COMES TO AN END (8:1–14)

1. God remembered "To remember," in the Bible, is not to retain or to recall a mental image. It is to focus on the object of memory that results in action.

Noah Like Adam, Noah is here the representative human being; therefore, he alone is mentioned.

God caused a wind to blow across the earth, and the waters subsided. 2The fountains of the deep and the floodgates of the sky were stopped up, and the rain from the sky was held back; 3the waters then receded steadily from the earth. At the end of one hundred and fifty days the waters diminished, 4so that in the seventh month, on the seventeenth day of the month, the ark came to rest on the mountains of Ararat. 5The waters went on diminishing until the tenth month; in the tenth month, on the first of the month, the tops of the mountains became visible.

6At the end of forty days, Noah opened the window of the ark that he had made 7and sent out the raven; it went to and fro until the waters had dried up from the earth. 8Then he sent out the dove to see whether the waters had decreased from the surface of the ground. 9But the dove could not find a resting place for its foot, and returned to him to the ark, for there was water over all the earth. So putting out his hand, he took it into the ark with him. 10He waited another seven days, and again sent out

אֲשֶׁר אִתּוֹ בַּתֵּבָה וַיַּעֲבֵר אֱלֹהִים רוּחַ עַל־
הָאָרֶץ וַיָּשֹׁכּוּ הַמָּיִם׃ 2 וַיִּסָּכְרוּ מַעְיְנֹת
תְּהוֹם וַאֲרֻבֹּת הַשָּׁמָיִם וַיִּכָּלֵא הַגֶּשֶׁם
מִן־הַשָּׁמָיִם׃ 3 וַיָּשֻׁבוּ הַמַּיִם מֵעַל הָאָרֶץ
הָלוֹךְ וָשׁוֹב וַיַּחְסְרוּ הַמַּיִם מִקְצֵה חֲמִשִּׁים
וּמְאַת יוֹם׃ 4 וַתָּנַח הַתֵּבָה בַּחֹדֶשׁ הַשְּׁבִיעִי
בְּשִׁבְעָה־עָשָׂר יוֹם לַחֹדֶשׁ עַל הָרֵי אֲרָרָט׃
5 וְהַמַּיִם הָיוּ הָלוֹךְ וְחָסוֹר עַד הַחֹדֶשׁ
הָעֲשִׂירִי בָּעֲשִׂירִי בְּאֶחָד לַחֹדֶשׁ נִרְאוּ
רָאשֵׁי הֶהָרִים׃
6 וַיְהִי מִקֵּץ אַרְבָּעִים יוֹם וַיִּפְתַּח נֹחַ אֶת־
חַלּוֹן הַתֵּבָה אֲשֶׁר עָשָׂה׃ 7 וַיְשַׁלַּח אֶת־
הָעֹרֵב וַיֵּצֵא יָצוֹא וָשׁוֹב עַד־יְבֹשֶׁת הַמַּיִם
מֵעַל הָאָרֶץ׃ 8 וַיְשַׁלַּח אֶת־הַיּוֹנָה מֵאִתּוֹ
לִרְאוֹת הֲקַלּוּ הַמַּיִם מֵעַל פְּנֵי הָאֲדָמָה׃
9 וְלֹא־מָצְאָה הַיּוֹנָה מָנוֹחַ לְכַף־רַגְלָהּ
וַתָּשָׁב אֵלָיו אֶל־הַתֵּבָה כִּי־מַיִם עַל־פְּנֵי
כָל־הָאָרֶץ וַיִּשְׁלַח יָדוֹ וַיִּקָּחֶהָ וַיָּבֵא אֹתָהּ
אֵלָיו אֶל־הַתֵּבָה׃ 10 וַיָּחֶל עוֹד שִׁבְעַת
יָמִים אֲחֵרִים וַיֹּסֶף שַׁלַּח אֶת־הַיּוֹנָה מִן־

caused a wind to blow As the waters symbolize chaos and the undoing of Creation, so the movement of the wind forecasts the return of order (see 1:2).

2. were stopped up The cosmic forces unleashed in 7:11 are halted abruptly, emphasizing God's absolute control over nature. In the Mesopotamian flood tales, the gods lost control over the forces they had set loose and were stricken with terror.

4. came to rest The ark was barely above the highest peak when the Flood crested (7:20). Hence a slight receding of the waters would cause the vessel to ground.

on the mountains of Ararat On the mountain range of Ararat, which refers to Armenia (as in 2 Kings 19:37, Isa. 37:38, and Jer. 51:27). In Akkadian it is called Urartu. In this region lie the sources of the Tigris and the Euphrates rivers. Today there is a mountain called Ararat near the conjunction of the Turkish, Armenian, and Iranian borders.

5. The waters went on diminishing The tops of other mountains in the area became visible 73 days after the ark grounded.

THE RELEASE OF THE BIRDS
(vv. 6–12)

Noah releases a raven 40 days later, then a dove and another dove. In ancient times, mariners would take birds aboard and use them to determine the ship's proximity to land. Both the raven and the dove are also featured in the Mesopotamian stories.

7. the raven This wild bird feeds on carrion as well as vegetation and thus could obtain its food from among the floating carcasses. That is why it made repeated forays from the ark. Noah could observe its movements over several days.

8. the dove A timid bird. Noah took it in his hand when it returned, probably to see if there was clay on its feet.

הַתֵּבָה׃ 11 וַתָּבֹא אֵלָיו הַיּוֹנָה לְעֵת עֶרֶב
וְהִנֵּה עֲלֵה־זַיִת טָרָף בְּפִיהָ וַיֵּדַע נֹחַ כִּי־
קַלּוּ הַמַּיִם מֵעַל הָאָרֶץ׃ 12 וַיִּיָּחֶל עוֹד
שִׁבְעַת יָמִים אֲחֵרִים וַיְשַׁלַּח אֶת־הַיּוֹנָה
וְלֹא־יָסְפָה שׁוּב־אֵלָיו עוֹד׃
13 וַיְהִי בְּאַחַת וְשֵׁשׁ־מֵאוֹת שָׁנָה בָּרִאשׁוֹן
בְּאֶחָד לַחֹדֶשׁ חָרְבוּ הַמַּיִם מֵעַל הָאָרֶץ
וַיָּסַר נֹחַ אֶת־מִכְסֵה הַתֵּבָה וַיַּרְא וְהִנֵּה
חָרְבוּ פְּנֵי הָאֲדָמָה׃ 14 וּבַחֹדֶשׁ הַשֵּׁנִי
בְּשִׁבְעָה וְעֶשְׂרִים יוֹם לַחֹדֶשׁ יָבְשָׁה
הָאָרֶץ׃ ס
רביעי 15 וַיְדַבֵּר אֱלֹהִים אֶל־נֹחַ לֵאמֹר׃ 16 צֵא מִן־
הַתֵּבָה אַתָּה וְאִשְׁתְּךָ וּבָנֶיךָ וּנְשֵׁי־בָנֶיךָ
אִתָּךְ׃ 17 כָּל־הַחַיָּה אֲשֶׁר־אִתְּךָ מִכָּל־בָּשָׂר
בָּעוֹף וּבַבְּהֵמָה וּבְכָל־הָרֶמֶשׂ הָרֹמֵשׂ עַל־
הָאָרֶץ הוצא הַיְצֵא אִתָּךְ וְשָׁרְצוּ בָאָרֶץ
וּפָרוּ וְרָבוּ עַל־הָאָרֶץ׃ 18 וַיֵּצֵא־נֹחַ וּבָנָיו

the dove from the ark. 11 The dove came back to him toward evening, and there in its bill was a plucked-off olive leaf! Then Noah knew that the waters had decreased on the earth. 12 He waited still another seven days and sent the dove forth; and it did not return to him any more.

13 In the six hundred and first year, in the first month, on the first of the month, the waters began to dry from the earth; and when Noah removed the covering of the ark, he saw that the surface of the ground was drying. 14 And in the second month, on the twenty-seventh day of the month, the earth was dry.

15 God spoke to Noah, saying, 16 "Come out of the ark, together with your wife, your sons, and your sons' wives. 17 Bring out with you every living thing of all flesh that is with you: birds, animals, and everything that creeps on earth; and let them swarm on the earth and be fertile and increase on earth." 18 So Noah came out, together with his sons, his wife, and his

11. toward evening Birds customarily return to their nests at this time. The fact that the dove had been out all day indicated that there were resting places.

plucked-off Better: "fresh" or "verdant." The fresh olive leaf is a sure sign that plant life had begun to renew itself.

olive leaf The olive tree, a sturdy evergreen that can live to 1,000 years, is one of the earliest trees cultivated in the Near East. It is a short tree, indicating that the waters had diminished greatly.

THE GROUND DRIES OUT (vv. 13–14)

13. In the six hundred and first year On New Year's Day of the Hebrew calendar, the ground was dry, meaning that no water was visible on the surface.

14. in the second month It took another 56 days for the earth to return to its condition on the third day of Creation.

THE DISEMBARKATION (vv. 15–19)

16. together with your wife The order here varies from that in Gen. 6:18 and 7:7, where husbands and wives are not listed together.

17. be fertile and increase The repetition of the divine blessing of Gen. 1:22 signals the regeneration of animal, insect, and bird life.

CHAPTER 8

11. A dove bearing an olive branch in its beak has become the symbol of the peaceful resolution of conflict. An olive branch, however, tastes bitter. Perhaps this should warn us that although victory is sweet, it sows in the soul of the defeated the desire for revenge. Compromise, which could leave a bitter taste, promises an end to conflict.

15. The Midrash describes Noah as reluctant to leave the ark, afraid that his descendants will again defile God's clean world and bring on themselves another deluge. God must com-

וְאִשְׁתּ֥וֹ וּנְשֵֽׁי־בָנָ֖יו אִתּֽוֹ׃ 19 כָּל־הַֽחַיָּ֗ה כָּל־
הָרֶ֙מֶשׂ֙ וְכָל־הָע֔וֹף כֹּ֖ל רוֹמֵ֣שׂ עַל־הָאָ֑רֶץ
לְמִשְׁפְּחֹ֣תֵיהֶ֔ם יָֽצְא֖וּ מִן־הַתֵּבָֽה׃
20 וַיִּ֥בֶן נֹ֛חַ מִזְבֵּ֖חַ לַֽיהוָ֑ה וַיִּקַּ֞ח מִכֹּ֣ל ׀
הַבְּהֵמָ֣ה הַטְּהוֹרָ֗ה וּמִכֹּל֙ הָע֣וֹף הַטָּהֹ֔ר
וַיַּ֥עַל עֹלֹ֖ת בַּמִּזְבֵּֽחַ׃ 21 וַיָּ֣רַח יְהוָה֮ אֶת־
רֵ֣יחַ הַנִּיחֹחַ֒ וַיֹּ֨אמֶר יְהוָ֜ה אֶל־לִבּ֗וֹ לֹֽא־
אֹ֠סִף לְקַלֵּ֨ל ע֤וֹד אֶת־הָֽאֲדָמָה֙ בַּעֲב֣וּר
הָֽאָדָ֔ם כִּ֠י יֵ֣צֶר לֵ֧ב הָאָדָ֛ם רַ֖ע מִנְּעֻרָ֑יו
וְלֹֽא־אֹסִ֥ף ע֛וֹד לְהַכּ֥וֹת אֶת־כָּל־חַ֖י כַּאֲשֶׁ֥ר
עָשִֽׂיתִי׃ 22 עֹ֖ד כָּל־יְמֵ֣י הָאָ֑רֶץ
זֶ֡רַע וְקָצִיר
וְקֹ֨ר וָחֹ֜ם
וְקַ֧יִץ וָחֹ֛רֶף
וְי֥וֹם וָלַ֖יְלָה
לֹ֥א יִשְׁבֹּֽתוּ׃

sons' wives. 19Every animal, every creeping
thing, and every bird, everything that stirs on
earth came out of the ark by families.

20Then Noah built an altar to the LORD and,
taking of every pure animal and of every pure
bird, he offered burnt offerings on the altar.
21The LORD smelled the pleasing odor, and
the LORD said to Himself: "Never again will I
doom the earth because of man, since the devisings of man's mind are evil from his youth;
nor will I ever again destroy every living being,
as I have done.

22So long as the earth endures,
Seedtime and harvest,
Cold and heat,
Summer and winter,
Day and night
Shall not cease."

19. by families That is, species by species.

NOAH'S SACRIFICE AND GOD'S RESPONSE (vv. 20–22)

Noah builds an altar and brings burnt offerings on his own initiative. Now that the earth has been purged of its evil, sacrifice symbolizes the restoration of harmony between God and humankind.

20. burnt offerings The Hebrew word *olah* means, literally, "that which ascends." It refers to sacrifices that, except for the hide, must be consumed entirely by fire on the altar. No part of them may be eaten by the worshiper, whereas both priest and worshiper partake of the sacrifices known as *z'vaḥim* (see Deut. 12:27).

21. smelled the pleasing odor This is a cultic term indicating the acceptance of the sacrifice.

the LORD said to Himself In Gen. 6:7 this statement of God's resolve was for the purpose of destruction; here it is for salvation. Similarly, the observation here on the nature of humankind echoes that of 6:5.

Never again will I . . . nor will I ever again The repetition of the promise, as in Gen. 9:11, gives it the force of a solemn oath.

the devisings of man's mind The comment is less a judgment than an observation that the inclination for evil is part of human nature. This pessimism about human nature is also found elsewhere in the Bible (see Jer. 17:9).

from his youth But not from conception or birth, thereby implying that the tendency to evil may be curbed and redirected through the discipline of law.

22. Shall not cease The orderly cycles of nature will never again be interrupted.

---

mand him to leave, promising never to send another flood (Gen. R. 34:6). A modern commentator reads Noah's behavior in precisely the opposite way, seeing him as eager to leave the ark and be relieved of responsibility for so many people and animals (Zornberg). Another teacher sees Noah's being enclosed in the ark for a year as punishment for not feeling more compassion for his drowning neighbors, like the person exiled to a city of refuge for inadvertently causing the death of another (Aaron Samuel Tameret).

21. from his youth Only when people leave childhood for adolescent responsibility can we speak of them as good or bad. Children can be only obedient or disobedient. That is why Juda-

9

God blessed Noah and his sons, and said to them, "Be fertile and increase, and fill the earth. ²The fear and the dread of you shall be upon all the beasts of the earth and upon all the birds of the sky—everything with which the earth is astir—and upon all the fish of the sea; they are given into your hand. ³Every creature that lives shall be yours to eat; as with the green grasses, I give you all these. ⁴You must not, however, eat flesh with its life-blood in it. ⁵But for your own life-blood I will require a reckoning: I will require it of every beast; of

ט וַיְבָ֣רֶךְ אֱלֹהִ֔ים אֶת־נֹ֖חַ וְאֶת־בָּנָ֑יו וַיֹּ֧אמֶר לָהֶ֛ם פְּר֥וּ וּרְב֖וּ וּמִלְא֥וּ אֶת־הָאָֽרֶץ: ² וּמוֹרַאֲכֶ֤ם וְחִתְּכֶם֙ יִֽהְיֶ֔ה עַ֚ל כָּל־חַיַּ֣ת הָאָ֔רֶץ וְעַ֖ל כָּל־ע֣וֹף הַשָּׁמָ֑יִם בְּכֹל֩ אֲשֶׁ֨ר תִּרְמֹ֧שׂ הָֽאֲדָמָ֛ה וּבְכָל־דְּגֵ֥י הַיָּ֖ם בְּיֶדְכֶ֥ם נִתָּֽנוּ: ³ כָּל־רֶ֙מֶשׂ֙ אֲשֶׁ֣ר הוּא־חַ֔י לָכֶ֥ם יִֽהְיֶ֖ה לְאָכְלָ֑ה כְּיֶ֣רֶק עֵ֔שֶׂב נָתַ֥תִּי לָכֶ֖ם אֶת־כֹּֽל: ⁴ אַךְ־בָּשָׂ֕ר בְּנַפְשׁ֥וֹ דָמ֖וֹ לֹ֥א תֹאכֵֽלוּ: ⁵ וְאַ֨ךְ אֶת־דִּמְכֶ֤ם לְנַפְשֹֽׁתֵיכֶם֙ אֶדְרֹ֔שׁ מִיַּ֥ד כָּל־חַיָּ֖ה אֶדְרְשֶׁ֑נּוּ וּמִיַּ֣ד

THE REGENERATION AND REORDERING OF SOCIETY (9:1–17)

Humankind must now be re-established on more secure moral foundations than before. New norms of behavior must be instituted. And the possibility of a future cataclysm must be laid to rest, lest it have a paralyzing effect on human progress.

THE NEW ORDER (vv. 1–7)

1. Be fertile This is a command. See Comment to Gen. 1:28. In the Mesopotamian flood tales, the people who are saved are granted immortality and removed from human society. Here, Noah and his family are not to withdraw from the world but are to be fertile and to use

the resources of nature for the benefit of humankind.

2. The fear and dread of you Human power over the animal kingdom is confirmed and enhanced. It is a concession to human wickedness, which God now tries to limit.

4. with its life-blood in it Eating the flesh of a living animal is prohibited. The creature must first be slaughtered.

5. I will require a reckoning It is God who calls the murderer to account. The repeated Hebrew verb meaning "require" (דרש) in this verse, with God as the subject, connotes relentless pursuit until punishment is meted out.

of every beast The killing of a human being by a beast disturbs the divinely ordered structure of relationships laid down in verse 2. The act

ism sets the age of entering moral responsibility at 12 or 13, the boundary between childhood and adolescence.

CHAPTER 9

1. After acknowledging the persistence of the evil impulse (the ego-centric impulse), God commands Noah's children to be fruitful. "For every human impulse, God provides a moral way of expressing it. The moral channel for sexual lust is the commitment to marriage and family" (Mid. Tad.).

2. Originally, God expected people to be vegetarians and not kill living creatures for their food (cf. Gen. 2:18–19). But this ideal became corrupted into the notion that there

are no qualitative differences between humans and animals, leading some people to the conclusion that they could behave like animals. God then compromised the vegetarian ideal, permitting the eating of meat but strenuously forbidding the shedding of *human* blood, as a way of emphasizing the distinction between humans and animals. The dietary laws (Lev. 11) provide ways of reminding ourselves that eating meat is a compromise. We refrain from eating certain animals, not because we and they are so similar but precisely because we are different, because we are capable of introducing religious guidelines into our eating habits.

5. Rashi understands these words as a biblical prohibition of suicide.

man, too, will I require a reckoning for human life, of every man for that of his fellow man!

⁶Whoever sheds the blood of man,

By man shall his blood be shed;

For in His image

Did God make man.

⁷Be fertile, then, and increase; abound on the earth and increase on it."

⁸And God said to Noah and to his sons with him, ⁹"I now establish My covenant with you and your offspring to come, ¹⁰and with every living thing that is with you—birds, cattle, and every wild beast as well—all that have come out of the ark, every living thing on earth. ¹¹I will maintain My covenant with you: never again shall all flesh be cut off by the waters of a flood, and never again shall there be a flood to destroy the earth."

¹²God further said, "This is the sign that I set for the covenant between Me and you, and every living creature with you, for all ages to come. ¹³I have set My bow in the clouds, and it

הָאָדָ֗ם מִיַּד֙ אִ֣ישׁ אָחִ֔יו אֶדְרֹ֖שׁ אֶת־נֶ֣פֶשׁ הָֽאָדָֽם׃

⁶ שֹׁפֵךְ֙ דַּ֣ם הָֽאָדָ֔ם בָּֽאָדָ֖ם דָּמ֣וֹ יִשָּׁפֵ֑ךְ כִּ֚י בְּצֶ֣לֶם אֱלֹהִ֔ים עָשָׂ֖ה אֶת־הָֽאָדָֽם׃

⁷ וְאַתֶּ֖ם פְּר֣וּ וּרְב֑וּ שִׁרְצ֥וּ בָאָ֖רֶץ וּרְבוּ־בָֽהּ׃ ס

⁸ וַיֹּ֤אמֶר אֱלֹהִים֙ אֶל־נֹ֔חַ וְאֶל־בָּנָ֥יו אִתּ֖וֹ לֵאמֹֽר׃ ⁹ וַאֲנִ֕י הִנְנִ֥י מֵקִ֛ים אֶת־בְּרִיתִ֖י אִתְּכֶ֑ם וְאֶֽת־זַרְעֲכֶ֖ם אַחֲרֵיכֶֽם׃ ¹⁰ וְאֵ֣ת כָּל־נֶ֣פֶשׁ הַֽחַיָּ֣ה אֲשֶׁ֣ר אִתְּכֶ֗ם בָּע֧וֹף בַּבְּהֵמָ֛ה וּֽבְכָל־חַיַּ֥ת הָאָ֖רֶץ אִתְּכֶ֑ם מִכֹּל֙ יֹצְאֵ֣י הַתֵּבָ֔ה לְכֹ֖ל חַיַּ֥ת הָאָֽרֶץ׃ ¹¹ וַהֲקִמֹתִ֤י אֶת־בְּרִיתִי֙ אִתְּכֶ֔ם וְלֹֽא־יִכָּרֵ֧ת כָּל־בָּשָׂ֛ר ע֖וֹד מִמֵּ֣י הַמַּבּ֑וּל וְלֹֽא־יִהְיֶ֥ה ע֛וֹד מַבּ֖וּל לְשַׁחֵ֥ת הָאָֽרֶץ׃ ¹² וַיֹּ֣אמֶר אֱלֹהִ֗ים זֹ֤את אֽוֹת־הַבְּרִית֙ אֲשֶׁר־אֲנִ֣י נֹתֵ֗ן בֵּינִי֙ וּבֵ֣ינֵיכֶ֔ם וּבֵ֛ין כָּל־נֶ֥פֶשׁ חַיָּ֖ה אֲשֶׁ֣ר אִתְּכֶ֑ם לְדֹרֹ֖ת עוֹלָֽם׃ ¹³ אֶת־קַשְׁתִּ֕י

itself, like murder, constitutes the destruction of the image of God. The creature must, therefore, be put to death (see Exod. 21:28).

of his fellow man Literally, "his brother." All homicide is fratricide (see Gen. 4:9).

6. Whoever sheds the blood of man The sanctity of human life is reaffirmed here.

By man Punishment is now the responsibility of humankind. A judiciary must be established to correct the condition of lawlessness that prevailed before the Flood (6:11). Murder is a crime against society.

shall his blood be shed By capital punishment.

For in His image Murder is the ultimate

crime because the dignity and sanctity of human life derive from the fact that every human being bears the stamp of the divine maker. Murderers may be put to death because their act has effaced the divine image in the victim.

image See Gen. 1:26 and 5:3.

THE COVENANT AND THE RAINBOW (vv. 8–17)

9. I now The same Hebrew phrase (*va-ani hin'ni*) was also used in 6:17 to introduce the original pronouncement of doom. The same supreme authority who executed the judgment stands behind the message of hope.

12. the sign A distinctive, visible object.

13. My bow Ramban points out that the

6. whoever sheds the blood of man The verse not only prohibits murder. It is understood to prohibit embarrassing a person in public, causing him or her to blush or turn pale as the blood rushes to or from the face (Ḥafetz Ḥayyim, based on BT BM 58b). Another com-

mentator reads it, "Whoever sheds human blood allegedly in the name of humanity defaces the divine image in every individual." If every human life is of infinite value, we cannot calculate that it is acceptable to sacrifice some lives for the good of others.

shall serve as a sign of the covenant between Me and the earth. 14When I bring clouds over the earth, and the bow appears in the clouds, 15I will remember My covenant between Me and you and every living creature among all flesh, so that the waters shall never again become a flood to destroy all flesh. 16When the bow is in the clouds, I will see it and remember the everlasting covenant between God and all living creatures, all flesh that is on earth. 17That," God said to Noah, "shall be the sign of the covenant that I have established between Me and all flesh that is on earth."

18The sons of Noah who came out of the ark were Shem, Ham, and Japheth—Ham being the father of Canaan. 19These three were the sons of Noah, and from these the whole world branched out.

20Noah, the tiller of the soil, was the first to plant a vineyard. 21He drank of the wine and

נָתַ֖תִּי בֶּֽעָנָ֑ן וְהָֽיְתָה֙ לְא֣וֹת בְּרִ֔ית בֵּינִ֖י וּבֵ֥ין
הָאָֽרֶץ׃ 14 וְהָיָ֕ה בְּעַֽנְנִ֥י עָנָ֖ן עַל־הָאָ֑רֶץ
וְנִרְאֲתָ֥ה הַקֶּ֖שֶׁת בֶּעָנָֽן׃ 15 וְזָכַרְתִּ֣י אֶת־
בְּרִיתִ֗י אֲשֶׁ֤ר בֵּינִי֙ וּבֵ֣ינֵיכֶ֔ם וּבֵ֛ין כָּל־נֶ֥פֶשׁ
חַיָּ֖ה בְּכָל־בָּשָׂ֑ר וְלֹֽא־יִהְיֶ֨ה ע֤וֹד הַמַּ֙יִם֙
לְמַבּ֔וּל לְשַׁחֵ֖ת כָּל־בָּשָֽׂר׃ 16 וְהָיְתָ֥ה
הַקֶּ֖שֶׁת בֶּעָנָ֑ן וּרְאִיתִ֗יהָ לִזְכֹּר֙ בְּרִ֣ית עוֹלָ֔ם
בֵּ֣ין אֱלֹהִ֔ים וּבֵין֙ כָּל־נֶ֣פֶשׁ חַיָּ֔ה בְּכָל־בָּשָׂ֖ר
אֲשֶׁ֥ר עַל־הָאָֽרֶץ׃ 17 וַיֹּ֥אמֶר אֱלֹהִ֖ים אֶל־
נֹ֑חַ זֹ֤את אֽוֹת־הַבְּרִית֙ אֲשֶׁ֣ר הֲקִמֹ֔תִי בֵּינִ֕י
וּבֵ֥ין כָּל־בָּשָׂ֖ר אֲשֶׁ֥ר עַל־הָאָֽרֶץ׃ פ
ששי 18 וַיִּהְי֣וּ בְנֵי־נֹ֗חַ הַיֹּֽצְאִים֙ מִן־הַתֵּבָ֔ה שֵׁ֖ם
וְחָ֣ם וָיָ֑פֶת וְחָ֕ם ה֖וּא אֲבִ֥י כְנָֽעַן׃
19 שְׁלֹשָׁ֥ה אֵ֖לֶּה בְּנֵי־נֹ֑חַ וּמֵאֵ֖לֶּה נָֽפְצָ֥ה
כָל־הָאָֽרֶץ׃
20 וַיָּ֥חֶל נֹ֖חַ אִ֣ישׁ הָֽאֲדָמָ֑ה וַיִּטַּ֖ע כָּֽרֶם׃
21 וַיֵּ֥שְׁתְּ מִן־הַיַּ֖יִן וַיִּשְׁכָּ֑ר וַיִּתְגַּ֖ל בְּת֥וֹךְ

rainbow, a phenomenon that already exists, is now invested with new symbolic significance as an eternal testimony to God's constancy and mercy. No other celestial body is similarly endowed in biblical literature. The bow, widespread in ancient Near Eastern mythology as the weapon favored by the gods, is here transformed into a symbol of reconciliation between God and humankind.

THE DEPRAVITY OF CANAAN (vv. 18–29)

Much time has elapsed since the Flood. Noah now has a grown grandson. The events depicted here are given in the barest outline. Apparently the original incidents, in all their detail, were well known to the biblical audience but for reasons of delicate sensibility were not preserved.

20. the tiller of the soil This phrase implies something well known about Noah (see 5:29).

was the first to plant a vineyard He was the initiator of orchard husbandry.

21. He drank of the wine Noah was involved not only in viticulture (the science and art of grape growing) but also in viniculture (the specific cultivation of grapes for wine making). (It is interesting to note that many historians believe that viniculture first began in the vicinity of Ararat.) Here again, as in 4:17–22, advances in the arts of civilization are human achieve-

---

13. The rainbow is the sign of God's covenant not to destroy the world again. The rainbow is a sign of peace in at least three ways: It represents the inverted bow, the weapon turned away so that it does not threaten (Maimonides). It represents all shades and colors joined side by side in a single entity, calling on different races and nations to do the same. And it represents the promise that, no matter how hard it may rain, the rain eventually will stop—and the sun will come out again. Therefore, the Sages teach us to recite a blessing whenever we see a rainbow: "Praised are You, LORD our God, Sovereign of the universe who remembers the Covenant, is faithful to it, and keeps promises" (BT Ber. 59a).

20–1. Overwhelmed by the task of rebuilding a destroyed world, finding himself virtually alone and friendless in a nearly empty world, or perhaps burdened by a sense of guilt at having

became drunk, and he uncovered himself within his tent. 22Ham, the father of Canaan, saw his father's nakedness and told his two brothers outside. 23But Shem and Japheth took a cloth, placed it against both their backs and, walking backward, they covered their father's nakedness; their faces were turned the other way, so that they did not see their father's nakedness. 24When Noah woke up from his wine and learned what his youngest son had done to him, 25he said,

אֹהֱלֹה אָהֳלֹֽו: 22וַיַּ֗רְא חָ֚ם אֲבִ֣י כְנַ֔עַן אֵ֖ת עֶרְוַ֣ת אָבִ֑יו וַיַּגֵּ֥ד לִשְׁנֵֽי־אֶחָ֖יו בַּחֽוּץ: 23וַיִּקַּח֩ שֵׁ֨ם וָיֶ֜פֶת אֶת־הַשִּׂמְלָ֗ה וַיָּשִׂ֙ימוּ֙ עַל־שְׁכֶ֣ם שְׁנֵיהֶ֔ם וַיֵּֽלְכוּ֙ אֲחֹ֣רַנִּ֔ית וַיְכַסּ֕וּ אֵ֖ת עֶרְוַ֣ת אֲבִיהֶ֑ם וּפְנֵיהֶם֙ אֲחֹ֣רַנִּ֔ית וְעֶרְוַ֥ת אֲבִיהֶ֖ם לֹ֥א רָאֽוּ: 24וַיִּ֣יקֶץ נֹ֔חַ מִיֵּינ֑וֹ וַיֵּ֕דַע אֵ֛ת אֲשֶׁר־עָֽשָׂה־ל֖וֹ בְּנ֥וֹ הַקָּטָֽן: 25וַיֹּ֖אמֶר

ments, not the work of gods or demigods as they generally were considered to be in the ancient world.

and became drunk No blame attaches to Noah for his drunkenness, because he was unaware of the intoxicating effects of his discovery.

he uncovered himself An act associated with shame and loss of dignity (see 3:7,21).

within his tent In the privacy of his dwelling, which makes Ham's behavior all the more contemptible.

THE BEHAVIOR OF THE SONS (vv. 22–23)

22. saw his father's nakedness Early traditional commentary takes this verse literally. Ham magnified his act of disrespect: He left his

father uncovered and told others what he had seen.

23. a cloth The Hebrew word *"simlah"* refers to a garment that also served as a covering at night.

24. woke up from his wine That is, when he had sobered up.

his youngest son This description makes Ham the youngest despite the five-times-repeated sequence: Shem, Ham, Japheth. Here Ramban points to Gen. 25:9 and Josh. 24:4 as proof that the order of listing need not always reflect the order of birth. In Gen. 10:21, the text explicitly states that Shem is the elder brother of Japheth.

had done to him Shem and Japheth had re-

survived when so many others perished, Noah turns to drink.

22. The severity of Noah's reaction led Rabbinic sources to suggest that the Torah may have suppressed the sordid details of some repugnant act.

23ff. One senses that originally there was more to the story than what we have here, that Ham (or Canaan) did something more reprehensible than look at Noah's nakedness. But the Sages find moral lessons about filial respect in the story as we have it, teaching that it is disrespectful for young people to see their parents or teachers unclothed, unless they need

help bathing (Hal. Ged. 56a). We lose a great deal if we come to see our parent or teacher as just another person. The Sages understood the Torah's description of Ham as Noah's smallest child, not because he was the youngest or shortest but because he was smallest in moral stature (Gen. R. 36:1).

Why was Canaan punished for his father Ham's sin? The Torah views the family as a corporate unit, so that punishing one is punishing all. Furthermore, because Ham's offense was a lack of respect for his father, a fitting punishment would be having a son who reflected badly on him.

HALAKHAH L'MA·ASEH
9:21 became drunk Wine is used in the rituals that celebrate Sabbaths, festivals, births, and weddings; and Jewish law permits drinking alcohol for pleasure. Drunkenness, however, is strongly opposed. The drunk person is fully responsible for any violations of the law committed while drunk (BT Er. 65a). Today we understand alcoholism, or any addiction, as an illness. With any illness, Jewish law generally obligates the ill to seek healing.

"Cursed be Canaan;
The lowest of slaves
Shall he be to his brothers."
26And he said,
"Blessed be the LORD,
The God of Shem;
Let Canaan be a slave to them.
27May God enlarge Japheth,
And let him dwell in the tents of Shem;
And let Canaan be a slave to them."
28Noah lived after the Flood 350 years. 29And all the days of Noah came to 950 years; then he died.

אָר֖וּר כְּנָ֑עַן
עֶ֥בֶד עֲבָדִ֖ים
יִֽהְיֶ֥ה לְאֶחָֽיו׃
26 וַיֹּ֕אמֶר
בָּר֥וּךְ יְהֹוָ֖ה
אֱלֹ֣הֵי שֵׁ֑ם
וִיהִ֥י כְנַ֖עַן עֶ֥בֶד לָֽמוֹ׃
27 יַ֤פְתְּ אֱלֹהִים֙ לְיֶ֔פֶת
וְיִשְׁכֹּ֖ן בְּאָֽהֳלֵי־שֵׁ֑ם
וִיהִ֥י כְנַ֖עַן עֶ֥בֶד לָֽמוֹ׃
28 וַֽיְחִי־נֹ֗חַ אַחַ֖ר הַמַּבּ֑וּל שְׁלֹ֤שׁ מֵאוֹת֙ שָׁנָ֔ה וַחֲמִשִּׁ֖ים שָׁנָֽה׃ 29 וַיִּֽהְיוּ֙* כׇּל־יְמֵי־נֹ֔חַ תְּשַׁ֤ע מֵאוֹת֙ שָׁנָ֔ה וַחֲמִשִּׁ֖ים שָׁנָ֑ה וַיָּמֹֽת׃ פ

10 These are the lines of Shem, Ham, and Japheth, the sons of Noah: sons were born to them after the Flood.

י וְאֵ֙לֶּה֙ תּֽוֹלְדֹ֣ת בְּנֵי־נֹ֔חַ שֵׁ֖ם חָ֣ם וָיָ֑פֶת וַיִּוָּלְד֥וּ לָהֶ֛ם בָּנִ֖ים אַחַ֥ר הַמַּבּֽוּל׃

v. 29. "וַיִּֽהְיוּ" לְפִי נֻסַּח סְפָרַד וְתֵימָן

ported the facts, whatever they were, to their father.

25. Canaan The text is silent as to why Canaan, not Ham, is cursed. Saadia and Ibn Janaḥ take the verse to mean, "Cursed be [the father of] Canaan." The phrase "the father of" has already appeared twice in this narrative. Perhaps in the fuller story Canaan, son of Ham, participated in the offense against Noah, and his deed was well known to the reader.

The lowest of slaves Literally, "a slave of slaves."

26. Blessed be the LORD Shem's virtuous behavior inspires Noah to bless the LORD, whose norms of conduct Shem upholds.

THE DEATH OF NOAH (vv. 28–29)

28. Noah lived This verse and the one following conclude the story of Noah. They belong to the pattern of the listings in chapter 5, and complement verse 32 there.

THE TABLE OF NATIONS (10:1–32)

The text now offers us a genealogy that shows how, after the Flood, all of humankind branched out from the three sons of Noah. Racial characteristics, physical types, and the color of skin play no role in this genealogy.

1. These are the lines of Shem After the digression about Noah's drunkenness, the text resumes the theme of 9:18–19.

after the Flood This same phrase functions in Mesopotamian texts to denote historical time.

According to some authorities, the name Canaan means "the low-lying land." Genesis consistently employs metaphors of "moral geography," in which high and low have moral as well as geographic connotations. Thus Sodom, the lowest point on earth, also represents

the depth of human depravity. Abraham finds God on mountaintops, but when he "goes down" to Egypt (in Gen. 12:10) he lowers himself to the moral level of the Egyptians. To this day, we speak of "going up" to Israel and to Jerusalem, regardless of our starting altitude.

2בְּנֵ֣י יֶ֔פֶת גֹּ֣מֶר וּמָג֔וֹג וּמָדַ֖י וְיָוָ֑ן וְתֻבָ֕ל
וּמֶ֖שֶׁךְ וְתִירָֽס׃ 3וּבְנֵ֖י גֹּ֑מֶר אַשְׁכְּנַ֥ז וְרִיפַ֖ת
וְתֹגַרְמָֽה׃ 4וּבְנֵ֥י יָוָ֖ן אֱלִישָׁ֣ה וְתַרְשִׁ֑ישׁ
כִּתִּ֖ים וְדֹדָנִֽים׃ 5מֵ֠אֵלֶּה נִפְרְד֞וּ אִיֵּ֤י
הַגּוֹיִם֙ בְּאַרְצֹתָ֔ם אִ֖ישׁ לִלְשֹׁנ֑וֹ לְמִשְׁפְּחֹתָ֖ם
בְּגוֹיֵהֶֽם׃
6וּבְנֵ֖י חָ֑ם כּ֥וּשׁ וּמִצְרַ֖יִם וּפ֥וּט וּכְנָֽעַן׃
7וּבְנֵ֣י כ֔וּשׁ סְבָא֙ וַחֲוִילָ֔ה וְסַבְתָּ֥ה וְרַעְמָ֖ה
וְסַבְתְּכָ֑א וּבְנֵ֥י רַעְמָ֖ה שְׁבָ֥א וּדְדָֽן׃
8וְכ֖וּשׁ יָלַ֣ד אֶת־נִמְרֹ֑ד ה֣וּא הֵחֵ֔ל לִהְי֥וֹת
גִּבֹּ֖ר בָּאָֽרֶץ׃ 9הֽוּא־הָיָ֥ה גִבֹּֽר־צַ֖יִד לִפְנֵ֣י
יְהוָ֑ה עַל־כֵּן֙ יֵֽאָמַ֔ר כְּנִמְרֹ֛ד גִּבּ֥וֹר צַ֖יִד
לִפְנֵ֥י יְהוָֽה׃ 10וַתְּהִ֨י רֵאשִׁ֤ית מַמְלַכְתּוֹ֙
בָּבֶ֔ל וְאֶ֖רֶךְ וְאַכַּ֣ד וְכַלְנֵ֑ה בְּאֶ֖רֶץ שִׁנְעָֽר׃

2The descendants of Japheth: Gomer, Magog,
Madai, Javan, Tubal, Meshech, and Tiras. 3The
descendants of Gomer: Ashkenaz, Riphath, and
Togarmah. 4The descendants of Javan: Elishah
and Tarshish, the Kittim and the Dodanim.
5From these the maritime nations branched
out. [These are the descendants of Japheth] by
their lands—each with its language—their clans
and their nations.

6The descendants of Ham: Cush, Mizraim,
Put, and Canaan. 7The descendants of Cush:
Seba, Havilah, Sabtah, Raamah, and Sabteca.
The descendants of Raamah: Sheba and Dedan.
8Cush also begot Nimrod, who was the first
man of might on earth. 9He was a mighty
hunter by the grace of the LORD; hence the
saying, "Like Nimrod a mighty hunter by the
grace of the LORD." 10The mainstays of his
kingdom were Babylon, Erech, Accad, and
Calneh in the land of Shinar. 11From that land

NIMROD (vv. 8–12)

This section shifts the focus of interest to Mesopotamia.

8. Nimrod He is not a historical figure. He may be based on an outstanding Mesopotamian personality (Tukulti-Ninurta I) whose exploits left their mark on the historical memory of Israel. His achievements were commemorated on steles, buildings, and inscriptions; and he was the subject of numerous tales and legends.

10. The mainstays of his kingdom These cities were the power base from which he expanded into Assyria.

Babylon The famous city on the river Euphrates, about 50 miles (80 km) south of modern Baghdad in Iraq.

Erech The Sumerian city-state Uruk, now Warka on the east side of the Euphrates, about 40 miles (64 km) up the river from Ur in southern Iraq.

Calneh The only name in this list that never appears in Akkadian inscriptions. A widely accepted suggestion is to read the word as *v'-khullanah,* meaning, "all of them being."

Shinar The land of Babylonia, embracing Sumer and Akkad and bounded on the north by Assyria, modern southern Iraq.

11. From that land That is, "From that land, he (Nimrod) went forth to Asshur." The

CHAPTER 10

2ff. These tables of the descendants of Noah's sons do not seem to conform to any identifiable racial or linguistic pattern. It has been suggested that they are divided by types of social organization: the sons of Japheth represent island communities (the Greek isles of the Mediterranean), the sons of Ham are city dwellers (which is why Egypt and Assyria are on the same list), while the sons of Shem are seminomadic shepherds.

8. Nimrod The name in Hebrew suggests rebelliousness. The Midrash sees Nimrod as the first person to take advantage of God's permission to kill animals for food. Then, having developed a taste for blood and the thrill of being able to take life, he killed human beings. Blessed by God with grace and skill, he misused his talents.

Asshur went forth and built Nineveh, Rehoboth-ir, Calah, [12]and Resen between Nineveh and Calah, that is the great city.

[13]And Mizraim begot the Ludim, the Anamim, the Lehabim, the Naphtuhim, [14]the Pathrusim, the Casluhim, and the Caphtorim, whence the Philistines came forth.

[15]Canaan begot Sidon, his first-born, and Heth; [16]and the Jebusites, the Amorites, the Girgashites, [17]the Hivites, the Arkites, the Sinites, [18]the Arvadites, the Zemarites, and the Hamathites. Afterward the clans of the Canaanites spread out. ([19]The [original] Canaanite territory extended from Sidon as far as Gerar, near Gaza, and as far as Sodom, Gomorrah, Admah, and Zeboiim, near Lasha.) [20]These

11 מִן־הָאָרֶץ הַהִוא יָצָא אַשּׁוּר וַיִּבֶן
אֶת־נִינְוֵה וְאֶת־רְחֹבֹת עִיר וְאֶת־כָּלַח׃
12 וְאֶת־רֶסֶן בֵּין נִינְוֵה וּבֵין כָּלַח הִוא
הָעִיר הַגְּדֹלָה׃
13 וּמִצְרַיִם יָלַד אֶת־לוּדִים וְאֶת־עֲנָמִים
וְאֶת־לְהָבִים וְאֶת־נַפְתֻּחִים׃ 14 וְאֶת־
פַּתְרֻסִים וְאֶת־כַּסְלֻחִים אֲשֶׁר יָצְאוּ
מִשָּׁם פְּלִשְׁתִּים וְאֶת־כַּפְתֹּרִים׃ ס
15 וּכְנַעַן יָלַד אֶת־צִידֹן בְּכֹרוֹ וְאֶת־חֵת׃
16 וְאֶת־הַיְבוּסִי וְאֶת־הָאֱמֹרִי וְאֵת
הַגִּרְגָּשִׁי׃ 17 וְאֶת־הַחִוִּי וְאֶת־הַעַרְקִי וְאֶת־
הַסִּינִי׃ 18 וְאֶת־הָאַרְוָדִי וְאֶת־הַצְּמָרִי
וְאֶת־הַחֲמָתִי וְאַחַר נָפֹצוּ מִשְׁפְּחוֹת
הַכְּנַעֲנִי׃ 19 וַיְהִי גְּבוּל הַכְּנַעֲנִי מִצִּידֹן

passage reflects the historical fact that, in its early period, Assyria was long under the domination of Sumer and Akkad, whose religious, linguistic, and cultural influence it freely acknowledged.

Asshur The region of the Upper Mesopotamian plain.

Nineveh Situated on the left bank of the Tigris, about 250 miles (400 km) northwest of Babylon, presently the mounds of Kuyunjik and Nebi Yunus ("the prophet Jonah") opposite Mosul.

Rehoboth-ir Literally, "broad places of the city," this is a Hebraized form of *rebit Ninua,* which refers to "the quarters of Nineveh."

Calah The famous Assyrian city Kalah, the site of which is presently known as Nimrud, located on the left bank of the Tigris near its juncture with the Great Zab.

12. Resen This may be related to the Assyrian city of *Resh-eni.*

that is the great city Nineveh.

THE DEPENDENCIES OF CANAAN
(vv. 15–19)

15. Sidon The famous Phoenician port city.

Heth The ancestor of the Hittites, an Indo-European people who settled in Asia Minor, took over the name of the earlier inhabitants, the Hatti, and ca. 1800 B.C.E. founded the Hittite Empire.

16. Jebusites Nothing is known about the origin of this people. In the period of Joshua's wars of conquest, and until David's time, they were located in Jerusalem.

Amorites A Semitic people who first appeared in Babylonia in significant numbers ca. 2000 B.C.E., having migrated from the fringes of the Syrian desert. In later centuries, successive waves of Amorites infiltrated the entire Fertile Crescent.

17–18. Arkites . . . Hamathites All these refer to the inhabitants of five Syrian cities, four on the coast and one inland.

Afterward This note corresponds to that in verse 5. The text recognizes that Phoenicia proper and Palestine constituted a cultural continuum.

19. Canaanite territory Here "Canaan" is not a person but a people. The Table of Nations is leading up to the forerunner of Abraham, whose descendants are to inherit the land; hence this interest in the boundaries of Canaan.

Gerar An important city in the western Negeb, situated west or northwest of Beer-sheba in a region sufficiently well watered to provide pasturing facilities for shepherds.

Gaza The regional capital of the Egyptian province of Canaan and the most southerly of the coastal cities, it was strategically situated along the main highway and trade route that linked Mesopotamia and Egypt.

Sodom . . . Zeboiim These are the "cities of the Plain" (mentioned again in Gen. 14:2 and Deut. 29:22) that were destroyed because of

בֹּאֲכָ֛ה גְּרָ֖רָה עַד־עַזָּ֑ה בֹּאֲכָ֞ה סְדֹ֛מָה
וַעֲמֹרָ֥ה וְאַדְמָ֖ה וּצְבֹיִ֑ם עַד־לָֽשַׁע׃ 20 אֵ֣לֶּה
בְנֵי־חָ֔ם לְמִשְׁפְּחֹתָ֖ם לִלְשֹׁנֹתָ֑ם בְּאַרְצֹתָ֖ם
בְּגוֹיֵהֶֽם׃ ס
21 וּלְשֵׁ֥ם יֻלַּ֖ד גַּם־ה֑וּא אֲבִי֙ כָּל־בְּנֵי־עֵ֔בֶר
אֲחִ֖י יֶ֥פֶת הַגָּדֽוֹל׃ 22 בְּנֵ֥י שֵׁ֖ם עֵילָ֣ם
וְאַשּׁ֑וּר וְאַרְפַּכְשַׁ֖ד וְל֥וּד וַאֲרָֽם׃ 23 וּבְנֵ֖י
אֲרָ֑ם ע֥וּץ וְח֖וּל וְגֶ֥תֶר וָמַֽשׁ׃ 24 וְאַרְפַּכְשַׁ֖ד
יָלַ֣ד אֶת־שָׁ֑לַח וְשֶׁ֖לַח יָלַ֥ד אֶת־עֵֽבֶר׃
25 וּלְעֵ֥בֶר יֻלַּ֖ד שְׁנֵ֣י בָנִ֑ים שֵׁ֣ם הָאֶחָ֞ד פֶּ֗לֶג
כִּ֤י בְיָמָיו֙ נִפְלְגָ֣ה הָאָ֔רֶץ וְשֵׁ֥ם אָחִ֖יו
יָקְטָֽן׃ 26 וְיָקְטָ֣ן יָלַ֔ד אֶת־אַלְמוֹדָ֖ד וְאֶת־
שָׁ֑לֶף וְאֶת־חֲצַרְמָ֖וֶת וְאֶת־יָֽרַח׃ 27 וְאֶת־
הֲדוֹרָ֥ם וְאֶת־אוּזָ֖ל וְאֶת־דִּקְלָֽה׃ 28 וְאֶת־
עוֹבָ֥ל וְאֶת־אֲבִֽימָאֵ֖ל וְאֶת־שְׁבָֽא׃ 29 וְאֶת־
אוֹפִ֥ר וְאֶת־חֲוִילָ֖ה וְאֶת־יוֹבָ֑ב כָּל־אֵ֖לֶּה
בְּנֵ֥י יָקְטָֽן׃ 30 וַיְהִ֥י מוֹשָׁבָ֖ם מִמֵּשָׁ֑א

are the descendants of Ham, according to their
clans and languages, by their lands and nations.
21 Sons were also born to Shem, ancestor of
all the descendants of Eber and older brother
of Japheth. 22 The descendants of Shem: Elam,
Asshur, Arpachshad, Lud, and Aram. 23 The
descendants of Aram: Uz, Hul, Gether, and
Mash. 24 Arpachshad begot Shelah, and Shelah
begot Eber. 25 Two sons were born to Eber: the
name of the first was Peleg, for in his days the
earth was divided; and the name of his brother
was Joktan. 26 Joktan begot Almodad, Sheleph,
Hazarmaveth, Jerah, 27 Hadoram, Uzal, Diklah,
28 Obal, Abimael, Sheba, 29 Ophir, Havilah, and
Jobab; all these were the descendants of Joktan.
30 Their settlements extended from Mesha as far
as Sephar, the hill country to the east. 31 These

their wickedness. They have not been identified, but their most likely location is in the area now covered by the southern extension of the Dead Sea below the Lisan.

Lasha Otherwise unknown. Rabbinic commentators identified it with Callirrhoe, a site of hot springs near the eastern shore of the Dead Sea.

THE SHEMITES (vv. 21–31)

21. all the descendants of Eber Eber, although he is the fourth generation from Shem, receives special mention here because he is the ancestor both of Israel and of a variety of peoples with whom Israelite history is linked: Arameans, Ammonites, Moabites, Midianites, the Ishmaelite tribes, and Edomites.

22. Elam The ancient name for modern Khūzestān in southwestern Iran in the Iranian Plateau east of Babylon and northeast of the Persian Gulf. Its capital was Susa, the biblical Shushan of Esther 1:2–5. Elam is the most easterly country in the Table of Nations.

Asshur The city of Asshur on the Tigris in Upper Mesopotamia gave its name to the surrounding territory, which became known as Assyria.

Arpachshad A tradition from Second Temple times connects this name to the ancestor of the Chaldeans, an Aramean tribe that inhabited the desert regions between northern Arabia and the Persian Gulf.

Lud Possibly Lydia, a region on the west coast of Asia Minor.

Aram It is unclear whether this term applies here to a specific tribe or to the wider confederation of Aramean tribes that were western Semites.

23. descendants of Aram Of the four subdivisions of Aram, only Uz is known from sources outside the Bible. See Gen. 22:21 and 1 Chron. 1:17.

25. Peleg Possibly in Syria. His descendants are listed in Gen. 11:18–28. The name can mean "water channel" and may refer to an area of land watered by irrigation canals.

the earth was divided Traditionally, this has been taken as a reference to the confusion of languages and the dispersal of mankind described in the next chapter. The "dividing of the earth" may also refer to the development of agriculture by irrigation canals, some historic split up of tribes, or even an earthquake.

are the descendants of Shem according to their clans and languages, by their lands, according to their nations.

32These are the groupings of Noah's descendants, according to their origins, by their nations; and from these the nations branched out over the earth after the Flood.

בֹּאֲכָה סְפָרָה הַר הַקֶּדֶם׃ 31 אֵלֶּה בְנֵי־
שֵׁם לְמִשְׁפְּחֹתָם לִלְשֹׁנֹתָם בְּאַרְצֹתָם
לְגוֹיֵהֶם׃
32 אֵלֶּה מִשְׁפְּחֹת בְּנֵי־נֹחַ לְתוֹלְדֹתָם
בְּגוֹיֵהֶם וּמֵאֵלֶּה נִפְרְדוּ הַגּוֹיִם בָּאָרֶץ
אַחַר הַמַּבּוּל׃ פ

11 Everyone on earth had the same language and the same words. 2And as they migrated from the east, they came upon a valley in the land of Shinar and settled there. 3They said

שביעי **יא** וַיְהִי כָל־הָאָרֶץ שָׂפָה אֶחָת
וּדְבָרִים אֲחָדִים׃ 2 וַיְהִי בְּנָסְעָם מִקֶּדֶם
וַיִּמְצְאוּ בִקְעָה בְּאֶרֶץ שִׁנְעָר וַיֵּשְׁבוּ שָׁם׃

THE TOWER OF BABEL (11:1–9)

The generation after the Flood proves to be out of harmony with God, who must then embark on a new effort to fulfill divine purposes on earth.

THE MAKING OF BABEL (vv. 1–4)

1. Everyone on earth This and the following verses emphasize repeatedly the involvement of all humankind in the offense. This point is vital to the proper understanding of this narrative, which closes the second universal epoch in human history. It indicates that humankind is still rebellious against God, having learned nothing from the past.

the same language Belief in an original universal human language seems to have been current in ancient Sumer as well. The Bible here portrays the disruption of communication between human beings as having been the consequence of humankind's deliberate disharmony with God.

2. migrated Humankind is seen as having been nomadic after the Flood.

from the east That is, from the vantage point of Canaan.

a valley The flat alluvial plain in southern Mesopotamia between the Tigris and the Euphrates rivers.

Shinar See Comment to Gen. 10:10. A similar tradition is preserved by the ancient historian Berosus, whose story of the Mesopotamian flood also has the survivors first going to Babylon.

there The Hebrew word "*sham,*" repeated five times, directs our attention to the crucial importance of the site.

CHAPTER 11

Commanded to disperse and settle the earth, Noah's descendants insist on clustering in one area. Commanded to submit to the will of God, they set out to make a name for themselves. The story of the Tower of Babel seems inspired by the Babylonian temple towers (ziggurats). Can we sense here the Torah's ambivalence about large cities, with the anonymity, crime, and lack of neighborliness they represent? Or its suspicion that technology, the celebration of human ingenuity, will often lead to idolatry, people worshiping the work of their own hands?

One writer distinguishes between "mountain cultures," which see the heart of the world in wilderness, revering nature and adapting to it, and "tower cultures," for whom the essence of the world is the city and the human-made environment, stripping the sense of awe from nature and attaching it to the social and technological order. Egypt, land of pyramids and treasure cities, will be a tower culture. Israel, from Mount Sinai to the Temple Mount, will be largely a mountain culture. The people of the Tower of Babel are a pre-eminent example of a tower culture. Although human beings have done many wonderful things to reshape their environment, there is always the danger

3וַיֹּאמְרוּ אִישׁ אֶל־רֵעֵהוּ הָבָה נִלְבְּנָה
לְבֵנִים וְנִשְׂרְפָה לִשְׂרֵפָה וַתְּהִי לָהֶם
הַלְּבֵנָה לְאָבֶן וְהַחֵמָר הָיָה לָהֶם לַחֹמֶר׃
4וַיֹּאמְרוּ הָבָה ׀ נִבְנֶה־לָּנוּ עִיר וּמִגְדָּל
וְרֹאשׁוֹ בַשָּׁמַיִם וְנַעֲשֶׂה־לָּנוּ שֵׁם פֶּן־נָפוּץ
עַל־פְּנֵי כָל־הָאָרֶץ׃ 5וַיֵּרֶד יְהוָה לִרְאֹת
אֶת־הָעִיר וְאֶת־הַמִּגְדָּל אֲשֶׁר בָּנוּ בְּנֵי
הָאָדָם׃ 6וַיֹּאמֶר יְהוָה הֵן עַם אֶחָד
וְשָׂפָה אַחַת לְכֻלָּם וְזֶה הַחִלָּם לַעֲשׂוֹת
וְעַתָּה לֹא־יִבָּצֵר מֵהֶם כֹּל אֲשֶׁר יָזְמוּ

to one another, "Come, let us make bricks and
burn them hard."—Brick served them as
stone, and bitumen served them as mortar.—
4And they said, "Come, let us build us a city,
and a tower with its top in the sky, to make a
name for ourselves; else we shall be scattered all
over the world." 5The LORD came down to look
at the city and tower that man had built, 6and
the LORD said, "If, as one people with one language for all, this is how they have begun to act,
then nothing that they may propose to do will

3. Come, let us make bricks The narrator, writing from the perspective of a foreign observer, nevertheless displays an accurate and detailed knowledge of Mesopotamian construction methods.

Brick . . . mortar This editorial aside expresses wonderment at construction techniques so different from those familiar to the narrator in Israel where stone was used for construction purposes. (The phrase "with bitumen and burnt-brick" is a standard formula in Babylonian building inscriptions.)

4. a tower The ziggurat—a lofty, massive, solid-brick, multistaged temple tower that symbolized a sacred mountain, a meeting point of heaven and earth. The outstanding feature of most Mesopotamian cities, it was regarded as the center of the universe, the arena of divine activity, where humankind and the gods might enter into direct contact with one another.

with its top in the sky This phrase is the name of the chief ziggurat of Babylon, the locus of the story and the very tower in question, Esagilah, "the house that lifts its head to heaven." This expression is also often found in other Mesopotamian building inscriptions, leading to the widespread interpretation that the aim of the tower builders was to storm heaven. Generally, the Bible considers tall towers to be symbols of human arrogance (see Isa. 2:12–15 and 30:25; Ezek. 26:4,9).

to make a name for ourselves "Name" here probably means "monument," as in Isa. 56:5. Important kings were associated with great building projects. Bricks inscribed with royal names were placed in the ziggurat's foundations to ensure the monarch's eternal fame.

else we shall be scattered The ziggurat, a source of civic pride, was expected to foster a spirit of unity. But the Torah interprets construction as a mark of human arrogance and a direct affront to God.

GOD'S COUNTERMEASURES (vv. 5–9)

5. The LORD came down To investigate humankind's doings.

man The biblical narrator stresses the strictly human nature of the entire enterprise. In Mesopotamian tradition, the gods erected the temple at Babylon.

had built Thus far; Gen. 11:8 tells us that the project was never completed.

---

of becoming so enamored of technology that human values are lost.

A rabbinic legend relates that people paid no mind if a worker on the tower fell to his death. If a brick fell, however, they lamented the delay in their building project (PRE 24). "The purpose of these awe-inspiring monuments erected by the technical skill of men was to enable people to forget their insignificance and transient nature" (N. Leibowitz).

4. God learns from experiences like these, "When I am gracious to decent people, they respond with gratitude and humility. When I am gracious to wicked people (like Nimrod and the builders of the Tower), they respond with arrogance" (BT Ḥul. 89a).

5. The LORD came down A *midrash* states that this passage is intended to teach us not to pass judgment on anyone without personally examining the situation (Tanḥ.).

לַעֲשֽׂוֹת׃ 7 הָ֚בָה נֵֽרְדָ֔ה וְנָבְלָ֥ה שָׁ֖ם שְׂפָתָ֑ם
אֲשֶׁר֙ לֹ֣א יִשְׁמְע֔וּ אִ֖ישׁ שְׂפַ֥ת רֵעֵֽהוּ׃
8 וַיָּ֨פֶץ יְהוָ֥ה אֹתָ֛ם מִשָּׁ֖ם עַל־פְּנֵ֣י כָל־
הָאָ֑רֶץ וַֽיַּחְדְּל֖וּ לִבְנֹ֥ת הָעִֽיר׃ 9 עַל־כֵּ֞ן קָרָ֤א
שְׁמָהּ֙ בָּבֶ֔ל כִּי־שָׁ֛ם בָּלַ֥ל יְהוָ֖ה שְׂפַ֣ת כָּל־
הָאָ֑רֶץ וּמִשָּׁם֙ הֱפִיצָ֣ם יְהוָ֔ה עַל־פְּנֵ֖י כָּל־
הָאָֽרֶץ׃ פ

10 אֵ֚לֶּה תּוֹלְדֹ֣ת שֵׁ֔ם שֵׁ֚ם בֶּן־מְאַ֣ת שָׁנָ֔ה
וַיּ֖וֹלֶד אֶת־אַרְפַּכְשָׁ֑ד שְׁנָתַ֖יִם אַחַ֥ר
הַמַּבּֽוּל׃ 11 וַֽיְחִי־שֵׁ֗ם אַֽחֲרֵי֙ הוֹלִיד֣וֹ אֶת־
אַרְפַּכְשָׁ֔ד חֲמֵ֥שׁ מֵא֖וֹת שָׁנָ֑ה וַיּ֥וֹלֶד בָּנִ֖ים
וּבָנֽוֹת׃ ס 12 וְאַרְפַּכְשַׁ֣ד חַ֔י חָמֵ֥שׁ
וּשְׁלֹשִׁ֖ים שָׁנָ֑ה וַיּ֖וֹלֶד אֶת־שָֽׁלַח׃ 13 וַיְחִ֣י
אַרְפַּכְשַׁ֗ד אַֽחֲרֵי֙ הוֹלִיד֣וֹ אֶת־שֶׁ֔לַח שָׁל֣שׁ
שָׁנִ֔ים וְאַרְבַּ֥ע מֵא֖וֹת שָׁנָ֑ה וַיּ֥וֹלֶד בָּנִ֖ים
וּבָנֽוֹת׃ ס 14 וְשֶׁ֥לַח חַ֖י שְׁלֹשִׁ֣ים שָׁנָ֑ה
וַיּ֖וֹלֶד אֶת־עֵֽבֶר׃ 15 וַֽיְחִי־שֶׁ֗לַח אַֽחֲרֵי֙

be out of their reach. [7]Let us, then, go down and confound their speech there, so that they shall not understand one another's speech." [8]Thus the LORD scattered them from there over the face of the whole earth; and they stopped building the city. [9]That is why it was called Babel, because there the LORD confounded the speech of the whole earth; and from there the LORD scattered them over the face of the whole earth.

[10]This is the line of Shem. Shem was 100 years old when he begot Arpachshad, two years after the Flood. [11]After the birth of Arpachshad, Shem lived 500 years and begot sons and daughters.

[12]When Arpachshad had lived 35 years, he begot Shelah. [13]After the birth of Shelah, Arpachshad lived 403 years and begot sons and daughters.

[14]When Shelah had lived 30 years, he be-

7. Let us, then Unless preventive measures are taken, there will be no limit to humankind's schemes. For the plural use of the verb, see Comment to 1:26.

confound The Hebrew word *"navlah"* is a form of the stem for "to confuse" (בלל).

8. they stopped building This narrative may have been inspired by the spectacle of Babylon and its ziggurat lying in ruins, which was the situation after the Hittite raid on the city ca. 1600 B.C.E.

the city That is, the ziggurat.

9. it was called Literally, "one called its name," an ironic echo of verse 4. They aspired to "make a name" for themselves, but succeeded only in attaching the name "confusion" to their handiwork.

Babel Neither the "gate of god," as the inhabitants of Babylon interpreted the name, nor the center of the earth, as they conceived their city to be—but a site of gibberish, radiating divisiveness and disastrous alienation from God.

The narrative of this chapter's opening is a parody belittling Babylon and its temple tower (ziggurat). Babylon ("the gate of the god," *bab-il*) becomes "babble." The ziggurat, the abode of the god, is unable to withstand the divine onslaught.

FROM SHEM TO ABRAHAM (11:10–32)

The narrative now focuses on one line of descent within the family tree of Shem. This line leads to Abraham, the 10th generation from Shem, just as Noah was the 10th generation from Adam. From the biblical point of view, the birth of Abraham constitutes a decisive turning point in the history of humankind.

10. This is the line The advent of Terah is a climactic event set off by the words translated here as "This is the line" (*eilleh tol'dot*). The Hebrew phrase appears another 10 times in Genesis. Here, the phrase establishes the transition from universal to patriarchal history.

100 This figure is approximate, because Shem would now have been 102, according to the data of 5:32 and 7:6.

Arpachshad Inexplicably, in 10:22 he is the third son of Shem, whereas here he seems to be the first-born.

got Eber. [15]After the birth of Eber, Shelah lived 403 years and begot sons and daughters.

[16]When Eber had lived 34 years, he begot Peleg. [17]After the birth of Peleg, Eber lived 430 years and begot sons and daughters.

[18]When Peleg had lived 30 years, he begot Reu. [19]After the birth of Reu, Peleg lived 209 years and begot sons and daughters.

[20]When Reu had lived 32 years, he begot Serug. [21]After the birth of Serug, Reu lived 207 years and begot sons and daughters.

[22]When Serug had lived 30 years, he begot Nahor. [23]After the birth of Nahor, Serug lived 200 years and begot sons and daughters.

[24]When Nahor had lived 29 years, he begot Terah. [25]After the birth of Terah, Nahor lived 119 years and begot sons and daughters.

[26]When Terah had lived 70 years, he begot Abram, Nahor, and Haran. [27]Now this is the

הוֹלִידוֹ אֶת־עֵ֫בֶר שָׁלֹ֤שׁ שָׁנִים֙ וְאַרְבַּ֣ע
מֵא֣וֹת שָׁנָ֔ה וַיּ֥וֹלֶד בָּנִ֖ים וּבָנֽוֹת: ס
[16]וַֽיְחִי־עֵ֕בֶר אַרְבַּ֥ע וּשְׁלֹשִׁ֖ים שָׁנָ֑ה וַיּ֖וֹלֶד
אֶת־פָּֽלֶג: [17]וַֽיְחִי־עֵ֗בֶר אַֽחֲרֵי֙ הֽוֹלִיד֣וֹ אֶת־
פֶּ֔לֶג שְׁלֹשִׁ֣ים שָׁנָ֔ה וְאַרְבַּ֥ע מֵא֖וֹת שָׁנָ֑ה
וַיּ֥וֹלֶד בָּנִ֖ים וּבָנֽוֹת: ס [18]וַֽיְחִי־פֶ֕לֶג
שְׁלֹשִׁ֣ים שָׁנָ֔ה וַיּ֖וֹלֶד אֶת־רְעֽוּ: [19]וַֽיְחִי־פֶ֗לֶג
אַֽחֲרֵי֙ הֽוֹלִיד֣וֹ אֶת־רְע֔וּ תֵּ֥שַׁע שָׁנִ֖ים
וּמָאתַ֣יִם שָׁנָ֑ה וַיּ֥וֹלֶד בָּנִ֖ים וּבָנֽוֹת: ס
[20]וַיְחִ֣י רְע֔וּ שְׁתַּ֥יִם וּשְׁלֹשִׁ֖ים שָׁנָ֑ה וַיּ֖וֹלֶד
אֶת־שְׂרֽוּג: [21]וַיְחִ֣י רְע֗וּ אַֽחֲרֵי֙ הֽוֹלִיד֣וֹ
אֶת־שְׂר֔וּג שֶׁ֥בַע שָׁנִ֖ים וּמָאתַ֣יִם שָׁנָ֑ה
וַיּ֥וֹלֶד בָּנִ֖ים וּבָנֽוֹת: ס [22]וַיְחִ֣י שְׂר֗וּג
שְׁלֹשִׁ֣ים שָׁנָ֑ה וַיּ֖וֹלֶד אֶת־נָחֽוֹר: [23]וַיְחִ֣י
שְׂר֗וּג אַֽחֲרֵי֙ הֽוֹלִיד֣וֹ אֶת־נָח֔וֹר מָאתַ֣יִם
שָׁנָ֑ה וַיּ֥וֹלֶד בָּנִ֖ים וּבָנֽוֹת: ס [24]וַיְחִ֣י נָח֗וֹר
תֵּ֥שַׁע וְעֶשְׂרִ֖ים שָׁנָ֑ה וַיּ֖וֹלֶד אֶת־תָּֽרַח:
[25]וַיְחִ֣י נָח֗וֹר אַֽחֲרֵי֙ הֽוֹלִיד֣וֹ אֶת־תֶּ֔רַח
תְּשַֽׁע־עֶשְׂרֵ֥ה שָׁנָ֖ה וּמְאַ֣ת שָׁנָ֑ה וַיּ֖וֹלֶד
בָּנִ֖ים וּבָנֽוֹת: ס [26]וַֽיְחִי־תֶ֖רַח שִׁבְעִ֣ים
שָׁנָ֑ה וַיּ֕וֹלֶד אֶת־אַבְרָ֖ם אֶת־נָח֥וֹר וְאֶת־
הָרָֽן: [27]וְאֵ֨לֶּה֙ תּֽוֹלְדֹ֣ת תֶּ֔רַח תֶּ֖רַח הוֹלִ֣יד

18. Reu Probably a shortened form of Reuel, meaning "friend of God." (Cf. Reuel, a name of Moses' father-in-law, in Exod. 2:18.)

20. Serug The well-known city of Sarugi, not far north of Haran in the Balīkh Valley.

22. Nahor An important site in the upper Balīkh Valley.

24. Terah Ancient sources mention a place-name *Til (sa) Turahi* situated on the Balīkh River not far from Haran and Nahor. The name may well be connected with *yarei·aḥ,* "moon." Several members of Terah's family, as well as some of the sites connected with him, bear names associated with moon worship. Josh. 24:2 explicitly describes Terah as an idolater. Note that both Haran and Ur were also associated with moon worship.

26. 70 years Terah begets children when he is about twice the age of all his predecessors in the line of Shem. This detail inserts into the nar-

rative the motif of protracted childlessness, a condition that will be a major factor in the lives of his descendants, the patriarchs of Israel.

Abram This form of the name is consistently used until it is expanded to Abraham in Gen. 17:5, after which it appears again only in Neh. 9:7 and 1 Chron. 1:26 as required by their respective contexts. The name Abram is west Semitic and attested in cuneiform sources. It could mean "exalted father," "the father is exalted," or "the (divine) father loves (him)."

Nahor Apparently named after his grandfather.

Haran A name derived from *har,* "a mountain," used in the sense of "mountain god" in ancient Semitic personal names.

THE FAMILY OF TERAH (vv. 27–32)

27. Now this is the line This *eilleh tol'dot* phrase introduces the biography of Abraham.

line of Terah: Terah begot Abram, Nahor, and
Haran; and Haran begot Lot. 28Haran died in
the lifetime of his father Terah, in his native
land, Ur of the Chaldeans. 29Abram and Nahor
took to themselves wives, the name of Abram's
wife being Sarai and that of Nahor's wife
Milcah, the daughter of Haran, the father of
Milcah and Iscah. 30Now Sarai was barren,
she had no child.

31Terah took his son Abram, his grandson Lot
the son of Haran, and his daughter-in-law Sarai,
the wife of his son Abram, and they set out together from Ur of the Chaldeans for the land
of Canaan; but when they had come as far as

אֶת־אַבְרָ֔ם אֶת־נָח֖וֹר וְאֶת־הָרָ֑ן וְהָרָ֖ן
הוֹלִ֥יד אֶת־לֽוֹט׃ 28וַיָּ֣מָת הָרָ֔ן עַל־פְּנֵ֖י
תֶּ֣רַח אָבִ֑יו בְּאֶ֥רֶץ מוֹלַדְתּ֖וֹ בְּא֥וּר כַּשְׂדִּֽים׃
מפטיר 29וַיִּקַּ֨ח אַבְרָ֧ם וְנָח֛וֹר לָהֶ֖ם נָשִׁ֑ים שֵׁ֤ם
אֵֽשֶׁת־אַבְרָם֙ שָׂרָ֔י וְשֵׁ֤ם אֵֽשֶׁת־נָחוֹר֙
מִלְכָּ֔ה בַּת־הָרָ֥ן אֲבִֽי־מִלְכָּ֖ה וַאֲבִ֥י יִסְכָּֽה׃
30וַתְּהִ֥י שָׂרַ֖י עֲקָרָ֑ה אֵ֥ין לָ֖הּ וָלָֽד׃
31וַיִּקַּ֨ח תֶּ֜רַח אֶת־אַבְרָ֣ם בְּנ֗וֹ וְאֶת־ל֤וֹט
בֶּן־הָרָן֙ בֶּן־בְּנ֔וֹ וְאֵת֙ שָׂרַ֣י כַּלָּת֔וֹ אֵ֖שֶׁת
אַבְרָ֣ם בְּנ֑וֹ וַיֵּצְא֨וּ אִתָּ֜ם מֵא֣וּר כַּשְׂדִּ֗ים
לָלֶ֙כֶת֙ אַ֣רְצָה כְּנַ֔עַן וַיָּבֹ֥אוּ עַד־חָרָ֖ן וַיֵּ֥שְׁבוּ

Lot The origin of this name is unknown.

28. Haran died A fact essential for understanding 12:4–5.

Ur of the Chaldeans Most scholars regard this mention of the Chaldeans as an anachronism. They were a Semitic people related to, but distinct from, the Arameans. Nothing excavated from the great city of Ur in southern Mesopotamia indicates the presence of Chaldeans until the 7th to 6th centuries B.C.E., long after the period of the patriarchs. Thus the Ur of our text may be one of the sites in Upper Mesopotamia, founded by citizens of the famous city in the south and named after it. An Upper Mesopotamian Ur would have been much closer to Haran, a city crucial to patriarchal narratives.

29. Sarai The name (changed to Sarah in 17:15) means "princess" in Hebrew. If it is based on the Akkadian word *"sharratu"* (a term used for the female consort of the moon god Sin, the principal god of Ur), it means "queen." The parentage of Nahor's wife is given, that of Sarai is not—a startling omission that must have been intentional. Perhaps the narrator withholds that information so as not to diminish the suspense in chapter 20 when Abraham, to extricate himself from an embarrassing predicament, reveals that Sarai is his half-sister.

Milcah The name is a variant form of Malcah, "queen." In Akkadian, *malkatu* is a title of the goddess Ishtar, known as Queen of Heaven, daughter of the moon god Sin.

Iscah The name may derive from the stem meaning "to see" (סכה) and may be a shortened form of a sentence name: "May God see [i.e., with favor] the child." Nothing is known of her; she may have been the central figure of traditions now lost.

30. barren The Hebrew word *akarah* simply means "childless," but not necessarily infertile.

31. they set out . . . as far as Haran Haran is situated some 550 miles (885 km) northwest of Ur, about 10 miles (16 km) north of the present-day Syrian–Turkish border on the left bank of the Balīkh River. The name means "route, journey, caravan," no doubt derived from the city's location as an important station on the main international trade routes from Mesopotamia to the Mediterranean Sea.

Nahor is not mentioned as included in the company, but he was closely associated with Haran. Indeed, the place is called "the city of Nahor" in Gen. 24:10. Perhaps he migrated at a later time.

---

31. They set out together from Ur We know from archeological sources that there was a great influx of population into Ur at about this time. But Abraham, the *Ivri,* from a word meaning "the other side," ever the contrarian, chose to leave Ur in pursuit of God.

they settled there So often in life, we set out with the best of intentions, only to give up halfway to our goal (*Arugat Ha-Bosem*).

Haran, they settled there. 32The days of Terah came to 205 years; and Terah died in Haran.

שָׁם׃ 32 וַיִּהְי֣וּ יְמֵי־תֶ֔רַח חָמֵ֥שׁ שָׁנִ֖ים וּמָאתַ֣יִם שָׁנָ֑ה וַיָּ֥מָת תֶּ֖רַח בְּחָרָֽן׃ ס

32. Terah died The Torah does not always tell its stories in strict time sequence. A calculation based on the data of 11:26 and 12:4 shows him to have been 145 years old when Abraham left Haran for Canaan. Thus Terah lived on in Haran for another 60 years after Abraham's departure.

---

32. Terah died in Haran Actually, Terah did not die for another 60 years. Therefore the Torah must be describing him here as "spiritually dead," having given his soul over to idol worship (Gen. R. 39:7).

As the previous *parashah* lightened the note of disappointment at its end by introducing the righteous Noah, this *parashah* tempers God's disappointment by anticipating the emergence of Abraham. "Whereas Noah remained fixed in Nature, Abraham sets out into history to proclaim God's dominion" (Buber).

הפטרת נח

HAFTARAH FOR NO·AḤ

ISAIAH 54:1–55:5 (*Ashk'nazim*)
ISAIAH 54:1–10 (*S'fardim*)

This *haftarah* presents a series of promises and assurances to Zion and its inhabitants. They constitute prophecies addressed to the city (Jerusalem) and to the nation, destroyed and defeated since the Babylonian conquest in 587–586 B.C.E. The prophet promises the restoration of divine mercy and covenantal guarantees. God's wrath will be replaced with kindness everlasting, recalling the oath sworn after the Flood in the time of Noah.

Figures of assurance dominate the prophet's style, as dramatized through expanding expressions of God's language and attributes. The opening proclamation ends simply with the words "said the LORD" (54:1). After several oracles of renewed kindness, however, the conclusion states, "said the LORD your Redeemer" (v. 8); and the finale to God's oath of permanent loyalty triumphantly proclaims, "said the LORD, who takes you back in love" (v. 10). From another perspective, the nation successively learns that "The Holy One of Israel" who "redeems" Zion is none other than the "God of all the Earth." Intimate love is expressed by the universal God.

The use of comparisons for the sake of rhetorical emphasis is another stylistic feature of this *haftarah*. In one instance, the prophet imagines the desolation and restoration of Zion as a ruptured and healed marriage relationship. "The LORD has called you back / As a wife forlorn and forsaken" (v. 6). She who once was "espoused" (*b'-ulah;* v. 1) will be espoused anew by her redeeming and loving Lord (*bo·alayikh;* v. 5). This language draws from older legal usage (Deut. 24:1) and prophetic tradition (Hos. 2 and Jer. 2:1 and 3:1, especially). In those cases, too, God's relation with Israel is that of husband and wife. Isaiah's emphasis that God will take His bride back in "love" (*riḥamtikh*) and "kindness everlasting" (*ḥesed olam;* v. 8) literally recalls the vows of new espousals as enunciated in Hos. 2:21. "And I [God] will espouse you forever (*l'olam*): / I will espouse you with . . . goodness and mercy (*ḥesed v'raḥamim*)." There is a notable difference, however. Isaiah speaks of a marriage between God and Zion, not between God and the people Israel. The city is a mystical embodiment of its inhabitants, a connection underscored by the imagery of barrenness and repopulation found throughout the prophecy. Nevertheless, the wider Near Eastern theme of a bond between a deity and its city is maintained here.

RELATION OF THE *HAFTARAH* TO THE *PARASHAH*

The primary connection between the *haftarah* and *parashah* is their common reference to the Flood in the days of Noah, the result of divine wrath. That event from earliest time, together with God's oath that followed, are invoked by Isaiah as part of God's promise of renewed loyalty to His people. A series of close verbal links establish a relationship between the present situation and the original event. In the ancient past, God made a "covenant" (*b'rit*) with Noah and his descendants (Gen. 9:9,11,15), swearing that "not again" (*lo . . . od*) will the earth and its inhabitants be destroyed (9:11,15). Now, too, God promises the nation (Isa. 54:10, 55:1) a renewed "covenant" (*b'rit*) and the hope that the nation's shame will "not again" (*lo od*) be recalled (Isa. 54:4).

The prophet transforms the language of the narrative in two respects. In the first case, a covenant guaranteeing the stability of nature becomes a guarantee of permanent divine loyalty toward Zion and Israel. The second instance in-

volves taking a pact made between God and all humans and applying it to a covenant with a particular people. These contrasts heighten the mythic proportions by which the nation experienced its destruction and will experience its restoration.

Another version of the divine oath in Genesis adds an additional dimension. In it, God swears: "Never again (*lo . . . od*) will I doom the earth because of man, since the devisings of man's mind are evil from his youth; nor will I ever again (*v'lo . . . od*) destroy every living being, as I have done" (Gen. 8:21). According to the prophet, the divine oath of restraint is not justified by this realization of the human propensity for evil. Rather, it is motivated by the return of God's love to His creatures and the decision to transform that love into an everlasting covenant.

The final section of the *haftarah* suggests that the human heart may be transformed through heeding the call for spiritual living that is God's gift to "all who are thirsty" (Isa. 55:1–3).

Two models of piety are offered by the *parashah* and *haftarah*. One model is the example of Noah, characterized as a "righteous man" (*tzaddik*) who was "blameless in his age" and "walked with God" (Gen. 6:9). This model of righteousness is focused on inner purity and divine-centered living. It is the way of spiritual aloneness, with all its inner demands and mysteries. The other model is that of the "disciples of the LORD" who establish their city "through righteousness (*bitzdakah*)" (Isa. 54:13–14). The focus of this model is the community and its collective transformation. Here the tasks are public and the demands are in full view. Maimonides perceptively identified a scriptural source for the duty of giving charity (*tz'dakah*) in 54:14, underscoring the importance of such personal piety for collective religious life.

54 Shout, O barren one,
You who bore no child!
Shout aloud for joy,
You who did not travail!
For the children of the wife forlorn
Shall outnumber those of the espoused
—said the LORD.
2Enlarge the site of your tent,
Extend the size of your dwelling,
Do not stint!
Lengthen the ropes, and drive the pegs firm.
3For you shall spread out to the right and the left;
Your offspring shall dispossess nations
And shall people the desolate towns.

4Fear not, you shall not be shamed;

נד רָנִּי עֲקָרָה
לֹא יָלָדָה
פִּצְחִי רִנָּה וְצַהֲלִי
לֹא־חָלָה
כִּי־רַבִּים בְּנֵי־שׁוֹמֵמָה
מִבְּנֵי בְעוּלָה
אָמַר יְהוָה׃
2 הַרְחִיבִי ׀ מְקוֹם אָהֳלֵךְ
וִירִיעוֹת מִשְׁכְּנוֹתַיִךְ יַטּוּ
אַל־תַּחְשֹׂכִי
הַאֲרִיכִי מֵיתָרַיִךְ וִיתֵדֹתַיִךְ חַזֵּקִי׃
3 כִּי־יָמִין וּשְׂמֹאול* תִּפְרֹצִי
וְזַרְעֵךְ גּוֹיִם יִירָשׁ
וְעָרִים נְשַׁמּוֹת יוֹשִׁיבוּ׃

4 אַל־תִּירְאִי כִּי־לֹא תֵבוֹשִׁי

v. 3. מלא ו׳

Do not cringe, you shall not be disgraced.
For you shall forget
The reproach of your youth,
And remember no more
The shame of your widowhood.
5For He who made you will espouse you—
His name is "LORD of Hosts."
The Holy One of Israel will redeem you—
He is called "God of all the Earth."

6The LORD has called you back
As a wife forlorn and forsaken.
Can one cast off the wife of his youth?
—said your God.
7For a little while I forsook you,
But with vast love I will bring you back.
8In slight anger, for a moment,
I hid My face from you;
But with kindness everlasting
I will take you back in love
—said the LORD your Redeemer.
9For this to Me is like the waters of Noah:
As I swore that the waters of Noah
Nevermore would flood the earth,
So I swear that I will not
Be angry with you or rebuke you.
10For the mountains may move
And the hills be shaken,
But my loyalty shall never move from you,
Nor My covenant of friendship be shaken
—said the LORD, who takes you back in love.

וְאַל־תִּכָּלְמִי כִּי לֹא תַחְפִּירִי
כִּי בֹשֶׁת עֲלוּמַיִךְ
תִּשְׁכָּחִי
וְחֶרְפַּת אַלְמְנוּתַיִךְ
לֹא תִזְכְּרִי־עוֹד׃
5 כִּי בֹעֲלַיִךְ עֹשַׂיִךְ
יְהוָה צְבָאוֹת שְׁמוֹ
וְגֹאֲלֵךְ קְדוֹשׁ יִשְׂרָאֵל
אֱלֹהֵי כָל־הָאָרֶץ יִקָּרֵא׃

6 כִּי־כְאִשָּׁה עֲזוּבָה וַעֲצוּבַת רוּחַ
קְרָאָךְ יְהוָה
וְאֵשֶׁת נְעוּרִים כִּי תִמָּאֵס
אָמַר אֱלֹהָיִךְ׃
7 בְּרֶגַע קָטֹן עֲזַבְתִּיךְ
וּבְרַחֲמִים גְּדֹלִים אֲקַבְּצֵךְ׃
8 בְּשֶׁצֶף קֶצֶף
הִסְתַּרְתִּי פָנַי רֶגַע מִמֵּךְ
וּבְחֶסֶד עוֹלָם
רִחַמְתִּיךְ
אָמַר גֹּאֲלֵךְ יְהוָה׃ ס
9 כִּי־מֵי נֹחַ זֹאת לִי
אֲשֶׁר נִשְׁבַּעְתִּי מֵעֲבֹר מֵי־נֹחַ
עוֹד עַל־הָאָרֶץ
כֵּן נִשְׁבַּעְתִּי
מִקְּצֹף עָלַיִךְ וּמִגְּעָר־בָּךְ׃
10 כִּי הֶהָרִים יָמוּשׁוּ
וְהַגְּבָעוֹת תְּמוּטֶנָה
וְחַסְדִּי מֵאִתֵּךְ לֹא־יָמוּשׁ
וּבְרִית שְׁלוֹמִי לֹא תָמוּט
אָמַר מְרַחֲמֵךְ יְהוָה׃ ס

Isaiah 54:6–8. The reference to Israel as "wife of his youth" (*n'urim*) recalls the terminology in other images of the marriage motif in prophetic literature (Hos. 2:17, Jer. 2:2, Ezek. 23:8,19–20). The idea of loyalty and commitment is conveyed by the word "*ḥesed*" (cf. Isa. 54:10; 2 Sam. 7:15; Ps. 89:34). The same word alludes to the covenant response found also in Hos. 2:21 and Jer. 2:2. Through *ḥesed* one deals faithfully or keeps faith with another; it is so used of divine–human and interpersonal relationships (Deut. 5:10, 1 Sam. 20:8).

11Unhappy, storm-tossed one, uncomforted!
I will lay carbuncles as your building stones
And make your foundations of sapphires.
12I will make your battlements of rubies,
Your gates of precious stones,
The whole encircling wall of gems.
13And all your children shall be disciples of the LORD,
And great shall be the happiness of your children;
14You shall be established through righteousness.
You shall be safe from oppression,
And shall have no fear;
From ruin, and it shall not come near you.
15Surely no harm can be done
Without My consent:
Whoever would harm you
Shall fall because of you.
16It is I who created the smith
To fan the charcoal fire
And produce the tools for his work;
So it is I who create
The instruments of havoc.
17No weapon formed against you
Shall succeed,
And every tongue that contends with you at law
You shall defeat.

11 עֲנִיָּה סֹעֲרָה לֹא נֻחָמָה
הִנֵּה אָנֹכִי מַרְבִּיץ בַּפּוּךְ אֲבָנַיִךְ
וִיסַדְתִּיךְ בַּסַּפִּירִים׃
12 וְשַׂמְתִּי כַּדְכֹד שִׁמְשֹׁתַיִךְ
וּשְׁעָרַיִךְ לְאַבְנֵי אֶקְדָּח
וְכָל־גְּבוּלֵךְ לְאַבְנֵי־חֵפֶץ׃
13 וְכָל־בָּנַיִךְ לִמּוּדֵי יְהוָה
וְרַב שְׁלוֹם בָּנָיִךְ׃
14 בִּצְדָקָה תִּכּוֹנָנִי
רַחֲקִי מֵעֹשֶׁק
כִּי־לֹא תִירָאִי
וּמִמְּחִתָּה כִּי לֹא־תִקְרַב אֵלָיִךְ׃
15 הֵן גּוֹר יָגוּר
אֶפֶס מֵאוֹתִי
מִי־גָר אִתָּךְ
עָלַיִךְ יִפּוֹל׃
16 הן הִנֵּה אָנֹכִי בָּרָאתִי חָרָשׁ
נֹפֵחַ בְּאֵשׁ פֶּחָם
וּמוֹצִיא כְלִי לְמַעֲשֵׂהוּ
וְאָנֹכִי בָּרָאתִי
מַשְׁחִית לְחַבֵּל׃
17 כָּל־כְּלִי יוּצַר עָלַיִךְ
לֹא יִצְלָח
וְכָל־לָשׁוֹן תָּקוּם־אִתָּךְ לַמִּשְׁפָּט
תַּרְשִׁיעִי

13. disciples Hebrew *limmudei*, a technical term (see 8:16, 50:4).

your children Hebrew: *banayikh*, spelled בניך. In a well-known *midrash*, the second instance of this word in v. 13 is reread as *bonayikh* (your builders); it became the basis for teaching that knowledgeable children are the culture builders of the next generation (BT Ber. 64a). The spelling is בוניכי in the large Isaiah scroll from Qumran (the "Dead Sea Scrolls"), which supports the midrashic vocalization *bonayikh*. However, this spelling may equally indicate that the original sense was "your learned ones" (from the root בינ, "to know"). If so, this noun would parallel "disciples of the LORD" in the first part of the verse.

14. You shall be established through righteousness This sentence recalls 1:27: "Zion shall be saved in the judgment; / Her repentant ones, in the retribution."

17. their triumph In Hebrew: *tzidkatam*. The force of the noun is justification in court. It counterpoints the opening clause (cf. Exod. 23:7; 2 Sam. 15:4; Isa. 5:23; Prov. 17:15). God

Such is the lot of the servants of the LORD,
Such their triumph through Me
—declares the LORD.

55 Ho, all who are thirsty,
Come for water,
Even if you have no money;
Come, buy food and eat:
Buy food without money,
Wine and milk without cost.
2 Why do you spend money for what is not bread,
Your earnings for what does not satisfy?
Give heed to Me,
And you shall eat choice food
And enjoy the richest viands.
3 Incline your ear and come to Me;
Hearken, and you shall be revived.
And I will make with you an everlasting covenant,
The enduring loyalty promised to David.
4 As I made him a leader of peoples,
A prince and commander of peoples,
5 So you shall summon a nation you did not know,
And a nation that did not know you
Shall come running to you—
For the sake of the LORD your God,
The Holy One of Israel who has glorified you.

זֹאת נַחֲלַת עַבְדֵי יְהוָה
וְצִדְקָתָם מֵאִתִּי
נְאֻם־יְהוָה׃ ס

נה הוֹי כָּל־צָמֵא
לְכוּ לַמַּיִם
וַאֲשֶׁר אֵין־לוֹ כָּסֶף
לְכוּ שִׁבְרוּ וֶאֱכֹלוּ
וּלְכוּ שִׁבְרוּ בְּלוֹא־כֶסֶף
וּבְלוֹא מְחִיר יַיִן וְחָלָב׃
2 לָמָּה תִשְׁקְלוּ־כֶסֶף בְּלוֹא־לֶחֶם
וִיגִיעֲכֶם בְּלוֹא לְשָׂבְעָה
שִׁמְעוּ שָׁמוֹעַ אֵלַי
וְאִכְלוּ־טוֹב
וְתִתְעַנַּג בַּדֶּשֶׁן נַפְשְׁכֶם׃
3 הַטּוּ אָזְנְכֶם וּלְכוּ אֵלַי
שִׁמְעוּ וּתְחִי נַפְשְׁכֶם
וְאֶכְרְתָה לָכֶם בְּרִית עוֹלָם
חַסְדֵי דָוִד הַנֶּאֱמָנִים׃
4 הֵן עֵד לְאוּמִּים נְתַתִּיו
נָגִיד וּמְצַוֵּה לְאֻמִּים׃
5 הֵן גּוֹי לֹא־תֵדַע תִּקְרָא
וְגוֹי לֹא־יְדָעוּךָ
אֵלֶיךָ יָרוּצוּ
לְמַעַן יְהוָה אֱלֹהֶיךָ
וְלִקְדוֹשׁ יִשְׂרָאֵל כִּי פֵאֲרָךְ׃ ס

is the vindicator of Israel and thus the one who brings them triumph.

Isaiah 55:1. all who are thirsty The appeal is either to those of Israel who are still far from the Lord or to the nations who follow foreign wisdom (Ibn Ezra). The imagery of hunger and thirst indicates the absence of divine instruction, as in Amos 8:11 (cf. Radak).

3. The enduring loyalty promised to David The royal covenant given to David (2 Sam. 7) is now transferred to the entire people. It employs *ḥesed* in the sense of covenant faithfulness. The divine pact with David promised unconditional commitment.

4. a leader of peoples The word translated here as "leader" (*ed*) has the literal meaning of "witness." The figure combines images of Israel's mission as a "light of nations" and "witness" to God's power for all (cf. Isa. 42:7, 43:10).

12 The LORD said to Abram, "Go forth יב וַיֹּאמֶר יְהוָה אֶל־אַבְרָם לֶךְ־לְךָ

GOD'S ELECTION OF ABRAHAM (12:1–13:18)

The first 75 years of Abraham's life are passed over in total silence. He still bears the name Abram when God's call comes. The patriarch's immediate response thrusts him onto the scene of history with astounding suddenness and marks the true beginning of his life.

Note that his wanderings in Canaan were later repeated by his descendants. This led Ramban to comment that Abraham's wanderings foreshadowed those of later generations.

THE DIVINE CALL AND THE PROMISES (vv. 1–3)

1. The LORD said to Abram The divine voice that first set Creation in motion resounds again after 10 generations of silence. This time it is at Haran, where the intended migration of Terah and his family from Ur to Canaan had come to a halt, for some unexplained reason.

Go forth Take leave of, separate.

CHAPTER 12

God, by giving Adam one command to follow, gave him the opportunity to be a moral, obedient person. The ultimate goal of God's creation was not a static world but a world in which people, having free choice between good and bad, would freely choose good. Adam and his descendants, however, were not up to the challenge. Just 10 generations later, God began again with a single righteous family. Noah had the advantage over Adam of having shown himself to be more righteous than his neighbors, but Noah and his descendants also disappointed God, who now changes the approach. Instead of asking one individual or one family to be good in isolation, God seeks to create a community, a people, descendants of a God-fearing couple, in the hope that the members of that community would sustain and reinforce each other. In that way, ordinary people would be capable of displaying extraordinary behavior.

The new venture begins with Abram and Sarai, later to be known as Abraham and Sarah. We were told that Noah was righteous, at least in comparison with his contemporaries, but we are not told directly why this couple is a worthy choice. The tradition, as usual, seeks to fill the gap, portraying Abraham as the first person to realize that the world is ruled by one God who demands righteous behavior of humanity. Abraham's descendants have been marked by a willingness to stand apart from conventional thinking.

A *midrash* pictures Abraham coming across a palace with all of its windows illuminated and musing to himself, "Is it possible that there is no lord of this palace?" At that moment, God appears and proclaims, "I am the lord of this palace!" (Gen. R. 39:1).

Another *midrash* portrays Abraham's father Terah as a manufacturer of idols. One night, Abraham smashed all his father's idols. The next morning his father, incensed, demanded to know who had destroyed his property. "They attacked each other," Abraham told him. "That's impossible!" cried Terah. "They are made of stone. There is no soul or spirit in them." "Then why do you worship them?" Abraham challenged him (Gen. R. 38:13).

The insistence that God is one is more than a mathematical statement. It is a prerequisite for a religion that demands righteousness, not merely obedience. It enables us to claim that there are fixed standards of right and wrong. In a world of many gods, the issue is not "what does God demand of me?" but "which god can best reward and protect me in exchange for my loyalty?" The revolutionary claim of monotheism is not only that one God alone exists but that God summons us to freely choose what is good.

1. God's first words to Abraham, translated

HALAKHAH L'MA·ASEH

12:1 the land I will show you This is the first verse of many in the Torah expressing the divine promise to the people of Israel that the land of Israel would be their homeland. It is permissible for Jews to live anywhere, but Jewish tradition prefers "going up" (*aliyah*) to live in Israel (MT Kings 5:7,12).

from your native land and from your father's house to the land that I will show you.

²I will make of you a great nation,
And I will bless you;
I will make your name great,
And you shall be a blessing.
³I will bless those who bless you
And curse him that curses you;
And all the families of the earth
Shall bless themselves by you."
⁴Abram went forth as the LORD had com-

מֵאַרְצְךָ֥ וּמִמּֽוֹלַדְתְּךָ֖ וּמִבֵּ֣ית אָבִ֑יךָ אֶל־
הָאָ֖רֶץ אֲשֶׁ֥ר אַרְאֶֽךָּ׃
²וְאֶֽעֶשְׂךָ֙ לְג֣וֹי גָּד֔וֹל
וַאֲבָ֣רֶכְךָ֔
וַאֲגַדְּלָ֖ה שְׁמֶ֑ךָ
וֶֽהְיֵ֖ה בְּרָכָֽה׃
³וַאֲבָֽרְכָה֙ מְבָ֣רְכֶ֔יךָ
וּמְקַלֶּלְךָ֖ אָאֹ֑ר
וְנִבְרְכ֣וּ בְךָ֔
כֹּ֖ל מִשְׁפְּחֹ֥ת הָאֲדָמָֽה׃

your native land The land of your kinsmen. The reference is to Haran, not Ur.

to the land God's word transforms the trek into a new venture, now with divine guidance and purpose. At this point, Abram may not have known the identity of the Promised Land, continuing the westward migration interrupted by his father (11:31), arriving in Canaan unaware of having reached his goal until so informed by God (12:2). Alternatively, God may have revealed the destination as soon as Abram accepted the call.

2. I will make of you a great nation Great in both number and significance.

I will bless you With material prosperity.

I will make your name great You will ac-

quire fame and be greatly esteemed as a man of superior character. In the ancient Near East, one's name was not merely a practical means of identification. It conveyed the very essence of an individual's being.

you shall be a blessing You will serve as the exemplar by which a blessing is invoked.

3. I will bless those who bless you Those who wish you well and show solidarity with you will enjoy My blessing of well-being.

And curse him that curses you Whoever mistreats you will reap misfortune.

And all the families of the earth / Shall bless themselves by you People will take your good fortune as the desired measure when they invoke a blessing on themselves.

as "Go forth" (*lekh l'kha*), literally mean, "betake yourself." A *midrash* interprets this to mean, "Go forth to find your authentic self, to learn who you are meant to be" (*Mei Ha-Shilo·ah*).

Physically we leave our home first, then our neighborhood, and finally our country. Emotionally, however, leaving one's geographic country of origin is easier than leaving one's family (Alshekh).

"For the first time, a journey is undertaken, not as an act of exile (Adam, Cain) or a quest for domination (the generation of Babel) but as a response to a divine imperative" (Zornberg).

the land I will show you The Midrash plays on the Hebrew and reads, "the land wherein I will *appear* to you." God cannot be found as readily in the opulent surroundings of Haran as in the pasture lands of Canaan (Mid. Ha-Gadol).

2. be a blessing Hirsch takes this not as a promise but as a command. To merit the promised reward, you must so live as to be a blessing to the world.

3. I will bless those who bless you / And curse him that curses you Lest Abraham be intimidated by God's summons, God reassures him that his admirers will be many and his detractors few (Ralbag). Why would anyone curse or hate Abraham, who is setting out to serve God and be a blessing to all humanity? There always have been individuals and societies that resent God's strenuous moral demands and direct their resentment toward those who strive to live up to them.

And all the families of the earth / Shall bless themselves by you History has borne out the validity of Hirsch's comment: "I will bless each nation in accordance with the respect it shows the Jewish spirit." Nations and empires that

4 וַיֵּ֣לֶךְ אַבְרָ֗ם כַּאֲשֶׁ֨ר דִּבֶּ֤ר אֵלָיו֙ יְהֹוָ֔ה וַיֵּ֥לֶךְ
אִתּ֖וֹ ל֑וֹט וְאַבְרָ֗ם בֶּן־חָמֵ֤שׁ שָׁנִים֙ וְשִׁבְעִ֣ים
שָׁנָ֔ה בְּצֵאת֖וֹ מֵחָרָֽן׃ 5 וַיִּקַּ֣ח אַבְרָם֩ אֶת־
שָׂרַ֨י אִשְׁתּ֜וֹ וְאֶת־ל֣וֹט בֶּן־אָחִ֗יו וְאֶת־כָּל־
רְכוּשָׁם֙ אֲשֶׁ֣ר רָכָ֔שׁוּ וְאֶת־הַנֶּ֖פֶשׁ אֲשֶׁר־
עָשׂ֣וּ בְחָרָ֑ן וַיֵּצְא֗וּ לָלֶ֙כֶת֙ אַ֣רְצָה כְּנַ֔עַן
וַיָּבֹ֖אוּ אַ֥רְצָה כְּנָֽעַן׃ 6 וַיַּעֲבֹ֤ר אַבְרָם֙
בָּאָ֔רֶץ עַ֚ד מְק֣וֹם שְׁכֶ֔ם עַ֖ד אֵל֣וֹן מוֹרֶ֑ה
וְהַֽכְּנַעֲנִ֖י אָ֥ז בָּאָֽרֶץ׃

manded him, and Lot went with him. Abram
was seventy-five years old when he left Haran.
5 Abram took his wife Sarai and his brother's son
Lot, and all the wealth that they had amassed,
and the persons that they had acquired in
Haran; and they set out for the land of Canaan.
When they arrived in the land of Canaan,
6 Abram passed through the land as far as the
site of Shechem, at the terebinth of Moreh. The
Canaanites were then in the land.

ABRAM'S RESPONSE (vv. 4–5)

In silent, unwavering obedience to God's will, the patriarch leaves Haran, accepting his new destiny in perfect faith.

4. Lot went with him The mention of Lot prepares the reader for the events to come in chapter 13.

seventy-five years old Abram's age is given here because he is at a crucial moment of his life.

5. his brother's son Lot The kinship description explains his presence in Abram's entourage. The oldest uncle assumed the guardianship of the child of his dead brother, which is clear in 14:12.

they set out The trek would have taken them near or through some of the great urban centers of the day. The narrative is silent about the precise route and the incidents on the journey, probably to avoid diverting our attention from the primary theme: the entry into the land and the first divine revelation that the patriarch experiences.

ABRAM IN THE LAND (vv. 6–9)

6. passed through the land Abram does not stop at Hazor, the major military and commercial center in the Upper Galilee, but continues along the central mountain range, avoiding the well-inhabited areas of northern Canaan and the coastal plain.

the site of Shechem The unusual Hebrew phrase for this (*m'kom Sh'chem*) probably refers to a sacred site. Such sites were desirable stopping places for travelers and pastoral nomads because of their proximity to springs and wells.

the terebinth of Moreh Some extraordinary tree. The Hebrew word *moreh* means "teacher, oracle giver." The tree (or a cluster of such trees) was so conspicuous and famous that it served as a landmark. The phenomenon of a sacred tree is well known in many cultures.

The Canaanites were then in the land "Canaanite" here, as often, designates all pre-Israelite inhabitants. The word "then" (*az*) seems to imply that at the time of the narrator, the Canaanites no longer existed—a situation that did

---

have treated the Jews well, from Moslem Spain to the United States, have flourished, owing in large measure to their openness to many peoples and to the specific contributions of their Jewish citizens. Nations that began by persecuting Jews, out of their hatred for the Jewish moral code, too often have gone on to bring destruction on themselves and their surroundings.

5. *the persons that they had acquired* The literal meaning is, "the persons they had made." The Midrash understands this anachronistically as referring to converts whom they had led to belief in the one true God (Gen. R. 39:14). For that reason, when converts to Judaism are given a Hebrew name they are called son or daughter "of Abraham and Sarah." According to the Sages, "One who brings a person to the Torah is regarded as having given birth to him or her" (BT Sanh. 99a). Although the women of Genesis seem to play a minor role in what are presented as patriarchal narratives, we find the Midrash pointing to the larger role they undoubtedly played. Sarah was every bit the pioneer and "soul-maker" that Abraham was.

[7]The LORD appeared to Abram and said, "I will assign this land to your offspring." And he built an altar there to the LORD who had appeared to him. [8]From there he moved on to the hill country east of Bethel and pitched his tent, with Bethel on the west and Ai on the east; and he built there an altar to the LORD and invoked the LORD by name. [9]Then Abram journeyed by stages toward the Negeb.

[10]There was a famine in the land, and Abram went down to Egypt to sojourn there, for the

7 וַיֵּרָא יְהוָה אֶל־אַבְרָם וַיֹּאמֶר לְזַרְעֲךָ
אֶתֵּן אֶת־הָאָרֶץ הַזֹּאת וַיִּבֶן שָׁם מִזְבֵּחַ
לַיהוָה הַנִּרְאֶה אֵלָיו׃ 8 וַיַּעְתֵּק מִשָּׁם
הָהָרָה מִקֶּדֶם לְבֵית־אֵל וַיֵּט אהלה אָהֳלוֹ
בֵּית־אֵל מִיָּם וְהָעַי מִקֶּדֶם וַיִּבֶן־שָׁם מִזְבֵּחַ
לַיהוָה וַיִּקְרָא בְּשֵׁם יְהוָה׃ 9 וַיִּסַּע אַבְרָם
הָלוֹךְ וְנָסוֹעַ הַנֶּגְבָּה׃ פ
10 וַיְהִי רָעָב בָּאָרֶץ וַיֵּרֶד אַבְרָם מִצְרַיְמָה

not become a reality until long after Joshua's conquest (see Ibn Ezra).

7. The LORD appeared This is the first divine revelation.

I will assign this land The identity of the land referred to in verse 1 is now established. This is one of the Torah's seminal texts. Hereafter, the history and destiny of Abram and his descendants, including the Jewish people of today, will be bound up inextricably with the promised land.

He built an altar there In gratitude for the promise of land. Among the patriarchs, acts of worship are always individual, never public. They do not take part in any existing religion, and they always build new altars or reuse those they previously erected.

8. From there he moved on Legal ownership of the land is not the same as actual possession. The nation does not yet exist, and the patriarch remains a wanderer.

Ai The site is identified with a mound known as et-Tell, about 1 mile (1.6 km) southeast of Bethel. It was a flourishing town in the early Bronze Age during the 3rd millennium B.C.E.

he built there an altar Bethel is identified with modern Baytīn, which lies about 10.5 miles (17 km) north of Jerusalem. It was the site of a Canaanite sanctuary to the god El.

9. toward the Negeb To southern and southeastern Judah around Beer-sheba, below the central hill country and the Shephelah. The name derives from a root meaning "dry, parched," indicating the sparse rainfall in the area and the arid terrain. By now, Abram has covered the length of the country from north to south.

ABRAM IN EGYPT (vv. 10–21)

The divine promises of nationhood and territory are abruptly endangered by famine.

10. There was a famine in the land This resulted from the prolonged failure of the seasonal rains, which was the primary cause of famine in Canaan.

Abram went down The standard phrase for travel from hilly Canaan to low-lying Egypt, just as one "goes up" in the reverse direction.

Egypt This is the first mention of Egypt in Israelite history, foreshadowing the ambiguous nature of their future relationships. On the one hand, it was a place of shelter in time of distress; on the other, a region of mortal danger.

to sojourn there The Hebrew stem meaning "to sojourn" (גור) indicates temporary residence. Everywhere in the ancient Near East, the resident alien (*ger*) was without legal rights and protection, depending entirely on the local community's goodwill.

---

10. Abram went down to Egypt He lowered himself to the moral level of that society. Even an Abraham is not immune to the influence of his surroundings. In a setting of danger and depravity, he can be vulnerable to fear and tempted to deceive others to save himself.

Clearly, to understand Abraham's motivation is not to justify it. The Torah continually portrays its leading figures with all of their flaws, perhaps to teach us that we too can be good people without being perfect people. Reading this and similar episodes, we can condemn Abraham's behavior while forgiving him even as Sarah forgives him.

famine was severe in the land. 11As he was about to enter Egypt, he said to his wife Sarai, "I know what a beautiful woman you are. 12If the Egyptians see you, and think, 'She is his wife,' they will kill me and let you live. 13Please say that you are my sister, that it may go well with me because of you, and that I may remain alive thanks to you."

14When Abram entered Egypt, the Egyptians saw how very beautiful the woman was. 15Pharaoh's courtiers saw her and praised her to Pharaoh, and the woman was taken into Pharaoh's palace. 16And because of her, it went well with Abram; he acquired sheep, oxen, asses, male and female slaves, she-asses, and camels.

לָגוּר שָׁם כִּי־כָבֵד הָרָעָב בָּאָרֶץ׃ 11 וַיְהִי
כַּאֲשֶׁר הִקְרִיב לָבוֹא מִצְרָיְמָה וַיֹּאמֶר
אֶל־שָׂרַי אִשְׁתּוֹ הִנֵּה־נָא יָדַעְתִּי כִּי אִשָּׁה
יְפַת־מַרְאֶה אָתְּ׃ 12 וְהָיָה כִּי־יִרְאוּ אֹתָךְ
הַמִּצְרִים וְאָמְרוּ אִשְׁתּוֹ זֹאת וְהָרְגוּ אֹתִי
וְאֹתָךְ יְחַיּוּ׃ 13 אִמְרִי־נָא אֲחֹתִי אָתְּ לְמַעַן
יִיטַב־לִי בַעֲבוּרֵךְ וְחָיְתָה נַפְשִׁי בִּגְלָלֵךְ׃
שני 14 וַיְהִי כְּבוֹא אַבְרָם מִצְרָיְמָה וַיִּרְאוּ
הַמִּצְרִים אֶת־הָאִשָּׁה כִּי־יָפָה הִוא מְאֹד׃
15 וַיִּרְאוּ אֹתָהּ שָׂרֵי פַרְעֹה וַיְהַלְלוּ אֹתָהּ
אֶל־פַּרְעֹה וַתֻּקַּח הָאִשָּׁה בֵּית פַּרְעֹה׃
16 וּלְאַבְרָם הֵיטִיב בַּעֲבוּרָהּ וַיְהִי־לוֹ צֹאן־
וּבָקָר וַחֲמֹרִים וַעֲבָדִים וּשְׁפָחֹת וַאֲתֹנֹת
וּגְמַלִּים׃

for the famine was severe Only so dire a situation would have driven Abram to leave the land.

THE SEIZURE OF SARAI (vv. 11–20)

Approaching the Egyptian border, Abram begins to fear that Sarai's beauty will lead to his murder and her abduction. Narratives about the kidnaping of the hero's beautiful wife are found in Canaanite and Greek epics, and it is reasonable to assume that similar sagas circulated about the matriarchs of Israel.

11. a beautiful woman Sarai is 65 at the time, 10 years younger than her husband.

12. and let you live Though in shame and dishonor.

13. Please say Although Abram's words are not an order, they convey a sense of urgency (through the Hebrew *na*).

you are my sister The dilemma confronting the patriarch is a very real moral conflict between human life and human dignity. Ramban comments: "Know that our father Abraham inadvertently committed a great sin by placing his virtuous wife in a compromising situation because of his fear of being killed. He should have trusted in God."

14. the Egyptians saw Clearly, Sarai did not generally veil her face. See Comments to 24:65 and 38:14–15.

15. Pharaoh This is the first appearance of this title in the Bible. The names of the pharaohs in Genesis and Exodus are not given, thereby making it difficult to fix the chronology of the patriarchal period. The title itself derives from an Egyptian word meaning "the great house" (*per-o*), a designation of the royal palace as early as 2500 B.C.E. In New Kingdom times (from the 16th century B.C.E. on), it came to be used for the king, in the same way as "the White House" can designate the American president or "the Crown," the British monarch.

the woman was taken This incident is illuminated by the ancient Egyptian *Tale of Two Brothers,* in which a beautiful woman comes to the attention of Pharaoh, who has her hunted down and brought to his palace. There he makes love to her, even though he knows she is married.

16. she-asses Possession of many she asses was a sign of great wealth. See Job 1:3 and 42:12.

camels This is an anachronism. The widespread domestication of the camel as a beast of burden did not take place before the 12th century B.C.E., long after the patriarchal period.

---

11. A *midrash* suggests that Abraham, after so many years of marriage, took his wife's beauty for granted until he became aware of how others regarded her (Tanḥ.).

17But the LORD afflicted Pharaoh and his household with mighty plagues on account of Sarai, the wife of Abram. 18Pharaoh sent for Abram and said, "What is this you have done to me! Why did you not tell me that she was your wife? 19Why did you say, 'She is my sister,' so that I took her as my wife? Now, here is your wife; take her and begone!" 20And Pharaoh put men in charge of him, and they sent him off with his wife and all that he possessed.

17וַיְנַגַּע יְהוָה | אֶת־פַּרְעֹה נְגָעִים גְּדֹלִים
וְאֶת־בֵּיתוֹ עַל־דְּבַר שָׂרַי אֵשֶׁת אַבְרָם׃
18וַיִּקְרָא פַרְעֹה לְאַבְרָם וַיֹּאמֶר מַה־זֹּאת
עָשִׂיתָ לִּי לָמָּה לֹא־הִגַּדְתָּ לִּי כִּי אִשְׁתְּךָ
הִוא׃ 19לָמָה אָמַרְתָּ אֲחֹתִי הִוא וָאֶקַּח
אֹתָהּ לִי לְאִשָּׁה וְעַתָּה הִנֵּה אִשְׁתְּךָ קַח
וָלֵךְ׃ 20וַיְצַו עָלָיו פַּרְעֹה אֲנָשִׁים וַיְשַׁלְּחוּ
אֹתוֹ וְאֶת־אִשְׁתּוֹ וְאֶת־כָּל־אֲשֶׁר־לוֹ׃

13 From Egypt, Abram went up into the Negeb, with his wife and all that he possessed, together with Lot. 2Now Abram was very rich in cattle, silver, and gold. 3And he proceeded by stages from the Negeb as far as Bethel, to the place where his tent had been formerly, between Bethel and Ai, 4the site of the altar that he had built there at first; and there Abram invoked the LORD by name.

5Lot, who went with Abram, also had flocks

יג וַיַּעַל אַבְרָם מִמִּצְרַיִם הוּא וְאִשְׁתּוֹ
וְכָל־אֲשֶׁר־לוֹ וְלוֹט עִמּוֹ הַנֶּגְבָּה׃ 2וְאַבְרָם
כָּבֵד מְאֹד בַּמִּקְנֶה בַּכֶּסֶף וּבַזָּהָב׃ 3וַיֵּלֶךְ
לְמַסָּעָיו מִנֶּגֶב וְעַד־בֵּית־אֵל עַד־הַמָּקוֹם
אֲשֶׁר־הָיָה שָׁם אהלה אָהֳלוֹ בַּתְּחִלָּה בֵּין
בֵּית־אֵל וּבֵין הָעָי׃ 4אֶל־מְקוֹם הַמִּזְבֵּחַ
אֲשֶׁר־עָשָׂה שָׁם בָּרִאשֹׁנָה וַיִּקְרָא שָׁם
אַבְרָם בְּשֵׁם יְהוָה׃
5וְגַם־לְלוֹט הַהֹלֵךְ אֶת־אַבְרָם הָיָה צֹאן־ שלישי

17. mighty plagues Their nature is not explained.

18. What is this you have done to me Pharaoh, suddenly made suspicious as a result of the affliction, must have interrogated Sarai, who admitted her true status. Abram makes no effort to justify his conduct.

20. put men in charge Ibn Ezra suggests that Pharaoh provided guards to accompany the pair across the border for their protection and as a sign of honor. Saadia maintains that it was to enforce their expulsion from the territory.

RETURN TO THE LAND (13:1–4)

1. went up See Comment to 12:10.

Lot Because he played no role in the events in Egypt, he has not been mentioned. He appears here because of the following episode.

2. Abram was very rich The divine blessing of 12:2 is beginning to be fulfilled.

silver, and gold It would not have been unusual for shepherds and herdsman in Canaan to possess precious metals. In time of famine, silver and gold were a significant source of security, being media of exchange.

3. by stages He moved from one watering place to another.

4. the site of the altar By returning to worship at the altar he had previously built (12:8), Abram renews his spiritual connection with the land.

THE SEPARATION OF LOT (vv. 5–13)

The affluence of Abram's family becomes a threat to its tranquility.

5. Lot His family is an independent sub-

CHAPTER 13

2. Abram was very rich The Hebrew word translated as "rich" (*kaved*) literally means "heavy, burdened." This has prompted the comment that, for a righteous person, great

וּבָקָר וְאֹהָלִים׃ 6 וְלֹא־נָשָׂא אֹתָם הָאָרֶץ
לָשֶׁבֶת יַחְדָּו כִּי־הָיָה רְכוּשָׁם רָב וְלֹא
יָכְלוּ לָשֶׁבֶת יַחְדָּו׃ 7 וַיְהִי־רִיב בֵּין רֹעֵי
מִקְנֵה־אַבְרָם וּבֵין רֹעֵי מִקְנֵה־לוֹט
וְהַכְּנַעֲנִי וְהַפְּרִזִּי אָז יֹשֵׁב בָּאָרֶץ׃ 8 וַיֹּאמֶר
אַבְרָם אֶל־לוֹט אַל־נָא תְהִי מְרִיבָה בֵּינִי
וּבֵינֶךָ וּבֵין רֹעַי וּבֵין רֹעֶיךָ כִּי־אֲנָשִׁים
אַחִים אֲנָחְנוּ׃ 9 הֲלֹא כָל־הָאָרֶץ לְפָנֶיךָ
הִפָּרֶד נָא מֵעָלָי אִם־הַשְּׂמֹאל וְאֵימִנָה
וְאִם־הַיָּמִין וְאַשְׂמְאִילָה׃ 10 וַיִּשָּׂא־לוֹט
אֶת־עֵינָיו וַיַּרְא אֶת־כָּל־כִּכַּר הַיַּרְדֵּן כִּי
כֻלָּהּ מַשְׁקֶה לִפְנֵי | שַׁחֵת יְהוָה אֶת־
סְדֹם וְאֶת־עֲמֹרָה כְּגַן־יְהוָה כְּאֶרֶץ

and herds and tents, [6]so that the land could not
support them staying together; for their possessions were so great that they could not remain together. [7]And there was quarreling between the herdsmen of Abram's cattle and
those of Lot's cattle.—The Canaanites and
Perizzites were then dwelling in the land.—
[8]Abram said to Lot, "Let there be no strife
between you and me, between my herdsmen
and yours, for we are kinsmen. [9]Is not the
whole land before you? Let us separate: if you
go north, I will go south; and if you go south, I
will go north." [10]Lot looked about him and saw
how well watered was the whole plain of the
Jordan, all of it—this was before the LORD had
destroyed Sodom and Gomorrah—all the way
to Zoar, like the garden of the LORD, like the

group within the larger clan, its wealth mostly in cattle.

6. the land Ecologic conditions, forcing a limit to the size of the herds, have begun to affect family harmony. Increasingly, there is friction over available pasturage and water.

7. between the herdsmen Abram acts quickly while the discord is still in its early stage and before it can embitter relationships among those involved.

The Canaanites Apparently, the natural resources would have been sufficient for two small pastoral nomadic clans. The area, however, already had a settled agricultural–urban community, which explains why both Abram and Lot have to leave the region.

Perizzites The name of a minor pre-Israelite people. It may mean "inhabitants of rural areas."

8. Let there be no strife Although he is the older man and the uncle, Abram does not insist on priority of rights, but instead selflessly offers his nephew first choice of grazing land and watering places.

9. north . . . south Literally, "left . . . right," from the customary viewpoint of one facing the rising sun.

10. looked about him From Bethel, which is on a hill, he would have had a magnificent view of the Jordan Valley.

well watered Fed by streams and brooks, not depending on seasonal rainfall for its fertility.

this was before A parenthetic note to explain the contrast between this depiction of the verdant land and its rutted barrenness during later Israelite history.

all the way to Zoar This refers back to the first clause: "Lot looked about him." Zoar was at the southern limit of the plain of Jordan (19:20–22).

like the garden of the LORD A perennially watered Eden.

---

wealth can sometimes be a burden, a challenge to use it wisely and responsibly.

6. Abram and Lot had been able to get along when they had relatively little. Was it prosperity that now caused conflict between them? Or was it Lot's growing recognition that he did not share Abram's values (Pes. R.)? The text emphasizes Abram's magnanimity, which is even more striking if we take into account what we learn only later (15:2), that Abram was concerned with his posterity. Lot's departure might have felt like losing a surrogate son.

land of Egypt. 11So Lot chose for himself the
whole plain of the Jordan, and Lot journeyed
eastward. Thus they parted from each other;
12Abram remained in the land of Canaan,
while Lot settled in the cities of the Plain, pitch-
ing his tents near Sodom. 13Now the inhabitants of Sodom were very wicked sinners
against the LORD.

14And the LORD said to Abram, after Lot had
parted from him, "Raise your eyes and look out
from where you are, to the north and south, to
the east and west, 15for I give all the land that
you see to you and your offspring forever. 16I
will make your offspring as the dust of the

מִצְרַיִם בֹּאֲכָה צֹעַר׃ 11 וַיִּבְחַר־לוֹ לוֹט
אֵת כָּל־כִּכַּר הַיַּרְדֵּן וַיִּסַּע לוֹט מִקֶּדֶם
וַיִּפָּרְדוּ אִישׁ מֵעַל אָחִיו׃ 12 אַבְרָם יָשַׁב
בְּאֶרֶץ־כְּנָעַן וְלוֹט יָשַׁב בְּעָרֵי הַכִּכָּר
וַיֶּאֱהַל עַד־סְדֹם׃ 13 וְאַנְשֵׁי סְדֹם רָעִים
וְחַטָּאִים לַיהוָה מְאֹד׃
14 וַיהוָה אָמַר אֶל־אַבְרָם אַחֲרֵי הִפָּרֶד־
לוֹט מֵעִמּוֹ שָׂא נָא עֵינֶיךָ וּרְאֵה מִן־
הַמָּקוֹם אֲשֶׁר־אַתָּה שָׁם צָפֹנָה וָנֶגְבָּה
וָקֵדְמָה וָיָמָּה׃ 15 כִּי אֶת־כָּל־הָאָרֶץ
אֲשֶׁר־אַתָּה רֹאֶה לְךָ אֶתְּנֶנָּה וּלְזַרְעֲךָ עַד־
עוֹלָם׃ 16 וְשַׂמְתִּי אֶת־זַרְעֲךָ כַּעֲפַר הָאָרֶץ

11. So Lot chose for himself He selects a setting of wealth and comfort, without concern for the nature of the morality of the inhabitants.

eastward From east of Bethel, where Abram was then encamped, as noted in 12:8 and 13:3.

Thus they parted Abram's swift action ensures that the quarrel is settled without rancor.

12. in the land of Canaan This seems to reflect a tradition that the "cities of the Plain" lay outside the borders of Canaan (see Comment to 10:19). To what period this applies is unknown, but verses 13:14–15 revise this situation.

13. very wicked sinners This brief addition to the narrative offers the reason for the coming destruction, referred to in verse 10. It also carries with it a judgment on Lot's character and prepares the reader for the events of chapter 19.

THE REAFFIRMATION OF THE BLESSINGS (vv. 14–17)

The earlier promise of national territory (12:7) is now reaffirmed in different terms. This language reflects legal formulas current throughout the ancient Near East from the middle of the 2nd millennium B.C.E.

14. after Lot had parted His departure and Abram's blessing are linked. Abram's last tie with his father's house is now severed and a new phase in his life begins.

15. all the land The future national territory will include the area in which Lot settles.

you and your offspring The blessings are invested solely in the patriarch and his direct lineal descendants. Abram is included, even though he, personally, cannot take possession. The language follows legal formulas used in Near Eastern royal land grant documents.

forever God gives the land to Abram and his descendants without any preconditions and in perpetuity.

16. as the dust of the earth An image of uncommon propagation and diffusion.

---

11. Lot journeyed eastward The Midrash reads the word for "eastward" (*mi-kedem*) as *mi-kadmono shel olam,* "away from the Ancient One." Lot chose to live closer to Sodom and further from God (Gen. R. 41:7).

13. wicked sinners against the LORD In Jewish tradition, the sin of Sodom referred to here was inhospitality to strangers and the wayfarer. (See Ezek. 16:49, "this was the sin of your sister Sodom. . . . she did not support the poor and the needy.") To mistreat a stranger is to sin against God, the patron and protector of the most vulnerable.

16. as the dust of the earth The biblical promise is of great numbers and abundance. After the *Shoah*—when so many Jews were murdered and their bodies cremated—the Yiddish poet Yaakov Glatstein bitterly noted that God's promise became fulfilled; Abraham's descendants had become like the dust of the earth.

earth, so that if one can count the dust of the
earth, then your offspring too can be counted.
17 Up, walk about the land, through its length
and its breadth, for I give it to you." 18 And
Abram moved his tent, and came to dwell at
the terebinths of Mamre, which are in Hebron;
and he built an altar there to the LORD.

אֲשֶׁר | אִם־יוּכַל אִישׁ לִמְנוֹת אֶת־עֲפַר
הָאָרֶץ גַּם־זַרְעֲךָ יִמָּנֶה׃ 17 קוּם הִתְהַלֵּךְ
בָּאָרֶץ לְאָרְכָּהּ וּלְרָחְבָּהּ כִּי לְךָ אֶתְּנֶנָּה׃
18 וַיֶּאֱהַל אַבְרָם וַיָּבֹא וַיֵּשֶׁב בְּאֵלֹנֵי
מַמְרֵא אֲשֶׁר בְּחֶבְרוֹן וַיִּבֶן־שָׁם מִזְבֵּחַ
לַיהוָה׃ פ

14 Now, when King Amraphel of Shinar,
King Arioch of Ellasar, King Chedorlaomer of
Elam, and King Tidal of Goiim 2 made war on
King Bera of Sodom, King Birsha of Gomorrah,
King Shinab of Admah, King Shemeber of
Zeboiim, and the king of Bela, which is Zoar,
3 all the latter joined forces at the Valley of

יד וַיְהִי בִּימֵי אַמְרָפֶל מֶלֶךְ־שִׁנְעָר רביעי
אַרְיוֹךְ מֶלֶךְ אֶלָּסָר כְּדָרְלָעֹמֶר מֶלֶךְ עֵילָם
וְתִדְעָל מֶלֶךְ גּוֹיִם׃ 2 עָשׂוּ מִלְחָמָה אֶת־
בֶּרַע מֶלֶךְ סְדֹם וְאֶת־בִּרְשַׁע מֶלֶךְ עֲמֹרָה
שִׁנְאָב | מֶלֶךְ אַדְמָה וְשֶׁמְאֵבֶר מֶלֶךְ צביים
צְבוֹיִם וּמֶלֶךְ בֶּלַע הִיא־צֹעַר׃ 3 כָּל־אֵלֶּה

17. walk about the land Ramban understood this traversing of the length and breadth of the land to be a symbolic act of legal acquisition. Egyptian and Hittite kings periodically would undertake a ceremonial walk around a field or a tour of the realm to symbolize renewal of their sovereignty over the land.

ABRAM'S DEPARTURE FOR HEBRON (v. 18)

18. the terebinths See Comment to 12:6.

Mamre According to 14:13,24, Mamre was a distinguished personage allied to Abram. In 23:19, Mamre is another name for the city of Hebron.

Hebron A strategically located city in the Judean heartland, about midway between Jerusalem to the north and Beer-sheba to the south. Situated about 3,050 feet (930 m) above sea level, Hebron is surrounded by a fertile countryside.

ABRAM'S RESCUE OF LOT (14:1–23)

This is the first biblical account of warfare. The narrative reveals a new side to Abram's character: He is a decisive, courageous, and skilled battle commander.

THE INVASION FROM THE EAST
(vv. 1–11)

1. Now, when Literally, "in the days of."

Amraphel Once thought to be King Hammurabi, his identity is unknown.

Shinar This is a Hurrian name. See Comment to 10:10.

Arioch Corresponding to Arriyuk/Arriwuk, this name is mentioned in some ancient Near Eastern archives.

Ellasar Probably the city of Asshur, the mother city of the land of Assyria.

Chedorlaomer This name consists of two Elamite words that mean "the servant of [the god] Lagamer." It does not appear among the lists of about 40 known Elamite kings.

Elam See Comment to 10:22.

Tidal A Semitic rendering of the Hittite royal name Tudhalias borne by four kings. The first king lived in the 17th century B.C.E.

Goiim A "king of Goiim" is mentioned in Josh. 12:23. The place-name is otherwise unknown.

2. Zoar Each of the five cities has its own king; an instance of the classic city-state system that prevailed in Canaan before the Israelite conquest.

Bela This seems to be the earlier or alternative name of Zoar. In Gen. 36:32, Bela is the name of a king.

3. joined forces In the face of the common threat, the rebellious cities formed a five-city confederacy.

Siddim, now the Dead Sea. 4Twelve years they
served Chedorlaomer, and in the thirteenth
year they rebelled. 5In the fourteenth year Chedorlaomer and the kings who were with him
came and defeated the Rephaim at Ashteroth-
karnaim, the Zuzim at Ham, the Emim at
Shaveh-kiriathaim, 6and the Horites in their hill
country of Seir as far as El-paran, which is by
the wilderness. 7On their way back they came
to En-mishpat, which is Kadesh, and subdued
all the territory of the Amalekites, and also the
Amorites who dwelt in Hazazon-tamar. 8Then

חָבְרוּ אֶל־עֵמֶק הַשִּׂדִּים הוּא יָם הַמֶּלַח׃
4 שְׁתֵּים עֶשְׂרֵה שָׁנָה עָבְדוּ אֶת־
כְּדָרְלָעֹמֶר וּשְׁלֹשׁ־עֶשְׂרֵה שָׁנָה מָרָדוּ׃
5 וּבְאַרְבַּע עֶשְׂרֵה שָׁנָה בָּא כְדָרְלָעֹמֶר
וְהַמְּלָכִים אֲשֶׁר אִתּוֹ וַיַּכּוּ אֶת־רְפָאִים
בְּעַשְׁתְּרֹת קַרְנַיִם וְאֶת־הַזּוּזִים בְּהָם וְאֵת
הָאֵימִים בְּשָׁוֵה קִרְיָתָיִם׃ 6 וְאֶת־הַחֹרִי
בְּהַרְרָם שֵׂעִיר עַד אֵיל פָּארָן אֲשֶׁר עַל־
הַמִּדְבָּר׃ 7 וַיָּשֻׁבוּ וַיָּבֹאוּ אֶל־עֵין מִשְׁפָּט
הִוא קָדֵשׁ וַיַּכּוּ אֶת־כָּל־שְׂדֵה הָעֲמָלֵקִי
וְגַם אֶת־הָאֱמֹרִי הַיֹּשֵׁב בְּחַצְצֹן תָּמָר׃

the Valley of Siddim Mentioned again in verse 10 and nowhere else.

now the Dead Sea This remark implies that the valley, which clearly existed at the time of Abraham, was no longer in existence at the time of the narrator. Indeed, centuries after Abraham, the Valley of Siddim was submerged by the encroaching waters of the Dead Sea.

Dead Sea The Hebrew name means "salt sea." The waters register the highest saline content of any body of water in the world: an average of 32 percent, compared to 3 percent in the oceans.

4. served The root of this word (עבד) occurs widely in Semitic languages in reference to the condition of being a vassal. See 2 Kings 18:7 and 24:1.

rebelled Rebellion by a vassal city or state began when it withheld payment of the annual tribute stipulated in the treaty between king and vassal.

5. the Rephaim Listed among the pre-Israelite inhabitants of the land in Gen. 15:20, these people were regarded as a race of giants by the popular imagination. In the Canaanite religion, they are the spirits of dead heroes. By the time of the Exodus, they had all but disappeared (see Deut. 2:20 and 3:11).

Ashteroth-karnaim Two originally distinct but closely neighboring cities. The first was the ancient capital of Bashan, mentioned in Deut. 1:4 and Josh. 9:10. When its fortunes declined, Karnaim took its place as the capital of Bashan.

Ham This may be the city of Huma referred to in an ancient Egyptian document.

Emim Like the Rephaim, the Emim too were a race of giants, according to Deut. 2:10ff. They received their name, which might mean "frightful," from the Moabites who dispossessed them.

Shaveh-kiriathaim The first part of the name, which appears again only in Gen. 14:17, may mean "level, plane." The latter part is a well-known city in the Moabite tableland and is identified with Khirbet el-Qureiye, about 6 miles (10 km) due west of Ma'daba.

6. The Horites Not easily identifiable with any of the known peoples in that region. Some scholars believe them to be the Hurrians.

Seir The name means "hairy, shaggy," that is, covered with brush or forest. The hill country stretches southeast of the Dead Sea alongside the 'Arabah.

El-paran Paran is the name for the wilderness of the eastern Sinai Peninsula, but the identity of El-paran is uncertain. It may be another name for Elath, on the Gulf of Aqaba.

7. En-mishpat, which is Kadesh The full name of Kadesh is Kadesh-barnea, an important oasis on the southern border of Canaan, which served the Israelites as a leading base during the wilderness wanderings. It is identified with a group of springs 46 miles (75 km) south of Beer-sheba and 15 miles (25 km) south of Nizzanah.

Amalekites A warlike nomadic tribe associated with the Edomites in 36:12. In later times the Amalekites became the hereditary enemy of Israel.

Amorites See Comment to 10:16.

Hazazon-tamar If Hazazon is the earlier name of Tamar or a nearby settlement, then the most likely location would be the strategically important site fortified by Solomon on the southern border of the land of Israel. It is best identified with Ain Husb, about 20 miles (32

the king of Sodom, the king of Gomorrah, the king of Admah, the king of Zeboiim, and the king of Bela, which is Zoar, went forth and engaged them in battle in the Valley of Siddim: ⁹King Chedorlaomer of Elam, King Tidal of Goiim, King Amraphel of Shinar, and King Arioch of Ellasar—four kings against those five.

¹⁰Now the Valley of Siddim was dotted with bitumen pits; and the kings of Sodom and Gomorrah, in their flight, threw themselves into them, while the rest escaped to the hill country. ¹¹[The invaders] seized all the wealth of Sodom and Gomorrah and all their provisions, and went their way. ¹²They also took Lot, the son of Abram's brother, and his possessions, and departed; for he had settled in Sodom.

¹³A fugitive brought the news to Abram the Hebrew, who was dwelling at the terebinths of Mamre the Amorite, kinsman of Eshkol and

8 וַיֵּצֵ֣א מֶֽלֶךְ־סְדֹם֩ וּמֶ֨לֶךְ עֲמֹרָ֜ה וּמֶ֣לֶךְ אַדְמָה֙ וּמֶ֣לֶךְ צְבֹייִ֔ם וּמֶ֥לֶךְ בֶּ֖לַע הִוא־צֹ֑עַר וַיַּֽעַרְכ֤וּ אִתָּם֙ מִלְחָמָ֔ה בְּעֵ֖מֶק הַשִּׂדִּֽים: 9 אֵ֣ת כְּדָרְלָעֹ֜מֶר מֶ֣לֶךְ עֵילָ֗ם וְתִדְעָל֙ מֶ֣לֶךְ גּוֹיִ֔ם וְאַמְרָפֶל֙ מֶ֣לֶךְ שִׁנְעָ֔ר וְאַרְי֖וֹךְ מֶ֣לֶךְ אֶלָּסָ֑ר אַרְבָּעָ֥ה מְלָכִ֖ים אֶת־הַֽחֲמִשָּֽׁה:

10 וְעֵ֣מֶק הַשִּׂדִּ֗ים בֶּֽאֱרֹ֤ת בֶּֽאֱרֹת֙ חֵמָ֔ר וַיָּנֻ֛סוּ מֶֽלֶךְ־סְדֹ֥ם וַֽעֲמֹרָ֖ה וַיִּפְּלוּ־שָׁ֑מָּה וְהַנִּשְׁאָרִ֖ים הֶ֥רָה נָּֽסוּ: 11 וַ֠יִּקְחוּ אֶת־כָּל־רְכֻ֨שׁ סְדֹ֧ם וַֽעֲמֹרָ֛ה וְאֶת־כָּל־אָכְלָ֖ם וַיֵּלֵֽכוּ: 12 וַיִּקְח֣וּ אֶת־ל֠וֹט וְאֶת־רְכֻשׁ֧וֹ בֶּן־אֲחִ֛י אַבְרָ֖ם וַיֵּלֵ֑כוּ וְה֥וּא יֹשֵׁ֖ב בִּסְדֹֽם:

13 וַיָּבֹא֙ הַפָּלִ֔יט וַיַּגֵּ֖ד לְאַבְרָ֣ם הָֽעִבְרִ֑י וְהוּא֩ שֹׁכֵ֨ן בְּאֵֽלֹנֵ֜י מַמְרֵ֣א הָֽאֱמֹרִ֗י אֲחִ֤י אֶשְׁכֹּל֙ וַֽאֲחִ֣י עָנֵ֔ר וְהֵ֖ם בַּֽעֲלֵ֥י בְרִית־

km) southwest of the Dead Sea, which is the most important highway junction in the northern 'Arabah.

9. four kings against . . . five Having disposed of any threat from the neighboring peoples, the invaders now engage the rebellious five cities, the main target of the campaign.

10. bitumen pits Bitumen and asphalt are native to the Dead Sea. Asphalt is found in heavy liquid form in the southern part of the sea.

ABRAM THE WARRIOR (vv. 12–16)

The city of Hebron, where Abram resided, lay outside the region of hostilities, and the patriarch had no reason to intervene—until the capture of his nephew Lot altered the situation.

13. Abram the Hebrew Israelites identify

themselves as "Hebrew" (*ivri*) when addressing foreigners. It is a term used by the latter when referring to Israelites. Many scholars relate the term to the nomadic mixed ethnic group called Hapiru in ancient Near Eastern documents. The origin and meaning of the term *"ivri"* is unknown.

Mamre . . . Eshkol and Aner The first name mentioned is also a place-name connected with Hebron in 13:18. The Hebrew word *eshkol* means "a cluster of grapes" and is the name of a wadi near Hebron (Num. 13:23). The meaning of Aner is unknown. Apparently, the three were heads of aristocratic families in Hebron.

Amorite . . . allies The Hebrew term *ba-alei b'rit* ("allies") means "those bound by treaty." Treaties regulating human relationships were a

---

CHAPTER 14

13. Abram the Hebrew The Midrash offers three possible explanations for this designation (Gen. R. 42:13). One connects the term "Hebrew" (*ivri*) with Eber, grandson of Noah, who

is mentioned in Gen. 10:24 and 11:4. Another derives it from the Hebrew word *eiver* (beyond), that is, "the one from beyond [the river Euphrates]." The third alludes to Abram's nonconformism: "All the world was on one side (*eiver*) and he on the other side."

Aner, these being Abram's allies. 14When
Abram heard that his kinsman had been taken
captive, he mustered his retainers, born into
his household, numbering three hundred
and eighteen, and went in pursuit as far as
Dan. 15At night, he and his servants deployed
against them and defeated them; and he pursued them as far as Hobah, which is north of
Damascus. 16He brought back all the possessions; he also brought back his kinsman Lot
and his possessions, and the women and the
rest of the people.

17When he returned from defeating Chedorlaomer and the kings with him, the king of
Sodom came out to meet him in the Valley of

אַבְרָם׃ 14 וַיִּשְׁמַע אַבְרָם כִּי נִשְׁבָּה אָחִיו
וַיָּרֶק אֶת־חֲנִיכָיו יְלִידֵי בֵיתוֹ שְׁמֹנָה
עָשָׂר וּשְׁלֹשׁ מֵאוֹת וַיִּרְדֹּף עַד־דָּן׃
15 וַיֵּחָלֵק עֲלֵיהֶם ׀ לַיְלָה הוּא וַעֲבָדָיו
וַיַּכֵּם וַיִּרְדְּפֵם עַד־חוֹבָה אֲשֶׁר מִשְּׂמֹאל
לְדַמָּשֶׂק׃ 16 וַיָּשֶׁב אֵת כָּל־הָרְכֻשׁ וְגַם
אֶת־לוֹט אָחִיו וּרְכֻשׁוֹ הֵשִׁיב וְגַם אֶת־
הַנָּשִׁים וְאֶת־הָעָם׃
17 וַיֵּצֵא מֶלֶךְ־סְדֹם לִקְרָאתוֹ אַחֲרֵי שׁוּבוֹ
מֵהַכּוֹת אֶת־כְּדָר־לָעֹמֶר וְאֶת־הַמְּלָכִים
אֲשֶׁר אִתּוֹ אֶל־עֵמֶק שָׁוֵה הוּא עֵמֶק

common feature of the ancient Near East. The treaty entered into by Abram and the three Amorites was one among equals and involved mutual military obligations. The attack on their own kin gave Abram's allies additional incentive to support him.

14. When Abram heard Although Lot had separated himself from his uncle, the ties of kinship remained intact.

retainers, born into his household These were slaves born of slaves, regarded as more reliable than purchased slaves.

three hundred and eighteen It is unclear if this is meant to be taken literally or as a symbolic number. From early correspondence between governors of the city-states of Canaan and Pharaoh, it appears that the number constituted a powerful force.

Dan The city at the northern extremity of the land of Israel (see Judg. 20:1 and 1 Sam. 3:20). It is identified with Tell Dan (Tell el-Qadi), about 4 miles (6.4 km) west of Baniyas, at the foot of Mount Hermon on the international trade route.

15. and defeated them Abram had the advantages of fresh troops and a night engagement against a battle-weary, depleted enemy. By dividing his forces and attacking from two sides, he achieved tactical surprise and neutralized the numerical superiority of his foe.

Hobah An unidentified site north of Damascus.

17. the king of Sodom came out It took several weeks for Abram's troops to reach beyond Damascus and then return. In the meantime, the ruler of Sodom has regained his kingdom and now comes out to meet the victorious patriarch. Although five cities were involved in the alliance, this king alone is mentioned because the rescue of Lot, who lived in Sodom, is the focal point of the narrative and because Sodom was the leader of the alliance and is always listed first (Gen. 14:2; 10:19).

the Valley of Shaveh Also named "the Valley of the King" (see 2 Sam. 18:18). It may be the broad, level valley formed by the junction of the Valley of Ben-hinnom, west and south of Jerusalem, with the Kidron Valley on the east side.

The later notion of Gehenna derives its name from the Valley of Hinnom (*Gei ben Hinnom*), a

---

14. This verse gives us another view of Abraham, the warrior who is prepared to do battle to redeem his kin. The redemption of captives (*pidyon sh'vuyim*) in later centuries became a prime responsibility taken on by the Jewish community, which ransomed Jews who had been captured by pirates, imprisoned, or enslaved. Some authorities were reluctant, fearful that this would encourage the kidnaping of Jews for ransom. Still, the basic practice has continued from earliest times to the efforts on behalf of Russian Jews and Ethiopian Jews in more recent times.

Shaveh, which is the Valley of the King. 18And
King Melchizedek of Salem brought out bread
and wine; he was a priest of God Most High.
19He blessed him, saying,

"Blessed be Abram of God Most High,
Creator of heaven and earth.
20And blessed be God Most High,
Who has delivered your foes into your hand."

And [Abram] gave him a tenth of everything.

21Then the king of Sodom said to Abram,
"Give me the persons, and take the possessions
for yourself." 22But Abram said to the king of
Sodom, "I swear to the LORD, God Most High,

הַמֶּלֶךְ׃ 18 וּמַלְכִּי־צֶדֶק מֶלֶךְ שָׁלֵם הוֹצִיא
לֶחֶם וָיָיִן וְהוּא כֹהֵן לְאֵל עֶלְיוֹן׃
19 וַיְבָרְכֵהוּ וַיֹּאמַר
בָּרוּךְ אַבְרָם לְאֵל עֶלְיוֹן
קֹנֵה שָׁמַיִם וָאָרֶץ׃
20 וּבָרוּךְ אֵל עֶלְיוֹן
אֲשֶׁר־מִגֵּן צָרֶיךָ בְּיָדֶךָ
וַיִּתֶּן־לוֹ מַעֲשֵׂר מִכֹּל׃
חמישי 21 וַיֹּאמֶר מֶלֶךְ־סְדֹם אֶל־אַבְרָם תֶּן־לִי
הַנֶּפֶשׁ וְהָרְכֻשׁ קַח־לָךְ׃ 22 וַיֹּאמֶר אַבְרָם
אֶל־מֶלֶךְ סְדֹם הֲרִימֹתִי יָדִי אֶל־יְהוָה אֵל

narrow gorge southeast of Jerusalem where idolatrous Israelites offered their children to Moloch (see 2 Kings 23:10). King Josiah defiled it and converted it into a dung heap, where garbage was burned. At about the same time, Jeremiah prophesied that the corpses of many of Israel's warriors would be left unburied there after they were slain by an invading army (Jer. 7:30–34).

THE MELCHIZEDEK EPISODE (vv. 18–20)

18. Salem Named after the Canaanite god Shalem, it is identified along with Zion (in Ps. 76:3) as the location of the Temple.

priest It is not known whether this fusion of royal and priestly offices was characteristic of Canaanite city-states or was peculiar to Salem. In ancient Israel, the two institutions were separate from the beginning (see 1 Sam. 2:35).

God Most High Hebrew: *el elyon*. In most Semitic languages, *el* means "god" or is a deity's proper name; in the Bible, it refers to the one God. The noun *elyon*, from the root עלה (ascend), expresses absolute transcendence.

19. He blessed him He invoked God's blessing on the patriarch.

Creator of heaven and earth This formula is an attested description of the deity in Phoenician sources. It is here adapted to describe the God of Israel.

20. gave him a tenth Abram gives Melchizedek a tithe of all the spoils of war. A tithe payable to the king is known from Canaanite documents and is listed among the prerogatives of Near Eastern kingship in 1 Sam. 8:15,17.

ABRAM AND THE KING OF SODOM
(vv. 21–24)

Having discharged his duty to his kinsman and paid his dues to the priest-king, the patriarch now wishes to have nothing more to do with Sodom and rejects any idea of personal gain.

22. I swear Literally, "I lift up my hand," the universal gesture that accompanies oath taking.

23. a thread or a sandal strap That is, "from a thin to a thick cord," a figure of speech

---

18. It is not clear exactly who Melchizedek is. The name may be taken to mean "righteous king," prompting the Midrash to suggest that living in Salem (Jerusalem) inspired him to be a righteous ruler (Gen. R. 43:6). Soloveitchik sees him as having been impressed not only by Abraham's lofty ideals but by his willingness to fight for them. The commentary *Or Ha-Ḥayyim* sets the generosity of Melchizedek in contrast to the cunning greed of the king of Sodom in v. 21.

21. The offer of the king of Sodom, translated literally, was "give me the soul(s) and take the property for yourself." This has been the bargain offered to the Jewish people in many countries of our dispersion: Become prosperous here but at the cost of your soul.

Creator of heaven and earth: 23I will not take so
much as a thread or a sandal strap of what is
yours; you shall not say, 'It is I who made
Abram rich.' 24For me, nothing but what my
servants have used up; as for the share of the
men who went with me—Aner, Eshkol, and
Mamre—let them take their share."

עֶלְיוֹן קֹנֵה שָׁמַיִם וָאָרֶץ׃ 23אִם־מִחוּט
וְעַד שְׂרוֹךְ־נַעַל וְאִם־אֶקַּח מִכָּל־אֲשֶׁר־לָךְ
וְלֹא תֹאמַר אֲנִי הֶעֱשַׁרְתִּי אֶת־אַבְרָם׃
24בִּלְעָדַי רַק אֲשֶׁר אָכְלוּ הַנְּעָרִים וְחֵלֶק
הָאֲנָשִׁים אֲשֶׁר הָלְכוּ אִתִּי עָנֵר אֶשְׁכֹּל
וּמַמְרֵא הֵם יִקְחוּ חֶלְקָם׃ ס

15 Some time later, the word of the LORD
came to Abram in a vision. He said,

"Fear not, Abram,
I am a shield to you;
Your reward shall be very great."

2But Abram said, "O Lord GOD, what can You

טו אַחַר ׀ הַדְּבָרִים הָאֵלֶּה הָיָה דְבַר־
יְהוָה אֶל־אַבְרָם בַּמַּחֲזֶה לֵאמֹר
אַל־תִּירָא אַבְרָם
אָנֹכִי מָגֵן לָךְ
שְׂכָרְךָ הַרְבֵּה מְאֹד׃
2וַיֹּאמֶר אַבְרָם אֲדֹנָי יֱהוִה מַה־תִּתֶּן־לִי

used to express totality. It means "not even the smallest thing." A similar expression in ancient Aramaic, used in the context of treaties, is "from a straw to a string."

It is I who made Abram rich Abram did not want it to appear that he had acted for mercenary reasons. Because part of the spoil had originally come from Sodom (Gen. 14:11), he did not want to benefit from tainted possessions.

24. my servants The Hebrew term here (*n'arim*) literally means "youths" and probably is used for "warriors." The word, borrowed from Canaanite, also appears in ancient Egyptian in the sense of "elite corps."

THE COVENANT BETWEEN THE PIECES (15:1–21)

THE PROMISE OF OFFSPRING (vv. 1–6)

1. Some time later The literal meaning of the Hebrew is "after these things." Here it means, very soon after the preceding events.

Fear not The patriarch is deeply concerned about the possibility of revenge by the defeated kings.

I am a shield This poetic phrase means "I am your protection."

Your reward Abram had refused to partake of the spoils of war (14:22ff.). The rejected material reward will be vastly exceeded by a compensation of a different kind.

2. Abram said Abram speaks to God for the first time.

O Lord GOD This Hebrew divine title is read aloud as *Adonai Elohim*. Rarely found in the Torah, it is used in a context of grievance, prayer, or request.

what can You give me No material reward can equal the blessing of having children.

I shall die Literally, "I shall go," from the Hebrew meaning "to walk, go" (הלך). In Ak-

---

CHAPTER 15

In a mysterious vision, God promises Abraham that, after several generations of adversity, his descendants will return to claim as their own the land through which he had passed as a wayfarer. This promise is cast as a covenant between God and Abraham. A covenant implies obligations on the part of both parties. God promises a special destiny for Abraham's descendants even as Abraham promises loyalty and obedience to God.

1. I am a shield to you We echo these words in the opening blessing of the Amidah, praising God as *magen Avraham,* "Abraham's shield," or protector.

give me, seeing that I shall die childless, and the
one in charge of my household is Dammesek
Eliezer!" 3Abram said further, "Since You have
granted me no offspring, my steward will be
my heir." 4The word of the LORD came to him in
reply, "That one shall not be your heir; none
but your very own issue shall be your heir."
5He took him outside and said, "Look toward
heaven and count the stars, if you are able to
count them." And He added, "So shall your
offspring be." 6And because he put his trust
in the LORD, He reckoned it to his merit.

7Then He said to him, "I am the LORD who
brought you out from Ur of the Chaldeans to

וְאָנֹכִי הוֹלֵךְ עֲרִירִי וּבֶן־מֶשֶׁק בֵּיתִי הוּא
דַּמֶּשֶׂק אֱלִיעֶזֶר׃ 3 וַיֹּאמֶר אַבְרָם הֵן לִי
לֹא נָתַתָּה זָרַע וְהִנֵּה בֶן־בֵּיתִי יוֹרֵשׁ
אֹתִי׃ 4 וְהִנֵּה דְבַר־יְהוָה אֵלָיו לֵאמֹר לֹא
יִירָשְׁךָ זֶה כִּי־אִם אֲשֶׁר יֵצֵא מִמֵּעֶיךָ הוּא
יִירָשֶׁךָ׃ 5 וַיּוֹצֵא אֹתוֹ הַחוּצָה וַיֹּאמֶר
הַבֶּט־נָא הַשָּׁמַיְמָה וּסְפֹר הַכּוֹכָבִים אִם־
תּוּכַל לִסְפֹּר אֹתָם וַיֹּאמֶר לוֹ כֹּה יִהְיֶה
זַרְעֶךָ׃ 6 וְהֶאֱמִן בַּיהוָה וַיַּחְשְׁבֶהָ לּוֹ
צְדָקָה׃

ששי 7 וַיֹּאמֶר אֵלָיו אֲנִי יְהוָה אֲשֶׁר הוֹצֵאתִיךָ
מֵאוּר כַּשְׂדִּים לָתֶת לְךָ אֶת־הָאָרֶץ הַזֹּאת

kadian, too, *"alaku"* is used as a euphemism for dying.

3. will be my heir In the ancient Near East, a servant who performed filial duties for a childless couple—paying them proper respect, maintaining their household, taking care of their physical needs and comforts in their old age—could become their adopted heir. The patriarch, despairing of having children, had decided to adopt his servant.

5. Look toward heaven The visual experience—a real or dream revelation—reinforces the oral promise.

6. he put his trust in the LORD The encounter with God, which had begun on a note of fear and depression, closes with a firm statement of Abram's faith in the LORD (see Hab. 2:4).

He reckoned it to his merit The subject of the verb is God; "it" refers to Abram's act of faith, which made him worthy of God's reward, about to be secured through a covenant. The Hebrew word *tz'dakah* (righteousness) can also have the sense of "merit."

THE PROMISE OF NATIONAL TERRITORY (vv. 7–21)

7. I am the LORD This first use of the solemn formula of self-identification emphasizes the unimpeachable authority behind the forthcoming declaration. The style "I am so-and-so" is known from Hittite and Akkadian treaties and Canaanite royal proclamations.

Ur of the Chaldeans See Comments to 11:28,31.

to assign this land God had said nothing to Abram in 12:1–3 about a gift of land, but apparently that was the original intent, unrevealed at the time.

---

5. count the stars From an earth-bound perspective, a star looks tiny. From the viewpoint of heaven, each star is a world by itself. The descendants of Abraham seem insignificant in terms of numbers and power, but each one is an indispensable part of God's plan (Ḥayyim of Tzantz). Each individual Jew, each individual human being, is a world by himself or herself.

6. An enigmatic verse. According to Moshe of Kobrin, Abraham felt that God had done him a favor, an act of *tz'dakah,* by giving him the capacity to have faith even when circumstances seemed bleak. Yaakov of Rakov understands the verse to mean instead that God credited Abraham with an act of *tz'dakah,* teaching people that there is a purpose to life, that life can be redeemed from futility. Or we might understand Abraham's putting "his trust in the LORD" to mean that he gave God the benefit of the doubt, believing not only in God's existence but in God's reliability, even when circumstances might have led him to think otherwise. The only thing we can do for God, the only thing for which God depends on us, is to hold on to our faith even when things do not go our way. This is Abraham's (and our) *tz'dakah* (favor) to God.

7. who brought you out from Ur The language anticipates the first pronouncement at

assign this land to you as a possession." 8And
he said, "O Lord GOD, how shall I know that
I am to possess it?" 9He answered, "Bring Me
a three-year-old heifer, a three-year-old she-
goat, a three-year-old ram, a turtledove, and
a young bird." 10He brought Him all these and
cut them in two, placing each half opposite the
other; but he did not cut up the bird. 11Birds
of prey came down upon the carcasses, and
Abram drove them away. 12As the sun was
about to set, a deep sleep fell upon Abram,
and a great dark dread descended upon him.
13And He said to Abram, "Know well that your
offspring shall be strangers in a land not theirs,
and they shall be enslaved and oppressed four
hundred years; 14but I will execute judgment

לְרִשְׁתָּהּ׃ 8 וַיֹּאמַר אֲדֹנָי יֱהוִה בַּמָּה אֵדַע
כִּי אִירָשֶׁנָּה׃ 9 וַיֹּאמֶר אֵלָיו קְחָה לִי עֶגְלָה
מְשֻׁלֶּשֶׁת וְעֵז מְשֻׁלֶּשֶׁת וְאַיִל מְשֻׁלָּשׁ וְתֹר
וְגוֹזָל׃ 10 וַיִּקַּח־לוֹ אֶת־כָּל־אֵלֶּה וַיְבַתֵּר
אֹתָם בַּתָּוֶךְ וַיִּתֵּן אִישׁ־בִּתְרוֹ לִקְרַאת
רֵעֵהוּ וְאֶת־הַצִּפֹּר לֹא בָתָר׃ 11 וַיֵּרֶד
הָעַיִט עַל־הַפְּגָרִים וַיַּשֵּׁב אֹתָם אַבְרָם׃
12 וַיְהִי הַשֶּׁמֶשׁ לָבוֹא וְתַרְדֵּמָה נָפְלָה
עַל־אַבְרָם וְהִנֵּה אֵימָה חֲשֵׁכָה גְדֹלָה
נֹפֶלֶת עָלָיו׃ 13 וַיֹּאמֶר לְאַבְרָם יָדֹעַ תֵּדַע
כִּי־גֵר ׀ יִהְיֶה זַרְעֲךָ בְּאֶרֶץ לֹא לָהֶם
וַעֲבָדוּם וְעִנּוּ אֹתָם אַרְבַּע מֵאוֹת שָׁנָה׃
14 וְגַם אֶת־הַגּוֹי אֲשֶׁר יַעֲבֹדוּ דָּן אָנֹכִי

8. how shall I know Abram, speaking not as an individual but as the personification of the future nation, asks: By what process will that nation take possession of its promised land?

9. He answered In response, God enters into a covenant with the patriarch. The covenant is modeled after the royal land-grant treaty common in the ancient Near East, by which a king bestowed a gift of land on an individual or vassal as a reward for loyal service. But here, for the first time in the history of religions, it is God who initiates the contract.

a three-year-old An animal of three years was considered to be full grown and most preferable for a religious rite.

a young bird Probably a pigeon.

10. cut them in two The cutting of the animals in Mesopotamian sources is a warning that the violator of the covenant treaty would be sliced in half, as criminals were.

the bird A collective noun referring to both birds. The fact that the birds were not cut in two may be due solely to their small size.

11. Birds of prey Carrion-eating falcons (see Isa. 18:6 and Ezek. 39:4).

12. a deep sleep An abnormal stupor is associated with the dread aroused by the awareness of the presence of God (see Job 4:13ff., 33:15ff).

13. Know well God's response to Abram's query in Gen. 15:8.

a land not theirs That is, a foreign land, other than the land of Israel.

four hundred years This is probably a round number. It does not accord with the "four generations" of verse 16, and it is not identical with the 430-year figure given in Exod. 12:40 as the entire period of time spent in Egypt.

14. I will execute judgment This refers to the plagues (see Exod. 6:6, 7:4, 12:12).

Sinai, "I am the LORD who brought you out of Egypt."

8. Abraham is the first person in the Bible to call God *Adonai,* "my Lord," the first person to understand that religion asks us not so much to believe in God as to serve God (BT Ber. 7a).

how shall I know that I am to possess it? Does this indicate a lack of faith on Abraham's part, two verses after he is described as putting his faith in God? Perhaps the earlier verse refers to Abraham's commitment to faith even without proof, and this verse is Abraham's plea: "I believe; can I know that my belief is reasonable and not merely wishful thinking? I believe but, I will continue to question and challenge, out of the context of my belief."

on the nation they shall serve, and in the end
they shall go free with great wealth. 15As for
you,

You shall go to your fathers in peace;
You shall be buried at a ripe old age.

16And they shall return here in the fourth
generation, for the iniquity of the Amorites is
not yet complete."

17When the sun set and it was very dark,
there appeared a smoking oven, and a flaming torch which passed between those pieces.
18On that day the LORD made a covenant with
Abram, saying, "To your offspring I assign
this land, from the river of Egypt to the great
river, the river Euphrates: 19the Kenites, the
Kenizzites, the Kadmonites, 20the Hittites, the
Perizzites, the Rephaim, 21the Amorites, the
Canaanites, the Girgashites, and the Jebusites."

וְאַחֲרֵי־כֵן יֵצְאוּ בִּרְכֻשׁ גָּדוֹל׃ 15וְאַתָּה
תָּבוֹא אֶל־אֲבֹתֶיךָ בְּשָׁלוֹם
תִּקָּבֵר בְּשֵׂיבָה טוֹבָה׃
16וְדוֹר רְבִיעִי יָשׁוּבוּ הֵנָּה כִּי לֹא־שָׁלֵם עֲוֺן
הָאֱמֹרִי עַד־הֵנָּה׃
17וַיְהִי הַשֶּׁמֶשׁ בָּאָה וַעֲלָטָה הָיָה וְהִנֵּה
תַנּוּר עָשָׁן וְלַפִּיד אֵשׁ אֲשֶׁר עָבַר בֵּין
הַגְּזָרִים הָאֵלֶּה׃ 18בַּיּוֹם הַהוּא כָּרַת
יְהוָה אֶת־אַבְרָם בְּרִית לֵאמֹר לְזַרְעֲךָ
נָתַתִּי אֶת־הָאָרֶץ הַזֹּאת מִנְּהַר מִצְרַיִם
עַד־הַנָּהָר הַגָּדֹל נְהַר־פְּרָת׃ 19אֶת־הַקֵּינִי
וְאֶת־הַקְּנִזִּי וְאֵת הַקַּדְמֹנִי׃ 20וְאֶת־הַחִתִּי
וְאֶת־הַפְּרִזִּי וְאֶת־הָרְפָאִים׃ 21וְאֶת־
הָאֱמֹרִי וְאֶת־הַכְּנַעֲנִי וְאֶת־הַגִּרְגָּשִׁי וְאֶת־
הַיְבוּסִי׃ ס

great wealth This was either restitution for the decades of slave labor or in accordance with the law in Deut. 15:13ff. to the effect that an emancipated slave must be liberally provisioned by the master.

15. You shall go to your fathers A term for dying that is unique within the Hebrew Bible. It originates from the belief that one is reunited with one's ancestors after death.

16. the fourth generation Exod. 6:16–20 presents the same tradition of "four generations" between Levi and Moses. Another tradition, in Gen. 15:13, refers to the bondage as lasting 400 years.

the iniquity of the Amorites The local peoples, here called "Amorites," have violated the universal moral law, thereby dooming themselves by their own corruption. But the limit of God's tolerance of evil—four generations—has not yet been reached, and the Israelites must wait until the time is ripe.

COMPLETING THE COVENANT
(vv. 18–21)

God, the principal party to the covenant, passes between the pieces. As in a legal document, the nature of the instrument of transfer is defined, its promissory clause is specified as concerning a land grant, and the extent of the territory involved is delineated.

18. a covenant See Comment to 6:18.

the river of Egypt Hebrew: *nahar.* This is not the Nile, called *y'or* in the Bible, but its most easterly arm, which emptied into Lake Sirbonis near Pelusium not far from Port Said. The southwestern border of Canaan is the "Wadi (Hebrew, *naḥal*) of Egypt," which is identified with Wadi Al 'Arīsh and marks the boundary between the settled land and the Sinai desert.

the great river The boundaries given here, which include Tyre-Sidon, Lebanon, and Byblos, are a generalized ideal.

19. Kenites A seminomadic tribe of metal workers in the southern region of the land.

Kenizzites These people had close ties with the Edomites and were later absorbed into the tribe of Judah.

Kadmonites They may be the Kedemites (*b'nei kedem*) or "easterners," a general term for the tribes that roamed the desert from Aram in the north down to the Red Sea. They were famous for their wisdom.

16 Sarai, Abram's wife, had borne him no
children. She had an Egyptian maidservant
whose name was Hagar. 2And Sarai said to
Abram, "Look, the LORD has kept me from
bearing. Consort with my maid; perhaps I shall
have a son through her." And Abram heeded
Sarai's request. 3So Sarai, Abram's wife, took
her maid, Hagar the Egyptian—after Abram
had dwelt in the land of Canaan ten years—and
gave her to her husband Abram as concubine.
4He cohabited with Hagar and she conceived;
and when she saw that she had conceived, her
mistress was lowered in her esteem. 5And Sarai
said to Abram, "The wrong done me is your

טז וְשָׂרַי֙ אֵ֣שֶׁת אַבְרָ֔ם לֹ֥א יָלְדָ֖ה
ל֑וֹ וְלָ֛הּ שִׁפְחָ֥ה מִצְרִ֖ית וּשְׁמָ֥הּ הָגָֽר׃
2 וַתֹּ֨אמֶר שָׂרַ֜י אֶל־אַבְרָ֗ם הִנֵּה־נָ֞א עֲצָרַ֤נִי
יְהוָה֙ מִלֶּ֔דֶת בֹּא־נָא֙ אֶל־שִׁפְחָתִ֔י אוּלַ֥י
אִבָּנֶ֖ה מִמֶּ֑נָּה וַיִּשְׁמַ֥ע אַבְרָ֖ם לְק֥וֹל שָׂרָֽי׃
3 וַתִּקַּ֞ח שָׂרַ֣י אֵֽשֶׁת־אַבְרָ֗ם אֶת־הָגָ֤ר
הַמִּצְרִית֙ שִׁפְחָתָ֔הּ מִקֵּץ֙ עֶ֣שֶׂר שָׁנִ֔ים
לְשֶׁ֥בֶת אַבְרָ֖ם בְּאֶ֣רֶץ כְּנָ֑עַן וַתִּתֵּ֥ן אֹתָ֛הּ
לְאַבְרָ֥ם אִישָׁ֖הּ ל֥וֹ לְאִשָּֽׁה׃ 4 וַיָּבֹ֥א אֶל־
הָגָ֖ר וַתַּ֑הַר וַתֵּ֙רֶא֙ כִּ֣י הָרָ֔תָה וַתֵּקַ֥ל
גְּבִרְתָּ֖הּ בְּעֵינֶֽיהָ׃ 5 וַתֹּ֨אמֶר שָׂרַ֣י אֶל־
אַבְרָם֮ חֲמָסִ֣י עָלֶ֒יךָ֒ אָנֹכִ֗י נָתַ֤תִּי שִׁפְחָתִי֙

SARAH, HAGAR, AND THE BIRTH OF ISHMAEL (16:1–16)

CONCUBINAGE (vv. 1–6)

It has been 10 years since Abram parted from his father in Haran (v. 3). Throughout that decade his wife, Sarai, endured her infertility in silence. Now, to present Abram with a son, she resorts to concubinage.

1. She had Apparently, the maid attended primarily to the personal needs of her mistress and was not the common property of husband and wife.

Hagar The name, related to the Arabic word *hajara,* "to flee," may mean "fugitive." A people called Hagrites, mentioned in Ps. 83:7 and 1 Chron. 5:10,19ff., were pastoralists who roamed the Syro-Arabian desert.

2. kept me from bearing In ancient times the woman, not the man, was regarded as the source of barrenness, although God was seen as its ultimate cause.

through her In the ancient Near East, it was customary for an infertile wife to provide her husband with a concubine to bear children.

Abram heeded Ramban points out that Abram took Hagar only in response to his wife's urging.

4. her mistress was lowered in her esteem This is a natural consequence of a situation in which barrenness is regarded as a disgrace and the social position of the wife is diminished.

5. is your fault By giving Hagar to Abram, Sarai has relinquished her exclusive authority over her. It is now Abram's responsibility to control her behavior.

CHAPTER 16

1. In a world with few avenues of fulfilment open to women except as wives and mothers, infertility was an especially cruel and frustrating fate. Even today, in a world of wider possibilities, many women who yearn to be mothers and have difficulty conceiving and bearing children feel the frustration articulated in the Torah by Sarah, Rebekah, and Rachel. In the Torah, God responds to their cries by granting them the experience of motherhood. In the modern world, God's response can be found sometimes in the marvels of medical technology and sometimes in the pursuit of other paths to personal fulfilment and the nourishing of others' lives.

5. The wrong done me is your fault "You heard me insulted and did not speak up on my

HALAKHAH L'MA·ASEH

16:1–2 borne him no children Jewish law is divided on whether surrogate motherhood is appropriate. The CJLS has approved two responsa on surrogate motherhood—one citing this passage in support of surrogacy, the other citing this passage to caution against relying on surrogacy as a response to infertility.

fault! I myself put my maid in your bosom; now that she sees that she is pregnant, I am lowered in her esteem. The LORD decide between you and me!" [6]Abram said to Sarai, "Your maid is in your hands. Deal with her as you think right." Then Sarai treated her harshly, and she ran away from her.

[7]An angel of the LORD found her by a spring of water in the wilderness, the spring on the road to Shur, [8]and said, "Hagar, slave of Sarai, where have you come from, and where are you going?" And she said, "I am running away from my mistress Sarai."

[9]And the angel of the LORD said to her, "Go back to your mistress, and submit to her harsh treatment." [10]And the angel of the LORD said to her,

"I will greatly increase your offspring,
And they shall be too many to count."
[11]The angel of the LORD said to her further,
"Behold, you are with child
And shall bear a son;

בְּחֵיקֶךָ וַתֵּרֶא כִּי הָרָתָה וָאֵקַל בְּעֵינֶיהָ
יִשְׁפֹּט יְהוָה בֵּינִי וּבֵינֶיךָ*׃ 6 וַיֹּאמֶר אַבְרָם
אֶל־שָׂרַי הִנֵּה שִׁפְחָתֵךְ בְּיָדֵךְ עֲשִׂי־לָהּ
הַטּוֹב בְּעֵינָיִךְ וַתְּעַנֶּהָ שָׂרַי וַתִּבְרַח
מִפָּנֶיהָ׃
7 וַיִּמְצָאָהּ מַלְאַךְ יְהוָה עַל־עֵין הַמַּיִם
בַּמִּדְבָּר עַל־הָעַיִן בְּדֶרֶךְ שׁוּר׃ 8 וַיֹּאמַר
הָגָר שִׁפְחַת שָׂרַי אֵי־מִזֶּה בָאת וְאָנָה
תֵלֵכִי וַתֹּאמֶר מִפְּנֵי שָׂרַי גְּבִרְתִּי אָנֹכִי
בֹּרַחַת׃
9 וַיֹּאמֶר לָהּ מַלְאַךְ יְהוָה שׁוּבִי אֶל־
גְּבִרְתֵּךְ וְהִתְעַנִּי תַּחַת יָדֶיהָ׃ 10 וַיֹּאמֶר
לָהּ מַלְאַךְ יְהוָה
הַרְבָּה אַרְבֶּה אֶת־זַרְעֵךְ
וְלֹא יִסָּפֵר מֵרֹב׃
11 וַיֹּאמֶר לָהּ מַלְאַךְ יְהוָה
הִנָּךְ הָרָה
וְיֹלַדְתְּ בֵּן

v. 5. נקוד על י׳ בתראה

6. Sarai treated her harshly The Laws of Hammurabi (numbers 146–147) deal with the problem of the female slave-concubine who bears children and claims equality with her mistress. They prescribe that the insolent concubine be reduced to slave status and again bear the slave mark. The Hebrew verb used here (*va-t'anneha*) implies that Sarai subjected Hagar to physical and psychological abuse and carries with it the nuance of a negative judgment of her actions. Ramban states: "The matriarch sinned by such maltreatment, and Abraham too by permitting it."

HAGAR AND THE ANGEL (vv. 7–14)

God appears to the lowly Egyptian maidservant, bringing her a message of hope and comfort. The narrator's sympathies are clearly with Hagar.

7. An angel of the LORD This is the first appearance of an angel in biblical literature.

on the road to Shur Hagar fled in the direction of her native land. Shur is elsewhere described as being "close to Egypt" (Gen. 25:18).

8. where have you come from A gentle way of opening a conversation. The angel knows who she is; this encounter with Hagar is deliberate.

10. the angel of the LORD said This is the first of several announcements by a divine messenger predicting the birth and destiny of one who is given a special role in God's design of history (see 25:23; Judg. 13:3).

increase your offspring Ishmael is to become the father of 12 tribes and a great nation. The fulfillment of this promise is recorded in Gen. 25:12–18.

behalf (Gen. R. 45:5). When Hagar was rude to me, you did not take my side." Sarah, quite humanly, blames Abraham, although the idea was hers to begin with.

8. Hagar, . . . where have you come from, and where are you going? This is the first time in the Torah that God speaks to a woman (and to a non-Israelite woman).

You shall call him Ishmael,
For the LORD has paid heed to your suffering.
12He shall be a wild ass of a man;
His hand against everyone,
And everyone's hand against him;
He shall dwell alongside of all his kinsmen."
13And she called the LORD who spoke to her,
"You Are El-roi," by which she meant, "Have I
not gone on seeing after He saw me!" 14There-
fore the well was called Beer-lahai-roi; it is
between Kadesh and Bered.—15Hagar bore a
son to Abram, and Abram gave the son that
Hagar bore him the name Ishmael. 16Abram
was eighty-six years old when Hagar bore Ishmael to Abram.

וְקָרָ֤את שְׁמוֹ֙ יִשְׁמָעֵ֔אל
כִּֽי־שָׁמַ֥ע יְהוָ֖ה אֶל־עָנְיֵֽךְ׃
12 וְה֤וּא יִהְיֶה֙ פֶּ֣רֶא אָדָ֔ם
יָד֣וֹ בַכֹּ֔ל
וְיַ֥ד כֹּ֖ל בּ֑וֹ
וְעַל־פְּנֵ֥י כָל־אֶחָ֖יו יִשְׁכֹּֽן׃
13 וַתִּקְרָ֤א שֵׁם־יְהוָה֙ הַדֹּבֵ֣ר אֵלֶ֔יהָ אַתָּ֖ה
אֵ֣ל רֳאִ֑י כִּ֣י אָֽמְרָ֗ה הֲגַ֥ם הֲלֹ֛ם רָאִ֖יתִי
אַחֲרֵ֥י רֹאִֽי׃ 14 עַל־כֵּן֙ קָרָ֣א לַבְּאֵ֔ר בְּאֵ֥ר
לַחַ֖י רֹאִ֑י הִנֵּ֥ה בֵין־קָדֵ֖שׁ וּבֵ֥ין בָּֽרֶד׃
15 וַתֵּ֧לֶד הָגָ֛ר לְאַבְרָ֖ם בֵּ֑ן וַיִּקְרָ֨א אַבְרָ֧ם
שֶׁם־בְּנ֛וֹ אֲשֶׁר־יָלְדָ֥ה הָגָ֖ר יִשְׁמָעֵֽאל׃
16 וְאַבְרָ֕ם בֶּן־שְׁמֹנִ֥ים שָׁנָ֖ה וְשֵׁ֣שׁ שָׁנִ֑ים
בְּלֶֽדֶת־הָגָ֥ר אֶת־יִשְׁמָעֵ֖אל לְאַבְרָֽם׃ ס

11. Ishmael The name (literally, "God hears") is here interpreted as "God has paid heed to your suffering."

12. a wild ass of a man Hagar, the slave woman subjected to the cruel discipline of her mistress, will produce a people free and undisciplined. They are to be among people as the wild ass is among beasts: sturdy, fearless, fleet-footed, like the Syrian onager (Hebrew, *pere*), who roams the wilderness and is almost impossible to domesticate.

His hand against everyone A prediction reflecting the unremitting tension between the sedentary and the nomadic populations in the Near East.

alongside of all his kinsmen Better: "in confrontation with his kinsmen."

13. she called the LORD Literally, "she called the name of *YHVH*." The name—from the Hebrew root meaning "to be"—is inextricably bound up with existence. Hagar gives expression to her personal discovery by referring to God with a name that recalls the particular aspect of divine providence that she has experienced. Hagar is the only individual in the Bible (male or female) who gives God a name.

El-roi Literally, "God of seeing," that is, the all-seeing God. Also, "God of my seeing," that is, whom I have seen; and "God who sees me." The several meanings are to be apprehended simultaneously.

Have I not gone on seeing Hagar is spiritually stirred by her revelatory experience. She has become conscious of God's concern for the downtrodden.

14. Beer-lahai-roi This is either a newly coined name or the reinterpretation of an old one whose original meaning is unknown.

15. Hagar bore a son The narrative assumes that Hagar returned to Sarai, as bidden. Significantly, it is Abram who named the child, not Hagar, thus implying that he legitimized him.

I am running away from my mistress Hagar can tell the angel only what she is running from. She has no destination in mind, she only wants to escape harsh treatment.

13. El-roi "The God who sees me." God is a God who notices the oppressed, the needy, the marginalized, those of whom human society takes no notice.

17 When Abram was ninety-nine years old, the Lord appeared to Abram and said to him, "I am El Shaddai. Walk in My ways and be blameless. [2]I will establish My covenant between Me and you, and I will make you exceedingly numerous."

[3]Abram threw himself on his face; and God spoke to him further, [4]"As for Me, this is My covenant with you: You shall be the father of a multitude of nations. [5]And you shall no longer be called Abram, but your name shall

יז וַיְהִי אַבְרָם בֶּן־תִּשְׁעִים שָׁנָה וְתֵשַׁע
שָׁנִים וַיֵּרָא יְהוָה אֶל־אַבְרָם וַיֹּאמֶר אֵלָיו
אֲנִי־אֵל שַׁדַּי הִתְהַלֵּךְ לְפָנַי וֶהְיֵה תָמִים׃
2 וְאֶתְּנָה בְרִיתִי בֵּינִי וּבֵינֶךָ וְאַרְבֶּה אוֹתְךָ
בִּמְאֹד מְאֹד׃
3 וַיִּפֹּל אַבְרָם עַל־פָּנָיו וַיְדַבֵּר אִתּוֹ אֱלֹהִים
לֵאמֹר׃ 4 אֲנִי הִנֵּה בְרִיתִי אִתָּךְ וְהָיִיתָ
לְאַב הֲמוֹן גּוֹיִם׃ 5 וְלֹא־יִקָּרֵא עוֹד אֶת־
שִׁמְךָ אַבְרָם וְהָיָה שִׁמְךָ אַבְרָהָם כִּי אַב־

THE COVENANT IN THE FLESH (17:1–27)

After 13 years, God's promises still remain unfulfilled. The narrator, focusing on events that bear on the destiny of the nation yet to be born, tells us nothing about Abram's activities during that period. Suddenly Abram experiences a series of divine communications.

THE CHANGE OF ABRAM'S NAME (vv. 1–8)

1. the Lord This sole appearance of the name *YHVH* in this chapter (*Elohim* is used nine times) is intended to link it with the name "El Shaddai" (see Exod. 6:2ff.). The use of the name *YHVH* also connects it to the covenant of Gen. 15 made by God under that name.

El Shaddai The meaning of this name of God remains unknown.

Walk in My ways Literally, "Walk before Me." The corresponding Akkadian phrase is a technical term for absolute loyalty to a king. In the Bible, to "walk before God" means to condition one's entire range of experience by the awareness of God's presence.

and be blameless This is a near synonym of the preceding clause.

3. threw himself on his face An expression of awe and submission in the presence of the Lord.

4. father of a multitude of nations The Edomites, Ishmaelites, Midianites, and several other peoples descended from Abraham, according to the genealogical lists of chapters 25 and 36. The phrase may also have a more universal meaning in that a segment of humanity much larger than those alluded to regards Abraham as its spiritual father.

5. your name In the Bible a change of name is of major significance. It symbolizes the transformation of character and destiny. See Comment to 1:5.

CHAPTER 17

1. El Shaddai The Midrash understands this name of God to mean: "the God who says, '*Dai* (Enough)!'" The people of the world have gone on long enough acting like children. It is time to demand righteous behavior of them, to proclaim that certain things are permitted and others forbidden (Tanḥ. B. 25). God's covenant of circumcision marks Abraham as committed to teaching humanity what the God-ordained life can mean.

walk in My ways Let all your actions be done in the knowledge that you do them in My presence.

blameless In the King James translation, the word translated here as "blameless" (*tamim*) is rendered "be perfect," an unrealistic demand. We might understand it to mean "be whole," "come before Me with your whole self: the parts of yourself you are proud of, and the parts you are ashamed of and wish were different." Thus do we come before God on Yom Kippur, not proclaiming our blamelessness but bringing to God our whole selves, our faults with our merits, to be told that we are acceptable in God's sight.

5. father of a multitude of nations May a convert, bringing an offering of first fruits, recite the formula, "the land which You swore to

הֲמוֹן גּוֹיִם נְתַתִּיךָ׃ 6 וְהִפְרֵתִי אֹתְךָ בִּמְאֹד
מְאֹד וּנְתַתִּיךָ לְגוֹיִם וּמְלָכִים מִמְּךָ יֵצֵאוּ׃
שביעי 7 וַהֲקִמֹתִי אֶת־בְּרִיתִי בֵּינִי וּבֵינֶךָ וּבֵין
זַרְעֲךָ אַחֲרֶיךָ לְדֹרֹתָם לִבְרִית עוֹלָם
לִהְיוֹת לְךָ לֵאלֹהִים וּלְזַרְעֲךָ אַחֲרֶיךָ׃
8 וְנָתַתִּי לְךָ וּלְזַרְעֲךָ אַחֲרֶיךָ אֵת ׀ אֶרֶץ
מְגֻרֶיךָ אֵת כָּל־אֶרֶץ כְּנַעַן לַאֲחֻזַּת עוֹלָם
וְהָיִיתִי לָהֶם לֵאלֹהִים׃
9 וַיֹּאמֶר אֱלֹהִים אֶל־אַבְרָהָם וְאַתָּה אֶת־
בְּרִיתִי תִשְׁמֹר אַתָּה וְזַרְעֲךָ אַחֲרֶיךָ
לְדֹרֹתָם׃ 10 זֹאת בְּרִיתִי אֲשֶׁר תִּשְׁמְרוּ
בֵּינִי וּבֵינֵיכֶם וּבֵין זַרְעֲךָ אַחֲרֶיךָ הִמּוֹל
לָכֶם כָּל־זָכָר׃ 11 וּנְמַלְתֶּם אֵת בְּשַׂר

be Abraham, for I make you the father of a multitude of nations. [6]I will make you exceedingly fertile, and make nations of you; and kings shall come forth from you. [7]I will maintain My covenant between Me and you, and your offspring to come, as an everlasting covenant throughout the ages, to be God to you and to your offspring to come. [8]I assign the land you sojourn in to you and your offspring to come, all the land of Canaan, as an everlasting holding. I will be their God."

[9]God further said to Abraham, "As for you, you and your offspring to come throughout the ages shall keep My covenant. [10]Such shall be the covenant between Me and you and your offspring to follow which you shall keep: every male among you shall be circumcised.

Abram . . . Abraham Henceforth the patriarch is referred to only by the expanded form of his name, which carries with it an intimation of his God-given destiny.

6. kings The same promise recurs in verse 16 and in 35:11. Kingship, in the context of the times, is the consummation of the process of national development. The Davidic dynasty is the fulfillment of this promise.

7. to be God to you So again in verse 8. This phrase belongs to the formal language of the covenant and recurs frequently in the Bible. God elects Israel to be His special people, demanding exclusive allegiance in return (see Exod. 19:5–6).

to you and to your offspring to come This legal terminology occurs six times in this chapter. It also appears in Gen. 35:12 and 48:4 in connection with the covenantal promises. The phrase is found in ancient Near Eastern documents relating to the transmission of property on the death of the owner; it ensured that the real estate would be passed from generation to generation without restriction.

8. an everlasting holding National ownership of the land is to be eternal, like the covenant itself.

I will be their God The indissoluble union of the people Israel, the land of Israel, and God is the foundation on which Jewish civilization is built.

THE LAW OF CIRCUMCISION
(vv. 9–14)

Circumcision is both a symbol of God's covenant and a mark of the commitment to a life lived in awareness of that covenant. The law of circumcision is the first mitzvah in the Torah addressed to Abraham and his descendants.

9. As for you This is the counterpart of "As for Me" in verse 4.

10. every male Only males, a restriction that excludes female circumcision, practiced in many parts of the world.

---

our forefathers [Deut. 26:4]"? The Sages rule that the convert may do so, because Abraham is the forefather of all righteous individuals (JT Bikk. 1:4).

10. The covenant (*b'rit*) of the night vision (see 15:18) is re-affirmed through the rite of circumcision. In Hebrew, the formal term for the covenant of circumcision is *b'rit milah*. But the rite is so highly charged and symbolic that the term *b'rit* (Yiddish: *bris*) by itself has become synonymous with the circumcision ritual. Note that Abraham is given a new name at his circumcision, even as a Jewish male child is given a name at his.

11You shall circumcise the flesh of your foreskin, and that shall be the sign of the covenant
between Me and you. 12And throughout the
generations, every male among you shall be
circumcised at the age of eight days. As for
the homeborn slave and the one bought from
an outsider who is not of your offspring,
13they must be circumcised, homeborn, and
purchased alike. Thus shall My covenant be
marked in your flesh as an everlasting pact.
14And if any male who is uncircumcised fails
to circumcise the flesh of his foreskin, that
person shall be cut off from his kin; he has
broken My covenant."
15And God said to Abraham, "As for your
wife Sarai, you shall not call her Sarai, but
her name shall be Sarah. 16I will bless her; indeed, I will give you a son by her. I will bless her
so that she shall give rise to nations; rulers of

עָרְלַתְכֶ֑ם וְהָיָה֙ לְא֣וֹת בְּרִ֔ית בֵּינִ֖י
וּבֵינֵיכֶֽם׃ 12 וּבֶן־שְׁמֹנַ֣ת יָמִ֗ים יִמּ֥וֹל לָכֶ֛ם
כׇּל־זָכָ֖ר לְדֹרֹתֵיכֶ֑ם יְלִ֣יד בָּ֔יִת וּמִקְנַת־כֶּ֙סֶף֙
מִכֹּ֣ל בֶּן־נֵכָ֔ר אֲשֶׁ֛ר לֹ֥א מִֽזַּרְעֲךָ֖ הֽוּא׃
13 הִמּ֧וֹל ׀ יִמּ֛וֹל יְלִ֥יד בֵּיתְךָ֖ וּמִקְנַ֣ת כַּסְפֶּ֑ךָ
וְהָיְתָ֧ה בְרִיתִ֛י בִּבְשַׂרְכֶ֖ם לִבְרִ֥ית עוֹלָֽם׃
14 וְעָרֵ֣ל ׀ זָכָ֗ר אֲשֶׁ֤ר לֹֽא־יִמּוֹל֙ אֶת־בְּשַׂ֣ר
עׇרְלָת֔וֹ וְנִכְרְתָ֛ה הַנֶּ֥פֶשׁ הַהִ֖וא מֵעַמֶּ֑יהָ
אֶת־בְּרִיתִ֖י הֵפַֽר׃ ס
15 וַיֹּ֤אמֶר אֱלֹהִים֙ אֶל־אַבְרָהָ֔ם שָׂרַ֣י
אִשְׁתְּךָ֔ לֹא־תִקְרָ֥א אֶת־שְׁמָ֖הּ שָׂרָ֑י כִּ֥י
שָׂרָ֖ה שְׁמָֽהּ׃ 16 וּבֵרַכְתִּ֣י אֹתָ֔הּ וְגַ֨ם נָתַ֧תִּי
מִמֶּ֛נָּה לְךָ֖ בֵּ֑ן וּבֵֽרַכְתִּ֙יהָ֙ וְהָיְתָ֣ה לְגוֹיִ֔ם

11. the sign An outward, physical reminder of the covenant, like the rainbow after the Flood.

12. eight days The reinterpretation of the common practice of circumcision from a pubertal or nuptial rite to a covenantal rite is reinforced by the transfer of the time of the operation to the eighth day after birth. The eighth day is especially significant because the seven-day unit of time completed by the newborn corresponds to the process of Creation.

13. marked in your flesh "Flesh" is here a euphemism for "penis," as in Lev. 15:2ff. and Ezek. 16:26, 23:20.

14. his foreskin That is, his own foreskin. When a father fails to fulfill his duty, the responsibility falls on the individual himself when he reaches maturity.

shall be cut off This punishment, known as *karet* (see Lev. 20:1–6), is largely confined to offenses connected to the system of Israelite worship and to deviant sexual behavior. The Torah gives no definition of *karet,* and no analogy to it exists in ancient Near Eastern sources. In rabbinic literature, *karet* means premature death. The general idea is that one who excludes himself from the religious community dooms himself and his line to extinction, because he cannot benefit from the covenantal blessings.

THE CHANGE OF SARAI'S NAME
(vv. 15–22)

15. Sarai . . . Sarah Actually, the revised form *sarah* is simply a later modernization of the archaic form *sarai,* the second syllable being an old Semitic female ending. In either case, the literal meaning of the name is "princess."

---

15. Sarah is given a new name as well, for she is a partner in the covenant. She merits, and receives, her own blessing. The letter *hei,* representing the name of God, is added both to her name and to Abram's name, as a reward for their pious behavior. To do good deeds is to link our name with the name of God (Mekh. Yitro).

HALAKHAH L'MA·ASEH

17:12 the age of eight days This is the origin of the obligation to circumcise infant boys on the eighth day of their life in a *b'rit milah* ceremony (see Exod. 4:24–25). This ceremony seals the covenant in the flesh of the male generative organ, to make that covenant permanent for us and for all future generations.

peoples shall issue from her." 17Abraham threw
himself on his face and laughed, as he said to
himself, "Can a child be born to a man a hundred years old, or can Sarah bear a child at
ninety?" 18And Abraham said to God, "O that
Ishmael might live by Your favor!" 19God said,
"Nevertheless, Sarah your wife shall bear you a
son, and you shall name him Isaac; and I will
maintain My covenant with him as an everlasting covenant for his offspring to come.
20As for Ishmael, I have heeded you. I hereby
bless him. I will make him fertile and exceedingly numerous. He shall be the father of
twelve chieftains, and I will make of him a
great nation. 21But My covenant I will maintain with Isaac, whom Sarah shall bear to you
atthis season next year." 22And when He was
done speaking with him, God was gone from
Abraham.

23Then Abraham took his son Ishmael, and
all his homeborn slaves and all those he had
bought, every male in Abraham's household,
and he circumcised the flesh of their foreskins

מַלְכֵי עַמִּים מִמֶּנָּה יִהְיוּ׃ 17 וַיִּפֹּל אַבְרָהָם
עַל־פָּנָיו וַיִּצְחָק וַיֹּאמֶר בְּלִבּוֹ הַלְּבֶן מֵאָה־
שָׁנָה יִוָּלֵד וְאִם־שָׂרָה הֲבַת־תִּשְׁעִים שָׁנָה
תֵּלֵד׃ 18 וַיֹּאמֶר אַבְרָהָם אֶל־הָאֱלֹהִים לוּ
יִשְׁמָעֵאל יִחְיֶה לְפָנֶיךָ׃ 19 וַיֹּאמֶר אֱלֹהִים
אֲבָל שָׂרָה אִשְׁתְּךָ יֹלֶדֶת לְךָ בֵּן וְקָרָאתָ
אֶת־שְׁמוֹ יִצְחָק וַהֲקִמֹתִי אֶת־בְּרִיתִי
אִתּוֹ לִבְרִית עוֹלָם לְזַרְעוֹ אַחֲרָיו׃
20 וּלְיִשְׁמָעֵאל שְׁמַעְתִּיךָ הִנֵּה ׀ בֵּרַכְתִּי
אֹתוֹ וְהִפְרֵיתִי אֹתוֹ וְהִרְבֵּיתִי אֹתוֹ בִּמְאֹד
מְאֹד שְׁנֵים־עָשָׂר נְשִׂיאִם יוֹלִיד וּנְתַתִּיו
לְגוֹי גָּדוֹל׃ 21 וְאֶת־בְּרִיתִי אָקִים אֶת־
יִצְחָק אֲשֶׁר תֵּלֵד לְךָ שָׂרָה לַמּוֹעֵד הַזֶּה
בַּשָּׁנָה הָאַחֶרֶת׃ 22 וַיְכַל לְדַבֵּר אִתּוֹ וַיַּעַל
אֱלֹהִים מֵעַל אַבְרָהָם׃
23 וַיִּקַּח אַבְרָהָם אֶת־יִשְׁמָעֵאל בְּנוֹ וְאֵת
כָּל־יְלִידֵי בֵיתוֹ וְאֵת כָּל־מִקְנַת כַּסְפּוֹ כָּל־
זָכָר בְּאַנְשֵׁי בֵּית אַבְרָהָם וַיָּמָל אֶת־בְּשַׂר

17. and laughed The laughter foretokens the name of the son of destiny that Sarah will bear Abraham (Gen. 17:19).

Can . . . or can The double question describes two conditions that together produce a state of affairs clearly inimical to any possibility of Abraham and Sarah producing a child.

18. by Your favor Abraham fears for the life of Ishmael because God's words appear to exclude the boy from the benefits of the covenant.

19. God said God reassures Abraham, point by point.

Isaac The Hebrew word *yitzhak* means "he laughs." All three biblical traditions relating to the birth of Isaac (17:19, 18:12, 21:6) mention laughter in connection with doubting God's power. Isaac's birth represents the triumph of God over the limitations of nature.

20. Ishmael . . . heeded Although Ishmael is not to be Abraham's spiritual heir, he receives God's blessing and will pursue his own destiny.

twelve chieftains Corresponding to the 12 tribes of Israel, listed in 25:12–16.

22. God was gone Literally, "went up," implying that God had "come down" to speak with Abraham. The latter verb occurs in a context of divine self-manifestation; thus "to go up" means the termination of divine communication.

20. as for Ishmael Abraham prays that Ishmael will grow up to be a good person. The reply received by Abraham implies that each individual has the responsibility to become a good person. It is not in God's power to make people good. As the Midrash teaches, everything is in the hands of Heaven except the fear of Heaven. God, however, will bless Ishmael with wealth and family, so that neither poverty nor lack of companionship will incline him to unrighteous behavior (Barukh of Gorelitz). Ishmael will be blessed with wealth and numbers, but Isaac will, in addition, be blessed with a unique relationship to God (Mid. Ha-Gadol).

on that very day, as God had spoken to him.
²⁴Abraham was ninety-nine years old when he
circumcised the flesh of his foreskin, ²⁵and his
son Ishmael was thirteen years old when he
was circumcised in the flesh of his foreskin.
²⁶Thus Abraham and his son Ishmael were cir-
cumcised on that very day; ²⁷and all his household, his homeborn slaves and those that had
been bought from outsiders, were circumcised
with him.

עָרְלָתָ֖ם בְּעֶ֥צֶם הַיּ֣וֹם הַזֶּ֑ה כַּאֲשֶׁ֛ר דִּבֶּ֥ר
פטיר אִתּ֖וֹ אֱלֹהִֽים: 24 וְאַ֨בְרָהָ֔ם בֶּן־תִּשְׁעִ֥ים
וָתֵ֖שַׁע שָׁנָ֑ה בְּהִמֹּל֖וֹ בְּשַׂ֥ר עָרְלָתֽוֹ:
25 וְיִשְׁמָעֵ֣אל בְּנ֔וֹ בֶּן־שְׁלֹ֥שׁ עֶשְׂרֵ֖ה שָׁנָ֑ה
בְּהִ֨מֹּל֔וֹ אֵ֖ת בְּשַׂ֥ר עָרְלָתֽוֹ: 26 בְּעֶ֨צֶם֙ הַיּ֣וֹם
הַזֶּ֔ה נִמּ֖וֹל אַבְרָהָ֑ם וְיִשְׁמָעֵ֖אל בְּנֽוֹ:
27 וְכָל־אַנְשֵׁ֤י בֵיתוֹ֙ יְלִ֣יד בָּ֔יִת וּמִקְנַת־כֶּ֖סֶף
מֵאֵ֣ת בֶּן־נֵכָ֑ר נִמֹּ֖לוּ אִתּֽוֹ: פ

THE LAW OF CIRCUMCISION
CARRIED OUT   (vv. 23–27)

23. *that very day*   Without delay, Abraham
fulfills God's command and circumcises the en-

tire male population of his household. Kinship
is defined here by the residential unit; this household becomes an inclusive community. Yet heirship to the new covenant with Abraham is to be
based only on a matrilineal principle (see. v. 21).

הפטרת לך לך

HAFTARAH FOR LEKH L'KHA

ISAIAH 40:27–41:16

This *haftarah* is a call to the people, seed of Abraham, to return from exile to their homeland. It was delivered in Babylon, sometime in the mid-6th century B.C.E. Isaiah emphasizes God's power and providential guidance to alleviate the nation's mood of despair and fear. Through their faithful response, the people would thus renew a redemptive journey begun by their great ancestor more than a millennium earlier.

The several oracles included in this *haftarah* presumably were uttered at different times to the people in exile, presenting diverse themes and using distinct styles. At one level, these divine prophecies were anthologized on the basis of external verbal links. Thus, for example, the language of God's proclamation to the people Israel, calling on them to "renew their strength" through trust in the Lord (40:31), is repeated ironically in the following chapter, where this call for renewal is part of a challenge to the nations (41:1).

Read as part of a liturgical whole (related to public worship), the verbal connections take on thematic substance. One notable example is provided by the repetition of the phrase "the ends of the earth." It is used to describe God as Creator "of the earth from end to end" (40:28), the foreign nations ("ends of earth") who behold God's victory in fear and trembling (41:5), and God's act of liberating Israel from "the ends of the earth" to be His servant (41:9). The repetition of this phrase includes all the themes of the *haftarah:* God as creator, victor over the nations, and redeemer of the people Israel.

As a unified liturgical teaching, the *haftarah* moves progressively from the realism of despair to a near surreal vision of victory. In the process, Israel's speech moves from lament to exhilaration. These two poles are marked by Israel's opening words, "My way is hid from the LORD" (40:27), and the final divine promise, "But you shall rejoice in the LORD" (41:16). The proof is formulated in between these two statements: God will arouse a victor who will destroy the nations and thereby help prepare the fulfillment of the divine promises. The initial cry of disbelief is countered with reasons for trust.

In an attempt to motivate the people, the prophet alludes to earlier occasions of divine support. Thus in the opening oracle, the promise that the faithful will renew their strength and soar homeward like eagles (40:31) counters the sense of being forgotten in exile. This promise echoes the people's redemption from Egypt, when God first "bore you [the Israelites] on eagles' wings" (Exod. 19:4). "Like an eagle . . . / . . . did He spread His wings and take [Israel], / Bear [them] along on His pinions" (Deut. 32:11). An even earlier event of divine guidance is alluded to in the reference to the nation as the "Seed of Abraham My friend" (Isa. 41:8). This patriarch faithfully followed God and was promised the blessing of the land for his "seed" (Gen. 15:5). So may Israel, "the Seed of Abraham," confidently anticipate its own restoration to the homeland. Designating the nation as God's "servant" whom He has "chosen" (Isa. 41:8–9) also underscores the special status of the people Israel.

RELATION OF THE *HAFTARAH* TO THE *PARASHAH*

Isaiah's reference to the people Israel as the "Seed (*zera*) of Abraham My friend" (Isa. 41:8) establishes a correlation between a late prophecy of renewal and the Torah narrative in which this patriarch was promised "offspring" (*zera*) as numerous as the stars on high (Gen. 15:5). Indeed, because of this the Judeans in Babylon may hope

that God will rescue them from Babylon just as he once "brought" Abraham "out from Ur of the Chaldeans" to the promised "land" (Gen. 15:7). At one level, therefore, the nation's restoration from its exile completes God's promises to Abraham. God's ancient assurance, "Fear not" (*al tira;* Gen. 15:1), rings in the people's ears as the prophet proclaims God's new word of trust "Fear not" (*al tira;* Isa. 41:10) to the patriarch's seed.

By this same means, the *haftarah* may also suggest the mystery of divine protection to later generations. The God who rewarded Abraham's faith with "merit" (*tz'dakah;* Gen. 15:6) speaks now to all the people with the promise of providential care: "I am your God . . . I uphold you with My victorious right hand" (*biymin tzidki;* Isa. 41:10). Here God's gracious might sustains His creatures, not their own merit. Isaiah seeks to awaken his audience to this reality, providing the hope that renews strength. By proclaiming that the impaired spirit may be revived through trust in God's creative vitality (40:28–31), the prophet offers a new theology of divine immanence (presence) and the renewal of creation.

40 27Why do you say, O Jacob,
Why declare, O Israel,
"My way is hid from the LORD,
My cause is ignored by my God"?
28Do you not know?
Have you not heard?
The LORD is God from of old,
Creator of the earth from end to end,
He never grows faint or weary,
His wisdom cannot be fathomed.
29He gives strength to the weary,
Fresh vigor to the spent.
30Youths may grow faint and weary,
And young men stumble and fall;
31But they who trust in the LORD shall renew their strength
As eagles grow new plumes:
They shall run and not grow weary,
They shall march and not grow faint.

מ 27 לָ֤מָּה תֹאמַר֙ יַֽעֲקֹ֔ב
וּתְדַבֵּ֖ר יִשְׂרָאֵ֑ל
נִסְתְּרָ֤ה דַרְכִּי֙ מֵֽיְהוָ֔ה
וּמֵאֱלֹהַ֖י מִשְׁפָּטִ֥י יַעֲבֽוֹר׃
28 הֲל֨וֹא יָדַ֜עְתָּ
אִם־לֹ֣א שָׁמַ֗עְתָּ
אֱלֹהֵ֨י עוֹלָ֤ם ׀ יְהוָה֙
בּוֹרֵא֙ קְצ֣וֹת הָאָ֔רֶץ
לֹ֥א יִיעַ֖ף וְלֹ֣א יִיגָ֑ע
אֵ֥ין חֵ֖קֶר לִתְבוּנָתֽוֹ׃
29 נֹתֵ֥ן לַיָּעֵ֖ף כֹּ֑חַ
וּלְאֵ֥ין אוֹנִ֖ים עָצְמָ֥ה יַרְבֶּֽה׃
30 וְיִעֲפ֥וּ נְעָרִ֖ים וְיִגָ֑עוּ
וּבַחוּרִ֖ים כָּשׁ֥וֹל יִכָּשֵֽׁלוּ׃
31 וְקוֹיֵ֤ יְהוָה֙ יַחֲלִ֣יפוּ כֹ֔חַ
יַעֲל֥וּ אֵ֖בֶר כַּנְּשָׁרִ֑ים
יָר֨וּצוּ֙ וְלֹ֣א יִיגָ֔עוּ
יֵלְכ֖וּ וְלֹ֥א יִיעָֽפוּ׃

Isaiah 40:27. My way is hid from the LORD This quote from a communal criticism or lament bemoans the lack of divine knowledge, a knowledge that would lead to divine involvement. Hence the prophet responds that God's "wisdom cannot be fathomed" (v. 28).

28. Do you not know? / Have you not heard? The questions introduce a glorification of God as creator. A subsequent section mocks the making of idols (41:6–7).

41 Stand silent before Me, coastlands,
And let nations renew their strength.
Let them approach to state their case;
Let us come forward together for argument.
2Who has roused a victor from the East,
Summoned him to His service?
Has delivered up nations to him,
And trodden sovereigns down?
Has rendered their swords like dust,
Their bows like wind-blown straw?
3He pursues them, he goes on unscathed;
No shackle is placed on his feet.
4Who has wrought and achieved this?
He who announced the generations from the start—
I, the LORD, who was first
And will be with the last as well.

5The coastlands look on in fear,
The ends of earth tremble.

They draw near and come;
6Each one helps the other,
Saying to his fellow, "Take courage!"
7The woodworker encourages the smith;
He who flattens with the hammer
[Encourages] him who pounds the anvil.
He says of the riveting, "It is good!"
And he fixes it with nails,
That it may not topple.

מא הַחֲרִישׁוּ אֵלַי אִיִּים
וּלְאֻמִּים יַחֲלִיפוּ כֹחַ
יִגְּשׁוּ אָז יְדַבֵּרוּ
יַחְדָּו לַמִּשְׁפָּט נִקְרָבָה׃
2מִי הֵעִיר מִמִּזְרָח צֶדֶק
יִקְרָאֵהוּ לְרַגְלוֹ
יִתֵּן לְפָנָיו גּוֹיִם
וּמְלָכִים יַרְדְּ
יִתֵּן כֶּעָפָר חַרְבּוֹ
כְּקַשׁ נִדָּף קַשְׁתּוֹ׃
3יִרְדְּפֵם יַעֲבוֹר שָׁלוֹם
אֹרַח בְּרַגְלָיו לֹא יָבוֹא׃
4מִי־פָעַל וְעָשָׂה
קֹרֵא הַדֹּרוֹת מֵרֹאשׁ
אֲנִי יְהוָה רִאשׁוֹן
וְאֶת־אַחֲרֹנִים אֲנִי־הוּא׃

5רָאוּ אִיִּים וְיִירָאוּ
קְצוֹת הָאָרֶץ יֶחֱרָדוּ

קָרְבוּ וַיֶּאֱתָיוּן׃
6אִישׁ אֶת־רֵעֵהוּ יַעְזֹרוּ
וּלְאָחִיו יֹאמַר חֲזָק׃
7וַיְחַזֵּק חָרָשׁ אֶת־צֹרֵף
מַחֲלִיק פַּטִּישׁ
אֶת־הוֹלֶם פָּעַם
אֹמֵר לַדֶּבֶק טוֹב הוּא
וַיְחַזְּקֵהוּ בְמַסְמְרִים
לֹא יִמּוֹט׃ ס

Isaiah 41:2. Who has roused a victor from the East Ibn Ezra understood this as referring to Cyrus the Mede, who is mentioned explicitly in 45:1.

4. He who announced the generations God's control of history and foreknowledge of events are crucial elements in Isaiah's theology. Israel's history is living testimony to God's prophetic power (43:9–10).

8–13. An oracle of confidence, similar in language and form to oracles presented elsewhere to motivate leaders (Deut. 31:6–8) and prophets (Jer. 1:8,17).

8 But you, Israel, My servant,
Jacob, whom I have chosen,
Seed of Abraham My friend—
9 You whom I drew from the ends of the earth
And called from its far corners,
To whom I said: You are My servant;
I chose you, I have not rejected you—
10 Fear not, for I am with you,
Be not frightened, for I am your God;
I strengthen you and I help you,
I uphold you with My victorious right hand.
11 Shamed and chagrined shall be
All who contend with you;
They who strive with you
Shall become as naught and shall perish.
12 You may seek, but shall not find
Those who struggle with you;
Less than nothing shall be
The men who battle against you.
13 For I the LORD am your God,
Who grasped your right hand,
Who say to you: Have no fear;
I will be your help.
14 Fear not, O worm Jacob,
O men of Israel:
I will help you
—declares the LORD—

8 וְאַתָּה֙ יִשְׂרָאֵ֣ל עַבְדִּ֔י
יַעֲקֹ֖ב אֲשֶׁ֣ר בְּחַרְתִּ֑יךָ
זֶ֖רַע אַבְרָהָ֥ם אֹהֲבִֽי׃
9 אֲשֶׁ֤ר הֶחֱזַקְתִּ֙יךָ֙ מִקְצ֣וֹת הָאָ֔רֶץ
וּמֵאֲצִילֶ֖יהָ קְרָאתִ֑יךָ
וָאֹ֤מַר לְךָ֙ עַבְדִּי־אַ֔תָּה
בְּחַרְתִּ֖יךָ וְלֹ֥א מְאַסְתִּֽיךָ׃
10 אַל־תִּירָא֙ כִּ֣י עִמְּךָ־אָ֔נִי
אַל־תִּשְׁתָּ֖ע כִּֽי־אֲנִ֣י אֱלֹהֶ֑יךָ
אִמַּצְתִּ֙יךָ֙ אַף־עֲזַרְתִּ֔יךָ
אַף־תְּמַכְתִּ֖יךָ בִּימִ֥ין צִדְקִֽי׃
11 הֵ֤ן יֵבֹ֙שׁוּ֙ וְיִכָּ֣לְמ֔וּ
כֹּ֖ל הַנֶּחֱרִ֣ים בָּ֑ךְ
יִהְי֧וּ כְאַ֛יִן וְיֹאבְד֖וּ
אַנְשֵׁ֥י רִיבֶֽךָ׃
12 תְּבַקְשֵׁם֙ וְלֹ֣א תִמְצָאֵ֔ם
אַנְשֵׁ֖י מַצֻּתֶ֑ךָ
יִהְי֧וּ כְאַ֛יִן וּכְאֶ֖פֶס
אַנְשֵׁ֥י מִלְחַמְתֶּֽךָ׃
13 כִּ֗י אֲנִ֛י יְהוָ֥ה אֱלֹהֶ֖יךָ
מַחֲזִ֣יק יְמִינֶ֑ךָ
הָאֹמֵ֥ר לְךָ֛ אַל־תִּירָ֖א
אֲנִ֥י עֲזַרְתִּֽיךָ׃ ס
14 אַל־תִּֽירְאִי֙ תּוֹלַ֣עַת יַעֲקֹ֔ב
מְתֵ֖י יִשְׂרָאֵ֑ל
אֲנִ֤י עֲזַרְתִּיךְ֙
נְאֻם־יְהוָ֔ה

8. Israel, My servant The "servant" here is understood to be the nation (apparently also in Isa. 42:19, 43:10, 45:4, and 48:20). The prophet transfers to the nation as a whole a designation used in older sources for specific individuals (e.g., Abraham in Gen. 26:24; Moses in Deut. 34:5; David in Ps. 89:4). In this context, the title "My servant" has a strong covenantal aspect.

Seed of Abraham My friend The Hebrew for "My friend" is *ohavi;* literally, "who loves Me." Ibn Ezra stressed the active force of the verb, distinguishing it sharply from the passive sense ("who is loved by Me").

14. O worm Jacob A rare designation of abject suffering (see Ps. 22:7). The next phrase refers to "men of Israel" (*m'tei Yisra·el*). The Hebrew vocalization may be an error. The Akkadian noun for "maggot" (*mutu*) could yield the reading *moti Yisra·el,* leading to the parallelism of worm/maggot. This harsh designation of Israel is turned into a more positive attribute in an old *midrash*: Just as the strength of a worm is in its mouth, so the strength of suffering Israel is in its prayers and repentance (*Tanḥ. B'shallaḥ* 9).

I your Redeemer, the Holy One of Israel.
15I will make of you a threshing board,
A new thresher, with many spikes;
You shall thresh mountains to dust,
And make hills like chaff.
16You shall winnow them
And the wind shall carry them off;
The whirlwind shall scatter them.
But you shall rejoice in the LORD,
And glory in the Holy One of Israel.

וְגֹאֲלֵךְ קְדוֹשׁ יִשְׂרָאֵל׃
15 הִנֵּה שַׂמְתִּיךְ לְמוֹרַג
חָרוּץ חָדָשׁ בַּעַל פִּיפִיּוֹת
תָּדוּשׁ הָרִים וְתָדֹק
וּגְבָעוֹת כַּמֹּץ תָּשִׂים׃
16 תִּזְרֵם
וְרוּחַ תִּשָּׂאֵם
וּסְעָרָה תָּפִיץ אוֹתָם
וְאַתָּה תָּגִיל בַּיהוָה
בִּקְדוֹשׁ יִשְׂרָאֵל תִּתְהַלָּל׃ פ

VA-YERA

וירא

18 The LORD appeared to him by the terebinths of Mamre; he was sitting at the entrance of the tent as the day grew hot. 2 Looking
up, he saw three men standing near him. As

יח וַיֵּרָא אֵלָיו יְהוָה בְּאֵלֹנֵי מַמְרֵא
וְהוּא יֹשֵׁב פֶּתַח־הָאֹהֶל כְּחֹם הַיּוֹם׃
2 וַיִּשָּׂא עֵינָיו וַיַּרְא וְהִנֵּה שְׁלֹשָׁה אֲנָשִׁים

DIVINE VISITORS (18:1–33)

HOSPITALITY TO STRANGERS (vv. 1–8)

1. The LORD appeared to him This revelation, unlike the previous revelations, is unaccompanied by a formal act of worship or the building of an altar.

the terebinths of Mamre These are trees in the area of Hebron. See Comment to 12:6.

the day grew hot Noontime was approaching. The Bible does not divide time into hours, minutes, and seconds. A specific time of the day may be marked by a cooling breeze, the heat of the sun, or the dawning of light (see Gen. 3:8).

2. Looking up, he saw The wayfarers appear suddenly at a time of the day when people normally would not be traveling.

three men There seems to be nothing unusual about their appearance. Abraham and the people of Sodom (19:5) see them as entirely human.

CHAPTER 18

Even as the opening notes of a symphony often sound a theme that will be developed in various ways throughout the piece, the opening word of this fourth *parashah* of Genesis proclaims the theme: *Va-yera,* "The LORD appeared/was seen." One incident after another involves people seeing or not seeing God. Hagar's eyes are opened to see the miraculous well God has provided for her in 21:19. Abraham sees God atop Mount Moriah (22:4), while the servants who were traveling with him do not. One of the gifts with which spiritually sensitive people are blessed is the ability to see the presence of God in their daily experiences. Others, sharing the same experiences, are blind to the divine presence.

1. By visiting Abraham to distract him from the pain of recovering from his circumcision, God provides us with an example of the mitzvah of visiting the sick, *bikkur ḥolim* (BT Sot. 14a). Visiting the sick may not physically alter the course of an illness, but the knowledge that people care may ease the suffering and discomfort of one who is ill or recuperating and dispel any fears that the suffering is deserved because he or she is a bad person. The presence of a caring friend lessens a sense of suffering. When the Sages envision God visiting Abraham to lessen his discomfort, they may be implying that sometimes all we can give an afflicted person is the gift of our caring presence, and when we do that, we are following God's ways.

By turning away from God to attend to the three strangers, Abraham teaches us that caring for others is a great mitzvah. "Hospitality to wayfarers is greater than welcoming the Divine Presence" (BT Shab. 127a). Aaron of Karlin taught that when we turn our attention from God to tend to the needs of people, we do God's will. Conversely, God is not pleased when we place such a great focus on God that we ignore needy human beings.

2. Perhaps Abraham, having benefited from God's show of concern, is no longer focused exclusively on his own problems and is moved to help others. A tradition has it that Abraham and Sarah's tent was open on all four sides to facilitate their extending hospitality to wayfarers.

It will become clear (in 19:1) that these travelers are angels in human guise. What is an angel? An agent. The Hebrew for "angel" (*mal·akh*) is related to the word for "task" (*m'lakhah*). We can think of an angel as a phys-

---

HALAKHAH L'MA·ASEH

18:1 The LORD appeared to him The *mitzvah* of *bikkur ḥolim,* visiting the sick, is motivated by our desire to emulate God's behavior here (BT Sot. 14a), for, as the last verses of the previous chapter indicate, Abraham had just been circumcised.

soon as he saw them, he ran from the entrance of the tent to greet them and, bowing to the ground, 3 he said, "My lords, if it please you, do not go on past your servant. 4 Let a little water be brought; bathe your feet and recline under the tree. 5 And let me fetch a morsel of bread that you may refresh yourselves; then go on—seeing that you have come your servant's way." They replied, "Do as you have said."

6 Abraham hastened into the tent to Sarah, and said, "Quick, three seahs of choice flour! Knead and make cakes!" 7 Then Abraham ran to the herd, took a calf, tender and choice, and gave it to a servant-boy, who hastened to prepare it. 8 He took curds and milk and the calf that had been prepared and set these before them; and he waited on them under the tree as they ate.

נִצָּבִים עָלָיו וַיַּרְא וַיָּרָץ לִקְרָאתָם מִפֶּתַח
הָאֹהֶל וַיִּשְׁתַּחוּ אָרְצָה׃ 3 וַיֹּאמַר אֲדֹנָי
אִם־נָא מָצָאתִי חֵן בְּעֵינֶיךָ אַל־נָא תַעֲבֹר
מֵעַל עַבְדֶּךָ׃ 4 יֻקַּח־נָא מְעַט־מַיִם וְרַחֲצוּ
רַגְלֵיכֶם וְהִשָּׁעֲנוּ תַּחַת הָעֵץ׃ 5 וְאֶקְחָה
פַת־לֶחֶם וְסַעֲדוּ לִבְּכֶם אַחַר תַּעֲבֹרוּ כִּי־
עַל־כֵּן עֲבַרְתֶּם עַל־עַבְדְּכֶם וַיֹּאמְרוּ כֵּן
תַּעֲשֶׂה כַּאֲשֶׁר דִּבַּרְתָּ׃
6 וַיְמַהֵר אַבְרָהָם הָאֹהֱלָה אֶל־שָׂרָה
וַיֹּאמֶר מַהֲרִי שְׁלֹשׁ סְאִים קֶמַח סֹלֶת
לוּשִׁי וַעֲשִׂי עֻגוֹת׃ 7 וְאֶל־הַבָּקָר רָץ
אַבְרָהָם וַיִּקַּח בֶּן־בָּקָר רַךְ וָטוֹב וַיִּתֵּן אֶל־
הַנַּעַר וַיְמַהֵר לַעֲשׂוֹת אֹתוֹ׃ 8 וַיִּקַּח חֶמְאָה
וְחָלָב וּבֶן־הַבָּקָר אֲשֶׁר עָשָׂה וַיִּתֵּן לִפְנֵיהֶם
וְהוּא־עֹמֵד עֲלֵיהֶם תַּחַת הָעֵץ וַיֹּאכֵלוּ׃

he ran Abraham begins his hospitality even before the strangers reach his tent.

bowing to the ground Abraham reinforces this gesture of honor and respect by referring to himself as "your servant."

3. My lords The word translated here as "My lords" (*adonai*), with a final long vowel, is a plural form otherwise used only for God. Rashi and Ibn Ezra understand it to mean "My lords." Maimonides renders it "My Lord" (referring to God). Because it is clear that the patriarch is unaware of the strangers' true identity, the unusual vocalization may be a signal to the reader that the three "men" are no ordinary wayfarers.

4. Let a little water be brought Water for bathing one's feet was a much-appreciated comfort to travelers with their sandal-like footwear and the pervasive dust of the roads.

under the tree Probably one of the famous local terebinths. See Comment to 12:6.

6. choice flour That is, the finest and choicest wheat flour, from which grain offerings in later times were brought to the sanctuary.

7. Abraham ran to the herd For the main dish, he himself selects the calf, a rare delicacy and a sign of princely hospitality among pastoralists.

8. curds and milk Staple products of a pastoral economy. Curds are similar to the modern leben or yogurt. Milk, regarded as a source of vitality, was also offered to the gods. Abraham personally serves the strangers this rich fare and then stands by, ready to attend to their needs.

as they ate The Talmud would not accept the notion that angels partook of food, understanding the phrase to mean that they only gave the appearance of eating (BT BM 86b).

---

ical manifestation of God's will and concern, appearing on earth to perform a specific task. As the chapter later discloses, when the task is completed, the angel disappears. This is also seen in the story of Samson (Judg. 13:2–21).

4. let a little water be brought God promises Abraham, "As you brought a little water to My emissaries, I will give your descendants water in the desert. As you brought them bread to eat, I will sustain your descendants with manna for forty years. As you gave them shade under a tree, I will give the Israelites a cover of clouds to protect them from the desert sun" (Gen. R. 48:10).

8. The verse is remarkable for describing the angels as eating. Also, they ate milk and meat together (which was forbidden only after the giving of the Torah at Sinai). A legend about

9They said to him, "Where is your wife Sarah?" And he replied, "There, in the tent."
10Then one said, "I will return to you next year,
and your wife Sarah shall have a son!" Sarah
was listening at the entrance of the tent, which
was behind him. 11Now Abraham and Sarah
were old, advanced in years; Sarah had stopped
having the periods of women. 12And Sarah
laughed to herself, saying, "Now that I am
withered, am I to have enjoyment—with my
husband so old?" 13Then the LORD said to
Abraham, "Why did Sarah laugh, saying, 'Shall
I in truth bear a child, old as I am?' 14Is anything
too wondrous for the LORD? I will return to you
at the same season next year, and Sarah shall
have a son." 15Sarah lied, saying, "I did not
laugh," for she was frightened. But He replied,
"You did laugh."

9 וַיֹּאמְרוּ אֵלָיו* אַיֵּה שָׂרָה אִשְׁתֶּךָ וַיֹּאמֶר
הִנֵּה בָאֹהֶל׃ 10 וַיֹּאמֶר שׁוֹב אָשׁוּב אֵלֶיךָ
כָּעֵת חַיָּה וְהִנֵּה־בֵן לְשָׂרָה אִשְׁתֶּךָ וְשָׂרָה
שֹׁמַעַת פֶּתַח הָאֹהֶל וְהוּא אַחֲרָיו׃
11 וְאַבְרָהָם וְשָׂרָה זְקֵנִים בָּאִים בַּיָּמִים
חָדַל לִהְיוֹת לְשָׂרָה אֹרַח כַּנָּשִׁים׃
12 וַתִּצְחַק שָׂרָה בְּקִרְבָּהּ לֵאמֹר אַחֲרֵי
בְלֹתִי הָיְתָה־לִּי עֶדְנָה וַאדֹנִי זָקֵן׃
13 וַיֹּאמֶר יְהוָה אֶל־אַבְרָהָם לָמָּה זֶּה
צָחֲקָה שָׂרָה לֵאמֹר הַאַף אֻמְנָם אֵלֵד
וַאֲנִי זָקַנְתִּי׃ 14 הֲיִפָּלֵא מֵיְהוָה דָּבָר
לַמּוֹעֵד אָשׁוּב אֵלֶיךָ כָּעֵת חַיָּה וּלְשָׂרָה
שני בֵן׃ 15 וַתְּכַחֵשׁ שָׂרָה ׀ לֵאמֹר לֹא צָחַקְתִּי
כִּי ׀ יָרֵאָה וַיֹּאמֶר ׀ לֹא כִּי צָחָקְתְּ׃

v. 9. נקוד על א׳ י׳ ו׳, ולפי נוסחים מקובלים אין נקוד על ל׳

THE ANNOUNCEMENT ABOUT SARAH
(vv. 9–15)

9. Where is your wife Sarah? Their question (as Rashbam notes) is merely a way of politely opening a conversation about Sarah.

10. next year The Hebrew phrase translated as "next year" (*ka-et ḥayyah*) is an idiom, meaning "next year at this time."

11. the periods of women Literally, "the way of women." The phrase refers to the menstrual cycle, as it does in 31:35.

12. Sarah laughed See Comments to 17:17,19.

enjoyment The Hebrew word translated as "enjoyment" (*ednah*) has a sexual connotation here. It means "abundant moisture" and is an exact antonym of "withered."

13. Then the LORD said God and the angels often speak interchangeably. In the Torah, an angel is often a manifestation of God in human form.

to Abraham The patriarch maintains a discreet silence.

15. Sarah lied The Bible does not gloss over the human failings of Israel's traditional heroes.

she was frightened The supernatural character of the visitors has become apparent. Even

the time of revelation at Mount Sinai presents the angels protesting against God's intention of giving the Torah to the people Israel, on the grounds that they inevitably would violate it. God silences them by reminding them that the angels themselves mixed milk and meat at Abraham's table.

12. Sarah's laughter may not be a response to the far-fetched notion of pregnancy at an advanced age, but the laughter of delight at the prospect of two elderly people resuming marital intimacy.

13. In the previous verse, Sarah laughed at the prospect of bearing a child "with my husband so old." God, in speaking with Abraham about this, deliberately misquotes Sarah as hav-

HALAKHAH L'MA·ASEH

18:13 And the LORD said to Abraham God rephrases Sarah's comment to refer to her own advanced age rather than Abraham's lest he be offended. Similarly, the Talmud states that one is not obligated to tell the whole truth if it will hurt someone's feelings (BT Ket. 16b–17a) and that one may even speak an untruth for the sake of peace (BT Yev. 65a).

[16]The men set out from there and looked down toward Sodom, Abraham walking with them to see them off. [17]Now the LORD had said, "Shall I hide from Abraham what I am about to do, [18]since Abraham is to become a great and populous nation and all the nations of the earth are to bless themselves by him? [19]For I have singled him out, that he may instruct his children and his posterity to keep the way of the LORD by doing what is just and right, in order that the LORD may bring about for Abraham what He has promised him." [20]Then the LORD said, "The outrage of Sodom and Gomorrah is so great, and their sin so grave! [21]I will go down to see whether they have acted altogether according to the outcry that has reached Me; if not, I will take note."

[22]The men went on from there to Sodom, while Abraham remained standing before the

16 וַיָּקֻמוּ מִשָּׁם הָאֲנָשִׁים וַיַּשְׁקִפוּ עַל־פְּנֵי
סְדֹם וְאַבְרָהָם הֹלֵךְ עִמָּם לְשַׁלְּחָם׃
17 וַיהוָה אָמָר הַמְכַסֶּה אֲנִי מֵאַבְרָהָם
אֲשֶׁר אֲנִי עֹשֶׂה׃ 18 וְאַבְרָהָם הָיוֹ יִהְיֶה
לְגוֹי גָּדוֹל וְעָצוּם וְנִבְרְכוּ בוֹ כֹּל גּוֹיֵי
הָאָרֶץ׃ 19 כִּי יְדַעְתִּיו לְמַעַן אֲשֶׁר יְצַוֶּה
אֶת־בָּנָיו וְאֶת־בֵּיתוֹ אַחֲרָיו וְשָׁמְרוּ דֶּרֶךְ
יְהוָה לַעֲשׂוֹת צְדָקָה וּמִשְׁפָּט לְמַעַן
הָבִיא יְהוָה עַל־אַבְרָהָם אֵת אֲשֶׁר־דִּבֶּר
עָלָיו׃ 20 וַיֹּאמֶר יְהוָה זַעֲקַת סְדֹם וַעֲמֹרָה
כִּי־רָבָּה וְחַטָּאתָם כִּי כָבְדָה מְאֹד׃
21 אֵרְדָה־נָּא וְאֶרְאֶה הַכְּצַעֲקָתָהּ הַבָּאָה
אֵלַי עָשׂוּ ׀ כָּלָה וְאִם־לֹא אֵדָעָה׃
22 וַיִּפְנוּ מִשָּׁם הָאֲנָשִׁים וַיֵּלְכוּ סְדֹמָה
וְאַבְרָהָם עוֹדֶנּוּ עֹמֵד לִפְנֵי יְהוָה׃ 23 וַיִּגַּשׁ

though Sarah had laughed to herself, not aloud, her innermost thoughts had been read!

16. The men set out This statement links the first scene in the chapter with the next.

looked down toward Sodom At some point they must have been within walking distance of Hebron from which the Dead Sea region was visible.

THE ANNOUNCEMENT ABOUT SODOM
(vv. 17–22)

God informs Abraham of the decision to destroy Sodom, and Abraham feels compelled to plead for people's lives.

19. instruct In the Bible, education of the young is the responsibility of parents.

20. their sin so grave Their wrongdoings are unspecified. They have been understood as being in the moral realm, including adultery, false dealings, arrogant disregard of human rights, and the encouragement of evildoers.

21. I will go down to see The fate of Sodom is not yet sealed. God personally will investigate the moral condition of the city. This statement of intent serves to vindicate the act of divine justice.

22. The men went on from there This note is connected with verse 16.

Abraham remained standing According to rabbinic tradition, this text is 1 of 18 instances in the Bible that required scribal corrections (*tikkunei sof'rim*). Thus it is assumed that the original text read: "God remained standing be-

---

ing said "old as I am," to spare her husband's feelings. Although truth is a major value in Judaism, sometimes truth has to be compromised to maintain love and harmony between husband and wife (Gen. R. 48:18). Using the principle of truth as an excuse cannot justify words that wound another person.

19. This is a "verse of supreme importance in the Book of Genesis" (N. Leibowitz). God promises to have a special relationship with Abraham and his progeny, so that they will be inspired to do what is right and just. The negotiation over the fate of Sodom is one result of that relationship and that commitment to what is right and just. "The descendants of Abraham are characterized by three traits: a capacity for kindness, a sense of shame, and a commitment to doing what is right" (BT Yev. 79a).

22. remained standing before the LORD A Rabbinic tradition maintains that Abraham instituted the morning service (*Shaharit*), inter-

Lord. 23 Abraham came forward and said,
"Will You sweep away the innocent along with
the guilty? 24 What if there should be fifty innocent within the city; will You then wipe out
the place and not forgive it for the sake of the
innocent fifty who are in it? 25 Far be it from You
to do such a thing, to bring death upon the
innocent as well as the guilty, so that innocent
and guilty fare alike. Far be it from You! Shall
not the Judge of all the earth deal justly?" 26 And
the Lord answered, "If I find within the city of
Sodom fifty innocent ones, I will forgive the
whole place for their sake." 27 Abraham spoke
up, saying, "Here I venture to speak to my Lord,
I who am but dust and ashes: 28 What if the fifty
innocent should lack five? Will You destroy the
whole city for want of the five?" And He answered, "I will not destroy if I find forty-five

אַבְרָהָם וַיֹּאמַר הַאַף תִּסְפֶּה צַדִּיק עִם־
רָשָׁע׃ 24 אוּלַי יֵשׁ חֲמִשִּׁים צַדִּיקִם בְּתוֹךְ
הָעִיר הַאַף תִּסְפֶּה וְלֹא־תִשָּׂא לַמָּקוֹם
לְמַעַן חֲמִשִּׁים הַצַּדִּיקִם אֲשֶׁר בְּקִרְבָּהּ׃
25 חָלִלָה לְּךָ מֵעֲשֹׂת ׀ כַּדָּבָר הַזֶּה
לְהָמִית צַדִּיק עִם־רָשָׁע וְהָיָה כַצַּדִּיק
כָּרָשָׁע חָלִלָה לָּךְ הֲשֹׁפֵט כָּל־הָאָרֶץ לֹא
יַעֲשֶׂה מִשְׁפָּט׃ 26 וַיֹּאמֶר יְהוָה אִם־
אֶמְצָא בִסְדֹם חֲמִשִּׁים צַדִּיקִם בְּתוֹךְ
הָעִיר וְנָשָׂאתִי לְכָל־הַמָּקוֹם בַּעֲבוּרָם׃
27 וַיַּעַן אַבְרָהָם וַיֹּאמַר הִנֵּה־נָא הוֹאַלְתִּי
לְדַבֵּר אֶל־אֲדֹנָי וְאָנֹכִי עָפָר וָאֵפֶר׃
28 אוּלַי יַחְסְרוּן חֲמִשִּׁים הַצַּדִּיקִם
חֲמִשָּׁה הֲתַשְׁחִית בַּחֲמִשָּׁה אֶת־כָּל־
הָעִיר וַיֹּאמֶר לֹא אַשְׁחִית אִם־אֶמְצָא

fore Abraham." The Scribes, deeming it disrespectful that God should have to wait for Abraham, reversed the subject and the object of the clause.

ABRAHAM ARGUES WITH GOD (vv. 22–33)

Abraham stands before God to plead for the lives of pagans who are depraved.

23. came forward As if in are courtroom, he came forward to present his case.

24. within the city The narrative concentrates on Sodom because, as the metropolis, it stood for all the other cities of the Plain.

25. Shall not the Judge Abraham's faith in God's justice apparently gives rise to his serious questions about God's morality in governing the world.

27. but dust and ashes Abraham approaches God with profound humility.

---

preting the verse to mean that he prayed when he rose early to face God (BT Ber. 26a).

24. fifty innocent within the city If a community can produce a subculture of righteous people, and if they involve themselves *within the city,* trying to change it, then there is hope for that community. But if the righteous are only isolated individuals who avoid or are barred from being involved in the affairs of the city, there is no hope. One can only extricate them and condemn the rest.

25. Shall not the Judge of all the earth deal justly? Abraham's challenge to God is rooted in the audacious claim that even God is subject to the moral standards divinely decreed for humans. If God is to be obeyed when commanding moral behavior, God must exemplify that moral behavior. A commentary takes this not as a question or a challenge, but as a demand: "Do not exact strict justice upon these people! You, Lord, know how weak human nature is. You know how hard it is to be a good person in Sodom. Treat them more leniently than strict justice would require" (*Meshekh Ḥokhmah*).

HALAKHAH L'MA·ASEH

18:25 Shall not the Judge of all the earth deal justly? Abraham's conviction that God must be just has provided theological grounds for Jewish commitments to justice and to social action, for just as God seeks justice and helps the poor, so must we (BT Sot. 14a).

there." 29But he spoke to Him again, and said,
"What if forty should be found there?" And He
answered, "I will not do it, for the sake of the
forty." 30And he said, "Let not my Lord be
angry if I go on: What if thirty should be found
there?" And He answered, "I will not do it if I
find thirty there." 31And he said, "I venture
again to speak to my Lord: What if twenty
should be found there?" And He answered, "I
will not destroy, for the sake of the twenty."
32And he said, "Let not my Lord be angry if I
speak but this last time: What if ten should be
found there?" And He answered, "I will not
destroy, for the sake of the ten."
33When the LORD had finished speaking to
Abraham, He departed; and Abraham returned to his place.

שָׁם אַרְבָּעִים וַחֲמִשָּׁה׃ 29 וַיֹּסֶף עוֹד לְדַבֵּר
אֵלָיו וַיֹּאמַר אוּלַי יִמָּצְאוּן שָׁם אַרְבָּעִים
וַיֹּאמֶר לֹא אֶעֱשֶׂה בַּעֲבוּר הָאַרְבָּעִים׃
30 וַיֹּאמֶר אַל־נָא יִחַר לַאדֹנָי וַאֲדַבֵּרָה
אוּלַי יִמָּצְאוּן שָׁם שְׁלֹשִׁים וַיֹּאמֶר לֹא
אֶעֱשֶׂה אִם־אֶמְצָא שָׁם שְׁלֹשִׁים׃
31 וַיֹּאמֶר הִנֵּה־נָא הוֹאַלְתִּי לְדַבֵּר אֶל־
אֲדֹנָי אוּלַי יִמָּצְאוּן שָׁם עֶשְׂרִים וַיֹּאמֶר
לֹא אַשְׁחִית בַּעֲבוּר הָעֶשְׂרִים׃ 32 וַיֹּאמֶר
אַל־נָא יִחַר לַאדֹנָי וַאֲדַבְּרָה אַךְ־הַפַּעַם
אוּלַי יִמָּצְאוּן שָׁם עֲשָׂרָה וַיֹּאמֶר לֹא
אַשְׁחִית בַּעֲבוּר הָעֲשָׂרָה׃
33 וַיֵּלֶךְ יְהוָה כַּאֲשֶׁר כִּלָּה לְדַבֵּר אֶל־
אַבְרָהָם וְאַבְרָהָם שָׁב לִמְקֹמוֹ׃

19 The two angels arrived in Sodom in
the evening, as Lot was sitting in the gate of
Sodom. When Lot saw them, he rose to greet
them and, bowing low with his face to the
ground, 2he said, "Please, my lords, turn aside

שלישי **יט** וַיָּבֹאוּ שְׁנֵי הַמַּלְאָכִים סְדֹמָה
בָּעֶרֶב וְלוֹט יֹשֵׁב בְּשַׁעַר־סְדֹם וַיַּרְא־לוֹט
וַיָּקָם לִקְרָאתָם וַיִּשְׁתַּחוּ אַפַּיִם אָרְצָה׃
2 וַיֹּאמֶר הִנֶּה נָּא־אֲדֹנַי סוּרוּ נָא אֶל־בֵּית

32. ten A round number that symbolizes totality, 10 is the number of adults who constitute the minimum effective social entity. Abraham has reached the limit of the ability of righteous individuals to outweigh the cumulative evil of a community.

33. returned to his place That is, to his tent near Hebron (18:1).

THE DESTRUCTION OF SODOM AND GOMORRAH (19:1–29)

ARRIVAL OF THE ANGELS AT SODOM (vv. 1–5)

1. sitting in the gate The gate area of an ancient Near Eastern city served as a civic center where the community's affairs could be conducted with the full participation of the citizens, in the sight of all.

---

32. Why does Abraham stop at 10? Perhaps it takes a critical mass to generate an alternative way of living; isolated individuals cannot. The number 10 may be psychologically related to the stipulation of 10 people for a *minyan*, the quorum for public worship, the point at which an assembly of individuals becomes a group, a congregation.

33. Presumably God knew that Sodom was beyond redemption but was pleased that Abraham, unlike Noah, argued on behalf of his contemporaries (Tanḥ. 8).

CHAPTER 19

1. Only two angels now remain. According to the Talmud, an angel exists to perform one

עַבְדְּכֶם וְלִינוּ וְרַחֲצוּ רַגְלֵיכֶם וְהִשְׁכַּמְתֶּם
וַהֲלַכְתֶּם לְדַרְכְּכֶם וַיֹּאמְרוּ לֹּא כִּי בָרְחוֹב
נָלִין׃ 3 וַיִּפְצַר־בָּם מְאֹד וַיָּסֻרוּ אֵלָיו וַיָּבֹאוּ
אֶל־בֵּיתוֹ וַיַּעַשׂ לָהֶם מִשְׁתֶּה וּמַצּוֹת אָפָה
וַיֹּאכֵלוּ׃
4 טֶרֶם יִשְׁכָּבוּ וְאַנְשֵׁי הָעִיר אַנְשֵׁי סְדֹם
נָסַבּוּ עַל־הַבַּיִת מִנַּעַר וְעַד־זָקֵן כָּל־הָעָם
מִקָּצֶה׃ 5 וַיִּקְרְאוּ אֶל־לוֹט וַיֹּאמְרוּ לוֹ
אַיֵּה הָאֲנָשִׁים אֲשֶׁר־בָּאוּ אֵלֶיךָ הַלָּיְלָה
הוֹצִיאֵם אֵלֵינוּ וְנֵדְעָה אֹתָם׃ 6 וַיֵּצֵא
אֲלֵהֶם לוֹט הַפֶּתְחָה וְהַדֶּלֶת סָגַר
אַחֲרָיו׃ 7 וַיֹּאמַר אַל־נָא אַחַי תָּרֵעוּ׃
8 הִנֵּה־נָא לִי שְׁתֵּי בָנוֹת אֲשֶׁר לֹא־יָדְעוּ

to your servant's house to spend the night, and
bathe your feet; then you may be on your way
early." But they said, "No, we will spend the
night in the square." 3 But he urged them
strongly, so they turned his way and entered
his house. He prepared a feast for them and
baked unleavened bread, and they ate.

4 They had not yet lain down, when the
townspeople, the men of Sodom, young and
old—all the people to the last man—gathered
about the house. 5 And they shouted to Lot and
said to him, "Where are the men who came to
you tonight? Bring them out to us, that we may
be intimate with them." 6 So Lot went out to
them to the entrance, shut the door behind
him, 7 and said, "I beg you, my friends, do not
commit such a wrong. 8 Look, I have two
daughters who have not known a man. Let

2. house Lot, who formerly lived in a tent near Sodom (13:12), has become a townsman, residing in a house within the city. Although he has changed his style of living, he has preserved the virtue of hospitality characteristic of a pastoral society.

be on your way early The strangers are urged to get out of town before the people of Sodom become aware of their presence.

No These messengers are unafraid. Moreover, they must test the inhabitants to learn whether or not their evil reputation is in fact deserved.

the square The Hebrew word *"r'ḥov,"* in the Bible, refers to a broad, open square or plaza.

3. unleavened bread A flat cake baked before the dough has had time to rise. It can be prepared very quickly for unexpected guests.

4. the men of Sodom The townspeople live up to their unsavory reputation; they are true men of Sodom, as described in 13:13 and 18:20ff.

young . . . to the last man Not one decent person can be found.

5. be intimate This means to commit rape (see Judg. 19:22).

LOT'S MORAL RESISTANCE (vv. 6–11)

Lot is faced with a dilemma, for his own morals defy the standards of Sodom. He adheres to his own code of honor. The sacred duty of hospitality gave a guest the right of asylum.

8. I have two daughters A patriarch possessed absolute power over the members of his clan. Lot's tactic mirrors a value system that held daughters in low esteem.

who have not known a man Verse 14 shows that the two girls were betrothed but not yet married. That is why they still lived in Lot's house. According to biblical law, a betrothed

---

specific task, after which the angel disappears. One angel was sent to announce the good news to Abraham and Sarah, one to destroy Sodom, and one to rescue Lot (Gen. R. 50:2). Unlike angels, we human beings have multiple tasks, continuing to live our lives even after we have achieved significant goals.

4. The sin of Sodom was not just that some people acted wickedly (people do that everywhere), but that wickedness became public policy, endorsed and approved by the authorities (PdRE 25).

8. Ramban condemns Lot for this proposal, declaring that a man should face death rather than permit his wife or daughters to be dishonored.

אִ֔ישׁ אוֹצִֽיאָה־נָּ֤א אֶתְהֶן֙ אֲלֵיכֶ֔ם וַעֲשׂ֣וּ
לָהֶ֔ן כַּטּ֖וֹב בְּעֵינֵיכֶ֑ם רַ֠ק לָֽאֲנָשִׁ֤ים הָאֵל֙
אַל־תַּעֲשׂ֣וּ דָבָ֔ר כִּֽי־עַל־כֵּ֥ן בָּ֖אוּ בְּצֵ֥ל
קֹרָתִֽי׃ 9 וַיֹּאמְר֣וּ ׀ גֶּשׁ־הָ֗לְאָה וַיֹּֽאמְרוּ֙
הָאֶחָ֤ד בָּֽא־לָגוּר֙ וַיִּשְׁפֹּ֣ט שָׁפ֔וֹט עַתָּ֕ה נָרַ֥ע
לְךָ֖ מֵהֶ֑ם וַיִּפְצְר֨וּ בָאִ֤ישׁ בְּלוֹט֙ מְאֹ֔ד וַֽיִּגְּשׁ֖וּ
לִשְׁבֹּ֥ר הַדָּֽלֶת׃ 10 וַיִּשְׁלְח֤וּ הָֽאֲנָשִׁים֙ אֶת־
יָדָ֔ם וַיָּבִ֧יאוּ אֶת־ל֛וֹט אֲלֵיהֶ֖ם הַבָּ֑יְתָה
וְאֶת־הַדֶּ֖לֶת סָגָֽרוּ׃ 11 וְֽאֶת־הָאֲנָשִׁ֞ים
אֲשֶׁר־פֶּ֣תַח הַבַּ֗יִת הִכּוּ֙ בַּסַּנְוֵרִ֔ים מִקָּטֹ֖ן
וְעַד־גָּד֑וֹל וַיִּלְא֖וּ לִמְצֹ֥א הַפָּֽתַח׃
12 וַיֹּאמְר֨וּ הָאֲנָשִׁ֜ים אֶל־ל֗וֹט עֹ֚ד מִֽי־לְךָ֣
פֹ֔ה חָתָן֙ וּבָנֶ֣יךָ וּבְנֹתֶ֔יךָ וְכֹ֥ל אֲשֶׁר־לְךָ֖
בָּעִ֑יר הוֹצֵ֖א מִן־הַמָּקֽוֹם׃ 13 כִּֽי־מַשְׁחִתִ֣ים
אֲנַ֔חְנוּ אֶת־הַמָּק֖וֹם הַזֶּ֑ה כִּֽי־גָדְלָ֤ה
צַעֲקָתָם֙ אֶת־פְּנֵ֣י יְהוָ֔ה וַיְשַׁלְּחֵ֥נוּ יְהוָ֖ה
לְשַׁחֲתָֽהּ׃ 14 וַיֵּצֵ֨א ל֜וֹט וַיְדַבֵּ֣ר ׀ אֶל־
חֲתָנָ֣יו ׀ לֹקְחֵ֣י בְנֹתָ֗יו וַיֹּ֙אמֶר֙ ק֤וּמוּ צְּאוּ֙
מִן־הַמָּק֣וֹם הַזֶּ֔ה כִּֽי־מַשְׁחִ֥ית יְהוָ֖ה אֶת־
הָעִ֑יר וַיְהִ֥י כִמְצַחֵ֖ק בְּעֵינֵ֥י חֲתָנָֽיו׃
15 וּכְמוֹ֙ הַשַּׁ֣חַר עָלָ֔ה וַיָּאִ֥יצוּ הַמַּלְאָכִ֖ים
בְּל֣וֹט לֵאמֹ֑ר קוּם֩ קַ֨ח אֶת־אִשְׁתְּךָ֜ וְאֶת־

me bring them out to you, and you may do to
them as you please; but do not do anything to
these men, since they have come under the
shelter of my roof." 9But they said, "Stand back!
The fellow," they said, "came here as an alien,
and already he acts the ruler! Now we will deal
worse with you than with them." And they
pressed hard against the person of Lot, and
moved forward to break the door. 10But the
men stretched out their hands and pulled Lot
into the house with them, and shut the door.
11And the people who were at the entrance of
the house, young and old, they struck with
blinding light, so that they were helpless to
find the entrance.

12Then the men said to Lot, "Whom else
have you here? Sons-in-law, your sons and
daughters, or anyone else that you have in the
city—bring them out of the place. 13For we are
about to destroy this place; because the outcry
against them before the LORD has become so
great that the LORD has sent us to destroy it."
14So Lot went out and spoke to his sons-in-law,
who had married his daughters, and said, "Up,
get out of this place, for the LORD is about to
destroy the city." But he seemed to his sons-in-
law as one who jests.

15As dawn broke, the angels urged Lot on,

woman is considered married, although the marriage has not been sexually consummated. The violator of such a woman incurs the death penalty. This is true in ancient Near Eastern law codes as well.

9. The fellow Literally, "the one," a remark laden with contempt. Lot is being reminded that he is a stranger, without legal rights and protection, entirely dependent on the goodwill of the local community.

11. blinding light A sudden, immobilizing, blazing flash of light.

THE DELIVERANCE OF LOT AND HIS FAMILY (vv. 12–16)

12. Sons-in-law They list possible relatives, not only Lot's immediate family.

13. the outcry The guilt of the city is now beyond all doubt, and its punishment is inevitable.

14. went out To where his intended sons-in-law lived.

who had married This rendering, which is that of the Septuagint (the ancient Greek translation), assumes that Lot had two married daughters in the city.

as one who jests Their lack of seriousness reveals their insensitivity to the moral evil about them.

15. two remaining daughters Literally, "your two daughters who are here."

saying, "Up, take your wife and your two remaining daughters, lest you be swept away because of the iniquity of the city." ¹⁶Still he delayed. So the men seized his hand, and the
hands of his wife and his two daughters—in
the LORD's mercy on him—and brought him
out and left him outside the city. ¹⁷When they
had brought them outside, one said, "Flee for
your life! Do not look behind you, nor stop
anywhere in the Plain; flee to the hills, lest
you be swept away." ¹⁸But Lot said to them,
"Oh no, my lord! ¹⁹You have been so gracious
to your servant, and have already shown me so
much kindness in order to save my life; but I
cannot flee to the hills, lest the disaster overtake
me and I die. ²⁰Look, that town there is near
enough to flee to; it is such a little place! Let me
flee there—it is such a little place—and let my
life be saved." ²¹He replied, "Very well, I will
grant you this favor too, and I will not annihilate the town of which you have spoken.
²²Hurry, flee there, for I cannot do anything
until you arrive there." Hence the town came
to be called Zoar.

²³As the sun rose upon the earth and Lot
entered Zoar, ²⁴the LORD rained upon Sodom
and Gomorrah sulfurous fire from the LORD

שְׁתֵּי בְנֹתֶ֙יךָ֙ הַנִּמְצָאֹ֔ת פֶּן־תִּסָּפֶ֖ה בַּעֲוֺ֣ן
הָעִֽיר: ¹⁶וַֽיִּתְמַהְמָ֓הּ ׀ וַיַּחֲזִ֨קוּ הָאֲנָשִׁ֜ים
בְּיָד֣וֹ וּבְיַד־אִשְׁתּ֗וֹ וּבְיַד֙ שְׁתֵּ֣י בְנֹתָ֔יו
בְּחֶמְלַ֥ת יְהֹוָ֖ה עָלָ֑יו וַיֹּצִאֻ֥הוּ וַיַּנִּחֻ֖הוּ
מִח֥וּץ לָעִֽיר: ¹⁷וַיְהִי֩ כְהוֹצִיאָ֨ם אֹתָ֜ם
הַח֗וּצָה וַיֹּ֙אמֶר֙ הִמָּלֵ֣ט עַל־נַפְשֶׁ֔ךָ אַל־
תַּבִּ֣יט אַחֲרֶ֗יךָ וְאַֽל־תַּעֲמֹ֖ד בְּכָל־הַכִּכָּ֑ר
הָהָ֥רָה הִמָּלֵ֖ט פֶּן־תִּסָּפֶֽה: ¹⁸וַיֹּ֥אמֶר ל֖וֹט
אֲלֵהֶ֑ם אַל־נָ֖א אֲדֹנָֽי: ¹⁹הִנֵּה־נָ֠א מָצָ֨א
עַבְדְּךָ֣ חֵן֮ בְּעֵינֶ֒יךָ֒ וַתַּגְדֵּ֣ל חַסְדְּךָ֗ אֲשֶׁ֤ר
עָשִׂ֙יתָ֙ עִמָּדִ֔י לְהַחֲי֖וֹת אֶת־נַפְשִׁ֑י וְאָנֹכִ֗י
לֹ֤א אוּכַל֙ לְהִמָּלֵ֣ט הָהָ֔רָה פֶּן־תִּדְבָּקַ֥נִי
הָרָעָ֖ה וָמַֽתִּי: ²⁰הִנֵּה־נָ֠א הָעִ֨יר הַזֹּ֧את
קְרֹבָ֛ה לָנ֥וּס שָׁ֖מָּה וְהִ֣יא מִצְעָ֑ר אִמָּלְטָ֙ה
נָּ֜א שָׁ֗מָּה הֲלֹ֥א מִצְעָ֛ר הִ֖וא וּתְחִ֥י נַפְשִֽׁי:
²¹וַיֹּ֣אמֶר אֵלָ֔יו הִנֵּה֙ נָשָׂ֣אתִי פָנֶ֔יךָ גַּ֖ם
לַדָּבָ֣ר הַזֶּ֑ה לְבִלְתִּ֛י הׇפְכִּ֥י אֶת־הָעִ֖יר
אֲשֶׁ֥ר דִּבַּֽרְתָּ: ²²מַהֵר֙ הִמָּלֵ֣ט שָׁ֔מָּה כִּ֣י לֹ֤א
אוּכַל֙ לַעֲשׂ֣וֹת דָּבָ֔ר עַד־בֹּאֲךָ֖ שָׁ֑מָּה עַל־כֵּ֛ן
קָרָ֥א שֵׁם־הָעִ֖יר צֽוֹעַר: ²³הַשֶּׁ֖מֶשׁ יָצָ֣א* עַל־הָאָ֑רֶץ וְל֖וֹט בָּ֥א
צֹֽעֲרָה: ²⁴וַֽיהֹוָ֗ה הִמְטִ֧יר עַל־סְדֹ֛ם וְעַל־

v. 23.   סבירין ומטעין "יצאה"

---

16. the LORD's mercy on him The deliverance of Lot is an act of divine grace, as verse 29
indicates.

17. Do not look behind you Do not linger.
the hills The highlands of Moab.

18. my lord This translation takes the Hebrew word *adonai* here as a nonsacred term.
Some commentators read it as a plural: "my
lords" or "sirs." Others understand it as a direct
plea to God.

20. a little place The Hebrew word translated as "a little place" (*mitz·ar*) is a play on the
place-name *tzo·ar* (Zoar) in verse 22. It is intended to explain, by popular etymology, the

change in Zoar's name from the original Bela
(14:2).

THE CATACLYSM (vv. 23–29)

The passage contains traces of historical memory
that the region was affected by earthquakes. Evidently, one of the last earthquakes had shaped
the lower Jordan Valley region by allowing heat
and gases to escape from the earth. Lightning
then ignited the sulfur and bitumen that were
there, obliterating everything in the area. According to geologic studies, this took place long
before the age of Abraham.

24. the LORD . . . the LORD The repetition

---

15. lest you be swept away "Once destruction begins, it does not discriminate between

the righteous and the wicked" (*Seikhel Tov*).

עֲמֹרָה גָּפְרִית וָאֵשׁ מֵאֵת יְהוָה מִן־
הַשָּׁמָיִם׃ 25 וַיַּהֲפֹךְ אֶת־הֶעָרִים הָאֵל
וְאֵת כָּל־הַכִּכָּר וְאֵת כָּל־יֹשְׁבֵי הֶעָרִים
וְצֶמַח הָאֲדָמָה׃ 26 וַתַּבֵּט אִשְׁתּוֹ מֵאַחֲרָיו
וַתְּהִי נְצִיב מֶלַח׃
27 וַיַּשְׁכֵּם אַבְרָהָם בַּבֹּקֶר אֶל־הַמָּקוֹם
אֲשֶׁר־עָמַד שָׁם אֶת־פְּנֵי יְהוָה׃ 28 וַיַּשְׁקֵף
עַל־פְּנֵי סְדֹם וַעֲמֹרָה וְעַל־כָּל־פְּנֵי אֶרֶץ
הַכִּכָּר וַיַּרְא וְהִנֵּה עָלָה קִיטֹר הָאָרֶץ
כְּקִיטֹר הַכִּבְשָׁן׃
29 וַיְהִי בְּשַׁחֵת אֱלֹהִים אֶת־עָרֵי הַכִּכָּר
וַיִּזְכֹּר אֱלֹהִים אֶת־אַבְרָהָם וַיְשַׁלַּח אֶת־
לוֹט מִתּוֹךְ הַהֲפֵכָה בַּהֲפֹךְ אֶת־הֶעָרִים
אֲשֶׁר־יָשַׁב בָּהֵן לוֹט׃
30 וַיַּעַל לוֹט מִצּוֹעַר וַיֵּשֶׁב בָּהָר וּשְׁתֵּי

out of heaven. 25 He annihilated those cities and
the entire Plain, and all the inhabitants of the
cities and the vegetation of the ground. 26 Lot's
wife looked back, and she thereupon turned
into a pillar of salt.

27 Next morning, Abraham hurried to the
place where he had stood before the LORD,
28 and, looking down toward Sodom and Gomorrah and all the land of the Plain, he saw the
smoke of the land rising like the smoke of a
kiln.

29 Thus it was that, when God destroyed the
cities of the Plain and annihilated the cities
where Lot dwelt, God was mindful of Abraham
and removed Lot from the midst of the upheaval.

30 Lot went up from Zoar and settled in the
hill country with his two daughters, for he was

of this word and the phrase "out of heaven" both emphasize the conviction that what occurred was not a random accident of nature but an instance of God's direct intervention in human affairs.

sulfurous fire "Sulfur" is Latin for "burning stone," or "brimstone" in Old English.

26. looked back She lingered in flight and was overwhelmed by the rapidly spreading devastation.

a pillar of salt This image must have been suggested by some unique salt-rock formation in the vicinity of the Dead Sea. The origin of the salt tradition no doubt lies in the presence of Mount Sodom (Jebel Usdum), the base of which is a ridge of rock salt that extends for about 5 miles (8 km).

27. Abraham hurried to the place His argument with God had ended on an uncertain note. Now he hastens to his vantage point (18:16) from which he sees immense destruction and realizes that Sodom did not have even 10 righteous men.

THE BIRTH OF MOAB AND AMMON
(vv. 30–38)

The concluding section of this chapter describes the incestuous origin of the peoples of Moab and Ammon. Yet the right of Moab and Ammon to live peaceably in their homelands is acknowledged as God-given in Deuteronomy (2:9,19). Furthermore, it should be recalled that King David was descended from a Moabite woman, as we are told in the Book of Ruth (4:17–22).

30. Lot went up from Zoar It is not known why Lot was afraid to stay in Zoar. Perhaps earth tremors continued to be felt there. Later sources have preserved a tradition that all five cities of the Plain—including Zoar—were destroyed. This would explain why Lot's daughters believed the catastrophe was universal.

---

26. she thereupon turned into a pillar of salt Why salt? Salt is a preservative. It keeps things from changing. Lot's wife sinned in her reluctance to break with immorality in the past, even as Lot himself "delayed" (v. 16), torn between rejection of where he was and fear of the unknown future. Lot's wife is judged more leniently by Ramban. As he sees it, she had difficulty leaving Sodom not because she was fond of the lifestyle there but because she had children there, her daughters and sons-in-law who chose not to leave.

afraid to dwell in Zoar; and he and his two
daughters lived in a cave. 31 And the older one
said to the younger, "Our father is old, and
there is not a man on earth to consort with us
in the way of all the world. 32 Come, let us make
our father drink wine, and let us lie with him,
that we may maintain life through our father."
33 That night they made their father drink wine,
and the older one went in and lay with her
father; he did not know when she lay down
or when she rose. 34 The next day the older
one said to the younger, "See, I lay with Father
last night; let us make him drink wine tonight
also, and you go and lie with him, that we may
maintain life through our father." 35 That night
also they made their father drink wine, and the
younger one went and lay with him; he did not
know when she lay down or when she rose.

36 Thus the two daughters of Lot came to be
with child by their father. 37 The older one bore
a son and named him Moab; he is the father of
the Moabites of today. 38 And the younger also
bore a son, and she called him Ben-ammi; he is
the father of the Ammonites of today.

בְנֹתָיו עִמּוֹ כִּי יָרֵא לָשֶׁבֶת בְּצוֹעַר וַיֵּשֶׁב
בַּמְּעָרָה הוּא וּשְׁתֵּי בְנֹתָיו׃ 31 וַתֹּאמֶר
הַבְּכִירָה אֶל־הַצְּעִירָה אָבִינוּ זָקֵן וְאִישׁ
אֵין בָּאָרֶץ לָבוֹא עָלֵינוּ כְּדֶרֶךְ כָּל־
הָאָרֶץ׃ 32 לְכָה נַשְׁקֶה אֶת־אָבִינוּ יַיִן
וְנִשְׁכְּבָה עִמּוֹ וּנְחַיֶּה מֵאָבִינוּ זָרַע׃
33 וַתַּשְׁקֶיןָ אֶת־אֲבִיהֶן יַיִן בַּלַּיְלָה הוּא
וַתָּבֹא הַבְּכִירָה וַתִּשְׁכַּב אֶת־אָבִיהָ וְלֹא־
יָדַע בְּשִׁכְבָהּ וּבְקוּמָהּ*׃ 34 וַיְהִי מִמָּחֳרָת
וַתֹּאמֶר הַבְּכִירָה אֶל־הַצְּעִירָה הֵן־
שָׁכַבְתִּי אֶמֶשׁ אֶת־אָבִי נַשְׁקֶנּוּ יַיִן גַּם־
הַלַּיְלָה וּבֹאִי שִׁכְבִי עִמּוֹ וּנְחַיֶּה מֵאָבִינוּ
זָרַע׃ 35 וַתַּשְׁקֶיןָ גַּם בַּלַּיְלָה הַהוּא אֶת־
אֲבִיהֶן יָיִן וַתָּקָם הַצְּעִירָה וַתִּשְׁכַּב עִמּוֹ
וְלֹא־יָדַע בְּשִׁכְבָהּ וּבְקֻמָהּ׃
36 וַתַּהֲרֶיןָ שְׁתֵּי בְנוֹת־לוֹט מֵאֲבִיהֶן׃
37 וַתֵּלֶד הַבְּכִירָה בֵּן וַתִּקְרָא שְׁמוֹ מוֹאָב
הוּא אֲבִי־מוֹאָב עַד־הַיּוֹם׃ 38 וְהַצְּעִירָה
גַם־הִוא יָלְדָה בֵּן וַתִּקְרָא שְׁמוֹ בֶּן־עַמִּי
הוּא אֲבִי בְנֵי־עַמּוֹן עַד־הַיּוֹם׃ ס

20 Abraham journeyed from there to the
region of the Negeb and settled between Ka-

כ וַיִּסַּע מִשָּׁם אַבְרָהָם אַרְצָה הַנֶּגֶב
וַיֵּשֶׁב בֵּין־קָדֵשׁ וּבֵין שׁוּר וַיָּגָר בִּגְרָר׃

v. 33. נקוד על ו'

32. drink wine The implication is clear: Lot never would have been a willing partner to such an act.

maintain life There is no way of knowing whether their intent was renewal of the entire human race or just the perpetuation of their father's name. The narrative does not explicitly condemn the actions of the two daughters, although the fact that they are not named implies censure.

37. Moab A popular etymology, based on the Hebrew word *me-avi,* "from [my] father."

38. Ben-ammi Literally, "son of my [paternal] kinsman." The name reflects the fact that the Ammonites are generally called *b'nei ammon* in the Bible.

ABRAHAM, SARAH, AND ABIMELECH (20:1–21:34)

THE SEIZURE OF SARAH (20:1–2)

1. Abraham journeyed from there That is, from the district of Mamre–Hebron, Abraham's only domicile since the separation from Lot.

the region of the Negeb The northern Negeb in the Beer-sheba Basin is the site of fertile soil and some vegetation.

settled Abraham made a prolonged stay in this region.

2 וַיֹּ֧אמֶר אַבְרָהָ֛ם אֶל־שָׂרָ֥ה אִשְׁתּ֖וֹ אֲחֹ֣תִי
ה֑וא וַיִּשְׁלַ֗ח אֲבִימֶ֙לֶךְ֙ מֶ֣לֶךְ גְּרָ֔ר וַיִּקַּ֖ח
אֶת־שָׂרָֽה׃ 3 וַיָּבֹ֧א אֱלֹהִ֛ים אֶל־אֲבִימֶ֖לֶךְ
בַּחֲל֣וֹם הַלָּ֑יְלָה וַיֹּ֣אמֶר ל֗וֹ הִנְּךָ֥ מֵת֙ עַל־
הָאִשָּׁ֣ה אֲשֶׁר־לָקַ֔חְתָּ וְהִ֖וא בְּעֻ֥לַת בָּֽעַל׃
4 וַאֲבִימֶ֕לֶךְ לֹ֥א קָרַ֖ב אֵלֶ֑יהָ וַיֹּאמַ֕ר אֲדֹנָ֕י
הֲג֥וֹי גַּם־צַדִּ֖יק תַּהֲרֹֽג׃ 5 הֲלֹ֨א ה֤וּא אָֽמַר־
לִי֙ אֲחֹ֣תִי הִ֔וא וְהִֽיא־גַם־ה֥וּא אָמְרָ֖ה אָחִ֣י
ה֑וּא בְּתָם־לְבָבִ֛י וּבְנִקְיֹ֥ן כַּפַּ֖י עָשִׂ֥יתִי זֹֽאת׃
6 וַיֹּאמֶר֩ אֵלָ֨יו הָאֱלֹהִ֜ים בַּחֲלֹ֗ם גַּ֣ם אָנֹכִ֤י
יָדַ֙עְתִּי֙ כִּ֤י בְתָם־לְבָֽבְךָ֙ עָשִׂ֣יתָ זֹּ֔את
וָאֶחְשֹׂ֧ךְ גַּם־אָנֹכִ֛י אֽוֹתְךָ֖ מֵחֲטוֹ*־לִ֑י עַל־כֵּ֥ן
לֹא־נְתַתִּ֖יךָ לִנְגֹּ֥עַ אֵלֶֽיהָ׃ 7 וְעַתָּ֗ה הָשֵׁ֞ב
אֵֽשֶׁת־הָאִישׁ֙ כִּֽי־נָבִ֣יא ה֔וּא וְיִתְפַּלֵּ֥ל

v. 6. חסר א׳

desh and Shur. While he was sojourning in Gerar, 2 Abraham said of Sarah his wife, "She is my sister." So King Abimelech of Gerar had Sarah brought to him. 3 But God came to Abimelech in a dream by night and said to him, "You are to die because of the woman that you have taken, for she is a married woman." 4 Now Abimelech had not approached her. He said, "O Lord, will You slay people even though innocent? 5 He himself said to me, 'She is my sister!' And she also said, 'He is my brother.' When I did this, my heart was blameless and my hands were clean." 6 And God said to him in the dream, "I knew that you did this with a blameless heart, and so I kept you from sinning against Me. That was why I did not let you touch her. 7 Therefore, restore the man's wife—since he is a prophet, he will intercede for you—to save your life. If you fail to restore

between Kadesh and Shur The line between the oasis of Kadesh on the southern border of Canaan and the Egyptian defense wall in the eastern Delta of the Nile. This is the southernmost limit of Abraham's wanderings.

sojourning in Gerar At some point, the patriarch left the Kadesh–Shur grazing region to visit the royal city of Gerar. Perhaps he wanted to trade pastoral products and purchase supplies in the city; perhaps he was attracted by the rich pasture lands in the vicinity. In Gerar he is an alien (*ger*), unprotected and subject to mistreatment.

2. She is my sister Abraham takes the initiative in passing off Sarah as his sister without asking her for permission to do so. This is unlike the case in Gen. 12:10–20ff.

GOD'S ADMONITION TO ABIMELECH
(vv. 3–7)

3. in a dream Dreams were accepted as media of divine communication throughout the ancient world. Here the reproach conveyed by the king's dream is clear and no interpreter is needed.

4. approached her This is a euphemism for sexual relations. The reason for Abimelech's abstention is withheld here, to be revealed only later (v. 6).

O Lord *Adonai* is used here, and not the divine name *YHVH*, probably because the king is not of the Abrahamic faith. See Comment to 18:3. *Adonai* very often is substituted for God's name *YHVH*, which is used more sparingly because of its great sanctity.

will You slay The king appeals to God's justice, which also was Abraham's approach in the story of Sodom and Gomorrah.

people That is, my household. The Hebrew word translated "people" (*goy*) usually means "nation," but on occasion it has the sense of "people," "folk," or "group."

5. heart . . . hands This refers to sincere intent and upright behavior.

6. ***And God said*** God affirms only that the possible adultery was unintended, nothing else.

I kept you from How this happened is not disclosed until verses 17–18.

sinning against Me Israelite law regards adultery as a violation of a husband's rights and as an offense against divinely given standards of morality. The former alone was the general view of the ancient Near Eastern law codes.

7. he is a prophet The Hebrew word for prophet (*navi*) appears here for the first time in the Bible. It means "one who receives the (divine) call," "one who proclaims," or "a spokesman." It is in the latter sense that Abraham is here designated a prophet whose role, as stated immediately, is to intercede on behalf of others.

בַּעַדְךָ וֶחְיֵה וְאִם־אֵינְךָ מֵשִׁיב דַּע כִּי־מוֹת
תָּמוּת אַתָּה וְכָל־אֲשֶׁר־לָךְ׃
8 וַיַּשְׁכֵּם אֲבִימֶלֶךְ בַּבֹּקֶר וַיִּקְרָא לְכָל־
עֲבָדָיו וַיְדַבֵּר אֶת־כָּל־הַדְּבָרִים הָאֵלֶּה
בְּאָזְנֵיהֶם וַיִּירְאוּ הָאֲנָשִׁים מְאֹד׃ 9 וַיִּקְרָא
אֲבִימֶלֶךְ לְאַבְרָהָם וַיֹּאמֶר לוֹ מֶה־עָשִׂיתָ
לָּנוּ וּמֶה־חָטָאתִי לָךְ כִּי־הֵבֵאתָ עָלַי וְעַל־
מַמְלַכְתִּי חֲטָאָה גְדֹלָה מַעֲשִׂים אֲשֶׁר לֹא־
יֵעָשׂוּ עָשִׂיתָ עִמָּדִי׃ 10 וַיֹּאמֶר אֲבִימֶלֶךְ
אֶל־אַבְרָהָם מָה רָאִיתָ כִּי עָשִׂיתָ אֶת־
הַדָּבָר הַזֶּה׃ 11 וַיֹּאמֶר אַבְרָהָם כִּי אָמַרְתִּי
רַק אֵין־יִרְאַת אֱלֹהִים בַּמָּקוֹם הַזֶּה
וַהֲרָגוּנִי עַל־דְּבַר אִשְׁתִּי׃ 12 וְגַם־אָמְנָה
אֲחֹתִי בַת־אָבִי הִוא אַךְ לֹא בַת־אִמִּי
וַתְּהִי־לִי לְאִשָּׁה׃ 13 וַיְהִי כַּאֲשֶׁר הִתְעוּ
אֹתִי אֱלֹהִים מִבֵּית אָבִי וָאֹמַר לָהּ זֶה
חַסְדֵּךְ אֲשֶׁר תַּעֲשִׂי עִמָּדִי אֶל כָּל־הַמָּקוֹם
אֲשֶׁר נָבוֹא שָׁמָּה אִמְרִי־לִי אָחִי הוּא׃

her, know that you shall die, you and all that are
yours."
8Early next morning, Abimelech called his
servants and told them all that had happened;
and the men were greatly frightened. 9Then
Abimelech summoned Abraham and said to
him, "What have you done to us? What wrong
have I done that you should bring so great a
guilt upon me and my kingdom? You have
done to me things that ought not to be done.
10What, then," Abimelech demanded of Abraham, "was your purpose in doing this thing?"
11"I thought," said Abraham, "surely there is
no fear of God in this place, and they will kill
me because of my wife. 12And besides, she is in
truth my sister, my father's daughter though
not my mother's; and she became my wife. 13So
when God made me wander from my father's
house, I said to her, 'Let this be the kindness
that you shall do me: whatever place we come
to, say there of me: He is my brother.'"

you shall die The excuse that there was no intent will no longer be credible.

ABRAHAM'S DEFENSE (vv. 8–13)

The dream makes such an impression on the king that he convokes his council of state, whose members are thoroughly alarmed by his report. Abraham is summoned. Confronted by Abimelech, he tries to defend himself.

9. ***so great a guilt*** Literally, "a great sin," a phrase that reflects legal terminology found in ancient Near Eastern documents. The "great sin" is adultery.

11. *they will kill me* Abraham believed that the king would have had him killed to avoid committing adultery. Adultery would be an offense far graver than the murder of a husband who, as an alien, was outside the protection of the law.

12. *she is in truth my sister* The statement must be derived from a tradition of great antiquity, because marrying a half-sister was forbidden in later Israel.

my father's daughter though not my mother's Although abhorrence of incest is nearly universal, the definition of prohibited kinship marriage varies widely among societies.

13. *made me wander* That is, gave me the command, "Go forth from your native land and from your father's house" (12:1).

whatever place The danger was seen as a recurring one. Kidnaping women for the royal

---

CHAPTER 20

11. there is no fear of God in this place. "Fear of God" is the closest term in the Bible for what we call "religion." It refers not to a theological position (e.g., belief in God's existence or nature) or to an emotional state (e.g., fear of punishment) but to an awareness that certain kinds of behavior are unconditionally wrong. A verse in Psalms (111:10), "the beginning of wisdom is the fear of the LORD," refers to that sort of awareness. The midwives in Exodus who disobey Pharaoh's edict to kill the Israelite babies are described as "fearing God" (Exod. 1:17).

[14]Abimelech took sheep and oxen, and male
and female slaves, and gave them to Abraham;
and he restored his wife Sarah to him. [15]And
Abimelech said, "Here, my land is before you;
settle wherever you please." [16]And to Sarah he
said, "I herewith give your brother a thousand
pieces of silver; this will serve you as vindication before all who are with you, and you
are cleared before everyone." [17]Abraham then
prayed to God, and God healed Abimelech and
his wife and his slave girls, so that they bore
children; [18]for the LORD had closed fast every
womb of the household of Abimelech because
of Sarah, the wife of Abraham.

14 וַיִּקַּח אֲבִימֶלֶךְ צֹאן וּבָקָר וַעֲבָדִים
וּשְׁפָחֹת וַיִּתֵּן לְאַבְרָהָם וַיָּשֶׁב לוֹ אֵת
שָׂרָה אִשְׁתּוֹ׃ 15 וַיֹּאמֶר אֲבִימֶלֶךְ הִנֵּה
אַרְצִי לְפָנֶיךָ בַּטּוֹב בְּעֵינֶיךָ שֵׁב׃
16 וּלְשָׂרָה אָמַר הִנֵּה נָתַתִּי אֶלֶף כֶּסֶף
לְאָחִיךְ הִנֵּה הוּא־לָךְ כְּסוּת עֵינַיִם לְכֹל
אֲשֶׁר אִתָּךְ וְאֵת כֹּל וְנֹכָחַת׃ 17 וַיִּתְפַּלֵּל
אַבְרָהָם אֶל־הָאֱלֹהִים וַיִּרְפָּא אֱלֹהִים
אֶת־אֲבִימֶלֶךְ וְאֶת־אִשְׁתּוֹ וְאַמְהֹתָיו
וַיֵּלֵדוּ׃ 18 כִּי־עָצֹר עָצַר יְהוָה בְּעַד כָּל־
רֶחֶם לְבֵית אֲבִימֶלֶךְ עַל־דְּבַר שָׂרָה
אֵשֶׁת אַבְרָהָם׃ ס

21 The LORD took note of Sarah as He had
promised, and the LORD did for Sarah as He

כא וַיהוָה פָּקַד אֶת־שָׂרָה כַּאֲשֶׁר
אָמָר וַיַּעַשׂ יְהוָה לְשָׂרָה כַּאֲשֶׁר דִּבֵּר׃

harem was feared to be widespread, not an exceptional experience. No special insult to Abimelech was intended.

He is my brother The absence of children would reinforce her claim.

ABIMELECH'S RESTITUTION, ABRAHAM'S INTERCESSION (vv. 14–18)

14. gave them to Abraham Abraham, considered to be the injured party, receives reparations from the king.

15. settle No longer will he be an alien in Abimelech's realm.

16. a thousand pieces of silver Either the worth of the gifts listed in verse 14 or a separate award granted for Sarah.

vindication The Hebrew phrase *k'sut einayim* means, literally, "a covering of eyes." The payment can be seen as a declaration that Sarah's honor was not violated, so that the eyes of others are henceforth closed to what occurred and she is not to be scorned.

17–18. bore children . . . closed fast every womb Abimelech and his household enjoy the restoration of sexual vigor.

THE BIRTH OF ISAAC (21:1–7)

Some time has passed since Abraham first heard the divine call promising him great posterity (12:2, 15:5). Although this pledge has been affirmed repeatedly, he has experienced constant disappointment and has faced periodic crises that threatened its fulfillment. God's word now comes to fruition.

1. took note The Hebrew stem פקד often is used to describe God's intervention in human

---

17. Though one could see Abimelech as the aggrieved party, the Midrash praises Abraham for so readily and wholeheartedly forgiving one who did him wrong and then sincerely apologized (*Midrash Ha-Gadol*). Similarly, the Sages condemn the person who refuses to forgive someone who sincerely apologizes (BT BK 93a). Only after Abraham prays for others are his prayers for his own needs answered.

CHAPTER 21

This chapter and the next make up the Torah readings for the two days of *Rosh ha-Shanah.* Why were these chapters chosen? Perhaps to

had spoken. ²Sarah conceived and bore a son to Abraham in his old age, at the set time of which God had spoken. ³Abraham gave his newborn son, whom Sarah had borne him, the name of Isaac. ⁴And when his son Isaac was eight days old, Abraham circumcised him, as God had commanded him. ⁵Now Abraham was a hundred years old when his son Isaac was born to him. ⁶Sarah said, "God has brought me laughter; everyone who hears will laugh with me." ⁷And she added,

"Who would have said to Abraham
That Sarah would suckle children!
Yet I have borne a son in his old age."

⁸The child grew up and was weaned, and Abraham held a great feast on the day that Isaac was weaned.

²וַתַּ֩הַר֩ וַתֵּ֨לֶד שָׂרָ֧ה לְאַבְרָהָ֛ם בֵּ֖ן לִזְקֻנָ֑יו לַמּוֹעֵ֕ד אֲשֶׁר־דִּבֶּ֥ר אֹת֖וֹ אֱלֹהִֽים׃ ³וַיִּקְרָ֨א אַבְרָהָ֜ם אֶֽת־שֶׁם־בְּנ֧וֹ הַנּֽוֹלַד־ל֛וֹ אֲשֶׁר־יָלְדָה־לּ֥וֹ שָׂרָ֖ה יִצְחָֽק׃ ⁴וַיָּ֤מָל אַבְרָהָם֙ אֶת־יִצְחָ֣ק בְּנ֔וֹ בֶּן־שְׁמֹנַ֖ת יָמִ֑ים כַּֽאֲשֶׁ֛ר צִוָּ֥ה אֹת֖וֹ אֱלֹהִֽים׃ ⁵וְאַבְרָהָ֖ם בֶּן־מְאַ֣ת שָׁנָ֑ה בְּהִוָּ֣לֶד ל֔וֹ אֵ֖ת יִצְחָ֥ק בְּנֽוֹ׃ ⁶וַתֹּ֣אמֶר שָׂרָ֔ה צְחֹ֕ק עָ֥שָׂה לִ֖י אֱלֹהִ֑ים כָּל־הַשֹּׁמֵ֖עַ יִֽצְחַק־לִֽי׃ ⁷וַתֹּ֗אמֶר מִ֤י מִלֵּל֙ לְאַבְרָהָ֔ם הֵינִ֥יקָה בָנִ֖ים שָׂרָ֑ה כִּֽי־יָלַ֥דְתִּי בֵ֖ן לִזְקֻנָֽיו׃ ⁸וַיִּגְדַּ֥ל הַיֶּ֖לֶד וַיִּגָּמַ֑ל וַיַּ֤עַשׂ אַבְרָהָם֙ מִשְׁתֶּ֣ה גָד֔וֹל בְּי֖וֹם הִגָּמֵ֥ל אֶת־יִצְחָֽק׃

חמישי

affairs. Here it connotes making good an unfulfilled promise. The birth of Isaac thus marks a new and momentous stage in biblical history.

as He had promised The reference is to 17:16.

2. at the set time See 17:21 and 18:10,14.

3. Isaac The name was chosen by God. Thus Isaac is the only patriarch who does not undergo a change of name. For the meaning of "Isaac," see Comment to 17:19.

4. eight days old He is the first person reported to have been circumcised at that age, thereby emphasizing his role as the one true heir to the Abrahamic covenant. (Ishmael was circumcised at the age of 13.)

had commanded Referring to 17:12.

5. a hundred years old This chronologic

note echoes the incredulity expressed by Abraham in 17:17.

6. brought me laughter The laughter is now joyous, in contrast to the skeptical laughter recorded in 17:17 and 18:12ff.

7. who would have said This utterance of Sarah, in Hebrew, has the form of a song consisting of three short clauses of three words each.

THE EXPULSION OF HAGAR AND ISHMAEL   (vv. 8–21)

8. was weaned Weaning at about age three marked the completion of the first significant stage in an infant's life cycle. It, therefore, was a festive occasion.

make the point that the real story of humanity is a story of parents and children, husbands and wives, not of kings and wars. Perhaps to emphasize that Judaism is meaningful not when it is a private faith but when it is passed from parent to child.

1. took note This is not only a statement about God's remembering and fulfilling a promise. It places Sarah at the center of events. Isaac, Sarah's child, rather than Ishmael, will be Abraham's true heir because God's covenant is with Abraham and Sarah. Many modern lit-

urgies include the Matriarchs in the opening blessing of the Amidah, and praise God as blessing Sarah as well as being "the shield of Abraham."

6. everyone who hears will laugh [rejoice] with me "My experience will give new hope to other childless couples" (Gen. R. 53:8).

7. That Sarah would suckle children The plural noun (rather than the singular "child") gave rise to a legend that Sarah's breasts overflowed with so much milk that she was able to nurse many infants in addition to Isaac. A tradi-

[9]Sarah saw the son whom Hagar the Egyptian had borne to Abraham playing. [10]She said to Abraham, "Cast out that slave-woman and her son, for the son of that slave shall not share in the inheritance with my son Isaac." [11]The matter distressed Abraham greatly, for it concerned a son of his. [12]But God said to Abraham, "Do not be distressed over the boy or your slave; whatever Sarah tells you, do as she says, for it is through Isaac that offspring shall be continued for you. [13]As for the son of the slave-woman, I will make a nation of him, too, for he is your seed."

[14]Early next morning Abraham took some bread and a skin of water, and gave them to Hagar. He placed them over her shoulder, together with the child, and sent her away. And

9 וַתֵּרֶא שָׂרָה אֶת־בֶּן־הָגָר הַמִּצְרִית אֲשֶׁר־
יָלְדָה לְאַבְרָהָם מְצַחֵק׃ 10 וַתֹּאמֶר
לְאַבְרָהָם גָּרֵשׁ הָאָמָה הַזֹּאת וְאֶת־בְּנָהּ
כִּי לֹא יִירַשׁ בֶּן־הָאָמָה הַזֹּאת עִם־בְּנִי
עִם־יִצְחָק׃ 11 וַיֵּרַע הַדָּבָר מְאֹד בְּעֵינֵי
אַבְרָהָם עַל אוֹדֹת בְּנוֹ׃ 12 וַיֹּאמֶר אֱלֹהִים
אֶל־אַבְרָהָם אַל־יֵרַע בְּעֵינֶיךָ עַל־הַנַּעַר
וְעַל־אֲמָתֶךָ כֹּל אֲשֶׁר תֹּאמַר אֵלֶיךָ שָׂרָה
שְׁמַע בְּקֹלָהּ כִּי בְיִצְחָק יִקָּרֵא לְךָ זָרַע׃
13 וְגַם אֶת־בֶּן־הָאָמָה לְגוֹי אֲשִׂימֶנּוּ כִּי
זַרְעֲךָ הוּא׃
14 וַיַּשְׁכֵּם אַבְרָהָם ׀ בַּבֹּקֶר וַיִּקַּח־לֶחֶם
וְחֵמַת מַיִם וַיִּתֵּן אֶל־הָגָר שָׂם עַל־שִׁכְמָהּ
וְאֶת־הַיֶּלֶד וַיְשַׁלְּחֶהָ וַתֵּלֶךְ וַתֵּתַע בְּמִדְבַּר

9. playing He either was amusing himself or was playing with Isaac.

10. Cast out that slave-woman Ishmael was entitled to a share of Abraham's estate. Inheritance rights, according to ancient Near Eastern law, are a legal consequence of a father's acceptance of an infant as his legitimate son. Abraham undoubtedly recognized Ishmael as such (16:15, 17:23,25ff.). The key to Sarah's demand lies in another ancient Near Eastern law, a stipulation that a father may grant freedom to a slave woman and the children she has borne him, in which case they forfeit all claims to his property (see Judg. 11:1–3). Sarah is asking Abraham to exercise that right.

11. The matter distressed Abraham Fatherly love and moral concerns inhibit Abraham from giving his consent.

12. God said to Abraham Apparently, this happened in a night vision, because it is immediately followed by "early next morning."

14. over her shoulder This refers only to the bread and water container. Ishmael could hardly have been carried by his mother.

child The Hebrew word translated here as "child" (*yeled*) can be used for a youth and is

---

tion suggests that all those who convert to Judaism are the descendants of those children nursed by Sarah.

9. Sarah fears that the danger of Ishmael corrupting his younger brother is greater than the prospect of Isaac being a good influence on Ishmael (Ḥafetz Ḥayyim). This is why she urges Abraham to banish Hagar and Ishmael. Some of the Sages try to justify Sarah's behavior by interpreting the word "playing" as a reference to Ishmael's cruelty and lewdness, perhaps even sexual molestation (Gen. R. 53:11). Alter suggests that Ishmael was *m'tzaḥek,* "playing at being Isaac," comporting himself as if he were Abraham's heir and continuer of the covenant.

11. One *midrash* says that this banishment of Abraham's firstborn son and the child's mother was the hardest of his many trials (PdRE 30:67a).

12. do as she says Literally, "listen to her voice." Hirsch takes that to mean, "don't only listen to her words, her demands; listen to your wife's anguish, her fear, the tone of pleading in the voice of the woman you have been married to for so many years."

Commentators who view Ishmael unfavorably note that the reference to him as "playing, laughing" (*m'tzaḥek*) is in the present tense, whereas Isaac's name, associated with laughter (*Yitzḥak*) is in the future tense. Although forces of evildoers may laugh now, the good will have cause to rejoice in the end.

בְּאֵר שָׁבַע׃ 15 וַיִּכְלוּ הַמַּיִם מִן־הַחֵמֶת
וַתַּשְׁלֵךְ אֶת־הַיֶּלֶד תַּחַת אַחַד הַשִּׂיחִם׃
16 וַתֵּלֶךְ וַתֵּשֶׁב לָהּ מִנֶּגֶד הַרְחֵק כִּמְטַחֲוֵי
קֶשֶׁת כִּי אָמְרָה אַל־אֶרְאֶה בְּמוֹת הַיָּלֶד
וַתֵּשֶׁב מִנֶּגֶד וַתִּשָּׂא אֶת־קֹלָהּ וַתֵּבְךְּ׃
17 וַיִּשְׁמַע אֱלֹהִים אֶת־קוֹל הַנַּעַר וַיִּקְרָא
מַלְאַךְ אֱלֹהִים ׀ אֶל־הָגָר מִן־הַשָּׁמַיִם
וַיֹּאמֶר לָהּ מַה־לָּךְ הָגָר אַל־תִּירְאִי כִּי־
שָׁמַע אֱלֹהִים אֶל־קוֹל הַנַּעַר בַּאֲשֶׁר הוּא־
שָׁם׃ 18 קוּמִי שְׂאִי אֶת־הַנַּעַר וְהַחֲזִיקִי
אֶת־יָדֵךְ בּוֹ כִּי־לְגוֹי גָּדוֹל אֲשִׂימֶנּוּ׃
19 וַיִּפְקַח אֱלֹהִים אֶת־עֵינֶיהָ וַתֵּרֶא בְּאֵר
מָיִם וַתֵּלֶךְ וַתְּמַלֵּא אֶת־הַחֵמֶת מַיִם
וַתַּשְׁקְ אֶת־הַנָּעַר׃ 20 וַיְהִי אֱלֹהִים אֶת־
הַנַּעַר וַיִּגְדָּל וַיֵּשֶׁב בַּמִּדְבָּר וַיְהִי רֹבֶה
קַשָּׁת׃ 21 וַיֵּשֶׁב בְּמִדְבַּר פָּארָן וַתִּקַּח־לוֹ
ששי אִמּוֹ אִשָּׁה מֵאֶרֶץ מִצְרָיִם׃ פ

she wandered about in the wilderness of Beer-
sheba. 15 When the water was gone from the
skin, she left the child under one of the bushes,
16 and went and sat down at a distance, a bow-
shot away; for she thought, "Let me not look on
as the child dies." And sitting thus afar, she
burst into tears.

17 God heard the cry of the boy, and an angel
of God called to Hagar from heaven and said to
her, "What troubles you, Hagar? Fear not, for
God has heeded the cry of the boy where he is.
18 Come, lift up the boy and hold him by the
hand, for I will make a great nation of him."
19 Then God opened her eyes and she saw a well
of water. She went and filled the skin with
water, and let the boy drink. 20 God was with
the boy and he grew up; he dwelt in the wilderness and became a bowman. 21 He lived in the
wilderness of Paran; and his mother got a wife
for him from the land of Egypt.

interchangeable with *na·ar,* which can also refer both to a baby and to a young man.

she wandered Presumably, she set out for her native Egypt but lost her way.

15. When the water was gone Had she not lost her way, her original supplies would have been sufficient.

17. God heard That is, heeded. The phrase has the same meaning as the name Ishmael.

called to Hagar from heaven Both sons of Abraham are saved at a critical moment by an angelic "voice from heaven" (see 22:11).

18. a great nation Unlike Isaac, Ishmael is promised only nationhood, not national territory.

20. a bowman The tradition that the Ishmaelites were professional marksmen is preserved in Isa. 21:17, which speaks of the bows of Kedar's warriors. Kedar is listed as a son of Ishmael in Gen. 25:13.

ABRAHAM'S PACT WITH ABIMELECH
(vv. 22–34)

Abraham makes his first acquisition—a well at Beer-sheba. His rights are acknowledged and guaranteed by the king.

---

17. God heard the cry of the boy But we never read that Ishmael cried aloud! Thus we learn that God can hear the silent cries of the anguished heart, even when no words are uttered (Mendel of Worka).

18. hold him by the hand Hagar need not feel helpless. She can at least be with her child, so that her presence will allay his fears. The literal meaning of the Hebrew here is, "make your hand strong in his." Often, when we are fearful or depressed, we gain strength and courage by taking someone else by the hand and helping that person.

19. God opened her eyes God performed a miracle, not by creating a well where none had been before, but by opening Hagar's eyes so that she could see what she previously had been blind to, the existence of life-sustaining resources in her world. Once again, we encounter the theme of seeing.

22 At that time Abimelech and Phicol, chief of his troops, said to Abraham, "God is with you in everything that you do. 23 Therefore swear to me here by God that you will not deal falsely with me or with my kith and kin, but will deal with me and with the land in which you have sojourned as loyally as I have dealt with you." 24 And Abraham said, "I swear it."

25 Then Abraham reproached Abimelech for the well of water which the servants of Abimelech had seized. 26 But Abimelech said, "I do not know who did this; you did not tell me, nor have I heard of it until today." 27 Abraham took sheep and oxen and gave them to Abimelech, and the two of them made a pact. 28 Abraham then set seven ewes of the flock by themselves, 29 and Abimelech said to Abraham, "What mean these seven ewes which you have set apart?" 30 He replied, "You are to accept these seven ewes from me as proof that I dug this well." 31 Hence that place was called Beer-sheba, for there the two of them swore an oath. 32 When they had concluded the pact at Beer-

ששי 22 וַיְהִי בָּעֵת הַהִוא וַיֹּאמֶר אֲבִימֶלֶךְ
וּפִיכֹל שַׂר־צְבָאוֹ אֶל־אַבְרָהָם לֵאמֹר
אֱלֹהִים עִמְּךָ בְּכֹל אֲשֶׁר־אַתָּה עֹשֶׂה:
23 וְעַתָּה הִשָּׁבְעָה לִּי בֵאלֹהִים הֵנָּה אִם־
תִּשְׁקֹר לִי וּלְנִינִי וּלְנֶכְדִּי כַּחֶסֶד אֲשֶׁר־
עָשִׂיתִי עִמְּךָ תַּעֲשֶׂה עִמָּדִי וְעִם־הָאָרֶץ
אֲשֶׁר־גַּרְתָּה בָּהּ: 24 וַיֹּאמֶר אַבְרָהָם אָנֹכִי
אִשָּׁבֵעַ:
25 וְהוֹכִחַ אַבְרָהָם אֶת־אֲבִימֶלֶךְ עַל־אֹדוֹת
בְּאֵר הַמַּיִם אֲשֶׁר גָּזְלוּ עַבְדֵי אֲבִימֶלֶךְ:
26 וַיֹּאמֶר אֲבִימֶלֶךְ לֹא יָדַעְתִּי מִי עָשָׂה
אֶת־הַדָּבָר הַזֶּה וְגַם־אַתָּה לֹא־הִגַּדְתָּ לִּי
וְגַם אָנֹכִי לֹא שָׁמַעְתִּי בִּלְתִּי הַיּוֹם:
27 וַיִּקַּח אַבְרָהָם צֹאן וּבָקָר וַיִּתֵּן
לַאֲבִימֶלֶךְ וַיִּכְרְתוּ שְׁנֵיהֶם בְּרִית: 28 וַיַּצֵּב
אַבְרָהָם אֶת־שֶׁבַע כִּבְשֹׂת הַצֹּאן לְבַדְּהֶן:
29 וַיֹּאמֶר אֲבִימֶלֶךְ אֶל־אַבְרָהָם מָה הֵנָּה
שֶׁבַע כְּבָשֹׂת הָאֵלֶּה אֲשֶׁר הִצַּבְתָּ לְבַדָּנָה:
30 וַיֹּאמֶר כִּי אֶת־שֶׁבַע כְּבָשֹׂת תִּקַּח מִיָּדִי
בַּעֲבוּר תִּהְיֶה־לִּי לְעֵדָה כִּי חָפַרְתִּי אֶת־
הַבְּאֵר הַזֹּאת: 31 עַל־כֵּן קָרָא לַמָּקוֹם
הַהוּא בְּאֵר שָׁבַע כִּי שָׁם נִשְׁבְּעוּ
שְׁנֵיהֶם: 32 וַיִּכְרְתוּ בְרִית בִּבְאֵר שָׁבַע

22. At that time Soon after the expulsion of Ishmael.

Abimelech The deliberate omission of his royal title emphasizes that he and Abraham are considered to be equals.

said to Abraham The entire action occurs in the Beer-sheba region. Hence, Abraham must have left Gerar for this place after the episode recounted in chapter 20.

God is with you This is an acknowledgment of Abraham's success and power.

23. not deal falsely Abimelech is suggesting a mutual nonaggression pact.

kith and kin The Hebrew phrase *nin v'nekhed*—literally, "son and grandson"—simply means "posterity" or "forever."

as loyally as This refers back to 20:14–16.

25. seized They had prevented Abraham from free access to water for his herds.

27. sheep and oxen The animals may have been part of the pact-making ceremony.

29. these seven ewes The seven ewes are not part of the traditional ceremony but a separate transaction. By accepting them as a gift, the king publicly acknowledges Abraham's ownership of the well.

31. Beer-sheba The name can mean either "well of oath" or "well of seven." The narrative,

---

22. After the birth of Isaac, Abimelech realizes that the clan of Abraham is there to stay.

sheba, Abimelech and Phicol, chief of his troops, departed and returned to the land of the Philistines. 33 [Abraham] planted a tamarisk at Beer-sheba, and invoked there the name of the LORD, the Everlasting God. 34 And Abraham resided in the land of the Philistines a long time.

וַיָּקָם אֲבִימֶלֶךְ וּפִיכֹל שַׂר־צְבָאוֹ וַיָּשֻׁבוּ
אֶל־אֶרֶץ פְּלִשְׁתִּים׃ 33 וַיִּטַּע אֶשֶׁל בִּבְאֵר
שָׁבַע וַיִּקְרָא־שָׁם בְּשֵׁם יְהוָה אֵל עוֹלָם׃
34 וַיָּגָר אַבְרָהָם בְּאֶרֶץ פְּלִשְׁתִּים יָמִים
רַבִּים׃ פ

22 Some time afterward, God put Abraham to the test. He said to him, "Abraham,"

יעי **כב** וַיְהִי אַחַר הַדְּבָרִים הָאֵלֶּה
וְהָאֱלֹהִים נִסָּה אֶת־אַבְרָהָם וַיֹּאמֶר אֵלָיו

like the parallel story in connection with Isaac (Gen. 26:23–33), fuses both meanings.

33. [Abraham] The name does not appear in the Hebrew here but is present in ancient versions of the text.

a tamarisk This tall, shady tree develops deep roots, requires little water, and is particularly suitable for the sandy soil of the northern Negeb area. We are not told why Abraham planted the tree.

THE AKEDAH: THE BINDING OF ISAAC (22:1–19)

This is the climactic event in Abraham's life. God asks the aged patriarch to offer his son Isaac as a sacrifice. This ultimate trial of faith has come to be known as "the *Akedah,*" from the Hebrew stem meaning "to bind" (עקד) in verse 9. With the *Akedah,* Abraham's spiritual odyssey, which began with God's call at Haran, comes to an end.

GOD TESTS ABRAHAM (vv. 1–2)

1. Some time afterward The phrase indicates an indefinite connection with previous

---

33. *tamarisk* The Hebrew word for this tree is *eshel.* This word has been taken to be an acronym signifying eating-drinking-lodging (*akhilah-sh'tiyah-linah*). The Vilna Gaon interpreted this tree as not only facilitating Abraham's practice of hospitality but symbolizing a new start for the world, to atone for the failures of Adam (eating), Noah (drinking), and Lot (incestuous relations).

CHAPTER 22

The narrative of the binding and near sacrifice of Isaac, the *Akedah,* is an unforgettably harrowing story that defies easy interpretation. God commands Abraham to sacrifice the child born to him after so many years of longing. Is this a test of Abraham's faith and readiness to obey, as the opening verse suggests? Is it a protest against the widely observed ancient practice of sacrificing firstborn children as the firstborn of the flocks were sacrificed? Is it to teach us that, for the believer, the voice of God must override the voice of human conscience—what Kierkegaard called the "teleological suspension of the ethical"?

The medieval philosopher Joseph Albo taught that God, who knew how Abraham would respond, wanted Abraham to discover the great depth of his faith. "The reward for potential good deeds is less than the reward for actual good deeds."

In an intriguing interpretation, Theodore Reik notes the parallel between the story of the *Akedah* and the coming-of-age ordeals imposed on adolescent boys in many primitive societies. A boy on the verge of outgrowing childhood is taken away from the company of women and made to undergo a life-threatening experience, which sometimes included a simulated death. Afterward, he is welcomed into the company of adult males and initiated into the lore of the tribe.

The *Akedah* was recalled from another perspective by persecuted Jews of later genera-

and he answered, "Here I am." 2And He said,
"Take your son, your favored one, Isaac, whom
you love, and go to the land of Moriah, and
offer him there as a burnt offering on one of
the heights that I will point out to you." 3So
early next morning, Abraham saddled his ass
and took with him two of his servants and his

אַבְרָהָם וַיֹּאמֶר הִנֵּנִי׃ 2 וַיֹּאמֶר קַח־נָא
אֶת־בִּנְךָ אֶת־יְחִידְךָ אֲשֶׁר־אָהַבְתָּ אֶת־
יִצְחָק וְלֶךְ־לְךָ אֶל־אֶרֶץ הַמֹּרִיָּה וְהַעֲלֵהוּ
שָׁם לְעֹלָה עַל אַחַד הֶהָרִים אֲשֶׁר אֹמַר
אֵלֶיךָ׃ 3 וַיַּשְׁכֵּם אַבְרָהָם בַּבֹּקֶר וַיַּחֲבֹשׁ
אֶת־חֲמֹרוֹ וַיִּקַּח אֶת־שְׁנֵי נְעָרָיו אִתּוֹ וְאֵת

events. No specific age is given for Isaac, but he is now old enough to carry a load of firewood and to ask an intelligent question based on experience and observation.

God put Abraham to the test This information is divulged to the reader, although not to Abraham, to remove any possible misunderstanding on the reader's part that God requires human sacrifice.

He said Abraham receives God's call in a night dream or a vision.

Here I am The Hebrew word *"hinneni,"* the only word Abraham utters to God during the entire episode, expresses an attitude of conscientious receptivity and response.

2. And He said The descriptive terms are listed in ascending order of endearment (son, favored one, Isaac, whom you love). This emphasizes the enormity of God's request and the agonizing nature of the decision Abraham must make (see 12:1).

Take your son The Hebrew adds the untranslated particle *na* to the imperative for "take." This makes it a strong, emphatic expression with a sense of urgency.

your favored one Literally, "your only one."

whom you love This is the first time that the Hebrew verb meaning "to love" (אהב) appears in the Bible, used here in connection with the parent–child relationship. It is next used (24:67) in the husband–wife relationship.

go Hebrew: *lekh l'kha.* This phrase echoes 12:1, and thus it serves here to close the narrative cycle about Abraham.

the land of Moriah The site remains unknown. In 2 Chron. 2:1 it is identified with Jerusalem.

that I will point out The manner of communication is not specified.

ABRAHAM MEETS THE CHALLENGE
(vv. 3–10)

3. early next morning The aged patriarch makes no verbal response, not even "Here I am!" (*hinneni*), but rises early to fulfill God's charge. Remarkably, Sarah is never even mentioned in this chapter.

two of his servants An eminent person such as Abraham would be accompanied by two attendants.

---

tions. Shalom Spiegel has written: "In the light of the historical reality of the second-century persecution under the Roman Empire, it seemed almost as though something of the splendor and awe of the biblical Akedah story was diminished. Who cares about some ancient, far off in time, who was merely *thought of* as a *possible* sacrifice on the altar, but who was delivered from danger, whom no misfortune overtook, when right before your eyes, in the immediate present, fathers and sons en masse ascend the executioner's block to be butchered and burned, literally butchered and burned?" Many medieval Jewish communities suffering persecution saw themselves as re-enacting the drama of the *Akedah* without the redemptive ending.

1. Here I am Abraham responds to God with a readiness to listen and serve. Abraham responds to Isaac with the same word (*hinneni*, v. 7), prompting the comment that Abraham was as responsive to the voice of his child as he was to the voice of God.

2. The Sages imagine a dialogue between God and Abraham:

"Take your son." / "I have two sons."

"Your only son." / "Each is an only son to his mother."

"Whom you love." / "I love them both."

Finally God is explicit: "Isaac" (BT Sanh. 89b).

3. The reader is struck by the contrast between Abraham's readiness to argue on behalf of the people of Sodom and Gomorrah (18:23ff.) and his reluctance to argue in defense of his own child.

son Isaac. He split the wood for the burnt offering, and he set out for the place of which God
had told him. 4On the third day Abraham
looked up and saw the place from afar. 5Then
Abraham said to his servants, "You stay here
with the ass. The boy and I will go up there; we
will worship and we will return to you."

6Abraham took the wood for the burnt offering and put it on his son Isaac. He himself
took the firestone and the knife; and the two
walked off together. 7Then Isaac said to his
father Abraham, "Father!" And he answered,
"Yes, my son." And he said, "Here are the firestone and the wood; but where is the sheep for
the burnt offering?" 8And Abraham said, "God
will see to the sheep for His burnt offering, my
son." And the two of them walked on together.

9They arrived at the place of which God had
told him. Abraham built an altar there; he laid

יִצְחָק בְּנוֹ וַיְבַקַּע עֲצֵי עֹלָה וַיָּקָם וַיֵּלֶךְ אֶל־
הַמָּקוֹם אֲשֶׁר־אָמַר־לוֹ הָאֱלֹהִים׃ 4 בַּיּוֹם
הַשְּׁלִישִׁי וַיִּשָּׂא אַבְרָהָם אֶת־עֵינָיו וַיַּרְא
אֶת־הַמָּקוֹם מֵרָחֹק׃ 5 וַיֹּאמֶר אַבְרָהָם
אֶל־נְעָרָיו שְׁבוּ־לָכֶם פֹּה עִם־הַחֲמוֹר וַאֲנִי
וְהַנַּעַר נֵלְכָה עַד־כֹּה וְנִשְׁתַּחֲוֶה וְנָשׁוּבָה
אֲלֵיכֶם׃

6 וַיִּקַּח אַבְרָהָם אֶת־עֲצֵי הָעֹלָה וַיָּשֶׂם
עַל־יִצְחָק בְּנוֹ וַיִּקַּח בְּיָדוֹ אֶת־הָאֵשׁ וְאֶת־
הַמַּאֲכֶלֶת וַיֵּלְכוּ שְׁנֵיהֶם יַחְדָּו׃ 7 וַיֹּאמֶר
יִצְחָק אֶל־אַבְרָהָם אָבִיו וַיֹּאמֶר אָבִי
וַיֹּאמֶר הִנֶּנִּי בְנִי וַיֹּאמֶר הִנֵּה הָאֵשׁ
וְהָעֵצִים וְאַיֵּה הַשֶּׂה לְעֹלָה׃ 8 וַיֹּאמֶר
אַבְרָהָם אֱלֹהִים יִרְאֶה־לּוֹ הַשֶּׂה לְעֹלָה בְּנִי
וַיֵּלְכוּ שְׁנֵיהֶם יַחְדָּו׃

9 וַיָּבֹאוּ אֶל־הַמָּקוֹם אֲשֶׁר אָמַר־לוֹ

He split the wood Because he does not know the precise destination, he cannot be certain he will find fuel there.

4. On the third day Three days, in the biblical worldview, constitute a period of significant duration, especially in connection with travel. The long trek allows Abraham the opportunity for sober reflection about his assent to God's request. His resolve, nevertheless, is not weakened.

saw the place from afar Perhaps it is an existing sacred site, or perhaps he instinctively recognizes it as the proper place.

5. we will return Abraham uses the plural form to conceal from Isaac the true purpose of the journey.

6. Abraham took the wood He removed it from the beast of burden. He himself carried the dangerous articles—the firestone and the knife—so that the boy would not be harmed on the way. Were Isaac to be injured, he could not be offered as a proper, unblemished sacrifice.

firestone A flint that produces fire.

the two walked off together There appears to be perfect harmony between father and son.

7. where is the sheep The oppressive silence is broken by Isaac's simple query. Is a suspicion of the awful truth beginning to dawn on him?

8. God will see to the sheep The father's feeble reply surely sustains whatever doubts Isaac now feels, especially in an age when human sacrifice is possible.

walked on together The repetition of these words from verse 6 heightens the tension. The bond between the father and the son remains unbroken.

9. They arrived at the place The narrative busies itself with the details of the preparatory

---

4. he saw the place Abraham saw the Presence of God on the mountaintop (*Makom*—meaning place—is one of God's names in Jewish tradition). He asked Isaac if he saw it as well, and he did. He asked the servants if they saw it, but they did not. Abraham, perceiving the distinction between those who are sensitive to God's presence and those who are blind to it, left the servants behind as he rose to a higher level with Isaac (Gen. R. 56:2).

8. God will see to the sheep Once again, we encounter the thematic verb of seeing. One suspects that Isaac, at this point, intuited that he himself was to be the offering. Both father

out the wood; he bound his son Isaac; he laid him on the altar, on top of the wood. [10]And Abraham picked up the knife to slay his son. [11]Then an angel of the LORD called to him from heaven: "Abraham! Abraham!" And he answered, "Here I am." [12]And he said, "Do not raise your hand against the boy, or do anything to him. For now I know that you fear God, since you have not withheld your son, your favored one, from Me." [13]When Abraham looked up, his eye fell upon a ram, caught in the thicket by its horns. So Abraham went and took the ram and offered it up as a burnt offering in place of his son. [14]And Abraham named that site Ado-

הָאֱלֹהִים֒ וַיִּ֤בֶן שָׁם֙ אַבְרָהָם֙ אֶת־הַמִּזְבֵּ֔חַ
וַיַּעֲרֹ֖ךְ אֶת־הָעֵצִ֑ים וַֽיַּעֲקֹד֙ אֶת־יִצְחָ֣ק בְּנ֔וֹ
וַיָּ֤שֶׂם אֹתוֹ֙ עַל־הַמִּזְבֵּ֔חַ מִמַּ֖עַל לָעֵצִֽים׃
[10]וַיִּשְׁלַ֤ח אַבְרָהָם֙ אֶת־יָד֔וֹ וַיִּקַּ֖ח אֶת־
הַֽמַּאֲכֶ֑לֶת לִשְׁחֹ֖ט אֶת־בְּנֽוֹ׃ וַיִּקְרָ֨א
אֵלָ֜יו מַלְאַ֤ךְ יְהֹוָה֙ מִן־הַשָּׁמַ֔יִם וַיֹּ֖אמֶר
אַבְרָהָ֣ם ׀ [11]אַבְרָהָ֑ם וַיֹּ֖אמֶר הִנֵּֽנִי׃
[12]וַיֹּ֗אמֶר אַל־תִּשְׁלַ֤ח יָֽדְךָ֙ אֶל־הַנַּ֔עַר וְאַל־
תַּ֥עַשׂ ל֖וֹ מְא֑וּמָה כִּ֣י ׀ עַתָּ֣ה יָדַ֗עְתִּי כִּֽי־
יְרֵ֤א אֱלֹהִים֙ אַ֔תָּה וְלֹ֥א חָשַׂ֛כְתָּ אֶת־בִּנְךָ֥
אֶת־יְחִֽידְךָ֖ מִמֶּֽנִּי׃ [13]וַיִּשָּׂ֨א אַבְרָהָ֜ם אֶת־
עֵינָ֗יו וַיַּרְא֙ וְהִנֵּה־אַ֔יִל אַחַר֙ נֶֽאֱחַ֣ז בַּסְּבַ֔ךְ
בְּקַרְנָ֑יו וַיֵּ֤לֶךְ אַבְרָהָם֙ וַיִּקַּ֣ח אֶת־הָאַ֔יִל
וַיַּעֲלֵ֥הוּ לְעֹלָ֖ה תַּ֥חַת בְּנֽוֹ׃ [14]וַיִּקְרָ֧א
אַבְרָהָ֛ם שֵֽׁם־הַמָּק֥וֹם הַה֖וּא יְהֹוָ֣ה ׀

v. 13. בנוסח אחר "אחד".

procedures. Both Abraham and Isaac are silent. The anguish of this moment is beyond words.

bound   The Hebrew stem of the word translated as "bound" (עקד) is found nowhere else in connection with sacrifices in the Bible.

GOD ACKNOWLEDGES ABRAHAM'S FIDELITY   (vv. 11–12)

11. called to him from heaven   Angels normally need to travel between heaven and earth (see 28:12), as well as from place to place on earth (see 18:22). The urgency of the moment, however, dictates an exceptional mode of angelic intervention, as it did in 21:17.

Abraham! Abraham!   The repetition conveys urgency and a special relationship between the one addressed and the one who calls.

12. And he said   In the Bible, God and His angels often interchange imperceptibly.

for now I know   In the biblical view, the genuinely righteous man must deserve that status through demonstrated action. The act might go

unfulfilled, but its value lies as much in the intention of the doer as in any final enactment.

THE SUBSTITUTION OF A RAM   (v. 13)

Abraham interprets the sudden appearance of a ram to mean that a substitute animal offering is desired in place of Isaac.

13. a ram   All contemporary printed editions and a few ancient renderings read here *ayil aḥar*, which can be taken to mean "a ram behind [him]" or "a ram, later [caught]." Many ancient versions and several medieval manuscripts read "a single ram" (*ayil eḥad*), which differs by only one similar-looking letter. This translation follows the latter tradition.

THE NAMING OF THE ALTAR   (v. 14)

In accordance with patriarchal practice, the site of a revelation becomes sacred and is given a name reminiscent of the occasion.

14. whence the present saying   A popular saying arose based on this event.

and son missed an opportunity for open conversation about a matter of supreme importance to each of them. This father and son never speak with each other again.

14. On the mount of the LORD there is vision   We can paraphrase the name that Abra-

ham gives the site as "the high point where I saw God." (This is an intriguing contrast to Gen. 16:14, where the name that Hagar gives the well that saved her life can be understood as "the low point where I saw God" [*B'.er la-Ḥai Ro·i*]. The *parashah*, which begins with Abra-

nai-yireh, whence the present saying, "On the mount of the LORD there is vision."

15The angel of the LORD called to Abraham a second time from heaven, 16and said, "By Myself I swear, the LORD declares: Because you have done this and have not withheld your son, your favored one, 17I will bestow My blessing upon you and make your descendants as numerous as the stars of heaven and the sands on the seashore; and your descendants shall seize the gates of their foes. 18All the nations of the earth shall bless themselves by your descendants, because you have obeyed My command." 19Abraham then returned to his servants, and they departed together for Beer-sheba; and Abraham stayed in Beer-sheba.

20Some time later, Abraham was told,

יִרְאֶה אֲשֶׁר יֵאָמֵר הַיּוֹם בְּהַר יְהוָה
יֵרָאֶה׃
15 וַיִּקְרָא מַלְאַךְ יְהוָה אֶל־אַבְרָהָם שֵׁנִית
מִן־הַשָּׁמָיִם׃ 16 וַיֹּאמֶר בִּי נִשְׁבַּעְתִּי נְאֻם־
יְהוָה כִּי יַעַן אֲשֶׁר עָשִׂיתָ אֶת־הַדָּבָר הַזֶּה
וְלֹא חָשַׂכְתָּ אֶת־בִּנְךָ אֶת־יְחִידֶךָ׃ 17 כִּי־
בָרֵךְ אֲבָרֶכְךָ וְהַרְבָּה אַרְבֶּה אֶת־זַרְעֲךָ
כְּכוֹכְבֵי הַשָּׁמַיִם וְכַחוֹל אֲשֶׁר עַל־שְׂפַת
הַיָּם וְיִרַשׁ זַרְעֲךָ אֵת שַׁעַר אֹיְבָיו׃
18 וְהִתְבָּרְכוּ בְזַרְעֲךָ כֹּל גּוֹיֵי הָאָרֶץ עֵקֶב
אֲשֶׁר שָׁמַעְתָּ בְּקֹלִי׃ 19 וַיָּשָׁב אַבְרָהָם
אֶל־נְעָרָיו וַיָּקֻמוּ וַיֵּלְכוּ יַחְדָּו אֶל־בְּאֵר
שָׁבַע וַיֵּשֶׁב אַבְרָהָם בִּבְאֵר שָׁבַע׃ פ

מפטיר 20 וַיְהִי אַחֲרֵי הַדְּבָרִים הָאֵלֶּה וַיֻּגַּד

there is vision The Hebrew word *yera·eh* literally means "He/it shall be seen," but here the subject of the verb is unclear. The Septuagint renders, "On the mount the LORD appears." Note that Mount Moriah is identified with the site of the ancient Temple Mount in 2 Chron. 3:1.

REAFFIRMATION OF THE BLESSINGS (vv. 15–18)

16. Because you have done this Because Abraham has demonstrated his willingness to forfeit his posterity in obedience to God's will, it is fitting that all previous promises now be reaffirmed as a reward for the patriarch's devotion to God.

THE OFFSPRING OF NAHOR (vv. 20–24)

These verses establish the genealogy of Abraham's brother Nahor and forge a link between the *Akedah* and chapter 24. If the blessings of Abraham are to be fulfilled, Isaac must marry and establish a family. The mention of Rebekah, Bethuel, Milcah, Nahor, and Aram, hints at Isaac's forthcoming marriage to Rebekah, daughter of Bethuel, son of Milcah, of the city of Nahor in Aram-naharaim.

---

ham encountering God in the form of three strangers, which contains so many references to seeing and not seeing, concludes with Abraham finding God in this searing experience. We come to see God not only in the daily experiences of the beauty and order of nature; the companionship of others; and our abilities to grow, to learn, and to share. We come to see God as well in our peak experiences—of love, marriage, parenthood, personal success, and being delivered from danger—and in our ability to survive and transcend misfortune.

17. your descendants shall seize the gates of their foes Hirsch chooses to see this blessing as something other than a military victory. He takes "gates" to mean the public forums where people sat to discuss significant matters. Thus Abraham is given the blessing that his ideas will prevail in many lands.

19. Abraham then returned to his servants Where was Isaac? Estranged from his father? The Sages suggest that he went to devote himself to the study of Torah at the *y'shivah* of Shem and Ever. Menaḥem Mendel of Kotzk taught that although it was hard for Abraham to bind Isaac on the altar, it was just as hard to release him. For Abraham realized that Isaac, for the rest of his life, would remember that his father had almost killed him.

לְאַבְרָהָם לֵאמֹר הִנֵּה יָלְדָה מִלְכָּה גַם־
הִוא בָּנִים לְנָחוֹר אָחִיךָ: 21 אֶת־עוּץ
בְּכֹרוֹ וְאֶת־בּוּז אָחִיו וְאֶת־קְמוּאֵל אֲבִי
אֲרָם: 22 וְאֶת־כֶּשֶׂד וְאֶת־חֲזוֹ וְאֶת־פִּלְדָּשׁ
וְאֶת־יִדְלָף וְאֵת בְּתוּאֵל: 23 וּבְתוּאֵל יָלַד
אֶת־רִבְקָה שְׁמֹנָה אֵלֶּה יָלְדָה מִלְכָּה
לְנָחוֹר אֲחִי אַבְרָהָם: 24 וּפִילַגְשׁוֹ וּשְׁמָהּ
רְאוּמָה וַתֵּלֶד גַּם־הִוא אֶת־טֶבַח וְאֶת־
גַּחַם וְאֶת־תַּחַשׁ וְאֶת־מַעֲכָה: ס

"Milcah too has borne children to your brother
Nahor: 21 Uz the first-born, and Buz his broth-
er, and Kemuel the father of Aram; 22 and
Chesed, Hazo, Pildash, Jidlaph, and
Bethuel"—23 Bethuel being the father of Re-
bekah. These eight Milcah bore to Nahor,
Abraham's brother. 24 And his concubine,
whose name was Reumah, also bore children:
Tebah, Gaham, Tahash, and Maacah.

This genealogic list echoes historical reality and represents a league of tribes tied to one another by kinship or treaty. Often, when such a list includes the words "wife" and "concubine," it is reflecting certain relationships within the tribal confederation. Thus wife tribes were most likely more influential and may have constituted the original core of a tribal league. The concubine tribes would then have been later affiliates, subordinates who were absorbed into the confederation of tribes. Such tribal organizations were common throughout the ancient Semitic world.

20. Milcah too has borne children The earlier genealogy of 11:29 mentions Milcah together with Sarah.

Nahor An important city in ancient Mesopotamia, situated in the upper Euphrates region in the Balīkh Valley. The derivation of all these tribes from Nahor implies that the city was the original center of the confederation.

21. Uz The attribution of "first-born" status to Uz means that this tribe constituted the oldest, or most powerful, element within the group (see 10:23). Of Milcah's eight sons, nothing at all is known about Kemuel, Pildash, or Jidlaph. They must have disappeared from the scene of history early in the 2nd millennium B.C.E.

Buz Situated in northern Arabia.

22. Chesed The supposed ancestor of the Chaldeans (Hebrew, *kasdim;* see 11:31).

Hazo A region in Arabia.

Bethuel A Semitic personal name. No tribe or geographic entity with this name is known.

23. Rebekah The wife-to-be of Isaac.

---

23. Rebekah Now that it is clear that Isaac will survive, Abraham's next concern will be finding a suitable wife for him, one who would share with him the responsibility of carrying on the faith of Abraham and Sarah.

Tradition identifies the site of the *Akedah* with Mount Moriah, the mountain on which Solomon's Temple was built. (The rock at the heart of Jerusalem's Dome of the Rock at the Mosque of Omar, built on the Temple's site, is alleged by the Sages to be the rock on which the *Akedah* took place.) Why was the Temple built there, rather than on Mount Sinai, the site of revelation? Because a place where an ancestor of Israel was prepared to offer his life for the sake of God is holier than the place where God gave the Torah to the people Israel (Ḥayyim of Tzanz).

הפטרת וירא

HAFTARAH FOR VA-YERA

2 KINGS 4:1–37 (*Ashk'nazim*)
2 KINGS 4:1–23 (*S'fardim*)

This *haftarah* presents two miracles performed by the prophet Elisha. In the first miracle, Elisha provides a poor widow with oil, so that she might redeem her children, taken in debt-bondage, and live on the proceeds of the remainder (4:1–7). In the second, he tells a barren woman that she will give birth to a child, as a reward for her charity. Later, after that child suffers a fatal illness, the prophet restores him to life (4:8–37). These wonders are part of a cycle of tales about help and healing that commence with the death of Elijah (mid-9th century B.C.E.) and the descent of his spirit upon his disciple, Elisha (2 Kings 2:1–15).

At first sight there seems to be little connection between the miracle of food for a debtor widow and the resurrection of a wealthy woman's son. Yet the two narratives are intertwined, with intriguing and complex relations. Food provides the first point of contact. Its absence in the first text is the reason for the miracle of plenty, and its presence in the second text (as charity) is the reason for the announcement of the woman's pregnancy and giving birth. Significantly, both narratives include the query "What can I/we do for you?" (4:2,13), and the subsequent fulfillment of a request. The second point of connection revolves around the restoration of children. In the first case, children who had been taken away are restored to their mother; in the second, a child given up for dead is restored to life. Furthermore, each story uses the same phrase about the enactment of a miracle. In the first, the woman is told to "go in and shut the door behind you" (v. 4). In the second account, Elisha himself "went in" to the child's room (actually his own guest room; cf. v. 21) and "shut the door behind the two of them" (v. 33).

Such thematic and verbal patterning suggests a close tie between the two tales. They may draw on a cluster of oral traditions with similar stylistic shaping. Such sharing of motifs within this miracle cycle extends beyond it. For Elisha repeats actions that had been performed by his teacher, Elijah (in 1 Kings 17:7–24).

This *haftarah,* in its present form, has the character of an artful narrative. Something like this tale of wonders must have circulated among the prophets' disciples—reworked as retold, restyled as reworked, and eventually written down for generations to come. Note the recounting of Elisha's miraculous deed in 2 Kings 8:4–6. Similarly, the great deeds of God, from the Exodus on, were told from mouth to ear, as memory and message, until the day they were collected and inscribed as sacred scripture for all time (see Exod. 10:1–2; Ps. 78:2–8, 106:2).

RELATION OF THE *HAFTARAH* TO THE *PARASHAH*

In the *parashah,* Abraham at Mamre extends hospitality to three unexpected visitors. Immediately thereafter, he receives the divine promise that "at the same season (*la-mo·ed*) next year (*ka-et ḥayyah*)" the barren Sarah will have a child (Gen. 18:14, cf. 18:10). There is no statement that this constitutes a reward for hospitality, but in the *haftarah,* reward for hospitality is an explicit theme. The wealthy woman of Shunem who provides food and lodging for Elisha is rewarded with the announcement that "at this season (*la-mo·ed ha-zeh*) next year (*ka-et ḥayyah*), you will be embracing a son" (2 Kings 4:15).

4 A certain woman, the wife of one of the
disciples of the prophets, cried out to Elisha:
"Your servant my husband is dead, and you
know how your servant revered the LORD.
And now a creditor is coming to seize my two
children as slaves." 2Elisha said to her, "What
can I do for you? Tell me, what have you in the
house?" She replied, "Your maidservant has
nothing at all in the house, except a jug of
oil." 3"Go," he said, "and borrow vessels outside, from all your neighbors, empty vessels, as
many as you can. 4Then go in and shut the door
behind you and your children, and pour [oil]
into all those vessels, removing each one as it is
filled."

5She went away and shut the door behind
her and her children. They kept bringing [ves-
sels] to her and she kept pouring. 6When the
vessels were full, she said to her son, "Bring me
another vessel." He answered her, "There are
no more vessels"; and the oil stopped. 7She
came and told the man of God, and he said,
"Go sell the oil and pay your debt, and you and
your children can live on the rest."

8One day Elisha visited Shunem. A wealthy
woman lived there, and she urged him to have a
meal; and whenever he passed by, he would
stop there for a meal. 9Once she said to her
husband, "I am sure it is a holy man of God
who comes this way regularly. 10Let us make a
small enclosed upper chamber and place a bed,
a table, a chair, and a lampstand there for him,
so that he can stop there whenever he comes to
us." 11One day he came there; he retired to the
upper chamber and lay down there. 12He said
to his servant Gehazi, "Call that Shunammite

ד וְאִשָּׁה אַחַת מִנְּשֵׁי בְנֵי־הַנְּבִיאִים
צָעֲקָה אֶל־אֱלִישָׁע לֵאמֹר עַבְדְּךָ אִישִׁי
מֵת וְאַתָּה יָדַעְתָּ כִּי עַבְדְּךָ הָיָה יָרֵא
אֶת־יְהוָה וְהַנֹּשֶׁה בָּא לָקַחַת אֶת־שְׁנֵי
יְלָדַי לוֹ לַעֲבָדִים׃ 2 וַיֹּאמֶר אֵלֶיהָ אֱלִישָׁע
מָה אֶעֱשֶׂה־לָּךְ הַגִּידִי לִי מַה־יֶּשׁ־לכי לָךְ
בַּבָּיִת וַתֹּאמֶר אֵין לְשִׁפְחָתְךָ כֹל בַּבַּיִת כִּי
אִם־אָסוּךְ שָׁמֶן׃ 3 וַיֹּאמֶר לְכִי שַׁאֲלִי־לָךְ
כֵּלִים מִן־הַחוּץ מֵאֵת כָּל־שכנכי שְׁכֵנָיִךְ
כֵּלִים רֵקִים אַל־תַּמְעִיטִי׃ 4 וּבָאת וְסָגַרְתְּ
הַדֶּלֶת בַּעֲדֵךְ וּבְעַד־בָּנַיִךְ וְיָצַקְתְּ עַל כָּל־
הַכֵּלִים הָאֵלֶּה וְהַמָּלֵא תַּסִּיעִי׃
5 וַתֵּלֶךְ מֵאִתּוֹ וַתִּסְגֹּר הַדֶּלֶת בַּעֲדָהּ וּבְעַד
בָּנֶיהָ הֵם מַגִּשִׁים אֵלֶיהָ וְהִיא מיצקת
מוֹצָקֶת׃ 6 וַיְהִי ׀ כִּמְלֹאת הַכֵּלִים וַתֹּאמֶר
אֶל־בְּנָהּ הַגִּישָׁה אֵלַי עוֹד כֶּלִי וַיֹּאמֶר
אֵלֶיהָ אֵין עוֹד כֶּלִי וַיַּעֲמֹד הַשָּׁמֶן׃ 7 וַתָּבֹא
וַתַּגֵּד לְאִישׁ הָאֱלֹהִים וַיֹּאמֶר לְכִי מִכְרִי
אֶת־הַשֶּׁמֶן וְשַׁלְּמִי אֶת־נשיכי נִשְׁיֵךְ וְאַתְּ
בניכי וּבָנַיִךְ תִּחְיִי בַּנּוֹתָר׃ פ

8 וַיְהִי הַיּוֹם וַיַּעֲבֹר אֱלִישָׁע אֶל־שׁוּנֵם וְשָׁם
אִשָּׁה גְדוֹלָה וַתַּחֲזֶק־בּוֹ לֶאֱכָל־לָחֶם וַיְהִי
מִדֵּי עָבְרוֹ יָסֻר שָׁמָּה לֶאֱכָל־לָחֶם׃
9 וַתֹּאמֶר אֶל־אִישָׁהּ הִנֵּה־נָא יָדַעְתִּי כִּי
אִישׁ אֱלֹהִים קָדוֹשׁ הוּא עֹבֵר עָלֵינוּ
תָּמִיד׃ 10 נַעֲשֶׂה־נָּא עֲלִיַּת־קִיר קְטַנָּה
וְנָשִׂים לוֹ שָׁם מִטָּה וְשֻׁלְחָן וְכִסֵּא
וּמְנוֹרָה וְהָיָה בְּבֹאוֹ אֵלֵינוּ יָסוּר שָׁמָּה׃
11 וַיְהִי הַיּוֹם וַיָּבֹא שָׁמָּה וַיָּסַר אֶל־
הָעֲלִיָּה וַיִּשְׁכַּב־שָׁמָּה׃ 12 וַיֹּאמֶר אֶל־גֵּיחֲזִי

2 Kings 4:1. A certain woman . . . cried out to Elisha This cry (*tza·akah*) denotes an appeal for legal aid. It is used here in the context of a creditor who has seized a widow's children for repayment of a debt. A biblical exhortation warns creditors against keeping debtors' garments as security overnight, noting that compassionate God will come to the poor person's rescue if such a one "cries out" (*yitz·ak*) to Him in distress (Exod. 22:24–26, cf. 22:20–22).

woman." He called her, and she stood before
him. 13He said to him, "Tell her, 'You have gone
to all this trouble for us. What can we do for
you? Can we speak in your behalf to the king or
to the army commander?'" She replied, "I live
among my own people." 14"What then can be
done for her?" he asked. "The fact is," said
Gehazi, "she has no son, and her husband is
old." 15"Call her," he said. He called her, and she
stood in the doorway. 16And Elisha said, "At
this season next year, you will be embracing a
son." She replied, "Please, my lord, man of
God, do not delude your maidservant."

17The woman conceived and bore a son at
the same season the following year, as Elisha
had assured her. 18The child grew up. One day,
he went out to his father among the reapers.
19[Suddenly] he cried to his father, "Oh, my
head, my head!" He said to a servant, "Carry
him to his mother." 20He picked him up and
brought him to his mother. And the child sat
on her lap until noon; and he died. 21She took
him up and laid him on the bed of the man of
God, and left him and closed the door. 22Then
she called to her husband: "Please, send me
one of the servants and one of the she-asses,
so I can hurry to the man of God and back."
23But he said, "Why are you going to him today? It is neither new moon nor sabbath." She
answered, "It's all right."

24She had the ass saddled, and said to her
servant, "Urge [the beast] on; see that I don't

נַעֲרוֹ קְרָא לַשּׁוּנַמִּית הַזֹּאת וַיִּקְרָא־לָהּ
וַתַּעֲמֹד לְפָנָיו׃ 13 וַיֹּאמֶר לוֹ אֱמָר־נָא
אֵלֶיהָ הִנֵּה חָרַדְתְּ ׀ אֵלֵינוּ אֶת־כָּל־
הַחֲרָדָה הַזֹּאת מֶה לַעֲשׂוֹת לָךְ הֲיֵשׁ
לְדַבֶּר־לָךְ אֶל־הַמֶּלֶךְ אוֹ אֶל־שַׂר הַצָּבָא
וַתֹּאמֶר בְּתוֹךְ עַמִּי אָנֹכִי יֹשָׁבֶת׃
14 וַיֹּאמֶר וּמֶה לַעֲשׂוֹת לָהּ וַיֹּאמֶר גֵּיחֲזִי
אֲבָל בֵּן אֵין־לָהּ וְאִישָׁהּ זָקֵן׃ 15 וַיֹּאמֶר
קְרָא־לָהּ וַיִּקְרָא־לָהּ וַתַּעֲמֹד בַּפָּתַח׃
16 וַיֹּאמֶר לַמּוֹעֵד הַזֶּה כָּעֵת חַיָּה אתי
אַתְּ חֹבֶקֶת בֵּן וַתֹּאמֶר אַל־אֲדֹנִי אִישׁ
הָאֱלֹהִים אַל־תְּכַזֵּב בְּשִׁפְחָתֶךָ׃
17 וַתַּהַר הָאִשָּׁה וַתֵּלֶד בֵּן לַמּוֹעֵד הַזֶּה
כָּעֵת חַיָּה אֲשֶׁר־דִּבֶּר אֵלֶיהָ אֱלִישָׁע׃
18 וַיִּגְדַּל הַיָּלֶד וַיְהִי הַיּוֹם וַיֵּצֵא אֶל־אָבִיו
אֶל־הַקֹּצְרִים׃ 19 וַיֹּאמֶר אֶל־אָבִיו רֹאשִׁי ׀
רֹאשִׁי וַיֹּאמֶר אֶל־הַנַּעַר שָׂאֵהוּ אֶל־אִמּוֹ׃
20 וַיִּשָּׂאֵהוּ וַיְבִיאֵהוּ אֶל־אִמּוֹ וַיֵּשֶׁב עַל־
בִּרְכֶּיהָ עַד־הַצָּהֳרַיִם וַיָּמֹת׃ 21 וַתַּעַל
וַתַּשְׁכִּבֵהוּ עַל־מִטַּת אִישׁ הָאֱלֹהִים
וַתִּסְגֹּר בַּעֲדוֹ וַתֵּצֵא׃ 22 וַתִּקְרָא אֶל־אִישָׁהּ
וַתֹּאמֶר שִׁלְחָה נָא לִי אֶחָד מִן־הַנְּעָרִים
וְאַחַת הָאֲתֹנוֹת וְאָרוּצָה עַד־אִישׁ
הָאֱלֹהִים וְאָשׁוּבָה׃ 23 וַיֹּאמֶר מַדּוּעַ אתי
אַתְּ הלכתי הֹלֶכֶת אֵלָיו הַיּוֹם לֹא־חֹדֶשׁ
וְלֹא שַׁבָּת וַתֹּאמֶר שָׁלוֹם׃
24 וַתַּחֲבֹשׁ הָאָתוֹן וַתֹּאמֶר אֶל־נַעֲרָהּ נְהַג
וָלֵךְ אַל־תַּעֲצָר־לִי לִרְכֹּב כִּי אִם־אָמַרְתִּי

16. At this season next year In Hebrew: *la-mo·ed ha-zeh ka-et ḥayyah.* The phrase translated as "next year" (*ka-et ḥayyah*) in the promise to the barren woman is also used when the pregnancy of Sarah is predicted (Gen. 18:10). The Hebrew may be more literally rendered "in a living (or viable) time"; that is, "in due course."

23. But he said, "Why are you going to him today?" After the woman announces that she wishes to see the "man of God" concerning her dead son (2 Kings 4:22), her husband asks this question and adds a complaint that "It is neither new moon nor sabbath." Presumably, it was on such sacred days that people customarily visited local shrines to consult the local man of God on various matters. Based on this passage, rabbinic tradition justified the custom of visiting one's teacher on the New Moon or *Shabbat* (BT Suk. 27b).

slow down unless I tell you." ²⁵She went on until she came to the man of God on Mount Carmel. When the man of God saw her from afar, he said to his servant Gehazi, "There is that Shunammite woman. ²⁶Go, hurry toward her and ask her, 'How are you? How is your husband? How is the child?'" "We are well," she replied. ²⁷But when she came up to the man of God on the mountain, she clasped his feet. Gehazi stepped forward to push her away; but the man of God said, "Let her alone, for she is in bitter distress; and the Lord has hidden it from me and has not told me." ²⁸Then she said, "Did I ask my lord for a son? Didn't I say: 'Don't mislead me'?"

²⁹He said to Gehazi, "Tie up your skirts, take my staff in your hand, and go. If you meet anyone, do not greet him; and if anyone greets you, do not answer him. And place my staff on the face of the boy." ³⁰But the boy's mother said, "As the Lord lives and as you live, I will not leave you!" So he arose and followed her.

³¹Gehazi had gone on before them and had placed the staff on the boy's face; but there was no sound or response. He turned back to meet him and told him, "The boy has not awakened." ³²Elisha came into the house, and there was the boy, laid out dead on his couch. ³³He went in, shut the door behind the two of them, and prayed to the Lord. ³⁴Then he mounted [the bed] and placed himself over the child. He put his mouth on its mouth, his eyes on its eyes, and his hands on its hands, as he bent over it. And the body of the child became warm. ³⁵He stepped down, walked once up and down the room, then mounted and bent over him. Thereupon, the boy sneezed seven times, and the boy opened his eyes. ³⁶[Elisha] called Gehazi and said, "Call the Shunammite woman," and he called her. When she came to him, he said, "Pick up your son." ³⁷She came and fell at his feet and bowed low to the ground; then she picked up her son and left.

לֵֽךְ׃ 25 וַתֵּ֙לֶךְ֙ וַתָּבֹ֞א אֶל־אִ֤ישׁ הָֽאֱלֹהִים֙ אֶל־הַ֣ר הַכַּרְמֶ֔ל וַ֠יְהִי כִּרְא֨וֹת אִישׁ־הָאֱלֹהִ֤ים אֹתָהּ֙ מִנֶּ֔גֶד וַיֹּ֙אמֶר֙ אֶל־גֵּיחֲזִ֣י נַעֲר֔וֹ הִנֵּ֖ה הַשּׁוּנַמִּ֥ית הַלָּֽז׃ 26 עַתָּ֞ה רֽוּץ־ נָ֣א לִקְרָאתָ֗הּ וֶאֱמָר־לָ֛הּ הֲשָׁל֥וֹם לָ֖ךְ הֲשָׁל֣וֹם לְאִישֵׁ֑ךְ הֲשָׁל֣וֹם לַיָּ֑לֶד וַתֹּ֖אמֶר שָׁלֽוֹם׃ 27 וַתָּבֹ֞א אֶל־אִ֤ישׁ הָֽאֱלֹהִים֙ אֶל־הָהָ֔ר וַֽתַּחֲזֵ֖ק בְּרַגְלָ֑יו וַיִּגַּ֨שׁ גֵּֽיחֲזִ֜י לְהָדְפָ֗הּ וַיֹּ֩אמֶר֩ אִ֨ישׁ הָאֱלֹהִ֤ים הַרְפֵּֽה־לָהּ֙ כִּֽי־ נַפְשָׁ֣הּ מָֽרָה־לָ֔הּ וַֽיהוָה֙ הֶעְלִ֣ים מִמֶּ֔נִּי וְלֹ֥א הִגִּ֖יד לִֽי׃ 28 וַתֹּ֕אמֶר הֲשָׁאַ֥לְתִּי בֵ֖ן מֵאֵ֣ת אֲדֹנִ֑י הֲלֹ֣א אָמַ֔רְתִּי לֹ֥א תַשְׁלֶ֖ה אֹתִֽי׃ 29 וַיֹּ֨אמֶר לְגֵֽיחֲזִ֜י חֲגֹ֣ר מָתְנֶ֗יךָ וְקַ֨ח מִשְׁעַנְתִּ֣י בְיָדְךָ֮ וָלֵךְ֒ כִּֽי־תִמְצָ֥א אִישׁ֙ לֹ֣א תְבָרְכֶ֔נּוּ וְכִֽי־יְבָרֶכְךָ֥ אִ֖ישׁ לֹ֣א תַעֲנֶ֑נּוּ וְשַׂמְתָּ֥ מִשְׁעַנְתִּ֖י עַל־פְּנֵ֥י הַנָּֽעַר׃ 30 וַתֹּ֙אמֶר֙ אֵ֣ם הַנַּ֔עַר חַי־יְהוָ֥ה וְחֵֽי־נַפְשְׁךָ֖ אִם־אֶעֶזְבֶ֑ךָּ וַיָּ֖קָם וַיֵּ֥לֶךְ אַחֲרֶֽיהָ׃ 31 וְגֵחֲזִ֞י עָבַ֣ר לִפְנֵיהֶ֗ם וַיָּ֤שֶׂם אֶת־ הַמִּשְׁעֶ֙נֶת֙ עַל־פְּנֵ֣י הַנַּ֔עַר וְאֵ֥ין ק֖וֹל וְאֵ֣ין קָ֑שֶׁב וַיָּ֣שָׁב לִקְרָאת֗וֹ וַיַּגֶּד־ל֣וֹ לֵאמֹ֔ר לֹ֥א הֵקִ֖יץ הַנָּֽעַר׃ 32 וַיָּבֹ֥א אֱלִישָׁ֖ע הַבָּ֑יְתָה וְהִנֵּ֤ה הַנַּ֙עַר֙ מֵ֔ת מֻשְׁכָּ֖ב עַל־מִטָּתֽוֹ׃ 33 וַיָּבֹ֕א וַיִּסְגֹּ֥ר הַדֶּ֖לֶת בְּעַ֣ד שְׁנֵיהֶ֑ם וַיִּתְפַּלֵּ֖ל אֶל־יְהוָֽה׃ 34 וַיַּ֜עַל וַיִּשְׁכַּ֣ב עַל־ הַיֶּ֗לֶד וַיָּ֩שֶׂם֩ פִּ֨יו עַל־פִּ֜יו וְעֵינָ֤יו עַל־עֵינָיו֙ וְכַפָּ֣יו עַל־כַּפָּ֔יו וַיִּגְהַ֖ר עָלָ֑יו וַיָּ֖חָם בְּשַׂ֥ר הַיָּֽלֶד׃ 35 וַיָּ֜שָׁב וַיֵּ֣לֶךְ בַּבַּ֗יִת אַחַ֥ת הֵ֙נָּה֙ וְאַחַ֣ת הֵ֔נָּה וַיַּ֖עַל וַיִּגְהַ֣ר עָלָ֑יו וַיְזוֹרֵ֤ר הַנַּ֙עַר֙ עַד־שֶׁ֣בַע פְּעָמִ֔ים וַיִּפְקַ֥ח הַנַּ֖עַר אֶת־עֵינָֽיו׃ 36 וַיִּקְרָ֣א אֶל־גֵּֽיחֲזִ֗י וַיֹּ֙אמֶר֙ קְרָא֙ אֶל־הַשֻּׁנַמִּ֣ית הַזֹּ֔את וַֽיִּקְרָאֶ֖הָ וַתָּב֣וֹא אֵלָ֑יו וַיֹּ֖אמֶר שְׂאִ֥י בְנֵֽךְ׃ 37 וַתָּבֹא֙ וַתִּפֹּ֣ל עַל־רַגְלָ֔יו וַתִּשְׁתַּ֖חוּ אָ֑רְצָה וַתִּשָּׂ֥א אֶת־בְּנָ֖הּ וַתֵּצֵֽא׃ פ

HAYYEI SARAH

חיי שרה

23 Sarah's lifetime—the span of Sarah's
life—came to one hundred and twenty-seven
years. 2Sarah died in Kiriath-arba—now Hebron—in the land of Canaan; and Abraham
proceeded to mourn for Sarah and to bewail
her. 3Then Abraham rose from beside his dead,
and spoke to the Hittites, saying, 4"I am a resident alien among you; sell me a burial site

כג וַיִּהְיוּ֙ חַיֵּ֣י שָׂרָ֔ה מֵאָ֥ה שָׁנָ֛ה
וְעֶשְׂרִ֥ים שָׁנָ֖ה וְשֶׁ֣בַע שָׁנִ֑ים שְׁנֵ֖י חַיֵּ֥י שָׂרָֽה׃
2 וַתָּ֣מָת שָׂרָ֗ה בְּקִרְיַ֥ת אַרְבַּ֛ע הִ֥וא חֶבְר֖וֹן
בְּאֶ֣רֶץ כְּנָ֑עַן וַיָּבֹא֙ אַבְרָהָ֔ם לִסְפֹּ֥ד לְשָׂרָ֖ה
וְלִבְכֹּתָֽהּ׃* 3 וַיָּ֙קָם֙ אַבְרָהָ֔ם מֵעַ֖ל פְּנֵ֣י מֵת֑וֹ
וַיְדַבֵּ֥ר אֶל־בְּנֵי־חֵ֖ת לֵאמֹֽר׃ 4 גֵּר־וְתוֹשָׁ֥ב

v. 2. כ׳ זעירא לפי נוסחים מקובלים

THE CAVE OF MACHPELAH (23:1–20)

Here are the first recorded death and burial in the history of the people Israel. The cave of Machpelah is the first parcel of real estate acquired by the founding father of the nation in the promised land.

THE DEATH OF SARAH (vv. 1–2)

1. Sarah's lifetime—the span of Sarah's life This repetition that emphasizes a woman's age at her death is unique in the Bible. It testifies to Sarah's importance as the first Matriarch.

2. Kiriath-arba An explanation offered for the name is "city of four," referring to the four settlements that confederated and received the name "Hebron," meaning "confederation" (see 13:18). Arba may also be a proper name (see Josh. 14:15, 15:10), which would make it "the city of Arba."

THE APPEAL TO THE HITTITES (vv. 3–9)

3. rose Mourners would sit on the ground.

Hittites See Comment to Gen. 10:15.

4. a resident alien The Hebrew phrase, literally "alien and resident" (*ger v'toshav*), is a figure of speech in which two terms express a single notion. Abraham mentions his status because it is the underlying reason for the request that follows. A resident alien was unable to purchase real estate.

sell me The Hebrew verb translated here as

CHAPTER 23

This *parashah* marks the transition from one generation to the next. It begins with Sarah's death and concludes with Abraham's. But its major theme is arranging a marriage for Isaac, the effort to find the right wife and partner so that the special tradition of Abraham and Sarah will continue beyond their lifetimes and the life of their son.

Although the Torah never explicitly makes the connection, many commentators connect Sarah's death with Isaac's narrow escape from tragedy at the *Akedah,* because it follows immediately after that in the narrative. Some see Sarah dying of shock either because Abraham was prepared to slay their son without informing her or because of the alarming news of his near death. According to one legend, Sarah is told that Abraham has killed Isaac at God's command. Believing it, she dies on the spot. One commentator sees her death, even after learning that Isaac has survived, as an inability to live in a world as dangerous and unreliable as she has found this world to be, a world where life hangs by such a fragile thread (Zornberg).

1. one hundred and twenty-seven years In the words of the Midrash, Sarah retained the innocence of a 7-year-old when she was 20, and the beauty of a 20-year-old when she was 100 (Gen. R. 58:1).

4. resident alien Abraham is uncertain

HALAKHAH L'MA·ASEH

23:3–4 Abraham rose . . . that I may remove my dead for burial Mourning does not eclipse the need to make arrangements for the prompt burial of the deceased, as required under Jewish law (S.A. YD 357:1). See Deut. 21:23 for a discussion about extenuating circumstances affecting immediate burial.

among you, that I may remove my dead for
burial." 5And the Hittites replied to Abraham,
saying to him, 6"Hear us, my lord: you are the
elect of God among us. Bury your dead in the
choicest of our burial places; none of us will
withhold his burial place from you for burying
your dead." 7Thereupon Abraham bowed low
to the people of the land, the Hittites, 8and he
said to them, "If it is your wish that I remove my
dead for burial, you must agree to intercede for
me with Ephron son of Zohar. 9Let him sell me
the cave of Machpelah that he owns, which is at
the edge of his land. Let him sell it to me, at the
full price, for a burial site in your midst."
10Ephron was present among the Hittites; so
Ephron the Hittite answered Abraham in the

אָנֹכִי עִמָּכֶם תְּנוּ לִי אֲחֻזַּת־קֶבֶר עִמָּכֶם
וְאֶקְבְּרָה מֵתִי מִלְּפָנָי׃ 5 וַיַּעֲנוּ בְנֵי־חֵת
אֶת־אַבְרָהָם לֵאמֹר לוֹ׃ 6 שְׁמָעֵנוּ ׀ אֲדֹנִי
נְשִׂיא אֱלֹהִים אַתָּה בְּתוֹכֵנוּ בְּמִבְחַר
קְבָרֵינוּ קְבֹר אֶת־מֵתֶךָ אִישׁ מִמֶּנּוּ אֶת־
קִבְרוֹ לֹא־יִכְלֶה מִמְּךָ מִקְּבֹר מֵתֶךָ׃ 7 וַיָּקָם
אַבְרָהָם וַיִּשְׁתַּחוּ לְעַם־הָאָרֶץ לִבְנֵי־חֵת׃
8 וַיְדַבֵּר אִתָּם לֵאמֹר אִם־יֵשׁ אֶת־נַפְשְׁכֶם
לִקְבֹּר אֶת־מֵתִי מִלְּפָנַי שְׁמָעוּנִי וּפִגְעוּ־לִי
בְּעֶפְרוֹן בֶּן־צֹחַר׃ 9 וְיִתֶּן־לִי אֶת־מְעָרַת
הַמַּכְפֵּלָה אֲשֶׁר־לוֹ אֲשֶׁר בִּקְצֵה שָׂדֵהוּ
בְּכֶסֶף מָלֵא יִתְּנֶנָּה לִּי בְּתוֹכְכֶם לַאֲחֻזַּת־
קָבֶר׃
10 וְעֶפְרוֹן יֹשֵׁב בְּתוֹךְ בְּנֵי־חֵת וַיַּעַן עֶפְרוֹן

"sell" (נתן) can mean "to give, sell, or pay." Its ambiguity permitted the dialogue to be conducted in an atmosphere of delicate and dignified, if somewhat contrived, politeness.

a burial site The Hebrew term *"aḥuzzat kever"* denotes an inheritable tomb. This element is vital to the transaction, because the cave is to serve future generations of the family of Abraham.

6. Bury your dead Abraham receives permission to bury his dead within the municipal boundaries of Hebron. Now he must acquire a plot of land.

7. bowed low In gratitude.

the people of the land Abraham may not approach the landowner directly. First he must deal with "the people of the land," which refers either to the general body of citizens or to the group of rulers who served as the town council. Their approval was necessary for an alien to acquire real estate and before a citizen could agree to negotiate the sale of property.

8. Ephron son of Zohar Because the Bible rarely records the father's name in the case of a non-Israelite, its presence here suggests that Ephron was a man of high nobility.

9. Machpelah It is traditionally identified with the site the Arabs call *ḥaram el-khalil* (in present-day Hebron), "the sacred precinct of the friend (of God)," referring to Abraham. Tradition has it that Sarah and Abraham were buried there, as were Isaac, Rebekah, Jacob, and Leah.

at the edge of his land Legal procedure naturally requires specification of the plot's locale.

at the full price Literally, "at full silver" (*b'khesef malei*). The silver *shekel*, a weight of about 0.4 ounces (12 g), was the most common medium of exchange in business transactions. (Coinage, invented at about the end of the 8th century B.C.E. by the Lydians, was not found in the land of Israel until the end of the biblical period.) The phrase appears in ancient Near Eastern commercial documents.

---

whether his neighbors accept him as a fellow resident or tolerate him as an alien in their midst. Their answer surprises him, going beyond both acceptance and toleration. Rather, they admire him for the quality of his faith: "you are the elect of God among us" (v. 6).

Much of Jewish history has seen the majority of Jews living as "resident aliens" in the midst of other nations. The descendants of this resident alien, the people Israel, will be extraordinarily creative when living in their own land, giving the world such spiritual treasures as the Psalms and the Prophets. The same spirit of creativity will mark their presence in the lands of the Diaspora.

הַחִתִּי אֶת־אַבְרָהָם בְּאָזְנֵי בְנֵי־חֵת לְכֹל
בָּאֵי שַׁעַר־עִירוֹ לֵאמֹר׃ 11 לֹא־אֲדֹנִי
שְׁמָעֵנִי הַשָּׂדֶה נָתַתִּי לָךְ וְהַמְּעָרָה אֲשֶׁר־
בּוֹ לְךָ נְתַתִּיהָ לְעֵינֵי בְנֵי־עַמִּי נְתַתִּיהָ לָּךְ
קְבֹר מֵתֶךָ׃ 12 וַיִּשְׁתַּחוּ אַבְרָהָם לִפְנֵי עַם
הָאָרֶץ׃ 13 וַיְדַבֵּר אֶל־עֶפְרוֹן בְּאָזְנֵי עַם־
הָאָרֶץ לֵאמֹר אַךְ אִם־אַתָּה לוּ שְׁמָעֵנִי
נָתַתִּי כֶּסֶף הַשָּׂדֶה קַח מִמֶּנִּי וְאֶקְבְּרָה
אֶת־מֵתִי שָׁמָּה׃ 14 וַיַּעַן עֶפְרוֹן אֶת־
אַבְרָהָם לֵאמֹר לוֹ׃ 15 אֲדֹנִי שְׁמָעֵנִי אֶרֶץ
אַרְבַּע מֵאֹת שֶׁקֶל־כֶּסֶף בֵּינִי וּבֵינְךָ מַה־
הִוא וְאֶת־מֵתְךָ קְבֹר׃ 16 וַיִּשְׁמַע אַבְרָהָם
אֶל־עֶפְרוֹן וַיִּשְׁקֹל אַבְרָהָם לְעֶפְרֹן אֶת־
הַכֶּסֶף אֲשֶׁר דִּבֶּר בְּאָזְנֵי בְנֵי־חֵת אַרְבַּע
מֵאוֹת שֶׁקֶל כֶּסֶף עֹבֵר לַסֹּחֵר׃ שני

hearing of the Hittites, all who entered the gate
of his town, saying, 11"No, my lord, hear me: I
give you the field and I give you the cave that is
in it; I give it to you in the presence of my
people. Bury your dead." 12Then Abraham
bowed low before the people of the land,
13and spoke to Ephron in the hearing of the
people of the land, saying, "If only you would
hear me out! Let me pay the price of the land;
accept it from me, that I may bury my dead
there." 14And Ephron replied to Abraham, saying to him, 15"My lord, do hear me! A piece of
land worth four hundred shekels of silver—
what is that between you and me? Go and bury
your dead." 16Abraham accepted Ephron's
terms. Abraham paid out to Ephron the money
that he had named in the hearing of the Hittites—four hundred shekels of silver at the
going merchants' rate.

THE NEGOTIATIONS WITH EPHRON
(vv. 10–16)

The assembly must have indicated its assent to Abraham's request. His negotiations with Ephron take place at the city gate, which served as a center of civic activity. The sale is given the widest possible publicity, to avoid any likelihood of litigation in the future.

10. all who entered the gate of his town The phrase seems to mean "all who had free access to the town," that is, the body of free citizens. It could also be an ancient term for the town council.

11. I give you the field Abraham seems to have had in mind only the cave. Ephron offers the cave together with the field as a gift. It is either a sincere offer or the opening gambit in the usual manner of Near Eastern bargaining.

12. bowed low A gesture of gratitude (see v. 7).

15. four hundred shekels of silver The price is introduced by Ephron with an air of seeming nonchalance. In the absence of any information about contemporary land values and the size and quality of the property, it is not possible to know whether or not the price quoted was exorbitant. (Three texts from the city of Ugarit in northern Syria, dating from the 14th to 13th centuries B.C.E. and written in Akkadian, do record real estate transactions involving a purchase price of 400 shekels of silver.)

16. paid out Literally, "weighed." The term was regularly used of payment in commercial transactions because the metal was weighed each time on a pair of scales.

at the going merchants' rate A similar expression appears in Akkadian, referring to the rate that is current among merchants, a specification necessary and important in view of the variations in the shekel weight. There was a common weight and a royal weight (2 Sam. 14:26); and within each class, also a light standard and a heavy standard.

10–16. Ephron may be pretending to give Abraham the land while hinting at a steep price for it. Such bargaining seems devious and hypocritical; however, custom may have deemed it dishonorable to sell ancestral land but acceptable to give it as a present to a close friend (who, presumably, would give you a present of equal value). Although Abraham has God's promise

[17]So Ephron's land in Machpelah, near Mamre—the field with its cave and all the trees anywhere within the confines of that field—passed [18]to Abraham as his possession, in the presence of the Hittites, of all who entered the gate of his town. [19]And then Abraham buried his wife Sarah in the cave of the field of Machpelah, facing Mamre—now Hebron—in the land of Canaan. [20]Thus the field with its cave passed from the Hittites to Abraham, as a burial site.

שני 17 וַיָּקָם | שְׂדֵה עֶפְרוֹן אֲשֶׁר בַּמַּכְפֵּלָה
אֲשֶׁר לִפְנֵי מַמְרֵא הַשָּׂדֶה וְהַמְּעָרָה
אֲשֶׁר־בּוֹ וְכָל־הָעֵץ אֲשֶׁר בַּשָּׂדֶה אֲשֶׁר
בְּכָל־גְּבֻלוֹ סָבִיב׃ 18 לְאַבְרָהָם לְמִקְנָה
לְעֵינֵי בְנֵי־חֵת בְּכֹל בָּאֵי שַׁעַר־עִירוֹ׃
19 וְאַחֲרֵי־כֵן קָבַר אַבְרָהָם אֶת־שָׂרָה
אִשְׁתּוֹ אֶל־מְעָרַת שְׂדֵה הַמַּכְפֵּלָה עַל־
פְּנֵי מַמְרֵא הִוא חֶבְרוֹן בְּאֶרֶץ כְּנָעַן׃
20 וַיָּקָם הַשָּׂדֶה וְהַמְּעָרָה אֲשֶׁר־בּוֹ
לְאַבְרָהָם לַאֲחֻזַּת־קָבֶר מֵאֵת בְּנֵי־חֵת׃ ס

24 Abraham was now old, advanced in years, and the LORD had blessed Abraham in

כד וְאַבְרָהָם זָקֵן בָּא בַּיָּמִים וַיהוָה
בֵּרַךְ אֶת־אַבְרָהָם בַּכֹּל׃ 2 וַיֹּאמֶר אַבְרָהָם

A LEGAL SUMMATION (vv. 17–20)

The final passage reads like a legal document. The act of burial completes the transaction, makes the sale absolute and incontestable, and confers the power to dispose of the property by testament or will.

17. Mamre This ancient and influential family in Hebron seems to have lent its name to one of the town's important quarters (see Gen. 13:18).

and all the trees The specification of the trees in land sale contracts is widespread in the ancient Near East.

19. Abraham buried his wife This terse statement echoes the simplicity and lack of ostentation with which Abraham buried Sarah.

20. passed Literally, "arose." The stem קום is a legal term used in connection with property transfers.

from the Hittites Because the ultimate control of land was vested in the community, mention of the Hittites in the legal summation was essential.

A WIFE FOR ISAAC (24:1–67)

ABRAHAM COMMISSIONS HIS SERVANT (vv. 1–9)

1. old, advanced in years Abraham's extreme old age adds urgency to his search for a wife for Isaac. That is why he is about to request that his servant take an oath rather than give him a simple order.

blessed . . . in all things Abraham's wealth

---

that the land will belong to his descendants, it is important for him to pay full price for it.

CHAPTER 24

1. After Sarah's death, Abraham, perhaps confronting his own loneliness and mortality, turns his attention to finding a wife for Isaac. As long as Isaac is unmarried, the divine promise of posterity will remain unfulfilled. He does not want Isaac to marry a Canaanite woman, so he sends his servant back to Aram to find a bride from among Abraham's relatives. The commentators wonder about this, because the Arameans were idol worshipers no less than the Canaanites. *Ḥizz'kuni* says that had Isaac married a Canaanite, people might attribute his claim to the land to his wife's inheritance, not to God's promise. Hirsch sees Abraham concerned about the influence of Canaanite neighbors and relatives on Isaac. Rabbenu Nissim attributes Abraham's rejection of a Canaanite bride not to Canaanite idolatry but to Canaanite moral depravity.

Abraham was now old Before Abraham, although people lived for many years, none

all things. 2And Abraham said to the senior
servant of his household, who had charge of
all that he owned, "Put your hand under my
thigh 3and I will make you swear by the LORD,
the God of heaven and the God of the earth,
that you will not take a wife for my son from the
daughters of the Canaanites among whom I
dwell, 4but will go to the land of my birth and
get a wife for my son Isaac." 5And the servant
said to him, "What if the woman does not consent to follow me to this land, shall I then take
your son back to the land from which you
came?" 6Abraham answered him, "On no account must you take my son back there! 7The
LORD, the God of heaven, who took me from

אֶל־עַבְדּוֹ זְקַן בֵּיתוֹ הַמֹּשֵׁל בְּכָל־אֲשֶׁר־לוֹ
שִׂים־נָא יָדְךָ תַּחַת יְרֵכִי׃ 3 וְאַשְׁבִּיעֲךָ
בַּיהוָה אֱלֹהֵי הַשָּׁמַיִם וֵאלֹהֵי הָאָרֶץ
אֲשֶׁר לֹא־תִקַּח אִשָּׁה לִבְנִי מִבְּנוֹת
הַכְּנַעֲנִי אֲשֶׁר אָנֹכִי יוֹשֵׁב בְּקִרְבּוֹ׃ 4 כִּי
אֶל־אַרְצִי וְאֶל־מוֹלַדְתִּי תֵּלֵךְ וְלָקַחְתָּ
אִשָּׁה לִבְנִי לְיִצְחָק׃ 5 וַיֹּאמֶר אֵלָיו הָעֶבֶד
אוּלַי לֹא־תֹאבֶה הָאִשָּׁה לָלֶכֶת אַחֲרַי אֶל־
הָאָרֶץ הַזֹּאת הֶהָשֵׁב אָשִׁיב אֶת־בִּנְךָ אֶל־
הָאָרֶץ אֲשֶׁר־יָצָאתָ מִשָּׁם׃ 6 וַיֹּאמֶר אֵלָיו
אַבְרָהָם הִשָּׁמֶר לְךָ פֶּן־תָּשִׁיב אֶת־בְּנִי
שָׁמָּה׃ 7 יְהוָה ׀ אֱלֹהֵי הַשָּׁמַיִם אֲשֶׁר
לְקָחַנִי מִבֵּית אָבִי וּמֵאֶרֶץ מוֹלַדְתִּי וַאֲשֶׁר

will be a decisive factor in gaining consent to the marriage and to the bride's journey to a distant land.

2. senior servant Possibly Eliezer, mentioned in 15:2. The chief servant in an aristocratic household held considerable power and responsibility.

Put your hand under my thigh Gestures that accompany oath taking were universal in the ancient world. The "thigh" here refers to the genital organ, in which the power of procreation resides (see 47:29 for the same expression). Abraham is thereby invoking the presence and the power of God as the guarantor of the oath.

3. swear by the LORD In light of the fact that the mission involves travel to a distant land, Abraham invokes God's universal sovereignty, using a title ("the LORD, the God of heaven and the God of the earth") that is unique in biblical literature. It may be a monotheistic version of an ancient Near Eastern oath formula in which the gods of heaven and earth were invoked as witnesses.

4. get a wife The Hebrew verb לקח literally means "to take." It defines the marriage institution from the perspective of the groom.

6. Abraham answered him This verse and the following two verses are the last words of the patriarch.

---

was described as "old," with its connotations of wisdom and maturity, not just chronologic length of days. In Jewish tradition, the Hebrew word for "old" (*zaken*) is associated with wisdom because it forms an acronym meaning "this one has acquired wisdom" (*zeh kanah hokhmah*). Abraham was the first person in history to grow wiser as he grew older (Gen. R. 59:6). Another *midrash* comments that Abraham began to feel old only when Sarah died (Tanḥ.).

2. Why is the genital organ involved in this oath taking? According to the Sages, it acquired sanctity because it was marked by the covenant of circumcision (*b'rit milah*). We know of similar involvement in other cultures, as the words "testify" and "testimony" (derived from "testes") indicate.

3. The God of heaven and the God of the earth The Midrash suggests that, before the time of Abraham, God ruled in heaven but was unknown on earth. Abraham brought God's sovereignty down to earth (Sifrei Deut. 313).

HALAKHAH L'MA·ASEH

24:3 that you will not take a wife This is the first indication of the Jewish norm of endogamy, of marrying within the clan. Jewish law requires that Jews marry Jews (see Gen. 26:35, 28:1; Deut. 7:3).

דִּבֶּר־לִי וַאֲשֶׁר נִשְׁבַּע־לִי לֵאמֹר לְזַרְעֲךָ
אֶתֵּן אֶת־הָאָרֶץ הַזֹּאת הוּא יִשְׁלַח
מַלְאָכוֹ לְפָנֶיךָ וְלָקַחְתָּ אִשָּׁה לִבְנִי מִשָּׁם׃
8 וְאִם־לֹא תֹאבֶה הָאִשָּׁה לָלֶכֶת אַחֲרֶיךָ
וְנִקִּיתָ מִשְּׁבֻעָתִי זֹאת רַק אֶת־בְּנִי לֹא
תָשֵׁב שָׁמָּה׃ 9 וַיָּשֶׂם הָעֶבֶד אֶת־יָדוֹ
תַּחַת יֶרֶךְ אַבְרָהָם אֲדֹנָיו וַיִּשָּׁבַע לוֹ עַל־
הַדָּבָר הַזֶּה׃
שלישי 10 וַיִּקַּח הָעֶבֶד עֲשָׂרָה גְמַלִּים מִגְּמַלֵּי
אֲדֹנָיו וַיֵּלֶךְ וְכָל־טוּב אֲדֹנָיו בְּיָדוֹ וַיָּקָם
וַיֵּלֶךְ אֶל־אֲרַם נַהֲרַיִם אֶל־עִיר נָחוֹר׃
11 וַיַּבְרֵךְ הַגְּמַלִּים מִחוּץ לָעִיר אֶל־בְּאֵר
הַמָּיִם לְעֵת עֶרֶב לְעֵת צֵאת הַשֹּׁאֲבֹת׃
12 וַיֹּאמַר ׀ יְהוָה אֱלֹהֵי אֲדֹנִי אַבְרָהָם

my father's house and from my native land, who promised me on oath, saying, 'I will assign this land to your offspring'—He will send His angel before you, and you will get a wife for my son from there. 8And if the woman does not consent to follow you, you shall then be clear of this oath to me; but do not take my son back there." 9So the servant put his hand under the thigh of his master Abraham and swore to him as bidden.

10Then the servant took ten of his master's camels and set out, taking with him all the bounty of his master; and he made his way to Aram-naharaim, to the city of Nahor. 11He made the camels kneel down by the well outside the city, at evening time, the time when women come out to draw water. 12And he said, "O Lord, God of my master Abraham, grant

7. His angel God's providence is here personified as a heavenly being.

8. clear of this oath Free of further obligation.

THE SERVANT'S PRAYER (vv. 10–14)

10. and set out The details of the journey are ignored; only the goal and its realization are described.

ten of his master's camels Concerning the presence of camels in the patriarchal narratives, see Comment to 12:16. Here, the sizable convoy is intended to make a strong impression on the future bride and her family, to serve as the means for testing her character, and to provide transportation back to Canaan for her and her entourage.

Aram-naharaim The Septuagint took the second word of the name to mean "two rivers," and so arose the name "Mesopotamia": literally, the land "between the two rivers." These were the Tigris and the Euphrates, or the Euphrates and its tributary Balīkh. The Aramaic translation rendered "Aram-naharaim" as "Aram which is on the Euphrates," referring to the territory bounded on three sides by the great bend of the Euphrates, within which lay the kingdom of Mitanni, called Naharain in ancient Near Eastern texts.

11. by the well Public wells served as a meeting place for townsfolk and shepherds. Newly arrived strangers could restock their water supplies, gather information about the town, and make useful contacts there.

at evening time When the chores are done and the day has cooled, the young women go out to draw water and can lounge about and engage in leisurely conversation.

12. And he said This unnamed servant of Abraham is the first person whom Scripture records as praying for personal guidance at a critical moment.

grant me good fortune The Hebrew verb here (*hakrei*) literally means "make it occur." What appears to be the result of chance (*mikreh*) may, in reality, be a deliberate determination of

---

12ff. Some of the Sages criticize the servant for his prayer. Conceivably, an unsuitable young woman might have come along to offer him water. Furthermore, although miracles do happen, a person may not demand a miracle. Others see the content of the prayer as a brilliantly intuitive realization that the qualities Isaac most needed in a wife, and might not have known that he needed, were kindness and generosity.

me good fortune this day, and deal graciously with my master Abraham: [13] Here I stand by the spring as the daughters of the townsmen come out to draw water; [14] let the maiden to whom I say, 'Please, lower your jar that I may drink,' and who replies, 'Drink, and I will also water your camels'—let her be the one whom You have decreed for Your servant Isaac. Thereby shall I know that You have dealt graciously with my master."

[15] He had scarcely finished speaking, when Rebekah, who was born to Bethuel, the son of Milcah the wife of Abraham's brother Nahor, came out with her jar on her shoulder. [16] The maiden was very beautiful, a virgin whom no man had known. She went down to the spring, filled her jar, and came up. [17] The servant ran toward her and said, "Please, let me sip a little water from your jar." [18] "Drink, my lord," she said, and she quickly lowered her jar upon her hand and let him drink. [19] When she had let him drink his fill, she said, "I will also draw for your camels, until they finish

הַקְרֵה־נָ֥א לְפָנַ֖י הַיּ֑וֹם וַעֲשֵׂה־חֶ֕סֶד עִ֖ם אֲדֹנִ֥י אַבְרָהָֽם: 13 הִנֵּ֛ה אָנֹכִ֥י נִצָּ֖ב עַל־עֵ֣ין הַמָּ֑יִם וּבְנוֹת֙ אַנְשֵׁ֣י הָעִ֔יר יֹצְאֹ֖ת לִשְׁאֹ֥ב מָֽיִם: 14 וְהָיָ֣ה הַֽנַּעֲרָ֗ אֲשֶׁ֨ר אֹמַ֤ר אֵלֶ֙יהָ֙ הַטִּי־נָ֤א כַדֵּךְ֙ וְאֶשְׁתֶּ֔ה וְאָמְרָ֣ה שְׁתֵ֔ה וְגַם־גְּמַלֶּ֖יךָ אַשְׁקֶ֑ה אֹתָ֤הּ הֹכַ֙חְתָּ֙ לְעַבְדְּךָ֣ לְיִצְחָ֔ק וּבָ֣הּ אֵדַ֔ע כִּי־עָשִׂ֥יתָ חֶ֖סֶד עִם־אֲדֹנִֽי:

15 וַֽיְהִי־ה֗וּא טֶ֘רֶם֮ כִּלָּ֣ה לְדַבֵּר֒ וְהִנֵּ֧ה רִבְקָ֣ה יֹצֵ֗את אֲשֶׁ֤ר יֻלְּדָה֙ לִבְתוּאֵ֔ל בֶּן־מִלְכָּ֔ה אֵ֥שֶׁת נָח֖וֹר אֲחִ֣י אַבְרָהָ֑ם וְכַדָּ֖הּ עַל־שִׁכְמָֽהּ: 16 וְהַֽנַּעֲרָ֗ טֹבַ֤ת מַרְאֶה֙ מְאֹ֔ד בְּתוּלָ֕ה וְאִ֖ישׁ לֹ֣א יְדָעָ֑הּ וַתֵּ֣רֶד הָעַ֔יְנָה וַתְּמַלֵּ֥א כַדָּ֖הּ וַתָּֽעַל: 17 וַיָּ֥רָץ הָעֶ֖בֶד לִקְרָאתָ֑הּ וַיֹּ֕אמֶר הַגְמִיאִ֥ינִי נָ֛א מְעַט־מַ֖יִם מִכַּדֵּֽךְ: 18 וַתֹּ֖אמֶר שְׁתֵ֣ה אֲדֹנִ֑י וַתְּמַהֵ֗ר וַתֹּ֤רֶד כַּדָּהּ֙ עַל־יָדָ֔הּ וַתַּשְׁקֵֽהוּ: 19 וַתְּכַ֖ל לְהַשְׁקֹת֑וֹ וַתֹּ֗אמֶר גַּ֤ם לִגְמַלֶּ֙יךָ֙

God. Nothing is more characteristic of the biblical outlook than the conviction about the role of divine providence in everyday human affairs.

14. water your camels A single camel (and here there were 10!) requires at least 25 gallons of water to regain the weight it loses in the course of a long journey. It takes a camel about 10 minutes to drink this amount of water.

let her be the one Because she possesses nobility of character, is hospitable to strangers, and is kind to animals.

THE ENCOUNTER WITH REBEKAH
(vv. 15–27)

The servant's prayer is answered at once.

15. born to Bethuel Her full genealogy is given because Nahor also had children from a concubine (related in 22:20–24). The child of a chief wife enjoyed higher social prestige. The relationship to Abraham is given to emphasize the providential nature of what occurred.

16. a virgin That is, a sexually mature young girl of marriageable age.

went down . . . filled . . . came up She went about her business briskly and conscientiously, not wasting time in gossip. This made a great impression on the servant.

17. let me sip To test her, he refrains from asking for water for the animals.

19. until they finish Her offer is not a hollow gesture but an act of generosity given in full knowledge of the labor involved.

---

16. Rebekah is described as beautiful and chaste, but her distinguishing characteristic is her kindness, offering to draw water not only for this stranger but for his train of camels as well. Abraham and Sarah, for all of their pioneering religious achievements, were sometimes insensitive to members of their own household. Rebekah's kindness and generosity may have been what was needed to correct those family dynamics.

drinking." 20Quickly emptying her jar into the trough, she ran back to the well to draw, and she drew for all his camels.

21The man, meanwhile, stood gazing at her, silently wondering whether the LORD had made his errand successful or not. 22When the camels had finished drinking, the man took a gold nose-ring weighing a half-shekel, and two gold bands for her arms, ten shekels in weight. 23"Pray tell me," he said, "whose daughter are you? Is there room in your father's house for us to spend the night?" 24She replied, "I am the daughter of Bethuel the son of Milcah, whom she bore to Nahor." 25And she went on, "There is plenty of straw and feed at home, and also room to spend the night." 26The man bowed low in homage to the LORD 27and said, "Blessed be the LORD, the God of my master Abraham, who has not withheld His steadfast faithfulness from my master. For I have been guided on my errand by the LORD, to the house of my master's kinsmen."

28The maiden ran and told all this to her mother's household. 29Now Rebekah had a brother whose name was Laban. Laban ran out to the man at the spring— 30when he saw

אֶשְׁאָב עַד אִם־כִּלּוּ לִשְׁתֹּת׃ 20 וַתְּמַהֵר
וַתְּעַר כַּדָּהּ אֶל־הַשֹּׁקֶת וַתָּרָץ עוֹד אֶל־
הַבְּאֵר לִשְׁאֹב וַתִּשְׁאַב לְכָל־גְּמַלָּיו׃
21 וְהָאִישׁ מִשְׁתָּאֵה לָהּ מַחֲרִישׁ לָדַעַת
הַהִצְלִיחַ יְהוָה דַּרְכּוֹ אִם־לֹא׃ 22 וַיְהִי
כַּאֲשֶׁר כִּלּוּ הַגְּמַלִּים לִשְׁתּוֹת וַיִּקַּח
הָאִישׁ נֶזֶם זָהָב בֶּקַע מִשְׁקָלוֹ וּשְׁנֵי
צְמִידִים עַל־יָדֶיהָ עֲשָׂרָה זָהָב מִשְׁקָלָם׃
23 וַיֹּאמֶר בַּת־מִי אַתְּ הַגִּידִי נָא לִי הֲיֵשׁ
בֵּית־אָבִיךְ מָקוֹם לָנוּ לָלִין׃ 24 וַתֹּאמֶר
אֵלָיו בַּת־בְּתוּאֵל אָנֹכִי בֶּן־מִלְכָּה אֲשֶׁר
יָלְדָה לְנָחוֹר׃ 25 וַתֹּאמֶר אֵלָיו גַּם־
תֶּבֶן גַּם־מִסְפּוֹא רַב עִמָּנוּ גַּם־מָקוֹם
לָלוּן׃ 26 וַיִּקֹּד הָאִישׁ וַיִּשְׁתַּחוּ לַיהוָה׃
רביעי 27 וַיֹּאמֶר בָּרוּךְ יְהוָה אֱלֹהֵי אֲדֹנִי אַבְרָהָם
אֲשֶׁר לֹא־עָזַב חַסְדּוֹ וַאֲמִתּוֹ מֵעִם אֲדֹנִי
אָנֹכִי בַּדֶּרֶךְ נָחַנִי יְהוָה בֵּית אֲחֵי אֲדֹנִי׃
28 וַתָּרָץ הנער הַנַּעֲרָה וַתַּגֵּד לְבֵית אִמָּהּ
כַּדְּבָרִים הָאֵלֶּה׃ 29 וּלְרִבְקָה אָח וּשְׁמוֹ
לָבָן וַיָּרָץ לָבָן אֶל־הָאִישׁ הַחוּצָה אֶל־
הָעָיִן׃ 30 וַיְהִי ׀ כִּרְאֹת אֶת־הַנֶּזֶם וְאֶת־

22. a gold nose-ring Partly in return for her arduous labors and partly to win her goodwill and to impress her family, the servant lavishes rich gifts on the girl—even before learning her identity! Rashi understands the servant's action to be an expression of faith in God's response to his prayer. Most Jewish commentators reverse the order of events (he asks her name, then gives the gifts), citing verse 47 as proof.

ten shekels in weight The weight is specified because items of jewelry were cast according to fixed standards and used as media of exchange.

24. I am the daughter of Bethuel She has no reason to include her father's relationship to Abraham, as the narrator did in verse 15.

25. plenty of straw To offer food and shelter for the camels is a most generous act.

27. kinsmen Literally, the "brothers of [my master]."

THE BETROTHAL (vv. 28–61)

28. her mother's household This indicates that her father probably was not alive. (The lone reference to him in verse 50 may be the result of a scribal error.) That is why her brother Laban is introduced immediately in the next verse.

29. Rebekah had a brother Not included in the genealogy of 22:23, he needs to be introduced now.

Laban In Hebrew the word *lavan* means "white." The feminine form *l'vanah,* "the white one," is a poetic term for the moon. This association is in keeping with other names in Abraham's family that are connected with lunar worship, such as Terah, which has been connected with *yarei·aḥ,* "moon."

30. when he saw the nose-ring Laban's hospitality appears to match that of his sister, but

the nose-ring and the bands on his sister's
arms, and when he heard his sister Rebekah
say, "Thus the man spoke to me." He went up
to the man, who was still standing beside the
camels at the spring. 31 "Come in, O blessed of
the LORD," he said, "why do you remain outside, when I have made ready the house and a
place for the camels?" 32 So the man entered the
house, and the camels were unloaded. The
camels were given straw and feed, and water
was brought to bathe his feet and the feet of the
men with him. 33 But when food was set before
him, he said, "I will not eat until I have told my
tale." He said, "Speak, then."
34 "I am Abraham's servant," he began.
35 "The LORD has greatly blessed my master,
and he has become rich: He has given him
sheep and cattle, silver and gold, male and
female slaves, camels and asses. 36 And Sarah,
my master's wife, bore my master a son in her
old age, and he has assigned to him everything
he owns. 37 Now my master made me swear,
saying, 'You shall not get a wife for my son from
the daughters of the Canaanites in whose land I
dwell; 38 but you shall go to my father's house,
to my kindred, and get a wife for my son.' 39 And
I said to my master, 'What if the woman does
not follow me?' 40 He replied to me, 'The LORD,
whose ways I have followed, will send His angel
with you and make your errand successful; and
you will get a wife for my son from my kindred,
from my father's house. 41 Thus only shall you
be freed from my adjuration: if, when you
come to my kindred, they refuse you—only
then shall you be freed from my adjuration.'

הַצְּמִדִים עַל־יְדֵי אֲחֹתוֹ וּכְשָׁמְעוֹ אֶת־
דִּבְרֵי רִבְקָה אֲחֹתוֹ לֵאמֹר כֹּה־דִבֶּר אֵלַי
הָאִישׁ וַיָּבֹא אֶל־הָאִישׁ וְהִנֵּה עֹמֵד עַל־
הַגְּמַלִּים עַל־הָעָיִן׃ 31 וַיֹּאמֶר בּוֹא בְּרוּךְ
יְהוָה לָמָּה תַעֲמֹד בַּחוּץ וְאָנֹכִי פִּנִּיתִי
הַבַּיִת וּמָקוֹם לַגְּמַלִּים׃ 32 וַיָּבֹא הָאִישׁ
הַבַּיְתָה וַיְפַתַּח הַגְּמַלִּים וַיִּתֵּן תֶּבֶן
וּמִסְפּוֹא לַגְּמַלִּים וּמַיִם לִרְחֹץ רַגְלָיו
וְרַגְלֵי הָאֲנָשִׁים אֲשֶׁר אִתּוֹ׃ 33 ויישם
וַיּוּשַׂם לְפָנָיו לֶאֱכֹל וַיֹּאמֶר לֹא אֹכַל עַד
אִם־דִּבַּרְתִּי דְּבָרָי וַיֹּאמֶר דַּבֵּר׃
34 וַיֹּאמַר עֶבֶד אַבְרָהָם אָנֹכִי׃ 35 וַיהוָה
בֵּרַךְ אֶת־אֲדֹנִי מְאֹד וַיִּגְדָּל וַיִּתֶּן־לוֹ צֹאן
וּבָקָר וְכֶסֶף וְזָהָב וַעֲבָדִם וּשְׁפָחֹת
וּגְמַלִּים וַחֲמֹרִים׃ 36 וַתֵּלֶד שָׂרָה אֵשֶׁת
אֲדֹנִי בֵן לַאדֹנִי אַחֲרֵי זִקְנָתָהּ וַיִּתֶּן־לוֹ
אֶת־כָּל־אֲשֶׁר־לוֹ׃ 37 וַיַּשְׁבִּעֵנִי אֲדֹנִי
לֵאמֹר לֹא־תִקַּח אִשָּׁה לִבְנִי מִבְּנוֹת
הַכְּנַעֲנִי אֲשֶׁר אָנֹכִי יֹשֵׁב בְּאַרְצוֹ׃ 38 אִם־
לֹא אֶל־בֵּית־אָבִי תֵּלֵךְ וְאֶל־מִשְׁפַּחְתִּי
וְלָקַחְתָּ אִשָּׁה לִבְנִי׃ 39 וָאֹמַר אֶל־אֲדֹנִי
אֻלַי לֹא־תֵלֵךְ הָאִשָּׁה אַחֲרָי׃ 40 וַיֹּאמֶר
אֵלָי יְהוָה אֲשֶׁר־הִתְהַלַּכְתִּי לְפָנָיו יִשְׁלַח
מַלְאָכוֹ אִתָּךְ וְהִצְלִיחַ דַּרְכֶּךָ וְלָקַחְתָּ
אִשָּׁה לִבְנִי מִמִּשְׁפַּחְתִּי וּמִבֵּית אָבִי׃
41 אָז תִּנָּקֶה מֵאָלָתִי כִּי תָבוֹא אֶל־
מִשְׁפַּחְתִּי וְאִם־לֹא יִתְּנוּ לָךְ וְהָיִיתָ נָקִי
מֵאָלָתִי׃

we are given the impression that he is motivated by greed.

Thus the man spoke to me Referring to verse 23.

34. I am Abraham's servant The servant recounts his experiences in a long and detailed speech. This type of repetition, which has its origins in orally transmitted literature, is characteristic of ancient Near Eastern epics and is found in various kinds of biblical prose narrative.

41. my adjuration The Hebrew word *alah* refers to the curse—the penalty for noncompliance—attached to an oath.

42"I came today to the spring, and I said: O
LORD, God of my master Abraham, if You
would indeed grant success to the errand on
which I am engaged! 43As I stand by the spring
of water, let the young woman who comes out
to draw and to whom I say, 'Please, let me drink
a little water from your jar,' 44and who answers,
'You may drink, and I will also draw for your
camels'—let her be the wife whom the LORD
has decreed for my master's son.' 45I had scarcely finished praying in my heart, when Rebekah came out with her jar on her shoulder,
and went down to the spring and drew. And I
said to her, 'Please give me a drink.' 46She
quickly lowered her jar and said, 'Drink, and
I will also water your camels.' So I drank, and
she also watered the camels. 47I inquired of her,
'Whose daughter are you?' And she said, 'The
daughter of Bethuel, son of Nahor, whom Milcah bore to him.' And I put the ring on her nose
and the bands on her arms. 48Then I bowed low
in homage to the LORD and blessed the LORD,
the God of my master Abraham, who led me on
the right way to get the daughter of my master's
brother for his son. 49And now, if you mean to
treat my master with true kindness, tell me;
and if not, tell me also, that I may turn right
or left."

50Then Laban and Bethuel answered, "The
matter was decreed by the LORD; we cannot
speak to you bad or good. 51Here is Rebekah
before you; take her and go, and let her be a wife
to your master's son, as the LORD has spoken."

42 וָאָבֹא הַיּוֹם אֶל־הָעָיִן וָאֹמַר יְהוָה
אֱלֹהֵי אֲדֹנִי אַבְרָהָם אִם־יֶשְׁךָ־נָּא מַצְלִיחַ
דַּרְכִּי אֲשֶׁר אָנֹכִי הֹלֵךְ עָלֶיהָ׃ 43 הִנֵּה
אָנֹכִי נִצָּב עַל־עֵין הַמָּיִם וְהָיָה הָעַלְמָה
הַיֹּצֵאת לִשְׁאֹב וְאָמַרְתִּי אֵלֶיהָ הַשְׁקִינִי־
נָא מְעַט־מַיִם מִכַּדֵּךְ׃ 44 וְאָמְרָה אֵלַי גַּם־
אַתָּה שְׁתֵה וְגַם לִגְמַלֶּיךָ אֶשְׁאָב הִוא
הָאִשָּׁה אֲשֶׁר־הֹכִיחַ יְהוָה לְבֶן־אֲדֹנִי׃
45 אֲנִי טֶרֶם אֲכַלֶּה לְדַבֵּר אֶל־לִבִּי וְהִנֵּה
רִבְקָה יֹצֵאת וְכַדָּהּ עַל־שִׁכְמָהּ וַתֵּרֶד
הָעַיְנָה וַתִּשְׁאָב וָאֹמַר אֵלֶיהָ הַשְׁקִינִי
נָא׃ 46 וַתְּמַהֵר וַתּוֹרֶד כַּדָּהּ מֵעָלֶיהָ
וַתֹּאמֶר שְׁתֵה וְגַם־גְּמַלֶּיךָ אַשְׁקֶה וָאֵשְׁתְּ
וְגַם הַגְּמַלִּים הִשְׁקָתָה׃ 47 וָאֶשְׁאַל אֹתָהּ
וָאֹמַר בַּת־מִי אַתְּ וַתֹּאמֶר בַּת־בְּתוּאֵל
בֶּן־נָחוֹר אֲשֶׁר יָלְדָה־לּוֹ מִלְכָּה וָאָשִׂם
הַנֶּזֶם עַל־אַפָּהּ וְהַצְּמִידִים עַל־יָדֶיהָ׃
48 וָאֶקֹּד וָאֶשְׁתַּחֲוֶה לַיהוָה וָאֲבָרֵךְ אֶת־
יְהוָה אֱלֹהֵי אֲדֹנִי אַבְרָהָם אֲשֶׁר הִנְחַנִי
בְּדֶרֶךְ אֱמֶת לָקַחַת אֶת־בַּת־אֲחִי אֲדֹנִי
לִבְנוֹ׃ 49 וְעַתָּה אִם־יֶשְׁכֶם עֹשִׂים חֶסֶד
וֶאֱמֶת אֶת־אֲדֹנִי הַגִּידוּ לִי וְאִם־לֹא
הַגִּידוּ לִי וְאֶפְנֶה עַל־יָמִין אוֹ עַל־שְׂמֹאל׃
50 וַיַּעַן לָבָן וּבְתוּאֵל וַיֹּאמְרוּ מֵיְהוָה יָצָא
הַדָּבָר לֹא נוּכַל דַּבֵּר אֵלֶיךָ רַע אוֹ־טוֹב׃
51 הִנֵּה־רִבְקָה לְפָנֶיךָ קַח וָלֵךְ וּתְהִי אִשָּׁה

47. I inquired of her See Comment to verse 22. The order of events is not the same as previously recorded. But had the servant not reported as he did, he would have been open to the charge of contradicting his assertion that he came specifically to find a wife from among Abraham's family.

48. my master's brother "Brother" here simply means "kinsman," as it does in 29:12,15.

50. Laban and Bethuel The father plays no further role in the proceedings. Numerous ancient Near Eastern texts demonstrate that in a patriarchal society a brother had important duties and powers in regard to his sisters.

bad or good That is, anything at all; we have no choice in the matter. The combination of opposites expresses a totality. See Comment to 2:9.

52When Abraham's servant heard their words, he bowed low to the ground before the LORD. 53The servant brought out objects of silver and gold, and garments, and gave them to Rebekah; and he gave presents to her brother and her mother. 54Then he and the men with him ate and drank, and they spent the night. When they arose next morning, he said, "Give me leave to go to my master." 55But her brother and her mother said, "Let the maiden remain with us some ten days; then you may go." 56He said to them, "Do not delay me, now that the LORD has made my errand successful. Give me leave that I may go to my master." 57And they said, "Let us call the girl and ask for her reply." 58They called Rebekah and said to her, "Will you go with this man?" And she said, "I will." 59So they sent off their sister Rebekah and her nurse along with Abraham's servant and his men. 60And they blessed Rebekah and said to her,

"O sister!
May you grow
Into thousands of myriads;
May your offspring seize
The gates of their foes."

לְבֶן־אֲדֹנֶיךָ כַּאֲשֶׁר דִּבֶּר יְהוָה׃ 52וַיְהִי
כַּאֲשֶׁר שָׁמַע עֶבֶד אַבְרָהָם אֶת־דִּבְרֵיהֶם
חמישי וַיִּשְׁתַּחוּ אַרְצָה לַיהוָה׃ 53וַיּוֹצֵא הָעֶבֶד
כְּלֵי־כֶסֶף וּכְלֵי זָהָב וּבְגָדִים וַיִּתֵּן לְרִבְקָה
וּמִגְדָּנֹת נָתַן לְאָחִיהָ וּלְאִמָּהּ׃ 54וַיֹּאכְלוּ
וַיִּשְׁתּוּ הוּא וְהָאֲנָשִׁים אֲשֶׁר־עִמּוֹ וַיָּלִינוּ
וַיָּקוּמוּ בַבֹּקֶר וַיֹּאמֶר שַׁלְּחֻנִי לַאדֹנִי׃
55וַיֹּאמֶר אָחִיהָ וְאִמָּהּ תֵּשֵׁב הנער
הַנַּעֲרָ אִתָּנוּ יָמִים אוֹ עָשׂוֹר אַחַר תֵּלֵךְ׃
56וַיֹּאמֶר אֲלֵהֶם אַל־תְּאַחֲרוּ אֹתִי וַיהוָה
הִצְלִיחַ דַּרְכִּי שַׁלְּחוּנִי וְאֵלְכָה לַאדֹנִי׃
57וַיֹּאמְרוּ נִקְרָא לנער לַנַּעֲרָ וְנִשְׁאֲלָה
אֶת־פִּיהָ׃ 58וַיִּקְרְאוּ לְרִבְקָה וַיֹּאמְרוּ
אֵלֶיהָ הֲתֵלְכִי עִם־הָאִישׁ הַזֶּה וַתֹּאמֶר
אֵלֵךְ׃ 59וַיְשַׁלְּחוּ אֶת־רִבְקָה אֲחֹתָם וְאֶת־
מֵנִקְתָּהּ וְאֶת־עֶבֶד אַבְרָהָם וְאֶת־אֲנָשָׁיו׃
60וַיְבָרְכוּ אֶת־רִבְקָה וַיֹּאמְרוּ לָהּ
אֲחֹתֵנוּ
אַתְּ הֲיִי
לְאַלְפֵי רְבָבָה
וְיִירַשׁ זַרְעֵךְ
אֵת שַׁעַר שֹׂנְאָיו׃

53. objects of silver and gold The two types of gifts—one for Rebekah, the other for her family—correspond to the "bride-price" and "gifts" mentioned in 34:12. The first was a fixed amount paid by the groom to the bride. The second consisted of ceremonial marriage gifts to the bride's family.

55. But her brother and her mother said At issue here is not consent to the marriage—it has already been given and its formalities completed—but agreement to leave the family at once for a distant land, without the customary elaborate leave-taking ceremonies Laban describes in 31:27.

59. her nurse The Hebrew word *"meneket"* refers to a wet nurse. In Mesopotamia the wet nurse frequently had the duties of bringing up the child and acting as guardian. The nurse, having attended and reared Rebekah from birth, must have remained as a member of the household and now will accompany her as a chaperon (see 35:8).

60. they blessed Rebekah She receives the same kind of blessing that God bestowed on Abraham after the *Akedah.*

---

57. The Sages cite this verse when they rule that the consent of a woman is required before she may be married.

60. These words are used today at the veiling of the bride (Yiddish: *bedeken*) that customarily precedes the Jewish wedding ceremony.

61Then Rebekah and her maids arose, mounted the camels, and followed the man. So the servant took Rebekah and went his way.

62Isaac had just come back from the vicinity of Beer-lahai-roi, for he was settled in the region of the Negeb. 63And Isaac went out walking in the field toward evening and, looking up, he saw camels approaching. 64Raising her eyes, Rebekah saw Isaac. She alighted from the camel 65and said to the servant, "Who is that man walking in the field toward us?" And the servant said, "That is my master." So she took her veil and covered herself. 66The servant told Isaac all the things that he had done. 67Isaac then brought her into the tent of his mother Sarah, and he took Rebekah as his wife. Isaac loved her, and thus found comfort after his mother's death.

61וַתָּקָם רִבְקָה וְנַעֲרֹתֶיהָ וַתִּרְכַּבְנָה עַל־
הַגְּמַלִּים וַתֵּלַכְנָה אַחֲרֵי הָאִישׁ וַיִּקַּח
הָעֶבֶד אֶת־רִבְקָה וַיֵּלַךְ׃
62וְיִצְחָק בָּא מִבּוֹא בְּאֵר לַחַי רֹאִי וְהוּא
יוֹשֵׁב בְּאֶרֶץ הַנֶּגֶב׃ 63וַיֵּצֵא יִצְחָק לָשׂוּחַ
בַּשָּׂדֶה לִפְנוֹת עָרֶב וַיִּשָּׂא עֵינָיו וַיַּרְא
וְהִנֵּה גְמַלִּים בָּאִים׃ 64וַתִּשָּׂא רִבְקָה
אֶת־עֵינֶיהָ וַתֵּרֶא אֶת־יִצְחָק וַתִּפֹּל מֵעַל
הַגָּמָל׃ 65וַתֹּאמֶר אֶל־הָעֶבֶד מִי־הָאִישׁ
הַלָּזֶה הַהֹלֵךְ בַּשָּׂדֶה לִקְרָאתֵנוּ וַיֹּאמֶר
הָעֶבֶד הוּא אֲדֹנִי וַתִּקַּח הַצָּעִיף וַתִּתְכָּס׃
66וַיְסַפֵּר הָעֶבֶד לְיִצְחָק אֵת כָּל־הַדְּבָרִים
אֲשֶׁר עָשָׂה׃ 67וַיְבִאֶהָ יִצְחָק הָאֹהֱלָה
שָׂרָה אִמּוֹ וַיִּקַּח אֶת־רִבְקָה וַתְּהִי־לוֹ
לְאִשָּׁה וַיֶּאֱהָבֶהָ וַיִּנָּחֵם יִצְחָק אַחֲרֵי
ששי אִמּוֹ׃ פ

61. her maids Having maids was a mark of social status. In the ancient world, occasionally one gave a maid to one's daughter at her wedding.

REBEKAH AND ISAAC (vv. 62–67)

62. Beer-lahai-roi The name of a well located in the Negeb (16:14), probably part of an oasis to which sheep breeders came for water and pasturage. Isaac later settled there (25:11).

63. walking This translation of the Hebrew *lasu·aḥ* is based on the Arabic word *saḥa,* "to take a stroll." Another translation, from the Hebrew word *si·aḥ,* "to talk, to meditate, to pray," has Isaac "chatting" with his friends.

63–64. saw The Hebrew text, using identical phrases for the actions of Isaac and of Rebekah, conveys an impression of simultaneity. Their eyes met in instant recognition; each knew instinctively who the other was.

64. She alighted Some Jewish commentators observe that this phrase properly belongs after verse 65.

65. my master He merits this title because he is his father's sole heir.

her veil Israelite women normally were not veiled. In the ancient Near East, the veiling of the bride was part of the marriage ceremony, but wives generally went about unveiled. By veiling herself now, as a sign of modesty, Rebekah signals Isaac that she is his bride.

67. into the tent of his mother Thereby she formally became the successor to Sarah the matriarch, ensuring the continuity of the generations.

as his wife Literally, "and she became his wife." The marriage was consummated and her status was recognized by all.

loved her The first reference to love in the Bible (22:2) concerned the tie between parent and child. This, the second reference to love, relates to the bond between husband and wife.

---

63. walking The Talmud takes the word to mean "praying." Rebekah saw Isaac praying and was impressed by the piety of her future husband. The Sages maintain that Isaac instituted the afternoon service of *Minḥah* (BT Ber. 26a–b).

67. Isaac comes to love Rebekah *after* he marries her. Their love is the result, not the prerequisite, of their relationship.

after his mother's death "As long as Sarah was alive, a light shone over her tent (signifying the divine Presence). When she died, it disap-

25 Abraham took another wife, whose
name was Keturah. 2She bore him Zimran,
Jokshan, Medan, Midian, Ishbak, and Shuah.
3Jokshan begot Sheba and Dedan. The descendants of Dedan were the Asshurim, the Letushim, and the Leummim. 4The descendants of
Midian were Ephah, Epher, Enoch, Abida,
and Eldaah. All these were descendants of Keturah. 5Abraham willed all that he owned to
Isaac; 6but to Abraham's sons by concubines
Abraham gave gifts while he was still living,

ששי **כה** וַיֹּסֶף אַבְרָהָם וַיִּקַּח אִשָּׁה וּשְׁמָהּ
קְטוּרָה׃ 2וַתֵּלֶד לוֹ אֶת־זִמְרָן וְאֶת־יָקְשָׁן
וְאֶת־מְדָן וְאֶת־מִדְיָן וְאֶת־יִשְׁבָּק וְאֶת־
שׁוּחַ׃ 3וְיָקְשָׁן יָלַד אֶת־שְׁבָא וְאֶת־דְּדָן
וּבְנֵי דְדָן הָיוּ אַשּׁוּרִם וּלְטוּשִׁים וּלְאֻמִּים׃
4וּבְנֵי מִדְיָן עֵיפָה וָעֵפֶר וַחֲנֹךְ וַאֲבִידָע
וְאֶלְדָּעָה כָּל־אֵלֶּה בְּנֵי קְטוּרָה׃ 5וַיִּתֵּן
אַבְרָהָם אֶת־כָּל־אֲשֶׁר־לוֹ לְיִצְחָק׃
6וְלִבְנֵי הַפִּילַגְשִׁים אֲשֶׁר לְאַבְרָהָם נָתַן

THE GENEALOGIES OF ABRAHAM (25:1–18)

After Isaac's marriage, the biblical text reports nothing more of Abraham's activities, even though he lived for another 35 years. His death and burial are now recorded, preceded and followed by lists of his descendants: two groupings of nomadic tribes or peoples, mostly identifiable as Arab. Many of the names are known from cuneiform sources. The two lists represent in reality two confederations of tribes that once enjoyed kinship, trade, or political ties with the early Israelites. In keeping with common biblical practice, these relationships are expressed in family terms and arranged in a genealogic pattern.

THE DESCENDANTS OF KETURAH (vv. 1–6)

The "sons" of Keturah, six in number, are to be regarded as the original core of the tribal confederation to which others, here referred to as "grandsons" and "great-grandsons," later adhered.

1. Abraham took another wife Verse 6 refers to Keturah as a "concubine," not a wife. Abraham probably had children with her during Sarah's lifetime.

Keturah Neither her parentage nor her origin is given. The name Keturah is related to the Hebrew word for "spices" (*k'toret*). The "sons" of Keturah were probably a tribal confederation that traded in spices, the source of which was southern Arabia.

2. she bore him

Of the six names listed, the first three have not been identified with any degree of confidence, but most likely they refer to peoples or oases along the international trade routes.

Midian The Midianites traded in frankincense. Their land lay along the territory east of the Gulf of Aqaba in northwestern Arabia.

3. Sheba A source of frankincense and other spices, it is situated in the southwestern part of the Arabian Peninsula.

Dedan This major center of the spice trade is identified with the modern oasis of 'el 'Ulla in the northwestern part of the peninsula.

Asshurim, Letushim, Leummim Possibly obscure tribes that fell under the domination of the Dedanites or that were associated with them.

4. The descendants of Midian The Midianites were a confederation of five tribes, here called "sons" in Hebrew (*b'nei midyan*). Ephah is mentioned in Assyrian sources. The others are unknown.

5. Abraham willed Isaac is formally declared to be the sole heir of Abraham. In this period, unlike the Torah legislation of a later age (Deut. 21:15–17), the father had the absolute right to designate his own successor, regardless of the birth order of his sons.

6. Abraham gave gifts A gesture of generos-

---

peared. When Rebekah arrived, it returned" (Gen. R. 60:16). Rebekah does not replace Isaac's mother; she fills the emotional void in his life.

CHAPTER 25

5–6. Translated literally, the verse tells us that "Abraham gave everything he had to Isaac,

אַבְרָהָם מַתָּנֹת וַיְשַׁלְּחֵם מֵעַל יִצְחָק בְּנוֹ
בְּעוֹדֶנּוּ חַי קֵדְמָה אֶל־אֶרֶץ קֶדֶם׃
7 וְאֵלֶּה יְמֵי שְׁנֵי־חַיֵּי אַבְרָהָם אֲשֶׁר־חָי
מְאַת שָׁנָה וְשִׁבְעִים שָׁנָה וְחָמֵשׁ שָׁנִים׃
8 וַיִּגְוַע וַיָּמָת אַבְרָהָם בְּשֵׂיבָה טוֹבָה זָקֵן
וְשָׂבֵעַ וַיֵּאָסֶף אֶל־עַמָּיו׃ 9 וַיִּקְבְּרוּ אֹתוֹ
יִצְחָק וְיִשְׁמָעֵאל בָּנָיו אֶל־מְעָרַת
הַמַּכְפֵּלָה אֶל־שְׂדֵה עֶפְרֹן בֶּן־צֹחַר הַחִתִּי
אֲשֶׁר עַל־פְּנֵי מַמְרֵא׃ 10 הַשָּׂדֶה אֲשֶׁר־קָנָה
אַבְרָהָם מֵאֵת בְּנֵי־חֵת שָׁמָּה קֻבַּר
אַבְרָהָם וְשָׂרָה אִשְׁתּוֹ׃ 11 וַיְהִי אַחֲרֵי

and he sent them away from his son Isaac eastward, to the land of the East.

7 This was the total span of Abraham's life: one hundred and seventy-five years. 8 And Abraham breathed his last, dying at a good ripe age, old and contented; and he was gathered to his kin. 9 His sons Isaac and Ishmael buried him in the cave of Machpelah, in the field of Ephron son of Zohar the Hittite, facing Mamre, 10 the field that Abraham had bought from the Hittites; there Abraham was buried, and Sarah his wife. 11 After the death of Abraham, God

ity on his part to secure the goodwill of the other sons toward Isaac or to compensate for their surrender of future claims.

sent them away Isaac's portion is secured by the separation of the half-brothers from the clan of Abraham and their migration to another land.

concubines Hagar and Keturah.

the land of the East In the Bible, the word *kedem* (east) covers a wide territorial expanse east of the land of Israel from the Aramean area of the Middle Euphrates down to northern Arabia.

THE DEATH AND BURIAL OF ABRAHAM
(vv. 7–11)

7. the total span According to the chronology of Genesis, Abraham resided in the land 100 years and lived to see the 50th birthday of his twin grandsons Esau and Jacob.

8. old and contented The phrase denotes a full life.

he was gathered to his kin Death is regarded as a transition to an afterlife where one is united with one's ancestors in Sheol, envisioned as a huge cavern under the earth.

9. Isaac and Ishmael In order of importance, not birth.

Machpelah This refers to the transaction described in Gen. 23. The cave now becomes a family tomb.

11. After the death of Literally, "It was after the death of." The Hebrew expression occurs again in Josh. 1:1, Judg. 1:1, and 2 Sam. 1:1 in connection with the death of Moses, of Joshua, and of Saul, respectively. In each instance, it indicates that a historic turning point has been reached. An era has come to an end, but the continuity of leadership has been ensured.

God blessed . . . Isaac He made him the

---

and gave presents to the sons by the concubines." Abraham gave his other children material gifts, but to Isaac he gave himself. As a result, Isaac became his true heir; the other children were only footnotes in his biography.

9. Isaac and Ishmael are reunited at their father's funeral, a sign that Ishmael changed his ways as he matured (BT BB 16b). Although he could not have forgotten how his father treated him and how his brother supplanted him, he seems to have forgiven Abraham for having been a less-than-perfect father. Isaac too seems to have come to terms with his father's nearly killing him on Mount Moriah.

Might these reconciliations have occurred in Abraham's lifetime and be the reason for the Torah's describing him as "contented" in his old age (Gen. R. 38:12)? Can we see this as a model for family reconciliations, forgiving old hurts? And can it not be a model for the descendants of Ishmael and Isaac, contemporary Arabs and Israeli Jews, to find grounds for forgiveness and reconciliation?

11. after the death of Abraham, God blessed his son Isaac God teaches us by example the importance of the mitzvah of comforting a mourner, *niḥum avelim*.

The next years will be critical in determining whether the faith of Abraham will survive his death and become the heritage of his descendants or whether it will die with him, remaining the insight of one remarkable individual.

blessed his son Isaac. And Isaac settled near Beer-lahai-roi.

12This is the line of Ishmael, Abraham's son, whom Hagar the Egyptian, Sarah's slave, bore to Abraham. 13These are the names of the sons of Ishmael, by their names, in the order of their birth: Nebaioth, the first-born of Ishmael, Kedar, Adbeel, Mibsam, 14Mishma, Dumah, Massa, 15Hadad, Tema, Jetur, Naphish, and Kedmah. 16These are the sons of Ishmael and these are their names by their villages and by their encampments: twelve chieftains of as many tribes.—17These were the years of the life of Ishmael: one hundred and thirty-seven years; then he breathed his last and died, and was gathered to his kin.—18They dwelt from Havilah, by Shur, which is close to Egypt, all the way to Asshur; they camped alongside all their kinsmen.

מוֹת אַבְרָהָם וַיְבָ֣רֶךְ אֱלֹהִ֔ים אֶת־יִצְחָ֖ק
בְּנ֑וֹ וַיֵּ֣שֶׁב יִצְחָ֔ק עִם־בְּאֵ֥ר לַחַ֖י רֹאִֽי: ס
12 וְאֵ֛לֶּה תֹּלְדֹ֥ת יִשְׁמָעֵ֖אל בֶּן־אַבְרָהָ֑ם
אֲשֶׁ֨ר יָלְדָ֜ה הָגָ֧ר הַמִּצְרִ֛ית שִׁפְחַ֥ת שָׂרָ֖ה
לְאַבְרָהָֽם: 13 וְאֵ֗לֶּה שְׁמוֹת֙ בְּנֵ֣י יִשְׁמָעֵ֔אל
בִּשְׁמֹתָ֖ם לְתוֹלְדֹתָ֑ם בְּכֹ֤ר יִשְׁמָעֵאל֙ נְבָיֹ֔ת
וְקֵדָ֥ר וְאַדְבְּאֵ֖ל וּמִבְשָֽׂם: 14 וּמִשְׁמָ֣ע
וְדוּמָ֖ה וּמַשָּֽׂא: 15 חֲדַ֣ד וְתֵימָ֔א יְט֥וּר נָפִ֖ישׁ
וָקֵֽדְמָה: 16 אֵ֣לֶּה הֵ֞ם בְּנֵ֤י יִשְׁמָעֵאל֙ וְאֵ֣לֶּה
שְׁמֹתָ֔ם בְּחַצְרֵיהֶ֖ם וּבְטִֽירֹתָ֑ם שְׁנֵים־עָשָׂ֥ר
נְשִׂיאִ֖ם לְאֻמֹּתָֽם: 17 וְאֵ֗לֶּה שְׁנֵי֙ חַיֵּ֣י
יִשְׁמָעֵ֔אל מְאַ֥ת שָׁנָ֛ה וּשְׁלֹשִׁ֥ים שָׁנָ֖ה
וְשֶׁ֣בַע שָׁנִ֑ים וַיִּגְוַ֣ע וַיָּ֔מׇת וַיֵּאָ֖סֶף אֶל־
עַמָּֽיו: 18 וַיִּשְׁכְּנ֨וּ מֵֽחֲוִילָ֜ה עַד־שׁ֗וּר אֲשֶׁר֙
עַל־פְּנֵ֣י מִצְרַ֔יִם בֹּאֲכָ֖ה אַשּׁ֑וּרָה עַל־פְּנֵ֥י
כׇל־אֶחָ֖יו נָפָֽל: פ

recipient of the covenant, in fulfillment of the promise of 17:21.

near Beer-lahai-roi This is mentioned in Gen. 16:14 as the site of God's promise of a son—Ishmael—to Hagar.

THE LINE OF ISHMAEL   (vv. 12–18)

13. Nebaioth Ancient Near Eastern documents refer to an Arab people called Nabaiati. Some identify this people with the later Nabateans, who lived in the former Edomite homeland.

Kedar The Kedarites are depicted as herders of sheep and goats who pursued a seminomadic existence and lived scattered over a wide area of the desert region east of the land of Israel.

16. villages These were unfortified encampments, often dependent on neighboring towns.

twelve chieftains The phrase indicates that God's promise (17:20) has been fulfilled. The "chieftain" (nasi) was the leader of the tribe. The 12 are taken to be the historical personalities from whom the tribes and places of the Ishmaelite confederacy received their names.

tribes The Hebrew word *ummah* denotes here a large nomadic tribal unit. The word usually means "a nation."

17. the life of Ishmael From the patriarchal period on, the Bible records only the life spans of the heroes of Israel. This notice about Ishmael is exceptional and appears because of two earlier chronologic notes: Abraham's age at his birth and the boy's age when he was circumcised.

18. They dwelt The territorial boundaries of the Ishmaelite confederation, or the geographic limits of their settlement and migration patterns, are now given.

Havilah Its location is uncertain because there was more than one site with this name.

Shur The line of Egyptian fortifications in the eastern delta discussed in connection with 16:7.

Asshur Not Assyria but some place in the northern Sinai desert.

they camped . . . their kinsmen The Hebrew has the singular "he . . . his" because it harks back to the prediction of 16:12, which speaks of Ishmael, the person.

הפטרת חיי שרה

HAFTARAH FOR ḤAYYEI SARAH

1 KINGS 1:1–31

This *haftarah* begins with an account of the last days of King David (c. 965 B.C.E.), which yield anything but a harvest of honor. It records the power struggle for seizing the crown of the king, even as his blood is turning cold (1:1–4). It seems that David never could escape the plots of his advisers and of his sons, in this case the scheming of his son Adonijah, who wanted to be king, versus the advisers who backed his son Solomon, the intended heir to the throne.

The narrative is structured and developed around pairs: David and Abishag (in the prologue), Nathan and Bathsheba, and Nathan and David (in the middle sections), and David and Bathsheba (in the epilogue). The pivotal scene of the narrative is the encounter between David and Bathsheba, with Abishag present (vv. 15–21). The text initially states that the king "did not know" Abishag the Shunammite maiden (v. 4). Bathsheba must now tell her husband what he "does not know"—that Adonijah has claimed the throne (v. 18).

The narrator, clearly a master of thematic intonation, connects and counterpoises various other episodes as well, with consummate skill. Another example of the subtle texture of this *haftarah* is provided by the threads linking the verb *shava* (to swear an oath) with the name Bathsheba (Hebrew: *Bat-sheva*) (as in 1:28–29).

RELATION OF THE *HAFTARAH* TO THE *PARASHAH*

The *parashah* and the *haftarah* are linked by the expression "old, advanced in years" (*zaken ba bayamim*) found in both Gen. 24:1 and 1 Kings 1:1, and by the theme of old age. Abraham and David represent two distinct models of aging. The Abrahamic type enters old age with all the religious and moral integrity of his life intact. Thus we see that Abraham, after the death of Sarah and the purchase of a family tomb (Gen. 23), "became old" and prepared for succession in his family. He directed his servant to "swear" (*v'ashbi·akha*) that he would not allow Isaac to marry one of the Canaanite women but, rather, would procure a wife for him from Abraham's homeland (Gen. 24:1–4). The patriarch was active in securing a future that would continue the past. Being blessed by God with "all things" (*ba-kol;* 24:1), Abraham passed on to Isaac "all" (*kol*) he had (25:5). This was his deposition before death, along with "gifts" to the children of his concubines (v. 6). Eliminating contention over the inheritance and preparing for new generations, Abraham died "in good ripe age" (*seivah*), "old and contented" (*savei·a*). The harmony between a good old age and contentment (v. 8) suggests an integrated aging, a balance between his physical person and his spiritual self.

David entered old age in the atmosphere of a catastrophe. He spoke too soon when he boasted, in a poetic testament, "Is not my House established before God? / For He has granted me an eternal pact, / Drawn up in full (*ba-kol*) and secured. / Will He not cause all (*kol*) my success / And [my] every desire to blossom?" (2 Sam. 23:5) The story of David's aging focuses on his physical debility and on the schemes of his dependents for securing their own stake in the future. Succumbing to infirmity, he did not "know" what was going on. His courtiers seem self-serving, and he himself represents all the frustrations of defunct power. David was a manipulator for most of his life, but his memory and pride were manipulated in his old age. Stung by the disclosures of Nathan and of Bathsheba, David "swears" (*va-yishava*) that he will fulfill his "former" oath (1 Kings 1:29). Something of the old David has thus returned. Giving final vent to

his complex personality, he transmits to Solomon some advice for survival: Observe the Torah, so that God will fulfill His promises to the dynasty, and kill the renegade soldier Joab, to secure the realm (2:1–5). Both theological and political sensibilities marked the man. But his was a "fullness" (kol) of will and conceit, far removed from the noble "wholeness" of Abraham.

---

1 King David was now old, advanced in years; and though they covered him with bedclothes, he never felt warm. ²His courtiers said to him, "Let a young virgin be sought for my lord the king, to wait upon Your Majesty and be his attendant; and let her lie in your bosom, and my lord the king will be warm." ³So they looked for a beautiful girl throughout the territory of Israel. They found Abishag the Shunammite and brought her to the king. ⁴The girl was exceedingly beautiful. She became the king's attendant and waited upon him; but the king was not intimate with her.

⁵Now Adonijah son of Haggith went about boasting, "I will be king!" He provided himself with chariots and horses, and an escort of fifty outrunners. ⁶His father had never scolded him: "Why did you do that?" He was the one born after Absalom and, like him, was very handsome.

⁷He conferred with Joab son of Zeruiah and with the priest Abiathar, and they supported Adonijah; ⁸but the priest Zadok, Benaiah son of Jehoiada, the prophet Nathan, Shimei and Rei, and David's own fighting men did not side

א וְהַמֶּ֤לֶךְ דָּוִד֙ זָקֵ֔ן בָּ֖א בַּיָּמִ֑ים וַיְכַסֻּ֙הוּ֙ בַּבְּגָדִ֔ים וְלֹ֥א יִחַ֖ם ל֑וֹ: ²וַיֹּ֧אמְרוּ ל֣וֹ עֲבָדָ֗יו יְבַקְשׁ֞וּ לַאדֹנִ֤י הַמֶּ֙לֶךְ֙ נַעֲרָ֣ה בְתוּלָ֔ה וְעָֽמְדָה֙ לִפְנֵ֣י הַמֶּ֔לֶךְ וּתְהִי־ל֖וֹ סֹכֶ֑נֶת וְשָֽׁכְבָ֣ה בְחֵיקֶ֔ךָ וְחַ֖ם לַאדֹנִ֥י הַמֶּֽלֶךְ: ³וַיְבַקְשׁוּ֙ נַעֲרָ֣ה יָפָ֔ה בְּכֹ֖ל גְּב֣וּל יִשְׂרָאֵ֑ל וַֽיִּמְצְא֗וּ אֶת־אֲבִישַׁג֙ הַשּׁ֣וּנַמִּ֔ית וַיָּבִ֥אוּ אֹתָ֖הּ לַמֶּֽלֶךְ: ⁴וְהַֽנַּעֲרָ֖ה יָפָ֣ה עַד־מְאֹ֑ד וַתְּהִ֤י לַמֶּ֙לֶךְ֙ סֹכֶ֔נֶת וַתְּשָׁ֣רְתֵ֔הוּ וְהַמֶּ֖לֶךְ לֹ֥א יְדָעָֽהּ:

⁵וַאֲדֹנִיָּ֧ה בֶן־חַגִּ֛ית מִתְנַשֵּׂ֥א לֵאמֹ֖ר אֲנִ֣י אֶמְלֹ֑ךְ וַיַּ֣עַשׂ ל֗וֹ רֶ֚כֶב וּפָ֣רָשִׁ֔ים וַחֲמִשִּׁ֥ים אִ֖ישׁ רָצִ֥ים לְפָנָֽיו: ⁶וְלֹֽא־עֲצָב֨וֹ אָבִ֤יו מִיָּמָיו֙ לֵאמֹ֔ר מַדּ֖וּעַ כָּ֣כָה עָשִׂ֑יתָ וְגַם־ה֤וּא טֽוֹב־תֹּ֙אַר֙ מְאֹ֔ד וְאֹת֥וֹ יָלְדָ֖ה אַחֲרֵ֥י אַבְשָׁלֽוֹם: ⁷וַיִּהְי֣וּ דְבָרָ֔יו עִ֚ם יוֹאָ֣ב בֶּן־צְרוּיָ֔ה וְעִ֖ם אֶבְיָתָ֣ר הַכֹּהֵ֑ן וַֽיַּעְזְר֔וּ אַחֲרֵ֖י אֲדֹנִיָּֽה: ⁸וְצָד֣וֹק הַ֠כֹּהֵן וּבְנָיָ֨הוּ בֶן־יְהוֹיָדָ֜ע וְנָתָ֣ן הַנָּבִ֗יא וְשִׁמְעִ֤י וְרֵעִי֙ וְהַגִּבּוֹרִ֔ים אֲשֶׁ֖ר

---

1 Kings 1:2. wait upon Your Majesty Literally, "stand before (*am'dah lifnei*) [the king]." In royal contexts, the idiom means to "serve at court" (cf. 1 Kings 12:8).

7–8. Joab, who was David's longtime faithful commander-in-chief (2 Sam. 8:16), now becomes a follower of the rebel Adonijah. Benaiah, who had served David as head of the elite guard (8:18), becomes the new commander-in-chief (1 Kings 4:4) with the succession of Solomon, who instructs him to kill Joab (2:28–34), in fulfillment of David's wishes.

The priests Zadok and Abiathar were descended from Aaron, although they were not brothers. Both served David and were frequently paired (cf. 2 Sam. 15:29,35; 20:25); but Abiathar supported Adonijah, and Zadok sided with the supporters of Solomon. After Solomon's succession, Zadok replaced Abiathar (1 Kings 2:35), who was dismissed from his office and banished to Anathoth. He was not killed, however, because of his past loyal service to David (2:26–27).

with Adonijah. 9Adonijah made a sacrificial
feast of sheep, oxen, and fatlings at the Zohe-
leth stone which is near En-rogel; he invited all
his brother princes and all the king's courtiers
of the tribe of Judah; 10but he did not invite the
prophet Nathan, or Benaiah, or the fighting
men, or his brother Solomon.

11Then Nathan said to Bathsheba, Solomon's mother, "You must have heard that Adonijah son of Haggith has assumed the kingship
without the knowledge of our lord David.
12Now take my advice, so that you may save
your life and the life of your son Solomon.
13Go immediately to King David and say to
him, 'Did not you, O lord king, swear to your
maidservant: "Your son Solomon shall succeed me as king, and he shall sit upon my
throne"? Then why has Adonijah become
king?' 14While you are still there talking with
the king, I will come in after you and confirm
your words."

15So Bathsheba went to the king in his chamber.—The king was very old, and Abishag
the Shunammite was waiting on the king.—
16Bathsheba bowed low in homage to the king;
and the king asked, "What troubles you?"
17She answered him, "My lord, you yourself
swore to your maidservant by the LORD your
God: 'Your son Solomon shall succeed me as
king, and he shall sit upon my throne.' 18Yet
now Adonijah has become king, and you, my
lord the king, know nothing about it. 19He has
prepared a sacrificial feast of a great many oxen,
fatlings, and sheep, and he has invited all the
king's sons and Abiathar the priest and Joab
commander of the army; but he has not invited
your servant Solomon. 20And so the eyes of all
Israel are upon you, O lord king, to tell them
who shall succeed my lord the king on the

לְדָוִד לֹא הָיוּ עִם־אֲדֹנִיָּהוּ׃ 9 וַיִּזְבַּח
אֲדֹנִיָּהוּ צֹאן וּבָקָר וּמְרִיא עִם אֶבֶן
הַזֹּחֶלֶת אֲשֶׁר־אֵצֶל עֵין רֹגֵל וַיִּקְרָא אֶת־
כָּל־אֶחָיו בְּנֵי הַמֶּלֶךְ וּלְכָל־אַנְשֵׁי יְהוּדָה
עַבְדֵי הַמֶּלֶךְ׃ 10 וְאֶת־נָתָן הַנָּבִיא וּבְנָיָהוּ
וְאֶת־הַגִּבּוֹרִים וְאֶת־שְׁלֹמֹה אָחִיו לֹא
קָרָא׃

11 וַיֹּאמֶר נָתָן אֶל־בַּת־שֶׁבַע אֵם־שְׁלֹמֹה
לֵאמֹר הֲלוֹא שָׁמַעַתְּ כִּי מָלַךְ אֲדֹנִיָּהוּ בֶן־
חַגִּית וַאֲדֹנֵינוּ דָוִד לֹא יָדָע׃ 12 וְעַתָּה לְכִי
אִיעָצֵךְ נָא עֵצָה וּמַלְּטִי אֶת־נַפְשֵׁךְ וְאֶת־
נֶפֶשׁ בְּנֵךְ שְׁלֹמֹה׃ 13 לְכִי וּבֹאִי ׀ אֶל־
הַמֶּלֶךְ דָּוִד וְאָמַרְתְּ אֵלָיו הֲלֹא־אַתָּה
אֲדֹנִי הַמֶּלֶךְ נִשְׁבַּעְתָּ לַאֲמָתְךָ לֵאמֹר כִּי־
שְׁלֹמֹה בְנֵךְ יִמְלֹךְ אַחֲרַי וְהוּא יֵשֵׁב עַל־
כִּסְאִי וּמַדּוּעַ מָלַךְ אֲדֹנִיָּהוּ׃ 14 הִנֵּה עוֹדָךְ
מְדַבֶּרֶת שָׁם עִם־הַמֶּלֶךְ וַאֲנִי אָבוֹא
אַחֲרַיִךְ וּמִלֵּאתִי אֶת־דְּבָרָיִךְ׃

15 וַתָּבֹא בַת־שֶׁבַע אֶל־הַמֶּלֶךְ הַחַדְרָה
וְהַמֶּלֶךְ זָקֵן מְאֹד וַאֲבִישַׁג הַשּׁוּנַמִּית
מְשָׁרַת אֶת־הַמֶּלֶךְ׃ 16 וַתִּקֹּד בַּת־שֶׁבַע
וַתִּשְׁתַּחוּ לַמֶּלֶךְ וַיֹּאמֶר הַמֶּלֶךְ מַה־לָּךְ׃
17 וַתֹּאמֶר לוֹ אֲדֹנִי אַתָּה נִשְׁבַּעְתָּ בַּיהוָה
אֱלֹהֶיךָ לַאֲמָתֶךָ כִּי־שְׁלֹמֹה בְנֵךְ יִמְלֹךְ
אַחֲרָי וְהוּא יֵשֵׁב עַל־כִּסְאִי׃ 18 וְעַתָּה
הִנֵּה אֲדֹנִיָּה מָלָךְ וְעַתָּה* אֲדֹנִי הַמֶּלֶךְ
לֹא יָדָעְתָּ׃ 19 וַיִּזְבַּח שׁוֹר וּמְרִיא־וְצֹאן
לָרֹב וַיִּקְרָא לְכָל־בְּנֵי הַמֶּלֶךְ וּלְאֶבְיָתָר
הַכֹּהֵן וּלְיֹאָב שַׂר הַצָּבָא וְלִשְׁלֹמֹה עַבְדְּךָ
לֹא קָרָא׃ 20 וְאַתָּה אֲדֹנִי הַמֶּלֶךְ עֵינֵי כָל־
יִשְׂרָאֵל עָלֶיךָ לְהַגִּיד לָהֶם מִי יֵשֵׁב עַל־

v. 18. בנוסח אחר "ואתה"

13. Did not you . . . swear to your maidservant This appears to be a ruse, because there is no record of such a conversation between them.

18. you As in many manuscripts and ancient versions; the usual editions have "now" [Transl.].

throne. 21Otherwise, when my lord the king lies down with his fathers, my son Solomon and I will be regarded as traitors."

22She was still talking to the king when the prophet Nathan arrived. 23They announced to the king, "The prophet Nathan is here," and he entered the king's presence. Bowing low to the king with his face to the ground, 24Nathan said, "O lord king, you must have said, 'Adonijah shall succeed me as king and he shall sit upon my throne.' 25For he has gone down today and prepared a sacrificial feast of a great many oxen, fatlings, and sheep. He invited all the king's sons and the army officers and Abiathar the priest. At this very moment they are eating and drinking with him, and they are shouting, 'Long live King Adonijah!' 26But he did not invite me your servant, or the priest Zadok, or Benaiah son of Jehoiada, or your servant Solomon. 27Can this decision have come from my lord the king, without your telling your servant who is to succeed to the throne of my lord the king?"

28King David's response was: "Summon Bathsheba!" She entered the king's presence and stood before the king. 29And the king took an oath, saying, "As the LORD lives, who has rescued me from every trouble: 30The oath I swore to you by the LORD, the God of Israel, that your son Solomon should succeed me as king and that he should sit upon my throne in my stead, I will fulfill this very day!" 31Bathsheba bowed low in homage to the king with her face to the ground, and she said, "May my lord King David live forever!"

כִּסֵּא אֲדֹנִי־הַמֶּלֶךְ אַחֲרָיו׃ 21 וְהָיָה כִּשְׁכַב
אֲדֹנִי־הַמֶּלֶךְ עִם־אֲבֹתָיו וְהָיִיתִי אֲנִי וּבְנִי
שְׁלֹמֹה חַטָּאִים׃
22 וְהִנֵּה עוֹדֶנָּה מְדַבֶּרֶת עִם־הַמֶּלֶךְ וְנָתָן
הַנָּבִיא בָּא׃ 23 וַיַּגִּידוּ לַמֶּלֶךְ לֵאמֹר הִנֵּה
נָתָן הַנָּבִיא וַיָּבֹא לִפְנֵי הַמֶּלֶךְ וַיִּשְׁתַּחוּ
לַמֶּלֶךְ עַל־אַפָּיו אָרְצָה׃ 24 וַיֹּאמֶר נָתָן
אֲדֹנִי הַמֶּלֶךְ אַתָּה אָמַרְתָּ אֲדֹנִיָּהוּ יִמְלֹךְ
אַחֲרָי וְהוּא יֵשֵׁב עַל־כִּסְאִי׃ 25 כִּי ׀ יָרַד
הַיּוֹם וַיִּזְבַּח שׁוֹר וּמְרִיא־וְצֹאן לָרֹב
וַיִּקְרָא לְכָל־בְּנֵי הַמֶּלֶךְ וּלְשָׂרֵי הַצָּבָא
וּלְאֶבְיָתָר הַכֹּהֵן וְהִנָּם אֹכְלִים וְשֹׁתִים
לְפָנָיו וַיֹּאמְרוּ יְחִי הַמֶּלֶךְ אֲדֹנִיָּהוּ׃ 26 וְלִי
אֲנִי־עַבְדֶּךָ וּלְצָדֹק הַכֹּהֵן וְלִבְנָיָהוּ בֶן־
יְהוֹיָדָע וְלִשְׁלֹמֹה עַבְדְּךָ לֹא קָרָא׃ 27 אִם
מֵאֵת אֲדֹנִי הַמֶּלֶךְ נִהְיָה הַדָּבָר הַזֶּה וְלֹא
הוֹדַעְתָּ אֶת־עבדיך עַבְדְּךָ מִי יֵשֵׁב עַל־
כִּסֵּא אֲדֹנִי־הַמֶּלֶךְ אַחֲרָיו׃ ס
28 וַיַּעַן הַמֶּלֶךְ דָּוִד וַיֹּאמֶר קִרְאוּ־לִי לְבַת־
שָׁבַע וַתָּבֹא לִפְנֵי הַמֶּלֶךְ וַתַּעֲמֹד לִפְנֵי
הַמֶּלֶךְ׃ 29 וַיִּשָּׁבַע הַמֶּלֶךְ וַיֹּאמַר חַי־יְהוָה
אֲשֶׁר־פָּדָה אֶת־נַפְשִׁי מִכָּל־צָרָה׃ 30 כִּי
כַּאֲשֶׁר נִשְׁבַּעְתִּי לָךְ בַּיהוָה אֱלֹהֵי
יִשְׂרָאֵל לֵאמֹר כִּי־שְׁלֹמֹה בְנֵךְ יִמְלֹךְ
אַחֲרַי וְהוּא יֵשֵׁב עַל־כִּסְאִי תַּחְתָּי כִּי כֵּן
אֶעֱשֶׂה הַיּוֹם הַזֶּה׃ 31 וַתִּקֹּד בַּת־שֶׁבַע
אַפַּיִם אֶרֶץ* וַתִּשְׁתַּחוּ לַמֶּלֶךְ וַתֹּאמֶר יְחִי
אֲדֹנִי הַמֶּלֶךְ דָּוִד לְעֹלָם׃ פ

v. 31. סבירין ומטעין "ארצה"

21. traitors Literally, "offenders" (*ḥata·im*).

TOL'DOT

[19]This is the story of Isaac, son of Abraham.
Abraham begot Isaac. [20]Isaac was forty years
old when he took to wife Rebekah, daughter of
Bethuel the Aramean of Paddan-aram, sister of
Laban the Aramean. [21]Isaac pleaded with the
LORD on behalf of his wife, because she was
barren; and the LORD responded to his plea,
and his wife Rebekah conceived. [22]But the children struggled in her womb, and she said, "If

תולדות

19 וְאֵ֛לֶּה תּוֹלְדֹ֥ת יִצְחָ֖ק בֶּן־אַבְרָהָ֑ם
אַבְרָהָ֖ם הוֹלִ֥יד אֶת־יִצְחָֽק׃ 20 וַיְהִ֤י יִצְחָק֙
בֶּן־אַרְבָּעִ֣ים שָׁנָ֔ה בְּקַחְתּ֣וֹ אֶת־רִבְקָ֗ה בַּת־
בְּתוּאֵל֙ הָֽאֲרַמִּ֔י מִפַּדַּ֖ן אֲרָ֑ם אֲח֛וֹת לָבָ֥ן
הָאֲרַמִּ֖י ל֥וֹ לְאִשָּֽׁה׃ 21 וַיֶּעְתַּ֨ר יִצְחָ֤ק
לַֽיהוָה֙ לְנֹ֣כַח אִשְׁתּ֔וֹ כִּ֥י עֲקָרָ֖ה הִ֑וא
וַיֵּעָ֤תֶר לוֹ֙ יְהוָ֔ה וַתַּ֖הַר רִבְקָ֥ה אִשְׁתּֽוֹ׃

ISAAC, FATHER OF TWO NATIONS (25:19–34)

THE BIRTH OF JACOB AND ESAU (vv. 19–26)

19. This is the story of Isaac This introductory formula serves as the general title for the narrative cycle that concludes with 35:29.

Abraham begot Isaac This note, seemingly redundant after the foregoing "Isaac son of Abraham," actually serves to emphasize Isaac's role as the sole successor to Abraham, in fulfillment of the promise of 21:12: "it is through Isaac that offspring shall be continued for you."

20. Isaac was forty years old Rebekah's age is omitted because, unlike Sarah, she was not beyond the age of childbearing.

Bethuel the Aramean According to 22:22, Bethuel was one of the Nahorite tribes, and Aram was his nephew.

Paddan-aram This place-name is found only in Genesis. It is either another name for Aram-naharaim, mentioned in 24:10, or a town within that region.

21. she was barren Once again we encounter the motif of the barren wife of the patriarch.

22. struggled in her womb Rebekah experiences an unusually difficult pregnancy. The fetal movements are spasmodic and she has fears of miscarrying.

If so, why do I exist? The Hebrew, an incomplete sentence, is saying something like, "Why then did I yearn and pray to become pregnant?" or "Why do I go on living?"

She went to inquire of the LORD She sought divine guidance in a moment of great perplexity and anguish. Generally, one would go to a spe-

---

CHAPTER 25

The sixth *parashah* of Genesis tells about the birth and early years of Isaac and Rebekah's twin sons, Jacob and Esau. Often in ancient tales, twins who are not identical are complementary, each twin representing one-half of a complete personality, each having qualities the other lacks and lacking qualities the other possesses. Jacob represents the gentle, cerebral side of a person, reaching goals by persuasion or cleverness. Esau represents the active, physical side. When the Torah describes them as struggling within Rebekah's womb and continues to portray them as rivals growing up, it may be telling us that these two sides of many people are struggling within each individual for dominance.

19. Isaac, son of Abraham Isaac's life is defined by his being Abraham's son more than by any other single factor (*Ha·amek Davar*).

Abraham begot Isaac As Isaac was proud of his father, Abraham was proud of his son (Gen. R. 63:2).

21. Isaac does not pray for himself, for the fulfilment of his own needs, but for his wife. Rather than urging her to be content with her lot, he prays that she find fulfilment where it means most to her.

HALAKHAH L'MA·ASEH

25:21 Isaac pleaded . . . because she was barren The tragedy of infertility need not be borne alone. The Conservative Movement has created a ritual for coping with infertility, published in its *Moreih Derekh,* to provide the infertile couple the support of their community (see Gen. 1:28, 30:14).

22 וַיִּתְרֹצְצוּ הַבָּנִים בְּקִרְבָּהּ וַתֹּאמֶר אִם־
כֵּן לָמָּה זֶּה אָנֹכִי וַתֵּלֶךְ לִדְרֹשׁ אֶת־
יְהוָה׃ 23 וַיֹּאמֶר יְהוָה לָהּ
שְׁנֵי גיים גוֹיִם בְּבִטְנֵךְ
וּשְׁנֵי לְאֻמִּים מִמֵּעַיִךְ יִפָּרֵדוּ
וּלְאֹם מִלְאֹם יֶאֱמָץ
וְרַב יַעֲבֹד צָעִיר׃
24 וַיִּמְלְאוּ יָמֶיהָ לָלֶדֶת וְהִנֵּה תוֹמִם*
בְּבִטְנָהּ׃ 25 וַיֵּצֵא הָרִאשׁוֹן אַדְמוֹנִי כֻּלּוֹ
כְּאַדֶּרֶת שֵׂעָר וַיִּקְרְאוּ שְׁמוֹ עֵשָׂו׃
26 וְאַחֲרֵי־כֵן יָצָא אָחִיו וְיָדוֹ אֹחֶזֶת בַּעֲקֵב
עֵשָׂו וַיִּקְרָא שְׁמוֹ יַעֲקֹב וְיִצְחָק בֶּן־שִׁשִּׁים
שָׁנָה בְּלֶדֶת אֹתָם׃
27 וַיִּגְדְּלוּ הַנְּעָרִים וַיְהִי עֵשָׂו אִישׁ יֹדֵעַ צַיִד
אִישׁ שָׂדֶה וְיַעֲקֹב אִישׁ תָּם יֹשֵׁב אֹהָלִים׃
28 וַיֶּאֱהַב יִצְחָק אֶת־עֵשָׂו כִּי־צַיִד בְּפִיו

v. 24. חסר א׳ ר׳

so, why do I exist?" She went to inquire of the
Lord, 23and the Lord answered her,

"Two nations are in your womb,
Two separate peoples shall issue from your body;
One people shall be mightier than the other,
And the older shall serve the younger."

24When her time to give birth was at hand,
there were twins in her womb. 25The first one
emerged red, like a hairy mantle all over; so
they named him Esau. 26Then his brother
emerged, holding on to the heel of Esau; so
they named him Jacob. Isaac was sixty years
old when they were born.
27When the boys grew up, Esau became a
skillful hunter, a man of the outdoors; but Jacob was a mild man who stayed in camp.
28Isaac favored Esau because he had a taste

cific sanctuary or to some charismatic personage of recognized authority.

23. the Lord answered her God's response is oracular in style and poetic in form, and the message is conveyed in four concise phrases.

25. red A ruddy complexion. The Hebrew term *"admoni"* is also used—admiringly—in descriptions of David (1 Sam. 16:12, 17:14).

like a hairy mantle Hairiness was popularly taken as a sign of uncouthness. The Hebrew word *sa·ir* (hairy) is a wordplay on Seir, the name of Edom, associated with Esau.

Esau "The mantled one," possibly from the Arabic verb *gh-s-w,* "to cover, envelop."

26. holding on to the heel This has been understood as an attempt to thwart the prior birth of his twin.

Jacob The name is here derived, by folk etymology, from the Hebrew noun *akev,* "heel." In reality, however, the Hebrew name *ya·akov* stems from a Semitic verb עקב, "to protect." Thus, in its origin, the name Jacob is a plea for divine protection of the newly born.

THE SALE OF THE BIRTHRIGHT (vv. 27–34)

The struggle between the twins for seniority continues into adulthood. Jacob seizes a chance to pressure Esau into transferring the birthright to him. In the ancient Near East, an heir could barter away his inheritance. A tablet records how a man parted with his birthright in return for three sheep he received immediately from his brother.

27. When the boys grew up The description of Esau as a hunter and as one who lives by the sword (Gen. 27:40) reflects an early stage in the history of Edom. Hunting as a way of life was held in low esteem in ancient Israel, where sacrifice was restricted to domesticated animals.

a mild man Jacob, a quiet man, does not carry weapons.

who stayed in camp Literally, "who dwelt in tents." He is a pastoralist.

---

23. the Lord answered her God charges Rebekah with the responsibility of seeing to it that the Covenant is entrusted to the more worthy, not necessarily the elder, child.

28. Isaac favored Esau Perhaps he raised Esau to do many of the things he had never been able to do when he was growing up, asking Esau to fill in the blank spaces in his own life, and he

וְרִבְקָה אֹהֶבֶת אֶת־יַעֲקֹב׃ 29 וַיָּזֶד יַעֲקֹב
נָזִיד וַיָּבֹא עֵשָׂו מִן־הַשָּׂדֶה וְהוּא עָיֵף׃
30 וַיֹּאמֶר עֵשָׂו אֶל־יַעֲקֹב הַלְעִיטֵנִי נָא מִן־
הָאָדֹם הָאָדֹם הַזֶּה כִּי עָיֵף אָנֹכִי עַל־כֵּן
קָרָא־שְׁמוֹ אֱדוֹם׃ 31 וַיֹּאמֶר יַעֲקֹב מִכְרָה
כַיּוֹם אֶת־בְּכֹרָתְךָ לִי׃ 32 וַיֹּאמֶר עֵשָׂו הִנֵּה
אָנֹכִי הוֹלֵךְ לָמוּת וְלָמָּה־זֶּה לִי בְּכֹרָה׃
33 וַיֹּאמֶר יַעֲקֹב הִשָּׁבְעָה לִּי כַּיּוֹם וַיִּשָּׁבַע
לוֹ וַיִּמְכֹּר אֶת־בְּכֹרָתוֹ לְיַעֲקֹב׃ 34 וְיַעֲקֹב
נָתַן לְעֵשָׂו לֶחֶם וּנְזִיד עֲדָשִׁים וַיֹּאכַל
וַיֵּשְׁתְּ וַיָּקָם וַיֵּלַךְ וַיִּבֶז עֵשָׂו אֶת־הַבְּכֹרָה׃ ס

for game; but Rebekah favored Jacob. 29 Once
when Jacob was cooking a stew, Esau came in
from the open, famished. 30 And Esau said to
Jacob, "Give me some of that red stuff to gulp
down, for I am famished"—which is why he
was named Edom. 31 Jacob said, "First sell me
your birthright." 32 And Esau said, "I am at the
point of death, so of what use is my birthright
to me?" 33 But Jacob said, "Swear to me first." So
he swore to him, and sold his birthright to
Jacob. 34 Jacob then gave Esau bread and lentil
stew; he ate and drank, and he rose and went
away. Thus did Esau spurn the birthright.

28. but Rebekah favored Jacob No reason is given for her preference.

29. cooking a stew The nature of the dish is at first left vague and is disclosed only in stages—first as "red stuff," then as "lentil stew."

famished The Hebrew word *ayef,* traditionally rendered "faint," actually means to be in desperate need of food and drink.

30. Give me . . . to gulp down This is an indication of Esau's boorish manners.

red stuff The Hebrew *"adom"* (red) is a wordplay on Edom.

31. sell Jacob exploits his brother's misery to gain what he thought an accident of birth had denied him. The Bible uses the verb translated as "sell" (מכר) for both sale and barter.

32. I am at the point of death Literally, "I am going to die." His statement is an exaggerated report of his condition.

33. Swear to me first Esau's reply indicates that he agrees to the transaction. But Jacob, not trusting his brother, wants an oath. In the ancient world, an oath was a sacred act that rendered a transaction irrevocable.

34. lentil One of the first plants cultivated in the Near East and an important staple in the daily diet. The color of the lentil is normally yellowish red or light brown.

he ate and drank, and he rose and went away. Thus did Esau spurn This is a translation of five short Hebrew verbs in abrupt succession, which effectively reproduce the chilling, sullen atmosphere.

Thus did Esau spurn the birthright These words express the feelings of the narrator. Having finished the broth, Esau does not quarrel with Jacob but goes about his business, with no apparent regard for the sacred institution of the firstborn.

---

loved his physically gifted son for being what he had never been.

The Sages envision a day when God will come to judge the Jewish people for their sins, and Isaac will rise to defend them. Why Isaac? Because he will be entitled to say to God, "I had a wicked child and I loved him. Can You not do the same?" (BT Shab. 89a).

29. famished Soloveitchik sees Esau as desperately tired and hungry, not just because of the exertion of hunting but because he lacks a sustaining faith to give meaning to his life on bleak days. He is weary of the pointlessness of life and the inevitability of death. Or it may simply be that a person who is very hungry lacks the capacity to be concerned with covenants and religious obligations.

The reader may wonder why Jacob exacts a price for the stew rather than act like a brother and give Esau what he needs. Jacob may resent Esau's privileges, based on his being older by a matter of minutes. Or he may have felt (encouraged perhaps by his mother and the prophecy she recalls) that he was more worthy of being Isaac's heir.

32. I am at the point of death Some people, contemplating their mortality, are moved to live their lives thoughtfully, to invest their energies in things that truly matter. Others, like Esau, say, "Why need I worry about morality

כו וַיְהִי רָעָב בָּאָרֶץ מִלְּבַד הָרָעָב
הָרִאשׁוֹן אֲשֶׁר הָיָה בִּימֵי אַבְרָהָם וַיֵּלֶךְ
יִצְחָק אֶל־אֲבִימֶלֶךְ מֶלֶךְ־פְּלִשְׁתִּים
גְּרָרָה׃ 2 וַיֵּרָא אֵלָיו יְהוָה וַיֹּאמֶר אַל־תֵּרֵד
מִצְרָיְמָה שְׁכֹן בָּאָרֶץ אֲשֶׁר אֹמַר אֵלֶיךָ׃
3 גּוּר בָּאָרֶץ הַזֹּאת וְאֶהְיֶה עִמְּךָ וַאֲבָרְכֶךָּ
כִּי־לְךָ וּלְזַרְעֲךָ אֶתֵּן אֶת־כָּל־הָאֲרָצֹת
הָאֵל וַהֲקִמֹתִי אֶת־הַשְּׁבֻעָה אֲשֶׁר
נִשְׁבַּעְתִּי לְאַבְרָהָם אָבִיךָ׃ 4 וְהִרְבֵּיתִי
אֶת־זַרְעֲךָ כְּכוֹכְבֵי הַשָּׁמַיִם וְנָתַתִּי לְזַרְעֲךָ
אֵת כָּל־הָאֲרָצֹת הָאֵל וְהִתְבָּרְכוּ בְזַרְעֲךָ
כֹּל גּוֹיֵי הָאָרֶץ׃ 5 עֵקֶב אֲשֶׁר־שָׁמַע

26 There was a famine in the land—aside
from the previous famine that had occurred in
the days of Abraham—and Isaac went to Abimelech, king of the Philistines, in Gerar. 2 The
LORD had appeared to him and said, "Do not
go down to Egypt; stay in the land which I point
out to you. 3 Reside in this land, and I will be
with you and bless you; I will assign all these
lands to you and to your heirs, fulfilling the
oath that I swore to your father Abraham. 4 I
will make your heirs as numerous as the stars of
heaven, and assign to your heirs all these lands,
so that all the nations of the earth shall bless
themselves by your heirs— 5 inasmuch as

THE ADVENTURES OF ISAAC (26:1–35)

REAFFIRMATION OF THE COVENANT (vv. 1–5)

The desperate need for forage and water forces Isaac to undertake a journey through the land of the Philistines to Egypt. Along the way, he stops at Gerar, a Philistine royal city certain to have storage facilities.

1. Abimelech This king bears the same name as the king Abraham dealt with more than 75 years earlier.

2. stay The verb translated as "stay" (שכן) means, literally, "to tent."

3. Reside The Hebrew root translated as "reside" (גור) refers to one who has the status of an alien, devoid of legal rights and wholly dependent on the goodwill of the local community (see 23:4).

I will be with you It is to Isaac's alien status that this promise of God's protection is addressed.

and bless you You will prosper even in time of famine.

all these lands The use of the plural is unusual and may reflect the idealized boundaries of the promised land as set forth in 15:18–21 and elsewhere: the territories of Sidon, Tyre, Byblos, the Hermon, and Lebanon, as well as the land of the Philistines.

4. shall bless themselves by your heirs This is one of the major themes of Genesis and is repeated to each of the patriarchs in turn: The well-being of humanity is intertwined with the destiny of the people Israel.

5. Abraham obeyed Me By his fidelity, Abraham represents the ideal standard of obedience to the will of God.

---

and religion since I will die soon anyway?" (Ḥafetz Ḥayyim).

CHAPTER 26

Isaac, who was introduced in the opening words of the *parashah* as "son of Abraham," finds himself reliving many of the events of his father's life: traveling south in time of famine, passing his wife off as his sister out of fear for his own safety, coming into conflict with his neighbors, and being reconciled with them. Verse 18 describes him as redigging the same wells his father had dug and calling them by the same names. Isaac's pilgrimage is a familiar one to many middle-aged men and women who find themselves coming more and more to resemble their parents in appearance and behavior as they mature and coming to understand why their parents did some of the things they did.

Abraham obeyed Me and kept My charge: My commandments, My laws, and My teachings."

[6]So Isaac stayed in Gerar. [7]When the men of the place asked him about his wife, he said, "She is my sister," for he was afraid to say "my wife," thinking, "The men of the place might kill me on account of Rebekah, for she is beautiful." [8]When some time had passed, Abimelech king of the Philistines, looking out of the window, saw Isaac fondling his wife Rebekah. [9]Abimelech sent for Isaac and said, "So she is your wife! Why then did you say: 'She is my sister?'" Isaac said to him, "Because I thought I might lose my life on account of her." [10]Abimelech said, "What have you done to us! One of the people might have lain with your wife, and you would have brought guilt upon us." [11]Abimelech then charged all the people, saying, "Anyone who molests this man or his wife shall be put to death."

[12]Isaac sowed in that land and reaped a hundredfold the same year. The LORD blessed him, [13]and the man grew richer and richer until he was very wealthy: [14]he acquired flocks and herds, and a large household, so that the Phil-

אַבְרָהָם בְּקֹלִי וַיִּשְׁמֹר מִשְׁמַרְתִּי מִצְוֺתַי
חֻקּוֹתַי וְתוֹרֹתָי׃
שני 6 וַיֵּשֶׁב יִצְחָק בִּגְרָר׃ 7 וַיִּשְׁאֲלוּ אַנְשֵׁי
הַמָּקוֹם לְאִשְׁתּוֹ וַיֹּאמֶר אֲחֹתִי הִוא כִּי
יָרֵא לֵאמֹר אִשְׁתִּי פֶּן־יַהַרְגֻנִי אַנְשֵׁי
הַמָּקוֹם עַל־רִבְקָה כִּי־טוֹבַת מַרְאֶה הִיא׃
8 וַיְהִי כִּי אָרְכוּ־לוֹ שָׁם הַיָּמִים וַיַּשְׁקֵף
אֲבִימֶלֶךְ מֶלֶךְ פְּלִשְׁתִּים בְּעַד הַחַלּוֹן
וַיַּרְא וְהִנֵּה יִצְחָק מְצַחֵק אֵת רִבְקָה
אִשְׁתּוֹ׃ 9 וַיִּקְרָא אֲבִימֶלֶךְ לְיִצְחָק וַיֹּאמֶר
אַךְ הִנֵּה אִשְׁתְּךָ הִוא וְאֵיךְ אָמַרְתָּ אֲחֹתִי
הִוא וַיֹּאמֶר אֵלָיו יִצְחָק כִּי אָמַרְתִּי פֶּן־
אָמוּת עָלֶיהָ׃ 10 וַיֹּאמֶר אֲבִימֶלֶךְ מַה־
זֹּאת עָשִׂיתָ לָּנוּ כִּמְעַט שָׁכַב אַחַד הָעָם
אֶת־אִשְׁתֶּךָ וְהֵבֵאתָ עָלֵינוּ אָשָׁם׃ 11 וַיְצַו
אֲבִימֶלֶךְ אֶת־כָּל־הָעָם לֵאמֹר הַנֹּגֵעַ
בָּאִישׁ הַזֶּה וּבְאִשְׁתּוֹ מוֹת יוּמָת׃
12 וַיִּזְרַע יִצְחָק בָּאָרֶץ הַהִוא וַיִּמְצָא
בַּשָּׁנָה הַהִוא מֵאָה שְׁעָרִים וַיְבָרְכֵהוּ
שלישי יְהוָה׃ 13 וַיִּגְדַּל הָאִישׁ וַיֵּלֶךְ הָלוֹךְ וְגָדֵל
עַד כִּי־גָדַל מְאֹד׃ 14 וַיְהִי־לוֹ מִקְנֵה־צֹאן
וּמִקְנֵה בָקָר וַעֲבֻדָּה רַבָּה וַיְקַנְאוּ אֹתוֹ

POSSIBLE PERIL TO REBEKAH (vv. 6–11)

The episode that follows must have occurred before the birth of the twins. Otherwise it is hardly likely that Rebekah could have been passed off as a sister.

7. She is my sister The meaning of this stratagem is discussed in the Comment to 12:13.

8. fondling The verb translated as fondling" (*m'tzahek*) is a wordplay on the name Isaac (*yitzhak*), and refers to sexual dalliance.

10. might have lain In reproving Isaac, the king inadvertently confirms the patriarch's assessment of the low moral standards of the local inhabitants.

brought guilt upon us The entire community would have been blamed, as in the two previous stories about a matriarch in peril (12:17, 20:7–9).

11. who molests The Hebrew verb נגע has the sense of "causing harm," "coming into physical contact with," or "sexually harassing."

ISAAC'S PROSPERITY (vv. 12–16)

Isaac reaps a bountiful harvest in a time of famine, clearly a fulfillment of God's blessing. His prosperity provokes the envy of some of the local people.

12. Isaac sowed Pastoral nomads engaged in small-scale agriculture from time to time. Isaac's experience was probably occasioned by the famine and encouraged by the favorable agricultural conditions in the low-lying plains of the region of Gerar, situated between the settled country and the grazing land of the nomads.

reaped a hundredfold The crop yield in relation to the unit of seed planted was 100 for 1.

פְּלִשְׁתִּים׃ 15 וְכָל־הַבְּאֵרֹת אֲשֶׁר חָפְרוּ
עַבְדֵי אָבִיו בִּימֵי אַבְרָהָם אָבִיו סִתְּמוּם
פְּלִשְׁתִּים וַיְמַלְאוּם עָפָר׃ 16 וַיֹּאמֶר
אֲבִימֶלֶךְ אֶל־יִצְחָק לֵךְ מֵעִמָּנוּ כִּי־
עָצַמְתָּ־מִמֶּנּוּ מְאֹד׃
17 וַיֵּלֶךְ מִשָּׁם יִצְחָק וַיִּחַן בְּנַחַל־גְּרָר וַיֵּשֶׁב
שָׁם׃ 18 וַיָּשָׁב יִצְחָק וַיַּחְפֹּר ׀ אֶת־בְּאֵרֹת
הַמַּיִם אֲשֶׁר חָפְרוּ בִּימֵי אַבְרָהָם אָבִיו
וַיְסַתְּמוּם פְּלִשְׁתִּים אַחֲרֵי מוֹת אַבְרָהָם
וַיִּקְרָא לָהֶן שֵׁמוֹת כַּשֵּׁמֹת אֲשֶׁר־קָרָא
לָהֶן אָבִיו׃ 19 וַיַּחְפְּרוּ עַבְדֵי־יִצְחָק בַּנָּחַל
וַיִּמְצְאוּ־שָׁם בְּאֵר מַיִם חַיִּים׃ 20 וַיָּרִיבוּ
רֹעֵי גְרָר עִם־רֹעֵי יִצְחָק לֵאמֹר לָנוּ הַמָּיִם
וַיִּקְרָא שֵׁם־הַבְּאֵר עֵשֶׂק כִּי הִתְעַשְּׂקוּ
עִמּוֹ׃ 21 וַיַּחְפְּרוּ בְּאֵר אַחֶרֶת וַיָּרִיבוּ גַּם־
עָלֶיהָ וַיִּקְרָא שְׁמָהּ שִׂטְנָה׃ 22 וַיַּעְתֵּק
מִשָּׁם וַיַּחְפֹּר בְּאֵר אַחֶרֶת וְלֹא רָבוּ עָלֶיהָ
וַיִּקְרָא שְׁמָהּ רְחֹבוֹת וַיֹּאמֶר כִּי־עַתָּה
הִרְחִיב יְהוָה לָנוּ וּפָרִינוּ בָאָרֶץ׃ רביעי

istines envied him. 15 And the Philistines stopped up all the wells which his father's servants had dug in the days of his father Abraham, filling them with earth. 16 And Abimelech said to Isaac, "Go away from us, for you have become far too big for us."

17 So Isaac departed from there and encamped in the wadi of Gerar, where he settled. 18 Isaac dug anew the wells which had been dug in the days of his father Abraham and which the Philistines had stopped up after Abraham's death; and he gave them the same names that his father had given them. 19 But when Isaac's servants, digging in the wadi, found there a well of spring water, 20 the herdsmen of Gerar quarreled with Isaac's herdsmen, saying, "The water is ours." He named that well Esek, because they contended with him. 21 And when they dug another well, they disputed over that one also; so he named it Sitnah. 22 He moved from there and dug yet another well, and they did not quarrel over it; so he called it Rehoboth, saying, "Now at last the LORD has granted us ample space to increase in the land."

15. the Philistines stopped up Prevented by the king from physically abusing Isaac, the townsfolk attempt to force him out by denying him access to water.

in the days of . . . Abraham See 21:25,30. The digging of wells or cisterns, usually in the dry beds of rivers, streams, and brooks, was essential to the survival of the pastoralists. After the winter floods would silt them up, they would have to be cleaned out. The Philistines spitefully refilled them with dirt.

16. Go away from us Given the hostility of his subjects to the foreigners, the king feels that he can no longer guarantee the safety of his guests and so requests their departure.

ISAAC'S WELLS (vv. 17–22)

Isaac submits to the expulsion order and moves his family beyond the urban limits of Gerar to the same region in which his father had once made a prolonged stay (21:34).

19. A well of spring water A well of this type was especially valuable. In this instance it should belong to the finder, because there was no memory of its owner.

20. Esek Literally, "contention."

21. Sitnah Literally, "hostility" or "harassment."

22. He moved from there Once again Isaac avoids strife and moves away from the communal grazing ground.

Rehoboth The present-day town of Ruheibeh, located about 19 miles (30.5 km) southwest of Beer-sheba. There are wells of great antiquity in the area and traces of early agricultural settlements.

---

15. One commentator understands that the Philistines stopping up the wells was symbolic, not physical. They tried to block the dissemination of Abraham's ideas about God and human behavior—the need for human beings to live righteously (*Ha-K'tav V'ha-Kabbalah*).

23 From there he went up to Beer-sheba. 24 That night the LORD appeared to him and said, "I am the God of your father Abraham. Fear not, for I am with you, and I will bless you and increase your offspring for the sake of My servant Abraham." 25 So he built an altar there and invoked the LORD by name. Isaac pitched his tent there and his servants started digging a well. 26 And Abimelech came to him from Gerar, with Ahuzzath his councilor and Phicol chief of his troops. 27 Isaac said to them, "Why have you come to me, seeing that you have been hostile to me and have driven me away from you?" 28 And they said, "We now see plainly that the LORD has been with you, and we thought: Let there be a sworn treaty between our two parties, between you and us. Let us make a pact with you 29 that you will not do us harm, just as we have not molested you but have always dealt kindly with you and sent you away in peace. From now on, be you blessed of the LORD!"

רביעי 23 וַיַּעַל מִשָּׁם בְּאֵר שָׁבַע׃ 24 וַיֵּרָא אֵלָיו
יְהוָה בַּלַּיְלָה הַהוּא וַיֹּאמֶר אָנֹכִי אֱלֹהֵי
אַבְרָהָם אָבִיךָ אַל־תִּירָא כִּי־אִתְּךָ אָנֹכִי
וּבֵרַכְתִּיךָ וְהִרְבֵּיתִי אֶת־זַרְעֲךָ בַּעֲבוּר
אַבְרָהָם עַבְדִּי׃ 25 וַיִּבֶן שָׁם מִזְבֵּחַ וַיִּקְרָא
בְּשֵׁם יְהוָה וַיֶּט־שָׁם אָהֳלוֹ וַיִּכְרוּ־שָׁם
עַבְדֵי־יִצְחָק בְּאֵר׃ 26 וַאֲבִימֶלֶךְ הָלַךְ
אֵלָיו מִגְּרָר וַאֲחֻזַּת מֵרֵעֵהוּ וּפִיכֹל שַׂר־
צְבָאוֹ׃ 27 וַיֹּאמֶר אֲלֵהֶם יִצְחָק מַדּוּעַ
בָּאתֶם אֵלָי וְאַתֶּם שְׂנֵאתֶם אֹתִי
וַתְּשַׁלְּחוּנִי מֵאִתְּכֶם׃ 28 וַיֹּאמְרוּ רָאוֹ
רָאִינוּ כִּי־הָיָה יְהוָה ׀ עִמָּךְ וַנֹּאמֶר תְּהִי
נָא אָלָה בֵּינוֹתֵינוּ בֵּינֵינוּ וּבֵינֶךָ וְנִכְרְתָה
בְרִית עִמָּךְ׃ 29 אִם־תַּעֲשֵׂה עִמָּנוּ רָעָה
כַּאֲשֶׁר לֹא נְגַעֲנוּךָ וְכַאֲשֶׁר עָשִׂינוּ עִמְּךָ
רַק־טוֹב וַנְּשַׁלֵּחֲךָ בְּשָׁלוֹם אַתָּה עַתָּה

A REVELATION AT BEER-SHEBA (vv. 23–25)

Isaac finally abandons the region of Gerar and returns to Beer-sheba.

24. I am See Comment to 15:7.

the God of your father The designation affirms God's role as the guarantor of the promises: He is the same one who spoke with Abraham.

My servant This title is used in the Torah only of the Patriarchs, Moses, and Caleb; and, later, only of David and Job.

for the sake of . . . Abraham Here, for the first time, we encounter the notion of "the merit of the fathers" (*z'khut avot*). The righteousness of ancestors creates a fund of spiritual credit that may sustain their descendants.

ISAAC'S PACT WITH ABIMELECH (vv. 26–33)

Abimelech, uneasy over the presence of a powerful clan of pastoralists on the fringes of his kingdom, seeks to regulate his relationship with Isaac. Because Isaac is now the stronger party, the king initiates the pact.

26. his councilor Literally "his friend." The title "king's friend" has no emotional allusion and refers to one who counseled the king in matters of state. Here the king has brought along his chief civilian and military officers.

28. the LORD has been with you He ascribes Isaac's success in agriculture to God.

a sworn treaty The Hebrew term for "a sworn treaty" (*alah*) is also the word used for the curse that accompanies a treaty sealed by an oath. It constitutes its sanction and is meant to ensure fidelity to the treaty's terms.

29. as we have not molested you The king cites the incident described in verses 7–11 and boasts that no harm had befallen Isaac.

be you blessed of the LORD A final greeting of goodwill, intended to allay the bitterness produced by the previous expulsion order.

24. Why does God appear to Isaac now? From God's message, it would seem that Isaac was discouraged, perhaps because of the repeated conflicts with neighbors, perhaps with the resigned recognition of a middle-aged man that he would never match the achievements of his father. God assures him that his life is still rich with meaning and purpose.

מישי בְּר֖וּךְ יְהוָֽה׃ 30 וַיַּ֤עַשׂ לָהֶם֙ מִשְׁתֶּ֔ה וַיֹּאכְל֖וּ
וַיִּשְׁתּֽוּ׃
31 וַיַּשְׁכִּ֣ימוּ בַבֹּ֔קֶר וַיִּשָּׁבְע֖וּ אִ֣ישׁ לְאָחִ֑יו
וַיְשַׁלְּחֵ֣ם יִצְחָ֔ק וַיֵּלְכ֥וּ מֵאִתּ֖וֹ בְּשָׁלֽוֹם׃
32 וַיְהִ֣י ׀ בַּיּ֣וֹם הַה֗וּא וַיָּבֹ֙אוּ֙ עַבְדֵ֣י יִצְחָ֔ק
וַיַּגִּ֣דוּ ל֔וֹ עַל־אֹד֥וֹת הַבְּאֵ֖ר אֲשֶׁ֣ר חָפָ֑רוּ
וַיֹּ֥אמְרוּ ל֖וֹ מָצָ֥אנוּ מָֽיִם׃ 33 וַיִּקְרָ֥א אֹתָ֖הּ
שִׁבְעָ֑ה עַל־כֵּ֤ן שֵׁם־הָעִיר֙ בְּאֵ֣ר שֶׁ֔בַע עַ֖ד
הַיּ֥וֹם הַזֶּֽה׃ ס

34 וַיְהִ֤י עֵשָׂו֙ בֶּן־אַרְבָּעִ֣ים שָׁנָ֔ה וַיִּקַּ֥ח אִשָּׁ֛ה
אֶת־יְהוּדִ֔ית בַּת־בְּאֵרִ֖י הַֽחִתִּ֑י וְאֶת־
בָּ֣שְׂמַ֔ת בַּת־אֵילֹ֖ן הַֽחִתִּֽי׃ 35 וַתִּהְיֶ֖יןָ מֹ֣רַת
ר֑וּחַ לְיִצְחָ֖ק וּלְרִבְקָֽה׃ ס

30Then he made for them a feast, and they ate
and drank.
31Early in the morning, they exchanged
oaths. Isaac then bade them farewell, and they
departed from him in peace. 32That same day
Isaac's servants came and told him about the
well they had dug, and said to him, "We have
found water!" 33He named it Shibah; therefore
the name of the city is Beer-sheba to this day.

34When Esau was forty years old, he took to
wife Judith daughter of Beeri the Hittite, and
Basemath daughter of Elon the Hittite; 35and
they were a source of bitterness to Isaac and
Rebekah.

כז וַיְהִי֙ כִּֽי־זָקֵ֣ן יִצְחָ֔ק וַתִּכְהֶ֥יןָ עֵינָ֖יו
מֵֽרְאֹ֑ת וַיִּקְרָ֞א אֶת־עֵשָׂ֣ו ׀ בְּנ֣וֹ הַגָּדֹ֗ל

27 When Isaac was old and his eyes were
too dim to see, he called his older son Esau and

30. a feast In the ancient world, treaty making often was accompanied by a ceremonial meal, to create an atmosphere of harmony and fellowship for the pact to go into effect.

31. they exchanged oaths The pact is concluded by oaths that most likely also embodied the curse mentioned in verse 28.

32. That same day This narrative about Isaac, Shibah, and Beer-sheba contains wordplay on *shivah* (seven, as in v. 33) and *sh'vu·ah* (oath). The wordplay is best understood in the context of the earlier account involving Abraham and Abimelech (21:22–34), in which the number seven figures prominently.

ESAU'S HITTITE WIVES (vv. 34–35)

This passage reinforces the idea of Esau's unworthiness to be Isaac's heir. He commits two offenses. He breaks with social convention by contracting the marriage himself rather than leaving the initiative to his parents, and he marries outside the kinship group.

34. Esau was forty years old On the basis of 25:20,26.

Judith She is not mentioned in the second list of Esau's wives found in 36:2–3, and no offspring of hers is recorded.

35. they were a source of bitterness The reason is not stated, but the fact is important for the development of the narrative (27:46ff.).

JACOB DECEITFULLY ACQUIRES THE BLESSING (27:1–28:9)

Birthright and blessing were separate institutions. Esau rightly expected to receive the blessing even though he admitted losing the birthright.

ISAAC AND ESAU (27:1–4)

1. When Isaac was old He is 100 years old.

his eyes were too dim His blindness, or perhaps some illness, prompts him to decide on his

HALAKHAH L'MA·ASEH
26:35 they were a source of bitterness See Comment to 24:3.

said to him, “My son.” He answered, “Here I am.” 2And he said, “I am old now, and I do not know how soon I may die. 3Take your gear, your quiver and bow, and go out into the open and hunt me some game. 4Then prepare a dish for me such as I like, and bring it to me to eat, so that I may give you my innermost blessing before I die.”

5Rebekah had been listening as Isaac spoke to his son Esau. When Esau had gone out into the open to hunt game to bring home, 6Rebe-

וַיֹּאמֶר אֵלָיו בְּנִי וַיֹּאמֶר אֵלָיו הִנֵּנִי:
2 וַיֹּאמֶר הִנֵּה־נָא זָקַנְתִּי לֹא יָדַעְתִּי יוֹם
מוֹתִי: 3 וְעַתָּה שָׂא־נָא כֵלֶיךָ תֶּלְיְךָ
וְקַשְׁתֶּךָ וְצֵא הַשָּׂדֶה וְצוּדָה לִּי צידה צָיִד:
4 וַעֲשֵׂה־לִי מַטְעַמִּים כַּאֲשֶׁר אָהַבְתִּי
וְהָבִיאָה לִּי וְאֹכֵלָה בַּעֲבוּר תְּבָרֶכְךָ נַפְשִׁי
בְּטֶרֶם אָמוּת:
5 וְרִבְקָה שֹׁמַעַת בְּדַבֵּר יִצְחָק אֶל־עֵשָׂו בְּנוֹ
וַיֵּלֶךְ עֵשָׂו הַשָּׂדֶה לָצוּד צַיִד לְהָבִיא:

successor at this time. The loss of vision is crucial to the narrative.

his older son The narrator avoids calling Esau the “firstborn” because the term carries with it social and legal implications that Esau no longer has because he sold his birthright.

3. gear A general term for “quiver and bow.” The arrow was kept in a lightweight container, a quiver, that hung over the hunter's shoulder.

4. prepare a dish The repeated emphasis given to the meal suggests inducing not just a means of physical well-being and the proper mood for the occasion but also a ritual closely connected with the act of blessing.

my innermost blessing Literally, “that my being (*nefesh*) may bless you.” Isaac summons from the depths of his soul all the vitality and energy at his command to invoke God's blessing on his son. The literal meaning of *nefesh* is “throat,” “appetite.” That is, Isaac's vitality will be strengthened by food, making his blessing more forceful.

REBEKAH AND JACOB (vv. 5–17)

5. Rebekah had been listening Rebekah, alert to the interests of her favorite son, makes it her business to know what is going on when Isaac summons Esau.

CHAPTER 27

1. his eyes were too dim to see Several commentators understand Isaac's blindness as emotional, not physical. Because he loved and envied Esau, he was blind to Esau's faults. He could not recognize that Esau's shortcomings disqualified him from being the heir to Abraham's teachings. One *midrash* connects this incident to the passage (in Deut. 16:19) warning judges not to accept gifts, lest they distort the clarity of the judges' vision (Tanḥ.). Isaac's judgment is clouded by Esau's bringing him his favorite foods. Another *midrash* recalls Isaac lying on his back on the altar at the time of the *Akedah,* glimpsing the light of heaven when the angel appears to spare his life, and suggests that Isaac was never able to see events on earth clearly after that (Gen. R. 65:10). Having been afforded a glimpse of heaven, Isaac was naively blind to lying and deceit on earth. He could no more recognize the transparent lies of Jacob than he could recognize the unworthiness of Esau.

Rebekah resorts to duplicity because she has no other way of bringing about what she knows is right and what God told her (in Gen. 25:23). She cannot persuade Isaac that he is wrong about the respective merits of their two sons. Once again, as so often in the Torah, God's

HALAKHAH L'MA·ASEH

27:2 I am old now Those who tend to the dying must ask them whether they have put their affairs in order. In order not to be discouraging, caregivers should emphasize that they hope for recovery and are just taking precautions in case recovery does not occur (S.A. YD 335:7). In addition to arranging for the disbursement of their assets, people should be encouraged to fill out an Advanced Directive for Health Care, as approved by the CJLS, and to compose an ethical will for their relatives, recounting their life story and expressing their convictions, hopes, and love.

kah said to her son Jacob, "I overheard your
father speaking to your brother Esau, saying,
7'Bring me some game and prepare a dish for
me to eat, that I may bless you, with the LORD's
approval, before I die.' 8Now, my son, listen
carefully as I instruct you. 9Go to the flock
and fetch me two choice kids, and I will make
of them a dish for your father, such as he likes.
10Then take it to your father to eat, in order that
he may bless you before he dies." 11Jacob answered his mother Rebekah, "But my brother
Esau is a hairy man and I am smooth-skinned.
12If my father touches me, I shall appear to him
as a trickster and bring upon myself a curse, not
a blessing." 13But his mother said to him, "Your
curse, my son, be upon me! Just do as I say and
go fetch them for me."

14He got them and brought them to his
mother, and his mother prepared a dish such
as his father liked. 15Rebekah then took the best
clothes of her older son Esau, which were there
in the house, and had her younger son Jacob
put them on; 16and she covered his hands and
the hairless part of his neck with the skins of the
kids. 17Then she put in the hands of her son
Jacob the dish and the bread that she had prepared.

18He went to his father and said, "Father."
And he said, "Yes, which of my sons are you?"

6 וְרִבְקָה֙ אָֽמְרָ֔ה אֶל־יַעֲקֹ֥ב בְּנָ֖הּ לֵאמֹ֑ר הִנֵּ֤ה
שָׁמַ֙עְתִּי֙ אֶת־אָבִ֔יךָ מְדַבֵּ֛ר אֶל־עֵשָׂ֥ו אָחִ֖יךָ
לֵאמֹֽר׃ 7 הָבִ֨יאָה לִּ֥י צַ֛יִד וַעֲשֵׂה־לִ֥י
מַטְעַמִּ֖ים וְאֹכֵ֑לָה וַאֲבָרֶכְכָ֛ה לִפְנֵ֥י יְהוָ֖ה
לִפְנֵ֥י מוֹתִֽי׃ 8 וְעַתָּ֥ה בְנִ֖י שְׁמַ֣ע בְּקֹלִ֑י
לַאֲשֶׁ֥ר אֲנִ֖י מְצַוָּ֥ה אֹתָֽךְ׃ 9 לֶךְ־נָא֙ אֶל־
הַצֹּ֔אן וְקַֽח־לִ֣י מִשָּׁ֗ם שְׁנֵ֛י גְּדָיֵ֥י עִזִּ֖ים טֹבִ֑ים
וְאֶעֱשֶׂ֨ה אֹתָ֧ם מַטְעַמִּ֛ים לְאָבִ֖יךָ כַּאֲשֶׁ֥ר
אָהֵֽב׃ 10 וְהֵבֵאתָ֥ לְאָבִ֖יךָ וְאָכָ֑ל בַּעֲבֻ֛ר
אֲשֶׁ֥ר יְבָרֶכְךָ֖ לִפְנֵ֥י מוֹתֽוֹ׃ 11 וַיֹּ֣אמֶר יַעֲקֹ֔ב
אֶל־רִבְקָ֖ה אִמּ֑וֹ הֵ֚ן עֵשָׂ֣ו אָחִ֔י אִ֣ישׁ שָׂעִ֔ר
וְאָנֹכִ֖י אִ֥ישׁ חָלָֽק׃ 12 אוּלַ֤י יְמֻשֵּׁ֙נִי֙ אָבִ֔י
וְהָיִ֥יתִי בְעֵינָ֖יו כִּמְתַעְתֵּ֑עַ וְהֵבֵאתִ֥י עָלַ֛י
קְלָלָ֖ה וְלֹ֥א בְרָכָֽה׃ 13 וַתֹּ֤אמֶר לוֹ֙ אִמּ֔וֹ עָלַ֥י
קִלְלָֽתְךָ֖ בְּנִ֑י אַ֛ךְ שְׁמַ֥ע בְּקֹלִ֖י וְלֵ֥ךְ קַֽח־לִֽי׃
14 וַיֵּ֙לֶךְ֙ וַיִּקַּ֔ח וַיָּבֵ֖א לְאִמּ֑וֹ וַתַּ֤עַשׂ אִמּוֹ֙
מַטְעַמִּ֔ים כַּאֲשֶׁ֖ר אָהֵ֥ב אָבִֽיו׃ 15 וַתִּקַּ֣ח
רִ֠בְקָה אֶת־בִּגְדֵ֨י עֵשָׂ֜ו בְּנָ֤הּ הַגָּדֹל֙
הַחֲמֻדֹ֔ת אֲשֶׁ֥ר אִתָּ֖הּ בַּבָּ֑יִת וַתַּלְבֵּ֥שׁ אֶת־
יַעֲקֹ֖ב בְּנָ֥הּ הַקָּטָֽן׃ 16 וְאֵ֗ת עֹרֹת֙ גְּדָיֵ֣י
הָֽעִזִּ֔ים הִלְבִּ֖ישָׁה עַל־יָדָ֑יו וְעַ֖ל חֶלְקַ֥ת
צַוָּארָֽיו׃ 17 וַתִּתֵּ֧ן אֶת־הַמַּטְעַמִּ֛ים וְאֶת־
הַלֶּ֖חֶם אֲשֶׁ֣ר עָשָׂ֑תָה בְּיַ֖ד יַעֲקֹ֥ב בְּנָֽהּ׃
18 וַיָּבֹ֥א אֶל־אָבִ֖יו וַיֹּ֣אמֶר אָבִ֑י וַיֹּ֣אמֶר הִנֶּ֔נִּי

7. with the LORD's approval Literally, "in the presence of the LORD." Rebekah adds this phrase to Isaac's words to impress on Jacob the importance and solemnity of the occasion.

12. a trickster Jacob seems to be more concerned with the consequences of detection than with the morality of the act.

13. his mother said Rebekah, recalling the oracle she received that the older son was destined to serve the younger (25:23), confidently brushes aside Jacob's fears.

14. He got them and brought them The Hebrew here is a staccato succession of three short verbs: "He went, he took, he brought." The effect is a picture of Jacob performing the deed with nervous haste.

15. the best clothes These probably were reserved for special occasions.

ISAAC AND JACOB (vv. 18–20)

18. Father Jacob, deeply apprehensive, can utter only a single word.

which of my sons are you? Either Jacob's attempt to mime Esau is not quite successful or

---

work is carried out by the least powerful members of society, women and younger sons.

18. The Hebrew literally asks, "Who are you, my son?" This can be understood to mean

19 Jacob said to his father, "I am Esau, your first-
born; I have done as you told me. Pray sit up
and eat of my game, that you may give me your
innermost blessing." 20 Isaac said to his son,
"How did you succeed so quickly, my son?"
And he said, "Because the LORD your God
granted me good fortune." 21 Isaac said to Jacob, "Come closer that I may feel you, my
son—whether you are really my son Esau or
not." 22 So Jacob drew close to his father Isaac,
who felt him and wondered. "The voice is the
voice of Jacob, yet the hands are the hands of
Esau." 23 He did not recognize him, because his
hands were hairy like those of his brother Esau;
and so he blessed him.

24 He asked, "Are you really my son Esau?"
And when he said, "I am," 25 he said, "Serve me
and let me eat of my son's game that I may give
you my innermost blessing." So he served him

מִי אַתָּה בְּנִי׃ 19 וַיֹּאמֶר יַעֲקֹב אֶל־אָבִיו
אָנֹכִי עֵשָׂו בְּכֹרֶךָ עָשִׂיתִי כַּאֲשֶׁר דִּבַּרְתָּ
אֵלָי קוּם־נָא שְׁבָה וְאָכְלָה מִצֵּידִי בַּעֲבוּר
תְּבָרְכַנִּי נַפְשֶׁךָ׃ 20 וַיֹּאמֶר יִצְחָק אֶל־בְּנוֹ
מַה־זֶּה מִהַרְתָּ לִמְצֹא בְּנִי וַיֹּאמֶר כִּי
הִקְרָה יְהוָה אֱלֹהֶיךָ לְפָנָי׃ 21 וַיֹּאמֶר
יִצְחָק אֶל־יַעֲקֹב גְּשָׁה־נָּא וַאֲמֻשְׁךָ בְּנִי
הַאַתָּה זֶה בְּנִי עֵשָׂו אִם־לֹא׃ 22 וַיִּגַּשׁ
יַעֲקֹב אֶל־יִצְחָק אָבִיו וַיְמֻשֵּׁהוּ וַיֹּאמֶר
הַקֹּל קוֹל יַעֲקֹב וְהַיָּדַיִם יְדֵי עֵשָׂו׃ 23 וְלֹא
הִכִּירוֹ כִּי־הָיוּ יָדָיו כִּידֵי עֵשָׂו אָחִיו שְׂעִרֹת
וַיְבָרְכֵהוּ׃
24 וַיֹּאמֶר אַתָּה זֶה בְּנִי עֵשָׂו וַיֹּאמֶר אָנִי׃
25 וַיֹּאמֶר הַגִּשָׁה לִּי וְאֹכְלָה מִצֵּיד בְּנִי
לְמַעַן תְּבָרֶכְךָ נַפְשִׁי וַיַּגֶּשׁ־לוֹ וַיֹּאכַל

Isaac is so suspicious that he has to verify which one of his sons is before him.

20. the LORD your God Jacob invokes God's name in an outright lie!

21. Come closer Deprived of his eyesight, Isaac summons to his aid the remaining senses of hearing, touch, taste, and smell.

22. the voice The distinctive quality of Jacob's voice puts his impersonation of Esau in jeopardy, but the skin disguise is effective and saves the day. Isaac decides to bless his son.

24. He asked At the last moment Isaac renews his probing, once again seized by a vague disquiet.

I am Again at the critical moment, Jacob can utter only a single word.

25. Serve me In demanding the meal at this point, Isaac imposes the test of taste. His repeated emphasis on the meat being prepared in accordance with his special preference suggests a recipe used with skill by Esau that helped endear him to his father.

---

not only "which of my sons are you?" but "what sort of person are you?" Jacob will spend many years pondering that question: "Who are you?"

20. the LORD your God granted me good fortune This answer troubles Isaac. Esau usually did not speak that way, thanking God for his good fortune. Indeed, when Esau arrives (in v. 31), he speaks in a very different tone. (The translation cannot quite capture the flavor of Esau's speech: short, blunt, demanding words.) The reader cannot help but suspect that Isaac realizes it is Jacob before him and either acquiesces to the substitution (for when did Isaac ever protest when others determined the course of his life?) or else realizes that Jacob does indeed deserve the blessing.

22. The voice is the voice of Jacob This familiar verse has prompted many comments, some on the essential differences between the descendants of Jacob and the descendants of Esau, others on the hypocrisy of people whose deeds do not match their words. "So long as the voice of Jacob is heard in prayer and study, the hands of Esau are powerless against him" (Gen. R. 65:20). "Esau wields power with his hands, with physical force, so he can only have an effect on what he can reach. But Jacob's power is in his words, his ideas, which can reach anywhere on earth" (Tanḥ. B.).

and he ate, and he brought him wine and he
drank. 26 Then his father Isaac said to him,
"Come close and kiss me, my son"; 27 and he
went up and kissed him. And he smelled his
clothes and he blessed him, saying, "Ah, the
smell of my son is like the smell of the fields
that the LORD has blessed.

28 "May God give you
Of the dew of heaven and the fat of the
earth,
Abundance of new grain and wine.
29 Let peoples serve you,
And nations bow to you;
Be master over your brothers,
And let your mother's sons bow to you.
Cursed be they who curse you,
Blessed they who bless you."

30 No sooner had Jacob left the presence of
his father Isaac—after Isaac had finished blessing Jacob—than his brother Esau came back
from his hunt. 31 He too prepared a dish and
brought it to his father. And he said to his
father, "Let my father sit up and eat of his son's
game, so that you may give me your innermost
blessing." 32 His father Isaac said to him, "Who
are you?" And he said, "I am your son, Esau,
your first-born!" 33 Isaac was seized with very
violent trembling. "Who was it then," he de-

וַיָּבֵא לוֹ יַיִן וַיֵּשְׁתְּ׃ 26 וַיֹּאמֶר אֵלָיו יִצְחָק
אָבִיו גְּשָׁה־נָּא וּשְׁקָה־לִּי בְּנִי׃ 27 וַיִּגַּשׁ
וַיִּשַּׁק־לוֹ וַיָּרַח אֶת־רֵיחַ בְּגָדָיו וַיְבָרְכֵהוּ
וַיֹּאמֶר רְאֵה רֵיחַ בְּנִי כְּרֵיחַ שָׂדֶה אֲשֶׁר
בֵּרֲכוֹ יְהוָה׃

ששי 28 וְיִתֶּן־לְךָ הָאֱלֹהִים
מִטַּל הַשָּׁמַיִם וּמִשְׁמַנֵּי הָאָרֶץ
וְרֹב דָּגָן וְתִירֹשׁ׃
29 יַעַבְדוּךָ עַמִּים
וישתחו וְיִשְׁתַּחֲוּוּ לְךָ לְאֻמִּים
הֱוֵה גְבִיר לְאַחֶיךָ
וְיִשְׁתַּחֲוּוּ לְךָ בְּנֵי אִמֶּךָ
אֹרְרֶיךָ אָרוּר
וּמְבָרְכֶיךָ בָּרוּךְ׃

30 וַיְהִי כַּאֲשֶׁר כִּלָּה יִצְחָק לְבָרֵךְ אֶת־
יַעֲקֹב וַיְהִי אַךְ יָצֹא יָצָא יַעֲקֹב מֵאֵת פְּנֵי
יִצְחָק אָבִיו וְעֵשָׂו אָחִיו בָּא מִצֵּידוֹ׃
31 וַיַּעַשׂ גַּם־הוּא מַטְעַמִּים וַיָּבֵא לְאָבִיו
וַיֹּאמֶר לְאָבִיו יָקֻם אָבִי וְיֹאכַל מִצֵּיד בְּנוֹ
בַּעֲבֻר תְּבָרְכַנִּי נַפְשֶׁךָ׃ 32 וַיֹּאמֶר לוֹ יִצְחָק
אָבִיו מִי־אָתָּה וַיֹּאמֶר אֲנִי בִּנְךָ בְכֹרְךָ
עֵשָׂו׃ 33 וַיֶּחֱרַד יִצְחָק חֲרָדָה גְּדֹלָה עַד־
מְאֹד וַיֹּאמֶר מִי־אֵפוֹא הוּא הַצָּד־צַיִד

27. he smelled his clothes The clothes of the shepherd reek of the flock and the herd, whereas those of the hunter are redolent of the fields, which Isaac relished.

and he blessed him Isaac now communicates the decisive blessing, which really relates to national destiny rather than to the fate of an individual. It is unique in the patriarchal narratives thus far, in that it contains no promises of progeny or land. For this reason, it may better be viewed as Isaac's personal blessing rather than a covenantal blessing. For that, see 28:3–4.

28. the dew of heaven This is a metaphor for abundance, reinvigoration, and God's beneficence. Throughout most of the rainless summer months, it is dew that serves as the major source of moisture for crops in many places in the land of Israel.

the fat of the earth The finest fruits of the soil.

29. master over your brothers Israel's military might and political power will give it preeminence over its hostile neighbors.

Cursed In the ancient Near East, the curse was considered a powerful weapon against an enemy.

ISAAC AND ESAU (vv. 30–41)

There can be no doubt that the sympathies of the narrator are with Esau, portrayed here as the innocent victim of a cruel scheme.

32. Who are you This time, Isaac does not

manded, "that hunted game and brought it to
me? Moreover, I ate of it before you came, and I
blessed him; now he must remain blessed!"
34When Esau heard his father's words, he burst
into wild and bitter sobbing, and said to his
father, "Bless me too, Father!" 35But he answered, "Your brother came with guile and
took away your blessing." 36[Esau] said, "Was
he, then, named Jacob that he might supplant
me these two times? First he took away my
birthright and now he has taken away my blessing!" And he added, "Have you not reserved a
blessing for me?" 37Isaac answered, saying to
Esau, "But I have made him master over you: I
have given him all his brothers for servants,
and sustained him with grain and wine. What,
then, can I still do for you, my son?" 38And Esau
said to his father, "Have you but one blessing,
Father? Bless me too, Father!" And Esau wept
aloud. 39And his father Isaac answered, saying
to him,

וַיָּבֵא לִי וָאֹכַל מִכֹּל בְּטֶרֶם תָּבוֹא
וָאֲבָרְכֵהוּ גַּם־בָּרוּךְ יִהְיֶה׃ 34 כִּשְׁמֹעַ עֵשָׂו
אֶת־דִּבְרֵי אָבִיו וַיִּצְעַק צְעָקָה גְּדֹלָה
וּמָרָה עַד־מְאֹד וַיֹּאמֶר לְאָבִיו בָּרְכֵנִי גַם־
אָנִי אָבִי׃ 35 וַיֹּאמֶר בָּא אָחִיךָ בְּמִרְמָה
וַיִּקַּח בִּרְכָתֶךָ׃ 36 וַיֹּאמֶר הֲכִי קָרָא שְׁמוֹ
יַעֲקֹב וַיַּעְקְבֵנִי זֶה פַעֲמַיִם אֶת־בְּכֹרָתִי
לָקָח וְהִנֵּה עַתָּה לָקַח בִּרְכָתִי וַיֹּאמַר
הֲלֹא־אָצַלְתָּ לִּי בְּרָכָה׃ 37 וַיַּעַן יִצְחָק
וַיֹּאמֶר לְעֵשָׂו הֵן גְּבִיר שַׂמְתִּיו לָךְ וְאֶת־
כָּל־אֶחָיו נָתַתִּי לוֹ לַעֲבָדִים וְדָגָן וְתִירֹשׁ
סְמַכְתִּיו וּלְכָה אֵפוֹא מָה אֶעֱשֶׂה בְּנִי׃
38 וַיֹּאמֶר עֵשָׂו אֶל־אָבִיו הַבְרָכָה אַחַת
הִוא־לְךָ אָבִי בָּרְכֵנִי גַם־אָנִי אָבִי וַיִּשָּׂא
עֵשָׂו קֹלוֹ וַיֵּבְךְּ׃ 39 וַיַּעַן יִצְחָק אָבִיו
וַיֹּאמֶר אֵלָיו

call the speaker "my son" because he cannot conceive of having been deceived by his own offspring.

33. he must remain blessed Isaac is overwhelmed with dismay but then realizes, in keeping with the concept of the time, that the blessing he has given now possesses a potency and dynamism all its own. The destiny that has been conferred on his younger son is irreversible (v. 37). For that reason, Esau does not ask his father to rescind the blessing, only to bless him as well.

36. Was he, then, named Jacob In his misery, Esau resorts to bitter sarcasm that expresses itself in wordplays. He reinterprets the name Jacob (*ya·akov*) as deriving from the stem עקב, meaning "to supplant" (see 25:26). He also puns on *b'khorah,* "birthright," and *b'rakhah,* "blessing."

he took away my birthright Esau blurts out the loss of his birthright, which Isaac apparently does not yet know.

39. saying to him The pronouncement is strangely enigmatic and ambiguous. The prefix letter *mem* in each of the two key words for "fat" and "dew" can mean that Esau will *share in* the richness of the earth. It can also mean, "your abode shall be *far from* the fat of the earth, / And *far from* the dew of heaven above." The land of Edom was never very fruitful, and the nature of its topography deprives it of all but negligible rain.

40. by your sword Edom's sustenance shall

---

34. wild and bitter sobbing The Sages generally regarded Esau as a villain and the archetypical anti-Semite, the spiritual ancestor of Imperial Rome and all the other European persecutors of Jews. Here, however, they sympathize with his tears and his pain at being cheated and are uncomfortable with Jacob's having gained the blessing by fraudulent means. "Years later, our people will have to shed tears for what the descendants of Esau (the Edomites who helped destroy the First Temple and the Romans who destroyed the Second Temple) did to them, as retribution for the day Jacob made Esau cry" (Gen. R. 67:4).

"See, your abode shall enjoy the fat of the earth
And the dew of heaven above.
40Yet by your sword you shall live,
And you shall serve your brother;
But when you grow restive,
You shall break his yoke from your neck."

41Now Esau harbored a grudge against Jacob because of the blessing which his father had given him, and Esau said to himself, "Let but the mourning period of my father come, and I will kill my brother Jacob." 42When the words of her older son Esau were reported to Rebekah, she sent for her younger son Jacob and said to him, "Your brother Esau is consoling himself by planning to kill you. 43Now, my son, listen to me. Flee at once to Haran, to my brother Laban. 44Stay with him a while, until your brother's fury subsides—45until your brother's anger against you subsides—and he forgets what you have done to him. Then I will fetch you from there. Let me not lose you both in one day!"

46Rebekah said to Isaac, "I am disgusted with my life because of the Hittite women. If Jacob marries a Hittite woman like these, from among the native women, what good will life

הִנֵּה מִשְׁמַנֵּי הָאָרֶץ יִהְיֶה מוֹשָׁבֶךָ
וּמִטַּל הַשָּׁמַיִם מֵעָל׃
40 *וְעַל־חַרְבְּךָ תִחְיֶה
וְאֶת־אָחִיךָ תַּעֲבֹד
וְהָיָה כַּאֲשֶׁר תָּרִיד
וּפָרַקְתָּ עֻלּוֹ מֵעַל צַוָּארֶךָ׃
41 וַיִּשְׂטֹם עֵשָׂו אֶת־יַעֲקֹב עַל־הַבְּרָכָה
אֲשֶׁר בֵּרְכוֹ אָבִיו וַיֹּאמֶר עֵשָׂו בְּלִבּוֹ
יִקְרְבוּ יְמֵי אֵבֶל אָבִי וְאַהַרְגָה אֶת־יַעֲקֹב
אָחִי׃ 42 וַיֻּגַּד לְרִבְקָה אֶת־דִּבְרֵי עֵשָׂו
בְּנָהּ הַגָּדֹל וַתִּשְׁלַח וַתִּקְרָא לְיַעֲקֹב בְּנָהּ
הַקָּטָן וַתֹּאמֶר אֵלָיו הִנֵּה עֵשָׂו אָחִיךָ
מִתְנַחֵם לְךָ לְהָרְגֶךָ׃ 43 וְעַתָּה בְנִי שְׁמַע
בְּקֹלִי וְקוּם בְּרַח־לְךָ אֶל־לָבָן אָחִי חָרָנָה׃
44 וְיָשַׁבְתָּ עִמּוֹ יָמִים אֲחָדִים עַד אֲשֶׁר־
תָּשׁוּב חֲמַת אָחִיךָ׃ 45 עַד־שׁוּב אַף־אָחִיךָ
מִמְּךָ וְשָׁכַח אֵת אֲשֶׁר־עָשִׂיתָ לּוֹ וְשָׁלַחְתִּי
וּלְקַחְתִּיךָ מִשָּׁם לָמָה אֶשְׁכַּל גַּם־שְׁנֵיכֶם
יוֹם אֶחָד׃
46 וַתֹּאמֶר רִבְקָה אֶל־יִצְחָק קַצְתִּי* בְּחַיַּי
מִפְּנֵי בְּנוֹת חֵת אִם־לֹקֵחַ יַעֲקֹב אִשָּׁה
מִבְּנוֹת־חֵת כָּאֵלֶּה מִבְּנוֹת הָאָרֶץ לָמָּה

v. 40. למדינחאי חצי הספר בפסוקים

v. 46. ק׳ זעירא לפי נוסחים מקובלים

come not from pastoral or agricultural pursuits but from violence and pillage, raiding its neighbors and plundering the caravans that pass through its land.

serve your brother Edom will be a vassal of Israel for a long time.

break his yoke Eventually, however, it will free itself of Israelite domination.

41. Esau said to himself The Hebrew simply means that his mind was made up, not that he kept his thoughts to himself.

the mourning period Out of filial respect, Esau employs a euphemism for death.

REBEKAH AND JACOB (vv. 42–45)

Rebekah seems to have misjudged the intensity of Esau's outrage. She is now clearly alarmed.

42. she sent for . . . Jacob He may have been in hiding.

REBEKAH AND ISAAC (v. 46)

Rebekah realizes that Jacob must be sent away at once. But to do that she will need her husband's agreement. She dare not divulge the true reason: She wishes to spare Isaac further anguish, and she fears that her own involvement in the deception might be exposed. She hits on the pretext of Jacob's need to get married.

46. I am disgusted Her argument is decisive, because, as 26:34–35 have already informed us, Esau's union with the local women has become intolerable to his parents.

28

be to me?" 1 So Isaac sent for Jacob
and blessed him. He instructed him,
saying, "You shall not take a wife from among
the Canaanite women. 2 Up, go to Paddan-
aram, to the house of Bethuel, your mother's
father, and take a wife there from among the
daughters of Laban, your mother's brother,
3 May El Shaddai bless you, make you fertile
and numerous, so that you become an assembly of peoples. 4 May He grant the blessing of
Abraham to you and your offspring, that you
may possess the land where you are sojourning, which God assigned to Abraham."
5 Then Isaac sent Jacob off, and he went to
Paddan-aram, to Laban the son of Bethuel the
Aramean, the brother of Rebekah, mother of
Jacob and Esau.

כח

לִי חַיִּים: 1 וַיִּקְרָא יִצְחָק אֶל־
יַעֲקֹב וַיְבָרֶךְ אֹתוֹ וַיְצַוֵּהוּ
וַיֹּאמֶר לוֹ לֹא־תִקַּח אִשָּׁה מִבְּנוֹת כְּנָעַן:
2 קוּם לֵךְ פַּדֶּנָה אֲרָם בֵּיתָה בְתוּאֵל אֲבִי
אִמֶּךָ וְקַח־לְךָ מִשָּׁם אִשָּׁה מִבְּנוֹת לָבָן
אֲחִי אִמֶּךָ: 3 וְאֵל שַׁדַּי יְבָרֵךְ אֹתְךָ וְיַפְרְךָ
וְיַרְבֶּךָ וְהָיִיתָ לִקְהַל עַמִּים: 4 וְיִתֶּן־לְךָ
אֶת־בִּרְכַּת אַבְרָהָם לְךָ וּלְזַרְעֲךָ אִתָּךְ
לְרִשְׁתְּךָ אֶת־אֶרֶץ מְגֻרֶיךָ אֲשֶׁר־נָתַן
אֱלֹהִים לְאַבְרָהָם:
שביעי 5 וַיִּשְׁלַח יִצְחָק אֶת־יַעֲקֹב וַיֵּלֶךְ פַּדֶּנָה
אֲרָם אֶל־לָבָן בֶּן־בְּתוּאֵל הָאֲרַמִּי אֲחִי
רִבְקָה אֵם יַעֲקֹב וְעֵשָׂו:

ISAAC AND JACOB (28:1–5)

1. and blessed him By this act, Isaac confirms Jacob's title to the birthright. Jacob is now recognized as the true heir to the Abrahamic covenant, which is why he must not marry outside the family.

2. Up, go Isaac knows nothing of the real reason for Jacob's journey. That is why he uses "go" in contrast to Rebekah's "flee" in 27:43.

Paddan-aram See Comment to 25:20.

take a wife there The patriarch has the right to decide whom the members of his clan shall marry.

3. bless you This blessing adds to the earlier one the dimensions of nationhood and national territory. It cites the divine promises to Abraham as given in chapter 17, even to the extent of using the divine name El Shaddai with which that section begins.

5. mother of Jacob and Esau Jacob is given precedence. At the same time, Esau is mentioned in order to smooth the connection with the following verses.

CHAPTER 28

4. Now that Isaac knows for a certainty which of his sons he is blessing, his words to Jacob invoke the promises (see 12:7, 13:14–17, and 17:8) to Abraham.

5. Why does the text emphasize that Rebekah was the mother of Jacob and Esau, something we already knew? She sends Jacob away not only to spare his life but to save Esau from becoming a murderer. Although she favored Jacob for the blessing, they were both her children and she loved them both (*Tzeidah La-Derekh*).

If the reader is left troubled by Jacob's apparently getting away with lying and deceit, fooling his father, and fraudulently depriving his brother of the intended blessing, one need only read on in the next *parashah* to see Jacob's punishment. It is not the way of the Torah to moralize over questionable behavior but rather to show its consequences in people's lives. Jacob soon will find out what it feels like to be deceived and defrauded.

HALAKHAH L'MA·ASEH

28:1 from among the Canaanite women See Comment to 24:3.

6When Esau saw that Isaac had blessed Jacob and sent him off to Paddan-aram to take a wife from there, charging him, as he blessed him, "You shall not take a wife from among the Canaanite women," 7and that Jacob had obeyed his father and mother and gone to Paddan-aram, 8Esau realized that the Canaanite women displeased his father Isaac. 9So Esau went to Ishmael and took to wife, in addition to the wives he had, Mahalath the daughter of Ishmael son of Abraham, sister of Nebaioth.

6וַיַּ֣רְא עֵשָׂ֗ו כִּֽי־בֵרַ֣ךְ יִצְחָק֮ אֶֽת־יַעֲקֹב֒ וְשִׁלַּ֤ח אֹתוֹ֙ פַּדֶּ֣נָֽה אֲרָ֔ם לָקַֽחַת־ל֥וֹ מִשָּׁ֖ם אִשָּׁ֑ה בְּבָרֲכ֣וֹ אֹת֔וֹ וַיְצַ֤ו עָלָיו֙ לֵאמֹ֔ר לֹֽא־תִקַּ֥ח אִשָּׁ֖ה מִבְּנ֥וֹת כְּנָֽעַן: 7וַיִּשְׁמַ֣ע יַעֲקֹ֔ב מפטיר אֶל־אָבִ֖יו וְאֶל־אִמּ֑וֹ וַיֵּ֖לֶךְ פַּדֶּ֥נָֽה אֲרָֽם: 8וַיַּ֣רְא עֵשָׂ֔ו כִּ֥י רָע֖וֹת בְּנ֣וֹת כְּנָ֑עַן בְּעֵינֵ֖י יִצְחָ֥ק אָבִֽיו: 9וַיֵּ֥לֶךְ עֵשָׂ֖ו אֶל־יִשְׁמָעֵ֑אל וַיִּקַּ֡ח אֶֽת־מָחֲלַ֣ת ׀ בַּת־יִשְׁמָעֵ֨אל בֶּן־אַבְרָהָ֜ם אֲח֧וֹת נְבָי֛וֹת עַל־נָשָׁ֖יו ל֥וֹ לְאִשָּֽׁה: ס

ESAU'S ISHMAELITE WIFE   (vv. 6–9)

6. When Esau saw Realizing that his marriages outside the kinship group and his alliances with the native women have contributed to his loss of the blessing, Esau now weds the daughter of his father's brother. That act will later be paralleled by Jacob's marriage to the daughter of his mother's brother.

9. Ishmael The tribe; the man himself was no longer alive.

Mahalath She is not mentioned among Esau's wives in 36:2–3. There, Basemath is cited as the daughter of Ishmael and sister of Nebaioth. The two names may have belonged to the same person. The Aramaic stem חלא means "sweetness," a more appropriate meaning than "sickness," which is the usual understanding derived from the Hebrew.

Nebaioth The firstborn of Ishmael. The clan with that name was pre-eminent in the Ishmaelite tribal league.

הפטרת תולדות

HAFTARAH FOR TOL'DOT

MALACHI 1:1–2:7

This *haftarah* recalls the rivalry between Jacob and Esau, as it focuses on the ongoing historical strife between their descendants—Israel and Edom. The prophet, speaking in the 5th century B.C.E., illustrates some aspects of religion and culture in the early years of the Second Temple.

The overall ritual content of the *haftarah* leaves little room for moral rebuke. Morality is not entirely outside of Malachi's message (see 3:5), but it is not the focus of his concern here. Indeed, even when he expresses antagonism over the people's theft of animals (along with their deception and disobedience), the emphasis is on ritual faults (1:13). Malachi puts special stress on the priests' duties of piety and purity before the Lord. In a striking statement, the prophet contrasts the perversity of the priests of Israel with the faithful among the nations who offer "incense and pure oblation" to the Lord—thus doing Him honor throughout the world, "from where the sun rises to where it sets" (1:10–13). The piety of pagans is also a feature of the late book of Jonah (1:14; 3:5–9).

RELATION OF THE *HAFTARAH* TO THE *PARASHAH*

A link between the *haftarah* and the *parashah* is established at the outset. Malachi announces that God has "accepted," (i.e., loved) Jacob, but "rejected" Esau (1:2–3). He notes that "Esau is Jacob's brother" (v. 2) and presents them as the ancestors of the nations of Israel and Edom (vv. 4–5). In similar fashion, the *parashah* emphasizes Rebekah's love for Jacob (Gen. 25:25), whom she prefers over Esau. These two fraternal "nations" in her womb (v. 23) are later designated Israel and Edom (Gen. 36:1,43). A divine oracle guarantees the superiority of the younger brother; it vindicates Rebekah's scheme in patriarchal times as well as God's choice in Malachi's day. The divine word in the prophetic text reinforces and actualizes the promise made ages before. At the same time, just as Esau "spurned" (*va-yivez;* stem בזה) his birthright through an imprudent act involving food (Gen. 25:34), the latter-day heirs of Jacob "scorn" (*bozei*) God through impious treatment of the food of sacrifice (Mal. 1:6–7). The use of the same Hebrew verb in both texts subtly suggests that Jacob has become like his hated twin.

Since the 2nd century C.E. (specifically, since the time of Hadrian's edicts and the revolt at Bethar, 132–35 C.E.), Edom has been a symbol for Rome in Jewish tradition. Thus Simeon bar Yoḥai interpreted "the voice of Jacob" and "the hands of Esau" in the *parashah* (Gen. 27:22) with reference to the screams of Jews being slaughtered in Bethar at the hands of Romans. The promised destruction of the "wild oxen" (*r'emim*) of Edom in Isa. 34:7 was interpreted by Meir to allude to Rome (*romiyyim*). Clearly, biblical interpretation was exploited for political protest. Another trenchant homily, on the divine oracle concerning the "two nations" (*shnei goyyim*) in Rebekah's womb (Gen. 25:23), declares that this predicts the future of "two proud" (*ge·im*) kingdoms (the Jews, typified by Solomon, and the Romans, typified by Hadrian). One of the "two" (*shnei*) will be "rejected" (*sanuy*). By invoking Mal. 1:3—"I . . . have rejected" (*saneiti*)—the preacher further informs his audience that the hated one is Edom-Rome (Gen. R. 63:7). The *haftarah* thus provided scriptural assurance that Edom and all its evil historical incarnations were condemned by God.

The annual recitation of this *haftarah* as interpreted throughout the ages thus serves to reinforce national and religious hope. Jews could rest assured in the promise of God's ancient and eter-

nal love for Israel, as Joshua ibn Shu'eib of 14th-century Spain pointedly preached. Through the mouth of Malachi, then, divine love expresses an absolute confirmation of Israel's covenantal destiny, with reverence for God and loyalty in His service being the fitting response.

1 A pronouncement: The word of the LORD
to Israel through Malachi.

2I have shown you love, said the LORD. But
you ask, "How have You shown us love?" After
all—declares the LORD—Esau is Jacob's brother; yet I have accepted Jacob 3and have rejected
Esau. I have made his hills a desolation, his
territory a home for beasts of the desert. 4If
Edom thinks, "Though crushed, we can build
the ruins again," thus said the LORD of Hosts:
They may build, but I will tear down. And so
they shall be known as the region of wickedness, the people damned forever of the LORD.
5Your eyes shall behold it, and you shall declare, "Great is the LORD beyond the borders
of Israel!"

6A son should honor his father, and a slave
his master. Now if I am a father, where is the
honor due Me? And if I am a master, where is
the reverence due Me?—said the LORD of
Hosts to you, O priests who scorn My name.
But you ask, "How have we scorned Your
name?" 7You offer defiled food on My altar.
But you ask, "How have we defiled You?" By
saying, "The table of the LORD can be treated
with scorn." 8When you present a blind animal

א מַשָּׂא דְבַר־יְהוָה אֶל־יִשְׂרָאֵל בְּיַד
מַלְאָכִי׃

2 אָהַבְתִּי אֶתְכֶם אָמַר יְהוָה וַאֲמַרְתֶּם
בַּמָּה אֲהַבְתָּנוּ הֲלוֹא־אָח עֵשָׂו לְיַעֲקֹב
נְאֻם־יְהוָה וָאֹהַב אֶת־יַעֲקֹב׃ 3 וְאֶת־עֵשָׂו
שָׂנֵאתִי וָאָשִׂים אֶת־הָרָיו שְׁמָמָה וְאֶת־
נַחֲלָתוֹ לְתַנּוֹת מִדְבָּר׃ 4 כִּי־תֹאמַר אֱדוֹם
רֻשַּׁשְׁנוּ וְנָשׁוּב וְנִבְנֶה חֳרָבוֹת כֹּה אָמַר
יְהוָה צְבָאוֹת הֵמָּה יִבְנוּ וַאֲנִי אֶהֱרוֹס
וְקָרְאוּ לָהֶם גְּבוּל רִשְׁעָה וְהָעָם אֲשֶׁר־
זָעַם יְהוָה עַד־עוֹלָם׃ 5 וְעֵינֵיכֶם תִּרְאֶינָה
וְאַתֶּם תֹּאמְרוּ יִגְדַּל יְהוָה מֵעַל לִגְבוּל
יִשְׂרָאֵל׃

6 בֵּן יְכַבֵּד אָב וְעֶבֶד אֲדֹנָיו וְאִם־אָב אָנִי
אַיֵּה כְבוֹדִי וְאִם־אֲדוֹנִים אָנִי אַיֵּה מוֹרָאִי
אָמַר ׀ יְהוָה צְבָאוֹת לָכֶם הַכֹּהֲנִים
בּוֹזֵי שְׁמִי וַאֲמַרְתֶּם בַּמֶּה בָזִינוּ אֶת־
שְׁמֶךָ׃ 7 מַגִּישִׁים עַל־מִזְבְּחִי לֶחֶם מְגֹאָל
וַאֲמַרְתֶּם בַּמֶּה גֵאַלְנוּךָ בֶּאֱמָרְכֶם שֻׁלְחַן
יְהוָה נִבְזֶה הוּא׃ 8 וְכִי־תַגִּשׁוּן עִוֵּר לִזְבֹּחַ

Malachi 1:1. A pronouncement Hebrew: *massa;* often translated "burden," on the assumption that this is the word that the prophet had to "carry" to the people (Rashi). The term refers to prophecy (Ibn Ezra) and is used to indicate the taking up of a speech (Num. 23:7,18; 24:3).

2. accepted Literally, "I loved" (*va-ohav*). This term continues the theme of favor for Jacob, as against the hatred and disfavor of Esau. In this context, the love is expressed through the giving of the land (Rashi, Radak).

6. A son should honor his father All the terms of this passage (father–son, master–slave, honor–reverence), which recur throughout the book of Malachi, have extended overtones: The father–son pair alludes to the divine–human relationship (cf. Mal. 2:10; 3:17), the master–slave pair alludes to the divine–worshiper relationship (3:1,14,17), and the honor–reverence pair sets the terms of positive piety against which the language of scorn and curse are counterposed, often through puns (see *mora,* "reverence," and *m'erah,* "curse," in 2:2).

for sacrifice—it doesn't matter! When you present a lame or sick one—it doesn't matter! Just offer it to your governor: Will he accept you? Will he show you favor?—said the LORD of Hosts. 9And now implore the favor of God! Will He be gracious to us? This is what you have done—will He accept any of you?

The LORD of Hosts has said: 10If only you would lock My doors, and not kindle fire on My altar to no purpose! I take no pleasure in you—said the LORD of Hosts—and I will accept no offering from you. 11For from where the sun rises to where it sets, My name is honored among the nations, and everywhere incense and pure oblation are offered to My name; for My name is honored among the nations—said the LORD of Hosts. 12But you profane it when you say, "The table of the Lord is defiled and the meat, the food, can be treated with scorn." 13You say, "Oh, what a bother!" And so you degrade it—said the LORD of Hosts—and you bring the stolen, the lame, and the sick; and you offer such as an oblation. Will I accept it from you?—said the LORD.

14A curse on the cheat who has [an unblemished] male in his flock, but for his vow sacrifices a blemished animal to the Lord! For I am a great King—said the LORD of Hosts—and My name is revered among the nations.

אֵין רָע וְכִי תַגִּישׁוּ פִּסֵּחַ וְחֹלֶה אֵין רָע
הַקְרִיבֵהוּ נָא לְפֶחָתֶךָ הֲיִרְצְךָ אוֹ הֲיִשָּׂא
פָנֶיךָ אָמַר יְהוָה צְבָאוֹת׃ 9 וְעַתָּה חַלּוּ־נָא
פְנֵי־אֵל וִיחָנֵנוּ מִיֶּדְכֶם הָיְתָה זֹּאת הֲיִשָּׂא
מִכֶּם פָּנִים
אָמַר יְהוָה צְבָאוֹת׃ 10 מִי גַם־בָּכֶם וְיִסְגֹּר
דְּלָתַיִם וְלֹא־תָאִירוּ מִזְבְּחִי חִנָּם אֵין־לִי
חֵפֶץ בָּכֶם אָמַר יְהוָה צְבָאוֹת וּמִנְחָה
לֹא־אֶרְצֶה מִיֶּדְכֶם׃ 11 כִּי מִמִּזְרַח־שֶׁמֶשׁ
וְעַד־מְבוֹאוֹ גָּדוֹל שְׁמִי בַּגּוֹיִם וּבְכָל־מָקוֹם
מֻקְטָר מֻגָּשׁ לִשְׁמִי וּמִנְחָה טְהוֹרָה כִּי־
גָדוֹל שְׁמִי בַּגּוֹיִם אָמַר יְהוָה צְבָאוֹת׃
12 וְאַתֶּם מְחַלְּלִים אוֹתוֹ בֶּאֱמָרְכֶם שֻׁלְחַן
אֲדֹנָי מְגֹאָל הוּא וְנִיבוֹ נִבְזֶה אָכְלוֹ׃
13 וַאֲמַרְתֶּם הִנֵּה מַתְּלָאָה וְהִפַּחְתֶּם
אוֹתוֹ אָמַר יְהוָה צְבָאוֹת וַהֲבֵאתֶם גָּזוּל
וְאֶת־הַפִּסֵּחַ וְאֶת־הַחוֹלֶה וַהֲבֵאתֶם אֶת־
הַמִּנְחָה הַאֶרְצֶה אוֹתָהּ מִיֶּדְכֶם אָמַר
יְהוָה׃ ס
14 וְאָרוּר נוֹכֵל וְיֵשׁ בְּעֶדְרוֹ זָכָר וְנֹדֵר וְזֹבֵחַ
מָשְׁחָת לַאדֹנָי כִּי מֶלֶךְ גָּדוֹל אָנִי אָמַר
יְהוָה צְבָאוֹת וּשְׁמִי נוֹרָא בַגּוֹיִם׃

2 And now, O priests, this charge is for you: 2Unless you obey and unless you lay it to heart, and do honor to My name—said the LORD of Hosts—I will send a curse and turn your blessings into curses. (Indeed, I have turned them into curses, because you do not lay it to heart.) 3I will put your seed under a ban, and I will strew dung upon your faces, the dung of your festal sacrifices, and you shall be carried out to its [heap].

ב וְעַתָּה אֲלֵיכֶם הַמִּצְוָה הַזֹּאת
הַכֹּהֲנִים׃ 2 אִם־לֹא תִשְׁמְעוּ וְאִם־לֹא
תָשִׂימוּ עַל־לֵב לָתֵת כָּבוֹד לִשְׁמִי אָמַר
יְהוָה צְבָאוֹת וְשִׁלַּחְתִּי בָכֶם אֶת־הַמְּאֵרָה
וְאָרוֹתִי אֶת־בִּרְכוֹתֵיכֶם וְגַם אָרוֹתִיהָ כִּי
אֵינְכֶם שָׂמִים עַל־לֵב׃ 3 הִנְנִי גֹעֵר לָכֶם
אֶת־הַזֶּרַע וְזֵרִיתִי פֶרֶשׁ עַל־פְּנֵיכֶם פֶּרֶשׁ
חַגֵּיכֶם וְנָשָׂא אֶתְכֶם אֵלָיו׃

⁴Know, then, that I have sent this charge to you that My covenant with Levi may endure—said the LORD of Hosts. ⁵I had with him a covenant of life and well-being, which I gave to him, and of reverence, which he showed Me. For he stood in awe of My name.

⁶Proper rulings were in his mouth,
And nothing perverse was on his lips;
He served Me with complete loyalty
And held the many back from iniquity.
⁷For the lips of a priest guard knowledge,
And men seek rulings from his mouth;
For he is a messenger of the LORD of Hosts.

4 וִידַעְתֶּ֗ם כִּ֚י שִׁלַּ֣חְתִּי אֲלֵיכֶ֔ם אֵ֖ת הַמִּצְוָ֣ה הַזֹּ֑את לִהְי֤וֹת בְּרִיתִי֙ אֶת־לֵוִ֔י אָמַ֖ר יְהוָ֥ה צְבָאֽוֹת: 5 בְּרִיתִ֣י ׀ הָיְתָ֣ה אִתּ֗וֹ הַֽחַיִּים֙ וְהַ֣שָּׁל֔וֹם וָאֶתְּנֵֽם־ל֥וֹ מוֹרָ֛א וַיִּֽירָאֵ֖נִי וּמִפְּנֵ֥י שְׁמִ֖י נִחַ֥ת הֽוּא:

6 תּוֹרַ֣ת אֱמֶת֙ הָיְתָ֣ה בְּפִ֔יהוּ
וְעַוְלָ֖ה לֹא־נִמְצָ֣א בִשְׂפָתָ֑יו
בְּשָׁל֤וֹם וּבְמִישׁוֹר֙ הָלַ֣ךְ אִתִּ֔י
וְרַבִּ֖ים הֵשִׁ֥יב מֵעָוֹֽן:
7 כִּֽי־שִׂפְתֵ֤י כֹהֵן֙ יִשְׁמְרוּ־דַ֔עַת
וְתוֹרָ֖ה יְבַקְשׁ֣וּ מִפִּ֑יהוּ
כִּ֛י מַלְאַ֥ךְ יְהוָֽה־צְבָא֖וֹת הֽוּא:

Malachi 2:4. My covenant with Levi The priest is exalted for the perfection of his service and reverence for God's holy name—the opposite of the situation here (cf. 1:6). The precise "covenant" is not specified. Num. 25:12–13 refers to a pact with the Aaronid clan, descendants of the priest Phinehas. A covenant of peace is mentioned, both in Numbers and here. The text here, however, has the whole tribe of Levi in mind (note the variant "covenant of the Levites" in Mal. 2:8), not just one priestly line.

6. Proper rulings Literally, "the Law of truth" (*Torat emet*). The priestly role in instruction is emphasized here and in verse 7. Instruction in ritual matters is found in Lev. 10:10–11. The role of the priests is extended to jurisprudence in Deut. 17:8–10. Ezekiel combines both functions (Ezek. 44:23–24). The tribe of Levi received the blessing of instruction in Deut. 33:8,10.

7. a messenger of the LORD of Hosts The exalted perfection of the true priests gave them the status of a "messenger" or an "angel" of God (*mal·akh*). This notion is dramatically portrayed in a postexilic vision of Zechariah (Zech. 3:1–7).

[10]Jacob left Beer-sheba, and set out for Haran. [11]He came upon a certain place and stopped there for the night, for the sun had set. Taking one of the stones of that place, he put it under his head and lay down in that place. [12]He had a dream; a stairway was set on the ground and its top reached to the sky, and angels of God were going up and down on it. [13]And the LORD was standing beside him

10 וַיֵּצֵא יַעֲקֹב מִבְּאֵר שָׁבַע וַיֵּלֶךְ חָרָנָה׃
11 וַיִּפְגַּע בַּמָּקוֹם וַיָּלֶן שָׁם כִּי־בָא הַשֶּׁמֶשׁ
וַיִּקַּח מֵאַבְנֵי הַמָּקוֹם וַיָּשֶׂם מְרַאֲשֹׁתָיו
וַיִּשְׁכַּב בַּמָּקוֹם הַהוּא׃ 12 וַיַּחֲלֹם וְהִנֵּה
סֻלָּם מֻצָּב אַרְצָה וְרֹאשׁוֹ מַגִּיעַ הַשָּׁמָיְמָה
וְהִנֵּה מַלְאֲכֵי אֱלֹהִים עֹלִים וְיֹרְדִים בּוֹ׃
13 וְהִנֵּה יְהוָה נִצָּב עָלָיו וַיֹּאמַר אֲנִי יְהוָה

JACOB'S ENCOUNTER WITH GOD (28:10–22)

Jacob has embarked on a long, perilous journey that will take him from Beer-sheba in southern Canaan to Haran in northern Mesopotamia.

THE DREAM REVELATION (vv. 11–15)

10. Jacob left Beer-sheba We are given no details about anything that happened to Jacob in the course of his trek; we are told only of his encounter with God.

11. He came upon a certain place Jacob stops at an unnamed "place" because it is impossible to travel in this region after sunset. The Hebrew word for "place" (*makom*) frequently has the connotation of "a sacred site" in later interpretations, but to Jacob it is a place with no tradition of holiness, and he treats it with indifference.

12. He had a dream While Jacob sleeps, he has a dream revelation.

a stairway The Hebrew term *"sullam"* is related to the Akkadian word *"simmiltu,"* which means "ladder" or "steps." *Sullam* could, therefore, be a ladder or a stairway ramp. The image of a ladder ascending to heaven is also known from Egyptian and Hittite sources.

angels of God They play no role in the dream and probably reflect the notion of angelic beings who patrol the earth and report back to God.

13. beside him Or "it," the stairway.

CHAPTER 28

In this *parashah,* Jacob leaves home to spend the next 20 years at the home of his mother's brother Laban (whom we met briefly in chapter 24). He marries two wives and fathers several children there. Jacob's journey begins with a setting sun and concludes (Gen. 32:27) with a rising sun. This has prompted one contemporary commentator to consider the 20 years at Laban's house as a "dark night of the soul," years spent struggling with the dark forces represented by Laban's treachery and Jacob's confronting his own attraction to deceit (Zornberg). When the Sages attribute to Jacob the institution of the evening prayer (*Ma·ariv*), they may be crediting him as the first person able to find God in the midst of darkness.

10. Jacob left Beer-Sheba Why does the Torah, ordinarily so sparing of words, include this detail? When a good person leaves a community, it is no longer the same place (Gen. R. 68:6).

12. a stairway We ascend toward God one step at a time, making one small change in our lives and stabilizing it before we take another step. Sometimes we slip and miss a step, falling back, but we recover and keep climbing. Most people do not leap toward God in one great burst of enthusiasm.

angels of God were going up and down on it From this we learn that one set of angels was leaving Jacob and a different set would accompany him outside the Land (Gen. R. 68:12). Jews have different concerns and different priorities outside the Land than they do when living in it. We need different "angels" to guide us (Mordecai Kaplan).

13. We can speculate that Jacob was a frightened young man, away from home for the first time and embarrassed by the circumstances that forced him to leave. To have God appear

and He said, "I am the LORD, the God of your
father Abraham and the God of Isaac: the
ground on which you are lying I will assign to
you and to your offspring. 14Your descendants
shall be as the dust of the earth; you shall spread
out to the west and to the east, to the north and
to the south. All the families of the earth shall
bless themselves by you and your descendants.
15Remember, I am with you: I will protect you
wherever you go and will bring you back to this
land. I will not leave you until I have done what
I have promised you."

16Jacob awoke from his sleep and said,
"Surely the LORD is present in this place, and
I did not know it!" 17Shaken, he said, "How
awesome is this place! This is none other than
the abode of God, and that is the gateway to

אֱלֹהֵי אַבְרָהָם אָבִיךָ וֵאלֹהֵי יִצְחָק הָאָרֶץ
אֲשֶׁר אַתָּה שֹׁכֵב עָלֶיהָ לְךָ אֶתְּנֶנָּה
וּלְזַרְעֶךָ׃ 14 וְהָיָה זַרְעֲךָ כַּעֲפַר הָאָרֶץ
וּפָרַצְתָּ יָמָּה וָקֵדְמָה וְצָפֹנָה וָנֶגְבָּה
וְנִבְרְכוּ בְךָ כָּל־מִשְׁפְּחֹת הָאֲדָמָה
וּבְזַרְעֶךָ׃ 15 וְהִנֵּה אָנֹכִי עִמָּךְ וּשְׁמַרְתִּיךָ
בְּכֹל אֲשֶׁר־תֵּלֵךְ וַהֲשִׁבֹתִיךָ אֶל־הָאֲדָמָה
הַזֹּאת כִּי לֹא אֶעֱזָבְךָ עַד אֲשֶׁר אִם־
עָשִׂיתִי אֵת אֲשֶׁר־דִּבַּרְתִּי לָךְ׃
16 וַיִּיקַץ יַעֲקֹב מִשְּׁנָתוֹ וַיֹּאמֶר אָכֵן יֵשׁ
יְהוָה בַּמָּקוֹם הַזֶּה וְאָנֹכִי לֹא יָדָעְתִּי׃
17 וַיִּירָא וַיֹּאמַר מַה־נּוֹרָא הַמָּקוֹם הַזֶּה
אֵין זֶה כִּי אִם־בֵּית אֱלֹהִים וְזֶה שַׁעַר

I am the LORD For this self-identifying formula, see Comment to 15:7. The use of the divine name *YHVH* has special importance here, because it serves to disengage the revelation from any connection with El, the head of the Canaanite pantheon, whose name is a component of Bethel, the name soon to be given to the place.

Abraham . . . Isaac The revelation confirms Jacob as the heir to the divine promises made to his father and grandfather.

the ground on which you are lying Just as he is about to leave the Land, his title to it is affirmed.

14. Your descendants The wording of these divine promises shows a clear affinity with the promises made to Abraham in 13:14–17.

15. I am with you The national promises that project into the distant future end on a personal note directed to Jacob.

BETHEL (vv. 16–19)

The next morning Jacob gives the site a name and makes a vow to God. The sanctuary at Bethel was of major importance in the later history of Israel.

17. Shaken Jacob is profoundly affected by the overwhelming mystery of the encounter with God.

abode of God The site where He has manifested His presence. The building or consecration of a sanctuary is not mentioned.

the gateway to heaven The place where the angels ascend to and descend from heaven. The notion that such "gateways" existed was widespread. One of the titles of the high priest of

---

reassuringly, promising him a successful journey and a safe return home, must have been what Jacob needed most at that moment. Years later, at the end of his life (48:3), this is one of only two incidents that Jacob recalls, cherishing the memory that when he was young and afraid, God assured him that he would achieve great things in his life.

16. and I did not know it How often do we find ourselves in the presence of God, not only in synagogue sanctuaries but at crucial moments of our lives or in the midst of natural beauty, and remain unaware of it?

17. Shaken We tend to speak casually of coming into God's presence. Jacob's response here reminds us that to truly encounter God in our lives is a soul-shattering experience. We are shaken to the core of our souls, and we are never the same person afterward. Jacob's encounter changes him from a frightened young man to a man prepared to take responsibility for his life.

הַשָּׁמָֽיִם׃ 18 וַיַּשְׁכֵּ֨ם יַעֲקֹ֜ב בַּבֹּ֗קֶר וַיִּקַּ֤ח
אֶת־הָאֶ֙בֶן֙ אֲשֶׁר־שָׂ֣ם מְרַֽאֲשֹׁתָ֔יו וַיָּ֥שֶׂם
אֹתָ֖הּ מַצֵּבָ֑ה וַיִּצֹ֥ק שֶׁ֖מֶן עַל־רֹאשָֽׁהּ׃
19 וַיִּקְרָ֛א אֶת־שֵֽׁם־הַמָּק֥וֹם הַה֖וּא בֵּֽית־
אֵ֑ל וְאוּלָ֛ם ל֥וּז שֵׁם־הָעִ֖יר לָרִאשֹׁנָֽה׃
20 וַיִּדַּ֥ר יַעֲקֹ֖ב נֶ֣דֶר לֵאמֹ֑ר אִם־יִהְיֶ֨ה
אֱלֹהִ֜ים עִמָּדִ֗י וּשְׁמָרַ֙נִי֙ בַּדֶּ֤רֶךְ הַזֶּה֙ אֲשֶׁ֣ר
אָנֹכִ֣י הוֹלֵ֔ךְ וְנָֽתַן־לִ֥י לֶ֛חֶם לֶאֱכֹ֖ל וּבֶ֥גֶד
לִלְבֹּֽשׁ׃ 21 וְשַׁבְתִּ֥י בְשָׁל֖וֹם אֶל־בֵּ֣ית אָבִ֑י
וְהָיָ֧ה יְהוָ֛ה לִ֖י לֵאלֹהִֽים׃ 22 וְהָאֶ֣בֶן הַזֹּ֗את
אֲשֶׁר־שַׂ֙מְתִּי֙ מַצֵּבָ֔ה יִהְיֶ֖ה בֵּ֣ית אֱלֹהִ֑ים
וְכֹל֙ אֲשֶׁ֣ר תִּתֶּן־לִ֔י עַשֵּׂ֖ר אֲעַשְּׂרֶ֥נּוּ לָֽךְ׃ שני

heaven." 18Early in the morning, Jacob took the stone that he had put under his head and set it up as a pillar and poured oil on the top of it. 19He named that site Bethel; but previously the name of the city had been Luz.

20Jacob then made a vow, saying, "If God remains with me, if He protects me on this journey that I am making, and gives me bread to eat and clothing to wear, 21and if I return safe to my father's house—the LORD shall be my God. 22And this stone, which I have set up as a pillar, shall be God's abode; and of all that You give me, I will set aside a tithe for You."

Thebes in Egypt was "the Opener of the Gates of Heavens," and the name of the city of Babylon was interpreted by the Semites as derived from *bab-ilim,* "gate of the god."

18. a pillar The Hebrew *"matzevah"* derives from the stem meaning "to take a firm position" (נצב). It denotes a single, upright slab of stone. Because the stone is by Jacob's head while he sleeps, it not only marks the spot but also functions as a sort of witness to the dream and the accompanying divine promises.

and poured oil on the top of it Oil was used in the ancient Near East in international treaty relationships and business contracts as a token of peace, friendship, and assumed obligation. Here the anointing is a symbolic act of dedication that establishes a contractual bond between Jacob and God.

19. Luz The name may mean "an almond tree," as in 30:37; the region is ideal fruit and nut country. Or it may derive from the Arabic *laudh,* "a place of refuge," a name highly appropriate to the present circumstances.

THE VOW (vv. 20–22)

At this critical moment, still under the effect of his dream experience, Jacob takes on certain obligations. His vow is best understood not as a bargaining with God, because all that he asks for has already been promised (v. 15). Rather, he pledges himself to a certain course of action as an expression of gratitude to God after the promises will be fulfilled.

21. the LORD shall be my God Jacob obligates himself to exclusive allegiance to *YHVH.*

22. And this stone The stone shall function as a witness to Jacob's vow. An 8th-century-B.C.E. Aramaic treaty inscription terms each upright stone on which the treaty is inscribed as *ntzb,* the same as the Hebrew *"matzevah"* (see v. 18).

a tithe The institution of tithe giving to temples and the royal court is known throughout the ancient Near East. The text is silent on who is to receive the tithe and what is to be done with it. Normally, one offers the tithe only to a king or to a sanctuary with an established clergy.

20–21. This is one of the first instances of someone making a promise to God in return for God's blessings. Does it represent a posture of gratitude or is it an attempt to manipulate God with promises of worship and generosity? Is Jacob excessive in his demands, asking that God give him everything he will ever need and grant him a life free of problems? Or is he simply asking for food, clothing, and safety, the minimum he needs to survive? Although Jewish prayer is predominantly about thanking and praising God for what we have, Judaism is not so other-worldly as to be embarrassed by prayers for material sustenance.

Several commentators are troubled by Jacob's saying, "if [God] protects me" when God has just promised to do so in his dream. Also, how can Jacob say "the LORD shall be my God" only if God helps him prosper? The first comment may reflect Jacob's doubts about the validity of his dream. Was it real or just wishful thinking? Can Jacob, like his grandfather Abra-

29

Jacob resumed his journey and came
to the land of the Easterners. 2There before his
eyes was a well in the open. Three flocks of
sheep were lying there beside it, for the flocks
were watered from that well. The stone on the
mouth of the well was large. 3When all the
flocks were gathered there, the stone would
be rolled from the mouth of the well and the
sheep watered; then the stone would be put
back in its place on the mouth of the well.

4Jacob said to them, "My friends, where are
you from?" And they said, "We are from Haran." 5He said to them, "Do you know Laban the
son of Nahor?" And they said, "Yes, we do." 6He
continued, "Is he well?" They answered, "Yes,
he is; and there is his daughter Rachel, coming
with the flock." 7He said, "It is still broad daylight, too early to round up the animals; water
the flock and take them to pasture." 8But
they said, "We cannot, until all the flocks are

כט

שני וַיִּשָּׂא יַעֲקֹב רַגְלָיו וַיֵּלֶךְ אַרְצָה
בְנֵי־קֶדֶם׃ 2 וַיַּרְא וְהִנֵּה בְאֵר בַּשָּׂדֶה וְהִנֵּה־
שָׁם שְׁלֹשָׁה עֶדְרֵי־צֹאן רֹבְצִים עָלֶיהָ כִּי
מִן־הַבְּאֵר הַהִוא יַשְׁקוּ הָעֲדָרִים וְהָאֶבֶן
גְּדֹלָה עַל־פִּי הַבְּאֵר׃ 3 וְנֶאֶסְפוּ־שָׁמָּה כָל־
הָעֲדָרִים וְגָלֲלוּ אֶת־הָאֶבֶן מֵעַל פִּי הַבְּאֵר
וְהִשְׁקוּ אֶת־הַצֹּאן וְהֵשִׁיבוּ אֶת־הָאֶבֶן
עַל־פִּי הַבְּאֵר לִמְקֹמָהּ׃
4 וַיֹּאמֶר לָהֶם יַעֲקֹב אַחַי מֵאַיִן אַתֶּם
וַיֹּאמְרוּ מֵחָרָן אֲנָחְנוּ׃ 5 וַיֹּאמֶר לָהֶם
הַיְדַעְתֶּם אֶת־לָבָן בֶּן־נָחוֹר וַיֹּאמְרוּ
יָדָעְנוּ׃ 6 וַיֹּאמֶר לָהֶם הֲשָׁלוֹם לוֹ וַיֹּאמְרוּ
שָׁלוֹם וְהִנֵּה רָחֵל בִּתּוֹ בָּאָה עִם־הַצֹּאן׃
7 וַיֹּאמֶר הֵן עוֹד הַיּוֹם גָּדוֹל לֹא־עֵת
הֵאָסֵף הַמִּקְנֶה הַשְׁקוּ הַצֹּאן וּלְכוּ רְעוּ׃
8 וַיֹּאמְרוּ לֹא נוּכַל עַד אֲשֶׁר יֵאָסְפוּ כָּל־

JACOB'S MARRIAGES (29:1–30)

Jacob's arrival at the well is reminiscent of what had occurred many years earlier (in chapter 26) when Abraham's servant came to this same place intent on finding a wife for Isaac. What a glaring contrast between the well-laden camel train of the grandfather's servant and the lonely, empty-handed Jacob who arrives on foot!

1. resumed his journey Literally, "lifted up his feet," a Hebrew phrase found nowhere else in this connection. It has been interpreted to mean: (a) the going was now easier; (b) he directed his feet, that is, he went with resolve and confidence; or (c) he had to force himself to leave the site of the revelation.

the Easterners In Hebrew: *b'nei kedem*. The word *"kedem"* refers to the Syrian-Arabian desert east of the land of Israel.

3. the stone would be rolled The stone restricted the use of the well to a closed group, and outsiders were required to pay for water. At the same time, the cover would serve as a protection against dust and filth and as a guard against accidental fall by person or beast.

4. where are you from Jacob does not realize that he has arrived at his destination.

5. Laban the son of Nahor Bethuel, Laban's actual father, is ignored here, as he largely is in chapter 24. The grandfather, Nahor, was the head of the clan and its most notable figure.

6. Rachel Her name means "a ewe lamb."

7. and take them to pasture Quite likely, Jacob wants the shepherds out of the way so that he can greet Rachel and converse with her alone.

8. But they said The shepherds suddenly become talkative, for Jacob touches a raw nerve when he insinuates that they are shirking their duties.

---

ham, trust God to fulfill the divine promise? The Midrash resolves the second question by taking the words "the LORD shall be my God" as part of Jacob's prayer, not as a promise. Along with food and safety, Jacob is praying for a sense of God's presence (Sifrei Deut. 31).

הָעֲדָרִ֔ים וְגָֽלֲלוּ֙ אֶת־הָאֶ֔בֶן מֵעַ֖ל פִּ֣י הַבְּאֵ֑ר
וְהִשְׁקִ֖ינוּ הַצֹּֽאן׃
9 עוֹדֶ֖נּוּ מְדַבֵּ֣ר עִמָּ֑ם וְרָחֵ֣ל ׀ בָּ֗אָה עִם־
הַצֹּאן֙ אֲשֶׁ֣ר לְאָבִ֔יהָ כִּ֛י רֹעָ֖ה הִֽוא׃
10 וַיְהִ֡י כַּאֲשֶׁ֣ר רָאָה֩ יַעֲקֹ֨ב אֶת־רָחֵ֜ל בַּת־
לָבָן֙ אֲחִ֣י אִמּ֔וֹ וְאֶת־צֹ֖אן לָבָ֣ן אֲחִ֣י אִמּ֑וֹ
וַיִּגַּ֣שׁ יַעֲקֹ֗ב וַיָּ֤גֶל אֶת־הָאֶ֙בֶן֙ מֵעַל֙ פִּ֣י
הַבְּאֵ֔ר וַיַּ֕שְׁקְ אֶת־צֹ֖אן לָבָ֥ן אֲחִ֥י אִמּֽוֹ׃
11 וַיִּשַּׁ֥ק יַעֲקֹ֖ב לְרָחֵ֑ל וַיִּשָּׂ֥א אֶת־קֹל֖וֹ
וַיֵּֽבְךְּ׃ 12 וַיַּגֵּ֨ד יַעֲקֹ֜ב לְרָחֵ֗ל כִּ֣י אֲחִ֤י אָבִ֙יהָ֙
ה֔וּא וְכִ֥י בֶן־רִבְקָ֖ה ה֑וּא וַתָּ֖רׇץ וַתַּגֵּ֥ד
לְאָבִֽיהָ׃ 13 וַיְהִי֩ כִשְׁמֹ֨עַ לָבָ֜ן אֶת־שֵׁ֣מַע ׀
יַעֲקֹ֣ב בֶּן־אֲחֹת֗וֹ וַיָּ֤רׇץ לִקְרָאתוֹ֙ וַיְחַבֶּק־לוֹ֙
וַיְנַשֶּׁק־ל֔וֹ וַיְבִיאֵ֖הוּ אֶל־בֵּית֑וֹ וַיְסַפֵּ֣ר לְלָבָ֔ן
אֵ֥ת כׇּל־הַדְּבָרִ֖ים הָאֵֽלֶּה׃ 14 וַיֹּ֤אמֶר לוֹ֙
לָבָ֔ן אַ֛ךְ עַצְמִ֥י וּבְשָׂרִ֖י אָ֑תָּה

rounded up; then the stone is rolled off the
mouth of the well and we water the sheep."
9While he was still speaking with them, Rachel came with her father's flock; for she was a
shepherdess. 10And when Jacob saw Rachel,
the daughter of his uncle Laban, and the
flock of his uncle Laban, Jacob went up and
rolled the stone off the mouth of the well,
and watered the flock of his uncle Laban.
11Then Jacob kissed Rachel, and broke into
tears. 12Jacob told Rachel that he was her
father's kinsman, that he was Rebekah's son;
and she ran and told her father. 13On hearing
the news of his sister's son Jacob, Laban ran to
greet him; he embraced him and kissed him,
and took him into his house. He told Laban all
that had happened, 14and Laban said to him,
"You are truly my bone and flesh."

10. his uncle Literally, "his mother's brother." The repetition of this phrase links the incident to the instructions of his parents (27:43, 28:2) and contains a hint that this is the girl who is to become his wife.

rolled the stone Single-handedly, apparently as the result of a surge of strength he experienced at the sight of Rachel and in the knowledge that he is meeting with his own kin at last.

watered the flock Rachel is certainly dumbfounded by this preferential treatment at the well (see Exod. 2:16–19). And by a total stranger! Jacob's act establishes a bond between them.

11. kissed Because Jacob already knows her to be his cousin, his kiss, even before he discloses his identity, is a natural and innocent act. Kissing is mentioned twice in The Song of Songs (1:2, 8:1), but this is the only instance in a biblical narrative of a man kissing a woman who is neither his mother nor his wife.

12. and told her father Either because her mother was dead or because it was the duty of the father to welcome strangers.

13. the news Of Jacob's arrival.

all that had happened It is hardly likely that Jacob reported that he had deceived his brother and father. Probably, he told how his parents had sent him to find a wife from among his kinfolk and that misadventures on the journey had left him empty-handed.

14. You are truly my bone and flesh Re-

CHAPTER 29

9. One commentator, reading between the lines, deduces that at this point, Laban's flocks were so few that a young girl could manage them alone. Only under Jacob's guidance did Laban's affairs flourish (*Or Ha-Ḥayyim*).

13. The Midrash interprets Laban's excitement at the news of Jacob's arrival as issuing from his greed. Remembering how Abraham's servant brought many gifts, he imagined Abraham's grandson coming even more heavily laden. Seeing Jacob empty-handed, Laban kisses him, thinking he may have hidden jewels in his mouth to foil robbers. Upon hearing the circumstances of Jacob's leaving home, he says resignedly, "you are my relative and I must let you in." One month later, Laban puts him to work (Gen. R. 70:13). When Laban, hearing of Jacob's difficulties at home, calls him "truly my bone and flesh," is he thinking, "You are a deceiver even as I am"?

When he had stayed with him a month's
time, [15]Laban said to Jacob, "Just because you
are a kinsman, should you serve me for nothing? Tell me, what shall your wages be?" [16]Now
Laban had two daughters; the name of the older one was Leah, and the name of the younger
was Rachel. [17]Leah had weak eyes; Rachel was
shapely and beautiful. [18]Jacob loved Rachel; so
he answered, "I will serve you seven years for
your younger daughter Rachel." [19]Laban said,
"Better that I give her to you than that I should
give her to an outsider. Stay with me." [20]So
Jacob served seven years for Rachel and they
seemed to him but a few days because of his
love for her.

וַיֵּשֶׁב עִמּוֹ חֹדֶשׁ יָמִים׃ 15 וַיֹּאמֶר לָבָן
לְיַעֲקֹב הֲכִי־אָחִי אַתָּה וַעֲבַדְתַּנִי חִנָּם
הַגִּידָה לִּי מַה־מַּשְׂכֻּרְתֶּךָ׃ 16 וּלְלָבָן שְׁתֵּי
בָנוֹת שֵׁם הַגְּדֹלָה לֵאָה וְשֵׁם הַקְּטַנָּה
רָחֵל׃ 17 וְעֵינֵי לֵאָה רַכּוֹת וְרָחֵל הָיְתָה
שלישי יְפַת־תֹּאַר וִיפַת מַרְאֶה׃ 18 וַיֶּאֱהַב יַעֲקֹב
אֶת־רָחֵל וַיֹּאמֶר אֶעֱבָדְךָ שֶׁבַע שָׁנִים
בְּרָחֵל בִּתְּךָ הַקְּטַנָּה׃ 19 וַיֹּאמֶר לָבָן טוֹב
תִּתִּי אֹתָהּ לָךְ מִתִּתִּי אֹתָהּ לְאִישׁ אַחֵר
שְׁבָה עִמָּדִי׃ 20 וַיַּעֲבֹד יַעֲקֹב בְּרָחֵל שֶׁבַע
שָׁנִים וַיִּהְיוּ בְעֵינָיו כְּיָמִים אֲחָדִים
בְּאַהֲבָתוֹ אֹתָהּ׃

cognition of kinship involved formal obligations of solidarity and determined social behavior. It meant acceptance of Jacob as a member of Laban's household.

15. serve This word, which occurs seven times in the narrative, is the essential term in the blessing that Jacob fought so desperately to obtain. The original oracle to the pregnant Rebekah forecast that "the older shall *serve* the younger" (Gen. 25:23). The stolen blessing contained the phrase, "Let peoples *serve* you" (27:29), which Isaac confirmed, saying to Esau, "I have given him all his brothers for *servants*" (27:37) and "You shall *serve* your brother" (27:40). Now—what irony!—it is Jacob who must serve.

16. Now Laban Jacob's response is delayed by the narrator to provide us with background information essential to the understanding of subsequent developments.

Leah The name may mean "cow" or "weak."

Rachel She is mentioned again only because it was necessary to introduce Leah and to explain the order of birth, an item of vital importance to the narrative.

17. weak eyes This does not describe poor vision, but eyes lacking in luster or lacking in tenderness and sensitivity.

18. seven years The seven years of service are to be in place of the usual "bride-price," known as *mohar* in Hebrew and *terhatum* in Akkadian, an institution discussed in the Comment to 24:53. Jacob, working to pay off the bride-price, will have the status of an indentured laborer (see Exod. 21:2–3).

19. Laban said Laban's reply is a statement of consummate ambiguity naively accepted by Jacob as a binding commitment.

Better that I give her to you Marriage between relatives was regarded as highly desirable: It safeguarded tribal property and the welfare of the daughter.

20. but a few days An echo of Gen. 27:44, where Jacob's mother sends her son to Laban "for a short while" (literally, "a few days") on the pretext of finding a wife. Grim reality now mocks her words.

---

17. Leah had weak eyes This was the result of weeping after she heard a rumor that she would be married off to Esau, Rebekah's older son, while her younger sister would marry Jacob (Gen. R. 70:16).

18. Jacob loved Rachel This is an unusual instance of romantic love in a world where marriage was typically an economic arrangement between two families.

20. they seemed . . . but a few days We might think that the time would pass all too slowly. A person looking forward to attaining a goal, though, welcomes everything that brings him or her a step closer to that goal.

21וַיֹּ֨אמֶר יַעֲקֹ֤ב אֶל־לָבָן֙ הָבָ֣ה אֶת־אִשְׁתִּ֔י
כִּ֥י מָלְא֖וּ יָמָ֑י וְאָב֖וֹאָה אֵלֶֽיהָ׃ 22וַיֶּאֱסֹ֥ף
לָבָ֛ן אֶת־כָּל־אַנְשֵׁ֥י הַמָּק֖וֹם וַיַּ֥עַשׂ
מִשְׁתֶּֽה׃ 23וַיְהִ֣י בָעֶ֔רֶב וַיִּקַּח֙ אֶת־לֵאָ֣ה
בִתּ֔וֹ וַיָּבֵ֥א אֹתָ֖הּ אֵלָ֑יו וַיָּבֹ֖א אֵלֶֽיהָ׃
24וַיִּתֵּ֤ן לָבָן֙ לָ֔הּ אֶת־זִלְפָּ֖ה שִׁפְחָת֑וֹ
לְלֵאָ֥ה בִתּ֖וֹ שִׁפְחָֽה׃ 25וַיְהִ֣י בַבֹּ֔קֶר וְהִנֵּה־
הִ֖וא לֵאָ֑ה וַיֹּ֣אמֶר אֶל־לָבָ֗ן מַה־זֹּאת֙ עָשִׂ֣יתָ
לִּ֔י הֲלֹ֤א בְרָחֵל֙ עָבַ֣דְתִּי עִמָּ֔ךְ וְלָ֖מָּה
רִמִּיתָֽנִי׃ 26וַיֹּ֣אמֶר לָבָ֔ן לֹא־יֵעָשֶׂ֥ה כֵ֖ן
בִּמְקוֹמֵ֑נוּ לָתֵ֥ת הַצְּעִירָ֖ה לִפְנֵ֥י הַבְּכִירָֽה׃
27מַלֵּ֖א שְׁבֻ֣עַ זֹ֑את וְנִתְּנָ֨ה לְךָ֜ גַּם־אֶת־

21Then Jacob said to Laban, "Give me my wife, for my time is fulfilled, that I may cohabit with her." 22And Laban gathered all the people of the place and made a feast. 23When evening came, he took his daughter Leah and brought her to him; and he cohabited with her.—24Laban had given his maidservant Zilpah to his daughter Leah as her maid.—25When morning came, there was Leah! So he said to Laban, "What is this you have done to me? I was in your service for Rachel! Why did you deceive me?" 26Laban said, "It is not the practice in our place to marry off the younger before the older. 27Wait until the bridal week of this one is over and we will give you that one too, provided you

21. my wife A betrothed woman has the status of a wife in the laws of Hammurabi as well as in Deut. 20:7 and 22:23–24.

23. When evening came Either it was the custom to hold weddings in the evening or Laban deliberately chose that time of the day.

he took his daughter Leah This is intelligible only if Leah wore a veil; in the ancient Near East, the bride was indeed veiled when presented to her husband.

24. his maidservant In ancient Mesopotamia it was the custom for a father to present his daughter with a maid on her marriage.

Zilpah The name has been connected with the Arabic word *zulfah*, "dignity," or *dhulifa*, "to be small" (said of a nose).

25. there was Leah Jacob's masquerading as his brother meets its counterstroke in the substitution of Leah for her sister.

Why did you deceive me? The Hebrew stem "רמה" (for "deceive") is the same used by Isaac in 27:35 to describe Jacob's own act of deception.

26. It is not the practice Laban feigns outrage, as though Jacob were the guilty one! In justification of his conduct, he invokes the importance of tradition.

younger . . . older This remark, an instance of dramatic irony, whose underlying meaning is perceived by Jacob and the reader, returns us sharply to the Jacob–Esau rivalry. It so stuns Jacob that he doesn't even reprove Laban for never having informed him about that local custom.

27. the bridal week Literally, "the week of

25. there was Leah A Rabbinic *midrash* tells of Jacob and Rachel devising a code to make sure that the deceitful Laban could not substitute Leah for Rachel. But on the wedding night, Rachel, feeling compassion for Leah and not wanting her to be shamed, shares the code with her sister (BT Meg. 13b). As a result, Jacob is deceived in the darkness, even as his father Isaac had been fooled in his blindness.

26. It is not the practice in our place That is, I have heard stories of younger siblings rushing ahead of older ones as you yourself did, but we don't do that here. Jacob has just learned why it was wrong for him to deceive his father. Rather than moralize, the Torah lets Jacob discover that people who give themselves permission to lie and cheat find themselves in a world where no one can be trusted.

HALAKHAH L'MA·ASEH

29:27 bridal week On each of the seven nights after a wedding, it is traditional to invite at least one new individual to join family and friends at a festive meal with the bride and groom. If at least 10 adults are present, grace after meals culminates with the recitation of the *sheva b'rakhot* (the seven blessings pronounced during the wedding ceremony) with the blessing over the wine recited last.

serve me another seven years." 28Jacob did so;
he waited out the bridal week of the one, and
then he gave him his daughter Rachel as
wife.— 29Laban had given his maidservant Bilhah to his daughter Rachel as her maid.—
30And Jacob cohabited with Rachel also; indeed, he loved Rachel more than Leah. And
he served him another seven years.

31The LORD saw that Leah was unloved and
he opened her womb; but Rachel was barren.
32Leah conceived and bore a son, and named
him Reuben; for she declared, "It means: 'The

זֹאת בַּעֲבֹדָה אֲשֶׁר תַּעֲבֹד עִמָּדִי עוֹד
שֶׁבַע־שָׁנִים אֲחֵרוֹת׃ 28וַיַּעַשׂ יַעֲקֹב כֵּן
וַיְמַלֵּא שְׁבֻעַ זֹאת וַיִּתֶּן־לוֹ אֶת־רָחֵל בִּתּוֹ
לוֹ לְאִשָּׁה׃ 29וַיִּתֵּן לָבָן לְרָחֵל בִּתּוֹ אֶת־
בִּלְהָה שִׁפְחָתוֹ לָהּ לְשִׁפְחָה׃ 30וַיָּבֹא גַּם
אֶל־רָחֵל וַיֶּאֱהַב גַּם־אֶת־רָחֵל מִלֵּאָה
וַיַּעֲבֹד עִמּוֹ עוֹד שֶׁבַע־שָׁנִים אֲחֵרוֹת׃
31וַיַּרְא יְהוָה כִּי־שְׂנוּאָה לֵאָה וַיִּפְתַּח
אֶת־רַחְמָהּ וְרָחֵל עֲקָרָה׃ 32וַתַּהַר לֵאָה
וַתֵּלֶד בֵּן וַתִּקְרָא שְׁמוֹ רְאוּבֵן כִּי אָמְרָה

this one," that is, the seven days of feasting in celebration of a marriage, also mentioned in connection with Samson's wedding (Judg. 14:12,17).

28. Jacob did so His action violates the law of Lev. 18:18, which prohibits a man from marrying a sister of his wife during the latter's lifetime. No attempt was made to rewrite this ancient narrative in the light of the morality and law of a later age.

29. Bilhah The Arabic word *baliha* means "innocent, foolish, unconcerned."

THE BIRTH OF JACOB'S CHILDREN (29:31–30:43)

LEAH'S FOUR SONS (29:31–35)

Jacob's greater love of Rachel is understandable in the context of his experience with Laban, but that makes the lesser-loved Leah the innocent victim of her father's duplicity. For this reason, it would appear, she is the beneficiary of God's compassion and is blessed with many children.

31. unloved The Hebrew word translated here as "unloved" (*s'nu·ah*) literally means "hated." When paired with the word meaning "beloved" (*ahuvah*) in a context of a husband's relationship to his co-wives, it does not mean "hated" as against "beloved." It refers to a degree of preference (see Deut. 21:15).

opened her womb Apparently, she had been childless for a while.

Rachel was barren This remark prepares us for the next episode.

32. Reuben The simplest explanation of

---

31. unloved The word translated here as "unloved" (*s'nu·ah*) generally means "hated." Did Jacob hate Leah or only love her less than he loved Rachel? One commentator suggests that Leah hated herself for having tricked Jacob into marrying her. Knowing what we know of human psychology, we can also suspect that Jacob did indeed hate Leah because, by reminding him of the fraudulent circumstances of their wedding, she reminded him of his most shameful memory, the time he deceived his father. We often hate people for confronting us with what we like least about ourselves.

The LORD saw that Leah was unloved Some human beings abandon their friends when misfortune strikes, but God draws closer to the rejected, the marginalized, the unloved (Tanḥ. B.) We can only imagine the complicated relationship between the sisters, bound to each other by family ties but competing for the love

HALAKHAH L'MA·ASEH

29:32 named him In the biblical period, the name of a child was chosen for its symbolic meaning. Nowadays, Ashkenazic Jews customarily name children after deceased relatives; and Sephardic Jews, after relatives who are still alive.

LORD has seen my affliction'; it also means: 'Now my husband will love me.'" [33] She conceived again and bore a son, and declared, "This is because the LORD heard that I was unloved and has given me this one also"; so she named him Simeon. [34] Again she conceived and bore a son and declared, "This time my husband will become attached to me, for I have borne him three sons." Therefore he was named Levi. [35] She conceived again and bore a son, and declared, "This time I will praise the LORD." Therefore she named him Judah. Then she stopped bearing.

30
When Rachel saw that she had borne Jacob no children, she became envious of her sister; and Rachel said to Jacob, "Give me chil-

כִּי־רָאָ֤ה יְהֹוָה֙ בְּעָנְיִ֔י כִּ֥י עַתָּ֖ה יֶאֱהָבַ֣נִי אִישִׁ֑י: [33] וַתַּ֣הַר עוֹד֮ וַתֵּ֣לֶד בֵּן֒ וַתֹּ֗אמֶר כִּֽי־שָׁמַ֤ע יְהֹוָה֙ כִּֽי־שְׂנוּאָ֣ה אָנֹ֔כִי וַיִּתֶּן־לִ֖י גַּם־אֶת־זֶ֑ה וַתִּקְרָ֥א שְׁמ֖וֹ שִׁמְעֽוֹן: [34] וַתַּ֣הַר עוֹד֮ וַתֵּ֣לֶד בֵּן֒ וַתֹּ֗אמֶר עַתָּ֤ה הַפַּ֙עַם֙ יִלָּוֶ֤ה אִישִׁי֙ אֵלַ֔י כִּֽי־יָלַ֥דְתִּי ל֖וֹ שְׁלֹשָׁ֣ה בָנִ֑ים עַל־כֵּ֥ן קָרָֽא־שְׁמ֖וֹ לֵוִֽי: [35] וַתַּ֨הַר ע֜וֹד וַתֵּ֣לֶד בֵּ֗ן וַתֹּ֙אמֶר֙ הַפַּ֙עַם֙ אוֹדֶ֣ה אֶת־יְהֹוָ֔ה עַל־כֵּ֛ן קָרְאָ֥ה שְׁמ֖וֹ יְהוּדָ֑ה וַֽתַּעֲמֹ֖ד מִלֶּֽדֶת:

ל וַתֵּ֣רֶא רָחֵ֗ל כִּ֣י לֹ֤א יָֽלְדָה֙ לְיַעֲקֹ֔ב וַתְּקַנֵּ֥א רָחֵ֖ל בַּֽאֲחֹתָ֑הּ וַתֹּ֤אמֶר אֶֽל־יַעֲקֹב֙

the name derives it from two Hebrew words: *r'u ben*, "See, a son!"—a joyous exclamation by parents at the time of birth. Here the name is given a folk etymology that roots it in a Hebrew phrase that sounds like the name: *ra·ah b'onyi*, "He (God) has seen my affliction."

it also means This is the force of the Hebrew word *"ki"* in this context. The double explanation of a name is a recurring feature in the Torah's birth narratives.

will love me The last two syllables of the Hebrew word *"ye·ehavani"* (*vani*) echo the final syllable of *"r'uven,"* thereby revealing Leah's as-

piration to become the *ahuvah,* "the preferred wife."

33. Simeon The narrative here connects this name with the Hebrew stem שמע, "to hear."

34. Levi A similar word in inscriptions from the ancient Near East designates a special class of temple slaves, but here the name carries no sacred nuances and simply articulates the mother's yearning for her husband's companionship. The name itself means "attached to."

35. she stopped bearing No reason for this is given, but 30:14–15 indicate that Jacob had ceased sleeping with her.

of the same man. One sister had his love but was infertile, the other had his children but longed for his love. Each diminished the value of what she was blessed with and focused on what she lacked.

35. This time I will praise the LORD The names of Leah's first three sons reflect her frustrating rivalry with her sister for the love of the husband they share. The reasons given for her choice of names for the first three children say nothing about her hopes for them but focus solely on how the births will affect her marriage. Now, with a fourth son, her mood changes from rivalry to gratitude, so she names him Judah (*Y'hudah*), from a Hebrew root

meaning "to praise." In the future, the descendants of Jacob will be known as Judeans, or Jews (*Y'hudim*). Yoḥanan stated, "From the beginning of time, no one ever thanked God as Leah did" (BT Ber. 7b). Her heartfelt prayer of thanks reflects her having grown from self-concern and a focus on what she lacked to a genuine sense of appreciation for what was hers.

CHAPTER 30

1. Give me children, or I shall die Is this simply exaggeration, born out of Rachel's rivalry with Leah? Or is she saying that, without the vicarious immortality conferred by children, her life will disappear when she dies?

dren, or I shall die." 2Jacob was incensed at Rachel, and said, "Can I take the place of God, who has denied you fruit of the womb?" 3She said, "Here is my maid Bilhah. Consort with her, that she may bear on my knees and that through her I too may have children." 4So she gave him her maid Bilhah as concubine, and Jacob cohabited with her. 5Bilhah conceived and bore Jacob a son. 6And Rachel said, "God has vindicated me; indeed, He has heeded my plea and given me a son." Therefore she named him Dan. 7Rachel's maid Bilhah conceived again and bore Jacob a second son. 8And Rachel said, "A fateful contest I waged with my sister; yes, and I have prevailed." So she named him Naphtali.

הָבָה־לִּי בָנִים וְאִם־אַיִן מֵתָה אָנֹכִי׃
2 וַיִּחַר־אַף יַעֲקֹב בְּרָחֵל וַיֹּאמֶר הֲתַחַת
אֱלֹהִים אָנֹכִי אֲשֶׁר־מָנַע מִמֵּךְ פְּרִי־בָטֶן׃
3 וַתֹּאמֶר הִנֵּה אֲמָתִי בִלְהָה בֹּא אֵלֶיהָ
וְתֵלֵד עַל־בִּרְכַּי וְאִבָּנֶה גַם־אָנֹכִי מִמֶּנָּה׃
4 וַתִּתֶּן־לוֹ אֶת־בִּלְהָה שִׁפְחָתָהּ לְאִשָּׁה
וַיָּבֹא אֵלֶיהָ יַעֲקֹב׃ 5 וַתַּהַר בִּלְהָה וַתֵּלֶד
לְיַעֲקֹב בֵּן׃ 6 וַתֹּאמֶר רָחֵל דָּנַנִּי אֱלֹהִים
וְגַם שָׁמַע בְּקֹלִי וַיִּתֶּן־לִי בֵּן עַל־כֵּן קָרְאָה
שְׁמוֹ דָּן׃ 7 וַתַּהַר עוֹד וַתֵּלֶד בִּלְהָה שִׁפְחַת
רָחֵל בֵּן שֵׁנִי לְיַעֲקֹב׃ 8 וַתֹּאמֶר רָחֵל
נַפְתּוּלֵי אֱלֹהִים ׀ נִפְתַּלְתִּי עִם־אֲחֹתִי
גַּם־יָכֹלְתִּי וַתִּקְרָא שְׁמוֹ נַפְתָּלִי׃
9 וַתֵּרֶא לֵאָה כִּי עָמְדָה מִלֶּדֶת וַתִּקַּח אֶת־

THE FOUR SONS OF THE HANDMAIDS (vv. 1–13)

1. or I shall die My life is worthless without children.

3. Here is my maid Rachel, like Sarah before her, resorts to the device of concubinage. See Comments to 16:1–3.

that she may bear on my knees In the ancient Near East, as well as in ancient Greece and Rome, placing a child on or near the knees of another signified acknowledgment of physical parenthood or adoption. Here, because Bilhah is to act as a surrogate mother for Rachel, her offspring have to be accepted and legitimated, which calls for the appropriate symbolic gesture on Rachel's part.

4. as concubine The text reads literally "as a wife," but in 35:22 Bilhah is called "a concubine" (*pilegesh*). Zilpah is designated "concubine" in 30:9, and both women are termed "wives" in 37:2. The difference between a concubine and a wife is that no bride-price (*mohar*) is paid for the former. The interchange of terminology shows that in the course of time the distinction in social status between the two often tended to diminish or disappear.

5. Jacob The word *l'ya·akov,* "to Jacob," which does not appear in the account of the birth of the previous sons, is placed in an emphatic position in the word order because the paternity of a child born to a maidservant may be uncertain.

6. Dan The name is derived from the stem דין, "to judge, vindicate, or to bring victory" (see 49:16).

8. Naphtali The name is explained by a unique noun, *naftulim,* usually understood to mean "contest." The rendering "fateful contest" is based on the occasional use of *elohim,* "God," to intensify a word. The phrase could also mean "a contest for God," that is, for divine favor.

9. she had stopped bearing This connects with 29:35. Leah's resort to concubinage is un-

---

Ironically, Rachel is destined to die in the act of giving birth to a second child.

2. The Sages criticize Jacob for his insensitive response (Gen. R. 71:10). Might it be that Jacob is disappointed to learn that his love is not enough to satisfy Rachel, that Rachel's primary passion is to be a mother, not just a wife? (Sforno). Compare the response of another husband, Elkanah, to his wife Hannah in a similar situation, centuries later: "Am I not more devoted to you than ten sons?" (1 Sam. 1:8, in the *haftarah* for the first day of *Rosh ha-Shanah*). The Midrash pictures Rachel reminding Jacob that he was born only after his father Isaac had prayed that his mother be blessed with children (Gen. 25:21; Gen. R. 71:7).

זִלְפָּ֥ה שִׁפְחָתָ֖הּ וַתִּתֵּ֥ן אֹתָ֛הּ לְיַעֲקֹ֖ב
לְאִשָּֽׁה׃ 10 וַתֵּ֗לֶד זִלְפָּ֛ה שִׁפְחַ֥ת לֵאָ֖ה
לְיַעֲקֹ֥ב בֵּֽן׃ 11 וַתֹּ֥אמֶר לֵאָ֖ה בגד בָּ֣א גָ֑ד
וַתִּקְרָ֥א אֶת־שְׁמ֖וֹ גָּֽד׃ 12 וַתֵּ֗לֶד זִלְפָּה֙
שִׁפְחַ֣ת לֵאָ֔ה בֵּ֥ן שֵׁנִ֖י לְיַעֲקֹֽב׃ 13 וַתֹּ֣אמֶר
לֵאָ֔ה בְּאָשְׁרִ֕י כִּ֥י אִשְּׁר֖וּנִי בָּנ֑וֹת וַתִּקְרָ֥א
אֶת־שְׁמ֖וֹ אָשֵֽׁר׃
רביעי 14 וַיֵּ֨לֶךְ רְאוּבֵ֜ן בִּימֵ֣י קְצִיר־חִטִּ֗ים וַיִּמְצָ֤א
דֽוּדָאִים֙ בַּשָּׂדֶ֔ה וַיָּבֵ֣א אֹתָ֔ם אֶל־לֵאָ֖ה
אִמּ֑וֹ וַתֹּ֤אמֶר רָחֵל֙ אֶל־לֵאָ֔ה תְּנִי־נָ֣א לִ֔י
מִדּוּדָאֵ֖י בְּנֵֽךְ׃ 15 וַתֹּ֣אמֶר לָ֗הּ הַמְעַט֙
קַחְתֵּ֣ךְ אֶת־אִישִׁ֔י וְלָקַ֕חַת גַּ֥ם אֶת־דּוּדָאֵ֖י
בְּנִ֑י וַתֹּ֣אמֶר רָחֵ֗ל לָכֵן֙ יִשְׁכַּ֤ב עִמָּךְ֙ הַלַּ֔יְלָה
תַּ֖חַת דּוּדָאֵ֥י בְנֵֽךְ׃ 16 וַיָּבֹ֨א יַעֲקֹ֣ב מִן־
הַשָּׂדֶה֮ בָּעֶ֒רֶב֒ וַתֵּצֵ֨א לֵאָ֜ה לִקְרָאת֗וֹ
וַתֹּ֙אמֶר֙ אֵלַ֣י תָּב֔וֹא כִּ֛י שָׂכֹ֥ר שְׂכַרְתִּ֔יךָ

[9]When Leah saw that she had stopped bearing, she took her maid Zilpah and gave her to Jacob as concubine. [10]And when Leah's maid Zilpah bore Jacob a son, [11]Leah said, "What luck!" So she named him Gad. [12]When Leah's maid Zilpah bore Jacob a second son, [13]Leah declared, "What fortune!" meaning, "Women will deem me fortunate." So she named him Asher.

[14]Once, at the time of the wheat harvest, Reuben came upon some mandrakes in the field and brought them to his mother Leah. Rachel said to Leah, "Please give me some of your son's mandrakes." [15]But she said to her, "Was it not enough for you to take away my husband, that you would also take my son's mandrakes?" Rachel replied, "I promise, he shall lie with you tonight, in return for your son's mandrakes." [16]When Jacob came home from the field in the evening, Leah went out to

explained. Perhaps she sensed that Jacob wanted more children. Convinced that Rachel could not provide them and facing the fact that her husband did not find her desirable, Leah was prepared to sacrifice her pride and gave her maid for that purpose.

11. Gad The name of the god of fortune and good luck in several ancient Near Eastern cultures. To Leah it is simply a word meaning "luck."

13. Asher This name is derived from the Hebrew stem meaning "happy" (אשר).

THE FOUR SONS OF RACHEL AND LEAH (vv. 14–24)

THE MANDRAKES (vv. 14–16)

The chronicle of births is briefly interrupted by a minor episode.

14. at the time of the wheat harvest Around May. The dating of events by agricultural seasons is common in the Bible. Ancient Near Eastern archives provide abundant evidence for the involvement of pastoralist nomads in seasonal agricultural activity in the fields near their grazing grounds.

mandrakes The Hebrew term *duda·im* has long been identified with the mandrake—a small, yellow, tomato-like fruit that grows wild in the fields and ripens during March and April. It contains purgative and narcotic substances and was widely used for medicinal purposes in ancient times. It was also believed to have aphrodisiac powers.

15. my husband . . . mandrakes The pairing of these two words intimates that the fruit was to be used to induce Jacob to resume his conjugal duty.

he shall lie with you The nature of this barter arrangement is underlined by the fact that in Genesis when the verb "to lie with" (שכב) is used with a sexual nuance, it never connotes a relationship of marital love but one that takes place under unsavory circumstances.

16. I have hired you The Hebrew word for

HALAKHAH L'MA·ASEH

30:14 mandrakes Rachel apparently wants Reuben's mandrakes as a means to overcome infertility. The CJLS has approved several rulings about current treatments to help infertile couples.

meet him and said, "You are to sleep with me,
for I have hired you with my son's mandrakes."
And he lay with her that night. 17 God heeded
Leah, and she conceived and bore him a fifth
son. 18 And Leah said, "God has given me my
reward for having given my maid to my husband." So she named him Issachar. 19 When
Leah conceived again and bore Jacob a sixth
son, 20 Leah said, "God has given me a choice
gift; this time my husband will exalt me, for I
have borne him six sons." So she named him
Zebulun. 21 Last, she bore him a daughter, and
named her Dinah.

22 Now God remembered Rachel; God
heeded her and opened her womb. 23 She conceived and bore a son, and said, "God has taken
away my disgrace." 24 So she named him Joseph, which is to say, "May the LORD add another son for me."

25 After Rachel had borne Joseph, Jacob said
to Laban, "Give me leave to go back to my own

בְּדוּדָאֵ֖י בְּנִ֑י וַיִּשְׁכַּ֥ב עִמָּ֖הּ בַּלַּ֥יְלָה הֽוּא׃
17 וַיִּשְׁמַ֥ע אֱלֹהִ֖ים אֶל־לֵאָ֑ה וַתַּ֛הַר וַתֵּ֥לֶד
לְיַעֲקֹ֖ב בֵּ֥ן חֲמִישִֽׁי׃ 18 וַתֹּ֣אמֶר לֵאָ֗ה נָתַ֤ן
אֱלֹהִים֙ שְׂכָרִ֔י אֲשֶׁר־נָתַ֥תִּי שִׁפְחָתִ֖י
לְאִישִׁ֑י וַתִּקְרָ֥א שְׁמ֖וֹ יִשָּׂשכָֽר׃ 19 וַתַּ֤הַר
עוֹד֙ לֵאָ֔ה וַתֵּ֥לֶד בֵּן־שִׁשִּׁ֖י לְיַעֲקֹֽב׃
20 וַתֹּ֣אמֶר לֵאָ֗ה זְבָדַ֨נִי אֱלֹהִ֥ים ׀ אֹתִי֮ זֵ֣בֶד
ט֒וֹב֒ הַפַּ֙עַם֙ יִזְבְּלֵ֣נִי אִישִׁ֔י כִּֽי־יָלַ֥דְתִּי ל֖וֹ
שִׁשָּׁ֣ה בָנִ֑ים וַתִּקְרָ֥א אֶת־שְׁמ֖וֹ זְבֻלֽוּן׃
21 וְאַחַ֖ר יָ֣לְדָה בַּ֑ת וַתִּקְרָ֥א אֶת־שְׁמָ֖הּ
דִּינָֽה׃
22 וַיִּזְכֹּ֥ר אֱלֹהִ֖ים אֶת־רָחֵ֑ל וַיִּשְׁמַ֤ע אֵלֶ֙יהָ֙
אֱלֹהִ֔ים וַיִּפְתַּ֖ח אֶת־רַחְמָֽהּ׃ 23 וַתַּ֖הַר
וַתֵּ֣לֶד בֵּ֑ן וַתֹּ֕אמֶר אָסַ֥ף אֱלֹהִ֖ים אֶת־
חֶרְפָּתִֽי׃ 24 וַתִּקְרָ֧א אֶת־שְׁמ֛וֹ יוֹסֵ֖ף לֵאמֹ֑ר
יֹסֵ֧ף יְהוָ֛ה לִ֖י בֵּ֥ן אַחֵֽר׃
25 וַיְהִ֕י כַּאֲשֶׁ֛ר יָלְדָ֥ה רָחֵ֖ל אֶת־יוֹסֵ֑ף
וַיֹּ֤אמֶר יַעֲקֹב֙ אֶל־לָבָ֔ן שַׁלְּחֵ֙נִי֙ וְאֵֽלְכָ֔ה אֶל־

"hire" (שכר) points to a folk etymology for Issachar, who is to issue from this rendezvous.

18. Issachar This explanation connects the name with the action of verse 9 and suggests "there is a reward" (*yesh sakhar*), an affirmation of belief in divine providence.

20. Zebulun Two folk etymologies are given for this name. The first is based on similarity of sound with the two initial consonants of the stem זבד, "to give, grant." It appears as a verb only here in the Bible but is known from Syriac and Arabic. The second connects the name with the stem זבל, which is now known from Ugaritic and means "to raise up."

this time Leah's yearning for her husband's attention and esteem following the birth of her sixth son echoes her plea after the arrival of the third son (29:34).

21. Dinah Her birth is announced in an offhand manner and no explanation is given for her name.

22. God remembered For the significance of this phrase, see Comment to 8:1.

23–24. Joseph The two Hebrew verbs *"asaf"* (take away) and *"yosef"* (add) provide a double etymology for the name. The first looks back to the past years of shame and anguish, the second looks forward to an even greater measure of joy. With the announcement about Joseph, the birth narrative, which opens and closes with the use of the divine name *YHVH* (29:31, 30:24), is completed.

JACOB AND LABAN: A NEW CONTRACT
(vv. 25–43)

25. Give me leave to go back Jacob formally asks Laban to permit him to return with his wives and children to his native land. By the

---

24. When Rachel finally bears a child, her response to one of the most physically painful experiences a person can undergo is to pray to undergo it again.

25–43. What does this complicated narrative represent? Jacob and Laban agree to a wager to determine Jacob's compensation. The terms favor Laban, but Jacob relies on God to sustain

homeland. 26Give me my wives and my children, for whom I have served you, that I may go; for well you know what services I have rendered you." 27But Laban said to him, "If you will indulge me, I have learned by divination that the LORD has blessed me on your account." 28And he continued, "Name the wages due from me, and I will pay you." 29But he said, "You know well how I have served you and how your livestock has fared with me. 30For the little you had before I came has grown to much, since the LORD has blessed you wherever I turned. And now, when shall I make provision for my own household?" 31He said, "What shall I pay you?" And Jacob said, "Pay me nothing! If you will do this thing for me, I will again pasture and keep your flocks: 32let me pass through your whole flock today, removing from there every speckled and spotted animal—every dark-colored sheep and every spotted and speckled goat. Such shall be my wages. 33In the future when you go over my wages, let my honesty toward you testify for me: if there are among my goats any that are not speckled or spotted or any sheep that are not dark-colored, they got

מְקוֹמִי וּלְאַרְצִי׃ 26 תְּנָה אֶת־נָשַׁי וְאֶת־
יְלָדַי אֲשֶׁר עָבַדְתִּי אֹתְךָ בָּהֵן וְאֵלֵכָה כִּי
אַתָּה יָדַעְתָּ אֶת־עֲבֹדָתִי אֲשֶׁר עֲבַדְתִּיךָ׃
27 וַיֹּאמֶר אֵלָיו לָבָן אִם־נָא מָצָאתִי חֵן
בְּעֵינֶיךָ נִחַשְׁתִּי וַיְבָרְכֵנִי יְהוָה בִּגְלָלֶךָ׃
חמישי 28 וַיֹּאמַר נָקְבָה שְׂכָרְךָ עָלַי וְאֶתֵּנָה׃
29 וַיֹּאמֶר אֵלָיו אַתָּה יָדַעְתָּ אֵת אֲשֶׁר
עֲבַדְתִּיךָ וְאֵת אֲשֶׁר־הָיָה מִקְנְךָ אִתִּי׃
30 כִּי מְעַט אֲשֶׁר־הָיָה לְךָ לְפָנַי וַיִּפְרֹץ
לָרֹב וַיְבָרֶךְ יְהוָה אֹתְךָ לְרַגְלִי וְעַתָּה
מָתַי אֶעֱשֶׂה גַם־אָנֹכִי לְבֵיתִי׃ 31 וַיֹּאמֶר
מָה אֶתֶּן־לָךְ וַיֹּאמֶר יַעֲקֹב לֹא־תִתֶּן־
לִי מְאוּמָה אִם־תַּעֲשֶׂה־לִּי הַדָּבָר הַזֶּה
אָשׁוּבָה אֶרְעֶה צֹאנְךָ אֶשְׁמֹר׃ 32 אֶעֱבֹר
בְּכָל־צֹאנְךָ הַיּוֹם הָסֵר מִשָּׁם כָּל־שֶׂה ׀
נָקֹד וְטָלוּא וְכָל־שֶׂה־חוּם בַּכְּשָׂבִים
וְטָלוּא וְנָקֹד בָּעִזִּים וְהָיָה שְׂכָרִי׃
33 וְעָנְתָה־בִּי צִדְקָתִי בְּיוֹם מָחָר כִּי־תָבוֹא
עַל־שְׂכָרִי לְפָנֶיךָ כֹּל אֲשֶׁר־אֵינֶנּוּ נָקֹד

terms of the original contract with Laban (as explained in the Comment to 29:18), Jacob's status was that of an indentured servant paying off a debt. In this case, the debt was the bride-price for his employer's two daughters.

27. I have learned by divination This is the traditional rendering of the Hebrew word *niḥashti.* But there is an Akkadian verb *naḥashu*, which means "to prosper"; and Laban is probably saying here, "I have become prosperous, seeing that God has blessed me on your account."

28. Name the wages Laban is reluctant to lose the skilled services of Jacob, so he ignores the request to depart and pretends to understand Jacob's remarks as the opening bid in a haggle over the price of future service.

29. how I have served you Jacob disregards Laban's question and astutely drives home the point about his own decisive role in Laban's success.

32. every dark-colored sheep In the Near East, sheep are generally white and goats are dark brown or black. A minority of sheep may have dark patches, and goats white markings. It is these uncommon types to be born in the future that Jacob demands as wages for his unpaid services.

---

him. Laban, unsatisfied with natural advantage, tries to trick Jacob. Jacob responds with trickery to protect his interests. After 20 years of living with Laban, Jacob has come to resemble Laban as a master of guile.

there by theft." [34]And Laban said, "Very well, let it be as you say."

[35]But that same day he removed the streaked and spotted he-goats and all the speckled and spotted she-goats—every one that had white on it—and all the dark-colored sheep, and left them in the charge of his sons. [36]And he put a distance of three days' journey between himself and Jacob, while Jacob was pasturing the rest of Laban's flock.

[37]Jacob then got fresh shoots of poplar, and of almond and plane, and peeled white stripes in them, laying bare the white of the shoots. [38]The rods that he had peeled he set up in front of the goats in the troughs, the water receptacles, that the goats came to drink from. Their mating occurred when they came to drink, [39]and since the goats mated by the rods, the goats brought forth streaked, speckled, and spotted young. [40]But Jacob dealt separately with the sheep; he made these animals face the streaked or wholly dark-colored animals in Laban's flock. And so he produced special flocks for himself, which he did not put with Laban's flocks. [41]Moreover, when the sturdier animals were mating, Jacob would place the rods in the troughs, in full view of the animals, so that they mated by the rods; [42]but with the feebler animals he would not place them there. Thus the feeble ones went to Laban and the sturdy to Jacob. [43]So the man grew exceedingly prosperous, and came to own large flocks, maidservants and menservants, camels and asses.

וְטָל֤וּא בֶּֽעִזִּים֙ וְח֣וּם בַּכְּשָׂבִ֔ים גָּנ֥וּב ה֖וּא אִתִּֽי: [34]וַיֹּ֣אמֶר לָבָ֑ן הֵ֖ן ל֥וּ יְהִ֖י כִדְבָרֶֽךָ: [35]וַיָּ֣סַר בַּיּוֹם֩ הַה֨וּא אֶת־הַתְּיָשִׁ֜ים הָֽעֲקֻדִּ֣ים וְהַטְּלֻאִ֗ים וְאֵ֤ת כָּל־הָֽעִזִּים֙ הַנְּקֻדּ֣וֹת וְהַטְּלֻאֹ֔ת כֹּ֤ל אֲשֶׁר־לָבָן֙ בּ֔וֹ וְכָל־ח֖וּם בַּכְּשָׂבִ֑ים וַיִּתֵּ֖ן בְּיַד־בָּנָֽיו: [36]וַיָּ֡שֶׂם דֶּ֩רֶךְ֩ שְׁלֹ֨שֶׁת יָמִ֜ים בֵּינ֣וֹ וּבֵ֣ין יַֽעֲקֹ֑ב וְיַֽעֲקֹ֗ב רֹעֶ֛ה אֶת־צֹ֥אן לָבָ֖ן הַנּֽוֹתָרֹֽת: [37]וַיִּֽקַּֽח־ל֣וֹ יַֽעֲקֹ֗ב מַקַּ֥ל לִבְנֶ֛ה לַ֖ח וְל֣וּז וְעַרְמ֑וֹן וַיְפַצֵּ֤ל בָּהֵן֙ פְּצָל֣וֹת לְבָנ֔וֹת מַחְשֹׂף֙ הַלָּבָ֔ן אֲשֶׁ֖ר עַל־הַמַּקְלֽוֹת: [38]וַיַּצֵּ֗ג אֶת־הַמַּקְלוֹת֙ אֲשֶׁ֣ר פִּצֵּ֔ל בָּֽרְהָטִ֖ים בְּשִֽׁקֲת֣וֹת הַמָּ֑יִם אֲשֶׁר֩ תָּבֹ֨אןָ הַצֹּ֤אן לִשְׁתּוֹת֙ לְנֹ֣כַח הַצֹּ֔אן וַיֵּחַ֖מְנָה בְּבֹאָ֥ן לִשְׁתּֽוֹת: [39]וַיֶּֽחֱמ֥וּ הַצֹּ֖אן אֶל־הַמַּקְל֑וֹת וַתֵּלַ֣דְןָ הַצֹּ֔אן עֲקֻדִּ֥ים נְקֻדִּ֖ים וּטְלֻאִֽים: [40]וְהַכְּשָׂבִים֮ הִפְרִ֣יד יַֽעֲקֹב֒ וַ֠יִּתֵּ֠ן פְּנֵ֨י הַצֹּ֜אן אֶל־עָקֹ֗ד וְכָל־ח֖וּם בְּצֹ֣אן לָבָ֑ן וַיָּֽשֶׁת־ל֤וֹ עֲדָרִים֙ לְבַדּ֔וֹ וְלֹ֥א שָׁתָ֖ם עַל־צֹ֥אן לָבָֽן: [41]וְהָיָ֗ה בְּכָל־יַחֵם֙ הַצֹּ֣אן הַֽמְקֻשָּׁר֔וֹת וְשָׂ֧ם יַֽעֲקֹ֛ב אֶת־הַמַּקְל֗וֹת לְעֵינֵ֥י הַצֹּ֖אן בָּֽרְהָטִ֑ים לְיַחְמֵ֖נָּה בַּמַּקְלֽוֹת: [42]וּבְהַֽעֲטִיף֙* הַצֹּ֔אן לֹ֖א יָשִׂ֑ים וְהָיָ֤ה הָֽעֲטֻפִים֙ לְלָבָ֔ן וְהַקְּשֻׁרִ֖ים לְיַֽעֲקֹֽב: [43]וַיִּפְרֹ֥ץ הָאִ֖ישׁ מְאֹ֣ד מְאֹ֑ד וַֽיְהִי־לוֹ֙ צֹ֣אן רַבּ֔וֹת וּשְׁפָחוֹת֙ וַֽעֲבָדִ֔ים וּגְמַלִּ֖ים וַֽחֲמֹרִֽים:

v. 42. ‏ק׳ רבתי לפי מהדורת לעטעריס

34. Very well Laban readily agrees, believing that he is getting a bargain on account of their rarity.

36. three days' journey See Comment to 22:4.

38. The rods that he had peeled The folklore of the time believed that sheep seeing striped rods would bear striped young.

43. exceedingly prosperous God's promise has been fulfilled.

came to own Jacob was able to barter the rare sheep and goats for these other possessions.

31 Now he heard the things that Laban's
sons were saying: "Jacob has taken all that was
our father's, and from that which was our
father's he has built up all this wealth." 2 Jacob
also saw that Laban's manner toward him was
not as it had been in the past. 3 Then the LORD
said to Jacob, "Return to the land of your fathers
where you were born, and I will be with you."
4 Jacob had Rachel and Leah called to the field,
where his flock was, 5 and said to them, "I see
that your father's manner toward me is not as it
has been in the past. But the God of my father
has been with me. 6 As you know, I have served
your father with all my might; 7 but your father
has cheated me, changing my wages time and
again. God, however, would not let him do me
harm. 8 If he said thus, 'The speckled shall be
your wages,' then all the flocks would drop
speckled young; and if he said thus, 'The
streaked shall be your wages,' then all the flocks
would drop streaked young. 9 God has taken
away your father's livestock and given it to me.

לא וַיִּשְׁמַע אֶת־דִּבְרֵי בְנֵי־לָבָן
לֵאמֹר לָקַח יַעֲקֹב אֵת כָּל־אֲשֶׁר לְאָבִינוּ
וּמֵאֲשֶׁר לְאָבִינוּ עָשָׂה אֵת כָּל־הַכָּבֹד
הַזֶּה׃ 2 וַיַּרְא יַעֲקֹב אֶת־פְּנֵי לָבָן וְהִנֵּה
אֵינֶנּוּ עִמּוֹ כִּתְמוֹל שִׁלְשׁוֹם׃ 3 וַיֹּאמֶר
יְהוָה אֶל־יַעֲקֹב שׁוּב אֶל־אֶרֶץ אֲבוֹתֶיךָ
וּלְמוֹלַדְתֶּךָ וְאֶהְיֶה עִמָּךְ׃ 4 וַיִּשְׁלַח יַעֲקֹב
וַיִּקְרָא לְרָחֵל וּלְלֵאָה הַשָּׂדֶה אֶל־צֹאנוֹ׃
5 וַיֹּאמֶר לָהֶן רֹאֶה אָנֹכִי אֶת־פְּנֵי אֲבִיכֶן
כִּי־אֵינֶנּוּ אֵלַי כִּתְמֹל שִׁלְשֹׁם וֵאלֹהֵי אָבִי
הָיָה עִמָּדִי׃ 6 וְאַתֵּנָה יְדַעְתֶּן כִּי בְּכָל־כֹּחִי
עָבַדְתִּי אֶת־אֲבִיכֶן׃ 7 וַאֲבִיכֶן הֵתֶל בִּי
וְהֶחֱלִף אֶת־מַשְׂכֻּרְתִּי עֲשֶׂרֶת מֹנִים וְלֹא־
נְתָנוֹ אֱלֹהִים לְהָרַע עִמָּדִי׃ 8 אִם־כֹּה
יֹאמַר נְקֻדִּים יִהְיֶה שְׂכָרֶךָ וְיָלְדוּ כָל־
הַצֹּאן נְקֻדִּים וְאִם־כֹּה יֹאמַר עֲקֻדִּים
יִהְיֶה שְׂכָרֶךָ וְיָלְדוּ כָל־הַצֹּאן עֲקֻדִּים׃
9 וַיַּצֵּל אֱלֹהִים אֶת־מִקְנֵה אֲבִיכֶם וַיִּתֶּן־לִי׃

JACOB AND LABAN: THE FINALE (31:1–32:3)

JACOB CONSULTS WITH HIS WIVES
(vv. 1–16)

1. he heard the things Jacob hears what is being said about him, and observes Laban's changed attitude.

3. the LORD said Any doubt as to his proper course of action is now dispelled by God's command and reassurance of protection.

4. called to the field While shepherding his flock in the open field, Jacob can summon Rachel and Leah without arousing suspicion. At the same time, the locale affords protection from eavesdroppers. He must consult with his wives. The concubines are excluded because their lower social status makes it unnecessary for Jacob to seek their agreement to his plan.

7. time and again The Hebrew phrase *aseret monim,* literally, "10 times," is used here in the sense of "repeatedly."

9. taken away The verb *va-yatzel,* a form of *hitzil,* usually means "saved" but here it is used in the sense of "taking back."

CHAPTER 31

5–7. Jacob credits God for his good fortune, even as he did in Gen. 27:20. There this manner of speaking was deemed "the voice of Jacob" by his father, Isaac (27:22).

HALAKHAH L'MA·ASEH

31:4 Rachel and Leah Whenever the two sisters are listed together in the Bible, Rachel is listed first. Consequently, Rachel is also listed before Leah in the parental blessing recited over daughters on Friday night, and in other prayers whenever the Matriarchs are included in Conservative movement liturgy.

[10]"Once, at the mating time of the flocks, I had a dream in which I saw that the he-goats mating with the flock were streaked, speckled, and mottled. [11]And in the dream an angel of God said to me, 'Jacob!' 'Here,' I answered. [12]And he said, 'Note well that all the he-goats which are mating with the flock are streaked, speckled, and mottled; for I have noted all that Laban has been doing to you. [13]I am the God of Bethel, where you anointed a pillar and where you made a vow to Me. Now, arise and leave this land and return to your native land.'"

[14]Then Rachel and Leah answered him, saying, "Have we still a share in the inheritance of our father's house? [15]Surely, he regards us as outsiders, now that he has sold us and has used up our purchase price. [16]Truly, all the wealth that God has taken away from our father belongs to us and to our children. Now then, do just as God has told you."

[17]Thereupon Jacob put his children and wives on camels; [18]and he drove off all his livestock and all the wealth that he had amassed,

10 וַיְהִי בְּעֵת יַחֵם הַצֹּאן וָאֶשָּׂא עֵינַי וָאֵרֶא
בַּחֲלוֹם וְהִנֵּה הָעַתֻּדִים הָעֹלִים עַל־הַצֹּאן
עֲקֻדִּים נְקֻדִּים וּבְרֻדִּים׃ 11 וַיֹּאמֶר אֵלַי
מַלְאַךְ הָאֱלֹהִים בַּחֲלוֹם יַעֲקֹב וָאֹמַר
הִנֵּנִי׃ 12 וַיֹּאמֶר שָׂא־נָא עֵינֶיךָ וּרְאֵה כָּל־
הָעַתֻּדִים הָעֹלִים עַל־הַצֹּאן עֲקֻדִּים
נְקֻדִּים וּבְרֻדִּים כִּי רָאִיתִי אֵת כָּל־אֲשֶׁר
לָבָן עֹשֶׂה לָּךְ׃ 13 אָנֹכִי הָאֵל בֵּית־אֵל
אֲשֶׁר מָשַׁחְתָּ שָּׁם מַצֵּבָה אֲשֶׁר נָדַרְתָּ לִּי
שָׁם נֶדֶר עַתָּה קוּם צֵא מִן־הָאָרֶץ הַזֹּאת
וְשׁוּב אֶל־אֶרֶץ מוֹלַדְתֶּךָ׃
14 וַתַּעַן רָחֵל וְלֵאָה וַתֹּאמַרְנָה לוֹ הַעוֹד
לָנוּ חֵלֶק וְנַחֲלָה בְּבֵית אָבִינוּ׃ 15 הֲלוֹא
נָכְרִיּוֹת נֶחְשַׁבְנוּ לוֹ כִּי מְכָרָנוּ וַיֹּאכַל גַּם־
אָכוֹל אֶת־כַּסְפֵּנוּ׃ 16 כִּי כָל־הָעֹשֶׁר אֲשֶׁר
הִצִּיל אֱלֹהִים מֵאָבִינוּ לָנוּ הוּא וּלְבָנֵינוּ
וְעַתָּה כֹּל אֲשֶׁר אָמַר אֱלֹהִים אֵלֶיךָ עֲשֵׂה׃
17 וַיָּקָם יַעֲקֹב וַיִּשָּׂא אֶת־בָּנָיו וְאֶת־נָשָׁיו ששי
עַל־הַגְּמַלִּים׃ 18 וַיִּנְהַג אֶת־כָּל־מִקְנֵהוּ

10. I had a dream Jacob credits his sheep-breeding strategy to the inspiration of a dream vision.

12. for I have noted Literally, "saw," a term frequently used to express God's compassionate response to a suffering victim.

13. I am the God of Bethel The title is not intended to limit God to a specific locale but to call to mind the original revelation to Jacob, specifically the promise of constant protection and safe return.

14. Have we still a share A rhetorical question.

15. as outsiders By not giving them their share of the bride-price (*mohar*), Laban treated them from the beginning as though they were not part of the clan. Hence, they considered themselves as "being sold," rather than married off.

and has used up our purchase price Literally, "and has eaten up our money." A similar statement is found in Akkadian sources, with the same meaning.

16. belongs to us The wives fully agree with Jacob's claim of good title to his wealth.

THE ESCAPE (vv. 17–21)

18. that he had amassed . . . in his possession that he had acquired This cluster of phrases underscores Jacob's claim to absolute and rightful ownership of all his possessions.

13. The angel's message to Jacob is, "Once you dreamed of stairways leading to heaven. Now you dream of how to increase the number of sheep and goats you own. You have been corrupted by the values of Laban's world. The time has come for you to leave this place and return to the Land."

15. he regards us as outsiders He did not treat us as daughters when he bartered us for 14 years of unpaid labor.

the livestock in his possession that he had acquired in Paddan-aram, to go to his father Isaac
in the land of Canaan.
19Meanwhile Laban had gone to shear his
sheep, and Rachel stole her father's household
idols. 20Jacob kept Laban the Aramean in the
dark, not telling him that he was fleeing, 21and
fled with all that he had. Soon he was across the
Euphrates and heading toward the hill country
of Gilead.
22On the third day, Laban was told that Jacob
had fled. 23So he took his kinsmen with him
and pursued him a distance of seven days,
catching up with him in the hill country of
Gilead. 24But God appeared to Laban the Aramean in a dream by night and said to him,
"Beware of attempting anything with Jacob,
good or bad."
25Laban overtook Jacob. Jacob had pitched
his tent on the Height, and Laban with his kins-

וְאֶת־כָּל־רְכֻשׁוֹ אֲשֶׁר רָכָשׁ מִקְנֵה קִנְיָנוֹ
אֲשֶׁר רָכַשׁ בְּפַדַּן אֲרָם לָבוֹא אֶל־יִצְחָק
אָבִיו אַרְצָה כְּנָעַן׃
19 וְלָבָן הָלַךְ לִגְזֹז אֶת־צֹאנוֹ וַתִּגְנֹב רָחֵל
אֶת־הַתְּרָפִים אֲשֶׁר לְאָבִיהָ׃ 20 וַיִּגְנֹב
יַעֲקֹב אֶת־לֵב לָבָן הָאֲרַמִּי עַל־בְּלִי הִגִּיד
לוֹ כִּי בֹרֵחַ הוּא׃ 21 וַיִּבְרַח הוּא וְכָל־
אֲשֶׁר־לוֹ וַיָּקָם וַיַּעֲבֹר אֶת־הַנָּהָר וַיָּשֶׂם
אֶת־פָּנָיו הַר הַגִּלְעָד׃
22 וַיֻּגַּד לְלָבָן בַּיּוֹם הַשְּׁלִישִׁי כִּי בָרַח
יַעֲקֹב׃ 23 וַיִּקַּח אֶת־אֶחָיו עִמּוֹ וַיִּרְדֹּף
אַחֲרָיו דֶּרֶךְ שִׁבְעַת יָמִים וַיַּדְבֵּק אֹתוֹ
בְּהַר הַגִּלְעָד׃ 24 וַיָּבֹא אֱלֹהִים אֶל־לָבָן
הָאֲרַמִּי בַּחֲלֹם הַלָּיְלָה וַיֹּאמֶר לוֹ הִשָּׁמֶר
לְךָ פֶּן־תְּדַבֵּר עִם־יַעֲקֹב מִטּוֹב עַד־רָע׃
25 וַיַּשֵּׂג לָבָן אֶת־יַעֲקֹב וְיַעֲקֹב תָּקַע אֶת־
אָהֳלוֹ בָּהָר וְלָבָן תָּקַע אֶת־אֶחָיו בְּהַר

19. to shear his sheep In Mesopotamia, sheep shearing took place in the spring. It entailed much hard work on the part of a large number of men who often had to labor at a considerable distance from their homes for extended periods of time. Thus Laban, his sons, and his menfolk would all be far away and busily preoccupied—an ideal time for Jacob to make his departure.

Rachel stole The text clearly describes her act as thievery.

household idols They are called *t'rafim* in Hebrew, derived from the Hittite word *"tarpi."* Ancient versions of the text, such as the Aramaic Targums and the Greek Septuagint, translate the word as "idols." They are believed to have been the household gods who ensured the well-being of the family.

20. the Aramean The emphasis on Laban's ethnic affiliation, here and again in verse 24, alerts the reader to the fact that Laban and Jacob are now totally alienated from each other and represent two distinct peoples.

21. the hill country of Gilead This designation is very general. Apparently it covers the entire plateau region east of the river Jordan between the Yarmuk, which flows into the Jordan just below the Sea of Galilee, and the northern shore of the Dead Sea.

LABAN IN HOT PURSUIT (vv. 22–35)

22–23. third day . . . seven days These are symbolic numbers that indicate significant segments of time. The distance of 400 miles (640 km) between Haran and Gilead could not have been covered by Jacob and his large entourage in 10 days. That would have involved an average rate of travel of about 40 miles (64 km) a day, and evidence from the ancient Near East suggests that a daily progress of no more than about 6 miles (9.65 km) could be expected in these circumstances.

24. attempting anything Once he has Jacob in sight, Laban encamps for the night without making contact. He then experiences the dream.

25. on the Height . . . in the hill country The contrast suggests two separate and adjacent

---

19. Although Rachel probably took the *t'rafim* because she believed in their power, the Sages credit her with taking them to prevent her father from continuing to worship them.

men encamped in the hill country of Gilead. ²⁶And Laban said to Jacob, "What did you mean by keeping me in the dark and carrying off my daughters like captives of the sword? ²⁷Why did you flee in secrecy and mislead me and not tell me? I would have sent you off with festive music, with timbrel and lyre. ²⁸You did not even let me kiss my sons and daughters good-by! It was a foolish thing for you to do. ²⁹I have it in my power to do you harm; but the God of your father said to me last night, 'Beware of attempting anything with Jacob, good or bad.' ³⁰Very well, you had to leave because you were longing for your father's house; but why did you steal my gods?"

³¹Jacob answered Laban, saying, "I was afraid because I thought you would take your daughters from me by force. ³²But anyone with whom you find your gods shall not remain alive! In the presence of our kinsmen, point out what I have of yours and take it." Jacob, of course, did not know that Rachel had stolen them.

הַגִּלְעָֽד׃ 26 וַיֹּ֤אמֶר לָבָן֙ לְיַעֲקֹ֔ב מֶ֣ה עָשִׂ֔יתָ וַתִּגְנֹ֖ב אֶת־לְבָבִ֑י וַתְּנַהֵג֙ אֶת־בְּנֹתַ֔י כִּשְׁבֻי֖וֹת חָֽרֶב׃ 27 לָ֤מָּה נַחְבֵּ֙אתָ֙ לִבְרֹ֔חַ וַתִּגְנֹ֖ב אֹתִ֑י וְלֹא־הִגַּ֣דְתָּ לִּ֔י וָֽאֲשַׁלֵּֽחֲךָ֛ בְּשִׂמְחָ֥ה וּבְשִׁרִ֖ים בְּתֹ֥ף וּבְכִנּֽוֹר׃ 28 וְלֹ֣א נְטַשְׁתַּ֔נִי לְנַשֵּׁ֥ק לְבָנַ֖י וְלִבְנֹתָ֑י עַתָּ֖ה הִסְכַּ֥לְתָּֽ עֲשֽׂוֹ׃ 29 יֶשׁ־לְאֵ֣ל יָדִ֔י לַעֲשׂ֥וֹת עִמָּכֶ֖ם רָ֑ע וֵֽאלֹהֵ֨י אֲבִיכֶ֜ם אֶ֣מֶשׁ ׀ אָמַ֧ר אֵלַ֣י לֵאמֹ֗ר הִשָּׁ֧מֶר לְךָ֛ מִדַּבֵּ֥ר עִֽם־יַעֲקֹ֖ב מִטּ֥וֹב עַד־רָֽע׃ 30 וְעַתָּה֙ הָלֹ֣ךְ הָלַ֔כְתָּ כִּֽי־נִכְסֹ֥ף נִכְסַ֖פְתָּה לְבֵ֣ית אָבִ֑יךָ לָ֥מָּה גָנַ֖בְתָּ אֶת־אֱלֹהָֽי׃ 31 וַיַּ֥עַן יַעֲקֹ֖ב וַיֹּ֣אמֶר לְלָבָ֑ן כִּ֣י יָרֵ֔אתִי כִּ֣י אָמַ֔רְתִּי פֶּן־תִּגְזֹ֥ל אֶת־בְּנוֹתֶ֖יךָ מֵעִמִּֽי׃ 32 עִ֠ם אֲשֶׁ֨ר תִּמְצָ֣א אֶת־אֱלֹהֶיךָ֮ לֹ֣א יִֽחְיֶה֒ נֶ֣גֶד אַחֵ֧ינוּ הַֽכֶּר־לְךָ֛ מָ֥ה עִמָּדִ֖י וְקַֽח־לָ֑ךְ וְלֹֽא־יָדַ֣ע יַעֲקֹ֔ב כִּ֥י רָחֵ֖ל גְּנָבָֽתַם׃

sites that face one another, possibly Mizpah and Mount Gilead.

26. What did you mean Literally, "What have you done?" Laban opens with a phrase that invariably introduces an accusation of wrongdoing (see 29:25).

27. with festive music Laban is referring either to a farewell of a social nature or to some formal, ceremonious leave-taking procedure.

29. I have it in my power Laban apparently regards Jacob as a member of his clan who deserves punishment for violating its rules and mores. In deference to the divine admonition, however, he will not exact retribution.

30. why did you steal my gods In the first part of the verse, Laban reinforces his false magnanimity with a show of empathy. Having lulled Jacob into a false sense of relief, he then proceeds to deliver the most serious charge of all: theft of his gods.

31. Jacob answered His flight was justified, Jacob claims, by his fear that Laban might have robbed him of his wives by force. To Jacob, this was a more realistic prospect than the joyous send-off that Laban had described in v. 27.

32. shall not remain alive Outright rejection of the final charge takes the form of a fearful condemnation. It is uncertain whether the phrase here has judicial or merely rhetorical force. Sacrilege was severely dealt with in the an-

30. why did you steal my gods When Jews imitate the religious practices of their neighbors, the neighbors may not be flattered. They may resent seeing things that are sacred to them used in a nonreligious manner (Israel H. Levinthal).

32. anyone with whom you find your gods

shall not remain alive Jacob's curse will find its fulfilment in Rachel's death in childbirth (35:19). On the other hand, the Ḥatam Sofer interprets the verse as "anyone who finds your idols will realize that they, the idols, are not alive and there is no reason to be upset about their disappearance."

[33]So Laban went into Jacob's tent and Leah's tent and the tents of the two maidservants; but he did not find them. Leaving Leah's tent, he entered Rachel's tent. [34]Rachel, meanwhile, had taken the idols and placed them in the camel cushion and sat on them; and Laban rummaged through the tent without finding them. [35]For she said to her father, "Let not my lord take it amiss that I cannot rise before you, for the period of women is upon me." Thus he searched, but could not find the household idols.

[36]Now Jacob became incensed and took up his grievance with Laban. Jacob spoke up and said to Laban, "What is my crime, what is my guilt that you should pursue me? [37]You rummaged through all my things; what have you found of all your household objects? Set it here, before my kinsmen and yours, and let them decide between us two.

[38]"These twenty years I have spent in your

33 וַיָּבֹא לָבָן בְּאֹהֶל יַעֲקֹב ׀ וּבְאֹהֶל לֵאָה
וּבְאֹהֶל שְׁתֵּי הָאֲמָהֹת וְלֹא מָצָא וַיֵּצֵא
מֵאֹהֶל לֵאָה וַיָּבֹא בְּאֹהֶל רָחֵל׃ 34 וְרָחֵל
לָקְחָה אֶת־הַתְּרָפִים וַתְּשִׂמֵם בְּכַר הַגָּמָל
וַתֵּשֶׁב עֲלֵיהֶם וַיְמַשֵּׁשׁ לָבָן אֶת־כָּל־
הָאֹהֶל וְלֹא מָצָא׃ 35 וַתֹּאמֶר אֶל־אָבִיהָ
אַל־יִחַר בְּעֵינֵי אֲדֹנִי כִּי לוֹא* אוּכַל לָקוּם
מִפָּנֶיךָ כִּי־דֶרֶךְ נָשִׁים לִי וַיְחַפֵּשׂ וְלֹא מָצָא
אֶת־הַתְּרָפִים׃
36 וַיִּחַר לְיַעֲקֹב וַיָּרֶב בְּלָבָן וַיַּעַן יַעֲקֹב
וַיֹּאמֶר לְלָבָן מַה־פִּשְׁעִי מַה חַטָּאתִי כִּי
דָלַקְתָּ אַחֲרָי׃ 37 כִּי־מִשַּׁשְׁתָּ אֶת־כָּל־כֵּלַי
מַה־מָּצָאתָ מִכֹּל כְּלֵי־בֵיתֶךָ שִׂים כֹּה נֶגֶד
אַחַי וְאַחֶיךָ וְיוֹכִיחוּ בֵּין שְׁנֵינוּ׃
38 זֶה עֶשְׂרִים שָׁנָה אָנֹכִי עִמָּךְ רְחֵלֶיךָ

v. 35. מלא ו

cient Near East, but it did not always incur the death penalty.

34. camel cushion In a relief uncovered in northern Syria, dating from 900 B.C.E., a camel driver is shown seated on a boxlike object that serves as a riding saddle and as a pack saddle. It is secured to the camel by straps.

I cannot rise before you Rachel apologizes that her indisposition prevents her from paying her father proper filial respect.

the period of women Rachel's condition deters Laban from searching the camel cushion. He cannot approach her, and he cannot imagine that she would ever sit on his "gods" in a state of menstrual impurity. The ancients regarded menstrual flow as a potently contaminating substance, and the menstruant was thought to be possessed by evil spirits, thus requiring her separation from other persons.

JACOB'S RESPONSE (vv. 36–43)

According to ancient law, the futility of Laban's search for his property is proof of Jacob's innocence. At that, 20 years of suppressed anger suddenly find expression in Jacob's outpouring of righteous indignation.

36. became incensed By searching Jacob's tent, Laban had shown that he really believed him to be guilty of theft.

took up his grievance It is Jacob who now becomes the aggrieved party, and Laban the accused.

37. What have you found Jacob believes that Laban used the issue of the *t'rafim* as a pretext and that he really suspected his son-in-law of stealing much more from him.

let them decide Jacob calls on the kinsmen of each side to form a tribunal and to decide which of the rivals is the real thief.

38–42 As Jacob finally stands up for himself to his father-in-law, our sympathies are enlisted on behalf of the laborer cheated by his master. Although there were laws protecting the worker in Aramean society, there was no one to whom Jacob could appeal. The Torah consistently portrays God as protector of the weak and the vulnerable (cf. Lev. 19:13).

וְעִזֶּיךָ לֹא שִׁכֵּלוּ וְאֵילֵי צֹאנְךָ לֹא אָכָלְתִּי׃
39 טְרֵפָה לֹא־הֵבֵאתִי אֵלֶיךָ אָנֹכִי אֲחַטֶּנָּה
מִיָּדִי תְּבַקְשֶׁנָּה גְּנֻבְתִי יוֹם וּגְנֻבְתִי לָיְלָה׃
40 הָיִיתִי בַיּוֹם אֲכָלַנִי חֹרֶב וְקֶרַח בַּלָּיְלָה
וַתִּדַּד שְׁנָתִי מֵעֵינָי׃ 41 זֶה־לִּי עֶשְׂרִים שָׁנָה
בְּבֵיתֶךָ עֲבַדְתִּיךָ אַרְבַּע־עֶשְׂרֵה שָׁנָה
בִּשְׁתֵּי בְנֹתֶיךָ וְשֵׁשׁ שָׁנִים בְּצֹאנֶךָ וַתַּחֲלֵף
אֶת־מַשְׂכֻּרְתִּי עֲשֶׂרֶת מֹנִים׃ 42 לוּלֵי
אֱלֹהֵי אָבִי אֱלֹהֵי אַבְרָהָם וּפַחַד יִצְחָק
הָיָה לִי כִּי עַתָּה רֵיקָם שִׁלַּחְתָּנִי אֶת־
עָנְיִי וְאֶת־יְגִיעַ כַּפַּי רָאָה אֱלֹהִים וַיּוֹכַח
אָמֶשׁ׃
שביעי 43 וַיַּעַן לָבָן וַיֹּאמֶר אֶל־יַעֲקֹב הַבָּנוֹת בְּנֹתַי
וְהַבָּנִים בָּנַי וְהַצֹּאן צֹאנִי וְכֹל אֲשֶׁר־אַתָּה
רֹאֶה לִי־הוּא וְלִבְנֹתַי מָה־אֶעֱשֶׂה לָאֵלֶּה
הַיּוֹם אוֹ לִבְנֵיהֶן אֲשֶׁר יָלָדוּ׃ 44 וְעַתָּה
לְכָה נִכְרְתָה בְרִית אֲנִי וָאָתָּה וְהָיָה לְעֵד
בֵּינִי וּבֵינֶךָ׃ 45 וַיִּקַּח יַעֲקֹב אָבֶן וַיְרִימֶהָ
מַצֵּבָה׃ 46 וַיֹּאמֶר יַעֲקֹב לְאֶחָיו לִקְטוּ

service, your ewes and she-goats never miscarried, nor did I feast on rams from your flock. 39That which was torn by beasts I never brought to you; I myself made good the loss; you exacted it of me, whether snatched by day or snatched by night. 40Often, scorching heat ravaged me by day and frost by night; and sleep fled from my eyes. 41Of the twenty years that I spent in your household, I served you fourteen years for your two daughters, and six years for your flocks; and you changed my wages time and again. 42Had not the God of my father, the God of Abraham and the Fear of Isaac, been with me, you would have sent me away empty-handed. But God took notice of my plight and the toil of my hands, and He gave judgment last night."

43Then Laban spoke up and said to Jacob, "The daughters are my daughters, the children are my children, and the flocks are my flocks; all that you see is mine. Yet what can I do now about my daughters or the children they have borne? 44Come, then, let us make a pact, you and I, that there may be a witness between you and me." 45Thereupon Jacob took a stone and set it up as a pillar. 46And Jacob said to his kins-

38. never miscarried This is another way of saying, "I was never negligent but always exercised tender care and due diligence with the flock."

39. I myself made good the loss Jacob is accusing Laban of violating ancient Near Eastern law and custom, which stipulated that a shepherd under contract was liable for only lost or stolen sheep.

42. the God of my father On this title, see Comment to 26:24.

the Fear of Isaac This unique title of God, *"Paḥad Yitzḥak,"* found also in verse 53, conveys a double meaning: "The One Whom Isaac Reveres" and "The One of Isaac Who Caused Terror." This latter nuance is a reference to Laban's dream, the source of which he recognized to be the God of Jacob's father (v. 29). It may also mean "the kinsman of Isaac."

43. Then Laban spoke up Exposed as a scoundrel, Laban tries to cover his loss of face with empty rhetoric. It is as though he were saying, "All the same, were it not for me, you would still be a nobody possessing nothing. Besides, how could you think I might harm my own offspring?"

THE PACT BETWEEN LABAN AND JACOB
(vv. 44–54)

To show good faith, Laban now proposes that he and Jacob conclude a pact of mutual nonaggression. In legal terms, it means that he tacitly acknowledges Jacob as constituting a separate, independent social entity of equal status.

44. that there may be a witness Literally, "It shall constitute." The pact itself is testimony to the state of relationships between the parties.

45. pillar See Comment to 28:18.

46. his kinsmen The term apparently embraces all present on both sides (see v. 54).

men, "Gather stones." So they took stones and made a mound; and they partook of a meal there by the mound. ⁴⁷Laban named it Yegar-sahadutha, but Jacob named it Gal-ed. ⁴⁸And Laban declared, "This mound is a witness between you and me this day." That is why it was named Gal-ed; ⁴⁹and [it was called] Mizpah, because he said, "May the Lord watch between you and me, when we are out of sight of each other. ⁵⁰If you ill-treat my daughters or take other wives besides my daughters—though no one else be about, remember, God Himself will be witness between you and me."

⁵¹And Laban said to Jacob, "Here is this mound and here the pillar which I have set up between you and me: ⁵²this mound shall be witness and this pillar shall be witness that I am not to cross to you past this mound, and that you are not to cross to me past this mound and this pillar, with hostile intent. ⁵³May the God of Abraham and the god of Nahor"—their ancestral deities—"judge between us." And Jacob swore by the Fear of his father Isaac. ⁵⁴Jacob then offered up a sacrifice on the Height, and invited his kinsmen to partake of the meal. After the meal, they spent the night on the Height.

אֲבָנִ֖ים וַיִּקְח֤וּ אֲבָנִים֙ וַיַּֽעֲשׂוּ־גָ֔ל וַיֹּ֥אכְלוּ שָׁ֖ם עַל־הַגָּֽל׃ ⁴⁷וַיִּקְרָא־ל֣וֹ לָבָ֔ן יְגַ֖ר שָׂהֲדוּתָ֑א וְיַ֣עֲקֹ֔ב קָ֥רָא ל֖וֹ גַּלְעֵֽד׃ ⁴⁸וַיֹּ֣אמֶר לָבָ֔ן הַגַּ֨ל הַזֶּ֥ה עֵ֛ד בֵּינִ֥י וּבֵֽינְךָ֖ הַיּ֑וֹם עַל־כֵּ֥ן קָרָֽא־שְׁמ֖וֹ גַּלְעֵֽד׃ ⁴⁹וְהַמִּצְפָּה֙ אֲשֶׁ֣ר אָמַ֔ר יִ֥צֶף יְהֹוָ֖ה בֵּינִ֣י וּבֵינֶ֑ךָ כִּ֥י נִסָּתֵ֖ר אִ֥ישׁ מֵרֵעֵֽהוּ׃ ⁵⁰אִם־תְּעַנֶּ֣ה אֶת־בְּנֹתַ֗י וְאִם־תִּקַּ֤ח נָשִׁים֙ עַל־בְּנֹתַ֔י אֵ֥ין אִ֖ישׁ עִמָּ֑נוּ רְאֵ֕ה אֱלֹהִ֥ים עֵ֖ד בֵּינִ֥י וּבֵינֶֽךָ׃

⁵¹וַיֹּ֥אמֶר לָבָ֖ן לְיַֽעֲקֹ֑ב הִנֵּ֣ה ׀ הַגַּ֣ל הַזֶּ֗ה וְהִנֵּה֙ הַמַּצֵּבָ֔ה אֲשֶׁ֥ר יָרִ֖יתִי בֵּינִ֥י וּבֵינֶֽךָ׃ ⁵²עֵ֚ד הַגַּ֣ל הַזֶּ֔ה וְעֵדָ֖ה הַמַּצֵּבָ֑ה אִם־אָ֗נִי לֹֽא־אֶֽעֱבֹ֤ר אֵלֶ֙יךָ֙ אֶת־הַגַּ֣ל הַזֶּ֔ה וְאִם־אַ֠תָּ֠ה לֹֽא־תַֽעֲבֹ֨ר אֵלַ֜י אֶת־הַגַּ֥ל הַזֶּ֛ה וְאֶת־הַמַּצֵּבָ֥ה הַזֹּ֖את לְרָעָֽה׃ ⁵³אֱלֹהֵ֨י אַבְרָהָ֜ם וֵֽאלֹהֵ֤י נָחוֹר֙ יִשְׁפְּט֣וּ בֵינֵ֔ינוּ אֱלֹהֵ֖י אֲבִיהֶ֑ם וַיִּשָּׁבַ֣ע יַֽעֲקֹ֔ב בְּפַ֖חַד אָבִ֥יו יִצְחָֽק׃ ⁵⁴וַיִּזְבַּ֨ח יַֽעֲקֹ֥ב זֶ֙בַח֙ בָּהָ֔ר וַיִּקְרָ֥א לְאֶחָ֖יו לֶֽאֱכָל־לָ֑חֶם וַיֹּ֣אכְלוּ לֶ֔חֶם וַיָּלִ֖ינוּ בָּהָֽר׃

---

they partook of a meal See Comment to 26:30. It is likely that only the principals, Laban and Jacob, ate at this time.

47. Yegar-sahadutha This is the first appearance of Aramaic in the Bible.

48. And Laban declared Having initiated the pact, he speaks first.

This mound is a witness See Comment to 28:18.

Gal-ed A folk etymology for the regional name Gilead, the site of the treaty making as recorded in verses 21, 23, and 25. The name probably comes from the Arabic word *jal'ad*, "hard, rough," referring to the local limestone.

49. Mizpah See Comment to 31:25.

May the Lord watch Deities were appealed to as the highest authority for monitoring the enforcement of treaties in the ancient Near East.

50. or take other wives The restrictions imposed by Laban to safeguard the status of his

daughters are not found elsewhere in the Bible but are similar to those in other Near Eastern texts.

53. May the God of Abraham and the god of Nahor . . . judge Everywhere in the ancient Near East, the national god was regarded as the protector of the boundary. The plural verb for "judge" in Hebrew indicates that Laban is invoking two separate deities.

their ancestral deities This phrase is the narrator's explanatory comment. Literally, the Hebrew means "the deities of their father," perhaps referring to Terah, who, according to Josh. 24:2, "worshiped other gods."

Jacob swore In response, Jacob ignores Laban's formula and invokes only the "Fear of his father Isaac."

54. the meal The entire treaty-making process is sealed by a sacrificial meal in which all partake.

32 Early in the morning, Laban kissed his
sons and daughters and bade them good-by;
then Laban left on his journey homeward. 2 Jacob went on his way, and angels of God encountered him. 3 When he saw them, Jacob
said, "This is God's camp." So he named that
place Mahanaim.

מפטיר לב וַיַּשְׁכֵּם לָבָן בַּבֹּקֶר וַיְנַשֵּׁק לְבָנָיו
וְלִבְנוֹתָיו וַיְבָרֶךְ אֶתְהֶם וַיֵּלֶךְ וַיָּשָׁב לָבָן
לִמְקֹמוֹ׃ 2 וְיַעֲקֹב הָלַךְ לְדַרְכּוֹ וַיִּפְגְּעוּ־בוֹ
מַלְאֲכֵי אֱלֹהִים׃ 3 וַיֹּאמֶר יַעֲקֹב כַּאֲשֶׁר
רָאָם מַחֲנֵה אֱלֹהִים זֶה וַיִּקְרָא שֵׁם־
הַמָּקוֹם הַהוּא מַחֲנָיִם׃ פ

ANGELS AT MAHANAIM (vv. 1–3)

The next morning, Jacob and Laban part, thus ending forever the patriarchal connection with Mesopotamia.

1. his sons That is, his grandsons (see Gen. 31:28,43).

3. God's camp In 1 Chron. 12:22 this phrase connotes a vast throng.

Mahanaim According to other biblical references, the site is located in Transjordan (see 1 Chron. 6:65). Gen. 32:23 suggests that it is on the Jabbok River.

CHAPTER 32

2. Angels appear as Jacob prepares to cross the border into Canaan, as they appeared at the beginning of the *parashah* (28:12), as if setting the account of Jacob's 20 years in the house of Laban within parentheses. Have angels been accompanying Jacob throughout those 20 years, so that he prospered in all that he did; and only now as they take their leave of him is he able to see them?

הפטרת ויצא

HAFTARAH FOR VA-YETZEI

HOSEA 12:13–14:10 (*Ashk'nazim*)

The opening of this *haftarah* recounts Jacob's flight to Aram after deceiving his brother Esau. The first verses (12:13–15) are actually the end of a larger section of Hosea dealing with the northern kingdom of Israel (Ephraim), the patriarch Jacob, and similarities between events in the patriarch's life and current national life (during the reign of King Jeroboam II, 784–748 B.C.E.).

Originally this *haftarah* consisted of distinct and unrelated units, as we can see from the diversity of content, theme, and literary form in its verses. In their present form these units nevertheless have a certain cohesion, because they reflect a sequence of events from the patriarchal period to the monarchy. Thus the recollection of Jacob's flight to Aram and his labors there is followed by references to the Exodus, divine sustenance in the wilderness, and the sin of Baal worship. This is succeeded by the worship of idols and calves (in Bethel and Samaria) and the people's desire for a king. The people of the nation, having substituted a subversive religious history for God's providential guidance, are threatened with dire punishments unless they repent.

The effect of concluding these proclamations of doom with an exhortation to repent is to reverse the tone of the *haftarah* and inject a mood of hope into the cycle of sin and punishment. The freedom for new spiritual possibilities erupts unexpectedly through a proclamation of repentance. In turning from the false gods of nature and politics, the people are promised renewal and revival from the divine source of life.

A series of verbal echoes dramatizes this. The divine "plagues" (*d'varekha*) of death for sin (13:14) will be reversed when Israel takes "words" (*d'varim*) of confession and returns to God alone (14:3). Then Israel will not be destroyed "Like dew (*tal*) so early gone" (13:3) but will be nourished by God, who "will be to Israel as dew (*tal*)" (14:6).

The concluding call to heed the prophet's message (14:10) reinforces the need for spiritual awareness and humility. For Hosea, sin arises through pride and forgetting one's divine roots (13:6). This folly is resisted by the religiously alert, who follow the path of piety and are renewed in the shade of God's sustenance (14:7–8). The presumptions of self-sufficiency are rejected when the people renounce calling "our handiwork our god" (14:4). "He who is prudent will take note." This ringing conclusion to the *haftarah* calls out to all who hearken to Hosea's words.

RELATION OF THE *HAFTARAH* TO THE *PARASHAH*

The *haftarah* refers to the flight of Jacob to Aram and his service there for a wife. The vocabulary of the *parashah* recurs in the prophet. In the Torah, Jacob "served" (*va-ya·avod*) for Rachel (Gen. 29:20,30) by "guarding" (*eshmor*) Laban's sheep (Gen. 30:31). Hosea states that Israel (i.e., Jacob) "served" (*va-ya·avod*) for his wife by guarding (*shamar*) sheep (Hos. 12:13).

This verbal connection may be extended in two directions. First, the prophet uses the theme of Jacob's guarding to emphasize the theme of divine care. God's providence is first directed to the patriarch and then to the entire nation through a prophet who helped deliver the nation from servitude and guarded (*shamar*) them during their wilderness sojourn (12:14). Indeed, God's care for the person Jacob/Israel during his servitude in Aram is a prototype for God's protection of the people Israel in Egypt. Similarly, the patriarch's act of guarding is a prototype for God's providence for the people through Moses in the wilderness; and Jacob's flight from Aram prefigures the Israelite exodus from Egypt. The deeds of the fathers anticipate the history of their descendants in unexpected ways.

12

13Then Jacob had to flee to the land of Aram;
There Israel served for a wife,
For a wife he had to guard [sheep].
14But when the LORD
Brought Israel up from Egypt,
It was through a prophet;
Through a prophet they were guarded.
15Ephraim gave bitter offense,
And his Lord cast his crimes upon him
And requited him for his mockery.

יב

13 וַיִּבְרַח יַעֲקֹב שְׂדֵה אֲרָם
וַיַּעֲבֹד יִשְׂרָאֵל בְּאִשָּׁה
וּבְאִשָּׁה שָׁמָר׃
14 וּבְנָבִיא
הֶעֱלָה יְהוָה
אֶת־יִשְׂרָאֵל מִמִּצְרָיִם
וּבְנָבִיא נִשְׁמָר׃
15 הִכְעִיס אֶפְרַיִם תַּמְרוּרִים
וְדָמָיו עָלָיו יִטּוֹשׁ
וְחֶרְפָּתוֹ יָשִׁיב לוֹ אֲדֹנָיו׃

13

When Ephraim spoke piety,
He was exalted in Israel;
But he incurred guilt through Baal,
And so he died.
2And now they go on sinning;
They have made them molten images,
Idols, by their skill, from their silver,
Wholly the work of craftsmen.
Yet for these they appoint men to sacrifice;
They are wont to kiss calves!
3Assuredly,
They shall be like morning clouds,

יג

כְּדַבֵּר אֶפְרַיִם רְתֵת
נָשָׂא הוּא בְּיִשְׂרָאֵל
וַיֶּאְשַׁם בַּבַּעַל
וַיָּמֹת׃
2 וְעַתָּה ׀ יוֹסִפוּ לַחֲטֹא
וַיַּעֲשׂוּ לָהֶם מַסֵּכָה
מִכַּסְפָּם כִּתְבוּנָם עֲצַבִּים
מַעֲשֵׂה חָרָשִׁים כֻּלֹּה
לָהֶם הֵם אֹמְרִים זֹבְחֵי אָדָם
עֲגָלִים יִשָּׁקוּן׃
3 לָכֵן
יִהְיוּ כַּעֲנַן־בֹּקֶר

Hosea 12:14. Through a prophet Namely, Moses. This is the first attribution of the title to him. The designation of Moses as the prophet who brought Israel from Egypt and guarded (*nishmar*) it in the wilderness may be a polemical rejection of the Torah tradition that God sent an angel to guard the people (*lishmorkha*) in their wanderings (Exod. 23:20).

15. cast his crimes upon him Literally, "held him liable for his blood guilt." Presumably, the prophet means that God will leave the blood on the guilty one, thereby holding him accountable.

Hosea 13:1. When Ephraim spoke The prophet surveys the history of the northern kingdom, from its powerful rise to pre-eminence among all the Israelites to its physical and spiritual collapse. Through seduction to Canaanite worship and pride in their own accomplishments, the people of Ephraim rejected their divine savior and faced destruction.

piety The word translated "piety" (*retet*) occurs only here. The Hebrew has the sense of trembling.

2. kiss calves At the division of the United Monarchy, Jeroboam I built a shrine in Shechem, in the hills of Ephraim (1 Kings 12:25), where golden bulls were made and were venerated through liturgical proclamations (v. 28) and sacrifices (v. 32; cf. Hosea 11:2). Kissing the image of the bulls was undoubtedly an act of ritual piety in Hosea's day, as was the act of kissing images of Baal in the days of Elijah (1 Kings 19:18). It is condemned.

3. morning clouds This image signals the swift extinction of Israel for their unfaithful-

Like dew so early gone;
Like chaff whirled away from the threshing floor.
And like smoke from a lattice.
4Only I the LORD have been your God
Ever since the land of Egypt;
You have never known a [true] God but Me,
You have never had a helper other than Me.
5I looked after you in the desert,
In a thirsty land.
6When they grazed, they were sated;
When they were sated, they grew haughty;
And so they forgot Me.
7So I am become like a lion to them,
Like a leopard I lurk on the way;
8Like a bear robbed of her young I attack them
And rip open the casing of their hearts;
I will devour them there like a lion,
The beasts of the field shall mangle them.

9You are undone, O Israel!
You had no help but Me.
10Where now is your king?
Let him save you!
Where are the chieftains in all your towns
From whom you demanded:
"Give me a king and officers"?
11I give you kings in my ire,
And take them away in My wrath.

וְכַטַּל מַשְׁכִּים הֹלֵךְ
כְּמֹץ יְסֹעֵר מִגֹּרֶן
וּכְעָשָׁן מֵאֲרֻבָּה׃
4 וְאָנֹכִי יְהוָה אֱלֹהֶיךָ
מֵאֶרֶץ מִצְרָיִם
וֵאלֹהִים זוּלָתִי לֹא תֵדָע
וּמוֹשִׁיעַ אַיִן בִּלְתִּי׃
5 אֲנִי יְדַעְתִּיךָ בַּמִּדְבָּר
בְּאֶרֶץ תַּלְאֻבוֹת׃
6 כְּמַרְעִיתָם וַיִּשְׂבָּעוּ
שָׂבְעוּ וַיָּרָם לִבָּם
עַל־כֵּן שְׁכֵחוּנִי׃
7 וָאֱהִי לָהֶם כְּמוֹ־שָׁחַל
כְּנָמֵר עַל־דֶּרֶךְ אָשׁוּר׃
8 אֶפְגְּשֵׁם כְּדֹב שַׁכּוּל
וְאֶקְרַע סְגוֹר לִבָּם
וְאֹכְלֵם שָׁם כְּלָבִיא
חַיַּת הַשָּׂדֶה תְּבַקְּעֵם׃

9 שִׁחֶתְךָ יִשְׂרָאֵל
כִּי־בִי בְעֶזְרֶךָ׃
10 אֱהִי מַלְכְּךָ אֵפוֹא
וְיוֹשִׁיעֲךָ
בְּכָל־עָרֶיךָ וְשֹׁפְטֶיךָ
אֲשֶׁר אָמַרְתָּ
תְּנָה־לִּי מֶלֶךְ וְשָׂרִים׃
11 אֶתֶּן־לְךָ מֶלֶךְ בְּאַפִּי
וְאֶקַּח בְּעֶבְרָתִי׃ ס

ness. It ironically echoes Hos. 6:4, where the people fail in their efforts to repent and are mocked by God, who states that Israel's "goodness is like morning clouds, / Like dew so early gone."

4–5. I the LORD This emphasis on the Lord as the historical redeemer from Egyptian bondage is an important theme in early classical prophecy and an early witness to the theological and historical assertion embodied in the opening words of the Decalogue (Exod. 20:2).

7–15. Verses 7–11 contain a series of images projecting retributive doom on Israel. Punishment is also delineated in 13:15–14:1.

12Ephraim's guilt is bound up,
His sin is stored away.
13Pangs of childbirth assail him,
And the babe is not wise—
For this is no time to survive
At the birthstool of babes.

12 צָר֙וּר עֲוֺ֣ן אֶפְרָ֔יִם
צְפוּנָ֖ה חַטָּאתֽוֹ׃
13 חֶבְלֵ֥י יוֹלֵדָ֖ה יָבֹ֣אוּ ל֑וֹ
הוּא־בֵן֙ לֹ֣א חָכָ֔ם
כִּֽי־עֵ֥ת לֹֽא־יַעֲמֹ֖ד
בְּמִשְׁבַּ֥ר בָּנִֽים׃

14From Sheol itself I will save them,
Redeem them from very Death.
Where, O Death, are your plagues?
Your pestilence where, O Sheol?
Revenge shall be far from My thoughts.
15For though he flourish among reeds,
A blast, a wind of the LORD,
Shall come blowing up from the wilderness;
His fountain shall be parched,
His spring dried up.
That [wind] shall plunder treasures,
Every lovely object.

14 מִיַּ֤ד שְׁאוֹל֙ אֶפְדֵּ֔ם
מִמָּ֖וֶת אֶגְאָלֵ֑ם
אֱהִ֨י דְבָרֶ֜יךָ מָ֗וֶת
אֱהִ֤י קָֽטָבְךָ֙ שְׁא֔וֹל
נֹ֖חַם יִסָּתֵ֥ר מֵעֵינָֽי׃
15 כִּ֣י ה֔וּא בֵּ֥ן אַחִ֖ים יַפְרִ֑יא
יָב֣וֹא קָדִ֡ים ר֣וּחַ יְהוָ֩ה
מִמִּדְבָּ֨ר
עֹלֶ֜ה וְיֵב֤וֹשׁ מְקוֹרוֹ֙
וְיֶחֱרַ֣ב מַעְיָנ֔וֹ
ה֣וּא יִשְׁסֶ֔ה אוֹצַ֖ר
כָּל־כְּלִ֥י חֶמְדָּֽה׃

14 Samaria must bear her guilt,
For she has defied her God.
They shall fall by the sword,
Their infants shall be dashed to death,
And their women with child ripped open.

יד תֶּאְשַׁם֙ שֹֽׁמְר֔וֹן
כִּ֥י מָרְתָ֖ה בֵּאלֹהֶ֑יהָ
בַּחֶ֣רֶב יִפְּל֔וּ
עֹלְלֵיהֶ֣ם יְרֻטָּ֔שׁוּ
וְהָרִיּוֹתָ֖יו יְבֻקָּֽעוּ׃ פ

2Return, O Israel, to the LORD your God,
For you have fallen because of your sin.
3Take words with you
And return to the LORD.
Say to Him:

2 שׁ֚וּבָה יִשְׂרָאֵ֔ל עַ֖ד יְהוָ֣ה אֱלֹהֶ֑יךָ
כִּ֥י כָשַׁ֖לְתָּ בַּעֲוֺנֶֽךָ׃
3 קְח֤וּ עִמָּכֶם֙ דְּבָרִ֔ים
וְשׁ֖וּבוּ אֶל־יְהוָ֑ה
אִמְר֣וּ אֵלָ֔יו

Hosea 14:2–4. Hosea calls on the nation to repent, counterpointing the preceding oracles of doom and concluding the *haftarah* (and the entire book) on a note of hope. The elements include recognition of guilt (vv. 2,4), repentance (v. 2), confession and an appeal to mercy (v. 3), and rejection of past practices and the decision never to engage in them again (vv. 4,9).

3. Take words with you The prophet instructs the people with appropriate words of confession (Ibn Ezra, Radak), appealing that they ask God to "Forgive all guilt" (*kol tissa avon*). This phrase alludes to the same attribute

"Forgive all guilt
And accept what is good;
Instead of bulls we will pay
[The offering of] our lips.
4Assyria shall not save us,
No more will we ride on steeds;
Nor ever again will we call
Our handiwork our god,
Since in You alone orphans find pity!"
5I will heal their affliction,
Generously will I take them back in love;
For My anger has turned away from them.
6I will be to Israel like dew;
He shall blossom like the lily,
He shall strike root like a Lebanon tree.
7His boughs shall spread out far,
His beauty shall be like the olive tree's,
His fragrance like that of Lebanon.
8They who sit in his shade shall be revived:
They shall bring to life new grain,
They shall blossom like the vine;
His scent shall be like the wine of Lebanon.
9Ephraim [shall say]:
"What more have I to do with idols?
When I respond and look to Him,
I become like a verdant cypress."
Your fruit is provided by Me.

כָּל־תִּשָּׂא עָוֺן
וְקַח־טוֹב
וּנְשַׁלְּמָה פָרִים
שְׂפָתֵינוּ׃
4 אַשּׁוּר ׀ לֹא יוֹשִׁיעֵנוּ
עַל־סוּס לֹא נִרְכָּב
וְלֹא־נֹאמַר עוֹד
אֱלֹהֵינוּ לְמַעֲשֵׂה יָדֵינוּ
אֲשֶׁר־בְּךָ יְרֻחַם יָתוֹם׃
5 אֶרְפָּא מְשׁוּבָתָם
אֹהֲבֵם נְדָבָה
כִּי שָׁב אַפִּי מִמֶּנּוּ׃
6 אֶהְיֶה כַטַּל לְיִשְׂרָאֵל
יִפְרַח כַּשּׁוֹשַׁנָּה
וְיַךְ שָׁרָשָׁיו כַּלְּבָנוֹן׃
7 יֵלְכוּ יֹנְקוֹתָיו
וִיהִי כַזַּיִת הוֹדוֹ
וְרֵיחַ לוֹ כַּלְּבָנוֹן׃
8 יָשֻׁבוּ יֹשְׁבֵי בְצִלּוֹ
יְחַיּוּ דָגָן
וְיִפְרְחוּ כַגָּפֶן
זִכְרוֹ כְּיֵין לְבָנוֹן׃ ס
9 אֶפְרַיִם
מַה־לִּי עוֹד לָעֲצַבִּים
אֲנִי עָנִיתִי וַאֲשׁוּרֶנּוּ
אֲנִי כִּבְרוֹשׁ רַעֲנָן
מִמֶּנִּי פֶּרְיְךָ נִמְצָא׃

of divine mercy known from Exod. 34:7 ("forgiving iniquity," *nosei avon*).

And accept what is good Hebrew, *v'kaḥ tov.* The meaning is obscure. It may indicate a request that God accept the good deeds done (Kara), or the good heart (Radak), or even the words of contrition (Ibn Ezra).

5–9. I will heal their affliction Or "their backsliding." In response to Israel's confession, God forgoes His wrath. Sensuous images of earthly bounty replace images of rapine and drought in Hos. 13:7–15. Israel will be restored to renewed vigor. This renewal is as much spiritual as it is physical. The double restoration balances that which is announced at the beginning of the book (2:20–25).

The language of repentance or return dominates the passage. Thus the prophet twice calls on Israel to "return" (*shuvah* and *shuvu*) to the Lord (vv. 2–3). In response to this act, God promises that He will heal their affliction, "for My anger has turned away (*shav*) from them" (v. 5). The consequence will be total renewal: "They who sit (*yosh'vei*) in his shade shall be revived (*yashuvu*)" (v. 8).

9. Ephraim [shall say] The last part of verse

[10]He who is wise will consider these words,
He who is prudent will take note of them.
For the paths of the LORD are smooth;
The righteous can walk on them,
While sinners stumble on them.

10 מִי חָכָם֙ וְיָבֵ֣ן אֵ֔לֶּה
נָב֖וֹן וְיֵדָעֵ֑ם
כִּֽי־יְשָׁרִ֞ים דַּרְכֵ֣י יְהוָ֗ה
וְצַדִּקִים֙ יֵ֣לְכוּ בָ֔ם
וּפֹשְׁעִ֖ים יִכָּ֥שְׁלוּ בָֽם׃

9 brings the confession to a climax. The verse is a fitting conclusion to the prophet's call. In it, the main point is affirmed: Spiritual fidelity leads to a thorough transformation of earthly life.

10. consider . . . take note A concluding exhortation.

these words . . . of them If "these" refers to the preceding counsel to repent (Rashi), then v. 10a is the rhetorical conclusion to the unit 14:2–9. Alternatively, if "these" refers to the "paths of the LORD" in the following phrase (Ibn Ezra), then the reference is to the justice of God ("path," or "way," indicates divine providence; cf. Exod. 33:13). By contrast, Radak understood "these" as referring to the prophet's earlier words of reproof. By this view, the exhortation calls on the people to take heed of God's judgment.

הפטרת ויצא

HAFTARAH FOR VA-YETZEI

HOSEA 11:7–12:12 (*S'fardim*)

This *haftarah* is dominated by the recurrent denunciation of the religious and moral behavior of Ephraim (a designation for the northern tribes). Ephraim is judged for continuous defection from God. Counterpointing this human trait, God's love for His people is proclaimed (11:8–9): He cannot and will not destroy them like the ancient cities of the Plain (Admah and Zeboiim, ruined along with Sodom and Gomorrah in ancient times, although not mentioned in Gen. 19:23ff; cf. Deut. 29:22). The vaunted mark of divinity is the ability to transcend wrath, to love with an unrequited and unconditional grace. Yet in a later passage (Hos. 12:7), reconciliation with God depends not on God's unilateral grace but on the people's transformation of their moral and spiritual lives.

The *haftarah* begins in the middle of chapter 11, with a proclamation of Ephraim's defection from God (v. 7). It is part of the prophet's overall rebuke of Israelite behavior during the reign of King Jeroboam II (784–748 B.C.E.).

The prophet's words begin and end with condemnations of Ephraim's ongoing sins. The guile of father Jacob in the past provides a pivotal perspective. The nation is reminded of their ancestor's deeds and of how he was requited for his acts. This historical reference serves to warn the descendants of Jacob/Israel that they will also suffer punishment if they do not change their ways and return to a life of goodness and trust in God.

God's attitude is not in doubt. Despite the people's sinful behavior, divine punishment is aborted: "I will not act on My wrath," says the Lord, "Will not turn (*lo ashuv*) to destroy Ephraim" (11:9). Indeed, God's love will prevail; He will "roar like a lion" and will "settle" (*v'hoshavtim*) His people "in their homes" (11:11). This promise precedes God's second rebuke of Ephraim and His call that they "return (*tashuv*) to your God" (12:7). It also precedes the ensuing (third) denunciation of Ephraimite overreaching (12:8), and God's declaration in judgment that He will "let you dwell (*oshiyv'kha*) in your tents again as in days of old" (12:10). The linguistic play on the verb *shuv* (return, repent) and the variations on the verb *yashav* (dwell, settle) point to the positive and the negative consequences of Israel's behavior.

As for the return itself, the prophet is direct and precise: "Practice goodness (*ḥesed*) and justice (*mishpat*), / And constantly trust (*kavveh*) in your God" (12:7). The first part articulates the social-moral dimension of the covenant, enacting on the human plane precisely those values articulated by God Himself in His promised betrothal of the people: "And I will espouse you with righteousness and justice (*mishpat*), / And with goodness (*ḥesed*) and mercy" (2:21). Israel's covenantal actions thus mirror God's constancy, but inevitably they are expressed through human fulfillment of His just and good laws.

The second part of Hosea's demand transcends the human realm and has an exclusively transcendent focus. Trust in God is an entirely theological attitude, a commitment to a source of power and truth beyond human calculation. But it does not cancel the activist demands of justice, even as goodness in the social realm does not invalidate a theological orientation toward reality.

RELATION OF THE *HAFTARAH* TO THE *PARASHAH*

The *haftarah* illustrates various episodes in the Book of Genesis, beginning with Jacob's birth and continuing through his return to the land and the shrine of Bethel. Hosea emphasizes the theme of strife: Jacob's struggle with his brother Esau and his night combat with the angel at the

Jabbok ford. These actions follow a denunciation of the Israelites as a people surrounding God with "guile" (*mirmah*, Hos. 12:1). This term recalls Isaac's use of it to describe Jacob's act of deceit, when he stole Esau's blessing (Gen. 27:35). Jacob also alludes to it when he reproves Laban for deceiving him with Leah, but the patriarch was reproved in turn (Gen. 29:25–26). Given this strategic recurrence, one may conclude that the term *"mirmah"* (and its derivatives) is used to suggest the continuity of Jacob's deceitful character. A relationship is thereby established between the acts of the patriarch and of his descendants. The intergenerational continuity of guile thus underscores an ancient flaw in father Jacob and its disastrous ramifications for later generations. Such a family trait must be confronted, to be halted or removed. Toward this end, the prophet calls on the people to repent and perform good deeds. The *haftarah,* however, leaves little hope that self-examination will result. The reader thus confronts the destructive possibilities of unexamined character traits and their insidious affect on later generations.

11 7For My people persists
In its defection from Me;
When it is summoned upward,
It does not rise at all.

8How can I give you up, O Ephraim?
How surrender you, O Israel?
How can I make you like Admah,
Render you like Zeboiim?
I have had a change of heart,
All My tenderness is stirred.
9I will not act on My wrath,
Will not turn to destroy Ephraim.
For I am God, not man,
The Holy One in your midst:
I will not come in fury.

10The LORD will roar like a lion,
And they shall march behind Him;

יא 7 וְעַמִּי תְלוּאִים
לִמְשׁוּבָתִי
וְאֶל־עַל יִקְרָאֻהוּ
יַחַד לֹא יְרוֹמֵם׃

8 אֵיךְ אֶתֶּנְךָ אֶפְרַיִם
אֲמַגֶּנְךָ יִשְׂרָאֵל
אֵיךְ אֶתֶּנְךָ כְאַדְמָה
אֲשִׂימְךָ כִּצְבֹאיִם*
נֶהְפַּךְ עָלַי לִבִּי
יַחַד נִכְמְרוּ נִחוּמָי׃
9 לֹא אֶעֱשֶׂה חֲרוֹן אַפִּי
לֹא אָשׁוּב לְשַׁחֵת אֶפְרָיִם
כִּי אֵל אָנֹכִי וְלֹא־אִישׁ
בְּקִרְבְּךָ קָדוֹשׁ
וְלֹא אָבוֹא בְּעִיר׃

10 אַחֲרֵי יְהוָה יֵלְכוּ
כְּאַרְיֵה יִשְׁאָג

v. 8. יתיר א׳

Hosea 11:7. When it is summoned upward The word translated "summoned" (*yikra·uhu*) is a plural verb with the literal meaning of "they have summoned him." Presumably this refers to the prophets who have called Israel to heed their message (Rashi).

8. Ephraim This common designation for the northern kingdom of Israel stands in contradistinction to Judah, a designation for the south.

10. The LORD will roar An abrupt shift to the third person, with the unexpected use of an image of terror. The verse presumably refers to God's awesome manifestation to the nation in exile, inspiring them with terror and the urge to follow Him (Rashi, Ibn Ezra).

When He roars, His children shall come
Fluttering out of the west.
11 They shall flutter from Egypt like sparrows,
From the land of Assyria like doves;
And I will settle them in their homes
—declares the LORD.

כִּי־הוּא יִשְׁאַג
וְיֶחֶרְדוּ בָנִים מִיָּם׃
11 יֶחֶרְדוּ כְצִפּוֹר מִמִּצְרַיִם
וּכְיוֹנָה מֵאֶרֶץ אַשּׁוּר
וְהוֹשַׁבְתִּים עַל־בָּתֵּיהֶם
נְאֻם־יְהוָה׃ ס

12 Ephraim surrounds Me with deceit,
The House of Israel with guile.
(But Judah stands firm with God
And is faithful to the Holy One.)
2 Ephraim tends the wind
And pursues the gale;
He is forever adding
Illusion to calamity.
Now they make a covenant with Assyria,
Now oil is carried to Egypt.

יב סְבָבֻנִי בְכַחַשׁ אֶפְרַיִם
וּבְמִרְמָה בֵּית יִשְׂרָאֵל
וִיהוּדָה עֹד רָד עִם־אֵל
וְעִם־קְדוֹשִׁים נֶאֱמָן׃
2 אֶפְרַיִם רֹעֶה רוּחַ
וְרֹדֵף קָדִים
כָּל־הַיּוֹם
כָּזָב וָשֹׁד יַרְבֶּה
וּבְרִית עִם־אַשּׁוּר יִכְרֹתוּ
וְשֶׁמֶן לְמִצְרַיִם יוּבָל׃

3 The LORD once indicted Judah,
And punished Jacob for his conduct,
Requited him for his deeds.
4 In the womb he tried to supplant his brother;
Grown to manhood, he strove with a divine being,
5 He strove with an angel and prevailed—
The other had to weep and implore him.
At Bethel [Jacob] would meet him,
There to commune with him.
6 Yet the LORD, the God of Hosts,
Must be invoked as "LORD."
7 You must return to your God!
Practice goodness and justice,
And constantly trust in your God.

3 וְרִיב לַיהוָה עִם־יְהוּדָה
וְלִפְקֹד עַל־יַעֲקֹב כִּדְרָכָיו
כְּמַעֲלָלָיו יָשִׁיב לוֹ׃
4 בַּבֶּטֶן עָקַב אֶת־אָחִיו
וּבְאוֹנוֹ שָׂרָה אֶת־אֱלֹהִים׃
5 וַיָּשַׂר אֶל־מַלְאָךְ וַיֻּכָל
בָּכָה וַיִּתְחַנֶּן־לוֹ
בֵּית־אֵל יִמְצָאֶנּוּ
וְשָׁם יְדַבֵּר עִמָּנוּ׃
6 וַיהוָה אֱלֹהֵי הַצְּבָאוֹת
יְהוָה זִכְרוֹ׃
7 וְאַתָּה בֵּאלֹהֶיךָ תָשׁוּב
חֶסֶד וּמִשְׁפָּט שְׁמֹר
וְקַוֵּה אֶל־אֱלֹהֶיךָ תָּמִיד׃

Hosea 12:5. commune with him Literally, "commune with us" (*immanu*). The Hebrew form may be influenced by the preceding *yimtza·ennu* (would meet him).

7. Practice goodness and justice The call for repentance is followed by an exhortation to "Practice goodness and righteousness" (*hesed u-mishpat*). These traits of human allegiance cor-

8A trader who uses false balances,	8 כְּנַעַן בְּיָדוֹ מֹאזְנֵי מִרְמָה
Who loves to overreach,	לַעֲשֹׁק אָהֵב:
9Ephraim thinks,	9 וַיֹּאמֶר* אֶפְרַיִם
"Ah, I have become rich;	אַךְ עָשַׁרְתִּי
I have gotten power!	מָצָאתִי אוֹן לִי
All my gains do not amount	כָּל־יְגִיעַי לֹא יִמְצְאוּ־לִי
To an offense which is real guilt."	עָוֺן אֲשֶׁר־חֵטְא:
10I the LORD have been your God	10 וְאָנֹכִי יְהוָה אֱלֹהֶיךָ
Ever since the land of Egypt.	מֵאֶרֶץ מִצְרָיִם
I will let you dwell in your tents again	עֹד אוֹשִׁיבְךָ בָאֳהָלִים
As in the days of old,	כִּימֵי מוֹעֵד:
11When I spoke to the prophets;	11 וְדִבַּרְתִּי עַל־הַנְּבִיאִים
For I granted many visions,	וְאָנֹכִי חָזוֹן הִרְבֵּיתִי
And spoke parables through the prophets.	וּבְיַד הַנְּבִיאִים אֲדַמֶּה:
12As for Gilead, it is worthless;	12 אִם־גִּלְעָד אָוֶן
And to no purpose have they	אַךְ־שָׁוְא הָיוּ
Been sacrificing oxen in Gilgal:	בַּגִּלְגָּל שְׁוָרִים זִבֵּחוּ
The altars of these are also	גַּם מִזְבְּחוֹתָם
Like stone heaps upon a plowed field.	כְּגַלִּים עַל תַּלְמֵי שָׂדָי:

v. 9. סביריו ומטעין לשון רבים

respond to God's own promise of covenantal commitment in Hos. 2:21, "I will espouse you with righteousness and justice (*mishpat*), / And with goodness (*ḥesed*) and mercy."

10. I will let you dwell in your tents again The verse may be translated, "I will yet again make you to dwell in tents." This verse thus may be speaking less of a reward than of a reversal of fate, given Hosea's condemnation of Ephraim's greed. It restores Israel to its ancient desert condition when it depended on God.

11. When I spoke to the prophets One may construe the passage to mean, "I also spoke to the prophets." This rendition has the advantage of separating the period of the wilderness (when God spoke from the tent) from the subsequent times of prophecy. It further suggests that Hosea mentions the prophets because they (like him) brought God's word of judgment to the people. This reading also provides a transition to the judgment in verse 12.

spoke parables Hebrew: *adammeh.* This passage played a central role in Jewish philosophical arguments that the prophets spoke of God figuratively—in ways that do not depict His indescribable essence (cf. *Guide*, Intro.)

12. As for Gilead, it is worthless The concluding verse, taken literally, articulates a strong judgment.

VA-YISHLAḤ

וישלח

4Jacob sent messengers ahead to his brother
Esau in the land of Seir, the country of Edom,
5and instructed them as follows, "Thus shall
you say, 'To my lord Esau, thus says your servant Jacob: I stayed with Laban and remained
until now; 6I have acquired cattle, asses, sheep,
and male and female slaves; and I send this
message to my lord in the hope of gaining your
favor.'" 7The messengers returned to Jacob, saying, "We came to your brother Esau; he himself
is coming to meet you, and there are four hun-

4וַיִּשְׁלַ֨ח יַעֲקֹ֤ב מַלְאָכִים֙ לְפָנָ֔יו אֶל־עֵשָׂ֖ו
אָחִ֑יו אַ֥רְצָה שֵׂעִ֖יר שְׂדֵ֥ה אֱדֽוֹם׃ 5וַיְצַ֤ו
אֹתָם֙ לֵאמֹ֔ר כֹּ֣ה תֹאמְר֔וּן לַֽאדֹנִ֖י לְעֵשָׂ֑ו
כֹּ֤ה אָמַר֙ עַבְדְּךָ֣ יַעֲקֹ֔ב עִם־לָבָ֣ן גַּ֔רְתִּי
וָאֵחַ֖ר עַד־עָֽתָּה׃ 6וַֽיְהִי־לִי֙ שׁ֣וֹר וַחֲמ֔וֹר
צֹ֖אן וְעֶ֣בֶד וְשִׁפְחָ֑ה וָֽאֶשְׁלְחָה֙ לְהַגִּ֣יד
לַֽאדֹנִ֔י לִמְצֹא־חֵ֖ן בְּעֵינֶֽיךָ׃ 7וַיָּשֻׁ֙בוּ֙
הַמַּלְאָכִ֔ים אֶֽל־יַעֲקֹ֖ב לֵאמֹ֑ר בָּ֤אנוּ אֶל־
אָחִ֙יךָ֙ אֶל־עֵשָׂ֔ו וְגַם֙ הֹלֵ֣ךְ לִקְרָֽאתְךָ֔

JACOB AND ESAU: THE CONFRONTATION (32:4–33:20)

Jacob resumes his homeward journey. Long-suppressed memories begin to haunt his consciousness. The specter of a vengeful Esau looms before him.

JACOB'S PREPARATIONS (vv. 4–22)

GATHERING INFORMATION (vv. 4–7)

4. Seir The narrative assumes that Esau/Edom by this time had migrated east of the Jordan, having dispossessed from Seir the aboriginal Horites or being engaged in dispossessing them.

5. To my lord Esau This opening phrase identifying the recipient is part of the message. It conforms to the standard letter-writing style of the ancient Near East.

lord . . . servant This normally deferential mode of address, used by a vassal speaking to his lord, is motivated here by fear and intended to be conciliatory.

I stayed with Laban The Hebrew verb for "stayed with" (גור) here connotes both temporary residence and loss of protection. As to his reasons for going to Laban in the first place, Jacob says nothing.

and remained until now This explains why he had not contacted Esau previously.

6. I have acquired Jacob hints that he can pay off his brother, if the need arises. Listing each item, he omits mention of the camels, the most valuable of all his livestock, even though they are listed in verse 8 and are part of the gift in verse 16. Probably, he understates his possessions so that the gift will be that much more of a surprise and delight to Esau.

7. The messengers returned They report back that Esau seems to have obtained independent intelligence about Jacob's movements.

coming to meet The phrase can convey either amity or enmity. Jacob is thus unable to decipher Esau's intentions.

four hundred men The standard size of a militia and, therefore, ominous (see 1 Sam. 22:2, 25:13, 30:10,17).

As this *parashah* opens, Jacob's return to the Land from Laban's house brings him to the same boundary where he dreamed and prayed 20 years earlier. Here he will undergo the single most important event in his life, the nighttime struggle with a mysterious stranger that concludes with his being given a new name, Israel, and a new sense of who he is as reflected by that name. He will be reunited with his brother Esau, as Isaac and Ishmael were reunited late in life (25:9) and as Joseph and his brothers will be reunited in the next generation.

5. *I stayed with Laban* The letters of the Hebrew word גרתי ("I stayed," *garti*) are the same as those in תרי״ג ("*taryag*") with the numerical value of 613, recalling the 613 commandments of the Torah. This prompted Rashi to interpret Jacob's words to mean "I stayed with Laban but maintained my integrity; I was not corrupted by him."

7. *your brother Esau* Esau is viewed as the ancestor of the Edomites (36:1) who sided with the Babylonians in destroying the First Temple and as the prototype of later Roman and Euro-

dred men with him." [8]Jacob was greatly frightened; in his anxiety, he divided the people with him, and the flocks and herds and camels, into two camps, [9]thinking, "If Esau comes to the one camp and attacks it, the other camp may yet escape."

[10]Then Jacob said, "O God of my father Abraham and God of my father Isaac, O LORD, who said to me, 'Return to your native land and I will deal bountifully with you'! [11]I am unworthy of all the kindness that You have so steadfastly shown Your servant: with my staff alone I crossed this Jordan, and now I have become two camps. [12]Deliver me, I pray, from the hand of my brother, from the hand of Esau; else, I fear, he may come and strike me down, mothers and children alike. [13]Yet You have said, 'I will deal bountifully with you and make your offspring as the sands of the sea, which are too numerous to count.'"

וְאַרְבַּע־מֵאוֹת אִישׁ עִמּוֹ׃ 8 וַיִּירָא יַעֲקֹב
מְאֹד וַיֵּצֶר לוֹ וַיַּחַץ אֶת־הָעָם אֲשֶׁר־אִתּוֹ
וְאֶת־הַצֹּאן וְאֶת־הַבָּקָר וְהַגְּמַלִּים לִשְׁנֵי
מַחֲנוֹת׃ 9 וַיֹּאמֶר אִם־יָבוֹא עֵשָׂו אֶל־
הַמַּחֲנֶה הָאַחַת וְהִכָּהוּ וְהָיָה הַמַּחֲנֶה
הַנִּשְׁאָר לִפְלֵיטָה׃
10 וַיֹּאמֶר יַעֲקֹב אֱלֹהֵי אָבִי אַבְרָהָם וֵאלֹהֵי
אָבִי יִצְחָק יְהוָה הָאֹמֵר אֵלַי שׁוּב לְאַרְצְךָ
וּלְמוֹלַדְתְּךָ וְאֵיטִיבָה עִמָּךְ׃ 11 קָטֹנְתִּי
מִכֹּל הַחֲסָדִים וּמִכָּל־הָאֱמֶת אֲשֶׁר עָשִׂיתָ
אֶת־עַבְדֶּךָ כִּי בְמַקְלִי עָבַרְתִּי אֶת־הַיַּרְדֵּן
הַזֶּה וְעַתָּה הָיִיתִי לִשְׁנֵי מַחֲנוֹת׃
12 הַצִּילֵנִי נָא מִיַּד אָחִי מִיַּד עֵשָׂו כִּי־יָרֵא
אָנֹכִי אֹתוֹ פֶּן־יָבוֹא וְהִכַּנִי אֵם עַל־בָּנִים׃
13 וְאַתָּה אָמַרְתָּ הֵיטֵב אֵיטִיב עִמָּךְ
וְשַׂמְתִּי אֶת־זַרְעֲךָ כְּחוֹל הַיָּם אֲשֶׁר לֹא־
שני יִסָּפֵר מֵרֹב׃

DEFENSIVE MEASURES (vv. 8–9)

8. Jacob was greatly frightened He is aware that retreat would violate his pact with Laban, and he cannot flee because he is encumbered with small children and much livestock.

two camps Jacob decides to minimize his losses in the event of an attack.

PRAYER (vv. 10–13)

10. Then Jacob said The opening words combine quotations from revelations at Bethel and Haran, which mark the beginning and end of Jacob's 20-year exile (see 28:13–15, 31:3).

I will deal bountifully with you This phrase, which does not appear in God's promises, is likely an interpretation of "I will be with you" (31:3).

11. this Jordan Standing on the banks of the Jabbok River, Jacob can point to the Jordan, clearly visible in the distance.

12. Deliver me The plea lays bare the terror that seizes Jacob at this moment.

13. Yet You have said The prayer concludes with a recollection of God's promises. At the moment of crisis, it is his concern with descendants that is uppermost in Jacob's mind.

---

pean anti-Semites. One *midrash*, perhaps influenced by later Israelite encounters with Esau's biologic and ideologic descendants, reads, "we went looking for a brother, but instead found Esau, armed and hostile in a very non-brotherly manner" (Gen. R. 75:7). Another has the opposite view: "We met him, and though he is Esau, he is still your brother" (Gen. R. 75:4).

8. frightened . . . anxiety Hebrew: *va-yiyra . . . va-yeitzer*, lit., "he was frightened and upset." Jacob both feared that he and his family might be harmed and was upset that he might harm his brother in self-defense (Gen. R. 76:2).

10–13. Years before, as a young man leaving the land of Canaan, Jacob had prayed (Gen. 28:20–22). Some commentators see that youthful prayer as essentially a bargaining with God. "If God protects me and brings me home safely, then I will set up a shrine to God and set aside a tithe of all that God gives me." Now he prays a more mature prayer. In place of bargaining, there is the realization that he has nothing to offer God and that God has already blessed him

[14]After spending the night there, he selected from what was at hand these presents for his brother Esau: [15]200 she-goats and 20 he-goats; 200 ewes and 20 rams; [16]30 milch camels with their colts; 40 cows and 10 bulls; 20 she-asses and 10 he-asses. [17]These he put in the charge of his servants, drove by drove, and he told his servants, "Go on ahead, and keep a distance between droves." [18]He instructed the one in front as follows, "When my brother Esau meets you and asks you, 'Whose man are you? Where are you going? And whose [animals] are these ahead of you?' [19]you shall answer, 'Your servant Jacob's; they are a gift sent to my lord Esau; and [Jacob] himself is right behind us.'" [20]He gave similar instructions to the second one, and the third, and all the others who followed the droves, namely, "Thus and so shall you say to Esau when you reach him. [21]And you shall add, 'And your servant Jacob himself is right behind us.'" For he reasoned, "If I propitiate him with presents in advance, and then face him, perhaps he will show me favor." [22]And so the gift went on ahead, while he remained in camp that night.

[23]That same night he arose, and taking his two wives, his two maidservants, and his eleven

שני 14 וַיָּ֥לֶן שָׁ֖ם בַּלַּ֣יְלָה הַה֑וּא וַיִּקַּ֞ח מִן־הַבָּ֧א
בְיָד֛וֹ מִנְחָ֖ה לְעֵשָׂ֥ו אָחִֽיו׃ 15 עִזִּ֣ים מָאתַ֔יִם
וּתְיָשִׁ֖ים עֶשְׂרִ֑ים רְחֵלִ֥ים מָאתַ֖יִם וְאֵילִ֥ים
עֶשְׂרִֽים׃ 16 גְּמַלִּ֧ים מֵינִיק֛וֹת וּבְנֵיהֶ֖ם
שְׁלֹשִׁ֑ים פָּר֤וֹת אַרְבָּעִים֙ וּפָרִ֣ים עֲשָׂרָ֔ה
אֲתֹנֹ֣ת עֶשְׂרִ֔ים וַעְיָרִ֖ם עֲשָׂרָֽה׃ 17 וַיִּתֵּן֙
בְּיַד־עֲבָדָ֔יו עֵ֥דֶר עֵ֖דֶר לְבַדּ֑וֹ וַיֹּ֤אמֶר אֶל־
עֲבָדָיו֙ עִבְר֣וּ לְפָנַ֔י וְרֶ֣וַח תָּשִׂ֔ימוּ בֵּ֥ין עֵ֖דֶר
וּבֵ֥ין עֵֽדֶר׃ 18 וַיְצַ֥ו אֶת־הָרִאשׁ֖וֹן לֵאמֹ֑ר כִּ֣י
יִֽפְגָּשְׁךָ֞ עֵשָׂ֣ו אָחִ֗י וּשְׁאֵֽלְךָ֙ לֵאמֹ֔ר לְמִי־
אַ֙תָּה֙ וְאָ֣נָה תֵלֵ֔ךְ וּלְמִ֖י אֵ֥לֶּה לְפָנֶֽיךָ׃
19 וְאָמַרְתָּ֙ לְעַבְדְּךָ֣ לְיַעֲקֹ֔ב מִנְחָ֥ה הִוא֙
שְׁלוּחָ֔ה לַֽאדֹנִ֖י לְעֵשָׂ֑ו וְהִנֵּ֥ה גַם־ה֖וּא
אַחֲרֵֽינוּ׃ 20 וַיְצַ֞ו גַּ֣ם אֶת־הַשֵּׁנִ֗י גַּ֚ם אֶת־
הַשְּׁלִישִׁ֔י גַּ֚ם אֶת־כָּל־הַהֹ֣לְכִ֔ים אַחֲרֵ֥י
הָעֲדָרִ֖ים לֵאמֹ֑ר כַּדָּבָ֤ר הַזֶּה֙ תְּדַבְּר֣וּן אֶל־
עֵשָׂ֔ו בְּמֹצַאֲכֶ֖ם אֹתֽוֹ׃ 21 וַאֲמַרְתֶּ֕ם גַּ֛ם הִנֵּ֥ה
עַבְדְּךָ֥ יַעֲקֹ֖ב אַחֲרֵ֑ינוּ כִּֽי־אָמַ֞ר אֲכַפְּרָ֣ה
פָנָ֗יו בַּמִּנְחָה֙ הַהֹלֶ֣כֶת לְפָנָ֔י וְאַחֲרֵי־כֵן֙
אֶרְאֶ֣ה פָנָ֔יו אוּלַ֖י יִשָּׂ֥א פָנָֽי׃ 22 וַתַּעֲבֹ֥ר
הַמִּנְחָ֖ה עַל־פָּנָ֑יו וְה֛וּא לָ֥ן בַּלַּֽיְלָה־הַה֖וּא
בַּֽמַּחֲנֶֽה׃
23 וַיָּ֣קָם ׀ בַּלַּ֣יְלָה ה֗וּא וַיִּקַּ֞ח אֶת־שְׁתֵּ֣י

THE GIFT (vv. 14–22)

14. spending the night there At Mahanaim.

presents The Hebrew word *minḥah* may mean a gift expressing friendship and respect—or a tribute in recognition of the donor's subordinate status. The ambiguity in its use here is intentional. Esau is free to interpret it as he wishes.

15–16. There are 550 beasts, a lavish gift.

17. drove by drove Each time, Esau is barely able to scrutinize the animals and interrogate the men, when the next drove arrives.

THE MYSTERIOUS ASSAILANT (vv. 23–33)

The narrative of Jacob's encounter with Esau is suddenly interrupted. The restless Jacob gets up during the night and decides to transfer his entire camp to the other side of the Jabbok.

23. his eleven children Jacob is about to become Israel, the personification of the tribal

---

with more than he had any right to claim—love, family, and material wealth. Jacob asks now only for God's help and protection, on two grounds: (a) God once promised him that he would be the father of a multitude, and that will not happen if Esau kills him. He has to survive to carry out God's plan for him. (b) Because what he has to do is too hard for him to do unaided, he needs God's help.

נָשָׁיו וְאֶת־שְׁתֵּי שִׁפְחֹתָיו וְאֶת־אַחַד עָשָׂר
יְלָדָיו וַיַּעֲבֹר אֵת מַעֲבַר יַבֹּק׃ 24 וַיִּקָּחֵם
וַיַּעֲבִרֵם אֶת־הַנָּחַל וַיַּעֲבֵר אֶת־אֲשֶׁר־לוֹ׃
25 וַיִּוָּתֵר יַעֲקֹב לְבַדּוֹ וַיֵּאָבֵק אִישׁ עִמּוֹ עַד
עֲלוֹת הַשָּׁחַר׃ 26 וַיַּרְא כִּי לֹא יָכֹל לוֹ וַיִּגַּע
בְּכַף־יְרֵכוֹ וַתֵּקַע כַּף־יֶרֶךְ יַעֲקֹב בְּהֵאָבְקוֹ
עִמּוֹ׃ 27 וַיֹּאמֶר שַׁלְּחֵנִי כִּי עָלָה הַשָּׁחַר

children, he crossed the ford of the Jabbok.
24 After taking them across the stream, he sent
across all his possessions. 25 Jacob was left
alone. And a man wrestled with him until the
break of dawn. 26 When he saw that he had not
prevailed against him, he wrenched Jacob's hip
at its socket, so that the socket of his hip was
strained as he wrestled with him. 27 Then he
said, "Let me go, for dawn is breaking." But

confederation. Only those directly involved in the evolution of the nation are mentioned. Dinah and the rest of his household are omitted.

the ford of the Jabbok This river, called by the Arabs "Blue River" (Nahr ez-Zerqa), is one of the most important rivers east of the Jordan. Flowing through a deep ravine on a meandering course, it joins the Jordan River at right angles about 20 miles (32 km) north of the Dead Sea. To cross at night with a vast entourage is dangerous. Flat stones or timber would be laid across the shallowest and narrowest part to afford passage.

25. Jacob was left alone He crossed the river repeatedly until all his people and possessions had been safely transported. Now he is alone in the dead of night.

a man In verses 29 and 31 the person is described as "a divine being" (*elohim*). In the prophet Hosea's account, he is identified as an angel (Hos. 12:4). These terms are often interchangeable in passages dealing with angels.

the break of dawn As dawn approaches, the assailant, trying desperately to disengage himself, delivers a sudden, powerful blow.

26. Jacob's hip at its socket This is the cup-shaped socket in the hip bone that receives the head of the thigh bone.

was strained Or "dislocated."

27. dawn is breaking At this point, Jacob

---

23. the ford of the Jabbok The Torah may be punning on the term *ma·avar Yabbok*, the crossing or transit point of the Jabbok—and the transition of Jacob to becoming a different person. Also note the wordplay between Jabbok (*Yabbok*) and the word for "he wrestled" (*ye·avek*).

25. a man wrestled with him Who is this mysterious being? The classic commentaries are nearly unanimous in seeing him as evil, a malign force. He may have been Esau's guardian angel (Gen. R. 77:3). "Before encountering Esau in the flesh, his spirit struggled with the spirit of Esau" (N. Leibowitz). He may have been the demonic guardian of the river. His purpose seems to have been to weaken Jacob on the eve of his confrontation with Esau.

Or this may be an account of Jacob's wrestling with his conscience, torn between his human tendency to avoid an unpleasant encounter and the divine impulse in him that urges him to do the difficult but right thing. This position may find support in the text, "you have striven with beings divine and human" (v. 29), which can also be translated, "you have striven with God and with men." We can imagine Jacob saying to himself, "Until now, I have responded to difficult situations by lying and running. I deceived my father. I ran away from Esau. I left Laban's house stealthily instead of confronting him. I hate myself for being a person who lies and runs. But I'm afraid of facing up to the situation." By not defeating his conscience, Jacob wins. He outgrows his Jacob identity as the trickster and becomes Israel, the one who contends with God and people instead of avoiding or manipulating them. At the end of the struggle, he is physically wounded and emotionally depleted. Nevertheless, the Torah describes him (in 33:18) as *shalem,* translated "safe" with connotations of "whole," at peace with himself (*shalem* is related to the word *"shalom"*), possessing an integrity he never had before (*S'fat Emet*).

Rashbam sees God as sending an angel to wrestle with Jacob to prevent him from running away as he may have been tempted to do, compelling him to do the right thing. And B. Jacob writes, "God answers a person's prayers if the person prays by searching himself, becoming his own opponent."

וַיֹּאמֶר לֹא אֲשַׁלֵּחֲךָ כִּי אִם־בֵּרַכְתָּנִי׃
28 וַיֹּאמֶר אֵלָיו מַה־שְּׁמֶךָ וַיֹּאמֶר יַעֲקֹב׃
29 וַיֹּאמֶר לֹא יַעֲקֹב יֵאָמֵר עוֹד שִׁמְךָ כִּי
אִם־יִשְׂרָאֵל כִּי־שָׂרִיתָ עִם־אֱלֹהִים וְעִם־
אֲנָשִׁים וַתּוּכָל׃ 30 וַיִּשְׁאַל יַעֲקֹב וַיֹּאמֶר
הַגִּידָה־נָּא שְׁמֶךָ וַיֹּאמֶר לָמָּה זֶּה תִּשְׁאַל
לִשְׁמִי וַיְבָרֶךְ אֹתוֹ שָׁם׃ 31 וַיִּקְרָא יַעֲקֹב שלישי
שֵׁם הַמָּקוֹם פְּנִיאֵל כִּי־רָאִיתִי אֱלֹהִים
פָּנִים אֶל־פָּנִים וַתִּנָּצֵל נַפְשִׁי׃ 32 וַיִּזְרַח־לוֹ
הַשֶּׁמֶשׁ כַּאֲשֶׁר עָבַר אֶת־פְּנוּאֵל וְהוּא

he answered, "I will not let you go, unless you
bless me." 28 Said the other, "What is your
name?" He replied, "Jacob." 29 Said he, "Your
name shall no longer be Jacob, but Israel, for
you have striven with beings divine and human, and have prevailed." 30 Jacob asked, "Pray
tell me your name." But he said, "You must not
ask my name!" And he took leave of him there.
31 So Jacob named the place Peniel, meaning, "I
have seen a divine being face to face, yet my life
has been preserved." 32 The sun rose upon him

realizes that his opponent is a supernatural being.

28. What is your name? A rhetorical question that affords opportunity for the names "Jacob" and "Israel" to be mentioned together.

29. Israel Names in the Bible are intertwined with character and destiny. Jacob, purged of the name *ya·akov* and its negative associations, is assured that he will become the patriarch of a nation named Israel. The bestowal of the new name is the core of the blessing and the climax of the episode.

with beings divine and human The humans were Esau and Laban.

and have prevailed The name "Israel" in the Bible was popularly derived from *sarita* (you struggled), referring to Jacob's struggle and triumph in the face of overwhelming odds in this story. Its actual meaning is "God is superior."

The earliest two documents outside the Bible to mention Israel give ironic testimony of prevailing against the odds. The first, the victory hymn of King Merneptah of Egypt (ca. 1207 B.C.E.), reports that "Israel is laid waste, his seed is not." The second earliest document, the victory inscription of King Mesha of Moab (ca. 830 B.C.E.), declares "Israel has perished forever."

30. You must not ask my name! In the period before the Babylonian exile (586 B.C.E.) all angels are anonymous (see Judg. 13:17–18).

31. Peniel Literally, "Face of God."

meaning Hebrew: *ki.* See Comment to 4:25.

a divine being Hebrew: *elohim.* In Judg. 13, the one repeatedly called "an angel" is also referred to in Hebrew as *elohim* (v. 22).

I have seen . . . face to face The idiom "face to face," used only of divine–human encounters, may describe either an adversarial experience or one of extraordinary intimacy. Here the deliberate ambiguity reflects the menace and the promise inherent in the furious struggle. This is the biblical way of expressing the intensity of an encounter with the divine presence—the overwhelming nature of the mysterious contact with God.

32. The sun rose Jacob's flight from home was marked by the setting of the sun (see Gen. 28:11). Fittingly, the sunrise greets him as he crosses back into his native land.

27–28. unless you bless me The blessing must be one I will have earned in my own right, not by guile (Rashi). The angel asks Jacob, "What is your name?" The last time he sought a blessing—when his father asked him "Who are you?"—he answered that question falsely. "Now that you are prepared to testify truthfully as to who you are, you have shed that previous identity and are prepared to take on a new one, Israel."

The name *Yisra·el* may be interpreted to mean "one who struggles with God." Through the ages, Jews have struggled to understand what God means in their lives and have con-

HALAKHAH L'MA·ASEH

32:33 to this day This biblical verse underlies the requirement in kosher slaughter that the sciatic nerve be extracted (Sephardic practice) or that the entire hind quarter of the animal be considered unfit for consumption by Jews (Ashkenazic practice).

צֹלֵ֖עַ עַל־יְרֵכֽוֹ׃ 33 עַל־כֵּ֞ן לֹֽא־יֹאכְל֨וּ בְנֵֽי־
יִשְׂרָאֵ֜ל אֶת־גִּ֣יד הַנָּשֶׁ֗ה אֲשֶׁר֙ עַל־כַּ֣ף
הַיָּרֵ֔ךְ עַ֖ד הַיּ֣וֹם הַזֶּ֑ה כִּ֤י נָגַע֙ בְּכַף־יֶ֣רֶךְ
יַעֲקֹ֔ב בְּגִ֖יד הַנָּשֶֽׁה׃

as he passed Penuel, limping on his hip. 33That
is why the children of Israel to this day do not
eat the thigh muscle that is on the socket of the
hip, since Jacob's hip socket was wrenched at
the thigh muscle.

לג וַיִּשָּׂ֨א יַעֲקֹ֜ב עֵינָ֗יו וַיַּרְא֙ וְהִנֵּ֣ה
עֵשָׂ֣ו בָּ֔א וְעִמּ֕וֹ אַרְבַּ֥ע מֵא֖וֹת אִ֑ישׁ וַיַּ֣חַץ
אֶת־הַיְלָדִ֗ים עַל־לֵאָה֙ וְעַל־רָחֵ֔ל וְעַ֖ל
שְׁתֵּ֥י הַשְּׁפָחֽוֹת׃ 2 וַיָּ֧שֶׂם אֶת־הַשְּׁפָח֛וֹת
וְאֶת־יַלְדֵיהֶ֖ן רִֽאשֹׁנָ֑ה וְאֶת־לֵאָ֤ה וִֽילָדֶ֙יהָ֙
אַחֲרֹנִ֔ים וְאֶת־רָחֵ֥ל וְאֶת־יוֹסֵ֖ף אַחֲרֹנִֽים׃
3 וְה֖וּא עָבַ֣ר לִפְנֵיהֶ֑ם וַיִּשְׁתַּ֤חוּ אַ֙רְצָה֙
שֶׁ֣בַע פְּעָמִ֔ים עַד־גִּשְׁתּ֖וֹ עַד־אָחִֽיו׃ 4 וַיָּ֨רָץ
עֵשָׂ֤ו לִקְרָאתוֹ֙ וַֽיְחַבְּקֵ֔הוּ וַיִּפֹּ֥ל על־צוארו

33 Looking up, Jacob saw Esau coming,
accompanied by four hundred men. He divided the children among Leah, Rachel, and
the two maids, 2putting the maids and their
children first, Leah and her children next,
and Rachel and Joseph last. 3He himself went
on ahead and bowed low to the ground seven
times until he was near his brother. 4Esau ran
to greet him. He embraced him and, falling on
his neck, he kissed him; and they wept. 5Look-

33. the children of Israel The reference is to the entire people, not only to Jacob's sons. This is the first time that the phrase occurs in the Bible.

to this day These words are written from the perspective of a later age.

the thigh muscle Jewish tradition identifies this term (*gid ha-nasheh*) with the sciatic nerve.

RECONCILIATION (vv. 1–11)

1. four hundred men A reminder of Esau's possible hostile intentions. The earlier report is now reality.

He divided The division of people and effects, mentioned in 32:8, had been a tactical precaution in case of flight. Now Jacob is arranging mothers with their children for formal presentation to Esau.

3. bowed low . . . seven times This symbolic act in the ancient Near East denotes submission to a superior authority. Ironically, this is the reversal of Isaac's blessing to Jacob that his mother's sons would bow to him (27:29).

4. he kissed him Esau's undoubtedly sincere kiss—he seems genuinely moved by Jacob's extravagant gesture—signals the conclusion of the chain of events precipitated by that other kiss, Jacob's deceitful kiss, recounted in 27:27, which played a crucial role in the original blessing.

and they wept Jacob's tears are a release from emotional tension, although his anxieties are not entirely eased.

---

tended with God, insisting that God live up to the divinely proclaimed standards of justice and kindness.

CHAPTER 33

1–2. In this arrangement, Jacob betrays his feelings of whom he is prepared to sacrifice if necessary and whom he is determined to protect. This favoritism toward Rachel and Rachel's son Joseph will lead to serious problems in subsequent chapters. But can any parent hide his or her predilection for treating some children differently from others? Children long to have their parents recognize their individual strengths and talents, to be treated uniquely, not equally.

4. he kissed him The commentators are divided as to whether Esau's hugs and kisses and kind words were genuine. (The Masoretic text has dots over the words "he kissed him," indicating that there is something unusual about them.) Some are reluctant to credit Esau with any decent motives (Gen. R. 78:9). One *midrash* says, "everything Esau ever did was motivated by hatred, except for this one occasion which was motivated by love" (ARN 34).

ing about, he saw the women and the children.
"Who," he asked, "are these with you?" He
answered, "The children with whom God has
favored your servant." 6Then the maids, with
their children, came forward and bowed low;
7next Leah, with her children, came forward
and bowed low; and last, Joseph and Rachel
came forward and bowed low. 8And he asked,
"What do you mean by all this company which
I have met?" He answered, "To gain my lord's
favor." 9Esau said, "I have enough, my brother;
let what you have remain yours." 10But Jacob
said, "No, I pray you; if you would do me this
favor, accept from me this gift; for to see your
face is like seeing the face of God, and you have
received me favorably. 11Please accept my present which has been brought to you, for God
has favored me and I have plenty." And when he
urged him, he accepted.

עַל־צַוָּארָיו וַיִּשָּׁקֵהוּ* וַיִּבְכּוּ׃ 5וַיִּשָּׂא אֶת־
עֵינָיו וַיַּרְא אֶת־הַנָּשִׁים וְאֶת־הַיְלָדִים
וַיֹּאמֶר מִי־אֵלֶּה לָּךְ וַיֹּאמַר הַיְלָדִים
רביעי אֲשֶׁר־חָנַן אֱלֹהִים אֶת־עַבְדֶּךָ׃ 6וַתִּגַּשְׁןָ
הַשְּׁפָחוֹת הֵנָּה וְיַלְדֵיהֶן וַתִּשְׁתַּחֲוֶיןָ׃
7וַתִּגַּשׁ גַּם־לֵאָה וִילָדֶיהָ וַיִּשְׁתַּחֲווּ וְאַחַר
נִגַּשׁ יוֹסֵף וְרָחֵל וַיִּשְׁתַּחֲווּ׃ 8וַיֹּאמֶר מִי לְךָ
כָּל־הַמַּחֲנֶה הַזֶּה אֲשֶׁר פָּגָשְׁתִּי וַיֹּאמֶר
לִמְצֹא־חֵן בְּעֵינֵי אֲדֹנִי׃ 9וַיֹּאמֶר עֵשָׂו יֶשׁ־
לִי רָב אָחִי יְהִי לְךָ אֲשֶׁר־לָךְ׃ 10וַיֹּאמֶר
יַעֲקֹב אַל־נָא אִם־נָא מָצָאתִי חֵן בְּעֵינֶיךָ
וְלָקַחְתָּ מִנְחָתִי מִיָּדִי כִּי עַל־כֵּן רָאִיתִי
פָנֶיךָ כִּרְאֹת פְּנֵי אֱלֹהִים וַתִּרְצֵנִי׃ 11קַח־
נָא אֶת־בִּרְכָתִי אֲשֶׁר הֻבָאת לָךְ כִּי־חַנַּנִי
אֱלֹהִים וְכִי יֶשׁ־לִי־כֹל וַיִּפְצַר־בּוֹ וַיִּקָּח׃

v. 4. נקוד על ו׳ י׳ ש׳ ק׳ ה׳ ו׳

5. your servant Jacob continues to address his brother as an inferior in the presence of a superior.

6–7. Then the maids The maids and the wives are presented in ascending order of social status and affection.

8. all this company The servants and droves who had gone on ahead.

9. I have enough Ancient Near Eastern etiquette requires Esau to make a show of refusing the gift, and Jacob to press it on him. The recipient must appear to accept it with reluctance.

my brother In contrast to Jacob's mode of address.

10. like seeing the face of God Jacob might be saying to Esau: I have been admitted to your presence; you have been graciously indulgent of me; my encounter with you is like that with a divine being, or like a pilgrimage to a shrine, which one does not make empty-handed.

11. accept my present By changing his terminology for "present" from the Hebrew word *minḥah* (which he had used five times) to *b'ra-khah,* "blessing, gift," Jacob signals to Esau that

---

Hirsch comments, "Even Esau gradually relinquishes the sword and begins to feel the chords of human love." Zornberg sees the brothers' embrace as resembling Jacob's encounter with the angel. Their embrace is a combination of hugging in love and grappling in struggle, as each one wants to merge with the other but also to defeat him.

Both Jacob and Esau realize that the mental images each has been carrying of the other for 20 years are no longer accurate.

9. I have enough, my brother For whatever reason, Esau is presented as being unable to accept a gift from Jacob graciously. There is an art to accepting gifts and compliments, even as there is an art to extending them.

10. like seeing the face of God I have seen the face of God. As a result, I am not the same person I was years ago, the one who tricked you and stole your blessing. I have learned to see you not as an intimidating rival, but as a person fashioned in God's image. The Midrash understands Jacob's words about seeing God's face as an attempt to make an impression: "I have seen the face of God, who is my patron and protector, so you had better respect me" (Gen. R. 75:10).

11. accept my present The literal meaning of Jacob's words is, "take my blessing," as if this

12And [Esau] said, "Let us start on our journey, and I will proceed at your pace." 13But he
said to him, "My lord knows that the children
are frail and that the flocks and herds, which
are nursing, are a care to me; if they are driven
hard a single day, all the flocks will die. 14Let my
lord go on ahead of his servant, while I travel
slowly, at the pace of the cattle before me and at
the pace of the children, until I come to my lord
in Seir."

15Then Esau said, "Let me assign to you
some of the men who are with me." But he said,
"Oh no, my lord is too kind to me!" 16So Esau
started back that day on his way to Seir. 17But
Jacob journeyed on to Succoth, and built a
house for himself and made stalls for his cattle;
that is why the place was called Succoth.

18Jacob arrived safe in the city of Shechem

12 וַיֹּאמֶר נִסְעָה וְנֵלֵכָה וְאֵלְכָה לְנֶגְדֶּךָ׃
13 וַיֹּאמֶר אֵלָיו אֲדֹנִי יֹדֵעַ כִּי־הַיְלָדִים
רַכִּים וְהַצֹּאן וְהַבָּקָר עָלוֹת עָלָי וּדְפָקוּם
יוֹם אֶחָד וָמֵתוּ כָּל־הַצֹּאן׃ 14 יַעֲבָר־נָא
אֲדֹנִי לִפְנֵי עַבְדּוֹ וַאֲנִי אֶתְנָהֲלָה לְאִטִּי
לְרֶגֶל הַמְּלָאכָה אֲשֶׁר־לְפָנַי וּלְרֶגֶל
הַיְלָדִים עַד אֲשֶׁר־אָבֹא אֶל־אֲדֹנִי
שֵׂעִירָה׃

15 וַיֹּאמֶר עֵשָׂו אַצִּיגָה־נָּא עִמְּךָ מִן־הָעָם
אֲשֶׁר אִתִּי וַיֹּאמֶר לָמָּה זֶּה אֶמְצָא־חֵן
בְּעֵינֵי אֲדֹנִי׃ 16 וַיָּשָׁב בַּיּוֹם הַהוּא עֵשָׂו
לְדַרְכּוֹ שֵׂעִירָה׃ 17 וְיַעֲקֹב נָסַע סֻכֹּתָה
וַיִּבֶן לוֹ בָּיִת וּלְמִקְנֵהוּ עָשָׂה סֻכֹּת עַל־כֵּן
קָרָא שֵׁם־הַמָּקוֹם סֻכּוֹת׃ ס

18 וַיָּבֹא יַעֲקֹב שָׁלֵם עִיר שְׁכֶם אֲשֶׁר

the present is a kind of reparation for the theft of the paternal blessing 20 years earlier. On that occasion, both Isaac and Esau (27:35,36) had referred to the theft of the blessing with the identical Hebrew term now employed by Jacob.

he accepted Esau does not reciprocate, thereby clearly indicating that this is the settling of an old score, not a polite exchange of civilities.

DISENGAGEMENT (vv. 12–17)

12. Let us start on our journey Esau assumes that Jacob was on his way to pay him a visit, so he suggests that they travel together.

14. while I travel From one watering place to another.

16. So Esau started back He now fades from the scene of recorded history, reappearing briefly for Isaac's funeral (35:29). Esau's genealogies are given in chapter 36.

17. Succoth Esau departs southward for Seir and Jacob turns northward, recrossing the Jabbok. He no doubt wants to reach the east–west road that connected Canaan with the north–south artery that led from Damascus. Succoth is now identified with a large tell situated in the Jordan Valley, Deir Allah.

built a house The construction of a dwelling for himself and stalls (*sukkot*) for his cattle indicates an intended prolonged stay at this place before crossing the Jordan into Canaan.

JACOB'S RETURN TO CANAAN
(vv. 18–20)

After a stay at Succoth, Jacob finally returns to his native land—a momentous event recorded with a minimum of detail.

18. arrived Jacob no doubt forded the Jordan near the biblical city Adam (mentioned in Josh. 3:16), situated about 16 miles (27.75 km) up the river from Jericho, from which a road leads to Shechem.

safe The Hebrew word *shalem* may here mean "safe and sound," or "in friendship" toward the inhabitants. The ancient versions as well as some medieval commentators take *shalem* to be a place-name referring to the village of Salim, about 4 miles (6.5 km) east of Shechem.

the city of Shechem The next verse and

---

would undo what happened 20 years earlier ("he has taken away my blessing," Gen. 27:36).

12–17. Despite the reconciliation, wariness remains. Perhaps it is too much to hope that 20 years of estrangement can be erased in a few minutes, but this represents a start.

which is in the land of Canaan—having come thus from Paddan-aram—and he encamped before the city. [19]The parcel of land where he pitched his tent he purchased from the children of Hamor, Shechem's father, for a hundred *kesitah*s. [20]He set up an altar there, and called it El-elohe-yisrael.

בְּאֶרֶץ כְּנַעַן בְּבֹאוֹ מִפַּדַּן אֲרָם וַיִּחַן אֶת־
פְּנֵי הָעִיר׃ 19 וַיִּקֶן אֶת־חֶלְקַת הַשָּׂדֶה
אֲשֶׁר נָטָה־שָׁם אָהֳלוֹ מִיַּד בְּנֵי־חֲמוֹר אֲבִי
שְׁכֶם בְּמֵאָה קְשִׂיטָה׃ 20 וַיַּצֶּב־שָׁם מִזְבֵּחַ
וַיִּקְרָא־לוֹ אֵל אֱלֹהֵי יִשְׂרָאֵל׃ ס

34 Now Dinah, the daughter whom Leah had borne to Jacob, went out to visit the daugh-

חמישי **לד** וַתֵּצֵא דִינָה בַּת־לֵאָה אֲשֶׁר
יָלְדָה לְיַעֲקֹב לִרְאוֹת בִּבְנוֹת הָאָרֶץ׃

Gen. 34 make clear that Shechem is here a personal name.

encamped before the city The patriarchs generally would stay at the fringes of cities, entering them only rarely.

19. he purchased Jacob, now Israel, purchases a plot of ground, his first acquisition in the future land of Israel. His purpose is not stated. Perhaps, like Abraham (23:1–20), he wishes to establish a family burial ground.

the children of Hamor Because the sale involves permanent separation from their ancestral holdings, the entire clan needs to be involved in the transaction (see chapter 23).

a hundred kesitahs The exact price is stated, as in the purchase of Machpelah in chapter 23, because the real estate is to be acquired in perpetuity and the sale must be final and incontestable. *K'sitah* (mentioned again only in Job 42:11) is not a coin but an unknown unit of weight; coinage does not appear in the Bible until after the period of the monarchy.

20. He set up an altar Unlike the other altars erected by the patriarchs, this altar is neither in response to a revelation nor for use in worship. Rather, it is a pillar celebrating the safe arrival home after a prolonged absence filled with peril and crises and commemorating the change of name from Jacob to Israel.

El-elohe-yisrael Literally, "God, God of Israel." "Israel" in this name refers to the patriarch, not the people.

THE RAVISHING OF DINAH (34:1–31)

THE ASSAULT (vv. 1–7)

1. Dinah The information about her parentage, known from Gen. 30:21, is repeated here to clarify the role that Simeon and Levi, her full brothers, will play in the ensuing tragic drama.

went out Girls of marriageable age normally would not leave a rural encampment to venture alone into an alien city. The narrative subtly criticizes Dinah's highly unconventional behavior through its use of the Hebrew stem meaning "to go out" (יצא). This has been interpreted by some medieval and modern commentators as a reference to some coquettish or promiscuous conduct.

the daughters of the land This phrase too carries undertones of disapproval, as is clear from 24:3,37.

CHAPTER 34

1. Incidents like the rape of Dinah were probably not uncommon, yet Jacob's family seems unprepared for such an event and does not know how to react. Dinah, an only daughter raised in a family of men, was seeking the company of other young women. Although some commentators blame her for leaving the security of her home to consort with strangers, the modern reader will likely reject this effort to blame the victim and minimize the responsibility of the assailant. Characteristically, the narrative describes the actions of men, but never tells us what Dinah thought nor how she felt about what happened.

ters of the land. [2]Shechem son of Hamor the Hivite, chief of the country, saw her, and took her and lay with her by force. [3]Being strongly drawn to Dinah daughter of Jacob, and in love with the maiden, he spoke to the maiden tenderly. [4]So Shechem said to his father Hamor, "Get me this girl as a wife."

[5]Jacob heard that he had defiled his daughter Dinah; but since his sons were in the field with his cattle, Jacob kept silent until they came home. [6]Then Shechem's father Hamor came out to Jacob to speak to him. [7]Meanwhile Jacob's sons, having heard the news, came in from the field. The men were distressed and

2 וַיַּרְא אֹתָהּ שְׁכֶם בֶּן־חֲמוֹר הַחִוִּי נְשִׂיא
הָאָרֶץ וַיִּקַּח אֹתָהּ וַיִּשְׁכַּב אֹתָהּ וַיְעַנֶּהָ׃
3 וַתִּדְבַּק נַפְשׁוֹ בְּדִינָה בַּת־יַעֲקֹב וַיֶּאֱהַב
אֶת־הנער הַנַּעֲרָה וַיְדַבֵּר עַל־לֵב הנער
הַנַּעֲרָה׃ 4 וַיֹּאמֶר שְׁכֶם אֶל־חֲמוֹר אָבִיו
לֵאמֹר קַח־לִי אֶת־הַיַּלְדָּה הַזֹּאת לְאִשָּׁה׃
5 וְיַעֲקֹב שָׁמַע כִּי טִמֵּא אֶת־דִּינָה בִתּוֹ
וּבָנָיו הָיוּ אֶת־מִקְנֵהוּ בַּשָּׂדֶה וְהֶחֱרִשׁ
יַעֲקֹב עַד־בֹּאָם׃ 6 וַיֵּצֵא חֲמוֹר אֲבִי־שְׁכֶם
אֶל־יַעֲקֹב לְדַבֵּר אִתּוֹ׃ 7 וּבְנֵי יַעֲקֹב בָּאוּ
מִן־הַשָּׂדֶה כְּשָׁמְעָם וַיִּתְעַצְּבוּ הָאֲנָשִׁים

2. Shechem son of Hamor The city-state of Shechem appears to have had a mixed population and may have been established through a confederacy of various clans.

chief Hamor is called "chief" (*nasi*), whereas the head of a Canaanite city-state generally was called "king." Hamor's unusual title reflects the fact that the ruler of Shechem had dominion over rural—that is, tribal—territory as well as the urban center, in this case a confederacy of various ethnic elements. Such a complex situation did not permit the absolute power of a king.

of the country Not "the city," because the city-state of Shechem in pre-Israelite times extended its control over a vast area. At one time, it governed the central hill country as far as the borders of Jerusalem and Gezer to the south and Megiddo to the north, a domain of about 1,000 square miles.

took . . . lay . . . force Three Hebrew verbs of increasing severity underscore the brutality of Shechem's assault on Dinah.

3. drawn . . . love . . . spoke Three expressions of affection describe Shechem's feelings after the deed. He is hopelessly enamored of Dinah.

4. to his father Marriage arrangements were negotiated by a father on behalf of the son.

Get me Literally, "take for me." The same Hebrew stem, לקח, is used in verse 2 for the abduction. This "taking" is to make amends for the other.

5. that he had defiled The subject is Shechem of verse 4. He was guilty not only of an offense against the dignity of the girl but of an assault on the honor of the family.

Jacob kept silent The need to exercise restraint, pending the arrival of his sons, is understandable, but his passivity throughout the entire incident is noteworthy.

6. Hamor came out Apparently, Hamor arrives before the brothers and is left cooling his heels until they come home. Shechem has accompanied his father, but remains in the background until it is opportune for him to appear.

to speak to him To begin marriage negotiations.

7. having heard the news It seems that Jacob urgently summoned his sons.

an outrage The Hebrew word *"n'valah"* is a powerful noun describing offenses of such profound abhorrence that they threaten to tear apart the fabric of Israelite society. For society's own self-protection, such atrocities can never be tolerated or left unpunished.

Israel This is an anachronism. The narrator may be saying that the sacred, inviolable norms that constituted the moral underpinnings of the later people of Israel were already prevalent at this time.

HALAKHAH L'MA·ASEH

34:2 by force Jewish law prohibits forcing sexual relations on another (e.g., BT Ket. 39a–b; see also Comments to Deut. 22:23–25,28–29.)

וַיִּחַר לָהֶם מְאֹד כִּי־נְבָלָה עָשָׂה בְיִשְׂרָאֵל
לִשְׁכַּב אֶת־בַּת־יַעֲקֹב וְכֵן לֹא יֵעָשֶׂה׃
8 וַיְדַבֵּר חֲמוֹר אִתָּם לֵאמֹר שְׁכֶם בְּנִי
חָשְׁקָה נַפְשׁוֹ בְּבִתְּכֶם תְּנוּ נָא אֹתָהּ לוֹ
לְאִשָּׁה׃ 9 וְהִתְחַתְּנוּ אֹתָנוּ בְּנֹתֵיכֶם
תִּתְּנוּ־לָנוּ וְאֶת־בְּנֹתֵינוּ תִּקְחוּ לָכֶם׃
10 וְאִתָּנוּ תֵּשֵׁבוּ וְהָאָרֶץ תִּהְיֶה לִפְנֵיכֶם
שְׁבוּ וּסְחָרוּהָ וְהֵאָחֲזוּ בָּהּ׃ 11 וַיֹּאמֶר
שְׁכֶם אֶל־אָבִיהָ וְאֶל־אַחֶיהָ אֶמְצָא־חֵן
בְּעֵינֵיכֶם וַאֲשֶׁר תֹּאמְרוּ אֵלַי אֶתֵּן׃
12 הַרְבּוּ עָלַי מְאֹד מֹהַר וּמַתָּן וְאֶתְּנָה
כַּאֲשֶׁר תֹּאמְרוּ אֵלָי וּתְנוּ־לִי אֶת־הנער
הַנַּעֲרָ לְאִשָּׁה׃
13 וַיַּעֲנוּ בְנֵי־יַעֲקֹב אֶת־שְׁכֶם וְאֶת־חֲמוֹר
אָבִיו בְּמִרְמָה וַיְדַבֵּרוּ אֲשֶׁר טִמֵּא אֵת
דִּינָה אֲחֹתָם׃ 14 וַיֹּאמְרוּ אֲלֵיהֶם לֹא
נוּכַל לַעֲשׂוֹת הַדָּבָר הַזֶּה לָתֵת אֶת־
אֲחֹתֵנוּ לְאִישׁ אֲשֶׁר־לוֹ עָרְלָה כִּי־חֶרְפָּה
הִוא לָנוּ׃ 15 אַךְ־בְּזֹאת נֵאוֹת לָכֶם אִם

very angry, because he had committed an outrage in Israel by lying with Jacob's daughter—
a thing not to be done.
8 And Hamor spoke with them, saying, "My
son Shechem longs for your daughter. Please
give her to him in marriage. 9 Intermarry with
us: give your daughters to us, and take our
daughters for yourselves: 10 You will dwell
among us, and the land will be open before
you; settle, move about, and acquire holdings
in it." 11 Then Shechem said to her father and
brothers, "Do me this favor, and I will pay
whatever you tell me. 12 Ask of me a bride-price
ever so high, as well as gifts, and I will pay what
you tell me; only give me the maiden for a wife."
13 Jacob's sons answered Shechem and his
father Hamor—speaking with guile because
he had defiled their sister Dinah—14 and said
to them, "We cannot do this thing, to give our
sister to a man who is uncircumcised, for that is
a disgrace among us. 15 Only on this condition
will we agree with you; that you will become

a thing not to be done Not among the people Israel, not in any civilized society.

THE SPEECHES OF HAMOR AND SHECHEM (vv. 8–12)

Jacob, an alien seminomad, probably cannot claim redress against the ruler of the city. Hamor deals with the family only because his son wishes to marry Dinah. The terms he offers are intended to induce Jacob and his sons to let the incident be forgotten.

10. move about To trade and barter and to have unlimited grazing rights.

acquire holdings Certainly the most valuable of the privileges offered and also a pointed reminder to Jacob of his disadvantaged position as an alien.

12. bride-price The Hebrew word *mohar* refers to the payment made by the prospective husband in return for the bride. The amount is usually fixed by custom. Shechem's readiness to pay far beyond that is a tacit recognition of the need to make reparations.

gifts The ceremonial gifts made to the bride's family.

THE BROTHERS' RESPONSE (vv. 13–17)

Although outwardly polite, Hamor, in effect, has attributed to Jacob and his sons a sordid, mercenary concern that adds insult to injury.

13. with guile The narrator informs us that the brothers' acceptance of intermarriage with the Shechemites is a ruse. Dinah, who is still being held by the perpetrator (vv. 17,26), cannot be liberated by a tiny minority in the face of overwhelming odds—except by cunning.

he had defiled This reminder of the enormity of the offense places the brothers' "guile" in its proper perspective.

their sister In verses 1 and 5 Dinah is described as the daughter of Jacob. Here and in verse 27 she is linked to her brothers. The phrase serves to dissociate the patriarch from their plans and to stress the obligation that falls on brothers in this type of society.

14. uncircumcised Circumcision is the essential precondition for admittance into the community of Israel; see 17:9–14 and Exod. 12:43–49.

תִּהְיוּ כָמֹנוּ לְהִמֹּל לָכֶם כָּל־זָכָר׃ 16 וְנָתַנּוּ
אֶת־בְּנֹתֵינוּ לָכֶם וְאֶת־בְּנֹתֵיכֶם נִקַּח־לָנוּ
וְיָשַׁבְנוּ אִתְּכֶם וְהָיִינוּ לְעַם אֶחָד׃
17 וְאִם־לֹא תִשְׁמְעוּ אֵלֵינוּ לְהִמּוֹל
וְלָקַחְנוּ אֶת־בִּתֵּנוּ וְהָלָכְנוּ׃
18 וַיִּיטְבוּ דִבְרֵיהֶם בְּעֵינֵי חֲמוֹר וּבְעֵינֵי
שְׁכֶם בֶּן־חֲמוֹר׃ 19 וְלֹא־אֵחַר הַנַּעַר
לַעֲשׂוֹת הַדָּבָר כִּי חָפֵץ בְּבַת־יַעֲקֹב וְהוּא
נִכְבָּד מִכֹּל בֵּית אָבִיו׃ 20 וַיָּבֹא חֲמוֹר
וּשְׁכֶם בְּנוֹ אֶל־שַׁעַר עִירָם וַיְדַבְּרוּ אֶל־
אַנְשֵׁי עִירָם לֵאמֹר׃ 21 הָאֲנָשִׁים הָאֵלֶּה
שְׁלֵמִים הֵם אִתָּנוּ וְיֵשְׁבוּ בָאָרֶץ וְיִסְחֲרוּ
אֹתָהּ וְהָאָרֶץ הִנֵּה רַחֲבַת־יָדַיִם לִפְנֵיהֶם
אֶת־בְּנֹתָם נִקַּח־לָנוּ לְנָשִׁים וְאֶת־בְּנֹתֵינוּ
נִתֵּן לָהֶם׃ 22 אַךְ־בְּזֹאת יֵאֹתוּ לָנוּ
הָאֲנָשִׁים לָשֶׁבֶת אִתָּנוּ לִהְיוֹת לְעַם אֶחָד
בְּהִמּוֹל לָנוּ כָּל־זָכָר כַּאֲשֶׁר הֵם נִמֹּלִים׃
23 מִקְנֵהֶם וְקִנְיָנָם וְכָל־בְּהֶמְתָּם הֲלוֹא

like us in that every male among you is circumcised. 16Then we will give our daughters to you
and take your daughters to ourselves; and we
will dwell among you and become as one kindred. 17But if you will not listen to us and
become circumcised, we will take our daughter and go."

18Their words pleased Hamor and Hamor's
son Shechem. 19And the youth lost no time in
doing the thing, for he wanted Jacob's daughter. Now he was the most respected in his
father's house. 20So Hamor and his son Shechem went to the public place of their town and
spoke to their fellow townsmen, saying,
21"These people are our friends; let them settle
in the land and move about in it, for the land is
large enough for them; we will take their
daughters to ourselves as wives and give our
daughters to them. 22But only on this condition will the men agree with us to dwell among
us and be as one kindred: that all our males
become circumcised as they are circumcised.
23Their cattle and substance and all their beasts
will be ours, if we only agree to their terms, so

RESPONSE OF THE SHECHEMITES
(vv. 18–24)

19. lost no time The narrative is anticipating developments to indicate Shechem's furious ardor. He hardly could have appeared at the public assembly had he just been circumcised.

the most respected As a role model for others, who were soon influenced by his initiative.

20. public place Literally, "the gate," which served as the civic center.

their fellow townsmen Literally, "the men of their city," the popular assembly of free citizens who must rule on major items of public business, such as granting special privileges to an alien group. Such assemblies are well documented in ancient Near Eastern texts.

21. our friends The reference may be to some existing treaty arrangement between the city of Shechem and the clan of Jacob. City-states that dominated a wide area usually regulated their relationships with the nomadic groups within their domain by means of formal treaties.

23. will be ours Hamor here has omitted the promise of landed property rights for the newcomers and has inserted the assurance of dispossessing them of their belongings. As the occasion is a public ratification of the agreement, he is clearly guilty of double-dealing.

HALAKHAH L'MA·ASEH

34:15 circumcised This is the earliest source stating that non-Jewish males require circumcision for conversion to Judaism. According to traditional Jewish standards affirmed in the Conservative Movement, all converts to Judaism must undergo immersion and males must undergo circumcision (*b'rit milah*) prior to immersion. In addition, males who have been circumcised medically must complete the requirements of the ritual by having a drop of blood drawn from the same site (*hatafat dam b'rit*).

that they will settle among us." 24All who went
out of the gate of his town heeded Hamor and
his son Shechem, and all males, all those who
went out of the gate of his town, were circumcised.
25On the third day, when they were in pain,
Simeon and Levi, two of Jacob's sons, brothers
of Dinah, took each his sword, came upon the
city unmolested, and slew all the males. 26They
put Hamor and his son Shechem to the sword,
took Dinah out of Shechem's house, and went
away. 27The other sons of Jacob came upon the
slain and plundered the town, because their
sister had been defiled. 28They seized their
flocks and herds and asses, all that was inside
the town and outside; 29all their wealth, all
their children, and their wives, all that was in
the houses, they took as captives and booty.

לָנוּ הֵם אַךְ נֵאוֹתָה לָהֶם וְיֵשְׁבוּ אִתָּנוּ׃
24 וַיִּשְׁמְעוּ אֶל־חֲמוֹר וְאֶל־שְׁכֶם בְּנוֹ כָּל־
יֹצְאֵי שַׁעַר עִירוֹ וַיִּמֹּלוּ כָּל־זָכָר כָּל־יֹצְאֵי
שַׁעַר עִירוֹ׃
25 וַיְהִי בַיּוֹם הַשְּׁלִישִׁי בִּהְיוֹתָם כֹּאֲבִים
וַיִּקְחוּ שְׁנֵי־בְנֵי־יַעֲקֹב שִׁמְעוֹן וְלֵוִי אֲחֵי
דִינָה אִישׁ חַרְבּוֹ וַיָּבֹאוּ עַל־הָעִיר בֶּטַח
וַיַּהַרְגוּ כָּל־זָכָר׃ 26 וְאֶת־חֲמוֹר וְאֶת־שְׁכֶם
בְּנוֹ הָרְגוּ לְפִי־חָרֶב וַיִּקְחוּ אֶת־דִּינָה
מִבֵּית שְׁכֶם וַיֵּצֵאוּ׃ 27 בְּנֵי יַעֲקֹב בָּאוּ
עַל־הַחֲלָלִים וַיָּבֹזּוּ הָעִיר אֲשֶׁר טִמְּאוּ
אֲחוֹתָם׃ 28 אֶת־צֹאנָם וְאֶת־בְּקָרָם וְאֶת־
חֲמֹרֵיהֶם וְאֵת אֲשֶׁר־בָּעִיר וְאֶת־אֲשֶׁר
בַּשָּׂדֶה לָקָחוּ׃ 29 וְאֶת־כָּל־חֵילָם וְאֶת־
כָּל־טַפָּם וְאֶת־נְשֵׁיהֶם שָׁבוּ וַיָּבֹזּוּ וְאֵת
כָּל־אֲשֶׁר בַּבָּיִת׃

24. All who went out of the gate The phrase might refer to all the free citizens of the city or, in this instance, the males of military age—the group available for intermarriage with Jacob's clan.

THE RETRIBUTION (vv. 25–29)

25. On the third day By now all the males have been circumcised.

Simeon and Levi Dinah's full brothers, who would feel most keenly her brutal humiliation.

took each his sword To avenge the violence of Shechem, who "took" Dinah (Gen. 34:2).

unmolested The Hebrew word translated as "unmolested" (*betaḥ*) may here have the sense of "meeting no resistance" or "confidently." Or it may refer to the city as "unsuspecting, caught off guard."

26. took Dinah . . . went away The entire affair began with Dinah "going out" and being "taken" (vv. 1,2). It concludes with the same two Hebrew verbs, but in reverse order. As far as Simeon and Levi are concerned, their account with Shechem is settled. They take no part in the plunder of the city.

27. The other sons The other brothers seize the opportunity to pillage, but they do not destroy the city.

because The narrator stresses the point that the brothers were stirred to action because of the defilement of their sister, not for the sake of booty. See, however, 49:5 where Jacob denounces them for this act.

---

25. This unsavory episode, coming after Jacob's struggle with the angel and his reconciliation with Esau, might warn us that although Jacob may have outgrown his tendency to deceive, his children were shaped by the person he had been during their formative years. Maimonides justifies the slaughter of the men of Shechem on the grounds that they became implicated in the serious crime of the rapist by not punishing him (MT Kings 9:14). Others posit that the Shechemites were all guilty of similar behavior and deserving of death. Hirsch calls the behavior of Simeon and Levi "acts which are deserving of censure and for which we are under no obligation to find an excuse." We can understand the wish for revenge against a numerically superior people without having to justify the tactics of Jacob's sons.

30Jacob said to Simeon and Levi, "You have brought trouble on me, making me odious among the inhabitants of the land, the Canaanites and the Perizzites; my men are few in number, so that if they unite against me and attack me, I and my house will be destroyed." 31But they answered, "Should our sister be treated like a whore?"

30 וַיֹּאמֶר יַעֲקֹב אֶל־שִׁמְעוֹן וְאֶל־לֵוִי
עֲכַרְתֶּם אֹתִי לְהַבְאִישֵׁנִי בְּיֹשֵׁב הָאָרֶץ
בַּכְּנַעֲנִי וּבַפְּרִזִּי וַאֲנִי מְתֵי מִסְפָּר
וְנֶאֶסְפוּ עָלַי וְהִכּוּנִי וְנִשְׁמַדְתִּי אֲנִי
וּבֵיתִי׃ 31 וַיֹּאמְרוּ הַכְזוֹנָה* יַעֲשֶׂה אֶת־
אֲחוֹתֵנוּ׃ פ

35 God said to Jacob, "Arise, go up to Bethel and remain there; and build an altar there to the God who appeared to you when you were fleeing from your brother Esau." 2So Jacob said to his household and to all who were with him, "Rid yourselves of the alien gods in

לה וַיֹּאמֶר אֱלֹהִים אֶל־יַעֲקֹב קוּם
עֲלֵה בֵית־אֵל וְשֶׁב־שָׁם וַעֲשֵׂה־שָׁם מִזְבֵּחַ
לָאֵל הַנִּרְאֶה אֵלֶיךָ בְּבָרְחֲךָ מִפְּנֵי עֵשָׂו
אָחִיךָ׃ 2 וַיֹּאמֶר יַעֲקֹב אֶל־בֵּיתוֹ וְאֶל כָּל־
אֲשֶׁר עִמּוֹ הָסִרוּ אֶת־אֱלֹהֵי הַנֵּכָר אֲשֶׁר

v. 31. ז׳ רבתי לפי מהדורת לעטעריס

JACOB'S REACTION (vv. 30–31)

Jacob intervenes for the first time, berating Simeon and Levi.

30. brought trouble Literally, "muddied (the waters)."

making me odious Literally, "making my breath to stink."

31. But they answered The two brothers have the last word. The women of the Israelites are not to be dishonored.

THE BETHEL TRADITION (35:1–15)

The narratives with Jacob at the center come to a close with this chapter. From now on his life will be intertwined with that of Joseph.

THE PILGRIMAGE TO BETHEL (vv. 1–7)

Jacob, seized with panic after his sons' massacre of the Shechemites, fears reprisals from the neighboring peoples, who may have been bound to Shechem by treaty obligations. God's intervention transforms the patriarch's flight into a dignified pilgrimage to Bethel.

1. Arise, go up The words befit the dignified pace of a pilgrimage and the fact that Bethel lies about 1,000 feet (300 m) higher than Shechem.

remain there For as long as he chooses. Jacob does not remain long in Bethel, though. He soon continues to journey southward.

build an altar The construction of altars by the Patriarchs is an act of homage and loyalty to God. Building an altar at a site known as sacred to pagans indicates that the patriarch is dissociating the sanctity of the site from its pagan antecedents. Bethel had a long Canaanite prehistory.

the God The Hebrew name *el,* and not the regular *elohim,* is deliberately used here because it evokes Bethel, as in 31:13. Jacob is reminded that he has not yet fulfilled the vow made at Bethel (28:20–22).

2. all who were with him Including the captives taken at Shechem.

Rid yourselves Jacob vowed at Bethel that if he returned safely from his exile, "the Lord shall be my God." Thus, before embarking on the pilgrimage to that city, he formally renounces

CHAPTER 35

2. Alien gods in your midst Jacob's directive comes after his sons' massacre at Shechem (34:25–29). Might he be referring here to his sons' taste for extrajudicial vengeance?

your midst, purify yourselves, and change your
clothes. 3Come, let us go up to Bethel, and I will
build an altar there to the God who answered
me when I was in distress and who has been
with me wherever I have gone." 4They gave to
Jacob all the alien gods that they had, and the
rings that were in their ears, and Jacob buried
them under the terebinth that was near Shechem. 5As they set out, a terror from God fell
on the cities round about, so that they did not
pursue the sons of Jacob.

6Thus Jacob came to Luz—that is, Bethel—
in the land of Canaan, he and all the people
who were with him. 7There he built an altar
and named the site El-bethel, for it was there
that God had revealed Himself to him when he
was fleeing from his brother.

8Deborah, Rebekah's nurse, died, and was

בְּתֹכְכֶם וְהִטַּהֲרוּ וְהַחֲלִיפוּ שִׂמְלֹתֵיכֶם׃
3 וְנָקוּמָה וְנַעֲלֶה בֵּית־אֵל וְאֶעֱשֶׂה־שָּׁם
מִזְבֵּחַ לָאֵל הָעֹנֶה אֹתִי בְּיוֹם צָרָתִי וַיְהִי
עִמָּדִי בַּדֶּרֶךְ אֲשֶׁר הָלָכְתִּי׃ 4 וַיִּתְּנוּ אֶל־
יַעֲקֹב אֵת כָּל־אֱלֹהֵי הַנֵּכָר אֲשֶׁר בְּיָדָם
וְאֶת־הַנְּזָמִים אֲשֶׁר בְּאָזְנֵיהֶם וַיִּטְמֹן אֹתָם
יַעֲקֹב תַּחַת הָאֵלָה אֲשֶׁר עִם־שְׁכֶם׃
5 וַיִּסָּעוּ וַיְהִי ׀ חִתַּת אֱלֹהִים עַל־הֶעָרִים
אֲשֶׁר סְבִיבוֹתֵיהֶם וְלֹא רָדְפוּ אַחֲרֵי בְּנֵי
יַעֲקֹב׃
6 וַיָּבֹא יַעֲקֹב לוּזָה אֲשֶׁר בְּאֶרֶץ כְּנַעַן הִוא
בֵּית־אֵל הוּא וְכָל־הָעָם אֲשֶׁר־עִמּוֹ׃ 7 וַיִּבֶן
שָׁם מִזְבֵּחַ וַיִּקְרָא לַמָּקוֹם אֵל בֵּית־אֵל כִּי
שָׁם נִגְלוּ אֵלָיו הָאֱלֹהִים בְּבָרְחוֹ מִפְּנֵי
אָחִיו׃
8 וַתָּמָת דְּבֹרָה מֵינֶקֶת רִבְקָה וַתִּקָּבֵר

"alien gods." For the first time in the Bible, there is tension between the religion of Israel and that of its neighbors.

alien gods These were probably household gods found among the spoils of Shechem or carried by the captives. Perhaps they included the *t'rafim* that Rachel stole (31:19).

purify yourselves They were to immerse themselves in water, to remove the bodily impurity acquired through contact with corpses at Shechem and to prepare them for the impending pilgrimage to Bethel, where they will enter sacred space.

change your clothes Laundering is a precondition of purification. Putting on fresh clothes is a stricter requirement and signifies a transition from one state to another.

3. who answered me when I was in distress Jacob omits the unpleasant details mentioned in verse 1. As befits the occasion, his language is a poetic acknowledgment of God's beneficence.

4. the rings These were no ordinary pieces of jewelry but apparently talismans adorned with pagan symbols.

buried them This procedure is found nowhere else in the Bible's laws and narratives relating to the disposal of pagan images. The method prescribed in Deut. 7:5,25 is not burial but utter destruction.

5. a terror Jacob's earlier fears turn out to be groundless. The nearby city-states are themselves petrified.

6. Luz The earlier name of the city, according to Gen. 28:19.

7. the site The Hebrew word *makom* here means "sacred site."

El-bethel Literally, "the God of Bethel," that is, the one whose associations with Jacob were repeatedly bound up with Bethel.

THE DEATH OF DEBORAH (v. 8)

8. Deborah, Rebekah's nurse, died The demise of a woman is reported only in exceptional cases in the Torah. It is likely that traditions about Deborah (which would make the context of the present notice intelligible) were

---

8. Deborah, Rebekah's nurse, died Ramban sees this as a veiled announcement of Rebekah's death (which is unmentioned in the Torah). Rashi cites a tradition that Rebekah had sent Deborah to Aram to tell Jacob that it was now safe to return.

buried under the oak below Bethel; so it was
named Allon-bacuth.
9 God appeared again to Jacob on his arrival
from Paddan-aram, and He blessed him.
10 God said to him,
"You whose name is Jacob,
You shall be called Jacob no more,
But Israel shall be your name."
Thus He named him Israel.
11 And God said to him,
"I am El Shaddai.
Be fertile and increase;
A nation, yea an assembly of nations,
Shall descend from you.
Kings shall issue from your loins.
12 The land that I assigned to Abraham
and Isaac
I assign to you;
And to your offspring to come
Will I assign the land."
13 God parted from him at the spot where He
had spoken to him; 14 and Jacob set up a pillar at
the site where He had spoken to him, a pillar of
stone, and he offered a libation on it and
poured oil upon it. 15 Jacob gave the site, where
God had spoken to him, the name of Bethel.

מִתַּ֣חַת לְבֵֽית־אֵ֔ל תַּ֖חַת הָֽאַלּ֑וֹן וַיִּקְרָ֥א
שְׁמ֖וֹ אַלּ֥וֹן בָּכֽוּת׃ פ
9 וַיֵּרָ֨א אֱלֹהִ֤ים אֶֽל־יַעֲקֹב֙ ע֔וֹד בְּבֹא֖וֹ מִפַּדַּ֣ן
אֲרָ֑ם וַיְבָ֖רֶךְ אֹתֽוֹ׃ 10 וַיֹּֽאמֶר־ל֥וֹ אֱלֹהִ֖ים
שִׁמְךָ֣ יַעֲקֹ֑ב
לֹֽא־יִקָּרֵא֩ שִׁמְךָ֨ ע֜וֹד יַעֲקֹ֗ב
כִּ֤י אִם־יִשְׂרָאֵל֙ יִהְיֶ֣ה שְׁמֶ֔ךָ
וַיִּקְרָ֥א אֶת־שְׁמ֖וֹ יִשְׂרָאֵֽל׃
11 וַיֹּאמֶר֩ ל֨וֹ אֱלֹהִ֜ים
אֲנִ֨י אֵ֤ל שַׁדַּי֙
פְּרֵ֣ה וּרְבֵ֔ה
גּ֛וֹי וּקְהַ֥ל גּוֹיִ֖ם
יִהְיֶ֣ה מִמֶּ֑ךָּ
וּמְלָכִ֖ים מֵחֲלָצֶ֥יךָ יֵצֵֽאוּ׃
ששי 12 וְאֶת־הָאָ֗רֶץ אֲשֶׁ֥ר נָתַ֛תִּי לְאַבְרָהָ֥ם
וּלְיִצְחָ֖ק
לְךָ֣ אֶתְּנֶ֑נָּה
וּֽלְזַרְעֲךָ֥ אַחֲרֶ֖יךָ
אֶתֵּ֥ן אֶת־הָאָֽרֶץ׃
13 וַיַּ֥עַל מֵעָלָ֖יו אֱלֹהִ֑ים בַּמָּק֖וֹם אֲשֶׁר־דִּבֶּ֥ר
אִתּֽוֹ׃ 14 וַיַּצֵּ֨ב יַעֲקֹ֜ב מַצֵּבָ֗ה בַּמָּק֛וֹם אֲשֶׁר־
דִּבֶּ֥ר אִתּ֖וֹ מַצֶּ֣בֶת אָ֑בֶן וַיַּסֵּ֤ךְ עָלֶ֨יהָ֙ נֶ֔סֶךְ
וַיִּצֹ֥ק עָלֶ֖יהָ שָֽׁמֶן׃ 15 וַיִּקְרָ֨א יַעֲקֹ֜ב אֶת־
שֵׁ֣ם הַמָּק֗וֹם אֲשֶׁר֩ דִּבֶּ֨ר אִתּ֥וֹ שָׁ֛ם אֱלֹהִ֖ים
בֵּֽית־אֵֽל׃

widely known to reader and narrator alike in biblical times but for some reason were not included in the Torah.

THE REVELATION AT BETHEL (vv. 9–15)

Jacob has fulfilled the divine charge given in verse 1. God now answers the prayer offered by Isaac in 28:3–4, as Jacob departs for Haran. The words of God echo the promises made to Abraham, as recorded in 17:1–8.

10. called Jacob no more The name change was not effected by God but by an angelic being on the other side of the Jordan (32:28–29). God now validates his new name (Israel) in the promised land.

11. I am El Shaddai As in 17:1.

Be fertile and increase See 17:2,6.

A nation, yea an assembly of nations See 17:4–6.

Kings shall issue from your loins See 17:6.

12. The land See 17:8.

13. God parted from him Literally, "God ascended from upon him," that is, the revelation came to an end.

14. Jacob set up a pillar This stone pillar commemorates the experience. It is either a rededication of the original pillar (28:18) or a new one.

15. Bethel No interpretation of the name is given. A *beit el* was a specific type of stone pillar: a monitor and witness commemorating the divine presence. See Comments to 28:17–18.

[16]They set out from Bethel; but when they were still some distance short of Ephrath, Rachel was in childbirth, and she had hard labor. [17]When her labor was at its hardest, the midwife said to her, "Have no fear, for it is another boy for you." [18]But as she breathed her last—for she was dying—she named him Ben-oni; but his father called him Benjamin. [19]Thus Rachel died. She was buried on the road to Ephrath—now Bethlehem. [20]Over her grave Jacob set up a pillar; it is the pillar at Rachel's grave to this day. [21]Israel journeyed on, and pitched his tent beyond Migdal-eder.

16 וַיִּסְעוּ֙ מִבֵּ֣ית אֵ֔ל וַֽיְהִי־ע֥וֹד כִּבְרַת־
הָאָ֖רֶץ לָב֣וֹא אֶפְרָ֑תָה וַתֵּ֥לֶד רָחֵ֖ל וַתְּקַ֥שׁ
בְּלִדְתָּֽהּ׃ 17 וַיְהִ֥י בְהַקְשֹׁתָ֖הּ בְּלִדְתָּ֑הּ
וַתֹּ֨אמֶר לָ֤הּ הַמְיַלֶּ֙דֶת֙ אַל־תִּ֣ירְאִ֔י כִּֽי־גַם־
זֶ֥ה לָ֖ךְ בֵּֽן׃ 18 וַיְהִ֞י בְּצֵ֤את נַפְשָׁהּ֙ כִּ֣י מֵ֔תָה
וַתִּקְרָ֥א שְׁמ֖וֹ בֶּן־אוֹנִ֑י וְאָבִ֖יו קָֽרָא־ל֥וֹ
בִנְיָמִֽין׃ 19 וַתָּ֖מָת רָחֵ֑ל וַתִּקָּבֵר֙ בְּדֶ֣רֶךְ
אֶפְרָ֔תָה הִ֖וא בֵּ֥ית לָֽחֶם׃ 20 וַיַּצֵּ֧ב יַעֲקֹ֛ב
מַצֵּבָ֖ה עַל־קְבֻרָתָ֑הּ הִ֛וא מַצֶּ֥בֶת קְבֻֽרַת־
רָחֵ֖ל עַד־הַיּֽוֹם׃ 21 וַיִּסַּ֖ע יִשְׂרָאֵ֑ל וַיֵּ֣ט אהלה
אָֽהֳלֹ֔ו מֵהָ֖לְאָה לְמִגְדַּל־עֵֽדֶר׃

THE DEATH OF RACHEL;
THE BIRTH OF BENJAMIN (vv. 16–20)

17. Have no fear Rachel is comforted in her dying moments by the knowledge that God answered the prayer she had uttered after the birth of Joseph: "May the LORD add another son for me."

18. Ben-oni The name is understood to mean "son of my sorrow."

THE TOMB OF RACHEL (vv. 19–20)

20. Jacob set up a pillar A stone memorial to mark her grave. "The tomb of Rachel" was a famous landmark from the time of Samuel, ca. 1020 B.C.E. (1 Sam. 10:2). The traditional site lies about 4 miles (6.5 km) south of Jerusalem and 1 mile (1.6 km) north of Bethlehem.

REUBEN'S WANTON CHALLENGE
(vv. 21–22)

21. Migdal-eder The name means "herd tower" and designates a structure built to provide protection against raiders of the flocks.

---

19. Rachel wants to name the child Ben-Oni, "child of pain" or (according to Maimonides) "child of mourning." Jacob overrules her deathbed wish and names him Benjamin, "child of strength" (or perhaps "child of long life"). He wants the child to remind him of Rachel's strength and courage, not of her pain and death, and does not want Benjamin to grow up feeling responsible for his mother's death.

on the road to Ephrath—now Bethlehem But Bethlehem is only a short distance from Hebron and the burial tomb of the Patriarchs at Machpelah! Perhaps Jacob realized that burying Rachel in Machpelah, leaving only one grave for himself, would stir the jealous rage of Leah with whom he would still have to live for many years. The apocryphal Book of Jubilees would have us believe that Jacob grew to love Leah in the course of time and grieved deeply for her when she died. On his deathbed, Jacob will remember with rueful guilt having buried Rachel by the roadside near Ephrath (Gen. 48:7).

Centuries later, when Babylonia conquered the Land of Israel and sent its population into exile, the road that the Judeans took out of Jerusalem led past the site of Rachel's burial. The prophet Jeremiah pictured Rachel calling out to God from her grave, imploring God to forgive

HALAKHAH L'MA·ASEH

35:20 pillar It is Jewish custom to mark the grave with a monument. An unveiling ceremony to dedicate the monument, while not universally observed, may be held any time after *shiv·ah* (the first week after the funeral). Customs vary: *S'fardim* commonly dedicate the stone at the end of *sh'loshim* (the first 30 days of mourning), and many *Ashk'nazim* in Israel follow that practice as well; *Ashk'nazim* in the Diaspora usually dedicate the monument sometime near the first *yortsayt* (*yahrzeit*; Yiddish for the anniversary of death).

[22]While Israel stayed in that land, Reuben went and lay with Bilhah, his father's concubine; and Israel found out.

Now the sons of Jacob were twelve in number. [23]The sons of Leah: Reuben—Jacob's first-born—Simeon, Levi, Judah, Issachar, and Zebulun. [24]The sons of Rachel: Joseph and Benjamin. [25]The sons of Bilhah, Rachel's maid: Dan and Naphtali. [26]And the sons of Zilpah, Leah's maid: Gad and Asher. These are the sons of Jacob who were born to him in Paddan-aram.

[27]And Jacob came to his father Isaac at Mamre, at Kiriath-arba—now Hebron—where Abraham and Isaac had sojourned. [28]Isaac was a hundred and eighty years old [29]when he breathed his last and died. He was gathered to his kin in ripe old age; and he was buried by his sons Esau and Jacob.

22 וַיְהִי בִּשְׁכֹּן יִשְׂרָאֵל בָּאָרֶץ הַהִוא וַיֵּלֶךְ
רְאוּבֵן וַיִּשְׁכַּב אֶת־בִּלְהָה פִּילֶגֶשׁ אָבִיו
וַיִּשְׁמַע יִשְׂרָאֵל* פ
וַיִּהְיוּ בְנֵי־יַעֲקֹב שְׁנֵים עָשָׂר׃ 23 בְּנֵי לֵאָה
בְּכוֹר יַעֲקֹב רְאוּבֵן וְשִׁמְעוֹן וְלֵוִי וִיהוּדָה
וְיִשָּׂשכָר וּזְבֻלוּן׃ 24 בְּנֵי רָחֵל יוֹסֵף
וּבִנְיָמִן׃ 25 וּבְנֵי בִלְהָה שִׁפְחַת רָחֵל דָּן
וְנַפְתָּלִי׃ 26 וּבְנֵי זִלְפָּה שִׁפְחַת לֵאָה גָּד
וְאָשֵׁר אֵלֶּה בְּנֵי יַעֲקֹב אֲשֶׁר יֻלַּד־לוֹ בְּפַדַּן
אֲרָם׃

27 וַיָּבֹא יַעֲקֹב אֶל־יִצְחָק אָבִיו מַמְרֵא
קִרְיַת הָאַרְבַּע הִוא חֶבְרוֹן אֲשֶׁר־גָּר־שָׁם
אַבְרָהָם וְיִצְחָק׃ 28 וַיִּהְיוּ יְמֵי יִצְחָק מְאַת
שָׁנָה וּשְׁמֹנִים שָׁנָה׃ 29 וַיִּגְוַע יִצְחָק וַיָּמָת
וַיֵּאָסֶף אֶל־עַמָּיו זָקֵן וּשְׂבַע יָמִים וַיִּקְבְּרוּ
אֹתוֹ עֵשָׂו וְיַעֲקֹב בָּנָיו׃ פ

v. 22. למדינחאי סוף פסוק, ולמערבאי פיסקא באמצע פסוק

22. Reuben went and lay with Bilhah In the ancient Near East, possession of the concubine(s) of one's father bestowed legitimacy on the assumption of heirship. Reuben's move—a calculated challenge to his father's authority—is a political, not a lustful act.

Israel found out Literally, "heard." One expects an immediate reaction to the offense, but none occurs. There is certainly much more to this story than is revealed here, but the narrator chose to omit the unpleasant details. The episode ends abruptly.

Now the sons of Jacob were twelve With the birth of Benjamin, the family of Jacob is complete, and it is appropriate to list it in full, particularly because a following passage will feature the genealogies of Esau. The roster also indicates that, despite Reuben's misdeed, the unity of the family remained intact.

26. in Paddan-aram The reader is expected to exclude Benjamin, who was not born there.

THE DEATH OF ISAAC (vv. 27–29)

The report of Isaac's death, which is not in chronologic sequence, is placed here to reintroduce Esau and provide a connective with the next chapter.

27. Hebron The family moved here from Beer-sheba (Gen. 28:10).

29. he was buried The place of interment was the cave of Machpelah, where Rebekah had been buried, as is made clear in 49:29–32.

Esau and Jacob Here the names are in order of seniority. In the account of Abraham's burial (25:9), the order of the sons is reversed, because Ishmael was the son of a handmaid.

Israel's turning to rival idols even as she had been willing to share her husband's love with a rival. God promises Rachel that her children will one day return to their own land (Jer. 31:15–17, part of the *haftarah* for the second day of *Rosh ha-Shanah*).

36 This is the line of Esau—that is, Edom.
2Esau took his wives from among the Canaanite women—Adah daughter of Elon the
Hittite, and Oholibamah daughter of Anah
daughter of Zibeon the Hivite—3and also
Basemath daughter of Ishmael and sister of
Nebaioth. 4Adah bore to Esau Eliphaz; Basemath bore Reuel; 5and Oholibamah bore
Jeush, Jalam, and Korah. Those were the sons
of Esau, who were born to him in the land of
Canaan.
6Esau took his wives, his sons and daughters,
and all the members of his household, his cattle
and all his livestock, and all the property that he
had acquired in the land of Canaan, and went
to another land because of his brother Jacob.
7For their possessions were too many for them
to dwell together, and the land where they sojourned could not support them because of
their livestock. 8So Esau settled in the hill country of Seir—Esau being Edom.

לו וְאֵ֛לֶּה תֹּלְד֥וֹת עֵשָׂ֖ו ה֥וּא אֱדֽוֹם׃
2 עֵשָׂ֛ו לָקַ֥ח אֶת־נָשָׁ֖יו מִבְּנ֣וֹת כְּנָ֑עַן אֶת־
עָדָ֗ה בַּת־אֵילוֹן֙ הַֽחִתִּ֔י וְאֶת־אָהֳלִֽיבָמָה֙
בַּת־עֲנָ֔ה בַּת־צִבְע֖וֹן הַֽחִוִּֽי׃ 3 וְאֶת־בָּשְׂמַ֥ת
בַּת־יִשְׁמָעֵ֖אל אֲח֥וֹת נְבָיֽוֹת׃ 4 וַתֵּ֧לֶד עָדָ֛ה
לְעֵשָׂ֖ו אֶת־אֱלִיפָ֑ז וּבָ֣שְׂמַ֔ת יָלְדָ֖ה אֶת־
רְעוּאֵֽל׃ 5 וְאָהֳלִֽיבָמָה֙ יָֽלְדָ֔ה אֶת־יעיש
יְע֥וּשׁ וְאֶת־יַעְלָ֖ם וְאֶת־קֹ֑רַח אֵ֚לֶּה בְּנֵ֣י
עֵשָׂ֔ו אֲשֶׁ֥ר יֻלְּדוּ־ל֖וֹ בְּאֶ֥רֶץ כְּנָֽעַן׃
6 וַיִּקַּ֣ח עֵשָׂ֡ו אֶת־נָ֠שָׁיו וְאֶת־בָּנָ֣יו וְאֶת־
בְּנֹתָיו֮ וְאֶת־כָּל־נַפְשׁ֣וֹת בֵּיתוֹ֒ וְאֶת־מִקְנֵ֣הוּ
וְאֶת־כָּל־בְּהֶמְתּ֗וֹ וְאֵת֙ כָּל־קִנְיָנ֔וֹ אֲשֶׁ֥ר
רָכַ֖שׁ בְּאֶ֣רֶץ כְּנָ֑עַן וַיֵּ֣לֶךְ אֶל־אֶ֔רֶץ מִפְּנֵ֖י
יַעֲקֹ֥ב אָחִֽיו׃ 7 כִּֽי־הָיָ֧ה רְכוּשָׁ֛ם רָ֖ב מִשֶּׁ֣בֶת
יַחְדָּ֑ו וְלֹ֨א יָֽכְלָ֜ה אֶ֤רֶץ מְגֽוּרֵיהֶם֙ לָשֵׂ֣את
אֹתָ֔ם מִפְּנֵ֖י מִקְנֵיהֶֽם׃ 8 וַיֵּ֤שֶׁב עֵשָׂו֙ בְּהַ֣ר
שֵׂעִ֔יר עֵשָׂ֖ו ה֥וּא אֱדֽוֹם׃

THE LINE OF ESAU (36:1–43)

In this chapter all mention of Esau in the Book of Genesis is brought to an end with the listing of his descendants. The genealogic tables here also show how the divine oracle and patriarchal blessing bestowed on Esau (25:23; 27:39–40) were fulfilled.

ESAU'S WIVES AND SONS IN CANAAN (vv. 1–5)

The text, a detailed list of Esau's three wives and the five sons they bore him in Canaan, reflects a confederation of three tribal groupings. Historically, the marriage notices tell the reader about the various ethnic relationships among the tribes and record the absorption of Canaanite clans into the sphere of Edom.

1. Edom The name, which is repeated another 10 times in this chapter, functions as the name of a person, a people, and a national territory.

2. Adah This is also the name of Lamech's first wife (4:19–20).

Elon the Hittite According to 26:34, he had a daughter Basemath.

3. Basemath The name, like that of Ishmael's son Mibsam (25:13) and of Abraham's second wife Keturah (25:1), means "spice." Like them, it suggests an involvement of the clan in the spice trade of the ancient Near East.

sister of Nebaioth In 28:9 the daughter of Ishmael whom Esau married, and who bears this same description, is named Mahalath.

THE MIGRATION TO SEIR (vv. 6–8)

Esau now moves his entire household and all his livestock out of Canaan and into the hill country of Seir, a territory southeast of the Dead Sea alongside the Arabah, which becomes the national territory of Esau/Edom.

6. went to another land The word "another," not in the Hebrew text, is supplied by the Aramaic translations. The Syriac translation adds: "The land of Seir."

because of his brother Jacob Esau recognizes Jacob's right to the other side of the Jordan. Otherwise, he could have insisted that Jacob be the one to leave.

7. could not support them Esau's migration

9 וְאֵ֗לֶּה תֹּלְד֥וֹת עֵשָׂ֖ו אֲבִ֣י אֱד֑וֹם בְּהַ֖ר
שֵׂעִֽיר׃
10 אֵ֖לֶּה שְׁמ֣וֹת בְּנֵֽי־עֵשָׂ֑ו אֱלִיפַ֗ז בֶּן־עָדָה֙
אֵ֣שֶׁת עֵשָׂ֔ו רְעוּאֵ֕ל בֶּן־בָּשְׂמַ֖ת אֵ֥שֶׁת עֵשָֽׂו׃
11 וַיִּהְי֖וּ בְּנֵ֣י אֱלִיפָ֑ז תֵּימָ֣ן אוֹמָ֔ר צְפ֖וֹ
וְגַעְתָּ֥ם וּקְנַֽז׃ 12 וְתִמְנַ֣ע ׀ הָיְתָ֣ה פִילֶ֗גֶשׁ
לֶֽאֱלִיפַז֙ בֶּן־עֵשָׂ֔ו וַתֵּ֥לֶד לֶֽאֱלִיפַ֖ז אֶת־
עֲמָלֵ֑ק אֵ֕לֶּה בְּנֵ֖י עָדָ֥ה אֵ֥שֶׁת עֵשָֽׂו׃
13 וְאֵ֙לֶּה֙ בְּנֵ֣י רְעוּאֵ֔ל נַ֥חַת וָזֶ֖רַח שַׁמָּ֣ה
וּמִזָּ֑ה אֵ֣לֶּה הָי֔וּ בְּנֵ֥י בָשְׂמַ֖ת אֵ֥שֶׁת עֵשָֽׂו׃
14 וְאֵ֣לֶּה הָי֗וּ בְּנֵ֨י אָהֳלִיבָמָ֧ה בַת־עֲנָ֛ה
בַּת־צִבְע֖וֹן אֵ֣שֶׁת עֵשָׂ֑ו וַתֵּ֣לֶד לְעֵשָׂ֗ו אֶת־
יעיש יְע֥וּשׁ וְאֶת־יַעְלָ֖ם וְאֶת־קֹֽרַח׃
15 אֵ֖לֶּה אַלּוּפֵ֣י בְנֵֽי־עֵשָׂ֑ו בְּנֵ֤י אֱלִיפַז֙ בְּכ֣וֹר
עֵשָׂ֔ו אַלּ֤וּף תֵּימָן֙ אַלּ֣וּף אוֹמָ֔ר אַלּ֥וּף צְפ֖וֹ
אַלּ֥וּף קְנַֽז׃ 16 אַלּֽוּף־קֹ֛רַח אַלּ֥וּף גַּעְתָּ֖ם
אַלּ֣וּף עֲמָלֵ֑ק אֵ֜לֶּה אַלּוּפֵ֤י אֱלִיפַז֙ בְּאֶ֣רֶץ

9This, then, is the line of Esau, the ancestor of
the Edomites, in the hill country of Seir.

10These are the names of Esau's sons: Eliphaz, the son of Esau's wife Adah; Reuel, the
son of Esau's wife Basemath. 11The sons of
Eliphaz were Teman, Omar, Zepho, Gatam,
and Kenaz. 12Timna was a concubine of Esau's
son Eliphaz; she bore Amalek to Eliphaz.
Those were the descendants of Esau's wife
Adah. 13And these were the sons of Reuel: Nahath, Zerah, Shammah, and Mizzah. Those
were the descendants of Esau's wife Basemath.
14And these were the sons of Esau's wife Oholibamah, daughter of Anah daughter of Zibeon: she bore to Esau Jeush, Jalam, and
Korah.

15These are the clans of the children of Esau.
The descendants of Esau's first-born Eliphaz:
the clans Teman, Omar, Zepho, Kenaz, 16Ko-
rah, Gatam, and Amalek; these are the clans of
Eliphaz in the land of Edom. Those are the

is determined by social and economic factors: overcrowding and insufficient natural resources.

ESAU'S DESCENDANTS IN SEIR (vv. 9–14)

This second genealogy of Esau repeats the details of the preceding one but continues the line to the third generation for Adah and Basemath. Only in this list is Amalek noted to be the son of a concubine and, as such, of inferior status. Excluding Amalek, there are 12 legitimate descendants in all, intimating a 12-tribe confederation, just like that of the Nahorites (22:20–24); the Ishmaelites (17:20; 25:13–16); and, of course, the Israelites, as recounted in 35:22–26.

11. Teman The name is the same as one of the most important places in Edom, identified with Tawilan, northeast of the Arab village of Elji on the eastern outskirts of Petra. It bears no relation to the Hebrew name *teiman* for Yemen.

12. Timna . . . Amalek According to verse 22, Timna was "the sister of Lotan," an indigenous Horite. In historical terms, this means that the Edomites who migrated to Seir began to intermarry with the natives and that such alliances were not socially acceptable. This explains Timna's inferior status here as a concubine rather than as a wife.

THE ALLUFIM OF ESAU (vv. 15–19)

This is the third genealogy of Esau. Here Amalek is on a par with the other sons of Eliphaz, although in last place, which probably reflects a political development in Edomite tribal history. A section of the Korahites may have split off from the Oholibamah group and attached itself to the Eliphaz confederation, into which Amalek too was incorporated.

15. the clans The Hebrew word *elef* refers to a social unit, a subdivision of a tribe, most likely a clan. The term was meaningful in the premonarchic period (1200–1000 B.C.E.) before the breakdown of the tribal system.

THE INDIGENOUS HORITES OF SEIR (vv. 20–30)

The information given in this chapter, taken in conjunction with the report of Deut. 2:12, adds up to a picture of a violent invasion of Seir by the Esau clan, followed by a process of gradual absorption of the native Horites into the "descendants of Esau." We are now given a genealogy of Seir, who is regarded as the name-giving patriarch of the leading native clans, numbering seven in all.

descendants of Adah. [17]And these are the descendants of Esau's son Reuel: the clans Nahath, Zerah, Shammah, and Mizzah; these are the clans of Reuel in the land of Edom. Those are the descendants of Esau's wife Basemath. [18]And these are the descendants of Esau's wife Oholibamah: the clans Jeush, Jalam, and Korah; these are the clans of Esau's wife Oholibamah, the daughter of Anah. [19]Those were the sons of Esau—that is, Edom—and those are their clans.

[20]These were the sons of Seir the Horite, who were settled in the land: Lotan, Shobal, Zibeon, Anah, [21]Dishon, Ezer, and Dishan. Those are the clans of the Horites, the descendants of Seir, in the land of Edom.

[22]The sons of Lotan were Hori and Hemam; and Lotan's sister was Timna. [23]The sons of Shobal were these: Alvan, Manahath, Ebal, Shepho, and Onam. [24]The sons of Zibeon were these: Aiah and Anah—that was the Anah who discovered the hot springs in the wilderness while pasturing the asses of his father Zibeon. [25]The children of Anah were these: Dishon and Anah's daughter Oholibamah. [26]The sons of Dishon were these: Hemdan, Eshban, Ithran, and Cheran. [27]The sons of Ezer were these: Bilhan, Zaavan, and Akan. [28]And the sons of Dishan were these: Uz and Aran.

[29]These are the clans of the Horites: the clans Lotan, Shobal, Zibeon, Anah, [30]Dishon, Ezer, and Dishan. Those are the clans of the Horites, clan by clan, in the land of Seir.

אֱד֖וֹם אֵ֥לֶּה בְנֵֽי־עָדָֽה׃ 17 וְאֵ֗לֶּה בְּנֵ֣י רְעוּאֵ֔ל בֶּן־עֵשָׂ֑ו אַלּ֤וּף נַ֙חַת֙ אַלּ֣וּף זֶ֔רַח אַלּ֥וּף שַׁמָּ֖ה אַלּ֣וּף מִזָּ֑ה אֵ֣לֶּה אַלּוּפֵ֤י רְעוּאֵל֙ בְּאֶ֣רֶץ אֱד֔וֹם אֵ֕לֶּה בְּנֵ֥י בָשְׂמַ֖ת אֵ֥שֶׁת עֵשָֽׂו׃ 18 וְאֵ֗לֶּה בְּנֵ֤י אָהֳלִֽיבָמָה֙ אֵ֣שֶׁת עֵשָׂ֔ו אַלּ֥וּף יְע֛וּשׁ אַלּ֥וּף יַעְלָ֖ם אַלּ֣וּף קֹ֑רַח אֵ֣לֶּה אַלּוּפֵ֞י אָהֳלִֽיבָמָ֛ה בַּת־עֲנָ֖ה אֵ֥שֶׁת עֵשָֽׂו׃ 19 אֵ֧לֶּה בְנֵי־עֵשָׂ֛ו וְאֵ֥לֶּה אַלּוּפֵיהֶ֖ם ה֥וּא אֱדֽוֹם׃ ס

שביעי 20 אֵ֤לֶּה בְנֵֽי־שֵׂעִיר֙ הַחֹרִ֔י יֹשְׁבֵ֖י הָאָ֑רֶץ לוֹטָ֥ן וְשׁוֹבָ֖ל וְצִבְע֥וֹן וַעֲנָֽה׃ 21 וְדִשׁ֥וֹן וְאֵ֖צֶר וְדִישָׁ֑ן אֵ֣לֶּה אַלּוּפֵ֧י הַחֹרִ֛י בְּנֵ֥י שֵׂעִ֖יר בְּאֶ֥רֶץ אֱדֽוֹם׃

22 וַיִּהְי֥וּ בְנֵֽי־לוֹטָ֖ן חֹרִ֣י וְהֵימָ֑ם וַאֲח֥וֹת לוֹטָ֖ן תִּמְנָֽע׃ 23 וְאֵ֙לֶּה֙ בְּנֵ֣י שׁוֹבָ֔ל עַלְוָ֥ן וּמָנַ֖חַת וְעֵיבָ֑ל שְׁפ֖וֹ וְאוֹנָֽם׃ 24 וְאֵ֥לֶּה בְנֵֽי־צִבְע֖וֹן וְאַיָּ֣ה וַעֲנָ֑ה ה֣וּא עֲנָ֗ה אֲשֶׁ֨ר מָצָ֤א אֶת־הַיֵּמִם֙ בַּמִּדְבָּ֔ר בִּרְעֹת֥וֹ אֶת־הַחֲמֹרִ֖ים לְצִבְע֥וֹן אָבִֽיו׃ 25 וְאֵ֥לֶּה בְנֵֽי־עֲנָ֖ה דִּשֹׁ֑ן וְאָהֳלִֽיבָמָ֖ה בַּת־עֲנָֽה׃ 26 וְאֵ֖לֶּה בְּנֵ֣י דִישָׁ֑ן חֶמְדָּ֥ן וְאֶשְׁבָּ֖ן וְיִתְרָ֥ן וּכְרָֽן׃ 27 אֵ֖לֶּה בְּנֵי־אֵ֑צֶר בִּלְהָ֥ן וְזַעֲוָ֖ן וַעֲקָֽן׃ 28 אֵ֥לֶּה בְנֵֽי־דִישָׁ֖ן ע֥וּץ וַאֲרָֽן׃

29 אֵ֖לֶּה אַלּוּפֵ֣י הַחֹרִ֑י אַלּ֤וּף לוֹטָן֙ אַלּ֣וּף שׁוֹבָ֔ל אַלּ֥וּף צִבְע֖וֹן אַלּ֥וּף עֲנָֽה׃ 30 אַלּ֥וּף דִּשֹׁ֛ן אַלּ֥וּף אֵ֖צֶר אַלּ֣וּף דִּישָׁ֑ן אֵ֣לֶּה אַלּוּפֵ֧י הַחֹרִ֛י לְאַלֻּפֵיהֶ֖ם בְּאֶ֥רֶץ שֵׂעִֽיר׃ פ

---

20. the Horite This ethnic term is discussed in the Comment to Gen. 14:6.

22. Lotan's sister was Timna She is the concubine of Eliphaz (36:12).

24. Anah The mention of his discovery presupposes the reader's knowledge of the adventure. Obviously, there once was a widely known tale about this person.

the hot springs Another possible translation

of the unique Hebrew word translated as "the hot springs" (*ha-yeimim*) is "mules." This would make Anah the first to crossbreed the horse with the donkey to produce the hybrid mule.

25. Anah's daughter Oholibamah This note serves to differentiate this Oholibamah from Zibeon's granddaughter of the same name who married Esau (see v. 2).

28. Uz See Comment to 10:23.

31These are the kings who reigned in the land
of Edom before any king reigned over the Israelites. 32Bela son of Beor reigned in Edom,
and the name of his city was Dinhabah.
33When Bela died, Jobab son of Zerah, from
Bozrah, succeeded him as king. 34When Jobab
died, Husham of the land of the Temanites
succeeded him as king. 35When Husham died,
Hadad son of Bedad, who defeated the Midianites in the country of Moab, succeeded him
as king; the name of his city was Avith. 36When
Hadad died, Samlah of Masrekah succeeded
him as king. 37When Samlah died, Saul of Rehoboth-on-the-river succeeded him as king.
38When Saul died, Baal-hanan son of Achbor
succeeded him as king. 39And when Baal-hanan son of Achbor died, Hadar succeeded him
as king; the name of his city was Pau, and
his wife's name was Mehetabel daughter of
Matred daughter of Me-zahab.

31 וְאֵ֗לֶּה הַמְּלָכִ֔ים אֲשֶׁ֥ר מָלְכ֖וּ בְּאֶ֣רֶץ
אֱד֑וֹם לִפְנֵ֥י מְלָךְ־מֶ֖לֶךְ לִבְנֵ֥י יִשְׂרָאֵֽל׃
32 וַיִּמְלֹ֣ךְ בֶּֽאֱד֔וֹם בֶּ֖לַע בֶּן־בְּע֑וֹר וְשֵׁ֥ם
עִיר֖וֹ דִּנְהָֽבָה׃ 33 וַיָּ֖מָת בָּ֑לַע וַיִּמְלֹ֣ךְ
תַּחְתָּ֔יו יוֹבָ֥ב בֶּן־זֶ֖רַח מִבָּצְרָֽה׃ 34 וַיָּ֖מָת
יוֹבָ֑ב וַיִּמְלֹ֣ךְ תַּחְתָּ֔יו חֻשָׁ֖ם מֵאֶ֥רֶץ
הַתֵּימָנִֽי׃ 35 וַיָּ֖מָת חֻשָׁ֑ם וַיִּמְלֹ֣ךְ תַּחְתָּ֗יו
הֲדַ֤ד בֶּן־בְּדַד֙ הַמַּכֶּ֤ה אֶת־מִדְיָן֙ בִּשְׂדֵ֣ה
מוֹאָ֔ב וְשֵׁ֥ם עִיר֖וֹ עֲוִֽית׃ 36 וַיָּ֖מָת הֲדָ֑ד
וַיִּמְלֹ֣ךְ תַּחְתָּ֔יו שַׂמְלָ֖ה מִמַּשְׂרֵקָֽה׃
37 וַיָּ֖מָת שַׂמְלָ֑ה וַיִּמְלֹ֣ךְ תַּחְתָּ֔יו שָׁא֖וּל
מֵרְחֹב֥וֹת הַנָּהָֽר׃ 38 וַיָּ֖מָת שָׁא֑וּל וַיִּמְלֹ֣ךְ
תַּחְתָּ֔יו בַּ֥עַל חָנָ֖ן בֶּן־עַכְבּֽוֹר׃ 39 וַיָּ֗מָת
בַּ֣עַל חָנָ֣ן בֶּן־עַכְבּוֹר֒ וַיִּמְלֹ֣ךְ תַּחְתָּיו֮ הֲדַ֔ר
וְשֵׁ֥ם עִיר֖וֹ פָּ֑עוּ וְשֵׁ֨ם אִשְׁתּ֤וֹ מְהֵֽיטַבְאֵל֙
בַּת־מַטְרֵ֔ד בַּ֖ת מֵ֥י זָהָֽב׃

THE EDOMITE KINGS (vv. 31–39)

This list, which is not a genealogy, details eight kings who reigned in Edom before the establishment of the monarchy in Israel. The narrator probably used Edomite records as the source for the list.

31. before any king reigned over the Israelites That is, before the reign of Saul, first king of Israel, through whom the divine promises of kingship for Israel, recorded in 17:6 and 35:11, were first fulfilled.

33. Jobab In the Bible's ancient Jewish translation into Greek (Septuagint), the Book of Job carries an addendum that identifies Jobab with Job.

Bozrah This city was of such importance that it is sometimes equated with Edom as a whole. It is identified with modern Butseirah, some 30 miles (45 km) south-southeast of the Dead Sea and 35 miles (56 km) north of Petra.

34. the land of the Temanites See Comment to verse 11.

35. Hadad The name of an ancient Semitic storm god, later identified with Baal, head of the Canaanite pantheon.

Midianites This nomadic people, descendant of Abraham according to 25:2, spread out in an arc from the Sinai Peninsula through the Negeb and northwestern Arabia.

36. Masrekah The name seems to indicate a grape-growing region, possibly the site known today as Jebel el-Mushrak.

37. Rehoboth-on-the-river "The river" in the Bible usually is the Euphrates, but this is very far from Edom. Here it may refer to Wadi el-Hesa, the border between Edom and Moab.

38. Baal-hanan He is the only king whose place-name is not given. The Edomite source material used by the narrator may have been defective here.

39. Hadar In the parallel list in 1 Chron. 1:50–57, as well as in numerous Hebrew manuscripts, the name appears as Hadad. This eighth Edomite king could have been an older contemporary of King Saul. By the time of David, Saul's successor, dynastic kingship existed in Edom.

his wife's name His father is not named, but the mention of his wife's mother and grandmother indicates that she had a very distinguished ancestry.

EDOMITE ALLUFIM (vv. 40–43)

This list, arranged by localities that are identical with the clan names, reflects administrative arrangements in Edom.

[40]These are the names of the clans of Esau, each with its families and locality, name by name: the clans Timna, Alvah, Jetheth, [41]Oholibamah, Elah, Pinon, [42]Kenaz, Teman, Mibzar, [43]Magdiel, and Iram. Those are the clans of Edom—that is, of Esau, father of the Edomites—by their settlements in the land which they hold.

מפטיר 40 וְאֵ֩לֶּה֩ שְׁמ֨וֹת אַלּוּפֵ֤י עֵשָׂו֙ לְמִשְׁפְּחֹתָ֔ם
לִמְקֹמֹתָ֖ם בִּשְׁמֹתָ֑ם אַלּ֥וּף תִּמְנָ֛ע אַלּ֥וּף
עַלְוָ֖ה אַלּ֥וּף יְתֵֽת׃ 41 אַלּ֧וּף אָהֳלִיבָמָ֛ה
אַלּ֥וּף אֵלָ֖ה אַלּ֥וּף פִּינֹֽן׃ 42 אַלּ֥וּף קְנַ֛ז אַלּ֥וּף
תֵּימָ֖ן אַלּ֥וּף מִבְצָֽר׃ 43 אַלּ֥וּף מַגְדִּיאֵ֖ל אַלּ֣וּף
עִירָ֑ם אֵ֣לֶּה ׀ אַלּוּפֵ֣י אֱד֗וֹם לְמֹֽשְׁבֹתָם֙
בְּאֶ֣רֶץ אֲחֻזָּתָ֔ם ה֥וּא עֵשָׂ֖ו אֲבִ֥י אֱדֽוֹם׃ פ

41. Elah Elath on the Gulf of Aqaba. According to Deut. 2:8, this marked the southernmost boundary of Edom.

Pinon Punon, mentioned in Num. 33:42–43 as one of the stations of the Israelites during the wilderness wanderings. It is identified with Feinan, an important copper-mining area on the slopes of the hills of Edom, east of the ʿArabah, about 20 miles (35 km) south of the Dead Sea.

42. Mibzar The name means "fortification" and is probably the same as Bozrah in verse 33.

43. which they hold Esau's story closes on this note. His death is not recorded.

הפטרת וישלח

HAFTARAH FOR VA-YISHLAḤ

OBADIAH 1:1–21

The entire brief book of Obadiah is the *haftarah.* The prophecy is a message of judgment and promise.

The judgment focuses on the nation of Edom, whose downfall is proclaimed for their treachery against their "brother Israel" during the siege and destruction of the First Temple. Because Edom participated in the plunder, they shall be plundered in turn (v. 15). Given these allusions, most modern scholars concur that the work was written sometime after the fall of Jerusalem in 587–586 B.C.E.

The theme of promise is addressed to Israel (the House of Jacob). On the day of doom they "shall wreak judgment on Mount Esau" (v. 21), inheriting its lands as part of a national resettlement in the promised land. The renewal of the ancient rivalry between Esau/Edom and Jacob/Israel will again result in the loss of the elder brother's patrimony.

RELATION OF THE *HAFTARAH* TO THE *PARASHAH*

The narrative in the *parashah* and the prophecy in the *haftarah* stand at two opposite points in the historical spectrum of relations between Jacob (Israel) and Esau (Edom). The Torah narrative continues the account of the brothers' relationship that began with embryonic and natal strife and assumed consequential proportions when Jacob deceived his father, Isaac, to obtain the blessing of the firstborn. As a result of the enmity engendered, Jacob fled to Paddan-aram where he married Leah and Rachel, assembled great wealth, and eventually made plans to return to his homeland at the divine behest. The *parashah* opens with Jacob sending messengers to Esau to placate his twin who is marching toward him with an army. Unexpectedly, Esau receives his brother with a noble and generous spirit. The brothers separate in peace, each to his own land. National conflicts between their descendants lie in the distant future.

The *haftarah* takes us to the end of the biblical period, after Judah was exiled from its homeland and Edom participated in the downfall of the nation (cf. Ps. 137:7). The prophet indicts the elder "brother" for duplicity and arraigns him on charges of passive and active deceit. The roles of deceiver–deceived are now reversed, with fatal consequences for Edom. Obadiah predicts Edom's destruction and dispossession. As a triumphant nation, Israel will consume Edom and resettle its homeland. What is more, this destruction is part of a scenario at "the end of days," that will result in the restoration of God's dominion over all.

It is not clear if the prophet saw Israelite restoration in world historical terms or as a case of national liberation. His rabbinic heirs clearly regarded the defeat of Edom as the end of historical tyranny and the onset of God's universal kingship. This is because Edom had become a standard name for the hated Roman Empire. As a result, the prophecy of Obadiah fostered hopes for an end to this brutal domination and a restoration of national religious service. In due course, when Christendom assumed the mantle and the might of Rome, the name Edom received a new identity.

The encounter between Jacob and Esau marked by the *parashah* was dramatized in political terms through exemplifying Edom as imperial or medieval Rome and in religious terms through exemplifying Edom as the civil cult of Rome or as Christianity. For all postbiblical readers, Obadiah's prophecy of liberators ascending Mount Zion to destroy Edom, and the anticipation of God's dominion, was crucial. It was the

consolation preached by ancient Sages and recited by synagogue poets. Exemplary in this regard is the thematic centrality of Obad. 1:21 in Jewish liturgy, because it serves as one of the climactic verses in part of the *Rosh ha-Shanah Musaf* service (known as *Malkhuyot*), celebrating and proclaiming God's future kingdom or dominion. The verse also has a climactic presence in the daily morning liturgy, where it occurs at the conclusion of *P'sukei d'Zimra* (an opening selection of biblical psalms and hymns before the call to worship [*Bar'khu*]). In both contexts, Obad. 1:21 is cited along with the prophecy of divine dominion in Zech. 14:9 ("And the LORD shall be king over all the earth; in that day there shall be one LORD with one name.")

1 The prophecy of Obadiah.

We have received tidings from the LORD,
And an envoy has been sent out among the nations:
"Up! Let us rise up against her for battle."

Thus said my Lord GOD concerning Edom:
2 I will make you least among nations,
You shall be most despised.
3 Your arrogant heart has seduced you,
You who dwell in clefts of the rock,
In your lofty abode.
You think in your heart,
"Who can pull me down to earth?"
4 Should you nest as high as the eagle,
Should your eyrie be lodged 'mong the stars,
Even from there I will pull you down
—declares the LORD.

5 If thieves were to come to you,
Marauders by night,
They would steal no more than they needed.

א חֲזוֹן עֹבַדְיָה

כֹּה־אָמַר אֲדֹנָי יְהוִה לֶאֱדוֹם
שְׁמוּעָה שָׁמַעְנוּ מֵאֵת יְהוָה
וְצִיר בַּגּוֹיִם שֻׁלָּח
קוּמוּ וְנָקוּמָה עָלֶיהָ לַמִּלְחָמָה׃
2 הִנֵּה קָטֹן נְתַתִּיךָ בַּגּוֹיִם
בָּזוּי אַתָּה מְאֹד׃
3 זְדוֹן לִבְּךָ הִשִּׁיאֶךָ
שֹׁכְנִי בְחַגְוֵי־סֶּלַע
מְרוֹם שִׁבְתּוֹ
אֹמֵר בְּלִבּוֹ
מִי יוֹרִדֵנִי אָרֶץ׃
4 אִם־תַּגְבִּיהַּ כַּנֶּשֶׁר
וְאִם־בֵּין כּוֹכָבִים שִׂים קִנֶּךָ
מִשָּׁם אוֹרִידְךָ
נְאֻם־יְהוָה׃

5 אִם־גַּנָּבִים בָּאוּ־לְךָ
אִם־שׁוֹדְדֵי לַיְלָה
אֵיךְ נִדְמֵיתָה

Obadiah 1:1. The prophecy of Obadiah The word translated as "prophecy" (*ḥazon*) literally means "vision."

We have received The plural form of the word translated as "we have received" (*shamanu*) is unexpected because there is only one speaker. Ibn Ezra suggested that this reflects Obadiah's identification with other prophets like "Jeremiah, Isaiah, and Amos who prophesied against Edom."

3. You who dwell in clefts of the rock This image of living in a remote mountain fastness,

If vintagers came to you,
They would surely leave some gleanings.
How utterly you are destroyed!
6How thoroughly rifled is Esau,
How ransacked his hoards!
7All your allies turned you back
At the frontier;
Your own confederates
Have duped and overcome you;
[Those who ate] your bread
Have planted snares under you.

He is bereft of understanding.
8In that day
—declares the LORD—
I will make the wise vanish from Edom,
Understanding from Esau's mount.
9Your warriors shall lose heart, O Teman,
And not a man on Esau's mount
Shall survive the slaughter.

10For the outrage to your brother Jacob,
Disgrace shall engulf you,
And you shall perish forever.
11On that day when you stood aloof,
When aliens carried off his goods,
When foreigners entered his gates
And cast lots for Jerusalem,
You were as one of them.

12How could you gaze with glee
On your brother that day,
On his day of calamity!
How could you gloat
Over the people of Judah

הֲלוֹא יִגְנְבוּ דַּיָּם
אִם־בֹּצְרִים בָּאוּ לָךְ
הֲלוֹא יַשְׁאִירוּ עֹלֵלוֹת׃
6 אֵיךְ נֶחְפְּשׂוּ עֵשָׂו
נִבְעוּ מַצְפֻּנָיו׃
7 עַד־הַגְּבוּל
שִׁלְּחוּךָ כֹּל אַנְשֵׁי בְרִיתֶךָ
הִשִּׁיאוּךָ יָכְלוּ לְךָ
אַנְשֵׁי שְׁלֹמֶךָ
לַחְמְךָ
יָשִׂימוּ מָזוֹר תַּחְתֶּיךָ
אֵין תְּבוּנָה בּוֹ׃
8 הֲלוֹא בַּיּוֹם הַהוּא
נְאֻם־יְהוָה
וְהַאֲבַדְתִּי חֲכָמִים מֵאֱדוֹם
וּתְבוּנָה מֵהַר עֵשָׂו׃
9 וְחַתּוּ גִבּוֹרֶיךָ תֵּימָן
לְמַעַן יִכָּרֶת־אִישׁ מֵהַר עֵשָׂו
מִקָּטֶל׃
10 מֵחֲמַס אָחִיךָ יַעֲקֹב
תְּכַסְּךָ בוּשָׁה
וְנִכְרַתָּ לְעוֹלָם׃
11 בְּיוֹם עֲמָדְךָ מִנֶּגֶד
בְּיוֹם שְׁבוֹת זָרִים חֵילוֹ
וְנָכְרִים בָּאוּ שערו שְׁעָרָיו
וְעַל־יְרוּשָׁלִַם יַדּוּ גוֹרָל
גַּם־אַתָּה כְּאַחַד מֵהֶם׃
12 וְאַל־תֵּרֶא
בְיוֹם־אָחִיךָ
בְּיוֹם נָכְרוֹ
וְאַל־תִּשְׂמַח
לִבְנֵי־יְהוּדָה

and thus beyond danger, portrays Edom's pride.

9. Teman A city and region in Edom (southeast of the Dead Sea), used here to designate Edom as a whole.

On that day of ruin!
How could you loudly jeer
On a day of anguish!
13 How could you enter the gate of My people
On its day of disaster,
Gaze in glee with the others
On its misfortune
On its day of disaster,
And lay hands on its wealth
On its day of disaster!
14 How could you stand at the passes
To cut down its fugitives!
How could you betray those who fled
On that day of anguish!
15 As you did, so shall it be done to you;
Your conduct shall be requited.

Yea, against all nations
The day of the LORD is at hand.
16 That same cup that you drank on My Holy Mount
Shall all nations drink evermore,
Drink till their speech grows thick,
And they become as though they had never been.
17 But on Zion's mount a remnant shall survive,
And it shall be holy.
The House of Jacob shall dispossess
Those who dispossessed them.
18 The House of Jacob shall be fire,
And the House of Joseph flame,
And the House of Esau shall be straw;
They shall burn it and devour it,

בְּיוֹם אׇבְדָם
וְאַל־תַּגְדֵּל פִּיךָ
בְּיוֹם צָרָה׃
13 אַל־תָּבוֹא בְשַׁעַר־עַמִּי
בְּיוֹם אֵידָם
אַל־תֵּרֶא גַם־אַתָּה
בְּרָעָתוֹ
בְּיוֹם אֵידוֹ
וְאַל־תִּשְׁלַחְנָה בְחֵילוֹ
בְּיוֹם אֵידוֹ׃
14 וְאַל־תַּעֲמֹד עַל־הַפֶּרֶק
לְהַכְרִית אֶת־פְּלִיטָיו
וְאַל־תַּסְגֵּר שְׂרִידָיו
בְּיוֹם צָרָה׃
15 כִּי־קָרוֹב יוֹם־יְהוָה
עַל־כׇּל־הַגּוֹיִם
כַּאֲשֶׁר עָשִׂיתָ יֵעָשֶׂה לָּךְ
גְּמֻלְךָ יָשׁוּב בְּרֹאשֶׁךָ׃
16 כִּי כַּאֲשֶׁר שְׁתִיתֶם עַל־הַר קׇדְשִׁי
יִשְׁתּוּ כׇל־הַגּוֹיִם תָּמִיד
וְשָׁתוּ וְלָעוּ
וְהָיוּ כְּלוֹא הָיוּ׃
17 וּבְהַר צִיּוֹן תִּהְיֶה פְלֵיטָה
וְהָיָה קֹדֶשׁ
וְיָרְשׁוּ בֵּית יַעֲקֹב
אֵת מוֹרָשֵׁיהֶם׃
18 וְהָיָה בֵית־יַעֲקֹב אֵשׁ
וּבֵית יוֹסֵף לֶהָבָה
וּבֵית עֵשָׂו לְקַשׁ
וְדָלְקוּ בָהֶם וַאֲכָלוּם

15. day of the LORD An anticipated time of judgment against Israel and the nations. It is first mentioned in Amos 5:18,20 and is usually depicted as accompanied by violent terrestrial and atmospheric disturbances (cf. this idiom in Ezek. 30:3 and Joel 1:15).

17. holy That is, inviolate. Compare Jer. 2:3, "Israel was holy to the LORD, / The first fruits of His harvest. / All who ate of it were held guilty."

And no survivor shall be left of the House of Esau
—for the LORD has spoken.

[19]Thus they shall possess the Negeb and Mount Esau as well, the Shephelah and Philistia. They shall possess the Ephraimite country and the district of Samaria, and Benjamin along with Gilead. [20]And that exiled force of Israelites [shall possess] what belongs to the Phoenicians as far as Zarephath, while the Jerusalemite exile community of Sepharad shall possess the towns of the Negeb. [21]For liberators shall march up on Mount Zion to wreak judgment on Mount Esau; and dominion shall be the LORD's.

וְלֹֽא־יִֽהְיֶ֤ה שָׂרִיד֙ לְבֵ֣ית עֵשָׂ֔ו
כִּ֥י יְהוָ֖ה דִּבֵּֽר׃

19 וְיָרְשׁ֨וּ הַנֶּ֜גֶב אֶת־הַ֣ר עֵשָׂ֗ו וְהַשְּׁפֵלָה֙
אֶת־פְּלִשְׁתִּ֔ים וְיָֽרְשׁוּ֙ אֶת־שְׂדֵ֣ה אֶפְרַ֔יִם
וְאֵ֖ת שְׂדֵ֣ה שֹׁמְר֑וֹן וּבִנְיָמִ֖ן אֶת־הַגִּלְעָֽד׃
20 וְגָלֻ֣ת הַֽחֵל־הַ֠זֶּה לִבְנֵ֨י יִשְׂרָאֵ֤ל אֲשֶׁר־
כְּנַעֲנִים֙ עַד־צָ֣רְפַ֔ת וְגָלֻ֥ת יְרוּשָׁלִַ֖ם אֲשֶׁ֣ר
בִּסְפָרַ֑ד יִרְשׁ֕וּ אֵ֖ת עָרֵ֥י הַנֶּֽגֶב׃ 21 וְעָל֤וּ
מֽוֹשִׁעִים֙ בְּהַ֣ר צִיּ֔וֹן לִשְׁפֹּ֖ט אֶת־הַ֣ר עֵשָׂ֑ו
וְהָיְתָ֥ה לַֽיהוָ֖ה הַמְּלוּכָֽה׃

18. for the LORD has spoken Hebrew: *ki pi YHVH dibber* (literally, "the mouth of the LORD has spoken"). This formula gives divine authority to the prophet's words and was used to cite earlier prophecies at the time of their reapplication to new circumstances. In this case, the reference is to the oracle against Edom recited by Balaam, in Num. 24:17. The same terms for dispossession and survival link the passages.

20. Zarephath A town on the Phoenician coast, also mentioned in 1 Kings 17:9 as being in the vicinity of Sidon.

Sepharad The Aramaic form of Sardis, a city in Asia Minor, as evidenced by an Aramaic–Lydian bilingual inscription. Targum Jonathan and all later Jewish interpreters understood this place as Spain. On this basis, the Jews of Iberian descent are called *S'fardim*.

21. For liberators shall march up This concluding allusion to the "liberators" (*moshi·im*) of Israel, who will "wreak judgment" (*lishpot*) on the enemy, makes use of the old language of saviors and judgment found in the Book of Judges (cf. Ibn Ezra). The liberators here came to be understood as the Messiah and his companions (Radak).

37 Now Jacob was settled in the land
where his father had sojourned, the land of
Canaan. 2This, then, is the line of Jacob:
At seventeen years of age, Joseph tended the
flocks with his brothers, as a helper to the sons
of his father's wives Bilhah and Zilpah. And
Joseph brought bad reports of them to their
father. 3Now Israel loved Joseph best of all his

לז וַיֵּשֶׁב יַעֲקֹב בְּאֶרֶץ מְגוּרֵי אָבִיו
בְּאֶרֶץ כְּנָעַן׃ 2 אֵלֶּה ׀ תֹּלְדוֹת יַעֲקֹב
יוֹסֵף בֶּן־שְׁבַע־עֶשְׂרֵה שָׁנָה הָיָה רֹעֶה אֶת־
אֶחָיו בַּצֹּאן וְהוּא נַעַר אֶת־בְּנֵי בִלְהָה
וְאֶת־בְּנֵי זִלְפָּה נְשֵׁי אָבִיו וַיָּבֵא יוֹסֵף
אֶת־דִּבָּתָם רָעָה אֶל־אֲבִיהֶם׃ 3 וְיִשְׂרָאֵל
אָהַב אֶת־יוֹסֵף מִכָּל־בָּנָיו כִּי־בֶן־זְקֻנִים

PROLOGUE TO THE JOSEPH STORY (37:1–36)

The story of Joseph and his brothers initiates the chain of events that leads to the descent to Egypt. It is the prelude to the drama of oppression and redemption that constitutes the central motif of biblical theology.

THE BEGINNING OF HOSTILITY (vv. 1–4)

1. *Now Jacob was settled in the land* In contrast to Esau, who had migrated. The specific reference is to the Hebron region (see v. 14).

where his father had sojourned That is, the land of Canaan. Only Isaac, of the three Patriarchs, had never left it.

2. *This, then, is the line of Jacob* Mention of Joseph and his brothers here is, in effect, an abbreviated genealogy, the full version of which was already listed in 35:22–26.

as a helper to the sons of He was an assistant to Dan, Naphtali, Gad, and Asher. The word translated as "to" (*et*) often means "with." Here it has the meaning of "subordinate to."

Bilhah and Zilpah The order of the wives is here reversed, because Joseph would have been closer to Bilhah, his late mother's maid. The concubines, until now referred to as "maidservants" when mentioned together with Rachel and Leah, are here called "wives." This may indicate a new status acquired after their mistresses had died, as Ramban suggests.

bad reports of them The content of the "reports" is not given. This is the first of several causes of simmering enmity between Joseph and his brothers.

3. *Israel loved Joseph best* Jacob's favoritism is understandable, because Joseph was the

---

CHAPTER 37

The story of Joseph occupies the last four *parashiyyot* of Genesis, the longest single narrative in the book. It is the story of a young man blessed by God with a special grace, so that no matter what misfortunes befall him, he is able to surmount them. But it is also a story of unintended consequences, of an effort to do harm that ended up doing good and of an apparent triumph that set the stage for the Israelites' descent into slavery. "On the surface, the actors in the story make their own way in life. In fact, however, it transpires that it is Divine Providence that is carrying out, through mankind, its own predestined plan" (N. Leibowitz).

1. *Jacob was settled* Jacob thought he was going to settle down after all he had been through, but events would not permit him to (Rashi). We often think that, once we reach a certain milestone, we will be able to settle down to a life free of challenges. But life never promised to be tranquil. The Sages see this "settling" (*va-yeishev*), as an effort to disengage from the problems of living. Zornberg comments, "The full tension of composure and discomposure, of order and disorder in the world is felt most acutely by the righteous, by those whose sense of beauty and desire for order exposes them to the shock of reality." Esau, by contrast, "settles" in the land of Seir without incident (Gen. 36:8).

Joseph, the favored child, apparently felt closer to his father than to his siblings. A *midrash* suggests that the "bad reports" had to do with the sons of Leah mistreating the sons of the lower-caste wives (Gen. R. 84:7).

הוּא לוֹ וְעָשָׂה לוֹ כְּתֹנֶת פַּסִּים: 4 וַיִּרְאוּ
אֶחָיו כִּי־אֹתוֹ אָהַב אֲבִיהֶם מִכָּל־אֶחָיו
וַיִּשְׂנְאוּ אֹתוֹ וְלֹא יָכְלוּ דַּבְּרוֹ לְשָׁלֹם:
5 וַיַּחֲלֹם יוֹסֵף חֲלוֹם וַיַּגֵּד לְאֶחָיו וַיּוֹסִפוּ
עוֹד שְׂנֹא אֹתוֹ: 6 וַיֹּאמֶר אֲלֵיהֶם שִׁמְעוּ־
נָא הַחֲלוֹם הַזֶּה אֲשֶׁר חָלָמְתִּי: 7 וְהִנֵּה
אֲנַחְנוּ מְאַלְּמִים אֲלֻמִּים בְּתוֹךְ הַשָּׂדֶה
וְהִנֵּה קָמָה אֲלֻמָּתִי וְגַם־נִצָּבָה וְהִנֵּה
תְסֻבֶּינָה אֲלֻמֹּתֵיכֶם וַתִּשְׁתַּחֲוֶיןָ
לַאֲלֻמָּתִי: 8 וַיֹּאמְרוּ לוֹ אֶחָיו הֲמָלֹךְ
תִּמְלֹךְ עָלֵינוּ אִם־מָשׁוֹל תִּמְשֹׁל בָּנוּ

sons, for he was the child of his old age; and he
had made him an ornamented tunic. 4 And
when his brothers saw that their father loved
him more than any of his brothers, they hated
him so that they could not speak a friendly
word to him.

5 Once Joseph had a dream which he told to
his brothers; and they hated him even more.
6 He said to them, "Hear this dream which I
have dreamed: 7 There we were binding sheaves
in the field, when suddenly my sheaf stood up
and remained upright; then your sheaves gathered around and bowed low to my sheaf." 8 His

son of his beloved wife Rachel, born after years of heartbreaking frustration. This partiality is the second cause of enmity between Joseph and his brothers.

Israel Throughout the narrative the two names of the patriarch are interchanged indiscriminately.

the child of his old age He was the last of the sons to be born in Paddan-aram.

an ornamented tunic Such a tunic was a mark of high social standing, as is known from Assyrian inscriptions. Egyptian tomb paintings show Semitic men and women wearing multicolored tunics draped over one shoulder and reaching below the knees. Syrian ambassadors dressed in elaborately designed long robes wrapped around the body and over the shoulders. Others interpret it as a sleeved garment, a tunic reaching the wrists and the ankles.

4. speak a friendly word They rebuffed every attempt by Joseph to be friendly.

JOSEPH'S DREAMS (vv. 5–11)

Everywhere in the ancient Near East dreams were recognized as a means of divine communication. It was assumed that dreams foretold events.

THE FIRST DREAM (vv. 5–8)

5. to his brothers He did not tell his father, who does not figure in the first dream.

7. stood up . . . bowed low A clear assertion of authority by Joseph and of submission on the part of his brothers.

---

3. child of his old age Benjamin was in fact younger, causing Rashi to understand these words (*ben z'kunim*) as "a child with the mature wisdom of an older person." Or possibly, Joseph could be playful with children and mature in the company of adults (*K'li Yakar*).

Israel loved Joseph best "See the consequences of favoring one child over another. Because of those few ounces of wool [the 'coat of many colors' Jacob gave Joseph], our people were enslaved in Egypt" (BT Shab. 10b). One would expect Jacob of all people, having suffered the consequences of parental favoritism, to avoid repeating his parents' mistake. Perhaps it is easier for us to see a problem intellectually than to free ourselves of the tendency to imitate our parents.

5. Why does Joseph tell his brothers his dream, which will only inflame their jealousy? Because he was too young and naive to anticipate their reaction (Sforno; also Hirsch, who sees Joseph's immaturity as the result of growing up without a mother)? Because he thought they would respect him more if they knew that his eminence was God's will (*Ḥizz'kuni*)? Or perhaps because he thought the dream was a message from God, and a prophet may not withhold God's message, whatever the consequences for him personally (Vilna Gaon). Zornberg sees the adolescent Joseph "behaving with the narcissism of youth, with a dangerous unawareness of the feelings of others." Years later, the vicissitudes of life will have matured him to the point where he could look at a person's face and ask, "Why do you appear downcast today?" (Gen. 40:7).

וַיּוֹסִפוּ עוֹד שְׂנֹא אֹתוֹ עַל־חֲלֹמֹתָיו וְעַל־
דְּבָרָיו׃
9 וַיַּחֲלֹם עוֹד חֲלוֹם אַחֵר וַיְסַפֵּר אֹתוֹ
לְאֶחָיו וַיֹּאמֶר הִנֵּה חָלַמְתִּי חֲלוֹם עוֹד
וְהִנֵּה הַשֶּׁמֶשׁ וְהַיָּרֵחַ וְאַחַד עָשָׂר
כּוֹכָבִים מִשְׁתַּחֲוִים לִי׃ 10 וַיְסַפֵּר אֶל־
אָבִיו וְאֶל־אֶחָיו וַיִּגְעַר־בּוֹ אָבִיו וַיֹּאמֶר לוֹ
מָה הַחֲלוֹם הַזֶּה אֲשֶׁר חָלָמְתָּ הֲבוֹא
נָבוֹא אֲנִי וְאִמְּךָ וְאַחֶיךָ לְהִשְׁתַּחֲוֺת לְךָ
אָרְצָה׃ 11 וַיְקַנְאוּ־בוֹ אֶחָיו וְאָבִיו שָׁמַר
אֶת־הַדָּבָר׃
שני 12 וַיֵּלְכוּ אֶחָיו לִרְעוֹת אֶת*־צֹאן אֲבִיהֶם
בִּשְׁכֶם׃ 13 וַיֹּאמֶר יִשְׂרָאֵל אֶל־יוֹסֵף הֲלוֹא
אַחֶיךָ רֹעִים בִּשְׁכֶם לְכָה וְאֶשְׁלָחֲךָ

v. 12. נקוד על א׳ ת׳

brothers answered, "Do you mean to reign over us? Do you mean to rule over us?" And they hated him even more for his talk about his dreams.

9He dreamed another dream and told it to his brothers, saying, "Look, I have had another dream: And this time, the sun, the moon, and eleven stars were bowing down to me." 10And when he told it to his father and brothers, his father berated him. "What," he said to him, "is this dream you have dreamed? Are we to come, I and your mother and your brothers, and bow low to you to the ground?" 11So his brothers were wrought up at him, and his father kept the matter in mind.

12One time, when his brothers had gone to pasture their father's flock at Shechem, 13Israel said to Joseph, "Your brothers are pasturing at Shechem. Come, I will send you to them." He

8. And they hated him The phrase is repeated three times, suggesting an increasing hostility.

for his talk about his dreams Some commentators believe that this refers to the boastful way he recounted them.

dreams The plural either anticipates the second dream or implies a previous, unreported history of similar dreams.

THE SECOND DREAM (vv. 9–11)

9. another dream In the literature of the ancient Near East there are descriptions of repeated dreams in which one symbol is successively substituted for another, although the basic meaning and theme remain the same. In the Joseph narratives, dreams come in pairs to demonstrate their seriousness.

the sun This dream, with its celestial setting, presents Joseph's innermost thoughts and aspirations in a clear and distinct manner, and includes his parents among those who are to be subservient to him.

stars The symbolism is probably suggested by the repeated image comparing the Israelites to the stars of the heavens.

10. and brothers For the second time, Joseph recounts his dream, this time in the presence of his father as well. On both occasions, the brothers are ominously silent.

berated him This was done publicly, in the hope of easing the tension and curbing Joseph's sense of self-importance.

your mother To reconcile this with the death of Rachel (35:19), some see this either as a dream distortion or as a reference to Joseph's stepmother Bilhah.

to the ground Joseph did not utter this phrase. Jacob, in adding it, echoes the manner in which he himself made obeisance to his brother Esau (33:3).

11. his brothers were wrought up The repetition of the dream has validated its message. The brothers now look on Joseph with hatred.

THE SALE OF JOSEPH (vv. 12–36)

12. his brothers Joseph did not go with them, perhaps because he was exempt from labor.

at Shechem Being pastoral nomads, the brothers move from one area to another to secure pasturage for their livestock. The region around Shechem has rich soil and an adequate water supply.

13. I will send you to them The brothers had hidden their true feelings about Joseph. Otherwise, Jacob would not have sent him to them—and Joseph would not have gone so eagerly.

answered, "I am ready." [14]And he said to him, "Go and see how your brothers are and how the flocks are faring, and bring me back word." So he sent him from the valley of Hebron.

When he reached Shechem, [15]a man came upon him wandering in the fields. The man asked him, "What are you looking for?" [16]He answered, "I am looking for my brothers. Could you tell me where they are pasturing?" [17]The man said, "They have gone from here, for I heard them say: Let us go to Dothan." So Joseph followed his brothers and found them at Dothan.

[18]They saw him from afar, and before he came close to them they conspired to kill him. [19]They said to one another, "Here comes that dreamer! [20]Come now, let us kill him and

אֲלֵיהֶ֖ם וַיֹּ֥אמֶר ל֖וֹ הִנֵּֽנִי׃ 14 וַיֹּ֤אמֶר לוֹ֙ לֶךְ־
נָ֣א רְאֵ֞ה אֶת־שְׁל֤וֹם אַחֶ֙יךָ֙ וְאֶת־שְׁל֣וֹם
הַצֹּ֔אן וַהֲשִׁבֵ֖נִי דָּבָ֑ר וַיִּשְׁלָחֵ֙הוּ֙ מֵעֵ֣מֶק
חֶבְר֔וֹן
וַיָּבֹ֖א שְׁכֶֽמָה׃ 15 וַיִּמְצָאֵ֣הוּ אִ֔ישׁ וְהִנֵּ֥ה
תֹעֶ֖ה בַּשָּׂדֶ֑ה וַיִּשְׁאָלֵ֧הוּ הָאִ֛ישׁ לֵאמֹ֖ר
מַה־תְּבַקֵּֽשׁ׃ 16 וַיֹּ֕אמֶר אֶת־אַחַ֖י אָנֹכִ֣י
מְבַקֵּ֑שׁ הַגִּֽידָה־נָּ֣א לִ֔י אֵיפֹ֖ה הֵ֥ם רֹעִֽים׃
17 וַיֹּ֤אמֶר הָאִישׁ֙ נָסְע֣וּ מִזֶּ֔ה כִּ֤י שָׁמַ֙עְתִּי֙
אֹֽמְרִ֔ים נֵלְכָ֖ה דֹּתָ֑יְנָה וַיֵּ֤לֶךְ יוֹסֵף֙ אַחַ֣ר
אֶחָ֔יו וַיִּמְצָאֵ֖ם בְּדֹתָֽן׃
18 וַיִּרְא֥וּ אֹת֖וֹ מֵֽרָחֹ֑ק וּבְטֶ֙רֶם֙ יִקְרַ֣ב אֲלֵיהֶ֔ם
וַיִּֽתְנַכְּל֥וּ אֹת֖וֹ לַהֲמִיתֽוֹ׃ 19 וַיֹּֽאמְר֖וּ אִ֣ישׁ
אֶל־אָחִ֑יו הִנֵּ֗ה בַּ֛עַל הַחֲלֹמ֥וֹת הַלָּזֶ֖ה בָּֽא׃
20 וְעַתָּ֣ה ׀ לְכ֣וּ וְנַֽהַרְגֵ֗הוּ וְנַשְׁלִכֵ֙הוּ֙ בְּאַחַ֣ד

---

14. bring me back word Jacob is anxious about the well-being of his sons.

valley of Hebron A name found nowhere else. Hebron itself was located on a hill. The cave of Machpelah, in which Abraham was buried, was in a field outside the city and the text may be referring to that area.

Hebron . . . Shechem A distance of some 50 miles (80 km). The south–north watershed road that traversed the central hill country connected these two cities. It split into two at Shechem, one branch turning northwest to Dothan (v. 17).

When he reached Shechem A journey of about five days by foot.

15. a man The exchange between Joseph and the man is reported only in briefest outline. The stranger surely must have asked for the identity of the brothers, if only to be of help.

17. Dothan An ancient fortress town about 13 miles (21 km) northwest of Shechem, lying in a valley known for its rich pasture land.

18. They saw him from afar The mere glimpse of Joseph incites the murderous hatred of the brothers, who are now far away from their father's restraining presence.

20. kill him The verb translated as "kill" (הרג), which connotes ruthless violence, is the same verb used when Cain slays Abel.

---

14. see how your brothers are Literally, "see the *shalom* (the integrity and the peacefulness) of your brothers." Why does Jacob send his favorite son on this dangerous venture? "You who complained about them and brought back bad reports (v. 2), go and discover their admirable qualities" (Simḥah Bunem).

15. a man Maimonides takes this stranger to be an angel, sent to make sure that Joseph would not give up on his mission when he could not find his brothers immediately. A modern scholar has noted that Dothan (v. 17) was a city, not a place of pasture. Perhaps Joseph discovered that his brothers were neglecting the sheep to explore the pleasures of the city, and it was to

hide this embarrassing disclosure as well as for reasons of jealousy that they were moved to get rid of him.

We never hear of this man again. Yet if Joseph had not met him, he never would have found his brothers. He never would have been sold into slavery. The family would not have followed him into Egypt. There would have been no Exodus. The history of the world would have been so different! Could that man have known how his chance encounter changed history? Do we ever know the consequences of the little acts of thoughtfulness we perform?

throw him into one of the pits; and we can say, 'A savage beast devoured him.' We shall see what comes of his dreams!" 21But when Reuben heard it, he tried to save him from them. He said, "Let us not take his life." 22And Reuben went on, "Shed no blood! Cast him into that pit out in the wilderness, but do not touch him yourselves"—intending to save him from them and restore him to his father. 23When Joseph came up to his brothers, they stripped Joseph of his tunic, the ornamented tunic that he was wearing, 24and took him and cast him into the pit. The pit was empty; there was no water in it.

25Then they sat down to a meal. Looking up, they saw a caravan of Ishmaelites coming from

הַבֹּרוֹת וְאָמַרְנוּ חַיָּה רָעָה אֲכָלָתְהוּ
וְנִרְאֶה מַה־יִּהְיוּ חֲלֹמֹתָיו׃ 21 וַיִּשְׁמַע
רְאוּבֵן וַיַּצִּלֵהוּ מִיָּדָם וַיֹּאמֶר לֹא נַכֶּנּוּ
נָפֶשׁ׃ 22 וַיֹּאמֶר אֲלֵהֶם ׀ רְאוּבֵן אַל־
תִּשְׁפְּכוּ־דָם הַשְׁלִיכוּ אֹתוֹ אֶל־הַבּוֹר הַזֶּה
אֲשֶׁר בַּמִּדְבָּר וְיָד אַל־תִּשְׁלְחוּ־בוֹ לְמַעַן
הַצִּיל אֹתוֹ מִיָּדָם לַהֲשִׁיבוֹ אֶל־אָבִיו׃
שלישי 23 וַיְהִי כַּאֲשֶׁר־בָּא יוֹסֵף אֶל־אֶחָיו
וַיַּפְשִׁיטוּ אֶת־יוֹסֵף אֶת־כֻּתָּנְתּוֹ אֶת־
כְּתֹנֶת הַפַּסִּים אֲשֶׁר עָלָיו׃ 24 וַיִּקָּחֻהוּ
וַיַּשְׁלִכוּ אֹתוֹ הַבֹּרָה וְהַבּוֹר רֵק אֵין בּוֹ
מָיִם׃
25 וַיֵּשְׁבוּ לֶאֱכָל־לֶחֶם וַיִּשְׂאוּ עֵינֵיהֶם

one of the pits These were cisterns hewn out of rock intended for gathering and storing water in the rainy season. At times murderers may have slaughtered their victims near such pits, which varied in depth from 16 to 24 feet, to dispose of the corpses there.

21. when Reuben heard it Being the firstborn, he would surely bear the main share of blame for any misfortune that befell Joseph.

he tried to save him The Hebrew verb *vayatzileihu,* "he saved him," also can mean "he came to the rescue."

Let us not That is, "We shall not!" Reuben speaks with a decisiveness that tolerates no opposition. The use of the first person plural makes clear that this is to be their collective decision. Indeed, the brothers do not say another word.

22. Reuben went on He pauses for his words to take effect and then continues.

Shed no blood By using the Hebrew second person plural in addressing them, he dissociates himself from them and emphasizes his loathing for the idea.

out in the wilderness The abundant, uninhabited pasture land in the region of Dothan. The brothers believe that Joseph will die of hunger and exposure; Reuben thinks he can rescue him somehow without their noticing.

23. the ornamented tunic The explanatory comment is necessary in light of verse 33.

24. cast him into the pit The narrative tells us nothing here of Joseph's reactions to their deeds, although it is clear from 42:21 that he pleaded to be released.

no water in it This is a necessary observation, because such pits were dug largely for water storage.

25. sat down to a meal They ate in callous indifference to their brother's anguished pleas. Reuben, in the meantime, leaves (v. 29).

a caravan of Ishmaelites Apparently, they buy Joseph, take him down to Egypt (v. 28), and sell him to Potiphar (39:1). In verse 28, however, it is Midianite traders (or "Medanites") who are said to have sold Joseph to Potiphar (v. 36). Rashi suggests that Joseph probably was traded several times. Some modern commentators explain the discrepancy as being the result of different traditions.

---

21. Reuben's relationship with Joseph may have been the most complicated of any of the brothers. As the eldest son, he would be held responsible for what happened. Moreover, Joseph, as the firstborn son of the favored wife, would be Reuben's chief rival for family supremacy (Hirsch).

25. they sat down to a meal This detail not only conveys the callousness of the brothers but foreshadows the consequences of their action.

וַיִּרְאוּ וְהִנֵּה אֹרְחַת יִשְׁמְעֵאלִים בָּאָה
מִגִּלְעָד וּגְמַלֵּיהֶם נֹשְׂאִים נְכֹאת וּצְרִי
וָלֹט הוֹלְכִים לְהוֹרִיד מִצְרָיְמָה׃ 26 וַיֹּאמֶר
יְהוּדָה אֶל־אֶחָיו מַה־בֶּצַע כִּי נַהֲרֹג אֶת־
אָחִינוּ וְכִסִּינוּ אֶת־דָּמוֹ׃ 27 לְכוּ וְנִמְכְּרֶנּוּ
לַיִּשְׁמְעֵאלִים וְיָדֵנוּ אַל־תְּהִי־בוֹ כִּי־אָחִינוּ
בְשָׂרֵנוּ הוּא וַיִּשְׁמְעוּ אֶחָיו׃ 28 וַיַּעַבְרוּ
אֲנָשִׁים מִדְיָנִים סֹחֲרִים וַיִּמְשְׁכוּ וַיַּעֲלוּ
אֶת־יוֹסֵף מִן־הַבּוֹר וַיִּמְכְּרוּ אֶת־יוֹסֵף
לַיִּשְׁמְעֵאלִים בְּעֶשְׂרִים כָּסֶף וַיָּבִיאוּ אֶת־
יוֹסֵף מִצְרָיְמָה׃
29 וַיָּשָׁב רְאוּבֵן אֶל־הַבּוֹר וְהִנֵּה אֵין־יוֹסֵף
בַּבּוֹר וַיִּקְרַע אֶת־בְּגָדָיו׃ 30 וַיָּשָׁב אֶל־אֶחָיו
וַיֹּאמַר הַיֶּלֶד אֵינֶנּוּ וַאֲנִי אָנָה אֲנִי־בָא׃

Gilead, their camels bearing gum, balm, and ladanum to be taken to Egypt. 26 Then Judah said to his brothers, "What do we gain by killing our brother and covering up his blood? 27 Come, let us sell him to the Ishmaelites, but let us not do away with him ourselves. After all, he is our brother, our own flesh." His brothers agreed. 28 When Midianite traders passed by, they pulled Joseph up out of the pit. They sold Joseph for twenty pieces of silver to the Ishmaelites, who brought Joseph to Egypt.

29 When Reuben returned to the pit and saw that Joseph was not in the pit, he rent his clothes. 30 Returning to his brothers, he said, "The boy is gone! Now, what am I to do?" 31 Then they took Joseph's tunic, slaughtered

from Gilead The central mountainous region east of the river Jordan.

camels See Comment to 12:16.

gum Gums and resins were vital to the economy of Egypt, where they constituted the ingredients of perfumes, cosmetics, and medicines, all of which were used in the worship of the gods, in embalming the dead, as sanitizing and deodorizing agents, as insect repellents, and for cleansing the body.

26. killing Leaving him to die in the pit would be the same as killing him. It is also possible that in Reuben's absence the idea of murdering Joseph had been revived.

covering up his blood In the language of the Bible, the blood of a murder victim is said to "cry out" for justice (see 4:10). Uncovered blood was a constant reminder of a crime and an incitement to revenge.

27. flesh This is a metaphor for kinship relationship.

agreed Literally, "heard." The Hebrew verb here may connote listening in stony silence as well as willing assent.

28. Midianite See Comment to 37:25.

twenty pieces of silver The 20 shekels is the average price of a male slave between 15 and 20 years of age (see Lev. 27:5).

to Egypt They intended to sell him in the slave market. There is pictorial evidence for the presence of a brisk trade with Egypt in Asian slaves.

29. he rent his clothes This was a sign of grief. Clearly, Reuben knows nothing about the sale and believes Joseph to be dead.

30. to his brothers They had left the scene after the sale.

is gone Or "is no more!"—perhaps meaning that Joseph must be dead.

what am I to do? An agonized cry. Literally, "as for me, where can I go?"—to escape my father's grief.

Because they will sell Joseph into slavery, Israelites and Egyptians will have food to eat during the famine.

27. Though Judah saves Joseph's life with this suggestion, the Sages condemn him. One is not to be praised merely for being less wicked than one's companions (BT Sanh. 6b).

30. Reuben despairs that despite his best efforts, Joseph may have died. In fact, Reuben's suggestion (v. 22) saved his life. Often, we despair that the good deeds we have done have made no difference, when in fact they have made a great difference (*S'fat Emet*).

31. Jacob, who had deceived his father with goatskins and borrowed clothing (Gen. 27:15–16), is deceived by his children with stolen clothing and goat's blood. Maimonides suggests that the goat sent to destruction in the

a kid, and dipped the tunic in the blood. 32They
had the ornamented tunic taken to their father,
and they said, "We found this. Please examine
it; is it your son's tunic or not?" 33He recognized it, and said, "My son's tunic! A savage
beast devoured him! Joseph was torn by a
beast!" 34Jacob rent his clothes, put sackcloth
on his loins, and observed mourning for his
son many days. 35All his sons and daughters
sought to comfort him; but he refused to be
comforted, saying, "No, I will go down mourning to my son in Sheol." Thus his father bewailed him.

36The Midianites, meanwhile, sold him in

31 וַיִּקְחוּ אֶת־כְּתֹנֶת יוֹסֵף וַיִּשְׁחֲטוּ שְׂעִיר
עִזִּים וַיִּטְבְּלוּ אֶת־הַכֻּתֹּנֶת בַּדָּם׃
32 וַיְשַׁלְּחוּ אֶת־כְּתֹנֶת הַפַּסִּים וַיָּבִיאוּ
אֶל־אֲבִיהֶם וַיֹּאמְרוּ זֹאת מָצָאנוּ הַכֶּר־
נָא הַכְּתֹנֶת בִּנְךָ הִוא אִם־לֹא׃ 33 וַיַּכִּירָהּ
וַיֹּאמֶר כְּתֹנֶת בְּנִי חַיָּה רָעָה אֲכָלָתְהוּ
טָרֹף טֹרַף יוֹסֵף׃ 34 וַיִּקְרַע יַעֲקֹב שִׂמְלֹתָיו
וַיָּשֶׂם שַׂק בְּמָתְנָיו וַיִּתְאַבֵּל עַל־בְּנוֹ יָמִים
רַבִּים׃ 35 וַיָּקֻמוּ כָל־בָּנָיו וְכָל־בְּנֹתָיו
לְנַחֲמוֹ וַיְמָאֵן לְהִתְנַחֵם וַיֹּאמֶר כִּי־אֵרֵד
אֶל־בְּנִי אָבֵל שְׁאֹלָה וַיֵּבְךְּ אֹתוֹ אָבִיו׃
36 וְהַמְּדָנִים מָכְרוּ אֹתוֹ אֶל־מִצְרָיִם

32. ornamented That distinctive feature is what establishes for Jacob the identity of its owner.

and they said The brothers now use the explanation they originally had planned to use (Gen. 37:20).

is it your son's tunic It is not the brothers who ask this, but those with whom they sent the tunic.

33. He recognized it Jacob becomes aware of the full horror of the situation only in stages. First he recognizes the tunic. Then its bloody and tattered condition leads him to infer that a wild beast had devoured his son. Then he has a vivid mental image of his beloved Joseph actually being torn to pieces.

Joseph was torn by a beast Jacob has been maneuvered into uttering the very words the brothers originally had planned to say (v. 20).

34. rent his clothes A symbol of grief. See Comment to verse 29.

sackcloth The wearing of sackcloth, a coarse material probably made of goat hair or camel hair, is another symbol of grief.

many days His inconsolable sorrow was no doubt intensified by feelings of guilt at having sent Joseph alone on such a long and perilous journey.

35. daughters Both his daughter Dinah and his daughters-in-law.

go down mourning That is, he never will cease to mourn until the day of his death.

Sheol This is the most frequently used term in biblical Hebrew for the abode of the spirits of the dead. The region was imagined as situated deep beneath the earth, enclosed with gates. It was a place of unrelieved gloom and silence; it received everyone, good and bad, great and small. All were equal there, and none who entered it could leave. There is no concept of "heaven" and "hell" in the Hebrew Bible.

36. the Midianites In 39:1, those who sell Joseph are called "Ishmaelites."

Potiphar The name of Joseph's master is almost identical with that of his future father-in-law, Poti-phera (41:45). This latter name has been explained as the Egyptian *Pa-di-pa-re*, meaning "he whom Re (the sun god) has given."

courtier The term translated as "courtier" (*saris*) means "the one at the head," that is, a high officer of the realm.

chief steward The literal meaning of the word translated as "steward" (*tabbaḥ*) is either "cook" or "slaughterer" (i.e., executioner). The full title refers to persons attached to the services of nobles, princes, and kings.

---

wilderness on Yom Kippur is meant to be an atonement for the sin of hatred of one Israelite for another (*Guide* III:46).

35. he refused to be comforted Was this because he felt guilty for having sent Joseph on that doomed mission (Gen. R. 84:13)? Or was it because at some level he intuited that Joseph might still be alive (Gen. R. 84:21)? The Hebrew word translated as "to be comforted" (*l'hitnaḥem*) is reflexive; he refused to comfort himself.

לְפֽוֹטִיפַר֙ סְרִ֣יס פַּרְעֹ֔ה שַׂ֖ר הַטַּבָּחִֽים׃ פ

Egypt to Potiphar, a courtier of Pharaoh and his chief steward.

רביעי **לח** וַיְהִי֙ בָּעֵ֣ת הַהִ֔וא וַיֵּ֥רֶד יְהוּדָ֖ה
מֵאֵ֣ת אֶחָ֑יו וַיֵּ֛ט עַד־אִ֥ישׁ עֲדֻלָּמִ֖י וּשְׁמ֥וֹ
חִירָֽה׃ 2 וַיַּרְא־שָׁ֧ם יְהוּדָ֛ה בַּת־אִ֥ישׁ
כְּנַעֲנִ֖י וּשְׁמ֣וֹ שׁ֑וּעַ וַיִּקָּחֶ֖הָ וַיָּבֹ֥א אֵלֶֽיהָ׃
3 וַתַּ֖הַר וַתֵּ֣לֶד בֵּ֑ן וַיִּקְרָ֥א אֶת־שְׁמ֖וֹ עֵֽר׃
4 וַתַּ֥הַר ע֖וֹד וַתֵּ֣לֶד בֵּ֑ן וַתִּקְרָ֥א אֶת־שְׁמ֖וֹ

38 About that time Judah left his brothers
and camped near a certain Adullamite whose
name was Hirah. 2 There Judah saw the daughter of a certain Canaanite whose name was
Shua, and he married her and cohabited with
her. 3 She conceived and bore a son, and he
named him Er. 4 She conceived again and bore
a son, and named him Onan. 5 Once again she

JUDAH AND TAMAR (38:1–30)

The story of Joseph is interrupted by a narrative about Judah. Modern scholars point out that although the Joseph narratives describe the rise of Joseph, they also subtly register the ascendancy of Judah, the fourth son, over Reuben, the firstborn. Two kingdoms resulted from God's promises to Abraham (17:6) and to Jacob (35:11): Judah became the name of the southern kingdom, and the northern kingdom of Israel became known as Joseph (Zech. 10:6). This chapter alludes to the future Joseph–Judah polarity in the history of the people Israel (see 1 Chron. 5:1–2).

JUDAH'S MARRIAGE (vv. 1–5)

1. left his brothers The literal meaning of the word translated here as "left" (*va-yeired*) is "went down from," that is, from the hill country of Hebron (Gen. 37:12,14).

Adullamite A man of the city of Adullam, which is in the northern sector of the Judean lowland, about 9 miles (14.4 km) northeast of modern Beit Guvrin.

2. Canaanite The wife herself is identified as a Canaanite in 1 Chron. 2:3. Simeon also had a Canaanite wife. In both cases, the foreign woman is absorbed into the Israelite tribe. Conscious of the later prohibition on intermarriage with Canaanites (Deut. 7:1,3), traditional Jewish commentators have understood the word for "Canaanite" (*k'na·ani*) here in the sense of "merchant."

daughter . . . Shua The daughter's name is not recorded. She is called "Shua's daughter" (*bat-shu·a*) in Gen. 38:12. In 1 Chron. 2:3 she is called "Bath-Shua the Canaanite woman."

3. he named him In some manuscripts, as well as in the Samaritan version and in an Aramaic translation, the reading here is "she named"—that is, the mother named all three sons.

Er No interpretation is given for the names of Judah's sons. Er probably was understood to mean "watchful, vigilant."

4. Onan This possibly was understood to mean "vigorous."

We can never truly comfort a mourner, even when we have known a similar loss. We can only surround the mourners with a sense of being cared about, in the hope that this will bring them to the point of comforting themselves (Hirsch).

CHAPTER 38

What is this story doing here, interrupting the Joseph narrative? There are thematic connections and there are parallels of language (e.g., "examine it/these," *hakker na,* in 37:32 and 38:25). Another connection is suggested by a *midrash.* It imagines God saying to Judah, "How could you have done such a thing to your father? Don't you realize how a parent feels when a child dies? You will come to know that feeling" (Tanḥ.).

1. Judah left his brothers He left either out of feelings of guilt for what he had done with Joseph, or because his brothers blamed him (Tanḥ. B.).

bore a son, and named him Shelah; he was at Chezib when she bore him.

⁶Judah got a wife for Er his first-born; her name was Tamar. ⁷But Er, Judah's first-born, was displeasing to the Lord, and the Lord took his life. ⁸Then Judah said to Onan, "Join with your brother's wife and do your duty by her as a brother-in-law, and provide offspring for your brother." ⁹But Onan, knowing that the seed would not count as his, let it go to waste whenever he joined with his brother's wife, so as not to provide offspring for his brother. ¹⁰What he did was displeasing to the Lord, and He took his life also. ¹¹Then Judah said to his daughter-in-law Tamar, "Stay as a widow in your father's

אוֹנָ֑ן: ⁵וַתֹּ֤סֶף עוֹד֙ וַתֵּ֣לֶד בֵּ֔ן וַתִּקְרָ֥א אֶת־
שְׁמ֖וֹ שֵׁלָ֑ה וְהָיָ֥ה בִכְזִ֖יב בְּלִדְתָּ֥הּ אֹתֽוֹ:
⁶וַיִּקַּ֧ח יְהוּדָ֛ה אִשָּׁ֖ה לְעֵ֣ר בְּכוֹר֑וֹ וּשְׁמָ֖הּ
תָּמָֽר: ⁷וַיְהִ֗י עֵ֚ר בְּכ֣וֹר יְהוּדָ֔ה רַ֖ע בְּעֵינֵ֣י
יְהֹוָ֑ה וַיְמִתֵ֖הוּ יְהֹוָֽה: ⁸וַיֹּ֤אמֶר יְהוּדָה֙
לְאוֹנָ֔ן בֹּ֛א אֶל־אֵ֥שֶׁת אָחִ֖יךָ וְיַבֵּ֣ם אֹתָ֑הּ
וְהָקֵ֥ם זֶ֖רַע לְאָחִֽיךָ: ⁹וַיֵּ֣דַע אוֹנָ֔ן כִּ֛י לֹּ֥א ל֖וֹ
יִהְיֶ֣ה הַזָּ֑רַע וְהָיָ֞ה אִם־בָּ֨א אֶל־אֵ֤שֶׁת אָחִיו֙
וְשִׁחֵ֣ת אַ֔רְצָה לְבִלְתִּ֥י נְתָן־זֶ֖רַע לְאָחִֽיו:
¹⁰וַיֵּ֛רַע בְּעֵינֵ֥י יְהֹוָ֖ה אֲשֶׁ֣ר עָשָׂ֑ה וַיָּ֖מֶת גַּם־
אֹתֽוֹ: ¹¹וַיֹּ֣אמֶר יְהוּדָה֩ לְתָמָ֨ר כַּלָּת֜וֹ שְׁבִ֧י
אַלְמָנָ֣ה בֵית־אָבִ֗יךְ עַד־יִגְדַּל֙ שֵׁלָ֣ה בְנִ֔י כִּ֣י

---

5. Shelah   Perhaps this means "drawn out" (namely, out of the womb).

Chezib   Elsewhere this city is called Achzib. It was situated in the territory of Judah, southwest of Adullam.

THE LEVIRATE OBLIGATION   (vv. 6–11)

6. got a wife   Judah, the father, selects a bride for his son, as was the custom in biblical times.

Tamar   The word means "a palm tree."

7. displeasing   The text does not specify the sin.

8. Join with your brother's wife   The marriage of a man and his brother's wife is forbidden by the Torah (see Lev. 18:16, 20:21). An exception is made only when a married brother dies without a son. According to Deut. 25:5, the brother of the deceased is obligated to take the widow as his wife. This institution is known in Hebrew as *yibbum*. In English it is called "levi-

rate marriage" (from Latin *levir*, "a husband's brother").

provide offspring for your brother   There was no requirement to name the son of such a union after the dead brother. The child, however, was considered to be the dead man's heir.

9. would not count as his   With the death of the firstborn, Onan stood to inherit one-half of his father's estate, because his brother left no heir. Should he provide an heir to his brother, however, his own portion would be less.

let it go to waste   Literally, "he let it spoil on the ground." Apparently, there was no provision at that time for the kind of voluntary renunciation of the levirate duty that is permitted in Deut. (25:7–9).

10. What he did was displeasing   Onan incurs the anger of God because he evades his obligation to his dead brother, not because of the manner in which he acts. The issue here is the levirate obligation, not birth control.

11. as a widow in your father's house   She was not free to remarry, but she could return to

---

7. displeasing to the Lord   Early levels of the biblical narrative could understand the untimely death of a young person only as being caused by some sin on that person's part. Other-

wise, the world would make no sense. Later in the biblical period, and in the time of the Talmud, a more nuanced, less judgmental approach to misfortune emerges.

HALAKHAH L'MA·ASEH

38:9 let it go to waste   Jewish law permits various forms of contraception for medical and other reasons but prefers methods that do not destroy the generative seed (MT Forbidden Intercourse 21:18). Using gametes in infertility treatments does not constitute wasting them.

house until my son Shelah grows up"—for he thought, "He too might die like his brothers." So Tamar went to live in her father's house.

[12]A long time afterward, Shua's daughter, the wife of Judah, died. When his period of mourning was over, Judah went up to Timnah to his sheepshearers, together with his friend Hirah the Adullamite. [13]And Tamar was told, "Your father-in-law is coming up to Timnah for the sheepshearing." [14]So she took off her widow's garb, covered her face with a veil, and, wrapping herself up, sat down at the entrance to Enaim, which is on the road to Timnah; for she saw that Shelah was grown up, yet she had not been given to him as wife. [15]When Judah saw her, he took her for a harlot; for she had covered her face. [16]So he turned aside to her by the road and said, "Here, let me sleep with you"—for he did not know that she was his

אָמַר פֶּן־יָמוּת גַּם־הוּא כְּאֶחָיו וַתֵּלֶךְ תָּמָר
וַתֵּשֶׁב בֵּית אָבִיהָ׃
12 וַיִּרְבּוּ הַיָּמִים וַתָּמָת בַּת־שׁוּעַ אֵשֶׁת־
יְהוּדָה וַיִּנָּחֶם יְהוּדָה וַיַּעַל עַל־גֹּזְזֵי צֹאנוֹ
הוּא וְחִירָה רֵעֵהוּ הָעֲדֻלָּמִי תִּמְנָתָה׃
13 וַיֻּגַּד לְתָמָר לֵאמֹר הִנֵּה חָמִיךְ עֹלֶה
תִמְנָתָה לָגֹז צֹאנוֹ׃ 14 וַתָּסַר בִּגְדֵי
אַלְמְנוּתָהּ מֵעָלֶיהָ וַתְּכַס בַּצָּעִיף
וַתִּתְעַלָּף וַתֵּשֶׁב בְּפֶתַח עֵינַיִם אֲשֶׁר עַל־
דֶּרֶךְ תִּמְנָתָה כִּי רָאֲתָה כִּי־גָדַל שֵׁלָה
וְהִוא לֹא־נִתְּנָה לוֹ לְאִשָּׁה׃ 15 וַיִּרְאֶהָ
יְהוּדָה וַיַּחְשְׁבֶהָ לְזוֹנָה כִּי כִסְּתָה פָּנֶיהָ׃
16 וַיֵּט אֵלֶיהָ אֶל־הַדֶּרֶךְ וַיֹּאמֶר הָבָה־נָּא
אָבוֹא אֵלַיִךְ כִּי לֹא יָדַע כִּי כַלָּתוֹ הִוא
וַתֹּאמֶר מַה־תִּתֶּן־לִּי כִּי תָבוֹא אֵלָי׃

live with her parents while still subject to the authority of her father-in-law.

for he thought Judah had no intention of marrying her to Shelah.

THE DECEPTION OF JUDAH (vv. 12–26)

12. A long time afterward About one year has elapsed.

died The death of Judah's wife is mentioned as an extenuating circumstance to account for his consorting with a harlot.

his period of mourning was over Literally, "he was comforted." The official mourning rites had ended.

went up In contrast to "went down" (Gen. 38:1).

Timnah This is west of Beth-Shemesh.

sheepshearers The shearing season was filled with joy and revelry.

14. her widow's garb This was the kind of clothing worn by a widow in mourning.

a veil Tamar normally was not veiled. She simply wanted to conceal her identity, as is clear from verses 15 and 19.

Enaim Probably the village Enam in the territory of Judah.

Shelah Nothing more is reported of him here, but his clan is mentioned in Num. 26:20.

she had not been given Apparently, Tamar has no claim against Shelah, only against Judah. The responsibility for the enforcement of the levirate obligation here, as in the Hittite and Assyrian laws, seems to have rested with the widow's father-in-law. Deut. 25:5–10 modified the levirate institution by restricting responsibility to the brothers of the deceased.

Tamar was unafraid to assert herself in the face of social disapproval. Because of this, she is considered to be a heroine, like Ruth, and like Ruth she is worthy of being an ancestress of David.

15. she had covered her face The narrator, conscious of the contradiction between the moral standards of a later age and the fact that the offspring of Judah's venture with his daughter-in-law bore no stigma of illegitimacy, is care-

14. Tamar is another in the line of biblical women who long to be mothers and who are rewarded by becoming the mother of a special person (in this case, an ancestor of King David and the messianic line).

daughter-in-law. "What," she asked, "will you pay for sleeping with me?" 17He replied, "I will send a kid from my flock." But she said, "You must leave a pledge until you have sent it." 18And he said, "What pledge shall I give you?" She replied, "Your seal and cord, and the staff which you carry." So he gave them to her and slept with her, and she conceived by him. 19Then she went on her way. She took off her veil and again put on her widow's garb.

20Judah sent the kid by his friend the Adullamite, to redeem the pledge from the woman; but he could not find her. 21He inquired of the people of that town, "Where is the cult prostitute, the one at Enaim, by the road?" But they said, "There has been no prostitute here." 22So he returned to Judah and said, "I could not find her; moreover, the townspeople said: There has been no prostitute here." 23Judah said, "Let her keep them, lest we become a laughingstock. I did send her this kid, but you did not find her."

24About three months later, Judah was told, "Your daughter-in-law Tamar has played the harlot; in fact, she is with child by harlotry." "Bring her out," said Judah, "and let her be burned." 25As she was being brought out, she

17 וַיֹּאמֶר אָנֹכִי אֲשַׁלַּח גְּדִי־עִזִּים מִן־הַצֹּאן
וַתֹּאמֶר אִם־תִּתֵּן עֵרָבוֹן עַד שָׁלְחֶךָ׃
18 וַיֹּאמֶר מָה הָעֵרָבוֹן אֲשֶׁר אֶתֶּן־לָּךְ
וַתֹּאמֶר חֹתָמְךָ וּפְתִילֶךָ וּמַטְּךָ אֲשֶׁר בְּיָדֶךָ
וַיִּתֶּן־לָהּ וַיָּבֹא אֵלֶיהָ וַתַּהַר לוֹ׃ 19 וַתָּקָם
וַתֵּלֶךְ וַתָּסַר צְעִיפָהּ מֵעָלֶיהָ וַתִּלְבַּשׁ בִּגְדֵי
אַלְמְנוּתָהּ׃
20 וַיִּשְׁלַח יְהוּדָה אֶת־גְּדִי הָעִזִּים בְּיַד
רֵעֵהוּ הָעֲדֻלָּמִי לָקַחַת הָעֵרָבוֹן מִיַּד
הָאִשָּׁה וְלֹא מְצָאָהּ׃ 21 וַיִּשְׁאַל אֶת־אַנְשֵׁי
מְקֹמָהּ לֵאמֹר אַיֵּה הַקְּדֵשָׁה הִוא בָעֵינַיִם
עַל־הַדָּרֶךְ וַיֹּאמְרוּ לֹא־הָיְתָה בָזֶה קְדֵשָׁה׃
22 וַיָּשָׁב אֶל־יְהוּדָה וַיֹּאמֶר לֹא מְצָאתִיהָ
וְגַם אַנְשֵׁי הַמָּקוֹם אָמְרוּ לֹא־הָיְתָה בָזֶה
קְדֵשָׁה׃ 23 וַיֹּאמֶר יְהוּדָה תִּקַּח־לָהּ פֶּן
נִהְיֶה לָבוּז הִנֵּה שָׁלַחְתִּי הַגְּדִי הַזֶּה
וְאַתָּה לֹא מְצָאתָהּ׃
24 וַיְהִי ׀ כְּמִשְׁלֹשׁ חֳדָשִׁים וַיֻּגַּד לִיהוּדָה
לֵאמֹר זָנְתָה תָּמָר כַּלָּתֶךָ וְגַם הִנֵּה
הָרָה לִזְנוּנִים וַיֹּאמֶר יְהוּדָה הוֹצִיאוּהָ
וְתִשָּׂרֵף׃ 25 הִוא מוּצֵאת וְהִיא שָׁלְחָה אֶל־

ful to emphasize that had Judah known the identity of the woman, he never would have had relations with her.

17. a kid from my flock Judah carried nothing at that moment with which to pay for the woman's services—a clear indication that he acted on impulse.

a pledge This is security to be held until the fulfillment of the obligation.

18. seal and cord Judah gave Tamar his cylinder seal, a small object made of a hard material and engraved with distinctive ornamentation. Its center was hollowed out and a cord passed through so that it could be worn around the neck. This highly personal object performed the function of a signature in modern society.

staff It must have had some distinguishing sign. Scepter heads, some incised with names, have been discovered over a wide area of the Near East.

20. the woman The relationship was so casual that he had not even bothered to find out her name.

24. Judah was told He had not seen her himself because she had returned to her father's house (Gen. 38:11).

Bring her out To the city gate, where justice was administered. Judah, as head of the family, exercises his power of life and death here, even though Tamar lives with her parents.

let her be burned The tie between the childless widow and the levir exists automatically from the moment of widowhood. Thus a sexual relationship with anyone other than the levir would be adulterous, an offense punishable by the death penalty, according to Lev. 20:10 and Deut. 22:22.

25. Examine these Tamar, who has maintained her self-restraint until the last moment, confronts Judah with unimpeachable evidence.

חָמִיהָ לֵאמֹר לְאִישׁ אֲשֶׁר־אֵלֶּה לּוֹ אָנֹכִי
הָרָה וַתֹּאמֶר הַכֶּר־נָא לְמִי הַחֹתֶמֶת
וְהַפְּתִילִים וְהַמַּטֶּה הָאֵלֶּה׃ 26 וַיַּכֵּר
יְהוּדָה וַיֹּאמֶר צָדְקָה מִמֶּנִּי כִּי־עַל־כֵּן
לֹא־נְתַתִּיהָ לְשֵׁלָה בְנִי וְלֹא־יָסַף עוֹד
לְדַעְתָּהּ׃
27 וַיְהִי בְּעֵת לִדְתָּהּ וְהִנֵּה תְאוֹמִים
בְּבִטְנָהּ׃ 28 וַיְהִי בְלִדְתָּהּ וַיִּתֶּן־יָד וַתִּקַּח
הַמְיַלֶּדֶת וַתִּקְשֹׁר עַל־יָדוֹ שָׁנִי לֵאמֹר זֶה
יָצָא רִאשֹׁנָה׃ 29 וַיְהִי ׀ כְּמֵשִׁיב יָדוֹ וְהִנֵּה
יָצָא אָחִיו וַתֹּאמֶר מַה־פָּרַצְתָּ עָלֶיךָ פָּרֶץ
וַיִּקְרָא שְׁמוֹ פָּרֶץ׃ 30 וְאַחַר יָצָא אָחִיו
אֲשֶׁר עַל־יָדוֹ הַשָּׁנִי וַיִּקְרָא שְׁמוֹ זָרַח׃ ס חמישי

sent this message to her father-in-law, "I am with child by the man to whom these belong." And she added, "Examine these: whose seal and cord and staff are these?" 26 Judah recognized them, and said, "She is more in the right than I, inasmuch as I did not give her to my son Shelah." And he was not intimate with her again.

27 When the time came for her to give birth, there were twins in her womb! 28 While she was in labor, one of them put out his hand, and the midwife tied a crimson thread on that hand, to signify: This one came out first. 29 But just then he drew back his hand, and out came his brother; and she said, "What a breach you have made for yourself!" So he was named Perez. 30 Afterward his brother came out, on whose hand was the crimson thread; he was named Zerah.

Her tactic of indirect accusation results in a minimum of embarrassment and so elicits a noble response.

26. he was not intimate with her again There is a distinction between this incident and the levirate law of Deut. 25:5. There, the widow becomes her brother-in-law's wife. Here, it would appear that Tamar has only a clear right to conceive a child but no claim on marriage. Again, the present narrative reflects a much earlier society than that of Deuteronomy.

THE BIRTH OF THE TWINS (vv. 27–30)

27. When the time came . . . twins Unlike the case with Rebekah (as told in Gen. 25:24), twins apparently were not expected here.

28. came out first The narrative seems to echo a history of rivalry between the two clans (see 25:22–23).

29. she said That is, the midwife.

breach From the Hebrew *peretz*. Perez is the only name in this chapter for which an explanation is given, a fact that reflects the pre-eminence of the Perezite clan within the tribe of Judah. The birth of Perez is taken to be a historic turning point; 10 generations separate him from King David (see Ruth 4:18–22).

he was named Literally, "he called his name;" that is, Judah did, on the basis of the midwife's words.

30. Zerah No interpretation of the name is given. The Hebrew stem means "brightness," suggesting an allusion to the crimson thread. The Zerahites were a clan of Judah.

---

26. Tamar does not embarrass Judah publicly. Her life is spared because Judah recognizes and admits his guilt when he could have denied it. Judah, as a man who can accept responsibility, steps forward to heal the breach between Joseph and his brothers in chapter 44.

חמישי

לט וְיוֹסֵף הוּרַד מִצְרָיְמָה וַיִּקְנֵהוּ
פּוֹטִיפַר סְרִיס פַּרְעֹה שַׂר הַטַּבָּחִים אִישׁ
מִצְרִי מִיַּד הַיִּשְׁמְעֵאלִים אֲשֶׁר הוֹרִדֻהוּ
שָׁמָּה: 2 וַיְהִי יְהוָה אֶת־יוֹסֵף וַיְהִי אִישׁ
מַצְלִיחַ וַיְהִי בְּבֵית אֲדֹנָיו הַמִּצְרִי: 3 וַיַּרְא
אֲדֹנָיו כִּי יְהוָה אִתּוֹ וְכֹל אֲשֶׁר־הוּא עֹשֶׂה
יְהוָה מַצְלִיחַ בְּיָדוֹ: 4 וַיִּמְצָא יוֹסֵף חֵן
בְּעֵינָיו וַיְשָׁרֶת אֹתוֹ וַיַּפְקִדֵהוּ עַל־בֵּיתוֹ
וְכָל־יֶשׁ־לוֹ נָתַן בְּיָדוֹ: 5 וַיְהִי מֵאָז הִפְקִיד

39 When Joseph was taken down to
Egypt, a certain Egyptian, Potiphar, a courtier
of Pharaoh and his chief steward, bought him
from the Ishmaelites who had brought him
there. 2The LORD was with Joseph, and he
was a successful man; and he stayed in the
house of his Egyptian master. 3And when his
master saw that the LORD was with him and
that the LORD lent success to everything he
undertook, 4he took a liking to Joseph. He
made him his personal attendant and put
him in charge of his household, placing in his
hands all that he owned. 5And from the time

JOSEPH IN POTIPHAR'S HOUSEHOLD (39:1–23)

1. When Joseph The narrator resumes the story of Joseph, returning to the events in the last verses of chapter 37.

a certain Egyptian The national identity of Joseph's master is repeated three times for emphasis (vv. 1,2,5), probably because the sale of Joseph into Egyptian slavery sets the stage for the enslavement and redemption of the Israelites. The prophecy to Abraham (15:13) is being fulfilled.

Potiphar The name and titles of the master are here given to draw attention to the aristocratic nature of the household into which Joseph is sold, a detail essential to the development of the story.

2. The LORD was with Joseph This crucial phrase appears four times in this chapter. It is intended to impart meaning to events that appear to be merely random. At the same time, it enables the reader to understand how the spoiled lad of 17, alone in a foreign land and in dire adversity, suddenly begins to mature and acquire great strength of character.

a successful man The phrase expresses the idea that innate gifts of intelligence and skill cannot achieve fruition without divine support.

he stayed in the house This is the first of four stages in the rise of Joseph: he is not sent to work in the fields.

3. when his master saw Joseph's competence in fulfilling his duties—not here specified—is visible proof to the master of divine support for his slave.

4. he took a liking Literally, "Joseph found favor in his eyes." He wins the esteem and confidence of his master—the second stage in his rise.

his personal attendant This is the third stage.

in charge of his household The fourth and final rung on the ladder of success. Joseph is now overseer of the entire estate, a function fre-

---

CHAPTER 39

1. Joseph was taken down to Egypt Of both Abraham (Gen. 12:10) and Judah (Gen. 38:1), it is said that they "went down." This implies that they lowered the moral level of their behavior. Joseph, however, did not lower himself; he was transported against his will. The episode in this chapter shows him maintaining a high moral standard.

2. The verse can be read, "The LORD was with Joseph when he was a successful man and also when he stayed in the house of his Egyptian master." Some people are conscious of God's presence in their lives only when they are successful. When adversity strikes, they believe God has abandoned them. Joseph felt God's presence in his life both in good times and in bad times.

that the Egyptian put him in charge of his
household and of all that he owned, the LORD
blessed his house for Joseph's sake, so that the
blessing of the LORD was upon everything that
he owned, in the house and outside. 6He left all
that he had in Joseph's hands and, with him
there, he paid attention to nothing save the
food that he ate. Now Joseph was well built
and handsome.

7After a time, his master's wife cast her eyes
upon Joseph and said, "Lie with me." 8But he
refused. He said to his master's wife, "Look,
with me here, my master gives no thought to
anything in this house, and all that he owns he
has placed in my hands. 9He wields no more

אֹתוֹ בְּבֵיתוֹ וְעַל כָּל־אֲשֶׁר יֶשׁ־לוֹ וַיְבָרֶךְ
יְהוָה אֶת־בֵּית הַמִּצְרִי בִּגְלַל יוֹסֵף וַיְהִי
בִּרְכַּת יְהוָה בְּכָל־אֲשֶׁר יֶשׁ־לוֹ בַּבַּיִת
וּבַשָּׂדֶה׃ 6וַיַּעֲזֹב כָּל־אֲשֶׁר־לוֹ בְּיַד־יוֹסֵף
וְלֹא־יָדַע אִתּוֹ מְאוּמָה כִּי אִם־הַלֶּחֶם
אֲשֶׁר־הוּא אוֹכֵל וַיְהִי יוֹסֵף יְפֵה־תֹאַר
וִיפֵה מַרְאֶה׃

ששי 7וַיְהִי אַחַר הַדְּבָרִים הָאֵלֶּה וַתִּשָּׂא אֵשֶׁת־
אֲדֹנָיו אֶת־עֵינֶיהָ אֶל־יוֹסֵף וַתֹּאמֶר
שִׁכְבָה עִמִּי׃ 8וַיְמָאֵן | וַיֹּאמֶר אֶל־אֵשֶׁת
אֲדֹנָיו הֵן אֲדֹנִי לֹא־יָדַע אִתִּי מַה־בַּבָּיִת
וְכֹל אֲשֶׁר־יֶשׁ־לוֹ נָתַן בְּיָדִי׃ 9אֵינֶנּוּ גָּדוֹל

quently referred to in Egyptian texts as "comptroller" (*mer-per*).

5. the LORD blessed God brought great prosperity to the master.

in the house and outside Literally, "in the house and in the field." The phrase is a figure of speech that combines two contrasting elements to express totality.

6. in Joseph's hands Joseph has now reached the pinnacle of his career as a servant.

the food that he ate Egyptians did not eat with strangers (43:32). Thus early commentators understood the phrase as a euphemism for "wife."

well built and handsome No other male is so described in Scripture. Its insertion here serves solely to introduce the next episode.

THE ATTEMPTED SEDUCTION (vv. 7–20)

7. After a time Sufficient time has elapsed for Joseph's high position to be accepted by him as normal and routine.

his master's wife She remains nameless.

cast her eyes upon With longing, lasciviously. There is irony here. The mistress of the house has become a slave to her lust for her husband's slave.

Lie with me There are no preliminaries, no words of love. Her demand reflects her awareness of Joseph's slave status.

8. he refused Sexual promiscuity was commonplace in all slave societies, and an ambitious person might have considered that the woman was presenting him with a chance to advance his personal interests.

He said to his master's wife Joseph explains his personal reasons for refusing her advances. First he points to the abuse of trust that would be involved, then to the violation of the husband's proprietary rights over his wife, then to the religious and moral nature of the offense.

---

6. Joseph was well built and handsome He inherited his good looks from his mother, Rachel, who is described in identical Hebrew terms in Gen. 29:17. The Midrash pictures Joseph as immersed in vanity and concerned with his appearance. This prompted God to say, "Your father is grieving and you comport yourself thus!" Immediately, his good looks get him into trouble and cause him to be cast into prison (Tanḥ.).

8. The Sages imagine Joseph about to yield to the enticements of Potiphar's wife when the image of his father appears before him and strengthens his resolve to say no (BT Sot. 36b). Although Jacob had schemed and cheated when he was young, he never was guilty of sexual impropriety. The cantillation note for the word translated as "but he refused" (*va-y'ma·en*) is the rare note *"shalshelet,"* which appears only four times in the Torah. It is a wavering, back-and-forth note, suggesting indecision and ambivalence on Joseph's part.

authority in this house than I, and he has withheld nothing from me except yourself, since
you are his wife. How then could I do this most
wicked thing, and sin before God?" [10]And
much as she coaxed Joseph day after day, he
did not yield to her request to lie beside her,
to be with her.

[11]One such day, he came into the house to do
his work. None of the household being there
inside, [12]she caught hold of him by his garment
and said, "Lie with me!" But he left his garment
in her hand and got away and fled outside.
[13]When she saw that he had left it in her hand
and had fled outside, [14]she called out to her
servants and said to them, "Look, he had to
bring us a Hebrew to dally with us! This one
came to lie with me; but I screamed loud.

בַּבַּ֣יִת הַזֶּה֮ מִמֶּ֒נִּי֒ וְלֹֽא־חָשַׂ֤ךְ מִמֶּ֙נִּי֙ מְא֔וּמָה
כִּ֣י אִם־אוֹתָ֖ךְ בַּאֲשֶׁ֣ר אַתְּ־אִשְׁתּ֑וֹ וְאֵ֞יךְ
אֶֽעֱשֶׂ֤ה הָֽרָעָה֙ הַגְּדֹלָ֣ה הַזֹּ֔את וְחָטָ֖אתִי
לֵֽאלֹהִֽים׃ [10]וַיְהִ֕י כְּדַבְּרָ֥הּ אֶל־יוֹסֵ֖ף י֣וֹם ׀
י֑וֹם וְלֹֽא־שָׁמַ֥ע אֵלֶ֛יהָ לִשְׁכַּ֥ב אֶצְלָ֖הּ
לִֽהְי֥וֹת עִמָּֽהּ׃
[11]וַיְהִי֙ כְּהַיּ֣וֹם הַזֶּ֔ה וַיָּבֹ֥א הַבַּ֖יְתָה לַעֲשׂ֣וֹת
מְלַאכְתּ֑וֹ וְאֵ֨ין אִ֜ישׁ מֵאַנְשֵׁ֧י הַבַּ֛יִת שָׁ֖ם
בַּבָּֽיִת׃ [12]וַתִּתְפְּשֵׂ֧הוּ בְּבִגְד֛וֹ לֵאמֹ֖ר שִׁכְבָ֣ה
עִמִּ֑י וַיַּעֲזֹ֤ב בִּגְדוֹ֙ בְּיָדָ֔הּ וַיָּ֖נׇס וַיֵּצֵ֥א הַחֽוּצָה׃
[13]וַיְהִי֙ כִּרְאוֹתָ֔הּ כִּֽי־עָזַ֥ב בִּגְד֖וֹ בְּיָדָ֑הּ וַיָּ֖נׇס
הַחֽוּצָה׃ [14]וַתִּקְרָ֞א לְאַנְשֵׁ֣י בֵיתָ֗הּ וַתֹּ֤אמֶר
לָהֶם֙ לֵאמֹ֔ר רְא֗וּ הֵ֤בִיא לָ֙נוּ֙ אִ֣ישׁ עִבְרִ֔י
לְצַ֥חֶק בָּ֑נוּ בָּ֤א אֵלַי֙ לִשְׁכַּ֣ב עִמִּ֔י וָאֶקְרָ֖א

9. you are his wife The second of these reasons reflects pagan legal theory that adultery
was largely a private injury, an affront and indignity to the husband.

and sin before God The third line of argument conforms to the Israelite concept of morality as having its source and sanction in divine
will, not in social convention or utilitarian considerations.

10. she coaxed She does not reply to Joseph's arguments and attempts to wear down his
resistance.

11. into the house Literally, "into the interior of the house."

to do his work Early commentaries have Joseph attending to his master's accounts.

there inside In that part of the house. Servants were present elsewhere (v. 14).

12. she caught hold Her pleas having failed
to achieve their end, she resorts to physical aggression.

garment The loose-fitting outer garment of
the well-to-do.

got away and fled Literally, "he fled (va-ya-
nos) and went out (va-yetzei) to the outside."
The first verb describes his abrupt withdrawal
from the room; the second suggests the assump-

tion of a normal gait, once outside, in order not
to attract attention.

13. When she saw She must have been
stricken with terror over the possibility of the
truth getting out. Furious over having been refused, she was hungry for revenge.

14. to her servants Literally, "the people of
her house," who were in another part of the
building.

Look She may have held up the coat for all
to see.

he had to bring She is referring to her husband.

a Hebrew There is a clear derogatory intent
here. In addressing her domestics, who are probably Egyptians, she appeals to their instinctive
suspicion of foreigners, who were looked down
on by the Egyptians.

to dally The Hebrew stem translated here as
"dally" (צחק) can also mean "to mock us, insult
us."

I screamed The scream was regarded as evidence of resistance to attempted rape. Hence it
was a sign of innocence. She knows that none
of those to whom she speaks had been close
enough to hear her (v. 11).

12. Once again, a distinctive garment gets
Joseph into difficulty. Once again, as in Gen.

37:23, he is stripped of his garment and thrown
into a pit.

15 And when he heard me screaming at the top
of my voice, he left his garment with me and got
away and fled outside." 16 She kept his garment
beside her, until his master came home. 17 Then
she told him the same story, saying, "The Hebrew slave whom you brought into our house
came to me to dally with me; 18 but when I
screamed at the top of my voice, he left his
garment with me and fled outside."

19 When his master heard the story that his
wife told him, namely, "Thus and so your slave
did to me," he was furious. 20 So Joseph's master
had him put in prison, where the king's prisoners were confined. But even while he was there
in prison, 21 the Lord was with Joseph: He extended kindness to him and disposed the chief
jailer favorably toward him. 22 The chief jailer
put in Joseph's charge all the prisoners who

בְּקוֹל גָּדוֹל׃ 15 וַיְהִי כְשָׁמְעוֹ כִּי־הֲרִימֹתִי
קוֹלִי וָאֶקְרָא וַיַּעֲזֹב בִּגְדוֹ אֶצְלִי וַיָּנָס
וַיֵּצֵא הַחוּצָה׃ 16 וַתַּנַּח בִּגְדוֹ אֶצְלָהּ עַד־
בּוֹא אֲדֹנָיו אֶל־בֵּיתוֹ׃ 17 וַתְּדַבֵּר אֵלָיו
כַּדְּבָרִים הָאֵלֶּה לֵאמֹר בָּא־אֵלַי הָעֶבֶד
הָעִבְרִי אֲשֶׁר־הֵבֵאתָ לָּנוּ לְצַחֶק בִּי׃
18 וַיְהִי כַּהֲרִימִי קוֹלִי וָאֶקְרָא וַיַּעֲזֹב בִּגְדוֹ
אֶצְלִי וַיָּנָס הַחוּצָה׃
19 וַיְהִי כִשְׁמֹעַ אֲדֹנָיו אֶת־דִּבְרֵי אִשְׁתּוֹ
אֲשֶׁר דִּבְּרָה אֵלָיו לֵאמֹר כַּדְּבָרִים הָאֵלֶּה
עָשָׂה לִי עַבְדֶּךָ וַיִּחַר אַפּוֹ׃ 20 וַיִּקַּח אֲדֹנֵי
יוֹסֵף אֹתוֹ וַיִּתְּנֵהוּ אֶל־בֵּית הַסֹּהַר מְקוֹם
אֲשֶׁר־אסורי אֲסִירֵי הַמֶּלֶךְ אֲסוּרִים וַיְהִי־
שָׁם בְּבֵית הַסֹּהַר׃ 21 וַיְהִי יְהוָה אֶת־יוֹסֵף
וַיֵּט אֵלָיו חָסֶד וַיִּתֵּן חִנּוֹ בְּעֵינֵי שַׂר בֵּית־
הַסֹּהַר׃ 22 וַיִּתֵּן שַׂר בֵּית־הַסֹּהַר בְּיַד־יוֹסֵף

15. with me The same phraseology as in the report to her husband (v. 18), but she avoids mentioning that the garment was left in her hand (vv. 12,13).

and fled outside See Comment to 39:12. Again she is cautious in her formulation, because someone might have seen Joseph leaving her room and walking normally.

16. his master Not "her husband," because it was in the capacity of slave master that she would confront him.

17. Hebrew slave This time she emphasizes Joseph's slave status.

into our house She does not repeat to her husband the charge of attempted rape, an omission that probably saved Joseph from the executioner.

20. had him put Literally, "took him and put him." High government officials in ancient Egypt also performed judicial functions.

in prison Imprisonment is well attested in Egypt, where each town of any size had a prison that served as a penal institution for convicted criminals, as a labor camp for those forced into slave labor, and as the seat of the criminal court. In the present instance, the prison is under the jurisdiction of Joseph's master and is housed on his property.

where the king's prisoners Being an officer of the court, Potiphar puts Joseph in the section reserved for royal prisoners. There are many stories in ancient literature about the blameless man who repels the amorous advances of a married woman and escapes death.

IMPRISONMENT (vv. 20–23)

20. But even while Here in prison Joseph is at the lowest point of his fortunes. According to Psalms (105:17–18), his feet were fettered and an iron collar was put around his neck.

22. The chief jailer The jailer who is responsible to the chief steward.

put in Joseph's charge He assigns Joseph duties not here specified.

---

19. he was furious With Joseph? Or with his wife, whom he suspected of fabricating her story (Gen. R. 87:9)? If Potiphar believed his wife's account, it seems strange that Joseph's punishment was only imprisonment in a facility for high-ranking offenders.

22. Once again, as with Potiphar and as will happen with Pharaoh, God's favor and Joseph's personal qualities bring him to the attention of powerful patrons.

were in that prison, and he was the one to carry
out everything that was done there. 23The chief
jailer did not supervise anything that was in
Joseph's charge, because the LORD was with
him, and whatever he did the LORD made successful.

אֵת כָּל־הָאֲסִירִם אֲשֶׁר בְּבֵית הַסֹּהַר וְאֵת
כָּל־אֲשֶׁר עֹשִׂים שָׁם הוּא הָיָה עֹשֶׂה׃
23 אֵין ׀ שַׂר בֵּית־הַסֹּהַר רֹאֶה אֶת־כָּל־
מְאוּמָה בְּיָדוֹ בַּאֲשֶׁר יְהוָה אִתּוֹ וַאֲשֶׁר־
הוּא עֹשֶׂה יְהוָה מַצְלִיחַ׃ ס

40 Some time later, the cupbearer and the
baker of the king of Egypt gave offense to their
lord the king of Egypt. 2Pharaoh was angry
with his two courtiers, the chief cupbearer
and the chief baker, 3and put them in custody,
in the house of the chief steward, in the same
prison house where Joseph was confined. 4The
chief steward assigned Joseph to them, and he
attended them.

When they had been in custody for some
time, 5both of them—the cupbearer and the
baker of the king of Egypt, who were confined
in the prison—dreamed in the same night,
each his own dream and each dream with its
own meaning. 6When Joseph came to them in
the morning, he saw that they were distraught.
7He asked Pharaoh's courtiers, who were with

שביעי **מ** וַיְהִי אַחַר הַדְּבָרִים הָאֵלֶּה חָטְאוּ
מַשְׁקֵה מֶלֶךְ־מִצְרַיִם וְהָאֹפֶה לַאֲדֹנֵיהֶם
לְמֶלֶךְ מִצְרָיִם׃ 2 וַיִּקְצֹף פַּרְעֹה עַל שְׁנֵי
סָרִיסָיו עַל שַׂר הַמַּשְׁקִים וְעַל שַׂר
הָאוֹפִים׃ 3 וַיִּתֵּן אֹתָם בְּמִשְׁמַר בֵּית שַׂר
הַטַּבָּחִים אֶל־בֵּית הַסֹּהַר מְקוֹם אֲשֶׁר
יוֹסֵף אָסוּר שָׁם׃ 4 וַיִּפְקֹד שַׂר הַטַּבָּחִים
אֶת־יוֹסֵף אִתָּם וַיְשָׁרֶת אֹתָם
וַיִּהְיוּ יָמִים בְּמִשְׁמָר׃ 5 וַיַּחַלְמוּ חֲלוֹם
שְׁנֵיהֶם אִישׁ חֲלֹמוֹ בְּלַיְלָה אֶחָד אִישׁ
כְּפִתְרוֹן חֲלֹמוֹ הַמַּשְׁקֶה וְהָאֹפֶה אֲשֶׁר
לְמֶלֶךְ מִצְרַיִם אֲשֶׁר אֲסוּרִים בְּבֵית
הַסֹּהַר׃ 6 וַיָּבֹא אֲלֵיהֶם יוֹסֵף בַּבֹּקֶר וַיַּרְא
אֹתָם וְהִנָּם זֹעֲפִים׃ 7 וַיִּשְׁאַל אֶת־סְרִיסֵי

JOSEPH IN PRISON (40:1–23)

1. Some time later Joseph is now 28 years old; 11 years have gone by since his sale into slavery. There is no way of knowing how many of those years he spent in the service of Potiphar and how many in prison.

the cupbearer and the baker The following verse identifies them as the chief officials of their professions in the royal household. The cupbearer, who is crucial to the narrative, is always mentioned first. Because he personally served wine to the king, he was an important official in the royal court. Ancient Egyptian documents attest to the wealth and power of such officials.

gave offense The details, being irrelevant to the narrative, are ignored.

3. in custody That is, in detention pending final disposition of their case.

4. The chief steward Joseph's own master, on whose estate the prison was situated.

for some time The Hebrew word *yamim* may indicate either indefinite time or "a year."

5. both of them On the subject of dreams, see the Comment to Gen. 37:9. In this case, the two dreams are needed to establish Joseph's reputation as an interpreter of dreams.

each dream with its own meaning Literally, "each according to the interpretation of his dream." The Hebrew can be taken to mean that the interpretation turned out to be appropriate to the content or that each dreamed as if his dream were a prediction.

6. distraught The anxiety normally brought on by dreams is intensified for the prisoners by the uncertainty of their fate and because they are being denied access to a professional dream interpreter. The odd coincidence of the two officials having simultaneous dreams no doubt heightens their tension.

him in custody in his master's house, saying, "Why do you appear downcast today?" 8And they said to him, "We had dreams, and there is no one to interpret them." So Joseph said to them, "Surely God can interpret! Tell me [your dreams]."

9Then the chief cupbearer told his dream to Joseph. He said to him, "In my dream, there was a vine in front of me. 10On the vine were three branches. It had barely budded, when out came its blossoms and its clusters ripened into grapes. 11Pharaoh's cup was in my hand, and I took the grapes, pressed them into Pharaoh's cup, and placed the cup in Pharaoh's hand." 12Joseph said to him, "This is its interpretation: The three branches are three days. 13In three days Pharaoh will pardon you and restore you to your post; you will place Pharaoh's cup in his hand, as was your custom formerly when you were his cupbearer. 14But think of me when all is well with you again, and do me the kindness of mentioning me to Pharaoh, so as to free me from this place. 15For in truth, I was kidnapped from the land of the

פַּרְעֹה אֲשֶׁר אִתּוֹ בְמִשְׁמַר בֵּית אֲדֹנָיו
לֵאמֹר מַדּוּעַ פְּנֵיכֶם רָעִים הַיּוֹם׃
8 וַיֹּאמְרוּ אֵלָיו חֲלוֹם חָלַמְנוּ וּפֹתֵר אֵין
אֹתוֹ וַיֹּאמֶר אֲלֵהֶם יוֹסֵף הֲלוֹא לֵאלֹהִים
פִּתְרֹנִים סַפְּרוּ־נָא לִי׃
9 וַיְסַפֵּר שַׂר־הַמַּשְׁקִים אֶת־חֲלֹמוֹ לְיוֹסֵף
וַיֹּאמֶר לוֹ בַּחֲלוֹמִי וְהִנֵּה־גֶפֶן לְפָנָי׃
10 וּבַגֶּפֶן שְׁלֹשָׁה שָׂרִיגִם וְהִוא כְפֹרַחַת
עָלְתָה נִצָּהּ הִבְשִׁילוּ אַשְׁכְּלֹתֶיהָ עֲנָבִים׃
11 וְכוֹס פַּרְעֹה בְּיָדִי וָאֶקַּח אֶת־הָעֲנָבִים
וָאֶשְׂחַט אֹתָם אֶל־כּוֹס פַּרְעֹה וָאֶתֵּן אֶת־
הַכּוֹס עַל־כַּף פַּרְעֹה׃ 12 וַיֹּאמֶר לוֹ יוֹסֵף
זֶה פִּתְרֹנוֹ שְׁלֹשֶׁת הַשָּׂרִגִים שְׁלֹשֶׁת יָמִים
הֵם׃ 13 בְּעוֹד ׀ שְׁלֹשֶׁת יָמִים יִשָּׂא פַרְעֹה
אֶת־רֹאשֶׁךָ וַהֲשִׁיבְךָ עַל־כַּנֶּךָ וְנָתַתָּ כוֹס־
פַּרְעֹה בְּיָדוֹ כַּמִּשְׁפָּט הָרִאשׁוֹן אֲשֶׁר הָיִיתָ
מַשְׁקֵהוּ׃ 14 כִּי אִם־זְכַרְתַּנִי אִתְּךָ כַּאֲשֶׁר
יִיטַב לָךְ וְעָשִׂיתָ־נָּא עִמָּדִי חָסֶד
וְהִזְכַּרְתַּנִי אֶל־פַּרְעֹה וְהוֹצֵאתַנִי מִן־
הַבַּיִת הַזֶּה׃ 15 כִּי־גֻנֹּב גֻּנַּבְתִּי מֵאֶרֶץ

8. there is no one Here in prison.

Tell me "And perhaps God will reveal the meaning to me," implies Joseph.

THE CUPBEARER'S DREAM (vv. 9–15)

9. The chief cupbearer told his dream The dream is recounted in a rapid series of scenes: the grape-growing season, the production process, the serving of the finished wine.

12. This is its interpretation Joseph deciphers the dream by a scheme of equivalences. The rapidity of the action suggests imminent fulfillment. The recurrence of the number three (three days, three branches, three stages of growth, three actions performed) and the fact that both "Pharaoh" and his "cup" are mentioned three times, all indicate specifically three days.

13. pardon you Literally, "lift up your head," that is, you will regain your dignity and honor.

14. this place The word translated here as "place" (*bayit*) means "house." Here it is short for *beit ha-sohar,* "prison," or "the house of my master" (v. 7, 41:10). The professional diviner and dream interpreter expected to be paid for his services. Joseph, therefore, feels free to request a personal favor instead.

15. kidnapped Joseph is referring to the events in 37:28,36, stating in effect that it was the Midianites, not his brothers, who drew him up from the pit. He may have put it this way,

---

CHAPTER 40

8. When Joseph lived in the Land, he dreamed of his own future greatness. In exile, he would only interpret the dreams of others (Soloveitchik).

Hebrews; nor have I done anything here that they should have put me in the dungeon."

16When the chief baker saw how favorably he had interpreted, he said to Joseph, "In my dream, similarly, there were three openwork baskets on my head. 17In the uppermost basket were all kinds of food for Pharaoh that a baker prepares; and the birds were eating it out of the basket above my head." 18Joseph answered, "This is its interpretation: The three baskets are three days. 19In three days Pharaoh will lift off your head and impale you upon a pole; and the birds will pick off your flesh."

20On the third day—his birthday—Pharaoh made a banquet for all his officials, and he singled out his chief cupbearer and his chief

הָעִבְרִ֑ים וְגַם־פֹּה֙ לֹא־עָשִׂ֣יתִי מְא֔וּמָה כִּֽי־
שָׂמ֥וּ אֹתִ֖י בַּבּֽוֹר׃
16 וַיַּ֥רְא שַׂר־הָאֹפִ֖ים כִּ֣י ט֣וֹב פָּתָ֑ר וַיֹּ֙אמֶר֙
אֶל־יוֹסֵ֔ף אַף־אֲנִי֙ בַּחֲלוֹמִ֔י וְהִנֵּ֗ה שְׁלֹשָׁ֛ה
סַלֵּ֥י חֹרִ֖י עַל־רֹאשִֽׁי׃ 17 וּבַסַּ֣ל הָֽעֶלְי֔וֹן
מִכֹּ֛ל מַאֲכַ֥ל פַּרְעֹ֖ה מַעֲשֵׂ֣ה אֹפֶ֑ה וְהָע֗וֹף
אֹכֵ֥ל אֹתָ֛ם מִן־הַסַּ֖ל מֵעַ֥ל רֹאשִֽׁי׃ 18 וַיַּ֤עַן
יוֹסֵף֙ וַיֹּ֔אמֶר זֶ֖ה פִּתְרֹנ֑וֹ שְׁלֹ֙שֶׁת֙ הַסַּלִּ֔ים
שְׁלֹ֥שֶׁת יָמִ֖ים הֵֽם׃ 19 בְּע֣וֹד ׀ שְׁלֹ֣שֶׁת
יָמִ֗ים יִשָּׂ֤א פַרְעֹה֙ אֶת־רֹֽאשְׁךָ֙ מֵֽעָלֶ֔יךָ
וְתָלָ֥ה אוֹתְךָ֖ עַל־עֵ֑ץ וְאָכַ֥ל הָע֛וֹף אֶת־
בְּשָׂרְךָ֖ מֵעָלֶֽיךָ׃
מפטיר 20 וַיְהִ֣י ׀ בַּיּ֣וֹם הַשְּׁלִישִׁ֗י י֚וֹם הֻלֶּ֣דֶת אֶת־
פַּרְעֹ֔ה וַיַּ֥עַשׂ מִשְׁתֶּ֖ה לְכָל־עֲבָדָ֑יו וַיִּשָּׂ֞א
אֶת־רֹ֣אשׁ ׀ שַׂ֣ר הַמַּשְׁקִ֗ים וְאֶת־רֹ֖אשׁ שַׂ֥ר

though, because he was ashamed to tell others that his own brothers had sold him into slavery.

land of the Hebrews That is, the land in which the Hebrews sojourn, either Canaan or the Hebron area in which they were concentrated and were buried.

nor have I done anything Joseph assures the cupbearer that he would be intervening on behalf of an innocent man.

dungeon The word *bor* means "pit," another term for "prison," deriving from the subterranean nature of the place of detention (see 38:24).

THE BAKER'S DREAM (vv. 16–19)

16. openwork The Hebrew term for this (*ḥori*) has been explained as "a hole" or "white." Here it describes either the baskets—"perforated," "wickerwork"—or their contents, "white bread."

on my head Repeated in verse 17 and of special significance for the interpretation.

17. uppermost basket The contents of only this basket are described because it was the one accessible to the birds.

all kinds The dream reflects Egyptian foods. No less than 57 varieties of bread and 38 different types of cake are known from hieroglyphic texts.

birds The baker has neither the strength nor the presence of mind to drive them away—an ominous detail.

18. This is its interpretation Joseph notes that, unlike the cupbearer, the baker in his dream does not prepare the delicacies himself; nor does he personally serve Pharaoh. In fact, the food does not even reach Pharaoh, for it is eaten by the birds.

19. will lift off your head The idiom "to raise the head" (נשא ראש) has the meaning of "call to account" or "bring to justice."

impale you Impaling, not hanging, was a widely used mode of execution in the ancient Near East.

pick off your flesh The ancient Egyptians paid special attention to the preservation of the body after death. Hence, the punishment foretold here is particularly loathsome.

FULFILLMENT AND DISAPPOINTMENT (vv. 20–23)

20. singled out Literally, "lifted the head." See Comments to 40:13,19.

---

16. The baker waited until he heard Joseph give the chief cupbearer a favorable interpretation and then related (or invented) a similar dream.

baker from among his officials. [21]He restored the chief cupbearer to his cupbearing, and he placed the cup in Pharaoh's hand; [22]but the chief baker he impaled—just as Joseph had interpreted to them.

[23]Yet the chief cupbearer did not think of Joseph; he forgot him.

הָאֹפִ֖ים בְּת֥וֹךְ עֲבָדָֽיו׃ 21 וַיָּ֛שֶׁב אֶת־שַׂ֥ר
הַמַּשְׁקִ֖ים עַל־מַשְׁקֵ֑הוּ וַיִּתֵּ֥ן הַכּ֖וֹס עַל־כַּ֥ף
פַּרְעֹֽה׃ 22 וְאֵ֛ת שַׂ֥ר הָאֹפִ֖ים תָּלָ֑ה כַּאֲשֶׁ֥ר
פָּתַ֛ר לָהֶ֖ם יוֹסֵֽף׃
23 וְלֹֽא־זָכַ֧ר שַֽׂר־הַמַּשְׁקִ֛ים אֶת־יוֹסֵ֖ף
וַיִּשְׁכָּחֵֽהוּ׃ פ

22. just as Joseph had interpreted The narration uses the very words of Joseph to indicate the precision with which his predictions were fulfilled.

23. did not think of Joseph; he forgot him The negative–positive wording is idiomatic and simply means "he completely forgot him."

23. The chief cupbearer finds himself so busy dealing with important and demanding people that he forgets his anonymous prisonmate until the circumstances of the next chapter lead him to remember. Perhaps because the chief cupbearer believed that he was innocent and deserved to be released, he minimized his obligation to Joseph.

הפטרת וישב

HAFTARAH FOR VA-YEISHEV

AMOS 2:6–3:8

This *haftarah* elaborates on the wrongs of Israel during the reign of King Jeroboam II (784–748 B.C.E.) and calls the people to account for their deeds. The prophet Amos thunders against the transgressions of Israel, denouncing their economic greed and their desecrations. The nation will pay the penalty.

The *haftarah* opens with a strong indictment of the northern kingdom of Israel for its transgressions. The passages that precede the *haftarah* indict six surrounding nations (Amos 1:3–2:3) as well as the southern kingdom of Judah (2:4–5). In the case of the nations and Judah, God will send a devouring fire against transgressors. The indictment against the northern kingdom of Israel emphasizes that punishment on the day of doom is inescapable (2:14–16), with no mention of fire. Also distinctive is the fact that the indictment against foreigners is for breach of international commitments, not for transgressions of divine law—as is the case with Judah and Israel.

The opening list of Israel's crimes focuses on their unethical nature, particularly their expression of corruption and greed. Hence the references to matters such as reclining (at altars) on garments taken in pledge, and drinking (in the temple of the Lord) wine bought with money from imposed fines do not describe religious transgressions per se. There is nothing inherently wrong with lying on garments or drinking wine in the environs of a shrine (presumably during pilgrimages and family sacrifices). It is rather the people's utter disregard of how they attained these objects that raises the prophet's ire. Amos is against oppression, first and foremost; but he is also against all types of blind formalism, in the realms of civil law and cultic behavior.

God's arraignment of the nation's faithlessness is juxtaposed to acts of divine beneficence in the wilderness (Amos 2:9–10). Later prophets, like Jeremiah, also refer to divine guidance and favor in the past as a counterpoint to the nation's failure to reciprocate with loyalty (cf. Jer. 2:4–8, 9–12). Amos specifically refers to the Exodus (in 3:1) as a prelude to a demand of accountability: "You alone have I singled out (*yadati*) / Of all the families of the earth— / That is why I will call you to account / For all your iniquities" (3:2). The implications of the verb *yadati* suggest that Israel's singular status goes beyond the deliverance from Egypt. The verb *yadati* means literally "I have known." It was used as a technical term for recognition of partners in ancient Near Eastern treaties. This suggests that God alludes here to the covenantal chosenness of Israel. It was because of this relationship, then, not only because of the Exodus, that the people are held liable for their iniquities.

The rhetorical touch is deft. The image of the lion's roar is found at the beginning of Amos as well as at the beginning of this rhetorical chain (3:4). As his opening word to the people, breaking the silence of their complacency, Amos proclaimed that "the LORD roars from Zion" and that "the pastures of the shepherds shall languish" (1:2).

RELATION OF THE *HAFTARAH* TO THE *PARASHAH*

Amos mentions the crime of both "father and son" going "to the same girl" (2:6–7). Readers of the *parashah* will call to mind Judah, who had intercourse with his son's wife Tamar (Gen. 38).

Verbal congruity also links the sale of Joseph by his brothers in the *parashah* with Amos's condemnation of unjust practices in the *haftarah*. In the former, the sons of Jacob "sold (*va-yimk'ru*) Joseph for twenty pieces of silver (*kesef*) to the Ishmaelites" (Gen. 37:28). According to the latter, the unjust "have sold [*mikhram*] for silver [*ba-kesef*] / Those whose cause was just [*tzaddik*, an

innocent person], / And the needy for a pair of sandals" (Amos 2:6). These similarities suggest that Amos not only rebuked his contemporaries for their immoral practices but also alluded to the grave sin of their ancestors in patriarchal times.

Rabbinic interpretations of the sale of Joseph led to a *midrash* known as *Eilleh Ezk'rah* (These I Recall). In its view, 10 sages whom the Roman occupation put to death were an atonement for the long-ago crime of the 10 brothers who sold Joseph into slavery. A poetic version of this *midrash* is included in the *Musaf* service of *Yom Kippur.* According to that text, the Roman governor tells the scholars about their ancestors "who sold their brother . . . for a pair of sandals" and condemns them to death as vicarious punishment, complying with Exod. 21:16 ("He who kidnaps a man . . . shall be put to death"). The divine words in Amos, declaring that the punishment for selling a *tzaddik* would not be revoked, may have contributed to the notion that the ancient crime of the brothers needed atonement. According to one midrashic tradition, although the penalty was paid by the 10 martyrs of old, the sin is requited "in every generation" and "is still pending."

2 6Thus said the LORD:
For three transgressions of Israel,
For four, I will not revoke it:
Because they have sold for silver
Those whose cause was just,
And the needy for a pair of sandals.
7[Ah,] you who trample the heads of the
poor
Into the dust of the ground,
And make the humble walk a twisted course!
Father and son go to the same girl,
And thereby profane My holy name.
8They recline by every altar
On garments taken in pledge,

ב 6 כֹּה אָמַר יְהוָה
עַל־שְׁלֹשָׁה פִּשְׁעֵי יִשְׂרָאֵל
וְעַל־אַרְבָּעָה לֹא אֲשִׁיבֶנּוּ
עַל־מִכְרָם בַּכֶּסֶף
צַדִּיק
וְאֶבְיוֹן בַּעֲבוּר נַעֲלָיִם׃
7 הַשֹּׁאֲפִים עַל־עֲפַר־אֶרֶץ
בְּרֹאשׁ דַּלִּים
וְדֶרֶךְ עֲנָוִים יַטּוּ
וְאִישׁ וְאָבִיו יֵלְכוּ אֶל־הַנַּעֲרָה
לְמַעַן חַלֵּל אֶת־שֵׁם קָדְשִׁי׃
8 וְעַל־בְּגָדִים חֲבֻלִים
יַטּוּ אֵצֶל כָּל־מִזְבֵּחַ

Amos 2:6–7. For three transgressions . . . For four The graded sequence in these two verses constitutes a rhetorical pattern that is preceded by seven other examples in Amos 1:3–2:5. This structuring device, with a pattern of three elements climaxed by a fourth element also appears in the oracles of Balaam (Num. 23–24), the temptations of Samson (Judg. 16:6–20), and the disasters of Job (Job 1:14–19).

sold for silver Either the bribery of judges (Ibn Ezra) or the sale of persons into debt bondage on false charges.

And the needy for a pair of sandals This clause is linked to the preceding clause stylistically. Once more the charge seems to be some type of corruption.

And make the humble walk a twisted course Rashi understands the phrase to mean that the weak turn from their path to a twisted one out of fear.

profane My holy name Hebrew: *ḥallel et shem kodshi.* In the later speeches of Ezekiel (20:39, 36:20–22) and in the Holiness Code (Lev. 17–26; see 20:3, 22:2,32), this expression refers to cultic offenses that desecrate God's name; whereas in Amos, the expression appears in the context of moral perversions. In classical rabbinic sources, the desecration of God's name (*ḥillul ha-shem*) has a larger sense—the result of disgracing the Jewish religion through acts of immorality and falsehood.

8. garments taken in pledge This prohibi-

And drink in the House of their God
Wine bought with fines they imposed.
9Yet I
Destroyed the Amorite before them,
Whose stature was like the cedar's
And who was stout as the oak,
Destroying his boughs above
And his trunk below!
10And I
Brought you up from the land of Egypt
And led you through the wilderness forty years,
To possess the land of the Amorite!
11And I raised up prophets from among your sons
And nazirites from among your young men.
Is that not so, O people of Israel?
—says the LORD.
12But you made the nazirites drink wine
And ordered the prophets not to prophesy.
13Ah, I will slow your movements
As a wagon is slowed
When it is full of cut grain.
14Flight shall fail the swift,
The strong shall find no strength,
And the warrior shall not save his life.
15The bowman shall not hold his ground,
And the fleet-footed shall not escape,
Nor the horseman save his life.
16Even the most stouthearted warrior

וְיֵין עֲנוּשִׁים
יִשְׁתּוּ בֵּית אֱלֹהֵיהֶם׃
9 וְאָנֹכִי
הִשְׁמַדְתִּי אֶת־הָאֱמֹרִי מִפְּנֵיהֶם
אֲשֶׁר כְּגֹבַהּ אֲרָזִים גָּבְהוֹ
וְחָסֹן הוּא כָּאַלּוֹנִים
וָאַשְׁמִיד פִּרְיוֹ מִמַּעַל
וְשָׁרָשָׁיו מִתָּחַת׃
10 וְאָנֹכִי
הֶעֱלֵיתִי אֶתְכֶם מֵאֶרֶץ מִצְרָיִם
וָאוֹלֵךְ אֶתְכֶם בַּמִּדְבָּר אַרְבָּעִים שָׁנָה
לָרֶשֶׁת אֶת־אֶרֶץ הָאֱמֹרִי׃
11 וָאָקִים מִבְּנֵיכֶם לִנְבִיאִים
וּמִבַּחוּרֵיכֶם לִנְזִרִים
הַאַף אֵין־זֹאת בְּנֵי יִשְׂרָאֵל
נְאֻם־יְהוָה׃
12 וַתַּשְׁקוּ אֶת־הַנְּזִרִים יָיִן
וְעַל־הַנְּבִיאִים צִוִּיתֶם לֵאמֹר לֹא
תִּנָּבְאוּ׃
13 הִנֵּה אָנֹכִי מֵעִיק תַּחְתֵּיכֶם
כַּאֲשֶׁר תָּעִיק הָעֲגָלָה
הַמְלֵאָה לָהּ עָמִיר׃
14 וְאָבַד מָנוֹס מִקָּל
וְחָזָק לֹא־יְאַמֵּץ כֹּחוֹ
וְגִבּוֹר לֹא־יְמַלֵּט נַפְשׁוֹ׃
15 וְתֹפֵשׂ הַקֶּשֶׁת לֹא יַעֲמֹד
וְקַל בְּרַגְלָיו לֹא יְמַלֵּט
וְרֹכֵב הַסּוּס לֹא יְמַלֵּט נַפְשׁוֹ׃
16 וְאַמִּיץ לִבּוֹ בַּגִּבּוֹרִים

tion is stated in the Torah (Exod. 22:25–26; Deut. 24:17). In the words of the prophet, however, these cases and others suggest that Amos objects to something more than an object taken as security for a loan. Rather, the charge is against the confiscation of persons (Job 24:9) or goods (Prov. 20:16) taken when a debtor defaults on a loan.

9–11. Divine beneficence is stated repeatedly in the first person, with the pronoun "I" (*anokhi*) dramatically emphasized in verses 9 and 10. God's guidance in history contrasts with Israelite faithlessness. In verse 11, the prophets symbolize obedience to the divine will as addressed to them, and the nazirites symbolize the voluntary assumption of an exceptional divine discipline (including abstinence from wine, see Num. 6:3–4).

Shall run away unarmed that day
—declares the LORD.

3 Hear this word, O people of Israel,
That the LORD has spoken concerning you,
Concerning the whole family that I brought up from the land of Egypt:
2You alone have I singled out
Of all the families of the earth—
That is why I will call you to account
For all your iniquities.

3Can two walk together
Without having met?
4Does a lion roar in the forest
When he has no prey?
Does a great beast let out a cry from its den
Without having made a capture?
5Does a bird drop on the ground—in a trap—
With no snare there?
Does a trap spring up from the ground
Unless it has caught something?
6When a ram's horn is sounded in a town,
Do the people not take alarm?
Can misfortune come to a town
If the LORD has not caused it?
7Indeed, my Lord GOD does nothing
Without having revealed His purpose
To His servants the prophets.
8A lion has roared,
Who can but fear?
My Lord GOD has spoken,
Who can but prophesy?

עָרוֹם יָנוּס בַּיּוֹם־הַהוּא
נְאֻם־יְהוָה׃ פ

ג שִׁמְעוּ אֶת־הַדָּבָר הַזֶּה
אֲשֶׁר דִּבֶּר יְהוָה עֲלֵיכֶם בְּנֵי יִשְׂרָאֵל
עַל כָּל־הַמִּשְׁפָּחָה אֲשֶׁר הֶעֱלֵיתִי
מֵאֶרֶץ מִצְרַיִם לֵאמֹר׃
2 רַק אֶתְכֶם יָדַעְתִּי
מִכֹּל מִשְׁפְּחוֹת הָאֲדָמָה
עַל־כֵּן אֶפְקֹד עֲלֵיכֶם
אֵת כָּל־עֲוֹנֹתֵיכֶם׃

3 הֲיֵלְכוּ שְׁנַיִם יַחְדָּו
בִּלְתִּי אִם־נוֹעָדוּ׃
4 הֲיִשְׁאַג אַרְיֵה בַּיַּעַר
וְטֶרֶף אֵין לוֹ
הֲיִתֵּן כְּפִיר קוֹלוֹ מִמְּעֹנָתוֹ
בִּלְתִּי אִם־לָכָד׃
5 הֲתִפֹּל צִפּוֹר עַל־פַּח הָאָרֶץ
וּמוֹקֵשׁ אֵין לָהּ
הֲיַעֲלֶה־פַּח מִן־הָאֲדָמָה
וְלָכוֹד לֹא יִלְכּוֹד׃
6 אִם־יִתָּקַע שׁוֹפָר בְּעִיר
וְעָם לֹא יֶחֱרָדוּ
אִם־תִּהְיֶה רָעָה בְּעִיר
וַיהוָה לֹא עָשָׂה׃
7 כִּי לֹא יַעֲשֶׂה אֲדֹנָי יְהוִה דָּבָר
כִּי אִם־גָּלָה סוֹדוֹ
אֶל־עֲבָדָיו הַנְּבִיאִים׃
8 אַרְיֵה שָׁאָג
מִי לֹא יִירָא
אֲדֹנָי יְהוִה דִּבֶּר
מִי לֹא יִנָּבֵא׃

Amos 3:3–8. This unit legitimizes Amos's prophetic word. He will speak because he must. His final words, "Who can but prophesy?" (*mi lo yinnavei*), contrast sharply with the earlier charge that the people "ordered earlier prophets not to prophesy" (*lo tinnav'u*). The unit thus also functions to distinguish Amos from earlier prophets. He will not be silenced.

MI-KETZ

41 After two years' time, Pharaoh
dreamed that he was standing by the Nile,
2when out of the Nile there came up seven
cows, handsome and sturdy, and they grazed
in the reed grass. 3But presently, seven other
cows came up from the Nile close behind them,
ugly and gaunt, and stood beside the cows on
the bank of the Nile; 4and the ugly gaunt cows
ate up the seven handsome sturdy cows. And
Pharaoh awoke.

5He fell asleep and dreamed a second time:
Seven ears of grain, solid and healthy, grew on a

מקץ

מא וַיְהִי מִקֵּץ שְׁנָתַיִם יָמִים
וּפַרְעֹה חֹלֵם וְהִנֵּה עֹמֵד עַל־הַיְאֹר׃
2וְהִנֵּה מִן־הַיְאֹר עֹלֹת שֶׁבַע פָּרוֹת יְפוֹת
מַרְאֶה וּבְרִיאֹת בָּשָׂר וַתִּרְעֶינָה בָּאָחוּ׃
3וְהִנֵּה שֶׁבַע פָּרוֹת אֲחֵרוֹת עֹלוֹת
אַחֲרֵיהֶן מִן־הַיְאֹר רָעוֹת מַרְאֶה וְדַקּוֹת
בָּשָׂר וַתַּעֲמֹדְנָה אֵצֶל הַפָּרוֹת עַל־שְׂפַת
הַיְאֹר׃ 4וַתֹּאכַלְנָה הַפָּרוֹת רָעוֹת
הַמַּרְאֶה וְדַקֹּת הַבָּשָׂר אֵת שֶׁבַע הַפָּרוֹת
יְפֹת הַמַּרְאֶה וְהַבְּרִיאֹת וַיִּיקַץ פַּרְעֹה׃
5וַיִּישָׁן וַיַּחֲלֹם שֵׁנִית וְהִנֵּה ׀ שֶׁבַע שִׁבֳּלִים

JOSEPH'S LIBERATION AND RISE TO POWER (41:1–56)

Dreams, the cause of Joseph's misfortunes, become the means of his rise to power.

PHARAOH'S DREAMS (vv. 1–8)

1. After two years' time Literally, "at the end of two years of days." Two complete years have elapsed since the release of the cupbearer.

the Nile A fateful setting for Pharaoh's dream. The river was the lifeline of Egypt, the fountainhead of its entire economy.

2. seven cows Cows were abundant in Egypt and important to the economy. The motif of seven cows is found in Egyptian paintings and texts.

3. close behind them That is, in time.

5. on a single stalk A clear symbol of abundance.

CHAPTER 41

This *parashah* is almost always read during the week of *Ḥanukkah*. Although that is only a coincidence of the calendar, we can find thematic connections. Just as *Ḥanukkah* celebrates the victory of the weak over the powerful, the *parashah* begins with Pharaoh's dream of the lean cows conquering the well-fed ones. As the *parashah* begins with Joseph in prison and ends with Joseph as ruler, the story of *Ḥanukkah* begins with Israel oppressed and ends with Israel triumphant and independent.

1. standing by the Nile The literal meaning is "over the Nile." This prompted the Rabbinic comment that Jews see themselves as subservient to God and dependent on God, whereas idolaters see themselves as superior to their gods. (The Nile was a god to the Egyptians, source of life and food.) Judaism teaches us how to serve God. Pagan religions teach their followers how to use and manipulate their gods (Gen. R. 89:4).

4. This must be every tyrant's nightmare, that one day the weak will rise up and overthrow the powerful.

5ff. One of the lessons of the Joseph story, reinforced by its being read as autumn gives way to winter, is that life is cyclical. Good years are followed by lean years, adversity is followed by success, rejection yields to connection, winter gives way to spring and summer, only to return again. "What can be learned from this *parashah* to prepare ourselves in good days, days in which holiness is revealed, to set the light in our hearts, to be there in times when holiness seems far off?" The author of *S'fat Emet* answers his own question: We must store up resources of faith, even as the Egyptians stored grain, to nourish us spiritually when events turn against us.

single stalk. ⁶But close behind them sprouted seven ears, thin and scorched by the east wind. ⁷And the thin ears swallowed up the seven solid and full ears. Then Pharaoh awoke: it was a dream!

⁸Next morning, his spirit was agitated, and he sent for all the magicians of Egypt, and all its wise men; and Pharaoh told them his dreams, but none could interpret them for Pharaoh.

⁹The chief cupbearer then spoke up and said to Pharaoh, "I must make mention today of my offenses. ¹⁰Once Pharaoh was angry with his servants, and placed me in custody in the house of the chief steward, together with the chief baker. ¹¹We had dreams the same night, he and I, each of us a dream with a meaning of its own. ¹²A Hebrew youth was there with us, a servant of the chief steward; and when we told him our dreams, he interpreted them for us, telling each of the meaning of his dream. ¹³And as he interpreted for us, so it came to pass: I was restored to my post, and the other was impaled."

עֹלֹות בְּקָנֶ֖ה אֶחָ֑ד בְּרִיא֖וֹת וְטֹבֽוֹת: ⁶וְהִנֵּ֞ה שֶׁ֤בַע שִׁבֳּלִים֙ דַּקּ֣וֹת וּשְׁדוּפֹ֣ת קָדִ֔ים צֹמְח֖וֹת אַחֲרֵיהֶֽן: ⁷וַתִּבְלַ֙עְנָה֙ הַשִּׁבֳּלִ֣ים הַדַּקּ֔וֹת אֵ֚ת שֶׁ֣בַע הַֽשִּׁבֳּלִ֔ים הַבְּרִיא֖וֹת וְהַמְּלֵא֑וֹת וַיִּיקַ֥ץ פַּרְעֹ֖ה וְהִנֵּ֥ה חֲלֽוֹם: ⁸וַיְהִ֤י בַבֹּ֙קֶר֙ וַתִּפָּ֣עֶם רוּח֔וֹ וַיִּשְׁלַ֗ח וַיִּקְרָ֛א אֶת־כָּל־חַרְטֻמֵּ֥י מִצְרַ֖יִם וְאֶת־כָּל־חֲכָמֶ֑יהָ וַיְסַפֵּ֨ר פַּרְעֹ֤ה לָהֶם֙ אֶת־חֲלֹמ֔וֹ וְאֵין־פּוֹתֵ֥ר אוֹתָ֖ם לְפַרְעֹֽה: ⁹וַיְדַבֵּר֙ שַׂ֣ר הַמַּשְׁקִ֔ים אֶת־פַּרְעֹ֖ה לֵאמֹ֑ר אֶת־חֲטָאַ֕י אֲנִ֖י מַזְכִּ֥יר הַיּֽוֹם: ¹⁰פַּרְעֹ֖ה קָצַ֣ף עַל־עֲבָדָ֑יו וַיִּתֵּ֨ן אֹתִ֜י בְּמִשְׁמַ֗ר בֵּ֚ית שַׂ֣ר הַטַּבָּחִ֔ים אֹתִ֕י וְאֵ֖ת שַׂ֥ר הָאֹפִֽים: ¹¹וַנַּֽחַלְמָ֥ה חֲל֛וֹם בְּלַ֥יְלָה אֶחָ֖ד אֲנִ֣י וָה֑וּא אִ֛ישׁ כְּפִתְר֥וֹן חֲלֹמ֖וֹ חָלָֽמְנוּ: ¹²וְשָׁ֨ם אִתָּ֜נוּ נַ֣עַר עִבְרִ֗י עֶ֚בֶד לְשַׂ֣ר הַטַּבָּחִ֔ים וַנְּ֨סַפֶּר־ל֔וֹ וַיִּפְתָּר־לָ֖נוּ אֶת־חֲלֹמֹתֵ֑ינוּ אִ֥ישׁ כַּחֲלֹמ֖וֹ פָּתָֽר: ¹³וַיְהִ֛י כַּאֲשֶׁ֥ר פָּֽתַר־לָ֖נוּ כֵּ֣ן הָיָ֑ה אֹתִ֛י הֵשִׁ֥יב עַל־כַּנִּ֖י וְאֹת֥וֹ תָלָֽה:

---

6. scorched by the east wind This is the sirocco that blows in from the desert.

7. it was a dream This was much to Pharaoh's surprise, for it all seemed so vivid.

8. his spirit was agitated Apparently, Pharaoh spent a sleepless night after his dreams, anxiously awaiting the dawn.

magicians Magic was a feature of Egyptian life. Although Israel shared with its pagan neighbors a belief in the reality of dreams as a medium of divine communication, it never developed a class of magicians or dream interpreters, as Egypt and Mesopotamia did.

wise men This is a translation of *ḥakhamim*, the first use of the stem חכם in the Bible. Here the term refers to those who possessed specialized knowledge and skill in the magic arts.

none could interpret them for Pharaoh It is inconceivable that the professional dream interpreters were unable to provide any interpretations. Their interpretations, however, did not satisfy the king in a manner that he found convincing.

THE CUPBEARER REMEMBERS JOSEPH (vv. 9–13)

9. I must make mention The stem of the word for "making mention" (*mazkir*) is used by Joseph in his plea in 40:14 and by the narrator in reporting the ingratitude of the cupbearer in 40:23. The use of the same verbal root in both incidents is intended to draw our attention to the relationship between the two.

of my offenses Against Pharaoh and against Joseph.

12. A Hebrew youth The cupbearer stops short of recommending that Joseph, a servant, be brought to Pharaoh.

---

12. The chief cupbearer tries to justify his forgetfulness by emphasizing Joseph's unworthiness, describing him as a youth, a foreigner, and a servant.

14Thereupon Pharaoh sent for Joseph, and he was rushed from the dungeon. He had his hair cut and changed his clothes, and he appeared before Pharaoh. 15And Pharaoh said to Joseph, "I have had a dream, but no one can interpret it. Now I have heard it said of you that for you to hear a dream is to tell its meaning." 16Joseph answered Pharaoh, saying, "Not I! God will see to Pharaoh's welfare."

17Then Pharaoh said to Joseph, "In my dream, I was standing on the bank of the Nile, 18when out of the Nile came up seven sturdy and well-formed cows and grazed in the reed grass. 19Presently there followed them seven other cows, scrawny, ill-formed, and emaciated—never had I seen their likes for ugliness in all the land of Egypt! 20And the seven lean and ugly cows ate up the first seven cows, the sturdy ones; 21but when they had consumed them, one could not tell that they had consumed them, for they looked just as bad as before. And I awoke. 22In my other dream, I

14 וַיִּשְׁלַ֤ח פַּרְעֹה֙ וַיִּקְרָ֣א אֶת־יוֹסֵ֔ף וַיְרִיצֻ֖הוּ
מִן־הַבּ֑וֹר וַיְגַלַּח֙ וַיְחַלֵּ֣ף שִׂמְלֹתָ֔יו וַיָּבֹ֖א אֶל־
שני פַּרְעֹֽה׃ 15 וַיֹּ֤אמֶר פַּרְעֹה֙ אֶל־יוֹסֵ֔ף חֲל֣וֹם
חָלַ֔מְתִּי וּפֹתֵ֖ר אֵ֣ין אֹת֑וֹ וַאֲנִ֗י שָׁמַ֤עְתִּי
עָלֶ֙יךָ֙ לֵאמֹ֔ר תִּשְׁמַ֥ע חֲל֖וֹם לִפְתֹּ֥ר אֹתֽוֹ׃
16 וַיַּ֨עַן יוֹסֵ֧ף אֶת־פַּרְעֹ֛ה לֵאמֹ֖ר בִּלְעָדָ֑י
אֱלֹהִ֕ים יַעֲנֶ֖ה אֶת־שְׁל֥וֹם פַּרְעֹֽה׃
17 וַיְדַבֵּ֥ר פַּרְעֹ֖ה אֶל־יוֹסֵ֑ף בַּחֲלֹמִ֕י הִנְנִ֥י
עֹמֵ֖ד עַל־שְׂפַ֥ת הַיְאֹֽר׃ 18 וְהִנֵּ֣ה מִן־הַיְאֹ֗ר
עֹלֹת֙ שֶׁ֣בַע פָּר֔וֹת בְּרִיא֥וֹת בָּשָׂ֖ר וִיפֹ֣ת
תֹּ֑אַר וַתִּרְעֶ֖ינָה בָּאָֽחוּ׃ 19 וְהִנֵּ֞ה שֶֽׁבַע־
פָּר֤וֹת אֲחֵרוֹת֙ עֹל֣וֹת אַחֲרֵיהֶ֔ן דַּלּ֨וֹת
וְרָע֥וֹת תֹּ֛אַר מְאֹ֖ד וְרַקּ֣וֹת בָּשָׂ֑ר לֹֽא־
רָאִ֧יתִי כָהֵ֛נָּה בְּכָל־אֶ֥רֶץ מִצְרַ֖יִם לָרֹֽעַ׃
20 וַתֹּאכַ֙לְנָה֙ הַפָּר֔וֹת הָֽרַקּ֖וֹת וְהָֽרָע֑וֹת
אֵ֣ת שֶׁ֧בַע הַפָּר֛וֹת הָרִֽאשֹׁנ֖וֹת הַבְּרִיאֹֽת׃
21 וַתָּבֹ֣אנָה אֶל־קִרְבֶּ֗נָה וְלֹ֤א נוֹדַע֙ כִּי־בָ֣אוּ
אֶל־קִרְבֶּ֔נָה וּמַרְאֵיהֶ֣ן רַ֔ע כַּאֲשֶׁ֖ר בַּתְּחִלָּ֑ה
וָאִיקָֽץ׃ 22 וָאֵ֖רֶא בַּחֲלֹמִ֑י וְהִנֵּ֣ה ׀ שֶׁ֣בַע

JOSEPH'S DREAM INTERPRETATION
(vv. 14–32)

14. he was rushed The verbs in this verse indicate a series of actions performed in swift succession in the atmosphere of urgency created when Pharaoh's wishes are to be satisfied.

dungeon See Comment to 40:15.

his hair cut The verb meaning "to shave" (גלח) applies to both the head and the face. Egyptian men shaved both areas.

his clothes Clothes have consistently been a key element in Joseph's misfortunes. This change of clothing marks the beginning of his liberation.

15. no one can interpret See Comment to verse 8.

for you to hear a dream Pharaoh believes that Joseph is endowed with magical power.

16. God will see Joseph is saying, in effect, "God will respond to me and grant Pharaoh's welfare." He is certain that the sudden turn of events that has brought him into the presence of Pharaoh is providential for him. And he believes that he will receive a dream interpretation from God that will satisfy Pharaoh entirely.

17. Then Pharaoh said The repetition of the dreams to Joseph contains differences from the original narration. Such variations between an initial version and a repeat of it are a recurring feature of biblical discourse.

19. never had I seen This previously unstated personal observation points to the real meaning of the dream.

21. but when This entire verse is not in Pharaoh's original narrative. Here, it directs attention to the key element (see vv. 30ff.).

22. In my other dream Significantly, the phrase (v. 5) "a second time" is omitted, as though Pharaoh himself realized that the two dreams are really one.

---

14. Joseph, who twice was stripped of his clothes and thrown into a pit, is twice (here and in v. 42) elevated in status and given new clothes to mark his new position.

saw seven ears of grain, full and healthy, growing on a single stalk; 23but right behind them
sprouted seven ears, shriveled, thin, and
scorched by the east wind. 24And the thin ears
swallowed the seven healthy ears. I have told
my magicians, but none has an explanation for
me."

25And Joseph said to Pharaoh, "Pharaoh's
dreams are one and the same: God has told
Pharaoh what He is about to do. 26The seven
healthy cows are seven years, and the seven
healthy ears are seven years; it is the same
dream. 27The seven lean and ugly cows that
followed are seven years, as are also the seven
empty ears scorched by the east wind; they are
seven years of famine. 28It is just as I have told
Pharaoh: God has revealed to Pharaoh what
He is about to do. 29Immediately ahead are
seven years of great abundance in all the land
of Egypt. 30After them will come seven years of
famine, and all the abundance in the land of
Egypt will be forgotten. As the land is ravaged
by famine, 31no trace of the abundance will be
left in the land because of the famine thereafter,
for it will be very severe. 32As for Pharaoh having had the same dream twice, it means that the
matter has been determined by God, and that
God will soon carry it out.

33"Accordingly, let Pharaoh find a man of

שִׁבֳּלִים עֹלֹת בְּקָנֶה אֶחָד מְלֵאֹת וְטֹבוֹת׃
23 וְהִנֵּה שֶׁבַע שִׁבֳּלִים צְנֻמוֹת דַּקּוֹת
שְׁדֻפוֹת קָדִים צֹמְחוֹת אַחֲרֵיהֶם׃
24 וַתִּבְלַעְןָ הַשִּׁבֳּלִים הַדַּקֹּת אֵת שֶׁבַע
הַשִּׁבֳּלִים הַטֹּבוֹת וָאֹמַר אֶל־הַחַרְטֻמִּים
וְאֵין מַגִּיד לִי׃
25 וַיֹּאמֶר יוֹסֵף אֶל־פַּרְעֹה חֲלוֹם פַּרְעֹה
אֶחָד הוּא אֵת אֲשֶׁר הָאֱלֹהִים עֹשֶׂה הִגִּיד
לְפַרְעֹה׃ 26 שֶׁבַע פָּרֹת הַטֹּבֹת שֶׁבַע שָׁנִים
הֵנָּה וְשֶׁבַע הַשִּׁבֳּלִים הַטֹּבֹת שֶׁבַע שָׁנִים
הֵנָּה חֲלוֹם אֶחָד הוּא׃ 27 וְשֶׁבַע הַפָּרוֹת
הָרַקּוֹת וְהָרָעֹת הָעֹלֹת אַחֲרֵיהֶן שֶׁבַע
שָׁנִים הֵנָּה וְשֶׁבַע הַשִּׁבֳּלִים הָרֵקוֹת
שְׁדֻפוֹת הַקָּדִים יִהְיוּ שֶׁבַע שְׁנֵי רָעָב׃
28 הוּא הַדָּבָר אֲשֶׁר דִּבַּרְתִּי אֶל־פַּרְעֹה
אֲשֶׁר הָאֱלֹהִים עֹשֶׂה הֶרְאָה אֶת־פַּרְעֹה׃
29 הִנֵּה שֶׁבַע שָׁנִים בָּאוֹת שָׂבָע גָּדוֹל
בְּכָל־אֶרֶץ מִצְרָיִם׃ 30 וְקָמוּ שֶׁבַע שְׁנֵי
רָעָב אַחֲרֵיהֶן וְנִשְׁכַּח כָּל־הַשָּׂבָע בְּאֶרֶץ
מִצְרָיִם וְכִלָּה הָרָעָב אֶת־הָאָרֶץ׃ 31 וְלֹא־
יִוָּדַע הַשָּׂבָע בָּאָרֶץ מִפְּנֵי הָרָעָב הַהוּא
אַחֲרֵי־כֵן כִּי־כָבֵד הוּא מְאֹד׃ 32 וְעַל
הִשָּׁנוֹת הַחֲלוֹם אֶל־פַּרְעֹה פַּעֲמָיִם כִּי־
נָכוֹן הַדָּבָר מֵעִם הָאֱלֹהִים וּמְמַהֵר
הָאֱלֹהִים לַעֲשֹׂתוֹ׃
33 וְעַתָּה יֵרֶא פַרְעֹה אִישׁ נָבוֹן וְחָכָם

24. none has an explanation The phrase refers to what was related in verses 8 and 15.

25. one and the same Both dreams, though separate and successive, constitute a single whole and express the identical phenomenon.

has told That is, "has disclosed."

31. no trace The reserves of food set aside for the famine will be used up completely.

32. determined It is established beyond doubt.

soon The seven-year cycle begins at once.

JOSEPH'S ADVICE (vv. 33–36)

Unsolicited by Pharaoh, Joseph offers advice on how to avert the famine.

33. Accordingly Joseph presents his advice

---

33. Joseph's interpretation strikes Pharaoh as valid because its message of impending disaster seems to fit the mood of the dream and because he not only interprets the dream but gives Pharaoh advice on how to deal with its message.

discernment and wisdom, and set him over the land of Egypt. [34]And let Pharaoh take steps to appoint overseers over the land, and organize the land of Egypt in the seven years of plenty. [35]Let all the food of these good years that are coming be gathered, and let the grain be collected under Pharaoh's authority as food to be stored in the cities. [36]Let that food be a reserve for the land for the seven years of famine which will come upon the land of Egypt, so that the land may not perish in the famine."

[37]The plan pleased Pharaoh and all his courtiers. [38]And Pharaoh said to his courtiers, "Could we find another like him, a man in whom is the spirit of God?" [39]So Pharaoh said to Joseph, "Since God has made all this known to you, there is none so discerning and wise as you. [40]You shall be in charge of my court, and by your command shall all my people be directed; only with respect to the throne shall I be superior to you." [41]Pharaoh further said to Joseph, "See, I put you in charge of all the land of Egypt." [42]And removing his signet ring from

וִישִׁיתֵהוּ עַל־אֶרֶץ מִצְרָיִם׃ 34 יַעֲשֶׂה
פַרְעֹה וְיַפְקֵד פְּקִדִים עַל־הָאָרֶץ וְחִמֵּשׁ
אֶת־אֶרֶץ מִצְרַיִם בְּשֶׁבַע שְׁנֵי הַשָּׂבָע׃
35 וְיִקְבְּצוּ אֶת־כָּל־אֹכֶל הַשָּׁנִים הַטֹּבֹת
הַבָּאֹת הָאֵלֶּה וְיִצְבְּרוּ־בָר תַּחַת יַד־
פַּרְעֹה אֹכֶל בֶּעָרִים וְשָׁמָרוּ׃ 36 וְהָיָה
הָאֹכֶל לְפִקָּדוֹן לָאָרֶץ לְשֶׁבַע שְׁנֵי הָרָעָב
אֲשֶׁר תִּהְיֶיןָ בְּאֶרֶץ מִצְרָיִם וְלֹא־תִכָּרֵת
הָאָרֶץ בָּרָעָב׃
37 וַיִּיטַב הַדָּבָר בְּעֵינֵי פַרְעֹה וּבְעֵינֵי כָּל־
עֲבָדָיו׃ 38 וַיֹּאמֶר פַּרְעֹה אֶל־עֲבָדָיו
הֲנִמְצָא כָזֶה אִישׁ אֲשֶׁר רוּחַ אֱלֹהִים בּוֹ׃
39 וַיֹּאמֶר פַּרְעֹה אֶל־יוֹסֵף אַחֲרֵי הוֹדִיעַ שלישי
אֱלֹהִים אוֹתְךָ אֶת־כָּל־זֹאת אֵין־נָבוֹן
וְחָכָם כָּמוֹךָ׃ 40 אַתָּה תִּהְיֶה עַל־בֵּיתִי
וְעַל־פִּיךָ יִשַּׁק כָּל־עַמִּי רַק הַכִּסֵּא אֶגְדַּל
מִמֶּךָּ׃ 41 וַיֹּאמֶר פַּרְעֹה אֶל־יוֹסֵף רְאֵה
נָתַתִּי אֹתְךָ עַל כָּל־אֶרֶץ מִצְרָיִם׃ 42 וַיָּסַר
פַּרְעֹה אֶת־טַבַּעְתּוֹ מֵעַל יָדוֹ וַיִּתֵּן אֹתָהּ

not as part of the dream message but as a personal suggestion.

34. let Pharaoh Not wishing to raise any suspicion that he is suggesting the creation of a new focus of power, Joseph repeatedly emphasizes "Pharaoh," thereby stressing the ubiquitous, omniscient, and omnipotent nature of the king in ancient Egypt.

35. good years Joseph sensibly suggests that grain be stockpiled during the plentiful years against the forthcoming years of famine.

JOSEPH'S APPOINTMENT AS VIZIER
(vv. 37–46)

37. The plan pleased Pharaoh Pharaoh and his courtiers are impressed by Joseph's perception that the two dreams are actually one, by his relating them to national affairs rather than to the king's personal interests, and by the social concern that he displays in his advice.

38. Could we find Pharaoh's question to his courtiers is rhetorical. He knows at once what he must do.

in whom is the spirit of God This is the first biblical mention of an individual so endowed. Possession of the "spirit of God" impels one to undertake a mission (Num. 27:18), imparts extraordinary energy and drive (Judg. 3:10, 11:29), and produces uncommon intelligence and practical wisdom.

39. discerning and wise Pharaoh repeats Joseph's own words (v. 33).

40. in charge of my court This function probably refers to the position of "overseer of the domain of the palace," one of the known Egyptian bureaucratic titles. Most likely, Joseph is given control over the king's personal estates.

41. Pharaoh further said Joseph does not utter a word in response to Pharaoh's announcement.

in charge of all the land The function reflects the Egyptian title "chief of the entire land."

42. removing Pharaoh now performs a series of ceremonial acts that confirm Joseph's position as "grand vizier of Egypt."

signet ring The transfer of the ring bearing the royal seal from the finger of Pharaoh to that of Joseph signifies the delegation of authority; it

his hand, Pharaoh put it on Joseph's hand; and he had him dressed in robes of fine linen, and put a gold chain about his neck. ⁴³He had him ride in the chariot of his second-in-command, and they cried before him, "Abrek!" Thus he placed him over all the land of Egypt.

⁴⁴Pharaoh said to Joseph, "I am Pharaoh; yet without you, no one shall lift up hand or foot in all the land of Egypt." ⁴⁵Pharaoh then gave Joseph the name Zaphenath-paneah; and he gave him for a wife Asenath daughter of Poti-phera, priest of On. Thus Joseph emerged in

עַל־יַ֣ד יוֹסֵ֑ף וַיַּלְבֵּ֨שׁ אֹתוֹ֙ בִּגְדֵי־שֵׁ֔שׁ וַיָּ֛שֶׂם רְבִ֥ד הַזָּהָ֖ב עַל־צַוָּארֽוֹ: ⁴³וַיַּרְכֵּ֣ב אֹת֗וֹ בְּמִרְכֶּ֤בֶת הַמִּשְׁנֶה֙ אֲשֶׁר־ל֔וֹ וַיִּקְרְא֥וּ לְפָנָ֖יו אַבְרֵ֑ךְ וְנָת֣וֹן אֹת֔וֹ עַ֖ל כָּל־אֶ֥רֶץ מִצְרָֽיִם: ⁴⁴וַיֹּ֧אמֶר פַּרְעֹ֛ה אֶל־יוֹסֵ֖ף אֲנִ֣י פַרְעֹ֑ה וּבִלְעָדֶ֗יךָ לֹֽא־יָרִ֨ים אִ֧ישׁ אֶת־יָד֛וֹ וְאֶת־רַגְל֖וֹ בְּכָל־אֶ֥רֶץ מִצְרָֽיִם: ⁴⁵וַיִּקְרָ֨א פַרְעֹ֥ה שֵׁם־יוֹסֵף֮ צָֽפְנַ֣ת פַּעְנֵחַ֒ וַיִּתֶּן־ל֣וֹ אֶת־אָֽסְנַ֗ת בַּת־פּ֥וֹטִי פֶ֛רַע כֹּהֵ֥ן אֹ֖ן לְאִשָּׁ֑ה וַיֵּצֵ֥א יוֹסֵ֖ף

enables the new official to validate documents in the king's name. The title "royal seal bearer" was well known in ancient Egypt.

fine linen   The term translated as "fine linen" (*shesh*) is an Egyptian loan word for cloth of exceptional quality.

a gold chain   The giving of a gold chain was one of the highest distinctions the king could bestow upon his favorites.

43. chariot   This is the first reference to a chariot in the Bible. The Hyksos invasion of Egypt in the 18th century B.C.E. introduced the chariot to that country as an instrument of warfare.

second-in-command   That is, viceroy.

they cried before him   The practice of having heralds declaim in front of the chariot rider is recorded in Esther 6:9.

Abrek!   An exclamation found nowhere else in the Bible. In Akkadian, *abarakku* is the term for a steward of the temple and the chief steward of a private or royal household.

44. I am Pharaoh   That is, I speak with the full authority of my royal office.

lift up hand or foot   A figure of speech meaning "no action shall be taken."

45. gave Joseph the name   The change of name signifies a new identity and a fresh start in life. The king probably wanted to "Egyptianize" the name Joseph.

Zaphenath-paneah   The Egyptian words mean "God speaks; he lives," or "the creator/sustainer of life." During this period in Egypt, it was not unusual for foreigners, and Semites in particular, to be welcomed by the court and to rise to positions of responsibility and power in the government.

Asenath   The Egyptian name means "she who belongs to (the goddess) Neith."

Poti-phera   See Comment to 37:36.

priest of On   This city, located seven miles northeast of modern Cairo, was the worship center of the sun god Re. It was called Beit Shemesh in Hebrew (Jer. 43:13) and Heliopolis in

---

45. Is Poti-phera identical with Potiphar, whom Joseph served in chapter 39? The Talmud thinks he is and understands his giving his daughter to Joseph in marriage as an acknowledgment that Joseph was innocent of the charge brought against him (BT Sot. 13b).

A Rabbinic legend identifies Asenath as the daughter who was born to Dinah, Jacob's daughter, after she had been violated by Shechem (Gen. 34). Subsequently, she was adopted by the childless Potiphar. Thus Joseph, like the other Patriarchs, marries a relative.

HALAKHAH L'MA·ASEH

41:45 the name   This is the first instance in Jewish tradition of having more than one name, one of them Hebrew. For purposes of religious honors (such as an *aliyah* to the Torah) and religious documents (such as for marriage and divorce), one is identified by one's Hebrew name, the son or daughter of (*ben* or *bat*) one's father's Hebrew name. In prayers for the ill, one is traditionally identified by one's mother's name. Conservative practice increasingly uses both the mother's and father's Hebrew names in all circumstances, as an expression of honoring both parents in accordance with the Decalogue (see Exod. 20:12).

עַל־אֶ֥רֶץ מִצְרָֽיִם׃ 46 וְיוֹסֵף֙ בֶּן־שְׁלֹשִׁ֣ים
שָׁנָ֔ה בְּעָמְד֕וֹ לִפְנֵ֖י פַּרְעֹ֣ה מֶֽלֶךְ־מִצְרָ֑יִם
וַיֵּצֵ֤א יוֹסֵף֙ מִלִּפְנֵ֣י פַרְעֹ֔ה וַיַּעֲבֹ֖ר בְּכָל־
אֶ֥רֶץ מִצְרָֽיִם׃
47 וַתַּ֣עַשׂ הָאָ֔רֶץ בְּשֶׁ֖בַע שְׁנֵ֣י הַשָּׂבָ֑ע
לִקְמָצִֽים׃ 48 וַיִּקְבֹּ֞ץ אֶת־כָּל־אֹ֣כֶל ׀ שֶׁ֣בַע
שָׁנִ֗ים אֲשֶׁ֤ר הָיוּ֙ בְּאֶ֣רֶץ מִצְרַ֔יִם וַיִּתֶּן־אֹ֖כֶל
בֶּעָרִ֑ים אֹ֧כֶל שְׂדֵה־הָעִ֛יר אֲשֶׁ֥ר סְבִיבֹתֶ֖יהָ
נָתַ֥ן בְּתוֹכָֽהּ׃ 49 וַיִּצְבֹּ֨ר יוֹסֵ֥ף בָּ֛ר כְּח֥וֹל הַיָּ֖ם
הַרְבֵּ֣ה מְאֹ֑ד עַ֛ד כִּי־חָדַ֥ל לִסְפֹּ֖ר כִּי־אֵ֥ין
מִסְפָּֽר׃
50 וּלְיוֹסֵ֤ף יֻלַּד֙ שְׁנֵ֣י בָנִ֔ים בְּטֶ֥רֶם תָּב֖וֹא
שְׁנַ֣ת הָרָעָ֑ב אֲשֶׁ֤ר יָֽלְדָה־לּוֹ֙ אָֽסְנַ֔ת בַּת־
פּ֥וֹטִי פֶ֖רַע כֹּהֵ֥ן אֽוֹן׃ 51 וַיִּקְרָ֥א יוֹסֵ֛ף אֶת־

charge of the land of Egypt.—46 Joseph was thirty years old when he entered the service of Pharaoh king of Egypt.—Leaving Pharaoh's presence, Joseph traveled through all the land of Egypt.

47 During the seven years of plenty, the land produced in abundance. 48 And he gathered all the grain of the seven years that the land of Egypt was enjoying, and stored the grain in the cities; he put in each city the grain of the fields around it. 49 So Joseph collected produce in very large quantity, like the sands of the sea, until he ceased to measure it, for it could not be measured.

50 Before the years of famine came, Joseph became the father of two sons, whom Asenath daughter of Poti-phera, priest of On, bore to him. 51 Joseph named the first-born Manasseh,

Greek. The high priest at On held the title "greatest of seers." Joseph thus marries into clerical nobility. Moses would later do the same.

emerged in charge of Literally, "went out over." The clause probably should be understood as short for "he left Pharaoh's presence to be in charge of the land of Egypt."

46. Joseph was thirty This note, given at the time Joseph's ordeals end, corresponds to the recording of his age as 17 when they began (37:2) and provides a framework for the narrative.

entered the service of Literally, "stood before."

Joseph traveled Joseph begins to familiarize himself with local conditions to prepare for the task of enabling the Egyptians to survive the expected famine.

THE SEVEN YEARS OF PLENTY (vv. 47–49)

47. in abundance The word translated as "in abundance" (*likmatzim*) means, literally, "by handfuls," i.e., "bumper crops."

48. he gathered all the grain From Joseph's activities it is clear that he holds the well-known Egyptian office of "overseer of the granaries of Upper and Lower Egypt," whose duties included the collection of tax payments on field produce, the storage of an adequate supply of food in years of plenty, and the distribution of food during years of famine. He was, in effect, minister of agriculture.

JOSEPH'S TWO SONS (vv. 50–52)

50. years Literally, "year." The sons were born either before the first year of the famine or before the year when its effect first became severe—i.e., toward the end of the famine's second year, when the migration of Jacob and his family took place.

51. Manasseh Joseph adapts the name,

---

50. Before the years of famine came Once the famine arrived, however, people stopped having children, so as not to have additional mouths to feed (BT Ta·an. 11a).

51. By calling his first son Manasseh, Joseph is not saying that he has forgotten the circumstances of his coming to Egypt. He is saying that he remembers them but that the memory no longer oppresses him.

HALAKHAH L'MA·ASEH

41:51 Joseph named the first-born See Comment to Gen. 29:32.

meaning, "God has made me forget completely my hardship and my parental home."
52And the second he named Ephraim, meaning, "God has made me fertile in the land of my affliction."

53The seven years of abundance that the land of Egypt enjoyed came to an end,
54and the seven years of famine set in, just as Joseph had foretold. There was famine in all lands, but throughout the land of Egypt there was bread.
55And when all the land of Egypt felt the hunger, the people cried out to Pharaoh for bread; and Pharaoh said to all the Egyptians, "Go to Joseph; whatever he tells you, you shall do."—
56Accordingly, when the famine became severe in the land of Egypt, Joseph laid open all that was within, and rationed out grain to the Egyptians. The famine, however, spread over the whole world.
57So all the world came to Joseph in Egypt to procure rations, for the famine had become severe throughout the world.

שֵׁם הַבְּכוֹר מְנַשֶּׁה כִּי־נַשַּׁנִי אֱלֹהִים אֶת־
כָּל־עֲמָלִי וְאֵת כָּל־בֵּית אָבִי׃ 52וְאֵת שֵׁם
הַשֵּׁנִי קָרָא אֶפְרָיִם כִּי־הִפְרַנִי אֱלֹהִים
בְּאֶרֶץ עָנְיִי׃

רביעי 53וַתִּכְלֶינָה שֶׁבַע שְׁנֵי הַשָּׂבָע אֲשֶׁר הָיָה
בְּאֶרֶץ מִצְרָיִם׃ 54וַתְּחִלֶּינָה שֶׁבַע שְׁנֵי
הָרָעָב לָבוֹא כַּאֲשֶׁר אָמַר יוֹסֵף וַיְהִי רָעָב
בְּכָל־הָאֲרָצוֹת וּבְכָל־אֶרֶץ מִצְרַיִם הָיָה
לָחֶם׃ 55וַתִּרְעַב כָּל־אֶרֶץ מִצְרַיִם וַיִּצְעַק
הָעָם אֶל־פַּרְעֹה לַלָּחֶם וַיֹּאמֶר פַּרְעֹה
לְכָל־מִצְרַיִם לְכוּ אֶל־יוֹסֵף אֲשֶׁר־יֹאמַר
לָכֶם תַּעֲשׂוּ׃ 56וְהָרָעָב הָיָה עַל כָּל־פְּנֵי
הָאָרֶץ וַיִּפְתַּח יוֹסֵף אֶת־כָּל־אֲשֶׁר בָּהֶם
וַיִּשְׁבֹּר לְמִצְרַיִם וַיֶּחֱזַק הָרָעָב בְּאֶרֶץ
מִצְרָיִם׃ 57וְכָל־הָאָרֶץ בָּאוּ מִצְרַיְמָה
לִשְׁבֹּר אֶל־יוֹסֵף כִּי־חָזַק הָרָעָב בְּכָל־
הָאָרֶץ׃

which means "he who causes to forget," to his own situation.

meaning Hebrew: *ki,* "because."

my hardship and my parental home This is an instance of a single idea expressed by two terms. It means, "my suffering in my parental home."

52. Ephraim The name must have meant either "fertile land," from the stem פרה, or "pastureland," from *"afar."* Either meaning would suitably describe the future territory of the tribe bearing this name, which was located in the central region of the Land of Israel and blessed with good soil and rainfall.

made me fertile The Hebrew verb *hifrani,* a wordplay on the name Ephraim, refers to the blessing of abundant descendants.

the land of my affliction That is, where I spent 13 years in captivity.

THE ONSET OF FAMINE (vv. 53–57)

The entire agricultural economy of Lower Egypt, the northern, virtually rainless area of the country, has always depended on the Nile floods caused by the river's periodic rise during three summer months. There are years when the rains in the southern Sudan are insufficient. A shortfall of only a few inches could bring famine to Egypt. This phenomenon and the motif of seven-year famines are well documented in Egyptian and other Near Eastern texts.

54. in all lands In actuality, there could not be any natural connection between the famine in Egypt and that in neighboring countries. The situation in Canaan resulted from a prolonged lack of rainfall that had nothing to do with the failure of the Nile to rise.

55. Go to Joseph This verse, which anticipates the next episode, explains why the brothers have to appear in person before Joseph (v. 57).

56. Accordingly For the sake of clarity and for continuity with verse 55, the translation inverts the order of the Hebrew clauses.

within The Hebrew word *ba-hem,* literally, "in them," has no antecedent. The ancient versions variously rendered "all the granaries," "all the granaries in which was grain," and "everything in which was grain." These either reflect a different text or are attempts to interpret the difficult Hebrew.

over the whole world Literally, "over all the face of the land."

מב וַיַּ֣רְא יַעֲקֹ֔ב כִּ֥י יֶשׁ־שֶׁ֖בֶר
בְּמִצְרָ֑יִם וַיֹּ֤אמֶר יַעֲקֹב֙ לְבָנָ֔יו לָ֖מָּה
תִּתְרָאֽוּ׃ 2 וַיֹּ֕אמֶר הִנֵּ֣ה שָׁמַ֔עְתִּי כִּ֥י יֶשׁ־
שֶׁ֖בֶר בְּמִצְרָ֑יִם רְדוּ־שָׁ֙מָּה֙ וְשִׁבְרוּ־לָ֣נוּ
מִשָּׁ֔ם וְנִחְיֶ֖ה וְלֹ֥א נָמֽוּת׃ 3 וַיֵּרְד֥וּ אֲחֵֽי־
יוֹסֵ֖ף עֲשָׂרָ֑ה לִשְׁבֹּ֥ר בָּ֖ר מִמִּצְרָֽיִם׃ 4 וְאֶת־
בִּנְיָמִין֙ אֲחִ֣י יוֹסֵ֔ף לֹא־שָׁלַ֥ח יַעֲקֹ֖ב אֶת־
אֶחָ֑יו כִּ֣י אָמַ֔ר פֶּן־יִקְרָאֶ֖נּוּ אָסֽוֹן׃ 5 וַיָּבֹ֙אוּ֙
בְּנֵ֣י יִשְׂרָאֵ֔ל לִשְׁבֹּ֖ר בְּת֣וֹךְ הַבָּאִ֑ים כִּֽי־הָיָ֥ה
הָרָעָ֖ב בְּאֶ֥רֶץ כְּנָֽעַן׃
6 וְיוֹסֵ֗ף ה֚וּא הַשַּׁלִּ֣יט עַל־הָאָ֔רֶץ ה֥וּא

42 When Jacob saw that there were food
rations to be had in Egypt, he said to his sons,
"Why do you keep looking at one another?
2 Now I hear," he went on, "that there are rations to be had in Egypt. Go down and procure rations for us there, that we may live and not
die." 3 So ten of Joseph's brothers went down to
get grain rations in Egypt; 4 for Jacob did not
send Joseph's brother Benjamin with his brothers, since he feared that he might meet
with disaster. 5 Thus the sons of Israel were
among those who came to procure rations, for the famine extended to the land of Canaan.
6 Now Joseph was the vizier of the land; it was

JOSEPH AND HIS BROTHERS—ONCE AGAIN (42:1–38)

Joseph, having reached a time in his life when he no longer wishes to be reminded of his past, suddenly finds himself once again face to face with his brothers.

THE BROTHERS' JOURNEY TO EGYPT (vv. 1–5)

1. saw More than 20 years have passed since we last observed Jacob as an inconsolable father mourning his lost son. Now we see him noticing his countrymen as they return from Egypt laden with supplies.

looking at one another Helplessly, inactive.

2. Go down and procure rations The old Patriarch once again exercises authority and initiative in a critical situation.

3. ten of Joseph's brothers Not "Joseph's 10 brothers," because there were 11 in all. The rations in Egypt must have been available on a limited per capita basis, so that the presence and services of all 10 were needed to purchase and transport sufficient supplies for their large households. Reasons of security may also have dictated the need to travel as a convoy on the journey, which lasted one week each way.

4. Joseph's brother Benjamin The description explains the special status of Benjamin, Joseph's full brother, who has replaced Joseph as his father's favorite (Gen. 44:20).

meet with disaster Benjamin's mother, Rachel—as well as his brother—had encountered misfortune during a journey.

5. among those who came They were just one among many such groups who came from neighboring countries—yet they alone attract attention.

THE FIRST ENCOUNTER WITH JOSEPH (vv. 6–17)

6. vizier This title of Joseph's, in addition to "seller of corn," explains in what capacity he interrogated and accused the brothers. A man

---

CHAPTER 42

1. The availability of food in Egypt sets in motion a series of events that will bring Joseph's family to Egypt, where they will be reunited with him. There they will prosper at first, before being reduced to slavery.

5. This is the first mention of the people Israel (*b'nei Yisra·el*) in the Bible. (The translation reads "sons of Israel," because Israel is another name for Jacob.)

6ff. The purpose of Joseph's elaborate ruse is not to torment or embarrass his brothers but to see whether they indeed had changed. Repentance (*t'shuvah*) is more than regret. It includes finding oneself in a similar situation and responding differently. Joseph needs to know whether the brothers will leave Simeon and/or

הַמַּשְׁבִּיר לְכָל־עַם הָאָרֶץ וַיָּבֹאוּ אֲחֵי
יוֹסֵף וַיִּשְׁתַּחֲווּ־לוֹ אַפַּיִם אָרְצָה׃ 7וַיַּרְא
יוֹסֵף אֶת־אֶחָיו וַיַּכִּרֵם וַיִּתְנַכֵּר אֲלֵיהֶם
וַיְדַבֵּר אִתָּם קָשׁוֹת וַיֹּאמֶר אֲלֵהֶם מֵאַיִן
בָּאתֶם וַיֹּאמְרוּ מֵאֶרֶץ כְּנַעַן לִשְׁבָּר־
אֹכֶל׃ 8וַיַּכֵּר יוֹסֵף אֶת־אֶחָיו וְהֵם לֹא
הִכִּרֻהוּ׃ 9וַיִּזְכֹּר יוֹסֵף אֵת הַחֲלֹמוֹת
אֲשֶׁר חָלַם לָהֶם וַיֹּאמֶר אֲלֵהֶם מְרַגְּלִים
אַתֶּם לִרְאוֹת אֶת־עֶרְוַת הָאָרֶץ בָּאתֶם׃
10וַיֹּאמְרוּ אֵלָיו לֹא אֲדֹנִי וַעֲבָדֶיךָ בָּאוּ
לִשְׁבָּר־אֹכֶל׃ 11כֻּלָּנוּ בְּנֵי אִישׁ־אֶחָד נָחְנוּ
כֵּנִים אֲנַחְנוּ לֹא־הָיוּ עֲבָדֶיךָ מְרַגְּלִים׃
12וַיֹּאמֶר אֲלֵהֶם לֹא כִּי־עֶרְוַת הָאָרֶץ
בָּאתֶם לִרְאוֹת׃ 13וַיֹּאמְרוּ שְׁנֵים עָשָׂר
עֲבָדֶיךָ אַחִים ׀ אֲנַחְנוּ בְּנֵי אִישׁ־אֶחָד

he who dispensed rations to all the people of
the land. And Joseph's brothers came and
bowed low to him, with their faces to the
ground. 7When Joseph saw his brothers, he
recognized them; but he acted like a stranger
toward them and spoke harshly to them. He
asked them, "Where do you come from?" And
they said, "From the land of Canaan, to procure food." 8For though Joseph recognized his
brothers, they did not recognize him. 9Recal-
ling the dreams that he had dreamed about
them, Joseph said to them, "You are spies,
you have come to see the land in its nakedness."
10But they said to him, "No, my lord! Truly,
your servants have come to procure food.
11We are all of us sons of the same man; we
are honest men; your servants have never been
spies!" 12And he said to them, "No, you have
come to see the land in its nakedness!" 13And
they replied, "We your servants were twelve
brothers, sons of a certain man in the land of

who was solely the dispenser of rations would not normally be concerned with matters of state security.

bowed low Joseph's boyhood dreams (Gen. 37:7,9ff.) are being fulfilled.

7. he acted like a stranger toward them The Hebrew may also be translated, "he hid his identity from them." Joseph schemes against the former schemers.

to procure food To each question the brothers respond with unsolicited information.

8. Joseph recognized The repetition of this fact is simply due to the stylistic need for a counterbalance to the new fact: "they did not recognize him."

they did not recognize him It has been more than two decades since they last saw Joseph. He has developed into mature manhood. In addition, his language, his dress, his position, and his name have become Egyptianized.

9. Recalling the dreams The sight of his brothers prostrating themselves before him suddenly reminds Joseph of those long-forgotten dreams, and he realizes that they actually had presaged his future. At the same time, recalling how deeply his brothers hated him, he feels that he must find out conclusively whether or not they regret their actions.

You are spies They were foreigners who had entered Egypt from the northeast, the land's most vulnerable border. Incursions by Asians coming from Canaan were fairly common. The discovery of spies might herald an imminent attack.

the land in its nakedness This figure of speech refers to uncovering any hidden weaknesses in Egypt's fortifications.

11. We are all of us We are one family unit and would not jeopardize all of our lives by collectively engaging in such a dangerous occupation.

Benjamin to languish in prison, as they once had abandoned him.

11. we are all of us sons of the same man They spoke the truth to their brother Joseph without realizing it: "You and we have the same father" (Gen. R. 91:7).

בְּאֶרֶץ כְּנַעַן וְהִנֵּה הַקָּטֹן אֶת־אָבִינוּ הַיּוֹם
וְהָאֶחָד אֵינֶנּוּ׃ 14 וַיֹּאמֶר אֲלֵהֶם יוֹסֵף הוּא
אֲשֶׁר דִּבַּרְתִּי אֲלֵכֶם לֵאמֹר מְרַגְּלִים
אַתֶּם׃ 15 בְּזֹאת תִּבָּחֵנוּ חֵי פַרְעֹה אִם־
תֵּצְאוּ מִזֶּה כִּי אִם־בְּבוֹא אֲחִיכֶם הַקָּטֹן
הֵנָּה׃ 16 שִׁלְחוּ מִכֶּם אֶחָד וְיִקַּח אֶת־
אֲחִיכֶם וְאַתֶּם הֵאָסְרוּ וְיִבָּחֲנוּ דִּבְרֵיכֶם
הַאֱמֶת אִתְּכֶם וְאִם־לֹא חֵי פַרְעֹה כִּי
מְרַגְּלִים אַתֶּם׃ 17 וַיֶּאֱסֹף אֹתָם אֶל־
מִשְׁמָר שְׁלֹשֶׁת יָמִים׃
18 וַיֹּאמֶר אֲלֵהֶם יוֹסֵף בַּיּוֹם הַשְּׁלִישִׁי זֹאת
עֲשׂוּ וִחְיוּ אֶת־הָאֱלֹהִים אֲנִי יָרֵא׃ 19 אִם־ חמישי
כֵּנִים אַתֶּם אֲחִיכֶם אֶחָד יֵאָסֵר בְּבֵית
מִשְׁמַרְכֶם וְאַתֶּם לְכוּ הָבִיאוּ שֶׁבֶר רַעֲבוֹן
בָּתֵּיכֶם׃ 20 וְאֶת־אֲחִיכֶם הַקָּטֹן תָּבִיאוּ
אֵלַי וְיֵאָמְנוּ דִבְרֵיכֶם וְלֹא תָמוּתוּ וַיַּעֲשׂוּ־
כֵן׃ 21 וַיֹּאמְרוּ אִישׁ אֶל־אָחִיו אֲבָל

Canaan; the youngest, however, is now with
our father, and one is no more." 14 But Joseph
said to them, "It is just as I have told you: You
are spies! 15 By this you shall be put to the test:
unless your youngest brother comes here, by
Pharaoh, you shall not depart from this place!
16 Let one of you go and bring your brother,
while the rest of you remain confined, that
your words may be put to the test whether there
is truth in you. Else, by Pharaoh, you are nothing but spies!" 17 And he confined them in the
guardhouse for three days.

18 On the third day Joseph said to them, "Do
this and you shall live, for I am a God-fearing
man. 19 If you are honest men, let one of you
brothers be held in your place of detention,
while the rest of you go and take home rations
for your starving households; 20 but you must
bring me your youngest brother, that your
words may be verified and that you may not
die." And they did accordingly. 21 They said to
one another, "Alas, we are being punished on

13. one is no more The phrasing either reflects their uncertainty as to Joseph's fate or is a delicate way of saying that he was dead.

14. It is just as I have told you In a show of despotic arbitrariness, Joseph imperiously rejects their defense. The burden of disproof is on the brothers.

15. by Pharaoh Literally, "the life of Pharaoh." This phrase gives the following statement the character of an oath, validated and sanctioned by the awesome power of the king. It was common practice in the ancient world to swear by the life of the king. Israelites also swore by God.

16. Let one of you go This is the first of the tests Joseph imposes. How would they endure the strain of imprisonment? What rivalries would surface as a result of their awareness that only one would return to Canaan and that the fate of the others depended on that one?

THE SECOND ENCOUNTER WITH JOSEPH (vv. 18–26)

18. On the third day Had Joseph intended only a three-day imprisonment, or does he now change his mind? If the latter, then he must have become aware of the terrible, perhaps fatal suffering that he would be inflicting on his father by detaining nine of the brothers. Furthermore, how would the starving families back home obtain food?

a God-fearing man Fear of God is the ultimate restraint on treachery.

20. that you may not die Joseph has forced the brothers into a situation in which they have no choice but to bring Benjamin to avoid dying of hunger.

And they did accordingly They agreed to Joseph's conditions.

21. we are being punished The word

---

21. we are being punished on account of our brother There was no logical reason for them to connect their predicament with what they had done to Joseph so many years earlier. Ap-

account of our brother, because we looked on at his anguish, yet paid no heed as he pleaded with us. That is why this distress has come upon us." 22Then Reuben spoke up and said to them, "Did I not tell you, 'Do no wrong to the boy'? But you paid no heed. Now comes the reckoning for his blood." 23They did not know that Joseph understood, for there was an interpreter between him and them. 24He turned away from them and wept. But he came back to them and spoke to them; and he took Simeon from among them and had him bound before their eyes. 25Then Joseph gave orders to fill their bags with grain, return each one's money to his sack, and give them provisions for the journey; and this was done for them. 26So they loaded their asses with the rations and departed from there.

27As one of them was opening his sack to give feed to his ass at the night encampment, he saw his money right there at the mouth of his bag. 28And he said to his brothers, "My money has been returned! It is here in my bag!" Their

אֲשֵׁמִים ׀ אֲנַחְנוּ עַל־אָחִינוּ אֲשֶׁר רָאִינוּ
צָרַת נַפְשׁוֹ בְּהִתְחַנְנוֹ אֵלֵינוּ וְלֹא שָׁמָעְנוּ
עַל־כֵּן בָּאָה אֵלֵינוּ הַצָּרָה הַזֹּאת׃ 22 וַיַּעַן
רְאוּבֵן אֹתָם לֵאמֹר הֲלוֹא אָמַרְתִּי
אֲלֵיכֶם ׀ לֵאמֹר אַל־תֶּחֶטְאוּ בַיֶּלֶד וְלֹא
שְׁמַעְתֶּם וְגַם־דָּמוֹ הִנֵּה נִדְרָשׁ׃ 23 וְהֵם
לֹא יָדְעוּ כִּי שֹׁמֵעַ יוֹסֵף כִּי הַמֵּלִיץ
בֵּינֹתָם׃ 24 וַיִּסֹּב מֵעֲלֵיהֶם וַיֵּבְךְּ וַיָּשָׁב
אֲלֵהֶם וַיְדַבֵּר אֲלֵהֶם וַיִּקַּח מֵאִתָּם אֶת־
שִׁמְעוֹן וַיֶּאֱסֹר אֹתוֹ לְעֵינֵיהֶם׃ 25 וַיְצַו
יוֹסֵף וַיְמַלְאוּ אֶת־כְּלֵיהֶם בָּר וּלְהָשִׁיב
כַּסְפֵּיהֶם אִישׁ אֶל־שַׂקּוֹ וְלָתֵת לָהֶם צֵדָה
לַדָּרֶךְ וַיַּעַשׂ לָהֶם כֵּן׃ 26 וַיִּשְׂאוּ אֶת־
שִׁבְרָם עַל־חֲמֹרֵיהֶם וַיֵּלְכוּ מִשָּׁם׃
27 וַיִּפְתַּח הָאֶחָד אֶת־שַׂקּוֹ לָתֵת מִסְפּוֹא
לַחֲמֹרוֹ בַּמָּלוֹן וַיַּרְא אֶת־כַּסְפּוֹ וְהִנֵּה־
הוּא בְּפִי אַמְתַּחְתּוֹ׃ 28 וַיֹּאמֶר אֶל־אֶחָיו
הוּשַׁב כַּסְפִּי וְגַם הִנֵּה בְאַמְתַּחְתִּי וַיֵּצֵא

ashem (the singular of the adjective *ashemim,* translated as "we are being punished") can mean both guilt and its consequent punishment (Ps. 34:22), for the two are inseparable in Israelite thought. In this moment of common adversity, the brothers' tortured consciences suddenly erupt.

22. the reckoning for his blood Reuben had warned his brothers (37:22), "Shed no blood!" Apparently, he thinks Joseph is dead.

23. an interpreter This is the only instance in the patriarchal narratives when direct communication is impeded by differences in language.

24. and wept Joseph is deeply affected by the genuine contrition he hears in the words of his brothers, but for the present he must conceal his emotions.

Simeon Having overheard that Reuben, the eldest, tried to save his life, Joseph selects the next in seniority to be detained.

before their eyes To show that his threats were to be taken seriously and to test their solidarity.

25. each one's money Did Joseph mean to test their integrity or to intensify their torment? His motive is unclear.

THE RETURN TO CANAAN (vv. 27–38)

27. night encampment Pastoral nomads did not lodge in inns but in crude tent encampments.

bag The bag or pack was inside a sack.

28. Their hearts sank The surprising find arouses their apprehension. They know they

---

parently, they had been burdened by guilt for all those years.

24. *He turned away from them and wept* For 20 years, Joseph had dreamed of getting even with his brothers. Now that he has that power, now that his youthful dream of having them bow to him has come true, Joseph realizes that he does not really want revenge. He wants

hearts sank; and, trembling, they turned to one another, saying, "What is this that God has done to us?"

²⁹When they came to their father Jacob in the land of Canaan, they told him all that had befallen them, saying, ³⁰"The man who is lord of the land spoke harshly to us and accused us of spying on the land. ³¹We said to him, 'We are honest men; we have never been spies! ³²There were twelve of us brothers, sons by the same father; but one is no more, and the youngest is now with our father in the land of Canaan.' ³³But the man who is lord of the land said to us, 'By this I shall know that you are honest men: leave one of your brothers with me, and take something for your starving households and be off. ³⁴And bring your youngest brother to me, that I may know that you are not spies but honest men. I will then restore your brother to you, and you shall be free to move about in the land.'"

³⁵As they were emptying their sacks, there, in each one's sack, was his money-bag! When they and their father saw their money-bags, they were dismayed. ³⁶Their father Jacob said to them, "It is always me that you bereave: Joseph is no more and Simeon is no more, and now you would take away Benjamin. These

לָבָּם וַיֶּחֶרְד֡וּ אִ֣ישׁ אֶל־אָחִיו֙ לֵאמֹ֔ר מַה־
זֹּ֛את עָשָׂ֥ה אֱלֹהִ֖ים לָֽנוּ׃
29 וַיָּבֹ֛אוּ אֶל־יַעֲקֹ֥ב אֲבִיהֶ֖ם אַ֣רְצָה כְּנָ֑עַן
וַיַּגִּ֣ידוּ ל֔וֹ אֵ֛ת כָּל־הַקֹּרֹ֥ת אֹתָ֖ם לֵאמֹֽר׃
30 דִּ֠בֶּר הָאִ֨ישׁ אֲדֹנֵ֧י הָאָ֛רֶץ אִתָּ֖נוּ קָשׁ֑וֹת
וַיִּתֵּ֣ן אֹתָ֔נוּ כִּֽמְרַגְּלִ֖ים אֶת־הָאָֽרֶץ׃
31 וַנֹּ֥אמֶר אֵלָ֖יו כֵּנִ֣ים אֲנָ֑חְנוּ לֹ֥א הָיִ֖ינוּ
מְרַגְּלִֽים׃ 32 שְׁנֵים־עָשָׂ֥ר אֲנַ֛חְנוּ אַחִ֖ים בְּנֵ֣י
אָבִ֑ינוּ הָאֶחָ֣ד אֵינֶ֔נּוּ וְהַקָּטֹ֥ן הַיּ֛וֹם אֶת־
אָבִ֖ינוּ בְּאֶ֥רֶץ כְּנָֽעַן׃ 33 וַיֹּ֣אמֶר אֵלֵ֗ינוּ
הָאִישׁ֙ אֲדֹנֵ֣י הָאָ֔רֶץ בְּזֹ֣את אֵדַ֔ע כִּ֥י כֵנִ֖ים
אַתֶּ֑ם אֲחִיכֶ֤ם הָֽאֶחָד֙ הַנִּ֣יחוּ אִתִּ֔י וְאֶת־
רַעֲב֥וֹן בָּתֵּיכֶ֖ם קְח֥וּ וָלֵֽכוּ׃ 34 וְ֠הָבִ֠יאוּ אֶת־
אֲחִיכֶ֨ם הַקָּטֹ֜ן אֵלַ֗י וְאֵֽדְעָ֞ה כִּ֣י לֹ֤א מְרַגְּלִים֙
אַתֶּ֔ם כִּ֥י כֵנִ֖ים אַתֶּ֑ם אֶת־אֲחִיכֶם֙ אֶתֵּ֣ן
לָכֶ֔ם וְאֶת־הָאָ֖רֶץ תִּסְחָֽרוּ׃
35 וַיְהִ֗י הֵ֚ם מְרִיקִ֣ים שַׂקֵּיהֶ֔ם וְהִנֵּה־אִ֥ישׁ
צְרֽוֹר־כַּסְפּ֖וֹ בְּשַׂקּ֑וֹ וַיִּרְא֞וּ אֶת־צְרֹר֧וֹת
כַּסְפֵּיהֶ֛ם הֵ֥מָּה וַאֲבִיהֶ֖ם וַיִּירָֽאוּ׃
36 וַיֹּ֤אמֶר אֲלֵהֶם֙ יַעֲקֹ֣ב אֲבִיהֶ֔ם אֹתִ֖י
שִׁכַּלְתֶּ֑ם יוֹסֵ֣ף אֵינֶ֗נּוּ וְשִׁמְע֤וֹן אֵינֶ֔נּוּ וְאֶת־

must return to Egypt for further supplies and the release of their brother.

What is this The words convey their sense of helplessness.

29. When they came to their father The brothers tell their father only what is minimally necessary to explain Simeon's absence and to emphasize the importance of sending Benjamin next time. They say nothing of the three days in detention, of the shackling of Simeon, or of finding the money.

33. and take something for your starving households Literally, "and take the starvation of your households."

35. they were dismayed The brothers must have dipped into their packs for food during the return journey; each discovered his money long before they reached Canaan.

36. It is always me that you bereave Jacob, crushed with sorrow, laments, "It is I who suffer; it is my sons who disappear!"

---

his family back. Revenge is almost always sweeter in the contemplation than in the realization.

36. It is always me that you bereave Does Jacob suspect that they were responsible for Joseph's disappearance (Sforno)?

things always happen to me!" 37Then Reuben
said to his father, "You may kill my two sons if I
do not bring him back to you. Put him in my
care, and I will return him to you." 38But he
said, "My son must not go down with you,
for his brother is dead and he alone is left. If
he meets with disaster on the journey you are
taking, you will send my white head down to
Sheol in grief."

43 But the famine in the land was severe.
2And when they had eaten up the rations which
they had brought from Egypt, their father said
to them, "Go again and procure some food for
us." 3But Judah said to him, "The man warned
us, 'Do not let me see your faces unless your
brother is with you.' 4If you will let our brother
go with us, we will go down and procure food
for you; 5but if you will not let him go, we will
not go down, for the man said to us, 'Do not let
me see your faces unless your brother is with
you.'" 6And Israel said, "Why did you serve me
so ill as to tell the man that you had another
brother?" 7They replied, "But the man kept

בִּנְיָמִן תִּקָּחוּ עָלַי הָיוּ כֻלָּנָה׃ 37 וַיֹּאמֶר
רְאוּבֵן אֶל־אָבִיו לֵאמֹר אֶת־שְׁנֵי בָנַי
תָּמִית אִם־לֹא אֲבִיאֶנּוּ אֵלֶיךָ תְּנָה אֹתוֹ
עַל־יָדִי וַאֲנִי אֲשִׁיבֶנּוּ אֵלֶיךָ׃ 38 וַיֹּאמֶר
לֹא־יֵרֵד בְּנִי עִמָּכֶם כִּי־אָחִיו מֵת וְהוּא
לְבַדּוֹ נִשְׁאָר וּקְרָאָהוּ אָסוֹן בַּדֶּרֶךְ אֲשֶׁר
תֵּלְכוּ־בָהּ וְהוֹרַדְתֶּם אֶת־שֵׂיבָתִי בְּיָגוֹן
שְׁאוֹלָה׃

מג וְהָרָעָב כָּבֵד בָּאָרֶץ׃ 2 וַיְהִי
כַּאֲשֶׁר כִּלּוּ לֶאֱכֹל אֶת־הַשֶּׁבֶר אֲשֶׁר
הֵבִיאוּ מִמִּצְרָיִם וַיֹּאמֶר אֲלֵיהֶם אֲבִיהֶם
שֻׁבוּ שִׁבְרוּ־לָנוּ מְעַט־אֹכֶל׃ 3 וַיֹּאמֶר אֵלָיו
יְהוּדָה לֵאמֹר הָעֵד הֵעִד בָּנוּ הָאִישׁ
לֵאמֹר לֹא־תִרְאוּ פָנַי בִּלְתִּי אֲחִיכֶם
אִתְּכֶם׃ 4 אִם־יֶשְׁךָ מְשַׁלֵּחַ אֶת־אָחִינוּ
אִתָּנוּ נֵרְדָה וְנִשְׁבְּרָה לְךָ אֹכֶל׃ 5 וְאִם־
אֵינְךָ מְשַׁלֵּחַ לֹא נֵרֵד כִּי־הָאִישׁ אָמַר
אֵלֵינוּ לֹא־תִרְאוּ פָנַי בִּלְתִּי אֲחִיכֶם
אִתְּכֶם׃ 6 וַיֹּאמֶר יִשְׂרָאֵל לָמָה הֲרֵעֹתֶם
לִי לְהַגִּיד לָאִישׁ הַעוֹד לָכֶם אָח׃

37. Reuben He assumes leadership for the last time.

38. is left That is, from his mother.

disaster on the journey Reuben's self-confidence leaves Jacob unimpressed. Deeply concerned about the perils of the journey, Jacob does not see that Reuben is trying to assure him of an ultimate positive outcome—that the viceroy of Egypt will keep his promise.

THE SECOND JOURNEY TO EGYPT (43:1–34)

Jacob rejects Reuben's plea and offer. But the brothers know that the fear of starvation will ultimately overcome their father's resistance.

2. when they had eaten up There remains only food enough to enable their families to survive while the brothers travel to Egypt and back.

3. Judah He is the spokesman from now on. Reuben is not heard from again, even though he is the firstborn. The incident described in 35:22 shows that he has lost his position of honor in the family.

The man Abbreviated from "the man who is lord of the land" (42:30,33). Joseph is henceforth called "the man," while the brothers are correspondingly termed "the men." This is an artful device of the narrator as events move toward the climactic moment when Joseph discloses his true identity to his brothers.

7. They replied The report the brothers now give to their father does not correspond to the account of the interrogation in chapter 42, when the brothers seemed to offer unsolicited information about themselves quite freely (vv. 11,13). However, from 44:19 it is clear that Jo-

asking about us and our family, saying, 'Is your father still living? Have you another brother?' And we answered him accordingly. How were we to know that he would say, 'Bring your brother here'?"

⁸Then Judah said to his father Israel, "Send the boy in my care, and let us be on our way, that we may live and not die—you and we and our children. ⁹I myself will be surety for him; you may hold me responsible: if I do not bring him back to you and set him before you, I shall stand guilty before you forever. ¹⁰For we could have been there and back twice if we had not dawdled."

¹¹Then their father Israel said to them, "If it must be so, do this: take some of the choice products of the land in your baggage, and carry them down as a gift for the man—some balm

⁷וַיֹּאמְרוּ שָׁא֣וֹל שָֽׁאַל־הָאִ֜ישׁ לָ֣נוּ וּלְמֽוֹלַדְתֵּ֗נוּ לֵאמֹר֙ הַע֨וֹד אֲבִיכֶ֥ם חַי֙ הֲיֵ֣שׁ לָכֶ֣ם אָ֔ח וַנַּ֨גֶּד־ל֔וֹ עַל־פִּ֖י הַדְּבָרִ֣ים הָאֵ֑לֶּה הֲיָד֣וֹעַ נֵדַ֔ע כִּ֣י יֹאמַ֔ר הוֹרִ֖ידוּ אֶת־אֲחִיכֶֽם:

⁸וַיֹּ֨אמֶר יְהוּדָ֜ה אֶל־יִשְׂרָאֵ֣ל אָבִיו֮ שִׁלְחָ֣ה הַנַּ֣עַר אִתִּי֒ וְנָק֣וּמָה וְנֵלֵ֔כָה וְנִֽחְיֶה֙ וְלֹ֣א נָמ֔וּת גַּם־אֲנַ֖חְנוּ גַם־אַתָּ֥ה גַּם־טַפֵּֽנוּ:

⁹אָֽנֹכִי֙ אֶֽעֶרְבֶ֔נּוּ מִיָּדִ֖י תְּבַקְשֶׁ֑נּוּ אִם־לֹ֣א הֲבִֽיאֹתִ֤יו אֵלֶ֙יךָ֙ וְהִצַּגְתִּ֣יו לְפָנֶ֔יךָ וְחָטָ֥אתִי לְךָ֖ כָּל־הַיָּמִֽים: ¹⁰כִּ֖י לוּלֵ֣א הִתְמַהְמָ֑הְנוּ כִּֽי־עַתָּ֥ה שַׁ֖בְנוּ זֶ֥ה פַעֲמָֽיִם:

¹¹וַיֹּ֨אמֶר אֲלֵהֶ֜ם יִשְׂרָאֵ֣ל אֲבִיהֶם֮ אִם־כֵּ֣ן ׀ אֵפוֹא֮ זֹ֣את עֲשׂוּ֒ קְח֞וּ מִזִּמְרַ֤ת הָאָ֙רֶץ֙ בִּכְלֵיכֶ֔ם וְהוֹרִ֥ידוּ לָאִ֖ישׁ מִנְחָ֑ה מְעַ֤ט צֳרִי֙

seph had indeed asked the specific questions referred to here. It must, therefore, be assumed that chapter 42 represents a very abbreviated account.

our family The word *moledet* is used here in the sense of "kindred."

8. Then Judah said The argument has reached a dead end. Judah steps in to save the situation.

you and we and our children In Hebrew, the order is "we and you and our children." Judah lists them in ascending order of importance to himself.

the boy The word *na·ar* can be used of any male from infancy (Exod. 2:6) to marriageable age (Gen. 34:19). The probability of Benjamin's youthfulness accords with, and renders especially poignant, Jacob's fears and reluctance to let him undertake the journey to Egypt.

9. I myself Meaning, "I personally."

be surety The Hebrew stem ערב most frequently refers to the acceptance of legal responsibility for a debt contracted by another. The guarantor undertakes to ensure that the bor-

rower will not disappear or to repay the loan should the borrower default.

hold me responsible The Hebrew phrase *l'vakkesh mi-yad*, "to hold responsible," "to require an accounting for," is particularly used with respect to bloodshed.

forever Personal guilt and blame would weigh on him always.

11. If it must be so Judah's forceful speech has its effect. The aged Jacob offers no further resistance and resigns himself to the inevitable.

do this The Egyptian vizier must be placated with a gift, and the payments for the grain are to be returned.

choice products of the land The noun *zimrah* in this verse, derived from a similar word in Ugaritic, corresponds to *ko·ah* (strength), which also is used in the sense of "yield, produce" (Gen. 4:12; Hos. 7:9; Job 31:39).

gift The word *minḥah* signifies a gift brought as a token of submission.

honey Biblical *d'vash* refers to the thick, intensely sweet syrup made from dates and grapes or figs and is called *dibs* by the Arabs.

CHAPTER 43

8. Reuben had spoken rashly and foolishly to Jacob (42:37—Why would Jacob want to kill

his own grandchildren?). Judah, who had himself experienced the loss of two children (Gen. 38:6–10), is now able to speak convincingly to Jacob's heart.

and some honey, gum, ladanum, pistachio
nuts, and almonds. 12 And take with you double the money, carrying back with you the
money that was replaced in the mouths of your
bags; perhaps it was a mistake. 13 Take your
brother too; and go back at once to the man.
14 And may El Shaddai dispose the man to
mercy toward you, that he may release to you
your other brother, as well as Benjamin. As for
me, if I am to be bereaved, I shall be bereaved."

15 So the men took that gift, and they took
with them double the money, as well as Benjamin. They made their way down to Egypt,
where they presented themselves to Joseph.
16 When Joseph saw Benjamin with them, he
said to his house steward, "Take the men into
the house; slaughter and prepare an animal, for
the men will dine with me at noon." 17 The man
did as Joseph said, and he brought the men into
Joseph's house. 18 But the men were frightened
at being brought into Joseph's house. "It must
be," they thought, "because of the money replaced in our bags the first time that we have
been brought inside, as a pretext to attack us
and seize us as slaves, with our pack animals."
19 So they went up to Joseph's house steward
and spoke to him at the entrance of the house.
20 "If you please, my lord," they said, "we came
down once before to procure food. 21 But when

וּמְעַט דְּבַשׁ נְכֹאת וָלֹט בָּטְנִים וּשְׁקֵדִים׃
12 וְכֶסֶף מִשְׁנֶה קְחוּ בְיֶדְכֶם וְאֶת־הַכֶּסֶף
הַמּוּשָׁב בְּפִי אַמְתְּחֹתֵיכֶם תָּשִׁיבוּ בְיֶדְכֶם
אוּלַי מִשְׁגֶּה הוּא׃ 13 וְאֶת־אֲחִיכֶם קָחוּ
וְקוּמוּ שׁוּבוּ אֶל־הָאִישׁ׃ 14 וְאֵל שַׁדַּי יִתֵּן
לָכֶם רַחֲמִים לִפְנֵי הָאִישׁ וְשִׁלַּח לָכֶם
אֶת־אֲחִיכֶם אַחֵר וְאֶת־בִּנְיָמִין וַאֲנִי
כַּאֲשֶׁר שָׁכֹלְתִּי שָׁכָלְתִּי׃
15 וַיִּקְחוּ הָאֲנָשִׁים אֶת־הַמִּנְחָה הַזֹּאת
וּמִשְׁנֶה־כֶּסֶף לָקְחוּ בְיָדָם וְאֶת־בִּנְיָמִן
וַיָּקֻמוּ וַיֵּרְדוּ מִצְרַיִם וַיַּעַמְדוּ לִפְנֵי יוֹסֵף׃
ששי 16 וַיַּרְא יוֹסֵף אִתָּם אֶת־בִּנְיָמִין וַיֹּאמֶר
לַאֲשֶׁר עַל־בֵּיתוֹ הָבֵא אֶת־הָאֲנָשִׁים
הַבָּיְתָה וּטְבֹחַ טֶבַח וְהָכֵן כִּי אִתִּי יֹאכְלוּ
הָאֲנָשִׁים בַּצָּהֳרָיִם׃ 17 וַיַּעַשׂ הָאִישׁ כַּאֲשֶׁר
אָמַר יוֹסֵף וַיָּבֵא הָאִישׁ אֶת־הָאֲנָשִׁים
בֵּיתָה יוֹסֵף׃ 18 וַיִּירְאוּ הָאֲנָשִׁים כִּי
הוּבְאוּ בֵּית יוֹסֵף וַיֹּאמְרוּ עַל־דְּבַר הַכֶּסֶף
הַשָּׁב בְּאַמְתְּחֹתֵינוּ בַּתְּחִלָּה אֲנַחְנוּ
מוּבָאִים לְהִתְגֹּלֵל עָלֵינוּ וּלְהִתְנַפֵּל עָלֵינוּ
וְלָקַחַת אֹתָנוּ לַעֲבָדִים וְאֶת־חֲמֹרֵינוּ׃
19 וַיִּגְּשׁוּ אֶל־הָאִישׁ אֲשֶׁר עַל־בֵּית יוֹסֵף
וַיְדַבְּרוּ אֵלָיו פֶּתַח הַבָּיִת׃ 20 וַיֹּאמְרוּ בִּי
אֲדֹנִי יָרֹד יָרַדְנוּ בַּתְּחִלָּה לִשְׁבָּר־אֹכֶל׃

12. double the money The second clause of this verse clarifies the reason for the double amount. One part is for the purchase of food; the other is to return the sum of money placed in their bags.

a mistake Jacob appears to be trying to convince himself that the return of the money by the Egyptians has no sinister motives.

13. Take your brother The aged patriarch leaves the most painful matter till the end. His use of the words "your brother," rather than Benjamin, appears to emphasize their fraternal responsibilities.

14. As for me Having done all that is humanly possible, Jacob now leaves the rest to God, whose blessing he invokes.

if I am to be bereaved Jacob's words opened (v. 11) and now close on a note of sorrowful resignation.

THE BROTHERS IN JOSEPH'S HOUSE
(vv. 15–34)

16. his house steward Literally, "the one who is over his house."

18. frightened Because they alone, of all the buyers of grain, are singled out for this treatment. The brothers are probably aware that high Egyptian officials maintained private dungeons in their homes.

19. at the entrance They lose no time in deterring an accusation.

we arrived at the night encampment and opened our bags, there was each one's money in the mouth of his bag, our money in full. So we have brought it back with us. 22And we have brought down with us other money to procure food. We do not know who put the money in our bags." 23He replied, "All is well with you; do not be afraid. Your God, the God of your father, must have put treasure in your bags for you. I got your payment." And he brought out Simeon to them.

24Then the man brought the men into Joseph's house; he gave them water to bathe their feet, and he provided feed for their asses. 25They laid out their gifts to await Joseph's arrival at noon, for they had heard that they were to dine there.

26When Joseph came home, they presented to him the gifts that they had brought with them into the house, bowing low before him to the ground. 27He greeted them, and he said, "How is your aged father of whom you spoke? Is he still in good health?" 28They replied, "It is well with your servant our father; he is still in

21וַיְהִ֗י כִּֽי־בָ֙אנוּ֙ אֶל־הַמָּל֔וֹן וַנִּפְתְּחָה֙ אֶת־אַמְתְּחֹתֵ֔ינוּ וְהִנֵּ֤ה כֶֽסֶף־אִישׁ֙ בְּפִ֣י אַמְתַּחְתּ֔וֹ כַּסְפֵּ֖נוּ בְּמִשְׁקָל֑וֹ וַנָּ֥שֶׁב אֹת֖וֹ בְּיָדֵֽנוּ: 22וְכֶ֧סֶף אַחֵ֛ר הוֹרַ֥דְנוּ בְיָדֵ֖נוּ לִשְׁבָּר־אֹ֑כֶל לֹ֣א יָדַ֔עְנוּ מִי־שָׂ֥ם כַּסְפֵּ֖נוּ בְּאַמְתְּחֹתֵֽינוּ: 23וַיֹּאמֶר֩ שָׁל֨וֹם לָכֶ֜ם אַל־תִּירָ֗אוּ אֱלֹֽהֵיכֶ֞ם וֵֽאלֹהֵ֤י אֲבִיכֶם֙ נָתַ֨ן לָכֶ֤ם מַטְמוֹן֙ בְּאַמְתְּחֹ֣תֵיכֶ֔ם כַּסְפְּכֶ֖ם בָּ֣א אֵלָ֑י וַיּוֹצֵ֥א אֲלֵהֶ֖ם אֶת־שִׁמְעֽוֹן: 24וַיָּבֵ֥א הָאִ֛ישׁ אֶת־הָאֲנָשִׁ֖ים בֵּ֣יתָה יוֹסֵ֑ף וַיִּתֶּן־מַ֙יִם֙ וַיִּרְחֲצ֣וּ רַגְלֵיהֶ֔ם וַיִּתֵּ֥ן מִסְפּ֖וֹא לַחֲמֹֽרֵיהֶֽם: 25וַיָּכִ֙ינוּ֙ אֶת־הַמִּנְחָ֔ה עַד־בּ֥וֹא יוֹסֵ֖ף בַּֽצׇּהֳרָ֑יִם כִּ֣י שָֽׁמְע֔וּ כִּי־שָׁ֖ם יֹ֥אכְלוּ לָֽחֶם: 26וַיָּבֹ֤א יוֹסֵף֙ הַבַּ֔יְתָה וַיָּבִ֥יאוּ* ל֛וֹ אֶת־הַמִּנְחָ֥ה אֲשֶׁר־בְּיָדָ֖ם הַבָּ֑יְתָה וַיִּשְׁתַּחֲווּ־ל֖וֹ אָֽרְצָה: 27וַיִּשְׁאַ֤ל לָהֶם֙ לְשָׁל֔וֹם וַיֹּ֗אמֶר הֲשָׁל֛וֹם אֲבִיכֶ֥ם הַזָּקֵ֖ן אֲשֶׁ֣ר אֲמַרְתֶּ֑ם הַעוֹדֶ֖נּוּ חָֽי: 28וַיֹּ֣אמְר֔וּ שָׁל֛וֹם לְעַבְדְּךָ֥

v. 26. א׳ דגושה

21. in full Literally, "by its weight."
23. All is well This reassurance on the part of the steward is intelligible only if it is assumed that he is privy to Joseph's scheme. His purpose is to lull them into a false sense of security, bolstered by the release of Simeon.
I got your payment Literally, "your money came to me," a legal formula used by ancient Near Eastern traders to confirm receipt of full payment and implying renunciation of any claim.

27. your aged father The adjective was not reported in the account of the brothers' first meeting with Joseph, but 44:20 shows that it had indeed been used.
28. bowed and made obeisance Either as a sign of appreciation to Joseph for his solicitude in asking about their father's welfare or as a gesture of gratitude to God, a physical equivalent of the verbal "Thank God."

23. Your God, the God of your father, must have put treasure Joseph has taught the steward and his other servants to see the hand of God in life's unexpected blessings.

HALAKHAH L'MA·ASEH
43:27 How is your aged father Asking about a person's well-being became an expected norm in rabbinic Judaism, both as an act of friendship and as a way of knowing when to fulfill the commandment of visiting the sick (*bikkur ḥolim*) (BT Ned. 39b–40a). We also recite the *Mi she-Berakh* prayer for the sick in the synagogue, in part to beseech God's aid in healing and in part to notify the congregation of who is ill and in need of the support of the community.

good health." And they bowed and made obeisance.

29 Looking about, he saw his brother Benjamin, his mother's son, and asked, "Is this your youngest brother of whom you spoke to me?" And he went on, "May God be gracious to you, my boy." 30 With that, Joseph hurried out, for he was overcome with feeling toward his brother and was on the verge of tears; he went into a room and wept there. 31 Then he washed his face, reappeared, and—now in control of himself—gave the order, "Serve the meal." 32 They served him by himself, and them by themselves, and the Egyptians who ate with him by themselves; for the Egyptians could not dine with the Hebrews, since that would be abhorrent to the Egyptians. 33 As they were seated by his direction, from the oldest in the order of his seniority to the youngest in the order of his youth, the men looked at one another in astonishment. 34 Portions were served them from his table; but Benjamin's portion was several times that of anyone else. And they drank their fill with him.

לְאָבִ֖ינוּ עוֹדֶ֣נּוּ חָ֑י וַֽיִּקְּד֖וּ וישתחו וַיִּֽשְׁתַּחֲוּֽוּ׃
29 וַיִּשָּׂ֣א עֵינָ֗יו וַיַּ֞רְא אֶת־בִּנְיָמִ֣ין אָחִיו֮ בֶּן־
אִמּוֹ֒ וַיֹּ֗אמֶר הֲזֶה֙ אֲחִיכֶ֣ם הַקָּטֹ֔ן אֲשֶׁ֥ר
אֲמַרְתֶּ֖ם אֵלָ֑י וַיֹּאמַ֕ר אֱלֹהִ֥ים יָחְנְךָ֖ בְּנִֽי׃
שביעי 30 וַיְמַהֵ֣ר יוֹסֵ֗ף כִּֽי־נִכְמְר֤וּ רַחֲמָיו֙ אֶל־
אָחִ֔יו וַיְבַקֵּ֖שׁ לִבְכּ֑וֹת וַיָּבֹ֥א הַחַ֖דְרָה וַיֵּ֥בְךְּ
שָֽׁמָּה׃ 31 וַיִּרְחַ֥ץ פָּנָ֖יו וַיֵּצֵ֑א וַיִּ֨תְאַפַּ֔ק
וַיֹּ֖אמֶר שִׂ֥ימוּ לָֽחֶם׃ 32 וַיָּשִׂ֥ימוּ ל֛וֹ לְבַדּ֖וֹ
וְלָהֶ֣ם לְבַדָּ֑ם וְלַמִּצְרִ֞ים הָאֹכְלִ֤ים אִתּוֹ֙
לְבַדָּ֔ם כִּי֩ לֹ֨א יוּכְל֜וּן הַמִּצְרִ֗ים לֶאֱכֹ֤ל
אֶת־הָֽעִבְרִים֙ לֶ֔חֶם כִּֽי־תוֹעֵבָ֥ה הִ֖וא
לְמִצְרָֽיִם׃ 33 וַיֵּשְׁב֣וּ לְפָנָ֔יו הַבְּכֹר֙ כִּבְכֹ֣רָת֔וֹ
וְהַצָּעִ֖יר כִּצְעִרָת֑וֹ
וַיִּתְמְה֥וּ הָאֲנָשִׁ֖ים אִ֥ישׁ אֶל־רֵעֵֽהוּ׃
34 וַיִּשָּׂ֨א מַשְׂאֹ֜ת מֵאֵ֣ת פָּנָיו֮ אֲלֵהֶם֒ וַתֵּ֜רֶב
מַשְׂאַ֧ת בִּנְיָמִ֛ן מִמַּשְׂאֹ֥ת כֻּלָּ֖ם חָמֵ֣שׁ יָד֑וֹת
וַיִּשְׁתּ֥וּ וַֽיִּשְׁכְּר֖וּ עִמּֽוֹ׃

30. overcome with feeling The sight of Benjamin arouses overwhelming tenderness and affection in Joseph. He can find relief only through tears.

31. Serve the meal Joseph hosts a meal for his brothers, who years before had callously sat down to eat while he languished in a pit.

32. They served him by himself Joseph eats alone because of his august status. The Hebrews were segregated because the Egyptians, believing themselves racially and religiously superior to all other peoples, were generally contemptuous of foreigners.

could not dine That is, were prohibited from dining.

33. were seated by his direction Literally, "they sat before him." Saadia and Rashbam point out that the seating arrangement by descending order of seniority could only be at Joseph's direction. This surprises the brothers. The Egyptians, too, are astonished that the vizier should invite foreigners—especially shepherds, an abhorrent profession (46:34)—to dine at his house.

34. several Literally, "five." Joseph is perhaps testing his brothers to see whether this obvious favoritism would arouse their envy or expose any hostile feelings that they might harbor against the one who is now their father's favorite and Joseph's as well.

THE BROTHERS' LAST TRIAL (44:1–34)

After their reception at Joseph's house, the brothers set out on their homeward journey, undoubtedly in high spirits. Their light mood is shattered, however, as Joseph employs his final stratagem.

44

44 Then he instructed his house steward as follows, "Fill the men's bags with food, as much as they can carry, and put each one's money in the mouth of his bag. 2Put my silver goblet in the mouth of the bag of the youngest one, together with his money for the rations." And he did as Joseph told him.

3With the first light of morning, the men were sent off with their pack animals. 4They had just left the city and had not gone far, when Joseph said to his steward, "Up, go after the men! And when you overtake them, say to them, 'Why did you repay good with evil? 5It is the very one from which my master drinks and which he uses for divination. It was a wicked thing for you to do!'"

6He overtook them and spoke those words to them. 7And they said to him, "Why does my lord say such things? Far be it from your servants to do anything of the kind! 8Here we brought back to you from the land of Canaan the money that we found in the mouths of our bags. How then could we have stolen any silver or gold from your master's house! 9Whichever

מד וַיְצַו אֶת־אֲשֶׁר עַל־בֵּיתוֹ לֵאמֹר
מַלֵּא אֶת־אַמְתְּחֹת הָאֲנָשִׁים אֹכֶל כַּאֲשֶׁר
יוּכְלוּן שְׂאֵת וְשִׂים כֶּסֶף־אִישׁ בְּפִי
אַמְתַּחְתּוֹ׃ 2 וְאֶת־גְּבִיעִי גְּבִיעַ הַכֶּסֶף
תָּשִׂים בְּפִי אַמְתַּחַת הַקָּטֹן וְאֵת כֶּסֶף
שִׁבְרוֹ וַיַּעַשׂ כִּדְבַר יוֹסֵף אֲשֶׁר דִּבֵּר׃
3 הַבֹּקֶר אוֹר וְהָאֲנָשִׁים שֻׁלְּחוּ הֵמָּה
וַחֲמֹרֵיהֶם׃ 4 הֵם יָצְאוּ אֶת־הָעִיר לֹא
הִרְחִיקוּ וְיוֹסֵף אָמַר לַאֲשֶׁר עַל־בֵּיתוֹ קוּם
רְדֹף אַחֲרֵי הָאֲנָשִׁים וְהִשַּׂגְתָּם וְאָמַרְתָּ
אֲלֵהֶם לָמָּה שִׁלַּמְתֶּם רָעָה תַּחַת טוֹבָה׃
5 הֲלוֹא זֶה אֲשֶׁר יִשְׁתֶּה אֲדֹנִי בּוֹ וְהוּא
נַחֵשׁ יְנַחֵשׁ בּוֹ הֲרֵעֹתֶם אֲשֶׁר עֲשִׂיתֶם׃
6 וַיַּשִּׂגֵם וַיְדַבֵּר אֲלֵהֶם אֶת־הַדְּבָרִים
הָאֵלֶּה׃ 7 וַיֹּאמְרוּ אֵלָיו לָמָּה יְדַבֵּר אֲדֹנִי
כַּדְּבָרִים הָאֵלֶּה חָלִילָה לַעֲבָדֶיךָ מֵעֲשׂוֹת
כַּדָּבָר הַזֶּה׃ 8 הֵן כֶּסֶף אֲשֶׁר מָצָאנוּ בְּפִי
אַמְתְּחֹתֵינוּ הֱשִׁיבֹנוּ אֵלֶיךָ מֵאֶרֶץ כְּנָעַן
וְאֵיךְ נִגְנֹב מִבֵּית אֲדֹנֶיךָ כֶּסֶף אוֹ זָהָב׃
9 אֲשֶׁר יִמָּצֵא אִתּוֹ מֵעֲבָדֶיךָ וָמֵת וְגַם־

JOSEPH'S INSTRUCTIONS (vv. 1–5)

1. Then he instructed These preparations no doubt take place during the night while the brothers sleep.

Fill the men's bags By supplying them in excess of what their money can buy, Joseph makes them appear all the more ungrateful when they are apprehended for alleged theft.

put each one's money The restoration of their money this time is puzzling, because it plays no role in the accusation that is soon to be made against them.

2. goblet A "libation vessel" for wine, larger than an ordinary cup and used also as a receptacle for oil in the menorah of the Tabernacle. Here, the goblet serves both as a drinking vessel and as a divining instrument (v. 5).

3. the first light of morning This explains why Joseph is still at home when the brothers later return (v. 14).

4. the city The city is said to be situated "in the region of Goshen." See Comment to 45:10.

repay good with evil In verse 50:20, Joseph tells his brothers that God used their evil intentions to good end.

5. It is the very one The one they saw him using at dinner. They cannot claim it is their own property.

he uses for divination It is not stated that Joseph actually believes in divination, but he wants the brothers to think he does.

THE STEWARD'S ACCUSATION AND SEARCH (vv. 6–12)

8. How then could we have stolen This inference from a minor premise ("Here") to a major one ("How then") is known in rabbinic terminology as *kal va-ḥomer.* There are 10 instances of this type of reasoning in the Bible, listed in Gen. R. 92:7.

אֲנַ֖חְנוּ נִהְיֶ֥ה לַֽאדֹנִ֖י לַעֲבָדִֽים׃ 10 וַיֹּ֕אמֶר
גַּם־עַתָּ֥ה כְדִבְרֵיכֶ֖ם כֶּן־ה֑וּא אֲשֶׁ֨ר יִמָּצֵ֤א
אִתּוֹ֙ יִהְיֶה־לִּ֣י עָ֔בֶד וְאַתֶּ֖ם תִּהְי֥וּ נְקִיִּֽם׃
11 וַֽיְמַהֲר֗וּ וַיּוֹרִ֛דוּ אִ֥ישׁ אֶת־אַמְתַּחְתּ֖וֹ
אָ֑רְצָה וַֽיִּפְתְּח֖וּ אִ֥ישׁ אַמְתַּחְתּֽוֹ׃
12 וַיְחַפֵּ֕שׂ בַּגָּד֣וֹל הֵחֵ֔ל וּבַקָּטֹ֖ן כִּלָּ֑ה וַיִּמָּצֵא֙
הַגָּבִ֔יעַ בְּאַמְתַּ֖חַת בִּנְיָמִֽן׃ 13 וַֽיִּקְרְע֖וּ
שִׂמְלֹתָ֑ם וַֽיַּעֲמֹס֙ אִ֣ישׁ עַל־חֲמֹר֔וֹ וַיָּשֻׁ֖בוּ
הָעִֽירָה׃
מפטיר 14 וַיָּבֹ֨א יְהוּדָ֤ה וְאֶחָיו֙ בֵּ֣יתָה יוֹסֵ֔ף וְה֖וּא
עוֹדֶ֣נּוּ שָׁ֑ם וַיִּפְּל֥וּ לְפָנָ֖יו אָֽרְצָה׃ 15 וַיֹּ֤אמֶר
לָהֶם֙ יוֹסֵ֔ף מָֽה־הַמַּעֲשֶׂ֥ה הַזֶּ֖ה אֲשֶׁ֣ר
עֲשִׂיתֶ֑ם הֲל֣וֹא יְדַעְתֶּ֔ם כִּֽי־נַחֵ֥שׁ יְנַחֵ֖שׁ
אִ֥ישׁ אֲשֶׁ֥ר כָּמֹֽנִי׃ 16 וַיֹּ֣אמֶר יְהוּדָ֗ה מַה־

of your servants it is found with shall die; the rest of us, moreover, shall become slaves to my lord." 10He replied, "Although what you are proposing is right, only the one with whom it is found shall be my slave; but the rest of you shall go free."

11So each one hastened to lower his bag to the ground, and each one opened his bag. 12He searched, beginning with the oldest and ending with the youngest; and the goblet turned up in Benjamin's bag. 13At this they rent their clothes. Each reloaded his pack animal, and they returned to the city.

14When Judah and his brothers reentered the house of Joseph, who was still there, they threw themselves on the ground before him. 15Joseph said to them, "What is this deed that you have done? Do you not know that a man like me practices divination?" 16Judah replied,

9. shall die The proposed punishments reflect no known Egyptian law. It is possible that because the brothers are convinced of their innocence, they propose a penalty for themselves that is harsher than the law actually requires.

the rest of us The brothers accept the principle of collective responsibility.

10. what you are proposing The opening words of the steward's response—literally, "also now according to your words so it is"—could mean, "The penalties you invoke are indeed the law, but I shall be lenient," or, "I accept the logic of your argument to the effect that you are generally honest."

shall go free The word *n'kiyim* is a legal term for "cleared of offense or obligation."

11. hastened Their haste is a demonstration of innocence as well as an attempt to dispose of the entire business as quickly as possible.

12. He searched The steward adroitly manipulates the situation. One can imagine the rising self-confidence of the brothers after each successive search yielded nothing.

THE RETURN TO JOSEPH (vv. 13–17)

13. they rent their clothes The horror of their predicament leaves them speechless. They can only do what they caused their father to do years before (37:34).

14. Judah He takes the lead, because he took on the safety of Benjamin as his personal obligation.

who was still there Joseph has not yet left the house for his place of work because it is still very early in the morning (v. 3). His presence, therefore, does not raise any suspicion of trickery.

on the ground This addition to the usual phrase expresses their state of utter despair.

15. Joseph said Feigning anger, he addresses them collectively, implying that they are all involved in the theft. His "leniency," soon to

CHAPTER 44

12. Benjamin's mother, Rachel, had stolen Laban's idols and hidden them in her baggage. Will Benjamin be accused of acting similarly (Gen. R. 92:8)? Joseph's trap is now set. How will the brothers respond? Will they abandon Benjamin out of resentment of Jacob's favoring him? Or have they learned how to be brothers?

“What can we say to my lord? How can we plead, how can we prove our innocence? God has uncovered the crime of your servants. Here we are, then, slaves of my lord, the rest of us as much as he in whose possession the goblet was found.” 17But he replied, “Far be it from me to act thus! Only he in whose possession the goblet was found shall be my slave; the rest of you go back in peace to your father.”

נֹּאמַר֙ לַֽאדֹנִ֔י מַה־נְּדַבֵּ֖ר וּמַה־נִּצְטַדָּ֑ק
הָאֱלֹהִ֗ים מָצָא֙ אֶת־עֲוֺ֣ן עֲבָדֶ֔יךָ הִנֶּ֤נּוּ
עֲבָדִים֙ לַֽאדֹנִ֔י גַּם־אֲנַ֕חְנוּ גַּ֛ם אֲשֶׁר־נִמְצָ֥א
הַגָּבִ֖יעַ בְּיָדֽוֹ׃ 17 וַיֹּ֕אמֶר חָלִ֣ילָה לִּ֔י
מֵעֲשׂ֖וֹת זֹ֑את הָאִ֡ישׁ אֲשֶׁר֩ נִמְצָ֨א הַגָּבִ֜יעַ
בְּיָד֗וֹ ה֚וּא יִהְיֶה־לִּ֣י עָ֔בֶד וְאַתֶּ֕ם עֲל֥וּ
לְשָׁל֖וֹם אֶל־אֲבִיכֶֽם׃ פ

be displayed (v. 17), thus appears to be all the more generous.

practices divination See Comment to verse 5. Because no mention is made of the goblet, it may be assumed that Joseph simply boasts of his ability to detect a thief by divination.

16. the crime of your servants Judah is perhaps falsely confessing collective guilt regarding the theft of the goblet to save Benjamin from being singled out for punishment. Alternatively, he is expressing the ancient belief that suffering is divine punishment for sin, even if the sin could not be identified, and his words are a resignation to misfortune. It also could be a veiled reference to their sale of Joseph.

slaves Judah wisely makes no reference to his earlier rash statement regarding the death penalty (v. 9).

17. Far be it from me Joseph now confronts the brothers with a dilemma. They can save their own lives, but that would be an act of disloyalty to Benjamin and a disaster to their father. Or they can remain with Benjamin, but they would then be unable to bring food to their father and their families, who would die of starvation.

הפטרת מקץ

HAFTARAH FOR MI-KETZ

1 KINGS 3:15–4:1

This *haftarah*, which takes place c. 965 B.C.E. at the start of King Solomon's reign, begins abruptly. "Then Solomon awoke: it was a dream" (3:15). This concludes the preceding account of his dream at Gibeon, in which the king requests and receives divine wisdom to judge the nation (3:5–14). Verse 15 continues with a transition that moves the action to Jerusalem, where the king performs an exemplary act of justice using his divinely inspired wisdom to determine a child's maternity.

RELATION OF THE *HAFTARAH* TO THE *PARASHAH*

Solomon's waking from a dream was undoubtedly chosen as the prologue here because the Hebrew verb used to open this passage (*va-yiykatz*) is the same one used to describe Pharaoh's waking from a dream at the outset of the *parashah* (Gen. 41:4). The importance of royal dreams for national and individual destiny further connects the two readings.

Each text leads to the public awareness of an individual gifted with divine wisdom. Pharaoh, after his dream, fruitlessly consults his court magicians for an interpretation, only to learn subsequently of "a Hebrew youth" with proven skill in dream interpretation. Joseph decodes the dream, much to Pharaoh's approval (Gen. 41:37), and the king exclaims to his courtiers that this is surely "a man in whom is the spirit of God" (*ruaḥ elohim*, v. 38). In his direct praise of Joseph he declares, "there is none so discerning (*navon*) and wise (*ḥakham*) as you (*kamokha*)" (v. 39). In the *haftarah,* Solomon received in a dream God's promise of "a wise (*ḥakham*) and discerning (*navon*) mind," so exceptional that "there has never been anyone like you (*kamokha*) before," nor will there ever again be another as wise (1 Kings 3:12). This aptitude was demonstrated fully in his judgment of the two prostitutes, with the result that "all Israel" recognized that their king "possessed divine wisdom (*ḥokhmat elohim*) to execute justice" (v. 28).

Both Joseph and Solomon were blessed with divine wisdom and discernment, but each applied it to a different realm. Joseph decoded the hidden language of dreams. Solomon determined the truth claims of conflicting testimony.

ג 15 וַיִּקַץ* שְׁלֹמֹה וְהִנֵּה חֲלוֹם וַיָּבוֹא
יְרוּשָׁלַם וַיַּעֲמֹד ׀ לִפְנֵי ׀ אֲרוֹן בְּרִית־
אֲדֹנָי וַיַּעַל עֹלוֹת וַיַּעַשׂ שְׁלָמִים וַיַּעַשׂ
מִשְׁתֶּה לְכָל־עֲבָדָיו׃ פ

v. 15. חסר י׳ בשורש

3 15Then Solomon awoke: it was a dream! He went to Jerusalem, stood before the Ark of the Covenant of the Lord, and sacrificed burnt offerings and presented offerings of well-being; and he made a banquet for all his courtiers.

1 Kings 3:15. He went to Jerusalem The king returned to Jerusalem from Gibeon, an ancient site of worship where he had sacrificed and had received a divine revelation (3:4–14). Worship was not then centralized in Jerusalem.

16Later two prostitutes came to the king and stood before him. 17The first woman said, "Please, my lord! This woman and I live in the same house; and I gave birth to a child while she was in the house. 18On the third day after I was delivered, this woman also gave birth to a child. We were alone; there was no one else with us in the house, just the two of us in the house. 19During the night this woman's child died, because she lay on it. 20She arose in the night and took my son from my side while your maidservant was asleep, and laid him in her bosom; and she laid her dead son in my bosom. 21When I arose in the morning to nurse my son, there he was, dead; but when I looked at him closely in the morning, it was not the son I had borne."

22The other woman spoke up, "No, the live one is my son, and the dead one is yours!" But the first insisted, "No, the dead boy is yours; mine is the live one!" And they went on arguing before the king.

23The king said, "One says, 'This is my son, the live one, and the dead one is yours'; and the other says, 'No, the dead boy is yours, mine is the live one.' 24So the king gave the order, "Fetch me a sword." A sword was brought before the king, 25and the king said, "Cut the live child in two, and give half to one and half to the other."

26But the woman whose son was the live one pleaded with the king, for she was overcome with compassion for her son. "Please, my lord," she cried, "give her the live child; only don't kill it!" The other insisted, "It shall be neither yours nor mine; cut it in two!" 27Then

16 אָ֣ז תָּבֹ֗אנָה שְׁתַּ֛יִם נָשִׁ֥ים זֹנ֖וֹת אֶל־
הַמֶּ֑לֶךְ וַֽתַּעֲמֹ֖דְנָה לְפָנָֽיו׃ 17 וַתֹּ֜אמֶר
הָאִשָּׁ֤ה הָֽאַחַת֙ בִּ֣י אֲדֹנִ֔י אֲנִי֙ וְהָאִשָּׁ֣ה
הַזֹּ֔את יֹשְׁבֹ֖ת בְּבַ֣יִת אֶחָ֑ד וָאֵלֵ֥ד עִמָּ֖הּ
בַּבָּֽיִת׃ 18 וַיְהִ֞י בַּיּ֤וֹם הַשְּׁלִישִׁי֙ לְלִדְתִּ֔י
וַתֵּ֖לֶד גַּם־הָאִשָּׁ֣ה הַזֹּ֑את וַאֲנַ֣חְנוּ יַחְדָּ֗ו
אֵֽין־זָ֤ר אִתָּ֙נוּ֙ בַּבַּ֔יִת זוּלָתִ֥י שְׁתַּֽיִם־אֲנַ֖חְנוּ
בַּבָּֽיִת׃ 19 וַיָּ֛מָת בֶּן־הָאִשָּׁ֥ה הַזֹּ֖את לָ֑יְלָה
אֲשֶׁ֥ר שָׁכְבָ֖ה עָלָֽיו׃ 20 וַתָּ֨קָם בְּת֜וֹךְ
הַלַּ֗יְלָה וַתִּקַּ֨ח אֶת־בְּנִ֤י מֵֽאֶצְלִי֙ וַאֲמָ֣תְךָ֔
יְשֵׁנָ֔ה וַתַּשְׁכִּיבֵ֖הוּ בְּחֵיקָ֑הּ וְאֶת־בְּנָ֥הּ
הַמֵּ֖ת הִשְׁכִּ֥יבָה בְחֵיקִֽי׃ 21 וָאָקֻ֥ם בַּבֹּ֛קֶר
לְהֵינִ֥יק אֶת־בְּנִ֖י וְהִנֵּה־מֵ֑ת וָאֶתְבּוֹנֵ֤ן אֵלָיו֙
בַּבֹּ֔קֶר וְהִנֵּ֛ה לֹֽא־הָיָ֥ה בְנִ֖י אֲשֶׁ֥ר יָלָֽדְתִּי׃
22 וַתֹּ֨אמֶר הָאִשָּׁ֜ה הָאַחֶ֗רֶת לֹ֤א כִי֙ בְּנִ֣י
הַחַ֔י וּבְנֵ֖ךְ הַמֵּ֑ת וְזֹ֤את אֹמֶ֙רֶת֙ לֹ֣א
כִ֔י בְּנֵ֥ךְ הַמֵּ֖ת וּבְנִ֣י הֶחָ֑י וַתְּדַבֵּ֖רְנָה לִפְנֵ֥י
הַמֶּֽלֶךְ׃
23 וַיֹּ֣אמֶר הַמֶּ֔לֶךְ זֹ֣את אֹמֶ֔רֶת זֶה־בְּנִ֥י הַחַ֖י
וּבְנֵ֣ךְ הַמֵּ֑ת וְזֹ֤את אֹמֶ֙רֶת֙ לֹ֣א כִ֔י בְּנֵ֥ךְ הַמֵּ֖ת
וּבְנִ֥י הֶחָֽי׃ פ 24 וַיֹּ֥אמֶר הַמֶּ֖לֶךְ קְח֣וּ
לִי־חָ֑רֶב וַיָּבִ֥אוּ הַחֶ֖רֶב לִפְנֵ֥י הַמֶּֽלֶךְ׃
25 וַיֹּ֣אמֶר הַמֶּ֔לֶךְ גִּזְר֛וּ אֶת־הַיֶּ֥לֶד הַחַ֖י
לִשְׁנָ֑יִם וּתְנ֤וּ אֶֽת־הַחֲצִי֙ לְאַחַ֔ת וְאֶֽת־
הַחֲצִ֖י לְאֶחָֽת׃
26 וַתֹּ֣אמֶר הָאִשָּׁה֩ אֲשֶׁר־בְּנָ֨הּ הַחַ֜י אֶל־
הַמֶּ֗לֶךְ כִּֽי־נִכְמְר֣וּ רַחֲמֶיהָ֮ עַל־בְּנָהּ֒
וַתֹּ֣אמֶר ׀ בִּ֣י אֲדֹנִ֗י תְּנוּ־לָהּ֙ אֶת־הַיָּל֣וּד
הַחַ֔י וְהָמֵ֖ת אַל־תְּמִית֑וּהוּ וְזֹ֣את אֹמֶ֗רֶת
גַּם־לִ֥י גַם־לָ֛ךְ לֹ֥א יִהְיֶ֖ה גְּזֹֽרוּ׃ 27 וַיַּ֨עַן

16. and stood before him The text reveals features of legal protocol: (a) the claimants standing before the judge (v. 16), (b) the claim of the plaintiff (vv. 17–21), (c) the rebuttal by the defendant (v. 22), (d) the response of the plaintiff (v. 22), (e) the summary of arguments by the judge (v. 23), (f) the adjudication (here an ordeal, in the absence of witnesses, vv. 24–25), (g) the plea bargaining by the claimants (v. 26), and (h) the final settlement (v. 27). This is followed by a statement of the salutary effects of publicized justice (v. 28).

the king spoke up. "Give the live child to her," he said, "and do not put it to death; she is its mother."
28When all Israel heard the decision that the king had rendered, they stood in awe of the king; for they saw that he possessed divine wisdom to execute justice.

הַמֶּ֜לֶךְ וַיֹּ֗אמֶר תְּנוּ־לָהּ֙ אֶת־הַיָּל֣וּד הַחַ֔י
וְהָמֵ֖ת לֹ֣א תְמִיתֻ֑הוּ הִ֖יא אִמּֽוֹ׃
28 וַיִּשְׁמְע֣וּ כָל־יִשְׂרָאֵ֗ל אֶת־הַמִּשְׁפָּט֙ אֲשֶׁ֣ר
שָׁפַ֣ט הַמֶּ֔לֶךְ וַיִּרְא֖וּ מִפְּנֵ֣י הַמֶּ֑לֶךְ כִּ֣י
רָא֔וּ כִּֽי־חָכְמַ֧ת אֱלֹהִ֛ים בְּקִרְבּ֖וֹ לַעֲשׂ֥וֹת
מִשְׁפָּֽט׃ ס

4 1King Solomon was now king over all Israel.

ד 1 וַיְהִי֙ הַמֶּ֣לֶךְ שְׁלֹמֹ֔ה מֶ֖לֶךְ עַל־כָּל־
יִשְׂרָאֵֽל׃ ס

27. she is its mother Solomon's adjudication involves a psychological "ordeal" and attention to the mothers' responses. According to a talmudic tradition, Solomon's judgment ("Give the live child to her . . ." v. 27) was confirmed by a heavenly voice (*bat kol*) from the divine court (saying: "she is its mother," v. 27).

28. divine wisdom Hebrew: *ḥokhmat elohim*. Solomon had a divine gift "to execute justice," much as he also had divine wisdom for composing parables (1 Kings 5:9–13) and answering riddles (10:1–4). God's gift of the spirit of wisdom" in judgment became a messianic ideal for Davidic kings (see Isa. 11:1–5).

VA-YIGGASH

18 Then Judah went up to him and said, "Please, my lord, let your servant appeal to my lord, and do not be impatient with your servant, you who are the equal of Pharaoh. 19 My lord asked his servants, 'Have you a father or another brother?' 20 We told my lord, 'We have an old father, and there is a child of his old age, the youngest; his full brother is dead, so that he alone is left of his mother, and his father dotes on him.' 21 Then you said to your servants, 'Bring him down to me, that I may set eyes on him.' 22 We said to my lord, 'The boy cannot leave his father; if he were to leave him, his father would die.' 23 But you said to your servants, 'Unless your youngest brother comes down with you, do not let me see your faces.' 24 When we came back to your servant my father, we reported my lord's words to him.

25 "Later our father said, 'Go back and pro-

ויגש

18 וַיִּגַּשׁ אֵלָיו יְהוּדָה וַיֹּאמֶר בִּי אֲדֹנִי
יְדַבֶּר־נָא עַבְדְּךָ דָבָר בְּאָזְנֵי אֲדֹנִי וְאַל־
יִחַר אַפְּךָ בְּעַבְדֶּךָ כִּי כָמוֹךָ כְּפַרְעֹה׃
19 אֲדֹנִי שָׁאַל אֶת־עֲבָדָיו לֵאמֹר הֲיֵשׁ־
לָכֶם אָב אוֹ־אָח׃ 20 וַנֹּאמֶר אֶל־אֲדֹנִי יֶשׁ־
לָנוּ אָב זָקֵן וְיֶלֶד זְקֻנִים קָטָן וְאָחִיו מֵת
וַיִּוָּתֵר הוּא לְבַדּוֹ לְאִמּוֹ וְאָבִיו אֲהֵבוֹ׃
21 וַתֹּאמֶר אֶל־עֲבָדֶיךָ הוֹרִדֻהוּ אֵלָי
וְאָשִׂימָה עֵינִי עָלָיו׃ 22 וַנֹּאמֶר אֶל־אֲדֹנִי
לֹא־יוּכַל הַנַּעַר לַעֲזֹב אֶת־אָבִיו וְעָזַב
אֶת־אָבִיו וָמֵת׃ 23 וַתֹּאמֶר אֶל־עֲבָדֶיךָ
אִם־לֹא יֵרֵד אֲחִיכֶם הַקָּטֹן אִתְּכֶם לֹא
תֹסִפוּן לִרְאוֹת פָּנָי׃ 24 וַיְהִי כִּי עָלִינוּ אֶל־
עַבְדְּךָ אָבִי וַנַּגֶּד־לוֹ אֵת דִּבְרֵי אֲדֹנִי׃
25 וַיֹּאמֶר אָבִינוּ שֻׁבוּ שִׁבְרוּ־לָנוּ מְעַט־

THE BROTHERS' LAST TRIAL (*continued*)

JUDAH'S SPEECH (44:18–34)

The encounter between Joseph and his brothers reaches its climactic moment.

18. appeal to Literally "speak in the ears of," which is idiomatic for "have a hearing."

the equal of Pharaoh The phrase is not mere flattery but a subtle reminder of Joseph's power to grant a pardon by virtue of his exalted position.

20. his full brother is dead In 42:13, they said, ambiguously referring to Joseph, "one is no more." Now Judah cites Jacob's words of 42:38.

21. I may set eyes on him Judah had inferred from Joseph's request to bring Benjamin an assurance that no harm would befall the lad. He now may be subtly calling into question Joseph's integrity and fair play.

CHAPTER 44

The reconciliation between Joseph and his brothers is one of the great scenes in all of literature. It is preceded by a deeply moving speech by Judah, who uses the word "father" 14 times in 17 verses. Joseph is moved to tears and to self-revelation by Judah's words. He realizes that his keeping Benjamin in prison would be doing to his brother and father what the brothers had done to him and their father years ago.

18. Judah went up to him He drew close emotionally as well as physically (Gen. R. 93:4). The author of *S'fat Emet* understands these words to mean, "Judah approached himself." He discovered who he really was, not the compromiser who had said "Let us sell him . . . not do away with him ourselves" (Gen. 37:27), causing his father boundless grief, but the advocate for compassion and family harmony. Judah knows that his father still favors one brother, Benjamin, over the other brothers. Such knowledge, however, no longer drives him to jealousy. He understands that he cannot change his father; he can only change his reaction to his father's deeds. Judah, although not the eldest of the brothers, emerges as the family spokesman and leader.

cure some food for us.' [26]We answered, 'We cannot go down; only if our youngest brother is with us can we go down, for we may not show our faces to the man unless our youngest brother is with us.' [27]Your servant my father said to us, 'As you know, my wife bore me two sons. [28]But one is gone from me, and I said: Alas, he was torn by a beast! And I have not seen him since. [29]If you take this one from me, too, and he meets with disaster, you will send my white head down to Sheol in sorrow.'

[30]"Now, if I come to your servant my father and the boy is not with us—since his own life is so bound up with his—[31]when he sees that the boy is not with us, he will die, and your servants will send the white head of your servant our father down to Sheol in grief. [32]Now your servant has pledged himself for the boy to my father, saying, 'If I do not bring him back to you, I shall stand guilty before my father forever.' [33]Therefore, please let your servant remain as a slave to my lord instead of the boy, and let the boy go back with his brothers. [34]For how can I go back to my father unless the boy is with me? Let me not be witness to the woe that would overtake my father!"

אֹכֶל׃ 26 וַנֹּאמֶר לֹא נוּכַל לָרֶדֶת אִם־יֵשׁ
אָחִינוּ הַקָּטֹן אִתָּנוּ וְיָרַדְנוּ כִּי־לֹא נוּכַל
לִרְאוֹת פְּנֵי הָאִישׁ וְאָחִינוּ הַקָּטֹן אֵינֶנּוּ
אִתָּנוּ׃ 27 וַיֹּאמֶר עַבְדְּךָ אָבִי אֵלֵינוּ אַתֶּם
יְדַעְתֶּם כִּי שְׁנַיִם יָלְדָה־לִּי אִשְׁתִּי׃ 28 וַיֵּצֵא
הָאֶחָד מֵאִתִּי וָאֹמַר אַךְ טָרֹף טֹרָף וְלֹא
רְאִיתִיו עַד־הֵנָּה׃ 29 וּלְקַחְתֶּם גַּם־אֶת־זֶה
מֵעִם פָּנַי וְקָרָהוּ* אָסוֹן וְהוֹרַדְתֶּם אֶת־
שֵׂיבָתִי בְּרָעָה שְׁאֹלָה׃
30 וְעַתָּה כְּבֹאִי אֶל־עַבְדְּךָ אָבִי וְהַנַּעַר
אֵינֶנּוּ אִתָּנוּ וְנַפְשׁוֹ קְשׁוּרָה בְנַפְשׁוֹ׃
שני 31 וְהָיָה כִּרְאוֹתוֹ כִּי־אֵין הַנַּעַר וָמֵת
וְהוֹרִידוּ עֲבָדֶיךָ אֶת־שֵׂיבַת עַבְדְּךָ אָבִינוּ
בְּיָגוֹן שְׁאֹלָה׃ 32 כִּי עַבְדְּךָ עָרַב אֶת־
הַנַּעַר מֵעִם אָבִי לֵאמֹר אִם־לֹא אֲבִיאֶנּוּ
אֵלֶיךָ וְחָטָאתִי לְאָבִי כָּל־הַיָּמִים׃
33 וְעַתָּה יֵשֶׁב־נָא עַבְדְּךָ תַּחַת הַנַּעַר עֶבֶד
לַאדֹנִי וְהַנַּעַר יַעַל עִם־אֶחָיו׃ 34 כִּי־אֵיךְ
אֶעֱלֶה אֶל־אָבִי וְהַנַּעַר אֵינֶנּוּ אִתִּי פֶּן
אֶרְאֶה בָרָע אֲשֶׁר יִמְצָא אֶת־אָבִי׃

45 Joseph could no longer control himself before all his attendants, and he cried out,

מה 1 וְלֹא־יָכֹל יוֹסֵף לְהִתְאַפֵּק לְכֹל
הַנִּצָּבִים עָלָיו וַיִּקְרָא הוֹצִיאוּ כָל־אִישׁ

v. 29. חסר א׳

28. and I said That is, "I had to admit."

31. with us These words are an addition to the Hebrew text (*ein ha-na·ar*), required by the context. The addition is also found in many of the ancient versions.

your servants will send Judah is in essence saying to Joseph, "You will be responsible for his death."

32. has pledged himself Judah explains why he is acting as the spokesman, because Joseph knows that he is not the oldest brother (43:33).

33. remain as a slave The brother responsible for the sale of Joseph into slavery (37:26ff.) now unwittingly offers to become the slave of his own victim!

THE RECONCILIATION (vv. 1–28)

JOSEPH REVEALS HIMSELF (vv. 1–3)

1. before all his attendants Literally, "before all who were standing by him," i.e., his entourage.

מֵעָלָי וְלֹא־עָמַד אִישׁ אִתּוֹ בְּהִתְוַדַּע יוֹסֵף
אֶל־אֶחָיו׃ 2וַיִּתֵּן אֶת־קֹלוֹ בִּבְכִי וַיִּשְׁמְעוּ
מִצְרַיִם וַיִּשְׁמַע בֵּית פַּרְעֹה׃
3וַיֹּאמֶר יוֹסֵף אֶל־אֶחָיו אֲנִי יוֹסֵף הַעוֹד
אָבִי חָי וְלֹא־יָכְלוּ אֶחָיו לַעֲנוֹת אֹתוֹ כִּי
נִבְהֲלוּ מִפָּנָיו׃
4וַיֹּאמֶר יוֹסֵף אֶל־אֶחָיו גְּשׁוּ־נָא אֵלַי
וַיִּגָּשׁוּ וַיֹּאמֶר אֲנִי יוֹסֵף אֲחִיכֶם אֲשֶׁר־
מְכַרְתֶּם אֹתִי מִצְרָיְמָה׃ 5וְעַתָּה ׀ אַל־
תֵּעָצְבוּ וְאַל־יִחַר בְּעֵינֵיכֶם כִּי־מְכַרְתֶּם
אֹתִי הֵנָּה כִּי לְמִחְיָה שְׁלָחַנִי אֱלֹהִים
לִפְנֵיכֶם׃ 6כִּי־זֶה שְׁנָתַיִם הָרָעָב בְּקֶרֶב
הָאָרֶץ וְעוֹד חָמֵשׁ שָׁנִים אֲשֶׁר אֵין־חָרִישׁ

"Have everyone withdraw from me!" So there
was no one else about when Joseph made himself known to his brothers. 2His sobs were so
loud that the Egyptians could hear, and so the
news reached Pharaoh's palace.
3Joseph said to his brothers, "I am Joseph. Is
my father still well?" But his brothers could not
answer him, so dumfounded were they on account of him.
4Then Joseph said to his brothers, "Come
forward to me." And when they came forward,
he said, "I am your brother Joseph, he whom
you sold into Egypt. 5Now, do not be distressed
or reproach yourselves because you sold me
hither; it was to save life that God sent me
ahead of you. 6It is now two years that there
has been famine in the land, and there are still
five years to come in which there shall be no

no one else about No outsider may share this intensely intimate moment of reconciliation. Furthermore, Joseph would not want the Egyptians to know that his own brothers had sold him into slavery.

2. the news reached Pharaoh's palace Literally, "the house of Pharaoh heard." The report quickly reached the royal court.

3. I am Joseph. Is my father still well? The terrifying picture Judah has painted of the aged father makes Joseph cry out. His words are more exclamation than inquiry, for he already knew the answer (43:27).

REASSURANCE (vv. 4–8)

4. your brother Joseph, he whom you sold His words are both reassurance and rebuke: I shall behave as a brother should—even though you were not brotherly.

5. you sold The brothers had indeed acted with evil intent.

God sent The hidden, guiding hand of divine providence had been behind it all.

to save life That I should be the agency of your survival.

6. no yield from tilling Literally, "no plowing and harvesting."

CHAPTER 45

3. Is my father still well? Why had Joseph not communicated with his father during his years of authority in Egypt? Was he angry at his father, whose favoritism had put him through so much? Or was he reluctant to shame his brothers by telling his father what had happened? (For that matter, there is no record of Jacob having been in touch with his own parents during his years at Laban's house. Did Jacob resent his father Isaac's favoritism as well?)

5. it was to save life The narrative here makes an important theological statement. God could not prevent the brothers from choosing to do something cruel. God's role was to sustain Joseph and guide him to bring something good and life affirming out of the unfairness inflicted on him. Abravanel notes that, although God used the sale of Joseph to further the divine plan, the brothers were still accountable for what they did. The verse seems to imply that the move was not intended to be permanent but would last only for the duration of the famine. The Israelites, however, became comfortable amid the material pleasures of Egypt.

yield from tilling. 7God has sent me ahead of
you to ensure your survival on earth, and to
save your lives in an extraordinary deliverance.
8So, it was not you who sent me here, but God;
and He has made me a father to Pharaoh, lord
of all his household, and ruler over the whole
land of Egypt.

9"Now, hurry back to my father and say to
him: Thus says your son Joseph, 'God has made
me lord of all Egypt; come down to me without
delay. 10You will dwell in the region of Goshen,
where you will be near me—you and your
children and your grandchildren, your flocks
and herds, and all that is yours. 11There I will
provide for you—for there are yet five years of
famine to come—that you and your household and all that is yours may not suffer want.'
12You can see for yourselves, and my brother
Benjamin for himself, that it is indeed I who am
speaking to you. 13And you must tell my father
everything about my high station in Egypt and
all that you have seen; and bring my father here
with all speed."

14With that he embraced his brother Benjamin around the neck and wept, and Benjamin
wept on his neck. 15He kissed all his brothers

וְקָצִיר׃ 7 וַיִּשְׁלָחֵנִי אֱלֹהִים֙ לִפְנֵיכֶ֔ם לָשׂ֥וּם
לָכֶ֛ם שְׁאֵרִ֖ית בָּאָ֑רֶץ וּלְהַחֲי֣וֹת לָכֶ֔ם
לִפְלֵיטָ֖ה גְּדֹלָֽה׃ 8 וְעַתָּ֗ה לֹֽא־אַתֶּ֞ם שלישי
שְׁלַחְתֶּ֤ם אֹתִי֙ הֵ֔נָּה כִּ֖י הָאֱלֹהִ֑ים וַיְשִׂימֵ֨נִי
לְאָ֜ב לְפַרְעֹ֗ה וּלְאָדוֹן֙ לְכָל־בֵּית֔וֹ וּמֹשֵׁ֖ל
בְּכָל־אֶ֥רֶץ מִצְרָֽיִם׃
9 מַהֲרוּ֮ וַעֲל֣וּ אֶל־אָבִי֒ וַאֲמַרְתֶּ֣ם אֵלָ֗יו כֹּ֤ה
אָמַר֙ בִּנְךָ֣ יוֹסֵ֔ף שָׂמַ֧נִי אֱלֹהִ֛ים לְאָד֖וֹן לְכָל־
מִצְרָ֑יִם רְדָ֥ה אֵלַ֖י אַֽל־תַּעֲמֹֽד׃ 10 וְיָשַׁבְתָּ֣
בְאֶֽרֶץ־גֹּ֗שֶׁן וְהָיִ֤יתָ קָרוֹב֙ אֵלַ֔י אַתָּ֕ה וּבָנֶ֖יךָ
וּבְנֵ֣י בָנֶ֑יךָ וְצֹאנְךָ֥ וּבְקָרְךָ֖ וְכָל־אֲשֶׁר־לָֽךְ׃
11 וְכִלְכַּלְתִּ֤י אֹֽתְךָ֙ שָׁ֔ם כִּי־ע֛וֹד חָמֵ֥שׁ
שָׁנִ֖ים רָעָ֑ב פֶּן־תִּוָּרֵ֛שׁ אַתָּ֥ה וּבֵיתְךָ֖ וְכָל־
אֲשֶׁר־לָֽךְ׃ 12 וְהִנֵּ֤ה עֵינֵיכֶם֙ רֹא֔וֹת וְעֵינֵ֖י
אָחִ֣י בִנְיָמִ֑ין כִּי־פִ֖י הַֽמְדַבֵּ֥ר אֲלֵיכֶֽם׃
13 וְהִגַּדְתֶּ֣ם לְאָבִ֗י אֶת־כָּל־כְּבוֹדִי֙ בְּמִצְרַ֔יִם
וְאֵ֖ת כָּל־אֲשֶׁ֣ר רְאִיתֶ֑ם וּמִֽהַרְתֶּ֛ם
וְהוֹרַדְתֶּ֥ם אֶת־אָבִ֖י הֵֽנָּה׃
14 וַיִּפֹּ֛ל עַל־צַוְּארֵ֥י בִנְיָמִֽן־אָחִ֖יו וַיֵּ֑בְךְּ
וּבִנְיָמִ֔ן בָּכָ֖ה עַל־צַוָּארָֽיו׃ 15 וַיְנַשֵּׁ֥ק לְכָל־

8. who sent me For the third time, Joseph repeats his understanding of the true significance of his life. He no longer accuses the brothers of having sold him but says they "sent" him, thereby substituting the beneficial result for their evil purpose.

father to Pharaoh No such title is known from ancient Egypt. The term "father" appears in some biblical passages as a title of honor for a prophet, a king, or a high administrator.

ruler The word translated as "ruler" (*moshel*) here reminds us of the brothers' reaction to Joseph's dreams. They had scornfully asked, "Do you mean to rule over us?"

INSTRUCTIONS TO THE FAMILY (vv. 9–13)

10. You will dwell Joseph clearly has in mind a long-term migration from Canaan to Egypt.

Goshen Goshen is most likely located in the area of Wadi Tumeilat, which stretches from the eastern arm of the Nile to the Great Bitter Lake. Egyptian texts confirm the presence of Semites and other Asians in the northeastern part of the country both at the end of the Sixth Dynasty (ca. 2250 B.C.E.) and ca. 1700 B.C.E. in the wake of the Hyksos invasion.

11. for there are yet five years of famine This parenthetical note is inserted to overcome Jacob's anticipated resistance to a massive migration from Canaan.

12. You can see These words are intended for the brothers, not the father.

I who am speaking Face-to-face, in your language, without an interpreter.

13. all that you have seen That is, your awareness of my situation is not derived from rumor but is firsthand.

and wept upon them; only then were his brothers able to talk to him.

16 The news reached Pharaoh's palace: "Joseph's brothers have come." Pharaoh and his courtiers were pleased. 17 And Pharaoh said to Joseph, "Say to your brothers, 'Do as follows: load up your beasts and go at once to the land of Canaan. 18 Take your father and your households and come to me; I will give you the best of the land of Egypt and you shall live off the fat of the land.' 19 And you are bidden [to add], 'Do as follows: take from the land of Egypt wagons for your children and your wives, and bring your father here. 20 And never mind your belongings, for the best of all the land of Egypt shall be yours.'"

21 The sons of Israel did so; Joseph gave them wagons as Pharaoh had commanded, and he supplied them with provisions for the journey. 22 To each of them, moreover, he gave a change of clothing; but to Benjamin he gave three hundred pieces of silver and several changes of

אֶחָיו וַיֵּבְךְּ עֲלֵהֶם וְאַחֲרֵי כֵן דִּבְּרוּ אֶחָיו
אִתּוֹ׃
16 וְהַקֹּל נִשְׁמַע בֵּית פַּרְעֹה לֵאמֹר בָּאוּ
אֲחֵי יוֹסֵף וַיִּיטַב בְּעֵינֵי פַרְעֹה וּבְעֵינֵי
עֲבָדָיו׃ 17 וַיֹּאמֶר פַּרְעֹה אֶל־יוֹסֵף אֱמֹר
אֶל־אַחֶיךָ זֹאת עֲשׂוּ טַעֲנוּ אֶת־בְּעִירְכֶם
וּלְכוּ־בֹאוּ אַרְצָה כְּנָעַן׃ 18 וּקְחוּ אֶת־
אֲבִיכֶם וְאֶת־בָּתֵּיכֶם וּבֹאוּ אֵלָי וְאֶתְּנָה
לָכֶם אֶת־טוּב אֶרֶץ מִצְרַיִם וְאִכְלוּ אֶת־
רביעי חֵלֶב הָאָרֶץ׃ 19 וְאַתָּה צֻוֵּיתָה זֹאת עֲשׂוּ
קְחוּ־לָכֶם מֵאֶרֶץ מִצְרַיִם עֲגָלוֹת לְטַפְּכֶם
וְלִנְשֵׁיכֶם וּנְשָׂאתֶם אֶת־אֲבִיכֶם וּבָאתֶם׃
20 וְעֵינְכֶם אַל־תָּחֹס עַל־כְּלֵיכֶם כִּי־טוּב
כָּל־אֶרֶץ מִצְרַיִם לָכֶם הוּא׃
21 וַיַּעֲשׂוּ־כֵן בְּנֵי יִשְׂרָאֵל וַיִּתֵּן לָהֶם יוֹסֵף
עֲגָלוֹת עַל־פִּי פַרְעֹה וַיִּתֵּן לָהֶם צֵדָה
לַדָּרֶךְ׃ 22 לְכֻלָּם נָתַן לָאִישׁ חֲלִפוֹת
שְׂמָלֹת וּלְבִנְיָמִן נָתַן שְׁלֹשׁ מֵאוֹת כֶּסֶף

15. only then So far the brothers have not uttered a word. It is only after the embrace that they are able to communicate with Joseph, something they were unable to do when he lived among them as a boy (Gen. 37:4).

PHARAOH'S INVITATION (vv. 16–20)

16. The news reached The point made in verse 2 is now repeated and expanded.

17. Pharaoh said Joseph's invitation to his family to settle in Egypt is now endorsed by the king himself.

18. the fat of the land The choicest products of the soil.

19. you are bidden [to add] The order is given to Joseph to relay to his brothers. The previous instructions could be carried out with no outside assistance. This one, however, requires official authorization, the effect of which is to accord Jacob's clan the special status of wards of the king.

20. never mind Do not be concerned about leaving behind personal possessions that will cause inconvenience if you take them along; do not allow such considerations to delay you.

RETURN TO JACOB (vv. 21–28)

22. a change of clothing The term *halifot* (literally, "a change [of clothes]") is specifically employed for a gift of clothing as a valued prize or a token of affection or honor.

several Literally, "five" (see 43:34, 45:6,11).

---

22. a change of clothing To replace the clothes they tore in their grief (Gen. 44:13)? Or as a reversal of what happened years ago, when they stripped Joseph of his clothes and threw him into a pit (Gen. 37:23)?

but to Benjamin Despite the risk of rekindling feelings of jealousy, Joseph displays his special closeness to his only full brother, repeating the favoritism that caused problems for his father and grandfather (BT Meg. 16b). Ramban views Joseph's public favoring of Benjamin as yet another test of the depth and authenticity of the brothers' repentance.

clothing. 23And to his father he sent the following: ten he-asses laden with the best things of
Egypt, and ten she-asses laden with grain,
bread, and provisions for his father on the journey. 24As he sent his brothers off on their way, he
told them, "Do not be quarrelsome on the way."
25They went up from Egypt and came to
their father Jacob in the land of Canaan.
26And they told him, "Joseph is still alive; yes,
he is ruler over the whole land of Egypt." His
heart went numb, for he did not believe them.
27But when they recounted all that Joseph had
said to them, and when he saw the wagons that
Joseph had sent to transport him, the spirit of
their father Jacob revived. 28"Enough!" said
Israel. "My son Joseph is still alive! I must go
and see him before I die."

וַחֲמֵשׁ חֲלִפֹת שְׂמָלֹת׃ 23וּלְאָבִיו שָׁלַח
כְּזֹאת עֲשָׂרָה חֲמֹרִים נֹשְׂאִים מִטּוּב
מִצְרָיִם וְעֶשֶׂר אֲתֹנֹת נֹשְׂאֹת בָּר וָלֶחֶם
וּמָזוֹן לְאָבִיו לַדָּרֶךְ׃ 24וַיְשַׁלַּח אֶת־אֶחָיו
וַיֵּלֵכוּ וַיֹּאמֶר אֲלֵהֶם אַל־תִּרְגְּזוּ בַּדָּרֶךְ׃
25וַיַּעֲלוּ מִמִּצְרָיִם וַיָּבֹאוּ אֶרֶץ* כְּנַעַן אֶל־
יַעֲקֹב אֲבִיהֶם׃ 26וַיַּגִּדוּ לוֹ לֵאמֹר עוֹד
יוֹסֵף חַי וְכִי־הוּא מֹשֵׁל בְּכָל־אֶרֶץ
מִצְרָיִם וַיָּפָג לִבּוֹ כִּי לֹא־הֶאֱמִין לָהֶם׃
27וַיְדַבְּרוּ אֵלָיו אֵת כָּל־דִּבְרֵי יוֹסֵף אֲשֶׁר
דִּבֶּר אֲלֵהֶם וַיַּרְא אֶת־הָעֲגָלוֹת אֲשֶׁר־
שָׁלַח יוֹסֵף לָשֵׂאת אֹתוֹ וַתְּחִי רוּחַ יַעֲקֹב
חמישי אֲבִיהֶם׃ 28וַיֹּאמֶר יִשְׂרָאֵל רַב עוֹד־יוֹסֵף
בְּנִי חָי אֵלְכָה וְאֶרְאֶנּוּ בְּטֶרֶם אָמוּת׃

46 So Israel set out with all that was his,
and he came to Beer-sheba, where he offered

מו וַיִּסַּע יִשְׂרָאֵל וְכָל־אֲשֶׁר־לוֹ וַיָּבֹא
בְּאֵרָה שָּׁבַע וַיִּזְבַּח זְבָחִים לֵאלֹהֵי אָבִיו

v. 25. סבירין ומטעין "ארצה"

The number five, the number of fingers on each hand, is used throughout the Bible to express completeness or "a small abundance."

24. quarrelsome The Hebrew stem רגז means "trembling" and carries overtones of agitation, profound concern, or rage. The translation understands Joseph's words to mean: Do not engage in mutual recrimination. But the text can also be saying: Have no fear for your safety on the journey to Canaan and back.

28. go and see him Jacob does not mention the famine and is not concerned with Joseph's power and glory. His only desire is to visit his son, not to settle in Egypt.

THE MIGRATION TO EGYPT (46:1–47:10)

Jacob's descent to Egypt follows the route of Abraham, which is now laden with national significance.

JACOB AT BEER-SHEBA (vv. 1–4)

1. Israel set out Presumably from Hebron, which was his last specified location (37:14).

Beer-sheba An important north–south road linked Hebron to this city, a distance of about 25 miles (40 km). Jacob stops here as he did before leaving for Aram-Naharaim (28:11) and as Isaac had done earlier (26:23–25).

offered sacrifices Because no mention is made of an altar, it must be assumed that Jacob

---

24. Do not be quarrelsome on the way Do not enter into recriminations over who said "Kill him" and who said "Sell him." The past is past and cannot be undone, and we all have to live with each other.

26. he did not believe them This is the fate of a liar; even when telling the truth, a liar is not believed (ARN 30).

יִצְחָק׃ 2 וַיֹּאמֶר אֱלֹהִים ׀ לְיִשְׂרָאֵל
בְּמַרְאֹת הַלַּיְלָה וַיֹּאמֶר יַעֲקֹב ׀ יַעֲקֹב
וַיֹּאמֶר הִנֵּנִי׃ 3 וַיֹּאמֶר אָנֹכִי הָאֵל אֱלֹהֵי
אָבִיךָ אַל־תִּירָא מֵרְדָה מִצְרַיְמָה כִּי־לְגוֹי
גָּדוֹל אֲשִׂימְךָ שָׁם׃ 4 אָנֹכִי אֵרֵד עִמְּךָ
מִצְרַיְמָה וְאָנֹכִי אַעַלְךָ גַם־עָלֹה וְיוֹסֵף
יָשִׁית יָדוֹ עַל־עֵינֶיךָ׃
5 וַיָּקָם יַעֲקֹב מִבְּאֵר שָׁבַע וַיִּשְׂאוּ בְנֵי־
יִשְׂרָאֵל אֶת־יַעֲקֹב אֲבִיהֶם וְאֶת־טַפָּם
וְאֶת־נְשֵׁיהֶם בָּעֲגָלוֹת אֲשֶׁר־שָׁלַח פַּרְעֹה
לָשֵׂאת אֹתוֹ׃ 6 וַיִּקְחוּ אֶת־מִקְנֵיהֶם וְאֶת־
רְכוּשָׁם אֲשֶׁר רָכְשׁוּ בְּאֶרֶץ כְּנַעַן וַיָּבֹאוּ
מִצְרָיְמָה יַעֲקֹב וְכָל־זַרְעוֹ אִתּוֹ׃ 7 בָּנָיו
וּבְנֵי בָנָיו אִתּוֹ בְּנֹתָיו וּבְנוֹת בָּנָיו וְכָל־
זַרְעוֹ הֵבִיא אִתּוֹ מִצְרָיְמָה׃ ס

sacrifices to the God of his father Isaac. 2 God
called to Israel in a vision by night: "Jacob!
Jacob!" He answered, "Here." 3 And He said,
"I am God, the God of your father. Fear not
to go down to Egypt, for I will make you there
into a great nation. 4 I Myself will go down with
you to Egypt, and I Myself will also bring you
back; and Joseph's hand shall close your eyes."
5 So Jacob set out from Beer-sheba. The sons
of Israel put their father Jacob and their children and their wives in the wagons that Pharaoh had sent to transport him; 6 and they took
along their livestock and the wealth that they
had amassed in the land of Canaan. Thus Jacob
and all his offspring with him came to Egypt:
7 he brought with him to Egypt his sons and
grandsons, his daughters and granddaughters—all his offspring.

uses the one that Isaac constructed at this place (26:25). This sacrificial rite was probably an offering of thanks to God that Joseph was still alive.

the God of his father Isaac Isaac is invoked here because he built the altar at Beer-sheba and experienced a revelation there (26:24–25).

2. by night The usual time of divine communication to the Patriarchs.

3. I am God See Comment to 15:7.

the God of your father This echoes verse 1 and suggests that when he performed the sacrifice Jacob recited some invocation that mentioned Isaac by name.

Fear not The same reassurance was given to Abraham and to Isaac. It is never preceded by a statement revealing human disquiet. The idea is that a person's unexpressed inner anxieties and fears are known to God.

a great nation Another point of contact with the first revelation to the patriarchs (12:2). Now it is explained that the divine promise of peoplehood is to be fulfilled in Egypt. The patriarch is told that the migration to Egypt is to be total and of long duration. A family visit is thereby transformed into an event of national significance.

4. I Myself will go down with you Meaning, I shall protect you on the journey and in Egypt.

will also bring you back The promise is both personal and national. Jacob himself will be brought back for burial in the grave of his fathers (47:29ff., 50:5–13). His offspring will return to possess the Land of Israel.

Joseph's hand shall close your eyes Literally, "Joseph shall place his hand on your eyes," understood as a reference to the custom that the eldest son or nearest relative would gently close the eyes of the deceased.

DEPARTURE FOR EGYPT (vv. 5–7)

5. The sons of Israel The action is carried out by his sons because Jacob is too weak.

6. and the wealth Mention of the all-inclusive nature of the migration is meant to draw attention, once again, to the national significance of the event.

CHAPTER 46

2. Jacob has another reassuring dream, recalling his dream when he prepared to leave the Land the first time. He is the only one of the Patriarchs to whom God speaks only at night.

3. Fear not to go down to Egypt God tells Jacob: do not fear that your descendants will be

8These are the names of the Israelites, Jacob and his descendants, who came to Egypt.

Jacob's first-born Reuben; 9Reuben's sons: Enoch, Pallu, Hezron, and Carmi. 10Simeon's sons: Jemuel, Jamin, Ohad, Jachin, Zohar, and Saul the son of a Canaanite woman. 11Levi's sons: Gershon, Kohath, and Merari. 12Judah's sons: Er, Onan, Shelah, Perez, and Zerah—but Er and Onan had died in the land of Canaan; and Perez's sons were Hezron and Hamul. 13Issachar's sons: Tola, Puvah, Iob, and Shimron. 14Zebulun's sons: Sered, Elon, and Jahleel. 15Those were the sons whom Leah bore to Jacob in Paddan-aram, in addition to his daughter Dinah. Persons in all, male and female: 33.

16Gad's sons: Ziphion, Haggi, Shuni, Ezbon, Eri, Arodi, and Areli. 17Asher's sons: Imnah, Ishvah, Ishvi, and Beriah, and their sister Serah. Beriah's sons: Heber and Malchiel. 18These

8וְאֵ֗לֶּה שְׁמ֤וֹת בְּנֵֽי־יִשְׂרָאֵל֙ הַבָּאִ֣ים מִצְרַ֔יְמָה יַעֲקֹ֖ב וּבָנָ֑יו בְּכֹ֥ר יַעֲקֹ֖ב רְאוּבֵֽן: 9וּבְנֵ֣י רְאוּבֵ֔ן חֲנ֥וֹךְ וּפַלּ֖וּא וְחֶצְרֹ֥ן וְכַרְמִֽי: 10וּבְנֵ֣י שִׁמְע֗וֹן יְמוּאֵ֧ל וְיָמִ֛ין וְאֹ֖הַד וְיָכִ֣ין וְצֹ֑חַר וְשָׁא֖וּל בֶּן־הַֽכְּנַעֲנִֽית: 11וּבְנֵ֣י לֵוִ֔י גֵּרְשׁ֖וֹן קְהָ֥ת וּמְרָרִֽי: 12וּבְנֵ֣י יְהוּדָ֗ה עֵ֧ר וְאוֹנָ֛ן וְשֵׁלָ֖ה וָפֶ֣רֶץ וָזָ֑רַח וַיָּ֨מׇת עֵ֤ר וְאוֹנָן֙ בְּאֶ֣רֶץ כְּנַ֔עַן וַיִּֽהְי֥וּ בְנֵי־פֶ֖רֶץ חֶצְרֹ֥ן וְחָמֽוּל: 13וּבְנֵ֣י יִשָּׂשכָ֔ר תּוֹלָ֥ע וּפֻוָּ֖ה וְי֥וֹב וְשִׁמְרֹֽן: 14וּבְנֵ֣י זְבֻל֔וּן סֶ֥רֶד וְאֵל֖וֹן וְיַחְלְאֵֽל: 15אֵ֣לֶּה ׀ בְּנֵ֣י לֵאָ֗ה אֲשֶׁ֨ר יָֽלְדָ֤ה לְיַעֲקֹב֙ בְּפַדַּ֣ן אֲרָ֔ם וְאֵ֖ת דִּינָ֣ה בִתּ֑וֹ כׇּל־נֶ֧פֶשׁ בָּנָ֛יו וּבְנוֹתָ֖יו שְׁלֹשִׁ֥ים וְשָׁלֹֽשׁ: 16וּבְנֵ֣י גָ֗ד צִפְי֤וֹן וְחַגִּי֙ שׁוּנִ֣י וְאֶצְבֹּ֔ן עֵרִ֥י וַֽאֲרוֹדִ֖י וְאַרְאֵלִֽי: 17וּבְנֵ֣י אָשֵׁ֗ר יִמְנָ֧ה וְיִשְׁוָ֛ה וְיִשְׁוִ֥י וּבְרִיעָ֖ה וְשֶׂ֣רַח אֲחֹתָ֑ם וּבְנֵ֣י

THE GENEALOGY OF JACOB   (vv. 8–27)

A census of the Israelite clans interrupts the narrative. It lists names according to the Matriarch with whom they are associated.

8. the Israelites An imperceptible transformation has occurred. The children of the Patriarch Israel are now "the Israelites," a national entity.

9. Reuben's sons The four sons of Reuben listed here are identical to those in the parallel genealogies of Exod. 6:14, Num. 26:5–6, and 1 Chron. 5:3.

10. Zohar As in Exod. 6:15. In Num. 26:13 and 1 Chron. 4:24 it is replaced by Zerah. Both names mean "shining, brightness."

12. Er, Onan See 38:3–10.

died in the land of Canaan As in Num. 26:19.

Perez's sons were Only Perez's sons are named because his was the most important of the clans: David was his descendant.

15. Dinah Although she is not included in the computation, Dinah is mentioned because of the narrative about her in Gen. 34.

17. their sister Serah She is also mentioned in Num. 26:46 and 1 Chron. 7:30. It is inconceivable that Jacob's 12 sons should have had 53 sons and only 1 daughter. In light of the general biblical tendency to omit women from the genealogies, there must be some extraordinary reason for her mention here, although no hint is given in the text. A similar notice about a sister is found in Gen. 4:22 and 36:22.

---

absorbed into the Egyptian way of life. I will be with them in Egypt to keep them distinctive, and I will lead them out (Ha-amek Davar).

17. their sister Serah This unique mention of one—and only one—of Jacob's granddaughters moves the Sages to speculate on who Serah was. They picture her first as a beautiful and talented young girl who breaks the news of

Joseph's survival to Jacob in a way that will not shock him. She survives into old age, and at the time of the Exodus, she tells Moses where to find the grave of Joseph. As a reward, according to one tradition, she never dies but enters Paradise alive, like the prophet Elijah (Seifer Ha-Yashar 166,203; BT Sot. 13a).

were the descendants of Zilpah, whom Laban had given to his daughter Leah. These she bore to Jacob—16 persons.

[19]The sons of Jacob's wife Rachel were Joseph and Benjamin. [20]To Joseph were born in the land of Egypt Manasseh and Ephraim, whom Asenath daughter of Poti-phera priest of On bore to him. [21]Benjamin's sons: Bela, Becher, Ashbel, Gera, Naaman, Ehi, Rosh, Muppim, Huppim, and Ard. [22]These were the descendants of Rachel who were born to Jacob—14 persons in all.

[23]Dan's son: Hushim. [24]Naphtali's sons: Jahzeel, Guni, Jezer, and Shillem. [25]These were the descendants of Bilhah, whom Laban had given to his daughter Rachel. These she bore to Jacob—7 persons in all.

[26]All the persons belonging to Jacob who came to Egypt—his own issue, aside from the wives of Jacob's sons—all these persons numbered 66. [27]And Joseph's sons who were born to him in Egypt were two in number. Thus the total of Jacob's household who came to Egypt was seventy persons.

בְרִיעָה חֶבֶר וּמַלְכִּיאֵל׃ 18 אֵלֶּה בְּנֵי זִלְפָּה
אֲשֶׁר־נָתַן לָבָן לְלֵאָה בִתּוֹ וַתֵּלֶד אֶת־
אֵלֶּה לְיַעֲקֹב שֵׁשׁ עֶשְׂרֵה נָפֶשׁ׃
19 בְּנֵי רָחֵל אֵשֶׁת יַעֲקֹב יוֹסֵף וּבִנְיָמִן׃
20 וַיִּוָּלֵד לְיוֹסֵף בְּאֶרֶץ מִצְרַיִם אֲשֶׁר
יָלְדָה־לּוֹ אָסְנַת בַּת־פּוֹטִי פֶרַע כֹּהֵן אֹן
אֶת־מְנַשֶּׁה וְאֶת־אֶפְרָיִם׃ 21 וּבְנֵי בִנְיָמִן
בֶּלַע וָבֶכֶר וְאַשְׁבֵּל גֵּרָא וְנַעֲמָן אֵחִי
וָרֹאשׁ מֻפִּים וְחֻפִּים וָאָרְדְּ׃ 22 אֵלֶּה בְּנֵי
רָחֵל אֲשֶׁר יֻלַּד לְיַעֲקֹב כָּל־נֶפֶשׁ אַרְבָּעָה
עָשָׂר׃
23 וּבְנֵי־דָן חֻשִׁים׃ 24 וּבְנֵי נַפְתָּלִי יַחְצְאֵל
וְגוּנִי וְיֵצֶר וְשִׁלֵּם׃ 25 אֵלֶּה בְּנֵי בִלְהָה
אֲשֶׁר־נָתַן לָבָן לְרָחֵל בִּתּוֹ וַתֵּלֶד אֶת־
אֵלֶּה לְיַעֲקֹב כָּל־נֶפֶשׁ שִׁבְעָה׃
26 כָּל־הַנֶּפֶשׁ הַבָּאָה לְיַעֲקֹב מִצְרַיְמָה
יֹצְאֵי יְרֵכוֹ מִלְּבַד נְשֵׁי בְנֵי־יַעֲקֹב כָּל־נֶפֶשׁ
שִׁשִּׁים וָשֵׁשׁ׃ 27 וּבְנֵי יוֹסֵף אֲשֶׁר־יֻלַּד־לוֹ
בְמִצְרַיִם נֶפֶשׁ שְׁנָיִם כָּל־הַנֶּפֶשׁ לְבֵית־
ששי יַעֲקֹב הַבָּאָה מִצְרַיְמָה שִׁבְעִים׃ פ

18. of Zilpah The 16 descendants of Zilpah consist of 2 sons, 11 grandsons, 1 granddaughter, and 2 great-grandsons.

19. The sons of Jacob's wife Rachel Of the four Matriarchs, only Rachel is called "wife." The title affirms Rachel's superior status.

20. Manasseh and Ephraim See Comment to 41:50.

21. Benjamin's sons Here, 10 sons are listed. Num. 26:38–40 records 5 sons (and 2 grandsons); 1 Chron. 7:6 notes 3 sons; 1 Chron. 8:1ff. mentions 5 sons. Moreover, the names and the order of seniority differ in the various lists. The divergences reflect different periods in biblical history as well as variant textual and historical traditions.

23. Dan's son The Hebrew reads *b'nei,* "sons"; the plural noun simply follows the stereotyped formulaic pattern "sons," despite the single name that follows.

Hushim In Num. 26:42 he is called Shuham, an inversion of the consonants.

24. Naphtali's sons The same list is given in Num. 26:48ff. and 1 Chron. 7:13, except that in the latter source Jahzeel appears as Jahziel and Shillem as Shallum.

26. his own issue Literally, "that came out of his loin." In the Bible, the loins are the locale of procreative power. It is possible that the word appears in the singular here as a euphemism for the reproductive organ.

numbered 66 Because this is not a symbolic number in the Bible, it must represent a genuine calculation based on the data just recorded. The key phrase is "who came to Egypt." Accordingly, Er and Onan must be omitted because they died in Canaan. Verse 27 indicates that Manasseh and Ephraim are not included among the 66. They were born in Egypt and cannot be said to have come there. The computation would then be Leah 31 + Zilpah 16 + Rachel 12 + Bilhah 7 = 66.

27. the total . . . 70 persons The number 70 here, as elsewhere in biblical literature, is

²⁸He had sent Judah ahead of him to Joseph, to point the way before him to Goshen. So when they came to the region of Goshen, ²⁹Joseph ordered his chariot and went to Goshen to meet his father Israel; he presented himself to him and, embracing him around the neck, he wept on his neck a good while. ³⁰Then Israel said to Joseph, "Now I can die, having seen for myself that you are still alive."

³¹Then Joseph said to his brothers and to his father's household, "I will go up and tell the news to Pharaoh, and say to him, 'My brothers and my father's household, who were in the land of Canaan, have come to me. ³²The men are shepherds; they have always been breeders of livestock, and they have brought with them

שׁשׁי 28וְאֶת־יְהוּדָ֞ה שָׁלַ֤ח לְפָנָיו֙ אֶל־יוֹסֵ֔ף לְהוֹרֹ֥ת לְפָנָ֖יו גֹּ֑שְׁנָה וַיָּבֹ֖אוּ אַ֥רְצָה גֹּֽשֶׁן: 29וַיֶּאְסֹ֤ר יוֹסֵף֙ מֶרְכַּבְתּ֔וֹ וַיַּ֛עַל לִקְרַֽאת־יִשְׂרָאֵ֥ל אָבִ֖יו גֹּ֑שְׁנָה וַיֵּרָ֣א אֵלָ֗יו וַיִּפֹּל֙ עַל־צַוָּארָ֔יו וַיֵּ֥בְךְּ עַל־צַוָּארָ֖יו עֽוֹד: 30וַיֹּ֧אמֶר יִשְׂרָאֵ֛ל אֶל־יוֹסֵ֖ף אָמ֣וּתָה הַפָּ֑עַם אַֽחֲרֵ֥י רְאוֹתִ֣י אֶת־פָּנֶ֔יךָ כִּ֥י עֽוֹדְךָ֖ חָֽי: 31וַיֹּ֨אמֶר יוֹסֵ֤ף אֶל־אֶחָיו֙ וְאֶל־בֵּ֣ית אָבִ֔יו אֶֽעֱלֶ֖ה וְאַגִּ֣ידָה לְפַרְעֹ֑ה וְאֹֽמְרָ֣ה אֵלָ֗יו אַחַ֧י וּבֵית־אָבִ֛י אֲשֶׁ֥ר בְּאֶֽרֶץ־כְּנַ֖עַן בָּ֥אוּ אֵלָֽי: 32וְהָֽאֲנָשִׁים֙ רֹ֣עֵי צֹ֔אן כִּֽי־אַנְשֵׁ֥י מִקְנֶ֖ה הָי֑וּ וְצֹאנָ֧ם וּבְקָרָ֛ם וְכָל־אֲשֶׁ֥ר

---

symbolic, expressing totality. The number 70 is the base of 10 multiplied by 7, a number expressing completeness. It reiterates the point made in verses 1 and 6–7, emphasizing the comprehensive nature of the descent to Egypt, because this event is seen as the fulfillment of Gen. 15:13. Note that the Greek Septuagint, as well as the Exodus Qumran text, has a tradition of 75, which is not a stock number.

JACOB AND JOSEPH REUNITED (vv. 28–30)

28. *He had sent*   This verse belongs immediately after verse 7, from which it was detached by the genealogy.

Judah   It is only fitting that Judah, who bore responsibility for separating Joseph from Jacob (37:26–27), should now be charged with arranging the reunion.

29. *ordered his chariot*   The literal meaning of the Hebrew is "hitched." Although it was cer-

tainly not done by Joseph himself, attributing it to him heightens the impression of Joseph excitedly rushing forth to Goshen to greet his father. Despite his exalted position, Joseph does not wait for his father to come to him.

30. *Now I can die*   I am ready for death now that my dearest wish has been fulfilled.

PREPARATIONS FOR THE AUDIENCE WITH PHARAOH (vv. 31–34)

Joseph had designated Goshen as the family's proposed dwelling place (45:10). Pharaoh, in confirming the invitation to settle in Egypt, left the place unspecified (45:17–20). Joseph must now obtain clear royal authorization for Israelite settlement in Goshen.

32.   This verse is part of Joseph's address to be made to Pharaoh.

breeders of livestock   Another way of saying "shepherds."

---

29. *he presented himself*   The verb used here (*va-yera*) is used elsewhere in the Torah only for appearances by God or an angel. One commentator suggests that Joseph's appearance after so many years of being thought dead verged on being a miraculous, supernatural event, like the manifestation of an angel.

he wept   It is not clear from the text who wept. Ramban believes that it was Jacob who wept. "By whom are tears more easily shed? By

the aged parent who finds his long-lost son alive, or by the young man who is a ruler?" Rashi thinks that Joseph wept out of a mixture of strong, conflicting feelings, while Jacob offered a prayer of thanks to God.

30. *Now I can die*   The word translated "now" (*ha-pa·am*) can also mean "once." Jacob may be saying "Now I will only die once, physically, but achieve immortality through Joseph."

their flocks and herds and all that is theirs.' 33So when Pharaoh summons you and asks, 'What is your occupation?' 34you shall answer, 'Your servants have been breeders of livestock from the start until now, both we and our fathers'—so that you may stay in the region of Goshen. For all shepherds are abhorrent to Egyptians."

לָהֶ֖ם הֵבִֽיאוּ׃ 33 וְהָיָ֕ה כִּֽי־יִקְרָ֥א לָכֶ֖ם
פַּרְעֹ֑ה וְאָמַ֖ר מַה־מַּעֲשֵׂיכֶֽם׃ 34 וַאֲמַרְתֶּ֗ם
אַנְשֵׁ֨י מִקְנֶ֜ה הָי֤וּ עֲבָדֶ֙יךָ֙ מִנְּעוּרֵ֣ינוּ וְעַד־
עַ֔תָּה גַּם־אֲנַ֖חְנוּ גַּם־אֲבֹתֵ֑ינוּ בַּעֲב֗וּר
תֵּשְׁבוּ֙ בְּאֶ֣רֶץ גֹּ֔שֶׁן כִּֽי־תוֹעֲבַ֥ת מִצְרַ֖יִם
כָּל־רֹ֥עֵה צֹֽאן׃

47

Then Joseph came and reported to Pharaoh, saying, "My father and my brothers, with their flocks and herds and all that is theirs, have come from the land of Canaan and are now in the region of Goshen." 2And selecting a few of his brothers, he presented them to Pharaoh. 3Pharaoh said to his brothers, "What is your occupation?" They answered Pharaoh, "We your servants are shepherds, as were also

מז

וַיָּבֹ֣א יוֹסֵף֮ וַיַּגֵּ֣ד לְפַרְעֹה֒ וַיֹּ֗אמֶר
אָבִ֨י וְאַחַ֜י וְצֹאנָ֤ם וּבְקָרָם֙ וְכָל־אֲשֶׁ֣ר לָהֶ֔ם
בָּ֖אוּ מֵאֶ֣רֶץ כְּנָ֑עַן וְהִנָּ֖ם בְּאֶ֥רֶץ גֹּֽשֶׁן׃
2 וּמִקְצֵ֣ה אֶחָ֔יו לָקַ֖ח חֲמִשָּׁ֣ה אֲנָשִׁ֑ים
וַיַּצִּגֵ֖ם לִפְנֵ֥י פַרְעֹֽה׃ 3 וַיֹּ֧אמֶר פַּרְעֹ֛ה אֶל־
אֶחָ֖יו מַה־מַּעֲשֵׂיכֶ֑ם וַיֹּאמְר֣וּ אֶל־פַּרְעֹ֗ה
רֹעֵ֥ה צֹאן֙ עֲבָדֶ֔יךָ גַּם־אֲנַ֖חְנוּ גַּם־

34. shepherds are abhorrent to Egyptians This remark was occasioned by the fact that the townsfolk held the shepherd in low social esteem. Nevertheless, they were valued because they did the necessary work ordinary Egyptians did not want to do.

PHARAOH AND JOSEPH'S BROTHERS (47:1–6)

1. reported to Pharaoh Joseph must personally inform Pharaoh of his family's arrival because it was through Joseph that Pharaoh originally had extended the invitation to them (45:16–20).

are now in the region of Goshen Joseph selected this location from the beginning (45:10, 46:34). He now prepares Pharaoh for the brothers' formal request (v. 4), hoping to predispose him in its favor.

2. a few of his brothers The first clause means, literally, "and from the extremity of his brothers (i.e., from the best among them) he took five men" (see Judg. 18:2).

3. What is your occupation Pharaoh had not yet been told anything about the brothers,

---

CHAPTER 47

3. We your servants are shepherds Joseph had asked his brothers to stress that they were breeders of livestock (46:33–34), because Egyptians held shepherds in low esteem. When Pharaoh asks the brothers about their occupation, they answer that they are shepherds, like their fathers. Why did they ignore Joseph's request? At one level, we can speculate that Joseph was the first of Abraham's line to grow up outside the Land and be integrated in the highest levels of a foreign society. His brothers, by contrast, grew up in the Land and see nothing embarrassing about being shepherds. (For that matter, neither does Pharaoh, who responds to their professional pride by putting them in charge of the royal flocks and herds.) We can see this passage as reflecting the healthy self-esteem of a people raised in their own land, in contrast to the concern of Diaspora Jews as to what their neighbors think of them. Joseph, despite his prominence and power, does not seem completely secure about his place in Egyptian society and finds it necessary to conceal part of his identity. At the same time, however, we can

our fathers. 4We have come," they told Pharaoh, "to sojourn in this land, for there is no
pasture for your servants' flocks, the famine
being severe in the land of Canaan. Pray, then,
let your servants stay in the region of Goshen."
5Then Pharaoh said to Joseph, "As regards your
father and your brothers who have come to
you, 6the land of Egypt is open before you:
settle your father and your brothers in the best
part of the land; let them stay in the region of
Goshen. And if you know any capable men
among them, put them in charge of my livestock."

7Joseph then brought his father Jacob and
presented him to Pharaoh; and Jacob greeted
Pharaoh. 8Pharaoh asked Jacob, "How many
are the years of your life?" 9And Jacob answered
Pharaoh, "The years of my sojourn [on earth]
are one hundred and thirty. Few and hard have

אֲבוֹתֵינוּ׃ 4וַיֹּאמְרוּ אֶל־פַּרְעֹה לָגוּר
בָּאָרֶץ בָּאנוּ כִּי־אֵין מִרְעֶה לַצֹּאן אֲשֶׁר
לַעֲבָדֶיךָ כִּי־כָבֵד הָרָעָב בְּאֶרֶץ כְּנָעַן
וְעַתָּה יֵשְׁבוּ־נָא עֲבָדֶיךָ בְּאֶרֶץ גֹּשֶׁן׃
5וַיֹּאמֶר פַּרְעֹה אֶל־יוֹסֵף לֵאמֹר אָבִיךָ
וְאַחֶיךָ בָּאוּ אֵלֶיךָ׃ 6אֶרֶץ מִצְרַיִם לְפָנֶיךָ
הִוא בְּמֵיטַב הָאָרֶץ הוֹשֵׁב אֶת־אָבִיךָ
וְאֶת־אַחֶיךָ יֵשְׁבוּ בְּאֶרֶץ גֹּשֶׁן וְאִם־יָדַעְתָּ
וְיֶשׁ־בָּם אַנְשֵׁי־חַיִל וְשַׂמְתָּם שָׂרֵי מִקְנֶה
עַל־אֲשֶׁר־לִי׃

7וַיָּבֵא יוֹסֵף אֶת־יַעֲקֹב אָבִיו וַיַּעֲמִדֵהוּ
לִפְנֵי פַרְעֹה וַיְבָרֶךְ יַעֲקֹב אֶת־פַּרְעֹה׃
8וַיֹּאמֶר פַּרְעֹה אֶל־יַעֲקֹב כַּמָּה יְמֵי שְׁנֵי
חַיֶּיךָ׃ 9וַיֹּאמֶר יַעֲקֹב אֶל־פַּרְעֹה יְמֵי שְׁנֵי
מְגוּרַי שְׁלֹשִׁים וּמְאַת שָׁנָה מְעַט וְרָעִים

so his question is not surprising and was anticipated by Joseph (46:33).

4. to sojourn The use of the verb *gur* (translated "sojourn") links the migration to Egypt with the divine prophecy to Abraham, "Know well that your offspring shall be strangers (*gerim,* plural of *ger*) in a land not theirs" (15:13).

5. Then Pharaoh said He makes a simple statement that acknowledges and legitimates the Israelite presence on Egyptian soil.

6. in the best part of the land The king is true to his word (45:18).

capable men Hebrew *anshei ḥayil,* literally "men of substance."

in charge of my livestock The literal meaning of the phrase *sarei mikneh* is "officers of cattle," referring to superintendents of the royal cattle, an office mentioned frequently in Egyptian inscriptions. This appointment makes some of Joseph's brothers officers of the crown and grants them legal protection not usually accorded aliens.

PHARAOH AND JACOB (vv. 7–10)

Joseph presents his father to Pharaoh in a separate, private audience, probably because he felt it would not be dignified for the aged Patriarch to appear publicly in the role of a supplicant.

7. greeted The word translated as "greeted" (*va-y'varekh,* literally "and he blessed") here probably means "he saluted." The content of the greeting is not given, but it was customary in the ancient Near East to wish the king long life (as in 2 Sam. 16:16 and 1 Kings 1:31).

8. the years of your life Pharaoh may be wondering if Jacob has exceeded the ideal Egyptian life span of 110 years.

9. my sojourn Jacob responds by telling of his "sojournings." He uses the term either as a reference to the unsettled and turbulent nature of his life or as a figure of speech for "life's journey."

hard Jacob recalls the unbroken chain of suffering and misfortunes he has endured.

---

appreciate Joseph's sensitivity to the feelings of his Egyptian neighbors. Jewish law and custom legitimates adjusting our behavior "for the sake of ways of peace" (*mi-p'nei darkhei shalom*), furthering good relations with those around us by avoiding giving offense to their values and sensibilities.

9. Few and hard One would not expect

הָיוּ יְמֵי שְׁנֵי חַיַּי וְלֹא הִשִּׂיגוּ אֶת־יְמֵי שְׁנֵי
חַיֵּי אֲבֹתַי בִּימֵי מְגוּרֵיהֶם: 10 וַיְבָרֶךְ יַעֲקֹב
אֶת־פַּרְעֹה וַיֵּצֵא מִלִּפְנֵי פַרְעֹה:
11 וַיּוֹשֵׁב יוֹסֵף אֶת־אָבִיו וְאֶת־אֶחָיו וַיִּתֵּן שביעי
לָהֶם אֲחֻזָּה בְּאֶרֶץ מִצְרַיִם בְּמֵיטַב
הָאָרֶץ בְּאֶרֶץ רַעְמְסֵס כַּאֲשֶׁר צִוָּה
פַרְעֹה: 12 וַיְכַלְכֵּל יוֹסֵף אֶת־אָבִיו וְאֶת־
אֶחָיו וְאֵת כָּל־בֵּית אָבִיו לֶחֶם לְפִי הַטָּף:

13 וְלֶחֶם אֵין בְּכָל־הָאָרֶץ כִּי־כָבֵד הָרָעָב
מְאֹד וַתֵּלַהּ אֶרֶץ מִצְרַיִם וְאֶרֶץ כְּנַעַן
מִפְּנֵי הָרָעָב: 14 וַיְלַקֵּט יוֹסֵף אֶת־כָּל־
הַכֶּסֶף הַנִּמְצָא בְאֶרֶץ־מִצְרַיִם וּבְאֶרֶץ
כְּנַעַן בַּשֶּׁבֶר אֲשֶׁר־הֵם שֹׁבְרִים וַיָּבֵא יוֹסֵף
אֶת־הַכֶּסֶף בֵּיתָה פַרְעֹה: 15 וַיִּתֹּם הַכֶּסֶף
מֵאֶרֶץ מִצְרַיִם וּמֵאֶרֶץ כְּנַעַן וַיָּבֹאוּ כָל־
מִצְרַיִם אֶל־יוֹסֵף לֵאמֹר הָבָה־לָּנוּ לֶחֶם
וְלָמָּה נָמוּת נֶגְדֶּךָ כִּי אָפֵס כָּסֶף:

been the years of my life, nor do they come up to the life spans of my fathers during their sojourns." 10 Then Jacob bade Pharaoh farewell, and left Pharaoh's presence.

11 So Joseph settled his father and his brothers, giving them holdings in the choicest part of the land of Egypt, in the region of Rameses, as Pharaoh had commanded. 12 Joseph sustained his father, and his brothers, and all his father's household with bread, down to the little ones.

13 Now there was no bread in all the world, for the famine was very severe; both the land of Egypt and the land of Canaan languished because of the famine. 14 Joseph gathered in all the money that was to be found in the land of Egypt and in the land of Canaan, as payment for the rations that were being procured, and Joseph brought the money into Pharaoh's palace. 15 And when the money gave out in the land of Egypt and in the land of Canaan, all the Egyptians came to Joseph and said, "Give us bread, lest we die before your very eyes; for

my fathers In the mouth of Jacob the term refers only to Isaac and Abraham. The former lived to 180 (35:28), the latter to 175 (25:7).

10. Jacob bade Pharaoh farewell He saluted the king, as in verse 7.

and left Pharaoh's presence The patriarchal period in the history of the people Israel has now come to an end.

JOSEPH'S AGRARIAN POLICIES (57:11–27)

11. Joseph settled his father His role as provider for his family reminds the reader that the famine is still raging.

the region of Rameses This is another name for Goshen. The pharaoh Ramses II, in the 13th century B.C.E., enlarged the city of Tanis and made it his capital. Thereafter, his royal name was attached to it. The use of the name here in Joseph's time is anachronistic.

13. there was no bread The severity of the remaining years of famine is such that the people become wholly dependent on the state for their survival.

14. gathered in Joseph averts disaster through a series of drastic measures that, in effect, nationalize the land and livestock and turn the populace into tenant farmers of the state.

Jacob to sound so bitter about his life. He has been reunited with his beloved son, whom he thought dead, and has been promised a life of ease in Egypt. Jacob's life has been described as "a story with a happy ending that withholds any simple feeling of happiness at the end. . . . Although he gets everything he wanted, it is not in the way he would have wanted. Everything has been a struggle" (Alter).

16 וַיֹּאמֶר יוֹסֵף הָבוּ מִקְנֵיכֶם וְאֶתְּנָה לָכֶם
בְּמִקְנֵיכֶם אִם־אָפֵס כָּסֶף׃ 17 וַיָּבִיאוּ אֶת־
מִקְנֵיהֶם אֶל־יוֹסֵף וַיִּתֵּן לָהֶם יוֹסֵף לֶחֶם
בַּסּוּסִים וּבְמִקְנֵה הַצֹּאן וּבְמִקְנֵה הַבָּקָר
וּבַחֲמֹרִים וַיְנַהֲלֵם בַּלֶּחֶם בְּכָל־מִקְנֵהֶם
בַּשָּׁנָה הַהִוא׃ 18 וַתִּתֹּם הַשָּׁנָה הַהִוא
וַיָּבֹאוּ אֵלָיו בַּשָּׁנָה הַשֵּׁנִית וַיֹּאמְרוּ לוֹ
לֹא־נְכַחֵד מֵאֲדֹנִי כִּי אִם־תַּם הַכֶּסֶף
וּמִקְנֵה הַבְּהֵמָה אֶל־אֲדֹנִי לֹא נִשְׁאַר
לִפְנֵי אֲדֹנִי בִּלְתִּי אִם־גְּוִיָּתֵנוּ וְאַדְמָתֵנוּ׃
19 לָמָּה נָמוּת לְעֵינֶיךָ גַּם־אֲנַחְנוּ גַּם
אַדְמָתֵנוּ קְנֵה־אֹתָנוּ וְאֶת־אַדְמָתֵנוּ בַּלָּחֶם
וְנִהְיֶה אֲנַחְנוּ וְאַדְמָתֵנוּ עֲבָדִים לְפַרְעֹה
וְתֶן־זֶרַע וְנִחְיֶה וְלֹא נָמוּת וְהָאֲדָמָה לֹא
תֵשָׁם׃
20 וַיִּקֶן יוֹסֵף אֶת־כָּל־אַדְמַת מִצְרַיִם
לְפַרְעֹה כִּי־מָכְרוּ מִצְרַיִם אִישׁ שָׂדֵהוּ כִּי־
חָזַק עֲלֵהֶם הָרָעָב וַתְּהִי הָאָרֶץ לְפַרְעֹה׃

the money is gone!" 16 And Joseph said, "Bring
your livestock, and I will sell to you against your
livestock, if the money is gone." 17 So they
brought their livestock to Joseph, and Joseph
gave them bread in exchange for the horses, for
the stocks of sheep and cattle, and the asses;
thus he provided them with bread that year
in exchange for all their livestock. 18 And when
that year was ended, they came to him the next
year and said to him, "We cannot hide from my
lord that, with all the money and animal stocks
consigned to my lord, nothing is left at my
lord's disposal save our persons and our farmland. 19 Let us not perish before your eyes, both
we and our land. Take us and our land in exchange for bread, and we with our land will be
serfs to Pharaoh; provide the seed, that we may
live and not die, and that the land may not
become a waste."

20 So Joseph gained possession of all the farm
land of Egypt for Pharaoh, every Egyptian having sold his field because the famine was too
much for them; thus the land passed over to

into Pharaoh's palace Joseph took nothing for himself.

16. sell He will sell to them the "bread" mentioned in verse 15.

17. horses This is the first time the Bible mentions the horse, which was widespread in the Near East by the middle of the 16th century B.C.E. Its place at the head of the list marks its high value.

18. the next year Literally, "the second year." This could refer to the second year of the famine, to two years after the arrival of Jacob, to the second of the remaining five years of famine, or to the seventh year of the famine. The last might explain why the people ask for seed. The predicted end of the famine is at hand, and it is time to prepare for next year's harvest. Farmers continue to sow their fields in years of famine.

19. Take us and our land The suggestion to barter livestock for food had come from Joseph. Now the Egyptians initiate the proposal to surrender their land and become serfs of the crown.

provide the seed Egyptian sources document the practice of the state lending seed corn to farmers for repayment at harvest time.

20. Joseph gained possession Private landed property existed in all periods of Egyptian history, but after the expulsion of the Hyksos in the middle of the 16th century B.C.E., the major part of the land became the actual property of the state.

HALAKHAH L'MA·ASEH

47:19 serfs The Sages placed so many restrictions on slave owners that slavery became economically disadvantageous (e.g., BT Kid. 20a). In any case, the Torah requires us to help the poor so that they should not have to sell themselves into slavery in order to repay a debt (cf. Lev. 25:25,35).

Pharaoh. 21And he removed the population
town by town, from one end of Egypt's border
to the other. 22Only the land of the priests he
did not take over, for the priests had an allotment from Pharaoh, and they lived off the
allotment which Pharaoh had made to them;
therefore they did not sell their land.

23Then Joseph said to the people, "Whereas I
have this day acquired you and your land for
Pharaoh, here is seed for you to sow the land.
24And when harvest comes, you shall give one-
fifth to Pharaoh, and four-fifths shall be yours
as seed for the fields and as food for you and
those in your households, and as nourishment
for your children." 25And they said, "You have
saved our lives! We are grateful to my lord, and
we shall be serfs to Pharaoh." 26And Joseph
made it into a land law in Egypt, which is still
valid, that a fifth should be Pharaoh's; only the
land of the priests did not become Pharaoh's.

21 וְאֶת־הָעָם הֶעֱבִיר אֹתוֹ לֶעָרִים מִקְצֵה
גְבוּל־מִצְרַיִם וְעַד־קָצֵהוּ׃ 22 רַק אַדְמַת
הַכֹּהֲנִים לֹא קָנָה כִּי חֹק לַכֹּהֲנִים מֵאֵת
פַּרְעֹה וְאָכְלוּ אֶת־חֻקָּם אֲשֶׁר נָתַן לָהֶם
פַּרְעֹה עַל־כֵּן לֹא מָכְרוּ אֶת־אַדְמָתָם׃
23 וַיֹּאמֶר יוֹסֵף אֶל־הָעָם הֵן קָנִיתִי אֶתְכֶם
הַיּוֹם וְאֶת־אַדְמַתְכֶם לְפַרְעֹה הֵא־לָכֶם
זֶרַע וּזְרַעְתֶּם אֶת־הָאֲדָמָה׃ 24 וְהָיָה
בַּתְּבוּאֹת וּנְתַתֶּם חֲמִישִׁית לְפַרְעֹה
וְאַרְבַּע הַיָּדֹת יִהְיֶה לָכֶם לְזֶרַע הַשָּׂדֶה
וּלְאָכְלְכֶם וְלַאֲשֶׁר בְּבָתֵּיכֶם וְלֶאֱכֹל
מפטיר לְטַפְּכֶם׃ 25 וַיֹּאמְרוּ הֶחֱיִתָנוּ נִמְצָא־חֵן
בְּעֵינֵי אֲדֹנִי וְהָיִינוּ עֲבָדִים לְפַרְעֹה׃
26 וַיָּשֶׂם אֹתָהּ יוֹסֵף לְחֹק עַד־הַיּוֹם הַזֶּה
עַל־אַדְמַת מִצְרַיִם לְפַרְעֹה לַחֹמֶשׁ רַק
אַדְמַת הַכֹּהֲנִים לְבַדָּם לֹא הָיְתָה
לְפַרְעֹה׃

21. he removed the population town by town The text is generally understood as referring to a population transfer on a large scale, probably to remove farmers from nationalized lands.

22. the land of the priests Because the temples received fixed royal endowments, they were under no pressure to barter their lands for food or seed.

23. here is seed The provision of seed depends on the barter of the peasants' land for food.

24. one-fifth to Pharaoh The state-controlled land is cultivated by the former landowners, who pay a tax of 20 percent of the harvest in return for the privilege and for the seed allotment. Such an interest rate was not considered excessive in the ancient Near East.

25. grateful Joseph's actions must be judged in the context of the ancient Near Eastern world, by whose norms Joseph emerges here as a shrewd, successful, and highly admirable administrator.

26. still valid The Hebrew formula meaning "until this day" (*ad ha-yom ha-zeh*) is used here in a legal context (as in 1 Sam. 30:25). The narrator here bears witness to the fact that the ancient laws described in verses 22 and 24 were still in use in his day. The statement reflects the fact that at various periods of Egyptian history individual temple estates were exempt from taxation by royal decree.

---

22. Only the land of the priests Among Israelites, priests and Levites owned no land (Num. 18:23–24). They depended on the tithes and gifts of worshipers, which led them to identify with the poor among the people. In Egypt, by contrast, the priests were a privileged class, likely to be sympathetic to other privileged elements in Egyptian society.

23–24. Rashbam criticizes Joseph as ruthless, comparing his dispossessing the people of their lands to the actions of Sennacherib (infamous Assyrian king; 2 Kings 18, esp. vv.31–32).

25. we shall be serfs to Pharaoh A generation later, the Egyptians would take their revenge on Joseph for having reduced them to slavery, by enslaving his people.

27 וַיֵּשֶׁב יִשְׂרָאֵל בְּאֶרֶץ מִצְרַיִם בְּאֶרֶץ גֹּשֶׁן
וַיֵּאָחֲזוּ בָהּ וַיִּפְרוּ וַיִּרְבּוּ מְאֹד׃

[27]Thus Israel settled in the country of Egypt, in the region of Goshen; they acquired holdings in it, and were fertile and increased greatly.

27. Thus Israel Following the digression, the narrative resumes the story of the Israelites. This verse is closely connected with verse 11.

settled This verb is in the singular, whereas the succeeding three verbs are each plural. The inconsistency is deliberate. Israel the individual Patriarch merges with the national entity. See Comments to 46:3ff.

and were fertile and increased greatly God's blessing, bestowed on Jacob on his return from Haran (35:11) and repeated as he was about to go down to Egypt (46:3), is now being fulfilled.

הפטרת ויגש

HAFTARAH FOR VA-YIGGASH

EZEKIEL 37:15–28

The verses of this *haftarah* are an independent unit of divine revelation that continues the theme of national restoration that was expressed dramatically in the vision of the resurrected dry bones in verses 1–14. Verses 15–28 focus on the promised reunification of the northern and the southern tribes, the renewal of the Davidic royal lineage, and the re-establishment of the covenant between God and the people Israel. Ezekiel 37 as a whole progresses from physical revival and national ingathering (vv. 1–14) to political unification and spiritual restoration (vv. 15–28).

The *haftarah* itself is composed of two parts. In the first, the prophet performs a symbolic act that anticipates the unification of the tribes of Judah and Israel in the homeland, followed by an explanation of its significance (vv. 15–23). The second part develops the themes of this explanation (vv. 24–28). The prophecy was delivered in the Babylonian exile, sometime after the destruction of the Temple in 587–586 B.C.E.

The central concern of the first part is national unification and the ascension of one king over all. It is built on the structure of act, inquiry, and explanation. The second part further develops the theme of monarchy (adding such terms as "shepherd" and "prince") and national purification. It focuses on settlement in the Land, and the new sanctuary. The elements of ingathering, monarchy, repurification, and Temple building constitute the main configuration of messianic hope for ancient Israel and for subsequent Jewish generations.

The themes of the *haftarah* are underscored by recurrent terminology. In a striking manner, they reflect the concerns and hopes of the nation. The first of these is "unity," expressed through variations of the word *eḥad* (one). Another recurrent theme is "permanence," expressed as a permanent change from the past and as a vision of a permanent future. The idioms used are *lo od* (never again, vv. 22,23) and *l'olam* (forever, vv. 25,26,28).

Through these repeated terms and ideas, the *haftarah* achieves an intensity of focus and emphasis. Indeed, through them the dispersed nation is given hope in a new future, unsullied by the defilements of sin, and restored to their land and God, one people forever. This is the new covenant of peace prophesied to the people. It is an unconditional promise.

RELATION OF THE *HAFTARAH* TO THE *PARASHAH*

What the Torah portrays as a family event, the prophet Ezekiel projects as a national hope: the reconciliation and reunification of all the people Israel. In the *parashah,* Judah assumes a leadership role among his brothers and negotiates with Joseph for the redemption of his brethren (Gen. 44:18–34). This leads to the restoration of family unity and the collective ingathering of Jacob's offspring in Egypt during the time of drought. In the *haftarah,* God prophesies the unification of the northern and the southern tribes, symbolized respectively by Judah and Joseph, along with their national ingathering to the ancestral homeland. In the Torah, the initiation of reconciliation starts on the human plane and requires bilateral human understanding for its fulfillment. In Ezek. 37:15–28, the initiation of redemption belongs to God alone, as does its consummation: a divine grace transforming human hopelessness. Joined together, the Torah episode of reconciled brothers is a portent of the redeemed and reunited nation prophesied in the *haftarah*. Put in the manner of the classic rabbinic epigram, "the acts of the fathers are a sign for the children."

37 [15]The word of the LORD came to me:
[16]And you, O mortal, take a stick and write on it,
"Of Judah and the Israelites associated with
him"; and take another stick and write on it,
"Of Joseph—the stick of Ephraim—and all
the House of Israel associated with him."
[17]Bring them close to each other, so that they
become one stick, joined together in your hand.
[18]And when any of your people ask you, "Won't
you tell us what these actions of yours mean?"
[19]answer them, "Thus said the Lord GOD: I am
going to take the stick of Joseph—which is in
the hand of Ephraim—and of the tribes of Israel
associated with him, and I will place the stick of
Judah upon it and make them into one stick;
they shall be joined in My hand." [20]You shall
hold up before their eyes the sticks which you
have inscribed, [21]and you shall declare to them:
Thus said the Lord GOD: I am going to take the
Israelite people from among the nations they
have gone to, and gather them from every quarter, and bring them to their own land. [22]I will
make them a single nation in the land, on the
hills of Israel, and one king shall be king of them
all. Never again shall they be two nations, and
never again shall they be divided into two kingdoms. [23]Nor shall they ever again defile themselves by their fetishes and their abhorrent
things, and by their other transgressions. I will
save them in all their settlements where they
sinned, and I will purify them. Then they shall
be My people, and I will be their God.

לז 15 וַיְהִ֥י דְבַר־יְהוָ֖ה אֵלַ֥י לֵאמֹֽר׃
16 וְאַתָּ֣ה בֶן־אָדָ֗ם קַח־לְךָ֙ עֵ֣ץ אֶחָ֔ד וּכְתֹ֣ב
עָלָ֔יו לִֽיהוּדָ֔ה וְלִבְנֵ֥י יִשְׂרָאֵ֖ל חברו חֲבֵרָ֑יו
וּלְקַח֙ עֵ֣ץ אֶחָ֔ד וּכְת֣וֹב עָלָ֗יו לְיוֹסֵף֙ עֵ֣ץ
אֶפְרַ֔יִם וְכָל־בֵּ֥ית יִשְׂרָאֵ֖ל חברו חֲבֵרָֽיו׃
17 וְקָרַ֨ב אֹתָ֜ם אֶחָ֧ד אֶל־אֶחָ֛ד לְךָ֖ לְעֵ֣ץ
אֶחָ֑ד וְהָי֥וּ לַאֲחָדִ֖ים בְּיָדֶֽךָ׃ 18 וְכַֽאֲשֶׁר֙
יֹאמְר֣וּ אֵלֶ֔יךָ בְּנֵ֥י עַמְּךָ֖ לֵאמֹ֑ר הֲלֽוֹא־
תַגִּ֥יד לָ֖נוּ מָה־אֵ֥לֶּה לָּֽךְ׃ 19 דַּבֵּ֣ר אֲלֵהֶ֗ם
כֹּֽה־אָמַר֮ אֲדֹנָ֣י יְהוִה֒ הִנֵּ֨ה אֲנִ֜י לֹקֵ֣חַ אֶת־
עֵ֤ץ יוֹסֵף֙ אֲשֶׁ֣ר בְּיַד־אֶפְרַ֔יִם וְשִׁבְטֵ֥י יִשְׂרָאֵ֖ל
חברו חֲבֵרָ֑יו וְנָתַתִּ֨י אוֹתָ֜ם עָלָ֗יו אֶת־
עֵ֤ץ יְהוּדָה֙ וַעֲשִׂיתִם֙ לְעֵ֣ץ אֶחָ֔ד וְהָי֥וּ
אֶחָ֖ד בְּיָדִֽי׃ 20 וְהָי֨וּ הָעֵצִ֜ים אֲשֶׁר־תִּכְתֹּ֧ב
עֲלֵיהֶ֛ם בְּיָדְךָ֖ לְעֵינֵיהֶֽם׃ 21 וְדַבֵּ֣ר אֲלֵיהֶ֗ם
כֹּֽה־אָמַר֮ אֲדֹנָ֣י יְהוִה֒ הִנֵּ֨ה אֲנִ֤י לֹקֵ֙חַ֙ אֶת־
בְּנֵ֣י יִשְׂרָאֵ֔ל מִבֵּ֥ין הַגּוֹיִ֖ם אֲשֶׁ֣ר הָֽלְכוּ־שָׁ֑ם
וְקִבַּצְתִּ֤י אֹתָם֙ מִסָּבִ֔יב וְהֵבֵאתִ֥י אוֹתָ֖ם
אֶל־אַדְמָתָֽם׃ 22 וְעָשִׂ֨יתִי אֹתָ֜ם לְג֤וֹי אֶחָד֙
בָּאָ֙רֶץ֙ בְּהָרֵ֣י יִשְׂרָאֵ֔ל וּמֶ֥לֶךְ אֶחָ֛ד יִהְיֶ֥ה
לְכֻלָּ֖ם לְמֶ֑לֶךְ וְלֹ֤א יהיה יִֽהְיוּ־עוֹד֙ לִשְׁנֵ֣י
גוֹיִ֔ם וְלֹ֨א יֵחָ֥צוּ ע֛וֹד לִשְׁתֵּ֥י מַמְלָכ֖וֹת
עֽוֹד׃ 23 וְלֹ֧א יִֽטַּמְּא֣וּ ע֗וֹד בְּגִלּֽוּלֵיהֶם֙
וּבְשִׁקּ֣וּצֵיהֶ֔ם וּבְכֹ֖ל פִּשְׁעֵיהֶ֑ם וְהוֹשַׁעְתִּ֣י
אֹתָ֗ם מִכֹּ֤ל מוֹשְׁבֹֽתֵיהֶם֙ אֲשֶׁ֣ר חָטְא֣וּ
בָהֶ֔ם וְטִהַרְתִּ֤י אוֹתָם֙ וְהָיוּ־לִ֣י לְעָ֔ם וַאֲנִ֕י
אֶהְיֶ֥ה לָהֶ֖ם לֵאלֹהִֽים׃

Ezekiel 37:16. O mortal The Hebrew is, literally, "son of man." The Hebrew phrase recurs repeatedly in Ezekiel and frequently as here: "and you, O son of man." The phrase emphasizes the mortality of the prophet who, at his commission, beheld God transcendent in the heavens.

take a stick . . . and write on it Each stick has an inscription referring to Judah (representing the southern tribes) or to Joseph (representing the northern tribes), and the Israelites associated with them (see Rashi).

16–22. Ezekiel frequently dramatized his oracles through symbolic actions (see Ezek. 4:1–2,9–11, 5:1–2, 12:3).

23. I will purify them Ezekiel's priestly concerns lead him to regard the people's sins and restoration in cultic terms: Idolatry is described as ritually defiling, and salvation is presented in terms of purification.

they shall be My people, and I shall be their God This is a formulaic expression of the covenantal bond and its reciprocity. It is also found in Ezek. 11:20 and 14:11, with alternate for-

24 וְעַבְדִּי דָוִד מֶלֶךְ עֲלֵיהֶם וְרוֹעֶה אֶחָד
יִהְיֶה לְכֻלָּם וּבְמִשְׁפָּטַי יֵלֵכוּ וְחֻקֹּתַי
יִשְׁמְרוּ וְעָשׂוּ אוֹתָם׃ 25 וְיָשְׁבוּ עַל־הָאָרֶץ
אֲשֶׁר נָתַתִּי לְעַבְדִּי לְיַעֲקֹב אֲשֶׁר יָשְׁבוּ־בָהּ
אֲבוֹתֵיכֶם וְיָשְׁבוּ עָלֶיהָ הֵמָּה וּבְנֵיהֶם
וּבְנֵי בְנֵיהֶם עַד־עוֹלָם וְדָוִד עַבְדִּי נָשִׂיא
לָהֶם לְעוֹלָם׃ 26 וְכָרַתִּי לָהֶם בְּרִית שָׁלוֹם
בְּרִית עוֹלָם יִהְיֶה אוֹתָם וּנְתַתִּים
וְהִרְבֵּיתִי אוֹתָם וְנָתַתִּי אֶת־מִקְדָּשִׁי
בְּתוֹכָם לְעוֹלָם׃ 27 וְהָיָה מִשְׁכָּנִי עֲלֵיהֶם
וְהָיִיתִי לָהֶם לֵאלֹהִים וְהֵמָּה יִהְיוּ־לִי
לְעָם׃ 28 וְיָדְעוּ הַגּוֹיִם כִּי אֲנִי יְהוָה
מְקַדֵּשׁ אֶת־יִשְׂרָאֵל בִּהְיוֹת מִקְדָּשִׁי
בְּתוֹכָם לְעוֹלָם׃ ס

24 My servant David shall be king over them;
there shall be one shepherd for all of them.
They shall follow My rules and faithfully obey
My laws. 25 Thus they shall remain in the land
which I gave to My servant Jacob and in which
your fathers dwelt; they and their children and
their children's children shall dwell there forever, with My servant David as their prince for
all time. 26 I will make a covenant of friendship
with them—it shall be an everlasting covenant
with them—I will establish them and multiply
them, and I will place My Sanctuary among
them forever. 27 My Presence shall rest over
them; I will be their God and they shall be
My people. 28 And when My Sanctuary abides
among them forever, the nations shall know
that I the Lord do sanctify Israel.

mulations in 36:28 and 37:27. The formulary is common in other prophetic writings (cf. Hos. 2:25) and in the Torah (cf. Lev. 26:12; Deut. 29:12).

24. My servant David That is, a descendant of the Davidic dynasty. The expression goes back to the founding of the dynasty (see 2 Sam. 7:5, and its citation in Ps. 89:4,21; cf. 1 Kings 11:13,32,34,36,38). Ezekiel anticipates a restoration of the United Monarchy of Davidic times.

27. My Presence shall rest over them "My Presence" is the translation here for *mishkani*. The prophet uses the old vocabulary of the wilderness Tabernacle (*mishkan*) to indicate the renewal of the divine Presence among the people (cf. Exod. 25:8–9). Ancient Jewish tradition (*Targum*) interpreted *mishkani* (My tabernacle) as "My (indwelling) Presence," or *Sh'khinah*. Eliezer of Beaugency emphasized the protective aspect of the symbolism.

VA-Y'ḤI

28Jacob lived seventeen years in the land of
Egypt, so that the span of Jacob's life came to
one hundred and forty-seven years. 29And
when the time approached for Israel to die,
he summoned his son Joseph and said to
him, "Do me this favor, place your hand under
my thigh as a pledge of your steadfast loyalty:
please do not bury me in Egypt. 30When I lie
down with my fathers, take me up from Egypt
and bury me in their burial-place." He replied,
"I will do as you have spoken." 31And he said,
"Swear to me." And he swore to him. Then
Israel bowed at the head of the bed.

ויחי

28וַיְחִי יַעֲקֹב בְּאֶרֶץ מִצְרַיִם שְׁבַע עֶשְׂרֵה
שָׁנָה וַיְהִי יְמֵי־יַעֲקֹב שְׁנֵי חַיָּיו שֶׁבַע שָׁנִים
וְאַרְבָּעִים וּמְאַת שָׁנָה׃ 29וַיִּקְרְבוּ יְמֵי־
יִשְׂרָאֵל לָמוּת וַיִּקְרָא ׀ לִבְנוֹ לְיוֹסֵף
וַיֹּאמֶר לוֹ אִם־נָא מָצָאתִי חֵן בְּעֵינֶיךָ
שִׂים־נָא יָדְךָ תַּחַת יְרֵכִי וְעָשִׂיתָ עִמָּדִי
חֶסֶד וֶאֱמֶת אַל־נָא תִקְבְּרֵנִי בְּמִצְרָיִם׃
30וְשָׁכַבְתִּי עִם־אֲבֹתַי וּנְשָׂאתַנִי מִמִּצְרַיִם
וּקְבַרְתַּנִי בִּקְבֻרָתָם וַיֹּאמַר אָנֹכִי אֶעֱשֶׂה
כִדְבָרֶךָ׃ 31וַיֹּאמֶר הִשָּׁבְעָה לִי וַיִּשָּׁבַע לוֹ
וַיִּשְׁתַּחוּ יִשְׂרָאֵל עַל־רֹאשׁ הַמִּטָּה׃ פ

JACOB PREPARES FOR DEATH (47:28–48:22)

Jacob is aware that he will die outside the Land of Israel. Burial in his ancestral grave, in accordance with his wishes, will involve a major effort and elaborate arrangements, all of which must be carefully described.

28. seventeen years The Patriarch had thought that his time with Joseph would be brief. Instead, he has enjoyed many more years, precisely as many years as Joseph had lived with his father in Canaan (37:2). There was a similar pattern for Abraham, who lived exactly as many years in his father's home (12:4) as in the lifetime of his son Isaac (21:5, 25:7).

29. place your hand See Comment to 24:2.

do not bury me in Egypt Similarly, Joseph later requests of his brothers that they rebury him in the land of Canaan (50:25). The deathbed requests are bound up with the divine promise of redemption and nationhood in the Land of Israel (48:21, 50:24ff.).

30. When I lie down with my fathers An idiomatic expression for death, not burial, and analogous to "going to one's fathers" or being "gathered to one's kin." See Comment to 15:15 and 25:8.

in their burial-place The cave of Machpelah.

31. Swear to me Jacob exacts this solemn oath, in addition to a promise, to bolster Joseph's position when he will request the royal authorization needed to fulfill the difficult task of reinterment.

bowed at the head of the bed The aged Patriarch, being an invalid, can make only some bodily gesture symbolic of bowing, either as a

---

This final *parashah* of Genesis brings to a close the age of the Patriarchs. Jacob dies after blessing his sons. Some years later, Joseph dies. Genesis ends on that note. In contrast, Exodus will not deal with a family, but with a nation.

The account of Jacob's death begins with "Jacob lived" (*va-y'ḥi*), from which the *parashah* derives its name. The achievements of Jacob's life are emphasized, not the fact of his death.

28. Jacob lived He spent his last years in honor and dignity, rather than simply waiting to die.

29. do me this favor We sense the poignancy of the role reversal, as an aging parent becomes dependent on his adult child.

steadfast loyalty In later Hebrew, the words for this phrase come to mean "true kindness" (*ḥesed v'emet*). Jewish tradition defines "true kindness" as a good deed for which no reciprocal favor can be anticipated, such as tending to the needs of the dead. Adherence to this sacred practice is one reason why the volunteer burial society in a community is known as *ḥevra kaddisha,* the sacred society.

do not bury me in Egypt For Jacob, as for many others, Egypt was a land of graves, domi-

48

Some time afterward, Joseph was told,
"Your father is ill." So he took with him his two
sons, Manasseh and Ephraim. 2When Jacob
was told, "Your son Joseph has come to see
you," Israel summoned his strength and sat
up in bed.
3And Jacob said to Joseph, "El Shaddai appeared to me at Luz in the land of Canaan, and
He blessed me, 4and said to me, 'I will make
you fertile and numerous, making of you a
community of peoples; and I will assign this

מח וַיְהִ֗י אַחֲרֵי֙ הַדְּבָרִ֣ים הָאֵ֔לֶּה
וַיֹּ֣אמֶר לְיוֹסֵ֔ף הִנֵּ֥ה אָבִ֖יךָ חֹלֶ֑ה וַיִּקַּ֞ח
אֶת־שְׁנֵ֤י בָנָיו֙ עִמּ֔וֹ אֶת־מְנַשֶּׁ֖ה וְאֶת־
אֶפְרָֽיִם׃ 2 וַיַּגֵּ֣ד לְיַעֲקֹ֔ב וַיֹּ֕אמֶר הִנֵּ֛ה בִּנְךָ֥
יוֹסֵ֖ף בָּ֣א אֵלֶ֑יךָ וַיִּתְחַזֵּק֙ יִשְׂרָאֵ֔ל וַיֵּ֖שֶׁב
עַל־הַמִּטָּֽה׃
3 וַיֹּ֤אמֶר יַעֲקֹב֙ אֶל־יוֹסֵ֔ף אֵ֥ל שַׁדַּ֛י נִרְאָֽה־
אֵלַ֥י בְּל֖וּז בְּאֶ֣רֶץ כְּנָ֑עַן וַיְבָ֖רֶךְ אֹתִֽי׃
4 וַיֹּ֣אמֶר אֵלַ֗י הִנְנִ֤י מַפְרְךָ֙ וְהִרְבִּיתִ֔ךָ
וּנְתַתִּ֖יךָ לִקְהַ֣ל עַמִּ֑ים וְנָ֨תַתִּ֜י אֶת־הָאָ֧רֶץ

token of gratitude to Joseph or as an expression of thanks and praise to God.

EPHRAIM AND MANASSEH (48:1–20)

Joseph's two sons are elevated to the status of Israelite tribes, retaining the number 12 for the landed tribes when Levi is not assigned any territory. Ephraim's elevation in status over Manasseh reflects the political realities of later Israel.

THE ADOPTION (vv. 1–12)

1. Some time afterward That is, following the oath ceremony described in the preceding four verses and within the final year of Jacob's life.

So he took with him The narrative leaves the destination and arrival to the reader's imagination. The ancient Greek translation (Septuagint) adds, "He came to Jacob."

2. sat up Out of respect for the office that Joseph represented.

3. El Shaddai See Comment to 17:1.

Luz This is the original name of Bethel according to 28:19. See chapter 35.

4. and said to me Jacob now establishes the legal basis for his subsequent actions. As heir to the blessings, Jacob has the sole right to decide who is to be included in the "community of peoples" that will be known as Israel. Only the one who receives the divine blessing directly has the right to bestow it on another. Hence, Jo-

---

nated by the pyramids and by the cult of the dead. Jacob fears that Egypt will become a graveyard for the vision and special purpose of the line of Abraham.

CHAPTER 48

1. Joseph was told, "Your father is ill." Was Joseph too busy with his responsibilities to be aware of his father's failing health? Or was he still ambivalent about his feelings toward his father? Or, as a *midrash* suggests, was he avoiding his father so that Jacob would not ask him how he came to be in Egypt in the first place (Pesik. R.)? The Talmud notes that Jacob is the first person in the Bible to be described as ill. Previously, the Sages imagine, people simply grew older and one day died. They picture Jacob praying for a sign about the number of his days, so that he would have time to bless his children and grandchildren, reflect on the lessons of his life, and articulate his hopes and wishes for his family's future (BT BM 87a).

2. Joseph has come to see you One should never enter the room of a sick or elderly person unannounced, lest they be embarrassed, indisposed, or not fit to receive visitors.

3–7. Jacob on his deathbed remembers two incidents from his long and full life: When he was young, God appeared to him and told him that he would become a special person; and Rachel, the woman he loved, died young. Ramban and Ibn Ezra understand the reference to Rachel's burial on the road to Ephrath as an apology to Joseph for not having buried his mother in the family crypt at Machpelah. Jacob fears that Joseph, resenting the treatment of his mother, will not honor his own request to be

land to your offspring to come for an everlasting possession.' 5Now, your two sons, who were born to you in the land of Egypt before I came to you in Egypt, shall be mine; Ephraim and Manasseh shall be mine no less than Reuben and Simeon. 6But progeny born to you after them shall be yours; they shall be recorded instead of their brothers in their inheritance. 7I [do this because], when I was returning from Paddan, Rachel died, to my sorrow, while I was journeying in the land of Canaan, when still some distance short of Ephrath; and I buried her there on the road to Ephrath"—now Bethlehem.

8Noticing Joseph's sons, Israel asked, "Who are these?" 9And Joseph said to his father, "They are my sons, whom God has given me here." "Bring them up to me," he said, "that I

הַזֹּאת לְזַרְעֲךָ אַחֲרֶיךָ אֲחֻזַּת עוֹלָם׃
5 וְעַתָּה שְׁנֵי־בָנֶיךָ הַנּוֹלָדִים לְךָ בְּאֶרֶץ
מִצְרַיִם עַד־בֹּאִי אֵלֶיךָ מִצְרַיְמָה לִי־הֵם
אֶפְרַיִם וּמְנַשֶּׁה כִּרְאוּבֵן וְשִׁמְעוֹן יִהְיוּ־לִי׃
6 וּמוֹלַדְתְּךָ אֲשֶׁר־הוֹלַדְתָּ אַחֲרֵיהֶם לְךָ
יִהְיוּ עַל שֵׁם אֲחֵיהֶם יִקָּרְאוּ בְּנַחֲלָתָם׃
7 וַאֲנִי ׀ בְּבֹאִי מִפַּדָּן מֵתָה עָלַי רָחֵל
בְּאֶרֶץ כְּנַעַן בַּדֶּרֶךְ בְּעוֹד כִּבְרַת־אֶרֶץ
לָבֹא אֶפְרָתָה וָאֶקְבְּרֶהָ שָּׁם בְּדֶרֶךְ אֶפְרָת
הִוא בֵּית לָחֶם׃
8 וַיַּרְא יִשְׂרָאֵל אֶת־בְּנֵי יוֹסֵף וַיֹּאמֶר מִי־
אֵלֶּה׃ 9 וַיֹּאמֶר יוֹסֵף אֶל־אָבִיו בָּנַי הֵם
אֲשֶׁר־נָתַן־לִי אֱלֹהִים בָּזֶה וַיֹּאמַר קָחֶם־

seph, who never experienced a divine revelation, cannot endow his sons with tribal territory.

an everlasting possession The only inalienable "possession" of territory is the Land of Israel. Only God can grant such a possession. Pharaoh's gift is temporary.

5. shall be mine Jacob formally adopts his two grandchildren through a legal process that elevates them to full membership in the Israelite tribal league. The first stage of the process is this declaration of intent. Intrafamily adoptions are well attested in the ancient Near East.

Ephraim and Manasseh Jacob mentions the younger son first, in contrast to the order in verse 1—a hint of impending developments.

Reuben and Simeon The parallel drawn between the two sons of Joseph and the two oldest sons of Jacob marks the new legal status of the former.

6. born to you The verb *holad'ta* means, literally, "you have begotten." The past tense of this verb is confirmed by the word meaning "who were born" (*ha-noladim*) in verse 5. It appears that we have here a fragment of a lost tradition, not otherwise referred to in the Bible, concerning other children born to Joseph, i.e., clans who adhered to the "House of Joseph."

shall be yours They shall not constitute separate tribal entities, but shall share the inheritance of either Manasseh or Ephraim.

7. Rachel died On his deathbed, Jacob recalls his beloved wife, who died so young and for whom he endured so much.

Paddan The full place-name is Paddan-aram, as in 25:20, 35:9.

8. Israel This name, rather than Jacob, is used hereafter until the end of the chapter to reflect the change of name (35:10) on which

---

buried in Machpelah. Sforno imagines Jacob pleading that he was too overcome with grief to make proper burial arrangements for Rachel, whom he loved so desperately, and stating that he has felt guilty about it ever since.

8. Who are these? Jacob, who has just spoken so extravagantly about his closeness to Ephraim and Manasseh (v. 5), does not recognize them. Has his vision begun to fail, as happened to his father, Isaac, in similar circumstances? Or did he fail to recognize Ephraim and Manasseh because, having been born and raised in Egypt, they were indistinguishable from Egyptian youths? Tradition has it that they reassured him by reciting the *Sh'ma*—"Hear, O Israel" (i.e., Jacob)—we may look like Egyptians but we affirm the same God as our father and grandfather.

may bless them." [10]Now Israel's eyes were dim with age; he could not see. So [Joseph] brought them close to him, and he kissed them and embraced them. [11]And Israel said to Joseph, "I never expected to see you again, and here God has let me see your children as well."

[12]Joseph then removed them from his knees, and bowed low with his face to the ground. [13]Joseph took the two of them, Ephraim with his right hand—to Israel's left—and Manasseh with his left hand—to Israel's right—and brought them close to him. [14]But Israel stretched out his right hand and laid it on Ephraim's head, though he was the younger, and his left hand on Manasseh's head—thus crossing his hands—although Manasseh was the first-born. [15]And he blessed Joseph, saying,

"The God in whose ways my fathers Abraham and Isaac walked,
The God who has been my shepherd from my birth to this day—

שני נָ֥א אֵלַ֖י וַאֲבָרְכֵֽם׃ 10 וְעֵינֵ֤י יִשְׂרָאֵל֙ כָּבְד֣וּ
מִזֹּ֔קֶן לֹ֥א יוּכַ֖ל לִרְא֑וֹת וַיַּגֵּ֤שׁ אֹתָם֙ אֵלָ֔יו
וַיִּשַּׁ֥ק לָהֶ֖ם וַיְחַבֵּ֥ק לָהֶֽם׃ 11 וַיֹּ֤אמֶר
יִשְׂרָאֵל֙ אֶל־יוֹסֵ֔ף רְאֹ֥ה פָנֶ֖יךָ לֹ֣א פִלָּ֑לְתִּי
וְהִנֵּ֨ה הֶרְאָ֥ה אֹתִ֛י אֱלֹהִ֖ים גַּ֥ם אֶת־זַרְעֶֽךָ׃
12 וַיּוֹצֵ֥א יוֹסֵ֛ף אֹתָ֖ם מֵעִ֣ם בִּרְכָּ֑יו וַיִּשְׁתַּ֥חוּ
לְאַפָּ֖יו אָֽרְצָה׃ 13 וַיִּקַּ֣ח יוֹסֵף֮ אֶת־שְׁנֵיהֶם֒
אֶֽת־אֶפְרַ֤יִם בִּֽימִינוֹ֙ מִשְּׂמֹ֣אל יִשְׂרָאֵ֔ל
וְאֶת־מְנַשֶּׁ֥ה בִשְׂמֹאל֖וֹ מִימִ֣ין יִשְׂרָאֵ֑ל
וַיַּגֵּ֖שׁ אֵלָֽיו׃ 14 וַיִּשְׁלַח֩ יִשְׂרָאֵ֨ל אֶת־יְמִינ֜וֹ
וַיָּ֨שֶׁת עַל־רֹ֤אשׁ אֶפְרַ֙יִם֙ וְה֣וּא הַצָּעִ֔יר
וְאֶת־שְׂמֹאל֖וֹ עַל־רֹ֣אשׁ מְנַשֶּׁ֑ה שִׂכֵּל֙ אֶת־
יָדָ֔יו כִּ֥י מְנַשֶּׁ֖ה הַבְּכֽוֹר׃ 15 וַיְבָ֥רֶךְ אֶת־יוֹסֵ֖ף
וַיֹּאמַ֑ר
הָֽאֱלֹהִ֡ים אֲשֶׁר֩ הִתְהַלְּכ֨וּ אֲבֹתַ֤י לְפָנָיו֙
אַבְרָהָ֣ם וְיִצְחָ֔ק
הָֽאֱלֹהִים֙ הָרֹעֶ֣ה אֹתִ֔י מֵעוֹדִ֖י עַד־הַיּ֥וֹם
הַזֶּֽה׃

this episode depends. Furthermore, the name Israel is more appropriate because the narrative concludes with tribal history.

10. Israel's eyes The statement explains Joseph's reaction in the following scene. He attributes his father's unusual act to his impaired vision.

12. from his knees The knees of Jacob, on or between which the two boys were placed. This is another symbolic gesture that marks acceptance and legitimation as son and heir. See Comment to 30:3.

and bowed low The Hebrew verb is singular and refers to Joseph.

THE GRANDFATHER'S BLESSING
(vv. 13–16)

13. Joseph took the two of them Joseph positions the boys before their grandfather in such a way as to ensure that Jacob's right hand, the symbol of action and power, will naturally rest on Manasseh, the firstborn.

14. on Ephraim's head Placing the hand on the head establishes physical contact between the parties to the blessing, heightening the sense of intimacy and communication.

15. he blessed Joseph The mention of Joseph is surprising because the blessing is directed entirely to the grandsons. The Septuagint reads "he blessed them," and the Latin reads "the sons of Joseph."

my fathers Abraham and Isaac walked Jacob, out of modesty, does not include himself.

my shepherd The image for the deity as a shepherd, common throughout ancient Near Eastern literature and found frequently in the Bible, expresses the idea of God as guide, provider, and protector (see Ps. 23).

---

14. crossing his hands Onkelos translates the verb for "crossing" (*sikkel*) as "acting wisely," acting with *seikhel,* "good sense." We are reminded of the lengths which Jacob himself went to in moving the patriarchal blessing from the older to the younger brother. Throughout the Torah, there is a preference for younger brothers over older ones. This is a way of saying that eminence is a function of individual character rather than birth order.

15. he blessed Joseph One blesses people best by blessing their children (*Zohar* I:227b).

¹⁶The Angel who has redeemed me from
all harm—
Bless the lads.
In them may my name be recalled,
And the names of my fathers Abraham
and Isaac,
And may they be teeming multitudes upon
the earth."

¹⁷When Joseph saw that his father was plac-
ing his right hand on Ephraim's head, he
thought it wrong; so he took hold of his father's hand to move it from Ephraim's head to
Manasseh's. ¹⁸"Not so, Father," Joseph said to
his father, "for the other is the first-born; place
your right hand on his head." ¹⁹But his father
objected, saying, "I know, my son, I know. He
too shall become a people, and he too shall be
great. Yet his younger brother shall be greater
than he, and his offspring shall be plentiful
enough for nations." ²⁰So he blessed them that
day, saying, "By you shall Israel invoke blessings, saying: God make you like Ephraim

16 הַמַּלְאָךְ֙ הַגֹּאֵ֣ל אֹתִי֙ מִכָּל־רָ֔ע
יְבָרֵךְ֮ אֶת־הַנְּעָרִים֒
וְיִקָּרֵ֤א בָהֶם֙ שְׁמִ֔י
וְשֵׁ֥ם אֲבֹתַ֖י אַבְרָהָ֣ם וְיִצְחָ֑ק
וְיִדְגּ֥וּ לָרֹ֖ב בְּקֶ֥רֶב הָאָֽרֶץ׃
שלישי 17 וַיַּ֣רְא יוֹסֵ֗ף כִּֽי־יָשִׁ֨ית אָבִ֧יו יַד־יְמִינ֛וֹ עַל־
רֹ֥אשׁ אֶפְרַ֖יִם וַיֵּ֣רַע בְּעֵינָ֑יו וַיִּתְמֹ֣ךְ יַד־אָבִ֗יו
לְהָסִ֥יר אֹתָ֛הּ מֵעַ֥ל רֹאשׁ־אֶפְרַ֖יִם עַל־רֹ֥אשׁ
מְנַשֶּֽׁה׃ 18 וַיֹּ֧אמֶר יוֹסֵ֛ף אֶל־אָבִ֖יו לֹא־כֵ֣ן
אָבִ֑י כִּי־זֶ֣ה הַבְּכֹ֔ר שִׂ֥ים יְמִֽינְךָ֖ עַל־רֹאשֽׁוֹ׃
19 וַיְמָאֵ֣ן אָבִ֗יו וַיֹּ֙אמֶר֙ יָדַ֤עְתִּֽי בְנִי֙ יָדַ֔עְתִּי
גַּם־ה֥וּא יִֽהְיֶה־לְּעָ֖ם וְגַם־ה֣וּא יִגְדָּ֑ל
וְאוּלָ֗ם אָחִ֤יו הַקָּטֹן֙ יִגְדַּ֣ל מִמֶּ֔נּוּ וְזַרְע֖וֹ
יִהְיֶ֥ה מְלֹֽא־הַגּוֹיִֽם׃ 20 וַיְבָ֨רֲכֵ֜ם בַּיּ֣וֹם
הַה֗וּא לֵאמוֹר֙ בְּךָ֗ יְבָרֵ֤ךְ יִשְׂרָאֵל֙ לֵאמֹ֔ר

16. *In them may my name be recalled* "May
my name be perpetuated through Ephraim and
Manasseh." That is, may they ever be part of the
Israelite tribal confederation, identifying themselves with the history, traditions, and values of
their Patriarchs.

teeming multitudes At the start of the wilderness wandering period, Ephraim and Manasseh together will number 72,700 male adults
(Num. 1:32–35); 40 years later, the figure will
be 85,200 (Num. 26:28–37), exceeding the
combined population of Reuben and Simeon.

REVERSAL OF SENIORITY (vv. 17–20)

17. *he thought it wrong* That is, to disre-

gard the status of the firstborn. He attributes the
"error" to his father's failing eyesight (v. 10).

19. *I know* I know who is the real firstborn
and how you placed your two sons before me.

shall be greater than he Moses' farewell address (Deut. 33:17) reflects the numerical superiority of Ephraim.

plentiful enough for nations Jacob transfers to Ephraim the contents of the blessing that
he himself had received (48:4, 35:11).

20. *he blessed them* Jacob's blessing of
Ephraim and Manasseh (v. 16), interrupted by
Joseph, is now resumed.

Israel See Comment to 47:27.

**16. *In them may my name be recalled,* /*And
the names of my fathers Abraham and Isaac***
May God bless them as long as they call themselves by traditional, biblical names. The most
valuable legacy we can leave our children and
grandchildren is bequeathing to them the faith
that sustained us (Shneur Zalman of Lyady).

20. *By you shall Israel invoke blessings* To
this day, Jewish parents bless their children on
Shabbat eve, usually before *kiddush* or right
after candle lighting). Before blessing all children with the priestly blessing (Num. 6:24–26),
they bless their daughters, "May God make you
as Sarah, Rebekah, Rachel, and Leah." And they

and Manasseh." Thus he put Ephraim before Manasseh.

21 Then Israel said to Joseph, "I am about to die; but God will be with you and bring you back to the land of your fathers. 22 And now, I assign to you one portion more than to your brothers, which I wrested from the Amorites with my sword and bow."

יְשִׂמְךָ אֱלֹהִים כְּאֶפְרַיִם וְכִמְנַשֶּׁה וַיָּשֶׂם
אֶת־אֶפְרַיִם לִפְנֵי מְנַשֶּׁה׃
21 וַיֹּאמֶר יִשְׂרָאֵל אֶל־יוֹסֵף הִנֵּה אָנֹכִי מֵת
וְהָיָה אֱלֹהִים עִמָּכֶם וְהֵשִׁיב אֶתְכֶם אֶל־
אֶרֶץ אֲבֹתֵיכֶם׃ 22 וַאֲנִי נָתַתִּי לְךָ שְׁכֶם
אַחַד עַל־אַחֶיךָ אֲשֶׁר לָקַחְתִּי מִיַּד
הָאֱמֹרִי בְּחַרְבִּי וּבְקַשְׁתִּי׃ פ

49 And Jacob called his sons and said, "Come together that I may tell you what is to befall you in days to come.

רביעי **מט** וַיִּקְרָא יַעֲקֹב אֶל־בָּנָיו וַיֹּאמֶר
הֵאָסְפוּ וְאַגִּידָה לָכֶם אֵת אֲשֶׁר־יִקְרָא
אֶתְכֶם בְּאַחֲרִית הַיָּמִים׃

A GIFT TO JOSEPH (vv. 21–22)

21. I am about to die; but God will be with you These apparently unrelated clauses allude to the contrast between the present situation that permits Jacob to be buried in the Promised Land and the impending bondage in Egypt. Yet future redemption is ensured, because God wills it.

with you The Hebrew pronoun for "you" is in the plural. Jacob speaks through Joseph to the entire people.

22. one portion This translation of *sh'khem*, which agrees with many ancient versions, is accepted by traditional Jewish commentators. It means that Jacob is giving Joseph a double share, thus elevating him to the status of firstborn. It is likely, however, that *sh'khem* here does not mean "portion" but is connected with the city of Shechem, a place closely associated with Jacob and Joseph (Gen. 33:18ff.; Josh. 24:32). In that understanding, the passage refers to some tradition in the life of Jacob (other than the one in chapter 34) concerning his participation in a war against Shechem, which the Bible has not otherwise preserved. The Book of Joshua contains no report of the conquest of that city, although Joshua delivered his farewell address and conducted a covenant ceremony there. It is likely, therefore, that there was a pre-Mosaic Israelite conquest of Shechem. Possibly the city was razed in such a conquest and remained largely in ruins until it was reoccupied by Joshua without a fight.

from the Amorites This is a generic name for the pre-Israelite peoples of Canaan.

THE TESTAMENT OF JACOB (49:1–33)

Jacob summons his sons to his bedside to hear his farewell words. He addresses each son individually in poetic form. Traditional Jewish commentators treated these blessings and curses as prophetic. Modern scholars view them as reflections of later historical reality.

A PROSE INTRODUCTION (v. 1)

1. called That is, he sent for his sons.

what is to befall you This refers to the distant future. Jacob is speaking to the individual tribes personified as his sons.

---

bless their sons, "May God make you as Ephraim and Manasseh." Why Ephraim and Manasseh? Perhaps because they were the first children who had to maintain their identity in a foreign land. Or perhaps because they were the first brothers in the Bible to get along peaceably, after the conflicts that marred the lives of Cain and Abel, Isaac and Ishmael, Jacob and Esau, and Joseph and his brothers. Now that siblings have learned to get along, the story of the Jewish people can move to the next stage.

CHAPTER 49

1. Jacob summons his children, promising to tell them what will happen to them in the future. Instead, he speaks to each of his sons

2Assemble and hearken, O sons of Jacob; Hearken to Israel your father:	2 הִקָּבְצ֥וּ וְשִׁמְע֖וּ בְּנֵ֣י יַעֲקֹ֑ב וְשִׁמְע֖וּ אֶל־יִשְׂרָאֵ֥ל אֲבִיכֶֽם׃
3Reuben, you are my first-born, My might and first fruit of my vigor, Exceeding in rank And exceeding in honor. 4Unstable as water, you shall excel no longer; For when you mounted your father's bed, You brought disgrace—my couch he mounted!	3 רְאוּבֵן֙ בְּכֹ֣רִי אַ֔תָּה כֹּחִ֖י וְרֵאשִׁ֣ית אוֹנִ֑י יֶ֥תֶר שְׂאֵ֖ת וְיֶ֥תֶר עָֽז׃ 4 פַּ֤חַז כַּמַּ֙יִם֙ אַל־תּוֹתַ֔ר כִּ֥י עָלִ֖יתָ מִשְׁכְּבֵ֣י אָבִ֑יךָ אָ֥ז חִלַּ֖לְתָּ יְצוּעִ֥י עָלָֽה׃ פ

in days to come The phrase *b'aḥarit ha-yamim* means simply "in the future," a time without precise definition.

THE POEM (vv. 2–27)

2. hearken . . . Hearken The repetition of a word at the beginning of two parallel clauses is a feature of biblical Hebrew poetry.

REUBEN (vv. 3–4)

Reuben is censured for the flaws in his character and for his moral failing (see Comment to verse 4). Reuben's place at the head of the tribal lists in the Bible must echo the actual state of affairs that existed in dim antiquity. Behind Reuben's loss of his firstborn status is a legal reality during an early period of Israelite history when it still was possible for a father to annul the birthright of his firstborn son, in contrast to the later legislation of Deut. 21:15–17.

3. My might That is, "my virility."

my vigor The Hebrew word *on* refers here to the powers of procreation.

Exceeding The literal meaning of the word translated as "exceeding" (*yeter*) is "excellence." The meaning: Being the firstborn, you should have pre-eminence over your brothers.

4. Unstable as water Jacob censures Reuben for acting irresponsibly and impetuously, with no moral restraint, just as a torrent of water rushes along wildly.

shall excel no longer You have lost your pre-eminence.

mounted . . . bed This refers to Reuben's act of incest, recorded in 35:22 and mentioned again in 1 Chron. 5:1.

bed The word translated here as "bed" (*mishk'vei*) is plural, always so used in the context of carnal relations (see Lev. 18:22, 20:13). Here the phrase "your father's bed" stands for "the bed of your father's wife."

You brought disgrace The Hebrew stem חלל "to pollute, defile, profane," is used in connection with sexual depravity, as in Lev. 19:29 and 21:9.

my couch he mounted This is an aside addressed to the assembled sons.

SIMEON AND LEVI (vv. 5–7)

These two brothers are strongly censured for acts of cruelty and violence, alluding to their attack

---

about that son's character and special gifts. The Midrash suggests that this is because the spirit of prophecy departed from Jacob (Gen. R. 98:2). Perhaps we are not meant to know the future lest it lead us to despair or complacency. Perhaps, when Jacob looked into the future, he saw the quarreling and bloodshed that would befall his descendants, and the spirit of prophecy cannot abide where there is grief and sadness (Naftali of Ropshitz). The modern reader may understand the passage to mean that a person's future depends on his or her character. There is no preordained script that we are fated to follow.

4. You brought disgrace What sort of blessing is this? Perhaps the greatest blessing is to have someone who cares about you point out your faults.

5 Simeon and Levi are a pair;
Their weapons are tools of lawlessness.
6 Let not my person be included in their council,
Let not my being be counted in their assembly.
For when angry they slay men,
And when pleased they maim oxen.
7 Cursed be their anger so fierce,
And their wrath so relentless.
I will divide them in Jacob,
Scatter them in Israel.

8 You, O Judah, your brothers shall praise;
Your hand shall be on the nape of your foes;

5 שִׁמְעוֹן וְלֵוִי אַחִים
כְּלֵי חָמָס מְכֵרֹתֵיהֶם׃
6 בְּסֹדָם אַל־תָּבֹא נַפְשִׁי
בִּקְהָלָם אַל־תֵּחַד כְּבֹדִי
כִּי בְאַפָּם הָרְגוּ אִישׁ
וּבִרְצֹנָם עִקְּרוּ־שׁוֹר׃
7 אָרוּר אַפָּם כִּי עָז
וְעֶבְרָתָם כִּי קָשָׁתָה
אֲחַלְּקֵם בְּיַעֲקֹב
וַאֲפִיצֵם בְּיִשְׂרָאֵל׃ ס

8 יְהוּדָה אַתָּה יוֹדוּךָ אַחֶיךָ
יָדְךָ בְּעֹרֶף אֹיְבֶיךָ

on the city of Shechem, described in chapter 34. Neither Levi nor Simeon, next in line of seniority after Reuben, inherited the mantle of leadership. Levi, next after Simeon, is here depicted as a warlike tribe, with no hint of the sacred status it would later have (Exod. 32:26ff.; Deut. 33:11). Very likely, these verses echo an early, independent tradition.

5. a pair The Hebrew word *aḥim* literally means "brothers," i.e., partners and allies.

Their weapons The Hebrew word translated as "their weapons" (*m'kheroteihem*) appears only here, and any translation is guesswork.

6. council . . . assembly The Hebrew for these words (*sod . . . kahal*) refer to the tribal gatherings at which decisions are made.

Let not my being Jacob dissociates himself from these two tribes because of their disregard for human values. The word translated here as "being" (*kavod*) means "presence," as in "the Presence of the LORD" (*k'vod Adonai*). A derivative meaning is "honor." It is the God-endowed quality that distinguishes human beings from other forms of life.

angry . . . pleased That is, in any mood, as the whim strikes them.

maim According to 34:28ff., the cattle in Shechem were not mutilated but carried off as spoil. Jacob's reproach, therefore, may refer to some other acts of cruelty perpetrated by these two tribes, the record of which has not been preserved.

7. I will It is Jacob who pronounces their fate.

divide them These two tribes are cursed with the loss of independence and territorial integrity. The future condition of the tribes is explained in terms of the punitive ban decreed on their original ancestors.

JUDAH (vv. 8–12)

In striking contrast to Simeon and Levi, Judah is lavishly praised and blessed. The tribe of Judah attained leadership in the time of David, the period referred to in these verses.

8. You You alone, in contrast to the others.

hand . . . on the nape The enemies, turning their backs in flight, will be seized by the nape before they can escape.

your foes The tribe of Judah, constantly be-

---

5. *Their weapons are tools of lawlessness* The Midrash reads: "their weapons are stolen." It was Esau who was ordained to live by the sword; Jacob and his descendants were to flourish through their piety. When Simeon and Levi resorted to violence, they appropriated Esau's method of dealing with conflict (Gen. R. 99:6).

7. *Cursed be their anger* Even in his displeasure, Jacob does not curse his sons; he curses their unacceptable behavior. A com-

Your father's sons shall bow low to you.
9 Judah is a lion's whelp;
On prey, my son, have you grown.
He crouches, lies down like a lion,
Like the king of beasts—who dare rouse him?
10 The scepter shall not depart from Judah,
Nor the ruler's staff from between his feet;
So that tribute shall come to him
And the homage of peoples be his.

11 He tethers his ass to a vine,
His ass's foal to a choice vine;
He washes his garment in wine,
His robe in blood of grapes.
12 His eyes are darker than wine;
His teeth are whiter than milk.

יִשְׁתַּחֲווּ לְךָ בְּנֵי אָבִיךָ׃
9 גּוּר אַרְיֵה יְהוּדָה
מִטֶּרֶף בְּנִי עָלִיתָ
כָּרַע רָבַץ כְּאַרְיֵה
וּכְלָבִיא מִי יְקִימֶנּוּ׃
10 לֹא־יָסוּר שֵׁבֶט מִיהוּדָה
וּמְחֹקֵק מִבֵּין רַגְלָיו
עַד כִּי־יָבֹא שילה שִׁילוֹ
וְלוֹ יִקְּהַת עַמִּים׃

11 אֹסְרִי לַגֶּפֶן עירה עִירוֹ
וְלַשֹּׂרֵקָה בְּנִי אֲתֹנוֹ
כִּבֵּס בַּיַּיִן לְבֻשׁוֹ
וּבְדַם־עֲנָבִים סותה סוּתוֹ׃
12 חַכְלִילִי עֵינַיִם מִיָּיִן
וּלְבֶן־שִׁנַּיִם מֵחָלָב׃ פ

set by the Philistines to the west, Amalekites in the Negeb, and Edomites to the east, was for a long time isolated from the northern tribes by Canaanite enclaves and forced to expand southward.

9. a lion's whelp A metaphor of strength, daring, and invincibility.

have you grown An allusion to the later heroic and expansionist campaigns of David.

10. The scepter An emblem of sovereignty. Judah will always enjoy authority over the other tribes. From the tribe of Judah came the royal house of David.

from between his feet The phrase conjures up the picture of a ruler holding the staff of office between his legs when seated in formal session.

tribute shall come to him This translation understands the Hebrew word *shiloh* as a combination of *shai* (tribute) and *loh* (to him).

peoples Either the other tribes (i.e., "kinsmen") or an allusion to foreign peoples conquered by David.

11. He tethers This is an exaggerated image of the fertility of the tribal territory of Judah.

choice vine The Hebrew word is *"sorekah."* A place named Wadi Sorek, in the territory of Judah, is located in Timnah, a region rich in vineyards.

He washes his garment in wine Either this is another exaggerated image for the abundance of wine or it may poetically relate to the stained garments of those engaged in the manufacture of wine, as mentioned in Isa. 63:2ff.

blood of grapes A poetic term for wine.

12. darker than wine . . . whiter than milk The phrases express an ideal of beauty: sparkling eyes and shining white teeth.

---

mentator interprets his words to mean, "May they be unsuccessful in their anger and violence. May such behavior not prove effective, so that they not be encouraged to use it" (*Ḥizz'kuni*).

10. So that tribute shall come to him Sforno understands *Shiloh* as related to *shalom,* so that the verse would mean "till the time of total peace arrives." The Midrash and Rashi take the verse as a reference to the Messianic Era, when nations will pay tribute to the ruler from the seed of Judah.

13Zebulun shall dwell by the seashore;
He shall be a haven for ships,
And his flank shall rest on Sidon.

14Issachar is a strong-boned ass,
Crouching among the sheepfolds.
15When he saw how good was security,
And how pleasant was the country,
He bent his shoulder to the burden,
And became a toiling serf.

16Dan shall govern his people,
As one of the tribes of Israel.

13 זְבוּלֻן לְחוֹף יַמִּים יִשְׁכֹּן
וְהוּא לְחוֹף אֳנִיֹּת
וְיַרְכָתוֹ עַל־צִידֹן׃ ס

14 יִשָּׂשכָר חֲמֹר גָּרֶם
רֹבֵץ בֵּין הַמִּשְׁפְּתָיִם׃
15 וַיַּרְא מְנֻחָה כִּי טוֹב
וְאֶת־הָאָרֶץ כִּי נָעֵמָה
וַיֵּט שִׁכְמוֹ לִסְבֹּל
וַיְהִי לְמַס־עֹבֵד׃ ס

16 דָּן יָדִין עַמּוֹ
כְּאַחַד שִׁבְטֵי יִשְׂרָאֵל׃

ZEBULUN (v. 13)

The usual order, Issachar–Zebulun, is here reversed, very likely reflecting a time when the tribe of Zebulun was in the ascendancy.

13. the seashore The Mediterranean.

Sidon A port city in Phoenicia, about 25 miles (40 km) north of Tyre. See 2 Sam. 24:6, according to which this was the northernmost limit of David's empire.

ISSACHAR (vv. 14–15)

The tribe is not even mentioned in the list of Judg. 1, which indicates that it played an insignificant role in the conquest of the Land of Israel. Here it is chided for passively submitting to servitude as the price of peace with its Canaanite neighbors.

14. a strong-boned ass The idiom for this (*ḥamor gerem*) appears only here. This translation implies a criticism of the tribe for placing its strength at the service of the Canaanites.

Crouching among the sheepfolds That is, inactive, content to enjoy its safety at the expense of its freedom.

15. security The word *m'nuḥah* means "resting place" and is used here in the sense of "haven, settled home."

good . . . pleasant The territory of the tribe lay in a fertile plateau in Lower Galilee.

to the burden . . . a toiling serf The verb סבל and the following word, *mas,* both refer to "corvée," enforced hard labor imposed on a subservient people. These very terms are used that way in Akkadian documents from Syria and Canaan. It would seem that until the final overthrow of the Canaanite city-states in the time of Deborah, the tribe was content to perform corvée labor for the local overlords in return for a quiet existence.

DAN (vv. 16–17)

Dan is the first of the tribes descended from concubines to be addressed. During the settlement period, it was a small tribe in a precarious position. All attempts on the part of the Danites to settle in their originally assigned territory were unsuccessful, and they migrated northward (see Judg. 18:1ff.). The testament of Jacob is referring either to the premigration period or to events after the settlement in the north.

16. shall govern The tribe of Dan will maintain its independence, despite its tribulations and failures.

the tribes of Israel This is the first use of the phrase.

13–14. There is a rabbinic tradition that members of the tribe of Zebulun were prosperous merchants who subsidized the members of the tribe of Issachar, enabling them to engage in study. Jacob gives precedence to Zebulun (another younger brother favored over an older one) as a way of commending them for their actions (Gen. R. 99:9). Similarly, at the end of the Torah, Moses in his farewell address blesses "Zebulun in your excursions and Issachar in your tents" (Deut. 33:18).

17 Dan shall be a serpent by the road,
A viper by the path,
That bites the horse's heels
So that his rider is thrown backward.

18 I wait for Your deliverance, O LORD!

19 Gad shall be raided by raiders,
But he shall raid at their heels.

20 Asher's bread shall be rich,
And he shall yield royal dainties.

17 יְהִי־דָן֙ נָחָ֣שׁ עֲלֵי־דֶ֔רֶךְ
שְׁפִיפֹ֖ן עֲלֵי־אֹ֑רַח
הַנֹּשֵׁךְ֙ עִקְּבֵי־ס֔וּס
וַיִּפֹּ֥ל רֹכְב֖וֹ אָחֽוֹר׃

18 לִישׁוּעָתְךָ֖ קִוִּ֥יתִי יְהוָֽה׃

ששי 19 גָּ֖ד גְּד֣וּד יְגוּדֶ֑נּוּ
וְה֖וּא יָגֻ֥ד עָקֵֽב׃ ס

20 מֵאָשֵׁ֖ר שְׁמֵנָ֣ה לַחְמ֑וֹ
וְה֥וּא יִתֵּ֖ן מַֽעֲדַנֵּי־מֶֽלֶךְ׃ ס

17. viper The image may allude to the form of guerrilla warfare to which the tribe of Dan was forced to resort in its struggle for survival against its neighbors during the period of settlement.

horse's . . . rider The word for "rider" (*rokhev*) can also be used of a charioteer, as in Exod. 15:2 and Jer. 51:21. Hence the likely reference here is to Canaanite chariots, which for a long time constituted the primary obstacle to Israelite penetration into the lowlands and caused the migration of the Danites (Josh. 17:18; Judg. 1:19, 4:3).

A PRAYER (v. 18)

18. I wait for Your deliverance Most likely, this is a prayer invoked by Jacob for the tribe of Dan in its desperate struggle for a territorial foothold in the land of Canaan. It also could be a prayer uttered by Jacob who, in a sudden moment of weakness, calls for strength to finish the testament.

GAD (v. 19)

This tribe's territory was east of the Jordan. Gad was engaged in a series of wars with its neighbors—Ammonites, Moabites, and Arameans—for most of its history. No particular historic situation can be pinpointed as the background to this aphorism.

19. Gad . . . raided The Hebrew contains a play on the name: *Gad* is associated with *g'dud*, "a troop," and the verb formed from it, *y'gudennu*, "shall be raided."

ASHER (v. 20)

This tribe settled in western Galilee between Carmel and Phoenicia (Josh. 19:24–31), an area famed for its fertility, and inside the Canaanite–Phoenician sphere of political and commercial activity. Asher, which did not succeed in capturing the most important cities in its allotted territory, seems to have thrown in its lot with the local city-states from which it derived its prosperity. The testament thus refers to the period of the Judges, before the final defeat of the Canaanites in the north under Deborah's leadership.

20. Asher The name, which means "fortune, happiness" (Gen. 30:13), contains an allusion to the prosperity of the tribe.

bread The word translated as "bread" (*leḥem*) can mean food in general. This is its meaning in Arabic, where it often refers to meat.

royal dainties The phrase may either be figurative, "delicacies fit for a king," or literal—i.e., Asher serviced the petty Canaanite kingdoms with gifts of oil.

NAPHTALI (v. 21)

The territory of this tribe lay in Upper Galilee and ran parallel to the Jordan from the south shore of the Sea of Galilee to an unspecified line in the north beyond Lake Huleh, with its western boundary bordering on Asher (Josh.

---

17. This rather violent prediction about the tribe of Dan is commonly related to the career of Samson, a warlike leader who came from that tribe. It may also refer to Dan's later relocation to the north when it was a border tribe.

21 נַפְתָּלִי אַיָּלָה שְׁלֻחָה
הַנֹּתֵן אִמְרֵי־שָׁפֶר׃ ס

22 בֵּן פֹּרָת יוֹסֵף
בֵּן פֹּרָת עֲלֵי־עָיִן
בָּנוֹת צָעֲדָה עֲלֵי־שׁוּר׃

23 וַיְמָרְרֻהוּ וָרֹבּוּ
וַיִּשְׂטְמֻהוּ בַּעֲלֵי חִצִּים׃
24 וַתֵּשֶׁב בְּאֵיתָן קַשְׁתּוֹ
וַיָּפֹזּוּ זְרֹעֵי יָדָיו
מִידֵי אֲבִיר יַעֲקֹב
מִשָּׁם רֹעֶה אֶבֶן יִשְׂרָאֵל׃
25 מֵאֵל אָבִיךָ וְיַעְזְרֶךָּ
וְאֵת שַׁדַּי וִיבָרְכֶךָּ
בִּרְכֹת שָׁמַיִם מֵעָל
בִּרְכֹת תְּהוֹם רֹבֶצֶת תָּחַת

21 Naphtali is a hind let loose,
Which yields lovely fawns.

22 Joseph is a wild ass,
A wild ass by a spring
—Wild colts on a hillside.

23 Archers bitterly assailed him;
They shot at him and harried him.
24 Yet his bow stayed taut,
And his arms were made firm
By the hands of the Mighty One of Jacob—
There, the Shepherd, the Rock of Israel—
25 The God of your father who helps you,
And Shaddai who blesses you
With blessings of heaven above,
Blessings of the deep that couches below,

19:32–39). It played a glorious role in the war against the Canaanites.

21. a hind The word *ayyalah,* a symbol of beauty, also typifies fleet-footedness.

let loose The literal meaning of the word *sh'luḥah* is "unrestrained."

lovely fawns Perhaps a reference to the beauty, openness, and fruitfulness of its tribal territory.

JOSEPH (vv. 22–26)

Lavish blessing is showered upon Joseph in a passage of exceptional length, equaled only by that to Judah.

22. Joseph The name "Joseph" is here used for the two tribes of Ephraim and Manasseh. Such usage is rare. Normally, "Joseph" designates the entire northern kingdom of ancient Israel, and the two tribes are known as "the House of Joseph" or "the sons of Joseph."

wild ass This may allude to the freedom and independence of the Joseph tribes, which occupied an area that had been sparsely populated (see Josh. 17:14–18).

23. Archers The Bible nowhere else records attacks by archers on Joseph. This may refer to some unreported episode in his life or to attacks on Ephraim and Manasseh by neighboring tribes or Canaanite armies.

24. his bow stayed taut Joseph remained steadfast in the face of adversity and drew his strength from God, who championed his cause.

Mighty One of Jacob The phrase *"Avir Ya·akov"* is a rare title for God. It corresponds to the Akkadian divine title *bel abari*, "endowed with strength."

Jacob . . . Israel Do these refer to the Patriarch—or to the people Israel? The ambiguity is probably deliberate. The Patriarch and the people are now as one.

There The Hebrew vocalization *mi-sham* (literally, "from there") may be a scribal error for the word *mi-shem* (literally, "by the name of").

the Shepherd For the image of God as a shepherd, see Comment to 48:15.

the Rock of Israel This image expresses strength, permanence, and protection.

25. The God of your father This title stresses the continuity of the generations, the unbroken chain of religious tradition that alone makes the dying Patriarch's blessing meaningful and effective. The testament to Joseph now shifts from the miseries of the past to the promise of the future.

blessings These consist of rain and dew and abundance of water resources, all of which symbolize fruitfulness of the soil and the fecundity of animals and humans.

the deep that couches below The Hebrew word translated as "the deep" (*t'hom*) refers to

Blessings of the breast and womb.
26 The blessings of your father
Surpass the blessings of my ancestors,
To the utmost bounds of the eternal hills.
May they rest on the head of Joseph,
On the brow of the elect of his brothers.

בִּרְכֹת שָׁדַיִם וָרָחַם׃
26 בִּרְכֹת אָבִיךָ
גָּבְרוּ עַל־בִּרְכֹת הוֹרַי
עַד־תַּאֲוַת גִּבְעֹת עוֹלָם
תִּהְיֶיןָ לְרֹאשׁ יוֹסֵף
וּלְקָדְקֹד נְזִיר אֶחָיו׃ פ

27 Benjamin is a ravenous wolf;
In the morning he consumes the foe,
And in the evening he divides the spoil."

ששי 27 בִּנְיָמִין זְאֵב יִטְרָף
בַּבֹּקֶר יֹאכַל עַד
וְלָעֶרֶב יְחַלֵּק שָׁלָל׃

28 All these were the tribes of Israel, twelve in number, and this is what their father said to them as he bade them farewell, addressing to each a parting word appropriate to him.

29 Then he instructed them, saying to them, "I am about to be gathered to my kin. Bury me

28 כָּל־אֵלֶּה שִׁבְטֵי יִשְׂרָאֵל שְׁנֵים עָשָׂר
וְזֹאת אֲשֶׁר־דִּבֶּר לָהֶם אֲבִיהֶם וַיְבָרֶךְ
אוֹתָם אִישׁ אֲשֶׁר כְּבִרְכָתוֹ בֵּרַךְ אֹתָם׃
29 וַיְצַו אוֹתָם וַיֹּאמֶר אֲלֵהֶם אֲנִי נֶאֱסָף
אֶל־עַמִּי קִבְרוּ אֹתִי אֶל־אֲבֹתָי אֶל־

the ancient notion of the subterranean source of uncontrollable waters that rise to the earth's surface (see Gen. 1:2).

26. Surpass Joseph is assured that the blessings he is receiving from his father exceed the blessings his father received from his own forebears.

BENJAMIN (v. 27)

The image of Benjamin as a warrior and a predator is that of a tribe, not an individual. The belligerence of the Benjaminites resulted from their geographic situation: a narrow strip of land so strategically located that the important north–south central highway, as well as a main east–west road leading to Transjordan, passed through it. As a result, the territory of Benjamin became an arena for wars. The testament of Jacob reflects this general historical situation. (See the anti-Benjamin war in Judg. 20–21.)

27. morning . . . evening The two contrasting terms express continual action. They could also describe the wolf as prowling among the sheep at night, snatching its prey and returning to its lair to share it with its young, with enough left over for the morning.

PROSE EPILOGUE: THE DEATH OF JACOB (vv. 28–33)

28. the tribes of Israel See Comment to verse 16. The phrase expresses the collective awareness of a national unity and common identity that is "Israel," even though each tribe is individually addressed in the testament and regarded as an autonomous entity.

twelve in number This is the first reference in the Bible to the 12 tribes of Israel, a number that is maintained in all tribal lists.

as he bade them farewell The Hebrew verb *va-y'varekh,* usually understood as "bless," here is rendered "bade farewell" because not all the tribes received blessings.

29. Bury me Jacob imposes on all his sons the obligation to bury him in Canaan, but he does not make them swear to that effect, as he did with Joseph (47:29–31), because only Jo-

---

25. blessings of heaven above, / Blessings of the deep that couches below Some of Joseph's remarkable achievements came about because he was fortunate to be blessed with good qualities from birth ("blessings of heaven above"). At the same time, he encountered chaos and misfortune ("the deep that couches below") and overcame them.

הַמְּעָרָ֕ה אֲשֶׁ֥ר בִּשְׂדֵ֖ה עֶפְר֥וֹן הַחִתִּֽי׃
30 בַּמְּעָרָ֞ה אֲשֶׁ֨ר בִּשְׂדֵ֧ה הַמַּכְפֵּלָ֛ה אֲשֶׁר
עַל־פְּנֵי־מַמְרֵ֖א בְּאֶ֣רֶץ כְּנָ֑עַן אֲשֶׁר֩ קָנָ֨ה
אַבְרָהָ֜ם אֶת־הַשָּׂדֶ֗ה מֵאֵ֛ת עֶפְרֹ֥ן הַחִתִּ֖י
לַאֲחֻזַּת־קָֽבֶר׃ 31 שָׁ֣מָּה קָֽבְר֞וּ אֶת־
אַבְרָהָ֗ם וְאֵת֙ שָׂרָ֣ה אִשְׁתּ֔וֹ שָׁ֚מָּה קָבְר֣וּ
אֶת־יִצְחָ֔ק וְאֵ֖ת רִבְקָ֣ה אִשְׁתּ֑וֹ וְשָׁ֥מָּה
קָבַ֖רְתִּי אֶת־לֵאָֽה׃ 32 מִקְנֵ֧ה הַשָּׂדֶ֛ה
וְהַמְּעָרָ֥ה אֲשֶׁר־בּ֖וֹ מֵאֵ֥ת בְּנֵי־חֵֽת׃ 33 וַיְכַ֤ל
יַעֲקֹב֙ לְצַוֺּ֣ת אֶת־בָּנָ֔יו וַיֶּאֱסֹ֥ף רַגְלָ֖יו אֶל־
הַמִּטָּ֑ה וַיִּגְוַ֖ע וַיֵּאָ֥סֶף אֶל־עַמָּֽיו׃

with my fathers in the cave which is in the field
of Ephron the Hittite, 30the cave which is in the
field of Machpelah, facing Mamre, in the land
of Canaan, the field that Abraham bought
from Ephron the Hittite for a burial site—
31there Abraham and his wife Sarah were buried; there Isaac and his wife Rebekah were
buried; and there I buried Leah—32the field
and the cave in it, bought from the Hittites."
33When Jacob finished his instructions to his
sons, he drew his feet into the bed and, breathing his last, he was gathered to his people.

נ וַיִּפֹּ֥ל יוֹסֵ֖ף עַל־פְּנֵ֣י אָבִ֑יו וַיֵּ֥בְךְּ עָלָ֖יו
וַיִּשַּׁק־לֽוֹ׃ 2 וַיְצַ֨ו יוֹסֵ֤ף אֶת־עֲבָדָיו֙ אֶת־
הָרֹ֣פְאִ֔ים לַחֲנֹ֖ט אֶת־אָבִ֑יו וַיַּחַנְט֥וּ

50 Joseph flung himself upon his father's
face and wept over him and kissed him. 2Then
Joseph ordered the physicians in his service to
embalm his father, and the physicians em-

seph had the capability, and access to the Egyptian authorities, necessary to implement the Patriarch's wish.

30. the cave The description of the burial site follows that of 23:17–20.

33. he drew his feet into the bed A figurative expression for dying.

MOURNING AND BURIAL (50:1–14)

1. Joseph flung himself upon his father's face The usual phrase for such an emotional embrace is "to fall on the neck," but this would be appropriate only when the parties involved are in an upright position.

and kissed him An act of farewell. See Gen. 31:28, 32:1 and Ruth 1:9,14.

2. the physicians in his service The text dissociates the embalming procedure from any connection with pagan rites by having Joseph entrust the task to his own physicians and not to professional mortuary priests.

to embalm his father Joseph, too, was embalmed at death (v. 26). Such a practice is never again referred to in the Bible. It is well known that mummification was bound up with the Egyptian worship of Osiris and conceptions of the afterlife. The embalming of Jacob and Jo-

---

33. he drew his feet into the bed Jacob is described as "lifting his feet" to begin his journey after his dream of the ladder at Bethel (see Comment to 29:1). His journey will have taken him to three countries. He has loved, he has fought, he has known bereavement. Now, after many years, Jacob can finally stop wandering and struggling. We may see Jacob as perhaps the most fascinating of the Patriarchs. He is many different people in the course of a long and eventful life. He grows and changes over the years, from the "mild man" (Gen. 25:27) who stays home, to Jacob the trickster who deceives and is deceived, and finally to Israel the mortal who struggles with God. He spends much of the last part of his life burdened by grief and perhaps guilt, ending his days as an old man who is dependent on his favorite son. We can see him as the exemplar of the flawed person who can outgrow his flaws. He seeks contentment and

הָרֹפְאִ֖ים אֶת־יִשְׂרָאֵֽל׃ 3 וַיִּמְלְאוּ־ל֙וֹ
אַרְבָּעִ֣ים י֔וֹם כִּ֛י כֵּ֥ן יִמְלְא֖וּ יְמֵ֣י הַחֲנֻטִ֑ים
וַיִּבְכּ֥וּ אֹת֛וֹ מִצְרַ֖יִם שִׁבְעִ֥ים יֽוֹם׃ 4 וַיַּֽעַבְרוּ֙
יְמֵ֣י בְכִית֔וֹ וַיְדַבֵּ֣ר יוֹסֵ֔ף אֶל־בֵּ֥ית פַּרְעֹ֖ה
לֵאמֹ֑ר אִם־נָ֨א מָצָ֤אתִי חֵן֙ בְּעֵ֣ינֵיכֶ֔ם
דַּבְּרוּ־נָ֕א בְּאָזְנֵ֥י פַרְעֹ֖ה לֵאמֹֽר׃ 5 אָבִ֞י
הִשְׁבִּיעַ֣נִי לֵאמֹ֗ר הִנֵּ֣ה אָנֹכִי֮ מֵת֒ בְּקִבְרִ֗י
אֲשֶׁ֨ר כָּרִ֤יתִי לִי֙ בְּאֶ֣רֶץ כְּנַ֔עַן שָׁ֖מָּה
תִּקְבְּרֵ֑נִי וְעַתָּ֗ה אֶֽעֱלֶה־נָּ֛א וְאֶקְבְּרָ֥ה אֶת־
אָבִ֖י וְאָשֽׁוּבָה׃ 6 וַיֹּ֖אמֶר פַּרְעֹ֑ה עֲלֵ֛ה וּקְבֹ֥ר
אֶת־אָבִ֖יךָ כַּאֲשֶׁ֥ר הִשְׁבִּיעֶֽךָ׃
7 וַיַּ֥עַל יוֹסֵ֖ף לִקְבֹּ֣ר אֶת־אָבִ֑יו וַיַּעֲל֨וּ אִתּ֜וֹ
כָּל־עַבְדֵ֤י פַרְעֹה֙ זִקְנֵ֣י בֵית֔וֹ וְכֹ֖ל זִקְנֵ֥י
אֶֽרֶץ־מִצְרָֽיִם׃ 8 וְכֹל֙ בֵּ֣ית יוֹסֵ֔ף וְאֶחָ֖יו
וּבֵ֣ית אָבִ֑יו רַ֗ק טַפָּם֙ וְצֹאנָ֣ם וּבְקָרָ֔ם עָזְב֖וּ

balmed Israel. 3 It required forty days, for such
is the full period of embalming. The Egyptians
bewailed him seventy days; 4 and when the
wailing period was over, Joseph spoke to Pharaoh's court, saying, "Do me this favor, and lay
this appeal before Pharaoh: 5 'My father made
me swear, saying, "I am about to die. Be sure to
bury me in the grave which I made ready for
myself in the land of Canaan." Now, therefore,
let me go up and bury my father; then I shall
return.'" 6 And Pharaoh said, "Go up and bury
your father, as he made you promise on oath."
7 So Joseph went up to bury his father; and
with him went up all the officials of Pharaoh,
the senior members of his court, and all of
Egypt's dignitaries, 8 together with all of Joseph's household, his brothers, and his father's
household; only their children, their flocks,
and their herds were left in the region of

seph, however, was a purely practical measure, for Jacob is to be buried far from his place of death, and Joseph is to be reinterred many years later (v. 25).

3. forty days . . . seventy days Embalming required 40 days, followed by another 30 days of mourning.

4. the wailing period That is, the period fixed by convention.

to Pharaoh's court Joseph does not approach the king directly, probably because a mourner, regarded as unclean, was not permitted into the presence of Pharaoh.

5. I made ready From the verb *kariti,* "I dug" or "I purchased." In 2 Chron. 16:14, the Hebrew stem כרה has the sense of "to prepare a grave in advance."

7. all the officials of Pharaoh The elite of the court and the government participate in the funeral procession.

---

never succeeds in finding it because there is always one more challenge to be overcome. To be a Jew is to be a descendant of Jacob/Israel.

CHAPTER 50

4. lay this appeal before Pharaoh Was Joseph concerned that Pharaoh would not let him leave the country to bury his father? Is that why he emphasizes the solemnity of his father's deathbed oath and refers to "the grave (he) made ready" (which must have been a telling argument in the land of the pyramids)? Did the large delegation of horsemen and chariots accompany Joseph to protect and honor him or to ensure that he would return from Canaan? And is that why the children and flocks remained behind? Joseph may have been a promi-

HALAKHAH L'MA·ASEH

50:2 embalm Rabbinic authorities forbade embalming as an indignity to the dead (*nivvul ha-met*) and an infringement on the honor due the dead (*kvod ha-met*). However, when civil law requires it or when it is necessary to protect the body from offensive odors while being moved long distances for burial, means necessary to preserve the body may be permitted.

Goshen. 9Chariots, too, and horsemen went
up with him; it was a very large troop.

10When they came to Goren ha-Atad, which
is beyond the Jordan, they held there a very
great and solemn lamentation; and he observed
a mourning period of seven days for his father.
11And when the Canaanite inhabitants of the
land saw the mourning at Goren ha-Atad, they
said, "This is a solemn mourning on the part of
the Egyptians." That is why it was named Abel-
mizraim, which is beyond the Jordan. 12Thus
his sons did for him as he had instructed them.
13His sons carried him to the land of Canaan,
and buried him in the cave of the field of Machpelah, the field near Mamre, which Abraham
had bought for a burial site from Ephron the
Hittite. 14After burying his father, Joseph returned to Egypt, he and his brothers and all
who had gone up with him to bury his father.

בְּאֶרֶץ גֹּשֶׁן׃ 9 וַיַּעַל עִמּוֹ גַּם־רֶכֶב גַּם־
פָּרָשִׁים וַיְהִי הַמַּחֲנֶה כָּבֵד מְאֹד׃
10 וַיָּבֹאוּ עַד־גֹּרֶן הָאָטָד אֲשֶׁר בְּעֵבֶר
הַיַּרְדֵּן וַיִּסְפְּדוּ־שָׁם מִסְפֵּד גָּדוֹל וְכָבֵד
מְאֹד וַיַּעַשׂ לְאָבִיו אֵבֶל שִׁבְעַת יָמִים׃
11 וַיַּרְא יוֹשֵׁב הָאָרֶץ הַכְּנַעֲנִי אֶת־הָאֵבֶל
בְּגֹרֶן הָאָטָד וַיֹּאמְרוּ אֵבֶל־כָּבֵד זֶה
לְמִצְרָיִם עַל־כֵּן קָרָא שְׁמָהּ אָבֵל מִצְרַיִם
אֲשֶׁר בְּעֵבֶר הַיַּרְדֵּן׃ 12 וַיַּעֲשׂוּ בָנָיו לוֹ כֵּן
כַּאֲשֶׁר צִוָּם׃ 13 וַיִּשְׂאוּ אֹתוֹ בָנָיו אַרְצָה
כְּנַעַן וַיִּקְבְּרוּ אֹתוֹ בִּמְעָרַת שְׂדֵה
הַמַּכְפֵּלָה אֲשֶׁר קָנָה אַבְרָהָם אֶת־
הַשָּׂדֶה לַאֲחֻזַּת־קֶבֶר מֵאֵת עֶפְרֹן הַחִתִּי
עַל־פְּנֵי מַמְרֵא׃ 14 וַיָּשָׁב יוֹסֵף מִצְרַיְמָה
הוּא וְאֶחָיו וְכָל־הָעֹלִים אִתּוֹ לִקְבֹּר אֶת־
אָבִיו אַחֲרֵי קָבְרוֹ אֶת־אָבִיו׃

15When Joseph's brothers saw that their
father was dead, they said, "What if Joseph still

15 וַיִּרְאוּ אֲחֵי־יוֹסֵף כִּי־מֵת אֲבִיהֶם
וַיֹּאמְרוּ לוּ יִשְׂטְמֵנוּ יוֹסֵף וְהָשֵׁב יָשִׁיב

9. Chariots The charioteers, not usually depicted in Egyptian tomb paintings of such events, are most likely present for security reasons, because the burial is to take place beyond the borders of the land.

10. Goren ha-Atad Probably Tell el-Ajjul (Beth Eglaim), situated 4.5 miles (7 km) southwest of Gaza on the eastern Mediterranean coast. A little to the south of the town lies a Late Bronze Age cemetery, which was a burial ground for high-ranking Egyptians serving in Canaan and for Egyptianized Canaanite rulers and dignitaries. That would explain why the cortege halted at Abel-mizraim for public homage to Jacob in his own country.

seven days An ancient custom found as far back as one of the earliest of writings, the *Gilgamesh* epic.

13. His sons carried him The brothers participated in the fulfillment of their father's last request (49:29–32) by completing the final segment of the journey to Hebron.

JOSEPH AND HIS BROTHERS: THE FINALE (50:15–21)

Death has removed the commanding presence of the Patriarch. Family cohesion disintegrates as the brothers wait for Joseph to take revenge for the crime they committed against him.

15. When Joseph's brothers saw When the reality of the situation struck them on their return to Egypt.

What if The brothers tell each other, "If Joseph should harbor a grudge, what would become of us?"

---

nent and powerful official in Egypt, but if he was not free to leave the country, we may sense that the enslavement of Jacob's children, the children of Israel, has begun.

10. seven days From this we see that the Jewish mourning tradition of *shiv·ah* (literally, seven) has ancient roots.

15. When Joseph's brothers saw According

bears a grudge against us and pays us back for all the wrong that we did him!" 16 So they sent this message to Joseph, "Before his death your father left this instruction: 17 So shall you say to Joseph, 'Forgive, I urge you, the offense and guilt of your brothers who treated you so harshly.' Therefore, please forgive the offense of the servants of the God of your father." And Joseph was in tears as they spoke to him.

18 His brothers went to him themselves, flung themselves before him, and said, "We are prepared to be your slaves." 19 But Joseph said to them, "Have no fear! Am I a substitute for God? 20 Besides, although you intended me harm, God intended it for good, so as to bring about the present result—the survival of many people. 21 And so, fear not. I will sustain you and your children." Thus he reassured them, speaking kindly to them.

22 So Joseph and his father's household remained in Egypt. Joseph lived one hundred

לָ֫נוּ אֵ֣ת כָּל־הָ֣רָעָ֔ה אֲשֶׁ֥ר גָּמַ֖לְנוּ אֹתֽוֹ׃
16 וַיְצַוּ֕וּ אֶל־יוֹסֵ֖ף לֵאמֹ֑ר אָבִ֣יךָ צִוָּ֔ה לִפְנֵ֥י
מוֹת֖וֹ לֵאמֹֽר׃ 17 כֹּֽה־תֹאמְר֣וּ לְיוֹסֵ֗ף אָ֣נָּ֡א
שָׂ֣א נָ֡א פֶּ֣שַׁע אַחֶ֣יךָ וְחַטָּאתָם֮ כִּֽי־רָעָ֣ה
גְמָל֒וּךָ֒ וְעַתָּ֗ה שָׂ֣א נָא֙ לְפֶ֣שַׁע עַבְדֵ֖י אֱלֹהֵ֣י
אָבִ֑יךָ וַיֵּ֥בְךְּ יוֹסֵ֖ף בְּדַבְּרָ֥ם אֵלָֽיו׃
18 וַיֵּלְכוּ֙ גַּם־אֶחָ֔יו וַֽיִּפְּל֖וּ לְפָנָ֑יו וַיֹּ֣אמְר֔וּ
הִנֶּ֥נּֽוּ לְךָ֖ לַעֲבָדִֽים׃ 19 וַיֹּ֧אמֶר אֲלֵהֶ֣ם יוֹסֵ֗ף
אַל־תִּירָ֑אוּ כִּ֛י הֲתַ֥חַת אֱלֹהִ֖ים אָֽנִי׃
20 וְאַתֶּ֕ם חֲשַׁבְתֶּ֥ם עָלַ֖י רָעָ֑ה אֱלֹהִים֙
חֲשָׁבָ֣הּ לְטֹבָ֔ה לְמַ֗עַן עֲשֹׂ֛ה כַּיּ֥וֹם הַזֶּ֖ה
בִּיעִי לְהַחֲיֹ֥ת עַם־רָֽב׃ 21 וְעַתָּה֙ אַל־תִּירָ֔אוּ
אָנֹכִ֛י אֲכַלְכֵּ֥ל אֶתְכֶ֖ם וְאֶֽת־טַפְּכֶ֑ם וַיְנַחֵ֣ם
אוֹתָ֔ם וַיְדַבֵּ֖ר עַל־לִבָּֽם׃

22 וַיֵּ֤שֶׁב יוֹסֵף֙ בְּמִצְרַ֔יִם ה֖וּא וּבֵ֣ית אָבִ֑יו

---

16. they sent this message Rather than risk a personal confrontation, the brothers send Joseph a message through a third party.

17. God of your father As Abravanel observes, they do not appeal to the claim of brotherliness because they forfeited it by their own actions. Hence they appeal to Joseph's respect and love for his father and to the religion that unites them all.

18. His brothers went to him When they learn of Joseph's emotional reaction they feel free to approach him in person.

19. Have no fear Their anxiety is eased at once. Joseph has no interest in seeking revenge; the very idea offends him.

Am I a substitute for God Human beings dare not usurp the prerogative of God, who alone has the right of punitive retaliation (see Lev. 19:18).

22. one hundred and ten years This was

---

to a *midrash*, when Jacob's body was brought to Hebron for burial, the brothers saw Joseph make a side trip to the pit into which he had been thrown as a child. Joseph went there to reflect on the wondrous deliverance he had experienced since that day, but the brothers feared that he was harboring thoughts of revenge (Tanḥ. 17).

16. Before his death We have no reason to believe that Jacob ever learned the truth about how Joseph came to Egypt. If he had, would he not have rebuked them for what they did, as he rebuked Reuben, Simeon, and Levi? Joseph weeps (v. 17) at the discovery that his brothers

still do not trust him. Although the brothers might have justified their invention as a white lie in the interests of family peace, even as God misquoted Sarah's words to spare Abraham's feelings (Gen. 18:12–13), their situation is different. They shaded the truth not to spare another's feelings but to protect themselves from the possible consequences of what they had done (Gen. R. 100:8).

21. I will sustain you This can be seen as the brothers' ultimate punishment. Having hated Joseph for his dreams of lording it over them, they will now depend on him for their daily bread.

and ten years. 23Joseph lived to see children of
the third generation of Ephraim; the children
of Machir son of Manasseh were likewise born
upon Joseph's knees. 24At length, Joseph said to
his brothers, "I am about to die. God will surely
take notice of you and bring you up from this
land to the land that He promised on oath to
Abraham, to Isaac, and to Jacob." 25So Joseph
made the sons of Israel swear, saying, "When
God has taken notice of you, you shall carry up
my bones from here."

מפטיר וַיְחִי יוֹסֵף מֵאָה וָעֶשֶׂר שָׁנִים׃ 23 וַיַּרְא
יוֹסֵף לְאֶפְרַיִם בְּנֵי שִׁלֵּשִׁים* גַּם בְּנֵי
מָכִיר בֶּן־מְנַשֶּׁה יֻלְּדוּ עַל־בִּרְכֵּי יוֹסֵף׃
24 וַיֹּאמֶר יוֹסֵף אֶל־אֶחָיו אָנֹכִי מֵת
וֵאלֹהִים פָּקֹד יִפְקֹד אֶתְכֶם וְהֶעֱלָה
אֶתְכֶם מִן־הָאָרֶץ הַזֹּאת אֶל־הָאָרֶץ אֲשֶׁר
נִשְׁבַּע לְאַבְרָהָם לְיִצְחָק וּלְיַעֲקֹב׃
25 וַיַּשְׁבַּע יוֹסֵף אֶת־בְּנֵי יִשְׂרָאֵל לֵאמֹר
פָּקֹד יִפְקֹד אֱלֹהִים אֶתְכֶם וְהַעֲלִתֶם אֶת־
עַצְמֹתַי מִזֶּה׃

v. 23. ם׳ רבתי לפי מהדורת לעטעריס

regarded as the ideal life span in ancient Egypt. In Israel it seems to have been 120 years.

23. children of Machir Machir, the most important of the clans of Manasseh, at one time was identified with the tribe as a whole.

24. his brothers "Brothers" here has the same sense as "sons of Israel" in the next verse.

God will surely take notice of you This profession of faith, made 54 years after Jacob's death, seems to carry with it resonances of a serious deterioration in the circumstances of the Israelites in Egypt. The repetition of the statement in verse 25 heightens its importance. It is used as a rallying cry in Exod. 3:16 when Moses appears as the national savior.

Abraham . . . Isaac . . . Jacob This clustering of the three Patriarchs for the first time sets the pattern for all such subsequent citations in the Torah, which are invariably in a context of the divine promises of national territory for the people Israel.

25. you shall carry up my bones Why Joseph does not request immediate interment in the land of his fathers is not explained; no doubt he knows that present conditions are unfavorable. The oath he extracts was carried out at the time of the Exodus (reported in Exod. 13:19) and he is laid to rest in a plot of land that Jacob once bought in Shechem (see Josh. 24:32; Gen. 33:19).

---

26. Looking back at Joseph's long and full life, what are we to make of it? On the surface, it was crowned with success. His childhood dream of having his father and brothers bow down to him was fulfilled. He came to know wealth and power and the satisfaction of having saved many people's lives. At the same time, though, his success frequently provoked jealousy and resentment, from his brothers and from the Egyptians who had to sell themselves into serfdom for food. He prospered as an Israelite in a foreign land, but to what extent did he have to compromise his Israelite identity in the process? Jewish tradition will speak of him as Joseph the *tzaddik,* the righteous one, because of his moral restraint with Potiphar's wife and his foregoing revenge against his brothers. Our evaluation may be more ambivalent.

a coffin in Egypt The last words of the Book of Genesis, "a coffin in Egypt," foreshadow the events of the opening chapter of Exodus, the enslavement of the Hebrews, the killing of the Hebrew babies, and the birth of Moses who will be placed in a coffin-like basket on the Nile. The last words in each of the five books of the Torah, "Egypt, journeys, Sinai, Jericho, Israel," are a virtual summary of the Torah's narrative about the people Israel, from slavery to Sinai to the Promised Land.

HALAKHAH L'MA·ASEH

50:25 swear The last wishes of the dying must be obeyed as long as they do not contravene Jewish law. Deathbed instructions have the same force as a legal contract duly delivered under Jewish law (BT Git. 13a).

26וַיָּ֣מָת יוֹסֵ֔ף בֶּן־מֵאָ֥ה וָעֶ֖שֶׂר שָׁנִ֑ים וַיַּחַנְט֣וּ אֹת֔וֹ וַיִּ֥ישֶׂם בָּאָר֖וֹן בְּמִצְרָֽיִם׃*

[26]Joseph died at the age of one hundred and ten years; and he was embalmed and placed in a coffin in Egypt.

v. 26. למדינחאי סכום הפסוקים של 1,534 הספר וחציו 27:40

חֲזַק חֲזַק וְנִתְחַזֵּק

26. a coffin The use of a coffin is uniquely Egyptian and is never again mentioned in the Bible. In sharp contrast to the honors accorded Jacob, no ritual or time of mourning is recorded with the death of Joseph. The formative period in the history of ancient Israel has come to an end.

HALAKHAH L'MA·ASEH

50:26 Joseph died In accordance with Prov. 10:7, we say of an individual we remember with love and respect, "May his or her memory be a blessing": *Zikhrono/Zikhronah livrakhah.*

הפטרת ויחי

HAFTARAH FOR VA-Y'ḤI

1 KINGS 2:1–12

This *haftarah* contains David's last will and testament to Solomon. The dying king instructs his son and heir about the religious and political pursuits he should follow to be successful (1 Kings 2:1–4,5–9). A concluding note states that Solomon's sovereignty was well established (v. 12), even though he had not yet carried out the ruthless acts advised by his father (cf. 2:28–35).

David died in ca. 965 B.C.E. The David portrayed here is both a pious believer in the Law and a shrewd politician who knows what it will take to secure Solomon's throne, which had just been won through intrigue and duplicity (1 Kings 1).

The aged King David speaks to Solomon in the language of religious rhetoric. The pious speech artfully attributed to him is also reflected in the high style of his learned language. This is illustrated, for example, by citations ("as recorded in the Teaching of Moses," 1 Kings 2:3) and by motivation clauses (introduced by *l'-ma·an*, "in order that," vv. 3–4; see Deut. 4:1,5, 5:16). David, a man of the Covenant, fully versed in the language of Torah, urges Solomon to obey its precepts.

The tone and content of the political section of David's directives, by contrast, is less polished and more in tune with realpolitik. David's advice to his son is based on personal considerations, and the language he uses recalls private grudges and other matters that the dying king wants his son to know, taking him into his confidence. The king's tactics are crafty. He simultaneously colludes with Solomon (saying "you know," vv. 5,9), appeals to his son's pride and cleverness ("your wisdom," "for you are . . . wise," vv. 6,9), and lets him know that death in Sheol is the only way to treat dangerous rivals (vv. 6,9). Moreover, knowing that his son will understand the hint contained in his comment that "*I* swore" that "*I* will not put [Shimei] to the sword," David can die in peace knowing that Solomon will attend to unsavory tasks that David has left for him. And this he does, through the agency of Benaiah (2:46). Significantly, the narrator's remark about the security of Solomon's throne in 1 Kings 2:12 recurs in verse 46, just after the murder of Shimei.

RELATION OF THE *HAFTARAH* TO THE *PARASHAH*

The *parashah* and the *haftarah* both deal with the approaching death of a leader (Jacob and David) and with a final pronouncement delivered to his son(s) (the 12 sons of Jacob, and Solomon). Both episodes begin alike, with the phrase "When [Jacob's/David's] life was drawing to a close" (*va-yikr'vu y'mei . . . lamut*). The technical term "he instructed" (*va-y'tzav*) also occurs in both instances (Gen. 49:29; 1 Kings 2:1), leading to the final instructions. Jacob requests that he be buried in the family tomb in the cave of Machpelah (Gen. 49:29–32), a request that subsequently is fulfilled (50:12–13).

Joseph's brothers, fearing that he would take revenge because they had sold him into servitude, "sent this message" (*va-y'tzavvu*). "Before his death your father left this instruction (*tzivvah*): So shall you say to Joseph, 'Forgive, I urge you, the offense and guilt of your brothers who treated you so harshly'" (Gen. 50:16–17). Whether this was true or concocted, Joseph accepts their testimony and assures them of his good intentions (50:19–21).

Jacob's final request of his sons in the *parashah* repeats the more personal account made to Joseph alone (Gen. 47:29). It is here that the full moral force of being an agent for the dead is articulated. After supplicating the son, the father refers to the burial in Canaan as an act of "stead-

fast loyalty" (*ḥesed v'emet*). More particularly, it is best understood as an act of gratuitous kindness (*ḥesed shel emet;* Gen. R. 96:5).

The agency of Solomon in fulfilling David's last will is more complicated. For David's requests do not involve what a person never could do for himself (burial), but that which he intentionally delegates. In an effort to give the act of agency moral and legal force, rabbinic tradition articulated the overall principle that "the agent of a person is as himself" (BT Kid. 41b). But in a further attempt to eliminate the double evasion of responsibility, they further stated that "there is no agent for enacting a sin" (BT Kid. 42b). From this perspective, David is culpable for the deaths of Joab and Shimei. Unlike Joseph, he is not magnanimous, but reaches beyond the grave to strike at his enemies.

2 When David's life was drawing to a close, he instructed his son Solomon as follows: 2"I am going the way of all the earth; be strong and show yourself a man. 3Keep the charge of the LORD your God, walking in His ways and following His laws, His commandments, His rules, and His admonitions as recorded in the Teaching of Moses, in order that you may succeed in whatever you undertake and wherever you turn. 4Then the LORD will fulfill the promise that He made concerning me: 'If your descendants are scrupulous in their conduct, and walk before Me faithfully, with all their heart and soul, your line on the throne of Israel shall never end!'

5"Further, you know what Joab son of Zeruiah did to me, what he did to the two commanders of Israel's forces, Abner son of Ner and Amasa son of Jether: he killed them, shedding blood of war in peacetime, staining the girdle of his loins and the sandals on his feet

ב וַיִּקְרְב֣וּ יְמֵֽי־דָוִ֖ד לָמ֑וּת וַיְצַ֛ו אֶת־
שְׁלֹמֹ֥ה בְנ֖וֹ לֵאמֹֽר׃ 2 אָנֹכִ֣י הֹלֵ֔ךְ בְּדֶ֖רֶךְ
כׇּל־הָאָ֑רֶץ וְחָזַקְתָּ֖ וְהָיִ֥יתָֽ לְאִֽישׁ׃
3 וְשָׁמַרְתָּ֞ אֶת־מִשְׁמֶ֣רֶת ׀ יְהֹוָ֣ה אֱלֹהֶ֗יךָ
לָלֶ֤כֶת בִּדְרָכָיו֙ לִשְׁמֹ֤ר חֻקֹּתָיו֙ מִצְוֺתָ֣יו
וּמִשְׁפָּטָ֣יו וְעֵדְוֺתָ֔יו כַּכָּת֖וּב בְּתוֹרַ֣ת מֹשֶׁ֑ה
לְמַ֣עַן תַּשְׂכִּ֗יל אֵ֤ת כׇּל־אֲשֶׁר֙ תַּֽעֲשֶׂ֔ה וְאֵ֖ת
כׇּל־אֲשֶׁ֥ר תִּפְנֶ֖ה שָֽׁם׃ 4 לְמַעַן֩ יָקִ֨ים יְהֹוָ֜ה
אֶת־דְּבָר֗וֹ אֲשֶׁ֨ר דִּבֶּ֣ר עָלַי֮ לֵאמֹר֒ אִם־
יִשְׁמְר֨וּ בָנֶ֜יךָ אֶת־דַּרְכָּ֗ם לָלֶ֤כֶת לְפָנַי֙
בֶּאֱמֶ֔ת בְּכׇל־לְבָבָ֖ם וּבְכׇל־נַפְשָׁ֑ם לֵאמֹ֗ר
לֹֽא־יִכָּרֵ֤ת לְךָ֙ אִ֔ישׁ מֵעַ֖ל כִּסֵּ֥א יִשְׂרָאֵֽל׃
5 וְגַ֣ם אַתָּ֣ה יָדַ֗עְתָּ אֵת֩ אֲשֶׁר־עָ֨שָׂה לִ֜י
יוֹאָ֣ב בֶּן־צְרוּיָ֗ה אֲשֶׁ֣ר עָשָׂ֣ה לִשְׁנֵֽי־שָׂרֵ֣י
צִבְא֣וֹת יִשְׂרָאֵ֡ל לְאַבְנֵ֣ר בֶּן־נֵר֩ וְלַעֲמָשָׂ֨א
בֶן־יֶ֤תֶר וַיַּ֣הַרְגֵ֔ם וַיָּ֥שֶׂם דְּמֵֽי־מִלְחָמָ֖ה
בְּשָׁלֹ֑ם וַיִּתֵּ֞ן דְּמֵ֣י מִלְחָמָ֗ה בַּחֲגֹֽרָתוֹ֙ אֲשֶׁ֣ר

1 Kings 2:1. he instructed The word translated as "he instructed" (*va-y'tzav*) literally means "he commanded." The term is used for final pronouncements. As used here, the verb has a double entendre, combining the force of an exhortation (Deut. 31:23) with the urgency of a final request (Gen. 49:29).

3-4. The references to obeying the Torah and commandments interrupt David's practical and political exhortation. In a similar manner, Josh. 1:7-8 interrupt the exhortation of national courage in vv. 6 and 9. Later notions of Torah piety thus transform older injunctions.

3. Keep the charge of the LORD The word translated as "charge" (*mishmeret*) is a technical term for observing the Covenant, in the tradition of Deuteronomy. Elsewhere it has the sense of maintaining a watch, especially over priestly objects of sanctity.

4. your line ... shall never end The promise that the royal line will not cease, or be cut off, is cited from the divine promise to David in 2 Sam. 7:12-16. Generational continuity is promised "forever" (v. 16).

with blood of war. 6So act in accordance with
your wisdom, and see that his white hair does
not go down to Sheol in peace.

7"But deal graciously with the sons of Bar-
zillai the Gileadite, for they befriended me
when I fled from your brother Absalom; let
them be among those that eat at your table.

8"You must also deal with Shimei son of
Gera, the Benjaminite from Bahurim. He insulted me outrageously when I was on my way
to Mahanaim; but he came down to meet me at
the Jordan, and I swore to him by the LORD: 'I
will not put you to the sword.' 9So do not let
him go unpunished; for you are a wise man and
you will know how to deal with him and send
his gray hair down to Sheol in blood."

10So David slept with his fathers, and he was
buried in the City of David. 11The length of
David's reign over Israel was forty years: he
reigned seven years in Hebron, and he reigned
thirty-three years in Jerusalem. 12And Solomon sat upon the throne of his father David,
and his rule was firmly established.

בְּמָתְנָיו וּבְנַעֲלוֹ אֲשֶׁר בְּרַגְלָיו׃ 6 וְעָשִׂיתָ
כְּחָכְמָתֶךָ וְלֹא־תוֹרֵד שֵׂיבָתוֹ בְּשָׁלֹם
שְׁאֹל׃ ס
7 וְלִבְנֵי בַרְזִלַּי הַגִּלְעָדִי תַּעֲשֶׂה־חֶסֶד וְהָיוּ
בְּאֹכְלֵי שֻׁלְחָנֶךָ כִּי־כֵן קָרְבוּ אֵלַי בְּבָרְחִי
מִפְּנֵי אַבְשָׁלוֹם אָחִיךָ׃
8 וְהִנֵּה עִמְּךָ שִׁמְעִי בֶן־גֵּרָא בֶן־הַיְמִינִי
מִבַּחֻרִים וְהוּא קִלְלַנִי קְלָלָה נִמְרֶצֶת
בְּיוֹם לֶכְתִּי מַחֲנָיִם וְהוּא־יָרַד לִקְרָאתִי
הַיַּרְדֵּן וָאֶשָּׁבַע לוֹ בַיהוָה לֵאמֹר אִם־
אֲמִיתְךָ בֶּחָרֶב׃ 9 וְעַתָּה אַל־תְּנַקֵּהוּ כִּי
אִישׁ חָכָם אָתָּה וְיָדַעְתָּ אֵת אֲשֶׁר
תַּעֲשֶׂה־לּוֹ וְהוֹרַדְתָּ אֶת־שֵׂיבָתוֹ בְּדָם
שְׁאוֹל׃
10 וַיִּשְׁכַּב דָּוִד עִם־אֲבֹתָיו וַיִּקָּבֵר בְּעִיר
דָּוִד׃ פ 11 וְהַיָּמִים אֲשֶׁר מָלַךְ דָּוִד
עַל־יִשְׂרָאֵל אַרְבָּעִים שָׁנָה בְּחֶבְרוֹן מָלַךְ
שֶׁבַע שָׁנִים וּבִירוּשָׁלַם מָלַךְ שְׁלֹשִׁים
וְשָׁלֹשׁ שָׁנִים׃ 12 וּשְׁלֹמֹה יָשַׁב עַל־כִּסֵּא
דָּוִד אָבִיו וַתִּכֹּן מַלְכֻתוֹ מְאֹד׃

12. and his rule was firmly established This concluding line of the *haftarah* indicates Solomon's success.

שמות

EXODUS

שמות

וארא

בא

בשלח

יתרו

משפטים

תרומה

תצוה

כי תשא

ויקהל

פקודי

EXODUS

NAHUM M. SARNA

In ancient times, this second book of the Bible had four titles: (a) *Sh'mot,* shortened from its initial Hebrew words; (b) *Seifer Y'tzi·at Mitzrayim,* "The Book of the Departure from Egypt," expressing its central theme; (c) *Exodus Aigyptous,* given by Greek-speaking Jews of Alexandria in Egypt, a title that was adopted in the Latin versions; and (d) its abbreviated form, *Exodus,* which passed into European languages. The practice of dividing the book into 40 chapters was adopted by Jews in the Middle Ages, when they were forced to engage in disputations with Christians who already had such an arrangement.

The geography of the Exodus narrative reveals a tripartite separation: (a) Chapters 1–15:21 deal with the Egyptian oppression of Israel, the struggle for liberation, and its achievement; (b) the events recorded in chapters 15:22–18:27 take place on the way from the Sea of Reeds to Mount Sinai (the location in chapter 18 is debatable); and (c) chapters 19–40 have their setting at Sinai itself. However, this simple classification obscures the rich variety of the subject matter.

Exodus is the great seminal text of biblical literature; its central topic, which shaped and informed the future development of the culture and religion of Israel, is mentioned here no less than 120 times. It profoundly influenced ethical and social consciousness so significantly that it is frequently invoked as the motivation for protecting and providing the interests and rights of the stranger and the disadvantaged of society.

Examination of the constituent elements of Exodus indicates an episodic account in an extremely limited time frame. Although one tradition has 140 years elapsing between the death of Joseph (Exod. 1:6) and the construction of the tabernacle, the last dated occurrence (Exod. 40:2), the book actually covers the events of only 2 years. Details relating to the period of oppression are sparse; there is no mention of the inner life and communal existence of the people. This limitation suggests a high degree of selectivity, and the intent of the selective focus is didactic. In Exodus, God is the sole actor, the initiator of events. The various episodes project Israelite concepts of God and His relations to the world.

The different aspects of the divine personality, as told in Exodus, express a conception of a single God who demands exclusive service and fidelity. God is presented as the Creator of all existence, wholly independent of His creations and totally beyond the constraints of the world of nature. Hence, any attempt to depict or represent God in material or pictorial form is inevitably a falsification and is strictly prohibited.

The Book of Exodus also affirms that God is deeply involved in human affairs and human history is the deliberate, purposeful plan of divine intelligence. Furthermore, God chooses to enter into an eternally valid covenantal relationship with Israel, a legal reality that entails immutable and inescapable obligations on Israel's part, as spelled out in a series of laws.

Finally, the religious calendar of Israel becomes transformed though the Exodus experience. Formerly an expression of the rhythms of the seasons, the sacred times become reinterpreted in terms of that great historical event. They become commemorations of God's benefactions upon Israel in Egypt and in the wilderness and are emancipated from the phenomena of nature.

1 These are the names of the sons of Israel who
came to Egypt with Jacob, each coming with his
household: 2Reuben, Simeon, Levi, and Judah;
3Issachar, Zebulun, and Benjamin; 4Dan and

א וְאֵ֗לֶּה שְׁמוֹת֙ בְּנֵ֣י יִשְׂרָאֵ֔ל הַבָּאִ֖ים
מִצְרָ֑יְמָה אֵ֣ת יַעֲקֹ֔ב אִ֥ישׁ וּבֵית֖וֹ בָּֽאוּ׃
2 רְאוּבֵ֣ן שִׁמְע֔וֹן לֵוִ֖י וִיהוּדָֽה׃ 3 יִשָּׂשכָ֥ר

REVERSAL OF FORTUNE (1:1–22)

Joseph dies, with his generation; the Israelites multiply in Egypt; and a new pharaoh suddenly enslaves them. The barest of details concerning slavery and suffering are offered. The narrative becomes expansive only when it begins to describe the liberation.

AN INTRODUCTORY SUMMARY (vv. 1–7)

The sons of Jacob—the tribes of Israel—are listed in an order based on Gen. 35:23–26. That chapter includes the divine blessing to Jacob: "Be fertile and increase; / A nation, yea an assembly of nations, / Shall descend from you" (35:11). This promise of increase has been fulfilled, as we read in 1:7.

1. These are The initial Hebrew letter of the verse that begins Exodus (*vav,* usually translated "and") is a link to Genesis, because the letter suggests continuity with what precedes it.

Israel The name here refers to the patriarch Jacob. The name is used to refer to the nation for the first time in verse 9.

We read in the Book of Genesis the story of a family living out its relationship to God in the midst of sibling jealousies and marital strife. Exodus is the story of a people encountering God in the course of their journey from slavery to freedom.

CHAPTER 1

"The historian asks, What political, economic or religious factors inclined Pharaoh to enslave the Israelites? The Midrash asks, Why is Israel persecuted and enslaved more than any other nation of the world?" (N. Leibowitz).

The Sages of the Midrash, writing more than a thousand years after the events and living under the harsh rule of the Romans, tried to interpret the experience of slavery in Egypt as a way of understanding their own experience. Some said that slavery was a punishment for assimilating into the Egyptian way of life and wanting to be like the Egyptians. They interpreted the words "the land was filled with them" (1:7) to mean "the theaters and circuses were filled with them." The Israelites adopted the Egyptian way of life in all of its crudeness and superficiality. Thus psychological enslavement, the notion that being an Egyptian was better than being an Israelite, preceded physical enslavement, even as psychological liberation will later precede physical liberation. These commentators describe the Israelites as devoid of redeeming qualities, and see the Exodus as resulting from God's unearned grace and God's promise to the patriarchs (Tanḥ. B. Sh'mot 6).

Others saw enslavement in Egypt as part of God's long-range plan, foreshadowed in Gen. 15:13, to take the descendants of Abraham and teach them, through the experience of being enslaved and redeemed, to be sensitive to the oppressed in every age (Exod. 22:20: "You shall not wrong a stranger . . . for you were strangers in the land of Egypt") and to be grateful to God for intervening to free them. On the opening words of the book, "These are the names," the Sages commented (again with later generations in mind) that "the Israelites were worthy of being redeemed precisely because they did not assimilate. Through all the years of slavery, they did not change their names, their language, or their mode of dress" (Mekh. Bo 5).

Striving not only to understand the Torah but to understand the phenomenon of gentile hatred of the Jewish people, the commentators carefully studied Pharaoh's words in verses 9 and 10. They note that he objects not so much to the behavior of the Israelites as to their very existence. Like many enemies of the Jewish people, he exaggerates their numbers and power (they could not have been more than a small fraction of the Egyptian population). He uses the same words ("they are much too numerous for us") that the king of the Philistines used for Isaac's lone family in Gen. 26:16.

1. the sons of Israel When they were growing up, they were the sons of Jacob, not Israel.

זְבוּלֻ֖ן וּבִנְיָמִֽן׃ 4 דָּ֥ן וְנַפְתָּלִ֖י גָּ֥ד וְאָשֵֽׁר׃
5 וַֽיְהִ֗י כׇּל־נֶ֛פֶשׁ יֹצְאֵ֥י יֶֽרֶךְ־יַעֲקֹ֖ב שִׁבְעִ֣ים
נָ֑פֶשׁ וְיוֹסֵ֖ף הָיָ֥ה בְמִצְרָֽיִם׃ 6 וַיָּ֤מׇת יוֹסֵף֙
וְכׇל־אֶחָ֔יו וְכֹ֖ל הַדּ֥וֹר הַהֽוּא׃ 7 וּבְנֵ֣י
יִשְׂרָאֵ֗ל פָּר֧וּ וַֽיִּשְׁרְצ֛וּ וַיִּרְבּ֥וּ וַיַּֽעַצְמ֖וּ בִּמְאֹ֣ד
מְאֹ֑ד וַתִּמָּלֵ֥א הָאָ֖רֶץ אֹתָֽם׃ פ
8 וַיָּ֥קׇם מֶֽלֶךְ־חָדָ֖שׁ עַל־מִצְרָ֑יִם אֲשֶׁ֥ר לֹֽא־
יָדַ֖ע אֶת־יוֹסֵֽף׃ 9 וַיֹּ֖אמֶר אֶל־עַמּ֑וֹ הִנֵּ֗ה עַ֚ם
בְּנֵ֣י יִשְׂרָאֵ֔ל רַ֥ב וְעָצ֖וּם מִמֶּֽנּוּ׃ 10 הָ֥בָה

Naphtali, Gad and Asher.
5 The total number of persons that were of Jacob's issue came to seventy, Joseph being already in Egypt.
6 Joseph died, and all his brothers, and all that generation.
7 But the Israelites were fertile and prolific; they multiplied and increased very greatly, so that the land was filled with them.

8 A new king arose over Egypt who did not know Joseph.
9 And he said to his people, "Look, the Israelite people are much too numerous for us.
10 Let us deal shrewdly with them, so that they

5. Jacob's issue Literally, "that came out of Jacob's loin." In the Bible, the Hebrew for "thigh, loin," (*yerekh*) is a euphemism for the male organ of procreation.

seventy The number 70 in the Bible usually is not meant to be taken literally. It evokes the idea of totality, of being all-inclusive, on a large scale. Here, it is a round number.

6. The entire immigrant generation had died out by the time the oppression began.

7. This description of the Israelites' extraordinary fertility (in language that is also used in the Creation narrative of Gen. 1:20,28) suggests the concept of the community of Israel in Egypt as a miniature universe, self-contained and apart from the larger Egyptian society. It is the nucleus of a new humanity, spiritually speaking.

the land Not the whole of Egypt, but the area of Israelite settlement known as Goshen.

THE OPPRESSION (vv. 8–14)

The Israelites experience sudden cataclysmic change. The most reasonable explanation for the Israelites' change in fortune lies in the policies adopted by pharaohs of the Nineteenth Dynasty (ca. 1304–1200 B.C.E.), especially by Ramses II (1290–1224 B.C.E.), who shifted Egypt's administrative and strategic center to the eastern delta of the Nile, where he undertook building projects that required a huge local labor force. "A new king" may also refer to a new dynasty.

8. who did not know Joseph He was ignorant of or indifferent to the extraordinary service that Joseph had rendered to Egypt and the crown.

know This is the first appearance in Exodus of the verb ידע, a key term in the Exodus narratives, occurring more than 20 times in the first 14 chapters. The usual rendering, "to know," hardly does justice to the richness of its meanings, which include emotions and relatedness as well as the intellect. The use of the word here to describe Pharaoh may anticipate "that you [Pharaoh] may know" in 9:29.

9–10. The historical situation that prompted his fears may plausibly be reconstructed if it is assumed that the text refers to Ramses II. The eastern delta of the Nile was vulnerable to penetration from Asia. In the middle of the 18th century B.C.E., it had been infiltrated by the Hyksos, an Egyptian term meaning "rulers of foreign lands." The Hyksos were a conglomeration of ethnic groups among whom Semites predominated. They gradually took over Lower Egypt and ruled it until their expulsion in the second half of the 16th century B.C.E. After that, the delta was neglected by the central government, although many Semites remained in the region. A revival of interest in that part of Egypt began with the reign of Haremheb (ca. 1330–1306 B.C.E.) and accelerated under his successors. It probably heightened sensitivity to the presence of a large body of foreigners in that strategic area.

Israelite people The unique Hebrew phrase *am b'nei yisra·el* (the nation of the descendants of Israel) is found only here. It tells us that the family of the patriarch Israel (Jacob) has become the people Israel and hence are a threat to the Egyptians.

deal shrewdly Literally, "wisely." To control

Jacob had to wrestle and change to become Israel; and his children, the children of Jacob, also had to struggle to outgrow their less admirable traits to become the children of Israel.

8. who did not know Joseph Pharaoh knew that Joseph had saved Egypt, but did not care. He did not let the information change his outlook (MRE 7:137). Through much of Jewish history, the people's well-being depended on the goodwill of a ruler. When the leadership changed, the fortunes of the Jewish community often changed as well. Pharaoh begins by

נִתְחַכְּמָה לוֹ פֶּן־יִרְבֶּה וְהָיָה כִּי־תִקְרֶאנָה
מִלְחָמָה וְנוֹסַף גַּם־הוּא עַל־שֹׂנְאֵינוּ
וְנִלְחַם־בָּנוּ וְעָלָה מִן־הָאָרֶץ׃ 11 וַיָּשִׂימוּ
עָלָיו שָׂרֵי מִסִּים לְמַעַן עַנֹּתוֹ בְּסִבְלֹתָם
וַיִּבֶן עָרֵי מִסְכְּנוֹת לְפַרְעֹה אֶת־פִּתֹם
וְאֶת־רַעַמְסֵס׃ 12 וְכַאֲשֶׁר יְעַנּוּ אֹתוֹ כֵּן
יִרְבֶּה וְכֵן יִפְרֹץ וַיָּקֻצוּ מִפְּנֵי בְּנֵי
יִשְׂרָאֵל׃
13 וַיַּעֲבִדוּ מִצְרַיִם אֶת־בְּנֵי יִשְׂרָאֵל בְּפָרֶךְ׃
14 וַיְמָרְרוּ אֶת־חַיֵּיהֶם בַּעֲבֹדָה קָשָׁה
בְּחֹמֶר וּבִלְבֵנִים וּבְכָל־עֲבֹדָה בַּשָּׂדֶה אֵת
כָּל־עֲבֹדָתָם אֲשֶׁר־עָבְדוּ בָהֶם בְּפָרֶךְ׃

may not increase; otherwise in the event of war
they may join our enemies in fighting against
us and rise from the ground." 11 So they set taskmasters over them to oppress them with forced
labor; and they built garrison cities for Pharaoh:
Pithom and Rameses. 12 But the more they were
oppressed, the more they increased and spread
out, so that the [Egyptians] came to dread the
Israelites.

13 The Egyptians ruthlessly imposed upon the
Israelites 14 the various labors that they made
them perform. Ruthlessly they made life bitter
for them with harsh labor at mortar and bricks
and with all sorts of tasks in the field.

the growth of the Israelite population. Pharaoh unwittingly challenges the will of God, for the divine promise to Abraham (Gen. 22:17 and elsewhere) had pledged that his descendants would be as numerous as the stars of the heaven and the sands of the seashore.

and rise from the ground The literal meaning of the Hebrew (*v'alah min ha-aretz*) may come from a forgotten idiom that means "to rise from a lowly state," or "to gain ascendancy over" (see Hos. 2:2). Or it may simply mean "leave the land."

11. The Israelites are conscripted for compulsory unpaid labor on public works projects for indefinite periods.

they built The Hebrew may refer to founding new cities as well as to rebuilding those that existed.

Pharaoh The title combines two Egyptian words, *per-'o* (literally, "the great house"). They originally applied to the royal palace and court; later, during the Nineteenth Dynasty (ca. 1304–1200 B.C.E.), it was an honorific title for the reigning monarch. It is analogous to present-day use of "the Palace" or "the White House."

Pithom and Rameses Both names are well known in Egyptian sources, but their precise location has not been fixed. Pithom is never again mentioned in the Bible. It was identified with a location in the eastern Nile delta (Tell er-Ratabah, in the east of Wadi Tumilat). The name derives from the Egyptian *per-atum,* which means "the House of (the sun god) Atum," indicating the presence of a major temple dedicated to the primeval creator god of that name. Raamses can be none other than the famous delta residence built by and named after Pharaoh Ramses II; its beauty and glory are extolled in poems still extant. The city was situated in "the region of Goshen," a phrase that is synonymous with "the region of Rameses," where the Israelites lived.

13–14. The Israelites now are subjected to forced labor in construction and agriculture, as opposed to the labor exacted from them earlier

---

refusing to acknowledge Joseph, and later refusing to acknowledge God, saying, "Who is the LORD that I should heed Him?" (Exod. 5:2).

14. *harsh labor* One of the Sages reads "harsh labor" (*b'farekh*) as "with soft words" (*b'feh rakh*). Instead of confronting the Israelites with threats and demands, the Egyptians hid their evil intent behind soft, innocuous words, assuring the Israelites that this was for their own good. The word *"b'farekh"* occurs one other time in the Torah. In Lev. 25:46, the Israelites are told never to treat their own slaves *b'farekh.* Some oppressed people, given the opportunity, would be eager to reverse the roles and oppress others. We are taught that, because we know how it feels, we should never oppress others. Abraham Lincoln reflected the teaching of the Torah in his statement: "As I

HALAKHAH L'MA·ASEH

1:14. they made life bitter for them The *Haggadah* of *Pesaḥ* connects to this verse the practice of eating bitter herbs at the *Seider.*

15 וַיֹּ֨אמֶר֙ מֶ֣לֶךְ מִצְרַ֔יִם לַֽמְיַלְּדֹ֖ת הָֽעִבְרִיֹּ֑ת
אֲשֶׁ֨ר שֵׁ֤ם הָֽאַחַת֙ שִׁפְרָ֔ה וְשֵׁ֥ם הַשֵּׁנִ֖ית
פּוּעָֽה׃ 16 וַיֹּ֗אמֶר בְּיַלֶּדְכֶן֙ אֶת־הָֽעִבְרִיּ֔וֹת
וּרְאִיתֶ֖ן עַל־הָאָבְנָ֑יִם אִם־בֵּ֥ן הוּא֙ וַהֲמִתֶּ֣ן
אֹת֔וֹ וְאִם־בַּ֥ת הִ֖יא וָחָֽיָה׃ 17 וַתִּירֶ֤אןָ
הַֽמְיַלְּדֹת֙ אֶת־הָ֣אֱלֹהִ֔ים וְלֹ֣א עָשׂ֔וּ כַּאֲשֶׁ֛ר
דִּבֶּ֥ר אֲלֵיהֶ֖ן מֶ֣לֶךְ מִצְרָ֑יִם וַתְּחַיֶּ֖יןָ אֶת־
הַיְלָדִֽים׃ 18 וַיִּקְרָ֤א מֶֽלֶךְ־מִצְרַ֙יִם֙ לַֽמְיַלְּדֹ֔ת שני
וַיֹּ֣אמֶר לָהֶ֔ן מַדּ֥וּעַ עֲשִׂיתֶ֖ן הַדָּבָ֣ר
הַזֶּ֑ה וַתְּחַיֶּ֖יןָ אֶת־הַיְלָדִֽים׃ 19 וַתֹּאמַ֤רְןָ

15 The king of Egypt spoke to the Hebrew midwives, one of whom was named Shiphrah and the other Puah, 16 saying, "When you deliver the Hebrew women, look at the birthstool: if it is a boy, kill him; if it is a girl, let her live." 17 The midwives, fearing God, did not do as the king of Egypt had told them; they let the boys live. 18 So the king of Egypt summoned the midwives and said to them, "Why have you done this thing, letting the boys live?" 19 The midwives said to Pharaoh, "Because the Hebrew women

together with the other inhabitants of Egypt. In the consciousness of Israel, this experience indelibly stamped Egypt as the "house of bondage." The word translated as "forced labor" also connotes ruthless behavior on the part of those in charge.

THE MIDWIVES (vv. 15–22)

In response to the failure of his scheme, Pharaoh issues a barbarous decree to reduce the Israelite population.

15. Hebrew The Hebrew word *ivri* first appears in Gen. 14:13, as a descriptive term for Abram. It is used in the Bible when non-Israelites refer to Israelites or when the latter identify themselves to others. (A class of wandering people known as *apiru* is found in a variety of Near Eastern texts.) The origin of the term is a puzzle.

midwives It is possible that the two names given here are not of individuals but guilds of midwives.

Shiphrah The name appears in a list of slaves attached to an Egyptian estate and is indicated as Asiatic. It comes from a Semitic root meaning "beauty."

Puah This name, apparently meaning "young girl," is attested on documents at Ugarit (an ancient Canaanite city whose buried library was discovered in 1929). Midrashic tradition has identified the two women with Jochebed and Miriam.

16. birthstool Literally, "two stones," most likely the two bricks on which women in labor squatted opposite the midwife during childbirth.

19. The midwives respond evasively out of a sense of self-preservation and their desire to continue to save lives.

---

would not be a slave, so would I not be a master." An ancient rabbi taught: What made the work so unbearable? Not only that it was hard but that it seemed pointless. People are capable of working hard, but they burn out from a sense of futility, a sense that nothing will come of what they are doing.

16. if it is a boy Pharaoh assumed that the only threat to his power would be physical resistance by Israelite males. He could not conceive of the power of spiritual resistance, exemplified by the role women play in the Exodus narrative.

17. The midwives, fearing God The phrase translated as "the fear of God" (*yir·at Elohim*) is the closest the Torah comes to having a word for religion. The case of the midwives suggests that the essence of religion is not belief in the existence of God or any other theological precept, but belief that certain things are wrong because God has built standards of moral behavior into the universe. (In Gen. 20:11, Abraham is afraid that the Philistines will murder him and abduct his wife because "there is no fear of God in this place.") The midwives not only believed in God but also understood that God demands a high level of moral behavior. They were willing to risk punishment at the hands of Pharaoh rather than betray their allegiance to God. This is the first recorded case of civil disobedience, challenging government in the name of a higher authority. It would find an echo in the thousands of righteous gentiles who risked their own lives to protect Jews from the Nazis. The midwives begin a pattern that is continued in the story of Moses, whose life is repeatedly threatened by men and saved by women (his mother; Pharaoh's daughter; his sister, Miriam; his wife, Zipporah). "It was through righteous women that Israel was redeemed" (Exod. R. 1:12).

19. the Hebrew women are not like the

are not like the Egyptian women: they are vigorous. Before the midwife can come to them,
they have given birth." 20And God dealt well
with the midwives; and the people multiplied
and increased greatly. 21And because the midwives feared God, He established households
for them. 22Then Pharaoh charged all his people, saying, "Every boy that is born you shall
throw into the Nile, but let every girl live."

הַמְיַלְּדֹת אֶל־פַּרְעֹה כִּי לֹא כַנָּשִׁים
הַמִּצְרִיֹּת הָעִבְרִיֹּת כִּי־חָיוֹת הֵנָּה בְּטֶרֶם
תָּבוֹא אֲלֵהֶן הַמְיַלֶּדֶת וְיָלָדוּ׃ 20 וַיֵּיטֶב
אֱלֹהִים לַמְיַלְּדֹת וַיִּרֶב הָעָם וַיַּעַצְמוּ
מְאֹד׃ 21 וַיְהִי כִּי־יָרְאוּ הַמְיַלְּדֹת אֶת־
הָאֱלֹהִים וַיַּעַשׂ לָהֶם בָּתִּים׃ 22 וַיְצַו פַּרְעֹה
לְכָל־עַמּוֹ לֵאמֹר כָּל־הַבֵּן הַיִּלּוֹד הַיְאֹרָה
תַּשְׁלִיכֻהוּ וְכָל־הַבַּת תְּחַיּוּן׃ ס

2 A certain man of the house of Levi went
and married a Levite woman. 2The woman con-

ב וַיֵּלֶךְ אִישׁ מִבֵּית לֵוִי וַיִּקַּח אֶת־בַּת־
לֵוִי׃ 2 וַתַּהַר הָאִשָּׁה וַתֵּלֶד בֵּן וַתֵּרֶא אֹתוֹ

20. multiplied and increased The narrative closes as it began (1:7), suggesting divine providence. Pharaoh's diabolical measures have not changed the situation.

21. established households Or families. God rewarded their virtue by blessing them with large families.

22. All else having failed, Pharaoh issues a final decree. He mobilizes "all his people," the entire apparatus of the state, to annihilate the Israelites.

THE BIRTH AND YOUTH OF MOSES (2:1–25)

THE ABANDONMENT AND SALVATION OF MOSES (vv. 1–10)

1. man . . . woman This refers to Amram and Jochebed. Note the lack of personal names in this part of the story, except for Moses at the end.

married The Hebrew root לקח (literally, "to take"), is frequently used of marriage. The narrative focuses on the role of the mother.

2. she saw how beautiful he was The word *tov* usually means "good." Here it might also convey the sense of "robust, healthy."

Egyptian women Why does Pharaoh choose to believe this improbable excuse? The Hebrew word here translated "vigorous" literally means "like animals." Pharaoh is ready to believe that the Israelites are virtually a different species, less human and less deserving of life than are the Egyptians, so that he can proceed with his program of persecution and slaughter.

22. all his people Why did Pharaoh involve all the people rather than leave it to the authorities or the army? Persecution cannot be successful without the complicity of the community.

CHAPTER 2

The story of Moses' birth and early years contains many elements common to hero legends: The special child, endangered at birth but rescued, undergoes a period of separation and then returns as a changed person with a mission. But there is one notable difference. The typical hero, of noble birth, is raised by peasants and ultimately returns to his lofty origins. Moses, an Israelite raised in Pharaoh's palace, returns to his people, as if to suggest that it was nobler to be a common Israelite than an Egyptian prince.

1. A certain man of the house of Levi The text implied that Moses was born shortly after his parents married. But we know that they had two older children, Miriam and Aaron. The Midrash resolves the problem in this way: Moses' parents already had two children when Pharaoh decreed that all Israelite males would be killed. His father and mother divorced, his father declaring, "What is the point of having another child only to see him killed?" But Miriam reproached her father, saying, "You are worse than Pharaoh. Pharaoh only threatens the males; you eliminate the possibility of any child. Pharaoh's decree may not be carried out, but your decision not to have children cer-

ceived and bore a son; and when she saw how beautiful he was, she hid him for three months.
3When she could hide him no longer, she got a wicker basket for him and caulked it with bitumen and pitch. She put the child into it and placed it among the reeds by the bank of the Nile.
4And his sister stationed herself at a distance, to learn what would befall him.

5The daughter of Pharaoh came down to bathe in the Nile, while her maidens walked along the Nile. She spied the basket among the reeds and sent her slave girl to fetch it.
6When she opened it, she saw that it was a child, a boy crying. She took pity on it and said, "This must

כִּי־ט֖וֹב ה֑וּא וַֽתִּצְפְּנֵ֖הוּ שְׁלֹשָׁ֥ה יְרָחִֽים׃
3 וְלֹא־יָכְלָ֣ה עוֹד֮ הַצְּפִינוֹ֒ וַתִּֽקַּֽח־לוֹ֙ תֵּ֣בַת
גֹּ֔מֶא וַתַּחְמְרָ֥ה בַחֵמָ֖ר וּבַזָּ֑פֶת וַתָּ֤שֶׂם בָּהּ֙
אֶת־הַיֶּ֔לֶד וַתָּ֥שֶׂם בַּסּ֖וּף עַל־שְׂפַ֥ת הַיְאֹֽר׃
4 וַתֵּתַצַּ֥ב אֲחֹת֖וֹ מֵרָחֹ֑ק לְדֵעָ֕ה מַה־יֵּעָשֶׂ֖ה
לֽוֹ׃
5 וַתֵּ֤רֶד בַּת־פַּרְעֹה֙ לִרְחֹ֣ץ עַל־הַיְאֹ֔ר
וְנַעֲרֹתֶ֥יהָ הֹלְכֹ֖ת עַל־יַ֣ד הַיְאֹ֑ר וַתֵּ֤רֶא
אֶת־הַתֵּבָה֙ בְּת֣וֹךְ הַסּ֔וּף וַתִּשְׁלַ֥ח אֶת־
אֲמָתָ֖הּ וַתִּקָּחֶֽהָ׃ 6 וַתִּפְתַּח֙ וַתִּרְאֵ֣הוּ אֶת־
הַיֶּ֔לֶד וְהִנֵּה־נַ֖עַר בֹּכֶ֑ה וַתַּחְמֹ֣ל עָלָ֔יו
וַתֹּ֕אמֶר מִיַּלְדֵ֥י הָֽעִבְרִ֖ים זֶֽה׃ 7 וַתֹּ֣אמֶר

3. The desperate mother, because of the decree, takes every possible precaution to ensure the baby's safety.

a wicker basket The receptacle is called *tevah*. The word appears elsewhere in the Bible only as the ark in which Noah and his family were saved from the waters of the Flood (Gen. 6:14). The use of the word here heightens our awareness of the infant's vulnerability and of divine protection. The reminder of the Flood tells us once again that the birth of Moses signals a new era in history.

wicker The Hebrew word *gome* is the "papyrus plant," once abundant in the marshlands of the Nile delta. Its huge stems, often more than 10 feet high, were used by the Egyptians for a variety of purposes, especially for the construction of light boats. Both *gome* and *tevah* are Egyptian words, giving local color to the story.

reeds The Hebrew word *suf,* also borrowed from Egyptian, is a "reed thicket." By placing the basket among the reeds, the mother prevented it from being carried downstream.

4. his sister Miriam.

at a distance Thus she was inconspicuous and would not arouse suspicions that the child was not really abandoned.

5. to bathe in the Nile An Egyptian princess would not have bathed publicly in the mighty, crocodile-infested river itself. This bathing place was no doubt one of the Nile's many rivulets, where privacy and safety could be ensured. The mother of Moses probably selected that spot after observing the princess's character and habits.

---

tainly will be." She persuaded her parents to reunite, and Moses was born shortly afterward. The other Israelites followed both decisions of her parents, divorcing and reuniting. Because of her action, the Sages call Miriam a redeemer of Israel every bit as much as her brothers (BT Sot. 12a).

The names of Moses' parents are not revealed to us until 6:20. Why does the Torah not mention their names at this point? To teach us that any Jewish family can give rise to a great person. In the same way, we set aside a chair for Elijah, the forerunner of the Messiah, whenever a Jewish baby is brought into the Covenant, as if to say: "Perhaps this will be the one to make the world into the kingdom of God."

2. The mother's delight at seeing her newborn child echoes God's delight at contemplating the newly created world: "Behold it was good" (B. Jacob).

5. The daughter of Pharaoh came down to bathe in the Nile Would not the daughter of Pharaoh have servants to bring water for her bath? Bar Yoḥai suggests that she (perhaps an idealistic adolescent) opposed her father's policy of murdering the Israelite children; she went to bathe in the Nile as a way of simultaneously identifying with Israel at the place of its suffering and cleansing herself of her father's defiling policies (BT Sot. 12b). Another commentator sees Pharaoh's daughter as going along with her father's policies until she saw the endangered Hebrew child. Until that moment, the Israelites had been an abstraction, and she was prepared to believe the worst about them. Once she encountered an innocent, vul-

be a Hebrew child.” 7Then his sister said to Pharaoh’s daughter, “Shall I go and get you a Hebrew nurse to suckle the child for you?” 8And Pharaoh’s daughter answered, “Yes.” So the girl went and called the child’s mother. 9And Pharaoh’s daughter said to her, “Take this child and nurse it for me, and I will pay your wages.” So the woman took the child and nursed it. 10When the child grew up, she brought him to Pharaoh’s daughter, who made him her son. She named him Moses, explaining, “I drew him out of the water.”

11Some time after that, when Moses had

אֲחֹתוֹ אֶל־בַּת־פַּרְעֹה הַאֵלֵךְ וְקָרָאתִי לָךְ
אִשָּׁה מֵינֶקֶת מִן הָעִבְרִיֹּת וְתֵינִק לָךְ
אֶת־הַיָּלֶד׃ 8 וַתֹּאמֶר־לָהּ בַּת־פַּרְעֹה לֵכִי
וַתֵּלֶךְ הָעַלְמָה וַתִּקְרָא אֶת־אֵם הַיָּלֶד׃
9 וַתֹּאמֶר לָהּ בַּת־פַּרְעֹה הֵילִיכִי אֶת־
הַיֶּלֶד הַזֶּה וְהֵינִקִהוּ לִי וַאֲנִי אֶתֵּן אֶת־
שְׂכָרֵךְ וַתִּקַּח הָאִשָּׁה הַיֶּלֶד וַתְּנִיקֵהוּ׃
10 וַיִּגְדַּל הַיֶּלֶד וַתְּבִאֵהוּ לְבַת־פַּרְעֹה וַיְהִי־
לָהּ לְבֵן וַתִּקְרָא שְׁמוֹ מֹשֶׁה וַתֹּאמֶר כִּי
מִן־הַמַּיִם מְשִׁיתִהוּ׃

שלישי 11 וַיְהִי | בַּיָּמִים הָהֵם וַיִּגְדַּל מֹשֶׁה וַיֵּצֵא

MOSES IS RETURNED TO HIS MOTHER (vv. 7–10)

Ironically, the evil intentions of Pharaoh are unknowingly thwarted by his own daughter. The arrangements she makes follow a pattern found in Mesopotamian legal documents relating to the adoption of foundlings. These “wet nurse contracts” specify payment for the services of nursing and rearing the infant; they stipulate that, after weaning, the right of possession belongs to the one who paid for the child’s upbringing. That the princess can personally execute such a contract accords with the relatively high social and legal position of women in ancient Egypt. She possessed rights of inheritance and disposal of property and enjoyed a fair measure of economic independence.

10. The high infant mortality rate in the ancient world dictated that formal adoption and naming by the adoptive parent be postponed until after weaning, which took place at a much later age than in modern societies.

Moses The Hebrew *Moshe* is of Egyptian origin. Its verbal stem *ms'i* means “to be born,” and the noun *ms* means “a child, son.” It is a frequent part of ancient Egyptian personal names, usually with the addition of the name of a god, as illustrated by Ahmose, Ptahmose, Ramose, and Thotmose. Two papyri from the time of Ramses II mention officials named Mose.

explaining A Hebrew origin for the name is attributed to the Egyptian princess. Through wordplay, the Egyptian *Mose* is connected with Hebrew משה, “to draw up/out (of water).” Note the ironic wordplay. She intended it as “the one who is drawn out (of the water).” *Moshe* is active in form and means “one who draws out,” a name that fits his future situation better than his present one.

THE CHARACTER OF MOSES (vv. 11–15)

How did Moses spend his days in the royal palace, and how long did he remain there? The Bible is not interested in such details. Like other privileged boys in court and bureaucratic circles in Egypt, Moses at an early age would have begun his formal education, which lasted about 12 years. Concentrating largely on basic skills and knowledge, it would have been conducted under a regimen of strict discipline, with drill and memorization as the basic teaching techniques. The Bible is concerned with Moses’ character and commitments, which are illustrated by three incidents that display his moral passion and his inability to tolerate injustice: 2:11–12, 13, and 16–17. These qualities mark him as being worthy to lead the struggle for the liberation of the Israelites.

---

nerable Israelite, however, she had to recognize her common humanity with them. “Only one who can hear the cry of Moses the infant will be able to properly understand the words of Moses the lawgiver” (Isaac Luria). A rabbinic tradition has it that Pharaoh’s daughter later joined the Israelite people at the time of the Exodus and that she stood at Sinai with them.

11. when Moses had grown up An ancient rabbi taught: The phrase “he grew up” occurs twice (vv. 10–11), once referring to physical maturity, the second time to a sense of re-

אֶל־אֶחָיו וַיַּרְא בְּסִבְלֹתָם וַיַּרְא אִישׁ מִצְרִי
מַכֶּה אִישׁ־עִבְרִי מֵאֶחָיו׃ 12 וַיִּפֶן כֹּה וָכֹה
וַיַּרְא כִּי אֵין אִישׁ וַיַּךְ אֶת־הַמִּצְרִי
וַיִּטְמְנֵהוּ בַּחוֹל׃ 13 וַיֵּצֵא בַּיּוֹם הַשֵּׁנִי וְהִנֵּה
שְׁנֵי־אֲנָשִׁים עִבְרִים נִצִּים וַיֹּאמֶר לָרָשָׁע
לָמָּה תַכֶּה רֵעֶךָ׃ 14 וַיֹּאמֶר מִי שָׂמְךָ לְאִישׁ
שַׂר וְשֹׁפֵט עָלֵינוּ הַלְהָרְגֵנִי אַתָּה אֹמֵר
כַּאֲשֶׁר הָרַגְתָּ אֶת־הַמִּצְרִי וַיִּירָא מֹשֶׁה
וַיֹּאמַר אָכֵן נוֹדַע הַדָּבָר׃ 15 וַיִּשְׁמַע פַּרְעֹה
אֶת־הַדָּבָר הַזֶּה וַיְבַקֵּשׁ לַהֲרֹג אֶת־מֹשֶׁה
וַיִּבְרַח מֹשֶׁה מִפְּנֵי פַרְעֹה וַיֵּשֶׁב בְּאֶרֶץ־
מִדְיָן וַיֵּשֶׁב עַל־הַבְּאֵר׃

grown up, he went out to his kinsfolk and witnessed their labors. He saw an Egyptian beating
a Hebrew, one of his kinsmen. 12 He turned this
way and that and, seeing no one about, he struck
down the Egyptian and hid him in the sand.
13 When he went out the next day, he found two
Hebrews fighting; so he said to the offender,
"Why do you strike your fellow?" 14 He retorted,
"Who made you chief and ruler over us? Do you
mean to kill me as you killed the Egyptian?" Moses was frightened, and thought: Then the matter is known! 15 When Pharaoh learned of the
matter, he sought to kill Moses; but Moses fled
from Pharaoh. He arrived in the land of Midian,
and sat down beside a well.

11. his kinsfolk Literally, "his brethren." In the Hebrew of this verse, the word for "his brethren" (*eḥav*) is repeated, perhaps to emphasize that the years Moses spent in court circles did not alienate him from his people.

witnessed their labors Not as a detached observer but as one who identifies wholeheartedly with their suffering.

12. Outraged, Moses goes to the aid of the victim. He hesitates for a moment because he is aware that, by Egyptian law, he is about to commit an act that will forever cut his ties to the aristocratic society in which he was raised. Note that he takes action before God does (see 2:25). His looking "this way and that" indicates that he is calculating the cost and proceeding with deliberation.

he struck down The same verb, *"makkeh,"* is used in v. 11 for the action of the Egyptian assailant. It can be a technical term for killing, as here.

15. Now an outcast, Moses flees for his life to the "land of Midian," where he takes refuge. (The Midianites are described as the nomadic descendants of Abraham and Keturah in Gen. 25:2). "The land of Midian" was under the control of one or more of the five seminomadic tribes that, according to biblical sources, made up the Midianite confederation. There was an early history of close and friendly relations between Israel and the Midianites. The two peoples became enemies, however, in the period that followed the conquest of Canaan (see Num. 31).

a well In the ancient Near East, wells were meeting places for shepherds, wayfarers, and townsfolk. It was most natural for newcomers to head for them.

---

sponsibility, going out to join his kinsmen and take responsibility for righting the wrongs of society. It is not uncommon for a leader of an oppressed people to come from a privileged background: One thinks of Theodore Herzl, Mahatma Gandhi, and Martin Luther King Jr. Such a person may be psychologically freer to act, and will be taken more seriously both by his followers and by his opponents.

"Witnessing an injustice and degradation of another, Moses feels the blow dealt to the other as though it were directed against himself. Breaking through the selfishness of his own ego, he discovers his neighbor. It is this discovery that, in the last resort, brings about the Exodus. The estrangement between men has disappeared. Before, all men were strangers, bearing not even the slightest resemblance to himself. Now all men are neighbors" (André Neher).

12. seeing no one about Not because Moses wanted to act furtively but to indicate that because there was no one to administer justice, he had to take the law into his own hands.

14. Moses was frightened When Moses learned that there were bullies and talebearers among the Israelites, he was afraid that they were unworthy of being saved (Mekh.). Suffering and persecution can bring forth nobility of spirit in some victims, and meanness of spirit in others. Moses shows his maturity as a leader by devoting his efforts to helping his people even though they are less than perfect.

16 וּלְכֹהֵן מִדְיָן שֶׁבַע בָּנוֹת וַתָּבֹאנָה
וַתִּדְלֶנָה וַתְּמַלֶּאנָה אֶת־הָרְהָטִים
לְהַשְׁקוֹת צֹאן אֲבִיהֶן׃ 17 וַיָּבֹאוּ הָרֹעִים
וַיְגָרְשׁוּם וַיָּקָם מֹשֶׁה וַיּוֹשִׁעָן וַיַּשְׁקְ אֶת־
צֹאנָם׃ 18 וַתָּבֹאנָה אֶל־רְעוּאֵל אֲבִיהֶן
וַיֹּאמֶר מַדּוּעַ מִהַרְתֶּן בֹּא הַיּוֹם׃
19 וַתֹּאמַרְןָ אִישׁ מִצְרִי הִצִּילָנוּ מִיַּד
הָרֹעִים וְגַם־דָּלֹה דָלָה לָנוּ וַיַּשְׁקְ אֶת־
הַצֹּאן׃ 20 וַיֹּאמֶר אֶל־בְּנֹתָיו וְאַיּוֹ לָמָּה זֶּה
עֲזַבְתֶּן אֶת־הָאִישׁ קִרְאֶן לוֹ וְיֹאכַל לָחֶם׃
21 וַיּוֹאֶל מֹשֶׁה לָשֶׁבֶת אֶת־הָאִישׁ וַיִּתֵּן
אֶת־צִפֹּרָה בִתּוֹ לְמֹשֶׁה׃ 22 וַתֵּלֶד בֵּן
וַיִּקְרָא אֶת־שְׁמוֹ גֵּרְשֹׁם כִּי אָמַר גֵּר הָיִיתִי
בְּאֶרֶץ נָכְרִיָּה׃ פ

23 וַיְהִי בַיָּמִים הָרַבִּים הָהֵם וַיָּמָת מֶלֶךְ

16Now the priest of Midian had seven daughters. They came to draw water, and filled the
troughs to water their father's flock; 17but shepherds came and drove them off. Moses rose to
their defense, and he watered their flock.
18When they returned to their father Reuel, he
said, "How is it that you have come back so soon
today?" 19They answered, "An Egyptian rescued
us from the shepherds; he even drew water for
us and watered the flock." 20He said to his
daughters, "Where is he then? Why did you
leave the man? Ask him in to break bread."
21Moses consented to stay with the man, and
he gave Moses his daughter Zipporah as wife.
22She bore a son whom he named Gershom, for
he said, "I have been a stranger in a foreign
land."

23A long time after that, the king of Egypt

MOSES IN MIDIAN (vv. 16–22)

Once again, Moses reveals his intolerance of injustice. Although himself a fugitive, and alone in a strange land, he comes to the aid of others.

16. to draw water A common occupation of young women in that part of the world.

18. their father Reuel The name may mean "friend of God." The title "priest of Midian" is attached only to Jethro (Hebrew *Yitro*) who, in other texts, is also referred to as Moses' father-in-law. This raises the possibility that *Yitro* (*yeter*) is not a proper name but an honorific meaning "His Excellency." Thus His Excellency (*yitro*) Reuel would be the father of the shepherdesses and the father-in-law of Moses. Tradition also refers to him as Hobab (Num. 10:29).

How is it Apparently, the girls experienced constant mistreatment at the hands of male shepherds, causing them to arrive home late regularly.

19. an Egyptian Identified by his garb.

21. he gave A father had the power to make such decisions.

Zipporah The name means "a bird."

22. Gershom The name is explained as a composite of the Hebrew words *ger sham,* "a stranger there," signifying "a stranger in a foreign land." This echoes God's covenant with Abraham: "Your offspring shall be strangers in a land not theirs." The "land" is Egypt, not Midian. The prediction of slavery that was made to Abraham had been fulfilled; the liberation is now at hand. The birth of the child is symbolic of the regeneration of Israel.

A TRANSITIONAL POSTSCRIPT (vv. 23–25)

These verses return us to the plight of the Israelites in Egypt and serve as a transition to the next development. God breaks His silence and directly

17. "Three times Moses intervenes on behalf of a weak person oppressed by a stronger one: first an Israelite beaten by an Egyptian, then an Israelite beaten by another Israelite, and finally the Midianite women harassed by shepherds. Had we been told only of the first clash, we might have doubted the unselfishness of his motives. Perhaps he had been motivated by the sense of solidarity with his own people. . . . Had we been faced with the second example, we might still have had our doubts. Perhaps he was revolted by the disgrace of witnessing internal strife among his own folk. Came the third clash, where both parties were outsiders . . . his sense of justice and fair play was exclusively involved" (N. Leibowitz).

23. A close reading of the text would seem to indicate that the Israelites were not crying

died. The Israelites were groaning under the bondage and cried out; and their cry for help from the bondage rose up to God. 24God heard their moaning, and God remembered His covenant with Abraham and Isaac and Jacob. 25God looked upon the Israelites, and God took notice of them.

מִצְרַ֔יִם וַיֵּאָנְח֧וּ בְנֵֽי־יִשְׂרָאֵ֛ל מִן־הָעֲבֹדָ֖ה
וַיִּזְעָ֑קוּ וַתַּ֧עַל שַׁוְעָתָ֛ם אֶל־הָאֱלֹהִ֖ים מִן־
הָעֲבֹדָֽה׃ 24 וַיִּשְׁמַ֥ע אֱלֹהִ֖ים אֶת־נַאֲקָתָ֑ם
וַיִּזְכֹּ֤ר אֱלֹהִים֙ אֶת־בְּרִית֔וֹ אֶת־אַבְרָהָ֖ם
אֶת־יִצְחָ֥ק וְאֶֽת־יַעֲקֹֽב׃ 25 וַיַּ֥רְא אֱלֹהִ֖ים
אֶת־בְּנֵ֣י יִשְׂרָאֵ֑ל וַיֵּ֖דַע אֱלֹהִֽים׃ ס

3 Now Moses, tending the flock of his father-in-law Jethro, the priest of Midian, drove

רביעי ג וּמֹשֶׁ֗ה הָיָ֥ה רֹעֶ֛ה אֶת־צֹ֛אן יִתְר֥וֹ חֹתְנ֖וֹ
כֹּהֵ֣ן מִדְיָ֑ן וַיִּנְהַ֤ג אֶת־הַצֹּאן֙ אַחַ֣ר הַמִּדְבָּ֔ר

intervenes in Israel's history. It was established practice in Egypt for a new king to celebrate his accession to the throne by granting amnesty to those guilty of crimes, by releasing prisoners, and by freeing slaves. The Israelites had good reason to expect that the change in regime would bring with it some easing of their condition. But this was not to be. Hence, the emphasis on the intensity of their misery. Moses, however, did benefit from the amnesty, as 4:19 confirms. Four terms give expression to Israel's suffering: "groaning," "cried out," "cry for help," "moaning"; and four verbs express God's response: "heard," "remembered," "looked upon," "took notice."

24. remembered The Hebrew stem זכר connotes much more than merely the remembrance of things past. It means "to be mindful, to pay heed" and signifies a sharp focusing of attention on someone or something. It embraces concern and involvement, and always leads to action.

His covenant The repeated promises to the patriarchs of nationhood and national territory.

THE COMMISSIONING OF MOSES (3:1–4:17)

The appointment of a leader to rally the demoralized people and represent them before the Egyptian authorities is the first stage in the process of liberation.

REVELATION AT THE BURNING BUSH (3:1–6)

1. into the wilderness He traveled westward, in the direction of Egypt from Midian. The term "wilderness" (*midbar*) indicates a region of uninhabited and unirrigated pastureland.

Horeb Some traditions seem to identify this location with Sinai, but they may not be identical. Horeb may have been the name of a wider region in which Mount Sinai, a specific peak, was located; perhaps that peak eventually lent its name

---

out to God. They were groaning in their misery, with no certainty that anyone would hear them. (The Hebrew for "cry for help" is used in Job 24:12 in reference to the last groan of a dying person.) God responds to the Israelites, not because they besought divine help but because God sees their suffering. Heschel defined Jewish religion as "the awareness of God's interest in Man."

25. God looked upon the Israelites An ancient rabbi taught: What God saw was that despite their misery, the Israelites tried to help each other. For example, instead of each man looking out for himself, when one would finish making his quota of bricks, he would help out a weaker neighbor. Similar testimony from the Nazi death camps tells of how some prisoners would share their meager rations of food and clothing with the sick and needy.

and God took notice of them Unlike Pharaoh, who "did not know [i.e., care about] Joseph," God is not only informed about Israel's plight but is moved to sympathy. God feels the tension between compassion for the suffering of innocent people and the commitment to a long-range plan calling for their continuing to suffer until the time of redemption arrives, until the people are psychologically ready to claim their freedom.

CHAPTER 3

1. drove the flock into the wilderness Why

the flock into the wilderness, and came to Horeb, the mountain of God. 2An angel of the LORD
appeared to him in a blazing fire out of a bush.
He gazed, and there was a bush all aflame, yet
the bush was not consumed. 3Moses said, "I
must turn aside to look at this marvelous sight;
why doesn't the bush burn up?" 4When the
LORD saw that he had turned aside to look, God
called to him out of the bush: "Moses! Moses!"
He answered, "Here I am." 5And He said, "Do
not come closer. Remove your sandals from
your feet, for the place on which you stand is

וַיָּבֹא אֶל־הַר הָאֱלֹהִים חֹרֵבָה׃ 2 וַיֵּרָא
מַלְאַךְ יְהוָה אֵלָיו בְּלַבַּת־אֵשׁ מִתּוֹךְ הַסְּנֶה
וַיַּרְא וְהִנֵּה הַסְּנֶה בֹּעֵר בָּאֵשׁ וְהַסְּנֶה אֵינֶנּוּ
אֻכָּל׃ 3 וַיֹּאמֶר מֹשֶׁה אָסֻרָה־נָּא וְאֶרְאֶה
אֶת־הַמַּרְאֶה הַגָּדֹל הַזֶּה מַדּוּעַ לֹא־יִבְעַר
הַסְּנֶה׃ 4 וַיַּרְא יְהוָה כִּי סָר לִרְאוֹת וַיִּקְרָא
אֵלָיו אֱלֹהִים מִתּוֹךְ הַסְּנֶה וַיֹּאמֶר מֹשֶׁה
מֹשֶׁה וַיֹּאמֶר הִנֵּנִי׃ 5 וַיֹּאמֶר אַל־תִּקְרַב
הֲלֹם שַׁל־נְעָלֶיךָ מֵעַל רַגְלֶיךָ כִּי הַמָּקוֹם
אֲשֶׁר אַתָּה עוֹמֵד עָלָיו אַדְמַת־קֹדֶשׁ הוּא׃

to the entire area. Horeb (Hebrew *Ḥorev*) means "desolate, dry." Its precise location is unknown.

mountain of God Clearly, Moses is unaware of any sanctity attached to that site.

2. an angel of the LORD The messenger here, like the angels in Genesis, has no independent being. It is the sudden appearance of the fire that attracts Moses before God speaks.

in a blazing fire Fire, being nonmaterial, formless, mysterious, and luminous, is often used to describe the external manifestation of God.

a bush Hebrew *s'neh* occurs only here and in Deut. 33:16, where God is named "the Presence in the Bush." *S'neh* is most likely a wordplay on "Sinai" and an intimation of the Sinaitic revelation alluded to in verse 12. The bush has been identified as the thorny desert plant *Rubus sanctus* that grows near wadis and in moist soil.

not consumed The self-sustaining fire, requiring no other substance for its existence, is a clear representation of the divine Presence. To see that a bush is on fire is easy; to see that it is not consumed takes time and patience, another necessary quality of leadership that Moses displays here. The bush that remains intact in the face of flames may symbolize the people Israel surviving Egyptian oppression.

4. Moses! Moses! In the Bible, repetition of a name often characterizes a direct divine call.

Here I am Hebrew: *hinneni*, the spontaneous, unhesitating response to a divine call (see Gen. 22:1,11; 1 Sam. 3:4).

"into the wilderness"? Rashi suggests that this was necessary to prevent the flocks from grazing on someone else's land, for that would be theft. Sforno says that it was to be free of distractions, so that Moses could meditate. The Midrash tells a story of a lamb running away and Moses chasing it into the wilderness. God, taking notice, decides that this is a man of compassion, fit to be the leader of the people. The first interpretation emphasizes Moses' commitment to justice and ethical behavior. The second sees him as a mystic, a man in search of God's presence. The third describes his compassion.

2. An angel of the LORD appeared to him Why did God appear to Moses in a thornbush? (*a*) The bush that burns but is not consumed symbolizes the Jewish people, perpetually attacked and endangered but perpetually surviving (Philo). (*b*) The thornbush is the humblest, least impressive of trees and plants. God, who will take note of a tiny, oppressed people, chooses to appear in this lowly bush. "No place is devoid of God's presence, not even a thornbush" (Exod. R. 2:5). (*c*) For the Midrash, the thornbush symbolizes Israel's experience in Egypt (and many other situations in life). It is easier to put one's hand into a thornbush than to extricate it; so Israel's arrival in Egypt was comfortable compared to the difficulties and pain of their departure (Mekh. of bar Yoḥai). How long must one watch a burning bush before realizing that it is not being consumed by the flames? How many miracles might be happening around us but we, in our haste, never stop to notice them?

5. Remove your sandals from your feet Shoes not only carry the dirt and defilement of the world into the presence of God. They symbolize the effort of the well-to-do to shield themselves from the pain felt by the poor. "Remove your shoes" may be a way of saying to

holy ground. 6I am," He said, "the God of your
father, the God of Abraham, the God of Isaac,
and the God of Jacob." And Moses hid his face,
for he was afraid to look at God.
7And the LORD continued, "I have marked
well the plight of My people in Egypt and have
heeded their outcry because of their taskmasters; yes, I am mindful of their sufferings. 8I have
come down to rescue them from the Egyptians
and to bring them out of that land to a good
and spacious land, a land flowing with milk and
honey, the region of the Canaanites, the Hit-

6 וַיֹּאמֶר אָנֹכִי אֱלֹהֵי אָבִיךָ אֱלֹהֵי אַבְרָהָם
אֱלֹהֵי יִצְחָק וֵאלֹהֵי יַעֲקֹב וַיַּסְתֵּר מֹשֶׁה
פָּנָיו כִּי יָרֵא מֵהַבִּיט אֶל־הָאֱלֹהִים׃
7 וַיֹּאמֶר יְהוָה רָאֹה רָאִיתִי אֶת־עֳנִי עַמִּי
אֲשֶׁר בְּמִצְרָיִם וְאֶת־צַעֲקָתָם שָׁמַעְתִּי
מִפְּנֵי נֹגְשָׂיו כִּי יָדַעְתִּי אֶת־מַכְאֹבָיו׃
8 וָאֵרֵד לְהַצִּילוֹ ׀ מִיַּד מִצְרַיִם וּלְהַעֲלֹתוֹ
מִן־הָאָרֶץ הַהִוא אֶל־אֶרֶץ טוֹבָה וּרְחָבָה
אֶל־אֶרֶץ זָבַת חָלָב וּדְבָשׁ אֶל־מְקוֹם
הַכְּנַעֲנִי וְהַחִתִּי וְהָאֱמֹרִי וְהַפְּרִזִּי וְהַחִוִּי

5. holy ground The sanctity of space is occasioned by the appearance of God. It does not depend on the inherent nature of the place, as in the pagan world. The idea of sanctified space also appears in Jacob's experience at Bethel (Gen. 28:10ff.).

Removal of footwear in the ancient Near East was a sign of respect and humility. (The sandals mentioned here probably were made of papyrus or leather.) Priests officiated barefoot in the sanctuary, and to this day *kohanim* remove their footwear before pronouncing the priestly benediction publicly during the synagogue service.

6. I am This solemn, self-identifying mode of address frequently introduces royal proclamations and inscriptions in the ancient Near East. It lends special weight to the ensuing announcement, which thereby becomes authoritative and unchallengeable.

God of your father This phrase, frequently used in the Book of Genesis, all but vanishes during the period of the Exodus, to be replaced by "the God of your fathers," i.e., the three patriarchs. Moses is commissioned here as a divine messenger, a prophet (see, e.g., Isa. 6; Jer. 1).

Moses hid his face His initial encounter with God is a terrifying experience, shared by others in the Bible.

THE DIVINE CALL (vv. 7–10)

The intimation of deliverance from bondage found in 2:24–25 becomes a clear message of hope and redemption.

8. I have come down A common figure of speech used to express God's descending from His heavenly abode to become involved in human affairs.

good and spacious land A depiction of the land of Israel, contrasting with the image of an oppressed people confined to the region of Goshen.

flowing with milk and honey This is a recurrent symbol of the land's fertility. Ancient Egyptian sources testify to the richness of the land. The combination of milk and honey implies that the land supports both agriculture (honey from dates) and pasturage (milk from goats). The phrase is never included in the divine promises made to the patriarchs, for whom famine was frequently a grim reality. Their faith did not need to be reinforced by stressing the attractiveness of the land. Such an enticement would carry weight for the demoralized, enslaved masses of Israelites.

Moses, "remove from yourself everything that would keep you from identifying with the suffering of your people."

6. I am . . . the God of your father According to the Midrash, when God appeared to him, Moses was but a novice in prophecy. God said, "If I reveal Myself to him in a thunderous voice, I will terrify him. If in a whisper, he may not hear Me." What did God do? God spoke in the voice of Moses' father, whereupon Moses answered, "Here I am, Father, what do you want of me?" God said, "I am not your father. I am the God of your father. I addressed you in a familiar voice so that you would not be afraid" (Exod. R. 3:1).

HALAKHAH L'MA·ASEH

3:6. the God of Abraham, the God of Isaac, and the God of Jacob This is the wording in the first blessing of the *Amidah.*

tites, the Amorites, the Perizzites, the Hivites, and the Jebusites. ⁹Now the cry of the Israelites has reached Me; moreover, I have seen how the Egyptians oppress them. ¹⁰Come, therefore, I will send you to Pharaoh, and you shall free My people, the Israelites, from Egypt."

¹¹But Moses said to God, "Who am I that I should go to Pharaoh and free the Israelites from Egypt?" ¹²And He said, "I will be with you; that shall be your sign that it was I who sent you. And when you have freed the people from Egypt, you shall worship God at this mountain."

¹³Moses said to God, "When I come to the Israelites and say to them, 'The God of your fathers has sent me to you,' and they ask me, 'What is His name?' what shall I say to them?"

וְהַיְבוּסִֽי: ⁹ וְעַתָּ֗ה הִנֵּ֛ה צַעֲקַ֥ת בְּנֵֽי־יִשְׂרָאֵ֖ל בָּ֣אָה אֵלָ֑י וְגַם־רָאִ֙יתִי֙ אֶת־הַלַּ֔חַץ אֲשֶׁ֥ר מִצְרַ֖יִם לֹחֲצִ֥ים אֹתָֽם: ¹⁰ וְעַתָּ֣ה לְכָ֔ה וְאֶֽשְׁלָחֲךָ֖ אֶל־פַּרְעֹ֑ה וְהוֹצֵ֛א אֶת־עַמִּ֥י בְנֵֽי־ יִשְׂרָאֵ֖ל מִמִּצְרָֽיִם: ¹¹ וַיֹּ֤אמֶר מֹשֶׁה֙ אֶל־הָ֣אֱלֹהִ֔ים מִ֣י אָנֹ֔כִי כִּ֥י אֵלֵ֖ךְ אֶל־פַּרְעֹ֑ה וְכִ֥י אוֹצִ֖יא אֶת־בְּנֵ֥י יִשְׂרָאֵ֖ל מִמִּצְרָֽיִם: ¹² וַיֹּ֙אמֶר֙ כִּֽי־אֶֽהְיֶ֣ה עִמָּ֔ךְ וְזֶה־לְּךָ֣ הָא֔וֹת כִּ֥י אָנֹכִ֖י שְׁלַחְתִּ֑יךָ בְּהוֹצִֽיאֲךָ֤ אֶת־הָעָם֙ מִמִּצְרַ֔יִם תַּֽעַבְדוּן֙ אֶת־הָ֣אֱלֹהִ֔ים עַ֖ל הָהָ֥ר הַזֶּֽה: ¹³ וַיֹּ֙אמֶר מֹשֶׁה֙ אֶל־הָ֣אֱלֹהִ֔ים הִנֵּ֣ה אָנֹכִ֣י בָא֮ אֶל־בְּנֵ֣י יִשְׂרָאֵל֒ וְאָמַרְתִּ֣י לָהֶ֔ם אֱלֹהֵ֥י אֲבֽוֹתֵיכֶ֖ם שְׁלָחַ֣נִי אֲלֵיכֶ֑ם וְאָֽמְרוּ־לִ֣י מַה־

Milk in the Bible is generally from the goat, "the little man's cow." A plentiful supply presupposes an abundance of goats, which in turn points to ample pasturage and the prospect of plentiful meat, hide, and wool. Honey in the Bible is predominantly the thick, sweet syrup produced from dates. The combination of milk and honey provides a highly nutritious diet. Some Arab tribes are known to subsist for months at a time solely on milk products and honey.

region of the Canaanites There are numerous biblical lists of the pre-Israelite inhabitants of Canaan. The most comprehensive is that of Gen. 15:19–21, which names 10 peoples. Other lists register 7, 6, 5, or 3 ethnic groups. The origin of these rosters is unknown, as is the reason for the variations in number, order, and content.

10. Come This is the pivotal moment of God's manifestation at the bush. God chooses Moses to be the emissary of the divine will, the human instrument by which the redemption of Israel is to be carried through. The biblical institution of the messenger prophet is established here.

MOSES' DIALOGUE WITH GOD (3:11–4:17)

11. Who am I His immediate reaction is a deep sense of personal unworthiness. The prophet

resisting his call is a universal theme in world prophecy (see Jer. 1:6). Moses carries it to an extreme, demonstrating his humility. This fits in with the biblical theme that God often chooses a weak vessel to exhibit His own power.

12. I will be with you God's "being with" someone, an assurance of His protection, usually coincides with critical moments of human fear and indecision.

that shall be your sign The Hebrew for "sign" (*ot*) functions to corroborate either a promise or an appointment to office. But to what does the Hebrew for "that" (*zeh*) refer? Is it the spectacle at the bush? This would mean that the Burning Bush itself is the sign that affirms the divinely appointed nature of Moses' mission. Or is it Moses' unique ability to negotiate freely and safely with the all-powerful Pharaoh that will authenticate his calling?

you shall worship This phrase is a subtle hint to Moses on how to handle negotiations with the Egyptians. The motif of the worship of God as an objective of the Exodus is uttered time and again before Pharaoh.

13. Moses' second objection revolves around his sense of being unable to represent Israel without a clear mandate from the people and without even knowing the name of the God for whom he

---

13. and they ask me, 'What is His name?' Abraham, Isaac, and Jacob did not need to know God's name because God was a living presence in their lives. For the Israelites in

Egypt, however, it was harder to believe in the reality of God. Therefore, they needed to have God introduced to them (MRE). Jews have involved themselves in theology, speculating on

14And God said to Moses, "Ehyeh-Asher-Ehyeh." He continued, "Thus shall you say to the Israelites, 'Ehyeh sent me to you.'" 15And God said further to Moses, "Thus shall you

שְׁמ֖וֹ מָ֥ה אֹמַ֖ר אֲלֵהֶֽם׃ 14 וַיֹּ֤אמֶר אֱלֹהִים֙
אֶל־מֹשֶׁ֔ה אֶֽהְיֶ֖ה אֲשֶׁ֣ר אֶֽהְיֶ֑ה וַיֹּ֗אמֶר כֹּ֤ה
תֹאמַר֙ לִבְנֵ֣י יִשְׂרָאֵ֔ל אֶֽהְיֶ֖ה שְׁלָחַ֥נִי
אֲלֵיכֶֽם׃ 15 וַיֹּאמֶר֩ ע֨וֹד אֱלֹהִ֜ים אֶל־מֹשֶׁ֗ה

is now asked to speak. By asking for God's name, Moses denies knowledge of it, as Rashbam notes.

14. Ehyeh-Asher-Ehyeh This phrase has been translated, "I Am That I Am," "I Am Who I Am," and "I Will Be What I Will Be." It evokes *YHVH,* the specific proper name of Israel's God, known also as the Tetragrammaton, "the four consonants." The phrase also indicates that the earliest recorded understanding of the divine name was as a verb derived from a stem meaning "to be" (הוה). Because it is the sound of wind and breath, the way in which we sense the invisible, it could express the quality of absolute Being, the eternal, unchanging, dynamic Presence. Or it could mean "He causes to be." *"YHVH"* is the third-person masculine singular; *"ehyeh"* is the corresponding first-person singular. The latter is used here because name giving in the ancient world implied the wielding of power over the one named; hence, the divine name can proceed only from God. God reveals to Moses a name symbolizing the help needed for his task, without offering a "real" name, which would put God under human control.

During the Second Temple period the Tetragrammaton (*Shem ha-M'forash*) came to be regarded as charged with sanctity and magical potency. Therefore, its pronunciation ceased. It was replaced in speech by *adonai,* "Lord." Often the vowels of *"adonai"* would accompany the letters of *"YHVH"* in written texts, which gave rise to the mistaken form "Jehovah" found in some Christian translations. The original pronunciation of *"YHVH"* was lost; modern attempts at recovery, such as "Yahweh," are conjectural and have no support from tradition.

Taken together with the statement in 6:3, it would appear that the name *YHVH* came into prominence only as the characteristic personal name of the God of Israel in the time of Moses. Whether it was known before that time or not is questionable. It is of interest, though, that the various divine names found in Genesis are not used in the later biblical books, except occasionally in poetic texts. A new stage in the history of Israelite monotheism begins with the revelation of the divine name *YHVH* to Moses.

15. My name . . . My appellation How I am addressed and referred to.

forever . . . for all eternity God's unvarying dependability ensures that His promises will be fulfilled.

---

the nature of God, mostly when they have had to understand the ways their faith differed from the faith of those around them.

14. Ehyeh-Asher-Ehyeh The phrase defies simple translation. It has been taken to mean "I am whatever I choose to be," "I am pure being," "I am more than you can comprehend." The psychologist Erich Fromm takes it to mean: I, God, am in the process of becoming; neither I nor human understanding of Me is yet complete. And you human beings, fashioned in the image of God, are also in the process of becoming.

The name is gender free, neither specifically masculine nor specifically feminine, as befits a God who embraces polarities of male and female, young and old, transcendent and near at hand. It may be connected to the phrase in verse 12, "I will be with you" (*ki ehyeh immakh*). In that case, God's name, God's essence, would imply "I am not a far-off God, a remote, uncaring philosophical conclusion. I am God who will be with you. You cannot understand My nature, but you will know Me by My presence, and you will walk with Me when you follow My commands." Buber understands it to mean, "I cannot be summoned or manipulated, as the magicians of Egypt invoke and manipulate their gods. In accordance with My character, again and again I stand by those whom I befriend."

It is significant that this name of God is not a noun but a verb. The essence of Jewish theology is not the nature of God ("what God is") but the actions of God ("what God does," the difference that God makes in our lives). What, then, does God's name mean? It may mean any or all of the following: God exists. God is more than we can comprehend. God, or our understanding of God, is constantly growing. God is present in our lives. God is with us in our efforts to do what is right but difficult.

speak to the Israelites: The LORD, the God of
your fathers, the God of Abraham, the God of
Isaac, and the God of Jacob, has sent me to you:

This shall be My name forever,
This My appellation for all eternity.

16“Go and assemble the elders of Israel and
say to them: the LORD, the God of your fathers,
the God of Abraham, Isaac, and Jacob, has appeared to me and said, ‘I have taken note of you
and of what is being done to you in Egypt, 17and
I have declared: I will take you out of the misery
of Egypt to the land of the Canaanites, the Hittites, the Amorites, the Perizzites, the Hivites,
and the Jebusites, to a land flowing with milk
and honey.’ 18They will listen to you; then you
shall go with the elders of Israel to the king of
Egypt and you shall say to him, ‘The LORD, the
God of the Hebrews, manifested Himself to us.
Now therefore, let us go a distance of three days
into the wilderness to sacrifice to the LORD our
God.’ 19Yet I know that the king of Egypt will
let you go only because of a greater might.

כֹּה־תֹאמַר אֶל־בְּנֵי יִשְׂרָאֵל יְהֹוָה אֱלֹהֵי
אֲבֹתֵיכֶם אֱלֹהֵי אַבְרָהָם אֱלֹהֵי יִצְחָק
וֵאלֹהֵי יַעֲקֹב שְׁלָחַנִי אֲלֵיכֶם

זֶה־שְּׁמִי לְעֹלָם
וְזֶה זִכְרִי לְדֹר דֹּר׃

חמישי 16 לֵךְ וְאָסַפְתָּ אֶת־זִקְנֵי יִשְׂרָאֵל וְאָמַרְתָּ
אֲלֵהֶם יְהֹוָה אֱלֹהֵי אֲבֹתֵיכֶם נִרְאָה
אֵלַי אֱלֹהֵי אַבְרָהָם יִצְחָק וְיַעֲקֹב לֵאמֹר
פָּקֹד פָּקַדְתִּי אֶתְכֶם וְאֶת־הֶעָשׂוּי לָכֶם
בְּמִצְרָיִם׃ 17 וָאֹמַר אַעֲלֶה אֶתְכֶם מֵעֳנִי
מִצְרַיִם אֶל־אֶרֶץ הַכְּנַעֲנִי וְהַחִתִּי וְהָאֱמֹרִי
וְהַפְּרִזִּי וְהַחִוִּי וְהַיְבוּסִי אֶל־אֶרֶץ זָבַת
חָלָב וּדְבָשׁ׃ 18 וְשָׁמְעוּ לְקֹלֶךְ וּבָאתָ אַתָּה
וְזִקְנֵי יִשְׂרָאֵל אֶל־מֶלֶךְ מִצְרַיִם וַאֲמַרְתֶּם
אֵלָיו יְהֹוָה אֱלֹהֵי הָעִבְרִיִּים נִקְרָה עָלֵינוּ
וְעַתָּה נֵלְכָה־נָּא דֶּרֶךְ שְׁלֹשֶׁת יָמִים
בַּמִּדְבָּר וְנִזְבְּחָה לַיהֹוָה אֱלֹהֵינוּ׃ 19 וַאֲנִי
יָדַעְתִּי כִּי לֹא־יִתֵּן אֶתְכֶם מֶלֶךְ מִצְרַיִם

16. elders Moses' first concern in his new role must be to win the confidence and support of the acknowledged leaders of the people. These are the elders (*z'kenim*) who are frequently mentioned in the Exodus narratives. The institution of elders is rooted in the tribal-patriarchal system that shaped the character of Israelite society in early times. Ancient Near Eastern archives show that the council of elders was entrusted with considerable judicial and political authority.

I have taken note Echoing the promise handed down from generation to generation and the dying words of Joseph (recorded in Gen. 50:24): “God will surely take notice of you and bring you up from this land to the land that He promised on oath to Abraham, to Isaac, and to Jacob.”

18. The LORD, the God of the Hebrews This name of God appears only in Exodus, invariably when Pharaoh is addressed and always with a demand for permission to worship in the wilderness. Although Pharaoh does not know *YHVH*, he never claims to be ignorant of “the God of the Hebrews.” Perhaps this name, like “the God of the father,” belongs to the pre-Mosaic history of Israelite religion and was widely used among the pastoral nomads of the region. That might be the reason Moses carefully identifies it with *YHVH* each time he uses it.

manifested Himself Hebrew *nikrah,* as opposed to the usual *nir'ah*, “appeared,” emphasizes the sudden and unexpected nature of the encounter with the divine and explains to Pharaoh why no such demand had been made before.

three days In the biblical consciousness, this is a significant length of time, particularly in connection with travel. Here it may indicate that the intended sacrifice, regarded with revulsion by the Egyptians (see Exod. 8:22), would take place well beyond the borders of Egypt.

to sacrifice In terms of the state-organized forced labor gangs of that time, this request was not exceptional, as is proved by entries in extant logs of Egyptian slave supervisors. There is also archaeological evidence for the custom among pastoral nomads of making periodic pilgrimages to sacred shrines in the wilderness. The denial of these reasonable demands of the Israelites reveals the brutal nature of Pharaoh's tyrannical rule.

19. a greater might Literally “a strong hand,” meaning the “hand” of God, mentioned again in verse 20, as opposed to the oppressive “hand of Egypt” of verse 8. It may simply mean

[20]So I will stretch out My hand and smite Egypt with various wonders which I will work upon them; after that he shall let you go. [21]And I will dispose the Egyptians favorably toward this people, so that when you go, you will not go away empty-handed. [22]Each woman shall borrow from her neighbor and the lodger in her house objects of silver and gold, and clothing, and you shall put these on your sons and daughters, thus stripping the Egyptians."

לַהֲלֹךְ וְלֹא בְּיָד חֲזָקָה׃ 20 וְשָׁלַחְתִּי אֶת־
יָדִי וְהִכֵּיתִי אֶת־מִצְרַיִם בְּכֹל נִפְלְאֹתַי
אֲשֶׁר אֶעֱשֶׂה בְּקִרְבּוֹ וְאַחֲרֵי־כֵן יְשַׁלַּח
אֶתְכֶם׃ 21 וְנָתַתִּי אֶת־חֵן הָעָם־הַזֶּה
בְּעֵינֵי מִצְרָיִם וְהָיָה כִּי תֵלֵכוּן לֹא תֵלְכוּ
רֵיקָם׃ 22 וְשָׁאֲלָה אִשָּׁה מִשְּׁכֶנְתָּהּ וּמִגָּרַת
בֵּיתָהּ כְּלֵי־כֶסֶף וּכְלֵי זָהָב וּשְׂמָלֹת
וְשַׂמְתֶּם עַל־בְּנֵיכֶם וְעַל־בְּנֹתֵיכֶם וְנִצַּלְתֶּם
אֶת־מִצְרָיִם׃

4 But Moses spoke up and said, "What if they do not believe me and do not listen to me, but say: The LORD did not appear to you?" [2]The LORD said to him, "What is that in your hand?"

ד וַיַּעַן מֹשֶׁה וַיֹּאמֶר וְהֵן לֹא־יַאֲמִינוּ
לִי וְלֹא יִשְׁמְעוּ בְּקֹלִי כִּי יֹאמְרוּ לֹא־נִרְאָה
אֵלֶיךָ יְהוָה׃ 2 וַיֹּאמֶר אֵלָיו יְהוָה מזה

"except by force," a prediction that God knows all attempts to leave will be unsuccessful until the Egyptians are forced to let them go.

20. wonders Hebrew: *nifla'ot,* almost always used of God's timely, direct intervention in human affairs—not necessarily expressed through the suspension of the laws of nature.

21. This fulfills the promise in Gen. 15:14.

22. borrow Hebrew: *sha·alah,* which here means "ask for." Early Jewish interpretations looked upon these spoils as well-deserved compensation to the Israelites for their centuries of unpaid forced labor (see Deut. 15:13).

4:1. Moses presents his third objection: He might be rejected by the Israelite masses. God had mentioned only the elders, not the people. Knowledge of the divine name might not be sufficient confirmation of a claim to be divinely commissioned.

THE SIGNS (4:2–9)

This time Moses' argument is not refuted. In-

20. Readers may be bothered by the aspects of God's plan that delay the redemption while slaves continue to suffer and die—and that manipulate Pharaoh's response, "hardening his heart" so that the Egyptian people are afflicted with 10 plagues. Part of the answer lies in the Torah's view that God wanted Israel to go through the experience of slavery and redemption, to teach them compassion for the oppressed and gratitude for their freedom. The purpose of the Exodus is not only to free the Israelites but to demonstrate the greatness of God over the idols and human rulers of Egypt. Had God moved Pharaoh to deal generously with Israel from the outset that lesson would not have been learned.

Moreover, just as paleontologists discover fossils of creatures that lived long ago and use them to study the process of physical evolution, it may be that here and in a few other places in the Bible, we have "remnants" of an earlier moral outlook that we can use to trace the evolution of Jewish moral thought in the Bible and in postbiblical commentaries. These remnants include the acceptance of slavery, the vulnerable position of women, capital punishment for *Shabbat* violators and disrespectful children, and the command to wipe out Canaanite women and children. In the Bible itself and among the rabbis of the Talmud and Midrash, there are signs that people who lived more than 2000 years ago were often as troubled by these passages as we are today and strove to understand or reinterpret them in ways that sustained the more evolved moral view of a later age without in any way diminishing their reverence for the Torah.

And he replied, "A rod." 3 He said, "Cast it on
the ground." He cast it on the ground and it
became a snake; and Moses recoiled from it.
4 Then the LORD said to Moses, "Put out your
hand and grasp it by the tail"—he put out his
hand and seized it, and it became a rod in his
hand—5 "that they may believe that the LORD,
the God of their fathers, the God of Abraham,
the God of Isaac, and the God of Jacob, did appear to you."

6 The LORD said to him further, "Put your
hand into your bosom." He put his hand into
his bosom; and when he took it out, his hand
was encrusted with snowy scales! 7 And He said,
"Put your hand back into your bosom."—He
put his hand back into his bosom; and when
he took it out of his bosom, there it was again
like the rest of his body.—8 "And if they do not
believe you or pay heed to the first sign, they
will believe the second. 9 And if they are not convinced by both these signs and still do not heed

מַה־זֶּה בְיָדֶךָ וַיֹּאמֶר מַטֶּה׃ 3 וַיֹּאמֶר
הַשְׁלִיכֵהוּ אַרְצָה וַיַּשְׁלִכֵהוּ אַרְצָה וַיְהִי
לְנָחָשׁ וַיָּנָס מֹשֶׁה מִפָּנָיו׃ 4 וַיֹּאמֶר יְהוָה
אֶל־מֹשֶׁה שְׁלַח יָדְךָ וֶאֱחֹז בִּזְנָבוֹ וַיִּשְׁלַח
יָדוֹ וַיַּחֲזֶק בּוֹ וַיְהִי לְמַטֶּה בְּכַפּוֹ׃ 5 לְמַעַן
יַאֲמִינוּ כִּי־נִרְאָה אֵלֶיךָ יְהוָה אֱלֹהֵי
אֲבֹתָם אֱלֹהֵי אַבְרָהָם אֱלֹהֵי יִצְחָק וֵאלֹהֵי
יַעֲקֹב׃
6 וַיֹּאמֶר יְהוָה לוֹ עוֹד הָבֵא־נָא יָדְךָ
בְּחֵיקֶךָ וַיָּבֵא יָדוֹ בְּחֵיקוֹ וַיּוֹצִאָהּ וְהִנֵּה
יָדוֹ מְצֹרַעַת כַּשָּׁלֶג׃ 7 וַיֹּאמֶר הָשֵׁב יָדְךָ
אֶל־חֵיקֶךָ וַיָּשֶׁב יָדוֹ אֶל־חֵיקוֹ וַיּוֹצִאָהּ
מֵחֵיקוֹ וְהִנֵּה־שָׁבָה כִּבְשָׂרוֹ׃ 8 וְהָיָה אִם־
לֹא יַאֲמִינוּ לָךְ וְלֹא יִשְׁמְעוּ לְקֹל הָאֹת
הָרִאשׁוֹן וְהֶאֱמִינוּ לְקֹל הָאֹת הָאַחֲרוֹן׃
9 וְהָיָה אִם־לֹא יַאֲמִינוּ גַּם לִשְׁנֵי הָאֹתוֹת
הָאֵלֶּה וְלֹא יִשְׁמְעוּן לְקֹלֶךָ וְלָקַחְתָּ מִמֵּימֵי

stead, he is instructed how to dispel popular skepticism should it materialize. It is not surprising that the signs Moses will produce in Egypt possess a distinctly Egyptian coloration, for magic was part of everyday life in Egypt. The signs taught to Moses are intended to validate his claim to be the divinely chosen instrument for the redemption of the Israelites. They also function to establish the superiority of Moses over the Egyptian magicians and to affirm the greater might of Israel's God over the gods of the Egyptians.

The First Sign (vv. 2–5)

2. What is that in your hand? The query serves to verify that the object is an ordinary shepherd's crook, not invested with magical powers.

3. Moses recoils before the transformed rod, thereby expressing his astonishment at the marvel, and intimating that God, not he, is in command of the situation.

a snake The rod in ancient Egypt was a symbol of royal authority and power; and the snake represented the patron cobra-goddess of Lower Egypt in the north. Worn over the forehead on the headdress of the pharaohs, the snake symbolized divinely protected sovereignty and served as a menacing emblem of death dealt to enemies of the crown.

4. by the tail Normally a foolhardy act, because snakes are picked up by their necks, it manifests Moses' faith in God.

The Second Sign (vv. 6–7)

6. encrusted The Hebrew word *tzara·at* is usually translated "leprosy." But it has none of the major symptoms of that malady, and the descriptions of it in Lev. 13–14 are incompatible with Hansen's disease. The comparison to snow is not in regard to its whiteness but to its flakiness. The appearance and disappearance of the encrustation is sudden and, therefore, quite startling. The Bible regards the affliction as an ominous sign of divine retribution for human wrongdoing.

The Third Sign (vv. 8–9)

8. pay heed to Literally, "listen to the voice of." The sign "speaks"; it testifies to the divine commission.

9. The third sign will become the first plague. The Nile—the life-blood of Egypt—was deified. Thus this sign, like the first, signifies God's sovereign rule over nature and the subordination of Egypt and its gods to *YHVH*.

הַיְאֹ֖ר וְשָׁפַכְתָּ֣ הַיַּבָּשָׁ֑ה וְהָי֤וּ הַמַּ֙יִם֙ אֲשֶׁ֣ר
תִּקַּ֣ח מִן־הַיְאֹ֔ר וְהָי֥וּ לְדָ֖ם בַּיַּבָּֽשֶׁת׃
10 וַיֹּ֨אמֶר מֹשֶׁ֣ה אֶל־יְהוָה֮ בִּ֣י אֲדֹנָי֒ לֹא֩
אִ֨ישׁ דְּבָרִ֜ים אָנֹ֗כִי גַּ֤ם מִתְּמוֹל֙ גַּ֣ם
מִשִּׁלְשֹׁ֔ם גַּ֛ם מֵאָ֥ז דַּבֶּרְךָ֖ אֶל־עַבְדֶּ֑ךָ כִּ֧י
כְבַד־פֶּ֛ה וּכְבַ֥ד לָשׁ֖וֹן אָנֹֽכִי׃ 11 וַיֹּ֨אמֶר
יְהוָ֜ה אֵלָ֗יו מִ֣י שָׂ֣ם פֶּה֮ לָֽאָדָם֒ א֚וֹ מִֽי־יָשׂ֣וּם
אִלֵּ֔ם א֣וֹ חֵרֵ֔שׁ א֥וֹ פִקֵּ֖חַ א֣וֹ עִוֵּ֑ר הֲלֹ֥א אָנֹכִ֖י
יְהוָֽה׃ 12 וְעַתָּ֖ה לֵ֑ךְ וְאָנֹכִי֙ אֶֽהְיֶ֣ה עִם־פִּ֔יךָ
וְהוֹרֵיתִ֖יךָ אֲשֶׁ֥ר תְּדַבֵּֽר׃ 13 וַיֹּ֖אמֶר בִּ֣י אֲדֹנָ֑י
שְֽׁלַֽח־נָ֖א בְּיַד־תִּשְׁלָֽח׃ 14 וַיִּֽחַר־אַ֨ף יְהוָ֜ה
בְּמֹשֶׁ֗ה וַיֹּ֙אמֶר֙ הֲלֹ֨א אַהֲרֹ֤ן אָחִ֙יךָ֙ הַלֵּוִ֔י
יָדַ֕עְתִּי כִּֽי־דַבֵּ֥ר יְדַבֵּ֖ר ה֑וּא וְגַ֤ם הִנֵּה־הוּא֙
יֹצֵ֣א לִקְרָאתֶ֔ךָ וְרָאֲךָ֖ וְשָׂמַ֥ח בְּלִבּֽוֹ׃
15 וְדִבַּרְתָּ֣ אֵלָ֔יו וְשַׂמְתָּ֥ אֶת־הַדְּבָרִ֖ים בְּפִ֑יו
וְאָנֹכִ֗י אֶֽהְיֶ֤ה עִם־פִּ֙יךָ֙ וְעִם־פִּ֔יהוּ וְהוֹרֵיתִ֣י
אֶתְכֶ֔ם אֵ֖ת אֲשֶׁ֥ר תַּעֲשֽׂוּן׃ 16 וְדִבֶּר־ה֥וּא
לְךָ֖ אֶל־הָעָ֑ם וְהָ֤יָה הוּא֙ יִֽהְיֶה־לְּךָ֣ לְפֶ֔ה
וְאַתָּ֖ה תִּֽהְיֶה־לּ֥וֹ לֵאלֹהִֽים׃ 17 וְאֶת־הַמַּטֶּ֥ה

you, take some water from the Nile and pour it on the dry ground, and it—the water that you take from the Nile—will turn to blood on the dry ground."

10But Moses said to the LORD, "Please, O Lord, I have never been a man of words, either in times past or now that You have spoken to Your servant; I am slow of speech and slow of tongue." 11And the LORD said to him, "Who gives man speech? Who makes him dumb or deaf, seeing or blind? Is it not I, the LORD? 12Now go, and I will be with you as you speak and will instruct you what to say." 13But he said, "Please, O Lord, make someone else Your agent." 14The LORD became angry with Moses, and He said, "There is your brother Aaron the Levite. He, I know, speaks readily. Even now he is setting out to meet you, and he will be happy to see you. 15You shall speak to him and put the words in his mouth—I will be with you and with him as you speak, and tell both of you what to do—16and he shall speak for you to the people. Thus he shall serve as your spokesman, with you playing the role of God to him, 17and take with

10. Moses puts forth his final objection: he is inadequate to the task of being God's spokesman before the Egyptian court. The precise nature of the deficiency is unclear, but it should be noted that other prophets, such as Jeremiah, made similar claims. Traditional commentators understood it as a speech defect. Prophetic eloquence is not an inborn talent but a divine gift granted for a special purpose.

14. Aaron Mentioned here for the first time, he is three years older than Moses.

the Levite A strange designation, because Moses too was from the tribe of Levi. The Hebrew can be translated as "your brother Levite."

16. your spokesman Hebrew: *peh,* literally "mouth," i.e., mouthpiece. Moses will be to Aaron as God is to Moses. It is the role of the prophet to speak the word of God (see Exod. 7:1).

CHAPTER 4

10. I am slow of speech and slow of tongue A Jewish legend tells that when the infant Moses was sitting on Pharaoh's lap, he reached up and took off Pharaoh's crown. Pharaoh feared that this was a sign that this child would one day try to replace him, so he devised a test. He set before Moses a crown and a hot coal, thinking, "If he reaches for the crown, I will have him killed." The baby Moses was about to reach for the shiny crown when an angel redirected his hand away from it toward the coal. Burning his fingers, he put his hand in his mouth and injured his tongue, rendering him "slow of tongue" ever after (Exod. R. 1:26). Perhaps the Torah is telling us that, whatever our limitations, God can use us to do great things.

14. he will be happy to see you This is a striking and welcome contrast to the accounts of sibling jealousy in the Book of Genesis.

you this rod, with which you shall perform the signs."

18Moses went back to his father-in-law Jether and said to him, "Let me go back to my kinsmen in Egypt and see how they are faring." And Jethro said to Moses, "Go in peace."

19The LORD said to Moses in Midian, "Go back to Egypt, for all the men who sought to kill you are dead." 20So Moses took his wife and sons, mounted them on an ass, and went back to the land of Egypt; and Moses took the rod of God with him.

21And the LORD said to Moses, "When you return to Egypt, see that you perform before Pharaoh all the marvels that I have put within your power. I, however, will stiffen his heart so that he will not let the people go. 22Then you shall say to Pharaoh, 'Thus says the LORD:

הַזֶּה תִּקַּח בְּיָדֶךָ אֲשֶׁר תַּעֲשֶׂה־בּוֹ אֶת־
הָאֹתֹת׃ פ
18 וַיֵּלֶךְ מֹשֶׁה וַיָּשָׁב ׀ אֶל־יֶתֶר חֹתְנוֹ וַיֹּאמֶר ששי
לוֹ אֵלְכָה נָּא וְאָשׁוּבָה אֶל־אַחַי אֲשֶׁר־
בְּמִצְרַיִם וְאֶרְאֶה הַעוֹדָם חַיִּים וַיֹּאמֶר
יִתְרוֹ לְמֹשֶׁה לֵךְ לְשָׁלוֹם׃
19 וַיֹּאמֶר יְהוָה אֶל־מֹשֶׁה בְּמִדְיָן לֵךְ שֻׁב
מִצְרָיִם כִּי־מֵתוּ כָּל־הָאֲנָשִׁים הַמְבַקְשִׁים
אֶת־נַפְשֶׁךָ׃ 20 וַיִּקַּח מֹשֶׁה אֶת־אִשְׁתּוֹ
וְאֶת־בָּנָיו וַיַּרְכִּבֵם עַל־הַחֲמֹר וַיָּשָׁב אַרְצָה
מִצְרָיִם וַיִּקַּח מֹשֶׁה אֶת־מַטֵּה הָאֱלֹהִים
בְּיָדוֹ׃
21 וַיֹּאמֶר יְהוָה אֶל־מֹשֶׁה בְּלֶכְתְּךָ לָשׁוּב
מִצְרַיְמָה רְאֵה כָּל־הַמֹּפְתִים אֲשֶׁר־שַׂמְתִּי
בְיָדֶךָ וַעֲשִׂיתָם לִפְנֵי פַרְעֹה וַאֲנִי אֲחַזֵּק
אֶת־לִבּוֹ וְלֹא יְשַׁלַּח אֶת־הָעָם׃ 22 וְאָמַרְתָּ
אֶל־פַּרְעֹה כֹּה אָמַר יְהוָה בְּנִי בְכֹרִי

THE CHALLENGE OF LEADERSHIP: INITIAL FAILURE (4:18–6:1)

This section covers the events between the two great divine manifestations of 3:1–4:17 and 6:2–8.

LEAVE-TAKING AND DEPARTURE (4:18–23)

18. Moses returns to Midian with the sheep. He needs to obtain his father-in-law's formal permission to leave his household (see 2:21). He does not reveal the true reason for returning to Egypt, probably because Jethro might think the mission to be impossible and withhold his consent.

my kinsmen The phrase links the return with the original flight, which was a consequence of his having gone out "to his kinsfolk" (2:11).

how they are faring Literally, "whether they are still alive."

19. Apparently still fearing for his personal safety, Moses delays; hence the divine directive and reassurance.

20. his wife and sons According to 18:2–5, Jethro brought Zipporah and the two sons from Midian to Sinai after the Exodus. This shows that they were not in Egypt all the while.

sons Only Gershom has so far been mentioned (2:22, but see 18:3–6). The ancient translations read "son" here.

rod of God The shepherd's crook mentioned in verses 2–4. In the ancient Near East, gods were depicted carrying rods as symbols of authority and as emblems of supernatural power.

21. stiffen his heart The motif of the stiffening, or hardening, of Pharaoh's heart appears exactly 20 times in Exodus. Half of the references are descriptions of Pharaoh's character (i.e., he hardens his own heart). Half of them are attributed to divine causality, a form of "measure for measure" (see *D'rash* to 7:3). In the biblical conception, psychological faculties are considered to be concentrated in the heart. Human behavior is determined in the heart, which is regarded as the seat of the intellectual, moral, and spiritual life of the individual. "Hardening of the heart" thus expresses a state of arrogant moral degeneracy, unresponsive to reason and incapable of compassion. Pharaoh's personal guilt is beyond question. Pharaoh's character is now his destiny. Deprived of any chance of relenting, he is irresistibly drawn to a doom of his own making. Note that repentance is not even considered a possibility here. It is a religious notion that evidently developed after the time of the Exodus story.

22. Thus says the LORD Hebrew: *koh amar YHVH*. This is the first use of what was to become

Israel is My first-born son. 23I have said to you, "Let My son go, that he may worship Me," yet you refuse to let him go. Now I will slay your first-born son.'"

יִשְׂרָאֵל׃ 23 וָאֹמַר אֵלֶיךָ שַׁלַּח אֶת־בְּנִי
וְיַעַבְדֵנִי וַתְּמָאֵן לְשַׁלְּחוֹ הִנֵּה אָנֹכִי הֹרֵג
אֶת־בִּנְךָ בְּכֹרֶךָ׃

24At a night encampment on the way, the Lord encountered him and sought to kill him. 25 So Zipporah took a flint and cut off her son's

24 וַיְהִי בַדֶּרֶךְ בַּמָּלוֹן וַיִּפְגְּשֵׁהוּ יְהוָה
וַיְבַקֵּשׁ הֲמִיתוֹ׃ 25 וַתִּקַּח צִפֹּרָה צֹר

the formula for introducing a prophetic address. It is the regular messenger formula (Gen. 32:5, 45:9), similar to the opening words of ancient Near Eastern royal heralds. It secures the attention of an audience while emphasizing the unimpeachable authority behind the ensuing proclamation. Moses is to approach the Egyptian king as the emissary of the sovereign Lord of the universe.

My first-born son The relationship of Israel to God is expressed poetically. All peoples are recognized as children under the universal fatherhood of God, but Israel has the singular status of the first to acknowledge *YHVH* and thus to enter into a special relationship with Him. As such, Israel enjoys God's devoted care and protection. It is this that lies behind the demand of verse 23 that the Israelites be allowed to worship in the wilderness. Denial of this right by Pharaoh will incur punishment.

23. your first-born son Pharaoh here stands for all Egyptians, parallel to the collective "Israel." The threat alludes to the 10th plague, the one that finally breaks the tyrant's obstinacy.

NIGHT ENCOUNTER AND CIRCUMCISION (vv. 24–26)

This strange story is not easily understood. It must echo an ancient myth whose background has been lost to us. The account of Moses' return to Egypt is interrupted by a three-verse story that seems disconnected from the previous narrative and makes no mention of Moses. Like Jacob's wrestling with the angel at the Jabbok River, the confrontation with God is so terrifying that it makes the confrontation with Pharaoh minor.

This sketchy tale of the mysterious night incident is not entirely dissociated from the larger context. The introductory phrase, "At a night encampment on the way," establishes a chronologic linkage with verse 20. It is connected with the passages that immediately precede and follow it by several verbal tie-ins. Thus the phrase "sought to kill" in verse 24 echoes "who sought to kill you" in verse 19; "her son's" in verse 25 recalls "sons," "My . . . son," "your . . . son" in verses 20, 22, and 23; and the Hebrew for "encountered him" (*va-yifg'sheihu*) in verse 24 is identical with that for "met him" in verse 27. There is also a correspondence between the blood of circumcision and the visible sign of blood on the paschal sacrifice. In both instances, God comes as a destroyer, and blood averts evil (4:26, 12:7,13,22–23). This brief narrative underscores the vital significance of the institution of circumcision and the serious consequences of its neglect.

24. kill him The sequence of verses suggests that it was Moses' firstborn, Gershom, whose life was imperiled. If it was Moses who was attacked, the purpose was to temper him, making him more prepared for the dangers that await him.

25. Zipporah As the daughter of a Midianite priest, she may have been familiar with the rite of circumcision, a practice found among the an-

---

22. Israel is My first-born Parents can love all of their children equally but differently and often invest their firstborn with special hopes, obligations, and responsibilities, so that younger children will be able to learn from the firstborn's example. This would seem to be the role that God chose for Israel.

25. Once again, it is a woman, this time Zipporah, who understands and does what has to be done to sustain life. If Zipporah, daughter

HALAKHAH L'MA·ASEH

4:25. cut off her son's foreskin According to Jewish law, the father bears primary responsibility to have his sons circumcised, but community authorities or, as here, the mother can arrange for the circumcision if the father fails to do so. Ultimately, if a Jewish man has not been circumcised, he bears the responsibility to have himself circumcised (BT Kid. 29a).

וַתִּכְרֹת֙ אֶת־עָרְלַ֣ת בְּנָ֔הּ וַתַּגַּ֖ע לְרַגְלָ֑יו
וַתֹּ֕אמֶר כִּ֧י חֲתַן־דָּמִ֛ים אַתָּ֖ה לִֽי׃ 26 וַיִּ֖רֶף
מִמֶּ֑נּוּ אָ֚ז אָֽמְרָ֔ה חֲתַ֥ן דָּמִ֖ים לַמּוּלֹֽת׃ פ

foreskin, and touched his legs with it, saying, "You are truly a bridegroom of blood to me!"
26And when He let him alone, she added, "A bridegroom of blood because of the circumcision."

27 וַיֹּ֤אמֶר יְהוָה֙ אֶֽל־אַהֲרֹ֔ן לֵ֛ךְ לִקְרַ֥את
מֹשֶׁ֖ה הַמִּדְבָּ֑רָה וַיֵּ֗לֶךְ וַֽיִּפְגְּשֵׁ֛הוּ בְּהַ֥ר
הָאֱלֹהִ֖ים וַיִּשַּׁק־לֽוֹ׃ 28 וַיַּגֵּ֤ד מֹשֶׁה֙ לְאַהֲרֹ֔ן
אֵ֛ת כָּל־דִּבְרֵ֥י יְהוָ֖ה אֲשֶׁ֣ר שְׁלָח֑וֹ וְאֵ֚ת
כָּל־הָאֹתֹ֖ת אֲשֶׁ֥ר צִוָּֽהוּ׃ 29 וַיֵּ֥לֶךְ מֹשֶׁ֖ה
וְאַהֲרֹ֑ן וַיַּ֣אַסְפ֔וּ אֶת־כָּל־זִקְנֵ֖י בְּנֵ֥י יִשְׂרָאֵֽל׃
30 וַיְדַבֵּ֣ר אַהֲרֹ֔ן אֵ֚ת כָּל־הַדְּבָרִ֔ים אֲשֶׁר־

27The LORD said to Aaron, "Go to meet Moses in the wilderness." He went and met him at the mountain of God, and he kissed him.
28Moses told Aaron about all the things that the LORD had committed to him and all the signs about which He had instructed him.
29Then Moses and Aaron went and assembled all the elders of the Israelites.
30Aaron repeated all the words

cient Semites and prevalent among the priestly classes in Egypt. It is not known how she came to attribute her son's illness to the fact that he was uncircumcised. Moses may have neglected this rite because of the danger of exposing a newly circumcised child to the rigors of a wilderness journey. Josh. 5:5,7 states that the generation born during the wilderness wanderings was not circumcised.

a flint Rather than a metal knife, even though the events occurred in the Late Bronze Age. A stone knife is still widely preferred in primitive societies that practice circumcision, because flint can be given a sharper edge than metal and the knife must be very sharp.

cut off Circumcision is called "the sign of the covenant" in Gen. 17:9–14. Gen. 17:14 states that whoever fails to fulfill that rite—the first command given to Abraham and his descendants—"shall be cut off from his kin; he has broken My covenant." An uncircumcised Israelite would be alienated from the community of Israel and excluded from the paschal sacrifice and the redemption from Egypt. Josh. 5:5 explicitly records that all the males who came out of Egypt had undergone the rite. It would have been paradoxical indeed had the son of the central figure in the story of the Exodus been an outsider.

touched his legs Whose legs is unclear, as is the symbolism of the gesture. "Legs" may be a euphemism for the genital organs, either of the child or of Moses. The act might signify that the foreskin has been cut off and that the requirement of circumcision has been fulfilled. Or it may be a reference to daubing the child with blood, for the Hebrew verb used here (rendered "touched") is the same as that used for daubing the blood of the paschal lamb on the lintel and doorposts in 12:22 (rendered "apply"). In both cases, the purpose would be the same: The blood would act as a protective sign against plague; the destroyer would not smite.

a bridegroom of blood This could refer either to Moses or to his son. It is the traditional English rendering of the unique Hebrew phrase *"ḥatan damim,"* for which no parallel has been found in ancient Near Eastern literature. In Arabic, the stem חתן denotes "to circumcise" as well as "to protect." Hence, the phrase could convey, "You are now circumcised [and so] protected for me by means of the blood of circumcision."

26. He let him alone The subject is God. The crisis has passed.

MOSES' LEADERSHIP IS ACCEPTED
(vv. 27–31)

27. he kissed him This was the usual biblical greeting between close relatives.

29. The directive given in 3:16 is carried out.

---

of a Midianite priest, joined herself to the people of Israel and to the God of Israel, she would be an early example of the convert to Judaism who takes its demands more seriously than the native-born Jew. Buber sees this strange incident as an "event of the night," which typically happens to religious leaders as a psychological reaction to their newly won certainty, an intuition that the task they have undertaken on God's behalf will be harder than they thought.

that the Lord had spoken to Moses, and he performed the signs in the sight of the people, ³¹and the people were convinced. When they heard that the Lord had taken note of the Israelites and that He had seen their plight, they bowed low in homage.

דִּבֶּ֤ר יְהוָה֙ אֶל־מֹשֶׁ֔ה וַיַּ֥עַשׂ הָאֹתֹ֖ת לְעֵינֵ֥י הָעָֽם: ³¹ וַֽיַּאֲמֵ֖ן הָעָ֑ם וַֽיִּשְׁמְע֞וּ כִּֽי־פָקַ֤ד יְהוָה֙ אֶת־בְּנֵ֣י יִשְׂרָאֵ֔ל וְכִ֥י רָאָ֖ה אֶת־עָנְיָ֑ם וַֽיִּקְּד֖וּ וַיִּֽשְׁתַּחֲוּֽוּ:

5

Afterward Moses and Aaron went and said to Pharaoh, "Thus says the Lord, the God of Israel: Let My people go that they may celebrate a festival for Me in the wilderness." ²But Pharaoh said, "Who is the Lord that I should heed Him and let Israel go? I do not know the Lord, nor will I let Israel go." ³They answered, "The God of the Hebrews has manifested Himself to us. Let us go, we pray, a distance of three days

שביעי ה וְאַחַ֗ר בָּ֚אוּ מֹשֶׁ֣ה וְאַהֲרֹ֔ן וַיֹּאמְר֖וּ אֶל־פַּרְעֹ֑ה כֹּֽה־אָמַ֤ר יְהוָה֙ אֱלֹהֵ֣י יִשְׂרָאֵ֔ל שַׁלַּח֙ אֶת־עַמִּ֔י וְיָחֹ֥גּוּ לִ֖י בַּמִּדְבָּֽר: ² וַיֹּ֣אמֶר פַּרְעֹ֔ה מִ֤י יְהוָה֙ אֲשֶׁ֣ר אֶשְׁמַ֣ע בְּקֹל֔וֹ לְשַׁלַּ֖ח אֶת־יִשְׂרָאֵ֑ל לֹ֤א יָדַ֙עְתִּי֙ אֶת־יְהוָ֔ה וְגַ֥ם אֶת־יִשְׂרָאֵ֖ל לֹ֥א אֲשַׁלֵּֽחַ: ³ וַיֹּ֣אמְר֔וּ אֱלֹהֵ֥י הָעִבְרִ֖ים נִקְרָ֣א עָלֵ֑ינוּ נֵ֣לֲכָה נָּ֡א

31. As predicted (vv. 8–9), the signs are accepted as testimony to the reliability of Moses and the truth of his message.

bowed low Here, this is a gesture of thanksgiving.

FIRST AUDIENCE WITH PHARAOH
(5:1–6:1)

The diplomatic approach attempted by Moses and Aaron ends in failure, leading to another new phase in the history of Israel in Egypt. The struggle for freedom begins in earnest. This chapter is also the introduction to the narrative of the plagues.

THE FIRST CONFRONTATION
WITH THE COURT (vv. 1–5)

1. Afterward Upon meeting with popular acceptance.

God of Israel This title more precisely defines the name *YHVH*.

celebrate a festival The Hebrew for "festi-

val" (*ḥag*) is a sacrificial feast associated with a pilgrimage to a sanctuary.

2. Who is the Lord? A contemptuous retort. It contrasts starkly with the humble response of Moses to the divine call: "Who am I?" In Egyptian doctrine, Pharaoh was the incarnation of a god, with unlimited power. Part of God's purpose is to make the divine name known.

I do not know I do not acknowledge His authority.

3. The reaction of Moses and Aaron is restrained. They seem surprised and cowed by the king's aggressive arrogance.

God of the Hebrews They use the language prescribed in 3:18, but they omit "the Lord" because the monarch already has denied any knowledge of Him.

lest He strike us For disregarding our obligation. Pharaoh should be concerned about this, because he will lose our labor. "Us" may be an intimation that the Egyptians too will be stricken.

CHAPTER 5

1. Moses and Aaron went What happened to the elders and leaders who were to go with them? A *midrash* tells us that the whole group set out to confront Pharaoh, but one by one, the others dropped out for reasons of timidity. Only Moses and Aaron remained, two old men standing against the power of the Egyptian empire (Exod. R. 5:14).

2. Pharaoh refuses to free the slaves, not because it is in his economic interest to keep them, but because he "does not know God," i.e., he does not recognize that certain kinds of behavior, such as abusing other people, are wrong. "Divine sovereignty is precisely what Pharaoh mocks at the outset of his power struggle with Moses. It is not a matter of oversize egos in battle but of the limits of human authority" (Schorsch).

into the wilderness to sacrifice to the LORD our God, lest He strike us with pestilence or sword." 4But the king of Egypt said to them, "Moses and Aaron, why do you distract the people from their tasks? Get to your labors!" 5And Pharaoh continued, "The people of the land are already so numerous, and you would have them cease from their labors!"

6That same day Pharaoh charged the taskmasters and foremen of the people, saying, 7"You shall no longer provide the people with straw for making bricks as heretofore; let them go and gather straw for themselves. 8But impose upon them the same quota of bricks as they have been making heretofore; do not reduce it, for they are shirkers; that is why they cry, 'Let us go and sacrifice to our God!' 9Let heavier work be laid upon the men; let them keep at it and not pay attention to deceitful promises."

10So the taskmasters and foremen of the people went out and said to the people, "Thus says

דֶּרֶךְ שְׁלֹשֶׁת יָמִים בַּמִּדְבָּר וְנִזְבְּחָה
לַיהוָה אֱלֹהֵינוּ פֶּן־יִפְגָּעֵנוּ בַּדֶּבֶר אוֹ
בֶחָרֶב׃ 4 וַיֹּאמֶר אֲלֵהֶם מֶלֶךְ מִצְרַיִם לָמָּה
מֹשֶׁה וְאַהֲרֹן תַּפְרִיעוּ אֶת־הָעָם מִמַּעֲשָׂיו
לְכוּ לְסִבְלֹתֵיכֶם׃ 5 וַיֹּאמֶר פַּרְעֹה הֵן־
רַבִּים עַתָּה עַם הָאָרֶץ וְהִשְׁבַּתֶּם אֹתָם
מִסִּבְלֹתָם׃
6 וַיְצַו פַּרְעֹה בַּיּוֹם הַהוּא אֶת־הַנֹּגְשִׂים
בָּעָם וְאֶת־שֹׁטְרָיו לֵאמֹר׃ 7 לֹא תֹאסִפוּן*
לָתֵת תֶּבֶן לָעָם לִלְבֹּן הַלְּבֵנִים כִּתְמוֹל
שִׁלְשֹׁם הֵם יֵלְכוּ וְקֹשְׁשׁוּ לָהֶם תֶּבֶן׃
8 וְאֶת־מַתְכֹּנֶת הַלְּבֵנִים אֲשֶׁר הֵם עֹשִׂים
תְּמוֹל שִׁלְשֹׁם תָּשִׂימוּ עֲלֵיהֶם לֹא תִגְרְעוּ
מִמֶּנּוּ כִּי־נִרְפִּים הֵם עַל־כֵּן הֵם צֹעֲקִים
לֵאמֹר נֵלְכָה נִזְבְּחָה לֵאלֹהֵינוּ׃ 9 תִּכְבַּד
הָעֲבֹדָה עַל־הָאֲנָשִׁים וְיַעֲשׂוּ־בָהּ וְאַל־
יִשְׁעוּ בְּדִבְרֵי־שָׁקֶר׃
10 וַיֵּצְאוּ נֹגְשֵׂי הָעָם וְשֹׁטְרָיו וַיֹּאמְרוּ אֶל־

v. 7. יתיר א׳

pestilence or sword These are conventional symbols of divine judgment that will make their appearance later in Egypt.

4. Pharaoh treats the request for time to worship as a scheme to avoid work.

5. This statement may explain the economic reasons for refusing the request: The Israelites are so numerous that any interruption of their labors would entail an enormous loss of productivity. It might also take up the original theme of Exod.1:7,9–10 that the huge population would constitute a power to be reckoned with were they to quit working. Either way, the second half of the verse is an exclamation.

people of the land Meaning the common laborers, perhaps a derisive term.

A PEREMPTORY REFUSAL (vv. 6–9)

Moses and Aaron are silent. The audience with the king is terminated abruptly. The tyrant loses no time in issuing orders designed to drive home to the Israelites the futility of entertaining any hope of easing their labors.

6. taskmasters and foremen In the Egyptian slave-labor system the workers were organized into manageable gangs, each headed by a foreman from among their own. He, in turn, was directly responsible to his superior, the "taskmaster." The foremen were Israelites; the taskmasters, Egyptian.

7–8. The new directive did not demand "bricks without straw," as the English saying goes. Rather, it ordered the brickmakers to collect their own straw; until then it had been supplied by the state. Chopped straw or stubble was a crucial ingredient in the manufacture of bricks. It was added to the mud from the Nile, then shaped in a mold and left to dry in the sun. The straw acted as a binder, and the acid released by the decay of the vegetable matter greatly enhanced the plastic and cohesive properties of the brick, thus preventing shrinking, cracking, and loss of shape.

to our God Pharaoh does not recognize the Lord and so refrains from using the divine name.

9. deceitful promises This refers back to 4:29–31. Egyptian intelligence must have reported about the promises of redemption.

THE OPPRESSION INTENSIFIES (vv. 10–14)

10. Thus says Pharaoh As opposed to "Thus

Pharaoh: I will not give you any straw. 11You must go and get the straw yourselves wherever you can find it; but there shall be no decrease whatever in your work." 12Then the people scattered throughout the land of Egypt to gather stubble for straw. 13And the taskmasters pressed them, saying, "You must complete the same work assignment each day as when you had straw." 14And the foremen of the Israelites, whom Pharaoh's taskmasters had set over them, were beaten. "Why," they were asked, "did you not complete the prescribed amount of bricks, either yesterday or today, as you did before?"

15Then the foremen of the Israelites came to Pharaoh and cried: "Why do you deal thus with your servants? 16No straw is issued to your servants, yet they demand of us: Make bricks! Thus your servants are being beaten, when the fault is with your own people." 17He replied, "You are shirkers, shirkers! That is why you say, 'Let us go and sacrifice to the LORD.' 18Be off now to your work! No straw shall be issued to you, but you must produce your quota of bricks!"

19Now the foremen of the Israelites found themselves in trouble because of the order, "You must not reduce your daily quantity of bricks." 20As they left Pharaoh's presence, they came upon Moses and Aaron standing in their path, 21and they said to them, "May the LORD look upon you and punish you for making us loathsome to Pharaoh and his courtiers—putting a sword in their hands to slay us." 22Then Moses returned to the LORD and said, "O Lord, why did You bring harm upon this

הָעָם לֵאמֹר כֹּה אָמַר פַּרְעֹה אֵינֶנִּי נֹתֵן
לָכֶם תֶּבֶן׃ 11 אַתֶּם לְכוּ קְחוּ לָכֶם תֶּבֶן
מֵאֲשֶׁר תִּמְצָאוּ כִּי אֵין נִגְרָע מֵעֲבֹדַתְכֶם
דָּבָר׃ 12 וַיָּפֶץ הָעָם בְּכָל־אֶרֶץ מִצְרָיִם
לְקֹשֵׁשׁ קַשׁ לַתֶּבֶן׃ 13 וְהַנֹּגְשִׂים אָצִים
לֵאמֹר כַּלּוּ מַעֲשֵׂיכֶם דְּבַר־יוֹם בְּיוֹמוֹ
כַּאֲשֶׁר בִּהְיוֹת הַתֶּבֶן׃ 14 וַיֻּכּוּ שֹׁטְרֵי בְּנֵי
יִשְׂרָאֵל אֲשֶׁר־שָׂמוּ עֲלֵהֶם נֹגְשֵׂי פַּרְעֹה
לֵאמֹר מַדּוּעַ לֹא כִלִּיתֶם חָקְכֶם לִלְבֹּן
כִּתְמוֹל שִׁלְשֹׁם גַּם־תְּמוֹל גַּם־הַיּוֹם׃
15 וַיָּבֹאוּ שֹׁטְרֵי בְּנֵי יִשְׂרָאֵל וַיִּצְעֲקוּ אֶל־
פַּרְעֹה לֵאמֹר לָמָּה תַעֲשֶׂה כֹה לַעֲבָדֶיךָ׃
16 תֶּבֶן אֵין נִתָּן לַעֲבָדֶיךָ וּלְבֵנִים אֹמְרִים
לָנוּ עֲשׂוּ וְהִנֵּה עֲבָדֶיךָ מֻכִּים וְחָטָאת
עַמֶּךָ׃ 17 וַיֹּאמֶר נִרְפִּים אַתֶּם נִרְפִּים עַל־כֵּן
אַתֶּם אֹמְרִים נֵלְכָה נִזְבְּחָה לַיהוָה׃
18 וְעַתָּה לְכוּ עִבְדוּ וְתֶבֶן לֹא־יִנָּתֵן לָכֶם
וְתֹכֶן לְבֵנִים תִּתֵּנוּ׃
19 וַיִּרְאוּ שֹׁטְרֵי בְנֵי־יִשְׂרָאֵל אֹתָם בְּרָע
לֵאמֹר לֹא־תִגְרְעוּ מִלִּבְנֵיכֶם דְּבַר־יוֹם
בְּיוֹמוֹ׃ 20 וַיִּפְגְּעוּ אֶת־מֹשֶׁה וְאֶת־אַהֲרֹן
נִצָּבִים לִקְרָאתָם בְּצֵאתָם מֵאֵת פַּרְעֹה׃
21 וַיֹּאמְרוּ אֲלֵהֶם יֵרֶא יְהוָה עֲלֵיכֶם
וְיִשְׁפֹּט אֲשֶׁר הִבְאַשְׁתֶּם אֶת־רֵיחֵנוּ בְּעֵינֵי
פַרְעֹה וּבְעֵינֵי עֲבָדָיו לָתֶת־חֶרֶב בְּיָדָם
לְהָרְגֵנוּ׃ 22 וַיָּשָׁב מֹשֶׁה אֶל־יְהוָה וַיֹּאמַר מפטיר
אֲדֹנָי לָמָה הֲרֵעֹתָה לָעָם הַזֶּה לָמָּה זֶּה

says the LORD" (4:22; 5:1). Pharaoh is now on a collision course with the God of Israel.

13–14. According to the chain of command, the pressure would have fallen on the Israelite foremen.

THE FOREMEN PROTEST (vv. 15–18)

16. the fault is with your own people We are being treated unfairly.

DEMORALIZATION (5:19–6:1)

21. making us loathsome Literally, "causing our breath to be malodorous in the eyes of." The mixed metaphor means "brought us into contempt" (see Gen. 34:30).

22–23. Moses' bitter disappointment at his initial failure points both to his unrealistic expectations of early success and to his original reluctance to accept the divine commission.

people? Why did You send me? 23Ever since I came to Pharaoh to speak in Your name, he has dealt worse with this people; and still You have not delivered Your people."

שְׁלַחְתָּנִי׃ 23 וּמֵאָ֞ז בָּ֤אתִי אֶל־פַּרְעֹה֙ לְדַבֵּ֣ר בִּשְׁמֶ֔ךָ הֵרַ֖ע לָעָ֣ם הַזֶּ֑ה וְהַצֵּ֥ל לֹא־הִצַּ֖לְתָּ אֶת־עַמֶּֽךָ׃

6 Then the LORD said to Moses, "You shall soon see what I will do to Pharaoh: he shall let them go because of a greater might; indeed, because of a greater might he shall drive them from his land."

ו וַיֹּ֤אמֶר יְהוָה֙ אֶל־מֹשֶׁ֔ה עַתָּ֣ה תִרְאֶ֔ה אֲשֶׁ֥ר אֶעֱשֶׂ֖ה לְפַרְעֹ֑ה כִּ֣י בְיָ֤ד חֲזָקָה֙ יְשַׁלְּחֵ֔ם וּבְיָ֣ד חֲזָקָ֔ה יְגָרְשֵׁ֖ם מֵאַרְצֽוֹ׃ ס

returned to the LORD He retreated into seclusion to commune with God.

6:1. a greater might Literally, "a strong hand." Note the irony. Pharaoh not only will let you go; he will force you to go. See Comment to Exod. 3:19.

הפטרת שמות

HAFTARAH FOR SH'MOT

ISAIAH 27:6–28:13, 29:22–23 (*Ashk'nazim*)

This *haftarah* alternates between promises of hope for the people Israel and threats of destruction. It opens with a vision of national renewal and it concludes the two sections of threats against Israel (27:7–11, 28:1–13) with passages promising redemption and renewal (27:12–13, 29:22–23). The prophet predicts fulfillment of the central hope for an ingathering of the people Israel from the distant reaches of Assyria and Egypt (Isa. 27:13). This will be a new exodus, a counterpoint to the original Exodus anticipated in the *parashah*.

The tension between hope and doom, between promises and threats, is expressed through the imagery of botany. The opening verse depicts Israel striking roots in the land, to sprout (*yatzitz*) and to blossom with a prodigious growth (27:6). By contrast, the faithless receiving punishment are depicted as broken boughs stripped of all growth, with no future (27:10–11). The people gathered from their exile are imagined as collected grain (27:12). The destruction of Ephraim—which symbolizes the northern kingdom—is imagined in terms of "an early fig / Before the fruit harvest" devoured by all comers (28:4). The "proud crowns" (*ateret gei·ut*) of "glorious beauty" (*tz'vi tif·arto*) on the head of Ephraim are likened to "wilted flowers" (*tzitzat novel*) "trampled underfoot" (28:1,4). This image is counterpoised to the splendor of God, who "shall become a crown of beauty (*ateret tz'vi*) and a diadem of glory (*tz'firat tif·arah*) for the remnant of His people" (28:5). The contrast provides a unifying figure for the overall proclamation and marks the difference between doom and divinity.

RELATION OF THE *HAFTARAH* TO THE *PARASHAH*

The Book of Exodus begins with a reference to "the sons of Israel who came (*ha-ba·im*) to Egypt with Jacob," where they settled and "increased very greatly, so that the land was filled (*va-timmalei*) with them" (Exod. 1:1,7). Similarly, the prophetic lesson opens with reference to the people of Jacob/Israel who "[in days] to come [*ha-ba·im*]" shall "strike root" in their homeland, and "the world shall be covered [*u-mal·u*] with fruit" (Isa. 27:6). Through such verbal echos, the Sages linked the promise of the *haftarah* to the descent of ancient Israelites to Egypt.

Just as Moses had beseeched Pharaoh to permit the Israelites to worship God in the wilderness (Exod. 5:1), Isaiah foresees service of the Lord as part of a new exodus: "in that day, a great ram's horn shall be sounded; and the strayed who are in the land of Assyria and the expelled who are in the land of Egypt shall come (*u-va·u*) and worship the LORD on the holy mount (*har ha-kodesh*), in Jerusalem" (Isa. 27:13). The physical restoration of the nation to its homeland will have a spiritual component as well. The final words of the prophecy add a more inward dimension, betokening a transformation of the spirit, with the promise that a future generation will perceive the presence of the Lord in its midst and "hallow (*yakdishu*) My name" (29:23).

The *parashah* states that God put His awesome signs "upon" or (literally) "in the midst" (*b'kirbo*) of the Egyptians, so that they might recognize His greatness and release the people Israel from bondage (Exod. 3:20). The *haftarah* (Isa. 29:23) complements that image, stating that the renewal of the people Israel will be realized through an awakening to God's mysterious work "in his midst" (*b'kirbo*). This will be a transformation of mind and heart, a release from mere earthliness to godly sensibility. This too will be a new exodus, that is, a re-rooting of the self in days to come (Isa. 27:6).

27 6[In days] to come Jacob shall strike root,
Israel shall sprout and blossom,
And the face of the world
Shall be covered with fruit.

7Was he beaten as his beater has been?
Did he suffer such slaughter as his slayers?
8Assailing them with fury unchained,
His pitiless blast bore them off
On a day of gale.

9Assuredly, by this alone
Shall Jacob's sin be purged away;
This is the only price
For removing his guilt:
That he make all the altar-stones
Like shattered blocks of chalk—
With no sacred post left standing,
Nor any incense altar.
10Thus fortified cities lie desolate,

כז 6 הַבָּאִים֙ יַשְׁרֵ֣שׁ יַעֲקֹ֔ב
יָצִ֥יץ וּפָרַ֖ח יִשְׂרָאֵ֑ל
וּמָלְא֥וּ פְנֵי־תֵבֵ֖ל
תְּנוּבָֽה׃ ס

7 הַכְּמַכַּ֥ת מַכֵּ֖הוּ הִכָּ֑הוּ
אִם־כְּהֶ֥רֶג הֲרֻגָ֖יו הֹרָֽג׃
8 בְּסַאסְּאָ֖ה בְּשַׁלְחָ֣הּ תְּרִיבֶ֑נָּה
הָגָ֛ה בְּרוּח֥וֹ הַקָּשָׁ֖ה
בְּי֥וֹם קָדִֽים׃

9 לָכֵ֗ן בְּזֹאת֙
יְכֻפַּ֣ר עֲוֺן־יַעֲקֹ֔ב
וְזֶ֕ה כָּל־פְּרִ֖י
הָסִ֣ר חַטָּאת֑וֹ
בְּשׂוּמ֣וֹ ׀ כָּל־אַבְנֵ֣י מִזְבֵּ֗חַ
כְּאַבְנֵי־גִר֙ מְנֻפָּצ֔וֹת
לֹא־יָקֻ֥מוּ אֲשֵׁרִ֖ים
וְחַמָּנִֽים׃
10 כִּ֣י עִ֤יר בְּצוּרָה֙ בָּדָ֔ד

Isaiah 27:6. [In days] to come The Hebrew word *ha-ba·im,* "coming," has been understood by many medieval (Ibn Ezra and Radak) and modern commentators as an abbreviation for *ba-yamim ha-ba·im* (in days to come). This reading aligns it with the formula *ba-yom ha-hu* (in that day) in verse 12 and 28:5. Alternatively, the word *ha-ba·im* has been understood as the "coming" or "ingathering" of Israel to its homeland (Septuagint and Targ.). Such a reading would juxtapose the Israelites' arrival in Egypt to their return from future exile and bondage.

7. Was he beaten as his beater had been? The Hebrew captures the alliterative sound of blows, *ha-k'makkat makkeihu hikkahu.* The phrase is obscure, and the beater here is not identified. Another version interprets the verse in terms of divine justice: "Has He smitten him as He smote those who smote him?" (OJPS). Alternatively, some medieval commentators identify the agent with Assyria (Ibn Ezra) or with Egypt (Radak).

8. Assailing them with fury unchained The Hebrew translated as "assailing them" (*t'rivennah*) means something like "striving with her." This suggests that when God contended with Israel, He sent it into exile as a punishment in full measure (*b'sass'ah*) for its crimes. This may allude to Assyria's devastation of the community in Samaria, Israel's ancient capital (722–721 B.C.E.). The Talmud and Targum understood *b'sass'ah* as referring to punishment measure for measure (from *se·ah,* "measure"). Israel would not be punished unfairly. Divine justice would fit the crime.

bore them off For this meaning of the verb *hagah,* see 2 Sam. 20:13.

9. This is the only price The nation's sin was to be expiated through banishment and the destruction of false worship. This is the required condition (see Ibn Ezra).

no sacred post The sacred post is proscribed most likely because of its association with Canaanite worship of the goddess Asherah.

10–11. What these verses refer to is difficult to determine. If the focus is on Israel, the verse projects the devastation that would accompany

Homesteads deserted, forsaken like a wilderness;
There calves graze, there they lie down
And consume its boughs.
11When its crown is withered, they break;
Women come and make fires with them.
For they are a people without understanding;
That is why
Their Maker will show them no mercy,
Their Creator will deny them grace.

נָוֶה מְשֻׁלָּח וְנֶעֱזָב כַּמִּדְבָּר
שָׁם יִרְעֶה עֵגֶל וְשָׁם יִרְבָּץ
וְכִלָּה סְעִפֶיהָ׃
11 בִּיבֹשׁ קְצִירָהּ תִּשָּׁבַרְנָה
נָשִׁים בָּאוֹת מְאִירוֹת אוֹתָהּ
כִּי לֹא עַם־בִּינוֹת הוּא
עַל־כֵּן
לֹא־יְרַחֲמֶנּוּ עֹשֵׂהוּ
וְיֹצְרוֹ לֹא יְחֻנֶּנּוּ׃ ס

12And in that day, the LORD will beat out [the
peoples like grain] from the channel of the Euphrates to the Wadi of Egypt; and you shall be
picked up one by one, O children of Israel!
13And in that day, a great ram's horn shall be
sounded; and the strayed who are in the land
of Assyria and the expelled who are in the land
of Egypt shall come and worship the LORD on
the holy mount, in Jerusalem.

12 וְהָיָה בַּיּוֹם הַהוּא יַחְבֹּט יְהוָה מִשִּׁבֹּלֶת
הַנָּהָר עַד־נַחַל מִצְרָיִם וְאַתֶּם תְּלֻקְּטוּ
לְאַחַד אֶחָד בְּנֵי יִשְׂרָאֵל׃ ס
13 וְהָיָה ׀ בַּיּוֹם הַהוּא יִתָּקַע בְּשׁוֹפָר גָּדוֹל
וּבָאוּ הָאֹבְדִים בְּאֶרֶץ אַשּׁוּר וְהַנִּדָּחִים
בְּאֶרֶץ מִצְרָיִם וְהִשְׁתַּחֲווּ לַיהוָה בְּהַר
הַקֹּדֶשׁ בִּירוּשָׁלִָם׃

28 Ah, the proud crowns of the drunkards of Ephraim,
Whose glorious beauty is but wilted flowers
On the heads of men bloated with rich food,
Who are overcome by wine!

2Lo, my Lord has something strong and mighty,
Like a storm of hail,
A shower of pestilence.

כח הוֹי עֲטֶרֶת גֵּאוּת שִׁכֹּרֵי אֶפְרַיִם
וְצִיץ נֹבֵל צְבִי תִפְאַרְתּוֹ
אֲשֶׁר עַל־רֹאשׁ גֵּיא־שְׁמָנִים
הֲלוּמֵי יָיִן׃

2 הִנֵּה חָזָק וְאַמִּץ לַאדֹנָי
כְּזֶרֶם בָּרָד
שַׂעַר קָטֶב

divine judgment (Ibn Ezra). If the focus is on Israel's enemy, the verse projects that foreign nation's doom after Israel abandons idolatry (Rashi). The decision as to which nation has "no understanding" would vary accordingly.

13. the strayed . . . and the expelled These terms, translations of *ov'dim* and *niddaḥim,* respectively, reflect a sense of loss and abandonment (see also Jer. 27:10 and Ezek. 34:11–16). The promise gives comfort to the scattered exiles that their restoration is near.

Isaiah 28. The prophet condemns Ephraim (the northern kingdom) for its besotted ways. The focus is on the nation at large; the reference to "these are also" (v. 7) extends the condemnation to priests and prophets. Some commentators have taken this reference to mark the inclusion of Judeans in the rebuke (Ibn Ezra). The projection of doom suggests that this unit precedes the destruction of Samaria in 722–721 B.C.E.

1. Ah Hebrew: *hoy.* Isaiah's cry of woe punctuates his oracles of doom in chapters 28–33.

Something like a storm of massive, torrential
    rain
Shall be hurled with force to the ground.
[3]Trampled underfoot shall be
The proud crowns of the drunkards of
    Ephraim,
[4]The wilted flowers—
On the heads of men bloated with rich
    food—
That are his glorious beauty.
They shall be like an early fig
Before the fruit harvest;
Whoever sees it devours it
While it is still in his hand.

[5]In that day, the LORD of Hosts shall become
a crown of beauty and a diadem of glory for the
remnant of His people, [6]and a spirit of judgment
for him who sits in judgment and of valor for
those who repel attacks at the gate.

[7]But these are also muddled by wine
And dazed by liquor:
Priest and prophet
Are muddled by liquor;
They are confused by wine,
They are dazed by liquor;
They are muddled in their visions,
They stumble in judgment.
[8]Yea, all tables are covered
With vomit and filth,
So that no space is left.

[9]"To whom would he give instruction?
To whom expound a message?
To those newly weaned from milk,
Just taken away from the breast?
[10]That same mutter upon mutter,

כְּזֶ֥רֶם מַ֖יִם כַּבִּירִ֣ים שֹׁטְפִ֑ים
הִנִּ֥יחַ לָאָ֖רֶץ בְּיָֽד:
3 בְּרַגְלַ֖יִם תֵּרָמַ֑סְנָה
עֲטֶ֥רֶת גֵּא֖וּת שִׁכּוֹרֵ֥י אֶפְרָֽיִם:
4 וְֽהָ֘יְתָ֤ה צִיצַ֨ת נֹבֵ֜ל
צְבִ֣י תִפְאַרְתּ֗וֹ
אֲשֶׁ֛ר עַל־רֹ֥אשׁ גֵּ֖יא שְׁמָנִ֑ים
כְּבִכּוּרָהּ֙ בְּטֶ֣רֶם קַ֔יִץ
אֲשֶׁ֨ר יִרְאֶ֤ה
הָרֹאֶ֣ה אוֹתָ֔הּ
בְּעוֹדָ֛הּ בְּכַפּ֖וֹ יִבְלָעֶֽנָּה: ס

5 בַּיּ֣וֹם הַה֗וּא יִֽהְיֶה֙ יְהוָ֣ה צְבָא֔וֹת לַעֲטֶ֖רֶת
צְבִ֑י וְלִצְפִירַ֖ת תִּפְאָרָ֑ה לִשְׁאָ֖ר עַמּֽוֹ:
6 וּלְר֙וּחַ֙ מִשְׁפָּ֔ט לַיּוֹשֵׁ֖ב עַל־הַמִּשְׁפָּ֑ט
וְלִ֨גְבוּרָ֔ה מְשִׁיבֵ֥י מִלְחָמָ֖ה שָֽׁעְרָה: ס

7 וְגַם־אֵ֙לֶּה֙ בַּיַּ֣יִן שָׁג֔וּ
וּבַשֵּׁכָ֖ר תָּע֑וּ
כֹּהֵ֣ן וְנָבִ֗יא
שָׁג֤וּ בַשֵּׁכָר֙
נִבְלְע֣וּ מִן־הַיַּ֔יִן
תָּעוּ֙ מִן־הַשֵּׁכָ֔ר
שָׁג֖וּ בָּרֹאֶ֑ה
פָּק֖וּ פְּלִילִיָּֽה:
8 כִּ֚י כָּל־שֻׁלְחָנ֔וֹת
מָלְא֖וּ קִ֣יא צֹאָ֑ה
בְּלִ֖י מָקֽוֹם: ס

9 אֶת־מִי֙ יוֹרֶ֣ה דֵעָ֔ה
וְאֶת־מִ֖י יָבִ֣ין שְׁמוּעָ֑ה
גְּמוּלֵי֙ מֵֽחָלָ֔ב
עַתִּיקֵ֖י מִשָּׁדָֽיִם:
10 כִּ֣י צַ֤ו לָצָו֙ צַ֣ו לָצָ֔ו

***10, 13. mutter upon mutter, / Murmur upon
murmur*** The prophet despairs of making sense
to the nation. He speaks to the people in a kind
of prattle, ironically alluding to divine law and

Murmur upon murmur,
Now here, now there!"

קַו לָקָו קַו לָקָו
זְעֵיר שָׁם זְעֵיר שָׁם׃

11Truly, as one who speaks to that people in
a stammering jargon and an alien tongue 12is
he who declares to them, "This is the resting
place, let the weary rest; this is the place of repose." They refuse to listen. 13To them the word
of the LORD is:

"Mutter upon mutter,
Murmur upon murmur,
Now here, now there."
And so they will march,
But they shall fall backward,
And be injured and snared and captured.

11 כִּי בְּלַעֲגֵי שָׂפָה וּבְלָשׁוֹן אַחֶרֶת יְדַבֵּר
אֶל־הָעָם הַזֶּה׃ 12 אֲשֶׁר | אָמַר אֲלֵיהֶם
זֹאת הַמְּנוּחָה הָנִיחוּ לֶעָיֵף וְזֹאת
הַמַּרְגֵּעָה וְלֹא אָבוּא* שְׁמוֹעַ׃ 13 וְהָיָה
לָהֶם דְּבַר־יְהוָה

צַו לָצָו צַו לָצָו
קַו לָקָו קַו לָקָו
זְעֵיר שָׁם זְעֵיר שָׁם
לְמַעַן יֵלְכוּ
וְכָשְׁלוּ אָחוֹר
וְנִשְׁבָּרוּ וְנוֹקְשׁוּ וְנִלְכָּדוּ׃ פ

29

22Assuredly, thus said the LORD to the
House of Jacob, Who redeemed Abraham:

כט

22 לָכֵן כֹּה־אָמַר יְהוָה אֶל־בֵּית
יַעֲקֹב אֲשֶׁר פָּדָה אֶת־אַבְרָהָם

No more shall Jacob be shamed,
No longer his face grow pale.

לֹא־עַתָּה יֵבוֹשׁ יַעֲקֹב
וְלֹא עַתָּה פָּנָיו יֶחֱוָרוּ׃

23For when he—that is, his children—behold
what My hands have wrought in his midst, they
will hallow My name.

23 כִּי בִרְאֹתוֹ יְלָדָיו מַעֲשֵׂה יָדַי בְּקִרְבּוֹ
יַקְדִּישׁוּ שְׁמִי

Men will hallow the Holy One of Jacob
And stand in awe of the God of Israel.

וְהִקְדִּישׁוּ אֶת־קְדוֹשׁ יַעֲקֹב
וְאֶת־אֱלֹהֵי יִשְׂרָאֵל יַעֲרִיצוּ׃

v. 12. יתיר א׳

punishment (cf. v. 11), apparently mocking the way God's words sound to the people. Thus the words "mutter and murmur" (*tzav l'tzav kav l'kav*) are playing with the notions of commandment (*tzav*) and measure (*kav*), both of which were ignored by the people. Alternatively, the prophet mockingly suggests that what the people hear as mere blather (*tzav/kav*) is in truth God's own command (*tzav*) and measure of judgment (*kav*) against them.

Isaiah 29:22–23. The prophecy concludes on a positive note. God, who redeemed Abraham, will redeem his descendants, and all will hallow the Lord for His mighty acts.

הפטרת שמות

HAFTARAH FOR SH'MOT

JEREMIAH 1:1–2:3 (S'fardim)

In this *haftarah,* Jeremiah is commissioned as a messenger to deliver God's word. Jeremiah's inauguration is reinforced by two visionary signs (1:11–12,13–15), which introduce the themes of divine providence and approaching doom.

The call to prophecy (1:4–10) is presented as an autobiographical fragment. God's word strikes terror in Jeremiah's heart, but his fear is countered by a promise of divine protection and verbal inspiration, a promise repeated at the end of the chapter in the image of an inviolable city (vv. 18–19). The prophet's cry of woe (*ahah*) and the divine exhortation not to fear capture the mood of anxiety.

A highly stylized literary pattern captures this private moment in Jeremiah's life, presenting him as a true prophet in the standard mode. The same pattern is also preserved in the prophetic call of Moses (see Exod. 3:10–12, 4:15; cf. Isa. 6:5–7; Ezek. 2:3–3:11). Like Moses before him, Jeremiah is sent forth to prophesy against his personal inclination but with divine assurances. The *haftarah* closes as usual with a hopeful assertion (2:1–3).

RELATION OF THE *HAFTARAH* TO THE *PARASHAH*

The *parashah* and the *haftarah* are linked through the prophetic commissions of Moses and Jeremiah, dramatizing the continuity of divine guidance throughout the generations and repeating a pattern of divine address, human resistance, and divine assurance. Moses and Jeremiah function as intermediaries between the divine spirit and the people. Through them it is taught that Israel's life is determined not by earthly political powers but by divine care and judgment. They thus challenge the peoples' perceptions of the everyday (the Israelites' weariness of spirit in the time of Moses and Israel's political vision in Jeremiah's day). The prophets, who sense the enormity of their task and their personal inadequacy, are strengthened by divine reassurances as they set out to confront the resistance of others.

1 The words of Jeremiah son of Hilkiah, one of the priests at Anathoth in the territory of Benjamin. ²The word of the LORD came to him in the days of King Josiah son of Amon of Judah, in the thirteenth year of his reign, ³and through-

אֶ דִּבְרֵי יִרְמְיָהוּ בֶּן־חִלְקִיָּהוּ מִן־הַכֹּהֲנִים֙ אֲשֶׁ֣ר בַּעֲנָת֔וֹת בְּאֶ֖רֶץ בִּנְיָמִֽן: ² אֲשֶׁ֨ר הָיָ֤ה דְבַר־יְהוָה֙ אֵלָ֔יו בִּימֵ֖י יֹאשִׁיָּ֣הוּ בֶן־אָמ֛וֹן מֶ֥לֶךְ יְהוּדָ֖ה בִּשְׁלֹשׁ־עֶשְׂרֵ֥ה שָׁנָ֖ה

Jeremiah 1:1. Jeremiah The Hebrew vocalization (*yirmiyahu*) is derived from either the root רמה or the root רום. Thus the name "Jeremiah" means "The LORD loosens," or "the LORD is exalted." The name is attested in Hebrew seals from the 8th century and in letters (written on potsherds) found in the city of Lachish shortly before the destruction of Jerusalem.

Anathoth A levitical city in the territory of Benjamin (see Josh. 21:18). The oracles of Jeremiah, who was a resident of Anathoth (Jer. 29:27), incurred the wrath of the local people (11:21). His family also had land holdings there (32:7).

2. in the thirteenth year of his reign The reign of King Josiah. This corresponds to 627 B.C.E., a volatile time when King Nebuchadrezzar of Babylon rebelled against his Assyrian overlord. That was the first stage in Babylon's gradual rise to political dominance in the region.

out the days of King Jehoiakim son of Josiah of Judah, and until the end of the eleventh year of King Zedekiah son of Josiah of Judah, when Jerusalem went into exile in the fifth month.

לְמַלְכוֹ׃ 3 וַיְהִ֗י בִּימֵ֨י יְהוֹיָקִ֤ים בֶּן־יֹאשִׁיָּ֙הוּ֙
מֶ֣לֶךְ יְהוּדָ֔ה עַד־תֹּם֙ עַשְׁתֵּ֣י עֶשְׂרֵ֣ה שָׁנָ֔ה
לְצִדְקִיָּ֥הוּ בֶן־יֹאשִׁיָּ֖הוּ מֶ֣לֶךְ יְהוּדָ֑ה עַד־
גְּל֥וֹת יְרוּשָׁלִַ֖ם בַּחֹ֥דֶשׁ הַחֲמִישִֽׁי׃ ס

4The word of the LORD came to me:

4 וַיְהִ֥י דְבַר־יְהוָ֖ה אֵלַ֥י לֵאמֹֽר׃

5Before I created you in the womb, I selected you;
Before you were born, I consecrated you;
I appointed you a prophet concerning the nations.

5 בְּטֶ֨רֶם אצורך אֶצָּרְךָ֤ בַבֶּ֙טֶן֙ יְדַעְתִּ֔יךָ
וּבְטֶ֛רֶם תֵּצֵ֥א מֵרֶ֖חֶם הִקְדַּשְׁתִּ֑יךָ
נָבִ֥יא לַגּוֹיִ֖ם נְתַתִּֽיךָ׃

6I replied:
Ah, Lord GOD!
I don't know how to speak,
For I am still a boy.
7And the LORD said to me:
Do not say, "I am still a boy,"
But go wherever I send you
And speak whatever I command you.
8Have no fear of them,
For I am with you to deliver you
—declares the LORD.

6 וָאֹמַ֗ר
אֲהָהּ֙ אֲדֹנָ֣י יְהוִ֔ה
הִנֵּ֥ה לֹא־יָדַ֖עְתִּי דַּבֵּ֑ר
כִּי־נַ֖עַר אָנֹֽכִי׃ פ
7 וַיֹּ֤אמֶר יְהוָה֙ אֵלַ֔י
אַל־תֹּאמַ֖ר נַ֣עַר אָנֹ֑כִי
כִּ֠י עַל־כָּל־אֲשֶׁ֤ר אֶֽשְׁלָחֲךָ֙ תֵּלֵ֔ךְ
וְאֵ֛ת כָּל־אֲשֶׁ֥ר אֲצַוְּךָ֖ תְּדַבֵּֽר׃
8 אַל־תִּירָ֖א מִפְּנֵיהֶ֑ם
כִּֽי־אִתְּךָ֥ אֲנִ֛י לְהַצִּלֶ֖ךָ
נְאֻם־יְהוָֽה׃

9The LORD put out His hand and touched my mouth, and the LORD said to me: Herewith I put My words into your mouth.
10See, I appoint you this day
Over nations and kingdoms:
To uproot and to pull down,

9 וַיִּשְׁלַ֤ח יְהוָה֙ אֶת־יָד֔וֹ וַיַּגַּ֖ע עַל־פִּ֑י וַיֹּ֤אמֶר
יְהוָה֙ אֵלַ֔י הִנֵּ֛ה נָתַ֥תִּי דְבָרַ֖י בְּפִֽיךָ׃
10 רְאֵ֞ה הִפְקַדְתִּ֣יךָ ׀ הַיּ֣וֹם הַזֶּ֗ה
עַל־הַגּוֹיִם֙ וְעַל־הַמַּמְלָכ֔וֹת
לִנְת֥וֹשׁ וְלִנְת֖וֹץ

3. until the end of the eleventh year . . . in the fifth month Jerusalem actually fell on the ninth day of the fourth month of Zedekiah's 11th year (Jer. 39:2, 52:5–6).

5. Before I created you This translation follows the version of the Hebrew text as read (*k'rei*). This yields the word *"etzorkha,"* which is derived from the root יצר (create). The motif of creation in the womb occurs in ancient Near Eastern royal annals (Assyrian and Egyptian), where it indicates the divine appointment of a king. The version of the Hebrew text as written (*k'tiv*) yields the word *"atzurkha,"* derived from צור and translated as "I formed you" (Rashi, Kara).

a prophet concerning the nations This phrase has long puzzled commentators, because Jeremiah often speaks to the Israelites—not only to the nations. Rashi and Radak refer to verse 7 to maintain that both Israel and the gentiles were included in Jeremiah's mission. However, one could maintain that only foreign nations are referred to in this verse, because the commission re-

To destroy and to overthrow,
To build and to plant.

11 The word of the LORD came to me: What
do you see, Jeremiah? I replied: I see a branch
of an almond tree.
12 The LORD said to me:
You have seen right,
For I am watchful to bring My word to pass.

13 And the word of the LORD came to me a sec-
ond time: What do you see? I replied:
I see a steaming pot,
Tipped away from the north.
14 And the LORD said to me:
From the north shall disaster break loose
Upon all the inhabitants of the land!
15 For I am summoning all the peoples
Of the kingdoms of the north
—declares the LORD.
They shall come, and shall each set up a throne
Before the gates of Jerusalem,
Against its walls roundabout,
And against all the towns of Judah.
16 And I will argue My case against them
For all their wickedness:
They have forsaken Me
And sacrificed to other gods
And worshiped the works of their hands.

17 So you, gird up your loins,
Arise and speak to them
All that I command you.
Do not break down before them,
Lest I break you before them.

וּלְהַאֲבִיד וְלַהֲרוֹס
לִבְנוֹת וְלִנְטוֹעַ׃ פ

11 וַיְהִי דְבַר־יְהוָה אֵלַי לֵאמֹר מָה־אַתָּה
רֹאֶה יִרְמְיָהוּ וָאֹמַר מַקֵּל שָׁקֵד אֲנִי רֹאֶה׃
12 וַיֹּאמֶר יְהוָה אֵלַי
הֵיטַבְתָּ לִרְאוֹת
כִּי־שֹׁקֵד אֲנִי עַל־דְּבָרִי לַעֲשֹׂתוֹ׃ פ

13 וַיְהִי דְבַר־יְהוָה ׀ אֵלַי שֵׁנִית לֵאמֹר מָה
אַתָּה רֹאֶה וָאֹמַר
סִיר נָפוּחַ אֲנִי רֹאֶה
וּפָנָיו מִפְּנֵי צָפוֹנָה׃
14 וַיֹּאמֶר יְהוָה אֵלָי
מִצָּפוֹן תִּפָּתַח הָרָעָה
עַל כָּל־יֹשְׁבֵי הָאָרֶץ׃
15 כִּי ׀ הִנְנִי קֹרֵא לְכָל־מִשְׁפְּחוֹת
מַמְלְכוֹת צָפוֹנָה
נְאֻם־יְהוָה
וּבָאוּ וְנָתְנוּ אִישׁ כִּסְאוֹ
פֶּתַח ׀ שַׁעֲרֵי יְרוּשָׁלַםִ
וְעַל כָּל־חוֹמֹתֶיהָ סָבִיב
וְעַל כָּל־עָרֵי יְהוּדָה׃
16 וְדִבַּרְתִּי מִשְׁפָּטַי אוֹתָם
עַל כָּל־רָעָתָם
אֲשֶׁר עֲזָבוּנִי
וַיְקַטְּרוּ לֵאלֹהִים אֲחֵרִים
וַיִּשְׁתַּחֲווּ לְמַעֲשֵׂי יְדֵיהֶם׃

17 וְאַתָּה תֶּאְזֹר מָתְנֶיךָ
וְקַמְתָּ וְדִבַּרְתָּ אֲלֵיהֶם
אֵת כָּל־אֲשֶׁר אָנֹכִי אֲצַוֶּךָּ
אַל־תֵּחַת מִפְּנֵיהֶם
פֶּן־אֲחִתְּךָ לִפְנֵיהֶם׃

fers to the nations who will exact judgment on Israel (vv. 5,10), a theme that dominates the vision of the pot (vv. 13–15).

13–14. steaming pot The translation states that the "steaming" (*nafu·ah*) pot is "tipped away from the north" (v. 13), thereby symbolizing the

18 וַאֲנִ֞י הִנֵּ֧ה נְתַתִּ֣יךָ הַיּ֗וֹם
לְעִ֣יר מִבְצָ֞ר
וּלְעַמּ֥וּד בַּרְזֶ֛ל וּלְחֹמ֥וֹת נְחֹ֖שֶׁת
עַל־כָּל־הָאָ֑רֶץ
לְמַלְכֵ֤י יְהוּדָה֙ לְשָׂרֶ֔יהָ
לְכֹהֲנֶ֖יהָ וּלְעַ֥ם הָאָֽרֶץ׃
19 וְנִלְחֲמ֥וּ אֵלֶ֖יךָ
וְלֹא־י֣וּכְלוּ לָ֑ךְ
כִּֽי־אִתְּךָ֥ אֲנִ֛י נְאֻם־יְהוָ֖ה לְהַצִּילֶֽךָ׃ פ

ב 2 וַיְהִ֥י דְבַר־יְהוָ֖ה אֵלַ֥י לֵאמֹֽר׃ הָלֹ֡ךְ
וְקָרָ֩אתָ֩ בְאָזְנֵ֨י יְרוּשָׁלַ֜͏ִם לֵאמֹ֗ר כֹּ֚ה אָמַ֣ר
יְהוָ֔ה
זָכַ֤רְתִּי לָךְ֙
חֶ֣סֶד נְעוּרַ֔יִךְ
אַהֲבַ֖ת כְּלוּלֹתָ֑יִךְ
לֶכְתֵּ֤ךְ אַחֲרַי֙ בַּמִּדְבָּ֔ר
בְּאֶ֖רֶץ לֹ֥א זְרוּעָֽה׃
3 קֹ֤דֶשׁ יִשְׂרָאֵל֙ לַֽיהוָ֔ה
רֵאשִׁ֖ית תְּבוּאָתֹ֑ה
כָּל־אֹכְלָ֣יו יֶאְשָׁ֔מוּ
רָעָ֛ה תָּבֹ֥א אֲלֵיהֶ֖ם
נְאֻם־יְהוָֽה׃ פ

18 I make you this day
A fortified city,
And an iron pillar,
And bronze walls
Against the whole land—
Against Judah's kings and officers,
And against its priests and citizens.
19 They will attack you,
But they shall not overcome you;
For I am with you—declares the LORD—to
save you.

2 The word of the LORD came to me, saying, **2** Go proclaim to Jerusalem: Thus said the LORD:
I accounted to your favor
The devotion of your youth,
Your love as a bride—
How you followed Me in the wilderness,
In a land not sown.
3 Israel was holy to the LORD,
The first fruits of His harvest.
All who ate of it were held guilty;
Disaster befell them
—declares the LORD.

outbreak (*tippatah*) of the destruction from that region (v. 14). But the Hebrew formulation is unclear, and commentators have suggested, with good reason, that the pot was actually facing north to receive the evil (Radak, Kara, Luzzatto).

Jeremiah 2:2. The positive portrayal of Israel's youthful past and the marital symbolism of the Covenant contradict the repeated episodes of Israel's faithlessness found in the Torah. The various depictions of Israel's relationship with God reflect different streams of tradition.

3. Jeremiah's depiction of the nation as a holy people articulates the theology of Deuteronomy (see Deut. 7:6), which revises the conditional nature of the people's holy status found in Exod. 19:4–6. In that context of Exodus, Israel may become holy if it observes God's teachings. The revision in Deuteronomy deems Israel holy per se and, therefore, obligated to fulfill its covenantal obligations.

[2]God spoke to Moses and said to him, "I am
the LORD. [3]I appeared to Abraham, Isaac, and
Jacob as El Shaddai, but I did not make Myself

2 וַיְדַבֵּר אֱלֹהִים אֶל־מֹשֶׁה וַיֹּאמֶר אֵלָיו
אֲנִי יְהוָה׃ 3 וָאֵרָא אֶל־אַבְרָהָם אֶל־יִצְחָק
וְאֶל־יַעֲקֹב בְּאֵל שַׁדָּי וּשְׁמִי יְהוָה לֹא

DIVINE REAFFIRMATION (6:2–7:13)

Moses and the Israelites are demoralized because their situation has deteriorated sharply. God reappears to Moses and reveals the essential nature of the divine name and its relation to the promises made to the patriarchs.

3. I did not make Myself known An enigmatic phrase. It cannot mean that a previously unknown divine name—*YHVH*—is about to be revealed for the first time. A divine promise is of little credibility if it is made by an unknown deity.

In this *parashah,* Pharaoh continues his refusal to grant the Israelites their freedom. God threatens to continue to harden Pharaoh's heart, so that only after several terrible plagues will he relent. Moses and Aaron do not succeed in impressing Pharaoh and his court magicians with their wonders. The first 7 of the Ten Plagues are called down on the Egyptians. The confrontation between Moses and Aaron on the one hand and Pharaoh on the other, between God's emissaries and those who defy God, becomes sharper. Even Pharaoh's new order that the slaves gather their own straw for making bricks fits this process of escalation. The situation for both the Egyptians and the Israelites must become unbearable to overcome the tendency of both sides to maintain the status quo.

Why is it necessary to prolong the process of liberation? It is not enough that the Israelites be freed. That might mistakenly be seen as an act of magnanimity on Pharaoh's part. They must be freed in such a way that they, the Egyptians, and all the nations of the world will understand that it was God's doing, not Pharaoh's goodwill. (This is important, not so much to burnish God's reputation but to establish the principle that it is unacceptable for one human being to reduce another human being to slavery, that freedom is the will of God and not the choice of a despot.)

CHAPTER 6

2. I am the LORD According to the Midrash, God has two attributes: justice (represented by the divine name *Elohim,* translated "God") and mercy (represented by the divine name *YHVH,* translated "the LORD"). This verse would seem to represent a conflict within God, in which the attribute of justice would chastise Moses for seeming to lose faith (5:22: "why did You bring harm upon this people?" Why have You waited while so many have suffered and died? When the Redemption occurs, it will be too late for them!). *Elohim,* the divine attribute of justice, wants to strike at Moses for speaking thus, but the attribute of mercy speaks out ("I am *YHVH*") and saves him, realizing that he was speaking in that tone on behalf of people who have suffered so much for so long (Exod. R. 6:1). This is the last time that the divine name *Elohim*/justice appears in any speech of God to Moses. Henceforth it will always be *YHVH*/mercy.

A modern midrashic interpretation: Why did God speak to Moses exclusively in the name of the attribute of mercy from this moment on? Hearing Moses' concern for those who would not live to see the liberation from slavery, God declared: "I cannot judge this man! He is as righteous a judge as I! Therefore I will speak to him only with the voice of Mercy, for the burden of caring for the Israelites is so great, and only Moses is merciful enough to do it." Another modern midrashic interpretation: "To the patriarchs, I revealed Myself as a nurturing, mothering God. [Some suggest that *Shaddai* may be related to the word *shadayim,* "breasts."] My relationship to them was that of a parent to a child, encouraging and forgiving, making few demands. But with this man Moses, I will speak face to face, as one adult to another. I will reveal to him My personal, intimate name, *YHVH.* Moreover, because Moses defends the cause of the Israelites so passionately, I will show this side of My nature to them as well: 'And you shall know that I, *YHVH,* am your God who freed you from the labors of the Egyptians' (6:7)." "God of your fathers" is the God of Genesis; *YHVH* is the God of Exodus (B. Jacob).

known to them by My name יהוה. 4I also established My covenant with them, to give them the
land of Canaan, the land in which they lived as
sojourners. 5I have now heard the moaning of
the Israelites because the Egyptians are holding
them in bondage, and I have remembered My
covenant. 6Say, therefore, to the Israelite people: I am the LORD. I will free you from the labors
of the Egyptians and deliver you from their

נוֹדַ֖עְתִּי לָהֶֽם׃ 4 וְגַ֨ם הֲקִמֹ֤תִי אֶת־בְּרִיתִי֙
אִתָּ֔ם לָתֵ֥ת לָהֶ֖ם אֶת־אֶ֣רֶץ כְּנָ֑עַן אֵ֛ת אֶ֥רֶץ
מְגֻרֵיהֶ֖ם אֲשֶׁר־גָּ֥רוּ בָֽהּ׃ 5 וְגַ֣ם ׀ אֲנִ֣י
שָׁמַ֗עְתִּי אֶֽת־נַאֲקַת֙ בְּנֵ֣י יִשְׂרָאֵ֔ל אֲשֶׁ֥ר
מִצְרַ֖יִם מַעֲבִדִ֣ים אֹתָ֑ם וָאֶזְכֹּ֖ר אֶת־בְּרִיתִֽי׃
6 לָכֵ֞ן אֱמֹ֥ר לִבְנֵֽי־יִשְׂרָאֵל֮ אֲנִ֣י יְהוָה֒
וְהוֹצֵאתִ֣י אֶתְכֶ֗ם מִתַּ֙חַת֙ סִבְלֹ֣ת מִצְרַ֔יִם

Nor would an unknown divine name serve to counteract the widespread demoralization of the Israelites. Furthermore, the phrase "I am *YHVH*" in verse 2 appears often in the Bible. It is similar to a form widespread in ancient Semitic royal inscriptions as a self-identification presentation formula, such as "I am Shalmaneser," "I am Mesha," or "I am Esarhaddon." It is not likely, therefore, that it is being used here to introduce a new name. On the contrary, it is precisely because the bearer of the name is well known and its mention evokes awe, reverence, honor, and fear, that its use as the source of a law or an edict encourages obedience.

What, then, does the phrase "I did not make Myself known" mean? In the ancient Near Eastern world names in general, and the name of a god in particular, possessed a dynamic quality and served to express character, attributes, and power. The names of gods were identified with their nature, status, and function. Thus to say, "I did not make Myself known to them by My name *YHVH*," is to state that the patriarchs did not experience the specific power that is associated with the name *YHVH*. That power—to be displayed in the coming process of redemption—belongs to the future. The repetition here of the promises made by El Shaddai to the patriarchs and now uttered in the name of *YHVH* means that their fulfillment is imminent.

El Shaddai The reference is to Gen. 17:1–8, 35:11–12. With the advent of Moses, the name El Shaddai becomes obsolete, preserved only in poetic texts.

4. to give them The patriarchs received ownership of the land; their descendants would receive possession of it.

5. My covenant With the patriarchs.

6. free you Literally, "bring you out."

6–8. I will free you . . . and deliver you. . . . I will redeem you. . . . I will take you. . . . I will bring you into the land The stages of Redemption: "I will free you" from physical enslavement in Egypt; I will "deliver you" from the psychological mind-set of being a slave, which might persist even after you have been physically liberated; "I will redeem you" so that you will think of yourselves as free people; and "I will take you" into a special relationship with Me, for that is the ultimate goal of your liberation. Finally, "I will bring you into the land which I swore to give Abraham." Only when the Israelites have their own land can they become the special people they are summoned to be. Only there will they have the duty and the opportunity to translate the ideals of the Torah into the realities of daily life and fashion the model society from which all nations will be able to learn. The promise of a land of their own is the Torah's ultimate promise; the threat of being cast out of that land is its ultimate punishment. It is not enough to remove the burden of slavery; they must also have the proper circumstances that will permit them to flourish as God's people.

labors of the Egyptians A Hasidic interpretation understands the Hebrew for "burdens" (*sivlot*) as "tolerance." What was the worst part of slavery? The Israelites became accustomed to it. They lost sight of the fact that one does not have to live in such conditions.

HALAKHAH L'MA·ASEH

6:6–8. I will free you . . . and deliver you. . . . I will redeem you. . . . I will take you to be My people These four phrases of redemption are one source for the four cups of wine that we use at the *Pesaḥ Seider* (JT Pes. 10:1). A fifth phrase in these verses—"I will bring you into the land"—is the basis for having on the *Seider* table a fifth cup reserved for Elijah, the prophet. See Mal. 3:23 (part of the *haftarah* for *Shabbat ha-Gadol* preceding *Pesaḥ*.

bondage. I will redeem you with an outstretched arm and through extraordinary chastisements. [7]And I will take you to be My people, and I will be your God. And you shall know that I, the LORD, am your God who freed you from the labors of the Egyptians. [8]I will bring you into the land which I swore to give to Abraham, Isaac, and Jacob, and I will give it to you for a possession, I the LORD." [9]But when Moses told this to the Israelites, they would not listen to Moses, their spirits crushed by cruel bondage.

[10]The LORD spoke to Moses, saying, [11]"Go and tell Pharaoh king of Egypt to let the Israelites depart from his land." [12]But Moses appealed to the LORD, saying, "The Israelites would not listen to me; how then should Phar-

וְהִצַּלְתִּי אֶתְכֶם מֵעֲבֹדָתָם וְגָאַלְתִּי אֶתְכֶם
בִּזְרוֹעַ נְטוּיָה וּבִשְׁפָטִים גְּדֹלִים: 7 וְלָקַחְתִּי
אֶתְכֶם לִי לְעָם וְהָיִיתִי לָכֶם לֵאלֹהִים
וִידַעְתֶּם כִּי אֲנִי יְהוָה אֱלֹהֵיכֶם הַמּוֹצִיא
אֶתְכֶם מִתַּחַת סִבְלוֹת מִצְרָיִם: 8 וְהֵבֵאתִי
אֶתְכֶם אֶל־הָאָרֶץ אֲשֶׁר נָשָׂאתִי אֶת־יָדִי
לָתֵת אֹתָהּ לְאַבְרָהָם לְיִצְחָק וּלְיַעֲקֹב
וְנָתַתִּי אֹתָהּ לָכֶם מוֹרָשָׁה אֲנִי יְהוָה:
9 וַיְדַבֵּר מֹשֶׁה כֵּן אֶל־בְּנֵי יִשְׂרָאֵל וְלֹא
שָׁמְעוּ אֶל־מֹשֶׁה מִקֹּצֶר רוּחַ וּמֵעֲבֹדָה
קָשָׁה: פ
10 וַיְדַבֵּר יְהוָה אֶל־מֹשֶׁה לֵּאמֹר: 11 בֹּא
דַבֵּר אֶל־פַּרְעֹה מֶלֶךְ מִצְרָיִם וִישַׁלַּח אֶת־
בְּנֵי־יִשְׂרָאֵל מֵאַרְצוֹ: 12 וַיְדַבֵּר מֹשֶׁה לִפְנֵי
יְהוָה לֵאמֹר הֵן בְּנֵי־יִשְׂרָאֵל לֹא־שָׁמְעוּ

redeem you The Hebrew stem here is גאל. In time, the abstract noun *g'ulah* (redemption) acquired messianic associations referring to God's ultimate redemption of Israel from exile.

outstretched arm A symbol of strength and power, the arm generally is understood as a metaphor in descriptions of God's mighty deeds related to the Exodus.

7. This declaration alludes to the covenant that is to be established at Sinai. The phraseology—"to take" and "to be [someone's]"—serves here as a covenantal adoption metaphor.

you shall know That is, "acknowledge." See Comment to 1:8.

8. I swore Literally, "I raised my hand." The phrase derives from the symbolic act that accompanies oath taking. The Bible repeatedly asserts that the land of Israel was pledged on oath by God to the patriarchs and their descendants.

MOSES TRANSMITS THE DIVINE MESSAGE (v. 9)

9. they would not listen Moses' message did not succeed in strengthening their morale, in contrast to the experience recorded in 4:31.

their spirits crushed by cruel bondage Literally, "from shortness of spirit." The word for "spirit" (*ru·aḥ*) here indicates the spiritual and psychic energy that motivates action. Its absence or diminishment indicates loss of will.

A first step toward liberation will be freeing themselves from their passivity and their tolerance of the intolerable (Menaḥem Mendel of Kotzk).

9. they would not listen to Moses, their spirits crushed by cruel bondage Literally, "because of impatience and hard work." Was it because slavery was so hard and exhausting and left them weary, unable even to envision the possibility of change? The Hebrew translated as "their spirits crushed" (*kotzer ru·aḥ*) can literally mean "their spirits were stunted." Or was it because they sensed that freedom would require hard work—that it would not happen quickly or easily? Or perhaps they would not listen to Moses, because he came from Midian and had not shared their labors and suffering. The gap between Moses and his people was great. They were slaves, whereas he had grown up in the palace and had lived in the freedom of Midian. It may be that only one whose spirit had not been crushed by slavery could be capable of leading the people to freedom. The generation that grew up in slavery ultimately would be unable to take advantage of their freedom, and it would perish in the wilderness. Only their children would inherit the Promised Land.

aoh heed me, a man of impeded speech!" 13So the LORD spoke to both Moses and Aaron in regard to the Israelites and Pharaoh king of Egypt, instructing them to deliver the Israelites from the land of Egypt.

14The following are the heads of their respective clans.

The sons of Reuben, Israel's first-born: Enoch and Pallu, Hezron and Carmi; those are the families of Reuben. 15The sons of Simeon: Jemuel, Jamin, Ohad, Jachin, Zohar, and Saul the son of a Canaanite woman; those are the families of Simeon. 16These are the names of Levi's sons by their lineage: Gershon, Kohath, and Merari; and the span of Levi's life was 137 years.

אֵלַי וְאֵיךְ יִשְׁמָעֵנִי פַרְעֹה וַאֲנִי עֲרַל
שְׂפָתָיִם׃ פ 13 וַיְדַבֵּר יְהוָה אֶל־מֹשֶׁה
וְאֶל־אַהֲרֹן וַיְצַוֵּם אֶל־בְּנֵי יִשְׂרָאֵל וְאֶל־
פַּרְעֹה מֶלֶךְ מִצְרָיִם לְהוֹצִיא אֶת־בְּנֵי־
יִשְׂרָאֵל מֵאֶרֶץ מִצְרָיִם׃ ס

שני 14 אֵלֶּה רָאשֵׁי בֵית־אֲבֹתָם
בְּנֵי רְאוּבֵן בְּכֹר יִשְׂרָאֵל חֲנוֹךְ וּפַלּוּא
חֶצְרוֹן וְכַרְמִי אֵלֶּה מִשְׁפְּחֹת רְאוּבֵן׃
15 וּבְנֵי שִׁמְעוֹן יְמוּאֵל וְיָמִין וְאֹהַד וְיָכִין
וְצֹחַר וְשָׁאוּל בֶּן־הַכְּנַעֲנִית אֵלֶּה מִשְׁפְּחֹת
שִׁמְעוֹן׃ 16 וְאֵלֶּה שְׁמוֹת בְּנֵי־לֵוִי לְתֹלְדֹתָם
גֵּרְשׁוֹן וּקְהָת וּמְרָרִי וּשְׁנֵי חַיֵּי לֵוִי שֶׁבַע

A RENEWED CALL TO ACTION
(vv. 10–13)

12. impeded speech Literally, "uncircumcised of lips," a synonym for "slow of speech and slow of tongue" (4:10). "Uncircumcised" is also used metaphorically of the heart and the ear. The organ involved is, so to speak, obstructed by a "foreskin" that prevents it from functioning properly.

13. Ignoring Moses' objections, God orders him and his brother to resume their mission to both the Israelites and Pharaoh. Aaron is mentioned here for two reasons. First, he is to act as spokesman and thereby offset Moses' disability; second, he is the focus of the following genealogy. His name thus serves to bridge the transition to the next section.

A GENEALOGY (vv. 14–25)

The insertion of a genealogy at this point is a literary device that separates the first stage in the process of liberation—futile human efforts—from the awesome intervention of God that will now ensue: the Ten Plagues. At the same time, it links the period of the Exodus with that of the patriarchs. (Note that it presents only four generations between Levi and Moses, in keeping with Gen. 15:16.) A genealogy symbolizes vigor and continuity. Its inclusion here injects a reassuring note into the prevailing mood of despair. The genealogy singles out the Levites from among the tribes of Israel and distinguishes the family of Aaron from among the levitical families. This anticipates later developments: the special status granted to the tribe of Levi, the appointment of the Aaronides to serve as priests, and the appointment of Aaron as high priest.

15. a Canaanite woman This exceptional notice most likely reflects the unfavorable view of intermarriage with Canaanites.

16. These three are the heads of levitical clans that later performed necessary menial duties in connection with the wilderness tabernacle. The names of the members of their families and the services assigned to them are listed in detail in Num. 3:17–39.

---

12. The Israelites would not listen to me Leaders derive their power and legitimacy from the willingness of people to listen to them.

14. Why does this genealogical list interrupt the narrative at this point? Perhaps to emphasize that Moses, despite having grown up in the palace, is of Israelite descent. Perhaps to connect the Israelite clans in Egypt (*beit avot*) with God's promise to the *avot,* the patriarchs, referred to in verses 3 and 8. Moses and Aaron may have questioned their own worthiness. This list would remind them that they confront Pharaoh not as two anonymous individuals but as the latest representatives of an illustrious ancestry.

17The sons of Gershon: Libni and Shimei, by their families. 18The sons of Kohath: Amram, Izhar, Hebron, and Uzziel; and the span of Kohath's life was 133 years. 19The sons of Merari: Mahli and Mushi. These are the families of the Levites by their lineage.

20Amram took to wife his father's sister Jochebed, and she bore him Aaron and Moses; and the span of Amram's life was 137 years. 21The sons of Izhar: Korah, Nepheg, and Zichri. 22The sons of Uzziel: Mishael, Elzaphan, and Sithri. 23Aaron took to wife Elisheba, daughter of Amminadab and sister of Nahshon, and she bore him Nadab and Abihu, Eleazar and Ithamar. 24The sons of Korah: Assir, Elkanah, and Abiasaph. Those are the families of the Korahites. 25And Aaron's son Eleazar took to wife one of Putiel's daughters, and she bore him Phinehas. Those are the heads of the fathers' houses of the Levites by their families.

26It is the same Aaron and Moses to whom the LORD said, "Bring forth the Israelites from the land of Egypt, troop by troop." 27It was they

וּשְׁלֹשִׁ֥ים וּמְאַ֖ת שָׁנָֽה׃ 17 בְּנֵ֥י גֵרְשׁ֛וֹן לִבְנִ֥י
וְשִׁמְעִ֖י לְמִשְׁפְּחֹתָֽם׃ 18 וּבְנֵ֣י קְהָ֔ת עַמְרָ֣ם
וְיִצְהָ֔ר וְחֶבְר֖וֹן וְעֻזִּיאֵ֑ל וּשְׁנֵי֙ חַיֵּ֣י קְהָ֔ת
שָׁלֹ֧שׁ וּשְׁלֹשִׁ֛ים וּמְאַ֖ת שָׁנָֽה׃ 19 וּבְנֵ֥י
מְרָרִ֖י מַחְלִ֣י וּמוּשִׁ֑י אֵ֛לֶּה מִשְׁפְּחֹ֥ת הַלֵּוִ֖י
לְתֹלְדֹתָֽם׃
20 וַיִּקַּ֨ח עַמְרָ֜ם אֶת־יוֹכֶ֤בֶד דֹּֽדָתוֹ֙ ל֣וֹ לְאִשָּׁ֔ה
וַתֵּ֣לֶד ל֔וֹ אֶֽת־אַהֲרֹ֖ן וְאֶת־מֹשֶׁ֑ה וּשְׁנֵי֙
חַיֵּ֣י עַמְרָ֔ם שֶׁ֛בַע וּשְׁלֹשִׁ֥ים וּמְאַ֖ת שָׁנָֽה׃
21 וּבְנֵ֖י יִצְהָ֑ר קֹ֥רַח וָנֶ֖פֶג וְזִכְרִֽי׃ 22 וּבְנֵ֖י
עֻזִּיאֵ֑ל מִֽישָׁאֵ֥ל וְאֶלְצָפָ֖ן וְסִתְרִֽי׃ 23 וַיִּקַּ֨ח
אַהֲרֹ֜ן אֶת־אֱלִישֶׁ֧בַע בַּת־עַמִּֽינָדָ֛ב אֲח֥וֹת
נַחְשׁ֖וֹן ל֣וֹ לְאִשָּׁ֑ה וַתֵּ֣לֶד ל֗וֹ אֶת־נָדָב֙
וְאֶת־אֲבִיה֔וּא אֶת־אֶלְעָזָ֖ר וְאֶת־אִיתָמָֽר׃
24 וּבְנֵ֣י קֹ֔רַח אַסִּ֥יר וְאֶלְקָנָ֖ה וַאֲבִיאָסָ֑ף אֵ֖לֶּה
מִשְׁפְּחֹ֥ת הַקָּרְחִֽי׃ 25 וְאֶלְעָזָ֨ר בֶּֽן־אַהֲרֹ֜ן
לָֽקַח־ל֨וֹ מִבְּנ֤וֹת פּֽוּטִיאֵל֙ ל֣וֹ לְאִשָּׁ֔ה וַתֵּ֥לֶד
ל֖וֹ אֶת־פִּֽינְחָ֑ס אֵ֗לֶּה רָאשֵׁ֛י אֲב֥וֹת הַלְוִיִּ֖ם
לְמִשְׁפְּחֹתָֽם׃
26 ה֥וּא אַהֲרֹ֖ן וּמֹשֶׁ֑ה אֲשֶׁ֨ר אָמַ֤ר יְהוָה֙
לָהֶ֔ם הוֹצִ֜יאוּ אֶת־בְּנֵ֧י יִשְׂרָאֵ֛ל מֵאֶ֥רֶץ

20. his father's sister Marriage to a paternal aunt is prohibited in the legislation of Lev. 18:12 and 20:19. Therefore, this notice must preserve a very ancient tradition.

Jochebed She is the anonymous "Levite woman" of Exod. 2:1 and the first biblical personage clearly to bear a name including *yo,* the shortened form of the divine name *YHVH*. Her name seems to mean "*YHVH* is glory."

24. The Korahite clan later became a guild of Temple singers to whom several psalms are attributed (e.g., Ps. 42,45–49,84–85,87–88). They are also listed as "guards of the threshold of the Tent" (1 Chron. 9:19) who performed tasks such as baking and gate keeping. An 8th-century bowl inscribed with the words "the sons of Korah" (*bny krḥ*) has been found in an Israelite shrine at Arad in the Negev.

25. Putiel's The text assumes that he was well known although he is not mentioned elsewhere. The name is a hybrid of Egyptian (*Puti*) and Hebrew (*el*), and means "the one whom God has given."

Phinehas This name is also Egyptian and means "the Nubian/dark-skinned one." It was fairly common in Egypt in the 13th century B.C.E. Other levitical figures also have Egyptian names, such as Hor, Merari, and Hophni, offering evidence to the historicity of the Exodus of the ancestors of that tribe from Egypt.

A RECAPITULATION (vv. 26–30)

Following the digression of the genealogy, this brief section summarizes and repeats verses 10–13. It also reconnects the genealogy with the account of the Exodus.

26. It is the same That is, the same Aaron and Moses mentioned in the genealogy.

troop by troop The narratives employ military terminology for the organization of the Israelites during the Exodus and the wilderness wanderings.

who spoke to Pharaoh king of Egypt to free the
Israelites from the Egyptians; these are the same
Moses and Aaron. 28For when the LORD spoke
to Moses in the land of Egypt 29and the LORD
said to Moses, "I am the LORD; speak to Pharaoh
king of Egypt all that I will tell you," 30Moses
appealed to the LORD, saying, "See, I am of
impeded speech; how then should Pharaoh
heed me!"

מִצְרַיִם עַל־צִבְאֹתָם׃ 27 הֵם הַֽמְדַבְּרִים
אֶל־פַּרְעֹה מֶֽלֶךְ־מִצְרַיִם לְהוֹצִיא אֶת־
בְּנֵי־יִשְׂרָאֵל מִמִּצְרָיִם הוּא מֹשֶׁה וְאַהֲרֹן׃
28 וַיְהִי בְּיוֹם דִּבֶּר יְהוָה אֶל־מֹשֶׁה בְּאֶרֶץ
שלישי מִצְרָיִם׃ פ 29 וַיְדַבֵּר יְהוָה אֶל־מֹשֶׁה
לֵּאמֹר אֲנִי יְהוָה דַּבֵּר אֶל־פַּרְעֹה מֶלֶךְ
מִצְרַיִם אֵת כָּל־אֲשֶׁר אֲנִי דֹּבֵר אֵלֶיךָ׃
30 וַיֹּאמֶר מֹשֶׁה לִפְנֵי יְהוָה הֵן אֲנִי עֲרַל
שְׂפָתַיִם וְאֵיךְ יִשְׁמַע אֵלַי פַּרְעֹה׃ פ

7 The LORD replied to Moses, "See, I place
you in the role of God to Pharaoh, with your
brother Aaron as your prophet. 2You shall repeat all that I command you, and your brother
Aaron shall speak to Pharaoh to let the Israelites

ז
וַיֹּאמֶר יְהוָה אֶל־מֹשֶׁה רְאֵה נְתַתִּיךָ
אֱלֹהִים לְפַרְעֹה וְאַהֲרֹן אָחִיךָ יִהְיֶה
נְבִיאֶךָ׃ 2 אַתָּה תְדַבֵּר אֵת כָּל־אֲשֶׁר אֲצַוֶּךָּ
וְאַהֲרֹן אָחִיךָ יְדַבֵּר אֶל־פַּרְעֹה וְשִׁלַּח

REAFFIRMATION AND RENEWAL OF MOSES' MISSION (7:1–7)

1. your prophet Your spokesman. The Hebrew word *navi* may well be derived from an Akkadian verb meaning "to call, proclaim"—the divine word, that is. Moses will thus expose the hollowness of Pharaoh's claim to divinity.

2. Moses and Aaron speak not on their own initiative but as agents of God's will.

CHAPTER 7

3. I will harden Pharaoh's heart The verse raises major moral and theological problems. If Pharaoh is foreordained to reject Moses' plea, if God will arrange for the confrontation to continue, how can Pharaoh be held responsible for his actions and how can we justify his being punished for what God causes him to do? "Although 'hardening of the heart' seems deterministic, events flow naturally from the ambitions and conflicts of a human being, Pharaoh, who is seized with the delusion of self-sufficiency. While events unfold under the providence of God, their unfolding is always according to the motives of the human beings through whom God's will is done without their realizing it. . . . Pharaoh conducted himself in conformity with his own motives and his own Godless view of his status. God made it so, but Pharaoh had only to be himself to do God's will" (Moshe Greenberg).

We note that for the first five plagues, the text reads: "Pharaoh's heart was hardened." That is, he himself chose to be stubborn. Only for the last five plagues do we read "God hardened Pharaoh's heart." In the beginning of the process, Pharaoh was equally free to be generous or to be stubborn. Every time he chose the option of stubbornness, however, he gave away some of his free will. Each choice made it more likely that he would choose similarly the next time, both to spare himself the embarrassment of admitting that he was wrong and because he now had the self-image of a person who would not yield to Moses' pleading. "At first, it was you who hardened your heart. Henceforth I shall contribute to the hardening."

Similarly, Maimonides writes: "Sometimes a man's offense is so grave that he forecloses the possibility of repentance. At first [Pharaoh] sinned repeatedly of his own free will, until he forfeited the capacity to repent." Erich Fromm has written, "Pharaoh's heart hardens because he keeps on doing evil. It hardens to a point where no more change or repentance is possible. . . . The longer he refuses to choose the right, the harder his heart becomes . . . until there is no longer any freedom of choice left him." God has structured the human heart in such a way that Pharaoh prevents himself from changing.

אֶת־בְּנֵי־יִשְׂרָאֵל מֵאַרְצוֹ׃ 3 וַאֲנִי אַקְשֶׁה
אֶת־לֵב פַּרְעֹה וְהִרְבֵּיתִי אֶת־אֹתֹתַי וְאֶת־
מוֹפְתַי בְּאֶרֶץ מִצְרָיִם׃ 4 וְלֹא־יִשְׁמַע
אֲלֵכֶם פַּרְעֹה וְנָתַתִּי אֶת־יָדִי בְּמִצְרָיִם
וְהוֹצֵאתִי אֶת־צִבְאֹתַי אֶת־עַמִּי בְנֵי־
יִשְׂרָאֵל מֵאֶרֶץ מִצְרַיִם בִּשְׁפָטִים גְּדֹלִים׃
5 וְיָדְעוּ מִצְרַיִם כִּי־אֲנִי יְהוָה בִּנְטֹתִי אֶת־
יָדִי עַל־מִצְרָיִם וְהוֹצֵאתִי אֶת־בְּנֵי־יִשְׂרָאֵל
מִתּוֹכָם׃ 6 וַיַּעַשׂ מֹשֶׁה וְאַהֲרֹן כַּאֲשֶׁר צִוָּה
יְהוָה אֹתָם כֵּן עָשׂוּ׃ 7 וּמֹשֶׁה בֶּן־שְׁמֹנִים
שָׁנָה וְאַהֲרֹן בֶּן־שָׁלֹשׁ וּשְׁמֹנִים שָׁנָה
בְּדַבְּרָם אֶל־פַּרְעֹה׃ פ
8 וַיֹּאמֶר יְהוָה אֶל־מֹשֶׁה וְאֶל־אַהֲרֹן ביעי
לֵאמֹר׃ 9 כִּי יְדַבֵּר אֲלֵכֶם פַּרְעֹה לֵאמֹר
תְּנוּ לָכֶם מוֹפֵת וְאָמַרְתָּ אֶל־אַהֲרֹן קַח
אֶת־מַטְּךָ וְהַשְׁלֵךְ לִפְנֵי־פַרְעֹה יְהִי לְתַנִּין׃

depart from his land. 3But I will harden Pharaoh's heart, that I may multiply My signs and marvels in the land of Egypt. 4When Pharaoh does not heed you, I will lay My hand upon Egypt and deliver My ranks, My people the Israelites, from the land of Egypt with extraordinary chastisements. 5And the Egyptians shall know that I am the LORD, when I stretch out My hand over Egypt and bring out the Israelites from their midst." 6This Moses and Aaron did; as the LORD commanded them, so they did. 7Moses was eighty years old and Aaron eighty-three, when they made their demand on Pharaoh.

8The LORD said to Moses and Aaron, 9"When Pharaoh speaks to you and says, 'Produce your marvel,' you shall say to Aaron, 'Take your rod and cast it down before Pharaoh.' It shall turn into a serpent." 10So Moses and Aaron came be-

3–4. These verses, which allude to the forthcoming plagues, are also God's response to Moses' protestations in 6:30, as though to say, "Of course Pharaoh will not be easily swayed, but not on account of your inadequacy. Rather, it is because I use his stubbornness to demonstrate My active Presence."

harden Pharaoh's heart See Comment to 4:21.

5. the Egyptians shall know This is the ultimate response to Pharaoh's contemptuous declaration, "I do not know the LORD." In time, as a result of these events, the entire world will come to "know the LORD."

7. eighty years old Moses commences his public leadership career at an age that in biblical times was seen as the completion of unusual longevity (see Ps. 90:10).

SIGNS BEFORE PHARAOH (vv. 8–13)

Moses, to authenticate his claim as a divinely appointed emissary to Israel, had performed his signs before the people. Now he must do the same before Pharaoh.

9. say to Aaron Henceforth, Aaron will perform the signs when the Egyptian magicians are present. This enables Moses to negotiate with Pharaoh as an equal and not be equated with the magicians.

a serpent In 4:3 the word for "serpent" is *naḥash.* Here it is *tannin,* a more general term for a large reptile. *Tannin* may have special relevance

---

7. *Moses was eighty years old* In Gen. 47:7–10, a previous Pharaoh was impressed by Jacob's advanced age. Moses and Aaron may have thought, "If Pharaoh doesn't respect our message, perhaps he will respect our advanced years." The reference to Moses' age might remind us of the potential contribution of the elderly to our society, the sharing of their wisdom and experience, and their ability to take on new challenges and responsibilities.

8. The confrontation here is not only between Moses and Pharaoh's magicians but also between miracles and magic. In magic, humans try to impose their will on God. Miracles demonstrate God's greatness beyond the limits of human power. Magic originates in the will of a human being to impress or fool other human beings. Miracles, although they may use a human instrument, are part of a larger divine design. A Hasidic comment takes the words "produce your marvel" (v. 9) to mean "produce a marvel that will astonish you as well." A magic trick astonishes the audience; a miracle astonishes even those who perform it with God's help.

10 וַיָּבֹ֨א מֹשֶׁ֤ה וְאַהֲרֹן֙ אֶל־פַּרְעֹ֔ה וַיַּ֣עֲשׂוּ כֵ֔ן
כַּאֲשֶׁ֖ר צִוָּ֣ה יְהוָ֑ה וַיַּשְׁלֵ֨ךְ אַהֲרֹ֜ן אֶת־מַטֵּ֗הוּ
לִפְנֵ֥י פַרְעֹ֛ה וְלִפְנֵ֥י עֲבָדָ֖יו וַיְהִ֥י לְתַנִּֽין׃
11 וַיִּקְרָא֙ גַּם־פַּרְעֹ֔ה לַֽחֲכָמִ֖ים וְלַֽמְכַשְּׁפִ֑ים
וַיַּֽעֲשׂ֨וּ גַם־הֵ֜ם חַרְטֻמֵּ֥י מִצְרַ֛יִם בְּלַהֲטֵיהֶ֖ם
כֵּֽן׃ 12 וַיַּשְׁלִ֙יכוּ֙ אִ֣ישׁ מַטֵּ֔הוּ וַיִּהְי֖וּ לְתַנִּינִ֑ם
וַיִּבְלַ֥ע מַטֵּֽה־אַהֲרֹ֖ן אֶת־מַטֹּתָֽם׃ 13 וַיֶּחֱזַק֙
לֵ֣ב פַּרְעֹ֔ה וְלֹ֥א שָׁמַ֖ע אֲלֵהֶ֑ם כַּאֲשֶׁ֖ר דִּבֶּ֥ר
יְהוָֽה׃ פ
14 וַיֹּ֤אמֶר יְהוָה֙ אֶל־מֹשֶׁ֔ה כָּבֵ֖ד לֵ֣ב פַּרְעֹ֑ה

fore Pharaoh and did just as the LORD had commanded: Aaron cast down his rod in the presence of Pharaoh and his courtiers, and it turned into a serpent. 11Then Pharaoh, for his part, summoned the wise men and the sorcerers; and the Egyptian magicians, in turn, did the same with their spells; 12each cast down his rod, and they turned into serpents. But Aaron's rod swallowed their rods. 13Yet Pharaoh's heart stiffened and he did not heed them, as the LORD had said.

14And the LORD said to Moses, "Pharaoh is

regarding Pharaoh, who is addressed as follows in Ezek. 29:3: "Thus says the Lord GOD: / I am going to deal with you, O Pharaoh, king of Egypt, / Mighty monster [*ha-tannin ha-gadol*]."

11. magicians Hebrew *ḥartumim* derives from an Egyptian term meaning "chief lector [reader] priest," a title bestowed on a learned scribe and priest whose skills included expertise in magic and dream interpretation.

with their spells The use of "spells" contrasts sharply with the simplicity of Aaron's act, which is unaccompanied by any incantation or unusual behavior. Such spells probably belonged to the magicians' repertoire of tricks.

12–13. After casting his rod down, Aaron does nothing further. The rod—a real one—appears to act on its own. Nevertheless, Pharaoh remains unmoved.

THE PLAGUES (7:14–11:10)

As foretold, Pharaoh's stubbornness sets in motion the "extraordinary chastisements" mentioned in verse 4. A total of 10 disasters—popularly known as the "Ten Plagues" (*Eser Makkot*)—strike Egypt in the course of a year.

There are three accounts of the plagues in the Hebrew Bible. The longest and most detailed is the version set forth in these chapters. Psalms 78:43–51 and 105:27–36 are shorter, poetic presentations. The narrative here is a sophisticated literary structure, with a pattern of three groups, each made up of 3 plagues. The climactic 10th plague has a character all its own. The first 2 afflictions in each group are preceded by a warning; the last affliction always strikes suddenly, unannounced. For the 1st, 4th, and 7th plagues, Pharaoh is informed in the morning and Moses is told to "station" himself before the king; in the second of each series, Moses is told to "come in before Pharaoh," that is, to confront him in the palace. In the first group of plagues, it is Aaron who is the effective agent; in the third, it is Moses. This symmetrical literary architecture emphasizes the idea that the 9 plagues are not random natural disasters, but deliberate acts of divine will—their purpose being to deliver retribution, to coerce, to educate. They are God's judgments on Egypt for the enslavement of the Israelites. They are meant to crush Pharaoh's resistance and demonstrate to Egypt the impotence of its gods and the uniqueness of *YHVH*, God of Israel, as the one supreme sovereign God of Creation, who uses the natural order for His own purposes.

FIRST PLAGUE: BLOODY WATERS (*dam*) (7:14–25)

The Nile is the most important natural feature in Egypt. In fact, it is Egypt's "life blood." How fitting, then, that it should be struck first by God to "make it bleed" from a mortal wound. This plague has been explained as the intensification of a phenomenon that occurs periodically in the Nile valley. The river is fed by melting snow and summer rains that pour down from the highlands of Ethiopia and carry with them sediment from the tropical red earth of that region. An abnormally heavy rainfall would lead to an excessively high rise of the Nile and wash down into it inordinate amounts of the red sediment. Thus the river, unable to absorb this substance as it would during a gradual rise of its waters, takes on a bloody hue. As a result, bacteria washed down from the high mountain lakes, together with the particles of red earth, disturb the river's oxygen

stubborn; he refuses to let the people go. 15Go
to Pharaoh in the morning, as he is coming out
to the water, and station yourself before him at
the edge of the Nile, taking with you the rod
that turned into a snake. 16And say to him, 'The
LORD, the God of the Hebrews, sent me to you
to say, "Let My people go that they may worship
Me in the wilderness." But you have paid no
heed until now. 17Thus says the LORD, "By this
you shall know that I am the LORD." See, I shall
strike the water in the Nile with the rod that is
in my hand, and it will be turned into blood;
18and the fish in the Nile will die. The Nile will
stink so that the Egyptians will find it impossible
to drink the water of the Nile.'"

19And the LORD said to Moses, "Say to Aaron:
Take your rod and hold out your arm over the
waters of Egypt—its rivers, its canals, its ponds,
all its bodies of water—that they may turn to
blood; there shall be blood throughout the land
of Egypt, even in vessels of wood and stone."

מֵאֵ֖ן לְשַׁלַּ֥ח הָעָֽם׃ 15 לֵ֣ךְ אֶל־פַּרְעֹ֞ה בַּבֹּ֗קֶר
הִנֵּה֙ יֹצֵ֣א הַמַּ֔יְמָה וְנִצַּבְתָּ֥ לִקְרָאת֖וֹ עַל־
שְׂפַ֣ת הַיְאֹ֑ר וְהַמַּטֶּ֛ה אֲשֶׁר־נֶהְפַּ֥ךְ לְנָחָ֖שׁ
תִּקַּ֥ח בְּיָדֶֽךָ׃ 16 וְאָמַרְתָּ֣ אֵלָ֗יו יְהֹוָ֞ה אֱלֹהֵ֤י
הָֽעִבְרִים֙ שְׁלָחַ֣נִי אֵלֶ֔יךָ לֵאמֹ֔ר שַׁלַּח֙ אֶת־
עַמִּ֔י וְיַֽעַבְדֻ֖נִי בַּמִּדְבָּ֑ר וְהִנֵּ֥ה לֹא־שָׁמַ֖עְתָּ
עַד־כֹּֽה׃ 17 כֹּ֚ה אָמַ֣ר יְהֹוָ֔ה בְּזֹ֣את תֵּדַ֔ע כִּ֖י
אֲנִ֣י יְהֹוָ֑ה הִנֵּ֨ה אָנֹכִ֜י מַכֶּ֣ה ׀ בַּמַּטֶּ֣ה
אֲשֶׁר־בְּיָדִ֗י עַל־הַמַּ֛יִם אֲשֶׁ֥ר בַּיְאֹ֖ר וְנֶהֶפְכ֥וּ
לְדָֽם׃ 18 וְהַדָּגָ֧ה אֲשֶׁר־בַּיְאֹ֛ר תָּמ֖וּת וּבָאַ֣שׁ
הַיְאֹ֑ר וְנִלְא֣וּ מִצְרַ֔יִם לִשְׁתּ֥וֹת מַ֖יִם מִן־
הַיְאֹֽר׃ ס
19 וַיֹּ֨אמֶר יְהֹוָ֜ה אֶל־מֹשֶׁ֗ה אֱמֹ֣ר אֶֽל־אַהֲרֹ֡ן
קַ֣ח מַטְּךָ֩ וּנְטֵֽה־יָדְךָ֨ עַל־מֵימֵ֜י מִצְרַ֗יִם
עַֽל־נַהֲרֹתָ֣ם ׀ עַל־יְאֹרֵיהֶ֣ם וְעַֽל־אַגְמֵיהֶ֗ם
וְעַ֛ל כָּל־מִקְוֵ֥ה מֵימֵיהֶ֖ם וְיִֽהְיוּ־דָ֑ם וְהָ֤יָה
דָם֙ בְּכָל־אֶ֣רֶץ מִצְרַ֔יִם וּבָעֵצִ֖ים וּבָאֲבָנִֽים׃

balance and begin to kill off the fish, producing a horrendous stench.

The Nile flooding, which crests in September or October, has a bearing on the next plague as well. The Egyptians personified and deified the Nile as the crocodile god Sobek, to whom offerings were made at the time of inundation. The flooding itself was regarded as a manifestation of the god Osiris. It is quite possible, then, that the contamination of the river served to discredit Egyptian polytheism. By beginning the series of plagues with the striking of the Nile, the text suggests an underlying notion of divine retribution for Pharaoh's decree that all newborn males be cast into the river. Although any one of the plagues can be explained naturally, their occurrence here is by divine intervention.

15. as he is coming out to the water The significance of Pharaoh's act is unexplained. It may involve a ceremony associated with his morning rituals or with worship of the god of the Nile during the inundation period. It is also possible that he may have gone out to measure the height of the river.

17. by this you shall know It is only by experiencing God's might that Pharaoh will be persuaded to let Israel go.

18. The Nile and its pools teemed with fish, an important element of the popular daily diet. The rotting of the fish, therefore, was a calamitous blow.

19. in vessels of wood and stone "Vessels" is not in the Hebrew text, but the phrase is so understood by medieval Jewish commentators.

---

16. Let My people go that they may worship Me The popular phrase is "Let My people go," but the Bible never uses that phrase without adding the reason and purpose for the Israelites' freedom. Freedom was more than release from bondage; it provided the opportunity to serve God. It was not only freedom from something; it was freedom for something.

The plagues emphasize that God is the God of all Creation. Water, weather, animals, and insects all bend to God's will. The Exodus narrative asserts that the God of Creation is also the God of history. The *Kiddush* recited on *Shabbat* describes *Shabbat* as a reminder both of the world's creation (God as Lord of nature) and of the Exodus (God as manifest in history).

19. Why was the first plague directed at the Nile? The Nile was the mainstay of Egyptian

20Moses and Aaron did just as the LORD commanded: he lifted up the rod and struck the water in the Nile in the sight of Pharaoh and his
courtiers, and all the water in the Nile was
turned into blood 21and the fish in the Nile died.
The Nile stank so that the Egyptians could not
drink water from the Nile; and there was blood
throughout the land of Egypt. 22But when the
Egyptian magicians did the same with their
spells, Pharaoh's heart stiffened and he did not
heed them—as the LORD had spoken. 23Pha-
raoh turned and went into his palace, paying
no regard even to this. 24And all the Egyptians
had to dig round about the Nile for drinking
water, because they could not drink the water
of the Nile.

25When seven days had passed after the LORD
struck the Nile, 26the LORD said to Moses, "Go
to Pharaoh and say to him, 'Thus says the LORD:
Let My people go that they may worship Me.
27If you refuse to let them go, then I will plague
your whole country with frogs. 28The Nile shall
swarm with frogs, and they shall come up and
enter your palace, your bedchamber and your
bed, the houses of your courtiers and your people, and your ovens and your kneading bowls.
29The frogs shall come up on you and on your
people and on all your courtiers.'"

20 וַיַּעֲשׂוּ־כֵן מֹשֶׁה וְאַהֲרֹן כַּאֲשֶׁר ׀ צִוָּה
יְהוָה וַיָּרֶם בַּמַּטֶּה וַיַּךְ אֶת־הַמַּיִם אֲשֶׁר
בַּיְאֹר לְעֵינֵי פַרְעֹה וּלְעֵינֵי עֲבָדָיו וַיֵּהָפְכוּ
כָּל־הַמַּיִם אֲשֶׁר־בַּיְאֹר לְדָם׃ 21 וְהַדָּגָה
אֲשֶׁר־בַּיְאֹר מֵתָה וַיִּבְאַשׁ הַיְאֹר וְלֹא־יָכְלוּ
מִצְרַיִם לִשְׁתּוֹת מַיִם מִן־הַיְאֹר וַיְהִי הַדָּם
בְּכָל־אֶרֶץ מִצְרָיִם׃ 22 וַיַּעֲשׂוּ־כֵן חַרְטֻמֵּי
מִצְרַיִם בְּלָטֵיהֶם וַיֶּחֱזַק לֵב־פַּרְעֹה וְלֹא־
שָׁמַע אֲלֵהֶם כַּאֲשֶׁר דִּבֶּר יְהוָה׃ 23 וַיִּפֶן
פַּרְעֹה וַיָּבֹא אֶל־בֵּיתוֹ וְלֹא־שָׁת לִבּוֹ גַּם־
לָזֹאת׃ 24 וַיַּחְפְּרוּ כָל־מִצְרַיִם סְבִיבֹת
הַיְאֹר מַיִם לִשְׁתּוֹת כִּי לֹא יָכְלוּ לִשְׁתֹּת
מִמֵּימֵי הַיְאֹר׃

25 וַיִּמָּלֵא שִׁבְעַת יָמִים אַחֲרֵי הַכּוֹת־יְהוָה
אֶת־הַיְאֹר׃ פ 26 וַיֹּאמֶר יְהוָה אֶל־מֹשֶׁה
בֹּא אֶל־פַּרְעֹה וְאָמַרְתָּ אֵלָיו כֹּה אָמַר
יְהוָה שַׁלַּח אֶת־עַמִּי וְיַעַבְדֻנִי׃ 27 וְאִם־
מָאֵן אַתָּה לְשַׁלֵּחַ הִנֵּה אָנֹכִי נֹגֵף אֶת־
כָּל־גְּבוּלְךָ בַּצְפַרְדְּעִים׃ 28 וְשָׁרַץ הַיְאֹר
צְפַרְדְּעִים וְעָלוּ וּבָאוּ בְּבֵיתֶךָ וּבַחֲדַר
מִשְׁכָּבְךָ וְעַל־מִטָּתֶךָ וּבְבֵית עֲבָדֶיךָ וּבְעַמֶּךָ
וּבְתַנּוּרֶיךָ וּבְמִשְׁאֲרוֹתֶיךָ׃ 29 וּבְכָה*
וּבְעַמְּךָ וּבְכָל־עֲבָדֶיךָ יַעֲלוּ הַצְפַרְדְּעִים׃

v. 29. יתיר ה׳

22. The magicians' success offsets the ominous effect of the plague.

SECOND PLAGUE: FROGS (*tz'fardei·a*)
(7:26–8:11)

Frogs, during their reproductive period, normally concentrate in ponds and lakes, and as the Nile begins to recede in September and October, they usually mass on land. Because their habitat was now polluted by putrefying fish, they were forced onto the land much earlier than usual. But the dead fish were a source of insect-borne infection, which killed off the frogs en masse. This plague, like the first one, may have been regarded as a judgment on the many gods of Egypt, for a frog-headed goddess named Hepat was the consort of the god

---

life. It provided water for drinking and irrigation; its periodic floods enriched the soil. In the *haftarah,* the prophet Ezekiel pictures Pharaoh saying, "The Nile is mine, I made it for myself." It also was the site of the Egyptians' great crime of slaying the Hebrew male children. One can speculate on the psychological effect on the Egyptians, who saw their source of life (that they had made an instrument of death for Israelite babies) turned into a river of blood. Why is Aaron the one to call down the plague on the Nile, not Moses? Because the Nile protected Moses when he was an infant, it would have been ungrateful on his part to afflict it (MRE).

8 And the LORD said to Moses, "Say to Aaron:
Hold out your arm with the rod over the rivers,
the canals, and the ponds, and bring up the frogs
on the land of Egypt." [2]Aaron held out his arm
over the waters of Egypt, and the frogs came up
and covered the land of Egypt. [3]But the magicians did the same with their spells, and brought
frogs upon the land of Egypt.

[4]Then Pharaoh summoned Moses and Aaron
and said, "Plead with the LORD to remove the
frogs from me and my people, and I will let the
people go to sacrifice to the LORD." [5]And Moses
said to Pharaoh, "You may have this triumph
over me: for what time shall I plead in behalf
of you and your courtiers and your people, that
the frogs be cut off from you and your houses,
to remain only in the Nile?" [6]"For tomorrow,"
he replied. And [Moses] said, "As you say—that
you may know that there is none like the LORD
our God; [7]the frogs shall retreat from you and
your courtiers and your people; they shall remain only in the Nile." [8]Then Moses and Aaron
left Pharaoh's presence, and Moses cried out to
the LORD in the matter of the frogs which He
had inflicted upon Pharaoh. [9]And the LORD did
as Moses asked; the frogs died out in the houses,
the courtyards, and the fields. [10]And they piled
them up in heaps, till the land stank. [11]But when

ח וַיֹּאמֶר יְהוָה אֶל־מֹשֶׁה אֱמֹר אֶל־
אַהֲרֹן נְטֵה אֶת־יָדְךָ בְּמַטֶּךָ עַל־הַנְּהָרֹת
עַל־הַיְאֹרִים וְעַל־הָאֲגַמִּים וְהַעַל אֶת־
הַצְפַרְדְּעִים עַל־אֶרֶץ מִצְרָיִם׃ 2 וַיֵּט
אַהֲרֹן אֶת־יָדוֹ עַל מֵימֵי מִצְרָיִם וַתַּעַל
הַצְפַרְדֵּעַ וַתְּכַס אֶת־אֶרֶץ מִצְרָיִם׃
3 וַיַּעֲשׂוּ־כֵן הַחַרְטֻמִּים בְּלָטֵיהֶם וַיַּעֲלוּ
אֶת־הַצְפַרְדְּעִים עַל־אֶרֶץ מִצְרָיִם׃
4 וַיִּקְרָא פַרְעֹה לְמֹשֶׁה וּלְאַהֲרֹן וַיֹּאמֶר
הַעְתִּירוּ אֶל־יְהוָה וְיָסֵר הַצְפַרְדְּעִים מִמֶּנִּי
וּמֵעַמִּי וַאֲשַׁלְּחָה אֶת־הָעָם וְיִזְבְּחוּ
לַיהוָה׃ 5 וַיֹּאמֶר מֹשֶׁה לְפַרְעֹה הִתְפָּאֵר
עָלַי לְמָתַי ׀ אַעְתִּיר לְךָ וְלַעֲבָדֶיךָ וּלְעַמְּךָ
לְהַכְרִית הַצְפַרְדְּעִים מִמְּךָ וּמִבָּתֶּיךָ רַק
בַּיְאֹר תִּשָּׁאַרְנָה׃ 6 וַיֹּאמֶר לְמָחָר וַיֹּאמֶר
כִּדְבָרְךָ לְמַעַן תֵּדַע כִּי־אֵין כַּיהוָה
חמישי אֱלֹהֵינוּ׃ 7 וְסָרוּ הַצְפַרְדְּעִים מִמְּךָ וּמִבָּתֶּיךָ
וּמֵעֲבָדֶיךָ וּמֵעַמֶּךָ רַק בַּיְאֹר תִּשָּׁאַרְנָה׃
8 וַיֵּצֵא מֹשֶׁה וְאַהֲרֹן מֵעִם פַּרְעֹה וַיִּצְעַק
מֹשֶׁה אֶל־יְהוָה עַל־דְּבַר הַצְפַרְדְּעִים
אֲשֶׁר־שָׂם לְפַרְעֹה׃ 9 וַיַּעַשׂ יְהוָה כִּדְבַר
מֹשֶׁה וַיָּמֻתוּ הַצְפַרְדְּעִים מִן־הַבָּתִּים מִן־
הַחֲצֵרֹת וּמִן־הַשָּׂדֹת׃ 10 וַיִּצְבְּרוּ אֹתָם
חֳמָרִם חֳמָרִם וַתִּבְאַשׁ הָאָרֶץ׃ 11 וַיַּרְא

Khnum, who was credited with having fashioned man out of clay. Hepat, associated with fertility, was believed to assist women at childbirth. Hence, the plague may have been taken as retribution for Pharaoh's decree ordering the midwives to kill newborn Israelite males at birth.

4. Plead with the LORD For the first time, Pharaoh acknowledges the existence of *YHVH*. He makes a sweeping concession, but soon rescinds it.

6. that you may know that there is none like the LORD Pharaoh now "knows" God. He has yet to learn of His uniqueness.

CHAPTER 8

3. Pharaoh's magicians cannot remove the frogs; they can only create more frogs, making matters even worse. Trying to spite Moses, they make their own lot worse. It is easier to augment a plague (whether conflict, gossip, or greed) than to end one. Note too that Moses summons the frogs in obedience to God's command. Pharaoh's courtiers summon frogs as a way of showing that they can command the gods to obey them.

Pharaoh saw that there was relief, he became stubborn and would not heed them, as the LORD had spoken.

12Then the LORD said to Moses, "Say to Aaron: Hold out your rod and strike the dust of the earth, and it shall turn to lice throughout the land of Egypt." 13And they did so. Aaron held out his arm with the rod and struck the dust of the earth, and vermin came upon man and beast; all the dust of the earth turned to lice throughout the land of Egypt. 14The magicians did the like with their spells to produce lice, but they could not. The vermin remained upon man and beast; 15and the magicians said to Pharaoh, "This is the finger of God!" But Pharaoh's heart stiffened and he would not heed them, as the LORD had spoken.

16And the LORD said to Moses, "Early in the morning present yourself to Pharaoh, as he is coming out to the water, and say to him, 'Thus says the LORD: Let My people go that they may worship Me. 17For if you do not let My people go, I will let loose swarms of insects against you

פַּרְעֹה כִּי הָיְתָה הָרְוָחָה וְהַכְבֵּד אֶת־לִבּוֹ
וְלֹא שָׁמַע אֲלֵהֶם כַּאֲשֶׁר דִּבֶּר יְהוָה׃ ס
12 וַיֹּאמֶר יְהוָה אֶל־מֹשֶׁה אֱמֹר אֶל־אַהֲרֹן
נְטֵה אֶת־מַטְּךָ וְהַךְ אֶת־עֲפַר הָאָרֶץ וְהָיָה
לְכִנִּם בְּכָל־אֶרֶץ מִצְרָיִם׃ 13 וַיַּעֲשׂוּ־כֵן וַיֵּט
אַהֲרֹן אֶת־יָדוֹ בְמַטֵּהוּ וַיַּךְ אֶת־עֲפַר
הָאָרֶץ וַתְּהִי הַכִּנָּם בָּאָדָם וּבַבְּהֵמָה כָּל־
עֲפַר הָאָרֶץ הָיָה כִנִּים בְּכָל־אֶרֶץ מִצְרָיִם׃
14 וַיַּעֲשׂוּ־כֵן הַחַרְטֻמִּים בְּלָטֵיהֶם לְהוֹצִיא
אֶת־הַכִּנִּים וְלֹא יָכֹלוּ וַתְּהִי הַכִּנָּם
בָּאָדָם וּבַבְּהֵמָה׃ 15 וַיֹּאמְרוּ הַחַרְטֻמִּם
אֶל־פַּרְעֹה אֶצְבַּע אֱלֹהִים הִוא וַיֶּחֱזַק
לֵב־פַּרְעֹה וְלֹא־שָׁמַע אֲלֵהֶם כַּאֲשֶׁר דִּבֶּר
יְהוָה׃ ס
16 וַיֹּאמֶר יְהוָה אֶל־מֹשֶׁה הַשְׁכֵּם בַּבֹּקֶר
וְהִתְיַצֵּב לִפְנֵי פַרְעֹה הִנֵּה יוֹצֵא הַמָּיְמָה
וְאָמַרְתָּ אֵלָיו כֹּה אָמַר יְהוָה שַׁלַּח עַמִּי
וְיַעַבְדֻנִי׃ 17 כִּי אִם־אֵינְךָ מְשַׁלֵּחַ אֶת־עַמִּי
הִנְנִי מַשְׁלִיחַ בְּךָ וּבַעֲבָדֶיךָ וּבְעַמְּךָ

THIRD PLAGUE: VERMIN (*kinnim*)
(vv. 12–15)

Without warning, the land is hit by an infestation of insects, identified by some as lice or mosquitoes. These carriers of deadly diseases, normally troublesome enough in Egypt during October and November, would now have multiplied astronomically in the wake of the prior plagues.

14–15. The magicians retire from the scene, their powers exhausted.

finger of God A supernatural phenomenon beyond human control.

FOURTH PLAGUE (*arov*) (vv. 16–28)

The second group of three plagues begins. Pharaoh is warned as he goes down to the river. The nature of this plague cannot be identified with certainty because the Hebrew word *arov* occurs only here. Different interpretations existed already in ancient times. Usually the word was taken to mean "mixture," and the most widely accepted understanding was "various kinds of wild animals." An alternative tradition explains it as "swarms of insects," specifically the dog fly, a bloodsucking insect that can multiply prodigiously in tropical and subtropical regions and is known to transmit anthrax and other animal diseases.

There are two unique features to this plague: (a) For the first time, a clear distinction is made between the Egyptians and the Israelites and (b) the day of the onset of the plague is fixed. The intent is to leave no doubt in Pharaoh that the

---

23. we must go a distance of three days Is Moses simply telling Pharaoh a justifiable lie, asking for less here in the hope of winning an agreement? (Sometimes deception appears to be the only tactic available to the powerless.) Or is he calculating that once the Israelites have tasted freedom and realized there is an alternative to the way that they have been living, there would be no possibility of their returning to Egypt?

and your courtiers and your people and your houses; the houses of the Egyptians, and the very ground they stand on, shall be filled with swarms of insects. 18But on that day I will set apart the region of Goshen, where My people dwell, so that no swarms of insects shall be there, that you may know that I the LORD am in the midst of the land. 19And I will make a distinction between My people and your people. Tomorrow this sign shall come to pass.'" 20And the LORD did so. Heavy swarms of insects invaded Pharaoh's palace and the houses of his courtiers; throughout the country of Egypt the land was ruined because of the swarms of insects.

21Then Pharaoh summoned Moses and Aaron and said, "Go and sacrifice to your God within the land." 22But Moses replied, "It would not be right to do this, for what we sacrifice to the LORD our God is untouchable to the Egyptians. If we sacrifice that which is untouchable to the Egyptians before their very eyes, will they not stone us! 23So we must go a distance of three days into the wilderness and sacrifice to the LORD our God as He may command us." 24Pharaoh said, "I will let you go to sacrifice to the LORD your God in the wilderness; but do

וּבְבָתֶּ֛יךָ אֶת־הֶעָרֹ֑ב וּמָ֨לְא֜וּ בָּתֵּ֤י מִצְרַ֙יִם֙
אֶת־הֶ֣עָרֹ֔ב וְגַ֥ם הָאֲדָמָ֖ה אֲשֶׁר־הֵ֥ם עָלֶֽיהָ׃
18 וְהִפְלֵיתִי֩ בַיּ֨וֹם הַה֜וּא אֶת־אֶ֣רֶץ גֹּ֗שֶׁן
אֲשֶׁ֤ר עַמִּי֙ עֹמֵ֣ד עָלֶ֔יהָ לְבִלְתִּ֥י הֱיֽוֹת־שָׁ֖ם
עָרֹ֑ב לְמַ֣עַן תֵּדַ֔ע כִּ֛י אֲנִ֥י יְהוָ֖ה בְּקֶ֥רֶב
הָאָֽרֶץ׃ 19 וְשַׂמְתִּ֣י פְדֻ֔ת בֵּ֥ין עַמִּ֖י וּבֵ֣ין עַמֶּ֑ךָ ששי
לְמָחָ֥ר יִהְיֶ֖ה הָאֹ֥ת הַזֶּֽה׃ 20 וַיַּ֤עַשׂ יְהוָה֙
כֵּ֔ן וַיָּבֹא֙ עָרֹ֣ב כָּבֵ֔ד בֵּ֥יתָה פַרְעֹ֖ה וּבֵ֣ית*
עֲבָדָ֑יו וּבְכָל־אֶ֧רֶץ מִצְרַ֛יִם תִּשָּׁחֵ֥ת הָאָ֖רֶץ
מִפְּנֵ֥י הֶעָרֹֽב׃
21 וַיִּקְרָ֣א פַרְעֹ֔ה אֶל־מֹשֶׁ֖ה וּֽלְאַהֲרֹ֑ן וַיֹּ֗אמֶר
לְכ֛וּ זִבְח֥וּ לֵאלֹהֵיכֶ֖ם בָּאָֽרֶץ׃ 22 וַיֹּ֣אמֶר
מֹשֶׁ֗ה לֹ֤א נָכוֹן֙ לַעֲשׂ֣וֹת כֵּ֔ן כִּ֚י תּוֹעֲבַ֣ת
מִצְרַ֔יִם נִזְבַּ֖ח לַיהוָ֣ה אֱלֹהֵ֑ינוּ הֵ֣ן נִזְבַּ֞ח
אֶת־תּוֹעֲבַ֥ת מִצְרַ֛יִם לְעֵינֵיהֶ֖ם וְלֹ֥א
יִסְקְלֻֽנוּ׃ 23 דֶּ֚רֶךְ שְׁלֹ֣שֶׁת יָמִ֔ים נֵלֵ֖ךְ בַּמִּדְבָּ֑ר
וְזָבַ֙חְנוּ֙ לַיהוָ֣ה אֱלֹהֵ֔ינוּ כַּאֲשֶׁ֖ר יֹאמַ֥ר
אֵלֵֽינוּ׃ 24 וַיֹּ֣אמֶר פַּרְעֹ֗ה אָנֹכִ֞י אֲשַׁלַּ֤ח
אֶתְכֶם֙ וּזְבַחְתֶּ֞ם לַיהוָ֤ה אֱלֹֽהֵיכֶם֙ בַּמִּדְבָּ֔ר

v. 20. סבירין ומטעין "ובבית"

source of the plague is not just a god (v. 15), but *YHVH*, God of Israel.

18. I will set apart the region of Goshen The Israelites also suffered the first three plagues. They will not suffer the rest.

Goshen In Gen. 45:10 this is the name given to the area of Israelite settlement in Egypt. Its precise location is unknown, although some evidence indicates it was in the region of Wadi Tumilat, which stretches from the eastern arm of the Nile to the Great Bitter Lake. Egyptian texts tell of the presence of Semites and other Asians in the northeastern part of the country, both at the end of the Sixth Dynasty (ca. 2250 B.C.E.) and ca. 1700 B.C.E. The concentration was especially strong in the New Kingdom from 1500 to 1000 B.C.E. Exodus 12:38 refers to a "mixed multitude" (that is, foreign tribes) dwelling in the area of Israelite settlement.

21. For the second time, Pharaoh makes a concession, this time more limited. He has reneged on his original promise and will do so again.

within the land Not in the wilderness.

22–23. The Israelites do not know what animal sacrifice the Lord will demand of them. It may turn out that Egyptians will regard it as a sacrilege, because their religion venerates gods in animal form.

untouchable A deliberate ambiguity: The Hebrew word *to·evah* can mean "that which is taboo" to the Egyptians and also "that which is an [Egyptian] abomination" in the sight of Israel, namely, their animal divinities.

three days See Comment to 3:18.

24. Pharaoh seems to accept Moses' reasoning and to relent.

I will let you go The Hebrew places the personal pronoun *anokhi,* "I," before the verb to em-

not go very far. Plead, then, for me." 25And Moses said, "When I leave your presence, I will plead with the LORD that the swarms of insects depart tomorrow from Pharaoh and his courtiers and his people; but let not Pharaoh again act deceitfully, not letting the people go to sacrifice to the LORD."

26So Moses left Pharaoh's presence and pleaded with the LORD. 27And the LORD did as Moses asked: He removed the swarms of insects from Pharaoh, from his courtiers, and from his people; not one remained. 28But Pharaoh became stubborn this time also, and would not let the people go.

רַק הַרְחֵק לֹא־תַרְחִיקוּ לָלֶכֶת הַעְתִּירוּ
בַּעֲדִי׃ 25 וַיֹּאמֶר מֹשֶׁה הִנֵּה אָנֹכִי יוֹצֵא
מֵעִמָּךְ וְהַעְתַּרְתִּי אֶל־יְהוָה וְסָר הֶעָרֹב
מִפַּרְעֹה מֵעֲבָדָיו וּמֵעַמּוֹ מָחָר רַק אַל־יֹסֵף
פַּרְעֹה הָתֵל לְבִלְתִּי שַׁלַּח אֶת־הָעָם לִזְבֹּחַ
לַיהוָה׃
26 וַיֵּצֵא מֹשֶׁה מֵעִם פַּרְעֹה וַיֶּעְתַּר אֶל־
יְהוָה׃ 27 וַיַּעַשׂ יְהוָה כִּדְבַר מֹשֶׁה וַיָּסַר
הֶעָרֹב מִפַּרְעֹה מֵעֲבָדָיו וּמֵעַמּוֹ לֹא נִשְׁאַר
אֶחָד׃ 28 וַיַּכְבֵּד פַּרְעֹה אֶת־לִבּוֹ גַּם בַּפַּעַם
הַזֹּאת וְלֹא שִׁלַּח אֶת־הָעָם׃ פ

9 The LORD said to Moses, "Go to Pharaoh and say to him, 'Thus says the LORD, the God of the Hebrews: Let My people go to worship Me. 2For if you refuse to let them go, and continue to hold them, 3then the hand of the LORD will strike your livestock in the fields—the horses, the asses, the camels, the cattle, and the sheep—with a very severe pestilence. 4But the LORD will make a distinction between the livestock of Israel and the livestock of the Egyptians, so that nothing shall die of all that belongs to the Israelites. 5The LORD has fixed the time: tomorrow the LORD will do this thing in the

ט וַיֹּאמֶר יְהוָה אֶל־מֹשֶׁה בֹּא אֶל־
פַּרְעֹה וְדִבַּרְתָּ אֵלָיו כֹּה־אָמַר יְהוָה אֱלֹהֵי
הָעִבְרִים שַׁלַּח אֶת־עַמִּי וְיַעַבְדֻנִי׃ 2 כִּי
אִם־מָאֵן אַתָּה לְשַׁלֵּחַ וְעוֹדְךָ מַחֲזִיק בָּם׃
3 הִנֵּה יַד־יְהוָה הוֹיָה בְּמִקְנְךָ אֲשֶׁר בַּשָּׂדֶה
בַּסּוּסִים בַּחֲמֹרִים בַּגְּמַלִּים בַּבָּקָר וּבַצֹּאן
דֶּבֶר כָּבֵד מְאֹד׃ 4 וְהִפְלָה יְהוָה בֵּין מִקְנֵה
יִשְׂרָאֵל וּבֵין מִקְנֵה מִצְרָיִם וְלֹא יָמוּת
מִכָּל־לִבְנֵי יִשְׂרָאֵל דָּבָר׃ 5 וַיָּשֶׂם יְהוָה
מוֹעֵד לֵאמֹר מָחָר יַעֲשֶׂה יְהוָה הַדָּבָר

phasize the subject. In this way Pharaoh asserts his superior authority even though he is making a concession.

FIFTH PLAGUE: PESTILENCE (*dever*) (9:1–7)

The notion of sacred animals in Egyptian religion is now rendered absurd. The God of Israel strikes the animals with pestilence. The soil, contaminated by enormous mounds of rotting frogs, most likely became the breeding ground of disease, probably the highly infectious anthrax, which affected the cattle in the fields. Once again, the animals of the Israelites go untouched, the time of the plague's onset is foretold, and Pharaoh is warned in his palace.

3. hand of the LORD As distinguished from the "finger of God" in 8:15. The "hand" is a symbol of power, used here both to punish and to coerce. In some ancient Near Eastern texts, diseases are described as "the hand of Ishtar," "the hand of Nergal," or "the hand" of other gods.

camels An anachronism. Camels were introduced to Egypt only later, during the Persian period (after 538 B.C.E.).

---

28. Human memories are so short. When Pharaoh was suffering, he could be compassionate toward his suffering slaves. When he recovered, he lost that sense of compassion. (And note that here, Pharaoh hardens his own heart.)

land.'" 6And the LORD did so the next day: all
the livestock of the Egyptians died, but of the
livestock of the Israelites not a beast died.
7When Pharaoh inquired, he found that not a
head of the livestock of Israel had died; yet Pharaoh remained stubborn, and he would not let
the people go.

8Then the LORD said to Moses and Aaron,
"Each of you take handfuls of soot from the kiln,
and let Moses throw it toward the sky in the sight
of Pharaoh. 9It shall become a fine dust all over
the land of Egypt, and cause an inflammation
breaking out in boils on man and beast throughout the land of Egypt." 10So they took soot of
the kiln and appeared before Pharaoh; Moses
threw it toward the sky, and it caused an
inflammation breaking out in boils on man and
beast. 11The magicians were unable to confront
Moses because of the inflammation, for the
inflammation afflicted the magicians as well as
all the other Egyptians. 12But the LORD stiffened
the heart of Pharaoh, and he would not heed
them, just as the LORD had told Moses.

13The LORD said to Moses, "Early in the
morning present yourself to Pharaoh and say

הַזֶּה בָּאָרֶץ׃ 6 וַיַּעַשׂ יְהוָה אֶת־הַדָּבָר הַזֶּה
מִמָּחֳרָת וַיָּמָת כֹּל מִקְנֵה מִצְרָיִם וּמִמִּקְנֵה
בְנֵי־יִשְׂרָאֵל לֹא־מֵת אֶחָד׃ 7 וַיִּשְׁלַח פַּרְעֹה
וְהִנֵּה לֹא־מֵת מִמִּקְנֵה יִשְׂרָאֵל עַד־
אֶחָד וַיִּכְבַּד לֵב פַּרְעֹה וְלֹא שִׁלַּח אֶת־
הָעָם׃ פ

8 וַיֹּאמֶר יְהוָה אֶל־מֹשֶׁה וְאֶל־אַהֲרֹן קְחוּ
לָכֶם מְלֹא חָפְנֵיכֶם פִּיחַ כִּבְשָׁן וּזְרָקוֹ
מֹשֶׁה הַשָּׁמַיְמָה לְעֵינֵי פַרְעֹה׃ 9 וְהָיָה
לְאָבָק עַל כָּל־אֶרֶץ מִצְרָיִם וְהָיָה עַל־
הָאָדָם וְעַל־הַבְּהֵמָה לִשְׁחִין פֹּרֵחַ
אֲבַעְבֻּעֹת בְּכָל־אֶרֶץ מִצְרָיִם׃ 10 וַיִּקְחוּ
אֶת־פִּיחַ הַכִּבְשָׁן וַיַּעַמְדוּ לִפְנֵי פַרְעֹה
וַיִּזְרֹק אֹתוֹ מֹשֶׁה הַשָּׁמָיְמָה וַיְהִי שְׁחִין
אֲבַעְבֻּעֹת פֹּרֵחַ בָּאָדָם וּבַבְּהֵמָה׃ 11 וְלֹא־
יָכְלוּ הַחַרְטֻמִּים לַעֲמֹד לִפְנֵי מֹשֶׁה מִפְּנֵי
הַשְּׁחִין כִּי־הָיָה הַשְּׁחִין בַּחַרְטֻמִּם וּבְכָל־
מִצְרָיִם׃ 12 וַיְחַזֵּק יְהוָה אֶת־לֵב פַּרְעֹה
וְלֹא שָׁמַע אֲלֵהֶם כַּאֲשֶׁר דִּבֶּר יְהוָה
אֶל־מֹשֶׁה׃ ס

13 וַיֹּאמֶר יְהוָה אֶל־מֹשֶׁה הַשְׁכֵּם בַּבֹּקֶר
וְהִתְיַצֵּב לִפְנֵי פַרְעֹה וְאָמַרְתָּ אֵלָיו כֹּה־

7. Pharaoh's need to learn whether the prediction made in verse 4 was fulfilled betrays a weakened self-confidence. Yet the clear evidence of God's power only reinforces his stubbornness.

SIXTH PLAGUE: BOILS (*sh'ḥin*) (vv. 8–12)

As the third in this group of three, this affliction arrives without warning. The plagues now become more intense. Words in Aramaic and Arabic from a root similar to *sh'ḥin* mean "to be hot; to be inflamed." Thus it probably refers to an inflammation. There is great irony in the fact that Pharaoh's magicians were themselves so afflicted by the disease as to be totally immobilized.

8. soot from the kiln The significance of this substance and of the accompanying action is unclear.

in the sight of Pharaoh So that he knows that this particular outbreak is not the familiar, common type but one that has been sent by God for a particular time and purpose.

9. breaking out This probably refers to the skin pustules and ulceration that characterize the disease known today as anthrax.

12. See 8:15, which implies that Pharaoh himself stiffened his heart.

SEVENTH PLAGUE: HAIL (*barad*) (vv. 13–35)

The third (and final) group of three plagues now begins. An escalation in terror and ruin will set

CHAPTER 9

12. But the LORD stiffened the heart of Pharaoh "Those in whom viciousness becomes second nature, those in whom brutality is linked with haughtiness, forfeit their ability and therefore their right" to the gift of free will (Heschel).

to him, 'Thus says the LORD, the God of the Hebrews: Let My people go to worship Me. ¹⁴For this time I will send all My plagues upon your person, and your courtiers, and your people, in order that you may know that there is none like Me in all the world. ¹⁵I could have stretched forth My hand and stricken you and your people with pestilence, and you would have been effaced from the earth. ¹⁶Nevertheless I have spared you for this purpose: in order to show you My power, and in order that My fame may resound throughout the world. ¹⁷Yet you continue to thwart My people, and do not let them go! ¹⁸This time tomorrow I will rain down a very heavy hail, such as has not been in Egypt from the day it was founded until now. ¹⁹There-fore, order your livestock and everything you have in the open brought under shelter; every man and beast that is found outside, not having been brought indoors, shall perish when the hail comes down upon them!'" ²⁰Those among Pharaoh's courtiers who feared the LORD's word brought their slaves and livestock indoors to safety; ²¹but those who paid no regard to the word of the LORD left their slaves and livestock in the open.

²²The LORD said to Moses, "Hold out your arm toward the sky that hail may fall on all the land of Egypt, upon man and beast and all the grasses of the field in the land of Egypt." ²³So Moses held out his rod toward the sky, and the LORD sent thunder and hail, and fire streamed down to the ground, as the LORD rained down hail upon the land of Egypt. ²⁴The hail was very heavy—fire flashing in the midst of the hail—such as had not fallen on the land of Egypt since it had become a nation. ²⁵Throughout the

אָמַ֨ר יְהֹוָ֜ה אֱלֹהֵ֤י הָֽעִבְרִים֙ שַׁלַּ֣ח אֶת־עַמִּ֔י וְיַֽעַבְדֻֽנִי׃ 14 כִּ֣י ׀ בַּפַּ֣עַם הַזֹּ֗את אֲנִ֨י שֹׁלֵ֜חַ אֶת־כׇּל־מַגֵּפֹתַי֙ אֶֽל־לִבְּךָ֔ וּבַעֲבָדֶ֖יךָ וּבְעַמֶּ֑ךָ בַּעֲב֣וּר תֵּדַ֔ע כִּ֛י אֵ֥ין כָּמֹ֖נִי בְּכׇל־הָאָֽרֶץ׃ 15 כִּ֤י עַתָּה֙ שָׁלַ֣חְתִּי אֶת־יָדִ֔י וָאַ֥ךְ אוֹתְךָ֛ וְאֶֽת־עַמְּךָ֖ בַּדָּ֑בֶר וַתִּכָּחֵ֖ד מִן־הָאָֽרֶץ׃ 16 וְאוּלָ֗ם בַּעֲב֥וּר זֹאת֙ הֶעֱמַדְתִּ֔יךָ בַּעֲב֖וּר הַרְאֹתְךָ֣ אֶת־כֹּחִ֑י וּלְמַ֛עַן סַפֵּ֥ר שְׁמִ֖י בְּכׇל־הָאָֽרֶץ׃ 17 עוֹדְךָ֖ מִסְתּוֹלֵ֣ל בְּעַמִּ֑י לְבִלְתִּ֖י שַׁלְּחָֽם׃ 18 הִנְנִ֤י מַמְטִיר֙ כָּעֵ֣ת מָחָ֔ר בָּרָ֖ד כָּבֵ֣ד מְאֹ֑ד אֲשֶׁ֨ר לֹא־הָיָ֤ה כָמֹ֙הוּ֙ בְּמִצְרַ֔יִם לְמִן־הַיּ֥וֹם הִוָּסְדָ֖ה וְעַד־עָֽתָּה׃ 19 וְעַתָּ֗ה שְׁלַ֤ח הָעֵז֙ אֶֽת־מִקְנְךָ֔ וְאֵ֛ת כׇּל־אֲשֶׁ֥ר לְךָ֖ בַּשָּׂדֶ֑ה כׇּל־הָאָדָ֨ם וְהַבְּהֵמָ֜ה אֲשֶֽׁר־יִמָּצֵ֣א בַשָּׂדֶ֗ה וְלֹ֤א יֵֽאָסֵף֙ הַבַּ֔יְתָה וְיָרַ֧ד עֲלֵהֶ֛ם הַבָּרָ֖ד וָמֵֽתוּ׃ 20 הַיָּרֵא֙ אֶת־דְּבַ֣ר יְהֹוָ֔ה מֵֽעַבְדֵ֖י פַּרְעֹ֑ה הֵנִ֛יס אֶת־עֲבָדָ֥יו וְאֶת־מִקְנֵ֖הוּ אֶל־הַבָּתִּֽים׃ 21 וַאֲשֶׁ֤ר לֹא־שָׂם֙ לִבּ֔וֹ אֶל־דְּבַ֖ר יְהֹוָ֑ה וַֽיַּעֲזֹ֛ב אֶת־עֲבָדָ֥יו וְאֶת־מִקְנֵ֖הוּ בַּשָּׂדֶֽה׃ פ

22 וַיֹּ֨אמֶר יְהֹוָ֜ה אֶל־מֹשֶׁ֗ה נְטֵ֤ה אֶת־יָֽדְךָ֙ עַל־הַשָּׁמַ֔יִם וִיהִ֥י בָרָ֖ד בְּכׇל־אֶ֣רֶץ מִצְרָ֑יִם עַל־הָֽאָדָ֣ם וְעַל־הַבְּהֵמָ֗ה וְעַ֛ל כׇּל־עֵ֥שֶׂב הַשָּׂדֶ֖ה בְּאֶ֥רֶץ מִצְרָֽיִם׃ 23 וַיֵּ֨ט מֹשֶׁ֣ה אֶת־מַטֵּ֘הוּ֮ עַל־הַשָּׁמַ֒יִם֒ וַֽיהֹוָ֗ה נָתַ֤ן קֹלֹת֙ וּבָרָ֔ד וַתִּ֥הֲלַךְ אֵ֖שׁ אָ֑רְצָה וַיַּמְטֵ֧ר יְהֹוָ֛ה בָּרָ֖ד עַל־אֶ֥רֶץ מִצְרָֽיִם׃ 24 וַיְהִ֣י בָרָ֔ד וְאֵ֕שׁ מִתְלַקַּ֖חַת בְּת֣וֹךְ הַבָּרָ֑ד כָּבֵ֣ד מְאֹ֔ד אֲשֶׁ֨ר לֹֽא־הָיָ֤ה כָמֹ֙הוּ֙ בְּכׇל־אֶ֣רֶץ מִצְרַ֔יִם מֵאָ֖ז הָיְתָ֥ה לְגֽוֹי׃ 25 וַיַּ֨ךְ הַבָּרָ֜ד בְּכׇל־אֶ֣רֶץ

שביעי

---

the stage for the climactic catastrophe. This accounts for the unusual length of the next warning to Pharaoh. For the first time, the Egyptians and their livestock will be offered the chance to take shelter, and some will avail themselves of it. Also for the first time, Pharaoh will openly admit to being at fault.

14. all My plagues This phrase either introduces the last four plagues or alludes to their overwhelming consequences.

land of Egypt the hail struck down all that were
in the open, both man and beast; the hail also
struck down all the grasses of the field and shattered all the trees of the field. 26Only in the region of Goshen, where the Israelites were, there
was no hail.

27Thereupon Pharaoh sent for Moses and
Aaron and said to them, "I stand guilty this time.
The LORD is in the right, and I and my people
are in the wrong. 28Plead with the LORD that
there may be an end of God's thunder and of
hail. I will let you go; you need stay no longer."
29Moses said to him, "As I go out of the city,
I shall spread out my hands to the LORD; the
thunder will cease and the hail will fall no more,
so that you may know that the earth is the
LORD's. 30But I know that you and your courtiers do not yet fear the LORD God."—31Now the
flax and barley were ruined, for the barley was
in the ear and the flax was in bud; 32but the
wheat and the emmer were not hurt, for they
ripen late.—33Leaving Pharaoh, Moses went
outside the city and spread out his hands to the
LORD: the thunder and the hail ceased, and no

מִצְרַיִם אֵת כׇּל־אֲשֶׁר בַּשָּׂדֶה מֵאָדָם וְעַד־
בְּהֵמָה וְאֵת כׇּל־עֵשֶׂב הַשָּׂדֶה הִכָּה הַבָּרָד
וְאֶת־כׇּל־עֵץ הַשָּׂדֶה שִׁבֵּר׃ 26 רַק בְּאֶרֶץ
גֹּשֶׁן אֲשֶׁר־שָׁם בְּנֵי יִשְׂרָאֵל לֹא הָיָה בָּרָד׃
27 וַיִּשְׁלַח פַּרְעֹה וַיִּקְרָא לְמֹשֶׁה וּלְאַהֲרֹן
וַיֹּאמֶר אֲלֵהֶם חָטָאתִי הַפָּעַם יְהוָה
הַצַּדִּיק וַאֲנִי וְעַמִּי הָרְשָׁעִים׃ 28 הַעְתִּירוּ
אֶל־יְהוָה וְרַב מִהְיֹת קֹלֹת אֱלֹהִים וּבָרָד
וַאֲשַׁלְּחָה אֶתְכֶם וְלֹא תֹסִפוּן לַעֲמֹד׃
29 וַיֹּאמֶר אֵלָיו מֹשֶׁה כְּצֵאתִי אֶת־הָעִיר
אֶפְרֹשׂ אֶת־כַּפַּי אֶל־יְהוָה הַקֹּלוֹת יֶחְדָּלוּן
וְהַבָּרָד לֹא יִהְיֶה־עוֹד לְמַעַן תֵּדַע כִּי
לַיהוָה הָאָרֶץ׃ 30 וְאַתָּה וַעֲבָדֶיךָ יָדַעְתִּי
כִּי טֶרֶם תִּירְאוּן מִפְּנֵי יְהוָה אֱלֹהִים׃
31 וְהַפִּשְׁתָּה וְהַשְּׂעֹרָה נֻכָּתָה כִּי הַשְּׂעֹרָה
אָבִיב וְהַפִּשְׁתָּה גִּבְעֹל׃ 32 וְהַחִטָּה
וְהַכֻּסֶּמֶת לֹא נֻכּוּ כִּי אֲפִילֹת הֵנָּה׃ 33 וַיֵּצֵא פטיר
מֹשֶׁה מֵעִם פַּרְעֹה אֶת־הָעִיר וַיִּפְרֹשׂ כַּפָּיו
אֶל־יְהוָה וַיַּחְדְּלוּ הַקֹּלוֹת וְהַבָּרָד וּמָטָר

27. this time Pharaoh echoes the identical phrase used by God in His forewarning in verse 14.

28. Pharaoh's concession now appears to be unqualified.

29. spread out my hands An attitude of prayer.

that the earth is the LORD's It is God, and not the Egyptian gods, who is sovereign over nature.

30. Moses senses that Pharaoh's confession of guilt consists only of empty words.

31–32. This note creates suspense, because it delays Moses' response to Pharaoh's plea in light of verse 30 and it explains why, despite the devastation of crops caused by the hail, there still remained a residue for the locusts in the next plague (10:5).

In Egypt, flax was normally sown at the beginning of January and was in bloom three weeks later; barley was sown in August and harvested in February.

emmer A species of wheat that, together with barley and winter wheat, made up the three chief cereals of Egypt.

ripen late Wheat and emmer are planted in August and harvested in March or April. Hence, they were less vulnerable than flax and barley.

---

27. The LORD is in the right, and I and my people are in the wrong Pharaoh's words can be punctuated to read, "The LORD is righteous and so am I, but my people are wicked." In other words, perhaps Pharaoh is trying to excuse himself, saying, "Don't blame me! I would have let the Israelites go, but my people would not have let me."

32. The wheat and the emmer were not hurt To leave something for the locusts to devour in the next plague? Or perhaps to teach the lesson that one should always leave an adversary with enough to live on, rather than leave that person with nothing to lose (*Yad Yosef*). Despite the battering, Pharaoh still refuses to give in. The worst of the plagues is yet to come.

rain came pouring down upon the earth. ³⁴But
when Pharaoh saw that the rain and the hail and
the thunder had ceased, he became stubborn
and reverted to his guilty ways, as did his courtiers. ³⁵So Pharaoh's heart stiffened and he
would not let the Israelites go, just as the Lord
had foretold through Moses.

לֹא־נִתַּ֖ךְ אָֽרְצָה׃ 34 וַיַּ֣רְא פַּרְעֹ֗ה כִּֽי־חָדַ֤ל
הַמָּטָ֤ר וְהַבָּרָד֙ וְהַקֹּלֹ֔ת וַיֹּ֖סֶף לַחֲטֹ֑א וַיַּכְבֵּ֥ד
לִבּ֖וֹ ה֥וּא וַעֲבָדָֽיו׃ 35 וַיֶּחֱזַק֙ לֵ֣ב פַּרְעֹ֔ה וְלֹ֥א
שִׁלַּ֖ח אֶת־בְּנֵ֣י יִשְׂרָאֵ֑ל כַּאֲשֶׁ֛ר דִּבֶּ֥ר יְהֹוָ֖ה
בְּיַד־מֹשֶֽׁה׃ פ

34. Once again Pharaoh yields to his treacherous impulses.
35. foretold through Moses This implies that

Moses had previously conveyed to the people
God's foreknowledge of Pharaoh's obstinacy (see
v. 30), a fact not explicitly stated.

הפטרת וארא

HAFTARAH FOR VA-ERA

EZEKIEL 28:25–29:21

This *haftarah* is drawn from Ezekiel's oracles against foreign nations (Ezek. 25–32). The main body of the reading is a series of pronouncements against Egypt. They are framed by two oracles of hope for the people Israel (28:25–26, 29:21), which anticipate their restoration from exile to the Land.

Ezekiel's opening prophecy against Egypt may be dated to the beginning of 586 B.C.E., when the nation Israel placed some hope in an alliance with Egypt during the final, fatal Babylonian siege of Jerusalem (see Jer. 37:5). Israel's vain hope is the basis of the prophet's vilification of an undependable Egypt (Ezek. 29:7). The oracle mocks Egypt, through its Pharaoh (29:3–5).

Key words in Hebrew underscore the themes of Israelite restoration and Egyptian doom. The cluster concerned with ingathering and dispersion, true security and false trust is particularly forceful. In the opening oracle (28:25–26), the house of Israel that has "been dispersed" (*nafotzu*) among the "peoples" (*ammim*) is promised that they will be "gathered" (*kabtzi*) by God to their homeland, where they will "dwell" (*yashvu*) in "security" (*la-vetaḥ*). By contrast, doomed Egypt (in the figure of the "pharaonic fish") will be caught and left "unburied" (*v'lo tikkavetz,* literally "ungathered") on its shores (29:5) or scattered by God (*v'hafitzoti*) among the nations (29:12). So great is their punishment that, although God "will gather" (*akabbetz*) the Egyptians from "the peoples" (*ha-ammim*) among whom they were dispersed (*nafotzu,* 29:13), they will not rise to their former greatness and will never again "be the trust" (*l'mivtaḥ*) of the house of Israel (29:16).

These acts of divine might will convince Israel and Egypt alike that the Lord is the true God. Both of them "shall know" (*v'yad'u*) that the Lord is God (28:26, 29:6,16, 21). This motif of recognition is a signature feature of the prophet Ezekiel, and it echoes the formula first found in the Book of Exodus. There too, by signs and wonders, the Lord promises that both Israel and the Egyptians will come to know (*v'yad'u, viyda·atem*) His awesome might. (On Egypt, see Exod. 7:5, 14:4,18. On Israel, see Exod. 6:7; 10:2) Such knowledge is born of direct experience, a theological assertion confirmed through the specific events of history.

To underscore the effect of divine victory, the Egyptian enemy is portrayed through a figure of mythic arrogance. The Pharaoh is identified with the "mighty monster" of the Nile who proclaims that "My Nile is my own; / I made it for myself" (or even: I have created myself; 29:3). The defeat of this monster (called *tannim,* like *tannin*) echoes God's destruction of ancient sea monsters. Ezekiel mocks the molester's claims of inviolable might. The arrogant king is humbled, flung like a rotten fish on the banks. In this victory God's providential power and might are exalted.

RELATION OF THE *HAFTARAH* TO THE *PARASHAH*

The *parashah* and the *haftarah* present an old and a new judgment against Egypt. As the first judgment came to pass with Israel's liberation, so the new judgment against Egypt is marked by promises of Israel's ingathering and the sprouting of its "horn" of strength, victory (29:21). History is thus seen as a recurrent pattern of divine acts of redemption. As a prophecy of future liberation, Ezekiel draws on the imagery of the first great act of divine salvation for Israel: the Exodus from Egypt. Through His saving acts God again will be recognized as the transcendent source of redemption and will vindicate human hopes in freedom from oppression. The *haftarah* taken from Ezekiel's prophecy is thus a counterpoint to his-

torical despair. The people are challenged to look beyond political alliances and the false confidences they bring (29:6–7,16). Only divine power will liberate the people.

A rich verbal and thematic tapestry links the two units. For example, there are judgments against enemies (*sh'fatim*) and a plagued Nile (*Y'or*), which yields dead fish (Exod. 7:4,20; Ezek. 28:26, 29:3–5,10). The linkage in the motif of both Israel and Egypt coming to know God was noted earlier.

כח 25 כֹּה־אָמַר֩ אֲדֹנָ֨י יְהֹוִ֜ה בְּקַבְּצִ֣י ׀ אֶת־בֵּ֣ית יִשְׂרָאֵ֗ל מִן־הָֽעַמִּים֙ אֲשֶׁ֣ר נָפֹ֣צוּ בָ֔ם וְנִקְדַּ֥שְׁתִּי בָ֖ם לְעֵינֵ֣י הַגּוֹיִ֑ם וְיָֽשְׁבוּ֙ עַל־אַדְמָתָ֔ם אֲשֶׁ֥ר נָתַ֖תִּי לְעַבְדִּ֥י לְיַעֲקֹֽב׃ 26 וְיָֽשְׁב֣וּ עָלֶ֘יהָ֮ לָבֶ֒טַח֒ וּבָנ֤וּ בָתִּים֙ וְנָטְע֣וּ כְרָמִ֔ים וְיָֽשְׁב֖וּ לָבֶ֑טַח בַּֽעֲשׂוֹתִ֣י שְׁפָטִ֗ים בְּכֹ֞ל הַשָּׁאטִ֤ים* אֹתָם֙ מִסְּבִ֣יבוֹתָ֔ם וְיָ֣דְע֔וּ כִּ֛י אֲנִ֥י יְהֹוָ֖ה אֱלֹֽהֵיהֶֽם׃ ס

כט בַּשָּׁנָ֣ה הָעֲשִׂירִ֗ית בָּעֲשִׂרִי֙ בִּשְׁנֵ֣ים עָשָׂ֣ר לַחֹ֔דֶשׁ הָיָ֥ה דְבַר־יְהֹוָ֖ה אֵלַ֥י לֵאמֹֽר׃ 2 בֶּן־אָדָ֕ם שִׂ֣ים פָּנֶ֔יךָ עַל־פַּרְעֹ֖ה מֶ֣לֶךְ מִצְרָ֑יִם וְהִנָּבֵ֣א עָלָ֔יו וְעַל־מִצְרַ֖יִם כֻּלָּֽהּ׃ 3 דַּבֵּ֨ר וְאָמַרְתָּ֜ כֹּה־אָמַ֣ר ׀ אֲדֹנָ֣י יְהֹוִ֗ה הִנְנִ֤י עָלֶ֨יךָ֙ פַּרְעֹ֣ה מֶֽלֶךְ־מִצְרַ֔יִם הַתַּנִּים֙ הַגָּד֔וֹל הָרֹבֵ֖ץ בְּת֣וֹךְ יְאֹרָ֑יו אֲשֶׁ֥ר אָמַ֖ר לִ֣י יְאֹרִ֑י וַאֲנִ֥י עֲשִׂיתִֽנִי׃

יתיר א׳   v. 26.

28 25Thus said the Lord GOD: When I have gathered the House of Israel from the peoples among which they have been dispersed, and have shown Myself holy through them in the sight of the nations, they shall settle on their own soil, which I gave to My servant Jacob, 26and they shall dwell on it in security. They shall build houses and plant vineyards, and shall dwell on it in security, when I have meted out punishment to all those about them who despise them. And they shall know that I the LORD am their God.

29 In the tenth year, on the twelfth day of the tenth month, the word of the LORD came to me: 2O mortal, turn your face against Pharaoh king of Egypt, and prophesy against him and against all Egypt. 3Speak these words:

Thus said the Lord GOD:

I am going to deal with you, O Pharaoh king of Egypt,

Mighty monster, sprawling in your channels,

Who said,

My Nile is my own;

I made it for myself.

Ezekiel 28:25. When I . . . have shown Myself holy through them   Ezekiel expresses the striking notion that God Himself is sanctified. God declares that His sanctity is manifest in His restoration of the people Israel to their homeland.

Ezekiel 29:1. In the tenth year   Dated from 597 B.C.E., the beginning of King Jehoiachin's exile to Babylon.

3. I made it for myself   Pharaoh boasts of having created the Nile. He thus claims self-sufficiency. Alternatively, the Hebrew verb here (*asitini*) means "I have made myself." This is the more radical mythic assertion, laden with the hubris of self-creation. It is so understood in many rabbinic *midrashim* and liturgical poems.

4I will put hooks in your jaws,
And make the fish of your channels
Cling to your scales;
I will haul you up from your channels,
With all the fish of your channels
Clinging to your scales.
5And I will fling you into the desert,
With all the fish of your channels.
You shall be left lying in the open,
Ungathered and unburied:
I have given you as food
To the beasts of the earth
And the birds of the sky.
6Then all the inhabitants of Egypt shall know
That I am the LORD.
Because you were a staff of reed
To the House of Israel:
7When they grasped you with the hand, you would splinter,
And wound all their shoulders,
And when they leaned on you, you would break,
And make all their loins unsteady.
8Assuredly, thus said the Lord GOD: Lo, I will
bring a sword against you, and will cut off man
and beast from you, 9so that the land of Egypt
shall fall into desolation and ruin. And they shall
know that I am the LORD—because he boasted,
"The Nile is mine, and I made it." 10Assuredly,
I am going to deal with you and your channels,
and I will reduce the land of Egypt to utter ruin
and desolation, from Migdol to Syene, all the
way to the border of Nubia. 11No foot of man
shall traverse it, and no foot of beast shall tra-

4 וְנָתַתִּי חחיים חַחִים בִּלְחָיֶיךָ
וְהִדְבַּקְתִּי דְגַת־יְאֹרֶיךָ
בְּקַשְׂקְשֹׂתֶיךָ
וְהַעֲלִיתִיךָ מִתּוֹךְ יְאֹרֶיךָ
וְאֵת כָּל־דְּגַת יְאֹרֶיךָ
בְּקַשְׂקְשֹׂתֶיךָ תִּדְבָּק׃
5 וּנְטַשְׁתִּיךָ הַמִּדְבָּרָה
אוֹתְךָ וְאֵת כָּל־דְּגַת יְאֹרֶיךָ
עַל־פְּנֵי הַשָּׂדֶה תִּפּוֹל
לֹא תֵאָסֵף וְלֹא תִקָּבֵץ
לְחַיַּת הָאָרֶץ
וּלְעוֹף הַשָּׁמַיִם
נְתַתִּיךָ לְאָכְלָה׃
6 וְיָדְעוּ כָּל־יֹשְׁבֵי מִצְרַיִם
כִּי אֲנִי יְהוָה
יַעַן הֱיוֹתָם מִשְׁעֶנֶת קָנֶה
לְבֵית יִשְׂרָאֵל׃
7 בְּתָפְשָׂם בְּךָ בככפך בַכַּף תֵּרוֹץ
וּבָקַעְתָּ לָהֶם כָּל־כָּתֵף
וּבְהִשָּׁעֲנָם עָלֶיךָ תִּשָּׁבֵר
וְהַעֲמַדְתָּ לָהֶם כָּל־מָתְנָיִם׃ ס
8 לָכֵן כֹּה אָמַר אֲדֹנָי יְהוִה הִנְנִי מֵבִיא
עָלַיִךְ חָרֶב וְהִכְרַתִּי מִמֵּךְ אָדָם וּבְהֵמָה׃
9 וְהָיְתָה אֶרֶץ־מִצְרַיִם לִשְׁמָמָה וְחָרְבָּה
וְיָדְעוּ כִּי־אֲנִי יְהוָה יַעַן אָמַר יְאֹר לִי וַאֲנִי
עָשִׂיתִי׃ 10 לָכֵן הִנְנִי אֵלֶיךָ וְאֶל־יְאֹרֶיךָ
וְנָתַתִּי אֶת־אֶרֶץ מִצְרַיִם לְחָרְבוֹת חֹרֶב
שְׁמָמָה מִמִּגְדֹּל סְוֵנֵה וְעַד־גְּבוּל כּוּשׁ׃
11 לֹא תַעֲבָר־בָּהּ רֶגֶל אָדָם וְרֶגֶל בְּהֵמָה
לֹא תַעֲבָר־בָּהּ וְלֹא תֵשֵׁב אַרְבָּעִים שָׁנָה׃

4. I will put hooks in your jaws This capture and destruction of a sea serpent allude to ancient mythic motifs of battles between God and the *tannin*-monster found elsewhere in the Bible (see Isa. 51:9; Ps. 74:13ff.; Job 26:12).

6. a staff of reed The portrayal of false confidence in political alliances as trust in a broken reed is first found in the prophecies of Isaiah, where an Assyrian envoy describes Israel's trust in Egypt in such terms (Isa. 36:6). By contrast, a postexilic prophecy portrays God's chosen servant as a reliable reed, an unbreakable source of divine instruction to the nations (Isa. 42:1–4).

10. from Migdol to Syene A comprehensive

12 וְנָתַתִּי אֶת־אֶרֶץ מִצְרַיִם שְׁמָמָה בְּתוֹךְ ׀
אֲרָצוֹת נְשַׁמּוֹת וְעָרֶיהָ בְּתוֹךְ עָרִים
מָחֳרָבוֹת תִּהְיֶיןָ שְׁמָמָה אַרְבָּעִים שָׁנָה
וַהֲפִצֹתִי אֶת־מִצְרַיִם בַּגּוֹיִם וְזֵרִיתִים
בָּאֲרָצוֹת׃ פ
13 כִּי כֹּה אָמַר אֲדֹנָי יְהוִה מִקֵּץ אַרְבָּעִים
שָׁנָה אֲקַבֵּץ אֶת־מִצְרַיִם מִן־הָעַמִּים
אֲשֶׁר־נָפֹצוּ שָׁמָּה׃ 14 וְשַׁבְתִּי אֶת־שְׁבוּת
מִצְרַיִם וַהֲשִׁבֹתִי אֹתָם אֶרֶץ פַּתְרוֹס
עַל־אֶרֶץ מְכוּרָתָם וְהָיוּ שָׁם מַמְלָכָה
שְׁפָלָה׃ 15 מִן־הַמַּמְלָכוֹת תִּהְיֶה שְׁפָלָה
וְלֹא־תִתְנַשֵּׂא עוֹד עַל־הַגּוֹיִם וְהִמְעַטְתִּים
לְבִלְתִּי רְדוֹת בַּגּוֹיִם׃ 16 וְלֹא יִהְיֶה־עוֹד
לְבֵית יִשְׂרָאֵל לְמִבְטָח מַזְכִּיר עָוֺן
בִּפְנוֹתָם אַחֲרֵיהֶם וְיָדְעוּ כִּי אֲנִי אֲדֹנָי
יְהוִה׃ פ

17 וַיְהִי בְּעֶשְׂרִים וָשֶׁבַע שָׁנָה בָּרִאשׁוֹן
בְּאֶחָד לַחֹדֶשׁ הָיָה דְבַר־יְהוָה אֵלַי
לֵאמֹר׃ 18 בֶּן־אָדָם נְבוּכַדְרֶאצַּר מֶלֶךְ־בָּבֶל
הֶעֱבִיד אֶת־חֵילוֹ עֲבֹדָה גְדֹלָה אֶל־צֹר
כָּל־רֹאשׁ מֻקְרָח וְכָל־כָּתֵף מְרוּטָה וְשָׂכָר
לֹא־הָיָה לוֹ וּלְחֵילוֹ מִצֹּר עַל־הָעֲבֹדָה
אֲשֶׁר־עָבַד עָלֶיהָ׃ ס 19 לָכֵן כֹּה אָמַר
אֲדֹנָי יְהוִה הִנְנִי נֹתֵן לִנְבוּכַדְרֶאצַּר מֶלֶךְ־
בָּבֶל אֶת־אֶרֶץ מִצְרָיִם וְנָשָׂא הֲמֹנָהּ וְשָׁלַל

verse it; and it shall remain uninhabited for forty
years. 12For forty years I will make the land of
Egypt the most desolate of desolate lands, and
its cities shall be the most desolate of ruined
cities. And I will scatter the Egyptians among
the nations and disperse them throughout the
countries.

13Further, thus said the Lord God: After a period of forty years I will gather the Egyptians
from the peoples among whom they were dispersed. 14I will restore the fortunes of the Egyptians and bring them back to the land of their
origin, the land of Pathros, and there they shall
be a lowly kingdom. 15It shall be the lowliest of
all the kingdoms, and shall not lord it over the
nations again. I will reduce the Egyptians, so
that they shall have no dominion over the nations. 16Never again shall they be the trust of
the House of Israel, recalling its guilt in having
turned to them. And they shall know that I am
the Lord God.

17In the twenty-seventh year, on the first day
of the first month, the word of the Lord came
to me: 18O mortal, King Nebuchadrezzar of
Babylon has made his army expend vast labor
on Tyre; every head is rubbed bald and every
shoulder scraped. But he and his army have had
no return for the labor he expended on Tyre.
19Assuredly, thus said the Lord God: I will give
the land of Egypt to Nebuchadrezzar, king of

geographic designation of Egypt, from north to south. (Cf. the designation of Israel as "from Dan to Beersheba" in Judg. 20:1.)

12. forty years The number 40 is well known in biblical literature as a comprehensive period of time, perhaps two generations. It is used to mark the number of years during which the Israelites wandered in the wilderness, in punishment for the period of 40 days in which the faithless spies scouted the land (Num. 14:33–34).

17ff. This oracle promises the spoils of Egypt to King Nebuchadrezzar of Babylon, as a reward for his siege against Tyre. This prophecy is dated to 571 B.C.E. (the 27th year of Jehoiachin's exile), 17 years after the announcement of Egypt's doom (29:1). This is a transformation of an older oracle against Tyre, in which it was predicted that Nebuchadrezzar would "plunder its wealth" (Ezek. 26:7–14). Because the prophecy did not come to pass, Ezekiel now promises Nebuchadrezzar the booty of Egypt. This is a classic example of reapplying a prophecy that failed to materialize in the specifics of its original form. Here it dramatizes the providential role of Israel's God in the fate of other nations.

18. Nebuchadrezzar This form corresponds to the Babylonian name. The better known biblical variant is "Nebuchadnezzar."

Babylon. He shall carry off her wealth and take her spoil and seize her booty; and she shall be the recompense of his army. 20As the wage for which he labored, for what they did for Me, I give him the land of Egypt—declares the Lord God.

21On that day I will endow the House of Israel with strength, and you shall be vindicated among them. And they shall know that I am the Lord.

שְׁלָלָהּ וּבָזַז בִּזָּהּ וְהָיְתָה שָׂכָר לְחֵילוֹ׃
20 פְּעֻלָּתוֹ אֲשֶׁר־עָבַד בָּהּ נָתַתִּי לוֹ אֶת־
אֶרֶץ מִצְרָיִם אֲשֶׁר עָשׂוּ לִי נְאֻם אֲדֹנָי
יְהוִה׃ ס
21 בַּיּוֹם הַהוּא אַצְמִיחַ קֶרֶן לְבֵית יִשְׂרָאֵל
וּלְךָ אֶתֵּן פִּתְחוֹן־פֶּה בְּתוֹכָם וְיָדְעוּ כִּי־
אֲנִי יְהוָה׃ פ

21. I will endow the House of Israel with strength, and you shall be vindicated among them Literally, "I will cause a horn to sprout for the House of Israel, and I will grant you an opening of the mouth." Some commentators understand the horn as referring to Cyrus, whose edict in 538 B.C.E. allowed Babylonian Jews to return to the land of Israel (Rashi, Radak).

BO

10 Then the LORD said to Moses, "Go to
Pharaoh. For I have hardened his heart and the
hearts of his courtiers, in order that I may display these My signs among them, 2and that you
may recount in the hearing of your sons and
of your sons' sons how I made a mockery of the
Egyptians and how I displayed My signs among
them—in order that you may know that I am
the LORD." 3So Moses and Aaron went to Pharaoh and said to him, "Thus says the LORD, the
God of the Hebrews, 'How long will you refuse
to humble yourself before Me? Let My people

בא

י וַיֹּ֣אמֶר יְהוָה֙ אֶל־מֹשֶׁ֔ה בֹּ֖א אֶל־פַּרְעֹ֑ה
כִּֽי־אֲנִ֞י הִכְבַּ֤דְתִּי אֶת־לִבּוֹ֙ וְאֶת־לֵ֣ב עֲבָדָ֔יו
לְמַ֗עַן שִׁתִ֛י אֹתֹתַ֥י אֵ֖לֶּה בְּקִרְבּֽוֹ׃ 2 וּלְמַ֡עַן
תְּסַפֵּר֩ בְּאָזְנֵ֨י בִנְךָ֜ וּבֶן־בִּנְךָ֗ אֵ֣ת אֲשֶׁ֤ר
הִתְעַלַּ֙לְתִּי֙ בְּמִצְרַ֔יִם וְאֶת־אֹתֹתַ֖י אֲשֶׁר־
שַׂ֣מְתִּי בָ֑ם וִידַעְתֶּ֖ם כִּֽי־אֲנִ֥י יְהוָֽה׃ 3 וַיָּבֹ֨א
מֹשֶׁ֣ה וְאַהֲרֹן֮ אֶל־פַּרְעֹה֒ וַיֹּאמְר֣וּ אֵלָ֗יו
כֹּֽה־אָמַ֤ר יְהוָה֙ אֱלֹהֵ֣י הָֽעִבְרִ֔ים עַד־מָתַ֣י
מֵאַ֔נְתָּ לֵעָנֹ֖ת מִפָּנָ֑י שַׁלַּ֥ח עַמִּ֖י וְיַֽעַבְדֻֽנִי׃

THE PLAGUES (*continued*)

EIGHTH PLAGUE: LOCUSTS (*arbeh*) (10:1–20)

The locust swarm is one of the worst scourges. An area of one square kilometer can contain 50 million such insects; in a single night they can devour 100,000 tons of vegetation. Unusually humid weather conditions contribute to their proliferation. A long section containing some new features introduces the plague. The courtiers boldly challenge Pharaoh, who makes concessions in advance of the actual plague. The plague serves not only to coerce the Egyptians but also to educate the Israelites.

1. I have hardened his heart See Comment to 4:21.

in order that The multiplication of these "signs" enhances the evidence pointing to God's power.

2. that you may recount Moses is addressed as the personification of the people Israel, for whom the message is really intended. Hence, in Hebrew the last verb (for "that you may know") is in the plural form. As the cycle of plagues draws to its inevitable conclusion, its larger historical significance is brought into view. The events are to be indelibly marked on the collective memory of the people Israel and thus become a permanent part of the lore that is transmitted from generation to generation.

I made a mockery This was done by humbling the mighty Egyptian state, by humiliating Pharaoh, its "divine" king, and by exposing the impotence of its gods.

The events of this *parashah* record the birth of the Israelite people. Three final plagues, each more devastating than the one before, force Pharaoh to relent. In anticipation of their leaving, the Israelites celebrate the first *Pesaḥ,* which will shape the annual celebration of the event for generations to come. Halfway through the *parashah,* the tone of the Torah changes from narrative to legislation, as the Israelites are given commands for marking *Pesaḥ* and for re-enacting it in future generations.

CHAPTER 10

1. I have hardened his heart Pharaoh's repeated refusals to let the slaves go have made it virtually impossible for him to change now. In effect, he has given away his freedom to decide. The talmudic sage Resh Lakish is quoted as saying, "When God warns someone once, twice, and even a third time and that person does not repent, then and only then does God close the person's heart against repentance and exact punishment for his sins." Nonetheless, the sensitive reader is bothered by this notion of God setting Pharaoh up for punishment by making inevitable a situation in which he will not be allowed to repent. Although the Torah may find it necessary to emphasize the Exodus as God's triumph over the forces of tyranny and idolatry, later texts will portray God as grieving for the Egyptians who are also God's children and suffer because of Pharaoh's stubbornness.

go that they may worship Me. [4]For if you refuse to let My people go, tomorrow I will bring locusts on your territory. [5]They shall cover the surface of the land, so that no one will be able to see the land. They shall devour the surviving remnant that was left to you after the hail; and they shall eat away all your trees that grow in the field. [6]Moreover, they shall fill your palaces and the houses of all your courtiers and of all the Egyptians—something that neither your fathers nor fathers' fathers have seen from the day they appeared on earth to this day.'" With that he turned and left Pharaoh's presence.

[7]Pharaoh's courtiers said to him, "How long shall this one be a snare to us? Let the men go to worship the LORD their God! Are you not yet aware that Egypt is lost?" [8]So Moses and Aaron were brought back to Pharaoh and he said to them, "Go, worship the LORD your God! Who are the ones to go?" [9]Moses replied, "We will all go, young and old: we will go with our sons and daughters, our flocks and herds; for we must observe the LORD's festival." [10]But he said to them, "The LORD be with you the same as I mean to let your children go with you! Clearly, you are bent on mischief. [11]No! You menfolk go and worship the LORD, since that is what you want." And they were expelled from Pharaoh's presence.

4 כִּ֛י אִם־מָאֵ֥ן אַתָּ֖ה לְשַׁלֵּ֣חַ אֶת־עַמִּ֑י הִנְנִ֨י
מֵבִ֥יא מָחָ֛ר אַרְבֶּ֖ה בִּגְבֻלֶֽךָ׃ 5 וְכִסָּ֣ה אֶת־
עֵ֣ין הָאָ֔רֶץ וְלֹ֥א יוּכַ֖ל לִרְאֹ֣ת אֶת־הָאָ֑רֶץ
וְאָכַ֣ל ׀ אֶת־יֶ֣תֶר הַפְּלֵטָ֗ה הַנִּשְׁאֶ֤רֶת לָכֶם֙
מִן־הַבָּרָ֔ד וְאָכַל֙ אֶת־כָּל־הָעֵ֔ץ הַצֹּמֵ֥חַ
לָכֶ֖ם מִן־הַשָּׂדֶֽה׃ 6 וּמָלְא֨וּ בָתֶּ֜יךָ וּבָתֵּ֣י
כָל־עֲבָדֶ֘יךָ֮ וּבָתֵּ֣י כָל־מִצְרַיִם֒ אֲשֶׁ֨ר לֹֽא־
רָא֤וּ אֲבֹתֶ֙יךָ֙ וַאֲב֣וֹת אֲבֹתֶ֔יךָ מִיּ֗וֹם הֱיוֹתָם֙
עַל־הָ֣אֲדָמָ֔ה עַ֖ד הַיּ֣וֹם הַזֶּ֑ה וַיִּ֖פֶן וַיֵּצֵ֥א
מֵעִ֥ם פַּרְעֹֽה׃
7 וַיֹּאמְר֜וּ עַבְדֵ֨י פַרְעֹ֜ה אֵלָ֗יו עַד־מָתַי֙ יִהְיֶ֨ה
זֶ֤ה לָ֙נוּ֙ לְמוֹקֵ֔שׁ שַׁלַּח֙ אֶת־הָ֣אֲנָשִׁ֔ים
וְיַֽעַבְד֖וּ אֶת־יְהוָ֣ה אֱלֹהֵיהֶ֑ם הֲטֶ֣רֶם תֵּדַ֔ע
כִּ֥י אָבְדָ֖ה מִצְרָֽיִם׃ 8 וַיּוּשַׁ֞ב אֶת־מֹשֶׁ֤ה
וְאֶֽת־אַהֲרֹן֙ אֶל־פַּרְעֹ֔ה וַיֹּ֣אמֶר אֲלֵהֶ֔ם
לְכ֖וּ עִבְד֣וּ אֶת־יְהוָ֣ה אֱלֹהֵיכֶ֑ם מִ֥י וָמִ֖י
הַהֹלְכִֽים׃ 9 וַיֹּ֣אמֶר מֹשֶׁ֔ה בִּנְעָרֵ֥ינוּ
וּבִזְקֵנֵ֖ינוּ נֵלֵ֑ךְ בְּבָנֵ֨ינוּ וּבִבְנוֹתֵ֜נוּ בְּצֹאנֵ֤נוּ
וּבִבְקָרֵ֙נוּ֙ נֵלֵ֔ךְ כִּ֥י חַג־יְהוָ֖ה לָֽנוּ׃ 10 וַיֹּ֣אמֶר
אֲלֵהֶ֗ם יְהִ֨י כֵ֤ן יְהוָה֙ עִמָּכֶ֔ם כַּאֲשֶׁ֛ר אֲשַׁלַּ֥ח
אֶתְכֶ֖ם וְאֶת־טַפְּכֶ֑ם רְא֕וּ כִּ֥י רָעָ֖ה נֶ֥גֶד
פְּנֵיכֶֽם׃ 11 לֹ֣א כֵ֗ן לְכוּ־נָ֤א הַגְּבָרִים֙ וְעִבְד֣וּ
אֶת־יְהוָ֔ה כִּ֥י אֹתָ֖הּ אַתֶּ֣ם מְבַקְשִׁ֑ים וַיְגָ֣רֶשׁ
אֹתָ֔ם מֵאֵ֖ת פְּנֵ֥י פַרְעֹֽה׃ פ שני

6. your . . . fathers' fathers A counterpoint to "your sons' sons" in verse 2. For Israel, the future is one of enduring inspiration and celebration. For Egypt, the past is recalled to paint a picture of impending catastrophe.

7. this one A disrespectful allusion to Moses.
a snare We are inviting disaster.

9. the LORD's festival Hebrew: *ḥag.* See Comment to 5:1.

10. you are bent on mischief The literal meaning of the Hebrew—"evil is before your faces"—has given rise to various interpretations: "You have evil intentions," i.e., you do not intend to return after three days, or "you are foredoomed to disaster," an understanding that would seem to be supported by 32:12.

11. The women and children are to be held hostage to ensure the return of the men.

9. young and old Why does Moses emphasize "young and old"? One commentator states, "because no celebration is complete without children." A second adds, "a child without parents is an orphan, but a nation without children is an orphan people." Still another takes the words to mean, "We will go with our old people who feel rejuvenated at the prospect of living in freedom."

12Then the LORD said to Moses, "Hold out your arm over the land of Egypt for the locusts, that they may come upon the land of Egypt and eat up all the grasses in the land, whatever the hail has left." 13So Moses held out his rod over the land of Egypt, and the LORD drove an east wind over the land all that day and all night; and when morning came, the east wind had brought the locusts. 14Locusts invaded all the land of Egypt and settled within all the territory of Egypt in a thick mass; never before had there been so many, nor will there ever be so many again. 15They hid all the land from view, and the land was darkened; and they ate up all the grasses of the field and all the fruit of the trees which the hail had left, so that nothing green was left, of tree or grass of the field, in all the land of Egypt.

16Pharaoh hurriedly summoned Moses and Aaron and said, "I stand guilty before the LORD your God and before you. 17Forgive my offense just this once, and plead with the LORD your God that He but remove this death from me." 18So he left Pharaoh's presence and pleaded with the LORD. 19The LORD caused a shift to a very strong west wind, which lifted the locusts and hurled them into the Sea of Reeds; not a single locust remained in all the territory of Egypt. 20But the LORD stiffened Pharaoh's heart, and he would not let the Israelites go.

21Then the LORD said to Moses, "Hold out

שני 12 וַיֹּאמֶר יְהוָה אֶל־מֹשֶׁה נְטֵה יָדְךָ עַל־
אֶרֶץ מִצְרַיִם בָּאַרְבֶּה וְיַעַל עַל־אֶרֶץ
מִצְרָיִם וְיֹאכַל אֶת־כָּל־עֵשֶׂב הָאָרֶץ אֵת
כָּל־אֲשֶׁר הִשְׁאִיר הַבָּרָד׃ 13 וַיֵּט מֹשֶׁה
אֶת־מַטֵּהוּ עַל־אֶרֶץ מִצְרַיִם וַיהוָה נִהַג
רוּחַ קָדִים בָּאָרֶץ כָּל־הַיּוֹם הַהוּא וְכָל־
הַלָּיְלָה הַבֹּקֶר הָיָה וְרוּחַ הַקָּדִים נָשָׂא
אֶת־הָאַרְבֶּה׃ 14 וַיַּעַל הָאַרְבֶּה עַל כָּל־
אֶרֶץ מִצְרַיִם וַיָּנַח בְּכֹל גְּבוּל מִצְרָיִם כָּבֵד
מְאֹד לְפָנָיו לֹא־הָיָה כֵן אַרְבֶּה כָּמֹהוּ
וְאַחֲרָיו לֹא יִהְיֶה־כֵּן׃ 15 וַיְכַס אֶת־עֵין
כָּל־הָאָרֶץ וַתֶּחְשַׁךְ הָאָרֶץ וַיֹּאכַל אֶת־
כָּל־עֵשֶׂב הָאָרֶץ וְאֵת כָּל־פְּרִי הָעֵץ אֲשֶׁר
הוֹתִיר הַבָּרָד וְלֹא־נוֹתַר כָּל־יֶרֶק בָּעֵץ
וּבְעֵשֶׂב הַשָּׂדֶה בְּכָל־אֶרֶץ מִצְרָיִם׃
16 וַיְמַהֵר פַּרְעֹה לִקְרֹא לְמֹשֶׁה וּלְאַהֲרֹן
וַיֹּאמֶר חָטָאתִי לַיהוָה אֱלֹהֵיכֶם וְלָכֶם׃
17 וְעַתָּה שָׂא נָא חַטָּאתִי אַךְ הַפַּעַם
וְהַעְתִּירוּ לַיהוָה אֱלֹהֵיכֶם וְיָסֵר מֵעָלַי רַק
אֶת־הַמָּוֶת הַזֶּה׃ 18 וַיֵּצֵא מֵעִם פַּרְעֹה
וַיֶּעְתַּר אֶל־יְהוָה׃ 19 וַיַּהֲפֹךְ יְהוָה רוּחַ־יָם
חָזָק מְאֹד וַיִּשָּׂא אֶת־הָאַרְבֶּה וַיִּתְקָעֵהוּ
יָמָּה סּוּף לֹא נִשְׁאַר אַרְבֶּה אֶחָד בְּכֹל
גְּבוּל מִצְרָיִם׃ 20 וַיְחַזֵּק יְהוָה אֶת־לֵב
פַּרְעֹה וְלֹא שִׁלַּח אֶת־בְּנֵי יִשְׂרָאֵל׃ פ
21 וַיֹּאמֶר יְהוָה אֶל־מֹשֶׁה נְטֵה יָדְךָ עַל־

13. an east wind A hot, dry, withering wind possibly originating in the Sahara, because Egypt was oriented southward to the source and headwaters of the Nile.

14–15. An overstatement to convey something of the magnitude of the plague.

18. Moses and Aaron, having been recalled by Pharaoh, make no response to his plea. Their silence must have been especially humiliating to Pharaoh, because he had dismissed them summarily only a short while before (v. 11).

NINTH PLAGUE: DARKNESS (*ḥoshekh*) (vv. 21–29)

As before, the third in the series of plagues strikes with no warning. For three days the land is enveloped in darkness. This affliction could be explained in terms of the hot, dry wind (*ḥamsin*)

---

21. The Midrash calls the plague of darkness "the darkness of Hell/*Geihinnom*" (Exod. R.14:2); and it connects the darkness that afflicted Egypt with the primordial darkness that existed before God said, "Let there be light!" Just as the light of *Shabbat* is a foretaste of the

your arm toward the sky that there may be darkness upon the land of Egypt, a darkness that can be touched." 22Moses held out his arm toward the sky and thick darkness descended upon all the land of Egypt for three days. 23People could not see one another, and for three days no one could get up from where he was; but all the Israelites enjoyed light in their dwellings.

24Pharaoh then summoned Moses and said, "Go, worship the LORD! Only your flocks and your herds shall be left behind; even your children may go with you." 25But Moses said, "You yourself must provide us with sacrifices and burnt offerings to offer up to the LORD our God; 26our own livestock, too, shall go along with us—not a hoof shall remain behind: for we must select from it for the worship of the LORD our God; and we shall not know with what we are to worship the LORD until we arrive there." 27But the LORD stiffened Pharaoh's heart and

הַשָּׁמַיִם וִיהִי חֹשֶׁךְ עַל־אֶרֶץ מִצְרָיִם וְיָמֵשׁ
חֹשֶׁךְ׃ 22 וַיֵּט מֹשֶׁה אֶת־יָדוֹ עַל־הַשָּׁמָיִם
וַיְהִי חֹשֶׁךְ־אֲפֵלָה בְּכָל־אֶרֶץ מִצְרַיִם
שְׁלֹשֶׁת יָמִים׃ 23 לֹא־רָאוּ אִישׁ אֶת־אָחִיו
וְלֹא־קָמוּ אִישׁ מִתַּחְתָּיו שְׁלֹשֶׁת יָמִים
וּלְכָל־בְּנֵי יִשְׂרָאֵל הָיָה אוֹר בְּמוֹשְׁבֹתָם׃
24 וַיִּקְרָא פַרְעֹה אֶל־מֹשֶׁה וַיֹּאמֶר לְכוּ שלישי
עִבְדוּ אֶת־יְהוָה רַק צֹאנְכֶם וּבְקַרְכֶם יֻצָּג
גַּם־טַפְּכֶם יֵלֵךְ עִמָּכֶם׃ 25 וַיֹּאמֶר מֹשֶׁה
גַּם־אַתָּה תִּתֵּן בְּיָדֵנוּ זְבָחִים וְעֹלֹת
וְעָשִׂינוּ לַיהוָה אֱלֹהֵינוּ׃ 26 וְגַם־מִקְנֵנוּ יֵלֵךְ
עִמָּנוּ לֹא תִשָּׁאֵר פַּרְסָה כִּי מִמֶּנּוּ נִקַּח
לַעֲבֹד אֶת־יְהוָה אֱלֹהֵינוּ וַאֲנַחְנוּ לֹא־נֵדַע
מַה־נַּעֲבֹד אֶת־יְהוָה עַד־בֹּאֵנוּ שָׁמָּה׃
27 וַיְחַזֵּק יְהוָה אֶת־לֵב פַּרְעֹה וְלֹא אָבָה

referred to in verse 13. The blotting out of sunlight for three days no doubt conveyed a powerful message to the Egyptians, for the sun was their supreme god. Its daily rising was seen as a triumph over the snake demon Apophis, the embodiment of darkness. The plague of darkness would have had the devastating psychological effect of revealing to the Egyptians the impotence of their supreme god, thereby forecasting imminent doom.

21. that can be touched This probably refers to sand, dust, and soil particles that filled the air.

25. You yourself He who contemptuously denied all knowledge of *YHVH* will, in the end, provide sacrifices for Him in acknowledgment of His reality and power.

---

world to come, the reward that awaits the righteous, the darkness of the ninth plague is a foretaste of *Geihinnom,* the punishment that awaits those who cannot truly see their neighbors, who cannot feel the pain and recognize the dignity of their afflicted neighbors.

23. During all the other plagues, the average Egyptian could do nothing to end them. During a plague of darkness, however, could Egyptians not light candles? Perhaps the plague was not a physical darkness, a sandstorm, or a solar eclipse (eclipses last for a few minutes, never for three days); perhaps it was a spiritual or psychological darkness, a deep depression. (The word "melancholy" comes from a Greek root meaning "dark mood.") People suffering from depression lack the energy to move about or to be concerned with anyone other than themselves, precisely as the Torah describes the Egyptians. Perhaps the Egyptians were depressed by the series of calamities that had struck them or by the realization of how much their own comfort depended on the enslavement of others. The person who cannot see his neighbor is incapable of spiritual growth, incapable of rising from where he is currently. In Jewish legal discussion defining how early one may recite the morning prayers, "dawn" is defined as "when one can recognize the face of a friend" (BT Ber. 9b). When one can see other people and recognize them as friends, the darkness has begun to lift.

26. we shall not know with what we are to worship the LORD until we arrive there God makes unique demands on each of us. We cannot know what God wants of us until we encounter God in each new stage of our lives.

לְשַׁלְּחָם׃ 28 וַיֹּאמֶר־לוֹ פַרְעֹה לֵךְ מֵעָלָי
הִשָּׁמֶר לְךָ אַל־תֹּסֶף רְאוֹת פָּנַי כִּי בְּיוֹם
רְאֹתְךָ פָנַי תָּמוּת׃ 29 וַיֹּאמֶר מֹשֶׁה כֵּן
דִּבַּרְתָּ לֹא־אֹסִף עוֹד רְאוֹת פָּנֶיךָ׃ פ

he would not agree to let them go. 28Pharaoh
said to him, "Be gone from me! Take care not
to see me again, for the moment you look upon
my face you shall die." 29And Moses replied,
"You have spoken rightly. I shall not see your
face again!"

יא וַיֹּאמֶר יְהוָה אֶל־מֹשֶׁה עוֹד נֶגַע
אֶחָד אָבִיא עַל־פַּרְעֹה וְעַל־מִצְרַיִם
אַחֲרֵי־כֵן יְשַׁלַּח אֶתְכֶם מִזֶּה כְּשַׁלְּחוֹ כָּלָה
גָּרֵשׁ יְגָרֵשׁ אֶתְכֶם מִזֶּה׃ 2 דַּבֶּר־נָא בְּאָזְנֵי
הָעָם וְיִשְׁאֲלוּ אִישׁ ׀ מֵאֵת רֵעֵהוּ וְאִשָּׁה
מֵאֵת רְעוּתָהּ כְּלֵי־כֶסֶף וּכְלֵי זָהָב׃ 3 וַיִּתֵּן
יְהוָה אֶת־חֵן הָעָם בְּעֵינֵי מִצְרָיִם גַּם ׀

11 And the LORD said to Moses, "I will bring
but one more plague upon Pharaoh and upon
Egypt; after that he shall let you go from here;
indeed, when he lets you go, he will drive you
out of here one and all. 2Tell the people to borrow, each man from his neighbor and each
woman from hers, objects of silver and gold."
3The LORD disposed the Egyptians favorably toward the people. Moreover, Moses himself was

ANNOUNCEMENT OF THE TENTH PLAGUE (11:1–10)

Pharaoh has closed the door on any further negotiations with Moses. The natural disasters have left the despot even more unyielding than before. A final blow, one wholly beyond nature or any previous human experience, is now about to descend on the Egyptians.

1–3. These verses seem parenthetical. It must be assumed that Moses received this message in the palace as he was about to leave, for verse 8 shows that he conveyed its content to Pharaoh.

1. he will drive you out The Exodus will no longer be a concession by Pharaoh. He will want your swift departure.

one and all Without restriction, exactly as Moses had demanded.

2. Tell the people Throughout the plagues, there has been no reported communication between Moses and the Israelites. Now that his mission to Pharaoh is concluded, he once again turns his attention to internal matters.

to borrow See Comment to 3:21–22.

3. disposed . . . favorably The Egyptians willingly part with their possessions.

CHAPTER 11

2. "During the plague of darkness, the Israelites could have plundered the homes of the Egyptians. When the Egyptians saw that the Israelites had not done so, they realized the moral greatness of that people and were inclined to give them the silver and gold they asked for" (Hirsch). One psychologist sees the message of the plagues as teaching Israel that "external forces can sometimes help us even when we cannot help ourselves." Thus we come to believe that, despite our prior experiences, the universe can be supportive of our hopes.

Pharaoh, who once decreed death for the Israelite male children, will now see the children of his own people struck down. God has tried everything to persuade Pharaoh to relent, to no avail. Of course, God could have struck Egypt with this plague first, but hoped that lesser punishments would bring about the desired result. It turned out that the society that benefited from slaying the Israelite children will now pay the price. Most modern readers are troubled by the sins of the parents being visited on their children, but the ancient mind did not have the concept of separate individual identities that we have today. The child was part of the parent, not a separate individual. To punish a child for a parent's sin was no more unjust than whipping a person's back for a crime his hand had committed. However, the later Israelite prophets Jeremiah and Ezekiel would repudiate this attitude in God's name, as would the Torah itself, in Deut. 24:16.

much esteemed in the land of Egypt, among Pharaoh's courtiers and among the people.

4Moses said, "Thus says the LORD: Toward midnight I will go forth among the Egyptians, 5and every first-born in the land of Egypt shall die, from the first-born of Pharaoh who sits on his throne to the first-born of the slave girl who is behind the millstones; and all the first-born of the cattle. 6And there shall be a loud cry in all the land of Egypt, such as has never been or will ever be again; 7but not a dog shall snarl at any of the Israelites, at man or beast—in order that you may know that the LORD makes a distinction between Egypt and Israel.

8"Then all these courtiers of yours shall come down to me and bow low to me, saying, 'Depart, you and all the people who follow you!' After that I will depart." And he left Pharaoh's presence in hot anger.

9Now the LORD had said to Moses, "Pharaoh will not heed you, in order that My marvels may be multiplied in the land of Egypt." 10Moses and Aaron had performed all these marvels before Pharaoh, but the LORD had stiffened the heart

הָאִישׁ מֹשֶׁה גָּדוֹל מְאֹד בְּאֶרֶץ מִצְרַיִם
בְּעֵינֵי עַבְדֵי־פַרְעֹה וּבְעֵינֵי הָעָם: ס
־ביעי 4 וַיֹּאמֶר מֹשֶׁה כֹּה אָמַר יְהוָה כַּחֲצֹת
הַלַּיְלָה אֲנִי יוֹצֵא בְּתוֹךְ מִצְרָיִם: 5 וּמֵת
כָּל־בְּכוֹר בְּאֶרֶץ מִצְרַיִם מִבְּכוֹר פַּרְעֹה
הַיֹּשֵׁב עַל־כִּסְאוֹ עַד בְּכוֹר הַשִּׁפְחָה אֲשֶׁר
אַחַר הָרֵחָיִם וְכֹל בְּכוֹר בְּהֵמָה: 6 וְהָיְתָה
צְעָקָה גְדֹלָה בְּכָל־אֶרֶץ מִצְרָיִם אֲשֶׁר
כָּמֹהוּ לֹא נִהְיָתָה וְכָמֹהוּ לֹא תֹסִף:
7 וּלְכֹל ׀ בְּנֵי יִשְׂרָאֵל לֹא יֶחֱרַץ־כֶּלֶב לְשֹׁנוֹ
לְמֵאִישׁ וְעַד־בְּהֵמָה לְמַעַן תֵּדְעוּן אֲשֶׁר
יַפְלֶה יְהוָה בֵּין מִצְרַיִם וּבֵין יִשְׂרָאֵל:
8 וְיָרְדוּ כָל־עֲבָדֶיךָ אֵלֶּה אֵלַי וְהִשְׁתַּחֲווּ־לִי
לֵאמֹר צֵא אַתָּה וְכָל־הָעָם אֲשֶׁר־בְּרַגְלֶיךָ
וְאַחֲרֵי־כֵן אֵצֵא וַיֵּצֵא מֵעִם־פַּרְעֹה בָּחֳרִי־
אָף: ס
9 וַיֹּאמֶר יְהוָה אֶל־מֹשֶׁה לֹא־יִשְׁמַע
אֲלֵיכֶם פַּרְעֹה לְמַעַן רְבוֹת מוֹפְתַי בְּאֶרֶץ
מִצְרָיִם: 10 וּמֹשֶׁה וְאַהֲרֹן עָשׂוּ אֶת־כָּל־
הַמֹּפְתִים הָאֵלֶּה לִפְנֵי פַרְעֹה וַיְחַזֵּק

Moses himself An additional reason for the Egyptian people's response.

4. Toward midnight When everyone would be at home. For psychological effect, the specific night is not disclosed.

5. For the first time, Pharaoh personally will be afflicted.

from . . . Pharaoh . . . to . . . the slave girl No one will be spared.

millstones The utensil with which grain was ground into flour. Grain was placed between two pieces of stone. The smaller, upper stone was moved back and forth by hand over the larger, stationary stone. This tedious, menial labor was performed by slave girls and captives.

first-born of the cattle These were included because they were objects of Egyptian worship. The Egyptians might have ascribed their misfortune to the work of their own animal-shaped gods instead of to *YHVH*.

6. a loud cry The Hebrew word *tz'akah* is the very term used to express Israel's misery under Egyptian enslavement. The anguished cry of the oppressed is now supplanted by the cry of their oppressors and tormentors.

7. By contrast, the departing Israelites will encounter no resistance.

8. in hot anger At Pharaoh's death threat (10:28).

9–10. These summarizing verses conclude the saga that began in chapter 7, just as the summarizing verses of chapter 6 bring to completion the first section of the book. Moses' negotiations with Pharaoh are over. He never speaks to him again. (Pharaoh, however, speaks to Moses for the last time in 12:31–32.)

---

5. first-born of the slave Non-Israelite slaves certainly did not have power in that society, so why would they be punished? Because they did not make common cause with the Israelites, saying, "let us join hands and rise together against our oppressors." Bad as their lives were, they took perverse satisfaction in knowing that there were others even worse off.

of Pharaoh so that he would not let the Israelites
go from his land.

יְהוָה֙ אֶת־לֵ֣ב פַּרְעֹ֔ה וְלֹֽא־שִׁלַּ֥ח אֶת־בְּנֵֽי־
יִשְׂרָאֵ֖ל מֵאַרְצֽוֹ׃ פ

12 The LORD said to Moses and Aaron in
the land of Egypt: 2This month shall mark for
you the beginning of the months; it shall be the
first of the months of the year for you. 3Speak
to the whole community of Israel and say that
on the tenth of this month each of them shall
take a lamb to a family, a lamb to a household.

יב וַיֹּ֤אמֶר יְהוָה֙ אֶל־מֹשֶׁ֣ה וְאֶֽל־אַהֲרֹ֔ן
בְּאֶ֥רֶץ מִצְרַ֖יִם לֵאמֹֽר׃ 2 הַחֹ֧דֶשׁ הַזֶּ֛ה לָכֶ֖ם
רֹ֣אשׁ חֳדָשִׁ֑ים רִאשׁ֥וֹן הוּא֙ לָכֶ֔ם לְחָדְשֵׁ֖י
הַשָּׁנָֽה׃ 3 דַּבְּר֗וּ אֶֽל־כָּל־עֲדַ֤ת יִשְׂרָאֵל֙
לֵאמֹ֔ר בֶּעָשֹׂ֖ר לַחֹ֣דֶשׁ הַזֶּ֑ה וְיִקְח֣וּ לָהֶ֗ם

THE LAST ACT (12:1–51)

This chapter, a composite of several strands of tradition, contains a number of literary units. Each unit centers on an aspect of the Exodus events. Some of these units deal with immediate concerns, such as the last-minute preparations for the departure from Egypt; others relate to the enduring effect of the events in shaping the future course of Israel's life as a people.

REFORM OF THE CALENDAR (v. 2)

The impending Exodus is visualized as the start of a new order of life that will be dominated by the consciousness of God's active presence in history. The religious calendar of Israel is henceforth to reflect this reality by numbering the months of the year from the month of the Exodus.

This month Elsewhere it is called "the month of Abib," meaning literally "when the ears of barley ripen," referring to the spring (March and April). The month of Abib is nowadays known as Nisan.

first of the months The Hebrew months, like the days of the week in Hebrew, are called by numbers. The absence of names may be due to the desire to avoid any connection with the ancient calendars that associated days and months with heavenly bodies or pagan deities and rituals. There is evidence that at least some Israelite months once had Canaanite-Phoenician names, because the Bible refers to the months of Ziv (1 Kings 6:1), Ethanim (1 Kings 8:2), and Bul (1 Kings 6:38). The names of months now used by Jews were borrowed from the Babylonian calendar during the first exile.

THE PASCHAL OFFERING (vv. 3–13)

The laws relating to the sacrificial meal that is to take place immediately before the Exodus are now set forth in detail.

3. community of Israel The word translated as "community" (*edah,* the feminine abstract from *ed* = "witness") was the term used to designate the people Israel acting as a covenant community, in relation to worship.

tenth of this month The completion of the first 10 days of the lunar month apparently held

---

CHAPTER 12

2. This month shall mark for you the beginning of the months One of the first steps in the process of liberation was for the Israelites to have their own calendar, their own way of keeping track of time and recalling the most important days of their people's history. A slave does not control his or her own time; it belongs to someone else. Hirsch wrote that "the Jewish calendar is the Jewish catechism," for it is the most concise summary of what we remember and what we stand for. Why does Israel count by the moon, with each month starting when the new moon emerges? Because the moon, unlike the sun, waxes and wanes, nearly disappears and then grows bright again. So the Jewish people go through cycles of prosperity and suffering, knowing that even in darkness there are brighter days ahead (*S'fat Emet*). "Just as God showed Noah the rainbow as a sign of the covenant, God shows Moses the sliver of the new moon as a symbol of Israel's capacity for constant renewal" (Hirsch).

3. The next step toward liberation was to slaughter a lamb publicly, something no Egyptian would do, and mark the doorpost with its blood. In this way, they would proclaim their

4But if the household is too small for a lamb,
let him share one with a neighbor who dwells
nearby, in proportion to the number of persons:
you shall contribute for the lamb according to
what each household will eat. 5Your lamb shall
be without blemish, a yearling male; you may
take it from the sheep or from the goats. 6You
shall keep watch over it until the fourteenth day

אִישׁ שֶׂה לְבֵית־אָבֹת שֶׂה לַבָּיִת׃ 4 וְאִם־
יִמְעַט הַבַּיִת מִהְיֹת מִשֶּׂה וְלָקַח הוּא
וּשְׁכֵנוֹ הַקָּרֹב אֶל־בֵּיתוֹ בְּמִכְסַת נְפָשֹׁת
אִישׁ לְפִי אָכְלוֹ תָּכֹסּוּ עַל־הַשֶּׂה׃ 5 שֶׂה
תָמִים זָכָר בֶּן־שָׁנָה יִהְיֶה לָכֶם מִן־
הַכְּבָשִׂים וּמִן־הָעִזִּים תִּקָּחוּ׃ 6 וְהָיָה לָכֶם
לְמִשְׁמֶרֶת עַד אַרְבָּעָה עָשָׂר יוֹם לַחֹדֶשׁ

some sort of special significance now lost to us. Yom Kippur, the most sacred day in the religious calendar, falls on the 10th of the seventh month, and in ancient times this same date ushered in the jubilee year. Joshua chose the 10th of the first month to cross the Jordan into the land of Canaan.

a lamb See verse 5 and Deut. 14:4. The Hebrew word *seh* can mean both "a lamb" and "a kid of the goats." In light of the fear expressed in Gen. 8:22, this act broke the sense of dread felt by the enslaved Israelites and removed the psychological barrier to liberation.

a family The Hebrew phrase *beit avot* literally means "a house of fathers" and is a subunit of a clan (the biblical *mishpaḥah*). It is made up of a husband, his wife or wives, his unmarried daughters and sons, and his married sons with their wives and unmarried children.

a household Originally, the paschal celebration was a domestic experience. Later it became a pilgrimage festival.

4. too small In Second Temple times, a minimum quorum of 10 participants was required for this ritual. The actual slaughtering of the animal was performed in the presence of no fewer than 30.

will eat The eating of the animal is an essential part of the ritual. By means of this sacrificial meal, kinship ties are strengthened, family and neighborly solidarity is promoted, and communion with God is established.

5. without blemish A defective gift is an insult to the recipient; hence the harmony between the one who brings the gift and God would be impaired by such a gift.

6. keep watch The animal, selected on the 10th of the month, is to be carefully protected

---

psychological liberation from fear of Egyptian opinion and from an eagerness to imitate Egyptian customs, a necessary prerequisite to physical liberation. The Sages see the lamb as a symbol of idol worship, and its public slaughter as a repudiation of idolatry. It has also been noted that in times of drastic change people need specific, action-oriented advice. This gives them a sense of control over a chaotic situation, as we see with mourning customs in the wake of a death.

The shared meal, with *matzah* and bitter herbs (v. 8), will become the prototype of the *Pesaḥ Seider,* when we not only remember but strive to re-enact our ancestors' deliverance from Egypt. Members of some communities come to the *Seider* table with sandals on their feet and a staff in their hand (v. 11), as if they were setting out on a journey to freedom.

Although we celebrate *Rosh ha-Shanah,* beginning a new year, in the fall, the Hebrew calendar actually begins in the spring with *Nisan,* the month of *Pesaḥ,* as the first month. *Tishrei,* the month of *Rosh ha-Shanah* and *Yom Kippur,* is the seventh month (see Lev. 23:23ff.). Some scholars see this as a compromise among ancient cultures, those who celebrated the beginning of the new year in the spring when the harsh winter rains were over and the plants and flowers re-emerged, versus those who celebrated the new year in the fall when the rains returned to replenish the land after summer's harsh drought. We can see it as analogous to our beginning a new calendar year in January but marking our personal age on our birthday. Thus *Rosh ha-Shanah* is seen as the anniversary of the creation of the world, marking our shared humanity with other peoples; *Pesaḥ* is the birthday of the people Israel, symbolizing our special destiny as Jews.

4. Like so much of Judaism, *Pesaḥ,* although a family celebration, is not to be observed in isolation. It is an occasion for families to join with other families and create a community. More than the poor need the rich, the rich need the poor. Let those whose households are too small to absorb all the blessings that God has given them seek out their neighbors and share the bounty with them (Hirsch).

of this month; and all the assembled congregation of the Israelites shall slaughter it at twilight. 7They shall take some of the blood and
put it on the two doorposts and the lintel of the
houses in which they are to eat it. 8They shall
eat the flesh that same night; they shall eat it
roasted over the fire, with unleavened bread and
with bitter herbs. 9Do not eat any of it raw, or
cooked in any way with water, but roasted—
head, legs, and entrails—over the fire. 10You
shall not leave any of it over until morning;
if any of it is left until morning, you shall
burn it.
11This is how you shall eat it: your loins
girded, your sandals on your feet, and your staff

הַזֶּה וְשָׁחֲטוּ אֹתוֹ כֹּל קְהַל עֲדַת־יִשְׂרָאֵל
בֵּין הָעַרְבָּיִם׃ 7 וְלָקְחוּ מִן־הַדָּם וְנָתְנוּ
עַל־שְׁתֵּי הַמְּזוּזֹת וְעַל־הַמַּשְׁקוֹף עַל
הַבָּתִּים אֲשֶׁר־יֹאכְלוּ אֹתוֹ בָּהֶם׃ 8 וְאָכְלוּ
אֶת־הַבָּשָׂר בַּלַּיְלָה הַזֶּה צְלִי־אֵשׁ וּמַצּוֹת
עַל־מְרֹרִים יֹאכְלֻהוּ׃ 9 אַל־תֹּאכְלוּ מִמֶּנּוּ
נָא וּבָשֵׁל מְבֻשָּׁל בַּמָּיִם כִּי אִם־צְלִי־אֵשׁ
רֹאשׁוֹ עַל־כְּרָעָיו וְעַל־קִרְבּוֹ׃ 10 וְלֹא־
תוֹתִירוּ מִמֶּנּוּ עַד־בֹּקֶר וְהַנֹּתָר מִמֶּנּוּ עַד־
בֹּקֶר בָּאֵשׁ תִּשְׂרֹפוּ׃
11 וְכָכָה תֹּאכְלוּ אֹתוֹ מָתְנֵיכֶם חֲגֻרִים
נַעֲלֵיכֶם בְּרַגְלֵיכֶם וּמַקֶּלְכֶם בְּיֶדְכֶם

from blemish for four days until it is slaughtered. No reason for the interval is given.

7. According to verses 13 and 23, the daubing at the entrances served to identify the houses of the Israelites, for the blood is designated "a sign." Blood was a readily available coloring substance; it also possessed symbolic significance because it was looked on as the life essence. The lintel and doorposts form the demarcation between the sacred Israelite interior and the profane world outside.

8–9. Unlike other offerings, this one (called *pesaḥ* in v.11) is roasted. Roasting may have been required here because it is the quickest means of preparation when time is short, or because it is the most effective way of extracting the blood. Deut. 16:7 instructs that this passover offering is to be boiled like a normal sacrifice.

8. unleavened bread The Hebrew for "unleavened bread" (*matzot,* singular *matzah*) is introduced without definition or explanation, implying that it is already well known and, hence, independent of the Exodus events. The contexts suggest a kind of flat cake that can be prepared quickly for unexpected guests (see Gen. 19:3). This verse witnesses the integration of the originally separate *matzot* festival with the Passover celebration. See Comments to Exod. 12:14–20.

bitter herbs The Hebrew word *m'rorim* (singular *maror*) probably referred originally to the kind of pungent condiment with which pastoral nomads habitually season their meals of roasted flesh. In rabbinic tradition, the plant referred to five different species of herbs, including lettuce (*ḥassah*), a vegetable known to have been cultivated in ancient Egypt.

10. A sacrificial animal is devoted in its entirety to a sacred purpose. This is so even when the offering is eaten by the worshipers and not wholly burned on the altar. The intentional act of eating at the designated time is an indispensable part of the ritual. Any leftovers retain their sacred status but may no longer be consumed and must be burned.

11. loins girded The standard dress consisted of a flowing shirtlike garment that was tightened by a sash wrapped around the waist when greater maneuverability was called for. The

7. Was the blood on the doorpost a sign that this family had the courage to defy their Egyptian neighbors and demonstrate an inner liberation? Was it perhaps a sign that this family has already suffered and should be spared? Or was it simply that this family had complied with God's command? Could God not distinguish between Israelite and Egyptian homes? The Talmud says that once a plague has begun, it does not distinguish between the righteous and the wicked (BT BK 60a). Some means was needed to mark the homes that merited being spared.

HALAKHAH L'MA·ASEH

12:8. night On the basis of this verse, the *Pesaḥ Seider* is held at night (BT Pes. 41b; 96a).

in your hand; and you shall eat it hurriedly: it
is a passover offering to the LORD. 12For that
night I will go through the land of Egypt and
strike down every first-born in the land of
Egypt, both man and beast; and I will mete out
punishments to all the gods of Egypt, I the LORD.
13And the blood on the houses where you are
staying shall be a sign for you: when I see the
blood I will pass over you, so that no plague will
destroy you when I strike the land of Egypt.

14This day shall be to you one of remembrance: you shall celebrate it as a festival to the

וַאֲכַלְתֶּם אֹתוֹ בְּחִפָּזוֹן פֶּסַח הוּא לַיהוָה׃
12 וְעָבַרְתִּי בְאֶרֶץ־מִצְרַיִם בַּלַּיְלָה הַזֶּה
וְהִכֵּיתִי כָל־בְּכוֹר בְּאֶרֶץ מִצְרַיִם מֵאָדָם
וְעַד־בְּהֵמָה וּבְכָל־אֱלֹהֵי מִצְרַיִם אֶעֱשֶׂה
שְׁפָטִים אֲנִי יְהוָה׃ 13 וְהָיָה הַדָּם לָכֶם
לְאֹת עַל הַבָּתִּים אֲשֶׁר אַתֶּם שָׁם וְרָאִיתִי
אֶת־הַדָּם וּפָסַחְתִּי עֲלֵכֶם וְלֹא־יִהְיֶה בָכֶם
נֶגֶף לְמַשְׁחִית בְּהַכֹּתִי בְּאֶרֶץ מִצְרָיִם׃
14 וְהָיָה הַיּוֹם הַזֶּה לָכֶם לְזִכָּרוֹן וְחַגֹּתֶם
אֹתוֹ חַג לַיהוָה לְדֹרֹתֵיכֶם חֻקַּת עוֹלָם

climactic moment of liberation is imminent, and the Israelites must be prepared for immediate departure.

a passover offering The Hebrew noun *"pesaḥ"* has given rise to the English adjective "paschal," used to designate the Passover lamb, the Passover holiday, and Easter. Like the word *"matzah," pesaḥ* is assumed in this narrative to be an immediately understandable term, so it too must have a history that predates the Exodus. The etymology of the word is uncertain, although it may be related to an Akkadian root meaning "to appease." Three traditions about the meaning of the stem פסח have survived: "to have compassion," "to protect," and "to skip over" (see 12:13). Strictly speaking, as noted in the Comments to verses 14–20, only the 14th day of the month can be called *Pesaḥ;* but in the course of time, this term was extended to cover the entire week of the festival.

12. I will go through An example of anthropomorphism, attributing a human activity to God. Here it may be used to make His active presence in history more vividly and dramatically perceived. Despite this emphatic statement, however, tradition frequently speaks of the Angel of Death, not God, as "the destroyer."

to all the gods of Egypt God's power to take Israel out of Egypt manifests His own exclusivity, mocks the professed divinity of Pharaoh, and exposes the deities of Egypt as non-gods.

13. The first section of the chapter concludes with an assurance that no harm will befall the Israelites. This is necessary because fulfillment of the preceding instructions is fraught with peril, and the coming period of inaction will allow anxiety to surface.

THE FESTIVAL OF *MATZOT* (vv. 14–20)

The previous rites deal with a specific time and situation—the Passover of Egypt. The Exodus now becomes an experience stamped for all time on Israel's memory and imagination, shaping forever its religious consciousness and traditions. Verse 14 establishes an annual festival of remembrance; the subsequent verses explain how it is to be observed.

The focus is on the festival of *matzot,* "unleavened bread." Without doubt, throughout the biblical period this celebration remained distinct from the one-day paschal rite. Indeed, the next chapter (13:6–8) establishes the laws of *matzot* and makes no mention of the paschal sacrifice. Lev. 23:5–6 similarly differentiates the one from the other: "In the first month, on the fourteenth day of the month, at twilight, there shall be a passover offering to the LORD, and on the fifteenth day of that month the LORD's Feast of Unleavened Bread." Special Passovers were celebrated in the reigns of Kings Hezekiah and Josiah of Judah, both of whom were associated with major reformations (see 2 Chron. 30, 35). We are told in Ezra 6:19–22 that when the exiles returned from Babylon they "celebrated the Passover on the fourteenth day of the first month," and then "joyfully celebrated the Feast of Unleavened Bread for seven days."

---

14. The topic and tone of the Torah narrative now shifts seamlessly but significantly from instructions to Moses' contemporaries to listing *mitzvot* to be followed by Jews in later generations—not so as to effect the Exodus but in order to remember it.

Lord throughout the ages; you shall celebrate
it as an institution for all time. 15Seven days you
shall eat unleavened bread; on the very first day
you shall remove leaven from your houses, for
whoever eats leavened bread from the first day
to the seventh day, that person shall be cut off
from Israel.
16You shall celebrate a sacred occasion on the
first day, and a sacred occasion on the seventh
day; no work at all shall be done on them; only
what every person is to eat, that alone may be

תְּחָגֻּהוּ: 15 שִׁבְעַת יָמִים מַצּוֹת תֹּאכֵלוּ
אַךְ בַּיּוֹם הָרִאשׁוֹן תַּשְׁבִּיתוּ שְּׂאֹר
מִבָּתֵּיכֶם כִּי | כָּל־אֹכֵל חָמֵץ וְנִכְרְתָה
הַנֶּפֶשׁ הַהִוא מִיִּשְׂרָאֵל מִיּוֹם הָרִאשֹׁן
עַד־יוֹם הַשְּׁבִעִי:
16 וּבַיּוֹם הָרִאשׁוֹן מִקְרָא־קֹדֶשׁ וּבַיּוֹם
הַשְּׁבִיעִי מִקְרָא־קֹדֶשׁ יִהְיֶה לָכֶם כָּל־
מְלָאכָה לֹא־יֵעָשֶׂה בָהֶם אַךְ אֲשֶׁר
יֵאָכֵל לְכָל־נֶפֶשׁ הוּא לְבַדּוֹ יֵעָשֶׂה לָכֶם:

14. throughout the ages That is, for future annual celebration.

15. The characteristics of the newly ordained festival are now stated: one week's duration, the eating of *matzot,* and the removal of leaven. It is a new season of the year and a new era for the people Israel. One should not enter it with yeast collected from a previous time.

unleavened bread Stringent regulations govern the manufacture of *matzot.* The only ingredients are flour and water. The flour may be made only from grains that are susceptible to fermentation: wheat, barley, emmer, rye, and oats.

on the very first day Because festivals begin in the evening, this injunction traditionally has been taken to mean that the leaven must have been removed on the previous evening, before the time for the paschal offering on the 14th of the month.

remove leaven The positive command to eat *matzah* is supplemented by the strict prohibition against retaining or eating leaven or leavened food throughout the entire festival. This rule is repeated below in verses 19–20 and again in 13:7. Leaven (*s'or*) is the leavening agent known as sourdough; "leavened food" (*ḥametz*) is food to which sourdough has been added to accelerate the rising of the dough.

shall be cut off This punishment, known as *karet,* is largely confined to those who transgress in certain matters of religious worship and sexual behavior. Its nature is uncertain. Various biblical passages lead to the conclusion that *karet* is not a penalty enforced by the courts but a punishment left to divine execution.

16. The first and the last days of the festival possess special sanctity, but not to the same degree

15. shall be cut off *Pesaḥ* is a fundamental statement of Jewish identity and the meaning and purpose of Jewish existence—so much so that those who choose not to observe it can be seen as cutting themselves off from the Jewish people.

HALAKHAH L'MA·ASEH

12:15. remove leaven On the night before the *Seider,* there is a ritual search of the home (*B'dikat Ḥametz*) by candlelight. A feather and a spoon are used to collect pieces of bread or other leaven that had been hidden to stimulate the search. The next morning, any leavened product not otherwise stored and sold is disposed of, traditionally by burning (*Bi·ur Ḥametz*) (see Lev. 2:11; Deut. 16:3).

12:16. the seventh day This last day is considered to be as holy as the first; all restrictions apply equally to both. Outside Israel, two days are traditionally observed for each day defined as a *mikra kodesh* (sacred occasion) in the Torah, except for *Yom Kippur* (because the Sages judged that fasting for two days would be too burdensome). Before the calendar was established, news of the *Sanhedrin*'s announcement of the new moon would not necessarily reach diaspora communities in time before a holiday, and so diaspora Jews observed a second day to be sure not to violate holy day prohibitions. Despite the subsequent creation of the Jewish calendar, adding a second day for each day the Torah designates as a sacred occasion remains the most widespread practice (MT Festivals 1:21). Therefore, the first and last days of *Pesaḥ* are each observed for two days (for a total of eight days); the first day of *Sukkot* and *Sh'mini Atzeret* are each observed for two days (for a total of nine days); and *Shavuot* is observed for two days. The intermediate days of *Pesaḥ* and *Sukkot* have some of the aspects of the festival's first and last days and some aspects of a weekday; hence the name *ḥol ha-mo·ed,* "the ordinary part of the festival." *Rosh ha-Shanah* is observed for two days even in Israel, because it occurs at the very beginning of the month and even the Jews of Jerusalem could not determine when the new moon would be sighted and the holiday would begin.

17 וּשְׁמַרְתֶּם אֶת־הַמַּצּוֹת כִּי בְּעֶצֶם הַיּוֹם
הַזֶּה הוֹצֵאתִי אֶת־צִבְאוֹתֵיכֶם מֵאֶרֶץ
מִצְרָיִם וּשְׁמַרְתֶּם אֶת־הַיּוֹם הַזֶּה
לְדֹרֹתֵיכֶם חֻקַּת עוֹלָם׃ 18 בָּרִאשֹׁן
בְּאַרְבָּעָה עָשָׂר יוֹם לַחֹדֶשׁ בָּעֶרֶב תֹּאכְלוּ
מַצֹּת עַד יוֹם הָאֶחָד וְעֶשְׂרִים לַחֹדֶשׁ
בָּעָרֶב׃ 19 שִׁבְעַת יָמִים שְׂאֹר לֹא יִמָּצֵא
בְּבָתֵּיכֶם כִּי ׀ כָּל־אֹכֵל מַחְמֶצֶת וְנִכְרְתָה
הַנֶּפֶשׁ הַהִוא מֵעֲדַת יִשְׂרָאֵל בַּגֵּר וּבְאֶזְרַח
הָאָרֶץ׃ 20 כָּל־מַחְמֶצֶת לֹא תֹאכֵלוּ בְּכֹל
מוֹשְׁבֹתֵיכֶם תֹּאכְלוּ מַצּוֹת׃ פ
21 וַיִּקְרָא מֹשֶׁה לְכָל־זִקְנֵי יִשְׂרָאֵל וַיֹּאמֶר מישי
אֲלֵהֶם מִשְׁכוּ וּקְחוּ לָכֶם צֹאן
לְמִשְׁפְּחֹתֵיכֶם וְשַׁחֲטוּ הַפָּסַח׃ 22 וּלְקַחְתֶּם
אֲגֻדַּת אֵזוֹב וּטְבַלְתֶּם בַּדָּם אֲשֶׁר־בַּסַּף

prepared for you. 17You shall observe the [Feast of] Unleavened Bread, for on this very day I brought your ranks out of the land of Egypt; you shall observe this day throughout the ages as an institution for all time. 18In the first month, from the fourteenth day of the month at evening, you shall eat unleavened bread until the twenty-first day of the month at evening. 19No leaven shall be found in your houses for seven days. For whoever eats what is leavened, that person shall be cut off from the community of Israel, whether he is a stranger or a citizen of the country. 20You shall eat nothing leavened; in all your settlements you shall eat unleavened bread.

21Moses then summoned all the elders of Israel and said to them, "Go, pick out lambs for your families, and slaughter the passover offering. 22Take a bunch of hyssop, dip it in the

as do *Shabbat* and the Day of Atonement. Hence the preparation of food on those festival days is permitted, exempted from the prohibition against labor.

17. The rationale for this springtime festival is now given.

You shall observe the* [*Feast of*] *Unleavened Bread Understanding the phrase *"u-sh'martem et ha-matzot"* (literally, "guard the *matzot*") in this way is based on the next phrase—"on this very day"—which takes the word *"matzot"* to mean the festival (*Ḥag ha-Matzot*). (For a parallel passage, see 23:15.)

I brought Better: "I am bringing."

18. As specified in Lev. 23:32, the duration of all festivals is from evening to evening.

19. a stranger The Hebrew word *ger* is a foreigner who has taken up permanent residence among the people Israel. Like his Israelite neighbor, he is required to abstain from possessing leaven for this one week, because its presence within the closely knit community interferes with the ability of others to fulfill their religious obligation. Only the Israelite, however, has the duty to eat *matzah*.

INSTRUCTIONS FOR THE *PESAḤ* ARE RELAYED (vv. 21–28)

Moses conveys to the people the divinely given instructions and supplements them with some clarifications.

21. Go, pick out Either select a lamb from your flock or purchase one.

22. a bunch of hyssop A brushlike plant. This explains how the directive of verse 7 is to be carried out. Three of the hyssop's thin, woody

---

17. observe the [Feast of] Unleavened Bread Literally, "guard the *matzot*" (pl. of *matzah*). Traditional postbiblical Jewish interpretation takes this to mean that one should supervise the process of making *matzot* to ensure that no fermentation occurs at any stage.

HALAKHAH L'MA·ASEH

12:19. No leaven shall be found Because disposing of foods prohibited on *Pesaḥ* could impose financial hardship, Jewish law permits food to be stored away in the home of the owner provided that for the duration of *Pesaḥ* it is neither seen nor used and its ownership is transferred to a non-Jew. This sale of *hametz* (*M'khirat Ḥametz*) can be arranged through a rabbi. All foods prohibited during *Pesaḥ* that are not sold in this manner must be disposed of before the holiday; otherwise they may not be used after *Pesaḥ* (*ḥametz she-avar alav ha-Pesaḥ*).

blood that is in the basin, and apply some of the blood that is in the basin to the lintel and to the two doorposts. None of you shall go outside the door of his house until morning.
23For when the LORD goes through to smite the Egyptians, He will see the blood on the lintel and the two doorposts, and the LORD will pass over the door and not let the Destroyer enter and smite your home.

24"You shall observe this as an institution for all time, for you and for your descendants.
25And when you enter the land that the LORD will give you, as He has promised, you shall observe this rite.
26And when your children ask you, 'What do you mean by this rite?'
27you shall say, 'It is the passover sacrifice to the LORD, because He passed over the houses of the Israelites in Egypt when He smote the Egyptians, but saved our houses.'"

The people then bowed low in homage.
28And the Israelites went and did so; just as the LORD had commanded Moses and Aaron, so they did.

וְהִגַּעְתֶּם אֶל־הַמַּשְׁקוֹף וְאֶל־שְׁתֵּי הַמְּזוּזֹת
מִן־הַדָּם אֲשֶׁר בַּסָּף וְאַתֶּם לֹא תֵצְאוּ
אִישׁ מִפֶּתַח־בֵּיתוֹ עַד־בֹּקֶר׃ 23 וְעָבַר יְהוָה
לִנְגֹּף אֶת־מִצְרַיִם וְרָאָה אֶת־הַדָּם עַל־
הַמַּשְׁקוֹף וְעַל שְׁתֵּי הַמְּזוּזֹת וּפָסַח יְהוָה
עַל־הַפֶּתַח וְלֹא יִתֵּן הַמַּשְׁחִית לָבֹא אֶל־
בָּתֵּיכֶם לִנְגֹּף׃
24 וּשְׁמַרְתֶּם אֶת־הַדָּבָר הַזֶּה לְחָק־לְךָ
וּלְבָנֶיךָ עַד־עוֹלָם׃ 25 וְהָיָה כִּי־תָבֹאוּ אֶל־
הָאָרֶץ אֲשֶׁר יִתֵּן יְהוָה לָכֶם כַּאֲשֶׁר דִּבֵּר
וּשְׁמַרְתֶּם אֶת־הָעֲבֹדָה הַזֹּאת׃ 26 וְהָיָה
כִּי־יֹאמְרוּ אֲלֵיכֶם בְּנֵיכֶם מָה הָעֲבֹדָה
הַזֹּאת לָכֶם׃ 27 וַאֲמַרְתֶּם זֶבַח־פֶּסַח הוּא
לַיהוָה אֲשֶׁר פָּסַח עַל־בָּתֵּי בְנֵי־יִשְׂרָאֵל
בְּמִצְרַיִם בְּנָגְפּוֹ אֶת־מִצְרַיִם וְאֶת־בָּתֵּינוּ
הִצִּיל
וַיִּקֹּד הָעָם וַיִּשְׁתַּחֲווּ׃ 28 וַיֵּלְכוּ וַיַּעֲשׂוּ בְּנֵי
יִשְׂרָאֵל כַּאֲשֶׁר צִוָּה יְהוָה אֶת־מֹשֶׁה
ששי וְאַהֲרֹן כֵּן עָשׂוּ׃ ס

branches make an ideal applicator. It is often used in rites of purification.

None . . . shall go outside On this night of danger and vigilance, the Israelites would be most secure inside their homes.

23. Destroyer The plague, although personified, is not an independent demonic being. It can operate only within the limits set by God.

24. observe this Ramban notes that this refers to the slaughter of the passover offering, not to the daubing of the blood.

25. when you enter the land Apart from the celebration on the first anniversary of the Exodus, as described in Num. 9:1–5, no further mention of the observance of Passover appears in the account of the wilderness wanderings until after the crossing of the river Jordan, as recorded in Josh. 5:2–12.

as He has promised To the patriarchs. See Comment to Exod. 6:8.

26–27. The ritual also serves a pedagogic function. Its oddities arouse the curiosity of children, presenting an opportunity to teach these traditions to the young.

our houses The passage of time never diminishes the significance of the events. The national culture is nurtured by their memory and by their repeated re-enactment, a theme later stressed in the *Pesaḥ Haggadah.*

---

26. when your children ask you This is the origin of the familiar *Seider* custom of having the children present ask the Four Questions. Three references in this *parashah* to telling the story to our children and another in Deuteronomy gave rise to the *Haggadah* passage about the Four Children. Exodus 13:8 ("And you shall explain to your son") emphasizes the parent's role in informing children even if they do not ask, gearing our information to the child's capacity for understanding. It is better to encourage children to ask questions while they are still at home and parents and teachers can respond to them, than to wait until others cause them to doubt and question.

²⁹In the middle of the night the Lord struck down all the first-born in the land of Egypt, from the first-born of Pharaoh who sat on the throne to the first-born of the captive who was in the dungeon, and all the first-born of the cattle. ³⁰And Pharaoh arose in the night, with all his courtiers and all the Egyptians—because there was a loud cry in Egypt; for there was no house where there was not someone dead. ³¹He summoned Moses and Aaron in the night and said, "Up, depart from among my people, you and the Israelites with you! Go, worship the Lord as you said! ³²Take also your flocks and your herds, as you said, and begone! And may you bring a blessing upon me also!"

³³The Egyptians urged the people on, impatient to have them leave the country, for they said, "We shall all be dead." ³⁴So the people took their dough before it was leavened, their kneading bowls wrapped in their cloaks upon their shoulders. ³⁵The Israelites had done Moses' bidding and borrowed from the Egyptians objects

ששי 29 וַיְהִ֣י | בַּחֲצִ֣י הַלַּ֗יְלָה וַֽיהוָה֮ הִכָּ֣ה כָל־בְּכוֹר֮ בְּאֶ֣רֶץ מִצְרַ֒יִם֒ מִבְּכֹ֤ר פַּרְעֹה֙ הַיֹּשֵׁ֣ב עַל־כִּסְא֔וֹ עַ֚ד בְּכ֣וֹר הַשְּׁבִ֔י אֲשֶׁ֖ר בְּבֵ֣ית הַבּ֑וֹר וְכֹ֖ל בְּכ֥וֹר בְּהֵמָֽה: 30 וַיָּ֨קָם פַּרְעֹ֜ה לַ֗יְלָה ה֤וּא וְכָל־עֲבָדָיו֙ וְכָל־מִצְרַ֔יִם וַתְּהִ֛י צְעָקָ֥ה גְדֹלָ֖ה בְּמִצְרָ֑יִם כִּֽי־אֵ֣ין בַּ֔יִת אֲשֶׁ֥ר אֵֽין־שָׁ֖ם מֵֽת: 31 וַיִּקְרָא֩ לְמֹשֶׁ֨ה וּֽלְאַהֲרֹ֜ן לַ֗יְלָה וַיֹּ֙אמֶר֙ ק֤וּמוּ צְּאוּ֙ מִתּ֣וֹךְ עַמִּ֔י גַּם־אַתֶּ֖ם גַּם־בְּנֵ֣י יִשְׂרָאֵ֑ל וּלְכ֛וּ עִבְד֥וּ אֶת־יְהוָ֖ה כְּדַבֶּרְכֶֽם: 32 גַּם־צֹאנְכֶ֨ם גַּם־בְּקַרְכֶ֥ם קְח֛וּ כַּאֲשֶׁ֥ר דִּבַּרְתֶּ֖ם וָלֵ֑כוּ וּבֵֽרַכְתֶּ֖ם גַּם־אֹתִֽי:

33 וַתֶּחֱזַ֤ק מִצְרַ֙יִם֙ עַל־הָעָ֔ם לְמַהֵ֖ר לְשַׁלְּחָ֣ם מִן־הָאָ֑רֶץ כִּ֥י אָמְר֖וּ כֻּלָּ֥נוּ מֵתִֽים: 34 וַיִּשָּׂ֥א הָעָ֛ם אֶת־בְּצֵק֖וֹ טֶ֣רֶם יֶחְמָ֑ץ מִשְׁאֲרֹתָ֛ם צְרֻרֹ֥ת בְּשִׂמְלֹתָ֖ם עַל־שִׁכְמָֽם: 35 וּבְנֵֽי־יִשְׂרָאֵ֥ל עָשׂ֖וּ כִּדְבַ֣ר מֹשֶׁ֑ה וַֽיִּשְׁאֲלוּ֙ מִמִּצְרַ֔יִם כְּלֵי־כֶ֥סֶף וּכְלֵ֥י זָהָ֖ב וּשְׂמָלֹֽת:

TENTH PLAGUE (*makkat b'khorot*)   (vv. 29–36)

All the preparations have been completed. The stage is set for the climactic plague, which will secure the release of the Israelites from bondage. The Torah recognizes that the entire Egyptian people is subject to judgment for having tolerated the perverse will of Pharaoh.

PHARAOH SURRENDERS   (vv. 30–32)

The king himself has to rise during the night, thereby adding to his humiliation at having to surrender unconditionally to Moses' demands. By summoning Moses and Aaron, he must retract the arrogant threat made at their last meet-

ing (10:28). He asks for their blessing, an ultimate humbling act.

31. Israelites   Pharaoh uses this term for the first time, thereby at last granting recognition to the Israelites as a national entity. The narrative of the oppression opened with this term (1:1), and now closes with it.

34. before it was leavened   In verse 39 this note is amplified in such a way as to provide a clear explanation for the eating of *matzot* on Passover. A similar reason is given in Deut. 16:3. Because the eating of the *matzot* was ordained and presumably carried out before the 10th plague struck (v. 8), the present rationale must be a reinterpretation of a pre-existing practice.

---

35.   The silver and gold given (not lent) by the Egyptians constituted a protest against the policies of the royal tyrant. They demonstrated a renewal of public conscience. Similar gifts were given to the Jews leaving Babylonia to return to Judea (Ezra 1:4). Had the Israelites left Egypt with nothing after so many years of suffering, the hatred in their hearts toward the Egyptians would have been never ending. The

Torah wanted the Egyptian people to send them off with gifts, so that it would be easier for the Israelites to fulfill the *mitzvah* "you shall not abhor an Egyptian" (Deut. 23:8). (This comment is by Benno Jacob, who was born and grew up in Germany and had to escape to England after the Nazis came to power. He understood that the purpose of the commandment was to cleanse our memory of bitterness and hatred.)

36 וַיהוָה נָתַן אֶת־חֵן הָעָם בְּעֵינֵי מִצְרַיִם
וַיַּשְׁאִלוּם וַיְנַצְּלוּ אֶת־מִצְרָיִם׃ פ
37 וַיִּסְעוּ בְנֵי־יִשְׂרָאֵל מֵרַעְמְסֵס סֻכֹּתָה
כְּשֵׁשׁ־מֵאוֹת אֶלֶף רַגְלִי הַגְּבָרִים לְבַד
מִטָּף׃ 38 וְגַם־עֵרֶב רַב עָלָה אִתָּם וְצֹאן
וּבָקָר מִקְנֶה כָּבֵד מְאֹד׃ 39 וַיֹּאפוּ אֶת־
הַבָּצֵק אֲשֶׁר הוֹצִיאוּ מִמִּצְרַיִם עֻגֹת מַצּוֹת
כִּי לֹא חָמֵץ כִּי־גֹרְשׁוּ מִמִּצְרַיִם וְלֹא יָכְלוּ
לְהִתְמַהְמֵהַּ וְגַם־צֵדָה לֹא־עָשׂוּ לָהֶם׃

of silver and gold, and clothing. 36And the LORD had disposed the Egyptians favorably toward the people, and they let them have their request; thus they stripped the Egyptians.

37The Israelites journeyed from Rameses to Succoth, about six hundred thousand men on foot, aside from children. 38Moreover, a mixed multitude went up with them, and very much livestock, both flocks and herds. 39And they baked unleavened cakes of the dough that they had taken out of Egypt, for it was not leavened, since they had been driven out of Egypt and could not delay; nor had they prepared any provisions for themselves.

THE EXODUS (vv. 37–42)

37. Raamses This city served as the assembly point for the departing Israelites. See Comment to 1:11.

Succoth A one day's journey from the royal palace at Raamses. This probably was the site known as Tjeku in Egyptian, the capital of the eighth province of Lower Egypt in the eastern part of the delta. The region is known to have served as pasture land for Semitic tribes and was the Egyptian gateway to and from Asia.

Six hundred thousand Women, children, and the elderly are not included. This number of men on foot would mean there was a total Israelite population of more than two million. The eastern part of the Nile delta or the peninsula of Sinai could not sustain such a vast population with water and food, not to mention the logistics involved in moving two million people together with their cattle and herds across the Sea of Reeds with the Egyptian chariots in hot pursuit. In response to these problems, it has been suggested that the Hebrew word *elef,* usually rendered "thousand," here means "clan" or that it signifies a small military unit—the number of fighting men levied from each tribe. Another theory construes the total number as envisaging the Israelite population at the close of the "Exodus era," which culminated with the completion of the Temple by King Solomon: 600,000 adult males would be a realistic statistic for that period.

38. a mixed multitude Varied groups of forced laborers seem to have taken advantage of the confused situation and fled the country with the Israelites. Note that the Hebrew word translated as "mixed multitude" (*eirev*) is from the same root (ערב) as the plague in 8:17, suggesting the rabbinic tradition that these people were a major source of the troubles in the desert.

This practice of the Egyptians sending the Israelites off with gifts of gold and jewels anticipates the law (Deut. 15:13) that one who frees a slave must not send him or her away empty handed. According to the Midrash, there were three kinds of people among the Egyptians. One third wanted to keep the Israelites as slaves. They died in the plagues. A second group supported Israel's bid for liberation and rose in revolt against Pharaoh's stubborn policies. These were the Egyptians who gave Israel gold, silver, and jewels as they prepared to leave. Their "lending" these gifts to the Israelites was part of the public nature of the Exodus. The Israelites did not sneak out furtively under cover of darkness. A third group of Egyptians celebrated the *Pesaḥ* with Israel and then left with them, as we read (v. 38), "a mixed multitude went up with them" (Exod. R. 18:8).

39. nor had they prepared They had two weeks to prepare for the Exodus. Does this suggest a certain lack of confidence that God would in fact redeem them? Or does it reflect the slaves' mentality of living day to day and not planning for the future? Perhaps it testifies to their faith, willing to march into the desert without having prepared food in advance.

40 The length of time that the Israelites lived in Egypt was four hundred and thirty years; 41 at the end of the four hundred and thirtieth year, to the very day, all the ranks of the LORD departed from the land of Egypt. 42 That was for the LORD a night of vigil to bring them out of the land of Egypt; that same night is the LORD's, one of vigil for all the children of Israel throughout the ages.

40 וּמוֹשַׁב֙ בְּנֵ֣י יִשְׂרָאֵ֔ל אֲשֶׁ֥ר יָשְׁב֖וּ בְּמִצְרָ֑יִם
שְׁלֹשִׁ֣ים שָׁנָ֔ה וְאַרְבַּ֥ע מֵא֖וֹת שָׁנָֽה׃ 41 וַיְהִ֗י
מִקֵּץ֙ שְׁלֹשִׁ֣ים שָׁנָ֔ה וְאַרְבַּ֥ע מֵא֖וֹת שָׁנָ֑ה
וַיְהִ֗י בְּעֶ֙צֶם֙ הַיּ֣וֹם הַזֶּ֔ה יָצְא֛וּ כָּל־צִבְא֥וֹת
יְהוָ֖ה מֵאֶ֥רֶץ מִצְרָֽיִם׃ 42 לֵ֣יל שִׁמֻּרִ֥ים הוּא֙
לַֽיהוָ֔ה לְהוֹצִיאָ֖ם מֵאֶ֣רֶץ מִצְרָ֑יִם הֽוּא־
הַלַּ֤יְלָה הַזֶּה֙ לַֽיהוָ֔ה שִׁמֻּרִ֛ים לְכָל־בְּנֵ֥י
יִשְׂרָאֵ֖ל לְדֹרֹתָֽם׃ פ

43 The LORD said to Moses and Aaron: This is the law of the passover offering: No foreigner shall eat of it. 44 But any slave a man has bought may eat of it once he has been circumcised. 45 No bound or hired laborer shall eat of it. 46 It shall be eaten in one house: you shall not take any of the flesh outside the house; nor shall you

43 וַיֹּ֤אמֶר יְהוָה֙ אֶל־מֹשֶׁ֣ה וְאַהֲרֹ֔ן זֹ֖את
חֻקַּ֣ת הַפָּ֑סַח כָּל־בֶּן־נֵכָ֖ר לֹא־יֹ֥אכַל בּֽוֹ׃
44 וְכָל־עֶ֥בֶד אִ֖ישׁ מִקְנַת־כָּ֑סֶף וּמַלְתָּ֣ה אֹת֔וֹ
אָ֖ז יֹ֥אכַל בּֽוֹ׃ 45 תּוֹשָׁ֥ב וְשָׂכִ֖יר לֹא־יֹ֥אכַל־
בּֽוֹ׃ 46 בְּבַ֤יִת אֶחָד֙ יֵאָכֵ֔ל לֹא־תוֹצִ֨יא

40–41. This historical summation does not accord precisely with the 400 years of Egyptian oppression predicted in Gen. 15:13. Perhaps that round number and its division into neatly symmetrical periods of time—as explained by some of the rabbis and medieval commentators—are intended to be rhetorical rather than literal; i.e., they underline the biblical concept of history as the fulfillment of God's design. In the worldview of the Bible, history is not a series of disconnected and haphazard incidents.

42. The final night in Egypt, the night of redemption, is described as one of vigil for both God and the Israelites.

EXCLUSIONARY REGULATIONS (vv. 43–49)

This final section has its own title: "The Law of the Passover Offering." It largely defines who is ineligible to celebrate the festival. The primary emphasis is on the practice of circumcision. As the physical token of God's covenant and a symbol of commitment to a life lived in the full awareness of that covenant, it is the indispensable prerequisite for males who wish to participate in the paschal offering. This requirement was forcefully expressed in 4:24–26, when Moses set out to return to Egypt to commence his mission of liberation, and it is stressed once again at the moment of the successful fulfillment of that mission.

43. foreigner The Hebrew term *ben nekhar* refers to a non-Israelite who resides in the land temporarily, usually for purposes of commerce. He does not profess the religion of Israel and does not identify with the community's historical experiences. He is, therefore, exempted from the religious obligations and restrictions imposed on Israelites.

44. Once the privately owned slave is circumcised (per the law of Gen. 17:12–13) he is treated as a member of the family and may participate fully in the paschal offering. The link between Passover and circumcision is also found in Josh. 5, a companion to this passage designated as the *haftarah* for the first day of *Pesaḥ*.

45. bound or hired laborer These are two categories of non-Israelite wage earners who do not have the status of members of a household.

46. in one house This logically connects with the preceding verses, which stress that only those included within a household may participate. None may leave the house because every Israelite must be accounted for and prepared when the signal is given to depart.

HALAKHAH L'MA·ASEH

12:43. No foreigner shall eat of it This rule applied only to the sacrifice of the paschal lamb in biblical times. It does not apply to non-Jewish guests at a *Seider* meal in our time.

break a bone of it. ⁴⁷The whole community of
Israel shall offer it. ⁴⁸If a stranger who dwells
with you would offer the passover to the LORD,
all his males must be circumcised; then he shall
be admitted to offer it; he shall then be as a citizen of the country. But no uncircumcised person may eat of it. ⁴⁹There shall be one law for
the citizen and for the stranger who dwells
among you.

50And all the Israelites did so; as the LORD had
commanded Moses and Aaron, so they did.

51That very day the LORD freed the Israelites
from the land of Egypt, troop by troop.

מִן־הַבַּ֫יִת מִן־הַבָּשָׂ֛ר ח֖וּצָה וְעֶ֥צֶם לֹ֣א
תִשְׁבְּרוּ־בֽוֹ׃ 47 כָּל־עֲדַ֥ת יִשְׂרָאֵ֖ל יַעֲשׂ֥וּ
אֹתֽוֹ׃ 48 וְכִֽי־יָג֨וּר אִתְּךָ֜ גֵּ֗ר וְעָ֣שָׂה פֶ֨סַח֩
לַֽיהוָ֜ה הִמּ֧וֹל ל֣וֹ כָל־זָכָ֗ר וְאָז֙ יִקְרַ֣ב
לַעֲשֹׂת֔וֹ וְהָיָ֖ה כְּאֶזְרַ֣ח הָאָ֑רֶץ וְכָל־עָרֵ֖ל
לֹֽא־יֹ֥אכַל בּֽוֹ׃ 49 תּוֹרָ֣ה אַחַ֔ת יִהְיֶ֖ה לָֽאֶזְרָ֑ח
וְלַגֵּ֖ר הַגָּ֥ר בְּתוֹכְכֶֽם׃
50 וַיַּֽעֲשׂ֖וּ כָּל־בְּנֵ֣י יִשְׂרָאֵ֑ל כַּאֲשֶׁ֨ר צִוָּ֤ה יְהוָה֙
אֶת־מֹשֶׁ֣ה וְאֶֽת־אַהֲרֹ֔ן כֵּ֖ן עָשֽׂוּ׃ ס
51 וַיְהִ֕י בְּעֶ֖צֶם הַיּ֣וֹם הַזֶּ֑ה הוֹצִ֨יא יְהוָ֜ה
אֶת־בְּנֵ֧י יִשְׂרָאֵ֛ל מֵאֶ֥רֶץ מִצְרַ֖יִם עַל־
שביעי צִבְאֹתָֽם׃ פ

---

break a bone Presumably, to suck out the
marrow.

48–49. These instructions relate to the situation envisaged above in verse 25. Strangers in ancient Israel enjoyed numerous rights and privileges, such as the benefits of *Shabbat* rest, the protection afforded by the cities of refuge, and access
to a share of certain tithes and to the produce of
the sabbatical year. They could even offer sacrifices if they so wished and participate in religious
festivals. They were obligated to refrain from certain actions that could undermine the social,
moral, and spiritual well-being of the dominant
society—such as immorality, idolatry, blasphemy,
and the consumption of blood. They were not

required to celebrate *Pesaḥ;* but if they desired to
do so, and thus identify themselves and their families with the national experience of Israel, the
men first had to undergo the rite of circumcision.
Having done so, no discrimination between them
and citizens was allowed. An uncircumcised
Israelite was also excluded from participation.

50. This refers to the eating of the paschal
offering.

51. This verse resumes the narrative of verses
37–41. It is connected to the next chapter by the
traditional scribal division of the Torah, to indicate that the subsequent law of the firstborn came
into effect on the very day of the Exodus.

---

48. The person of non-Jewish origin who
chooses to join the Jewish people, the *ger,* is
welcome to celebrate *Pesaḥ* even though his or
her ancestors were not literally slaves in Egypt
and did not leave with Moses, even as immi-
grants to the United States sing, "Land where
my fathers died."

49. This may be taken as a major statement
of the innate worth of all human beings and
their right to equal treatment under the law.

Every spring at the *Pesaḥ Seider,* every week

when we pause on *Shabbat* to demonstrate
that we are free people and not slaves (praising
Shabbat in the *Kiddush* as "a reminder of our
liberation from Egypt"), indeed every day, the
Jew is to recall that Jewish history began with
God's intervening on behalf of an enslaved people, leading them to freedom, and giving them
the Torah. That memory is to be personal, not
a fact of ancient history. (Exod. 13:8: "It is because of what the LORD did for me when I went
free from Egypt.")

HALAKHAH L'MA·ASEH
12:49. one law The non-Jew, though not subject to all the duties and privileges of Jewish law, must nevertheless
be treated fairly and justly in all business and legal dealings, and Jews are commanded to care for all who are
sick or poor, including non-Jews. (BT Git. 61a).

13 The Lord spoke further to Moses, saying, 2"Consecrate to Me every first-born; man
and beast, the first issue of every womb among
the Israelites is Mine."
3And Moses said to the people,
"Remember this day, on which you went free
from Egypt, the house of bondage, how the
Lord freed you from it with a mighty hand: no
leavened bread shall be eaten. 4You go free on

יג וַיְדַבֵּ֥ר יְהוָ֖ה אֶל־מֹשֶׁ֥ה לֵּאמֹֽר׃ ביעי
2 קַדֶּשׁ־לִ֨י כָל־בְּכ֜וֹר פֶּ֤טֶר כָּל־רֶ֙חֶם֙ בִּבְנֵ֣י
יִשְׂרָאֵ֔ל בָּאָדָ֖ם וּבַבְּהֵמָ֑ה לִ֖י הֽוּא׃
3 וַיֹּאמֶר֩ מֹשֶׁ֨ה אֶל־הָעָ֜ם
זָכ֞וֹר אֶת־הַיּ֣וֹם הַזֶּ֗ה אֲשֶׁ֨ר יְצָאתֶ֤ם
מִמִּצְרַ֙יִם֙ מִבֵּ֣ית עֲבָדִ֔ים כִּ֚י בְּחֹ֣זֶק יָ֔ד
הוֹצִ֧יא יְהוָ֛ה אֶתְכֶ֖ם מִזֶּ֑ה וְלֹ֥א יֵאָכֵ֖ל
חָמֵֽץ׃ 4 הַיּ֖וֹם אַתֶּ֣ם יֹצְאִ֑ים בְּחֹ֖דֶשׁ

COMMEMORATIVE RITUALS (13:1–16)

This section continues the process of connecting institutions of the present with the Exodus experience of the past. The revitalized ancient rituals, charged with new historical meaning, serve to perpetuate the memory of those events by making them living realities for subsequent generations. In this section, the key to linking historical and natural events is the coincidence that the liberation from Egypt occurred in the spring (v. 4), the season of nature's rebirth. It is the period of the new barley harvest and the time when animals begin their reproductive cycle.

CONSECRATION OF THE FIRSTBORN (vv. 1–2)

1. The Lord spoke further to Moses, saying This simple formula always introduces a specific instruction given to Moses personally, a communication not relayed to the people. It usually requires that he initiate some action—in this instance, consecrating the firstborn, which is juxtaposed to the slaying of the firstborn Egyptians.

2. In many ancient pagan cultures it was believed that the first fruits of the soil, and the first offspring of animals and humans, were endowed by nature with intrinsic holiness. The instruction that Moses consecrate the firstborn may be an aggressive attack against such notions. The firstborn belongs to God solely by reason of His divine will decreed at the time of the Exodus and not because of any inherent sanctity.

Consecrate to Me This instruction usually involves a rite of purification as well as an induction ceremony. The former requires bathing, laundering of clothes, and abstention from ritual defilement on the part of the initiate (see 19:10,14). The latter entails an investiture performed by a superior (see Lev. 8:6ff.).

beast Verse 12 below will restrict the requirement to the male animal, which would more likely be expendable, because animal breeding requires many females and few males. (Nothing is stated here concerning the law of the first fruits of the soil, because they cannot be connected with the events of the 10th plague and the Exodus, but only with the conquest and settlement of the Land. They are treated in later texts.)

first issue of every womb Some believe that this alludes to a pre-Israelite requirement that the firstborn child be offered as a sacrifice. It is clear from this text, however, that the notion is rejected by the Torah (see v. 13).

LAWS OF *MATZOT* AND *T'FILLIN* (vv. 3–10)

Israel's liberation from Egypt is to be an event forever imprinted on its memory, individually and collectively. A set of symbols is created to actualize the experiences.

3. Remember See Comment to 2:24.

this day The 15th of the first month.

house of bondage Literally, "house of slaves." This designation for Egypt, frequent in Deuteronomy, may derive from the Egyptian practice of settling the labor gangs in walled workmen's villages close to the site of the project for which they were conscripted. To the Israelites, such a village may have appeared to be a gigantic "slave house."

no leavened bread Denying oneself all benefit from anything containing leaven during *Pesaḥ* is one way of fulfilling the commandment to "remember."

HALAKHAH L'MA·ASEH

13:2. every first-born See Comment on Num. 3:13.

this day, in the month of Abib. 5 So, when the
Lord has brought you into the land of the Canaanites, the Hittites, the Amorites, the Hivites,
and the Jebusites, which He swore to your fathers to give you, a land flowing with milk and
honey, you shall observe in this month the following practice:
6 "Seven days you shall eat unleavened bread,
and on the seventh day there shall be a festival
of the Lord. 7 Throughout the seven days unleavened bread shall be eaten; no leavened bread
shall be found with you, and no leaven shall be
found in all your territory. 8 And you shall explain to your son on that day, 'It is because of
what the Lord did for me when I went free from
Egypt.'
9 "And this shall serve you as a sign on your
hand and as a reminder on your forehead—in
order that the Teaching of the Lord may be in
your mouth—that with a mighty hand the Lord
freed you from Egypt. 10 You shall keep this institution at its set time from year to year.

הָאָבִיב׃ 5 וְהָיָה כִי־יְבִיאֲךָ יְהוָה אֶל־אֶרֶץ
הַכְּנַעֲנִי וְהַחִתִּי וְהָאֱמֹרִי וְהַחִוִּי וְהַיְבוּסִי
אֲשֶׁר נִשְׁבַּע לַאֲבֹתֶיךָ לָתֶת לָךְ אֶרֶץ זָבַת
חָלָב וּדְבָשׁ וְעָבַדְתָּ אֶת־הָעֲבֹדָה הַזֹּאת
בַּחֹדֶשׁ הַזֶּה׃
6 שִׁבְעַת יָמִים תֹּאכַל מַצֹּת וּבַיּוֹם
הַשְּׁבִיעִי חַג לַיהוָה׃ 7 מַצּוֹת יֵאָכֵל אֵת
שִׁבְעַת הַיָּמִים וְלֹא־יֵרָאֶה לְךָ חָמֵץ וְלֹא־
יֵרָאֶה לְךָ שְׂאֹר בְּכָל־גְּבֻלֶךָ׃ 8 וְהִגַּדְתָּ
לְבִנְךָ בַּיּוֹם הַהוּא לֵאמֹר בַּעֲבוּר זֶה עָשָׂה
יְהוָה לִי בְּצֵאתִי מִמִּצְרָיִם׃
9 וְהָיָה לְךָ לְאוֹת עַל־יָדְךָ וּלְזִכָּרוֹן בֵּין
עֵינֶיךָ לְמַעַן תִּהְיֶה תּוֹרַת יְהוָה בְּפִיךָ כִּי
בְּיָד חֲזָקָה הוֹצִאֲךָ יְהוָה מִמִּצְרָיִם׃
10 וְשָׁמַרְתָּ אֶת־הַחֻקָּה הַזֹּאת לְמוֹעֲדָהּ
מִיָּמִים יָמִימָה׃ ס

5. flowing with milk and honey See Comment to Exod. 3:8.

6. Another aid to memory, this one a positive action: the eating of *matzot.*

seventh day According to rabbinic tradition, it was on the seventh day after the Exodus that the pursuing Egyptians drowned in the Sea of Reeds. Nevertheless, the emphasis here—before the Exodus—on the special religious character of that day disconnects it from any celebration of Egypt's defeat.

8. you shall explain The word translated "you shall explain" (*v'higgadta,* literally, "you shall tell") is the source of the *Haggadah,* the name of the service containing rituals and readings for the *Pesaḥ* night ceremonials. Parents must take the initiative in instructing their children.

9. In rabbinic tradition, this verse has been interpreted as instituting the *t'fillin* (commonly known as "phylacteries" in English), worn during weekday morning prayers (see v. 16).

your hand Rabbinic tradition understands this as the left arm and hand.

forehead Literally, "between your eyes." The Hebrew, which has always been interpreted to refer to the forehead, is confirmed by Deut. 14:1.

Teaching of the Lord Hebrew: *torat YHVH.* This phrase first appears here. It cannot possibly refer to the canonized Torah, but it does presuppose a text that can be memorized and recited.

HALAKHAH L'MA·ASEH

13:8. you shall explain to your son The Hebrew word *ben* here is understood as a female as well as a male child. If no children are present, adults are obligated to ask the questions and recount the Exodus from Egypt each *Seider* night. It is especially praiseworthy to expound at length on the Exodus through discussion, debate, and additional readings.

13:9. as a sign See Comment on Deut. 6:8.

13:10. at its set time Because *Pesaḥ* must be celebrated in the spring, the lunar cycle that governs the Jewish calendar had to be adapted to the solar seasons. Therefore, the Jewish calendar adds an extra month before *Pesaḥ* during 7 designated years of a 19-year cycle to ensure that *Pesaḥ* remains a spring holiday, as required in Exod. 13:4 and Deut. 16:1.

11“And when the LORD has brought you into the land of the Canaanites, as He swore to you and to your fathers, and has given it to you, 12you shall set apart for the LORD every first issue of the womb: every male firstling that your cattle drop shall be the LORD’s. 13But every firstling ass you shall redeem with a sheep; if you do not redeem it, you must break its neck. And you must redeem every first-born male among your children. 14And when, in time to come, your son asks you, saying, ‘What does this mean?’ you shall say to him, ‘It was with a mighty hand that the LORD brought us out from Egypt, the house of bondage. 15When Pharaoh stubbornly refused to let us go, the LORD slew every first-born in the land of Egypt, the first-born of both man and beast. Therefore I sacrifice to the LORD every first male issue of the womb, but redeem every first-born among my sons.’

16“And so it shall be as a sign upon your hand

11 וְהָיָ֞ה כִּֽי־יְבִֽאֲךָ֤ יְהוָה֙ אֶל־אֶ֣רֶץ הַֽכְּנַעֲנִ֔י
כַּאֲשֶׁ֛ר נִשְׁבַּ֥ע לְךָ֖ וְלַאֲבֹתֶ֑יךָ וּנְתָנָ֖הּ לָֽךְ׃
12 וְהַעֲבַרְתָּ֥ כָל־פֶּֽטֶר־רֶ֖חֶם לַֽיהוָ֑ה וְכָל־
פֶּ֣טֶר ׀ שֶׁ֣גֶר בְּהֵמָ֗ה אֲשֶׁ֨ר יִהְיֶ֥ה לְךָ֛ הַזְּכָרִ֖ים
לַֽיהוָֽה׃ 13 וְכָל־פֶּ֤טֶר חֲמֹר֙ תִּפְדֶּ֣ה בְשֶׂ֔ה
וְאִם־לֹ֥א תִפְדֶּ֖ה וַעֲרַפְתּ֑וֹ וְכֹ֨ל בְּכ֥וֹר אָדָ֛ם
בְּבָנֶ֖יךָ תִּפְדֶּֽה׃ 14 וְהָיָ֞ה כִּֽי־יִשְׁאָלְךָ֥ בִנְךָ֛ פטיר
מָחָ֖ר לֵאמֹ֣ר מַה־זֹּ֑את וְאָמַרְתָּ֣ אֵלָ֔יו בְּחֹ֣זֶק
יָ֗ד הוֹצִיאָ֧נוּ יְהוָ֛ה מִמִּצְרַ֖יִם מִבֵּ֥ית עֲבָדִֽים׃
15 וַיְהִ֗י כִּֽי־הִקְשָׁ֣ה פַרְעֹה֮ לְשַׁלְּחֵנוּ֒ וַיַּהֲרֹ֨ג
יְהוָ֤ה כָּל־בְּכוֹר֙ בְּאֶ֣רֶץ מִצְרַ֔יִם מִבְּכֹ֥ר אָדָ֖ם
וְעַד־בְּכ֣וֹר בְּהֵמָ֑ה עַל־כֵּ֞ן אֲנִ֣י זֹבֵ֗חַ לַֽיהוָ֗ה
כָּל־פֶּ֤טֶר רֶ֙חֶם֙ הַזְּכָרִ֔ים וְכָל־בְּכ֥וֹר בָּנַ֖י
אֶפְדֶּֽה׃
16 וְהָיָ֤ה לְאוֹת֙ עַל־יָ֣דְכָ֔ה* וּלְטוֹטָפֹ֖ת בֵּ֣ין

v. 16. יתיר ה׳

REDEMPTION OF THE FIRSTBORN
(vv. 11–16)

Verse 2 ordains the immediate consecration of the firstborn. This section deals with the treatment of the firstborn after settlement in the Promised Land. The animal firstling is to retain its status; it belongs to God. The priestly status of the human firstborn, however, is to be revoked, their functions taken over by the tribe of Levi. Hence, the sanctity of the firstborn sons is to be removed by the process of “redemption,” which explains why this section does not immediately follow verse 2.

12. issue of the womb A firstborn by cesarean section is thus exempt from the redemption requirement.

13. firstling ass This is the only ritually impure animal that needs to be redeemed, in this case by giving a sheep to the priest as a replacement. The ass was the standard means of transport and a beast of burden. As Ibn Ezra observes, it was most likely the only ritually impure domestic animal possessed by the Israelites in Egypt.

break its neck According to rabbinic tradition, the neck was broken by a blow from behind with a hatchet. This exceptional form of slaughter was used to avoid the appearance of performing the ritual slaughter of an unclean animal.

redeem every first-born male The method of redemption is not given, presupposing a familiar, established practice. See Num. 18:16.

14. this The ceremony of redemption.

15. The “mighty hand” in the previous verse is here explained as referring to the slaying of the Egyptian firstborn.

16. See Comments to verse 9. (*Totafot* are identified as a pendant or headband, interpreted by later Jewish tradition as phylacteries.)

CHAPTER 13

16. sign upon your hand . . . symbol on your forehead It is striking that a people so recently released from bondage in Egypt should respond to their freedom not by wanting to live

HALAKHAH L’MA·ASEH

13:13. redeem every first-born male See Comment on Num. 3:13.

and as a symbol on your forehead that with a mighty hand the LORD freed us from Egypt."

עֵינֶ֑יךָ כִּ֚י בְּחֹ֣זֶק יָ֔ד הוֹצִיאָ֥נוּ יְהוָ֖ה מִמִּצְרָֽיִם׃ ס

without obligations but by willingly binding themselves to the God who freed them (in the symbolism of *t'fillin*).

Why are *t'fillin* placed on the left arm, which generally is the weaker arm? Because our arm was weak in Egypt and it was only by God's mighty hand that we were rescued (*K'li Yakar*). The word *totafot* ("symbol") is plural. The *t'fillin* worn on the arm has a single receptacle for the scriptural verses placed therein, whereas the *t'fillin* worn on the forehead is divided into four. This has prompted the comment that, although Jews may be divided in their beliefs and opinions, with no authority to compel their belief, they should be united in action. The Rabbinic imagination envisioned God as also wearing *t'fillin*. What is written inside God's *t'fillin*? A statement of God's love and admiration for the Jewish people, in words taken from 1 Chron. 17:21, "Who is like My people Israel!" (BT Ber. 6a).

HALAKHAH L'MA·ASEH

13:16. as a sign See Comment on Deut. 6:8.

הפטרת בא

HAFTARAH FOR BO

JEREMIAH 46:13–28

This *haftarah* is part of a series of prophecies against Egypt that begin with Jer. 46:2. They constitute the first group of Jeremiah's pronouncements against foreign nations, collected in chapters 46–51. The anti-Egyptian oracles in the *haftarah* (46:13–26), varying in content and in style, are followed by two positive oracles about Israel in verses 27–28. Jeremiah's doom oracles against Egypt are given a historical setting in verses 13 and 25–26, where King Nebuchadrezzar of Babylon is identified as the avenger. The *parashah* also presents a polarity of Egyptian doom and Israelite salvation.

Following the taunting proclamations of the Egyptian call to arms and the ensuing flight and fear (46:14–16), the assertive voice of the Lord, proclaiming doom and desolation, provides a counterpoint. This contrast is underscored by the mocking epithet for "Pharaoh king of Egypt: / 'Braggart who let the hour go by'" (v. 17). In contradistinction, God "the King, / Whose name is Lord of Hosts" swears by His own being that the words of doom "shall . . . come to pass" (v. 18). The aura of inevitability is reinforced by the repeated use of the Hebrew particle *ki,* with the sense of "for" and "surely" (vv. 14–15,18–19, 21–23).

In these oracles, "The Lord of Hosts, the God of Israel" is the universal Lord of history, inflicting punishment "on Egypt, her gods, and her kings" (v. 25). Total destruction will not be the outcome, however, because God's final word to the Egyptians prophesies their eventual restoration (v. 26).

The concluding oracles in verses 27 and 28 of the *haftarah* breathe another spirit. The prophet repeatedly exhorts the Israelites to overcome fear and loss though assurances that the Lord will deliver them from their land of captivity (v. 27). They will receive judgment in proper measure, without unilateral doom (v. 28). One senses here a consolation for the dismayed. The promise of calm and quiet is not yet a reality.

RELATION OF THE *HAFTARAH* TO THE *PARASHAH*

The theme of Israelite servitude in Egypt in the *parashah* is counterpoised with a promise of Egypt's destruction in the *haftarah* (vv. 14–24). The plague of locusts described in the *parashah* (Exod. 10:3–20) is echoed in Jeremiah's prophecy as a metaphor for the overwhelmingly numerous armies that will descend on Egypt in its hour of doom (Jer. 46:23). Nebuchadrezzar's "coming" in judgment against Pharaoh (v. 13) responds to Moses' ancient "coming" in supplication before Pharaoh (Exod. 10:1). God will wreak judgment on the gods of Egypt (Jer. 46:25), as He declared long ago ("I will mete out punishments to all the gods of Egypt," Exod. 12:12).

46 13The word which the Lord spoke to
the prophet Jeremiah about the coming of King
Nebuchadrezzar of Babylon to attack the land
of Egypt:

14Declare in Egypt, proclaim in Migdol,

מו 13 הַדָּבָר אֲשֶׁר דִּבֶּר יְהוָה אֶל־
יִרְמְיָהוּ הַנָּבִיא לָבוֹא נְבוּכַדְרֶאצַּר מֶלֶךְ
בָּבֶל לְהַכּוֹת אֶת־אֶרֶץ מִצְרָיִם׃

14 הַגִּידוּ בְמִצְרַיִם וְהַשְׁמִיעוּ בְמִגְדּוֹל

Proclaim in Noph and Tahpanhes!
Say: Take your posts and stand ready,
For the sword has devoured all around you!
15Why are your stalwarts swept away?
They did not stand firm,
For the LORD thrust them down;
16He made many stumble,
They fell over one another.

They said:
"Up! Let us return to our people,
To the land of our birth,
Because of the deadly sword."
17There they called Pharaoh king of Egypt:
"Braggart who let the hour go by."

18As I live—declares the King,
Whose name is LORD of Hosts—
As surely as Tabor is among the mountains
And Carmel is by the sea,
So shall this come to pass.
19Equip yourself for exile,
Fair Egypt, you who dwell secure!
For Noph shall become a waste,
Desolate, without inhabitants.
20Egypt is a handsome heifer—

וְהַשְׁמִיעוּ בְנֹף וּבְתַחְפַּנְחֵס
אִמְרוּ הִתְיַצֵּב וְהָכֵן לָךְ
כִּי־אָכְלָה חֶרֶב סְבִיבֶיךָ׃
15 מַדּוּעַ נִסְחַף אַבִּירֶיךָ
לֹא עָמַד
כִּי יְהוָה הֲדָפוֹ׃
16 הִרְבָּה כּוֹשֵׁל
גַּם־נָפַל אִישׁ אֶל־רֵעֵהוּ

וַיֹּאמְרוּ
קוּמָה ׀ וְנָשֻׁבָה אֶל־עַמֵּנוּ
וְאֶל־אֶרֶץ מוֹלַדְתֵּנוּ
מִפְּנֵי חֶרֶב הַיּוֹנָה׃
17 קָרְאוּ שָׁם פַּרְעֹה מֶלֶךְ־מִצְרַיִם
שָׁאוֹן הֶעֱבִיר הַמּוֹעֵד׃

18 חַי־אָנִי נְאֻם־הַמֶּלֶךְ
יְהוָה צְבָאוֹת שְׁמוֹ
כִּי כְּתָבוֹר בֶּהָרִים
וּכְכַרְמֶל בַּיָּם
יָבוֹא׃
19 כְּלֵי גוֹלָה עֲשִׂי לָךְ
יוֹשֶׁבֶת בַּת־מִצְרָיִם
כִּי־נֹף לְשַׁמָּה תִהְיֶה
וְנִצְּתָה מֵאֵין יוֹשֵׁב׃ ס
20 עֶגְלָה יְפֵה־פִיָּה מִצְרָיִם

Jeremiah 46:14. in Migdol . . . Noph and Tahpanhes The Egyptian place-names have been hebraized. Migdol is a Semitic name meaning "Tower." It was used for several frontier towns in the eastern delta. Noph is a corruption of Moph (see Hos. 9:6) or Memphis (Saqqara, in the lower Nile). Tahpanhes is derived from two words, meaning "fortress of the Nubian" (Tel Daphne).

16. Up! Let us return to our people This refers either to the mercenaries or to the foreign traders who flee from Egypt.

17. Braggart who let the hour go by The Hebrew phrase is difficult. The word translated "braggart" (*sha·on*, literally "uproar, tumult") is understood as "loudmouth." The Targum understands the term more literally, referring to Pharaoh as one who made a big tumult. The noun can also mean "desolation" or "destruction." On this basis, Radak dubbed Nebuchadrezzar "king of Destruction."

18. As surely as Tabor . . . / So shall this come to pass The simile is puzzling. As rendered here, the analogy suggests that as surely as Tabor is among the mountains the event will come to pass (Rashi and Radak). Alternatively, the verb ("will come") refers to the advent of Nebuchadrezzar (i.e., "he shall come").

20. Egypt is a handsome heifer This meta-

A gadfly from the north is coming, coming!
21 The mercenaries, too, in her midst
Are like stall-fed calves;
They too shall turn tail,
Flee as one, and make no stand.
Their day of disaster is upon them,
The hour of their doom.
22 She shall rustle away like a snake
As they come marching in force;
They shall come against her with axes,
Like hewers of wood.
23 They shall cut down her forest
—declares the LORD—
Though it cannot be measured;
For they are more numerous than locusts,
And cannot be counted.
24 Fair Egypt shall be shamed,
Handed over to the people of the north.

25 The LORD of Hosts, the God of Israel, has
said: I will inflict punishment on Amon of No
and on Pharaoh—on Egypt, her gods, and her
kings—on Pharaoh and all who rely on him. 26 I
will deliver them into the hands of those who
seek to kill them, into the hands of King Nebuchadrezzar of Babylon and into the hands of
his subjects. But afterward she shall be inhabited
again as in former days, declares the LORD.

קֶ֥רֶץ מִצָּפ֖וֹן בָּ֥א בָֽא׃
21 גַּם־שְׂכִרֶ֤יהָ בְקִרְבָּהּ֙
כְּעֶגְלֵ֣י מַרְבֵּ֔ק
כִּֽי־גַם־הֵ֙מָּה֙ הִפְנ֛וּ
נָ֥סוּ יַחְדָּ֖יו לֹ֣א עָמָ֑דוּ
כִּ֣י י֥וֹם אֵידָ֛ם בָּ֥א עֲלֵיהֶ֖ם
עֵ֥ת פְּקֻדָּתָֽם׃
22 קוֹלָ֖הּ כַּנָּחָ֣שׁ יֵלֵ֑ךְ
כִּֽי־בְחַ֣יִל יֵלֵ֔כוּ
וּבְקַרְדֻּמּוֹת֙ בָּ֣אוּ לָ֔הּ
כְּחֹטְבֵ֖י עֵצִֽים׃
23 כָּרְת֤וּ יַעְרָהּ֙
נְאֻם־יְהוָ֔ה
כִּ֖י לֹ֣א יֵחָקֵ֑ר
כִּ֤י רַבּוּ֙ מֵֽאַרְבֶּ֔ה
וְאֵ֥ין לָהֶ֖ם מִסְפָּֽר׃
24 הֹבִ֖ישָׁה בַּת־מִצְרָ֑יִם
נִתְּנָ֖ה בְּיַ֥ד עַם־צָפֽוֹן׃

25 אָמַר֩ יְהוָ֨ה צְבָא֜וֹת אֱלֹהֵ֣י יִשְׂרָאֵ֗ל הִנְנִ֤י
פוֹקֵד֙ אֶל־אָמ֣וֹן מִנֹּ֔א וְעַל־פַּרְעֹה֙ וְעַל־
מִצְרַ֔יִם וְעַל־אֱלֹהֶ֖יהָ וְעַל־מְלָכֶ֑יהָ וְעַל־
פַּרְעֹ֔ה וְעַ֖ל הַבֹּטְחִ֥ים בּֽוֹ׃ 26 וּנְתַתִּ֗ים בְּיַד֙
מְבַקְשֵׁ֣י נַפְשָׁ֔ם וּבְיַ֛ד נְבוּכַדְרֶאצַּ֥ר מֶֽלֶךְ־
בָּבֶ֖ל וּבְיַד־עֲבָדָ֑יו וְאַחֲרֵי־כֵ֛ן תִּשְׁכֹּ֥ן כִּֽימֵי־
קֶ֖דֶם נְאֻם־יְהוָֽה׃ ס

phor may have been chosen to allude to the Egyptian bull god, Apis.

from the north The reference to an enemy from the north here and in verse 24 is unspecified. Elsewhere in Jeremiah the designation of an enemy from the northland is similarly vague (see 3:18, 6:22, 10:22, 16:15). Only in 605 B.C.E. does the prophet identify this enemy with Babylon (Jer. 25:9).

25. inflict punishment Hebrew: *poked.* This summary statement is linked to "their day of disaster" (*et p'kudatam*) in verse 21. The verb *poked* has the sense of inflicting punishment for wrongdoing. It is used that way in the Decalogue (Exod. 20:5) and in the list of divine attributes (Exod. 34:7). Significantly, the phrase "I will not leave you unpunished" (*nakkei lo anakkeka*) in the last verse of the *haftarah* echoes the phrase in Exod. 34:7 which declares that God "does not remit all punishment" (*nakkei lo y'nakkeh*).

Amon Amon, or Amon Re, was the imperial god of Egypt. The chief center of his worship was the Temple of Karnak in Thebes.

No Thebes; *niwt* (The City) in Egyptian. It was the chief city of Upper Egypt, starting with the Middle Kingdom (2000 B.C.E.). Jeremiah lived during the time when the center of government shifted from Thebes to Sais, a city in the upper delta. Even so, Thebes and its Temple of Karnak remained prominent.

27 But you,
Have no fear, My servant Jacob,
Be not dismayed, O Israel!
I will deliver you from far away,
Your folk from their land of captivity;
And Jacob again shall have calm
And quiet, with none to trouble him.
28 But you, have no fear,
My servant Jacob
—declares the LORD—
For I am with you.
I will make an end of all the nations
Among which I have banished you,
But I will not make an end of you!
I will not leave you unpunished,
But I will chastise you in measure.

27 וְאַתָּה
אַל־תִּירָא עַבְדִּי יַעֲקֹב
וְאַל־תֵּחַת יִשְׂרָאֵל
כִּי הִנְנִי מוֹשִׁעֲךָ מֵרָחוֹק
וְאֶת־זַרְעֲךָ מֵאֶרֶץ שִׁבְיָם
וְשָׁב יַעֲקוֹב* וְשָׁקַט
וְשַׁאֲנַן וְאֵין מַחֲרִיד׃ ס
28 אַתָּה אַל־תִּירָא
עַבְדִּי יַעֲקֹב
נְאֻם־יְהוָה
כִּי אִתְּךָ אָנִי
כִּי אֶעֱשֶׂה כָלָה בְּכָל־הַגּוֹיִם ׀
אֲשֶׁר הִדַּחְתִּיךָ שָׁמָּה
וְאֹתְךָ לֹא־אֶעֱשֶׂה כָלָה
וְיִסַּרְתִּיךָ לַמִּשְׁפָּט
וְנַקֵּה לֹא אֲנַקֶּךָּ׃ ס

v. 27. מלא ו'

27–28. Have no fear . . . have no fear These oracles exhort the people to courage and hope. The same usage is found in prophecies addressed to the nation in exile (Isa. 43:1, 44:2).

17Now when Pharaoh let the people go, God
did not lead them by way of the land of the Philistines, although it was nearer; for God said,
"The people may have a change of heart

17 וַיְהִ֗י בְּשַׁלַּ֣ח פַּרְעֹה֮ אֶת־הָעָם֒ וְלֹא־נָחָ֣ם
אֱלֹהִ֗ים דֶּ֚רֶךְ אֶ֣רֶץ פְּלִשְׁתִּ֔ים כִּ֥י קָר֖וֹב ה֑וּא
כִּ֣י ׀ אָמַ֣ר אֱלֹהִ֗ים פֶּֽן־יִנָּחֵ֥ם הָעָ֛ם בִּרְאֹתָ֥ם

THE EXODUS (13:17–14:31)

INTO THE WILDERNESS (13:17–22)

The narrative, interrupted at 12:42 by laws related to *Pesaḥ,* now continues.

17. God . . . lead them God, not Moses, is the protagonist here.

by way of the land of the Philistines The shortest land route from the Nile delta to Canaan. It was the southern segment of the 1000-mile international artery of transportation that led from the Egyptian fortress city of Tjaru (Sile) to the Canaanite city of Megiddo, and from there into Asia Minor and on to Mesopotamia. The "land of the Philistines" is the name given here to the stretch of territory in Canaan alongside the highway. The "Sea of Philistia" in 23:31 is the section of the Mediterranean adjacent to it. These apparently anachronistic names attest to the dominant role played in later centuries by the Philistines in that part of the country. They were part of a vast confederacy of "sea peoples"—so named by the Egyptians—and were first mentioned in historical records that date from the time of Ramses III (1183–1152 B.C.E.). They invaded Egypt from the region of Crete in the eighth year of that king's reign.

a change of heart Preferring Egyptian slavery to war.

---

17. God did not lead them by way of the land of the Philistines, although it was nearer The Hebrew word translated here as "although" (*ki*) has several different meanings. The commentators differ in their understanding of the word and of God's purpose in leading Israel by a longer, less direct route. Some see it as an act of kindness and consideration on God's part. One commentator translates *ki karov hu* as "because God was near to them" and loved them and, therefore, did not want to risk having some of them killed in a battle with the Philistines (*Minḥah B'lulah*). Others give it a psychological interpretation. Thus Rashi: God did not lead Israel through Philistine territory precisely because it was close, and it would have been too tempting to become discouraged and return to Egypt. Ramban: Although the way through the Philistine territory was more direct, God was afraid that the people would be discouraged if they had to fight their way through.

Finally, some see the long route as necessary for the Israelites to develop the qualities they would need to conquer and settle the Promised Land. Ibn Ezra: God did not want them to arrive at the Promised Land too soon. Having been slaves all their lives, they would not have been prepared to conquer Canaan until they had a lengthy experience of freedom. Maimonides: God wanted to accustom them to hardship, to prepare them for the task of conquering and settling Canaan. Some commentators specifically spell out the implication that sometimes the harder way of doing something turns out to be the better way. "There is a long way which is short and a short way which is long" (BT Er. 53b). When something comes to us too easily instead of being hard earned, we don't always appreciate it.

The Midrash understands the phrase "God did not lead them" as "God was not comforted," taking the word *naḥam* not as "lead" but as "was comforted" (Exod. R. 20:13). Although God rejoiced over the Israelites who were redeemed from Egypt, God was not comforted for those who died without seeing the deliverance.

מִלְחָמָה וְשָׁבוּ מִצְרָיְמָה׃ 18 וַיַּסֵּב אֱלֹהִים ׀
אֶת־הָעָם דֶּרֶךְ הַמִּדְבָּר יַם־סוּף
וַחֲמֻשִׁים עָלוּ בְנֵי־יִשְׂרָאֵל מֵאֶרֶץ מִצְרָיִם׃
19 וַיִּקַּח מֹשֶׁה אֶת־עַצְמוֹת יוֹסֵף עִמּוֹ כִּי
הַשְׁבֵּעַ הִשְׁבִּיעַ אֶת־בְּנֵי יִשְׂרָאֵל לֵאמֹר
פָּקֹד יִפְקֹד אֱלֹהִים אֶתְכֶם וְהַעֲלִיתֶם
אֶת־עַצְמֹתַי מִזֶּה אִתְּכֶם׃
20 וַיִּסְעוּ מִסֻּכֹּת וַיַּחֲנוּ בְאֵתָם בִּקְצֵה
הַמִּדְבָּר׃ 21 וַיהוָה הֹלֵךְ לִפְנֵיהֶם יוֹמָם
בְּעַמּוּד עָנָן לַנְחֹתָם הַדֶּרֶךְ וְלַיְלָה בְּעַמּוּד
אֵשׁ לְהָאִיר לָהֶם לָלֶכֶת יוֹמָם וָלָיְלָה׃

when they see war, and return to Egypt." 18So
God led the people roundabout, by way of the
wilderness at the Sea of Reeds.

Now the Israelites went up armed out of the
land of Egypt. 19And Moses took with him the
bones of Joseph, who had exacted an oath from
the children of Israel, saying, "God will be sure
to take notice of you: then you shall carry up
my bones from here with you."

20They set out from Succoth, and encamped
at Etham, at the edge of the wilderness. 21The
LORD went before them in a pillar of cloud by
day, to guide them along the way, and in a pillar
of fire by night, to give them light, that they

when they see war Since the days of Pharaoh Seti I (ca. 1305–1290 B.C.E.), the coastal road to Canaan had been heavily fortified by the Egyptians. A chain of strongholds, way stations, reservoirs, and wells dotted the area as far as Gaza, the provincial capital.

18. by way of the wilderness This must refer to one of the ancient, natural tracks that cross the Sinai peninsula. The vagueness of the designation and the inability to identify and locate most of the many wilderness stations recorded in the Torah make it impossible to chart the route followed by the departing Israelites.

Sea of Reeds Literal translation of *yam suf.* The Red Sea, its usual but incorrect translation, is more than 120 miles from the probable site of Goshen, where the Israelites lived in Egypt—too great a distance to cover even in one week in those days. The Hebrew word *suf* is derived from the Egyptian word for the papyrus reed, which grows in fresh water; therefore, *yam suf* would not be an appropriate designation for the present Red Sea, because its water is saline and does not favor the growth of that plant. This stage of the march probably took the Israelites to the far northeastern corner of Egypt, to one of the lagoons near the shore of the Mediterranean Sea.

19. Joseph's dying request is fulfilled. His words here are almost precisely those given in Gen. 50:25.

20. Succoth See Comment to Exod. 12:37.

Etham The site, mentioned again in Num. 33:6–8, has not been identified; nor are we given the distance between it and Succoth.

21–22. The dynamic presence of God is a recurring theme throughout the narratives of the wilderness wanderings. It is symbolized by the mysterious, intangible elements of fire and cloud—a storm cloud shot through with flashes of lightning (see Ezek. 1:4). During the day, the dark cloud was most visible; at night, the fiery flashes were (see Exod. 40:38). The cloud escorts

19. Moses took with him the bones of Joseph While the others were busy packing their belongings in preparation for the journey, Moses was busy keeping a promise. Gen. 50:25 expresses Joseph's dying wish: "When God has taken notice of you, you shall carry up my bones from here" (Mekh.). A later comment understands the passage symbolically: To be a proper leader of Israel, Moses acquired the strengths of Joseph, his ability to provide people with food as well as with spiritual guidance and his capacity to forgive people who had wronged him.

HALAKHAH L'MA·ASEH

13:19. Moses took with him the bones of Joseph Some Jews who do not live in Israel arrange to be buried there. Some Jews who are buried outside of Israel arrange that some earth from Israel be buried with them. These customs express the Jewish commitment to the land of Israel. They also reflect the *midrash* that Israel will be the site of resurrection, even for those who died in the Diaspora (JT Ket. 35b).

might travel day and night. 22The pillar of cloud
by day and the pillar of fire by night did not depart from before the people.

22 לֹא־יָמִישׁ עַמּוּד הֶעָנָן יוֹמָם וְעַמּוּד
הָאֵשׁ לָיְלָה לִפְנֵי הָעָם׃ פ

14 The LORD said to Moses: 2Tell the Israelites to turn back and encamp before
Pi-hahiroth, between Migdol and the sea, before Baal-zephon; you shall encamp facing it,
by the sea. 3Pharaoh will say of the Israelites,
"They are astray in the land; the wilderness has
closed in on them." 4Then I will stiffen Pharaoh's heart and he will pursue them, that I may
gain glory through Pharaoh and all his host; and
the Egyptians shall know that I am the LORD.
And they did so.
5When the king of Egypt was told that the
people had fled, Pharaoh and his courtiers had

יד וַיְדַבֵּר יְהוָה אֶל־מֹשֶׁה לֵּאמֹר׃
2 דַּבֵּר אֶל־בְּנֵי יִשְׂרָאֵל וְיָשֻׁבוּ וְיַחֲנוּ לִפְנֵי
פִּי הַחִירֹת בֵּין מִגְדֹּל וּבֵין הַיָּם לִפְנֵי בַּעַל
צְפֹן נִכְחוֹ תַחֲנוּ עַל־הַיָּם׃ 3 וְאָמַר פַּרְעֹה
לִבְנֵי יִשְׂרָאֵל נְבֻכִים הֵם בָּאָרֶץ סָגַר
עֲלֵיהֶם הַמִּדְבָּר׃ 4 וְחִזַּקְתִּי אֶת־לֵב־פַּרְעֹה
וְרָדַף אַחֲרֵיהֶם וְאִכָּבְדָה בְּפַרְעֹה וּבְכָל־
חֵילוֹ וְיָדְעוּ מִצְרַיִם כִּי־אֲנִי יְהוָה
וַיַּעֲשׂוּ־כֵן׃
5 וַיֻּגַּד לְמֶלֶךְ מִצְרַיִם כִּי בָרַח הָעָם וַיֵּהָפֵךְ

and guides the people through the untamed wilderness, signals the beginning and end of each day's journey, and provides a protective screen in times of peril. Although God is portrayed as speaking "from the midst of the cloud," as in Exod. 24:16, this should always be understood as figurative language. There never is a question of His actually residing inside the cloud or being identified with it. This is clear from 19:20, when God "came down" on Mount Sinai only after it had been enveloped in cloud (19:16).

THE MIRACLE AT THE SEA (14:1–31)

The liberated Israelites, having reached the edge of the wilderness, suddenly were ordered to change course. This new direction, fraught with great danger, was actually a tactic to mislead the Egyptians and lure them to their doom, the culminating defeat of Pharaoh. Egypt does not appear in Israelite history again for three centuries, in the time of King Solomon. The miracle of the parting, or splitting, of the sea (*k'ri·at yam suf*) left a profound impression on all subsequent Hebrew literature and became the paradigm for Israel's future redemption from exile. Most of the biblical passages that celebrate the crossing of the sea relate solely to God's sovereign control over nature and history and do not mention the drowning of the Egyptians.

REASON TO CHANGE COURSE (vv. 1–4)

2. Some of the place-names mentioned here, and repeated in Num. 33:7–8, cannot be identified with certainty. Baal-zephon was a port on the Mediterranean coast, suggesting a northern route from Succot for the Exodus.

3. astray The word translated as "astray" (*n'vukhim*) here has the sense of "disoriented" or "hopelessly confused." The Israelites, at God's behest (v. 2), have taken up a position where they are hemmed in on all sides—by Egyptian border fortresses, by the wilderness, and by the sea.

4. Pharaoh will be irresistibly drawn to give chase.

stiffen Pharaoh's heart See Comment to 4:21.

that I may gain glory Or "and I will . . ." The Hebrew is unclear whether this is the purpose of the tactic or its consequence. Destruction of the wicked reaffirms the fundamental biblical principle that the world is governed by a divinely ordained moral order that ultimately must prevail. God is thereby glorified. (For a similar notion that God takes "glory" by humbling a foe, see Ezekiel's war of Gog, Ezek. 38–39.)

THE EGYPTIANS HAVE A CHANGE OF HEART AND GIVE CHASE (vv. 5–9)

5. the people had fled It is clear that the Israelites are not coming back, for the "three-day

a change of heart about the people and said, "What is this we have done, releasing Israel from our service?" 6He ordered his chariot and took his men with him; 7he took six hundred of his picked chariots, and the rest of the chariots of Egypt, with officers in all of them. 8The LORD stiffened the heart of Pharaoh king of Egypt, and he gave chase to the Israelites. As the Israelites were departing defiantly, 9the Egyptians gave chase to them, and all the chariot horses of Pharaoh, his horsemen, and his warriors overtook them encamped by the sea, near Pi-hahiroth, before Baal-zephon.

10As Pharaoh drew near, the Israelites caught sight of the Egyptians advancing upon them. Greatly frightened, the Israelites cried out to the LORD. 11And they said to Moses, "Was it for want of graves in Egypt that you brought us to

לְבַ֞ב פַּרְעֹ֤ה וַעֲבָדָיו֙ אֶל־הָעָ֔ם וַיֹּֽאמְרוּ֙
מַה־זֹּ֣את עָשִׂ֔ינוּ כִּֽי־שִׁלַּ֥חְנוּ אֶת־יִשְׂרָאֵ֖ל
מֵעָבְדֵֽנוּ׃ 6 וַיֶּאְסֹ֖ר אֶת־רִכְבּ֑וֹ וְאֶת־עַמּ֖וֹ
לָקַ֥ח עִמּֽוֹ׃ 7 וַיִּקַּ֗ח שֵׁשׁ־מֵא֥וֹת רֶ֙כֶב֙ בָּח֔וּר
וְכֹ֖ל רֶ֣כֶב מִצְרָ֑יִם וְשָׁלִשִׁ֖ם עַל־כֻּלּֽוֹ׃
8 וַיְחַזֵּ֣ק יְהוָ֗ה אֶת־לֵ֤ב פַּרְעֹה֙ מֶ֣לֶךְ מִצְרַ֔יִם
וַיִּרְדֹּ֕ף אַחֲרֵ֖י בְּנֵ֣י יִשְׂרָאֵ֑ל וּבְנֵ֣י יִשְׂרָאֵ֔ל
שני יֹצְאִ֖ים בְּיָ֥ד רָמָֽה׃ 9 וַיִּרְדְּפ֨וּ מִצְרַ֜יִם
אַחֲרֵיהֶ֗ם וַיַּשִּׂ֤יגוּ אוֹתָם֙ חֹנִ֣ים עַל־הַיָּ֔ם
כָּל־סוּס֙ רֶ֣כֶב פַּרְעֹ֔ה וּפָרָשָׁ֖יו וְחֵיל֑וֹ עַל־פִּי֙
הַֽחִירֹ֔ת לִפְנֵ֖י בַּ֥עַל צְפֹֽן׃
10 וּפַרְעֹ֖ה הִקְרִ֑יב וַיִּשְׂא֩וּ בְנֵֽי־יִשְׂרָאֵ֨ל אֶת־
עֵינֵיהֶ֜ם וְהִנֵּ֥ה מִצְרַ֣יִם ׀ נֹסֵ֣עַ אַחֲרֵיהֶ֗ם
וַיִּֽירְאוּ֙ מְאֹ֔ד וַיִּצְעֲק֥וּ בְנֵֽי־יִשְׂרָאֵ֖ל אֶל־
יְהוָֽה׃ 11 וַיֹּאמְרוּ֮ אֶל־מֹשֶׁה֒ הֲֽמִבְּלִ֤י אֵין־
קְבָרִים֙ בְּמִצְרַ֔יִם לְקַחְתָּ֖נוּ לָמ֣וּת בַּמִּדְבָּ֑ר

journey" that Moses repeatedly requested has come and gone, and they have not returned.

6. took his men The word translated here as "men" (*am*) usually means "people." It can also mean an "armed force."

7. Pharaoh himself leads an elite corps of 600 chariots, apparently the standard military unit.

and the rest of the chariots The Hebrew reads, literally, "every chariot/all the chariots/all the chariotry of Egypt"—i.e., in addition to the elite corps. The chariot, a powerful and revolutionary innovation in the art of warfare, was introduced into Egypt from Canaan. Among the Hittites and Assyrians, the chariot crew was composed of a driver, a warrior, and a shieldbearer; but Egyptian chariots generally had only a two-man team. Drawn by two horses, it was used for massed charges. The charioteers, well trained and highly skilled, enjoyed high social standing and became a military aristocracy.

8. departing defiantly Literally, "with upraised hand," a metaphor drawn from the depiction of ancient Near Eastern gods menacingly brandishing a weapon in the upraised right hand. The confident Israelites are oblivious of the renewed Egyptian threat.

9. his horsemen Horseback riding was introduced into Egypt only in the 14th century B.C.E., and the use of mounted cavalry in warfare was unknown before the end of the 11th century B.C.E. Hence, the word understood here as "horseman" (*parash*) probably means "steed," as in other biblical texts. It also could be a term for "charioteer," one skilled at handling a horse.

THE PEOPLE'S REACTION; MOSES' RESPONSE (vv. 10–14)

10. cried out to the LORD The self-assurance mentioned in verse 8 suddenly vanishes. Now only God can save them.

11. This rebuke is uttered with bitter irony, for Egypt was the classic land of tombs.

CHAPTER 14

10. the Israelites caught sight of the Egyptians advancing Often in life, we think we can escape our problems by running away, only to find our problems running after us (Baal Shem Tov).

Greatly frightened The Israelites still have a slave mentality, despite their having experienced God's redemptive power during the Ten Plagues (Ibn Ezra). No matter how much God has done for them, they still lack confidence in God's saving power.

die in the wilderness? What have you done to us, taking us out of Egypt? [12]Is this not the very thing we told you in Egypt, saying, 'Let us be, and we will serve the Egyptians, for it is better for us to serve the Egyptians than to die in the wilderness'?" [13]But Moses said to the people, "Have no fear! Stand by, and witness the deliverance which the LORD will work for you today; for the Egyptians whom you see today you will never see again. [14]The LORD will battle for you; you hold your peace!"

[15]Then the LORD said to Moses, "Why do you cry out to Me? Tell the Israelites to go forward. [16]And you lift up your rod and hold out your arm over the sea and split it, so that the Israelites may march into the sea on dry ground. [17]And I will stiffen the hearts of the Egyptians so that they go in after them; and I will gain glory through Pharaoh and all his warriors, his chariots and his horsemen. [18]Let the Egyptians know that I am LORD, when I gain glory through Pharaoh, his chariots, and his horsemen."

[19]The angel of God, who had been going ahead of the Israelite army, now moved and followed behind them; and the pillar of cloud shifted from in front of them and took up a place

מַה־זֹּאת֙ עָשִׂ֣יתָ לָּ֔נוּ לְהוֹצִיאָ֖נוּ מִמִּצְרָֽיִם׃
12 הֲלֹא־זֶ֣ה הַדָּבָ֗ר אֲשֶׁ֨ר דִּבַּ֨רְנוּ אֵלֶ֤יךָ
בְמִצְרַ֙יִם֙ לֵאמֹ֔ר חֲדַ֥ל מִמֶּ֖נּוּ וְנַעַבְדָ֣ה אֶת־
מִצְרָ֑יִם כִּ֣י ט֥וֹב לָ֙נוּ֙ עֲבֹ֣ד אֶת־מִצְרַ֔יִם
מִמֻּתֵ֖נוּ בַּמִּדְבָּֽר׃ 13 וַיֹּ֨אמֶר מֹשֶׁ֣ה אֶל־הָעָם֮
אַל־תִּירָאוּ֒ הִֽתְיַצְּב֗וּ וּרְאוּ֙ אֶת־יְשׁוּעַ֣ת
יְהוָ֔ה אֲשֶׁר־יַעֲשֶׂ֥ה לָכֶ֖ם הַיּ֑וֹם כִּ֗י אֲשֶׁ֨ר
רְאִיתֶ֤ם אֶת־מִצְרַ֙יִם֙ הַיּ֔וֹם לֹ֥א תֹסִ֛פוּ
לִרְאֹתָ֥ם ע֖וֹד עַד־עוֹלָֽם׃ 14 יְהוָ֖ה יִלָּחֵ֣ם
לָכֶ֑ם וְאַתֶּ֖ם תַּחֲרִשֽׁוּן׃ פ
שׁי 15 וַיֹּ֤אמֶר יְהוָה֙ אֶל־מֹשֶׁ֔ה מַה־תִּצְעַ֖ק אֵלָ֑י
דַּבֵּ֥ר אֶל־בְּנֵֽי־יִשְׂרָאֵ֖ל וְיִסָּֽעוּ׃ 16 וְאַתָּ֞ה
הָרֵ֣ם אֶֽת־מַטְּךָ֗ וּנְטֵ֧ה אֶת־יָדְךָ֛ עַל־הַיָּ֖ם
וּבְקָעֵ֑הוּ וְיָבֹ֧אוּ בְנֵֽי־יִשְׂרָאֵ֛ל בְּת֥וֹךְ הַיָּ֖ם
בַּיַּבָּשָֽׁה׃ 17 וַאֲנִ֗י הִנְנִי֙ מְחַזֵּק֙ אֶת־לֵ֣ב
מִצְרַ֔יִם וְיָבֹ֖אוּ אַחֲרֵיהֶ֑ם וְאִכָּבְדָ֤ה בְּפַרְעֹה֙
וּבְכָל־חֵיל֔וֹ בְּרִכְבּ֖וֹ וּבְפָרָשָֽׁיו׃ 18 וְיָדְע֥וּ
מִצְרַ֖יִם כִּֽי־אֲנִ֣י יְהוָ֑ה בְּהִכָּֽבְדִ֣י בְּפַרְעֹ֔ה
בְּרִכְבּ֖וֹ וּבְפָרָשָֽׁיו׃
19 וַיִּסַּ֞ע מַלְאַ֣ךְ הָאֱלֹהִ֗ים הַהֹלֵךְ֙ לִפְנֵי֙
מַחֲנֵ֣ה יִשְׂרָאֵ֔ל וַיֵּ֖לֶךְ מֵאַחֲרֵיהֶ֑ם וַיִּסַּ֞ע
עַמּ֤וּד הֶֽעָנָן֙ מִפְּנֵיהֶ֔ם וַיַּעֲמֹ֖ד מֵאַחֲרֵיהֶֽם׃

12. This statement is not found in the two previous repudiations of Moses by the Israelites (in 5:21 and 6:9). Therefore, it must reflect some incident not otherwise recorded in the Torah. A rebellion by the Israelites at the Sea of Reeds is reported in Ps. 106:7.

13–14. Moses ignores their rebuke; he attempts to calm them and allay their fears.

GOD'S RESPONSE (vv. 15–20)

15. Why do you cry out to Me This was the first of many times that Moses interceded for the people. Here he is told by God: It is time for action, not for prayer.

16. Moses is not instructed to strike the sea. In verse 21 the action of Moses with his rod is the signal for the strong wind to blow back the waters. It is God who splits the sea.

19. The symbol of God's indwelling Presence, the luminous pillar of cloud mentioned in 13:21 as leading and guiding the people, now serves as a protective screen separating the Egyptians and the Israelites.

---

14. The LORD will battle for you; you hold your peace! Sometimes quiet confidence can be a form of prayer. Another interpretation: God will support and defend you—but only when you stop quarreling among yourselves. A united people merits God's intervention.

20 וַיָּבֹא בֵּין ׀ מַחֲנֵה מִצְרַיִם וּבֵין מַחֲנֵה
יִשְׂרָאֵל וַיְהִי הֶעָנָן וְהַחֹשֶׁךְ וַיָּאֶר אֶת־
הַלָּיְלָה וְלֹא־קָרַב זֶה אֶל־זֶה כָּל־הַלָּיְלָה׃
21 וַיֵּט מֹשֶׁה אֶת־יָדוֹ עַל־הַיָּם וַיּוֹלֶךְ יְהוָה ׀
אֶת־הַיָּם בְּרוּחַ קָדִים עַזָּה כָּל־הַלַּיְלָה
וַיָּשֶׂם אֶת־הַיָּם לֶחָרָבָה וַיִּבָּקְעוּ הַמָּיִם׃
22 וַיָּבֹאוּ בְנֵי־יִשְׂרָאֵל בְּתוֹךְ הַיָּם בַּיַּבָּשָׁה
וְהַמַּיִם לָהֶם חוֹמָה מִימִינָם וּמִשְּׂמֹאלָם׃
23 וַיִּרְדְּפוּ מִצְרַיִם וַיָּבֹאוּ אַחֲרֵיהֶם כֹּל סוּס
פַּרְעֹה רִכְבּוֹ וּפָרָשָׁיו אֶל־תּוֹךְ הַיָּם׃ 24 וַיְהִי
בְּאַשְׁמֹרֶת הַבֹּקֶר וַיַּשְׁקֵף יְהוָה אֶל־מַחֲנֵה
מִצְרַיִם בְּעַמּוּד אֵשׁ וְעָנָן וַיָּהָם אֵת מַחֲנֵה
מִצְרָיִם׃ 25 וַיָּסַר אֵת אֹפַן מַרְכְּבֹתָיו

behind them, 20and it came between the army of the Egyptians and the army of Israel. Thus there was the cloud with the darkness, and it cast a spell upon the night, so that the one could not come near the other all through the night.

21Then Moses held out his arm over the sea and the LORD drove back the sea with a strong east wind all that night, and turned the sea into dry ground. The waters were split, 22and the Israelites went into the sea on dry ground, the waters forming a wall for them on their right and on their left. 23The Egyptians came in pursuit after them into the sea, all of Pharaoh's horses, chariots, and horsemen. 24At the morning watch, the LORD looked down upon the Egyptian army from a pillar of fire and cloud, and threw the Egyptian army into panic. 25He locked the wheels of their chariots so that they

THE PARTING OF THE SEA
(vv. 21–29)

21. Moses fulfills the instructions detailed in verse 16. But God is the immediate cause of what is about to take place.

a strong east wind See Comment to 10:13.

23. Pressing forward in an uncontrollable frenzy, the Egyptian forces plunge into the turbulent waters.

24. morning watch In ancient Israel, the night was divided into three watches: 6 to 10 P.M., 10 P.M. to 2 A.M., and the morning watch between the hours of 2 and 6 A.M. These hours would vary, according to the season.

25. He locked The wheels became bogged down in the mud.

---

21. Like many of us, the rabbis of old had difficulty accepting the literal veracity of the splitting of the sea, the classic example of God working a miracle for Israel's sake. They believed in the divine miracle but were reluctant to accept the suspension of natural law. They fasten on the apparently superfluous words "a strong east wind" as a hint that the splitting of the sea was accomplished through natural, rather than supernatural, means. Similarly, in the 19th century, Levi Yitzḥak of Berdichev translated the words *ru·aḥ kadim* not as "east wind" but as "an ancient wind," explaining, "God does not change or suspend the laws of nature in order to work miracles. The wind that divided the sea had been created for that purpose at the time of the creation of the world."

According to one *midrash,* the sea would not part until the Israelites showed enough faith to march into the waters. They were reluctant to do so, waiting for God to work a miracle first. Finally, Naḥshon son of Amminadab, of the tribe of Judah, was bold enough to march into the sea. Only at that point did the sea respond to his act of faith by separating, allowing the Israelites to cross on dry land (BT Sot. 37a). Another legend would have it that Pharaoh alone, of all the Egyptians, survived. Because he had learned his lesson, he was appointed king of Nineveh. In that capacity, he led his people in penitential prayer and fasting to avert the decree of the prophet Jonah. When he died, he was stationed at the gates of the underworld, where he would greet tyrants of a later generation with the words "Why did you not learn from my example?" (Mekh.).

moved forward with difficulty. And the Egyptians said, "Let us flee from the Israelites, for the LORD is fighting for them against Egypt."

26Then the LORD said to Moses, "Hold out your arm over the sea, that the waters may come back upon the Egyptians and upon their chariots and upon their horsemen." 27Moses held out his arm over the sea, and at daybreak the sea returned to its normal state, and the Egyptians fled at its approach. But the LORD hurled the Egyptians into the sea. 28The waters turned back and covered the chariots and the horsemen—Pharaoh's entire army that followed them into the sea; not one of them remained. 29But the Israelites had marched through the sea on dry ground, the waters forming a wall for them on their right and on their left.

30Thus the LORD delivered Israel that day from the Egyptians. Israel saw the Egyptians dead on the shore of the sea. 31And when Israel saw the wondrous power which the LORD had wielded against the Egyptians, the people feared the LORD; they had faith in the LORD and His servant Moses.

וַיְנַהֲגֵהוּ בִּכְבֵדֻת וַיֹּאמֶר* מִצְרַיִם אָנוּסָה
מִפְּנֵי יִשְׂרָאֵל כִּי יְהוָה נִלְחָם לָהֶם
בְּמִצְרָיִם: פ
ביעי 26 וַיֹּאמֶר יְהוָה אֶל־מֹשֶׁה נְטֵה אֶת־יָדְךָ
עַל־הַיָּם וְיָשֻׁבוּ הַמַּיִם עַל־מִצְרַיִם עַל־
רִכְבּוֹ וְעַל־פָּרָשָׁיו: 27 וַיֵּט מֹשֶׁה אֶת־יָדוֹ
עַל־הַיָּם וַיָּשָׁב הַיָּם לִפְנוֹת בֹּקֶר לְאֵיתָנוֹ
וּמִצְרַיִם נָסִים לִקְרָאתוֹ וַיְנַעֵר יְהוָה אֶת־
מִצְרַיִם בְּתוֹךְ הַיָּם: 28 וַיָּשֻׁבוּ הַמַּיִם וַיְכַסּוּ
אֶת־הָרֶכֶב וְאֶת־הַפָּרָשִׁים לְכֹל חֵיל
פַּרְעֹה הַבָּאִים אַחֲרֵיהֶם בַּיָּם לֹא־נִשְׁאַר
בָּהֶם עַד־אֶחָד: 29 וּבְנֵי יִשְׂרָאֵל הָלְכוּ
בַיַּבָּשָׁה בְּתוֹךְ הַיָּם וְהַמַּיִם לָהֶם חֹמָה
מִימִינָם וּמִשְּׂמֹאלָם:
30 וַיּוֹשַׁע יְהוָה בַּיּוֹם הַהוּא אֶת־יִשְׂרָאֵל
מִיַּד מִצְרָיִם וַיַּרְא יִשְׂרָאֵל אֶת־מִצְרַיִם מֵת
עַל־שְׂפַת הַיָּם: 31 וַיַּרְא יִשְׂרָאֵל אֶת־הַיָּד
הַגְּדֹלָה אֲשֶׁר עָשָׂה יְהוָה בְּמִצְרַיִם וַיִּירְאוּ
הָעָם אֶת־יְהוָה וַיַּאֲמִינוּ בַּיהוָה וּבְמֹשֶׁה
עַבְדּוֹ: פ

v. 25. סבירין ומטעין לשון רבים

the LORD is fighting for them The fulfillment of the prediction in verse 14.

27. hurled . . . into the sea They were buffeted about in the sea.

RECAPITULATION (vv. 30–31)

These two verses round out the preceding narrative and preface the following "Song at the Sea."

31. wondrous power Literally, the "great hand" of God that cut off the tyrannous "hand of Egypt." The word for "hand" (*yad*) is a key word in this chapter, occurring seven times.

they had faith In the Hebrew Bible, "faith" does not mean belief in a doctrine or a creed. It refers to trust and loyalty expressed through commitment and obedience.

His servant Moses As the faithful instrument of God's will, it is fitting that Moses receives the title "servant of the LORD/of God." He is referred to by this title more than 30 times in the Hebrew Bible and is unquestionably Israel's greatest leader.

טו אָ֣ז יָשִֽׁיר־מֹשֶׁה֩ וּבְנֵ֨י יִשְׂרָאֵ֜ל אֶת־הַשִּׁירָ֤ה הַזֹּאת֙ לַֽיהוָ֔ה וַיֹּאמְר֖וּ
לֵאמֹ֑ר* אָשִׁ֤ירָה לַֽיהוָה֙ כִּֽי־גָאֹ֣ה גָּאָ֔ה ס֥וּס
וְרֹכְב֖וֹ רָמָ֥ה בַיָּֽם׃ 2 עָזִּ֤י וְזִמְרָת֙ יָ֔הּ וַֽיְהִי־לִ֖י
לִֽישׁוּעָ֑ה זֶ֤ה אֵלִי֙ וְאַנְוֵ֔הוּ אֱלֹהֵ֥י

v. 1. צורת השירה לפי כתב היד שלנו, והיא כהלכה

THE DEFEAT OF THE EGYPTIANS (vv. 1–10)

1. I will sing The "I" here can refer only to Moses.

for This gives the occasion of the song.

driver The word translated as "driver" (*rokhev*) here means the rider in the chariot, not one on horseback. See Comment to 14:9.

2. The Lord The Hebrew word *yah* is an abbreviation of the divine name *YHVH*. This form of the name is used exclusively in poetry. It also appears as an element in proper names such as Jeremiah (*yirmi-yahu*) and has survived in English in "hallelujah" (*hall'lu-yah*, "praise the Lord").

my strength and might The source of my survival.

will enshrine Him Build Him a shrine or temple. Psalms 118:28, which seems to quote this verse, reads "I will praise You" (*odeka*).

---

the other hand, maintained the position that people who want to connect with God in the good or the bad moments of their lives but don't know how, can be given the words to recite along with those who know.

Horse and driver He has hurled into the sea The driver says, "Why punish me? I could not have pursued the Israelites if the horse had not carried me so swiftly." The horse says, "Why punish me? I only did the driver's bidding." What does God do? God judges the driver and the horse together. Similarly, in the world to come the soul will plead, "Why punish me? It was the body that sinned." And the body will say, "I would have done nothing, but the soul directed me to act." What will God do? God will reject the duality that separates body from soul and judge both together (Mekh.). Another rabbinic tradition describes the angels as wishing to break into song when they saw the Egyptian pursuers drowning. God silenced them, declaring, "How dare you sing for joy when My creatures are perishing!" (BT Meg. 10b). This is the source of our custom to spill drops of wine from our cups at the *Pesaḥ Seider*. Our cup of deliverance and rejoicing cannot be full when we recall that innocent Egyptians had to suffer because of their ruler's stubbornness. A similar outlook is behind the custom of breaking a glass at the conclusion of a wedding, to remind us of the destruction of the Temple and other mournful events of Jewish history. Our personal happiness should never leave us unmindful of the sorrows and misfortunes afflicting others (BT Ber. 31a).

2. This is my God "A common woman at the Sea saw God more clearly than any of the prophets did." This is why she could proclaim, "This is my God!" (Mekh.). For those who experienced God's saving power as they left Egypt, God was unmistakably real, not the subject of abstract speculation.

I will enshrine Him Hebrew: *anveihu*; "I will build Him a permanent sanctuary." The moments in our lives when God seems so real to us are overpowering but fleeting. To keep those memories accessible, we need to establish places where we can reconnect with those feelings of being in God's presence. *Anveihu* can also be translated as "I will glorify Him." "God has made us known among the nations, and we will make God known among the nations." How can a human being glorify God when all glory is already God's? Ishmael says, by performing religious acts in a particularly glorious manner, with an especially beautiful *sukkah* or an especially handsome *tallit*. Abba Saul says, by imitating God. Even as God is gracious and compassionate, so we should be gracious and compassionate (BT Shab. 133b).

15 Then Moses and the Israelites sang this song to the LORD. They said:
I will sing to the LORD, for He has triumphed gloriously;
Horse and driver He has hurled into the sea.
2The LORD is my strength and might;
He is become my deliverance.
This is my God and I will enshrine Him;

THE SONG AT THE SEA (*Shirat ha-Yam*) (15:1–21)

After the narrative account of the extraordinary events at the Sea of Reeds, there follows one of the two oldest extended poems in the Hebrew Bible. (The other poem is the Song of Deborah in Judg. 5, designated as the *haftarah* for this *parashah.*) Its date is debated. Exod. 15:21 links it to Miriam's song, which may have predated it. It is a lyrical outpouring of emotion on the part of the people who experienced the great events of the Exodus. Carefully crafted, the song celebrates the mighty acts of God as He intervenes in human affairs. It uses strong poetic metaphor. Thus in place of the naturalistic "strong east wind" that blew through the night (14:21), there is the poetic "blast of [God's] nostrils" (15:8)—a sudden, brief, yet devastatingly effective breath that humbles human arrogance. Moses plays no active role, for he does not hold out his arm over the sea, as in 14:16,21. Rather, it is the "right hand" of God that is extended (15:12). Nor is there any mention of the angel, the cloud, or the darkness, all so prominent in 14:19–20 and all serving as intermediaries that mark the distance between God and Israel.

CHAPTER 15

14:31–15:1. They had faith in the LORD. . . . Then Moses . . . sang Moses' song does not celebrate the splitting of the sea. It celebrates the Israelites' commitment to faith in God after experiencing the splitting of the sea. The crossing of the sea is the prototype of the biblical miracle, the one to which Jews have always looked to recall God's intervention on our people's behalf. We can scarcely imagine what is must have felt like for the Israelites, whose lives to this point had been a tale of unrelieved misery, to have events conspire to favor them so spectacularly. Moses' song of triumph is traditionally read in the Torah service with a special chant, both in sequence as part of the Book of Exodus and on the seventh day of *Pesaḥ,* the day on which tradition maintains that it was sung. The miracle of crossing the sea is recalled in the prayer book just before the *Amidah* prayer on weekdays and on *Shabbat* and festivals. Its placement in the prayer service suggests to the worshiper that prayers may well be answered, as they were for our ancestors at the shores of the sea. It is referred to in the Book of Psalms as proof of God's caring for the people Israel.

Then Moses and the Israelites sang From the day that God created the world until this moment, no one had sung praises to God—not Adam after having been created, not Abraham after being delivered from the fiery furnace, not Isaac when he was spared the knife, or Jacob when he escaped from wrestling with an angel and from Esau. But when Israel came to the sea and it parted for them, "Then Moses and the Israelites sang this song to the LORD." And God said, "for this I have been waiting" (Exod. R. 23:4).

Legend has it that the angels wanted to sing songs of praise, but God told them, "Wait, and let Israel sing first. Humans are able to praise only when they are inspired. If we do not give them the opportunity, the desire will pass" (David of Kotzk). "Sometimes 'then' (as in 'then Moses sang') refers to the past, and sometimes to the future" (Mekh.). We believe that times will come when Israel will once again have cause to break into a grateful song of praise to God.

In the Mishnah (Sot. 5:4), Nehemiah suggests that Moses and the Israelites all sang the song together. Akiva suggests that Moses sang it line by line, with the people repeating each line. Their disagreement might be understood as follows: Nehemiah would welcome only those who know the words of prayer. Akiva, on

אָבִי וַאֲרֹמְמֶנְהוּ׃ 3 יְהוָה אִישׁ מִלְחָמָה יְהוָה
שְׁמוֹ׃ 4 מַרְכְּבֹת פַּרְעֹה וְחֵילוֹ יָרָה בַיָּם וּמִבְחַר
שָׁלִשָׁיו טֻבְּעוּ בְיַם־סוּף׃ 5 תְּהֹמֹת יְכַסְיֻמוּ יָרְדוּ בִמְצוֹלֹת כְּמוֹ־
אָבֶן׃ 6 יְמִינְךָ יְהוָה נֶאְדָּרִי בַּכֹּחַ יְמִינְךָ
יְהוָה תִּרְעַץ אוֹיֵב׃ 7 וּבְרֹב גְּאוֹנְךָ תַּהֲרֹס
קָמֶיךָ תְּשַׁלַּח חֲרֹנְךָ יֹאכְלֵמוֹ כַּקַּשׁ׃ 8 וּבְרוּחַ
אַפֶּיךָ נֶעֶרְמוּ מַיִם נִצְּבוּ כְמוֹ־נֵד
נֹזְלִים קָפְאוּ תְהֹמֹת בְּלֶב־יָם׃ 9 אָמַר
אוֹיֵב אֶרְדֹּף אַשִּׂיג אֲחַלֵּק שָׁלָל תִּמְלָאֵמוֹ
נַפְשִׁי אָרִיק חַרְבִּי תּוֹרִישֵׁמוֹ יָדִי׃ 10 נָשַׁפְתָּ
בְרוּחֲךָ כִּסָּמוֹ יָם צָלֲלוּ כַּעוֹפֶרֶת בְּמַיִם
אַדִּירִים׃ 11 מִי־כָמֹכָה* בָּאֵלִם יְהוָה מִי

v. 11. יתיר ה׳

the enemies of Israel are the enemies of God, so that Israel's wars for survival are portrayed as the battles of the Lord.

Lord is His name! The statement evokes the power of God with which the name is associated (see Comment to 6:3). This divine name is the one that is repeated in the liturgical recitation of the *Sh'ma.*

5. deeps The Hebrew word *t'homot* is the term for the vast ocean of waters, which was believed to lie beneath the earth, as mentioned in Gen. 1:2.

7. fury The word translated as "fury" (*ḥaron*) is a term used only of divine anger. Here the word carries its original sense of "burning."

8. blast of Your nostrils Poetic imagery for the wind.

froze They formed a solid mass.

9. The poet mimics the arrogant self-confidence of the foe.

I will divide the spoil This promise is an inducement for reluctant soldiers to give chase.

shall subdue Literally, "my hand shall dispossess them," here meaning "I shall force them into slavery once again." Note the staccato effect of the Hebrew verbs, implying the overconfident pride of the Egyptians.

10. The first section of the Song at the Sea closes with a recital of God's effortless act that exposes the empty rhetoric of the enemy. The waters do not act on their own accord but only when God energizes them.

wind blow One brief, light puff, and the sea engulfs the Egyptians.

THE INCOMPARABILITY OF *YHVH* (vv. 11–13)

11. The song and its theme of God's sovereign control over nature ends with an affirmation of His uniqueness through a rhetorical question: "Who is like You, O Lord?"

celestials These are the hosts of ministering angels imagined as surrounding God's throne, waiting to be of service.

---

4. God's justice is meted out measure for measure. As the Egyptians drowned Israelite babies, so they themselves were drowned. As they immersed the Israelites in mud-like mortar, so they now sank in the mud. In short, all of us eventually pay for what we have done wrong.

The God of my father, and I will exalt Him.
3The LORD, the Warrior—
LORD is His name!
4Pharaoh's chariots and his army
He has cast into the sea;
And the pick of his officers
Are drowned in the Sea of Reeds.
5The deeps covered them;
They went down into the depths like a stone.
6Your right hand, O LORD, glorious in power,
Your right hand, O LORD, shatters the foe!
7In Your great triumph You break Your opponents;
You send forth Your fury, it consumes them like straw.
8At the blast of Your nostrils the waters piled up,
The floods stood straight like a wall;
The deeps froze in the heart of the sea.
9The foe said,
"I will pursue, I will overtake,
I will divide the spoil;
My desire shall have its fill of them.
I will bare my sword—
My hand shall subdue them."
10You made Your wind blow, the sea covered them;
They sank like lead in the majestic waters.
11Who is like You, O LORD, among the celestials;

God of my father See Comment to Exod. 3:6.

3. Warrior This description of God reflects 14:14, "The LORD will battle for you" and verse 25, "the Egyptians said . . . the LORD is fighting for them against Egypt." Because the Egyptians came against Israel as an armed force, the Lord—to whom alone victory is attributed—metaphorically is described as a warrior. In the biblical view,

---

God of my father, and I will exalt Him It is as great a spiritual commitment to honor God because your ancestors did as it as to do so because you have experienced God in your own life (Aaron of Belz). Others, however, taught that it is not enough to inherit a faith. One must discover and experience the reality of God in one's own life.

כָּמֹכָה* נֶאְדָּר בַּקֹּדֶשׁ נוֹרָא תְהִלֹּת עֹשֵׂה
פֶלֶא׃ 12 נָטִיתָ יְמִינְךָ תִּבְלָעֵמוֹ אָרֶץ׃ 13 נָחִיתָ
בְחַסְדְּךָ עַם־זוּ גָּאָלְתָּ נֵהַלְתָּ בְעָזְּךָ אֶל־נְוֵה
קָדְשֶׁךָ׃ 14 שָׁמְעוּ עַמִּים יִרְגָּזוּן חִיל
אָחַז יֹשְׁבֵי פְּלָשֶׁת׃ 15 אָז נִבְהֲלוּ אַלּוּפֵי
אֱדוֹם אֵילֵי מוֹאָב יֹאחֲזֵמוֹ רָעַד נָמֹגוּ
כֹּל יֹשְׁבֵי כְנָעַן׃ 16 תִּפֹּל עֲלֵיהֶם אֵימָתָה
וָפַחַד בִּגְדֹל זְרוֹעֲךָ יִדְּמוּ כָּאָבֶן עַד־
יַעֲבֹר עַמְּךָ יְהוָה עַד־יַעֲבֹר עַם־זוּ
קָנִיתָ׃ 17 תְּבִאֵמוֹ וְתִטָּעֵמוֹ בְּהַר נַחֲלָתְךָ מָכוֹן
לְשִׁבְתְּךָ פָּעַלְתָּ יְהוָה מִקְּדָשׁ אֲדֹנָי כּוֹנְנוּ
יָדֶיךָ׃ 18 יְהוָה ׀ יִמְלֹךְ לְעֹלָם וָעֶד׃

v. 11. יתיר ה׳

the Israelites: from south to north and then westward across the Jordan.

15. Edom The Edomites were descendants of Esau, brother of Jacob, also known as Edom. They occupied the southernmost part of Transjordan and later became perpetual enemies of the Israelites.

Moab The plateau east of the Dead Sea between the wadis Arnon and Zered. It was occupied by the Moabites, who are traced back to Abraham's nephew Lot. The alarm felt by the Moabites at the appearance of the Israelites close to their border is described in Num. 22:1–7.

are aghast Literally, "melt away." They are demoralized.

16. The Israelites are perceived as a threat by the peoples who dwell in the vicinity of the wilderness route and who fear that they may be struck by God who accompanies and protects Israel.

Your people The one whom You selected for a unique relationship and destiny.

THE GRAND FINALE (vv. 17–18)

The Song at the Sea closes with an affirmation of confidence in the promise that God's redemption of Israel from Egypt will culminate in the building of a Temple. The theme parallels the traditional Canaanite theme that Baal will build a palace after defeating his foes.

17. place The dais on which the divine throne rests.

18. The song closes, as it opens, with the exaltation of God, now expressed in terms of sovereignty. This is the earliest biblical use of this metaphor of God as King, found elsewhere in the Torah in Num. 23:21, another poetic passage. This finale is the climax of the basic themes of the poem: God's absolute sovereignty over nature and history.

Who is like You, majestic in holiness,
Awesome in splendor, working wonders!
12You put out Your right hand,
The earth swallowed them.
13In Your love You lead the people You redeemed;
In Your strength You guide them to Your holy abode.
14The peoples hear, they tremble;
Agony grips the dwellers in Philistia.
15Now are the clans of Edom dismayed;
The tribes of Moab—trembling grips them;
All the dwellers in Canaan are aghast.
16Terror and dread descend upon them;
Through the might of Your arm they are still as stone—
Till Your people cross over, O LORD,
Till Your people cross whom You have ransomed.
17You will bring them and plant them in Your own mountain,
The place You made to dwell in, O LORD,
The sanctuary, O LORD, which Your hands established.
18The LORD will reign for ever and ever!

12. earth swallowed them This is poetic language for "They met their death." "The earth" here refers to the underworld, as in the story of Korah (Num. 16:32).

13. With the Egyptian menace finally eliminated, the poem moves away from the events that occurred at the sea to focus on the march to the Promised Land.

In Your love The word translated as "love" (*ḥesed*) means "loyalty." A crucial term in the Bible, it can express intimate relationship, covenantal obligation, or even undeserved benevolence. It is one of God's supreme attributes.

Your holy abode This phrase refers either to the entire Land of Israel or to the Temple on Mount Zion.

THE EFFECT ON NEIGHBORING PEOPLES
(vv. 14–16)

God's mighty deeds on Israel's behalf strike terror in the hearts of Israel's neighbors, their potential enemies. These are listed in the order that Israel would have encountered them. The Philistines are mentioned first because they were closest to the northeastern border of Egypt and because they were the most formidable. The other three appear in proper geographic and chronologic order, according to the circuitous route followed by

19For the horses of Pharaoh, with his chariots and horsemen, went into the sea; and the LORD turned back on them the waters of the sea; but the Israelites marched on dry ground in the midst of the sea.

19 כִּ֣י בָא֩ ס֨וּס פַּרְעֹ֜ה בְּרִכְבּ֤וֹ וּבְפָרָשָׁיו֙ בַּיָּ֔ם
וַיָּ֧שֶׁב יְהוָ֛ה עֲלֵהֶ֖ם אֶת־מֵ֣י הַיָּ֑ם וּבְנֵ֧י
יִשְׂרָאֵ֛ל הָלְכ֥וּ בַיַּבָּשָׁ֖ה בְּת֥וֹךְ הַיָּֽם׃ פ

20Then Miriam the prophetess, Aaron's sister, took a timbrel in her hand, and all the women went out after her in dance with timbrels. 21And Miriam chanted for them:

Sing to the LORD, for He has triumphed gloriously;
Horse and driver He has hurled into the sea.

20 וַתִּקַּח֩ מִרְיָ֨ם הַנְּבִיאָ֜ה אֲח֧וֹת אַהֲרֹ֛ן
אֶת־הַתֹּ֖ף בְּיָדָ֑הּ וַתֵּצֶ֤אןָ כָֽל־הַנָּשִׁים֙
אַחֲרֶ֔יהָ בְּתֻפִּ֖ים וּבִמְחֹלֹֽת׃ 21 וַתַּ֥עַן לָהֶ֖ם
מִרְיָ֑ם

שִׁ֤ירוּ לַֽיהוָה֙ כִּֽי־גָאֹ֣ה גָּאָ֔ה
ס֥וּס וְרֹכְב֖וֹ רָמָ֥ה בַיָּֽם׃ ס

22Then Moses caused Israel to set out from

22 וַיַּסַּ֨ע מֹשֶׁ֤ה אֶת־יִשְׂרָאֵל֙ מִיַּם־ס֔וּף

A CODA (v. 19)

A brief prose summary of the occasion for celebration closes the composition and reconnects it with verse 1.

THE SONG OF MIRIAM (vv. 20–21)

These verses affirm the custom (chronicled in Judg. 11:34 and 1 Sam. 18:6) of women going forth with music and dance to hail a returning victorious hero, although here God and not man is the victor.

20. Miriam No longer anonymous as in Exod. 2:4,7–8; she is here given two titles.

prophetess The other women with whom she shares this designation are Deborah, Huldah (see 2 Kings 22:14), and Noadiah (see Neh. 6:14). Rabbinic tradition adds another three—Hannah, Abigail, and Esther—for a total of seven prophetesses in ancient Israel.

timbrel Most likely a portable percussion instrument constructed of two parallel membranes stretched over a loop or frame.

CRISES IN THE WILDERNESS (15:22–17:16)

Freed from the Egyptian threat, the people begin the long trek through the wilderness toward the Promised Land. The rest of the Book of Exodus relates some major events of the first year of these

---

20ff. After crossing the sea, the Israelites promised to be faithful to God forever. A mere three days later, however, they were complaining, yearning to be back in Egypt. Although they had been slaves in Egypt, they had been free of the responsibilities of making choices, ordering their lives, and providing food for their families. While life now offered more possibilities, it made new demands.

It may be that it is hard to sustain one's faith without enough food to eat. Or it may be that it is hard to nourish one's faith today on the basis of yesterday's miracle. Yesterday's miracle, however spectacular it may have been, grows stale overnight. The miracle does not last; only the daily triumph over adversity endures. Jewish faith is not rooted in miracles; the generation that crossed the sea did not maintain their faith for more than three days after that event. Jewish faith is rooted in the daily experience of God's reality and God's goodness. Thus God changes tactics here. Instead of a spectacular miracle once in a generation, God works a small miracle, the manna, every day. The Talmud equates the two: "Providing everyone with enough to eat is as great a miracle as splitting the Sea" (BT Pes. 118a).

20–21. Where did Miriam and the other women obtain timbrels in the wilderness? These righteous women were so confident that God would work miracles for them that they had brought timbrels along from Egypt, antic-

וַיֵּצְא֖וּ אֶל־מִדְבַּר־שׁ֑וּר וַיֵּלְכ֧וּ שְׁלֹֽשֶׁת־יָמִ֛ים
בַּמִּדְבָּ֖ר וְלֹא־מָ֥צְאוּ מָֽיִם׃ 23 וַיָּבֹ֣אוּ מָרָ֔תָה
וְלֹ֣א יָֽכְל֗וּ לִשְׁתֹּ֥ת מַ֙יִם֙ מִמָּרָ֔ה כִּ֥י מָרִ֖ים
הֵ֑ם עַל־כֵּ֥ן קָרָֽא־שְׁמָ֖הּ מָרָֽה׃ 24 וַיִּלֹּ֧נוּ הָעָ֛ם
עַל־מֹשֶׁ֥ה לֵּאמֹ֖ר מַה־נִּשְׁתֶּֽה׃ 25 וַיִּצְעַ֣ק
אֶל־יְהוָ֗ה וַיּוֹרֵ֤הוּ יְהוָה֙ עֵ֔ץ וַיַּשְׁלֵךְ֙ אֶל־
הַמַּ֔יִם וַיִּמְתְּק֖וּ הַמָּ֑יִם
שָׁ֣ם שָׂ֥ם ל֛וֹ חֹ֥ק וּמִשְׁפָּ֖ט וְשָׁ֥ם נִסָּֽהוּ׃
26 וַיֹּ֨אמֶר אִם־שָׁמ֨וֹעַ תִּשְׁמַ֜ע לְק֣וֹל ׀ יְהוָ֣ה
אֱלֹהֶ֗יךָ וְהַיָּשָׁ֤ר בְּעֵינָיו֙ תַּעֲשֶׂ֔ה וְהַאֲזַנְתָּ֙
לְמִצְוֺתָ֔יו וְשָׁמַרְתָּ֖ כָּל־חֻקָּ֑יו כָּֽל־הַמַּחֲלָ֞ה

the Sea of Reeds. They went on into the wilderness of Shur; they traveled three days in the
wilderness and found no water. 23They came to
Marah, but they could not drink the water of
Marah because it was bitter; that is why it was
named Marah. 24And the people grumbled
against Moses, saying, "What shall we drink?"
25So he cried out to the LORD, and the LORD
showed him a piece of wood; he threw it into
the water and the water became sweet.

There He made for them a fixed rule, and
there He put them to the test. 26He said, "If you
will heed the LORD your God diligently, doing
what is upright in His sight, giving ear to His
commandments and keeping all His laws, then
I will not bring upon you any of the diseases

wanderings, the central event being the experience at Sinai. On the way to that mountain, four crises occur, which reflect the harsh realities of life in the wilderness brought on by nature's cruelties and human brutality.

BITTER WATERS AT MARAH (15:22–27)

This section resumes the narrative interrupted at 14:29.

22. A location called Shur, the site of an oasis between the Negeb and Egypt, is mentioned several times in biblical texts. The name means "a wall" and probably refers to the wall of fortifications built by the pharaohs in the eastern delta of the Nile along the line of the present-day isthmus of Suez.

three days If intended literally, this implies a distance of 45 miles at most. Often "three days" is a literary convention (see Comment to 3:18).

24. the people grumbled Their seemingly innocent and justifiable question was accusatory and confrontational.

25. Moses is not a wonder worker; he can do nothing except by divine instruction.

a fixed rule Apparently the verse is a parenthetic note that reflects a now-lost tradition about some law(s) given to Israel at this site.

He put them to the test Rashbam explains that the lack of drinking water was a test of Israel's faith in God.

26. diseases Not the plagues, but maladies endemic in Egypt, referred to elsewhere in Torah as "the dreadful diseases of Egypt," "Egyptian inflammation," and "the sicknesses of Egypt."

---

ipating that God would give them cause to celebrate (Mekh.).

22. they traveled three days in the wilderness and found no water Later Sages took water to be a symbol of Torah and taught that just as the body cannot go three days without water, the soul cannot go three days without the refreshing, life-sustaining contact with Torah. Thus they instituted the practice of several public readings from the Torah each week—on *Shabbat,* Monday, and Thursday.

23. they could not drink the water . . . because it was bitter Literally, "they could not drink the waters . . . because they were bitter" ("water" is plural in Hebrew). Were the waters bitter? Or was it the people who were bitter, full of self-pity at having to travel through a wilderness (Exod. R. 50:3)? One of the Sages interprets the words "found no water" (v. 22) to mean that water was there (see the oasis nearby in Elim, v. 27) but the people did not notice it because they were so busy complaining.

25. the water became sweet The purpose of religion is not to explain life's bitterness but to sweeten it, to make it more palatable. The Midrash envisions Moses asking God, "Why did You create brackish water in Your world, a liquid that serves no purpose?" God replies, "Instead of asking philosophical questions, do something to make the bitter waters sweet."

that I brought upon the Egyptians, for I the LORD am your healer."

27 And they came to Elim, where there were twelve springs of water and seventy palm trees; and they encamped there beside the water.

אֲשֶׁר־שַׂמְתִּי בְמִצְרַיִם לֹא־אָשִׂים עָלֶיךָ
כִּי אֲנִי יְהוָה רֹפְאֶךָ׃ ס
חמישי 27 וַיָּבֹאוּ אֵילִמָה וְשָׁם שְׁתֵּים עֶשְׂרֵה עֵינֹת
מַיִם וְשִׁבְעִים תְּמָרִים וַיַּחֲנוּ־שָׁם עַל־
הַמָּיִם׃

16 Setting out from Elim, the whole Israelite community came to the wilderness of Sin, which is between Elim and Sinai, on the fifteenth day of the second month after their departure from the land of Egypt. 2 In the wilderness, the whole Israelite community grumbled against Moses and Aaron. 3 The Israelites said to them, "If only we had died by the hand of the LORD in the land of Egypt, when we sat by the fleshpots, when we ate our fill of bread! For you have brought us out into this wilderness to starve this whole congregation to death."

4 And the LORD said to Moses, "I will rain down bread for you from the sky, and the people shall go out and gather each day that day's

טז וַיִּסְעוּ מֵאֵילִם וַיָּבֹאוּ כָּל־עֲדַת
בְּנֵי־יִשְׂרָאֵל אֶל־מִדְבַּר־סִין אֲשֶׁר בֵּין־
אֵילִם וּבֵין סִינָי בַּחֲמִשָּׁה עָשָׂר יוֹם לַחֹדֶשׁ
הַשֵּׁנִי לְצֵאתָם מֵאֶרֶץ מִצְרָיִם׃ 2 וילינו
וַיִּלּוֹנוּ כָּל־עֲדַת בְּנֵי־יִשְׂרָאֵל עַל־מֹשֶׁה
וְעַל־אַהֲרֹן בַּמִּדְבָּר׃ 3 וַיֹּאמְרוּ אֲלֵהֶם בְּנֵי
יִשְׂרָאֵל מִי־יִתֵּן מוּתֵנוּ בְיַד־יְהוָה בְּאֶרֶץ
מִצְרַיִם בְּשִׁבְתֵּנוּ עַל־סִיר הַבָּשָׂר בְּאָכְלֵנוּ
לֶחֶם לָשֹׂבַע כִּי־הוֹצֵאתֶם אֹתָנוּ אֶל־
הַמִּדְבָּר הַזֶּה לְהָמִית אֶת־כָּל־הַקָּהָל הַזֶּה
בָּרָעָב׃ ס
4 וַיֹּאמֶר יְהוָה אֶל־מֹשֶׁה הִנְנִי מַמְטִיר לָכֶם
לֶחֶם מִן־הַשָּׁמָיִם וְיָצָא הָעָם וְלָקְטוּ דְבַר־

your healer God is the ultimate source of all healing. Just as He cured the waters at Marah, so will He heal the ills of obedient Israelites. Here, a great deed of God is cited to support an injunction to the Israelites. Until now, God's miracles were directed to convincing Pharaoh to let Israel go.

27. Elim A wooded, freshwater oasis.

SHORTAGE OF FOOD—MANNA AND QUAIL (16:1–20)

It is now six weeks after the Exodus. With the oasis at Elim behind them and the provisions brought from Egypt exhausted, the people face a severe food shortage. Conditions in the wilderness make it impossible to secure fresh supplies. Popular discontent flares, and harsh accusations are hurled against Moses and Aaron.

THE COMPLAINT (vv. 1–3)

The hardships of wilderness life arouse nostalgia for life in Egypt.

2. whole Israelite community The suffering is more severe and widespread than in the previous crisis, for there the grumblers were described simply as "the people" (15:24).

3. died by the hand of the LORD That is, from natural causes. Death in old age in slavery is preferable to early death by starvation in freedom.

fleshpots . . . bread Because the people left Egypt with their flocks and herds, they could not have been in danger of starvation. Livestock, however, is the most valuable possession of the pastoralist, and the people would not have wanted to slaughter their cattle for food. Also, the lack of adequate pasturage no doubt had caused considerable losses among the flocks, adding to the people's hardships.

THE DIVINE RESPONSE (vv. 4–5)

Even before Moses can "cry out to the LORD," as in the preceding crisis (15:25), God responds to Israel's needs.

4. the LORD said to Moses God reveals His intentions to Moses but does not instruct him to divulge the information to the people.

each day The fixed daily allotment of manna to each individual ensured fair and equal distri-

יוֹם בְּיוֹמוֹ לְמַעַן אֲנַסֶּנּוּ הֲיֵלֵךְ בְּתוֹרָתִי
אִם־לֹא׃ 5 וְהָיָה בַּיּוֹם הַשִּׁשִּׁי וְהֵכִינוּ אֵת
אֲשֶׁר־יָבִיאוּ וְהָיָה מִשְׁנֶה עַל אֲשֶׁר־יִלְקְטוּ
יוֹם ׀ יוֹם׃ ס 6 וַיֹּאמֶר מֹשֶׁה וְאַהֲרֹן
אֶל־כָּל־בְּנֵי יִשְׂרָאֵל עֶרֶב וִידַעְתֶּם כִּי יְהוָה
הוֹצִיא אֶתְכֶם מֵאֶרֶץ מִצְרָיִם׃ 7 וּבֹקֶר
וּרְאִיתֶם אֶת־כְּבוֹד יְהוָה בְּשָׁמְעוֹ אֶת־
תְּלֻנֹּתֵיכֶם עַל־יְהוָה וְנַחְנוּ מָה כִּי תלונו
תַלִּינוּ עָלֵינוּ׃ 8 וַיֹּאמֶר מֹשֶׁה בְּתֵת יְהוָה
לָכֶם בָּעֶרֶב בָּשָׂר לֶאֱכֹל וְלֶחֶם בַּבֹּקֶר
לִשְׂבֹּעַ בִּשְׁמֹעַ יְהוָה אֶת־תְּלֻנֹּתֵיכֶם אֲשֶׁר־
אַתֶּם מַלִּינִם עָלָיו וְנַחְנוּ מָה לֹא־עָלֵינוּ
תְלֻנֹּתֵיכֶם כִּי עַל־יְהוָה׃

portion—that I may thus test them, to see
whether they will follow My instructions or not.
[5]But on the sixth day, when they apportion what
they have brought in, it shall prove to be double
the amount they gather each day." [6]So Moses
and Aaron said to all the Israelites, "By evening
you shall know it was the LORD who brought
you out from the land of Egypt; [7]and in the
morning you shall behold the Presence of the
LORD, because He has heard your grumblings
against the LORD. For who are we that you
should grumble against us? [8]Since it is the
LORD," Moses continued, "who will give you
flesh to eat in the evening and bread in the
morning to the full, because the LORD has heard
the grumblings you utter against Him, what is
our part? Your grumbling is not against us, but
against the LORD!"

bution of this scarce commodity. The insecurity of the people's day-to-day existence, wholly dependent on this unfamiliar substance, heightens their absolute reliance on God's beneficence.

that I may thus test them There are two interpretations of this phrase: (a) The gift of manna is itself to be subject to restrictions that will test Israel's obedience and trust, and (b) God deliberately subjects the Israelites to hunger to demonstrate their absolute dependence on Him for sustenance.

5. sixth day Of the week.

THE PEOPLE ARE INFORMED (vv. 6–10)

Even though Moses and Aaron are not commanded to transmit God's message, they do so anyway to pacify the populace. But they speak in generalities and say nothing about the sixth day. That is why, according to verse 22, the chieftains are later puzzled about the purpose of the double portion of manna.

6. Aaron He is included here because the people directed their complaint against both Moses and Aaron.

it was the LORD And not we, who took you out of Egypt.

7. Presence of the LORD This is the first biblical usage of the crucial Hebrew phrase *"k'vod YHVH."* It refers to a fiery phenomenon radiating a bright light (see Ezek. 1:28; and cf. Exod. 3:2, 19:18).

against the LORD The grumbling against Moses and Aaron is really a grievance against God, from whom their mission and authority derived.

For who are we . . . This self-deprecating question is intensified by the Hebrew word *mah,* literally, "what"—used of things rather than persons.

8. Moses repeats the sentiment he has just voiced and expands it to emphasize that the people's complaint is in fact a challenge to God.

to eat . . . to the full The varying expres-

CHAPTER 16

4. that I may thus test them In what way is the manna a test? Some commentators see it as a deprivation, being confined to the same limited menu day after day. Others interpret it differently: If people are assured of food to eat without any effort on their part, will they remember to be grateful to God (Dov Ber of Mezeritch)? Are wealthy people more likely to follow God's ways, out of gratitude? Or are poor people more likely to do so, because their awareness of their dependence on God is greater? Perhaps the test was to see whether people would content themselves with one day's supply, truly believing that God could be counted on to renew their food supply on the morrow.

9Then Moses said to Aaron, "Say to the whole Israelite community: Advance toward the LORD, for He has heard your grumbling." 10And as Aaron spoke to the whole Israelite community, they turned toward the wilderness, and there, in a cloud, appeared the Presence of the LORD.

11The LORD spoke to Moses: 12"I have heard the grumbling of the Israelites. Speak to them and say: By evening you shall eat flesh, and in the morning you shall have your fill of bread; and you shall know that I the LORD am your God."

13In the evening quail appeared and covered the camp; in the morning there was a fall of dew about the camp. 14When the fall of dew lifted, there, over the surface of the wilderness, lay a fine and flaky substance, as fine as frost on the ground. 15When the Israelites saw it, they said to one another, "What is it?"—for they did not know what it was. And Moses said to them, "That is the bread which the LORD has given you to eat. 16This is what the LORD has commanded: Gather as much of it as each of you requires to

9 וַיֹּ֤אמֶר מֹשֶׁה֙ אֶֽל־אַהֲרֹ֔ן אֱמֹ֗ר אֶֽל־כָּל־עֲדַת֙ בְּנֵ֣י יִשְׂרָאֵ֔ל קִרְב֖וּ לִפְנֵ֣י יְהֹוָ֑ה כִּ֣י שָׁמַ֔ע אֵ֖ת תְּלֻנֹּתֵיכֶֽם: 10 וַיְהִ֗י כְּדַבֵּ֤ר אַהֲרֹן֙ אֶל־כָּל־עֲדַ֣ת בְּנֵֽי־יִשְׂרָאֵ֔ל וַיִּפְנ֖וּ אֶל־הַמִּדְבָּ֑ר וְהִנֵּה֙ כְּב֣וֹד יְהֹוָ֔ה נִרְאָ֖ה בֶּֽעָנָֽן: פ

11 שׁשׁי וַיְדַבֵּ֥ר יְהֹוָ֖ה אֶל־מֹשֶׁ֥ה לֵּאמֹֽר: 12 שָׁמַ֗עְתִּי אֶת־תְּלוּנֹּת֮ בְּנֵ֣י יִשְׂרָאֵל֒ דַּבֵּ֨ר אֲלֵהֶ֜ם לֵאמֹ֗ר בֵּ֤ין הָֽעַרְבַּ֙יִם֙ תֹּֽאכְל֣וּ בָשָׂ֔ר וּבַבֹּ֖קֶר תִּשְׂבְּעוּ־לָ֑חֶם וִֽידַעְתֶּ֕ם כִּ֛י אֲנִ֥י יְהֹוָ֖ה אֱלֹֽהֵיכֶֽם:

13 וַיְהִ֣י בָעֶ֔רֶב וַתַּ֣עַל הַשְּׂלָ֔ו וַתְּכַ֖ס אֶת־הַֽמַּחֲנֶ֑ה וּבַבֹּ֗קֶר הָֽיְתָה֙ שִׁכְבַ֣ת הַטַּ֔ל סָבִ֖יב לַֽמַּחֲנֶֽה: 14 וַתַּ֖עַל שִׁכְבַ֣ת הַטָּ֑ל וְהִנֵּ֞ה עַל־פְּנֵ֤י הַמִּדְבָּר֙ דַּ֣ק מְחֻסְפָּ֔ס דַּ֥ק כַּכְּפֹ֖ר עַל־הָאָֽרֶץ: 15 וַיִּרְא֣וּ בְנֵֽי־יִשְׂרָאֵ֗ל וַיֹּ֨אמְר֜וּ אִ֤ישׁ אֶל־אָחִיו֙ מָ֣ן ה֔וּא כִּ֛י לֹ֥א יָֽדְע֖וּ מַה־ה֑וּא וַיֹּ֤אמֶר מֹשֶׁה֙ אֲלֵהֶ֔ם ה֣וּא הַלֶּ֔חֶם אֲשֶׁ֨ר נָתַ֧ן יְהֹוָ֛ה לָכֶ֖ם לְאָכְלָֽה: 16 זֶ֤ה הַדָּבָר֙ אֲשֶׁ֣ר צִוָּ֣ה יְהֹוָ֔ה לִקְט֣וּ מִמֶּ֔נּוּ אִ֖ישׁ לְפִ֥י

sions—"flesh to eat," and "bread . . . to the full"—seem to indicate that God will satisfy the cravings for both flesh and bread.

9. Aaron again acts as Moses' spokesman, this time to the Israelites rather than to Pharaoh.

toward the LORD Literally, "before the LORD." Here, as Rashi notes, it must refer to the direction of the cloud.

10. *in a cloud* That is, in the luminous cloud that symbolizes God's active, dynamic, indwelling Presence in Israel during the wilderness period. The sudden appearance of the cloud affirms the announcement just made by Aaron. See Comment to 13:21–22.

THE QUAIL AND MANNA ARRIVE
(vv. 11–20)

God fulfills His promise. The narrative offers a detailed description of the manna, but says little about the quail. Perhaps this is because the cry for bread was considered reasonable and the craving for meat was not. The Torah describes the

provision of manna as a supernatural phenomenon; the quail, except for its timing, was entirely natural (see Num. 11:31–32). The manna was supplied continually for 40 years, whereas the quail appeared only occasionally.

12. *I have heard* The repetition of the complaint serves to introduce the account of the actual arrival of the quail and manna. They appear not by chance but as the result of divine deliberation.

you shall know Israel "knows" God by experiencing His actions on their behalf.

13. *quail* These small birds of the pheasant family migrate in vast flocks from central Europe to Africa in the autumn. To this day they are caught in large numbers in northern Sinai and Egypt.

a fall of dew Two layers of dew enveloped the manna, so that it remained clean until it was collected in the early morning. In biblical times, dew was thought to descend like rain from the sky; thus the manna could be called "bread from Heaven."

אָכְל֑וֹ עֹ֚מֶר לַגֻּלְגֹּ֔לֶת מִסְפַּר֙ נַפְשֹׁ֣תֵיכֶ֔ם
אִ֛ישׁ לַאֲשֶׁ֥ר בְּאָהֳל֖וֹ תִּקָּֽחוּ׃
17 וַיַּֽעֲשׂוּ־כֵ֖ן בְּנֵ֣י יִשְׂרָאֵ֑ל וַֽיִּלְקְט֔וּ הַמַּרְבֶּ֖ה
וְהַמַּמְעִֽיט׃ 18 וַיָּמֹ֣דּוּ בָעֹ֔מֶר וְלֹ֤א הֶעְדִּיף֙
הַמַּרְבֶּ֔ה וְהַמַּמְעִ֖יט לֹ֣א הֶחְסִ֑יר אִ֥ישׁ לְפִֽי־
אָכְל֖וֹ לָקָֽטוּ׃ 19 וַיֹּ֥אמֶר מֹשֶׁ֖ה אֲלֵהֶ֑ם אִ֕ישׁ
אַל־יוֹתֵ֥ר מִמֶּ֖נּוּ עַד־בֹּֽקֶר׃ 20 וְלֹא־שָׁמְע֣וּ
אֶל־מֹשֶׁ֗ה וַיּוֹתִ֨רוּ אֲנָשִׁ֤ים מִמֶּ֙נּוּ֙ עַד־בֹּ֔קֶר
וַיָּ֥רֻם תּוֹלָעִ֖ים וַיִּבְאַ֑שׁ וַיִּקְצֹ֥ף עֲלֵהֶ֖ם
מֹשֶֽׁה׃
21 וַיִּלְקְט֤וּ אֹתוֹ֙ בַּבֹּ֣קֶר בַּבֹּ֔קֶר אִ֖ישׁ כְּפִ֣י
אָכְל֑וֹ וְחַ֥ם הַשֶּׁ֖מֶשׁ וְנָמָֽס׃ 22 וַיְהִ֣י ׀ בַּיּ֣וֹם
הַשִּׁשִּׁ֗י לָֽקְטוּ֙ לֶ֣חֶם מִשְׁנֶ֔ה שְׁנֵ֥י הָעֹ֖מֶר
לָאֶחָ֑ד וַיָּבֹ֙אוּ֙ כָּל־נְשִׂיאֵ֣י הָֽעֵדָ֔ה וַיַּגִּ֖ידוּ
לְמֹשֶֽׁה׃ 23 וַיֹּ֣אמֶר אֲלֵהֶ֗ם ה֚וּא אֲשֶׁ֣ר דִּבֶּ֣ר
יְהוָ֔ה שַׁבָּת֧וֹן שַׁבַּת־קֹ֛דֶשׁ לַיהוָ֖ה מָחָ֑ר אֵ֣ת
אֲשֶׁר־תֹּאפ֞וּ אֵפ֗וּ וְאֵ֤ת אֲשֶׁר־תְּבַשְּׁלוּ֙

eat, an *omer* to a person for as many of you as there are; each of you shall fetch for those in his tent."

17The Israelites did so, some gathering much, some little. 18But when they measured it by the *omer*, he who had gathered much had no excess, and he who had gathered little had no deficiency: they had gathered as much as they needed to eat. 19And Moses said to them, "Let no one leave any of it over until morning." 20But they paid no attention to Moses; some of them left of it until morning, and it became infested with maggots and stank. And Moses was angry with them.

21So they gathered it every morning, each as much as he needed to eat; for when the sun grew hot, it would melt. 22On the sixth day they gathered double the amount of food, two *omer*s for each; and when all the chieftains of the community came and told Moses, 23he said to them, "This is what the LORD meant: Tomorrow is a day of rest, a holy sabbath of the LORD. Bake what you would bake and boil what you would

16. omer In this chapter, a dry measure of volume; elsewhere it means "a sheaf of grain."

19. Ibn Ezra understood this restriction as a test of faith that the manna would appear again the next day.

THE LAW OF *SHABBAT* (vv. 21–30)

God's abstention from creativity on the seventh day is the climax of the Creation, as narrated in Gen. 2:1–3. In describing that, the Hebrew stem שבת is used as a verb, with God as the subject. Now, for the first time, *"shabbat"* appears as a noun, to designate a fixed day that recurs regularly. Note that the Israelites are expected to observe *Shabbat* even before it has been commanded of them at Mount Sinai.

22. Presumably, the people had been told to collect double the usual daily amount on Fridays, but had not been told why. The tribal chiefs report to Moses that the order was followed, and they await clarification.

23. a day of rest Hebrew: *shabbaton*, an abstract term meaning "restfulness."

a holy sabbath The holiness of the day flows from God's blessing and sanctity, as related in Gen. 2:3. It is an integral part of the divinely ordained cosmic order. Its blessed and sacred character is independent of human initiative. Hence it is frequently referred to as "a sabbath of the LORD." See Comments to Exod. 20:8–11.

bake . . . boil The people would grind the manna between millstones or pound it in a mortar, boil it in a pot, and make it into cakes.

all that is left That is, what was neither baked nor boiled on Friday but remained in its original raw and still edible state.

17. some gathering much It was a violation of God's plan for the people that some should grab more of the good things of life than their neighbors, ostentatiously gorging themselves while others went hungry. God provides food for everyone, but some people insist on taking more than their share. For them, it is not sufficient to have plenty. To feel prosperous, they must have more than their neighbors.

22. double the amount of food The He-

בַּשֵּׁ֑לוּ וְאֵת֙ כׇּל־הָ֣עֹדֵ֔ף הַנִּ֧יחוּ לָכֶ֛ם
לְמִשְׁמֶ֖רֶת עַד־הַבֹּֽקֶר׃ 24 וַיַּנִּ֤יחוּ אֹתוֹ֙ עַד־
הַבֹּ֔קֶר כַּאֲשֶׁ֖ר צִוָּ֣ה מֹשֶׁ֑ה וְלֹ֣א הִבְאִ֔ישׁ
וְרִמָּ֖ה לֹא־הָ֥יְתָה בּֽוֹ׃ 25 וַיֹּ֤אמֶר מֹשֶׁה֙
אִכְלֻ֣הוּ הַיּ֔וֹם כִּֽי־שַׁבָּ֥ת הַיּ֖וֹם לַיהֹוָ֑ה הַיּ֕וֹם
לֹ֥א תִמְצָאֻ֖הוּ בַּשָּׂדֶֽה׃ 26 שֵׁ֥שֶׁת יָמִ֖ים
תִּלְקְטֻ֑הוּ וּבַיּ֧וֹם הַשְּׁבִיעִ֛י שַׁבָּ֖ת לֹ֥א יִֽהְיֶה־
בּֽוֹ׃
27 וַיְהִי֙ בַּיּ֣וֹם הַשְּׁבִיעִ֔י יָצְא֥וּ מִן־הָעָ֖ם
לִלְקֹ֑ט וְלֹ֖א מָצָֽאוּ׃ ס 28 וַיֹּ֥אמֶר יְהֹוָ֖ה
אֶל־מֹשֶׁ֑ה עַד־אָ֙נָה֙ מֵֽאַנְתֶּ֔ם לִשְׁמֹ֥ר מִצְוֺתַ֖י
וְתוֹרֹתָֽי׃ 29 רְא֗וּ כִּֽי־יְהֹוָה֮ נָתַ֣ן לָכֶ֣ם הַשַּׁבָּת֒
עַל־כֵּ֠ן ה֣וּא נֹתֵ֥ן לָכֶ֛ם בַּיּ֥וֹם הַשִּׁשִּׁ֖י לֶ֣חֶם
יוֹמָ֑יִם שְׁב֣וּ ׀ אִ֣ישׁ תַּחְתָּ֗יו אַל־יֵ֥צֵא אִ֛ישׁ
מִמְּקֹמ֖וֹ בַּיּ֥וֹם הַשְּׁבִיעִֽי׃ 30 וַיִּשְׁבְּת֥וּ הָעָ֖ם
בַּיּ֥וֹם הַשְּׁבִעִֽי׃
31 וַיִּקְרְא֧וּ בֵֽית־יִשְׂרָאֵ֛ל אֶת־שְׁמ֖וֹ מָ֑ן וְה֗וּא
כְּזֶ֤רַע גַּד֙ לָבָ֔ן וְטַעְמ֖וֹ כְּצַפִּיחִ֥ת בִּדְבָֽשׁ׃

boil; and all that is left put aside to be kept until
morning." 24So they put it aside until morning,
as Moses had ordered; and it did not turn foul,
and there were no maggots in it. 25Then Moses
said, "Eat it today, for today is a sabbath of the
LORD; you will not find it today on the plain.
26Six days you shall gather it; on the seventh day,
the sabbath, there will be none."

27Yet some of the people went out on the seventh day to gather, but they found nothing.
28And the LORD said to Moses, "How long will
you men refuse to obey My commandments
and My teachings? 29Mark that the LORD has
given you the sabbath; therefore He gives you
two days' food on the sixth day. Let everyone
remain where he is: let no one leave his place
on the seventh day." 30So the people remained
inactive on the seventh day.

31The house of Israel named it manna; it
was like coriander seed, white, and it tasted like

27. Some people were skeptical of Moses' prediction that no manna would fall on *Shabbat*, and they went out to test it.

29. has given you the sabbath The day is God's gift to Israel.

Let everyone remain where he is . . . his place And not go out to collect manna.

AN APPENDIX ON MANNA (vv. 31–36)

This appendix apparently was written at a time later than the events just narrated. It presupposes the erection of the tabernacle, the appointment of a priesthood, the cessation of the manna, the settlement in the Land, and the fact that the *omer* measure was no longer in use.

31. The manna has been identified with the sap of the tamarisk tree in the wilderness of northern Arabia. From the sap, a type of plant lice produces a yellowish white flake or ball, which melts during the warmth of the day but congeals when cold. It has a desirable sweet taste; is often gathered by the natives in the early morning; and when cooked, becomes a kind of bread. It decays rapidly. Its ephemeral nature and its undependability—appearing irregularly and only for several hours each day—would have stamped it as supernatural, originating in heaven.

coriander An herb; its seeds are used in flavoring.

wafers The word *"tzapiḥit"* appears nowhere else in the Bible. In Num. 11:8 the taste is compared to "cream of oil," i.e., rich cream. Perhaps the verse here describes the taste of the manna in its raw state and the passage in Numbers characterizes its flavor when cooked.

32. A sample of the manna—an amount

---

brew term for "double the amount of food" (*leḥem mishneh*) occurs in the Bible only here. This verse is the source for the Jewish custom of having two loaves of bread on the table when reciting *Kiddush* to inaugurate the main meals on *Shabbat* and festivals.

HALAKHAH L'MA·ASEH

16:23. put aside Cooking is one of the major categories of prohibited activity on *Shabbat*. Therefore, all cooked food for *Shabbat* meals must be prepared before *Shabbat* begins. Food already prepared may be kept warm in the oven or on a covered burner or hot plate kept on for that purpose throughout *Shabbat*.

wafers in honey. ³²Moses said, "This is what the Lord has commanded: Let one *omer* of it be kept throughout the ages, in order that they may see the bread that I fed you in the wilderness when I brought you out from the land of Egypt." ³³And Moses said to Aaron, "Take a jar, put one *omer* of manna in it, and place it before the Lord, to be kept throughout the ages." ³⁴As the Lord had commanded Moses, Aaron placed it before the Pact, to be kept. ³⁵And the Israelites ate manna forty years, until they came to a settled land; they ate the manna until they came to the border of the land of Canaan. ³⁶The *omer* is a tenth of an *ephah*.

³² וַיֹּ֣אמֶר מֹשֶׁ֗ה זֶ֤ה הַדָּבָר֙ אֲשֶׁ֣ר צִוָּ֣ה יְהֹוָ֔ה מְלֹ֤א הָעֹ֙מֶר֙ מִמֶּ֔נּוּ לְמִשְׁמֶ֖רֶת לְדֹרֹֽתֵיכֶ֑ם לְמַ֣עַן ׀ יִרְא֣וּ אֶת־הַלֶּ֗חֶם אֲשֶׁ֨ר הֶאֱכַ֤לְתִּי אֶתְכֶם֙ בַּמִּדְבָּ֔ר בְּהוֹצִיאִ֥י אֶתְכֶ֖ם מֵאֶ֥רֶץ מִצְרָֽיִם׃ ³³ וַיֹּ֨אמֶר מֹשֶׁ֜ה אֶֽל־אַהֲרֹ֗ן קַ֚ח צִנְצֶ֣נֶת אַחַ֔ת וְתֶן־שָׁ֥מָּה מְלֹֽא־הָעֹ֖מֶר מָ֑ן וְהַנַּ֤ח אֹתוֹ֙ לִפְנֵ֣י יְהֹוָ֔ה לְמִשְׁמֶ֖רֶת לְדֹרֹֽתֵיכֶֽם׃ ³⁴ כַּאֲשֶׁ֛ר צִוָּ֥ה יְהֹוָ֖ה אֶל־מֹשֶׁ֑ה וַיַּנִּיחֵ֧הוּ אַהֲרֹ֛ן לִפְנֵ֥י הָעֵדֻ֖ת לְמִשְׁמָֽרֶת׃ ³⁵ וּבְנֵ֣י יִשְׂרָאֵ֗ל אָֽכְל֤וּ אֶת־הַמָּן֙ אַרְבָּעִ֣ים שָׁנָ֔ה עַד־בֹּאָ֖ם אֶל־אֶ֣רֶץ נוֹשָׁ֑בֶת אֶת־הַמָּן֙ אָֽכְל֔וּ עַד־בֹּאָ֕ם אֶל־קְצֵ֖ה אֶ֥רֶץ כְּנָֽעַן׃ ³⁶ וְהָעֹ֕מֶר עֲשִׂרִ֥ית הָאֵיפָ֖ה הֽוּא׃ פ

17 From the wilderness of Sin the whole Israelite community continued by stages as the Lord would command. They encamped at Rephidim, and there was no water for the people to drink. ²The people quarreled with Moses.

שביעי **יז** ¹ וַ֠יִּסְע֠וּ כׇּל־עֲדַ֨ת בְּנֵֽי־יִשְׂרָאֵ֧ל מִמִּדְבַּר־סִ֛ין לְמַסְעֵיהֶ֖ם עַל־פִּ֣י יְהֹוָ֑ה וַֽיַּחֲנוּ֙ בִּרְפִידִ֔ים וְאֵ֥ין מַ֖יִם לִשְׁתֹּ֥ת הָעָֽם׃ ² וַיָּ֤רֶב הָעָם֙ עִם־מֹשֶׁ֔ה וַיֹּ֣אמְר֔וּ תְּנוּ־לָ֣נוּ

equal to an individual's daily ration—is to be preserved as a kind of cultural relic and serve future generations as a reminder of God's providential care of Israel throughout the wilderness period.

33. before the Lord That is, in front of the Ark in the Holy of Holies of the tabernacle, which was not erected until the first anniversary of the Exodus. Because the priesthood in Israel has not yet been established, the instruction to place the *omer* of manna "before the Lord" cannot be contemporaneous with the events described earlier.

34. the Pact That is, "the Ark of the Pact." The Ark housed the two tablets of stone on which the Decalogue was inscribed.

35. After the Israelites crossed the Jordan and celebrated the Passover in the land of Israel for the first time (Josh. 5:11–12), the manna ceased.

to the border of the land of Canaan This additional note is not consistent with the tradition that was just cited. Ibn Ezra thought "the border of the land" might refer to Gilgal, the first Israelite encampment west of the Jordan.

36. The note is needed here because the *omer*, which never recurs in the Bible as a measure, became obsolete and unintelligible to later generations. The *ephah* (*eifah*), a dry measure of Egyptian origin that approximately equals 1 bushel (35 L), is frequently mentioned in the Bible.

MASSAH AND MERIBAH (17:1–7)

For the third time the people grumble against Moses. This time they even question God's providence. The incident made a profound impression on Israel's historical memory. Its locale was called by a derogatory symbolic name: *Massah-M'rivah*, literally, "trial-quarrel." The frequent reference to this narrative in the Bible indicates that it was much talked about in ancient Israel.

1. Rephidim The last station on the journey from the Sea of Reeds to Sinai, according to Exod. 19:2 and Num. 33:14–15. Although its precise location is still uncertain, Exod. 17:6 shows that it was situated close to Horeb/Mount Sinai. A wilderness station would have water. Why, then, was there no water for the Israelites when they arrived at Rephidim? Either the area was affected by a severe drought or the Amalekites were in control of this region and blocked the approaches to the sources of water.

2. quarreled The narrative uses the Hebrew verb רִיב, "fight," a term that conjures up a picture of an angry, hostile confrontation.

"Give us water to drink," they said; and Moses
replied to them, "Why do you quarrel with me?
Why do you try the LORD?" 3But the people
thirsted there for water; and the people grumbled against Moses and said, "Why did you
bring us up from Egypt, to kill us and our children and livestock with thirst?" 4Moses cried
out to the LORD, saying, "What shall I do with
this people? Before long they will be stoning
me!" 5Then the LORD said to Moses, "Pass before the people; take with you some of the elders
of Israel, and take along the rod with which you
struck the Nile, and set out. 6I will be standing
there before you on the rock at Horeb. Strike
the rock and water will issue from it, and the
people will drink." And Moses did so in the sight
of the elders of Israel. 7The place was named
Massah and Meribah, because the Israelites
quarreled and because they tried the LORD, saying, "Is the LORD present among us or not?"

מַ֥יִם וְנִשְׁתֶּ֑ה וַיֹּ֤אמֶר לָהֶם֙ מֹשֶׁ֔ה מַה־
תְּרִיבוּן֙ עִמָּדִ֔י מַה־תְּנַסּ֖וּן אֶת־יְהוָֽה׃
3 וַיִּצְמָ֨א שָׁ֤ם הָעָם֙ לַמַּ֔יִם וַיָּ֥לֶן הָעָ֖ם
עַל־מֹשֶׁ֑ה וַיֹּ֗אמֶר לָ֤מָּה זֶּה֙ הֶֽעֱלִיתָ֣נוּ
מִמִּצְרַ֔יִם לְהָמִ֥ית אֹתִ֛י וְאֶת־בָּנַ֥י וְאֶת־
מִקְנַ֖י בַּצָּמָֽא׃ 4 וַיִּצְעַ֤ק מֹשֶׁה֙ אֶל־יְהוָ֣ה
לֵאמֹ֔ר מָ֥ה אֶעֱשֶׂ֖ה לָעָ֣ם הַזֶּ֑ה ע֥וֹד מְעַ֖ט
וּסְקָלֻֽנִי׃ 5 וַיֹּ֨אמֶר יְהוָ֜ה אֶל־מֹשֶׁ֗ה עֲבֹר֙
לִפְנֵ֣י הָעָ֔ם וְקַ֥ח אִתְּךָ֖ מִזִּקְנֵ֣י יִשְׂרָאֵ֑ל וּמַטְּךָ֗
אֲשֶׁ֨ר הִכִּ֤יתָ בּוֹ֙ אֶת־הַיְאֹ֔ר קַ֥ח בְּיָדְךָ֖
וְהָלָֽכְתָּ׃ 6 הִנְנִ֣י עֹמֵד֩ לְפָנֶ֨יךָ שָּׁ֥ם ׀ עַֽל־
הַצּוּר֮ בְּחֹרֵב֒ וְהִכִּ֣יתָ בַצּ֗וּר וְיָצְא֥וּ מִמֶּ֛נּוּ
מַ֖יִם וְשָׁתָ֣ה הָעָ֑ם וַיַּ֤עַשׂ כֵּן֙ מֹשֶׁ֔ה לְעֵינֵ֖י
זִקְנֵ֥י יִשְׂרָאֵֽל׃ 7 וַיִּקְרָא֙ שֵׁ֣ם הַמָּק֔וֹם מַסָּ֖ה
וּמְרִיבָ֑ה עַל־רִ֣יב ׀ בְּנֵ֣י יִשְׂרָאֵ֗ל וְעַ֨ל נַסֹּתָ֤ם
אֶת־יְהוָה֙ לֵאמֹ֔ר הֲיֵ֧שׁ יְהוָ֛ה בְּקִרְבֵּ֖נוּ
אִם־אָֽיִן׃ פ

8Amalek came and fought with Israel at

8 וַיָּבֹ֖א עֲמָלֵ֑ק וַיִּלָּ֥חֶם עִם־יִשְׂרָאֵ֖ל

Give us water The demand, in effect, is both a denunciation and an accusation.

3–4. The situation has deteriorated. The language of the people is unrestrained; their mood, explosive. A riot may break out any moment.

6. at Horeb At this site—known as "the mountain of God," another name for Mount Sinai—Moses first received the call to leadership and the promise of Israel's redemption.

Strike the rock Most likely, soft porous limestone, which can retain water. A sharp blow to such rock can crack its crust and release a flow of groundwater. The miracle is credited to God and not to Moses, a point emphasized several times in the Bible. Moses acts only as the agent of God's will, not on his own initiative.

THE BATTLE WITH AMALEK
(vv. 8–16)

According to the more detailed account given in Deut. 25:17–19, the Amalekites made a surprise rear attack on the famished and exhausted Israelites not long after the escape from Egypt. They cut down the stragglers—the elderly, the weak, and the infirm. Israel was forced to fight its first war of survival. The Amalekites were a tribe of

---

CHAPTER 17

3. The text reads literally, "Why did you bring us out of Egypt to kill me and my children?" When the Israelites were leaving Egypt in triumph and the future looked glorious, they thought in terms of "us," all of us together. But when times became hard and there was not enough to eat and drink, they stopped saying "us" and began to speak of "me and my children."

5. take along the rod with which you struck the Nile Thus the people might know that the rod that had been used to start a plague, to make the waters of the Nile undrinkable, could also be used to produce a blessing, to call forth water in the wilderness.

8. Amalek is the Torah's symbol of pure malice, attacking without cause. Some people commit crimes for profit or revenge, but Amalek acts that way for the sheer joy of hurting people. God's "war from generation to gener-

Rephidim. ⁹Moses said to Joshua, "Pick some men for us, and go out and do battle with Amalek. Tomorrow I will station myself on the top of the hill, with the rod of God in my hand." ¹⁰Joshua did as Moses told him and fought with Amalek, while Moses, Aaron, and Hur went up to the top of the hill. ¹¹Then, whenever Moses held up his hand, Israel prevailed; but whenever he let down his hand, Amalek prevailed. ¹²But Moses' hands grew heavy; so they took a stone and put it under him and he sat on it, while Aaron and Hur, one on each side, supported his hands; thus his hands remained steady until the sun set. ¹³And Joshua overwhelmed the people of Amalek with the sword.

¹⁴Then the Lord said to Moses, "Inscribe this in a document as a reminder, and read it aloud to Joshua: I will utterly blot out the memory of Amalek from under heaven!" ¹⁵And Moses

בִּרְפִידִֽם׃ ⁹ וַיֹּ֨אמֶר מֹשֶׁ֤ה אֶל־יְהוֹשֻׁ֙עַ֙ בְּחַר־
לָ֣נוּ אֲנָשִׁ֔ים וְצֵ֖א הִלָּחֵ֣ם בַּֽעֲמָלֵ֑ק מָחָ֗ר
אָֽנֹכִ֤י נִצָּב֙ עַל־רֹ֣אשׁ הַגִּבְעָ֔ה וּמַטֵּ֥ה
הָֽאֱלֹהִ֖ים בְּיָדִֽי׃ ¹⁰ וַיַּ֣עַשׂ יְהוֹשֻׁ֗עַ כַּֽאֲשֶׁ֤ר
אָֽמַר־לוֹ֙ מֹשֶׁ֔ה לְהִלָּחֵ֖ם בַּֽעֲמָלֵ֑ק וּמֹשֶׁ֤ה
אַֽהֲרֹן֙ וְח֔וּר עָל֖וּ רֹ֥אשׁ הַגִּבְעָֽה׃ ¹¹ וְהָיָ֗ה
כַּֽאֲשֶׁ֨ר יָרִ֥ים מֹשֶׁ֛ה יָד֖וֹ וְגָבַ֣ר יִשְׂרָאֵ֑ל
וְכַֽאֲשֶׁ֥ר יָנִ֛יחַ יָד֖וֹ וְגָבַ֥ר עֲמָלֵֽק׃ ¹² וִידֵ֤י מֹשֶׁה֙
כְּבֵדִ֔ים וַיִּקְחוּ־אֶ֛בֶן וַיָּשִׂ֥ימוּ תַחְתָּ֖יו וַיֵּ֣שֶׁב
עָלֶ֑יהָ וְאַֽהֲרֹ֨ן וְח֜וּר תָּֽמְכ֣וּ בְיָדָ֗יו מִזֶּ֤ה אֶחָד֙
וּמִזֶּ֣ה אֶחָ֔ד וַיְהִ֥י יָדָ֛יו אֱמוּנָ֖ה עַד־בֹּ֥א
הַשָּֽׁמֶשׁ׃ ¹³ וַיַּֽחֲלֹ֧שׁ יְהוֹשֻׁ֛עַ אֶת־עֲמָלֵ֥ק
וְאֶת־עַמּ֖וֹ לְפִי־חָֽרֶב׃ פ

מפטיר ¹⁴ וַיֹּ֨אמֶר יְהֹוָ֜ה אֶל־מֹשֶׁ֗ה כְּתֹ֨ב זֹ֤את זִכָּרוֹן֙
בַּסֵּ֔פֶר וְשִׂ֖ים בְּאָזְנֵ֣י יְהוֹשֻׁ֑עַ כִּֽי־מָחֹ֤ה
אֶמְחֶה֙ אֶת־זֵ֣כֶר עֲמָלֵ֔ק מִתַּ֖חַת הַשָּׁמָֽיִם׃

Edomite nomads whose home was the Negeb and the Sinai Peninsula. Interpreting the appearance of the Israelites in this region as a menacing encroachment on their territory and as a threat to their control of the oases and trading routes, the Amalekites savagely attacked them.

9. Joshua Although previously unmentioned, he is not identified here, which suggests that he was well known. He was Moses' faithful attendant and his designated successor. This incident is the only account in the Torah of Joshua's military skill.

rod of God   See Comment to 4:20.

10. Hur Like Joshua, he too must have been an important public figure at this time. A later tradition identifies him as the husband of Moses' sister, Miriam.

11. held up his hand The hand is viewed by the Sages as a symbol of action and power, not as a mysterious focusing of supernatural power on Israel.

12. remained steady The Hebrew root אמן means "to be firm," "to be established" (see 2 Sam. 7:16). The verse makes the point that Moses' steady arms and hands, which gave confidence to the people, had to be propped up. The power was God's, not his.

13. overwhelmed The use of the Hebrew חלש, "to be weak," seems to convey the notion of inflicting heavy casualties, rather than total victory. The Amalekites were forced to withdraw.

14. Inscribe This is the first reference in the Bible to the act of writing.

a reminder   See Comment to 2:24.

---

ation" is not only with the tribe of Amalek (which disappears early in the biblical period) but with those people in every generation who revel in cruelty and hatred.

11. When Moses raises his hands, Israel prevails because the victory is not the result of their prowess but of their faith in God, their thoughts being directed to heaven. Repeatedly in the first half of the Book of Exodus, God's "outstretched arm" smites the Egyptians in Egypt and at the sea. Similarly, Israel is de-

scribed as leaving Egypt *b'yad ramah* (boldly), literally "with arms raised high," and Moses commands the sea to split by lifting his arm and rod over it. The upraised arm, representing both God's power and Israel's attention directed heavenward, is a central image in the narrative.

14. I will utterly blot out the memory of Amalek A homiletic comment suggests that sometimes Amalek is like a mad dog, attacking without provocation. In those cases, God says

built an altar and named it Adonai-nissi. 16He said, "It means, 'Hand upon the throne of the LORD!' The LORD will be at war with Amalek throughout the ages."

15 וַיִּ֥בֶן מֹשֶׁ֖ה מִזְבֵּ֑חַ וַיִּקְרָ֥א שְׁמ֖וֹ יְהוָ֥ה ׀
נִסִּֽי׃ 16 וַיֹּ֗אמֶר כִּֽי־יָד֙ עַל־כֵּ֣ס יָ֔הּ מִלְחָמָ֥ה
לַֽיהוָ֖ה בַּֽעֲמָלֵ֑ק מִדֹּ֖ר דֹּֽר׃ פ

15. built an altar As an expression of gratitude to God and as a memorial and witness to the battle.

Adonai-nissi Literally, "The LORD is my standard."

16. This verse appears to be a citation from some ancient poetic text, now lost—perhaps the Book of the Wars of the Lord, mentioned in Num. 21:14, or the Book of Jashar, cited in Josh. 10:13 and 2 Sam. 1:18. These works apparently contained war songs and poetic accounts of battles. The verse may be an excerpt from a poetic version of the battle against Amalek.

He said, "It means, . . ." The passage is intended to be an explanation of the altar's name, but the relationship between the two is difficult to discern.

Hand upon the throne Some ancient and medieval Jewish commentators understood the unusual word *"kes,"* which appears only here, as *kissei,* "throne," and interpreted the phrase to be an oath uttered either by Moses or by God, reinforcing the promise of verse 14.

the LORD Hebrew: *yah.* See Comment to 15:2.

"*I* will deal with him." At times, however, Amalek is like a fly, appearing only where dirt and filth are. In those cases, the Torah says "you blot out his memory" (Deut. 25:19) by cleaning up the corruption that attracts him. We are commanded to combat Amalek in every generation, even as we wait for God to eradicate Amalek entirely. On Purim, when we make noise to blot out the name of Haman, considered a descendant of Amalek both biologically and spiritually, we are fulfilling this commandment.

16. The words translated as "throne of the LORD" (*kes Yah*) in the last verse of the *parashah,* are written "defective," with letters missing, as if to imply that God's sovereignty is incomplete as long as Amalek is at work in this world (Tanḥ. Ki Tetzei).

הפטרת בשלח

HAFTARAH FOR B'SHALLAḤ

JUDGES 4:4–5:31 (*Ashk'nazim*)
JUDGES 5:1–31 (*S'fardim*)

The battle between a coalition of northern Israelite tribes and the Canaanite armies is recounted in prose and in poetry in this *haftarah*. It was part of the wars that completed the conquest of the land begun by Joshua in the mid-12th century B.C.E. Both accounts praise the prowess and the initiative of two women: Deborah, a prophetess and judge in the region of Ephraim, and Jael, a tent dweller of the Kenite tribe.

Ashk'nazim recite both the prose and the poetic accounts. *S'fardim* recite only the poetic version, the focus of which is the praise of God, the participating tribes, and the individual heroes. As in military epics of other cultures, this song of glory is addressed to both contemporary and future generations.

Both versions of the victory over the Canaanites portray God's power on behalf of His people. Both versions omit the historical prologue (Judg. 4:1–3) that presents the Canaanite menace as divine punishment for Israelite offenses against God, and presents the divinely aided victory as a result of the people's return to Him in supplication.

Each version is distinctive in content, voice, style, and theological emphasis. The prose account uses the narrative voice, portraying Deborah as both charismatic leader—able to rouse the troops to battle—and prophetess. The events unfold within the framework of her prophecies, which charge the narrative with expectation. Details of the battle are meager, save for the concluding encounter between Jael and Sisera. The death of the Canaanite commander at the hands of the Kenite woman is a memorable moment of great glory. Jael's use of a ruse, by which military victory is ensured, is a characteristic feature of other narratives in the Book of Judges.

In the poetic version of these events, the hymn of praise in Judg. 5 is sung by the heroine ("I will sing," v. 3) with interjections by a song leader or chorus ("Awake, awake, O Deborah! / . . . strike up the chant! / . . . Take your captives, O son of Abinoam," v. 12). This poetic version, placed after the historical narrative, functions as a supplementary song of victory, although it must have been formulated originally as an independent epic. This is suggested by the fact that in this version seven tribal units answered the call to battle (not just Zebulun and Naphtali, as in Judg. 4). Also, other tribes are chided or cursed for not participating in the national call to arms (5:14–18,23).

Repetitions and puns give the song a structure as well as the tempo and tone of a living epic. For example, the adverb *az* (then) provides a recurrent punctuation of details and events (vv. 8,11,13,19, 22). The word *az* spelled with an *alef* also evokes a military term spelled with an *ayin,* namely: *oz* (courage, v. 21).

RELATION OF THE *HAFTARAH* TO THE *PARASHAH*

The Song of Deborah and Barak (Judg. 5) is read along with the Songs of Moses and Israel and of Miriam (Exod. 15) as two celebrations of divine salvation in history. Moses' Song of the Sea, which celebrates how the Lord "threw the Egyptian army into a panic" (*va-yaham,* Exod. 14:24), occurs at the beginning of national liberation and anticipates settlement in the Land and the building of the Temple (Exod. 15:15–17). It concludes with the climactic hope in God's enduring kingship (v. 18). Deborah's song, which celebrates how "the LORD threw Sisera and all his chariots and army into a panic" (*va-yaham,* Judg. 4:15), occurs within the period of settling the Land. It, too, concludes on a hopeful note (Judg. 5:31).

4

4 Deborah, wife of Lappidoth, was a prophetess; she led Israel at that time. 5 She used to sit under the Palm of Deborah, between Ramah and Bethel in the hill country of Ephraim, and the Israelites would come to her for decisions.

6 She summoned Barak son of Abinoam, of Kedesh in Naphtali, and said to him, "The LORD, the God of Israel, has commanded: Go, march up to Mount Tabor, and take with you ten thousand men of Naphtali and Zebulun. 7 And I will draw Sisera, Jabin's army commander, with his chariots and his troops, toward you up to the Wadi Kishon; and I will deliver him into your hands." 8 But Barak said to her, "If you will go with me, I will go; if not, I will not go." 9 "Very well, I will go with you," she answered. "However, there will be no glory for you in the course you are taking, for then the LORD will deliver Sisera into the hands of a woman." So Deborah went with Barak to Kedesh. 10 Barak then mustered Zebulun and Naphtali at Kedesh; ten thousand men marched up after him; and Deborah also went up with him.

11 Now Heber the Kenite had separated from the other Kenites, descendants of Hobab, father-in-law of Moses, and had pitched his tent at Elon-bezaanannim, which is near Kedesh.

12 Sisera was informed that Barak son of Abinoam had gone up to Mount Tabor. 13 So Sisera ordered all his chariots—nine hundred iron chariots—and all the troops he had to move from Harosheth-goiim to the Wadi Kishon.

ד

4 וּדְבוֹרָה אִשָּׁה נְבִיאָה אֵשֶׁת לַפִּידוֹת
הִיא שֹׁפְטָה אֶת־יִשְׂרָאֵל בָּעֵת הַהִיא׃
5 וְהִיא יוֹשֶׁבֶת תַּחַת־תֹּמֶר דְּבוֹרָה בֵּין
הָרָמָה וּבֵין בֵּית־אֵל בְּהַר אֶפְרָיִם וַיַּעֲלוּ
אֵלֶיהָ בְּנֵי יִשְׂרָאֵל לַמִּשְׁפָּט׃
6 וַתִּשְׁלַח וַתִּקְרָא לְבָרָק בֶּן־אֲבִינֹעַם
מִקֶּדֶשׁ נַפְתָּלִי וַתֹּאמֶר אֵלָיו הֲלֹא צִוָּה ׀
יְהוָה אֱלֹהֵי־יִשְׂרָאֵל לֵךְ וּמָשַׁכְתָּ בְּהַר
תָּבוֹר וְלָקַחְתָּ עִמְּךָ עֲשֶׂרֶת אֲלָפִים אִישׁ
מִבְּנֵי נַפְתָּלִי וּמִבְּנֵי זְבֻלוּן׃ 7 וּמָשַׁכְתִּי
אֵלֶיךָ אֶל־נַחַל קִישׁוֹן אֶת־סִיסְרָא שַׂר־
צְבָא יָבִין וְאֶת־רִכְבּוֹ וְאֶת־הֲמוֹנוֹ
וּנְתַתִּיהוּ בְּיָדֶךָ׃ 8 וַיֹּאמֶר אֵלֶיהָ בָּרָק אִם־
תֵּלְכִי עִמִּי וְהָלָכְתִּי וְאִם־לֹא תֵלְכִי עִמִּי
לֹא אֵלֵךְ׃ 9 וַתֹּאמֶר הָלֹךְ אֵלֵךְ עִמָּךְ אֶפֶס
כִּי לֹא תִהְיֶה תִּפְאַרְתְּךָ עַל־הַדֶּרֶךְ אֲשֶׁר
אַתָּה הוֹלֵךְ כִּי בְיַד־אִשָּׁה יִמְכֹּר יְהוָה
אֶת־סִיסְרָא וַתָּקָם דְּבוֹרָה וַתֵּלֶךְ עִם־בָּרָק
קֶדְשָׁה׃ 10 וַיַּזְעֵק בָּרָק אֶת־זְבוּלֻן וְאֶת־
נַפְתָּלִי קֶדְשָׁה וַיַּעַל בְּרַגְלָיו עֲשֶׂרֶת אַלְפֵי
אִישׁ וַתַּעַל עִמּוֹ דְּבוֹרָה׃
11 וְחֶבֶר הַקֵּינִי נִפְרָד מִקַּיִן מִבְּנֵי חֹבָב חֹתֵן
מֹשֶׁה וַיֵּט אָהֳלוֹ עַד־אֵלוֹן בצענים
בְּצַעֲנַנִּים אֲשֶׁר אֶת־קֶדֶשׁ׃
12 וַיַּגִּדוּ לְסִיסְרָא כִּי עָלָה בָּרָק בֶּן־אֲבִינֹעַם
הַר־תָּבוֹר׃ ס 13 וַיַּזְעֵק סִיסְרָא אֶת־כָּל־
רִכְבּוֹ תְּשַׁע מֵאוֹת רֶכֶב בַּרְזֶל וְאֶת־כָּל־

Judges 4:4. Deborah . . . a prophetess Deborah is portrayed with seerlike qualities and as a judge (v. 5). Rabbinic tradition lists her among seven female prophets in the Hebrew Bible, along with Sarah, Miriam, Hannah, Abigail, Hulda, and Esther (BT Meg. 14a).

7. Jabin A king of Canaan, with a large military force of 900 iron chariots (v. 13). See Comment on 4:23–4.

11. Kenites A nomadic tribe that associated with Israel (see Num. 24:22).

Hobab, father-in-law of Moses Here he is a Kenite, the ancestor of Heber (v. 11), but in Num. 10:29, Hobab is son of Reuel the Midianite. Exodus 2:18 speaks of Reuel as Moses' father-in-law, and Exod. 18:1 identifies him as Jethro, priest of Midian. Rabbinic tradition tried to resolve these variations by assuming that Jethro had seven names.

13–14. The battle took place in the Galilee, in the Valley of Jezreel. Harosheth-goiim was near Megiddo. The Wadi Kishon rises in the southeast of the valley and flows into the Mediterranean. Mount Tabor is also located there.

[14]Then Deborah said to Barak, "Up! This is the day on which the LORD will deliver Sisera into your hands: the LORD is marching before you." Barak charged down Mount Tabor, followed by the ten thousand men, [15]and the LORD threw Sisera and all his chariots and army into a panic before the onslaught of Barak. Sisera leaped from his chariot and fled on foot [16]as Barak pursued the chariots and the soldiers as far as Harosheth-goiim. All of Sisera's soldiers fell by the sword; not a man was left.

[17]Sisera, meanwhile, had fled on foot to the tent of Jael, wife of Heber the Kenite; for there was friendship between King Jabin of Hazor and the family of Heber the Kenite. [18]Jael came out to greet Sisera and said to him, "Come in, my lord, come in here, do not be afraid." So he entered her tent, and she covered him with a blanket. [19]He said to her, "Please let me have some water; I am thirsty." She opened a skin of milk and gave him some to drink; and she covered him again. [20]He said to her, "Stand at the entrance of the tent. If anybody comes and asks you if there is anybody here, say 'No.'" [21]Then Jael wife of Heber took a tent pin and grasped the mallet. When he was fast asleep from exhaustion, she approached him stealthily and drove the pin through his temple till it went down to the ground. Thus he died.

[22]Now Barak appeared in pursuit of Sisera. Jael went out to greet him and said, "Come, I will show you the man you are looking for." He went inside with her, and there Sisera was lying dead, with the pin in his temple.

[23]On that day God subdued King Jabin of Canaan before the Israelites. [24]The hand of the Israelites bore harder and harder on King Jabin of Canaan, until they destroyed King Jabin of Canaan.

הָעָם אֲשֶׁר אִתּוֹ מֵחֲרֹשֶׁת הַגּוֹיִם אֶל־נַחַל
קִישׁוֹן׃ 14 וַתֹּאמֶר דְּבֹרָה אֶל־בָּרָק קוּם
כִּי זֶה הַיּוֹם אֲשֶׁר נָתַן יְהוָה אֶת־סִיסְרָא
בְּיָדֶךָ הֲלֹא יְהוָה יָצָא לְפָנֶיךָ וַיֵּרֶד בָּרָק
מֵהַר תָּבוֹר וַעֲשֶׂרֶת אֲלָפִים אִישׁ אַחֲרָיו׃
15 וַיָּהָם יְהוָה אֶת־סִיסְרָא וְאֶת־כָּל־הָרֶכֶב
וְאֶת־כָּל־הַמַּחֲנֶה לְפִי־חֶרֶב לִפְנֵי בָרָק
וַיֵּרֶד סִיסְרָא מֵעַל הַמֶּרְכָּבָה וַיָּנָס בְּרַגְלָיו׃
16 וּבָרָק רָדַף אַחֲרֵי הָרֶכֶב וְאַחֲרֵי הַמַּחֲנֶה
עַד חֲרֹשֶׁת הַגּוֹיִם וַיִּפֹּל כָּל־מַחֲנֵה סִיסְרָא
לְפִי־חֶרֶב לֹא נִשְׁאַר עַד־אֶחָד׃ 17 וְסִיסְרָא
נָס בְּרַגְלָיו אֶל־אֹהֶל יָעֵל אֵשֶׁת חֶבֶר הַקֵּינִי
כִּי שָׁלוֹם בֵּין יָבִין מֶלֶךְ־חָצוֹר וּבֵין בֵּית
חֶבֶר הַקֵּינִי׃ 18 וַתֵּצֵא יָעֵל לִקְרַאת סִיסְרָא
וַתֹּאמֶר אֵלָיו סוּרָה אֲדֹנִי סוּרָה אֵלַי
אַל־תִּירָא וַיָּסַר אֵלֶיהָ הָאֹהֱלָה וַתְּכַסֵּהוּ
בַּשְּׂמִיכָה׃ 19 וַיֹּאמֶר אֵלֶיהָ הַשְׁקִינִי־נָא
מְעַט־מַיִם כִּי צָמֵאתִי וַתִּפְתַּח אֶת־נֹאוד
הֶחָלָב וַתַּשְׁקֵהוּ וַתְּכַסֵּהוּ׃ 20 וַיֹּאמֶר אֵלֶיהָ
עֲמֹד פֶּתַח הָאֹהֶל וְהָיָה אִם־אִישׁ יָבוֹא
וּשְׁאֵלֵךְ וְאָמַר הֲיֵשׁ־פֹּה אִישׁ וְאָמַרְתְּ אָיִן׃
21 וַתִּקַּח יָעֵל אֵשֶׁת־חֶבֶר אֶת־יְתַד הָאֹהֶל
וַתָּשֶׂם אֶת־הַמַּקֶּבֶת בְּיָדָהּ וַתָּבוֹא אֵלָיו
בַּלָּאט* וַתִּתְקַע אֶת־הַיָּתֵד בְּרַקָּתוֹ וַתִּצְנַח
בָּאָרֶץ וְהוּא־נִרְדָּם וַיָּעַף וַיָּמֹת׃
22 וְהִנֵּה בָרָק רֹדֵף אֶת־סִיסְרָא וַתֵּצֵא יָעֵל
לִקְרָאתוֹ וַתֹּאמֶר לוֹ לֵךְ וְאַרְאֶךָּ אֶת־
הָאִישׁ אֲשֶׁר־אַתָּה מְבַקֵּשׁ וַיָּבֹא אֵלֶיהָ
וְהִנֵּה סִיסְרָא נֹפֵל מֵת וְהַיָּתֵד בְּרַקָּתוֹ׃
23 וַיַּכְנַע אֱלֹהִים בַּיּוֹם הַהוּא אֵת יָבִין
מֶלֶךְ־כְּנָעַן לִפְנֵי בְּנֵי יִשְׂרָאֵל׃ 24 וַתֵּלֶךְ יַד
בְּנֵי־יִשְׂרָאֵל הָלוֹךְ וְקָשָׁה עַל יָבִין מֶלֶךְ־
כְּנָעַן עַד אֲשֶׁר הִכְרִיתוּ אֵת יָבִין מֶלֶךְ־
כְּנָעַן׃ פ

23–4. King Jabin of Canaan He is also called "King Jabin of Hazor" (v. 17, Josh. 11:1,

v. 21. א׳ נחה

ה *וַתָּשַׁר דְּבוֹרָה וּבָרָק בֶּן־אֲבִינֹעַם בַּיּוֹם הַהוּא
לֵאמֹר: 2 בִּפְרֹעַ פְּרָעוֹת בְּיִשְׂרָאֵל בְּהִתְנַדֵּב
עָם בָּרְכוּ יְהוָה: 3 שִׁמְעוּ מְלָכִים הַאֲזִינוּ
רֹזְנִים אָנֹכִי לַיהוָה אָנֹכִי אָשִׁירָה אֲזַמֵּר
לַיהוָה אֱלֹהֵי יִשְׂרָאֵל: 4 יְהוָה בְּצֵאתְךָ
מִשֵּׂעִיר בְּצַעְדְּךָ מִשְּׂדֵה אֱדוֹם אֶרֶץ
רָעָשָׁה גַּם־שָׁמַיִם נָטָפוּ גַּם־עָבִים נָטְפוּ
מָיִם: 5 הָרִים נָזְלוּ מִפְּנֵי יְהוָה זֶה
סִינַי מִפְּנֵי יְהוָה אֱלֹהֵי יִשְׂרָאֵל: 6 בִּימֵי שַׁמְגַּר בֶּן־
עֲנָת בִּימֵי יָעֵל חָדְלוּ אֳרָחוֹת וְהֹלְכֵי
נְתִיבוֹת יֵלְכוּ אֳרָחוֹת עֲקַלְקַלּוֹת: 7 חָדְלוּ פְרָזוֹן בְּיִשְׂרָאֵל
חָדֵלּוּ עַד שַׁקַּמְתִּי דְּבוֹרָה שַׁקַּמְתִּי אֵם בְּיִשְׂרָאֵל: 8 יִבְחַר
אֱלֹהִים חֲדָשִׁים אָז לָחֶם שְׁעָרִים מָגֵן אִם־יֵרָאֶה
וָרֹמַח בְּאַרְבָּעִים אֶלֶף בְּיִשְׂרָאֵל: 9 לִבִּי
לְחוֹקְקֵי יִשְׂרָאֵל הַמִּתְנַדְּבִים בָּעָם בָּרְכוּ
יְהוָה: 10 רֹכְבֵי אֲתֹנוֹת צְחֹרוֹת יֹשְׁבֵי
עַל־מִדִּין וְהֹלְכֵי עַל־דֶּרֶךְ שִׂיחוּ: 11 מִקּוֹל מְחַצְצִים בֵּין
מַשְׁאַבִּים שָׁם יְתַנּוּ צִדְקוֹת יְהוָה צִדְקֹת
פִּרְזֹנוֹ בְּיִשְׂרָאֵל אָז יָרְדוּ לַשְּׁעָרִים עַם־

v. 1. צורת השירה לפי כתר ארם צובה, כדי שחלוקת השירה כחלוקיה, והיא כהלכה

cf. Judg. 4:2). According to Judg. 5:19, Jabin was only one member of a coalition of kings of Canaan led by Sisera. The title "king of Canaan" is attested centuries earlier in the Mari tablets of northern Mesopotamia.

Judges 5:1. On that day Deborah and Barak . . . sang The victors sing a song of praise to God and the people. Rabbinic tradition records "Ten Songs" that span the sacred history of Israel. The 1st is sung during the Passover feast (Isa. 30:29), and the 2nd is the "Song of the Sea" in the *parashah* (Exod. 15). This song of Deborah and Barak is the 6th song. The 10th song will be the messianic song of the future (see Isa. 42:10; Mekh. B'shallaḥ 1).

2. When locks go untrimmed Apparently as an act of dedication (see Num. 6:5) [Transl.].

3–5. The Targum saw here an allusion to Mount Sinai and the giving of the Torah (see Rashi and Ps. 68).

6. Shamgar The previous chieftain to lead the people of Israel (see Judg. 3:31).

5 On that day Deborah and Barak son of Abinoam sang:

2When locks go untrimmed in Israel,
When people dedicate themselves—
Bless the LORD!

3Hear, O kings! Give ear, O potentates!
I will sing, will sing to the LORD,
Will hymn the LORD, the God of Israel.

4O LORD, when You came forth from Seir,
Advanced from the country of Edom,
The earth trembled;
The heavens dripped,
Yea, the clouds dripped water,
5The mountains quaked—
Before the LORD, Him of Sinai,
Before the LORD, God of Israel.

6In the days of Shamgar son of Anath,
In the days of Jael, caravans ceased,
And wayfarers went
By roundabout paths.
7Deliverance ceased,
Ceased in Israel,
Till you arose, O Deborah,
Arose, O mother, in Israel!
8When they chose new gods,
Was there a fighter then in the gates?
No shield or spear was seen
Among forty thousand in Israel!
9My heart is with Israel's leaders,
With the dedicated of the people—
Bless the LORD!
10You riders on tawny she-asses,
You who sit on saddle rugs,
And you wayfarers, declare it!
11Louder than the sound of archers,
There among the watering places
Let them chant the gracious acts of the LORD,
His gracious deliverance of Israel.
Then did the people of the LORD
March down to the gates!

יְהוָה׃ 12 עוּרִי עוּרִי דְּבוֹרָה עוּרִי
עוּרִי דַּבְּרִי־שִׁיר קוּם בָּרָק וּשֲׁבֵה שֶׁבְיְךָ בֶּן־
אֲבִינֹעַם׃ 13 אָז יְרַד שָׂרִיד לְאַדִּירִים עָם* יְהוָה
יְרַד־לִי בַּגִּבּוֹרִים׃ 14 מִנִּי אֶפְרַיִם שָׁרְשָׁם
בַּעֲמָלֵק אַחֲרֶיךָ בִנְיָמִין בַּעֲמָמֶיךָ מִנִּי
מָכִיר יָרְדוּ מְחֹקְקִים וּמִזְּבוּלֻן מֹשְׁכִים בְּשֵׁבֶט
סֹפֵר׃ 15 וְשָׂרַי בְּיִשָּׂשכָר עִם־דְּבֹרָה וְיִשָּׂשכָר
כֵּן בָּרָק בָּעֵמֶק שֻׁלַּח בְּרַגְלָיו בִּפְלַגּוֹת רְאוּבֵן גְּדֹלִים חִקְקֵי־
לֵב׃ 16 לָמָּה יָשַׁבְתָּ בֵּין הַמִּשְׁפְּתַיִם לִשְׁמֹעַ
שְׁרִקוֹת עֲדָרִים לִפְלַגּוֹת רְאוּבֵן גְּדוֹלִים חִקְרֵי־
לֵב׃ 17 גִּלְעָד בְּעֵבֶר הַיַּרְדֵּן שָׁכֵן וְדָן
לָמָּה יָגוּר אֳנִיּוֹת אָשֵׁר יָשַׁב לְחוֹף
יַמִּים וְעַל מִפְרָצָיו יִשְׁכּוֹן׃ 18 זְבֻלוּן
עַם חֵרֵף נַפְשׁוֹ לָמוּת וְנַפְתָּלִי עַל מְרוֹמֵי
שָׂדֶה׃ 19 בָּאוּ מְלָכִים נִלְחָמוּ אָז
נִלְחֲמוּ מַלְכֵי כְנַעַן בְּתַעְנַךְ עַל־מֵי
מְגִדּוֹ בֶּצַע כֶּסֶף לֹא לָקָחוּ׃ 20 מִן־
שָׁמַיִם נִלְחָמוּ הַכּוֹכָבִים מִמְּסִלּוֹתָם נִלְחֲמוּ עִם־
סִיסְרָא׃ 21 נַחַל קִישׁוֹן גְּרָפָם נַחַל
קְדוּמִים נַחַל קִישׁוֹן תִּדְרְכִי נַפְשִׁי
עֹז׃ 22 אָז הָלְמוּ עִקְּבֵי־סוּס מִדַּהֲרוֹת
דַּהֲרוֹת אַבִּירָיו׃ 23 אוֹרוּ מֵרוֹז אָמַר מַלְאַךְ יְהוָה אֹרוּ אָרוֹר

v. 13. בנוסח אחר ״עַם״ כלומר שני תנועה

13. The Lord's people Reading *"am* [with a *pataḥ* vowel] *Adonai,"* as in many Hebrew manuscripts [Transl.].

14. whose roots are in Amalek This is a puzzling comment about the origins of citizens of Ephraim. An old solution that continued into the Middle Ages interprets the passage as referring to heroes who stemmed from Ephraim and fought against Amalek; for example, Joshua (Exod. 17:8–13) and Saul (1 Sam. 15) (see Targ. Jon., Rashi, and Radak).

19. At Taanach, by Megiddo's waters In the Valley of Jezreel. The Canaanite kings came to this broad plain to stage the battle.

12Awake, awake, O Deborah!
Awake, awake, strike up the chant!
Arise, O Barak;
Take your captives, O son of Abinoam!

13Then was the remnant made victor over the mighty,
The LORD's people won my victory over the warriors.

14From Ephraim came they whose roots are in Amalek;
After you, your kin Benjamin;
From Machir came down leaders,
From Zebulun such as hold the marshal's staff.
15And Issachar's chiefs were with Deborah;
As Barak, so was Issachar—
Rushing after him into the valley.

Among the clans of Reuben
Were great decisions of heart.
16Why then did you stay among the sheepfolds
And listen as they pipe for the flocks?
Among the clans of Reuben
Were great searchings of heart!
17Gilead tarried beyond the Jordan;
And Dan—why did he linger by the ships?
Asher remained at the seacoast
And tarried at his landings.
18Zebulun is a people that mocked at death,
Naphtali—on the open heights.

19Then the kings came, they fought:
The kings of Canaan fought
At Taanach, by Megiddo's waters—
They got no spoil of silver.
20The stars fought from heaven,
From their courses they fought against Sisera.
21The torrent Kishon swept them away,
The raging torrent, the torrent Kishon.

March on, my soul, with courage!

22Then the horses' hoofs pounded
As headlong galloped the steeds.
23"Curse Meroz!" said the angel of the LORD.
"Bitterly curse its inhabitants,

יֹשְׁבֶ֑יהָ   כִּ֤י לֹֽא־בָ֙אוּ֙ לְעֶזְרַ֣ת יְהֹוָ֔ה   לְעֶזְרַ֖ת

יְהֹוָ֖ה בַּגִּבּוֹרִֽים: 24 תְּבֹרַךְ֙ מִנָּשִׁ֔ים יָעֵ֕ל אֵ֖שֶׁת חֶ֣בֶר

הַקֵּינִ֑י   מִנָּשִׁ֥ים בָּאֹ֖הֶל תְּבֹרָֽךְ: 25 מַ֤יִם

שָׁאַל֙ חָלָ֣ב נָתָ֔נָה   בְּסֵ֥פֶל אַדִּירִ֖ים הִקְרִ֥יבָה

חֶמְאָֽה: 26 יָדָהּ֙ לַיָּתֵ֣ד תִּשְׁלַ֔חְנָה   וִֽימִינָ֖הּ

לְהַלְמ֣וּת עֲמֵלִ֑ים   וְהָלְמָ֤ה סִֽיסְרָא֙ מָֽחֲקָ֣ה

רֹאשׁ֔וֹ   וּמָחֲצָ֥ה וְחָֽלְפָ֖ה רַקָּתֽוֹ: 27 בֵּ֣ין

רַגְלֶ֔יהָ כָּרַ֥ע נָפַ֖ל שָׁכָ֑ב   בֵּ֤ין רַגְלֶ֙יהָ֙ כָּרַ֣ע

נָפָ֔ל   בַּאֲשֶׁ֣ר כָּרַ֔ע שָׁ֖ם נָפַ֥ל שָׁדֽוּד: 28 בְּעַד֩

הַחַלּ֨וֹן נִשְׁקְפָ֤ה וַתְּיַבֵּב֙ אֵ֣ם סִֽיסְרָ֔א בְּעַ֖ד הָאֶשְׁנָ֑ב   מַדּ֗וּעַ בֹּ֤שֵֽׁשׁ רִכְבּוֹ֙

לָב֔וֹא   מַדּ֣וּעַ אֶחֱר֔וּ פַּעֲמֵ֖י מַרְכְּבוֹתָֽיו: 29 חַכְמ֥וֹת

שָׂרוֹתֶ֖יהָ תַּעֲנֶ֑ינָּה   אַף־הִ֕יא תָּשִׁ֥יב אֲמָרֶ֖יהָ

לָֽהּ: 30 הֲלֹ֙א יִמְצְא֜וּ יְחַלְּק֣וּ שָׁלָ֗ל   רַ֤חַם

רַחֲמָתַ֙יִם֙ לְרֹ֣אשׁ גֶּ֔בֶר   שְׁלַ֤ל צְבָעִים֙

לְסִ֣יסְרָ֔א   שְׁלַ֥ל צְבָעִ֖ים רִקְמָ֑ה   צֶ֥בַע

רִקְמָתַ֖יִם לְצַוְּארֵ֥י שָׁלָֽל: 31 כֵּ֠ן יֹאבְד֤וּ כׇל־אוֹיְבֶ֙יךָ֙ יְהֹוָ֔ה

וְאֹ֣הֲבָ֔יו כְּצֵ֥את הַשֶּׁ֖מֶשׁ בִּגְבֻרָת֑וֹ   וַתִּשְׁקֹ֥ט הָאָ֖רֶץ אַרְבָּעִ֥ים שָׁנָֽה: פ

---

27. At her feet he sank The phrases here have an intensifying redundancy, rhythmically echoing the violent hammering of the murder (Radak).

28. Through the window peered Sisera's mother The image of Sisera's mother on the rampart, peering through the window, is a conventional scene. Thus Michal, daughter of Saul, looks from her royal window at the processional bearing the Ark to Jerusalem. The particular phrase used with Michal (*nishk'fah b'ad ha-ḥallon*, 2 Sam. 6:16) is almost identical with that used of Sisera's mother. The portrait of (royal) women at the window is also represented in 8th-century-B.C.E. Phoenician ivories.

31. all Your enemies In the context of the *haftarah*, the refrain calling for the defeat of "all" God's enemies has an eschatologic ring, looking to "the end of days" (see Rashi and Kara, following Targ.).

His friends Hebrew: *ohavav*, literally "His loved ones." In Hebrew and its cognate equivalent in Akkadian, this is a standard designation for treaty partners.

Because they came not to the aid of the LORD,
To the aid of the LORD among the warriors."

24Most blessed of women be Jael,
Wife of Heber the Kenite,
Most blessed of women in tents.
25He asked for water, she offered milk;
In a princely bowl she brought him curds.
26Her [left] hand reached for the tent pin,
Her right for the workmen's hammer.
She struck Sisera, crushed his head,
Smashed and pierced his temple.
27At her feet he sank, lay outstretched,
At her feet he sank, lay still;
Where he sank, there he lay—destroyed.

28Through the window peered Sisera's mother,
Behind the lattice she whined:
"Why is his chariot so long in coming?
Why so late the clatter of his wheels?"
29The wisest of her ladies give answer;
She, too, replies to herself:
30"They must be dividing the spoil they have found:
A damsel or two for each man,
Spoil of dyed cloths for Sisera,
Spoil of embroidered cloths,
A couple of embroidered cloths
Round every neck as spoil."

31So may all Your enemies perish, O LORD!
But may His friends be as the sun rising in might!

And the land was tranquil forty years.

YITRO

18 Jethro priest of Midian, Moses' father-
in-law, heard all that God had done for Moses
and for Israel His people, how the LORD had
brought Israel out from Egypt. [2]So Jethro,
Moses' father-in-law, took Zipporah, Moses'
wife, after she had been sent home, [3]and her
two sons—of whom one was named Gershom,
that is to say, "I have been a stranger in a
foreign land"; [4]and the other was named Eliezer,
meaning, "The God of my father was my help,
and He delivered me from the sword of Phar-

יתרו

יח וַיִּשְׁמַע יִתְרוֹ כֹהֵן מִדְיָן חֹתֵן
מֹשֶׁה אֵת כָּל־אֲשֶׁר עָשָׂה אֱלֹהִים לְמֹשֶׁה
וּלְיִשְׂרָאֵל עַמּוֹ כִּי־הוֹצִיא יְהוָה אֶת־
יִשְׂרָאֵל מִמִּצְרָיִם׃ 2 וַיִּקַּח יִתְרוֹ חֹתֵן מֹשֶׁה
אֶת־צִפֹּרָה אֵשֶׁת מֹשֶׁה אַחַר שִׁלּוּחֶיהָ׃
3 וְאֵת שְׁנֵי בָנֶיהָ אֲשֶׁר שֵׁם הָאֶחָד גֵּרְשֹׁם
כִּי אָמַר גֵּר הָיִיתִי בְּאֶרֶץ נָכְרִיָּה׃ 4 וְשֵׁם
הָאֶחָד אֱלִיעֶזֶר כִּי־אֱלֹהֵי אָבִי בְּעֶזְרִי

JETHRO'S VISIT AND THE ORGANIZATION OF THE JUDICIARY (18:1–27)

A principle of traditional exegesis states that the Torah occasionally departs from chronologic order so as to make a special point (see, for example, Rashi on Num. 9:1). Jethro's visit must have taken place after the revelation at Mount Sinai—which is not described until chapter 20. Moses and the Israelites are described here (v. 5) encamped "at the mountain of God," i.e., Mount Sinai, but we read about their arrival at Sinai in 19:1–2. We read here (v. 12) that Jethro brings a burnt offering and sacrifices, but the altar for them was not built until after the revelation. The present passage is placed here to highlight Jethro's role in the creation of the Israelite judiciary.

THE ARRIVAL OF JETHRO (vv. 1–12)

2. after she had been sent home We are treated to a fleeting glimpse into the leader Moses' domestic life.

This *parashah* can be seen as "the hinge of the Torah," containing the pivotal event in the history of the Israelite people and indeed of all humanity. Through the revelation at Sinai, Israel is transformed from a band of freed slaves to a nation covenanted to God. The *parashah* describes the moment when God reached down to reveal the Torah to humanity or, more specifically, to the Israelites, that they might live by it and thereby reveal it to the rest of the world. A Rabbinic tradition has it that God created the world so that Israel would emerge as a model nation and all humanity would learn from their example (see Sifrei Deut. 346). Had Israel not accepted the Torah, the universe would have ceased to exist. That is, what purpose would there be to the world if the descendants of Abraham did not follow God's ways?

CHAPTER 18

1. Jethro . . . heard The Sages understand that the Torah reports this event right after the encounter with Amalek (Exod. 17:8ff.) to assure us that not all gentiles are wicked enemies of Israel. Although there are Amaleks, there are also Jethros (Ibn Ezra). The name of Jethro is perpetually linked with the reading that includes the giving of the Decalogue. We are a people who long remember the goodness of righteous gentiles. What did Jethro hear that moved him to associate himself with the people Israel? Some say he heard about their suffering in Egypt and was moved by pity. Some say he heard of their triumph over Pharaoh's army and wanted to associate himself with a victorious people. Others say he heard that the Israelites were on their way to a rendezvous with God, that they were destined to be a special people, and he wanted to share in their destiny (Mekh. Amalek 3:1). Did not everyone hear what Jethro heard? Yes, but some people hear and do not really hear.

all that God had done for Moses and for Israel Moses is named separately because he experienced the Exodus differently than did the rest of the Israelites. For them, it was liberation from slavery. For Moses, it was an opportunity to serve God (Elimelekh of Lyzhansk).

וַיַּצִּלֵנִי מֵחֶרֶב פַּרְעֹה׃ 5 וַיָּבֹא יִתְרוֹ חֹתֵן
מֹשֶׁה וּבָנָיו וְאִשְׁתּוֹ אֶל־מֹשֶׁה אֶל־הַמִּדְבָּר
אֲשֶׁר־הוּא חֹנֶה שָׁם הַר הָאֱלֹהִים׃
6 וַיֹּאמֶר אֶל־מֹשֶׁה אֲנִי חֹתֶנְךָ יִתְרוֹ בָּא
אֵלֶיךָ וְאִשְׁתְּךָ וּשְׁנֵי בָנֶיהָ עִמָּהּ׃ 7 וַיֵּצֵא
מֹשֶׁה לִקְרַאת חֹתְנוֹ וַיִּשְׁתַּחוּ וַיִּשַּׁק־
לוֹ וַיִּשְׁאֲלוּ אִישׁ־לְרֵעֵהוּ לְשָׁלוֹם וַיָּבֹאוּ
הָאֹהֱלָה׃
8 וַיְסַפֵּר מֹשֶׁה לְחֹתְנוֹ אֵת כָּל־אֲשֶׁר עָשָׂה
יְהוָה לְפַרְעֹה וּלְמִצְרַיִם עַל אוֹדֹת יִשְׂרָאֵל
אֵת כָּל־הַתְּלָאָה אֲשֶׁר מְצָאָתַם בַּדֶּרֶךְ
וַיַּצִּלֵם יְהוָה׃ 9 וַיִּחַדְּ יִתְרוֹ עַל כָּל־הַטּוֹבָה
אֲשֶׁר־עָשָׂה יְהוָה לְיִשְׂרָאֵל אֲשֶׁר הִצִּילוֹ
מִיַּד מִצְרָיִם׃ 10 וַיֹּאמֶר יִתְרוֹ בָּרוּךְ יְהוָה
אֲשֶׁר הִצִּיל אֶתְכֶם מִיַּד מִצְרַיִם וּמִיַּד
פַּרְעֹה אֲשֶׁר הִצִּיל אֶת־הָעָם מִתַּחַת
יַד־מִצְרָיִם׃ 11 עַתָּה יָדַעְתִּי כִּי־גָדוֹל יְהוָה
מִכָּל־הָאֱלֹהִים כִּי בַדָּבָר אֲשֶׁר זָדוּ
עֲלֵיהֶם׃ 12 וַיִּקַּח יִתְרוֹ חֹתֵן מֹשֶׁה עֹלָה
וּזְבָחִים לֵאלֹהִים וַיָּבֹא אַהֲרֹן וְכֹל ׀ זִקְנֵי

aoh." 5Jethro, Moses' father-in-law, brought
Moses' sons and wife to him in the wilderness, where he was encamped at the mountain
of God. 6He sent word to Moses, "I, your
father-in-law Jethro, am coming to you, with
your wife and her two sons." 7Moses went out
to meet his father-in-law; he bowed low and kissed him; each asked after the other's welfare, and they went into the tent.

8Moses then recounted to his father-in-law
everything that the LORD had done to Pharaoh and to the Egyptians for Israel's sake, all the hardships that had befallen them on the way,
and how the LORD had delivered them. 9And
Jethro rejoiced over all the kindness that the LORD had shown Israel when He delivered them
from the Egyptians. 10"Blessed be the LORD,"
Jethro said, "who delivered you from the Egyptians and from Pharaoh, and who delivered the people from under the hand of the Egyptians.
11Now I know that the LORD is greater than all gods, yes, by the result of their very schemes
against [the people]." 12And Jethro, Moses'
father-in-law, brought a burnt offering and

6. He sent word Literally, "He said." Jethro no doubt announced his arrival through a messenger.

7. Moses and Jethro engage in the formal civilities customary in the East.

10. Blessed be the LORD It is not uncommon in the Bible for a non-Israelite to invoke God as *YHVH* when dealing with Israelites (see 10:10). God in the Hebrew Bible is God for all people.

11. Now I know For Jethro, the divine superiority of *YHVH* has now been demonstrated through the disaster suffered by the Egyptians. The phrase appears elsewhere as a confirmation of faith (Josh. 2:9; 2 Kings 5:15).

***yes . . . against** [**the people**]* Most traditional Jewish commentators have understood this clause as an incomplete statement, its conclusion to be supplied by the imagination. Usually it is taken to mean that the Egyptians were punished measure for measure. They perished by drowning—the fate they had devised for the Israelites.

12. In the ancient Near East, the parties to treaties or pacts often participated in a solemn meal as part of the ratification ceremony (see 24:11).

a burnt offering and sacrifices These are the two main types of sacrifice offered in ancient Israel. The first, *olah,* was wholly consumed by fire on the altar as a tribute to God; the second, *zevah,* was partially offered up, and the major portion eaten at a festive meal. Here they are offered to

---

6. with your wife and her two sons Moses had sent them away, perhaps out of concern for their safety, perhaps to enable him to concentrate fully on his mission (Arama). In the text, however, Moses now seems to be ignoring his own family and relating to his father-in-law Jethro only as one dignitary to another. As sometimes happens with leaders, have his official duties caused him to neglect his family and to lose his capacity for intimacy?

sacrifices for God; and Aaron came with all the elders of Israel to partake of the meal before God with Moses' father-in-law.

[13]Next day, Moses sat as magistrate among the people, while the people stood about Moses from morning until evening. [14]But when Moses' father-in-law saw how much he had to do for the people, he said, "What is this thing that you are doing to the people? Why do you act alone, while all the people stand about you from morning until evening?" [15]Moses replied to his father-in-law, "It is because the people come to me to inquire of God. [16]When they have a dispute, it comes before me, and I decide between one person and another, and I make known the laws and teachings of God."

[17]But Moses' father-in-law said to him, "The thing you are doing is not right; [18]you will surely wear yourself out, and these people as well. For the task is too heavy for you; you cannot do it alone. [19]Now listen to me. I will give you counsel, and God be with you! You represent the people before God: you bring the disputes before God, [20]and enjoin upon them the laws and the teachings, and make known to them the way they are to go and the practices they are to fol-

יִשְׂרָאֵ֗ל לֶאֱכָל־לֶ֛חֶם עִם־חֹתֵ֥ן מֹשֶׁ֖ה לִפְנֵ֥י
הָאֱלֹהִֽים׃

שני 13 וַֽיְהִי֙ מִֽמָּחֳרָ֔ת וַיֵּ֥שֶׁב מֹשֶׁ֖ה לִשְׁפֹּ֣ט אֶת־
הָעָ֑ם וַיַּעֲמֹ֤ד הָעָם֙ עַל־מֹשֶׁ֔ה מִן־הַבֹּ֖קֶר
עַד־הָעָֽרֶב׃ 14 וַיַּרְא֙ חֹתֵ֣ן מֹשֶׁ֔ה אֵ֛ת כָּל־
אֲשֶׁר־ה֥וּא עֹשֶׂ֖ה לָעָ֑ם וַיֹּ֗אמֶר מָֽה־הַדָּבָ֤ר
הַזֶּה֙ אֲשֶׁ֨ר אַתָּ֤ה עֹשֶׂה֙ לָעָ֔ם מַדּ֗וּעַ אַתָּ֤ה
יוֹשֵׁב֙ לְבַדֶּ֔ךָ וְכָל־הָעָ֛ם נִצָּ֥ב עָלֶ֖יךָ מִן־בֹּ֥קֶר
עַד־עָֽרֶב׃ 15 וַיֹּ֥אמֶר מֹשֶׁ֖ה לְחֹתְנ֑וֹ כִּֽי־יָבֹ֥א
אֵלַ֛י הָעָ֖ם לִדְרֹ֥שׁ אֱלֹהִֽים׃ 16 כִּֽי־יִהְיֶ֨ה
לָהֶ֤ם דָּבָר֙ בָּ֣א אֵלַ֔י וְשָׁ֣פַטְתִּ֔י בֵּ֥ין אִ֖ישׁ וּבֵ֣ין
רֵעֵ֑הוּ וְהוֹדַעְתִּ֛י אֶת־חֻקֵּ֥י הָאֱלֹהִ֖ים וְאֶת־
תּוֹרֹתָֽיו׃
17 וַיֹּ֛אמֶר חֹתֵ֥ן מֹשֶׁ֖ה אֵלָ֑יו לֹא־טוֹב֙ הַדָּבָ֔ר
אֲשֶׁ֥ר אַתָּ֖ה עֹשֶֽׂה׃ 18 נָבֹ֣ל תִּבֹּ֔ל גַּם־אַתָּ֕ה
גַּם־הָעָ֥ם הַזֶּ֖ה אֲשֶׁ֣ר עִמָּ֑ךְ כִּֽי־כָבֵ֤ד מִמְּךָ֙
הַדָּבָ֔ר לֹא־תוּכַ֥ל עֲשֹׂ֖הוּ לְבַדֶּֽךָ׃ 19 עַתָּ֞ה
שְׁמַ֤ע בְּקֹלִי֙ אִיעָ֣צְךָ֔ וִיהִ֥י אֱלֹהִ֖ים עִמָּ֑ךְ
הֱיֵ֧ה אַתָּ֣ה לָעָ֗ם מ֚וּל הָֽאֱלֹהִ֔ים וְהֵבֵאתָ֥
אַתָּ֛ה אֶת־הַדְּבָרִ֖ים אֶל־הָאֱלֹהִֽים׃
20 וְהִזְהַרְתָּ֣ה אֶתְהֶ֔ם אֶת־הַחֻקִּ֖ים וְאֶת־
הַתּוֹרֹ֑ת וְהוֹדַעְתָּ֣ לָהֶ֗ם אֶת־הַדֶּ֙רֶךְ֙ יֵ֣לְכוּ

Elohim, the generic name for God, rather than to *YHVH,* the specific name of God revealed to Israel. This indicates that although Jethro made obeisance to the Deity he did not join the Israelites in their worship of *YHVH.*

ORGANIZATION OF THE JUDICIARY (vv. 13–27)

The new Israelite judicial system is shaped by a Midianite priest, who draws its personnel "from among all the people" (v. 21). The elders, who usually exercise judicial functions in a tribal-patriarchal society, are not mentioned. Tribal divisions are also ignored. Moses will act as the supreme judicial authority, mediating the will of God.

15. to inquire of God That is, to seek divine guidance in a situation for which human wisdom has exhausted itself.

18. The inefficiency of the system is bound to have a debilitating effect on Moses and on the public.

---

13. Note that while the Israelites learn about holiness from God, they do not hesitate to learn science, civics, and commerce from their gentile neighbors. As the sage Ben Zoma said, "Who is wise? One who learns from all people" (M Avot 4:1).

low. 21You shall also seek out from among all
the people capable men who fear God, trustworthy men who spurn ill-gotten gain. Set these
over them as chiefs of thousands, hundreds,
fifties, and tens, and 22let them judge the people
at all times. Have them bring every major dispute to you, but let them decide every minor
dispute themselves. Make it easier for yourself
by letting them share the burden with you. 23If
you do this—and God so commands you—you
will be able to bear up; and all these people too
will go home unwearied."

24Moses heeded his father-in-law and did just
as he had said. 25Moses chose capable men out
of all Israel, and appointed them heads over the
people—chiefs of thousands, hundreds, fifties,
and tens; 26and they judged the people at all
times: the difficult matters they would bring to
Moses, and all the minor matters they would
decide themselves. 27Then Moses bade his father-in-law farewell, and he went his way to his
own land.

בָּהּ וְאֶת־הַמַּעֲשֶׂה אֲשֶׁר יַעֲשׂוּן׃ 21 וְאַתָּה
תֶחֱזֶה מִכָּל־הָעָם אַנְשֵׁי־חַיִל יִרְאֵי
אֱלֹהִים אַנְשֵׁי אֱמֶת שֹׂנְאֵי בָצַע וְשַׂמְתָּ
עֲלֵהֶם שָׂרֵי אֲלָפִים שָׂרֵי מֵאוֹת שָׂרֵי
חֲמִשִּׁים וְשָׂרֵי עֲשָׂרֹת׃ 22 וְשָׁפְטוּ אֶת־
הָעָם בְּכָל־עֵת וְהָיָה כָּל־הַדָּבָר הַגָּדֹל
יָבִיאוּ אֵלֶיךָ וְכָל־הַדָּבָר הַקָּטֹן יִשְׁפְּטוּ־הֵם
וְהָקֵל מֵעָלֶיךָ וְנָשְׂאוּ אִתָּךְ׃ 23 אִם אֶת־
הַדָּבָר הַזֶּה תַּעֲשֶׂה וְצִוְּךָ אֱלֹהִים וְיָכָלְתָּ
עֲמֹד וְגַם כָּל־הָעָם הַזֶּה עַל־מְקֹמוֹ יָבֹא
בְשָׁלוֹם׃

שלישי 24 וַיִּשְׁמַע מֹשֶׁה לְקוֹל חֹתְנוֹ וַיַּעַשׂ כֹּל
אֲשֶׁר אָמָר׃ 25 וַיִּבְחַר מֹשֶׁה אַנְשֵׁי־חַיִל
מִכָּל־יִשְׂרָאֵל וַיִּתֵּן אֹתָם רָאשִׁים עַל־הָעָם
שָׂרֵי אֲלָפִים שָׂרֵי מֵאוֹת שָׂרֵי חֲמִשִּׁים
וְשָׂרֵי עֲשָׂרֹת׃ 26 וְשָׁפְטוּ אֶת־הָעָם בְּכָל־
עֵת אֶת־הַדָּבָר הַקָּשֶׁה יְבִיאוּן אֶל־מֹשֶׁה
וְכָל־הַדָּבָר הַקָּטֹן יִשְׁפּוּטוּ הֵם׃ 27 וַיְשַׁלַּח
רביעי מֹשֶׁה אֶת־חֹתְנוֹ וַיֵּלֶךְ לוֹ אֶל־אַרְצוֹ׃ פ

21. Jethro defines the ideal social, spiritual, and moral qualifications for judges—those necessary to create and maintain a healthy and just legal order.

chiefs of thousands The Israelites frequently are depicted in the Torah as an army marching out of Egypt and proceeding in military formation through the wilderness to the Promised Land.

22. at all times The new judiciary is to be a permanent, professional institution.

every major dispute In verse 26 this is defined as "the difficult matters." To act as supreme judge traditionally was the prerogative of the leader or the king.

23. will go home unwearied In contrast to the description in verse 18.

24. Moses heeded his father-in-law Early Israelites apparently lived under a system of common law that was prevalent among their neighbors, elements of which were later incorporated into the Torah as divine legislation.

---

21. capable men Men of sufficient wealth that they will be immune to bribes or financial considerations (Rashi).

who fear God Doing what is right in God's sight will be more important for them than popularity among their neighbors (Ibn Ezra). Ibn Ezra notes, however, that when Moses actually chooses these men, the text describes them as "capable," without referring to their fearing God (v. 25). Only God—not any human being—can know who is truly God-fearing.

HALAKHAH L'MA·ASEH

18:22. let them judge the people at all times See *D'rash* to Deut. 17:9.

19 On the third new moon after the Israelites had gone forth from the land of Egypt, on
that very day, they entered the wilderness of Sinai. 2Having journeyed from Rephidim, they
entered the wilderness of Sinai and encamped
in the wilderness. Israel encamped there in front
of the mountain, 3and Moses went up to God.

רביעי יט בַּחֹ֙דֶשׁ֙ הַשְּׁלִישִׁ֔י לְצֵ֥את בְּנֵֽי־
יִשְׂרָאֵ֖ל מֵאֶ֣רֶץ מִצְרָ֑יִם בַּיּ֣וֹם הַזֶּ֔ה בָּ֖אוּ
מִדְבַּ֥ר סִינָֽי׃ 2 וַיִּסְע֣וּ מֵרְפִידִ֗ים וַיָּבֹ֙אוּ֙
מִדְבַּ֣ר סִינַ֔י וַֽיַּחֲנ֖וּ בַּמִּדְבָּ֑ר וַיִּֽחַן־שָׁ֥ם
יִשְׂרָאֵ֖ל נֶ֥גֶד הָהָֽר׃ 3 וּמֹשֶׁ֥ה עָלָ֖ה אֶל־

THE COVENANT AT SINAI (19:1–20:23)

The arrival at Sinai inaugurates the final stage in the process of forging Israel's national identity and spiritual destiny. The great communal encounter with God gave ultimate meaning to the shared experiences of bondage and liberation. Henceforth, the people Israel are in a covenantal relationship with God, inextricably bound to Him by a treaty (*b'rit*).

NARRATIVE INTRODUCTION (19:1–3b)

1. On the third new moon . . . on that very day The more precise definition, "on that very day," shows that the word *ḥodesh*, which later came to mean "month," is here used in its original sense of "new moon."

2. Rephidim See Comment to 17:1.

mountain The one selected to be the site of the revelation.

ISRAEL'S DESTINY DEFINED (vv. 3c–6)

Written in poetic prose, these verses express the essence of the covenant idea. Israel is chosen to

---

CHAPTER 19

1. On the third new moon The Sages, noting that the zodiacal sign for the third month (*Sivan*) is Gemini, the twins, take it as symbolizing the equal importance of the written Torah and the oral Torah. According to another interpretation, this teaches us that should Jacob's twin brother, Esau, change his wicked ways and come to accept the Torah, he would be welcomed (PdRK). We may find it strange that the Sages refer to the signs of the zodiac. They were often used in synagogue decorations, for homiletic purposes, and possibly in poetry. (Some find traces of them in Jacob's blessing of his 12 sons in Gen. 49.) For example, Libra (the scales) is the sign for the High Holy Day season. (The signs of the zodiac are never used by the Sages to predict the future, nor do the Sages attribute to them any power to shape people's destiny.)

Why was the Torah not given as soon as the Israelites left Egypt? The Midrash compares the situation to that of a child who had fallen gravely ill. His father gave him several weeks to recuperate and only then did he let him return to school. So, too, when Israel went out of Egypt some Israelites had been disabled by the experience of slavery. God said, "I will wait until they are healed and then I will give them the Torah" (Tanḥ.). Levi Yitzḥak of Berdichev sees it slightly differently. Had Israel received the Torah immediately after the Exodus and the parting of the sea, it would have seemed that they accepted it out of gratitude for the miracles God had wrought for them. Instead, God waited until the effect of the miracles had worn off and they began to complain. Then their acceptance of the Torah was a completely voluntary act of commitment.

on that very day The Hebrew here literally means "on this day" (*ba-yom ha-zeh*), as if to suggest that on any day when a Jew accepts the obligations of the Torah, it is as if he or she were there that day, standing at Sinai and hearing the voice of God. Rashi takes the words to mean that every time a Jew reads the Torah, it should be as if for the first time. Heschel distinguishes between the giving of the Torah (*mattan Torah*), which was a one-time event in the Sinai wilderness, and the acceptance of the Torah as an authoritative voice in our lives, which can take place at any time. When a person of non-Jewish origin joins the Jewish people and accepts the Torah, it is as if he or she personally had been standing at Sinai.

2. wilderness According to rabbinic tradition, the Torah was given in the wilderness because it is free of distractions that might tempt the newly freed slaves, and to emphasize that

The LORD called to him from the mountain, saying, "Thus shall you say to the house of Jacob
and declare to the children of Israel: 4'You have
seen what I did to the Egyptians, how I bore you
on eagles' wings and brought you to Me. 5Now
then, if you will obey Me faithfully and keep My
covenant, you shall be My treasured possession
among all the peoples. Indeed, all the earth is
Mine, 6but you shall be to Me a kingdom of
priests and a holy nation.' These are the words
that you shall speak to the children of Israel."

הָאֱלֹהִים וַיִּקְרָא אֵלָיו יְהוָה מִן־הָהָר
לֵאמֹר כֹּה תֹאמַר לְבֵית יַעֲקֹב וְתַגֵּיד לִבְנֵי
יִשְׂרָאֵל׃ 4 אַתֶּם רְאִיתֶם אֲשֶׁר עָשִׂיתִי
לְמִצְרָיִם וָאֶשָּׂא אֶתְכֶם עַל־כַּנְפֵי נְשָׁרִים
וָאָבִא אֶתְכֶם אֵלָי׃ 5 וְעַתָּה אִם־שָׁמוֹעַ
תִּשְׁמְעוּ בְּקֹלִי וּשְׁמַרְתֶּם אֶת־בְּרִיתִי
וִהְיִיתֶם לִי סְגֻלָּה מִכָּל־הָעַמִּים כִּי־לִי
כָּל־הָאָרֶץ׃ 6 וְאַתֶּם תִּהְיוּ־לִי מַמְלֶכֶת
כֹּהֲנִים וְגוֹי קָדוֹשׁ אֵלֶּה הַדְּבָרִים אֲשֶׁר
חמישי תְּדַבֵּר אֶל־בְּנֵי יִשְׂרָאֵל׃

enter into a unique relationship with God, which imposes obligations and responsibilities.

4. on eagles' wings The image projects both God's power and love (see Deut. 32:10–11). The king of the birds, the eagle, impressed the biblical writers with the prodigious expanse of its outstretched wings, its way of protectively carrying its young on its back, and its ability to soar to great heights at considerable speed and to fly long distances.

to Me That I should be your God (Rashbam).

5. My covenant This is the first mention of the Covenant in the Exodus narrative. The stipulations are soon to be set forth.

My treasured possession The Hebrew word *s'gullah* originally denoted valued property to which one has exclusive right of possession. The biblical description of Israel as God's *s'gullah* or *am s'gullah* ("treasured people," Deut. 7:6, 14:2, 26:18–19), expresses God's special covenantal relationship with the Israelites and His love for them as His people. Here it is stated conditionally; in Deuteronomy it is presented as an established fact.

6. This statement further defines the implications of being God's "treasured people." National sovereignty, here expressed by "kingdom," is indispensable for the proper fulfillment of Israel's mission. Without it, the nation becomes the passive tool of historical forces beyond its control. At the same time, the priest's place and function within society must serve as the ideal model for Israel's self-understanding of its role among the nations. The priest is set apart by a distinctive way of life consecrated to the service of God and dedicated to ministering to the needs of the people. Striving for holiness as a people is to be the hallmark of Israel's existence.

---

the Torah is accessible to all who would claim it and live by it. Might it be that the noises of modern life make it hard for us to hear the divine message that God is constantly trying to communicate to us?

Israel encamped there Until now, all the verbs referring to Israel have been plural: "they journeyed," "they entered." Here, for the first time, the Hebrew verb for "encamped" is singular, suggesting that only when they transcended their differences and quarrels to become one people were they fit to receive the Torah (Rashi).

3. house of Jacob The Midrash interprets this as referring to wives, traditionally the keepers of the home. They, more than their husbands, will determine whether the spirit of Sinai fills their home (Exod. R. 28:2).

4. on eagles' wings God supports and sustains people who are too weak or weary to carry on by themselves. When the isolated Jews of Yemen, most of whom had never seen an airplane, were flown to the modern state of Israel, many of them understood the airplane flight to be a fulfilment of this verse.

5–6. Indeed all the earth is Mine, but you shall be to Me a kingdom of priests and a holy nation God, as Creator of the world, cares for all people. Israel has no monopoly on God. Israel, however, does have a special relationship to God. This is true not only when the rest of the world is pagan but will also be true in the future, even after all the nations will have turned to God. The notion that the people Israel have been chosen is not a claim of superiority. The Bible never hesitates to chronicle and condemn the Israelites' shortcomings and God's disappointment with them. To speak of

7Moses came and summoned the elders of the
people and put before them all that the LORD
had commanded him. 8All the people answered
as one, saying, "All that the LORD has spoken
we will do!" And Moses brought back the people's words to the LORD. 9And the LORD said to
Moses, "I will come to you in a thick cloud, in
order that the people may hear when I speak
with you and so trust you ever after." Then Moses reported the people's words to the LORD,
10and the LORD said to Moses, "Go to the people
and warn them to stay pure today and tomor-

חמישי 7 וַיָּבֹא מֹשֶׁה וַיִּקְרָא לְזִקְנֵי הָעָם וַיָּשֶׂם
לִפְנֵיהֶם אֵת כָּל־הַדְּבָרִים הָאֵלֶּה אֲשֶׁר
צִוָּהוּ יְהוָה׃ 8 וַיַּעֲנוּ כָל־הָעָם יַחְדָּו
וַיֹּאמְרוּ כֹּל אֲשֶׁר־דִּבֶּר יְהוָה נַעֲשֶׂה וַיָּשֶׁב
מֹשֶׁה אֶת־דִּבְרֵי הָעָם אֶל־יְהוָה׃ 9 וַיֹּאמֶר
יְהוָה אֶל־מֹשֶׁה הִנֵּה אָנֹכִי בָּא אֵלֶיךָ בְּעַב
הֶעָנָן בַּעֲבוּר יִשְׁמַע הָעָם בְּדַבְּרִי עִמָּךְ
וְגַם־בְּךָ יַאֲמִינוּ לְעוֹלָם וַיַּגֵּד מֹשֶׁה אֶת־
דִּבְרֵי הָעָם אֶל־יְהוָה׃ 10 וַיֹּאמֶר יְהוָה
אֶל־מֹשֶׁה לֵךְ אֶל־הָעָם וְקִדַּשְׁתָּם הַיּוֹם

THE POPULAR RESPONSE (vv. 7–8)

Moses conveys the divine message through the agency of the elders (See Comment to 3:16).

8. we will do The first of three affirmations of Israel's acceptance of the Covenant, this phrase is repeated at Exod. 24:3 and again with the climactic "we will faithfully do" at Exod. 24:7.

PREPARATIONS FOR THE THEOPHANY (vv. 9–25)

The preparations for the theophany (the appearance of God), which begin at once, include authentication of the role of Moses; purification—involving sexual abstinence and, most likely, bathing and laundering of clothes—and repeated warnings against encroachment on the sacred domain of the mountain. The divine revelation is presented in a way that dramatizes the overwhelming confusion the event must have produced in the minds of those present.

9. This passage may well allude to the declaration in 3:12 that the Sinai experience will be the ultimate validation of Moses' leadership.

a thick cloud See Comment to 13:21–22.

Then Moses reported This phrase refers not to what immediately precedes it but to the quote in verse 8.

10. to stay pure This is defined in verse 15. It most likely includes bathing, which is taken for granted.

Israel as God's Chosen People is a historical truth (it is through Israel that the Bible and the notion of ethical monotheism came into the world) and an assertion of divine power to select any people as the bearers of that revelation. An additional dimension in the notion of chosenness is that God's Torah belongs to an entire people, not only to professional clergy or an intellectual elite.

8. One tradition describes God as compelled to lift the mountain over their heads, threatening to crush them with it unless they accept the Torah (BT Shab. 88a). Another rabbinic tradition has Israel responding enthusiastically to God's demands. It sees the event as a wedding, with the uplifted mountain serving as the marriage canopy (*ḥuppah*). Yet another pictures God offering the Torah to the other nations (to forestall any charges of favoritism toward Israel), only to have them reject it when they learn of its demands. Only Israel is prepared to accept it. The divergence of traditional views may reflect an ambivalence toward the Torah's demands or the reality of their experiences later in history. The varying *midrashim* may reflect the truth that the *mitzvot* are both a joy and a burden. The prophets Hosea and Jeremiah look back on the wilderness years as a honeymoon period, the golden age when Israel was close to God and trusted God. The Torah's own account in subsequent chapters shows Israel as repeatedly rebellious and complaining.

10. warn them to stay pure today and tomorrow It is easy to be pure while standing at Sinai. Will the people be able to maintain that sense of purity tomorrow, when they return to the challenge of living in the world? An ancient rabbi taught: Not only literally tomorrow but in the distant future, Israel will be purified by this encounter with God.

row. Let them wash their clothes. 11Let them be
ready for the third day; for on the third day the
LORD will come down, in the sight of all the people, on Mount Sinai. 12You shall set bounds for
the people round about, saying, 'Beware of going up the mountain or touching the border of
it. Whoever touches the mountain shall be put
to death: 13no hand shall touch him, but he shall
be either stoned or shot; beast or man, he shall
not live.' When the ram's horn sounds a long
blast, they may go up on the mountain."

וּמָחָר וְכִבְּסוּ שִׂמְלֹתָם׃ 11 וְהָיוּ נְכֹנִים
לַיּוֹם הַשְּׁלִישִׁי כִּי ׀ בַּיּוֹם הַשְּׁלִישִׁי יֵרֵד
יְהוָה לְעֵינֵי כָל־הָעָם עַל־הַר סִינָי׃
12 וְהִגְבַּלְתָּ אֶת־הָעָם סָבִיב לֵאמֹר
הִשָּׁמְרוּ לָכֶם עֲלוֹת בָּהָר וּנְגֹעַ בְּקָצֵהוּ
כָּל־הַנֹּגֵעַ בָּהָר מוֹת יוּמָת׃ 13 לֹא־תִגַּע בּוֹ
יָד כִּי־סָקוֹל יִסָּקֵל אוֹ־יָרֹה יִיָּרֶה אִם־
בְּהֵמָה אִם־אִישׁ לֹא יִחְיֶה בִּמְשֹׁךְ הַיֹּבֵל
הֵמָּה יַעֲלוּ בָהָר׃

14Moses came down from the mountain to
the people and warned the people to stay pure,
and they washed their clothes. 15And he said to
the people, "Be ready for the third day: do not
go near a woman."

14 וַיֵּרֶד מֹשֶׁה מִן־הָהָר אֶל־הָעָם וַיְקַדֵּשׁ
אֶת־הָעָם וַיְכַבְּסוּ שִׂמְלֹתָם׃ 15 וַיֹּאמֶר
אֶל־הָעָם הֱיוּ נְכֹנִים לִשְׁלֹשֶׁת יָמִים אַל־
תִּגְּשׁוּ אֶל־אִשָּׁה׃

16On the third day, as morning dawned, there
was thunder, and lightning, and a dense cloud

16 וַיְהִי בַיּוֹם הַשְּׁלִישִׁי בִּהְיֹת הַבֹּקֶר
וַיְהִי קֹלֹת וּבְרָקִים וְעָנָן כָּבֵד עַל־הָהָר

11. third day In biblical consciousness, a three-day period has special significance. As with Abraham at the *Akedah* (Gen. 22:4), three days of preparation and self-restraint allow time for sober reflection, so that acceptance of the Covenant can be considered an unqualified act of free will. According to Jewish tradition, the third day fell on the sixth of *Sivan* and is identified with the harvest festival of *Shavuot*, which consequently came to commemorate the giving of the Torah (see Rashi).

will come down This fairly frequent figurative depiction of God's action in terms of human motion expresses at one and the same time God's infinite transcendence and personal, intimate involvement with humanity.

12. shall be put to death By human agency, as verse 13 makes clear.

13. no hand shall touch him The trespasser, who has intruded on sacred domain, shall not be seized, because this itself would bring another person to violate the restriction. He shall be executed when he is beyond the limits of the mountain.

ram's horn The Hebrew word *yovel* seems originally to have meant a sheep or a ram, as in Josh. 6:4,5. The word came to be restricted to the horn. *Yovel* lies behind the word "jubilee," which was inaugurated by a sounding of the ram's horn (Lev. 25:9).

they may go up Sinai possesses no inherent or "natural" holiness, nor does it acquire such by virtue of the theophany. Its sanctity and hence untouchability do not outlast the limited duration of the event.

15. do not go near a woman This refers to sexual contact, which would render men ritually unfit for an encounter with God. It is here implied, although not spelled out, that women were to comport themselves similarly (see Lev. 15:18).

16–19. Violent atmospheric disturbances are said to precede and accompany the theophany. The Bible frequently portrays upheavals of

---

15. do not go near a woman According to God's instructions, all the people, women as well as men, were to be present for the revelation at Sinai. Moses confuses that invitation by adding this prohibition; here, as in the incident of striking the rock at Meribah (Num. 20), he takes liberties in transmitting God's word. We might learn from this verse that, despite Judaism's emphasis on family and congregation as settings for fashioning holiness, sometimes we need distance from others, even from those with whom we are most intimate, to find God.

וְקֹ֨ל שֹׁפָ֜ר חָזָ֣ק מְאֹ֗ד וַיֶּחֱרַ֛ד כָּל־הָעָ֖ם
אֲשֶׁ֥ר בַּֽמַּחֲנֶֽה׃ 17 וַיּוֹצֵ֨א מֹשֶׁ֧ה אֶת־הָעָ֛ם
לִקְרַ֥את הָֽאֱלֹהִ֖ים מִן־הַֽמַּחֲנֶ֑ה וַיִּֽתְיַצְּב֖וּ
בְּתַחְתִּ֥ית הָהָֽר׃
18 וְהַ֤ר סִינַי֙ עָשַׁ֣ן כֻּלּ֔וֹ מִ֠פְּנֵי אֲשֶׁ֨ר יָרַ֥ד עָלָ֛יו
יְהוָ֖ה בָּאֵ֑שׁ וַיַּ֤עַל עֲשָׁנוֹ֙ כְּעֶ֣שֶׁן הַכִּבְשָׁ֔ן
וַיֶּחֱרַ֥ד כָּל־הָהָ֖ר מְאֹֽד׃ 19 וַיְהִי֙ ק֣וֹל הַשּׁוֹפָ֔ר
הוֹלֵ֖ךְ וְחָזֵ֣ק מְאֹ֑ד מֹשֶׁ֣ה יְדַבֵּ֔ר וְהָאֱלֹהִ֖ים
יַעֲנֶ֥נּוּ בְקֽוֹל׃ 20 וַיֵּ֧רֶד יְהוָ֛ה עַל־הַ֥ר סִינַ֖י ששי
אֶל־רֹ֣אשׁ הָהָ֑ר וַיִּקְרָ֨א יְהוָ֧ה לְמֹשֶׁ֛ה אֶל־
רֹ֥אשׁ הָהָ֖ר וַיַּ֥עַל מֹשֶֽׁה׃ 21 וַיֹּ֤אמֶר יְהוָה֙
אֶל־מֹשֶׁ֔ה רֵ֖ד הָעֵ֣ד בָּעָ֑ם פֶּן־יֶהֶרְס֤וּ אֶל־
יְהוָה֙ לִרְא֔וֹת וְנָפַ֥ל מִמֶּ֖נּוּ רָֽב׃ 22 וגם
הַכֹּהֲנִ֛ים הַנִּגָּשִׁ֥ים אֶל־יְהוָ֖ה יִתְקַדָּ֑שׁוּ פֶּן־

upon the mountain, and a very loud blast of the
horn; and all the people who were in the camp
trembled. 17 Moses led the people out of the
camp toward God, and they took their places
at the foot of the mountain.
18 Now Mount Sinai was all in smoke, for the
LORD had come down upon it in fire; the smoke
rose like the smoke of a kiln, and the whole
mountain trembled violently. 19 The blare of the
horn grew louder and louder. As Moses spoke,
God answered him in thunder. 20 The LORD
came down upon Mount Sinai, on the top of
the mountain, and the LORD called Moses to the
top of the mountain and Moses went up. 21 The
LORD said to Moses, "Go down, warn the people
not to break through to the LORD to gaze, lest
many of them perish. 22 The priests also, who
come near the LORD, must stay pure, lest the

nature in association with the self-manifestation of God. Apart from the present context, however, such imagery is always confined to poetic or prophetic texts. Here, the vivid, majestic, and terrifying depiction that draws its inspiration from natural phenomena, such as the storm, volcano, and earthquake, is meant to convey the awe-inspiring effect of the event on those who experienced it. The Elijah story in 1 Kings (19:12) emphasizes, however, that God manifests Himself in a "still, small voice," not in lightning and thunder.

17. toward God Toward the site of the theophany.

foot of the mountain The lowest part, on the level ground.

19. horn Hebrew for "horn" here is *shofar*, not *yovel* as in verse 13. The blasts of thunder are imagined as a celestial fanfare, heralding the arrival of the King.

20. Moses He alone is privileged to ascend to the top.

22. priests According to chapters 28 and 29, the priesthood was not established among the Israelites until after the Sinaitic revelation, which would make this, like their mention in verse 24, an anachronism. Many modern scholars believe that these verses reflect a different strand of tradition about the origins of the priestly institution. Jewish commentators have understood "priests" here as referring to firstborn males, who functioned as priests until they were replaced by the

---

17. out of the camp toward God At times we must leave the familiar places and habits with which we have grown comfortable, as Abraham did at the beginning of Israelite history, to grow to be the people we are capable of becoming.

19. blare of the horn grew louder Ordinarily, sounds grow more faint with time. The words spoken at Sinai, however, echo as loudly today as when they were spoken more than 3000 years ago.

21. lest many of them perish The Israelites, who had seen God smite the Egyptians with 10 plagues and again at the sea, had learned to see God as an awesome, terrifying power. Here, and elsewhere in the Torah, we read about the danger of approaching God carelessly. (See Exod. 20:16, the warning to the priests in Exod. 28:35, and the account of the death of Nadab and Abihu in Lev. 10:2.) If we today are less inclined to see God as dangerous or to see sudden deaths as "acts of God," punishments for violating the sanctity of God's precincts, do we lose some sense of God's awesome holiness in the process?

LORD break out against them." 23But Moses said
to the LORD, "The people cannot come up to
Mount Sinai, for You warned us saying, 'Set
bounds about the mountain and sanctify it.'"
24So the LORD said to him, "Go down, and come
back together with Aaron; but let not the priests
or the people break through to come up to the
LORD, lest He break out against them." 25And
Moses went down to the people and spoke to
them.

יִפְרֹץ בָּהֶם יְהוָה׃ 23 וַיֹּאמֶר מֹשֶׁה אֶל־
יְהוָה לֹא־יוּכַל הָעָם לַעֲלֹת אֶל־הַר סִינָי
כִּי־אַתָּה הַעֵדֹתָה בָּנוּ לֵאמֹר הַגְבֵּל אֶת־
הָהָר וְקִדַּשְׁתּוֹ׃ 24 וַיֹּאמֶר אֵלָיו יְהוָה לֶךְ־
רֵד וְעָלִיתָ אַתָּה וְאַהֲרֹן עִמָּךְ וְהַכֹּהֲנִים
וְהָעָם אַל־יֶהֶרְסוּ לַעֲלֹת אֶל־יְהוָה פֶּן־
יִפְרָץ־בָּם׃ 25 וַיֵּרֶד מֹשֶׁה אֶל־הָעָם וַיֹּאמֶר
אֲלֵהֶם׃ ס

20 God spoke all these words, saying:

כ וַיְדַבֵּר אֱלֹהִים אֵת כָּל־הַדְּבָרִים
הָאֵלֶּה לֵאמֹר׃ ס

family of Aaron, as recounted in Num. 3:12 and 8:16–18.

break out The verb, with God as the subject, connotes a visitation that is sudden, violent, and destructive, indicating the extreme care with which God's holiness must be approached even by the priests who serve Him.

THE DECALOGUE (20:1–14)

The title: The present passage carries no designation for this document. The popular English title "The Ten Commandments" is derived from the traditional, although inaccurate, English rendering of the Hebrew phrase *"aseret ha-d'varim,"* which appears in Exod. 34:28 and Deut. 4:13 and 10:4. In fact, the term "commandment" (*mitzvah,* pl. *mitzvot*) is not employed in the present context. The Hebrew, which means "The Ten Words/Statements/Pronouncements," was translated literally into Greek by the Jews of ancient Alexandria in Egypt as *deka logoi.* This gave rise to the more accurate English alternative "Decalogue." In Rabbinic texts, and generally in Hebrew down to modern times, the common designation is *aseret ha-dibrot.*

The tablets of stone: Several biblical passages (including Exod. 24:12; 32:15) testify to the inscribing of the Decalogue on two stone tablets. The practice of recording covenants on tablets was well rooted in the biblical world, as was the custom of depositing the document in a sanctuary (referred to as "Ark" in Exod. 25:16). Why two tablets were needed for the Decalogue is unclear; nor

---

24. Go down, and come back The path to God is rarely a steady climb upward. We climb, we fall back, and we climb higher again.

25. Moses went down to the people He went down to be included with them in accepting the Torah (*Kol Dodi*).

CHAPTER 20

1–14. What is unique about the Decalogue? Other ancient societies had laws against murder, theft, and adultery, but they invariably were phrased as conditional: "if . . . then." If someone murders another, this is the punishment. The statements in the Decalogue were unique in being phrased as absolutes: "You shall not." These things are not only illegal; they are wrong. They not only disrupt society; they violate universal principles. Furthermore, the Decalogue enshrines a fundamental principle of Judaism: How we treat one another is of concern to God.

What did the Israelites actually hear at Sinai? Some say they heard God proclaim all 10 of the utterances. Others say that God spoke only the first 2, declared in the divine "I," and that Moses added the remaining 8 in which God is referred to in the third person. One Hasidic master taught that the Israelites heard only the first letter of the first word (the *alef* in *anokhi,* which is a silent letter) and intuitively understood the rest (Menaḥem Mendel of Rymanov). That is, having encountered God in such a real and direct way, they understood the rightness and wrongness of certain modes of behavior without the need for words to be spoken. What God said is clear, how God com-

2I the Lord am your God who brought you

2*אָנֹכִי֙ יְהוָ֣ה אֱלֹהֶ֔יךָ אֲשֶׁ֧ר הוֹצֵאתִ֛יךָ

vv. 2–16. נדפס בטעם תחתון בלבד והוא למערבאי, והפסוקים ממוספרים לפי מהדורת לעטעריס. נדפס בטעם עליון בסוף התורה

do we know the arrangement of the text on the tablets. The most common understanding of the Sages assumes that five declarations were incised on each tablet (as attested by Philo and later *midrashim*). In the Jerusalem Talmud there is a tradition, given as the majority view, that each tablet contained the entire Decalogue. Saadia, among others, maintained that the two tablets featured the variant versions found in Exodus 20 and Deuteronomy 5, respectively.

The internal division: Context, style, and language suggest a basic division of the Decalogue into two distinct groups of commandments. The first group governs relations between God and the individual Israelite; the second regulates human relationships. The first group is characterized by the fivefold use of the phrase "the Lord your God"; the second contains no reference to God. The first group features obligations unique to the religion of Israel. The second group, consisting entirely of prohibitions, is of universal application with numerous parallels in other literature of the ancient world. Only in Israel, however, are these injunctions presented as divine in origin. It is striking that the document opens with "the Lord your God" and closes with "your neighbor."

Tradition provides two versions of the Decalogue's cantillation and verse division. (Thus the verses from 13 on are numbered differently in various editions of the Bible.) The version known as the "lower notes" is presented here; for the "upper notes," which are used in many synagogues on certain occasions, see p. 1509.

1. This introductory statement is unique in the Torah, for it does not indicate to whom the divine declaration is addressed—the individual Israelite or the entire community. On the one hand, it is "all the people" as a corporate entity who enter into the covenantal relationship with God. On the other hand, it is each individual as a member of the community who is addressed, as shown by the consistent use in Hebrew of the second person singular.

2. I the Lord am your God This type of royal formula occurs in "the historical prologue" of the ancient Near Eastern treaty form (see Comment to 3:6). Here it not only identifies the unimpeachable sovereign authority behind the ensuing pronouncements but emphasizes that the demands of the Decalogue have their source and sanction in the divine will, not in human wisdom. Hence they remain eternally valid and unaffected by temporal considerations. This is regarded as the first of the 10 divine pronouncements by most Jewish commentators, in contrast to the Christian perspective, which sees it exclusively as an introductory verse. See Comment to Deut. 5:6.

---

municated it to human beings remains a mystery. Many of us have had the experience of meeting someone in whose presence we found ourselves incapable of lying or gossiping, or someone whose very presence conveyed a message of compassion or courage. Perhaps coming into the presence of God at Sinai was an intensified experience of that sort. What God said will be the content of the rest of the Torah and generations of commentaries; that God communicated the divine will to human beings is a foundation stone of Judaism. Rosenzweig suggests that the single word actually spoken by God was the first word—*anokhi* ("I am"). From God's affirmation of existence and presence, all else flowed.

2. I the Lord am your God The Hebrew for "your" here is singular, because every person comes to understand God in his or her own way. "God is like a mirror. The mirror never changes, but everyone who looks at it sees a different face" (PdRK 12). Is this a commandment to believe in God? Maimonides holds that it is: "The first *mitzvah* is that [we] believe in God's existence, that there is a cause and motive force behind all that exists" (*Seifer Ha-Mitzvot* 1). Others disagree. Abravanel takes this first utterance as "a preface to subsequent injunctions, a declaration making known to the Israelites who was addressing them." Ḥasdai Crescas insists that a commandment can apply only to matters of free will and free choice; matters of belief cannot be commanded. The rabbis of the Talmud see this as a summons to Israel to "accept the yoke of God's sovereignty," to recognize God as the Supreme Authority. Only when they have done that can God give them laws and decrees. We re-enact this acceptance in the daily recitation of the *Sh'ma*.

out of the land of Egypt, the house of bondage:
3You shall have no other gods besides Me.
4You shall not make for yourself a sculptured
image, or any likeness of what is in the heavens
above, or on the earth below, or in the waters
under the earth. 5You shall not bow down to
them or serve them. For I the LORD your God
am an impassioned God, visiting the guilt of the

מֵאֶ֥רֶץ מִצְרַ֖יִם מִבֵּ֣ית עֲבָדִ֑ים 3 *לֹֽא־יִהְיֶ֥ה
לְךָ֛ אֱלֹהִ֥ים אֲחֵרִ֖ים עַל־פָּנָֽי׃
4 לֹ֣א תַֽעֲשֶׂה־לְךָ֥ פֶ֙סֶל֙ וְכָל־תְּמוּנָ֔ה אֲשֶׁ֣ר
בַּשָּׁמַ֣יִם ׀ מִמַּ֗עַל וַֽאֲשֶׁר֙ בָּאָ֣רֶץ מִתָּ֔חַת
וַאֲשֶׁ֥ר בַּמַּ֖יִם מִתַּ֣חַת לָאָֽרֶץ׃ 5 לֹֽא־
תִשְׁתַּחֲוֶ֥ה לָהֶ֖ם וְלֹ֣א תָעָבְדֵ֑ם כִּ֣י
אָֽנֹכִ֞י יְהוָ֤ה אֱלֹהֶ֙יךָ֙ אֵ֣ל קַנָּ֔א פֹּ֠קֵד עֲוֺ֨ן

v. 3. למערבאי לא נחשב פסוק נפרד

3–6. Rabbinic tradition generally treats these verses as a single unit.

You shall have no other gods besides Me The God of Israel demands uncompromising and exclusive loyalty, because He has redeemed them to serve Him.

You shall not make for yourself a sculptured image Later thinkers took this revolutionary Israelite concept to mean that God is wholly separate from the world of His creation and wholly other than what the human mind can conceive or the human imagination depict. Therefore, any material representation of divinity is forbidden. This does not prohibit artistic representation, only the use of images for worship.

an impassioned God The Hebrew word *kanna* is rendered here in its primitive sense, as "impassioned," referring to a zealous God emotionally involved in human affairs, who holds people accountable for their acts, capable of anger as well as compassion. The traditional translation, "a jealous God," understands the marriage bond

---

God is here proclaimed not as the God of Creation who made the world, but as the God of history who directed the Exodus. To the Israelites at the foot of the mountain, Creation was an abstract principle; the Exodus was the event that shaped their lives. Isaak Heinemann paraphrases the poet-philosopher Judah ha-Levi: "God as First Cause is a God reached by intellectual speculation, a God of metaphysics. But a God who acts in history, a God who frees the enslaved, is a God for whom the soul yearns." "Judaism is an elaborate way of relating to God as the Source of all existence and the provider of ultimate meaning. Nothing could be more fatuous than the all-too-common notion that observance is possible without faith. Hence the Decalogue begins with an affirmation of God's reality" (Schorsch).

out of the land of Egypt, the house of bondage For some, Egypt was the house of culture, science, and mathematics. For God and God's people, however, it was the house of bondage. Cultural and scientific accomplishments cannot make up for a nation's treating some of its people as less than human. "If freedom and culture cannot coexist, we should bid farewell to culture for the sake of freedom" (B. Jacob).

3. You shall have no other gods besides Me Some take the words translated as "besides Me" (*al panai*) to mean "in addition to" not only "in place of." It is forbidden to worship idols along with God. Arama takes this passage not as a prohibition but as a promise: As long as you have Me, you will not need any others.

4. You shall not make for yourself God is not merely invisible, i.e., possessing a shape that we cannot see. God has no physical form. It is only our limited human imagination that drives us to think of God as a heavenly being with bodily parts. To picture God is to limit God: male not female, old not young, of one specific race and skin color. Heschel suggests that we may not make an image of God because we ourselves bear the divine image in this world. We alone are God's agents, not any idol we might fashion. A homiletic interpretation of the same words comes to a contrasting conclusion: "You shall not make yourself into an idol, and come to believe that you are God."

5. visiting the guilt of the parents upon the children Children do benefit from, and suffer from, the choices of their parents when it comes to health, wealth, educational opportunities, and the fate of being born in a peaceful rather than in a war-torn land. Children are shaped by habits learned in their families of origin as to how they handle stress, quarrels, eat-

parents upon the children, upon the third and upon the fourth generations of those who reject Me, 6but showing kindness to the thousandth generation of those who love Me and keep My commandments.

7You shall not swear falsely by the name of the LORD your God; for the LORD will not clear one who swears falsely by His name.

אָבֹ֛ת עַל־בָּנִ֛ים עַל־שִׁלֵּשִׁ֥ים וְעַל־רִבֵּעִ֖ים
לְשֹׂנְאָֽי׃ 6 וְעֹ֥שֶׂה חֶ֖סֶד לַאֲלָפִ֑ים לְאֹהֲבַ֖י
וּלְשֹׁמְרֵ֥י מִצְוֺתָֽי׃ ס
7 לֹ֥א תִשָּׂ֛א אֶת־שֵׁם־יְהוָ֥ה אֱלֹהֶ֖יךָ לַשָּׁ֑וְא
כִּ֣י לֹ֤א יְנַקֶּה֙ יְהוָ֔ה אֵ֥ת אֲשֶׁר־יִשָּׂ֥א אֶת־
שְׁמ֖וֹ לַשָּֽׁוְא׃ פ

to be the implied metaphor for the covenant between God and the people Israel. God demands exclusive loyalty from His people. According to this interpretation, His reaction to their infidelity is expressed in terms of human jealousy. Whether one renders *kanna* as "jealous" or "impassioned," the term emphasizes that God is not indifferent to His creatures. God's anger or wrath usually is directed to those who flout His will, but at times it blazes forth against those who infringe on His holy domain. Most often, it serves to punish those who violate the moral world order or their covenantal responsibilities.

visiting the guilt of the parents upon the children Society is collectively responsible for its actions, and the individual is accountable for behavior that affects the life of the community. Conduct inevitably has an effect on succeeding generations. The doctrine that God visits the guilt of the parents on later generations was later modified by Jeremiah (31:29–30): "They shall no longer say, 'Parents have eaten sour grapes and children's teeth are blunted.' But every one shall die for his own sins: whosoever eats sour grapes, his teeth shall be blunted." His contemporary Ezekiel (18:2ff.) also felt compelled to deny cross-generational punishment. It is important to note that the statement concerning extension of punishment to later generations (see also Exod. 34:7) was never the concern of administering justice in Israel's legal system. Vicarious punishment is outlawed explicitly in Deut. 24:16.

who reject Me This phrase may modify "parents" or "children" or both.

thousandth generation God's boundless beneficence and the limited extent of punishment were emphasized by the Sages.

7. The Third Commandment deals with abuse of the divine name.

swear Literally, "lift up" (on your lips), "to utter" the divine name.

falsely Hebrew: *la-shav,* which can mean this as well as "for nothing, in vain." The ambiguity broadens the prohibition and allows for the proscription of both perjury (by the principals in a lawsuit, swearing falsely) and unnecessary or frivolous use of the divine name.

will not clear God will not allow the deed to go unpunished even though it may go undetected or not be actionable in a human court of law.

---

ing, and drinking. The Talmud interprets this verse to suggest that children who know that their parents are doing wrong but nonetheless choose to follow their example are held responsible for that choice (BT Ber. 7a). A modern writer understands the Hebrew verb *poked* ("visiting") as in Gen. 21:1 ("to take note"), reading the verse as "God takes note of the sins that parents inflict on their children"—and deals leniently with the children.

7. *You shall not swear falsely* You shall not resort to using God's name to make your lies more plausible. "If one does not keep one's word, that is tantamount to repudiating the name of God" (Ibn Ezra). It is especially important for a religiously committed Jew not to bring God's name into disrepute by false dealings. Some scholars interpret this verse to prohibit linking God's name to anything false, such as sorcery or fortune-telling.

HALAKHAH L'MA·ASEH

20:7. swear falsely The tradition demands that we neither swear falsely in court nor use God's name in vain. We, therefore, refrain from using the traditional names for God in secular writings or conversation, much less in voicing profanities. However, the English word "God" is not God's name or an English translation of it, but rather a description of God's role in our lives, as in the traditional formula for blessings, "Praised are you, LORD [God's name], our God, Sovereign of the universe." The CJLS has, therefore, ruled that Jews need not hyphenate the word "God."

8 Remember the sabbath day and keep it holy.
9 Six days you shall labor and do all your work,

8 זָכוֹר אֶת־יוֹם הַשַּׁבָּת לְקַדְּשׁוֹ׃ 9 שֵׁשֶׁת
יָמִים תַּעֲבֹד וְעָשִׂיתָ כָּל־מְלַאכְתֶּךָ׃ 10 וְיוֹם

8. The Fourth Commandment establishes *Shabbat* as a fixed weekly institution. With the Creation as its rationale (verse 11, reiterated in Exod. 31:13–17), the seventh day of each week is invested with special blessing and holiness. It is an integral part of the divinely ordained cosmic order and exists independent of human effort. For this reason it is described (verse 10) as "a sabbath of the LORD your God." There is nothing analogous to the Israelite *Shabbat* in the entire ancient Near Eastern world, where seven-day units of time were well known. *Shabbat* is the sole exception to the otherwise universal practice of basing all the major units of time—months and seasons as well as years—on the phases of the moon and the solar cycle. *Shabbat,* in other words, is completely dissociated from the movement of celestial bodies. This singularity, together with Creation as the basis for the institution, expresses the quintessential idea of Israel's monotheism: God is entirely outside of and sovereign over nature.

Remember Hebrew: *zakhor.* See Comment to 2:24. The narrative about the manna (Exod. 16:5,22–30) presupposes the existence of *Shabbat* as an institution before the Sinaitic revelation.

keep it holy Its intrinsic sacred character derives from God. Texts like Hos. 2:13 and Isa. 58:13–14 show that already in biblical times *Shabbat* was a day of rejoicing and delight.

8. Remember the sabbath day The commandment here calls on us to "remember" *Shabbat* in imitating God's rest; God created the world in six days and rested on the seventh. The wording of this commandment in Deut. 5:12 tells us to "keep" *Shabbat* as a weekly celebration of the fact that we are not slaves (Deut. 5:15); only free people own their own time and can choose to stop laboring. According to a *midrash* recalled in the Friday-night hymn *"L'khah Dodi,"* God at Sinai did what no human being can do: utter two distinct words ("remember" and "keep") at the same time. "Remember" is seen as a positive command to do things that make *Shabbat* special. "Keep" is a negative command to refrain from work and other activities that mar *Shabbat*. Israel of Modzhitz spoke of two modes of *Shabbat* observance: being and doing. The first is passive (not working, not making physical changes in the world). The second is active (praying, studying, spending time with family). One of the Sages strove each day of the week to fulfill the command to remember *Shabbat;* whenever he would find a particularly fine object or special food, he would put it aside for *Shabbat* (BT Betz. 16a). Those whose circumstances make it impossible to keep *Shabbat* as they would like to, should at least find ways to remind themselves that it is *Shabbat*.

9. Six days you shall labor Certain activity is as much a religious duty as resting on *Shabbat*. We are enjoined to labor over this world, to change it and to improve it. Idleness is a waste of the talents with which God has blessed us. Work, however, too often leads to economic competitiveness in which we see other people as rivals, obstacles to our success. *Shabbat* comes as a truce in those economic struggles. The rabbis of the talmudic period formulated rules governing *Shabbat* in systematic fashion. They were guided by the close proximity in the Torah of the prohibition of work on *Shabbat* and the instructions for building the tabernacle (Exod. 31:1–17, 35:1ff.). Acts that were essential in constructing the tabernacle are termed "principal" categories (*avot*); 39 such acts forbidden on *Shabbat* are listed in M Shab. 7:2. Other subcategories, analogous but not essential in constructing the tabernacle, are called "derivatives" (*toladot*). Elsewhere in the Bible, certain types of work are specified as off limits: "leaving one's place" (walking beyond a certain distance), agricultural activities, kindling fire, gathering wood, conducting business, carrying burdens, tread-

HALAKHAH L'MA·ASEH

20:8. Remember The Sages deduce from this verse the requirement to say *Kiddush* both Friday evening and during the day on Saturday as a way of marking and thus remembering the *Shabbat* (BT Pes. 106a). Maimonides (MT *Shabbat* 29:1) links it also to *Havdalah,* to end *Shabbat* and thereby distinguish it from the rest of the week (see Lev. 23:3; and especially Deut. 5:12). The Sages also deduce from this verse that rather than calling each day of the week by its own independent name, we should refer to each day by its number in the week before *Shabbat*—i.e., Sunday is the first day in [the week before] *Shabbat,* Monday the second day, and so on—so that the very names of the days remind us of *Shabbat* (Mekh.).

10but the seventh day is a sabbath of the LORD
your God: you shall not do any work—you,
your son or daughter, your male or female slave,
or your cattle, or the stranger who is within your
settlements. 11For in six days the LORD made
heaven and earth and sea, and all that is in them,
and He rested on the seventh day; therefore the
LORD blessed the sabbath day and hallowed it.
12Honor your father and your mother, that

הַשְּׁבִיעִ֗י שַׁבָּ֛ת לַיהֹוָ֥ה אֱלֹהֶ֖יךָ לֹֽא־תַעֲשֶׂ֣ה
כָל־מְלָאכָ֡ה אַתָּ֣ה ׀ וּבִנְךָֽ־וּבִתֶּ֗ךָ עַבְדְּךָ֤
וַאֲמָֽתְךָ֙ וּבְהֶמְתֶּ֔ךָ וְגֵרְךָ֖ אֲשֶׁ֥ר בִּשְׁעָרֶֽיךָ׃
11 כִּ֣י שֵֽׁשֶׁת־יָמִים֩ עָשָׂ֨ה יְהֹוָ֜ה אֶת־
הַשָּׁמַ֣יִם וְאֶת־הָאָ֗רֶץ אֶת־הַיָּם֙ וְאֶת־כָּל־
אֲשֶׁר־בָּ֔ם וַיָּ֖נַח בַּיּ֣וֹם הַשְּׁבִיעִ֑י עַל־כֵּ֗ן בֵּרַ֧ךְ
יְהֹוָ֛ה אֶת־י֥וֹם הַשַּׁבָּ֖ת וַֽיְקַדְּשֵֽׁהוּ׃ ס
12 כַּבֵּ֥ד אֶת־אָבִ֖יךָ וְאֶת־אִמֶּ֑ךָ לְמַ֙עַן֙

10. work The definition of prohibited labor (*m'lakhah*), which limits the commandment explicitly to Creation (Gen. 2:2), is not given here.

you . . . the stranger By proscribing work and creativity on the seventh day, and by ordering that nature be kept inviolate one day a week, the Torah places a limit on human autonomy and restores nature to its original state of pure freedom. Human liberty is immeasurably enhanced, human equality is strengthened, and the cause of social justice is promoted by legislating the inalienable right of every human being, irrespective of social class, and of draft animals as well, to 24 hours of complete rest every seven days. Appropriately, the list in this verse enumerates seven categories of God's creatures who benefit from rest on the seventh day. The "you" of the commandment includes both husbands and wives.

12. The Fifth Commandment forms a transition from the first to the second group of divine declarations, because it incorporates both religious and social dimensions. It shares with the preceding commandment the formula "the LORD your God." Also, the relationship of the people Israel to God is often expressed metaphorically in filial terms, and the same verbs of "honoring" and "revering" are used to express proper human attitudes to both God and parents. In fact, the Torah explicitly requires "respect" only in relation to God and parents. An offender in either instance is liable to the extreme penalty. The parallels point out the importance the Torah assigns to the integrity of the family, which can help ensure the stability of society as well as generational continuity.

father . . . mother The command, directed equally to son and daughter irrespective of age, holds for both parents.

---

ing the winepress, and loading asses. All *Shabbat* prohibitions are suspended when human life is at risk. In such a situation it is a religious duty to violate them to save a life (*pikku·aḥ nefesh*). This principle is grounded in Lev. 18:5: "You shall keep My laws and My rules, by the pursuit of which man shall live: I am the LORD."

and do all your work What if we cannot finish all our work by sundown on Friday? Then we should keep *Shabbat* as if we had completed it. Do not mar *Shabbat* by worrying about unfinished business (Rashi).

12. Honor your father and your mother Honoring parents is a way of honoring God, the ultimate source of all life and care. Lev. 19:3 reverses the order in commanding us to fear (i.e., revere) our parents, listing the mother first. The Talmud suggests that the Torah is seeking to balance the natural impulse to honor one's mother and fear one's father (BT Kid. 30b). Some societies and religious movements teach that people can be truly themselves only if they reject their parents. In Judaism, to reject one's parents is to reject all of one's ancestors and pretend that one has no past. It verges on rejecting the ultimate parent, God, from whom all life flows. Thus, although

HALAKHAH L'MA·ASEH

20:10. your son or daughter See Comment on 23:12.

20:12. Honor your father and your mother Honoring parents includes arranging necessary physical and financial assistance (BT Kid. 31a–b). Children are not required or permitted to violate Jewish law to conform to parental wishes (BT Yev. 5b), but children should always balance their Jewish commitments to other *mitzvot* with honor and respect for their parents. See also Comments on Lev. 19:3; Deut. 21:18–21.

you may long endure on the land that the LORD your God is assigning to you.
13You shall not murder.
You shall not commit adultery.

יַאֲרִכ֣וּן יָמֶ֔יךָ עַ֚ל הָֽאֲדָמָ֔ה אֲשֶׁר־יְהֹוָ֥ה אֱלֹהֶ֖יךָ נֹתֵ֥ן לָֽךְ׃ ס
13*לֹ֖א תִּֿרְצָֽח׃ ס
לֹ֖א תִּֿנְאָֽף׃ ס

v. 13. למערבאי פיסקא באמצע פסוק שלוש פעמים

long endure Respect for parents is regarded as vital for preservation of the social fabric. Dishonoring parents imperils the well-being of society and survival of the people Israel in the Land.

13. You shall not murder The stem of the word translated as "murder" (רצח) applies only to illegal killing. Unlike other verbs for the taking of life, it is never used in the administration of justice or for killing in war. The rationale for this prohibition is found in Gen. 9:6: "Whoever sheds the blood of man, / By man shall his blood be shed; / For in His image / Did God make man." In practice, at least in Second Temple times, imposition of the death penalty was a rare occurrence.

You shall not commit adultery The definition of adultery is sexual intercourse by mutual consent between a married or engaged woman and a man who is not her lawful husband. Because adultery is treated as both a public wrong and an offense against God, a husband has no legal power to pardon his faithless wife or her paramour. The gravity of adultery in Israelite law may be gauged both by its place in the Decalogue—between murder and theft—and by the extreme severity of the penalty.

---

a convert to Judaism is technically considered a new person with no past (lest he or she be embarrassed by past years of idol worship or unseemly behavior), most authorities would direct the convert to continue to honor his or her parents.

long endure Perhaps the intention here is that we will be able to look forward to a long life and not dread growing old, because we will have fashioned a society in which the elderly are honored and respected. The commandment is not addressed to children, telling them to heed their parents, but to adults, enjoining them to continue to honor their elderly parents even when there is no biologic need to. The Sages interpret this verse not to command feelings of affection but to command behavior. We are obliged to support and maintain our parents and to avoid shaming them. "Now that I have commanded you to acknowledge that I am the Creator of all, and to honor parents because they have joined Me in an act of creating life, guard against destroying the work of My hands in acts of murder" (Maimonides). Four things above all must be protected so that the community may stand firm: life, marriage, property and social honor (Buber).

13. You shall not murder The Hebrew text does not state "you shall not kill" (*lo taharog*) but "you shall not murder" (*lo tirtzaḥ*). The Sages understand "bloodshed" to include embarrassing a fellow human being in public so that the blood drains from his or her face, not providing safety for travelers, and causing anyone the loss of his or her livelihood. "One may murder with the hand or with the tongue, by talebearing or by character assassination. One may murder also by carelessness, by indifference, by the failure to save human life when it is in your power to do so" (Ibn Ezra).

You shall not commit adultery For the Torah, marriage is not only a private sexual or economic arrangement between two individuals. It is a holy covenant (*kiddushin*). Buber taught that "God is found in relationships." God is present when two people pledge themselves to each other; God is present in a home sustained by marital love. The Midrash suggests that

HALAKHAH L'MA·ASEH

20:13. adultery Until a man gives a Jewish writ of divorce (a *get*) to his wife, Jewish law considers both of them to be married, even if they are divorced under civil law. Although the Torah allowed polygamy, Rabbeinu Gershom (ca. 1000 C.E.) forbade it. We view marriage today as a monogamous relationship built on mutual trust, and so sex outside the marriage by either partner is forbidden by Jewish law and/or by Jewish moral norms. See Comment on Deut. 22:28–29.

לֹא תִּגְנֹב ס

לֹא־תַעֲנֶה בְרֵעֲךָ עֵד שָׁקֶר׃ ס

14 לֹא תַחְמֹד בֵּית רֵעֶךָ לֹא־תַחְמֹד אֵשֶׁת
רֵעֶךָ וְעַבְדּוֹ וַאֲמָתוֹ וְשׁוֹרוֹ וַחֲמֹרוֹ וְכֹל
אֲשֶׁר לְרֵעֶךָ׃ פ שביעי

You shall not steal.

You shall not bear false witness against your neighbor.

14You shall not covet your neighbor's house: you shall not covet your neighbor's wife, or his male or female slave, or his ox or his ass, or anything that is your neighbor's.

You shall not steal The precise application of this Eighth Commandment is complicated by the obvious lack of specifics. The Hebrew verb גנב may cover theft of property as well as kidnaping (Rashbam).

You shall not bear false witness This is not the same as "swearing falsely" in verse 7, for witnesses did not always testify under oath in ancient Israel. The prohibition here refers to judicial proceedings.

14. You shall not covet The meaning of this commandment has been a matter of dispute. Does it refer to a private mental state or only to acts directed toward acquiring the coveted object?

house The Hebrew word *bayit* here, as frequently elsewhere, means "household."

God's presence is diminished by infidelity, implying perhaps that the spiritual integrity of a marital relationship is diluted when a third party intrudes (Lev. R. 23:12, end). Hosea, a prophet of the 8th century B.C.E., described God's relationship to the people Israel in terms of a marriage bond, comparing God's pain over Israel's chasing after false gods to the sense of betrayal felt by a human being confronting the infidelity of his or her partner.

You shall not steal Rashi and other commentators understand this commandment to refer to kidnaping, stealing a person. They understand the last prohibition of the Decalogue to refer to stealing property. Later rabbinic interpretations clarify the notion of theft to include borrowing an object without permission, even with the intention of returning it, and keeping a lost object when you suspect that, with some effort, you could locate the rightful owner. Does the Torah compare the sanctity of private property to that of marriage or life itself? Perhaps the intent of this commandment is to avoid dividing society into two hostile camps—the very rich and the destitute—which might drive some of the poor to rebel against this economic inequity by striking at the property of others. In such a social order no one, however wealthy or prominent, would feel secure.

You shall not bear false witness Alshekh interprets this to mean "you shall not testify falsely on behalf of your neighbor," even to help an honest person win a case in which he lacks witnesses.

14. You shall not covet Many commentators are troubled by the apparent prohibition of a feeling, when the general pattern of the Torah is to command behavior, not thought. Can we control our feelings or are we responsible only for our actions? Some (e.g., Rashi) resolve the issue by taking the 8th commandment to apply to kidnaping and the 10th to stealing property. The same verb occurs in Exod. 34:24, assuring the Israelites of the security of their homes when they go on pilgrimage at festival time. There, it makes more sense to take it to mean "no one will confiscate your house" while you are away rather than "no one will covet it." Others (Maimonides) understand this commandment to prohibit action that could be the result of coveting, such as pressuring a person to sell you something you desire. But the majority understand it to apply to covetous thoughts. It may be difficult to control our emotions, but we may never excuse our behavior by claiming that our emotions overcame us so that we could not help doing what we did.

Some see a symmetrical arrangement in the entire passage. The Decalogue begins with an abstract principle concerning thought ("I the LORD am your God"), proceeds to prohibit verbal utterances (swearing falsely) and then focuses on deeds (*Shabbat*; honoring parents; re-

HALAKHAH L'MA·ASEH

20:14. covet This verse prohibits longing only for anything we cannot obtain honestly and legally (BT BM 5b).

15 All the people witnessed the thunder and lightning, the blare of the horn and the mountain smoking; and when the people saw it, they fell back and stood at a distance. 16 "You speak to us," they said to Moses, "and we will obey; but let not God speak to us, lest we die." 17 Moses answered the people, "Be not afraid; for God has come only in order to test you, and in order that the fear of Him may be ever with you, so that you do not go astray." 18 So the people remained at a distance, while Moses approached the thick cloud where God was.

שביעי 15 וְכָל־הָעָם רֹאִים אֶת־הַקּוֹלֹת וְאֶת־
הַלַּפִּידִם וְאֵת קוֹל הַשֹּׁפָר וְאֶת־הָהָר עָשֵׁן
וַיַּרְא הָעָם וַיָּנֻעוּ וַיַּעַמְדוּ מֵרָחֹק׃
16 וַיֹּאמְרוּ אֶל־מֹשֶׁה דַּבֵּר־אַתָּה עִמָּנוּ
וְנִשְׁמָעָה וְאַל־יְדַבֵּר עִמָּנוּ אֱלֹהִים פֶּן־
נָמוּת׃ 17 וַיֹּאמֶר מֹשֶׁה אֶל־הָעָם אַל־
תִּירָאוּ כִּי לְבַעֲבוּר נַסּוֹת אֶתְכֶם בָּא
הָאֱלֹהִים וּבַעֲבוּר תִּהְיֶה יִרְאָתוֹ עַל־
פְּנֵיכֶם לְבִלְתִּי תֶחֱטָאוּ׃ 18 וַיַּעֲמֹד הָעָם
מֵרָחֹק וּמֹשֶׁה נִגַּשׁ אֶל־הָעֲרָפֶל אֲשֶׁר־שָׁם
הָאֱלֹהִים׃ פ

19 The LORD said to Moses:

Thus shall you say to the Israelites: You yourselves saw that I spoke to you from the very heavens: 20 With Me, therefore, you shall not make any gods of silver, nor shall you make for yourselves any gods of gold. 21 Make for Me an altar of earth and sacrifice on it your burnt offerings and your sacrifices of well-being, your

מפטיר 19 וַיֹּאמֶר יְהוָה אֶל־מֹשֶׁה
כֹּה תֹאמַר אֶל־בְּנֵי יִשְׂרָאֵל אַתֶּם רְאִיתֶם
כִּי מִן־הַשָּׁמַיִם דִּבַּרְתִּי עִמָּכֶם׃ 20 לֹא
תַעֲשׂוּן אִתִּי אֱלֹהֵי כֶסֶף וֵאלֹהֵי זָהָב לֹא
תַעֲשׂוּ לָכֶם׃ 21 מִזְבַּח אֲדָמָה תַּעֲשֶׂה־לִּי
וְזָבַחְתָּ עָלָיו אֶת־עֹלֹתֶיךָ וְאֶת־שְׁלָמֶיךָ

THE PEOPLE'S REACTION (vv. 15–16)

15. witnessed The Hebrew verbal stem ראה (literally, "to see") here encompasses sound. The figurative language serves to indicate the profound awareness among the assembled throng of the overpowering majesty and mystery of God's self-manifestation. This experience cannot be described adequately by ordinary language applied to the senses.

18. thick cloud Hebrew: *arafel.* The dense, dark cloud poetically expresses God's mysteriously perceptible yet unseen Presence.

THE REGULATION OF WORSHIP (vv. 19–23)

These verses continue the narrative by featuring the instructions that Moses received as he "approached the thick cloud." They also serve to introduce the laws that follow in *Mishpatim.*

21. altar of earth This is an altar made by heaping up a mound of earth in an open field.

---

fraining from murder, adultery, and theft) before returning to the improper use of words (bearing false witness) and concluding with abstract thought (coveting). One Hasidic preacher takes this last commandment not as a prohibition but as a promise and reward: if you live by the first 9 commandments, you will have no reason to covet what anyone else possesses (Yeḥiel Michael of Zolochev).

15. All the people witnessed the thunder and lightning The text reads literally, "they *saw* the thunder . . . and the blare of the horn." The experience of Revelation was so uniquely intense and overwhelming that the senses overflowed their normal bounds. People felt that they were seeing sounds and hearing visions.

16. lest we die With the exception of rare individuals, human beings cannot endure direct contact with God. Thus every religion strives to mediate God's Presence. Through ritual, through study, through the performance of *mitzvot,* and through our encounters with people who embody what God stands for, we are able to "meet" God.

אֶת־צֹאנְךָ וְאֶת־בְּקָרֶךָ בְּכָל־הַמָּקוֹם אֲשֶׁר
אַזְכִּיר אֶת־שְׁמִי אָבוֹא אֵלֶיךָ וּבֵרַכְתִּיךָ׃
22 וְאִם־מִזְבַּח אֲבָנִים תַּעֲשֶׂה־לִּי לֹא־
תִבְנֶה אֶתְהֶן גָּזִית כִּי חַרְבְּךָ הֵנַפְתָּ עָלֶיהָ
וַתְּחַלְלֶהָ׃ 23 וְלֹא־תַעֲלֶה בְמַעֲלֹת עַל־
מִזְבְּחִי אֲשֶׁר לֹא־תִגָּלֶה עֶרְוָתְךָ עָלָיו׃ פ

sheep and your oxen; in every place where I
cause My name to be mentioned I will come to
you and bless you. 22And if you make for Me
an altar of stones, do not build it of hewn stones;
for by wielding your tool upon them you have
profaned them. 23Do not ascend My altar by
steps, that your nakedness may not be exposed
upon it.

in every place The word for "place" (*makom*) most likely means here "sacred site," a site rendered sacred by an altar to God, as in Gen. 12:7. This implies approval of numerous altars scattered throughout the land, in contrast with later laws in Deuteronomy that insist that all sacrificial worship take place exclusively in one official national-religious center.

22. This prohibition against hewn masonry is incorporated in Deut. 27:5–6 regarding instructions for the altar to be erected on Mount Ebal, which Joshua later strictly enforced (Josh. 8:30–31). In the construction of Solomon's Temple, "only finished stones cut at the quarry were used, so that no hammer or axe or any iron tool was heard in the House while it was being built" (1 Kings 6:7). Many centuries later, when Judah the Maccabee built a new altar after the liberation of Jerusalem, he was careful to use only uncut stones. Josephus, describing Herod's Temple, likewise reports that no iron was used in the construction of its altar.

tool Undefined here; Deut. 27:5 and 1 Kings 6:7 specify iron.

23. The instructions here must be directed to a layman at a private altar, because the uniform of the priests included linen breeches that covered their nakedness. This contrasts with many scenes in ancient Near Eastern art that depict priests officiating in the nude.

---

21. in every place A sense of God's presence is not limited to Mount Sinai. Wherever we turn our homes, schools, offices, and synagogues into places where God's name is invoked, God promises to be with us and bless us. The remainder of the Book of Exodus, and virtually the rest of the Torah, can be seen as a commentary on and expansion of the Sinai experience. An entire people has been addressed by God. Their lives and the lives of their descendants, their every daily moment, will henceforth be shaped by that encounter.

הפטרת יתרו

HAFTARAH FOR YITRO

ISAIAH 6:1–7:6, 9:5–6 (*Ashk'nazim*)
ISAIAH 6:1–13 (*S'fardim*)

The first part of this *haftarah* (6:1–13) takes place in the year of King Uzziah's death (733–732 B.C.E.). The second part (7:1–6) occurs during the regency of his successor King Ahaz, when an alliance between Syria and the northern kingdom of Israel threatened Jerusalem in the south. The reading concludes with a depiction of a royal figure who will rule in peace and justice (9:5–6).

The *haftarah* opens with Isaiah's commission to prophecy. He presumably is standing in the Temple courts when he experiences an ecstatic vision of God. At that moment, Isaiah is struck with a terrifying sense of impurity. Only after his mouth is purified by a heavenly coal does he return to his people to prophesy.

A common pattern shapes the structure and components of divine commissions of prophets (see Exod. 3:2–4,9–12, 4:10–12; Jer. 1:4–10; Ezek. 1:1–3:3). All of them are put to a divinely ordained task. Their expressions of awe and unworthiness underscore that the initiative comes from God. When we examine both Isaiah's and Ezekiel's throne visions, we see that neither event was induced by mystical preparations, but was unexpected. Likewise, neither vision serves as a mystical experience for its own sake, but functions as a prelude to God's commission of the prophet.

Isaiah's vision differs in one aspect: His commission occurs within both the earthly and the divine Temple. Indeed, the prophet experiences being raised into the heavenly court as a participant. Such heavenly ascensions for the sake of Israel's destiny became common in postbiblical literature.

A standard feature of prophetic commissions is God's promise of support. The messenger is told: "Do not be afraid" (*al tira,* cf. Jer. 1:8; Ezek. 2:6). Isaiah uses the same language when he tells Ahaz (in God's name) not to be terrorized by the alliance between Syria and Ephraim (Isa. 7:4). The trust expressed here is an important part of Isaiah's theology. He repeatedly contrasts spiritual truth with military might.

RELATION OF THE *HAFTARAH* TO THE *PARASHAH*

Thematic and verbal parallels connect the two readings. The *parashah* (Exod. 18–20) presents a blueprint for justice and judgment as well as a revelation of God's instruction to the entire nation (Exod. 19–20). The *haftarah* echoes these themes in more personal terms. Isaiah first receives a vision of God's majesty, and instruction to the people and its leader (Isa. 6:1–7:6). This is followed by the promise of a new era of national justice, to be inaugurated by a wondrous king. These two biblical passages are at two historical poles: the past time of the origin of the Covenant and the future time of messianic justice. What Moses inaugurates, the prophet Isaiah can only envisage: a kingdom of justice under God. What is more, the Covenant people, bidden to be a "kingdom of priests and a holy nation" (Exod. 19:6), have failed their task. They are now impure. Only in the future, after their punishment and purgation (Isa. 6:5,11–13), can they become a "holy seed." Then the ancient Covenant will be carried on by a remnant.

The two passages are intimately intertwined by language and imagery. Compare, for example, "wings of eagles" (*kanfei n'sharim*) and "holy nation" (*goy kadosh*) in Exod. 19:5–6 with "wings" (*k'nafayim*) and "holy" (*kadosh*) in Isaiah 6:2–3 as well as "smoke" (*ashan*) in both Exod. 19:18 and Isa. 6:4. Through shared vocabulary and imagery, the prophet Isaiah emerges as the historical disciple of Moses, first teacher of the divine cov-

enant. Like Moses, Isaiah is overawed by the revelation of God. He stands firm before the vision, however, and is brought to the depths of his own unworthiness. His confession of unfitness leads to heavenly purification, readying him to serve his people. But their spiritual life has been dulled, and the prophet must acknowledge their failure. Only

disaster and miraculous survival will generate the holy potential of the people. Can the holy seed again become a holy nation, or is it destined to remain but a trace of its sacred past? This is the silent question put before each reader of the *haftarah,* when Isaiah's prophecy is recited.

6 In the year that King Uzziah died, I beheld my Lord seated on a high and lofty throne; and the skirts of His robe filled the Temple. ²Seraphs stood in attendance on Him. Each of them had six wings: with two he covered his face, with two he covered his legs, and with two he would fly.

³And one would call to the other,

"Holy, holy, holy!

The LORD of Hosts!

His presence fills all the earth!"

⁴The doorposts would shake at the sound of the one who called, and the House kept filling with smoke. ⁵I cried,

ו בִּשְׁנַת־מוֹת֙ הַמֶּ֣לֶךְ עֻזִּיָּ֔הוּ וָאֶרְאֶ֧ה אֶת־אֲדֹנָ֛י יֹשֵׁ֥ב עַל־כִּסֵּ֖א רָ֣ם וְנִשָּׂ֑א וְשׁוּלָ֖יו מְלֵאִ֥ים אֶת־הַהֵיכָֽל: 2 שְׂרָפִ֨ים עֹמְדִ֤ים ׀ מִמַּ֙עַל֙ ל֔וֹ שֵׁ֣שׁ כְּנָפַ֞יִם שֵׁ֣שׁ כְּנָפַ֖יִם לְאֶחָ֑ד בִּשְׁתַּ֣יִם ׀ יְכַסֶּ֣ה פָנָ֗יו וּבִשְׁתַּ֛יִם יְכַסֶּ֥ה רַגְלָ֖יו וּבִשְׁתַּ֥יִם יְעוֹפֵֽף:

3 וְקָרָ֨א זֶ֤ה אֶל־זֶה֙ וְאָמַ֔ר
קָד֧וֹשׁ ׀ קָד֛וֹשׁ קָד֖וֹשׁ
יְהוָ֣ה צְבָא֑וֹת
מְלֹ֥א כָל־הָאָ֖רֶץ כְּבוֹדֽוֹ:

4 וַיָּנֻ֙עוּ֙ אַמּ֣וֹת הַסִּפִּ֔ים מִקּ֖וֹל הַקּוֹרֵ֑א וְהַבַּ֖יִת יִמָּלֵ֥א עָשָֽׁן: 5 וָאֹמַ֞ר

Isaiah 6:2. Seraphs stood in attendance Isaiah's vision resembles other scenes of God's heavenly enthronement amid a retinue of heavenly beings (1 Kings 22:19–23; Daniel 7:9–14).

3. And one would call to the other, / "Holy, holy, holy!" The translation suggests that each of the six seraphs enacted a threefold sanctification, although it is unclear whether they did so successively or in unison. Rashi observes that the calling is a mutual angelic invitation to sanctify God, performed in unison. Viewing and hearing this angelic sanctification was often deemed a climax of ancient mystical experience (see 1 Enoch 90:40).

Jewish tradition has adapted the sanctification in Isa. 6:3 to the formal liturgy (where it is called *K'dushah*). It is recited as part of the *Amidah* prayer and in other parts of the liturgy. Talmudic *midrash* claims that recitation of *K'dushah* by a congregation on earth parallels the praise of the angelic host. The Sages also stress that the human recitation precedes the angelic one and that this

leads to the coronation of God who ascends the highest throne in heaven. The visionary experience of Isaiah thus has become a communal ritual, uniting heaven and earth in a chorale of divine praise.

His presence fills all the earth The Hebrew word *kavod* (presence)—sometimes translated as "glory"—refers to the manifestation of the divine glory on earth (Lev. 10:3; Isa. 40:5). God's *kavod* is often described anthropomorphically, as in the visionary experiences of Moses (Exod. 33:22–23) and Ezekiel (Ezek. 1:28). The medieval philosophers intensely discussed how God, utterly beyond any anthropomorphic conception, could become manifest in such terms on earth. In mystical sources, such images were repeatedly depicted and often provided the basis for bold theological assertions. The "Hymn of Glory" (*Shir ha-Kavod*), recited during *Shabbat* services, articulates the tension between figurative human depiction of God and His absolute transcendence of all such forms.

"Woe is me; I am lost!
For I am a man of impure lips
And I live among a people
Of impure lips;
Yet my own eyes have beheld
The King LORD of Hosts."

אֽוֹי־לִ֣י כִֽי־נִדְמֵ֗יתִי
כִּ֣י אִ֤ישׁ טְמֵֽא־שְׂפָתַ֙יִם֙ אָנֹ֔כִי
וּבְתוֹךְ֙ עַם־טְמֵ֣א שְׂפָתַ֔יִם
אָנֹכִ֖י יוֹשֵׁ֑ב
כִּ֗י אֶת־הַמֶּ֛לֶךְ יְהוָ֥ה צְבָא֖וֹת
רָא֥וּ עֵינָֽי׃

6Then one of the seraphs flew over to me with
a live coal, which he had taken from the altar
with a pair of tongs. 7He touched it to my lips
and declared,

6 וַיָּ֣עָף אֵלַ֗י אֶחָד֙ מִן־הַשְּׂרָפִ֔ים וּבְיָד֖וֹ
רִצְפָּ֑ה בְּמֶ֨לְקַחַ֔יִם לָקַ֖ח מֵעַ֥ל הַמִּזְבֵּֽחַ׃
7 וַיַּגַּ֣ע עַל־פִּ֔י וַיֹּ֕אמֶר

"Now that this has touched your lips,
Your guilt shall depart
And your sin be purged away."

הִנֵּ֛ה נָגַ֥ע זֶ֖ה עַל־שְׂפָתֶ֑יךָ
וְסָ֣ר עֲוֺנֶ֔ךָ
וְחַטָּאתְךָ֖ תְּכֻפָּֽר׃

8Then I heard the voice of my Lord saying,
"Whom shall I send? Who will go for us?" And
I said, "Here am I; send me." 9And He said, "Go,
say to that people:
'Hear, indeed, but do not understand;
See, indeed, but do not grasp.'
10Dull that people's mind,
Stop its ears,
And seal its eyes—
Lest, seeing with its eyes
And hearing with its ears,
It also grasp with its mind,
And repent and save itself."

8 וָאֶשְׁמַ֞ע אֶת־ק֤וֹל אֲדֹנָי֙ אֹמֵ֔ר אֶת־מִ֥י
אֶשְׁלַ֖ח וּמִ֣י יֵֽלֶךְ־לָ֑נוּ וָאֹמַ֖ר הִנְנִ֥י שְׁלָחֵֽנִי׃
9 וַיֹּ֕אמֶר לֵ֖ךְ וְאָמַרְתָּ֣ לָעָ֣ם הַזֶּ֑ה
שִׁמְע֤וּ שָׁמ֙וֹעַ֙ וְאַל־תָּבִ֔ינוּ
וּרְא֥וּ רָא֖וֹ וְאַל־תֵּדָֽעוּ׃
10 הַשְׁמֵן֙ לֵב־הָעָ֣ם הַזֶּ֔ה
וְאָזְנָ֥יו הַכְבֵּ֖ד
וְעֵינָ֣יו הָשַׁ֑ע
פֶּן־יִרְאֶ֨ה בְעֵינָ֜יו
וּבְאָזְנָ֣יו יִשְׁמָ֗ע
וּלְבָב֛וֹ יָבִ֥ין
וָשָׁ֖ב וְרָ֥פָא לֽוֹ׃

11I asked, "How long, my Lord?" And He re-
plied:
"Till towns lie waste without inhabitants
And houses without people,

11 וָאֹמַ֕ר עַד־מָתַ֖י אֲדֹנָ֑י וַיֹּ֗אמֶר
עַ֣ד אֲשֶׁר֩ אִם־שָׁא֨וּ עָרִ֜ים מֵאֵ֣ין יוֹשֵׁ֗ב
וּבָתִּים֙ מֵאֵ֣ין אָדָ֔ם

9. Hear, indeed, but do not understand Isaiah's message is difficult, both stylistically and theologically. One interpretation suggests that the prophet was instructed to speak in such a way that the people would reject his message, thus ensuring divine punishment. In this reading, his word is designed explicitly to prevent repentance (v. 10). Alternatively, this passage can be read as a psychological description: "Hear, though you do not understand" (Rashi, Radak). Thus, although the people may hear, they have become too indifferent to respond to the divine word. In either reading, the people's inability to see or hear contrasts sharply with the prophet's clear vision.

And the ground lies waste and desolate—
12For the LORD will banish the population—
And deserted sites are many
In the midst of the land.
13"But while a tenth part yet remains in it, it shall repent. It shall be ravaged like the terebinth and the oak, of which stumps are left even when they are felled: its stump shall be a holy seed."

וְהָאֲדָמָה תִּשָּׁאֶה שְׁמָמָה׃
12 וְרִחַק יְהוָה אֶת־הָאָדָם
וְרַבָּה הָעֲזוּבָה
בְּקֶרֶב הָאָרֶץ׃
13 וְעוֹד בָּהּ עֲשִׂרִיָּה וְשָׁבָה וְהָיְתָה לְבָעֵר
כָּאֵלָה וְכָאַלּוֹן אֲשֶׁר בְּשַׁלֶּכֶת מַצֶּבֶת בָּם*
זֶרַע קֹדֶשׁ מַצַּבְתָּהּ׃ פ

7

In the reign of Ahaz son of Jotham son of Uzziah, king of Judah, King Rezin of Aram and King Pekah son of Remaliah of Israel marched upon Jerusalem to attack it; but they were not able to attack it.

2Now, when it was reported to the House of David that Aram had allied itself with Ephraim, their hearts and the hearts of their people trembled as trees of the forest sway before a wind. 3But the LORD said to Isaiah, "Go out with your son Shear-jashub to meet Ahaz at the end of the conduit of the Upper Pool, by the road of the Fuller's Field. 4And say to him: Be firm and be calm. Do not be afraid and do not lose heart on account of those two smoking stubs of firebrands, on account of the raging of Rezin and his Arameans and the son of Remaliah. 5Because the Arameans—with Ephraim and the son of Remaliah—have plotted against you, saying, 6'We will march against Judah and invade and conquer it, and we will set up as king in it the son of Tabeel,'

ז

וַיְהִי בִּימֵי אָחָז בֶּן־יוֹתָם בֶּן־עֻזִּיָּהוּ
מֶלֶךְ יְהוּדָה עָלָה רְצִין מֶלֶךְ־אֲרָם
וּפֶקַח בֶּן־רְמַלְיָהוּ מֶלֶךְ־יִשְׂרָאֵל יְרוּשָׁלַםִ
לַמִּלְחָמָה עָלֶיהָ וְלֹא יָכֹל לְהִלָּחֵם
עָלֶיהָ׃
2 וַיֻּגַּד לְבֵית דָּוִד לֵאמֹר נָחָה אֲרָם עַל־
אֶפְרָיִם וַיָּנַע לְבָבוֹ וּלְבַב עַמּוֹ כְּנוֹעַ עֲצֵי־
יַעַר מִפְּנֵי־רוּחַ׃ 3 וַיֹּאמֶר יְהוָה אֶל־
יְשַׁעְיָהוּ צֵא־נָא לִקְרַאת אָחָז אַתָּה וּשְׁאָר
יָשׁוּב בְּנֶךָ אֶל־קְצֵה תְּעָלַת הַבְּרֵכָה
הָעֶלְיוֹנָה אֶל־מְסִלַּת שְׂדֵה כוֹבֵס׃
4 וְאָמַרְתָּ אֵלָיו הִשָּׁמֵר וְהַשְׁקֵט אַל־תִּירָא
וּלְבָבְךָ אַל־יֵרַךְ מִשְּׁנֵי זַנְבוֹת הָאוּדִים
הָעֲשֵׁנִים הָאֵלֶּה בָּחֳרִי־אַף רְצִין וַאֲרָם
וּבֶן־רְמַלְיָהוּ׃ 5 יַעַן כִּי־יָעַץ עָלֶיךָ אֲרָם
רָעָה אֶפְרַיִם וּבֶן־רְמַלְיָהוּ לֵאמֹר׃ 6 נַעֲלֶה
בִיהוּדָה וּנְקִיצֶנָּה וְנַבְקִעֶנָּה אֵלֵינוּ וְנַמְלִיךְ
מֶלֶךְ בְּתוֹכָהּ אֵת בֶּן־טָבְאַל׃ ס

9

5Surely a child has been born to us,
A son has been given us.

ט

5 כִּי־יֶלֶד יֻלַּד־לָנוּ
בֵּן נִתַּן־לָנוּ

v. 13. סבירין ומטעין "בה"

13. a tenth part There will be repentance only for a small remnant, who are like a ravaged tree whose stump produces new growth. The 10th part will become a holy seed.

Isaiah 9:5. Surely Hebrew: *ki,* usually translated by "for," as in its original setting in Isaiah. Rendering *ki* as "surely" shows how this *haftarah* connects its two passages; it juxtaposes the plot-

And authority has settled on his shoulders.
He has been named
"The Mighty God is planning grace;
The Eternal Father, a peaceable ruler"—
6In token of abundant authority
And of peace without limit
Upon David's throne and kingdom,
That it may be firmly established
In justice and in equity
Now and evermore.
The zeal of the LORD of Hosts
Shall bring this to pass.

וַתְּהִי הַמִּשְׂרָה עַל־שִׁכְמוֹ
וַיִּקְרָא שְׁמוֹ
פֶּלֶא יוֹעֵץ אֵל גִּבּוֹר
אֲבִיעַד שַׂר־שָׁלוֹם׃
6 לסרבה לְמַרְבֵּה הַמִּשְׂרָה
וּלְשָׁלוֹם אֵין־קֵץ
עַל־כִּסֵּא דָוִד וְעַל־מַמְלַכְתּוֹ
לְהָכִין אֹתָהּ וּלְסַעֲדָהּ
בְּמִשְׁפָּט וּבִצְדָקָה
מֵעַתָּה וְעַד־עוֹלָם
קִנְאַת יְהוָה צְבָאוֹת
תַּעֲשֶׂה־זֹּאת׃ ס

ters' royal pretender (7:5–6) to a future messianic king picked by God (9:5–6).

The Mighty God is planning grace The first in a series of royal titles, similar to others in the ancient Near East (as found in modern times by archaeologists). For Rashi and Radak, this initial title refers to God, but Ibn Ezra understands it as the title of the powerful messianic king.

21 These are the rules that you shall set before them:

כא וְאֵ֙לֶּה֙ הַמִּשְׁפָּטִ֔ים אֲשֶׁ֥ר תָּשִׂ֖ים לִפְנֵיהֶֽם׃

THE BOOK OF THE COVENANT: THE LAWS (21:1–24:18)

These chapters, containing the first body of Torah legislation, are known in English as "The Book of the Covenant" (*seifer ha-b'rit*). The name is derived from 24:4,7, where we read that Moses wrote down the divine commands and then read aloud the covenant document to the people, who gave their assent. The Book of the Covenant has many similarities to other Near Eastern collections of law. The Israelite collection, however, is embedded in the Exodus narratives, which are crucial to its meaning and significance. The combination of civil, moral, and religious laws in a code is unique to the ancient Near East.

The Book of the Covenant falls into four distinct parts. The first part (21:2–22:16) deals with civil and criminal matters. The second part (22:17–23:19) treats a variety of topics, with special emphasis on humanitarian considerations. The third (23:20–33) affirms the divine promises to Israel and warns against the dangers of assimilation to paganism. The fourth part (chapter 24) concludes the Book of the Covenant with a description of how the document was ratified and an account of Moses ascending the mountain once again to receive the Decalogue incised in stone.

With this *parashah,* the tone of the Torah changes. Up to this point, it has been a narrative, with occasional references to laws such as those regarding circumcision and *Pesaḥ*. Now, the emphasis is reversed. From here on, the Torah will present the rules by which the Israelites are to live, with occasional narrative breaks.

JUDICIAL RULINGS (21:1–22:16)

1. This verse serves as a heading for the entire section.

These are The Hebrew word *v'eileh* is literally "And these are." The conjunction "and" indicates continuity. This connects the laws that follow with the preceding Decalogue, implicitly asserting that all are derived from the same source at Sinai.

rules The Hebrew word *mishpatim* originally referred to "specific judicial rulings" and then came to be used for enactments in general, authoritative statements of law regarding standards of conduct.

you shall set before them Knowledge of the law is to be the privilege and obligation of the entire people, not the prerogative of specialists or of an elite class.

The rules of forming a just society outlined at the beginning of this *parashah* follow the discussion about the design of the altar at the end of the previous one. "In time to come, when there will no longer be an altar, building a just society will be the equivalent of bringing sacrifices" (*Yalkut Sh.* 1:271). The laws of the Torah are not given in the names of kings or even in the name of Moses. They are religious and moral instructions given by God. Obeying the laws creates not only a harmonious society but a just and holy one. Violations are seen as offenses against God, not just against the violated person. Unlike the secular legal traditions of other societies, the laws of the Torah are cited not as the products of human wisdom and experience but as a reflection of divine principles built into the world. Thus the dignity of a human being is as much a permanent part of God's Creation as the law of gravity.

"Outside of Israel, you would have to go to three different addresses to get the material . . . in *Mishpatim*. The Torah combines law (as in the Code of Hammurabi), cultic instructions (as from a priestly manual), and moral exhortation (as found in wisdom literature). This is the only Near Eastern literature in which an amalgam of these three interests is found: law, cult and wisdom" (M. Greenberg). Judaism is based not only on the major pronouncements of the Decalogue but on the hundreds of minor ways in which we are called on to sanctify our relationships with other people. Ramban sees this *parashah* as an extension of the 10th commandment, "You shall not covet." To obey that commandment properly, we need to know what we are entitled to and what belongs to our neighbor. Our standards for how we treat others must be based not on social-utilitarian concerns, the desire for an orderly society, but on the recognition of the image of God in every person and the presence of God in every relationship.

2When you acquire a Hebrew slave, he shall serve six years; in the seventh year he shall go free, without payment. 3If he came single, he shall leave single; if he had a wife, his wife shall leave with him. 4If his master gave him a wife, and she has borne him children, the wife and her children shall belong to the master, and he shall leave alone. 5But if the slave declares, "I

2 כִּי תִקְנֶה עֶבֶד עִבְרִי שֵׁשׁ שָׁנִים יַעֲבֹד
וּבַשְּׁבִעִת יֵצֵא לַחָפְשִׁי חִנָּם׃ 3 אִם־בְּגַפּוֹ
יָבֹא בְּגַפּוֹ יֵצֵא אִם־בַּעַל אִשָּׁה הוּא וְיָצְאָה
אִשְׁתּוֹ עִמּוֹ׃ 4 אִם־אֲדֹנָיו יִתֶּן־לוֹ אִשָּׁה
וְיָלְדָה־לוֹ בָנִים אוֹ בָנוֹת הָאִשָּׁה וִילָדֶיהָ
תִּהְיֶה לַאדֹנֶיהָ וְהוּא יֵצֵא בְגַפּוֹ׃ 5 וְאִם־

LAWS CONCERNING SLAVES (vv. 2–11)

The list of enactments (*mishpatim*) begins with 10 laws regulating the institution of slavery. None of the other law collections from the ancient Near East opens with this topic. The emphasis given to it by the Torah has a clear historical explanation: Having recently experienced liberation from bondage, the Israelites are instructed to be especially sensitive to the condition of the slave. Yet the Torah does not abolish slavery. That was left to later generations.

The Male Slave (vv. 2–6)

2. When you acquire By self-sale, the desperately poor could gain a measure of security. People also could be sold by the courts. The labors of a debtor or a thief could serve to repay a debt or compensate for stolen property.

a Hebrew slave A fellow Israelite (Mekh.).

six years The slavery laws of Lev. 25:40 rule that this maximum limit on his term of service is shortened should the jubilee year occur in the meantime.

in the seventh year Rabbinic tradition understood this to mean the seventh year from the beginning of his indenture.

free, without payment Emancipation is his by right, and no compensation is due to the master. The law in Deut. 15:12–15 requires that the master make generous provisions for the slave who leaves his service.

3. if he had a wife The master would have been responsible for the maintenance of the slave's wife and children throughout the period of his service.

4. In the ancient Near East it was common practice for a master to mate a slave with a foreign bondwoman solely for the purpose of siring "house-born" slaves. The woman and her offspring remained the property of the master.

CHAPTER 21

2. The legal code begins with the treatment of slaves, even as the Decalogue begins with a reference to Israel's enslavement in Egypt. For many modern readers, the subject raises questions about the morality of the Torah's legislation. How could God countenance slavery? First, we must note that this passage does not refer to the Egyptian model of slavery, a condition of cruel, permanent bondage. It deals with people who find themselves obliged to sell their labor for a fixed time to repay a debt or as a result of bankruptcy. Second, the Torah's overall emphasis on human freedom and dignity, its insistence that humans are called to serve God and not a human master, in time led to a strengthening of the rules protecting the rights of slaves and, ultimately, to a rejection of slavery entirely. The status of a slave in the Torah was better than that of a slave in Egypt, but still fell short of the Torah's vision of innate human dignity. This chapter still considers the slave and his or her family as the master's property and calls for decent treatment. Deuteronomy, seen by most scholars as a later compilation, considers slaves as virtually members of the master's family, to be included in festival celebrations and sent off with gifts at the end of their period of service. This chapter simply states, "when you acquire a Hebrew slave." The parallel text in Deut. 15:12 begins, "If a fellow Hebrew [literally, "your brother"] . . . is sold to you." It would seem that the Israelites, newly freed from Egypt, could not imagine a society without slavery (any more than Plato or Aristotle could). But over the course of time, a more humane view of the slave evolved.

3. *single* The usual translation of the Hebrew here (*b'gapo*) is "unmarried." The Midrash understands it as "vigorous." If the slave was strong and able bodied when he entered your service, you were not to work him so hard that he was no longer vigorous when he completed his obligation to you (Mid. Ha-Ḥefetz).

אָמֹר֙ יֹאמַר֙ הָעֶ֔בֶד אָהַ֨בְתִּי֙ אֶת־אֲדֹנִ֔י
אֶת־אִשְׁתִּ֖י וְאֶת־בָּנָ֑י לֹ֥א אֵצֵ֖א חָפְשִֽׁי׃
6 וְהִגִּישׁ֤וֹ אֲדֹנָיו֙ אֶל־הָ֣אֱלֹהִ֔ים וְהִגִּישׁוֹ֙ אֶל־
הַדֶּ֔לֶת א֖וֹ אֶל־הַמְּזוּזָ֑ה וְרָצַ֨ע אֲדֹנָ֤יו אֶת־
אָזְנוֹ֙ בַּמַּרְצֵ֔עַ וַעֲבָד֖וֹ לְעֹלָֽם׃ ס
7 וְכִֽי־יִמְכֹּ֥ר אִ֛ישׁ אֶת־בִּתּ֖וֹ לְאָמָ֑ה לֹ֥א
תֵצֵ֖א כְּצֵ֥את הָעֲבָדִֽים׃ 8 אִם־רָעָ֞ה בְּעֵינֵ֧י
אֲדֹנֶ֛יהָ אֲשֶׁר־לא לֹ֥ו יְעָדָ֖הּ וְהֶפְדָּ֑הּ לְעַ֥ם
נָכְרִ֛י לֹא־יִמְשֹׁ֥ל לְמָכְרָ֖הּ בְּבִגְדוֹ־בָֽהּ׃
9 וְאִם־לִבְנ֖וֹ יִֽיעָדֶ֑נָּה כְּמִשְׁפַּ֥ט הַבָּנ֖וֹת
יַעֲשֶׂה־לָּֽהּ׃ 10 אִם־אַחֶ֖רֶת יִֽקַּֽח־ל֑וֹ שְׁאֵרָ֛הּ

love my master, and my wife and children: I do not wish to go free," 6his master shall take him before God. He shall be brought to the door or the doorpost, and his master shall pierce his ear with an awl; and he shall then remain his slave for life.

7When a man sells his daughter as a slave, she shall not be freed as male slaves are. 8If she proves to be displeasing to her master, who designated her for himself, he must let her be redeemed; he shall not have the right to sell her to outsiders, since he broke faith with her. 9And if he designated her for his son, he shall deal with her as is the practice with free maidens. 10If he marries another, he must not withhold from

6. To avoid any possibility of abuse by a master and to safeguard the rights of a slave, the change from temporary to permanent slavery must be carried out according to a procedure fixed by law.

before God This term (*elohim*) appears again in a legal context in 22:7–8. Neither here nor there can it mean "God" literally. This is so in chapter 22, because its accompanying verb is plural. Its use here parallels Mesopotamian court records, which frequently mention a litigant taking "an oath of the gods" while in the presence of, or perhaps by actually holding, figurines of the gods. According to Rabbinic interpretation, *elohim* in this verse means "judges."

door or the doorpost Of the sanctuary or of the house where, in Mesopotamia, household gods were found.

pierce his ear A sign of permanent slave status.

The Female Slave (vv. 7–11)

7. his daughter as a slave The Hebrew word *amah,* used here for "slave," indicates a status quite different from that of the male slave. In the ancient world, a father, driven by poverty, might sell his daughter to a wealthy family to ensure her future security. The sale presupposes marriage to the master or his son, with the Torah stipulating that the girl must be treated as a wife.

8. outsiders The Hebrew term *am nokhri* refers to people who are not of the same family.

9. the practice with free maidens The girl is to be raised within the family and given the status of a daughter. As such, she normally would be protected from sexual abuse, and a marriage would be arranged for her.

10. Ancient Mesopotamian laws similarly stipulate that if a man takes a second wife and she becomes his favorite, he must continue to support

5–6. Some slaves would be intimidated by the prospect of freedom (as some Israelites were when they left Egypt). The Torah accommodates their feelings, but marks that as the less desirable alternative. To be fully human, people must take responsibility for their own lives. Those who decide to stay are branded in the ear, because it was the ear that heard God declare at Sinai, "I have brought you out of the house of bondage" (Rashi). Why a doorpost? "Because a door was opened for him to go free, and he refused to go" (*K'li Yakar*).

for life According to Rabbinic interpretation, however, the new term of service ends at the next jubilee year or at the death of the master, whichever comes first.

HALAKHAH L'MA·ASEH

21:10. he must not withhold . . . her food, her clothing, or her conjugal rights According to Jewish law, both husband and wife have the right to sexual satisfaction within marriage (M Ket. 5:6–7).

this one her food, her clothing, or her conjugal rights. [11]If he fails her in these three ways, she shall go free, without payment.

[12]He who fatally strikes a man shall be put to death. [13]If he did not do it by design, but it came about by an act of God, I will assign you a place to which he can flee.

[14]When a man schemes against another and kills him treacherously, you shall take him from My very altar to be put to death.

כְּסוּתָהּ וְעֹנָתָהּ לֹא יִגְרָע׃ 11 וְאִם־שְׁלָשׁ־
אֵלֶּה לֹא יַעֲשֶׂה לָהּ וְיָצְאָה חִנָּם אֵין
כָּסֶף׃ ס
12 מַכֵּה אִישׁ וָמֵת מוֹת יוּמָת׃ 13 וַאֲשֶׁר
לֹא צָדָה וְהָאֱלֹהִים אִנָּה לְיָדוֹ וְשַׂמְתִּי לְךָ
מָקוֹם אֲשֶׁר יָנוּס שָׁמָּה׃ ס
14 וְכִי־יָזִד אִישׁ עַל־רֵעֵהוּ לְהָרְגוֹ בְעָרְמָה
מֵעִם מִזְבְּחִי תִּקָּחֶנּוּ לָמוּת׃ ס

his first wife. The Torah extends this protection to the slave girl and here specifies three basic necessities of life to which she is entitled.

her conjugal rights All the ancient translations of the Torah understood the word translated by this phrase (*onah*) as referring to a woman's conjugal rights, an interpretation that is also found in Rabbinic sources. If correct, this would be the only instance in the laws of the ancient Near East that stipulates that a wife is entitled to sexual gratification. Other commentators render *onah* as "dwelling, shelter," and still others as "oil, ointment." In many ancient Near Eastern texts, there are clauses that make provision for a wife's "food, clothing, and ointment."

11. in these three ways Any of the previously mentioned possibilities: marriage to the master, or to his son, or allowing her to be redeemed.

THREE CAPITAL OFFENSES (vv. 12–17)

Homicide (vv. 12–14)

Murder (v. 12): A homicide for which criminal intent has been proven beyond question. The same law appears in Lev. 24:17,21. (Deuteronomy 17:6 and 19:15 state that capital punishment is to be carried out only on the evidence of two witnesses. Numbers 35:30–31 prohibit monetary compensation in lieu of execution. In contrast, other ancient Near Eastern law collections view murder only in terms of economic loss to the family or clan.) Although the text does not prescribe the mode of execution, Rabbinic sources specify decapitation.

Asylum (vv. 13–14): Unintentional homicide is treated differently from murder. With the development of the concept that crime should be punished by the community and not by means of personal vengeance, it became imperative to control the ancient and widespread phenomenon of the blood feud. These measures are designed to protect the manslayer and allow established legal procedure to take its course.

13. by design With premeditation.

by an act of God Literally, "and God caused it to happen by His hand." The manslayer was the unwitting agent.

I will assign you The manslayer is to be guaranteed temporary asylum pending judicial disposition of the case. This is the only instance in the presentation of enactments (*mishpatim*) in which the people Israel are addressed directly, thereby emphasizing the Torah's profound concern for the protection of life.

a place The Hebrew word *makom* here probably means "sacred site" (as in 20:21), a sanctuary whose precincts are inviolable. The other biblical sources dealing with this topic specifically mention "cities of refuge."

14. Even the sacred domain of the altar will not provide protection for a willful murderer. Its

---

12. Transgressions calling for capital punishment not only define legal parameters but indicate a society's core values, those whose violation is seen as striking at the foundations of the society. In verses 12–17, the Torah identifies some of those core values as the infinite worth of a human life, the dignity of the human being, and the honoring of parents. It distinguishes between murder—the ultimate crime for which the murderer must receive the ultimate punishment—and inadvertent killing, which cannot justify taking the life of the manslayer.

14. The Sages derive from this text the rule that a priest convicted of murder is to be re-

15He who strikes his father or his mother shall be put to death.

16He who kidnaps a man—whether he has sold him or is still holding him—shall be put to death.

17He who insults his father or his mother shall be put to death.

18When men quarrel and one strikes the other with stone or fist, and he does not die but has to take to his bed—19if he then gets up and walks outdoors upon his staff, the assailant shall go unpunished, except that he must pay for his idleness and his cure.

15 וּמַכֵּ֥ה אָבִ֛יו וְאִמּ֖וֹ מ֥וֹת יוּמָֽת׃
16 וְגֹנֵ֨ב אִ֧ישׁ וּמְכָר֛וֹ וְנִמְצָ֥א בְיָד֖וֹ מ֥וֹת
יוּמָֽת׃ ס
17 וּמְקַלֵּ֥ל אָבִ֛יו וְאִמּ֖וֹ מ֥וֹת יוּמָֽת׃ ס
18 וְכִֽי־יְרִיבֻ֣ן אֲנָשִׁ֔ים וְהִכָּה־אִישׁ֙ אֶת־
רֵעֵ֔הוּ בְּאֶ֖בֶן א֣וֹ בְאֶגְרֹ֑ף וְלֹ֥א יָמ֖וּת וְנָפַ֥ל
לְמִשְׁכָּֽב׃ 19 אִם־יָק֞וּם וְהִתְהַלֵּ֥ךְ בַּח֛וּץ
עַל־מִשְׁעַנְתּ֖וֹ וְנִקָּ֣ה הַמַּכֶּ֑ה רַ֥ק שִׁבְתּ֛וֹ יִתֵּ֖ן
שני וְרַפֹּ֥א יְרַפֵּֽא׃ ס

sanctuary is extended only to the perpetrators of accidental homicide.

Abuse of Parents (vv. 15,17)

Although separated by the law of the kidnaper, these two verses belong together. Verse 15 concerns violent assault on a parent by a child; verse 17 deals with verbal abuse. The analogous law in the ancient Near Eastern Hammurabi collection orders that the hand of a son who strikes his father be amputated. The mother as victim is not mentioned there.

15. strikes According to the Sages, only the actual infliction of physical injury by an adult son or daughter results in the death penalty.

Kidnaping (v. 16)

16. Unlike other ancient law codes, biblical law never punishes theft by death, except for kidnaping and stealing property that has been dedicated to God (*ḥeirem*).

17. insults "Insult" is too weak a rendering for the Hebrew stem קלל. The kind of behavior understood here includes uttering a curse. The horrendous nature of this offense is intensified in a culture that believed a curse possessed potent force and took on a devastating life of its own, especially if uttered in the name of God. The term קלל also means "to treat with contempt," the direct opposite of כבד, "to honor."

BODILY INJURY INFLICTED BY PERSONS
(vv. 18–27)

These laws deal with the compensation for personal injuries caused by physical attack. The basic principle is the question of intent—whether or not the assailant intended to inflict injury.

18. quarrel What begins as an exchange of words abruptly degenerates into a brawl as one person strikes a blow that temporarily incapacitates another. The aggressor must compensate the victim for loss of income, here called "idleness," and for medical expenses.

19. unpunished Presumably, if the victim dies, then the laws set forth in verses 12–14 become operative. Rabbinic tradition required the assailant to be held in custody until the victim recovered fully.

---

moved from the Temple even if he is in the midst of his sacred duties.

15. shall be put to death The same verb is used in Lev. 24:15, prohibiting blaspheming against God. This prompted the Midrash to comment, "God holds the honor due to parents as dear as the honor due to God."

19. and his cure Hebrew *v'rapo y'rapei;* literally, "he shall certainly cure him." Even though ultimately God is our healer (Exod. 15:26), it is religiously proper for doctors to cure the sick, because they are thus doing the work of God (BT BK 85a). A religious person is not to say, "If God wants me to be ill, I will be

HALAKHAH L'MA·ASEH

21:19. pay for his idleness and his cure A person who injures another is liable for five types of restitution: for the injury itself, for pain, for medical expenses, for absence from work, and for humiliation and mental anguish (M BK 8:1).

20When a man strikes his slave, male or female, with a rod, and he dies there and then, he must be avenged. 21But if he survives a day or two, he is not to be avenged, since he is the other's property.

22When men fight, and one of them pushes a pregnant woman and a miscarriage results, but no other damage ensues, the one responsible shall be fined according as the woman's hus-

שני 20 וְכִֽי־יַכֶּה אִישׁ אֶת־עַבְדּוֹ אוֹ אֶת־אֲמָתוֹ
בַּשֵּׁבֶט וּמֵת תַּחַת יָדוֹ נָקֹם יִנָּקֵם׃ 21 אַךְ
אִם־יוֹם אוֹ יוֹמַיִם יַעֲמֹד לֹא יֻקַּם כִּי כַסְפּוֹ
הוּא׃ ס
22 וְכִֽי־יִנָּצוּ אֲנָשִׁים וְנָגְפוּ אִשָּׁה הָרָה
וְיָצְאוּ יְלָדֶיהָ וְלֹא יִהְיֶה אָסוֹן עָנוֹשׁ יֵעָנֵשׁ
כַּאֲשֶׁר יָשִׁית עָלָיו בַּעַל הָאִשָּׁה וְנָתַן

Injury to a Slave (vv. 20–21)

This law—the protection of slaves from maltreatment by their masters—helps make the system more humane.

20. his slave The final clause of the next verse indicated to the Sages that the slave in question is a foreigner. An Israelite never could be considered the property of another Israelite, because all were equally bound by the Covenant.

a rod The right of a master to discipline his slave is recognized. According to the Sages, however, the instrument must never be one that normally is lethal, and it may not be applied to a part of the body considered to be especially vulnerable.

there and then Because the master unlawfully has used deadly force, homicidal intent is assumed.

he must be avenged The master, criminally liable, faces execution.

21. Should the beaten slave linger more than a day before succumbing, the intent of the master appears less likely to have been homicidal and more likely to have been disciplinary. He is given the benefit of the doubt, especially because he is losing his financial investment (the price of the slave). This lenient ruling does not apply to anyone other than the master (Mekh.).

Unintended Harm to a Pregnant Woman
(vv. 22–25)

Unlike the earlier instance of a verbal quarrel that was not lawful at the start (vv. 18–19), this quarrel involves physical violence. Because the possibility of indirect damage was foreseeable, the antagonists are liable for injury caused to an innocent bystander, in this case a pregnant woman.

22. fight The Hebrew verb implies the use of physical force.

damage The word translated as "damage" (*ason*) elsewhere always signifies a major calamity;

---

ill, and if God wants me to recover, God will heal me without medical intervention." Maimonides, a physician as well as a philosopher, wrote: "If a person eats to cure his hunger, do we say that he has abandoned his trust in God? Just as I thank God for providing me with food to sustain life, I thank God for providing me with that which heals my sickness." The Talmud teaches that one must not live in a city that has no physician (BT Sanh. 17b).

20. To harm a slave is to inflict harm on a human being, a bearer of God's image. No other ancient society, and few premodern societies, granted slaves this measure of humanity. In most cases, even in the United States in the 19th century, slaves were considered property. The Torah repeatedly insists on the fundamental human dignity of the poor, the slave, and even the criminal.

HALAKHAH L'MA·ASEH

21:22. a miscarriage results Applying this text to all forms of miscarriage, Jewish law requires different forms of mourning for a fetus than for someone born alive. Full mourning rites are not appropriate for a fetal loss; but the CJLS, understanding the emotional and physical pain of a couple experiencing a miscarriage, has ruled that the community should offer them support through prayer and the *mitzvah* of visiting the sick (*bikkur ḥolim*).

but no other damage Because the Torah demands only a monetary payment for the fetus in contrast to "life for life" for the woman, the fetus is not considered to be a full-fledged human being, and abortion is not murder (M Oho. 7:6). It is, however, an injury to the woman; and as such, abortion is generally prohibited. It is allowed only to save the physical or mental health of the mother. Many authorities, including the CJLS, permit abortion to prevent maternal anguish over the prospect of giving birth to a child with severe defects. Abortion is not permitted as a retroactive form of birth control.

בִּפְלִלִים׃ 23 וְאִם־אָסוֹן יִהְיֶה וְנָתַתָּה נֶפֶשׁ
תַּחַת נָפֶשׁ׃ 24 עַיִן תַּחַת עַיִן שֵׁן תַּחַת שֵׁן
יָד תַּחַת יָד רֶגֶל תַּחַת רָגֶל׃ 25 כְּוִיָּה תַּחַת
כְּוִיָּה פֶּצַע תַּחַת פָּצַע חַבּוּרָה תַּחַת
חַבּוּרָה׃ ס

band may exact from him, the payment to be
based on reckoning. 23But if other damage ensues, the penalty shall be life for life, 24eye for
eye, tooth for tooth, hand for hand, foot for foot,
25burn for burn, wound for wound, bruise for
bruise.

therefore, the most likely issue here is whether or not death ensues. Rabbinic tradition understands this as referring to the woman. The ancient Greek translation of the Bible, the Septuagint, takes it as damage to the fetus.

based on reckoning The husband makes a claim based on some standard set by the court, perhaps the age of the fetus.

Lex Talionis (vv. 23–25)

23. other damage Presumably the death of the mother, in which case the principle of "life for life" is invoked, not a monetary fine.

The principle of retaliation in kind for bodily injury—talion—was introduced by King Hammurabi of Babylonia (1792–1750 B.C.E.). Before this, monetary compensation was the penalty, because assault and battery were considered private wrongs to be settled between the families of the assailant and the victim. With the growth of urbanization and centralized government, physical violence became an issue of public welfare, and the state commenced to regulate the payments for various types of injuries. In a revolutionary development, Hammurabi categorized assault and battery as criminal conduct to be prosecuted by the state.

The talion principle (Latin: *lex talionis*) is based on the assumption that the guilty party should suffer precisely the same harm as the victim: Only one life for a life, only one eye for an eye, and so forth. The Babylonian laws, however, allowed physical retaliation and vicarious punishment, which were applied according to the social class of those involved. Although biblical law accepted the principle that assault and battery are public crimes, not simply private wrongs, the context of the surrounding laws makes it clear that the Torah prescribed monetary compensation rather than physical retaliation for bodily injury. It also insisted on equal justice for all citizens regardless of social class (including the slave; see vv. 20,26–27) and outlawed vicarious punishment.

---

23. penalty shall be life for life Other Near Eastern societies permitted the family of a murderer to accept a monetary settlement from the murderer; the Torah forbids it. "The guilt of a murderer is infinite because the murdered life is invaluable. By contrast, the Torah never requires the death penalty for crimes against property. In biblical law, life and property are incommensurable; taking of life cannot be made up for by any amount of property, nor can any property offense be considered as amounting to the value of a life" (M. Greenberg). From this passage the Sages derived the ruling that a fetus is not a full-fledged human being. The mother's life has precedence over the life of the fetus (M Oho. 7:6).

24. The passage concerning "an eye for an eye" is one of the best known, and most misunderstood, in the entire Bible. The Sages deduced that "an eye for an eye" does not mean that one lost an eye for injuring another's eye (one person's eye may be more valuable in his work than another's, and intentional maiming is not the same as accidental injury). Instead, one paid to the injured party the value of that eye in monetary compensation. Ibn Ezra endorses this interpretation: "If we do not trust the Sages' interpretation, we will be unable to understand the Torah's demands. Just as we received the written Torah from our ancestors, so did we receive its oral interpretation. The two are inseparable." Maimonides writes, "There never was any Rabbi, from the time of Moses . . . who ruled, based on 'an eye for an eye,' that he who blinds another should himself be blinded." In all likelihood, "an eye for an eye" is a graphic way of expressing the abstract idea that the punishment should not be too lenient ("a scolding for an eye") or too harsh ("a life for an eye") but should fit the crime and the circumstances.

26When a man strikes the eye of his slave, male
or female, and destroys it, he shall let him go
free on account of his eye. 27If he knocks out
the tooth of his slave, male or female, he shall
let him go free on account of his tooth.

28When an ox gores a man or a woman to
death, the ox shall be stoned and its flesh shall
not be eaten, but the owner of the ox is not to
be punished. 29If, however, that ox has been in
the habit of goring, and its owner, though
warned, has failed to guard it, and it kills a man
or a woman—the ox shall be stoned and its
owner, too, shall be put to death. 30If ransom
is laid upon him, he must pay whatever is laid
upon him to redeem his life. 31So, too, if it gores
a minor, male or female, [the owner] shall be
dealt with according to the same rule. 32But if
the ox gores a slave, male or female, he shall pay

26 וְכִֽי־יַכֶּ֨ה אִ֜ישׁ אֶת־עֵ֥ין עַבְדּ֛וֹ אֽוֹ־אֶת־
עֵ֥ין אֲמָת֖וֹ וְשִֽׁחֲתָ֑הּ לַֽחָפְשִׁ֥י יְשַׁלְּחֶ֖נּוּ תַּ֥חַת
עֵינֽוֹ׃ ס 27 וְאִם־שֵׁ֥ן עַבְדּ֛וֹ אֽוֹ־שֵׁ֥ן אֲמָת֖וֹ
יַפִּ֑יל לַֽחָפְשִׁ֥י יְשַׁלְּחֶ֖נּוּ תַּ֥חַת שִׁנּֽוֹ׃ פ
28 וְכִֽי־יִגַּ֨ח שׁ֥וֹר אֶת־אִ֛ישׁ א֥וֹ אֶת־אִשָּׁ֖ה
וָמֵ֑ת סָק֨וֹל יִסָּקֵ֜ל הַשּׁ֗וֹר וְלֹ֤א יֵאָכֵל֙ אֶת־
בְּשָׂר֔וֹ וּבַ֥עַל הַשּׁ֖וֹר נָקִֽי׃ 29 וְאִ֡ם שׁ֣וֹר נַגָּ֩ח
ה֨וּא מִתְּמֹ֜ל שִׁלְשֹׁ֗ם וְהוּעַ֤ד בִּבְעָלָיו֙ וְלֹ֣א
יִשְׁמְרֶ֔נּוּ וְהֵמִ֥ית אִ֖ישׁ א֣וֹ אִשָּׁ֑ה הַשּׁוֹר֙
יִסָּקֵ֔ל וְגַם־בְּעָלָ֖יו יוּמָֽת׃ 30 אִם־כֹּ֖פֶר יוּשַׁ֣ת
עָלָ֑יו וְנָתַן֙ פִּדְיֹ֣ן נַפְשׁ֔וֹ כְּכֹ֥ל אֲשֶׁר־יוּשַׁ֖ת
עָלָֽיו׃ 31 אוֹ־בֵ֥ן יִגָּ֖ח אוֹ־בַ֣ת יִגָּ֑ח כַּמִּשְׁפָּ֥ט
הַזֶּ֖ה יֵעָ֥שֶׂה לּֽוֹ׃ 32 אִם־עֶ֛בֶד יִגַּ֥ח הַשּׁ֖וֹר א֣וֹ

Injury by a Master to His Slave (vv. 26–27)

A master who causes his slave irreparable bodily injury is guilty of aggravated assault. He has robbed his slave of his humanity and dignity; for that the slave gains his or her freedom. This biblical law, like that of verses 20–21, has no parallel in other ancient Near Eastern legislation.

26. his slave This refers to a non-Israelite, according to the Sages, because an Israelite slave is to be treated like all other Israelites when injured by another, even his master.

26–27. eye . . . tooth Or any other of the chief external parts of the body.

THE HOMICIDAL BEAST (vv. 28–32)

This section contains three cases involving the attack of a beast—here, an ox—on human beings. They concern (a) the beast that has no previous record of viciousness, (b) the beast that has such a previous history and whose owner has been so informed, and (c) the beast that gores a slave.

28. the ox shall be stoned The killer ox is not destroyed solely because it is dangerous. This is clear from the fact that it is not destroyed when the victim is another ox and from the prescribed mode of its destruction, which is not ordinary slaughter but stoning. The ox was to be executed in the presence of the entire community, implying that the killing of a human being is a source of mass pollution and that the death of the ox served as a cleansing atonement.

not to be punished This is in contrast to the next case. Here there is no implicit negligence.

29. This is a case of either incompetence or criminal negligence. Because the owner has been warned that the animal is dangerous, he is culpable if it harms someone. Rabbinic tradition interprets the death penalty mentioned here to mean "death by the hand of Heaven," not by a human court.

30. ransom Num. 35:31 forbids the acceptance of ransom for the life of one found guilty of murder. This man, however, is not a murderer, strictly speaking, because he did not directly cause the homicide and did not have such intent; the sentence is, therefore, mitigated. Because no fine is stipulated, he must pay whatever is demanded.

whatever is laid upon him Presumably by the victim's family (cf. v. 22).

32. thirty shekels The evaluation, for purposes of vows, of a woman between the ages of 20 and 60 (Lev. 27:4). On the shekel, see Comment to Gen. 23:9.

HALAKHAH L'MA·ASEH

21:29. though warned This is one of the sources for rabbinic laws on negligence. The Mishnah states: "If I am responsible to care for something, I am the one who makes possible any injury it may do. . . . [Therefore] I must make restitution for that injury" (M BK 1:2).

אָמָה כֶּסֶף | שְׁלֹשִׁים שְׁקָלִים יִתֵּן לַאדֹנָיו
וְהַשּׁוֹר יִסָּקֵל׃ ס
33 וְכִֽי־יִפְתַּח אִישׁ בּוֹר אוֹ כִּֽי־יִכְרֶה אִישׁ
בֹּר וְלֹא יְכַסֶּנּוּ וְנָֽפַל־שָׁמָּה שּׁוֹר אוֹ חֲמוֹר׃
34 בַּעַל הַבּוֹר יְשַׁלֵּם כֶּסֶף יָשִׁיב לִבְעָלָיו
וְהַמֵּת יִֽהְיֶה־לּוֹ׃ ס
35 וְכִֽי־יִגֹּף שׁוֹר־אִישׁ אֶת־שׁוֹר רֵעֵהוּ וָמֵת
וּמָכְרוּ אֶת־הַשּׁוֹר הַחַי וְחָצוּ אֶת־כַּסְפּוֹ
וְגַם אֶת־הַמֵּת יֶחֱצוּן׃ 36 אוֹ נוֹדַע כִּי שׁוֹר
נַגָּח הוּא מִתְּמוֹל שִׁלְשֹׁם וְלֹא יִשְׁמְרֶנּוּ
בְּעָלָיו שַׁלֵּם יְשַׁלֵּם שׁוֹר תַּחַת הַשּׁוֹר
וְהַמֵּת יִֽהְיֶה־לּוֹ׃ ס
37 כִּי יִגְנֹב־אִישׁ שׁוֹר אוֹ־שֶׂה וּטְבָחוֹ אוֹ
מְכָרוֹ חֲמִשָּׁה בָקָר יְשַׁלֵּם תַּחַת הַשּׁוֹר
וְאַרְבַּע־צֹאן תַּחַת הַשֶּׂה׃ 1 אִם־
כב בַּמַּחְתֶּרֶת יִמָּצֵא הַגַּנָּב וְהֻכָּה

thirty shekels of silver to the master, and the ox shall be stoned.

33When a man opens a pit, or digs a pit and
does not cover it, and an ox or an ass falls into
it, 34the one responsible for the pit must make
restitution; he shall pay the price to the owner, but shall keep the dead animal.

35When a man's ox injures his neighbor's ox and it dies, they shall sell the live ox and divide its price; they shall also divide the dead animal.
36If, however, it is known that the ox was in the habit of goring, and its owner has failed to guard it, he must restore ox for ox, but shall keep the dead animal.

37When a man steals an ox or a sheep, and slaughters it or sells it, he shall pay five oxen for
22 the ox, and four sheep for the sheep.—
1If the thief is seized while tunneling, and he is beaten to death, there is no bloodguilt

DAMAGE TO LIVESTOCK (vv. 33–36)

33–34. The presumption is that the pit or cistern was located on public property or that there was unobstructed access to it from public property. For this act of negligence, the offender must make restitution for the value of the animal.

THE LAW OF THEFT (21:37–22:3)

The case of a thief who is surprised in the act of breaking and entering is injected parenthetically into the more general law dealing with theft, interrupting the connection between 21:37 and 22:2b. That is, 21:37 must be understood as followed immediately by 22:2b and 22:3.

37. This verse is numbered 22:1 in some other editions of the Bible.

22:1–2a. The condition "If the sun has risen" shows that the phrase "while tunneling" presupposes a nighttime setting. Because a nighttime burglar is likely to encounter the occupants and must anticipate that they will use force, his nocturnal intrusion carries with it a presumption of homicidal intent. The condition of imminent threat, necessary to satisfy a householder's claim

---

37. We are told that stealing an ox incurs greater punishment than stealing a sheep because a sheep is not a beast of burden. Meir states, "Physical labor is precious to the one who created the world" (Mekh.). The ox, a laboring animal, is more valuable. Similarly, a commentary on Rashi adds, "When one steals an ox, the Torah requires the thief to compensate the owner for time lost due to the ox's absence. This teaches that work is considered as important as money." Although the probable reason for the discrepancy is the greater value of the ox and the greater loss to its owner, the Sages of the Midrash offer another reason: A stolen ox can be led away but a stolen sheep must be carried, an unpleasant and humiliating task. This degrading experience lessens the thief's punishment. The Torah stresses the innate dignity of human beings, even of a robber; all humans are fashioned in God's image. Postbiblical laws limit the degree to which criminals can be punished, lest their essential humanity be compromised.

HALAKHAH L'MA·ASEH

22:1. no bloodguilt This verse is a source for justifying self-defense under Jewish law (BT Sanh. 72a) and the principle that saving a life takes precedence over most other Jewish laws (BT Yoma 85b). See Lev. 18:5.

in his case. [2]If the sun has risen on him, there is bloodguilt in that case.—He must make restitution; if he lacks the means, he shall be sold for his theft. [3]But if what he stole—whether ox or ass or sheep—is found alive in his possession, he shall pay double.

[4]When a man lets his livestock loose to graze in another's land, and so allows a field or a vineyard to be grazed bare, he must make restitution for the impairment of that field or vineyard.

[5]When a fire is started and spreads to thorns, so that stacked, standing, or growing grain is consumed, he who started the fire must make restitution.

[6]When a man gives money or goods to another for safekeeping, and they are stolen from

וָמֵ֥ת אֵ֖ין ל֥וֹ דָּמִֽים׃ 2 אִם־זָרְחָ֥ה הַשֶּׁ֛מֶשׁ
עָלָ֖יו דָּמִ֣ים ל֑וֹ שַׁלֵּ֣ם יְשַׁלֵּ֔ם אִם־אֵ֣ין ל֔וֹ
וְנִמְכַּ֖ר בִּגְנֵבָתֽוֹ׃ 3 אִֽם־הִמָּצֵא֩ תִמָּצֵ֨א בְיָד֜וֹ
הַגְּנֵבָ֗ה מִשּׁ֛וֹר עַד־חֲמ֥וֹר עַד־שֶׂ֖ה חַיִּ֑ים
שְׁנַ֖יִם יְשַׁלֵּֽם׃ ס
שלישי 4 כִּ֤י יַבְעֶר־אִישׁ֙ שָׂדֶ֣ה אוֹ־כֶ֔רֶם וְשִׁלַּח֙
אֶת־בעירה בְּעִיר֔וֹ וּבִעֵ֖ר בִּשְׂדֵ֣ה אַחֵ֑ר מֵיטַ֥ב
שָׂדֵ֛הוּ וּמֵיטַ֥ב כַּרְמ֖וֹ יְשַׁלֵּֽם׃ ס
5 כִּֽי־תֵצֵ֨א אֵ֜שׁ וּמָצְאָ֤ה קֹצִים֙ וְנֶאֱכַ֣ל גָּדִ֔ישׁ
א֥וֹ הַקָּמָ֖ה א֣וֹ הַשָּׂדֶ֑ה שַׁלֵּ֣ם יְשַׁלֵּ֔ם הַמַּבְעִ֖ר
אֶת־הַבְּעֵרָֽה׃ ס
6 כִּֽי־יִתֵּן֩ אִ֨ישׁ אֶל־רֵעֵ֜הוּ כֶּ֤סֶף אֽוֹ־כֵלִים֙
לִשְׁמֹ֔ר וְגֻנַּ֖ב מִבֵּ֣ית הָאִ֑ישׁ אִם־יִמָּצֵ֥א הַגַּנָּ֖ב

of lawful self-defense, is thus fulfilled. Hence, no bloodguilt is incurred should the intruder be killed.

If the break-in occurred in broad daylight, however, there is no presumption of imminent homicidal intent. The use of deadly force in such an instance, therefore, is deemed to be unwarranted, and bloodguilt would ensue upon its use. This is another example of the biblical scale of values, which gives priority to the protection of life—including even the life of a burglar—over property.

DAMAGE TO CROPS (vv. 4–5)

Two cases are under consideration: the destruction of crops by livestock and by fire. The first case is treated more severely—the cattle owner must compensate for the choice crops of the field because he carelessly, although without malicious intent, allowed his beast to stray into another's field. In the second case, restitution of choice produce is not required because the damage was wholly accidental. These two cases are wedged between laws relating to theft because all are viewed under the broad heading of damage to property.

4. for the impairment The Sages considered it unclear whether the compensation imposed on the owner of the beast is calculated according to the best property of the defendant or of the plaintiff.

5. When a fire is started For legitimate purposes, but winds send the flames into someone else's property.

thorns These would be collected and used as fuel by the poor and for the construction of hedges.

THE LAW OF BAILMENT (vv. 6–14)

Movable Goods (vv. 6–7)

A bailee (guardian) claims that movable goods entrusted to him for safekeeping have been stolen. If the thief is not caught, the bailee must clear himself of suspicion by taking an oath before the proper authorities. As a gratuitous bailee (one not paid for his services), he is not liable for loss or theft that does not result from his own negligence.

6. they are stolen So the bailee claims.

pay double In accordance with the rule of verse 3.

CHAPTER 22

2. If the sun has risen on him Ishmael takes the words figuratively, to mean "if it is clear as day" that the thief is only after your possessions and means no physical harm, he may be stopped but he may not be killed (Mekh.).

6. The Talmud elaborates on this brief discussion (BT BM 3), delineating four categories of bailees (guardians): (a) one who is paid to care for the owner's goods and, therefore, assumes the highest level of responsibility for their well-being; (b) one who agrees to care for the owner's goods as a favor and

the man's house—if the thief is caught, he shall pay double; [7] if the thief is not caught, the owner of the house shall depose before God that he has not laid hands on the other's property. [8] In all charges of misappropriation—pertaining to an ox, an ass, a sheep, a garment, or any other loss, whereof one party alleges, "This is it"—the case of both parties shall come before God: he whom God declares guilty shall pay double to the other.

[9] When a man gives to another an ass, an ox, a sheep or any other animal to guard, and it dies or is injured or is carried off, with no witness about, [10] an oath before the LORD shall decide between the two of them that the one has not laid hands on the property of the other; the owner must acquiesce, and no restitution shall be made. [11] But if [the animal] was stolen from him, he shall make restitution to its owner. [12] If it was torn by beasts, he shall bring it as evidence; he need not replace what has been torn by beasts.

[13] When a man borrows [an animal] from an-

יְשַׁלֵּם שְׁנָֽיִם: 7 אִם־לֹא יִמָּצֵא הַגַּנָּב וְנִקְרַב בַּֽעַל־הַבַּיִת אֶל־הָֽאֱלֹהִים אִם־לֹא שָׁלַח יָדוֹ בִּמְלֶאכֶת רֵעֵֽהוּ: 8 עַל־כָּל־דְּבַר־פֶּשַׁע עַל־שׁוֹר עַל־חֲמוֹר עַל־שֶׂה עַל־שַׂלְמָה עַל־כָּל־אֲבֵדָה אֲשֶׁר יֹאמַר כִּי־הוּא זֶה עַד הָֽאֱלֹהִים יָבֹא דְּבַר־שְׁנֵיהֶם אֲשֶׁר יַרְשִׁיעֻן אֱלֹהִים יְשַׁלֵּם שְׁנַיִם לְרֵעֵֽהוּ: ס

9 כִּי־יִתֵּן אִישׁ אֶל־רֵעֵהוּ חֲמוֹר אוֹ־שׁוֹר אוֹ־שֶׂה וְכָל־בְּהֵמָה לִשְׁמֹר וּמֵת אוֹ־נִשְׁבַּר אוֹ־נִשְׁבָּה אֵין רֹאֶה: 10 שְׁבֻעַת יְהֹוָה תִּֽהְיֶה בֵּין שְׁנֵיהֶם אִם־לֹא שָׁלַח יָדוֹ בִּמְלֶאכֶת רֵעֵהוּ וְלָקַח בְּעָלָיו וְלֹא יְשַׁלֵּם: 11 וְאִם־גָּנֹב יִגָּנֵב מֵֽעִמּוֹ יְשַׁלֵּם לִבְעָלָֽיו: 12 אִם־טָרֹף יִטָּרֵף יְבִאֵהוּ עֵד הַטְּרֵפָה לֹא יְשַׁלֵּֽם: פ

13 וְכִֽי־יִשְׁאַל אִישׁ מֵעִם רֵעֵהוּ וְנִשְׁבַּר

---

7. laid hands on That is, misappropriated. If he made use of the deposit for his own benefit, he has become a paid bailee and thus liable for theft or loss.

property Money and goods.

Wrongful Use of Another's Property (v. 8)

8. This is it The plaintiff claims to identify his property.

whom God declares guilty The word translated as "God" (*elohim*) traditionally is interpreted here as "judges." Elohim meaning "God" takes a singular verb, and the verb used here is plural (see Comment to 21:6).

shall pay double The livestock or movable property has remained intact in the possession of the guilty party, so the rule of 22:3 applies.

Livestock (vv. 9–12)

Unlike the case of "money or goods," safeguarding animals is complicated because they are out in the fields and require a lot of attention and labor. It may be assumed, therefore, that the bailee of livestock is paid for his services. This increases the degree of responsibility that is expected of him.

9. carried off This is a case of cattle rustling, not the same as ordinary theft mentioned in verse 11.

10. between the two of them It is uncertain whether both parties have to swear.

12. he shall bring it as evidence He needs to present at least some part of the torn animal as evidence against the charge of negligence (cf. Gen. 37:32–33).

Borrowing and Hiring (vv. 13–14)

The act of borrowing falls within the category of bailment. Because the use of the object is obtained gratis, entirely for the borrower's benefit, his or

---

is expected only to provide reasonable care; (c) one who borrows the owner's goods and assumes a fairly high degree of care; and (d) one who pays for the use of another's goods and, therefore, assumes a relatively low level of responsibility.

אוֹ־מֵ֑ת בְּעָלָ֥יו אֵין־עִמּ֖וֹ שַׁלֵּ֥ם יְשַׁלֵּֽם׃
14 אִם־בְּעָלָ֥יו עִמּ֖וֹ לֹ֣א יְשַׁלֵּ֑ם אִם־שָׂכִ֣יר
ה֔וּא בָּ֖א בִּשְׂכָרֽוֹ׃ ס
15 וְכִֽי־יְפַתֶּ֣ה אִ֗ישׁ בְּתוּלָ֛ה אֲשֶׁ֥ר לֹא־
אֹרָ֖שָׂה וְשָׁכַ֣ב עִמָּ֑הּ מָהֹ֛ר יִמְהָרֶ֥נָּה לּ֖וֹ
לְאִשָּֽׁה׃ 16 אִם־מָאֵ֥ן יְמָאֵ֛ן אָבִ֖יהָ לְתִתָּ֣הּ
ל֑וֹ כֶּ֣סֶף יִשְׁקֹ֔ל כְּמֹ֖הַר הַבְּתוּלֹֽת׃ ס
17 מְכַשֵּׁפָ֖ה לֹ֥א תְחַיֶּֽה׃ ס

other and it dies or is injured, its owner not being with it, he must make restitution. [14]If its owner was with it, no restitution need be made; but if it was hired, he is entitled to the hire.

[15]If a man seduces a virgin for whom the bride-price has not been paid, and lies with her, he must make her his wife by payment of a bride-price. [16]If her father refuses to give her to him, he must still weigh out silver in accordance with the bride-price for virgins.

[17]You shall not tolerate a sorceress.

her degree of responsibility and liability exceeds that in the previous cases.

13. borrows The verb here (*yish·al*) has no object. The theme of verses 9–12 and the phrase "it dies or is injured" make it certain that an animal, most likely a work animal, is meant.

14. If its owner was with it This provision may assume that the services of the owner were borrowed together with his animal.

he is entitled to the hire The owner who hired out his animal—which then suffered misfortune—is not compensated for the animal but is entitled to receive only the hiring fee.

THE LAW OF SEDUCTION (vv. 15–16)

The Book of the Covenant does not regulate the laws of marriage. Long established by custom among the Israelites, they were transmitted orally over the generations.

A man has seduced an unattached virgin. Ordinarily, her father would receive the bride-price customarily paid by the husband-to-be in compensation for the loss of the daughter's services and her potential value to the family. But the bride-price was predicated on the woman's virginity, considered essential to her family's honor. The deflowering of the girl caused a loss of social status for her whole family so that they could no longer require a good bride-price. Consequently, the seducer had to make good the lost sum, regardless of whether the father permitted him to marry his daughter.

15. seduces By persuasion or deception, but not by coercion. For the law of rape, see Deut. 22:22–29.

bride-price has not been paid Literally, "she was not betrothed." Biblical marriage comprised two separate stages. First, the girl's hand was asked in marriage. Once the bride-price was paid, the girl was considered betrothed (*m'orasah*) and had the legal status of a married woman even though she still was entirely under the care and authority of her father. Somewhat later she was escorted to her husband's home to take up residence there.

16. bride-price for virgins The amount is not specified, no doubt because the existing practice was well known.

CATEGORICAL COMMANDS
(22:17–23:19)

The second section of The Book of the Covenant now begins. It comprises a miscellany of social, ethical, moral and religious stipulations that fall under the rubric of divine commands, *d'varim.* These are formulated in the categorical style ("You shall not . . . ") characteristic of the Decalogue, not in the hypothetical style ("If . . . ") of the preceding laws. Many of these matters are of the sort that do not come within the scope of a court of law. Their enforcement is left to human conscience, to one fully aware that these laws are imposed by a transcendent divine will and are not merely the product of human experience and wisdom.

---

15. The Torah views seduction as a form of theft, connecting this verse to the preceding verses (v. 6ff.). The Sages refer to the sin of "stealing someone's opinion" (*g'neivat da·at*) by misleading a person with false information or false impressions.

16. The verb "refuses" is doubled in the Hebrew (*ma·en y'ma·en*). According to the Talmud, this teaches us that the young woman as well as the father may reject the match. (See Rashi on Gen. 24:57, concerning Rebecca's prospective marriage to Isaac.)

17. The literal translation, "You shall not let a witch (or a sorceress) live," was the basis

18 Whoever lies with a beast shall be put to death.
19 Whoever sacrifices to a god other than the LORD alone shall be proscribed.
20 You shall not wrong a stranger or oppress him, for you were strangers in the land of Egypt.

18 כָּל־שֹׁכֵ֥ב עִם־בְּהֵמָ֖ה מ֥וֹת יוּמָֽת׃ ס
19 זֹבֵ֥חַ לָאֱלֹהִ֖ים יָֽחֳרָ֑ם בִּלְתִּ֥י לַיהֹוָ֖ה
לְבַדּֽוֹ׃
20 וְגֵ֥ר לֹא־תוֹנֶ֖ה וְלֹ֣א תִלְחָצֶ֑נּוּ כִּֽי־גֵרִ֥ים
הֱיִיתֶ֖ם בְּאֶ֥רֶץ מִצְרָֽיִם׃

THE PROHIBITION OF SORCERY (v. 17)

The belief in and practice of magic was universal in the ancient world. Elaborate techniques were developed to activate and manipulate natural and supernatural forces. Biblical religion fought to eliminate such practices.

17. You shall not tolerate a sorceress Literally, "You shall not let a sorceress live." The same penalty certainly applies to a male practitioner. The feminine specification here probably reflects the historical reality that most of those who practiced this outlawed cult were women. Apparently, sorcery was a body of knowledge preserved in female circles, as certain types of priestly lore were maintained by males.

THE PROHIBITION OF BESTIALITY (v. 18)

18. This particular perversion is also prohibited in Lev. 18:23 and 20:15–16, where it is presented as one of the abominations of the pre-Israelite inhabitants of Canaan. Possibly, the biblical allusions are aimed at otherwise unrecorded official or popular practices.

THE PROHIBITION OF APOSTASY (v. 19)

19. To a god Literally, "to the gods"—of other nations.

proscribed The Hebrew verb חרם literally means "shall be devoted to God." Here it implies total annihilation and includes the destruction of the person and his or her property.

CONCERN FOR THE DISADVANTAGED OF SOCIETY (vv. 20–26)

The law, which addresses people in the singular and in the plural, recognizes that the individual and society are equally responsible and accountable for the terms of the covenantal relationship between God and the people Israel. Social evil is thus a sin against both humanity and God.

The Stranger (v. 20)

The Hebrew word *ger* (stranger, alien) denotes a foreign-born permanent resident whose status was intermediate between that of the native-born citizen (*ezraḥ*) and the foreigner temporarily residing outside the community (*nokhri*). Because the *ger* could not fall back on local family and clan ties, he or she could easily fall victim to discrimination and exploitation.

In addition to the numerous biblical prohibitions against the mistreatment of strangers, there are commands to love them, even as God does (cf. Deut. 10:18–19). That includes caring for their basic needs and extending to them the same social services to which disadvantaged Israelites were entitled. Over time, many strangers wishing to become part of the people Israel began to take on themselves the obligations and duties of the covenantal society. Hence, in postbiblical Hebrew the term *ger* (feminine *giyyoret*) came to be synonymous with "proselyte."

20. wrong . . . oppress The employment

---

for executing innocent women in 17th-century Salem, Massachusetts, and elsewhere in the Western world. A commentator suggests that we understand the text to mean: "you shall not provide a witch with a livelihood," i.e., we are to drive her out of the practice of witchcraft without taking her life.

20. The Sages, connecting this verse to the preceding verse, forbid belittling sincere converts by reminding them of their idol-worshiping days. The Talmud points out that the Torah cautions us 36 times about proper behavior toward a stranger (BT BM 59b). Similarly, as the Israelites were asked to recall what it felt like to be aliens in Egypt (even in later times, when these were ancestral memories, not something that actually had happened to them), they are asked in verse 23 to imagine what it would feel like to be a widow or an orphan. We are to treat aliens, widows, orphans, and other marginal members of society as we would want to be treated in similar circumstances. The decency of a society is measured by how it cares for its least powerful members.

21 כָּל־אַלְמָנָ֥ה וְיָת֖וֹם לֹ֥א תְעַנּֽוּן׃ 22 אִם־
עַנֵּ֥ה תְעַנֶּ֖ה אֹת֑וֹ כִּ֣י אִם־צָעֹ֤ק יִצְעַק֙ אֵלַ֔י
שָׁמֹ֥עַ אֶשְׁמַ֖ע צַעֲקָתֽוֹ׃ 23 וְחָרָ֣ה אַפִּ֔י
וְהָרַגְתִּ֥י אֶתְכֶ֖ם בֶּחָ֑רֶב וְהָי֤וּ נְשֵׁיכֶם֙
אַלְמָנ֔וֹת וּבְנֵיכֶ֖ם יְתֹמִֽים׃ פ
24 אִם־כֶּ֣סֶף ׀ תַּלְוֶ֣ה אֶת־עַמִּ֗י אֶת־הֶֽעָנִי֙
עִמָּ֔ךְ לֹא־תִהְיֶ֥ה ל֖וֹ כְּנֹשֶׁ֑ה לֹֽא־תְשִׂימ֥וּן
עָלָ֖יו נֶֽשֶׁךְ׃ 25 אִם־חָבֹ֥ל תַּחְבֹּ֖ל שַׂלְמַ֣ת
רֵעֶ֑ךָ עַד־בֹּ֥א הַשֶּׁ֖מֶשׁ תְּשִׁיבֶ֥נּוּ לֽוֹ׃ 26 כִּ֣י
הִ֤וא כסותה כְסוּתוֹ֙ לְבַדָּ֔הּ הִ֥וא שִׂמְלָת֖וֹ

21 You shall not ill-treat any widow or orphan.
22 If you do mistreat them, I will heed their outcry as soon as they cry out to Me, 23 and My anger
shall blaze forth and I will put you to the sword,
and your own wives shall become widows and
your children orphans.

24 If you lend money to My people, to the poor
among you, do not act toward them as a creditor; exact no interest from them. 25 If you take
your neighbor's garment in pledge, you must
return it to him before the sun sets; 26 it is his
only clothing, the sole covering for his skin. In

of two verbs here heightens the strictness of the prohibition.

The Widow and the Orphan (vv. 21–23)

21. widow or orphan God watches out for the widow, the orphan, and the stranger because they have no property of their own and there is no one to look after them (cf. Deut. 14:29, 27:19, Ps. 68:6).

23. the sword That is, in warfare. Social injustice leads to social disaster.

The Poor and Loans (vv. 24–26)

These laws, aimed at protecting the poor from exploitation, are the first of several such examples in the Torah that regulate loans and forbid the taking of interest. The others are Lev. 25:35–38 and Deut. 23:20–21, 24:10–13. In all the ancient Near East, only biblical law imposes an absolute ban on lending with interest to members of one's own society.

24. If you lend No penalties are specified for not lending.

to My people See Deut. 23:20–21, which permits taking interest on loans made to a "foreigner" (*nokhri*).

act . . . as a creditor That is, harass the borrower.

25. garment Hebrew: *salmah* (also *simlah*); a large piece of cloth wrapped around the body. For the poor it also served as a blanket at night and might have been such a person's only possession.

in pledge Although the exaction of interest is prohibited, taking a pledge to secure repayment of a loan is permitted.

---

24. My people Among human beings, the rich and powerful are embarrassed by their poor relatives. God is not embarrassed to call the poor "My people" (Exod. R. 31:5).

to the poor among you "The poor among your relatives take precedence over other poor; the poor of your town over the poor of other towns" (Tanḥ.; S.A. YD 251:3). For all of our universalistic commitment, we must take care of our own first. Indeed, by practicing fair treatment on those closest to us (which may be harder than extending fair treatment to those far off), we form a habit that we can then extend to strangers.

HALAKHAH L'MA·ASEH

22:24. exact no interest Cf. also Lev. 25:36; Deut. 23:20. Because most business assumes the acceptability of charging interest, the Sages instituted the *heter iska* (permission to do business), which treats such commercial transactions as partnerships, thereby making both parties subject to both profit and loss and transforming prohibited interest into the permitted form of added capital value (BT BM 104b). In addition, it is a *mitzvah* to lend to the poor without interest (Lev. 25:36).

22:25. you must return it to him Based on Exod. 22:20,25–6 (and verses in Lev. 25 and Deut. 15), Jewish law requires care for the poor and homeless.

what else shall he sleep? Therefore, if he cries out to Me, I will pay heed, for I am compassionate.

27You shall not revile God, nor put a curse upon a chieftain among your people.

28You shall not put off the skimming of the first yield of your vats. You shall give Me the first-born among your sons. 29You shall do the same with your cattle and your flocks: seven days it shall remain with its mother; on the eighth day you shall give it to Me.

30You shall be holy people to Me: you must not eat flesh torn by beasts in the field; you shall cast it to the dogs.

לְעֹרוֹ בַּמֶּה יִשְׁכָּב וְהָיָה כִּי־יִצְעַק אֵלַי
וְשָׁמַעְתִּי כִּי־חַנּוּן אָנִי׃ ס
רביעי 27 *אֱלֹהִים לֹא תְקַלֵּל וְנָשִׂיא בְעַמְּךָ לֹא
תָאֹר׃
28 מְלֵאָתְךָ וְדִמְעֲךָ לֹא תְאַחֵר בְּכוֹר בָּנֶיךָ
תִּתֶּן־לִּי׃ 29 כֵּן־תַּעֲשֶׂה לְשֹׁרְךָ לְצֹאנֶךָ
שִׁבְעַת יָמִים יִהְיֶה עִם־אִמּוֹ בַּיּוֹם הַשְּׁמִינִי
תִּתְּנוֹ־לִי׃
30 וְאַנְשֵׁי־קֹדֶשׁ תִּהְיוּן לִי וּבָשָׂר בַּשָּׂדֶה
טְרֵפָה לֹא תֹאכֵלוּ לַכֶּלֶב תַּשְׁלִכוּן
אֹתוֹ׃ ס

23 You must not carry false rumors; you

כג לֹא תִשָּׂא שֵׁמַע שָׁוְא אַל־תָּשֶׁת

v. 27. למערבאי חצי הספר בפסוקים

DUTIES TO GOD (vv. 27–30)

The characterization of God in verse 26 is followed by laws that regulate the proper attitude toward Him.

27. not revile God The judicial issue involved in reviling God is mentioned in Lev. 24:10–23, where the penalty is death by stoning.

chieftain Hebrew: *nasi;* the title given to the chief of a clan or a tribe in the period before the monarchy.

28. you shall give Me the first-born This may be an archaic legal formula from pre-Israelite times, understood among the Israelites to mean that the firstborn had special status in the performance of sacred duties (cf. Num. 8:16–19).

29. You shall do the same That is, dedicate the firstborn animals for sacred purposes.

seven days The dedication of the first fruits of the soil is not to be delayed. For the firstborn of animals, however, there is a minimum waiting period of seven days.

30. holy people This is the ideal that was set forth at Sinai (19:6). In pursuit of holiness, one must—among other things—avoid polluting substances and defiling actions, for these disrupt the relationship with God. Adherence to dietary laws (*kashrut*) as an essential element of holy living is found in Lev. 11:44–45 and Deut. 14:21, where a different motivation is presented.

JUDICIAL INTEGRITY (23:1–3)

1. The first clause addresses the litigants; the witnesses; and by implication, the judge. Giving unsubstantiated hearsay testimony in judicial proceedings is prohibited; such testimony is in-

---

27. You shall not revile God Akiva understands the words as prohibiting blasphemy against God. Ishmael takes them to refer to judges (as in Exod. 21:6). The rich and powerful are not to curse a judicial system that prevents them from exploiting the poor.

30. You shall be holy people to Me "Be holy in a human way, be holy while dealing with the temptations of normal people. God already has enough angels" (Menaḥem Mendel of Kotzk). The distinguishing mark of the holy person, unlike the animal, is the ability to control appetite.

CHAPTER 23

1. You must not carry A *midrash* interprets this to prohibit receiving as well as spreading false and damaging rumors. Even to listen to such a rumor is to participate in its circulation and thereby participate in hurting another human being.

false rumors The literal meaning of this

shall not join hands with the guilty to act as a
malicious witness: 2You shall neither side with
the mighty to do wrong—you shall not give perverse testimony in a dispute so as to pervert it
in favor of the mighty —3nor shall you show
deference to a poor man in his dispute.

4When you encounter your enemy's ox or ass
wandering, you must take it back to him.

5When you see the ass of your enemy lying

יָדְךָ֙ עִם־רָשָׁ֔ע לִהְיֹ֖ת עֵ֥ד חָמָֽס׃ ס 2 לֹֽא־
תִהְיֶ֥ה אַחֲרֵֽי־רַבִּ֖ים לְרָעֹ֑ת וְלֹא־תַעֲנֶ֣ה
עַל־רִ֗ב לִנְטֹ֛ת אַחֲרֵ֥י רַבִּ֖ים לְהַטֹּֽת׃ 3 וְדָ֕ל
לֹ֥א תֶהְדַּ֖ר בְּרִיבֽוֹ׃ ס

4 כִּ֣י תִפְגַּ֞ע שׁ֧וֹר אֹֽיִבְךָ֛ א֥וֹ חֲמֹר֖וֹ תֹּעֶ֑ה
הָשֵׁ֥ב תְּשִׁיבֶ֖נּוּ לֽוֹ׃ ס

5 כִּֽי־תִרְאֶ֞ה חֲמ֣וֹר שֹׂנַאֲךָ֗ רֹבֵץ֙ תַּ֣חַת

admissible. The second clause outlaws the collusion of a witness and one of the involved parties for a deceitful purpose.

2. Some have taken this to mean that in the interest of impartial justice, no consideration should be given to the social standing of the litigants. More likely, it expresses a warning not to pervert justice by deferring to the majority view if one is convinced that it is erroneous.

3. This verse forbids showing favor to the poor in a court of law. After so many directives to support and care for the poor, the Torah is concerned lest judges distort the law in a poor person's favor.

HUMANE TREATMENT OF THE ENEMY
(vv. 4–5)

4. This verse enjoins us to help our enemy and teaches that just behavior should not be distorted by either love or hate.

5. This case involves humanitarian considerations and the prevention of cruelty to animals. The latter, an important biblical and Rabbinic principle, is known in Hebrew as "[prevention of] pain to living things," *tza·ar ba·alei ḥayyim* (see BT BM 32a–b).

---

phrase in Hebrew (*sheima shav*) is "worthless utterance." One *midrash* understands it as referring to the utterance of rote prayers without proper feeling.

3. The Talmud presents the case of a judge who is tempted to say, "The poor claimant has no case, but he needs the money more than the rich defendant does." He is forbidden to rule in the poor person's favor for that reason. Instead, he is told to find for the rich defendant as the law requires and help the poor out of his own pocket (BT Ḥul. 134a). The Sages fear that if nonlegal considerations are permitted to distort legal judgments, people will lose faith in the fairness of the courts, and the poor will suffer more from that loss of faith. "The first requirement to a civilization is Justice, the assurance that a law once made will not be broken in favor of an individual" (S. Freud).

4–5. The Torah commands us neither to love nor to hate our enemy. Generally, the Torah commands behavior, not feelings. Its goal is justice, which is attainable—as opposed to loving everyone, which is an emotion-based attitude that cannot be commanded. We are to avoid malicious acts and treat everyone decently.

HALAKHAH L'MA·ASEH

23:1. rumors Jewish law prohibits three kinds of speech: *sheker* "falsehoods" (Exod. 23:7); *l'shon ha-ra* (literally, evil language, or slander), that is, negative truths about a person communicated to those who have no practical need to know of the person's weakness; and *r'khilut,* "gossip, rumors," that is, truths about a person that are not defamatory but are communicated to those who have no need to know the information (MT Ethics [*De·ot*] 7:1–3). See Lev. 19:16.

23:2. with the mighty Translating *rabbim* here as "majority," the Sages of the *Sanhedrin* and of all subsequent courts have determined legal matters by a majority vote of the judges on the court (BT Sanh. 3b).

23:3. nor . . . show deference See Comment on Deut. 1:17.

under its burden and would refrain from raising it, you must nevertheless raise it with him.

⁶You shall not subvert the rights of your needy in their disputes. ⁷Keep far from a false charge; do not bring death on those who are innocent and in the right, for I will not acquit the wrongdoer. ⁸Do not take bribes, for bribes blind the clear-sighted and upset the pleas of those who are in the right.

⁹You shall not oppress a stranger, for you know the feelings of the stranger, having yourselves been strangers in the land of Egypt.

¹⁰Six years you shall sow your land and gather in its yield; ¹¹but in the seventh you shall let it rest and lie fallow. Let the needy among your people eat of it, and what they leave let the wild beasts eat. You shall do the same with your vineyards and your olive groves.

מַשָּׂא֥וֹ וְחָדַלְתָּ֖ מֵעֲזֹ֣ב ל֑וֹ עָזֹ֥ב תַּֽעֲזֹ֖ב עִמּֽוֹ: ס

חמישי ⁶ לֹ֥א תַטֶּ֛ה מִשְׁפַּ֥ט אֶבְיֹֽנְךָ֖ בְּרִיבֽוֹ: ⁷ מִדְּבַר־שֶׁ֖קֶר תִּרְחָ֑ק וְנָקִ֤י וְצַדִּיק֙ אַל־תַּהֲרֹ֔ג כִּ֥י לֹֽא־אַצְדִּ֖יק רָשָֽׁע: ⁸ וְשֹׁ֖חַד לֹ֣א תִקָּ֑ח כִּ֤י הַשֹּׁ֙חַד֙ יְעַוֵּ֣ר פִּקְחִ֔ים וִֽיסַלֵּ֖ף דִּבְרֵ֥י צַדִּיקִֽים: ⁹ וְגֵ֖ר לֹ֣א תִלְחָ֑ץ וְאַתֶּ֗ם יְדַעְתֶּם֙ אֶת־נֶ֣פֶשׁ הַגֵּ֔ר כִּֽי־גֵרִ֥ים הֱיִיתֶ֖ם בְּאֶ֥רֶץ מִצְרָֽיִם: ¹⁰ וְשֵׁ֥שׁ שָׁנִ֖ים תִּזְרַ֣ע אֶת־אַרְצֶ֑ךָ וְאָסַפְתָּ֖ אֶת־תְּבֽוּאָתָֽהּ: ¹¹ וְהַשְּׁבִיעִ֗ת תִּשְׁמְטֶ֣נָּה וּנְטַשְׁתָּ֗הּ וְאָֽכְלוּ֙ אֶבְיֹנֵ֣י עַמֶּ֔ךָ וְיִתְרָ֕ם תֹּאכַ֖ל חַיַּ֣ת הַשָּׂדֶ֑ה כֵּֽן־תַּעֲשֶׂ֥ה לְכַרְמְךָ֖ לְזֵיתֶֽךָ:

A SERIES OF MISCELLANEOUS LAWS
(vv. 6–9)

6. your needy Those who depend on you for justice.

7. Keep far from a false charge A judge should have nothing to do with a claim he knows to be fraudulent.

do not bring death The final clause affirms that God will punish the guilty, including judges who act wickedly. Note the Hebrew wordplay of *"tzaddik"* and *"rasha."* The first means both "innocent" and "righteous"; the last means both "guilty" and "wicked."

8. Corruption of the judicial process by bribery is frequently mentioned in the Bible. It is emphasized that God "shows no favor and takes no bribe." A person who takes bribes is included in

the list of those who are under a divine curse. A judge who accepts a bribe is subject to the penalty of flogging.

9. The law concerning strangers in 22:20 is directed to the individual Israelite; this law is directed to judges. In verse 8 the perversion of justice resulted from familiarity between litigant and judge; here it issues from estrangement.

THE AGRICULTURAL PRESCRIPTIONS
(vv. 10–13a)

10–11. Concern for the unfortunates of society links these verses with the topic of verses 6–9 and 12–13.

let it rest and lie fallow Note the concern for wildlife as well as for the poor.

---

7. Only here does the Torah go beyond prohibiting an act and command us to distance ourselves from it. The Sages go to great lengths to explore the ways in which falsehood can infiltrate our thinking.

9. having yourselves been strangers Nathan deduced from this that we must not reproach another with our own faults (Mekh.).

11. The land of Israel is seen as different from other lands. It is a sacred space, the ap-

---

HALAKHAH L'MA·ASEH

23:5. of your enemy Noting that the parallel provision in Deut. 22:4 speaks of the fallen animal of one's friend, the Sages required that one tend first to the animal of one's enemy so as "to subdue one's evil inclination" (BT BM 32b).

23:7. Keep far from a false charge See *Halakhah l'Ma·aseh* on Exod. 23:1; Lev. 19:36.

[12]Six days you shall do your work, but on the seventh day you shall cease from labor, in order that your ox and your ass may rest, and that your bondman and the stranger may be refreshed.

[13]Be on guard concerning all that I have told you. Make no mention of the names of other gods; they shall not be heard on your lips.

[14]Three times a year you shall hold a festival for Me: [15]You shall observe the Feast of Unleavened Bread—eating unleavened bread for seven days as I have commanded you—at the set time in the month of Abib, for in it you went forth from Egypt; and none shall appear before

12 שֵׁשֶׁת יָמִים תַּעֲשֶׂה מַעֲשֶׂיךָ וּבַיּוֹם
הַשְּׁבִיעִי תִּשְׁבֹּת לְמַעַן יָנוּחַ שׁוֹרְךָ וַחֲמֹרֶךָ
וְיִנָּפֵשׁ בֶּן־אֲמָתְךָ וְהַגֵּר׃
13 וּבְכֹל אֲשֶׁר־אָמַרְתִּי אֲלֵיכֶם תִּשָּׁמֵרוּ
וְשֵׁם אֱלֹהִים אֲחֵרִים לֹא תַזְכִּירוּ לֹא
יִשָּׁמַע עַל־פִּיךָ׃
14 שָׁלֹשׁ רְגָלִים תָּחֹג לִי בַּשָּׁנָה׃ 15 אֶת־חַג
הַמַּצּוֹת תִּשְׁמֹר שִׁבְעַת יָמִים תֹּאכַל
מַצּוֹת כַּאֲשֶׁר צִוִּיתִךָ לְמוֹעֵד חֹדֶשׁ הָאָבִיב
כִּי־בוֹ יָצָאתָ מִמִּצְרָיִם וְלֹא־יֵרָאוּ פָנַי

12. in order that . . . may rest This expands on the motivation expressed in the commandment concerning *Shabbat* in 20:10.

OBLIGATIONS TO GOD (vv. 13b–19)

13. The first clause closes the preceding legislation, which concentrates on human relationships. The second clause opens the final section of the Book of the Covenant, focusing on obligations to God. The prohibition against mentioning the names of pagan gods is relevant because the rest of the section deals with celebrations of the seasonal cycle. The Israelites and their neighbors had seasonal festivals celebrating harvests at the same time of the year. This section thus begins by prohibiting the mention of names of gods, to emphasize that Israel's festivals must be devoted to Israel's God alone. Note the emphatic "festival for Me" in the next verse, meaning "for Me exclusively."

The Religious Calendar (vv. 14–17)

These verses present the three agricultural festivals that form the core of Israel's sacred calendar. *Rosh ha-Shanah, Yom Kippur,* and the *Pesaḥ* sacrifice do not appear here because they are not rooted in the life of the soil. Israel's festivals are distinctive in being both celebrations of history and acknowledgments of God's bounty. Thus, for example, the commemoration of the Exodus is interwoven with agricultural elements. Each festival is called *ḥag,* a term that indicates that the festival involves an obligatory pilgrimage to a sanctuary. The same meaning endures in the Muslim institution of the *haj,* the religious duty to make a pilgrimage to Mecca. The sequence of festivals listed here conforms to the rule of 12:2 that the religious year begins with the spring.

14. Three times Hebrew: *shalosh r'galim,* synonymous with *"shalosh p'amim"* in verse 17. In postbiblical Hebrew, *"shalosh r'galim"* began to signify the three pilgrimage festivals. The singular of *r'galim* is *regel,* literally "foot"; it became interchangeable with *ḥag,* "festival," and came to be used for a pilgrimage in general.

for Me Exclusively.

15. Feast of Unleavened Bread That is, the beginning of the barley harvest. *Pesaḥ* day, with the offering of the paschal lamb on the eve of the fourteenth of the month, is not mentioned here because it was not originally celebrated as an agricultural festival.

as I have commanded you In Exod. 12:14–20.

Abib Literally, "barley ear." It was renamed Nisan in postexilic times.

you went forth The agricultural festival is invested with historical significance.

---

propriate place for a special people to lead a special way of life. Just as a sacred people deserves a *Shabbat,* so does this consecrated Land. Other places on earth may tolerate depraved behavior, but the Land of Israel will spew out people who behave immorally within its boundaries.

HALAKHAH L'MA·ASEH

23:12. ox . . . and the stranger may be refreshed One is obligated to make sure that one's family, workers, and animals can also refrain from work on *Shabbat* (see also Exod. 20:10).

Me empty-handed; [16]and the Feast of the Harvest, of the first fruits of your work, of what you sow in the field; and the Feast of Ingathering at the end of the year, when you gather in the results of your work from the field. [17]Three times a year all your males shall appear before the Sovereign, the LORD.

[18]You shall not offer the blood of My sacrifice with anything leavened; and the fat of My festal offering shall not be left lying until morning.

[19]The choice first fruits of your soil you shall bring to the house of the LORD your God.

You shall not boil a kid in its mother's milk.

[20]I am sending an angel before you to guard you on the way and to bring you to the place

רֵיקָם׃ 16 וְחַג הַקָּצִיר בִּכּוּרֵי מַעֲשֶׂיךָ אֲשֶׁר
תִּזְרַע בַּשָּׂדֶה וְחַג הָאָסִף בְּצֵאת הַשָּׁנָה
בְּאָסְפְּךָ אֶת־מַעֲשֶׂיךָ מִן־הַשָּׂדֶה׃ 17 שָׁלֹשׁ
פְּעָמִים בַּשָּׁנָה יֵרָאֶה כָּל־זְכוּרְךָ אֶל־פְּנֵי
הָאָדֹן ׀ יְהוָה׃
18 לֹא־תִזְבַּח עַל־חָמֵץ דַּם־זִבְחִי וְלֹא־יָלִין
חֵלֶב־חַגִּי עַד־בֹּקֶר׃
19 רֵאשִׁית בִּכּוּרֵי אַדְמָתְךָ תָּבִיא בֵּית
יְהוָה אֱלֹהֶיךָ
לֹא־תְבַשֵּׁל גְּדִי בַּחֲלֵב אִמּוֹ׃ ס
ששי 20 הִנֵּה אָנֹכִי שֹׁלֵחַ מַלְאָךְ לְפָנֶיךָ לִשְׁמָרְךָ
בַּדָּרֶךְ וְלַהֲבִיאֲךָ אֶל־הַמָּקוֹם אֲשֶׁר

empty-handed Without bringing the appropriate offerings.

16. Feast of the Harvest This is better known as "Feast of Weeks," *Shavuot.*

According to Lev. 23:15–16, it falls on "the day after the seventh week—fifty days" from "the day after the sabbath" of *Pesaḥ* (which is interpreted by the Sages as the first day of *Pesaḥ*).

Feast of Ingathering Also known as *Sukkot.* The name here derives from the harvest and thanksgiving character of the festival—the celebration of the final ingathering of the yield of the fields and orchards and its storage in barns before the onset of the rainy season.

at the end of the year At the close of the agricultural year.

17. all your males The passages in Deuteronomy (16:11,14) that include women and children among those who are to appear "before the LORD" represent a later practice.

Sovereign The word translated as "Sovereign" (*adon*) literally means "master" and often was used as a royal title. It is applied to God as sovereign of the universe to whom all Creation is subordinate and to whom all owe homage.

19. a kid in its mother's milk This rule is stated twice more in the Torah (Exod. 34:26 and Deut. 14:21). In Deuteronomy, the prohibition appears in the context of the dietary laws, but the two sources in Exodus indicate that its origin lies in the overall context of the festivals. Many scholars, medieval and modern, follow the suggestion of Maimonides that this law prohibits a pagan rite, although no such rite is known.

RENEWAL OF THE DIVINE PROMISES
(vv. 20–33)

20. an angel See Comment to 3:2.

place that I have made ready Apparently, a reference to the land of Canaan.

---

19. a kid in its mother's milk Consistent with its view that eating meat is a compromise (see Gen. 9:3–5), the Torah forbids eating the flesh of the animal together with the milk that was meant to sustain it.

20. I am sending an angel before you That is, know that your journey is divinely guided. That knowledge will enable you to overcome the hardships of the journey, knowing that you are following a divine purpose in your wanderings. According to one interpretation, the angel (*mal·akh*) will not be a supernatural creature

HALAKHAH L'MA·ASEH

23:19. You shall not boil a kid in its mother's milk Expanding on this verse, Jewish law prohibits preparing, eating, serving, or benefiting from a mixture of meat and dairy together. Separate utensils are used for cooking and serving meat and dairy foods. One rinses the mouth, and some wait one half hour after eating dairy before eating meat; one waits three hours or six hours after eating meat before eating dairy, according to variant regional customs.

that I have made ready. 21Pay heed to him and
obey him. Do not defy him, for he will not pardon your offenses, since My Name is in him;
22but if you obey him and do all that I say, I
will be an enemy to your enemies and a foe to
your foes.

23When My angel goes before you and brings
you to the Amorites, the Hittites, the Perizzites,
the Canaanites, the Hivites, and the Jebusites,
and I annihilate them, 24you shall not bow down
to their gods in worship or follow their practices, but shall tear them down and smash their
pillars to bits. 25You shall serve the Lord your
God, and He will bless your bread and your water. And I will remove sickness from your midst.
26No woman in your land shall miscarry or be
barren. I will let you enjoy the full count of your
days.

27I will send forth My terror before you, and

הֲכִנֹתִי׃ 21 הִשָּׁמֶר מִפָּנָיו וּשְׁמַע בְּקֹלוֹ
אַל־תַּמֵּר בּוֹ כִּי לֹא יִשָּׂא לְפִשְׁעֲכֶם כִּי
שְׁמִי בְּקִרְבּוֹ׃ 22 כִּי אִם־שָׁמוֹעַ תִּשְׁמַע
בְּקֹלוֹ וְעָשִׂיתָ כֹּל אֲשֶׁר אֲדַבֵּר וְאָיַבְתִּי
אֶת־אֹיְבֶיךָ וְצַרְתִּי אֶת־צֹרְרֶיךָ׃
23 כִּי־יֵלֵךְ מַלְאָכִי לְפָנֶיךָ וֶהֱבִיאֲךָ אֶל־
הָאֱמֹרִי וְהַחִתִּי וְהַפְּרִזִּי וְהַכְּנַעֲנִי הַחִוִּי
וְהַיְבוּסִי וְהִכְחַדְתִּיו׃ 24 לֹא־תִשְׁתַּחֲוֶה
לֵאלֹהֵיהֶם וְלֹא תָעָבְדֵם וְלֹא תַעֲשֶׂה
כְּמַעֲשֵׂיהֶם כִּי הָרֵס תְּהָרְסֵם וְשַׁבֵּר
תְּשַׁבֵּר מַצֵּבֹתֵיהֶם׃ 25 וַעֲבַדְתֶּם אֵת יְהוָה
אֱלֹהֵיכֶם וּבֵרַךְ אֶת־לַחְמְךָ וְאֶת־מֵימֶיךָ
וַהֲסִרֹתִי מַחֲלָה מִקִּרְבֶּךָ׃ 26 לֹא תִהְיֶה ביעי
מְשַׁכֵּלָה וַעֲקָרָה בְּאַרְצֶךָ אֶת־מִסְפַּר יָמֶיךָ
אֲמַלֵּא׃
27 אֶת־אֵימָתִי אֲשַׁלַּח לְפָנֶיךָ וְהַמֹּתִי אֶת־

21. My Name is in him The divine will and power manifests itself through this Heaven-sent messenger (see 14:19).

22. Similar statements are found in a number of peace treaties from the ancient Near East.

24. Worshiping their gods is forbidden, as is adopting their religious practices—even in the service of the God of Israel. All objects used in their worship are to be destroyed.

pillars The Hebrew word *matzevah* (plural *matzevot*) derives from the stem meaning "to stand" (נצב). It refers to a single, upright slab of stone. Believed to be the dwelling of a divinity or spirit, it often was seen as an object of religious worship and, therefore, was considered to be idolatrous by Israelite religion (cf. Gen. 28:18; Exod. 24:4).

27. My terror That is, He will cause the enemy to be struck with terror.

---

but a human prophet to guide Israel on its path and keep the people from straying (Mekh. of bar Yoḥai).

25. He will bless The verse can also be read, "and you shall bless." From this reading the Sages derived the obligation for each of us to offer a blessing over food before eating it (BT Ber. 48b). The Sages go so far as to say that anyone who enjoys the goods of this world without thanking God for them is like a thief.

remove sickness from your midst The "sickness" of dissatisfaction. By following God's ways, we are cured of the "disease" of envying others who happen to have more material possessions than we do.

26. No woman in your land shall miscarry Here and in several other passages (e.g., Lev. 26:3ff.), the Torah promises health and prosperity as a reward for living an observant life. Yet, too often we see that health, wealth, and fertility are not the lot of the religiously committed. Because the Torah is here addressing members of the young Israelite nation, so new to freedom and responsibility, it is understandable that the message is couched in the idiom they can understand best, so that matters of right and wrong are explained in terms of reward and punishment, even as one would speak to young children. By the time of the Talmud, however, the Sages would acknowledge, "We cannot account for the sufferings of the righteous" (M Avot 4:15).

HALAKHAH L'MA·ASEH

23:25. You shall serve According to Maimonides, this verse obligates all Jews to daily prayer (MT Prayer 1:1).

I will throw into panic all the people among whom you come, and I will make all your enemies turn tail before you. 28I will send a plague ahead of you, and it shall drive out before you the Hivites, the Canaanites, and the Hittites. 29I will not drive them out before you in a single year, lest the land become desolate and the wild beasts multiply to your hurt. 30I will drive them out before you little by little, until you have increased and possess the land. 31I will set your borders from the Sea of Reeds to the Sea of Philistia, and from the wilderness to the Euphrates; for I will deliver the inhabitants of the land into your hands, and you will drive them out before you. 32You shall make no covenant with them and their gods. 33They shall not remain in your land, lest they cause you to sin against Me; for you will serve their gods—and it will prove a snare to you.

כָּל־הָעָ֔ם אֲשֶׁ֥ר תָּבֹ֖א בָּהֶ֑ם וְנָתַתִּ֧י אֶת־
כָּל־אֹיְבֶ֛יךָ אֵלֶ֖יךָ עֹֽרֶף׃ 28 וְשָׁלַחְתִּ֥י אֶת־
הַצִּרְעָ֖ה לְפָנֶ֑יךָ וְגֵרְשָׁ֗ה אֶת־הַֽחִוִּ֛י אֶת־
הַֽכְּנַעֲנִ֥י וְאֶת־הַֽחִתִּ֖י מִלְּפָנֶֽיךָ׃ 29 לֹ֧א
אֲגָרְשֶׁ֛נּוּ מִפָּנֶ֖יךָ בְּשָׁנָ֣ה אֶחָ֑ת פֶּן־תִּהְיֶ֤ה
הָאָ֙רֶץ֙ שְׁמָמָ֔ה וְרַבָּ֥ה עָלֶ֖יךָ חַיַּ֥ת הַשָּׂדֶֽה׃
30 מְעַ֥ט מְעַ֛ט אֲגָרְשֶׁ֖נּוּ מִפָּנֶ֑יךָ עַ֚ד אֲשֶׁ֣ר
תִּפְרֶ֔ה וְנָחַלְתָּ֖ אֶת־הָאָֽרֶץ׃ 31 וְשַׁתִּ֣י אֶת־
גְּבֻלְךָ֗ מִיַּם־סוּף֙ וְעַד־יָ֣ם פְּלִשְׁתִּ֔ים
וּמִמִּדְבָּ֖ר עַד־הַנָּהָ֑ר כִּ֣י ׀ אֶתֵּ֣ן בְּיֶדְכֶ֗ם
אֵ֚ת יֹשְׁבֵ֣י הָאָ֔רֶץ וְגֵרַשְׁתָּ֖מוֹ מִפָּנֶֽיךָ׃
32 לֹא־תִכְרֹ֥ת לָהֶ֛ם וְלֵאלֹהֵיהֶ֖ם בְּרִֽית׃
33 לֹ֤א יֵשְׁבוּ֙ בְּאַרְצְךָ֔ פֶּן־יַחֲטִ֥יאוּ אֹתְךָ֖ לִ֑י
כִּ֤י תַעֲבֹד֙ אֶת־אֱלֹ֣הֵיהֶ֔ם כִּֽי־יִהְיֶ֥ה לְךָ֖
לְמוֹקֵֽשׁ׃ פ

24 Then He said to Moses, "Come up to the LORD, with Aaron, Nadab and Abihu, and

כד וְאֶל־מֹשֶׁ֨ה אָמַ֜ר עֲלֵ֣ה אֶל־יְהוָ֗ה
אַתָּה֙ וְאַהֲרֹ֔ן נָדָ֣ב וַאֲבִיה֔וּא וְשִׁבְעִ֖ים

throw into panic The effect of the "terror."

31. The ideal boundaries of the Land are set forth. At no time in Israelite history, even at the height of the Davidic-Solomonic empire, were these boundaries a reality. They are believed to have their origin in the pre-Israelite Egyptian province of Canaan, which included Palestine and Syria as a single political and geographic entity.

Sea of Reeds Here, undoubtedly, the Gulf of Elat (also known as the Gulf of Aqaba).

Sea of Philistia The Mediterranean Sea.

the wilderness Probably a general term for the desert and the steppes.

32–33. The Covenant demands exclusive recognition of *YHVH* as the sovereign king to whom is owed uncompromising loyalty. Hence, a warning against making covenants with the inhabitants is appropriate.

POPULAR ASSENT (24:1–11)

The very first step in the centuries-long process of canonizing the Torah literature (considering it binding as the word of God) is recorded in 19:8: "All that the LORD has spoken we will do!" Then Moses reiterated the commandments orally to the entire people assembled at the foot of Mount Sinai. Having heard the stipulations, they now bind themselves vocally, using the same formula of affirmation as before (24:3).

1. Then He said to Moses This emphasizes that the instruction here pertains only to Moses and not to the assembled Israelites.

Nadab and Abihu Their abrupt introduc-

---

31. you will drive them out The young nation, still struggling to form its identity as God's covenanted people, remained too vulnerable to the temptations of paganism. Later in Israelite and Jewish history, the people will gain much from the nations in whose midst they live—and will teach them much as well.

seventy elders of Israel, and bow low from afar.
2 Moses alone shall come near the LORD; but the
others shall not come near, nor shall the people
come up with him."

3 Moses went and repeated to the people all
the commands of the LORD and all the rules; and
all the people answered with one voice, saying,
"All the things that the LORD has commanded
we will do!" 4 Moses then wrote down all the
commands of the LORD.

Early in the morning, he set up an altar at the
foot of the mountain, with twelve pillars for the
twelve tribes of Israel. 5 He designated some
young men among the Israelites, and they
offered burnt offerings and sacrificed bulls as

מִזִּקְנֵי יִשְׂרָאֵל וְהִשְׁתַּחֲוִיתֶם מֵרָחֹק׃
2 וְנִגַּשׁ מֹשֶׁה לְבַדּוֹ אֶל־יְהוָה וְהֵם לֹא
יִגָּשׁוּ וְהָעָם לֹא יַעֲלוּ עִמּוֹ׃
3 וַיָּבֹא מֹשֶׁה וַיְסַפֵּר לָעָם אֵת כָּל־דִּבְרֵי
יְהוָה וְאֵת כָּל־הַמִּשְׁפָּטִים וַיַּעַן כָּל־הָעָם
קוֹל אֶחָד וַיֹּאמְרוּ כָּל־הַדְּבָרִים אֲשֶׁר־דִּבֶּר
יְהוָה נַעֲשֶׂה׃ 4 וַיִּכְתֹּב מֹשֶׁה אֵת כָּל־דִּבְרֵי
יְהוָה

וַיַּשְׁכֵּם בַּבֹּקֶר וַיִּבֶן מִזְבֵּחַ תַּחַת הָהָר
וּשְׁתֵּים עֶשְׂרֵה מַצֵּבָה לִשְׁנֵים עָשָׂר שִׁבְטֵי
יִשְׂרָאֵל׃ 5 וַיִּשְׁלַח אֶת־נַעֲרֵי בְּנֵי יִשְׂרָאֵל
וַיַּעֲלוּ עֹלֹת וַיִּזְבְּחוּ זְבָחִים שְׁלָמִים לַיהוָה

tion without any prior description or identification presupposes knowledge of Aaron's genealogy, given in 6:23.

bow low from afar This idiom is found in ancient Near Eastern letters to royalty, suggesting a conventional courtesy on the part of a vassal who bows repeatedly as he approaches, starting at a distance from the suzerain's presence.

2. Moses alone Mount Sinai is divided into three zones, each of which has restricted access. Moses alone reaches the summit; a site partway up is reserved for Aaron and his delegation; the people are confined to the foot of the mountain.

3. commands . . . rules The Hebrew words—*d'varim* and *mishpatim,* respectively—distinguish the two types of laws in the foregoing legal code. The "commands" are those formulated in concise, categorical style ("You shall"), including the Decalogue and the bulk of 22:17–23:19. Their enforcement is left to God. The "rules" or "enactments" contained in 21:1–22:16, are given in conditional style ("If" or "When") and are to be enforced by the state and the law courts.

4. wrote down This is the document termed "the record of the covenant" (*seifer ha-b'rit*) in verse 7 (see introduction to chapter 21 and Comment to 24:7). Setting down the terms of the covenant in writing was an essential part of the ratification process of treaties in the ancient Near East. It made the treaty a legal reality.

set up an altar Doubtless in accord with the provisions of 20:21. This altar was not only the site for sacrifices (v. 5) but also was the symbolic locus of the divine Presence, just as the 12 pillars represented the other party to the contract: the 12 tribes.

twelve pillars It is likely that dashing the blood "on the people" described in verse 8 meant sprinkling it over the pillars. In Gen. 31:45–54 an upright pillar served as a silent witness to a treaty between Jacob and Laban.

5. young men The strenuous task of slaughtering bulls and preparing them for the altar could be accomplished only by young men.

they offered The two types of sacrifice are burnt offerings (*olah*) and offerings of well-being (*sh'lamim*). The first was wholly consumed by fire on the altar. The second was shared, certain parts being burnt and the remainder eaten by the worshipers in a sacred meal.

CHAPTER 24

3. All the commands . . . and all the rules All rules of the just society have the same divine origin as the Decalogue (Mekh. of bar Yoḥai). In the 1st century, recitation of the Decalogue was part of the daily prayer service. This was dropped from the service "because of the arguments of sectarians," perhaps early Christians, who claimed that only the Ten Commandments were divinely ordained and that the other rules could be ignored because they were of human origin. "No one Jew can fulfill all the commandments of the Torah. Some are directed only to *kohanim* (priests), some to women, some to farmers in the Land of Israel. Only all Jews together can do God's will completely" (Vilna Gaon).

offerings of well-being to the LORD. 6 Moses took one part of the blood and put it in basins, and the other part of the blood he dashed against the altar. 7 Then he took the record of the covenant and read it aloud to the people. And they said, "All that the LORD has spoken we will faithfully do!" 8 Moses took the blood and dashed it on the people and said, "This is the blood of the covenant that the LORD now makes with you concerning all these commands."

9 Then Moses and Aaron, Nadab and Abihu, and seventy elders of Israel ascended; 10 and they saw the God of Israel: under His feet there was the likeness of a pavement of sapphire, like the

פָּרִים׃ 6 וַיִּקַּח מֹשֶׁה֙ חֲצִ֣י הַדָּ֔ם וַיָּ֖שֶׂם
בָּאַגָּנֹ֑ת וַחֲצִ֣י הַדָּ֔ם זָרַ֖ק עַל־הַמִּזְבֵּֽחַ׃
7 וַיִּקַּח֙ סֵ֣פֶר הַבְּרִ֔ית וַיִּקְרָ֖א בְּאָזְנֵ֣י הָעָ֑ם
וַיֹּ֣אמְר֔וּ כֹּ֛ל אֲשֶׁר־דִּבֶּ֥ר יְהוָ֖ה נַעֲשֶׂ֥ה
וְנִשְׁמָֽע׃ 8 וַיִּקַּ֤ח מֹשֶׁה֙ אֶת־הַדָּ֔ם וַיִּזְרֹ֖ק
עַל־הָעָ֑ם וַיֹּ֗אמֶר הִנֵּ֤ה דַֽם־הַבְּרִית֙ אֲשֶׁ֨ר
כָּרַ֤ת יְהוָה֙ עִמָּכֶ֔ם עַ֥ל כָּל־הַדְּבָרִ֖ים
הָאֵֽלֶּה׃
9 וַיַּ֥עַל מֹשֶׁ֖ה וְאַהֲרֹ֑ן נָדָב֙ וַאֲבִיה֔וּא
וְשִׁבְעִ֖ים מִזִּקְנֵ֥י יִשְׂרָאֵֽל׃ 10 וַיִּרְא֕וּ אֵ֖ת
אֱלֹהֵ֣י יִשְׂרָאֵ֑ל וְתַ֣חַת רַגְלָ֗יו כְּמַעֲשֵׂה֙ לִבְנַ֣ת

6. The blood of the *olah* and the *sh'lamim* always was collected and dashed against the sides of the altar. Here Moses performs this standard ritual with only part of the blood (literally, "half the blood"); he stored the other half in basins for sprinkling on the people later (v. 8). The two halves were for the two parties to the covenant, God and the people Israel. The use of blood in a covenant is not found elsewhere in the Bible. The ordination of Aaron as High Priest (Lev. 8:23) also involved daubing blood of the sacrificial lamb of ordination on parts of his body and on the altar. It is possible that blood in both these ceremonies—covenant and ordination—functions mysteriously to cement the bond between the involved parties. It is also possible that its function was purgation, intended to keep impurity at bay.

basins Hebrew: *aggan* (singular); a large and deep two-handled bowl.

7. record of the covenant Public reading and popular assent were necessary elements of the ratification process. Some ancient Near Eastern treaties required periodic public recital before the vassal and his people, as does the Torah in Deut. 31:10–13.

we will faithfully do Because this is the last act of public participation, the formula of consent in verse 3 is expanded to give it finality.

8. concerning all these commands The essence of the Covenant is obedience to the laws of the Torah.

10. God of Israel The name befits the context of the special relationship now being forged between God and Israel.

---

7. we will faithfully do The literal meaning of the two words *na·aseh v'nishma* is "we will do and we will obey." This famous reply represents the Israelites' faithful acceptance of their role as God's chosen people. The Sages were impressed by the eagerness with which the Israelites accepted the burdens of being God's people and following God's laws. To say "I will do" even before one understands is to say, "I have faith that God will lead me in the proper path." According to a talmudic legend, the angels were so impressed with this show of faith that they came down from heaven and placed two crowns on the head of each Israelite, one for doing (*na·aseh*) and one for obeying, or seeking to understand (*v'nishma*). The Israelites could have responded, as most would today, "We will seek to understand and, if we are persuaded, we will agree to do them." Instead, having met God in Egypt, at the sea, and at Mount Sinai, the Israelites trusted that God's demands would be reasonable and in their best interest. Just as we accept medicine from our physician on trust, without understanding what it is or how it works, and commit ourselves to marriage, to parenthood, and to a career as acts of faith before we fully understand what they entail, so too the Israelites accepted God's will. There are many things in life that we cannot appreciate before we have lived them and come to appreciate their value. We must do them first (*na·aseh*) and only afterward realize why (*nishma*).

10. they saw the God of Israel What does this strange passage mean? Could it be that 70 elders "saw" God, while "eating and drink-

very sky for purity. 11 Yet He did not raise His hand against the leaders of the Israelites; they beheld God, and they ate and drank.

12 The LORD said to Moses, "Come up to Me on the mountain and wait there, and I will give you the stone tablets with the teachings and commandments which I have inscribed to instruct them." 13 So Moses and his attendant Joshua arose, and Moses ascended the mountain of God. 14 To the elders he had said, "Wait here for us until we return to you. You have Aaron and Hur with you; let anyone who has a legal matter approach them."

15 When Moses had ascended the mountain,

הַסַּפִּיר וּכְעֶצֶם הַשָּׁמַיִם לָטֹהַר׃ 11 וְאֶל־
אֲצִילֵי בְּנֵי יִשְׂרָאֵל לֹא שָׁלַח יָדוֹ וַיֶּחֱזוּ
אֶת־הָאֱלֹהִים וַיֹּאכְלוּ וַיִּשְׁתּוּ׃ ס
12 וַיֹּאמֶר יְהוָה אֶל־מֹשֶׁה עֲלֵה אֵלַי הָהָרָה
וֶהְיֵה־שָׁם וְאֶתְּנָה לְךָ אֶת־לֻחֹת הָאֶבֶן
וְהַתּוֹרָה וְהַמִּצְוָה אֲשֶׁר כָּתַבְתִּי לְהוֹרֹתָם׃
13 וַיָּקָם מֹשֶׁה וִיהוֹשֻׁעַ מְשָׁרְתוֹ וַיַּעַל מֹשֶׁה
אֶל־הַר הָאֱלֹהִים׃ 14 וְאֶל־הַזְּקֵנִים אָמַר
שְׁבוּ־לָנוּ בָזֶה עַד אֲשֶׁר־נָשׁוּב אֲלֵיכֶם
וְהִנֵּה אַהֲרֹן וְחוּר עִמָּכֶם מִי־בַעַל דְּבָרִים
יִגַּשׁ אֲלֵהֶם׃
15 וַיַּעַל מֹשֶׁה אֶל־הָהָר וַיְכַס הֶעָנָן אֶת־

pavement of sapphire A decorative floor area of covered bricks or tiles. What is meant by the Hebrew word *sappir,* rendered "sapphire," is not the modern blue gemstone (corundum), which was unknown in the ancient Near East, but the widely used, deep blue lapis lazuli (see also Ezek. 1:26, describing the throne of God).

11. did not raise His hand They survived the experience.

they beheld God Verse 10 has already told us that "they saw the God of Israel." The repetition here points up the extraordinary nature of the experience.

they ate and drank This describes a formal part of the ceremony, concluding the Covenant.

MOSES RECEIVES THE TABLETS (vv. 12–18)

These verses prepare us for the account of the building of the tabernacle and the episode of the Golden Calf.

12. Come up to Me Either Moses had descended with the entire delegation and is now instructed to ascend once again, or he is still on the mountain and is directed to ascend to its highest level. The former is favored by verses 13–14, which imply that he has been down among the people. The latter is supported by the parallel account in Deut. 5:28 in which Moses is told, "But you remain here with Me." Two strands of tradition appear to have been interwoven here in this account.

stone tablets This follows the widespread Near Eastern practice of recording important public documents, particularly treaties, on imperishable materials.

13. mountain of God The site is identified as Mount Sinai in verse 16.

14. for us Even though only Moses is mentioned in verses 13 and 15, the plural used here (*lanu*) indicates that Joshua too had ascended to a certain level.

Hur See Comment to 17:10.

ing"? What happens to people who experience the presence of God in an unusually intense and vivid way? The Talmud chooses not to take the passage literally, understanding it to mean that experiencing God took the place of eating and drinking for these elders, as it did for Moses during his 40 days on the mountaintop. In the presence of God, ordinary physical needs are transcended, and one forgets about the need to eat and drink. In a similar vein, Maimonides maintains that "seeing God" refers to intellectual perception rather than sensory experience. They did not actually see anything; they came to understand the reality of God more clearly (as one might say, "I see"). The references to eating and drinking may be the Torah's way of suggesting that the encounter with God was more than an intellectual encounter; it engaged all of the senses. Or it may reflect the anti-ascetic side of Judaism: We need not turn our back on the material experience of this world in the quest for God's presence. God may be found in eating and drinking as readily as in praying.

the cloud covered the mountain. 16The Presence of the LORD abode on Mount Sinai, and the cloud hid it for six days. On the seventh day He called to Moses from the midst of the cloud. 17Now the Presence of the LORD appeared in the sight of the Israelites as a consuming fire on the top of the mountain. 18Moses went inside the cloud and ascended the mountain; and Moses remained on the mountain forty days and forty nights.

מפטיר הָהָר: 16 וַיִּשְׁכֹּן כְּבוֹד־יְהוָה֙ עַל־הַר סִינַ֔י וַיְכַסֵּהוּ הֶעָנָ֖ן שֵׁשֶׁת יָמִ֑ים וַיִּקְרָ֧א אֶל־מֹשֶׁ֛ה בַּיּ֥וֹם הַשְּׁבִיעִ֖י מִתּ֥וֹךְ הֶעָנָֽן: 17 וּמַרְאֵה֙ כְּב֣וֹד יְהוָ֔ה כְּאֵ֥שׁ אֹכֶ֖לֶת בְּרֹ֣אשׁ הָהָ֑ר לְעֵינֵ֖י בְּנֵ֥י יִשְׂרָאֵֽל: 18 וַיָּבֹ֨א מֹשֶׁ֤ה בְּת֣וֹךְ הֶֽעָנָ֔ן וַיַּ֖עַל אֶל־הָהָ֑ר וַיְהִ֤י מֹשֶׁה֙ בָּהָ֔ר אַרְבָּעִ֣ים י֔וֹם וְאַרְבָּעִ֖ים לָֽיְלָה: פ

16. Presence Hebrew: *kavod;* the glory or majesty of God, a manifest Presence. See Comment to 16:7.

six days. On the seventh day This is an example of a well-known literary convention—the climactic use of numbers. It appears in ancient Near Eastern literature and often in the Bible. An action continues for six consecutive days, and then a new event will occur on the seventh. Here the six days are probably intended for spiritual preparation.

18. *forty days and forty nights* Repeated several times in the Bible. The number 40 often is used as a symbolic number, and 40 days expresses a significant period of time, frequently connected with purification and purging of sin.

הפטרת משפטים

HAFTARAH FOR MISHPATIM

JEREMIAH 34:8–22, 33:25–26

The final siege of Jerusalem, begun in 588 B.C.E. by Nebuchadrezzar, king of Babylon, is the historical setting of the *haftarah*. Jeremiah 34 opened with Jeremiah's prophetic word to King Zedekiah of Judah that Jerusalem would fall. The king, prompted perhaps by the national threat, had ordered the release of male and female slaves (vv. 8–9). A practical benefit of this release would have been the addition of manpower for the defense of Jerusalem. Slave owners had initially complied with this edict, but then "forced them into slavery again" (vv. 10–11).

This reversal may have taken place during a respite between sieges, after the Babylonian withdrawal (v. 22), which was due in part to the Babylonian fear of an Egyptian attack on its rear flank. Biblical sources indicate the makings of an alliance between the Egyptians and the Israelites against the Babylonians (Ezek. 17:11–18). The Egyptian support proved ineffective (Ezek. 30:20–21), and Nebuchadrezzar soon returned to the walls of Jerusalem. Jeremiah envisioned this turn of events (Jer. 37:8), and proclaimed it as God's judgment for the people's violation of the decree to free slaves (34:13–22). A final word of hope envisions reconciliation between Israel and God (33:25–26), but only after the "desolation" (34:22).

The *haftarah* focuses on three "covenants." The first covenant is made between the people and Zedekiah, in the present, for the release of Hebrew slaves. The second is that made between God and Israel at Mount Sinai, in the past, after they were delivered from Egyptian bondage. The third is God's "covenant with day and night" (Jer. 33:25), in token of which He promises never to reject the offspring of Jacob and even promises to restore them in love.

These three covenants comprise Israel's present, past, and future; the second and third evoke Creation, Revelation, and Redemption. Revelation and its consequences stand at the center of the *haftarah* (Jer. 34:8–22), while Creation and Redemption are the two poles of the concluding verses (33:25–26). There the language is that of a unilateral oath, because God acts alone as the sovereign agent in Creation and Redemption. By contrast, because God and Israel are partners in the covenant's Revelation, the passage from Jer. 34 reflects bilateral accountability and judgment. It is full of wordplays that underscore the inherent link between sin and punishment.

Variations on the verb *shuv* bring this dynamic into focus. Jeremiah points out that the slaveholders who properly "turned about" (*va-tashuvu*) and released their slaves have now "turned back" (*va-tashuvu*) and "brought back" (*va-tashivu*) the freed people into slavery again (vv. 15–16), thus violating the covenant (v. 18). As a result, God will "bring . . . back" (*va-hashivotim*) the Babylonian host to besiege and destroy the towns of Judah and all their inhabitants (v. 22).

A prophetic counterpoint reverses this bleak conclusion, for the language of promise precisely echoes the terms of judgment. God swears that His allegiance to Israel will endure as the "laws of heaven and earth"—and that He "will restore" (*ashiv*) the "fortunes" (*sh'vutam*) of the nation, taking them back in love. Throughout the *haftarah,* the term *shuv* serves as a leitmotif of the ongoing relationship between God and Israel in history. For the prophet, the covenant with God has conditions and consequences. Ultimately, however, God's love transcends them both. And just this, in the end, is the healing consolation of the *haftarah*.

RELATION OF THE *HAFTARAH* TO THE *PARASHAH*

The *parashah* and the *haftarah* are linked by their citation of rules that deal with the liberation of

Hebrew slaves. The divine concern to limit debt bondage is an expression of the Bible's overall concern for human dignity rooted in economic freedom. Virtually all the Torah's rules of slavery, debts, and indenture complicate or frustrate the desire for economic enrichment at the expense of other persons (see Exod. 21:2–6, 23:9–12; Lev. 25; Deut. 15). Toward this end, the rules repeatedly invoke the periodic restoration of land and release from debts. These social benefits, which derive from divine authority, depend on social enactment and enforcement. Jeremiah's rebuke suggests that the people's disregard for human freedom violates their ancient covenant with God, who "brought them out of . . . the house of bondage" (Jer. 34:13, see also Exod. 20:2).

34 8The word which came to Jeremiah from the LORD after King Zedekiah had made a covenant with all the people in Jerusalem to proclaim a release among them—9that everyone should set free his Hebrew slaves, both male and female, and that no one should keep his fellow Judean enslaved.

10Everyone, officials and people, who had entered into the covenant agreed to set their male and female slaves free and not keep them enslaved any longer; they complied and let them go. 11But afterward they turned about and brought back the men and women they had set free, and forced them into slavery again. 12Then it was that the word of the LORD came to Jeremiah from the LORD:

13Thus said the LORD, the God of Israel: I made a covenant with your fathers when I brought them out of the land of Egypt, the house of bondage, saying: 14"In the seventh year each of you must let go any fellow Hebrew who may be sold to you; when he has served you six years, you must set him free." But your fathers would not obey Me or give ear. 15Lately you turned about and did what is proper in My sight, and each of you proclaimed a release to his coun-

לד
8 הַדָּבָר אֲשֶׁר־הָיָה אֶל־יִרְמְיָהוּ
מֵאֵת יְהוָה אַחֲרֵי כְּרֹת הַמֶּלֶךְ צִדְקִיָּהוּ
בְּרִית אֶת־כָּל־הָעָם אֲשֶׁר בִּירוּשָׁלִַם לִקְרֹא
לָהֶם דְּרוֹר׃ 9 לְשַׁלַּח אִישׁ אֶת־עַבְדּוֹ וְאִישׁ
אֶת־שִׁפְחָתוֹ הָעִבְרִי וְהָעִבְרִיָּה חָפְשִׁים
לְבִלְתִּי עֲבָד־בָּם בִּיהוּדִי אָחִיהוּ אִישׁ׃
10 וַיִּשְׁמְעוּ כָּל־הַשָּׂרִים וְכָל־הָעָם אֲשֶׁר־
בָּאוּ בַבְּרִית לְשַׁלַּח אִישׁ אֶת־עַבְדּוֹ וְאִישׁ
אֶת־שִׁפְחָתוֹ חָפְשִׁים לְבִלְתִּי עֲבָד־בָּם
עוֹד וַיִּשְׁמְעוּ וַיְשַׁלֵּחוּ׃ 11 וַיָּשׁוּבוּ אַחֲרֵי־
כֵן וַיָּשִׁבוּ אֶת־הָעֲבָדִים וְאֶת־הַשְּׁפָחוֹת
אֲשֶׁר שִׁלְּחוּ חָפְשִׁים ויכבישום וַיִּכְבְּשׁוּם
לַעֲבָדִים וְלִשְׁפָחוֹת׃ ס 12 וַיְהִי דְבַר־
יְהוָה אֶל־יִרְמְיָהוּ מֵאֵת יְהוָה לֵאמֹר׃
13 כֹּה־אָמַר יְהוָה אֱלֹהֵי יִשְׂרָאֵל אָנֹכִי
כָּרַתִּי בְרִית אֶת־אֲבוֹתֵיכֶם בְּיוֹם הוֹצִאִי
אוֹתָם מֵאֶרֶץ מִצְרַיִם מִבֵּית עֲבָדִים
לֵאמֹר׃ 14 מִקֵּץ שֶׁבַע שָׁנִים תְּשַׁלְּחוּ אִישׁ
אֶת־אָחִיו הָעִבְרִי אֲשֶׁר־יִמָּכֵר לְךָ וַעֲבָדְךָ
שֵׁשׁ שָׁנִים וְשִׁלַּחְתּוֹ חָפְשִׁי מֵעִמָּךְ וְלֹא־
שָׁמְעוּ אֲבוֹתֵיכֶם אֵלַי וְלֹא הִטּוּ אֶת־
אָזְנָם׃ 15 וַתָּשֻׁבוּ אַתֶּם הַיּוֹם וַתַּעֲשׂוּ אֶת־
הַיָּשָׁר בְּעֵינַי לִקְרֹא דְרוֹר אִישׁ לְרֵעֵהוּ

Jeremiah 34:8. to proclaim a release This idiom is also found in Lev. 25:10 in connection with the restitution of property and freedom in the jubilee year (see Ezek. 46:17). Zedekiah's proclamation may thus be part of a sabbatical amnesty.

14. In the seventh year "That is to say, from the beginning of the seventh year" (Abravanel). For this phrase, see Deut. 15:1. Similarly, the legal terms in this verse ("fellow Hebrew," "who may be sold to you," "and set him free") are Deuteronomic formulations (see Deut. 15:12–13,18).

trymen; and you made a covenant accordingly
before Me in the House which bears My name.
16But now you have turned back and have profaned My name; each of you has brought back
the men and women whom you had given their
freedom, and forced them to be your slaves
again.

17Assuredly, thus said the LORD: You would
not obey Me and proclaim a release, each to his
kinsman and countryman. Lo! I proclaim your
release—declares the LORD—to the sword, to
pestilence, and to famine; and I will make you
a horror to all the kingdoms of the earth. 18I
will make the men who violated My covenant,
who did not fulfill the terms of the covenant
which they made before Me, [like] the calf
which they cut in two so as to pass between the
halves: 19The officers of Judah and Jerusalem,
the officials, the priests, and all the people of
the land who passed between the halves of the
calf 20shall be handed over to their enemies, to
those who seek to kill them. Their carcasses shall
become food for the birds of the sky and the
beasts of the earth. 21I will hand over King Zedekiah of Judah and his officers to their enemies,
who seek to kill them—to the army of the king
of Babylon which has withdrawn from you.
22I hereby give the command—declares the
LORD—by which I will bring them back against
this city. They shall attack it and capture it, and
burn it down. I will make the towns of Judah
a desolation, without inhabitant.

וַתִּכְרְת֤וּ בְרִית֙ לְפָנַ֔י בַּבַּ֕יִת אֲשֶׁר־נִקְרָ֥א
שְׁמִ֖י עָלָֽיו׃ 16 וַתָּשֻׁ֗בוּ וַתְּחַלְּל֣וּ אֶת־
שְׁמִ֔י וַתָּשִׁ֗בוּ אִ֤ישׁ אֶת־עַבְדּוֹ֙ וְאִ֣ישׁ אֶת־
שִׁפְחָת֔וֹ אֲשֶׁר־שִׁלַּחְתֶּ֥ם חָפְשִׁ֖ים לְנַפְשָׁ֑ם
וַתִּכְבְּשׁ֣וּ אֹתָ֔ם לִֽהְי֣וֹת לָכֶ֔ם לַעֲבָדִ֖ים
וְלִשְׁפָחֽוֹת׃ ס
17 לָכֵ֞ן כֹּֽה־אָמַ֣ר יְהוָ֗ה אַתֶּם֙ לֹא־שְׁמַעְתֶּ֣ם
אֵלַ֔י לִקְרֹ֣א דְר֔וֹר אִ֥ישׁ לְאָחִ֖יו וְאִ֣ישׁ
לְרֵעֵ֑הוּ הִנְנִ֣י קֹרֵא֩ לָכֶ֨ם דְּר֜וֹר נְאֻם־יְהוָ֗ה
אֶל־הַחֶ֙רֶב֙ אֶל־הַדֶּ֣בֶר וְאֶל־הָֽרָעָ֔ב וְנָתַתִּ֤י
אֶתְכֶם֙ לזועה לְזַעֲוָ֔ה לְכֹ֖ל מַמְלְכ֥וֹת
הָאָֽרֶץ׃ 18 וְנָתַתִּ֣י אֶת־הָאֲנָשִׁ֗ים הָעֹֽבְרִים֙
אֶת־בְּרִתִ֔י אֲשֶׁ֤ר לֹא־הֵקִ֙ימוּ֙ אֶת־דִּבְרֵ֣י
הַבְּרִ֔ית אֲשֶׁ֥ר כָּרְת֖וּ לְפָנָ֑י הָעֵ֙גֶל֙ אֲשֶׁ֣ר
כָּרְת֣וּ לִשְׁנַ֔יִם וַיַּעַבְר֖וּ בֵּ֥ין בְּתָרָֽיו׃ 19 שָׂרֵ֨י
יְהוּדָ֜ה וְשָׂרֵ֣י יְרוּשָׁלִַ֗ם הַסָּֽרִסִים֙ וְהַכֹּ֣הֲנִ֔ים
וְכֹ֖ל עַ֣ם הָאָ֑רֶץ הָעֹ֣בְרִ֔ים בֵּ֖ין בִּתְרֵ֥י
הָעֵֽגֶל׃ 20 וְנָתַתִּ֣י אוֹתָ֗ם בְּיַ֤ד אֹֽיְבֵיהֶם֙ וּבְיַ֖ד
מְבַקְשֵׁ֣י נַפְשָׁ֑ם וְהָיְתָ֤ה נִבְלָתָם֙ לְמַֽאֲכָ֔ל
לְע֥וֹף הַשָּׁמַ֖יִם וּלְבֶהֱמַ֥ת הָאָֽרֶץ׃ 21 וְאֶת־
צִדְקִיָּ֨הוּ מֶֽלֶךְ־יְהוּדָ֜ה וְאֶת־שָׂרָ֗יו אֶתֵּן֙ בְּיַ֣ד
אֹֽיְבֵיהֶ֔ם וּבְיַ֖ד מְבַקְשֵׁ֣י נַפְשָׁ֑ם וּבְיַד֙ חֵ֣יל
מֶ֣לֶךְ בָּבֶ֔ל הָעֹלִ֖ים מֵעֲלֵיכֶֽם׃ 22 הִנְנִ֨י מְצַוֶּ֜ה
נְאֻם־יְהוָ֗ה וַהֲשִׁ֨בֹתִ֜ים אֶל־הָעִ֣יר הַזֹּ֗את
וְנִלְחֲמ֣וּ עָלֶ֔יהָ וּלְכָד֖וּהָ וּשְׂרָפֻ֣הָ בָאֵ֑שׁ
וְאֶת־עָרֵ֧י יְהוּדָ֛ה אֶתֵּ֥ן שְׁמָמָ֖ה מֵאֵ֥ין
יֹשֵֽׁב׃ פ

16. have profaned My name Jeremiah uses the verb for "profane" or "desecrate" (*ḥillel*) elsewhere with "land" as the object (Jer. 16:18). The verb is also frequently used with the divine name (see Lev. 18:21, 19:12) and in prophetic sources influenced by priestly traditions (cf. Ezek. 20:39, 36:20–23; Mal. 1:12). Here it refers to a desecration of the covenant performed "before Me in the House which bears My name" (v. 15). It may allude to an oath sworn by God's name. From early rabbinic times, the phrase *"ḥillul ha-shem"* has been used to indicate a desecration of God's name consonant with disgracing the Jewish religion as such (Tosef. Yoma 5:8).

forced them The Hebrew verb used here (*kavash*) is a technical term for economic oppression (see Neh. 5:5). It can also be used to indicate the physical subjugation of land (Gen. 1:28) or of women (Esther 7:8).

18. [like] the calf This translation infers a comparison, much as if *ha-eigel* (the calf) were *ka-eigel* (like the calf). Near Eastern pacts threat-

33 ²⁵Thus said the LORD: As surely as I have established My covenant with day and night—the laws of heaven and earth—²⁶so I will never reject the offspring of Jacob and My servant David; I will never fail to take from his offspring rulers for the descendants of Abraham, Isaac, and Jacob. Indeed, I will restore their fortunes and take them back in love.

לג ²⁵ כֹּ֣ה אָמַ֣ר יְהֹוָ֔ה אִם־לֹ֥א בְרִיתִ֖י יוֹמָ֣ם וָלָ֑יְלָה חֻקּ֛וֹת שָׁמַ֥יִם וָאָ֖רֶץ לֹא־ שָֽׂמְתִּי: ²⁶ גַּם־זֶ֣רַע יַֽעֲק֞וֹב וְדָוִ֣ד עַבְדִּ֗י אֶמְאַ֞ס מִקַּ֣חַת מִזַּרְע֗וֹ מֹֽשְׁלִים֙ אֶל־זֶ֔רַע אַבְרָהָ֖ם יִשְׂחָ֣ק וְיַֽעֲקֹ֑ב כִּֽי־אָשִׁ֥יב אֶת־שְׁבוּתָ֖ם וְרִֽחַמְתִּֽים: ס

---

ened offenders with becoming "like" the animal whose parts were cut for the ceremony that established the agreement (see 1 Sam. 11:7). Moreover, parties to the agreement would often (actually or symbolically) "pass between" the animal parts. Various terms in this verse echo God's covenant with Abram (Gen. 15:9–10).

Jeremiah 33. The concluding consolation skips back to the preceding chapter, to end the prophetic message on a positive note.

T'RUMAH

תרומה

25 The Lord spoke to Moses, saying: [2]Tell

כה וַיְדַבֵּר יְהוָה אֶל־מֹשֶׁה לֵּאמֹר׃

THE TABERNACLE, PART I: INSTRUCTIONS (25:1–31:17)

The narrative that describes the building and the functioning of this sanctuary is divided into two parts: a series of detailed instructions (25:1–31:17) and an account of its construction (35:1–40:38). Between these two sections is the episode of the Golden Calf.

The tabernacle (see diagram, p. 1520) is an oblong structure comprising the Holy of Holies, the Holy Place, and the Outer Court. A perimeter demarcates this entire sacred area, which is divided into two equal squares. The first two zones—the Holy of Holies and the Holy Place—lie in one square; the Outer Court constitutes the other. From the ark in the Holy of Holies, God reaches out to the Israelites; from the altar of sacrifice in the Outer Court, the Israelites reach out to God.

MATERIALS (25:1–9)

The account opens with a list of the basic materials needed for the construction and operation of the tabernacle. All are to be acquired through public donations.

1. The Lord spoke to Moses During the 40 days he was on Mount Sinai.

The last third of the Book of Exodus concerns itself entirely (except for the incident of the Golden Calf) with the construction of the tabernacle, a portable shrine to house the Ark and the Tablets of the Pact. After the life-altering experience of standing at Sinai, how does one keep the feeling of Sinai present? It can be maintained with sacred deeds, daily acts of justice, and compassion as outlined in the previous *parashah, Mishpatim*. It can be accomplished by maintaining the observance of sacred time, on *Shabbat* and holy days. Or it can be maintained with sacred space, fashioning a physical site to represent the presence of God in the midst of the community. Typically, the Torah and later Jewish usage will blend all three modes—sacred deeds, space, and time—into an integrated way of life. "The ultimate goal is to break through the barriers and come into the presence of God. But that goal is not attained in an instant. There is a ladder of spiritual ascent . . . alluded to in the prayer which precedes the *Sh'ma* in our morning service, where the text moves from the study of Torah to the performance of *mitzvot* to bonding with God" (Schorsch).

Mount Sinai does not retain its holiness after the Israelites move on. It does not become a site of pilgrimage. The mountain is not holy; God is holy, and God's Presence is what makes a place holy. When the people leave Sinai, they do not leave God. God accompanies them on their journey, and the tabernacle is to be a symbol of that. The later Temples, built in Jerusalem by Solomon and by the Jews returning from Babylonia, did not follow the plan given here. Different generations build their houses of worship in ways appropriate to their own times and needs.

Abravanel suggests that one purpose of the tabernacle was to combat the idea that God had forsaken the earth, choosing to reside exclusively in heaven, remote from humanity. The Sages calculated that the command to build a tabernacle was given on *Yom Kippur,* the 10th of *Tishrei* (Tanḥ. 8). The tabernacle would be a "tent of witness" to the fact that God was still in Israel's midst even when they fall short of what they had promised to be. There is also a tradition that the instructions to fashion a tabernacle actually were given after the events recounted in Exod. 32, when the Israelites made the Golden Calf. (The Torah does not always present events in strict chronologic order.) The tabernacle would then serve as a Tent of Witness to the reality of penitence and forgiveness. The incident of the Golden Calf becomes less of a threat to sever the relationship between God and Israel when we know beforehand that reconciliation will follow.

Following the latter tradition stated above, Levi Yitzḥak of Berdichev suggests that God has to command Moses to speak to the Israelites, because Moses is so angry at them after the incident of the Golden Calf. God has to remind him that a leader should never give up on his people, no matter how much they may disappoint him.

2 דַּבֵּר֙ אֶל־בְּנֵ֣י יִשְׂרָאֵ֔ל וְיִקְחוּ־לִ֖י תְּרוּמָ֑ה
מֵאֵ֤ת כָּל־אִישׁ֙ אֲשֶׁ֣ר יִדְּבֶ֣נּוּ לִבּ֔וֹ תִּקְח֖וּ
אֶת־תְּרוּמָתִֽי׃ 3 וְזֹאת֙ הַתְּרוּמָ֔ה אֲשֶׁ֥ר
תִּקְח֖וּ מֵאִתָּ֑ם זָהָ֥ב וָכֶ֖סֶף וּנְחֹֽשֶׁת׃
4 וּתְכֵ֧לֶת וְאַרְגָּמָ֛ן וְתוֹלַ֥עַת שָׁנִ֖י וְשֵׁ֥שׁ
וְעִזִּֽים׃ 5 וְעֹרֹ֨ת אֵילִ֧ם מְאָדָּמִ֛ים וְעֹרֹ֥ת

the Israelite people to bring Me gifts; you shall
accept gifts for Me from every person whose
heart so moves him. 3 And these are the gifts that
you shall accept from them: gold, silver, and
copper; 4 blue, purple, and crimson yarns, fine
linen, goats' hair; 5 tanned ram skins, dolphin

2. the Israelite people Because the sanctuary will serve the entire community, its construction is to be made possible through the generosity of all the people.

gifts The Hebrew word *t'rumah* refers specifically to that which is set aside by its owner and dedicated for sacred use.

3. The metals are listed in descending order of value. The closer the object is to the Holy of Holies, the more valuable the metal of which it is made.

copper Better: bronze (a stronger alloy of copper and tin), used extensively in the Near East as early as the 3rd millennium B.C.E.; as in English, the Hebrew term comprises both substances.

4. blue, purple, and crimson yarns These were the most expensive dyed yarns in the ancient world. They were to be used for the tabernacle hangings and coverings and for the priestly vestments.

blue In the Bible, the Hebrew word *t'kheilet* (blue) often is paired with the word *"argaman"* (purple). Both were dyes produced from a marine snail that exudes a yellow fluid, which becomes a dye in the red-purple range when exposed to sunlight. Thousands of snails were required to produce sufficient dye for one robe. Possession of those dyed fabrics was a mark of wealth, nobility, and royalty.

crimson Hebrew: *tola·at shani*. The first word means "a worm"; the second signifies the color. The two words together designate the brilliant red dye produced from the eggs of certain insects that feed on oak trees.

fine linen Hebrew: *shesh;* Egyptian in origin, refers to cloth of exceptional quality.

goats' hair It grows in long locks and was left undyed. The spinning of goat's hair was a highly specialized skill of women.

5. tanned ram skins The use of animal hides and skins for human needs is ancient. The Bible refers to leather quite often, although it never describes the technique of its production.

CHAPTER 25

2. to bring Me gifts Hebrew: *v'yikḥu li.* Gifts from what was originally Mine, and which I shared with you. The gold, silver, and jewels that the Israelites would give were taken from the Egyptians when they left Egypt. They were not to be used for personal benefit but for something holy and transcendent. The verb here translated "bring" (*v'yikḥu*) literally means "take." One who gives receives something in return—the sense of being generous and making a worthy undertaking possible, the sense of sharing with others in an important venture, the sense of self-worth that comes from knowing that we can give away something of value without feeling diminished.

The word *t'rumah* (gift, offering) comes from a root meaning "to elevate." It originally referred to the physical act of lifting up that which was being offered. It can also imply that the act of offering a gift to God elevates the donor to a higher level as well (Levi Yitzḥak of Berdichev). Those who collect for charitable purposes must do so with only pure and noble purposes in mind, but those who give to charity may do so even for less worthy reasons; the act of giving will purify them (Shalom of Kaminka). One commentator asks why the laws of *Mishpatim* directly precede the offering of *T'rumah* and suggests it teaches that only after we make our living honestly can we give any proceeds to charity.

8. I may dwell among them God's presence is not found in a building. It is found in the hearts and souls of the people who fashion and sanctify the building. A *midrash* suggests that the tabernacle was fashioned to meet God's needs as well as Israel's. It tells of a king who gave his only daughter in marriage to a prince from another country. He told his daughter, "I cannot prevent you from moving away with your husband, but it grieves me to have you leave. Do this for me, then. Wherever you live, build an apartment for me so that I can come and visit you." Thus God says to Israel, "Wherever you travel, build a shrine for Me that I may dwell among you" (Exod. R. 33:1).

skins, and acacia wood; 6oil for lighting, spices
for the anointing oil and for the aromatic incense; 7lapis lazuli and other stones for setting,
for the ephod and for the breastpiece. 8And let
them make Me a sanctuary that I may dwell
among them. 9Exactly as I show you—the pattern of the Tabernacle and the pattern of all its
furnishings—so shall you make it.

10They shall make an ark of acacia wood, two
and a half cubits long, a cubit and a half wide,
and a cubit and a half high. 11Overlay it with
pure gold—overlay it inside and out—and

תְּחָשִׁים וַעֲצֵי שִׁטִּים׃ 6 שֶׁמֶן לַמָּאֹר
בְּשָׂמִים לְשֶׁמֶן הַמִּשְׁחָה וְלִקְטֹרֶת
הַסַּמִּים׃ 7 אַבְנֵי־שֹׁהַם וְאַבְנֵי מִלֻּאִים
לָאֵפֹד וְלַחֹשֶׁן׃ 8 וְעָשׂוּ לִי מִקְדָּשׁ וְשָׁכַנְתִּי
בְּתוֹכָם׃ 9 כְּכֹל אֲשֶׁר אֲנִי מַרְאֶה אוֹתְךָ
אֵת תַּבְנִית הַמִּשְׁכָּן וְאֵת תַּבְנִית כָּל־כֵּלָיו
וְכֵן תַּעֲשׂוּ׃ ס
10 וְעָשׂוּ אֲרוֹן עֲצֵי שִׁטִּים אַמָּתַיִם וָחֵצִי
אָרְכּוֹ וְאַמָּה וָחֵצִי רָחְבּוֹ וְאַמָּה וָחֵצִי
קֹמָתוֹ׃ 11 וְצִפִּיתָ אֹתוֹ זָהָב טָהוֹר מִבַּיִת

dolphin skins The Hebrew word *t'ḥashim* more likely means "dyed sheep or goat leather."

acacia wood There are about 800 species of acacias. Only a few have a straight trunk suitable for cutting timbers used in construction. These yield hard, durable planks that are lightweight.

6. oil Later specified as olive oil.

for lighting This oil was used only in the lamps, not for food preparation or anointing.

spices The aromatic oil was to be used to consecrate the tabernacle, its vessels, and its personnel for the service of God.

7. These semiprecious stones are to adorn the vestments of the priests.

8. All these materials are being collected for use in the construction of a sanctuary (*mikdash*), a term that defines an area clearly enclosed and recognized as sacred space. In later Hebrew, the term *Mikdash*—or *Beit ha-Mikdash*—became the familiar designation for the Temple in Jerusalem.

dwell among them Note that for His "indwelling" God had specific requirements that needed to be followed precisely. The text does not tell of God dwelling "in it," i.e., in the sanctuary, but "among them," i.e., among the people Israel. The literal meaning of *shakhan* is "to rest," not "to dwell." The sanctuary is not meant to be taken literally as God's abode; God dwells in heaven. The sanctuary makes tangible the concept of the indwelling of the divine Presence, God's immanence, in the camp of Israel, a presence to which the people may direct their hearts and minds.

9. Exactly as I show you The tabernacle and its furnishings are conceived of as earthly replicas of heavenly archetypes or as constructions based on divinely given blueprints and pictorial representations. Both notions are found earlier in the ancient Near East and elsewhere in the Bible (see 1 Chron. 28:11–19; Ezek. 40–42).

THE ARK (vv. 10–16)

The directions for constructing the tabernacle commence with the order to fashion an ark. It will permanently house the two stone tablets of the Decalogue that God is giving to Moses (24:12). The ark, therefore, is the focus of the entire enterprise. It is the ark and its contents, the symbol of the covenant between God and Israel, that give meaning to the tabernacle.

10. an ark A wooden chest open at the top. The Hebrew *aron* here is not the same word used for Noah's ark, which is *tevah*.

cubits One cubit is the distance between the elbow and the tip of the middle finger of an average-size person. The standard biblical cubit is about 18 inches (45 cm.). Thus the ark's external dimensions were approximately 3¾ feet (110 cm.) long, 2¼ feet (70 cm.) wide, and 2¼ feet (70 cm.) high.

11. Overlay it Some of the Sages described it as a nest of three separate chests of varying dimensions; one of wood and two of gold. The main, wooden chest, referred to in verse 10, was inserted inside one gold chest, which became its

---

10. make an ark The Sages find numerous linguistic and thematic parallels between the making of the tabernacle and the creation of the world, as if the tabernacle were a microcosm of the universe. To fashion sacred space is to create a separate world within God's universe. Here the Sages play on the similarity of the Hebrew words for "light" (*or*) and "ark" (*aron*).

11. The Ark was fashioned of gold and wood. Gold is beautiful, durable, and precious, symbolizing the enduring value and beauty of

make upon it a gold molding round about. 12Cast four gold rings for it, to be attached to its four feet, two rings on one of its side walls and two on the other. 13Make poles of acacia wood and overlay them with gold; 14then insert the poles into the rings on the side walls of the ark, for carrying the ark. 15The poles shall remain in the rings of the ark: they shall not be removed from it. 16And deposit in the Ark [the tablets of] the Pact which I will give you.

17You shall make a cover of pure gold, two and a half cubits long and a cubit and a half wide. 18Make two cherubim of gold—make them of hammered work—at the two ends of the cover.

וּמִח֖וּץ תְּצַפֶּ֑נּוּ וְעָשִׂ֧יתָ עָלָ֛יו זֵ֥ר זָהָ֖ב סָבִֽיב׃
12 וְיָצַ֣קְתָּ לּ֗וֹ אַרְבַּע֙ טַבְּעֹ֣ת זָהָ֔ב וְנָ֣תַתָּ֔ה
עַ֖ל אַרְבַּ֣ע פַּעֲמֹתָ֑יו וּשְׁתֵּ֣י טַבָּעֹ֗ת עַל־צַלְעוֹ֙
הָֽאֶחָ֔ת וּשְׁתֵּי֙ טַבָּעֹ֔ת עַל־צַלְע֖וֹ הַשֵּׁנִֽית׃
13 וְעָשִׂ֥יתָ בַדֵּ֖י עֲצֵ֣י שִׁטִּ֑ים וְצִפִּיתָ֥ אֹתָ֖ם
זָהָֽב׃ 14 וְהֵבֵאתָ֤ אֶת־הַבַּדִּים֙ בַּטַּבָּעֹ֔ת עַ֖ל
צַלְעֹ֣ת הָאָרֹ֑ן לָשֵׂ֥את אֶת־הָאָרֹ֖ן בָּהֶֽם׃
15 בְּטַבְּעֹת֙ הָאָרֹ֔ן יִהְי֖וּ הַבַּדִּ֑ים לֹ֥א יָסֻ֖רוּ
מִמֶּֽנּוּ׃ 16 וְנָתַתָּ֖ אֶל־הָאָרֹ֑ן אֵ֚ת הָעֵדֻ֔ת אֲשֶׁ֥ר
אֶתֵּ֖ן אֵלֶֽיךָ׃
שני 17 וְעָשִׂ֥יתָ כַפֹּ֖רֶת זָהָ֣ב טָה֑וֹר אַמָּתַ֤יִם וָחֵ֙צִי֙
אָרְכָּ֔הּ וְאַמָּ֥ה וָחֵ֖צִי רָחְבָּֽהּ׃ 18 וְעָשִׂ֛יתָ
שְׁנַ֥יִם כְּרֻבִ֖ים זָהָ֑ב מִקְשָׁה֙ תַּעֲשֶׂ֣ה אֹתָ֔ם

jacket; the other gold chest was fitted inside the wooden chest as a lining. Another tradition has the wooden chest simply overlaid with gold inside and out.

pure gold Such gold has undergone many steps in the refining process, which frees it of all impurities so that it becomes of the highest grade.

molding The top of the chest is to be rimmed by a gold band that slightly overlaps its perimeter.

12–15. The Ark is to be transported in the wilderness from station to station by means of gold-plated wooden poles inserted through gold rings attached to its sides.

16. [the tablets of] the Pact The function of the Ark is to house the stone tablets of the Decalogue.

The practice of depositing legal documents in a sacred place was widespread in the ancient Near East. It heightened the importance of the document and delivered the message that the deity constantly guarded it and was witnessing its implementation.

THE *KAPPORET* AND THE CHERUBIM (vv. 17–22)

A solid slab of pure gold is to be placed above the Ark, which was open at the top. The dimensions of the slab correspond exactly to those of the Ark. This object is called *kapporet* in Hebrew. At either end of the *kapporet* a cherub—a creature with human, animal, and birdlike features—was hammered out. The two cherubim faced each other. Their outstretched wings were turned upward, sheltering the main body of the lid and the Ark below it and forming a throne for God when He descends to earth. The voice of God was thought to issue from the space above the lid and between the two cherubim.

---

the commandments that would be housed in the Ark. Wood is alive and can grow (even as the Torah is called "a tree of life"), symbolizing the importance of the contents of God's Revelation, which continues to grow with the times.

pure gold . . . inside and out Even if no mortal ever sees the inside of the Ark, it must nevertheless be pure. "Any scholar who is not the same kind of person in private as in public is not a true scholar" (BT Yoma 72b).

15. The poles were never removed from the Ark, perhaps to make sure that the Ark was not touched needlessly or inadvertently. The Ark, the focus of holiness, simultaneously draws the worshiper to it and inspires fear and awe, keeping one at a distance. The Midrash notes that the *kohanim* (priests) may have thought that they were carrying the Ark, when in reality the Ark was carrying them. People do not sustain religion as much as religion sustains the people.

17. cover Hebrew: *kapporet*. The same root כפר is believed to be the source of the term *Yom Kippur.* The Ark will function to "cover" Israel's sins. The cover is made of gold to atone for the sin of the Golden Calf, reminding us that gold can be used as an idol or as an instrument of holiness (JT Shek. 1:1).

19Make one cherub at one end and the other
cherub at the other end; of one piece with the
cover shall you make the cherubim at its two
ends. 20The cherubim shall have their wings
spread out above, shielding the cover with their
wings. They shall confront each other, the faces
of the cherubim being turned toward the cover.
21Place the cover on top of the Ark, after depositing inside the Ark the Pact that I will give
you. 22There I will meet with you, and I will impart to you—from above the cover, from between the two cherubim that are on top of the
Ark of the Pact—all that I will command you
concerning the Israelite people.

23You shall make a table of acacia wood, two
cubits long, one cubit wide, and a cubit and a
half high. 24Overlay it with pure gold, and make
a gold molding around it. 25Make a rim of a
hand's breadth around it, and make a gold
molding for its rim round about. 26Make four
gold rings for it, and attach the rings to the four

מִשְּׁנֵי קְצוֹת הַכַּפֹּרֶת׃ 19 וַעֲשֵׂה כְּרוּב אֶחָד
מִקָּצָה מִזֶּה וּכְרוּב־אֶחָד מִקָּצָה מִזֶּה
מִן־הַכַּפֹּרֶת תַּעֲשׂוּ אֶת־הַכְּרֻבִים עַל־שְׁנֵי
קְצוֹתָיו׃ 20 וְהָיוּ הַכְּרֻבִים פֹּרְשֵׂי כְנָפַיִם
לְמַעְלָה סֹכְכִים בְּכַנְפֵיהֶם עַל־הַכַּפֹּרֶת
וּפְנֵיהֶם אִישׁ אֶל־אָחִיו אֶל־הַכַּפֹּרֶת יִהְיוּ
פְּנֵי הַכְּרֻבִים׃ 21 וְנָתַתָּ אֶת־הַכַּפֹּרֶת עַל־
הָאָרֹן מִלְמָעְלָה וְאֶל־הָאָרֹן תִּתֵּן אֶת־
הָעֵדֻת אֲשֶׁר אֶתֵּן אֵלֶיךָ׃ 22 וְנוֹעַדְתִּי
לְךָ שָׁם וְדִבַּרְתִּי אִתְּךָ מֵעַל הַכַּפֹּרֶת
מִבֵּין שְׁנֵי הַכְּרֻבִים אֲשֶׁר עַל־אֲרוֹן הָעֵדֻת
אֵת כָּל־אֲשֶׁר אֲצַוֶּה אוֹתְךָ אֶל־בְּנֵי
יִשְׂרָאֵל׃ פ
23 וְעָשִׂיתָ שֻׁלְחָן עֲצֵי שִׁטִּים אַמָּתַיִם אָרְכּוֹ
וְאַמָּה רָחְבּוֹ וְאַמָּה וָחֵצִי קֹמָתוֹ׃ 24 וְצִפִּיתָ
אֹתוֹ זָהָב טָהוֹר וְעָשִׂיתָ לּוֹ זֵר זָהָב סָבִיב׃
25 וְעָשִׂיתָ לּוֹ מִסְגֶּרֶת טֹפַח סָבִיב וְעָשִׂיתָ
זֵר־זָהָב לְמִסְגַּרְתּוֹ סָבִיב׃ 26 וְעָשִׂיתָ לּוֹ
אַרְבַּע טַבְּעֹת זָהָב וְנָתַתָּ אֶת־הַטַּבָּעֹת עַל
אַרְבַּע הַפֵּאֹת אֲשֶׁר לְאַרְבַּע רַגְלָיו׃

22. The ornamented footstool (here, the ark), like the throne (here, the wings of the cherubim), was a sign of power in the ancient Near East. In this verse, the imagery of the footstool and the throne evoke the conception of God as King who issues His royal decrees to the people Israel through Moses.

THE TABLE AND ITS APPURTENANCES (vv. 23–30)

Specialized furniture and utensils are to be housed in the Holy Place, the second sacred zone of the tabernacle.

The table is presented first, because in holiness it is second only to the ark. Made of acacia wood and overlaid with pure gold, the table is supported by four wooden legs to which golden rings are attached. Poles are inserted into these rings when the table is to be transported. Its main function was to accommodate the bread of display (v. 30), and its proper location was on the north side of the Holy Place in the tabernacle.

---

20. The cherubim shall have their wings spread out The cherubim "confront" one another, even as a religious person must always be connected to other people and may never turn away from them to be concerned only with God.

23. The table and the *m'norah* can be considered to symbolize the two halves of a human being, the physical-material half and the spiritual-intellectual half. The bread on the table represents a person's physical needs, and the *m'norah* represents the light of learning and conscience. The *m'norah* is placed facing the table so that when we go forth to "earn our bread" the light of the *m'norah* will help us know the proper way to do it.

24. pure gold This refers not to the quality of the gold but to the manner of its being acquired. Gold can be sanctified or it can be contaminated, depending on the way in which it is earned and the way in which it is used.

corners at its four legs. [27]The rings shall be next to the rim, as holders for poles to carry the table. [28]Make the poles of acacia wood, and overlay them with gold; by these the table shall be carried. [29]Make its bowls, ladles, jars and jugs with which to offer libations; make them of pure gold. [30]And on the table you shall set the bread of display, to be before Me always.

[31]You shall make a lampstand of pure gold; the lampstand shall be made of hammered work; its base and its shaft, its cups, calyxes, and petals shall be of one piece. [32]Six branches shall

27 לְעֻמַּת הַמִּסְגֶּרֶת תִּהְיֶיןָ הַטַּבָּעֹת
לְבָתִּים לְבַדִּים לָשֵׂאת אֶת־הַשֻּׁלְחָן׃
28 וְעָשִׂיתָ אֶת־הַבַּדִּים עֲצֵי שִׁטִּים וְצִפִּיתָ
אֹתָם זָהָב וְנִשָּׂא־בָם אֶת־הַשֻּׁלְחָן׃
29 וְעָשִׂיתָ קְעָרֹתָיו וְכַפֹּתָיו וּקְשׂוֹתָיו
וּמְנַקִּיֹּתָיו אֲשֶׁר יֻסַּךְ בָּהֵן זָהָב טָהוֹר
תַּעֲשֶׂה אֹתָם׃ 30 וְנָתַתָּ עַל־הַשֻּׁלְחָן לֶחֶם
פָּנִים לְפָנַי תָּמִיד׃ פ
31 וְעָשִׂיתָ מְנֹרַת זָהָב טָהוֹר מִקְשָׁה תֵּעָשֶׂה
הַמְּנוֹרָה יְרֵכָהּ וְקָנָהּ גְּבִיעֶיהָ כַּפְתֹּרֶיהָ

29. Four utensils were displayed on the table. These are referred to in other texts as "service vessels" and as "sacred utensils."

bowls The Talmud understood these to be the molds in which the loaves of bread were placed after baking so that they would retain their shape.

ladles These palm-shaped vessels contained the frankincense that was placed on the table of the bread of display and burned when the loaves were removed each *Shabbat.*

jars In the Talmud they are defined as "props" for the loaves of bread on display. One medieval commentator thought they might be containers for water used in kneading the dough.

jugs Hebrew: *m'nakkiyyot;* literally, "cleansers." One of the traditional commentators took them to be utensils for clearing ashes from the oven and for cleaning the table.

30. bread of display Referred to as such because it was displayed in a special way. According to the Talmud, 12 of these flat, oblong loaves were set out on the table in two equal rows (see Lev. 24:6). They were undisturbed for the entire week until *Shabbat,* when they were replaced by freshly baked loaves. The old loaves were eaten by the priests inside the sacred precincts.

THE *M'NORAH* (vv. 31–40)

The second sacred item of furniture in the Holy Place was the lampstand, the seven-branched *m'norah,* positioned on the south side of the tabernacle opposite the table. We are not told whether the lamps on the six side branches were level with the lamp of the central shaft; and there is no information about the material from which the lamps were to be made. The dimensions of the lampstand also are not given. The primary function of the *m'norah* was to illuminate the area around it at nighttime. For some early commentators the *m'norah* symbolized the tree of life. Aaron and his sons had the exclusive responsibility for lighting and tending the lamps.

31. a lampstand The biblical word *m'norah* is sometimes erroneously translated "candlestick" or "candelabrum." There were no candles, however, until the Roman period.

base Hebrew: *yarekh;* literally, "loins, thigh." Ancient Near Eastern lampstands featured a gradual increase in width toward the bottom. Probably this type of flared base is referred to here.

shaft Hebrew: *kaneh,* literally, "cane, reed"; refers to the six branches of the lampstand.

cups Hebrew: *g'vi·a;* refers to a goblet, a bulbous-shaped receptacle.

calyxes Hebrew: *kaftor;* an architectural term that designates the capital of a column. Such capitals were ornamented with a leaflike motif.

petals The Hebrew word *peraḥ,* usually meaning "flower," is here rendered "lily" in the Greek and Latin translations of the Torah. In the ancient world, the water lily (the lotus blossom) symbolized newborn life and was highly popular as a floral decoration on columns.

of one piece All these elements, together with the central shaft, are to be made from a single block of gold, not assembled from separate parts.

---

37. The seven lamps of the *m'norah* symbolize the seven days of Creation (PR 8), honoring God who created the world, and highlighting the tabernacle as a world of its own. Although this was the lamp that burned miraculously in the story of *Ḥanukkah,* a *Ḥanukkah m'norah* has eight branches rather than seven, to commemorate the eight days of the *Ḥanukkah* miracle.

issue from its sides; three branches from one
side of the lampstand and three branches from
the other side of the lampstand. 33On one
branch there shall be three cups shaped like
almond-blossoms, each with calyx and petals,
and on the next branch there shall be three cups
shaped like almond-blossoms, each with calyx
and petals; so for all six branches issuing from
the lampstand. 34And on the lampstand itself
there shall be four cups shaped like almond-
blossoms, each with calyx and petals: 35a calyx,
of one piece with it, under a pair of branches;
and a calyx, of one piece with it, under the second pair of branches, and a calyx, of one piece
with it, under the last pair of branches; so for
all six branches issuing from the lampstand.
36Their calyxes and their stems shall be of one
piece with it, the whole of it a single hammered
piece of pure gold. 37Make its seven lamps—the
lamps shall be so mounted as to give the light
on its front side—38and its tongs and fire pans
of pure gold. 39It shall be made, with all these
furnishings, out of a talent of pure gold. 40Note
well, and follow the patterns for them that are
being shown you on the mountain.

וּפְרָחֶיהָ מִמֶּנָּה יִהְיוּ׃ 32 וְשִׁשָּׁה קָנִים
יֹצְאִים מִצִּדֶּיהָ שְׁלֹשָׁה ׀ קְנֵי מְנֹרָה
מִצִּדָּהּ הָאֶחָד וּשְׁלֹשָׁה קְנֵי מְנֹרָה מִצִּדָּהּ
הַשֵּׁנִי׃ 33 שְׁלֹשָׁה גְבִעִים מְשֻׁקָּדִים בַּקָּנֶה
הָאֶחָד כַּפְתֹּר וָפֶרַח וּשְׁלֹשָׁה גְבִעִים
מְשֻׁקָּדִים בַּקָּנֶה הָאֶחָד כַּפְתֹּר וָפָרַח כֵּן
לְשֵׁשֶׁת הַקָּנִים הַיֹּצְאִים מִן־הַמְּנֹרָה׃
34 וּבַמְּנֹרָה אַרְבָּעָה גְבִעִים מְשֻׁקָּדִים
כַּפְתֹּרֶיהָ וּפְרָחֶיהָ׃ 35 וְכַפְתֹּר תַּחַת שְׁנֵי
הַקָּנִים מִמֶּנָּה וְכַפְתֹּר תַּחַת שְׁנֵי הַקָּנִים
מִמֶּנָּה וְכַפְתֹּר תַּחַת־שְׁנֵי הַקָּנִים מִמֶּנָּה
לְשֵׁשֶׁת הַקָּנִים הַיֹּצְאִים מִן־הַמְּנֹרָה׃
36 כַּפְתֹּרֵיהֶם וּקְנֹתָם מִמֶּנָּה יִהְיוּ כֻּלָּהּ
מִקְשָׁה אַחַת זָהָב טָהוֹר׃ 37 וְעָשִׂיתָ
אֶת־נֵרֹתֶיהָ שִׁבְעָה וְהֶעֱלָה אֶת־נֵרֹתֶיהָ
וְהֵאִיר עַל־עֵבֶר פָּנֶיהָ׃ 38 וּמַלְקָחֶיהָ
וּמַחְתֹּתֶיהָ זָהָב טָהוֹר׃ 39 כִּכַּר זָהָב טָהוֹר
יַעֲשֶׂה אֹתָהּ אֵת כָּל־הַכֵּלִים הָאֵלֶּה׃
40 וּרְאֵה וַעֲשֵׂה בְּתַבְנִיתָם אֲשֶׁר־אַתָּה
מָרְאֶה בָּהָר׃ ס

26 As for the Tabernacle, make it of ten
strips of cloth; make these of fine twisted linen,

שי **כו** וְאֶת־הַמִּשְׁכָּן תַּעֲשֶׂה עֶשֶׂר יְרִיעֹת
שֵׁשׁ מָשְׁזָר וּתְכֵלֶת וְאַרְגָּמָן וְתֹלַעַת שָׁנִי

35. lampstand The central shaft. Its ornamentation is to be located just beneath the points from which the six side branches emerge.

37. lamps The containers for the wick and oil.

on its front side The lamps are to be arranged in such a way that the light shines toward the facing table.

38. tongs and fire pans These nouns are objects of the verb "make" in verse 37. The tongs were used to remove the burned wicks; the fire pans, to receive them.

39. a talent Hebrew: *kikkar*. This is the largest unit of weight mentioned in the Bible, equivalent to 3000 shekels (see 38:24).

THE TABERNACLE COVERINGS (26:1–14)

The text turns to the four layers of coverings that serve as the tabernacle roof.

THE LOWEST LAYER (vv. 1–6)

The lowest layer is made of 10 multicolored sheets of fine linen decorated with the cherubim motif. They are sewn into paired sets of 5, i.e., two long sheets. A total of 50 blue loops are fixed along one edge of each sheet. The two sets are then fastened together by gold clasps inserted into the loops.

1. Tabernacle Here, the text refers specifically to the two sacred zones, the Holy of Holies

of blue, purple, and crimson yarns, with a design of cherubim worked into them. 2The length of each cloth shall be twenty-eight cubits, and the width of each cloth shall be four cubits, all the cloths to have the same measurements. 3Five of the cloths shall be joined to one another, and the other five cloths shall be joined to one another. 4Make loops of blue wool on the edge of the outermost cloth of the one set; and do likewise on the edge of the outermost cloth of the other set: 5make fifty loops on the one cloth, and fifty loops on the edge of the end cloth of the other set, the loops to be opposite one another. 6And make fifty gold clasps, and couple the cloths to one another with the clasps, so that the Tabernacle becomes one whole.

7You shall then make cloths of goats' hair for a tent over the Tabernacle; make the cloths eleven in number. 8The length of each cloth

כְּרֻבִים מַעֲשֵׂה חֹשֵׁב תַּעֲשֶׂה אֹתָם׃
2 אֹרֶךְ ׀ הַיְרִיעָה הָאַחַת שְׁמֹנֶה וְעֶשְׂרִים
בָּאַמָּה וְרֹחַב אַרְבַּע בָּאַמָּה הַיְרִיעָה
הָאֶחָת מִדָּה אַחַת לְכָל־הַיְרִיעֹת׃ 3 חֲמֵשׁ
הַיְרִיעֹת תִּהְיֶיןָ חֹבְרֹת אִשָּׁה אֶל־אֲחֹתָהּ
וְחָמֵשׁ יְרִיעֹת חֹבְרֹת אִשָּׁה אֶל־אֲחֹתָהּ׃
4 וְעָשִׂיתָ לֻלְאֹת תְּכֵלֶת עַל שְׂפַת הַיְרִיעָה
הָאֶחָת מִקָּצָה בַּחֹבָרֶת וְכֵן תַּעֲשֶׂה בִּשְׂפַת
הַיְרִיעָה הַקִּיצוֹנָה בַּמַּחְבֶּרֶת הַשֵּׁנִית׃
5 חֲמִשִּׁים לֻלָאֹת תַּעֲשֶׂה בַּיְרִיעָה הָאֶחָת
וַחֲמִשִּׁים לֻלָאֹת תַּעֲשֶׂה בִּקְצֵה הַיְרִיעָה
אֲשֶׁר בַּמַּחְבֶּרֶת הַשֵּׁנִית מַקְבִּילֹת הַלֻּלָאֹת
אִשָּׁה אֶל־אֲחֹתָהּ׃ 6 וְעָשִׂיתָ חֲמִשִּׁים קַרְסֵי
זָהָב וְחִבַּרְתָּ אֶת־הַיְרִיעֹת אִשָּׁה אֶל־
אֲחֹתָהּ בַּקְּרָסִים וְהָיָה הַמִּשְׁכָּן אֶחָד׃ פ
7 וְעָשִׂיתָ יְרִיעֹת עִזִּים לְאֹהֶל עַל־הַמִּשְׁכָּן
עַשְׁתֵּי־עֶשְׂרֵה יְרִיעֹת תַּעֲשֶׂה אֹתָם׃
8 אֹרֶךְ ׀ הַיְרִיעָה הָאַחַת שְׁלֹשִׁים בָּאַמָּה

and the Holy Place, both of which were covered by the lowest of the tabernacle's covers.

strips of cloth The Hebrew word *y'ri·ah* always pertains to the fabrics of which tents are made.

twisted The lowest layer is to be made of a fine grade of linen woven of twisted yarns.

a design of cherubim Hebrew: *k'ruvim ma·asei ḥoshev;* literally, "cherubs, the work of a thinker/designer," a creative and imaginative artist. A highly specialized technique of weaving apparently is referred to here, different from that mentioned later in verse 36 and 28:32.

3. joined Stitched together with needle and thread.

6. clasps Probably S-shaped, the clasps are to be inserted through the two parallel sets of loops.

one whole The 10 separate fabrics covering the section of the tabernacle that contains the Holy of Holies and the Holy Place become a single entity.

THE SECOND LAYER (vv. 7–13)

A coarser covering, made of 11 strips of goats' hair, was to be laid above the linen fabric. A unit of 5 strips and one of 6 strips were to be stitched together and then secured by loops and clasps. The text does not specify the color of the loops, which suggests that they were not dyed. The clasps were made of bronze. The long fabric was to be spread lengthwise over the entire area of the tabernacle, starting from the eastern entrance and extending toward the rear. The outermost strip, called "the sixth," which began at the entrance, was to be doubled over. On the north and south sides, the coverings of goats' hair just reached the ground. On the west side, the fabric would trail along the ground.

7. goats' hair See Comment to 25:4.

for a tent As a protective shield over the ornamented linen cover.

eleven One strip more than the number of linen cloths.

CHAPTER 26

6. so that the Tabernacle becomes one whole The tabernacle is symbolic of the Israelites. They too are composed of many parts, but they must form one harmonious whole.

shall be thirty cubits, and the width of each cloth shall be four cubits, the eleven cloths to have the same measurements. 9Join five of the cloths by themselves, and the other six cloths by themselves; and fold over the sixth cloth at the front of the tent. 10Make fifty loops on the edge of the outermost cloth of the one set, and fifty loops on the edge of the cloth of the other set. 11Make fifty copper clasps, and fit the clasps into the loops, and couple the tent together so that it becomes one whole. 12As for the overlapping excess of the cloths of the tent, the extra half-cloth shall overlap the back of the Tabernacle, 13while the extra cubit at either end of each length of tent cloth shall hang down to the bottom of the two sides of the Tabernacle and cover it. 14And make for the tent a covering of tanned ram skins, and a covering of dolphin skins above.

15You shall make the planks for the Tabernacle of acacia wood, upright. 16The length of each plank shall be ten cubits and the width of each plank a cubit and a half. 17Each plank shall

וְרֹ֙חַב֙ אַרְבַּ֣ע בָּֽאַמָּ֔ה הַיְרִיעָ֖ה הָאֶחָ֑ת מִדָּ֣ה אַחַ֔ת לְעַשְׁתֵּ֥י עֶשְׂרֵ֖ה יְרִיעֹֽת׃ 9וְחִבַּרְתָּ֞ אֶת־חֲמֵ֤שׁ הַיְרִיעֹת֙ לְבָ֔ד וְאֶת־שֵׁ֤שׁ הַיְרִיעֹת֙ לְבָ֑ד וְכָפַלְתָּ֙ אֶת־הַיְרִיעָ֣ה הַשִּׁשִּׁ֔ית אֶל־מ֖וּל פְּנֵ֥י הָאֹֽהֶל׃ 10וְעָשִׂ֜יתָ חֲמִשִּׁ֣ים לֻֽלָאֹ֗ת עַ֣ל שְׂפַ֤ת הַיְרִיעָה֙ הָֽאֶחָ֔ת הַקִּיצֹנָ֖ה בַּחֹבָ֑רֶת וַחֲמִשִּׁ֣ים לֻֽלָאֹ֗ת עַ֚ל שְׂפַ֣ת הַיְרִיעָ֔ה הַחֹבֶ֖רֶת הַשֵּׁנִֽית׃ 11וְעָשִׂ֛יתָ קַרְסֵ֥י נְחֹ֖שֶׁת חֲמִשִּׁ֑ים וְהֵבֵאתָ֤ אֶת־הַקְּרָסִים֙ בַּלֻּ֣לָאֹ֔ת וְחִבַּרְתָּ֥ אֶת־הָאֹ֖הֶל וְהָיָ֥ה אֶחָֽד׃ 12וְסֶ֙רַח֙ הָעֹדֵ֔ף בִּֽירִיעֹ֖ת הָאֹ֑הֶל חֲצִ֤י הַיְרִיעָה֙ הָעֹדֶ֔פֶת תִּסְרַ֕ח עַ֖ל אֲחֹרֵ֥י הַמִּשְׁכָּֽן׃ 13וְהָאַמָּ֨ה מִזֶּ֜ה וְהָאַמָּ֤ה מִזֶּה֙ בָּעֹדֵ֔ף בְּאֹ֖רֶךְ יְרִיעֹ֣ת הָאֹ֑הֶל יִֽהְיֶ֙ה סָר֜וּחַ עַל־צִדֵּ֧י הַמִּשְׁכָּ֛ן מִזֶּ֥ה וּמִזֶּ֖ה לְכַסֹּתֽוֹ׃ 14וְעָשִׂ֤יתָ מִכְסֶה֙ לָאֹ֔הֶל עֹרֹ֥ת אֵילִ֖ם מְאָדָּמִ֑ים וּמִכְסֵ֛ה עֹרֹ֥ת תְּחָשִׁ֖ים מִלְמָֽעְלָה׃ פ
15וְעָשִׂ֥יתָ אֶת־הַקְּרָשִׁ֖ים לַמִּשְׁכָּ֑ן עֲצֵ֥י שִׁטִּ֖ים עֹמְדִֽים׃ 16עֶ֥שֶׂר אַמּ֖וֹת אֹ֣רֶךְ הַקָּ֑רֶשׁ וְאַמָּה֙ וַחֲצִ֣י הָֽאַמָּ֔ה רֹ֖חַב הַקֶּ֥רֶשׁ הָאֶחָֽד׃ 17שְׁתֵּ֣י יָד֗וֹת לַקֶּ֙רֶשׁ֙ הָֽאֶחָ֔ד מְשֻׁלָּבֹ֕ת אִשָּׁ֖ה

---

11. copper   See Comment to 25:3.
12. tent   The covering.

THE THIRD AND FOURTH LAYERS   (v. 14)

The text does not give the measurements of the two uppermost leather coverings.
14. dolphin skins   See Comment to 25:5.

THE WOODEN STRUCTURE   (vv. 15–30)

The instructions now outline the structure that is to hold the cloths. Three walls are to be con-

structed of timber planks or frames cut from acacia trees. The northern and southern walls are made up of 20 such planks or frames, for a total of 40; the western wall requires 8; the eastern side has none. The tabernacle was exactly half the size of Solomon's Temple in length and width, and one-third its height, according to the dimensions given in 1 Kings 6:2.
15. acacia   See Comment to 25:5.
upright   This refers to the placement of the planks.

---

15.   Why was the acacia tree chosen to be the exclusive source of wood for the Ark and for the tabernacle? The Midrash suggests that it was chosen because it is not a fruit-bearing tree. God did not want to destroy the future fruit harvests of a tree even to build the Ark. Where did these acacia trees come from?

They are not native to the Sinai wilderness. Legend has it that the patriarch Jacob planted them on his way to Egypt, foreseeing that one day his grandchildren would need them. He did something of no immediate use to himself, for the benefit of future generations (Tanḥ.).

have two tenons, parallel to each other; do the same with all the planks of the Tabernacle. 18Of the planks of the Tabernacle, make twenty planks on the south side: 19making forty silver sockets under the twenty planks, two sockets under the one plank for its two tenons and two sockets under each following plank for its two tenons; 20and for the other side wall of the Tabernacle, on the north side, twenty planks, 21with their forty silver sockets, two sockets under the one plank and two sockets under each following plank. 22And for the rear of the Tabernacle, to the west, make six planks; 23and make two planks for the corners of the Tabernacle at the rear. 24They shall match at the bottom, and terminate alike at the top inside one ring; thus shall it be with both of them: they shall form the two corners. 25Thus there shall be eight planks with their sockets of silver: sixteen sockets, two sockets under the first plank, and two sockets under each of the other planks.

26You shall make bars of acacia wood: five for the planks of the one side wall of the Tabernacle, 27five bars for the planks of the other side wall of the Tabernacle, and five bars for the planks of the wall of the Tabernacle at the rear to the west. 28The center bar halfway up the planks shall run from end to end. 29Overlay the planks with gold, and make their rings of gold, as holders for the bars; and overlay the bars with gold. 30Then set up the Tabernacle according

אֶל־אֲחֹתָהּ כֵּן תַּעֲשֶׂה לְכֹל קַרְשֵׁי
הַמִּשְׁכָּן׃ 18 וְעָשִׂיתָ אֶת־הַקְּרָשִׁים לַמִּשְׁכָּן
עֶשְׂרִים קֶרֶשׁ לִפְאַת נֶגְבָּה תֵימָנָה׃
19 וְאַרְבָּעִים אַדְנֵי־כֶסֶף תַּעֲשֶׂה תַּחַת
עֶשְׂרִים הַקָּרֶשׁ שְׁנֵי אֲדָנִים תַּחַת־הַקֶּרֶשׁ
הָאֶחָד לִשְׁתֵּי יְדֹתָיו וּשְׁנֵי אֲדָנִים תַּחַת־
הַקֶּרֶשׁ הָאֶחָד לִשְׁתֵּי יְדֹתָיו׃ 20 וּלְצֶלַע
הַמִּשְׁכָּן הַשֵּׁנִית לִפְאַת צָפוֹן עֶשְׂרִים
קָרֶשׁ׃ 21 וְאַרְבָּעִים אַדְנֵיהֶם כָּסֶף שְׁנֵי
אֲדָנִים תַּחַת הַקֶּרֶשׁ הָאֶחָד וּשְׁנֵי אֲדָנִים
תַּחַת הַקֶּרֶשׁ הָאֶחָד׃ 22 וּלְיַרְכְּתֵי הַמִּשְׁכָּן
יָמָּה תַּעֲשֶׂה שִׁשָּׁה קְרָשִׁים׃ 23 וּשְׁנֵי
קְרָשִׁים תַּעֲשֶׂה לִמְקֻצְעֹת הַמִּשְׁכָּן
בַּיַּרְכָתָיִם׃ 24 וְיִהְיוּ תֹאֲמִם מִלְּמַטָּה
וְיַחְדָּו יִהְיוּ תַמִּים עַל־רֹאשׁוֹ אֶל־הַטַּבַּעַת
הָאֶחָת כֵּן יִהְיֶה לִשְׁנֵיהֶם לִשְׁנֵי הַמִּקְצֹעֹת
יִהְיוּ׃ 25 וְהָיוּ שְׁמֹנָה קְרָשִׁים וְאַדְנֵיהֶם
כֶּסֶף שִׁשָּׁה עָשָׂר אֲדָנִים שְׁנֵי אֲדָנִים תַּחַת
הַקֶּרֶשׁ הָאֶחָד וּשְׁנֵי אֲדָנִים תַּחַת הַקֶּרֶשׁ
הָאֶחָד׃

26 וְעָשִׂיתָ בְרִיחִם עֲצֵי שִׁטִּים חֲמִשָּׁה
לְקַרְשֵׁי צֶלַע־הַמִּשְׁכָּן הָאֶחָד׃ 27 וַחֲמִשָּׁה
בְרִיחִם לְקַרְשֵׁי צֶלַע־הַמִּשְׁכָּן הַשֵּׁנִית
וַחֲמִשָּׁה בְרִיחִם לְקַרְשֵׁי צֶלַע הַמִּשְׁכָּן
לַיַּרְכָתַיִם יָמָּה׃ 28 וְהַבְּרִיחַ הַתִּיכֹן בְּתוֹךְ
הַקְּרָשִׁים מַבְרִחַ מִן־הַקָּצֶה אֶל־הַקָּצֶה׃
29 וְאֶת־הַקְּרָשִׁים תְּצַפֶּה זָהָב וְאֶת־
טַבְּעֹתֵיהֶם תַּעֲשֶׂה זָהָב בָּתִּים לַבְּרִיחִם
וְצִפִּיתָ אֶת־הַבְּרִיחִם זָהָב׃ 30 וַהֲקֵמֹתָ

22. to the west Hebrew: *yammah*; literally, "seaward," i.e., toward the Mediterranean.

23. corners The Hebrew word *m'kutz·ot* (*miktzo·ot* in v. 24 and elsewhere) is an architectural term for some kind of special corner structure. Here it seems to involve two extra supports, one at each corner of the western wall.

24. Apparently, according to this verse, the corner buttresses are to be perfectly aligned and secured at both top and bottom.

26. bars A crossbar, usually one that secures doors and gates. The precise location and arrangement of the bars here are uncertain.

30. This refers back to 25:9.

to the manner of it that you were shown on the mountain.

אֶת־הַמִּשְׁכָּן כְּמִשְׁפָּטוֹ אֲשֶׁר הָרְאֵיתָ
בָּהָר׃ ס

[31]You shall make a curtain of blue, purple, and crimson yarns, and fine twisted linen; it shall have a design of cherubim worked into it. [32]Hang it upon four posts of acacia wood overlaid with gold and having hooks of gold, [set] in four sockets of silver. [33]Hang the curtain under the clasps, and carry the Ark of the Pact there, behind the curtain, so that the curtain shall serve you as a partition between the Holy and the Holy of Holies. [34]Place the cover upon the Ark of the Pact in the Holy of Holies. [35]Place the table outside the curtain, and the lampstand by the south wall of the Tabernacle opposite the table, which is to be placed by the north wall.

מישי 31 וְעָשִׂיתָ פָרֹכֶת תְּכֵלֶת וְאַרְגָּמָן וְתוֹלַעַת
שָׁנִי וְשֵׁשׁ מָשְׁזָר מַעֲשֵׂה חֹשֵׁב יַעֲשֶׂה אֹתָהּ
כְּרֻבִים׃ 32 וְנָתַתָּה אֹתָהּ עַל־אַרְבָּעָה
עַמּוּדֵי שִׁטִּים מְצֻפִּים זָהָב וָוֵיהֶם זָהָב
עַל־אַרְבָּעָה אַדְנֵי־כָסֶף׃ 33 וְנָתַתָּה אֶת־
הַפָּרֹכֶת תַּחַת הַקְּרָסִים וְהֵבֵאתָ שָׁמָּה
מִבֵּית לַפָּרֹכֶת אֵת אֲרוֹן הָעֵדוּת וְהִבְדִּילָה
הַפָּרֹכֶת לָכֶם בֵּין הַקֹּדֶשׁ וּבֵין קֹדֶשׁ
הַקֳּדָשִׁים׃ 34 וְנָתַתָּ אֶת־הַכַּפֹּרֶת עַל אֲרוֹן
הָעֵדֻת בְּקֹדֶשׁ הַקֳּדָשִׁים׃ 35 וְשַׂמְתָּ אֶת־
הַשֻּׁלְחָן מִחוּץ לַפָּרֹכֶת וְאֶת־הַמְּנֹרָה נֹכַח
הַשֻּׁלְחָן עַל צֶלַע הַמִּשְׁכָּן תֵּימָנָה וְהַשֻּׁלְחָן
תִּתֵּן עַל־צֶלַע צָפוֹן׃

[36]You shall make a screen for the entrance of the Tent, of blue, purple, and crimson yarns, and fine twisted linen, done in embroidery. [37]Make five posts of acacia wood for the screen and overlay them with gold—their hooks being of gold—and cast for them five sockets of copper.

36 וְעָשִׂיתָ מָסָךְ לְפֶתַח הָאֹהֶל תְּכֵלֶת
וְאַרְגָּמָן וְתוֹלַעַת שָׁנִי וְשֵׁשׁ מָשְׁזָר מַעֲשֵׂה
רֹקֵם׃ 37 וְעָשִׂיתָ לַמָּסָךְ חֲמִשָּׁה עַמּוּדֵי
שִׁטִּים וְצִפִּיתָ אֹתָם זָהָב וָוֵיהֶם זָהָב
שי וְיָצַקְתָּ לָהֶם חֲמִשָּׁה אַדְנֵי נְחֹשֶׁת׃ ס

THE INNER CURTAIN (*PAROKHET*) (vv. 31–35)

The tabernacle is to be partitioned into two unequal sections by a curtain, or a veil (Hebrew: *parokhet*). The inner section will form a perfect cube measuring 10 cubits (15 ft.; 4.6 m.) on each side. This is the Holy of Holies, which will contain the ark and the *kapporet,* as prescribed in 25:17. The outer section will measure 10 cubits in width, 20 cubits in length, and 10 cubits in height (15 by 30 by 15 ft.). It is called the "Holy Place" and will receive the table, the *m'norah,* and the altar of incense. The *parokhet* is made from the same fabric and designed with the same colors as the lowest coverings. It, too, is adorned with figures of cherubim. Its size is not given.

33. Ramban notes that the sequence presented here is not the same as that of the actual construction and assembly described in 40:3, where we are told the ark was put in place first and the curtain later.

THE OUTER CURTAIN (vv. 36–37)

A second screen separated the entrance of the Holy Place on the eastern side from the outer court. It was made of the same multicolored fabric as the *parokhet* but was not decorated with cherubs. Other differences: It was embroidered and it rested on five pillars instead of four; its pillars fitted into bronze rather than silver sockets.

36. done in embroidery The Hebrew phrase *ma·asei rokem* refers to another type of specialized weaving, one that required less skill than that needed for the coverings of the tabernacle and the *parokhet*.

37. copper Better: bronze. See Comment to 25:3.

27 You shall make the altar of acacia wood,
five cubits long and five cubits wide—the altar
is to be square—and three cubits high. 2Make
its horns on the four corners, the horns to be
of one piece with it; and overlay it with copper.
3Make the pails for removing its ashes, as well
as its scrapers, basins, flesh hooks, and fire
pans—make all its utensils of copper. 4Make for
it a grating of meshwork in copper; and on the
mesh make four copper rings at its four corners.
5Set the mesh below, under the ledge of the altar,
so that it extends to the middle of the altar. 6And
make poles for the altar, poles of acacia wood,
and overlay them with copper. 7The poles shall
be inserted into the rings, so that the poles remain on the two sides of the altar when it is car-

ששי **כז** וְעָשִׂיתָ אֶת־הַמִּזְבֵּחַ עֲצֵי שִׁטִּים
חָמֵשׁ אַמּוֹת אֹרֶךְ וְחָמֵשׁ אַמּוֹת רֹחַב רָבוּעַ
יִהְיֶה הַמִּזְבֵּחַ וְשָׁלֹשׁ אַמּוֹת קֹמָתוֹ:
2 וְעָשִׂיתָ קַרְנֹתָיו עַל אַרְבַּע פִּנֹּתָיו מִמֶּנּוּ
תִּהְיֶיןָ קַרְנֹתָיו וְצִפִּיתָ אֹתוֹ נְחֹשֶׁת:
3 וְעָשִׂיתָ סִּירֹתָיו לְדַשְּׁנוֹ וְיָעָיו וּמִזְרְקֹתָיו
וּמִזְלְגֹתָיו וּמַחְתֹּתָיו לְכָל־כֵּלָיו תַּעֲשֶׂה
נְחֹשֶׁת: 4 וְעָשִׂיתָ לּוֹ מִכְבָּר מַעֲשֵׂה רֶשֶׁת
נְחֹשֶׁת וְעָשִׂיתָ עַל־הָרֶשֶׁת אַרְבַּע טַבְּעֹת
נְחֹשֶׁת עַל אַרְבַּע קְצוֹתָיו: 5 וְנָתַתָּה אֹתָהּ
תַּחַת כַּרְכֹּב הַמִּזְבֵּחַ מִלְּמָטָּה וְהָיְתָה
הָרֶשֶׁת עַד חֲצִי הַמִּזְבֵּחַ: 6 וְעָשִׂיתָ בַדִּים
לַמִּזְבֵּחַ בַּדֵּי עֲצֵי שִׁטִּים וְצִפִּיתָ אֹתָם
נְחֹשֶׁת: 7 וְהוּבָא אֶת־בַּדָּיו בַּטַּבָּעֹת וְהָיוּ
הַבַּדִּים עַל־שְׁתֵּי צַלְעֹת הַמִּזְבֵּחַ בִּשְׂאֵת

THE OUTER ALTAR OF SACRIFICES AND ITS ACCESSORIES (27:1–8)

The text moves from the Holy Place to the courtyard of the tabernacle, beginning with the most important item there, the altar of burnt offering. The details of its construction are quite complicated and imperfectly understood, and its precise location is not given. It was carried by means of bronzed poles inserted, when necessary, into rings affixed to its sides.

1. altar The patriarchs frequently built altars, and Moses built two of them. Because an altar was an indispensable part of worship and ritual, its presence in the tabernacle is taken for granted—hence, the use of the definite article. Stone altars with "horns" at the four corners have been discovered at several Israelite sites.

2. The horn-shaped projections at the upper corners were to be carved out of the wooden structure and then bronzed, to become integral parts of the altar. They were not to be made separately and then attached to it.

2–19. copper Better: bronze. See Comment to 25:3.

3. The text lists five accessories needed for the performance of the sacrificial rites. No quantity is given for any of them.

pails Hebrew: *sir;* usually refers to a large vessel with a wide mouth.

scrapers Hebrew: *ya·eh;* designates a kind of shovel with which the refuse on the altar is gathered up and placed in the pails for removal.

basins Hebrew: *mizrak,* from the stem זרק (to sprinkle); refers to the vessel in which the blood of the sacrificial animal is collected for sprinkling on the altar. Blood, in the biblical view, constitutes the essence of life and, therefore, belongs only to God, the giver of all life. The act of sprinkling the blood on the altar or its base, a vital part of the sacrificial ritual, symbolizes its return to God.

flesh hooks Hebrew: *mizlagah;* an implement, probably a large, three-pronged fork, with which the flesh is turned over while it is being burnt on the altar.

4. grating A kind of sieve, placed beneath a ledge that runs all around the altar, perhaps to catch falling embers.

5. ledge According to some of the Sages, the ledge was a projection that served as a walkway for the priests officiating on the altar.

middle Depending on the category of sacrifice, the blood had to be sprinkled either above or below this line.

6–7. poles For carrying.

ried. [8]Make it hollow, of boards. As you were shown on the mountain, so shall they be made.

[9]You shall make the enclosure of the Tabernacle:

On the south side, a hundred cubits of hangings of fine twisted linen for the length of the enclosure on that side—[10]with its twenty posts and their twenty sockets of copper, the hooks and bands of the posts to be of silver.

[11]Again a hundred cubits of hangings for its length along the north side—with its twenty posts and their twenty sockets of copper, the hooks and bands of the posts to be of silver.

[12]For the width of the enclosure, on the west side, fifty cubits of hangings, with their ten posts and their ten sockets.

[13]For the width of the enclosure on the front, or east side, fifty cubits: [14]fifteen cubits of hangings on the one flank, with their three posts and their three sockets; [15]fifteen cubits of hangings on the other flank, with their three posts and their three sockets; [16]and for the gate of the enclosure, a screen of twenty cubits, of blue, purple, and crimson yarns, and fine twisted linen, done in embroidery, with their four posts and their four sockets.

[17]All the posts round the enclosure shall be banded with silver and their hooks shall be of silver; their sockets shall be of copper.

[18]The length of the enclosure shall be a hundred cubits, and the width fifty throughout; and the height five cubits—[with hangings] of fine twisted linen. The sockets shall be of copper: [19]all the utensils of the Tabernacle, for all its

8 נָב֥וּב לֻחֹ֖ת תַּעֲשֶׂ֣ה אֹת֑וֹ כַּאֲשֶׁ֨ר הֶרְאָ֥ה אֹתְךָ֛ בָּהָ֖ר כֵּ֥ן יַעֲשֽׂוּ׃ ס

שביעי 9 וְעָשִׂ֕יתָ אֵ֖ת חֲצַ֣ר הַמִּשְׁכָּ֑ן לִפְאַ֣ת נֶֽגֶב־תֵּימָ֜נָה קְלָעִ֤ים לֶֽחָצֵר֙ שֵׁ֣שׁ מׇשְׁזָ֔ר מֵאָ֣ה בָֽאַמָּ֔ה אֹ֖רֶךְ לַפֵּאָ֥ה הָאֶחָֽת׃ 10 וְעַמֻּדָ֣יו עֶשְׂרִ֔ים וְאַדְנֵיהֶ֥ם עֶשְׂרִ֖ים נְחֹ֑שֶׁת וָוֵ֧י הָעַמֻּדִ֛ים וַחֲשֻׁקֵיהֶ֖ם כָּֽסֶף׃ 11 וְכֵ֨ן לִפְאַ֤ת צָפוֹן֙ בָּאֹ֔רֶךְ קְלָעִ֖ים מֵאָ֣ה אֹ֑רֶךְ וְעַמֻּדָ֣ו עֶשְׂרִ֗ים וְאַדְנֵיהֶ֤ם עֶשְׂרִים֙ נְחֹ֔שֶׁת וָוֵ֧י הָֽעַמֻּדִ֛ים וַחֲשֻׁקֵיהֶ֖ם כָּֽסֶף׃ 12 וְרֹ֤חַב הֶֽחָצֵר֙ לִפְאַת־יָ֔ם קְלָעִ֖ים חֲמִשִּׁ֣ים אַמָּ֑ה עַמֻּדֵיהֶ֣ם עֲשָׂרָ֔ה וְאַדְנֵיהֶ֖ם עֲשָׂרָֽה׃ 13 וְרֹ֣חַב הֶֽחָצֵ֗ר לִפְאַ֛ת קֵ֥דְמָה מִזְרָ֖חָה חֲמִשִּׁ֥ים אַמָּֽה׃ 14 וַחֲמֵ֨שׁ עֶשְׂרֵ֥ה אַמָּ֛ה קְלָעִ֖ים לַכָּתֵ֑ף עַמֻּדֵיהֶ֣ם שְׁלֹשָׁ֔ה וְאַדְנֵיהֶ֖ם שְׁלֹשָֽׁה׃ 15 וְלַכָּתֵף֙ הַשֵּׁנִ֔ית חֲמֵ֥שׁ עֶשְׂרֵ֖ה קְלָעִ֑ים עַמֻּדֵיהֶ֣ם שְׁלֹשָׁ֔ה וְאַדְנֵיהֶ֖ם שְׁלֹשָֽׁה׃ 16 וּלְשַׁ֨עַר הֶֽחָצֵ֜ר מָסָ֣ךְ ׀ עֶשְׂרִ֣ים אַמָּ֗ה תְּכֵ֨לֶת וְאַרְגָּמָ֜ן וְתוֹלַ֧עַת שָׁנִ֣י וְשֵׁ֣שׁ מׇשְׁזָ֗ר מַעֲשֵׂ֣ה רֹקֵ֔ם עַמֻּדֵיהֶ֣ם אַרְבָּעָ֔ה וְאַדְנֵיהֶ֖ם אַרְבָּעָֽה׃ 17 כׇּל־עַמּוּדֵ֨י הֶֽחָצֵ֤ר סָבִיב֙ מְחֻשָּׁקִ֣ים כֶּ֔סֶף וָוֵיהֶ֖ם כָּ֑סֶף וְאַדְנֵיהֶ֖ם נְחֹֽשֶׁת׃ 18 אֹ֣רֶךְ הֶֽחָצֵר֩ מֵאָ֨ה בָֽאַמָּ֜ה וְרֹ֣חַב ׀ חֲמִשִּׁ֣ים בַּֽחֲמִשִּׁ֗ים וְקֹמָ֛ה חָמֵ֥שׁ אַמּ֖וֹת שֵׁ֣שׁ מׇשְׁזָ֑ר וְאַדְנֵיהֶ֖ם נְחֹֽשֶׁת׃ 19 לְכֹל֙ כְּלֵ֣י

THE ENCLOSURE   (vv. 9–19)

As in all temples and sanctuaries, the sacred area of the tabernacle must be clearly separated from the profane space outside. The instructions now deal with the enclosure of the entire tabernacle compound, termed ḥatzer in Hebrew.

10. posts According to 38:17, the bronze posts had silver tops.

bands These are some type of connecting rods. The root of the word for "band" (ḥashuk) means "to be attached to."

13. on the front, or east side Hebrew: kedmah mizraḥah; literally, "on the front toward the rising sun."

A SUMMATION   (vv. 18–19)

19. Tabernacle Here, the Hebrew mishkan

service, as well as all its pegs and all the pegs of the court, shall be of copper.

הַמִּשְׁכָּ֖ן בְּכֹ֣ל עֲבֹדָת֑וֹ וְכָל־יְתֵדֹתָ֛יו וְכָל־
יִתְדֹ֥ת הֶחָצֵ֖ר נְחֹֽשֶׁת׃ ס

means the entire tabernacle compound. In the tabernacle proper, the accessories of the Holy of Holies and of the Holy Place were made of gold, not bronze. The requirements for the Solomonic Temple are found in 1 Kings 6–7. It should be noted that all of the specifications that the Torah prescribes in such detail were generally considered to be secret in other ancient Near Eastern sources.

הפטרת תרומה

HAFTARAH FOR T'RUMAH

1 KINGS 5:26–6:13

The beginning of the construction of the Temple by Solomon, dated by scholars at around 958 B.C.E., is described in this *haftarah*. To accomplish his task, Solomon came to an agreement with the king of Tyre, Hiram, whereby cedars and cypress trees from Lebanon would be exchanged for Judean wheat and beaten olive oil. This arrangement, detailed in the verses preceding the *haftarah*, is summed up in the prologue (1 Kings 5:26–27). These verses suggest that the divine wisdom granted to Solomon (3:12) includes political and executive acumen (Ralbag).

The preparations for and the beginnings of the Temple building are framed by references to two divine promises: the bequest of wisdom to Solomon, in the prologue (5:26–27), and the conditional grant of divine favor to David's lineage, in the epilogue (6:11–13). The religious covenant with God protects the realm, not the political alliance with Hiram. If the king will obey the divine commandments, the dynasty will be secure and God "will abide among the children of Israel" and "never forsake" them (6:13). Solomon could hardly be surprised by this revelation, for he heard a similar exhortation directly from his father, David, on his deathbed (1 Kings 2:2–4).

RELATION OF THE *HAFTARAH* TO THE *PARASHAH*

The *haftarah* and the *parashah* present the sites of two major phases of Israelite worship: God's portable tent in the desert and the stable shrine of the mighty empire. Solomon is the heir to Moses' leadership, establishing a space of holiness in the midst of the community.

The Torah reading contains a divinely revealed blueprint of the tabernacle, along with detailed specifications for its construction (Exod. 25:9 ff). The people contribute free-will donations for the construction of the shrine (25:2). God further tells Moses (25:8): "Let them [the people] make Me a sanctuary that I may dwell (*v'shakhanti*) among them (*b'tokham*)." The very building of the shrine is the condition for divine indwelling. In the *haftarah*, by contrast, there is no divine blueprint. God's presence in Solomon's Temple depends on the fulfillment of legal preconditions: "if you follow My law and observe My rules and faithfully keep My commandments, I will fulfill for you the promise that I gave to your father David: I will abide (*v'shakhanti*) among (*b'tokh*) the children of Israel, and I will never forsake My people Israel" (1 Kings 6:12–13). God is drawn into the human realm through covenantal obedience and service. Indeed, God's presence in the shrine is the sign of His presence in the heart and actions of the faithful.

Both *parashah* and *haftarah* thus evoke a concern for sacred space. In the Torah, it is a portable tabernacle, where the Lord could dwell as He chose. In 1 Kings, it is a permanent house, the Lord's earthly dwelling. Together, they establish two poles of the religious spirit, the ever new journey of a spiritual search and the always present embodiment of tradition. Impermanent forms depend again and again on the prompting of the heart, whereas stable structures draw on the wisdom of the world. Moses built God's tabernacle through the gifts of the inspired hearts of the people (Exod. 25:2); Solomon fulfilled his father's dream through deliberation and advice. One is not required to choose between these models but to be aware of their interaction and differences.

5 26The LORD had given Solomon wisdom, as He had promised him. There was friendship between Hiram and Solomon, and the two of them made a treaty.

ה 26 וַיהוָה נָתַן חָכְמָה לִשְׁלֹמֹה כַּאֲשֶׁר
דִּבֶּר־לוֹ וַיְהִי שָׁלֹם בֵּין חִירָם וּבֵין שְׁלֹמֹה
וַיִּכְרְתוּ בְרִית שְׁנֵיהֶם׃

27King Solomon imposed forced labor on all Israel; the levy came to 30,000 men. 28He sent them to the Lebanon in shifts of 10,000 a month: they would spend one month in the Lebanon and two months at home. Adoniram was in charge of the forced labor. 29Solomon also had 70,000 porters and 80,000 quarriers in the hills, 30apart from Solomon's 3,300 officials who were in charge of the work and supervised the gangs doing the work.

31The king ordered huge blocks of choice stone to be quarried, so that the foundations of the house might be laid with hewn stones. 32Solomon's masons, Hiram's masons, and the men of Gebal shaped them. Thus the timber and the stones for building the house were made ready.

27 וַיַּעַל הַמֶּלֶךְ שְׁלֹמֹה מַס מִכָּל־יִשְׂרָאֵל
וַיְהִי הַמַּס שְׁלֹשִׁים אֶלֶף אִישׁ׃ 28 וַיִּשְׁלָחֵם
לְבָנוֹנָה עֲשֶׂרֶת אֲלָפִים בַּחֹדֶשׁ חֲלִיפוֹת
חֹדֶשׁ יִהְיוּ בַלְּבָנוֹן שְׁנַיִם חֳדָשִׁים בְּבֵיתוֹ
וַאֲדֹנִירָם עַל־הַמַּס׃ ס 29 וַיְהִי לִשְׁלֹמֹה
שִׁבְעִים אֶלֶף נֹשֵׂא סַבָּל וּשְׁמֹנִים אֶלֶף
חֹצֵב בָּהָר׃ 30 לְבַד מִשָּׂרֵי הַנִּצָּבִים
לִשְׁלֹמֹה אֲשֶׁר עַל־הַמְּלָאכָה שְׁלֹשֶׁת
אֲלָפִים וּשְׁלֹשׁ מֵאוֹת הָרֹדִים בָּעָם
הָעֹשִׂים בַּמְּלָאכָה׃
31 וַיְצַו הַמֶּלֶךְ וַיַּסִּעוּ אֲבָנִים גְּדֹלוֹת אֲבָנִים
יְקָרוֹת לְיַסֵּד הַבָּיִת אַבְנֵי גָזִית׃ 32 וַיִּפְסְלוּ
בֹּנֵי שְׁלֹמֹה וּבֹנֵי חִירוֹם וְהַגִּבְלִים וַיָּכִינוּ
הָעֵצִים וְהָאֲבָנִים לִבְנוֹת הַבָּיִת׃ פ

6 In the four hundred and eightieth year after the Israelites left the land of Egypt, in the month of Ziv—that is, the second month—in the fourth year of his reign over Israel, Solomon began to build the House of the LORD. 2The House which King Solomon built for the LORD was 60 cubits long, 20 cubits wide, and 30 cubits high. 3The portico in front of the Great Hall of the House was 20 cubits long—along the width of

ו וַיְהִי בִשְׁמוֹנִים שָׁנָה וְאַרְבַּע מֵאוֹת
שָׁנָה לְצֵאת בְּנֵי־יִשְׂרָאֵל מֵאֶרֶץ־מִצְרַיִם
בַּשָּׁנָה הָרְבִיעִית בְּחֹדֶשׁ זִו הוּא הַחֹדֶשׁ
הַשֵּׁנִי לִמְלֹךְ שְׁלֹמֹה עַל־יִשְׂרָאֵל וַיִּבֶן
הַבַּיִת לַיהוָה׃ 2 וְהַבַּיִת אֲשֶׁר בָּנָה הַמֶּלֶךְ
שְׁלֹמֹה לַיהוָה שִׁשִּׁים־אַמָּה אָרְכּוֹ
וְעֶשְׂרִים רָחְבּוֹ וּשְׁלֹשִׁים אַמָּה קוֹמָתוֹ׃
3 וְהָאוּלָם עַל־פְּנֵי הֵיכַל הַבַּיִת עֶשְׂרִים

1 Kings 5:26. friendship Hebrew: *shalom.* The technical sense of this term indicates the loyalty and accord that are basic to treaties. This verse adds that Hiram and Solomon "made a treaty" (*va-yikhr'tu b'rit*). The term *b'rit* is regularly used to indicate political pacts as well as covenants.

1 Kings 6:1. In the four hundred and eightieth year This biblical dating has been justified in Rabbinic historical works (*Seider Olam Rabbah* 15). If correct, this dating would set the time of the Exodus at about 1440 B.C.E. Modern historians find this dating problematic, principally on the basis of Egyptian records claiming that the people of "Israel" were "laid waste" in Canaan some time in the fifth year of the reign of Merneptah (1207 B.C.E.). Thus the Israelites were in Canaan by the last third of the 13th century B.C.E. Modern chronology sets the construction of the Temple at around 958 B.C.E.

3–5. The Temple was built along an axis that

אַמָּה אָרְכּוֹ עַל־פְּנֵי רֹחַב הַבָּיִת עֶשֶׂר
בָּאַמָּה רָחְבּוֹ עַל־פְּנֵי הַבָּיִת׃ 4 וַיַּעַשׂ לַבָּיִת
חַלּוֹנֵי שְׁקֻפִים אֲטֻמִים׃ 5 וַיִּבֶן עַל־קִיר
הַבַּיִת יצוע יָצִיעַ סָבִיב אֶת־קִירוֹת הַבַּיִת
סָבִיב לַהֵיכָל וְלַדְּבִיר וַיַּעַשׂ צְלָעוֹת סָבִיב׃
6 היצוע הַיָּצִיעַ הַתַּחְתֹּנָה חָמֵשׁ בָּאַמָּה
רָחְבָּהּ וְהַתִּיכֹנָה שֵׁשׁ בָּאַמָּה רָחְבָּהּ
וְהַשְּׁלִישִׁית שֶׁבַע בָּאַמָּה רָחְבָּהּ כִּי
מִגְרָעוֹת נָתַן לַבַּיִת סָבִיב חוּצָה לְבִלְתִּי
אֲחֹז בְּקִירוֹת־הַבָּיִת׃
7 וְהַבַּיִת בְּהִבָּנֹתוֹ אֶבֶן־שְׁלֵמָה מַסָּע נִבְנָה
וּמַקָּבוֹת וְהַגַּרְזֶן כָּל־כְּלִי בַרְזֶל לֹא־נִשְׁמַע
בַּבַּיִת בְּהִבָּנֹתוֹ׃
8 פֶּתַח הַצֵּלָע הַתִּיכֹנָה אֶל־כֶּתֶף הַבַּיִת
הַיְמָנִית וּבְלוּלִּים יַעֲלוּ עַל־הַתִּיכֹנָה וּמִן־
הַתִּיכֹנָה אֶל־הַשְּׁלִשִׁים׃ 9 וַיִּבֶן אֶת־הַבַּיִת
וַיְכַלֵּהוּ וַיִּסְפֹּן אֶת־הַבַּיִת גֵּבִים וּשְׂדֵרֹת
בָּאֲרָזִים׃ 10 וַיִּבֶן אֶת־היצוע הַיָּצִיעַ עַל־
כָּל־הַבַּיִת חָמֵשׁ אַמּוֹת קוֹמָתוֹ וַיֶּאֱחֹז
אֶת־הַבַּיִת בַּעֲצֵי אֲרָזִים׃ פ
11 וַיְהִי דְּבַר־יְהוָה אֶל־שְׁלֹמֹה לֵאמֹר׃
12 הַבַּיִת הַזֶּה אֲשֶׁר־אַתָּה בֹנֶה אִם־תֵּלֵךְ
בְּחֻקֹּתַי וְאֶת־מִשְׁפָּטַי תַּעֲשֶׂה וְשָׁמַרְתָּ

the House—and 10 cubits deep to the front of the House. 4He made windows for the House, recessed and latticed. 5Against the outside wall of the House—the outside walls of the House enclosing the Great Hall and the Shrine—he built a storied structure; and he made side chambers all around. 6The lowest story was 5 cubits wide, the middle one 6 cubits wide, and the third 7 cubits wide; for he had provided recesses around the outside of the House so as not to penetrate the walls of the House.

7When the House was built, only finished stones cut at the quarry were used, so that no hammer or ax or any iron tool was heard in the House while it was being built.

8The entrance to the middle [story of] the side chambers was on the right side of the House; and winding stairs led up to the middle chambers, and from the middle chambers to the third story. 9When he finished building the House, he paneled the House with beams and planks of cedar. 10He built the storied structure against the entire House—each story 5 cubits high, so that it encased the House with timbers of cedar.

11Then the word of the LORD came to Solomon, 12"With regard to this House you are building—if you follow My laws and observe

included an outer portico (*ulam*), an inner sanctuary (*heikhal*), and a hidden area of supreme holiness (*d'vir*). A similar threefold structure characterized the tabernacle as well as temple structures in the Canaanite-Phoenician region at that time.

7. only finished stones With this comment, the writer interrupts his document (v. 6 describes the lower story, v. 8 describes the middle one). This intrusion and the comment that no iron tool was heard in the Temple during its construction seem gratuitous. These phrases, however, are precise allusions to the Torah, which states that an altar must be made of undressed stone (Deut. 27:5–7), without the use of any iron implement (Exod. 20:22).

9. When he finished . . . he paneled The verb "he finished" (*va-y'khalleihu*) recalls the statement at the completion of the construction of the tabernacle that "Moses finished" (*va-y'khal*) "the work" (Exod. 40:33). In turn, both cases echo the earlier statement that "God finished" (*va-y'khal*) His work of Creation on the seventh day (Gen. 2:2). Meanwhile, mention of the cedar-paneled house of God alludes to 2 Sam. 7:2 and David's initial motivation to build a permanent dwelling for the Ark.

11. the word of the LORD came The Hebrew word *davar* (word) is regularly used in prophetic sources to indicate a divine revelation. In this case, it appears to be a direct revelation to the king.

12. if you follow Three conditions are given for divine benefits. If the king will (a) "follow My laws," (b) "observe My rules," and (c) "faithfully keep My commandments," then God will (a) "fulfill for you the promise that I gave to your father David," (b) "abide among the children of Israel," and (c) "never forsake My people Israel." Note that the conditions are for Solomon alone.

My rules and faithfully keep My commandments, I will fulfill for you the promise that I gave to your father David: 13I will abide among the children of Israel, and I will never forsake My people Israel."

אֶת־כָּל־מִצְוֺתַ֖י לָלֶ֣כֶת בָּהֶ֑ם וַהֲקִמֹתִ֤י אֶת־
דְּבָרִי֙ אִתָּ֔ךְ אֲשֶׁ֥ר דִּבַּ֖רְתִּי אֶל־דָּוִ֥ד אָבִֽיךָ׃
13 וְשָׁ֣כַנְתִּ֔י בְּת֖וֹךְ בְּנֵ֣י יִשְׂרָאֵ֑ל וְלֹ֥א אֶעֱזֹ֖ב
אֶת־עַמִּ֥י יִשְׂרָאֵֽל׃ ס

20You shall further instruct the Israelites to
bring you clear oil of beaten olives for lighting,

20 וְאַתָּ֞ה תְּצַוֶּ֣ה ׀ אֶת־בְּנֵ֣י יִשְׂרָאֵ֗ל וְיִקְח֨וּ
אֵלֶ֜יךָ שֶׁ֣מֶן זַ֥יִת זָ֛ךְ כָּתִ֖ית לַמָּא֑וֹר לְהַעֲלֹ֥ת

THE TABERNACLE, PART 1: INSTRUCTIONS (*continued*)

THE OIL FOR LIGHTING (27:20–21)

"Oil for lighting" the *m'norah* is first listed in 25:6, but the kind of oil is not specified. Here the text specifies the fuel to be used in the *m'norah* to provide illumination.

20. to bring you The Israelites had no facilities in the wilderness for acquiring olives and extracting oil. The same is true for many of the other objects listed in this chapter. That is why many scholars view the description of the tabernacle here as the presentation of a later idealization.

clear oil of beaten olives The oil and other items mentioned in 25:6 constituted a one-time donation for the construction of the tabernacle. The instruction in this verse presents an ongoing obligation. The text specifies oil extracted from olives because oil used in the tabernacle had to be "clear," or so refined as to be free of dregs. This distinguished it from oil made from other sources, including sesame seed, flax, and animal fats, which were used in the ancient Near East.

regularly The Hebrew words *ner tamid* can refer to a lamp that burns without interruption or to one that is regularly kindled. Verse 21 and Lev. 24:3 explicitly state that the lamps are to burn from evening until morning.

This *parashah* continues the theme of furnishing the tabernacle as the place that will represent God's presence in the midst of the Israelite camp. It then describes the role and the investiture of Aaron and his sons as *kohanim,* ministering priests in the tabernacle. This *parashah* is the only one in the last four books of the Torah in which the name of Moses does not appear. Noting this literary curiosity, some commentators explain it as Moses' generously stepping aside to let the spotlight fall on Aaron and his priestly functions. Others point out that the traditional date of Moses' death, the 7th of *Adar,* always falls during the week in which *T'tzavveh* is read; they see his absence from the Torah reading, like his virtual absence from the *Haggadah,* as part of an effort to ensure that no cult of Moses worship would ever arise.

CHAPTER 27

The first section of the *parashah* deals with the lighting of the *m'norah.* This tradition is reflected in today's Eternal Light, the only commanded practice associated with the ancient tabernacle that is still with us (see *Halakhah l'Ma·aseh,* below). Why has light been such a favorite symbol of God? Perhaps because light itself cannot be seen. We become aware of its presence when it enables us to see other things. Similarly, we cannot see God, but we become aware of God's presence when we see the beauty of the world, when we experience love and the goodness of our fellow human beings. Similarly, fire has been used to symbolize God's presence. Like light, fire is not an object. It is the process of liberating the energy hidden in a log of wood or a lump of coal, even as God becomes real in our lives in the process of liberating the potential energy in each of us to be good, generous, and self-controlled. If light is the symbol of God, then fire—the product of human technology—represents human efforts to bring the reality of God into our world.

20. clear oil of beaten olives That which fuels the *m'norah* must be pure, uncontaminated by jealousy, selfishness, pride, or greed. Why olive oil? In antiquity as today, the olive branch was a sign of peace. Olive trees mature slowly, so only when there was an extended time of peace, with agriculture left undisturbed, could the olive tree produce its fruit. "Even as the oil of the olive does not mix with

HALAKHAH L'MA·ASEH

27:20. kindling lamps regularly Or "to cause a lamp to burn continually." This is the source for the Eternal Light (*Ner Tamid*) that hangs above the Ark in the synagogue, one of many symbols identifying the synagogue as a miniature sanctuary (*mikdash m'at*).

נֵר תָּמִיד׃ 21 בְּאֹהֶל מוֹעֵד מִחוּץ לַפָּרֹכֶת
אֲשֶׁר עַל־הָעֵדֻת יַעֲרֹךְ אֹתוֹ אַהֲרֹן וּבָנָיו
מֵעֶרֶב עַד־בֹּקֶר לִפְנֵי יְהוָה חֻקַּת עוֹלָם
לְדֹרֹתָם מֵאֵת בְּנֵי יִשְׂרָאֵל׃ ס

for kindling lamps regularly. 21Aaron and his
sons shall set them up in the Tent of Meeting, outside the curtain which is over [the Ark of] the Pact, [to burn] from evening to morning before the LORD. It shall be a due from the Israelites for all time, throughout the ages.

כח וְאַתָּה הַקְרֵב אֵלֶיךָ אֶת־אַהֲרֹן
אָחִיךָ וְאֶת־בָּנָיו אִתּוֹ מִתּוֹךְ בְּנֵי יִשְׂרָאֵל

28 You shall bring forward your brother Aaron, with his sons, from among the Israelites,

21. Aaron and his sons This verse preserves the tradition that any priest of Aaron's lineage may perform the ritual of lighting the lamps. In other biblical passages, however (Exod. 30:7–8; Lev. 24:3; Num. 8:1–3) the duty of attending to the lamps seems to be the exclusive prerogative of Aaron, i.e., the High Priest.

Tent of Meeting The place where God communicates with Moses.

outside the curtain That is, in the Holy Place.

a due Provision of the oil is now to become a permanent public obligation.

THE PRIESTHOOD AND THE PRIESTLY VESTMENTS (28:1–43)

A sanctuary requires officiating priests. God orders Moses to appoint Aaron and his sons to fill this role. The office is to be hereditary. Just as sacred space must be separated from profane space, so the occupants of the sacred office must be distinguishable from all others. Hence special attire—the insignia of office—is ordained for Aaron, the archetypal High Priest, and his sons, the priests of lower rank, when officiating inside the tabernacle. The ceremonial clothing of the High Priest is the main concern of this chapter. The garments of ordinary priests are detailed only in verses 40 and 42. No mention is made of footwear, because the priests officiated barefoot.

THE HIGH PRIEST (vv. 1–39)

The attire of the High Priest is colorful, distinguished by the prominent use of gold, except on Yom Kippur, the Day of Atonement, when he performed his duties clothed in white linen garments.

1. You shall bring forward You shall induct into office. Until now, Moses has acted as chief officiant; hence he is the one who is to "bring forward"—to the Tent of Meeting, once it is erected—the newly appointed chief priest.

Nadab and Abihu Aaron's four sons are first listed in 6:23. We read of them accompanying

---

other liquids with which it comes in contact, so has the people Israel kept its own identity when it has come in contact with other nations" (Exod. R. 36:1).

CHAPTER 28

This chapter deals with the priestly garments. Again drawing a parallel between the creation of the world and the fashioning of the tabernacle, commentators have noted that God made garments for Adam and Eve after creating the world and that God describes the special garments to be worn by the priests after fashioning the tabernacle. "Just as humans are the only creatures in the universe who do not rest content with their natural skin . . . the sons of Aaron who minister in their priestly office in the House of the Lord do not serve God in their ordinary, everyday garments" (N. Leibowitz). A uniform simultaneously invests the wearer with special authority (only special people can wear it) and diminishes the person's personal authority (anyone wearing it acquires the sense of being special). "Without these prescribed garments, the *kohen* is merely an ordinary individual and his ritual act becomes a personal gesture" (Hirsch).

1. Although some people may be bothered by the idea of a hereditary priestly class, which could easily include the unworthy children of a *kohen* and exclude those who would want to serve, it did have advantages. It kept the priesthood free of ambitious outsiders who would seek it for personal advantage, and it permitted children to be trained for a life of service and responsibility from birth. The Sages taught

to serve Me as priests: Aaron, Nadab and Abihu, Eleazar and Ithamar, the sons of Aaron. 2Make sacral vestments for your brother Aaron, for dignity and adornment. 3Next you shall instruct all who are skillful, whom I have endowed with the gift of skill, to make Aaron's vestments, for consecrating him to serve Me as priest. 4These are the vestments they are to make: a breastpiece, an ephod, a robe, a fringed tunic, a headdress, and a sash. They shall make those sacral vestments for your brother Aaron and his sons, for priestly service to Me; 5they, therefore, shall receive the gold, the blue, purple, and crimson yarns, and the fine linen.

6They shall make the ephod of gold, of blue, purple, and crimson yarns, and of fine twisted

לְכַהֲנוֹ־לִ֑י אַהֲרֹ֕ן נָדָ֥ב וַאֲבִיה֛וּא אֶלְעָזָ֥ר
וְאִיתָמָ֖ר בְּנֵ֥י אַהֲרֹֽן׃ 2 וְעָשִׂ֥יתָ בִגְדֵי־קֹ֖דֶשׁ
לְאַהֲרֹ֣ן אָחִ֑יךָ לְכָב֖וֹד וּלְתִפְאָֽרֶת׃ 3 וְאַתָּ֗ה
תְּדַבֵּר֙ אֶל־כָּל־חַכְמֵי־לֵ֔ב אֲשֶׁ֥ר מִלֵּאתִ֖יו
ר֣וּחַ חָכְמָ֑ה וְעָשׂ֞וּ אֶת־בִּגְדֵ֧י אַהֲרֹ֛ן לְקַדְּשׁ֖וֹ
לְכַהֲנוֹ־לִֽי׃ 4 וְאֵ֨לֶּה הַבְּגָדִ֜ים אֲשֶׁ֣ר יַעֲשׂ֗וּ
חֹ֤שֶׁן וְאֵפוֹד֙ וּמְעִ֔יל וּכְתֹ֥נֶת תַּשְׁבֵּ֖ץ מִצְנֶ֣פֶת
וְאַבְנֵ֑ט וְעָשׂ֨וּ בִגְדֵי־קֹ֜דֶשׁ לְאַהֲרֹ֥ן אָחִ֛יךָ
וּלְבָנָ֖יו לְכַהֲנוֹ־לִֽי׃ 5 וְהֵם֙ יִקְח֣וּ אֶת־הַזָּהָ֔ב
וְאֶת־הַתְּכֵ֖לֶת וְאֶת־הָֽאַרְגָּמָ֑ן וְאֶת־תּוֹלַ֥עַת
הַשָּׁנִ֖י וְאֶת־הַשֵּֽׁשׁ׃ פ
6 וְעָשׂ֖וּ אֶת־הָאֵפֹ֑ד זָהָ֡ב תְּכֵ֨לֶת וְאַרְגָּמָ֜ן
תּוֹלַ֧עַת שָׁנִ֛י וְשֵׁ֥שׁ מָשְׁזָ֖ר מַעֲשֵׂ֥ה חֹשֵֽׁב׃

their father and the elders partway up Mount Sinai (24:1–11). The death of Nadab and Abihu is described in Lev. 10:1–2. Eleazar and Ithamar continued to exercise their priestly functions, with Eleazar succeeding to the High Priesthood after Aaron's death (Num. 20:25–28).

2. Make That is, you are responsible for having them made.

sacral vestments So-called either because the High Priest wore them while officiating in the Holy Place or because the vestments were regarded as endowed with sanctity since they were anointed with the sacred oil.

for dignity and adornment As befits the exalted office.

4. Only six of the eight articles of clothing are listed. The other two—the frontlet and the breeches—are prescribed in verses 36–38 and 42–43.

5. These elements are made of the same materials as the tabernacle fabrics.

they . . . shall receive That is, the skilled craftsmen are to receive these contributions directly from the people.

The Ephod (vv. 6–12)

Following the pattern of the prescriptions for building the tabernacle, the instructions for the priestly vestments begin with the most important item, a long vest—the ephod. Its pre-eminence is indicated by the fact that it uses all five colors. The ephod is mentioned several times in the Bible, on occasion in connection with household gods and also with sculptured and molten images,

---

that "though the crown of priesthood is limited to the descendants of Aaron and the crown of royalty to the descendants of David, the crown of learning is available to anyone who would earn it" (Gen. R. 34:2).

3. *skillful* The literal meaning of the phrase translated as "skillful" (*ḥakhmei lev*) is "wise of heart." There is a wisdom of the heart, an emotional maturity born of age and experience, that is different from intellectual knowledge and is specially suited to fashioning holiness.

4. The Talmud understands the priestly vestments as designed to protect human beings against the sins to which they are prone. Thus the breastpiece—called "the breastpiece of judgment" (*mishpat*) in 28:15—was meant to prevent miscarriages of justice. The jacket (*m'il,* similar to the word for betrayal, *ma·al*) would discourage gossip. The ephod (a coat also used to decorate idols, as in Hos. 3:4) would protect them against the danger of succumbing to idolatry. The fringed tunic (the same Hebrew phrase used for Joseph's coat in Gen. 37) would protect against bloodshed (as the brothers nearly killed Joseph). The robe, covering the entire body, would protect them against sins of unchastity; and the headdress, against prideful, arrogant thoughts (BT Zev. 88b).

linen, worked into designs. 7It shall have two shoulder-pieces attached; they shall be attached at its two ends. 8And the decorated band that is upon it shall be made like it, of one piece with it: of gold, of blue, purple, and crimson yarns, and of fine twisted linen. 9Then take two lazuli stones and engrave on them the names of the sons of Israel: 10six of their names on the one stone, and the names of the remaining six on the other stone, in the order of their birth. 11On the two stones you shall make seal engravings—the work of a lapidary—of the names of the sons of Israel. Having bordered them with frames of gold, 12attach the two stones to the shoulder-pieces of the ephod, as stones for remembrance of the Israelite people, whose names Aaron shall carry upon his two shoulder-pieces for remembrance before the Lord.

13Then make frames of gold 14and two chains

7 שְׁתֵּי כְתֵפֹת חֹבְרֹת יִהְיֶה־לּוֹ אֶל־שְׁנֵי
קְצוֹתָיו וְחֻבָּר׃ 8 וְחֵשֶׁב אֲפֻדָּתוֹ אֲשֶׁר עָלָיו
כְּמַעֲשֵׂהוּ מִמֶּנּוּ יִהְיֶה זָהָב תְּכֵלֶת וְאַרְגָּמָן
וְתוֹלַעַת שָׁנִי וְשֵׁשׁ מָשְׁזָר׃ 9 וְלָקַחְתָּ אֶת־
שְׁתֵּי אַבְנֵי־שֹׁהַם וּפִתַּחְתָּ עֲלֵיהֶם שְׁמוֹת
בְּנֵי יִשְׂרָאֵל׃ 10 שִׁשָּׁה מִשְּׁמֹתָם עַל הָאֶבֶן
הָאֶחָת וְאֶת־שְׁמוֹת הַשִּׁשָּׁה הַנּוֹתָרִים
עַל־הָאֶבֶן הַשֵּׁנִית כְּתוֹלְדֹתָם׃ 11 מַעֲשֵׂה
חָרַשׁ אֶבֶן פִּתּוּחֵי חֹתָם תְּפַתַּח אֶת־שְׁתֵּי
הָאֲבָנִים עַל־שְׁמֹת בְּנֵי יִשְׂרָאֵל מֻסַבֹּת
מִשְׁבְּצוֹת זָהָב תַּעֲשֶׂה אֹתָם׃ 12 וְשַׂמְתָּ
אֶת־שְׁתֵּי הָאֲבָנִים עַל כִּתְפֹת הָאֵפֹד אַבְנֵי
זִכָּרֹן לִבְנֵי יִשְׂרָאֵל וְנָשָׂא אַהֲרֹן אֶת־
שְׁמוֹתָם לִפְנֵי יְהוָה עַל־שְׁתֵּי כְתֵפָיו
לְזִכָּרֹן׃ ס
שני 13 וְעָשִׂיתָ מִשְׁבְּצֹת זָהָב׃ 14 וּשְׁתֵּי שַׁרְשְׁרֹת
זָהָב טָהוֹר מִגְבָּלֹת תַּעֲשֶׂה אֹתָם מַעֲשֵׂה

all of which are illegitimate in the religion of Israel. The ephod was used to ascertain the divine will, which is particularly pertinent to understanding the function of the ephod as a vestment of the High Priest. The "breastpiece" attached to it (v. 29) served a similar purpose. The biblical description of the priest's ephod includes four elements: the main body of the garment, two shoulder straps, and a richly decorated band. It is unclear whether the ephod covered the lower and/or upper parts of the body and the back and/or front.

9. engrave on them The technique of miniature engraving on precious stones was highly developed in the ancient Near East. The names of all the tribes engraved on the gems and affixed to the High Priest's vestments are to serve as a perpetual and humbling reminder to him that he is the representative of the entire community of Israel before God.

10. in the order of their birth As recounted in Gen. 30 and 35:16–18.

12. for remembrance These twice-repeated words point to the dual function of the engraved stones: a reminder to the High Priest of his role as the representative of the community and an invocation to God to be mindful of His people Israel, with whom He has entered into a covenant.

The Breastpiece and the Urim and Thummim
(vv. 13–30)

Fastened to the ephod, and made of the same fine multicolored fabric, was a pouch about 9 inches square worn over the breast. Affixed to it were 12 different gemstones, each engraved with the name of one of the tribes of Israel. These stones were arranged in four rows of three. The pouch (Hebrew: *ḥoshen*) contained the Urim and Thummim, discussed in verse 30.

13–14. These two verses prescribe the means

12. Aaron the High Priest was to carry the names of Israel's tribes on his shoulders "like a father carrying a young child on his shoulders to keep the child safe" (*B'er Mayim Ḥayyim*). Aaron is told to wear the names over his heart (vv. 29–30). When Aaron had to make a decision regarding a fellow Israelite, he was to consult not only the rule book but his heart as well. "The heart that rejoiced so unreservedly at his brother's good fortune (Exod. 4:14) is worthy to wear this emblem before God" (Tanḥ. Sh'mot 27).

עֲבֹ֑ת וְנָתַתָּ֛ה אֶת־שַׁרְשְׁרֹ֥ת הָעֲבֹתֹ֖ת עַל־
הַמִּשְׁבְּצֹֽת׃ ס
15 וְעָשִׂ֜יתָ חֹ֤שֶׁן מִשְׁפָּט֙ מַעֲשֵׂ֣ה חֹשֵׁ֔ב
כְּמַעֲשֵׂ֥ה אֵפֹ֖ד תַּעֲשֶׂ֑נּוּ זָ֠הָב תְּכֵ֨לֶת וְאַרְגָּמָ֜ן
וְתוֹלַ֧עַת שָׁנִ֛י וְשֵׁ֥שׁ מָשְׁזָ֖ר תַּעֲשֶׂ֥ה אֹתֽוֹ׃
16 רָב֛וּעַ יִהְיֶ֖ה כָּפ֑וּל זֶ֥רֶת אָרְכּ֖וֹ וְזֶ֥רֶת
רָחְבּֽוֹ׃ 17 וּמִלֵּאתָ֥ בוֹ֙ מִלֻּ֣אַת אֶ֔בֶן אַרְבָּעָ֖ה
טוּרִ֣ים אָ֑בֶן ט֗וּר אֹ֤דֶם פִּטְדָה֙ וּבָרֶ֔קֶת
הַטּ֖וּר הָאֶחָֽד׃ 18 וְהַטּ֖וּר הַשֵּׁנִ֑י נֹ֥פֶךְ סַפִּ֖יר
וְיָהֲלֹֽם׃ 19 וְהַטּ֖וּר הַשְּׁלִישִׁ֑י לֶ֥שֶׁם שְׁב֖וֹ
וְאַחְלָֽמָה׃ 20 וְהַטּוּר֙ הָֽרְבִיעִ֔י תַּרְשִׁ֥ישׁ
וְשֹׁ֖הַם וְיָשְׁפֵ֑ה מְשֻׁבָּצִ֥ים זָהָ֛ב יִהְי֖וּ
בְּמִלּוּאֹתָֽם׃ 21 וְ֠הָאֲבָנִים תִּהְיֶ֜יןָ עַל־שְׁמֹ֣ת
בְּנֵֽי־יִשְׂרָאֵ֗ל שְׁתֵּ֥ים עֶשְׂרֵ֖ה עַל־שְׁמֹתָ֑ם
פִּתּוּחֵ֤י חוֹתָם֙ אִ֣ישׁ עַל־שְׁמ֔וֹ תִּֽהְיֶ֔יןָ לִשְׁנֵ֥י
עָשָׂ֖ר שָֽׁבֶט׃
22 וְעָשִׂ֧יתָ עַל־הַחֹ֛שֶׁן שַֽׁרְשֹׁ֥ת גַּבְלֻ֖ת

of pure gold; braid these like corded work, and
fasten the corded chains to the frames.
15 You shall make a breastpiece of decision,
worked into a design; make it in the style of the
ephod: make it of gold, of blue, purple, and
crimson yarns, and of fine twisted linen. 16 It
shall be square and doubled, a span in length
and a span in width. 17 Set in it mounted stones,
in four rows of stones. The first row shall be a
row of carnelian, chrysolite, and emerald; 18 the
second row: a turquoise, a sapphire, and an amethyst; 19 the third row: a jacinth, an agate, and
a crystal; 20 and the fourth row: a beryl, a lapis
lazuli, and a jasper. They shall be framed with
gold in their mountings. 21 The stones shall correspond [in number] to the names of the sons
of Israel: twelve, corresponding to their names.
They shall be engraved like seals, each with its
name, for the twelve tribes.
22 On the breastpiece make braided chains of

by which the *ḥoshen* is to be attached to the ephod. The braiding provides it with great strength.

15. a breastpiece of decision The Hebrew for this term (*ḥoshen mishpat*) usually has been translated "breastplate of judgment." It was not a plate, however. All available sources indicate that it was some sort of device for determining divine will.

16. square and doubled By doubling over the piece of cloth, it became a square, taking the form of a pouch.

span Hebrew: *zeret;* the maximum distance between the top of the little finger and the thumb, approximately 9 inches, or half a cubit.

17–20. The 12 stones have not been identified with certainty.

21. The insignia of office symbolize the role of the High Priest as representing the entire community, personifying its historic ideals.

22–28. The instructions for fastening the breastpiece to the ephod and keeping it in position employ the items mentioned in verses 13–14.

---

17. The 2 stones on the robe (*ephod*) bear the collective names of the tribes, six on each stone (vv. 9–10). Each of the 12 stones on the breastpiece (*ḥoshen*) bears the name of a single tribe. Religion, like so much of life, oscillates between the poles of individual and collective activity.

Hirsch notes that "the linen (v. 42), representing the vegetative domain, is white, the color of purity. The wool, symbol of the animal world, is dyed red, with a paler purple (*shani,* v. 6) representing the lower, animal stage of life and a darker crimson (*argaman,* v. 6) the human level. Blue, the color of the sky, directs us to the Godliness that has been revealed to us." A modern thinker expands on those comments: "Human beings reflect a combination of those four levels. At one time or another, an individual may be living at the lowest level of existence, just getting by. Or an individual may be mobile, not just vegetative, able to impose some order on life. Then there is the individual who lives with full humanity, behaving in a moral and ethical way. Finally, there are those who sense God continually. When the priest wears all the colors together, when the Israelites see all the colors together, they are reminded that the people Israel comprises all these individuals, that the priests serve them all, and that at any time any one of us may be in any one of those four stages."

corded work in pure gold. 23Make two rings of
gold on the breastpiece, and fasten the two rings
at the two ends of the breastpiece, 24attaching
the two golden cords to the two rings at the ends
of the breastpiece. 25Then fasten the two ends
of the cords to the two frames, which you shall
attach to the shoulder-pieces of the ephod, at
the front. 26Make two rings of gold and attach
them to the two ends of the breastpiece, at its
inner edge, which faces the ephod. 27And make
two other rings of gold and fasten them on the
front of the ephod, low on the two shoulder-
pieces, close to its seam above the decorated
band. 28The breastpiece shall be held in place
by a cord of blue from its rings to the rings of
the ephod, so that the breastpiece rests on the
decorated band and does not come loose from
the ephod. 29Aaron shall carry the names of the
sons of Israel on the breastpiece of decision over
his heart, when he enters the sanctuary, for remembrance before the LORD at all times. 30In-
side the breastpiece of decision you shall place
the Urim and Thummim, so that they are over
Aaron's heart when he comes before the LORD.
Thus Aaron shall carry the instrument of decision for the Israelites over his heart before the
LORD at all times.
31You shall make the robe of the ephod of

מַעֲשֵׂה עֲבֹת זָהָב טָהוֹר׃ 23 וְעָשִׂיתָ עַל־
הַחֹשֶׁן שְׁתֵּי טַבְּעוֹת זָהָב וְנָתַתָּ אֶת־שְׁתֵּי
הַטַּבָּעוֹת עַל־שְׁנֵי קְצוֹת הַחֹשֶׁן׃ 24 וְנָתַתָּה
אֶת־שְׁתֵּי עֲבֹתֹת הַזָּהָב עַל־שְׁתֵּי הַטַּבָּעֹת
אֶל־קְצוֹת הַחֹשֶׁן׃ 25 וְאֵת שְׁתֵּי קְצוֹת שְׁתֵּי
הָעֲבֹתֹת תִּתֵּן עַל־שְׁתֵּי הַמִּשְׁבְּצוֹת
וְנָתַתָּה עַל־כִּתְפוֹת הָאֵפֹד אֶל־מוּל פָּנָיו׃
26 וְעָשִׂיתָ שְׁתֵּי טַבְּעוֹת זָהָב וְשַׂמְתָּ אֹתָם
עַל־שְׁנֵי קְצוֹת הַחֹשֶׁן עַל־שְׂפָתוֹ אֲשֶׁר
אֶל־עֵבֶר הָאֵפֹד בָּיְתָה׃ 27 וְעָשִׂיתָ שְׁתֵּי
טַבְּעוֹת זָהָב וְנָתַתָּה אֹתָם עַל־שְׁתֵּי
כִתְפוֹת הָאֵפוֹד מִלְּמַטָּה מִמּוּל פָּנָיו
לְעֻמַּת מַחְבַּרְתּוֹ מִמַּעַל לְחֵשֶׁב הָאֵפוֹד׃
28 וְיִרְכְּסוּ אֶת־הַחֹשֶׁן מטבעתו מִטַּבְּעֹתָיו
אֶל־טַבְּעֹת הָאֵפֹד בִּפְתִיל תְּכֵלֶת לִהְיוֹת
עַל־חֵשֶׁב הָאֵפוֹד וְלֹא־יִזַּח הַחֹשֶׁן מֵעַל
הָאֵפוֹד׃ 29 וְנָשָׂא אַהֲרֹן אֶת־שְׁמוֹת בְּנֵי־
יִשְׂרָאֵל בְּחֹשֶׁן הַמִּשְׁפָּט עַל־לִבּוֹ בְּבֹאוֹ
אֶל־הַקֹּדֶשׁ לְזִכָּרֹן לִפְנֵי־יְהוָה תָּמִיד׃
30 וְנָתַתָּ אֶל־חֹשֶׁן הַמִּשְׁפָּט אֶת־הָאוּרִים
וְאֶת־הַתֻּמִּים וְהָיוּ עַל־לֵב אַהֲרֹן בְּבֹאוֹ
לִפְנֵי יְהוָה וְנָשָׂא אַהֲרֹן אֶת־מִשְׁפַּט בְּנֵי־
יִשְׂרָאֵל עַל־לִבּוֹ לִפְנֵי יְהוָה תָּמִיד׃ ס
שלישי 31 וְעָשִׂיתָ אֶת־מְעִיל הָאֵפוֹד כְּלִיל תְּכֵלֶת׃

30. Urim and Thummim It is clear from the association with "the breastpiece of decision" and "the instrument of decision" that these two items constituted a device for determining the will of God in specific matters that were beyond human ability to decide. Although the function of this device is clear, nowhere in the Torah is there a description of it or of the technique employed in its use. (It has been suggested that two sacred lots were drawn out of the *hoshen* in the process of consulting God; see 1 Sam. 14:41–42, 23:6,9–11.) It remained in the exclusive possession of the priest and was used only on behalf of the leader of the people in matters of vital national importance. This mode of discovering the divine will disappeared from ancient Israel after the age of King David (see Ezra 2:63).

The Robe (vv. 31–35)

Beneath the ephod and the *hoshen* the High Priest is to wear a long robe woven of woolen thread dyed the aristocratic color *t'kheilet* (see Comment to 25:4). It seems to have been ankle length and free flowing, with armholes but no sleeves. The neck opening is reinforced to prevent fraying. The hem of the robe is fringed with tassels of three

29. for remembrance "Remembering is the source of redemption, while forgetting leads to exile" (Baal Shem Tov). Our identities have been shaped by those who came before us.

32 וְהָיָה פִי־רֹאשׁוֹ בְּתוֹכוֹ שָׂפָה יִהְיֶה לְפִיו
סָבִיב מַעֲשֵׂה אֹרֵג כְּפִי תַחְרָא יִהְיֶה־
לּוֹ לֹא יִקָּרֵעַ׃ 33 וְעָשִׂיתָ עַל־שׁוּלָיו רִמֹּנֵי
תְּכֵלֶת וְאַרְגָּמָן וְתוֹלַעַת שָׁנִי עַל־שׁוּלָיו
סָבִיב וּפַעֲמֹנֵי זָהָב בְּתוֹכָם סָבִיב׃ 34 פַּעֲמֹן
זָהָב וְרִמּוֹן פַּעֲמֹן זָהָב וְרִמּוֹן עַל־שׁוּלֵי
הַמְּעִיל סָבִיב׃ 35 וְהָיָה עַל־אַהֲרֹן לְשָׁרֵת
וְנִשְׁמַע קוֹלוֹ בְּבֹאוֹ אֶל־הַקֹּדֶשׁ לִפְנֵי יְהוָה
וּבְצֵאתוֹ וְלֹא יָמוּת׃ ס
36 וְעָשִׂיתָ צִּיץ זָהָב טָהוֹר וּפִתַּחְתָּ עָלָיו
פִּתּוּחֵי חֹתָם קֹדֶשׁ לַיהוָה׃ 37 וְשַׂמְתָּ
אֹתוֹ עַל־פְּתִיל תְּכֵלֶת וְהָיָה עַל־הַמִּצְנֶפֶת

pure blue. [32]The opening for the head shall be in the middle of it; the opening shall have a binding of woven work round about—it shall be like the opening of a coat of mail—so that it does not tear. [33]On its hem make pomegranates of blue, purple, and crimson yarns, all around the hem, with bells of gold between them all around: [34]a golden bell and a pomegranate, a golden bell and a pomegranate, all around the hem of the robe. [35]Aaron shall wear it while officiating, so that the sound of it is heard when he comes into the sanctuary before the LORD and when he goes out—that he may not die.

[36]You shall make a frontlet of pure gold and engrave on it the seal inscription: "Holy to the LORD." [37]Suspend it on a cord of blue, so that it may remain on the headdress; it shall remain

colors, representing pomegranates, and with gold bells.

31. of pure blue With no admixture of the other two colors listed in 25:4.

32. binding Like a turnover collar.

coat of mail This is probably the leather collar that protected the neck, a feature of the armor worn by Canaanite charioteers.

33. pomegranates The pomegranate was one of the seven characteristic fruits of the land of Israel (see Deut. 8:8).

35. sound of it is heard The specific role of the bells is to announce his approach to the deity.

that he may not die Any deviation from the prescribed rules places the priest in the category of an unauthorized person and invalidates his service. He thus becomes an encroacher (*zar*) in the sacred precincts, a most serious offense.

The Frontlet (vv. 36–38)

The text now turns to the High Priest's headgear. Once again, it begins with the most important and most sacred element. In this instance, it is the gold plate worn on the forehead over the headdress and bearing the Hebrew inscription *kodesh l'YHVH,* "Holy to the LORD."

36. Holy to the LORD It is not clear how the Hebrew words were inscribed on the frontlet. In addition to signifying the sacred nature of the office and the person of the High Priest (who is consecrated to God's service all his life), the inscription served to remind God, so to speak, that the High Priest had been assigned to gain atonement for Israel.

37. cord of blue This cord apparently was threaded through holes punched in the frontlet and served to hold it in place.

---

35. that the sound of it is heard From this we learn that it is forbidden to enter anyone's room without first announcing your presence (Lev. R. 21:8).

36. The gold template marked "Holy to the LORD" was to remind him to direct his thoughts to God when he officiated and to protect him against feelings of excessive pride (BT Zev. 88b). This awareness is reflected today in the practice of wearing *t'fillin* on the forehead and of wrapping a *t'fillin* strap around the arm and hand in a way that spells out God's name *Shaddai* (Almighty). Not only the High Priest is consecrated to God but every Israelite man and woman is. The development of Jewish law and observance has produced numerous instances of obligations and prohibitions that originally were intended only for *kohanim* (priests) democratically extended to all Jews. This is to help us fulfill our mandate to be "a kingdom of priests" (*mamlekhet kohanim*) (Exod. 19:6).

on the front of the headdress. ³⁸It shall be on Aaron's forehead, that Aaron may take away any sin arising from the holy things that the Israelites consecrate, from any of their sacred donations; it shall be on his forehead at all times, to win acceptance for them before the LORD.

³⁹You shall make the fringed tunic of fine linen.

You shall make the headdress of fine linen.

You shall make the sash of embroidered work.

⁴⁰And for Aaron's sons also you shall make tunics, and make sashes for them, and make turbans for them, for dignity and adornment. ⁴¹Put these on your brother Aaron and on his sons as well; anoint them, and ordain them and consecrate them to serve Me as priests.

אֶל־מ֥וּל פְּנֵֽי־הַמִּצְנֶ֖פֶת יִהְיֶֽה׃ 38 וְהָיָה֮ עַל־מֵ֣צַח אַהֲרֹן֒ וְנָשָׂ֣א אַהֲרֹ֗ן אֶת־עֲוֺ֣ן הַקֳּדָשִׁ֗ים אֲשֶׁ֤ר יַקְדִּ֙ישׁוּ֙ בְּנֵ֣י יִשְׂרָאֵ֔ל לְכׇֽל־מַתְּנֹ֖ת קׇדְשֵׁיהֶ֑ם וְהָיָ֤ה עַל־מִצְחוֹ֙ תָּמִ֔יד לְרָצ֥וֹן לָהֶ֖ם לִפְנֵ֥י יְהֹוָֽה׃

39 וְשִׁבַּצְתָּ֙ הַכְּתֹ֣נֶת שֵׁ֔שׁ

וְעָשִׂ֖יתָ מִצְנֶ֣פֶת שֵׁ֑שׁ

וְאַבְנֵ֥ט תַּעֲשֶׂ֖ה מַעֲשֵׂ֥ה רֹקֵֽם׃

40 וְלִבְנֵ֤י אַהֲרֹן֙ תַּעֲשֶׂ֣ה כֻתֳּנֹ֔ת וְעָשִׂ֥יתָ לָהֶ֖ם אַבְנֵטִ֑ים וּמִגְבָּעוֹת֙ תַּעֲשֶׂ֣ה לָהֶ֔ם לְכָב֖וֹד וּלְתִפְאָֽרֶת׃ 41 וְהִלְבַּשְׁתָּ֤ אֹתָם֙ אֶת־אַהֲרֹ֣ן אָחִ֔יךָ וְאֶת־בָּנָ֖יו אִתּ֑וֹ וּמָשַׁחְתָּ֨ אֹתָ֜ם וּמִלֵּאתָ֧ אֶת־יָדָ֛ם וְקִדַּשְׁתָּ֥ אֹתָ֖ם וְכִהֲנ֥וּ לִֽי׃

---

headdress The Hebrew word *mitznefet* literally means "a turban," a symbol of royalty.

38. It shall be on Aaron's forehead The instruction is repeated later in this same verse with the addition of the Hebrew word *tamid,* "at all times," meaning "whenever the High Priest performs the service."

may take away any sin The High Priest is responsible for any infraction of the rules governing the sacred offerings. Wearing the frontlet inscribed with the words *kodesh l'YHVH,* "Holy to the LORD," helps him concentrate his thoughts on his duties and on his accountability. At the same time, this awareness effectively secures atonement from God for such offenses.

The Tunic (v. 39)

The Hebrew for "tunic" (*kuttonet*) appears often in the Bible. Both men and women wore such clothing, mainly as an ankle-length undergarment, usually next to the skin. Some types of outer tunic were clearly marks of prestige, such as the garment that Jacob gave to Joseph, described in Gen. 37:3. A tunic was standard fashionable dress in the ancient Near East.

The Headdress (v. 39)

See Comment to verse 37.

The Sash (v. 39)

In 39:29 the sash is described as made of "fine twisted linen, blue, purple, and crimson yarns, done in embroidery." This sash was girded over the tunic.

THE VESTMENTS OF ORDINARY PRIESTS
(vv. 40–43)

Four articles of clothing are mandated.

40. turbans No description is given, but they probably differ from the High Priest's headdress because a different Hebrew word (*migba·ot*) is used.

41. This verse and the following chapter prescribe how priests are to be officially installed into office once the tabernacle is erected.

Put these That is, the vestments, as they apply, respectively, to Aaron and to his sons.

anoint them The formula for compounding the special aromatic oil for this rite is specified in 30:22–25. It was forbidden to use that oil for any other purpose. The oil was sprinkled on the vestments to be worn by Aaron and by his sons; it also was poured over the head of the High Priest. The tabernacle vessels also were anointed. This ceremony served to bring about the transition from the profane to the sacred. Note that the verb for anoint (משח) is used more frequently in the Bible for anointing kings. Individuals or objects that are anointed are set apart for the service of God.

consecrate them This probably does not refer to another distinct ceremony but sums up the consequence of performing all the previously enumerated rituals.

42You shall also make for them linen breeches
to cover their nakedness; they shall extend from
the hips to the thighs. 43They shall be worn
by Aaron and his sons when they enter the Tent
of Meeting or when they approach the altar
to officiate in the sanctuary, so that they do
not incur punishment and die. It shall be a law
for all time for him and for his offspring to
come.

42 וַעֲשֵׂה לָהֶם מִכְנְסֵי־בָד לְכַסּוֹת בְּשַׂר
עֶרְוָה מִמָּתְנַיִם וְעַד־יְרֵכַיִם יִהְיוּ׃ 43 וְהָיוּ
עַל־אַהֲרֹן וְעַל־בָּנָיו בְּבֹאָם ׀ אֶל־אֹהֶל
מוֹעֵד אוֹ בְגִשְׁתָּם אֶל־הַמִּזְבֵּחַ לְשָׁרֵת
בַּקֹּדֶשׁ וְלֹא־יִשְׂאוּ עָוֺן וָמֵתוּ חֻקַּת עוֹלָם
לוֹ וּלְזַרְעוֹ אַחֲרָיו׃ ס

29 This is what you shall do to them in consecrating them to serve Me as priests: Take a
young bull of the herd and two rams without
blemish; 2also unleavened bread, unleavened
cakes with oil mixed in, and unleavened wafers
spread with oil—make these of choice wheat
flour. 3Place these in one basket and present
them in the basket, along with the bull and the
two rams. 4Lead Aaron and his sons up to the
entrance of the Tent of Meeting, and wash them
with water. 5Then take the vestments, and

ביעי כט וְזֶה הַדָּבָר אֲשֶׁר־תַּעֲשֶׂה לָהֶם
לְקַדֵּשׁ אֹתָם לְכַהֵן לִי לְקַח פַּר אֶחָד
בֶּן־בָּקָר וְאֵילִם שְׁנַיִם תְּמִימִם׃ 2 וְלֶחֶם
מַצּוֹת וְחַלֹּת מַצֹּת בְּלוּלֹת בַּשֶּׁמֶן וּרְקִיקֵי
מַצּוֹת מְשֻׁחִים בַּשָּׁמֶן סֹלֶת חִטִּים תַּעֲשֶׂה
אֹתָם׃ 3 וְנָתַתָּ אוֹתָם עַל־סַל אֶחָד
וְהִקְרַבְתָּ אֹתָם בַּסָּל וְאֶת־הַפָּר וְאֵת שְׁנֵי
הָאֵילִם׃ 4 וְאֶת־אַהֲרֹן וְאֶת־בָּנָיו תַּקְרִיב
אֶל־פֶּתַח אֹהֶל מוֹעֵד וְרָחַצְתָּ אֹתָם
בַּמָּיִם׃ 5 וְלָקַחְתָּ אֶת־הַבְּגָדִים וְהִלְבַּשְׁתָּ

42. Hebrew: *mikhnasayim* (breeches), a word that occurs in the Bible only in connection with priestly attire. Here they are listed separately, because they clearly are not the sort of vestments worn "for dignity and adornment" (v. 40). This is also because, to avoid unseemliness, the priest put them on by himself; others helped him into the vestments.

to cover their nakedness See Comment to 20:23.

43. This instruction probably refers to all of the vestments together, not only to the last item.

INSTALLATION OF THE PRIESTS (29:1–46)

Moses is to preside over the installation of the priests, during which he will act as the sole priest. The installation rituals, lasting seven days, comprise animal sacrifices, meal offerings, washing the body, robing, and anointing. The installation is reported and described in Lev. 8–9, where it includes purification, preparation, and ordination.

ANIMALS AND MATERIALS (vv. 1–3)

First these are listed (as in 25:1–7) and then their functions are specified.

1. to them To Aaron and his sons.

without blemish Literally, "whole." This requirement applies to all three animals.

2. The grain offerings are to consist of three varieties of *matzah:* "unleavened bread," made of choice wheat flour: (a) plain oven baked, (b) with the dough mixed and kneaded with oil, and (c) with oil smeared on top after the baking. The significance of the variations is unknown. These unleavened breads are for use only with the ram of ordination.

3. present Literally, "bring forward," i.e., to the Tent of Meeting.

THE WASHING (v. 4)

Before Aaron and his sons are dressed in the sacred garments of office for the first time, they must undergo ritual purification by total immersion in water.

THE ROBING AND ANOINTING OF AARON ALONE (vv. 5–7)

The linen breeches are not mentioned for reasons of delicacy, because Aaron puts on this undergarment by himself. It is not known why the order

אֶת־אַהֲרֹן֙ אֶת־הַכֻּתֹּ֔נֶת וְאֵת֙ מְעִ֣יל הָֽאֵפֹ֔ד
וְאֶת־הָאֵפֹ֖ד וְאֶת־הַחֹ֑שֶׁן וְאָפַדְתָּ֣ ל֔וֹ בְּחֵ֖שֶׁב
הָאֵפֹֽד׃ 6 וְשַׂמְתָּ֥ הַמִּצְנֶ֖פֶת עַל־רֹאשׁ֑וֹ
וְנָתַתָּ֛ אֶת־נֵ֥זֶר הַקֹּ֖דֶשׁ עַל־הַמִּצְנָֽפֶת׃
7 וְלָקַחְתָּ֙ אֶת־שֶׁ֣מֶן הַמִּשְׁחָ֔ה וְיָצַקְתָּ֖ עַל־
רֹאשׁ֑וֹ וּמָשַׁחְתָּ֖ אֹתֽוֹ׃ 8 וְאֶת־בָּנָ֖יו תַּקְרִ֑יב
וְהִלְבַּשְׁתָּ֖ם כֻּתֳּנֹֽת׃ 9 וְחָגַרְתָּ֨ אֹתָ֜ם אַבְנֵ֗ט
אַהֲרֹ֣ן וּבָנָ֔יו וְחָבַשְׁתָּ֤ לָהֶם֙ מִגְבָּעֹ֔ת וְהָיְתָ֥ה
לָהֶ֛ם כְּהֻנָּ֖ה לְחֻקַּ֣ת עוֹלָ֑ם
וּמִלֵּאתָ֥ יַד־אַהֲרֹ֖ן וְיַד־בָּנָֽיו׃ 10 וְהִקְרַבְתָּ֙
אֶת־הַפָּ֔ר לִפְנֵ֖י אֹ֣הֶל מוֹעֵ֑ד וְסָמַ֨ךְ
אַהֲרֹ֧ן וּבָנָ֛יו אֶת־יְדֵיהֶ֖ם עַל־רֹ֥אשׁ הַפָּֽר׃
11 וְשָׁחַטְתָּ֥ אֶת־הַפָּ֖ר לִפְנֵ֣י יְהוָ֑ה פֶּ֖תַח
אֹ֥הֶל מוֹעֵֽד׃ 12 וְלָקַחְתָּ֙ מִדַּ֣ם הַפָּ֔ר וְנָתַתָּ֛ה
עַל־קַרְנֹ֥ת הַמִּזְבֵּ֖חַ בְּאֶצְבָּעֶ֑ךָ וְאֶת־כָּל־
הַדָּ֣ם תִּשְׁפֹּ֔ךְ אֶל־יְס֖וֹד הַמִּזְבֵּֽחַ׃ 13 וְלָקַחְתָּ֗
אֶֽת־כָּל־הַחֵ֘לֶב֮ הַֽמְכַסֶּ֣ה אֶת־הַקֶּ֒רֶב֒ וְאֵ֗ת
הַיֹּתֶ֙רֶת֙ עַל־הַכָּבֵ֔ד וְאֵת֙ שְׁתֵּ֣י הַכְּלָיֹ֔ת
וְאֶת־הַחֵ֖לֶב אֲשֶׁ֣ר עֲלֵיהֶ֑ן וְהִקְטַרְתָּ֖
הַמִּזְבֵּֽחָה׃ 14 וְאֶת־בְּשַׂ֤ר הַפָּר֙ וְאֶת־עֹר֣וֹ

clothe Aaron with the tunic, the robe of the
ephod, the ephod, and the breastpiece, and gird
him with the decorated band of the ephod. 6Put
the headdress on his head, and place the holy
diadem upon the headdress. 7Take the anointing oil and pour it on his head and anoint him.
8Then bring his sons forward; clothe them with
tunics 9and wind turbans upon them. And gird
both Aaron and his sons with sashes. And so
they shall have priesthood as their right for all
time.

You shall then ordain Aaron and his sons.
10Lead the bull up to the front of the Tent of
Meeting, and let Aaron and his sons lay their
hands upon the head of the bull. 11Slaughter the
bull before the LORD, at the entrance of the Tent
of Meeting, 12and take some of the bull's blood
and put it on the horns of the altar with your
finger; then pour out the rest of the blood at
the base of the altar. 13Take all the fat that covers
the entrails, the protuberance on the liver, and
the two kidneys with the fat on them, and turn
them into smoke upon the altar. 14The rest of

of robing found here differs from that in Lev. 8:7–9.

7. This verse implies that Aaron alone is to be anointed. Other biblical passages, however, make it clear that ordinary priests were also anointed. The differing texts may reflect different traditions.

THE ROBING OF AARON AND HIS SONS (vv. 8–9)

The instructions deal in turn with the vestments of the ordinary priests and with the items that are worn by them and by Aaron. For the sake of clarity, the English translation slightly rearranges the order of the clauses in the Hebrew text.

9. sashes The sash of the High Priest, described in 28:4,39, is not mentioned in the instructions of 29:5–6.

THE ANIMAL SACRIFICES (vv. 10–26)

Immediately before slaughtering each of the three animals listed in verse 1, the priests are to perform "the laying on of the hands." The text does not explain how this is to be done, or the meaning of the ceremony. Originally it may have been a legal, not a ritual, act intended to mark the animal or person for a specific role or fate; at times, too, it served to identify and affirm ownership of the animals to be sacrificed. In a number of places in the Bible, the act seems to signify the transfer of authority.

The Bull of Purification Offering (vv. 10–14)

This is essentially a purificatory and expiatory sacrifice.

12. See Comment to 24:6. The reason for daubing the horns of the altar specifically may be that blood was used to purify holy objects (see v. 20).

13. protuberance on the liver The requirement to remove and burn this part is quite likely a reaction against the great importance attached to the liver in ancient Near Eastern divination. Numerous clay models of the liver have been uncovered in Mesopotamia, some divided into 50 sections and inscribed with omens and magical formulas. These models guided the trained priests in divining the intentions of the gods.

the flesh of the bull, its hide, and its dung shall be put to the fire outside the camp; it is a purification offering.

[15]Next take the one ram, and let Aaron and his sons lay their hands upon the ram's head. [16]Slaughter the ram, and take its blood and dash it against all sides of the altar. [17]Cut up the ram into sections, wash its entrails and legs, and put them with its quarters and its head. [18]Turn all of the ram into smoke upon the altar. It is a burnt offering to the LORD, a pleasing odor, a gift to the LORD.

[19]Then take the other ram, and let Aaron and his sons lay their hands upon the ram's head. [20]Slaughter the ram, and take some of its blood and put it on the ridge of Aaron's right ear and on the ridges of his sons' right ears, and on the thumbs of their right hands, and on the big toes of their right feet; and dash the rest of the blood against every side of the altar round about. [21]Take some of the blood that is on the altar and

וְאֶת־פִּרְשׁוֹ תִּשְׂרֹף בָּאֵשׁ מִחוּץ לַמַּחֲנֶה
חַטָּאת הוּא׃
15 וְאֶת־הָאַיִל הָאֶחָד תִּקָּח וְסָמְכוּ אַהֲרֹן
וּבָנָיו אֶת־יְדֵיהֶם עַל־רֹאשׁ הָאָיִל׃
16 וְשָׁחַטְתָּ אֶת־הָאָיִל וְלָקַחְתָּ אֶת־דָּמוֹ
וְזָרַקְתָּ עַל־הַמִּזְבֵּחַ סָבִיב׃ 17 וְאֶת־הָאַיִל
תְּנַתֵּחַ לִנְתָחָיו וְרָחַצְתָּ קִרְבּוֹ וּכְרָעָיו
וְנָתַתָּ עַל־נְתָחָיו וְעַל־רֹאשׁוֹ׃ 18 וְהִקְטַרְתָּ
אֶת־כָּל־הָאַיִל הַמִּזְבֵּחָה עֹלָה הוּא לַיהוָה
רֵיחַ נִיחוֹחַ אִשֶּׁה לַיהוָה הוּא׃
19 וְלָקַחְתָּ אֵת הָאַיִל הַשֵּׁנִי וְסָמַךְ אַהֲרֹן מישי
וּבָנָיו אֶת־יְדֵיהֶם עַל־רֹאשׁ הָאָיִל׃
20 וְשָׁחַטְתָּ אֶת־הָאַיִל וְלָקַחְתָּ מִדָּמוֹ
וְנָתַתָּה עַל־תְּנוּךְ אֹזֶן אַהֲרֹן וְעַל־תְּנוּךְ
אֹזֶן בָּנָיו הַיְמָנִית וְעַל־בֹּהֶן יָדָם הַיְמָנִית
וְעַל־בֹּהֶן רַגְלָם הַיְמָנִית וְזָרַקְתָּ אֶת־הַדָּם
עַל־הַמִּזְבֵּחַ סָבִיב׃ 21 וְלָקַחְתָּ מִן־הַדָּם

The Ram of Burnt Offering (vv. 15–18)

The first of the rams is to be an *olah* offering, to be consumed completely by fire on the altar.

16. against all sides The blood, which had been collected in a vessel, was dashed against the altar from diagonally opposite corners in such a way that each of the two sprinklings spattered two of the sides, signifying the return of the animal to God.

18. pleasing odor In verses that deal with technical matters involving the sacrificial system, this phrase means that the sacrifice has been accepted by God.

The Ram of Ordination (vv. 19–26)

This ram comes under the category of the *zevaḥ sh'lamim,* "an offering of well-being" or (according to B. Levine) "a sacred gift of greeting." That is, the slaughtered ram is only partly burned on the altar. The rest of it belongs to the priests and those who offered it. This offering, which concludes the ceremony of installation, is accompanied by elaborate rites.

20. This daubing of the blood most likely has a purificatory function.

ridge It is uncertain whether the part of the ear denoted by the Hebrew word *t'nukh* refers to the cartilage or to the lobe.

21. As the text explains, and as the description of Lev. 8:30 repeats, this ritual effectuated the consecration of the priests.

CHAPTER 29

20. The Midrash understands the anointing of the ear, thumb, and big toe of the *kohen* (priest) as teaching that a *kohen* must listen to the people, act on their behalf, and go forth among them. Another *midrash* sees the ceremony as helping Aaron atone for his role in the incident of the Golden Calf. "The ear that heard the words 'You shall have no other gods beside Me' and then listened to the people's demand for a calf; the hands which had pledged to serve God and then fashioned a calf; the feet that climbed Mount Sinai and then hastened to do that which was wrong"—all of these had to be cleansed and rededicated to the service of God.

some of the anointing oil and sprinkle upon Aaron and his vestments, and also upon his sons and his sons' vestments. Thus shall he and his vestments be holy, as well as his sons and his sons' vestments.

22You shall take from the ram the fat parts—the broad tail, the fat that covers the entrails, the protuberance on the liver, the two kidneys with the fat on them—and the right thigh; for this is a ram of ordination. 23Add one flat loaf of bread, one cake of oil bread, and one wafer, from the basket of unleavened bread that is before the LORD. 24Place all these on the palms of Aaron and his sons, and offer them as an elevation offering before the LORD. 25Take them from their hands and turn them into smoke upon the altar with the burnt offering, as a pleasing odor before the LORD; it is a gift to the LORD.

26Then take the breast of Aaron's ram of ordination and offer it as an elevation offering before the LORD; it shall be your portion. 27You shall consecrate the breast that was offered as an elevation offering and the thigh that was offered as a gift offering from the ram of ordination—from that which was Aaron's and from that which was his sons'—28and those parts shall be a due for all time from the Israelites to Aaron and his descendants. For they are a gift; and so shall they be a gift from the Israelites, their gift to the LORD out of their sacrifices of well-being.

29The sacral vestments of Aaron shall pass on

אֲשֶׁר עַל־הַמִּזְבֵּחַ וּמִשֶּׁמֶן הַמִּשְׁחָה וְהִזֵּיתָ
עַל־אַהֲרֹן וְעַל־בְּגָדָיו וְעַל־בָּנָיו וְעַל־בִּגְדֵי
בָנָיו אִתּוֹ וְקָדַשׁ הוּא וּבְגָדָיו וּבָנָיו וּבִגְדֵי
בָנָיו אִתּוֹ׃
22 וְלָקַחְתָּ מִן־הָאַיִל הַחֵלֶב וְהָאַלְיָה
וְאֶת־הַחֵלֶב ׀ הַמְכַסֶּה אֶת־הַקֶּרֶב וְאֵת
יֹתֶרֶת הַכָּבֵד וְאֵת ׀ שְׁתֵּי הַכְּלָיֹת וְאֶת־
הַחֵלֶב אֲשֶׁר עֲלֵיהֶן וְאֵת שׁוֹק הַיָּמִין כִּי
אֵיל מִלֻּאִים הוּא׃ 23 וְכִכַּר לֶחֶם אַחַת
וְחַלַּת לֶחֶם שֶׁמֶן אַחַת וְרָקִיק אֶחָד מִסַּל
הַמַּצּוֹת אֲשֶׁר לִפְנֵי יְהוָה׃ 24 וְשַׂמְתָּ הַכֹּל
עַל כַּפֵּי אַהֲרֹן וְעַל כַּפֵּי בָנָיו וְהֵנַפְתָּ אֹתָם
תְּנוּפָה לִפְנֵי יְהוָה׃ 25 וְלָקַחְתָּ אֹתָם מִיָּדָם
וְהִקְטַרְתָּ הַמִּזְבֵּחָה עַל־הָעֹלָה לְרֵיחַ
נִיחוֹחַ לִפְנֵי יְהוָה אִשֶּׁה הוּא לַיהוָה׃
26 וְלָקַחְתָּ אֶת־הֶחָזֶה מֵאֵיל הַמִּלֻּאִים
אֲשֶׁר לְאַהֲרֹן וְהֵנַפְתָּ אֹתוֹ תְּנוּפָה לִפְנֵי
יְהוָה וְהָיָה לְךָ לְמָנָה׃ 27 וְקִדַּשְׁתָּ אֵת ׀
חֲזֵה הַתְּנוּפָה וְאֵת שׁוֹק הַתְּרוּמָה אֲשֶׁר
הוּנַף וַאֲשֶׁר הוּרָם מֵאֵיל הַמִּלֻּאִים מֵאֲשֶׁר
לְאַהֲרֹן וּמֵאֲשֶׁר לְבָנָיו׃ 28 וְהָיָה לְאַהֲרֹן
וּלְבָנָיו לְחָק־עוֹלָם מֵאֵת בְּנֵי יִשְׂרָאֵל
כִּי תְרוּמָה הוּא* וּתְרוּמָה יִהְיֶה מֵאֵת
בְּנֵי־יִשְׂרָאֵל מִזִּבְחֵי שַׁלְמֵיהֶם תְּרוּמָתָם
לַיהוָה׃
29 וּבִגְדֵי הַקֹּדֶשׁ אֲשֶׁר לְאַהֲרֹן יִהְיוּ לְבָנָיו

v. 28. סבירין ומטעין "היא"

22. for this is a ram of ordination Normally the right thigh of the animal is assigned to the priest and not, as here, offered up in smoke on the altar.

24. elevation offering An offering that undergoes the special ritual of being "raised up."

26. Here, because the installation ceremonies are not quite completed and because Moses serves in the capacity of a priest, he is entitled to that which routinely would be the priest's portion in the future.

THE INSTALLATION OF FUTURE PRIESTS
(vv. 27–30)

These verses briefly interrupt the theme of installation to explain that the foregoing applies only to the present inaugural and that different rules will govern the installation of future priests.

28. their gift to the LORD God assigns these parts to the priests.

29–30. The eight garments that are the uniform of the High Priest (as described in 28:3–

to his sons after him, for them to be anointed
and ordained in. 30 He among his sons who becomes priest in his stead, who enters the Tent
of Meeting to officiate within the sanctuary,
shall wear them seven days.
31 You shall take the ram of ordination and
boil its flesh in the sacred precinct; 32 and Aaron
and his sons shall eat the flesh of the ram, and
the bread that is in the basket, at the entrance
of the Tent of Meeting. 33 These things shall be
eaten only by those for whom expiation was
made with them when they were ordained and
consecrated; they may not be eaten by a layman,
for they are holy. 34 And if any of the flesh of
ordination, or any of the bread, is left until
morning, you shall put what is left to the fire;
it shall not be eaten, for it is holy.
35 Thus you shall do to Aaron and his sons,
just as I have commanded you. You shall ordain
them through seven days, 36 and each day you
shall prepare a bull as a purification offering
for expiation; you shall purify the altar by performing purification upon it, and you shall
anoint it to consecrate it. 37 Seven days you shall
perform purification for the altar to consecrate
it, and the altar shall become most holy; whatever touches the altar shall become consecrated.
38 Now this is what you shall offer upon the

אַחֲרָיו לְמָשְׁחָה בָהֶם וּלְמַלֵּא־בָם אֶת־
יָדָם׃ 30 שִׁבְעַת יָמִים יִלְבָּשָׁם הַכֹּהֵן
תַּחְתָּיו מִבָּנָיו אֲשֶׁר יָבֹא אֶל־אֹהֶל מוֹעֵד
לְשָׁרֵת בַּקֹּדֶשׁ׃
31 וְאֵת אֵיל הַמִּלֻּאִים תִּקָּח וּבִשַּׁלְתָּ אֶת־
בְּשָׂרוֹ בְּמָקֹם קָדֹשׁ׃ 32 וְאָכַל אַהֲרֹן וּבָנָיו
אֶת־בְּשַׂר הָאַיִל וְאֶת־הַלֶּחֶם אֲשֶׁר בַּסָּל
פֶּתַח אֹהֶל מוֹעֵד׃ 33 וְאָכְלוּ אֹתָם אֲשֶׁר
כֻּפַּר בָּהֶם לְמַלֵּא אֶת־יָדָם לְקַדֵּשׁ אֹתָם
וְזָר לֹא־יֹאכַל כִּי־קֹדֶשׁ הֵם׃ 34 וְאִם־יִוָּתֵר
מִבְּשַׂר הַמִּלֻּאִים וּמִן־הַלֶּחֶם עַד־הַבֹּקֶר
וְשָׂרַפְתָּ אֶת־הַנּוֹתָר בָּאֵשׁ לֹא יֵאָכֵל כִּי־
קֹדֶשׁ הוּא׃
35 וְעָשִׂיתָ לְאַהֲרֹן וּלְבָנָיו כָּכָה כְּכֹל אֲשֶׁר־
צִוִּיתִי אֹתָכָה שִׁבְעַת יָמִים תְּמַלֵּא יָדָם׃
36 וּפַר חַטָּאת תַּעֲשֶׂה לַיּוֹם עַל־הַכִּפֻּרִים
וְחִטֵּאתָ עַל־הַמִּזְבֵּחַ בְּכַפֶּרְךָ עָלָיו וּמָשַׁחְתָּ
אֹתוֹ לְקַדְּשׁוֹ׃ 37 שִׁבְעַת יָמִים תְּכַפֵּר עַל־
הַמִּזְבֵּחַ וְקִדַּשְׁתָּ אֹתוֹ וְהָיָה הַמִּזְבֵּחַ קֹדֶשׁ
קָדָשִׁים כָּל־הַנֹּגֵעַ בַּמִּזְבֵּחַ יִקְדָּשׁ׃ ס
ששי 38 וְזֶה אֲשֶׁר תַּעֲשֶׂה עַל־הַמִּזְבֵּחַ כְּבָשִׂים

4,42) are to be handed down from father to son and worn for each successor's installation ceremony, which is also to last for seven days.

THE SACRIFICIAL MEAL (vv. 31–34)

Instructions for the installation of Aaron and his sons resume.

31. in the sacred precinct In the enclosed court of the tabernacle.

32–33. The ritual of the *sh'lamim* offering involves a sacrificial meal, as prescribed in Lev. 7:15.

layman Hebrew: *zar,* literally, "strange, alien, removed"; used in describing rituals to refer to an outsider or a person or thing unauthorized to participate in certain religious roles or functions.

A WEEK-LONG OBSERVANCE (vv. 35–37)

These verses appear to mean that the entire installation ceremony is to be repeated each day for seven days.

36. The altar is assumed to possess a natural impurity, because it is a piece of furniture fashioned by human beings. It must, therefore, be anointed, purged of defilement and consecrated before it can be used for a sacred function.

37. most holy Hebrew: *kodesh kodashim,* literally, "holy of holies"; normally designates the inner sanctum of the tabernacle but is also used, as here, to denote superior holiness.

whatever touches The holiness of the altar is contagious.

THE REGULAR BURNT OFFERING (vv. 38–42)

The repeated mention of the altar in the previous two verses makes this an appropriate occasion for introducing its basic function: to accommodate

altar: two yearling lambs each day, regularly.
39You shall offer the one lamb in the morning,
and you shall offer the other lamb at twilight.
40There shall be a tenth of a measure of choice
flour with a quarter of a *hin* of beaten oil mixed
in, and a libation of a quarter *hin* of wine for
one lamb; 41and you shall offer the other lamb
at twilight, repeating with it the grain offering
of the morning with its libation—a gift for a
pleasing odor to the LORD, 42a regular burnt
offering throughout the generations, at the entrance of the Tent of Meeting before the LORD.

For there I will meet with you, and there I
will speak with you, 43and there I will meet with
the Israelites, and it shall be sanctified by My
Presence. 44I will sanctify the Tent of Meeting
and the altar, and I will consecrate Aaron and
his sons to serve Me as priests. 45I will abide

בְּנֵי־שָׁנָה שְׁנַיִם לַיּוֹם תָּמִיד׃ 39 אֶת־
הַכֶּבֶשׂ הָאֶחָד תַּעֲשֶׂה בַבֹּקֶר וְאֵת הַכֶּבֶשׂ
הַשֵּׁנִי תַּעֲשֶׂה בֵּין הָעַרְבָּיִם׃ 40 וְעִשָּׂרֹן
סֹלֶת בָּלוּל בְּשֶׁמֶן כָּתִית רֶבַע הַהִין וְנֵסֶךְ
רְבִיעִת הַהִין יָיִן לַכֶּבֶשׂ הָאֶחָד׃ 41 וְאֵת
הַכֶּבֶשׂ הַשֵּׁנִי תַּעֲשֶׂה בֵּין הָעַרְבָּיִם כְּמִנְחַת
הַבֹּקֶר וּכְנִסְכָּהּ תַּעֲשֶׂה־לָּהּ לְרֵיחַ נִיחֹחַ
אִשֶּׁה לַיהוָה׃ 42 עֹלַת תָּמִיד לְדֹרֹתֵיכֶם
פֶּתַח אֹהֶל־מוֹעֵד לִפְנֵי יְהוָה
אֲשֶׁר אִוָּעֵד לָכֶם שָׁמָּה לְדַבֵּר אֵלֶיךָ שָׁם׃
43 וְנֹעַדְתִּי שָׁמָּה לִבְנֵי יִשְׂרָאֵל וְנִקְדַּשׁ
בִּכְבֹדִי׃ 44 וְקִדַּשְׁתִּי אֶת־אֹהֶל מוֹעֵד וְאֶת־
הַמִּזְבֵּחַ וְאֶת־אַהֲרֹן וְאֶת־בָּנָיו אֲקַדֵּשׁ
לְכַהֵן לִי׃ 45 וְשָׁכַנְתִּי בְּתוֹךְ בְּנֵי יִשְׂרָאֵל

the daily burnt offering. Twice daily, a lamb was wholly burned on the altar. Called "the regular burnt offering" (*olat ha-tamid*), it was the core of the whole sacrificial system.

40. hin A liquid measure of Egyptian origin, approximately 1½ gallons (6 L).

42. there This refers back to the Tent of Meeting, not to the entrance.

A SUMMATION (vv. 43–46)

The chapter closes with an emphatic reaffirmation of the religious and spiritual significance of the tabernacle.

43. it shall be sanctified That is, the Tent of Meeting. The verb קדשׁ means "to set apart," from that which is mundane, from that which is ugly or impure (see Lev. 19:2).

44. The tabernacle as such and its regimen of rituals possess no innate sanctity. No effective magic derives from them. The sacred status of the priests and the edifice, with its furniture and utensils, flows entirely from the will of God.

---

42. Until now, holiness was manifest only occasionally and sporadically in the world. Once Israel received the Torah, the world would know holiness on a regular, daily basis. The daily offering (*tamid*) was to represent this (Kook).

44. Aaron is bequeathing not only material goods to his children but is passing on to them an ethical imperative to see themselves as consecrated to the service of God and of the people Israel.

45. The people Israel did not have the power to summon God's Presence by performing these rituals. It was an act of grace on God's part to choose to be present in their midst. Nonetheless, in postbiblical times, Jews developed the belief that by performing a *mitzvah* and reciting a blessing that addresses God directly ("Praised are You, O LORD"), they would feel God's presence in the moment. The Talmud asks a strange question: If a priest's body is inside the Tent but his head remains outside, is he considered having entered the Tent and may he perform the service? The answer is that he may not; he must be totally within (BT Zev. 26a). One is tempted to understand the question in spiritual rather than purely physical terms. A person can be physically present at a service but emotionally and spiritually absent. One's head may be elsewhere. Such a person is not considered a true participant.

among the Israelites, and I will be their God.
⁴⁶And they shall know that I the LORD am their
God, who brought them out from the land of
Egypt that I might abide among them, I the
LORD their God.

וְהָיִ֣יתִי לָהֶם֮ לֵֽאלֹהִים֒ ٤٦ וְיָ֣דְע֗וּ כִּ֣י אֲנִ֤י
יְהֹוָה֙ אֱלֹ֣הֵיהֶ֔ם אֲשֶׁ֨ר הוֹצֵ֤אתִי אֹתָם֙
מֵאֶ֣רֶץ מִצְרַ֔יִם לְשׇׁכְנִ֖י בְתוֹכָ֑ם אֲנִ֖י יְהֹוָ֥ה
אֱלֹהֵיהֶֽם׃ פ

30

You shall make an altar for burning incense; make it of acacia wood. ²It shall be a cubit
long and a cubit wide—it shall be square—and
two cubits high, its horns of one piece with it.
³Overlay it with pure gold: its top, its sides
round about, and its horns; and make a gold
molding for it round about. ⁴And make two
gold rings for it under its molding; make them
on its two side walls, on opposite sides. They
shall serve as holders for poles with which to
carry it. ⁵Make the poles of acacia wood, and
overlay them with gold.

⁶Place it in front of the curtain that is over
the Ark of the Pact—in front of the cover that
is over the Pact—where I will meet with you.
⁷On it Aaron shall burn aromatic incense: he
shall burn it every morning when he tends the
lamps, ⁸and Aaron shall burn it at twilight when

שְׁבִיעִי
לְ וְעָשִׂ֣יתָ מִזְבֵּ֖חַ מִקְטַ֣ר קְטֹ֑רֶת עֲצֵ֥י
שִׁטִּ֖ים תַּעֲשֶׂ֥ה אֹתֽוֹ׃ ² אַמָּ֨ה אׇרְכּ֜וֹ וְאַמָּ֣ה
רׇחְבּ֗וֹ רָב֤וּעַ יִֽהְיֶה֙ וְאַמָּתַ֣יִם קֹֽמָת֔וֹ מִמֶּ֖נּוּ
קַרְנֹתָֽיו׃ ³ וְצִפִּיתָ֨ אֹת֜וֹ זָהָ֣ב טָה֗וֹר אֶת־גַּגּ֤וֹ
וְאֶת־קִֽירֹתָיו֙ סָבִ֔יב וְאֶת־קַרְנֹתָ֑יו וְעָשִׂ֥יתָ
לּ֛וֹ זֵ֥ר זָהָ֖ב סָבִֽיב׃ ⁴ וּשְׁתֵּי֩ טַבְּעֹ֨ת זָהָ֜ב
תַּֽעֲשֶׂה־לּ֣וֹ ׀ מִתַּ֣חַת לְזֵר֗וֹ עַ֚ל שְׁתֵּ֣י
צַלְעֹתָ֔יו תַּעֲשֶׂ֖ה עַל־שְׁנֵ֣י צִדָּ֑יו וְהָיָה֙
לְבָתִּ֣ים לְבַדִּ֔ים לָשֵׂ֥את אֹת֖וֹ בָּהֵֽמָּה׃
⁵ וְעָשִׂ֥יתָ אֶת־הַבַּדִּ֖ים עֲצֵ֣י שִׁטִּ֑ים וְצִפִּיתָ֥
אֹתָ֖ם זָהָֽב׃

⁶ וְנָתַתָּ֣ה אֹת֗וֹ לִפְנֵ֣י הַפָּרֹ֒כֶת֒ אֲשֶׁ֖ר עַל־אֲרֹ֣ן
הָעֵדֻ֑ת לִפְנֵ֣י הַכַּפֹּ֗רֶת אֲשֶׁר֙ עַל־הָ֣עֵדֻ֔ת
אֲשֶׁ֛ר אִוָּעֵ֥ד לְךָ֖ שָֽׁמָּה׃ ⁷ וְהִקְטִ֥יר עָלָ֛יו
אַהֲרֹ֖ן קְטֹ֣רֶת סַמִּ֑ים בַּבֹּ֣קֶר בַּבֹּ֗קֶר בְּהֵיטִיב֛וֹ
אֶת־הַנֵּרֹ֖ת יַקְטִירֶֽנָּה׃ ⁸ וּבְהַעֲלֹ֨ת אַהֲרֹ֧ן טִיר

45. I will be their God See Comment to 6:7.
46. they shall know See Comment to 1:8.
God's presence is manifest and meaningful to the
people Israel through His intervention in the
events of history.

AN APPENDIX TO THE INSTRUCTIONS (30:1–38)

This chapter consists of supplementary instructions relating to the construction of the tabernacle
and its rituals.

THE INCENSE ALTAR (vv. 1–10)

The use of incense in rites of worship was widespread and had a long history in the ancient world.
Given the number of animals slaughtered, incense
was used not only to disperse noxious odors but
to prevent people from being overcome by the
fumes. The cloud of aromatic incense in the tabernacle was later perceived to be a reminder of the
invisible Presence of God, as was the cloud that

accompanied the Israelites during the Exodus and
the wilderness wanderings. The importance attached to the incense altar is shown by its placement in the Holy Place just outside the curtain
that veils the Holy of Holies. It measured 1.5 feet
(0.45 m.) square at the top and stood 3 feet (0.9
m.) high. Unlike the Ark and the table, it was embellished with a molding; like them, it was transported by means of poles inserted through rings
affixed to its sides.

1. an altar Hebrew: *mizbe·aḥ*, literally, a
"place of slaughter"; applicable only to an altar
for animal sacrifice. It is used here for the incense
altar because its shape was similar to that of a sacrificial altar.

7–8. These verses seem to indicate that offering incense and tending and lighting the lamps
are to be the prerogatives of the High Priest. We
know, however, that the daily performance of
these rituals was carried out by ordinary priests
as well (see M Yoma 4:4; Tamid 6:3).

אֶת־הַנֵּרֹת בֵּין הָעַרְבַּיִם יַקְטִירֶנָּה קְטֹרֶת
תָּמִיד לִפְנֵי יְהוָה לְדֹרֹתֵיכֶם׃ 9 לֹא־תַעֲלוּ
עָלָיו קְטֹרֶת זָרָה וְעֹלָה וּמִנְחָה וְנֵסֶךְ לֹא
תִסְּכוּ עָלָיו׃ 10 וְכִפֶּר אַהֲרֹן עַל־קַרְנֹתָיו
אַחַת בַּשָּׁנָה מִדַּם חַטַּאת הַכִּפֻּרִים אַחַת
בַּשָּׁנָה יְכַפֵּר עָלָיו לְדֹרֹתֵיכֶם קֹדֶשׁ־
קָדָשִׁים הוּא לַיהוָה׃ פ

he lights the lamps—a regular incense offering
before the LORD throughout the ages.
9 You shall
not offer alien incense on it, or a burnt offering
or a grain offering; neither shall you pour a
libation on it.
10 Once a year Aaron shall purge
its horns with blood of the purification offering;
it shall be purged once a year throughout the
ages. It is most holy to the LORD.

aromatic incense Hebrew: *k'toret sammim.* The noun *k'toret* derives from a stem meaning "to burn, smoke"; it eventually became the term for the substance that produces the aroma.

tends Literally, "makes good," i.e., cleans the lamps of refuse and replaces the wicks and the oil.

9. alien incense Hebrew: *k'toret zarah;* See Comment to 29:33. Any incense not precisely compounded according to the formula of verses 34–36 is invalid.

or a burnt offering It is to be used exclusively for the incense offering.

10. The only exception to the preceding rule occurs on Yom Kippur when the High Priest performs the rites of purification to reconsecrate the altar, as prescribed in Lev. 16:16–19.

הפטרת תצוה

HAFTARAH FOR T'TZAVVEH

EZEKIEL 43:10–27

In 587–586 B.C.E., Jerusalem was destroyed, the Temple was burned, and most of the population was deported to Babylon. Ezekiel continued to prophesy and offer consolation within this exilic community. Through visions of resurrected bones and apocalyptic wars, he projected the nation's restoration to Zion (Ezek. 35–39). The climax of these prophecies provides a blueprint of the future Temple and its new order of worship as well as a plan for resettlement in the homeland (Ezek. 40–48).

This *haftarah* is one of three *haftarah* selections taken from those chapters. It is a transition between the prophet's vision of God's Presence returning to the Temple (Ezek. 43:1–9) and the presentation of rules for priests in the Temple (Ezek. 44–46). In this *haftarah*, God tells Ezekiel to describe the Temple and the details of its consecration to the nation. Thus Ezekiel, like Moses before him, emerges as the mediator of a new order of worship.

The first three verses of the *haftarah* constitute a prologue that makes national contrition a precondition for learning details of the new Temple's construction. Presumably, just proclaiming the new order and describing the new Temple was thought sufficient to induce repentance and remorse for past sins. The announcement itself would show God's reconciliation with the people (Rashi).

The rest of the *haftarah* describes the altar and its consecration. The prominence of the sacrificial altar in the instructions and in the service points to its central role in priestly religion. It connects heaven and earth through the offerings brought to it by both the penitent and the pious, offerings that are transformed into gifts for God by being consumed there. Divine and human dimensions are aligned, atonement is sought, thanksgiving is expressed. God's own instruction about the offerings gives the people confidence in their efficacy, which requires the proper purification of both the personnel and the sacral objects involved in the service.

RELATION OF THE *HAFTARAH* TO THE *PARASHAH*

Readers of the *parashah,* with its account of the dedication of the wilderness altar fresh in mind, will sense a symmetry between founding events there with the tabernacle and future events in the new Temple described in the *haftarah.* This is a symmetry of continuity and renewal.

Both the tabernacle (built after the Exodus) and Ezekiel's Temple (to be built after the exile) are sacred sites for God's Presence on earth. It is on earth that the rites of sanctity are performed. These two constructions also mark the arena of divine immanence (indwelling on earth) at the beginning and at the end of the biblical era.

Later generations, in exile and without a Temple, would add their own hopes to Ezekiel's vision of restoration, which symbolized a renewal of time and space yet to come and a hope for purification and atonement before God. According to an old *midrash,* even hopes for the future have a redemptive dimension. God tells the people that when the nation in exile is engaged in "the reading" of the "plan of the Temple" they shall be considered "as if they were [in fact] occupied with the building of the Temple [itself]" (Tanḥ. Tzav 14).

The sanctity and the atoning power of the ancient Temple service were activated in another way as well. Noting that the great altar is called both "altar" (Ezek. 43:13) and "table" (41:22), Yoḥanan and Eleazar both taught: "As long as the Temple existed, the altar provided atonement for

Israel, but now (when the Temple is destroyed) a person's table provides atonement" (BT Ber. 55a). Other Sages focused on spiritual sustenance. Noting the same conjunction of altar and table in Ezek. 41:22, Simeon taught that when three people sit at a table and discuss Torah, it is "as if they ate from the table of the Presence [of God]" (M Avot 3:3).

43 10[Now] you, O mortal, describe the Temple to the House of Israel, and let them measure its design. But let them be ashamed of their iniquities: 11When they are ashamed of all they have done, make known to them the plan of the Temple and its layout, its exits and entrances—its entire plan, and all the laws and instructions pertaining to its entire plan. Write it down before their eyes, that they may faithfully follow its entire plan and all its laws. 12Such are the instructions for the Temple on top of the mountain: the entire area of its enclosure shall be most holy. Thus far the instructions for the Temple.

13And these are the dimensions of the altar, in cubits where each is a cubit and a handbreadth. The trench shall be a cubit deep and a cubit wide, with a rim one span high around its edge. And the height shall be as follows: 14From the trench in the ground to the lower ledge, which shall be a cubit wide: 2 cubits; from the lower ledge to the upper ledge, which shall likewise be a cubit wide: 4 cubits; 15and the height of the altar hearth shall be 4 cubits, with

מג 10 אַתָּה בֶן־אָדָם הַגֵּד אֶת־בֵּית־
יִשְׂרָאֵל אֶת־הַבַּיִת וְיִכָּלְמוּ מֵעֲוֺנוֹתֵיהֶם
וּמָדְדוּ אֶת־תָּכְנִית: 11 וְאִם־נִכְלְמוּ מִכֹּל
אֲשֶׁר־עָשׂוּ צוּרַת הַבַּיִת וּתְכוּנָתוֹ וּמוֹצָאָיו
וּמוֹבָאָיו וְכָל־צורתו צוּרֹתָיו וְאֵת כָּל־
חֻקֹּתָיו וְכָל־צורתי צוּרֹתָיו וְכָל־תורתו
תּוֹרֹתָיו הוֹדַע אוֹתָם וּכְתֹב לְעֵינֵיהֶם
וְיִשְׁמְרוּ אֶת־כָּל־צוּרָתוֹ וְאֶת־כָּל־חֻקֹּתָיו
וְעָשׂוּ אוֹתָם: 12 זֹאת תּוֹרַת הַבָּיִת עַל־
רֹאשׁ הָהָר כָּל־גְּבֻלוֹ סָבִיב ׀ סָבִיב קֹדֶשׁ
קָדָשִׁים הִנֵּה־זֹאת תּוֹרַת הַבָּיִת:
13 וְאֵלֶּה מִדּוֹת הַמִּזְבֵּחַ בָּאַמּוֹת אַמָּה
אַמָּה וָטֹפַח וְחֵיק הָאַמָּה וְאַמָּה־רֹחַב
וּגְבוּלָהּ אֶל־שְׂפָתָהּ סָבִיב זֶרֶת הָאֶחָד וְזֶה
גַּב הַמִּזְבֵּחַ: 14 וּמֵחֵיק הָאָרֶץ עַד־הָעֲזָרָה
הַתַּחְתּוֹנָה שְׁתַּיִם אַמּוֹת וְרֹחַב אַמָּה
אֶחָת וּמֵהָעֲזָרָה הַקְּטַנָּה עַד־הָעֲזָרָה
הַגְּדוֹלָה אַרְבַּע אַמּוֹת וְרֹחַב הָאַמָּה:
15 וְהַהַרְאֵל אַרְבַּע אַמּוֹת ומהאראיל
וּמֵהָאֲרִיאֵל וּלְמַעְלָה הַקְּרָנוֹת אַרְבַּע:

Ezekiel 43:12. Such are the instructions Literally, "this is the instruction." This conclusion of the Temple blueprint uses a formula common to priestly instructions in the Torah (see Lev. 11:46–47, 14:32,57). Such formulas (as here) routinely refer to the instructions as a *torah* and provide a brief summary of the content of the instruction.

most holy Hebrew: *kodesh kodoshim*, which is used here for the entire Temple area—not just the holiest recess of the Temple. This use underscores the high emphasis on sanctity attributed to Ezekiel's Temple.

13. cubit Hebrew: *amah*. This ancient measure of length is based on the forearm and is equal to 18 to 22 inches. The handbreadth is another measure based on the body.

15–16. altar hearth The altar resembles a tower or a mountain, which may explain the depiction of the top-most hearth (*ha-ari·el*) as a "mountain of God" (*har·el*). Possibly this is a punning variation. The meaning of *ari·el* has been debated; possible renderings include "lion of God" and "(fire-)hearth of God." The latter would support the function of the object as a ritual hearth (cf. Targ.). The prophet Isaiah refers to the city of Jerusalem as *ari·el* (29:1ff.,7), presumably as a term for the (altar hearth of the) Temple.

4 horns projecting upward from the hearth: 4 cubits. 16Now the hearth shall be 12 cubits long and 12 broad, square, with 4 equal sides. 17Hence, the [upper] base shall be 14 cubits broad, with 4 equal sides. The surrounding rim shall be half a cubit [high], and the surrounding trench shall measure one cubit. And the ramp shall face east.

18Then he said to me: O mortal, thus said the Lord God: These are the directions for the altar on the day it is erected, so that burnt offerings may be offered up on it and blood dashed against it. 19You shall give to the levitical priests who are of the stock of Zadok, and so eligible to minister to Me—declares the Lord God—a young bull of the herd for a purification offering. 20You shall take some of its blood and apply it to the four horns [of the altar], to the four corners of the base, and to the surrounding rim; thus you shall purify it and purge it. 21Then you shall take the bull of purification offering and burn it in the designated area of the Temple, outside the Sanctuary.

22On the following day, you shall offer a goat without blemish as a purification offering; and the altar shall be purified [with it] just as it was purified with the bull. 23When you have completed the ritual of purification, you shall offer a bull of the herd without blemish and a ram of the flock without blemish. 24Offer them to the Lord; let the priests throw salt on them and offer them up as a burnt offering to the Lord.

16 והאראיל וְהָאֲרִיאֵל שְׁתֵּים עֶשְׂרֵה אֹרֶךְ
בִּשְׁתֵּים עֶשְׂרֵה רֹחַב רָבוּעַ אֶל אַרְבַּעַת
רְבָעָיו׃ 17 וְהָעֲזָרָה אַרְבַּע עֶשְׂרֵה אֹרֶךְ
בְּאַרְבַּע עֶשְׂרֵה רֹחַב אֶל אַרְבַּעַת רְבָעֶיהָ
וְהַגְּבוּל סָבִיב אוֹתָהּ חֲצִי הָאַמָּה וְהַחֵיק־
לָהּ אַמָּה סָבִיב וּמַעֲלֹתֵהוּ פְּנוֹת קָדִים׃
18 וַיֹּאמֶר אֵלַי בֶּן־אָדָם כֹּה אָמַר אֲדֹנָי
יְהוִה אֵלֶּה חֻקּוֹת הַמִּזְבֵּחַ בְּיוֹם הֵעָשׂוֹתוֹ
לְהַעֲלוֹת עָלָיו עוֹלָה וְלִזְרֹק עָלָיו דָּם׃
19 וְנָתַתָּה אֶל־הַכֹּהֲנִים הַלְוִיִּם אֲשֶׁר הֵם
מִזֶּרַע צָדוֹק הַקְּרֹבִים אֵלַי נְאֻם אֲדֹנָי יְהוִה
לְשָׁרְתֵנִי פַּר בֶּן־בָּקָר לְחַטָּאת׃ 20 וְלָקַחְתָּ
מִדָּמוֹ וְנָתַתָּה עַל־אַרְבַּע קַרְנֹתָיו וְאֶל־
אַרְבַּע פִּנּוֹת הָעֲזָרָה וְאֶל־הַגְּבוּל סָבִיב
וְחִטֵּאתָ אוֹתוֹ וְכִפַּרְתָּהוּ׃ 21 וְלָקַחְתָּ אֵת
הַפָּר הַחַטָּאת וּשְׂרָפוֹ בְּמִפְקַד הַבַּיִת
מִחוּץ לַמִּקְדָּשׁ׃
22 וּבַיּוֹם הַשֵּׁנִי תַּקְרִיב שְׂעִיר־עִזִּים תָּמִים
לְחַטָּאת וְחִטְּאוּ אֶת־הַמִּזְבֵּחַ כַּאֲשֶׁר
חִטְּאוּ בַּפָּר׃ 23 בְּכַלּוֹתְךָ מֵחַטֵּא תַּקְרִיב
פַּר בֶּן־בָּקָר תָּמִים וְאַיִל מִן־הַצֹּאן
תָּמִים׃ 24 וְהִקְרַבְתָּם לִפְנֵי יְהוָה וְהִשְׁלִיכוּ
הַכֹּהֲנִים עֲלֵיהֶם מֶלַח וְהֶעֱלוּ אוֹתָם עֹלָה

18–24. The ceremony of consecration deals with expiation and purgation. The emphasis on purification offerings underscores the mood of purification pervading the ritual. Blood rites for decontamination are especially central (v. 20). A new divine address provides directions for the ritual preparation of the altar. Two different purification offerings are required on succeeding days—a bull from the herd, then a goat from the flock—for the rites of purgation and purification. These rites are followed by a concluding burnt offering of a bull and a ram.

19. the stock of Zadok Ezekiel regarded the Zadokite priests as the only legitimate priestly line (see 40:46). All other levitical priests were demoted to gatekeepers and cultic servants (44:9–16). The priest Zadok served David during his reign and supported him during the rebellion of Absalom (2 Sam. 15:24–29,35, 17:15, 19:12). He also sided with Solomon in the struggle for David's throne (against Aviathar, who supported Adoniah for king; see 1 Kings 1:8,32). In preferring the Zadokite line, Ezekiel bypassed the line of Aaron's son Ithamar.

לַיהוָה׃ 25 שִׁבְעַת יָמִים תַּעֲשֶׂה שְׂעִיר־
חַטָּאת לַיּוֹם וּפַר בֶּן־בָּקָר וְאַיִל מִן־הַצֹּאן
תְּמִימִים יַעֲשׂוּ׃ 26 שִׁבְעַת יָמִים יְכַפְּרוּ
אֶת־הַמִּזְבֵּחַ וְטִהֲרוּ אֹתוֹ וּמִלְאוּ ידו יָדָיו׃
27 וִיכַלּוּ אֶת־הַיָּמִים ס וְהָיָה בַיּוֹם
הַשְּׁמִינִי וָהָלְאָה יַעֲשׂוּ הַכֹּהֲנִים עַל־
הַמִּזְבֵּחַ אֶת־עוֹלוֹתֵיכֶם וְאֶת־שַׁלְמֵיכֶם
וְרָצֵאתִי* אֶתְכֶם נְאֻם אֲדֹנָי יְהוִה׃ ס

v. 27. א׳ במקום י׳

25Every day, for seven days, you shall present a goat of purification offering, as well as a bull of the herd and a ram of the flock; you shall present unblemished ones. 26Seven days they shall purge the altar and purify it; thus shall it be consecrated.

27And when these days are over, then from the eighth day onward the priests shall offer your burnt offerings and your offerings of well-being on the altar; and I will extend My favor to you—declares the Lord God.

25–27. This pattern of sacrifices differs from that in verses 18–24. The ritual here includes a bull from the herd and a goat from the flock. Both are offered all seven days and serve as purification offerings and for the rites of purgation and cleansing. After this procedure, on the 8th day, the altar would be ready for regular service. A week of consecration agrees with the regulation in Exod. 29:37.

26. shall it be consecrated This ancient idiom (literally, "shall fill its hands"), is usually used to designate the appointment of individuals to a special task (see Exod. 28:41). This is the only place in the Bible where the idiom refers to an object. Ezekiel's prescription of sacrifices for the seven-day consecration contradicts the laws of the Torah (see Exod. 29:37; Lev. 8:33,35). This is one of several discrepancies evident between the passage and regulations found in the Torah. For example, 43:22 legislates the use of he-goats as a purification offering for the purging of the altar, but this "did not occur in the tabernacle" (Rashi). Such difficulties almost led the early Sages to withdraw the book of Ezekiel from circulation. Only a legendary tour de force of reconciliation prevented this from occurring (BT Shab. 13b). There are also contradictions between the measurements of the altar described by Ezekiel and the measurements in the Second Temple (as reported in 2 Chron. 4:1; M Middot 3:1). Such matters led Radak to assert that Ezekiel's vision was intended for the Third Temple at the end of days (see his comment on Ezek. 43:11).

KI TISSA

כי תשא

11The LORD spoke to Moses, saying: 12When you take a census of the Israelite people according to their enrollment, each shall pay the LORD a ransom for himself on being enrolled, that no plague may come upon them through their be-

11 וַיְדַבֵּ֥ר יְהוָ֖ה אֶל־מֹשֶׁ֥ה לֵּאמֹֽר׃ 12 כִּ֣י
תִשָּׂ֞א אֶת־רֹ֣אשׁ בְּנֵֽי־יִשְׂרָאֵל֮ לִפְקֻדֵיהֶם֒
וְנָ֨תְנ֜וּ אִ֣ישׁ כֹּ֧פֶר נַפְשׁ֛וֹ לַיהוָ֖ה בִּפְקֹ֣ד אֹתָ֑ם

THE TABERNACLE, PART 1: INSTRUCTIONS (*continued*)

APPENDIX TO INSTRUCTIONS (*continued*)

THE CENSUS AND THE POLL TAX (30:11–16)

God orders Moses to take a census. Males above the age of 20 are to be entered into the records. Census taking in the ancient world, regarded as a necessary administrative measure, was believed to be fraught with danger to the public. Almost invariably it preceded a war or a new tax. The head counts recorded in the Bible are usually related to army service and warfare. Hence, each male in this census is to pay a poll tax of one-half shekel as a ransom for his life and to avert the possibility of a plague. The poll tax here is a one-time imposition for the building of the tabernacle, not an annual obligation. The expiatory function of the tax connects this topic with that of the verses immediately preceding it.

12. take a census Literally, "raise the head," i.e., take a head count. Other censuses are reported in the Torah (e.g., Num. 1,3:14ff.).

a ransom for himself Hebrew: *kofer;* refers to a monetary payment made to offset an incurred physical penalty. Apparently, it was taken for granted that a census jeopardizes the lives of those counted; therefore, each individual must redeem his life through payment of a half-shekel. (See 2 Sam. 24, where a plague follows a census undertaken by David.)

At the heart of this *parashah* stands the incident of the Golden Calf, the classic example of Israel's angering God by worshiping an idol (or, more likely, worshiping God in the form of a physical being, which is forbidden by the 2nd commandment). God is prepared to renounce the covenant with Israel, and Moses has to prevail on God not to do so. The incident of the Golden Calf is preceded by several brief matters involving a census of the people, further details about building the tabernacle, and an additional injunction to keep *Shabbat*. Following the destruction of the Calf, God's reconciliation with the people is symbolized by the carving of a second set of tablets, because Moses had broken the original set.

CHAPTER 30

12. It has been pointed out that the Hebrew word translated as "each shall pay" (ונתנו) is a palindrome, spelled the same way from right to left as from left to right. This suggests that charity is a two-way process. One receives even as one gives. This should remind us, according to the Vilna Gaon, that one who gives today may have to receive tomorrow.

This indirect manner of taking a census, having everyone give a standard coin and then counting coins instead of people, originally may have been rooted in a superstitious fear of the "evil eye." (If you take pride in how many people are in your family, some disaster will befall one or more of them.) It is reflected in the custom, still observed in some communities, of counting indirectly for a *minyan* rather than numbering people. This custom is given a moral interpretation by traditional and contemporary teachers: (*a*) Coins are interchangeable but people are not. Every human being is unique and cannot be reduced to a number. (*b*) "Let each person give a ransom for himself." Life is a gift and we owe God something just for being alive. We can never take life for granted. Benno Jacob sees the census as a preparation for battle and the half-shekel as an anticipatory atonement for the possibility of shedding blood in battle. (*c*) The half-shekel should teach us that a person is incomplete, becoming whole only by joining with others. Perhaps it served to remind the male warriors that the women and children who would not be going into battle represented half of the community. (*d*) After being counted, the shekels were to be used for services in the Tent of Meeting. "Now that there is no Temple with animal offerings, we show our grati-

ing enrolled. ¹³This is what everyone who is entered in the records shall pay: a half-shekel by the sanctuary weight—twenty *gerah*s to the shekel—a half-shekel as an offering to the LORD. ¹⁴Everyone who is entered in the records, from the age of twenty years up, shall give the LORD's offering: ¹⁵the rich shall not pay more and the poor shall not pay less than half a shekel when giving the LORD's offering as expiation for your persons. ¹⁶You shall take the expiation money from the Israelites and assign it to the service of the Tent of Meeting; it shall serve the Israelites as a reminder before the LORD, as expiation for your persons.

¹⁷The LORD spoke to Moses, saying: ¹⁸Make

וְלֹא־יִהְיֶ֥ה בָהֶ֛ם נֶ֖גֶף בִּפְקֹ֥ד אֹתָֽם׃ 13 זֶ֣ה ׀ יִתְּנ֗וּ כָּל־הָעֹבֵר֙ עַל־הַפְּקֻדִ֔ים מַחֲצִ֥ית הַשֶּׁ֖קֶל בְּשֶׁ֣קֶל הַקֹּ֑דֶשׁ עֶשְׂרִ֤ים גֵּרָה֙ הַשֶּׁ֔קֶל מַחֲצִ֣ית הַשֶּׁ֔קֶל תְּרוּמָ֖ה לַֽיהֹוָֽה׃ 14 כֹּ֗ל הָעֹבֵר֙ עַל־הַפְּקֻדִ֔ים מִבֶּ֛ן עֶשְׂרִ֥ים שָׁנָ֖ה וָמָ֑עְלָה יִתֵּ֖ן תְּרוּמַ֥ת יְהֹוָֽה׃ 15 הֶֽעָשִׁ֣יר לֹֽא־יַרְבֶּ֗ה וְהַדַּל֙ לֹ֣א יַמְעִ֔יט מִֽמַּחֲצִ֖ית הַשָּׁ֑קֶל לָתֵת֙ אֶת־תְּרוּמַ֣ת יְהֹוָ֔ה לְכַפֵּ֖ר עַל־נַפְשֹׁתֵיכֶֽם׃ 16 וְלָקַחְתָּ֞ אֶת־כֶּ֣סֶף הַכִּפֻּרִ֗ים מֵאֵת֙ בְּנֵ֣י יִשְׂרָאֵ֔ל וְנָתַתָּ֣ אֹת֔וֹ עַל־עֲבֹדַ֖ת אֹ֣הֶל מוֹעֵ֑ד וְהָיָה֩ לִבְנֵ֨י יִשְׂרָאֵ֤ל לְזִכָּרוֹן֙ לִפְנֵ֣י יְהֹוָ֔ה לְכַפֵּ֖ר עַל־נַפְשֹׁתֵיכֶֽם׃ פ

17 וַיְדַבֵּ֥ר יְהֹוָ֖ה אֶל־מֹשֶׁ֥ה לֵּאמֹֽר׃ 18 וְעָשִׂ֜יתָ

---

13. *half-shekel* See Comment to Gen. 23:9.

14. *twenty years* The age at which an Israelite male became subject to military service.

15. The contribution of the half-shekel has two purposes: to support the work of the tabernacle and to effect expiation for each individual. The tabernacle belongs equally to every Israelite, without regard to social status or wealth. As all human beings are equal before God, there is to be one standard contribution from all, to be neither exceeded nor reduced.

16. *service of the Tent* The Hebrew word *avodah* can refer both to the maintenance of wor-

ship and to the work of construction. It has the latter meaning in 39:32. Because silver was used in casting sockets for the sanctuary and for the manufacture of other items (38:25–28), *avodah* here must refer to the work of construction.

THE BRONZE LAVER   (vv. 17–21)

This vessel was not included in the earlier instructions for several reasons: (a) It was not used in a specific act of divine worship but in preparation for it; (b) because the laver was solely for washing hands and feet, it was not needed for the installation ceremony, which required immersion of

---

tude for being alive by giving to the poor" (Mid. Lekaḥ Tov). (*e*) In the early 20th century, the Zionist movement revived the custom of contributing a shekel to establish membership in a Zionist organization as a way of measuring how many people could be counted on to support it.

13. *This is what everyone . . . shall pay* Prompted by the word "this," the Sages conjecture that God showed Moses a flame in the shape of a half-shekel. Why a flame? Because money is like fire; it can warm and comfort—

or it can consume and destroy (Elimelekh of Lyzhansk).

14. *from the age of twenty years up* Judaism has always believed that religion, first and foremost, is not for children, although there is much in it that children can join in and appreciate. Primarily, it is for adults who alone can begin to appreciate its breadth and profundity (Hirsch). Children who see their parents taking Jewish obligation seriously are more likely to see it as something they will want to do as adults.

HALAKHAH L'MA·ASEH

30:13. everyone . . . shall pay: a half-shekel This is sometimes cited as the source for collecting the equivalent of half the common currency (in the United States and Canada, a half dollar) from everyone on *Purim*. Whereas this was given to the Temple in biblical times, we now use it for the upkeep of the synagogue or for the poor.

a laver of copper and a stand of copper for it, for washing; and place it between the Tent of Meeting and the altar. Put water in it, 19and let Aaron and his sons wash their hands and feet [in water drawn] from it. 20When they enter the Tent of Meeting they shall wash with water, that they may not die; or when they approach the altar to serve, to turn into smoke a gift to the LORD, 21they shall wash their hands and feet, that they may not die. It shall be a law for all time for them—for him and his offspring—throughout the ages.

22The LORD spoke to Moses, saying: 23Next take choice spices: five hundred weight of solidified myrrh, half as much—two hundred and fifty—of fragrant cinnamon, two hundred

כִּיּ֥וֹר נְח֛שֶׁת וְכַנּ֥וֹ נְח֖שֶׁת לְרָחְצָ֑ה וְנָתַתָּ֣
אֹת֗וֹ בֵּֽין־אֹ֤הֶל מוֹעֵד֙ וּבֵ֣ין הַמִּזְבֵּ֔חַ וְנָתַתָּ֥
שָׁ֖מָּה מָֽיִם׃ 19 וְרָחֲצ֛וּ אַהֲרֹ֥ן וּבָנָ֖יו מִמֶּ֑נּוּ
אֶת־יְדֵיהֶ֖ם וְאֶת־רַגְלֵיהֶֽם׃ 20 בְּבֹאָ֞ם אֶל־
אֹ֧הֶל מוֹעֵ֛ד יִרְחֲצוּ־מַ֖יִם וְלֹ֣א יָמֻ֑תוּ א֣וֹ
בְגִשְׁתָּ֤ם אֶל־הַמִּזְבֵּ֙חַ֙ לְשָׁרֵ֔ת לְהַקְטִ֥יר
אִשֶּׁ֖ה לַיהוָֽה׃ 21 וְרָחֲצ֛וּ יְדֵיהֶ֥ם וְרַגְלֵיהֶ֖ם
וְלֹ֣א יָמֻ֑תוּ וְהָיְתָ֨ה לָהֶ֧ם חָק־עוֹלָ֛ם ל֥וֹ
וּלְזַרְע֖וֹ לְדֹרֹתָֽם׃ פ

22 וַיְדַבֵּ֥ר יְהוָ֖ה אֶל־מֹשֶׁ֥ה לֵּאמֹֽר׃ 23 וְאַתָּ֣ה
קַח־לְךָ֮ בְּשָׂמִ֣ים רֹאשׁ֒ מָר־דְּרוֹר֙ חֲמֵ֣שׁ
מֵא֔וֹת וְקִנְּמָן־בֶּ֥שֶׂם מַחֲצִית֖וֹ חֲמִשִּׁ֣ים
וּמָאתָ֑יִם וּקְנֵה־בֹ֖שֶׂם חֲמִשִּׁ֥ים וּמָאתָֽיִם׃

the entire body; and (c) it was not fashioned with materials provided by public donations but from bronze mirrors of the women who served at the entrance of the tabernacle. For practical reasons, the laver was placed between the entrance of the tabernacle and the altar of sacrifice, enabling the priest to enter the sanctuary in a state of ritual purity and bodily cleanliness. A measure of the laver's importance is its inclusion among the vessels consecrated by being anointed with oil (v. 28).

18. copper Better: bronze. See Comment to 25:3.

20. that they may not die See Comment to 28:35. The washing is an essential requirement; its neglect renders the priest's service invalid.

THE AROMATIC ANOINTING OIL (vv. 22–33)

The anointing oil and the spices needed for it are mentioned in 25:6. Spices and perfumes were rare in the ancient world. They were very costly because of the huge amounts of raw materials needed to manufacture the desired quantity and the great distances transversed in transport—by land caravan or by sea—from Arabia, Somaliland, India, and China. The highly specialized art of perfumery required an exceptional level of skill and experience.

23. The list is set out in order of decreasing value.

solidified myrrh Southern Arabia and Somaliland were the sources of this aromatic gum resin. It exudes as globules from the ducts of the trunk and branches of the trees and flows freely if one makes a cut in the bark. It hardens slowly when exposed to air.

fragrant cinnamon The tree is indigenous to Sri Lanka but was also cultivated elsewhere in Asia.

---

18. Tradition tells us that the bronze laver and its stand were fashioned from the bronze mirrors formerly used by the Israelite women in Egypt to help make themselves attractive to their husbands. These mirrors enabled Israelite spouses to come together and produce children even in the midst of Pharaoh's disheartening oppression. When Moses protested their use in the tabernacle, regarding mirrors as symbols of vanity, God reminded him that they had been used to preserve the Israelite nation.

HALAKHAH L'MA·ASEH

30:19. wash their hands and feet See Comments on Num. 6:23, 18:23.

24 וְקִדָּ֕ה חֲמֵ֥שׁ מֵא֖וֹת בְּשֶׁ֣קֶל הַקֹּ֑דֶשׁ וְשֶׁ֥מֶן
זַ֖יִת הִֽין׃ 25 וְעָשִׂ֣יתָ אֹת֗וֹ שֶׁ֚מֶן מִשְׁחַת־
קֹ֔דֶשׁ רֹ֥קַח מִרְקַ֖חַת מַעֲשֵׂ֣ה רֹקֵ֑חַ שֶׁ֥מֶן
מִשְׁחַת־קֹ֖דֶשׁ יִהְיֶֽה׃ 26 וּמָשַׁחְתָּ֥ ב֖וֹ אֶת־
אֹ֣הֶל מוֹעֵ֑ד וְאֵ֖ת אֲר֥וֹן הָעֵדֻֽת׃ 27 וְאֶת־
הַשֻּׁלְחָן֙ וְאֶת־כָּל־כֵּלָ֔יו וְאֶת־הַמְּנֹרָ֖ה וְאֶת־
כֵּלֶ֑יהָ וְאֵ֖ת מִזְבַּ֥ח הַקְּטֹֽרֶת׃ 28 וְאֶת־מִזְבַּ֥ח
הָעֹלָ֖ה וְאֶת־כָּל־כֵּלָ֑יו וְאֶת־הַכִּיֹּ֖ר וְאֶת־
כַּנּֽוֹ׃ 29 וְקִדַּשְׁתָּ֣ אֹתָ֔ם וְהָי֖וּ קֹ֣דֶשׁ קָֽדָשִׁ֑ים
כָּל־הַנֹּגֵ֥עַ בָּהֶ֖ם יִקְדָּֽשׁ׃ 30 וְאֶת־אַהֲרֹ֥ן וְאֶת־
בָּנָ֖יו תִּמְשָׁ֑ח וְקִדַּשְׁתָּ֥ אֹתָ֖ם לְכַהֵ֥ן לִֽי׃
31 וְאֶל־בְּנֵ֥י יִשְׂרָאֵ֖ל תְּדַבֵּ֣ר לֵאמֹ֑ר שֶׁ֠מֶן
מִשְׁחַת־קֹ֨דֶשׁ֙ יִהְיֶ֥ה זֶ֛ה לִ֖י לְדֹרֹתֵיכֶֽם׃
32 עַל־בְּשַׂ֤ר אָדָם֙ לֹ֣א יִיסָ֔ךְ וּבְמַ֨תְכֻּנְתּ֔וֹ לֹ֥א
תַעֲשׂ֖וּ כָּמֹ֑הוּ קֹ֣דֶשׁ ה֔וּא קֹ֖דֶשׁ יִהְיֶ֥ה לָכֶֽם׃
33 אִ֚ישׁ אֲשֶׁ֣ר יִרְקַ֣ח כָּמֹ֔הוּ וַאֲשֶׁ֥ר יִתֵּ֛ן מִמֶּ֖נּוּ
עַל־זָ֑ר וְנִכְרַ֖ת מֵעַמָּֽיו׃ ס
34 וַיֹּאמֶר֩ יְהוָ֨ה אֶל־מֹשֶׁ֜ה קַח־לְךָ֣ סַמִּ֗ים
נָטָ֤ף ׀ וּשְׁחֵ֨לֶת֙ וְחֶלְבְּנָ֔ה סַמִּ֖ים וּלְבֹנָ֣ה זַכָּ֑ה
בַּ֥ד בְּבַ֖ד יִהְיֶֽה׃ 35 וְעָשִׂ֤יתָ אֹתָהּ֙ קְטֹ֔רֶת
רֹ֖קַח מַעֲשֵׂ֣ה רוֹקֵ֑חַ מְמֻלָּ֖ח טָה֥וֹר קֹֽדֶשׁ׃
36 וְשָֽׁחַקְתָּ֣ מִמֶּנָּה֮ הָדֵק֒ וְנָתַתָּ֨ה מִמֶּ֜נָּה לִפְנֵ֤י
הָעֵדֻת֙ בְּאֹ֣הֶל מוֹעֵ֔ד אֲשֶׁ֛ר אִוָּעֵ֥ד לְךָ֖ שָׁ֑מָּה

and fifty of aromatic cane, 24five hundred—by the sanctuary weight—of cassia, and a *hin* of olive oil. 25Make of this a sacred anointing oil, a compound of ingredients expertly blended, to serve as sacred anointing oil. 26With it anoint the Tent of Meeting, the Ark of the Pact, 27the table and all its utensils, the lampstand and all its fittings, the altar of incense, 28the altar of burnt offering and all its utensils, and the laver and its stand. 29Thus you shall consecrate them so that they may be most holy; whatever touches them shall be consecrated. 30You shall also anoint Aaron and his sons, consecrating them to serve Me as priests.

31And speak to the Israelite people, as follows: This shall be an anointing oil sacred to Me throughout the ages. 32It must not be rubbed on any person's body, and you must not make anything like it in the same proportions; it is sacred, to be held sacred by you. 33Whoever compounds its like, or puts any of it on a layman, shall be cut off from his kin.

34And the LORD said to Moses: Take the herbs stacte, onycha, and galbanum—these herbs together with pure frankincense; let there be an equal part of each. 35Make them into incense, a compound expertly blended, refined, pure, sacred. 36Beat some of it into powder, and put some before the Pact in the Tent of Meeting,

24. hin See Comment to 29:40.

26–28. The sacred aromatic oil is to be applied to the priests, to the articles of furniture, and to the utensils. The act of anointing consecrates them to divine service. Henceforth, their holiness is contagious. See Comment to 29:37.

31–33. This sacred aromatic anointing oil, with its specific ingredients blended in the appropriate proportions, must never be duplicated or used for any purpose other than that stated here.

THE INGREDIENTS OF THE INCENSE
(vv. 34–38)

The incense to be offered on the golden altar consists of four ingredients.

34. stacte A resin of balsam or persimmon.

onycha The classic Greek and Latin translations render this as "onyx."

galbanum A gum resin extracted from a plant that grows in Turkistan, Persia, and Crete. It emits a disagreeable odor when burned. This is diffused, however, when the substance is blended with the other aromatics, and it has the effect of making the latter more pungent.

frankincense A gum resin extracted from trees that are native to southern Arabia and northern Somaliland.

35. refined Hebrew: *m'mullaḥ;* literally, "salted." In the ancient world, salt was added to incense to enhance the rate of burning and smoking.

36. Each day, morning and evening, some of the blended and pulverized incense is to be placed on the golden altar for the incense offerings.

קֹדֶשׁ קָדָשִׁים תִּהְיֶה לָכֶם׃ 37 וְהַקְּטֹרֶת
אֲשֶׁר תַּעֲשֶׂה בְּמַתְכֻּנְתָּהּ לֹא תַעֲשׂוּ
לָכֶם קֹדֶשׁ תִּהְיֶה לְךָ לַיהוָה׃ 38 אִישׁ
אֲשֶׁר־יַעֲשֶׂה כָמוֹהָ לְהָרִיחַ בָּהּ וְנִכְרַת
מֵעַמָּיו׃ ס

where I will meet with you; it shall be most holy to you. 37But when you make this incense, you must not make any in the same proportions for yourselves; it shall be held by you sacred to the Lord. 38Whoever makes any like it, to smell of it, shall be cut off from his kin.

לא

וַיְדַבֵּר יְהוָה אֶל־מֹשֶׁה לֵּאמֹר׃
2 רְאֵה קָרָאתִי בְשֵׁם בְּצַלְאֵל בֶּן־אוּרִי
בֶן־חוּר לְמַטֵּה יְהוּדָה׃ 3 וָאֲמַלֵּא אֹתוֹ רוּחַ
אֱלֹהִים בְּחָכְמָה וּבִתְבוּנָה וּבְדַעַת וּבְכָל־
מְלָאכָה׃ 4 לַחְשֹׁב מַחֲשָׁבֹת לַעֲשׂוֹת
בַּזָּהָב וּבַכֶּסֶף וּבַנְּחֹשֶׁת׃ 5 וּבַחֲרֹשֶׁת אֶבֶן
לְמַלֹּאת וּבַחֲרֹשֶׁת עֵץ לַעֲשׂוֹת בְּכָל־
מְלָאכָה׃ 6 וַאֲנִי הִנֵּה נָתַתִּי אִתּוֹ אֵת
אָהֳלִיאָב בֶּן־אֲחִיסָמָךְ לְמַטֵּה־דָן וּבְלֵב
כָּל־חֲכַם־לֵב נָתַתִּי חָכְמָה וְעָשׂוּ אֵת
כָּל־אֲשֶׁר צִוִּיתִךָ׃ 7 אֵת ׀ אֹהֶל מוֹעֵד
וְאֶת־הָאָרֹן לָעֵדֻת וְאֶת־הַכַּפֹּרֶת אֲשֶׁר

31

The Lord spoke to Moses: 2See, I have singled out by name Bezalel son of Uri son of Hur, of the tribe of Judah. 3I have endowed him with a divine spirit of skill, ability, and knowledge in every kind of craft; 4to make designs for work in gold, silver, and copper, 5to cut stones for setting and to carve wood—to work in every kind of craft. 6Moreover, I have assigned to him Oholiab son of Ahisamach, of the tribe of Dan; and I have also granted skill to all who are skillful, that they may make everything that I have commanded you: 7the Tent of Meeting, the Ark for the Pact and the cover upon it, and all the

37–38. Like the aromatic oil (vv. 31–33), the incense must not be produced for use in any but its prescribed ritual.

CONCLUSION OF INSTRUCTIONS FOR THE TABERNACLE (31:1–17)

APPOINTMENT OF CONSTRUCTION PERSONNEL (vv. 1–11)

The final instruction to Moses relating to the work of the tabernacle concerns the appointment of a supervisory master craftsman named Bezalel, from the tribe of Judah, and his associate Oholiab, from the tribe of Dan. Presumably, Moses, Bezalel, and Oholiab are to recruit the subordinate workers, here described as those "who are skillful."

2. singled out by name Commissioned for the task.

7–11. These verses summarize the components of the tabernacle, its furnishings, and appurtenances in an order that differs slightly from that of the previous instructions.

pure lampstand See Comment to 25:31.

CHAPTER 31

3. I have endowed him with a divine spirit Moses had been assuming that he would have to build the items of the tabernacle himself. God now informs him that, despite his great gifts of the spirit, there are other Israelites with unique gifts who can fashion artifacts of holiness capable of bringing people to God (Exod. R. 40:2). To construct most things, one needs only a set of specific instructions. But to fashion something holy—something that will move others to prayer—being able to follow instructions is not enough. A measure of divine inspiration is required.

6. Bezalel comes from the tribe of Judah, the largest and most prominent of the tribes. Oholiab is from Dan, the smallest tribe. All parts of Israelite society were to be involved in fashioning the Ark (Tanḥ. 13). Similarly, the recipe for the incense (30:34) includes the foul-smelling galbanum, to teach us that even marginal, disagreeable people have to be included in the community (Rashi).

furnishings of the Tent; 8the table and its utensils, the pure lampstand and all its fittings, and
the altar of incense; 9the altar of burnt offering
and all its utensils, and the laver and its stand;
10the service vestments, the sacral vestments
of Aaron the priest and the vestments of his
sons, for their service as priests; 11as well as the
anointing oil and the aromatic incense for the
sanctuary. Just as I have commanded you, they
shall do.

12And the LORD said to Moses: 13Speak to the
Israelite people and say: Nevertheless, you must
keep My sabbaths, for this is a sign between Me
and you throughout the ages, that you may
know that I the LORD have consecrated you.
14You shall keep the sabbath, for it is holy for
you. He who profanes it shall be put to death:
whoever does work on it, that person shall be
cut off from among his kin. 15Six days may work
be done, but on the seventh day there shall be
a sabbath of complete rest, holy to the LORD;

עָלָיו וְאֵת כָּל־כְּלֵי הָאֹהֶל׃ 8 וְאֶת־הַשֻּׁלְחָן
וְאֶת־כֵּלָיו וְאֶת־הַמְּנֹרָה הַטְּהֹרָה וְאֶת־
כָּל־כֵּלֶיהָ וְאֵת מִזְבַּח הַקְּטֹרֶת׃ 9 וְאֶת־
מִזְבַּח הָעֹלָה וְאֶת־כָּל־כֵּלָיו וְאֶת־הַכִּיּוֹר
וְאֶת־כַּנּוֹ׃ 10 וְאֵת בִּגְדֵי הַשְּׂרָד וְאֶת־בִּגְדֵי
הַקֹּדֶשׁ לְאַהֲרֹן הַכֹּהֵן וְאֶת־בִּגְדֵי בָנָיו
לְכַהֵן׃ 11 וְאֵת שֶׁמֶן הַמִּשְׁחָה וְאֶת־
קְטֹרֶת הַסַּמִּים לַקֹּדֶשׁ כְּכֹל אֲשֶׁר־צִוִּיתִךָ
יַעֲשׂוּ׃ פ
12 וַיֹּאמֶר יְהוָה אֶל־מֹשֶׁה לֵּאמֹר׃ 13 וְאַתָּה
דַּבֵּר אֶל־בְּנֵי יִשְׂרָאֵל לֵאמֹר אַךְ אֶת־
שַׁבְּתֹתַי תִּשְׁמֹרוּ כִּי אוֹת הִוא בֵּינִי
וּבֵינֵיכֶם לְדֹרֹתֵיכֶם לָדַעַת כִּי אֲנִי יְהוָה
מְקַדִּשְׁכֶם׃ 14 וּשְׁמַרְתֶּם אֶת־הַשַּׁבָּת כִּי
קֹדֶשׁ הִוא לָכֶם מְחַלְלֶיהָ מוֹת יוּמָת כִּי
כָּל־הָעֹשֶׂה בָהּ מְלָאכָה וְנִכְרְתָה הַנֶּפֶשׁ
הַהִוא מִקֶּרֶב עַמֶּיהָ׃ 15 שֵׁשֶׁת יָמִים יֵעָשֶׂה
מְלָאכָה וּבַיּוֹם הַשְּׁבִיעִי שַׁבַּת שַׁבָּתוֹן

THE OBSERVANCE OF *SHABBAT* (vv. 12–17) The concluding—and, appropriately, the seventh—literary unit within the section of instructions for the tabernacle is devoted to the observance of *Shabbat.*

13. Nevertheless Even though building the tabernacle is a divine command, it does not supplant observance of *Shabbat.*

My sabbaths This phrase is defined in verses 15 and 17. *Shabbat,* i.e., the sanctity of the seventh day of the week, is an integral part of the cosmic order ordained by God.

a sign The idea of *Shabbat* as a sign is repeated in verse 17. Its observance is a declaration of faith, an affirmation of several tenets at once: that Israel is a holy nation by an act of divine will, not inherently; that the relationship between God and Israel is governed by a covenant; and that the universe is wholly the purposeful product of divine intelligence, the work of a transcendent being outside nature and sovereign over space and time.

15. a sabbath of complete rest See Comment to 16:23.

---

13. Nevertheless, you must keep My sabbaths Based on this phrase and the passage that precedes it, the Sages derived their definition of work that is forbidden on *Shabbat* from the tasks involved in constructing the tabernacle. If there is a conflict between the holiness of space and the holiness of time, the holiness of time takes precedence. Time came first; the first thing that God sanctified was *Shabbat*. It is accessible to everyone. One cannot defer it or return to it. If one misses the moment, it is gone forever. Based on Akiva's rule that the word translated here as "nevertheless" (*akh*) is intended to limit the applicability of a law, the Talmud teaches that in some situations *Shabbat* prohibitions must be set aside. These situations include saving a life and circumcising a baby boy on the eighth day of his life (JT Yoma 8:5).

this is a sign Because keeping *Shabbat* is called a sign (*ot*) of our bond to God, on *Shabbat* we do not wear *t'fillin,* which are also called *ot,* in Deut. 6:8 (BT Er. 96a). It is as much a religious obligation to be scrupulous in the way we work six days a week as it is to be scrupulous about refraining from work on the seventh day.

whoever does work on the sabbath day shall be put to death.
16The Israelite people shall keep the sabbath, observing the sabbath throughout the ages as a covenant for all time:
17it shall be a sign for all time between Me and the people of Israel. For in six days the LORD made heaven and earth, and on the seventh day He ceased from work and was refreshed.

קֹ֣דֶשׁ לַֽיהוָ֑ה כָּל־הָעֹשֶׂ֧ה מְלָאכָ֛ה בְּי֥וֹם
הַשַּׁבָּ֖ת מ֥וֹת יוּמָֽת׃ 16 וְשָׁמְר֥וּ בְנֵֽי־יִשְׂרָאֵ֖ל
אֶת־הַשַּׁבָּ֑ת לַעֲשׂ֧וֹת אֶת־הַשַּׁבָּ֛ת לְדֹרֹתָ֖ם
בְּרִ֥ית עוֹלָֽם׃ 17 בֵּינִ֗י וּבֵין֙ בְּנֵ֣י יִשְׂרָאֵ֔ל א֥וֹת
הִ֖וא לְעֹלָ֑ם כִּי־שֵׁ֣שֶׁת יָמִ֗ים עָשָׂ֤ה יְהוָה֙
אֶת־הַשָּׁמַ֣יִם וְאֶת־הָאָ֔רֶץ וּבַיּוֹם֙ הַשְּׁבִיעִ֔י
שָׁבַ֖ת וַיִּנָּפַֽשׁ׃ ס

18When He finished speaking with him on Mount Sinai, He gave Moses the two tablets of the Pact, stone tablets inscribed with the finger of God.

שני 18 וַיִּתֵּ֣ן אֶל־מֹשֶׁ֗ה כְּכַלֹּתוֹ֙ לְדַבֵּ֤ר אִתּוֹ֙ בְּהַ֣ר
סִינַ֔י שְׁנֵ֖י לֻחֹ֣ת הָעֵדֻ֑ת לֻחֹ֣ת אֶ֔בֶן כְּתֻבִ֖ים
בְּאֶצְבַּ֥ע אֱלֹהִֽים׃

32 When the people saw that Moses was so long in coming down from the mountain,

לב וַיַּ֣רְא הָעָ֔ם כִּֽי־בֹשֵׁ֥שׁ מֹשֶׁ֖ה לָרֶ֣דֶת
מִן־הָהָ֑ר וַיִּקָּהֵ֨ל הָעָ֜ם עַל־אַהֲרֹ֗ן וַיֹּאמְר֤וּ

16. The observance of *Shabbat* is the eternal obligation of those who participate in the covenant with God.

17. and was refreshed The Hebrew word *va-yinnafash* is derived from the noun *nefesh,* a term that can refer to a person's life essence, vitality, psychic energy, or essential character. The verbal form used here conveys the notion of a fresh infusion of spiritual and physical vigor, the revival of one's total being. Although the word here ascribes human characteristics to God, the language is intended to impress on the Israelite an awareness of the transcendent value of *Shabbat* observance.

A CODA (v. 18)

This concluding verse, which tells of Moses receiving the tablets of stone, picks up where the last narrative left off—Moses' ascent of Mount Sinai to acquire those tokens of the Covenant (24:12–18). It also serves as the transition to the next episode, which involves the smashing of those tablets.

18. He finished The Midrash notes the similarity of the Hebrew for "He finished" (*kalloto*) and "his bride" (*kallato*), suggesting that when Moses received the Torah he was as joyous as a bridegroom on his wedding day (Exod. R. 41:6). The metaphor of giving the Torah as solemnizing a marriage between God and the Jewish people, with the Torah serving as the marriage document (*k'tubah*), occurs frequently in the Midrash. So does the metaphor of Israel's disobedience being like marital infidelity rather than simply the breaking of a law. Another *midrash* fastens on the similarity of the Hebrew words for "He finished" (*kalloto*) and "rule" (*k'lal*); it suggests that at Sinai God gave Moses general rules or principles from which Moses derived the specific details of the Torah's laws (Exod. R. 41:6). This would seem to point to a human element in the development of laws of the Torah. See Comment to 34:1. A *midrash* reads the Hebrew word for "stone" in "stone tablets" (*even*) as *av–ben* (father to son). The Torah was not given to one generation alone, nor was it given only to scholars and leaders. It was meant to be passed on from parent to child.

HALAKHAH L'MA·ASEH

31:16. shall keep Verses 16–17 are part of the Friday evening and Saturday morning liturgy, and they are recited in the Saturday morning *Kiddush.*

the people gathered against Aaron and said to him, "Come, make us a god who shall go before us, for that man Moses, who brought us from the land of Egypt—we do not know what has happened to him." [2]Aaron said to them, "Take off the gold rings that are on the ears of your wives, your sons, and your daughters, and bring them to me." [3]And all the people took off the gold rings that were in their ears and brought

אֵלָיו֙ ק֣וּם ׀ עֲשֵׂה־לָ֣נוּ אֱלֹהִ֗ים אֲשֶׁ֤ר יֵֽלְכוּ֙
לְפָנֵ֔ינוּ כִּי־זֶ֣ה ׀ מֹשֶׁ֣ה הָאִ֗ישׁ אֲשֶׁ֤ר הֶֽעֱלָ֙נוּ֙
מֵאֶ֣רֶץ מִצְרַ֔יִם לֹ֥א יָדַ֖עְנוּ מֶה־הָ֥יָה לֽוֹ׃
2 וַיֹּ֣אמֶר אֲלֵהֶם֙ אַהֲרֹ֔ן פָּֽרְקוּ֙ נִזְמֵ֣י הַזָּהָ֔ב
אֲשֶׁר֙ בְּאָזְנֵ֣י נְשֵׁיכֶ֔ם בְּנֵיכֶ֖ם וּבְנֹתֵיכֶ֑ם
וְהָבִ֖יאוּ אֵלָֽי׃ 3 וַיִּתְפָּֽרְקוּ֙ כָּל־הָעָ֔ם אֶת־
נִזְמֵ֥י הַזָּהָ֖ב אֲשֶׁ֣ר בְּאָזְנֵיהֶ֑ם וַיָּבִ֖יאוּ אֶל־

VIOLATION OF THE COVENANT: THE GOLDEN CALF (32:1–33:23)

The account of the tabernacle is briefly interrupted.

THE MAKING OF THE GOLDEN CALF (32:1–6)

1. This verse must be understood in reference to 24:18, which tells of Moses' ascent of the cloud-enveloped mountain and his seclusion there for 40 days and nights. Because Moses has been the exclusive mediator between God and Israel—at the urgent request of the people, as told in 20:15–18—his prolonged absence now causes deep anxiety, a mood made worse by the awareness of the impending departure from Sinai.

make us a god Something to serve as a symbol of God's presence in their midst. Rashbam suggests that they had in mind some instrument for determining the divine will as a replacement for Moses, the absent human medium of divine revelation.

who brought us And now has abandoned us. Even though Moses always stressed that he is only God's agent, they cannot feel God's presence without him.

3. gold rings These may have been among the items the Israelites received from neighbors when they left Egypt, as related in 11:2–3 and 12:35–36.

CHAPTER 32

1. The people—who only a few weeks earlier had been slaves in Egypt where they had witnessed Egyptian idolatry—could not comprehend a God without physical form, as the 2nd commandment called on them to do. (Moses later, in v. 11, refers to "Your people, whom You delivered from the land of Egypt," as if to remind God of the influences to which they had been subjected there. The Midrash compares the situation to that of a man who bought his son a store in a notoriously corrupt neighborhood and then blames the son for having been corrupted there.) The people needed a visible, tangible symbol of God's presence. They had just come from Egypt where everything, even death, was rendered visible (through pyramids and mummies). It was extremely hard for them to grasp the idea that the greatest reality of all is intangible. The text seems to imply that at least some of the people, who saw Moses as an embodiment of God, wanted the Golden Calf to replace the vanished Moses, without whom they felt abandoned. According to Hirsch, the people did not understand that God had taken the initiative in reaching down to them, believing that Moses had the power to summon God. Without Moses, how would they ever be able to experience God's presence again?

Aaron is consistently portrayed in Jewish lore as a peacemaker and conciliator. Moses was the lawgiver proclaiming standards and prohibitions, the prophet who denounced those who fell short of those standards. Aaron in his priestly aspect met and accepted people where they were. Moses proclaimed, "You shall not!" Aaron welcomed people who brought their purification offerings to atone for their violations. Legends tell of Aaron's efforts to reconcile feuding individuals. In this instance, however, Aaron's inclination to accept, rather than to challenge, popular will led to misfortune.

3. The Talmud says of Israel: "What a peculiar people! When solicited to build the tabernacle, they give generously. When solicited to fashion an idol, they give equally generously" (JT Shek. 1:1).

them to Aaron. 4This he took from them and
cast in a mold, and made it into a molten calf.
And they exclaimed, "This is your god, O Israel,
who brought you out of the land of Egypt!"
5When Aaron saw this, he built an altar before
it; and Aaron announced: "Tomorrow shall be
a festival of the LORD!" 6Early next day, the people offered up burnt offerings and brought
sacrifices of well-being; they sat down to eat and
drink, and then rose to dance.

7The LORD spoke to Moses, "Hurry down, for
your people, whom you brought out of the land

אַהֲרֹן׃ 4 וַיִּקַּח מִיָּדָם וַיָּצַר אֹתוֹ בַּחֶרֶט
וַיַּעֲשֵׂהוּ עֵגֶל מַסֵּכָה וַיֹּאמְרוּ אֵלֶּה אֱלֹהֶיךָ
יִשְׂרָאֵל אֲשֶׁר הֶעֱלוּךָ מֵאֶרֶץ מִצְרָיִם׃
5 וַיַּרְא אַהֲרֹן וַיִּבֶן מִזְבֵּחַ לְפָנָיו וַיִּקְרָא
אַהֲרֹן וַיֹּאמַר חַג לַיהוָה מָחָר׃ 6 וַיַּשְׁכִּימוּ
מִמָּחֳרָת וַיַּעֲלוּ עֹלֹת וַיַּגִּשׁוּ שְׁלָמִים וַיֵּשֶׁב
הָעָם לֶאֱכֹל וְשָׁתוֹ וַיָּקֻמוּ לְצַחֵק׃ פ
7 וַיְדַבֵּר יְהוָה אֶל־מֹשֶׁה לֶךְ־רֵד כִּי שִׁחֵת
עַמְּךָ אֲשֶׁר הֶעֱלֵיתָ מֵאֶרֶץ מִצְרָיִם׃ 8 סָרוּ

4. molten Most likely a wooden model was overlaid with gold.

calf Hebrew: *eigel;* refers to a young bull. The bull in the ancient Near East was a symbol of lordship, leadership, strength, vital energy, and fertility and was either deified and worshiped or used to represent divinity. The Bible views the making of a calf as an idolatrous act. This is clearly shown by the Hebrew plural (*eileh elohekha;* literally, "these are your gods") in this verse and in verse 8 (translated here as "This is your god").

The reference here may be to the Canaanite god El, who was represented by a bull. Often, however, the bull, or another animal, served as a pedestal on which the god stood, elevated above humankind. The young bull made by Aaron may then have been a pedestal on which the invisible God of Israel was believed to be standing. His presence would be left to the imagination. Clearly, the people associated the manufactured image with the God who directs history, not with a deity possessing mythologic associations, for Aaron proclaimed (v. 5) that the following day would be "a festival of the LORD" (*YHVH*). The people, in demanding "a god" because of Moses' disappearance, wanted an appropriate visible object that would recall the divine presence in their midst (see also Jeroboam's bulls in 1 Kings 12:26–30).

they exclaimed The ringleaders of the people, not Aaron.

6. Aaron plays no further role in this narrative.

GOD'S ANGER AND MOSES' INTERCESSION (vv. 7–14)

When the boisterous revelry has reached its height, God informs Moses of what is happening in the camp below.

7. your people A strong intimation of their alienation from God, in contrast to "My people," repeatedly employed until now in divine speech.

5. In an effort to minimize Aaron's culpability, the Talmud vowelizes the Hebrew words for "he built an altar" (*va-yiven mizbei·aḥ*) so that they mean "he understood because of the one who was killed" (*va-yaven mi-zavu·aḥ*). The talmudic sages envision an episode in which a leader who stood up to the mob (Hur, referred to in Exod. 17:10 and 24:14) was killed by them. In this interpretation, Aaron pretended to accede to the people's demands not solely to save his life but to prevent the people from committing another grave sin (BT Sanh. 7a).

7. Hurry down . . . from your exalted position on this mountaintop to be with your people at this perilous moment (BT Ber. 32a). "Hurry down," God tells Moses, "even as I did at Sodom, to see for yourself—rather than condemn them from afar" (Exod. R. 42:5). The Midrash asks why Moses was not angry at the Israelites as soon as God told him what they had done but waited until he had seen for himself. Did he doubt the veracity of God? The answer: One should never condemn another on the basis of hearsay, no matter how reliable the source (Exod. R. 46:1).

your people These words not only minimize God's relationship to them, they emphasize Moses' close relationship to them. "Moses devoted his life to three things: the Torah, the people Israel, and the pursuit of justice. As a reward, his name was permanently attached to all three: the Law of Moses, 'your people,' and 'you shall appoint judges like yourself'" (Mekh. Shirata 1).

מַהֵר מִן־הַדֶּרֶךְ אֲשֶׁר צִוִּיתִם עָשׂוּ לָהֶם
עֵגֶל מַסֵּכָה וַיִּשְׁתַּחֲווּ־לוֹ וַיִּזְבְּחוּ־לוֹ
וַיֹּאמְרוּ אֵלֶּה אֱלֹהֶיךָ יִשְׂרָאֵל אֲשֶׁר הֶעֱלוּךָ
מֵאֶרֶץ מִצְרָיִם׃
9 וַיֹּאמֶר יְהוָה אֶל־מֹשֶׁה רָאִיתִי אֶת־הָעָם
הַזֶּה וְהִנֵּה עַם־קְשֵׁה־עֹרֶף הוּא׃ 10 וְעַתָּה
הַנִּיחָה לִּי וְיִחַר־אַפִּי בָהֶם וַאֲכַלֵּם
וְאֶעֱשֶׂה אוֹתְךָ לְגוֹי גָּדוֹל׃ 11 וַיְחַל מֹשֶׁה
אֶת־פְּנֵי יְהוָה אֱלֹהָיו וַיֹּאמֶר לָמָה יְהוָה
יֶחֱרֶה אַפְּךָ בְּעַמֶּךָ אֲשֶׁר הוֹצֵאתָ מֵאֶרֶץ
מִצְרַיִם בְּכֹחַ גָּדוֹל וּבְיָד חֲזָקָה׃ 12 לָמָּה
יֹאמְרוּ מִצְרַיִם לֵאמֹר בְּרָעָה הוֹצִיאָם
לַהֲרֹג אֹתָם בֶּהָרִים וּלְכַלֹּתָם מֵעַל פְּנֵי

of Egypt, have acted basely. 8They have been quick to turn aside from the way that I enjoined upon them. They have made themselves a molten calf and bowed low to it and sacrificed to it, saying: 'This is your god, O Israel, who brought you out of the land of Egypt!'"

9The LORD further said to Moses, "I see that this is a stiffnecked people. 10Now, let Me be, that My anger may blaze forth against them and that I may destroy them, and make of you a great nation." 11But Moses implored the LORD his God, saying, "Let not Your anger, O LORD, blaze forth against Your people, whom You delivered from the land of Egypt with great power and with a mighty hand. 12Let not the Egyptians say, 'It was with evil intent that He delivered them, only to kill them off in the mountains and an-

8. to turn aside from the way The text does not say "from Me"; the people have adopted pagan modes of worship, but still they worship the God of Israel.

9. I see Divine "seeing" as opposed to Aaron's "seeing" in verse 5.

stiffnecked A frequent image of obstinacy, derived from the farmer's experience with work animals. When an animal's neck is stiff, it is hard for the driver using the reins to turn it in any direction.

10. a great nation The phrase evokes the divine promises made by God to Abraham and is seized on at once by Moses.

11. Moses rejects God's offer to make his own descendants the sole heirs to the promises made to the patriarchs. This unselfish characteristic is again displayed in verse 32.

12. The effect of the events of the Exodus would now be undone, for the basic objective of the events in Egypt was that the Egyptians might "know" the Lord, i.e., recognize His incomparable nature.

---

9. a stiffnecked people Ami is quoted in the Midrash: "Is that a criticism? Rather it is to their credit. That stubbornness is what has permitted us to remain Jews" (Exod. R. 42:9). According to Abravanel, to be stiffnecked means to be unable to turn one's head and look down the road to see the consequences of one's actions.

10. let Me be In the words of the Midrash: Who is stopping God—that God must say, "Let Me be"? It seems to be a hint that God wants to be talked out of such fierce anger (Exod. R. 42:9). This may have encouraged Moses' intercession on the people's behalf. A striking *midrash* pictures God as a wife and Moses as God's husband (*ish ha-elohim,* "the man of God" [Deut. 33:1], understood as "the husband of God") exercising his right to cancel God's vow, as a husband in ancient times could annul a vow that had been made by his wife in his hearing; see Num. 30:14 (Exod. R. 43:4). The Midrash envisions God saying, "Whenever I win an argument with My children, as at the time of the Flood or of Sodom and Gomorrah, I lose" (i.e., God ends up destroying culpable human beings). "Whenever I lose an argument, I win" (as here, when Moses persuades God not to punish Israel) (PR 21).

11. Moses implored The unusual Hebrew verb translated as "implore" (*va-y'ḥal*) resembles the verb meaning "to be sick," which prompted the Midrash to suggest that Moses became physically ill when he realized what the people had done. God then responded, not so much to Moses' argument as to the strength of his love for and identification with his people (Exod. R. 43:4).

12. Let not the Egyptians say Should God renounce the people now, not only Israel will suffer but God's reputation, so to speak, would be diminished as well.

הָאֲדָמָה שׁוּב מֵחֲרוֹן אַפֶּךָ וְהִנָּחֵם עַל־
הָרָעָה לְעַמֶּךָ׃ 13 זְכֹר לְאַבְרָהָם לְיִצְחָק
וּלְיִשְׂרָאֵל עֲבָדֶיךָ אֲשֶׁר נִשְׁבַּעְתָּ לָהֶם בָּךְ
וַתְּדַבֵּר אֲלֵהֶם אַרְבֶּה אֶת־זַרְעֲכֶם כְּכוֹכְבֵי
הַשָּׁמָיִם וְכָל־הָאָרֶץ הַזֹּאת אֲשֶׁר אָמַרְתִּי
אֶתֵּן לְזַרְעֲכֶם וְנָחֲלוּ לְעֹלָם׃ 14 וַיִּנָּחֶם
יְהוָה עַל־הָרָעָה אֲשֶׁר דִּבֶּר לַעֲשׂוֹת
לְעַמּוֹ׃ פ
15 וַיִּפֶן וַיֵּרֶד מֹשֶׁה מִן־הָהָר וּשְׁנֵי לֻחֹת
הָעֵדֻת בְּיָדוֹ לֻחֹת כְּתֻבִים מִשְּׁנֵי עֶבְרֵיהֶם
מִזֶּה וּמִזֶּה הֵם כְּתֻבִים׃ 16 וְהַלֻּחֹת מַעֲשֵׂה
אֱלֹהִים הֵמָּה וְהַמִּכְתָּב מִכְתַּב אֱלֹהִים
הוּא חָרוּת עַל־הַלֻּחֹת׃ 17 וַיִּשְׁמַע יְהוֹשֻׁעַ
אֶת־קוֹל הָעָם ברעה בְּרֵעוֹ וַיֹּאמֶר אֶל־
מֹשֶׁה קוֹל מִלְחָמָה בַּמַּחֲנֶה׃ 18 וַיֹּאמֶר

אֵין קוֹל עֲנוֹת גְּבוּרָה
וְאֵין קוֹל עֲנוֹת חֲלוּשָׁה
קוֹל עַנּוֹת אָנֹכִי שֹׁמֵעַ׃

19 וַיְהִי כַּאֲשֶׁר קָרַב אֶל־הַמַּחֲנֶה וַיַּרְא

nihilate them from the face of the earth.' Turn from Your blazing anger, and renounce the plan to punish Your people. 13Remember Your servants, Abraham, Isaac, and Israel, how You swore to them by Your Self and said to them: I will make your offspring as numerous as the stars of heaven, and I will give to your offspring this whole land of which I spoke, to possess forever." 14And the LORD renounced the punishment He had planned to bring upon His people.

15Thereupon Moses turned and went down from the mountain bearing the two tablets of the Pact, tablets inscribed on both their surfaces: they were inscribed on the one side and on the other. 16The tablets were God's work, and the writing was God's writing, incised upon the tablets. 17When Joshua heard the sound of the people in its boisterousness, he said to Moses, "There is a cry of war in the camp." 18But he answered,

"It is not the sound of the tune of triumph,
Or the sound of the tune of defeat;
It is the sound of song that I hear!"

19As soon as Moses came near the camp and saw the calf and the dancing, he became en-

13. Remember See Comment to 2:24.

14. the LORD renounced Moses' intercession succeeded in averting the threatened punishment.

MOSES SMASHES THE TABLETS AND DESTROYS THE CALF (vv. 15–20)

15. bearing the two tablets Although their size is not recorded here, their maximum dimensions can be determined by the size of the Ark in which they were to repose, as presented in 25:10.

16. God's work . . . God's writing This verse amplifies God's instruction to Moses in 24:12.

incised Hebrew: *ḥarut;* found in the Bible only here.

17. Joshua He was stationed partway up the mountain awaiting Moses' return, as told in 24:13; thus he could hear the rising din but could not view the scene.

18. But he answered Verses 7 and 8 tell us that Moses has already been informed.

19. As Moses approaches the camp and wit-

13. Remember Your servants, Abraham, Isaac, and Israel The reference to the patriarchs here involves the concept known as "the merit of the ancestors" (*z'khut avot*). Our own failings are balanced in part by the remembered virtues of our forebears. Solomon Schechter translated this concept felicitously as "original virtue," in contrast to the notion of "original sin" inherited from one's ancestors. The Midrash here compares Israel to a grapevine. Just as branches bearing new grapes support themselves on earlier, dead branches, so the Israelites and later generations of Jews are supported and sustained by the example and memory of their departed ancestors (Exod. R. 44:1).

19. A Rabbinic legend describes Moses, a man of advanced age, carrying the heavy stone tablets down the mountainside with ease. But

אֶת־הָעֵגֶל וּמְחֹלֹת וַיִּחַר־אַף מֹשֶׁה וַיַּשְׁלֵךְ
מידו מִיָּדָיו אֶת־הַלֻּחֹת וַיְשַׁבֵּר אֹתָם תַּחַת
הָהָר׃ 20 וַיִּקַּח אֶת־הָעֵגֶל אֲשֶׁר עָשׂוּ
וַיִּשְׂרֹף בָּאֵשׁ וַיִּטְחַן עַד אֲשֶׁר־דָּק וַיִּזֶר
עַל־פְּנֵי הַמַּיִם וַיַּשְׁקְ אֶת־בְּנֵי יִשְׂרָאֵל׃
21 וַיֹּאמֶר מֹשֶׁה אֶל־אַהֲרֹן מֶה־עָשָׂה לְךָ
הָעָם הַזֶּה כִּי־הֵבֵאתָ עָלָיו חֲטָאָה גְדֹלָה׃
22 וַיֹּאמֶר אַהֲרֹן אַל־יִחַר אַף אֲדֹנִי אַתָּה
יָדַעְתָּ אֶת־הָעָם כִּי בְרָע הוּא׃ 23 וַיֹּאמְרוּ
לִי עֲשֵׂה־לָנוּ אֱלֹהִים אֲשֶׁר יֵלְכוּ לְפָנֵינוּ

raged; and he hurled the tablets from his hands
and shattered them at the foot of the mountain.
20He took the calf that they had made and
burned it; he ground it to powder and strewed
it upon the water and so made the Israelites
drink it.
21Moses said to Aaron, "What did this people
do to you that you have brought such great sin
upon them?" 22Aaron said, "Let not my lord be
enraged. You know that this people is bent on
evil. 23They said to me, 'Make us a god to lead
us; for that man Moses, who brought us from

nesses the scene, he realizes the full extent of the people's degradation and recognizes the enormity of their sin. He no longer is thinking of appeasing God. He, too, burns with anger.

he hurled the tablets This was not an impetuous act; rather, it quite deliberately signified the abrogation of the Covenant. In ancient Near Eastern legal terminology "to break the tablet" means to invalidate or repudiate a document or agreement.

at the foot of the mountain Where the people were assembled.

20. The same series of destructive acts is found in the description of the annihilation of the god Mot, god of the underworld, in Ugaritic literature. It conveys a picture of the total annihilation of the obnoxious object.

water Unidentified here, the water is described in Deut. 9:21 as "the brook that comes down from the mountain." This implies a single source of water for the entire camp so that, apparently, no individual could escape drinking the mixture.

made the Israelites drink it And thereby to identify the transgressors (cf. the trial by ordeal in Num. 5:12–31).

AARON'S APOLOGIA (vv. 21–24)

Moses breaks his silence. The question he puts to Aaron is actually a harsh rebuke.

21. great sin This is a legal term. Found in ancient Near Eastern marriage contracts, it always refers to adultery, suggesting here that the worship of the Golden Calf is an act of gross infidelity.

22–24. Aaron excuses himself by reviling the people and glossing over his involvement in the making of the calf image. He also claims that he did not fashion it, implying divine approval!

---

when he sees the Israelites dancing around the Golden Calf, the letters fly off the tablets, which become two large blank stones. At that point, they become too much for Moses to carry; they fall from his grasp and break. When Moses felt he was bringing God's word to a people eager to receive it, he was capable of doing something difficult and demanding. When he had reason to suspect that his efforts were in vain, the task became too hard for him (PdRE 45). Another *midrash* pictures Moses deliberately breaking the tablets of stone, not out of anger or a sense that Israel was not worthy of them but to destroy the evidence that Israel had ever been commanded not to worship idols (Exod. R. 43:1). "Sometimes, canceling the Torah is the only way to save it" (BT Men. 99b).

A 19th-century commentator observes that Moses here makes the point that there is no intrinsic holiness in things. Only God is intrinsically holy. Physical objects can be holy only insofar as they lead people to God. When Israel disregards the words on the stone tablets, they become mere stones (*Meshekh Ḥokhmah*).

Hirsch asks why Moses broke the tablets in despair only when he saw the Israelites dancing around the Calf (v. 19)—and not earlier, when he learned of their transgression (v. 8). He answers his own question: "When false conceptions of idolatry are rooted merely in the intellect, they can be eradicated by intellectual argument and instruction." When the attachment to wrongdoing reaches the emotional level, however, it becomes nearly impossible to talk people out of it.

the land of Egypt—we do not know what has happened to him.' 24So I said to them, 'Whoever has gold, take it off!' They gave it to me and I hurled it into the fire and out came this calf!"

25Moses saw that the people were out of control—since Aaron had let them get out of control—so that they were a menace to any who might oppose them. 26Moses stood up in the gate of the camp and said, "Whoever is for the LORD, come here!" And all the Levites rallied to him. 27He said to them, "Thus says the LORD, the God of Israel: Each of you put sword on thigh, go back and forth from gate to gate throughout the camp, and slay brother, neighbor, and kin." 28The Levites did as Moses had bidden; and some three thousand of the people fell that day. 29And Moses said, "Dedicate yourselves to the LORD this day—for each of you has been against son and brother—that He may bestow a blessing upon you today."

30The next day Moses said to the people, "You

כִּי־זֶ֣ה ׀ מֹשֶׁ֣ה הָאִ֗ישׁ אֲשֶׁ֤ר הֶֽעֱלָ֙נוּ֙ מֵאֶ֣רֶץ מִצְרַ֔יִם לֹ֥א יָדַ֖עְנוּ מֶה־הָ֥יָה לֽוֹ׃ 24וָאֹמַ֤ר לָהֶם֙ לְמִ֣י זָהָ֔ב הִתְפָּרָ֖קוּ וַיִּתְּנוּ־לִ֑י וָאַשְׁלִכֵ֣הוּ בָאֵ֔שׁ וַיֵּצֵ֖א הָעֵ֥גֶל הַזֶּֽה׃ 25וַיַּ֤רְא מֹשֶׁה֙ אֶת־הָעָ֔ם כִּ֥י פָרֻ֖עַ ה֑וּא כִּֽי־פְרָעֹ֣ה אַהֲרֹ֔ן לְשִׁמְצָ֖ה בְּקָמֵיהֶֽם׃ 26וַיַּעֲמֹ֤ד מֹשֶׁה֙ בְּשַׁ֣עַר הַֽמַּחֲנֶ֔ה וַיֹּ֕אמֶר מִ֥י לַֽיהֹוָ֖ה אֵלָ֑י וַיֵּאָסְפ֥וּ אֵלָ֖יו כָּל־בְּנֵ֥י לֵוִֽי׃ 27וַיֹּ֣אמֶר לָהֶ֗ם כֹּֽה־אָמַ֤ר יְהֹוָה֙ אֱלֹהֵ֣י יִשְׂרָאֵ֔ל שִׂ֥ימוּ אִישׁ־חַרְבּ֖וֹ עַל־יְרֵכ֑וֹ עִבְר֨וּ וָשׁ֜וּבוּ מִשַּׁ֤עַר לָשַׁ֙עַר֙ בַּֽמַּחֲנֶ֔ה וְהִרְג֧וּ אִֽישׁ־אֶת־אָחִ֛יו וְאִ֥ישׁ אֶת־רֵעֵ֖הוּ וְאִ֥ישׁ אֶת־קְרֹבֽוֹ׃ 28וַיַּֽעֲשׂ֥וּ בְנֵֽי־לֵוִ֖י כִּדְבַ֣ר מֹשֶׁ֑ה וַיִּפֹּ֤ל מִן־הָעָם֙ בַּיּ֣וֹם הַה֔וּא כִּשְׁלֹ֥שֶׁת אַלְפֵ֖י אִֽישׁ׃ 29וַיֹּ֣אמֶר מֹשֶׁ֗ה מִלְא֨וּ יֶדְכֶ֤ם הַיּוֹם֙ לַֽיהֹוָ֔ה כִּ֛י אִ֥ישׁ בִּבְנ֖וֹ וּבְאָחִ֑יו וְלָתֵ֧ת עֲלֵיכֶ֛ם הַיּ֖וֹם בְּרָכָֽה׃ 30וַיְהִי֙ מִֽמָּחֳרָ֔ת וַיֹּ֤אמֶר מֹשֶׁה֙ אֶל־הָעָ֔ם

---

out came this calf As though it produced itself.

SELECTION OF THE LEVITES (vv. 25–29)
The destruction of the Golden Calf sparks a riot among its worshipers. The Levites are called in to suppress it and to punish the guilty ones.

25. since Aaron . . . out of control This is a clear rejection of Aaron's lame excuse and a condemnation of his action.

26. all the Levites Moses' own tribe. They remained faithful to the Covenant and maintained the purity of Israel's worship. This is the foundation story for the special place of the Levites in Israelite religion.

27. Thus says the LORD This solemn formula is employed here to signify that the assignment to the Levites is beyond the right of any human authority to impose. It cannot be taken as a precedent for the disposition of future cases.

slay brother They must be absolutely impartial while carrying out their grim task.

MOSES' SECOND INTERCESSION (vv. 30–34)

Moses, through his first intercession with God, secured the annulment of the divine decree to destroy Israel. Now he attempts to gain complete forgiveness for the people.

30. The next day After the carnage.

---

27. This is indeed a harsh measure, made intelligible by the realization that the idolatry of the calf worshipers very nearly caused God to give up on everyone, ending the Israelite enterprise almost as soon as it had begun. The Midrash recalls that the Levites' eponymous ancestor, Levi son of Jacob, did something similar when he slaughtered the men of Shechem to avenge the dishonoring of his sister, Dinah; see Gen. 34 (Sifrei Deut. 349). The tribe of Levi

would soon be asked to sublimate its fierce passion in the task of guarding and transporting the portable shrine. Just as the people have to learn not to treat an idol as an embodiment of God, God has to learn not to expect the average person to comprehend a totally abstract, invisible deity. The answer to the quest for a representation is not a Golden Calf but the tabernacle, as discussed in the previous and subsequent *parashiyyot*.

have been guilty of a great sin. Yet I will now
go up to the LORD; perhaps I may win forgiveness for your sin." 31Moses went back to the
LORD and said, "Alas, this people is guilty of a
great sin in making for themselves a god of gold.
32Now, if You will forgive their sin [well and
good]; but if not, erase me from the record
which You have written!" 33But the LORD said
to Moses, "He who has sinned against Me, him
only will I erase from My record. 34Go now, lead
the people where I told you. See, My angel shall
go before you. But when I make an accounting,
I will bring them to account for their sins."
35Then the LORD sent a plague upon the people, for what they did with the calf that Aaron
made.

33 Then the LORD said to Moses, "Set out
from here, you and the people that you have

אַתֶּם חֲטָאתֶם חֲטָאָה גְדֹלָה וְעַתָּה אֶעֱלֶה
אֶל־יְהוָה אוּלַי אֲכַפְּרָה בְּעַד חַטַּאתְכֶם׃
31 וַיָּשָׁב מֹשֶׁה אֶל־יְהוָה וַיֹּאמַר אָנָּא חָטָא
הָעָם הַזֶּה חֲטָאָה גְדֹלָה וַיַּעֲשׂוּ לָהֶם אֱלֹהֵי
זָהָב׃ 32 וְעַתָּה אִם־תִּשָּׂא חַטָּאתָם וְאִם־
אַיִן מְחֵנִי נָא מִסִּפְרְךָ אֲשֶׁר כָּתָבְתָּ׃
33 וַיֹּאמֶר יְהוָה אֶל־מֹשֶׁה מִי אֲשֶׁר חָטָא־
לִי אֶמְחֶנּוּ מִסִּפְרִי׃ 34 וְעַתָּה לֵךְ ׀ נְחֵה
אֶת־הָעָם אֶל אֲשֶׁר־דִּבַּרְתִּי לָךְ הִנֵּה*
מַלְאָכִי יֵלֵךְ לְפָנֶיךָ וּבְיוֹם פָּקְדִי וּפָקַדְתִּי
עֲלֵהֶם חַטָּאתָם׃
35 וַיִּגֹּף יְהוָה אֶת־הָעָם עַל אֲשֶׁר עָשׂוּ
אֶת־הָעֵגֶל אֲשֶׁר עָשָׂה אַהֲרֹן׃ ס

לג וַיְדַבֵּר יְהוָה אֶל־מֹשֶׁה לֵךְ
עֲלֵה מִזֶּה אַתָּה וְהָעָם אֲשֶׁר הֶעֱלִיתָ

v. 34. סבירין ומטעין "והנה"

go up To the summit of Sinai.

31–32. The prayer blends confession with a plea for pardon. And another element is introduced: Moses ties his personal destiny to his people's fate. There can hardly be a more impressive example of selfless "love of Israel."

erase me from the record This request seems to reflect a widespread ancient Near Eastern popular belief in the existence of heavenly "books." Here, Moses' request is framed in the figurative language of the book of life. He is asking to die if Israel is not forgiven.

33–34. God responds to Moses' entreaty, demanding individual accountability. In addition, the people as a whole bear collective responsibility. Divine promises of national territory made to the people of Israel are unalterable, but total absolution for the sin of the Golden Calf cannot be given. The Israelites receive a suspended sentence; they are on probation. The punishment, however, will come in due time (see Ezek. 20).

35. This verse belongs after verse 20, where it would indicate that the water ordeal caused the guilty ones to be stricken—the goal of a similar procedure to be followed in the case of a suspected adulteress (Num. 5). The calf worshipers thus would have been readily identifiable to the Levites.

for what they did This difficult phrase seems to mean that Aaron and the people shared the blame equally; they, for demanding a visible "god"; he, for yielding to them.

MOSES SEEKS GOD'S CONTINUED PRESENCE (33:1–23)

Although Moses' intercession saves the people from annihilation, the Israelites have not yet secured full pardon and reconciliation with God. The unifying theme of this chapter is Moses' concern for the continued presence of God in the midst of His people, as symbolized by the mobile sanctuary.

WITHDRAWAL OF THE DIVINE PRESENCE (vv. 1–6)

Implementation of the punishment decreed in 32:10 has been suspended, only because of God's promise to the patriarchs (32:13), not because of the people's merit.

1. Set out Hebrew: *lekh alei;* literally "go, ascend." This is in contrast to 32:7, *lekh red,* "go,

brought up from the land of Egypt, to the land of which I swore to Abraham, Isaac, and Jacob, saying, 'To your offspring will I give it'—[2]I will send an angel before you, and I will drive out the Canaanites, the Amorites, the Hittites, the Perizzites, the Hivites, and the Jebusites—[3]a land flowing with milk and honey. But I will not go in your midst, since you are a stiffnecked people, lest I destroy you on the way."

[4]When the people heard this harsh word, they went into mourning, and none put on his finery.

[5]The LORD said to Moses, "Say to the Israelite people, 'You are a stiffnecked people. If I were to go in your midst for one moment, I would destroy you. Now, then, leave off your finery, and I will consider what to do to you.'" [6]So the Israelites remained stripped of the finery from Mount Horeb on.

[7]Now Moses would take the Tent and pitch it outside the camp, at some distance from the camp. It was called the Tent of Meeting, and

מֵאֶ֣רֶץ מִצְרָ֑יִם אֶל־הָאָ֗רֶץ אֲשֶׁ֣ר נִ֠שְׁבַּ֠עְתִּי לְאַבְרָהָ֨ם לְיִצְחָ֤ק וּֽלְיַעֲקֹב֙ לֵאמֹ֔ר לְזַרְעֲךָ֖ אֶתְּנֶ֑נָּה: 2 וְשָׁלַחְתִּ֥י לְפָנֶ֖יךָ מַלְאָ֑ךְ וְגֵרַשְׁתִּ֗י אֶת־הַֽכְּנַעֲנִי֙ הָֽאֱמֹרִ֔י וְהַֽחִתִּי֙ וְהַפְּרִזִּ֔י הַחִוִּ֖י וְהַיְבוּסִֽי: 3 אֶל־אֶ֛רֶץ זָבַ֥ת חָלָ֖ב וּדְבָ֑שׁ כִּי֩ לֹ֨א אֶֽעֱלֶ֜ה בְּקִרְבְּךָ֗ כִּ֤י עַם־קְשֵׁה־עֹ֙רֶף֙ אַ֔תָּה פֶּן־אֲכֶלְךָ֖ בַּדָּֽרֶךְ: 4 וַיִּשְׁמַ֣ע הָעָ֗ם אֶת־הַדָּבָ֥ר הָרָ֖ע הַזֶּ֑ה וַיִּתְאַבָּ֑לוּ וְלֹא־שָׁ֛תוּ אִ֥ישׁ עֶדְי֖וֹ עָלָֽיו: 5 וַיֹּ֨אמֶר יְהוָ֜ה אֶל־מֹשֶׁ֗ה אֱמֹ֤ר אֶל־בְּנֵֽי־יִשְׂרָאֵל֙ אַתֶּ֣ם עַם־קְשֵׁה־עֹ֔רֶף רֶ֥גַע אֶחָ֛ד אֶֽעֱלֶ֥ה בְקִרְבְּךָ֖ וְכִלִּיתִ֑יךָ וְעַתָּ֗ה הוֹרֵ֤ד עֶדְיְךָ֙ מֵֽעָלֶ֔יךָ וְאֵדְעָ֖ה מָ֥ה אֶֽעֱשֶׂה־לָּֽךְ: 6 וַיִּֽתְנַצְּל֧וּ בְנֵֽי־יִשְׂרָאֵ֛ל אֶת־עֶדְיָ֖ם מֵהַ֥ר חוֹרֵֽב:

7 וּמֹשֶׁה֩ יִקַּ֨ח אֶת־הָאֹ֜הֶל וְנָֽטָה־ל֣וֹ | מִח֣וּץ לַֽמַּחֲנֶ֗ה הַרְחֵק֙ מִן־הַֽמַּחֲנֶ֔ה וְקָ֥רָא ל֖וֹ אֹ֣הֶל

descend," signifying that there has been a reversal of fate.

you Moses' request in the last part of 32:32 is emphatically denied.

the people It is no longer "your people" as God said to Moses in 32:7. The shift connotes some softening of the effect of Israel's alienation from God.

2. an angel The promise of 23:20–33 and 32:34 is repeated, but here the emissary is not designated "My" angel. The change is ominous.

3. I will not go . . . lest I destroy you Paradoxically, God's withdrawal of His Presence is a merciful measure; it is intended to avert the inevitable destructive consequences of another episode such as that of the Golden Calf.

4. This decision has a shattering effect on the people, for it was the absence of a representation of God's immanence that had provoked the demand for a material image in the first place.

5. leave off The people have already done this. Hence, it is best to invert the order of verses 4–5, taking verse 4 as the response to the divine command.

6. from Mount Horeb on From that time on, throughout the wilderness wanderings. It is

a sign of the people's remorse over their transgression. See Comment to 3:1.

MOSES' EXCEPTIONAL STATUS   (vv. 7–11)

This section continues the theme of God's presence and connects with verse 3. Because God withholds His indwelling in the camp of Israel, Moses employs an extraordinary stratagem. He pitches "the Tent" outside the camp. This is not the tabernacle—which has not yet been constructed—but a private tent where he might commune with God.

7. the Tent The definite article seems to indicate a well-known, specific tent, although one has not yet been mentioned. Apparently, it was the site of Moses' previous dialogues with God. It is possible that there were two different traditions regarding a "tent," with the tabernacle in the heart of the camp serving as a shrine for sacrifices without speech, and the Tent outside serving as a place for inquiring of God.

outside the camp, at some distance The description draws attention to the Israelites' alienation from God. The camp has become polluted spiritually through the impurity brought on by the episode of the Golden Calf.

whoever sought the LORD would go out to the
Tent of Meeting that was outside the camp.
8Whenever Moses went out to the Tent, all the
people would rise and stand, each at the entrance of his tent, and gaze after Moses until he
had entered the Tent. 9And when Moses entered
the Tent, the pillar of cloud would descend and
stand at the entrance of the Tent, while He spoke
with Moses. 10When all the people saw the pillar
of cloud poised at the entrance of the Tent, all
the people would rise and bow low, each at the
entrance of his tent. 11The LORD would speak
to Moses face to face, as one man speaks to another. And he would then return to the camp;
but his attendant, Joshua son of Nun, a youth,
would not stir out of the Tent.

12Moses said to the LORD, "See, You say to
me, 'Lead this people forward,' but You have
not made known to me whom You will send
with me. Further, You have said, 'I have singled
you out by name, and you have, indeed, gained
My favor.' 13Now, if I have truly gained Your
favor, pray let me know Your ways, that I may
know You and continue in Your favor. Con-

מוֹעֵד וְהָיָה כָּל־מְבַקֵּשׁ יְהוָה יֵצֵא אֶל־
אֹהֶל מוֹעֵד אֲשֶׁר מִחוּץ לַמַּחֲנֶה׃ 8 וְהָיָה
כְּצֵאת מֹשֶׁה אֶל־הָאֹהֶל יָקוּמוּ כָּל־הָעָם
וְנִצְּבוּ אִישׁ פֶּתַח אָהֳלוֹ וְהִבִּיטוּ אַחֲרֵי
מֹשֶׁה עַד־בֹּאוֹ הָאֹהֱלָה׃ 9 וְהָיָה כְּבֹא
מֹשֶׁה הָאֹהֱלָה יֵרֵד עַמּוּד הֶעָנָן וְעָמַד
פֶּתַח הָאֹהֶל וְדִבֶּר עִם־מֹשֶׁה׃ 10 וְרָאָה
כָל־הָעָם אֶת־עַמּוּד הֶעָנָן עֹמֵד פֶּתַח
הָאֹהֶל וְקָם כָּל־הָעָם וְהִשְׁתַּחֲווּ אִישׁ
פֶּתַח אָהֳלוֹ׃ 11 וְדִבֶּר יְהוָה אֶל־מֹשֶׁה פָּנִים
אֶל־פָּנִים כַּאֲשֶׁר יְדַבֵּר אִישׁ אֶל־רֵעֵהוּ
וְשָׁב אֶל־הַמַּחֲנֶה וּמְשָׁרְתוֹ יְהוֹשֻׁעַ בִּן־נוּן
נַעַר לֹא יָמִישׁ מִתּוֹךְ הָאֹהֶל׃ ס

שלישי 12 וַיֹּאמֶר מֹשֶׁה אֶל־יְהוָה רְאֵה אַתָּה אֹמֵר
אֵלַי הַעַל אֶת־הָעָם הַזֶּה וְאַתָּה לֹא
הוֹדַעְתַּנִי אֵת אֲשֶׁר־תִּשְׁלַח עִמִּי וְאַתָּה
אָמַרְתָּ יְדַעְתִּיךָ בְשֵׁם וְגַם־מָצָאתָ חֵן
בְּעֵינָי׃ 13 וְעַתָּה אִם־נָא מָצָאתִי חֵן
בְּעֵינֶיךָ הוֹדִעֵנִי נָא אֶת־דְּרָכֶךָ וְאֵדָעֲךָ

9. at the entrance of the Tent Not inside the tabernacle, where the divine Presence is said to rest continuously and where God converses with Moses from within the Holy of Holies. The place of communication here is at the entrance, where God's self-manifestation is intermittent.

11. face to face The same expression is used in Deut. 34:10, whereas in Num. 12:6–8 it is said that God communicated with Moses "mouth to mouth." This figurative language is intended to convey the pre-eminence and uniqueness of Moses as a prophetic figure who experiences a special mode of revelation. His experience is personal and direct, not mediated through visions or dreams, and the message always is plain and straightforward, free of cryptic utterances.

Joshua He remained inside the tent and did not share in Moses' direct experience with God.

DIALOGUE WITH GOD (vv. 12–23)

This section depicts how Moses and God engage in the intimate talk mentioned in verse 11.

12. Moses now reverts to the subject matter of 32:34 and 33:1–3—the order to proceed to the Promised Land without the tabernacle, the token of God's immediate presence in the camp of Israel. He complains that the aforementioned "angel" is unidentified. Is it to be human or celestial? Is God's name to "be in him," as is promised in 23:21, or not?

I have singled you out by name Literally, "I know you by name." This Hebrew idiom, with God as the subject, is applied to no one else in the Bible. It signifies a close, exclusive, and unique association with God.

13. let me know Your ways Moses asks for comprehension of God's essential being—the attributes that guide His actions in dealing with humankind, the norms by which He operates in His governance of the world. "Ways" here is a play on the literal and the figurative meanings of Hebrew word *derekh*; it means both the right path through the wilderness and also God's way of acting, His nature.

sider, too, that this nation is Your people." [14]And He said, "I will go in the lead and will lighten your burden." [15]And he said to Him, "Unless You go in the lead, do not make us leave this place. [16]For how shall it be known that Your people have gained Your favor unless You go with us, so that we may be distinguished, Your people and I, from every people on the face of the earth?"

[17]And the LORD said to Moses, "I will also do this thing that you have asked; for you have truly gained My favor and I have singled you out by name." [18]He said, "Oh, let me behold Your Presence!" [19]And He answered, "I will make all My goodness pass before you, and I will proclaim before you the name LORD, and the grace that I grant and the compassion that I show. [20]But," He said, "you cannot see My face, for man may

לְמַ֤עַן אֶמְצָא־חֵן֙ בְּעֵינֶ֔יךָ וּרְאֵ֕ה כִּ֥י עַמְּךָ֖ הַגּ֥וֹי הַזֶּֽה: [14] וַיֹּאמַ֑ר פָּנַ֥י יֵלֵ֖כוּ וַהֲנִחֹ֥תִי לָֽךְ: [15] וַיֹּ֣אמֶר אֵלָ֑יו אִם־אֵ֤ין פָּנֶ֙יךָ֙ הֹלְכִ֔ים אַֽל־תַּעֲלֵ֖נוּ מִזֶּֽה: [16] וּבַמֶּ֣ה | יִוָּדַ֣ע אֵפ֗וֹא כִּֽי־מָצָ֨אתִי חֵ֤ן בְּעֵינֶ֙יךָ֙ אֲנִ֣י וְעַמֶּ֔ךָ הֲל֖וֹא בְּלֶכְתְּךָ֣ עִמָּ֑נוּ וְנִפְלֵ֜ינוּ אֲנִ֣י וְעַמְּךָ֗ מִכָּל־הָעָ֔ם אֲשֶׁ֖ר עַל־פְּנֵ֥י הָאֲדָמָֽה: פ

[17] וַיֹּ֤אמֶר יְהוָה֙ אֶל־מֹשֶׁ֔ה גַּ֣ם אֶת־הַדָּבָ֥ר הַזֶּ֛ה אֲשֶׁ֥ר דִּבַּ֖רְתָּ אֶֽעֱשֶׂ֑ה כִּֽי־מָצָ֤אתָ חֵן֙ בְּעֵינַ֔י וָאֵדָעֲךָ֖ בְּשֵֽׁם: [18] וַיֹּאמַ֑ר הַרְאֵ֥נִי נָ֖א אֶת־כְּבֹדֶֽךָ: [19] וַיֹּ֡אמֶר אֲנִ֣י אַעֲבִ֣יר כָּל־טוּבִי֩ עַל־פָּנֶ֜יךָ וְקָרָ֤אתִי בְשֵׁ֤ם יְהוָה֙ לְפָנֶ֔יךָ וְחַנֹּתִי֙ אֶת־אֲשֶׁ֣ר אָחֹ֔ן וְרִחַמְתִּ֖י אֶת־אֲשֶׁ֥ר אֲרַחֵֽם: [20] וַיֹּ֕אמֶר לֹ֥א תוּכַ֖ל לִרְאֹ֣ת אֶת־

this nation Moses stresses that the people Israel, and none other, constitute God's people. He wants to extend God's favor to embrace Israel as well as himself.

14. God does not yet respond to Moses' last point but addresses only his immediate personal concerns.

lighten your burden Literally, "I will give you rest." This phrase is normally found in a context of giving relief from national enemies, especially in relation to the occupation of the Land. The Hebrew word for "rest," *m'nuḥah*, probably means "camping places," a pun on Hebrew for "camp" (*maḥaneh*) (see Num. 10:33).

15–16. Moses, sensitive to God's omission of any mention of Israel, reacts immediately by stressing the people's interests, thereby affirming once again that he sees his own reputation inextricably bound up with the fate of his people. Note his repetition of "us" and "Your people."

we may be distinguished Israel's distinctiveness lies in its unique relationship with God.

18. *Oh, let me behold Your Presence!* Hebrew: *kavod* (Presence); one of the most impor-

tant concepts in biblical theology. See Comment to 16:7. Here Moses is pleading for an exclusively individual experience, one close at hand and immediate, as a response to his personal request there and then.

19. *all My goodness* This refers to the compassionate attributes that God reveals in dealing with His creatures (see 34:6–7).

proclaim . . . the name LORD This name is *YHVH*; see Comment to 3:14. This clause parallels the immediately preceding one—"I will make all My goodness pass before you." It reaffirms God's intention of voluntarily disclosing to Moses His defining characteristics. This is fulfilled in 34:5.

and the grace Literally, "I shall be gracious to whomever I am gracious and I shall show mercy to whomever I show mercy." The syntax indicates indefiniteness, as in 3:14. God is reminding Moses that He is a free agent. There is no magical practice that is automatically effective in influencing His behavior.

20. Moses' second plea is only partially granted. By virtue of their humanity, human beings, in-

---

CHAPTER 33

19. *I will make all My goodness pass before you* We encounter the reality of God when we experience goodness in the world, from the gift of life itself to the discovery of the capacity

to do good in our own souls, and the love and generosity of people around us whom God has inspired to do good.

20–23. What does it mean that a human being cannot see God's face—but can see God's back? In the words of the Ḥatam Sofer, we can-

not see Me and live." 21And the LORD said, "See,
there is a place near Me. Station yourself on the
rock 22and, as My Presence passes by, I will put
you in a cleft of the rock and shield you with
My hand until I have passed by. 23Then I will
take My hand away and you will see My back;
but My face must not be seen."

פָּנָ֑י כִּ֛י לֹֽא־יִרְאַ֥נִי הָאָדָ֖ם וָחָֽי׃ 21 וַיֹּ֣אמֶר
יְהוָ֔ה הִנֵּ֥ה מָק֖וֹם אִתִּ֑י וְנִצַּבְתָּ֖ עַל־הַצּֽוּר׃
22 וְהָיָה֙ בַּעֲבֹ֣ר כְּבֹדִ֔י וְשַׂמְתִּ֖יךָ בְּנִקְרַ֣ת
הַצּ֑וּר וְשַׂכֹּתִ֥י כַפִּ֛י עָלֶ֖יךָ עַד־עָבְרִֽי׃
23 וַהֲסִרֹתִי֙ אֶת־כַּפִּ֔י וְרָאִ֖יתָ אֶת־אֲחֹרָ֑י
וּפָנַ֖י לֹ֥א יֵרָאֽוּ׃ ס

34 The LORD said to Moses: "Carve two
tablets of stone like the first, and I will inscribe
upon the tablets the words that were on the
first tablets, which you shattered. 2Be ready
by morning, and in the morning come up to
Mount Sinai and present yourself there to Me,
on the top of the mountain. 3No one else shall
come up with you, and no one else shall be seen

חמישי
לד וַיֹּ֤אמֶר יְהוָה֙ אֶל־מֹשֶׁ֔ה פְּסָל־לְךָ֛
שְׁנֵֽי־לֻחֹ֥ת אֲבָנִ֖ים כָּרִאשֹׁנִ֑ים וְכָתַבְתִּי֙ עַל־
הַלֻּחֹ֔ת אֶת־הַדְּבָרִ֔ים אֲשֶׁ֥ר הָי֛וּ עַל־הַלֻּחֹ֥ת
הָרִאשֹׁנִ֖ים אֲשֶׁ֥ר שִׁבַּֽרְתָּ׃ 2 וֶהְיֵ֥ה נָכ֖וֹן
לַבֹּ֑קֶר וְעָלִ֤יתָ בַבֹּ֙קֶר֙ אֶל־הַ֣ר סִינַ֔י וְנִצַּבְתָּ֥
לִ֛י שָׁ֖ם עַל־רֹ֥אשׁ הָהָֽר׃ 3 וְאִישׁ֙ לֹא־יַעֲלֶ֣ה
עִמָּ֔ךְ וְגַם־אִ֥ישׁ אַל־יֵרָ֖א בְּכָל־הָהָ֑ר גַּם־

cluding Moses, cannot directly and closely observe God.

21. on the rock At the top of Mount Sinai (see 34:2). For a similar scene, see 1 Kings 19.

22. My Presence passes by Rashbam notes that God's action is characteristic of covenant making, as in Gen. 15:17 and Jer. 34:18,19. The manifestation of God here would then be a ceremony that signals renewal of the Covenant.

23. My back This daring human image for God, contrasted with the usual biblical term *panim,* "face, presence," refers to the traces of the divine Presence, the afterglow of His supernatural radiance.

must not be seen No human being can ever penetrate the ultimate mystery of God's Being. Only a glimpse of the divine reality is possible, even for Moses.

RENEWAL OF THE COVENANT (34:1–35)

PREPARATORY MEASURES (vv. 1–3)

Moses, assured that God will manifest His Presence privately to him, is instructed to prepare for the experience, which actually initiates the reinstatement of the Covenant.

1. Carve God had given the first set to Moses.

words They are identified as the Decalogue in verse 28.

3. No one else This time Aaron is excluded, because of his role in the episode of the Golden Calf.

---

not see God directly. We can only see the difference that God has made after the fact. We can recognize God's reality by seeing the difference God has made in people's lives.

CHAPTER 34

1. The first set of tablets was fashioned by God alone. Moses passively received them. The second set will be a joint divine–human effort (Y. Nissenbaum). This second set was written with a greater knowledge of human weakness, at the hand of an imperfect human being, rather than by a perfect deity. Heschel taught that God revealed the Torah to Moses in all its fullness; and Moses, a finite human being, wrote down what he could comprehend. The Talmud tells us that the fragments of the first set of tablets were carried in the Ark along with the replacement set (BT Ber. 8b). That which was once holy retains its holiness even when it is broken. So too the elderly, the senile, and the infirm may not be cast aside. They must be accorded the reverence they have earned in their lives.

anywhere on the mountain; neither shall the flocks and the herds graze at the foot of this mountain."

[4]So Moses carved two tablets of stone, like the first, and early in the morning he went up on Mount Sinai, as the LORD had commanded him, taking the two stone tablets with him. [5]The LORD came down in a cloud; He stood with him there, and proclaimed the name LORD. [6]The LORD passed before him and proclaimed: "The LORD! the LORD! a God compassionate and gracious, slow to anger, abounding in kindness and faithfulness, [7]extending kindness to the thousandth generation, forgiving iniquity, transgression, and sin; yet He does not remit all punishment, but visits the iniquity of parents upon children and children's children, upon the third and fourth generations."

הַצֹּאן וְהַבָּקָר אַל־יִרְעוּ אֶל־מוּל הָהָר
הַהוּא׃
4 וַיִּפְסֹל שְׁנֵי־לֻחֹת אֲבָנִים כָּרִאשֹׁנִים
וַיַּשְׁכֵּם מֹשֶׁה בַבֹּקֶר וַיַּעַל אֶל־הַר סִינַי
כַּאֲשֶׁר צִוָּה יְהוָה אֹתוֹ וַיִּקַּח בְּיָדוֹ שְׁנֵי
לֻחֹת אֲבָנִים׃ 5 וַיֵּרֶד יְהוָה בֶּעָנָן וַיִּתְיַצֵּב
עִמּוֹ שָׁם וַיִּקְרָא בְשֵׁם יְהוָה׃ 6 וַיַּעֲבֹר
יְהוָה ׀ עַל־פָּנָיו וַיִּקְרָא יְהוָה ׀ יְהוָה אֵל
רַחוּם וְחַנּוּן אֶרֶךְ אַפַּיִם וְרַב־חֶסֶד וֶאֱמֶת׃
7 נֹצֵר* חֶסֶד לָאֲלָפִים נֹשֵׂא עָוֺן וָפֶשַׁע
וְחַטָּאָה וְנַקֵּה לֹא יְנַקֶּה פֹּקֵד ׀ עֲוֺן אָבוֹת
עַל־בָּנִים וְעַל־בְּנֵי בָנִים עַל־שִׁלֵּשִׁים וְעַל־
רִבֵּעִים׃

v. 7. נ׳ רבתי לפי נוסחים מקובלים

GOD'S SELF-DISCLOSURE (vv. 4–9)

5. stood . . . proclaimed The text is ambiguous. The subject of the two verbs may be either Moses, as verses 2 and 33:21 indicate, or God, as the first clause and 33:19 would suggest. Or perhaps the first verb is governed by Moses and the second by God.

THE DIVINE RESPONSE (vv. 6–7)

These verses are the divine response to Moses' two requests—that he "know" God's ways (33:13) and that he "behold" God's Presence (33:18). God's mysterious passing before Moses answers to the second; the recital of the divine attributes, to the first. God's self-disclosure is confined to a proclamation of His moral qualities. To "know" them is to achieve a higher conception of Deity.

6. The LORD! the LORD! The Hebrew text also allows the first *YHVH* to be taken as the subject of the antecedent verb; thus "And the LORD proclaimed."

compassionate and gracious In the Decalogue (20:5–6) the order of attributes, unlike here, presents judgment before kindness. Emphasis and priority are here given to God's magnanimous qualities rather than to His judgmental actions.

kindness and faithfulness The Hebrew words *ḥesed v'emet* appear frequently together to express a single concept. *Ḥesed* involves acts of beneficence and obligation that flow from a legal relationship. See Comment to 15:13. *Emet,* usually translated "truth," encompasses the notions of reliability, durability, and faithfulness. When used together, the two words express God's absolute and eternal dependability in dispensing His benefactions.

7. extending kindness The phrase may express either God's continuous *ḥesed* or the idea that merit for the *ḥesed* that people perform endures beyond their own generation.

He does not remit Divine mercy does not mean that sinners can expect wholly to escape the consequences of their wrongs.

6–7. These two verses contain a passage recited and chanted on the High Holy Days and the Festivals. This summary of God's compassionate qualities is known as the "Thirteen Attributes of God" or the "Covenant of the Thirteen" (*b'rit sh'losh esrei*).

visits the iniquity of parents upon children and children's children Bothered by the apparent unfairness of the text, a Hasidic interpretation takes it to mean that God holds parents responsible for not giving their children a proper religious and moral upbringing. We recognize the unfairness of such punishment, yet it is true that the bad habits of parents are too often repeated by their children, for whom parents are the primary role models.

8 וַיְמַהֵר מֹשֶׁה וַיִּקֹּד אַרְצָה וַיִּשְׁתָּחוּ׃
9 וַיֹּאמֶר אִם־נָא מָצָאתִי חֵן בְּעֵינֶיךָ אֲדֹנָי
יֵלֶךְ־נָא אֲדֹנָי בְּקִרְבֵּנוּ כִּי עַם־קְשֵׁה־
עֹרֶף הוּא וְסָלַחְתָּ לַעֲוֺנֵנוּ וּלְחַטָּאתֵנוּ
וּנְחַלְתָּנוּ׃
ששי 10 וַיֹּאמֶר הִנֵּה אָנֹכִי כֹּרֵת בְּרִית נֶגֶד
כָּל־עַמְּךָ אֶעֱשֶׂה נִפְלָאֹת אֲשֶׁר לֹא־נִבְרְאוּ
בְכָל־הָאָרֶץ וּבְכָל־הַגּוֹיִם וְרָאָה כָל־הָעָם
אֲשֶׁר־אַתָּה בְקִרְבּוֹ אֶת־מַעֲשֵׂה יְהוָה כִּי־
נוֹרָא הוּא אֲשֶׁר אֲנִי עֹשֶׂה עִמָּךְ׃ 11 שְׁמָר־
לְךָ אֵת אֲשֶׁר אָנֹכִי מְצַוְּךָ הַיּוֹם הִנְנִי
גֹרֵשׁ מִפָּנֶיךָ אֶת־הָאֱמֹרִי וְהַכְּנַעֲנִי וְהַחִתִּי
וְהַפְּרִזִּי וְהַחִוִּי וְהַיְבוּסִי׃ 12 הִשָּׁמֶר לְךָ
פֶּן־תִּכְרֹת בְּרִית לְיוֹשֵׁב הָאָרֶץ אֲשֶׁר אַתָּה
בָּא עָלֶיהָ פֶּן־יִהְיֶה לְמוֹקֵשׁ בְּקִרְבֶּךָ׃
13 כִּי אֶת־מִזְבְּחֹתָם תִּתֹּצוּן וְאֶת־מַצֵּבֹתָם
תְּשַׁבֵּרוּן וְאֶת־אֲשֵׁרָיו תִּכְרֹתוּן׃ 14 כִּי לֹא
תִשְׁתַּחֲוֶה לְאֵל אַחֵר* כִּי יְהוָה קַנָּא שְׁמוֹ

[8]Moses hastened to bow low to the ground in homage, [9]and said, "If I have gained Your favor, O Lord, pray, let the Lord go in our midst, even though this is a stiffnecked people. Pardon our iniquity and our sin, and take us for Your own!"

[10]He said: I hereby make a covenant. Before all your people I will work such wonders as have not been wrought on all the earth or in any nation; and all the people who are with you shall see how awesome are the LORD's deeds which I will perform for you. [11]Mark well what I command you this day. I will drive out before you the Amorites, the Canaanites, the Hittites, the Perizzites, the Hivites, and the Jebusites. [12]Beware of making a covenant with the inhabitants of the land against which you are advancing, lest they be a snare in your midst. [13]No, you must tear down their altars, smash their pillars, and cut down their sacred posts; [14]for you must not worship any other god, because the LORD, whose name is Impassioned, is an impassioned

v. 14. ר׳ רבתי לפי נוסחים מקובלים

9. Moses emphasizes God's merciful qualities in asking that the punishment in 33:3 be set aside.

even though Allow for human frailty.

INAUTHENTIC AND AUTHENTIC WORSHIP (vv. 10–26)

This section concentrates on two fundamental issues that flow directly from the people's sin: false modes of worship (vv. 10–17) and the legitimate festivals and ritual obligations to God (vv. 18–26).

APOSTASY (vv. 10–17)

Mindful of the act of apostasy, the renewed covenant contains stricter admonitions than those given before (23:23,24) regarding the inroads of foreign forms of worship into the religion of Israel. If the people Israel is to be "distinguished . . . from every people on the face of the earth" (33:16), they must make themselves unique by exclusive loyalty to their covenantal relationship with God.

13. sacred posts Hebrew: *asherim* (singular *asherah*); pagan objects of worship often mentioned in the Bible. These wooden poles derive their name from the Canaanite fertility goddess Asherah, whom they symbolized.

14. any other god This Hebrew phrase in the singular—*el aḥer*—appears nowhere else in the

---

10. The Decalogue proclaims universal laws applicable to all humanity. This supplemental covenant deals with the specific rituals of the Israelite people. Our calendar and our kitchens would keep the Jewish people distinctive.

13. Why this troubling emphasis on destroying the holy places of the Canaanites and shunning their sacrificial occasions? The Israelites were a young, impressionable nation, and the Torah is concerned that the highly sexualized, orgiastic fertility cult of the Canaanites would be irresistibly seductive for them (as the incident of Baal-peor in Num. 25 attests). Even decent people can be vulnerable to sexual temptation, which is why the Torah speaks out in such extreme, uncompromising terms against the Canaanite cult.

God. 15You must not make a covenant with the
inhabitants of the land, for they will lust after
their gods and sacrifice to their gods and invite
you, and you will eat of their sacrifices. 16And
when you take wives from among their daughters for your sons, their daughters will lust after
their gods and will cause your sons to lust after
their gods.

17You shall not make molten gods for yourselves.

18You shall observe the Feast of Unleavened
Bread—eating unleavened bread for seven days,
as I have commanded you—at the set time of
the month of Abib, for in the month of Abib
you went forth from Egypt.

19Every first issue of the womb is Mine, from
all your livestock that drop a male as firstling,
whether cattle or sheep. 20But the firstling of an
ass you shall redeem with a sheep; if you do not
redeem it, you must break its neck. And you
must redeem every first-born among your sons.

None shall appear before Me empty-handed.

אֵל קַנָּא הוּא׃ 15 פֶּן־תִּכְרֹת בְּרִית לְיוֹשֵׁב
הָאָרֶץ וְזָנוּ ׀ אַחֲרֵי אֱלֹהֵיהֶם וְזָבְחוּ
לֵאלֹהֵיהֶם וְקָרָא לְךָ וְאָכַלְתָּ מִזִּבְחוֹ׃
16 וְלָקַחְתָּ מִבְּנֹתָיו לְבָנֶיךָ וְזָנוּ בְנֹתָיו אַחֲרֵי
אֱלֹהֵיהֶן וְהִזְנוּ אֶת־בָּנֶיךָ אַחֲרֵי אֱלֹהֵיהֶן׃
17 אֱלֹהֵי מַסֵּכָה לֹא תַעֲשֶׂה־לָּךְ׃
18 אֶת־חַג הַמַּצּוֹת תִּשְׁמֹר שִׁבְעַת יָמִים
תֹּאכַל מַצּוֹת אֲשֶׁר צִוִּיתִךָ לְמוֹעֵד
חֹדֶשׁ הָאָבִיב כִּי בְּחֹדֶשׁ הָאָבִיב יָצָאתָ
מִמִּצְרָיִם׃
19 כָּל־פֶּטֶר רֶחֶם לִי וְכָל־מִקְנְךָ תִּזָּכָר פֶּטֶר
שׁוֹר וָשֶׂה׃ 20 וּפֶטֶר חֲמוֹר תִּפְדֶּה בְשֶׂה
וְאִם־לֹא תִפְדֶּה וַעֲרַפְתּוֹ כֹּל בְּכוֹר בָּנֶיךָ
תִּפְדֶּה
וְלֹא־יֵרָאוּ פָנַי רֵיקָם׃

Bible. The Hebrew word *aḥer* in the text of the Torah has an enlarged letter *resh* to avoid confusion with the similar-looking letter *dalet,* which would make the word read *eḥad,* meaning "one."

impassioned Emphasis on the punitive aspect of the divine personality is prompted by the apostasy of the Golden Calf.

16. lust after The Hebrew verb זנה, literally "to engage in prostitution," is often used figuratively to express the people's infidelity to the covenant with God. Its use here may allude to the sexual immorality often associated with pagan worship, particularly with the popular excesses in connection with the Golden Calf, as mentioned in 32:6.

17–28. The laws that follow are referred to by scholars as "The Cultic Decalogue," though they differ among themselves as to the precise enumeration of the laws. Like the actual Decalogue (Exod. 20:2–14), these laws are considered to be terms of the Covenant (v. 27). Unlike them, they incorporate the requirement of observing the three pilgrimage festivals.

17. molten gods The warnings against idolatry in all its forms conclude with this prohibition because the Golden Calf is frequently referred to in the Bible as a molten image.

FESTIVALS AND RELATED RELIGIOUS OBLIGATIONS (vv. 18–26)

The topics in this section are associated with those of the preceding because the narrative about the Golden Calf recounts that a "festival of the LORD" was proclaimed and burnt offerings and sacrifices were brought (32:5–6). Hence, there is now a need to restate briefly the list of the legitimate festivals of the Israelites, previously set forth in 23:12–19.

18. Feast of Unleavened Bread The list begins with this feast rather than with *Shabbat* because the Golden Calf had been identified with the God of the Exodus and because the beginning of the ancient Israelite calendar occurs in the spring. See Comment to 12:2.

19–20. The law of the firstborn follows because it too is grounded in the Exodus (13:2,11–15). The text presupposes our familiarity with that passage. See Comments to 13:13 and 22:29.

None shall appear See Comment to 23:15.

21Six days you shall work, but on the seventh
day you shall cease from labor; you shall cease
from labor even at plowing time and harvest
time.

22You shall observe the Feast of Weeks, of the
first fruits of the wheat harvest; and the Feast
of Ingathering at the turn of the year. 23Three
times a year all your males shall appear before
the Sovereign LORD, the God of Israel. 24I will
drive out nations from your path and enlarge
your territory; no one will covet your land when
you go up to appear before the LORD your God
three times a year.

25You shall not offer the blood of My sacrifice
with anything leavened; and the sacrifice of the
Feast of Passover shall not be left lying until
morning.

26The choice first fruits of your soil you shall
bring to the house of the LORD your God.

You shall not boil a kid in its mother's milk.

27And the LORD said to Moses: Write down

21 שֵׁשֶׁת יָמִים תַּעֲבֹד וּבַיּוֹם הַשְּׁבִיעִי
תִּשְׁבֹּת בֶּחָרִישׁ וּבַקָּצִיר תִּשְׁבֹּת׃
22 וְחַג שָׁבֻעֹת תַּעֲשֶׂה לְךָ בִּכּוּרֵי קְצִיר
חִטִּים וְחַג הָאָסִיף תְּקוּפַת הַשָּׁנָה׃
23 שָׁלֹשׁ פְּעָמִים בַּשָּׁנָה יֵרָאֶה כָּל־זְכוּרְךָ
אֶת־פְּנֵי הָאָדֹן ׀ יְהוָה אֱלֹהֵי יִשְׂרָאֵל׃
24 כִּי־אוֹרִישׁ גּוֹיִם מִפָּנֶיךָ וְהִרְחַבְתִּי אֶת־
גְּבוּלֶךָ וְלֹא־יַחְמֹד אִישׁ אֶת־אַרְצְךָ
בַּעֲלֹתְךָ לֵרָאוֹת אֶת־פְּנֵי יְהוָה אֱלֹהֶיךָ
שָׁלֹשׁ פְּעָמִים בַּשָּׁנָה׃
25 לֹא־תִשְׁחַט עַל־חָמֵץ דַּם־זִבְחִי וְלֹא־
יָלִין לַבֹּקֶר זֶבַח חַג הַפָּסַח׃
26 רֵאשִׁית בִּכּוּרֵי אַדְמָתְךָ תָּבִיא בֵּית
יְהוָה אֱלֹהֶיךָ
לֹא־תְבַשֵּׁל גְּדִי בַּחֲלֵב אִמּוֹ׃ פ
שביעי 27 וַיֹּאמֶר יְהוָה אֶל־מֹשֶׁה כְּתָב־לְךָ אֶת־

As Rashi notes, this statement is a separate injunction, unconnected to the law of the firstborn. It belongs after verse 23.

21. The inclusion of the law of *Shabbat* here, after *Pesaḥ* and the firstborn, presupposes a view that the institution of *Shabbat* is based on the Exodus, as in Deut. 5:15, and not on Creation, as in Exod. 20:11.

work The soil.

even at plowing time and harvest time The busiest times of the agricultural year must give way to the commandment to observe sacred time. This sacrifice becomes a true test of faith.

22. Feast of Weeks See Comment to 23:16.

23. See Comment to 23:17. The formulation in the verse here is an expansion of the parallel text.

24. Another test of faith. This injunction clearly does not refer to local shrines but assumes the existence of some central or, at least, regional sanctuary that, for many, will be far from home and will require a pilgrimage.

covet See Comment to 20:14.

when you go up It is assumed that the central shrine will be situated on an elevation.

25. sacrifice of the Feast of Passover See Comment to 12:11.

26. See Comment to 23:19.

EPILOGUE: MOSES REACHES THE PINNACLE OF EMINENCE (vv. 27–35)

The narrative returns to the role and the status of Moses. The episode of apostasy began with a disparaging reference to him in verse 32:1; it closes with an account of his glorification. Apparently, Moses is instructed to write down the commandments contained in the foregoing (vv. 11–26), just as, following the original covenant, he wrote down "all the commands of the LORD" (24:4).

---

24. no one will covet your land The verb translated as "covet" is the same one used in the 10th commandment (Exod. 20:14), leading some scholars to surmise that in both locations it refers to seizing by force rather than simply envy.

these commandments, for in accordance with
these commandments I make a covenant with
you and with Israel.
28 And he was there with the LORD forty days
and forty nights; he ate no bread and drank no
water; and he wrote down on the tablets the
terms of the covenant, the Ten Commandments.

29 So Moses came down from Mount Sinai.
And as Moses came down from the mountain
bearing the two tablets of the Pact, Moses was
not aware that the skin of his face was radiant,
since he had spoken with Him. 30 Aaron and all
the Israelites saw that the skin of Moses' face
was radiant; and they shrank from coming near

הַדְּבָרִים הָאֵלֶּה כִּי עַל־פִּי ׀ הַדְּבָרִים
הָאֵלֶּה כָּרַתִּי אִתְּךָ בְּרִית וְאֶת־יִשְׂרָאֵל׃
28 וַיְהִי־שָׁם עִם־יְהוָה אַרְבָּעִים יוֹם
וְאַרְבָּעִים לַיְלָה לֶחֶם לֹא אָכַל וּמַיִם לֹא
שָׁתָה וַיִּכְתֹּב עַל־הַלֻּחֹת אֵת דִּבְרֵי הַבְּרִית
עֲשֶׂרֶת הַדְּבָרִים׃

29 וַיְהִי בְּרֶדֶת מֹשֶׁה מֵהַר סִינַי וּשְׁנֵי לֻחֹת
הָעֵדֻת בְּיַד־מֹשֶׁה בְּרִדְתּוֹ מִן־הָהָר וּמֹשֶׁה
לֹא־יָדַע כִּי קָרַן עוֹר פָּנָיו בְּדַבְּרוֹ אִתּוֹ׃
30 וַיַּרְא אַהֲרֹן וְכָל־בְּנֵי יִשְׂרָאֵל אֶת־מֹשֶׁה
וְהִנֵּה קָרַן עוֹר פָּנָיו וַיִּירְאוּ מִגֶּשֶׁת אֵלָיו׃

27. with you and with Israel This unexpected placing of Moses before Israel reflects his role as the dominant figure in dealing with the apostasy and in successfully interceding with God on Israel's behalf. It signals the transition to the final episode, which concentrates on Moses' exaltation.

28. The first half of this verse is the scriptural way of describing Moses' withdrawal into solitude at the onset of his experience on the mountain.

forty A symbolic number in the Bible, often associated with purification and the purging of sin.

wrote down In light of verse 1, the subject of the verb may be God.

the Ten Commandments The Hebrew phrase *aseret ha-d'varim* is also the formal title given in Deut. 4:13 and 10:4. See the introduction to Exod. 20.

THE RADIANCE OF MOSES' FACE (vv. 29–35)

Moses descends the mountain carrying the two inscribed tablets that bear witness to the renewal of the covenant between God and the people Israel. On his face is an awe-inspiring radiance emitted as the afterglow of his encounter with the splendor of the divine Presence. It reaffirms his role as the unique intimate of God, the sole and singular mediator between God and His people; it also testifies to the restoration of divine favor to Israel. As such, the narrative forms a fitting conclusion to the entire episode of the Golden Calf. It further serves as an appropriate transition to the last segment of the Book of Exodus—the account of the construction of the tabernacle that is to symbolize the presence of God in the midst of the people Israel.

29. tablets of the Pact See Comment to 25:16.

was radiant A unique phenomenon conveyed by a unique Hebrew verb *karan.* The word *keren* means both "a ray of light" and "a horn." The latter is the source of Michelangelo's portrayal of a "horned" Moses. (It is interesting to note that horns were associated with divinity in Mesopotamia and Canaan, where the gods were portrayed with horned helmets.) Numerous biblical passages bear witness to a widespread poetic notion of God enveloped in light. Moses' radiance is a reflection of the divine radiance.

27. in accordance with Hebrew: *al pi,* literally "by the mouth of"; understood by the Sages to mean "orally" and to refer to an oral Torah that accompanied the written Torah. This oral Torah (*torah she-b'al peh*) serves to illuminate obscurities, harmonize contradictions, and, in general, make possible the practical application of the written Torah's laws in everyday life.

28. forty days and forty nights The Midrash tells the story of a prominent rabbi named Yoḥanan who sold his family's vineyard to finance his studies of Torah. He explained, "I exchanged something that took six days to fashion (real property in this world, as described in Gen. 1) for something that took forty days to fashion" (Exod. R. 47:5).

him. 31But Moses called to them, and Aaron and all the chieftains in the assembly returned to him, and Moses spoke to them. 32Afterward all the Israelites came near, and he instructed them concerning all that the LORD had imparted to him on Mount Sinai. 33And when Moses had finished speaking with them, he put a veil over his face.

34Whenever Moses went in before the LORD to speak with Him, he would leave the veil off until he came out; and when he came out and told the Israelites what he had been commanded, 35the Israelites would see how radiant the skin of Moses' face was. Moses would then put the veil back over his face until he went in to speak with Him.

31 וַיִּקְרָ֤א אֲלֵהֶם֙ מֹשֶׁ֔ה וַיָּשֻׁ֥בוּ אֵלָ֛יו אַהֲרֹ֥ן
וְכָל־הַנְּשִׂאִ֖ים בָּעֵדָ֑ה וַיְדַבֵּ֥ר מֹשֶׁ֖ה אֲלֵהֶֽם׃
32 וְאַחֲרֵי־כֵ֥ן נִגְּשׁ֖וּ כָּל־בְּנֵ֣י יִשְׂרָאֵ֑ל וַיְצַוֵּ֗ם
אֵת֩ כָּל־אֲשֶׁ֨ר דִּבֶּ֧ר יְהוָ֛ה אִתּ֖וֹ בְּהַ֥ר סִינָֽי׃
מפטיר 33 וַיְכַ֣ל מֹשֶׁ֔ה מִדַּבֵּ֖ר אִתָּ֑ם וַיִּתֵּ֥ן עַל־פָּנָ֖יו
מַסְוֶֽה׃
34 וּבְבֹ֨א מֹשֶׁ֜ה לִפְנֵ֤י יְהוָה֙ לְדַבֵּ֣ר אִתּ֔וֹ יָסִ֥יר
אֶת־הַמַּסְוֶ֖ה עַד־צֵאת֑וֹ וְיָצָ֗א וְדִבֶּר֙ אֶל־בְּנֵ֣י
יִשְׂרָאֵ֔ל אֵ֖ת אֲשֶׁ֥ר יְצֻוֶּֽה׃ 35 וְרָא֤וּ בְנֵֽי־
יִשְׂרָאֵל֙ אֶת־פְּנֵ֣י מֹשֶׁ֔ה כִּ֣י קָרַ֔ן ע֖וֹר פְּנֵ֣י
מֹשֶׁ֑ה וְהֵשִׁ֨יב מֹשֶׁ֤ה אֶת־הַמַּסְוֶה֙ עַל־פָּנָ֔יו
עַד־בֹּא֖וֹ לְדַבֵּ֥ר אִתּֽוֹ׃ ס

31–35. In the immediate presence of God, Moses' radiance is replenished. When he mediates the word of God to the people, his radiance serves to authenticate the divine source of the message. On neither occasion would a veil be appropriate, for it would interfere with his effectiveness as a leader. In his capacity as a private individual, however, Moses veils his face as a matter of course.

הפטרת כי תשא

HAFTARAH FOR KI TISSA

1 KINGS 18:1–39 (*Ashk'nazim*)
1 KINGS 18:20–39 (*S'fardim*)

This *haftarah* focuses on a dramatic contest between the prophet Elijah and the prophets of Baal. It is the climax to three years of drought brought upon the land as punishment for the pagan practices fostered by King Ahab (871–852 B.C.E.) and his wife, Jezebel. Elijah, to conclusively dramatize before the nation the superiority of God and the folly of pagan nature worship, challenges Ahab to gather the prophets of Baal and of Asherah on Mount Carmel. These prophets beseech Baal to ignite their altar, ranting and raving without success. When the ancestral God of Israel miraculously answers Elijah with fire, the people twice proclaim: "The LORD alone is God."

The *haftarah* ends with this liturgical credo. It does not include the subsequent verses (18:40–45) about the slaughter of the false prophets or the downpour that fulfills the opening prophecy. In this way the reading emphasizes the defeat of false worship and the ecstatic conversion of the people back to God alone.

Ashk'nazim read both the contest and its prologue as the *haftarah* (18:1–39). *S'fardim* read only the contest of faith (18:20–39).

By first pouring water on the altar, Elijah heightens the drama and apparently also mocks a magical practice of pouring water on the ground to induce rain. Thus a divine miracle, contrasted with a magical ritual, highlights the power of God over nature. In a similar contrast, the prophets of Baal cut themselves and spill their blood as a means of manipulating their god. The God of Israel is moved by the words of prayer, not by the wounds of the flesh.

The word *kol* (voice) is used ironically in this text. Elijah (18:27) mocks his prophetic foes by telling them to "shout louder" (*kir·u v'kol gadol*), for perhaps Baal is asleep or otherwise occupied. But there is no sound (*kol*) from Baal, no response. This pun hinges on the fact that *kol* also means "thunderclap," the very signature in sound of Baal, the god of rain, who is said to ride the clouds as his chariot. The phrase *ein kol* (there was no sound) thus makes a polemical point: There is no god of thunder.

The contrasting positive credal formula, "The LORD alone is God" (*YHVH hu ha-Elohim*), is the climax of the drama. Elijah tauntingly plays with words in this phrase when he urges the pagan priests to "Shout louder! After all, he is a god" (*ki elohim hu,* v. 27). This contrasts sharply with Elijah's appeal to the Lord, "Let it be known (*yivada*) that you are God (*ki attah elohim*) in Israel" (v. 37), as well as with the people's credo of faith in the God of Israel (*YHVH hu ha-Elohim*) in verse 39. Similar credos are found in Ps. 100:3 and 1 Kings 8:60.

The spiritual fickleness of the people and the struggle of their leaders to teach them to know and acknowledge God are themes that permeate the Hebrew Bible. In this *haftarah,* the credo and renewed faith are asserted only after the people, who have been hopping between theologies like a bird among branches (1 Kings 18:21), overcome their ambivalence.

RELATION OF THE *HAFTARAH* TO THE *PARASHAH*

These readings from the Torah and from the Prophets join two moments of betrayal in ancient Israelite religious history: The apostasy of the people before the Golden Calf in the wilderness and the later worship of the Baals of the Land. Both required the intercession of a leader to restore true worship. Both Moses and Elijah ascend a mountain and zealously fight apostasy, invoking ancestors in prayer (Exod. 32:13; 1 Kings 18:20–

21,36). Both are the agents of a covenantal affirmation by the people (Exod. 24:7; 1 Kings 18:39), and both force the people to make a choice for God and to destroy the sinners (Exod. 32:26–29; 1 Kings 18:40).

In linking the *parashah* and the *haftarah,* the Sages produced a searing indictment of idolatry. The Torah narrative mocks the impatience of the crowd, and juxtaposes the words on the Tablets with the visible form of the Calf. The prophetic passage derides the indecision of the masses and contrasts the prayer of the pagans with Elijah's prophetic voice. Through this connection of the two texts, the Sages stress that the sin at Sinai was not only a perversion of the past but also endures as an ever present danger. In both cases, the anxieties caused by divine absence and earthly needs may threaten monotheism at its core. These liturgical readings are a warning and a proclamation of divine transcendence for the community of faith.

18 Much later, in the third year, the word
of the LORD came to Elijah: "Go, appear before
Ahab; then I will send rain upon the earth."
2 Thereupon Elijah set out to appear before
Ahab.

The famine was severe in Samaria. 3 Ahab had
summoned Obadiah, the steward of the palace.
(Obadiah revered the LORD greatly. 4 When Jezebel was killing off the prophets of the LORD,
Obadiah had taken a hundred prophets and
hidden them, fifty to a cave, and provided them
with food and drink.) 5 And Ahab had said to
Obadiah, "Go through the land, to all the
springs of water and to all the wadis. Perhaps
we shall find some grass to keep horses and
mules alive, so that we are not left without
beasts."

6 They divided the country between them to
explore it, Ahab going alone in one direction
and Obadiah going alone in another direction.
7 Obadiah was on the road, when Elijah suddenly
confronted him. [Obadiah] recognized him
and flung himself on his face, saying, "Is that
you, my lord Elijah?" 8 "Yes, it is I," he answered.
"Go tell your lord: Elijah is here!" 9 But he said,
"What wrong have I done, that you should hand
your servant over to Ahab to be killed? 10 As the
LORD your God lives, there is no nation or kingdom to which my lord has not sent to look for
you; and when they said, 'He is not here,' he
made that kingdom or nation swear that you

יח וַיְהִי֙ יָמִ֣ים רַבִּ֔ים וּדְבַר־יְהוָ֗ה הָיָה֙
אֶל־אֵ֣לִיָּ֔הוּ בַּשָּׁנָ֥ה הַשְּׁלִישִׁ֖ית לֵאמֹ֑ר לֵ֚ךְ
הֵרָאֵ֣ה אֶל־אַחְאָ֔ב וְאֶתְּנָ֥ה מָטָ֖ר עַל־פְּנֵ֥י
הָאֲדָמָֽה׃ 2 וַיֵּ֙לֶךְ֙ אֵֽלִיָּ֔הוּ לְהֵרָא֖וֹת אֶל־
אַחְאָ֑ב
וְהָרָעָ֖ב חָזָ֥ק בְּשֹׁמְרֽוֹן׃ 3 וַיִּקְרָ֣א אַחְאָ֔ב
אֶל־עֹבַדְיָ֖הוּ אֲשֶׁ֣ר עַל־הַבָּ֑יִת וְעֹבַדְיָ֗הוּ
הָיָ֥ה יָרֵ֛א אֶת־יְהוָ֖ה מְאֹֽד׃ 4 וַיְהִי֙ בְּהַכְרִ֣ית
אִיזֶ֔בֶל אֵ֖ת נְבִיאֵ֣י יְהוָ֑ה וַיִּקַּ֨ח עֹבַדְיָ֜הוּ
מֵאָ֣ה נְבִאִ֗ים וַֽיַּחְבִּיאֵ֞ם חֲמִשִּׁ֥ים אִישׁ֙
בַּמְּעָרָ֔ה וְכִלְכְּלָ֖ם לֶ֥חֶם וָמָֽיִם׃ 5 וַיֹּ֤אמֶר
אַחְאָב֙ אֶל־עֹ֣בַדְיָ֔הוּ לֵ֤ךְ בָּאָ֙רֶץ֙ אֶל־כָּל־
מַעְיְנֵ֣י הַמַּ֔יִם וְאֶ֖ל כָּל־הַנְּחָלִ֑ים אוּלַ֣י ׀
נִמְצָ֣א חָצִ֗יר וּנְחַיֶּה֙ ס֣וּס וָפֶ֔רֶד וְל֥וֹא נַכְרִ֖ית
מֵהַבְּהֵמָֽה׃
6 וַיְחַלְּק֣וּ לָהֶ֔ם אֶת־הָאָ֖רֶץ לַעֲבָר־בָּ֑הּ
אַחְאָ֞ב הָלַ֙ךְ בְּדֶ֤רֶךְ אֶחָד֙ לְבַדּ֔וֹ וְעֹבַדְיָ֛הוּ
הָלַ֥ךְ בְּדֶרֶךְ־אֶחָ֖ד לְבַדּֽוֹ׃ 7 וַיְהִ֤י עֹבַדְיָ֙הוּ֙
בַּדֶּ֔רֶךְ וְהִנֵּ֥ה אֵלִיָּ֖הוּ לִקְרָאת֑וֹ וַיַּכִּרֵ֙הוּ֙ וַיִּפֹּ֣ל
עַל־פָּנָ֔יו וַיֹּ֕אמֶר הַאַתָּ֥ה זֶ֖ה אֲדֹנִ֥י אֵלִיָּֽהוּ׃
8 וַיֹּ֥אמֶר ל֖וֹ אָ֑נִי לֵ֛ךְ אֱמֹ֥ר לַאדֹנֶ֖יךָ הִנֵּ֥ה
אֵלִיָּֽהוּ׃ 9 וַיֹּ֖אמֶר מֶ֣ה חָטָ֑אתִי כִּֽי־אַתָּ֞ה
נֹתֵ֧ן אֶֽת־עַבְדְּךָ֛ בְּיַד־אַחְאָ֖ב לַהֲמִיתֵֽנִי׃
10 חַ֣י ׀ יְהוָ֣ה אֱלֹהֶ֗יךָ אִם־יֶשׁ־גּ֤וֹי וּמַמְלָכָה֙
אֲשֶׁ֨ר לֹא־שָׁלַ֤ח אֲדֹנִי֙ שָׁ֣ם לְבַקֶּשְׁךָ֔ וְאָמְר֖וּ
אָ֑יִן וְהִשְׁבִּ֤יעַ אֶת־הַמַּמְלָכָה֙ וְאֶת־הַגּ֔וֹי כִּ֖י

could not be found. 11And now you say, 'Go tell
your lord: Elijah is here!' 12When I leave you,
the spirit of the LORD will carry you off I don't
know where; and when I come and tell Ahab
and he does not find you, he will kill me. Yet
your servant has revered the LORD from my
youth. 13My lord has surely been told what I
did when Jezebel was killing the prophets of
the LORD, how I hid a hundred of the prophets
of the LORD, fifty men to a cave, and provided
them with food and drink. 14And now you say,
'Go tell your lord: Elijah is here.' Why, he will
kill me!"

15Elijah replied, "As the LORD of Hosts lives,
whom I serve, I will appear before him this very
day."

16Obadiah went to find Ahab, and informed
him; and Ahab went to meet Elijah. 17When
Ahab caught sight of Elijah, Ahab said to him,
"Is that you, you troubler of Israel?" 18He retorted, "It is not I who have brought trouble on
Israel, but you and your father's House, by forsaking the commandments of the LORD and going after the Baalim. 19Now summon all Israel
to join me at Mount Carmel, together with the
four hundred and fifty prophets of Baal and the
four hundred prophets of Asherah, who eat at
Jezebel's table."

20Ahab sent orders to all the Israelites and
gathered the prophets at Mount Carmel. 21Eli-
jah approached all the people and said, "How
long will you keep hopping between two opinions? If the LORD is God, follow Him; and if Baal,
follow him!" But the people answered him not
a word. 22Then Elijah said to the people, "I am
the only prophet of the LORD left, while the
prophets of Baal are four hundred and fifty men.
23Let two young bulls be given to us. Let them
choose one bull, cut it up, and lay it on the wood,

לֹא יִמְצָאֶכָּה*׃ 11 וְעַתָּה אַתָּה אֹמֵר לֵךְ
אֱמֹר לַאדֹנֶיךָ הִנֵּה אֵלִיָּהוּ׃ 12 וְהָיָה אֲנִי ׀
אֵלֵךְ מֵאִתָּךְ וְרוּחַ יְהוָה ׀ יִשָּׂאֲךָ עַל אֲשֶׁר
לֹא־אֵדָע וּבָאתִי לְהַגִּיד לְאַחְאָב וְלֹא
יִמְצָאֲךָ וַהֲרָגָנִי וְעַבְדְּךָ יָרֵא אֶת־יְהוָה
מִנְּעֻרָי׃ 13 הֲלֹא־הֻגַּד לַאדֹנִי אֵת אֲשֶׁר־
עָשִׂיתִי בַּהֲרֹג אִיזֶבֶל אֵת נְבִיאֵי יְהוָה
וָאַחְבִּא מִנְּבִיאֵי יְהוָה מֵאָה אִישׁ חֲמִשִּׁים
חֲמִשִּׁים אִישׁ בַּמְּעָרָה וָאֲכַלְכְּלֵם לֶחֶם
וָמָיִם׃ 14 וְעַתָּה אַתָּה אֹמֵר לֵךְ אֱמֹר
לַאדֹנֶיךָ הִנֵּה אֵלִיָּהוּ וַהֲרָגָנִי׃ ס
15 וַיֹּאמֶר אֵלִיָּהוּ חַי יְהוָה צְבָאוֹת אֲשֶׁר
עָמַדְתִּי לְפָנָיו כִּי הַיּוֹם אֵרָאֶה אֵלָיו׃
16 וַיֵּלֶךְ עֹבַדְיָהוּ לִקְרַאת אַחְאָב וַיַּגֶּד־לוֹ
וַיֵּלֶךְ אַחְאָב לִקְרַאת אֵלִיָּהוּ׃ 17 וַיְהִי
כִּרְאוֹת אַחְאָב אֶת־אֵלִיָּהוּ וַיֹּאמֶר אַחְאָב
אֵלָיו הַאַתָּה זֶה עֹכֵר יִשְׂרָאֵל׃ 18 וַיֹּאמֶר
לֹא עָכַרְתִּי אֶת־יִשְׂרָאֵל כִּי אִם־אַתָּה
וּבֵית אָבִיךָ בַּעֲזָבְכֶם אֶת־מִצְוֺת יְהוָה
וַתֵּלֶךְ אַחֲרֵי הַבְּעָלִים׃ 19 וְעַתָּה שְׁלַח קְבֹץ
אֵלַי אֶת־כָּל־יִשְׂרָאֵל אֶל־הַר הַכַּרְמֶל
וְאֶת־נְבִיאֵי הַבַּעַל אַרְבַּע מֵאוֹת וַחֲמִשִּׁים
וּנְבִיאֵי הָאֲשֵׁרָה אַרְבַּע מֵאוֹת אֹכְלֵי
שֻׁלְחַן אִיזָבֶל׃

20 וַיִּשְׁלַח אַחְאָב בְּכָל־בְּנֵי יִשְׂרָאֵל וַיִּקְבֹּץ
אֶת־הַנְּבִיאִים אֶל־הַר הַכַּרְמֶל׃ 21 וַיִּגַּשׁ
אֵלִיָּהוּ אֶל־כָּל־הָעָם וַיֹּאמֶר עַד־מָתַי אַתֶּם
פֹּסְחִים עַל־שְׁתֵּי הַסְּעִפִּים אִם־יְהוָה
הָאֱלֹהִים לְכוּ אַחֲרָיו וְאִם־הַבַּעַל לְכוּ
אַחֲרָיו וְלֹא־עָנוּ הָעָם אֹתוֹ דָּבָר׃ 22 וַיֹּאמֶר
אֵלִיָּהוּ אֶל־הָעָם אֲנִי נוֹתַרְתִּי נָבִיא
לַיהוָה לְבַדִּי וּנְבִיאֵי הַבַּעַל אַרְבַּע־מֵאוֹת
וַחֲמִשִּׁים אִישׁ׃ 23 וְיִתְּנוּ־לָנוּ שְׁנַיִם פָּרִים

v. 10. יתיר ה׳

but let them not apply fire; I will prepare the other bull, and lay it on the wood, and will not apply fire. 24You will then invoke your god by name, and I will invoke the LORD by name; and let us agree: the god who responds with fire, that one is God." And all the people answered, "Very good!"

25Elijah said to the prophets of Baal, "Choose one bull and prepare it first, for you are the majority; invoke your god by name, but apply no fire." 26They took the bull that was given them; they prepared it, and invoked Baal by name from morning until noon, shouting, "O Baal, answer us!" But there was no sound, and none who responded; so they performed a hopping dance about the altar that had been set up. 27When noon came, Elijah mocked them, saying, "Shout louder! After all, he is a god. But he may be in conversation, he may be detained, or he may be on a journey, or perhaps he is asleep and will wake up." 28So they shouted louder, and gashed themselves with knives and spears, according to their practice, until the blood streamed over them. 29When noon passed, they kept raving until the hour of presenting the grain offering. Still there was no sound, and none who responded or heeded.

30Then Elijah said to all the people, "Come closer to me"; and all the people came closer to him. He repaired the damaged altar of the LORD. 31Then Elijah took twelve stones, corresponding to the number of the tribes of the sons of Jacob—to whom the word of the LORD had come: "Israel shall be your name"—32and with the stones he built an altar in the name of the LORD. Around the altar he made a trench large enough for two *seah*s of seed. 33He laid out the wood, and he cut up the bull and laid it on the

וְיִבְחֲרוּ לָהֶם הַפָּר הָאֶחָד וִינַתְּחֻהוּ
וְיָשִׂימוּ עַל־הָעֵצִים וְאֵשׁ לֹא יָשִׂימוּ וַאֲנִי
אֶעֱשֶׂה ׀ אֶת־הַפָּר הָאֶחָד וְנָתַתִּי עַל־
הָעֵצִים וְאֵשׁ לֹא אָשִׂים׃ 24 וּקְרָאתֶם בְּשֵׁם
אֱלֹהֵיכֶם וַאֲנִי אֶקְרָא בְשֵׁם־יְהֹוָה וְהָיָה
הָאֱלֹהִים אֲשֶׁר־יַעֲנֶה בָאֵשׁ הוּא הָאֱלֹהִים
וַיַּעַן כָּל־הָעָם וַיֹּאמְרוּ טוֹב הַדָּבָר׃
25 וַיֹּאמֶר אֵלִיָּהוּ לִנְבִיאֵי הַבַּעַל בַּחֲרוּ לָכֶם
הַפָּר הָאֶחָד וַעֲשׂוּ רִאשֹׁנָה כִּי אַתֶּם
הָרַבִּים וְקִרְאוּ בְּשֵׁם אֱלֹהֵיכֶם וְאֵשׁ לֹא
תָשִׂימוּ׃ 26 וַיִּקְחוּ אֶת־הַפָּר אֲשֶׁר־נָתַן
לָהֶם וַיַּעֲשׂוּ וַיִּקְרְאוּ בְשֵׁם־הַבַּעַל מֵהַבֹּקֶר
וְעַד־הַצָּהֳרַיִם לֵאמֹר הַבַּעַל עֲנֵנוּ וְאֵין
קוֹל וְאֵין עֹנֶה וַיְפַסְּחוּ עַל־הַמִּזְבֵּחַ אֲשֶׁר
עָשָׂה׃ 27 וַיְהִי בַצָּהֳרַיִם וַיְהַתֵּל בָּהֶם
אֵלִיָּהוּ וַיֹּאמֶר קִרְאוּ בְקוֹל־גָּדוֹל כִּי־
אֱלֹהִים הוּא כִּי שִׂיחַ וְכִי־שִׂיג לוֹ וְכִי־
דֶרֶךְ לוֹ אוּלַי יָשֵׁן הוּא וְיִקָץ*׃ 28 וַיִּקְרְאוּ
בְּקוֹל גָּדוֹל וַיִּתְגֹּדְדוּ כְּמִשְׁפָּטָם בַּחֲרָבוֹת
וּבָרְמָחִים עַד־שְׁפָךְ־דָּם עֲלֵיהֶם׃ 29 וַיְהִי
כַּעֲבֹר הַצָּהֳרַיִם וַיִּתְנַבְּאוּ עַד לַעֲלוֹת
הַמִּנְחָה וְאֵין־קוֹל וְאֵין־עֹנֶה וְאֵין קָשֶׁב׃
30 וַיֹּאמֶר אֵלִיָּהוּ לְכָל־הָעָם גְּשׁוּ אֵלַי
וַיִּגְּשׁוּ כָל־הָעָם אֵלָיו וַיְרַפֵּא אֶת־מִזְבַּח
יְהֹוָה הֶהָרוּס׃ 31 וַיִּקַּח אֵלִיָּהוּ שְׁתֵּים
עֶשְׂרֵה אֲבָנִים כְּמִסְפַּר שִׁבְטֵי בְנֵי־יַעֲקֹב
אֲשֶׁר הָיָה דְבַר־יְהֹוָה אֵלָיו לֵאמֹר יִשְׂרָאֵל
יִהְיֶה שְׁמֶךָ׃ 32 וַיִּבְנֶה אֶת־הָאֲבָנִים מִזְבֵּחַ
בְּשֵׁם יְהֹוָה וַיַּעַשׂ תְּעָלָה כְּבֵית סָאתַיִם
זֶרַע סָבִיב לַמִּזְבֵּחַ׃ 33 וַיַּעֲרֹךְ אֶת־הָעֵצִים

v. 27. חסר י׳ בשורש

1 Kings 18:24. I will invoke the LORD by name In Scripture, Abraham is the first to call upon God by His name (Gen. 12:8). Such invocations are repeatedly referred to in the Book of Psalms in connection with an appeal for divine aid (see Ps. 3:5, 102:3).

wood. ³⁴And he said, "Fill four jars with water and pour it over the burnt offering and the wood." Then he said, "Do it a second time"; and they did it a second time. "Do it a third time," he said; and they did it a third time. ³⁵The water ran down around the altar, and even the trench was filled with water.

³⁶When it was time to present the grain offering, the prophet Elijah came forward and said, "O Lord, God of Abraham, Isaac, and Israel! Let it be known today that You are God in Israel and that I am Your servant, and that I have done all these things at Your bidding. ³⁷Answer me, O Lord, answer me, that this people may know that You, O Lord, are God; for You have turned their hearts backward."

³⁸Then fire from the Lord descended and consumed the burnt offering, the wood, the stones, and the earth; and it licked up the water that was in the trench. ³⁹When they saw this, all the people flung themselves on their faces and cried out: "The Lord alone is God, The Lord alone is God!"

וַיְנַתַּח֙ אֶת־הַפָּ֔ר וַיָּ֖שֶׂם עַל־הָעֵצִֽים: ³⁴ וַיֹּ֗אמֶר מִלְא֨וּ אַרְבָּעָ֤ה כַדִּים֙ מַ֔יִם וְיִֽצְק֖וּ עַל־הָֽעֹלָ֖ה וְעַל־הָעֵצִ֑ים וַיֹּ֤אמֶר שְׁנוּ֙ וַיִּשְׁנ֔וּ וַיֹּ֥אמֶר שַׁלֵּ֖שׁוּ וַיְשַׁלֵּֽשׁוּ: ³⁵ וַיֵּלְכ֣וּ הַמַּ֔יִם סָבִ֖יב לַמִּזְבֵּ֑חַ וְגַ֥ם אֶת־הַתְּעָלָ֖ה מִלֵּא־מָֽיִם: ³⁶ וַיְהִ֣י | בַּעֲל֣וֹת הַמִּנְחָ֗ה וַיִּגַּ֨שׁ אֵלִיָּ֣הוּ הַנָּבִיא֮ וַיֹּאמַר֒ יְהֹוָ֗ה אֱלֹהֵי֙ אַבְרָהָם֙ יִצְחָ֣ק וְיִשְׂרָאֵ֔ל הַיּ֣וֹם יִוָּדַ֗ע כִּֽי־אַתָּ֧ה אֱלֹהִ֛ים בְּיִשְׂרָאֵ֖ל וַאֲנִ֣י עַבְדֶּ֑ךָ ובדבריך [וּבִדְבָֽרְךָ֔] עָשִׂ֕יתִי אֵ֥ת כָּל־הַדְּבָרִ֖ים הָאֵֽלֶּה: ³⁷ עֲנֵ֤נִי יְהֹוָה֙ עֲנֵ֔נִי וְיֵֽדְעוּ֙ הָעָ֣ם הַזֶּ֔ה כִּֽי־אַתָּ֥ה יְהֹוָ֖ה הָאֱלֹהִ֑ים וְאַתָּ֛ה הֲסִבֹּ֥תָ אֶת־לִבָּ֖ם אֲחֹרַנִּֽית: ³⁸ וַתִּפֹּ֣ל אֵשׁ־יְהֹוָ֗ה וַתֹּ֤אכַל אֶת־הָֽעֹלָה֙ וְאֶת־הָ֣עֵצִ֔ים וְאֶת־הָאֲבָנִ֖ים וְאֶת־הֶֽעָפָ֑ר וְאֶת־הַמַּ֥יִם אֲשֶׁר־בַּתְּעָלָ֖ה לִחֵֽכָה: ³⁹ וַיַּרְא֙ כָּל־הָעָ֔ם וַֽיִּפְּל֖וּ עַל־פְּנֵיהֶ֑ם וַיֹּ֣אמְר֔וּ יְהֹוָה֙ ה֣וּא הָאֱלֹהִ֔ים יְהֹוָ֖ה ה֥וּא הָאֱלֹהִֽים:

36. **Let it be known today that You are God** The Lord is challenged to manifest His power publicly, thereby showing the supremacy of Israel's national God. Similar language is found in the famous ordeal between the young David and the giant Goliath (1 Sam. 17:46).

37. **that this people may know** Specific actions that point convincingly to divine power constitute a form of proof throughout the Bible. Best known is the repeated idea that the plagues will convince both Israelite and Egyptian: They "shall know" that "I am the Lord" (see Exod. 6:7, 7:5, 10:2, 14:4).

for You have turned their hearts backward This phrase is theologically difficult, because it suggests that God was the cause of Israel's waywardness. Rabbinic tradition resisted the plain sense of this passage—reinterpreting the phrase to say that, despite divine efforts, the people bear responsibility for their actions. Thus: God "turned their hearts" for goodness, but (reading the text as elliptical) the people rebelliously turned "backward." Alternatively, perhaps the prophet's re-

mark is an expression of despair, when faced with the unfathomable mystery of human sin and resistance to repentance (M. Greenberg).

39. **The Lord alone is God** Hebrew: *YHVH hu ha-Elohim*. This proclamation is the quintessential expression of monotheism. The pronoun ("He") has an emphatic thrust. Its force is dramatized in the divine assertions found in late prophecy, where God Himself vaunts His power with the words: "Understand that I am He (*hu*); before Me no god was formed, and after Me none shall exist" (Isa. 43:10, cf. v. 13). The exclusivist emphasis is also found in other passages (Deut. 4:35; Isa. 45:5). This concept and this language entered Jewish liturgy. Every service of prayer, weekdays or holy days, ends with the words of *Aleinu* in which the Jew proclaims allegiance to God alone and anticipates a messianic time when all people will do likewise. At the end of the final service of *Yom Kippur* faithful Jews repeat their ancestors' words, publicly proclaiming seven times, "The Lord alone is God."

VA-YAK·HEL

35 Moses then convoked the whole Israelite community and said to them:

These are the things that the LORD has commanded you to do: 2On six days work may be done, but on the seventh day you shall have a sabbath of complete rest, holy to the LORD; whoever does any work on it shall be put to death.

ויקהל

לה וַיַּקְהֵ֣ל מֹשֶׁ֗ה אֶֽת־כָּל־עֲדַ֛ת בְּנֵ֥י
יִשְׂרָאֵ֖ל וַיֹּ֣אמֶר אֲלֵהֶ֑ם
אֵ֚לֶּה הַדְּבָרִ֔ים אֲשֶׁר־צִוָּ֥ה יְהוָ֖ה לַעֲשֹׂ֥ת
אֹתָֽם׃ 2 שֵׁ֣שֶׁת יָמִים֮ תֵּעָשֶׂ֣ה מְלָאכָה֒
וּבַיּ֣וֹם הַשְּׁבִיעִ֗י יִהְיֶ֨ה לָכֶ֥ם קֹ֛דֶשׁ שַׁבַּ֥ת
שַׁבָּת֖וֹן לַיהוָ֑ה כָּל־הָעֹשֶׂ֥ה ב֛וֹ מְלָאכָ֖ה

THE TABERNACLE, PART II: CONSTRUCTION (35:1–40:38)

See Comment prior to the start of Part I (25:1).

THE CONVENING OF THE PEOPLE (35:1–19)

The covenant between God and Israel has been renewed (Exod. 34), and the construction of the tabernacle proceeds. God's previous instructions about constructing the tabernacle concluded with the law of *Shabbat* rest (31:12ff.). That narrative now continues with the same theme. See Comments to 31:12–17.

1. whole Israelite community The construction of the tabernacle is to be an enterprise that will involve all the Israelites.

2–3. The injunction is a repetition, with slight variations, of 31:15.

This relatively brief *parashah* is almost entirely a recapitulation of the instructions for fashioning the tabernacle and its furnishings. This is puzzling to commentators, who are accustomed to the Torah being sparing in its use of words. One commentator suggests that God so loved the idea of having a permanent home amid the Israelites that the details were repeated. Another suggests that the earlier version of the instructions represents God's commands, reflecting the enthusiasm descending from on high for this link with God; and that this version represents Israel's carrying out those commands, showing the corresponding enthusiasm welling up from below.

There is a tradition that the sin of the Golden Calf and God's forgiving the people happened on *Yom Kippur,* the great annual day of forgiveness and reconciliation. Based on that tradition, Rashi sees the events of *Va-yak·hel* taking place on the day after *Yom Kippur.* Moses urges the people to translate their sense of a renewed relationship with God, of having been cleansed and forgiven, into action by keeping *Shabbat* (vv. 2–3), and by contributing to the fashioning of the tabernacle (v. 5ff.).

CHAPTER 35

1. convoked The verb translated here as "convoked" (*hak·hel*) is used only for assembling human beings. Other verbs are used for gathering herds of animals.

the whole Israelite community This is to restore the sense of unity and shared purpose that had existed at Mount Sinai, before the incident of the Golden Calf introduced divisiveness and disillusionment (*Eretz Ḥemdah*). Rabbinic tradition has it that the Second Temple was destroyed because of baseless hatred of one Jew for another (*sin·at ḥinnam*). Moses gathers the people together for the enterprise of establishing the sanctuary so that it will rest on a base of Jewish unity. "Every Jew depends on . . . fellow Jews for the energy, resources, and courage wherewith to be a Jew" (M. Kaplan).

2. shall be put to death One commentator would not take these words literally. He understood them to mean that those who ignore *Shabbat* forfeit their souls. That is, they become dead to the spiritual dimension of life (J. Eybeschütz). According to Jewish lore, on *Shabbat* a person acquires an additional, deeper soul (*n'shamah y'terah*). At *Shabbat*'s end, it is taken away, to be restored the following *Shabbat.* A person who makes no distinction between *Shabbat* and the weekday forfeits that gift.

3You shall kindle no fire throughout your settlements on the sabbath day.

4Moses said further to the whole community of Israelites:

This is what the LORD has commanded: 5Take from among you gifts to the LORD; everyone whose heart so moves him shall bring them— gifts for the LORD: gold, silver, and copper; 6blue, purple, and crimson yarns, fine linen, and goats' hair; 7tanned ram skins, dolphin skins, and acacia wood; 8oil for lighting, spices for the anointing oil and for the aromatic incense; 9lapis lazuli and other stones for setting, for the ephod and the breastpiece.

10And let all among you who are skilled come and make all that the LORD has commanded: 11the Tabernacle, its tent and its covering, its clasps and its planks, its bars, its posts, and its sockets; 12the ark and its poles, the cover, and the curtain for the screen; 13the table, and its poles and all its utensils; and the bread of display; 14the lampstand for lighting, its furnish-

יוּמָת: 3 לֹא־תְבַעֲר֣וּ אֵ֔שׁ בְּכֹ֖ל מֹשְׁבֹֽתֵיכֶ֑ם
בְּי֖וֹם הַשַּׁבָּֽת: פ

4 וַיֹּ֣אמֶר מֹשֶׁ֔ה אֶל־כָּל־עֲדַ֥ת בְּנֵֽי־יִשְׂרָאֵ֖ל
לֵאמֹֽר

זֶ֣ה הַדָּבָ֔ר אֲשֶׁר־צִוָּ֥ה יְהֹוָ֖ה לֵאמֹֽר: 5 קְח֣וּ
מֵֽאִתְּכֶ֤ם תְּרוּמָה֙ לַֽיהֹוָ֔ה כֹּ֚ל נְדִ֣יב לִבּ֔וֹ
יְבִיאֶ֕הָ אֵ֖ת תְּרוּמַ֣ת יְהֹוָ֑ה זָהָ֥ב וָכֶ֖סֶף
וּנְחֹֽשֶׁת: 6 וּתְכֵ֧לֶת וְאַרְגָּמָ֛ן וְתוֹלַ֥עַת שָׁנִ֖י
וְשֵׁ֥שׁ וְעִזִּֽים: 7 וְעֹרֹ֨ת אֵילִ֧ם מְאׇדָּמִ֛ים
וְעֹרֹ֥ת תְּחָשִׁ֖ים וַעֲצֵ֥י שִׁטִּֽים: 8 וְשֶׁ֖מֶן
לַמָּא֑וֹר וּבְשָׂמִים֙ לְשֶׁ֣מֶן הַמִּשְׁחָ֔ה וְלִקְטֹ֖רֶת
הַסַּמִּֽים: 9 וְאַבְנֵי־שֹׁ֔הַם וְאַבְנֵ֖י מִלֻּאִ֑ים
לָאֵפ֖וֹד וְלַחֹֽשֶׁן:

10 וְכׇל־חֲכַם־לֵ֖ב בָּכֶ֑ם יָבֹ֣אוּ וְיַעֲשׂ֔וּ אֵ֖ת
כׇּל־אֲשֶׁ֥ר צִוָּ֖ה יְהֹוָֽה: 11 אֶת־הַמִּשְׁכָּ֕ן אֶת־
אׇהֳל֖וֹ וְאֶת־מִכְסֵ֑הוּ אֶת־קְרָסָיו֙ וְאֶת־
קְרָשָׁ֔יו אֶת־בְּרִיחָ֕ו אֶת־עַמֻּדָ֖יו
וְאֶת־אֲדָנָֽיו: 12 אֶת־הָאָרֹ֥ן וְאֶת־בַּדָּ֖יו אֶת־
הַכַּפֹּ֑רֶת וְאֵ֖ת פָּרֹ֥כֶת הַמָּסָֽךְ: 13 אֶת־
הַשֻּׁלְחָ֥ן וְאֶת־בַּדָּ֖יו וְאֶת־כׇּל־כֵּלָ֑יו וְאֵ֖ת
לֶ֥חֶם הַפָּנִֽים: 14 וְאֶת־מְנֹרַ֧ת הַמָּא֛וֹר וְאֶת־

---

throughout your settlements Abravanel suggests that the intent of this clause is to apply the prohibition universally, wherever Jews reside.

A CALL FOR CONTRIBUTIONS (vv. 4–19)

4–9. Moses issues a call for donations of materials in accordance with 25:1–9. He specifies the various materials and explains how they are to be used.

12. curtain for the screen See 26:31–33.

---

3. You shall kindle no fire This is interpreted to include the fire of anger. Arguments and angry shouts are as much a disruption of *Shabbat* as working and spending money.

5. everyone whose heart so moves him shall

bring them The last words of this citation read literally, "shall bring it." This prompted a comment that the people did not only bring material gifts, but brought their willing hearts (*S'fat Emet*).

HALAKHAH L'MA·ASEH
35:3. kindle no fire Lighting, extinguishing, or transferring a fire on *Shabbat* is forbidden under Jewish law. Some scholars liken electricity to fire, therefore prohibiting turning on or off all electrical devices on *Shabbat*. Others in the Conservative movement maintain that electricity is not fire according to either science or Jewish law and that it does not violate the prohibition of building on *Shabbat* (*boneh*) either, for the electrician who installed the switch is the one who built it. They, therefore, permit switching on and off a light, likening it to the permitted action of tying a temporary knot. Nevertheless, activities prohibited on other grounds—such as shaving, cooking, or doing laundry—remain prohibited even if done electrically.

כֵּלֶ֖יהָ וְאֶת־נֵרֹתֶ֑יהָ וְאֵ֖ת שֶׁ֥מֶן הַמָּאֽוֹר׃
15 וְאֶת־מִזְבַּ֤ח הַקְּטֹ֙רֶת֙ וְאֶת־בַּדָּ֔יו וְאֵת֙
שֶׁ֣מֶן הַמִּשְׁחָ֔ה וְאֵ֖ת קְטֹ֣רֶת הַסַּמִּ֑ים וְאֶת־
מָסַ֥ךְ הַפֶּ֖תַח לְפֶ֥תַח הַמִּשְׁכָּֽן׃ 16 אֵ֣ת ׀
מִזְבַּ֣ח הָעֹלָ֗ה וְאֶת־מִכְבַּ֤ר הַנְּחֹ֙שֶׁת֙ אֲשֶׁר־
ל֔וֹ אֶת־בַּדָּ֖יו וְאֶת־כָּל־כֵּלָ֑יו אֶת־הַכִּיֹּ֖ר
וְאֶת־כַּנּֽוֹ׃ 17 אֵ֣ת קַלְעֵ֤י הֶֽחָצֵר֙ אֶת־עַמֻּדָ֣יו
וְאֶת־אֲדָנֶ֑יהָ וְאֵ֕ת מָסַ֖ךְ שַׁ֥עַר הֶחָצֵֽר׃
18 אֶת־יִתְדֹ֤ת הַמִּשְׁכָּן֙ וְאֶת־יִתְדֹ֥ת הֶחָצֵ֖ר
וְאֶת־מֵיתְרֵיהֶֽם׃ 19 אֶת־בִּגְדֵ֥י הַשְּׂרָ֖ד
לְשָׁרֵ֣ת בַּקֹּ֑דֶשׁ אֶת־בִּגְדֵ֤י הַקֹּ֙דֶשׁ֙ לְאַהֲרֹ֣ן
הַכֹּהֵ֔ן וְאֶת־בִּגְדֵ֥י בָנָ֖יו לְכַהֵֽן׃
20 וַיֵּצְא֛וּ כָּל־עֲדַ֥ת בְּנֵֽי־יִשְׂרָאֵ֖ל מִלִּפְנֵ֥י
שני מֹשֶֽׁה׃ 21 וַיָּבֹ֕אוּ כָּל־אִ֖ישׁ אֲשֶׁר־נְשָׂא֣וֹ לִבּ֑וֹ
וְכֹ֡ל אֲשֶׁר֩ נָדְבָ֨ה רוּח֜וֹ אֹת֗וֹ הֵ֠בִיאוּ אֶת־
תְּרוּמַ֨ת יְהוָ֜ה לִמְלֶ֨אכֶת אֹ֤הֶל מוֹעֵד֙
וּלְכָל־עֲבֹ֣דָת֔וֹ וּלְבִגְדֵ֖י הַקֹּֽדֶשׁ׃ 22 וַיָּבֹ֥אוּ
הָאֲנָשִׁ֖ים עַל־הַנָּשִׁ֑ים כֹּ֣ל ׀ נְדִ֣יב לֵ֗ב הֵ֠בִיאוּ
חָ֣ח וָנֶ֜זֶם וְטַבַּ֤עַת וְכוּמָז֙ כָּל־כְּלִ֣י זָהָ֔ב
וְכָל־אִ֕ישׁ אֲשֶׁ֥ר הֵנִ֛יף תְּנוּפַ֥ת זָהָ֖ב לַיהוָֽה׃
23 וְכָל־אִ֞ישׁ אֲשֶׁר־נִמְצָ֣א אִתּ֗וֹ תְּכֵ֧לֶת
וְאַרְגָּמָ֛ן וְתוֹלַ֥עַת שָׁנִ֖י וְשֵׁ֣שׁ וְעִזִּ֑ים וְעֹרֹ֨ת
אֵילִ֧ם מְאָדָּמִ֛ים וְעֹרֹ֥ת תְּחָשִׁ֖ים הֵבִֽיאוּ׃
24 כָּל־מֵרִ֗ים תְּר֤וּמַת כֶּ֙סֶף֙ וּנְחֹ֔שֶׁת הֵבִ֕יאוּ
אֵ֖ת תְּרוּמַ֣ת יְהוָ֑ה וְכֹ֡ל אֲשֶׁר֩ נִמְצָ֨א אִתּ֜וֹ
עֲצֵ֥י שִׁטִּ֛ים לְכָל־מְלֶ֥אכֶת הָעֲבֹדָ֖ה הֵבִֽיאוּ׃
25 וְכָל־אִשָּׁ֥ה חַכְמַת־לֵ֖ב בְּיָדֶ֣יהָ טָו֑וּ
וַיָּבִ֣יאוּ מַטְוֶ֗ה אֶֽת־הַתְּכֵ֙לֶת֙ וְאֶת־הָֽאַרְגָּמָ֔ן

ings and its lamps, and the oil for lighting; 15the altar of incense and its poles; the anointing oil and the aromatic incense; and the entrance screen for the entrance of the Tabernacle; 16the altar of burnt offering, its copper grating, its poles, and all its furnishings; the laver and its stand; 17the hangings of the enclosure, its posts and its sockets, and the screen for the gate of the court; 18the pegs for the Tabernacle, the pegs for the enclosure, and their cords; 19the service vestments for officiating in the sanctuary, the sacral vestments of Aaron the priest and the vestments of his sons for priestly service.

20So the whole community of the Israelites left Moses' presence. 21And everyone who excelled in ability and everyone whose spirit moved him came, bringing to the LORD his offering for the work of the Tent of Meeting and for all its service and for the sacral vestments. 22Men and women, all whose hearts moved them, all who would make an elevation offering of gold to the LORD, came bringing brooches, earrings, rings, and pendants—gold objects of all kinds. 23And everyone who had in his possession blue, purple, and crimson yarns, fine linen, goats' hair, tanned ram skins, and dolphin skins, brought them; 24everyone who would make gifts of silver or copper brought them as gifts for the LORD; and everyone who had in his possession acacia wood for any work of the service brought that. 25And all the skilled women spun with their own hands, and brought what they had spun, in blue, purple,

15. entrance screen The curtain that partitions off the Holy Place (the outer sanctum) from the outer court (see 26:36–37).

17. screen for the gate of the court The curtain on the east side, at the entrance from the outer perimeter (see 27:9–19; especially v. 16).

THE PEOPLE'S RESPONSE (vv. 20–29)

The people—men and women alike—respond with great generosity to Moses' call and freely contribute their most precious possessions as well as their skilled services.

---

25. skilled women Throughout our history, devoted Jewish women have contributed to *hiddur mitzvah*—the practice of giving the *mitzvot* an esthetically pleasing context in their homes and synagogues—through the skilled and creative work of their hands.

[8]Then all the skilled among those engaged in the work made the Tabernacle of ten strips of cloth, which they made of fine twisted linen, blue, purple, and crimson yarns; into these they worked a design of cherubim. [9]The length of each cloth was twenty-eight cubits, and the width of each cloth was four cubits, all cloths having the same measurements. [10]They joined five of the cloths to one another, and they joined the other five cloths to one another. [11]They made loops of blue wool on the edge of the outermost cloth of the one set, and did the same on the edge of the outermost cloth of the other set: [12]they made fifty loops on the one cloth, and they made fifty loops on the edge of the end cloth of the other set, the loops being opposite one another. [13]And they made fifty gold clasps and coupled the units to one another with the clasps, so that the Tabernacle became one whole.

[14]They made cloths of goats' hair for a tent over the Tabernacle; they made the cloths eleven in number. [15]The length of each cloth was thirty cubits, and the width of each cloth was four cubits, the eleven cloths having the same measurements. [16]They joined five of the cloths by themselves, and the other six cloths by themselves. [17]They made fifty loops on the edge of the outermost cloth of the one set, and they made fifty loops on the edge of the end cloth of the other set. [18]They made fifty copper clasps to couple the Tent together so that it might become one whole. [19]And they made a covering of tanned ram skins for the tent, and a covering of dolphin skins above.

רביעי 8 וַיַּעֲשׂוּ כָל־חֲכַם־לֵב בְּעֹשֵׂי הַמְּלָאכָה
אֶת־הַמִּשְׁכָּן עֶשֶׂר יְרִיעֹת שֵׁשׁ מָשְׁזָר
וּתְכֵלֶת וְאַרְגָּמָן וְתוֹלַעַת שָׁנִי כְּרֻבִים
מַעֲשֵׂה חֹשֵׁב עָשָׂה אֹתָם׃ 9 אֹרֶךְ הַיְרִיעָה
הָאַחַת שְׁמֹנֶה וְעֶשְׂרִים בָּאַמָּה וְרֹחַב
אַרְבַּע בָּאַמָּה הַיְרִיעָה הָאֶחָת מִדָּה
אַחַת לְכָל־הַיְרִיעֹת׃ 10 וַיְחַבֵּר אֶת־חֲמֵשׁ
הַיְרִיעֹת אַחַת אֶל־אֶחָת וְחָמֵשׁ יְרִיעֹת
חִבַּר אַחַת אֶל־אֶחָת׃ 11 וַיַּעַשׂ לֻלְאֹת
תְּכֵלֶת עַל שְׂפַת הַיְרִיעָה הָאֶחָת מִקָּצָה
בַּמַּחְבָּרֶת כֵּן עָשָׂה בִּשְׂפַת הַיְרִיעָה
הַקִּיצוֹנָה בַּמַּחְבֶּרֶת הַשֵּׁנִית׃ 12 חֲמִשִּׁים
לֻלָאֹת עָשָׂה בַּיְרִיעָה הָאֶחָת וַחֲמִשִּׁים
לֻלָאֹת עָשָׂה בִּקְצֵה הַיְרִיעָה אֲשֶׁר
בַּמַּחְבֶּרֶת הַשֵּׁנִית מַקְבִּילֹת הַלֻּלָאֹת אַחַת
אֶל־אֶחָת׃ 13 וַיַּעַשׂ חֲמִשִּׁים קַרְסֵי זָהָב
וַיְחַבֵּר אֶת־הַיְרִיעֹת אַחַת אֶל־אַחַת
בַּקְּרָסִים וַיְהִי הַמִּשְׁכָּן אֶחָד׃ ס
14 וַיַּעַשׂ יְרִיעֹת עִזִּים לְאֹהֶל עַל־הַמִּשְׁכָּן
עַשְׁתֵּי־עֶשְׂרֵה יְרִיעֹת עָשָׂה אֹתָם׃ 15 אֹרֶךְ
הַיְרִיעָה הָאַחַת שְׁלֹשִׁים בָּאַמָּה וְאַרְבַּע
אַמּוֹת רֹחַב הַיְרִיעָה הָאֶחָת מִדָּה אַחַת
לְעַשְׁתֵּי עֶשְׂרֵה יְרִיעֹת׃ 16 וַיְחַבֵּר אֶת־
חֲמֵשׁ הַיְרִיעֹת לְבָד וְאֶת־שֵׁשׁ הַיְרִיעֹת
לְבָד׃ 17 וַיַּעַשׂ לֻלָאֹת חֲמִשִּׁים עַל שְׂפַת
הַיְרִיעָה הַקִּיצֹנָה בַּמַּחְבָּרֶת וַחֲמִשִּׁים
לֻלָאֹת עָשָׂה עַל־שְׂפַת הַיְרִיעָה הַחֹבֶרֶת
הַשֵּׁנִית׃ 18 וַיַּעַשׂ קַרְסֵי נְחֹשֶׁת חֲמִשִּׁים
לְחַבֵּר אֶת־הָאֹהֶל לִהְיֹת אֶחָד׃ 19 וַיַּעַשׂ
מִכְסֶה לָאֹהֶל עֹרֹת אֵלִים מְאָדָּמִים
חמישי וּמִכְסֵה עֹרֹת תְּחָשִׁים מִלְמָעְלָה׃ ס

THE WORK OF CONSTRUCTION
(36:8–38:20)

This lengthy and detailed account of the work repeats the instructions already given. The account here differs from the account in Exod. 26 in that the verbs used here indicate completed action. Furthermore, the various items listed are presented in a different sequence. The earlier instructions began with the furnishings and ended with the structure of the tabernacle; here the order is reversed.

20They made the planks for the Tabernacle
of acacia wood, upright. 21The length of each
plank was ten cubits, the width of each plank
a cubit and a half. 22Each plank had two tenons,
parallel to each other; they did the same with
all the planks of the Tabernacle. 23Of the planks
of the Tabernacle, they made twenty planks
for the south side, 24making forty silver sockets
under the twenty planks, two sockets under
one plank for its two tenons and two sockets
under each following plank for its two tenons; 25and for the other side wall of the Tabernacle, the north side, twenty planks, 26with
their forty silver sockets, two sockets under one
plank and two sockets under each following
plank. 27And for the rear of the Tabernacle, to
the west, they made six planks; 28and they made
two planks for the corners of the Tabernacle at
the rear. 29They matched at the bottom, but
terminated as one at the top into one ring;
they did so with both of them at the two corners. 30Thus there were eight planks with their
sockets of silver: sixteen sockets, two under
each plank.

31They made bars of acacia wood, five for the
planks of the one side wall of the Tabernacle,
32five bars for the planks of the other side wall
of the Tabernacle, and five bars for the planks
of the wall of the Tabernacle at the rear, to the
west; 33they made the center bar to run, halfway
up the planks, from end to end. 34They overlaid
the planks with gold, and made their rings of
gold, as holders for the bars; and they overlaid
the bars with gold.

חמישי 20 וַיַּעַשׂ אֶת־הַקְּרָשִׁים לַמִּשְׁכָּן עֲצֵי שִׁטִּים
עֹמְדִים: 21 עֶשֶׂר אַמֹּת אֹרֶךְ הַקָּרֶשׁ וְאַמָּה
וַחֲצִי הָאַמָּה רֹחַב הַקֶּרֶשׁ הָאֶחָד: 22 שְׁתֵּי
יָדֹת לַקֶּרֶשׁ הָאֶחָד מְשֻׁלָּבֹת אַחַת אֶל־
אֶחָת כֵּן עָשָׂה לְכֹל קַרְשֵׁי הַמִּשְׁכָּן:
23 וַיַּעַשׂ אֶת־הַקְּרָשִׁים לַמִּשְׁכָּן עֶשְׂרִים
קְרָשִׁים לִפְאַת נֶגֶב תֵּימָנָה: 24 וְאַרְבָּעִים
אַדְנֵי־כֶסֶף עָשָׂה תַּחַת עֶשְׂרִים הַקְּרָשִׁים
שְׁנֵי אֲדָנִים תַּחַת־הַקֶּרֶשׁ הָאֶחָד לִשְׁתֵּי
יְדֹתָיו וּשְׁנֵי אֲדָנִים תַּחַת־הַקֶּרֶשׁ הָאֶחָד
לִשְׁתֵּי יְדֹתָיו: 25 וּלְצֶלַע הַמִּשְׁכָּן הַשֵּׁנִית
לִפְאַת צָפוֹן עָשָׂה עֶשְׂרִים קְרָשִׁים:
26 וְאַרְבָּעִים אַדְנֵיהֶם כָּסֶף שְׁנֵי אֲדָנִים
תַּחַת הַקֶּרֶשׁ הָאֶחָד וּשְׁנֵי אֲדָנִים תַּחַת
הַקֶּרֶשׁ הָאֶחָד: 27 וּלְיַרְכְּתֵי הַמִּשְׁכָּן יָמָּה
עָשָׂה שִׁשָּׁה קְרָשִׁים: 28 וּשְׁנֵי קְרָשִׁים
עָשָׂה לִמְקֻצְעֹת הַמִּשְׁכָּן בַּיַּרְכָתָיִם:
29 וְהָיוּ תוֹאֲמִם מִלְּמַטָּה וְיַחְדָּו יִהְיוּ תַמִּים
אֶל־רֹאשׁוֹ אֶל־הַטַּבַּעַת הָאֶחָת כֵּן עָשָׂה
לִשְׁנֵיהֶם לִשְׁנֵי הַמִּקְצֹעֹת: 30 וְהָיוּ שְׁמֹנָה
קְרָשִׁים וְאַדְנֵיהֶם כֶּסֶף שִׁשָּׁה עָשָׂר אֲדָנִים
שְׁנֵי אֲדָנִים שְׁנֵי אֲדָנִים תַּחַת הַקֶּרֶשׁ
הָאֶחָד:
31 וַיַּעַשׂ בְּרִיחֵי עֲצֵי שִׁטִּים חֲמִשָּׁה לְקַרְשֵׁי
צֶלַע־הַמִּשְׁכָּן הָאֶחָת: 32 וַחֲמִשָּׁה בְרִיחִם
לְקַרְשֵׁי צֶלַע־הַמִּשְׁכָּן הַשֵּׁנִית וַחֲמִשָּׁה
בְרִיחִם לְקַרְשֵׁי הַמִּשְׁכָּן לַיַּרְכָתַיִם יָמָּה:
33 וַיַּעַשׂ אֶת־הַבְּרִיחַ הַתִּיכֹן לִבְרֹחַ בְּתוֹךְ
הַקְּרָשִׁים מִן־הַקָּצֶה אֶל־הַקָּצֶה: 34 וְאֶת־
הַקְּרָשִׁים צִפָּה זָהָב וְאֶת־טַבְּעֹתָם עָשָׂה
זָהָב בָּתִּים לַבְּרִיחִם וַיְצַף אֶת־הַבְּרִיחִם
זָהָב:

26. The word for "sockets" (*adanim*) is like the name of God (*Adonai*). This similarity hints to us that just as those sockets served to hold the upper and the lower sections of the tabernacle together, the divine Presence holds the upper (i.e., spiritual) and the lower (i.e., material) worlds together (Menaḥem Naḥum of Chernobyl).

8Then all the skilled among those engaged in the work made the Tabernacle of ten strips of cloth, which they made of fine twisted linen, blue, purple, and crimson yarns; into these they worked a design of cherubim. 9The length of each cloth was twenty-eight cubits, and the width of each cloth was four cubits, all cloths having the same measurements. 10They joined five of the cloths to one another, and they joined the other five cloths to one another. 11They made loops of blue wool on the edge of the outermost cloth of the one set, and did the same on the edge of the outermost cloth of the other set: 12they made fifty loops on the one cloth, and they made fifty loops on the edge of the end cloth of the other set, the loops being opposite one another. 13And they made fifty gold clasps and coupled the units to one another with the clasps, so that the Tabernacle became one whole.

14They made cloths of goats' hair for a tent over the Tabernacle; they made the cloths eleven in number. 15The length of each cloth was thirty cubits, and the width of each cloth was four cubits, the eleven cloths having the same measurements. 16They joined five of the cloths by themselves, and the other six cloths by themselves. 17They made fifty loops on the edge of the outermost cloth of the one set, and they made fifty loops on the edge of the end cloth of the other set. 18They made fifty copper clasps to couple the Tent together so that it might become one whole. 19And they made a covering of tanned ram skins for the tent, and a covering of dolphin skins above.

רביעי 8 וַיַּעֲשׂוּ כָל־חֲכַם־לֵב בְּעֹשֵׂי הַמְּלָאכָה
אֶת־הַמִּשְׁכָּן עֶשֶׂר יְרִיעֹת שֵׁשׁ מָשְׁזָר
וּתְכֵלֶת וְאַרְגָּמָן וְתוֹלַעַת שָׁנִי כְּרֻבִים
מַעֲשֵׂה חֹשֵׁב עָשָׂה אֹתָם׃ 9 אֹרֶךְ הַיְרִיעָה
הָאַחַת שְׁמֹנֶה וְעֶשְׂרִים בָּאַמָּה וְרֹחַב
אַרְבַּע בָּאַמָּה הַיְרִיעָה הָאֶחָת מִדָּה
אַחַת לְכָל־הַיְרִיעֹת׃ 10 וַיְחַבֵּר אֶת־חֲמֵשׁ
הַיְרִיעֹת אַחַת אֶל־אֶחָת וְחָמֵשׁ יְרִיעֹת
חִבַּר אַחַת אֶל־אֶחָת׃ 11 וַיַּעַשׂ לֻלְאֹת
תְּכֵלֶת עַל שְׂפַת הַיְרִיעָה הָאֶחָת מִקָּצָה
בַּמַּחְבָּרֶת כֵּן עָשָׂה בִּשְׂפַת הַיְרִיעָה
הַקִּיצוֹנָה בַּמַּחְבֶּרֶת הַשֵּׁנִית׃ 12 חֲמִשִּׁים
לֻלָאֹת עָשָׂה בַּיְרִיעָה הָאֶחָת וַחֲמִשִּׁים
לֻלָאֹת עָשָׂה בִּקְצֵה הַיְרִיעָה אֲשֶׁר
בַּמַּחְבֶּרֶת הַשֵּׁנִית מַקְבִּילֹת הַלֻּלָאֹת אַחַת
אֶל־אֶחָת׃ 13 וַיַּעַשׂ חֲמִשִּׁים קַרְסֵי זָהָב
וַיְחַבֵּר אֶת־הַיְרִיעֹת אַחַת אֶל־אַחַת
בַּקְּרָסִים וַיְהִי הַמִּשְׁכָּן אֶחָד׃ ס
14 וַיַּעַשׂ יְרִיעֹת עִזִּים לְאֹהֶל עַל־הַמִּשְׁכָּן
עַשְׁתֵּי־עֶשְׂרֵה יְרִיעֹת עָשָׂה אֹתָם׃ 15 אֹרֶךְ
הַיְרִיעָה הָאַחַת שְׁלֹשִׁים בָּאַמָּה וְאַרְבַּע
אַמּוֹת רֹחַב הַיְרִיעָה הָאֶחָת מִדָּה אַחַת
לְעַשְׁתֵּי עֶשְׂרֵה יְרִיעֹת׃ 16 וַיְחַבֵּר אֶת־
חֲמֵשׁ הַיְרִיעֹת לְבָד וְאֶת־שֵׁשׁ הַיְרִיעֹת
לְבָד׃ 17 וַיַּעַשׂ לֻלָאֹת חֲמִשִּׁים עַל שְׂפַת
הַיְרִיעָה הַקִּיצֹנָה בַּמַּחְבָּרֶת וַחֲמִשִּׁים
לֻלָאֹת עָשָׂה עַל־שְׂפַת הַיְרִיעָה הַחֹבֶרֶת
הַשֵּׁנִית׃ 18 וַיַּעַשׂ קַרְסֵי נְחֹשֶׁת חֲמִשִּׁים
לְחַבֵּר אֶת־הָאֹהֶל לִהְיֹת אֶחָד׃ 19 וַיַּעַשׂ
מִכְסֶה לָאֹהֶל עֹרֹת אֵילִם מְאָדָּמִים
חמישי וּמִכְסֵה עֹרֹת תְּחָשִׁים מִלְמָעְלָה׃ ס

THE WORK OF CONSTRUCTION (36:8–38:20)

This lengthy and detailed account of the work repeats the instructions already given. The account here differs from the account in Exod. 26 in that the verbs used here indicate completed action. Furthermore, the various items listed are presented in a different sequence. The earlier instructions began with the furnishings and ended with the structure of the tabernacle; here the order is reversed.

20They made the planks for the Tabernacle of acacia wood, upright. 21The length of each plank was ten cubits, the width of each plank a cubit and a half. 22Each plank had two tenons, parallel to each other; they did the same with all the planks of the Tabernacle. 23Of the planks of the Tabernacle, they made twenty planks for the south side, 24making forty silver sockets under the twenty planks, two sockets under one plank for its two tenons and two sockets under each following plank for its two tenons; 25and for the other side wall of the Tabernacle, the north side, twenty planks, 26with their forty silver sockets, two sockets under one plank and two sockets under each following plank. 27And for the rear of the Tabernacle, to the west, they made six planks; 28and they made two planks for the corners of the Tabernacle at the rear. 29They matched at the bottom, but terminated as one at the top into one ring; they did so with both of them at the two corners. 30Thus there were eight planks with their sockets of silver: sixteen sockets, two under each plank.

31They made bars of acacia wood, five for the planks of the one side wall of the Tabernacle, 32five bars for the planks of the other side wall of the Tabernacle, and five bars for the planks of the wall of the Tabernacle at the rear, to the west; 33they made the center bar to run, halfway up the planks, from end to end. 34They overlaid the planks with gold, and made their rings of gold, as holders for the bars; and they overlaid the bars with gold.

חמישי 20 וַיַּעַשׂ אֶת־הַקְּרָשִׁים לַמִּשְׁכָּן עֲצֵי שִׁטִּים
עֹמְדִים׃ 21 עֶשֶׂר אַמֹּת אֹרֶךְ הַקָּרֶשׁ וְאַמָּה
וַחֲצִי הָאַמָּה רֹחַב הַקֶּרֶשׁ הָאֶחָד׃ 22 שְׁתֵּי
יָדֹת לַקֶּרֶשׁ הָאֶחָד מְשֻׁלָּבֹת אַחַת אֶל־
אֶחָת כֵּן עָשָׂה לְכֹל קַרְשֵׁי הַמִּשְׁכָּן׃
23 וַיַּעַשׂ אֶת־הַקְּרָשִׁים לַמִּשְׁכָּן עֶשְׂרִים
קְרָשִׁים לִפְאַת נֶגֶב תֵּימָנָה׃ 24 וְאַרְבָּעִים
אַדְנֵי־כֶסֶף עָשָׂה תַּחַת עֶשְׂרִים הַקְּרָשִׁים
שְׁנֵי אֲדָנִים תַּחַת־הַקֶּרֶשׁ הָאֶחָד לִשְׁתֵּי
יְדֹתָיו וּשְׁנֵי אֲדָנִים תַּחַת־הַקֶּרֶשׁ הָאֶחָד
לִשְׁתֵּי יְדֹתָיו׃ 25 וּלְצֶלַע הַמִּשְׁכָּן הַשֵּׁנִית
לִפְאַת צָפוֹן עָשָׂה עֶשְׂרִים קְרָשִׁים׃
26 וְאַרְבָּעִים אַדְנֵיהֶם כָּסֶף שְׁנֵי אֲדָנִים
תַּחַת הַקֶּרֶשׁ הָאֶחָד וּשְׁנֵי אֲדָנִים תַּחַת
הַקֶּרֶשׁ הָאֶחָד׃ 27 וּלְיַרְכְּתֵי הַמִּשְׁכָּן יָמָּה
עָשָׂה שִׁשָּׁה קְרָשִׁים׃ 28 וּשְׁנֵי קְרָשִׁים
עָשָׂה לִמְקֻצְעֹת הַמִּשְׁכָּן בַּיַּרְכָתָיִם׃
29 וְהָיוּ תוֹאֲמִם מִלְּמַטָּה וְיַחְדָּו יִהְיוּ תַמִּים
אֶל־רֹאשׁוֹ אֶל־הַטַּבַּעַת הָאֶחָת כֵּן עָשָׂה
לִשְׁנֵיהֶם לִשְׁנֵי הַמִּקְצֹעֹת׃ 30 וְהָיוּ שְׁמֹנָה
קְרָשִׁים וְאַדְנֵיהֶם כֶּסֶף שִׁשָּׁה עָשָׂר אֲדָנִים
שְׁנֵי אֲדָנִים שְׁנֵי אֲדָנִים תַּחַת הַקֶּרֶשׁ
הָאֶחָד׃
31 וַיַּעַשׂ בְּרִיחֵי עֲצֵי שִׁטִּים חֲמִשָּׁה לְקַרְשֵׁי
צֶלַע־הַמִּשְׁכָּן הָאֶחָת׃ 32 וַחֲמִשָּׁה בְרִיחִם
לְקַרְשֵׁי צֶלַע־הַמִּשְׁכָּן הַשֵּׁנִית וַחֲמִשָּׁה
בְרִיחִם לְקַרְשֵׁי הַמִּשְׁכָּן לַיַּרְכָתַיִם יָמָּה׃
33 וַיַּעַשׂ אֶת־הַבְּרִיחַ הַתִּיכֹן לִבְרֹחַ בְּתוֹךְ
הַקְּרָשִׁים מִן־הַקָּצֶה אֶל־הַקָּצֶה׃ 34 וְאֶת־
הַקְּרָשִׁים צִפָּה זָהָב וְאֶת־טַבְּעֹתָם עָשָׂה
זָהָב בָּתִּים לַבְּרִיחִם וַיְצַף אֶת־הַבְּרִיחִם
זָהָב׃

26. The word for "sockets" (*adanim*) is like the name of God (*Adonai*). This similarity hints to us that just as those sockets served to hold the upper and the lower sections of the tabernacle together, the divine Presence holds the upper (i.e., spiritual) and the lower (i.e., material) worlds together (Menaḥem Naḥum of Chernobyl).

35They made the curtain of blue, purple, and crimson yarns, and fine twisted linen, working into it a design of cherubim. 36They made for it four posts of acacia wood and overlaid them with gold, with their hooks of gold; and they cast for them four silver sockets.

37They made the screen for the entrance of the Tent, of blue, purple, and crimson yarns, and fine twisted linen, done in embroidery; 38and five posts for it with their hooks. They overlaid their tops and their bands with gold; but the five sockets were of copper.

35 וַיַּעַשׂ אֶת־הַפָּרֹכֶת תְּכֵלֶת וְאַרְגָּמָן
וְתוֹלַעַת שָׁנִי וְשֵׁשׁ מָשְׁזָר מַעֲשֵׂה חֹשֵׁב
עָשָׂה אֹתָהּ כְּרֻבִים׃ 36 וַיַּעַשׂ לָהּ אַרְבָּעָה
עַמּוּדֵי שִׁטִּים וַיְצַפֵּם זָהָב וָוֵיהֶם זָהָב וַיִּצֹק
לָהֶם אַרְבָּעָה אַדְנֵי־כָסֶף׃
37 וַיַּעַשׂ מָסָךְ לְפֶתַח הָאֹהֶל תְּכֵלֶת
וְאַרְגָּמָן וְתוֹלַעַת שָׁנִי וְשֵׁשׁ מָשְׁזָר מַעֲשֵׂה
רֹקֵם׃ 38 וְאֶת־עַמּוּדָיו חֲמִשָּׁה וְאֶת־וָוֵיהֶם
וְצִפָּה רָאשֵׁיהֶם וַחֲשֻׁקֵיהֶם זָהָב וְאַדְנֵיהֶם
חֲמִשָּׁה נְחֹשֶׁת׃ פ

37

Bezalel made the ark of acacia wood, two and a half cubits long, a cubit and a half wide, and a cubit and a half high. 2He overlaid it with pure gold, inside and out; and he made a gold molding for it round about. 3He cast four gold rings for it, for its four feet: two rings on one of its side walls and two rings on the other. 4He made poles of acacia wood, overlaid them with gold, 5and inserted the poles into the rings on the side walls of the ark for carrying the ark.

6He made a cover of pure gold, two and a half cubits long and a cubit and a half wide. 7He made two cherubim of gold; he made them of hammered work, at the two ends of the cover: 8one cherub at one end and the other cherub at the other end; he made the cherubim of one piece with the cover, at its two ends. 9The cherubim had their wings spread out above, shielding the cover with their wings. They faced each

לז

וַיַּעַשׂ בְּצַלְאֵל אֶת־הָאָרֹן עֲצֵי
שִׁטִּים אַמָּתַיִם וָחֵצִי אָרְכּוֹ וְאַמָּה וָחֵצִי
רָחְבּוֹ וְאַמָּה וָחֵצִי קֹמָתוֹ׃ 2 וַיְצַפֵּהוּ זָהָב
טָהוֹר מִבַּיִת וּמִחוּץ וַיַּעַשׂ לוֹ זֵר זָהָב
סָבִיב׃ 3 וַיִּצֹק לוֹ אַרְבַּע טַבְּעֹת זָהָב עַל
אַרְבַּע פַּעֲמֹתָיו וּשְׁתֵּי טַבָּעֹת עַל־צַלְעוֹ
הָאֶחָת וּשְׁתֵּי טַבָּעוֹת עַל־צַלְעוֹ הַשֵּׁנִית׃
4 וַיַּעַשׂ בַּדֵּי עֲצֵי שִׁטִּים וַיְצַף אֹתָם זָהָב׃
5 וַיָּבֵא אֶת־הַבַּדִּים בַּטַּבָּעֹת עַל צַלְעֹת
הָאָרֹן לָשֵׂאת אֶת־הָאָרֹן׃
6 וַיַּעַשׂ כַּפֹּרֶת זָהָב טָהוֹר אַמָּתַיִם וָחֵצִי
אָרְכָּהּ וְאַמָּה וָחֵצִי רָחְבָּהּ׃ 7 וַיַּעַשׂ שְׁנֵי
כְרֻבִים זָהָב מִקְשָׁה עָשָׂה אֹתָם מִשְּׁנֵי
קְצוֹת הַכַּפֹּרֶת׃ 8 כְּרוּב־אֶחָד מִקָּצָה מִזֶּה
וּכְרוּב־אֶחָד מִקָּצָה מִזֶּה מִן־הַכַּפֹּרֶת
עָשָׂה אֶת־הַכְּרֻבִים מִשְּׁנֵי קצוותו קְצוֹתָיו׃
9 וַיִּהְיוּ הַכְּרֻבִים פֹּרְשֵׂי כְנָפַיִם לְמַעְלָה
סֹכְכִים בְּכַנְפֵיהֶם עַל־הַכַּפֹּרֶת וּפְנֵיהֶם

THE MANUFACTURE OF THE FURNITURE AND ACCESSORIES (37:1–38:20)

The order of narration reflects descending gradations of holiness. The Ark, to be located in the Holy of Holies, comes first, followed by the three items that belong in the Holy Place—the table, the *m'norah,* and the altar of incense. Next are the anointing oil and aromatic incense, because both are needed in the Holy Place. And last are the altar of burnt offering and the laver, both of which are placed in the outer court.

1–9. Construction of the ark, which corresponds to 25:10–21, where the instruction reads, "They shall make an ark."

other; the faces of the cherubim were turned toward the cover.

10He made the table of acacia wood, two cubits long, one cubit wide, and a cubit and a half high; 11he overlaid it with pure gold and made a gold molding around it. 12He made a rim of a hand's breadth around it and made a gold molding for its rim round about. 13He cast four gold rings for it and attached the rings to the four corners at its four legs. 14The rings were next to the rim, as holders for the poles to carry the table. 15He made the poles of acacia wood for carrying the table, and overlaid them with gold. 16The utensils that were to be upon the table—its bowls, ladles, jugs, and jars with which to offer libations—he made of pure gold.

17He made the lampstand of pure gold. He made the lampstand—its base and its shaft—of hammered work; its cups, calyxes, and petals were of one piece with it. 18Six branches issued from its sides: three branches from one side of the lampstand, and three branches from the other side of the lampstand. 19There were three cups shaped like almond-blossoms, each with calyx and petals, on one branch; and there were three cups shaped like almond-blossoms, each with calyx and petals, on the next branch; so for all six branches issuing from the lampstand. 20On the lampstand itself there were four cups shaped like almond-blossoms, each with calyx and petals: 21a calyx, of one piece with it, under a pair of branches; and a calyx, of one piece with it, under the second pair of branches; and a calyx, of one piece with it, under the last pair of branches; so for all six branches issuing from it. 22Their calyxes and their stems were of one piece with it, the whole of it a single hammered piece of pure gold. 23He made its seven lamps,

אִישׁ אֶל־אָחִיו אֶל־הַכַּפֹּרֶת הָיוּ פְּנֵי
הַכְּרֻבִים׃ פ
10 וַיַּעַשׂ אֶת־הַשֻּׁלְחָן עֲצֵי שִׁטִּים אַמָּתַיִם
אָרְכּוֹ וְאַמָּה רָחְבּוֹ וְאַמָּה וָחֵצִי קֹמָתוֹ׃
11 וַיְצַף אֹתוֹ זָהָב טָהוֹר וַיַּעַשׂ לוֹ זֵר זָהָב
סָבִיב׃ 12 וַיַּעַשׂ לוֹ מִסְגֶּרֶת טֹפַח סָבִיב
וַיַּעַשׂ זֵר־זָהָב לְמִסְגַּרְתּוֹ סָבִיב׃ 13 וַיִּצֹק
לוֹ אַרְבַּע טַבְּעֹת זָהָב וַיִּתֵּן אֶת־הַטַּבָּעֹת
עַל אַרְבַּע הַפֵּאֹת אֲשֶׁר לְאַרְבַּע רַגְלָיו׃
14 לְעֻמַּת הַמִּסְגֶּרֶת הָיוּ הַטַּבָּעֹת בָּתִּים
לַבַּדִּים לָשֵׂאת אֶת־הַשֻּׁלְחָן׃ 15 וַיַּעַשׂ אֶת־
הַבַּדִּים עֲצֵי שִׁטִּים וַיְצַף אֹתָם זָהָב לָשֵׂאת
אֶת־הַשֻּׁלְחָן׃ 16 וַיַּעַשׂ אֶת־הַכֵּלִים ׀ אֲשֶׁר
עַל־הַשֻּׁלְחָן אֶת־קְעָרֹתָיו וְאֶת־כַּפֹּתָיו
וְאֵת מְנַקִּיֹּתָיו וְאֶת־הַקְּשָׂוֹת אֲשֶׁר יֻסַּךְ
בָּהֵן זָהָב טָהוֹר׃ פ
ששי [שלישי] 17 וַיַּעַשׂ אֶת־הַמְּנֹרָה זָהָב טָהוֹר מִקְשָׁה
עָשָׂה אֶת־הַמְּנֹרָה יְרֵכָהּ וְקָנָהּ גְּבִיעֶיהָ
כַּפְתֹּרֶיהָ וּפְרָחֶיהָ מִמֶּנָּה הָיוּ׃ 18 וְשִׁשָּׁה
קָנִים יֹצְאִים מִצִּדֶּיהָ שְׁלֹשָׁה ׀ קְנֵי מְנֹרָה
מִצִּדָּהּ הָאֶחָד וּשְׁלֹשָׁה קְנֵי מְנֹרָה מִצִּדָּהּ
הַשֵּׁנִי׃ 19 שְׁלֹשָׁה גְבִעִים מְשֻׁקָּדִים בַּקָּנֶה
הָאֶחָד כַּפְתֹּר וָפֶרַח וּשְׁלֹשָׁה גְבִעִים
מְשֻׁקָּדִים בְּקָנֶה אֶחָד כַּפְתֹּר וָפָרַח כֵּן
לְשֵׁשֶׁת הַקָּנִים הַיֹּצְאִים מִן־הַמְּנֹרָה׃
20 וּבַמְּנֹרָה אַרְבָּעָה גְבִעִים מְשֻׁקָּדִים
כַּפְתֹּרֶיהָ וּפְרָחֶיהָ׃ 21 וְכַפְתֹּר תַּחַת שְׁנֵי
הַקָּנִים מִמֶּנָּה וְכַפְתֹּר תַּחַת שְׁנֵי
הַקָּנִים מִמֶּנָּה וְכַפְתֹּר תַּחַת־שְׁנֵי הַקָּנִים
מִמֶּנָּה לְשֵׁשֶׁת הַקָּנִים הַיֹּצְאִים מִמֶּנָּה׃
22 כַּפְתֹּרֵיהֶם וּקְנֹתָם מִמֶּנָּה הָיוּ כֻּלָּהּ
מִקְשָׁה אַחַת זָהָב טָהוֹר׃ 23 וַיַּעַשׂ אֶת־
נֵרֹתֶיהָ שִׁבְעָה וּמַלְקָחֶיהָ וּמַחְתֹּתֶיהָ זָהָב

10–16. Construction of the table, which corresponds to 25:23–30.

17–24. Construction of the *m'norah,* which corresponds to 25:31–40.

its tongs, and its fire pans of pure gold. 24He made it and all its furnishings out of a talent of pure gold.

25He made the incense altar of acacia wood, a cubit long and a cubit wide—square—and two cubits high; its horns were of one piece with it. 26He overlaid it with pure gold: its top, its sides round about, and its horns; and he made a gold molding for it round about. 27He made two gold rings for it under its molding, on its two walls—on opposite sides—as holders for the poles with which to carry it. 28He made the poles of acacia wood, and overlaid them with gold. 29He prepared the sacred anointing oil and the pure aromatic incense, expertly blended.

38

He made the altar for burnt offering of acacia wood, five cubits long and five cubits wide—square—and three cubits high. 2He made horns for it on its four corners, the horns being of one piece with it; and he overlaid it with copper. 3He made all the utensils of the altar—the pails, the scrapers, the basins, the flesh hooks, and the fire pans; he made all these utensils of copper. 4He made for the altar a grating of meshwork in copper, extending below, under its ledge, to its middle. 5He cast four rings, at the four corners of the copper grating, as holders for the poles. 6He made the poles of acacia wood and overlaid them with copper; 7and he inserted the poles into the rings on the side walls of the altar, to carry it by them. He made it hollow, of boards.

טָהֽוֹר: 24 כִּכָּ֛ר זָהָ֥ב טָה֖וֹר עָשָׂ֣ה אֹתָ֑הּ וְאֵ֖ת כָּל־כֵּלֶֽיהָ: פ

25 וַיַּ֛עַשׂ אֶת־מִזְבַּ֥ח הַקְּטֹ֖רֶת עֲצֵ֣י שִׁטִּ֑ים אַמָּ֣ה אָרְכּ֣וֹ וְאַמָּ֣ה רָחְבּוֹ֮ רָב֒וּעַ֒ וְאַמָּתַ֣יִם קֹֽמָת֔וֹ מִמֶּ֖נּוּ הָי֥וּ קַרְנֹתָֽיו: 26 וַיְצַ֨ף אֹת֜וֹ זָהָ֣ב טָה֗וֹר אֶת־גַּגּ֧וֹ וְאֶת־קִֽירֹתָ֛יו סָבִ֖יב וְאֶת־קַרְנֹתָ֑יו וַיַּ֥עַשׂ ל֛וֹ זֵ֥ר זָהָ֖ב סָבִֽיב: 27 וּשְׁתֵּי֩ טַבְּעֹ֨ת זָהָ֜ב עָֽשָׂה־ל֣וֹ | מִתַּ֣חַת לְזֵר֗וֹ עַ֚ל שְׁתֵּ֣י צַלְעֹתָ֔יו עַ֖ל שְׁנֵ֣י צִדָּ֑יו לְבָתִּ֣ים לְבַדִּ֔ים לָשֵׂ֥את אֹת֖וֹ בָּהֶֽם: 28 וַיַּ֥עַשׂ אֶת־הַבַּדִּ֖ים עֲצֵ֣י שִׁטִּ֑ים וַיְצַ֥ף אֹתָ֖ם זָהָֽב: 29 וַיַּ֜עַשׂ אֶת־שֶׁ֤מֶן הַמִּשְׁחָה֙ קֹ֔דֶשׁ וְאֶת־קְטֹ֥רֶת הַסַּמִּ֖ים טָה֑וֹר מַעֲשֵׂ֖ה רֹקֵֽחַ: פ

לח וַיַּ֛עַשׂ אֶת־מִזְבַּ֥ח הָעֹלָ֖ה עֲצֵ֣י שִׁטִּ֑ים חָמֵשׁ֩ אַמּ֨וֹת אָרְכּ֜וֹ וְחָֽמֵשׁ־אַמּ֣וֹת רָחְבּוֹ֮ רָב֒וּעַ֒ וְשָׁלֹ֥שׁ אַמּ֖וֹת קֹמָתֽוֹ: 2 וַיַּ֣עַשׂ קַרְנֹתָ֗יו עַ֚ל אַרְבַּ֣ע פִּנֹּתָ֔יו מִמֶּ֖נּוּ הָי֣וּ קַרְנֹתָ֑יו וַיְצַ֥ף אֹת֖וֹ נְחֹֽשֶׁת: 3 וַיַּ֜עַשׂ אֶת־כָּל־כְּלֵ֣י הַמִּזְבֵּ֗חַ אֶת־הַסִּירֹ֤ת וְאֶת־הַיָּעִים֙ וְאֶת־הַמִּזְרָקֹ֣ת אֶת־הַמִּזְלָגֹ֔ת וְאֶת־הַמַּחְתֹּ֑ת כָּל־כֵּלָ֖יו עָשָׂ֥ה נְחֹֽשֶׁת: 4 וַיַּ֣עַשׂ לַמִּזְבֵּ֗חַ מִכְבָּר֙ מַעֲשֵׂ֣ה רֶ֣שֶׁת נְחֹ֔שֶׁת תַּ֣חַת כַּרְכֻּבּ֛וֹ מִלְּמַ֖טָּה עַד־חֶצְיֽוֹ: 5 וַיִּצֹ֞ק אַרְבַּ֣ע טַבָּעֹ֗ת בְּאַרְבַּ֛ע הַקְּצָוֹ֖ת לְמִכְבַּ֣ר הַנְּחֹ֑שֶׁת בָּתִּ֖ים לַבַּדִּֽים: 6 וַיַּ֥עַשׂ אֶת־הַבַּדִּ֖ים עֲצֵ֣י שִׁטִּ֑ים וַיְצַ֥ף אֹתָ֖ם נְחֹֽשֶׁת: 7 וַיָּבֵ֨א אֶת־הַבַּדִּ֜ים בַּטַּבָּעֹ֗ת עַ֚ל צַלְעֹ֣ת הַמִּזְבֵּ֔חַ לָשֵׂ֥את אֹת֖וֹ בָּהֶ֑ם נְב֥וּב לֻחֹ֖ת עָשָׂ֥ה אֹתֽוֹ: ס

25–28. Construction of the altar of incense, which corresponds to 30:1–10.

29. Preparation of the anointing oil and the

incense; this verse summarizes 30:22–33,34–37.

38:1–7. Construction of the altar of burnt offering, which corresponds to 27:1–8.

8 He made the laver of copper and its stand of copper, from the mirrors of the women who performed tasks at the entrance of the Tent of Meeting.

9 He made the enclosure:

On the south side, a hundred cubits of hangings of fine twisted linen for the enclosure—
10 with their twenty posts and their twenty sockets of copper, the hooks and bands of the posts being silver.

11 On the north side, a hundred cubits—with their twenty posts and their twenty sockets of copper, the hooks and bands of the posts being silver.

12 On the west side, fifty cubits of hangings—with their ten posts and their ten sockets, the hooks and bands of the posts being silver.

13 And on the front side, to the east, fifty cubits:
14 fifteen cubits of hangings on the one flank, with their three posts and their three sockets,
15 and fifteen cubits of hangings on the other flank—on each side of the gate of the enclosure—with their three posts and their three sockets.

16 All the hangings around the enclosure were of fine twisted linen.
17 The sockets for the posts were of copper, the hooks and bands of the posts were of silver, the overlay of their tops was of silver; all the posts of the enclosure were banded with silver.—
18 The screen of the gate of the en-

8 וַיַּ֗עַשׂ אֵ֚ת הַכִּיּ֣וֹר נְחֹ֔שֶׁת וְאֵ֖ת כַּנּ֣וֹ נְחֹ֑שֶׁת
בְּמַרְאֹת֙ הַצֹּ֣בְאֹ֔ת אֲשֶׁ֣ר צָֽבְא֔וּ פֶּ֖תַח אֹ֥הֶל
מוֹעֵֽד׃ ס
9 וַיַּ֖עַשׂ אֶת־הֶחָצֵ֑ר
לִפְאַ֣ת ׀ נֶ֣גֶב תֵּימָ֗נָה קַלְעֵ֤י הֶֽחָצֵר֙ שֵׁ֣שׁ
מָשְׁזָ֔ר מֵאָ֖ה בָּאַמָּֽה׃ 10 עַמּֽוּדֵיהֶ֣ם עֶשְׂרִ֔ים
וְאַדְנֵיהֶ֥ם עֶשְׂרִ֖ים נְחֹ֑שֶׁת וָוֵ֧י הָֽעַמֻּדִ֛ים
וַחֲשֻֽׁקֵיהֶ֖ם כָּֽסֶף׃
11 וְלִפְאַ֤ת צָפוֹן֙ מֵאָ֣ה בָֽאַמָּ֔ה עַמּֽוּדֵיהֶ֣ם
עֶשְׂרִ֔ים וְאַדְנֵיהֶ֥ם עֶשְׂרִ֖ים נְחֹ֑שֶׁת וָוֵ֧י
הָֽעַמּוּדִ֛ים וַחֲשֻׁקֵיהֶ֖ם כָּֽסֶף׃
12 וְלִפְאַת־יָ֗ם קְלָעִים֙ חֲמִשִּׁ֣ים בָּֽאַמָּ֔ה
עַמּֽוּדֵיהֶ֥ם עֲשָׂרָ֖ה וְאַדְנֵיהֶ֣ם עֲשָׂרָ֑ה וָוֵ֧י
הָעַמֻּדִ֛ים וַחֲשׁוּקֵיהֶ֖ם כָּֽסֶף׃
13 וְלִפְאַ֛ת קֵ֥דְמָה מִזְרָ֖חָה חֲמִשִּׁ֥ים אַמָּֽה׃
14 קְלָעִ֛ים חֲמֵשׁ־עֶשְׂרֵ֥ה אַמָּ֖ה אֶל־הַכָּתֵ֑ף
עַמּוּדֵיהֶ֥ם שְׁלֹשָׁ֖ה וְאַדְנֵיהֶ֥ם שְׁלֹשָֽׁה׃
15 וְלַכָּתֵ֣ף הַשֵּׁנִ֗ית מִזֶּ֤ה וּמִזֶּה֙ לְשַׁ֣עַר הֶֽחָצֵ֔ר
קְלָעִ֕ים חֲמֵ֥שׁ עֶשְׂרֵ֖ה אַמָּ֑ה עַמֻּדֵיהֶ֣ם
שְׁלֹשָׁ֔ה וְאַדְנֵיהֶ֖ם שְׁלֹשָֽׁה׃
16 כָּל־קַלְעֵ֧י הֶחָצֵ֛ר סָבִ֖יב שֵׁ֥שׁ מָשְׁזָֽר׃
17 וְהָאֲדָנִ֣ים לָֽעַמֻּדִים֮ נְחֹשֶׁת֒ וָוֵ֨י הָֽעַמּוּדִ֜ים
וַחֲשׁוּקֵיהֶם֙ כֶּ֔סֶף וְצִפּ֥וּי רָאשֵׁיהֶ֖ם כָּ֑סֶף
וְהֵם֙ מְחֻשָּׁקִ֣ים כֶּ֔סֶף כֹּ֖ל עַמֻּדֵ֥י הֶחָצֵֽר׃
מפטיר 18 וּמָסַ֞ךְ שַׁ֤עַר הֶֽחָצֵר֙ מַעֲשֵׂ֣ה רֹקֵ֔ם תְּכֵ֥לֶת

8. This verse summarizes 30:17–21 and provides additional information about the material of which the laver was made as well as the source of the donation.

copper Better: bronze. See Comment to 25:3.

mirrors In the ancient world, mirrors were mainly hand-held, highly polished disks of metal (copper or bronze), fitted with handles made of metal, wood, faience, or ivory. Egypt was the center of their manufacture for the entire Near East. Because of the high cost of metal in Egypt, metal objects were not discarded but were melted down and reused, as is done here.

women who performed tasks Nothing is known about this class of women, who are mentioned again only in 1 Sam. 2:22. It is likely that they performed a range of duties, including menial labor. Even women at the bottom of the occupational and social scale displayed unselfish generosity and devotion in donating their valuable mirrors for the tabernacle.

entrance of the Tent of Meeting At this stage, however, the tent had not yet been erected. Ramban understood this as referring to Moses' private tent (described in 33:7), which was situated outside the camp.

9–20. Construction of the enclosure, which corresponds to 27:9–19. These verses mark the completion of the report about construction of the edifice, furniture, and appurtenances.

closure, done in embroidery, was of blue, purple, and crimson yarns, and fine twisted linen. It was twenty cubits long. Its height—or width—was five cubits, like that of the hangings of the enclosure. 19The posts were four; their four sockets were of copper, their hooks of silver; and the overlay of their tops was of silver, as were also their bands.—20All the pegs of the Tabernacle and of the enclosure round about were of copper.

וְאַרְגָּמָ֔ן וְתוֹלַ֥עַת שָׁנִ֖י וְשֵׁ֣שׁ מָשְׁזָ֑ר
וְעֶשְׂרִ֤ים אַמָּה֙ אֹ֔רֶךְ וְקוֹמָ֤ה בְרֹ֙חַב֙ חָמֵ֣שׁ
אַמּ֔וֹת לְעֻמַּ֖ת קַלְעֵ֥י הֶחָצֵֽר׃ 19 וְעַמֻּֽדֵיהֶם֙
אַרְבָּעָ֔ה וְאַדְנֵיהֶ֥ם אַרְבָּעָ֖ה נְחֹ֑שֶׁת וָוֵיהֶ֣ם
כֶּ֔סֶף וְצִפּ֥וּי רָאשֵׁיהֶ֖ם וַחֲשֻׁקֵיהֶ֥ם כָּֽסֶף׃
20 וְכָל־הַיְתֵדֹ֞ת לַמִּשְׁכָּ֧ן וְלֶחָצֵ֛ר סָבִ֖יב
נְחֹֽשֶׁת׃* ס

* *For the* haftarah *for this Torah portion, see selections starting on p. 573.*

21These are the records of the Tabernacle, the
Tabernacle of the Pact, which were drawn up
at Moses' bidding—the work of the Levites under the direction of Ithamar son of Aaron the
priest. 22Now Bezalel, son of Uri son of Hur,
of the tribe of Judah, had made all that the LORD
had commanded Moses; 23at his side was
Oholiab son of Ahisamach, of the tribe of Dan,
carver and designer, and embroiderer in blue,
purple, and crimson yarns and in fine linen.
24All the gold that was used for the work, in
all the work of the sanctuary—the elevation
offering of gold—came to 29 talents and 730
shekels by the sanctuary weight. 25The silver of

21 אֵלֶּה פְקוּדֵי הַמִּשְׁכָּן מִשְׁכַּן הָעֵדֻת אֲשֶׁר
פֻּקַּד עַל־פִּי מֹשֶׁה עֲבֹדַת הַלְוִיִּם בְּיַד
אִיתָמָר בֶּן־אַהֲרֹן הַכֹּהֵן׃ 22 וּבְצַלְאֵל בֶּן־
אוּרִי בֶן־חוּר לְמַטֵּה יְהוּדָה עָשָׂה אֵת
כָּל־אֲשֶׁר־צִוָּה יְהוָה אֶת־מֹשֶׁה׃ 23 וְאִתּוֹ
אָהֳלִיאָב בֶּן־אֲחִיסָמָךְ לְמַטֵּה־דָן חָרָשׁ
וְחֹשֵׁב וְרֹקֵם בַּתְּכֵלֶת וּבָאַרְגָּמָן וּבְתוֹלַעַת
הַשָּׁנִי וּבַשֵּׁשׁ׃ ס
24 כָּל־הַזָּהָב הֶעָשׂוּי לַמְּלָאכָה בְּכֹל
מְלֶאכֶת הַקֹּדֶשׁ וַיְהִי ׀ זְהַב הַתְּנוּפָה תֵּשַׁע
וְעֶשְׂרִים כִּכָּר וּשְׁבַע מֵאוֹת וּשְׁלֹשִׁים שֶׁקֶל
בְּשֶׁקֶל הַקֹּדֶשׁ׃ 25 וְכֶסֶף פְּקוּדֵי הָעֵדָה

THE TABERNACLE, PART II: CONSTRUCTION *(continued)*

A TALLY OF THE METALS (38:21–31)

Moses orders an inventory of the metals, to be undertaken by the Levites under the direction of Aaron's son Ithamar. The tally is prefaced by a restatement of the roles of the two master craftsmen Bezalel and Oholiab. The inventory described here is similar to that found among the Egyptians, whose art depicts scenes of metalworking in which a master is weighing the metals on scales, with the scribes recording the results in their ledgers, before the materials are given to the artisans.

21. Tabernacle of the Pact This once again emphasizes that the symbol of the covenant with God is the focal point of the entire tabernacle.

Ithamar His birth was recorded in Exod. 6:23, and his nomination to be installed as a priest, in 28:1. Throughout the wilderness wanderings he directed the work of the levitical clans in connection with the tabernacle.

23. These qualifications of Oholiab repeat 35:35 and include some additional material.

24–30. The metals are listed in descending order of value.

shekel See Comment to Gen. 23:9.

half-shekel Hebrew: *beka,* mentioned as a weight in Gen. 24:22. The stem means "to split"—here, in half. Several weights from the time of the First Temple have been found inscribed in the old-Hebrew script with the word *beka* or its abbreviation, *"b."* Their average weight is 0.210 ounces (6.019 grams).

a head The reference is to the census that was ordered in 30:11–16.

In this *parashah,* Moses gives a detailed accounting of the expenditures for fashioning the tabernacle and its furnishings. Why did Moses feel obliged to give this detailed account? Some Israelites knew that they would have taken advantage of handling all that gold and silver for their own enrichment. They suspected Moses of being no better than they were. Thus the Midrash emphasizes that leaders of the community must be above any suspicion of personal aggrandizement. The family that prepared the incense for the Temple services would never let their relatives wear perfume, lest some people suspect them of using Temple incense for their personal benefit. The official who supervised the shekel offering would wear a special garment with no pockets and no long sleeves when he did so, so that no one could suspect him of pocketing public funds (Song R. 3:7). "A person should strive to please people as strenuously as one strives to please God" (Exod. R. 51:2).

those of the community who were recorded
came to 100 talents and 1,775 shekels by the
sanctuary weight: 26a half-shekel a head, half
a shekel by the sanctuary weight, for each one
who was entered in the records, from the age
of twenty years up, 603,550 men. 27The 100 talents of silver were for casting the sockets of the
sanctuary and the sockets for the curtain, 100
sockets to the 100 talents, a talent a socket.
28And of the 1,775 shekels he made hooks for
the posts, overlay for their tops, and bands
around them.

29The copper from the elevation offering
came to 70 talents and 2,400 shekels. 30Of it he
made the sockets for the entrance of the Tent
of Meeting; the copper altar and its copper grating and all the utensils of the altar; 31the sockets
of the enclosure round about and the sockets
of the gate of the enclosure; and all the pegs of
the Tabernacle and all the pegs of the enclosure
round about.

מְאַת כִּכָּר וְאֶלֶף וּשְׁבַע מֵאוֹת וַחֲמִשָּׁה
וְשִׁבְעִים שֶׁקֶל בְּשֶׁקֶל הַקֹּדֶשׁ׃ 26 בֶּקַע
לַגֻּלְגֹּלֶת מַחֲצִית הַשֶּׁקֶל בְּשֶׁקֶל הַקֹּדֶשׁ
לְכֹל הָעֹבֵר עַל־הַפְּקֻדִים מִבֶּן עֶשְׂרִים
שָׁנָה וָמַעְלָה לְשֵׁשׁ־מֵאוֹת אֶלֶף וּשְׁלֹשֶׁת
אֲלָפִים וַחֲמֵשׁ מֵאוֹת וַחֲמִשִּׁים׃ 27 וַיְהִי
מְאַת כִּכַּר הַכֶּסֶף לָצֶקֶת אֵת אַדְנֵי הַקֹּדֶשׁ
וְאֵת אַדְנֵי הַפָּרֹכֶת מְאַת אֲדָנִים לִמְאַת
הַכִּכָּר כִּכָּר לָאָדֶן׃ 28 וְאֶת־הָאֶלֶף וּשְׁבַע
הַמֵּאוֹת וַחֲמִשָּׁה וְשִׁבְעִים עָשָׂה וָוִים
לָעַמּוּדִים וְצִפָּה רָאשֵׁיהֶם וְחִשַּׁק אֹתָם׃
29 וּנְחֹשֶׁת הַתְּנוּפָה שִׁבְעִים כִּכָּר וְאַלְפַּיִם
וְאַרְבַּע־מֵאוֹת שָׁקֶל׃ 30 וַיַּעַשׂ בָּהּ אֶת־
אַדְנֵי פֶּתַח אֹהֶל מוֹעֵד וְאֵת מִזְבַּח
הַנְּחֹשֶׁת וְאֶת־מִכְבַּר הַנְּחֹשֶׁת אֲשֶׁר־לוֹ
וְאֵת כָּל־כְּלֵי הַמִּזְבֵּחַ׃ 31 וְאֶת־אַדְנֵי
הֶחָצֵר סָבִיב וְאֶת־אַדְנֵי שַׁעַר הֶחָצֵר וְאֵת
כָּל־יִתְדֹת הַמִּשְׁכָּן וְאֶת־כָּל־יִתְדֹת הֶחָצֵר
סָבִיב׃

39 Of the blue, purple, and crimson yarns
they also made the service vestments for officiating in the sanctuary; they made Aaron's sacral vestments—as the LORD had commanded
Moses.

2The ephod was made of gold, blue, purple,
and crimson yarns, and fine twisted linen. 3They
hammered out sheets of gold and cut threads
to be worked into designs among the blue, the
purple, and the crimson yarns, and the fine
linen. 4They made for it attaching shoulder-

לט וּמִן־הַתְּכֵלֶת וְהָאַרְגָּמָן וְתוֹלַעַת
הַשָּׁנִי עָשׂוּ בִגְדֵי־שְׂרָד לְשָׁרֵת בַּקֹּדֶשׁ
וַיַּעֲשׂוּ אֶת־בִּגְדֵי הַקֹּדֶשׁ אֲשֶׁר לְאַהֲרֹן
כַּאֲשֶׁר צִוָּה יְהוָה אֶת־מֹשֶׁה׃ פ
2 וַיַּעַשׂ אֶת־הָאֵפֹד זָהָב תְּכֵלֶת וְאַרְגָּמָן שני [חמישי]
וְתוֹלַעַת שָׁנִי וְשֵׁשׁ מָשְׁזָר׃ 3 וַיְרַקְּעוּ אֶת־
פַּחֵי הַזָּהָב וְקִצֵּץ פְּתִילִם לַעֲשׂוֹת בְּתוֹךְ
הַתְּכֵלֶת וּבְתוֹךְ הָאַרְגָּמָן וּבְתוֹךְ תּוֹלַעַת
הַשָּׁנִי וּבְתוֹךְ הַשֵּׁשׁ מַעֲשֵׂה חֹשֵׁב׃ 4 כְּתֵפֹת

THE MAKING OF THE PRIESTLY VESTMENTS (39:1–31)

This section corresponds to Exod. 28. It contains some additional information and affirms—seven times in all—that each item was made in accordance with God's instructions.

1. The omission of the fine linen from the list is especially puzzling because it is included in verses 2, 3, and 5.

3. The process described here is typically Egyptian. The highly malleable gold was hammered over a stone into a thin sheet from which very narrow strips were cut to make fine gold wire. Gold thread was created by cutting the sheet in spiral form.

עָשׂוּ־לוֹ חֹבְרֹת עַל־שְׁנֵי קצוותו קְצוֹתָיו
חֻבָּר׃ 5 וְחֵשֶׁב אֲפֻדָּתוֹ אֲשֶׁר עָלָיו מִמֶּנּוּ
הוּא כְּמַעֲשֵׂהוּ זָהָב תְּכֵלֶת וְאַרְגָּמָן
וְתוֹלַעַת שָׁנִי וְשֵׁשׁ מָשְׁזָר כַּאֲשֶׁר צִוָּה
יְהוָה אֶת־מֹשֶׁה׃
6 וַיַּעֲשׂוּ אֶת־אַבְנֵי הַשֹּׁהַם מֻסַבֹּת מִשְׁבְּצֹת
זָהָב מְפֻתָּחֹת פִּתּוּחֵי חוֹתָם עַל־שְׁמוֹת
בְּנֵי יִשְׂרָאֵל׃ 7 וַיָּשֶׂם אֹתָם עַל כִּתְפֹת
הָאֵפֹד אַבְנֵי זִכָּרוֹן לִבְנֵי יִשְׂרָאֵל כַּאֲשֶׁר
צִוָּה יְהוָה אֶת־מֹשֶׁה׃ פ
8 וַיַּעַשׂ אֶת־הַחֹשֶׁן מַעֲשֵׂה חֹשֵׁב כְּמַעֲשֵׂה
אֵפֹד זָהָב תְּכֵלֶת וְאַרְגָּמָן וְתוֹלַעַת שָׁנִי
וְשֵׁשׁ מָשְׁזָר׃ 9 רָבוּעַ הָיָה כָּפוּל עָשׂוּ
אֶת־הַחֹשֶׁן זֶרֶת אָרְכּוֹ וְזֶרֶת רָחְבּוֹ כָּפוּל׃
10 וַיְמַלְאוּ־בוֹ אַרְבָּעָה טוּרֵי אָבֶן טוּר אֹדֶם
פִּטְדָה וּבָרֶקֶת הַטּוּר הָאֶחָד׃ 11 וְהַטּוּר
הַשֵּׁנִי נֹפֶךְ סַפִּיר וְיָהֲלֹם׃ 12 וְהַטּוּר
הַשְּׁלִישִׁי לֶשֶׁם שְׁבוֹ וְאַחְלָמָה׃ 13 וְהַטּוּר
הָרְבִיעִי תַּרְשִׁישׁ שֹׁהַם וְיָשְׁפֵה מוּסַבֹּת
מִשְׁבְּצוֹת זָהָב בְּמִלֻּאֹתָם׃ 14 וְהָאֲבָנִים
עַל־שְׁמֹת בְּנֵי־יִשְׂרָאֵל הֵנָּה שְׁתֵּים עֶשְׂרֵה
עַל־שְׁמֹתָם פִּתּוּחֵי חֹתָם אִישׁ עַל־שְׁמוֹ
לִשְׁנֵים עָשָׂר שָׁבֶט׃
15 וַיַּעֲשׂוּ עַל־הַחֹשֶׁן שַׁרְשְׁרֹת גַּבְלֻת
מַעֲשֵׂה עֲבֹת זָהָב טָהוֹר׃ 16 וַיַּעֲשׂוּ שְׁתֵּי
מִשְׁבְּצֹת זָהָב וּשְׁתֵּי טַבְּעֹת זָהָב וַיִּתְּנוּ
אֶת־שְׁתֵּי הַטַּבָּעֹת עַל־שְׁנֵי קְצוֹת הַחֹשֶׁן׃
17 וַיִּתְּנוּ שְׁתֵּי הָעֲבֹתֹת הַזָּהָב עַל־שְׁתֵּי
הַטַּבָּעֹת עַל־קְצוֹת הַחֹשֶׁן׃ 18 וְאֵת שְׁתֵּי
קְצוֹת שְׁתֵּי הָעֲבֹתֹת נָתְנוּ עַל־שְׁתֵּי
הַמִּשְׁבְּצֹת וַיִּתְּנֻם עַל־כִּתְפֹת הָאֵפֹד אֶל־
מוּל פָּנָיו׃ 19 וַיַּעֲשׂוּ שְׁתֵּי טַבְּעֹת זָהָב
וַיָּשִׂימוּ עַל־שְׁנֵי קְצוֹת הַחֹשֶׁן עַל־שְׂפָתוֹ
אֲשֶׁר אֶל־עֵבֶר הָאֵפֹד בָּיְתָה׃ 20 וַיַּעֲשׂוּ
שְׁתֵּי טַבְּעֹת זָהָב וַיִּתְּנֻם עַל־שְׁתֵּי כִתְפֹת

pieces; they were attached at its two ends. 5The decorated band that was upon it was made like it, of one piece with it; of gold, blue, purple, and crimson yarns, and fine twisted linen—as the LORD had commanded Moses.

6They bordered the lazuli stones with frames of gold, engraved with seal engravings of the names of the sons of Israel. 7They were set on the shoulder-pieces of the ephod, as stones of remembrance for the Israelites—as the LORD had commanded Moses.

8The breastpiece was made in the style of the ephod: of gold, blue, purple, and crimson yarns, and fine twisted linen. 9It was square; they made the breastpiece doubled—a span in length and a span in width, doubled. 10They set in it four rows of stones. The first row was a row of carnelian, chrysolite, and emerald; 11the second row: a turquoise, a sapphire, and an amethyst; 12the third row: a jacinth, an agate, and a crystal; 13and the fourth row: a beryl, a lapis lazuli, and a jasper. They were encircled in their mountings with frames of gold. 14The stones corresponded [in number] to the names of the sons of Israel: twelve, corresponding to their names; engraved like seals, each with its name, for the twelve tribes.

15On the breastpiece they made braided chains of corded work in pure gold. 16They made two frames of gold and two rings of gold, and fastened the two rings at the two ends of the breastpiece, 17attaching the two golden cords to the two rings at the ends of the breastpiece. 18They then fastened the two ends of the cords to the two frames, attaching them to the shoulder-pieces of the ephod, at the front. 19They made two rings of gold and attached them to the two ends of the breastpiece, at its inner edge, which faced the ephod. 20They made two other rings of gold and fastened them on the front of the ephod, low on the two

shoulder-pieces, close to its seam above the decorated band. [21]The breastpiece was held in place by a cord of blue from its rings to the rings of the ephod, so that the breastpiece rested on the decorated band and did not come loose from the ephod—as the LORD had commanded Moses.

[22]The robe for the ephod was made of woven work, of pure blue. [23]The opening of the robe, in the middle of it, was like the opening of a coat of mail, with a binding around the opening, so that it would not tear. [24]On the hem of the robe they made pomegranates of blue, purple, and crimson yarns, twisted. [25]They also made bells of pure gold, and attached the bells between the pomegranates, all around the hem of the robe, between the pomegranates: [26]a bell and a pomegranate, a bell and a pomegranate, all around the hem of the robe for officiating in—as the LORD had commanded Moses.

[27]They made the tunics of fine linen, of woven work, for Aaron and his sons; [28]and the headdress of fine linen, and the decorated turbans of fine linen, and the linen breeches of fine twisted linen; [29]and sashes of fine twisted linen, blue, purple, and crimson yarns, done in embroidery—as the LORD had commanded Moses.

[30]They made the frontlet for the holy diadem of pure gold, and incised upon it the seal inscription: "Holy to the LORD." [31]They attached to it a cord of blue to fix it upon the headdress above—as the LORD had commanded Moses.

[32]Thus was completed all the work of the Tab-

הָאֵפֹד מִלְּמַטָּה מִמּוּל פָּנָיו לְעֻמַּת
מַחְבַּרְתּוֹ מִמַּעַל לְחֵשֶׁב הָאֵפֹד׃ 21 וַיִּרְכְּסוּ
אֶת־הַחֹשֶׁן מִטַּבְּעֹתָיו אֶל־טַבְּעֹת הָאֵפֹד
בִּפְתִיל תְּכֵלֶת לִהְיֹת עַל־חֵשֶׁב הָאֵפֹד
וְלֹא־יִזַּח הַחֹשֶׁן מֵעַל הָאֵפֹד כַּאֲשֶׁר צִוָּה
יְהוָה אֶת־מֹשֶׁה׃
22 וַיַּעַשׂ אֶת־מְעִיל הָאֵפֹד מַעֲשֵׂה אֹרֵג שלישי [ששי]
כְּלִיל תְּכֵלֶת׃ 23 וּפִי־הַמְּעִיל בְּתוֹכוֹ כְּפִי
תַחְרָא שָׂפָה לְפִיו סָבִיב לֹא יִקָּרֵעַ׃
24 וַיַּעֲשׂוּ עַל־שׁוּלֵי הַמְּעִיל רִמּוֹנֵי תְּכֵלֶת
וְאַרְגָּמָן וְתוֹלַעַת שָׁנִי מָשְׁזָר׃ 25 וַיַּעֲשׂוּ
פַעֲמֹנֵי זָהָב טָהוֹר וַיִּתְּנוּ אֶת־הַפַּעֲמֹנִים
בְּתוֹךְ הָרִמֹּנִים עַל־שׁוּלֵי הַמְּעִיל סָבִיב
בְּתוֹךְ הָרִמֹּנִים׃ 26 פַּעֲמֹן וְרִמֹּן פַּעֲמֹן וְרִמֹּן
עַל־שׁוּלֵי הַמְּעִיל סָבִיב לְשָׁרֵת כַּאֲשֶׁר
צִוָּה יְהוָה אֶת־מֹשֶׁה׃ ס
27 וַיַּעֲשׂוּ אֶת־הַכָּתְנֹת שֵׁשׁ מַעֲשֵׂה אֹרֵג
לְאַהֲרֹן וּלְבָנָיו׃ 28 וְאֵת הַמִּצְנֶפֶת שֵׁשׁ
וְאֶת־פַּאֲרֵי הַמִּגְבָּעֹת שֵׁשׁ וְאֶת־מִכְנְסֵי
הַבָּד שֵׁשׁ מָשְׁזָר׃ 29 וְאֶת־הָאַבְנֵט שֵׁשׁ
מָשְׁזָר וּתְכֵלֶת וְאַרְגָּמָן וְתוֹלַעַת שָׁנִי
מַעֲשֵׂה רֹקֵם כַּאֲשֶׁר צִוָּה יְהוָה אֶת־
מֹשֶׁה׃ ס
30 וַיַּעֲשׂוּ אֶת־צִיץ נֵזֶר־הַקֹּדֶשׁ זָהָב טָהוֹר
וַיִּכְתְּבוּ עָלָיו מִכְתַּב פִּתּוּחֵי חוֹתָם קֹדֶשׁ
לַיהוָה׃ 31 וַיִּתְּנוּ עָלָיו פְּתִיל תְּכֵלֶת לָתֵת
עַל־הַמִּצְנֶפֶת מִלְמָעְלָה כַּאֲשֶׁר צִוָּה יְהוָה
אֶת־מֹשֶׁה׃ ס

32 וַתֵּכֶל כָּל־עֲבֹדַת מִשְׁכַּן אֹהֶל מוֹעֵד

CHAPTER 39

21. the breastpiece . . . did not come loose from the ephod The breastpiece was the symbol of justice (thus it is referred to as "the breastpiece of judgment" in Exod. 28:15), of proper relations between people and their neighbors. The ephod was the symbol of worship, i.e., of a proper relationship between people and God. When religion is properly understood, justice and worship can never be separated from each other (N. Bloch).

ernacle of the Tent of Meeting. The Israelites
did so; just as the LORD had commanded Moses,
so they did.
33Then they brought the Tabernacle to Moses, with the Tent and all its furnishings: its
clasps, its planks, its bars, its posts, and its sockets; 34the covering of tanned ram skins, the covering of dolphin skins, and the curtain for the
screen; 35the Ark of the Pact and its poles, and
the cover; 36the table and all its utensils, and
the bread of display; 37the pure lampstand, its
lamps—lamps in due order—and all its fittings,
and the oil for lighting; 38the altar of gold, the
oil for anointing, the aromatic incense, and the
screen for the entrance of the Tent; 39the copper
altar with its copper grating, its poles and all its
utensils, and the laver and its stand; 40the hangings of the enclosure, its posts and its sockets,
the screen for the gate of the enclosure, its cords
and its pegs—all the furnishings for the service
of the Tabernacle, the Tent of Meeting; 41the
service vestments for officiating in the sanctuary, the sacral vestments of Aaron the priest, and
the vestments of his sons for priestly service.
42Just as the LORD had commanded Moses, so
the Israelites had done all the work. 43And when
Moses saw that they had performed all the

וַֽיַּעֲשׂוּ֙ בְּנֵ֣י יִשְׂרָאֵ֔ל כְּכֹ֨ל אֲשֶׁ֨ר צִוָּ֧ה יְהוָ֛ה
אֶת־מֹשֶׁ֖ה כֵּ֥ן עָשֽׂוּ׃ פ
רביעי 33 וַיָּבִ֤יאוּ אֶת־הַמִּשְׁכָּן֙ אֶל־מֹשֶׁ֔ה אֶת־
הָאֹ֖הֶל וְאֶת־כׇּל־כֵּלָ֑יו קְרָסָ֣יו קְרָשָׁ֔יו בריחו
בְּרִיחָ֖יו וְעַמֻּדָ֥יו וַאֲדָנָֽיו׃ 34 וְאֶת־מִכְסֵ֞ה
עוֹרֹ֤ת הָֽאֵילִם֙ הַמְאׇדָּמִ֔ים וְאֶת־מִכְסֵ֖ה
עֹרֹ֣ת הַתְּחָשִׁ֑ים וְאֵ֖ת פָּרֹ֥כֶת הַמָּסָֽךְ׃
35 אֶת־אֲר֥וֹן הָעֵדֻ֖ת וְאֶת־בַּדָּ֑יו וְאֵ֖ת
הַכַּפֹּֽרֶת׃ 36 אֶת־הַשֻּׁלְחָן֙ אֶת־כׇּל־כֵּלָ֔יו
וְאֵ֖ת לֶ֥חֶם הַפָּנִֽים׃ 37 אֶת־הַמְּנֹרָ֨ה
הַטְּהֹרָ֜ה אֶת־נֵרֹתֶ֗יהָ נֵרֹ֛ת הַמַּעֲרָכָ֖ה וְאֶת־
כׇּל־כֵּלֶ֑יהָ וְאֵ֖ת שֶׁ֥מֶן הַמָּאֽוֹר׃ 38 וְאֵת֙
מִזְבַּ֣ח הַזָּהָ֔ב וְאֵת֙ שֶׁ֣מֶן הַמִּשְׁחָ֔ה וְאֵ֖ת
קְטֹ֣רֶת הַסַּמִּ֑ים וְאֵ֕ת מָסַ֖ךְ פֶּ֥תַח הָאֹֽהֶל׃
39 אֵ֣ת ׀ מִזְבַּ֣ח הַנְּחֹ֗שֶׁת וְאֶת־מִכְבַּ֤ר
הַנְּחֹ֙שֶׁת֙ אֲשֶׁר־ל֔וֹ אֶת־בַּדָּ֖יו וְאֶת־כׇּל־כֵּלָ֑יו
אֶת־הַכִּיֹּ֖ר וְאֶת־כַּנּֽוֹ׃ 40 אֵת֩ קַלְעֵ֨י הֶחָצֵ֜ר
אֶת־עַמֻּדֶ֣יהָ וְאֶת־אֲדָנֶ֗יהָ וְאֶת־הַמָּסָךְ֙
לְשַׁ֣עַר הֶחָצֵ֔ר אֶת־מֵיתָרָ֖יו וִיתֵדֹתֶ֑יהָ וְאֵ֗ת
כׇּל־כְּלֵ֛י עֲבֹדַ֥ת הַמִּשְׁכָּ֖ן לְאֹ֥הֶל מוֹעֵֽד׃
41 אֶת־בִּגְדֵ֥י הַשְּׂרָ֖ד לְשָׁרֵ֣ת בַּקֹּ֑דֶשׁ אֶת־
בִּגְדֵ֤י הַקֹּ֙דֶשׁ֙ לְאַהֲרֹ֣ן הַכֹּהֵ֔ן וְאֶת־בִּגְדֵ֥י בָנָ֖יו
לְכַהֵֽן׃ 42 כְּכֹ֛ל אֲשֶׁר־צִוָּ֥ה יְהוָ֖ה אֶת־מֹשֶׁ֑ה
כֵּ֤ן עָשׂוּ֙ בְּנֵ֣י יִשְׂרָאֵ֔ל אֵ֖ת כׇּל־הָעֲבֹדָֽה׃
43 וַיַּ֨רְא מֹשֶׁ֜ה אֶת־כׇּל־הַמְּלָאכָ֗ה וְהִנֵּה֙

COMPLETION AND INSPECTION (vv. 32–43)

The tabernacle in all its several parts and with all its appurtenances is completed and brought to Moses for inspection. The text does not record how long the work took or the dates involved.

32. Tabernacle of the Tent of Meeting A combination of the two distinct terms for the sanctuary. Together they express its dual function as the symbol of the indwelling of the divine Presence in the camp of the Israelites and as the site of communication between God and Moses.

42. the Israelites The entire project is presented as an enterprise of all the Israelites (cf. v. 32).

43. This finale is patterned after the Creation narrative of Genesis, in which the completion of the work evoked divine approval followed by a blessing.

---

43. The Midrash supplies the words with which Moses blessed the people: "May it be God's will that the divine Presence rest upon the work of your hands" (Tanḥ.).

tasks—as the LORD had commanded, so they had done—Moses blessed them.

40 And the LORD spoke to Moses, saying: 2On the first day of the first month you shall set up the Tabernacle of the Tent of Meeting. 3Place there the Ark of the Pact, and screen off the ark with the curtain. 4Bring in the table and lay out its due setting; bring in the lampstand and light its lamps; 5and place the gold altar of incense before the Ark of the Pact. Then put up the screen for the entrance of the Tabernacle.

6You shall place the altar of burnt offering before the entrance of the Tabernacle of the Tent of Meeting. 7Place the laver between the Tent of Meeting and the altar, and put water in it. 8Set up the enclosure round about, and put in place the screen for the gate of the enclosure.

9You shall take the anointing oil and anoint the Tabernacle and all that is in it to consecrate it and all its furnishings, so that it shall be holy. 10Then anoint the altar of burnt offering and all its utensils to consecrate the altar, so that the altar shall be most holy. 11And anoint the laver and its stand to consecrate it.

12You shall bring Aaron and his sons forward to the entrance of the Tent of Meeting and wash them with the water. 13Put the sacral vestments on Aaron, and anoint him and consecrate him,

עָשׂוּ אֹתָהּ כַּאֲשֶׁר צִוָּה יְהוָה כֵּן עָשׂוּ
וַיְבָרֶךְ אֹתָם מֹשֶׁה׃ פ

חמישי [שביעי] **מ** וַיְדַבֵּר יְהוָה אֶל־מֹשֶׁה לֵּאמֹר׃
2 בְּיוֹם־הַחֹדֶשׁ הָרִאשׁוֹן בְּאֶחָד לַחֹדֶשׁ
תָּקִים אֶת־מִשְׁכַּן אֹהֶל מוֹעֵד׃ 3 וְשַׂמְתָּ
שָׁם אֵת אֲרוֹן הָעֵדוּת וְסַכֹּתָ עַל־הָאָרֹן
אֶת־הַפָּרֹכֶת׃ 4 וְהֵבֵאתָ אֶת־הַשֻּׁלְחָן
וְעָרַכְתָּ אֶת־עֶרְכּוֹ וְהֵבֵאתָ אֶת־הַמְּנֹרָה
וְהַעֲלֵיתָ אֶת־נֵרֹתֶיהָ׃ 5 וְנָתַתָּה אֶת־מִזְבַּח
הַזָּהָב לִקְטֹרֶת לִפְנֵי אֲרוֹן הָעֵדֻת וְשַׂמְתָּ
אֶת־מָסַךְ הַפֶּתַח לַמִּשְׁכָּן׃
6 וְנָתַתָּה אֵת מִזְבַּח הָעֹלָה לִפְנֵי פֶּתַח
מִשְׁכַּן אֹהֶל־מוֹעֵד׃ 7 וְנָתַתָּ אֶת־הַכִּיֹּר בֵּין־
אֹהֶל מוֹעֵד וּבֵין הַמִּזְבֵּחַ וְנָתַתָּ שָׁם מָיִם׃
8 וְשַׂמְתָּ אֶת־הֶחָצֵר סָבִיב וְנָתַתָּ אֶת־מָסַךְ
שַׁעַר הֶחָצֵר׃
9 וְלָקַחְתָּ אֶת־שֶׁמֶן הַמִּשְׁחָה וּמָשַׁחְתָּ
אֶת־הַמִּשְׁכָּן וְאֶת־כָּל־אֲשֶׁר־בּוֹ וְקִדַּשְׁתָּ
אֹתוֹ וְאֶת־כָּל־כֵּלָיו וְהָיָה קֹדֶשׁ׃
10 וּמָשַׁחְתָּ אֶת־מִזְבַּח הָעֹלָה וְאֶת־כָּל־
כֵּלָיו וְקִדַּשְׁתָּ אֶת־הַמִּזְבֵּחַ וְהָיָה הַמִּזְבֵּחַ
קֹדֶשׁ קָדָשִׁים׃ 11 וּמָשַׁחְתָּ אֶת־הַכִּיֹּר וְאֶת־
כַּנּוֹ וְקִדַּשְׁתָּ אֹתוֹ׃
12 וְהִקְרַבְתָּ אֶת־אַהֲרֹן וְאֶת־בָּנָיו אֶל־
פֶּתַח אֹהֶל מוֹעֵד וְרָחַצְתָּ אֹתָם בַּמָּיִם׃
13 וְהִלְבַּשְׁתָּ אֶת־אַהֲרֹן אֵת בִּגְדֵי הַקֹּדֶשׁ

ASSEMBLY AND DEDICATION
(40:1–15)

1–8. Moses is instructed by God to set up the tabernacle and put each item in its assigned place. The order of emplacement of the furnishings is from the interior outward, from the most sacred to the less sacred. The tabernacle is to be erected just two weeks short of the first anniversary of the Exodus from Egypt, and exactly nine months since the arrival at Sinai. This is New Year's day, a date that forges another link with the Creation narrative.

3. curtain See Comments to 26:31–35.

4. lay out its due setting The 12 loaves of the bread of display set out in two rows. See Comment to 25:30.

9–11. During the next stage every item is anointed with the sacred aromatic anointing oil. See Comments to 30:22–33.

12–15. The priests are installed. See Comments to 29:1–9.

that he may serve Me as priest. 14Then bring his sons forward, put tunics on them, 15and anoint them as you have anointed their father, that they may serve Me as priests. This their anointing shall serve them for everlasting priesthood throughout the ages.

16This Moses did; just as the LORD had commanded him, so he did.

17In the first month of the second year, on the first of the month, the Tabernacle was set up. 18Moses set up the Tabernacle, placing its sockets, setting up its planks, inserting its bars, and erecting its posts. 19He spread the tent over the Tabernacle, placing the covering of the tent on top of it—just as the LORD had commanded Moses.

20He took the Pact and placed it in the ark; he fixed the poles to the ark, placed the cover on top of the ark, 21and brought the ark inside the Tabernacle. Then he put up the curtain for screening, and screened off the Ark of the Pact—just as the LORD had commanded Moses.

וּמָשַׁחְתָּ֥ אֹת֛וֹ וְקִדַּשְׁתָּ֥ אֹת֖וֹ וְכִהֵ֥ן לִֽי׃
14 וְאֶת־בָּנָ֖יו תַּקְרִ֑יב וְהִלְבַּשְׁתָּ֥ אֹתָ֖ם
כֻּתֳּנֹֽת׃ 15 וּמָשַׁחְתָּ֣ אֹתָ֗ם כַּאֲשֶׁ֤ר מָשַׁ֙חְתָּ֙
אֶת־אֲבִיהֶ֔ם וְכִהֲנ֖וּ לִ֑י וְֽהָיְתָ֡ה לִהְיֹ֨ת לָהֶ֧ם
מָשְׁחָתָ֛ם לִכְהֻנַּ֥ת עוֹלָ֖ם לְדֹרֹתָֽם׃
16 וַיַּ֖עַשׂ מֹשֶׁ֑ה כְּ֠כֹל אֲשֶׁ֨ר צִוָּ֧ה יְהֹוָ֛ה אֹת֖וֹ
כֵּ֥ן עָשָֽׂה׃ ס

ששי 17 וַיְהִ֞י בַּחֹ֧דֶשׁ הָרִאשׁ֛וֹן בַּשָּׁנָ֥ה הַשֵּׁנִ֖ית
בְּאֶחָ֣ד לַחֹ֑דֶשׁ הוּקַ֖ם הַמִּשְׁכָּֽן׃ 18 וַיָּ֨קֶם
מֹשֶׁ֜ה אֶת־הַמִּשְׁכָּ֗ן וַיִּתֵּן֙ אֶת־אֲדָנָ֔יו
וַיָּ֙שֶׂם֙ אֶת־קְרָשָׁ֔יו וַיִּתֵּ֖ן אֶת־בְּרִיחָ֑יו וַיָּ֖קֶם
אֶת־עַמּוּדָֽיו׃ 19 וַיִּפְרֹ֤שׂ אֶת־הָאֹ֙הֶל֙ עַל־
הַמִּשְׁכָּ֔ן וַיָּ֜שֶׂם אֶת־מִכְסֵ֥ה הָאֹ֛הֶל עָלָ֖יו
מִלְמָ֑עְלָה כַּאֲשֶׁ֛ר צִוָּ֥ה יְהֹוָ֖ה אֶת־
מֹשֶֽׁה׃ ס
20 וַיִּקַּ֞ח וַיִּתֵּ֤ן אֶת־הָעֵדֻת֙ אֶל־הָ֣אָרֹ֔ן וַיָּ֥שֶׂם
אֶת־הַבַּדִּ֖ים עַל־הָאָרֹ֑ן וַיִּתֵּ֧ן אֶת־הַכַּפֹּ֛רֶת
עַל־הָאָרֹ֖ן מִלְמָֽעְלָה׃ 21 וַיָּבֵ֣א אֶת־הָאָרֹן֮
אֶל־הַמִּשְׁכָּן֒ וַיָּ֗שֶׂם אֵ֚ת פָּרֹ֣כֶת הַמָּסָ֔ךְ וַיָּ֕סֶךְ
עַ֖ל אֲר֣וֹן הָעֵד֑וּת כַּאֲשֶׁ֛ר צִוָּ֥ה יְהֹוָ֖ה אֶת־
מֹשֶֽׁה׃ ס

FULFILLING THE INSTRUCTIONS
(vv. 16–33)

16. This Moses did This affirmation applies to all the foregoing instructions. The details are spelled out, item by item, as though to emphasize the point.

CHAPTER 40

15. as you have anointed their father When Moses anointed Aaron as High Priest, he had no reason to be jealous of Aaron. Moses' role was at least as prominent as Aaron's. When Moses was called on to anoint Aaron's sons to follow him as priests, however, God was concerned that Moses might be jealous. He would never see his sons succeed him in his role as leader. Therefore, God commands Moses to show his greatness of character and his love for his brother by anointing Aaron's sons in the same wholehearted fashion as he had anointed their father. We show true love when we can rejoice in the good fortune of another even though it is an experience that we ourselves will never know.

HALAKHAH L'MA·ASEH

40:16. as the LORD had commanded him, so he did As Conservative Jews, we are motivated in our commitment to Jewish observance as an expression of our allegiance to God as the divine commander with whom we live in covenant.

[22]He placed the table in the Tent of Meeting,
outside the curtain, on the north side of the Tabernacle. [23]Upon it he laid out the setting of bread
before the LORD—as the LORD had commanded
Moses. [24]He placed the lampstand in the Tent
of Meeting opposite the table, on the south side
of the Tabernacle. [25]And he lit the lamps before
the LORD—as the LORD had commanded Mo-
ses. [26]He placed the altar of gold in the Tent of
Meeting, before the curtain. [27]On it he burned
aromatic incense—as the LORD had commanded Moses.

[28]Then he put up the screen for the entrance
of the Tabernacle. [29]At the entrance of the Tabernacle of the Tent of Meeting he placed the altar
of burnt offering. On it he offered up the burnt
offering and the grain offering—as the LORD
had commanded Moses. [30]He placed the laver
between the Tent of Meeting and the altar, and
put water in it for washing. [31]From it Moses and
Aaron and his sons would wash their hands
and feet; [32]they washed when they entered the
Tent of Meeting and when they approached
the altar—as the LORD had commanded Moses.
[33]And he set up the enclosure around the Tabernacle and the altar, and put up the screen for
the gate of the enclosure.

When Moses had finished the work, [34]the
cloud covered the Tent of Meeting, and the
Presence of the LORD filled the Tabernacle.
[35]Moses could not enter the Tent of Meeting,

22 וַיִּתֵּן אֶת־הַשֻּׁלְחָן בְּאֹהֶל מוֹעֵד עַל יֶרֶךְ
הַמִּשְׁכָּן צָפֹנָה מִחוּץ לַפָּרֹכֶת׃ 23 וַיַּעֲרֹךְ
עָלָיו עֵרֶךְ לֶחֶם לִפְנֵי יְהוָה כַּאֲשֶׁר
צִוָּה יְהוָה אֶת־מֹשֶׁה׃ ס 24 וַיָּשֶׂם אֶת־
הַמְּנֹרָה בְּאֹהֶל מוֹעֵד נֹכַח הַשֻּׁלְחָן עַל
יֶרֶךְ הַמִּשְׁכָּן נֶגְבָּה׃ 25 וַיַּעַל הַנֵּרֹת לִפְנֵי
יְהוָה כַּאֲשֶׁר צִוָּה יְהוָה אֶת־מֹשֶׁה׃ ס
26 וַיָּשֶׂם אֶת־מִזְבַּח הַזָּהָב בְּאֹהֶל מוֹעֵד
לִפְנֵי הַפָּרֹכֶת׃ 27 וַיַּקְטֵר עָלָיו קְטֹרֶת סַמִּים
כַּאֲשֶׁר צִוָּה יְהוָה אֶת־מֹשֶׁה׃ פ
שביעי 28 וַיָּשֶׂם אֶת־מָסַךְ הַפֶּתַח לַמִּשְׁכָּן׃ 29 וְאֵת
מִזְבַּח הָעֹלָה שָׂם פֶּתַח מִשְׁכַּן אֹהֶל־
מוֹעֵד וַיַּעַל עָלָיו אֶת־הָעֹלָה וְאֶת־
הַמִּנְחָה כַּאֲשֶׁר צִוָּה יְהוָה אֶת־מֹשֶׁה׃ ס
30 וַיָּשֶׂם אֶת־הַכִּיֹּר בֵּין־אֹהֶל מוֹעֵד וּבֵין
הַמִּזְבֵּחַ וַיִּתֵּן שָׁמָּה מַיִם לְרָחְצָה׃
31 וְרָחֲצוּ מִמֶּנּוּ מֹשֶׁה וְאַהֲרֹן וּבָנָיו אֶת־
יְדֵיהֶם וְאֶת־רַגְלֵיהֶם׃ 32 בְּבֹאָם אֶל־אֹהֶל
מוֹעֵד וּבְקָרְבָתָם אֶל־הַמִּזְבֵּחַ יִרְחָצוּ
כַּאֲשֶׁר צִוָּה יְהוָה אֶת־מֹשֶׁה׃ ס 33 וַיָּקֶם
אֶת־הֶחָצֵר סָבִיב לַמִּשְׁכָּן וְלַמִּזְבֵּחַ וַיִּתֵּן
אֶת־מָסַךְ שַׁעַר הֶחָצֵר
מפטיר וַיְכַל מֹשֶׁה אֶת־הַמְּלָאכָה׃ פ 34 וַיְכַס
הֶעָנָן אֶת־אֹהֶל מוֹעֵד וּכְבוֹד יְהוָה מָלֵא
אֶת־הַמִּשְׁכָּן׃ 35 וְלֹא־יָכֹל מֹשֶׁה לָבוֹא

29. he offered up The subject is either Moses or Aaron and his sons.

33. When Moses had finished the work The Hebrew word for "finished" (*va-y'khal*) echoes the same word in a different form (*va-y'khullu*) at the close of the story of Creation (Gen. 2:1). This is significant, because the link between shrines and Creation was traditional in the ancient world. It is echoed both in the structure of the tabernacle and in the procedure entailed in its construction.

APPEARANCE OF THE DIVINE PRESENCE
(vv. 34–38)

34. cloud . . . Presence The tabernacle was to function as a portable Sinai, a means by which a continued channel of communication with God could be maintained. As the people move away from the mountain of Revelation, they need a visible, tangible symbol of God's abiding presence in their midst. Thus the phenomenon that oc-

35. At this point, there are two embodiments of holiness in the Israelite camp: the Tent of Meeting (*Ohel Mo·ed*) and the tabernacle (*mishkan*). We can think of them as rep-

אֶל־אֹהֶל מוֹעֵד כִּי־שָׁכַן עָלָיו הֶעָנָן וּכְבוֹד
יְהֹוָה מָלֵא אֶת־הַמִּשְׁכָּן׃ 36 וּבְהֵעָלוֹת
הֶעָנָן מֵעַל הַמִּשְׁכָּן יִסְעוּ בְּנֵי יִשְׂרָאֵל בְּכֹל
מַסְעֵיהֶם׃ 37 וְאִם־לֹא יֵעָלֶה הֶעָנָן וְלֹא
יִסְעוּ עַד־יוֹם הֵעָלֹתוֹ׃ 38 כִּי עֲנַן יְהֹוָה
עַל־הַמִּשְׁכָּן יוֹמָם וְאֵשׁ תִּהְיֶה לַיְלָה בּוֹ
לְעֵינֵי כָל־בֵּית־יִשְׂרָאֵל בְּכָל־מַסְעֵיהֶם׃*

v. 38. למערבאי סכום הפסוקים של הספר 1,209 וחציו 22:27

because the cloud had settled upon it and the Presence of the LORD filled the Tabernacle.
36When the cloud lifted from the Tabernacle, the Israelites would set out, on their various journeys; 37but if the cloud did not lift, they would not set out until such time as it did lift.
38For over the Tabernacle a cloud of the LORD rested by day, and fire would appear in it by night, in the view of all the house of Israel throughout their journeys.

חֲזַק חֲזַק וְנִתְחַזֵּק

curred at Mount Sinai (see 24:15–17) now repeats itself.

35. It is unclear whether entry is literally blocked or is not permissible or that Moses simply dared not enter.

36–38. Henceforth, Israel's wanderings and encampments in the wilderness on the way to the Promised Land are determined by the movements of the luminous cloud.

The Book of Exodus, which opened with a narrative of misery and oppression, closes on a note of confidence and hope. Israel is assured that, day and night, the divine spirit hovers over it, guiding and controlling its destiny (see Num. 9:15–23).

---

resenting a theology of encounter and a theology of presence. There are moments (a wedding, the birth of a child, an escape from danger) when God erupts into our lives with a special intensity that transforms us but that is too intense to be lived constantly. Then there are times when God is a constant presence in our lives (marriage, parenthood, years of good health) in an equally real but less intense manner. The challenge is to recognize God's constant presence in our lives without its becoming so ordinary that we take it for granted. After all of this dedicated effort—taking up four-and-a-half *parashiyyot* of the Book of Exodus—God comes down and approves of the work. The Book of Exodus ends on that note. "Our book which began in darkness concludes in the brilliant illumination of God's glory before the eyes of the entire House of Israel" (B. Jacob).

הפטרת ויקהל

HAFTARAH FOR VA-YAK·HEL

1 KINGS 7:40–50 (*Ashk'nazim*)

הפטרת פקודי

HAFTARAH FOR P'KUDEI

1 KINGS 7:40–50 (*S'fardim*)

This *haftarah* includes a summary of constructing furnishings for the house of the Lord. It comes after an account of building the Temple and a trade agreement for goods and services made with Hiram, king of Tyre (1 Kings 5:15–26, 6:1–7:12), as well as a description of the copper work cast for the Temple executed by another Hiram, a master craftsman also from Tyre (1 Kings 7:13–46).

The contrast between the craftsman Hiram, who works in bronze for objects found outside the most sacred area, and Solomon, the (inspired) Judean who works in gold on objects having more sacred or special status, is not accidental. In the wilderness tabernacle, degrees of sanctity are correlated with the value of metals used; the same is true in the Temple. Moreover, both the furniture and objects of the Outer Court were bronzed, whereas those in the inner holy space were plated with "pure" or refined gold. In the tabernacle, the Ark in the Holy of Holies was gold plated inside and out, whereas the Ark cover (*kaporet*) was a solid slab of pure gold. Correspondingly (according to an earlier report) King Solomon overlaid "the entire House" and its "floor" with gold, including "the entire altar of the Shrine"; "the cherubim"; and even the cherubim, palms, and calyxes on the walls of the house and on the double doors of the entrance of the Shrine and Great Hall (1 Kings 6:21–22,28–29,32,35).

Pilgrims rejoiced at the thought of ascending to the Temple in Jerusalem (Ps. 122:1); the pious yearned for its glories and its spiritual benefits. Speaking for many, one psalmist prayed: "One thing I ask of the LORD, / only that do I seek: / to live in the house of the LORD / all the days of my life, / to gaze upon the beauty of the LORD, / [and] to frequent His Temple" (Ps. 27:4).

RELATION OF THE *HAFTARAH* TO THE *PARASHAH*

This *haftarah* is recited by *Ashk'nazim* and *S'fardim* for Torah portions that focus on construction details of the tabernacle erected in the wilderness. In the *haftarah,* the language that describes the building of the Temple echoes that which described the building of the tabernacle. The tabernacle was built by Bezalel, who was "singled out" by God and "endowed" with "a divine spirit of skill (*ḥokhmah*), ability (*t'vunah*), and knowledge (*da·at*) in every kind of craft (*u-v'khol m'lakhah*)" (Exod. 35:31). Likewise, the brass work of the Temple is the work of Hiram, "endowed with skill (*ḥokhmah*), ability (*t'vunah*), and talent (*da·at*) for executing all work (*kol m'lakhah*) in bronze" (1 Kings 7:14).

The *haftarah* contains other linguistic echoes of the Torah portions *Va-yak·hel* and *P'kudei.* Thus the verb used about Bezalel in his work on the tabernacle objects and Hiram and Solomon in their work on the Temple is *va-ya·as* (he made). This verb also echoes part of the Creation account in Genesis (1:7,16,25). This suggests a link between the Creation, the tabernacle, and the Tem-

ple. The correlation is reinforced by the repetition of other keywords. The tabernacle report concludes with the comment that "Moses finished (*va-y'khal*) the work (*et ha-m'lakhah*)" (Exod. 40:33). The Temple description notes that "Hiram finished (*va-y'khal la·asot*) all the work (*et kol ha-m'lakhah*) he had been doing (*asher asah*) for King Solomon" (7:40). Both of these recall summaries of the Creation account: "On the seventh day God finished (*va-y'khal*) the work (*m'lakhto*) He had been doing (*asher asah*)" (Gen. 2:2). It may be added that "God blessed" (*va-y'varekh*) that day "and declared it holy" (*va-y'kaddesh*, 2:3). Correspondingly, "when Moses saw that [the people] had performed all the tasks (*kol ha-m'lakhah*) . . . Moses blessed (*va-y'varekh*) them" (Exod. 39:43), and "declared holy" (*va-y'kaddesh*) the tabernacle immediately upon its completion (Num. 7:1).

The sages of old, aware of such linguistic patterns, offered rich developments on the theme. A *midrash* suggests that the features of the tabernacle fully corresponded to the works of Creation (Tanḥ. P'kudei 2). Included are correlations of the curtains with the heavens; the brazen tank with the waters of the sea, the golden candlesticks with the lights in the firmament, and the winged cherubs with the fowl in the firmament of heaven. A more elaborate example of this symbolism occurs later in *Midrash Tadshei*, which conflates the tabernacle and the Temple into one ensemble. This establishes a correlation of the Creation, the tabernacle, and the Temple. Using other recurrent terms, a *midrash* extends this correlation to include the future Temple at the end of days (Tanḥ. Va-yak·hel 5).

7 40Hiram also made the lavers, the scrapers,
and the sprinkling bowls.

So Hiram finished all the work that he had
been doing for King Solomon on the House of
the LORD: 41the two columns, the two globes of
the capitals upon the columns; and the two
pieces of network to cover the two globes of the
capitals upon the columns; 42the four hundred
pomegranates for the two pieces of network,
two rows of pomegranates for each network, to
cover the two globes of the capitals upon the
columns; 43the ten stands and the ten lavers
upon the stands; 44the one tank with the twelve

ז 40 וַיַּעַשׂ חִירוֹם אֶת־הַכִּיֹּרוֹת וְאֶת־
הַיָּעִים וְאֶת־הַמִּזְרָקוֹת

וַיְכַל חִירָם לַעֲשׂוֹת אֶת־כָּל־הַמְּלָאכָה
אֲשֶׁר עָשָׂה לַמֶּלֶךְ שְׁלֹמֹה בֵּית יְהוָה׃
41 עַמֻּדִים שְׁנַיִם וְגֻלֹּת הַכֹּתָרֹת אֲשֶׁר־עַל־
רֹאשׁ הָעַמֻּדִים שְׁתָּיִם וְהַשְּׂבָכוֹת שְׁתַּיִם
לְכַסּוֹת אֶת־שְׁתֵּי גֻּלֹּת הַכֹּתָרֹת אֲשֶׁר
עַל־רֹאשׁ הָעַמּוּדִים׃ 42 וְאֶת־הָרִמֹּנִים
אַרְבַּע מֵאוֹת לִשְׁתֵּי הַשְּׂבָכוֹת שְׁנֵי־טוּרִים
רִמֹּנִים לַשְּׂבָכָה הָאֶחָת לְכַסּוֹת אֶת־שְׁתֵּי
גֻּלֹּת הַכֹּתָרֹת אֲשֶׁר עַל־פְּנֵי הָעַמּוּדִים׃
43 וְאֶת־הַמְּכֹנוֹת עֶשֶׂר וְאֶת־הַכִּיֹּרֹת
עֲשָׂרָה עַל־הַמְּכֹנוֹת׃ 44 וְאֶת־הַיָּם הָאֶחָד

1 Kings 7:40. Hiram The son of a widow from the tribe of Naphtali, whose father was a Tyrian coppersmith. Called Huram in 2 Chron. 2:12. According to 2 Chron. 2:13, he was "the son of a Danite woman, his father a Tyrian." In the Midrash, the genealogy in Chronicles served as the basis for a comparison between the artisans of the tabernacle and of the Temple. Just as Bezalel the Judean, and his assistant Oholiab, from the tribe of Dan (Exod. 31:2,6), were the chief craftsmen in the construction of the tabernacle, Solomon the Judean and Hiram the Danite were responsible for the artwork of the Temple. The "two tribes [Judah and Dan] were [thus] partners" in both affairs (PR 6).

44. the . . . tank Hebrew: *ha-yam*, literally,

oxen underneath the tank; 45the pails, the scrapers, and the sprinkling bowls. All those vessels
in the House of the LORD that Hiram made for
King Solomon were of burnished bronze. 46The
king had them cast in earthen molds, in the plain
of the Jordan between Succoth and Zarethan.
47Solomon left all the vessels [unweighed] because of their very great quantity; the weight of
the bronze was not reckoned.

וְאֶת־הַבָּקָר שְׁנֵים־עָשָׂר תַּחַת הַיָּם׃
45 וְאֶת־הַסִּירוֹת וְאֶת־הַיָּעִים וְאֶת־
הַמִּזְרָקוֹת וְאֵת כָּל־הַכֵּלִים האהל הָאֵלֶּה
אֲשֶׁר עָשָׂה חִירָם לַמֶּלֶךְ שְׁלֹמֹה בֵּית יְהוָה
נְחֹשֶׁת מְמֹרָט׃ 46 בְּכִכַּר הַיַּרְדֵּן יְצָקָם
הַמֶּלֶךְ בְּמַעֲבֵה הָאֲדָמָה בֵּין סֻכּוֹת וּבֵין
צָרְתָן׃ 47 וַיַּנַּח שְׁלֹמֹה אֶת־כָּל־הַכֵּלִים
מֵרֹב מְאֹד מְאֹד לֹא נֶחְקַר מִשְׁקַל
הַנְּחֹשֶׁת׃

48And Solomon made all the furnishings that
were in the House of the LORD: the altar, of gold;
the table for the bread of display, of gold; 49the
lampstands—five on the right side and five on
the left—in front of the Shrine, of solid gold;
and the petals, lamps, and tongs, of gold; 50the
basins, snuffers, sprinkling bowls, ladles, and
fire pans, of solid gold; and the hinge sockets
for the doors of the innermost part of the House,
the Holy of Holies, and for the doors of the Great
Hall of the House, of gold.

48 וַיַּעַשׂ שְׁלֹמֹה אֵת כָּל־הַכֵּלִים אֲשֶׁר בֵּית
יְהוָה אֵת מִזְבַּח הַזָּהָב וְאֶת־הַשֻּׁלְחָן אֲשֶׁר
עָלָיו לֶחֶם הַפָּנִים זָהָב׃ 49 וְאֶת־הַמְּנֹרוֹת
חָמֵשׁ מִיָּמִין וְחָמֵשׁ מִשְּׂמֹאול לִפְנֵי הַדְּבִיר
זָהָב סָגוּר וְהַפֶּרַח וְהַנֵּרֹת וְהַמֶּלְקַחַיִם
זָהָב׃ 50 וְהַסִּפּוֹת וְהַמְזַמְּרוֹת וְהַמִּזְרָקוֹת
וְהַכַּפּוֹת וְהַמַּחְתּוֹת זָהָב סָגוּר וְהַפֹּתוֹת
לְדַלְתוֹת הַבַּיִת הַפְּנִימִי לְקֹדֶשׁ הַקֳּדָשִׁים
לְדַלְתֵי הַבַּיִת לַהֵיכָל זָהָב׃ פ

"the sea." This was an enormous drum, about 18 feet (10 cubits) in diameter and about 9 feet (5 cubits) deep. There were also 10 smaller basins (v. 43), each called *kiyor.* The large tank was supported by 12 brazen oxen, 3 facing each of the cardinal points (vv. 23–26). Moreover, the separate basins had insets engraved with images of lions, oxen, and cherubim (vv. 28–29) and were set on the likes of "chariot wheels" (v. 33). This iconography recalls the chariot of the divine glory in Ezek. 1, supported at the corners by four beings with four faces: human, lion, bull, and eagle (1:10–11). Ezekiel calls the beings "cherubim" (10:1ff). In ancient Near Eastern art it was common for such animals, or composites of human shapes with animal faces, to serve as pedestals for images of gods or supports for divine or royal chariots. It is possible that "the sea" and its supports symbolically refer to the lower world, whereas the Throne and its supports refer to the upper realm. Alternatively, given the existence of an upper sea in ancient Israelite cosmology (Gen. 1:7), "the sea" may have cosmic symbolism and refer to the supports and waters of the heavenly realm.

48. the altar, of gold This is the altar of incense, which was gilded.

49. the lampstands—five on the right side and five on the left According to tradition, these lampstands were set to the right and to the left of the original candelabrum of the tabernacle made by Moses (Rashi, Radak).

lamps These were receptacles for the oil and wicks (Rashi).

tongs For the removal of the wicks (Rashi).

50. sprinkling bowls Hebrew: *mizrakot.* These were the receptacles for the blood of the sacrifices (Rashi, Ralbag).

fire pans Used to carry the glowing coals from the outer altar to the inner one, on which the incense was burned (Rashi, Ralbag).

הפטרת ויקהל

HAFTARAH FOR VA-YAK·HEL

1 KINGS 7:13–26 (*S'fardim*)

This *haftarah* delineates in detail some of the brasswork done for the Temple by the craftsman Hiram of Tyre as commissioned by King Solomon. The text presents Hiram as a person of extraordinary skill—like Bezalel, the grand artisan of the tabernacle, although he lacks Bezalel's divine inspiration (Exod. 35:31). The details of Hiram's work described in the *haftarah* attest to the high level of design and brasswork he and his guild had achieved.

A large tank was supported by 12 brazen oxen, 3 facing each of the cardinal points (1 Kings 7:23–26). The separate lavers (not mentioned in the *haftarah*) had inserts engraved with images of lions, oxen, and cherubim (vv. 28–29) and were set on the likes of "chariot wheels" (v. 33). This imagery recalls the chariot of the divine glory in Ezekiel 1, supported at the corners by four beings with four faces: human, lion, bull, and eagle (1:1–11). Thus the large tank (literally, "sea," *yam*) may symbolize the lower earthly realm and its supports, just as the divine Throne in the upper realm had its supports. Alternatively, given the existence of an upper sea in ancient Israelite cosmology (Gen. 1:7), "the sea" may have cosmic symbolism and refer to the supports and waters of the heavenly realm.

RELATION OF THE *HAFTARAH* TO THE *PARASHAH*

The Sages found a deep connection between the Creation (divine wisdom), the tabernacle (Bezalel's wisdom), Solomon's Temple (Hiram's wisdom), and the new Temple to be built in the end of days (Tanḥ. Va-yak·hel 5). This connection is based on the themes and words of the respective texts. The tradition further connects the basin of the tabernacle described in the *parashah* with the gathered waters of Creation (Tanḥ. P'kudei 2). This basin (Exod. 38:8) corresponds to the giant tank ("sea") in the Temple, set on 12 oxen (1 Kings 7:23–26). An extended interpretation relates the solid "sea" to the world itself, and correlates its dimensions to various old Rabbinic accounts about the distance between the earth and the firmament (Mid. Tad. 2). In a further comment, the 12 oxen are deemed to symbolize "the twelve constellations by which the earth is governed."

7 13King Solomon sent for Hiram and
brought him down from Tyre. 14He was the son
of a widow of the tribe of Naphtali, and his father had been a Tyrian, a coppersmith. He was
endowed with skill, ability, and talent for executing all work in bronze. He came to King Solomon and executed all his work. 15He cast two

ז 13 וַיִּשְׁלַח הַמֶּלֶךְ שְׁלֹמֹה וַיִּקַּח אֶת־
חִירָם מִצֹּר׃ 14 בֶּן־אִשָּׁה אַלְמָנָה הוּא
מִמַּטֵּה נַפְתָּלִי וְאָבִיו אִישׁ־צֹרִי חֹרֵשׁ
נְחֹשֶׁת וַיִּמָּלֵא אֶת־הַחָכְמָה וְאֶת־
הַתְּבוּנָה וְאֶת־הַדַּעַת לַעֲשׂוֹת כָּל־
מְלָאכָה בַּנְּחֹשֶׁת וַיָּבוֹא אֶל־הַמֶּלֶךְ שְׁלֹמֹה

1 Kings 7:14. Hiram . . . son of a widow of the tribe of Naphtali In 2 Chron. 2:12 this same individual is called Huram, described in 2:13 as the "son of a Danite woman, his father a Tyrian." Rabbinic tradition preferred the second genealogy traced to the tribe of Dan, because

columns of bronze; one column was 18 cubits high and measured 12 cubits in circumference, [and similarly] the other column. ¹⁶He made two capitals, cast in bronze, to be set upon the two columns, the height of each of the two capitals being 5 cubits; ¹⁷also nets of meshwork with festoons of chainwork for the capitals that were on the top of the columns, seven for each of the two capitals. ¹⁸He made the columns so that there were two rows [of pomegranates] encircling the top of the one network, to cover the capitals that were on the top of the pomegranates; and he did the same for [the network on] the second capital. ¹⁹The capitals upon the columns of the portico were of lily design, 4 cubits high; ²⁰so also the capitals upon the two columns extended above and next to the bulge that was beside the network. There were 200 pomegranates in rows around the top of the second capital.

²¹He set up the columns at the portico of the Great Hall; he set up one column on the right and named it Jachin, and he set up the other column on the left and named it Boaz. ²²Upon the top of the columns there was a lily design. Thus the work of the columns was completed.

15 וַיַּעַשׂ אֶת־כָּל־מְלַאכְתּֽוֹ: וַיָּ֙צַר֙ אֶת־שְׁנֵ֣י הָעַמּוּדִ֔ים נְחֹ֕שֶׁת שְׁמֹנֶ֨ה עֶשְׂרֵ֤ה אַמָּה֙ קוֹמַת֙ הָעַמּ֣וּד הָֽאֶחָ֔ד וְח֣וּט שְׁתֵּים־עֶשְׂרֵ֥ה אַמָּ֖ה יָסֹ֛ב אֶת־הָעַמּ֥וּד הַשֵּׁנִֽי: 16 וּשְׁתֵּ֨י כֹֽתָרֹ֜ת עָשָׂ֗ה לָתֵ֛ת עַל־רָאשֵׁ֥י הָעַמּוּדִ֖ים מֻצַ֣ק נְחֹ֑שֶׁת חָמֵ֣שׁ אַמּ֗וֹת קוֹמַת֙ הַכֹּתֶ֣רֶת הָֽאֶחָ֔ת וְחָמֵ֣שׁ אַמּ֔וֹת קוֹמַ֖ת הַכֹּתֶ֥רֶת הַשֵּׁנִֽית: 17 שְׂבָכִ֞ים מַעֲשֵׂ֣ה שְׂבָכָ֗ה גְּדִלִים֙ מַעֲשֵׂ֣ה שַׁרְשְׁר֔וֹת לַכֹּ֣תָרֹ֔ת אֲשֶׁ֖ר עַל־רֹ֣אשׁ הָעַמּוּדִ֑ים שִׁבְעָה֙ לַכֹּתֶ֣רֶת הָֽאֶחָ֔ת וְשִׁבְעָ֖ה לַכֹּתֶ֥רֶת הַשֵּׁנִֽית: 18 וַיַּ֖עַשׂ אֶת־הָעַמּוּדִ֑ים וּשְׁנֵי֩ טוּרִ֨ים סָבִ֜יב עַל־הַשְּׂבָכָ֣ה הָֽאֶחָ֗ת לְכַסּ֤וֹת אֶת־הַכֹּֽתָרֹת֙ אֲשֶׁ֣ר עַל־רֹ֣אשׁ הָֽרִמֹּנִ֔ים וְכֵ֣ן עָשָׂ֔ה לַכֹּתֶ֖רֶת הַשֵּׁנִֽית: 19 וְכֹֽתָרֹ֗ת אֲשֶׁר֙ עַל־רֹ֣אשׁ הָעַמּוּדִ֔ים מַעֲשֵׂ֥ה שׁוּשַׁ֛ן בָּֽאוּלָ֖ם אַרְבַּ֥ע אַמּֽוֹת: 20 וְכֹֽתָרֹ֗ת עַל־שְׁנֵי֙ הָעַמּוּדִ֔ים גַּם־מִמַּ֙עַל֙ מִלְּעֻמַּ֣ת הַבֶּ֔טֶן אֲשֶׁ֖ר לְעֵ֣בֶר שבכה הַשְּׂבָכָ֑ה וְהָרִמּוֹנִ֤ים מָאתַ֙יִם֙ טֻרִ֣ים סָבִ֔יב עַ֖ל הַכֹּתֶ֥רֶת הַשֵּׁנִֽית: 21 וַיָּ֙קֶם֙ אֶת־הָֽעַמֻּדִ֔ים לְאֻלָ֖ם הַהֵיכָ֑ל וַיָּ֜קֶם אֶת־הָעַמּ֣וּד הַיְמָנִ֗י וַיִּקְרָ֤א אֶת־שְׁמוֹ֙ יָכִ֔ין וַיָּ֙קֶם֙ אֶת־הָעַמּ֣וּד הַשְּׂמָאלִ֔י וַיִּקְרָ֥א אֶת־שְׁמ֖וֹ בֹּֽעַז: 22 וְעַ֛ל רֹ֥אשׁ הָעַמּוּדִ֖ים מַעֲשֵׂ֣ה שׁוֹשָׁ֑ן וַתִּתֹּ֖ם מְלֶ֥אכֶת הָעַמּוּדִֽים:

it establishes a connection between the tabernacle and the Temple. Bezalel the Judean and his assistant Oholiab the Danite (Exod. 31:2,6), were the chief craftsmen in the construction of the tabernacle. Correspondingly, Solomon the Judean and Hiram the Danite were responsible for the artwork of the Temple. According to the Midrash, the "two tribes [Judah and Dan] were [thus] partners" in both institutions (PR 6).

21. Jachin . . . Boaz The names of the two monumental pillars, set up to the right and the left of the portico. Their exact nature is unclear, because of uncertainties about the meaning of the terms and the various formulations found in the Bible and ancient translations. Nevertheless, it is known that freestanding columns were part of an-

cient Temple architecture. Cultic objects of clay have been unearthed from the Israelite (Middle) Bronze period (10th to 9th century B.C.E.), with pillars represented outside the portal.

The significance of the names Jachin and Boaz in ancient Judea is unknown. Midrashic expositors, attempting to portray the Temple as a microcosm of the world, give the names symbolic significance. It has been suggested that Jachin (*yakhin*, "he establishes") stands for the moon, because the moon establishes (*mekhin*) the festivals of Israel, and that Boaz (*bo-az*) corresponds to the sun, which comes out in power and in strength (*b'oz*) (Mid. Tad.). Others attempted to correlate the Temple objects to the human body (as microcosm), associating the pillars with eyes, for

23Then he made the tank of cast metal, 10 cubits across from brim to brim, completely
round; it was 5 cubits high, and it measured 30
cubits in circumference. 24There were gourds
below the brim completely encircling it—ten to
a cubit, encircling the tank; the gourds were in
two rows, cast in one piece with it. 25It stood
upon twelve oxen: three facing north, three facing west, three facing south, and three facing
east, with the tank resting upon them; their
haunches were all turned inward. 26It was a
handbreadth thick, and its brim was made like
that of a cup, like the petals of a lily. Its capacity
was 2,000 *baths*.

23 וַיַּעַשׂ אֶת־הַיָּם מוּצָק עֶשֶׂר בָּאַמָּה
מִשְּׂפָתוֹ עַד־שְׂפָתוֹ עָגֹל ׀ סָבִיב וְחָמֵשׁ
בָּאַמָּה קוֹמָתוֹ וקוה וְקָו שְׁלֹשִׁים בָּאַמָּה
יָסֹב אֹתוֹ סָבִיב׃ 24 וּפְקָעִים מִתַּחַת
לִשְׂפָתוֹ ׀ סָבִיב סֹבְבִים אֹתוֹ עֶשֶׂר בָּאַמָּה
מַקִּפִים אֶת־הַיָּם סָבִיב שְׁנֵי טוּרִים
הַפְּקָעִים יְצֻקִים בִּיצֻקָתוֹ׃ 25 עֹמֵד עַל־שְׁנֵי
עָשָׂר בָּקָר שְׁלֹשָׁה פֹנִים ׀ צָפוֹנָה וּשְׁלֹשָׁה
פֹנִים ׀ יָמָּה וּשְׁלֹשָׁה ׀ פֹּנִים נֶגְבָּה וּשְׁלֹשָׁה
פֹּנִים מִזְרָחָה וְהַיָּם עֲלֵיהֶם מִלְמָעְלָה
וְכָל־אֲחֹרֵיהֶם בָּיְתָה׃ 26 וְעָבְיוֹ טֶפַח
וּשְׂפָתוֹ כְּמַעֲשֵׂה שְׂפַת־כּוֹס פֶּרַח שׁוֹשָׁן
אַלְפַּיִם בַּת יָכִיל׃ פ

"just as eyes are placed high in the head, so were these pillars high."

23. the tank Hebrew: *ha-yam,* literally, "the sea." This was an enormous drum, about 18 feet (10 cubits) in diameter and about 9 feet (5 cubits) deep. The object was supported by 12 brazen oxen. It served for the priests to wash in, according to 2 Chron. 4:6.

24. gourds These were beneath the brim. The Targum describes them as egg shaped, but according to 2 Chron. 4:3 "beneath were figures of oxen set all around it." Radak synthesizes the two, stating that the body was round like an egg and the head resembled an ox.

26. baths A "bath" (*bat*) is a liquid measure equivalent to about 8 gallons (30 L).

הפטרת פקודי

HAFTARAH FOR P'KUDEI

1 KINGS 7:51–8:21 (*Ashk'nazim*)

(Ashk'nazim *also read this* haftarah *whenever the Torah portions* Va-yak·hel *and* P'kudei *are combined.* S'fardim *read the passage starting on p. 573 with* P'kudei, *or whenever* Va-yak·hel *and* P'kudei *are combined.*)

This *haftarah* describes a momentous event in ancient Israel. After the completion of the Temple, Solomon transfers to it the ancient Ark and the Tent of Meeting and its holy vessels. With the transfer of these objects, and the sacred vessels from the city of David, to the Temple of Solomon, the period of the wilderness wandering—symbolized by the moveable tabernacle—is formally brought to a close. With the symbols of Sinai deposited in its midst, Jerusalem becomes the sacred center of the nation.

Two events that stand behind the depiction of Solomon's ceremony give it an added aura of authority. First, the processional. The account of the Ark's transfer from Zion to the accompaniment of royal sacrifices echoes David's ceremonious participation in the events that first brought the Ark to Zion (2 Sam. 6:12–19). The other event takes us back to the initial construction of the Ark in the time of Moses. According to the ancient report at the end of this week's *parashah,* when the work was done "the cloud covered the Tent of Meeting, and the Presence of the LORD filled the Tabernacle" (Exod. 40:34), making it clear that the Lord had accepted the work of human hands as a fit place for divine dwelling. Similarly, the *haftarah* announces that after the Ark was deposited in the Holy of Holies, "the cloud had filled the House of the LORD . . . for the Presence of the LORD filled the House of the LORD" (1 Kings 8:10–11). Thus Solomon is deemed the true heir of Moses as well as of David. To underscore this point the text notes that Solomon's Temple housed "the two tablets of stone," which were hewn by Moses on Sinai (v. 9).

The indwelling of the divine Presence or glory (*kavod*) in the shrine is a particular mark of priestly theology. It manifests God's presence in tangible terms. The *kavod* appeared before the entire congregation at the conclusion of the initiation of Aaron and his sons into the priesthood (Lev. 9:23), and it is this divine reality that will return to the shrine in the rebuilt new Temple described by Ezekiel (Ezek. 10:18–22, 43:2–4). In other accounts, the *kavod* also appears with an anthropomorphic shape. Thus when Moses at Mount Sinai asks God to reveal His *kavod,* he is graced with a glimpse of a receding figure that passes by and casts a hand over him, that he not see the divine face and die (Exod. 33:18–23). Similarly, Ezekiel in his inaugural vision discerned a "semblance of a human form" that "was the appearance of the semblance of the Presence (*kavod*) of the LORD" (Ezek. 1:26,28). Accordingly, the descent of the *kavod* into the tabernacle and the Temple conveys a visual concreteness of the divine presence. Solomon's words of prayer at this moment are a fitting sequel to that manifestation: "I have now built for You / . . . / A place where You may dwell (*makhon l'shivt'kha*) forever" (1 Kings 8:13).

The *haftarah* concludes with the fact that the holy Ark within the Temple contained the covenant that God made with the nation at Mount Sinai (1 Kings 8:21). This is of great theological significance. Following ancient tradition (Exod. 34:29, 40:20; Deut. 10:5), the Ark is no mere throne for God's indwelling Presence but the repository of a divine–human compact that binds both parties. Situated at the center of sacred space, the Covenant is concretely and symbolically the link between heaven and earth.

RELATION OF THE *HAFTARAH* TO THE *PARASHAH*

The *haftarah* makes a connection between the ancient tabernacle and the Temple. The first, built by Moses, served as the moveable pavilion of service during the wilderness wandering and through the initial phase of settlement in the land. The second, built by Solomon with all the grandeur of oriental opulence, was designed as a place where God "may dwell forever." The Ark's transfer into the Temple from the tabernacle was a public sign of continuity, proclaiming that with the end of the period of unstable settlement, the Ark could rest from its service in the vanguard of the armies of God. Perhaps this is hinted at in the language chosen to indicate the end of the two labors. Of Moses we read that he "finished the work" (*va-y'khal . . . et ha-m'lakhah,* Exod. 40:33). This is a distinct allusion to God's own ceasing from labor in Gen. 2:2 and a theological suggestion that the tabernacle finished the work of Creation. By contrast, we read of Solomon that he "completed the work" (*va-tishlam kol ha-m'lakhah,* 1 Kings 7:51). The Hebrew is a clear play on his name (*Sh'lomo*) and a reference to the fact that in his day there was "peace" (*shalom*) in the region so that the king could build the house of God (1 Kings 5:4).

The difference between the two shrines is notable. Whereas the ancient pavilion led the people in their temporal wanderings accompanied by God (Exod. 40:37–38), the great Temple in Jerusalem marked the people's settlement in space and the desire for God's indwelling forever (1 Kings 8:12–13). Moreover, a movable and a permanent shrine evoke different spiritual realities. The first evokes dynamic and changing circumstances, in accordance with the symbolism of religious life as a journey. The other evokes fixed and dependable stability, in accordance with the symbolism of religiosity directed toward a sacred center. The incorporation of the ancient Tent (of Moses) within the Temple of Solomon symbolically joins these two realities, making concrete a dialectic at the heart of the religious imagination.

7 51 When all the work that King Solomon had done in the House of the LORD was completed, Solomon brought in the sacred donations of his father David—the silver, the gold, and the vessels—and deposited them in the treasury of the House of the LORD.

ז 51 וַתִּשְׁלַם֙ כָּל־הַמְּלָאכָ֔ה אֲשֶׁ֥ר עָשָׂ֛ה
הַמֶּ֥לֶךְ שְׁלֹמֹ֖ה בֵּ֣ית יְהוָ֑ה וַיָּבֵ֨א שְׁלֹמֹ֜ה
אֶת־קָדְשֵׁ֣י ׀ דָּוִ֣ד אָבִ֗יו אֶת־הַכֶּ֤סֶף וְאֶת־
הַזָּהָב֙ וְאֶת־הַכֵּלִ֔ים נָתַ֕ן בְּאֹצְר֖וֹת בֵּ֥ית
יְהוָֽה׃ פ

8 Then Solomon convoked the elders of Israel—all the heads of the tribes and the ancestral chieftains of the Israelites—before King Solomon in Jerusalem, to bring up the Ark of the Covenant of the LORD from the City of David, that is, Zion.

ח אָ֣ז יַקְהֵ֣ל שְׁלֹמֹ֣ה אֶת־זִקְנֵ֣י יִשְׂרָאֵ֡ל
אֶת־כָּל־רָאשֵׁ֣י הַמַּטּוֹת֩ נְשִׂיאֵ֨י הָאָב֜וֹת
לִבְנֵ֧י יִשְׂרָאֵ֛ל אֶל־הַמֶּ֥לֶךְ שְׁלֹמֹ֖ה יְרוּשָׁלִָ֑ם
לְהַעֲל֞וֹת אֶת־אֲר֧וֹן בְּרִית־יְהוָ֛ה מֵעִ֥יר דָּוִ֖ד
הִ֥יא צִיּֽוֹן׃

1 Kings 7:51. the sacred donations of his father David Rabbinic tradition was troubled by the plain sense of this passage, which notes the enrichment of the Temple treasuries through David's donations. Several interpretations highlight Solomon's ethical integrity in refusing to use David's wealth in the actual building of his Temple. According to one view, David should have used this money to buy food for the hungry during the famine in his day (2 Sam. 24). Because he did not, his money was tainted (Rashi). Another opinion stressed that, because David's gain was ill-gotten,

2All the men of Israel gathered before King Solomon at the Feast, in the month of Ethanim—that is, the seventh month. 3When all the elders of Israel had come, the priests lifted the Ark 4and carried up the Ark of the LORD. Then the priests and the Levites brought the Tent of Meeting and all the holy vessels that were in the Tent. 5Meanwhile, King Solomon and the whole community of Israel, who were assembled with him before the Ark, were sacrificing sheep and oxen in such abundance that they could not be numbered or counted.

6The priests brought the Ark of the LORD's Covenant to its place underneath the wings of the cherubim, in the Shrine of the House, in the Holy of Holies; 7for the cherubim had their wings spread out over the place of the Ark, so that the cherubim shielded the Ark and its poles from above. 8The poles projected so that the ends of the poles were visible in the sanctuary in front of the Shrine, but they could not be seen outside; and there they remain to this day. 9There was nothing inside the Ark but the two tablets of stone which Moses placed there at Horeb, when the LORD made [a covenant] with the Israelites after their departure from the land of Egypt.

10When the priests came out of the sanctuary—for the cloud had filled the House of the LORD 11and the priests were not able to remain

2 וַיִּקָּהֲל֞וּ אֶל־הַמֶּ֣לֶךְ שְׁלֹמֹ֗ה כָּל־אִ֣ישׁ יִשְׂרָאֵ֜ל בְּיֶ֣רַח הָאֵֽתָנִ֛ים בֶּחָ֖ג ה֣וּא הַחֹ֥דֶשׁ הַשְּׁבִיעִֽי׃ 3 וַיָּבֹ֕אוּ כֹּ֖ל זִקְנֵ֣י יִשְׂרָאֵ֑ל וַיִּשְׂא֥וּ הַכֹּהֲנִ֖ים אֶת־הָאָרֽוֹן׃ 4 וַֽיַּעֲל֞וּ אֶת־אֲר֤וֹן יְהוָה֙ וְאֶת־אֹ֣הֶל מוֹעֵ֔ד וְאֶֽת־כָּל־כְּלֵ֥י הַקֹּ֖דֶשׁ אֲשֶׁ֣ר בָּאֹ֑הֶל וַיַּעֲל֣וּ אֹתָ֔ם הַכֹּהֲנִ֖ים וְהַלְוִיִּֽם׃ 5 וְהַמֶּ֣לֶךְ שְׁלֹמֹ֗ה וְכָל־עֲדַ֤ת יִשְׂרָאֵל֙ הַנּוֹעָדִ֣ים עָלָ֔יו אִתּ֖וֹ לִפְנֵ֣י הָֽאָר֑וֹן מְזַבְּחִים֙ צֹ֣אן וּבָקָ֔ר אֲשֶׁ֧ר לֹֽא־יִסָּפְר֛וּ וְלֹ֥א יִמָּנ֖וּ מֵרֹֽב׃

6 וַיָּבִ֣אוּ הַ֠כֹּהֲנִ֠ים אֶת־אֲר֨וֹן בְּרִית־יְהוָ֧ה אֶל־מְקוֹמ֛וֹ אֶל־דְּבִ֥יר הַבַּ֖יִת אֶל־קֹ֣דֶשׁ הַקֳּדָשִׁ֑ים אֶל־תַּ֖חַת כַּנְפֵ֥י הַכְּרוּבִֽים׃ 7 כִּ֤י הַכְּרוּבִים֙ פֹּרְשִׂ֣ים כְּנָפַ֔יִם אֶל־מְק֖וֹם הָֽאָר֑וֹן וַיָּסֹ֧כּוּ הַכְּרֻבִ֛ים עַל־הָאָר֥וֹן וְעַל־בַּדָּ֖יו מִלְמָֽעְלָה׃ 8 וַֽיַּאֲרִכוּ֮ הַבַּדִּים֒ וַיֵּרָאוּ֩ רָאשֵׁ֨י הַבַּדִּ֤ים מִן־הַקֹּ֙דֶשׁ֙ עַל־פְּנֵ֣י הַדְּבִ֔יר וְלֹ֥א יֵרָא֖וּ הַח֑וּצָה וַיִּ֣הְיוּ שָׁ֔ם עַ֖ד הַיּ֥וֹם הַזֶּֽה׃ 9 אֵ֚ין בָּֽאָר֔וֹן רַ֗ק שְׁנֵי֙ לֻח֣וֹת הָֽאֲבָנִ֔ים אֲשֶׁ֨ר הִנִּ֥חַ שָׁ֛ם מֹשֶׁ֖ה בְּחֹרֵ֑ב אֲשֶׁ֨ר כָּרַ֤ת יְהוָה֙ עִם־בְּנֵ֣י יִשְׂרָאֵ֔ל בְּצֵאתָ֖ם מֵאֶ֥רֶץ מִצְרָֽיִם׃

10 וַיְהִ֗י בְּצֵ֤את הַכֹּֽהֲנִים֙ מִן־הַקֹּ֔דֶשׁ וְהֶעָנָ֥ן מָלֵ֖א אֶת־בֵּ֥ית יְהוָֽה׃ 11 וְלֹֽא־יָכְל֧וּ

Solomon deferred his building project for years, until he could finance it on his own (Ralbag).

1 Kings 8:2. Feast The festival of Booths, or *Sukkot* (see Lev. 23:34). 1 Kings 8:2–21 is recited as the *haftarah* for the second day of *Sukkot*.

Ethanim Here identified with the seventh month, later called *Tishrei*.

4. Tent of Meeting The term used in the *parashah* for the tabernacle.

9. nothing inside the Ark Nothing but the "two tablets of stone (*avanim*)." This follows the tradition in Deut. 10:1–5. In the language of Exodus (25:16, 34:29, 40:20), Moses put into the Ark the two Tablets of the Pact (*edut*). Some Sages suggested that both the first (broken) and second

tablets were in the Ark (BT BB 14a–b). In the ancient Near East, treaty texts were regularly deposited at the feet of the gods, in the shrine. This is the custom that stands behind the deposit of the Tablets of *edut* (Exod. 25:16) or *b'rit* (Deut. 9:11,15) in the Ark of the tabernacle and the Temple. According to Deut. 31:9–13,26–29, the Torah (transcribed by Moses) was given to the levitical priests to place beside the "Ark of the Covenant of the LORD"—to be periodically read aloud and so serve as a warning and a witness to future generations. A copy of this document was to be copied by all kings as well, that they might read it and serve God with knowledge and reverence (Deut. 17:18–20).

and perform the service because of the cloud, for the Presence of the LORD filled the House of the LORD—12then Solomon declared:

"The LORD has chosen
To abide in a thick cloud:
13I have now built for You
A stately House,
A place where You
May dwell forever."

14Then, with the whole congregation of Israel standing, the king faced about and blessed the whole congregation of Israel. 15He said:

"Praised be the LORD, the God of Israel, who has fulfilled with deeds the promise He made to my father David. For He said, 16'Ever since I brought My people Israel out of Egypt, I have not chosen a city among all the tribes of Israel for building a House where My name might abide; but I have chosen David to rule My people Israel.'

17"Now my father David had intended to build a House for the name of the LORD, the God of Israel. 18But the LORD said to my father David, 'As regards your intention to build a House for My name, you did right to have that intention. 19However, you shall not build the House yourself; instead, your son, the issue of your loins, shall build the House for My name.'

20"And the LORD has fulfilled the promise that He made: I have succeeded my father David and have ascended the throne of Israel, as the LORD promised. I have built the House for the name of the LORD, the God of Israel; 21and I have set a place there for the Ark, containing the covenant which the LORD made with our fathers when He brought them out from the land of Egypt."

הַכֹּהֲנִים לַעֲמֹד לְשָׁרֵת מִפְּנֵי הֶעָנָן כִּֽי־
מָלֵא כְבוֹד־יְהֹוָה אֶת־בֵּית יְהֹוָֽה׃ פ
12 אָז אָמַר שְׁלֹמֹה
יְהֹוָה אָמַר
לִשְׁכֹּן בָּעֲרָפֶֽל׃
13 בָּנֹה בָנִיתִי
בֵּית זְבֻל לָךְ
מָכוֹן לְשִׁבְתְּךָ
עוֹלָמִֽים׃
14 וַיַּסֵּב הַמֶּלֶךְ אֶת־פָּנָיו וַיְבָרֶךְ אֵת כָּל־
קְהַל יִשְׂרָאֵל וְכָל־קְהַל יִשְׂרָאֵל עֹמֵֽד׃
15 וַיֹּאמֶר
בָּרוּךְ יְהֹוָה אֱלֹהֵי יִשְׂרָאֵל אֲשֶׁר דִּבֶּר בְּפִיו
אֵת דָּוִד אָבִי וּבְיָדוֹ מִלֵּא לֵאמֹֽר׃ 16 מִן־
הַיּוֹם אֲשֶׁר הוֹצֵאתִי אֶת־עַמִּי אֶת־יִשְׂרָאֵל
מִמִּצְרַיִם לֹֽא־בָחַרְתִּי בְעִיר מִכֹּל שִׁבְטֵי
יִשְׂרָאֵל לִבְנוֹת בַּיִת לִהְיוֹת שְׁמִי שָׁם
וָאֶבְחַר בְּדָוִד לִהְיוֹת עַל־עַמִּי יִשְׂרָאֵֽל׃
17 וַיְהִי עִם־לְבַב דָּוִד אָבִי לִבְנוֹת בַּיִת
לְשֵׁם יְהֹוָה אֱלֹהֵי יִשְׂרָאֵֽל׃ 18 וַיֹּאמֶר יְהֹוָה
אֶל־דָּוִד אָבִי יַעַן אֲשֶׁר הָיָה עִם־לְבָבְךָ
לִבְנוֹת בַּיִת לִשְׁמִי הֱטִיבֹתָ כִּי הָיָה עִם־
לְבָבֶֽךָ׃ 19 רַק אַתָּה לֹא תִבְנֶה הַבָּיִת כִּי
אִם־בִּנְךָ הַיֹּצֵא מֵֽחֲלָצֶיךָ הֽוּא־יִבְנֶה הַבַּיִת
לִשְׁמִֽי׃
20 וַיָּקֶם יְהֹוָה אֶת־דְּבָרוֹ אֲשֶׁר דִּבֵּר וָאָקֻם
תַּחַת דָּוִד אָבִי וָאֵשֵׁב עַל־כִּסֵּא יִשְׂרָאֵל
כַּאֲשֶׁר דִּבֶּר יְהֹוָה וָאֶבְנֶה הַבַּיִת לְשֵׁם
יְהֹוָה אֱלֹהֵי יִשְׂרָאֵֽל׃ 21 וָאָשִׂם שָׁם
מָקוֹם לָֽאָרוֹן אֲשֶׁר־שָׁם בְּרִית יְהֹוָה אֲשֶׁר
כָּרַת עִם־אֲבֹתֵינוּ בְּהוֹצִיאוֹ אֹתָם מֵאֶרֶץ
מִצְרָֽיִם׃ ס

ויקרא

LEVITICUS

ויקרא

צו

שמיני

תזריע

מצרע

אחרי מות

קדשים

אמר

בהר

בחקתי

LEVITICUS

BARUCH A. LEVINE

Popularly called by the Hebrew name *Vayikra,* "He called," which is its first word, Leviticus is known formally as *Torat Kohanim,* "instructions for the priests" (M Meg. 1:5). This title defines Leviticus as a prescription for the proper worship of the God of Israel.

The Hebrew Bible reflects the central concerns of the ancient Israelites: Perhaps the most vital of these was to know how they were to express their loyalty to the Lord. This very question is posed by the prophet Micah (6:6), who answers it by emphasizing the primacy of justice and love, ultimately desired by God more than sacrifice. Leviticus 19:2 gives a more specifically priestly answer to Micah's question: "You shall be holy, for I, the LORD your God, am holy." How Israel was to live as a holy nation is the burden of Leviticus.

The contents of Leviticus are diverse but unified by the theme of holiness. The first seven chapters delineate the major types of sacrifices undertaken by Israelites individually and as a community. Chapters 8 to 10 record the emergence of sacred worship in ancient Israel by describing the initiation of the Aaronide priesthood and its first performance on the sanctuary altar. As a stern admonition, chapter 10 records an instance of improper officiating by two of Aaron's sons, who met their death at the hands of the Lord.

Leviticus 11 is one of two major sources in the Torah for *kashrut,* or the dietary laws (cf. Deut. 14). The subject of purity informs chapters 12 to 15, which specify procedures for expiating impurity and susceptibility to danger. Continuing this theme, chapter 16 prescribes the rites of *Yom Kippur* aimed at the periodic cleansing of the sanctuary and the Israelite people.

Leviticus 17 to 26 cohere as a literary unit, referred to as "the Holiness Code," because of the frequent use of the term *kadosh*, "holy." This section begins by ordaining the place and form of proper worship of the God of Israel. It then defines the Israelite family and details improper sexual behavior, including incest (Lev. 18). Perhaps the best known part of Leviticus is chapter 19, which resonates with the Decalogue, combining ritual and ethical teachings. It is here that we read "Love your fellow as yourself." Chapters 20 to 22 contain more on the Israelite family and ordain specifically priestly duties and prerogatives. In chapter 23, the festivals and other holy days of the year are scheduled in a calendar of sacred time. The rest of the Holiness Code (ch. 24–26) and its appendix (ch. 27) add instructions to the priests about administration of the sanctuary and laws governing ownership of land and indebtedness. Here the source for the inscription on the Liberty Bell proclaims the inalienable right of the Israelite people to its land: "You shall proclaim release throughout the land for all its inhabitants" (25:10). In an epilogue (26:3–26), the Israelites are admonished to obey God and are forewarned of the consequences of disobedience, the most dire being exile from the land.

Two concepts embody the primary message of Leviticus. First, the Israelites are one community (*edah*), united by a common destiny and by a holy way of life—as commanded by the Lord Himself. They are forbidden to worship any other deity or follow the impure ways of other nations (19:4, 20:1–3,6). Second, the Israelites were granted the Promised Land as an eternal estate (*aḥuzzah*) on condition that they follow the laws of God and remain faithful to His covenant. In Leviticus, the priests of Israel are instructed in the ways of holiness, and the Israelites are told what the Lord requires of them.

1 The LORD called to Moses and spoke to him

א וַיִּקְרָא* אֶל־מֹשֶׁה וַיְדַבֵּר יְהוָה אֵלָיו

v. 1. א׳ זעירא לפי נוסחים מקובלים

THE PRINCIPAL TYPES OF SACRIFICE (1:1–7:38)

Chapters 1–7 outline the biblical sacrificial system, as the Israelite priesthood administered it. The laws of the Torah did not permit Israelites to atone for intentional or premeditated offenses by bringing a sacrifice. There was no ritual remedy for such violations. In such instances, the law dealt directly with the offender, imposing punishments and acting to prevent recurrences. Gaining atonement through ritual sacrifice was restricted to situations in which a reasonable doubt existed about the willfulness of the offense. Even then, restitution was required if another person had suffered any loss or injury.

These chapters describe the basic kinds of sacrifices and list the several classes of offerings to be presented to God in the sanctuary. Chapters 1–5, addressed to individual Israelites and their leaders, recount what may be offered—including animals, birds, and grain. They establish the proper procedures for presenting the various sacrifices, a function performed primarily by priests but that occasionally required the participation of those who brought the sacrifices. Chapters 6 and 7 constitute a professional manual for the priesthood and provide "an instruction" (a *torah*) for each of the major classes of sacrifices. In most cases, sacrifices served to remove the charges against the offenders, restoring them to a proper relationship with God and to membership in the religious community.

In most ancient societies it was believed that gods required food for their sustenance, relying on sacrifices for energy and strength. The Torah preserves the idiom common to ancient religions. However, it has a different understanding of the process: God desires sacrifices not out of the need for sustenance but out of longing for the devotion and fellowship of worshipers.

THE BURNT OFFERING (*olah*) (1:1–17)

Chapter 1 deals with the sacrifice called "burnt offering" (*olah*), which was burned to ashes in its entirety (except for its hide) on the altar of burnt offerings. It was brought on various occasions, of-

---

Leviticus is a difficult book for a modern person to read with reverence and appreciation. Its main subject matter—animal offerings and ritual impurity—seems remote from contemporary concerns. Yet almost half of the 613 *mitzvot* of the Torah are found in this book, the text with which young children traditionally began their Jewish education. Our concern in reading Leviticus should be more than historical ("this is what our ancestors used to believe and practice"). It should be an effort to understand the religious needs that were met by these practices in ancient times, needs that we still confront today, and the religious ideas that were taught in the process.

The modern temper tends to discount prescribed ritual in favor of spontaneous religious expression. Yet something in the human soul responds to ritual, whether it be the formality of a traditional wedding or the rituals of a sporting event or a public meeting. There is something comforting about the familiar, the recognizable, the predictable. There is something deeply moving about performing a rite that is older than we are, one that goes back beyond the time of our parents and grandparents. At crucial times, it is important for us to know that we are "doing it right." There is power in the knowledge that we are doing what generations of people before us have done in similar situations, something that other people in other places are doing at the same time and in the same way. And rituals, including prescribed prayers, tell us what to do and say at times when we cannot rely on our own powers of inspiration to know what to do or say. "Ritual is a way of giving voice to ultimate values. Each of us needs a sense of holiness to navigate the relentless secularity of our lives" (Schorsch). For the Israelites of biblical times, it must have been gratifying to know what to do when they wanted to approach God at crucial moments of their lives, in need or in gratitude.

Discomfort with sacrificing animals as a way of worshiping God is hardly a modern phenomenon. The biblical prophets criticized the sacrificial system for its tendency to deteriorate into form without feeling. The Midrash

envisions God saying "Better that they bring their offerings to My table than that they bring them before idols" (Lev. R. 22:8). All religions of biblical time were based on sacrificial worship, and the Israelites could not conceive of religion without it.

Maimonides believed that God did not savor this manner of worship, lest people assume that they were feeding God—who would go hungry without their gifts. Abravanel, too, suggests that God never intended to call for animal offerings. After the Israelites worshiped the Golden Calf, however, God recognized the inability of people to deal with a totally abstract notion of the divine and at that point ordained the details of the sacrificial system. Just as God does not need our prayers although we need to pray, God does not need our sacrifices although we need to offer them to feel God's nearness. We recognize this feeling in the eagerness of people to offer donations to charity to accompany their prayers or memorial observances. "The cult [i.e., organized worship through sacrifice] is not man's kindness to God but God's kindness to man" (Kaufmann).

Although Leviticus outlines the technical procedures for the various offerings, the Book of Psalms offers us insights into the spiritual-emotional dimension of the sacrificial system. In Psalms, it becomes clear how privileged the Israelite worshiper felt to be able to come into God's presence. "O God, deliver me by Your name; / by Your power vindicate me. / . . . Then I will offer You a freewill sacrifice" (Ps. 54:3,8). "O people, bless our God, / . . . I enter Your house with burnt offerings, / I pay my vows to You" (Ps. 66:8,13). "One thing I ask of the LORD, / . . . to live in the house of the LORD / all the days of my life, / . . . I sacrifice in His tent with shouts of joy" (Ps. 27:4,6).

The destruction of the Second Temple and the abrupt end of the sacrificial system in 70 C.E. was traumatic for Jews, depriving them of the accustomed way of reaching out to God. By that time, however, the synagogue had already evolved as a place for worshiping God through prayer and study. Piety, good deeds, and obedience to the Covenant would take the place of animal offerings. Over the course of centuries, Jews learned to invest their prayer and religious deeds with the same feeling of nearness to God that the temple altar had evoked. Today, hardly any liberal Jew would choose a return to the sacrificial system.

It may well be that animal offerings were an instinctive gesture on the part of human beings to express gratitude, reverence, or regret. The Bible pictures Cain, Abel, and Noah offering sacrifices without being commanded to do so. People must have felt that their prayers of gratitude or petition would seem more sincerely offered if they gave up something of their own in the process. Presumably, this is why game and fish were unacceptable as offerings. "I cannot sacrifice to the LORD my God burnt offerings that have cost me nothing" (2 Sam. 24:24). The offerings of first fruit, the firstborn of the flocks, and the symbolic redemption of the firstborn son may have been ways of recognizing that these gifts ultimately came from God, ways of conveying the faith that more blessings would be forthcoming so that these could be given up.

Why did young children begin their Jewish studies with Leviticus? "Children are pure; therefore let them study laws of purity" (Lev. R. 7:3). It also has been suggested that Jewish learning began here to teach from the outset that life involves sacrifice. One contemporary writer suggests, "In sacrifice, we could for a fleeting moment imagine *our own* death and yet go on living. . . . No other form of worship can so effectively liberate a person from the fear of living in the shadow of death."

Some scholars believe that Leviticus was originally a set of instructions for *kohanim,* priests officiating at the altar and presiding over rituals of purification, detailing how they were to perform their duties properly. This professional guide became one of the five books of the Torah as part of the process of democratizing the Israelite faith, making all Israel "a kingdom of priests and a holy nation" (Exod. 19:6). There would be no secret lore accessible only to the clergy.

CHAPTER 1

1. The LORD called to Moses Moses was afraid to approach the Tent of Meeting, intimidated by its holiness. God had to call him and reassure him that, although the Tent and the tabernacle were holy and had to be treated with due reverence, they existed to benefit Israel, not to threaten them (Ramban). In another interpretation, Moses thinks that his mission has been completed. The Israelites are out of Egypt, he has brought the tablets of the Pact down from the mountain and has supervised the construction of the Tabernacle. God summons him to declare that much more must be done, guiding the Israelites to sanctify their daily lives.

Even the religion of the Torah is not com-

from the Tent of Meeting, saying: 2Speak to the Israelite people, and say to them:

When any of you presents an offering of cattle to the LORD, he shall choose his offering from the herd or from the flock.

3If his offering is a burnt offering from the herd, he shall make his offering a male

מֵאֹ֥הֶל מוֹעֵ֖ד לֵאמֹֽר׃ 2 דַּבֵּ֞ר אֶל־בְּנֵ֤י
יִשְׂרָאֵל֙ וְאָמַרְתָּ֣ אֲלֵהֶ֔ם
אָדָ֗ם כִּֽי־יַקְרִ֥יב מִכֶּ֛ם קָרְבָּ֖ן לַֽיהוָ֑ה מִן־
הַבְּהֵמָ֗ה מִן־הַבָּקָר֙ וּמִן־הַצֹּ֔אן תַּקְרִ֖יבוּ
אֶת־קָרְבַּנְכֶֽם׃
3 אִם־עֹלָ֤ה קָרְבָּנוֹ֙ מִן־הַבָּקָ֔ר זָכָ֥ר תָּמִ֖ים

ten together with other offerings. No part of it was eaten, either by priests or by donors. The *olah* could consist of male herd cattle (vv. 3–9), male flock animals (vv. 10–13), or certain birds (vv. 14–17). This range of choices—from expensive to inexpensive—enabled Israelites of modest means to participate in religious life, because they could present less costly offerings at the sanctuary.

The procedures for all burnt offerings were similar. The sacrifice was presented at the entrance to the Tent of Meeting, the donor laid his or her hand on the creature (thereby designating it for a particular rite), and blood from the sacrificed animal or fowl was dashed on the altar in appropriate ways.

1. Tent of Meeting Hebrew: *ohel mo·ed,* the portable tent structure that housed the Ark and the objects connected to the sacrificial system (see Exod. 25:1–27:21, Exod. 35–40). In other texts, this complex is called *mishkan.*

2. the Israelite people Hebrew: *b'nei yisra·el,* often translated literally as "the children of Israel." "The Israelite people" reflects the concept of peoplehood basic to the biblical idea that nations, like families, are descendants of common ancestors with a common genealogy.

offering Hebrew: *korban,* which designates anything presented to God as one approaches the sanctuary. A *korban* could consist of artifacts and vessels, votive objects (brought in fulfillment of a vow), or sacrificial animals and fowl, as is the case here.

cattle . . . herd . . . flock In many of the Bible's legal statements, a general category is given first, followed by particulars. Here the general category is livestock (*b'hemah*), further specified by the two usual classes: "from the herd (*bakar*) or from the flock (*tzon*)."

3. If his offering is a burnt offering The conditional word "if" (*im*) frequently introduces cultic laws (rules for organized religious worship) in the Book of Leviticus. Here it precedes each of the options available to those who offer sacrifices—the choice of which type of sacrifice to bring as well as the choice of which animal, fowl, or grain will constitute the offering. "Burnt offering" is designated by the Hebrew word *olah,* derived from the verb meaning "to ascend" (עלה). This offering may have been called *olah* because its flames and smoke "ascended" to heaven. The sacrifice, in its altered form, reaches God who was perceived as breathing its aromatic smoke, so to speak. Its purpose was to offer a gift to God to secure a favorable response. Frequently, the *olah*

---

plete. Each generation must find new ways to make God present in new situations that the Torah could not have foreseen.

2. When any of you presents an offering Literally, "When a man (*adam*) presents an offering." May your offerings be like those of Adam, belonging to you and not stolen, offered solely to express your love of God and not to impress your neighbors (Lev. R. 2:7). The word for "offering" (*korban*) comes from the Hebrew root קרב, meaning "to bring close" or "to come close." When we give a gift to someone we feel close to, we feel even closer for having given the gift. The *korban* both reflects and reinforces the Israelite's bond to God. The point of the sacrifice is not to feed or to bribe God but to come close to God.

The opening words of the Hebrew text are singular, but the Torah soon shifts to plural. This reflects the essence of the religious experience. A Hasidic master taught that we enter the sanctuary as individuals but the experience of worship leads us to transcend our separateness and become part of the community.

3. The *olah* is purely a gift to God, with no specific benefit to the donor anticipated, except the satisfaction of having brought the offering to God. Whether brought out of a sense of reverence or out of a sense of guilt, it expresses the idea that everything we have comes

without blemish. He shall bring it to the entrance of the Tent of Meeting, for acceptance in
his behalf before the LORD. 4He shall lay his hand
upon the head of the burnt offering, that it may
be acceptable in his behalf, in expiation for him.
5The bull shall be slaughtered before the LORD;
and Aaron's sons, the priests, shall offer the
blood, dashing the blood against all sides of the
altar which is at the entrance of the Tent of Meeting. 6The burnt offering shall be flayed and cut
up into sections. 7The sons of Aaron the priest
shall put fire on the altar and lay out wood upon
the fire; 8and Aaron's sons, the priests, shall lay
out the sections, with the head and the suet, on
the wood that is on the fire upon the altar. 9Its
entrails and legs shall be washed with water, and
the priest shall turn the whole into smoke on

יַקְרִיבֶנּוּ אֶל־פֶּתַח אֹהֶל מוֹעֵד יַקְרִיב אֹתוֹ
לִרְצֹנוֹ לִפְנֵי יְהוָה׃ 4 וְסָמַךְ יָדוֹ עַל רֹאשׁ
הָעֹלָה וְנִרְצָה לוֹ לְכַפֵּר עָלָיו׃ 5 וְשָׁחַט
אֶת־בֶּן הַבָּקָר לִפְנֵי יְהוָה וְהִקְרִיבוּ בְּנֵי
אַהֲרֹן הַכֹּהֲנִים אֶת־הַדָּם וְזָרְקוּ אֶת־
הַדָּם עַל־הַמִּזְבֵּחַ סָבִיב אֲשֶׁר־פֶּתַח אֹהֶל
מוֹעֵד׃ 6 וְהִפְשִׁיט אֶת־הָעֹלָה וְנִתַּח אֹתָהּ
לִנְתָחֶיהָ׃ 7 וְנָתְנוּ בְּנֵי אַהֲרֹן הַכֹּהֵן אֵשׁ
עַל־הַמִּזְבֵּחַ וְעָרְכוּ עֵצִים עַל־הָאֵשׁ׃
8 וְעָרְכוּ בְּנֵי אַהֲרֹן הַכֹּהֲנִים אֵת הַנְּתָחִים
אֶת־הָרֹאשׁ וְאֶת־הַפָּדֶר עַל־הָעֵצִים אֲשֶׁר
עַל־הָאֵשׁ אֲשֶׁר עַל־הַמִּזְבֵּחַ׃ 9 וְקִרְבּוֹ
וּכְרָעָיו יִרְחַץ בַּמָּיִם וְהִקְטִיר הַכֹּהֵן אֶת־

was the first sacrifice in rites that included other offerings as well. In many instances, the *olah* was followed by the shared sacred meal (*zevaḥ*).

for acceptance in his behalf The sacrifice is accredited to the donor as proper. When a sacrifice is not considered proper, the opposite is said of it: "not acceptable, discredited."

before the LORD This refers to a defined sacred area. Sometimes it was the zone beginning at the rear of the altar of burnt offerings in the sanctuary courtyard that continued to the interior of the tent; at times it was a large space near the entrance of the courtyard. Priestly law strictly limits sacrifice to a particular area and to the legitimate altar.

4. He shall lay his hand This symbolic act, "the laying on" of hands (known in later Hebrew as *s'mikhah*), indicated ownership and served to assign a sacrificial animal or fowl solely for use in a specific rite. The offering, once assigned in this way, was sacred and belonged solely to God.

that it may be acceptable in his behalf The *olah* sacrifice served as protection from God's wrath. Proximity to God was dangerous for both the worshipers and the priests, even in the absence of a particular offense. The favorable acceptance of the *olah* signaled God's willingness to be approached.

5. against all sides of the altar This refers to the altar of burnt offerings (mentioned by name in Lev. 4:7, and described in Exod. 27:1–8).

6. shall be flayed and cut up into sections Sacrificial animals usually were sectioned before being placed on the altar. The only exception was the paschal lamb. It was roasted whole (Exod. 12:9).

8. with the head and the suet The head of the animal had been severed. Suet is a type of hard organ fat.

9. turn the whole into smoke The burned parts of the sacrifice rise as smoke when they are consumed by the altar fire. Likewise, the word for

---

from God, given to us only on loan (Tanḥ. Tzav). It is called *olah* (from the root "to go up," as in *aliyah*) not only because it goes up in smoke but because it elevates the soul of the person who performs this act of generosity.

without blemish What renders an animal unfit in the sight of God does not disqualify the human being who offers it. The offering must be unblemished, as a sign of respect for God's altar and to discourage people from bringing their lame and sick animals in a pretense of piety. An afflicted, broken soul, though, could bring an offering and might even be closer to God for having experienced pain and rejection. "The LORD is close to the brokenhearted" (Ps. 34:19). "You will not despise / a contrite and crushed heart" (Ps. 51:19, cited in Lev. R. 7:2).

9. of pleasing odor to the LORD The notion that God actually smells the aroma of the offering is rejected emphatically by rabbinic

the altar as a burnt offering, a gift of pleasing odor to the LORD.

10If his offering for a burnt offering is from the flock, of sheep or of goats, he shall make his offering a male without blemish. 11It shall be slaughtered before the LORD on the north side of the altar, and Aaron's sons, the priests, shall dash its blood against all sides of the altar. 12When it has been cut up into sections, the priest shall lay them out, with the head and the suet, on the wood that is on the fire upon the altar. 13The entrails and the legs shall be washed with water; the priest shall offer up and turn the whole into smoke on the altar. It is a burnt offering, a gift, of pleasing odor to the LORD.

14If his offering to the LORD is a burnt offering of birds, he shall choose his offering from turtledoves or pigeons. 15The priest shall bring it to the altar, pinch off its head, and turn it into smoke on the altar; and its blood shall be drained out against the side of the altar. 16He shall remove its crop with its contents, and cast it into the place of the ashes, at the east side of

הַכֹּל הַמִּזְבֵּחָה עֹלָה אִשֵּׁה רֵיחַ־נִיחוֹחַ
לַיהוָה׃ ס
10 וְאִם־מִן־הַצֹּאן קָרְבָּנוֹ מִן־הַכְּשָׂבִים אוֹ
מִן־הָעִזִּים לְעֹלָה זָכָר תָּמִים יַקְרִיבֶנּוּ׃
11 וְשָׁחַט אֹתוֹ עַל יֶרֶךְ הַמִּזְבֵּחַ צָפֹנָה לִפְנֵי
יְהוָה וְזָרְקוּ בְּנֵי אַהֲרֹן הַכֹּהֲנִים אֶת־דָּמוֹ
עַל־הַמִּזְבֵּחַ סָבִיב׃ 12 וְנִתַּח אֹתוֹ לִנְתָחָיו
וְאֶת־רֹאשׁוֹ וְאֶת־פִּדְרוֹ וְעָרַךְ הַכֹּהֵן אֹתָם
עַל־הָעֵצִים אֲשֶׁר עַל־הָאֵשׁ אֲשֶׁר עַל־
הַמִּזְבֵּחַ׃ 13 וְהַקֶּרֶב וְהַכְּרָעַיִם יִרְחַץ בַּמָּיִם
וְהִקְרִיב הַכֹּהֵן אֶת־הַכֹּל וְהִקְטִיר
הַמִּזְבֵּחָה עֹלָה הוּא אִשֵּׁה רֵיחַ נִיחֹחַ
לַיהוָה׃ פ
שני 14 וְאִם מִן־הָעוֹף עֹלָה קָרְבָּנוֹ לַיהוָה
וְהִקְרִיב מִן־הַתֹּרִים אוֹ מִן־בְּנֵי הַיּוֹנָה
אֶת־קָרְבָּנוֹ׃ 15 וְהִקְרִיבוֹ הַכֹּהֵן אֶל־הַמִּזְבֵּחַ
וּמָלַק אֶת־רֹאשׁוֹ וְהִקְטִיר הַמִּזְבֵּחָה
וְנִמְצָה דָמוֹ עַל קִיר הַמִּזְבֵּחַ׃ 16 וְהֵסִיר
אֶת־מֻרְאָתוֹ בְּנֹצָתָהּ וְהִשְׁלִיךְ אֹתָהּ אֵצֶל

incense (*k'toret*), in Hebrew and in other Semitic languages, derives from the word for smoke because it rises in the form of smoke.

gift Hebrew: *isheh,* translated in the past as "offering by fire"—as if derived from *esh* (fire). Based on an Ugaritic cognate, we now know the meaning of the biblical term more accurately.

pleasing odor Hebrew: *rei·aḥ niḥo·aḥ* (a pleasant aroma). Aromatic substances were used routinely in the sacrificial system. This description, anthropomorphic in origin, is the Torah's way of stating that the sacrifice is accepted.

15. pinch off its head The Hebrew verb used for this here means "to break the nape of the neck." According to rabbinic tradition, the priest did this with his fingernail, after which he severed the neck.

16. remove its crop The crop (an enlargement of the gullet, or esophagus) was too dirty to be placed on the altar. Therefore, it was consigned to the ash heap, near the altar. The entrails of animals sacrificed as burnt offerings had to be washed before being placed on the altar, to ensure that nothing offensive was offered to God (see v. 9).

---

commentators. "Far be it that the Almighty should smell or eat. The verse would tell us that the worshiper is as pleasing to God as a sweet odor is to a human being" (Ibn Ezra). "What is pleasing to God is not the aroma but the fact that Israel is doing God's will" (Rashi). Cassuto takes the phrase to mean that God accepts with pleasure the motives of the donor. According to Eliezer Ashkenazi, "Should the worshipers imagine that they have atoned for their sins by bringing a sacrifice, the Torah informs them that the sacrifice is merely a foretaste of proper behavior in the future, even as the smell of food is only an anticipation of the meal." And in an ancient passage that chillingly foreshadows 20th-century events, the Midrash states: "God smells the odor . . . of the burning flesh of Jewish martyrs" and is moved by that expression of their devotion (Gen. R. 34:9).

the altar. 17The priest shall tear it open by its
wings, without severing it, and turn it into
smoke on the altar, upon the wood that is on
the fire. It is a burnt offering, a gift, of pleasing
odor to the LORD.

הַמִּזְבֵּ֔חַ קֵ֣דְמָה אֶל־מְק֖וֹם הַדָּֽשֶׁן׃ 17 וְשִׁסַּ֨ע
אֹת֣וֹ בִכְנָפָיו֮ לֹ֣א יַבְדִּיל֒ וְהִקְטִ֨יר אֹת֤וֹ
הַכֹּהֵן֙ הַמִּזְבֵּ֔חָה עַל־הָעֵצִ֖ים אֲשֶׁ֣ר עַל־
הָאֵ֑שׁ עֹלָ֣ה ה֗וּא אִשֵּׁ֛ה רֵ֥יחַ נִיחֹ֖חַ
לַיהוָֽה׃ ס

2 When a person presents an offering of grain
to the LORD, his offering shall be of choice flour;
he shall pour oil upon it, lay frankincense on
it, 2and present it to Aaron's sons, the priests.
The priest shall scoop out of it a handful of its
choice flour and oil, as well as all of its frankincense; and this token portion he shall turn
into smoke on the altar, as a gift, of pleasing odor

ב וְנֶ֗פֶשׁ כִּֽי־תַקְרִ֞יב קָרְבַּ֤ן מִנְחָה֙ לַֽיהוָ֔ה
סֹ֖לֶת יִהְיֶ֣ה קָרְבָּנ֑וֹ וְיָצַ֤ק עָלֶ֙יהָ֙ שֶׁ֔מֶן וְנָתַ֥ן
עָלֶ֖יהָ לְבֹנָֽה׃ 2 וֶֽהֱבִיאָ֗הּ אֶל־בְּנֵ֣י אַהֲרֹן֮
הַכֹּהֲנִים֒ וְקָמַ֨ץ מִשָּׁ֜ם מְלֹ֣א קֻמְצ֗וֹ מִסָּלְתָּהּ֙
וּמִשַּׁמְנָ֔הּ עַ֖ל כָּל־לְבֹנָתָ֑הּ וְהִקְטִ֨יר הַכֹּהֵ֜ן
אֶת־אַזְכָּרָתָהּ֙ הַמִּזְבֵּ֔חָה אִשֵּׁ֛ה רֵ֥יחַ נִיחֹ֖חַ

THE GRAIN OFFERING (*minḥah*) (2:1–16)

Appropriate for a variety of occasions, the grain offering (*minḥah*) often served as a less costly alternative to animal sacrifices. Both the *minḥah* and the burnt offering were regarded as "a most sacred offering," a status that imposed special restrictions.

Various types of *minḥah* offerings, usually with the same ingredients, are listed according to their methods of preparation. The *minḥah* was made of the choice part of wheat taken from the inner kernels (semolina). Olive oil was mixed into the dough or smeared on it, and frankincense—a costly fragrant resin native to a tree in southern Arabia and Somaliland—was applied, to enhance the taste. The *minḥah* could be prepared on a griddle, in a pan, or in an oven. A fistful of the dough, with the oil and frankincense added, was burned on the altar. The rest of the *minḥah* was prepared in one of the accepted ways, to be eaten by the priests in the sacred precincts of the sanctuary.

Verses 14–16 digress somewhat from the pattern of the chapter as a whole. They ordain a special *minḥah* of first fruits (*bikkurim*), which consisted of nearly ripe grain from the new crop. This grain was roasted and made into groats.

1. a person Hebrew: *nefesh,* here an individual as part of a group.

offering of grain The primary meaning of the term *minḥah* is "tribute" or "gift." It is used in the Bible to reflect the subservient relationship of the worshiper toward God and to convey the notion that it is a duty to present gifts to God, often in the form of sacrifices.

2. handful A minute quantity.

token portion The fistful of dough represents the complete offering from which it was taken.

CHAPTER 2

In Lev. 1:2, the text reads, "when any of you (*adam*) presents an offering." In chapter 2, introducing the grain offering, typically brought by a poor person, the text reads "When a person (*nefesh*) presents an offering." The Hebrew word *nefesh,* a synonym for "person" in biblical Hebrew, later came to mean "soul." This prompted a comment in the Talmud: "When poor people bring an offering, however meager, God credits them as if they had offered their own soul" (BT Men. 104b). What sort of sacrifice does a soul offer? When we give up our unworthy dreams and ambitions, or when a person yearning for wealth decides to be content with a modest income rather than gain riches by unethical means, that is the sacrifice the soul brings to God's altar (Lev. R. 3:1).

Kook, a chief rabbi of Palestine and a vegetarian, envisioned a time when the Temple would be rebuilt and only the grain offering would be brought, for no animals would be slaughtered in God's name: "None shall hurt or destroy in all My holy mountain" (Isa. 11:9).

to the Lord. ³And the remainder of the grain offering shall be for Aaron and his sons, a most holy portion from the Lord's gifts.

⁴When you present an offering of grain baked in the oven, [it shall be of] choice flour: unleavened cakes with oil mixed in, or unleavened wafers spread with oil.

⁵If your offering is a grain offering on a griddle, it shall be of choice flour with oil mixed in, unleavened. ⁶Break it into bits and pour oil on it; it is a grain offering.

⁷If your offering is a grain offering in a pan, it shall be made of choice flour in oil.

⁸When you present to the Lord a grain offering that is made in any of these ways, it shall be brought to the priest who shall take it up to the altar. ⁹The priest shall remove the token portion from the grain offering and turn it into smoke on the altar as a gift, of pleasing odor to the Lord. ¹⁰And the remainder of the grain offering shall be for Aaron and his sons, a most holy portion from the Lord's gifts.

¹¹No grain offering that you offer to the Lord shall be made with leaven, for no leaven or

לַֽיהוָֽה׃ 3 וְהַנּוֹתֶ֙רֶת֙ מִן־הַמִּנְחָ֔ה לְאַהֲרֹ֖ן
וּלְבָנָ֑יו קֹ֥דֶשׁ קָֽדָשִׁ֖ים מֵאִשֵּׁ֥י יְהוָֽה׃ ס
4 וְכִֽי־תַקְרִ֣ב קָרְבַּ֥ן מִנְחָ֖ה מַאֲפֵ֣ה תַנּ֑וּר
סֹ֣לֶת חַלּ֤וֹת מַצֹּת֙ בְּלוּלֹ֣ת בַּשֶּׁ֔מֶן וּרְקִיקֵ֥י
מַצּ֖וֹת מְשֻׁחִ֥ים בַּשָּֽׁמֶן׃ ס
5 וְאִם־מִנְחָ֥ה עַל־הַֽמַּחֲבַ֖ת קָרְבָּנֶ֑ךָ סֹ֣לֶת
בְּלוּלָ֥ה בַשֶּׁ֖מֶן מַצָּ֥ה תִהְיֶֽה׃ 6 פָּת֤וֹת
אֹתָהּ֙ פִּתִּ֔ים וְיָצַקְתָּ֥ עָלֶ֖יהָ שָׁ֑מֶן מִנְחָ֖ה
הִֽוא׃ ס
7 וְאִם־מִנְחַ֥ת מַרְחֶ֖שֶׁת קָרְבָּנֶ֑ךָ סֹ֥לֶת בַּשֶּׁ֖מֶן
תֵּעָשֶֽׂה׃
8 וְהֵבֵאתָ֣ אֶת־הַמִּנְחָ֗ה אֲשֶׁ֥ר יֵעָשֶׂ֛ה מֵאֵ֖לֶּה
לַֽיהוָ֑ה וְהִקְרִיבָהּ֙ אֶל־הַכֹּהֵ֔ן וְהִגִּישָׁ֖הּ אֶל־
הַמִּזְבֵּֽחַ׃ 9 וְהֵרִ֨ים הַכֹּהֵ֤ן מִן־הַמִּנְחָה֙ אֶת־
אַזְכָּ֣רָתָ֔הּ וְהִקְטִ֖יר הַמִּזְבֵּ֑חָה אִשֵּׁ֛ה רֵ֥יחַ
נִיחֹ֖חַ לַֽיהוָֽה׃ 10 וְהַנּוֹתֶ֙רֶת֙ מִן־הַמִּנְחָ֔ה
לְאַהֲרֹ֖ן וּלְבָנָ֑יו קֹ֥דֶשׁ קָֽדָשִׁ֖ים מֵאִשֵּׁ֥י
יְהוָֽה׃
11 כָּל־הַמִּנְחָ֗ה אֲשֶׁ֤ר תַּקְרִ֙יבוּ֙ לַֽיהוָ֔ה לֹ֥א
תֵעָשֶׂ֖ה חָמֵ֑ץ כִּ֤י כָל־שְׂאֹר֙ וְכָל־דְּבַ֔שׁ לֹֽא־

---

3. a most holy portion Hebrew: *kodesh kodashim*; literally, "most holy of the holy offerings."

4. baked ... unleavened cakes ... unleavened wafers The law here distinguishes between the two customary varieties of baked goods: *ḥallah*, "a thick, round cake" (Ibn Ezra), and *rakik*, "a thin cake, cookie, or wafer."

5. on a griddle Cakes prepared on a griddle became crisp and could be broken into "bits," *pittim*, the plural of the Hebrew word for a slice of dry bread (*pat*).

7. in a pan The cakes were prepared in a pan with a lid and deep-fried, becoming soft in the process.

9. The priest shall remove This parallels the statement of verse 2: "The priest shall scoop out of it." Verses 8–10 recapitulate the provisions given earlier in verses 2–3. It is not uncommon for codes of law, as well as narratives, to include some repetition for clarity and for emphasis.

10. And the remainder ... for Aaron and his sons This rule refers to a basic feature of the Israelite sacrificial system and that of most ancient

Near Eastern religions. In a few cases, the complete sacrifice was consumed by the altar fire. Quite often, however, large portions of the offerings were to be eaten by the priests and, in some cases, by the donors of the offerings as well. This was regarded as indispensable to the ritual process, because it was important to celebrate a sacred meal in the presence of God. Failure to eat the appropriate portion of the sacrifices in the proper place and within the proper span of time would render the sacrifices ineffectual. Thus there were two dimensions to a sacrifice (other than the *olah*, which was completely burned): the portions on the altar or table that were received by the deity, and the portions later consumed by the priests and the donors. Without both dimensions, the sacrifice was incomplete.

11. no leaven or honey "Leaven" refers to food that has fermented. "Honey" most likely is from the nectar of trees, such as date palms, or from fruit, not the honey of bees. It is not clear why these products were forbidden on the altar, whereas wine, which was fermented, was used in

honey may be turned into smoke as a gift to the
LORD. 12You may bring them to the LORD as an
offering of choice products; but they shall not
be offered up on the altar for a pleasing odor.
13You shall season your every offering of grain
with salt; you shall not omit from your grain
offering the salt of your covenant with God;
with all your offerings you must offer salt.

14If you bring a grain offering of first fruits
to the LORD, you shall bring new ears parched
with fire, grits of the fresh grain, as your grain
offering of first fruits. 15You shall add oil to it
and lay frankincense on it; it is a grain offering.
16And the priest shall turn a token portion of
it into smoke: some of the grits and oil, with
all of the frankincense, as a gift to the LORD.

תַקְטִירוּ מִמֶּנּוּ אִשֶּׁה לַיהוָה׃ 12 קָרְבַּן
רֵאשִׁית תַּקְרִיבוּ אֹתָם לַיהוָה וְאֶל־
הַמִּזְבֵּחַ לֹא־יַעֲלוּ לְרֵיחַ נִיחֹחַ׃ 13 וְכָל־
קָרְבַּן מִנְחָתְךָ בַּמֶּלַח תִּמְלָח וְלֹא תַשְׁבִּית
מֶלַח בְּרִית אֱלֹהֶיךָ מֵעַל מִנְחָתֶךָ עַל
כָּל־קָרְבָּנְךָ תַּקְרִיב מֶלַח׃ ס
14 וְאִם־תַּקְרִיב מִנְחַת בִּכּוּרִים לַיהוָה
אָבִיב קָלוּי בָּאֵשׁ גֶּרֶשׂ כַּרְמֶל תַּקְרִיב
אֵת מִנְחַת בִּכּוּרֶיךָ׃ 15 וְנָתַתָּ עָלֶיהָ
שֶׁמֶן וְשַׂמְתָּ עָלֶיהָ לְבֹנָה מִנְחָה הִוא׃
16 וְהִקְטִיר הַכֹּהֵן אֶת־אַזְכָּרָתָהּ מִגִּרְשָׂהּ
וּמִשַּׁמְנָהּ עַל כָּל־לְבֹנָתָהּ אִשֶּׁה
לַיהוָה׃ פ

3 If his offering is a sacrifice of well-being—
If he offers of the herd, whether a male or a

רביעי **ג** וְאִם־זֶבַח שְׁלָמִים קָרְבָּנוֹ
אִם מִן־הַבָּקָר הוּא מַקְרִיב אִם־זָכָר אִם־

libations poured over the altar and consumed by fire.

12. choice products Literally, "first fruits." Although honey and leaven are unsuitable as burned altar offerings, they are suitable as offerings set before God. The Israelites were permitted to enjoy the bounty of the land, but first they were required to offer God some of what was His. Such offerings were simply given to the priest rather than burned on the altar.

13. the salt of your covenant with God Salt was the preservative par excellence in antiquity. According to priestly law, all sacrifices had to be salted. In the case of meat, salt functioned to remove whatever blood remained after slaughter. The unexpected use of salt in grain offerings probably reflects the normal tendency toward uniformity in ritual.

14. first fruits Hebrew: *bikkurim,* from the same root as the word for "firstborn" (*b'khor*), which refers to both animals and humans. Birth and growth were perceived as dimensions of the same process in all of nature.

new ears Hebrew: *aviv,* grain just before ripening, when the kernels, not yet darkened, are still greenish in color. *Aviv* is also the name of the spring month when grains ripen.

THE OFFERING OF WELL-BEING
(*zevaḥ sh'lamim*) (3:1–17)

This chapter deals with the third type of offering in Israelite worship, *zevaḥ*. The most frequent *zevaḥ* was *zevaḥ sh'lamim* (designated by Baruch Levine as the "sacred gift of greeting" and rendered here as "offering of well-being").

Some of the same animals used for the burnt offering (Lev. 1) could also be used for *zevaḥ.* The same altar was used for both types of offerings as well as for the grain offering (Lev. 2). *Zevaḥ,* however, had a special character. Whereas the burnt offering (*olah*) was completely consumed by the altar fire, entirely given over to God, *zevaḥ* was

HALAKHAH L'MA·ASEH

2:11 leaven Throughout *Pesaḥ* we are commanded to refrain from eating or benefiting from leavened food (*ḥametz*). "*Ḥametz*" is defined as food prepared from any of five species of grain—wheat, barley, oats, spelt, and rye—that has been allowed to rise through contact with a liquid for more than 18 minutes or with a leavening agent, such as yeast. Among *Ashk'nazim,* many rabbis added restrictions forbidding the use of rice, millet, corn, and legumes (*kitniyot*), although their derivatives (such as oil) are permitted by most authorities. See Comment to Deut. 16:3.

female, he shall bring before the LORD one without blemish. 2He shall lay his hand upon the
head of his offering and slaughter it at the entrance of the Tent of Meeting; and Aaron's sons,
the priests, shall dash the blood against all sides
of the altar. 3He shall then present from the
sacrifice of well-being, as a gift to the LORD, the
fat that covers the entrails and all the fat that
is about the entrails; 4the two kidneys and the
fat that is on them, that is at the loins; and the
protuberance on the liver, which he shall remove with the kidneys. 5Aaron's sons shall turn
these into smoke on the altar, with the burnt
offering which is upon the wood that is on the
fire, as a gift, of pleasing odor to the LORD.

נְקֵבָה תָּמִים יַקְרִיבֶנּוּ לִפְנֵי יְהוָה׃ 2 וְסָמַךְ
יָדוֹ עַל־רֹאשׁ קָרְבָּנוֹ וּשְׁחָטוֹ פֶּתַח אֹהֶל
מוֹעֵד וְזָרְקוּ בְּנֵי אַהֲרֹן הַכֹּהֲנִים אֶת־
הַדָּם עַל־הַמִּזְבֵּחַ סָבִיב׃ 3 וְהִקְרִיב מִזֶּבַח
הַשְּׁלָמִים אִשֶּׁה לַיהוָה אֶת־הַחֵלֶב
הַמְכַסֶּה אֶת־הַקֶּרֶב וְאֵת כָּל־הַחֵלֶב אֲשֶׁר
עַל־הַקֶּרֶב׃ 4 וְאֵת שְׁתֵּי הַכְּלָיֹת וְאֶת־
הַחֵלֶב אֲשֶׁר עֲלֵהֶן אֲשֶׁר עַל־הַכְּסָלִים
וְאֶת־הַיֹּתֶרֶת עַל־הַכָּבֵד עַל־הַכְּלָיוֹת
יְסִירֶנָּה׃ 5 וְהִקְטִירוּ אֹתוֹ בְנֵי־אַהֲרֹן
הַמִּזְבֵּחָה עַל־הָעֹלָה אֲשֶׁר עַל־הָעֵצִים
אֲשֶׁר עַל־הָאֵשׁ אִשֵּׁה רֵיחַ נִיחֹחַ
לַיהוָה׃ פ

a sacred meal shared by the priests and by donors of the offering. Only certain fatty portions of the animal were burned on the altar, as God's share. The grain offering (*minḥah*) could be eaten only by priests. Thus *zevaḥ* represents a distinctive mode of sacrifice, affording worshipers the experience of sharing a sacred meal with the priests.

1. sacrifice of well-being The term translated as "well-being" (*sh'lamim*) has various meanings, like the verb שלם from which it is derived. The usual translation, "sacrifice of well-being," is based on the meaning of *shalom* as "well-being, wholeness." Another view, understanding it as "sacred gift of greeting," reflects the specific role of this sacrifice as an offering made when one came to greet God at a sacred meal.

3. fat The Hebrew word *ḥeilev* here refers specifically to fat that covers or surrounds the kidneys, the liver, and the entrails—not to ordinary fat that adheres to the flesh of an animal. Like blood, *ḥeilev* is forbidden for human consumption. From the perspective of the sacrificial system, a food's desirability depends entirely on its symbolic value. Hence, although normally not regarded as choice food for humans, *ḥeilev* was considered to be a desirable gift for God.

4. protuberance on the liver The "protuberance" refers to the fingerlike projection from the liver, close to the right kidney.

5. with the burnt offering The altar of burnt offerings was used for both the *olah* and the *zevaḥ sh'lamim.*

CHAPTER 3

This category of offering was brought by a person who had something to celebrate. Hoffman emphasizes that *zevaḥ sh'lamim* is always an individual, never a communal, offering because the feelings of gratitude and well-being from which it flows are very personal. It is called *sh'lamim* (from *shalem,* "whole," and *shalom,* "harmony"), because it is motivated not by guilt or obligation but by a sense of wholeness in the donor's life, a sense of being at peace with one's family, with the priests of the Temple, and with God. One commentator derives the name from the fact that "it brings peace between the individual and neighbors who are invited to join in the feast."

Some readers of the chapters describing the sacrifices might conclude that they were all meant to atone for guilt, with the animal brought to the altar serving as a vicarious substitute for the person who might feel deserving of death for the sin. But as we see in the first three chapters of Leviticus, the first major categories of offering are motivated by profound reverence and overflowing happiness, not only by guilt.

Later injunctions of the Torah impose the rule that the *sh'lamim* be eaten on the day when it is brought or the following day at the latest, and that it must be discarded by the morning of the third day (Lev. 7:15, 19:6). One suspects that this is to encourage the donor to invite more friends and poor people to join the celebration. The sense of joy increases with the number of participants.

6 And if his offering for a sacrifice of well-being to the LORD is from the flock, whether a male or a female, he shall offer one without blemish. 7 If he presents a sheep as his offering, he shall bring it before the LORD 8 and lay his hand upon the head of his offering. It shall be slaughtered before the Tent of Meeting, and Aaron's sons shall dash its blood against all sides of the altar. 9 He shall then present, as a gift to the LORD, the fat from the sacrifice of well-being: the whole broad tail, which shall be removed close to the backbone; the fat that covers the entrails and all the fat that is about the entrails; 10 the two kidneys and the fat that is on them, that is at the loins; and the protuberance on the liver, which he shall remove with the kidneys. 11 The priest shall turn these into smoke on the altar as food, a gift to the LORD.

12 And if his offering is a goat, he shall bring it before the LORD 13 and lay his hand upon its head. It shall be slaughtered before the Tent of Meeting, and Aaron's sons shall dash its blood against all sides of the altar. 14 He shall then present as his offering from it, as a gift to the LORD, the fat that covers the entrails and all the fat that is about the entrails; 15 the two kidneys and the fat that is on them, that is at the loins; and the protuberance on the liver, which he shall remove with the kidneys. 16 The priest shall turn these into smoke on the altar as food, a gift, of pleasing odor.

All fat is the LORD's. 17 It is a law for all time throughout the ages, in all your settlements: you must not eat any fat or any blood.

6 וְאִם־מִן־הַצֹּאן קָרְבָּנ֛וֹ לְזֶ֥בַח שְׁלָמִ֖ים
לַיהוָ֑ה זָכָר֙ א֣וֹ נְקֵבָ֔ה תָּמִ֖ים יַקְרִיבֶֽנּוּ׃
7 אִם־כֶּ֥שֶׂב הֽוּא־מַקְרִ֖יב אֶת־קָרְבָּנ֑וֹ
וְהִקְרִ֥יב אֹת֖וֹ לִפְנֵ֥י יְהוָֽה׃ 8 וְסָמַ֤ךְ אֶת־יָדוֹ֙
עַל־רֹ֣אשׁ קָרְבָּנ֔וֹ וְשָׁחַ֣ט אֹת֔וֹ לִפְנֵ֖י אֹ֣הֶל
מוֹעֵ֑ד וְ֠זָרְקוּ בְּנֵ֨י אַהֲרֹ֧ן אֶת־דָּמ֛וֹ עַל־
הַמִּזְבֵּ֖חַ סָבִֽיב׃ 9 וְהִקְרִ֨יב מִזֶּ֣בַח הַשְּׁלָמִים֮
אִשֶּׁ֣ה לַֽיהוָה֒ חֶלְבּוֹ֙ הָֽאַלְיָ֣ה תְמִימָ֔ה
לְעֻמַּ֥ת הֶעָצֶ֖ה יְסִירֶ֑נָּה וְאֶת־הַחֵ֙לֶב֙
הַֽמְכַסֶּ֣ה אֶת־הַקֶּ֔רֶב וְאֵת֙ כָּל־הַחֵ֔לֶב אֲשֶׁ֖ר
עַל־הַקֶּֽרֶב׃ 10 וְאֵת֙ שְׁתֵּ֣י הַכְּלָיֹ֔ת וְאֶת־
הַחֵ֙לֶב֙ אֲשֶׁ֣ר עֲלֵהֶ֔ן אֲשֶׁ֖ר עַל־הַכְּסָלִ֑ים
וְאֶת־הַיֹּתֶ֙רֶת֙ עַל־הַכָּבֵ֔ד עַל־הַכְּלָיֹ֖ת
יְסִירֶֽנָּה׃ 11 וְהִקְטִיר֥וֹ הַכֹּהֵ֖ן הַמִּזְבֵּ֑חָה לֶ֥חֶם
אִשֶּׁ֖ה לַיהוָֽה׃ פ
12 וְאִ֖ם עֵ֣ז קָרְבָּנ֑וֹ וְהִקְרִיב֖וֹ לִפְנֵ֥י יְהוָֽה׃
13 וְסָמַ֤ךְ אֶת־יָדוֹ֙ עַל־רֹאשׁ֔וֹ וְשָׁחַ֣ט אֹת֔וֹ
לִפְנֵ֖י אֹ֣הֶל מוֹעֵ֑ד וְ֠זָרְקוּ בְּנֵ֧י אַהֲרֹ֛ן אֶת־
דָּמ֥וֹ עַל־הַמִּזְבֵּ֖חַ סָבִֽיב׃ 14 וְהִקְרִ֤יב מִמֶּ֙נּוּ֙
קָרְבָּנ֔וֹ אִשֶּׁ֖ה לַֽיהוָ֑ה אֶת־הַחֵ֙לֶב֙ הַֽמְכַסֶּ֣ה
אֶת־הַקֶּ֔רֶב וְאֵת֙ כָּל־הַחֵ֔לֶב אֲשֶׁ֖ר עַל־
הַקֶּֽרֶב׃ 15 וְאֵת֙ שְׁתֵּ֣י הַכְּלָיֹ֔ת וְאֶת־הַחֵ֙לֶב֙
אֲשֶׁ֣ר עֲלֵהֶ֔ן אֲשֶׁ֖ר עַל־הַכְּסָלִ֑ים וְאֶת־
הַיֹּתֶ֙רֶת֙ עַל־הַכָּבֵ֔ד עַל־הַכְּלָיֹ֖ת יְסִירֶֽנָּה׃
16 וְהִקְטִירָ֥ם הַכֹּהֵ֖ן הַמִּזְבֵּ֑חָה לֶ֤חֶם אִשֶּׁה֙
לְרֵ֣יחַ נִיחֹ֔חַ
כָּל־חֵ֖לֶב לַיהוָֽה׃ 17 חֻקַּ֤ת עוֹלָם֙ לְדֹרֹ֣תֵיכֶ֔ם
בְּכֹ֖ל מוֹשְׁבֹתֵיכֶ֑ם כָּל־חֵ֥לֶב וְכָל־דָּ֖ם לֹ֥א
חמישי תֹאכֵֽלוּ׃ פ

6–8. See Comments to Lev. 1.

9. whole broad tail This refers to the large, broad tail of certain species of sheep that are still raised in Israel and neighboring countries.

11. as food Hebrew: *leḥem,* not only bread (its literal meaning) but food in general. The sacrifices are referred to as *leḥem elohim* (food for God) in Lev. 21:6. The priests present the offerings to God in the same way as food is served to humans.

17. law Hebrew: *ḥukkah,* from the root meaning "to inscribe, incise" (חקק). This reflects the practice of inscribing statutes on stone.

for all time The priestly codes often stipulate that a law or regulation applied to a specific instance is meant to be a permanent statute as well.

you must not eat any fat or any blood They belong to God as sacrificial offerings. For the main prohibition against the eating of blood, see 17:10–12.

4 The LORD spoke to Moses, saying: 2Speak
to the Israelite people thus:

When a person unwittingly incurs guilt in regard to any of the LORD's commandments about things not to be done, and does one of them—

חמישי ד וַיְדַבֵּר יְהוָה אֶל־מֹשֶׁה לֵּאמֹר׃ 2 דַּבֵּר
אֶל־בְּנֵי יִשְׂרָאֵל לֵאמֹר
נֶפֶשׁ כִּי־תֶחֱטָא בִשְׁגָגָה מִכֹּל מִצְוֹת יְהוָה אֲשֶׁר לֹא תֵעָשֶׂינָה וְעָשָׂה מֵאַחַת מֵהֵנָּה׃

THE EXPIATORY SACRIFICES (4:1–5:26)

Chapters 4 and 5 contain the laws governing the "purification offering" (*ḥattat*) and the "reparation offering" (*asham*), which are intended to secure atonement and forgiveness from God. These offerings are effective only for unintended offenses. They do not apply to defiant acts or premeditated crimes. Whenever an individual Israelite, a tribal leader, a priest, the High Priest, or the entire Israelite community is guilty of inadvertent wrongdoing or failure to do what the law requires, atonement through sacrifice is required.

The laws of these chapters reflect a deep concern for sanctity. They were intended to maintain the purity of the sanctuary against all forms of defilement that might be caused by the priests or by the people and to ensure the acceptability of all Israelites in God's sight. Inherent in these laws is a connection between sinfulness and impurity. As in many other ancient traditions, the levitical codes of the Torah associate legal innocence-and-guilt with purity-and-impurity, so that the guilty are also considered impure. Conversely, the forgiven are regarded as purified. Thus the *ḥattat* sacrifice can be viewed both as a form of purification and as a ritual for the removal of guilt. Also, sinful acts are frequently the very ones that cause impurity.

THE PURIFICATION OFFERING

For Sins Committed Unintentionally (4:1–35)

2. unwittingly incurs guilt Ignorance of the law is a mitigating circumstance in both the biblical and the rabbinic traditions. This is especially true in ritual matters. The presumption is that a fully aware and knowledgeable Israelite would seek to obey God's laws, not to violate them. Unwitting offenses, therefore, could be expiated by ritual means.

things not to be done, and does one of them In contrast to "sins of omission," when the fault lies in the failure to do what the law requires.

CHAPTER 4

Biblical religion had a prophetic as well as a priestly dimension. The prophet (represented in the Torah by Moses and developed later in the Bible by Amos, Isaiah, and Jeremiah, among others) set high standards for the people, emphasizing God's disappointment with them when they failed to meet those standards. The priest (represented by Aaron and his descendants) met people where they were and, by accepting them, helped them deal with their feelings of inadequacy for having fallen short of the Covenant's demands. If religion sets very high standards, people will inevitably fall short of those standards at one time or another. Indeed, the most devoted people will feel most troubled at falling short of the standards. Religion will then have to offer them a means of finding their way back to acceptability in God's sight.

The purpose of the *ḥattat* was not to bribe God to overlook the sin or to balance it with an act of generosity. Its purpose was to acquaint the donor with one's own more generous side, so that instead of seeing oneself as weak and rebellious, a person could say "sometimes I am weak and rebellious, but that is not the real me. Often I can be generous and obedient." It was an opportunity to clear one's conscience, not a penalty for having done wrong. We can compare it to our own feelings of having been cleansed and reconciled with God at the end of *Yom Kippur*, our prayers and fasting being the contemporary equivalent of a sacrifice. "In the inwardness of the act, the offering of man and the gift of God are indistinguishable. . . . God already answered us when He prompted our heart to pray" (Shalom Spiegel). In a sense, only a good person can recognize having sinned and be motivated to return to God's path. The willingness to bring a *ḥattat* was in itself a sign of virtue.

2. When a person unwittingly incurs guilt The Hebrew word *nefesh*, translated as "person" here and elsewhere in the Bible, is often taken to mean "soul" in postbiblical literature.

3If it is the anointed priest who has incurred
guilt, so that blame falls upon the people, he
shall offer for the sin of which he is guilty a bull
of the herd without blemish as a purification
offering to the Lord. 4He shall bring the bull
to the entrance of the Tent of Meeting, before
the Lord, and lay his hand upon the head of
the bull. The bull shall be slaughtered before the
Lord, 5and the anointed priest shall take some
of the bull's blood and bring it into the Tent
of Meeting. 6The priest shall dip his finger in
the blood, and sprinkle of the blood seven times
before the Lord, in front of the curtain of the
Shrine. 7The priest shall put some of the blood
on the horns of the altar of aromatic incense,

3 אִם הַכֹּהֵן הַמָּשִׁיחַ יֶחֱטָא לְאַשְׁמַת הָעָם
וְהִקְרִיב עַל חַטָּאתוֹ אֲשֶׁר חָטָא פַּר
בֶּן־בָּקָר תָּמִים לַיהוָה לְחַטָּאת׃ 4 וְהֵבִיא
אֶת־הַפָּר אֶל־פֶּתַח אֹהֶל מוֹעֵד לִפְנֵי יְהוָה
וְסָמַךְ אֶת־יָדוֹ עַל־רֹאשׁ הַפָּר וְשָׁחַט אֶת־
הַפָּר לִפְנֵי יְהוָה׃ 5 וְלָקַח הַכֹּהֵן הַמָּשִׁיחַ
מִדַּם הַפָּר וְהֵבִיא אֹתוֹ אֶל־אֹהֶל מוֹעֵד׃
6 וְטָבַל הַכֹּהֵן אֶת־אֶצְבָּעוֹ בַּדָּם וְהִזָּה
מִן־הַדָּם שֶׁבַע פְּעָמִים לִפְנֵי יְהוָה אֶת־פְּנֵי
פָּרֹכֶת הַקֹּדֶשׁ׃ 7 וְנָתַן הַכֹּהֵן מִן־הַדָּם
עַל־קַרְנוֹת מִזְבַּח קְטֹרֶת הַסַּמִּים לִפְנֵי

3. anointed priest According to the laws of Leviticus, the High Priest is the only priest anointed with oil. This accounts for his title here and in 6:15.

so that blame falls upon the people The entire community was affected by the errors and possible offenses of the individual in charge of the sanctuary and the priesthood. Here the law refers to offenses that occurred while the priest was performing priestly duties—not to the personal sins of the priest, for which he had to atone independently. Such inadvertent offenses, even where there was no intent to violate the commandments, might immediately arouse God's wrath and result in divine punishment. Preventing and mitigating that wrath is a major objective of the religious life.

4. lay his hand upon the head of the bull See Comment to 1:4.

6. in front of the curtain of the Shrine The blood rites prescribed here and in verses 16–21 are unusual. Elsewhere, they are reserved for the *Yom Kippur* ritual, as set forth in Lev. 16.

7. on the horns of the altar of aromatic incense For the design of the altar, see Exod. 30:1–10. For the ingredients of the incense to be used on it, see Exod. 30:34–38. Nothing but incense was to be offered on this altar, which stood inside the tent. Only in this instance, and in the ritual on *Yom Kippur* (see Lev. 16:18), was sac-

---

"It is in the soul that the impulse to do wrong begins" (Ramban). "When a person sins, intelligence departs and for the moment one behaves like an animal." It is an appropriate response to sacrifice an animal, which symbolizes the expulsion of one's animal nature (*Seifer Ha-Ḥinnukh*). The Midrash pictures God saying to the soul, "I created you as the most God-like part of the human being (able to distinguish between good and evil)! How could you choose to lead astray those other limbs and organs" (Lev. R. 4:4)?

The *ḥattat* is brought for unintentional violations. Why must we atone for inadvertent sins? Perhaps because we were insufficiently attentive to what we were doing (Hirsch). Carelessness is no excuse for violating God's commandments. Inadvertent sins may reflect a lowering of our guard against temptation. There is a part of us that is inclined to be selfish, to take advantage of others. We must constantly be vigilant against such inclinations. Perhaps we must atone for inadvertent sins because the misdeed, though inadvertent, weighs on our conscience until we do something to atone for it. Because verbal regrets do not strike us as adequate, we must give up something to show our remorse (*Seifer Ha-Ḥinnukh*).

3. The anointed priest must atone for his own inadvertent failings in office before he can guide the people to atone for their sins. He must personally be familiar with feelings of guilt and repentance. Therefore, the rule for the *ḥattat* of the priest is mentioned first here. The Torah and later Jewish law and custom consistently demand that leaders set an example for the community by holding themselves to a higher standard.

which is in the Tent of Meeting, before the
LORD; and all the rest of the bull's blood he shall
pour out at the base of the altar of burnt offering,
which is at the entrance of the Tent of Meeting.
8He shall remove all the fat from the bull of purification offering: the fat that covers the entrails
and all the fat that is about the entrails; 9the two
kidneys and the fat that is on them, that is at
the loins; and the protuberance on the liver,
which he shall remove with the kidneys—10just
as it is removed from the ox of the sacrifice of
well-being. The priest shall turn them into
smoke on the altar of burnt offering. 11But the
hide of the bull, and all its flesh, as well as its
head and legs, its entrails and its dung—12all the
rest of the bull—he shall carry to a pure place
outside the camp, to the ash heap, and burn it
up in a wood fire; it shall be burned on the ash
heap.

13If it is the whole community of Israel that
has erred and the matter escapes the notice of
the congregation, so that they do any of the
things which by the LORD's commandments
ought not to be done, and they realize their
guilt—14when the sin through which they incurred guilt becomes known, the congregation
shall offer a bull of the herd as a purification
offering, and bring it before the Tent of Meet-

יְהוָה אֲשֶׁר בְּאֹהֶל מוֹעֵד וְאֵת ׀ כָּל־דַּם
הַפָּר יִשְׁפֹּךְ אֶל־יְסוֹד מִזְבַּח הָעֹלָה אֲשֶׁר־
פֶּתַח אֹהֶל מוֹעֵד׃ 8 וְאֶת־כָּל־חֵלֶב פַּר
הַחַטָּאת יָרִים מִמֶּנּוּ אֶת־הַחֵלֶב הַמְכַסֶּה
עַל־הַקֶּרֶב וְאֵת כָּל־הַחֵלֶב אֲשֶׁר עַל־
הַקֶּרֶב׃ 9 וְאֵת שְׁתֵּי הַכְּלָיֹת וְאֶת־הַחֵלֶב
אֲשֶׁר עֲלֵיהֶן אֲשֶׁר עַל־הַכְּסָלִים וְאֶת־
הַיֹּתֶרֶת עַל־הַכָּבֵד עַל־הַכְּלָיוֹת יְסִירֶנָּה׃
10 כַּאֲשֶׁר יוּרַם מִשּׁוֹר זֶבַח הַשְּׁלָמִים
וְהִקְטִירָם הַכֹּהֵן עַל מִזְבַּח הָעֹלָה׃
11 וְאֶת־עוֹר הַפָּר וְאֶת־כָּל־בְּשָׂרוֹ עַל־
רֹאשׁוֹ וְעַל־כְּרָעָיו וְקִרְבּוֹ וּפִרְשׁוֹ׃
12 וְהוֹצִיא אֶת־כָּל־הַפָּר אֶל־מִחוּץ לַמַּחֲנֶה
אֶל־מָקוֹם טָהוֹר אֶל־שֶׁפֶךְ הַדֶּשֶׁן וְשָׂרַף
אֹתוֹ עַל־עֵצִים בָּאֵשׁ עַל־שֶׁפֶךְ הַדֶּשֶׁן
יִשָּׂרֵף׃ פ
13 וְאִם כָּל־עֲדַת יִשְׂרָאֵל יִשְׁגּוּ וְנֶעְלַם
דָּבָר מֵעֵינֵי הַקָּהָל וְעָשׂוּ אַחַת מִכָּל־
מִצְוֺת יְהוָה אֲשֶׁר לֹא־תֵעָשֶׂינָה וְאָשֵׁמוּ׃
14 וְנוֹדְעָה הַחַטָּאת אֲשֶׁר חָטְאוּ עָלֶיהָ
וְהִקְרִיבוּ הַקָּהָל פַּר בֶּן־בָּקָר לְחַטָּאת

rificial blood to be dabbed on the horns of the incense altar. All sacrifices other than *ḥattat* were to be burned on the altar that stood in the courtyard, facing the entrance to the tent.

10. just as it is removed from the ox of the sacrifice of well-being The same parts of the animal are placed on the altar for the *ḥattat* sacrifice as for the *sh'lamim* sacrifice. Unlike the latter sacrifice, however, here the rest of the animal is not eaten but destroyed.

11. This rite, like the *Yom Kippur* ritual, combines two methods of expiation: an offering by fire on the altar for the purpose of placating God, and a ritual by which impurity is removed from the Israelite camp and physically destroyed.

its dung The undigested contents of the stomach.

12. to the ash heap Outside the camp. (Another ash heap was located near the altar of burnt offerings; see 1:16).

13. community Hebrew: *edah,* referring in the priestly codes of the Torah to the Israelites as a whole. It conveys the sense that a shared history and a common religion unified the group as a community.

they realize their guilt A state of guilt exists because of the wrongdoing, whether the individual is aware of the misdeed or not.

---

13. If it is the whole community It is possible for an entire community to be misled or swept away by prejudice or emotion. The voice of the people is not necessarily the voice of God.

ing. 15The elders of the community shall lay their hands upon the head of the bull before the LORD, and the bull shall be slaughtered before the LORD. 16The anointed priest shall bring some of the blood of the bull into the Tent of Meeting, 17and the priest shall dip his finger in the blood and sprinkle of it seven times before the LORD, in front of the curtain. 18Some of the blood he shall put on the horns of the altar which is before the LORD in the Tent of Meeting, and all the rest of the blood he shall pour out at the base of the altar of burnt offering, which is at the entrance of the Tent of Meeting. 19He shall remove all its fat from it and turn it into smoke on the altar. 20He shall do with this bull just as is done with the [priest's] bull of purification offering; he shall do the same with it. Thus the priest shall make expiation for them, and they shall be forgiven. 21He shall carry the bull outside the camp and burn it as he burned the first bull; it is the purification offering of the congregation.

22In case it is a chieftain who incurs guilt by

וְהֵבִיאוּ אֹתוֹ לִפְנֵי אֹהֶל מוֹעֵד׃ 15 וְסָמְכוּ
זִקְנֵי הָעֵדָה אֶת־יְדֵיהֶם עַל־רֹאשׁ הַפָּר
לִפְנֵי יְהוָה וְשָׁחַט אֶת־הַפָּר לִפְנֵי יְהוָה׃
16 וְהֵבִיא הַכֹּהֵן הַמָּשִׁיחַ מִדַּם הַפָּר אֶל־
אֹהֶל מוֹעֵד׃ 17 וְטָבַל הַכֹּהֵן אֶצְבָּעוֹ מִן־
הַדָּם וְהִזָּה שֶׁבַע פְּעָמִים לִפְנֵי יְהוָה אֵת
פְּנֵי הַפָּרֹכֶת׃ 18 וּמִן־הַדָּם יִתֵּן ׀ עַל־קַרְנֹת
הַמִּזְבֵּחַ אֲשֶׁר לִפְנֵי יְהוָה אֲשֶׁר בְּאֹהֶל
מוֹעֵד וְאֵת כָּל־הַדָּם יִשְׁפֹּךְ אֶל־יְסוֹד
מִזְבַּח הָעֹלָה אֲשֶׁר־פֶּתַח אֹהֶל מוֹעֵד׃
19 וְאֵת כָּל־חֶלְבּוֹ יָרִים מִמֶּנּוּ וְהִקְטִיר
הַמִּזְבֵּחָה׃ 20 וְעָשָׂה לַפָּר כַּאֲשֶׁר עָשָׂה
לְפַר הַחַטָּאת כֵּן יַעֲשֶׂה־לּוֹ וְכִפֶּר עֲלֵהֶם
הַכֹּהֵן וְנִסְלַח לָהֶם׃ 21 וְהוֹצִיא אֶת־הַפָּר
אֶל־מִחוּץ לַמַּחֲנֶה וְשָׂרַף אֹתוֹ כַּאֲשֶׁר
שָׂרַף אֵת הַפָּר הָרִאשׁוֹן חַטַּאת הַקָּהָל
הוּא׃ פ
22 אֲשֶׁר נָשִׂיא יֶחֱטָא וְעָשָׂה אַחַת מִכָּל־

15. elders of the community The "elders" (*z'kenim*), an ancient institution in biblical Israel, were comparable to councils of elders known from other ancient Near Eastern societies. The elders here act on behalf of the Israelite community in expiating collective offenses against God, as they often were obliged to do.

16–19. The rites required to atone for the sins of the whole community are identical to those prescribed for the expiation of the anointed priest, as set forth in verses 3–12.

20. the priest shall make expiation for them Expiation by means of sacrificial blood rites is a prerequisite for securing God's forgiveness. It was formerly thought that the Hebrew word for expiate (*kipper*) meant "cover over, conceal," a well-known image (see Ps. 32:1). On the basis of Akkadian usage of the cognate (linguistically related word) *kuppuru,* it has been established that the verb *kipper* means "to wipe off, burnish, cleanse." Expiation is conceived of as cleansing, as wiping away impurity and contamination and, by extension, sinfulness itself. The purification comes from God in response to the proper performance of required rituals undertaken in good faith.

they shall be forgiven The word for forgiving (*salaḥ*) most likely derives from a verb meaning "to wash, to sprinkle with water" in Akkadian. The basic notion is that of cleansing with water, a concept then extended to connote God's forgiveness and acceptance of expiation.

21. congregation Hebrew: *kahal;* like *edah* in verse 13, this is a term for the Israelites as a whole. It characterizes a group living together.

22. a chieftain who incurs guilt The chieftain, unlike the priest, was a secular leader. He was not, therefore, held directly responsible for

---

22. In case it is a chieftain who incurs guilt Literally, "when a chieftain incurs guilt." A ruler must make so many difficult decisions that it is virtually impossible never to harm innocent people in the process. Yoḥanan ben Zakkai is quoted as saying, "Fortunate is the

מִצְוֺת יְהֹוָה אֱלֹהָיו אֲשֶׁר לֹא־תֵעָשֶׂינָה
בִּשְׁגָגָה וְאָשֵׁם׃ 23 אוֹ־הוֹדַע אֵלָיו חַטָּאתוֹ
אֲשֶׁר חָטָא בָּהּ וְהֵבִיא אֶת־קָרְבָּנוֹ שְׂעִיר
עִזִּים זָכָר תָּמִים׃ 24 וְסָמַךְ יָדוֹ עַל־רֹאשׁ
הַשָּׂעִיר וְשָׁחַט אֹתוֹ בִּמְקוֹם אֲשֶׁר־יִשְׁחַט
אֶת־הָעֹלָה לִפְנֵי יְהֹוָה חַטָּאת הוּא׃
25 וְלָקַח הַכֹּהֵן מִדַּם הַחַטָּאת בְּאֶצְבָּעוֹ
וְנָתַן עַל־קַרְנֹת מִזְבַּח הָעֹלָה וְאֶת־דָּמוֹ
יִשְׁפֹּךְ אֶל־יְסוֹד מִזְבַּח הָעֹלָה׃ 26 וְאֶת־כָּל־
חֶלְבּוֹ יַקְטִיר הַמִּזְבֵּחָה כְּחֵלֶב זֶבַח
הַשְּׁלָמִים וְכִפֶּר עָלָיו הַכֹּהֵן מֵחַטָּאתוֹ
וְנִסְלַח לוֹ׃ פ
ששי 27 וְאִם־נֶפֶשׁ אַחַת תֶּחֱטָא בִשְׁגָגָה מֵעַם
הָאָרֶץ בַּעֲשֹׂתָהּ אַחַת מִמִּצְוֺת יְהֹוָה אֲשֶׁר

doing unwittingly any of the things which by the commandment of the LORD his God ought not to be done, and he realizes his guilt—23or the sin of which he is guilty is brought to his knowledge—he shall bring as his offering a male goat without blemish. 24He shall lay his hand upon the goat's head, and it shall be slaughtered at the spot where the burnt offering is slaughtered before the LORD; it is a purification offering. 25The priest shall take with his finger some of the blood of the purification offering and put it on the horns of the altar of burnt offering; and the rest of its blood he shall pour out at the base of the altar of burnt offering. 26All its fat he shall turn into smoke on the altar, like the fat of the sacrifice of well-being. Thus the priest shall make expiation on his behalf for his sin, and he shall be forgiven.

27If any person from among the populace unwittingly incurs guilt by doing any of the things which by the LORD's commandments ought not

the religious offenses of the whole community, as the High Priest was. His sacrifice of expiation, consequently, was basically the same as that of any other Israelite.

23. a male goat Literally, "a hairy goat" (*sa·ir*). Goats frequently were used for purification offerings.

25–26. The same portions of the sacrificial animal are placed on the altar here as for the *sh'lamim* (prescribed in 3:3–4). Here, however, some of the sacrificial blood is daubed on the horns of the altar of burnt offerings and the rest is poured out at the base of the altar. All of the sacrificial blood involved in both the *olah* and the *sh'lamim* sacrifices is dashed against the sides of the altar.

27. any person From here to the end of chapter 4, the form of the *ḥattat* sacrifice is essentially the same as the one prescribed for the chieftain (*nasi*), with one difference: An individual Israelite shall offer a female goat or a female sheep instead of a male animal.

populace Hebrew: *am ha-aretz;* literally, "people of the land." In the Bible, it connotes landed gentry, "people of status," not the populace at large. (In Rabbinic times, *am ha-aretz* took on the pejorative meaning it has today—an untutored person, an ignoramus. This is probably because it came to refer to someone from the countryside who was unlettered. The Latin word *paganus* suffered a similar fate.)

---

generation whose leader recognizes having sinned and brings an offering of purification" (BT Hor. 10b, reading in this verse the word *asher,* "in case," as *ashrei,* "fortunate"). When the people see the ruler humbling himself to atone for mistakes, they will be more likely to do so themselves. But a leader who denies ever being wrong, who seeks to blame others, will teach the people to behave in the same way. Also, leaders who admit their own human weaknesses will be more compassionate toward the weaknesses of their followers.

27. If any person from among the populace unwittingly incurs guilt Literally, "if a single person sins." This prompted the comment that the person was led to sin by separating from the community and becoming an isolated individual (*Tiferet Sh'mu·el*).

to be done, and he realizes his guilt—28 or the sin of which he is guilty is brought to his knowledge—he shall bring a female goat without blemish as his offering for the sin of which he is guilty. 29 He shall lay his hand upon the head of the purification offering, and the purification offering shall be slaughtered at the place of the burnt offering. 30 The priest shall take with his finger some of its blood and put it on the horns of the altar of burnt offering; and all the rest of its blood he shall pour out at the base of the altar. 31 He shall remove all its fat, just as the fat is removed from the sacrifice of well-being; and the priest shall turn it into smoke on the altar, for a pleasing odor to the LORD. Thus the priest shall make expiation for him, and he shall be forgiven.

32 If the offering he brings as a purification offering is a sheep, he shall bring a female without blemish. 33 He shall lay his hand upon the head of the purification offering, and it shall be slaughtered as a purification offering at the spot where the burnt offering is slaughtered. 34 The priest shall take with his finger some of the blood of the purification offering and put it on the horns of the altar of burnt offering, and all the rest of its blood he shall pour out at the base of the altar. 35 And all its fat he shall remove just as the fat of the sheep of the sacrifice of well-being is removed; and this the priest shall turn into smoke on the altar, over the LORD's gift. Thus the priest shall make expiation on his behalf for the sin of which he is guilty, and he shall be forgiven.

לֹא־תֵעָשֶׂינָה וְאָשֵׁם׃ 28 אוֹ הוֹדַע אֵלָיו
חַטָּאתוֹ אֲשֶׁר חָטָא וְהֵבִיא קָרְבָּנוֹ שְׂעִירַת
עִזִּים תְּמִימָה נְקֵבָה עַל־חַטָּאתוֹ אֲשֶׁר
חָטָא׃ 29 וְסָמַךְ אֶת־יָדוֹ עַל רֹאשׁ הַחַטָּאת
וְשָׁחַט אֶת־הַחַטָּאת בִּמְקוֹם הָעֹלָה׃
30 וְלָקַח הַכֹּהֵן מִדָּמָהּ בְּאֶצְבָּעוֹ וְנָתַן עַל־
קַרְנֹת מִזְבַּח הָעֹלָה וְאֶת־כָּל־דָּמָהּ יִשְׁפֹּךְ
אֶל־יְסוֹד הַמִּזְבֵּחַ׃ 31 וְאֶת־כָּל־חֶלְבָּהּ יָסִיר
כַּאֲשֶׁר הוּסַר חֵלֶב מֵעַל זֶבַח הַשְּׁלָמִים
וְהִקְטִיר הַכֹּהֵן הַמִּזְבֵּחָה לְרֵיחַ נִיחֹחַ
לַיהוָה וְכִפֶּר עָלָיו הַכֹּהֵן וְנִסְלַח לוֹ׃ פ
32 וְאִם־כֶּבֶשׂ יָבִיא קָרְבָּנוֹ לְחַטָּאת נְקֵבָה
תְמִימָה יְבִיאֶנָּה׃ 33 וְסָמַךְ אֶת־יָדוֹ עַל
רֹאשׁ הַחַטָּאת וְשָׁחַט אֹתָהּ לְחַטָּאת
בִּמְקוֹם אֲשֶׁר יִשְׁחַט אֶת־הָעֹלָה׃ 34 וְלָקַח
הַכֹּהֵן מִדַּם הַחַטָּאת בְּאֶצְבָּעוֹ וְנָתַן עַל־
קַרְנֹת מִזְבַּח הָעֹלָה וְאֶת־כָּל־דָּמָהּ יִשְׁפֹּךְ
אֶל־יְסוֹד הַמִּזְבֵּחַ׃ 35 וְאֶת־כָּל־חֶלְבָּהּ יָסִיר
כַּאֲשֶׁר יוּסַר חֵלֶב־הַכֶּשֶׂב מִזֶּבַח הַשְּׁלָמִים
וְהִקְטִיר הַכֹּהֵן אֹתָם הַמִּזְבֵּחָה עַל אִשֵּׁי
יְהוָה וְכִפֶּר עָלָיו הַכֹּהֵן עַל־חַטָּאתוֹ אֲשֶׁר־
חָטָא וְנִסְלַח לוֹ׃ פ

28. female goat It is not certain why female animals were required for certain offerings and not for others. Most animal sacrifices consisted of males, probably because fewer males than females were necessary to reproduce the herds and flocks. This pattern is common to most ancient Near Eastern religions.

32–35. The procedures for a female sheep offered as a *ḥattat* sacrifice are identical to those for a female goat.

---

29. at the place of the burnt offering It is done there in order not to embarrass those bringing a *ḥattat* by identifying them as repentant sinners. It would not be apparent to an onlooker whether the individual was bringing a purification offering or a burnt offering.

5 If a person incurs guilt—

When he has heard a public imprecation and—although able to testify as one who has either seen or learned of the matter—he does not give information, so that he is subject to punishment;

²Or when a person touches any impure thing—be it the carcass of an impure beast or the carcass of impure cattle or the carcass of an impure creeping thing—and the fact has escaped him, and then, being impure, he realizes his guilt;

³Or when he touches human impurity—any such impurity whereby one becomes impure—and, though he has known it, the fact has escaped him, but later he realizes his guilt;

ה וְנֶ֣פֶשׁ כִּֽי־תֶחֱטָ֗א
וְשָֽׁמְעָה֙ ק֣וֹל אָלָ֔ה וְה֣וּא עֵ֔ד א֖וֹ רָאָ֣ה
א֣וֹ יָדָ֑ע אִם־ל֥וֹא יַגִּ֖יד וְנָשָׂ֥א עֲוֺנֽוֹ׃
2 א֣וֹ נֶ֗פֶשׁ אֲשֶׁ֣ר תִּגַּע֮ בְּכׇל־דָּבָ֣ר טָמֵא֒
א֣וֹ בְנִבְלַ֤ת חַיָּה֙ טְמֵאָ֔ה א֚וֹ בְּנִבְלַת֙
בְּהֵמָ֣ה טְמֵאָ֔ה א֕וֹ בְּנִבְלַ֖ת שֶׁ֣רֶץ טָמֵ֑א
וְנֶעְלַ֣ם מִמֶּ֔נּוּ וְה֥וּא טָמֵ֖א וְאָשֵֽׁם׃
3 א֣וֹ כִ֣י יִגַּע֮ בְּטֻמְאַ֣ת אָדָם֒ לְכֹל֙ טֻמְאָת֔וֹ
אֲשֶׁ֥ר יִטְמָ֖א בָּ֑הּ וְנֶעְלַ֣ם מִמֶּ֔נּוּ וְה֥וּא יָדַ֖ע
וְאָשֵֽׁם׃

For Unintended Sins of Omission (5:1–13)

1. public Hebrew: *kol;* literally, "voice, sound." Here it has the technical sense of "oral proclamation." The proclamation urged all who possessed information in a certain case to come forward and testify.

subject to punishment A person who heard the proclamation but who failed to assist the judicial process and withheld evidence was liable to a penalty. (In the ancient Near East, courts and archives generally were located on temple grounds, and this was most likely true of ancient Israel as well. An institutional connection links testimony and related juridical procedures, on the one hand, with expiation for what we usually refer to as religious sins, on the other.) The failure to come forth was a form of negligence; and the omission involved speech, not deed.

2. when a person touches any impure thing The main source for these prohibitions of contact is chapter 11, especially verses 24–31, where their significance is discussed.

then, being impure, he realizes his guilt Better: "insofar as he was impure, he had incurred guilt." Impurity is the basis of the offender's guilt.

3. human impurity Hebrew: *tum·at adam;* the forms of impurity that affect a woman after childbirth (12:2), a person who has a bodily discharge (15:2,19), or a man who engages in sexual intercourse with a menstruating woman (15:24). It also applies to a person who has eaten the meat of an animal that died naturally or was torn by beasts (17:15–16).

and, though he has known it, the fact has escaped him, but later he realizes his guilt Although the fact escaped him, ultimately he knew that he had been guilty; i.e., something originally was ignored or forgotten, then later recalled. Verses 2 and 3 serve to protect the sanctuary and all within it from any impurity carried by an impure person. If the offense had been intentional, contamination of the sanctuary would subject the offender to the more severe penalty of being cut off from the community (7:19–21).

CHAPTER 5

1. We are held responsible not only for the wrong things we do but for the things we should but do not do. During the *Sho·ah,* as well as in other circumstances, bystanders who did not act to oppose evil caused enormous, irreparable harm. In Jewish law, one who has knowledge about a crime or legal dispute and does not come forward to divulge it is "innocent before a human court but liable in the sight of God" (BT BK 56a). The *asham* (reparation offering) is how the Torah seeks to resolve that conflict.

4Or when a person utters an oath to bad
or good purpose—whatever a man may utter
in an oath—and, though he has known it, the
fact has escaped him, but later he realizes his
guilt in any of these matters—
5when he realizes his guilt in any of these matters, he shall confess that wherein he has sinned.
6And he shall bring as his penalty to the LORD,
for the sin of which he is guilty, a female from
the flock, sheep or goat, as a purification
offering; and the priest shall make expiation on
his behalf for his sin.
7But if his means do not suffice for a sheep,
he shall bring to the LORD, as his penalty for that
of which he is guilty, two turtledoves or two pigeons, one for a purification offering and the
other for a burnt offering. 8He shall bring them
to the priest, who shall offer first the one for the
purification offering, pinching its head at the
nape without severing it. 9He shall sprinkle

4 אָ֣וֹ נֶ֡פֶשׁ כִּ֣י תִשָּׁבַע֩ לְבַטֵּ֨א בִשְׂפָתַ֜יִם
לְהָרַ֣ע ׀ א֣וֹ לְהֵיטִ֗יב לְכֹל֩ אֲשֶׁ֨ר יְבַטֵּ֧א
הָאָדָ֛ם בִּשְׁבֻעָ֖ה וְנֶעְלַ֣ם מִמֶּ֑נּוּ וְהוּא־יָדַ֥ע
וְאָשֵׁ֖ם לְאַחַ֥ת מֵאֵֽלֶּה׃
5 וְהָיָ֥ה כִֽי־יֶאְשַׁ֖ם לְאַחַ֣ת מֵאֵ֑לֶּה וְהִתְוַדָּ֕ה
אֲשֶׁ֥ר חָטָ֖א עָלֶֽיהָ׃ 6 וְהֵבִ֣יא אֶת־אֲשָׁמ֣וֹ
לַיהוָ֡ה עַ֣ל חַטָּאתוֹ֩ אֲשֶׁ֨ר חָטָ֜א נְקֵבָ֨ה
מִן־הַצֹּ֥אן כִּשְׂבָּ֛ה אֽוֹ־שְׂעִירַ֥ת עִזִּ֖ים
לְחַטָּ֑את וְכִפֶּ֥ר עָלָ֛יו הַכֹּהֵ֖ן מֵחַטָּאתֽוֹ׃
7 וְאִם־לֹ֨א תַגִּ֣יעַ יָדוֹ֮ דֵּ֣י שֶׂה֒ וְהֵבִ֨יא אֶת־
אֲשָׁמ֜וֹ אֲשֶׁ֣ר חָטָ֗א שְׁתֵּ֥י תֹרִ֛ים אֽוֹ־שְׁנֵ֥י
בְנֵי־יוֹנָ֖ה לַֽיהוָ֑ה אֶחָ֥ד לְחַטָּ֖את וְאֶחָ֥ד
לְעֹלָֽה׃ 8 וְהֵבִ֤יא אֹתָם֙ אֶל־הַכֹּהֵ֔ן וְהִקְרִ֛יב
אֶת־אֲשֶׁ֥ר לַחַטָּ֖את רִאשׁוֹנָ֑ה וּמָלַ֧ק אֶת־
רֹאשׁ֛וֹ מִמּ֥וּל עָרְפּ֖וֹ וְלֹ֥א יַבְדִּֽיל׃ 9 וְהִזָּ֞ה

4. an oath One who neglects to fulfill an oath, or allows the matter to escape notice, offends not only those affected by the oath but also God, in whose name the oath was taken.

5. he shall confess that wherein he has sinned This is the only explicit reference to confession in all of chapters 4 and 5—for a good reason. In the other cases, which involve second parties, there are indications that the offender was prompted to undertake expiation either by individuals or by the situation. Here, however, we are dealing with private acts and the failure to act, which might never have come to light had the offender not come forth to confess. The motivation for confessing was religious and moral—the desire to be purified and to avert God's wrath for having failed to fulfill one's commitments. It was also related to the judicial process.

6. a purification offering The sacrifice prescribed in this instance consisted of a female from the flock. This was for "sins of omission," just as the sacrifice prescribed in 4:27–35 was for "sins of commission." Here, the offender had the option of offering either a sheep or a goat. One who could afford the full *ḥattat* sacrifice was to offer it even for sins of omission, which were deemed less severe.

8–9. pinching its head at the nape without severing The use of sacrificial blood here is similar to the procedure for the *ḥattat* generally (as prescribed in 4:25,30), except that in this instance the blood was not sprinkled on the horns of the altar of burnt offerings but on its side (*kir*).

---

4. Jewish thought, taking words seriously, warns us against uttering oaths, lest we find ourselves unable to fulfill them. "It is better not to vow at all than to vow and not fulfill" (Eccles. 5:4). "Say little and do much" (M Avot 1:15).

5. he shall confess The Hebrew verb is reflexive, as if to say "one shall admit to oneself" having done wrong.

7. if his means do not suffice Throughout this detailed presentation of the rules of animal offerings, emphasizing that everything must be done in a prescribed manner, the Torah tells us that a person who cannot afford the prescribed offering may bring a more modest one, with the same result. There is nothing magical or automatic about the rituals. It is the attitude of the worshiper that matters most, not the details of the ceremony.

8. The purification offering is presented first, so that the burnt offering (*olah*) that follows will be offered by a cleansed and forgiven worshiper.

some of the blood of the purification offering on the side of the altar, and what remains of the blood shall be drained out at the base of the altar; it is a purification offering. 10And the second he shall prepare as a burnt offering, according to regulation. Thus the priest shall make expiation on his behalf for the sin of which he is guilty, and he shall be forgiven.

11And if his means do not suffice for two turtledoves or two pigeons, he shall bring as his offering for that of which he is guilty a tenth of an *ephah* of choice flour for a purification offering; he shall not add oil to it or lay frankincense on it, for it is a purification offering. 12He shall bring it to the priest, and the priest shall scoop out of it a handful as a token portion of it and turn it into smoke on the altar, with the LORD's gifts; it is a purification offering. 13Thus the priest shall make expiation on his behalf for whichever of these sins he is guilty, and he shall be forgiven. It shall belong to the priest, like the grain offering.

מִדַּם הַחַטָּאת֙ עַל־קִ֣יר הַמִּזְבֵּ֔חַ וְהַנִּשְׁאָ֣ר בַּדָּ֔ם יִמָּצֵ֖ה אֶל־יְס֣וֹד הַמִּזְבֵּ֑חַ חַטָּ֖את הֽוּא׃ 10 וְאֶת־הַשֵּׁנִ֛י יַעֲשֶׂ֥ה עֹלָ֖ה כַּמִּשְׁפָּ֑ט וְכִפֶּ֨ר עָלָ֧יו הַכֹּהֵ֛ן מֵחַטָּאת֥וֹ אֲשֶׁר־חָטָ֖א וְנִסְלַ֥ח לֽוֹ׃ ס

11 וְאִם־לֹ֨א תַשִּׂ֣יג יָדוֹ֮ לִשְׁתֵּ֣י תֹרִים֒ א֤וֹ לִשְׁנֵ֣י בְנֵֽי־יוֹנָה֒ וְהֵבִ֨יא אֶת־קׇרְבָּנ֜וֹ אֲשֶׁ֣ר חָטָ֗א עֲשִׂירִ֧ת הָאֵפָ֛ה סֹ֖לֶת לְחַטָּ֑את לֹא־יָשִׂ֨ים עָלֶ֜יהָ שֶׁ֗מֶן וְלֹא־יִתֵּ֤ן עָלֶ֙יהָ֙ לְבֹנָ֔ה כִּ֥י חַטָּ֖את הִֽיא׃ 12 וֶהֱבִיאָהּ֮ אֶל־הַכֹּהֵן֒ וְקָמַ֣ץ הַכֹּהֵ֣ן ׀ מִ֠מֶּ֠נָּה מְל֨וֹא קֻמְצ֜וֹ אֶת־אַזְכָּֽרָתָהּ֙ וְהִקְטִ֣יר הַמִּזְבֵּ֔חָה עַ֖ל אִשֵּׁ֣י יְהֹוָ֑ה חַטָּ֖את הִֽוא׃ 13 וְכִפֶּר֩ עָלָ֨יו הַכֹּהֵ֜ן עַל־חַטָּאת֧וֹ אֲשֶׁר־חָטָ֛א מֵֽאַחַ֥ת מֵאֵ֖לֶּה וְנִסְלַ֣ח ל֑וֹ וְהָֽיְתָ֥ה לַכֹּהֵ֖ן כַּמִּנְחָֽה׃ ס

14 וַיְדַבֵּ֥ר יְהֹוָ֖ה אֶל־מֹשֶׁ֥ה לֵּאמֹֽר׃
15 נֶ֚פֶשׁ כִּֽי־תִמְעֹ֣ל מַ֔עַל וְחָֽטְאָה֙ בִּשְׁגָגָ֔ה

14And the LORD spoke to Moses, saying:
15When a person commits a trespass, being

---

11. Embellishments of oil and frankincense, prescribed for the grain offering in 2:1 and elsewhere, are not included here. The reason is not entirely clear. Possibly the elimination of costly ingredients was intended to lower the cost of the offering so that all in need of expiation could afford it. Then, too, it might not be appropriate for an offering brought by a sinful person to be so embellished.

ephah See Comment to Exod. 16:36.

THE REPARATION OFFERING (vv. 14–26)
For Sins against the Sanctuary (vv. 14–16)
The law of verses 14–16 applies only to uninten-

tional misuse or destruction of sanctuary property. (Intentional theft of sacred property or damage to it was a crime punishable by death.)

15. trespass Hebrew: *ma·al;* in the Bible, the word refers to ancient notions of sacrilege and impurity. Here it is an appropriate term for the theft of sanctuary property. The term may also relate to betrayal of trust, such as marital infidelity, acts of deceit, and violation of the covenant between God and the people Israel by the worship of alien gods.

any of the LORD's sacred things This refers to sanctuary property, not to priestly allocations or tithes, which belonged to the priests and Levites. Misappropriation of what belonged to the

---

15. Hirsch contrasts "inadvertent" trespass of sanctuary property with "deliberate" violation, commenting, "It is not deliberate desecration but indifference and apathy that the sanctuary need fear." People who are angry

at God or at religious institutions often display a passion that has a religious dimension. It is a way of caring deeply. People who do not care at all are the ones who commit the ultimate blasphemy.

unwittingly remiss about any of the LORD's sacred things, he shall bring as his penalty to the
LORD a ram without blemish from the flock,
convertible into payment in silver by the sanctuary weight, as a reparation offering. 16He shall
make restitution for that wherein he was remiss
about the sacred things, and he shall add a fifth
part to it and give it to the priest. The priest shall
make expiation on his behalf with the ram of
the reparation offering, and he shall be forgiven.
17And when a person, without knowing it,
sins in regard to any of the LORD's commandments about things not to be done, and then
realizes his guilt, he shall be subject to punishment. 18He shall bring to the priest a ram without blemish from the flock, or the equivalent,
as a reparation offering. The priest shall make
expiation on his behalf for the error that he
committed unwittingly, and he shall be forgiven. 19It is a reparation offering; he has incurred guilt before the LORD.
20The LORD spoke to Moses, saying: 21When

מִקָּדְשֵׁי יְהוָה וְהֵבִיא אֶת־אֲשָׁמוֹ לַיהוָה
אַיִל תָּמִים מִן־הַצֹּאן בְּעֶרְכְּךָ כֶּסֶף־
שְׁקָלִים בְּשֶׁקֶל־הַקֹּדֶשׁ לְאָשָׁם׃ 16 וְאֵת
אֲשֶׁר חָטָא מִן־הַקֹּדֶשׁ יְשַׁלֵּם וְאֶת־
חֲמִישִׁתוֹ יוֹסֵף עָלָיו וְנָתַן אֹתוֹ לַכֹּהֵן
וְהַכֹּהֵן יְכַפֵּר עָלָיו בְּאֵיל הָאָשָׁם וְנִסְלַח
לוֹ׃ פ
17 וְאִם־נֶפֶשׁ כִּי תֶחֱטָא וְעָשְׂתָה אַחַת
מִכָּל־מִצְוֺת יְהוָה אֲשֶׁר לֹא תֵעָשֶׂינָה
וְלֹא־יָדַע וְאָשֵׁם וְנָשָׂא עֲוֺנוֹ׃ 18 וְהֵבִיא אַיִל
תָּמִים מִן־הַצֹּאן בְּעֶרְכְּךָ לְאָשָׁם אֶל־הַכֹּהֵן
וְכִפֶּר עָלָיו הַכֹּהֵן עַל שִׁגְגָתוֹ אֲשֶׁר־שָׁגָג
וְהוּא לֹא־יָדַע וְנִסְלַח לוֹ׃ 19 אָשָׁם הוּא
אָשֹׁם אָשַׁם לַיהוָה׃ פ
20 וַיְדַבֵּר יְהוָה אֶל־מֹשֶׁה לֵּאמֹר׃ 21 נֶפֶשׁ
כִּי תֶחֱטָא וּמָעֲלָה מַעַל בַּיהוָה וְכִחֵשׁ
בַּעֲמִיתוֹ בְּפִקָּדוֹן אוֹ־בִתְשׂוּמֶת יָד אוֹ בְגָזֵל

priests (according to 22:14) required the offender to make restitution and to pay a penalty, but there is no mention of an *asham.*

convertible into payment in silver That is, the equivalent in silver. The offender had the option of either providing a ram of one's own or remitting the cost of one so that a proper sacrificial ram could be secured on one's behalf.

sanctuary weight Hebrew: *shekel ha-kodesh,* the prevailing standard in ancient Israel at certain periods.

16. add a fifth part to it The penalty of one fifth was a common feature of Temple administration. The provisions of this law are reformulated in verse 24.

For Contingency (vv. 17–19)

17. without knowing it, sins . . . and then realizes The person did not know for certain that he committed an offense; it was only a suspicion. Certain knowledge of an offense would invoke the law of 4:27–35. In cases of uncertainty, however, an *asham* consisting of a ram was prescribed to avert God's wrath.

For Deceit with False Oaths (vv. 20–26)

Unlike the careless taking of sanctuary property in 5:14–16, the offenses outlined here were intentional: persons who deliberately misappropriated property or funds entrusted to their safekeeping, or defrauded another, or failed to restore lost property they had located. When sued, these defendants then lied under oath and claimed no responsibility. Without witnesses, the aggrieved party had no further recourse and sustained a great loss. But what if the accused later admitted to having lied under oath—thus assuming liability for the unrecovered property? Such persons were given the opportunity to clear themselves by making restitution and by paying a fine of 20 per-

---

17. any of the LORD's commandments about things not to be done Levi Yitzḥak of Berdichev read this text literally: "one of the LORD's commandments which should not be done." Based on this reading, he taught, "sometimes it is possible to perform a *mitzvah* in such an improper manner that it would have been better not to do it at all."

a person sins and commits a trespass against the LORD by dealing deceitfully with his fellow in the matter of a deposit or a pledge, or through robbery, or by defrauding his fellow, 22 or by finding something lost and lying about it; if he swears falsely regarding any one of the various things that one may do and sin thereby— 23 when one has thus sinned and, realizing his guilt, would restore that which he got through robbery or fraud, or the deposit that was entrusted to him, or the lost thing that he found, 24 or anything else about which he swore falsely, he shall repay the principal amount and add a fifth part to it. He shall pay it to its owner when he realizes his guilt. 25 Then he shall bring to the priest, as his penalty to the LORD, a ram without blemish from the flock, or the equivalent, as a reparation offering. 26 The priest shall make expiation on his behalf before the LORD, and he shall be forgiven for whatever he may have done to draw blame thereby.

אוֹ עָשַׁק אֶת־עֲמִיתוֹ׃ 22 אוֹ־מָצָא אֲבֵדָה
וְכִחֶשׁ בָּהּ וְנִשְׁבַּע עַל־שָׁקֶר עַל־אַחַת
מִכֹּל אֲשֶׁר־יַעֲשֶׂה הָאָדָם לַחֲטֹא בָהֵנָּה׃
23 וְהָיָה כִּי־יֶחֱטָא וְאָשֵׁם וְהֵשִׁיב אֶת־
הַגְּזֵלָה אֲשֶׁר גָּזָל אוֹ אֶת־הָעֹשֶׁק אֲשֶׁר
עָשָׁק אוֹ אֶת־הַפִּקָּדוֹן אֲשֶׁר הָפְקַד אִתּוֹ
מפטיר אוֹ אֶת־הָאֲבֵדָה אֲשֶׁר מָצָא׃ 24 אוֹ מִכֹּל
אֲשֶׁר־יִשָּׁבַע עָלָיו לַשֶּׁקֶר וְשִׁלַּם אֹתוֹ
בְּרֹאשׁוֹ וַחֲמִשִׁתָיו יֹסֵף עָלָיו לַאֲשֶׁר הוּא
לוֹ יִתְּנֶנּוּ בְּיוֹם אַשְׁמָתוֹ׃ 25 וְאֶת־אֲשָׁמוֹ
יָבִיא לַיהוָה אַיִל תָּמִים מִן־הַצֹּאן בְּעֶרְכְּךָ
לְאָשָׁם אֶל־הַכֹּהֵן׃ 26 וְכִפֶּר עָלָיו הַכֹּהֵן
לִפְנֵי יְהוָה וְנִסְלַח לוֹ עַל־אַחַת מִכֹּל
אֲשֶׁר־יַעֲשֶׂה לְאַשְׁמָה בָהּ׃ פ

cent to the aggrieved party. Having lied under oath, they also had offended God and were obliged to offer an *asham* in expiation.

23. would restore Literally, "must restore." This expresses what criminals are required to do, not what they may prefer to do.

25–26. The provisions here are identical to those of the *asham* prescribed in verses 15–16.

---

21. trespass against the LORD by dealing deceitfully To cheat another person is to sin against God as well as against that person. "It is worse to rob a fellow human being than to steal from God" (BT BB 88b). Akiva taught that whenever two people enter into an agreement, each is relying on the divine dimension of the other, the part of a person that is the image of God and knows what is right and what is wrong, making God a witness to every transaction. To betray that trust is to deny the divine image in ourselves, and to deny God's participation in our activities.

robbery . . . defrauding According to the Talmud, robbery (*gezel*) is defined as taking something that belongs to another person, and fraud (*oshek*) refers to withholding from another person something that is owed (BT BM 111a). "The reparation offering may not be brought until the violator has returned the property to its rightful owner" (Maimonides).

26. and he shall be forgiven The *parashah* concludes on this affirming note. As a Hadisic master taught, "The gates of repentance open for anyone who does wrong and then realizes it and seeks to make amends."

הפטרת ויקרא

HAFTARAH FOR VA-YIKRA

ISAIAH 43:21–44:23

This prophecy was addressed to the Judeans living in exile in Babylon, sometime after 538 B.C.E., when Cyrus the Mede issued an edict allowing the exiles to return to their homeland. Many of these people hesitated to return, and Isaiah exhorted them repeatedly to trust in God's saving power (see Isa. 40–48).

The opening verse of this *haftarah* is actually the conclusion of an independent statement of promise (Isa. 43:16–21) in which the Lord asks the people not to recall what happened in the past, because He is "about to do something new." God will nurture and restore His chosen people. As read in context, the nation will proclaim divine glory as a result of God's new act of sustenance: ". . . the people I formed for Myself that they might declare My praise."

In the framework of the *haftarah* alone, however, verse 21 introduces what is to follow. It must, therefore, be read as God's unconditional proclamation: "The people I formed for Myself shall declare My praise!" This declaration now serves as a unilateral promise whose theme anticipates the redemption and fulfillment of the people Israel at the end of the *haftarah* (44:23). The transformation of Isa. 43:21 from its original context to its use in the *haftarah* is an instructive example of how the ancient Sages transformed words of a biblical prophecy into a synagogue recitation for new generations.

The *haftarah* contrasts past and future time, revolving around the theme of divine forgiveness. Addressing the nation in exile (in the present), the prophet opens his divine discourse with a rebuke of the people's failure to worship the Lord (in the past), which is the reason for the nation's present calamity. As the prophecy develops, however, the tone of accusation is replaced by the language of reconciliation and hope in the future (43:25). Israel is called on to "remember" its intimate bond with God (44:21). The language of the conclusion underscores the reality of divine forgiveness (44:22–23).

The *haftarah* develops thematically from judgment to redemption. The language of the opening rebuke (43:22–24) is a blunt and direct reprimand that criticizes the people for violating the sacrificial cult, but does not include any moral or social critique. In this respect, Isaiah's rebuke stands in sharp contrast to a characteristic feature of prophecy in the Bible.

Chapter 44 begins a dramatic turnabout, in which a new word of God announces divine grace. Echoing the opening promise, in which Israel is called the people "I formed for Myself" (*yatzarti li,* 43:21), Israel is now called the chosen nation whom "Your Creator (*yotzrekha*) . . . has helped . . . since birth" (44:2). This intimate relationship leads to God's unilateral promise to pour His spirit upon future offspring and a prophecy that this progeny will renew their loyalty to the Lord and to the nation (44:3–5).

To reinforce the theme of God's unique supremacy, the divine assertion in Isa. 44:6–8 is contrasted with an extended polemic against idol worship. With stylistic deftness, similar terms are used here to mark with ironic force the difference between the worship of God and the worship of idols.

The mocking tone of the polemic against idols widens the gap between the God of Israel and the gods of the foolish. Not only does God create His people and care for them, but He is their redeemer who forgives their sins. By contrast, the image makers are prey to their own desires. They create a form of wood and then pray to it, apparently not realizing the folly of their deeds. Indeed, for the prophet, the realization that all self-proclaimed divinities are "a fraud" (43:20) is the first stage of a purified religious consciousness.

RELATION OF THE *HAFTARAH* TO THE *PARASHAH*

The *parashah* details the forms of public sacrifice whereby one may sustain and renew a relationship with God. In the *haftarah,* the prophet decries the abandonment of these cultic offerings as well as the offenses of sin and iniquity (43:22–24). In a pun on the verb that commonly means "to perform religious service" (*avad*), God declares that He did not "burden" (*he·evadtikha*) Israel with demands for grain offerings. They, however, have "burdened" Him (*he·evadtani*) with their transgressions. This word play underscores the perversity of Israel, along with their inversion of true worship.

A specific verbal link between the *parashah* and the *haftarah* focuses reflection on the importance of witnesses in the realms of morality and theology. A rule in Lev. 5:1 states that a person who has heard a public imprecation and can serve as a "witness" (*ed*) to the offense incurs guilt by failing to do so, avoiding social responsibility. By contrast, Isa. 44:6–8 speaks of Israel's role as "witnesses" (*edai*) to God's incomparable ability to fulfill His prophetic word. This places human experience at the center of theological claims, for without human testimony, the reality of God and the wonder of His ways would have no significance. Rabbinic tradition, understanding this paradox, presented a remarkable transformation of Isaiah's words. God's words in Isaiah are exultant: "You [Israel] are My witnesses. Is there any god . . . but Me?" The Midrash boldly drives the lesson home. There may be no god other than *YHVH,* but He needs humankind to be known as such: "If 'you are My witnesses,' then I am God; but if you are not My witnesses, then, so to speak, I am not God" (Sifrei Deut. 346). This remarkable teaching presents theology as a form of human testimony to religious experience. Integrity is as vital here as in the social sphere, where honest testimony is crucial if the social fabric of the world is to be maintained.

43 21The people I formed for Myself
Shall declare My praise!

22But you have not worshiped Me, O Jacob,
That you should be weary of Me, O Israel.
23You have not brought Me your sheep for burnt offerings,
Nor honored Me with your sacrifices.
I have not burdened you with grain offerings,
Nor wearied you about frankincense.
24You have not bought Me fragrant reed with money,
Nor sated Me with the fat of your sacrifices.

מג 21 עַם־זוּ יָצַרְתִּי לִי
תְּהִלָּתִי יְסַפֵּרוּ׃ ס

22 וְלֹא־אֹתִי קָרָאתָ יַעֲקֹב
כִּי־יָגַעְתָּ בִּי יִשְׂרָאֵל׃
23 לֹא־הֵבֵיאתָ לִּי שֵׂה עֹלֹתֶיךָ
וּזְבָחֶיךָ לֹא כִבַּדְתָּנִי
לֹא הֶעֱבַדְתִּיךָ בְּמִנְחָה
וְלֹא הוֹגַעְתִּיךָ בִּלְבוֹנָה׃
24 לֹא־קָנִיתָ לִּי בַכֶּסֶף קָנֶה
וְחֵלֶב זְבָחֶיךָ לֹא הִרְוִיתָנִי

Isaiah 43:21. I formed Hebrew: *yatzarti.* This verb recurs as a theme word throughout the *haftarah,* underscoring the contrast between true and false creations.

22–24. The negative *lo* (not) occurs seven times; the verb *yaga* (weary) concludes each verse.

22. worshiped Me Literally, "called upon Me" in worship (see Gen. 12:8).

24. bought Me fragrant reed The Hebrew employs a pun: "bought" (*kanita*) . . . fragrant reed (*kaneh*)." See Exod. 30:23.

Instead, you have burdened Me with your sins,
You have wearied Me with your iniquities.
25It is I, I who—for My own sake—
Wipe your transgressions away
And remember your sins no more.
26Help me remember!
Let us join in argument,
Tell your version,
That you may be vindicated.
27Your earliest ancestor sinned,
And your spokesmen transgressed against Me.
28So I profaned the holy princes;
I abandoned Jacob to proscription
And Israel to mockery.

אַךְ הֶעֱבַדְתַּנִי בְּחַטֹּאותֶיךָ*
הוֹגַעְתַּנִי בַּעֲוֺנֹתֶיךָ׃ ס
25 אָנֹכִי אָנֹכִי הוּא
מֹחֶה פְשָׁעֶיךָ לְמַעֲנִי
וְחַטֹּאתֶיךָ לֹא אֶזְכֹּר׃
26 הַזְכִּירֵנִי
נִשָּׁפְטָה יָחַד
סַפֵּר אַתָּה
לְמַעַן תִּצְדָּק׃
27 אָבִיךָ הָרִאשׁוֹן חָטָא
וּמְלִיצֶיךָ פָּשְׁעוּ בִי׃
28 וַאֲחַלֵּל שָׂרֵי קֹדֶשׁ
וְאֶתְּנָה לַחֵרֶם יַעֲקֹב
וְיִשְׂרָאֵל לְגִדּוּפִים׃ ס

44 But hear, now, O Jacob My servant,
Israel whom I have chosen!
2Thus said the LORD, your Maker,
Your Creator who has helped you since birth:
Fear not, My servant Jacob,
Jeshurun whom I have chosen,

מד וְעַתָּה שְׁמַע יַעֲקֹב עַבְדִּי
וְיִשְׂרָאֵל בָּחַרְתִּי בוֹ׃
2 כֹּה־אָמַר יְהוָה עֹשֶׂךָ
וְיֹצֶרְךָ מִבֶּטֶן יַעְזְרֶךָּ
אַל־תִּירָא עַבְדִּי יַעֲקֹב
וִישֻׁרוּן בָּחַרְתִּי בוֹ׃

v. 24. מלא ו׳

25. for My own sake God acts with unilateral grace, and not because of Israel's merit.

26. Let us join in argument Literally, "let us enter judgment together." This is a formal petition for countertestimony so that the accused might be justified.

27. Your earliest ancestor Literally, "your first forefather." This obscure reference evokes the sin of Adam (Radak).

28. So I profaned the holy princes The Hebrew for "holy princes" (*sarei kodesh,* cf. 1 Chron. 24:5) makes the verse difficult, conceptually and theologically. The Septuagint (ancient Greek) translation seemed to understand the phrase to mean "Your rulers profaned My sanctuary" (presumably based on a Hebrew text that read *va-y'ḥall'lu sarekha kodshi*).

proscription The Hebrew word *ḥerem* is used most commonly to designate ritual extermination or devoting objects to the shrine (i.e., proscribing them from common use, as in Lev. 27). Either use of the cult term is odd here, especially in conjunction with the references to "mockery" (*giddufim*). Therefore, it has been suggested that one should read "I abandoned Jacob to insult" here (Hebrew: *ḥeref* instead of *ḥerem*). This verb is found frequently in parallelism with the word for "mock" (*gadaf*). Compare Ps. 44:7.

Isaiah 44:1–2. Jacob . . . Israel . . . Jeshurun whom I have chosen The theme of this nation as chosen occurs frequently in this prophetic collection (see Isa. 41:8–9, 43:10, 44:2). Deuteronomy (4:37–38, cf. 7:6, 14:2) first speaks of God's love for the patriarchs as the reason for choosing Israel, redeeming them from Egypt, and restoring them to the Promised Land.

3Even as I pour water on thirsty soil,
And rain upon dry ground,
So will I pour My spirit on your offspring,
My blessing upon your posterity.
4And they shall sprout like grass,
Like willows by watercourses.
5One shall say, "I am the LORD's,"
Another shall use the name of "Jacob,"
Another shall mark his arm "of the LORD"
And adopt the name of "Israel."

6Thus said the LORD, the King of Israel,
Their Redeemer, the LORD of Hosts:
I am the first and I am the last,
And there is no god but Me.
7Who like Me can announce,
Can foretell it—and match Me thereby?
Even as I told the future to an ancient people,
So let him foretell coming events to them.
8Do not be frightened, do not be shaken!
Have I not from of old predicted to you?
I foretold, and you are My witnesses.
Is there any god, then, but Me?
"There is no other rock; I know none!"

9The makers of idols
All work to no purpose;
And the things they treasure
Can do no good,

3 כִּי אֶצָּק־מַיִם עַל־צָמֵא
וְנֹזְלִים עַל־יַבָּשָׁה
אֶצֹּק רוּחִי עַל־זַרְעֶךָ
וּבִרְכָתִי עַל־צֶאֱצָאֶיךָ׃
4 וְצָמְחוּ בְּבֵין חָצִיר
כַּעֲרָבִים עַל־יִבְלֵי־מָיִם׃
5 זֶה יֹאמַר לַיהוָה אָנִי
וְזֶה יִקְרָא בְשֵׁם־יַעֲקֹב
וְזֶה יִכְתֹּב יָדוֹ לַיהוָה
וּבְשֵׁם יִשְׂרָאֵל יְכַנֶּה׃ פ

6 כֹּה־אָמַר יְהוָה מֶלֶךְ־יִשְׂרָאֵל
וְגֹאֲלוֹ יְהוָה צְבָאוֹת
אֲנִי רִאשׁוֹן וַאֲנִי אַחֲרוֹן
וּמִבַּלְעָדַי אֵין אֱלֹהִים׃
7 וּמִי־כָמוֹנִי יִקְרָא
וְיַגִּידֶהָ וְיַעְרְכֶהָ לִי
מִשּׂוּמִי עַם־עוֹלָם וְאֹתִיּוֹת
וַאֲשֶׁר תָּבֹאנָה יַגִּידוּ לָמוֹ׃
8 אַל־תִּפְחֲדוּ וְאַל־תִּרְהוּ
הֲלֹא מֵאָז הִשְׁמַעְתִּיךָ
וְהִגַּדְתִּי וְאַתֶּם עֵדָי
הֲיֵשׁ אֱלוֹהַּ מִבַּלְעָדַי
וְאֵין צוּר בַּל־יָדָעְתִּי׃

9 יֹצְרֵי־פֶסֶל
כֻּלָּם תֹּהוּ
וַחֲמוּדֵיהֶם
בַּל־יוֹעִילוּ

3. I pour My spirit Israel, revived as a people, will return to its God as in previous times.

5. One shall say A prophecy of renewal and identification. The threefold repetition of *zeh* (translated as "one," "another," "another") suggests three main types of connection: (*1*) proclaiming identity, "I am the LORD's"; (*2*) using the ancestral name "Israel" for identity; and (*3*) marking "of the LORD's" on the flesh, in the manner of a bound servant, and adopting the name "Israel."

6. I am the first God is incomparable, the only being worthy of worship. This is a dominant theological theme of Isaiah (see 43:10, 45:5–6,18,22).

7. Who like Me can announce Divine uniqueness is proclaimed on the basis of the fulfillment of prophecy.

9–20. The supreme folly is constructing an image from a tree, one half of which serves for fuel and the other for a divine figure to which one says "Save me, for you are my god," *eli attah*

As they themselves can testify.

They neither look nor think,

And so they shall be shamed.

10Who would fashion a god

Or cast a statue

That can do no good?

11Lo, all its adherents shall be shamed;

They are craftsmen, are merely human.

Let them all assemble and stand up!

They shall be cowed, and they shall be
   shamed.

12The craftsman in iron, with his tools,

Works it over charcoal

And fashions it by hammering,

Working with the strength of his arm.

Should he go hungry, his strength would ebb;

Should he drink no water, he would grow
   faint.

13The craftsman in wood measures with a line

And marks out a shape with a stylus;

He forms it with scraping tools,

Marking it out with a compass.

He gives it a human form,

The beauty of a man, to dwell in a shrine.

14For his use he cuts down cedars;

He chooses plane trees and oaks.

He sets aside trees of the forest;

Or plants firs, and the rain makes them grow.

15All this serves man for fuel:

He takes some to warm himself,

And he builds a fire and bakes bread.

He also makes a god of it and worships it,

וְעֵדֵיהֶ֤ם הֵ֙מָּה֙*

בַּל־יִרְא֖וּ וּבַל־יֵדְע֑וּ

לְמַ֖עַן יֵבֹֽשׁוּ׃

10 מִֽי־יָצַ֣ר אֵ֔ל

וּפֶ֖סֶל נָסָ֑ךְ

לְבִלְתִּ֖י הוֹעִֽיל׃

11 הֵ֤ן כָּל־חֲבֵרָיו֙ יֵבֹ֔שׁוּ

וְחָרָשִׁ֥ים הֵ֖מָּה מֵאָדָ֑ם

יִֽתְקַבְּצ֤וּ כֻלָּם֙ יַעֲמֹ֔דוּ

יִפְחֲד֖וּ יֵבֹ֥שׁוּ יָֽחַד׃

12 חָרַ֤שׁ בַּרְזֶל֙ מַֽעֲצָ֔ד

וּפָעַל֙ בַּפֶּחָ֔ם

וּבַמַּקָּב֖וֹת יִצְּרֵ֑הוּ

וַיִּפְעָלֵ֙הוּ֙ בִּזְר֣וֹעַ כֹּח֔וֹ

גַּם־רָעֵב֙ וְאֵ֣ין כֹּ֔חַ

לֹא־שָׁ֥תָה מַ֖יִם וַיִּיעָֽף׃

13 חָרַ֣שׁ עֵצִים֮ נָ֣טָה קָו֒

יְתָאֲרֵ֣הוּ בַשֶּׂ֔רֶד

יַעֲשֵׂ֙הוּ֙ בַּמַּקְצֻע֔וֹת

וּבַמְּחוּגָ֖ה יְתָאֳרֵ֑הוּ

וַֽיַּעֲשֵׂ֙הוּ֙ כְּתַבְנִ֣ית אִ֔ישׁ

כְּתִפְאֶ֥רֶת אָדָ֖ם לָשֶׁ֥בֶת בָּֽיִת׃

14 לִכְרָת־ל֣וֹ אֲרָזִ֔ים

וַיִּקַּ֤ח תִּרְזָה֙ וְאַלּ֔וֹן

וַיְאַמֶּץ־ל֖וֹ בַּעֲצֵי־יָ֑עַר

נָטַ֥ע אֹ֛רֶן* וְגֶ֖שֶׁם יְגַדֵּֽל׃

15 וְהָיָ֤ה לְאָדָם֙ לְבָעֵ֔ר

וַיִּקַּ֤ח מֵהֶם֙ וַיָּ֔חָם

אַף־יַשִּׂ֖יק וְאָ֣פָה לָ֑חֶם

אַף־יִפְעַל־אֵל֙ וַיִּשְׁתָּ֔חוּ

v. 9.   נקוד על ה' מ' ה'

v. 14.   ז' זעירא

(v. 17, cf. 42:17). Such a false formula of commitment counterpoints the positive allegiance
stated by Israel in v. 5: "I am the LORD's"

(la-YHVH ani). This is the language of legal commitment, used to indicate marriage or adoption
in ancient Israel and in the ancient Near East.

Fashions an idol and bows down to it!
16Part of it he burns in a fire:
On that part he roasts meat,
He eats the roast and is sated;
He also warms himself and cries, "Ah,
I am warm! I can feel the heat!"
17Of the rest he makes a god—his own carving!
He bows down to it, worships it;
He prays to it and cries,
"Save me, for you are my god!"

18They have no wit or judgment:
Their eyes are besmeared, and they see not;
Their minds, and they cannot think.
19They do not give thought,
They lack the wit and judgment to say:
"Part of it I burned in a fire;
I also baked bread on the coals,
I roasted meat and ate it—
Should I make the rest an abhorrence?
Should I bow to a block of wood?"
20He pursues ashes!
A deluded mind has led him astray,
And he cannot save himself;
He never says to himself,
"The thing in my hand is a fraud!"
21Remember these things, O Jacob
For you, O Israel, are My servant:
I fashioned you, you are My servant—
O Israel, never forget Me.
22I wipe away your sins like a cloud,
Your transgressions like mist—
Come back to Me, for I redeem you.

עָשָׂהוּ פֶסֶל וַיִּסְגָּד־לָמוֹ׃
16 חֶצְיוֹ שָׂרַף בְּמוֹ־אֵשׁ
עַל־חֶצְיוֹ בָּשָׂר יֹאכֵל
יִצְלֶה צָלִי וְיִשְׂבָּע
אַף־יָחֹם וְיֹאמַר הֶאָח
חַמּוֹתִי רָאִיתִי אוּר׃
17 וּשְׁאֵרִיתוֹ לְאֵל עָשָׂה לְפִסְלוֹ
יסגוד יִסְגָּד־לוֹ וְיִשְׁתַּחוּ
וְיִתְפַּלֵּל אֵלָיו וְיֹאמַר
הַצִּילֵנִי כִּי אֵלִי אָתָּה׃

18 לֹא יָדְעוּ וְלֹא יָבִינוּ
כִּי טַח מֵרְאוֹת עֵינֵיהֶם
מֵהַשְׂכִּיל לִבֹּתָם׃
19 וְלֹא־יָשִׁיב אֶל־לִבּוֹ
וְלֹא דַעַת וְלֹא־תְבוּנָה לֵאמֹר
חֶצְיוֹ שָׂרַפְתִּי בְמוֹ־אֵשׁ
וְאַף אָפִיתִי עַל־גֶּחָלָיו לֶחֶם
אֶצְלֶה בָשָׂר וְאֹכֵל
וְיִתְרוֹ לְתוֹעֵבָה אֶעֱשֶׂה
לְבוּל עֵץ אֶסְגּוֹד׃
20 רֹעֶה אֵפֶר
לֵב הוּתַל הִטָּהוּ
וְלֹא־יַצִּיל אֶת־נַפְשׁוֹ
וְלֹא יֹאמַר
הֲלוֹא שֶׁקֶר בִּימִינִי׃ ס
21 זְכָר־אֵלֶּה יַעֲקֹב
וְיִשְׂרָאֵל כִּי עַבְדִּי־אָתָּה
יְצַרְתִּיךָ עֶבֶד־לִי אַתָּה
יִשְׂרָאֵל לֹא תִנָּשֵׁנִי׃
22 מָחִיתִי כָעָב פְּשָׁעֶיךָ
וְכֶעָנָן חַטֹּאותֶיךָ
שׁוּבָה אֵלַי כִּי גְאַלְתִּיךָ׃

22. Come back to Me Hebrew: *shuvah elai.* In context, the call is for a physical return from the Babylonian exile to the homeland (Radak). Later commentators found here an appeal for spiritual renewal as well.

23 רָנּ֨וּ שָׁמַ֜יִם כִּֽי־עָשָׂ֣ה יְהֹוָ֗ה
הָרִ֙יעוּ֙ תַּחְתִּיּ֣וֹת אָ֔רֶץ
פִּצְח֤וּ הָרִים֙ רִנָּ֔ה
יַ֖עַר וְכׇל־עֵ֣ץ בּ֑וֹ
כִּֽי־גָאַ֤ל יְהֹוָה֙ יַעֲקֹ֔ב
וּבְיִשְׂרָאֵ֖ל יִתְפָּאָֽר׃ פ

23Shout, O heavens, for the LORD has acted;
Shout aloud, O depths of the earth!
Shout for joy, O mountains,
O forests with all your trees!
For the LORD has redeemed Jacob,
Has glorified Himself through Israel.

6 The LORD spoke to Moses, saying: [2]Command Aaron and his sons thus:

This is the ritual of the burnt offering: The burnt offering itself shall remain where it is burned upon the altar all night until morning, while the fire on the altar is kept going on it.

ו וַיְדַבֵּר יְהוָה אֶל־מֹשֶׁה לֵּאמֹר׃ 2 צַו
אֶת־אַהֲרֹן וְאֶת־בָּנָיו לֵאמֹר
זֹאת תּוֹרַת הָעֹלָה הִוא הָעֹלָה עַל
מוֹקְדָה* עַל־הַמִּזְבֵּחַ כָּל־הַלַּיְלָה עַד־

v. 2. מ׳ זעירא לפי נוסחים מקובלים

THE PRINCIPAL TYPES OF SACRIFICE (*continued*)

THE DISPOSITION OF SACRIFICES (6:1–7:38)

The rituals for each of the various sacrifices outlined in chapters 1–5 are presented in chapters 6 and 7. These chapters also offer us a unique glimpse into the participation of the priesthood in the sacred meals within the precincts of the sanctuary.

The important Hebrew word *torah,* which appears in these chapters, derives from the verb ירה, "to cast, shoot"—an arrow, for instance. The verb, in one of its forms, means "to aim, direct toward"—hence "to show the way, instruct." The word *torah* here is limited to the content of the instruction.

THE BURNT OFFERING (*olah*) (vv. 1–6)

For the preparation and presentation of this offering, see Lev. 1.

2. where it is burned On top of the altar grill, where the firewood was placed.

all night until morning The daily burnt offering consisted of two yearling lambs, one offered in the morning and one in the evening. The morning burnt offering, with its accompanying grain offering and libation, were the first offerings placed on the altar of burnt offerings each day. The evening burnt offering and its accompaniments were the final offerings each day. The evening offering was left burning on the altar during the night. First thing in the morning, the ashes of the previous day's sacrifices were removed and new firewood was added. Although the same altar was used for other sacrifices during the day, it was logical to provide instructions for tending the altar at this point, because public worship began and concluded each day with the burnt offering.

In this *parashah,* we can see why the book is thought to be a manual for *kohanim.* How the *kohen* carries out his part of the sacrificial service is the focus of most of the text.

Neḥama Leibowitz suggests that chapters 1–5 are addressed to the Israelite public. Therefore, they begin with voluntary offerings (*olah, minḥah,* and *sh'lamim*) and continue with those that apply only to certain individuals in certain circumstances (e.g., the purification offering of the *kohen*). Chapters 6–7 are directed to the officiating priests. For that reason, the sequence of offerings is changed, beginning with the offerings that have the highest degree of sanctity ("most holy") and continuing with those of a lesser level of sanctity.

CHAPTER 6

2. Command Aaron . . . This is the ritual of the burnt offering The Talmud reads the Hebrew word *torat* ("ritual of") as "Torah for": "In our day, the study of Torah takes the place of bringing animal offerings" (BT Men. 110a). If so, then why command Aaron? Because Aaron might be reluctant to tell the people that the study of Torah is equivalent to bringing sacrifices. That would make the role of the *kohanim* less prominent, as it would present the people with an alternative form of worship (Ḥatam Sofer).

the fire on the altar is kept going on it The last Hebrew word can also be read "within him" (instead of "on it"). This prompted the comment that the fire on the altar must be paralleled by a fire in the heart of the officiating priest, whose enthusiasm for the sacred nature of the work must never be lost. The congregation, for its part, must recognize its responsibility to see that the enthusiasm and dedication of the clergy is never extinguished.

3The priest shall dress in linen raiment, with linen breeches next to his body; and he shall take up the ashes to which the fire has reduced the burnt offering on the altar and place them beside the altar. 4He shall then take off his vestments and put on other vestments, and carry the ashes outside the camp to a pure place. 5The fire on the altar shall be kept burning, not to go out: every morning the priest shall feed wood to it, lay out the burnt offering on it, and turn into smoke the fat parts of the offerings of well-being. 6A perpetual fire shall be kept burning on the altar, not to go out.

7And this is the ritual of the grain offering: Aaron's sons shall present it before the LORD, in front of the altar. 8A handful of the choice flour and oil of the grain offering shall be taken from it, with all the frankincense that is on the grain offering, and this token portion shall be turned into smoke on the altar as a pleasing odor to the LORD. 9What is left of it shall be eaten by Aaron and his sons; it shall be eaten as unleavened cakes, in the sacred precinct; they shall eat it in the enclosure of the Tent of Meeting. 10It shall not be baked with leaven; I have given it as their portion from My gifts; it is most holy,

הַבֹּ֔קֶר וְאֵ֥שׁ הַמִּזְבֵּ֖חַ תּ֥וּקַד בּֽוֹ׃ 3 וְלָבַ֨שׁ
הַכֹּהֵ֜ן מִדּ֣וֹ בַ֗ד וּמִֽכְנְסֵי־בַד֮ יִלְבַּ֣שׁ עַל־
בְּשָׂרוֹ֒ וְהֵרִ֣ים אֶת־הַדֶּ֗שֶׁן אֲשֶׁ֨ר תֹּאכַ֥ל
הָאֵ֛שׁ אֶת־הָעֹלָ֖ה עַל־הַמִּזְבֵּ֑חַ וְשָׂמ֕וֹ אֵ֖צֶל
הַמִּזְבֵּֽחַ׃ 4 וּפָשַׁט֙ אֶת־בְּגָדָ֔יו וְלָבַ֖שׁ בְּגָדִ֣ים
אֲחֵרִ֑ים וְהוֹצִ֤יא אֶת־הַדֶּ֙שֶׁן֙ אֶל־מִח֣וּץ
לַֽמַּחֲנֶ֔ה אֶל־מָק֖וֹם טָהֽוֹר׃ 5 וְהָאֵ֨שׁ עַל־
הַמִּזְבֵּ֤חַ תּֽוּקַד־בּוֹ֙ לֹ֣א תִכְבֶּ֔ה וּבִעֵ֨ר עָלֶ֧יהָ
הַכֹּהֵ֛ן עֵצִ֖ים בַּבֹּ֣קֶר בַּבֹּ֑קֶר וְעָרַ֤ךְ עָלֶ֙יהָ֙
הָעֹלָ֔ה וְהִקְטִ֥יר עָלֶ֖יהָ חֶלְבֵ֥י הַשְּׁלָמִֽים׃
6 אֵ֗שׁ תָּמִ֛יד תּוּקַ֥ד עַל־הַמִּזְבֵּ֖חַ לֹ֥א
תִכְבֶּֽה׃ ס
7 וְזֹ֥את תּוֹרַ֖ת הַמִּנְחָ֑ה הַקְרֵ֨ב אֹתָ֤הּ בְּנֵֽי־
אַהֲרֹן֙ לִפְנֵ֣י יְהוָ֔ה אֶל־פְּנֵ֖י הַמִּזְבֵּֽחַ׃
8 וְהֵרִ֨ים מִמֶּ֜נּוּ* בְּקֻמְצ֗וֹ מִסֹּ֤לֶת הַמִּנְחָה֙
וּמִשַּׁמְנָ֔הּ וְאֵת֙ כָּל־הַלְּבֹנָ֔ה אֲשֶׁ֖ר עַל־
הַמִּנְחָ֑ה וְהִקְטִ֣יר הַמִּזְבֵּ֗חַ רֵ֧יחַ נִיחֹ֛חַ
אַזְכָּרָתָ֖הּ לַיהוָֽה׃ 9 וְהַנּוֹתֶ֣רֶת מִמֶּ֔נָּה
יֹאכְל֖וּ אַהֲרֹ֣ן וּבָנָ֑יו מַצּ֤וֹת תֵּֽאָכֵל֙ בְּמָק֣וֹם
קָדֹ֔שׁ בַּחֲצַ֥ר אֹֽהֶל־מוֹעֵ֖ד יֹאכְלֽוּהָ׃ 10 לֹ֤א
תֵאָפֶה֙ חָמֵ֔ץ חֶלְקָ֛ם נָתַ֥תִּי אֹתָ֖הּ מֵאִשָּׁ֑י

v. 8. סבירין ומטעין "ממנה"

4. take off his vestments The priestly vestments were to be worn only in the sanctuary precincts (Exod. 28:43).

outside the camp to a pure place Called "the ash heap" in 4:12. The spot near the eastern side of the altar where the ashes were dumped is called "the place for the ashes" in 1:16.

6. perpetual fire . . . on the altar, not to go out The requirement to keep the fire burning at all times is also implied in verse 2. Perpetual fire expressed the Israelites' devotion to God by showing that they were attendant on Him at all times in the sanctuary.

THE GRAIN OFFERING (*minḥah*)
(vv. 7–11)

For the preparation and presentation of this offering, see Lev. 2.

9. eaten by Aaron and his sons An important element not stressed in chapter 2: Participation of the priests is indispensable to the efficacy of this ritual.

enclosure of the Tent of Meeting The tabernacle had an enclosed courtyard (e.g., see Exod. 27:9–19, 35:17), an arrangement later duplicated at the temple in Jerusalem. This sacred area, here and in verse 19, is called "courtyard" (*ḥatzer*); usu-

---

3. The first act of the *kohen* every morning is to put on ordinary clothes and remove the ashes of the previous night's sacrifice. This ensures that he never forgets his link to the ordinary people who spend their days in mundane pursuits (Simḥah Bunem). Why were the ashes treated with such reverence? It symbolizes the idea that what was holy yesterday must be treated with respect today as well.

like the purification offering and the reparation offering. [11]Only the males among Aaron's descendants may eat of it, as their due for all time throughout the ages from the LORD's gifts. Anything that touches these shall become holy.

[12]The LORD spoke to Moses, saying: [13]This is the offering that Aaron and his sons shall offer to the LORD on the occasion of his anointment: a tenth of an *ephah* of choice flour as a regular grain offering, half of it in the morning and half of it in the evening, [14]shall be prepared with oil on a griddle. You shall bring it well soaked, and offer it as a grain offering of baked slices, of pleasing odor to the LORD. [15]And so shall the priest, anointed from among his sons to succeed him, prepare it; it is the LORD's—a law for all time—to be turned entirely into smoke. [16]So, too, every grain offering of a priest shall be a whole offering: it shall not be eaten.

קֹדֶשׁ קָדָשִׁים הִוא כַּחַטָּאת וְכָאָשָׁם׃
11 כָּל־זָכָר בִּבְנֵי אַהֲרֹן יֹאכְלֶנָּה חָק־עוֹלָם
לְדֹרֹתֵיכֶם מֵאִשֵּׁי יְהוָה כֹּל אֲשֶׁר־יִגַּע בָּהֶם
יִקְדָּשׁ׃ פ
שני 12 וַיְדַבֵּר יְהוָה אֶל־מֹשֶׁה לֵּאמֹר׃ 13 זֶה
קָרְבַּן אַהֲרֹן וּבָנָיו אֲשֶׁר־יַקְרִיבוּ לַיהוָה
בְּיוֹם הִמָּשַׁח אֹתוֹ עֲשִׂירִת הָאֵפָה סֹלֶת
מִנְחָה תָּמִיד מַחֲצִיתָהּ בַּבֹּקֶר וּמַחֲצִיתָהּ
בָּעָרֶב׃ 14 עַל־מַחֲבַת בַּשֶּׁמֶן תֵּעָשֶׂה
מֻרְבֶּכֶת תְּבִיאֶנָּה תֻּפִינֵי מִנְחַת פִּתִּים
תַּקְרִיב רֵיחַ־נִיחֹחַ לַיהוָה׃ 15 וְהַכֹּהֵן
הַמָּשִׁיחַ תַּחְתָּיו מִבָּנָיו יַעֲשֶׂה אֹתָהּ חָק־
עוֹלָם לַיהוָה כָּלִיל תָּקְטָר׃ 16 וְכָל־מִנְחַת
כֹּהֵן כָּלִיל תִּהְיֶה לֹא תֵאָכֵל׃ פ

ally it is referred to as "the entrance of the Tent of Meeting" (*petaḥ ohel mo·ed*), which included a large part of the courtyard.

11. Only the males among Aaron's descendants Any foods brought for sacrifices could be eaten only by the priests themselves. Other foodstuffs collected for their support and other forms of priestly revenue could be used to feed their families.

due Hebrew: *ḥok* (fem. *ḥukkah*), which signifies a law ordained by written statute. By extension, it connotes one's lawful share or amount, a rightful due.

Anything that touches these shall become holy The condition of holiness, unlike that of impurity, was not regarded as contagious. Thus it would be better to translate: "Anyone who is to touch these must be in a holy state." Only consecrated persons may have contact with sacrificial materials. This notion reinforces the opening of the verse: Only Aaronide priests may partake of the sacrifices. An act of consecration is required.

12. ephah See Comment to Exod. 16:36.

THE GRAIN OFFERING OF THE HIGH PRIEST (vv. 12–16)

13. offering Hebrew: *korban;* see *D'rash* to 1:2.

on the occasion of his anointment The rite of anointing (unction), described in 8:10ff., was essential to the status of the High Priest. The altar, too, was anointed.

regular Hebrew: *tamid,* used for the most part to characterize regular daily offerings.

16. every grain offering of a priest Every offering of grain brought by a priest on his own behalf, or on behalf of the priesthood, in expiation or as a voluntary offering, was to be burned entirely on the altar. This affirms the rule that priests could benefit only for services undertaken on behalf of other Israelites, not on their own behalf. When the offering served only the priests themselves, the usual share of the priests had to be surrendered to God.

---

10. The purification offerings and the reparation offerings are called "most holy." A greater degree of holiness is ascribed to the person who has struggled with sin and overcome it than to the person who never has been tempted.

11. only the males Most Conservative synagogues have extended the honor and responsibility of serving as religious officiants, rabbis, and cantors, to women as well.

13. as a regular grain offering The daily grain offering of the High Priest taught the poor not to be ashamed of their grain offering, which was the same size. It also taught the High Priest humility (Abravanel).

17The LORD spoke to Moses, saying: 18Speak to Aaron and his sons thus: This is the ritual of the purification offering: the purification offering shall be slaughtered before the LORD, at the spot where the burnt offering is slaughtered: it is most holy. 19The priest who offers it as a purification offering shall eat of it; it shall be eaten in the sacred precinct, in the enclosure of the Tent of Meeting. 20Anything that touches its flesh shall become holy; and if any of its blood is spattered upon a garment, you shall wash the bespattered part in the sacred precinct. 21An earthen vessel in which it was boiled shall be broken; if it was boiled in a copper vessel, [the vessel] shall be scoured and rinsed with water. 22Only the males in the priestly line may eat of it: it is most holy. 23But no purification offering may be eaten from which any blood is brought into the Tent of Meeting for expiation in the sanctuary; any such shall be consumed in fire.

17 וַיְדַבֵּ֥ר יְהֹוָ֖ה אֶל־מֹשֶׁ֥ה לֵּאמֹֽר׃ 18 דַּבֵּ֨ר אֶֽל־אַהֲרֹ֜ן וְאֶל־בָּנָ֣יו לֵאמֹ֗ר זֹ֚את תּוֹרַ֣ת הַֽחַטָּ֔את בִּמְק֡וֹם אֲשֶׁר֩ תִּשָּׁחֵ֨ט הָעֹלָ֜ה תִּשָּׁחֵ֤ט הַֽחַטָּאת֙ לִפְנֵ֣י יְהֹוָ֔ה קֹ֥דֶשׁ קׇֽדָשִׁ֖ים הִֽוא׃ 19 הַכֹּהֵ֛ן הַֽמְחַטֵּ֥א אֹתָ֖הּ יֹֽאכְלֶ֑נָּה בְּמָק֤וֹם קָדֹשׁ֙ תֵּֽאָכֵ֔ל בַּֽחֲצַ֖ר אֹ֥הֶל מוֹעֵֽד׃ 20 כֹּ֛ל אֲשֶׁר־יִגַּ֥ע בִּבְשָׂרָ֖הּ יִקְדָּ֑שׁ וַאֲשֶׁ֨ר יִזֶּ֤ה מִדָּמָהּ֙ עַל־הַבֶּ֔גֶד אֲשֶׁר֙ יִזֶּ֣ה עָלֶ֔יהָ תְּכַבֵּ֖ס בְּמָק֥וֹם קָדֹֽשׁ׃ 21 וּכְלִי־חֶ֛רֶשׂ אֲשֶׁ֥ר תְּבֻשַּׁל־בּ֖וֹ יִשָּׁבֵ֑ר וְאִם־בִּכְלִ֤י נְחֹ֙שֶׁת֙ בֻּשָּׁ֔לָה וּמֹרַ֥ק וְשֻׁטַּ֖ף בַּמָּֽיִם׃ 22 כׇּל־זָכָ֥ר בַּכֹּֽהֲנִ֖ים יֹאכַ֣ל אֹתָ֑הּ קֹ֥דֶשׁ קׇֽדָשִׁ֖ים הִֽוא׃ 23 וְכׇל־חַטָּ֡את אֲשֶׁר֩ יוּבָ֨א מִדָּמָ֜הּ אֶל־אֹ֧הֶל מוֹעֵ֛ד לְכַפֵּ֥ר בַּקֹּ֖דֶשׁ לֹ֣א תֵֽאָכֵ֑ל בָּאֵ֖שׁ תִּשָּׂרֵֽף׃ פ

7 This is the ritual of the reparation offering: it is most holy. 2The reparation offering shall

ז וְזֹ֖את תּוֹרַ֣ת הָֽאָשָׁ֑ם קֹ֥דֶשׁ קׇֽדָשִׁ֖ים הֽוּא׃ 2 בִּמְק֗וֹם אֲשֶׁ֤ר יִשְׁחֲטוּ֙ אֶת־הָ֣עֹלָ֔ה יִשְׁחֲט֖וּ

THE PURIFICATION OFFERING
(ḥattat) (6:17–23)

18. The burnt offering (olah) was to be slaughtered at the northern side of the altar (1:11). Here we are informed that this rule also applies to the purification offering.

most holy The purification offering is in the category of offerings that are "most sacred" (kodesh kodashim). This category, first encountered in 2:3, is mentioned in 6:10; it recurs in 6:22 and in 7:6.

19. enclosure of the Tent of Meeting The entire courtyard is sacred. See Comment to 6:9.

20. Anything that touches its flesh shall become holy Rather, anyone who is to touch its flesh must be in a holy state. See Comment to 6:11.

blood . . . spattered upon a garment Part of the blood of the purification offering was to be placed on the horns of the altar and the rest poured down its side, as ordained in 4:25. Should any sacrificial blood stain a garment, that garment must be laundered, because it would be improper for any of this blood to be used for anything other than its ordained purpose.

21. An earthen vessel in which it was boiled shall be broken Earthenware, being more porous than metal, absorbs particles of the flesh boiled in it. Some of the sacrificial flesh very likely would remain in the vessel. Such flesh would constitute "leftovers of the sacrifice" (notar), forbidden for consumption according to 7:15–17. If other foodstuffs were subsequently boiled in the same vessel, the forbidden sacrificial particles would contaminate the rest. To prevent this, the earthenware vessel had to be broken, because there was no possible way to purify it.

23. This rule refers to the priestly ḥattat as set forth in 4:1–12, to the rites prescribed in 8:17 for the investiture of the priests, and to the Yom Kippur ritual in chapter 16.

THE REPARATION OFFERING (asham) (7:1–10)

1. ritual of the reparation offering The procedures specified in verses 1–6 for the "reparation offering" (asham) correspond to those already mandated for the purification offering in 6:17.

be slaughtered at the spot where the burnt offering is slaughtered, and the blood shall be dashed on all sides of the altar. [3]All its fat shall be offered: the broad tail; the fat that covers the entrails; [4]the two kidneys and the fat that is on them at the loins; and the protuberance on the liver, which shall be removed with the kidneys. [5]The priest shall turn them into smoke on the altar as a gift to the LORD; it is a reparation offering. [6]Only the males in the priestly line may eat of it; it shall be eaten in the sacred precinct: it is most holy.

[7]The reparation offering is like the purification offering. The same rule applies to both: it shall belong to the priest who makes expiation thereby. [8]So, too, the priest who offers a man's burnt offering shall keep the skin of the burnt offering that he offered. [9]Further, any grain offering that is baked in an oven, and any that is prepared in a pan or on a griddle, shall belong to the priest who offers it. [10]But every other grain offering, with oil mixed in or dry, shall go to the sons of Aaron all alike.

[11]This is the ritual of the sacrifice of well-being that one may offer to the LORD:

[12]If he offers it for thanksgiving, he shall offer together with the sacrifice of thanksgiving un-

אֶת־הָאָשָׁם וְאֶת־דָּמוֹ יִזְרֹק עַל־הַמִּזְבֵּחַ
סָבִיב׃ 3 וְאֵת כָּל־חֶלְבּוֹ יַקְרִיב מִמֶּנּוּ אֵת
הָאַלְיָה וְאֶת־הַחֵלֶב הַמְכַסֶּה אֶת־הַקֶּרֶב׃
4 וְאֵת שְׁתֵּי הַכְּלָיֹת וְאֶת־הַחֵלֶב אֲשֶׁר
עֲלֵיהֶן אֲשֶׁר עַל־הַכְּסָלִים וְאֶת־הַיֹּתֶרֶת
עַל־הַכָּבֵד עַל־הַכְּלָיֹת יְסִירֶנָּה׃ 5 וְהִקְטִיר
אֹתָם הַכֹּהֵן הַמִּזְבֵּחָה אִשֶּׁה לַיהוָה אָשָׁם
הוּא׃ 6 כָּל־זָכָר בַּכֹּהֲנִים יֹאכְלֶנּוּ בְּמָקוֹם
קָדוֹשׁ יֵאָכֵל קֹדֶשׁ קָדָשִׁים הוּא׃
7 כַּחַטָּאת כָּאָשָׁם תּוֹרָה אַחַת לָהֶם הַכֹּהֵן
אֲשֶׁר יְכַפֶּר־בּוֹ לוֹ יִהְיֶה׃ 8 וְהַכֹּהֵן הַמַּקְרִיב
אֶת־עֹלַת אִישׁ עוֹר הָעֹלָה אֲשֶׁר הִקְרִיב
לַכֹּהֵן לוֹ יִהְיֶה׃ 9 וְכָל־מִנְחָה אֲשֶׁר תֵּאָפֶה
בַּתַּנּוּר וְכָל־נַעֲשָׂה בַמַּרְחֶשֶׁת וְעַל־מַחֲבַת
לַכֹּהֵן הַמַּקְרִיב אֹתָהּ לוֹ תִהְיֶה׃ 10 וְכָל־
מִנְחָה בְלוּלָה־בַשֶּׁמֶן וַחֲרֵבָה לְכָל־בְּנֵי
אַהֲרֹן תִּהְיֶה אִישׁ כְּאָחִיו׃ פ

ששי 11 וְזֹאת תּוֹרַת זֶבַח הַשְּׁלָמִים אֲשֶׁר יַקְרִיב
לַיהוָה׃
12 אִם עַל־תּוֹדָה יַקְרִיבֶנּוּ וְהִקְרִיב ׀ עַל־
זֶבַח הַתּוֹדָה חַלּוֹת מַצּוֹת בְּלוּלֹת בַּשֶּׁמֶן

7. it shall belong to the priest who makes expiation thereby Sacrifices of expiation eaten by the priests are actually their property.

8. The officiating priest, in most cases, could keep the hide as his own and profit from its value.

9–10. Verse 9 speaks of offerings prepared in an oven, in a pan, or on a griddle, all of which belong to the officiating priest. Verse 10 speaks of other offerings that belong to all priests. These verses are saying, in effect, that the parts of the grain offerings due to the priests are to go to the officiants at these rites.

THE SACRIFICE OF WELL-BEING
(*zevaḥ ha-sh'lamim*) (vv. 11–34)

11. As in chapter 3, this section uses the term *sh'lamim* in a general sense, referring to all sacrifices of the *zevaḥ* type.

12. for thanksgiving For expressing one's gratitude to God for deliverance from danger or misfortune.

sacrifice of thanksgiving Hebrew: *zevaḥ todah,* which refers here to the animal sacrifice ordained in chapter 3: a sheep or a goat of either gender. The ritual first considers the preparation

CHAPTER 7

12. An individual brings an offering of thanksgiving (*todah*) in response to having been spared from disaster, which produces probably one of the most profound emotions that person will ever know. The Talmud (BT Ber. 54b) identifies the circumstances in which a person

leavened cakes with oil mixed in, unleavened wafers spread with oil, and cakes of choice flour with oil mixed in, well soaked. [13]This offering, with cakes of leavened bread added, he shall offer along with his thanksgiving sacrifice of well-being. [14]Out of this he shall offer one of each kind as a gift to the LORD; it shall go to the priest who dashes the blood of the offering of well-being. [15]And the flesh of his thanksgiving sacrifice of well-being shall be eaten on the day that it is offered; none of it shall be set aside until morning.

[16]If, however, the sacrifice he offers is a votive

וּרְקִיקֵי מַצּוֹת מְשֻׁחִים בַּשָּׁמֶן וְסֹלֶת
מֻרְבֶּכֶת חַלֹּת בְּלוּלֹת בַּשָּׁמֶן׃ 13 עַל־חַלֹּת
לֶחֶם חָמֵץ יַקְרִיב קָרְבָּנוֹ עַל־זֶבַח תּוֹדַת
שְׁלָמָיו׃ 14 וְהִקְרִיב מִמֶּנּוּ אֶחָד מִכָּל־קָרְבָּן
תְּרוּמָה לַיהוָה לַכֹּהֵן הַזֹּרֵק אֶת־דַּם
הַשְּׁלָמִים לוֹ יִהְיֶה׃ 15 וּבְשַׂר זֶבַח תּוֹדַת
שְׁלָמָיו בְּיוֹם קָרְבָּנוֹ יֵאָכֵל לֹא־יַנִּיחַ מִמֶּנּוּ
עַד־בֹּקֶר׃
16 וְאִם־נֶדֶר ׀ אוֹ נְדָבָה זֶבַח קָרְבָּנוֹ בְּיוֹם

and disposition of the grain offerings of both unleavened and leavened cakes that accompanied the animal sacrifice, a matter not taken up elsewhere in Leviticus. It then deals with the animal sacrifice itself, the basic information for which is in chapter 3.

13. No leaven may be placed on the altar of burnt offerings (Lev. 2:11). Thus only the unleavened cakes are offered on the altar, not the leavened cakes.

with . . . added . . . along with Hebrew: *al;* literally, "on." This preposition occurs twice in this verse, where it means "in addition to."

14. one of each kind as a gift to the LORD Sacrificial procedures in biblical Israel, and in the ancient Near East generally, often dictated that the offering first be presented to the deity for acceptance, at which time it belonged entirely to that deity. Only then did the deity grant portions of the offering to the priests and, occasionally, to the donors as well. Consequently, even in this case, in which no part of the leavened grain offering was placed on the altar, it could be considered as an offering to the Lord.

15. The flesh must be eaten on the day the altar sacrifice is made. If not consumed then, it must be burned. This is yet another difference between the thanksgiving sacrifice (*todah*) and other *sh'lamim* sacrifices.

16. Except in the case of a thanksgiving offering (*todah*), the flesh of *sh'lamim* sacrifices may be eaten until the third day, a rule also stated in 19:5–8. There were no restrictions regarding where the donor of a *sh'lamim* could eat his or her portion of the offering, so long as no person in an impure state partook of the flesh (v. 19).

---

should bring a *todah:* when one has safely completed a dangerous journey, recovered from illness, been released from confinement, or survived other dangers. The custom continues to this day in the *Gomel* blessing offered in the synagogue, during the Torah reading, by a worshiper who has avoided or survived misfortune. The talmudic text states that people "need" (*tzrikhin*) to bring a *todah* rather than "are obliged" to bring one, perhaps to suggest that the grateful individual brings the *todah* to fulfill a psychological need rather than to meet a religious obligation.

15. Several commentators connect the requirement that the *todah* be eaten on the day it is offered and on the following evening to the fact that it is brought in response to a miracle in the life of the donor. Abravanel says that if it must be consumed in a single day, the owner will invite more people to share it, thus publicizing the miracle more widely. "On being asked what prompted this feast, the host will recount some good fortune and the divine wonder it represents." We should have confidence that each new day will produce its own miracle. Therefore, the feast celebrating a miraculous event should be confined to one day and not extended into the next. Tomorrow will bring its own miracle (Yitzḥak Meir Alter of Ger). "In time to come, there will be no sacrifices except for the offering of thanksgiving, and there will be no prayers except for prayers of thanksgiving" (Lev. R. 9:7).

הַקְרִיבוֹ אֶת־זִבְחוֹ יֵאָכֵל וּמִמָּחֳרָת
וְהַנּוֹתָר מִמֶּנּוּ יֵאָכֵל׃ 17 וְהַנּוֹתָר מִבְּשַׂר
הַזָּבַח בַּיּוֹם הַשְּׁלִישִׁי בָּאֵשׁ יִשָּׂרֵף׃ 18 וְאִם
הֵאָכֹל יֵאָכֵל מִבְּשַׂר־זֶבַח שְׁלָמָיו בַּיּוֹם
הַשְּׁלִישִׁי לֹא יֵרָצֶה הַמַּקְרִיב אֹתוֹ לֹא
יֵחָשֵׁב לוֹ פִּגּוּל יִהְיֶה וְהַנֶּפֶשׁ הָאֹכֶלֶת
מִמֶּנּוּ עֲוֺנָהּ תִּשָּׂא׃

19 וְהַבָּשָׂר אֲשֶׁר־יִגַּע בְּכָל־טָמֵא לֹא יֵאָכֵל
בָּאֵשׁ יִשָּׂרֵף וְהַבָּשָׂר כָּל־טָהוֹר יֹאכַל
בָּשָׂר׃ 20 וְהַנֶּפֶשׁ אֲשֶׁר־תֹּאכַל בָּשָׂר מִזֶּבַח
הַשְּׁלָמִים אֲשֶׁר לַיהוָה וְטֻמְאָתוֹ עָלָיו
וְנִכְרְתָה הַנֶּפֶשׁ הַהִוא מֵעַמֶּיהָ׃ 21 וְנֶפֶשׁ
כִּי־תִגַּע בְּכָל־טָמֵא בְּטֻמְאַת אָדָם אוֹ ׀
בִּבְהֵמָה טְמֵאָה אוֹ בְּכָל־שֶׁקֶץ טָמֵא וְאָכַל
מִבְּשַׂר־זֶבַח הַשְּׁלָמִים אֲשֶׁר לַיהוָה
וְנִכְרְתָה הַנֶּפֶשׁ הַהִוא מֵעַמֶּיהָ׃ פ

22 וַיְדַבֵּר יְהוָה אֶל־מֹשֶׁה לֵּאמֹר׃ 23 דַּבֵּר
אֶל־בְּנֵי יִשְׂרָאֵל לֵאמֹר כָּל־חֵלֶב שׁוֹר
וְכֶשֶׂב וָעֵז לֹא תֹאכֵלוּ׃ 24 וְחֵלֶב נְבֵלָה
וְחֵלֶב טְרֵפָה יֵעָשֶׂה לְכָל־מְלָאכָה וְאָכֹל
לֹא תֹאכְלֻהוּ׃ 25 כִּי כָּל־אֹכֵל חֵלֶב מִן־
הַבְּהֵמָה אֲשֶׁר יַקְרִיב מִמֶּנָּה אִשֶּׁה לַיהוָה

or a freewill offering, it shall be eaten on the day that he offers his sacrifice, and what is left of it shall be eaten on the morrow. 17What is then left of the flesh of the sacrifice shall be consumed in fire on the third day. 18If any of the flesh of his sacrifice of well-being is eaten on the third day, it shall not be acceptable; it shall not count for him who offered it. It is an offensive thing, and the person who eats of it shall bear his guilt.

19Flesh that touches anything impure shall not be eaten; it shall be consumed in fire. As for other flesh, only he who is pure may eat such flesh. 20But the person who, in a state of impurity, eats flesh from the LORD's sacrifices of well-being, that person shall be cut off from his kin. 21When a person touches anything impure, be it human impurity or an impure animal or any impure creature, and eats flesh from the LORD's sacrifices of well-being, that person shall be cut off from his kin.

22And the LORD spoke to Moses, saying: 23Speak to the Israelite people thus: You shall eat no fat of ox or sheep or goat. 24Fat from animals that died or were torn by beasts may be put to any use, but you must not eat it. 25If anyone eats the fat of animals from which gifts may be made to the LORD, the person who eats

freewill offering Hebrew: *n'davah,* which also serves as a general term for many types of voluntary contributions to the sanctuary. Like the *todah,* it expresses gratitude to God and is often mentioned together with the vow (*neder*).

18. Because the sacrificial meat was left uneaten for an improper length of time, the sacrifice itself was not efficacious. In this verse, the penalty for eating flesh remaining from the *sh'lamim* sacrifice after the third day is stated merely as "bearing one's guilt," whereas in 19:5–8 the same offense brings on the penalty of being cut off from the religious community.

19. Beginning with this verse, the text deals more explicitly with the subject of impurity, a concern particularly relevant to the *sh'lamim,* because parts of it were handled by ordinary Israelites outside the sanctuary.

23. You shall eat no fat See Comment to 3:3.

24. Fat from animals that died An animal torn by beasts (*t'refah*) and the carcass of a dead animal (*n'velah*) are forbidden in their entirety (Exod. 22:30, Lev. 17:15). Hence, any part of such an animal would also be forbidden. It is likely that this seemingly superfluous rule was included here for emphasis, to reinforce the ban on eating organ fat (*ḥeilev*) (see 3:16).

25. from which gifts may be made This clarifies the provisions of verse 23. The *ḥeilev* of large and small cattle is forbidden, because such animals are of the kind offered as sacrifices.

it shall be cut off from his kin. 26And you must not consume any blood, either of bird or of animal, in any of your settlements. 27Anyone who eats blood shall be cut off from his kin.

28And the LORD spoke to Moses, saying: 29Speak to the Israelite people thus: The offering to the LORD from a sacrifice of well-being must be presented by him who offers his sacrifice of well-being to the LORD: 30his own hands shall present the LORD's gifts. He shall present the fat with the breast, the breast to be elevated as an elevation offering before the LORD; 31the priest shall turn the fat into smoke on the altar, and the breast shall go to Aaron and his sons. 32And the right thigh from your sacrifices of well-being you shall present to the priest as a gift; 33he from among Aaron's sons who offers the blood and the fat of the offering of well-being shall get the right thigh as his portion. 34For I have taken the breast of elevation offering and the thigh of gift offering from the Israelites, from their sacrifices of well-being, and given them to Aaron the priest and to his sons as their due from the Israelites for all time.

35Those shall be the perquisites of Aaron and the perquisites of his sons from the LORD's gifts, once they have been inducted to serve the LORD as priests; 36these the LORD commanded to be given them, once they had been anointed, as a due from the Israelites for all time throughout the ages.

וְנִכְרְתָ֛ה הַנֶּ֥פֶשׁ הָאֹכֶ֖לֶת מֵעַמֶּֽיהָ׃ 26 וְכָל־
דָּם֙ לֹ֣א תֹאכְל֔וּ בְּכֹ֖ל מוֹשְׁבֹתֵיכֶ֑ם לָע֖וֹף
וְלַבְּהֵמָֽה׃ 27 כָּל־נֶ֖פֶשׁ אֲשֶׁר־תֹּאכַ֣ל כָּל־
דָּ֑ם וְנִכְרְתָ֛ה הַנֶּ֥פֶשׁ הַהִ֖וא מֵעַמֶּֽיהָ׃ פ

28 וַיְדַבֵּ֥ר יְהוָ֖ה אֶל־מֹשֶׁ֥ה לֵּאמֹֽר׃ 29 דַּבֵּ֛ר
אֶל־בְּנֵ֥י יִשְׂרָאֵ֖ל לֵאמֹ֑ר הַמַּקְרִ֞יב אֶת־זֶ֤בַח
שְׁלָמָיו֙ לַיהוָ֔ה יָבִ֧יא אֶת־קָרְבָּנ֛וֹ לַיהוָ֖ה
מִזֶּ֥בַח שְׁלָמָֽיו׃ 30 יָדָ֣יו תְּבִיאֶ֔ינָה אֵ֖ת אִשֵּׁ֣י
יְהוָ֑ה אֶת־הַחֵ֣לֶב עַל־הֶֽחָזֶה֙ יְבִיאֶ֔נּוּ אֵ֣ת
הֶחָזֶ֗ה לְהָנִ֥יף אֹת֛וֹ תְּנוּפָ֖ה לִפְנֵ֥י יְהוָֽה׃
31 וְהִקְטִ֧יר הַכֹּהֵ֛ן אֶת־הַחֵ֖לֶב הַמִּזְבֵּ֑חָה
וְהָיָה֙ הֶֽחָזֶ֔ה לְאַהֲרֹ֖ן וּלְבָנָֽיו׃ 32 וְאֵת֙ שׁ֣וֹק
הַיָּמִ֔ין תִּתְּנ֥וּ תְרוּמָ֖ה לַכֹּהֵ֑ן מִזִּבְחֵ֖י
שַׁלְמֵיכֶֽם׃ 33 הַמַּקְרִ֞יב אֶת־דַּ֧ם הַשְּׁלָמִ֛ים
וְאֶת־הַחֵ֖לֶב מִבְּנֵ֣י אַהֲרֹ֑ן ל֧וֹ תִֽהְיֶ֛ה שׁ֥וֹק
הַיָּמִ֖ין לְמָנָֽה׃ 34 כִּי֩ אֶת־חֲזֵ֨ה הַתְּנוּפָ֜ה
וְאֵ֣ת ׀ שׁ֣וֹק הַתְּרוּמָ֗ה לָקַ֙חְתִּי֙ מֵאֵ֣ת
בְּנֵֽי־יִשְׂרָאֵ֔ל מִזִּבְחֵ֖י שַׁלְמֵיהֶ֑ם וָאֶתֵּ֣ן אֹ֠תָם
לְאַהֲרֹ֨ן הַכֹּהֵ֜ן וּלְבָנָיו֙ לְחָק־עוֹלָ֔ם מֵאֵ֖ת
בְּנֵ֥י יִשְׂרָאֵֽל׃
35 זֹ֣את מִשְׁחַ֤ת אַהֲרֹן֙ וּמִשְׁחַ֣ת בָּנָ֔יו מֵאִשֵּׁ֖י
יְהוָ֑ה בְּיוֹם֙ הִקְרִ֣יב אֹתָ֔ם לְכַהֵ֖ן לַיהוָֽה׃
36 אֲשֶׁר֩ צִוָּ֨ה יְהוָ֜ה לָתֵ֣ת לָהֶ֗ם בְּיוֹם֙ מָשְׁח֣וֹ
אֹתָ֔ם מֵאֵ֖ת בְּנֵ֣י יִשְׂרָאֵ֑ל חֻקַּ֥ת עוֹלָ֖ם
לְדֹרֹתָֽם׃

29–30. The donor of the *sh'lamim* had to personally participate in the presentation of the offering. Because nonpriests could not actually place sacrifices on the altar—indeed, they were banned from the adjacent area—the rite of "presentation" (*t'nufah*) afforded them some measure of participation in sacrifices of lesser sanctity such as this one.

30. the breast to be elevated as an elevation offering before the LORD The offering was raised up, in dedication to God. "Elevation offering" here is the designation for *t'nufah,* derived from the verb *henif* (lift, raise).

31. the priest shall turn the fat into smoke The priest was entitled to take the breast and the right thigh of the sacrificial animal only after God's share of the offering (i.e., the fatty portions) had been burned on the altar.

34. the thigh of gift offering See Comment to 7:14.

[37]Such are the rituals of the burnt offering, the grain offering, the purification offering, the reparation offering, the offering of ordination, and the sacrifice of well-being, [38]with which the LORD charged Moses on Mount Sinai, when He commanded that the Israelites present their offerings to the LORD, in the wilderness of Sinai.

37 זֹאת הַתּוֹרָה לָעֹלָה לַמִּנְחָה וְלַחַטָּאת
וְלָאָשָׁם וְלַמִּלּוּאִים וּלְזֶבַח הַשְּׁלָמִים׃
38 אֲשֶׁר צִוָּה יְהוָה אֶת־מֹשֶׁה בְּהַר סִינָי
בְּיוֹם צַוֺּתוֹ אֶת־בְּנֵי יִשְׂרָאֵל לְהַקְרִיב
אֶת־קָרְבְּנֵיהֶם לַיהוָה בְּמִדְבַּר סִינָי׃ פ

8

The LORD spoke to Moses, saying: [2]Take Aaron along with his sons, and the vestments, the anointing oil, the bull of purification offering, the two rams, and the basket of unleavened bread; [3]and assemble the whole community at the entrance of the Tent of Meeting. [4]Moses did as the LORD commanded him. And when the community was assembled at the entrance of the Tent of Meeting, [5]Moses said to the community, "This is what the LORD has commanded to be done."

[6]Then Moses brought Aaron and his sons forward and washed them with water. [7]He put the

ביעי ח וַיְדַבֵּר יְהוָה אֶל־מֹשֶׁה לֵּאמֹר׃ 2 קַח
אֶת־אַהֲרֹן וְאֶת־בָּנָיו אִתּוֹ וְאֵת הַבְּגָדִים
וְאֵת שֶׁמֶן הַמִּשְׁחָה וְאֵת ׀ פַּר הַחַטָּאת
וְאֵת שְׁנֵי הָאֵילִים וְאֵת סַל הַמַּצּוֹת׃
3 וְאֵת כָּל־הָעֵדָה הַקְהֵל אֶל־פֶּתַח אֹהֶל
מוֹעֵד׃ 4 וַיַּעַשׂ מֹשֶׁה כַּאֲשֶׁר צִוָּה יְהוָה
אֹתוֹ וַתִּקָּהֵל הָעֵדָה אֶל־פֶּתַח אֹהֶל מוֹעֵד׃
5 וַיֹּאמֶר מֹשֶׁה אֶל־הָעֵדָה זֶה הַדָּבָר אֲשֶׁר־
צִוָּה יְהוָה לַעֲשׂוֹת׃
6 וַיַּקְרֵב מֹשֶׁה אֶת־אַהֲרֹן וְאֶת־בָּנָיו וַיִּרְחַץ
אֹתָם בַּמָּיִם׃ 7 וַיִּתֵּן עָלָיו אֶת־הַכֻּתֹּנֶת

SUMMARY (7:35–38)

37. Such are the rituals All of the rituals set forth in chapters 6–7.

the offering of ordination This probably refers to the grain offering burned on the altar by the High Priest, prescribed in 6:12–16. The ordination rites are presented in chapters 8–9.

38. This verse asserts that in the wilderness of Sinai, the Israelites already had worshiped God with sacrifices.

THE INITIATION OF FORMAL WORSHIP (8:1–9:24)

Chapters 8 and 9 offer a detailed description of the religious celebrations that mark the beginning of formal worship in ancient Israel. The origin of Israelite worship was of great importance to the priesthood because of the formidable role priests occupied in this area of Israelite life.

CONSECRATION OF PRIESTS AND TABERNACLE (8:1–36)

2. anointing oil See Exod. 30:22–25.

3. assemble the whole community The actual place of assembly was in the outer section of the courtyard, not directly in front of the tent. Only priests were permitted to advance beyond the altar of burnt offerings, which stood in the courtyard about halfway between the outer gate and the entrance to the tent proper.

6. washed them with water Washing is a universal feature of religious ritual. Beyond the obvious hygienic advantages of water, its use in ritual also serves as symbolic purification.

7. The High Priest wore a total of eight vest-

---

37. *Such are the rituals* Hebrew: *zot ha-torah;* Menaḥem Mendel of Kotzk reads "This is the Torah," and then renders the offerings by their root meanings: "the Torah leads some people to *olah* (rising higher) and *minḥah* (generosity), but leads other people to *ḥattat* and *asham* (feelings of guilt)." The summary list concludes with *sh'lamim,* even as so many Jewish prayers, including the *Amidah,* the priestly benediction, and the *Kaddish,* con-

וַיַּחְגֹּר אֹתוֹ בָּאַבְנֵט וַיַּלְבֵּשׁ אֹתוֹ אֶת־
הַמְּעִיל וַיִּתֵּן עָלָיו אֶת־הָאֵפֹד וַיַּחְגֹּר אֹתוֹ
בְּחֵשֶׁב הָאֵפֹד וַיֶּאְפֹּד לוֹ בּוֹ׃ 8 *וַיָּשֶׂם עָלָיו
אֶת־הַחֹשֶׁן וַיִּתֵּן אֶל־הַחֹשֶׁן אֶת־הָאוּרִים
וְאֶת־הַתֻּמִּים׃ 9 וַיָּשֶׂם אֶת־הַמִּצְנֶפֶת עַל־
רֹאשׁוֹ וַיָּשֶׂם עַל־הַמִּצְנֶפֶת אֶל־מוּל פָּנָיו
אֵת צִיץ הַזָּהָב נֵזֶר הַקֹּדֶשׁ כַּאֲשֶׁר צִוָּה
יְהוָה אֶת־מֹשֶׁה׃
10 וַיִּקַּח מֹשֶׁה אֶת־שֶׁמֶן הַמִּשְׁחָה וַיִּמְשַׁח
אֶת־הַמִּשְׁכָּן וְאֶת־כָּל־אֲשֶׁר־בּוֹ וַיְקַדֵּשׁ
אֹתָם׃ 11 וַיַּז מִמֶּנּוּ עַל־הַמִּזְבֵּחַ שֶׁבַע
פְּעָמִים וַיִּמְשַׁח אֶת־הַמִּזְבֵּחַ וְאֶת־כָּל־
כֵּלָיו וְאֶת־הַכִּיֹּר וְאֶת־כַּנּוֹ לְקַדְּשָׁם׃
12 וַיִּצֹק מִשֶּׁמֶן הַמִּשְׁחָה עַל רֹאשׁ אַהֲרֹן
וַיִּמְשַׁח אֹתוֹ לְקַדְּשׁוֹ׃ 13 וַיַּקְרֵב מֹשֶׁה
אֶת־בְּנֵי אַהֲרֹן וַיַּלְבִּשֵׁם כֻּתֳּנֹת וַיַּחְגֹּר
אֹתָם אַבְנֵט וַיַּחֲבֹשׁ לָהֶם מִגְבָּעוֹת כַּאֲשֶׁר
צִוָּה יְהוָה אֶת־מֹשֶׁה׃
חמישי 14 וַיַּגֵּשׁ אֵת פַּר הַחַטָּאת וַיִּסְמֹךְ אַהֲרֹן

tunic on him, girded him with the sash, clothed him with the robe, and put the ephod on him, girding him with the decorated band with which he tied it to him. 8He put the breastpiece on him, and put into the breastpiece the Urim and Thummim. 9And he set the headdress on his head; and on the headdress, in front, he put the gold frontlet, the holy diadem—as the LORD had commanded Moses.

10Moses took the anointing oil and anointed the Tabernacle and all that was in it, thus consecrating them. 11He sprinkled some of it on the altar seven times, anointing the altar, all its utensils, and the laver with its stand, to consecrate them. 12He poured some of the anointing oil upon Aaron's head and anointed him, to consecrate him. 13Moses then brought Aaron's sons forward, clothed them in tunics, girded them with sashes, and wound turbans upon them, as the LORD had commanded Moses.

14He led forward the bull of purification offering. Aaron and his sons laid their hands

v. 8. חצי התורה בפסוקים

ments, four of which were unique to him (see Exod. 28 and 39).

8. breastpiece Made of wool and linen, with gold threads woven into the fabric, and 12 gem stones were set into the cloth, with the name of a different tribe of Israel engraved on each stone.

Urim and Thummim These were flat stones used for the casting of lots. The act of casting lots was the only form of divination permitted in ancient Israelite official worship, which normally objected to the use of omens for predicting the future.

9. headdress Ordinary priests wore turbans; only the High Priest wore the royal headdress.

10–12. In these verses we read of two parallel acts: the consecration of Aaron, the High Priest, and the consecration of the altar and the tabernacle with its vessels. Both were accomplished by the same means—anointing with the same oil. In this way Aaron, too, became a sacred vessel.

13. After the sons of Aaron were robed, the sacrifices of ordination commenced.

14. Large cattle were used in purification offerings when the entire community, or the High Priest in particular, were affected.

---

clude with *shalom* "peace," the ultimate blessing.

CHAPTER 8

12. anointed him, to consecrate him The verb translated as "anointed" (*va-yimshaḥ*) is related to the noun *mashi·aḥ* (messiah), which originally meant "anointed one." It referred to a priest, and later to a king, who had been consecrated for special responsibility. Throughout the Bible, it refers only to a human priest or king. The prophets' vision of the Messiah was of a good and benevolent king who would earn peace and prosperity for the people by serving God wholeheartedly (see Isa. 11:1–9). Biblical and Rabbinic Judaism as a rule did not conceive of the Messiah as a superhuman redeemer.

upon the head of the bull of purification offering, [15]and it was slaughtered. Moses took the blood and with his finger put some on each of the horns of the altar, purifying the altar; then he poured out the blood at the base of the altar. Thus he consecrated it in order to make expiation upon it.

[16]Moses then took all the fat that was about the entrails, and the protuberance of the liver, and the two kidneys and their fat, and turned them into smoke on the altar. [17]The rest of the bull, its hide, its flesh, and its dung, he put to the fire outside the camp—as the LORD had commanded Moses.

[18]Then he brought forward the ram of burnt offering. Aaron and his sons laid their hands upon the ram's head, [19]and it was slaughtered. Moses dashed the blood against all sides of the altar. [20]The ram was cut up into sections and Moses turned the head, the sections, and the suet into smoke on the altar; [21]Moses washed the entrails and the legs with water and turned all of the ram into smoke. That was a burnt offering for a pleasing odor, a gift to the LORD—as the LORD had commanded Moses.

[22]He brought forward the second ram, the ram of ordination. Aaron and his sons laid their hands upon the ram's head, [23]and it was slaughtered. Moses took some of its blood and put it on the ridge of Aaron's right ear, and on the thumb of his right hand, and on the big toe of his right foot. [24]Moses then brought forward the sons of Aaron, and put some of the blood on the ridges of their right ears, and on the thumbs of their right hands, and on the big toes of their

וּבָנָיו אֶת־יְדֵיהֶם עַל־רֹאשׁ פַּר הַחַטָּאת׃
15 וַיִּשְׁחָט וַיִּקַּח מֹשֶׁה אֶת־הַדָּם וַיִּתֵּן
עַל־קַרְנוֹת הַמִּזְבֵּחַ סָבִיב בְּאֶצְבָּעוֹ וַיְחַטֵּא
אֶת־הַמִּזְבֵּחַ וְאֶת־הַדָּם יָצַק אֶל־יְסוֹד
הַמִּזְבֵּחַ וַיְקַדְּשֵׁהוּ לְכַפֵּר עָלָיו׃
16 וַיִּקַּח אֶת־כָּל־הַחֵלֶב אֲשֶׁר עַל־הַקֶּרֶב
וְאֵת יֹתֶרֶת הַכָּבֵד וְאֶת־שְׁתֵּי הַכְּלָיֹת
וְאֶת־חֶלְבְּהֶן וַיַּקְטֵר מֹשֶׁה הַמִּזְבֵּחָה׃
17 וְאֶת־הַפָּר וְאֶת־עֹרוֹ וְאֶת־בְּשָׂרוֹ וְאֶת־
פִּרְשׁוֹ שָׂרַף בָּאֵשׁ מִחוּץ לַמַּחֲנֶה כַּאֲשֶׁר
צִוָּה יְהוָה אֶת־מֹשֶׁה׃
18 וַיַּקְרֵב אֵת אֵיל הָעֹלָה וַיִּסְמְכוּ אַהֲרֹן
וּבָנָיו אֶת־יְדֵיהֶם עַל־רֹאשׁ הָאָיִל׃
19 וַיִּשְׁחָט וַיִּזְרֹק מֹשֶׁה אֶת־הַדָּם עַל־
הַמִּזְבֵּחַ סָבִיב׃ 20 וְאֶת־הָאַיִל נִתַּח
לִנְתָחָיו וַיַּקְטֵר מֹשֶׁה אֶת־הָרֹאשׁ וְאֶת־
הַנְּתָחִים וְאֶת־הַפָּדֶר׃ 21 וְאֶת־הַקֶּרֶב
וְאֶת־הַכְּרָעַיִם רָחַץ בַּמָּיִם וַיַּקְטֵר מֹשֶׁה
אֶת־כָּל־הָאַיִל הַמִּזְבֵּחָה עֹלָה הוּא לְרֵיחַ־
נִיחֹחַ אִשֶּׁה הוּא לַיהוָה כַּאֲשֶׁר צִוָּה יְהוָה
אֶת־מֹשֶׁה׃
22 וַיַּקְרֵב אֶת־הָאַיִל הַשֵּׁנִי אֵיל הַמִּלֻּאִים
וַיִּסְמְכוּ אַהֲרֹן וּבָנָיו אֶת־יְדֵיהֶם עַל־רֹאשׁ
הָאָיִל׃ 23 וַיִּשְׁחָט ׀ וַיִּקַּח מֹשֶׁה מִדָּמוֹ וַיִּתֵּן
עַל־תְּנוּךְ אֹזֶן־אַהֲרֹן הַיְמָנִית וְעַל־בֹּהֶן יָדוֹ
הַיְמָנִית וְעַל־בֹּהֶן רַגְלוֹ הַיְמָנִית׃ 24 וַיַּקְרֵב
אֶת־בְּנֵי אַהֲרֹן וַיִּתֵּן מֹשֶׁה מִן־הַדָּם עַל־
תְּנוּךְ אָזְנָם הַיְמָנִית וְעַל־בֹּהֶן יָדָם

15. he consecrated it in order to make expiation upon it Expiatory sacrifices required an altar.

18–21. The function of this sacrifice was to evoke a favorable response from God before making an approach with other sacrifices.

23. blood . . . Aaron's right ear Dabbing sacrificial blood on certain extremities of the body is essentially a rite of purification. In this manner Aaron and his sons were purified as they entered into their new status.

24. the rest of the blood Moses dashed against every side of the altar This is similar to what occurred during the covenantal ceremony at Sinai (Exod. 24:6–8). In the ordination of the priests, the sacrificial blood served a dual function. It purified the priests and also bound them in a covenant of service to God in the tabernacle.

right feet; and the rest of the blood Moses dashed against every side of the altar. 25 He took the fat—the broad tail, all the fat about the entrails, the protuberance of the liver, and the two kidneys and their fat—and the right thigh. 26 From the basket of unleavened bread that was before the LORD, he took one cake of unleavened bread, one cake of oil bread, and one wafer, and placed them on the fat parts and on the right thigh. 27 He placed all these on the palms of Aaron and on the palms of his sons, and elevated them as an elevation offering before the LORD. 28 Then Moses took them from their hands and turned them into smoke on the altar with the burnt offering. This was an ordination offering for a pleasing odor; it was a gift to the LORD. 29 Moses took the breast and elevated it as an elevation offering before the LORD; it was Moses' portion of the ram of ordination—as the LORD had commanded Moses.

30 And Moses took some of the anointing oil and some of the blood that was on the altar and sprinkled it upon Aaron and upon his vestments, and also upon his sons and upon their vestments. Thus he consecrated Aaron and his vestments, and also his sons and their vestments.

31 Moses said to Aaron and his sons: Boil the flesh at the entrance of the Tent of Meeting and eat it there with the bread that is in the basket of ordination—as I commanded: Aaron and his sons shall eat it; 32 and what is left over of the flesh and the bread you shall consume in fire. 33 You shall not go outside the entrance of the Tent of Meeting for seven days, until the

הַיְמָנִית וְעַל־בֹּהֶן רַגְלָם הַיְמָנִית וַיִּזְרֹק
מֹשֶׁה אֶת־הַדָּם עַל־הַמִּזְבֵּחַ סָבִיב׃
25 וַיִּקַּח אֶת־הַחֵלֶב וְאֶת־הָאַלְיָה וְאֶת־
כָּל־הַחֵלֶב אֲשֶׁר עַל־הַקֶּרֶב וְאֵת יֹתֶרֶת
הַכָּבֵד וְאֶת־שְׁתֵּי הַכְּלָיֹת וְאֶת־חֶלְבְּהֶן
וְאֵת שׁוֹק הַיָּמִין׃ 26 וּמִסַּל הַמַּצּוֹת אֲשֶׁר ׀
לִפְנֵי יְהוָה לָקַח חַלַּת מַצָּה אַחַת וְחַלַּת
לֶחֶם שֶׁמֶן אַחַת וְרָקִיק אֶחָד וַיָּשֶׂם עַל־
הַחֲלָבִים וְעַל שׁוֹק הַיָּמִין׃ 27 וַיִּתֵּן אֶת־
הַכֹּל עַל כַּפֵּי אַהֲרֹן וְעַל כַּפֵּי בָנָיו
וַיָּנֶף אֹתָם תְּנוּפָה לִפְנֵי יְהוָה׃ 28 וַיִּקַּח
מֹשֶׁה אֹתָם מֵעַל כַּפֵּיהֶם וַיַּקְטֵר הַמִּזְבֵּחָה
עַל־הָעֹלָה מִלֻּאִים הֵם לְרֵיחַ נִיחֹחַ
אִשֶּׁה הוּא לַיהוָה׃ 29 וַיִּקַּח מֹשֶׁה אֶת־
הֶחָזֶה וַיְנִיפֵהוּ תְנוּפָה לִפְנֵי יְהוָה מֵאֵיל
הַמִּלֻּאִים לְמֹשֶׁה הָיָה לְמָנָה כַּאֲשֶׁר צִוָּה
יְהוָה אֶת־מֹשֶׁה׃

שביעי 30 וַיִּקַּח מֹשֶׁה מִשֶּׁמֶן הַמִּשְׁחָה וּמִן־הַדָּם
אֲשֶׁר עַל־הַמִּזְבֵּחַ וַיַּז עַל־אַהֲרֹן עַל־בְּגָדָיו
וְעַל־בָּנָיו וְעַל־בִּגְדֵי בָנָיו אִתּוֹ וַיְקַדֵּשׁ
אֶת־אַהֲרֹן אֶת־בְּגָדָיו וְאֶת־בָּנָיו וְאֶת־בִּגְדֵי
בָנָיו אִתּוֹ׃

31 וַיֹּאמֶר מֹשֶׁה אֶל־אַהֲרֹן וְאֶל־בָּנָיו בַּשְּׁלוּ
אֶת־הַבָּשָׂר פֶּתַח אֹהֶל מוֹעֵד וְשָׁם תֹּאכְלוּ
אֹתוֹ וְאֶת־הַלֶּחֶם אֲשֶׁר בְּסַל הַמִּלֻּאִים
כַּאֲשֶׁר צִוֵּיתִי לֵאמֹר אַהֲרֹן וּבָנָיו יֹאכְלֻהוּ׃
32 וְהַנּוֹתָר בַּבָּשָׂר וּבַלָּחֶם בָּאֵשׁ תִּשְׂרֹפוּ׃
מפטיר 33 וּמִפֶּתַח אֹהֶל מוֹעֵד לֹא תֵצְאוּ שִׁבְעַת
יָמִים עַד יוֹם מְלֹאת יְמֵי מִלֻּאֵיכֶם כִּי

27. all these Included here among the parts of the sacrifice burned on the altar was the thigh, which belonged to the priests (Lev. 7:32). In the rites of ordination, the priests surrendered their own portion to God, because it would have been improper for them to benefit from what was offered on their own behalf. Moses, however, received his portion.

30. A mix of anointing oil and sacrificial blood was sprinkled on Aaron and his sons and on their vestments. This completed their ordination.

31. Moses instructed Aaron and his sons on how to dispose of Moses' own portion of the sacrifice. It was vital to the efficacy of the ordination sacrifice that the priests actually partake of it.

33. The priests were not inside the tent but,

day that your period of ordination is completed. For your ordination will require seven days. ³⁴Everything done today, the LORD has commanded to be done [seven days], to make expiation for you. ³⁵You shall remain at the entrance of the Tent of Meeting day and night for seven days, keeping the LORD's charge—that you may not die—for so I have been commanded.

³⁶And Aaron and his sons did all the things that the LORD had commanded through Moses.

שִׁבְעַ֤ת יָמִים֙ יְמַלֵּ֖א אֶת־יֶדְכֶֽם׃ 34 כַּאֲשֶׁ֨ר
עָשָׂ֜ה בַּיּ֤וֹם הַזֶּה֙ צִוָּ֣ה יְהֹוָ֔ה לַעֲשֹׂ֖ת
לְכַפֵּ֥ר עֲלֵיכֶֽם׃ 35 וּפֶ֩תַח֩ אֹ֨הֶל מוֹעֵ֜ד
תֵּשְׁב֣וּ יוֹמָ֣ם וָלַ֗יְלָה שִׁבְעַ֣ת יָמִ֔ים
וּשְׁמַרְתֶּ֞ם אֶת־מִשְׁמֶ֤רֶת יְהֹוָה֙ וְלֹ֣א תָמ֔וּתוּ
כִּי־כֵ֖ן צֻוֵּֽיתִי׃
36 וַיַּ֤עַשׂ אַהֲרֹן֙ וּבָנָ֔יו אֵ֥ת כׇּל־הַדְּבָרִ֑ים
אֲשֶׁר־צִוָּ֥ה יְהֹוָ֖ה בְּיַד־מֹשֶֽׁה׃ ס

rather, near its entrance, in the inner section of the tabernacle courtyard. They were not to leave this sanctified area for seven days, to avoid contact with anything or anyone impure.

35. the LORD's charge   To follow the instructions given on this occasion.

33. seven days   These days parallel the seven days of Creation. The existence of the tabernacle and its capacity to atone for human sinfulness and imperfection make it possible for an imperfect world to survive in the sight of a just God. The Midrash emphasizes that "if

God demands absolute justice, there can be no world. If God desires a world, there cannot be absolute justice" (Lev. R. 10:1).

36.   As is often true, the *parashah* concludes on a positive note—in this case, by highlighting the priests' faithful obedience to God.

הפטרת צו

HAFTARAH FOR TZAV

JEREMIAH 7:21–8:3; 9:22–23

The prophet Jeremiah delivered a Temple sermon (Jer. 7:1–20), in which he announced God's judgment of doom upon the Temple and upon the nation for the people's moral sins and for pagan worship. The first part of this *haftarah* follows that sermon as part of a series of prophetic rebukes. The last part of this *haftarah* skips ahead to the end of chapter 9 to conclude the reading on a positive note of religious instruction. The *haftarah* does not fulfill the usual requirement of having at least 21 verses. The Talmud justifies this situation with the laconic comment that the unit is brief because "the topic is concluded" (BT Meg. 23b).

Rhetorical forms of negation and contrast emphasize the theme of proper action that dominates the *haftarah*. Thus, in the opening critique of the nation, God first says "I did not speak with them or command them" concerning sacrifices. This is contrasted with the positive assertion about "what I commanded them" to do (vv. 22–23). In this rebuke, unbidden and excessive offerings are juxtaposed with the command to follow the divine way. Similarly, at a later point, God maligns the people's idolatrous and heinous acts of child-sacrifice, emphasizing in counterpoint that "I never commanded" such behavior (v. 31). A further example of this structure occurs in the concluding instruction of the *haftarah*. In it the prophet contrasts self-glorification through money and might with acts of kindness and justice. The rhetorical phrasing sharply juxtaposes false and worthless assertions of glory (*al yithallel*) with their positive counterpart (*yithallel*) and teaching (9:22–23). The harsh condemnation of cultic activity found in 7:21–22 goes far beyond the rejection of sacrifices found in 6:19–20. The people are told, in a mocking fashion, to act in a manner that blatantly contradicts the law in the Torah, which states explicitly that the burnt offerings (*olot*) are to be entirely consumed upon the altar (Lev. 1:1–9). Thus it is best to follow those commentators who regard Jeremiah's words as an altogether ironic "instruction," implying that the people may as well desecrate the burnt offering (*olah*) for all that it is worth, because God did not command them about burnt offerings or sacrifice during the wilderness sojourn.

This interpretation has evoked consternation and perplexity for generations of interpreters, because Lev. 7:37–38 (at the end of the *parashah*) states explicitly that the cultic instructions were given during the Sinai sojourn.

A solution to the problem posed by this apparent contradiction between Jeremiah and the Torah was proposed by Radak: Only the Decalogue (and not the sacrificial cult) was commanded at Mount Sinai, to teach the nation that the unconditional obligations of morality constitute the cornerstone of the Covenant. In this sense Jeremiah's words are historically accurate and reinforce a central covenantal concern. In light of the centrality of the Decalogue, the prophet's point would then be that voluntary (individual) sacrifices offered by people who commit acts of disobedience to the divine are as good as worthless. In fact, he suggests, they are no more efficacious than if they were offered incorrectly.

Strikingly, the final verse of the *haftarah* (9:23) echoes the prophet Hosea's statement of what God desires ("I desire goodness, not sacrifice; / Obedience to God, rather than burnt offerings," Hos. 6:6). One can hardly avoid the conclusion that the Sages selected Jeremiah's teaching in 9:22–23 as a climax to the *haftarah* in light of the earlier *haftarah* verses emphasizing God's will and the nullity of sacrifices. Indeed, by concluding the *haftarah* on this note, rabbinic tradition provides a strong contrast to the teachings of the *parashah,* and a sharp qualification of its status.

RELATION OF THE *HAFTARAH* TO THE *PARASHAH*

Both the *parashah* and the *haftarah* refer to the *olah* (burnt offering) and to the *zevaḥ* offering. Jeremiah stresses that the people were "not commanded" to offer sacrifices when they came out of Egypt. By contrast, the priestly rule ends with the specific emphasis that its regulations were "commanded" by God in the wilderness of Sinai (Lev. 7:38).

It may have been just this critique of sacrifices that attracted the Sages to Jeremiah's word. In the years following the destruction of the Second Temple (70 C.E.), the prophet's statement that the Sinaitic covenant did not enjoin sacrifices would assuage Jewish fears that without the cult of ritual sacrifice their relationship with God was permanently impaired. Indeed, responding to just this anxiety, Yoḥanan ben Zakkai radically reinterpreted Judaism for a later generation when he remarked that acts of loving kindness would effect atonement "just as" the ancient sacrifices did (ARN B 4). Similarly, Jeremiah earlier emphasized that the covenantal virtues of kindness, justice, and equity are the very basis for knowing God, and for imitating His ways. The prophet's teachings would resonate in subsequent centuries.

7 [21]Thus said the LORD of Hosts, the God of
Israel: Add your burnt offerings to your other
sacrifices and eat the meat! [22]For when I freed
your fathers from the land of Egypt, I did not
speak with them or command them concerning
burnt offerings or sacrifice. [23]But this is what
I commanded them: Do My bidding, that I may
be your God and you may be My people; walk
only in the way that I enjoin upon you, that it
may go well with you. [24]Yet they did not listen
or give ear; they followed their own counsels,
the willfulness of their evil hearts. They have
gone backward, not forward, [25]from the day
your fathers left the land of Egypt until today.
And though I kept sending all My servants, the
prophets, to them daily and persistently, [26]they
would not listen to Me or give ear. They stiffened their necks, they acted worse than their
fathers.

[27]You shall say all these things to them, but
they will not listen to you; you shall call to

ז 21 כֹּה אָמַר יְהוָה צְבָאוֹת אֱלֹהֵי יִשְׂרָאֵל
עֹלוֹתֵיכֶם סְפוּ עַל־זִבְחֵיכֶם וְאִכְלוּ בָשָׂר׃
22 כִּי לֹא־דִבַּרְתִּי אֶת־אֲבוֹתֵיכֶם וְלֹא
צִוִּיתִים בְּיוֹם הוציא הוֹצִיאִי אוֹתָם מֵאֶרֶץ
מִצְרָיִם עַל־דִּבְרֵי עוֹלָה וָזָבַח׃ 23 כִּי אִם־
אֶת־הַדָּבָר הַזֶּה צִוִּיתִי אוֹתָם לֵאמֹר
שִׁמְעוּ בְקוֹלִי וְהָיִיתִי לָכֶם לֵאלֹהִים וְאַתֶּם
תִּהְיוּ־לִי לְעָם וַהֲלַכְתֶּם בְּכָל־הַדֶּרֶךְ
אֲשֶׁר אֲצַוֶּה אֶתְכֶם לְמַעַן יִיטַב לָכֶם׃
24 וְלֹא שָׁמְעוּ וְלֹא־הִטּוּ אֶת־אָזְנָם וַיֵּלְכוּ
בְּמֹעֵצוֹת בִּשְׁרִרוּת לִבָּם הָרָע וַיִּהְיוּ
לְאָחוֹר וְלֹא לְפָנִים׃ 25 לְמִן־הַיּוֹם אֲשֶׁר
יָצְאוּ אֲבוֹתֵיכֶם מֵאֶרֶץ מִצְרַיִם עַד הַיּוֹם
הַזֶּה וָאֶשְׁלַח אֲלֵיכֶם אֶת־כָּל־עֲבָדַי
הַנְּבִיאִים יוֹם הַשְׁכֵּם וְשָׁלֹחַ׃ 26 וְלוֹא
שָׁמְעוּ אֵלַי וְלֹא הִטּוּ אֶת־אָזְנָם וַיַּקְשׁוּ
אֶת־עָרְפָּם הֵרֵעוּ מֵאֲבוֹתָם׃

27 וְדִבַּרְתָּ אֲלֵיהֶם אֶת־כָּל־הַדְּבָרִים הָאֵלֶּה
וְלֹא יִשְׁמְעוּ אֵלֶיךָ וְקָרָאתָ אֲלֵיהֶם וְלֹא

Jeremiah 7:23. that I may be your God For the covenantal formulary, see Exod. 6:7, 19:5; Lev. 26:12; Jer. 31:33.

them, but they will not respond to you. 28Then
say to them: This is the nation that would not obey the LORD their God, that would not accept rebuke. Faithfulness has perished, vanished from their mouths.

29Shear your locks and cast them away,
Take up a lament on the heights,
For the LORD has spurned and cast off
The brood that provoked His wrath.

30For the people of Judah have done what displeases Me—declares the LORD. They have set up their abominations in the House which is called by My name, and they have defiled it.
31And they have built the shrines of Topheth in the Valley of Ben-hinnom to burn their sons and daughters in fire—which I never commanded, which never came to My mind.

32Assuredly, a time is coming—declares the LORD—when men shall no longer speak of Topheth or the Valley of Ben-hinnom, but of the Valley of Slaughter; and they shall bury in Topheth until no room is left.
33The carcasses of this people shall be food for the birds of the sky and the beasts of the earth, with none to frighten them off.
34And I will silence in the towns of Judah and the streets of Jerusalem the sound of mirth and gladness, the voice of bridegroom and bride. For the whole land shall fall to ruin.

8 At that time—declares the LORD—the bones of the kings of Judah, of its officers, of

יַעֲנוּכָה*׃ 28 וְאָמַרְתָּ אֲלֵיהֶם זֶה הַגּוֹי
אֲשֶׁר לוֹא־שָׁמְעוּ בְּקוֹל יְהוָה אֱלֹהָיו וְלֹא
לָקְחוּ מוּסָר אָבְדָה הָאֱמוּנָה וְנִכְרְתָה
מִפִּיהֶם׃ ס

29 גָּזִּי נִזְרֵךְ וְהַשְׁלִיכִי
וּשְׂאִי עַל־שְׁפָיִם קִינָה
כִּי מָאַס יְהוָה וַיִּטֹּשׁ
אֶת־דּוֹר עֶבְרָתוֹ׃

30 כִּי־עָשׂוּ בְנֵי־יְהוּדָה הָרַע בְּעֵינַי נְאֻם־
יְהוָה שָׂמוּ שִׁקּוּצֵיהֶם בַּבַּיִת אֲשֶׁר־נִקְרָא־
שְׁמִי עָלָיו לְטַמְּאוֹ׃ 31 וּבָנוּ בָּמוֹת הַתֹּפֶת
אֲשֶׁר בְּגֵיא בֶן־הִנֹּם לִשְׂרֹף אֶת־בְּנֵיהֶם
וְאֶת־בְּנֹתֵיהֶם בָּאֵשׁ אֲשֶׁר לֹא צִוִּיתִי וְלֹא
עָלְתָה עַל־לִבִּי׃ ס
32 לָכֵן הִנֵּה־יָמִים בָּאִים נְאֻם־יְהוָה וְלֹא־
יֵאָמֵר עוֹד הַתֹּפֶת וְגֵיא בֶן־הִנֹּם כִּי אִם־
גֵּיא הַהֲרֵגָה וְקָבְרוּ בְתֹפֶת מֵאֵין מָקוֹם׃
33 וְהָיְתָה נִבְלַת הָעָם הַזֶּה לְמַאֲכָל לְעוֹף
הַשָּׁמַיִם וּלְבֶהֱמַת הָאָרֶץ וְאֵין מַחֲרִיד׃
34 וְהִשְׁבַּתִּי ׀ מֵעָרֵי יְהוּדָה וּמֵחֻצוֹת
יְרוּשָׁלִַם קוֹל שָׂשׂוֹן וְקוֹל שִׂמְחָה קוֹל חָתָן
וְקוֹל כַּלָּה כִּי לְחָרְבָּה תִּהְיֶה הָאָרֶץ׃

ח בָּעֵת הַהִיא נְאֻם־יְהוָה ויציאו
יוֹצִיאוּ אֶת־עַצְמוֹת מַלְכֵי־יְהוּדָה וְאֶת־

v. 27. יתיר ה׳

29–34. Lament and judgment for apostasy. Two crimes are named: setting abominations in the Temple and sacrificing children. Both are mentioned in connection with Manasseh (2 Kings 21:4–7).

29. The language of this statement of doom ("For the LORD has spurned [*ma·as*] and cast off [*va-yittosh*] / The brood that provoked His wrath [*evrato*]") is similar to the language bespeaking the divine rejection of the shrine of Shilo in Ps. 78:59. The common phraseology clearly derives from a rhetorical tradition of doom sayings.

33. Exposure of the dead was considered a great dishonor and desecration throughout the ancient world. The Assyrian king Ashurbanipal, recording his action against Susa, the capital of

the priests, of the prophets, and of the inhabitants of Jerusalem shall be taken out of their
graves 2and exposed to the sun, the moon, and
all the host of heaven which they loved and
served and followed, to which they turned and
bowed down. They shall not be gathered for re-
burial; they shall become dung upon the face
of the earth. 3And death shall be preferable to
life for all that are left of this wicked folk, in
all the other places to which I shall banish
them—declares the LORD of Hosts.

עַצְמוֹת־שָׂרָיו וְאֶת־עַצְמוֹת הַכֹּהֲנִים
וְאֵת ׀ עַצְמוֹת הַנְּבִיאִים וְאֵת עַצְמוֹת
יוֹשְׁבֵי־יְרוּשָׁלָ͏ִם מִקִּבְרֵיהֶם׃ 2 וּשְׁטָחוּם
לַשֶּׁמֶשׁ וְלַיָּרֵחַ וּלְכֹל ׀ צְבָא הַשָּׁמַיִם אֲשֶׁר
אֲהֵבוּם וַאֲשֶׁר עֲבָדוּם וַאֲשֶׁר הָלְכוּ
אַחֲרֵיהֶם וַאֲשֶׁר דְּרָשׁוּם וַאֲשֶׁר הִשְׁתַּחֲווּ
לָהֶם לֹא יֵאָסְפוּ וְלֹא יִקָּבֵרוּ לְדֹמֶן
עַל־פְּנֵי הָאֲדָמָה יִהְיוּ׃ 3 וְנִבְחַר מָוֶת
מֵחַיִּים לְכֹל הַשְּׁאֵרִית הַנִּשְׁאָרִים מִן־
הַמִּשְׁפָּחָה הָרָעָה הַזֹּאת בְּכָל־הַמְּקֹמוֹת
הַנִּשְׁאָרִים אֲשֶׁר הִדַּחְתִּים שָׁם נְאֻם יְהוָה
צְבָאוֹת׃ ס

9 22Thus said the LORD:
Let not the wise man glory in his wisdom;
Let not the strong man glory in his strength;
Let not the rich man glory in his riches.
23But only in this should one glory:
In his earnest devotion to Me.
For I the LORD act with kindness,
Justice, and equity in the world;
For in these I delight
—declares the LORD.

ט 22 כֹּה ׀ אָמַר יְהוָה
אַל־יִתְהַלֵּל חָכָם בְּחָכְמָתוֹ
וְאַל־יִתְהַלֵּל הַגִּבּוֹר בִּגְבוּרָתוֹ
אַל־יִתְהַלֵּל עָשִׁיר בְּעָשְׁרוֹ׃
23 כִּי אִם־בְּזֹאת יִתְהַלֵּל הַמִּתְהַלֵּל
הַשְׂכֵּל וְיָדֹעַ אוֹתִי
כִּי אֲנִי יְהוָה עֹשֶׂה חֶסֶד
מִשְׁפָּט וּצְדָקָה בָּאָרֶץ
כִּי־בְאֵלֶּה חָפַצְתִּי
נְאֻם־יְהוָה׃ ס

Elam, states that he "ravaged, tore down, and laid open to the sun" the tombs of the former kings of that place. In ancient Judah, during the same period, Josiah desecrated the tombs of the shrine of Bethel and exposed the bones (2 Kings 23:16).

Jeremiah 9:23. kindness, / Justice, and equity Hebrew: *ḥesed, mishpat,* and *tz'dakah*. The last two terms constitute a pair that recurs frequently in the Bible as both a human and a divine ideal (see, e.g., Gen. 18:19). The triad of elements is also found elsewhere for God (Ps. 33:5, 89:15) and for mortals (Isa. 16:5). This verse shows the link between these divine attributes and the covenant ideal. The triad is also recited as a core element of the covenant espousal in Hos. 2:21. Both texts link this brief covenantal summary to knowledge of God. See also Maimonides, *Guide* III:53.

SH'MINI

שמיני

ט וַיְהִי֙ בַּיּ֣וֹם הַשְּׁמִינִ֔י קָרָ֣א מֹשֶׁ֔ה
לְאַהֲרֹ֖ן וּלְבָנָ֑יו וּלְזִקְנֵ֖י יִשְׂרָאֵֽל׃ 2 וַיֹּ֣אמֶר
אֶֽל־אַהֲרֹ֗ן קַח־לְךָ֙ עֵ֧גֶל בֶּן־בָּקָ֛ר לְחַטָּ֖את
וְאַ֣יִל לְעֹלָ֑ה תְּמִימִ֕ם וְהַקְרֵ֖ב לִפְנֵ֥י יְהוָֽה׃
3 וְאֶל־בְּנֵ֥י יִשְׂרָאֵ֖ל תְּדַבֵּ֣ר לֵאמֹ֑ר קְח֤וּ
שְׂעִיר־עִזִּים֙ לְחַטָּ֔את וְעֵ֨גֶל וָכֶ֧בֶשׂ בְּנֵֽי־
שָׁנָ֛ה תְּמִימִ֖ם לְעֹלָֽה׃ 4 וְשׁ֨וֹר וָאַ֜יִל
לִשְׁלָמִ֗ים לִזְבֹּ֙חַ֙ לִפְנֵ֣י יְהוָ֔ה וּמִנְחָ֖ה בְּלוּלָ֣ה
בַשָּׁ֑מֶן כִּ֣י הַיּ֔וֹם יְהוָ֖ה נִרְאָ֥ה אֲלֵיכֶֽם׃
5 וַיִּקְח֗וּ אֵ֚ת אֲשֶׁ֣ר צִוָּ֣ה מֹשֶׁ֔ה אֶל־פְּנֵ֖י אֹ֣הֶל
מוֹעֵ֑ד וַֽיִּקְרְבוּ֙ כָּל־הָ֣עֵדָ֔ה וַיַּֽעַמְד֖וּ לִפְנֵ֥י
יְהוָֽה׃ 6 וַיֹּ֣אמֶר מֹשֶׁ֔ה זֶ֧ה הַדָּבָ֛ר אֲשֶׁר־צִוָּ֥ה
יְהוָ֖ה תַּעֲשׂ֑וּ וְיֵרָ֥א אֲלֵיכֶ֖ם כְּב֥וֹד יְהוָֽה׃
7 וַיֹּ֨אמֶר מֹשֶׁ֜ה אֶֽל־אַהֲרֹ֗ן קְרַ֤ב אֶל־הַמִּזְבֵּ֙חַ֙

9 On the eighth day Moses called Aaron and his sons, and the elders of Israel. [2]He said to Aaron: "Take a calf of the herd for a purification offering and a ram for a burnt offering, without blemish, and bring them before the LORD. [3]And speak to the Israelites, saying: Take a he-goat for a purification offering; a calf and a lamb, yearlings without blemish, for a burnt offering; [4]and an ox and a ram for an offering of well-being to sacrifice before the LORD; and a grain offering with oil mixed in. For today the LORD will appear to you."

[5]They brought to the front of the Tent of Meeting the things that Moses had commanded, and the whole community came forward and stood before the LORD. [6]Moses said: "This is what the LORD has commanded that you do, that the Presence of the LORD may ap-

THE INITIATION OF FORMAL WORSHIP (*continued*)

THE FIRST CELEBRATION OF SACRIFICE (9:1–24)

This chapter describes what took place after the seven days of ordination of Aaron and his sons as priests.

1. elders of Israel The "elders" (*z'kenim*) represented the people. See Comment to 4:15.

2. He said to Aaron: "Take a calf" See Comments to 8:14–18, where only the priesthood is involved. Here all of the people are involved. The sequence of purification offering and burnt offering was ordained both for the priesthood and for the people.

4. For today the LORD will appear to you The main purpose of the celebrations (v. 6).

5. that Moses had commanded Moses had an enhanced role in this celebration as the transmitter of God's commands. In Leviticus, it is usually God who commands, not Moses.

CHAPTER 9

This *parashah* begins by recalling a tragic incident that marred the installation ceremony of Aaron and his sons as *kohanim*. The focus of the text then shifts to the second of the major concerns of Leviticus, the avoidance of ritual impurity (*tum·ah*), which would separate the Israelite from contact with God and God's sanctuary.

1. eighth day The seven-day week symbolizes a complete unit, and an eighth day represents starting over at a new level, concluding an octave and leading to "a higher octave" (Hirsch). Thus a baby boy is circumcised and brought into the Covenant on the eighth day, beginning the second week of his life as a member of the Covenant. The Talmud compares the first seven days of celebrating the construction of the tabernacle to the seven days of Creation (BT Meg. 10b). On the eighth day, we are challenged to begin living in the day-to-day world of ordinary events.

6. All of our activities in the synagogue, not only at prayer but in classes and at meetings, should have a goal of experiencing the presence of God.

pear to you." 7Then Moses said to Aaron: "Come forward to the altar and sacrifice your purification offering and your burnt offering, making expiation for yourself and for the people; and sacrifice the people's offering and make expiation for them, as the LORD has commanded."

8Aaron came forward to the altar and slaughtered his calf of purification offering. 9Aaron's sons brought the blood to him; he dipped his finger in the blood and put it on the horns of the altar; and he poured out the rest of the blood at the base of the altar. 10The fat, the kidneys, and the protuberance of the liver from the purification offering he turned into smoke on the altar—as the LORD had commanded Moses; 11and the flesh and the skin were consumed in fire outside the camp. 12Then he slaughtered the burnt offering. Aaron's sons passed the blood to him, and he dashed it against all sides of the altar. 13They passed the burnt offering to him in sections, as well as the head, and he turned it into smoke on the altar. 14He washed the entrails and the legs, and turned them into smoke on the altar with the burnt offering.

15Next he brought forward the people's offering. He took the goat for the people's purification offering, and slaughtered it, and presented it as a purification offering like the previous one. 16He brought forward the burnt

וַעֲשֵׂה אֶת־חַטָּאתְךָ וְאֶת־עֹלָתֶךָ וְכַפֵּר
בַּעַדְךָ וּבְעַד הָעָם וַעֲשֵׂה אֶת־קָרְבַּן הָעָם
וְכַפֵּר בַּעֲדָם כַּאֲשֶׁר צִוָּה יְהוָה׃
8 וַיִּקְרַב אַהֲרֹן אֶל־הַמִּזְבֵּחַ וַיִּשְׁחַט אֶת־
עֵגֶל הַחַטָּאת אֲשֶׁר־לוֹ׃ 9 וַיַּקְרִבוּ בְּנֵי
אַהֲרֹן אֶת־הַדָּם אֵלָיו וַיִּטְבֹּל אֶצְבָּעוֹ בַּדָּם
וַיִּתֵּן עַל־קַרְנוֹת הַמִּזְבֵּחַ וְאֶת־הַדָּם יָצַק
אֶל־יְסוֹד הַמִּזְבֵּחַ׃ 10 וְאֶת־הַחֵלֶב וְאֶת־
הַכְּלָיֹת וְאֶת־הַיֹּתֶרֶת מִן־הַכָּבֵד מִן־
הַחַטָּאת הִקְטִיר הַמִּזְבֵּחָה כַּאֲשֶׁר צִוָּה
יְהוָה אֶת־מֹשֶׁה׃ 11 וְאֶת־הַבָּשָׂר וְאֶת־
הָעוֹר שָׂרַף בָּאֵשׁ מִחוּץ לַמַּחֲנֶה׃
12 וַיִּשְׁחַט אֶת־הָעֹלָה וַיַּמְצִאוּ בְּנֵי אַהֲרֹן
אֵלָיו אֶת־הַדָּם וַיִּזְרְקֵהוּ עַל־הַמִּזְבֵּחַ
סָבִיב׃ 13 וְאֶת־הָעֹלָה הִמְצִיאוּ אֵלָיו
לִנְתָחֶיהָ וְאֶת־הָרֹאשׁ וַיַּקְטֵר עַל־הַמִּזְבֵּחַ׃
14 וַיִּרְחַץ אֶת־הַקֶּרֶב וְאֶת־הַכְּרָעָיִם וַיַּקְטֵר
עַל־הָעֹלָה הַמִּזְבֵּחָה׃
15 וַיַּקְרֵב אֵת קָרְבַּן הָעָם וַיִּקַּח אֶת־שְׂעִיר
הַחַטָּאת אֲשֶׁר לָעָם וַיִּשְׁחָטֵהוּ וַיְחַטְּאֵהוּ
כָּרִאשׁוֹן׃ 16 וַיַּקְרֵב אֶת־הָעֹלָה וַיַּעֲשֶׂהָ

7. Come forward to the altar Moses turned over the conduct of the ritual to Aaron by inviting him to officiate at the altar for the first time.

making expiation for yourself and for the people The purification offering of the priesthood indirectly served the people as well; nevertheless, an additional purification offering on their behalf was required.

9. Aaron's sons brought the blood to him This procedural detail is missing elsewhere. Practically speaking, the officiant needed the assistance of another priest.

7. Moses said to Aaron: "Come forward" There is a tradition that Aaron had to be urged to bring his purification offering, a calf, because he was embarrassed. It reminded him of his role in fashioning the Golden Calf. Moses, however, assured him: "Your sin has been forgiven because you were ashamed" (*M'norat Ha-Ma·or*). The ability to feel shame is one of the defining characteristics of a moral human being. It arises from an awareness of the gap between who we are and who we might be. Furthermore, it recognizes the authority of God and the right of other people to judge us.

offering and sacrificed it according to regulation. 17He then brought forward the grain
offering and, taking a handful of it, he turned
it into smoke on the altar—in addition to the
burnt offering of the morning. 18He slaughtered
the ox and the ram, the people's sacrifice of
well-being. Aaron's sons passed the blood to
him—which he dashed against every side of the
altar—19and the fat parts of the ox and the ram:
the broad tail, the covering [fat], the kidneys,
and the protuberances of the livers. 20They laid
these fat parts over the breasts; and Aaron
turned the fat parts into smoke on the altar,
21and elevated the breasts and the right thighs
as an elevation offering before the LORD—as
Moses had commanded.

22Aaron lifted his hands toward the people
and blessed them; and he stepped down after
offering the purification offering, the burnt
offering, and the offering of well-being. 23Moses
and Aaron then went inside the Tent of Meeting. When they came out, they blessed the people; and the Presence of the LORD appeared to
all the people. 24Fire came forth from before the
LORD and consumed the burnt offering and the
fat parts on the altar. And all the people saw,
and shouted, and fell on their faces.

שני כַּמִּשְׁפָּט׃ 17 וַיַּקְרֵב אֶת־הַמִּנְחָה וַיְמַלֵּא
כַפּוֹ מִמֶּנָּה וַיַּקְטֵר עַל־הַמִּזְבֵּחַ מִלְּבַד עֹלַת
הַבֹּקֶר׃ 18 וַיִּשְׁחַט אֶת־הַשּׁוֹר וְאֶת־הָאַיִל
זֶבַח הַשְּׁלָמִים אֲשֶׁר לָעָם וַיַּמְצִאוּ בְּנֵי
אַהֲרֹן אֶת־הַדָּם אֵלָיו וַיִּזְרְקֵהוּ עַל־
הַמִּזְבֵּחַ סָבִיב׃ 19 וְאֶת־הַחֲלָבִים מִן־
הַשּׁוֹר וּמִן־הָאַיִל הָאַלְיָה וְהַמְכַסֶּה
וְהַכְּלָיֹת וְיֹתֶרֶת הַכָּבֵד׃ 20 וַיָּשִׂימוּ אֶת־
הַחֲלָבִים עַל־הֶחָזוֹת וַיַּקְטֵר הַחֲלָבִים
הַמִּזְבֵּחָה׃ 21 וְאֵת הֶחָזוֹת וְאֵת שׁוֹק הַיָּמִין
הֵנִיף אַהֲרֹן תְּנוּפָה לִפְנֵי יְהוָה כַּאֲשֶׁר
צִוָּה מֹשֶׁה׃
22 וַיִּשָּׂא אַהֲרֹן אֶת־ידו יָדָיו אֶל־הָעָם
וַיְבָרְכֵם וַיֵּרֶד מֵעֲשֹׂת הַחַטָּאת וְהָעֹלָה
וְהַשְּׁלָמִים׃ 23 וַיָּבֹא מֹשֶׁה וְאַהֲרֹן אֶל־
אֹהֶל מוֹעֵד וַיֵּצְאוּ וַיְבָרְכוּ אֶת־הָעָם וַיֵּרָא
שלישי כְבוֹד־יְהוָה אֶל־כָּל־הָעָם׃ 24 וַתֵּצֵא אֵשׁ
מִלִּפְנֵי יְהוָה וַתֹּאכַל עַל־הַמִּזְבֵּחַ אֶת־
הָעֹלָה וְאֶת־הַחֲלָבִים וַיַּרְא כָּל־הָעָם
וַיָּרֹנּוּ וַיִּפְּלוּ עַל־פְּנֵיהֶם׃

10 Now Aaron's sons Nadab and Abihu

י וַיִּקְחוּ בְנֵי־אַהֲרֹן נָדָב וַאֲבִיהוּא אִישׁ

18. The extent of the sacrifice was greater than usual on this occasion, requiring both an ox and a ram.

22. Aaron lifted his hands toward the people and blessed them Raising the hands toward God was a characteristic gesture of prayer. Here, Aaron faced the people and raised his hands over them as he blessed them.

23. Moses and Aaron then went inside the Tent of Meeting Perhaps they went in to pray for the anticipated appearance of God's Presence (*Sifra*) or for the miraculous ignition of the altar fire (Ibn Ezra).

24. Fire came forth from before the LORD The fire issued from God's Presence (the *Kavod*), which itself was a fire enveloped in a thick cloud that pervaded the tent.

ADMONITIONS ON PRIESTLY CONDUCT (10:1–20)

To emphasize the necessity of precise compliance with all the ritual laws and regulations for priestly conduct, this chapter begins with the untimely death of two of Aaron's sons, Nadab and Abihu, who made an improper incense offering.

each took his fire pan, put fire in it, and laid
incense on it; and they offered before the LORD
alien fire, which He had not enjoined upon
them. 2And fire came forth from the LORD and
consumed them; thus they died at the instance
of the LORD. 3Then Moses said to Aaron, "This
is what the LORD meant when He said:

Through those near to Me I show Myself holy,

מַחְתָּתוֹ וַיִּתְּנוּ בָהֵן֙ אֵ֔שׁ וַיָּשִׂ֥ימוּ עָלֶ֖יהָ
קְטֹ֑רֶת וַיַּקְרִ֜בוּ לִפְנֵ֤י יְהוָה֙ אֵ֣שׁ זָרָ֔ה אֲשֶׁ֥ר
לֹ֦א צִוָּ֖ה אֹתָֽם׃ 2 וַתֵּ֥צֵא אֵ֛שׁ מִלִּפְנֵ֥י יְהוָ֖ה
וַתֹּ֣אכַל אוֹתָ֑ם וַיָּמֻ֖תוּ לִפְנֵ֥י יְהוָֽה׃ 3 וַיֹּ֨אמֶר
מֹשֶׁ֜ה אֶֽל־אַהֲרֹ֗ן ה֩וּא אֲשֶׁר־דִּבֶּ֨ר יְהוָ֤ה ׀
לֵאמֹר֙

בִּקְרֹבַ֣י אֶקָּדֵ֔שׁ

THE DEATH OF NADAB AND ABIHU: A DRAMATIC PRECEDENT (vv. 1–7)

1. put fire in it Each placed coals or embers on his fire pan.

alien fire Hebrew: *esh zarah,* the incense itself. They brought "an alien [incense offering by] fire," one that had not been specifically ordained.

2. fire came forth from the LORD This may refer to the fire mentioned in 9:24, which came forth from inside the Tent of Meeting and consumed the sacrifices offered at the dedication of the tabernacle (Rashbam).

3. Through those near to Me I show Myself holy Priests who adhere to the regulations of their office and protect the purity of the sanctuary are "near" to and sanctify God; in turn, the sanctuary is favored by God's Presence. When, as in

---

CHAPTER 10

The Torah narrates the death of Nadab and Abihu very briefly, never telling us explicitly what they did to cause them to be struck down. Therefore, commentators over the generations have used their imaginations to speculate about what grave sin they might have committed. One explanation is that they brought the instruments for making a fire into the Tent, not realizing that on this special occasion God was going to send fire miraculously from heaven (9:24). Because they were too close to that fire, they were killed. Their sin, if any, was a lack of faith, trying to help God in a situation in which God did not need their help (Mekh.).

Most of the Sages, however, judge them less charitably. Some find them guilty of egotism (each took his own fire pan, consulting neither with each other nor with their father, Aaron) or of entering the sanctuary drunk (for which reason priests are told in verse 9 not to drink wine before entering the sanctuary, Lev. R. 12:1) or of entering so casually dressed that they showed disrespect for their surroundings (ibidem). Others accuse them of impatience to succeed Moses and Aaron as leaders of the people. The "strange fire" they bore was the fire of ambition, which prompted them to say, "When will these old men, our father and our uncle, die already so that we can take their place?" Based on the comment of the *Sifra* that their sin was not consulting with their father, Hirsch, champion of modern Orthodoxy, identifies their sin as making themselves the highest authority and disregarding the tradition of their elders.

One intriguing interpretation sees them as motivated by excessive piety. Out of their love for the divine, they tried to come too close to God who is like a raging fire (*Or Ha-Ḥayyim*). They were motivated by a passion for closeness to God that God did not command because it was too dangerous. (Nadab means "willing," and Abihu means "[God] is my Father.") They could not be satisfied with rituals and sacrifices but had to draw so close to God that they were consumed by the strange fire in their souls. Perhaps Aaron is warned so often and so sternly about when and how to enter the tabernacle lest he too be struck down in his desire to be one with God.

A homiletic interpretation fastens on the rabbinic legend (BT Sanh. 52a) that the fire consumed their souls but left their bodies intact. (Thus they could be removed from the site by dragging them by their garments, verse 5.) It suggests that their fate was to suffer a spiritual death in their lifetime. In direct contrast to the previous interpretation, it sees them as no longer feeling reverence or holiness in carrying out their sacred tasks. They were emotionally burned out. Their souls had shriveled even as they continued to go through the motions of religious ritual.

3. Through those near to Me I show Myself holy Hirsch pictures God as saying, "The more a person stands out from among the peo-

And gain glory before all the people."
And Aaron was silent.
4Moses called Mishael and Elzaphan, sons of
Uzziel the uncle of Aaron, and said to them,
"Come forward and carry your kinsmen away
from the front of the sanctuary to a place outside
the camp." 5They came forward and carried
them out of the camp by their tunics, as Moses
had ordered. 6And Moses said to Aaron and to
his sons Eleazar and Ithamar, "Do not bare your
heads and do not rend your clothes, lest you die
and anger strike the whole community. But
your kinsmen, all the house of Israel, shall bewail the burning that the LORD has wrought.
7And so do not go outside the entrance of the
Tent of Meeting, lest you die, for the LORD's
anointing oil is upon you." And they did as
Moses had bidden.

וְעַל־פְּנֵי כָל־הָעָם אֶכָּבֵד
וַיִּדֹּם אַהֲרֹן׃
4 וַיִּקְרָא מֹשֶׁה אֶל־מִישָׁאֵל וְאֶל אֶלְצָפָן
בְּנֵי עֻזִּיאֵל דֹּד אַהֲרֹן וַיֹּאמֶר אֲלֵהֶם קִרְבוּ*
שְׂאוּ אֶת־אֲחֵיכֶם מֵאֵת פְּנֵי־הַקֹּדֶשׁ אֶל־
מִחוּץ לַמַּחֲנֶה׃ 5 וַיִּקְרְבוּ וַיִּשָּׂאֻם בְּכֻתֳּנֹתָם
אֶל־מִחוּץ לַמַּחֲנֶה כַּאֲשֶׁר דִּבֶּר מֹשֶׁה׃
6 וַיֹּאמֶר מֹשֶׁה אֶל־אַהֲרֹן וּלְאֶלְעָזָר
וּלְאִיתָמָר ׀ בָּנָיו רָאשֵׁיכֶם אַל־תִּפְרָעוּ ׀
וּבִגְדֵיכֶם לֹא־תִפְרֹמוּ וְלֹא תָמֻתוּ וְעַל
כָּל־הָעֵדָה יִקְצֹף וַאֲחֵיכֶם כָּל־בֵּית יִשְׂרָאֵל
יִבְכּוּ אֶת־הַשְּׂרֵפָה אֲשֶׁר שָׂרַף יְהוָה׃
7 וּמִפֶּתַח אֹהֶל מוֹעֵד לֹא תֵצְאוּ פֶּן־תָּמֻתוּ
כִּי־שֶׁמֶן מִשְׁחַת יְהוָה עֲלֵיכֶם וַיַּעֲשׂוּ
כִּדְבַר מֹשֶׁה׃ פ

v. 4. שני טעמים

this case, priests flout the divine will, God exercises punitive power, compelling all to recognize God's authority.

Aaron was silent Hebrew: *va-yiddom Aharon.* The traditional interpretation has it that Aaron accepted God's harsh judgment and did not cry out or complain at his painful loss.

4. from the front of the sanctuary The two priests had entered the Tent of Meeting. They probably were struck down as they were departing, when they were already in the courtyard outside the tent.

to a place outside the camp The corpses had to be removed from the camp, a requirement for any ritually impure object. Relatively little is known of ancient Israelite burial customs, except that the dead were buried away from the settled areas, because their bodies were deemed ritually impure.

5. by their tunics Apparently, the bodies of the two priests were not completely consumed by God's fire. The flame that killed them probably blasted their faces and left their clothing intact.

6. bare Hebrew: *para,* "to dishevel" the hair, which involves baring the head as well.

lest you die At the hand of God, as a punishment.

and anger strike the whole community The circumstances surrounding the deaths of Nadab and Abihu—occurring at the time of their consecration and purification—prevented, indeed forbade, their father and brothers from mourning for them, because their sanctification took precedence over their bereavement. The rest of the people, however, were to mourn.

7. do not go outside the entrance of the Tent of Meeting The priests were forbidden to leave the sacred precinct of the inner court.

---

ple as a teacher and a leader, the less will I show indulgence when that person does wrong." Prominence leads not to privilege but to responsibility.

Aaron was silent The Torah usually does not call attention to someone's not speaking. What, then, is the unusual significance of Aaron's silence? That he accepted God's decree without protest? That his anguish was too great for him to put into words? That he was tempted to burst out in anger at the unfairness of what had happened to his family but was able to restrain himself? Perhaps the text is suggesting that there are more possibilities—and more power—in silence than in any words.

8And the Lord spoke to Aaron, saying: 9Drink no wine or other intoxicant, you or your sons, when you enter the Tent of Meeting, that you may not die. This is a law for all time throughout the ages, 10for you must distinguish between the sacred and the profane, and between the impure and the pure; 11and you must teach the Israelites all the laws which the Lord has imparted to them through Moses.

12Moses spoke to Aaron and to his remaining sons, Eleazar and Ithamar: Take the grain offering that is left over from the Lord's gifts and eat it unleavened beside the altar, for it is most holy. 13You shall eat it in the sacred precinct, inasmuch as it is your due, and that of your children, from the Lord's gifts; for so I have been commanded. 14But the breast of elevation offering and the thigh of gift offering you, and your sons and daughters with you, may eat in any pure place, for they have been assigned as a due to you and your children from the Israelites' sacrifices of well-being. 15Together with the fat of fire offering, they must present the thigh of gift offering and the breast of elevation offering, which are to be elevated as an elevation offering before the Lord, and which are to be your due and that of your children with you for all time—as the Lord has commanded.

16Then Moses inquired about the goat of purification offering, and it had already been

8 וַיְדַבֵּ֣ר יְהֹוָ֔ה אֶֽל־אַהֲרֹ֖ן לֵאמֹֽר׃ 9 יַ֣יִן וְשֵׁכָ֞ר אַל־תֵּ֣שְׁתְּ ׀ אַתָּ֣ה ׀ וּבָנֶ֣יךָ אִתָּ֗ךְ בְּבֹאֲכֶ֛ם אֶל־אֹ֥הֶל מוֹעֵ֖ד וְלֹ֣א תָמֻ֑תוּ חֻקַּ֥ת עוֹלָ֖ם לְדֹרֹֽתֵיכֶֽם׃ 10 וּֽלְהַבְדִּ֔יל בֵּ֥ין הַקֹּ֖דֶשׁ וּבֵ֣ין הַחֹ֑ל וּבֵ֥ין הַטָּמֵ֖א וּבֵ֥ין הַטָּהֽוֹר׃ 11 וּלְהוֹרֹ֖ת אֶת־בְּנֵ֣י יִשְׂרָאֵ֑ל אֵ֚ת כׇּל־הַ֣חֻקִּ֔ים אֲשֶׁ֨ר דִּבֶּ֧ר יְהֹוָ֛ה אֲלֵיהֶ֖ם בְּיַד־מֹשֶֽׁה׃ פ

רביעי 12 וַיְדַבֵּ֨ר מֹשֶׁ֜ה אֶֽל־אַהֲרֹ֗ן וְאֶ֣ל אֶלְעָזָר֩ וְאֶל־אִ֨יתָמָ֥ר ׀ בָּנָיו֮ הַנּֽוֹתָרִים֒ קְח֣וּ אֶת־הַמִּנְחָ֗ה הַנּוֹתֶ֙רֶת֙ מֵאִשֵּׁ֣י יְהֹוָ֔ה וְאִכְל֥וּהָ מַצּ֖וֹת אֵ֣צֶל הַמִּזְבֵּ֑חַ כִּ֛י קֹ֥דֶשׁ קׇֽדָשִׁ֖ים הִֽוא׃ 13 וַאֲכַלְתֶּ֤ם אֹתָהּ֙ בְּמָק֣וֹם קָדֹ֔שׁ כִּ֣י חׇקְךָ֤ וְחׇק־בָּנֶ֙יךָ֙ הִ֔וא מֵאִשֵּׁ֖י יְהֹוָ֑ה כִּי־כֵ֖ן צֻוֵּֽיתִי׃ 14 וְאֵת֩ חֲזֵ֨ה הַתְּנוּפָ֜ה וְאֵ֣ת ׀ שׁ֣וֹק הַתְּרוּמָ֗ה תֹּֽאכְלוּ֙ בְּמָק֣וֹם טָה֔וֹר אַתָּ֕ה וּבָנֶ֥יךָ וּבְנֹתֶ֖יךָ אִתָּ֑ךְ כִּֽי־חׇקְךָ֤ וְחׇק־בָּנֶ֙יךָ֙ נִתְּנ֔וּ מִזִּבְחֵ֖י שַׁלְמֵ֥י בְּנֵ֥י יִשְׂרָאֵֽל׃ 15 שׁ֣וֹק הַתְּרוּמָ֞ה וַחֲזֵ֣ה הַתְּנוּפָ֗ה עַ֣ל אִשֵּׁ֤י הַחֲלָבִים֙ יָבִ֔יאוּ לְהָנִ֥יף תְּנוּפָ֖ה לִפְנֵ֣י יְהֹוָ֑ה וְהָיָ֨ה לְךָ֜ וּלְבָנֶ֤יךָ אִתְּךָ֙ לְחׇק־עוֹלָ֔ם כַּאֲשֶׁ֖ר צִוָּ֥ה יְהֹוָֽה׃

שי 16 וְאֵ֣ת ׀ שְׂעִ֣יר הַֽחַטָּ֗את דָּרֹ֥שׁ* דָּרַ֛שׁ מֹשֶׁ֖ה וְהִנֵּ֣ה שֹׂרָ֑ף וַ֠יִּקְצֹ֠ף עַל־אֶלְעָזָ֤ר

v. 16.   במסורה מסומנת "חצי התורה בתיבות", ולא אמת היא אבל יש ב"דרש דרש" רמז על אופן קריאה של התורה

RULES FOR THE PRIESTHOOD   (vv. 8–15)

9–10. Drinking intoxicants would impair the faculties of the priests, who would then be unable to distinguish between the sacred and the profane.

MOSES MONITORS THE PRIESTS AND THE CULT   (vv. 16–20)

16. *Moses inquired about the goat of purification offering* This refers to the purification offering provided by the people as part of the ded-

9. drink no wine This prohibition resulted not from Nadab and Abihu having been drunk but from the danger that the bereaved relatives would drown their sorrows in intoxicants and not be fit to carry on their responsibilities (Hoffman). Although wine "cheers the heart"

(Ps. 104:15), *kohanim* were to avoid it. When we come before God, our joy should stem from serving God, without the use of external stimulants (Simḥah Bunem).

16. Moses inquired The word translated as "inquired" (*darash*) is said to be the middle

burned! He was angry with Eleazar and Ithamar,
Aaron's remaining sons, and said, 17"Why did
you not eat the purification offering in the sacred area? For it is most holy, and He has given
it to you to remove the guilt of the community
and to make expiation for them before the
LORD. 18Since its blood was not brought inside
the sanctuary, you should certainly have eaten
it in the sanctuary, as I commanded." 19And
Aaron spoke to Moses, "See, this day they
brought their purification offering and their
burnt offering before the LORD, and such things
have befallen me! Had I eaten purification offering today, would the LORD have approved?"
20And when Moses heard this, he approved.

וְעַל־אִיתָמָר בְּנֵי אַהֲרֹן הַנּוֹתָרִם לֵאמֹר׃
17 מַדּוּעַ לֹא־אֲכַלְתֶּם אֶת־הַחַטָּאת
בִּמְקוֹם הַקֹּדֶשׁ כִּי קֹדֶשׁ קָדָשִׁים הִוא
וְאֹתָהּ ׀ נָתַן לָכֶם לָשֵׂאת אֶת־עֲוֺן הָעֵדָה
לְכַפֵּר עֲלֵיהֶם לִפְנֵי יְהוָה׃ 18 הֵן לֹא־הוּבָא
אֶת־דָּמָהּ אֶל־הַקֹּדֶשׁ פְּנִימָה אָכוֹל
תֹּאכְלוּ אֹתָהּ בַּקֹּדֶשׁ כַּאֲשֶׁר צִוֵּיתִי׃
19 וַיְדַבֵּר אַהֲרֹן אֶל־מֹשֶׁה הֵן הַיּוֹם הִקְרִיבוּ
אֶת־חַטָּאתָם וְאֶת־עֹלָתָם לִפְנֵי יְהוָה
וַתִּקְרֶאנָה אֹתִי כָּאֵלֶּה וְאָכַלְתִּי חַטָּאת
הַיּוֹם הַיִיטַב בְּעֵינֵי יְהוָה׃ 20 וַיִּשְׁמַע מֹשֶׁה
וַיִּיטַב בְּעֵינָיו׃ פ

11 The LORD spoke to Moses and Aaron,

ששי **יא** וַיְדַבֵּר יְהוָה אֶל־מֹשֶׁה וְאֶל־אַהֲרֹן

ication rites in 9:3,15. Moses discovered that on this occasion the priestly portions of the purification offering had been burned on the altar—the priests had not eaten them as they were obliged to do. Having disobeyed instructions, they incurred Moses' anger. He spoke directly to Aaron's sons in deference to Aaron.

17. Although the blood rites incorporated in the purification offering (*ḥattat*) constituted the primary means of expiation, the sacred meals of the priests were also essential. It was the duty of the priests to eat their assigned portions of the *ḥattat* brought by the people.

18. Since its blood was not brought inside the sanctuary This refers to the rule in 6:23.

19. Aaron sought to excuse the failure of the priests to eat their portions of the sacrifice by explaining to Moses that his sons thought they should not eat of the sacrifice because they were in mourning.

---

word of the Torah. The essence of the Torah is continued inquiry and study. "The ideal Jew is not so much a *learned* Jew as a *learning* Jew" (*Emet Ve-Emunah*).

He was angry The Midrash teaches: Look at what anger can do, even to a person as wise and pious as Moses. When Moses became angry, his knowledge of the law left him, and he forgot that a priest in mourning was not permitted to eat of the sacrifice (Lev. R. 13:1). It may be that Moses was speaking out of his own pain and sense of loss or perhaps even out of a sense of guilt at not having been able to prevent the calamity. What Aaron needed at that moment, however, were not words of rebuke but words of comfort, validating his feelings of loss, pain, and even outrage. Jewish law counsels us against trying to comfort people immediately after they have suffered a loss ("when the dead body is still before them").

19. Had I eaten purification offering today Aaron responds that because his family had sinned and had been punished publicly, identifying them publicly as sinners, it was not appropriate for them to stand before God bearing the people's prayers for atonement.

20. Moses is not too proud to admit that he was wrong (Rashi). This exchange between Moses and Aaron reflects the conflict in the life of any person who must simultaneously be public servant, officiating at public ceremonies, and private individual with personal grief and concerns. Aaron must leave his public role temporarily to deal with his grief, whereas Moses, who sometimes seems to have compromised his personal life in favor of his public role (see Comments to Exod.18:6 and Num. 12:1), urges him to give his public responsibilities priority because people depend on him.

לֵאמֹר אֲלֵהֶם׃ 2 דַּבְּרוּ אֶל־בְּנֵי יִשְׂרָאֵל
לֵאמֹר
זֹאת הַחַיָּה אֲשֶׁר תֹּאכְלוּ מִכָּל־הַבְּהֵמָה
אֲשֶׁר עַל־הָאָרֶץ׃ 3 כֹּל ׀ מַפְרֶסֶת פַּרְסָה
וְשֹׁסַעַת שֶׁסַע פְּרָסֹת מַעֲלַת גֵּרָה בַּבְּהֵמָה
אֹתָהּ תֹּאכֵלוּ׃ 4 אַךְ אֶת־זֶה לֹא תֹאכְלוּ
מִמַּעֲלֵי הַגֵּרָה וּמִמַּפְרִיסֵי הַפַּרְסָה אֶת־

saying to them: 2Speak to the Israelite people
thus:
These are the creatures that you may eat from
among all the land animals: 3any animal that
has true hoofs, with clefts through the hoofs,
and that chews the cud—such you may eat. 4The
following, however, of those that either chew
the cud or have true hoofs, you shall not eat:

THE LAWS OF KASHRUT: PROPER FOODS AND VESSELS (11:1–47)

This chapter is one of two major collections of dietary laws in the Torah. The other collection is found in Deut. 14.

PERMITTED AND FORBIDDEN FOOD SOURCES (vv. 1–23)

LAND ANIMALS (vv. 2–8)

2. creatures . . . land animals Hebrew: *ḥayyah . . . b'hemah;* here the former is used as a general term, while the latter refers specifically to that which lives on the land.

3. any animal that has true hoofs To qualify as pure, an animal's hoofs must be split all the way through, producing two toes, of a sort, so that the animal in question does not walk on paws.

4. you shall not eat The list of four impure land animals comprises borderline cases, animals that exhibit one but not both of the required phys-

---

CHAPTER 11

The basis for one major pillar of the Jewish dietary code, the separation of meat and dairy products, is enunciated in Exod. 34:26. Now the Torah adds a second pillar, the distinction between the living creatures that may be eaten and those that are forbidden.

An attentive reading of this chapter clearly shows that the dietary laws are not based on considerations of health, neither in terms of the animals permitted or forbidden nor out of concern for meat spoiling in the desert heat. (Does one need a law that prohibits eating spoiled meat?) "There is nothing intrinsically 'impure' about pigs or camels, except that the Torah forbids them to Israelites" (Hoffman). There may be moral or aesthetic considerations for shunning some creatures because of undesirable traits, e.g., flesh-eating animals and birds of prey; if we are forbidden to ingest blood (Lev. 17), we should avoid the flesh of animals and fowl that ingest blood.

The overriding purpose of the dietary code is explicit: "You shall sanctify yourselves and be holy, for I am holy" (v. 44). The dietary laws constitute a way of sanctifying the act of eating. The eating of meat requires killing a living creature, constantly seen by the Torah as a compromise. These laws elevate the eating of meat to a level of sanctity by introducing categories of permitted and forbidden. For animals, eating is a matter of instinct; only human beings can choose on moral or religious grounds not to eat something otherwise available.

The dietary laws are given incrementally in the Torah, forbidding boiling a kid in its mother's milk; then prohibiting the ingestion of blood; then declaring certain species of mammal, fish, and fowl unfit for consumption. Similarly, many Jews who begin from a position of limited observance can commit themselves to sanctifying their mealtimes in an incremental manner. They may begin by avoiding pork and shellfish, continue by separating meat and dairy products, and so on. No one need feel like a hypocrite for not keeping all of the commandments immediately. What is important is to be on the path of observance, to be, in the words of *Emet Ve-Emunah,* a "striving" Jew.

HALAKHAH L'MA·ASEH

11:3. any animal For meat to be *kasher* ("kosher," fit for consumption under Jewish law), it must not only come from the animals designated in this chapter (e.g., cows, sheep, goats, buffalos, and deer) but must also be slaughtered, soaked, salted, and prepared according to Jewish law. See Comments to Lev. 17:10; Deut. 12:21, 14:7.

the camel—although it chews the cud, it has no
true hoofs: it is impure for you; 5the daman—
although it chews the cud, it has no true hoofs:
it is impure for you; 6the hare—although it
chews the cud, it has no true hoofs: it is impure
for you; 7and the swine—although it has true
hoofs, with the hoofs cleft through, it does not
chew the cud: it is impure for you. 8You shall
not eat of their flesh or touch their carcasses;
they are impure for you.

9These you may eat of all that live in water:
anything in water, whether in the seas or in the
streams, that has fins and scales—these you may
eat. 10But anything in the seas or in the streams
that has no fins and scales, among all the swarming things of the water and among all the other
living creatures that are in the water—they are
an abomination for you 11and an abomination

הַגָּמָל כִּֽי־מַעֲלֵה גֵרָה הוּא וּפַרְסָה אֵינֶנּוּ
מַפְרִיס טָמֵא הוּא לָכֶם׃ 5 וְאֶת־הַשָּׁפָן
כִּֽי־מַעֲלֵה גֵרָה הוּא וּפַרְסָה לֹא יַפְרִיס
טָמֵא הוּא לָכֶם׃ 6 וְאֶת־הָאַרְנֶבֶת כִּֽי־
מַעֲלַת גֵּרָה הִוא וּפַרְסָה לֹא הִפְרִיסָה
טְמֵאָה הִוא לָכֶם׃ 7 וְאֶת־הַחֲזִיר כִּֽי־
מַפְרִיס פַּרְסָה הוּא וְשֹׁסַע שֶׁסַע פַּרְסָה
וְהוּא גֵּרָה לֹא־יִגָּר טָמֵא הוּא לָכֶם׃
8 מִבְּשָׂרָם לֹא תֹאכֵלוּ וּבְנִבְלָתָם לֹא תִגָּעוּ
טְמֵאִים הֵם לָכֶם׃
9 אֶת־זֶה תֹּאכְלוּ מִכֹּל אֲשֶׁר בַּמָּיִם כֹּל
אֲשֶׁר־לוֹ סְנַפִּיר וְקַשְׂקֶשֶׂת בַּמַּיִם בַּיַּמִּים
וּבַנְּחָלִים אֹתָם תֹּאכֵלוּ׃ 10 וְכֹל אֲשֶׁר
אֵין־לוֹ סְנַפִּיר וְקַשְׂקֶשֶׂת בַּיַּמִּים וּבַנְּחָלִים
מִכֹּל שֶׁרֶץ הַמַּיִם וּמִכֹּל נֶפֶשׁ הַחַיָּה
אֲשֶׁר בַּמַּיִם שֶׁקֶץ הֵם לָכֶם׃ 11 וְשֶׁקֶץ יִהְיוּ

ical criteria. There was a likelihood of mistaking such creatures for pure animals.

camel The hoof of the camel (an English word that derives from the Semitic word *gamal*) is split in its upper part, but bound together in its lower part.

5. daman A small mammal, the Syrian hyrax. It does not actually chew its cud, but gives that impression because of the protrusions in its stomach, which suggest that its stomach might have compartments, as is characteristic of the ruminants (who chew their cud).

6. hare It gives the impression of being a ruminant because it munches its food noticeably.

7. swine Hebrew: *ḥazir* (pig, swine), widely domesticated in ancient Canaan and raised for food. It was the only domesticated animal used as food in biblical times that had a truly split hoof but did not chew its cud. No distinction is made here between wild and domesticated species.

8. One is prohibited not only from eating the meat of forbidden animals but also from touching or handling any part of their bodies, which normally would occur when preparing meat as food. This rule probably was intended as a safeguard against any possible situation that might inadvertently lead to the consumption of meat from such prohibited animals.

WATER CREATURES (vv. 9–12)

10. all the swarming things of the water All water creatures that do not swim by the usual means of using fins, but crawl instead, are considered impure.

11. As in verse 8, the prohibition affects both eating and touching.

---

7. Only twice in the Torah are we commanded not to eat pork, yet every Jew knows that it is forbidden. The Torah commands us many more times to refrain from gossip and hurtful speech, yet many observant Jews do not sense that they are violating the Torah when they speak ill of others (Salanter).

13. The forbidden seem to share certain

HALAKHAH L'MA·ASEH

11:7. swine Based on this verse, bacon, ham, and all pork by-products are forbidden. This includes baked goods containing lard.

11:9. fins and scales This is the source for the ruling that only sea creatures with fins and scales may be eaten.

לָכֶם מִבְּשָׂרָם לֹא תֹאכֵלוּ וְאֶת־נִבְלָתָם
תְּשַׁקֵּצוּ׃ 12 כֹּל אֲשֶׁר אֵין־לוֹ סְנַפִּיר
וְקַשְׂקֶשֶׂת בַּמָּיִם שֶׁקֶץ הוּא לָכֶם׃
13 וְאֶת־אֵלֶּה תְּשַׁקְּצוּ מִן־הָעוֹף לֹא יֵאָכְלוּ
שֶׁקֶץ הֵם אֶת־הַנֶּשֶׁר וְאֶת־הַפֶּרֶס וְאֵת
הָעָזְנִיָּה׃ 14 וְאֶת־הַדָּאָה וְאֶת־הָאַיָּה
לְמִינָהּ׃ 15 אֵת כָּל־עֹרֵב לְמִינוֹ׃ 16 וְאֵת
בַּת הַיַּעֲנָה וְאֶת־הַתַּחְמָס וְאֶת־הַשָּׁחַף
וְאֶת־הַנֵּץ לְמִינֵהוּ׃ 17 וְאֶת־הַכּוֹס וְאֶת־
הַשָּׁלָךְ וְאֶת־הַיַּנְשׁוּף׃ 18 וְאֶת־הַתִּנְשֶׁמֶת
וְאֶת־הַקָּאָת וְאֶת־הָרָחָם׃ 19 וְאֵת
הַחֲסִידָה הָאֲנָפָה לְמִינָהּ וְאֶת־הַדּוּכִיפַת
וְאֶת־הָעֲטַלֵּף׃
20 כֹּל שֶׁרֶץ הָעוֹף הַהֹלֵךְ עַל־אַרְבַּע שֶׁקֶץ
הוּא לָכֶם׃ ס 21 אַךְ אֶת־זֶה תֹּאכְלוּ
מִכֹּל שֶׁרֶץ הָעוֹף הַהֹלֵךְ עַל־אַרְבַּע אֲשֶׁר־
לא לוֹ כְרָעַיִם מִמַּעַל לְרַגְלָיו לְנַתֵּר בָּהֵן
עַל־הָאָרֶץ׃ 22 אֶת־אֵלֶּה מֵהֶם תֹּאכֵלוּ

for you they shall remain: you shall not eat of their flesh and you shall abominate their carcasses. 12Everything in water that has no fins and scales shall be an abomination for you.

13The following you shall abominate among the birds—they shall not be eaten, they are an abomination: the eagle, the vulture, and the black vulture; 14the kite, falcons of every variety; 15all varieties of raven; 16the ostrich, the nighthawk, the sea gull; hawks of every variety; 17the little owl, the cormorant, and the great owl; 18the white owl, the pelican, and the bustard; 19the stork; herons of every variety; the hoopoe, and the bat.

20All winged swarming things that walk on fours shall be an abomination for you. 21But these you may eat among all the winged swarming things that walk on fours: all that have, above their feet, jointed legs to leap with on the ground—22of these you may eat the following: locusts of every variety; all varieties of bald locust; crickets of every variety; and all varieties

CREATURES OF THE SKY (vv. 13–19)

13. The following . . . among the birds No overall physical criteria distinguish pure birds from impure birds. Rather, a long list of prohibited birds is provided, implying that all others would be permitted. The list of prohibited birds given here is virtually identical with that in Deut. 14. It does not correspond exactly to zoologic classifications and even includes a winged rodent, the bat (*atallef*). Virtually all of the impure birds are birds of prey.

WINGED INSECTS (vv. 20–23)

20. The section begins with a general statement, repeated with only slight variations in verse 23. Both are prohibitive, whereas the intervening two verses (vv. 21–22) state exceptions to the overall prohibition.

21. Four types of locusts, each in turn comprising several varieties, are permitted.

---

characteristics, including a sharp talon on their feet for hunting and a tendency to prey on living creatures. Hoffman adds that, because the translation of some of these names is uncertain, "we may eat only fowl that are traditionally eaten in Jewish homes."

16. The Sages offer homiletic explanations as to why certain birds are considered abominations. Thus the hawk is ruled out because of its excellent eyesight. "It can live in Babylon and see everything that people are doing wrong in the Land of Israel." The stork is called "the pious bird" (*ha-ḥasidah*) because it takes such solicitous care of its young. Why, then, is it listed among the abominations? Because it cares only for its own young and not for anyone else's (BT Ḥul. 63a).

HALAKHAH L'MA·ASEH

11:12. no fins and scales Shark, catfish, and all shellfish, for example, are prohibited. Authorities disagree on the permissibility of eating sturgeon and swordfish.

of grasshopper. [23]But all other winged swarming things that have four legs shall be an abomination for you.

[24]And the following shall make you impure—whoever touches their carcasses shall be
impure until evening, [25]and whoever carries the
carcasses of any of them shall wash his clothes
and be impure until evening—[26]every animal
that has true hoofs but without clefts through
the hoofs, or that does not chew the cud. They
are impure for you; whoever touches them shall
be impure. [27]Also all animals that walk on paws,
among those that walk on fours, are impure for
you; whoever touches their carcasses shall be
impure until evening. [28]And anyone who carries
their carcasses shall wash his clothes and remain
impure until evening. They are impure for you.

[29]The following shall be impure for you from
among the things that swarm on the earth: the
mole, the mouse, and great lizards of every variety; [30]the gecko, the land crocodile, the lizard,
the sand lizard, and the chameleon. [31]Those are
for you the impure among all the swarming
things; whoever touches them when they are
dead shall be impure until evening. [32]And anything on which one of them falls when dead
shall be impure: be it any article of wood, or a

אֶת־הָאַרְבֶּה לְמִינוֹ וְאֶת־הַסָּלְעָם לְמִינֵהוּ
וְאֶת־הַחַרְגֹּל לְמִינֵהוּ וְאֶת־הֶחָגָב
לְמִינֵהוּ׃ 23 וְכֹל שֶׁרֶץ הָעוֹף אֲשֶׁר־לוֹ
אַרְבַּע רַגְלָיִם שֶׁקֶץ הוּא לָכֶם׃
24 וּלְאֵלֶּה תִּטַּמָּאוּ כָּל־הַנֹּגֵעַ בְּנִבְלָתָם
יִטְמָא עַד־הָעָרֶב׃ 25 וְכָל־הַנֹּשֵׂא מִנִּבְלָתָם
יְכַבֵּס בְּגָדָיו וְטָמֵא עַד־הָעָרֶב׃ 26 לְכָל־
הַבְּהֵמָה אֲשֶׁר הִוא מַפְרֶסֶת פַּרְסָה וְשֶׁסַע ׀
אֵינֶנָּה שֹׁסַעַת וְגֵרָה אֵינֶנָּה מַעֲלָה טְמֵאִים
הֵם לָכֶם כָּל־הַנֹּגֵעַ בָּהֶם יִטְמָא׃ 27 וְכֹל ׀
הוֹלֵךְ עַל־כַּפָּיו בְּכָל־הַחַיָּה הַהֹלֶכֶת עַל־
אַרְבַּע טְמֵאִים הֵם לָכֶם כָּל־הַנֹּגֵעַ
בְּנִבְלָתָם יִטְמָא עַד־הָעָרֶב׃ 28 וְהַנֹּשֵׂא
אֶת־נִבְלָתָם יְכַבֵּס בְּגָדָיו וְטָמֵא עַד־הָעָרֶב
טְמֵאִים הֵמָּה לָכֶם׃ ס
29 וְזֶה לָכֶם הַטָּמֵא בַּשֶּׁרֶץ הַשֹּׁרֵץ עַל־
הָאָרֶץ הַחֹלֶד וְהָעַכְבָּר וְהַצָּב לְמִינֵהוּ׃
30 וְהָאֲנָקָה וְהַכֹּחַ וְהַלְּטָאָה וְהַחֹמֶט
וְהַתִּנְשָׁמֶת׃ 31 אֵלֶּה הַטְּמֵאִים לָכֶם בְּכָל־
הַשָּׁרֶץ כָּל־הַנֹּגֵעַ בָּהֶם בְּמֹתָם יִטְמָא
עַד־הָעָרֶב׃ 32 וְכֹל אֲשֶׁר־יִפֹּל־עָלָיו מֵהֶם ׀
בְּמֹתָם יִטְמָא מִכָּל־כְּלִי־עֵץ אוֹ בֶגֶד אוֹ־

THE CONDUCTIVITY OF IMPURITY
(vv. 24–40)

This part of chapter 11 deals with the impurity that results from several kinds of contact—such as touching, carrying, or containing—that render persons, vessels, and foodstuffs impure in varying degrees.

27. The body of a person who touches the carcass of an impure creature is rendered impure. The clothing of a person who carries something impure is rendered impure or contaminated as well.

29. The following Eight types of swarming land creatures are listed, including four types of lizards.

32–38. Under priestly law, vessels made of wood, leather, and certain types of cloth become impure by means of exterior contact with a contaminating substance, whereas ceramic vessels (with the exception of stoves and ovens) become impure only if that substance enters their interior space. (This later developed into an elaborate system of ritual purity in ancient rabbinic Judaism, affecting vessels and foodstuffs.)

32. article Any vessel of wood, cloth, skin, or sackcloth. Such vessels may be cleansed in water, and they remain impure only until evening.

HALAKHAH L'MA·ASEH

11:23. swarming things that have four legs The commandment not to eat insects includes taking care not to inadvertently ingest insects in our food. A careful washing of all fruits and vegetables, with special attention to leafy greens such as romaine lettuce and broccoli, is sufficient. *Hashgaḥah* (kosher supervision) of fruits and vegetables is not required.

עוֹר אוֹ שָׂק כָּל־כְּלִי אֲשֶׁר־יֵעָשֶׂה מְלָאכָה
בָּהֶם בַּמַּיִם יוּבָא וְטָמֵא עַד־הָעֶרֶב וְטָהֵר׃
שביעי 33 וְכָל־כְּלִי־חֶרֶשׂ אֲשֶׁר־יִפֹּל מֵהֶם אֶל־
תּוֹכוֹ כֹּל אֲשֶׁר בְּתוֹכוֹ יִטְמָא וְאֹתוֹ
תִשְׁבֹּרוּ׃ 34 מִכָּל־הָאֹכֶל אֲשֶׁר יֵאָכֵל אֲשֶׁר
יָבוֹא עָלָיו מַיִם יִטְמָא וְכָל־מַשְׁקֶה אֲשֶׁר
יִשָּׁתֶה בְּכָל־כְּלִי יִטְמָא׃ 35 וְכֹל אֲשֶׁר־יִפֹּל
מִנִּבְלָתָם ׀ עָלָיו יִטְמָא תַּנּוּר וְכִירַיִם יֻתָּץ
טְמֵאִים הֵם וּטְמֵאִים יִהְיוּ לָכֶם׃ 36 אַךְ
מַעְיָן וּבוֹר מִקְוֵה־מַיִם יִהְיֶה טָהוֹר וְנֹגֵעַ
בְּנִבְלָתָם יִטְמָא׃ 37 וְכִי יִפֹּל מִנִּבְלָתָם
עַל־כָּל־זֶרַע זֵרוּעַ אֲשֶׁר יִזָּרֵעַ טָהוֹר הוּא׃
38 וְכִי יֻתַּן־מַיִם עַל־זֶרַע וְנָפַל מִנִּבְלָתָם
עָלָיו טָמֵא הוּא לָכֶם׃ ס
39 וְכִי יָמוּת מִן־הַבְּהֵמָה אֲשֶׁר־הִיא לָכֶם
לְאָכְלָה הַנֹּגֵעַ בְּנִבְלָתָהּ יִטְמָא עַד־הָעָרֶב׃
40 וְהָאֹכֵל מִנִּבְלָתָהּ יְכַבֵּס בְּגָדָיו וְטָמֵא
עַד־הָעָרֶב וְהַנֹּשֵׂא אֶת־נִבְלָתָהּ יְכַבֵּס
בְּגָדָיו וְטָמֵא עַד־הָעָרֶב׃

cloth, or a skin, or a sack—any such article that
can be put to use shall be dipped in water, and
it shall remain impure until evening; then it
shall be pure. 33 And if any of those falls into an
earthen vessel, everything inside it shall be impure and [the vessel] itself you shall break. 34 As
to any food that may be eaten, it shall become
impure if it came in contact with water; as to
any liquid that may be drunk, it shall become
impure if it was inside any vessel. 35 Everything
on which the carcass of any of them falls shall
be impure: an oven or stove shall be smashed.
They are impure and impure they shall remain
for you. 36 However, a spring or cistern in which
water is collected shall be pure, but whoever
touches such a carcass in it shall be impure. 37 If
such a carcass falls upon seed grain that is to
be sown, it is pure; 38 but if water is put on the
seed and any part of a carcass falls upon it, it
shall be impure for you.

39 If an animal that you may eat has died, anyone who touches its carcass shall be impure until evening; 40 anyone who eats of its carcass
shall wash his clothes and remain impure until
evening; and anyone who carries its carcass
shall wash his clothes and remain impure until
evening.

Food contained in such contaminated vessels is also impure.

33. A ceramic vessel does not become impure until the dead swarming creatures are inside it; should this happen, there is no remedy but to smash the vessel.

34. Solid food that has been dampened by water and then comes into contact with dead swarming creatures becomes impure because water conducts impurity. Similarly, liquids inside contaminated vessels become impure.

35. Ceramic ovens and stoves—like vessels of wood, cloth, leather, and animal hair, but unlike ceramic vessels in general—become contaminated as soon as dead swarming creatures fall onto them. There is no remedy; impure stoves and ovens must be smashed. (Metal vessels may be purified in fire [Num. 31:22–23]. Stone vessels are not susceptible to impurity.)

36. Water that comes from a vessel that is detached from the earth generally renders foodstuffs susceptible to impurity. By contrast, neither rainwater in a cistern nor natural bodies of water transmit impurity.

38. Water renders seed susceptible to impurity. Dampened seed—but not dry seed—becomes impure if the dead body of a forbidden swarming creature falls onto it.

39. Physical contact with the carcass of even a permitted animal, renders a person impure until evening.

40. This statement repeats the prohibition (v. 8) against eating meat of any animal, even a permitted one, that has died a natural death. Similarly, carrying the carcass or any part of it transmits impurity. In both cases the clothes of the person involved must be laundered.

41All the things that swarm upon the earth are an abomination; they shall not be eaten. 42You shall not eat, among all things that swarm upon the earth, anything that crawls on its belly, or anything that walks on fours, or anything that has many legs; for they are an abomination. 43You shall not draw abomination upon yourselves through anything that swarms; you shall not make yourselves impure therewith and thus become impure. 44For I the LORD am your God: you shall sanctify yourselves and be holy, for I am holy. You shall not make yourselves impure through any swarming thing that moves upon the earth. 45For I the LORD am He who brought you up from the land of Egypt to be your God: you shall be holy, for I am holy.

46These are the instructions concerning animals, birds, all living creatures that move in water, and all creatures that swarm on earth, 47for distinguishing between the impure and the pure, between the living things that may be eaten and the living things that may not be eaten.

41 וְכָל־הַשֶּׁרֶץ הַשֹּׁרֵץ עַל־הָאָרֶץ שֶׁקֶץ
הוּא לֹא יֵאָכֵל׃ 42 כֹּל הוֹלֵךְ עַל־גָּחוֹן*
וְכֹל ׀ הוֹלֵךְ עַל־אַרְבַּע עַד כָּל־מַרְבֵּה
רַגְלַיִם לְכָל־הַשֶּׁרֶץ הַשֹּׁרֵץ עַל־הָאָרֶץ לֹא
תֹאכְלוּם כִּי־שֶׁקֶץ הֵם׃ 43 אַל־תְּשַׁקְּצוּ
אֶת־נַפְשֹׁתֵיכֶם בְּכָל־הַשֶּׁרֶץ הַשֹּׁרֵץ וְלֹא
תִטַּמְּאוּ בָּהֶם וְנִטְמֵתֶם* בָּם׃ 44 כִּי אֲנִי
יְהוָה אֱלֹהֵיכֶם וְהִתְקַדִּשְׁתֶּם וִהְיִיתֶם
קְדֹשִׁים כִּי קָדוֹשׁ אָנִי וְלֹא תְטַמְּאוּ אֶת־
נַפְשֹׁתֵיכֶם בְּכָל־הַשֶּׁרֶץ הָרֹמֵשׂ עַל־
הָאָרֶץ׃ 45 כִּי ׀ אֲנִי יְהוָה הַמַּעֲלֶה אֶתְכֶם מפטיר
מֵאֶרֶץ מִצְרַיִם לִהְיֹת לָכֶם לֵאלֹהִים
וִהְיִיתֶם קְדֹשִׁים כִּי קָדוֹשׁ אָנִי׃
46 זֹאת תּוֹרַת הַבְּהֵמָה וְהָעוֹף וְכֹל נֶפֶשׁ
הַחַיָּה הָרֹמֶשֶׂת בַּמָּיִם וּלְכָל־נֶפֶשׁ
הַשֹּׁרֶצֶת עַל־הָאָרֶץ׃ 47 לְהַבְדִּיל בֵּין
הַטָּמֵא וּבֵין הַטָּהֹר וּבֵין הַחַיָּה הַנֶּאֱכֶלֶת
וּבֵין הַחַיָּה אֲשֶׁר לֹא תֵאָכֵל׃ פ

v. 42. ו׳ רבתי, ובמסורה היא ״חצי התורה באותיות״

v. 43. חסר א׳

44. you shall sanctify yourselves and be holy, for I am holy See Comment to 19:2.

POSTSCRIPT (vv. 46–47)

46. These are the instructions This postscript typically appears at the conclusion of a major code of law.

47. for distinguishing between the impure and the pure A similar admonition occurs in 20:25.

---

42. crawls on . . . belly In the word translated as "belly" (*gaḥon*), the letter *vav* is written large, for it is said to be the middle letter of the entire Torah. The large *vav* symbolizes the unique upright posture of a human being. There is something repugnant about a person who crawls instead of standing up for what he or she believes, foregoing the unique upright posture of a human being which is symbolized by the enlarged letter *vav*.

The Book of Leviticus is concerned with our use of words (vows, false oaths, hurtful speech), teaching us to sanctify what goes forth from our mouths. In its exposition of the rules of *kashrut,* it teaches us to sanctify what goes into our mouths as well. It would also remind us that there is a moral difference between eating an apple and eating a slice of meat; the latter requires taking the life of one of God's creatures. The Jew who lives by the dietary laws is constantly kept aware of that.

הפטרת שמיני

HAFTARAH FOR SH'MINI

2 SAMUEL 6:1–7:17 (*Ashk'nazim*)
2 SAMUEL 6:1–19 (*S'fardim*)

This *haftarah* introduces a new phase in ancient Israelite religion and culture. King David decided to consolidate his national authority after his coronation (in about 1000 B.C.E.) in Hebron (2 Sam. 5:1–5), his conquest of Jerusalem (5:6–10), and his defeat of the Philistines. As a symbolic act, he brought the Ark up to Jerusalem from the home of Abinadav in Baalim, where it had been kept after earlier wars against the Philistines in the time of Samuel (1 Sam. 6:21–7:1). The transfer of the holy Ark to the ancient site of Jebus (Jerusalem) was designed to unify the tribes of Israel and Judea (in the north and in the south) around a sacred center. The transfer also marked a new moment of religious centralization, in distinct contrast to the time when the Ark had circulated among the tribes.

The ceremonious portage of the Ark to Jerusalem with David at the helm (and its unexpected disruption) constitutes the first part of the *haftarah* (2 Sam. 6:1–19). The king's desire to build a permanent shrine for the Ark (together with a postponement of fulfilling this request to one of his descendants) makes up the second part of the reading (2 Sam. 7:1–17). Among *S'fardim,* only the first part is recited; *Ashk'nazim* read both sections.

The *haftarah,* with its principal focus on the "Ark of the LORD," oscillates between two poles: stability and movement. Moving the Ark to Jerusalem, from a site where apparently it had been at rest for nearly two generations, was abruptly postponed when Uzza was struck dead after reaching out to steady the Ark when it seemed to be toppling. After three months, the transfer was reinitiated, and the Ark was brought to Jerusalem.

God initially deflected David's desire for a more fitting and permanent site for the Ark, noting (in chapter 7) that from the Exodus until now He always had "moved about" in a portable shrine and never had requested a stable "house." With these words, idealizing the ancient tabernacle–tent as the suitable site for God's earthly dwelling, movement is portrayed as the very core of the people's life with God, on their journeys in the wilderness and in the rotation of the Ark from shrine to shrine in the Promised Land. Thus the desire for a permanent temple constitutes a radical break, exchanging older nomadic ideals (the "tent") for the opulence of a monarchy (the "house").

A similar social-ideologic tension underlay Samuel's early rejection of the people's desire for a king (1 Sam. 8), which he believed to be a rejection of the older ideals of divine rule. God, however, overruled Samuel and gave permission for a monarchy to be established. In this *haftarah,* too, the initial insistence on maintaining older practices is subsequently compromised when God announces that a permanent dynasty should have a permanent shrine.

God promises the king that He will provide the people a place in which they will dwell in security (2 Sam. 7:10–11). Wandering and fear will cease. Security and permanence are also stressed for the royal dynasty of David. God promises that a covenant bond will forever link Him with the Davidic line (v. 13). All subsequent beliefs and hopes in the dynasty of David and its restoration derive from this source. This heavenly guarantee echoes David's reference to the fall of Saul's line earlier in the *haftarah,* during his sarcastic response to Michal's taunts about his behavior during the transfer of the Ark to Jerusalem (2 Sam. 6:21). This failure of Saul's dynasty serves here as the negative counterpoint to the positive promise to David.

The overall movement toward stability (for the Ark and for the dynasty) is potentially endangered at two points. The first involves the holy Ark itself. As the seat of divine Presence among the people, the Ark was a source of blessing and power for the nation—especially in war (1 Sam. 4:5–9). But if it fell into the wrong hands, disaster could result. This was certainly the case when the Ark was hijacked by the Philistines in the days of Samuel (4:11).

The trend toward stability for the Ark and dynasty was endangered on the road to Jerusalem in the incident with Uzza who was killed by God "for his indiscretion" in touching the holy object, which appeared to be toppling, and the journey was halted. The Ark was then placed in the house of Obed-edom, where it remained until the blessings that accrued to him convinced David that divine wrath had subsided. When the journey to Jerusalem was resumed, the Ark was carried forward by "bearers." These individuals are not identified, but later biblical tradition believed that David had corrected his error of allowing laymen to transport the Ark. It reported this change in transport protocol by saying that "David gave orders that none but the Levites were to carry the Ark of God"—as was their duty according to the law (1 Chron. 15:2). Boundaries between the sacred and the profane are inviolable, and the old warnings in the Torah against lay encroachment upon the sacred were now dramatically confirmed. Holy objects are a source of both life and death, through God's favor or fury. This point is underscored at the very moment when Jerusalem is transformed into a holy city.

The second source of danger evident in the *haftarah* lies within the dynasty itself. God offers a covenant of eternal commitment to David and his descendants (2 Sam. 7:13–14). This special bond, however, does not free the kings of responsibility. For if a king "does wrong, I will chastise him with the rod of man and the affliction of mortals" (v. 14). Nevertheless, says God, "I will never withdraw My favor (*ḥasdi*) from him" (v. 15). Disobedience has its dangers, but it will never result in divine rejection. Later generations relied on this promise and recalled to God the "covenant" sworn to David "for all generations" in times of danger (Ps. 89:4–5), reciting His commitment of a "steadfast love" or "favor" (*ḥasdi*) "for him always" (vv. 25,29,34).

The *haftarah* thus preserves the foundation document of the Davidic dynasty, which also came to serve as words of comfort and hope for future generations. The promise that a descendant of David would also build a temple (2 Sam. 7:13) gave the dynastic prophecy an added dimension. It not only legitimated a temple in the immediate future, but justified the hopes of later believers that the destroyed temple would be rebuilt by a descendant of David. The ideas of a new (or renewed) temple and Davidic kingship also became the twin pillars of biblical and Jewish messianic hope for centuries to come.

RELATION OF THE *HAFTARAH* TO THE *PARASHAH*

The connection between the *haftarah* and the *parashah* derives from the striking symmetry of the two readings. The *parashah* first celebrates the dedication of the tabernacle (Lev. 9) and then records the deaths of Nadab and Abihu when they brought "alien fire" into the shrine (Lev. 10:1–2). Correspondingly, the *haftarah* initially describes the joyful transport of the Ark to Jerusalem (2 Sam. 6:2–5) and then notes the abrupt death of Uzza when he reached out to grasp the holy object (vv. 6–7).

An old *midrash* observes that these two disasters caused the people to complain, because they assumed that both the smoky incense (which the priests offered) and the holy Ark (that Uzza touched) were objects of punishment and danger (Tanḥ. B'shallaḥ 21). For that reason, the *midrash* states, scripture goes on to record that the incense could also bring the people atonement and protection (during the plague after Korah's rebellion, Num. 17:12), and that the Ark could be the agent of great blessing (for the household of Obed-edom, 2 Sam. 6:11). Holy objects are presented as bivalent entities, affecting human life by the manner in which they are approached and used.

6 David again assembled all the picked men of Israel, thirty thousand strong. 2Then David and all the troops that were with him set out from Baalim of Judah to bring up from there the Ark of God to which the Name was attached, the name LORD of Hosts Enthroned on the Cherubim.

3They loaded the Ark of God onto a new cart and conveyed it from the house of Abinadab, which was on the hill; and Abinadab's sons, Uzza and Ahio, guided the new cart. 4They conveyed it from Abinadab's house on the hill, [Uzzah walking] alongside the Ark of God and Ahio walking in front of the Ark. 5Meanwhile, David and all the House of Israel danced before the LORD to [the sound of] all kinds of cypress wood [instruments], with lyres, harps, timbrels, sistrums, and cymbals.

6But when they came to the threshing floor of Nacon, Uzzah reached out for the Ark of God and grasped it, for the oxen had stumbled. 7The LORD was incensed at Uzzah. And God struck him down on the spot for his indiscretion, and he died there beside the Ark of God. 8David was distressed because the LORD had inflicted a breach upon Uzzah; and that place was named Perez-uzzah, as it is still called.

9David was afraid of the LORD that day; he said, "How can I let the Ark of the LORD come to me?" 10So David would not bring the Ark of the LORD to his place in the City of David; instead, David diverted it to the house of

ו וַיֹּסֶף עוֹד דָּוִד אֶת־כָּל־בָּחוּר בְּיִשְׂרָאֵל
שְׁלֹשִׁים אָלֶף׃ 2 וַיָּקָם ׀ וַיֵּלֶךְ דָּוִד וְכָל־
הָעָם אֲשֶׁר אִתּוֹ מִבַּעֲלֵי יְהוּדָה לְהַעֲלוֹת
מִשָּׁם אֵת אֲרוֹן הָאֱלֹהִים אֲשֶׁר־נִקְרָא שֵׁם
שֵׁם יְהוָה צְבָאוֹת יֹשֵׁב הַכְּרֻבִים עָלָיו׃
3 וַיַּרְכִּבוּ אֶת־אֲרוֹן הָאֱלֹהִים אֶל־עֲגָלָה
חֲדָשָׁה וַיִּשָּׂאֻהוּ מִבֵּית אֲבִינָדָב אֲשֶׁר
בַּגִּבְעָה וְעֻזָּא* וְאַחְיוֹ בְּנֵי אֲבִינָדָב נֹהֲגִים
אֶת־הָעֲגָלָה חֲדָשָׁה׃ 4 וַיִּשָּׂאֻהוּ מִבֵּית
אֲבִינָדָב אֲשֶׁר בַּגִּבְעָה עִם אֲרוֹן הָאֱלֹהִים
וְאַחְיוֹ הֹלֵךְ לִפְנֵי הָאָרוֹן׃ 5 וְדָוִד ׀ וְכָל־בֵּית
יִשְׂרָאֵל מְשַׂחֲקִים לִפְנֵי יְהוָה בְּכֹל עֲצֵי
בְרוֹשִׁים וּבְכִנֹּרוֹת וּבִנְבָלִים וּבְתֻפִּים
וּבִמְנַעַנְעִים וּבְצֶלְצֶלִים׃
6 וַיָּבֹאוּ עַד־גֹּרֶן נָכוֹן וַיִּשְׁלַח עֻזָּא* אֶל־
אֲרוֹן הָאֱלֹהִים וַיֹּאחֶז בּוֹ כִּי שָׁמְטוּ הַבָּקָר׃
7 וַיִּחַר־אַף יְהוָה בְּעֻזָּה* וַיַּכֵּהוּ שָׁם
הָאֱלֹהִים עַל־הַשַּׁל וַיָּמָת שָׁם עִם אֲרוֹן
הָאֱלֹהִים׃ 8 וַיִּחַר לְדָוִד עַל אֲשֶׁר פָּרַץ
יְהוָה פֶּרֶץ בְּעֻזָּה* וַיִּקְרָא לַמָּקוֹם הַהוּא
פֶּרֶץ עֻזָּה עַד הַיּוֹם הַזֶּה׃
9 וַיִּרָא דָוִד אֶת־יְהוָה בַּיּוֹם הַהוּא וַיֹּאמֶר
אֵיךְ יָבוֹא אֵלַי אֲרוֹן יְהוָה׃ 10 וְלֹא־אָבָה
דָוִד לְהָסִיר אֵלָיו אֶת־אֲרוֹן יְהוָה עַל־עִיר
דָּוִד וַיַּטֵּהוּ דָוִד בֵּית עֹבֵד־אֱדֹם הַגִּתִּי׃

vv. 3–8. בכתבי היד כתוב שמו גם ”עזא“ וגם ”עזה“

2 Samuel 6:2. Baalim of Judah Baalim, a place also referred to as Baalah, is identified with Kiriath-jearim (Josh. 15:9, 1 Chron. 13:6). The Ark remained here after it had been retrieved from the Philistine city of Ashdod (1 Sam. 6:21).

The LORD of Hosts Enthroned on the Cherubim This is a fuller form of the title found in 1 Sam. 4:4. The divine epithet "LORD of Hosts" refers to God's majesty over the heavenly armies, with which He fights human enemies. These "hosts" include the sun, moon, and stars as well as the atmospheric powers of nature (see Judg. 5:20–21; 2 Sam. 22:11–16). From heaven, the Lord of battles rides forth on cherub-like "wings of wind" (2 Sam. 22:11, cf. Ps. 68:5,19). On earth, the Ark represents His chariot of war. The Ark with cherubim on its cover was placed in the inner recesses of the tabernacle. It is from there that the divine Presence was manifest to Moses (Exod. 25:10–22).

Obed-edom the Gittite. [11]The Ark of the Lord remained in the house of Obed-edom the Gittite three months, and the Lord blessed Obed-edom and his whole household.

[12]It was reported to King David: "The Lord has blessed Obed-edom's house and all that belongs to him because of the Ark of God." Thereupon David went and brought up the Ark of God from the house of Obed-edom to the City of David, amid rejoicing. [13]When the bearers of the Ark of the Lord had moved forward six paces, he sacrificed an ox and a fatling. [14]David whirled with all his might before the Lord; David was girt with a linen ephod. [15]Thus David and all the House of Israel brought up the Ark of the Lord with shouts and with blasts of the horn.

[16]As the Ark of the Lord entered the City of David, Michal daughter of Saul looked out of the window and saw King David leaping and whirling before the Lord; and she despised him for it.

[17]They brought in the Ark of the Lord and set it up in its place inside the tent which David had pitched for it, and David sacrificed burnt offerings and offerings of well-being before the Lord. [18]When David finished sacrificing the burnt offerings and the offerings of well-being, he blessed the people in the name of the Lord of Hosts. [19]And he distributed among all the people—the entire multitude of Israel, man and woman alike—to each a loaf of bread, a cake made in a pan, and a raisin cake. Then all the people left for their homes.

[20]David went home to greet his household. And Michal daughter of Saul came out to meet David and said, "Didn't the king of Israel do himself honor today—exposing himself today in the sight of the slavegirls of his subjects, as one of the riffraff might expose himself!" [21]David answered Michal, "It was before the Lord

11 וַיֵּ֩שֶׁב֩ אֲר֨וֹן יְהֹוָ֜ה בֵּ֣ית עֹבֵ֥ד אֱדֹ֛ם הַגִּתִּ֖י שְׁלֹשָׁ֣ה חֳדָשִׁ֑ים וַיְבָ֧רֶךְ יְהֹוָ֛ה אֶת־עֹבֵ֥ד אֱדֹ֖ם וְאֶת־כׇּל־בֵּיתֽוֹ׃

12 וַיֻּגַּ֗ד לַמֶּ֣לֶךְ דָּוִד֮ לֵאמֹר֒ בֵּרַ֣ךְ יְהֹוָ֗ה אֶת־בֵּ֨ית עֹבֵ֤ד אֱדֹם֙ וְאֶת־כׇּל־אֲשֶׁר־ל֔וֹ בַּעֲב֖וּר אֲר֣וֹן הָאֱלֹהִ֑ים וַיֵּ֣לֶךְ דָּוִ֗ד וַיַּ֩עַל֩ אֶת־אֲר֨וֹן הָאֱלֹהִ֜ים מִבֵּ֨ית עֹבֵ֥ד אֱדֹ֛ם עִ֥יר דָּוִ֖ד בְּשִׂמְחָֽה׃ 13 וַיְהִ֗י כִּ֧י צָעֲד֛וּ נֹשְׂאֵ֥י אֲרוֹן־יְהֹוָ֖ה שִׁשָּׁ֣ה צְעָדִ֑ים וַיִּזְבַּ֥ח שׁ֖וֹר וּמְרִֽיא׃ 14 וְדָוִ֛ד מְכַרְכֵּ֥ר בְּכׇל־עֹ֖ז לִפְנֵ֣י יְהֹוָ֑ה וְדָוִ֕ד חָג֖וּר אֵפ֥וֹד בָּֽד׃ 15 וְדָוִד֙ וְכׇל־בֵּ֣ית יִשְׂרָאֵ֔ל מַעֲלִ֖ים אֶת־אֲר֣וֹן יְהֹוָ֑ה בִּתְרוּעָ֖ה וּבְק֥וֹל שׁוֹפָֽר׃

16 וְהָיָה֙ אֲר֣וֹן יְהֹוָ֔ה בָּ֖א עִ֣יר דָּוִ֑ד וּמִיכַ֨ל בַּת־שָׁא֜וּל נִשְׁקְפָ֣ה ׀ בְּעַ֣ד הַחַלּ֗וֹן וַתֵּ֨רֶא אֶת־הַמֶּ֤לֶךְ דָּוִד֙ מְפַזֵּ֤ז וּמְכַרְכֵּר֙ לִפְנֵ֣י יְהֹוָ֔ה וַתִּ֥בֶז ל֖וֹ בְּלִבָּֽהּ׃

17 וַיָּבִ֜אוּ אֶת־אֲר֣וֹן יְהֹוָ֗ה וַיַּצִּ֤גוּ אֹתוֹ֙ בִּמְק֣וֹמ֔וֹ בְּת֣וֹךְ הָאֹ֔הֶל אֲשֶׁ֥ר נָֽטָה־ל֖וֹ דָּוִ֑ד וַיַּ֨עַל דָּוִ֤ד עֹלוֹת֙ לִפְנֵ֣י יְהֹוָ֔ה וּשְׁלָמִֽים׃ 18 וַיְכַ֣ל דָּוִ֔ד מֵהַעֲל֥וֹת הָעוֹלָ֖ה וְהַשְּׁלָמִ֑ים וַיְבָ֣רֶךְ אֶת־הָעָ֔ם בְּשֵׁ֖ם יְהֹוָ֥ה צְבָאֽוֹת׃ 19 וַיְחַלֵּ֨ק לְכׇל־הָעָ֜ם לְכׇל־הֲמ֣וֹן יִשְׂרָאֵל֮ לְמֵאִ֣ישׁ וְעַד־אִשָּׁה֒ לְאִ֗ישׁ חַלַּ֥ת לֶ֙חֶם֙ אַחַ֔ת וְאֶשְׁפָּ֣ר אֶחָ֔ד וַאֲשִׁישָׁ֖ה אֶחָ֑ת וַיֵּ֥לֶךְ כׇּל־הָעָ֖ם אִ֥ישׁ לְבֵיתֽוֹ׃

20 וַיָּ֥שׇׁב דָּוִ֖ד לְבָרֵ֣ךְ אֶת־בֵּית֑וֹ וַתֵּצֵ֞א מִיכַ֣ל בַּת־שָׁא֗וּל לִקְרַ֣את דָּוִד֮ וַתֹּ֒אמֶר֒ מַה־נִּכְבַּ֨ד הַיּ֜וֹם מֶ֣לֶךְ יִשְׂרָאֵ֗ל אֲשֶׁ֨ר נִגְלָ֤ה הַיּוֹם֙ לְעֵינֵ֨י אַמְה֣וֹת עֲבָדָ֔יו כְּהִגָּל֥וֹת נִגְל֖וֹת אַחַ֥ד הָרֵקִֽים׃ 21 וַיֹּ֣אמֶר דָּוִד֮ אֶל־מִיכַל֒ לִפְנֵ֣י יְהֹוָ֗ה אֲשֶׁ֨ר בָּֽחַר־בִּ֤י מֵאָבִ֙יךְ֙ וּמִכׇּל־בֵּית֔וֹ

who chose me instead of your father and all his family and appointed me ruler over the LORD's people Israel! I will dance before the LORD 22and dishonor myself even more, and be low in my own esteem; but among the slavegirls that you speak of I will be honored." 23So to her dying day Michal daughter of Saul had no children.

לְצַוֺּת אֹתִי נָגִיד עַל־עַם יְהוָה עַל־יִשְׂרָאֵל
וְשִׂחַקְתִּי לִפְנֵי יְהוָה׃ 22 וּנְקַלֹּתִי עוֹד
מִזֹּאת וְהָיִיתִי שָׁפָל בְּעֵינָי וְעִם־הָאֲמָהוֹת
אֲשֶׁר אָמַרְתְּ עִמָּם אִכָּבֵדָה׃ 23 וּלְמִיכַל
בַּת־שָׁאוּל לֹא־הָיָה לָהּ יָלֶד עַד יוֹם
מוֹתָהּ׃ פ

7 When the king was settled in his palace and the LORD had granted him safety from all the enemies around him, 2the king said to the prophet Nathan: "Here I am dwelling in a house of cedar, while the Ark of the LORD abides in a tent!" 3Nathan said to the king, "Go and do whatever you have in mind, for the LORD is with you."

4But that same night the word of the LORD came to Nathan: 5"Go and say to My servant David: Thus said the LORD: Are you the one to build a house for Me to dwell in? 6From the day that I brought the people of Israel out of Egypt to this day I have not dwelt in a house, but have moved about in Tent and Tabernacle. 7As I moved about wherever the Israelites went, did I ever reproach any of the tribal leaders whom I appointed to care for My people Israel: Why have you not built Me a house of cedar?

8"Further, say thus to My servant David: Thus said the LORD of Hosts: I took you from the pasture, from following the flock, to be ruler of My people Israel, 9and I have been with you wherever you went, and have cut down all your enemies before you. Moreover, I will give you great

ז וַיְהִי כִּי־יָשַׁב הַמֶּלֶךְ בְּבֵיתוֹ וַיהוָה
הֵנִיחַ־לוֹ מִסָּבִיב מִכָּל־אֹיְבָיו׃ 2 וַיֹּאמֶר
הַמֶּלֶךְ אֶל־נָתָן הַנָּבִיא רְאֵה נָא אָנֹכִי
יוֹשֵׁב בְּבֵית אֲרָזִים וַאֲרוֹן הָאֱלֹהִים יֹשֵׁב
בְּתוֹךְ הַיְרִיעָה׃ 3 וַיֹּאמֶר נָתָן אֶל־הַמֶּלֶךְ
כֹּל אֲשֶׁר בִּלְבָבְךָ לֵךְ עֲשֵׂה כִּי יְהוָה
עִמָּךְ׃ ס
4 וַיְהִי בַּלַּיְלָה הַהוּא וַיְהִי דְּבַר־יְהוָה
אֶל־נָתָן לֵאמֹר׃ 5 לֵךְ וְאָמַרְתָּ אֶל־עַבְדִּי
אֶל־דָּוִד כֹּה אָמַר יְהוָה הַאַתָּה תִּבְנֶה־לִּי
בַיִת לְשִׁבְתִּי׃ 6 כִּי לֹא יָשַׁבְתִּי בְּבַיִת
לְמִיּוֹם הַעֲלֹתִי אֶת־בְּנֵי יִשְׂרָאֵל מִמִּצְרַיִם
וְעַד הַיּוֹם הַזֶּה וָאֶהְיֶה מִתְהַלֵּךְ בְּאֹהֶל
וּבְמִשְׁכָּן׃ 7 בְּכֹל אֲשֶׁר־הִתְהַלַּכְתִּי בְּכָל־
בְּנֵי יִשְׂרָאֵל הֲדָבָר דִּבַּרְתִּי אֶת־אַחַד שִׁבְטֵי
יִשְׂרָאֵל אֲשֶׁר צִוִּיתִי לִרְעוֹת אֶת־עַמִּי
אֶת־יִשְׂרָאֵל לֵאמֹר לָמָּה לֹא־בְנִיתֶם לִי
בֵּית אֲרָזִים׃
8 וְעַתָּה כֹּה־תֹאמַר לְעַבְדִּי לְדָוִד כֹּה אָמַר
יְהוָה צְבָאוֹת אֲנִי לְקַחְתִּיךָ מִן־הַנָּוֶה
מֵאַחַר הַצֹּאן לִהְיוֹת נָגִיד עַל־עַמִּי עַל־
יִשְׂרָאֵל׃ 9 וָאֶהְיֶה עִמְּךָ בְּכֹל אֲשֶׁר הָלַכְתָּ
וָאַכְרִתָה אֶת־כָּל־אֹיְבֶיךָ מִפָּנֶיךָ וְעָשִׂתִי

2 Samuel 7:1. safety Literally, "rest" (cf. v. 11). This reference alludes to Deut. 12:10–11. There Moses tells the people that when they achieve rest from their enemies they must bring their burnt offerings to the place that the Lord will choose. Tradition understood this place to be Jerusalem.

5. Are you the one The reason for David's rejection is not indicated. Later biblical tradition explained this as due to David's military past, because he had "shed much blood" (1 Chron. 22:8).

renown like that of the greatest men on earth.
10I will establish a home for My people Israel
and will plant them firm, so that they shall dwell
secure and shall tremble no more. Evil men shall
not oppress them any more as in the past, 11ever
since I appointed chieftains over My people Israel. I will give you safety from all your enemies.

"The LORD declares to you that He, the LORD,
will establish a house for you. 12When your days
are done and you lie with your fathers, I will
raise up your offspring after you, one of your
own issue, and I will establish his kingship. 13He
shall build a house for My name, and I will establish his royal throne forever. 14I will be a father to him, and he shall be a son to Me. When
he does wrong, I will chastise him with the
rod of men and the affliction of mortals; 15but
I will never withdraw My favor from him as I
withdrew it from Saul, whom I removed to
make room for you. 16Your house and your
kingship shall ever be secure before you; your
throne shall be established forever."

17Nathan spoke to David in accordance with
all these words and all this prophecy.

לְךָ֙ שֵׁ֣ם גָּד֔וֹל כְּשֵׁ֥ם הַגְּדֹלִ֖ים אֲשֶׁ֥ר בָּאָֽרֶץ׃
10 וְשַׂמְתִּ֣י מָ֠קוֹם לְעַמִּ֨י לְיִשְׂרָאֵ֤ל וּנְטַעְתִּיו֙
וְשָׁכַ֣ן תַּחְתָּ֔יו וְלֹ֥א יִרְגַּ֖ז ע֑וֹד וְלֹא־יֹסִ֤יפוּ
בְנֵֽי־עַוְלָה֙ לְעַנּוֹת֔וֹ כַּאֲשֶׁ֖ר בָּרִאשׁוֹנָֽה׃
11 וּלְמִן־הַיּ֗וֹם אֲשֶׁ֨ר צִוִּ֤יתִי שֹֽׁפְטִים֙ עַל־
עַמִּ֣י יִשְׂרָאֵ֔ל וַהֲנִיחֹ֥תִי לְךָ֖ מִכָּל־אֹיְבֶ֑יךָ
וְהִגִּ֤יד לְךָ֙ יְהוָ֔ה כִּי־בַ֖יִת יַעֲשֶׂה־לְּךָ֥ יְהוָֽה׃
12 כִּ֣י ׀ יִמְלְא֣וּ יָמֶ֗יךָ וְשָֽׁכַבְתָּ֙ אֶת־אֲבֹתֶ֔יךָ
וַהֲקִימֹתִ֤י אֶֽת־זַרְעֲךָ֙ אַחֲרֶ֔יךָ אֲשֶׁ֥ר יֵצֵ֖א
מִמֵּעֶ֑יךָ וַהֲכִינֹתִ֖י אֶת־מַמְלַכְתּֽוֹ׃ 13 ה֥וּא
יִבְנֶה־בַּ֖יִת לִשְׁמִ֑י וְכֹנַנְתִּ֛י אֶת־כִּסֵּ֥א
מַמְלַכְתּ֖וֹ עַד־עוֹלָֽם׃ 14 אֲנִי֙ אֶהְיֶה־לּ֣וֹ
לְאָ֔ב וְה֖וּא יִהְיֶה־לִּ֣י לְבֵ֑ן אֲשֶׁר֙ בְּהַ֣עֲוֺת֔וֹ
וְהֹֽכַחְתִּיו֙ בְּשֵׁ֣בֶט אֲנָשִׁ֔ים וּבְנִגְעֵ֖י בְּנֵ֥י
אָדָֽם׃ 15 וְחַסְדִּ֖י לֹא־יָס֣וּר מִמֶּ֑נּוּ כַּאֲשֶׁ֤ר
הֲסִרֹ֙תִי֙ מֵעִ֣ם שָׁא֔וּל אֲשֶׁ֥ר הֲסִרֹ֖תִי
מִלְּפָנֶֽיךָ׃ 16 וְנֶאְמַ֨ן בֵּיתְךָ֧ וּמַמְלַכְתְּךָ֛ עַד־
עוֹלָ֖ם לְפָנֶ֑יךָ כִּסְאֲךָ֕ יִהְיֶ֥ה נָכ֖וֹן עַד־
עוֹלָֽם׃
17 כְּכֹל֙ הַדְּבָרִ֣ים הָאֵ֔לֶּה וּכְכֹ֖ל הַחִזָּי֣וֹן הַזֶּ֑ה
כֵּ֚ן דִּבֶּ֣ר נָתָ֔ן אֶל־דָּוִֽד׃ ס

14. I will be a father to him This formulation of a royal covenant is alluded to in Ps. 2:7 and 89:27 and gives the royal bond the intimacy of an adoption. Prophets regularly evoke a similarly constructed formulation of marriage vows to give the national covenant a sense of familial commitment (see Hos. 2:18–22).

12 The Lord spoke to Moses, saying:

 וַיְדַבֵּר יְהוָה אֶל־מֹשֶׁה לֵּאמֹר׃

CHAPTER 12

After the previous chapter's discussion of how food entering our bodies can make us ritually impure, the Torah now discusses how that which comes out of our bodies can do the same.

Perhaps no concept in the Torah is less accessible to the modern reader than the notion of *tum·ah,* generally translated "uncleanness" (although it has no connection to one's physical sanitary condition) or "ritual impurity." One contracts *tum·ah* through contact with a dead body, by being afflicted with *tzara·at* ("leprosy," although not the disease known by that name today), or by contact with a bodily emission that touches on the generation of life, such as menstrual blood, semen, or a flow from the reproductive organs. A woman who has just given birth is likewise considered ritually impure. *Tum·ah* bars one from approaching God's sanctuary; *tzara·at* isolates one from human contact.

Tum·ah has unmistakable negative connotations. It is defined by what one may not do, and the Torah tells us how to be relieved of it. It need not, however, imply wrongdoing on the part of the affected person. (Admittedly, as some commentators have noted, the Torah itself provides a basis for that interpretation, when it calls for a purification offering to be part of its prescribed process of reintegration.) *Tum·ah* seems to be the result of coming in contact with an awesomely potent force that disqualifies one from approaching the sanctuary.

Proof that *tum·ah* is not a totally negative condition can be found not only in its association with such religiously affirmed activities as childbirth and caring for the dead but also from the rabbinic rule that scrolls of the biblical books convey *tum·ah* to those who touch them. (This finds its extension in the efforts we make today to avoid touching the Torah scroll with our bare hands, using a pointer when we read from it and a mantle when taking it from the Ark and returning it.)

It has been suggested that these categories of ritual impurity were a response to the anxiety triggered by death, serious illness, and the "leaking" of life-generating fluids from the body. It has been noted further that natural flows require less purification than unnatural flows, which might indicate the presence of disease.

Although *tum·ah* bars a woman from the sanctuary, we need not see that condition as negative and certainly not as punishment. There is no reason to believe that God ordained menstruation or childbirth as punishment. We might postulate that there are two types of holiness in life, two ways of encountering the divine. There is a natural holiness found in the miracles of pregnancy, birth, and recovery from illness. And there is a stipulated holiness—the arbitrary designation of certain times, places, and activities as sacred. One meets God in the experiences of birth and death, sickness and health. But they are not everyday occurrences. The person who yearns for contact with God on a regular basis must rely on sanctuaries, worship services, and prescribed rituals, all of which are holy only because we have chosen to designate them as holy. Israelite society may have seen the two types of holiness as being mutually exclusive, so that it would not be appropriate for the woman or man who had encountered the vital holiness of childbirth, menstruation, or contact with a dead body to seek the designated holiness of the sanctuary. A woman who had just given birth might feel the presence of God so strongly in that experience that she would feel no need to go to the sanctuary to find God (although we might be more comfortable with that decision being left to the new mother rather than being written into law).

We can see the notion of *tum·ah,* then, as growing out of a sense of reverence for the miraculous nature of birth, the awesome power of death, and the mysteries of illness and recuperation. That this reverence would later be contaminated by superstitious fears related to menstrual blood and contact with the dead need not detract from our efforts to understand and appreciate these chapters of biblical law.

²Speak to the Israelite people thus: When a woman at childbirth bears a male, she shall be impure seven days; she shall be impure as at the time of her menstrual infirmity.—³On the eighth day the flesh of his foreskin shall be circumcised.—⁴She shall remain in a state of blood purification for thirty-three days: she shall not touch any consecrated thing, nor enter the sanctuary until her period of purification is completed. ⁵If she bears a female, she shall be impure two weeks as during her menstruation, and she shall remain in a state of blood purification for sixty-six days.

²דַּבֵּ֞ר אֶל־בְּנֵ֤י יִשְׂרָאֵל֙ לֵאמֹ֔ר אִשָּׁה֙ כִּ֣י תַזְרִ֔יעַ וְיָלְדָ֖ה זָכָ֑ר וְטָֽמְאָה֙ שִׁבְעַ֣ת יָמִ֔ים כִּימֵ֛י נִדַּ֥ת דְּוֺתָ֖הּ תִּטְמָֽא׃ ³וּבַיּ֖וֹם הַשְּׁמִינִ֑י יִמּ֖וֹל בְּשַׂ֥ר עָרְלָתֽוֹ׃ ⁴וּשְׁלֹשִׁ֥ים יוֹם֙ וּשְׁלֹ֣שֶׁת יָמִ֔ים תֵּשֵׁ֖ב בִּדְמֵ֣י טׇהֳרָ֑ה בְּכׇל־קֹ֣דֶשׁ לֹֽא־תִגָּ֗ע וְאֶל־הַמִּקְדָּשׁ֙ לֹ֣א תָבֹ֔א עַד־מְלֹ֖את יְמֵ֥י טׇהֳרָֽהּ׃ ⁵וְאִם־נְקֵבָ֣ה תֵלֵ֔ד וְטָֽמְאָ֥ה שְׁבֻעַ֖יִם כְּנִדָּתָ֑הּ וְשִׁשִּׁ֥ים יוֹם֙ וְשֵׁ֣שֶׁת יָמִ֔ים תֵּשֵׁ֖ב עַל־דְּמֵ֥י טׇהֳרָֽה׃

REGULATIONS CONCERNING THE NEW MOTHER (12:1–8)

2. When a woman at childbirth bears a male Literally, "When a woman is inseminated and bears a male."

she shall be impure as at the time of her menstrual infirmity Not only the duration but the actual nature of the impurity resembles that of a menstruating woman (see 15:19–24).

3. Circumcision is first mandated in the context of the covenant between God and Abraham (Gen. 17:10–14).

4. blood purification Discharges of blood that occur after the initial period of impurity are unlike menstrual blood and are not regarded as impure.

until her period of purification is completed Although the new mother was no longer impure because of discharges, she was still barred from entry into the sanctuary and from contact with consecrated objects. She had to wait until a specific period of time had elapsed before she could be declared pure.

5. The time periods are doubled for a female, but the provisions are the same.

2. Is the normal period of impurity after giving birth one week, and is it doubled after the birth of a daughter because the new mother has given birth to a child who will herself contain the divine gift of nurturing and giving birth to a new life? Or is the normal period two weeks, only to be reduced after the birth of a son to allow the mother to attend the b'rit in a state of ritual purity, or because b'rit milah on the eighth day is a purifying rite?

3. The unique ceremony of b'rit milah is performed on the male infant's generative organ to symbolize that the Covenant is passed on from generation to generation, from father to son. Except in cases of conversion (e.g., when a non-Jewish mother wishes to raise the child as a Jew), circumcision does not make the child Jewish. It celebrates the fact that he is born into the Covenant. Ceremonies for the home and for the synagogue have been created to welcome newborn girls into the Covenant with the same sense of importance and celebration as welcoming boys. Many other societies circumcised young boys at adolescence, as an ordeal of passage and a preparation for marriage and sexual activity. By moving the ritual back to infancy, biblical tradition stripped it of its erotic element and transmuted it into a symbol of the Covenant.

HALAKHAH L'MA·ASEH

12:2. as at the time of her menstrual infirmity Traditionally, the woman waits for seven days after bleeding ceases and immerses in a *mikveh* (ritual bath) before resuming relations. Immersion in a *mikveh* is not required after caesarian births.

12:3. On the eighth day See Gen. 17:12. The covenant of circumcision (*b'rit milah*) takes place on the eighth day of the child's life. This includes *Shabbat* and holy days (S.A. YD 266:2), unless the child was born through caesarian section. The *b'rit milah* is postponed only out of consideration for the health of the child.

6On the completion of her period of purification, for either son or daughter, she shall bring to the priest, at the entrance of the Tent of Meeting, a lamb in its first year for a burnt offering, and a pigeon or a turtledove for a purification offering. 7He shall offer it before the LORD and make expiation on her behalf; she shall then be pure from her flow of blood. Such are the rituals concerning her who bears a child, male or female. 8If, however, her means do not suffice for a sheep, she shall take two turtledoves or two pigeons, one for a burnt offering and the other for a purification offering. The priest shall make expiation on her behalf, and she shall be pure.

6 וּבִמְלֹאת ׀ יְמֵי טָהֳרָהּ לְבֵן אוֹ לְבַת
תָּבִיא כֶּבֶשׂ בֶּן־שְׁנָתוֹ לְעֹלָה וּבֶן־יוֹנָה
אוֹ־תֹר לְחַטָּאת אֶל־פֶּתַח אֹהֶל־מוֹעֵד
אֶל־הַכֹּהֵן׃ 7 וְהִקְרִיבוֹ לִפְנֵי יְהוָה וְכִפֶּר
עָלֶיהָ וְטָהֲרָה מִמְּקֹר דָּמֶיהָ זֹאת תּוֹרַת
הַיֹּלֶדֶת לַזָּכָר אוֹ לַנְּקֵבָה׃ 8 וְאִם־לֹא
תִמְצָא יָדָהּ דֵּי שֶׂה וְלָקְחָה שְׁתֵּי־תֹרִים
אוֹ שְׁנֵי בְּנֵי יוֹנָה אֶחָד לְעֹלָה וְאֶחָד
לְחַטָּאת וְכִפֶּר עָלֶיהָ הַכֹּהֵן וְטָהֵרָה׃ פ

13 The LORD spoke to Moses and Aaron, saying:

יג וַיְדַבֵּר יְהוָה אֶל־מֹשֶׁה וְאֶל־אַהֲרֹן
לֵּאמֹר׃

6. On the completion of her period of purification After the termination of the second period, rites are performed to readmit her into the sanctuary and into the religious life of the community.

purification offering Hebrew: *ḥattat;* needed here solely to remove impurity. All impurity, however contracted, could lead to sinfulness if not attended to, and failure to deal properly with impurity aroused God's anger. The purification offering restored to the person the right of access to the sanctuary; and the burnt offering (*olah*) that followed immediately symbolized this renewed acceptability.

8. If, however, her means do not suffice The right to bring a less-expensive sacrifice is standard for a number of purifications and religious obligations. Without it, poor Israelites would have been deprived of expiation when they incurred impurity through no fault of their own.

THE PURIFICATION OF SKIN DISEASES (13:1–14:57)

Chapters 13 and 14 prescribe the role of the Israelite priesthood in diagnosing and purifying persons afflicted with a skin disease known as *tzara·at.* This disease also contaminated fabrics and leather as well as plastered or mud-covered building stones. The identification of biblical *tzara·at* with leprosy is unlikely, if by "leprosy" is meant Hansen's disease; the symptoms presented in this chapter do not conform to the nature or the course of that disease. The term *"tzara·at"* probably designated a complex of various ailments. The priest combined medical and ritual procedures in safeguarding the purity of the sanctuary and of the Israelite community. Precisely why skin diseases were singled out in the priestly codes is not certain. *Tzara·at* was preva-

---

6. The new mother's burnt offering is seen by some as a form of an offering of gratitude (*todah*) for having survived the experience of childbirth or on behalf of the newborn for having been released into life from the confinement of the womb (Lev. R. 14:3). Why a purification offering? Hoffman sees it as the sacrifice of one compelled by circumstance to stay away from the sanctuary, who now brings a dove to symbolize her return to her spiritual home like a dove to its nest. The Talmud speculates that some women, because of the pain of childbirth, may have vowed to abstain from further sexual relations to avoid such pain. The offering is part of the process that releases her from that rash vow (BT Nid. 31b).

2When a person has on the skin of his body a swelling, a rash, or a discoloration, and it develops into a scaly affection on the skin of his body, it shall be reported to Aaron the priest

2 אָדָ֗ם כִּֽי־יִהְיֶ֤ה בְעוֹר־בְּשָׂרוֹ֙ שְׂאֵ֤ת אֽוֹ־
סַפַּ֙חַת֙ א֣וֹ בַהֶ֔רֶת וְהָיָ֥ה בְעוֹר־בְּשָׂר֖וֹ לְנֶ֣גַע
צָרָ֑עַת וְהוּבָא֙ אֶל־אַהֲרֹ֣ן הַכֹּהֵ֔ן א֛וֹ אֶל־

lent in ancient Israel and was presumed to be contagious.

THE SYMPTOMS (13:1–8)

The priest's initial problem was to determine whether the sufferer had acute *tzara·at* or some less serious ailment with which it might be confused, but which would heal.

2. it shall be reported to Aaron the priest The afflicted person must be brought before the priest.

CHAPTER 13

At least three things are worthy of note regarding the role of the *kohen* in treating leprous afflictions. First, in biblical Israel, the *kohen* was both the religious and the medical authority. The biblical mind saw the connection between the physical and the spiritual dimensions of illness and recovery (perhaps more clearly than we see it today). When the *kohen* visited the afflicted person in isolation and examined the person's sores, the experience of being cared for by the most prestigious person in the community must have helped generate healing powers in the sick person.

Second, the role of the *kohen* was not simply to diagnose the ailment (and certainly not to treat it) but to reintegrate the person into the community as soon as possible. Religion sought to include, not to isolate, the afflicted person. If the laws of leprosy were fashioned for reasons of health and contagion, Hirsch notes, they would be stringent in borderline cases. Instead, doubtful cases are deemed ritually pure.

Finally, we note that the *kohen* performs the ritual only after the *tzara·at* has disappeared, to avoid the appearance of performing a magical cure.

2. Despite a posture of sympathy for afflicted persons and a commitment to ameliorate their condition, the Sages often could not resist the temptation to ask, "What moral or spiritual failing may have caused this illness?" They see the Torah's discussion of illness in the abstract as an opportunity to make a moral point, although they caution us that it is insensitive to tell an ailing person, "You are suffering because of your sins." Anticipating what we recently have come to know about the unity joining the physical and the emotional dimensions of illness, they could understand illness as the result of moral as well as physical causes. Their outlook has been summarized as seeing *tzara·at* "not as a bodily disease but as the physical manifestation of a spiritual malaise." The leper is isolated from human society not because of the contagious skin disease but as a punishment for antisocial behavior. Yet one of the Sages insists, "When a person is in pain, what does the divine Presence say? 'It is My own head that aches, it is My own arm that aches'" (M Sanh. 6:5).

Playing on the linguistic similarity of the Hebrew for "leper" (*m'tzora*) and the Hebrew for "one who gossips" (*motzi shem ra*), the Sages considered leprosy to be a punishment for the sins of slander and malicious gossip (Lev. R. 16:1). They teach that gossip is like leprosy because it is highly contagious. One infected person can spread a malicious rumor to many others. They designate seven types of antisocial behavior that God punishes with *tzara·at:* "haughty eyes, a lying tongue, hands that shed innocent blood in secret, a mind that hatches evil, feet quick to do wrong, a witness who testifies falsely, and one who incites brothers to quarrel" (citing Prov. 6:16–19). Those types of behavior share the attribute of being hard to punish in a court of law. God exacts punishment in a variety of appropriate ways: "As your rumors separated husband from wife and brother from brother, you will now be separated from all human contact." The Midrash adduces proof texts to show that people guilty of those misdeeds were punished with leprosy. Thus Miriam is stricken after speaking ill of her brother Moses (Num. 12:10). Even Moses is afflicted for speaking ill of the Israelites; when he is summoned by God at the Burning Bush to bring the Israelites news of their impending liberation, he hesitates, saying, "They will not believe me" (Exod. 4:1). As a result, his hand becomes leprous (4:6).

Today we recognize that it is medically inaccurate and psychologically cruel to tell someone that he or she is afflicted with illness as a punishment for behavior not organically related to the illness, or that failure to heal is

or to one of his sons, the priests. 3 The priest shall examine the affection on the skin of his body: if hair in the affected patch has turned white and the affection appears to be deeper than the skin of his body, it is a leprous affection; when the priest sees it, he shall pronounce him impure. 4 But if it is a white discoloration on the skin of his body which does not appear to be deeper than the skin and the hair in it has not turned white, the priest shall isolate the affected person for seven days. 5 On the seventh day the priest shall examine him, and if the affection has remained unchanged in color and the disease has not spread on the skin, the priest shall isolate him for another seven days. 6 On the seventh day the priest shall examine him again: if the affection has faded and has not spread on the skin, the priest shall pronounce him pure. It is a rash; he shall wash his clothes, and he shall be pure. 7 But if the rash should spread on the skin after he has presented himself to the priest and been pronounced pure, he shall present himself again to the priest. 8 And if the priest sees that the rash has spread on the skin, the priest shall pronounce him impure; it is leprosy.

9 When a person has a scaly affection, it shall

אַחַד מִבָּנָיו הַכֹּהֲנִים׃ 3 וְרָאָה הַכֹּהֵן אֶת־
הַנֶּגַע בְּעוֹר־הַבָּשָׂר וְשֵׂעָר בַּנֶּגַע הָפַךְ ׀
לָבָן וּמַרְאֵה הַנֶּגַע עָמֹק מֵעוֹר בְּשָׂרוֹ נֶגַע
צָרַעַת הוּא וְרָאָהוּ הַכֹּהֵן וְטִמֵּא אֹתוֹ׃
4 וְאִם־בַּהֶרֶת לְבָנָה הִוא בְּעוֹר בְּשָׂרוֹ
וְעָמֹק אֵין־מַרְאֶהָ מִן־הָעוֹר וּשְׂעָרָה לֹא־
הָפַךְ לָבָן וְהִסְגִּיר הַכֹּהֵן אֶת־הַנֶּגַע שִׁבְעַת
יָמִים׃ 5 וְרָאָהוּ הַכֹּהֵן בַּיּוֹם הַשְּׁבִיעִי וְהִנֵּה
הַנֶּגַע עָמַד בְּעֵינָיו לֹא־פָשָׂה הַנֶּגַע בָּעוֹר
וְהִסְגִּירוֹ הַכֹּהֵן שִׁבְעַת יָמִים שֵׁנִית׃
שני 6 וְרָאָה הַכֹּהֵן אֹתוֹ בַּיּוֹם הַשְּׁבִיעִי שֵׁנִית
וְהִנֵּה כֵּהָה הַנֶּגַע וְלֹא־פָשָׂה הַנֶּגַע בָּעוֹר
וְטִהֲרוֹ הַכֹּהֵן מִסְפַּחַת הִוא וְכִבֶּס בְּגָדָיו
וְטָהֵר׃ 7 וְאִם־פָּשֹׂה תִפְשֶׂה הַמִּסְפַּחַת
בָּעוֹר אַחֲרֵי הֵרָאֹתוֹ אֶל־הַכֹּהֵן לְטָהֳרָתוֹ
וְנִרְאָה שֵׁנִית אֶל־הַכֹּהֵן׃ 8 וְרָאָה הַכֹּהֵן
וְהִנֵּה פָּשְׂתָה הַמִּסְפַּחַת בָּעוֹר וְטִמְּאוֹ
הַכֹּהֵן צָרַעַת הִוא׃ פ
9 נֶגַע צָרַעַת כִּי תִהְיֶה בְּאָדָם וְהוּבָא

4. the priest shall isolate the affected person More precisely, "he shall confine, lock up" (*v'hisgir*) the affected person. A special dwelling was used for this purpose.

6. he shall wash his clothes Laundering one's garments was a procedure frequently included in purification rites.

8. it is leprosy That is, it is acute *tzara·at*.

CHRONIC AILMENTS (vv. 9–17)

If a person with a chronic ailment is brought to the priest, a different set of diagnostic criteria is applied. Exposed ("raw") flesh in an infected area indicates that the old ailment never healed prop-

---

to be blamed on a lack of will. It should be noted that the Torah itself presents *tzara·at* as an affliction to be cured, not as a punishment to be explained. We might ask: What actions or conditions cause an individual to be isolated from the community today? And what can religious institutions do to restore that person to the community?

Salanter taught that the laws of leprosy and gossip follow immediately after the dietary laws to teach us to be as scrupulous about what comes out of our mouths as we are about what goes into them. He saw the essential sin of gossip as focusing on the faults of others rather than looking to improve ourselves. Society says to the slanderer, "If you are so good at recognizing faults, go live by yourself and discover your own faults and shortcomings."

3. when the priest sees it One commentator reads this as "when the priest sees him" (*Meshekh Ḥokhmah*). The priest is to examine the whole person, not only the diseased limb. He is to see what is whole and healthy about the person, not only what is afflicted.

be reported to the priest. 10If the priest finds on the skin a white swelling which has turned some hair white, with a patch of undiscolored flesh in the swelling, 11it is chronic leprosy on the skin of his body, and the priest shall pronounce him impure; he need not isolate him, for he is impure. 12If the eruption spreads out over the skin so that it covers all the skin of the affected person from head to foot, wherever the priest can see—13if the priest sees that the eruption has covered the whole body—he shall pronounce the affected person pure; he is pure, for he has turned all white. 14But as soon as undiscolored flesh appears in it, he shall be impure; 15when the priest sees the undiscolored flesh, he shall pronounce him impure. The undiscolored flesh is impure; it is leprosy. 16But if the undiscolored flesh again turns white, he shall come to the priest, 17and the priest shall examine him: if the affection has turned white, the priest shall pronounce the affected person pure; he is pure.

18When an inflammation appears on the skin of one's body and it heals, 19and a white swelling

אֶל־הַכֹּהֵן׃ 10 וְרָאָה הַכֹּהֵן וְהִנֵּה שְׂאֵת־
לְבָנָה בָּעוֹר וְהִיא הָפְכָה שֵׂעָר לָבָן וּמִחְיַת
בָּשָׂר חַי בַּשְׂאֵת׃ 11 צָרַעַת נוֹשֶׁנֶת הִוא
בְּעוֹר בְּשָׂרוֹ וְטִמְּאוֹ הַכֹּהֵן לֹא יַסְגִּרֶנּוּ כִּי
טָמֵא הוּא׃ 12 וְאִם־פָּרוֹחַ תִּפְרַח הַצָּרַעַת
בָּעוֹר וְכִסְּתָה הַצָּרַעַת אֵת כָּל־עוֹר הַנֶּגַע
מֵרֹאשׁוֹ וְעַד־רַגְלָיו לְכָל־מַרְאֵה עֵינֵי
הַכֹּהֵן׃ 13 וְרָאָה הַכֹּהֵן וְהִנֵּה כִסְּתָה
הַצָּרַעַת אֶת־כָּל־בְּשָׂרוֹ וְטִהַר אֶת־הַנָּגַע
כֻּלּוֹ הָפַךְ לָבָן טָהוֹר הוּא׃ 14 וּבְיוֹם
הֵרָאוֹת בּוֹ בָּשָׂר חַי יִטְמָא׃ 15 וְרָאָה הַכֹּהֵן
אֶת־הַבָּשָׂר הַחַי וְטִמְּאוֹ הַבָּשָׂר הַחַי טָמֵא
הוּא צָרַעַת הוּא׃ 16 אוֹ כִי יָשׁוּב הַבָּשָׂר
הַחַי וְנֶהְפַּךְ לְלָבָן וּבָא אֶל־הַכֹּהֵן׃
17 וְרָאָהוּ הַכֹּהֵן וְהִנֵּה נֶהְפַּךְ הַנֶּגַע לְלָבָן
וְטִהַר הַכֹּהֵן אֶת־הַנֶּגַע טָהוֹר הוּא׃ פ
שלישי 18 וּבָשָׂר כִּי־יִהְיֶה בוֹ־בְעֹרוֹ שְׁחִין וְנִרְפָּא׃
19 וְהָיָה בִּמְקוֹם הַשְּׁחִין שְׂאֵת לְבָנָה אוֹ

erly. If, however, the exposed flesh is subsequently covered by new skin (referred to in the text as "turning completely white"), this indicates that the chronic *tzara·at* has healed.

9. When a person has a scaly affection That is, when a person shows the priest an old ailment of the skin that may represent the recurrence of chronic *tzara·at.*

10. a white swelling which has turned some hair white Literally, "a white inflammation, in which the hair has turned white."

undiscolored flesh That is, exposed flesh. When healing occurs, white, normal skin grows over the infected area. Recurrence of infection is indicated by the reappearance of raw flesh.

11. it is chronic leprosy . . . he need not isolate him No need for quarantine, because it is determined at the outset that acute *tzara·at* has recurred.

12. wherever the priest can see That is, after the priest's complete examination.

13. for he has turned all white Exposed, or raw, flesh is a reddish color—not white, like normal skin. This, then, is the criterion: Skin turned white is new skin that has grown over the raw area.

14. as soon as undiscolored flesh appears in it If exposed flesh reappears on it, the old infection has not been covered by new skin and will not heal properly, and the individual has chronic *tzara·at.*

16. if the undiscolored flesh again turns white If the exposed flesh recedes and resumes its whiteness, then new ("white") skin has grown over the infected, exposed flesh.

TZARA·AT AS COMPLICATION (vv. 18–46)

This section deals with *tzara·at* that arises as a complication, i.e., a secondary development, out of other conditions. These symptoms are (a) *sh'ḥin,* a term characterizing a number of conditions similar to dermatitis; (b) a burn that became infected; (c) diseases of the hair; (d) a skin condition identified as vitiligo; and (e) ailments of the scalp and forehead.

18. an inflammation appears on the skin . . . and it heals The primary condition, dermatitis, had healed, but a secondary infection had developed in the same area.

or a white discoloration streaked with red develops where the inflammation was, he shall present himself to the priest. 20If the priest finds that it appears lower than the rest of the skin and that the hair in it has turned white, the priest shall pronounce him impure; it is a leprous affection that has broken out in the inflammation. 21But if the priest finds that there is no white hair in it and it is not lower than the rest of the skin, and it is faded, the priest shall isolate him for seven days. 22If it should spread in the skin, the priest shall pronounce him impure; it is an affection. 23But if the discoloration remains stationary, not having spread, it is the scar of the inflammation; the priest shall pronounce him pure.

24When the skin of one's body sustains a burn by fire, and the patch from the burn is a discoloration, either white streaked with red, or white, 25the priest shall examine it. If some hair has turned white in the discoloration, which itself appears to go deeper than the skin, it is leprosy that has broken out in the burn. The priest shall pronounce him impure; it is a leprous affection. 26But if the priest finds that there is no white hair in the discoloration, and that it is not lower than the rest of the skin, and it is faded, the priest shall isolate him for seven days. 27On the seventh day the priest shall examine him: if it has spread in the skin, the priest shall pronounce him impure; it is a leprous affection. 28But if the discoloration has remained stationary, not having spread on the skin, and it is faded, it is the swelling from the burn. The priest shall pronounce him pure, for it is the scar of the burn.

29If a man or a woman has an affection on the head or in the beard, 30the priest shall ex-

בַהֶרֶת לְבָנָה אֲדַמְדָּמֶת וְנִרְאָה אֶל־הַכֹּהֵן׃
20 וְרָאָה הַכֹּהֵן וְהִנֵּה מַרְאֶהָ שָׁפָל מִן־
הָעוֹר וּשְׂעָרָהּ הָפַךְ לָבָן וְטִמְּאוֹ הַכֹּהֵן
נֶגַע־צָרַעַת הִוא בַּשְּׁחִין פָּרָחָה׃ 21 וְאִם ׀
יִרְאֶנָּה הַכֹּהֵן וְהִנֵּה אֵין־בָּהּ שֵׂעָר לָבָן
וּשְׁפָלָה אֵינֶנָּה מִן־הָעוֹר וְהִיא כֵהָה
וְהִסְגִּירוֹ הַכֹּהֵן שִׁבְעַת יָמִים׃ 22 וְאִם־
פָּשֹׂה תִפְשֶׂה בָּעוֹר וְטִמֵּא הַכֹּהֵן אֹתוֹ נֶגַע
הִוא׃ 23 וְאִם־תַּחְתֶּיהָ תַּעֲמֹד הַבַּהֶרֶת לֹא
פָשָׂתָה צָרֶבֶת הַשְּׁחִין הִוא וְטִהֲרוֹ
הַכֹּהֵן׃ ס
24 אוֹ בָשָׂר כִּי־יִהְיֶה בְעֹרוֹ מִכְוַת־אֵשׁ רביעי [שני]
וְהָיְתָה מִחְיַת הַמִּכְוָה בַּהֶרֶת לְבָנָה
אֲדַמְדֶּמֶת אוֹ לְבָנָה׃ 25 וְרָאָה אֹתָהּ הַכֹּהֵן
וְהִנֵּה נֶהְפַּךְ שֵׂעָר לָבָן בַּבַּהֶרֶת וּמַרְאֶהָ
עָמֹק מִן־הָעוֹר צָרַעַת הִוא בַּמִּכְוָה פָּרָחָה
וְטִמֵּא אֹתוֹ הַכֹּהֵן נֶגַע צָרַעַת הִוא׃
26 וְאִם ׀ יִרְאֶנָּה הַכֹּהֵן וְהִנֵּה אֵין־בַּבַּהֶרֶת
שֵׂעָר לָבָן וּשְׁפָלָה אֵינֶנָּה מִן־הָעוֹר וְהִוא
כֵהָה וְהִסְגִּירוֹ הַכֹּהֵן שִׁבְעַת יָמִים׃
27 וְרָאָהוּ הַכֹּהֵן בַּיּוֹם הַשְּׁבִיעִי אִם־פָּשֹׂה
תִפְשֶׂה בָּעוֹר וְטִמֵּא הַכֹּהֵן אֹתוֹ נֶגַע צָרַעַת
הִוא׃ 28 וְאִם־תַּחְתֶּיהָ תַעֲמֹד הַבַּהֶרֶת
לֹא־פָשְׂתָה בָעוֹר וְהִוא כֵהָה שְׂאֵת
הַמִּכְוָה הִוא וְטִהֲרוֹ הַכֹּהֵן כִּי־צָרֶבֶת
הַמִּכְוָה הִוא׃ פ
29 וְאִישׁ אוֹ אִשָּׁה כִּי־יִהְיֶה בוֹ נֶגַע בְּרֹאשׁ מישי
אוֹ בְזָקָן׃ 30 וְרָאָה הַכֹּהֵן אֶת־הַנֶּגַע וְהִנֵּה

20. The symptomatology here is essentially the same as that applicable to the diagnosis of an initial condition of *tzara·at,* in verses 1–8.

24. the patch from the burn is a discoloration The exposed skin is a pink or white shiny spot.

29. The hair, which is rooted in layers of the skin, is directly affected by conditions (such as acne) that disturb the hair follicles.

amine the affection. If it appears to go deeper
than the skin and there is thin yellow hair in
it, the priest shall pronounce him impure; it is
a scall, a scaly eruption in the hair or beard. [31]But
if the priest finds that the scall affection does
not appear to go deeper than the skin, yet there
is no black hair in it, the priest shall isolate the
person with the scall affection for seven days.
[32]On the seventh day the priest shall examine
the affection. If the scall has not spread and no
yellow hair has appeared in it, and the scall does
not appear to go deeper than the skin, [33]the person with the scall shall shave himself, but without shaving the scall; the priest shall isolate him
for another seven days. [34]On the seventh day
the priest shall examine the scall. If the scall has
not spread on the skin, and does not appear to
go deeper than the skin, the priest shall pronounce him pure; he shall wash his clothes, and
he shall be pure. [35]If, however, the scall should
spread on the skin after he has been pronounced
pure, [36]the priest shall examine him. If the scall
has spread on the skin, the priest need not look
for yellow hair: he is impure. [37]But if the scall
has remained unchanged in color, and black
hair has grown in it, the scall is healed; he is pure.
The priest shall pronounce him pure.

[38]If a man or a woman has the skin of the body

מַרְאֵהוּ עָמֹק מִן־הָעוֹר וּבוֹ שֵׂעָר צָהֹב דָּק
וְטִמֵּא אֹתוֹ הַכֹּהֵן נֶתֶק הוּא צָרַעַת הָרֹאשׁ
אוֹ הַזָּקָן הוּא׃ 31 וְכִי־יִרְאֶה הַכֹּהֵן אֶת־
נֶגַע הַנֶּתֶק וְהִנֵּה אֵין־מַרְאֵהוּ עָמֹק מִן־
הָעוֹר וְשֵׂעָר שָׁחֹר אֵין בּוֹ וְהִסְגִּיר הַכֹּהֵן
אֶת־נֶגַע הַנֶּתֶק שִׁבְעַת יָמִים׃ 32 וְרָאָה
הַכֹּהֵן אֶת־הַנֶּגַע בַּיּוֹם הַשְּׁבִיעִי וְהִנֵּה
לֹא־פָשָׂה הַנֶּתֶק וְלֹא־הָיָה בוֹ שֵׂעָר צָהֹב
וּמַרְאֵה הַנֶּתֶק אֵין עָמֹק מִן־הָעוֹר׃
33 וְהִתְגַּלָּח* וְאֶת־הַנֶּתֶק לֹא יְגַלֵּחַ
וְהִסְגִּיר הַכֹּהֵן אֶת־הַנֶּתֶק שִׁבְעַת יָמִים
שֵׁנִית׃ 34 וְרָאָה הַכֹּהֵן אֶת־הַנֶּתֶק בַּיּוֹם
הַשְּׁבִיעִי וְהִנֵּה לֹא־פָשָׂה הַנֶּתֶק בָּעוֹר
וּמַרְאֵהוּ אֵינֶנּוּ עָמֹק מִן־הָעוֹר וְטִהַר אֹתוֹ
הַכֹּהֵן וְכִבֶּס בְּגָדָיו וְטָהֵר׃ 35 וְאִם־פָּשֹׂה
יִפְשֶׂה הַנֶּתֶק בָּעוֹר אַחֲרֵי טָהֳרָתוֹ׃
36 וְרָאָהוּ הַכֹּהֵן וְהִנֵּה פָּשָׂה הַנֶּתֶק בָּעוֹר
לֹא־יְבַקֵּר הַכֹּהֵן לַשֵּׂעָר הַצָּהֹב טָמֵא הוּא׃
37 וְאִם־בְּעֵינָיו עָמַד הַנֶּתֶק וְשֵׂעָר שָׁחֹר
צָמַח־בּוֹ נִרְפָּא הַנֶּתֶק טָהוֹר הוּא וְטִהֲרוֹ
הַכֹּהֵן׃ ס
38 וְאִישׁ אוֹ־אִשָּׁה כִּי־יִהְיֶה בְעוֹר־בְּשָׂרָם

v. 33. ג׳ רבתי לפי נוסחים מקובלים

30–31. This passage is describing the progressive stages of a complication whose treatment differs somewhat from acute *tzara·at* because of the background condition involved. Verse 30 stipulates that if both positive symptoms appear, acute *tzara·at* is indicated. Verse 31 states that if only one symptom occurs—the absence of black, normal hair (which is equivalent to the presence of yellow, infected hair)—quarantine is imposed, because a final determination cannot yet be made.

thin yellow hair The symptoms are generally similar to those of skin ailments, except that yellow, not white, hair is the discoloration to be watched for.

scall Hebrew: *netek,* which refers to the condition of hair follicles, not of skin, and describes the follicles as being "torn" from the scalp after "splitting."

32. On the seventh day the priest shall examine the affection Three conditions must exist for a declaration of purity to be issued at this stage: no yellow hair, no enlargement of the lesions, and no recessed lesions. To allow for clearer observation, the hair is shaved around the infected areas, leaving the areas themselves unshaven.

36. the scall has spread on the skin Any enlargement of the lesions after 14 days is sufficient to warrant a diagnosis of acute *tzara·at.* The priest need look no further for yellow hair.

37. the scall has remained unchanged If normal-colored hair grows back in the infected area and there has been no subsequent enlargement of the lesions, the *netek* infection has healed.

streaked with white discolorations, ³⁹and the priest sees that the discolorations on the skin of the body are of a dull white, it is a tetter broken out on the skin; he is pure.

⁴⁰If a man loses the hair of his head and becomes bald, he is pure. ⁴¹If he loses the hair on the front part of his head and becomes bald at the forehead, he is pure. ⁴²But if a white affection streaked with red appears on the bald part in the front or at the back of the head, it is a scaly eruption that is spreading over the bald part in the front or at the back of the head. ⁴³The priest shall examine him: if the swollen affection on the bald part in the front or at the back of his head is white streaked with red, like the leprosy of body skin in appearance, ⁴⁴the man is leprous; he is impure. The priest shall pronounce him impure; he has the affection on his head.

⁴⁵As for the person with a leprous affection, his clothes shall be rent, his head shall be left bare, and he shall cover over his upper lip; and he shall call out, "Impure! Impure!" ⁴⁶He shall be impure as long as the disease is on him. Being impure, he shall dwell apart; his dwelling shall be outside the camp.

בֶּהֶ֖רֶת בְּהֹ֣ת לְבָנֹ֑ת : 39 וְרָאָ֣ה הַכֹּהֵ֗ן וְהִנֵּ֤ה בְעוֹר־בְּשָׂרָם֙ בֶּהָרֹ֣ת כֵּה֔וֹת לְבָנֹ֑ת בֹּ֣הַק ה֞וּא פָּרַ֥ח בָּע֖וֹר טָה֥וֹר הֽוּא : ס

40 וְאִ֕ישׁ כִּ֥י יִמָּרֵ֖ט רֹאשׁ֑וֹ קֵרֵ֥חַ ה֖וּא טָה֥וֹר הֽוּא : 41 וְאִם֙ מִפְּאַ֣ת פָּנָ֔יו יִמָּרֵ֖ט רֹאשׁ֑וֹ גִּבֵּ֥חַ ה֖וּא טָה֥וֹר הֽוּא : 42 וְכִֽי־יִהְיֶ֤ה בַקָּרַ֙חַת֙ א֣וֹ בַגַּבַּ֔חַת נֶ֖גַע לָבָ֣ן אֲדַמְדָּ֑ם צָרַ֤עַת פֹּרַ֙חַת֙ הִ֔וא בְּקָרַחְתּ֖וֹ א֥וֹ בְגַבַּחְתּֽוֹ : 43 וְרָאָ֣ה אֹת֣וֹ הַכֹּהֵ֗ן וְהִנֵּ֤ה שְׂאֵת־הַנֶּ֙גַע֙ לְבָנָ֣ה אֲדַמְדֶּ֔מֶת בְּקָרַחְתּ֖וֹ א֥וֹ בְגַבַּחְתּֽוֹ כְּמַרְאֵ֥ה צָרַ֖עַת ע֥וֹר בָּשָֽׂר : 44 אִישׁ־צָר֣וּעַ ה֖וּא טָמֵ֥א ה֑וּא טַמֵּ֧א יְטַמְּאֶ֛נּוּ הַכֹּהֵ֖ן בְּרֹאשׁ֥וֹ נִגְעֽוֹ :

45 וְהַצָּר֜וּעַ אֲשֶׁר־בּ֣וֹ הַנֶּ֗גַע בְּגָדָ֞יו יִהְי֤וּ פְרֻמִים֙ וְרֹאשׁוֹ֙ יִהְיֶ֣ה פָר֔וּעַ וְעַל־שָׂפָ֖ם יַעְטֶ֑ה וְטָמֵ֥א | טָמֵ֖א יִקְרָֽא : 46 כָּל־יְמֵ֞י אֲשֶׁ֨ר הַנֶּ֥גַע בּ֛וֹ יִטְמָ֖א טָמֵ֣א ה֑וּא בָּדָ֣ד יֵשֵׁ֔ב מִח֥וּץ לַֽמַּחֲנֶ֖ה מוֹשָׁבֽוֹ : ס

ששי
[שלישי]

38–39. These verses deal with an ailment known as *bohak* (brightness), identified by some medical authorities as vitiligo. It is a rash that is not acute.

40. If a man loses the hair of his head and becomes bald This section (vv. 40–44) deals with cases in which a person was bald before the outbreak of the ailment in question.

43. If the inflamed infection is whitish on the bald pate or on the forehead, the person is suffering from acute *tzara·at*.

45. the person with a leprous affection Namely, one who suffers from the acute condition stated in verse 8.

his head shall be left bare Baring the head so that the hair hung loose was a customary way of shaming a person, as was covering the upper lip.

and he shall call out, "Impure!" The sufferer must warn all who approach that he is impure.

46. as long as the disease is on him Thus, an individual suffering from acute *tzara·at* may be banished permanently.

---

45. he shall call out, "Impure! Impure!" According to the Talmud, one does this not only to warn others of the contagion but also to elicit compassion and prayers on one's behalf (BT MK 5a). It is the responsibility of an afflicted person to recognize the illness and ask for help; and it is the responsibility of the community to offer support and prayer rather than shun or ignore the afflicted.

One commentator reads, "the impure shall call out, 'Impure!'" That is, people tend to project their own failings onto others. A corrupt person sees corruption all around (BT Kid. 70a).

47When an eruptive affection occurs in a cloth of wool or linen fabric, 48in the warp or in the woof of the linen or the wool, or in a skin or in anything made of skin; 49if the affection in the cloth or the skin, in the warp or the woof, or in any article of skin, is streaky green or red, it is an eruptive affection. It shall be shown to the priest; 50and the priest, after examining the affection, shall isolate the affected article for seven days. 51On the seventh day he shall examine the affection: if the affection has spread in the cloth—whether in the warp or the woof, or in the skin, for whatever purpose the skin may be used—the affection is a malignant eruption; it is impure. 52The cloth—whether warp or woof in wool or linen, or any article of skin—in which the affection is found, shall be burned, for it is a malignant eruption; it shall be consumed in fire. 53But if the priest sees that the affection in the cloth—whether in warp or in woof, or in any article of skin—has not spread, 54the priest shall order the affected article washed, and he shall isolate it for another seven days. 55And if, after the affected article has been washed, the priest sees that the affection has not changed color and that it has not spread, it is impure. It shall be consumed in fire; it is a fret, whether on its inner side or on its outer side. 56But if the priest sees that the affected part, after it has been washed, is faded, he shall tear it out from the cloth or skin, whether in the warp or

47 וְהַבֶּ֗גֶד כִּֽי־יִהְיֶ֥ה ב֖וֹ נֶ֣גַע צָ֑רַעַת בְּבֶ֣גֶד
צֶ֔מֶר א֖וֹ בְּבֶ֥גֶד פִּשְׁתִּֽים׃ 48 א֤וֹ בִשְׁתִי֙ א֣וֹ
בְעֵ֔רֶב לַפִּשְׁתִּ֖ים וְלַצָּ֑מֶר א֣וֹ בְע֔וֹר א֖וֹ
בְּכָל־מְלֶ֥אכֶת עֽוֹר׃ 49 וְהָיָ֨ה הַנֶּ֜גַע יְרַקְרַ֣ק ׀
א֣וֹ אֲדַמְדָּ֗ם בַּבֶּ֨גֶד א֜וֹ בָע֗וֹר אֽוֹ־בַשְּׁתִ֤י
אֽוֹ־בָעֵ֙רֶב֙ א֣וֹ בְכָל־כְּלִי־ע֔וֹר נֶ֥גַע צָרַ֖עַת
ה֑וּא וְהָרְאָ֖ה אֶת־הַכֹּהֵֽן׃ 50 וְרָאָ֥ה הַכֹּהֵ֖ן
אֶת־הַנָּ֑גַע וְהִסְגִּ֥יר אֶת־הַנֶּ֖גַע שִׁבְעַ֥ת
יָמִֽים׃ 51 וְרָאָ֨ה אֶת־הַנֶּ֜גַע בַּיּ֣וֹם הַשְּׁבִיעִ֗י
כִּֽי־פָשָׂ֤ה הַנֶּ֙גַע֙ בַּ֠בֶּגֶד אֽוֹ־בַשְּׁתִ֤י אֽוֹ־
בָעֵ֙רֶב֙ א֣וֹ בָע֔וֹר לְכֹ֛ל אֲשֶׁר־יֵעָשֶׂ֥ה הָע֖וֹר
לִמְלָאכָ֑ה צָרַ֧עַת מַמְאֶ֛רֶת הַנֶּ֖גַע טָמֵ֥א
הֽוּא׃ 52 וְשָׂרַ֨ף אֶת־הַבֶּ֜גֶד א֥וֹ אֶת־הַשְּׁתִ֣י ׀
א֣וֹ אֶת־הָעֵ֗רֶב בַּצֶּ֙מֶר֙ א֣וֹ בַפִּשְׁתִּ֔ים א֚וֹ
אֶת־כָּל־כְּלִ֣י הָע֔וֹר אֲשֶׁר־יִהְיֶ֥ה ב֖וֹ הַנָּ֑גַע
כִּֽי־צָרַ֤עַת מַמְאֶ֙רֶת֙ הִ֔וא בָּאֵ֖שׁ תִּשָּׂרֵֽף׃
53 וְאִם֮ יִרְאֶ֣ה הַכֹּהֵן֒ וְהִנֵּה֙ לֹא־פָשָׂ֣ה הַנֶּ֔גַע
בַּבֶּ֕גֶד א֥וֹ בַשְּׁתִ֖י א֣וֹ בָעֵ֑רֶב א֖וֹ בְּכָל־כְּלִי־
עֽוֹר׃ 54 וְצִוָּה֙ הַכֹּהֵ֔ן וְכִ֨בְּס֔וּ אֵ֥ת אֲשֶׁר־
בּ֖וֹ הַנָּ֑גַע וְהִסְגִּיר֥וֹ שִׁבְעַת־יָמִ֖ים שֵׁנִֽית׃
55 וְרָאָ֨ה הַכֹּהֵ֜ן אַחֲרֵ֣י ׀ הֻכַּבֵּ֣ס אֶת־הַנֶּ֗גַע שביעי [רביעי]
וְ֠הִנֵּה לֹא־הָפַ֨ךְ הַנֶּ֤גַע אֶת־עֵינוֹ֙ וְהַנֶּ֣גַע
לֹא־פָשָׂ֔ה טָמֵ֣א ה֔וּא בָּאֵ֖שׁ תִּשְׂרְפֶ֑נּוּ
פְּחֶ֣תֶת הִ֔וא בְּקָרַחְתּ֖וֹ א֥וֹ בְגַבַּחְתּֽוֹ׃ 56 וְאִם֙
רָאָ֣ה הַכֹּהֵ֔ן וְהִנֵּה֙ כֵּהָ֣ה הַנֶּ֔גַע אַחֲרֵ֖י הֻכַּבֵּ֣ס
אֹת֑וֹ וְקָרַ֣ע אֹת֗וֹ מִן־הַבֶּ֙גֶד֙ א֣וֹ מִן־הָע֔וֹר

***TZARA·AT* IN FABRICS AND LEATHER**
(vv. 47–59)

This section deals with *tzara·at*-type infections that damage fabrics and worked leather. They may have been some kinds of fungoid or sporoid infections.

---

47. Although most medieval and modern commentators see the eruption of *tzara·at* in clothing as a natural phenomenon, a form of rot or fungus, Maimonides and Ramban see it as supernatural, something that could take place only in the Land of Israel. Because of that land's sensitivity to immorality, even the clothes one wears would bear witness to the moral decay of the person wearing them.

Although the laws of *tum·ah* seem very foreign to us, they flow directly from the Israelites' sense that being able to come into God's presence is an irreplaceable privilege. This led them to be profoundly concerned with anything that might estrange them from the divine presence.

in the woof; 57and if it occurs again in the cloth—whether in warp or in woof—or in any article of skin, it is a wild growth; the affected article shall be consumed in fire. 58If, however, the affection disappears from the cloth—warp or woof—or from any article of skin that has been washed, it shall be washed again, and it shall be pure.

59Such is the procedure for eruptive affections of cloth, woolen or linen, in warp or in woof, or of any article of skin, for pronouncing it pure or impure.

מפטיר אוֹ מִן־הַשְּׁתִי אוֹ מִן־הָעֵרֶב׃ 57 וְאִם־
תֵּרָאֶה עוֹד בַּבֶּגֶד אוֹ־בַשְּׁתִי אוֹ־בָעֵרֶב אוֹ
בְכָל־כְּלִי־עוֹר פֹּרַחַת הִוא בָּאֵשׁ תִּשְׂרְפֶנּוּ
אֵת אֲשֶׁר־בּוֹ הַנָּגַע׃ 58 וְהַבֶּגֶד אוֹ־הַשְּׁתִי
אוֹ־הָעֵרֶב אוֹ־כָל־כְּלִי הָעוֹר אֲשֶׁר תְּכַבֵּס
וְסָר מֵהֶם הַנָּגַע וְכֻבַּס שֵׁנִית וְטָהֵר׃
59 זֹאת תּוֹרַת נֶגַע־צָרַעַת בֶּגֶד הַצֶּמֶר ׀ אוֹ
הַפִּשְׁתִּים אוֹ הַשְּׁתִי אוֹ הָעֵרֶב אוֹ כָּל־
כְּלִי־עוֹר לְטַהֲרוֹ אוֹ לְטַמְּאוֹ׃* פ

* *For the* haftarah *for this portion, see p. 671.*

M'TZORA

מצרע

14 The LORD spoke to Moses, saying: 2This
shall be the ritual for a leper at the time that
he is to be purified.
When it has been reported to the priest, 3the
priest shall go outside the camp. If the priest sees
that the leper has been healed of his scaly
affection, 4the priest shall order two live pure
birds, cedar wood, crimson stuff, and hyssop to
be brought for him who is to be purified. 5The
priest shall order one of the birds slaughtered

יד וַיְדַבֵּר יְהוָה אֶל־מֹשֶׁה לֵּאמֹר:
2 זֹאת תִּהְיֶה תּוֹרַת הַמְּצֹרָע בְּיוֹם טָהֳרָתוֹ
וְהוּבָא אֶל־הַכֹּהֵן: 3 וְיָצָא הַכֹּהֵן אֶל־מִחוּץ
לַמַּחֲנֶה וְרָאָה הַכֹּהֵן וְהִנֵּה נִרְפָּא נֶגַע־
הַצָּרַעַת מִן־הַצָּרוּעַ: 4 וְצִוָּה הַכֹּהֵן וְלָקַח
לַמִּטַּהֵר שְׁתֵּי־צִפֳּרִים חַיּוֹת טְהֹרוֹת וְעֵץ
אֶרֶז וּשְׁנִי תוֹלַעַת וְאֵזֹב: 5 וְצִוָּה הַכֹּהֵן
וְשָׁחַט אֶת־הַצִּפּוֹר הָאֶחָת אֶל־כְּלִי־חֶרֶשׂ

THE PURIFICATION OF SKIN DISEASES *(continued)*

PURIFICATION RITES FOR INDIVIDUALS (14:1–32)

The rites ordained for the purification of a person who had suffered from *tzara·at* are among the most elaborate in the priestly laws. They demonstrate how seriously the *tzara·at* infections were regarded in ancient Israel.

2. ritual Hebrew: *torah,* which here means a manual of procedure for the priests, who administered the purification rites.

When it has been reported to the priest The priest went out to the afflicted person who could not enter the camp, having been declared impure.

4. two live pure birds The birds must be physically sound and of a pure species.

crimson stuff Hebrew: *sh'ni tola·at;* literally, "the scarlet of the worm." A crimson dye is extracted from the eggs of an insect that lives in the leaves of oak trees. The cloth, most likely, was wool.

5. over fresh water in an earthen vessel Blood of the slaughtered bird not collected in the vessel would flow down into the earth. The Hebrew for "fresh water" (*mayim ḥayyim*) literally

---

CHAPTER 14

This *parashah* (read together with *Tazri·a* in most non-leap years) describes the ritual of purifying and reintegrating the recovered leper. We can read it as a description of the Israelites' attitude to the experience of recovering from illness. The text also discusses the appearance of a "plague" in the stones of a person's house and the implications of menstrual blood and seminal emissions as they relate to ritual impurity (*tum·ah*).

The formal description of the cleansing ritual masks the deep and possibly conflicted feelings of the person who has recovered from a serious illness. These might include feelings of relief and happiness together with a new appreciation of good health, perhaps resentment over what had been gone through as well as envy of people who had remained healthy. The offering of the recovered leper is sometimes referred to as "the sacrifice of one who has returned from the dead," either because the illness was so grave or because a life cut off from all human contact, a life without friends and family, was not really a life.

3. the priest shall go outside the camp He is not to wait until people come to him with their concerns but must go to where the people are.

4. The offering included cedar wood, from the tallest and strongest of all plants, and hyssop, a kind of grass, the smallest and most vulnerable of all growing things. This was to symbolize the leveling power of illness, which afflicts the powerful and the powerless alike, and to teach the mighty a lesson about their vulnerability. The person recovered from illness may re-enter the camp but may not go home yet. Perhaps one who leaves the hospital or the isolation of serious illness with great relief is not yet fully oneself, not quite ready to resume the routines and responsibilities of normal life, home, and family.

over fresh water in an earthen vessel; ⁶and he shall take the live bird, along with the cedar wood, the crimson stuff, and the hyssop, and dip them together with the live bird in the blood of the bird that was slaughtered over the fresh water. ⁷He shall then sprinkle it seven times on him who is to be purified of the eruption and purify him; and he shall set the live bird free in the open country. ⁸The one to be purified shall wash his clothes, shave off all his hair, and bathe in water; then he shall be pure. After that he may enter the camp, but he must remain outside his tent seven days. ⁹On the seventh day he shall shave off all his hair—of head, beard, and eyebrows. When he has shaved off all his hair, he shall wash his clothes and bathe his body in water; then he shall be pure. ¹⁰On the eighth day he shall take two male lambs without blemish, one ewe lamb in its first year without blemish, three-tenths of a measure of choice flour with oil mixed in for a grain offering, and one *log* of oil. ¹¹These shall be presented before the Lord, with the man to be purified, at the entrance of the Tent of Meeting, by the priest who performs the purification.

¹²The priest shall take one of the male lambs and offer it with the *log* of oil as a reparation offering, and he shall elevate them as an elevation offering before the Lord. ¹³The lamb shall be slaughtered at the spot in the sacred area

עַל־מַ֣יִם חַיִּֽים: 6 אֶת־הַצִּפֹּ֥ר הַֽחַיָּ֖ה יִקַּ֣ח אֹתָ֑הּ וְאֶת־עֵ֣ץ הָאֶ֗רֶז וְאֶת־שְׁנִ֤י הַתּוֹלַ֙עַת֙ וְאֶת־הָ֣אֵזֹ֔ב וְטָבַ֣ל אוֹתָ֗ם וְאֵ֣ת ׀ הַצִּפֹּ֣ר הַֽחַיָּ֔ה בְּדַם֙ הַצִּפֹּ֣ר הַשְּׁחֻטָ֔ה עַ֖ל הַמַּ֥יִם הַֽחַיִּֽים: 7 וְהִזָּ֗ה עַ֧ל הַמִּטַּהֵ֛ר מִן־הַצָּרַ֖עַת שֶׁ֣בַע פְּעָמִ֑ים וְטִ֣הֲר֔וֹ וְשִׁלַּ֛ח אֶת־הַצִּפֹּ֥ר הַֽחַיָּ֖ה עַל־פְּנֵ֥י הַשָּׂדֶֽה: 8 וְכִבֶּס֩ הַמִּטַּהֵ֨ר אֶת־בְּגָדָ֜יו וְגִלַּ֣ח אֶת־כָּל־שְׂעָר֗וֹ וְרָחַ֤ץ בַּמַּ֙יִם֙ וְטָהֵ֔ר וְאַחַ֖ר יָב֣וֹא אֶל־הַֽמַּחֲנֶ֑ה וְיָשַׁ֛ב מִח֥וּץ לְאׇהֳל֖וֹ שִׁבְעַ֥ת יָמִֽים: 9 וְהָיָה֩ בַיּ֨וֹם הַשְּׁבִיעִ֜י יְגַלַּ֣ח אֶת־כָּל־שְׂעָר֗וֹ אֶת־רֹאשׁ֤וֹ וְאֶת־זְקָנוֹ֙ וְאֵת֙ גַּבֹּ֣ת עֵינָ֔יו וְאֶת־כָּל־שְׂעָר֖וֹ יְגַלֵּ֑חַ וְכִבֶּ֣ס אֶת־בְּגָדָ֗יו וְרָחַ֧ץ אֶת־בְּשָׂר֛וֹ בַּמַּ֖יִם וְטָהֵֽר: 10 וּבַיּ֣וֹם הַשְּׁמִינִ֗י יִקַּ֤ח שְׁנֵֽי־כְבָשִׂים֙ תְּמִימִ֔ם וְכַבְשָׂ֥ה אַחַ֖ת בַּת־שְׁנָתָ֣הּ תְּמִימָ֑ה וּשְׁלֹשָׁ֣ה עֶשְׂרֹנִ֗ים סֹ֤לֶת מִנְחָה֙ בְּלוּלָ֣ה בַשֶּׁ֔מֶן וְלֹ֥ג אֶחָ֖ד שָֽׁמֶן: 11 וְהֶעֱמִ֞יד הַכֹּהֵ֣ן הַֽמְטַהֵ֗ר אֵ֛ת הָאִ֥ישׁ הַמִּטַּהֵ֖ר וְאֹתָ֑ם לִפְנֵ֣י יְהֹוָ֔ה פֶּ֖תַח אֹ֥הֶל מוֹעֵֽד: 12 וְלָקַ֨ח הַכֹּהֵ֜ן אֶת־הַכֶּ֣בֶשׂ הָֽאֶחָ֗ד וְהִקְרִ֥יב אֹת֛וֹ לְאָשָׁ֖ם וְאֶת־לֹ֣ג הַשָּׁ֑מֶן וְהֵנִ֥יף אֹתָ֛ם שני תְּנוּפָ֖ה לִפְנֵ֥י יְהֹוָֽה: 13 וְשָׁחַ֣ט אֶת־הַכֶּ֗בֶשׂ בִּמְק֡וֹם אֲשֶׁ֣ר יִשְׁחַ֧ט אֶת־הַֽחַטָּ֛את וְאֶת־

---

means "living water." It is water that flows continually, like that of springs.

9. of head, beard, and eyebrows   It was normally forbidden to shave the beard or the sidelocks of the head (19:27). Exceptions are made for these rites of purification.

10. log   About 10 fluid ounces (0.3 L).

11.   The person undergoing purification is stationed near the entrance of the Tent of Meet-

ing, together with the material assembled for use in the purification.

12. reparation offering   This provided sacrificial blood to be sprinkled on the extremities of the individual who was being purified; blood from the burnt offering or from the purification offering could not be applied to the human body.

13. at the spot in the sacred area   That is, on the north side of the altar (see 1:11, 4:24, and 7:2).

---

9. bathe his body in water   This was not simply to cleanse oneself. It symbolized rebirth and re-creation—just as an infant is born out of water, just as a convert emerges out of water to a new life and a new identity, just as the

world was created out of water (Gen. 1:2). The experience of illness and recovery has made the leper a new person—that is, someone who now looks at life differently (*Seifer Ha-Ḥinnukh*).

where the purification offering and the burnt offering are slaughtered. For the reparation offering, like the purification offering, goes to the priest; it is most holy. 14The priest shall take some of the blood of the reparation offering, and the priest shall put it on the ridge of the right ear of him who is being purified, and on the thumb of his right hand, and on the big toe of his right foot. 15The priest shall then take some of the *log* of oil and pour it into the palm of his own left hand. 16And the priest shall dip his right finger in the oil that is in the palm of his left hand and sprinkle some of the oil with his finger seven times before the Lord. 17Some of the oil left in his palm shall be put by the priest on the ridge of the right ear of the one being purified, on the thumb of his right hand, and on the big toe of his right foot—over the blood of the reparation offering. 18The rest of the oil in his palm the priest shall put on the head of the one being purified. Thus the priest shall make expiation for him before the Lord. 19The priest shall then offer the purification offering and make expiation for the one being purified of his impurity. Last, the burnt offering shall be slaughtered, 20and the priest shall offer the burnt offering and the grain offering on the altar, and the priest shall make expiation for him. Then he shall be pure.

21If, however, he is poor and his means are insufficient, he shall take one male lamb for a reparation offering, to be elevated in expiation

הָעֹלָ֖ה בִּמְק֣וֹם הַקֹּ֑דֶשׁ כִּ֡י כַּ֠חַטָּ֜את הָאָשָׁ֥ם הוּא֙ לַכֹּהֵ֔ן קֹ֥דֶשׁ קָֽדָשִׁ֖ים הֽוּא: 14 וְלָקַ֣ח הַכֹּהֵן֮ מִדַּ֣ם הָֽאָשָׁם֒ וְנָתַן֙ הַכֹּהֵ֔ן עַל־תְּנ֛וּךְ אֹ֥זֶן הַמִּטַּהֵ֖ר הַיְמָנִ֑ית וְעַל־בֹּ֤הֶן יָדוֹ֙ הַיְמָנִ֔ית וְעַל־בֹּ֥הֶן רַגְל֖וֹ הַיְמָנִֽית: 15 וְלָקַ֥ח הַכֹּהֵ֖ן מִלֹּ֣ג הַשָּׁ֑מֶן וְיָצַ֛ק עַל־כַּ֥ף הַכֹּהֵ֖ן הַשְּׂמָאלִֽית: 16 וְטָבַ֤ל הַכֹּהֵן֙ אֶת־אֶצְבָּע֣וֹ הַיְמָנִ֔ית מִן־הַשֶּׁ֕מֶן אֲשֶׁ֥ר עַל־כַּפּ֖וֹ הַשְּׂמָאלִ֑ית וְהִזָּ֨ה מִן־הַשֶּׁ֧מֶן בְּאֶצְבָּע֛וֹ שֶׁ֥בַע פְּעָמִ֖ים לִפְנֵ֥י יְהֹוָֽה: 17 וּמִיֶּ֨תֶר הַשֶּׁ֜מֶן אֲשֶׁ֣ר עַל־כַּפּ֗וֹ יִתֵּ֤ן הַכֹּהֵן֙ עַל־תְּנ֞וּךְ אֹ֤זֶן הַמִּטַּהֵר֙ הַיְמָנִ֔ית וְעַל־בֹּ֥הֶן יָד֖וֹ הַיְמָנִ֑ית וְעַל־בֹּ֥הֶן רַגְל֖וֹ הַיְמָנִ֑ית עַ֖ל דַּ֥ם הָֽאָשָֽׁם: 18 וְהַנּוֹתָ֗ר בַּשֶּׁ֨מֶן֙ אֲשֶׁר֙ עַל־כַּ֣ף הַכֹּהֵ֔ן יִתֵּ֖ן עַל־רֹ֣אשׁ הַמִּטַּהֵ֑ר וְכִפֶּ֥ר עָלָ֛יו הַכֹּהֵ֖ן לִפְנֵ֥י יְהֹוָֽה: 19 וְעָשָׂ֤ה הַכֹּהֵן֙ אֶת־הַ֣חַטָּ֔את וְכִפֶּ֕ר עַל־הַמִּטַּהֵ֖ר מִטֻּמְאָת֑וֹ וְאַחַ֖ר יִשְׁחַ֥ט אֶת־הָֽעֹלָֽה: 20 וְהֶֽעֱלָ֧ה הַכֹּהֵ֛ן אֶת־הָֽעֹלָ֖ה וְאֶת־הַמִּנְחָ֖ה הַמִּזְבֵּ֑חָה וְכִפֶּ֥ר עָלָ֛יו הַכֹּהֵ֖ן וְטָהֵֽר: ס

21 וְאִם־דַּ֣ל ה֗וּא וְאֵ֣ין יָדוֹ֮ מַשֶּׂ֒גֶת֒ וְ֠לָקַ֠ח כֶּ֣בֶשׂ אֶחָ֥ד אָשָׁ֛ם לִתְנוּפָ֖ה לְכַפֵּ֥ר עָלָֽיו

שלישי
[חמישי]

---

14. on the ridge of the right ear The person was treated literally from head to foot.

18. The rites were essential to securing expiation, or purification. The purification offering and the burnt offering were also parts of the purification rites. The purification offering served to place the individual in good standing with God.

The burnt offering symbolized renewed acceptability as a worshiper and full reinstatement in the community.

21–32. These verses repeat the rites prescribed in verses 1–20, except that birds are substituted for animals in the burnt offering and in the purification offering.

---

17. The oil is placed on the leper's head, hand, and foot and sprinkled on the altar, to convey the idea that recovery from illness is the combined result of our actions, our attitudes, and divine grace.

for him, one-tenth of a measure of choice flour with oil mixed in for a grain offering, and a *log* of oil; 22and two turtledoves or two pigeons, depending on his means, the one to be the purification offering and the other the burnt offering. 23On the eighth day of his purification he shall bring them to the priest at the entrance of the Tent of Meeting, before the LORD. 24The priest shall take the lamb of reparation offering and the *log* of oil, and elevate them as an elevation offering before the LORD. 25When the lamb of reparation offering has been slaughtered, the priest shall take some of the blood of the reparation offering and put it on the ridge of the right ear of the one being purified, on the thumb of his right hand, and on the big toe of his right foot. 26The priest shall then pour some of the oil into the palm of his own left hand, 27and with the finger of his right hand the priest shall sprinkle some of the oil that is in the palm of his left hand seven times before the LORD. 28Some of the oil in his palm shall be put by the priest on the ridge of the right ear of the one being purified, on the thumb of his right hand, and on the big toe of his right foot, over the same places as the blood of the reparation offering; 29and what is left of the oil in his palm the priest shall put on the head of the one being purified, to make expiation for him before the LORD. 30He shall then offer one of the turtledoves or pigeons, depending on his means—31whichever he can afford—the one as a purification offering and the other as a burnt offering, together with the grain offering. Thus the priest shall make expiation before the LORD for the one being purified. 32Such is the ritual for him who has a scaly affection and whose means for his purification are limited.

33The LORD spoke to Moses and Aaron, saying:

וְעִשָּׂרוֹן סֹלֶת אֶחָד בָּלוּל בַּשֶּׁמֶן לְמִנְחָה
וְלֹג שָׁמֶן׃ 22 וּשְׁתֵּי תֹרִים אוֹ שְׁנֵי בְּנֵי יוֹנָה
אֲשֶׁר תַּשִּׂיג יָדוֹ וְהָיָה אֶחָד חַטָּאת וְהָאֶחָד
עֹלָה׃ 23 וְהֵבִיא אֹתָם בַּיּוֹם הַשְּׁמִינִי
לְטָהֳרָתוֹ אֶל־הַכֹּהֵן אֶל־פֶּתַח אֹהֶל־מוֹעֵד
לִפְנֵי יְהוָה׃ 24 וְלָקַח הַכֹּהֵן אֶת־כֶּבֶשׂ
הָאָשָׁם וְאֶת־לֹג הַשָּׁמֶן וְהֵנִיף אֹתָם הַכֹּהֵן
תְּנוּפָה לִפְנֵי יְהוָה׃ 25 וְשָׁחַט אֶת־כֶּבֶשׂ
הָאָשָׁם וְלָקַח הַכֹּהֵן מִדַּם הָאָשָׁם וְנָתַן
עַל־תְּנוּךְ אֹזֶן־הַמִּטַּהֵר הַיְמָנִית וְעַל־בֹּהֶן
יָדוֹ הַיְמָנִית וְעַל־בֹּהֶן רַגְלוֹ הַיְמָנִית׃
26 וּמִן־הַשֶּׁמֶן יִצֹק הַכֹּהֵן עַל־כַּף הַכֹּהֵן
הַשְּׂמָאלִית׃ 27 וְהִזָּה הַכֹּהֵן בְּאֶצְבָּעוֹ
הַיְמָנִית מִן־הַשֶּׁמֶן אֲשֶׁר עַל־כַּפּוֹ
הַשְּׂמָאלִית שֶׁבַע פְּעָמִים לִפְנֵי יְהוָה׃
28 וְנָתַן הַכֹּהֵן מִן־הַשֶּׁמֶן ׀ אֲשֶׁר עַל־כַּפּוֹ
עַל־תְּנוּךְ אֹזֶן הַמִּטַּהֵר הַיְמָנִית וְעַל־בֹּהֶן
יָדוֹ הַיְמָנִית וְעַל־בֹּהֶן רַגְלוֹ הַיְמָנִית עַל־
מְקוֹם דַּם הָאָשָׁם׃ 29 וְהַנּוֹתָר מִן־הַשֶּׁמֶן
אֲשֶׁר עַל־כַּף הַכֹּהֵן יִתֵּן עַל־רֹאשׁ הַמִּטַּהֵר
לְכַפֵּר עָלָיו לִפְנֵי יְהוָה׃ 30 וְעָשָׂה אֶת־
הָאֶחָד מִן־הַתֹּרִים אוֹ מִן־בְּנֵי הַיּוֹנָה
מֵאֲשֶׁר תַּשִּׂיג יָדוֹ׃ 31 אֵת אֲשֶׁר־תַּשִּׂיג יָדוֹ
אֶת־הָאֶחָד חַטָּאת וְאֶת־הָאֶחָד עֹלָה עַל־
הַמִּנְחָה וְכִפֶּר הַכֹּהֵן עַל הַמִּטַּהֵר לִפְנֵי
יְהוָה׃ 32 זֹאת תּוֹרַת אֲשֶׁר־בּוֹ נֶגַע צָרָעַת
אֲשֶׁר לֹא־תַשִּׂיג יָדוֹ בְּטָהֳרָתוֹ׃ פ
ביעי
33 וַיְדַבֵּר יְהוָה אֶל־מֹשֶׁה וְאֶל־אַהֲרֹן ששי]
לֵאמֹר׃

TZARA·AT IN BUILDING STONES (vv. 33–53)

This section deals with some sort of mold, blight, or rot, perhaps of a fungoid nature, that produced recessed lesions and discoloration in the plaster or mud used to cover building stones.

34When you enter the land of Canaan that I give you as a possession, and I inflict an eruptive plague upon a house in the land you possess, 35the owner of the house shall come and tell the priest, saying, "Something like a plague has appeared upon my house." 36The priest shall order the house cleared before the priest enters to examine the plague, so that nothing in the house may become impure; after that the priest shall enter to examine the house. 37If, when he examines the plague, the plague in the walls of the house is found to consist of greenish or reddish streaks that appear to go deep into the wall, 38the priest shall come out of the house to the entrance of the house, and close up the house for seven days. 39On the seventh day the priest shall return. If he sees that the plague has spread on the walls of the house, 40the priest shall order the stones with the plague in them to be pulled out and cast outside the city into an impure place. 41The house shall be scraped inside all around, and the coating that is scraped off shall

34 כִּ֤י תָבֹ֙אוּ֙ אֶל־אֶ֣רֶץ כְּנַ֔עַן אֲשֶׁ֥ר אֲנִ֛י נֹתֵ֥ן
לָכֶ֖ם לַאֲחֻזָּ֑ה וְנָתַתִּי֙ נֶ֣גַע צָרַ֔עַת בְּבֵ֖ית
אֶ֥רֶץ אֲחֻזַּתְכֶֽם׃ 35 וּבָא֙ אֲשֶׁר־ל֣וֹ הַבַּ֔יִת
וְהִגִּ֥יד לַכֹּהֵ֖ן לֵאמֹ֑ר כְּנֶ֕גַע נִרְאָ֥ה לִ֖י בַּבָּֽיִת׃
36 וְצִוָּ֨ה הַכֹּהֵ֜ן וּפִנּ֣וּ אֶת־הַבַּ֗יִת בְּטֶ֨רֶם יָבֹ֤א
הַכֹּהֵן֙ לִרְא֣וֹת אֶת־הַנֶּ֔גַע וְלֹ֥א יִטְמָ֖א כָּל־
אֲשֶׁ֣ר בַּבָּ֑יִת וְאַ֥חַר כֵּ֛ן יָבֹ֥א הַכֹּהֵ֖ן לִרְא֥וֹת
אֶת־הַבָּֽיִת׃ 37 וְרָאָ֣ה אֶת־הַנֶּ֗גַע וְהִנֵּ֤ה
הַנֶּ֙גַע֙ בְּקִירֹ֣ת הַבַּ֔יִת שְׁקַֽעֲרוּרֹת֙ יְרַקְרַקֹּ֔ת
א֖וֹ אֲדַמְדַּמֹּ֑ת וּמַרְאֵיהֶ֥ן שָׁפָ֖ל מִן־הַקִּֽיר׃
38 וְיָצָ֧א הַכֹּהֵ֛ן מִן־הַבַּ֖יִת אֶל־פֶּ֣תַח הַבָּ֑יִת
וְהִסְגִּ֥יר אֶת־הַבַּ֖יִת שִׁבְעַ֥ת יָמִֽים׃ 39 וְשָׁ֥ב
הַכֹּהֵ֖ן בַּיּ֣וֹם הַשְּׁבִיעִ֑י וְרָאָ֕ה וְהִנֵּ֛ה פָּשָׂ֥ה
הַנֶּ֖גַע בְּקִירֹ֥ת הַבָּֽיִת׃ 40 וְצִוָּה֙ הַכֹּהֵ֔ן וְחִלְּצוּ֙
אֶת־הָ֣אֲבָנִ֔ים אֲשֶׁ֥ר בָּהֵ֖ן הַנָּ֑גַע וְהִשְׁלִ֤יכוּ
אֶתְהֶן֙ אֶל־מִח֣וּץ לָעִ֔יר אֶל־מָק֖וֹם טָמֵֽא׃
41 וְאֶת־הַבַּ֛יִת יַקְצִ֥עַ מִבַּ֖יִת סָבִ֑יב וְשָֽׁפְכ֗וּ
אֶת־הֶֽעָפָר֙ אֲשֶׁ֣ר הִקְצ֔וּ אֶל־מִח֖וּץ לָעִ֑יר

36. Once the priest arrives and quarantines the house, everything inside it becomes impure as well.

37. streaks that appear to go deep into the wall Literally, "lesions that appear to be recessed within the surface of the wall."

38. close up the house A diseased person is closed up in a house. Here, the house itself is locked up to keep people out.

39. If the lesions became enlarged, it is likely that the blight, or fungus, has penetrated to the stones themselves.

41. The mud coating is scraped off the interior facing of the rest of the stones to ascertain whether the infection had penetrated the stones themselves.

---

34. The appearance of *tzara·at* in the stones of a house was a mysterious event. Some Sages doubted it ever happened, and others consigned it to a distant past. Commentators consider the afflicted house (*ha-bayit ha-m'nugga*) to be a moral warning rather than a natural occurrence, even more emphatically than they consider cases of skin disease to be a moral warning. They fasten on the word for "I inflict" to deduce that this was a plague sent by God. A home is a family's private refuge. Thus a home afflicted by plague represents the breakdown of the social values that kept a family safe and united. It was a cause for concern if the problems of society at large had come to infect the home. Most commentators suggest that the antisocial behavior that brought the plague to the house was selfishness, a blindness to the needs of others.

35. owner of the house Literally, "one whose house it is," leading the Sages to conclude that the owner sinned by saying, "the house and everything in it are mine and I don't have to share it with anyone else" (BT Yoma 11b). As punishment, the house is torn down. The Midrash pictures such owners claiming that they cannot help the poor because they are poor themselves. When their houses are dismantled, all will see what they were hoarding (Lev. R. 17:2).

40. stones . . . to be pulled out From the heart of the selfish owner.

be dumped outside the city in an impure place. 42They shall take other stones and replace those stones with them, and take other coating and plaster the house.

43If the plague again breaks out in the house, after the stones have been pulled out and after the house has been scraped and replastered, 44the priest shall come to examine: if the plague has spread in the house, it is a malignant eruption in the house; it is impure. 45The house shall be torn down—its stones and timber and all the coating on the house—and taken to an impure place outside the city.

46Whoever enters the house while it is closed up shall be impure until evening. 47Whoever sleeps in the house must wash his clothes, and whoever eats in the house must wash his clothes.

48If, however, the priest comes and sees that the plague has not spread in the house after the house was replastered, the priest shall pronounce the house pure, for the plague has healed. 49To purify the house, he shall take two birds, cedar wood, crimson stuff, and hyssop. 50He shall slaughter the one bird over fresh water in an earthen vessel. 51He shall take the cedar wood, the hyssop, the crimson stuff, and the live bird, and dip them in the blood of the slaughtered bird and the fresh water, and sprinkle on

אֶל־מָקוֹם טָמֵא׃ 42 וְלָקְחוּ אֲבָנִים אֲחֵרוֹת
וְהֵבִיאוּ אֶל־תַּחַת הָאֲבָנִים וְעָפָר אַחֵר
יִקַּח וְטָח אֶת־הַבָּיִת׃
43 וְאִם־יָשׁוּב הַנֶּגַע וּפָרַח בַּבַּיִת אַחַר חִלֵּץ
אֶת־הָאֲבָנִים וְאַחֲרֵי הִקְצוֹת אֶת־הַבַּיִת
וְאַחֲרֵי הִטּוֹחַ׃ 44 וּבָא הַכֹּהֵן וְרָאָה וְהִנֵּה
פָּשָׂה הַנֶּגַע בַּבָּיִת צָרַעַת מַמְאֶרֶת הִוא
בַּבַּיִת טָמֵא הוּא׃ 45 וְנָתַץ אֶת־הַבַּיִת
אֶת־אֲבָנָיו וְאֶת־עֵצָיו וְאֵת כָּל־עֲפַר
הַבָּיִת וְהוֹצִיא אֶל־מִחוּץ לָעִיר אֶל־מָקוֹם
טָמֵא׃
46 וְהַבָּא אֶל־הַבַּיִת כָּל־יְמֵי הִסְגִּיר אֹתוֹ
יִטְמָא עַד־הָעָרֶב׃ 47 וְהַשֹּׁכֵב בַּבַּיִת יְכַבֵּס
אֶת־בְּגָדָיו וְהָאֹכֵל בַּבַּיִת יְכַבֵּס אֶת־
בְּגָדָיו׃
48 וְאִם־בֹּא יָבֹא הַכֹּהֵן וְרָאָה וְהִנֵּה לֹא־
פָשָׂה הַנֶּגַע בַּבַּיִת אַחֲרֵי הִטֹּחַ אֶת־הַבָּיִת
וְטִהַר הַכֹּהֵן אֶת־הַבַּיִת כִּי נִרְפָּא הַנָּגַע׃
49 וְלָקַח לְחַטֵּא אֶת־הַבַּיִת שְׁתֵּי צִפֳּרִים
וְעֵץ אֶרֶז וּשְׁנִי תוֹלַעַת וְאֵזֹב׃ 50 וְשָׁחַט
אֶת־הַצִּפֹּר הָאֶחָת אֶל־כְּלִי־חֶרֶשׂ עַל־מַיִם
חַיִּים׃ 51 וְלָקַח אֶת־עֵץ־הָאֶרֶז וְאֶת־הָאֵזֹב
וְאֵת ׀ שְׁנִי הַתּוֹלַעַת וְאֵת הַצִּפֹּר הַחַיָּה
וְטָבַל אֹתָם בְּדַם הַצִּפֹּר הַשְּׁחוּטָה וּבַמַּיִם
הַחַיִּים וְהִזָּה אֶל־הַבַּיִת שֶׁבַע פְּעָמִים׃

42. take other coating and plaster the house The stones could be retained if the blight had not penetrated into them.

46–47. These verses deal with the transmission of an impurity that is present in a closed structure to people who are inside the structure while it is impure.

49. The procedures for purifying the house that has "healed," so to speak, are almost identical to those prescribed in verses 1–32 for purifying a diseased person. There is only one difference: Oil and blood are sprinkled on a person; water and blood are sprinkled on a house.

43–45. Is the problem superficial, easily cleared up, or has it entered the structure of the institution, so that the institution is beyond saving?

The house shall be torn down The Midrash sees this as an anticipation of the destruction of Solomon's temple, a house that will have been corrupted by the behavior of its inhabitants (Lev. R. 17:7). It then adds, "But it will not be forever, as it is stated, 'Behold, I am laying in Zion a foundation stone, a precious cornerstone, a sure foundation'" (Isa. 28:16).

the house seven times. 52Having purified the
house with the blood of the bird, the fresh water,
the live bird, the cedar wood, the hyssop, and
the crimson stuff, 53he shall set the live bird free
outside the city in the open country. Thus he
shall make expiation for the house, and it shall
be pure.

54Such is the ritual for every eruptive
affection—for scalls, 55for an eruption on a
cloth or a house, 56for swellings, for rashes, or
for discolorations—57to determine when they
are impure and when they are pure.

Such is the ritual concerning eruptions.

52 וְחִטֵּא אֶת־הַבַּיִת בְּדַם הַצִּפּוֹר וּבַמַּיִם
הַחַיִּים וּבַצִּפֹּר הַחַיָּה וּבְעֵץ הָאֶרֶז וּבָאֵזֹב
וּבִשְׁנִי הַתּוֹלָעַת׃ 53 וְשִׁלַּח אֶת־הַצִּפֹּר
הַחַיָּה אֶל־מִחוּץ לָעִיר אֶל־פְּנֵי הַשָּׂדֶה
וְכִפֶּר עַל־הַבַּיִת וְטָהֵר׃

חמישי 54 זֹאת הַתּוֹרָה לְכָל־נֶגַע הַצָּרַעַת וְלַנָּתֶק׃
55 וּלְצָרַעַת הַבֶּגֶד וְלַבָּיִת׃ 56 וְלַשְׂאֵת
וְלַסַּפַּחַת וְלַבֶּהָרֶת׃ 57 לְהוֹרֹת בְּיוֹם
הַטָּמֵא וּבְיוֹם הַטָּהֹר
זֹאת תּוֹרַת הַצָּרָעַת׃ ס

15

The Lord spoke to Moses and Aaron,
saying: 2Speak to the Israelite people and say to
them:

When any man has a discharge issuing from
his member, he is impure. 3The impurity
from his discharge shall mean the following—
whether his member runs with the discharge or
is stopped up so that there is no discharge, his
impurity means this: 4Any bedding on which
the one with the discharge lies shall be impure,
and every object on which he sits shall be im-

טו

וַיְדַבֵּר יְהוָה אֶל־מֹשֶׁה וְאֶל־אַהֲרֹן
לֵאמֹר׃ 2 דַּבְּרוּ אֶל־בְּנֵי יִשְׂרָאֵל וַאֲמַרְתֶּם
אֲלֵהֶם
אִישׁ אִישׁ כִּי יִהְיֶה זָב מִבְּשָׂרוֹ זוֹבוֹ טָמֵא
הוּא׃ 3 וְזֹאת תִּהְיֶה טֻמְאָתוֹ בְּזוֹבוֹ רָר
בְּשָׂרוֹ אֶת־זוֹבוֹ אוֹ־הֶחְתִּים בְּשָׂרוֹ מִזּוֹבוֹ
טֻמְאָתוֹ הִוא׃ 4 כָּל־הַמִּשְׁכָּב אֲשֶׁר יִשְׁכַּב
עָלָיו הַזָּב יִטְמָא וְכָל־הַכְּלִי אֲשֶׁר־יֵשֵׁב

54–57. These verses are a postscript to the entire contents of chapters 13 and 14.

DISCHARGES FROM SEXUAL ORGANS (15:1–33)

Most of this chapter deals with discharges from the sexual organs as a result of illness or infection, not the normal menstruation of females or seminal emissions of males. Little was known about their treatment, apart from bathing, laundering clothing, and carefully observing the course taken by the ailment itself. All the impurities dealt with in this chapter, like any prevailing impurity within the Israelite community, threatened, directly or indirectly, the purity of the sanctuary, which was located within the area of settlement.

THE ISRAELITE MALE (vv. 1–18)

2. member Hebrew: *basar* (body, flesh); here it is a euphemism for the male sex organ.

4. lies . . . sits Two sorts of objects are ren-

CHAPTER 15

2ff. Once again we encounter the notion of *tum·ah* not as uncleanness or contamination but as an encounter with the mysterious life-engendering power of certain bodily fluids and with the life-endangering dimension of disease. This encounter with the primal forces of life and death rule out (or may possibly replace) other ways of entering into the divine presence.

pure. 5Anyone who touches his bedding shall
wash his clothes, bathe in water, and remain impure until evening. 6Whoever sits on an object
on which the one with the discharge has sat shall
wash his clothes, bathe in water, and remain impure until evening. 7Whoever touches the body
of the one with the discharge shall wash his
clothes, bathe in water, and remain impure until
evening. 8If one with a discharge spits on one
who is pure, the latter shall wash his clothes,
bathe in water, and remain impure until evening. 9Any means for riding that one with a discharge has mounted shall be impure; 10whoever
touches anything that was under him shall be
impure until evening; and whoever carries such
things shall wash his clothes, bathe in water, and
remain impure until evening. 11If one with a discharge, without having rinsed his hands in water, touches another person, that person shall
wash his clothes, bathe in water, and remain
impure until evening. 12An earthen vessel that
one with a discharge touches shall be broken;
and any wooden implement shall be rinsed with
water.

13When one with a discharge becomes purified of his discharge, he shall count off seven
days for his purification, wash his clothes, and
bathe his body in fresh water; then he shall be
pure. 14On the eighth day he shall take two turtledoves or two pigeons and come before the
LORD at the entrance of the Tent of Meeting and

עָלָיו יִטְמָא׃ 5 וְאִישׁ אֲשֶׁר יִגַּע בְּמִשְׁכָּבוֹ
יְכַבֵּס בְּגָדָיו וְרָחַץ בַּמַּיִם וְטָמֵא עַד־
הָעָרֶב׃ 6 וְהַיֹּשֵׁב עַל־הַכְּלִי אֲשֶׁר־יֵשֵׁב
עָלָיו הַזָּב יְכַבֵּס בְּגָדָיו וְרָחַץ בַּמַּיִם וְטָמֵא
עַד־הָעָרֶב׃ 7 *וְהַנֹּגֵעַ בִּבְשַׂר הַזָּב יְכַבֵּס
בְּגָדָיו וְרָחַץ בַּמַּיִם וְטָמֵא עַד־הָעָרֶב׃
8 וְכִי־יָרֹק הַזָּב בַּטָּהוֹר וְכִבֶּס בְּגָדָיו וְרָחַץ
בַּמַּיִם וְטָמֵא עַד־הָעָרֶב׃ 9 וְכָל־הַמֶּרְכָּב
אֲשֶׁר יִרְכַּב עָלָיו הַזָּב יִטְמָא׃ 10 וְכָל־הַנֹּגֵעַ
בְּכֹל אֲשֶׁר יִהְיֶה תַחְתָּיו יִטְמָא עַד־הָעָרֶב
וְהַנּוֹשֵׂא אוֹתָם יְכַבֵּס בְּגָדָיו וְרָחַץ בַּמַּיִם
וְטָמֵא עַד־הָעָרֶב׃ 11 וְכֹל אֲשֶׁר יִגַּע־בּוֹ הַזָּב
וְיָדָיו לֹא־שָׁטַף בַּמָּיִם וְכִבֶּס בְּגָדָיו וְרָחַץ
בַּמַּיִם וְטָמֵא עַד־הָעָרֶב׃ 12 וּכְלִי־חֶרֶשׂ
אֲשֶׁר־יִגַּע־בּוֹ הַזָּב יִשָּׁבֵר וְכָל־כְּלִי־עֵץ
יִשָּׁטֵף בַּמָּיִם׃

13 וְכִי־יִטְהַר הַזָּב מִזּוֹבוֹ וְסָפַר לוֹ שִׁבְעַת
יָמִים לְטָהֳרָתוֹ וְכִבֶּס בְּגָדָיו וְרָחַץ בְּשָׂרוֹ
בְּמַיִם חַיִּים וְטָהֵר׃ 14 וּבַיּוֹם הַשְּׁמִינִי
יִקַּח־לוֹ שְׁתֵּי תֹרִים אוֹ שְׁנֵי בְּנֵי יוֹנָה
וּבָא ׀ לִפְנֵי יְהוָה אֶל־פֶּתַח אֹהֶל מוֹעֵד

v. 7. חצי הספר בפסוקים

dered impure by contact with a person who has a discharge: those on which one lies, and those on which one sits. These objects must be purified.

5. bathe in water One must bathe completely.

7. Direct contact with the affected person renders one impure.

8–9. Verses 8–9 deal with contact initiated by the affected person.

spits Spittle was thought to carry infection and disease.

means for riding Hebrew: *merkav,* denoting "an object on which one rides," such as a saddle or other appurtenance located under the rider. If someone with a discharge rides on these objects, they become impure.

10. whoever touches anything that was under him That is, under the affected person. In this case, the impurity extends only to the body of the person who touches such objects, not to the clothing.

whoever carries such things Contact by carrying objects entails the usual severe restrictions in response.

13. seven days for his purification Seven consecutive days must pass after the termination of the ailment before ritual purification can be undertaken.

וּנְתָנָם אֶל־הַכֹּהֵן׃ 15 וְעָשָׂה אֹתָם הַכֹּהֵן
אֶחָד חַטָּאת וְהָאֶחָד עֹלָה וְכִפֶּר עָלָיו
הַכֹּהֵן לִפְנֵי יְהוָה מִזּוֹבוֹ׃ ס
ששי [שביעי] 16 וְאִישׁ כִּי־תֵצֵא מִמֶּנּוּ שִׁכְבַת־זָרַע וְרָחַץ
בַּמַּיִם אֶת־כָּל־בְּשָׂרוֹ וְטָמֵא עַד־הָעָרֶב׃
17 וְכָל־בֶּגֶד וְכָל־עוֹר אֲשֶׁר־יִהְיֶה עָלָיו
שִׁכְבַת־זָרַע וְכֻבַּס בַּמַּיִם וְטָמֵא עַד־
הָעָרֶב׃ פ 18 וְאִשָּׁה אֲשֶׁר יִשְׁכַּב אִישׁ
אֹתָהּ שִׁכְבַת־זָרַע וְרָחֲצוּ בַמַּיִם וְטָמְאוּ
עַד־הָעָרֶב׃
19 וְאִשָּׁה כִּי־תִהְיֶה זָבָה דָּם יִהְיֶה זֹבָהּ
בִּבְשָׂרָהּ שִׁבְעַת יָמִים תִּהְיֶה בְנִדָּתָהּ
וְכָל־הַנֹּגֵעַ בָּהּ יִטְמָא עַד־הָעָרֶב׃ 20 וְכֹל
אֲשֶׁר תִּשְׁכַּב עָלָיו בְּנִדָּתָהּ יִטְמָא וְכֹל
אֲשֶׁר־תֵּשֵׁב עָלָיו יִטְמָא׃ 21 וְכָל־הַנֹּגֵעַ
בְּמִשְׁכָּבָהּ יְכַבֵּס בְּגָדָיו וְרָחַץ בַּמַּיִם וְטָמֵא
עַד־הָעָרֶב׃ 22 וְכָל־הַנֹּגֵעַ בְּכָל־כְּלִי אֲשֶׁר־
תֵּשֵׁב עָלָיו יְכַבֵּס בְּגָדָיו וְרָחַץ בַּמַּיִם וְטָמֵא
עַד־הָעָרֶב׃ 23 וְאִם עַל־הַמִּשְׁכָּב הוּא אוֹ
עַל־הַכְּלִי אֲשֶׁר־הִוא יֹשֶׁבֶת־עָלָיו בְּנָגְעוֹ־

give them to the priest. 15The priest shall offer
them, the one as a purification offering and the
other as a burnt offering. Thus the priest shall
make expiation on his behalf, for his discharge,
before the LORD.

16When a man has an emission of semen, he
shall bathe his whole body in water and remain
impure until evening. 17All cloth or leather on
which semen falls shall be washed in water and
remain impure until evening. 18And if a man has
carnal relations with a woman, they shall bathe
in water and remain impure until evening.

19When a woman has a discharge, her discharge being blood from her body, she shall remain in her menstrual impurity seven days;
whoever touches her shall be impure until evening. 20Anything that she lies on during her
menstrual impurity shall be impure; and anything that she sits on shall be impure. 21Anyone
who touches her bedding shall wash his clothes,
bathe in water, and remain impure until evening; 22and anyone who touches any object on
which she has sat shall wash his clothes, bathe
in water, and remain impure until evening. 23Be
it the bedding or be it the object on which she

15. A purification offering is required not because the person in question offended God by any act on his or her part, but because the impurity (i.e., the ailment) threatened the purity of the sanctuary.

18. Both the man and the woman are ritually impure after the sex act, and both must bathe.

THE ISRAELITE FEMALE (vv. 19–30)

The subjects of the law in this section are a woman's normal menstruation and her abnormal discharges of blood.

19. menstrual impurity Better: "menstrual condition." Hebrew: *niddah,* denoting the physiologic process of the flow of blood.

---

19. The enforced separation of husband and wife during her menstrual period parallels the dietary laws. Both sets of regulations inculcate holiness by introducing rules of what is permitted and what is forbidden into what are matters of instinct for all other living creatures. Once again, the Torah defines the uniqueness of the human being as the ability to control instinct instead of being controlled by it.

HALAKHAH L'MA·ASEH

15:19. discharge being blood This and the following verses are the basis for *taharat ha-mishpaḥah,* the "family purity" laws that prohibit sexual contact during a woman's menstrual period until after her subsequent immersion in a *mikveh* (ritual bath). The biblical requirement for a man to immerse after a seminal emission (Lev. 15:16–17) fell into disuse by talmudic times (BT Ber. 21b–22a).

15:20. shall be impure Jewish law places no restrictions on a menstruant's touching a Torah scroll or reciting or leading prayers.

has sat, on touching it he shall be unclean until
evening. 24And if a man lies with her, her
menstural impurity is communicated to him;
he shall be impure seven days, and any bedding
on which he lies shall become impure.

25When a woman has had a discharge of
blood for many days, not at the time of her menstrual impurity, or when she has a discharge beyond her period of menstrual impurity, she
shall be impure, as though at the time of her
menstrual impurity, as long as her discharge
lasts. 26Any bedding on which she lies while her
discharge lasts shall be for her like bedding during her menstural impurity; and any object on
which she sits shall become impure, as it does
during her menstrual impurity: 27whoever
touches them shall be impure; he shall wash his
clothes, bathe in water, and remain impure until
evening.

28When she becomes purified of her discharge, she shall count off seven days, and after
that she shall be pure. 29On the eighth day she
shall take two turtledoves or two pigeons, and
bring them to the priest at the entrance of the
Tent of Meeting. 30The priest shall offer the one
as a purification offering and the other as a burnt
offering; and the priest shall make expiation on
her behalf, for her impure discharge, before the
LORD.

31You shall put the Israelites on guard against
their impurity, lest they die through their im-

בּוֹ יִטְמָא עַד־הָעָרֶב׃ 24 וְאִם שָׁכֹב יִשְׁכַּב
אִישׁ אֹתָהּ וּתְהִי נִדָּתָהּ עָלָיו וְטָמֵא
שִׁבְעַת יָמִים וְכָל־הַמִּשְׁכָּב אֲשֶׁר־יִשְׁכַּב
עָלָיו יִטְמָא׃ פ
25 וְאִשָּׁה כִּי־יָזוּב זוֹב דָּמָהּ יָמִים רַבִּים
בְּלֹא עֶת־נִדָּתָהּ אוֹ כִי־תָזוּב עַל־נִדָּתָהּ
כָּל־יְמֵי זוֹב טֻמְאָתָהּ כִּימֵי נִדָּתָהּ תִּהְיֶה
טְמֵאָה הִוא׃ 26 כָּל־הַמִּשְׁכָּב אֲשֶׁר־תִּשְׁכַּב
עָלָיו כָּל־יְמֵי זוֹבָהּ כְּמִשְׁכַּב נִדָּתָהּ יִהְיֶה־
לָּהּ וְכָל־הַכְּלִי אֲשֶׁר תֵּשֵׁב עָלָיו טָמֵא
יִהְיֶה כְּטֻמְאַת נִדָּתָהּ׃ 27 וְכָל־הַנּוֹגֵעַ בָּם
יִטְמָא וְכִבֶּס בְּגָדָיו וְרָחַץ בַּמַּיִם וְטָמֵא
עַד־הָעָרֶב׃
28 וְאִם־טָהֲרָה מִזּוֹבָהּ וְסָפְרָה לָּהּ שִׁבְעַת
יָמִים וְאַחַר תִּטְהָר׃ 29 וּבַיּוֹם הַשְּׁמִינִי שביעי
תִּקַּח־לָהּ שְׁתֵּי תֹרִים אוֹ שְׁנֵי בְּנֵי יוֹנָה
וְהֵבִיאָה אוֹתָם אֶל־הַכֹּהֵן אֶל־פֶּתַח אֹהֶל
מוֹעֵד׃ 30 וְעָשָׂה הַכֹּהֵן אֶת־הָאֶחָד חַטָּאת
וְאֶת־הָאֶחָד עֹלָה וְכִפֶּר עָלֶיהָ הַכֹּהֵן לִפְנֵי
יְהוָה מִזּוֹב טֻמְאָתָהּ׃
31 וְהִזַּרְתֶּם אֶת־בְּנֵי־יִשְׂרָאֵל מִטֻּמְאָתָם פטיר

24. he shall be impure seven days He must bathe and launder his clothing after seven days.

25. A woman who has discharges of blood not caused by menstruation bears the same impurity as a menstruating woman for as long as the discharges last.

28. Like the male in verse 13, the female must count off seven days after the termination of her abnormal discharge of blood.

29–30. This is the essential difference between abnormal and normal conditions: Abnormalities ultimately require ritual expiation as part of the purification process, whereas normal conditions, though they induce impurity, require only bathing and laundering of clothing and observance of the proper period of waiting. Such normal conditions do not of themselves involve the sanctuary directly, unless a person in such a state actually enters the sacred precincts.

CONCLUSION (vv. 31–33)

31. lest they die through their impurity It is not the condition of impurity itself that brings on God's punishment, but the failure to correct that condition so as to restore a state of purity.

וְלֹ֤א יָמֻ֙תוּ֙ בְּטֻמְאָתָ֔ם בְּטַמְּאָ֥ם אֶת־מִשְׁכָּנִ֖י
אֲשֶׁ֥ר בְּתוֹכָֽם׃
32 זֹ֥את תּוֹרַ֖ת הַזָּ֑ב וַאֲשֶׁ֨ר תֵּצֵ֥א מִמֶּ֛נּוּ
שִׁכְבַת־זֶ֖רַע לְטָמְאָה־בָֽהּ׃ 33 וְהַדָּוָה֙
בְּנִדָּתָ֔הּ וְהַזָּב֙ אֶת־זוֹב֔וֹ לַזָּכָ֖ר וְלַנְּקֵבָ֑ה
וּלְאִ֕ישׁ אֲשֶׁ֥ר יִשְׁכַּ֖ב עִם־טְמֵאָֽה׃ פ

purity by defiling My Tabernacle which is among them.

32Such is the ritual concerning him who has a discharge: concerning him who has an emission of semen and becomes impure thereby, 33and concerning her who is in menstrual infirmity, and concerning anyone, male or female, who has a discharge, and concerning a man who lies with an impure woman.

31. My Tabernacle which is among them Even when Israelites are impure, God's presence is found among them. Abravanel understands "My Tabernacle" as referring to the human body. Thus "defiling My Tabernacle" refers to rendering our bodies impure. Because each person is created in God's image, his or her body is a temple of God.

הפטרת תזריע

HAFTARAH FOR TAZRI·A

2 KINGS 4:42–5:19

(*When* Tazri·a *and* M'tzora *are combined, recite the* haftarah *for* M'tzora.)

This *haftarah* comprises two episodes from a cycle of wonder-working tales about the activities of the northern prophet Elisha during the reign of King Jehoram (851–842 B.C.E.). They report the miraculous feeding of a multitude with only a small amount of bread (2 Kings 4:42–44) and the healing of an Aramean leper named Naaman (5:1–19). Earlier in chapter 4, before the start of the *haftarah,* these two episodes are preceded by accounts of the miracle of a jug of oil (4:1–7), the resurrection of a Shunammite boy (4:8–37), and making poisonous food in a pot edible (4:38–41). Passages after the *haftarah* present the miracle of a floating ax head (6:1–7) and the wondrous end to a famine caused by the Aramean siege of Samaria (7:1–20). The preservation of such an extensive collection of wonders proves the popularity of such tales among the people. Significantly, almost the entire anthology figures in *haftarah* readings: 2 Kings 4:1–37 is the selection for *Va-yera,* 4:42–5:19 is the portion for *Tazri·a,* and 7:3–20 is the text for *M'tzora*.

In the sparse narrative about the loaves of bread (4:42–44), the connecting thread is provided by the verb "to give" (*natan*). A man brings his votary gift to Elisha, who instructs his steward Gehazi to "give" (*ten*) it to the people. When the steward doubts how he could "give" (*etten*) this small amount of loaves to so many, the prophet reissues his command to "give" (*ten*) the food to the people. When the steward complied and "gave" (*va-yitten*) the food to the masses, there was more than enough to go around. The miracle is underscored as something promised and fulfilled by God. The text also indicates Elisha's magnanimity, dispensing to the people gifts he refused to take for himself.

The account of Naaman's miraculous cure is presented with greater detail and fuller dialogues. Indeed, the dialogues generate the stages of narrative action: The Israelite girl intervenes with her mistress, the Aramean commander begs leave of his king, the king of Israel misinterprets the letter of the king of Aram, and Elisha expresses readiness to perform the desired cure that Naaman might know the power of prophets in Israel. Finally, Elisha sends a message to Naaman with instructions for a cure, and Naaman presents Elisha with a theological statement recognizing the unique power of the God of Israel whom he now wants to worship exclusively.

When the Aramean commander expresses his gratitude for being cured by offering Elisha a gift (5:15), the man of God once again demonstrates his refusal to profit from his prophetic powers (v. 16). This leads to a poignant reversal, as Naaman then requests the gift of some loads of holy earth to build a shrine to God in Aram (v. 17).

Two features of popular piety may be singled out. First, people would seek out holy men for consultation on topics of health or wealth. On such occasions, they would provide gifts in payment and gratitude. Second, the story of an Aramean commander seeking out an Israelite wonder worker shows that in matters of health and healing, political and religious boundaries were of little concern. People wanted the best and most respected divine aid and would go to a recognized shrine or healer as necessary.

Elisha's cure is simple and straightforward. Naaman is told to dip seven times in holy water. Naaman apparently had expected something more elaborate and ceremonious. The seven ablutions, however, were the key. They recall the prophet Balaam's request for seven altars, seven rams, and seven bulls before delivering his oracles (Num. 23:1–6,29). They also remind us of the

seven priests with seven rams' horns who circumambulated Jericho seven times on the seventh day (Josh. 6:6–8,15–16). In other cases, the requisite number was three. Thus Elijah prostrated himself over the child three times before he revived (1 Kings 17:21) and ceremoniously doused the altar and wood three times with pails of water before calling on God for rain (1 Kings 18:34). The prophet Jeremiah, cursing King Jehoiachin for his evil with an incantation, called on the "earth" three times to hear the word of God and banish the king to foreign soil (Jer. 22:28–29). Both three and seven are well-known magical numbers in the ancient Near East and beyond.

RELATION OF THE *HAFTARAH* TO THE *PARASHAH*

The miraculous healing of leprosy in the *haftarah* links thematically to the diagnoses of leprosy found in the second half of the *parashah* (Lev. 13). The *haftarah* dramatizes the conversion of a leprous polytheist to Israelite worship. Two phrases (with liturgical overtones) make this clear. The first is recited by Naaman after his cure: "Now I know (*yadati*) that there is no God (*ein elohim*) in the whole world except (*ki im*) in Israel" (2 Kings 5:15). The second records Naaman's determination to serve God alone and his vow that he "will never again (*lo . . . od*) offer up a burnt offering or a sacrifice to any god (literally, "other gods," *elohim aḥerim*), except (*ki im*) the Lord" (v. 17). Significantly, when Moses' father-in-law, Jethro, a pagan priest of Midian, converted upon hearing "everything that the Lord had done to Pharaoh and the Egyptians for Israel's sake" he reportedly said, "Now I know (*yadati*) that the Lord is greater than all gods (*elohim*)" and then "brought a burnt offering and sacrifice to God" (Exod. 18:8–12).

The formal correspondence between the two passages is striking. Apparently, some pagan conversions in Israelite antiquity required merely a credal statement along with a commitment to sacrifice to the Lord. These avowals typically include reference to a new knowledge of the supremacy of the God of Israel, based on experience.

Naaman senses that it may prove difficult to maintain his exclusive allegiance to God in the complicated circumstances of his everyday life, when he must serve his king and help him bend in worship in pagan shrines (2 Kings 5:18). Elisha does not directly answer this concern, and simply says "Go in peace."

4 42A man came from Baal-shalishah and he
brought the man of God some bread of the first
reaping—twenty loaves of barley bread, and
some fresh grain in his sack. And [Elisha] said,
"Give it to the people and let them eat." 43His
attendant replied, "How can I set this before a
hundred men?" But he said, "Give it to the people and let them eat. For thus said the Lord:
They shall eat and have some left over." 44So
he set it before them; and when they had eaten,
they had some left over, as the Lord had said.

ד 42 וְאִישׁ בָּא מִבַּעַל שָׁלִשָׁה וַיָּבֵא
לְאִישׁ הָאֱלֹהִים לֶחֶם בִּכּוּרִים עֶשְׂרִים־
לֶחֶם שְׂעֹרִים וְכַרְמֶל בְּצִקְלֹנוֹ וַיֹּאמֶר תֵּן
לָעָם וְיֹאכֵלוּ׃ 43 וַיֹּאמֶר מְשָׁרְתוֹ מָה אֶתֵּן
זֶה לִפְנֵי מֵאָה אִישׁ וַיֹּאמֶר תֵּן לָעָם
וְיֹאכֵלוּ כִּי כֹה אָמַר יְהוָה אָכֹל וְהוֹתֵר׃
44 וַיִּתֵּן לִפְנֵיהֶם וַיֹּאכְלוּ וַיּוֹתִרוּ כִּדְבַר
יְהוָה׃ פ

2 Kings 4:42. A man came from Baal-shalishah The land of Shalishah is mentioned as part of the tribal lands of Benjamin in the region of Mount Ephraim, along with the lands of Shaalim and Zuph.

and he brought . . . bread of the first reaping In antiquity prophets received votary gifts for their oracular or divinatory services (1 Sam. 9:7; 1 Kings 14:3).

5 Naaman, commander of the army of the
king of Aram, was important to his lord and
high in his favor, for through him the LORD had
granted victory to Aram. But the man, though
a great warrior, was a leper. 2Once, when the
Arameans were out raiding, they carried off a
young girl from the land of Israel, and she became an attendant to Naaman's wife. 3She said
to her mistress, "I wish Master could come before the prophet in Samaria; he would cure him
of his leprosy." 4[Naaman] went and told his
lord just what the girl from the land of Israel
had said. 5And the king of Aram said, "Go to
the king of Israel, and I will send along a letter."

He set out, taking with him ten talents of
silver, six thousand shekels of gold, and ten
changes of clothing. 6He brought the letter to
the king of Israel. It read: "Now, when this letter
reaches you, know that I have sent my courtier
Naaman to you, that you may cure him of his
leprosy." 7When the king of Israel read the letter, he rent his clothes and cried, "Am I God,
to deal death or give life, that this fellow writes
to me to cure a man of leprosy? Just see for yourselves that he is seeking a pretext against me!"

8When Elisha, the man of God, heard that the
king of Israel had rent his clothes, he sent a message to the king: "Why have you rent your
clothes? Let him come to me, and he will learn
that there is a prophet in Israel."

9So Naaman came with his horses and chariots and halted at the door of Elisha's house.
10Elisha sent a messenger to say to him, "Go and
bathe seven times in the Jordan, and your flesh

ה וְנַעֲמָן שַׂר־צְבָא מֶלֶךְ־אֲרָם הָיָה
אִישׁ גָּדוֹל לִפְנֵי אֲדֹנָיו וּנְשֻׂא פָנִים כִּי־בוֹ
נָתַן־יְהוָה תְּשׁוּעָה לַאֲרָם וְהָאִישׁ הָיָה
גִּבּוֹר חַיִל מְצֹרָע׃ 2 וַאֲרָם יָצְאוּ גְדוּדִים
וַיִּשְׁבּוּ מֵאֶרֶץ יִשְׂרָאֵל נַעֲרָה קְטַנָּה וַתְּהִי
לִפְנֵי אֵשֶׁת נַעֲמָן׃ 3 וַתֹּאמֶר אֶל־גְּבִרְתָּהּ
אַחֲלֵי אֲדֹנִי לִפְנֵי הַנָּבִיא אֲשֶׁר בְּשֹׁמְרוֹן
אָז יֶאֱסֹף אֹתוֹ מִצָּרַעְתּוֹ׃ 4 וַיָּבֹא וַיַּגֵּד
לַאדֹנָיו לֵאמֹר כָּזֹאת וְכָזֹאת דִּבְּרָה
הַנַּעֲרָה אֲשֶׁר מֵאֶרֶץ יִשְׂרָאֵל׃ 5 וַיֹּאמֶר
מֶלֶךְ־אֲרָם לֶךְ־בֹּא וְאֶשְׁלְחָה סֵפֶר אֶל־
מֶלֶךְ יִשְׂרָאֵל

וַיֵּלֶךְ וַיִּקַּח בְּיָדוֹ עֶשֶׂר כִּכְּרֵי־כֶסֶף וְשֵׁשֶׁת
אֲלָפִים זָהָב וְעֶשֶׂר חֲלִיפוֹת בְּגָדִים׃ 6 וַיָּבֵא
הַסֵּפֶר אֶל־מֶלֶךְ יִשְׂרָאֵל לֵאמֹר וְעַתָּה
כְּבוֹא הַסֵּפֶר הַזֶּה אֵלֶיךָ הִנֵּה שָׁלַחְתִּי
אֵלֶיךָ אֶת־נַעֲמָן עַבְדִּי וַאֲסַפְתּוֹ מִצָּרַעְתּוֹ׃
7 וַיְהִי כִּקְרֹא מֶלֶךְ־יִשְׂרָאֵל אֶת־הַסֵּפֶר
וַיִּקְרַע בְּגָדָיו וַיֹּאמֶר הַאֱלֹהִים אָנִי לְהָמִית
וּלְהַחֲיוֹת כִּי־זֶה שֹׁלֵחַ אֵלַי לֶאֱסֹף אִישׁ
מִצָּרַעְתּוֹ כִּי אַךְ־דְּעוּ־נָא וּרְאוּ כִּי־מִתְאַנֶּה
הוּא לִי׃

8 וַיְהִי כִּשְׁמֹעַ ׀ אֱלִישָׁע אִישׁ־הָאֱלֹהִים
כִּי־קָרַע מֶלֶךְ־יִשְׂרָאֵל אֶת־בְּגָדָיו וַיִּשְׁלַח
אֶל־הַמֶּלֶךְ לֵאמֹר לָמָּה קָרַעְתָּ בְּגָדֶיךָ
יָבֹא־נָא אֵלַי וְיֵדַע כִּי יֵשׁ נָבִיא בְּיִשְׂרָאֵל׃
9 וַיָּבֹא נַעֲמָן בסוסו בְּסוּסָו וּבְרִכְבּוֹ וַיַּעֲמֹד
פֶּתַח־הַבַּיִת לֶאֱלִישָׁע׃ 10 וַיִּשְׁלַח אֵלָיו
אֱלִישָׁע מַלְאָךְ לֵאמֹר הָלוֹךְ וְרָחַצְתָּ שֶׁבַע־

2 Kings 5:1. important to his lord and high in his favor Naaman is identified with various titles and honorifics. The designation "high in favor" is a translation of *n'su fanim* (literally, "raised face").

leper Hebrew: *tzara·at;* refers to skin diseases on humans and to molds and fungi on clothes and buildings (Lev. 13–14).

10–14. The seven immersions that Elisha prescribes echo the Torah portion's repeated mention of seven days of quarantine (Lev. 13). According to the next Torah portion, the priest should sprinkle a recovered leper seven times with a liquid solution of holy ingredients; and also that person must bathe (*rahatz*) twice before being fully purified (14:7–9). This *haftarah*

shall be restored and you shall be pure." [11]But Naaman was angered and walked away. "I thought," he said, "he would surely come out to me, and would stand and invoke the LORD his God by name, and would wave his hand toward the spot, and cure the affected part. [12]Are not the Amanah and the Pharpar, the rivers of Damascus, better than all the waters of Israel? I could bathe in them and be pure!" And he stalked off in a rage.

[13]But his servants came forward and spoke to him. "Sir," they said, "if the prophet told you to do something difficult, would you not do it? How much more when he has only said to you, 'Bathe and be pure.'" [14]So he went down and immersed himself in the Jordan seven times, as the man of God had bidden; and his flesh became like a little boy's, and he was pure. [15]Returning with his entire retinue to the man of God, he stood before him and exclaimed, "Now I know that there is no God in the whole world except in Israel! So please accept a gift from your servant." [16]But he replied, "As the LORD lives, whom I serve, I will not accept anything." He pressed him to accept, but he refused. [17]And Naaman said, "Then at least let your servant be given two mule-loads of earth; for your servant will never again offer up burnt offering or sacrifice to any god, except the LORD. [18]But may the LORD pardon your servant for this: When my master enters the temple of Rimmon to bow low in worship there, and he is leaning on my arm so that I must bow low in the temple of Rimmon—when I bow low in the temple of Rimmon, may the LORD pardon your servant in this." [19]And he said to him, "Go in peace."

So [Naaman] left him and went some distance away.

פְּעָמִים֙ בַּיַּרְדֵּן֙ וְיָשֹׁ֧ב בְּשָׂרְךָ֛ לְךָ֖ וּטְהָֽר׃ [11] וַיִּקְצֹ֥ף נַעֲמָ֖ן וַיֵּלַ֑ךְ וַיֹּ֗אמֶר הִנֵּ֤ה אָמַ֙רְתִּי֙ אֵלַ֣י ׀ יֵצֵ֣א יָצ֗וֹא וְעָמַד֙ וְקָרָא֙ בְּשֵׁם־ יְהֹוָ֣ה אֱלֹהָ֔יו וְהֵנִ֥יף יָד֛וֹ אֶל־הַמָּק֖וֹם וְאָסַ֥ף הַמְּצֹרָֽע׃ [12] הֲלֹ֡א טוֹב֩ אבנה אֲמָנָ֙ה וּפַרְפַּ֜ר נַהֲר֣וֹת דַּמֶּ֗שֶׂק מִכֹּל֙ מֵימֵ֣י יִשְׂרָאֵ֔ל הֲלֹֽא־אֶרְחַ֥ץ בָּהֶ֖ם וְטָהָ֑רְתִּי וַיִּ֥פֶן וַיֵּ֖לֶךְ בְּחֵמָֽה׃

[13] וַיִּגְּשׁ֣וּ עֲבָדָיו֮ וַיְדַבְּר֣וּ אֵלָיו֒ וַיֹּאמְר֗וּ אָבִי֙ דָּבָ֣ר גָּד֗וֹל הַנָּבִ֛יא דִּבֶּ֥ר אֵלֶ֖יךָ הֲל֣וֹא תַעֲשֶׂ֑ה וְאַ֛ף כִּֽי־אָמַ֥ר אֵלֶ֖יךָ רְחַ֥ץ וּטְהָֽר׃ [14] וַיֵּ֗רֶד וַיִּטְבֹּ֤ל בַּיַּרְדֵּן֙ שֶׁ֣בַע פְּעָמִ֔ים כִּדְבַ֖ר אִ֣ישׁ הָאֱלֹהִ֑ים וַיָּ֣שׇׁב בְּשָׂר֗וֹ כִּבְשַׂ֛ר נַ֥עַר קָטֹ֖ן וַיִּטְהָֽר׃ [15] וַיָּשׇׁב֩ אֶל־אִ֨ישׁ הָאֱלֹהִ֜ים ה֣וּא וְכׇל־מַחֲנֵ֗הוּ וַיָּבֹא֙ וַיַּעֲמֹ֣ד לְפָנָ֔יו וַיֹּ֗אמֶר הִנֵּה־נָ֤א יָדַ֙עְתִּי֙ כִּ֣י אֵ֤ין אֱלֹהִים֙ בְּכׇל־ הָאָ֔רֶץ כִּ֖י אִם־בְּיִשְׂרָאֵ֑ל וְעַתָּ֛ה קַח־נָ֥א בְרָכָ֖ה מֵאֵ֥ת עַבְדֶּֽךָ׃ [16] וַיֹּ֗אמֶר חַי־יְהֹוָ֛ה אֲשֶׁר־עָמַ֥דְתִּי לְפָנָ֖יו אִם־אֶקָּ֑ח וַיִּפְצַר־בּ֥וֹ לָקַ֖חַת וַיְמָאֵֽן׃ [17] וַיֹּ֘אמֶר֮ נַעֲמָן֒ וָלֹ֕א יֻתַּן־נָ֣א לְעַבְדְּךָ֔ מַשָּׂ֥א צֶֽמֶד־פְּרָדִ֖ים אֲדָמָ֑ה כִּ֡י לֽוֹא־יַעֲשֶׂה֩ ע֨וֹד עַבְדְּךָ֜ עֹלָ֤ה וָזֶ֙בַח֙ לֵאלֹהִ֣ים אֲחֵרִ֔ים כִּ֖י אִם־לַיהֹוָֽה׃ [18] לַדָּבָ֣ר הַזֶּ֔ה יִסְלַ֥ח יְהֹוָ֖ה לְעַבְדֶּ֑ךָ בְּב֣וֹא אֲדֹנִ֣י בֵית־רִמּוֹן֩ לְהִשְׁתַּחֲוֺ֨ת שָׁ֜מָּה וְה֤וּא ׀ נִשְׁעָ֣ן עַל־יָדִ֗י וְהִֽשְׁתַּחֲוֵ֙יתִי֙ בֵּ֣ית רִמֹּ֔ן בְּהִֽשְׁתַּחֲוָיָ֙תִי֙ בֵּ֣ית רִמֹּ֔ן יִסְלַח־נא* יְהֹוָ֥ה לְעַבְדְּךָ֖ בַּדָּבָ֥ר הַזֶּֽה׃ [19] וַיֹּ֥אמֶר ל֖וֹ לֵ֣ךְ לְשָׁל֑וֹם וַיֵּ֥לֶךְ מֵאִתּ֖וֹ כִּבְרַת־אָֽרֶץ׃ ס

v. 18. כתיב ולא קריא

(vv. 10,12,13) uses the same Hebrew verbs to indicate both bathing and ritual purification.

14. So he went down and immersed himself in the Jordan Naaman performed the rites "as the man of God had bidden." A 5th-century tradition, as inscribed at Ḥammat Gader (hot springs in the Yarmuk Valley), links Elijah (not Elisha) with healing the lepers who bathed there.

הפטרת מצרע

HAFTARAH FOR M'TZORA

2 KINGS 7:3–20

(*When* Tazri·a *and* M'tzora *are combined, recite this* haftarah.)

The power of prophecy is a main teaching of this *haftarah,* as indicated by its conclusion (vv. 16–20). The story presented here is incomplete, however, because certain phrases ("as the LORD has spoken" and "just as the man of God had spoken" in vv. 16–17) refer to matters stated in the first verses of chapter 7, not included in the *haftarah*. Because of this, the symmetry of a complete narrative, with fulfillment following prediction, is lost because the *haftarah* is only part of a cycle of legends and prophecies related to the prophet Elisha and Israel's wars against Aram. The *haftarah* constitutes the final section of 2 Kings 6:24–7:20 that begins when "King Ben-hadad of Aram mustered his entire army and marched upon Samaria and besieged it" (6:24).

The siege is described as brutal. Famine and cannibalism were rampant, and the price of food was out of control. "A donkey's head sold for eighty [shekels] of silver and a quarter of a *kab* of [carob pods] for five shekels" (6:25). The king of Israel, utterly helpless, sent his messenger to threaten the prophet Elisha who replied that by "this time tomorrow" all would change (see 6:26–33). "A *seah* of choice flour shall sell for a shekel at the gate of Samaria, and two *seahs* of barley for a shekel" (7:1). The royal messenger scoffed at this prediction of plenty; and in response, Elisha swore that the aide would die before partaking of it (v. 2). It is important to remember that the *haftarah* begins only after this prologue.

Yet the *haftarah,* in and of itself, has its own literary drama, beginning in the midst of a crisis (famine and siege) and ending with its termination (food and the opening of the gates). The fulfillment formulas ("as," "just as" in 7:16–20, at the end of the *haftarah*) suggest that the external course of events is more than it seems: Hidden within is the fulfillment of divine predictions. Although one who reads only the *haftarah* is not aware of the predictions, the fulfillment of the divine word is announced at the end of it as the inner truth of the historical events. History is thus presented as the dramatic shape of divine will, as revealed through God's prophets.

Two themes frame the development of the story in the *haftarah.* One theme has to do with the location of the lepers, who at the beginning are "outside the gate" (*sha·ar*) of Samaria. Their location marks the boundary of the siege, as well as the tension between the hunger within the city walls and the provisions of the Aramean camp in the field. The other theme involves the lepers' split status. They belong both to the city and to the field, both to the starving (native) Israelites within the walls and to the (alien) world beyond the walls. Ritually contaminated and thus prohibited from entering the city, they choose to defect. Thus they move the action to the Aramean camp.

Among the empty tents of the enemy, the lepers find food and wealth; they repeatedly "ate and drank . . . carried off silver and gold . . . and buried it." The turning point of the narrative is the lepers' recognition that they "are not doing right [*ken*]." Thus they return to the city and inform its rulers of the Aramean flight. At first, only a few of the king's men follow the lepers out to the camp. With the return of the positive report, however, the whole population streams out of Samaria to fill their needs. With that, the boundaries determined by location are opened and the crisis of the lepers' status is resolved. Elisha's forecast concerning the low price of "barley" in the "gate" of Samaria is gradually fulfilled. In the end, food is in the gates—not only in the lepers. The scoffing

aide-de-camp is punished, "exactly (*ken*)" as the prophet had predicted.

The constant movement between the city and the camp gives the illusion of an extended time frame. This sense is reinforced by the variety of scenes that make up the account. Because the original situation had been grave, and Elisha's prophecy was meant to assuage the people's fears, he began his economic prediction with the words "This time tomorrow" (7:1). Accordingly, we must assume that the time narrated in 7:3–20 covers only one day. The many comings and goings are intended to dramatize the successive stages of transformation.

It is intriguing that the fulfillment of the divine oracle begins with the defection of the four lepers, who dramatize the polarities and precariousness of the situation as a whole. What is more, it is precisely their social and ritual marginality that puts them beyond the walls and in a position to flee to the Aramean camp. As aliens among the aliens, they bring "good news" back to the city once they overcome their private desires and think of their starving compatriots in Samaria. Their moral turning is at the core of the narrative.

RELATION OF THE *HAFTARAH* TO THE *PARASHAH*

The formal and explicit connection between the passages hinges on the term *m'tzora.* This is the Rabbinic title of the *parashah* and refers to a "leper" (Lev. 14:2) with "a leprous affection" (*tzara·at*) on the skin (Lev. 13:45) who must "dwell apart . . . outside the camp" (v. 46) until permitted to undergo the ritual of cleansing. The previous *parashah* (Lev. 12–13), which is sometimes combined with this one, includes the detailed diagnostics of the disease (Lev. 13); *M'tzora* (Lev. 14–15) focuses on the rites of personal purification (14:1–32), with an appendix on diagnosing and purging the plague in buildings (vv. 33–57).

7 [3]There were four men, lepers, outside the gate. They said to one another, "Why should we sit here waiting for death? [4]If we decide to go into the town, what with the famine in the town, we shall die there; and if we just sit here, still we die. Come, let us desert to the Aramean camp. If they let us live, we shall live; and if they put us to death, we shall but die."

[5]They set out at twilight for the Aramean camp; but when they came to the edge of the Aramean camp, there was no one there. [6]For the Lord had caused the Aramean camp to hear a sound of chariots, a sound of horses—the din of a huge army. They said to one another, "The king of Israel must have hired the kings of the Hittites and the kings of Mizraim to attack us!" [7]And they fled headlong in the twilight, aban-

ז 3 וְאַרְבָּעָה אֲנָשִׁים הָיוּ מְצֹרָעִים פֶּתַח
הַשָּׁעַר וַיֹּאמְרוּ אִישׁ אֶל־רֵעֵהוּ מָה אֲנַחְנוּ
יֹשְׁבִים פֹּה עַד־מָתְנוּ׃ 4 אִם־אָמַרְנוּ נָבוֹא
הָעִיר וְהָרָעָב בָּעִיר וָמַתְנוּ שָׁם וְאִם־
יָשַׁבְנוּ פֹה וָמָתְנוּ וְעַתָּה לְכוּ וְנִפְּלָה
אֶל־מַחֲנֵה אֲרָם אִם־יְחַיֻּנוּ נִחְיֶה וְאִם־
יְמִיתֻנוּ וָמָתְנוּ׃
5 וַיָּקוּמוּ בַנֶּשֶׁף לָבוֹא אֶל־מַחֲנֵה אֲרָם
וַיָּבֹאוּ עַד־קְצֵה מַחֲנֵה אֲרָם וְהִנֵּה אֵין־
שָׁם אִישׁ׃ 6 וַאדֹנָי הִשְׁמִיעַ | אֶת־מַחֲנֵה
אֲרָם קוֹל רֶכֶב קוֹל סוּס קוֹל חַיִל גָּדוֹל
וַיֹּאמְרוּ אִישׁ אֶל־אָחִיו הִנֵּה שָׂכַר־עָלֵינוּ
מֶלֶךְ יִשְׂרָאֵל אֶת־מַלְכֵי הַחִתִּים וְאֶת־
מַלְכֵי מִצְרַיִם לָבוֹא עָלֵינוּ׃ 7 וַיָּקוּמוּ

2 Kings 7:3. lepers, outside the gate Medical analysis indicates that the disease as described in the Bible is neither what we know as leprosy (Hansen's disease) nor what we know as psoriasis. The general term "scale disease" has been suggested. People who were diagnosed with active symptoms of this malady were segregated from society (Lev. 13:4–5).

doning their tents and horses and asses—the [entire] camp just as it was—as they fled for their lives.

8When those lepers came to the edge of the camp, they went into one of the tents and ate and drank; then they carried off silver and gold and clothing from there and buried it. They came back and went into another tent, and they carried off what was there and buried it. 9Then they said to one another, "We are not doing right. This is a day of good news, and we are keeping silent! If we wait until the light of morning, we shall incur guilt. Come, let us go and inform the king's palace." 10They went and called out to the gatekeepers of the city and told them, "We have been to the Aramean camp. There is not a soul there, nor any human sound; but the horses are tethered and the asses are tethered and the tents are undisturbed."

11The gatekeepers called out, and the news was passed on into the king's palace. 12The king rose in the night and said to his courtiers, "I will tell you what the Arameans have done to us. They know that we are starving, so they have gone out of camp and hidden in the fields, thinking: When they come out of the town, we will take them alive and get into the town." 13But one of the courtiers spoke up, "Let a few of the remaining horses that are still here be taken—they are like those that are left here of the whole multitude of Israel, out of the whole multitude of Israel that have perished—and let us send and find out."

14They took two teams of horses and the king sent them after the Aramean army, saying, "Go and find out." 15They followed them as far as the Jordan, and found the entire road full of clothing and gear which the Arameans had thrown away in their haste; and the messengers returned and told the king. 16The people then went out and plundered the Aramean camp. So a *seah* of choice flour sold for a shekel, and two

וַיָּנ֣וּסוּ בַנֶּ֗שֶׁף וַיַּעַזְב֣וּ אֶת־אָהֳלֵיהֶ֡ם וְאֶת־
סֽוּסֵיהֶם֙ וְאֶת־חֲמ֣רֵיהֶ֔ם הַֽמַּחֲנֶ֖ה כַּאֲשֶׁר־
הִ֑יא וַיָּנֻ֖סוּ אֶל־נַפְשָֽׁם׃
8 וַיָּבֹ֜אוּ הַֽמְצֹרָעִ֣ים הָאֵ֗לֶּה עַד־קְצֵ֣ה
הַֽמַּחֲנֶ֔ה וַיָּבֹ֜אוּ אֶל־אֹ֤הֶל אֶחָד֙ וַיֹּאכְל֣וּ
וַיִּשְׁתּ֔וּ וַיִּשְׂא֣וּ מִשָּׁ֗ם כֶּ֤סֶף וְזָהָב֙ וּבְגָדִ֔ים
וַיֵּלְכ֖וּ וַיַּטְמִ֑נוּ וַיָּשֻׁ֗בוּ וַיָּבֹ֙אוּ֙ אֶל־אֹ֣הֶל אַחֵ֔ר
וַיִּשְׂא֣וּ מִשָּׁ֔ם וַיֵּלְכ֖וּ וַיַּטְמִֽנוּ׃ 9 וַיֹּאמְר֞וּ אִ֣ישׁ
אֶל־רֵעֵ֗הוּ לֹֽא־כֵ֣ן ׀ אֲנַ֣חְנוּ עֹשִׂ֗ים הַיּ֤וֹם
הַזֶּה֙ יוֹם־בְּשֹׂרָ֣ה ה֔וּא וַאֲנַ֣חְנוּ מַחְשִׁ֗ים
וְחִכִּ֛ינוּ עַד־א֥וֹר הַבֹּ֖קֶר וּמְצָאָ֣נוּ עָו֑וֹן וְעַתָּה֙
לְכ֣וּ וְנָבֹ֔אָה וְנַגִּ֖ידָה בֵּ֥ית הַמֶּֽלֶךְ׃ 10 וַיָּבֹ֗אוּ
וַֽיִּקְרְאוּ֮ אֶל־שֹׁעֵ֣ר הָעִיר֒ וַיַּגִּ֤ידוּ לָהֶם֙ לֵאמֹ֔ר
בָּ֚אנוּ אֶל־מַחֲנֵ֣ה אֲרָ֔ם וְהִנֵּ֛ה אֵֽין־שָׁ֥ם אִ֖ישׁ
וְק֣וֹל אָדָ֑ם כִּ֣י אִם־הַסּ֤וּס אָסוּר֙ וְהַחֲמ֣וֹר
אָס֔וּר וְאֹהָלִ֖ים כַּאֲשֶׁר־הֵֽמָּה׃
11 וַיִּקְרָ֖א הַשֹּֽׁעֲרִ֑ים וַיַּגִּ֕ידוּ בֵּ֥ית הַמֶּ֖לֶךְ
פְּנִֽימָה׃ 12 וַיָּ֨קָם הַמֶּ֜לֶךְ לַ֗יְלָה וַיֹּ֙אמֶר֙
אֶל־עֲבָדָ֔יו אַגִּֽידָה־נָּ֣א לָכֶ֔ם אֵ֛ת אֲשֶׁר־עָ֥שׂוּ
לָ֖נוּ אֲרָ֑ם יָדְע֞וּ כִּי־רְעֵבִ֣ים אֲנַ֗חְנוּ וַיֵּצְא֤וּ
מִן־הַֽמַּחֲנֶה֙ לְהֵחָבֵ֤ה בהשדה בַשָּׂדֶה֙
לֵאמֹ֔ר כִּֽי־יֵצְא֤וּ מִן־הָעִיר֙ וְנִתְפְּשֵׂ֣ם חַיִּ֔ים
וְאֶל־הָעִ֖יר נָבֹֽא׃ 13 וַיַּעַן֩ אֶחָ֨ד מֵעֲבָדָ֜יו
וַיֹּ֗אמֶר וְיִקְחוּ־נָ֡א חֲמִשָּׁ֣ה מִן־הַסּוּסִים֩
הַנִּשְׁאָרִ֨ים אֲשֶׁ֤ר נִשְׁאֲרוּ־בָהּ֙ הִנָּ֗ם כְּכָל־
ההמון הֲמ֤וֹן יִשְׂרָאֵל֙ אֲשֶׁ֣ר נִשְׁאֲרוּ־בָ֔הּ הִנָּ֕ם
כְּכָל־הֲמ֥וֹן יִשְׂרָאֵ֖ל אֲשֶׁר־תָּ֑מּוּ וְנִשְׁלְחָ֖ה
וְנִרְאֶֽה׃
14 וַיִּקְח֕וּ שְׁנֵ֖י רֶ֣כֶב סוּסִ֑ים וַיִּשְׁלַ֨ח הַמֶּ֜לֶךְ
אַחֲרֵ֧י מַחֲנֵה־אֲרָ֛ם לֵאמֹ֖ר לְכ֥וּ וּרְאֽוּ׃
15 וַיֵּלְכ֣וּ אַחֲרֵיהֶם֮ עַד־הַיַּרְדֵּן֒ וְהִנֵּ֣ה כָל־
הַדֶּ֗רֶךְ מְלֵאָ֤ה בְגָדִים֙ וְכֵלִ֔ים אֲשֶׁר־
הִשְׁלִ֥יכוּ אֲרָ֖ם בהחפזם בְּחָפְזָ֑ם וַיָּשֻׁ֙בוּ֙
הַמַּלְאָכִ֔ים וַיַּגִּ֖דוּ לַמֶּֽלֶךְ׃ 16 וַיֵּצֵ֣א הָעָ֔ם
וַיָּבֹ֕זּוּ אֵ֖ת מַחֲנֵ֣ה אֲרָ֑ם וַיְהִ֨י סְאָה־סֹ֜לֶת

*seah*s of barley for a shekel—as the LORD had
spoken.
17 Now the king had put the aide on whose
arm he leaned in charge of the gate; and he was
trampled to death in the gate by the people—
just as the man of God had spoken, as he had
spoken when the king came down to him. 18 For
when the man of God said to the king, "This
time tomorrow two *seah*s of barley shall sell at
the gate of Samaria for a shekel, and a *seah* of
choice flour for a shekel," 19 the aide answered
the man of God and said, "Even if the LORD
made windows in the sky, could this come to
pass?" And he retorted, "You shall see it with
your own eyes, but you shall not eat of it." 20 That
is exactly what happened to him: The people
trampled him to death in the gate.

בְּשֶׁקֶל וְסָאתַיִם שְׂעֹרִים בְּשֶׁקֶל כִּדְבַר
יְהוָה׃
17 וְהַמֶּלֶךְ הִפְקִיד אֶת־הַשָּׁלִישׁ אֲשֶׁר־
נִשְׁעָן עַל־יָדוֹ עַל־הַשַּׁעַר וַיִּרְמְסֻהוּ הָעָם
בַּשַּׁעַר וַיָּמֹת כַּאֲשֶׁר דִּבֶּר אִישׁ הָאֱלֹהִים
אֲשֶׁר דִּבֶּר בְּרֶדֶת הַמֶּלֶךְ אֵלָיו׃ 18 וַיְהִי
כְּדַבֵּר אִישׁ הָאֱלֹהִים אֶל־הַמֶּלֶךְ לֵאמֹר
סָאתַיִם שְׂעֹרִים בְּשֶׁקֶל וְסְאָה־סֹלֶת
בְּשֶׁקֶל יִהְיֶה כָּעֵת מָחָר בְּשַׁעַר שֹׁמְרוֹן׃
19 וַיַּעַן הַשָּׁלִישׁ אֶת־אִישׁ הָאֱלֹהִים וַיֹּאמַר
וְהִנֵּה יְהוָה עֹשֶׂה אֲרֻבּוֹת בַּשָּׁמַיִם הֲיִהְיֶה
כַּדָּבָר הַזֶּה וַיֹּאמֶר הִנְּךָ רֹאֶה בְּעֵינֶיךָ
וּמִשָּׁם לֹא תֹאכֵל׃ 20 וַיְהִי־לוֹ כֵּן וַיִּרְמְסוּ
אֹתוֹ הָעָם בַּשַּׁעַר וַיָּמֹת׃ ס

16 טז

16 The Lord spoke to Moses after the death
of the two sons of Aaron who died when they
drew too close to the presence of the Lord. 2The
Lord said to Moses:

Tell your brother Aaron that he is not to come
at will into the Shrine behind the curtain, in
front of the cover that is upon the ark, lest he
die; for I appear in the cloud over the cover.
3Thus only shall Aaron enter the Shrine: with
a bull of the herd for a purification offering
and a ram for a burnt offering.—4He shall
be dressed in a sacral linen tunic, with linen

וַיְדַבֵּ֤ר יְהוָה֙ אֶל־מֹשֶׁ֔ה אַחֲרֵ֣י מ֔וֹת
שְׁנֵ֖י בְּנֵ֣י אַהֲרֹ֑ן בְּקָרְבָתָ֥ם לִפְנֵי־יְהוָ֖ה
וַיָּמֻֽתוּ׃ 2 וַיֹּ֨אמֶר יְהוָ֜ה אֶל־מֹשֶׁ֗ה
דַּבֵּר֮ אֶל־אַהֲרֹ֣ן אָחִיךָ֒ וְאַל־יָבֹ֤א בְכָל־עֵת֙
אֶל־הַקֹּ֔דֶשׁ מִבֵּ֖ית לַפָּרֹ֑כֶת אֶל־פְּנֵ֨י הַכַּפֹּ֜רֶת
אֲשֶׁ֤ר עַל־הָאָרֹן֙ וְלֹ֣א יָמ֔וּת כִּ֚י בֶּֽעָנָ֔ן אֵרָאֶ֖ה
עַל־הַכַּפֹּֽרֶת׃ 3 בְּזֹ֛את יָבֹ֥א אַהֲרֹ֖ן אֶל־
הַקֹּ֑דֶשׁ בְּפַ֧ר בֶּן־בָּקָ֛ר לְחַטָּ֖את וְאַ֥יִל לְעֹלָֽה׃
4 כְּתֹֽנֶת־בַּ֨ד קֹ֜דֶשׁ יִלְבָּ֗שׁ וּמִֽכְנְסֵי־בַד֮ יִהְי֣וּ

THE YOM KIPPUR RITUAL (16:1–34)

The primary objective of these expiatory rites is to maintain a pure sanctuary. An impure, or defiled, sanctuary would induce God to withdraw His Presence from the Israelite community.

Verses 1–2 introduce the rites by referring to the untimely deaths of Nadab and Abihu, the two sons of Aaron who suffered because they improperly entered the sanctuary (Lev. 10). This reference served as an admonition to the priesthood, because the purification of the sanctuary required the High Priest to enter its innermost part. If extreme care were not exercised in this endeavor, he would risk death.

2. into the Shrine behind the curtain That is, on the inward side of the curtain that divided the Shrine, or Holy of Holies, from the larger area first encountered on entering the sanctuary.

in front of the cover that is upon the ark See Exod. 25:17–22.

for I appear in the cloud over the cover God's Presence (*Kavod*) was depicted as a cloud with fire burning inside it. The cloud pervaded the sanctuary and was visible above it.

PREPARATIONS FOR PURIFICATION (vv. 3–10)

The main officiant in the purification of the sanctuary was the High Priest. Although he was assisted at certain points in the proceedings, the efficacy of the entire ritual depended primarily on him.

4. For the rites described here, the High Priest donned unadorned white linen vestments that were fashioned especially for the occasion.

CHAPTER 16

This is one of the *parashiyyot* whose name and opening words set the tone for all that follows. "After the death of the two sons of Aaron," we are drawn to confront our own mortality and to reflect on the direction of our lives, for the text proceeds by describing the *Yom Kippur* rituals of cleansing, self-scrutiny, and self-renewal. The rituals of the Day of Atonement are presented here rather than in the listing of holidays in Lev. 23, because their focus is not so much the public observance of *Yom Kippur.* Their focus is the priestly responsibility to cleanse and purify the sanctuary so that it will be a fit place for the atonement rituals. (*Aḥarei Mot* is read in the spring, six months before and after *Yom Kippur,* as if to suggest that any season is an appropriate time for self-scrutiny and atonement.)

3–5. For the Midrash (Lev. R. 21:11), the bull recalls the merit of Abraham's offering in Gen. 18:7, the ram is a reminder of Isaac's readiness to be sacrificed in Gen. 22:13, and the two

HALAKHAH L'MA·ASEH

16:4ff. This chapter's description of the *Yom Kippur* rite of expiation for the community's sins is the Torah reading for *Yom Kippur* morning and serves as the basis for the *Avodah* service on *Yom Kippur.*

עַל־בְּשָׂרוֹ וּבְאַבְנֵט בַּד יַחְגֹּר וּבְמִצְנֶפֶת בַּד
יִצְנֹף בִּגְדֵי־קֹדֶשׁ הֵם וְרָחַץ בַּמַּיִם אֶת־
בְּשָׂרוֹ וּלְבֵשָׁם: 5 וּמֵאֵת עֲדַת בְּנֵי יִשְׂרָאֵל
יִקַּח שְׁנֵי־שְׂעִירֵי עִזִּים לְחַטָּאת וְאַיִל אֶחָד
לְעֹלָה:

6 וְהִקְרִיב אַהֲרֹן אֶת־פַּר הַחַטָּאת אֲשֶׁר־לוֹ
וְכִפֶּר בַּעֲדוֹ וּבְעַד בֵּיתוֹ: 7 וְלָקַח אֶת־שְׁנֵי
הַשְּׂעִירִם וְהֶעֱמִיד אֹתָם לִפְנֵי יְהוָה פֶּתַח
אֹהֶל מוֹעֵד: 8 וְנָתַן אַהֲרֹן עַל־שְׁנֵי
הַשְּׂעִירִם גֹּרָלוֹת גּוֹרָל אֶחָד לַיהוָה וְגוֹרָל
אֶחָד לַעֲזָאזֵל: 9 וְהִקְרִיב אַהֲרֹן אֶת־
הַשָּׂעִיר אֲשֶׁר עָלָה עָלָיו הַגּוֹרָל לַיהוָה
וְעָשָׂהוּ חַטָּאת: 10 וְהַשָּׂעִיר אֲשֶׁר עָלָה
עָלָיו הַגּוֹרָל לַעֲזָאזֵל יָעֳמַד־חַי לִפְנֵי יְהוָה

breeches next to his flesh, and be girt with a linen sash, and he shall wear a linen turban. They are sacral vestments; he shall bathe his body in water and then put them on.—
5And from the Israelite community he shall take two he-goats for a purification offering and a ram for a burnt offering.

6Aaron is to offer his own bull of purification offering, to make expiation for himself and for his household.
7Aaron shall take the two he-goats and let them stand before the LORD at the entrance of the Tent of Meeting;
8and he shall place lots upon the two goats, one marked for the LORD and the other marked for Azazel.
9Aaron shall bring forward the goat designated by lot for the LORD, which he is to offer as a purification offering;
10while the goat designated by lot for Azazel shall be left standing alive be-

5. from the Israelite community . . . two he-goats Purification offerings on behalf of the entire community usually consisted of large cattle; those offered by individual Israelites were usually from the flocks, as in 4:22f. The *Yom Kippur* ritual was an exception. He-goats from the flocks served as purification offerings for the entire people.

7. The two he-goats were stationed near the altar so that one could be chosen by lot as a sacrifice and the other one could be selected as the scapegoat.

8. one marked for the LORD and the other marked for Azazel One lot bore the inscription "for the LORD" (*l'YHVH*) and the other bore the inscription "for Azazel" (*la-azazel*). The precise meaning of the Hebrew *azazel,* found nowhere else in the Bible, has been disputed since antiquity and remains uncertain.

9. offer as a purification offering He designates it as a purification offering. Assigning an animal as a sacrifice was a formal act accompanied by a declaration.

10. left standing alive The he-goat selected for Azazel was not slaughtered for a sacrifice, as was the other goat, but served as a different means of obtaining expiation.

---

goats (v. 5) symbolize the meal Jacob prepared for his father to receive his father's blessing (Gen. 27:9). The four linen garments (v. 4) represent Sarah, Rebecca, Rachel, and Leah. On *Yom Kippur,* we come before God armed not only with our own merit but also with that of our ancestors, extending through the generations.

6. The ritual of the High Priest that leads to atonement is rooted in the premise that the sanctuary, which represents the presence of God, is also a human institution, subject to the flaws and imperfections of any human institution. Religious leaders, however pious and devoted, are human beings. Thus Aaron begins the purgation process by bringing an offering on his own behalf and on behalf of his fellow *kohanim* for whatever they may have done wrong. The Midrash takes the words "for himself and his household" to mean that the High Priest must be married. He comes before God, not as a pious individual but as the representative of a flawed community aspiring to holiness. How could he bear their prayers and hopes unless he had learned to care for and share the hopes and dreams of another person?

8. one marked for the LORD and the other marked for Azazel A Hasidic comment interprets these words to teach us that we should spend as much time, money, and energy on God's purposes as we do on earthly pleasures.

10. If Azazel is taken to be the name of a demon, either the demon that entices people

fore the LORD, to make expiation with it and to send it off to the wilderness for Azazel.

¹¹Aaron shall then offer his bull of purification offering, to make expiation for himself and his household. He shall slaughter his bull of purification offering, ¹²and he shall take a panful of glowing coals scooped from the altar before the LORD, and two handfuls of finely ground aromatic incense, and bring this behind the curtain. ¹³He shall put the incense on the fire before the LORD, so that the cloud from the incense screens the cover that is over [the Ark of] the Pact, lest he die. ¹⁴He shall take some of the blood of the bull and sprinkle it with his finger over the cover on the east side; and in front of the cover he shall sprinkle some of the blood with his finger seven times. ¹⁵He shall then slaughter the people's goat of purification offer-

לְכַפֵּ֣ר עָלָ֔יו לְשַׁלַּ֥ח אֹת֛וֹ לַעֲזָאזֵ֖ל הַמִּדְבָּֽרָה׃
¹¹ וְהִקְרִ֨יב אַהֲרֹ֜ן אֶת־פַּ֤ר הַֽחַטָּאת֙ אֲשֶׁר־ל֔וֹ וְכִפֶּ֥ר בַּֽעֲד֖וֹ וּבְעַ֣ד בֵּית֑וֹ וְשָׁחַ֛ט אֶת־פַּ֥ר הַֽחַטָּ֖את אֲשֶׁר־לֽוֹ׃ ¹² וְלָקַ֣ח מְלֹֽא־הַ֠מַּחְתָּ֠ה גַּֽחֲלֵי־אֵ֞שׁ מֵעַ֤ל הַמִּזְבֵּ֙חַ֙ מִלִּפְנֵ֣י יְהֹוָ֔ה וּמְלֹ֣א חָפְנָ֔יו קְטֹ֥רֶת סַמִּ֖ים דַּקָּ֑ה וְהֵבִ֖יא מִבֵּ֥ית לַפָּרֹֽכֶת׃ ¹³ וְנָתַ֧ן אֶת־הַקְּטֹ֛רֶת עַל־הָאֵ֖שׁ לִפְנֵ֣י יְהֹוָ֑ה וְכִסָּ֣ה ׀ עֲנַ֣ן הַקְּטֹ֗רֶת אֶת־הַכַּפֹּ֛רֶת אֲשֶׁ֥ר עַל־הָֽעֵד֖וּת וְלֹ֥א יָמֽוּת׃ ¹⁴ וְלָקַח֙ מִדַּ֣ם הַפָּ֔ר וְהִזָּ֧ה בְאֶצְבָּע֛וֹ עַל־פְּנֵ֥י הַכַּפֹּ֖רֶת קֵ֑דְמָה וְלִפְנֵ֣י הַכַּפֹּ֗רֶת יַזֶּ֧ה שֶֽׁבַע־פְּעָמִ֛ים מִן־הַדָּ֖ם בְּאֶצְבָּעֽוֹ׃ ¹⁵ וְשָׁחַ֞ט אֶת־שְׂעִ֤יר הַֽחַטָּאת֙ אֲשֶׁ֣ר לָעָ֔ם וְהֵבִיא֙ אֶת־דָּמ֔וֹ אֶל־מִבֵּ֖ית

PURIFICATION OF THE SANCTUARY
(vv. 11–19)

The sanctuary was purified in two stages, represented first by the bull and then by the he-goat; i.e., by the purification offerings of priesthood and people, respectively. This is the only instance in the Torah's priestly laws in which sacrificial blood is brought into the Holy of Holies.

11. Nothing was placed on the altar at this point. The actual sacrifice is described in verse 25.

12. the altar before the LORD This designation must refer to the altar of burnt offerings in

the sanctuary courtyard, because only it had a perpetual fire burning, allowing the High Priest to bring the coals from there into the sanctuary.

finely ground aromatic incense The prescription for blending this incense is provided in Exod. 30:34–38.

13. the Pact The Ark is referred to in this way because the tablets of "the Pact" (*ha-Edut*), the covenant between God and Israel, were deposited in it (Exod. 40:20).

lest he die The incense cloud served to protect the High Priest while he stood in the immediate area of God's Presence.

---

to sin or the malign power that testifies against them on the Day of Atonement, then the scapegoat is cast into the wilderness (or in later interpretations, thrown off a cliff) rather than sacrificed in the usual manner, to avoid violating the ban against offering sacrifices to demons (Ibn Ezra). A *midrash* sees Israel offering the scapegoat to Azazel as a bribe to persuade him not to testify against Israel or as a distraction to keep him from his evil work (PdRE).

What can we see as the meaning of the scapegoat if we do not accept the Azazel-as-demon theory? It may be a symbol of the evil impulse itself, the tendency to be led astray by the animal part of our nature, by lust or appetite. It may have been believed that words alone were

not enough to rid the Israelites of the inclination to do wrong; something physical had to be expelled from their communal midst. Hirsch interprets the two goats homiletically: "We can follow our sensual instincts into the wilderness, leading to self-destruction, or we can sacrifice our instincts to the service of God."

13. The Talmud suggests that the offering of incense, which has scent but no physical presence, atones for sins of gossip and slander, which are also without physical reality but can be carried far and wide with serious consequences. There are more sins relating to improper speech in the *Yom Kippur* confessional than any other category of wrongdoing (BT Yoma 44a).

לַפָּרֹכֶת וְעָשָׂה אֶת־דָּמוֹ כַּאֲשֶׁר עָשָׂה לְדַם
הַפָּר וְהִזָּה אֹתוֹ עַל־הַכַּפֹּרֶת וְלִפְנֵי
הַכַּפֹּרֶת׃
16 וְכִפֶּר עַל־הַקֹּדֶשׁ מִטֻּמְאֹת בְּנֵי יִשְׂרָאֵל
וּמִפִּשְׁעֵיהֶם לְכָל־חַטֹּאתָם וְכֵן יַעֲשֶׂה
לְאֹהֶל מוֹעֵד הַשֹּׁכֵן אִתָּם בְּתוֹךְ טֻמְאֹתָם׃
17 וְכָל־אָדָם לֹא־יִהְיֶה ׀ בְּאֹהֶל מוֹעֵד
בְּבֹאוֹ לְכַפֵּר בַּקֹּדֶשׁ עַד־צֵאתוֹ
וְכִפֶּר בַּעֲדוֹ וּבְעַד בֵּיתוֹ וּבְעַד כָּל־קְהַל
יִשְׂרָאֵל׃ 18 וְיָצָא אֶל־הַמִּזְבֵּחַ אֲשֶׁר לִפְנֵי־ שני
יְהוָה וְכִפֶּר עָלָיו וְלָקַח מִדַּם הַפָּר וּמִדַּם
הַשָּׂעִיר וְנָתַן עַל־קַרְנוֹת הַמִּזְבֵּחַ סָבִיב׃
19 וְהִזָּה עָלָיו מִן־הַדָּם בְּאֶצְבָּעוֹ שֶׁבַע
פְּעָמִים וְטִהֲרוֹ וְקִדְּשׁוֹ מִטֻּמְאֹת בְּנֵי
יִשְׂרָאֵל׃
20 וְכִלָּה מִכַּפֵּר אֶת־הַקֹּדֶשׁ וְאֶת־אֹהֶל
מוֹעֵד וְאֶת־הַמִּזְבֵּחַ וְהִקְרִיב אֶת־הַשָּׂעִיר
הֶחָי׃ 21 וְסָמַךְ אַהֲרֹן אֶת־שְׁתֵּי ידו יָדָיו
עַל רֹאשׁ הַשָּׂעִיר הַחַי וְהִתְוַדָּה עָלָיו

ing, bring its blood behind the curtain, and do with its blood as he has done with the blood of the bull: he shall sprinkle it over the cover and in front of the cover.

16Thus he shall purge the Shrine of the impurity and transgression of the Israelites, whatever their sins; and he shall do the same for the Tent of Meeting, which abides with them in the midst of their impurity. 17When he goes in to make expiation in the Shrine, nobody else shall be in the Tent of Meeting until he comes out.

When he has made expiation for himself and his household, and for the whole congregation of Israel, 18he shall go out to the altar that is before the LORD and purge it: he shall take some of the blood of the bull and of the goat and apply it to each of the horns of the altar; 19and the rest of the blood he shall sprinkle on it with his finger seven times. Thus he shall purify it of the impurity of the Israelites and consecrate it.

20When he has finished purging the Shrine, the Tent of Meeting, and the altar, the live goat shall be brought forward. 21Aaron shall lay both his hands upon the head of the live goat

16. This was the concession made by God out of His love for Israel. He allowed His people to build an earthly residence for Him, on condition that its purity be strictly maintained.

17. nobody else shall be in the Tent of Meeting On the occasion of this ritual, only the High Priest, who had undergone meticulous purification for his role on *Yom Kippur* and who held a special status, was permitted inside the tent.

18. he shall go out to the altar that is before the LORD The High Priest did not leave the tent itself, but came out of the Holy of Holies to the outer chamber of the tent.

19. In this instance, purification was accomplished by the use of sacrificial blood from the purification offerings.

DISPATCH OF THE SCAPEGOAT (vv. 20–22)

After completing the purification of the sanctuary by means of the blood rites, the High Priest turned his attention to the second mode of purification, the rite of riddance that involved the scapegoat. (The name, from "escape goat," first appeared in Tyndale's English translation of the Bible in 1530.)

20. brought forward The scapegoat was brought near to the altar of burnt offerings and stood facing the entrance of the courtyard, from which it would depart.

21. confess over it The confessional enumerated the various sins to bring them out into the open. Once isolated in this way, the sins could be exorcised. Sinfulness, like impurity, was

---

21. iniquities and transgressions . . . their sins These three categories of wrongdoing are defined in the Talmud as follows: *Avon* (iniquity), "twisting," is a deviation from the straight path due to temptation. *Pesha* (transgression), "rebellion," is a rejection of the law and of the right of God to direct one's behavior. *Ḥet* (sin), "missing the mark," is a transgres-

and confess over it all the iniquities and transgressions of the Israelites, whatever their sins, putting them on the head of the goat; and it shall be sent off to the wilderness through a designated man. [22]Thus the goat shall carry on it all their iniquities to an inaccessible region; and the goat shall be set free in the wilderness.

[23]And Aaron shall go into the Tent of Meeting, take off the linen vestments that he put on when he entered the Shrine, and leave them there. [24]He shall bathe his body in water in the holy precinct and put on his vestments; then he shall come out and offer his burnt offering and the burnt offering of the people, making expiation for himself and for the people. [25]The fat of the purification offering he shall turn into smoke on the altar.

[26]He who set the Azazel-goat free shall wash his clothes and bathe his body in water; after that he may reenter the camp.

[27]The bull of purification offering and the goat of purification offering whose blood was brought in to purge the Shrine shall be taken outside the camp; and their hides, flesh, and dung shall be consumed in fire. [28]He who

אֶת־כָּל־עֲוֹנֹת֩ בְּנֵ֨י יִשְׂרָאֵ֜ל וְאֶת־כָּל־פִּשְׁעֵיהֶ֖ם לְכָל־חַטֹּאתָ֑ם וְנָתַ֤ן אֹתָם֙ עַל־רֹ֣אשׁ הַשָּׂעִ֔יר וְשִׁלַּ֛ח בְּיַד־אִ֥ישׁ עִתִּ֖י הַמִּדְבָּֽרָה: [22] וְנָשָׂ֨א הַשָּׂעִ֥יר עָלָ֛יו אֶת־כָּל־עֲוֹנֹתָ֖ם אֶל־אֶ֣רֶץ גְּזֵרָ֑ה וְשִׁלַּ֥ח אֶת־הַשָּׂעִ֖יר בַּמִּדְבָּֽר:

[23] וּבָ֤א אַהֲרֹן֙ אֶל־אֹ֣הֶל מוֹעֵ֔ד וּפָשַׁט֙ אֶת־בִּגְדֵ֣י הַבָּ֔ד אֲשֶׁ֥ר לָבַ֖שׁ בְּבֹא֣וֹ אֶל־הַקֹּ֑דֶשׁ וְהִנִּיחָ֖ם שָֽׁם: [24] וְרָחַ֤ץ אֶת־בְּשָׂרוֹ֙ בַמַּ֔יִם בְּמָק֣וֹם קָד֔וֹשׁ וְלָבַ֖שׁ אֶת־בְּגָדָ֑יו וְיָצָ֗א וְעָשָׂ֤ה אֶת־עֹֽלָתוֹ֙ וְאֶת־עֹלַ֣ת הָעָ֔ם וְכִפֶּ֥ר בַּעֲד֖וֹ וּבְעַ֥ד הָעָֽם: [25] וְאֵ֛ת חֵ֥לֶב הַֽחַטָּ֖את יַקְטִ֥יר הַמִּזְבֵּֽחָה:

[26] וְהַֽמְשַׁלֵּ֤חַ אֶת־הַשָּׂעִיר֙ לַֽעֲזָאזֵ֔ל יְכַבֵּ֣ס בְּגָדָ֔יו וְרָחַ֥ץ אֶת־בְּשָׂר֖וֹ בַּמָּ֑יִם וְאַחֲרֵי־כֵ֖ן יָב֥וֹא אֶל־הַֽמַּחֲנֶֽה: [27] וְאֵת֩ פַּ֨ר הַֽחַטָּ֜את וְאֵ֣ת ׀ שְׂעִ֣יר הַֽחַטָּ֗את אֲשֶׁ֨ר הוּבָ֤א אֶת־דָּמָם֙ לְכַפֵּ֣ר בַּקֹּ֔דֶשׁ יוֹצִ֖יא אֶל־מִח֣וּץ לַֽמַּחֲנֶ֑ה וְשָׂרְפ֣וּ בָאֵ֔שׁ אֶת־עֹֽרֹתָ֥ם וְאֶת־בְּשָׂרָ֖ם וְאֶת־פִּרְשָֽׁם: [28] וְהַשֹּׂרֵ֣ף אֹתָ֔ם

שְׁלִישִׁי [שֵׁנִי]

thought to be an external force that clings to people; it was necessary, therefore, to "drive out," or detach, sins.

22. The Bible does not provide any information on what was done with the scapegoat in the wilderness.

AFTER THE SCAPEGOAT'S DISPATCH
(vv. 23–28)

23. Aaron shall go into the Tent of Meeting Aaron was to approach the tent. It is hardly conceivable that he would enter the tent and disrobe inside, because Exod. 20:23 specifically

forbids the exposure of a priest's nakedness near the altar. After dispatching the scapegoat, the High Priest was standing in the courtyard near the altar of burnt offerings. He proceeded to a screened area, adjacent to the tent, where he disrobed, bathed, and donned his golden vestments.

24. he shall come out From the screened area.

25. The fatty portions of the two purification offerings—the bull and the he-goat—were burned on the altar. The rest was burned outside the camp.

26. bathe Before re-entering the camp.

sion as a result of ignorance of or forgetting of the law (BT Yoma 36b). Soloveitchik stresses the need for verbal confession of one's misdeeds: "As long as ideas are bottled up in one's mind, they are unclear. Unexpressed thoughts of t'shuvah [repentance] are meaningless.... A confession which is not just lip service, one that

emanates from an anguished soul and an aching heart, is counted as an offering on the altar."

24. expiation for himself and for the people "Yom Kippur atones for sins against God. For infractions against our neighbors, we must seek their forgiveness before we can ask God to forgive us" (M Yoma 8:9).

burned them shall wash his clothes and bathe
his body in water; after that he may re-enter the
camp.
29 And this shall be to you a law for all time:
In the seventh month, on the tenth day of the
month, you shall practice self-denial; and you
shall do no manner of work, neither the citizen
nor the alien who resides among you. 30 For on
this day expiation shall be made for you to purify you of all your sins; you shall be pure before
the LORD. 31 It shall be a sabbath of complete rest
for you, and you shall practice self-denial; it is

יְכַבֵּס בְּגָדָיו וְרָחַץ אֶת־בְּשָׂרוֹ בַּמָּיִם
וְאַחֲרֵי־כֵן יָבוֹא אֶל־הַמַּחֲנֶה׃
29 וְהָיְתָה לָכֶם לְחֻקַּת עוֹלָם בַּחֹדֶשׁ
הַשְּׁבִיעִי בֶּעָשׂוֹר לַחֹדֶשׁ תְּעַנּוּ אֶת־
נַפְשֹׁתֵיכֶם וְכָל־מְלָאכָה לֹא תַעֲשׂוּ
הָאֶזְרָח וְהַגֵּר הַגָּר בְּתוֹכְכֶם׃ 30 כִּי־בַיּוֹם
הַזֶּה יְכַפֵּר עֲלֵיכֶם לְטַהֵר אֶתְכֶם מִכֹּל
חַטֹּאתֵיכֶם לִפְנֵי יְהוָה תִּטְהָרוּ׃ 31 שַׁבַּת
שַׁבָּתוֹן הִיא לָכֶם וְעִנִּיתֶם אֶת־נַפְשֹׁתֵיכֶם

AN ANNUAL EXPIATION DAY (vv. 29–34)

Once the sanctuary was in operation, periodic purification was necessary. The laws in this section, addressed to the entire people not only to the priesthood, ordain an annual Day of Atonement.

29. a law for all time What is ordained here is to be practiced in all future generations.

the seventh month According to Exod. 12:2, the month of *Pesaḥ* was to be counted as the first month of the year. According to a Babylonian calendrical reckoning, also, the year began in the spring. The Mishnah (RH 1:1) refers to *Tishrei* as the month from which the years are to be reckoned, which is our practice today. When exactly this was instituted, we do not know.

you shall practice self-denial In biblical literature *"innah nefesh,"* the idiom for the practice of self-denial, almost always connotes fasting.

you shall do no manner of work This includes the alien, for if resident aliens, such as merchants and craftsmen, were to continue their daily pursuits, the Israelite community would be affected. Aliens were not, however, expected to practice self-denial, only to honor the day by abstaining from work.

30. This verse introduces the purification rite of the people.

31. sabbath of complete rest Hebrew: *shabbat shabbaton,* a doubling of the word *"shabbat."* This has the force of a superlative, indicating the prohibition of all manner of labor, even the preparation of food necessary for subsistence.

---

29. the alien who resides among you Each of us carries a "stranger" inside us, a part of us that is alien to our essential self. Each of us must confront this "stranger" as we examine ourselves on *Yom Kippur.*

30. expiation . . . purify Soloveitchik distinguishes between "atonement" (expiation), restoring our relationship to God, and "purification," removing the stain of sin from our personality. Atonement relies on God's readiness to love and to accept imperfect people. Purification involves the capacity of those imperfect people to improve. This verse is prominent in the *Yom Kippur* liturgy.

31. you shall practice self-denial This is the basis for the obligation to fast and to abstain on *Yom Kippur* from bathing, sexual activity, and wearing leather. Earlier translations rendered the verse as "you shall afflict your souls," conveying the idea that the purpose of the *Yom Kippur* fast is to punish ourselves, to make us uncomfortable, making up for the self-indulgence of the rest of the year. The translation used here teaches the purpose of the fast not as punishment but as a proclamation of our humanity.

Human beings are the only creatures who can control their appetites, who can be hungry and choose not to eat. By fasting on *Yom Kippur,* we proclaim that we are masters of our appetites, not slaves to them. In addition, fasting is meant to free us to focus on the spiritual

HALAKHAH L'MA·ASEH

16:31. self-denial Jewish law requires those who are ill or infirm to follow doctor's orders to eat, drink, and take medicine even on *Yom Kippur.* Even in the absence of doctor's orders, the infirm and ill are allowed on fast days to eat and drink if they feel the necessity (BT Yoma 83a).

a law for all time. 32 The priest who has been anointed and ordained to serve as priest in place of his father shall make expiation. He shall put on the linen vestments, the sacral vestments. 33 He shall purge the innermost Shrine; he shall purge the Tent of Meeting and the altar; and he shall make expiation for the priests and for all the people of the congregation.

34 This shall be to you a law for all time: to make expiation for the Israelites for all their sins once a year.

And Moses did as the LORD had commanded him.

חֻקַּת עוֹלָם׃ 32 וְכִפֶּר הַכֹּהֵן אֲשֶׁר־יִמְשַׁח
אֹתוֹ וַאֲשֶׁר יְמַלֵּא אֶת־יָדוֹ לְכַהֵן תַּחַת
אָבִיו וְלָבַשׁ אֶת־בִּגְדֵי הַבָּד בִּגְדֵי הַקֹּדֶשׁ׃
33 וְכִפֶּר אֶת־מִקְדַּשׁ הַקֹּדֶשׁ וְאֶת־אֹהֶל
מוֹעֵד וְאֶת־הַמִּזְבֵּחַ יְכַפֵּר וְעַל הַכֹּהֲנִים
וְעַל־כָּל־עַם הַקָּהָל יְכַפֵּר׃
34 וְהָיְתָה־זֹּאת לָכֶם לְחֻקַּת עוֹלָם לְכַפֵּר
עַל־בְּנֵי יִשְׂרָאֵל מִכָּל־חַטֹּאתָם אַחַת
בַּשָּׁנָה
וַיַּעַשׂ כַּאֲשֶׁר צִוָּה יְהוָה אֶת־מֹשֶׁה׃ פ

17 The LORD spoke to Moses, saying:

2 Speak to Aaron and his sons and to all the Israelite people and say to them:

This is what the LORD has commanded: 3 if anyone of the house of Israel slaughters an ox

רביעי **יז** וַיְדַבֵּר יְהוָה אֶל־מֹשֶׁה לֵּאמֹר׃
2 דַּבֵּר אֶל־אַהֲרֹן וְאֶל־בָּנָיו וְאֶל כָּל־בְּנֵי
יִשְׂרָאֵל וְאָמַרְתָּ אֲלֵיהֶם
זֶה הַדָּבָר אֲשֶׁר־צִוָּה יְהוָה לֵאמֹר׃ 3 אִישׁ
אִישׁ מִבֵּית יִשְׂרָאֵל אֲשֶׁר יִשְׁחַט שׁוֹר

33. purge the innermost Shrine The primary sense of the Hebrew for "purge" (*kipper*) is "to wipe off, cleanse," as in cleansing with detergents. In the biblical conception, expiation was not the automatic result of performing certain acts. Purification resulted when God accepted the acts of the priests and of the people and granted expiation.

The Pursuit of Holiness (17:1–26:46)

Chapters 17–26 form a distinct unit; its central idea is that the entire people Israel bears the responsibility of seeking to achieve holiness. For that reason, this section has come to be known as the Holiness Code.

PROLOGUE: PROPER WORSHIP (17:1–16)

2. to all the Israelite people God addresses these ordinances to the people as a whole not just to the leaders and the priesthood.

3. the house of Israel The delineation of the Israelite people as "the house of Israel" expresses the close relationship and common descent of all Israelites.

slaughters an ox or sheep or goat The Hebrew verb translated as "slaughter" (שחט) can re-

---

dimension of our lives rather than worry about our physical needs.

"By fasting on *Yom Kippur* we should deepen our sensitivity for those who lack food and drink. This is part of the meaning of passages from Isaiah which are read as the *haftarah* on *Yom Kippur*. Through fasting we should be inspired to feed the hungry and to clothe the naked, to loosen the fetters of those who are bound" (Seymour Siegel). Likewise, the avoidance of leather—obtained by killing an animal—is an expression of our compassion and reverence for life on a day when we pray to be inscribed in the Book of Life.

32. to serve as priest in place of his father "Every generation has its own particular complex of sins to which it is vulnerable. Therefore, every generation needs its own spiritual guide to show it the way to atonement and reconciliation" (Salanter).

אוֹ־כֶ֥שֶׂב אוֹ־עֵ֖ז בַּֽמַּחֲנֶ֑ה א֚וֹ אֲשֶׁ֣ר יִשְׁחַ֔ט
מִח֖וּץ לַֽמַּחֲנֶֽה׃ 4 וְאֶל־פֶּ֜תַח אֹ֣הֶל מוֹעֵד֮
לֹ֣א הֱבִיאוֹ֒ לְהַקְרִ֤יב קָרְבָּן֙ לַֽיהוָ֔ה לִפְנֵ֖י
מִשְׁכַּ֣ן יְהוָ֑ה דָּ֣ם יֵחָשֵׁ֞ב לָאִ֤ישׁ הַהוּא֙ דָּ֣ם
שָׁפָ֔ךְ וְנִכְרַ֛ת הָאִ֥ישׁ הַה֖וּא מִקֶּ֥רֶב עַמּֽוֹ׃
5 לְמַ֡עַן אֲשֶׁר֩ יָבִ֨יאוּ בְּנֵ֜י יִשְׂרָאֵ֗ל אֶת־
זִבְחֵיהֶם֮ אֲשֶׁ֣ר הֵ֣ם זֹבְחִים֮ עַל־פְּנֵ֣י הַשָּׂדֶה֒
וֶהֱבִיאֻ֣ם לַֽיהוָ֗ה אֶל־פֶּ֛תַח אֹ֥הֶל מוֹעֵ֖ד
אֶל־הַכֹּהֵ֑ן וְזָבְח֗וּ זִבְחֵ֧י שְׁלָמִ֛ים לַֽיהוָ֖ה
אוֹתָֽם׃ 6 וְזָרַ֨ק הַכֹּהֵ֤ן אֶת־הַדָּם֙ עַל־מִזְבַּ֣ח
יְהוָ֔ה פֶּ֖תַח אֹ֣הֶל מוֹעֵ֑ד וְהִקְטִ֣יר הַחֵ֔לֶב
לְרֵ֥יחַ נִיחֹ֖חַ לַֽיהוָֽה׃ 7 וְלֹא־יִזְבְּח֥וּ עוֹד֙
אֶת־זִבְחֵיהֶ֔ם לַשְּׂעִירִ֕ם אֲשֶׁ֛ר הֵ֥ם זֹנִ֖ים
אַחֲרֵיהֶ֑ם חֻקַּ֥ת עוֹלָ֛ם תִּֽהְיֶה־זֹּ֥את לָהֶ֖ם
חמישי [שלישי] לְדֹרֹתָֽם׃

or sheep or goat in the camp, or does so outside
the camp, 4and does not bring it to the entrance
of the Tent of Meeting to present it as an offering
to the LORD, before the LORD's Tabernacle,
bloodguilt shall be imputed to that man: he has
shed blood; that man shall be cut off from
among his people. 5This is in order that the Israelites may bring the sacrifices which they have
been making in the open—that they may bring
them before the LORD, to the priest, at the entrance of the Tent of Meeting, and offer them
as sacrifices of well-being to the LORD; 6that the
priest may dash the blood against the altar of
the LORD at the entrance of the Tent of Meeting,
and turn the fat into smoke as a pleasing odor
to the LORD; 7and that they may offer their
sacrifices no more to the goat-demons after
whom they stray. This shall be to them a law
for all time, throughout the ages.

fer to slaughter in the general sense. This implies that whenever an Israelite slaughtered an animal, even for food, that act had to be carried out at the one legitimate altar located at the entrance of the Tent of Meeting. The verb can also mean "to slaughter a sacrifice." Taken in that sense, the verse suggests that only ritual sacrifices had to be made at the legitimate altar. It is probable that the latter sense of the verb is intended. But there are scholars who believe that in an earlier stage in the history of Israelite worship, all slaughter of animals, even for food, had to be of a sacral character.

4. before the LORD's Tabernacle The place of sacrifice is to be restricted to the tabernacle altar.

has shed blood The Hebrew idiom for shedding blood (*shafakh dam*) usually refers to intentional murder. Its use here dramatizes the extreme seriousness of improper sacrifice.

5. in the open Formerly, the Israelites had offered their sacrifices outside the camp as well as within it.

bring them before the LORD, to the priest Sacrifices should be offered by a proper priest at the sole legitimate altar.

6. the priest may dash the blood Concern for the proper use of sacrificial blood is basic to the regulations of chapter 17. The designation of the tabernacle altar as "the altar of the LORD" is based on the view that there is only one legitimate altar at which the God of Israel may be worshiped.

7. offer their sacrifices no more to the goat-demons The law is intended to uproot prior religious customs and to enforce strict adherence to the monotheistic religion of Israel.

CHAPTER 17

4. These rules about bringing animals to the central altar to be dispatched rest on the premise that slaughtering animals for food should never be a callous or a casual act. The Torah inculcates in us a horror of shedding blood, even the blood of animals. It would seem that, for the Torah, vegetarianism is the human ideal (see Gen. 1:30, 9:1–7), and that eating meat, taking the life of a living creature for our dinner, is a concession to human appetite. These rules extend the Jewish dietary laws to forbid not only prohibited species but even permitted species that have been killed by other beasts or have died of natural causes. They also prohibit ingesting the blood even of properly slaughtered animals.

[8]Say to them further: If anyone of the house
of Israel or of the strangers who reside among
them offers a burnt offering or a sacrifice, [9]and
does not bring it to the entrance of the Tent of
Meeting to offer it to the LORD, that person shall
be cut off from his people.

[10]And if anyone of the house of Israel or of the
strangers who reside among them partakes of
any blood, I will set My face against the person
who partakes of the blood, and I will cut him off
from among his kin. [11]For the life of the flesh is
in the blood, and I have assigned it to you for
making expiation for your lives upon the altar;
it is the blood, as life, that effects expiation.
[12]Therefore I say to the Israelite people: No person among you shall partake of blood, nor shall
the stranger who resides among you partake of
blood.

[13]And if any Israelite or any stranger who resides among them hunts down an animal or a
bird that may be eaten, he shall pour out its
blood and cover it with earth. [14]For the life of
all flesh—its blood is its life. Therefore I say to
the Israelite people: You shall not partake of the
blood of any flesh, for the life of all flesh is
its blood. Anyone who partakes of it shall be
cut off.

[15]Any person, whether citizen or stranger,
who eats what has died or has been torn by

חמישי [שלישי]
8 וַאֲלֵהֶם תֹּאמַר אִישׁ אִישׁ מִבֵּית יִשְׂרָאֵל
וּמִן־הַגֵּר אֲשֶׁר־יָגוּר בְּתוֹכָם אֲשֶׁר־יַעֲלֶה
עֹלָה אוֹ־זָבַח׃ 9 וְאֶל־פֶּתַח אֹהֶל מוֹעֵד לֹא
יְבִיאֶנּוּ לַעֲשׂוֹת אֹתוֹ לַיהוָה וְנִכְרַת הָאִישׁ
הַהוּא מֵעַמָּיו׃
10 וְאִישׁ אִישׁ מִבֵּית יִשְׂרָאֵל וּמִן־הַגֵּר הַגָּר
בְּתוֹכָם אֲשֶׁר יֹאכַל כָּל־דָּם וְנָתַתִּי פָנַי
בַּנֶּפֶשׁ הָאֹכֶלֶת אֶת־הַדָּם וְהִכְרַתִּי אֹתָהּ
מִקֶּרֶב עַמָּהּ׃ 11 כִּי נֶפֶשׁ הַבָּשָׂר בַּדָּם הִוא
וַאֲנִי נְתַתִּיו לָכֶם עַל־הַמִּזְבֵּחַ לְכַפֵּר עַל־
נַפְשֹׁתֵיכֶם כִּי־הַדָּם הוּא בַּנֶּפֶשׁ יְכַפֵּר׃
12 עַל־כֵּן אָמַרְתִּי לִבְנֵי יִשְׂרָאֵל כָּל־נֶפֶשׁ
מִכֶּם לֹא־תֹאכַל דָּם וְהַגֵּר הַגָּר בְּתוֹכְכֶם
לֹא־יֹאכַל דָּם׃ ס
13 וְאִישׁ אִישׁ מִבְּנֵי יִשְׂרָאֵל וּמִן־הַגֵּר הַגָּר
בְּתוֹכָם אֲשֶׁר יָצוּד צֵיד חַיָּה אוֹ־עוֹף אֲשֶׁר
יֵאָכֵל וְשָׁפַךְ אֶת־דָּמוֹ וְכִסָּהוּ בֶּעָפָר׃ 14 כִּי־
נֶפֶשׁ כָּל־בָּשָׂר דָּמוֹ בְנַפְשׁוֹ הוּא וָאֹמַר
לִבְנֵי יִשְׂרָאֵל דַּם כָּל־בָּשָׂר לֹא תֹאכֵלוּ
כִּי נֶפֶשׁ כָּל־בָּשָׂר דָּמוֹ הִוא כָּל־אֹכְלָיו
יִכָּרֵת׃
15 וְכָל־נֶפֶשׁ אֲשֶׁר תֹּאכַל נְבֵלָה וּטְרֵפָה

8–9. Sacrifices are to be outlawed everywhere except at the tabernacle altar.

10. The blood is to be dashed against the altar.

11. For the life of the flesh is in the blood This is repeated in verse 14. Similar formulations occur in Gen. 9:4 and Deut. 12:23.

it is the blood, as life, that effects expiation Blood represents life; living beings cannot exist without blood. Thus the blood of the sacrifice offered on the altar is the "life" of the sacrifice. God accepts it in place of human life and grants expiation or refrains from wrath.

12. This is a restatement of the blood prohibition, for emphasis.

13. Animals and fowl could be hunted for sustenance, not sport. Their blood, however, had to be drained before the meat could be eaten.

15. Eating flesh of carcasses or torn animals is forbidden. Tactile contact with carcasses renders one impure and requires purificatory ablutions.

HALAKHAH L'MA·ASEH

17:10. partakes of any blood Blood must be removed from meat before it is fit for eating. This is done through a special method of slaughtering (*sh'ḥitah*); removing certain prohibited parts of the animal; and salting, soaking, and rinsing the meat. Kosher butchers usually salt and soak the meat, a procedure once performed at home. If meat is broiled, salting and soaking are unnecessary, and liver must be broiled to be kosher.

beasts shall wash his clothes, bathe in water, and
remain impure until evening; then he shall be
pure. 16But if he does not wash [his clothes] and
bathe his body, he shall bear his guilt.

בָּאֶזְרָח וּבַגֵּר וְכִבֶּס בְּגָדָיו וְרָחַץ בַּמַּיִם
וְטָמֵא עַד־הָעֶרֶב וְטָהֵר׃ 16 וְאִם לֹא יְכַבֵּס
וּבְשָׂרוֹ לֹא יִרְחָץ וְנָשָׂא עֲוֺנוֹ׃ פ

18 The LORD spoke to Moses, saying:
2Speak to the Israelite people and say to them:
I the LORD am your God. 3You shall not
copy the practices of the land of Egypt where
you dwelt, or of the land of Canaan to which
I am taking you; nor shall you follow their
laws. 4My rules alone shall you observe, and

יח וַיְדַבֵּר יְהוָה אֶל־מֹשֶׁה לֵּאמֹר׃
2 דַּבֵּר אֶל־בְּנֵי יִשְׂרָאֵל וְאָמַרְתָּ אֲלֵהֶם
אֲנִי יְהוָה אֱלֹהֵיכֶם׃ 3 כְּמַעֲשֵׂה אֶרֶץ־
מִצְרַיִם אֲשֶׁר יְשַׁבְתֶּם־בָּהּ לֹא תַעֲשׂוּ
וּכְמַעֲשֵׂה אֶרֶץ־כְּנַעַן אֲשֶׁר אֲנִי מֵבִיא
אֶתְכֶם שָׁמָּה לֹא תַעֲשׂוּ וּבְחֻקֹּתֵיהֶם
לֹא תֵלֵכוּ׃ 4 אֶת־מִשְׁפָּטַי תַּעֲשׂוּ וְאֶת־

DEFINITION OF THE FAMILY (18:1–30)

2. the Israelite people The regulations of this chapter are meant to govern the conduct of the entire people.

I the LORD am your God The commandments come directly from God and are to be obeyed with utmost strictness.

3. At certain periods in the history of ancient Egypt, it was the custom among the royal class to encourage brother-sister marriages. Other prohibited acts found in this chapter, such as homosexuality and bestiality, at times were apparently practiced in Canaanite culture.

4. faithfully follow My laws The Hebrew for "follow" (הלך) means "to go, walk." It often

---

CHAPTER 18

Incest laws, prohibiting people from sexual contact with their closest relatives and underscoring those prohibitions in the strongest terms, are virtually universal in all ancient and modern societies. What is the basis for these laws? One doubts that they grew out of an observation that marrying close relatives could lead to the birth of deformed children bearing the results of recessive genetic defects. There is no evidence that primitive societies, which had incest laws, understood physical deformity in genetic terms. Nor would such an observation have inspired the sense of profound disgust and perversion with which incestuous acts were regarded. Rather, one suspects that incest laws were meant to make it clear that members of the opposite sex in one's household are not to be considered as possible sexual partners. A household would become impossibly "overheated" if sexually mature brothers and sisters, parents and children could regard each other as sexually available. This would explain the anomaly in the text (18:12–14) that a woman may marry her uncle (indeed that was often a preferred match) although a man could not marry his aunt. The family relationship is the same, but presumably the unmarried aunt might live in the same household while the unmarried uncle would have his own home elsewhere.

3. nor shall you follow their laws One senses here the Torah's revulsion at the erotic component of pagan society. Some commentators take these words to mean that we may not imitate the gentile nations even in innocuous matters, such as the clothing we wear (*S'fat Emet*). Hirsch, on the other hand, maintains: "We may imitate the nations among whom we live in things that are based on reason but not on things relating to religion or superstition." The Sages of the Talmud make it clear that Jews are to obey the civil laws of the lands in which they live ("the law of the [gentile] government is binding," *dina d'malkhuta dina,* BT Git. 10b), even as we are to separate ourselves from their religious ways.

חֻקֹּתַי תִּשְׁמְרוּ לָלֶכֶת בָּהֶם אֲנִי יְהוָה
אֱלֹהֵיכֶם׃
5 וּשְׁמַרְתֶּם אֶת־חֻקֹּתַי וְאֶת־מִשְׁפָּטַי אֲשֶׁר
יַעֲשֶׂה אֹתָם הָאָדָם וָחַי בָּהֶם אֲנִי
יְהוָה׃ ס
ששי 6 אִישׁ אִישׁ אֶל־כָּל־שְׁאֵר בְּשָׂרוֹ לֹא
תִקְרְבוּ לְגַלּוֹת עֶרְוָה אֲנִי יְהוָה׃ ס
7 עֶרְוַת אָבִיךָ וְעֶרְוַת אִמְּךָ לֹא תְגַלֵּה אִמְּךָ
הִוא לֹא תְגַלֶּה עֶרְוָתָהּ׃ ס
8 עֶרְוַת אֵשֶׁת־אָבִיךָ לֹא תְגַלֵּה עֶרְוַת
אָבִיךָ הִוא׃ ס
9 עֶרְוַת אֲחוֹתְךָ בַת־אָבִיךָ אוֹ בַת־אִמֶּךָ

faithfully follow My laws: I the LORD am your God.

5You shall keep My laws and My rules, by the pursuit of which man shall live: I am the LORD.

6None of you shall come near anyone of his own flesh to uncover nakedness: I am the LORD.

7Your father's nakedness, that is, the nakedness of your mother, you shall not uncover; she is your mother—you shall not uncover her nakedness.

8Do not uncover the nakedness of your father's wife; it is the nakedness of your father.

9The nakedness of your sister—your father's daughter or your mother's, whether born into

is used to connote adherence to God's commandments.

7. This verse forbids sexual relations with one's natural mother (Ramban).

8. the nakedness of your father's wife This refers to one who has sexual relations with a wife of his father who is not his natural mother.

9. whether born into the household or outside The ancient Aramaic translation renders: "who is born from your father by another woman, or by your mother from another man" (Onk.). In other words, your father's daughter was born into your

5. by the pursuit of which man shall live This important verse later became the basis for defining the limits of martyrdom (BT Yoma 85b). Only in cases of murder, incest, adultery, or idolatry must a Jew give up his or her life rather than violate the commandments. In all other cases, one must violate the Torah to spare one's life—in order to live by the Torah afterward.

Maimonides gives the words a deeper meaning: The wicked are considered as dead even in their lifetimes because they are not fulfilling their innate mission to live by God's laws. They do not understand what it means to be truly alive. A 19th-century Hasidic master understood the words homiletically to mean, "Keep God's laws while you are young and vigorous. Do not wait to become pious when you are old and the urge to sin has fled."

6. In the Torah, "to uncover the nakedness" is a euphemism for sexual intercourse. It may also serve to imply that, in a society where people dressed modestly, seeing a person undressed would inevitably lead to sexual contact. Nakedness, and the uncovering of nakedness, is a category that applies only to human beings. Only humans wear clothing, because only human beings have a sense of shame, of being judged (cf. Gen. 3). Judaism traditionally calls for modesty in dress, not only to avoid temptation but as a statement about the holiness of the body and at the same time a rejection of the pagan worship of the naked human form. Only human beings are motivated to cover certain parts of their bodies out of reverence for the power of those organs to create and sustain life. Similarly, only human beings can think in terms of "suitable marriage partners."

HALAKHAH L'MA·ASEH

18:5. by the pursuit of which man shall live Except for the prohibitions against murder, incest and adultery, and idolatry, any commandment must be set aside for *pikku·aḥ nefesh,* to save a human life (BT Sanh. 74a). Thus one may violate *Shabbat* to take someone to the hospital in an emergency, and doctors must not hesitate to violate the laws of *Shabbat* to save a life. Israel's armed forces rely on this principle to defend Israel from attack on *Shabbat* and holy days. See Comment to Exod. 22:1.

18:9. your sister This verse is understood to prohibit relations with all siblings. The CJLS has ruled that sexual relations and marriages between adopted children raised in the same family are also prohibited.

the household or outside—do not uncover their nakedness.

¹⁰The nakedness of your son's daughter, or of your daughter's daughter—do not uncover their nakedness; for their nakedness is yours.

¹¹The nakedness of your father's wife's daughter, who has born into your father's household—she is your sister; do not uncover her nakedness.

¹²Do not uncover the nakedness of your father's sister; she is your father's flesh.

¹³Do not uncover the nakedness of your mother's sister; for she is your mother's flesh.

¹⁴Do not uncover the nakedness of your father's brother: do not approach his wife; she is your aunt.

¹⁵Do not uncover the nakedness of your daughter-in-law: she is your son's wife; you shall not uncover her nakedness.

¹⁶Do not uncover the nakedness of your brother's wife; it is the nakedness of your brother.

¹⁷Do not uncover the nakedness of a woman and her daughter; nor shall you marry her son's daughter or her daughter's daughter and uncover her nakedness: they are kindred; it is depravity.

¹⁸Do not marry a woman as a rival to her sister and uncover her nakedness in the other's lifetime.

¹⁹Do not come near a woman during her period of impurity to uncover her nakedness.

מוֹלֶ֣דֶת בַּ֗יִת א֚וֹ מוֹלֶ֣דֶת ח֔וּץ לֹ֥א תְגַלֶּ֖ה עֶרְוָתָֽן: ס

¹⁰ עֶרְוַ֤ת בַּת־בִּנְךָ֙ א֣וֹ בַֽת־בִּתְּךָ֔ לֹ֥א תְגַלֶּ֖ה עֶרְוָתָ֑ן כִּ֥י עֶרְוָתְךָ֖ הֵֽנָּה: ס

¹¹ עֶרְוַ֨ת בַּת־אֵ֤שֶׁת אָבִ֙יךָ֙ מוֹלֶ֣דֶת אָבִ֔יךָ אֲחוֹתְךָ֖ הִ֑וא לֹ֥א תְגַלֶּ֖ה עֶרְוָתָֽהּ: ס

¹² עֶרְוַ֥ת אֲחֽוֹת־אָבִ֖יךָ לֹ֣א תְגַלֵּ֑ה שְׁאֵ֥ר אָבִ֖יךָ הִֽוא: ס

¹³ עֶרְוַ֥ת אֲחֽוֹת־אִמְּךָ֖ לֹ֣א תְגַלֵּ֑ה כִּֽי־שְׁאֵ֥ר אִמְּךָ֖ הִֽוא: ס

¹⁴ עֶרְוַ֥ת אֲחִֽי־אָבִ֖יךָ לֹ֣א תְגַלֵּ֑ה אֶל־אִשְׁתּוֹ֙ לֹ֣א תִקְרָ֔ב דֹּדָֽתְךָ֖ הִֽוא: ס

¹⁵ עֶרְוַ֥ת כַּלָּֽתְךָ֖ לֹ֣א תְגַלֵּ֑ה אֵ֤שֶׁת בִּנְךָ֙ הִ֔וא לֹ֥א תְגַלֶּ֖ה עֶרְוָתָֽהּ: ס

¹⁶ עֶרְוַ֥ת אֵֽשֶׁת־אָחִ֖יךָ לֹ֣א תְגַלֵּ֑ה עֶרְוַ֥ת אָחִ֖יךָ הִֽוא: ס

¹⁷ עֶרְוַ֨ת אִשָּׁ֤ה וּבִתָּהּ֙ לֹ֣א תְגַלֵּ֔ה אֶֽת־בַּת־בְּנָ֞הּ וְאֶת־בַּת־בִּתָּ֗הּ לֹ֤א תִקַּח֙ לְגַלּ֣וֹת עֶרְוָתָ֔הּ שַֽׁאֲרָ֥ה הֵ֖נָּה זִמָּ֥ה הִֽוא:

¹⁸ וְאִשָּׁ֥ה אֶל־אֲחֹתָ֖הּ לֹ֣א תִקָּ֑ח לִצְרֹ֗ר לְגַלּ֧וֹת עֶרְוָתָ֛הּ עָלֶ֖יהָ בְּחַיֶּֽיהָ:

¹⁹ וְאֶל־אִשָּׁ֗ה בְּנִדַּ֖ת טֻמְאָתָ֑הּ לֹ֣א תִקְרַ֔ב לְגַלּ֖וֹת עֶרְוָתָֽהּ:

---

household, whereas your mother's daughter was born outside of it at a time when your mother was not part of your father's household.

10. It is not clear why the prohibition of union with one's own daughter was not made explicit, but for the Sages it was obvious that such a union would be incestuous.

11. *your father's wife's daughter* A half-sister with whom one shares a common father but not the same mother.

15. *daughter-in-law* The basic meaning of the Hebrew word *kallah* is "daughter-in-law." Usage, however, was fluid. Viewed from the perspective of the son's generation, *kallah* is "bride," just as the masculine counterpart *ḥatan* means both "son-in-law" and "bridegroom."

18. *a woman as a rival to her sister* In polygamous marriages, the interests of the several wives inevitably came into conflict.

in the other's lifetime Marrying two sisters would create a damaging rivalry. The prohibition continues as long as the first sister remains alive, even if divorced from the man in question.

19. *her period of impurity* This refers to her menstrual period.

20 Do not have carnal relations with your
neighbor's wife and defile yourself with her.
21 Do not allow any of your offspring to be
offered up to Molech, and do not profane the
name of your God: I am the LORD.
22 Do not lie with a male as one lies with a
woman; it is an abhorrence.
23 Do not have carnal relations with any beast
and defile yourself thereby; and let no woman
lend herself to a beast to mate with it; it is perversion.
24 Do not defile yourselves in any of those
ways, for it is by such that the nations that I am
casting out before you defiled themselves.
25 Thus the land became defiled; and I called it
to account for its iniquity, and the land spewed
out its inhabitants. 26 But you must keep My laws
and My rules, and you must not do any of those
abhorrent things, neither the citizen nor the
stranger who resides among you; 27 for all those
abhorrent things were done by the people who

20 וְאֶל־אֵשֶׁת עֲמִיתְךָ לֹא־תִתֵּן שְׁכָבְתְּךָ
לְזָרַע לְטָמְאָה־בָהּ׃
21 וּמִזַּרְעֲךָ לֹא־תִתֵּן לְהַעֲבִיר לַמֹּלֶךְ וְלֹא
תְחַלֵּל אֶת־שֵׁם אֱלֹהֶיךָ אֲנִי יְהוָה׃
22 וְאֶת־זָכָר לֹא תִשְׁכַּב מִשְׁכְּבֵי אִשָּׁה ביעי [ביעי]
תּוֹעֵבָה הִוא׃
23 וּבְכָל־בְּהֵמָה לֹא־תִתֵּן שְׁכָבְתְּךָ
לְטָמְאָה־בָהּ וְאִשָּׁה לֹא־תַעֲמֹד לִפְנֵי
בְהֵמָה לְרִבְעָהּ תֶּבֶל הוּא׃
24 אַל־תִּטַּמְּאוּ בְּכָל־אֵלֶּה כִּי בְכָל־אֵלֶּה
נִטְמְאוּ הַגּוֹיִם אֲשֶׁר־אֲנִי מְשַׁלֵּחַ מִפְּנֵיכֶם׃
25 וַתִּטְמָא הָאָרֶץ וָאֶפְקֹד עֲוֺנָהּ עָלֶיהָ
וַתָּקִא הָאָרֶץ אֶת־יֹשְׁבֶיהָ׃ 26 וּשְׁמַרְתֶּם
אַתֶּם אֶת־חֻקֹּתַי וְאֶת־מִשְׁפָּטַי וְלֹא תַעֲשׂוּ
מִכֹּל הַתּוֹעֵבֹת הָאֵלֶּה הָאֶזְרָח וְהַגֵּר הַגָּר
בְּתוֹכְכֶם׃ 27 כִּי אֶת־כָּל־הַתּוֹעֵבֹת הָאֵל
עָשׂוּ אַנְשֵׁי־הָאָרֶץ אֲשֶׁר לִפְנֵיכֶם וַתִּטְמָא

21. offered up to Molech Molech is the name given to a deity worshiped by some of Israel's ancient neighbors. Some scholars believe that this is intended to prohibit the sacrifice of children to the God of Israel.

22. Aside from this verse and its parallel in 20:13, the Bible mentions homosexuality only in the context of rape (Gen. 19:5, Judg. 19:22) and apparently with regard to prostitution (Deut. 23:18–19). In its condemnation here, the Torah uses the word *to·eivah,* which appears more than one hundred times in the Bible to describe an object or act as repulsive.

23. let no woman The only instance in this chapter where women are the subject of the commandment.

perversion Hebrew: *tevel,* derived from the root בלל (to mix), implying that sex with beasts is a forbidden "mixture" of species.

25. the land became defiled Those who violate the code of family life commit an outrage that defiles the land; and the angry land may, in turn, spew them out.

26. neither the citizen nor the stranger who resides among you The objective of establishing a holy community requires that all who live within it, both Israelites and aliens, uphold a standard of proper sexual behavior.

---

21. For Hirsch, Molech represents a vision of God as blind fate, a god who does not represent or demand righteousness but wants only obedience. We might take this prohibition as a warning against sacrificing the integrity of our children on the altars of fame or material success.

HALAKHAH L'MA·ASEH

18:22. Do not lie with a male The Torah prohibits male homosexual relations, and the Sages understand the Torah to forbid lesbian relations as well (*Sifra Aḥarei Mot* 9:8). These prohibitions have engendered considerable debate. Conservative Movement resolutions call on congregations to welcome gay and lesbian congregants in all congregational activities.

were in the land before you, and the land became defiled.
28So let not the land spew you out for defiling it, as it spewed out the nation that came before you.
29All who do any of those abhorrent things—such persons shall be cut off from their people.
30You shall keep My charge not to engage in any of the abhorrent practices that were carried on before you, and you shall not defile yourselves through them: I the LORD am your God.

מפטיר הָאָֽרֶץ׃ 28 וְלֹֽא־תָקִיא הָאָרֶץ אֶתְכֶם
בְּטַמַּאֲכֶם אֹתָהּ כַּאֲשֶׁר קָאָה אֶת־הַגּוֹי
אֲשֶׁר לִפְנֵיכֶֽם׃ 29 כִּי כָּל־אֲשֶׁר יַעֲשֶׂה מִכֹּל
הַתּוֹעֵבוֹת הָאֵלֶּה וְנִכְרְתוּ הַנְּפָשׁוֹת
הָעֹשֹׂת מִקֶּרֶב עַמָּֽם׃ 30 וּשְׁמַרְתֶּם אֶת־
מִשְׁמַרְתִּי לְבִלְתִּי עֲשׂוֹת מֵחֻקּוֹת
הַתּוֹעֵבֹת אֲשֶׁר נַעֲשׂוּ לִפְנֵיכֶם וְלֹא
תִטַּמְּאוּ בָּהֶם אֲנִי יְהוָה אֱלֹהֵיכֶֽם׃* פ

30. You shall keep My charge The Hebrew verb for "keep" can also be translated "guard/protect." That dimension of the command led the Sages to the concept of "making a fence around the Torah," expanding the domain of the prohibited to protect the Torah from inadvertent violation.

The theme of Leviticus has been the striving of human beings to come into God's presence in a state of holiness, through animal offerings, through the avoidance of contact with defiling substances or behavior associated with the pagan world. This focus on holiness reaches its peak in the next *parashah, K'doshim.*

* *For the* haftarah *for this Torah portion, see selections starting on p. 705.*

19 The Lord spoke to Moses, saying:	יט וַיְדַבֵּר יְהוָה אֶל־מֹשֶׁה לֵּאמֹר׃
2Speak to the whole Israelite community and say to them:	2 דַּבֵּר אֶל־כָּל־עֲדַת בְּנֵי־יִשְׂרָאֵל וְאָמַרְתָּ אֲלֵהֶם
You shall be holy, for I, the Lord your God, am holy.	קְדֹשִׁים תִּהְיוּ כִּי קָדוֹשׁ אֲנִי יְהוָה אֱלֹהֵיכֶם׃

The Pursuit of Holiness (*continued*)

LAWS OF HOLINESS (19:1–37)

This chapter, which echoes the Decalogue, states the duties incumbent on the Israelites as a people.

2. You shall be holy The Hebrew is quite emphatic: "You must be holy!"

CHAPTER 19

This *parashah,* one of the richest and most exalted in the Torah, begins with the words "you shall be holy" (*k'doshim tihyu*). What is holiness? The term can be applied to God, to good people, to a book, to a period of time, or to an animal offered as a sacrifice. To be holy is to be different, to be set apart from the ordinary. "Ordinary" (*ḥol*) is often used as the opposite of "holy" in rabbinic discourse. To be holy is to rise to partake in some measure of the special qualities of God, the source of holiness. Holiness is the highest level of human behavior, human beings at their most Godlike. Hirsch defines holiness as occurring "when a morally free human being has complete dominion over one's own energies and inclinations and the temptations associated with them, and places them at the service of God's will." For Buber, holiness is found not in rising above the level of one's neighbors but in relationships, in human beings recognizing the latent divinity of other people, even as God recognizes the latent divinity in each of us. God can make things holy, as in the case of *Shabbat* (Gen. 2:3). As human beings, we can be Godlike by exercising our power to sanctify moments and objects in our lives.

Time can be sanctified when it is used to draw closer to God. Objects can become holy when they help people rise toward God. The Torah is holy not only because it comes from God but because it leads to God.

It should also be noted that the *mitzvot* of Lev. 19, the laws of holiness, cut across all categories of life. They deal with ritual, with business ethics, with proper behavior toward the poor and the afflicted, and with family relations. The modern distinction between "religious" and "secular" is unknown to the Torah. Everything we do has the potential of being holy. Buber wrote that Judaism does not divide life into the holy and the profane, but into the holy and the not-yet-holy. Similarly, Finkelstein writes: "Judaism is a way of life that endeavors to transform virtually every human action into a means of communion with God."

The Talmud (BT Yev. 20a) enunciates the important principle of "achieve holiness within the realm of the permitted" (*kadesh et atzm'kha ba-muttar l'kha*). Go beyond obeying the letter of the law and refraining from what is forbidden by finding ways of sanctifying every moment of your life. We can be as holy as we allow ourselves to be. Ramban warns against the person who manages to lead an unworthy life without technically breaking any of the Torah's rules. Such a person is called *naval birshut ha-Torah,* "a scoundrel within the bounds of Torah."

2. You shall be holy In Hebrew, this summons is phrased in the plural, implying that the capacity for holiness is not restricted to spiritually gifted people; anyone may attain holiness. God does not demand the impossible. The plural phrasing suggests further that holiness is most easily achieved in the context of a community. It is difficult for a person to live a life of holiness without others. Noah wasn't able to do it; even Abraham lapsed into unworthy behavior when surrounded by people who were not striving for holiness as he was (cf. Gen. 12, 20). When a community dedicates itself to the pursuit of holiness, its members sup-

[3]You shall each revere his mother and his father, and keep My sabbaths: I the LORD am your God.

[4]Do not turn to idols or make molten gods for yourselves: I the LORD am your God.

[5]When you sacrifice an offering of well-being to the LORD, sacrifice it so that it may be accepted on your behalf. [6]It shall be eaten on the day you sacrifice it, or on the day following; but what is left by the third day must be consumed in fire. [7]If it should be eaten on the third day, it is an offensive thing, it will not be acceptable. [8]And he who eats of it shall bear his guilt, for he has profaned what is sacred to the LORD; that person shall be cut off from his kin.

[9]When you reap the harvest of your land, you shall not reap all the way to the edges of your

3 אִישׁ אִמּוֹ וְאָבִיו תִּירָאוּ וְאֶת־שַׁבְּתֹתַי
תִּשְׁמֹרוּ אֲנִי יְהוָה אֱלֹהֵיכֶם׃
4 אַל־תִּפְנוּ אֶל־הָאֱלִילִם וֵאלֹהֵי מַסֵּכָה לֹא
תַעֲשׂוּ לָכֶם אֲנִי יְהוָה אֱלֹהֵיכֶם׃
5 וְכִי תִזְבְּחוּ זֶבַח שְׁלָמִים לַיהוָה לִרְצֹנְכֶם
תִּזְבָּחֻהוּ׃ 6 בְּיוֹם זִבְחֲכֶם יֵאָכֵל וּמִמָּחֳרָת
וְהַנּוֹתָר עַד־יוֹם הַשְּׁלִישִׁי בָּאֵשׁ יִשָּׂרֵף׃
7 וְאִם הֵאָכֹל יֵאָכֵל בַּיּוֹם הַשְּׁלִישִׁי פִּגּוּל
הוּא לֹא יֵרָצֶה׃ 8 וְאֹכְלָיו עֲוֺנוֹ יִשָּׂא
כִּי־אֶת־קֹדֶשׁ יְהוָה חִלֵּל וְנִכְרְתָה הַנֶּפֶשׁ
הַהִוא מֵעַמֶּיהָ׃
9 וּבְקֻצְרְכֶם אֶת־קְצִיר אַרְצְכֶם לֹא תְכַלֶּה

3. mother and . . . father In the Fifth Commandment, father precedes mother. The two statements, when combined, amount to an equitable estimation of both parents.

5–8. These verses are addressed primarily to the individual Israelites who donated *sh'lamim* sacrifices to God.

9–10. These verses require that some pro-

---

port and reinforce each other. Historically, when Jewish communities have been at their best, the whole became greater than the sum of its parts. Ordinary people achieved an extraordinary measure of sanctity in their daily lives.

"You shall be holy" has been understood by some not as a command but as a promise: Live by these rules and your life will become special in the process. Your fundamental need for significance, for the assurance that your life has meaning, will be met thereby (Ḥatam Sofer). For Heschel, "Judaism is an attempt to prove that in order to be a man, you have to be more than a man, that in order to be a people, you have to be more than a people. Israel was made to be a holy people."

3. A person need not obey a parent's directive to violate the Torah. However, if it is found necessary to disobey parents in this way, it must be done with respect and reverence (*Sifra*). The fifth commandment of the Decalogue tells us to "honor your father and mother." This verse calls on us to "revere (one's) mother and father." Rashi suggests that the natural instinct is to revere (i.e., fear) one's father and to honor (i.e., love) one's mother. The Torah would have us regard each of our parents equally with reverence and love and would have each parent represent both discipline and forgiveness in the child's mind.

5–10. The command to consume the *sh'lamim* (offering of well-being) within two days is meant to encourage the donor to invite the poor to share in the meal. Similarly, the subsequent command to leave the corner of the field and the fallen fruit is motivated by the desire to have us share our bounty with the poor. Even a poor person, owner of a small field, must leave a corner of the harvest for others. The biblical story of Ruth, read on *Shavu·ot,* turns on Ruth's right to glean in the fields of her affluent neighbors. "To care for the poor, who are fashioned in God's image, is a form of worship" (Hoffman).

HALAKHAH L'MA·ASEH

19:3. revere his mother and his father According to the Talmud, this requires, for example, that we refrain from publicly challenging what our parents have said and from sitting in their chair (BT Kid. 31a–b). See Comments to Exod. 20:12; Deut. 21:18–21.

field, or gather the gleanings of your harvest. [10]You shall not pick your vineyard bare, or gather the fallen fruit of your vineyard; you shall leave them for the poor and the stranger: I the Lord am your God.

[11]You shall not steal; you shall not deal deceitfully or falsely with one another. [12]You shall not swear falsely by My name, profaning the name of your God: I am the Lord.

[13]You shall not defraud your fellow. You shall not commit robbery. The wages of a laborer shall not remain with you until morning.

[14]You shall not insult the deaf, or place a stumbling block before the blind. You shall fear your God: I am the Lord.

פְּאַ֤ת שָֽׂדְךָ֙ לִקְצֹ֔ר וְלֶ֥קֶט קְצִֽירְךָ֖ לֹ֥א תְלַקֵּֽט׃ [10]וְכַרְמְךָ֙ לֹ֣א תְעוֹלֵ֔ל וּפֶ֥רֶט כַּרְמְךָ֖ לֹ֣א תְלַקֵּ֑ט לֶֽעָנִ֤י וְלַגֵּר֙ תַּעֲזֹ֣ב אֹתָ֔ם אֲנִ֖י יְהֹוָ֥ה אֱלֹהֵיכֶֽם׃

[11]לֹ֖א תִּגְנֹ֑בוּ וְלֹא־תְכַחֲשׁ֥וּ וְלֹֽא־תְשַׁקְּר֖וּ אִ֥ישׁ בַּעֲמִיתֽוֹ׃ [12]וְלֹֽא־תִשָּׁבְע֥וּ בִשְׁמִ֖י לַשָּׁ֑קֶר וְחִלַּלְתָּ֛ אֶת־שֵׁ֥ם אֱלֹהֶ֖יךָ אֲנִ֥י יְהֹוָֽה׃

[13]לֹֽא־תַעֲשֹׁ֤ק אֶת־רֵֽעֲךָ֙ וְלֹ֣א תִגְזֹ֔ל לֹֽא־תָלִ֞ין פְּעֻלַּ֥ת שָׂכִ֛יר אִתְּךָ֖ עַד־בֹּֽקֶר׃

[14]לֹא־תְקַלֵּ֣ל חֵרֵ֔שׁ וְלִפְנֵ֣י עִוֵּ֔ר לֹ֥א תִתֵּ֖ן מִכְשֹׁ֑ל וְיָרֵ֥אתָ מֵֽאֱלֹהֶ֖יךָ אֲנִ֥י יְהֹוָֽה׃

[שני מישי]

---

duce from the harvest of field and vineyard be given to the poor and the stranger. Four types of gifts are specified: two from the grain harvest and two from the vineyards.

your vineyard Underdeveloped clusters of grapes must be left unpicked until they mature. At that time, only the poor and the stranger may pick them. Fruit that falls to the ground during picking is to be left ungathered.

11. You shall not steal This parallels the Eighth Commandment.

you shall not deal deceitfully or falsely with

one another This approximates the significance of the Ninth Commandment.

12. You shall not swear falsely by My name This parallels the Third Commandment.

profaning the name of your God Oaths are sworn in God's name, and one who swears falsely treats God's name as if it were not holy.

14. You shall not insult the deaf Speaking ill of the deaf is especially blameworthy because it involves taking unfair advantage of another's disability.

a stumbling block before the blind Cf. Deut.

---

11. The words "you shall not steal" follow directly after the laws of leaving part of the harvest for the poor. Does this teach that keeping everything for ourselves is a form of stealing (Ibn Ezra)? Or are we commanded to help the poor find enough to eat so that they will not be driven to steal (Kara)?

12–13. Hoffman notes that sometimes within a single verse, some verbs will be in the singular and others in the plural. He suggests that it is the obligation of the community as a whole to create a moral climate that will make it easier for an individual to do what is right and make it less socially acceptable for an individ-

ual to sin. The law can only forbid and punish; the knowledge that one's neighbors will disapprove may be a more effective deterrent.

14. You shall not insult the deaf You shall not insult anyone, even a deaf person whose feelings will not be hurt by your words (BT Shevu. 36a), because the use of coarse language diminishes you as a person. Maimonides, ever the rationalist, takes the words of the Torah as a warning, lest we see that our words do not affect the deaf person and we resort to physical violence.

stumbling block before the blind "The term 'blind' refers not only to one who is phys-

---

HALAKHAH L'MA·ASEH

19:10. for the poor and the stranger See Comments to Lev. 25:25,35.

19:13. You shall not defraud See Comments to Exod. 23:7; Lev. 19:36.

19:14. stumbling block before the blind The Sages understand this as a prohibition against creating conditions that might tempt another person to transgress the Commandments, including those governing rituals (e.g., BT Pes. 22b), moral interactions (e.g., BT MK 17b), and commercial matters (e.g., BT BM 75a). It also forbids knowingly giving bad advice (Sifra).

[15]You shall not render an unfair decision: do
not favor the poor or show deference to the rich;
judge your kinsman fairly. [16]Do not deal basely
with your countrymen. Do not profit by the
blood of your fellow: I am the LORD.

[17]You shall not hate your kinsfolk in your
heart. Reprove your kinsman but incur no guilt

שני [חמישי]

15 לֹא־תַעֲשׂוּ עָוֶל בַּמִּשְׁפָּט לֹא־תִשָּׂא פְנֵי־
דָל וְלֹא תֶהְדַּר פְּנֵי גָדוֹל בְּצֶדֶק תִּשְׁפֹּט
עֲמִיתֶךָ׃ 16 לֹא־תֵלֵךְ רָכִיל בְּעַמֶּיךָ לֹא
תַעֲמֹד עַל־דַּם רֵעֶךָ אֲנִי יְהוָה׃
17 לֹא־תִשְׂנָא אֶת־אָחִיךָ בִּלְבָבֶךָ הוֹכֵחַ
תּוֹכִיחַ אֶת־עֲמִיתֶךָ וְלֹא־תִשָּׂא עָלָיו

27:18: "Cursed be he who misdirects a blind person on his way."

15. do not favor the poor In the pursuit of justice there can be no bias, even toward those for whom we have innate sympathy and who otherwise deserve our aid.

16. Do not deal basely with your countrymen Literally, "Do not act as a merchant toward your own kinsmen." A traveling merchant has fairly easy access to secret information and gossip. Here, no one should traffic in such information.

Do not profit by the blood of your fellow This has been interpreted in various ways. The rendering that best fits the context is: Do not pursue one's livelihood in a way that endangers another or at the expense of another's well-being.

17. You shall not hate your kinsfolk in your heart Do not allow ill feelings to fester.

Reprove your kinsman but incur no guilt because of him In other words, admonish your neighbor for his or her wrongdoing so that you will not incur guilt on your neighbor's account.

---

ically blind but also to one who is intellectually deficient, lacking appropriate information, or morally blinded by emotions" (Hirsch). For example, one violates this law by deliberately giving bad advice (*Sifra*), by providing someone with the means to do wrong whom you know cannot resist the temptation (BT Pes. 22b), or by provoking a short-tempered person to lash out in anger (BT Kid. 32a).

You shall fear your God "Whenever this phrase is used, it refers to something entrusted to the conscience of the individual, to those acts that are beyond the jurisdiction of an earthly court. Only the individual conscience can know whether or not an act was committed in good faith" (N. Leibowitz, based on Rashi and *Sifra*).

15. do not favor the poor or show deference to the rich Once again, as in Exod. 23:3, the Torah emphasizes that the poor are better served by justice uncompromised by emotion. Hirsch sees this verse as directed to judges and verse 16 ("do not deal basely") directed to the community at large. Judges must adhere to the law and not favor the poor, and others are obliged to reach out to the poor in charity. Love and compassion can supplement the rule of law, but cannot replace it.

17. You shall not hate your kinsfolk in your heart The literal meaning of "your kinsfolk" is "your brother." The following verse speaks of loving one's neighbor, and this verse prohibits hating one's brother. Hirsch suggests that though we can lose the status of being a friend or a neighbor (by quarreling, by moving away), we can never stop being related to a brother, even if he hurts us. Therefore, we are forbidden to hate him. This is one of the rare instances when the Torah seems to command feelings rather than behavior.

Reprove your kinsman The Sages forbid carrying reproach to the point of embarrassing someone, thus incurring guilt because of that exchange, something that is forbidden by the Torah (*Sifra*). The obligation to reprove is limited to cases in which one has reason to believe the reproof will bring about a change in behavior. It should always be a loving rebuke, never an occasion to belittle another for errant behavior.

HALAKHAH L'MA·ASEH

19:16. Do not deal basely See Comment to Exod. 23:1.

Do not profit The Talmud understands this verse to prohibit "standing by the blood of your fellow," ruling it an obligation to help someone in distress, for example, a person drowning (BT Sanh. 73a). Based on this precedent, CJLS has ruled that Jews should donate blood regularly and arrange to have one's organs donated for transplant after death.

because of him. 18You shall not take vengeance
or bear a grudge against your countrymen. Love
your fellow as yourself: I am the LORD.
19You shall observe My laws.
You shall not let your cattle mate with a different kind; you shall not sow your field with two kinds of seed; you shall not put on cloth from a mixture of two kinds of material.

חֵטְא׃ 18 לֹא־תִקֹּם וְלֹא־תִטֹּר אֶת־בְּנֵי
עַמֶּךָ וְאָהַבְתָּ לְרֵעֲךָ כָּמוֹךָ אֲנִי יְהוָה׃
19 אֶת־חֻקֹּתַי תִּשְׁמֹרוּ
בְּהֶמְתְּךָ לֹא־תַרְבִּיעַ כִּלְאַיִם שָׂדְךָ לֹא־
תִזְרַע כִּלְאָיִם וּבֶגֶד כִּלְאַיִם שַׁעַטְנֵז לֹא
יַעֲלֶה עָלֶיךָ׃ פ

18. You shall not take vengeance or bear a grudge You must not keep alive the memory of another's offense against you.

Love your fellow as yourself The great sage Akiva referred to this as "a basic principle in the Torah."

19. You shall observe My laws This statement introduces the specific laws that follow.

a different kind Hebrew: *kil·ayim,* which has been explained on the basis of other Semitic languages as meaning "two kinds (together)." The term is used of animals, plants, grain, and cloth.

---

18. take vengeance . . . bear a grudge Vengeance has been defined as saying, "I will not lend you my hammer because you broke my saw," and bearing a grudge as saying, "I will lend you my hammer even though you broke my saw." It has been recalled that the Eastern European sage Saul Katzenellenbogen had such a prodigious memory that he never forgot anything he read or heard. Invariably, however, he would forget when someone offended him.

Love your fellow as yourself When Hillel was asked by a gentile to summarize the Torah in one sentence, he offered a version of this: "What is distasteful to you, don't do to another person. The rest is commentary; now go study the commentary" (BT Shab. 31a). Love your neighbor because he or she is like yourself, subject to the same temptations that you are. Just as we excuse our own behavior by seeing it in context, claiming that we were tired, angry, or misinformed and, therefore, guilty of nothing worse than poor judgment, we should be prepared to judge the behavior of others as charitably.

Buber understood this commandment as being connected to the preceding one, "you shall not take vengeance." Because all human beings are part of the same body, to hurt another person in an effort to get even is to hurt part of oneself. He compares it to a person whose hand slips while holding a knife and he stabs himself. Should he stab the offending hand that slipped, to get even with it for hurting him? He will only hurt himself a second time. So it is when we, in anger, hurt another person, not understanding that we are all connected. Anger and a thirst for vengeance corrode the soul.

19. The Sages understand *ḥukkim* (translated here as "laws") as referring to rules for which there seems to be no rational explanation. We follow them, not because they make sense (as do laws forbidding murder or commanding rest on *Shabbat*) but as opportunities to do God's will. When a Jew follows God's command without understanding the reason for it, we can understand the relationship in one of three ways: (*a*) as that of slave to master, with obedience compelled; (*b*) as that of pupil to teacher, in which the pupil assumes that the teacher knows what is right and necessary even if the pupil cannot see the point of it, although the pupil may hope one day to understand it; or (*c*) as that of people in love, in which one takes pleasure in knowing what he or she can do to please the beloved. Conservative Judaism tends to give the tradition the benefit of the doubt when it baffles us but does not morally offend us. When the tradition asks us to do something that does offend us morally, Conservative Judaism claims the right to challenge and, if necessary, change the tradition, not because we see our judgment as superior to that of the Torah but because our judgment has been shaped by the values of the Torah and we are in effect calling the Torah to judge itself. "We affirm that the halakhic process has striven to embody the highest moral principles. Where changing conditions produce what seem to be immoral consequences and human anguish, varying approaches exist within our community to rectify the situation" (*Emet Ve-Emunah*).

This verse contains three prohibitions on mixing categories, something the Torah often forbids as a way of tampering with the divinely

20If a man has carnal relations with a woman who is a slave and has been designated for another man, but has not been redeemed or given her freedom, there shall be an indemnity; they shall not, however, be put to death, since she has not been freed. 21But he must bring to the entrance of the Tent of Meeting, as his reparation offering to the LORD, a ram of reparation offering. 22With the ram of reparation offering the priest shall make expiation for him before the LORD for the sin that he committed; and the sin that he committed will be forgiven him.

23When you enter the land and plant any tree for food, you shall regard its fruit as forbidden. Three years it shall be forbidden for you, not to be eaten. 24In the fourth year all its fruit shall be set aside for jubilation before the LORD; 25and

20 וְאִ֗ישׁ כִּֽי־יִשְׁכַּ֨ב אֶת־אִשָּׁ֜ה שִׁכְבַת־זֶ֗רַע וְהִ֤וא שִׁפְחָה֙ נֶחֱרֶ֣פֶת לְאִ֔ישׁ וְהָפְדֵּה֙ לֹ֣א נִפְדָּ֔תָה א֖וֹ חֻפְשָׁ֣ה לֹ֣א נִתַּן־לָ֑הּ בִּקֹּ֧רֶת תִּֽהְיֶ֛ה לֹ֥א יֽוּמְת֖וּ כִּֽי־לֹ֥א חֻפָּֽשָׁה: 21 וְהֵבִ֤יא אֶת־אֲשָׁמוֹ֙ לַֽיהוָ֔ה אֶל־פֶּ֖תַח אֹ֣הֶל מוֹעֵ֑ד אֵ֖יל אָשָֽׁם: 22 וְכִפֶּר֩ עָלָ֨יו הַכֹּהֵ֜ן בְּאֵ֤יל הָֽאָשָׁם֙ לִפְנֵ֣י יְהוָ֔ה עַל־חַטָּאת֖וֹ אֲשֶׁ֣ר חָטָ֑א וְנִסְלַ֣ח ל֔וֹ מֵֽחַטָּאת֖וֹ אֲשֶׁ֥ר חָטָֽא: פ

שלישי 23 וְכִֽי־תָבֹ֣אוּ אֶל־הָאָ֗רֶץ וּנְטַעְתֶּם֙ כָּל־עֵ֣ץ מַֽאֲכָ֔ל וַֽעֲרַלְתֶּ֥ם עָרְלָת֖וֹ אֶת־פִּרְי֑וֹ שָׁלֹ֣שׁ שָׁנִ֗ים יִֽהְיֶ֥ה לָכֶ֛ם עֲרֵלִ֖ים לֹ֥א יֵֽאָכֵֽל: 24 וּבַשָּׁנָה֙ הָֽרְבִיעִ֔ת יִֽהְיֶ֖ה כָּל־פִּרְי֑וֹ קֹ֥דֶשׁ הִלּוּלִ֖ים לַֽיהוָֽה: 25 וּבַשָּׁנָ֣ה הַֽחֲמִישִׁ֗ת

20. carnal relations with a woman who is a slave The law of verses 20–22 is topically related to the Seventh Commandment because it hinges on the legalities of adultery, even though adultery is not directly involved here.

designated for another man That is, she has been pledged by her master, before her redemption, to another man.

an indemnity A payment is imposed on the responsible party because the girl, no longer a virgin, would be less desirable as a wife and the prospective husband would undoubtedly cancel the marriage.

21. A reparation offering (*asham*) is required

here in addition to the indemnity because an act of defilement has been committed: a violation of holiness. The woman had been promised to another, and even though the act was strictly speaking not adulterous, it was more than simply an act of seduction.

23. you shall regard its fruit as forbidden Literally, "You shall trim its fruit in the manner of a foreskin." The sense here is to "trim" or "remove" certain growths.

24. set aside Hebrew: *kodesh,* which carries that meaning as well as "holy."

jubilation Hebrew: *hillulim,* which may be an imitation of the sounds made during a time of joy.

ordained order of Creation. The parallel verse in Deut. 22:11 defines the word translated here as "mixture" (*sha·atnez*) as a garment made of linen and wool, a blending of vegetable and animal products. These three injunctions are among the classic examples of *ḥukkim,* rationally inexplicable rules. Hirsch offers the theory that, because wearing clothing is one of the things that separates humans from animals, the rule of *sha·atnez* teaches us to be holy in the way we dress, even as other apparently arbitrary rules teach us to be holy, to be different from animals. Animals are controlled by instinct, whereas human beings can learn to master their instincts.

20. Although this law may have represented an advance compared to the way in

which other ancient societies treated female slaves, the modern reader looks in vain for concern for the woman's feelings or dignity. Perhaps the clause "they shall not be put to death" can be seen as a leniency. If the young woman consented to the act, she is not treated as an adulteress because her arranged marriage had not been completed.

23. The Torah has a special rule for fruit trees. Because fruits of the first three years are generally inedible, it would be wrong to offer them to God (like sacrificing a blemished animal). Only fourth-year fruits are eligible for the offering of first fruits.

plant any tree for food This is in imitation of God, who filled the newly created world with every manner of tree for food (Lev. R. 25:3).

only in the fifth year may you use its fruit—that its yield to you may be increased: I the LORD am your God.

26 You shall not eat anything with its blood. You shall not practice divination or soothsaying. 27 You shall not round off the side-growth on your head, or destroy the side-growth of your beard. 28 You shall not make gashes in your flesh for the dead, or incise any marks on yourselves: I am the LORD.

29 Do not degrade your daughter and make her a harlot, lest the land fall into harlotry and the land be filled with depravity. 30 You shall keep My sabbaths and venerate My sanctuary: I am the LORD.

31 Do not turn to ghosts and do not inquire

תֹּאכְלוּ֙ אֶת־פִּרְי֔וֹ לְהוֹסִ֥יף לָכֶ֖ם תְּבוּאָת֑וֹ
אֲנִ֖י יְהוָ֥ה אֱלֹהֵיכֶֽם׃
26 לֹ֥א תֹאכְל֖וּ עַל־הַדָּ֑ם לֹ֥א תְנַחֲשׁ֖וּ וְלֹ֥א
תְעוֹנֵֽנוּ׃ 27 לֹ֣א תַקִּ֔פוּ פְּאַ֖ת רֹאשְׁכֶ֑ם וְלֹ֣א
תַשְׁחִ֔ית אֵ֖ת פְּאַ֥ת זְקָנֶֽךָ׃ 28 וְשֶׂ֣רֶט לָנֶ֗פֶשׁ
לֹ֤א תִתְּנוּ֙ בִּבְשַׂרְכֶ֔ם וּכְתֹ֣בֶת קַֽעֲקַ֔ע לֹ֥א
תִתְּנ֖וּ בָּכֶ֑ם אֲנִ֖י יְהוָֽה׃
29 אַל־תְּחַלֵּ֥ל אֶֽת־בִּתְּךָ֖ לְהַזְנוֹתָ֑הּ וְלֹא־
תִזְנֶ֣ה הָאָ֔רֶץ וּמָלְאָ֥ה הָאָ֖רֶץ זִמָּֽה׃ 30 אֶת־
שַׁבְּתֹתַ֣י תִּשְׁמֹ֔רוּ וּמִקְדָּשִׁ֖י תִּירָ֑אוּ אֲנִ֖י
יְהוָֽה׃
31 אַל־תִּפְנ֤וּ אֶל־הָאֹבֹת֙ וְאֶל־הַיִּדְּעֹנִ֔ים

26–28. These verses contain prohibitions that forbid practices characteristic of the pagan Canaanites and other idolaters.

destroy the side-growth of your beard Tearing out the hair of one's beard, as well as of the head, was a custom associated with mourning over the dead.

gashes in your flesh Pagan priests gashed themselves as they called upon their gods to answer their prayers (see 1 Kings 18:28).

incise any marks The reference is to some form of tattoo.

29. a harlot Harlotry was a violation of holiness that resulted in a status similar to that of defiled sacred objects.

land . . . land In biblical Hebrew, the word for "land" (*eretz,* here *ha-aretz*) may also connote the people on the land, which is the intent in this verse.

31. This refers to spiritualist communication

---

26. You shall not eat anything with its blood The verse may simply be a repetition of the prohibition in 17:10–14. Or, given the rest of this verse, it may refer to a Canaanite practice of divining the future by examining the bloody entrails of an animal (Hoffman). The Talmud derives from this verse the moral lesson that judges should fast on the day they sentence a criminal to death (BT Sanh. 63a).

divination or soothsaying These idolatrous practices are rooted in the idea that the future has already been determined and we can compel God to reveal it to us. Judaism insists that the course of the future is not set until human beings make free decisions about their behavior, determining their fate and the fate of the people around them.

28. gashes in your flesh for the dead Judaism teaches us to express this grief by tearing our garments rather than by wounding ourselves. Again we are taught that the quest for holiness includes respect for one's body, rather than a concentration on the spiritual at the body's expense.

HALAKHAH L'MA·ASEH

19:27. round off The Sages restricted this prohibition to shaving the sideburns and beard with a straight-edged razor (BT Mak. 21a). Scissors and many electric shavers are permitted because they cut facial hair in permissible ways.

19:28. incise any marks It is prohibited to inscribe a permanent tattoo on one's body (M Mak. 3:6). Nevertheless, a Jew who is tattooed may be buried in a Jewish cemetery, like any other Jew. The CJLS permits body piercing (e.g., for earrings) as long as it does not compromise a person's health and would not lead to exposing parts of the body that usually are covered in public.

of familiar spirits, to be defiled by them: I the
LORD am your God.
32You shall rise before the aged and show deference to the old; you shall fear your God: I am
the LORD.
33When a stranger resides with you in your
land, you shall not wrong him. 34The stranger
who resides with you shall be to you as one of
your citizens; you shall love him as yourself, for
you were strangers in the land of Egypt: I the
LORD am your God.
35You shall not falsify measures of length,
weight, or capacity. 36You shall have an honest
balance, honest weights, an honest *ephah*, and
an honest *hin*.
I the LORD am your God who freed you from
the land of Egypt. 37You shall faithfully observe
all My laws and all My rules: I am the LORD.

אַל־תְּבַקְשׁוּ לְטָמְאָה בָהֶם אֲנִי יְהוָה
אֱלֹהֵיכֶם׃
32 מִפְּנֵי שֵׂיבָה תָּקוּם וְהָדַרְתָּ פְּנֵי זָקֵן
וְיָרֵאתָ מֵּאֱלֹהֶיךָ אֲנִי יְהוָה׃ פ
רביעי [ששי] 33 וְכִי־יָגוּר אִתְּךָ גֵּר בְּאַרְצְכֶם לֹא תוֹנוּ
אֹתוֹ׃ 34 כְּאֶזְרָח מִכֶּם יִהְיֶה לָכֶם הַגֵּר ׀
הַגָּר אִתְּכֶם וְאָהַבְתָּ לוֹ כָּמוֹךָ כִּי־גֵרִים
הֱיִיתֶם בְּאֶרֶץ מִצְרָיִם אֲנִי יְהוָה
אֱלֹהֵיכֶם׃
35 לֹא־תַעֲשׂוּ עָוֶל בַּמִּשְׁפָּט בַּמִּדָּה בַּמִּשְׁקָל
וּבַמְּשׂוּרָה׃ 36 מֹאזְנֵי צֶדֶק אַבְנֵי־צֶדֶק
אֵיפַת צֶדֶק וְהִין צֶדֶק יִהְיֶה לָכֶם
אֲנִי יְהוָה אֱלֹהֵיכֶם אֲשֶׁר־הוֹצֵאתִי אֶתְכֶם
מֵאֶרֶץ מִצְרָיִם׃ 37 וּשְׁמַרְתֶּם אֶת־כָּל־
חֻקֹּתַי וְאֶת־כָּל־מִשְׁפָּטַי וַעֲשִׂיתֶם אֹתָם
חמישי אֲנִי יְהוָה׃ פ

with the dead in the netherworld through orac-ular inquiry or augury.

33. a stranger The "stranger" (*ger*) referred to in the Bible was most often a foreign merchant, craftsman, or mercenary soldier. The term never refers to the prior inhabitants of the land, who are identified by ethnologic groupings, such as Canaanites and Amorites, or by other specific terms of reference.

35. You shall not falsify measures Literally, "You shall not commit an injustice."

36. honest balance Ancient scales had an up-right, on which two cups or plates were balanced. In one was a stone or iron weight, and the other held the goods to be weighed.

ephah See Comment to Exod. 16:36.

hin See Comment to Exod. 29:40.

I the LORD am your God who freed you from the land of Egypt In its emphasis on the liber-ation from Egypt this statement resembles the First Commandment.

---

32. show deference to the old "What we owe the old is reverence, but all they ask for is consideration, attention, not to be discarded and forgotten. What they deserve is preference, yet we do not even grant them equality" (Heschel). Act in such a manner that you do not embarrass the old person you will one day be-come, by your behavior today. The Midrash tells of a king who would rise to honor an el-derly commoner, saying, "God has chosen to reward him (with long life); how can I not do the same?" (Lev. R. 25:5).

34. for you were strangers in the land of Egypt Remembering our Egyptian experience, we might wish to be like the Egyptians when we have the opportunity, oppressing the pow-erless in our midst. Therefore, the Torah warns us to use the memory of slavery in Egypt to learn empathy for the oppressed.

HALAKHAH L'MA·ASEH

19:36. honest weights Jewish law bans fraud and deception (see Exod. 23:7; Lev. 19:13) in both business and personal interactions. Jewish communities historically appointed inspectors to ensure that the weights and mea-sures of Jewish merchants were honest (S.A. Ḥ.M. 231:2).

20 And the LORD spoke to Moses: 2Say further to the Israelite people:

Anyone among the Israelites, or among the strangers residing in Israel, who gives any of his offspring to Molech, shall be put to death; the people of the land shall pelt him with stones. 3And I will set My face against that man and will cut him off from among his people, because he gave of his offspring to Molech and so defiled My sanctuary and profaned My holy name. 4And if the people of the land should shut their eyes to that man when he gives of his offspring to Molech, and should not put him to death, 5I Myself will set My face against that man and his kin, and will cut off from among their people both him and all who follow him in going astray after Molech. 6And if any person turns to ghosts and familiar spirits and goes astray after them, I will set My face against that person and cut him off from among his people.

7You shall sanctify yourselves and be holy, for I the LORD am your God. 8You shall faithfully observe My laws: I the LORD make you holy.

חמישי כ וַיְדַבֵּר יְהוָה אֶל־מֹשֶׁה לֵּאמֹר׃ 2 וְאֶל־
בְּנֵי יִשְׂרָאֵל תֹּאמַר
אִישׁ אִישׁ מִבְּנֵי יִשְׂרָאֵל וּמִן־הַגֵּר ׀ הַגָּר
בְּיִשְׂרָאֵל אֲשֶׁר יִתֵּן מִזַּרְעוֹ לַמֹּלֶךְ מוֹת
יוּמָת עַם הָאָרֶץ יִרְגְּמֻהוּ בָאָבֶן׃ 3 וַאֲנִי
אֶתֵּן אֶת־פָּנַי בָּאִישׁ הַהוּא וְהִכְרַתִּי אֹתוֹ
מִקֶּרֶב עַמּוֹ כִּי מִזַּרְעוֹ נָתַן לַמֹּלֶךְ לְמַעַן
טַמֵּא אֶת־מִקְדָּשִׁי וּלְחַלֵּל אֶת־שֵׁם קָדְשִׁי׃
4 וְאִם הַעְלֵם יַעְלִימוּ עַם הָאָרֶץ אֶת־
עֵינֵיהֶם מִן־הָאִישׁ הַהוּא בְּתִתּוֹ מִזַּרְעוֹ
לַמֹּלֶךְ לְבִלְתִּי הָמִית אֹתוֹ׃ 5 וְשַׂמְתִּי אֲנִי
אֶת־פָּנַי בָּאִישׁ הַהוּא וּבְמִשְׁפַּחְתּוֹ
וְהִכְרַתִּי אֹתוֹ וְאֵת ׀ כָּל־הַזֹּנִים אַחֲרָיו
לִזְנוֹת אַחֲרֵי הַמֹּלֶךְ מִקֶּרֶב עַמָּם׃ 6 וְהַנֶּפֶשׁ
אֲשֶׁר תִּפְנֶה אֶל־הָאֹבֹת וְאֶל־הַיִּדְּעֹנִים
לִזְנוֹת אַחֲרֵיהֶם וְנָתַתִּי אֶת־פָּנַי בַּנֶּפֶשׁ
הַהִוא וְהִכְרַתִּי אֹתוֹ מִקֶּרֶב עַמּוֹ׃
7 וְהִתְקַדִּשְׁתֶּם וִהְיִיתֶם קְדֹשִׁים כִּי אֲנִי
ששי ביעי] יְהוָה אֱלֹהֵיכֶם׃ 8 וּשְׁמַרְתֶּם אֶת־חֻקֹּתַי
וַעֲשִׂיתֶם אֹתָם אֲנִי יְהוָה מְקַדִּשְׁכֶם׃

THE FAMILY IN RELIGIOUS CONTEXT (20:1–27)

The laws in this chapter assume a connection between pagan worship and sexual degeneracy. Both are regarded as causes of exile.

2. among the strangers residing in Israel The worship of gods was forbidden to all who resided in the land of Israel, whether they were Israelites or not.

3. Any object involved in pagan worship placed in or near the sanctuary rendered the sanctuary impure. Furthermore, the very act of disobedience to God by members of the community effectively defiled the sanctuary, which stood within the settlement.

5. kin Hebrew: *mishpaḥah* (kin, clan), which refers to the basic sociologic unit in ancient Israelite society. The clan tended to act together in matters of worship, following the way of its leaders.

CHAPTER 20

5. Molech represents the demonic, destructive face of religion, the cult of death and human sacrifice (whereas Baal represents the orgiastic, fertility dimension of paganism). It is the polar opposite of everything the Holiness Code stands for. That may be why the Torah condemns it so vigorously.

6. The word translated as "going astray" (*liznot*) has the meaning of betraying one's marriage vows. The Torah uses this word in connection with worshiping idols and consulting ghosts, because the covenant between God and Israel is not a business contract but a relationship of love and loyalty. Violating this covenant is seen not as default but as betrayal.

[9]If anyone insults his father or his mother, he
shall be put to death; he has insulted his father
and his mother—his bloodguilt is upon him.
[10]If a man commits adultery with a married
woman, committing adultery with another
man's wife, the adulterer and the adulteress
shall be put to death. [11]If a man lies with his
father's wife, it is the nakedness of his father that
he has uncovered; the two shall be put to
death—their bloodguilt is upon them. [12]If a
man lies with his daughter-in-law, both of them
shall be put to death; they have committed
incest—their bloodguilt is upon them. [13]If a
man lies with a male as one lies with a woman,
the two of them have done an abhorrent thing;
they shall be put to death—their bloodguilt is
upon them. [14]If a man marries a woman and
her mother, it is depravity; both he and they
shall be put to the fire, that there be no depravity
among you. [15]If a man has carnal relations with
a beast, he shall be put to death; and you shall
kill the beast. [16]If a woman approaches any beast
to mate with it, you shall kill the woman and
the beast; they shall be put to death—their
bloodguilt is upon them.
[17]If a man marries his sister, the daughter of

9 כִּֽי־אִ֣ישׁ אִ֗ישׁ אֲשֶׁ֨ר יְקַלֵּ֧ל אֶת־אָבִ֛יו
וְאֶת־אִמּ֖וֹ מ֣וֹת יוּמָ֑ת אָבִ֧יו וְאִמּ֛וֹ קִלֵּ֖ל
דָּמָ֥יו בּֽוֹ׃
10 וְאִ֗ישׁ אֲשֶׁ֤ר יִנְאַף֙ אֶת־אֵ֣שֶׁת אִ֔ישׁ אֲשֶׁ֥ר
יִנְאַ֖ף אֶת־אֵ֣שֶׁת רֵעֵ֑הוּ מֽוֹת־יוּמַ֥ת הַנֹּאֵ֖ף
וְהַנֹּאָֽפֶת׃ 11 וְאִ֗ישׁ אֲשֶׁ֤ר יִשְׁכַּב֙ אֶת־אֵ֣שֶׁת
אָבִ֔יו עֶרְוַ֥ת אָבִ֖יו גִּלָּ֑ה מֽוֹת־יוּמְת֥וּ שְׁנֵיהֶ֖ם
דְּמֵיהֶ֥ם בָּֽם׃ 12 וְאִ֗ישׁ אֲשֶׁ֤ר יִשְׁכַּב֙ אֶת־
כַּלָּת֔וֹ מ֥וֹת יוּמְת֖וּ שְׁנֵיהֶ֑ם תֶּ֥בֶל עָשׂ֖וּ
דְּמֵיהֶ֥ם בָּֽם׃ 13 וְאִ֗ישׁ אֲשֶׁ֨ר יִשְׁכַּ֤ב אֶת־
זָכָר֙ מִשְׁכְּבֵ֣י אִשָּׁ֔ה תּוֹעֵבָ֥ה עָשׂ֖וּ שְׁנֵיהֶ֑ם
מ֥וֹת יוּמָ֖תוּ דְּמֵיהֶ֥ם בָּֽם׃ 14 וְאִ֗ישׁ אֲשֶׁ֨ר
יִקַּ֧ח אֶת־אִשָּׁ֛ה וְאֶת־אִמָּ֖הּ זִמָּ֣ה הִ֑וא
בָּאֵ֞שׁ יִשְׂרְפ֤וּ אֹתוֹ֙ וְאֶתְהֶ֔ן וְלֹא־תִהְיֶ֥ה
זִמָּ֖ה בְּתוֹכְכֶֽם׃ 15 וְאִ֗ישׁ אֲשֶׁ֨ר יִתֵּ֧ן שְׁכָבְתּ֛וֹ
בִּבְהֵמָ֖ה מ֣וֹת יוּמָ֑ת וְאֶת־הַבְּהֵמָ֖ה
תַּהֲרֹֽגוּ׃ 16 וְאִשָּׁ֗ה אֲשֶׁ֨ר תִּקְרַ֤ב אֶל־כָּל־
בְּהֵמָה֙ לְרִבְעָ֣ה אֹתָ֔הּ וְהָרַגְתָּ֥ אֶת־הָאִשָּׁ֖ה
וְאֶת־הַבְּהֵמָ֑ה מ֥וֹת יוּמָ֖תוּ דְּמֵיהֶ֥ם בָּֽם׃
17 וְאִ֨ישׁ אֲשֶׁר־יִקַּ֜ח אֶת־אֲחֹת֗וֹ בַּת־אָבִ֛יו

9. his bloodguilt is upon him The Hebrew word for "blood" (*dam*) and its plural (*damim*) often connote infractions punished by the death penalty.

FORBIDDEN SEXUAL UNIONS (vv. 10–21)

15. you shall kill the beast The punishment derives from the Israelite notion that animals, like humans, possess a moral sense and, therefore, also bear guilt.

17. marries Hebrew: לקח (to acquire [as a wife]); a legal term for marriage.

---

9. insults Hebrew: *kallel,* literally "to treat lightly"—that is, to not take seriously (from *kal,* meaning "lightweight"). It is the opposite of the verb used in the Fifth Commandment, *kabbed* (from a root meaning heavy in weight, translated as "honor"). The words and values of one's parents are weighty; they must be taken seriously even when one disagrees with them.

10ff. According to Hoffman, the laws of incest are repeated here to emphasize that they apply to all people, not only to Israelites. God demands a basic level of sexual morality from all human beings, and then summons Israel to a higher level of holiness in their sexual behavior and other aspects of life.

HALAKHAH L'MA·ASEH
20:13. See Comment to Lev. 18:22.

either his father or his mother, so that he sees
her nakedness and she sees his nakedness, it is
a disgrace; they shall be excommunicated in the
sight of their kinsfolk. He has uncovered the nakedness of his sister, he shall bear his guilt. 18If
a man lies with a woman in her infirmity and
uncovers her nakedness, he has laid bare her
flow and she has exposed her blood flow; both
of them shall be cut off from among their people. 19You shall not uncover the nakedness of
your mother's sister or of your father's sister,
for that is laying bare one's own flesh; they shall
bear their guilt. 20If a man lies with his uncle's
wife, it is his uncle's nakedness that he has uncovered. They shall bear their guilt: they shall
die childless. 21If a man marries the wife of his
brother, it is indecency. It is the nakedness of
his brother that he has uncovered; they shall remain childless.

22You shall faithfully observe all My laws and
all My regulations, lest the land to which I bring
you to settle in spew you out. 23You shall not
follow the practices of the nation that I am driving out before you. For it is because they did
all these things that I abhorred them 24and said
to you: You shall possess their land, for I will
give it to you to possess, a land flowing with milk

אוֹ בַת־אִמּוֹ וְרָאָה אֶת־עֶרְוָתָהּ וְהִיא־
תִרְאֶה אֶת־עֶרְוָתוֹ חֶסֶד הוּא וְנִכְרְתוּ
לְעֵינֵי בְּנֵי עַמָּם עֶרְוַת אֲחֹתוֹ גִּלָּה עֲוֺנוֹ
יִשָּׂא׃ 18 וְאִישׁ אֲשֶׁר־יִשְׁכַּב אֶת־אִשָּׁה דָּוָה
וְגִלָּה אֶת־עֶרְוָתָהּ אֶת־מְקֹרָהּ הֶעֱרָה וְהִוא
גִּלְּתָה אֶת־מְקוֹר דָּמֶיהָ וְנִכְרְתוּ שְׁנֵיהֶם
מִקֶּרֶב עַמָּם׃ 19 וְעֶרְוַת אֲחוֹת אִמְּךָ וַאֲחוֹת
אָבִיךָ לֹא תְגַלֵּה כִּי אֶת־שְׁאֵרוֹ הֶעֱרָה
עֲוֺנָם יִשָּׂאוּ׃ 20 וְאִישׁ אֲשֶׁר יִשְׁכַּב אֶת־
דֹּדָתוֹ עֶרְוַת דֹּדוֹ גִּלָּה חֶטְאָם יִשָּׂאוּ
עֲרִירִים יָמֻתוּ׃ 21 וְאִישׁ אֲשֶׁר יִקַּח אֶת־
אֵשֶׁת אָחִיו נִדָּה הִוא עֶרְוַת אָחִיו גִּלָּה
עֲרִירִים יִהְיוּ׃

22 וּשְׁמַרְתֶּם אֶת־כָּל־חֻקֹּתַי וְאֶת־כָּל־
מִשְׁפָּטַי וַעֲשִׂיתֶם אֹתָם וְלֹא־תָקִיא אֶתְכֶם
הָאָרֶץ אֲשֶׁר אֲנִי מֵבִיא אֶתְכֶם שָׁמָּה
לָשֶׁבֶת בָּהּ׃ 23 וְלֹא תֵלְכוּ בְּחֻקֹּת הַגּוֹי ביעי
אֲשֶׁר־אֲנִי מְשַׁלֵּחַ מִפְּנֵיכֶם כִּי אֶת־כָּל־
אֵלֶּה עָשׂוּ וָאָקֻץ בָּם׃ 24 וָאֹמַר לָכֶם אַתֶּם
תִּירְשׁוּ אֶת־אַדְמָתָם וַאֲנִי אֶתְּנֶנָּה לָכֶם
לָרֶשֶׁת אֹתָהּ אֶרֶץ זָבַת חָלָב וּדְבָשׁ אֲנִי

disgrace Hebrew: *ḥesed,* like the Aramaic word *ḥasda* (ignominy, disgrace). It should not be confused with its Hebrew homonym, which means "love, kindness."

they shall be excommunicated in the sight of their kinsfolk This is a way of expressing banishment.

18. in her infirmity While menstruating.

POSSESSION OF THE LAND (vv. 22–27)

22. You shall faithfully observe all My laws This statement introduces the closing admonition of this section.

24. flowing with milk and honey A well-known characterization of the land in biblical literature. It is depicted as abounding in milk-producing herds, flocks, and fruit trees, especially the date palm. The Hebrew word for "honey" (*d'vash*) usually refers to the nectar of trees. The word translated as "flowing" also means "oozing," which links this section with the verses concerned about bodily discharge.

24–25. You shall possess their land, for I will give it to you The literal meaning of "for" here is "and." One commentator took these words to mean, first you must claim the land, and only then will I, God, confirm it as yours. God's gifts are given permanently only to those who make the effort to claim them.

and honey. I the LORD am your God who has set you apart from other peoples. 25So you shall set apart the pure beast from the impure, the impure bird from the pure. You shall not draw abomination upon yourselves through beast or bird or anything with which the ground is alive, which I have set apart for you to treat as impure. 26You shall be holy to Me, for I the LORD am holy, and I have set you apart from other peoples to be Mine.

27A man or a woman who has a ghost or a familiar spirit shall be put to death; they shall be pelted with stones—their bloodguilt shall be upon them.

יְהוָ֣ה אֱלֹהֵיכֶ֔ם אֲשֶׁר־הִבְדַּ֥לְתִּי אֶתְכֶ֖ם
מפטיר מִן־הָֽעַמִּֽים׃ 25 וְהִבְדַּלְתֶּ֞ם בֵּֽין־הַבְּהֵמָ֤ה
הַטְּהֹרָה֙ לַטְּמֵאָ֔ה וּבֵין־הָע֥וֹף הַטָּמֵ֖א
לַטָּהֹ֑ר וְלֹֽא־תְשַׁקְּצ֨וּ אֶת־נַפְשֹׁתֵיכֶ֜ם
בַּבְּהֵמָ֣ה וּבָע֗וֹף וּבְכֹל֙ אֲשֶׁ֣ר תִּרְמֹ֣שׂ
הָֽאֲדָמָ֔ה אֲשֶׁר־הִבְדַּ֥לְתִּי לָכֶ֖ם לְטַמֵּֽא׃
26 וִהְיִ֤יתֶם לִי֙ קְדֹשִׁ֔ים כִּ֥י קָד֖וֹשׁ אֲנִ֣י יְהוָ֑ה
וָאַבְדִּ֥ל אֶתְכֶ֛ם מִן־הָֽעַמִּ֖ים לִהְי֥וֹת לִֽי׃
27 וְאִ֣ישׁ אֽוֹ־אִשָּׁ֗ה כִּֽי־יִהְיֶ֨ה בָהֶ֥ם א֛וֹב א֥וֹ
יִדְּעֹנִ֖י מ֣וֹת יוּמָ֑תוּ בָּאֶ֛בֶן יִרְגְּמ֥וּ אֹתָ֖ם
דְּמֵיהֶ֥ם בָּֽם׃ פ

who has set you apart from other peoples. So you shall set apart the pure beast from the impure The people Israel, by bringing the dimension of holiness not only into its ritual life but also into its ways of eating, dress, and sexual mores, will be a model for all humanity of how people can refine and transcend their animal nature and achieve holiness.

26. You shall be holy to Me, for I the LORD am holy The *parashah* concludes (in this penultimate verse) as it began.

הפטרת אחרי מות / קדשים

HAFTARAH 1 FOR AḤAREI MOT / K'DOSHIM

AMOS 9:7–15 (*Ashk'nazim*)

(*Instructions for* Ashk'nazim: *When* Aḥarei Mot *and* K'doshim *are read separately and no occasions coincide that have a special* haftarah *of their own* [*see below*], *some traditions recite this* haftarah *with* Aḥarei Mot *and the following* haftarah *with* K'doshim; *others reverse the order of these* haftarot.

When Aḥarei Mot *and* K'doshim *are combined, recite this* haftarah.

When Aḥarei Mot *is read separately on* Shabbat ha-Gadol *or on* Erev Rosh Ḥodesh, *recite this* haftarah *with* K'doshim. *When* K'doshim *will be read separately on* Rosh Ḥodesh, *recite this* haftarah *with* Aḥarei Mot.)

The prophet Amos is among the earliest of the classical prophets, flourishing in the reigns of King Jeroboam II of Israel (784–748 B.C.E.) and King Uzziah of Judah (769–733 B.C.E.). Speaking against Judah (in the south), but especially against the northern kingdom of Israel, Amos severely criticizes the people for cultic sins and moral insensitivity. His words are all doom and dire prediction, except for his final words, which constitute the last two verses of this *haftarah.* After opening with a judgment speech against sinful nations, his own people included, Amos promises hope and restoration to Israel and Judah in days to come.

Amos's final words of hope constitute a striking reversal of his opening speech to the northern kingdom of Israel, when, years earlier, he spoke God's word "Concerning the whole family that I [God] brought up from the land of Egypt: / You alone have I singled out / Of all the families of the earth— / That is why I call you to account / For all your iniquities" (3:1–2). Even this uniqueness seems to be neutralized in the *haftarah,* as the people are told that God will judge them because they are no different from the other nations (like the Philistines and the Arameans) whom the Lord delivered from other lands (9:7–8). Thus doom will befall Israel, although not because God holds it to special account or because of unique favor shown it in the past.

These new remarks were certainly designed to unsettle the listener and to undermine any false sense of trust or advantage. Indeed, for Amos, historical redemption is not the basis for the divine election of Israel, or for its survival. God's will and grace are the independent factors determining Israelite destiny. Israel always remains accountable to the Covenant. Only obedience or the humble acceptance of divine judgment is in the hands of the people; all else depends on God.

The special favor that God accords Israel is marked by the decision to save a remnant of the northern nation and to scatter them in foreign exile. This mitigated judgment is presented as an expression of divine favor, although unmerited; for the sins of the people should have led to their doom, as was the case for the other nations. To announce God's act, the prophet uses the image of a sieve that scatters some particles while catching others in the grating. The strewn elements are apparently the people who are saved, in contradistinction to the sinners who remain in the instrument and do not escape its mesh (vv. 8–9). In terms of the prophet's rhetoric, the survivors are simply those who do not boastfully deny divine judgment, not individuals who deserve acquittal for any other reason (cf. v. 10). For later readers, Amos's pronouncement seems to forecast the dispersion of the northern tribes, an event that still lay in the future (722–721 B.C.E.). However, the imminent aggression of the Assyrian Empire and its expansion are never explicitly mentioned by the prophet.

More perplexing is the ensuing forecast that God "will set up again the fallen booth of David" (v. 11). The obscurity of this image and the en-

suing references to widespread ruins have long perplexed readers of Amos, not least because the destruction of the Temple and of Judea lay nearly two centuries ahead (587–586 B.C.E.). At any rate, readers of these words are given hope to anticipate a restoration of the Davidic era, when expansion was at a height and national unity a reality. The dooms forecast against Judea will be wholly assuaged by an anticipation of a renewal of the "days of old" (see 2:4–5, 9:11). In those times, Judea dominated Edom. So it will again.

The restoration of Israel is the fitting complement to these hopes. Here, too, ancient messages of doom against the north will be reversed through a miraculous regeneration of life (9:13–15). The cycle of nature will be so bountiful as to overlap itself repeatedly; scarcely will the older harvests be gathered when the times for new planting will fall due. Even the people will partake of this revival. In a dramatic image, Amos speaks of the planters planted in the earth, nevermore to be uprooted from their homeland. As a sign of this new era, Israel will again be called "My people" (v. 14).

RELATION OF THE *HAFTARAH* TO THE *PARASHAH*

Both *Aḥarei Mot* and this *haftarah* emphasize that God will judge all peoples for their iniquities. Furthermore, divine acts of national liberation are no guarantee against punishment for sin.

Meanwhile, these words of Amos contrast dramatically with *K'doshim*. For its part, *K'doshim*

concludes boldly with a challenging proclamation: "You shall be holy to Me, for I the LORD am holy, and I have set you apart from other peoples to be Mine (*li-hyot li*)" (Lev. 20:26). Action is a responsibility for both parties to the Covenant. Two distinct acts are portrayed. God has made a unilateral choice of Israel to be His special people. Israel is called on to react by faithfully observing the covenantal laws and regulations to realize the divine call to be holy.

This *haftarah* stands in tension with such a teaching. The prophet's divine assertion that "To Me (*li*), O Israelites, you are just like the Ethiopians" (Amos 9:7) denies Israel's uniqueness and asserts a fixed reality. No divine election is proclaimed here and no special destiny is awaiting fulfillment. Israel is a nation among the nations, and its history is similar to that of its neighbors. This does not erase national memory, however, or the path of piety that is uniquely Israel's. It only means that Israel may not rely on divine grace shown it in the past as a guarantee of mercy in the present or in the future. Thus Israel must reflect deeply on its destiny and discover just how its unique covenantal path shapes its national–religious character. Then will it transform the triumphal assertion of uniqueness found in *K'doshim* into a new awareness of distinction and duty.

Kept separate, *K'doshim* and this *haftarah*'s lessons cancel each other's truth concerning election; brought together, they revise one another reciprocally and suggest a more inward and humble theology of chosenness.

9

7 To Me, O Israelites, you are
Just like the Ethiopians
    —declares the LORD.
True, I brought Israel up
From the land of Egypt,
But also the Philistines from Caphtor
And the Arameans from Kir.

ט ⁷ הֲל֣וֹא כִבְנֵי֩ כֻשִׁיִּ֨ים
אַתֶּ֥ם לִ֛י בְּנֵ֥י יִשְׂרָאֵ֖ל
נְאֻם־יְהֹוָ֑ה
הֲל֣וֹא אֶת־יִשְׂרָאֵ֗ל הֶעֱלֵ֨יתִי֙
מֵאֶ֣רֶץ מִצְרַ֔יִם
וּפְלִשְׁתִּיִּ֥ים מִכַּפְתּ֖וֹר
וַאֲרָ֥ם מִקִּֽיר׃

Amos 9:7. To Me, O Israelites In Hebrew grammar, this assertion is a question: "Are you not just like the Ethiopians to Me, O Israelites?"

Caphtor Most likely identified with Crete (see Jer. 47:4).

Kir In Amos 1:5, the people will be exiled

8 הִנֵּ֞ה עֵינֵ֣י ׀ אֲדֹנָ֣י יְהוִ֗ה

בַּמַּמְלָכָה֙ הַֽחַטָּאָ֔ה

וְהִשְׁמַדְתִּ֣י אֹתָ֔הּ

מֵעַ֖ל פְּנֵ֣י הָאֲדָמָ֑ה

אֶ֗פֶס כִּ֠י לֹ֣א הַשְׁמֵ֥יד אַשְׁמִ֛יד

אֶת־בֵּ֥ית יַעֲקֹ֖ב

נְאֻם־יְהוָֽה׃

9 כִּֽי־הִנֵּ֤ה אָֽנֹכִי֙ מְצַוֶּ֔ה

וַהֲנִע֥וֹתִי בְכָֽל־הַגּוֹיִ֖ם

אֶת־בֵּ֣ית יִשְׂרָאֵ֑ל

כַּאֲשֶׁ֤ר יִנּ֙וֹעַ֙ בַּכְּבָרָ֔ה

וְלֹֽא־יִפּ֥וֹל צְר֖וֹר אָֽרֶץ׃

10 בַּחֶ֣רֶב יָמ֔וּתוּ

כֹּ֖ל חַטָּאֵ֣י עַמִּ֑י

הָאֹֽמְרִ֗ים

לֹֽא־תַגִּ֧ישׁ

וְתַקְדִּ֛ים בַּעֲדֵ֖ינוּ הָרָעָֽה׃

11 בַּיּ֣וֹם הַה֔וּא

אָקִ֛ים אֶת־סֻכַּ֥ת דָּוִ֖יד הַנֹּפֶ֑לֶת

וְגָדַרְתִּ֣י אֶת־פִּרְצֵיהֶ֗ן וַהֲרִֽסֹתָיו֙ אָקִ֔ים

וּבְנִיתִ֖יהָ כִּימֵ֥י עוֹלָֽם׃

12 לְמַ֙עַן֙ יִֽירְשׁ֗וּ אֶת־שְׁאֵרִ֣ית אֱד֔וֹם

וְכָל־הַגּוֹיִ֕ם אֲשֶׁר־נִקְרָ֥א שְׁמִ֖י עֲלֵיהֶ֑ם

נְאֻם־יְהוָ֖ה עֹ֥שֶׂה זֹּֽאת׃ פ

13 הִנֵּ֙ה יָמִ֤ים בָּאִים֙

נְאֻם־יְהוָ֔ה

8Behold, the Lord GOD has His eye
Upon the sinful kingdom:
I will wipe it off
The face of the earth!

But, I will not wholly wipe out
The House of Jacob
          —declares the LORD.
9For I will give the order
And shake the House of Israel—
Through all the nations—
As one shakes [sand] in a sieve,
And not a pebble falls to the ground.
10All the sinners of My people
Shall perish by the sword,
Who boast,
"Never shall the evil
Overtake us or come near us."

11In that day,
I will set up again the fallen booth of David:
I will mend its breaches and set up its ruins anew.
I will build it firm as in the days of old,
12So that they shall possess the rest of Edom
And all the nations once attached to My name
        —declares the LORD who will bring this to pass.
13A time is coming
        —declares the LORD—

---

back to Kir. Cf. 2 Kings 16:9, which reports that the Assyrian king Tiglath-pileser III took Damascus "captive to Kir" (ca. 734 B.C.E.).

8. the Lord GOD has His eye Literally, "the eyes of the Lord GOD." Use of this idiom dramatizes the investigative character of divine justice (cf. Zech. 4:10). The image apparently derives from the older Near Eastern identification of royal investigators with the eyes of the king.

9. sieve Hebrew: *k'varah*. Apparently a coarse sieve, used to strain straw and stones.

10. Never shall the evil . . . A quotation exemplifying the boastful disdain of the people.

11. booth This image is unclear. Some commentators have interpreted the metaphor in terms of the fallen state of the Davidic (United) Monarchy (Rashi, Radak).

12. once attached to My name Hebrew: *asher nikra sh'mi aleihem*; literally, "upon whom My name is called." This idiom signifies ownership.

When the plowman shall meet the reaper,
And the treader of grapes
Him who holds the [bag of] seed;
When the mountains shall drip wine
And all the hills shall wave [with grain].
14I will restore My people Israel.
They shall rebuild ruined cities and inhabit them;
They shall plant vineyards and drink their wine;
They shall till gardens and eat their fruits.
15And I will plant them upon their soil,
Nevermore to be uprooted
From the soil I have given them
—said the LORD your God.

וְנִגַּ֤שׁ חוֹרֵשׁ֙ בַּקֹּצֵ֔ר
וְדֹרֵ֥ךְ עֲנָבִ֖ים
בְּמֹשֵׁ֣ךְ הַזָּ֑רַע
וְהִטִּ֤יפוּ הֶֽהָרִים֙ עָסִ֔יס
וְכָל־הַגְּבָע֖וֹת תִּתְמוֹגַֽגְנָה׃
14 וְשַׁבְתִּי֮ אֶת־שְׁב֣וּת עַמִּ֣י יִשְׂרָאֵל֒
וּבָנ֞וּ עָרִ֤ים נְשַׁמּוֹת֙ וְיָשָׁ֔בוּ
וְנָטְע֣וּ כְרָמִ֔ים וְשָׁת֖וּ אֶת־יֵינָ֑ם
וְעָשׂ֣וּ גַנּ֔וֹת וְאָכְל֖וּ אֶת־פְּרִיהֶֽם׃
15 וּנְטַעְתִּ֖ים עַל־אַדְמָתָ֑ם
וְלֹ֨א יִנָּתְשׁ֜וּ ע֗וֹד
מֵעַ֤ל אַדְמָתָם֙ אֲשֶׁ֣ר נָתַ֣תִּי לָהֶ֔ם
אָמַ֖ר יְהוָ֥ה אֱלֹהֶֽיךָ׃

13. the plowman shall meet the reaper This image, and the subsequent image of the "treader of grapes" meeting the sower, both dramatize the physical bounty anticipated. The produce will be so munificent as to extend into the ensuing planting season (Rashi, Radak).

15. I will plant them Like a firmly rooted tree, not to be moved. Compare Exod. 15:17.

הפטרת אחרי מות / קדשים

HAFTARAH 2 FOR AḤAREI MOT / K'DOSHIM

EZEKIEL 22:1–19 (*Ashk'nazim*)
EZEKIEL 22:1–16 (*S'fardim*)

(*For instructions for* Ashk'nazim, *see the introduction to the previous* haftarah. S'fardim *recite this* haftarah *with* Aḥarei Mot, *and the next* haftarah *with* K'doshim.)

In this *haftarah* the prophet Ezekiel addresses the city Jerusalem as "the city of bloodshed," accusing Jerusalem for "all her abhorrent deeds" (v. 2). These sins, listed in clusters, focus on moral and sexual crimes in family and society, with special emphasis on the oppression of socially dependent and powerless individuals. The prophet also charges the city with desecrating *Shabbat* and the sacral offices. For Ezekiel, the city symbolizes the outrages committed by all the people, judging them as a whole. This passage is dated sometime after Ezekiel's deportation to Babylon in 597 B.C.E. and before 587–586, when the Babylonians destroyed Jerusalem and the general population was exiled to Babylon.

In his role as God's prosecutor, Ezekiel accuses the people of crimes specified in the Torah, showing familiarity with a wide range of rules from the Covenant Code (Exod. 21–23), and especially from the Holiness Code (Lev. 18–20), as well as various laws from Deuteronomy. Thus the prophet's speech testifies to formulations of the laws of the Torah from the early 6th century B.C.E. This was long before Ezra's return from the exile and the beginning of the canonization of the Torah in the 5th century B.C.E.

The detailed list of sins reinforces the prophet's assertion that the people were utterly deserving of divine punishment. This accounts for Ezekiel's specification of moral misdemeanors from the legal collections cited above. Alongside these faults the prophet specifies violations drawn from earlier priestly traditions, including contempt for *Shabbat* and the holy offerings, and improper sexual relations.

Undoubtedly there was a basis for these accusations. But their comprehensive and schematic character should be taken into account in any assessment of the religious and moral state of the nation at the time. Ezekiel does not limit his critique to issues of ritual impurity, but absolutely condemns immoral and inconsiderate uses of power as well.

For such actions, the people are condemned to exile, where in due course their suffering and "dishonor" will "consume the impurity" from them (15–16). The polluting effect of idolatry and sexual misconduct is found elsewhere in Ezekiel (see 5:11, 20:7,18,31). The prophet's inclusion of moral and civil behavior in his judgment of impurity is also found in priestly sources (Num. 35:33–34). Nevertheless, Ezekiel's comprehensive emphasis is noteworthy, as is his view of the punishment of exile as purification through suffering. On this note of judgment (22:16) the *haftarah* concludes according to Sephardic tradition.

Askh'nazim traditionally add three more verses to conclude the *haftarah* with a message of hope (22:17–19). Ezekiel here extends the imagery of purification found in verse 15, offering the good news of restoration to the homeland. This message of the *haftarah* represents a remarkable and radical transformation of scripture by the Sages, for 22:17–22 constitutes an outright oracle of doom, in which God condemns Israel as "dross" and announces that He will gather them together in Jerusalem and melt them in the fire of His fury. The Sages, determining which verses would constitute the *haftarah,* decided to stop the prophecy of doom at verse 19. Their truncated passage gives the impression that God will transform the sinful dross of His people in exile, to restore them to Jerusalem in their new and purified state. It is this positive word that prevailed when rabbinic tradition radically transformed the teaching of God's

wrath. The prophecy of hope that concludes the *haftarah* is thus a revelation of Jewish hope and its triumph over despair—even against the divine dooms of scripture.

RELATION OF THE *HAFTARAH* TO THE *PARASHAH*

This *haftarah* stresses cultic and moral sins, many of which are directly connected to laws found in both *parashiyyot.* There is a clear link to the sexual prohibitions of Lev. 18 (*Aḥarei Mot*) and Lev. 20 (*K'doshim*). The prophet's diatribe also echoes passages found in Lev. 19 (*K'doshim*), including detailed similarities such as the profanation of *Shabbat* (Lev. 19:3; Ezek. 22:8), the economic oppression of compatriots (Lev. 19:13; Ezek. 22:12), and base activities leading to bloodshed (Lev. 19:16; Ezek. 22:9).

The instruction in *Aḥarei Mot,* stressing the point that observing the laws of the Covenant is something one lives in and through (Lev. 18:5), raises living by the laws of the Torah into a spiritual principle. This *haftarah,* in contrast, teaches that immorality vitiates and perverts the life and spirit of the perpetrator and of the victim, by emphasizing the point that maltreatment of the poor and needy is an act of bloodshed.

By presenting sin as an act of defilement, both this *haftarah* and the two *parashiyyot* present the Covenant as a means of purity or sanctification, for the earth and for its inhabitants. In this way, all actions prescribed by the Covenant constitute a kind of priestly service, transforming the mere natural into acts of holiness and the mere human into spiritual life.

22 The word of the LORD came to me: 2Fur-
ther, O mortal, arraign, arraign the city of
bloodshed; declare to her all her abhorrent
deeds! 3Say: Thus said the Lord GOD: O city in
whose midst blood is shed, so that your hour
is approaching; within which fetishes are made,
so that you have become impure! 4You stand
guilty of the blood you have shed, defiled by the
fetishes you have made. You have brought on
your day; you have reached your year. Therefore
I will make you the mockery of the nations and
the scorn of all the lands. 5Both the near and
the far shall scorn you, O besmirched of name,
O laden with iniquity!
6Every one of the princes of Israel in your

כב וַיְהִי דְבַר־יְהוָה אֵלַי לֵאמֹר׃
2 וְאַתָּה בֶן־אָדָם הֲתִשְׁפֹּט הֲתִשְׁפֹּט
אֶת־עִיר הַדָּמִים וְהוֹדַעְתָּהּ אֵת כָּל־
תּוֹעֲבוֹתֶיהָ׃ 3 וְאָמַרְתָּ כֹּה אָמַר אֲדֹנָי
יְהוִה עִיר שֹׁפֶכֶת דָּם בְּתוֹכָהּ לָבוֹא עִתָּהּ
וְעָשְׂתָה גִלּוּלִים עָלֶיהָ לְטָמְאָה׃ 4 בְּדָמֵךְ
אֲשֶׁר־שָׁפַכְתְּ אָשַׁמְתְּ וּבְגִלּוּלַיִךְ אֲשֶׁר־
עָשִׂית טָמֵאת וַתַּקְרִיבִי יָמַיִךְ וַתָּבוֹא
עַד־שְׁנוֹתָיִךְ עַל־כֵּן נְתַתִּיךְ חֶרְפָּה לַגּוֹיִם
וְקַלָּסָה לְכָל־הָאֲרָצוֹת׃ 5 הַקְּרֹבוֹת
וְהָרְחֹקוֹת מִמֵּךְ יִתְקַלְּסוּ־בָךְ טְמֵאַת הַשֵּׁם
רַבַּת הַמְּהוּמָה׃
6 הִנֵּה נְשִׂיאֵי יִשְׂרָאֵל אִישׁ לִזְרֹעוֹ הָיוּ בָךְ

Ezekiel 22:2. arraign, arraign In Hebrew, this is literally a question: "Will you arraign?" A verb repeated at the outset of a prophetic speech (see also Ezek. 20:4) gives it emphatic force, yielding the meaning here: "Surely you will arraign!"

3. fetishes Hebrew: *gillulim,* meaning "idols." Abravanel suggests that this is a metaphor for "all the other sins" besides bloodshed that the people have committed.

become impure Ezekiel's priestly orientation transforms Israel's civil–legal crimes into ritual, polluting ones (cf. vv. 3–5,10,15). In this he was particularly indebted to older priestly traditions that treated illicit sexual relations with relatives as impurity (see Lev. 18:7–20,24–25). Ezekiel includes bloodshed and economic oppression in his list.

5. O besmirched of name Alternatively, this phrase is the derogatory epithet spoken against them by the surrounding gentiles (Rashi).

midst used his strength for the shedding of blood. [7]Fathers and mothers have been humiliated within you; strangers have been cheated in your midst; orphans and widows have been wronged within you. [8]You have despised My holy things and profaned My sabbaths.

[9]Base men in your midst were intent on shedding blood; in you they have eaten upon the mountains; and they have practiced depravity in your midst. [10]In you they have uncovered their fathers' nakedness; in you they have ravished women during their menstrual impurity. [11]They have committed abhorrent acts with other men's wives; in their depravity they have defiled their own daughters-in-law; in you they have ravished their own sisters, daughters of their fathers. [12]They have taken bribes within you to shed blood. You have taken advance and accrued interest; you have defrauded your countrymen to your profit. You have forgotten Me—declares the Lord God.

[13]Lo, I will strike My hands over the ill-gotten gains that you have amassed, and over the bloodshed that has been committed in your midst. [14]Will your courage endure, will your hands remain firm in the days when I deal with you? I the Lord have spoken and I will act. [15]I will scatter you among the nations and disperse you through the lands; I will consume the impurity out of you. [16]You shall be dishonored in the sight of nations, and you shall know that I am the Lord.

[17]The word of the Lord came to me: [18]O mortal, the House of Israel has become dross to Me; they are all copper, tin, iron, and lead. But in

לְמַ֥עַן שְׁפָךְ־דָּֽם׃ 7 אָ֤ב וָאֵם֙ הֵקַ֣לּוּ בָ֔ךְ
לַגֵּ֛ר עָשׂ֥וּ בַעֹ֖שֶׁק בְּתוֹכֵ֑ךְ יָת֥וֹם וְאַלְמָנָ֖ה
ה֥וֹנוּ בָֽךְ׃ 8 קָֽדָשַׁ֖י בָּזִ֑ית וְאֶת־שַׁבְּתֹתַ֖י
חִלָּֽלְתְּ׃
9 אַנְשֵׁ֥י רָכִ֛יל הָ֥יוּ בָ֖ךְ לְמַ֣עַן שְׁפָךְ־דָּ֑ם
וְאֶל־הֶֽהָרִים֙ אָ֣כְלוּ בָ֔ךְ זִמָּ֖ה עָשׂ֥וּ בְתוֹכֵֽךְ׃
10 עֶרְוַת־אָ֖ב גִּלָּה־בָ֑ךְ טְמֵאַ֥ת הַנִּדָּ֖ה עִנּוּ־
בָֽךְ׃ 11 וְאִ֣ישׁ ׀ אֶת־אֵ֣שֶׁת רֵעֵ֗הוּ עָשָׂה֙
תּֽוֹעֵבָ֔ה וְאִ֥ישׁ אֶת־כַּלָּת֖וֹ טִמֵּ֣א בְזִמָּ֑ה
וְאִ֛ישׁ אֶת־אֲחֹת֥וֹ בַת־אָבִ֖יו עִנָּה־בָֽךְ׃
12 שֹׁ֥חַד לָֽקְחוּ־בָ֖ךְ לְמַ֣עַן שְׁפָךְ־דָּ֑ם נֶ֧שֶׁךְ
וְתַרְבִּ֣ית לָקַ֗חַתְּ וַתְּבַצְּעִ֤י רֵעַ֙יִךְ֙ בַּעֹ֔שֶׁק
וְאֹתִ֣י שָׁכַ֔חַתְּ נְאֻ֖ם אֲדֹנָ֥י יְהוִֽה׃
13 וְהִנֵּה֙ הִכֵּ֣יתִי כַפִּ֔י אֶל־בִּצְעֵ֖ךְ אֲשֶׁ֣ר
עָשִׂ֑ית וְעַל־דָּמֵ֔ךְ אֲשֶׁ֥ר הָי֖וּ בְּתוֹכֵֽךְ׃
14 הֲיַעֲמֹ֤ד לִבֵּךְ֙ אִם־תֶּחֱזַ֣קְנָה יָדַ֔יִךְ לַיָּמִ֕ים
אֲשֶׁ֥ר אֲנִ֖י עֹשֶׂ֣ה אוֹתָ֑ךְ אֲנִ֥י יְהוָ֖ה דִּבַּ֥רְתִּי
וְעָשִֽׂיתִי׃ 15 וַהֲפִיצוֹתִ֤י אוֹתָךְ֙ בַּגּוֹיִ֔ם
וְזֵרִיתִ֖יךְ בָּאֲרָצ֑וֹת וַהֲתִמֹּתִ֥י טֻמְאָתֵ֖ךְ
מִמֵּֽךְ׃ 16 וְנִחַ֥לְתְּ בָּ֖ךְ לְעֵינֵ֣י גוֹיִ֑ם וְיָדַ֖עַתְּ
כִּֽי־אֲנִ֥י יְהוָֽה׃ פ

17 וַיְהִ֥י דְבַר־יְהוָ֖ה אֵלַ֥י לֵאמֹֽר׃ 18 בֶּן־אָדָ֕ם
הָיוּ־לִ֥י בֵֽית־יִשְׂרָאֵ֖ל לסוג לְסִ֑יג כֻּלָּ֞ם
נְ֠חֹשֶׁת וּבְדִ֨יל וּבַרְזֶ֤ל וְעוֹפֶ֙רֶת֙ בְּת֣וֹךְ כּ֔וּר

10–11. The prophet details various sexual offenses (incest, adultery, and cohabitation with a menstruating woman). In terms of both its technical vocabulary and its use of the third person, this legal cluster follows Lev. 20:10–18.

14. I the Lord have spoken and I will act Promise and fulfillment are linked. Alternatively, "I am *YHVH*; what I have spoken I will do!" (Greenberg).

16. you shall be dishonored Hebrew: *v'niḥalt bakh;* a term linked to ritual desecration (see v. 8, and Lev. 18:21, 19:8).

18. dross Hebrew: *sig,* meaning unclear. Possibly it refers to an alloy of lead and silver. In this

a crucible, the dross shall turn into silver. [19]Assuredly, thus said the Lord GOD: Because you have all become dross, I will gather you into Jerusalem.

סְגִ֖ים כֶּ֥סֶף הָיֽוּ׃ ס 19 לָכֵ֗ן כֹּ֤ה אָמַר֙ אֲדֹנָ֣י יְהֹוִ֔ה יַ֛עַן הֱי֥וֹת כֻּלְּכֶ֖ם לְסִגִ֑ים לָכֵן֙ הִנְנִ֣י קֹבֵ֣ץ אֶתְכֶ֔ם אֶל־תּ֖וֹךְ יְרוּשָׁלָֽ͏ִם׃

figurative expression, the people who are "dross" will be refined in fire as a punishment. (In reality, dross is the scum that forms on the surface of molten metal during the process of liquefying.) For Ezekiel, the melting fire is both a proving of the people's guilt and their punishment.

הפטרת קדשים

HAFTARAH FOR K'DOSHIM

EZEKIEL 20:2–20 (*S'fardim*)

The verses of this *haftarah* (from 591 B.C.E.) are part of a long sermonic retrospective on Israel's sinful past and present that concludes with prophecies of restoration.

God commands Ezekiel to call the people to account: "Arraign, arraign them" (v. 4). In Hebrew, this command is in the form of a double question—"Will you arraign them, will you arraign?"—which has the effect of an urgent direct request to "arraign" them. In calling them to account, the prophet is commanded to declare to them (literally, "make known" to them) the details of their sins as a people in the past (v. 4). To counterpoint this derogatory information, the prophet uses the same verb to indicate God's past favor in having made Himself "known" to the Israelites and to the Egyptians (vv. 5,9). As a further expression of beneficence, God also "made known" His law to the nation (v. 11) and even gave them the holy *Shabbat* so that they might "know" Him (vv. 12,20). By such linguistic emphasis Ezekiel drives home the point that Israel has been a historical ingrate and that the stress on their sins is appropriate because of their ongoing apostasy.

The prophet shows himself to be well versed in Torah traditions. For example, Ezekiel recalls the Israelite rebellion in the wilderness and God's subsequent decision not to "make an end of them" (*l'khallotam,* v. 13) so that His name would "not be profaned" (*heḥel*) among the nations (v. 14). This, too, recalls a passage in the Torah: The sin of the Golden Calf and God's initial statement that "I may destroy them" (*va-akhallem*) in the wilderness, although He subsequently relented owing to Moses' entreaty (*va-y'ḥal*) for forgiveness (Exod. 32:10–12). Significantly, Ezekiel does not refer to Moses' intervention here or to Moses' response to God's decision to destroy the people after their lack of faith in His ability to bring them to the Land. In his sermon, Ezekiel repeatedly and solely portrays mercy as a unilateral divine act.

Yet the people deserve punishment for their continuous sin and rebellion in the past, as pointed out in vv. 7–8 and 11–13. Ezekiel, in his closing exhortation, refers to a second divine appeal to the nation in the wilderness—urging a new generation to reject the ways of their ancestors and to observe God's laws and sanctify *Shabbat* (vv. 18–20). Here, again, the choice is between the defilement of idolatry and rebelliousness versus the sanctifying power of divine instruction.

This conclusion produces a new teaching. In its original setting, Ezek. 20:18–20 is but another exhortation, urging the people to obey the laws before presenting another account of their rebellion and sin. The ancient Sages decided not to include in this *haftarah* the people's negative response found in subsequent verses. With this decision they transformed Ezekiel's historical arraignment into a divine instruction for all generations, not limited to the people of biblical times. Thus Ezekiel's prophetic word is transformed from an old lawsuit into an ever-new summons to heed and obey the Covenant.

RELATION OF THE *HAFTARAH* TO THE *PARASHAH*

Like Moses, Ezekiel emphasizes the centrality of God's law and the divine sanctification of the people by and through it. At the outset of the *parashah,* Moses speaks for God in calling on the people to "be holy" and to "keep My sabbaths" (Lev. 19:2–3). Thereupon a pattern of behavior is specified as leading to holiness in God's sight. This theme recurs at the end of the *parashah,* when God instructs the people: "You shall faithfully observe My laws; I the LORD make you holy" (Lev. 20:8). Ezekiel, correspondingly, repeats God's instruction that the people "Follow My laws and be careful to observe My rules" (Ezek. 20:19, cf. v. 11). They are further told that "I gave them My

sabbaths to serve as a sign . . . that it is I the LORD who sanctify [the people]" (v. 12).

The *parashah* and the *haftarah* share another phrase that also underscores the blessed nature of the divine instruction and Ezekiel's knowledge of Torah traditions. This is the emphasis that God gave the people "My laws" and "My rules . . . by the pursuit of which a man shall live" (Lev. 18:5; Ezek. 20:11,19,21).

The phrase that associates life with following God's laws stresses that one will attain the blessings of earthly life by means of the laws. Generations of postbiblical readers, however, have understood the true reward of following God's laws to be in the spiritual life such piety engenders, be that in and through a life of sanctity in this world, or in a blissful afterlife (see Targ. and Ibn Ezra on Lev. 18:5, and MT Sacrilege 8:8).

20 2The word of the LORD came to me:
3O mortal, speak to the elders of Israel and
say to them: Thus said the Lord GOD: Have you
come to inquire of Me? As I live, I will not respond to your inquiry—declares the Lord GOD.
4Arraign, arraign them, O mortal! Declare to
them the abhorrent deeds of their fathers. 5Say
to them: Thus said the Lord GOD:
On the day that I chose Israel, I gave My oath
to the stock of the House of Jacob; when I made
Myself known to them in the land of Egypt, I
gave my oath to them. When I said, "I the LORD
am your God," 6that same day I swore to them
to take them out of the land of Egypt into a land
flowing with milk and honey, a land which I had
sought out for them, the fairest of all lands.
7I also said to them: Cast away, every one of
you, the detestable things that you are drawn
to, and do not defile yourselves with the fetishes
of Egypt—I the LORD am your God. 8But they
defied Me and refused to listen to Me. They did
not cast away the detestable things they were
drawn to, nor did they give up the fetishes of
Egypt. Then I resolved to pour out My fury

כ 2 וַיְהִי דְבַר־יְהוָה אֵלַי לֵאמֹר׃
3 בֶּן־אָדָם דַּבֵּר אֶת־זִקְנֵי יִשְׂרָאֵל וְאָמַרְתָּ
אֲלֵהֶם כֹּה אָמַר אֲדֹנָי יְהוִה הֲלִדְרֹשׁ אֹתִי
אַתֶּם בָּאִים חַי־אָנִי אִם־אִדָּרֵשׁ לָכֶם נְאֻם
אֲדֹנָי יְהוִה׃
4 הֲתִשְׁפֹּט אֹתָם הֲתִשְׁפּוֹט בֶּן־אָדָם אֶת־
תּוֹעֲבֹת אֲבוֹתָם הוֹדִיעֵם׃ 5 וְאָמַרְתָּ
אֲלֵיהֶם כֹּה־אָמַר אֲדֹנָי יְהוִה
בְּיוֹם בָּחֳרִי בְיִשְׂרָאֵל וָאֶשָּׂא יָדִי לְזֶרַע
בֵּית יַעֲקֹב וָאִוָּדַע לָהֶם בְּאֶרֶץ מִצְרָיִם
וָאֶשָּׂא יָדִי לָהֶם לֵאמֹר אֲנִי יְהוָה
אֱלֹהֵיכֶם׃ 6 בַּיּוֹם הַהוּא נָשָׂאתִי יָדִי לָהֶם
לְהוֹצִיאָם מֵאֶרֶץ מִצְרָיִם אֶל־אֶרֶץ אֲשֶׁר־
תַּרְתִּי לָהֶם זָבַת חָלָב וּדְבַשׁ צְבִי הִיא
לְכָל־הָאֲרָצוֹת׃
7 וָאֹמַר אֲלֵהֶם אִישׁ שִׁקּוּצֵי עֵינָיו הַשְׁלִיכוּ
וּבְגִלּוּלֵי מִצְרַיִם אַל־תִּטַּמָּאוּ אֲנִי יְהוָה
אֱלֹהֵיכֶם׃ 8 וַיַּמְרוּ־בִי וְלֹא אָבוּ לִשְׁמֹעַ אֵלַי
אִישׁ אֶת־שִׁקּוּצֵי עֵינֵיהֶם לֹא הִשְׁלִיכוּ
וְאֶת־גִּלּוּלֵי מִצְרַיִם לֹא עָזָבוּ וָאֹמַר לִשְׁפֹּךְ

Ezekiel 20:2–3. Ezekiel was approached by a delegation of elders who wanted an oracular consultation with God. The prophet thus acts as a medium ("and the word of the LORD came to me") who provides the divine response (vv. 3,31, cf. 14:3,7). This use of the verb "inquire" (*darash*) has roots in oracular functions (cf. Gen. 25:22), often performed by Israelite and foreign prophets (1 Sam. 9:9; 1 Kings 22:5–8; 2 Kings 1:3,6). It is also found in connection with Jeremiah, Ezekiel's contemporary (Jer. 21:2).

5–7. The references to divine self-revelation in Egypt and the divine oath to bring the people to the Promised Land are drawn directly from Exod. 6:2–8. In Ezekiel's discourse, however, the revelation is to all the people (not just to Moses), and the divine oath to redeem the people is given to the nation in Egypt (not only to the patriarchs).

upon them, to vent all My anger upon them
there, in the land of Egypt. 9But I acted for the
sake of My name, that it might not be profaned
in the sight of the nations among whom they
were. For it was before their eyes that I had made
Myself known to Israel to bring them out of the
land of Egypt.

10I brought them out of the land of Egypt and
I led them into the wilderness. 11I gave them My
laws and taught them My rules, by the pursuit
of which a man shall live. 12Moreover, I gave
them My sabbaths to serve as a sign between
Me and them, that they might know that it is
I the LORD who sanctify them. 13But the House
of Israel rebelled against Me in the wilderness;
they did not follow My laws and they rejected
My rules—by the pursuit of which a man shall
live—and they grossly desecrated My sabbaths.
Then I thought to pour out My fury upon them
in the wilderness and to make an end of them;
14but I acted for the sake of My name, that it
might not be profaned in the sight of the nations
before whose eyes I had led them out. 15How-
ever, I swore to them in the wilderness that I
would not bring them into the land flowing with
milk and honey, the fairest of all lands, which
I had assigned [to them], 16for they had rejected
My rules, disobeyed My laws, and desecrated
My sabbaths; their hearts followed after their
fetishes. 17But I had pity on them and did not
destroy them; I did not make an end of them
in the wilderness.

18I warned their children in the wilderness:
Do not follow the practices of your fathers, do

חֲמָתִי עֲלֵיהֶם לְכַלּוֹת אַפִּי בָּהֶם בְּתוֹךְ
אֶרֶץ מִצְרָיִם׃ 9 וָאַעַשׂ לְמַעַן שְׁמִי לְבִלְתִּי
הֵחֵל לְעֵינֵי הַגּוֹיִם אֲשֶׁר־הֵמָּה בְתוֹכָם
אֲשֶׁר נוֹדַעְתִּי אֲלֵיהֶם לְעֵינֵיהֶם לְהוֹצִיאָם
מֵאֶרֶץ מִצְרָיִם׃

10 וָאוֹצִיאֵם מֵאֶרֶץ מִצְרָיִם וָאֲבִאֵם אֶל־
הַמִּדְבָּר׃ 11 וָאֶתֵּן לָהֶם אֶת־חֻקּוֹתַי וְאֶת־
מִשְׁפָּטַי הוֹדַעְתִּי אוֹתָם אֲשֶׁר יַעֲשֶׂה
אוֹתָם הָאָדָם וָחַי בָּהֶם׃ 12 וְגַם אֶת־
שַׁבְּתוֹתַי נָתַתִּי לָהֶם לִהְיוֹת לְאוֹת בֵּינִי
וּבֵינֵיהֶם לָדַעַת כִּי אֲנִי יְהוָה מְקַדְּשָׁם׃
13 וַיַּמְרוּ־בִי בֵית־יִשְׂרָאֵל בַּמִּדְבָּר בְּחֻקּוֹתַי
לֹא־הָלָכוּ וְאֶת־מִשְׁפָּטַי מָאָסוּ אֲשֶׁר
יַעֲשֶׂה אֹתָם הָאָדָם וָחַי בָּהֶם וְאֶת־
שַׁבְּתֹתַי חִלְּלוּ מְאֹד וָאֹמַר לִשְׁפֹּךְ חֲמָתִי
עֲלֵיהֶם בַּמִּדְבָּר לְכַלּוֹתָם׃ 14 וָאֶעֱשֶׂה
לְמַעַן שְׁמִי לְבִלְתִּי הֵחֵל לְעֵינֵי הַגּוֹיִם
אֲשֶׁר הוֹצֵאתִים לְעֵינֵיהֶם׃ 15 וְגַם־אֲנִי
נָשָׂאתִי יָדִי לָהֶם בַּמִּדְבָּר לְבִלְתִּי הָבִיא
אוֹתָם אֶל־הָאָרֶץ אֲשֶׁר־נָתַתִּי זָבַת חָלָב
וּדְבַשׁ צְבִי הִיא לְכָל־הָאֲרָצוֹת׃ 16 יַעַן
בְּמִשְׁפָּטַי מָאָסוּ וְאֶת־חֻקּוֹתַי לֹא־הָלְכוּ
בָהֶם וְאֶת־שַׁבְּתוֹתַי חִלֵּלוּ כִּי אַחֲרֵי
גִלּוּלֵיהֶם לִבָּם הֹלֵךְ׃ 17 וַתָּחָס עֵינִי
עֲלֵיהֶם מִשַּׁחֲתָם וְלֹא־עָשִׂיתִי אוֹתָם כָּלָה
בַּמִּדְבָּר׃

18 וָאֹמַר אֶל־בְּנֵיהֶם בַּמִּדְבָּר בְּחוּקֵּי
אֲבוֹתֵיכֶם אַל־תֵּלֵכוּ וְאֶת־מִשְׁפְּטֵיהֶם

Moreover, the references to Israelite idolatry in Egypt and to a divine warning to desist are traditions virtually unique to Ezekiel.

9. I acted for the sake of My name This motivation for divine restraint is that the name of God not be profaned among the nations (see also vv. 14,22). It has a parallel in Moses' intercessory appeal to God's self-interest in Exod. 32:11–13.

12. I gave them My sabbaths *Shabbat* is repeatedly singled out among the covenantal laws (see also vv. 16,20,21,24). This emphasis is a characteristic of late, postexilic biblical literature (see Isa. 56:2–6). Desecration of *Shabbat* came to be regarded as the archetypal sin that caused the exile (Neh. 13:18; cf. Jer. 17:19–27).

it is I the LORD who sanctify them The idea that *Shabbat* is a sign between God and Israel, so that the people may know that the Lord sanctifies them, is derived from Exod. 31:13.

not keep their ways, and do not defile yourselves
with their fetishes. 19I the LORD am your God:
Follow My laws and be careful to observe My
rules. 20And hallow My sabbaths, that they may
be a sign between Me and you, that you may
know that I the LORD am your God.

אַל־תִּשְׁמֹ֑רוּ וּבְגִלּוּלֵיהֶ֖ם אַל־תִּטַּמָּֽאוּ׃
19 אֲנִי֙ יְהוָ֣ה אֱלֹהֵיכֶ֔ם בְּחֻקּוֹתַ֖י לֵ֑כוּ וְאֶת־
מִשְׁפָּטַ֥י שִׁמְר֖וּ וַעֲשׂ֥וּ אוֹתָֽם׃ 20 וְאֶת־
שַׁבְּתוֹתַ֖י קַדֵּ֑שׁוּ וְהָי֤וּ לְאוֹת֙ בֵּינִ֣י וּבֵֽינֵיכֶ֔ם
לָדַ֕עַת כִּ֛י אֲנִ֥י יְהוָ֖ה אֱלֹהֵיכֶֽם׃

EMOR

21 The Lord said to Moses: Speak to the
priests, the sons of Aaron, and say to them:
None shall defile himself for any [dead] person among his kin, 2except for the relatives that
are closest to him: his mother, his father, his son,
his daughter, and his brother; 3also for a virgin
sister, close to him because she has not married,
for her he may defile himself. 4But he shall not
defile himself as a kinsman by marriage, and so
profane himself.

אמר

כא וַיֹּאמֶר יְהוָה אֶל־מֹשֶׁה אֱמֹר
אֶל־הַכֹּהֲנִים בְּנֵי אַהֲרֹן וְאָמַרְתָּ אֲלֵהֶם
לְנֶפֶשׁ לֹא־יִטַּמָּא בְּעַמָּיו׃ 2 כִּי אִם־לִשְׁאֵרוֹ
הַקָּרֹב אֵלָיו לְאִמּוֹ וּלְאָבִיו וְלִבְנוֹ וּלְבִתּוֹ
וּלְאָחִיו׃ 3 וְלַאֲחֹתוֹ הַבְּתוּלָה הַקְּרוֹבָה
אֵלָיו אֲשֶׁר לֹא־הָיְתָה לְאִישׁ לָהּ יִטַּמָּא׃
4 לֹא יִטַּמָּא בַּעַל בְּעַמָּיו לְהֵחַלּוֹ׃

The Pursuit of Holiness (*continued*)

LAWS GOVERNING THE PRIESTHOOD (21:1–22:33)

The laws of chapters 21 and 22 are directed specifically to the priesthood, not to the Israelite people as a whole.

RESTRICTIONS AND LIMITATIONS (21:1–24)

1–4. In these verses, the social context is the clan. An ordinary priest may not become defiled by contact with the dead of his clan, but he may be defiled for those members of his clan who are most closely related to him. Attending to the burial of clan relatives was a traditional duty.

a virgin sister, close to him because she has not married The sister is "close" until she marries and goes to live with her husband's family. After that, there are others who will attend to her burial.

a kinsman by marriage According to the

This *parashah* lives up to the book's alternative Hebrew title *Torat Kohanim,* the priests' manual. It focuses on special regulations of *kohanim* and then on the ritual aspects of the sacred calendar. The previous *parashah* describes the Israelites as being set apart from other nations, called on to attain holiness through their distinctive lifestyle. This *parashah* sets the *kohanim* apart from other Israelites by means of symbolic obligations, restrictions, and abstentions in their lives. As the Israelites are to represent the God-oriented life to the nations of the world, the *kohanim* are to represent a maximal level of devotion to God for their fellow Israelites. Every society needs a core of people who live by a more demanding code, to set an example for others of what is possible.

CHAPTER 21

1. the priests, the sons of Aaron Declare these rules to the *kohanim* because they are descendants of Aaron. Remind them that their distinctiveness is based on their forebears, not on their own merit. And let them pass on to their children the importance of that lineage and the obligation to be worthy of it (Hirsch). "Tell the *kohanim* to be sons of Aaron in deed and not only in descent, pursuers of peace and reconciliation as Aaron was" (Jacob Isaac of Lublin).

As public figures, the *kohanim* must be role models of dealing with grief and loss, balancing their personal sorrow with their commitment to serving the people and the obligation to accept death as part of God's plan for the world. A *kohen* may willingly acquire ritual impurity (*tum·ah*) by coming into contact with the dead body of a family member, for he owes his priestly status to his family of origin. He may not do so, however, for the corpse of a friend or for a relative by marriage.

HALAKHAH L'MA·ASEH

21:2. except for the relatives The Sages add that a *kohen* is required to defile himself for burying his deceased wife (BT Yev. 22b).

[5]They shall not shave smooth any part of their heads, or cut the side-growth of their beards, or make gashes in their flesh. [6]They shall be holy to their God and not profane the name of their God; for they offer the LORD's gifts, the food of their God, and so must be holy.

[7]They shall not marry a woman defiled by harlotry, nor shall they marry one divorced from her husband. For they are holy to their God [8]and you must treat them as holy, since they offer the food of your God; they shall be holy to you, for I the LORD who sanctify you am holy.

[9]When the daughter of a priest defiles herself through harlotry, it is her father whom she defiles; she shall be put to the fire.

[10]The priest who is exalted above his fellows, on whose head the anointing oil has been

5 לֹא־יקרחה יִקְרְחוּ קָרְחָה֙ בְּרֹאשָׁם וּפְאַת
זְקָנָם לֹא יְגַלֵּחוּ וּבִבְשָׂרָם לֹא יִשְׂרְטוּ
שָׂרָטֶת׃ 6 קְדֹשִׁים יִהְיוּ לֵאלֹהֵיהֶם וְלֹא
יְחַלְּלוּ שֵׁם אֱלֹהֵיהֶם כִּי אֶת־אִשֵּׁי יְהוָה
לֶחֶם אֱלֹהֵיהֶם הֵם מַקְרִיבִם וְהָיוּ קֹדֶשׁ׃
7 אִשָּׁה זֹנָה וַחֲלָלָה לֹא יִקָּחוּ וְאִשָּׁה
גְּרוּשָׁה מֵאִישָׁהּ לֹא יִקָּחוּ כִּי־קָדֹשׁ הוּא
לֵאלֹהָיו׃ 8 וְקִדַּשְׁתּוֹ כִּי־אֶת־לֶחֶם אֱלֹהֶיךָ
הוּא מַקְרִיב קָדֹשׁ יִהְיֶה־לָּךְ כִּי קָדוֹשׁ אֲנִי
יְהוָה מְקַדִּשְׁכֶם׃
9 וּבַת אִישׁ כֹּהֵן כִּי תֵחֵל לִזְנוֹת אֶת־אָבִיהָ
הִיא מְחַלֶּלֶת בָּאֵשׁ תִּשָּׂרֵף׃ ס
10 וְהַכֹּהֵן הַגָּדוֹל מֵאֶחָיו אֲשֶׁר־יוּצַק
עַל־רֹאשׁוֹ ׀ שֶׁמֶן הַמִּשְׁחָה וּמִלֵּא אֶת־יָדוֹ

Torah, a priest is not permitted to attend to the burial of his wife. (Although she is related to him through marriage, she is not his blood relative. Rabbinic law, however, permits this.)

5. They shall not shave smooth Shaving the hair and pulling it out were rites of mourning in ancient Canaan that the Torah and its followers sought to prevent.

6. the food of their God Offerings to God, often called "food" (*leḥem*), are considered food for God in a symbolic sense.

7. defiled by harlotry According to Rabbinic interpretation, the Hebrew term for "harlot" (*zonah*) refers to a woman habitually given to harlotry not to one who may have lapsed on a particular occasion.

9. The behavior of a priest's daughter reflects on her father's sacred office. Death by fire indicates the seriousness of the offense.

10. The priest who is exalted above his fellows This is the full title of the High Priest, whose distinction derives from the facts that he is the only priest to be anointed with the sacred oil and that he wears unique vestments.

---

8. you must treat them as holy Rabbis and cantors are no different from other Jews. They have no special powers; no obligations devolve on them that do not apply to all Jews. "Ten shoemakers can make a *minyan* but nine rabbis can't." Nonetheless, they are considered *k'lei kodesh*—"instruments of holiness"—because, through their knowledge and teaching and by life, character, and commitments they show the way to a life of holiness.

9. When the daughter of a priest defiles herself To mitigate the severity of this law, the Sages made it apply only to a married daughter who had committed adultery.

HALAKHAH L'MA·ASEH

21:6. be holy . . . not profane Beyond the specifics of Jewish law, we are obligated to act in a way that reflects well on God, the Jewish people, and our traditions (*kiddush ha-Shem*) and to refrain from acting in a way that would bring dishonor to God, our people, and its traditions (*ḥillul ha-Shem*) (MT Foundations of the Torah 5:1,10–11).

21:7. nor shall they marry one divorced Traditional Jewish law prohibits a *kohen* from marrying a divorcée or a convert (S.A. E.H. 6:1). Nevertheless, if such a marriage took place, the marriage is considered valid and the children are legitimate, although they do not inherit their father's priestly status. Because we no longer consider divorced women as impaired, CJLS has ruled to allow such marriages ab initio without any loss of priestly status for the man or his children.

poured and who has been ordained to wear the
vestments, shall not bare his head or rend his
vestments. 11He shall not go in where there is
any dead body; he shall not defile himself even
for his father or mother. 12He shall not go outside the sanctuary and profane the sanctuary of
his God, for upon him is the distinction of the
anointing oil of his God, Mine the LORD's. 13He
may marry only a woman who is a virgin. 14A
widow, or a divorced woman, or one who is degraded by harlotry—such he may not marry.
Only a virgin of his own kin may he take to
wife—15that he may not profane his offspring
among his kin, for I the LORD have sanctified
him.

16The LORD spoke further to Moses: 17Speak
to Aaron and say: No man of your offspring
throughout the ages who has a defect shall be
qualified to offer the food of his God. 18No one
at all who has a defect shall be qualified: no man
who is blind, or lame, or has a limb too short

לִלְבֹּ֣שׁ אֶת־הַבְּגָדִ֔ים אֶת־רֹאשׁוֹ֙ לֹ֣א יִפְרָ֔ע
וּבְגָדָ֖יו לֹ֥א יִפְרֹֽם׃ 11 וְעַ֛ל כָּל־נַפְשֹׁ֥ת מֵ֖ת
לֹ֣א יָבֹ֑א לְאָבִ֥יו וּלְאִמּ֖וֹ לֹ֥א יִטַּמָּֽא׃ 12 וּמִן־
הַמִּקְדָּשׁ֙ לֹ֣א יֵצֵ֔א וְלֹ֣א יְחַלֵּ֔ל אֵ֖ת מִקְדַּ֣שׁ
אֱלֹהָ֑יו כִּ֡י נֵ֠זֶר שֶׁ֣מֶן מִשְׁחַ֧ת אֱלֹהָ֛יו עָלָ֖יו
אֲנִ֥י יְהוָֽה׃ 13 וְה֕וּא אִשָּׁ֥ה בִבְתוּלֶ֖יהָ יִקָּֽח׃
14 אַלְמָנָ֤ה וּגְרוּשָׁה֙ וַחֲלָלָ֣ה זֹנָ֔ה אֶת־אֵ֖לֶּה
לֹ֣א יִקָּ֑ח כִּ֛י אִם־בְּתוּלָ֥ה מֵעַמָּ֖יו יִקַּ֥ח
אִשָּֽׁה׃ 15 וְלֹֽא־יְחַלֵּ֥ל זַרְע֖וֹ בְּעַמָּ֑יו כִּ֛י אֲנִ֥י
יְהוָ֖ה מְקַדְּשֽׁוֹ׃ פ
שני 16 וַיְדַבֵּ֥ר יְהוָ֖ה אֶל־מֹשֶׁ֥ה לֵּאמֹֽר׃ 17 דַּבֵּ֥ר
אֶל־אַהֲרֹ֖ן לֵאמֹ֑ר אִ֣ישׁ מִֽזַּרְעֲךָ֞ לְדֹרֹתָ֗ם
אֲשֶׁ֨ר יִהְיֶ֥ה ב֙וֹ מ֔וּם לֹ֣א יִקְרַ֔ב לְהַקְרִ֖יב
לֶ֥חֶם אֱלֹהָֽיו׃ 18 כִּ֥י כָל־אִ֛ישׁ אֲשֶׁר־בּ֥וֹ מ֖וּם
לֹ֣א יִקְרָ֑ב אִ֤ישׁ עִוֵּר֙ א֣וֹ פִסֵּ֔חַ א֥וֹ חָרֻ֖ם א֥וֹ

shall not bare his head or rend his vestments These are practices associated with mourning.

11. He shall not go in where there is any dead body Or, "He shall not enter [anywhere] on account of a dead body," namely, to attend to a dead body.

he shall not defile himself even for his father or mother The Hebrew word order is inverted for emphasis: "Even for his father or mother he shall not defile himself."

12. He shall not go outside the sanctuary The High Priest may not leave the sanctuary even for the purpose of attending to the burial of close relatives, including his own parents. He could never purify himself so completely as to avoid the danger of contaminating the Holy of Holies.

13–14. Only the High Priest must marry a virgin from a priestly family. If he were to marry outside the priestly kinship, his offspring would be unfit to serve as priests.

17. Priests who are physically unsound are deprived only of the right to officiate in the sacrificial system. They are still entitled to receive their various gratuities, because it is through no fault of their own that they suffer from such defects.

17–23. The reader may be troubled by these rules disqualifying physically handicapped *kohanim* from officiating in public. Perhaps their disfigurements would distract the worshipers from concentrating on the ritual and, like the offering of the blemished animal, would compromise the sanctuary's image as a place of perfection reflecting God's perfection (cf. Lev. 22:21–25, where similar language is used for the animals brought to the altar). In later texts, in the Psalms and the prophets, the Bible emphasizes that the broken in body and spirit, because they have been cured of the sin of arrogance, are specially welcome before God. "True sacrifice to God is a contrite spirit; / God, You will not despise / a contrite and crushed heart" (Ps. 51:19).

Today we might well consider the religious institution that is willing to admit its own imperfections and is willing to engage physically handicapped spiritual leaders as being better able to welcome worshipers who are painfully aware of their own physical or emotional imperfections. Many congregations have made special efforts to provide access for the handicapped.

or too long; 19no man who has a broken leg or
a broken arm; 20or who is a hunchback, or a
dwarf, or who has a growth in his eye, or who
has a boil-scar, or scurvy, or crushed testes. 21No
man among the offspring of Aaron the priest
who has a defect shall be qualified to offer the
LORD's gift; having a defect, he shall not be
qualified to offer the food of his God. 22He may
eat of the food of his God, of the most holy as
well as of the holy; 23but he shall not enter behind the curtain or come near the altar, for he
has a defect. He shall not profane these places
sacred to Me, for I the LORD have sanctified
them.

24Thus Moses spoke to Aaron and his sons
and to all the Israelites.

שָׂרֽוּעַ׃ 19 א֣וֹ אִ֔ישׁ אֲשֶׁר־יִהְיֶ֥ה ב֖וֹ שֶׁ֣בֶר
רָ֑גֶל א֖וֹ שֶׁ֥בֶר יָֽד׃ 20 אֽוֹ־גִבֵּ֣ן אוֹ־דַ֔ק א֖וֹ
תְּבַלֻּ֣ל בְּעֵינ֑וֹ א֤וֹ גָרָב֙ א֣וֹ יַלֶּ֔פֶת א֖וֹ מְר֥וֹחַ
אָֽשֶׁךְ׃ 21 כָּל־אִ֞ישׁ אֲשֶׁר־בּ֣וֹ מ֗וּם מִזֶּ֙רַע֙
אַהֲרֹ֣ן הַכֹּהֵ֔ן לֹ֣א יִגַּ֔שׁ לְהַקְרִ֖יב אֶת־אִשֵּׁ֣י
יְהוָ֑ה מ֣וּם בּ֔וֹ אֵ֚ת לֶ֣חֶם אֱלֹהָ֔יו לֹ֥א
יִגַּ֖שׁ לְהַקְרִֽיב׃ 22 לֶ֣חֶם אֱלֹהָ֔יו מִקָּדְשֵׁ֖י
הַקֳּדָשִׁ֑ים וּמִן־הַקֳּדָשִׁ֖ים יֹאכֵֽל׃ 23 אַ֣ךְ אֶל־
הַפָּרֹ֜כֶת לֹ֣א יָבֹ֗א וְאֶל־הַמִּזְבֵּ֛חַ לֹ֥א יִגַּ֖שׁ
כִּי־מ֣וּם בּ֑וֹ וְלֹ֤א יְחַלֵּל֙ אֶת־מִקְדָּשַׁ֔י כִּ֛י אֲנִ֥י
יְהוָ֖ה מְקַדְּשָֽׁם׃
24 וַיְדַבֵּ֣ר מֹשֶׁ֔ה אֶֽל־אַהֲרֹ֖ן וְאֶל־בָּנָ֑יו וְאֶל־
כָּל־בְּנֵ֖י יִשְׂרָאֵֽל׃ פ

22 The LORD spoke to Moses, saying: 2In-
struct Aaron and his sons to be scrupulous
about the sacred donations that the Israelite
people consecrate to Me, lest they profane My
holy name, Mine the LORD's. 3Say to them:

Throughout the ages, if any man among your
offspring, while in a state of impurity, partakes
of any sacred donation that the Israelite people
may consecrate to the LORD, that person shall
be cut off from before Me: I am the LORD. 4No
man of Aaron's offspring who has an eruption
or a discharge shall eat of the sacred donations

כב וַיְדַבֵּ֥ר יְהוָ֖ה אֶל־מֹשֶׁ֥ה לֵּאמֹֽר׃
2 דַּבֵּ֨ר אֶֽל־אַהֲרֹ֜ן וְאֶל־בָּנָ֗יו וְיִנָּֽזְרוּ֙ מִקָּדְשֵׁ֣י
בְנֵֽי־יִשְׂרָאֵ֔ל וְלֹ֥א יְחַלְּל֖וּ אֶת־שֵׁ֣ם קָדְשִׁ֑י
אֲשֶׁ֨ר הֵ֧ם מַקְדִּשִׁ֛ים לִ֖י אֲנִ֥י יְהוָֽה׃ 3 אֱמֹ֣ר
אֲלֵהֶ֗ם
לְדֹרֹתֵיכֶ֞ם כָּל־אִ֣ישׁ ׀ אֲשֶׁר־יִקְרַ֣ב מִכָּל־
זַרְעֲכֶ֗ם אֶל־הַקֳּדָשִׁים֙ אֲשֶׁ֨ר יַקְדִּ֤ישׁוּ בְנֵֽי־
יִשְׂרָאֵל֙ לַֽיהוָ֔ה וְטֻמְאָת֖וֹ עָלָ֑יו וְנִכְרְתָ֞ה
הַנֶּ֧פֶשׁ הַהִ֛וא מִלְּפָנַ֖י אֲנִ֥י יְהוָֽה׃ 4 אִ֨ישׁ
אִ֜ישׁ מִזֶּ֣רַע אַהֲרֹ֗ן וְה֤וּא צָר֙וּעַ֙ א֣וֹ זָ֔ב

19. Normally, such injuries would be permanent because broken limbs were not set properly in ancient times.

22. A physically defective priest was forbidden to officiate but was not denied his benefits.

24. In stating that these laws are addressed to all the Israelites, the spirit of inclusiveness so characteristic of the Holiness Code is retained, even though this chapter deals with matters of specific concern to the priesthood.

SACRED DONATIONS (22:1–33)

2. Aaron and his sons must separate themselves from the sacrifices at certain necessary times. The verses that follow provide the details of what such avoidance entails.

3. partakes of any sacred donation Impure priests are not allowed to partake of the consecrated offerings lest they defile them.

that person shall be cut off Normally, the phrase refers to being cut off from one's kin or people. Here, the idea is that God directly objects to the nearness of impure priests and does not wish them to stand in His presence.

I am the LORD This refrain in the Holiness Code often concludes a section of laws or commandments.

4. The final purification of an afflicted priest occurs only after sacrifices are offered on the eighth day.

until he is pure. If one touches anything made impure by a corpse, or if a man has an emission of semen, 5or if a man touches any swarming thing by which he is made impure or any human being by whom he is made impure—whatever his impurity—6the person who touches such shall be impure until evening and shall not eat of the sacred donations unless he has washed his body in water. 7As soon as the sun sets, he shall be pure; and afterward he may eat of the sacred donations, for they are his food. 8He shall not eat anything that died or was torn by beasts, thereby becoming impure: I am the LORD. 9They shall keep My charge, lest they incur guilt thereby and die for it, having committed profanation: I the LORD consecrate them.

10No lay person shall eat of the sacred donations. No bound or hired laborer of a priest shall eat of the sacred donations; 11but a person who is a priest's property by purchase may eat of them; and those that are born into his household may eat of his food. 12If a priest's daughter marries a layman, she may not eat of the sacred gifts; 13but if the priest's daughter is widowed or divorced and without offspring, and is back

בַּקֳּדָשִׁים֙ לֹ֣א יֹאכַ֔ל עַ֖ד אֲשֶׁ֣ר יִטְהָ֑ר וְהַנֹּגֵ֙עַ֙ בְּכָל־טְמֵא־נֶ֔פֶשׁ א֣וֹ אִ֔ישׁ אֲשֶׁר־תֵּצֵ֥א מִמֶּ֖נּוּ שִׁכְבַת־זָֽרַע׃ 5 אוֹ־אִ֗ישׁ אֲשֶׁ֤ר יִגַּע֙ בְּכָל־שֶׁ֙רֶץ֙ אֲשֶׁ֣ר יִטְמָא־ל֔וֹ א֤וֹ בְאָדָם֙ אֲשֶׁ֣ר יִטְמָא־ל֔וֹ לְכֹ֖ל טֻמְאָתֽוֹ׃ 6 נֶ֚פֶשׁ אֲשֶׁ֣ר תִּגַּע־בּ֔וֹ וְטָמְאָ֖ה עַד־הָעָ֑רֶב וְלֹ֤א יֹאכַל֙ מִן־הַקֳּדָשִׁ֔ים כִּ֛י אִם־רָחַ֥ץ בְּשָׂר֖וֹ בַּמָּֽיִם׃ 7 וּבָ֣א הַשֶּׁ֔מֶשׁ וְטָהֵ֑ר וְאַחַר֙ יֹאכַ֣ל מִן־הַקֳּדָשִׁ֔ים כִּ֥י לַחְמ֖וֹ הֽוּא׃ 8 נְבֵלָ֧ה וּטְרֵפָ֛ה לֹ֥א יֹאכַ֖ל לְטׇמְאָה־בָ֑הּ אֲנִ֖י יְהֹוָֽה׃ 9 וְשָׁמְר֣וּ אֶת־מִשְׁמַרְתִּ֗י וְלֹֽא־יִשְׂא֤וּ עָלָיו֙ חֵ֔טְא וּמֵ֥תוּ ב֖וֹ כִּ֣י יְחַלְּלֻ֑הוּ אֲנִ֥י יְהֹוָ֖ה מְקַדְּשָֽׁם׃ 10 וְכָל־זָ֖ר לֹא־יֹ֣אכַל קֹ֑דֶשׁ תּוֹשַׁ֥ב כֹּהֵ֛ן וְשָׂכִ֖יר לֹא־יֹ֥אכַל קֹֽדֶשׁ׃ 11 וְכֹהֵ֗ן כִּֽי־יִקְנֶ֥ה נֶ֙פֶשׁ֙ קִנְיַ֣ן כַּסְפּ֔וֹ ה֖וּא יֹ֣אכַל בּ֑וֹ וִילִ֣יד בֵּית֔וֹ הֵ֖ם יֹאכְל֥וּ בְלַחְמֽוֹ׃ 12 וּבַת־כֹּהֵ֔ן כִּ֥י תִהְיֶ֖ה לְאִ֣ישׁ זָ֑ר הִ֕וא בִּתְרוּמַ֥ת הַקֳּדָשִׁ֖ים לֹ֥א תֹאכֵֽל׃ 13 וּבַת־כֹּהֵן֩ כִּ֨י תִהְיֶ֜ה אַלְמָנָ֣ה וּגְרוּשָׁ֗ה וְזֶ֘רַע֮ אֵ֣ין לָהּ֒ וְשָׁבָה֙ אֶל־בֵּ֣ית

5. This law concerns a person, in this case a priest, who touches another person who is in a state of impurity for any of a variety of reasons.

6. A priest who touches people or vessels that are impure but who was not initially impure himself, needs only to bathe and wait until after sunset to be restored to a pure state.

7. As soon as the sun sets Literally, "the sun having entered." In ancient cosmology, at twilight the sun "enters" its house of the night and begins its underground journey to the east.

for they are his food It would be unfair to deprive priests of their daily bread any longer than absolutely necessary. The priests' partaking of sacrifices was considered indispensable to the efficacy of those offerings.

8. This prohibition is extended to apply to all Israelites in Deut. 14:21.

10. lay person Hebrew: *zar*, which has the basic sense of "outsider, stranger."

bound . . . laborer Hebrew: *toshav* (resident), which may refer to foreign residents as well. The *toshav* of a priest was not his property, but like an indentured servant.

hired laborer An employee, not a slave.

11. These are non-Israelites.

12. A priest's daughter derives the privilege of partaking of the priests' food from her father, who is responsible for her care as long as she resides in his home. If she marries outside the priesthood, she forfeits this privilege.

HALAKHAH L'MA·ASEH
22:12. a priest's daughter marries a layman Matrilineal descent transmits Jewish status, but one's tribal identity (*kohen*, *levi*, or *yisra·el*) is determined through the father. The CJLS has ruled that in those egalitarian congregations that call a *kohen* for the first *aliyah* to the Torah, the daughter of a priest may receive the *kohen*'s *aliyah* even if her husband is not a *kohen*. However, children born of that union inherit the tribal identity of their father. See Comment to Num. 6:23.

in her father's house as in her youth, she may eat of her father's food. No lay person may eat of it: [14]but if a man eats of a sacred donation unwittingly, he shall pay the priest for the sacred donation, adding one-fifth of its value. [15]But [the priests] must not allow the Israelites to profane the sacred donations that they set aside for the LORD, [16]or to incur guilt requiring a penalty payment, by eating such sacred donations: for it is I the LORD who make them sacred.

[17]The LORD spoke to Moses, saying: [18]Speak to Aaron and his sons, and to all the Israelite people, and say to them:

When any man of the house of Israel or of the strangers in Israel presents a burnt offering as his offering for any of the votive or any of the freewill offerings that they offer to the LORD, [19]it must, to be acceptable in your favor, be a male without blemish, from cattle or sheep or goats. [20]You shall not offer any that has a defect, for it will not be accepted in your favor.

[21]And when a man offers, from the herd or the flock, a sacrifice of well-being to the LORD for an explicit vow or as a freewill offering, it

אָבִיהָ כִּנְעוּרֶיהָ מִלֶּחֶם אָבִיהָ תֹּאכֵל
וְכָל־זָר לֹא־יֹאכַל בּוֹ׃ ס 14 וְאִישׁ כִּי־
יֹאכַל קֹדֶשׁ בִּשְׁגָגָה וְיָסַף חֲמִשִׁיתוֹ עָלָיו
וְנָתַן לַכֹּהֵן אֶת־הַקֹּדֶשׁ׃ 15 וְלֹא יְחַלְּלוּ
אֶת־קָדְשֵׁי בְּנֵי יִשְׂרָאֵל אֵת אֲשֶׁר־יָרִימוּ
לַיהוָה׃ 16 וְהִשִּׂיאוּ אוֹתָם עֲוֺן אַשְׁמָה
בְּאָכְלָם אֶת־קָדְשֵׁיהֶם כִּי אֲנִי יְהוָה
מְקַדְּשָׁם׃ פ
שלישי 17 וַיְדַבֵּר יְהוָה אֶל־מֹשֶׁה לֵּאמֹר׃ 18 דַּבֵּר
אֶל־אַהֲרֹן וְאֶל־בָּנָיו וְאֶל כָּל־בְּנֵי יִשְׂרָאֵל
וְאָמַרְתָּ אֲלֵהֶם
אִישׁ אִישׁ מִבֵּית יִשְׂרָאֵל וּמִן־הַגֵּר
בְּיִשְׂרָאֵל אֲשֶׁר יַקְרִיב קָרְבָּנוֹ לְכָל־נִדְרֵיהֶם
וּלְכָל־נִדְבוֹתָם אֲשֶׁר־יַקְרִיבוּ לַיהוָה
לְעֹלָה׃ 19 לִרְצֹנְכֶם תָּמִים זָכָר בַּבָּקָר
בַּכְּשָׂבִים וּבָעִזִּים׃ 20 כֹּל אֲשֶׁר־בּוֹ מוּם לֹא
תַקְרִיבוּ כִּי־לֹא לְרָצוֹן יִהְיֶה לָכֶם׃
21 וְאִישׁ כִּי־יַקְרִיב זֶבַח־שְׁלָמִים לַיהוָה
לְפַלֵּא־נֶדֶר אוֹ לִנְדָבָה בַּבָּקָר אוֹ בַצֹּאן

14. he shall pay the priest for the sacred donation The entire payment, including the penalty of one fifth of the estimated value of the misappropriated property, is referred to as "the sacred donation" (*ha-kodesh*). Once remitted, it all became the property of the priest.

15. As the ones responsible for maintaining proper storage and accurate accounting procedures, the priests were to police themselves to prevent priests who might be so tempted from dealing in sacred donations to their own advantage.

16. who make them sacred "Them" can refer either to the priests or to the donations.

18. of the strangers in Israel Non-Israelites also donated sacrificial offerings to the God of Israel. In the ancient Near East, it was customary to pay respect to the deity of the host country.

a burnt offering as his offering for any of the votive or any of the freewill offerings The burnt offering (*olah*), the mainstay of the sacrificial system, also served as an individual sacrifice, often brought as a votive, or freewill, offering.

CHAPTER 22

18. of the strangers Non-Israelites living among the Israelites will be motivated to worship the God of Israel, and their offerings will be welcome. Solomon prayed at the dedication of the temple in Jerusalem: "Or if a foreigner who is not of Your people . . . shall hear about Your great name and . . . comes to pray toward this House, oh, hear in Your heavenly abode. . . . Thus all the peoples of the earth will know Your name and revere You, as does Your people Israel" (1 Kings 8:41–43).

19. We are to offer God our best, not because God's vanity requires it but because that reflects our attitude toward God and toward the offering we bring. Even if the blemished animal is larger and more valuable, it is not acceptable (Sforno). God looks for wholeness rather than monetary worth.

must, to be acceptable, be without blemish; there must be no defect in it. 22Anything blind, or injured, or maimed, or with a wen, boil-scar, or scurvy—such you shall not offer to the LORD; you shall not put any of them on the altar as gifts to the LORD. 23You may, however, present as a freewill offering an ox or a sheep with a limb extended or contracted; but it will not be accepted for a vow. 24You shall not offer to the LORD anything [with its testes] bruised or crushed or torn or cut. You shall have no such practices in your own land, 25nor shall you accept such [animals] from a foreigner for offering as food for your God, for they are mutilated, they have a defect; they shall not be accepted in your favor.

26The LORD spoke to Moses, saying: 27When an ox or a sheep or a goat is born, it shall stay seven days with its mother, and from the eighth day on it shall be acceptable as a gift to the LORD. 28However, no animal from the herd or from the flock shall be slaughtered on the same day with its young.

29When you sacrifice a thanksgiving offering to the LORD, sacrifice it so that it may be acceptable in your favor. 30It shall be eaten on the same day; you shall not leave any of it until morning: I am the LORD.

31You shall faithfully observe My command-

תָּמִ֤ים יִהְיֶה֙ לְרָצ֔וֹן כָּל־מ֖וּם לֹ֥א יִֽהְיֶה־בּֽוֹ׃
22 עַוֶּרֶת֩ א֨וֹ שָׁב֜וּר אֽוֹ־חָר֣וּץ אֽוֹ־יַבֶּ֗לֶת א֤וֹ
גָרָב֙ א֣וֹ יַלֶּ֔פֶת לֹא־תַקְרִ֥יבוּ אֵ֖לֶּה לַיהוָ֑ה
וְאִשֶּׁ֗ה לֹא־תִתְּנ֥וּ מֵהֶ֛ם עַל־הַמִּזְבֵּ֖חַ
לַיהוָֽה׃ 23 וְשׁ֣וֹר וָשֶׂ֔ה שָׂר֖וּעַ וְקָל֑וּט נְדָבָה֙
תַּעֲשֶׂ֣ה אֹת֔וֹ וּלְנֵ֖דֶר לֹ֥א יֵרָצֶֽה׃ 24 וּמָע֤וּךְ
וְכָתוּת֙ וְנָת֣וּק וְכָר֔וּת לֹ֥א תַקְרִ֖יבוּ לַיהוָ֑ה
וּבְאַרְצְכֶ֖ם לֹ֥א תַעֲשֽׂוּ׃ 25 וּמִיַּ֣ד בֶּן־נֵכָ֗ר לֹ֥א
תַקְרִ֛יבוּ אֶת־לֶ֥חֶם אֱלֹהֵיכֶ֖ם מִכָּל־אֵ֑לֶּה
כִּ֣י מָשְׁחָתָ֤ם בָּהֶם֙ מ֣וּם בָּ֔ם לֹ֥א יֵרָצ֖וּ
לָכֶֽם׃ פ
26 וַיְדַבֵּ֥ר יְהוָ֖ה אֶל־מֹשֶׁ֥ה לֵּאמֹֽר׃ 27 שׁ֣וֹר
אוֹ־כֶ֤שֶׂב אוֹ־עֵז֙ כִּ֣י יִוָּלֵ֔ד וְהָיָ֛ה שִׁבְעַ֥ת
יָמִ֖ים תַּ֣חַת אִמּ֑וֹ וּמִיּ֤וֹם הַשְּׁמִינִי֙ וָהָ֔לְאָה
יֵרָצֶ֕ה לְקָרְבַּ֥ן אִשֶּׁ֖ה לַיהוָֽה׃ 28 וְשׁ֖וֹר אוֹ־
שֶׂ֑ה אֹת֣וֹ וְאֶת־בְּנ֔וֹ לֹ֥א תִשְׁחֲט֖וּ בְּי֥וֹם
אֶחָֽד׃
29 וְכִֽי־תִזְבְּח֥וּ זֶֽבַח־תּוֹדָ֖ה לַיהוָ֑ה לִֽרְצֹנְכֶ֖ם
תִּזְבָּֽחוּ׃ 30 בַּיּ֤וֹם הַהוּא֙ יֵאָכֵ֔ל לֹא־תוֹתִ֥ירוּ
מִמֶּ֖נּוּ עַד־בֹּ֑קֶר אֲנִ֖י יְהוָֽה׃
31 וּשְׁמַרְתֶּם֙ מִצְוֺתַ֔י וַעֲשִׂיתֶ֖ם אֹתָ֑ם אֲנִ֖י

22. There is a marked similarity between the physical defects that render a priest unfit to officiate and those that render an animal unfit for sacrifice.

23. freewill offering Because this offering is a gift to the sanctuary and is not intended for sacrifice, it need not be perfect.

28. The law forbids such sacrifice even after eight days.

29–30. These verses present a separate law for the thanksgiving offering, which is here treated as distinct from the *sh'lamim.*

27–28. Maimonides writes, "There is no distinction between the suffering of a human being and that of a beast in this respect, since feelings of maternal affection belong not to the intellectual faculty but to the emotional faculty, which is common to humans and animals alike." Recent research seems to indicate that animals do indeed have such feelings. Other scholars claim that the primary concern of the law is not with the animal's feelings but with the cultivation of kindness and compassion in the heart of the human being. "It is not because God pities the animal but in order that the people of Israel should not practice cruel habits" (B'khor Shor).

ments: I am the LORD. 32You shall not profane My holy name, that I may be sanctified in the midst of the Israelite people—I the LORD who sanctify you, 33I who brought you out of the land of Egypt to be your God, I the LORD.

יְהוָה׃ 32 וְלֹא תְחַלְּלוּ אֶת־שֵׁם קָדְשִׁי
וְנִקְדַּשְׁתִּי בְּתוֹךְ בְּנֵי יִשְׂרָאֵל אֲנִי יְהוָה
מְקַדִּשְׁכֶם׃ 33 הַמּוֹצִיא אֶתְכֶם מֵאֶרֶץ
מִצְרַיִם לִהְיוֹת לָכֶם לֵאלֹהִים אֲנִי
יְהוָה׃ פ

23 The LORD spoke to Moses, saying: 2Speak to the Israelite people and say to them:

These are My fixed times, the fixed times of the LORD, which you shall proclaim as sacred occasions.

3On six days work may be done, but on the seventh day there shall be a sabbath of complete

רביעי **כג** וַיְדַבֵּר יְהוָה אֶל־מֹשֶׁה לֵּאמֹר׃
2 דַּבֵּר אֶל־בְּנֵי יִשְׂרָאֵל וְאָמַרְתָּ אֲלֵהֶם
מוֹעֲדֵי יְהוָה אֲשֶׁר־תִּקְרְאוּ אֹתָם מִקְרָאֵי
קֹדֶשׁ אֵלֶּה הֵם מוֹעֲדָי׃
3 שֵׁשֶׁת יָמִים תֵּעָשֶׂה מְלָאכָה וּבַיּוֹם
הַשְּׁבִיעִי שַׁבַּת שַׁבָּתוֹן מִקְרָא־קֹדֶשׁ כָּל־

THE CALENDAR OF SACRED TIME (23:1–44)

Chapter 23 presents a calendar of the annual festivals celebrated in biblical times.

SHABBAT (vv. 1–3)

2. Speak to the Israelite people These sacred occasions are to be observed by all the people, not only by the priesthood.

which you shall proclaim as sacred occasions Although the dates of the festivals and the regularity of *Shabbat* were set by God, the Israelites also must proclaim them as sacred.

3. On six days work may be done This statement emphasizes three norms of conduct basic to the observance of *Shabbat:* (a) the prohibition of *m'lakhah* (work), (b) the sanctity of *Shabbat,* and (c) the requirement that *Shabbat* be observed in all Israelite settlements.

sabbath of complete rest Hebrew: *shabbat*

---

32. in the midst of the Israelite people The public performance of a *mitzvah* not only benefits the one who does it but has an effect on those who see it, even as a violation of the Torah in public is more damaging than similar behavior done privately (Hoffman). This lead the Sages to view the sanctifying of God's name (*Kiddush ha-Shem*) as essentially a public act. Thus, for example, a *minyan* is required for recitation of the mourner's *Kaddish* and for other prayers proclaiming God's holiness. The faith of the congregation is strengthened when a newly bereaved man or woman, who might have reason to feel angry with God, stands up in its midst to praise God. The Talmud states that there is no greater achievement for a Jew than acting in a way that causes others to praise and respect the God of Israel and the Torah's ways; and there is no graver sin for a Jew than acting in a way that causes people to think less of Israel's God and Israel's laws (BT Yoma 86a). The term *Kiddush ha-Shem,* sanctifying God's name in public, is often linked to, but not limited to, acts of martyrdom.

CHAPTER 23

2. The festivals of the Jewish year are listed first in Exod. 34. The list is repeated here to set out the special role and responsibilities of the *kohanim,* again in Num. 28–29 to present the special offerings brought on each festive occasion, and once more in Deut. 16 to emphasize the obligation of pilgrimage to the central shrine. The Israelites find the presence of God in the sanctuary, which represents the permanent holiness of sacred space, and on the festivals, which represent the recurring holiness of sacred time.

HALAKHAH L'MA·ASEH

23:3. do no work The Hebrew word *m'lakhah* (work) signifies any creative endeavor. One should refrain not only from paid labor but also from many actions that today may be considered leisure activities, such as gardening, cooking, sewing, arts and crafts, building, and writing.

מְלָאכָה לֹא תַעֲשׂוּ שַׁבָּת הִוא לַיהוָה
בְּכֹל מוֹשְׁבֹתֵיכֶם׃ פ
4 אֵלֶּה מוֹעֲדֵי יְהוָה מִקְרָאֵי קֹדֶשׁ אֲשֶׁר־
תִּקְרְאוּ אֹתָם בְּמוֹעֲדָם׃ 5 בַּחֹדֶשׁ הָרִאשׁוֹן
בְּאַרְבָּעָה עָשָׂר לַחֹדֶשׁ בֵּין הָעַרְבָּיִם פֶּסַח
לַיהוָה׃ 6 וּבַחֲמִשָּׁה עָשָׂר יוֹם לַחֹדֶשׁ הַזֶּה
חַג הַמַּצּוֹת לַיהוָה שִׁבְעַת יָמִים מַצּוֹת
תֹּאכֵלוּ׃ 7 בַּיּוֹם הָרִאשׁוֹן מִקְרָא־קֹדֶשׁ
יִהְיֶה לָכֶם כָּל־מְלֶאכֶת עֲבֹדָה לֹא תַעֲשׂוּ׃
8 וְהִקְרַבְתֶּם אִשֶּׁה לַיהוָה שִׁבְעַת יָמִים
בַּיּוֹם הַשְּׁבִיעִי מִקְרָא־קֹדֶשׁ כָּל־מְלֶאכֶת
עֲבֹדָה לֹא תַעֲשׂוּ׃ פ

9 וַיְדַבֵּר יְהוָה אֶל־מֹשֶׁה לֵּאמֹר׃ 10 דַּבֵּר
אֶל־בְּנֵי יִשְׂרָאֵל וְאָמַרְתָּ אֲלֵהֶם

rest, a sacred occasion. You shall do no work;
it shall be a sabbath of the LORD throughout
your settlements.
4These are the set times of the LORD, the sacred occasions, which you shall celebrate each
at its appointed time: 5In the first month, on
the fourteenth day of the month, at twilight,
there shall be a passover offering to the LORD,
6and on the fifteenth day of that month the
LORD's Feast of Unleavened Bread. You shall eat
unleavened bread for seven days. 7On the first
day you shall celebrate a sacred occasion: you
shall not work at your occupations. 8Seven days
you shall make gifts to the LORD. The seventh
day shall be a sacred occasion: you shall not
work at your occupations.

9The LORD spoke to Moses, saying: 10Speak
to the Israelite people and say to them:

shabbaton; literally, "the most restful cessation" from assigned tasks. The word *shabbat* means "to desist, cease, be idle."

sabbath of the LORD A day that belongs to God.

FEAST OF UNLEAVENED BREAD (vv. 4–8)

4. Each festival is to occur at the same time every year.

5. In the first month, on the fourteenth day of the month This is the dating system that was in use during much of the biblical period. The unit of time was the lunar month (*ḥodesh*), not the week; and the months of the year were designated by ordinal numbers: the first month, the second month, and so forth. The counting of months began in the spring.

twilight The period of time between sunset and nightfall, approximately 1 hour and 20 minutes in duration.

passover offering Here the term *"pesaḥ"* refers to the sacrifice, not to the festival (see Exod. 12:6).

7. On the first and seventh (or last) days of the festival, work is forbidden. The community celebrates together. During the intervening days, necessary normal work may be done, but the celebration continues.

NEW GRAIN CROP (vv. 9–14)

New grain is to be regarded as belonging to God and may not be eaten until certain offerings are taken from it and presented before God. Those offerings remove the sanctity from the crop, thereby releasing the remainder for ordinary human use.

7. you shall not work at your occupations The Jewish festivals challenge us: Do we define ourselves primarily by our work? Or do we define ourselves primarily by our total humanity, our ability to celebrate, to sanctify time, to share special moments with our families?

HALAKHAH L'MA·ASEH

23:6. seven days Traditionally, *Pesaḥ* is observed for eight days in the Diaspora. See Comment to Exod. 12:16.

23:7. not work at your occupations Most categories of *m'lakhah* (activities prohibited on *Shabbat* and *Yom Kippur*) are also prohibited on the three pilgrimage festivals and *Rosh ha-Shanah*; the permitted activities are those necessary for the preparation of food (*okhel nefesh*), such as cooking, carrying, and the transfer of fire (M Betz. 5:2).

כִּֽי־תָבֹ֣אוּ אֶל־הָאָ֗רֶץ אֲשֶׁ֤ר אֲנִי֙ נֹתֵ֣ן לָכֶ֔ם
וּקְצַרְתֶּ֖ם אֶת־קְצִירָ֑הּ וַהֲבֵאתֶ֥ם אֶת־עֹ֛מֶר
רֵאשִׁ֥ית קְצִירְכֶ֖ם אֶל־הַכֹּהֵֽן׃ 11 וְהֵנִ֧יף
אֶת־הָעֹ֛מֶר לִפְנֵ֥י יְהוָ֖ה לִֽרְצֹנְכֶ֑ם מִֽמָּחֳרַת֙
הַשַּׁבָּ֔ת יְנִיפֶ֖נּוּ הַכֹּהֵֽן׃ 12 וַעֲשִׂיתֶ֕ם בְּי֥וֹם
הֲנִיפְכֶ֖ם אֶת־הָעֹ֑מֶר כֶּ֣בֶשׂ תָּמִ֧ים בֶּן־שְׁנָת֛וֹ
לְעֹלָ֖ה לַיהוָֽה׃ 13 וּמִנְחָתוֹ֩ שְׁנֵ֨י עֶשְׂרֹנִ֜ים
סֹ֣לֶת בְּלוּלָ֥ה בַשֶּׁ֛מֶן אִשֶּׁ֥ה לַיהוָ֖ה רֵ֣יחַ
נִיחֹ֑חַ ונסכה וְנִסְכֹּ֖ו יַ֥יִן רְבִיעִ֥ת הַהִֽין׃
14 וְלֶחֶם֩ וְקָלִ֨י וְכַרְמֶ֜ל לֹ֤א תֹֽאכְלוּ֙ עַד־
עֶ֙צֶם֙ הַיּ֣וֹם הַזֶּ֔ה עַ֚ד הֲבִ֣יאֲכֶ֔ם אֶת־קָרְבַּ֖ן
אֱלֹהֵיכֶ֑ם חֻקַּ֤ת עוֹלָם֙ לְדֹרֹ֣תֵיכֶ֔ם בְּכֹ֖ל
מֹשְׁבֹתֵיכֶֽם׃ ס
15 וּסְפַרְתֶּ֤ם לָכֶם֙ מִמָּחֳרַ֣ת הַשַּׁבָּ֔ת מִיּוֹם֙
הֲבִ֣יאֲכֶ֔ם אֶת־עֹ֖מֶר הַתְּנוּפָ֑ה שֶׁ֥בַע
שַׁבָּת֖וֹת תְּמִימֹ֥ת תִּהְיֶֽינָה׃ 16 עַ֣ד מִֽמָּחֳרַ֤ת
הַשַּׁבָּת֙ הַשְּׁבִיעִ֔ת תִּסְפְּר֖וּ חֲמִשִּׁ֣ים י֑וֹם
וְהִקְרַבְתֶּ֛ם מִנְחָ֥ה חֲדָשָׁ֖ה לַיהוָֽה׃
17 מִמּוֹשְׁבֹ֨תֵיכֶ֜ם תָּבִ֣יאּוּ* ׀ לֶ֣חֶם תְּנוּפָ֗ה

v. 17. א׳ דגושה

When you enter the land that I am giving to
you and you reap its harvest, you shall bring the
first sheaf of your harvest to the priest. 11He shall
elevate the sheaf before the LORD for acceptance
in your behalf; the priest shall elevate it on the
day after the sabbath. 12On the day that you elevate the sheaf, you shall offer as a burnt offering
to the LORD a lamb of the first year without
blemish. 13The grain offering with it shall be
two-tenths of a measure of choice flour with oil
mixed in, a gift of pleasing odor to the LORD;
and the libation with it shall be of wine, a quarter
of a *hin.* 14Until that very day, until you have
brought the offering of your God, you shall eat
no bread or parched grain or fresh ears; it is a
law for all time throughout the ages in all your
settlements.

15And from the day on which you bring the
sheaf of elevation offering—the day after the
sabbath—you shall count off seven weeks. They
must be complete: 16you must count until the
day after the seventh week—fifty days; then you
shall bring an offering of new grain to the LORD.
17You shall bring from your settlements two

10. sheaf Hebrew: *omer,* a bundle of stalks bound together after reaping. Here, the reference is to barley, the first grain to ripen in the spring.

to the priest The particular priest who officiates at the rite in the sanctuary.

11. The purpose of such rites was to "show" the offering to God, so that it might be accepted.

12–13. The burnt offering (*olah*) was often accompanied by a grain offering (*minḥah*) and a libation (*nesekh*), as prescribed here. The measure of grain required here is twice the usual amount, to emphasize the importance of grain in this celebration.

14. Until God receives a share of the new grain crop, none of it may be used by humans.

SHAVU·OT FESTIVAL (vv. 15–22)

17. No leaven could be brought up on the

---

11. the day after the sabbath This starts the counting of the *Omer* (see *Halakhah l'Ma·aseh,* below). The Sages held that "the sabbath" here refers to the *Pesaḥ* festival. Explaining that interpretation, Arama writes, "If the *Omer* were tied to *Shabbat,* symbol of the creation of the world, then the wheat harvest would be seen purely as a natural phenomenon. Connecting it to the Exodus teaches us to see it, like the Exodus, as an instance of God's benevolence." It is through God's favor, not through our clever manipulation of nature, that the earth yields food for us to eat; that is why we cannot properly enjoy it until we have thanked God for it.

HALAKHAH L'MA·ASEH

23:15. you shall count From the second night of *Pesaḥ* until *Shavuot,* we count the 49 days of the *Omer.* Jewish communities hold varying segments of this time period, known as the *S'firah* (literally, "counting"), as a time of semimourning, during which weddings and festive occasions do not take place.

loaves of bread as an elevation offering; each
shall be made of two-tenths of a measure of
choice flour, baked after leavening, as first fruits
to the LORD. 18With the bread you shall present,
as burnt offerings to the LORD, seven yearling
lambs without blemish, one bull of the herd,
and two rams, with their grain offerings and libations, a gift of pleasing odor to the LORD.
19You shall also offer one he-goat as a purification offering and two yearling lambs as a
sacrifice of well-being. 20The priest shall elevate
these—the two lambs—together with the bread
of first fruits as an elevation offering before the
LORD; they shall be holy to the LORD, for the
priest. 21On that same day you shall hold a celebration; it shall be a sacred occasion for you;
you shall not work at your occupations. This
is a law for all time in all your settlements,
throughout the ages.

22And when you reap the harvest of your land,
you shall not reap all the way to the edges of
your field, or gather the gleanings of your harvest; you shall leave them for the poor and the
stranger: I the LORD am your God.

23The LORD spoke to Moses, saying: 24Speak
to the Israelite people thus: In the seventh

שְׁתַּ֣יִם שְׁנֵ֣י עֶשְׂרֹנִ֗ים סֹ֤לֶת תִּֽהְיֶ֙ינָה֙ חָמֵ֣ץ
תֵּאָפֶ֔ינָה בִּכּוּרִ֖ים לַיהוָֽה׃ 18 וְהִקְרַבְתֶּ֣ם
עַל־הַלֶּ֗חֶם שִׁבְעַ֨ת כְּבָשִׂ֤ים תְּמִימִם֙ בְּנֵ֣י
שָׁנָ֔ה וּפַ֧ר בֶּן־בָּקָ֛ר אֶחָ֖ד וְאֵילִ֣ם שְׁנָ֑יִם יִהְי֤וּ
עֹלָה֙ לַֽיהוָ֔ה וּמִנְחָתָם֙ וְנִסְכֵּיהֶ֔ם אִשֵּׁ֥ה
רֵֽיחַ־נִיחֹ֖חַ לַיהוָֽה׃ 19 וַעֲשִׂיתֶ֛ם שְׂעִיר־
עִזִּ֥ים אֶחָ֖ד לְחַטָּ֑את וּשְׁנֵ֧י כְבָשִׂ֛ים בְּנֵ֥י
שָׁנָ֖ה לְזֶ֥בַח שְׁלָמִֽים׃ 20 וְהֵנִ֣יף הַכֹּהֵ֣ן ׀
אֹתָ֡ם עַל֩ לֶ֨חֶם הַבִּכֻּרִ֤ים תְּנוּפָה֙ לִפְנֵ֣י
יְהוָ֔ה עַל־שְׁנֵ֖י כְּבָשִׂ֑ים קֹ֛דֶשׁ יִהְי֥וּ לַיהוָ֖ה
לַכֹּהֵֽן׃ 21 וּקְרָאתֶ֞ם בְּעֶ֣צֶם ׀ הַיּ֣וֹם הַזֶּ֗ה
מִֽקְרָא־קֹ֙דֶשׁ֙ יִהְיֶ֣ה לָכֶ֔ם כָּל־מְלֶ֥אכֶת
עֲבֹדָ֖ה לֹ֣א תַעֲשׂ֑וּ חֻקַּ֥ת עוֹלָ֛ם בְּכָל־
מוֹשְׁבֹתֵיכֶ֖ם לְדֹרֹתֵיכֶֽם׃

22 וּֽבְקֻצְרְכֶ֞ם אֶת־קְצִ֣יר אַרְצְכֶ֗ם לֹֽא־
תְכַלֶּ֞ה פְּאַ֤ת שָֽׂדְךָ֙ בְּקֻצְרֶ֔ךָ וְלֶ֥קֶט קְצִירְךָ֖
לֹ֣א תְלַקֵּ֑ט לֶֽעָנִ֤י וְלַגֵּר֙ תַּעֲזֹ֣ב אֹתָ֔ם אֲנִ֖י
יְהוָ֥ה אֱלֹהֵיכֶֽם׃ ס

ישי 23 וַיְדַבֵּ֥ר יְהוָ֖ה אֶל־מֹשֶׁ֥ה לֵּאמֹֽר׃ 24 דַּבֵּ֛ר
אֶל־בְּנֵ֥י יִשְׂרָאֵ֖ל לֵאמֹ֑ר בַּחֹ֨דֶשׁ הַשְּׁבִיעִ֜י

altar. Here, because no part of the offering presented before God ascends the altar, it could be made of "leavened dough" (*ḥametz*).

18–20. The offerings prescribed in these verses are typical of those included in public rites, in which several different sacrifices are offered together to constitute a more elaborate celebration. The animals, both small and large, are to be offered as burnt offerings and are accompanied by the grain offerings and libations.

20. The priest shall elevate these—the two lambs That is, the two yearling lambs.

they shall be holy to the LORD, for the priest In the first instance, these offerings are the Lord's, who, in turn, commands that they be allotted to the priests.

FIRST DAY OF THE SEVENTH MONTH (vv. 23–25)

This section ordains the celebration of three major sacred occasions occurring during the seventh month: (a) the first day of the seventh month (which in the later tradition became the Jewish New Year), (b) the Day of Atonement, and (c) the *Sukkot* festival.

24. Here, the day is presented as one of rest and sacred assembly. It is conceived of not as a new year but as an occasion before the Day of

---

22. Why are the gleanings of the harvest mentioned here, interrupting the list of festivals? Perhaps because they were gathered at the *Shavu·ot* harvest season, as we read in the Book of Ruth, or because, as the *Sifra* suggests, when one shares one's bounty with the poor, it is as if it were offered on God's altar.

24. The Torah never refers to the first day of the seventh month as *Rosh ha-Shanah.* That term first appears in Ezek. 40:1. In the Torah,

בְּאֶחָד לַחֹדֶשׁ יִהְיֶה לָכֶם שַׁבָּתוֹן זִכְרוֹן
תְּרוּעָה מִקְרָא־קֹדֶשׁ׃ 25 כָּל־מְלֶאכֶת
עֲבֹדָה לֹא תַעֲשׂוּ וְהִקְרַבְתֶּם אִשֶּׁה
לַיהוָה׃ ס
26 וַיְדַבֵּר יְהוָה אֶל־מֹשֶׁה לֵּאמֹר׃ 27 אַךְ
בֶּעָשׂוֹר לַחֹדֶשׁ הַשְּׁבִיעִי הַזֶּה יוֹם הַכִּפֻּרִים
הוּא מִקְרָא־קֹדֶשׁ יִהְיֶה לָכֶם וְעִנִּיתֶם
אֶת־נַפְשֹׁתֵיכֶם וְהִקְרַבְתֶּם אִשֶּׁה לַיהוָה׃
28 וְכָל־מְלָאכָה לֹא תַעֲשׂוּ בְּעֶצֶם הַיּוֹם
הַזֶּה כִּי יוֹם כִּפֻּרִים הוּא לְכַפֵּר עֲלֵיכֶם
לִפְנֵי יְהוָה אֱלֹהֵיכֶם׃ 29 כִּי כָל־הַנֶּפֶשׁ
אֲשֶׁר לֹא־תְעֻנֶּה בְּעֶצֶם הַיּוֹם הַזֶּה
וְנִכְרְתָה מֵעַמֶּיהָ׃ 30 וְכָל־הַנֶּפֶשׁ אֲשֶׁר
תַּעֲשֶׂה כָּל־מְלָאכָה בְּעֶצֶם הַיּוֹם הַזֶּה
וְהַאֲבַדְתִּי אֶת־הַנֶּפֶשׁ הַהִוא מִקֶּרֶב עַמָּהּ׃
31 כָּל־מְלָאכָה לֹא תַעֲשׂוּ חֻקַּת עוֹלָם
לְדֹרֹתֵיכֶם בְּכֹל מֹשְׁבֹתֵיכֶם׃ 32 שַׁבַּת
שַׁבָּתוֹן הוּא לָכֶם וְעִנִּיתֶם אֶת־נַפְשֹׁתֵיכֶם
בְּתִשְׁעָה לַחֹדֶשׁ בָּעֶרֶב מֵעֶרֶב עַד־עֶרֶב
ששי תִּשְׁבְּתוּ שַׁבַּתְּכֶם׃ פ

month, on the first day of the month, you shall observe complete rest, a sacred occasion commemorated with loud blasts. 25You shall not work at your occupations; and you shall bring a gift to the LORD.

26The LORD spoke to Moses, saying: 27Mark, the tenth day of this seventh month is the Day of Atonement. It shall be a sacred occasion for you: you shall practice self-denial, and you shall bring a gift to the LORD; 28you shall do no work throughout that day. For it is a Day of Atonement, on which expiation is made on your behalf before the LORD your God. 29Indeed, any person who does not practice self-denial throughout that day shall be cut off from his kin; 30and whoever does any work throughout that day, I will cause that person to perish from among his people. 31Do no work whatever; it is a law for all time, throughout the ages in all your settlements. 32It shall be a sabbath of complete rest for you, and you shall practice self-denial; on the ninth day of the month at evening, from evening to evening, you shall observe this your sabbath.

Atonement. The Hebrew term *zikhron t'ru·ah* means, literally, "commemoration by blasting" the *shofar.*

DAY OF ATONEMENT (vv. 26–32)

See Comments to 16:29–34.

27. you shall practice self-denial That is, you shall fast.

32. from evening to evening, you shall observe this This verse has been interpreted as setting the norm for every festival in the Jewish religious calendar, namely, that the celebration

---

it is called "a day of remembrance" or "a day of sounding the *shofar.*" Readers may be surprised to learn that *Rosh ha-Shanah* begins the seventh month of the Hebrew calendar rather than the first. It commemorates the creation of the world, which traditionally is believed to have happened in the fall, the beginning of the new agricultural cycle. But the people Israel date their calendar from the Exodus, which happened in the spring (cf. Exod. 12:2, designating the month of the Exodus as the first month of Israel's calendar).

32. on the ninth day . . . at evening The *Yom Kippur* fast does not start until the evening (after sunset, at night) after the ninth day. "Eating and drinking responsibly on the day before and the day after *Yom Kippur* are as much of a *mitzvah* as fasting on *Yom Kippur*" (BT Yoma 81b).

HALAKHAH L'MA·ASEH

23:24. commemorated with loud blasts This is the source for the ruling that the *shofar* is not sounded on *Rosh ha-Shanah* when it coincides with *Shabbat,* which is itself a commemoration (BT RH 29b). On such a *Shabbat,* we "remember the blasting" in our prayers. It is also the source for the practice during the *Musaf* service on *Rosh ha-Shanah* of reciting 10 biblical verses about each of the themes of God's kingship, God's remembrance, and the *shofar* (BT RH 32a).

³³The Lord spoke to Moses, saying: ³⁴Say to the Israelite people:

On the fifteenth day of this seventh month there shall be the Feast of Booths to the Lord, [to last] seven days. ³⁵The first day shall be a sacred occasion: you shall not work at your occupations; ³⁶seven days you shall bring gifts to the Lord. On the eighth day you shall observe a sacred occasion and bring a gift to the Lord; it is a solemn gathering: you shall not work at your occupations.

³⁷Those are the set times of the Lord that you shall celebrate as sacred occasions, bringing gifts to the Lord—burnt offerings, grain offerings, sacrifices, and libations, on each day what is proper to it—³⁸apart from the sabbaths of the Lord, and apart from your gifts and from all your votive offerings and from all your freewill offerings that you give to the Lord.

³⁹Mark, on the fifteenth day of the seventh month, when you have gathered in the yield of your land, you shall observe the festival of the Lord [to last] seven days: a complete rest on

שׁשׁי 33 וַיְדַבֵּ֥ר יְהֹוָ֖ה אֶל־מֹשֶׁ֥ה לֵּאמֹֽר: 34 דַּבֵּ֞ר אֶל־בְּנֵ֤י יִשְׂרָאֵל֙ לֵאמֹ֔ר בַּחֲמִשָּׁ֨ה עָשָׂ֜ר י֗וֹם לַחֹ֤דֶשׁ הַשְּׁבִיעִי֙ הַזֶּ֔ה חַ֧ג הַסֻּכּ֛וֹת שִׁבְעַ֥ת יָמִ֖ים לַֽיהֹוָֽה: 35 בַּיּ֥וֹם הָרִאשׁ֖וֹן מִקְרָא־קֹ֑דֶשׁ כָּל־מְלֶ֥אכֶת עֲבֹדָ֖ה לֹ֥א תַעֲשֽׂוּ: 36 שִׁבְעַ֥ת יָמִ֖ים תַּקְרִ֥יבוּ אִשֶּׁ֣ה לַֽיהֹוָ֑ה בַּיּ֣וֹם הַשְּׁמִינִ֡י מִקְרָא־קֹ֩דֶשׁ֩ יִֽהְיֶ֨ה לָכֶ֜ם וְהִקְרַבְתֶּ֥ם אִשֶּׁ֣ה לַֽיהֹוָ֗ה עֲצֶ֣רֶת הִ֔וא כָּל־מְלֶ֥אכֶת עֲבֹדָ֖ה לֹ֥א תַעֲשֽׂוּ:

37 אֵ֚לֶּה מֽוֹעֲדֵ֣י יְהֹוָ֔ה אֲשֶׁר־תִּקְרְא֥וּ אֹתָ֖ם מִקְרָאֵ֣י קֹ֑דֶשׁ לְהַקְרִ֨יב אִשֶּׁ֜ה לַֽיהֹוָ֗ה עֹלָ֧ה וּמִנְחָ֛ה זֶ֥בַח וּנְסָכִ֖ים דְּבַר־י֥וֹם בְּיוֹמֽוֹ: 38 מִלְּבַ֖ד שַׁבְּתֹ֣ת יְהֹוָ֑ה וּמִלְּבַ֣ד מַתְּנ֣וֹתֵיכֶ֗ם וּמִלְּבַ֤ד כָּל־נִדְרֵיכֶם֙ וּמִלְּבַד֙ כָּל־נִדְב֣וֹתֵיכֶ֔ם אֲשֶׁ֥ר תִּתְּנ֖וּ לַֽיהֹוָֽה:

39 אַ֡ךְ בַּחֲמִשָּׁה֩ עָשָׂ֨ר י֜וֹם לַחֹ֣דֶשׁ הַשְּׁבִיעִ֗י בְּאָסְפְּכֶם֙ אֶת־תְּבוּאַ֣ת הָאָ֔רֶץ תָּחֹ֥גּוּ אֶת־חַג־יְהֹוָ֖ה שִׁבְעַ֣ת יָמִ֑ים בַּיּ֧וֹם

commences on the evening (actually the night, after sunset) that precedes the day of the festival. Scheduling the Day of Atonement only a few days before the major pilgrimage festival of the year ensured that the sanctuary and the people would be restored to a state of fitness in time for the celebration of the autumn *Sukkot* observance.

SUKKOT FESTIVAL (vv. 33–44)

34. the Feast of Booths The Hebrew word *suk-* *kah,* "booth," derives from the verb סכך, "to cover over," as with branches. It designates a small, usually temporary, structure that is covered on top and only partially enclosed on its sides.

36. solemn gathering This term derives from the Hebrew verb עצר, "to detain, restrain, confine," and may refer to the fact that the people are kept together for an additional day.

35. first day Why is it called the "first day" when it is actually the fifteenth of the month? After the slate has been wiped clean on *Yom Kippur,* we begin our relationship with God anew on *Sukkot* (Lev. R. 30:7).

36. solemn gathering The word *atzeret* is usually understood as "concluding event" or "solemn gathering." But Hirsch here understands it as derived from a root meaning "to gather, to store up." Even as farmers gather up the harvest in the autumn to last through the winter months, even as animals store food for the winter, the Israelites are urged to store up the feelings of gratitude and dependence that mark the holiday season—to last them through the months that will follow, months without festival days. (In the biblical period, *Ḥanukkah* did not exist. It celebrates events that took place after the time of the Torah.)

the first day, and a complete rest on the eighth
day. 40On the first day you shall take the product
of *hadar* trees, branches of palm trees, boughs
of leafy trees, and willows of the brook, and you
shall rejoice before the LORD your God seven
days. 41You shall observe it as a festival of the
LORD for seven days in the year; you shall observe it in the seventh month as a law for all time,
throughout the ages. 42You shall live in booths
seven days; all citizens in Israel shall live in
booths, 43in order that future generations may
know that I made the Israelite people live in
booths when I brought them out of the land of
Egypt, I the LORD your God.
44So Moses declared to the Israelites the set
times of the LORD.

הָֽרִאשׁוֹן֙ שַׁבָּת֔וֹן וּבַיּ֥וֹם הַשְּׁמִינִ֖י שַׁבָּתֽוֹן׃
40 וּלְקַחְתֶּ֨ם לָכֶ֜ם בַּיּ֣וֹם הָרִאשׁ֗וֹן פְּרִ֨י עֵ֤ץ
הָדָר֙ כַּפֹּ֣ת תְּמָרִ֔ים וַעֲנַ֥ף עֵץ־עָבֹ֖ת וְעַרְבֵי־
נָ֑חַל וּשְׂמַחְתֶּ֗ם לִפְנֵ֛י יְהוָ֥ה אֱלֹהֵיכֶ֖ם
שִׁבְעַ֥ת יָמִֽים׃ 41 וְחַגֹּתֶ֤ם אֹתוֹ֙ חַ֣ג לַֽיהוָ֔ה
שִׁבְעַ֥ת יָמִ֖ים בַּשָּׁנָ֑ה חֻקַּ֤ת עוֹלָם֙ לְדֹרֹ֣תֵיכֶ֔ם
בַּחֹ֥דֶשׁ הַשְּׁבִיעִ֖י תָּחֹ֥גּוּ אֹתֽוֹ׃ 42 בַּסֻּכֹּ֥ת
תֵּשְׁב֖וּ שִׁבְעַ֣ת יָמִ֑ים כָּל־הָֽאֶזְרָח֙ בְּיִשְׂרָאֵ֔ל
יֵשְׁב֖וּ בַּסֻּכֹּֽת׃ 43 לְמַ֘עַן֮ יֵדְע֣וּ דֹרֹתֵיכֶ֒ם
כִּ֣י בַסֻּכּ֗וֹת הוֹשַׁ֙בְתִּי֙ אֶת־בְּנֵ֣י יִשְׂרָאֵ֔ל
בְּהוֹצִיאִ֥י אוֹתָ֖ם מֵאֶ֣רֶץ מִצְרָ֑יִם אֲנִ֖י יְהוָ֥ה
אֱלֹהֵיכֶֽם׃
44 וַיְדַבֵּ֣ר מֹשֶׁ֔ה אֶת־מֹעֲדֵ֖י יְהוָ֑ה אֶל־בְּנֵ֖י
יִשְׂרָאֵֽל׃ פ שביעי

40. hadar trees Literally, "beautiful trees." They symbolize the abundance of water and oases and the beauty of the land of Israel. In horticulture, there are no particular trees designated as *hadar*. Traditionally, the "product of *hadar* trees" has been taken to be the citron (*etrog*).

you shall rejoice Rejoicing is explicitly commanded in this chapter only for the celebration of *Sukkot.* The pressing of the grapes had been completed, and there was no labor to be done until the beginning of the next agricultural cycle. The people had leisure time as well as ample food and wine with which to rejoice.

43. I made the Israelite people live in booths According to Exod. 12:37, *Sukkot* (literally, Booths) is the name of the first stop on the Exodus route from Egypt.

---

40. The Midrash offers many interpretations of the symbolic meaning of the four species of *Sukkot.* The *lulav* (palm branch) represents the spine—erect but not rigid; the myrtle, the eyes; the willow, the lips; and the *etrog,* the heart. They summon us to use all of our limbs and organs to rejoice before the Lord. Yet another *midrash* compares the *etrog,* which tastes and smells good, to people who possess learning and also do good deeds; the *lulav,* which has taste but no fragrance, to people who have learning but do not do good; the myrtle, which has fragrance but no taste, to people who do good but lack learning; and the willow, with neither taste nor fragrance, to people who lack both learning and good deeds but who are still to be counted as members of the community in order for the community to be complete (Lev. R. 30:10–12).

HALAKHAH L'MA·ASEH

23:40. the product of hadar trees, branches of palm trees, boughs of leafy trees, and willows of the brook This is the source for the commandment to take the citron fruit (*etrog*) with the branches of willow (*aravah*) and myrtle (*hadas*) bound to a palm branch (*lulav*) to fulfill the *mitzvah* of waving the *lulav* during *Sukkot.*

23:42. live in booths seven days One can fulfill this commandment by either sleeping in the *sukkah* (booth) or eating one's meals there during the seven-day holiday. One is exempt from eating or dwelling in the *sukkah* if the weather or other factors cause undue hardship (BT Suk. 25b–26a,29a).

23:44. So Moses declared On festivals, this verse is recited aloud before the *Amidah* during the *Ma·ariv* service, and before the blessing over wine for the *Kiddush* preceding lunch.

24 The LORD spoke to Moses, saying:

2Command the Israelite people to bring you clear oil of beaten olives for lighting, for kindling lamps regularly. 3Aaron shall set them up in the Tent of Meeting outside the curtain of the Pact [to burn] from evening to morning before the LORD regularly; it is a law for all time throughout the ages. 4He shall set up the lamps on the pure lampstand before the LORD [to burn] regularly.

5You shall take choice flour and bake of it twelve loaves, two-tenths of a measure for each loaf. 6Place them on the pure table before the LORD in two rows, six to a row. 7With each row you shall place pure frankincense, which is to be a token offering for the bread, as a gift to the LORD. 8He shall arrange them before the LORD regularly every sabbath day—it is a commitment for all time on the part of the Israelites. 9They shall belong to Aaron and his sons, who shall eat them in the sacred precinct; for they are his as most holy things from the LORD's gifts, a due for all time.

שביעי **כד** וַיְדַבֵּר יְהוָה אֶל־מֹשֶׁה לֵּאמֹר׃
2 צַו אֶת־בְּנֵי יִשְׂרָאֵל וְיִקְחוּ אֵלֶיךָ שֶׁמֶן
זַיִת זָךְ כָּתִית לַמָּאוֹר לְהַעֲלֹת נֵר תָּמִיד׃
3 מִחוּץ לְפָרֹכֶת הָעֵדֻת בְּאֹהֶל מוֹעֵד יַעֲרֹךְ
אֹתוֹ אַהֲרֹן מֵעֶרֶב עַד־בֹּקֶר לִפְנֵי יְהוָה
תָּמִיד חֻקַּת עוֹלָם לְדֹרֹתֵיכֶם׃ 4 עַל
הַמְּנֹרָה הַטְּהֹרָה יַעֲרֹךְ אֶת־הַנֵּרוֹת לִפְנֵי
יְהוָה תָּמִיד׃ פ

5 וְלָקַחְתָּ סֹלֶת וְאָפִיתָ אֹתָהּ שְׁתֵּים עֶשְׂרֵה
חַלּוֹת שְׁנֵי עֶשְׂרֹנִים יִהְיֶה הַחַלָּה הָאֶחָת׃
6 וְשַׂמְתָּ אוֹתָם שְׁתַּיִם מַעֲרָכוֹת שֵׁשׁ
הַמַּעֲרָכֶת עַל הַשֻּׁלְחָן הַטָּהֹר לִפְנֵי יְהוָה׃
7 וְנָתַתָּ עַל־הַמַּעֲרֶכֶת לְבֹנָה זַכָּה וְהָיְתָה
לַלֶּחֶם לְאַזְכָּרָה אִשֶּׁה לַיהוָה׃ 8 בְּיוֹם
הַשַּׁבָּת בְּיוֹם הַשַּׁבָּת יַעַרְכֶנּוּ לִפְנֵי יְהוָה
תָּמִיד מֵאֵת בְּנֵי־יִשְׂרָאֵל בְּרִית עוֹלָם׃
9 וְהָיְתָה לְאַהֲרֹן וּלְבָנָיו וַאֲכָלֻהוּ בְּמָקוֹם
קָדֹשׁ כִּי קֹדֶשׁ קָדָשִׁים הוּא* לוֹ מֵאִשֵּׁי
יְהוָה חָק־עוֹלָם׃ ס

v. 9. סבירין ומטעין "היא"

A COLLECTION OF LAWS (24:1–23)

KINDLING THE *M'NORAH* (vv. 1–4)

2. regularly Hebrew: *tamid,* often mistranslated as "eternal," "forever," or "always." It conveys the sense of regularity, whether used as an adjective or as an adverb (see v. 3). The lamps in the sanctuary burned only from evening to morning (see v. 3).

3. the curtain of the Pact That is, the curtain of the Ark of the Pact. Behind the curtain stood the Ark, in which rested the tablets of the Pact.

TWO ROWS OF BREAD (vv. 5–9)

5. The bread presented as an offering on a table inside the sanctuary is known in Exodus as "the bread of display" (*leḥem ha-panim*). It was viewed and accepted by God.

8. every sabbath day Hebrew: *b'yom ha-shabbat, b'yom ha-shabbat;* literally, "on the sabbath day, on the sabbath day"). In Hebrew, repetition is a way of expressing regularity.

CHAPTER 24

2. for kindling lamps regularly A *midrash* (Lev. R. 31:4) pictures God saying, "As you shine your light on Me (i.e., teaching the world about Me), I will shine My light on you (make you special among the nations)."

5. The Talmud states that "a great miracle was performed in the Tent of Meeting; the sacred loaves of bread never grew stale" (BT Men. 29a). According to Hirsch, those words were not meant to be taken literally. They convey the idea that the sanctuary was immune to the process of boredom and habit that afflict many religious institutions. Rituals did not grow stale or obsolete there.

¹⁰There came out among the Israelites one whose mother was Israelite and whose father was Egyptian. And a fight broke out in the camp between that half-Israelite and a certain Israelite. ¹¹The son of the Israelite woman pronounced the Name in blasphemy, and he was brought to Moses—now his mother's name was Shelomith daughter of Dibri of the tribe of Dan—¹²and he was placed in custody, until the decision of the LORD should be made clear to them.

¹³And the LORD spoke to Moses, saying: ¹⁴Take the blasphemer outside the camp; and let all who were within hearing lay their hands upon his head, and let the whole community stone him.

¹⁵And to the Israelite people speak thus: Anyone who blasphemes his God shall bear his guilt; ¹⁶if he also pronounces the name LORD, he shall be put to death. The whole community shall stone him; stranger or citizen, if he has thus pronounced the Name, he shall be put to death.

¹⁷If anyone kills any human being, he shall

10 וַיֵּצֵא֙ בֶּן־אִשָּׁ֣ה יִשְׂרְאֵלִ֔ית וְהוּא֙ בֶּן־אִ֣ישׁ מִצְרִ֔י בְּת֖וֹךְ בְּנֵ֣י יִשְׂרָאֵ֑ל וַיִּנָּצוּ֙ בַּֽמַּחֲנֶ֔ה בֶּ֚ן הַיִּשְׂרְאֵלִ֔ית וְאִ֖ישׁ הַיִּשְׂרְאֵלִֽי׃ 11 וַ֠יִּקֹּב בֶּן־הָֽאִשָּׁ֨ה הַיִּשְׂרְאֵלִ֤ית אֶת־הַשֵּׁם֙ וַיְקַלֵּ֔ל וַיָּבִ֥יאוּ אֹת֖וֹ אֶל־מֹשֶׁ֑ה וְשֵׁ֥ם אִמּ֛וֹ שְׁלֹמִ֥ית בַּת־דִּבְרִ֖י לְמַטֵּה־דָֽן׃ 12 וַיַּנִּיחֻ֖הוּ בַּמִּשְׁמָ֑ר לִפְרֹ֥שׁ לָהֶ֖ם עַל־פִּ֥י יְהֹוָֽה׃ פ

13 וַיְדַבֵּ֥ר יְהֹוָ֖ה אֶל־מֹשֶׁ֥ה לֵּאמֹֽר׃ 14 הוֹצֵ֣א אֶת־הַֽמְקַלֵּ֗ל אֶל־מִחוּץ֙ לַֽמַּחֲנֶ֔ה וְסָמְכ֧וּ כׇל־הַשֹּׁמְעִ֛ים אֶת־יְדֵיהֶ֖ם עַל־רֹאשׁ֑וֹ וְרָֽגְמ֥וּ אֹת֖וֹ כׇּל־הָעֵדָֽה׃

15 וְאֶל־בְּנֵ֥י יִשְׂרָאֵ֖ל תְּדַבֵּ֣ר לֵאמֹ֑ר אִ֥ישׁ אִ֛ישׁ כִּֽי־יְקַלֵּ֥ל אֱלֹהָ֖יו וְנָשָׂ֥א חֶטְאֽוֹ׃ 16 וְנֹקֵ֤ב שֵׁם־יְהֹוָה֙ מ֣וֹת יוּמָ֔ת רָג֥וֹם יִרְגְּמוּ־ב֖וֹ כׇּל־הָעֵדָ֑ה כַּגֵּר֙ כָּֽאֶזְרָ֔ח בְּנׇקְבוֹ־שֵׁ֖ם יוּמָֽת׃

17 וְאִ֕ישׁ כִּ֥י יַכֶּ֖ה כׇּל־נֶ֣פֶשׁ אָדָ֑ם מ֖וֹת יוּמָֽת׃

BLASPHEMY AND OTHER SERIOUS CRIMES (vv. 10–23)

10–12. This brief narrative introduces the law concerning the crime of blasphemy in verse 14.

14. outside the camp Capital punishment took place outside the area of settlement. This was due, at least in part, to the impurity attached to a corpse.

all who were within hearing . . . the whole community The entire community has responsibility to root out blasphemy, because it adversely affects everyone, even though it is committed by a single individual.

16. stranger or citizen Non-Israelites are responsible for acts considered vital to maintaining the sacred nature of the community. Offenses that endanger that sanctity are punishable, even when committed by non-Israelite residents. The Sages later held that all resident aliens were required to observe the Noahide laws.

17. The law is stated here because of its relationship to the death penalty imposed for blasphemy.

10–16. This is a puzzling incident. Did the blasphemer curse God, curse someone else using the name of God, or simply pronounce God's name without due reverence? (*"M'kallel"* can mean "curse" or "show disrespect.") It fits Leviticus's commitment to taking words seriously. Words are ephemeral but real and have the power to hurt or to heal. Using the power of speech (with its potential for holiness unique to humans) to hurt another person is a grave offense, deeply disturbing to Leviticus with its emphasis on the holiness of the ordinary and the things that distinguish humans from beasts. The Torah emphasizes that the blasphemer's parents were of different ethnic-religious origins. Might this have been a home where no religious values were taught, because there was no religion shared by all members of the family?

be put to death. [18]One who kills a beast shall
make restitution for it: life for life. [19]If anyone
maims his fellow, as he has done so shall it be
done to him: [20]fracture for fracture, eye for eye,
tooth for tooth. The injury he inflicted on another shall be inflicted on him. [21]One who kills
a beast shall make restitution for it; but one who
kills a human being shall be put to death. [22]You
shall have one standard for stranger and citizen
alike: for I the LORD am your God.

[23]Moses spoke thus to the Israelites. And they
took the blasphemer outside the camp and
pelted him with stones. The Israelites did as the
LORD had commanded Moses.

18 וּמַכֵּה נֶפֶשׁ־בְּהֵמָה יְשַׁלְּמֶנָּה נֶפֶשׁ תַּחַת
נָפֶשׁ׃ 19 וְאִישׁ כִּי־יִתֵּן מוּם בַּעֲמִיתוֹ
כַּאֲשֶׁר עָשָׂה כֵּן יֵעָשֶׂה לּוֹ׃ 20 שֶׁבֶר תַּחַת
שֶׁבֶר עַיִן תַּחַת עַיִן שֵׁן תַּחַת שֵׁן כַּאֲשֶׁר
מפטיר יִתֵּן מוּם בָּאָדָם כֵּן יִנָּתֶן בּוֹ׃ 21 וּמַכֵּה
בְהֵמָה יְשַׁלְּמֶנָּה וּמַכֵּה אָדָם יוּמָת׃
22 מִשְׁפַּט אֶחָד יִהְיֶה לָכֶם כַּגֵּר כָּאֶזְרָח
יִהְיֶה כִּי אֲנִי יְהוָה אֱלֹהֵיכֶם׃
23 וַיְדַבֵּר מֹשֶׁה אֶל־בְּנֵי יִשְׂרָאֵל וַיּוֹצִיאוּ
אֶת־הַמְקַלֵּל אֶל־מִחוּץ לַמַּחֲנֶה וַיִּרְגְּמוּ
אֹתוֹ אָבֶן וּבְנֵי־יִשְׂרָאֵל עָשׂוּ כַּאֲשֶׁר צִוָּה
יְהוָה אֶת־מֹשֶׁה׃ פ

18. life for life That is, the assessed value of the animal destroyed or of another animal provided in place of the one killed.

19. maims Literally, "gives an injury." The Hebrew word for "blemish, injury" (*mum*) here refers to a permanent condition.

22. The same rules apply whether the offender or the victim are Israelites or resident non-Israelites.

---

19. as he has done so shall it be done to him Saadia sought to prove that the verse refers to monetary punishment, as the Sages suggested, rather than retaliation, by citing the story of Samson in Judges 15. Samson says of his attack on the Philistines, "as they did to me, I did to them." Yet what he did to them was not literally "as they did" but instead what they deserved.

הפטרת אמר

HAFTARAH FOR EMOR

EZEKIEL 44:15–31

This *haftarah* contains a list of regulations addressed to Zadokite priests, which is part of a larger blueprint for the restoration of worship articulated in Ezek. 40–48. Ezekiel's heavenly vision of the new temple's ground plan is dated to the beginning of the year 572 B.C.E., 14 years after the fall of Jerusalem (40:1). The Zadokite priests are the only levitical priests who may now serve within the sanctuary (vv. 15–16). Their rules and regulations (vv. 17–31) have a notable affinity with laws in the Book of Leviticus.

Since antiquity, though, it has been observed that a number of the priestly regulations promulgated by Ezekiel contradict their counterparts in the Torah. This led to a report that the Book of Ezekiel was to have been withdrawn from circulation. The contradictions were reconciled only through a heroic act of sustained interpretation by the sage Ḥanina ben Hezekiah (BT Shab. 13b).

Despite the manifest differences in style and stringency between Ezekiel's regulations and those in the laws of Moses, one must assume that the ancient Israelite transmitters of tradition believed that they had the instructions in the Book of Ezekiel on good divine authority (Ezek. 44:9). The fact that the revelation to the prophet appears to supplement or revise the Torah does not seem to have been a problem. New times could bring new divine specifications for priests, authorizing new priestly families and reauthorizing their duties. The language of Ezek. 44:17–31 in the *haftarah* became a problem apparently only in later Rabbinic times, when the prohibition in Deut. 13:1 against adding to or subtracting from God's law was understood to give exclusive authority to the rules and regulations found in the Torah.

The central concern of Ezekiel's instruction is the elevation and authorization of the priests descended from Zadok. As we are told in verses preceding the *haftarah,* this purpose is achieved not only by the prophet's denigration of the other levitical priests for having been lax in securing the sacral areas against alien encroachment (44:6–7) or by his smearing them with the taint of apostasy (v. 12). Ezekiel also accomplishes his intent by appropriating and revising older priestly language.

Thus in the Torah Moses speaks of the special status of the Aaronid lineage, appointed to "discharge the duties" of the shrine (tent) and its holy altar. Their brethren, the Levites, however, are enjoined to "serve" them without the right to encroach on the holy objects or the altar (Num. 18:1–4). The Levites are thus the servitors of the priests and their divine labor, but cannot serve as priests in their own right. Ezekiel, by contrast, promotes the Zadokite line as having the exclusive right to "discharge the duties" of the Temple and "serve" God as levitical priests. Only the Zadokites can serve in the sanctuary, discharging all priestly functions, whereas the other Levites were demoted to the rank of servitors, guarding the gates, doing menial tasks, or assisting the people in their sacrifices (44:11). The biblical sources do not indicate that this revolution was the result of a contest for priestly power in the Second Temple. Nevertheless, the attestation of more liberal priestly regulations at just this time (Isa. 56), suggests that Ezekiel's propaganda for the Zadokites was part of contemporary ideologic strife over the character and limits of the priesthood.

On a broader plane, the notable gaps in Ezekiel's regulations constitute another puzzle, because their manifest purpose was to constitute a self-standing messianic program. Particularly striking is the absence of any mention of the Ark and cherubim in the inner sanctuary, or the table for the showbread in the outer area, or the anointing oil in the Temple or the courts. Furthermore, there is no reference to the purgation of the Temple on *Yom Kippur* (Lev. 16), to the dramatic cer-

emonies of *Pesaḥ* eve (Exod. 12:1–14), or to the species used to celebrate the festival of Booths (Lev. 23:39–43). Ezekiel thus appears to reflect an independent strand of cultic tradition and information. For him, as for his colleagues, concern with priestly comportment and purity is uppermost.

At the center of the priestly activity, and crucial to the maintenance of the proper and sacred order of things, is the law that the priests must teach: separating what needs to be separated, judging sacral and civil matters according to God's word, and making sure that the holy days are properly safeguarded and sanctified. In this way, the priests stand at the center of the sacred system, mediating between heaven and earth so that God's teachings may be properly applied.

RELATION OF THE *HAFTARAH* TO THE *PARASHAH*

The complex relationship between the regulations linking the *parashah* and the *haftarah* exemplifies the process of tradition and change—the need to maintain continuity with the sacred practices of the past and the desire to preserve the integrity of the tradition through leaders who have proved ready to preserve its ideals. Ezekiel thus functions as a new Moses, a spokesman for God in specifying the proper actions required of priests.

In describing priestly deportment, the *parashah* opens with a warning to "the priests, the sons of Aaron," not to defile themselves by contact with the dead of their people, lest they thereby desecrate their holy status. The only exceptions are certain close blood relations (Lev. 21:1–4). Ezekiel speaks likewise to "the levitical priests descended from Zadok" (Ezek. 44:15) and provides the ritual process for the reincorporation of priests who have been so defiled (vv. 25–27).

The inevitable conflicts that arise between the priests' religious duties and their social or familial obligations is the corollary concern. There are acts of care in the everyday world that take precedence over every personal or ritual consideration. The Sages stress as much in their teaching that a priest must defile himself to honor and dispose of a corpse if he would be the only one who could perform this task (Tanḥ. 3).

44 15Now the levitical priests descended
from Zadok, who maintained the service of My
Sanctuary when the people of Israel went astray
from Me—they shall approach Me to minister
to Me; they shall stand before Me to offer Me
fat and blood—declares the Lord God. 16They

מד 15 וְהַכֹּהֲנִים הַלְוִיִּם בְּנֵי צָדוֹק
אֲשֶׁר שָׁמְרוּ אֶת־מִשְׁמֶרֶת מִקְדָּשִׁי בִּתְעוֹת
בְּנֵי־יִשְׂרָאֵל מֵעָלַי הֵמָּה יִקְרְבוּ אֵלַי
לְשָׁרְתֵנִי וְעָמְדוּ לְפָנַי לְהַקְרִיב לִי חֵלֶב
וָדָם נְאֻם אֲדֹנָי יְהוִה׃ 16 הֵמָּה יָבֹאוּ

Ezekiel 44:15. levitical priests This title refers to priests of the tribe of Levi (Rashi). The designation first occurs in Deut. 18:1 (although that is not a priestly source). The subsequent phrase, in Deut. 18:1, "the whole tribe of Levi," emphasizes that all the Levites are priests, eligible for service in the Temple. The phrase in Deuteronomy appears to counter the position in Leviticus and Numbers, where the priesthood is restricted to the family of Aaron. In Ezekiel, the priesthood is restricted to the Zadokites alone, as a reward for their faithful service.

Zadok This is the ancestral line of priests in Jerusalem. Zadok served as a bearer of the ark for David, along with Abiathar (2 Sam. 15:24–29,35, 17:15). Zadok supported Solomon for dynastic succession (1 Kings 1:8,32), whereas Abiathar backed Adonijah. Therefore, it was Zadok who anointed Solomon king (1 Kings 1:39–45). Eventually, Solomon banished Abiathar (1 Kings 2:27), and Zadok remained the sole priest of the king. It is this old Jerusalemite priesthood that Ezekiel designates for his new Temple program. According to biblical genealogies, priests of the Second Temple were of the Zadokite line up to the Hasmonean rebellion. The Hasmonean priests were not Zadokite. This led to internal divisions among the groups that constituted late Second Temple Jewry.

alone may enter My Sanctuary and they alone shall approach My table to minister to Me; and they shall keep My charge. 17And when they enter the gates of the inner court, they shall wear linen vestments: they shall have nothing woolen upon them when they minister inside the gates of the inner court. 18They shall have linen turbans on their heads and linen breeches on their loins; they shall not gird themselves with anything that causes sweat. 19When they go out to the outer court—the outer court where the people are—they shall remove the vestments in which they minister and shall deposit them in the sacred chambers; they shall put on other garments, lest they make the people consecrated by [contact with] their vestments. 20They shall neither shave their heads nor let their hair go untrimmed; they shall keep their hair trimmed. 21No priest shall drink wine when he enters into the inner court. 22They shall not marry widows or divorced women; they may marry only virgins of the stock of the House of Israel, or widows who are widows of priests.

23They shall declare to My people what is sacred and what is profane, and inform them what is pure and what is impure. 24In lawsuits, too, it is they who shall act as judges; they shall decide them in accordance with My rules. They shall preserve My teachings and My laws regarding all My fixed occasions; and they shall maintain the sanctity of My sabbaths.

25[A priest] shall not defile himself by entering [a house] where there is a dead person. He shall defile himself only for father or mother, son or daughter, brother or unmarried sister. 26After he has become pure, seven days shall be

אֶל־מִקְדָּשִׁי וְהֵמָּה יִקְרְבוּ אֶל־שֻׁלְחָנִי
לְשָׁרְתֵנִי וְשָׁמְרוּ אֶת־מִשְׁמַרְתִּי׃ 17 וְהָיָה
בְּבוֹאָם אֶל־שַׁעֲרֵי הֶחָצֵר הַפְּנִימִית בִּגְדֵי
פִשְׁתִּים יִלְבָּשׁוּ וְלֹא־יַעֲלֶה עֲלֵיהֶם צֶמֶר
בְּשָׁרְתָם בְּשַׁעֲרֵי הֶחָצֵר הַפְּנִימִית
וָבָיְתָה׃ 18 פַּאֲרֵי פִשְׁתִּים יִהְיוּ עַל־רֹאשָׁם
וּמִכְנְסֵי פִשְׁתִּים יִהְיוּ עַל־מָתְנֵיהֶם לֹא
יַחְגְּרוּ בַּיָּזַע׃ 19 וּבְצֵאתָם אֶל־הֶחָצֵר
הַחִיצוֹנָה אֶל־הֶחָצֵר הַחִיצוֹנָה אֶל־הָעָם
יִפְשְׁטוּ אֶת־בִּגְדֵיהֶם אֲשֶׁר־הֵמָּה מְשָׁרְתִם
בָּם וְהִנִּיחוּ אוֹתָם בְּלִשְׁכֹת הַקֹּדֶשׁ וְלָבְשׁוּ
בְּגָדִים אֲחֵרִים וְלֹא־יְקַדְּשׁוּ אֶת־הָעָם
בְּבִגְדֵיהֶם׃ 20 וְרֹאשָׁם לֹא יְגַלֵּחוּ וּפֶרַע לֹא
יְשַׁלֵּחוּ כָּסוֹם יִכְסְמוּ אֶת־רָאשֵׁיהֶם׃
21 וְיַיִן לֹא־יִשְׁתּוּ כָּל־כֹּהֵן בְּבוֹאָם אֶל־
הֶחָצֵר הַפְּנִימִית׃ 22 וְאַלְמָנָה וּגְרוּשָׁה
לֹא־יִקְחוּ לָהֶם לְנָשִׁים כִּי אִם־ בְּתוּלֹת
מִזֶּרַע בֵּית יִשְׂרָאֵל וְהָאַלְמָנָה אֲשֶׁר תִּהְיֶה
אַלְמָנָה מִכֹּהֵן יִקָּחוּ׃
23 וְאֶת־עַמִּי יוֹרוּ בֵּין קֹדֶשׁ לְחֹל וּבֵין־טָמֵא
לְטָהוֹר יוֹדִעֻם׃ 24 וְעַל־רִיב הֵמָּה יַעַמְדוּ
לשפט לְמִשְׁפָּט בְּמִשְׁפָּטַי ושפטהו יִשְׁפְּטֻהוּ
וְאֶת־תּוֹרֹתַי וְאֶת־חֻקֹּתַי בְּכָל־מוֹעֲדַי
יִשְׁמֹרוּ וְאֶת־שַׁבְּתוֹתַי יְקַדֵּשׁוּ׃
25 וְאֶל־מֵת אָדָם לֹא יָבוֹא לְטָמְאָה כִּי
אִם־לְאָב וּלְאֵם וּלְבֵן וּלְבַת לְאָח וּלְאָחוֹת
אֲשֶׁר־לֹא־הָיְתָה לְאִישׁ יִטַּמָּאוּ׃ 26 וְאַחֲרֵי
טָהֳרָתוֹ שִׁבְעַת יָמִים יִסְפְּרוּ־לוֹ׃ 27 וּבְיוֹם

16. My table This may refer to the altar itself and not to the table of the showbread (Targ. Jon., Radak).

19. lest they make the people consecrated The concern is to avoid the real transfer of the holy quality of the vestments to the laity; it is not to avoid the appearance that the people were holy like the priests (Radak).

25. He shall defile himself only for . . . Some ancient Sages noted the absence of the wife in this list and in Lev. 21:2–3. They resolved the matter by suggesting that the reference to near kin in Lev. 21:2 refers to her (cf. *Sifra;* BT Yev. 90b).

26–27. The rules of decontamination from corpse defilement in Ezek. 44:26–27 seem to dif-

counted off for him; 27and on the day that he
reenters the inner court of the Sanctuary to minister in the Sanctuary, he shall present his purification offering—declares the Lord God.
28This shall be their portion, for I am their
portion; and no holding shall be given them in
Israel, for I am their holding. 29The grain offerings, purification offerings, and guilt offerings shall be consumed by them. Everything
proscribed in Israel shall be theirs. 30All the
choice first fruits of every kind, and all the gifts
of every kind—of all your contributions—shall
go to the priests. You shall further give the first
of the yield of your baking to the priest, that a
blessing may rest upon your home.
31Priests shall not eat anything, whether bird
or animal, that died or was torn by beasts.

בֹּאוֹ֩ אֶל־הַקֹּ֨דֶשׁ אֶל־הֶחָצֵ֤ר הַפְּנִימִית֙
לְשָׁרֵ֣ת בַּקֹּ֔דֶשׁ יַקְרִ֖יב חַטָּאת֑וֹ נְאֻ֖ם אֲדֹנָ֥י
יְהוִֽה׃
28 וְהָיְתָ֤ה לָהֶם֙ לְֽנַחֲלָ֔ה אֲנִ֖י נַחֲלָתָ֑ם
וַאֲחֻזָּ֗ה לֹֽא־תִתְּנ֤וּ לָהֶם֙ בְּיִשְׂרָאֵ֔ל אֲנִ֖י
אֲחֻזָּתָֽם׃ 29 הַמִּנְחָה֙ וְהַחַטָּ֣את וְהָאָשָׁ֔ם
הֵ֖מָּה יֹֽאכְל֑וּם וְכָל־חֵ֥רֶם בְּיִשְׂרָאֵ֖ל לָהֶ֥ם
יִהְיֶֽה׃ 30 וְרֵאשִׁית֩ כָּל־בִּכּ֨וּרֵי כֹ֜ל וְכָל־
תְּר֣וּמַת כֹּ֗ל מִכֹּל֙ תְּרֽוּמוֹתֵיכֶ֔ם לַכֹּהֲנִ֖ים
יִהְיֶ֑ה וְרֵאשִׁ֤ית עֲרִסֽוֹתֵיכֶם֙ תִּתְּנ֣וּ לַכֹּהֵ֔ן
לְהָנִ֥יחַ בְּרָכָ֖ה אֶל־בֵּיתֶֽךָ׃
31 כָּל־נְבֵלָה֙ וּטְרֵפָ֔ה מִן־הָע֖וֹף וּמִן־
הַבְּהֵמָ֑ה לֹ֥א יֹאכְל֖וּ הַכֹּהֲנִֽים׃ פ

fer from those stated in Num. 19, where only a seven-day period of purification is prescribed. The added week here for priestly purification has been understood as a special stringency for the New Age (Eliezer of Beaugency; Radak).

28. This shall be their portion Ezekiel's references to priestly portions in verse 29 echo Num. 18:20,23–24 and Deut. 18:1–2. The idea that God is the priests' portion refers to their receipt of portions from the sacrifices offered (Josh. 13:14; see Ezek. 44:29), and to the Israelite tithes (Num. 18:24, see Ezek. 44:30–31).

B'HAR

25 The LORD spoke to Moses on Mount
Sinai: 2Speak to the Israelite people and say to
them:

When you enter the land that I assign to you,
the land shall observe a sabbath of the LORD.
3Six years you may sow your field and six years
you may prune your vineyard and gather in the
yield. 4But in the seventh year the land shall have

בהר

כה וַיְדַבֵּר יְהוָה אֶל־מֹשֶׁה בְּהַר סִינַי
לֵאמֹר׃ 2 דַּבֵּר אֶל־בְּנֵי יִשְׂרָאֵל וְאָמַרְתָּ
אֲלֵהֶם
כִּי תָבֹאוּ אֶל־הָאָרֶץ אֲשֶׁר אֲנִי נֹתֵן
לָכֶם וְשָׁבְתָה הָאָרֶץ שַׁבָּת לַיהוָה׃ 3 שֵׁשׁ
שָׁנִים תִּזְרַע שָׂדֶךָ וְשֵׁשׁ שָׁנִים תִּזְמֹר
כַּרְמֶךָ וְאָסַפְתָּ אֶת־תְּבוּאָתָהּ׃ 4 וּבַשָּׁנָה

The Pursuit of Holiness (*continued*)

PRINCIPLES OF LAND TENURE (25:1–26:2)

Chapter 25 is the only law code on the subject of land tenure in ancient Israel that is preserved in the Torah. It governs the permanent rights of landowners and the legalities of the sale and mortgaging of land. There are also laws regarding indebtedness and indenture, a system of repaying debts through one's labors, and the commandment regarding the jubilee year.

SABBATICAL YEAR AND JUBILEE (vv. 1–23)

2. the land shall observe a sabbath The land is personified. It, too, tires and requires rest (see Exod. 23:10–11).

3. six years you may prune your vineyard Pruning was essential for ensuring the growth of the grapes. There were two prunings each year: one in the winter, or rainy season, when the shoots that had not produced grapes the previous year were snipped off, and the second in June or July, when the new blossoms had already appeared.

4. Allowing the land to lie fallow every seventh year reduced the amount of sodium in the

---

At the heart of this *parashah* is the visionary concept of returning land to its original owner at the end of a 50-year cycle. This prevents the polarization of society into two classes: wealthy, powerful landowners on the one hand and permanently impoverished people on the other. In an agrarian society, a farmer who sold all the land to pay debts had no prospect of ever being anything other than a servant. Nor would a servant's sons ever rise above that level. Anticipating the human misery and social instability this would lead to, the Torah provides a plan. In the 50th year, families would reclaim the land they had held originally and later sold. Behind this plan are two religious assumptions. Because all the earth and all of its inhabitants belong to God, human beings cannot possess either the land or the people in perpetuity. And no human being should be condemned to permanent servitude. Some critics have seen this as a utopian plan that never was put into practice, but archaeologists have found records of deeds from the late biblical period containing references to the number of years remaining till the jubilee year.

Kook taught that the purpose of the jubilee was primarily spiritual, not economic. It came to restore the sense of unity that once prevailed in Israel and to restore self-respect to the person who had sunk into poverty and a sense of failure. Even as the weekly *Shabbat* enables people to define themselves in noneconomic terms, the sabbatical year and the jubilee enable an entire society to put aside economic competition and the practice of defining a person's value in economic terms alone.

CHAPTER 25

1. Why does the Torah emphasize that these agricultural laws were promulgated at Mount Sinai? Perhaps because at Sinai no one owned any land yet, and no one could object that the law deprived people of what they had worked to acquire. It is easier to propose a visionary system of equality when all start out equal. Another interpretation: Just as Sinai was the smallest of the mountains but the words spoken there changed the world, so the people Israel, among the smallest of the nations, presents a vision of social justice that has the power to change the world.

4. The Holy Land, like the holy people who

a sabbath of complete rest, a sabbath of the
LORD: you shall not sow your field or prune your
vineyard. 5You shall not reap the aftergrowth
of your harvest or gather the grapes of your untrimmed vines; it shall be a year of complete rest
for the land. 6But you may eat whatever the land
during its sabbath will produce—you, your
male and female slaves, the hired and bound laborers who live with you, 7and your cattle and
the beasts in your land may eat all its yield.

8You shall count off seven weeks of years—
seven times seven years—so that the period of
seven weeks of years gives you a total of forty-
nine years. 9Then you shall sound the horn
loud; in the seventh month, on the tenth day
of the month—the Day of Atonement—you
shall have the horn sounded throughout your
land 10and you shall hallow the fiftieth year. You

הַשְּׁבִיעִ֗ת שַׁבַּ֤ת שַׁבָּתוֹן֙ יִהְיֶ֣ה לָאָ֔רֶץ שַׁבָּ֖ת
לַיהוָ֑ה שָֽׂדְךָ֙ לֹ֣א תִזְרָ֔ע וְכַרְמְךָ֖ לֹ֥א תִזְמֹֽר׃
5 אֵ֣ת סְפִ֤יחַ קְצִֽירְךָ֙ לֹ֣א תִקְצ֔וֹר וְאֶת־עִנְּבֵ֥י
נְזִירֶ֖ךָ לֹ֣א תִבְצֹ֑ר שְׁנַ֥ת שַׁבָּת֖וֹן יִהְיֶ֥ה
לָאָֽרֶץ׃ 6 וְֽ֠הָיְתָה שַׁבַּ֨ת הָאָ֤רֶץ לָכֶם֙
לְאָכְלָ֔ה לְךָ֖ וּלְעַבְדְּךָ֣ וְלַאֲמָתֶ֑ךָ וְלִשְׂכִֽירְךָ֙
וּלְתוֹשָׁ֣בְךָ֔ הַגָּרִ֖ים עִמָּֽךְ׃ 7 וְלִ֙בְהֶמְתְּךָ֔
וְלַֽחַיָּ֖ה אֲשֶׁ֣ר בְּאַרְצֶ֑ךָ תִּהְיֶ֥ה כָל־תְּבוּאָתָ֖הּ
לֶאֱכֹֽל׃ ס
8 וְסָפַרְתָּ֣ לְךָ֗ שֶׁ֚בַע שַׁבְּתֹ֣ת שָׁנִ֔ים שֶׁ֥בַע
שָׁנִ֖ים שֶׁ֣בַע פְּעָמִ֑ים וְהָי֣וּ לְךָ֗ יְמֵי֙ שֶׁ֚בַע
שַׁבְּתֹ֣ת הַשָּׁנִ֔ים תֵּ֥שַׁע וְאַרְבָּעִ֖ים שָׁנָֽה׃
9 וְהַֽעֲבַרְתָּ֞ שׁוֹפַ֤ר תְּרוּעָה֙ בַּחֹ֣דֶשׁ הַשְּׁבִעִ֔י
בֶּעָשׂ֖וֹר לַחֹ֑דֶשׁ בְּיוֹם֙ הַכִּפֻּרִ֔ים תַּעֲבִ֥ירוּ
שׁוֹפָ֖ר בְּכָל־אַרְצְכֶֽם׃ 10 וְקִדַּשְׁתֶּ֗ם אֵ֣ת

soil, especially in areas where the land was irrigated.

5. aftergrowth of your harvest That which grows naturally the following season from seeds that fell to the ground during reaping.

untrimmed vines Hebrew: *nazir;* or "forbidden vines" (cf. Num. 2:11–12).

6. hired . . . laborers Hebrew: *sakhir,* which usually refers to a laborer who works for wages.

bound laborers Hebrew: *toshav,* which often designates a foreign "resident," a merchant or laborer.

7. The reference to beasts symbolizes the freedom characteristic of the sabbatical year: Humans and beast are free to roam about and gather their sustenance.

9. The sounding of the *shofar* five days before the autumn harvest festival of *Sukkot* (even on *Shabbat*) served to proclaim the advent of the jubilee.

10. hallow Hebrew: *kiddesh* (sanctify, hallow), customarily used to convey the sanctification of *Shabbat.* The use of this verb in connection with the jubilee creates a parallelism between the

will inhabit it, needs a *Shabbat* to replenish itself and bear witness to God's ownership of it. Chapter 26 threatens that if the people Israel do not live by God's ways, the Land will be devastated by enemies and "make up for its sabbath years" (Lev. 26:34). The prophet Jeremiah predicted 70 years of exile in Babylonia to make up for the 70 sabbatical years the people neglected during their approximately 500 years of living in Israel (see 2 Chron. 36:21).

6. you may eat whatever the land during its sabbath may produce Sometimes the wealthy don't believe that poor people are actually suffering, suspecting that they are just too lazy to provide for themselves. Let the wealthy undergo the experience of not knowing whether there will be enough to eat, and their attitudes will change.

HALAKHAH L'MA·ASEH

25:5. You shall not reap Restrictions on working the land and purchasing agricultural produce during sabbatical years refer solely to the Land of Israel. Some still observe these restrictions in Israel today. The *Va·ad Halakhah* (Law Committee) of the Masorti/Conservative Movement in Israel has ruled that in modern times the laws of the seventh-year produce (*sh'mittah*) are neither biblically nor rabbinically required but are considered a *middat ḥassidut* (an act of piety). The *Va·ad* recommends that *kibbutzim* observe some of the *sh'mittah* laws by letting one field lie fallow as the *sh'mittah* field, and that they give a percentage of their income to the poor, because that was the original purpose of the law.

shall proclaim release throughout the land for all its inhabitants. It shall be a jubilee for you: each of you shall return to his holding and each of you shall return to his family. ¹¹That fiftieth year shall be a jubilee for you: you shall not sow, neither shall you reap the aftergrowth or harvest the untrimmed vines, ¹²for it is a jubilee. It shall be holy to you: you may only eat the growth direct from the field.

¹³In this year of jubilee, each of you shall return to his holding. ¹⁴When you sell property to your neighbor, or buy any from your neighbor, you shall not wrong one another. ¹⁵In buying from your neighbor, you shall deduct only

שְׁנַ֣ת הַחֲמִשִּׁים֮ שָׁנָה֒ וּקְרָאתֶ֥ם דְּר֛וֹר בָּאָ֖רֶץ לְכָל־יֹשְׁבֶ֑יהָ יוֹבֵ֥ל הִוא֙ תִּהְיֶ֣ה לָכֶ֔ם וְשַׁבְתֶּ֗ם אִ֚ישׁ אֶל־אֲחֻזָּת֔וֹ וְאִ֖ישׁ אֶל־מִשְׁפַּחְתּ֥וֹ תָּשֻֽׁבוּ: 11 יוֹבֵ֣ל הִ֗וא שְׁנַ֛ת הַחֲמִשִּׁ֥ים שָׁנָ֖ה תִּהְיֶ֣ה לָכֶ֑ם לֹ֣א תִזְרָ֔עוּ וְלֹ֤א תִקְצְרוּ֙ אֶת־סְפִיחֶ֔יהָ וְלֹ֥א תִבְצְר֖וּ אֶת־נְזִרֶֽיהָ: 12 כִּ֚י יוֹבֵ֣ל הִ֔וא קֹ֖דֶשׁ תִּהְיֶ֣ה לָכֶ֑ם מִן־הַ֨שָּׂדֶ֔ה תֹּאכְל֖וּ אֶת־תְּבוּאָתָֽהּ: 13 בִּשְׁנַ֖ת הַיּוֹבֵ֣ל הַזֹּ֑את תָּשֻׁ֕בוּ אִ֖ישׁ אֶל־אֲחֻזָּתֽוֹ: 14 וְכִֽי־תִמְכְּר֤וּ מִמְכָּר֙ לַעֲמִיתֶ֔ךָ א֥וֹ קָנֹ֖ה מִיַּ֣ד עֲמִיתֶ֑ךָ אַל־תּוֹנ֖וּ אִ֥ישׁ אֶת־אָחִֽיו: 15 בְּמִסְפַּ֤ר שָׁנִים֙ אַחַ֣ר הַיּוֹבֵ֔ל תִּקְנֶ֖ה

---

two occasions. The jubilee year is to be hallowed just as *Shabbat* is hallowed.

release Hebrew: *d'ror*, usually translated "freedom, liberty." It is related to the ancient Akkadian word *anduraru*, which refers to an edict issued by Mesopotamian kings when they ascended the throne. As a gesture of royal benevolence and power, they would proclaim a moratorium on debts and indenture, thereby releasing those bound by servitude.

jubilee Hebrew: *yovel*, which means both "ram" and "ram's horn." The 50th year is called "jubilee" because its arrival is announced by sounding the ram's horn.

each of you shall return to his holding This refers primarily to families who had been unable to repay their loans and were evicted from their homes and farms due to foreclosure. This situation is projected in verses 13–17 and 25–28.

family Hebrew: *mishpaḥah* (clan). It is the basic socioeconomic unit in ancient Israel, more inclusive than the immediate family.

12. The owners of fields and groves are forbidden to harvest their yields in the usual way, but must leave it for all to eat. They may, of course, join others in gathering food but not in the status of owners.

13. This general introductory statement is followed by a delineation of the specific conditions under which a person was likely to lose possession of his or her land in the first place.

14. This law applies only to transfers of property among Israelites.

you shall not wrong one another The following verses explain how to avoid fraud in land transfers.

15. The value of leases on the land was to be computed in terms of crop years, because all land

---

10. proclaim release This clause is inscribed on the Liberty Bell. Some commentators derive the word *d'ror*, "release," from the Hebrew root *dar*, "to dwell," and understand it to mean the freedom to live wherever one wants.

for all its inhabitants The jubilee year brings freedom not only to the slaves but also to the slave owners, freeing them from the dehumanizing situation of having such power over other human beings (*P'nei Y'hoshu·a*). We find a similar insight in Eccles. 4:1: "I further observed . . . the tears of the oppressed, with none to comfort them; and the power of their oppressors—with none to comfort them." Hirsch understands the word the word for "ju-

bilee" (*yovel*) to mean "a summoning home" of the rightful owners of the land.

14. you shall not wrong one another This rule, specifically applied to real estate sales, is expanded by the Talmud to include all commercial transactions. Egregious overcharging is grounds for canceling an agreement (BT BM 47b). The Midrash extends the concept still further to include wronging a person with harmful words (Lev. R. 33:1). This includes reminding a repentant sinner of his or her former misdeeds and asking a merchant the price of something when you have no intention of buying. Pious persons do not deceive even themselves.

for the number of years since the jubilee; and in selling to you, he shall charge you only for the remaining crop years: 16the more such years, the higher the price you pay; the fewer such years, the lower the price; for what he is selling you is a number of harvests. 17Do not wrong one another, but fear your God; for I the LORD am your God.

18You shall observe My laws and faithfully keep My rules, that you may live upon the land in security; 19the land shall yield its fruit and you shall eat your fill, and you shall live upon it in security. 20And should you ask, "What are we to eat in the seventh year, if we may neither sow nor gather in our crops?" 21I will ordain My blessing for you in the sixth year, so that it shall yield a crop sufficient for three years. 22When you sow in the eighth year, you will still be eating old grain of that crop; you will be eating the old until the ninth year, until its crops come in.

23But the land must not be sold beyond reclaim, for the land is Mine; you are but strangers resident with Me. 24Throughout the land that you hold, you must provide for the redemption of the land.

מֵאֵת עֲמִיתֶךָ בְּמִסְפַּר שְׁנֵי־תְבוּאֹת יִמְכָּר־
לָךְ׃ 16 לְפִי ׀ רֹב הַשָּׁנִים תַּרְבֶּה מִקְנָתוֹ
וּלְפִי מְעֹט הַשָּׁנִים תַּמְעִיט מִקְנָתוֹ כִּי
מִסְפַּר תְּבוּאֹת הוּא מֹכֵר לָךְ׃ 17 וְלֹא תוֹנוּ
אִישׁ אֶת־עֲמִיתוֹ וְיָרֵאתָ מֵאֱלֹהֶיךָ כִּי אֲנִי
יְהוָה אֱלֹהֵיכֶם׃
18 וַעֲשִׂיתֶם אֶת־חֻקֹּתַי וְאֶת־מִשְׁפָּטַי
תִּשְׁמְרוּ וַעֲשִׂיתֶם אֹתָם וִישַׁבְתֶּם עַל־
הָאָרֶץ לָבֶטַח׃ 19 וְנָתְנָה הָאָרֶץ פִּרְיָהּ לישי [שני]
וַאֲכַלְתֶּם לָשֹׂבַע וִישַׁבְתֶּם לָבֶטַח עָלֶיהָ׃
20 וְכִי תֹאמְרוּ מַה־נֹּאכַל בַּשָּׁנָה הַשְּׁבִיעִת
הֵן לֹא נִזְרָע וְלֹא נֶאֱסֹף אֶת־תְּבוּאָתֵנוּ׃
21 וְצִוִּיתִי אֶת־בִּרְכָתִי לָכֶם בַּשָּׁנָה
הַשִּׁשִּׁית וְעָשָׂת אֶת־הַתְּבוּאָה לִשְׁלֹשׁ
הַשָּׁנִים׃ 22 וּזְרַעְתֶּם אֵת הַשָּׁנָה הַשְּׁמִינִת
וַאֲכַלְתֶּם מִן־הַתְּבוּאָה יָשָׁן עַד ׀ הַשָּׁנָה
הַתְּשִׁיעִת עַד־בּוֹא תְּבוּאָתָהּ תֹּאכְלוּ יָשָׁן׃
23 וְהָאָרֶץ לֹא תִמָּכֵר לִצְמִתֻת כִּי־לִי
הָאָרֶץ כִּי־גֵרִים וְתוֹשָׁבִים אַתֶּם עִמָּדִי׃
24 וּבְכֹל אֶרֶץ אֲחֻזַּתְכֶם גְּאֻלָּה תִּתְּנוּ
לָאָרֶץ׃ ס יעי

that was "sold" would revert to its original owners at the next jubilee.

17. The Israelites are urged to act out of fear of God, especially in matters whose norms are not easily enforced.

SECURITY AND ABUNDANCE (vv. 18–22)

This section interrupts the continuity of legislation governing the sabbatical and jubilee years. It is an exhortation to obey God's laws and commandments, with the promise of security and abundance as a reward for such obedience.

18. live upon the land in security That is, the people will not fear invasions.

19. Along with security will come fertility and abundance.

20. This verse projects the anxiety of the people.

21–22. The response to the people. Until the crop of the eighth year is harvested, you will have sufficient food from the "old" crop, namely, that of the sixth year.

23. The text returns to its original subject: the inalienable status of the land.

ADDITIONAL LAND TENURE AND INDENTURE LAWS (vv. 24–55)

24. This general statement is followed by a series of situations in which the rule applies. The effect of this law is to obligate the purchaser to accept the redemption payment of the original owner.

---

23. you are but strangers resident with Me Even the Israelites are but God's tenants, resident aliens in the Land. Only if they live up to the terms of the Covenant will they endure there.

25 If your kinsman is in straits and has to sell part of his holding, his nearest redeemer shall come and redeem what his kinsman has sold. 26 If a man has no one to redeem for him, but prospers and acquires enough to redeem with, 27 he shall compute the years since its sale, refund the difference to the man to whom he sold it, and return to his holding. 28 If he lacks sufficient means to recover it, what he sold shall remain with the purchaser until the jubilee; in the jubilee year it shall be released, and he shall return to his holding.

29 If a man sells a dwelling house in a walled city, it may be redeemed until a year has elapsed since its sale; the redemption period shall be a year. 30 If it is not redeemed before a full year has elapsed, the house in the walled city shall pass to the purchaser beyond reclaim throughout the ages; it shall not be released in the jubilee. 31 But houses in villages that have no encircling walls shall be classed as open country: they may be redeemed, and they shall be released through the jubilee. 32 As for the cities of the Levites, the houses in the cities they hold—the Levites shall forever have the right of redemption. 33 Such property as may be redeemed from the Levites—houses sold in a city they hold—shall be released through the jubi-

רביעי 25 כִּֽי־יָמוּךְ אָחִיךָ וּמָכַר מֵאֲחֻזָּתוֹ וּבָא
גֹֽאֲלוֹ הַקָּרֹב אֵלָיו וְגָאַל אֵת מִמְכַּר אָחִֽיו׃
26 וְאִישׁ כִּי לֹא יִֽהְיֶה־לּוֹ גֹּאֵל וְהִשִּׂיגָה יָדוֹ
וּמָצָא כְּדֵי גְאֻלָּתֽוֹ׃ 27 וְחִשַּׁב אֶת־שְׁנֵי
מִמְכָּרוֹ וְהֵשִׁיב אֶת־הָעֹדֵף לָאִישׁ אֲשֶׁר
מָֽכַר־לוֹ וְשָׁב לַאֲחֻזָּתֽוֹ׃ 28 וְאִם לֹא־מָֽצְאָה
יָדוֹ דֵּי הָשִׁיב לוֹ וְהָיָה מִמְכָּרוֹ בְּיַד הַקֹּנֶה
אֹתוֹ עַד שְׁנַת הַיּוֹבֵל וְיָצָא בַּיֹּבֵל וְשָׁב
לַאֲחֻזָּתֽוֹ׃
חמישי [שלישי] 29 וְאִישׁ כִּֽי־יִמְכֹּר בֵּית־מוֹשַׁב עִיר חוֹמָה
וְהָיְתָה גְּאֻלָּתוֹ עַד־תֹּם שְׁנַת מִמְכָּרוֹ יָמִים
תִּהְיֶה גְאֻלָּתֽוֹ׃ 30 וְאִם לֹֽא־יִגָּאֵל עַד־
מְלֹאת לוֹ שָׁנָה תְמִימָה וְקָם הַבַּיִת
אֲשֶׁר־בָּעִיר אֲשֶׁר־לא לוֹ חֹמָה לַצְּמִיתֻת
לַקֹּנֶה אֹתוֹ לְדֹרֹתָיו לֹא יֵצֵא בַּיֹּבֵֽל׃
31 וּבָתֵּי הַחֲצֵרִים אֲשֶׁר אֵין־לָהֶם חֹמָה
סָבִיב עַל־שְׂדֵה הָאָרֶץ יֵחָשֵׁב גְּאֻלָּה
תִּֽהְיֶה־לּוֹ וּבַיֹּבֵל יֵצֵֽא׃ 32 וְעָרֵי הַלְוִיִּם בָּתֵּי
עָרֵי אֲחֻזָּתָם גְּאֻלַּת עוֹלָם תִּהְיֶה לַלְוִיִּֽם׃
33 וַאֲשֶׁר יִגְאַל מִן־הַלְוִיִּם וְיָצָא מִמְכַּר־
בַּיִת וְעִיר אֲחֻזָּתוֹ בַּיֹּבֵל כִּי בָתֵּי עָרֵי

25. The object of redemption is to restore the property to one's relative, who would retain possession of the land within the clan. The redeemer himself or herself would not possess the land.

27. One who wished to redeem land he or she had sold was required to pay the purchaser the value of the rest of the lease.

29. In the ancient Near East, towns and cities had a special status in regard to tax exemptions and legal prerogatives. Arable land and pastureland were the economic mainstays of an agrarian society and accounted for most of the employment, in addition to their value as the source of food. The artisans and those we would today call members of the service professions, which often included members of priestly families, lived in the towns.

31. villages Hebrew: *ḥatzerim,* which refers to agricultural villages with houses and fields, not tents and pastureland.

32. The urban dwellings of the Levites within their cities are to be released on the jubilee. They are redeemable, unlike other urban dwellings, which are subject to a different law, according to verse 31.

33. This verse concerns urban dwellings that

HALAKHAH L'MA·ASEH

25:25. If your kinsman is in straits Jewish law requires extending help to people in financial straits so that their economic condition does not worsen. According to Maimonides, helping people help themselves become financially independent is the highest form of *tz'dakah* (charity, or literally, righteousness) (MT Gifts to the Poor 10:7–14).

lee; for the houses in the cities of the Levites are
their holding among the Israelites. 34But the unenclosed land about their cities cannot be sold,
for that is their holding for all time.

35If your kinsman, being in straits, comes under your authority, and you hold him as though
a resident alien, let him live by your side: 36do
not exact from him advance or accrued interest,
but fear your God. Let him live by your side as
your kinsman. 37Do not lend him your money
at advance interest, or give him your food at accrued interest. 38I the LORD am your God, who
brought you out of the land of Egypt, to give
you the land of Canaan, to be your God.

הַלְוִיִּם הִוא אֲחֻזָּתָם בְּתוֹךְ בְּנֵי יִשְׂרָאֵל׃
34 וּשְׂדֵה מִגְרַשׁ עָרֵיהֶם לֹא יִמָּכֵר כִּי־
אֲחֻזַּת עוֹלָם הוּא לָהֶם׃ ס
35 וְכִי־יָמוּךְ אָחִיךָ וּמָטָה יָדוֹ עִמָּךְ
וְהֶחֱזַקְתָּ בּוֹ גֵּר וְתוֹשָׁב וָחַי עִמָּךְ׃ 36 אַל־
תִּקַּח מֵאִתּוֹ נֶשֶׁךְ וְתַרְבִּית וְיָרֵאתָ
מֵאֱלֹהֶיךָ וְחֵי אָחִיךָ עִמָּךְ׃ 37 אֶת־כַּסְפְּךָ
לֹא־תִתֵּן לוֹ בְּנֶשֶׁךְ וּבְמַרְבִּית לֹא־תִתֵּן
אָכְלֶךָ׃ 38 אֲנִי יְהוָה אֱלֹהֵיכֶם אֲשֶׁר־
הוֹצֵאתִי אֶתְכֶם מֵאֶרֶץ מִצְרָיִם לָתֵת
לָכֶם אֶת־אֶרֶץ כְּנַעַן לִהְיוֹת לָכֶם
לֵאלֹהִים׃ ס שי
[יעי]

had been sold or mortgaged by Levites who found themselves in difficult financial straits.

34. the unenclosed land about their cities cannot be sold Perhaps the reason for this restriction was related to the sustenance that the Levites derived from such plots of land, the only ones they possessed.

their holding for all time The rights to the land conferred by God to the Israelites are permanent. The plots of the Levites remain always in the possession of the Levites.

INDEBTEDNESS AND INDENTURE (vv. 35–46)

A person with debts who possesses property that can be sold or mortgaged is still free, but a person who has no assets must work off the debts as an indentured servant.

35. you hold him as though a resident alien Those who mortgaged their land or sold it to another became, in a real sense, tenants on their own land.

let him live by your side The person involved may not be evicted from the land but must be allowed to continue to reside at your side as a member of the community.

38. The God who gave the Israelites a land of their own and freed them from the servitude of Egypt now commands them, in turn, to prevent conditions of servitude among their own people.

---

35. If your kinsman, being in straits Literally, "if your kinsman stumbles." This prompted the Sages to comment that it is easier to support a person and hold him or her up when the person first begins to stumble than it is to pick the person up after he or she has fallen (*Sifra*). It is easier to prevent poverty than to cure it.

36. Let him live by your side as your kinsman This verse is the source of the famous ruling by Akiva: If two men in a desert have enough water to keep only one of them alive, the possessor of the water may drink it all rather than share it and condemn both to die of thirst. Our neighbors are entitled to live alongside us, not instead of us (BT BM 62a).

38. Why the reference to God's bringing Israel out of Egypt? To remind us that we owe all we have to God and dare not keep it all for ourselves? Or perhaps to imply that God, having given us the land of the Canaanites, holds Israel to a higher moral standard than that practiced by the Canaanites (Hoffman).

HALAKHAH L'MA·ASEH

25:35. you hold him The Joint Social Action Commission of the Rabbinical Assembly and of the United Synagogue of Conservative Judaism has published a Rabbinic Letter to articulate the theological convictions underlying the Torah's concern for the poor and to apply them to modern measures for alleviating the plight of the poor (Dorff, *"You Shall Strengthen Them"*).

25:36. interest See Comments to Exod. 22:24; Deut. 23:20.

[39]If your kinsman under you continues in straits and must give himself over to you, do not subject him to the treatment of a slave. [40]He shall remain with you as a hired or bound laborer; he shall serve with you only until the jubilee year. [41]Then he and his children with him shall be free of your authority; he shall go back to his family and return to his ancestral holding.—[42]For they are My servants, whom I freed from the land of Egypt; they may not give themselves over into servitude.—[43]You shall not rule over him ruthlessly; you shall fear your God. [44]Such male and female slaves as you may have—it is from the nations round about you that you may acquire male and female slaves. [45]You may also buy them from among the children of aliens resident among you, or from their families that are among you, whom they begot in your land. These shall become your property: [46]you may keep them as a possession for your children after you, for them to inherit as property for all time. Such you may treat as slaves. But as for your Israelite kinsmen, no one shall rule ruthlessly over the other.

[47]If a resident alien among you has prospered, and your kinsman being in straits, comes under his authority and gives himself over to the res-

ששי [רביעי] 39 וְכִי־יָמוּךְ אָחִיךָ עִמָּךְ וְנִמְכַּר־לָךְ לֹא־
תַעֲבֹד בּוֹ עֲבֹדַת עָבֶד׃ 40 כְּשָׂכִיר כְּתוֹשָׁב
יִהְיֶה עִמָּךְ עַד־שְׁנַת הַיֹּבֵל יַעֲבֹד עִמָּךְ׃
41 וְיָצָא מֵעִמָּךְ הוּא וּבָנָיו עִמּוֹ וְשָׁב
אֶל־מִשְׁפַּחְתּוֹ וְאֶל־אֲחֻזַּת אֲבֹתָיו יָשׁוּב׃
42 כִּי־עֲבָדַי הֵם אֲשֶׁר־הוֹצֵאתִי אֹתָם
מֵאֶרֶץ מִצְרָיִם לֹא יִמָּכְרוּ מִמְכֶּרֶת עָבֶד׃
43 לֹא־תִרְדֶּה בוֹ בְּפָרֶךְ וְיָרֵאתָ מֵאֱלֹהֶיךָ׃
44 וְעַבְדְּךָ וַאֲמָתְךָ אֲשֶׁר יִהְיוּ־לָךְ מֵאֵת
הַגּוֹיִם אֲשֶׁר סְבִיבֹתֵיכֶם מֵהֶם תִּקְנוּ עֶבֶד
וְאָמָה׃ 45 וְגַם מִבְּנֵי הַתּוֹשָׁבִים הַגָּרִים
עִמָּכֶם מֵהֶם תִּקְנוּ וּמִמִּשְׁפַּחְתָּם אֲשֶׁר
עִמָּכֶם אֲשֶׁר הוֹלִידוּ בְּאַרְצְכֶם וְהָיוּ לָכֶם
לַאֲחֻזָּה׃ 46 וְהִתְנַחַלְתֶּם אֹתָם לִבְנֵיכֶם
אַחֲרֵיכֶם לָרֶשֶׁת אֲחֻזָּה לְעֹלָם בָּהֶם
תַּעֲבֹדוּ וּבְאַחֵיכֶם בְּנֵי־יִשְׂרָאֵל אִישׁ
בְּאָחִיו לֹא־תִרְדֶּה בוֹ בְּפָרֶךְ׃ ס
שביעי 47 וְכִי תַשִּׂיג יַד גֵּר וְתוֹשָׁב עִמָּךְ וּמָךְ אָחִיךָ
עִמּוֹ וְנִמְכַּר לְגֵר תּוֹשָׁב עִמָּךְ אוֹ לְעֵקֶר

39. An Israelite indentured to another Israelite must not be treated as a slave.

40. as a hired or bound laborer The indentured Israelite has the legal status of an employee.

only until the jubilee year The laws of Exod. 21:1–6 and Deut. 15:12–18, which deal with slavery, set 6 years as the limit of service. Indenture, however, may last as long as 50 years.

41. Indentured servants often lived on the estates of their masters. With the jubilee, land was restored to its original owners and indentured servants were released. Thus indentured Israelites had a home, once again, to which they could return.

42. For they are My servants By redeeming the Israelites from Egyptian bondage, God acquired them as "slaves." God's claim has priority.

45. your property In ancient law, slaves often were regarded as having a legal status parallel to that of land. Just as the land was a "holding" to be handed down within families, so were slaves.

46. The rights granted to Israelites over their non-Israelite slaves, like those they had over the Land, were permanent.

43. ruthlessly Hebrew: *b'farekh.* The word recurs in verses 46 and 53. Except in Ezek. 34:4, it appears nowhere else in the Bible outside of the account of Israel's enslavement in Egypt. It apparently means a particularly rigorous kind of work. Maimonides suggests that it refers to work done not to benefit the master but to exhaust and humiliate the slave, work done only to emphasize the master's power over the slave (MT Slaves 1:6).

ident alien among you, or to an offshoot of an
alien's family, 48he shall have the right of redemption even after he has given himself over.
One of his kinsmen shall redeem him, 49or his
uncle or his uncle's son shall redeem him, or
anyone of his family who is of his own flesh shall
redeem him; or, if he prospers, he may redeem
himself. 50He shall compute with his purchaser
the total from the year he gave himself over to
him until the jubilee year; the price of his sale
shall be applied to the number of years, as
though it were for a term as a hired laborer under the other's authority. 51If many years remain, he shall pay back for his redemption in
proportion to his purchase price; 52and if few
years remain until the jubilee year, he shall so
compute: he shall make payment for his redemption according to the years involved. 53He
shall be under his authority as a laborer hired
by the year; he shall not rule ruthlessly over him
in your sight. 54If he has not been redeemed in
any of those ways, he and his children with him
shall go free in the jubilee year. 55For it is to Me
that the Israelites are servants: they are My servants, whom I freed from the land of Egypt,
I the Lord your God.

מִשְׁפַּחַת גֵּר׃ 48 אַחֲרֵי נִמְכַּר גְּאֻלָּה תִּהְיֶה־
לּוֹ אֶחָד מֵאֶחָיו יִגְאָלֶנּוּ׃ 49 אוֹ־דֹדוֹ
אוֹ בֶן־דֹּדוֹ יִגְאָלֶנּוּ אוֹ־מִשְּׁאֵר בְּשָׂרוֹ
מִמִּשְׁפַּחְתּוֹ יִגְאָלֶנּוּ אוֹ־הִשִּׂיגָה יָדוֹ וְנִגְאָל׃
50 וְחִשַּׁב עִם־קֹנֵהוּ מִשְּׁנַת הִמָּכְרוֹ לוֹ עַד
שְׁנַת הַיֹּבֵל וְהָיָה כֶּסֶף מִמְכָּרוֹ בְּמִסְפַּר
שָׁנִים כִּימֵי שָׂכִיר יִהְיֶה עִמּוֹ׃ 51 אִם־עוֹד
רַבּוֹת בַּשָּׁנִים לְפִיהֶן יָשִׁיב גְּאֻלָּתוֹ מִכֶּסֶף
מִקְנָתוֹ׃ 52 וְאִם־מְעַט נִשְׁאַר בַּשָּׁנִים עַד־
שְׁנַת הַיֹּבֵל וְחִשַּׁב־לוֹ כְּפִי שָׁנָיו יָשִׁיב
אֶת־גְּאֻלָּתוֹ׃ 53 כִּשְׂכִיר שָׁנָה בְּשָׁנָה יִהְיֶה
עִמּוֹ לֹא־יִרְדֶּנּוּ בְּפֶרֶךְ לְעֵינֶיךָ׃ 54 וְאִם־לֹא
יִגָּאֵל בְּאֵלֶּה וְיָצָא בִּשְׁנַת הַיֹּבֵל הוּא וּבָנָיו
עִמּוֹ׃ 55 כִּי־לִי בְנֵי־יִשְׂרָאֵל עֲבָדִים עֲבָדַי מפטיר
הֵם אֲשֶׁר־הוֹצֵאתִי אוֹתָם מֵאֶרֶץ מִצְרָיִם
אֲנִי יְהוָה אֱלֹהֵיכֶם׃

INDENTURE TO A NON-ISRAELITE
(vv. 47–54)

48. right of redemption The clan of the Israelite indentured to a non-Israelite bears the responsibility for redeeming its kinsman.

One of his kinsmen shall redeem him This is the order of obligation to redeem kinsmen within the clan: brothers, then uncles and cousins, then other blood relatives. These could even include grandchildren, also considered blood relatives in the laws of Lev. 18:10.

49. of his own flesh A clan is usually a fairly large unit, and not all relatives within it are of the same blood.

50. compute The computation is in terms of wages over a period of years.

53. To allow a fellow Israelite to remain indentured to a gentile would be a cruel humiliation. One was not permitted to remain indifferent in such a situation, which could lead to the forfeiture of land that had been mortgaged to debts and its seizure by non-Israelites.

54. The last recourse is the jubilee, when all other efforts have failed.

---

48. The obligation of a kinsman to redeem a relative from bondage to a non-Israelite would become the source in postbiblical times of the obligation to ransom Jews taken captive (*pidyon sh'vuyyim*). Communities would go to great lengths to save their fellow Jews in that situation, even selling Torah scrolls to redeem hostages. In the last three decades of the 20th century, successful efforts were undertaken by the Jewish community to bring Jews out of Ethiopia, Syria, and the former Soviet Union. The guiding principle is "all Jews are responsible one for another" (*kol Yisra·el arevim zeh ba-zeh*).

26 You shall not make idols for yourselves, or set up for yourselves carved images or pillars, or place figured stones in your land to worship upon, for I the LORD am your God. 2You shall keep My sabbaths and venerate My sanctuary, Mine, the LORD's.

כו לֹא־תַעֲשׂוּ לָכֶם אֱלִילִם וּפֶסֶל
וּמַצֵּבָה לֹא־תָקִימוּ לָכֶם וְאֶבֶן מַשְׂכִּית
לֹא תִתְּנוּ בְּאַרְצְכֶם לְהִשְׁתַּחֲוֺת עָלֶיהָ
כִּי אֲנִי יְהֹוָה אֱלֹהֵיכֶם׃ 2 אֶת־שַׁבְּתֹתַי
תִּשְׁמֹרוּ וּמִקְדָּשִׁי תִּירָאוּ אֲנִי יְהֹוָה׃* ס

POSTSCRIPT (26:1–2)

2. Instead of worshiping improperly, Israelites should attend God's legitimate sanctuary.

CHAPTER 26

1–2. Why this denunciation of idolatry at this point? And why are *Shabbat* and the sanctuary mentioned as contrasts to idol worship? It is suggested that these verses raise the question: Is the visible world all there is? Or is that which is real but invisible ultimately the greatest reality? Hoffman considers these two verses, which seem to be an arbitrary postscript, as a deliberate echoing of the Decalogue, serving to introduce the theme of loyalty to the Covenant, which will be the subject of the book's concluding chapters.

* *For the* haftarah *for this portion, see p. 758.*

B'ḤUKKOTAI

בחקתי

3If you follow My laws and faithfully observe My commandments, 4I will grant your rains in their season, so that the earth shall yield its produce and the trees of the field their fruit. 5Your threshing shall overtake the vintage, and your vintage shall overtake the sowing; you shall eat your fill of bread and dwell securely in your land.

3 אִם־בְּחֻקֹּתַ֖י תֵּלֵ֑כוּ וְאֶת־מִצְוֺתַ֣י תִּשְׁמְר֔וּ
וַעֲשִׂיתֶ֖ם אֹתָֽם׃ 4 וְנָתַתִּ֥י גִשְׁמֵיכֶ֖ם בְּעִתָּ֑ם
וְנָתְנָ֤ה הָאָ֙רֶץ֙ יְבוּלָ֔הּ וְעֵ֥ץ הַשָּׂדֶ֖ה יִתֵּ֥ן
פִּרְיֽוֹ׃ 5 וְהִשִּׂ֨יג לָכֶ֥ם דַּ֙יִשׁ֙ אֶת־בָּצִ֔יר וּבָצִ֖יר
יַשִּׂ֣יג אֶת־זָ֑רַע וַאֲכַלְתֶּ֤ם לַחְמְכֶם֙ לָשֹׂ֔בַע
שני וִישַׁבְתֶּ֥ם לָבֶ֖טַח בְּאַרְצְכֶֽם׃

The Pursuit of Holiness (*continued*)

EPILOGUE TO THE HOLINESS CODE (26:3–46)

Two major principles of biblical religion find expression in this epilogue: the concept of free will and the doctrine of reward and punishment. Obedience to God's will brings great reward; disobedience brings dire punishment. The choice is left to the people Israel and its leaders.

THE BLESSING (vv. 3–13)

5. Your threshing shall overtake the vintage There will be so much grain to thresh that the threshing will continue into late summer when the vines are picked.

This *parashah* centers on a brief but eloquent promise of blessings for those who follow God's ways and a lengthy and chilling series of curses for those who reject God's ways. The curses are known as the *Tokheḥah* (Reproach). Several commentators, notably Ibn Ezra, insist that although more verses are dedicated to the *Tokheḥah,* the blessings promised in the opening section outweigh it in quality. The curses are spelled out at length in the hope that they will put fear into the hearts of those who cannot be persuaded to do what is right by any other means. In many synagogues, it is customary to read the *Tokheḥah* in an undertone, perhaps because its vision of disaster is so frightening—or perhaps in keeping with Leviticus's commitment to the reality of words; to say something aloud is halfway to making it happen.

3. If you follow My laws Some commentators have understood this as "the Laws that I Myself follow" (Lev. R. 35:3). The verb translated "follow" literally means "walk, go," prompting the comment that humans "walk" in God's ways but angels "stand" in the presence of God. Human beings, unlike angels, have the ability to grow and change after doing something wrong. Jewish law is known as *halakhah* and is sometimes understood as "the way to go." For Hoffman, these blessings emphasize the idea that God is not only a God of liberation and hope but also a God of peace and prosperity. Once settled in the Land, Israel will have no need to turn to pagan fertility gods to ensure an abundant harvest.

4. rains in their season The plain meaning here refers to the rainy season in Israel. Rashi, however, following the Midrash (Lev. R. 35:10), takes it to mean that God will make it rain only at times convenient for the people, e.g., on Friday nights when most people are at home and no one is traveling.

What is the modern reader to make of these threats and promises, aware of the fact that righteous people are not always rewarded and that wicked people are not invariably punished? We can see them as a vision of what the world will be like when it truly becomes God's kingdom. Or we can see them as a collective assurance: When most members of a community follow God's ways, the community as a whole will prosper even if some innocent individuals suffer illness or injustice. Alternatively, we can understand these verses as addressed to a still immature Israelite nation, not mature enough to do good for its own sake, capable of responding only to promises of reward and threats of punishment. Although these passages may be the word of God, they need not be God's last word on the subject.

5. When will the people be able to live securely? When there is enough food for every-

6I will grant peace in the land, and you shall
lie down untroubled by anyone; I will give the
land respite from vicious beasts, and no sword
shall cross your land. 7You shall give chase to
your enemies, and they shall fall before you by
the sword. 8Five of you shall give chase to a hundred, and a hundred of you shall give chase to
ten thousand; your enemies shall fall before you
by the sword.

9I will look with favor upon you, and make
you fertile and multiply you; and I will maintain
My covenant with you. 10You shall eat old grain
long stored, and you shall have to clear out the
old to make room for the new.

11I will establish My abode in your midst, and
I will not spurn you. 12I will be ever present in
your midst: I will be your God, and you shall
be My people. 13I the LORD am your God who
brought you out from the land of the Egyptians
to be their slaves no more, who broke the bars
of your yoke and made you walk erect.

14But if you do not obey Me and do not ob-

שני 6 וְנָתַתִּי שָׁלוֹם בָּאָרֶץ וּשְׁכַבְתֶּם וְאֵין
מַחֲרִיד וְהִשְׁבַּתִּי חַיָּה רָעָה מִן־הָאָרֶץ
וְחֶרֶב לֹא־תַעֲבֹר בְּאַרְצְכֶם׃ 7 וּרְדַפְתֶּם
אֶת־אֹיְבֵיכֶם וְנָפְלוּ לִפְנֵיכֶם לֶחָרֶב׃
8 וְרָדְפוּ מִכֶּם חֲמִשָּׁה מֵאָה וּמֵאָה מִכֶּם
רְבָבָה יִרְדֹּפוּ וְנָפְלוּ אֹיְבֵיכֶם לִפְנֵיכֶם
לֶחָרֶב׃
9 וּפָנִיתִי אֲלֵיכֶם וְהִפְרֵיתִי אֶתְכֶם
וְהִרְבֵּיתִי אֶתְכֶם וַהֲקִימֹתִי אֶת־בְּרִיתִי
שלישי [חמישי] אִתְּכֶם׃ 10 וַאֲכַלְתֶּם יָשָׁן נוֹשָׁן וְיָשָׁן מִפְּנֵי
חָדָשׁ תּוֹצִיאוּ׃
11 וְנָתַתִּי מִשְׁכָּנִי בְּתוֹכְכֶם וְלֹא־תִגְעַל
נַפְשִׁי אֶתְכֶם׃ 12 וְהִתְהַלַּכְתִּי בְּתוֹכְכֶם
וְהָיִיתִי לָכֶם לֵאלֹהִים וְאַתֶּם תִּהְיוּ־לִי
לְעָם׃ 13 אֲנִי יְהוָה אֱלֹהֵיכֶם אֲשֶׁר
הוֹצֵאתִי אֶתְכֶם מֵאֶרֶץ מִצְרַיִם מִהְיֹת
לָהֶם עֲבָדִים וָאֶשְׁבֹּר מֹטֹת עֻלְּכֶם וָאוֹלֵךְ
אֶתְכֶם קוֹמְמִיּוּת׃ פ
14 וְאִם־לֹא תִשְׁמְעוּ לִי וְלֹא תַעֲשׂוּ אֵת

9. When God turns toward His people, they are blessed with victory and prosperity; but when God turns away from them or turns against them, the result is disaster.

11. abode Hebrew: *mishkan,* which often refers to the tabernacle, here has the more general sense of "residence."

12. I will be your God, and you shall be My people This statement, which here presents the terms of adoption, defines the covenantal relationship between God and Israel.

13. who broke the bars of your yoke The bars of the yoke were tied to the neck of a work animal by means of thongs. Persons who are subjugated, upon whom a yoke is placed, are bent over. After the bars of the yoke are broken, they can stand straight.

---

one, so that no one is driven to crime or violence for lack of food. Ultimately, then, the question of whether our society will be blessed with peace or cursed with violence depends on how we share our resources.

6. vicious beasts According to one homiletic interpretation, the reference is to humans acting viciously. Thus "peace in the land" would mean internal peace, between neighbors, and between factions.

9. Maimonides, recognizing that people who follow God's ways are not always rewarded with peace and prosperity, compares this passage to a teacher who bribes children to do their lessons with gifts of nuts and candy. He adds, "This is deplorable but unavoidable because of people's limited insight. A good person should not ask 'If I perform these commandments, what reward will I get?'" (*Mishnah Commentary,* Intro. to Sanh. 10).

11. My abode in your midst Israel's greatest blessing will be the sense that they are living in the presence of God.

14–45. The Sages called this section the *Tokheḥah* (Reproach). Based on the phrase "sevenfold for your sins" (v. 18), the *Sifra* sees

serve all these commandments, 15 if you reject
My laws and spurn My rules, so that you do not
observe all My commandments and you break
My covenant, 16 I in turn will do this to you:
I will wreak misery upon you—consumption
and fever, which cause the eyes to pine and the
body to languish; you shall sow your seed to no
purpose, for your enemies shall eat it. 17 I will
set My face against you: you shall be routed by
your enemies, and your foes shall dominate you.
You shall flee though none pursues.

18 And if, for all that, you do not obey Me, I
will go on to discipline you sevenfold for your
sins, 19 and I will break your proud glory. I will
make your skies like iron and your earth like
copper, 20 so that your strength shall be spent
to no purpose. Your land shall not yield its produce, nor shall the trees of the land yield their
fruit.

21 And if you remain hostile toward Me and
refuse to obey Me, I will go on smiting you sev-

כָּל־הַמִּצְוֺת הָאֵלֶּה׃ 15 וְאִם־בְּחֻקֹּתַי
תִּמְאָסוּ וְאִם אֶת־מִשְׁפָּטַי תִּגְעַל נַפְשְׁכֶם
לְבִלְתִּי עֲשׂוֹת אֶת־כָּל־מִצְוֺתַי לְהַפְרְכֶם
אֶת־בְּרִיתִי׃ 16 אַף־אֲנִי אֶעֱשֶׂה־זֹּאת לָכֶם
וְהִפְקַדְתִּי עֲלֵיכֶם בֶּהָלָה אֶת־הַשַּׁחֶפֶת
וְאֶת־הַקַּדַּחַת מְכַלּוֹת עֵינַיִם וּמְדִיבֹת נָפֶשׁ
וּזְרַעְתֶּם לָרִיק זַרְעֲכֶם וַאֲכָלֻהוּ אֹיְבֵיכֶם׃
17 וְנָתַתִּי פָנַי בָּכֶם וְנִגַּפְתֶּם לִפְנֵי אֹיְבֵיכֶם
וְרָדוּ בָכֶם שֹׂנְאֵיכֶם וְנַסְתֶּם וְאֵין־רֹדֵף
אֶתְכֶם׃ ס
18 וְאִם־עַד־אֵלֶּה לֹא תִשְׁמְעוּ לִי וְיָסַפְתִּי
לְיַסְּרָה אֶתְכֶם שֶׁבַע עַל־חַטֹּאתֵיכֶם׃
19 וְשָׁבַרְתִּי אֶת־גְּאוֹן עֻזְּכֶם וְנָתַתִּי אֶת־
שְׁמֵיכֶם כַּבַּרְזֶל וְאֶת־אַרְצְכֶם כַּנְּחֻשָׁה׃
20 וְתַם לָרִיק כֹּחֲכֶם וְלֹא־תִתֵּן אַרְצְכֶם
אֶת־יְבוּלָהּ וְעֵץ הָאָרֶץ לֹא יִתֵּן פִּרְיוֹ׃
21 וְאִם־תֵּלְכוּ עִמִּי קֶרִי וְלֹא תֹאבוּ
לִשְׁמֹעַ לִי וְיָסַפְתִּי עֲלֵיכֶם מַכָּה שֶׁבַע

THE EXECRATION (vv. 14–45)

The execration, the curse brought on by disobedience, often employs the terms and idioms of the blessing to state the reverse, a literary technique that heightens the opposition of obedience and disobedience.

15. It is the people Israel who create the unfavorable situation, not God, who promised not to reject His people as long as they remain obedient.

16. which cause the eyes to pine Literally, "exhaust the eyes," so that the eyes can no longer see. They will have been worn out by anxiety and despair.

your enemies shall eat it In a situation of blessing, one enjoys the fruits of one's labors. It is tragic for a people to see its harvests ravaged by conquering hordes.

17. I will set My face against you This is the reverse of verse 9 of the blessing.

18. discipline you sevenfold The notion of sevenfold is proverbial in biblical literature.

19. I will break your proud glory The land, which was the pride of the people, will be destroyed.

---

the process of falling away from God's ordained path occurring in seven steps, hinted at by proof texts in the Torah's warnings: (*a*) People will stop studying Torah. (*b*) Without the foundation of study, they will come to see the commandments as matters of personal choice rather than moral obligation. (*c*) They will resent people who do study and practice and who make them feel guilty for not doing so. (*d*) They will try to stop others from fulfilling the commandments, so they will feel less guilty themselves. (*e*) They will deny that the commandments come from God. (*f*) They will deny the existence of a covenant between God and Israel. (*g*) They will deny the existence of God.

21–41. hostile Hebrew: *keri,* a word found nowhere else in the Bible, characterizing the Israelites' attitude of disobedience. It has prompted several interpretations. Hoffman takes it to mean "at cross purposes," doing the opposite of what God commands, in the way that adolescents will often do the opposite of what they are told, to proclaim their autonomy. Rashi and Ibn Ezra relate it to the word

enfold for your sins. ²²I will loose wild beasts against you, and they shall bereave you of your children and wipe out your cattle. They shall decimate you, and your roads shall be deserted.

²³And if these things fail to discipline you for Me, and you remain hostile to Me, ²⁴I too will remain hostile to you: I in turn will smite you sevenfold for your sins. ²⁵I will bring a sword against you to wreak vengeance for the covenant; and if you withdraw into your cities, I will send pestilence among you, and you shall be delivered into enemy hands. ²⁶When I break your staff of bread, ten women shall bake your bread in a single oven; they shall dole out your bread by weight, and though you eat, you shall not be satisfied.

²⁷But if, despite this, you disobey Me and remain hostile to Me, ²⁸I will act against you in wrathful hostility; I, for My part, will discipline you sevenfold for your sins. ²⁹You shall eat the flesh of your sons and the flesh of your daughters. ³⁰I will destroy your cult places and cut down your incense stands, and I will heap your carcasses upon your lifeless fetishes.

I will spurn you. ³¹I will lay your cities in ruin and make your sanctuaries desolate, and I will not savor your pleasing odors. ³²I will make the

כְּחַטֹּאתֵיכֶֽם: ²² וְהִשְׁלַחְתִּ֨י בָכֶ֜ם אֶת־חַיַּ֣ת הַשָּׂדֶ֗ה וְשִׁכְּלָ֤ה אֶתְכֶם֙ וְהִכְרִ֣יתָה֙ אֶת־בְּהֶמְתְּכֶ֔ם וְהִמְעִ֖יטָה אֶתְכֶ֑ם וְנָשַׁ֖מּוּ דַּרְכֵיכֶֽם:

²³ וְאִם־בְּאֵ֣לֶּה לֹ֤א תִוָּֽסְרוּ֙ לִ֔י וַהֲלַכְתֶּ֥ם עִמִּ֖י קֶֽרִי: ²⁴ וְהָלַכְתִּ֧י אַף־אֲנִ֛י עִמָּכֶ֖ם בְּקֶ֑רִי וְהִכֵּיתִ֤י אֶתְכֶם֙ גַּם־אָ֔נִי שֶׁ֖בַע עַל־חַטֹּאתֵיכֶֽם: ²⁵ וְהֵבֵאתִ֨י עֲלֵיכֶ֜ם חֶ֗רֶב נֹקֶ֙מֶת֙ נְקַם־בְּרִ֔ית וְנֶאֱסַפְתֶּ֖ם אֶל־עָרֵיכֶ֑ם וְשִׁלַּ֤חְתִּי דֶ֙בֶר֙ בְּתֽוֹכְכֶ֔ם וְנִתַּתֶּ֖ם בְּיַד־אוֹיֵֽב: ²⁶ בְּשִׁבְרִ֣י לָכֶם֮ מַטֵּה־לֶחֶם֒ וְ֠אָפ֠וּ עֶ֣שֶׂר נָשִׁ֤ים לַחְמְכֶם֙ בְּתַנּ֣וּר אֶחָ֔ד וְהֵשִׁ֧יבוּ לַחְמְכֶ֛ם בַּמִּשְׁקָ֖ל וַאֲכַלְתֶּ֖ם וְלֹ֥א תִשְׂבָּֽעוּ: ס

²⁷ וְאִ֨ם־בְּזֹ֔את לֹ֥א תִשְׁמְע֖וּ לִ֑י וַהֲלַכְתֶּ֥ם עִמִּ֖י בְּקֶֽרִי: ²⁸ וְהָלַכְתִּ֥י עִמָּכֶ֖ם בַּחֲמַת־קֶ֑רִי וְיִסַּרְתִּ֤י אֶתְכֶם֙ אַף־אָ֔נִי שֶׁ֖בַע עַל־חַטֹּאתֵיכֶֽם: ²⁹ וַאֲכַלְתֶּ֖ם בְּשַׂ֣ר בְּנֵיכֶ֑ם וּבְשַׂ֥ר בְּנֹתֵיכֶ֖ם תֹּאכֵֽלוּ: ³⁰ וְהִשְׁמַדְתִּ֞י אֶת־בָּמֹֽתֵיכֶ֗ם וְהִכְרַתִּי֙ אֶת־חַמָּ֣נֵיכֶ֔ם וְנָֽתַתִּי֙ אֶת־פִּגְרֵיכֶ֔ם עַל־פִּגְרֵ֖י גִּלּֽוּלֵיכֶ֑ם וְגָעֲלָ֥ה נַפְשִׁ֖י אֶתְכֶֽם: ³¹ וְנָֽתַתִּ֤י אֶת־עָֽרֵיכֶם֙ חָרְבָּ֔ה וַהֲשִׁמּוֹתִ֖י אֶת־מִקְדְּשֵׁיכֶ֑ם וְלֹ֣א אָרִ֔יחַ בְּרֵ֖יחַ נִיחֹֽחֲכֶֽם: ³² וַהֲשִׁמֹּתִ֥י

I will make your skies like iron   The rains will cease and the artesian springs of the earth will become dry.

22. I will loose wild beasts against you   This is the reverse of verse 6 of the blessing.

25.   It will not help you to seek refuge in cities, because pestilence will spread quickly through the crowded towns under siege.

30.   The Israelite warriors and citizenry will be slain at the very altars where they worshiped foreign gods.

31. I will not savor your pleasing odors   God will refuse to accept the sacrificial offerings of those who have angered Him by violating His commandments.

32. I will make the land desolate   The He-

---

for "chance" (*mikreh*), following God's ways only when convenient, only if things happen to work out favorably, rather than out of a sense of obligation or love. Salanter relates it to *kor* (cold), so that it would mean "calculated, without passion." These curses will occur not only if the people Israel violate God's laws but

even if they obey them in a spirit that drains them of religious value. If the people Israel follow the commands without love, in a calculating manner, God says, "I will act toward you coldly (*b'keri*, v. 24), without the love that makes forgiveness for misbehavior possible."

32–33.   As the Promised Land was the re-

אֲנִי אֶת־הָאָרֶץ וְשָׁמְמוּ עָלֶיהָ אֹיְבֵיכֶם
הַיֹּשְׁבִים בָּהּ׃ 33 וְאֶתְכֶם אֱזָרֶה בַגּוֹיִם
וַהֲרִיקֹתִי אַחֲרֵיכֶם חָרֶב וְהָיְתָה אַרְצְכֶם
שְׁמָמָה וְעָרֵיכֶם יִהְיוּ חָרְבָּה׃
34 אָז תִּרְצֶה הָאָרֶץ אֶת־שַׁבְּתֹתֶיהָ כֹּל
יְמֵי הֳשַׁמָּה וְאַתֶּם בְּאֶרֶץ אֹיְבֵיכֶם אָז
תִּשְׁבַּת הָאָרֶץ וְהִרְצָת אֶת־שַׁבְּתֹתֶיהָ׃
35 כָּל־יְמֵי הָשַּׁמָּה תִּשְׁבֹּת אֵת אֲשֶׁר לֹא־
שָׁבְתָה בְּשַׁבְּתֹתֵיכֶם בְּשִׁבְתְּכֶם עָלֶיהָ׃
36 וְהַנִּשְׁאָרִים בָּכֶם וְהֵבֵאתִי מֹרֶךְ בִּלְבָבָם
בְּאַרְצֹת אֹיְבֵיהֶם וְרָדַף אֹתָם קוֹל עָלֶה
נִדָּף וְנָסוּ מְנֻסַת־חֶרֶב וְנָפְלוּ וְאֵין רֹדֵף׃
37 וְכָשְׁלוּ אִישׁ־בְּאָחִיו כְּמִפְּנֵי־חֶרֶב וְרֹדֵף
אָיִן וְלֹא־תִהְיֶה לָכֶם תְּקוּמָה לִפְנֵי
אֹיְבֵיכֶם׃ 38 וַאֲבַדְתֶּם בַּגּוֹיִם וְאָכְלָה
אֶתְכֶם אֶרֶץ אֹיְבֵיכֶם׃
39 וְהַנִּשְׁאָרִים בָּכֶם יִמַּקּוּ בַּעֲוֺנָם בְּאַרְצֹת

land desolate, so that your enemies who settle
in it shall be appalled by it. 33And you I will scatter among the nations, and I will unsheath the
sword against you. Your land shall become a
desolation and your cities a ruin.

34Then shall the land make up for its sabbath
years throughout the time that it is desolate and
you are in the land of your enemies; then shall
the land rest and make up for its sabbath years.
35Throughout the time that it is desolate, it shall
observe the rest that it did not observe in your
sabbath years while you were dwelling upon it.
36As for those of you who survive, I will cast a
faintness into their hearts in the land of their
enemies. The sound of a driven leaf shall put
them to flight. Fleeing as though from the
sword, they shall fall though none pursues.
37With no one pursuing, they shall stumble over
one another as before the sword. You shall not
be able to stand your ground before your enemies, 38but shall perish among the nations; and
the land of your enemies shall consume you.

39Those of you who survive shall be heartsick
over their iniquity in the land of your enemies;

brew is emphatic: "I, Myself, will make the land desolate."

your enemies ... shall be appalled They will interpret the desolation as punishment for a horrid offense the Israelites committed against their God.

36. The sound of a driven leaf A leaf "blown away" (*niddaf*) by the wind. The slightest sound will alarm the people, so great is their fear.

38. The exiled community, swallowed up by the land of exile, will become extinct.

39. heartsick The people will experience deep remorse.

---

ward for upholding the Covenant, the loss of the Land will be the ultimate punishment for neglecting the Covenant. As living in the presence of God as a distinctive people was the reward for following in God's ways, so exile and living far from God's sanctuary, becoming a number of unconnected individuals instead of a special people, will be the worst punishment imaginable.

Some medieval commentators, fastening on the principle that "even God's curses contain within them the possibility of being turned into a blessing," would interpret Israel's being scattered among the nations as a good thing. When enemies attacked and destroyed one Jewish community, others would still flourish. Some universally minded 19th-century thinkers saw the Diaspora as part of God's plan to have the people Israel bring its message to all humanity by being scattered to so many different countries.

Rashi took this verse as an implicit promise that, once the Land has been laid waste, it would not return to life for any of its gentile occupiers. It would wait for the Jewish people to return and reclaim it. Only then would it yield its blessings.

36. faintness into their hearts Not only will the Israelites be defeated in battle; they will not care enough about their people's fate even to put up a fight on its behalf. They will have given up even before the battle is joined.

more, they shall be heartsick over the iniquities of their fathers; 40and they shall confess their iniquity and the iniquity of their fathers, in that they trespassed against Me, yea, were hostile to Me. 41When I, in turn, have been hostile to them and have removed them into the land of their enemies, then at last shall their obdurate heart humble itself, and they shall atone for their iniquity. 42Then will I remember My covenant with Jacob; I will remember also My covenant with Isaac, and also My covenant with Abraham; and I will remember the land.

43For the land shall be forsaken of them, making up for its sabbath years by being desolate of them, while they atone for their iniquity; for the abundant reason that they rejected My rules and spurned My laws. 44Yet, even then, when they are in the land of their enemies, I will not reject them or spurn them so as to destroy them, annulling My covenant with them: for I the LORD am their God. 45I will remember in their favor the covenant with the ancients, whom I freed from the land of Egypt in the sight of the nations to be their God: I, the LORD.

46These are the laws, rules, and instructions

אֹיְבֵיכֶם וְאַף בַּעֲוֺנֹת אֲבֹתָם אִתָּם יִמָּקּוּ׃
40 וְהִתְוַדּוּ אֶת־עֲוֺנָם וְאֶת־עֲוֺן אֲבֹתָם
בְּמַעֲלָם אֲשֶׁר מָעֲלוּ־בִי וְאַף אֲשֶׁר־הָלְכוּ
עִמִּי בְּקֶרִי׃ 41 אַף־אֲנִי אֵלֵךְ עִמָּם בְּקֶרִי
וְהֵבֵאתִי אֹתָם בְּאֶרֶץ אֹיְבֵיהֶם אוֹ־אָז
יִכָּנַע לְבָבָם הֶעָרֵל וְאָז יִרְצוּ אֶת־עֲוֺנָם׃
42 וְזָכַרְתִּי אֶת־בְּרִיתִי יַעֲקוֹב וְאַף אֶת־
בְּרִיתִי יִצְחָק וְאַף אֶת־בְּרִיתִי אַבְרָהָם
אֶזְכֹּר וְהָאָרֶץ אֶזְכֹּר׃
43 וְהָאָרֶץ תֵּעָזֵב מֵהֶם וְתִרֶץ אֶת־
שַׁבְּתֹתֶיהָ בָּהְשַׁמָּה מֵהֶם וְהֵם יִרְצוּ אֶת־
עֲוֺנָם יַעַן וּבְיַעַן בְּמִשְׁפָּטַי מָאָסוּ וְאֶת־
חֻקֹּתַי גָּעֲלָה נַפְשָׁם׃ 44 וְאַף־גַּם־זֹאת
בִּהְיוֹתָם בְּאֶרֶץ אֹיְבֵיהֶם לֹא־מְאַסְתִּים
וְלֹא־גְעַלְתִּים לְכַלֹּתָם לְהָפֵר בְּרִיתִי אִתָּם
כִּי אֲנִי יְהוָה אֱלֹהֵיהֶם׃ 45 וְזָכַרְתִּי לָהֶם
בְּרִית רִאשֹׁנִים אֲשֶׁר הוֹצֵאתִי־אֹתָם
מֵאֶרֶץ מִצְרַיִם לְעֵינֵי הַגּוֹיִם לִהְיֹת לָהֶם
לֵאלֹהִים אֲנִי יְהוָה׃

46 אֵלֶּה הַחֻקִּים וְהַמִּשְׁפָּטִים וְהַתּוֹרֹת

the iniquities of their fathers The realization that they are suffering for the sins of past generations is even more distressing to the exiles.

41. their obdurate heart Literally, "their uncircumcised heart." In exile, the people will submit to God's will, and their contrition will prompt God to remember the covenant with Israel.

42. I will remember the land This statement is unique in Scripture. The personification of the land is a frequent theme, but nowhere else is it said that God remembers the land.

43. the land shall be forsaken of them Both the land and the people must atone: the land, through its desolation and the loss of its inhabitants; the people, through exile.

for the abundant reason that The Hebrew is emphatic: "For the very reason that."

45. the ancients Hebrew: *rishonim;* literally, "the former ones," referring here to the Israelites who left Egypt.

in the sight of the nations To allow Israel to be destroyed, even though the punishment is deserved, would diminish God's renown. Hence, if Israel shows remorse and mends its ways, God will not cause the entire people to perish.

POSTSCRIPT (v. 46)

All that is commanded in chapters 17–26, the Holiness Code, comes from the Lord and was transmitted through Moses on Mount Sinai.

---

40. Although God proclaims the divine readiness to accept penitents and meet them more than halfway, the first turning must come from the errant people. God does not impose repentance (*t'shuvah*) on an unwilling people.

that the LORD established, through Moses on Mount Sinai, between Himself and the Israelite people.

אֲשֶׁר נָתַן יְהוָה בֵּינוֹ וּבֵין בְּנֵי יִשְׂרָאֵל
בְּהַר סִינַי בְּיַד־מֹשֶׁה׃ פ

27 The LORD spoke to Moses, saying: 2 Speak to the Israelite people and say to them: When anyone explicitly vows to the LORD the equivalent for a human being, 3 the following scale shall apply: If it is a male from twenty to sixty years of age, the equivalent is fifty shekels of silver by the sanctuary weight; 4 if it is a female, the equivalent is thirty shekels. 5 If the age is from five years to twenty years, the equivalent is twenty shekels for a male and ten shekels for a female. 6 If the age is from one month to five years, the equivalent for a male is five shekels of silver, and the equivalent for a female is three

רביעי [ששי]

כז וַיְדַבֵּר יְהוָה אֶל־מֹשֶׁה לֵּאמֹר׃
2 דַּבֵּר אֶל־בְּנֵי יִשְׂרָאֵל וְאָמַרְתָּ אֲלֵהֶם אִישׁ
כִּי יַפְלִא נֶדֶר בְּעֶרְכְּךָ נְפָשֹׁת לַיהוָה׃
3 וְהָיָה עֶרְכְּךָ הַזָּכָר מִבֶּן עֶשְׂרִים שָׁנָה
וְעַד בֶּן־שִׁשִּׁים שָׁנָה וְהָיָה עֶרְכְּךָ חֲמִשִּׁים
שֶׁקֶל כֶּסֶף בְּשֶׁקֶל הַקֹּדֶשׁ׃ 4 וְאִם־נְקֵבָה
הִוא וְהָיָה עֶרְכְּךָ שְׁלֹשִׁים שָׁקֶל׃ 5 וְאִם
מִבֶּן־חָמֵשׁ שָׁנִים וְעַד בֶּן־עֶשְׂרִים שָׁנָה
וְהָיָה עֶרְכְּךָ הַזָּכָר עֶשְׂרִים שְׁקָלִים
וְלַנְּקֵבָה עֲשֶׂרֶת שְׁקָלִים׃ 6 וְאִם מִבֶּן־חֹדֶשׁ
וְעַד בֶּן־חָמֵשׁ שָׁנִים וְהָיָה עֶרְכְּךָ הַזָּכָר
חֲמִשָּׁה שְׁקָלִים כָּסֶף וְלַנְּקֵבָה עֶרְכְּךָ

FUNDING THE SANCTUARY (27:1–34)

Maintaining the sanctuary was costly. It was necessary to provide the materials used in public sacrifice and to support the clergy. The goal of the system of funding prescribed in this chapter was to secure silver for the sanctuary and its related needs. What was donated could be redeemed; it was the redemption payment, the silver, that was sought for the sanctuary in most cases.

VOTARY PLEDGES OF SILVER (vv. 1–8)

The custom of promising one's value in silver to the sanctuary goes back to the actual dedication of oneself, or one's child, to Temple service. Pledging the equivalent of one's life, according to a scale established by the priesthood, served two ends: the spirit of the ancient tradition was satisfied and, in practical terms, the sanctuary received necessary funds.

3. On the shekel, see Comment to Gen. 23:9; its silver content is specified in verse 25. The age factor reflects productive ability. At the age of one month, a child was considered viable and likely to survive the perils of infant mortality.

4. Gender differentiation may be linked to productivity, it being presumed that a male could earn more than a female. Note that women could participate freely in the votive system.

CHAPTER 27

Why is this chapter on pledging to the sanctuary appended to the end of Leviticus? Hoffman sees it as continuing the theme of raising ordinary objects to the status of holiness, a major theme of the entire book. One commentator sees this connection: Even after all the calamities predicted in Lev. 26 have befallen the Jewish people, they will still be dedicated to God and to God's sanctuary. Jews will strive for a life of holiness, not because it brings them rewards and comfort but because it brings them into the presence of God.

3. How do we measure the value of a person? The world at large values rich people more than poor people, economically productive people more than less productive, fertile women more than childless women, clever and attractive people more than others. In God's temple, however, people are evaluated "by the sanctuary weight" (*b'shekel ha-kodesh*). God views our worth differently than the world does.

shekels of silver. [7]If the age is sixty years or over, the equivalent is fifteen shekels in the case of a male and ten shekels for a female. [8]But if one cannot afford the equivalent, he shall be presented before the priest, and the priest shall assess him; the priest shall assess him according to what the vower can afford.

[9]If [the vow concerns] any animal that may be brought as an offering to the LORD, any such that may be given to the LORD shall be holy. [10]One may not exchange or substitute another for it, either good for bad, or bad for good; if one does substitute one animal for another, the thing vowed and its substitute shall both be holy. [11]If [the vow concerns] any impure animal that may not be brought as an offering to the LORD, the animal shall be presented before the priest, [12]and the priest shall assess it. Whether high or low, whatever assessment is set by the priest shall stand; [13]and if he wishes to redeem it, he must add one-fifth to its assessment.

[14]If anyone consecrates his house to the LORD,

שְׁלֹ֥שֶׁת שְׁקָלִ֖ים כָּֽסֶף׃ 7 וְאִ֠ם מִבֶּן־שִׁשִּׁ֨ים
שָׁנָ֤ה וָמַ֙עְלָה֙ אִם־זָכָ֔ר וְהָיָ֣ה עֶרְכְּךָ֔ חֲמִשָּׁ֥ה
עָשָׂ֖ר שָׁ֑קֶל וְלַנְּקֵבָ֖ה עֲשָׂרָ֥ה שְׁקָלִֽים׃
8 וְאִם־מָ֥ךְ הוּא֙ מֵֽעֶרְכֶּ֔ךָ וְהֶֽעֱמִידוֹ֙ לִפְנֵ֣י
הַכֹּהֵ֔ן וְהֶעֱרִ֥יךְ אֹת֖וֹ הַכֹּהֵ֑ן עַל־פִּ֗י אֲשֶׁ֤ר
תַּשִּׂיג֙ יַ֣ד הַנֹּדֵ֔ר יַעֲרִיכֶ֖נּוּ הַכֹּהֵֽן׃ ס
9 וְאִם־בְּהֵמָ֔ה אֲשֶׁ֨ר יַקְרִ֧יבוּ מִמֶּ֛נָּה קָרְבָּ֖ן
לַיהוָ֑ה כֹּל֩ אֲשֶׁ֨ר יִתֵּ֥ן מִמֶּ֛נּוּ* לַיהוָ֖ה
יִֽהְיֶה־קֹּֽדֶשׁ׃ 10 לֹ֣א יַחֲלִיפֶ֗נּוּ וְלֹֽא־יָמִ֥יר
אֹת֛וֹ ט֥וֹב בְּרָ֖ע אוֹ־רַ֣ע בְּט֑וֹב וְאִם־הָמֵ֨ר
יָמִ֤יר בְּהֵמָה֙ בִּבְהֵמָ֔ה וְהָֽיָה־ה֥וּא
וּתְמוּרָת֖וֹ יִֽהְיֶה־קֹּֽדֶשׁ׃ 11 וְאִם֙ כָּל־בְּהֵמָ֣ה
טְמֵאָ֔ה אֲשֶׁ֛ר לֹא־יַקְרִ֥יבוּ מִמֶּ֛נָּה קָרְבָּ֖ן
לַיהוָ֑ה וְהֶעֱמִ֥יד אֶת־הַבְּהֵמָ֖ה לִפְנֵ֥י הַכֹּהֵֽן׃
12 וְהֶעֱרִ֤יךְ הַכֹּהֵן֙ אֹתָ֔הּ בֵּ֥ין ט֖וֹב וּבֵ֣ין רָ֑ע
כְּעֶרְכְּךָ֥ הַכֹּהֵ֖ן כֵּ֥ן יִהְיֶֽה׃ 13 וְאִם־גָּאֹ֖ל
יִגְאָלֶ֑נָּה וְיָסַ֥ף חֲמִישִׁת֖וֹ עַל־עֶרְכֶּֽךָ׃
14 וְאִ֗ישׁ כִּֽי־יַקְדִּ֨שׁ אֶת־בֵּית֥וֹ קֹ֙דֶשׁ֙ לַֽיהוָ֔ה

v. 9. סבירין ומטעין "ממנה"

8. Allowance was made for reductions when the inability to afford the standard cost of an offering or donation would either deprive an Israelite of expiation or, as in this case, preclude a pious act.

VOTARY PLEDGES OF ANIMALS (vv. 9–13)

One who gave of his or her own property to the sanctuary received public thanks. Then, too, what was devoted had already become sacred. Accordingly, a surcharge of 20 percent was imposed on the donor who sought to undo the act, allowing the sanctuary to profit from the transaction.

9. If the donor pledged a ritually pure animal, it was presumed that he or she intended it as a sacrifice. The donation constituted a valid assignment to the altar, and no redemption was possible.

11. An impure animal is unfit for sacrifice. Therefore, it is presumed that the donor really intended to pledge the assessed value of the animal. By paying the 20 percent surcharge, one could retrieve it.

12. The assessment of the priest stands, even if it exceeds the market price of the animal.

13. The law is stated conditionally, although in actual practice it was usually expected that the donor would redeem what had been pledged.

CONSECRATIONS (vv. 14–25)

14. According to Lev. 25:29ff., urban dwellings are not subject to the jubilee; if sold but not redeemed within a year, they become the permanent property of the purchaser. Here, nothing is said about a time limit, because consecration differs from an ordinary sale.

---

14. If anyone consecrates his house to the LORD "True holiness sanctifies the seemingly mundane activities of running a household. One who behaves in an elevated manner in one's own house is truly a holy person" (Menaḥem Mendel of Kotzk). The home is a small sanctuary (*mikdash m'at*).

the priest shall assess it. Whether high or low, as the priest assesses it, so it shall stand; 15and if he who has consecrated his house wishes to redeem it, he must add one-fifth to the sum at which it was assessed, and it shall be his.

16If anyone consecrates to the LORD any land that he holds, its assessment shall be in accordance with its seed requirement: fifty shekels of silver to a *ḥomer* of barley seed. 17If he consecrates his land as of the jubilee year, its assessment stands. 18But if he consecrates his land after the jubilee, the priest shall compute the price according to the years that are left until the jubilee year, and its assessment shall be so reduced; 19and if he who consecrated the land wishes to redeem it, he must add one-fifth to the sum at which it was assessed, and it shall pass to him. 20But if he does not redeem the land, and the land is sold to another, it shall no longer be redeemable: 21when it is released in the jubilee, the land shall be holy to the LORD, as land proscribed; it becomes the priest's holding.

22If he consecrates to the LORD land that he purchased, which is not land of his holding, 23the priest shall compute for him the proportionate assessment up to the jubilee year, and he shall pay the assessment as of that day, a sa-

וְהֶעֱרִיכוֹ הַכֹּהֵן בֵּין טוֹב וּבֵין רָע כַּאֲשֶׁר
יַעֲרִיךְ אֹתוֹ הַכֹּהֵן כֵּן יָקוּם׃ 15 וְאִם־
הַמַּקְדִּישׁ יִגְאַל אֶת־בֵּיתוֹ וְיָסַף חֲמִישִׁית
כֶּסֶף־עֶרְכְּךָ עָלָיו וְהָיָה לוֹ׃
חמישי [שביעי] 16 וְאִם ׀ מִשְּׂדֵה אֲחֻזָּתוֹ יַקְדִּישׁ אִישׁ
לַיהוָה וְהָיָה עֶרְכְּךָ לְפִי זַרְעוֹ זֶרַע חֹמֶר
שְׂעֹרִים בַּחֲמִשִּׁים שֶׁקֶל כָּסֶף׃ 17 אִם־
מִשְּׁנַת הַיֹּבֵל יַקְדִּישׁ שָׂדֵהוּ כְּעֶרְכְּךָ יָקוּם׃
18 וְאִם־אַחַר הַיֹּבֵל יַקְדִּישׁ שָׂדֵהוּ וְחִשַּׁב־
לוֹ הַכֹּהֵן אֶת־הַכֶּסֶף עַל־פִּי הַשָּׁנִים
הַנּוֹתָרֹת עַד שְׁנַת הַיֹּבֵל וְנִגְרַע מֵעֶרְכֶּךָ׃
19 וְאִם־גָּאֹל יִגְאַל אֶת־הַשָּׂדֶה הַמַּקְדִּישׁ
אֹתוֹ וְיָסַף חֲמִשִׁית כֶּסֶף־עֶרְכְּךָ עָלָיו וְקָם
לוֹ׃ 20 וְאִם־לֹא יִגְאַל אֶת־הַשָּׂדֶה וְאִם־
מָכַר אֶת־הַשָּׂדֶה לְאִישׁ אַחֵר לֹא יִגָּאֵל
עוֹד׃ 21 וְהָיָה הַשָּׂדֶה בְּצֵאתוֹ בַיֹּבֵל קֹדֶשׁ
לַיהוָה כִּשְׂדֵה הַחֵרֶם לַכֹּהֵן תִּהְיֶה
אֲחֻזָּתוֹ׃
ששי 22 וְאִם אֶת־שְׂדֵה מִקְנָתוֹ אֲשֶׁר לֹא מִשְּׂדֵה
אֲחֻזָּתוֹ יַקְדִּישׁ לַיהוָה׃ 23 וְחִשַּׁב־לוֹ הַכֹּהֵן
אֵת מִכְסַת הָעֶרְכְּךָ עַד שְׁנַת הַיֹּבֵל וְנָתַן
אֶת־הָעֶרְכְּךָ בַּיּוֹם הַהוּא קֹדֶשׁ לַיהוָה׃

16. any land that he holds This chapter differentiates between land belonging to an original owner and acquired land that had been transferred to someone other than the original owner.

seed requirement The method of delineating plots of arable land by reference to the quantity of seed required in their planting was common to many ancient Near Eastern societies.

ḥomer A dry measure of Egyptian origin, approximately 6 bushels (220 L).

17. At the jubilee, tenured land reverted to its original owners, as mandated in 25:10,13ff. All transfers of such property were, in fact, not final sales, but long-term leases that expired at the next jubilee.

20. The priesthood sold the land when it became apparent that its donor had no intention of redeeming it. Once this occurred, the donor forever lost the right of redemption.

21. If the donor fails to redeem the land before the next jubilee, the initial consecration is considered permanently binding, and the land remains the property of the sanctuary forever.

22. This reflects the provisions of 25:25ff. If a man is compelled to sell any part of his tenured land, it reverts to him at the next jubilee, even if he has been unable to redeem it in the interim. Anyone who purchased such land from him, therefore, was not a full owner. If he subsequently consecrated such acquired land, he had to be prepared to remit its value in silver to the sanctuary at the time of its consecration, plus the surcharge of 20 percent. Otherwise, his consecration could not be accepted because the field could not be collateral for his donation.

24 בִּשְׁנַת הַיּוֹבֵל יָשׁוּב הַשָּׂדֶה לַאֲשֶׁר קָנָהוּ
מֵאִתּוֹ לַאֲשֶׁר־לוֹ אֲחֻזַּת הָאָרֶץ׃ 25 וְכָל־
עֶרְכְּךָ יִהְיֶה בְּשֶׁקֶל הַקֹּדֶשׁ עֶשְׂרִים גֵּרָה
יִהְיֶה הַשָּׁקֶל׃ ס

26 אַךְ־בְּכוֹר אֲשֶׁר־יְבֻכַּר לַיהוָה בִּבְהֵמָה
לֹא־יַקְדִּישׁ אִישׁ אֹתוֹ אִם־שׁוֹר אִם־שֶׂה
לַיהוָה הוּא׃ 27 וְאִם בַּבְּהֵמָה הַטְּמֵאָה
וּפָדָה בְעֶרְכֶּךָ וְיָסַף חֲמִשִׁתוֹ עָלָיו וְאִם־לֹא
יִגָּאֵל וְנִמְכַּר בְּעֶרְכֶּךָ׃

28 אַךְ־כָּל־חֵרֶם אֲשֶׁר יַחֲרִם אִישׁ לַיהוָה
מִכָּל־אֲשֶׁר־לוֹ מֵאָדָם וּבְהֵמָה וּמִשְּׂדֵה
אֲחֻזָּתוֹ לֹא יִמָּכֵר וְלֹא יִגָּאֵל כָּל־חֵרֶם
קֹדֶשׁ־קָדָשִׁים הוּא לַיהוָה׃ 29 כָּל־חֵרֶם שביעי
אֲשֶׁר יָחֳרַם מִן־הָאָדָם לֹא יִפָּדֶה מוֹת
יוּמָת׃

30 וְכָל־מַעְשַׂר הָאָרֶץ מִזֶּרַע הָאָרֶץ מִפְּרִי
הָעֵץ לַיהוָה הוּא קֹדֶשׁ לַיהוָה׃ 31 וְאִם־
גָּאֹל יִגְאַל אִישׁ מִמַּעַשְׂרוֹ חֲמִשִׁיתוֹ יֹסֵף
עָלָיו׃ 32 וְכָל־מַעְשַׂר בָּקָר וָצֹאן כֹּל אֲשֶׁר־ מפטיר

cred donation to the LORD. 24In the jubilee year the land shall revert to him from whom it was bought, whose holding the land is. 25All assessments shall be by the sanctuary weight, the shekel being twenty *gerahs*.

26A firstling of animals, however, which—as a firstling—is the LORD's, cannot be consecrated by anybody; whether ox or sheep, it is the LORD's. 27But if it is of impure animals, it may be ransomed as its assessment, with one-fifth added; if it is not redeemed, it shall be sold at its assessment.

28But of all that anyone owns, be it man or beast or land of his holding, nothing that he has proscribed for the LORD may be sold or redeemed; every proscribed thing is totally consecrated to the LORD. 29No human being who has been proscribed can be ransomed: he shall be put to death.

30All tithes from the land, whether seed from the ground or fruit from the tree, are the LORD's; they are holy to the LORD. 31If anyone wishes to redeem any of his tithes, he must add one-fifth to them. 32All tithes of the herd or

24. The consecration of the land by one who had purchased it from its original owner does not affect the primary rights of the original owner.

FIRSTLINGS (vv. 26–27)

The firstborn males of humans and beasts are consecrated to God at the moment of birth. One may not consecrate them to the sanctuary, for one may consecrate only what one owns.

26. This refers to pure animals, suitable for sacrifice.

27. The firstlings of impure animals, unsuitable for sacrifice, may be redeemed on the usual basis. If they are not redeemed, the sanctuary may sell them for silver. No time limit is stipulated.

PROSCRIBED PROPERTY (vv. 28–29)

28. owns . . . man A non-Israelite slave, considered to be the owner's property.

proscribed thing Hebrew: *ḥeirem;* the related verb means "to set apart, denote, restrict." In the Bible, it seems always to have a negative or prohibitive connotation; it describes what is to be avoided, destroyed, or forbidden. To designate something as *ḥeirem* may mean either that it is to be destroyed completely or that it is reserved for purposes associated with the sanctuary.

29. This law reflects, in part, the provisions of Exod. 22:19, which ordain that anyone who worships another god shall be condemned to death, proscribed (see Exod. 20:3).

TITHES (vv. 30–33)

This section speaks of two kinds of tithes: 1/10 of the yield of the land and 1/10 of the flocks and herds.

30. Israelites are required to set aside a tithe from the produce of the fields and to bring it each year to the central Temple. There, they are to consume it "in the presence of the LORD" as a sacred meal. Those distant from the Temple were to convert the ritual produce into silver and to use that silver to purchase offerings when they arrived at the Temple, with which they would then celebrate in God's presence. This was in addition to the tithe given locally to the Levites.

יַעֲבֹ֖ר תַּ֣חַת הַשָּׁ֑בֶט הָֽעֲשִׂירִ֕י יִֽהְיֶה־קֹּ֖דֶשׁ
לַיהוָֽה׃ 33 לֹ֧א יְבַקֵּ֛ר בֵּין־ט֖וֹב לָרַ֑ע וְלֹ֖א
יְמִירֶ֑נּוּ וְאִם־הָמֵ֣ר יְמִירֶ֔נּוּ וְהָֽיָה־ה֧וּא
וּתְמוּרָת֛וֹ יִֽהְיֶה־קֹּ֖דֶשׁ לֹ֥א יִגָּאֵֽל׃

34 אֵ֣לֶּה הַמִּצְוֺ֗ת אֲשֶׁ֨ר צִוָּ֧ה יְהוָ֛ה אֶת־מֹשֶׁ֖ה
אֶל־בְּנֵ֣י יִשְׂרָאֵ֑ל בְּהַ֖ר סִינָֽי׃*

flock—of all that passes under the shepherd's staff, every tenth one—shall be holy to the LORD.
33He must not look out for good as against bad, or make substitution for it. If he does make substitution for it, then it and its substitute shall both be holy: it cannot be redeemed.

34These are the commandments that the LORD gave Moses for the Israelite people on Mount Sinai.

v. 34. סכום הפסוקים של הספר 859 וחציו 15:7

חֲזַק חֲזַק וְנִתְחַזֵּק

33. The actual 10th animal is to be counted as the tithe, whatever its condition. It can be neither substituted nor redeemed.

POSTSCRIPT (v. 34)

Likewise, the opening verse of chapter 25 reads: "The LORD spoke to Moses on Mount Sinai." Both at the beginning and at the end of major sections, or books, of the Torah, it was customary to state where and when the revelation from God had occurred.

34. on Mount Sinai Not all the laws, however, were literally given to Moses at Sinai! The opening verse of Leviticus describes the laws that follow as having been given at the Tent of Meeting. Sinai is not a geographic location. It is a symbol of Israel's awareness of having stood in the presence of God and having come to understand what God requires of them. Whenever a person hears the commanding voice of God and commits himself or herself to live by that voice, that person can be considered to be standing at Sinai. "The greatest single event in the history of God's revelation took place at Sinai, but was not limited to it. God's communication continued in the teaching of the Prophets and the biblical Sages, and in the activity of the Rabbis of the Talmud. It remains alive in the Codes and Responsa to the present day" (*Emet Ve-Emunah*).

הפטרת בהר

HAFTARAH FOR B'HAR

JEREMIAH 32:6–27 (*Ashk'nazim*)
JEREMIAH 32:6–22 (*S'fardim*)

(*When* B'har *and* B'ḥukkotai *are combined, recite the* haftarah *for* B'ḥukkotai.)

This *haftarah* focuses on a symbolic action performed by the prophet Jeremiah. He was bidden by God to purchase the field of his cousin Hanamel "in the tenth year of King Zedekiah" (588–587 B.C.E.), when "the army of the king of Babylon was besieging Jerusalem" (32:1–2). At that time, Jeremiah was confined to a prison compound, charged with having uttered a seditious oracle about the fall of Jerusalem and the exile of its king, Zedekiah (vv. 3–5, cf. 34:2–5). The purpose of the divinely initiated performance was to dramatize the future restoration of the nation to its homeland on the very eve of its forthcoming destruction (in 586 B.C.E.).

Accordingly, the purchase and sale agreement negotiated by Jeremiah (32:9–12) was explicitly written down and stored against a future time when "houses, fields, and vineyards shall again be purchased in this land" (v. 15). Jeremiah's public action is followed by a private prayer in which the prophet struggles to comprehend the drama of hope, which is symbolized in what he has just done. God's response ("Is anything too wondrous for Me?") addresses his concern.

Under normal conditions, lands taken due to their owners' economic duress could be reclaimed before the jubilee year through the intervention of relatives who would pay the outstanding premium (Lev. 25:25–27). There is thus a strong resemblance between this reappropriation of ancestral lands by uncles and cousins (Lev. 25:49) and Jeremiah's action with his cousin Hanamel, as Ramban observed.

Jeremiah's prayer, which follows his act of obedience, expresses amazement glorifying divine justice and power (vv. 17–19) and recalls God's great wonders on behalf of the people Israel (vv. 20–23). The people's rejection of God's law, however, inevitably results in their punishment (vv. 23–24). Given this reality of doom, the prophet is astonished at God's word of redemptive hope (v. 25). The divine answer declares that there is nothing too wondrous for God, using language that echoes the opening words of praise in Jeremiah's prayer (Kara).

Threefold repetition of the Hebrew word *hinnei* (usually translated "behold") establishes the rhythm of this passage as it moves from human amazement to divine assertion. The word appears near the beginning of the prophet's prayer ("[Behold!] You made heaven and earth," v. 17), as he shifts from uttering declarations as a spokesman for God to uttering God's praise. Subsequently, *hinnei* ("Here," v. 24) provides a dramatic shift to the people's punishment and Jeremiah's wonder at what God told him to do. Finally, through the use of language recalling Jeremiah's words in verse 17, God seemingly cites the prophet, responding in a counterpoint to Jeremiah's words of concern with a rhetorical question: "Behold (*hinnei*) I am the LORD, the God of all flesh. Is there anything too wondrous for Me?" (v. 27). The question hangs in suspension. With ironic concision, the divine promise of redemption is posed as an unexpected challenge to religious faith.

RELATION OF THE *HAFTARAH* TO THE *PARASHAH*

The legal theme of land redemption by near kin is the common element in the *parashah* (Lev. 25:25–55) and in the *haftarah* (Jer. 32:6–12). The purpose of such a transaction was to safeguard the preservation of property within family

groups (see Ramban on Lev. 25:33). Redemption (*g'ullah*) is a legal term that takes on spiritually and nationally redemptive overtones in the process. Implied in the figure of Jeremiah's use of this term is the promise of God's own restorative *g'ul-lah* of His people to their homeland. One must marvel at the bold act of hope, much as Jeremiah himself did (32:24–25).

32 6Jeremiah said: The word of the LORD came to me: 7Hanamel, the son of your uncle Shallum, will come to you and say, "Buy my land in Anathoth, for you are next in succession to redeem it by purchase." 8And just as the LORD had said, my cousin Hanamel came to me in the prison compound and said to me, "Please buy my land in Anathoth, in the territory of Benjamin; for the right of succession is yours, and you have the duty of redemption. Buy it." Then I knew that it was indeed the word of the LORD.

9So I bought the land in Anathoth from my cousin Hanamel. I weighed out the money to him, seventeen shekels of silver. 10I wrote a deed, sealed it, and had it witnessed; and I weighed out the silver on a balance. 11I took the deed of purchase, the sealed text and the open one according to rule and law, 12and gave the deed to Baruch son of Neriah son of Mahseiah in the presence of my kinsman Hanamel, of the witnesses who were named in the deed, and all the Judeans who were sitting in the prison compound. 13In their presence I charged Baruch as follows: 14Thus said the LORD of Hosts, the God of Israel: "Take these documents, this deed of purchase, the sealed text and the open one, and

לב 6 וַיֹּ֖אמֶר יִרְמְיָ֑הוּ הָיָ֥ה דְבַר־יְהֹוָ֖ה
אֵלַ֥י לֵאמֹֽר׃ 7 הִנֵּ֣ה חֲנַמְאֵ֗ל בֶּן־שַׁלֻּם֙ דֹּֽדְךָ֔
בָּ֥א אֵלֶ֖יךָ לֵאמֹ֑ר קְנֵ֣ה לְךָ֗ אֶת־שָׂדִי֙ אֲשֶׁ֣ר
בַּעֲנָת֔וֹת כִּ֥י לְךָ֛ מִשְׁפַּ֥ט הַגְּאֻלָּ֖ה לִקְנֽוֹת׃
8 וַיָּבֹ֣א אֵ֠לַי חֲנַמְאֵ֨ל בֶּן־דֹּדִ֜י כִּדְבַ֣ר יְהֹוָ֗ה
אֶל־חֲצַ֣ר הַמַּטָּרָה֒ וַיֹּ֣אמֶר אֵלַ֡י קְנֵ֣ה נָ֠א
אֶת־שָׂדִ֨י אֲשֶׁר־בַּעֲנָת֜וֹת אֲשֶׁ֣ר ׀ בְּאֶ֣רֶץ
בִּנְיָמִ֗ין כִּֽי־לְךָ֞ מִשְׁפַּ֧ט הַיְרֻשָּׁ֛ה וּלְךָ֥ הַגְּאֻלָּ֖ה
קְנֵה־לָ֑ךְ וָאֵדַ֕ע כִּ֥י דְבַר־יְהֹוָ֖ה הֽוּא׃
9 וָאֶקְנֶה֙ אֶת־הַשָּׂדֶ֔ה מֵאֵ֛ת חֲנַמְאֵ֥ל בֶּן־דֹּדִ֖י
אֲשֶׁ֣ר בַּעֲנָת֑וֹת וָאֶשְׁקֲלָה־לּוֹ֙ אֶת־הַכֶּ֔סֶף
שִׁבְעָ֥ה שְׁקָלִ֖ים וַעֲשָׂרָ֥ה הַכָּֽסֶף׃ 10 וָאֶכְתֹּ֤ב
בַּסֵּ֙פֶר֙ וָאֶחְתֹּ֔ם וָאָעֵ֖ד עֵדִ֑ים וָאֶשְׁקֹ֥ל הַכֶּ֖סֶף
בְּמֹאזְנָֽיִם׃ 11 וָאֶקַּ֖ח אֶת־סֵ֣פֶר הַמִּקְנָ֑ה
אֶת־הֶחָת֛וּם הַמִּצְוָ֥ה וְהַחֻקִּ֖ים וְאֶת־
הַגָּלֽוּי׃ 12 וָאֶתֵּ֞ן אֶת־הַסֵּ֣פֶר הַמִּקְנָ֗ה אֶל־
בָּר֣וּךְ בֶּן־נֵרִיָּה֮ בֶּן־מַחְסֵיָה֒ לְעֵינֵי֙ חֲנַמְאֵ֣ל
דֹּדִ֔י וּלְעֵינֵי֙ הָֽעֵדִ֔ים הַכֹּתְבִ֖ים* בְּסֵ֣פֶר
הַמִּקְנָ֑ה לְעֵינֵי֙ כָּל־הַיְּהוּדִ֔ים הַיֹּשְׁבִ֖ים
בַּחֲצַ֥ר הַמַּטָּרָֽה׃ 13 וָאֲצַוֶּה֙ אֶת־בָּר֔וּךְ
לְעֵינֵיהֶ֖ם לֵאמֹֽר׃ 14 כֹּה־אָמַ֞ר יְהֹוָ֣ה
צְבָא֗וֹת אֱלֹהֵ֣י יִשְׂרָאֵ֮ל לָק֣וֹחַ אֶת־הַסְּפָרִ֣ים

v. 12. בנוסח אחר "הכתובים"

Jeremiah 32:8. you have the duty of redemption Hanamel is saying: "If I die without sons, you [Jeremiah] could be my heir; and if I were to sell [the property] to another, you would have the legal right to redeem [it] from the purchaser even if you were not to inherit it . . . as it is written, '[redemption may be performed by a kinsman] or his uncle or his uncle's son' (Lev. 25:49)" (Kara).

12. gave the deed to Baruch Baruch (ben Neriah) functions as Jeremiah's aide, disciple, agent, and personal scribe. This is especially the case in Jer. 36.

who were named Rendered according to the text of many mss. and ancient versions; so ancient Near Eastern practice. The Hebrew text above, like other mss. and the editions, reads "who wrote" (i.e., signed their names) [Transl.].

14. the sealed text and the open one The Mishnah refers to two types of documents: a "plain document whose witnesses signed within

put them into an earthen jar, so that they may last a long time." [15]For thus said the LORD of Hosts, the God of Israel: "Houses, fields, and vineyards shall again be purchased in this land."

[16]But after I had given the deed to Baruch son of Neriah, I prayed to the LORD: [17]"Ah, Lord GOD! You made heaven and earth with Your great might and outstretched arm. Nothing is too wondrous for You! [18]You show kindness to the thousandth generation, but visit the guilt of the fathers upon their children after them. O great and mighty God whose name is LORD of Hosts, [19]wondrous in purpose and mighty in deed, whose eyes observe all the ways of men, so as to repay every man according to his ways, and with the proper fruit of his deeds! [20]You displayed signs and marvels in the land of Egypt with lasting effect, and won renown in Israel and among mankind to this very day. [21]You freed

הָאֵ֨לֶּה אֵ֜ת סֵ֤פֶר הַמִּקְנָה֙ הַזֶּ֔ה וְאֵ֖ת
הֶֽחָת֑וּם וְאֵ֨ת סֵ֤פֶר הַגָּלוּי֙ הַזֶּ֔ה וּנְתַתָּ֖ם
בִּכְלִי־חָ֑רֶשׂ לְמַ֛עַן יַֽעַמְד֖וּ יָמִ֥ים רַבִּֽים׃ ס
‏15 כִּ֣י כֹ֣ה אָמַ֞ר יְהוָ֤ה צְבָאוֹת֙ אֱלֹהֵ֣י יִשְׂרָאֵ֔ל
ע֚וֹד יִקָּנ֣וּ בָתִּ֔ים וְשָׂד֥וֹת וּכְרָמִ֖ים בָּאָ֥רֶץ
הַזֹּֽאת׃ פ

‏16 וָאֶתְפַּלֵּ֣ל אֶל־יְהוָ֑ה אַֽחֲרֵ֤י תִתִּי֙ אֶת־
סֵ֣פֶר הַמִּקְנָ֔ה אֶל־בָּר֥וּךְ בֶּן־נֵֽרִיָּ֖ה לֵאמֹֽר׃
‏17 אֲהָהּ֙ אֲדֹנָ֣י יְהוִ֔ה הִנֵּ֣ה ׀ אַתָּ֣ה עָשִׂ֗יתָ
אֶת־הַשָּׁמַ֙יִם֙ וְאֶת־הָאָ֔רֶץ בְּכֹֽחֲךָ֙ הַגָּד֔וֹל
וּבִֽזְרֹֽעֲךָ֖ הַנְּטוּיָ֑ה לֹֽא־יִפָּלֵ֥א מִמְּךָ֖ כָּל־דָּבָֽר׃
‏18 עֹ֤שֶׂה חֶ֙סֶד֙ לַֽאֲלָפִ֔ים וּמְשַׁלֵּם֙ עֲוֺ֣ן אָב֔וֹת
אֶל־חֵ֥יק בְּנֵיהֶ֖ם אַֽחֲרֵיהֶ֑ם הָאֵ֤ל הַגָּדוֹל֙
הַגִּבּ֔וֹר יְהוָ֥ה צְבָא֖וֹת שְׁמֽוֹ׃ ‏19 גְּדֹל֙ הָ֣עֵצָ֔ה
וְרַ֖ב הָֽעֲלִֽילִיָּ֑ה אֲשֶׁר־עֵינֶ֣יךָ פְקֻח֗וֹת עַל־
כָּל־דַּרְכֵי֙ בְּנֵ֣י אָדָ֔ם לָתֵ֤ת לְאִישׁ֙ כִּדְרָכָ֔יו
וְכִפְרִ֖י מַֽעֲלָלָֽיו׃ ‏20 אֲשֶׁר־שַׂ֣מְתָּ אֹת֣וֹת
וּמֹֽפְתִים֩ בְּאֶֽרֶץ־מִצְרַ֨יִם עַד־הַיּ֤וֹם הַזֶּה֙
וּבְיִשְׂרָאֵ֣ל וּבָֽאָדָ֔ם וַתַּֽעֲשֶׂה־לְּךָ֥ שֵׁ֖ם כַּיּ֥וֹם

and a tied-up one in which they signed on the back" (M BB 10:1).

15. Houses, fields, and vineyards In the present setting, these three elements constitute a promise for the future. In the broadest terms, the rebuilding and replanting alludes to Jer. 1:10. More specifically, they are thematically linked to Jeremiah's prophetic letter to the exiles of 597 B.C.E. In that document, the prophet wrote to his compatriots in exile telling them to build, plant, and marry in Babylon, because redemption has not come (Jer. 29:5–6, cf. 28). Jeremiah's statement here counterpoints that letter: The redemption will come, and the people will again build and plant in their homeland.

17. Ah, Lord GOD! The Hebrew word *ahah* (Ah) is used in connection with cries of amazement, concern, or despair.

18. O great and mighty God In his prayer, Jeremiah extols God with two attributes: "great" (*ha-gadol*) and "mighty" (*ha-gibbor*). By contrast, Daniel praised God as "great" and "awesome" (*nora*), not using the epithet "mighty" (Dan. 9:4). All three attributes are combined in a praise for-

mula that praises "the great, the mighty, and the awesome God" (*ha-el ha-gadol ha-gibbor v'ha-nora*) (Deut. 10:17).

The Sages pondered these variations and tried to understand why the full formula enunciated by Moses (in Deut. 10:17) was subsequently changed. They emerged with the understanding that Jeremiah and Daniel wished to ascribe to God only those attributes that they could honestly affirm on the basis of their personal experience. In the context of the suffering and the destruction that they had experienced, they found it impossible to ascribe all three of the attributes to God. Therefore, each of them omitted one of the attributes. The Sages justify their liturgical revisions by stating that because "God insists on truth, these pious ones would not ascribe false things to Him" (JT Ber. 7:3; BT Yoma 69b). The full formula from Deuteronomy was restored to the liturgy by the men of the Great Assembly, according to talmudic tradition. It is now recited in the opening passage of the collection of blessings known as the *Amidah*.

הַזֶּה׃ 21 וַתֹּצֵא אֶת־עַמְּךָ אֶת־יִשְׂרָאֵל
מֵאֶרֶץ מִצְרָיִם בְּאֹתוֹת וּבְמוֹפְתִים וּבְיָד
חֲזָקָה וּבְאֶזְרוֹעַ נְטוּיָה וּבְמוֹרָא גָּדוֹל׃
22 וַתִּתֵּן לָהֶם אֶת־הָאָרֶץ הַזֹּאת אֲשֶׁר־
נִשְׁבַּעְתָּ לַאֲבוֹתָם לָתֵת לָהֶם אֶרֶץ זָבַת
חָלָב וּדְבָשׁ׃ 23 וַיָּבֹאוּ וַיִּרְשׁוּ אֹתָהּ וְלֹא־
שָׁמְעוּ בְקוֹלֶךָ ובתרותך וּבְתוֹרָתְךָ לֹא־
הָלָכוּ אֵת כָּל־אֲשֶׁר צִוִּיתָה לָהֶם לַעֲשׂוֹת
לֹא עָשׂוּ וַתַּקְרֵא אֹתָם אֵת כָּל־הָרָעָה
הַזֹּאת׃ 24 הִנֵּה הַסֹּלְלוֹת בָּאוּ הָעִיר
לְלָכְדָהּ וְהָעִיר נִתְּנָה בְּיַד הַכַּשְׂדִּים
הַנִּלְחָמִים עָלֶיהָ מִפְּנֵי הַחֶרֶב וְהָרָעָב
וְהַדָּבֶר וַאֲשֶׁר דִּבַּרְתָּ הָיָה וְהִנְּךָ רֹאֶה׃
25 וְאַתָּה אָמַרְתָּ אֵלַי אֲדֹנָי יְהוִה קְנֵה־לְךָ
הַשָּׂדֶה בַּכֶּסֶף וְהָעֵד עֵדִים וְהָעִיר נִתְּנָה
בְּיַד הַכַּשְׂדִּים׃
26 וַיְהִי דְּבַר־יְהוָה אֶל־יִרְמְיָהוּ לֵאמֹר׃
27 הִנֵּה אֲנִי יְהוָה אֱלֹהֵי כָּל־בָּשָׂר הֲמִמֶּנִּי
יִפָּלֵא כָּל־דָּבָר׃

Your people Israel from the land of Egypt with signs and marvels, with a strong hand and an outstretched arm, and with great terror. 22You gave them this land that You had sworn to their fathers to give them, a land flowing with milk and honey, 23and they came and took possession of it. But they did not listen to You or follow Your Teaching; they did nothing of what You commanded them to do. Therefore you have caused all this misfortune to befall them. 24Here are the siegemounds, raised against the city to storm it; and the city, because of sword and famine and pestilence, is at the mercy of the Chaldeans who are attacking it. What You threatened has come to pass—as You see. 25Yet You, Lord God, said to me: Buy the land for money and call in witnesses—when the city is at the mercy of the Chaldeans!"

26Then the word of the Lord came to Jeremiah:

27"Behold I am the Lord, the God of all flesh. Is anything too wondrous for Me?"

הפטרת בחקתי

HAFTARAH FOR B'ḤUKKOTAI

JEREMIAH 16:19–17:14

(*When* B'har *and* B'ḥukkotai *are combined, recite this* haftarah.)

This *haftarah* comprises a series of sayings by the prophet, spoken in Judea sometime in the late 7th to the early 6th century B.C.E. They include personal prayers of proclamation and petition, divine indictments and instructions, and impersonal maxims of a general and national character. The reality of divine punishment for false worship and for immorality and the overwhelming importance of proper trust in God constitute the general themes that bind the verses together. Sin occurs in the open and in the hiddenness of the human heart. Both are observed by God, and the offenders are brought to justice. One must, therefore, hope in the "Hope of Israel," the only source and font of life. Jeremiah exemplifies true piety by his own personal assertions of theological trust and dependence.

This passage establishes a contrast between the faithfulness of the prophet and the sins of his contemporaries. Jeremiah's trust is dramatized by his extraordinary prayers of reliance on God as his refuge and redeemer (16:19, 17:14). The sinners' folly, by contrast, lies in their flagrant disregard of the divine way. They serve "no-gods," hoping for fertility and success, not realizing that they rely on objects "futile and worthless" (vv. 19–20). They act with deception and stealth, hoping to increase unjust gain, not realizing that God who probes the heart undoes injustice and deceit. Thus will their projects be perverted: The verdant trees worshiped in their alien rites will be transformed into dry bushes of the wilderness. Abandoning the "Hope of Israel" (17:13), they reject the true source of living waters. Indeed, their blatant apostasy is marked on their cult objects, even as their rejection of true piety is written on the earth. There is no escape: God knows the inner heart and the outward acts of all.

Trust in God, unlike trust in idols, bestows on its bearers the blessings of heaven. In the language of natural growth and sustenance, the faithful are promised deep roots in flowing waters, bearing fruit despite external circumstances (17:7–8). This trust enables devoted individuals to overcome the destructive forces of the natural world. They withstand oppression by being rooted in divine reality. Accordingly, Jeremiah's teaching is a counsel to choose the "the Fount of living waters" (v. 13) for the sake of such inner power. Hence God's blessing is not external to this decision but at its very root. The wholly natural attitude that worships the forces of nature and the semblances of self-reliance is thus proclaimed a sham, a deceptive blindness to the divine source of life. Only through trust in God may this folly be transcended and one's life transformed.

RELATION OF THE *HAFTARAH* TO THE *PARASHAH*

The *parashah* concludes the Book of Leviticus with a series of blessings and curses that may befall an individual, depending on obedience or disobedience to God and His covenant (Lev. 26:3, 14–15). These rewards and punishments are set forth in detail, and correspond to the central image of the *haftarah:* blessings for those who trust in God and curses for those who spurn His ways (Jer. 17:5–8). Read independently, Jeremiah's exhortation of trust marks a spiritual or theological disposition and does not speak explicitly about covenantal observance as such. Nevertheless, in the wider context of the *haftarah,* which condemns false religious practice (17:1–4), Jeremiah's words on trust serve as an exhortation to covenantal commitments. This is emphasized when the *haftarah* is read in conjunction with the *parashah.* Through this pairing, the prophet's teaching serves to reinforce the concerns of Mo-

ses. Together they exhort the people to choose the blessed path of faithfulness to God and His Torah.

In diverse ways, the *parashah* and the *haftarah* emphasize that no aspect of life is immune to divine judgment: Inner deception yields external results that destroy one's life on the Land, and outward behavior affects a person's inner strength and spiritual resilience to life. Put theologically, the texts affirm a deep correlation between spiritual trust and behavior on the one hand, and renewed stability and productivity on the other. Using natural images of earthly bounty and being rooted in the Land, the Torah and the *haftarah* foster a consciousness of this correlation and invite meditation on its truth.

16 19O LORD, my strength and my stronghold,
My refuge in a day of trouble,
To You nations shall come
From the ends of the earth and say:
Our fathers inherited utter delusions,
Things that are futile and worthless.
20Can a man make gods for himself?
No-gods are they!
21Assuredly, I will teach them,
Once and for all I will teach them
My power and My might.
And they shall learn that My name is LORD.

טז 19 יְהֹוָ֞ה עֻזִּ֧י וּמָעֻזִּ֛י
וּמְנוּסִ֖י בְּי֣וֹם צָרָ֑ה
אֵלֶ֗יךָ גּוֹיִ֤ם יָבֹ֙אוּ֙
מֵֽאַפְסֵי־אָ֔רֶץ וְיֹאמְר֗וּ
אַךְ־שֶׁ֙קֶר֙ נָחֲל֣וּ אֲבוֹתֵ֔ינוּ
הֶ֖בֶל וְאֵֽין־בָּ֥ם מוֹעִֽיל׃
20 הֲיַעֲשֶׂה־לּ֥וֹ אָדָ֖ם אֱלֹהִ֑ים
וְהֵ֖מָּה לֹ֥א אֱלֹהִֽים׃
21 לָכֵן֙ הִנְנִ֣י מֽוֹדִיעָ֔ם
בַּפַּ֣עַם הַזֹּ֔את אוֹדִיעֵ֥ם
אֶת־יָדִ֖י וְאֶת־גְּבֽוּרָתִ֑י
וְיָדְע֖וּ כִּֽי־שְׁמִ֥י יְהֹוָֽה׃ ס

17 The guilt of Judah is inscribed
With a stylus of iron,
Engraved with an adamant point
On the tablet of their hearts,
And on the horns of their altars,

יז חַטַּ֣את יְהוּדָ֗ה כְּתוּבָ֛ה
בְּעֵ֥ט בַּרְזֶ֖ל
בְּצִפֹּ֣רֶן שָׁמִ֑יר חֲרוּשָׁה֙
עַל־ל֣וּחַ לִבָּ֔ם
וּלְקַרְנ֖וֹת מִזְבְּחוֹתֵיכֶֽם׃

Jeremiah 16:19. The underlying metaphor here is based on the fortresses that served as a fortified place of refuge (cf. Isa. 17:9). This accounts for the use of the term *m'nusi* (My refuge), presumably derived from the verb *nus,* "to run." It thus evokes a sense of sanctuary, insofar as just this verb is used in connection with the right of an accidental manslayer to flee to the protective custody of a city of refuge (Num. 35:6; Deut. 4:42).

20. No-gods are they The opprobrium "no-god" has polemical force (Deut. 32:17,21), and was often used rhetorically to signal Israel's rejection of the covenant with God (Deut. 32:21; Hos. 1:9).

21. I will teach them Or "inform them" (*odi·em*). A critique of the nations for idolatry is unusual in pre-exilic sources; Jeremiah is the first to enunciate this view (cf. Jer. 10:11, 50:35–39). By contrast, the Torah never condemns the nations for pagan worship but only for such perversions as child sacrifice (Deut. 12:29–31). Indeed, Deut. 4:19 even presents the worship of the sun, the moon, and the stars as the divine portion for all nations except Israel. However, the nations are always arraigned for immorality (cf. Amos 1).

Jeremiah 17:1. The guilt of Judah . . . on the horns of their altars Hebrew: *ḥattat Y'hudah.* Normally, the purging blood of the purification offering (*ḥattat*) was put on the horns of the altar.

2While their children remember
Their altars and sacred posts,
By verdant trees,
Upon lofty hills.
3Because of the sin of your shrines
Throughout your borders,
I will make your rampart a heap in the field,
And all your treasures a spoil.
4You will forfeit, by your own act,
The inheritance I have given you;
I will make you a slave to your enemies
In a land you have never known.
For you have kindled the flame of My wrath
Which shall burn for all time.

5Thus said the LORD:
Cursed is he who trusts in man,
Who makes mere flesh his strength,
And turns his thoughts from the LORD.
6He shall be like a bush in the desert,
Which does not sense the coming of good:
It is set in the scorched places of the wilderness,
In a barren land without inhabitant.
7Blessed is he who trusts in the LORD,
Whose trust is the LORD alone.
8He shall be like a tree planted by waters,
Sending forth its roots by a stream:
It does not sense the coming of heat,
Its leaves are ever fresh;
It has no care in a year of drought,
It does not cease to yield fruit.

2 כִּזְכֹּר בְּנֵיהֶם
מִזְבְּחוֹתָם וַאֲשֵׁרֵיהֶם
עַל־עֵץ רַעֲנָן
עַל גְּבָעוֹת הַגְּבֹהוֹת׃
3 הֲרָרִי בַּשָּׂדֶה
חֵילְךָ כָל־אוֹצְרוֹתֶיךָ לָבַז אֶתֵּן
בָּמֹתֶיךָ בְּחַטָּאת
בְּכָל־גְּבוּלֶיךָ׃
4 וְשָׁמַטְתָּה וּבְךָ
מִנַּחֲלָתְךָ אֲשֶׁר נָתַתִּי לָךְ
וְהַעֲבַדְתִּיךָ אֶת־אֹיְבֶיךָ
בָּאָרֶץ אֲשֶׁר לֹא־יָדָעְתָּ
כִּי־אֵשׁ קְדַחְתֶּם בְּאַפִּי
עַד־עוֹלָם תּוּקָד׃ ס

5 כֹּה ׀ אָמַר יְהוָה
אָרוּר הַגֶּבֶר אֲשֶׁר יִבְטַח בָּאָדָם
וְשָׂם בָּשָׂר זְרֹעוֹ
וּמִן־יְהוָה יָסוּר לִבּוֹ׃
6 וְהָיָה כְּעַרְעָר בָּעֲרָבָה
וְלֹא יִרְאֶה כִּי־יָבוֹא טוֹב
וְשָׁכַן חֲרֵרִים בַּמִּדְבָּר
אֶרֶץ מְלֵחָה וְלֹא תֵשֵׁב׃ ס
7 בָּרוּךְ הַגֶּבֶר אֲשֶׁר יִבְטַח בַּיהוָה
וְהָיָה יְהוָה מִבְטַחוֹ׃
8 וְהָיָה כְּעֵץ ׀ שָׁתוּל עַל־מַיִם
וְעַל־יוּבַל יְשַׁלַּח שָׁרָשָׁיו
וְלֹא ירא יִרְאֶה כִּי־יָבֹא חֹם
וְהָיָה עָלֵהוּ רַעֲנָן
וּבִשְׁנַת בַּצֹּרֶת לֹא יִדְאָג
וְלֹא יָמִישׁ מֵעֲשׂוֹת פֶּרִי׃

This was done to purify the shrine (Lev. 8:15; cf. M Shev. 1:4–7). It was also performed in cases of accidental sin by the individual (Lev. 4:25,30). Jeremiah thus mocks Israel's practices by punning. It is their guilt, he implies, that is on their altars and not the blood of the expunging sacrifice.

8. like a tree planted by waters Jeremiah's image of the regenerative bounty of one who trusts God echoes Ps. 1:3, where the beneficiary is the student of Torah. Jeremiah extends the metaphor with the words that the tree's "leaves are ever fresh (*ra·anan*)." This provides a powerful counterpoint to the critique of the sinners who worship "By verdant (*ra·anan*) trees" (17:2).

9Most devious is the heart;
It is perverse—who can fathom it?
10I the LORD probe the heart,
Search the mind—
To repay every man according to his ways,
With the proper fruit of his deeds.

9 עָקֹב הַלֵּב מִכֹּל
וְאָנֻשׁ הוּא מִי יֵדָעֶנּוּ׃
10 אֲנִי יְהוָה חֹקֵר לֵב
בֹּחֵן כְּלָיוֹת
וְלָתֵת לְאִישׁ כדרכו כִּדְרָכָיו
כִּפְרִי מַעֲלָלָיו׃ ס

11Like a partridge hatching what she did not lay,
So is one who amasses wealth by unjust means;
In the middle of his life it will leave him,
And in the end he will be proved a fool.

11 קֹרֵא דָגַר וְלֹא יָלָד
עֹשֶׂה עֹשֶׁר וְלֹא בְמִשְׁפָּט
בַּחֲצִי ימו יָמָיו יַעַזְבֶנּוּ
וּבְאַחֲרִיתוֹ יִהְיֶה נָבָל׃

12O Throne of Glory exalted from of old,
Our Sacred Shrine!
13O Hope of Israel! O LORD!
All who forsake You shall be put to shame,
Those in the land who turn from You
Shall be doomed men,
For they have forsaken the LORD,
The Fount of living waters.

12 כִּסֵּא כָבוֹד מָרוֹם מֵרִאשׁוֹן
מְקוֹם מִקְדָּשֵׁנוּ׃
13 מִקְוֵה יִשְׂרָאֵל יְהוָה
כָּל־עֹזְבֶיךָ יֵבֹשׁוּ
יסורי וְסוּרַי בָּאָרֶץ
יִכָּתֵבוּ
כִּי עָזְבוּ
מְקוֹר מַיִם־חַיִּים אֶת־יְהוָה׃ ס

14Heal me, O LORD, and let me be healed;
Save me, and let me be saved;
For You are my glory.

14 רְפָאֵנִי יְהוָה וְאֵרָפֵא
הוֹשִׁיעֵנִי וְאִוָּשֵׁעָה
כִּי תְהִלָּתִי אָתָּה׃

10. fruit of his deeds A deft pun linking verses 9–10 to the tree imagery of verses 5–8.

12. O Throne of Glory In modern times, the phrase has also been understood as an oath sworn "[By the] Throne" that "Israel's hope is the LORD."

13. O Hope of Israel! O LORD! Jeremiah's cry of pathos. God is not only the focus of trust but the source of hope and "Font of living waters (*m'kor mayyim ḥayyim*)." Calling God "Hope" (*Mikveh*) condenses both theological ideas, insofar as this noun is a pun on the pool for ritual immersion (*mikveh*). Thus it also conveys the notion of divine purification. Akiva taught this idea powerfully, interpreting the phrase as "The LORD is the *mikveh* (ritual pool) of Israel," adding: "Just as the *mikveh* purifies the impure, so the Holy One purifies Israel" (M Yoma 8:9).

14. Heal me, O LORD The *haftarah* closes with this request. In context, it initiates a separate prayer of the prophet that concludes, after the *haftarah,* with a wish for the destruction of his enemies (Jer. 17:18). The Sages thus truncated this prayer for the *haftarah,* leaving only this line. The result is a powerful appeal for divine aid that balances the opening line (16:19). Subsequent Jewish tradition incorporated this prayer into the 8th blessing of the weekday *Amidah.* In an adaptation appropriate for communal worship, the compilers changed the singular personal pronoun ("me," in "Heal me" and "Save me") to the collective plural ("us," in "Heal us" and "Save us").

במדבר

NUMBERS

במדבר
נשא
בהעלתך
שלח לך
קרח
חקת
בלק
פינחס
מטות
מסעי

NUMBERS

JACOB MILGROM

The Book of Exodus described how at Mount Sinai God revealed to Israel its basic laws. Whereas Leviticus further instructed Israel on the laws of sacrifice, purity, and ethics that would enable it to remain on its Land, Numbers now chronicles Israel's journey, from Sinai to the Jordan River, the edge of its Promised Land, where it will live out these laws.

The form of the book mirrors this striking shift in the narrative. In Numbers, the law (L) and narrative (N) alternate regularly as follows: 1:1–10:10 L, 10:11–14:45 N, 15 L, 16–17 N, 18–19 L, 20–25 N, 25:1–27:11 L, 27:12–23 N, 28–30 L, 31:1–33:49 N, 33:50–56, 34–36 L.

The principal actor in the Book of Numbers is the Lord. Even under extreme provocation, God keeps His covenant with the Israelites, guides them through the wilderness, and provides for their needs.

Numbers records the movement of God's presence, which is visible as a cloud by day and as fire by night (9:15–16), from the stationary center of Sinai to the mobile Tabernacle, exemplifying the developing relationship between God and God's people. Its starts and stops determine Israel's stages and stations. Its constant visibility is a sign to Israel and the nations "that You, O LORD, are in the midst of this people; that You, O LORD, appear in plain sight when Your cloud rests over them and when You go before them in a pillar of cloud by day and in a pillar of fire by night" (14:14). Thus the divine presence mandates the purity of God's camp (5:1–4, 31:19,24), so God's presence in the Land mandates that Israel not pollute the Land (35:34).

The climax of this relationship is articulated in Balaam's praise of Israel when he exclaims: "Lo, there is no augury in Jacob, / No divining in Israel: / Jacob is told at once, / Yea Israel, what God has planned" (23:23). Israel, Balaam explains, is unique among the nations. Having direct access to God, Israel needs neither diviners nor divination to understand the deity's will. As Balaam proceeds and blesses Israel, he discovers that complex techniques are not needed to approach the Lord. In Numbers, unique among the books, we see the realization of God's relationship with Israel in ways heretofore only promised or imagined.

As God's fire cloud descends on the Ark whenever God wishes to address Moses (7:89), the Ark serves as a tangible witness to the divine presence. The sight of the Ark in battle holds out the promise that Israel will be victorious over its enemies (10:32–36, 31:6), and its absence is a sure sign that Israel will be defeated (14:43–44). The Ark is flanked by winged cherubim, symbolizing that God is not confined to the Ark except when God descends on it to communicate with the people of Israel. During the march, the Ark, distinguished by its blue cover (4:6), occupies the very center of the camp (10:21); although according to another tradition, it is placed at the head of the camp to lead the march (10:33).

God supplies Israel with all its nutritional needs: manna, quail (11:4–34), and water, even when spurned by the people at large or by its leaders (20:12–13; 21:5). When the scouts bring back a negative report denying the possibility that Israel can conquer the Land (13:28–37), the people panic and want to return to Egypt. God is willing to destroy Israel but concedes to Moses that although this desert generation will be punished, God will bring their children safely into the Promised Land (14:14–15).

B'MIDBAR

1 On the first day of the second month, in the second year following the exodus from the land of Egypt, the Lord spoke to Moses in the wilderness of Sinai, in the Tent of Meeting, saying:

במדבר

א וַיְדַבֵּר יְהוָה אֶל־מֹשֶׁה בְּמִדְבַּר סִינַי
בְּאֹהֶל מוֹעֵד בְּאֶחָד לַחֹדֶשׁ הַשֵּׁנִי בַּשָּׁנָה
הַשֵּׁנִית לְצֵאתָם מֵאֶרֶץ מִצְרַיִם לֵאמֹר׃

The Generation of the Exodus: The Wilderness Camp (1:1–10:10)

CENSUS IN THE WILDERNESS (1:1–54)

The march of the Israelites through the wilderness, from Mount Sinai to the Promised Land, will take them through hostile environments, both natural and human. To meet those dangers, the people must be organized into a military camp, which requires a census.

1. first day In ancient times, the first day of each month was a holiday that provided an opportunity to bring the people together for important announcements.

wilderness Hebrew: *midbar;* it does not mean "desert." Although the scant rainfall in the Sinai cannot support agriculture, it can provide adequate pasturage for flocks.

The Lord spoke . . . in the Tent of Meeting As Moses had been permitted to ascend to the

---

This fourth book of the Torah is known as "Numbers" in English, because of the census recorded in the opening chapter. In some Rabbinic texts it is called "The Book of the Census" (*Seifer Ha-P'kudim*). Its proper Hebrew designation, from its first significant word, is *B'midbar* (In the Wilderness), and it describes a people wandering through a spiritual as well as a geographic wilderness.

What must it have been like to experience the transition from the grand events of Sinai and the Sea of Reeds to the daily routine of the wilderness? The answer might lead us to the lesson that life is lived, not so much in the grand moments as in uncelebrated ordinary times. In Numbers, the focus of leadership passes from the prophet Moses to the priest Aaron, perhaps because the prophet issues great demands from the mountaintop, whereas the priest is involved with the people in the complexities and routines of daily life.

Throughout this book, the Israelites, who had experienced the Exodus, the crossing of the sea, and the revelation at Sinai, are described as a petulant, complaining people, constantly trying the patience of God and of Moses. In Hirsch's words, *B'midbar* contrasts "the people of Israel as it actually is" to "the ideal to which it was summoned in *Va-yikra.*"

The generation of the wilderness dies off in the course of the 38 years covered by this book. At its conclusion, a new generation of Israelites who had never known slavery, a generation for whom the revelation at Sinai was tradition rather than personal experience, stands poised to enter the Promised Land.

CHAPTER 1

This first *parashah* deals mainly with two subjects: the census of Israelite adult males in preparation for the battles to reach and conquer the Promised Land, and the physical arrangement of the various tribes as they marched and as they camped.

1. in the Tent of Meeting "The Lord transferred the divine Presence from Sinai to the tabernacle, from a sanctuary established by God to one fashioned by the people Israel. The tabernacle was a portable Mount Sinai, the heavens transplanted and brought down to earth" (B. Jacob). The Israelites never felt lost in the wilderness because they were able to focus on the tabernacle at the center of their encampment.

The Jewish calendar arranges for these opening chapters of the Book of Numbers (which begin with God speaking to the people in the wilderness of Sinai) to be read every year on the *Shabbat* before the festival that celebrates the giving of the Torah, *Shavu·ot.* According to the Sages, this should remind us that the Torah was given in a wilderness, a place accessible to all, a site that belonged to no one people, and that it was given to a people with no real property and few possessions. "One should be as open as a wilderness to receive the Torah" (BT Ned. 55a). It is intimidating to open oneself to the demands of God, to a new and morally de-

2Take a census of the whole Israelite community by the clans of its ancestral houses, listing the names, every male, head by head. 3You and Aaron shall record them by their groups, from the age of twenty years up, all those in Israel who are able to bear arms. 4Associated with you shall be a man from each tribe, each one the head of his ancestral house.

5These are the names of the men who shall assist you:

From Reuben, Elizur son of Shedeur.

2 שְׂאוּ אֶת־רֹאשׁ כָּל־עֲדַת בְּנֵי־יִשְׂרָאֵל
לְמִשְׁפְּחֹתָם לְבֵית אֲבֹתָם בְּמִסְפַּר שֵׁמוֹת
כָּל־זָכָר לְגֻלְגְּלֹתָם: 3 מִבֶּן עֶשְׂרִים שָׁנָה
וָמַעְלָה כָּל־יֹצֵא צָבָא בְּיִשְׂרָאֵל תִּפְקְדוּ
אֹתָם לְצִבְאֹתָם אַתָּה וְאַהֲרֹן: 4 וְאִתְּכֶם
יִהְיוּ אִישׁ אִישׁ לַמַּטֶּה אִישׁ רֹאשׁ לְבֵית־
אֲבֹתָיו הוּא:
5 וְאֵלֶּה שְׁמוֹת הָאֲנָשִׁים אֲשֶׁר יַעַמְדוּ
אִתְּכֶם
לִרְאוּבֵן אֱלִיצוּר בֶּן־שְׁדֵיאוּר:

Presence of God atop the mountain, so might he enter the Tent of Meeting—a Mount Sinai on earth, so to speak. The Lord's voice came from within, from between the two cherubim facing each other atop the Ark.

2. The census described here follows the procedures of censuses in other ancient Near Eastern cultures. It even uses the same terminology. The census was indispensable for military conscription and for any government levy on persons or property. From 10:11, it is clear that the census was completed in less than 20 days.

3. twenty years up The age of conscription in ancient Israel. No upper limit is given here.

able to bear arms The previous statement with no age limit is now qualified.

5–15. Tribal lists throughout the Bible may vary in the names and the order of the tribes, but they share in common the concern for preserving the number 12. These lists can be divided roughly into two groups: those that include the tribe of Levi and those that omit it. All the tribal lists in Numbers fall into the latter category, because the tribe of Levi was exempt from military conscription.

These are the names The census supervisors, mandatory according to verse 4, are named by God.

---

manding way of life. The Torah portrays the people Israel as periodically wishing they were back in the predictable, morally undemanding servitude of Egypt. Yet Israel's willingness to accept the Torah, to be "as open as a wilderness" to let the Torah's morality fill the moral vacuum in the lives of former slaves, was the essential first step in God's remaking the world. For the first time, God's world will contain a model people, guided by the Torah to live a God-oriented life.

The wilderness, untouched by human settlement, offered a contrast to Egypt, which was dominated by monuments fashioned by human hands. Thus it was a fitting stage for God's being proclaimed sovereign of the world. We may even see a parallel between the revelation at Sinai (when God imposed moral order in the midst of a wilderness) and the creation of the world (when God imposed natural order on chaos).

2. Take a census Literally, "lift the head." This prompted the comment, "Let the Israelites hold their heads high in pride as they contemplate who their ancestors were" (Menaḥem Naḥum of Chernobyl). Although the purpose of the census was purely functional, mustering the Israelites for battle, the Midrash uncovers another dimension to it, by comparing God to a person who had a store of precious jewels. From time to time, this individual would take out the jewels and count them to take pleasure in their beauty and to be reassured that they were all safely there (Num. R. 4:2). For Ramban, the census testifies to the miracle of Israel's survival and increase despite the efforts of Pharaoh and Amalek and the rigors of the wilderness journey. He points to the enduring lesson of Jewish history: We have not succumbed in spite of devastating losses and persecution. Levi Yitzḥak of Berdichev connects the final total of 603,550 Israelites (v. 46) to a tradition that there are 603,550 letters in the Torah. Just as the absence of one letter renders a Torah scroll unfit for use, the loss of even one Jew prevents Israel from fulfilling its divine mission.

6 From Simeon, Shelumiel son of Zurishaddai.
7 From Judah, Nahshon son of Amminadab.
8 From Issachar, Nethanel son of Zuar.
9 From Zebulun, Eliab son of Helon.
10 From the sons of Joseph:
from Ephraim, Elishama son of Ammihud;
from Manasseh, Gamaliel son of Pedahzur.
11 From Benjamin, Abidan son of Gideoni.
12 From Dan, Ahiezer son of Ammishaddai.
13 From Asher, Pagiel son of Ochran.
14 From Gad, Eliasaph son of Deuel.
15 From Naphtali, Ahira son of Enan.
16 Those are the elected of the assembly, the chieftains of their ancestral tribes: they are the heads of the contingents of Israel.

17 So Moses and Aaron took those men, who were designated by name, 18 and on the first day of the second month they convoked the whole community, who were registered by the clans of their ancestral houses—the names of those aged twenty years and over being listed head by head. 19 As the LORD had commanded Moses, so he recorded them in the wilderness of Sinai.

20 They totaled as follows:

The descendants of Reuben, Israel's first-born, the registration of the clans of their ancestral house, as listed by name, head by head, all males aged twenty years and over, all who were able to bear arms—21 those enrolled from the tribe of Reuben: 46,500.

22 Of the descendants of Simeon, the registration of the clans of their ancestral house, their enrollment as listed by name, head by head, all males aged twenty years and over, all who were able to bear arms—23 those enrolled from the tribe of Simeon: 59,300.

6 לְשִׁמְעוֹן שְׁלֻמִיאֵל בֶּן־צוּרִישַׁדָּי׃
7 לִיהוּדָה נַחְשׁוֹן בֶּן־עַמִּינָדָב׃
8 לְיִשָּׂשכָר נְתַנְאֵל בֶּן־צוּעָר׃
9 לִזְבוּלֻן אֱלִיאָב בֶּן־חֵלֹן׃
10 לִבְנֵי יוֹסֵף
לְאֶפְרַיִם אֱלִישָׁמָע בֶּן־עַמִּיהוּד
לִמְנַשֶּׁה גַּמְלִיאֵל בֶּן־פְּדָהצוּר׃
11 לְבִנְיָמִן אֲבִידָן בֶּן־גִּדְעֹנִי׃
12 לְדָן אֲחִיעֶזֶר בֶּן־עַמִּישַׁדָּי׃
13 לְאָשֵׁר פַּגְעִיאֵל בֶּן־עָכְרָן׃
14 לְגָד אֶלְיָסָף בֶּן־דְּעוּאֵל׃
15 לְנַפְתָּלִי אֲחִירַע בֶּן־עֵינָן׃
16 אֵלֶּה קריאי קְרוּאֵי הָעֵדָה נְשִׂיאֵי מַטּוֹת
אֲבוֹתָם רָאשֵׁי אַלְפֵי יִשְׂרָאֵל הֵם׃
17 וַיִּקַּח מֹשֶׁה וְאַהֲרֹן אֵת הָאֲנָשִׁים הָאֵלֶּה
אֲשֶׁר נִקְּבוּ בְּשֵׁמוֹת׃ 18 וְאֵת כָּל־הָעֵדָה
הִקְהִילוּ בְּאֶחָד לַחֹדֶשׁ הַשֵּׁנִי וַיִּתְיַלְדוּ
עַל־מִשְׁפְּחֹתָם לְבֵית אֲבֹתָם בְּמִסְפַּר
שֵׁמוֹת מִבֶּן עֶשְׂרִים שָׁנָה וָמַעְלָה
לְגֻלְגְּלֹתָם׃ 19 כַּאֲשֶׁר צִוָּה יְהוָה אֶת־מֹשֶׁה
וַיִּפְקְדֵם בְּמִדְבַּר סִינָי׃ פ
שני 20 וַיִּהְיוּ בְנֵי־רְאוּבֵן בְּכֹר יִשְׂרָאֵל תּוֹלְדֹתָם
לְמִשְׁפְּחֹתָם לְבֵית אֲבֹתָם בְּמִסְפַּר שֵׁמוֹת
לְגֻלְגְּלֹתָם כָּל־זָכָר מִבֶּן עֶשְׂרִים שָׁנָה
וָמַעְלָה כֹּל יֹצֵא צָבָא׃ 21 פְּקֻדֵיהֶם לְמַטֵּה
רְאוּבֵן שִׁשָּׁה וְאַרְבָּעִים אֶלֶף וַחֲמֵשׁ
מֵאוֹת׃ פ 22 לִבְנֵי שִׁמְעוֹן תּוֹלְדֹתָם
לְמִשְׁפְּחֹתָם לְבֵית אֲבֹתָם פְּקֻדָיו בְּמִסְפַּר
שֵׁמוֹת לְגֻלְגְּלֹתָם כָּל־זָכָר מִבֶּן עֶשְׂרִים
שָׁנָה וָמַעְלָה כֹּל יֹצֵא צָבָא׃ 23 פְּקֻדֵיהֶם
לְמַטֵּה שִׁמְעוֹן תִּשְׁעָה וַחֲמִשִּׁים אֶלֶף

18. and on the first day The date of verse 1 is repeated to emphasize that the census was begun on the very day it was commanded.

were registered Hebrew: *va-yityaldu;* literally, "declared their lineage," according to their households and clans (Onk., Targ. Jon.).

20. Israel's first-born Reuben's title is given to account for the fact that he heads the list even though Judah is to lead the march (see 1 Chron. 5:1–2).

24 Of the descendants of Gad, the registration of the clans of their ancestral house, as listed by name, aged twenty years and over, all who were able to bear arms—25 those enrolled from the tribe of Gad: 45,650.

26 Of the descendants of Judah, the registration of the clans of their ancestral house, as listed by name, aged twenty years and over, all who were able to bear arms—27 those enrolled from the tribe of Judah: 74,600.

28 Of the descendants of Issachar, the registration of the clans of their ancestral house, as listed by name, aged twenty years and over, all who were able to bear arms—29 those enrolled from the tribe of Issachar: 54,400.

30 Of the descendants of Zebulun, the registration of the clans of their ancestral house, as listed by name, aged twenty years and over, all who were able to bear arms—31 those enrolled from the tribe of Zebulun: 57,400.

32 Of the descendants of Joseph:

Of the descendants of Ephraim, the registration of the clans of their ancestral house, as listed by name, aged twenty years and over, all who were able to bear arms—33 those enrolled from the tribe of Ephraim: 40,500.

34 Of the descendants of Manasseh, the registration of the clans of their ancestral house, as listed by name, aged twenty years and over, all who were able to bear arms—35 those enrolled from the tribe of Manasseh: 32,200.

36 Of the descendants of Benjamin, the registration of the clans of their ancestral house, as listed by name, aged twenty years and over, all who were able to bear arms—37 those enrolled from the tribe of Benjamin: 35,400.

38 Of the descendants of Dan, the registration of the clans of their ancestral house, as listed by name, aged twenty years and over, all who were able to bear arms—39 those enrolled from the tribe of Dan: 62,700.

וּשְׁלֹ֥שׁ מֵאֽוֹת׃ פ 24 לִבְנֵ֣י גָ֔ד תּוֹלְדֹתָ֖ם
לְמִשְׁפְּחֹתָ֣ם לְבֵ֣ית אֲבֹתָ֑ם בְּמִסְפַּ֣ר שֵׁמ֗וֹת
מִבֶּ֨ן עֶשְׂרִ֤ים שָׁנָה֙ וָמַ֔עְלָה כֹּ֖ל יֹצֵ֥א צָבָֽא׃
25 פְּקֻדֵיהֶ֖ם לְמַטֵּ֣ה גָ֑ד חֲמִשָּׁ֤ה וְאַרְבָּעִים֙
אֶ֔לֶף וְשֵׁ֥שׁ מֵא֖וֹת וַחֲמִשִּֽׁים׃ פ 26 לִבְנֵ֣י
יְהוּדָ֔ה תּוֹלְדֹתָ֥ם לְמִשְׁפְּחֹתָ֖ם לְבֵ֣ית
אֲבֹתָ֑ם בְּמִסְפַּ֣ר שֵׁמֹ֗ת מִבֶּ֨ן עֶשְׂרִ֤ים שָׁנָה֙
וָמַ֔עְלָה כֹּ֖ל יֹצֵ֥א צָבָֽא׃ 27 פְּקֻדֵיהֶ֖ם לְמַטֵּ֣ה
יְהוּדָ֑ה אַרְבָּעָ֧ה וְשִׁבְעִ֛ים אֶ֖לֶף וְשֵׁ֥שׁ
מֵאֽוֹת׃ פ 28 לִבְנֵ֣י יִשָּׂשכָ֔ר תּוֹלְדֹתָ֖ם
לְמִשְׁפְּחֹתָ֣ם לְבֵ֣ית אֲבֹתָ֑ם בְּמִסְפַּ֣ר שֵׁמֹ֗ת
מִבֶּ֨ן עֶשְׂרִ֤ים שָׁנָה֙ וָמַ֔עְלָה כֹּ֖ל יֹצֵ֥א
צָבָֽא׃ 29 פְּקֻדֵיהֶ֖ם לְמַטֵּ֣ה יִשָּׂשכָ֑ר אַרְבָּעָ֧ה
וַחֲמִשִּׁ֛ים אֶ֖לֶף וְאַרְבַּ֥ע מֵאֽוֹת׃ פ
30 לִבְנֵ֣י זְבוּלֻ֔ן תּוֹלְדֹתָ֥ם לְמִשְׁפְּחֹתָ֖ם לְבֵ֣ית
אֲבֹתָ֑ם בְּמִסְפַּ֣ר שֵׁמֹ֗ת מִבֶּ֨ן עֶשְׂרִ֤ים שָׁנָה֙
וָמַ֔עְלָה כֹּ֖ל יֹצֵ֥א צָבָֽא׃ 31 פְּקֻדֵיהֶ֖ם לְמַטֵּ֣ה
זְבוּלֻ֑ן שִׁבְעָ֧ה וַחֲמִשִּׁ֛ים אֶ֖לֶף וְאַרְבַּ֥ע
מֵאֽוֹת׃ פ 32 לִבְנֵ֤י יוֹסֵף֙ לִבְנֵ֣י אֶפְרַ֔יִם
תּוֹלְדֹתָ֥ם לְמִשְׁפְּחֹתָ֖ם לְבֵ֣ית אֲבֹתָ֑ם
בְּמִסְפַּ֣ר שֵׁמֹ֗ת מִבֶּ֨ן עֶשְׂרִ֤ים שָׁנָה֙ וָמַ֔עְלָה
כֹּ֖ל יֹצֵ֥א צָבָֽא׃ 33 פְּקֻדֵיהֶ֖ם לְמַטֵּ֣ה אֶפְרָ֑יִם
אַרְבָּעִ֥ים אֶ֖לֶף וַחֲמֵ֥שׁ מֵאֽוֹת׃ פ 34 לִבְנֵ֣י
מְנַשֶּׁ֔ה תּוֹלְדֹתָ֥ם לְמִשְׁפְּחֹתָ֖ם לְבֵ֣ית
אֲבֹתָ֑ם בְּמִסְפַּ֣ר שֵׁמ֗וֹת מִבֶּ֨ן עֶשְׂרִ֤ים
שָׁנָה֙ וָמַ֔עְלָה כֹּ֖ל יֹצֵ֥א צָבָֽא׃ 35 פְּקֻדֵיהֶ֖ם
לְמַטֵּ֣ה מְנַשֶּׁ֑ה שְׁנַ֧יִם וּשְׁלֹשִׁ֛ים אֶ֖לֶף
וּמָאתָֽיִם׃ פ 36 לִבְנֵ֣י בִנְיָמִ֔ן תּוֹלְדֹתָ֥ם
לְמִשְׁפְּחֹתָ֖ם לְבֵ֣ית אֲבֹתָ֑ם בְּמִסְפַּ֣ר שֵׁמֹ֗ת
מִבֶּ֨ן עֶשְׂרִ֤ים שָׁנָה֙ וָמַ֔עְלָה כֹּ֖ל יֹצֵ֥א צָבָֽא׃
37 פְּקֻדֵיהֶ֖ם לְמַטֵּ֣ה בִנְיָמִ֑ן חֲמִשָּׁ֧ה וּשְׁלֹשִׁ֛ים
אֶ֖לֶף וְאַרְבַּ֥ע מֵאֽוֹת׃ פ 38 לִבְנֵ֣י דָ֔ן
תּוֹלְדֹתָ֥ם לְמִשְׁפְּחֹתָ֖ם לְבֵ֣ית אֲבֹתָ֑ם
בְּמִסְפַּ֣ר שֵׁמֹ֗ת מִבֶּ֨ן עֶשְׂרִ֤ים שָׁנָה֙ וָמַ֔עְלָה
כֹּ֖ל יֹצֵ֥א צָבָֽא׃ 39 פְּקֻדֵיהֶ֖ם לְמַטֵּ֣ה דָ֑ן שְׁנַ֧יִם

[40]Of the descendants of Asher, the registration of the clans of their ancestral house, as listed by name, aged twenty years and over, all who were able to bear arms—[41]those enrolled from the tribe of Asher: 41,500.

[42][Of] the descendants of Naphtali, the registration of the clans of their ancestral house as listed by name, aged twenty years and over, all who were able to bear arms—[43]those enrolled from the tribe of Naphtali: 53,400.

[44]Those are the enrollments recorded by Moses and Aaron and by the chieftains of Israel, who were twelve in number, one man to each ancestral house. [45]All the Israelites, aged twenty years and over, enrolled by ancestral houses, all those in Israel who were able to bear arms—[46]all who were enrolled came to 603,550.

[47]The Levites, however, were not recorded among them by their ancestral tribe. [48]For the LORD had spoken to Moses, saying: [49]Do not on any account enroll the tribe of Levi or take a census of them with the Israelites. [50]You shall put the Levites in charge of the Tabernacle of the Pact, all its furnishings, and everything that pertains to it: they shall carry the Tabernacle and all its furnishings, and they shall tend it; and they

וְשִׁשִּׁים אֶלֶף וּשְׁבַע מֵאוֹת׃ פ 40 לִבְנֵי
אָשֵׁר תּוֹלְדֹתָם לְמִשְׁפְּחֹתָם לְבֵית אֲבֹתָם
בְּמִסְפַּר שֵׁמֹת מִבֶּן עֶשְׂרִים שָׁנָה וָמַעְלָה
כֹּל יֹצֵא צָבָא׃ 41 פְּקֻדֵיהֶם לְמַטֵּה אָשֵׁר
אֶחָד וְאַרְבָּעִים אֶלֶף וַחֲמֵשׁ מֵאוֹת׃ פ
42 בְּנֵי נַפְתָּלִי תּוֹלְדֹתָם לְמִשְׁפְּחֹתָם לְבֵית
אֲבֹתָם בְּמִסְפַּר שֵׁמֹת מִבֶּן עֶשְׂרִים שָׁנָה
וָמַעְלָה כֹּל יֹצֵא צָבָא׃ 43 פְּקֻדֵיהֶם לְמַטֵּה
נַפְתָּלִי שְׁלֹשָׁה וַחֲמִשִּׁים אֶלֶף וְאַרְבַּע
מֵאוֹת׃ פ
44 אֵלֶּה הַפְּקֻדִים אֲשֶׁר פָּקַד מֹשֶׁה וְאַהֲרֹן
וּנְשִׂיאֵי יִשְׂרָאֵל שְׁנֵים עָשָׂר אִישׁ אִישׁ־
אֶחָד לְבֵית־אֲבֹתָיו הָיוּ׃ 45 וַיִּהְיוּ כָּל־
פְּקוּדֵי בְנֵי־יִשְׂרָאֵל לְבֵית אֲבֹתָם מִבֶּן
עֶשְׂרִים שָׁנָה וָמַעְלָה כָּל־יֹצֵא צָבָא
בְּיִשְׂרָאֵל׃ 46 וַיִּהְיוּ כָּל־הַפְּקֻדִים שֵׁשׁ־
מֵאוֹת אֶלֶף וּשְׁלֹשֶׁת אֲלָפִים וַחֲמֵשׁ מֵאוֹת
וַחֲמִשִּׁים׃
47 וְהַלְוִיִּם לְמַטֵּה אֲבֹתָם לֹא הָתְפָּקְדוּ
בְּתוֹכָם׃ פ 48 וַיְדַבֵּר יְהוָה אֶל־מֹשֶׁה
לֵּאמֹר׃ 49 אַךְ אֶת־מַטֵּה לֵוִי לֹא תִפְקֹד
וְאֶת־רֹאשָׁם לֹא תִשָּׂא בְּתוֹךְ בְּנֵי יִשְׂרָאֵל׃
50 וְאַתָּה הַפְקֵד אֶת־הַלְוִיִּם עַל־מִשְׁכַּן
הָעֵדֻת וְעַל כָּל־כֵּלָיו וְעַל כָּל־אֲשֶׁר־לוֹ
הֵמָּה יִשְׂאוּ אֶת־הַמִּשְׁכָּן וְאֶת־כָּל־כֵּלָיו
וְהֵם יְשָׁרְתֻהוּ וְסָבִיב לַמִּשְׁכָּן יַחֲנוּ׃

46. 603,550 This figure is identical to that obtained by an earlier census of Israelite men over 20, taken during the 1st year in the wilderness (Exod. 30:12–16, 38:26). Another census taken in the 40th year netted a total of 601,730 (Num. 26:51). These figures presuppose a population of more than 2 million supporting itself for 40 years in the Sinai peninsula. The numbers are impossibly large. Some say that they reflect King David's census (see 2 Sam. 24). Others suggest that *"elef"* here does not mean "1,000" but a military unit averaging 5 or 6 men. The number would then be 60 units made up of 3,550 men.

DUTIES OF THE LEVITES (vv. 47–54)

This summary of the Levites' encampment and guard duties for the sanctuary anticipates the details in chapters 3–4.

48. had spoken Hebrew: *va-y'dabber,* usually "spoke." But the order not to count the Levites must have been given before Moses took the census.

50. You Literally, "But you." The Levites are assigned to the tabernacle instead of serving in the regular militia.

tend it By guarding it.

shall camp around the Tabernacle. 51 When the Tabernacle is to set out, the Levites shall take it down, and when the Tabernacle is to be pitched, the Levites shall set it up; any outsider who encroaches shall be put to death. 52 The Israelites shall encamp troop by troop, each man with his division and each under his standard. 53 The Levites, however, shall camp around the Tabernacle of the Pact, that wrath may not strike the Israelite community; the Levites shall stand guard around the Tabernacle of the Pact.

54 The Israelites did accordingly; just as the LORD had commanded Moses, so they did.

51 וּבִנְסֹעַ הַמִּשְׁכָּן יוֹרִידוּ אֹתוֹ הַלְוִיִּם
וּבַחֲנֹת הַמִּשְׁכָּן יָקִימוּ אֹתוֹ הַלְוִיִּם וְהַזָּר
הַקָּרֵב יוּמָת׃ 52 וְחָנוּ בְּנֵי יִשְׂרָאֵל אִישׁ
עַל־מַחֲנֵהוּ וְאִישׁ עַל־דִּגְלוֹ לְצִבְאֹתָם׃
53 וְהַלְוִיִּם יַחֲנוּ סָבִיב לְמִשְׁכַּן הָעֵדֻת
וְלֹא־יִהְיֶה קֶצֶף עַל־עֲדַת בְּנֵי יִשְׂרָאֵל
וְשָׁמְרוּ הַלְוִיִּם אֶת־מִשְׁמֶרֶת מִשְׁכַּן
הָעֵדוּת׃
54 וַיַּעֲשׂוּ בְּנֵי יִשְׂרָאֵל כְּכֹל אֲשֶׁר צִוָּה יְהוָה
אֶת־מֹשֶׁה כֵּן עָשׂוּ׃ פ

2 The LORD spoke to Moses and Aaron, saying: 2 The Israelites shall camp each with his standard, under the banners of their ancestral

שלישי ב וַיְדַבֵּר יְהוָה אֶל־מֹשֶׁה וְאֶל־אַהֲרֹן
לֵאמֹר׃ 2 אִישׁ עַל־דִּגְלוֹ בְאֹתֹת לְבֵית

51. take it down Dismantle it.

outsider An unauthorized person, in this case any Israelite not in the tribe of Levi.

53. shall stand guard around the Tabernacle Effective guard duty will prevent the outbreak of God's wrath.

THE ARRANGEMENT OF THE CAMP (2:1–34)

The men in the military are deployed to defend the camp when it is at rest.

ORDER OF THE TRIBES (vv. 1–31)

The tribes are ordered in military divisions around the tabernacle, each under its chieftain.

2. standard Hebrew: *degel;* by extension, it refers to an army division or a tribal military unit.

banners Hebrew: *otot.* Each ancestral house had its own, displayed by smaller military units.

---

52. encamp troop by troop Many commentators note the details here of tribal encampments as a way of emphasizing the need for order and organization in achieving a spiritual life. Simḥah Zissel Ziv writes, "A person disorderly in behavior is also confused in thought, incapable of stable, consistent work."

53. that wrath may not strike The Israelites are warned repeatedly that the awesome holiness of God can be destructive (see the story of Nadab and Abihu in Lev. 10:1–2; also Num. 3:10 and elsewhere). God is like a fire, capable of warming and comforting, but capable of burning as well.

CHAPTER 2

The key to the physical deployment of the Israelites as they camped and as they marched was the setting of the Ark at the center of the camp. Every individual Israelite was located in relation to the Ark and the tabernacle. The tabernacle was the first thing one saw on leaving home and the first thing one looked for on returning home. Gradually, this physical centrality must have led to the Ark's gaining a central place in the Israelite soul.

A tradition has it that the tribe of Judah, situated at the eastern edge of the camp, marched backward when the Israelites broke camp and traveled eastward, to avoid turning their backs on the Ark. Thus they found their path to the future by orienting themselves to their past.

2. each with his standard A person's identity consists of three elements: the self (the standard), the family (the ancestral banners), and the community (the Tent of Meeting).

house; they shall camp around the Tent of Meeting at a distance.

3Camped on the front, or east side: the standard of the division of Judah, troop by troop.
Chieftain of the Judites: Nahshon son of Amminadab. 4His troop, as enrolled: 74,600.
5Camping next to it:
The tribe of Issachar.
Chieftain of the Issacharites: Nethanel son of Zuar. 6His troop, as enrolled: 54,400.
7The tribe of Zebulun.
Chieftain of the Zebulunites: Eliab son of Helon. 8His troop, as enrolled: 57,400.
9The total enrolled in the division of Judah: 186,400, for all troops. These shall march first.

10On the south: the standard of the division of Reuben, troop by troop.
Chieftain of the Reubenites: Elizur son of Shedeur. 11His troop, as enrolled: 46,500.
12Camping next to it:
The tribe of Simeon.
Chieftain of the Simeonites: Shelumiel son of Zurishaddai.
13His troop, as enrolled: 59,300.
14And the tribe of Gad.
Chieftain of the Gadites: Eliasaph son of Reuel. 15His troop, as enrolled: 45,650.
16The total enrolled in the division of Reuben: 151,450, for all troops. These shall march second.

אֲבֹתָם יַחֲנוּ בְּנֵי יִשְׂרָאֵל מִנֶּגֶד סָבִיב
לְאֹהֶל־מוֹעֵד יַחֲנוּ׃

3 וְהַחֹנִים֙ קֵדְמָה מִזְרָחָה דֶּגֶל מַחֲנֵה
יְהוּדָה לְצִבְאֹתָם וְנָשִׂיא֙ לִבְנֵי יְהוּדָה
נַחְשׁוֹן בֶּן־עַמִּינָדָב׃ 4 וּצְבָאוֹ וּפְקֻדֵיהֶם
אַרְבָּעָה וְשִׁבְעִים אֶלֶף וְשֵׁשׁ מֵאוֹת׃
5 וְהַחֹנִים עָלָיו מַטֵּה יִשָּׂשכָר וְנָשִׂיא֙
לִבְנֵי יִשָּׂשכָר נְתַנְאֵל בֶּן־צוּעָר׃ 6 וּצְבָאוֹ
וּפְקֻדָיו אַרְבָּעָה וַחֲמִשִּׁים אֶלֶף וְאַרְבַּע
מֵאוֹת׃ ס
7 מַטֵּה זְבוּלֻן וְנָשִׂיא֙ לִבְנֵי זְבוּלֻן אֱלִיאָב
בֶּן־חֵלֹן׃ 8 וּצְבָאוֹ וּפְקֻדָיו שִׁבְעָה וַחֲמִשִּׁים
אֶלֶף וְאַרְבַּע מֵאוֹת׃
9 כָּל־הַפְּקֻדִים לְמַחֲנֵה יְהוּדָה מְאַת אֶלֶף
וּשְׁמֹנִים אֶלֶף וְשֵׁשֶׁת־אֲלָפִים וְאַרְבַּע־
מֵאוֹת לְצִבְאֹתָם רִאשֹׁנָה יִסָּעוּ׃ ס

10 דֶּגֶל מַחֲנֵה רְאוּבֵן תֵּימָנָה לְצִבְאֹתָם
וְנָשִׂיא֙ לִבְנֵי רְאוּבֵן אֱלִיצוּר בֶּן־שְׁדֵיאוּר׃
11 וּצְבָאוֹ וּפְקֻדָיו שִׁשָּׁה וְאַרְבָּעִים אֶלֶף
וַחֲמֵשׁ מֵאוֹת׃
12 וְהַחוֹנִם עָלָיו מַטֵּה שִׁמְעוֹן וְנָשִׂיא֙ לִבְנֵי
שִׁמְעוֹן שְׁלֻמִיאֵל בֶּן־צוּרִי־שַׁדָּי׃ 13 וּצְבָאוֹ
וּפְקֻדֵיהֶם תִּשְׁעָה וַחֲמִשִּׁים אֶלֶף וּשְׁלֹשׁ
מֵאוֹת׃ 14 וּמַטֵּה גָּד וְנָשִׂיא֙ לִבְנֵי גָד אֶלְיָסָף
בֶּן־רְעוּאֵל׃ 15 וּצְבָאוֹ וּפְקֻדֵיהֶם חֲמִשָּׁה
וְאַרְבָּעִים אֶלֶף וְשֵׁשׁ מֵאוֹת וַחֲמִשִּׁים׃
16 כָּל־הַפְּקֻדִים לְמַחֲנֵה רְאוּבֵן מְאַת אֶלֶף
וְאֶחָד וַחֲמִשִּׁים אֶלֶף וְאַרְבַּע־מֵאוֹת
וַחֲמִשִּׁים לְצִבְאֹתָם וּשְׁנִיִּם יִסָּעוּ׃ ס

at a distance It was necessary to make room for the levitical encampment, which was set up between the sanctuary and the Israelite camp.

3. Nahshon His sister, Elisheba, was the wife of Aaron.

4. His troop Literally, "As for his troop, its enrollment was." The chieftain is always associated with his troop.

17Then, midway between the divisions, the Tent of Meeting, the division of the Levites, shall move. As they camp, so they shall march, each in position, by their standards.

18On the west: the standard of the division of Ephraim, troop by troop.

Chieftain of the Ephraimites: Elishama son of Ammihud. 19His troop, as enrolled: 40,500. 20Next to it:

The tribe of Manasseh.

Chieftain of the Manassites: Gamaliel son of Pedahzur. 21His troop, as enrolled: 32,200. 22And the tribe of Benjamin.

Chieftain of the Benjaminites: Abidan son of Gideoni. 23His troop, as enrolled: 35,400. 24The total enrolled in the division of Ephraim: 108,100 for all troops. These shall march third.

25On the north: the standard of the division of Dan, troop by troop.

Chieftain of the Danites: Ahiezer son of Ammishaddai. 26His troop, as enrolled: 62,700.

27Camping next to it:

The tribe of Asher.

Chieftain of the Asherites: Pagiel son of Ochran. 28His troop, as enrolled: 41,500. 29And the tribe of Naphtali.

Chieftain of the Naphtalites: Ahira son of

17 וְנָסַ֞ע אֹֽהֶל־מוֹעֵ֧ד מַחֲנֵ֛ה הַלְוִיִּ֖ם בְּת֣וֹךְ הַֽמַּחֲנֹ֑ת כַּאֲשֶׁ֤ר יַחֲנוּ֙ כֵּ֣ן יִסָּ֔עוּ אִ֥ישׁ עַל־יָד֖וֹ לְדִגְלֵיהֶֽם׃ ס

18 דֶּ֣גֶל מַחֲנֵ֥ה אֶפְרַ֛יִם לְצִבְאֹתָ֖ם יָ֑מָּה וְנָשִׂיא֙ לִבְנֵ֣י אֶפְרַ֔יִם אֱלִישָׁמָ֖ע בֶּן־עַמִּיהֽוּד׃ 19 וּצְבָא֖וֹ וּפְקֻדֵיהֶ֑ם אַרְבָּעִ֥ים אֶ֖לֶף וַחֲמֵ֥שׁ מֵאֽוֹת׃

20 וְעָלָ֖יו מַטֵּ֣ה מְנַשֶּׁ֑ה וְנָשִׂיא֙ לִבְנֵ֣י מְנַשֶּׁ֔ה גַּמְלִיאֵ֖ל בֶּן־פְּדָהצֽוּר׃ 21 וּצְבָא֖וֹ וּפְקֻדֵיהֶ֑ם שְׁנַ֧יִם וּשְׁלֹשִׁ֛ים אֶ֖לֶף וּמָאתָֽיִם׃ 22 וּמַטֵּ֖ה בִּנְיָמִ֑ן וְנָשִׂיא֙ לִבְנֵ֣י בִנְיָמִ֔ן אֲבִידָ֖ן בֶּן־גִּדְעֹנִֽי׃ 23 וּצְבָא֖וֹ וּפְקֻדֵיהֶ֑ם חֲמִשָּׁ֧ה וּשְׁלֹשִׁ֛ים אֶ֖לֶף וְאַרְבַּ֥ע מֵאֽוֹת׃

24 כׇּל־הַפְּקֻדִ֞ים לְמַחֲנֵ֣ה אֶפְרַ֗יִם מְאַ֥ת אֶ֙לֶף֙ וּשְׁמֹנַ֤ת־אֲלָפִים֙ וּמֵאָ֔ה לְצִבְאֹתָ֑ם וּשְׁלִשִׁ֖ים יִסָּֽעוּ׃ ס

25 דֶּ֣גֶל מַחֲנֵ֥ה דָ֛ן צָפֹ֖נָה לְצִבְאֹתָ֑ם וְנָשִׂיא֙ לִבְנֵ֣י דָ֔ן אֲחִיעֶ֖זֶר בֶּן־עַמִּֽישַׁדָּֽי׃ 26 וּצְבָא֖וֹ וּפְקֻדֵיהֶ֑ם שְׁנַ֧יִם וְשִׁשִּׁ֛ים אֶ֖לֶף וּשְׁבַ֥ע מֵאֽוֹת׃

27 וְהַחֹנִ֥ים עָלָ֖יו מַטֵּ֣ה אָשֵׁ֑ר וְנָשִׂיא֙ לִבְנֵ֣י אָשֵׁ֔ר פַּגְעִיאֵ֖ל בֶּן־עׇכְרָֽן׃ 28 וּפְקֻדֵיהֶ֑ם אֶחָ֧ד וְאַרְבָּעִ֛ים אֶ֖לֶף וַחֲמֵ֥שׁ מֵאֽוֹת׃ 29 וּמַטֵּ֖ה נַפְתָּלִ֑י וְנָשִׂיא֙ לִבְנֵ֣י נַפְתָּלִ֔י אֲחִירַ֖ע בֶּן־עֵינָֽן׃ 30 וּצְבָא֖וֹ

---

17. midway between That is, in the midst of (see 10:17). The tabernacle and its levitical guards were divided into two groups during the march. The dismantled structure was transported by the Gershonites and Merarites who marched between the first and second divisions, whereas everything else was carried by the Kohathites in the very center of the column, between the second and third divisions.

the Tent of Meeting, the division of the Le- **vites** These two phrases should be understood as connected by "and."

As they camp, so shall they march The Levites are broken into two units during the march, but the Israelite troops remain intact at all times.

20. Next to it That is, camping next to it, referring to the two tribes associated with a leader.

25. Dan was made head of this division because Dan was the firstborn of Jacob's children from his concubines (see Gen. 30:1–13).

---

17. As they camp, so they shall march The verse is interpreted homiletically to teach that one should be the same person at home as away from home, in private as in public.

Enan. [30]His troop, as enrolled: 53,400. [31]The total enrolled in the division of Dan: 157,600. These shall march last, by their standards.

[32]Those are the enrollments of the Israelites by ancestral houses. The total enrolled in the divisions, for all troops: 603,550. [33]The Levites, however, were not recorded among the Israelites, as the LORD had commanded Moses.

[34]The Israelites did accordingly; just as the LORD had commanded Moses, so they camped by their standards, and so they marched, each with his clan according to his ancestral house.

וּפְקֻדֵיהֶם שְׁלֹשָׁה וַחֲמִשִּׁים אֶלֶף וְאַרְבַּע
מֵאוֹת׃
31 כׇּל־הַפְּקֻדִים לְמַחֲנֵה דָן מְאַת אֶלֶף
וְשִׁבְעָה וַחֲמִשִּׁים אֶלֶף וְשֵׁשׁ מֵאוֹת
לָאַחֲרֹנָה יִסְעוּ לְדִגְלֵיהֶם׃ פ
32 אֵלֶּה פְּקוּדֵי בְנֵי־יִשְׂרָאֵל לְבֵית אֲבֹתָם
כׇּל־פְּקוּדֵי הַמַּחֲנֹת לְצִבְאֹתָם שֵׁשׁ־מֵאוֹת
אֶלֶף וּשְׁלֹשֶׁת אֲלָפִים וַחֲמֵשׁ מֵאוֹת
וַחֲמִשִּׁים׃ 33 וְהַלְוִיִּם לֹא הׇתְפָּקְדוּ בְּתוֹךְ
בְּנֵי יִשְׂרָאֵל כַּאֲשֶׁר צִוָּה יְהֹוָה אֶת־מֹשֶׁה׃
34 וַיַּעֲשׂוּ בְּנֵי יִשְׂרָאֵל כְּכֹל אֲשֶׁר־צִוָּה יְהֹוָה
אֶת־מֹשֶׁה כֵּן־חָנוּ לְדִגְלֵיהֶם וְכֵן נָסָעוּ
אִישׁ לְמִשְׁפְּחֹתָיו עַל־בֵּית אֲבֹתָיו׃

3 This is the line of Aaron and Moses at the time that the LORD spoke with Moses on Mount Sinai. [2]These were the names of Aaron's sons: Nadab, the first-born, and Abihu, Eleazar and Ithamar; [3]those were the names of Aaron's sons, the anointed priests who were ordained for priesthood. [4]But Nadab and Abihu died by the

רביעי **ג** וְאֵלֶּה תּוֹלְדֹת אַהֲרֹן וּמֹשֶׁה בְּיוֹם דִּבֶּר
יְהֹוָה אֶת־מֹשֶׁה בְּהַר סִינָי׃ 2 וְאֵלֶּה שְׁמוֹת
בְּנֵי־אַהֲרֹן הַבְּכֹר ׀ נָדָב וַאֲבִיהוּא אֶלְעָזָר
וְאִיתָמָר׃ 3 אֵלֶּה שְׁמוֹת בְּנֵי אַהֲרֹן
הַכֹּהֲנִים הַמְּשֻׁחִים אֲשֶׁר־מִלֵּא יָדָם לְכַהֵן׃
4 וַיָּמׇת נָדָב וַאֲבִיהוּא לִפְנֵי יְהֹוָה בְּהַקְרִבָם

THE FIRST CENSUS OF LEVITES (3:1–51)

The events in verses 1–13 take place at Mount Sinai, where the Levites are designated as the guards and porters of the tabernacle. Verses 14–51 relate what occurs in the wilderness of Sinai, where the Levites are counted and assigned their guard duties in transit.

AT MOUNT SINAI (vv. 1–13)

The priestly genealogy properly precedes that of the Levites and also serves to identify Aaron's sons under whom the Levites will serve.

THE PRIESTS (vv. 1–4)

1. Moses, whose encampment is alongside that of Aaron, is counted with Aaron and not with the Levites. He is mentioned after Aaron because Aaron was the firstborn.

Mount Sinai As distinct from the wilderness of Sinai.

2. These were the names That is, when they were at Mount Sinai, for Nadab and Abihu died a while later (see Exod. 24:1; Lev. 10:1–2).

3. anointed The anointing of Aaron's sons as priests by the sprinkling of sanctified oil and blood is described in Exod. 29:21 and Lev. 8:30.

ordained Their anointing and ordination entitles them to the priesthood and to authority over the Levites.

---

34. It is noteworthy that there was no struggle for rank here, no argument over who went first or who camped where. They accepted God's word without rancor or jealousy (Sorotzkin).

CHAPTER 3

4. Nadab and Abihu died by the will of the LORD They died, literally, "before the LORD, in God's presence" (i.e., within the sanctuary)

will of the Lord, when they offered alien fire before the Lord in the wilderness of Sinai; and they left no sons. So it was Eleazar and Ithamar who served as priests in the lifetime of their father Aaron.

⁵The Lord spoke to Moses, saying: ⁶Advance the tribe of Levi and place them in attendance upon Aaron the priest to serve him. ⁷They shall perform duties for him and for the whole community before the Tent of Meeting, doing the work of the Tabernacle. ⁸They shall take charge of all the furnishings of the Tent of Meeting—a duty on behalf of the Israelites—doing the work of the Tabernacle. ⁹You shall assign the Levites to Aaron and to his sons: they are formally assigned to him from among the Israelites. ¹⁰You shall make Aaron and his sons responsible for observing their priestly duties; and any outsider who encroaches shall be put to death.

¹¹The Lord spoke to Moses, saying: ¹²I hereby take the Levites from among the Israelites in place of all the first-born, the first issue of the

אֵ֣שׁ זָרָ֗ה לִפְנֵ֤י יְהוָה֙ בְּמִדְבַּ֣ר סִינַ֔י וּבָנִ֖ים לֹא־הָי֣וּ לָהֶ֑ם וַיְכַהֵ֤ן אֶלְעָזָר֙ וְאִ֣יתָמָ֔ר עַל־פְּנֵ֖י אַהֲרֹ֥ן אֲבִיהֶֽם׃ פ

⁵ וַיְדַבֵּ֥ר יְהוָ֖ה אֶל־מֹשֶׁ֥ה לֵּאמֹֽר׃ ⁶ הַקְרֵב֙ אֶת־מַטֵּ֣ה לֵוִ֔י וְהַֽעֲמַדְתָּ֣ אֹת֔וֹ לִפְנֵ֖י אַהֲרֹ֣ן הַכֹּהֵ֑ן וְשֵׁרְת֖וּ אֹתֽוֹ׃ ⁷ וְשָׁמְר֣וּ אֶת־מִשְׁמַרְתּ֗וֹ וְאֶת־מִשְׁמֶ֙רֶת֙ כָּל־הָ֣עֵדָ֔ה לִפְנֵ֖י אֹ֣הֶל מוֹעֵ֑ד לַעֲבֹ֖ד אֶת־עֲבֹדַ֥ת הַמִּשְׁכָּֽן׃ ⁸ וְשָׁמְר֗וּ אֶֽת־כָּל־כְּלֵי֙ אֹ֣הֶל מוֹעֵ֔ד וְאֶת־מִשְׁמֶ֖רֶת בְּנֵ֣י יִשְׂרָאֵ֑ל לַעֲבֹ֖ד אֶת־עֲבֹדַ֥ת הַמִּשְׁכָּֽן׃ ⁹ וְנָתַתָּה֙ אֶת־הַלְוִיִּ֔ם לְאַהֲרֹ֖ן וּלְבָנָ֑יו נְתוּנִ֨ם נְתוּנִ֥ם הֵ֙מָּה֙ ל֔וֹ מֵאֵ֖ת בְּנֵ֥י יִשְׂרָאֵֽל׃ ¹⁰ וְאֶת־אַהֲרֹ֤ן וְאֶת־בָּנָיו֙ תִּפְקֹ֔ד וְשָׁמְר֖וּ אֶת־כְּהֻנָּתָ֑ם וְהַזָּ֥ר הַקָּרֵ֖ב יוּמָֽת׃ פ

¹¹ וַיְדַבֵּ֥ר יְהוָ֖ה אֶל־מֹשֶׁ֥ה לֵּאמֹֽר׃ ¹² וַאֲנִ֗י הִנֵּ֤ה לָקַ֙חְתִּי֙ אֶת־הַלְוִיִּ֔ם מִתּוֹךְ֙ בְּנֵ֣י יִשְׂרָאֵ֔ל תַּ֕חַת כָּל־בְּכ֥וֹר פֶּ֛טֶר רֶ֖חֶם מִבְּנֵ֣י

SUBORDINATION OF THE LEVITES (vv. 5–13)

7–8. Guard duty was incumbent on the Levites when the camp was at rest (v. 7) and in transit (v. 8). Guard duty constituted half of their work; their labors of removal, the other half.

duties The term *mishmeret*, in connection with the tabernacle, means "guard duty." The levitical cordon around the tabernacle guards it from incursion by the ordinary Israelite and protects the people from suffering what would be the consequent wrath of God.

and for the whole community By replacing the firstborn, as commanded in verses 11–13.

before the Tent of Meeting The Levites guarded outside the sacred area, whereas the priests were stationed within.

8. The Levites guarded the "furnishings of the Tent" while transporting them during the

march but had no access to them when they were set up in camp, where they were under the sole supervision of the priests.

on behalf of the Israelites By replacing their firstborn (see vv. 11–13).

doing Rather, "in doing" or "in addition to doing" or "while doing." This phrase is also in verse 7 (about levitical guard duty when the camp was at rest); it may be a mistaken repetition by the copyist, a dittography.

9. assigned The root נתן implies dedication. By replacing the firstborn, the Levites are dedicated to the Lord.

10. observing their priestly duties That is, guarding their priesthood against encroachment.

12. first issue of the womb Replacement of the firstborn by the Levites indicates that the former once held some kind of sacred status. It was the firstborn of the mother who held that status,

as well as "in the lifetime of their father." This prompted the comment of the Midrash that "God grieves for the death of the young as deeply as their parents do" (Num. R. 2:24). The Torah mentions the death of these two young

kohanim several times after it occurs (e.g., Lev. 16:1; Num. 26:61), as if to hint that God too was having difficulty accepting their tragic death.

12. I hereby take the Levites Just as the first fruits of the harvest belong to God, both

יִשְׂרָאֵל וְהָיוּ לִי הַלְוִיִּם׃ 13 כִּי לִי כָּל־בְּכוֹר
בְּיוֹם הַכֹּתִי כָל־בְּכוֹר בְּאֶרֶץ מִצְרַיִם
הִקְדַּשְׁתִּי לִי כָל־בְּכוֹר בְּיִשְׂרָאֵל מֵאָדָם
עַד־בְּהֵמָה לִי יִהְיוּ אֲנִי יְהוָה׃ ס
חמישי 14 וַיְדַבֵּר יְהוָה אֶל־מֹשֶׁה בְּמִדְבַּר סִינַי
לֵאמֹר׃ 15 פְּקֹד אֶת־בְּנֵי לֵוִי לְבֵית אֲבֹתָם
לְמִשְׁפְּחֹתָם כָּל־זָכָר מִבֶּן־חֹדֶשׁ וָמַעְלָה
תִּפְקְדֵם׃ 16 וַיִּפְקֹד אֹתָם מֹשֶׁה עַל־פִּי
יְהוָה כַּאֲשֶׁר צֻוָּה׃ 17 וַיִּהְיוּ־אֵלֶּה בְנֵי־לֵוִי
בִּשְׁמֹתָם גֵּרְשׁוֹן וּקְהָת וּמְרָרִי׃ 18 וְאֵלֶּה
שְׁמוֹת בְּנֵי־גֵרְשׁוֹן לְמִשְׁפְּחֹתָם לִבְנִי
וְשִׁמְעִי׃ 19 וּבְנֵי קְהָת לְמִשְׁפְּחֹתָם עַמְרָם
וְיִצְהָר חֶבְרוֹן וְעֻזִּיאֵל׃ 20 וּבְנֵי מְרָרִי
לְמִשְׁפְּחֹתָם מַחְלִי וּמוּשִׁי
אֵלֶּה הֵם מִשְׁפְּחֹת הַלֵּוִי לְבֵית אֲבֹתָם׃
21 לְגֵרְשׁוֹן מִשְׁפַּחַת הַלִּבְנִי וּמִשְׁפַּחַת
הַשִּׁמְעִי אֵלֶּה הֵם מִשְׁפְּחֹת הַגֵּרְשֻׁנִּי׃
22 פְּקֻדֵיהֶם בְּמִסְפַּר כָּל־זָכָר מִבֶּן־חֹדֶשׁ
וָמַעְלָה פְּקֻדֵיהֶם שִׁבְעַת אֲלָפִים וַחֲמֵשׁ
מֵאוֹת׃ 23 מִשְׁפְּחֹת הַגֵּרְשֻׁנִּי אַחֲרֵי

womb among the Israelites: the Levites shall be Mine. [13]For every first-born is Mine: at the time that I smote every first-born in the land of Egypt, I consecrated every first-born in Israel, man and beast, to Myself, to be Mine, the LORD's.

[14]The LORD spoke to Moses in the wilderness of Sinai, saying: [15]Record the Levites by ancestral house and by clan; record every male among them from the age of one month up. [16]So Moses recorded them at the command of the LORD, as he was bidden. [17]These were the sons of Levi by name: Gershon, Kohath, and Merari. [18]These were the names of the sons of Gershon by clan: Libni and Shimei. [19]The sons of Kohath by clan: Amram and Izhar, Hebron and Uzziel. [20]The sons of Merari by clan: Mahli and Mushi.

These were the clans of the Levites within their ancestral houses:

[21]To Gershon belonged the clan of the Libnites and the clan of the Shimeites; those were the clans of the Gershonites. [22]The recorded entries of all their males from the age of one month up, as recorded, came to 7,500. [23]The clans of the Gershonites were to camp be-

whereas the firstborn of the father had the rights of inheritance (see Exod. 13:2).

the Levites shall be Mine That is, to serve Me.

13. God spared Israel's firstborn and thereby acquired them (see Exod. 13:15).

IN THE WILDERNESS OF SINAI (vv. 14–51)

These verses concern the first census of Levites and the assignment of guard duty for the tabernacle furnishings while in transit.

15. one month up The census of Levites begins at the age of one month, the age at which redemption of the firstborn is required.

16. at the command of Rather: according to the oracle of. The two censuses of Levites in chapters 3 and 4, in contrast to the Israelite census in chapter 1, are taken by God. Moses is merely to record the totals and the work assignments.

23. camp Wherever the three levitical clans camped (south, west, and north, respectively), they presumably performed their guard duty for the tabernacle.

---

as a gesture of gratitude and as an expression of confidence that more fruit will be coming, the firstborn child "belongs to God."

15. from the age of one month For purposes of military readiness, Israelites were counted only from the age of 20. Spiritual training, however, must begin virtually at birth. A second census in chapter 4 will ascertain the number of adult Levites available for transporting the various parts of the tabernacle.

HALAKHAH L'MA·ASEH

3:13. For every first-born is Mine The ceremony of redeeming a firstborn son (*Pidyon ha-Ben*) is based on the Torah's assertion here that all firstborn belong to God (see Exod. 13:2) but should be redeemed because the Levites serve in their place. See Comment on Num. 18:15. It is through this ceremony of grateful acknowledgement that parents can claim the child for themselves.

hind the Tabernacle, to the west. 24The chieftain of the ancestral house of the Gershonites was Eliasaph son of Lael. 25The duties of the Gershonites in the Tent of Meeting comprised: the Tabernacle, the tent, its covering, and the screen for the entrance of the Tent of Meeting; 26the hangings of the enclosure, the screen for the entrance of the enclosure which surrounds the Tabernacle, the cords thereof, and the altar—all the service connected with these.

27To Kohath belonged the clan of the Amramites, the clan of the Izharites, the clan of the Hebronites, and the clan of the Uzzielites; those were the clans of the Kohathites. 28All the listed males from the age of one month up came to 8,600, attending to the duties of the sanctuary. 29The clans of the Kohathites were to camp along the south side of the Tabernacle. 30The chieftain of the ancestral house of the Kohathite clans was Elizaphan son of Uzziel. 31Their duties comprised: the ark, the table, the lampstand, the altars, and the sacred utensils that were used with them, and the screen—all the service connected with these. 32The head chieftain of the Levites

הַמִּשְׁכָּ֛ן יַחֲנ֖וּ יָֽמָּה׃ 24 וּנְשִׂ֥יא בֵֽית־אָ֖ב לַגֵּרְשֻׁנִּ֑י אֶלְיָסָ֖ף בֶּן־לָאֵֽל׃ 25 וּמִשְׁמֶ֜רֶת בְּנֵֽי־גֵרְשׁ֗וֹן בְּאֹ֣הֶל מוֹעֵד֙ הַמִּשְׁכָּ֣ן וְהָאֹ֔הֶל מִכְסֵ֕הוּ וּמָסַ֕ךְ פֶּ֖תַח אֹ֥הֶל מוֹעֵֽד׃ 26 וְקַלְעֵ֣י הֶֽחָצֵ֗ר וְאֶת־מָסַךְ֙ פֶּ֣תַח הֶֽחָצֵ֔ר אֲשֶׁ֥ר עַל־הַמִּשְׁכָּ֛ן וְעַל־הַמִּזְבֵּ֖חַ סָבִ֑יב וְאֵת֙ מֵֽיתָרָ֔יו לְכֹ֖ל עֲבֹדָתֽוֹ׃

27 וְלִקְהָ֗ת מִשְׁפַּ֤חַת הַֽעַמְרָמִי֙ וּמִשְׁפַּ֣חַת הַיִּצְהָרִ֔י וּמִשְׁפַּ֙חַת֙ הַֽחֶבְרֹנִ֔י וּמִשְׁפַּ֖חַת הָֽעׇזִּֽיאֵלִ֑י אֵ֥לֶּה הֵ֖ם מִשְׁפְּחֹ֥ת הַקְּהָתִֽי׃ 28 בְּמִסְפַּר֙ כׇּל־זָכָ֔ר מִבֶּן־חֹ֖דֶשׁ וָמָ֑עְלָה שְׁמֹנַ֤ת אֲלָפִים֙ וְשֵׁ֣שׁ מֵא֔וֹת שֹׁמְרֵ֖י מִשְׁמֶ֥רֶת הַקֹּֽדֶשׁ׃ 29 מִשְׁפְּחֹ֥ת בְּנֵֽי־קְהָ֖ת יַחֲנ֑וּ עַ֛ל יֶ֥רֶךְ הַמִּשְׁכָּ֖ן תֵּימָֽנָה׃ 30 וּנְשִׂ֥יא בֵֽית־אָ֖ב לְמִשְׁפְּחֹ֣ת הַקְּהָתִ֑י אֶלִֽיצָפָ֖ן בֶּן־עֻזִּיאֵֽל׃ 31 וּמִשְׁמַרְתָּ֗ם הָאָרֹ֤ן וְהַשֻּׁלְחָן֙ וְהַמְּנֹרָ֣ה וְהַֽמִּזְבְּחֹ֔ת וּכְלֵ֣י הַקֹּ֔דֶשׁ אֲשֶׁ֥ר יְשָׁרְת֖וּ בָּהֶ֑ם וְהַ֨מָּסָ֔ךְ וְכֹ֖ל עֲבֹדָתֽוֹ׃ 32 וּנְשִׂיא֩ נְשִׂיאֵ֨י הַלֵּוִ֜י אֶלְעָזָ֣ר בֶּן־אַהֲרֹ֣ן הַכֹּהֵ֑ן פְּקֻדַּ֕ת שֹׁמְרֵ֖י מִשְׁמֶ֥רֶת הַקֹּֽדֶשׁ׃

24. ancestral house Here, the larger unit of the clans making up the Gershonites, Kohathites, and Merarites.

25. duties That is, guard duty. The tabernacle furnishings placed in the custody of the Gershonites and Merarites are clearly delineated. The former are to guard the fabrics; the latter, the planks and posts.

Tabernacle The innermost tent covering composed of 10 finely twisted linen and woolen cloths with a design of cherubim worked into them.

tent A second covering made up of 11 cloths of goat's hair.

its covering The outermost covering made of tanned ram skins and yellow-orange skins.

screen The entrance to the tent was of lesser sanctity than the inner curtains, because the screen could be seen by anyone in the tabernacle court, whereas the inner curtains could not be seen from the outside.

27. Amramites To which the descendants of Moses would belong.

28. attending to the duties of the sanctuary It was the responsibility of the Kohathites to transport and to guard the most sacred objects, as itemized in verse 31.

29. south side Starting with the east, which is the most prestigious position (see v. 38), the position next in importance, rotating to the right (clockwise), is the south. The Kohathites merited this because it was their honored task to carry the most sacred objects. Note the proximity of Kohath to the tribe of Reuben (see 2:10), which possibly accounts for their collaboration in chapter 16.

32. Although Eleazar was chief officer, he was given a great deal of physical labor (4:16). "There is no special privilege in the palace of the king" (JT Shab. 10:3); there is no room for an "honorary" position in the service of God.

was Eleazar son of Aaron the priest, in charge of those attending to the duties of the sanctuary.

33To Merari belonged the clan of the Mahlites and the clan of the Mushites; those were the clans of Merari. 34The recorded entries of all their males from the age of one month up came to 6,200. 35The chieftain of the ancestral house of the clans of Merari was Zuriel son of Abihail. They were to camp along the north side of the Tabernacle. 36The assigned duties of the Merarites comprised: the planks of the Tabernacle, its bars, posts, and sockets, and all its furnishings—all the service connected with these; 37also the posts around the enclosure and their sockets, pegs, and cords.

38Those who were to camp before the Tabernacle, in front—before the Tent of Meeting, on the east—were Moses and Aaron and his sons, attending to the duties of the sanctuary, as a duty on behalf of the Israelites; and any outsider who encroached was to be put to death. 39All the Levites who were recorded, whom at the LORD's command Moses and Aaron recorded by their clans, all the males from the age of one month up, came to 22,000.

40The LORD said to Moses: Record every first-born male of the Israelite people from the age of one month up, and make a list of their names; 41and take the Levites for Me, the LORD, in place of every first-born among the Israelite

33 לִמְרָרִ֕י מִשְׁפַּ֙חַת֙ הַמַּחְלִ֔י וּמִשְׁפַּ֖חַת
הַמּוּשִׁ֑י אֵ֥לֶּה הֵ֖ם מִשְׁפְּחֹ֥ת מְרָרִֽי׃
34 וּפְקֻדֵיהֶם֙ בְּמִסְפַּ֣ר כָּל־זָכָ֔ר מִבֶּן־חֹ֖דֶשׁ
וָמָ֑עְלָה שֵׁ֥שֶׁת אֲלָפִ֖ים וּמָאתָֽיִם׃ 35 וּנְשִׂ֤יא
בֵֽית־אָב֙ לְמִשְׁפְּחֹ֣ת מְרָרִ֔י צוּרִיאֵ֖ל בֶּן־
אֲבִיחָ֑יִל עַ֣ל יֶ֧רֶךְ הַמִּשְׁכָּ֛ן יַחֲנ֖וּ צָפֹֽנָה׃
36 וּפְקֻדַּ֣ת מִשְׁמֶ֘רֶת֮ בְּנֵ֣י מְרָרִי֒ קַרְשֵׁי֙
הַמִּשְׁכָּ֔ן וּבְרִיחָ֖יו וְעַמֻּדָ֣יו וַאֲדָנָ֑יו וְכָל־כֵּלָ֕יו
וְכֹ֖ל עֲבֹדָתֽוֹ׃ 37 וְעַמֻּדֵ֧י הֶחָצֵ֛ר סָבִ֖יב
וְאַדְנֵיהֶ֑ם וִיתֵדֹתָ֖ם וּמֵיתְרֵיהֶֽם׃
38 וְהַחֹנִ֣ים לִפְנֵ֣י הַ֠מִּשְׁכָּן קֵ֡דְמָה לִפְנֵ֨י
אֹֽהֶל־מוֹעֵ֜ד ׀ מִזְרָ֗חָה מֹשֶׁ֣ה ׀ וְאַהֲרֹ֣ן וּבָנָ֔יו
שֹׁמְרִים֙ מִשְׁמֶ֣רֶת הַמִּקְדָּ֔שׁ לְמִשְׁמֶ֖רֶת בְּנֵ֣י
יִשְׂרָאֵ֑ל וְהַזָּ֥ר הַקָּרֵ֖ב יוּמָֽת׃ 39 כָּל־פְּקוּדֵ֨י
הַלְוִיִּ֜ם אֲשֶׁ֨ר פָּקַ֥ד מֹשֶׁ֛ה וְאַהֲרֹ֛ן* עַל־פִּ֥י
יְהוָ֖ה לְמִשְׁפְּחֹתָ֑ם כָּל־זָכָר֙ מִבֶּן־חֹ֣דֶשׁ
וָמַ֔עְלָה שְׁנַ֥יִם וְעֶשְׂרִ֖ים אָֽלֶף׃ ס
ששי 40 וַיֹּ֨אמֶר יְהוָ֜ה אֶל־מֹשֶׁ֗ה פְּקֹ֨ד כָּל־בְּכֹ֤ר
זָכָר֙ לִבְנֵ֣י יִשְׂרָאֵ֔ל מִבֶּן־חֹ֖דֶשׁ וָמָ֑עְלָה וְשָׂ֕א
אֵ֖ת מִסְפַּ֥ר שְׁמֹתָֽם׃ 41 וְלָקַחְתָּ֨ אֶת־הַלְוִיִּ֥ם
לִי֙ אֲנִ֣י יְהוָ֔ה תַּ֥חַת כָּל־בְּכֹ֖ר בִּבְנֵ֣י יִשְׂרָאֵ֑ל

v. 39. נקוד על ו׳ א׳ ה׳ ר׳ ן׳

32. attending to the duties That is, performing the guard duty.

38. to camp Because the priests had no watch posts outside the sacred area, their encampment in the east was also the place of their watch. This is to be expected, for the entrance to the tabernacle was in the east, which made that zone most vulnerable to encroachment.

on behalf of the Israelites By replacing their firstborn.

REPLACING THE ISRAELITE FIRSTBORN (vv. 40–51)

The number of Israelite firstborn exceeds that of the Levites by 273. The latter, chosen by lot, are redeemed by the payment of 5 shekels per person to the priests. This procedure became the standard for the redemption of all Israelite firstborn.

40. one month up An infant younger than 30 days was not considered a viable person, presumably because of the high rate of infant mortality.

---

39. The Levites were by far the smallest of the tribes. This was fitting, because they owned no large tracts of land and had to be supported by the gifts and tithes of their fellow Israelites. Their small numbers reduced the burden of support imposed on their neighbors.

people, and the cattle of the Levites in place of every first-born among the cattle of the Israelites. 42So Moses recorded all the first-born among the Israelites, as the LORD had commanded him. 43All the first-born males as listed by name, recorded from the age of one month up, came to 22,273.

44The LORD spoke to Moses, saying: 45Take the Levites in place of all the first-born among the Israelite people, and the cattle of the Levites in place of their cattle; and the Levites shall be Mine, the LORD's. 46And as the redemption price of the 273 Israelite first-born over and above the number of the Levites, 47take five shekels per head—take this by the sanctuary weight, twenty *gerah*s to the shekel—48and give the money to Aaron and his sons as the redemption price for those who are in excess. 49So Moses took the redemption money from those over and above the ones redeemed by the Levites; 50he took the money from the first-born of the Israelites, 1,365 sanctuary shekels. 51And Moses gave the redemption money to Aaron and his sons at the LORD's bidding, as the LORD had commanded Moses.

וְאֶת֙ בֶּהֱמַ֣ת הַלְוִיִּ֔ם תַּ֣חַת כָּל־בְּכ֔וֹר
בְּבֶהֱמַ֖ת בְּנֵ֥י יִשְׂרָאֵֽל׃ 42 וַיִּפְקֹ֣ד מֹשֶׁ֔ה
כַּאֲשֶׁ֛ר צִוָּ֥ה יְהוָ֖ה אֹת֑וֹ אֶת־כָּל־בְּכֹ֖ר בִּבְנֵ֥י
יִשְׂרָאֵֽל׃ 43 וַיְהִ֨י כָל־בְּכ֜וֹר זָכָ֨ר בְּמִסְפַּ֥ר
שֵׁמֹ֛ת מִבֶּן־חֹ֥דֶשׁ וָמַ֖עְלָה לִפְקֻדֵיהֶ֑ם
שְׁנַ֤יִם וְעֶשְׂרִים֙ אֶ֔לֶף שְׁלֹשָׁ֥ה וְשִׁבְעִ֖ים
וּמָאתָֽיִם׃ פ
44 וַיְדַבֵּ֥ר יְהוָ֖ה אֶל־מֹשֶׁ֥ה לֵּאמֹֽר׃ 45 קַ֣ח
אֶת־הַלְוִיִּ֗ם תַּ֤חַת כָּל־בְּכוֹר֙ בִּבְנֵ֣י יִשְׂרָאֵ֔ל
וְאֶת־בֶּהֱמַ֥ת הַלְוִיִּ֖ם תַּ֣חַת בְּהֶמְתָּ֑ם וְהָיוּ־
לִ֥י הַלְוִיִּ֖ם אֲנִ֥י יְהוָֽה׃ 46 וְאֵת֙ פְּדוּיֵ֣י
הַשְּׁלֹשָׁ֗ה וְהַשִּׁבְעִ֛ים וְהַמָּאתָ֖יִם הָעֹדְפִ֑ים
עַל־הַלְוִיִּ֔ם מִבְּכ֖וֹר בְּנֵ֥י יִשְׂרָאֵֽל׃ 47 וְלָקַחְתָּ֗
חֲמֵ֧שֶׁת חֲמֵ֛שֶׁת שְׁקָלִ֖ים לַגֻּלְגֹּ֑לֶת בְּשֶׁ֨קֶל
הַקֹּ֜דֶשׁ תִּקָּ֗ח עֶשְׂרִ֥ים גֵּרָ֖ה הַשָּֽׁקֶל׃
48 וְנָתַתָּ֣ה הַכֶּ֔סֶף לְאַהֲרֹ֖ן וּלְבָנָ֑יו פְּדוּיֵ֕י
הָעֹדְפִ֖ים בָּהֶֽם׃ 49 וַיִּקַּ֣ח מֹשֶׁ֔ה אֵ֖ת כֶּ֣סֶף
הַפִּדְי֑וֹם מֵאֵת֙ הָעֹ֣דְפִ֔ים עַ֖ל פְּדוּיֵ֥י הַלְוִיִּֽם׃
50 מֵאֵ֗ת בְּכ֛וֹר בְּנֵ֥י יִשְׂרָאֵ֖ל לָקַ֣ח אֶת־הַכָּ֑סֶף
חֲמִשָּׁ֨ה וְשִׁשִּׁ֜ים וּשְׁלֹ֥שׁ מֵא֛וֹת וָאֶ֖לֶף בְּשֶׁ֥קֶל
הַקֹּֽדֶשׁ׃ 51 וַיִּתֵּ֨ן מֹשֶׁ֜ה אֶת־כֶּ֥סֶף הַפְּדֻיִ֛ם*
לְאַהֲרֹ֥ן וּלְבָנָ֖יו עַל־פִּ֣י יְהוָ֑ה כַּאֲשֶׁ֛ר צִוָּ֥ה
יְהוָ֖ה אֶת־מֹשֶֽׁה׃ פ

4 The LORD spoke to Moses and Aaron, saying:

2Take a [separate] census of the Kohathites among the Levites, by the clans of their ancestral house, 3from the age of thirty years up to the

שביעי **ד** וַיְדַבֵּ֣ר יְהוָ֔ה אֶל־מֹשֶׁ֥ה וְאֶֽל־אַהֲרֹ֖ן
לֵאמֹֽר׃
2 נָשֹׂ֗א אֶת־רֹאשׁ֙ בְּנֵ֣י קְהָ֔ת מִתּ֖וֹךְ בְּנֵ֣י לֵוִ֑י
לְמִשְׁפְּחֹתָ֖ם לְבֵ֥ית אֲבֹתָֽם׃ 3 מִבֶּ֨ן שְׁלֹשִׁ֥ים

v. 51. חסר ו'

41. every first-born among the cattle of the Israelites The firstborn of pure animals automatically belonged to the Lord. They must be sacrificed on the altar and may not be redeemed (according to Lev. 27:26 and Num. 18:15,17). Therefore the Sages concluded that any Israelite animal that was redeemed must have been impure, ineligible for the altar (BT Bek. 4b).

45. their cattle That is, the cattle of the Israelite firstborn. Just as the firstborn Israelites must be redeemed, so must their cattle. The cattle of the Levites release the animals of the firstborn from their sacred status.

47. shekel See Comment to Gen. 23:9.

by the sanctuary weight See Comment to Exod. 30:13.

age of fifty, all who are subject to service, to perform tasks for the Tent of Meeting. 4This is the
responsibility of the Kohathites in the Tent of
Meeting: the most sacred objects.

5At the breaking of camp, Aaron and his sons
shall go in and take down the screening curtain
and cover the Ark of the Pact with it. 6They
shall lay a covering of dolphin skin over it and
spread a cloth of pure blue on top; and they shall
put its poles in place.

7Over the table of display they shall spread a
blue cloth; they shall place upon it the bowls,
the ladles, the jars, and the libation jugs; and
the regular bread shall rest upon it. 8They shall
spread over these a crimson cloth which they
shall cover with a covering of dolphin skin; and
they shall put the poles in place.

שָׁנָה֙ וָמַ֔עְלָה וְעַ֖ד בֶּן־חֲמִשִּׁ֣ים שָׁנָ֑ה כָּל־בָּא֙
לַצָּבָ֔א לַעֲשׂ֥וֹת מְלָאכָ֖ה בְּאֹ֥הֶל מוֹעֵֽד׃ 4 זֹ֛את עֲבֹדַ֥ת בְּנֵֽי־קְהָ֖ת בְּאֹ֣הֶל מוֹעֵ֑ד קֹ֖דֶשׁ
הַקֳּדָשִֽׁים׃

5 וּבָ֣א אַהֲרֹ֤ן וּבָנָיו֙ בִּנְסֹ֣עַ הַֽמַּחֲנֶ֔ה וְהוֹרִ֕דוּ
אֵ֖ת פָּרֹ֣כֶת הַמָּסָ֑ךְ וְכִסּוּ־בָ֕הּ אֵ֖ת אֲרֹ֥ן
הָעֵדֻֽת׃ 6 וְנָתְנ֣וּ עָלָ֗יו כְּס֚וּי ע֣וֹר תַּ֔חַשׁ
וּפָרְשׂ֧וּ בֶֽגֶד־כְּלִ֛יל תְּכֵ֖לֶת מִלְמָ֑עְלָה וְשָׂמ֖וּ
בַּדָּֽיו׃

7 וְעַ֣ל ׀ שֻׁלְחַ֣ן הַפָּנִ֗ים יִפְרְשׂוּ֙ בֶּ֣גֶד תְּכֵ֔לֶת
וְנָתְנ֣וּ עָ֠לָיו אֶת־הַקְּעָרֹ֤ת וְאֶת־הַכַּפֹּת֙
וְאֶת־הַמְּנַקִּיֹּ֔ת וְאֵ֖ת קְשׂ֣וֹת הַנָּ֑סֶךְ וְלֶ֥חֶם
הַתָּמִ֖יד עָלָ֥יו יִהְיֶֽה׃ 8 וּפָרְשׂ֣וּ עֲלֵיהֶ֗ם בֶּ֚גֶד
תּוֹלַ֣עַת שָׁנִ֔י וְכִסּ֣וּ אֹת֔וֹ בְּמִכְסֵ֖ה ע֣וֹר תָּ֑חַשׁ
וְשָׂמ֖וּ אֶת־בַּדָּֽיו׃

THE SECOND CENSUS OF LEVITES (4:1–49)

A second census of the Levites between the ages
of 30 and 50 is taken to determine the size of the
work force necessary to transport the sanctuary
during the wilderness march.

REMOVAL DUTIES OF THE KOHATHITES
(vv. 1–20)

The Kohathites are listed first, even though
Kohath is not the firstborn, because the work of
the Kohathites involved greater responsibility:
They transported the most sacred objects, and
their work was more hazardous because they
risked their lives (see vv. 15–20).

4. The specific job of the Kohathites is the
porterage of the most sacred objects by shoulder.
Only the priests, who were sacred, were qualified
to handle the Ark and the other sacred objects.
The Kohathites had no sacred status; hence their
touching and even seeing the uncovered objects
could be fatal. Thus Aaron and his sons had to
cover the objects before the Kohathites could enter the sacred area to attend to their transport.

5. screening curtain   It separated the Holy of
Holies from the rest of the sanctuary.

Ark   The most sacred of the objects is covered
first.

6. cloth   Hebrew: *beged*; literally, "garment."
In the Hebrew Bible, *"beged"* usually covers only
human beings, yet here all the sacred objects are
initially covered by a *beged*. They are treated with
the same respect as human beings. Indeed, they
are treated like royalty—dressed in regal garb of
violet or purple.

put its poles in place   The Ark, the display
table, and the altars were fitted with rings into
which poles were inserted for carrying, whereas
the lampstand, some utensils, and probably the
laver were set into carrying frames.

7. table of display   The full term is the "table
of display bread"; every *Shabbat*, 12 loaves of
bread arranged in two rows were displayed on it
before God in the sanctuary.

regular bread   The 12 loaves of bread regularly changed every *Shabbat*.

CHAPTER 4

3.   A Levite male, in the prime of his life,
during the years from 30 to 50, would be given
responsibility for the arduous tasks of main-

taining the tabernacle (and later the Temple).
After age 50, his new tasks would require more
wisdom and less physical strength: singing the
Psalms, opening and closing the gates, and acting as mentor to younger Levites.

9Then they shall take a blue cloth and cover the lampstand for lighting, with its lamps, its tongs, and its fire pans, as well as all the oil vessels that are used in its service. 10They shall put it and all its furnishings into a covering of dolphin skin, which they shall then place on a carrying frame.

11Next they shall spread a blue cloth over the altar of gold and cover it with a covering of dolphin skin; and they shall put its poles in place. 12They shall take all the service vessels with which the service in the sanctuary is performed, put them into a blue cloth and cover them with a covering of dolphin skin, which they shall then place on a carrying frame. 13They shall remove the ashes from the [copper] altar and spread a purple cloth over it. 14Upon it they shall place all the vessels that are used in its service: the fire pans, the flesh hooks, the scrapers, and the basins—all the vessels of the altar—and over it they shall spread a covering of dolphin skin; and they shall put its poles in place.

15When Aaron and his sons have finished covering the sacred objects and all the furnishings of the sacred objects at the breaking of camp, only then shall the Kohathites come and lift them, so that they do not come in contact with the sacred objects and die. These things in

9 וְלָקְח֣וּ ׀ בֶּ֣גֶד תְּכֵ֗לֶת וְכִסּ֞וּ אֶת־מְנֹרַ֤ת
הַמָּאוֹר֙ וְאֶת־נֵ֣רֹתֶ֔יהָ וְאֶת־מַלְקָחֶ֖יהָ וְאֶת־
מַחְתֹּתֶ֑יהָ וְאֵת֙ כָּל־כְּלֵ֣י שַׁמְנָ֔הּ אֲשֶׁ֥ר
יְשָֽׁרְתוּ־לָ֖הּ בָּהֶֽם׃ 10 וְנָתְנ֣וּ אֹתָהּ֙ וְאֶת־
כָּל־כֵּלֶ֔יהָ אֶל־מִכְסֵ֖ה ע֣וֹר תָּ֑חַשׁ וְנָתְנ֖וּ
עַל־הַמּֽוֹט׃

11 וְעַ֣ל ׀ מִזְבַּ֣ח הַזָּהָ֗ב יִפְרְשׂוּ֙ בֶּ֣גֶד תְּכֵ֔לֶת
וְכִסּ֣וּ אֹת֔וֹ בְּמִכְסֵ֖ה ע֣וֹר תָּ֑חַשׁ וְשָׂמ֖וּ
אֶת־בַּדָּֽיו׃ 12 וְלָקְח֞וּ אֶת־כָּל־כְּלֵ֣י הַשָּׁרֵ֗ת
אֲשֶׁ֨ר יְשָֽׁרְתוּ־בָם֮ בַּקֹּדֶשׁ֒ וְנָתְנוּ֙ אֶל־בֶּ֣גֶד
תְּכֵ֔לֶת וְכִסּ֣וּ אוֹתָ֔ם בְּמִכְסֵ֖ה ע֣וֹר תָּ֑חַשׁ
וְנָתְנ֖וּ עַל־הַמּֽוֹט׃ 13 וְדִשְּׁנ֖וּ אֶת־הַמִּזְבֵּ֑חַ
וּפָֽרְשׂ֣וּ עָלָ֔יו בֶּ֖גֶד אַרְגָּמָֽן׃ 14 וְנָתְנ֣וּ עָ֠לָיו
אֶֽת־כָּל־כֵּלָ֞יו אֲשֶׁ֣ר יְשָֽׁרְת֧וּ עָלָ֣יו בָּהֶ֗ם
אֶת־הַמַּחְתֹּ֤ת אֶת־הַמִּזְלָגֹת֙ וְאֶת־הַיָּעִ֣ים
וְאֶת־הַמִּזְרָקֹ֔ת כֹּ֖ל כְּלֵ֣י הַמִּזְבֵּ֑חַ וּפָרְשׂ֣וּ
עָלָ֗יו כְּס֛וּי ע֥וֹר תַּ֖חַשׁ וְשָׂמ֥וּ בַדָּֽיו׃

15 וְכִלָּ֣ה אַֽהֲרֹן־וּ֠בָנָיו לְכַסֹּ֨ת אֶת־הַקֹּ֜דֶשׁ
וְאֶת־כָּל־כְּלֵ֣י הַקֹּדֶשׁ֮ בִּנְסֹ֣עַ הַֽמַּחֲנֶה֒
וְאַֽחֲרֵי־כֵ֗ן יָבֹ֙אוּ֙ בְנֵֽי־קְהָת֙ לָשֵׂ֔את וְלֹֽא־

9. lampstand Hebrew: *m'norah;* see Exod. 25:31–40.

lamps The lamps and the lampstand are separate objects.

fire pans For removing the ashes from the lamps.

10. carrying frame The *m'norah* and its utensils, which could not be suspended on poles like the Ark and table, required the construction of a special carrying frame.

11. altar of gold Also known as the altar of incense, it was carried on poles.

12. service vessels Whatever additional vessels are used inside the tent, especially with the incense altar, which is too small to hold any utensils.

13. altar The text turns to the bronze sacrificial altar of the courtyard, because all the sacred objects inside the sanctuary have been covered.

purple cloth Actually, red-purple. In distinction to the objects of the sanctuary whose covering was made of violet or blue-purple, the outer altar was wrapped in red-purple, a mark of the decreasing degree of holiness in moving from the shrine out into the courtyard.

15. Aaron and his sons have finished This concludes the priestly assignment that began in verse 5 with "Aaron and his sons shall go in."

come That is, go in.

contact . . . and die The Kohathites' contact with the covered objects can be as fatal as seeing them uncovered. Their removal labor is appropriately termed "skilled labor" (v. 3).

the Tent of Meeting shall be the porterage of
the Kohathites.
16Responsibility shall rest with Eleazar son of
Aaron the priest for the lighting oil, the aromatic incense, the regular grain offering, and
the anointing oil—responsibility for the whole
Tabernacle and for everything consecrated that
is in it or in its vessels.
17The LORD spoke to Moses and Aaron, saying: 18Do not let the group of Kohathite clans
be cut off from the Levites. 19Do this with them,
that they may live and not die when they approach the most sacred objects: let Aaron and
his sons go in and assign each of them to his
duties and to his porterage. 20But let not [the
Kohathites] go inside and witness the dismantling of the sanctuary, lest they die.

יִגְּעוּ אֶל־הַקֹּדֶשׁ וָמֵתוּ אֵלֶּה מַשָּׂא בְנֵי־
קְהָת בְּאֹהֶל מוֹעֵד׃
16 וּפְקֻדַּת אֶלְעָזָר ׀ בֶּן־אַהֲרֹן הַכֹּהֵן שֶׁמֶן
הַמָּאוֹר וּקְטֹרֶת הַסַּמִּים וּמִנְחַת הַתָּמִיד
וְשֶׁמֶן הַמִּשְׁחָה פְּקֻדַּת כָּל־הַמִּשְׁכָּן וְכָל־
אֲשֶׁר־בּוֹ בְּקֹדֶשׁ וּבְכֵלָיו׃ ס
מפטיר 17 וַיְדַבֵּר יְהֹוָה אֶל־מֹשֶׁה וְאֶל־אַהֲרֹן
לֵאמֹר׃ 18 אַל־תַּכְרִיתוּ אֶת־שֵׁבֶט מִשְׁפְּחֹת
הַקְּהָתִי מִתּוֹךְ הַלְוִיִּם׃ 19 וְזֹאת ׀ עֲשׂוּ
לָהֶם וְחָיוּ וְלֹא יָמֻתוּ בְּגִשְׁתָּם אֶת־קֹדֶשׁ
הַקֳּדָשִׁים אַהֲרֹן וּבָנָיו יָבֹאוּ וְשָׂמוּ אוֹתָם
אִישׁ אִישׁ עַל־עֲבֹדָתוֹ וְאֶל־מַשָּׂאוֹ׃
20 וְלֹא־יָבֹאוּ לִרְאוֹת כְּבַלַּע אֶת־הַקֹּדֶשׁ
וָמֵתוּ׃ פ

porterage The dismantling and reassembling of the sacred objects is performed by the priests; the Kohathites are responsible only as porters.

16. Eleazar the priest, who personally is in charge of the sacred ingredients used with the objects carried by the Kohathites, must scrupulously supervise their porterage by reliable Kohathites. In addition, he supervises the Gershonite and Merarite clans, as well as his own clan, and is the chief of the Levites' labor battalions.

regular grain offering This probably refers to the private daily offering of the anointed priest.

18. cut off The penalty of being "cut off" (*karet*) is inflicted only by God. Because the Kohathites face divine wrath for any mishap with the sacred objects, this term is quite appropriate here.

from the Levites Only the Kohathites, who carry the sacred objects, are in mortal danger, not the Gershonites or Merarites.

19. approach Literally, "have access, handle," implying direct contact. Except for the Ark, there is no prohibition against approaching the sacred objects, only against encroaching on them.

to his duties and to his porterage Better: "to his porterage work." The Kohathites have no duties in the sanctuary removal except the transport of sacred objects.

20. inside Into the tent.

witness the dismantling of the sanctuary Literally, "look at the sacred objects even for a moment." Even the chance viewing of exposed objects inside the sanctuary could prove fatal.

---

20. There were special restrictions on the Levites who would handle the most sacred articles. Abravanel understood this verse to express concern lest the clans of Kohath become so fascinated by staring at the sacred objects that they would fall into a mystic trance, unable to do their work. Hirsch offers an opposite view; for him, the Torah's concern is that the Kohathites might become too accustomed to the routine of seeing the sacred objects packed and unpacked: "lest they die" spiritually, losing their capacity to see the tabernacle as holy.

הפטרת במדבר

HAFTARAH FOR B'MIDBAR

HOSEA 2:1–22

Hosea (8th century B.C.E.) was the first prophet to portray the covenantal bond between God and the people Israel in terms of a marriage. In chapter 1, before the opening of this *haftarah,* Hosea is bidden to marry a "wife of whoredom" who will bear "children of whoredom" with her many lovers. These acts symbolize the apostasy of the people Israel, turning away from God and pursuing other gods.

God now calls on Hosea and his fellow northern Israelites to rebuke their "mother" (the embodiment of the nation) who has gone astray after false lovers (i.e., gods), producing children conceived shamelessly through acts of promiscuity (i.e., apostasy).

Apostasy will not go unpunished, yet hope for the people Israel's future is proclaimed from the outset, a sign that divine mercy transcends judgment for sin. The covenant, perverted by national sin, will be renewed for the straying people.

The prophet marks these shifts of attitude with symbolic changes of names. The shifts of status are underscored by the negative particle *lo* (not) and by its absence. Thus the rejected people called "Not-My-People" (*lo ammi,* 2:1, also 1:9) and "Not-accepted" (*lo ruḥamah,* 1:6) will in the end be called "My People" (*ammi*). Removal of *lo* is the symbolic removal of distance between the nation and its God. Renewal of the covenant does not depend on Israel's repentance or initiative. It is a transformation initiated and guided by God; through His commitment to justice, mercy, and faithfulness, the nation will be devoted to the Lord (2:21–22). God's moral attributes stand at the center of the covenant.

Hosea's perception of the covenant, grounded in the sanctity of love and marriage, led to the Sages' understanding the Song of Songs as a dialogue of spiritual love between God and Israel. The Midrash underscored this theme and gave permanent status to Hosea's bold motif.

Covenant renewal is the climax of the *haftarah,* culminating the divine longing for reconciliation through entreaty and patient love. Through the divine attributes of justice, righteousness, and mercy—which make up the essence of the Covenant and covenantal living—Israel is promised knowledge of the Lord, overcoming the forgetfulness and unknowing that has characterized its recent behavior (2:10,15). Hosea implores the nation to transcend the seductions of nature and recognize God as the one and only source of life (2:10). Speaking for God, Hosea regards this new religious consciousness as an essential transformation, the prerequisite for any covenant renewed in faithfulness and truth.

RELATION OF THE *HAFTARAH* TO THE *PARASHAH*

The *parashah* inaugurates the period of wandering in the wilderness with a census of the Israelite nation. Their wandering with the Ark of the Covenant, following their apostasy with the Golden Calf, could be perceived as a time of purification and regeneration before entry into the Promised Land (see Maimonides, *Guide* III:24).

The wilderness serves a similar function in the *haftarah.* Hosea details how the seductions of idolatry once again perverted Israel's worship, corrupting their religious consciousness. Transformation will come about only through God's coaxing and tender speech to the people in the "wilderness," a symbolic image for the destroyed land (Ibn Ezra). This healing will inaugurate a period in which the rejected nation is restored in its homeland, regenerated beyond all measure or counting (Hos. 2:1). It will be a time of unification of the entire nation under one "head" (*rosh,* 2:2), a glorious transformation of the ancient past when each tribe was accounted for by its own head man (*rosh*) in the wilderness (Num. 1:4).

The wilderness is also a symbolic realm marking a spiritual journey of birth and rebirth. Later
generations, reading Hosea 2:1–22 in association
with the *parashah*, readily imagined the original

wandering as a prototype for all generations conscious of their religious failures and of their need
for covenantal renewal.

2 The number of the people of Israel shall be
like that of the sands of the sea, which cannot
be measured or counted; and instead of being
told, "You are Not-My-People," they shall be
called Children-of-the-Living-God. ²The people of Judah and the people of Israel shall assemble together and appoint one head over
them; and they shall rise from the ground—for
marvelous shall be the day of Jezreel!

³Oh, call your brothers "My People,"
And your sisters "Lovingly Accepted!"

⁴Rebuke your mother, rebuke her—
For she is not My wife
And I am not her husband—
And let her put away her harlotry from her
    face
And her adultery from between her breasts.

⁵Else will I strip her naked
And leave her as on the day she was born:
And I will make her like a wilderness,
Render her like desert land,
And let her die of thirst.

⁶I will also disown her children;
For they are now a harlot's brood,

בַ וְֽהָיָ֞ה מִסְפַּ֣ר בְּנֵֽי־יִשְׂרָאֵל֮ כְּח֣וֹל הַיָּם֒
אֲשֶׁ֥ר לֹֽא־יִמַּ֖ד וְלֹ֣א יִסָּפֵ֑ר וְֽהָיָ֞ה בִּמְק֣וֹם
אֲשֶׁר־יֵאָמֵ֤ר לָהֶם֙ לֹֽא־עַמִּ֣י אַתֶּ֔ם יֵאָמֵ֥ר
לָהֶ֖ם בְּנֵ֥י אֵל־חָֽי׃ ²וְ֠נִקְבְּצ֠וּ בְּנֵֽי־יְהוּדָ֤ה
וּבְנֵֽי־יִשְׂרָאֵל֙ יַחְדָּ֔ו וְשָׂמ֥וּ לָהֶ֖ם רֹ֣אשׁ אֶחָ֑ד
וְעָל֣וּ מִן־הָאָ֔רֶץ כִּ֥י גָד֖וֹל י֥וֹם יִזְרְעֶֽאל׃
³אִמְר֥וּ לַאֲחֵיכֶ֖ם עַמִּ֑י
וְלַאֲחֽוֹתֵיכֶ֖ם רֻחָֽמָה׃

⁴רִ֤יבוּ בְאִמְּכֶם֙ רִ֔יבוּ
כִּי־הִיא֙ לֹ֣א אִשְׁתִּ֔י
וְאָנֹכִ֖י לֹ֣א אִישָׁ֑הּ
וְתָסֵ֤ר זְנוּנֶ֙יהָ֙ מִפָּנֶ֔יהָ
וְנַאֲפוּפֶ֖יהָ מִבֵּ֥ין שָׁדֶֽיהָ׃
⁵פֶּן־אַפְשִׁיטֶ֣נָּה עֲרֻמָּ֔ה
וְהִ֨צַּגְתִּ֔יהָ כְּי֖וֹם הִוָּֽלְדָ֑הּ
וְשַׂמְתִּ֣יהָ כַמִּדְבָּ֗ר
וְשַׁתִּ֙הָ֙ כְּאֶ֣רֶץ צִיָּ֔ה
וַהֲמִתִּ֖יהָ בַּצָּמָֽא׃
⁶וְאֶת־בָּנֶ֖יהָ לֹ֣א אֲרַחֵ֑ם
כִּי־בְנֵ֥י זְנוּנִ֖ים הֵֽמָּה׃

Hosea 2:1. like . . . the sands of the sea This
image recalls God's promise of numerous descendants to Abraham (Gen. 15:5). The sharp contrast of this promise with the verse preceding the
haftarah ("you are not My people, and I will not
be your [God]") anticipates divine mercy and restoration.

2. rise from the ground The image seems to
point to rejuvenation of the national condition,
particularly through a rise in population (see
Exod. 1:10).

4. Rebuke your mother God urges the Israelites (i.e., the children) to rebuke their mother Israel for her spiritual harlotry (Radak).

she is not My wife / And I am not her husband
Hosea uses legal and covenantal formulas to
dramatize the divine–human relationship. Here,
the wife's guilt is emphasized by this divorce formula. Likewise, in Hos. 1:9, a repudiation formula ("I will not be your [God]") reverses the
opening of the Decalogue ("I the LORD am your
God," Exod. 20:2) and positive covenantal asser-

7In that their mother has played the harlot,
She that conceived them has acted shame-
lessly—
Because she thought,
"I will go after my lovers,
Who supply my bread and my water,
My wool and my linen,
My oil and my drink."

8Assuredly,
I will hedge up her roads with thorns
And raise walls against her,
And she shall not find her paths.
9Pursue her lovers as she will,
She shall not overtake them;
And seek them as she may,
She shall never find them.
Then she will say,
"I will go and return
To my first husband,
For then I fared better than now."
10And she did not consider this:
It was I who bestowed on her
The new grain and wine and oil;
I who lavished silver on her
And gold—which they used for Baal.
11Assuredly,
I will take back My new grain in its time
And My new wine in its season,
And I will snatch away My wool and My linen
That serve to cover her nakedness.

7 כִּי זָנְתָה אִמָּם
הֹבִישָׁה הוֹרָתָם
כִּי אָמְרָה
אֵלְכָה אַחֲרֵי מְאַהֲבַי
נֹתְנֵי לַחְמִי וּמֵימַי
צַמְרִי וּפִשְׁתִּי
שַׁמְנִי וְשִׁקּוּיָי׃

8 לָכֵן
הִנְנִי־שָׂךְ אֶת־דַּרְכֵּךְ בַּסִּירִים
וְגָדַרְתִּי אֶת־גְּדֵרָהּ
וּנְתִיבוֹתֶיהָ לֹא תִמְצָא׃
9 וְרִדְּפָה אֶת־מְאַהֲבֶיהָ
וְלֹא־תַשִּׂיג אֹתָם
וּבִקְשָׁתַם
וְלֹא תִמְצָא
וְאָמְרָה
אֵלְכָה וְאָשׁוּבָה
אֶל־אִישִׁי הָרִאשׁוֹן
כִּי טוֹב לִי אָז מֵעָתָּה׃
10 וְהִיא לֹא יָדְעָה
כִּי אָנֹכִי נָתַתִּי לָהּ
הַדָּגָן וְהַתִּירוֹשׁ וְהַיִּצְהָר
וְכֶסֶף הִרְבֵּיתִי לָהּ
וְזָהָב עָשׂוּ לַבָּעַל׃
11 לָכֵן
אָשׁוּב וְלָקַחְתִּי דְגָנִי בְּעִתּוֹ
וְתִירוֹשִׁי בְּמוֹעֲדוֹ
וְהִצַּלְתִּי צַמְרִי וּפִשְׁתִּי
לְכַסּוֹת אֶת־עֶרְוָתָהּ׃

tions ("I will take you to be My people, and I will be your God," Exod. 6:7; cf. Lev. 26:45, Deut. 26:17–18).

7. The mother's own thoughts (or words) are cited as self- incriminating evidence and proof of infidelity.

9. seek them . . . never find them Hosea uses the verbs "seek" and "find" to stress the failure of pursuing false gods. Elsewhere this pattern is used in positive terms, emphasizing God's readiness to respond to Israelite repentance or supplication (see Deut. 4:29: "you will find Him, if only you seek Him with all your heart").

10. gold—which they used for Baal Israel misuses the bounty of God for idolatrous rites.

11–12. The punishment of stripping and

12 Now will I uncover her shame
In the very sight of her lovers,
And none shall save her from Me.
13 And I will end all her rejoicing:
Her festivals, new moons, and sabbaths—
All her festive seasons.
14 I will lay waste her vines and her fig trees,
Which she thinks are a fee
She received from her lovers;
I will turn them into brushwood,
And beasts of the field shall devour them.
15 Thus will I punish her
For the days of the Baalim,
On which she brought them offerings;
When, decked with earrings and jewels,
She would go after her lovers,
Forgetting Me
—declares the LORD.
16 Assuredly,
I will speak coaxingly to her
And lead her through the wilderness
And speak to her tenderly.
17 I will give her her vineyards from there,
And the Valley of Achor as a plowland of hope.
There she shall respond as in the days of her youth,
When she came up from the land of Egypt.

12 וְעַתָּה אֲגַלֶּה אֶת־נַבְלֻתָהּ
לְעֵינֵי מְאַהֲבֶיהָ
וְאִישׁ לֹא־יַצִּילֶנָּה מִיָּדִי׃
13 וְהִשְׁבַּתִּי כָּל־מְשׂוֹשָׂהּ
חַגָּהּ חָדְשָׁהּ וְשַׁבַּתָּהּ
וְכֹל מוֹעֲדָהּ׃
14 וַהֲשִׁמֹּתִי גַּפְנָהּ וּתְאֵנָתָהּ
אֲשֶׁר אָמְרָה אֶתְנָה הֵמָּה לִי
אֲשֶׁר נָתְנוּ־לִי מְאַהֲבָי
וְשַׂמְתִּים לְיַעַר
וַאֲכָלָתַם חַיַּת הַשָּׂדֶה׃
15 וּפָקַדְתִּי עָלֶיהָ
אֶת־יְמֵי הַבְּעָלִים
אֲשֶׁר תַּקְטִיר לָהֶם
וַתַּעַד נִזְמָהּ וְחֶלְיָתָהּ
וַתֵּלֶךְ אַחֲרֵי מְאַהֲבֶיהָ
וְאֹתִי שָׁכְחָה
נְאֻם־יְהוָה׃ פ
16 לָכֵן
הִנֵּה אָנֹכִי מְפַתֶּיהָ
וְהֹלַכְתִּיהָ הַמִּדְבָּר
וְדִבַּרְתִּי עַל־לִבָּהּ׃
17 וְנָתַתִּי לָהּ אֶת־כְּרָמֶיהָ מִשָּׁם
וְאֶת־עֵמֶק עָכוֹר לְפֶתַח תִּקְוָה
וְעָנְתָה שָּׁמָּה כִּימֵי נְעוּרֶיהָ
וּכְיוֹם עֲלֹתָהּ מֵאֶרֶץ־מִצְרָיִם׃ ס

shaming is a featured motif elsewhere as well (Ezek. 16:36–39). These elements may have been part of common law or practice in ancient Israel.

14. fee Hebrew: *etnah,* a harlot's fee, like the *etnan* paid to a harlot in Hos. 9:1 and Deut. 23:19. The word puns on the payment itself (*t'enatah,* "her fig trees"). It also alludes to sexual passion (*ta·anatah,* Jer. 2:24).

15. days of the Baalim The plural "Baalim," here and in verse 19, presumably is used to correspond to the many "lovers" (see 2:7,9,12,14). Baal was the Canaanite god of the storm and of vegetation.

16. through the wilderness Or, "into the desert"; a metaphor for the exile (Rashi, Radak, Eliezer of Beaugency) or for the devastated homeland (Ibn Ezra) where God will comfort the nation and begin the process of renewal. Alternatively, it is a figure for God's revelation (cf. Hos. 13:5) and the place where Israel demonstrated its faithfulness to God (Jer. 2:2).

17. her vineyards Restored vineyards are a counterpoint to the destruction of vines in verse 14 (Ibn Ezra, Radak). Similarly, the covenant with the beasts of the field (v. 20) constitutes a counterpoint to their former destructive rapacity (v. 14).

Valley of Achor This may refer to the scene of Achan's sin at the beginning of the conquest of the Promised Land (Josh. 7:24–26; Radak).

¹⁸And in that day

—declares the LORD—

You will call [Me] Ishi,

And no more will you call Me Baali.

¹⁹For I will remove the names of the Baalim
from her mouth,

And they shall nevermore be mentioned by
name.

²⁰In that day, I will make a covenant for them
with the beasts of the field, the birds of the air,
and the creeping things of the ground; I will also
banish bow, sword, and war from the land. Thus
I will let them lie down in safety.

²¹And I will espouse you forever:

I will espouse you with righteousness and
justice,

And with goodness and mercy,

²²And I will espouse you with faithfulness;

Then you shall be devoted to the LORD.

18 וְהָיָ֤ה בַיּֽוֹם־הַהוּא֙
נְאֻם־יְהֹוָ֔ה
תִּקְרְאִ֖י אִישִׁ֑י
וְלֹא־תִקְרְאִי־לִ֥י ע֖וֹד בַּעְלִֽי:
19 וַהֲסִֽרֹתִ֛י אֶת־שְׁמ֥וֹת הַבְּעָלִ֖ים מִפִּ֑יהָ
וְלֹֽא־יִזָּכְר֥וּ ע֖וֹד בִּשְׁמָֽם:

20 וְכָרַתִּ֣י לָהֶ֣ם בְּרִית֮ בַּיּ֣וֹם הַהוּא֒ עִם־חַיַּ֣ת
הַשָּׂדֶ֗ה וְעִם־ע֤וֹף הַשָּׁמַ֨יִם֙ וְרֶ֣מֶשׂ הָֽאֲדָמָ֔ה
וְקֶ֨שֶׁת וְחֶ֤רֶב וּמִלְחָמָה֙ אֶשְׁבּ֣וֹר מִן־הָאָ֔רֶץ
וְהִשְׁכַּבְתִּ֖ים לָבֶֽטַח:

21 וְאֵֽרַשְׂתִּ֥יךְ לִ֖י לְעוֹלָ֑ם
וְאֵֽרַשְׂתִּ֥יךְ לִי֙ בְּצֶ֣דֶק וּבְמִשְׁפָּ֔ט
וּבְחֶ֖סֶד וּֽבְרַחֲמִֽים:
22 וְאֵֽרַשְׂתִּ֥יךְ לִ֖י בֶּאֱמוּנָ֑ה
וְיָדַ֖עַתְּ אֶת־יְהֹוָֽה: ס

That ancient site of infidelity will now become a
gateway of renewal.

18. Ishi The term for "my husband," used
figuratively for God in verse 9 and as part of the
divorce formula in verse 4. Here it is a counterpoint to the term "Baali" (my Baal). The latter
designation for a husband evokes the Canaanite
god of that name, with whom the people sinned;
hence that term will be avoided.

19. Unilaterally God will produce a religious
transformation, not only by removing pagan
terms from the nation's mouth, but also through
words of loving-kindness (v. 16) and gifts of espousal (vv. 21–22). No human act of repentance
is indicated.

21–22. God promises an everlasting, unalterable commitment. This act of espousal includes gifts by God as the bride-price. These gifts,
the central terms of covenantal fidelity and social
ethics, are the means by which the people shall
renew their relationship with God (cf. Jer. 9:23).

This espousal formula is recited by faithful Jews
daily, while binding the strap of the hand *t'fillin*
around the fingers of one hand. Thus they pledge
to show their commitment to God through the
covenantal behavior of justice and loving-kindness. It is the human response to God's spiritual
initiative as proclaimed in the *haftarah*.

be devoted The Hebrew *v'yada·at* (literally,
"know") echoes Near Eastern treaty terminology.

21The LORD spoke to Moses: 22Take a census
of the Gershonites also, by their ancestral house
and by their clans. 23Record them from the age
of thirty years up to the age of fifty, all who are
subject to service in the performance of tasks
for the Tent of Meeting. 24These are the duties
of the Gershonite clans as to labor and porterage: 25they shall carry the cloths of the Tabernacle, the Tent of Meeting with its covering, the
covering of dolphin skin that is on top of it, and
the screen for the entrance of the Tent of Meeting; 26the hangings of the enclosure, the screen
at the entrance of the gate of the enclosure that
surrounds the Tabernacle, the cords thereof,
and the altar, and all their service equipment
and all their accessories; and they shall perform
the service. 27All the duties of the Gershonites,
all their porterage and all their service, shall be
performed on orders from Aaron and his sons;
you shall make them responsible for attending
to all their porterage. 28Those are the duties of
the Gershonite clans for the Tent of Meeting;

21 וַיְדַבֵּ֥ר יְהוָ֖ה אֶל־מֹשֶׁ֥ה לֵּאמֹֽר׃ 22 נָשֹׂ֗א
אֶת־רֹ֛אשׁ בְּנֵ֥י גֵרְשׁ֖וֹן גַּם־הֵ֑ם לְבֵ֥ית אֲבֹתָ֖ם
לְמִשְׁפְּחֹתָֽם׃ 23 מִבֶּן֩ שְׁלֹשִׁ֨ים שָׁנָ֜ה וָמַ֗עְלָה
עַ֛ד בֶּן־חֲמִשִּׁ֥ים שָׁנָ֖ה תִּפְקֹ֣ד אוֹתָ֑ם כָּל־
הַבָּא֙ לִצְבֹ֣א צָבָ֔א לַעֲבֹ֥ד עֲבֹדָ֖ה בְּאֹ֥הֶל
מוֹעֵֽד׃ 24 זֹ֣את עֲבֹדַ֔ת מִשְׁפְּחֹ֖ת הַגֵּרְשֻׁנִּ֑י
לַעֲבֹ֖ד וּלְמַשָּֽׂא׃ 25 וְנָ֨שְׂא֜וּ אֶת־יְרִיעֹ֤ת
הַמִּשְׁכָּן֙ וְאֶת־אֹ֣הֶל מוֹעֵ֔ד מִכְסֵ֕הוּ וּמִכְסֵ֥ה
הַתַּ֛חַשׁ אֲשֶׁר־עָלָ֖יו מִלְמָ֑עְלָה וְאֶ֨ת־מָסַ֔ךְ
פֶּ֖תַח אֹ֥הֶל מוֹעֵֽד׃ 26 וְאֵת֩ קַלְעֵ֨י הֶחָצֵ֜ר
וְאֶת־מָסַ֣ךְ ׀ פֶּ֣תַח ׀ שַׁ֣עַר הֶחָצֵ֗ר אֲשֶׁ֨ר
עַל־הַמִּשְׁכָּ֤ן וְעַל־הַמִּזְבֵּ֙חַ֙ סָבִ֔יב וְאֵת֙
מֵיתְרֵיהֶ֔ם וְאֶת־כָּל־כְּלֵ֖י עֲבֹדָתָ֑ם וְאֵ֨ת כָּל־
אֲשֶׁ֧ר יֵעָשֶׂ֛ה לָהֶ֖ם וְעָבָֽדוּ׃ 27 עַל־פִּי֩ אַהֲרֹ֨ן
וּבָנָ֜יו תִּהְיֶ֗ה כָּל־עֲבֹדַת֙ בְּנֵ֣י הַגֵּרְשֻׁנִּ֔י
לְכָל־מַשָּׂאָ֖ם וּלְכֹ֣ל עֲבֹדָתָ֑ם וּפְקַדְתֶּ֤ם
עֲלֵהֶם֙ בְּמִשְׁמֶ֔רֶת אֵ֖ת כָּל־מַשָּׂאָֽם׃ 28 זֹ֣את
עֲבֹדַ֗ת מִשְׁפְּחֹת֙ בְּנֵ֣י הַגֵּרְשֻׁנִּ֔י בְּאֹ֖הֶל

The Generation of the Exodus: The Wilderness Camp (*continued*)

THE SECOND CENSUS OF LEVITES (*continued*)

REMOVAL DUTIES OF THE GERSHONITES AND MERARITES (4:21–33)

The Gershonites are assigned to the tabernacle curtains; the Merarites are responsible for the tabernacle structure.

24. The Gershonites and Merarites are limited here to dismantling and assembling the tabernacle. During the march they serve as guards (v. 27).

25. carry Transport by packing and loading the curtains onto the wagons.

26. cords That held up the enclosure curtains. (The curtains of the tent needed no cords; they simply were draped over the frame.)

accessories Refers either to the tabernacle curtains or to the work tools needed for their repair.

27. Aaron and his sons They assign the Gershonites to their tasks. But it is Aaron's son Ithamar who is their supervisor.

attending That is, guarding. Because the tabernacle curtains dismantled by the Gershonites and the tabernacle structure dismantled by the Merarites are to be transported by carts, these clans of Levites have no labor as such during the march; their duties are limited to guarding.

This is the longest *parashah* in the Torah. Most of its first half deals with circumstances when one's place in the community is in question because of unusual behavior. The second half deals with the offerings brought by each tribe as the sanctuary's dedication concludes.

they shall attend to them under the direction
of Ithamar son of Aaron the priest.

29As for the Merarites, you shall record them
by the clans of their ancestral house; 30you shall
record them from the age of thirty years up to
the age of fifty, all who are subject to service in
the performance of the duties for the Tent of
Meeting. 31These are their porterage tasks in
connection with their various duties for the
Tent of Meeting: the planks, the bars, the posts,
and the sockets of the Tabernacle; 32the posts
around the enclosure and their sockets, pegs,
and cords—all these furnishings and their service: you shall list by name the objects that are
their porterage tasks. 33Those are the duties of
the Merarite clans, pertaining to their various
duties in the Tent of Meeting under the direction of Ithamar son of Aaron the priest.

34So Moses, Aaron, and the chieftains of the
community recorded the Kohathites by the
clans of their ancestral house, 35from the age of
thirty years up to the age of fifty, all who were
subject to service for work relating to the Tent
of Meeting. 36Those recorded by their clans
came to 2,750. 37That was the enrollment of the
Kohathite clans, all those who performed duties
relating to the Tent of Meeting, whom Moses
and Aaron recorded at the command of the
LORD through Moses.

38The Gershonites who were recorded by the
clans of their ancestral house, 39from the age of
thirty years up to the age of fifty, all who were
subject to service for work relating to the Tent
of Meeting—40those recorded by the clans of
their ancestral house came to 2,630. 41That was

מוֹעֵד וּמִשְׁמַרְתָּם בְּיַד אִיתָמָר בֶּן־אַהֲרֹן
הַכֹּהֵן: פ
29 בְּנֵי מְרָרִי לְמִשְׁפְּחֹתָם לְבֵית־אֲבֹתָם
תִּפְקֹד אֹתָם: 30 מִבֶּן שְׁלֹשִׁים שָׁנָה וָמַעְלָה
וְעַד בֶּן־חֲמִשִּׁים שָׁנָה תִּפְקְדֵם כָּל־הַבָּא
לַצָּבָא לַעֲבֹד אֶת־עֲבֹדַת אֹהֶל מוֹעֵד:
31 וְזֹאת מִשְׁמֶרֶת מַשָּׂאָם לְכָל־עֲבֹדָתָם
בְּאֹהֶל מוֹעֵד קַרְשֵׁי הַמִּשְׁכָּן וּבְרִיחָיו
וְעַמּוּדָיו וַאֲדָנָיו: 32 וְעַמּוּדֵי הֶחָצֵר סָבִיב
וְאַדְנֵיהֶם וִיתֵדֹתָם וּמֵיתְרֵיהֶם לְכָל־
כְּלֵיהֶם וּלְכֹל עֲבֹדָתָם וּבְשֵׁמֹת תִּפְקְדוּ
אֶת־כְּלֵי מִשְׁמֶרֶת מַשָּׂאָם: 33 זֹאת עֲבֹדַת
מִשְׁפְּחֹת בְּנֵי מְרָרִי לְכָל־עֲבֹדָתָם בְּאֹהֶל
מוֹעֵד בְּיַד אִיתָמָר בֶּן־אַהֲרֹן הַכֹּהֵן:
34 וַיִּפְקֹד מֹשֶׁה וְאַהֲרֹן וּנְשִׂיאֵי הָעֵדָה
אֶת־בְּנֵי הַקְּהָתִי לְמִשְׁפְּחֹתָם וּלְבֵית
אֲבֹתָם: 35 מִבֶּן שְׁלֹשִׁים שָׁנָה וָמַעְלָה
וְעַד בֶּן־חֲמִשִּׁים שָׁנָה כָּל־הַבָּא לַצָּבָא
לַעֲבֹדָה בְּאֹהֶל מוֹעֵד: 36 וַיִּהְיוּ פְקֻדֵיהֶם
לְמִשְׁפְּחֹתָם אַלְפַּיִם שְׁבַע מֵאוֹת
וַחֲמִשִּׁים: 37 אֵלֶּה פְקוּדֵי מִשְׁפְּחֹת הַקְּהָתִי
כָּל־הָעֹבֵד בְּאֹהֶל מוֹעֵד אֲשֶׁר פָּקַד מֹשֶׁה
וְאַהֲרֹן עַל־פִּי יְהוָה בְּיַד־מֹשֶׁה: ס
38 וּפְקוּדֵי בְּנֵי גֵּרְשׁוֹן לְמִשְׁפְּחוֹתָם וּלְבֵית שני
אֲבֹתָם: 39 מִבֶּן שְׁלֹשִׁים שָׁנָה וָמַעְלָה
וְעַד בֶּן־חֲמִשִּׁים שָׁנָה כָּל־הַבָּא לַצָּבָא
לַעֲבֹדָה בְּאֹהֶל מוֹעֵד: 40 וַיִּהְיוּ פְּקֻדֵיהֶם
לְמִשְׁפְּחֹתָם לְבֵית אֲבֹתָם אַלְפַּיִם וְשֵׁשׁ
מֵאוֹת וּשְׁלֹשִׁים: 41 אֵלֶּה פְּקוּדֵי מִשְׁפְּחֹת

28. and they shall attend to them Literally, "and their guard duty" (*u-mishmartam*). This phrase belongs to the preceding clause. In this way, their task is parallel to that of the Merarites outlined in verse 33.

32. posts . . . pegs, and cords The cords are used to fasten the posts to the pegs. No pegs are mentioned in connection with the tabernacle curtains; they are not needed because the tabernacle frame gives the curtains sufficient stability.

by name It was essential to label the numerous objects under Merarite charge, such as sockets, pegs, bars, and cords. Four wagons were needed to transport them all.

34–49. These verses describe how the second

בְּנֵי גֵרְשׁוֹן כָּל־הָעֹבֵד בְּאֹהֶל מוֹעֵד אֲשֶׁר
פָּקַד מֹשֶׁה וְאַהֲרֹן עַל־פִּי יְהוָה׃
42 וּפְקוּדֵי מִשְׁפְּחֹת בְּנֵי מְרָרִי לְמִשְׁפְּחֹתָם
לְבֵית אֲבֹתָם׃ 43 מִבֶּן שְׁלֹשִׁים שָׁנָה
וָמַעְלָה וְעַד בֶּן־חֲמִשִּׁים שָׁנָה כָּל־הַבָּא
לַצָּבָא לַעֲבֹדָה בְּאֹהֶל מוֹעֵד׃ 44 וַיִּהְיוּ
פְקֻדֵיהֶם לְמִשְׁפְּחֹתָם שְׁלֹשֶׁת אֲלָפִים
וּמָאתָיִם׃ 45 אֵלֶּה פְּקוּדֵי מִשְׁפְּחֹת בְּנֵי
מְרָרִי אֲשֶׁר פָּקַד מֹשֶׁה וְאַהֲרֹן עַל־פִּי
יְהוָה בְּיַד־מֹשֶׁה׃
46 כָּל־הַפְּקֻדִים אֲשֶׁר פָּקַד מֹשֶׁה וְאַהֲרֹן
וּנְשִׂיאֵי יִשְׂרָאֵל אֶת־הַלְוִיִּם לְמִשְׁפְּחֹתָם
וּלְבֵית אֲבֹתָם׃ 47 מִבֶּן שְׁלֹשִׁים שָׁנָה
וָמַעְלָה וְעַד בֶּן־חֲמִשִּׁים שָׁנָה כָּל־הַבָּא
לַעֲבֹד עֲבֹדַת עֲבֹדָה וַעֲבֹדַת מַשָּׂא בְּאֹהֶל
מוֹעֵד׃ 48 וַיִּהְיוּ פְּקֻדֵיהֶם שְׁמֹנַת אֲלָפִים
וַחֲמֵשׁ מֵאוֹת וּשְׁמֹנִים׃ 49 עַל־פִּי יְהוָה
פָּקַד אוֹתָם בְּיַד־מֹשֶׁה אִישׁ אִישׁ עַל־
עֲבֹדָתוֹ וְעַל־מַשָּׂאוֹ וּפְקֻדָיו אֲשֶׁר־צִוָּה
יְהוָה אֶת־מֹשֶׁה׃ פ

the enrollment of the Gershonite clans, all those performing duties relating to the Tent of Meeting whom Moses and Aaron recorded at the command of the LORD.

42The enrollment of the Merarite clans by the clans of their ancestral house, 43from the age of thirty years up to the age of fifty, all who were subject to service for work relating to the Tent of Meeting—44those recorded by their clans came to 3,200. 45That was the enrollment of the Merarite clans which Moses and Aaron recorded at the command of the LORD through Moses.

46All the Levites whom Moses, Aaron, and the chieftains of Israel recorded by the clans of their ancestral houses, 47from the age of thirty years up to the age of fifty, all who were subject to duties of service and porterage relating to the Tent of Meeting—48those recorded came to 8,580. 49Each one was given responsibility for his service and porterage at the command of the LORD through Moses, and each was recorded as the LORD had commanded Moses.

ששי ה וַיְדַבֵּר יְהוָה אֶל־מֹשֶׁה לֵּאמֹר׃ 2 צַו
אֶת־בְּנֵי יִשְׂרָאֵל וִישַׁלְּחוּ מִן־הַמַּחֲנֶה כָּל־

5 The LORD spoke to Moses, saying: 2Instruct the Israelites to remove from camp anyone with

census of Levites was carried out with the assistance of the tribal chieftains.

49. each was recorded The work assignment was by God's direct command to Moses.

PURIFICATION OF THE CAMP (5:1–6:27)

Chapters 5 and 6 consist of several laws inserted into the account of the preparations for the march through the wilderness. They deal with the prevention and elimination of impurity in the camp of the Israelites. These laws have in common the figure of the priest, who plays a prominent role in each case.

REMOVAL OF SEVERELY IMPURE PERSONS (5:1–4)

The camp of Israel is sacred and must retain its purity. Any man or woman who bears or contracts impurity must eliminate it by ritual means of purification and sacrifice.

CHAPTER 5

2. For the Midrash, the expulsion of diseased Israelites is not a hygienic measure. It imagines that many of the Israelites who left Egypt were physically blemished as the result of their hard labor. When they arrived at Mount Sinai, they miraculously were made whole, so

an eruption or a discharge and anyone defiled by a corpse. [3]Remove male and female alike; put them outside the camp so that they do not defile the camp of those in whose midst I dwell.

[4]The Israelites did so, putting them outside the camp; as the LORD had spoken to Moses, so the Israelites did.

[5]The LORD spoke to Moses, saying: [6]Speak to the Israelites: When a man or woman commits any wrong toward a fellow man, thus breaking faith with the LORD, and that person realizes his guilt, [7]he shall confess the wrong that he has

צָר֖וּעַ וְכָל־זָ֑ב וְכֹ֖ל טָמֵ֥א לָנָֽפֶשׁ׃ 3 מִזָּכָ֤ר עַד־נְקֵבָה֙ תְּשַׁלֵּ֔חוּ אֶל־מִח֥וּץ לַֽמַּחֲנֶ֖ה תְּשַׁלְּח֑וּם וְלֹ֤א יְטַמְּאוּ֙ אֶת־מַ֣חֲנֵיהֶ֔ם אֲשֶׁ֥ר אֲנִ֖י שֹׁכֵ֥ן בְּתוֹכָֽם׃ 4 וַיַּֽעֲשׂוּ־כֵן֙ בְּנֵ֣י יִשְׂרָאֵ֔ל וַיְשַׁלְּח֣וּ אוֹתָ֔ם אֶל־מִח֖וּץ לַֽמַּחֲנֶ֑ה כַּֽאֲשֶׁ֨ר דִּבֶּ֤ר יְהֹוָה֙ אֶל־מֹשֶׁ֔ה כֵּ֥ן עָשׂ֖וּ בְּנֵ֥י יִשְׂרָאֵֽל׃ פ

5 וַיְדַבֵּ֥ר יְהֹוָ֖ה אֶל־מֹשֶׁ֥ה לֵּאמֹֽר׃ 6 דַּבֵּ֞ר אֶל־בְּנֵ֣י יִשְׂרָאֵ֗ל אִ֣ישׁ אֽוֹ־אִשָּׁ֞ה כִּ֤י יַֽעֲשׂוּ֙ מִכָּל־חַטֹּ֣את הָֽאָדָ֔ם לִמְעֹ֥ל מַ֖עַל בַּֽיהֹוָ֑ה וְאָֽשְׁמָ֖ה הַנֶּ֥פֶשׁ הַהִֽוא׃ 7 וְהִתְוַדּ֗וּ אֶת־

---

2. an eruption or a discharge See Lev. 13–15.

corpse For the rules concerning this impurity, see Num. 19.

3. outside the camp "Outside" differs from "within" in one respect only: It is out of the contamination range of the sanctuary, so that impurities there cannot pollute the sanctuary.

dwell The Lord's consent to dwell in the tabernacle must be matched by Israel's scrupulousness in keeping the camp pure. Any impurity in the camp threatens the purity of the tabernacle.

THE ASHAM FOR A FALSE OATH   (vv. 5–8)

6. thus breaking faith with the LORD Literally, "whereby he commits sacrilege against the LORD." The crime consists of defrauding another person and then committing sacrilege against God by denying it in a false oath.

realizes his guilt The feeling of guilt is the necessary requirement for the reduced penalty.

7. confess The penitent's remorse must be articulated.

---

that their physical perfection reflected the integrity of their souls. Thus the Torah describes all the Israelites as "standing" at the foot of the mountain, implying that none was crippled; "hearing" the words of God, implying that none was deaf; "seeing" the thunder and lightning, suggesting that none was blind. As they distanced themselves from Sinai and began to grumble about the hardships of the journey, the effect of the miracle began to wear off. Their blemished souls began to be reflected in physically blemished bodies (Num. R. 7:1); note that other Sages were sensitive to the danger of identifying physical infirmity with spiritual impurity.

6. This passage about confession and atonement for theft has prompted sages and commentators to offer several profound and important insights.

any wrong toward a fellow man, thus breaking faith with the LORD Any breach of faith toward another is an offense against God, who commands justice and whose image is found in every human being. Why is the principle of expiation associated here with a case of misappropriation of property? Every breach of faith is a form of theft, stealing another's trust under false pretenses, using one's God-given talents for a purpose other than that which God intended (Yitzḥak Meir Alter of Ger).

7. he shall confess Hebrew: *hitvadu;* the reflexive mode suggests that we must confess to ourselves the wrong that we have done, rather than go through the motions of an expiation ritual while privately believing we have done nothing wrong. Commentators distinguish between the "confession," made to cleanse the wrongdoer's soul, and the "resti-

---

HALAKHAH L'MA·ASEH

5:7. confess There is no atonement for sins against God without confession of sins. Similarly, when we have injured another human being, the process of return (*t'shuvah*) to the proper path and to good standing before God and the community requires that we first confess our transgression to those whom we have wronged and from whom we ask forgiveness (MT Repentance 2:3,5). See Comment on Deut. 30:2.

done. He shall make restitution in the principal
amount and add one-fifth to it, giving it to him
whom he has wronged. 8If the man has no kinsman to whom restitution can be made, the
amount repaid shall go to the LORD for the
priest—in addition to the ram of expiation with
which expiation is made on his behalf. 9So, too,
any gift among the sacred donations that the
Israelites offer shall be the priest's. 10And each
shall retain his sacred donations: each priest
shall keep what is given to him.

חַטָּאתָם֮ אֲשֶׁר עָשׂוּ֒ וְהֵשִׁיב אֶת־אֲשָׁמוֹ֙
בְּרֹאשׁוֹ וַחֲמִישִׁתוֹ יֹסֵף עָלָיו וְנָתַן לַאֲשֶׁר
אָשַׁם לוֹ׃ 8 וְאִם־אֵין לָאִישׁ גֹּאֵל לְהָשִׁיב
הָאָשָׁם֙ אֵלָיו הָאָשָׁם הַמּוּשָׁב לַיהוָה לַכֹּהֵן
מִלְּבַד אֵיל הַכִּפֻּרִים אֲשֶׁר יְכַפֶּר־בּוֹ עָלָיו׃
9 וְכָל־תְּרוּמָה לְכָל־קָדְשֵׁי בְנֵי־יִשְׂרָאֵל
אֲשֶׁר־יַקְרִיבוּ לַכֹּהֵן לוֹ יִהְיֶה׃ 10 וְאִישׁ
אֶת־קֳדָשָׁיו לוֹ יִהְיוּ אִישׁ אֲשֶׁר־יִתֵּן לַכֹּהֵן
לוֹ יִהְיֶה׃ פ ביעי

restitution Hebrew: *asham;* normally the name of a sacrifice. In verses 7 and 8 "*asham*" is used specifically for the restitution paid to the victim.

in the principal amount In its entirety.

one-fifth In Exod. 22:3 and 21:37, the penalty for an apprehended theft is double the value of the stolen article or more. This penalty is sharply reduced to 20 percent here to encourage the voluntary surrender of what was stolen.

whom he has wronged That is, to whom he has incurred liability.

8. kinsman Literally, "redeemer" (*go·el*). The law of redemption is given in Lev. 25:48–49.

go to the LORD for the priest In the absence of a kinsman, the sanctuary is the beneficiary—specifically, the officiating priest, chosen by the offerer. The monetary restitution is added to the reparation of the sacrificial ram to expiate for the trespass against the Lord. The sacrifice could also be in monetary equivalents.

in addition to The restitution to the defrauded man or his kin precedes the sacrificial restitution to God, as Lev. 5:24–25 makes clear.

ram of expiation Hebrew: *eil ha-kippurim,* used here as the name of the sacrifice. The proper name of the sacrifice (*asham*) is not used because the word was already used to denote "restitution" in verse 7.

THE PRIEST OF CHOICE (vv. 9–10)

9. gift Hebrew: *t'rumah;* literally, "that which is lifted" for the sanctuary, i.e., dedicated to it.

10. each That is, each priest. A person who makes a donation to the sanctuary has the right to determine which priest will receive it. The donation must be an item of food; nonperishables cannot become the property of any single priest and would be retained by the sanctuary.

---

tution," made to restore the stolen property to its rightful owner. A person found guilty must restore that property even if insisting on innocence.

8. has no kinsman One tradition understands that this refers to a convert to Judaism who has been cheated. (How else would a Jew have no Jewish relatives, however remote?) The *midrash* elaborates on God's love for the convert and on the seriousness of cheating him or her. The convert may have been attracted to the Jewish faith because of its emphasis on social justice. To cheat a fellow Jew is not just a crime but is a breach of faith with God, profaning God's name and robbing someone of the ability to believe in the goodness of God's world and in the decency of one's fellow Jews. The *midrash* offers a parable of the stag that came to graze among the king's flocks of sheep. The king ordered his servants to be especially generous to the stag "for it left its own kind to come and join my flock" (Num. R. 8:2).

By contrast, Moshe Feinstein suggests that the text refers to a situation in which people persuade themselves that it is not a sin to cheat a wealthy individual who is childless, because he has enough money for himself and has no heirs whose inheritance will be diminished.

to the LORD for the priest The priest is considered a member of every Israelite's family, taking the place here of the nonexistent relatives. Or perhaps this implies that God is kin to every Israelite, including the orphan and the childless.

10. each priest shall keep what is given to him Literally, "what a man gives to the priest shall be his." This prompted the comment that "his" refers to the donor, not to the priest (BT Ber. 63a). What we keep for ourselves may ultimately be taken from us. Only when we give something away does the gift, and the good deed it represents, become permanently ours.

11The LORD spoke to Moses, saying: 12Speak
to the Israelite people and say to them:

If any man's wife has gone astray and broken
faith with him 13in that a man has had carnal
relations with her unbeknown to her husband,
and she keeps secret the fact that she has defiled
herself without being forced, and there is no witness against her—14but a fit of jealousy comes
over him and he is wrought up about the wife
who has defiled herself; or if a fit of jealousy
comes over one and he is wrought up about his
wife although she has not defiled herself—15the
man shall bring his wife to the priest. And he
shall bring as an offering for her one-tenth of

רביעי 11 וַיְדַבֵּ֥ר יְהוָ֖ה אֶל־מֹשֶׁ֥ה לֵּאמֹֽר׃ 12 דַּבֵּר֙
אֶל־בְּנֵ֣י יִשְׂרָאֵ֔ל וְאָמַרְתָּ֖ אֲלֵהֶ֑ם
אִ֥ישׁ אִישׁ֙ כִּֽי־תִשְׂטֶ֣ה אִשְׁתּ֔וֹ וּמָעֲלָ֥ה ב֖וֹ
מָֽעַל׃ 13 וְשָׁכַ֨ב אִ֣ישׁ אֹתָהּ֮ שִׁכְבַת־זֶ֒רַע֒
וְנֶעְלַם֙ מֵעֵינֵ֣י אִישָׁ֔הּ וְנִסְתְּרָ֖ה וְהִ֣יא
נִטְמָ֑אָה וְעֵד֙ אֵ֣ין בָּ֔הּ וְהִ֖וא לֹ֥א נִתְפָּֽשָׂה׃
14 וְעָבַ֨ר עָלָ֧יו רֽוּחַ־קִנְאָ֛ה וְקִנֵּ֥א אֶת־אִשְׁתּ֖וֹ
וְהִ֣וא נִטְמָ֑אָה אוֹ־עָבַ֨ר עָלָ֤יו רֽוּחַ־קִנְאָה֙
וְקִנֵּ֣א אֶת־אִשְׁתּ֔וֹ וְהִ֖יא לֹ֥א נִטְמָֽאָה׃
15 וְהֵבִ֨יא הָאִ֣ישׁ אֶת־אִשְׁתּוֹ֮ אֶל־הַכֹּהֵן֒
וְהֵבִ֤יא אֶת־קָרְבָּנָהּ֙ עָלֶ֔יהָ עֲשִׂירִ֥ת הָאֵיפָ֖ה

THE SUSPECTED ADULTERESS (vv. 11–31)

An irate husband suspects that his wife has been unfaithful and accuses her of conjugal infidelity. Having no proof, his only recourse is to bring her to the sanctuary where she is subjected to an ordeal.

12. broken faith Hebrew: *ma·alah … ma·al,* which denotes betrayal. It is often applied to straying after gods. Here it is extended to refer to marital infidelity.

13. unbeknown Literally, "hidden from the eyes of." The husband was unaware of his wife's act or had no proof beyond his own suspicion.

defiled herself In a moral, not a ritual, sense.

PROCEDURE: OATH, SACRIFICE, AND ORDEAL (vv. 15–26)

15. the man shall bring his wife Only a woman's husband can press charges, not the community.

for her Because she is under suspicion of being a brazen, unrepentant sinner, she is not qualified to bring her own sacrifice. Hence, her husband brings her offering on her behalf.

11–31. The ordeal of the *sotah,* the woman suspected of betraying her husband, involves a strange and, at first reading, demeaning ritual. At one level, it reflects the immense seriousness with which the Torah regards marital infidelity. "All other transgressions recorded in the Torah can, if committed, be put right. If a man steals, he can return what he stole. If one withholds the wages of a laborer, he can pay him. But one who cohabits with a married woman … is unable to restore her marriage to what it was previously" (Num. R. 9:6).

Rashi connects *"sotah"* (literally, "deviant") to *shoteh* (fool), reflecting the talmudic dictum that "no one sins unless overcome by foolishness" (BT Sot. 3a). If we could clearly see the consequences of what we are tempted to do, we would never sin. People sin, not out of calculation but in a spirit of folly, losing control of their reasoning faculty. The Talmud tells us that the ordeal of the *sotah* worked only in an age when people believed in its power to expose the guilty and exonerate the innocent. In the more cynical period of the Second Temple, it had to be discontinued (M Sot. 9:9).

14. It would seem that the Sages understood the ordeal of the *sotah* less as a way of ferreting out adulteresses and more as a way of "proving" to the husband that his suspicions were groundless. A man who might not be satisfied with a court's finding of "not guilty in the absence of proof" would have to accept the judgment of Heaven. Because it is unlikely that the ritual would produce a guilty verdict (unless through the psychosomatic reaction of a truly guilty wife), its purpose may well have been to alleviate the husband's suspicion and restore domestic harmony.

We can understand the promise of v. 28, that if the woman is found innocent, she will be able to "retain seed," as foreseeing that she will be restored to a life of love with her husband. But even if the ordeal and a subsequent pregnancy turn the husband's heart back to his wife, what will it take to restore her trust in him and affection for him?

an *ephah* of barley flour. No oil shall be poured upon it and no frankincense shall be laid on it, for it is a grain offering of jealousy, a grain offering of remembrance which recalls wrongdoing.

16The priest shall bring her forward and have her stand before the Lord. 17The priest shall take sacral water in an earthen vessel and, taking some of the earth that is on the floor of the Tabernacle, the priest shall put it into the water. 18After he has made the woman stand before the Lord, the priest shall bare the woman's head and place upon her hands the grain offering of remembrance, which is a grain offering of jealousy. And in the priest's hands shall be the water of bitterness that induces the spell. 19The priest shall adjure the woman, saying to her, "If no man has lain with you, if you have not gone astray in defilement while married to your husband, be immune to harm from this water of bitterness that induces the spell. 20But if you have gone astray while married to your husband

קֶ֥מַח שְׂעֹרִ֑ים לֹֽא־יִצֹ֨ק עָלָ֜יו שֶׁ֗מֶן וְלֹֽא־יִתֵּ֤ן
עָלָיו֙ לְבֹנָ֔ה כִּֽי־מִנְחַ֤ת קְנָאֹת֙ ה֔וּא* מִנְחַ֥ת
זִכָּר֖וֹן מַזְכֶּ֥רֶת עָוֺֽן׃
16 וְהִקְרִ֥יב אֹתָ֖הּ הַכֹּהֵ֑ן וְהֶֽעֱמִדָ֖הּ לִפְנֵ֥י
יְהוָֽה׃ 17 וְלָקַ֧ח הַכֹּהֵ֛ן מַ֥יִם קְדֹשִׁ֖ים בִּכְלִי־
חָ֑רֶשׂ וּמִן־הֶֽעָפָ֗ר אֲשֶׁ֤ר יִהְיֶה֙ בְּקַרְקַ֣ע
הַמִּשְׁכָּ֔ן יִקַּ֥ח הַכֹּהֵ֖ן וְנָתַ֥ן אֶל־הַמָּֽיִם׃
18 וְהֶעֱמִ֨יד הַכֹּהֵ֥ן אֶֽת־הָאִשָּׁה֮ לִפְנֵ֣י יְהוָה֒
וּפָרַע֙ אֶת־רֹ֣אשׁ הָֽאִשָּׁ֔ה וְנָתַ֣ן עַל־כַּפֶּ֗יהָ
אֵ֚ת מִנְחַ֣ת הַזִּכָּר֔וֹן מִנְחַ֥ת קְנָאֹ֖ת הִ֑וא
וּבְיַ֤ד הַכֹּהֵן֙ יִהְי֔וּ מֵ֥י הַמָּרִ֖ים הַמְאָֽרְרִֽים׃
19 וְהִשְׁבִּ֨יעַ אֹתָ֜הּ הַכֹּהֵ֗ן וְאָמַ֤ר אֶל־הָֽאִשָּׁה֙
אִם־לֹ֨א שָׁכַ֥ב אִישׁ֙ אֹתָ֔ךְ וְאִם־לֹ֥א שָׂטִ֛ית
טֻמְאָ֖ה תַּ֣חַת אִישֵׁ֑ךְ הִנָּקִ֕י מִמֵּ֛י הַמָּרִ֥ים
הַמְאָרְרִ֖ים הָאֵֽלֶּה׃ 20 וְאַ֗תְּ כִּ֥י שָׂטִ֛ית תַּ֥חַת
אִישֵׁ֖ךְ וְכִ֣י נִטְמֵ֑את וַיִּתֵּ֨ן אִ֥ישׁ בָּךְ֙ אֶת־

v. 15. סבירין ומטעין "היא"

ephah See Comment to Exod. 16:36.

barley flour The grain offering (*minḥah*) normally consisted of fine wheat flour. Neither oil nor frankincense is added, for these ingredients were associated with joy. Their absence signifies that the occasion is one of real or suspected wrongdoing.

which recalls wrongdoing A remembrance offering is always for the benefit of the offerer. Thus the text must add this clause to explain the unusual situation.

16. before the Lord She stands before the altar so that the condemnation she takes upon herself will most certainly be effective.

17. take The items enumerated in this verse were prepared earlier.

sacral water Probably taken from the consecrated basin.

earth . . . on the floor The ground of the sacred area was regarded as having potency.

is Hebrew: *yihyeh;* better: "will be." Because the tabernacle was on the move constantly, the earthen floor could never be the same.

18. bare the woman's head Literally, "loosen the hair." An indication that the woman was in disgrace.

place upon her hands It was her sacrifice, even though her husband brought it, and it was she who had to present it to the priest.

water of bitterness Some attribute this description to the effect of the waters on the woman; others conjecture that a bitter ingredient was added.

20. while married to Hebrew: *taḥat;* literally, "under." The idiom refers to the husband's authority.

---

15. barley flour This usually is food for animals. It is used here because the woman is accused of behaving like an animal, giving in to lustful instinct instead of controlling it (*Sifrei*).

18. water of bitterness The water was not bitter; the bitterness was in the domestic conflict that led to the ordeal (*Sifrei*). Making the accused drink the bitter potion recalls Moses forcing a similar drink on those Israelites who had worshiped the Golden Calf (Exod. 32:20), worship understood by the Torah and later tradition as a classic example of unfaithfulness to God (Num. R. 9:49).

שְׁכָבְתּ֔וֹ מִֽבַּלְעֲדֵ֖י אִישֵֽׁךְ׃ 21 וְהִשְׁבִּ֨יעַ
הַכֹּהֵ֥ן אֶת־הָֽאִשָּׁה֮ בִּשְׁבֻעַ֣ת הָאָלָה֒ וְאָמַ֤ר
הַכֹּהֵן֙ לָֽאִשָּׁ֔ה יִתֵּ֨ן יְהוָ֥ה אוֹתָ֛ךְ לְאָלָ֥ה
וְלִשְׁבֻעָ֖ה בְּת֣וֹךְ עַמֵּ֑ךְ בְּתֵ֨ת יְהוָ֤ה אֶת־
יְרֵכֵךְ֙ נֹפֶ֔לֶת וְאֶת־בִּטְנֵ֖ךְ צָבָֽה׃ 22 וּ֠בָאוּ
הַמַּ֨יִם הַמְאָרְרִ֤ים הָאֵ֙לֶּה֙ בְּֽמֵעַ֔יִךְ לַצְבּ֥וֹת
בֶּ֖טֶן וְלַנְפִּ֣ל יָרֵ֑ךְ וְאָמְרָ֥ה הָאִשָּׁ֖ה אָמֵ֥ן ׀
אָמֵֽן׃
23 וְ֠כָתַב אֶת־הָאָלֹ֥ת הָאֵ֛לֶּה הַכֹּהֵ֖ן בַּסֵּ֑פֶר
וּמָחָ֖ה אֶל־מֵ֥י הַמָּרִֽים׃ 24 וְהִשְׁקָה֙ אֶת־
הָֽאִשָּׁ֔ה אֶת־מֵ֥י הַמָּרִ֖ים הַמְאָרֲרִ֑ים וּבָ֥אוּ
בָ֛הּ הַמַּ֥יִם הַמְאָרֲרִ֖ים לְמָרִֽים׃ 25 וְלָקַ֣ח
הַכֹּהֵן֙ מִיַּ֣ד הָֽאִשָּׁ֔ה אֵ֖ת מִנְחַ֣ת הַקְּנָאֹ֑ת
וְהֵנִ֤יף אֶת־הַמִּנְחָה֙ לִפְנֵ֣י יְהוָ֔ה וְהִקְרִ֥יב
אֹתָ֖הּ אֶל־הַמִּזְבֵּֽחַ׃ 26 וְקָמַ֨ץ הַכֹּהֵ֤ן מִן־
הַמִּנְחָה֙ אֶת־אַזְכָּ֣רָתָ֔הּ וְהִקְטִ֖יר הַמִּזְבֵּ֑חָה
וְאַחַ֛ר יַשְׁקֶ֥ה אֶת־הָאִשָּׁ֖ה אֶת־הַמָּֽיִם׃

and have defiled yourself, if a man other than
your husband has had carnal relations with
you"—21here the priest shall administer the
curse of adjuration to the woman, as the priest
goes on to say to the woman—"may the LORD
make you a curse and an imprecation among
your people, as the LORD causes your thigh to
sag and your belly to distend; 22may this water
that induces the spell enter your body, causing
the belly to distend and the thigh to sag." And
the woman shall say, "Amen, amen!"
23The priest shall put these curses down in
writing and rub it off into the water of bitterness.
24He is to make the woman drink the water of
bitterness that induces the spell, so that the
spell-inducing water may enter into her to bring
on bitterness. 25Then the priest shall take from
the woman's hand the grain offering of jealousy,
elevate the grain offering before the LORD, and
present it on the altar. 26The priest shall scoop
out of the grain offering a token part of it and
turn it into smoke on the altar. Last, he shall
make the woman drink the water.

21. a curse . . . among your people "All the women will use you in their imprecations; when they curse each other they will say, 'If you have done such a thing may your end be like that of so-and-so'" (Num. R. 9:18).

as the LORD causes The punishment suffered by the guilty woman is not to be attributed to any inherent magical powers of the water but to the sovereign will of God.

thigh to sag . . . belly to distend There is disagreement among scholars concerning the significance of these symptoms. "Thigh" probably is a euphemism for the procreative organs, and refers here to a miscarriage.

22. Amen Confirms the acceptance of the curse.

23. curses There is only one curse. Perhaps the plural refers to the two symptoms of the punishment: the sagging thigh and the distended belly. Perhaps it refers to the punishment and its effect, through which she will become an object of derision.

in writing and rub it off into the water This example of sympathetic magic illustrates a belief in the power of the curse when it is written down, read aloud, and then carried out—even in symbolic form.

24. He is to make The offering of the sacrifice precedes the drinking of the potion in verses 25–27; hence this verse anticipates what occurs later.

25. elevate In this special dedicatory rite of elevation offering (*t'nufah*), the offering is brought to the special attention of God before it can be brought to the altar.

---

23. The commentaries focus on the extraordinary detail that, during the ritual, a document bearing the name of God is dissolved in the potion from which the accused wife drinks. Ordinarily such a document would be considered too holy to destroy, and would have to be deposited in a proper storage place, a *g'nizah.* "For the sake of peace between husband and wife, God has ordered that the divine name be blotted out" (Num. R. 9:36). After all, "Peace" is considered to be one of God's names, and the establishment of peace replaces the effaced name.

27Once he has made her drink the water—if
she has defiled herself by breaking faith with her
husband, the spell-inducing water shall enter
into her to bring on bitterness, so that her belly
shall distend and her thigh shall sag; and the
woman shall become a curse among her people.
28But if the woman has not defiled herself and
is pure, she shall be unharmed and able to retain seed.

29This is the ritual in cases of jealousy, when
a woman goes astray while married to her husband and defiles herself, 30or when a fit of jealousy comes over a man and he is wrought up
over his wife: the woman shall be made to stand
before the LORD and the priest shall carry out
all this ritual with her. 31The man shall be clear
of guilt; but that woman shall suffer for her guilt.

27 וְהִשְׁקָהּ אֶת־הַמַּיִם וְהָיְתָה אִם־נִטְמְאָה
וַתִּמְעֹל מַעַל בְּאִישָׁהּ וּבָאוּ בָהּ הַמַּיִם
הַמְאָרְרִים לְמָרִים וְצָבְתָה בִטְנָהּ וְנָפְלָה
יְרֵכָהּ וְהָיְתָה הָאִשָּׁה לְאָלָה בְּקֶרֶב עַמָּהּ׃
28 וְאִם־לֹא נִטְמְאָה הָאִשָּׁה וּטְהֹרָה הִוא
וְנִקְּתָה וְנִזְרְעָה זָרַע׃
29 זֹאת תּוֹרַת הַקְּנָאֹת אֲשֶׁר תִּשְׂטֶה אִשָּׁה
תַּחַת אִישָׁהּ וְנִטְמָאָה׃ 30 אוֹ אִישׁ אֲשֶׁר
תַּעֲבֹר עָלָיו רוּחַ קִנְאָה וְקִנֵּא אֶת־אִשְׁתּוֹ
וְהֶעֱמִיד אֶת־הָאִשָּׁה לִפְנֵי יְהוָה וְעָשָׂה
לָהּ הַכֹּהֵן אֵת כָּל־הַתּוֹרָה הַזֹּאת׃ 31 וְנִקָּה
הָאִישׁ מֵעָוֺן וְהָאִשָּׁה הַהִוא תִּשָּׂא אֶת־
עֲוֺנָהּ׃ פ

6 The LORD spoke to Moses, saying: 2Speak
to the Israelites and say to them: If anyone, man

ו וַיְדַבֵּר יְהוָה אֶל־מֹשֶׁה לֵּאמֹר׃ 2 דַּבֵּר
אֶל־בְּנֵי יִשְׂרָאֵל וְאָמַרְתָּ אֲלֵהֶם אִישׁ אוֹ־

28. pure That is, the waters had no effect.
able to retain seed That is, she will be able to have children, as opposed to the punishment of sterility inflicted on a guilty wife.
29. The ritual allayed the husband's suspicions and restored a harmonious relationship to the family. Note that Yoḥanan ben Zakkai abolished the practice of this ritual, considering it to be one sided (M Sot. 9:9).
31. man That is, the husband.
clear of guilt The husband is free from punishment.
suffer for her guilt The wife must endure her punishment, i.e., the awful consequence of the ordeal-oath.

THE LAW OF THE NAZIRITE (6:1–21)

One becomes a nazirite by means of a vow. This law deals only with a nazirite whose vow is for a limited period, not a lifelong nazirite, like Samson. The temporary nazirite's need for the services of a priest and the sanctuary probably accounts for the addition of this section to the law of the suspected adulteress.

---

31. The man shall be clear of guilt Hirsch comments, "Only if the husband has never been guilty of unchastity can he impose this ordeal on his wife." God's laws of morality do not give men license to behave immorally in ways forbidden to women.

CHAPTER 6

Opinions are strongly divided concerning the nazirite. Is he or she a saint, aspiring voluntarily to higher levels of holiness, or a person with trouble controlling his or her impulses, who therefore has to impose limits on behavior beyond what normal people do? Thus Ibn Ezra derives the verb meaning "to utter explicitly" (*yafli,* in v. 2) from *pele* (a wonder). He considered it a wonder that a person could control appetites so completely. The Torah calls for the nazirite to bring a purification offering at the conclusion of the self-imposed period of abstinence. Ramban identifies the sin for which the offering is brought as the nazirite's readiness to return to a less demanding life, "defiling himself with worldly passion." In this view, a com-

אִשָּׁה כִּי יַפְלִא לִנְדֹּר נֶדֶר נָזִיר לְהַזִּיר
לַיהוָה׃ 3 מִיַּיִן וְשֵׁכָר יַזִּיר חֹמֶץ יַיִן וְחֹמֶץ
שֵׁכָר לֹא יִשְׁתֶּה וְכָל־מִשְׁרַת עֲנָבִים לֹא
יִשְׁתֶּה וַעֲנָבִים לַחִים וִיבֵשִׁים לֹא יֹאכֵל׃
4 כֹּל יְמֵי נִזְרוֹ מִכֹּל אֲשֶׁר יֵעָשֶׂה מִגֶּפֶן
הַיַּיִן מֵחַרְצַנִּים וְעַד־זָג לֹא יֹאכֵל׃

or woman, explicitly utters a nazirite's vow, to
set himself apart for the LORD, 3he shall abstain
from wine and any other intoxicant; he shall not drink vinegar of wine or of any other intoxicant, neither shall he drink anything in which grapes have been steeped, nor eat grapes fresh or dried.
4Throughout his term as nazirite, he may not eat anything that is obtained from the grapevine, even seeds or skin.

2. or woman The inclusion of a woman indicates that the nazirite vow was widely practiced. As with all other vows, however, before marriage a woman needed her father's acquiescence, and a married woman needed that of her husband (30:4–9).

explicitly utters Perhaps: "sets [oneself] apart by pronouncing [a vow]." The vow must be spoken aloud.

nazirite Hebrew: *nazir;* from the verb נזר (to separate oneself), and related to the verb נדר (to take an oath). Only by separating oneself, abstaining from certain acts permitted to all others, can one be totally sanctified to God.

PROHIBITIONS FOR THE NAZIRITE (vv. 3–8)

3. vinegar Wine turned sour, used as food by the poor.

grapes . . . dried Pressed into a cake, raisins were a common food item.

---

munity is blessed by having in its midst a handful of individuals who commit themselves to a more strenuous religious regimen.

On the other hand, Simon the Just, a high priest in the days of the Second Temple, made it a practice never to eat of the offerings brought by a nazirite. He felt the nazirite's vows were made in a moment of excessive guilt or excessive enthusiasm and, therefore, were not wholehearted (Num. R. 10:7). Maimonides, uncomfortable with the nazirite's extremism, urged the path of moderation in food, drink, and other matters. He cited the words of the Sages, "Is it not sufficient for you to abstain from what the Torah has forbidden, that you seek to forbid yourself other things as well!" Indeed, the talmudic sage Rav taught, "In the World to Come, people will have to account for all the good food God put in the world which they refused to eat" (JT Kid. 4:12). The sin for which the nazirite brings an offering of atonement would then be the sin of seeing the pleasures of God's world as a source of evil and temptation.

We today might feel a similar ambivalence toward the religious enthusiast. We can admire the fervor and readiness to refrain from ordinary pleasures, appreciating the person as a role model of religious seriousness. We can be grateful that there is a place in Judaism for such a person, and yet be concerned with the danger of extremism and fanaticism to which such enthusiasm can sometimes lead.

Astruc offers yet another view, that the nazirite's sin was neither abstinence nor the ending of abstinence, but rather the life of self-indulgence that preceded and led to his or her vow.

Why does the Torah place the laws of the nazirite immediately after the ordeal of the *sotah*? The Midrash suggests that the nazirite-to-be saw a *sotah* commit adultery while she was drunk and realized the power of liquor to lead people into sin (Num. R. 10:1). People with difficulty controlling their impulses may be so upset by the example of another person ruining his or her life by giving in to temptation that they set strenuous limits on themselves, to avoid a similar fate.

3. Why must the nazirite avoid grapes and raisins, which are not intoxicating? This is an instance of "making a fence around the law," establishing a safety zone of prohibition to keep one from approaching the boundary of the forbidden and perhaps inadvertently crossing it. (Thus we begin *Shabbat* by lighting candles 18 minutes before sunset rather than at the moment of sunset, and we avoid carrying money on *Shabbat* lest we find ourselves spending it.) Or the purpose of this rule may be the avoidance of giving others a wrong impression. People who see a nazirite eating grapes might suspect that he or she would drink grape wine as well. "Avoid unseemliness and the appearance of unseemliness" (Num. R. 10:8).

5 Throughout the term of his vow as nazirite, no razor shall touch his head; it shall remain consecrated until the completion of his term as nazirite of the LORD, the hair of his head being left to grow untrimmed. 6 Throughout the term that he has set apart for the LORD, he shall not go in where there is a dead person. 7 Even if his father or mother, or his brother or sister should die, he must not defile himself for them, since hair set apart for his God is upon his head: 8 throughout his term as nazirite he is consecrated to the LORD.

9 If a person dies suddenly near him, defiling his consecrated hair, he shall shave his head on the day he becomes pure; he shall shave it on the seventh day. 10 On the eighth day he shall bring two turtledoves or two pigeons to the priest, at the entrance of the Tent of Meeting. 11 The priest shall offer one as a purification

5 כָּל־יְמֵי֙ נֶ֣דֶר נִזְר֔וֹ תַּ֖עַר לֹא־יַעֲבֹ֣ר עַל־
רֹאשׁ֑וֹ עַד־מְלֹ֨את הַיָּמִ֜ם אֲשֶׁר־יַזִּ֤יר לַֽיהוָה֙
קָדֹ֣שׁ יִהְיֶ֔ה גַּדֵּ֥ל פֶּ֖רַע שְׂעַ֥ר רֹאשֽׁוֹ׃ 6 כָּל־
יְמֵ֛י הַזִּיר֥וֹ לַֽיהוָ֖ה עַל־נֶ֥פֶשׁ מֵ֖ת לֹ֥א יָבֹֽא׃
7 לְאָבִ֣יו וּלְאִמּ֗וֹ לְאָחִיו֙ וּלְאַ֣חֹת֔וֹ לֹֽא־
יִטַּמָּ֥א לָהֶ֖ם בְּמֹתָ֑ם כִּ֛י נֵ֥זֶר אֱלֹהָ֖יו עַל־
רֹאשֽׁוֹ׃ 8 כֹּ֖ל יְמֵ֣י נִזְר֑וֹ קָדֹ֥שׁ ה֖וּא לַֽיהוָֽה׃
9 וְכִֽי־יָמ֨וּת מֵ֤ת עָלָיו֙ בְּפֶ֣תַע פִּתְאֹ֔ם וְטִמֵּ֖א
רֹ֣אשׁ נִזְר֑וֹ וְגִלַּ֤ח רֹאשׁוֹ֙ בְּי֣וֹם טָהֳרָת֔וֹ בַּיּ֥וֹם
הַשְּׁבִיעִ֖י יְגַלְּחֶֽנּוּ׃ 10 וּבַיּ֣וֹם הַשְּׁמִינִ֗י יָבִא֙
שְׁתֵּ֣י תֹרִ֔ים א֥וֹ שְׁנֵ֖י בְּנֵ֣י יוֹנָ֑ה אֶל־הַכֹּהֵ֔ן
אֶל־פֶּ֖תַח אֹ֥הֶל מוֹעֵֽד׃ 11 וְעָשָׂ֣ה הַכֹּהֵ֗ן

5. shall touch Literally, "shall press over." Not only shaving is prohibited but any form of trimming.

it That is, the hair. The nazirite's most distinctive trait is uncut hair.

6. go in Defilement results from being under the same roof as the corpse.

8. consecrated The above restrictions have the sole function of consecrating the nazirite, who is thus endowed with a status equivalent to priesthood.

CONTAMINATION BY CORPSE (vv. 9–12)

9. The ordinary person is contaminated by a corpse only through direct contact or being under the same roof; the nazirite is contaminated merely by being in its proximity.

suddenly The occurrence was accidental. Indeed, if the contamination had been deliberate, sacrificial expiation would be impossible.

near Such is the added power of the nazirite's holiness that he or she contracts impurity at a distance.

defiling . . . consecrated hair Only the hair is permanently sanctified, in contrast to the person, which is desanctified at the termination of one's vow.

shave . . . head The shaved hair was buried, probably to prevent it from polluting other objects.

shave it on the seventh day After having been sprinkled on the third and seventh days with the purificatory waters.

10. turtledoves . . . pigeons The most inexpensive animal offerings.

---

7. A *kohen* may attend to the funerals of his parents because his priestly status derives from them. Because a nazirite's status is self-imposed, however, he may not do so. Perhaps the real significance of the institution of the nazirite is found in giving troubled, self-doubting people a way of dealing with their upsetting thoughts and impulses within a religious framework. It turns those thoughts to the service of God instead of allowing them to become a source of discomfort and guilt. A commentator asks why some people can drink wine while others cannot. His answer: Wine lays bare the inner essence of a person's soul. The pure of heart can drink and not worry about what will be revealed, but those who are struggling against their lower instincts would do well to avoid strong drink lest their unseemly side be exposed. The normative view of Judaism is that nothing created by God, including wine, sex, and wealth, is intrinsically evil. All can be sanctified if used properly.

offering and the other as a burnt offering, and
make expiation on his behalf for the guilt that
he incurred through the corpse. That same day
he shall reconsecrate his head ¹²and rededicate
to the LORD his term as nazirite; and he shall
bring a lamb in its first year as a penalty offering.
The previous period shall be void, since his consecrated hair was defiled.

¹³This is the ritual for the nazirite: On the day
that his term as nazirite is completed, he shall
be brought to the entrance of the Tent of Meeting. ¹⁴As his offering to the LORD he shall present: one male lamb in its first year, without
blemish, for a burnt offering; one ewe lamb in
its first year, without blemish, for a purification
offering; one ram without blemish for an
offering of well-being; ¹⁵a basket of unleavened
cakes of choice flour with oil mixed in, and unleavened wafers spread with oil; and the proper
grain offerings and libations.

¹⁶The priest shall present them before the
LORD and offer the purification offering and the
burnt offering. ¹⁷He shall offer the ram as a
sacrifice of well-being to the LORD, together
with the basket of unleavened cakes; the priest
shall also offer the grain offerings and the libations. ¹⁸The nazirite shall then shave his consecrated hair, at the entrance of the Tent of
Meeting, and take the locks of his consecrated

אֶחָד לְחַטָּאת֙ וְאֶחָ֣ד לְעֹלָ֔ה וְכִפֶּ֣ר עָלָ֔יו
מֵאֲשֶׁ֣ר חָטָ֖א עַל־הַנָּ֑פֶשׁ וְקִדַּ֥שׁ אֶת־רֹאשׁ֖וֹ
בַּיּ֥וֹם הַהֽוּא׃ 12 וְהִזִּ֤יר לַֽיהוָה֙ אֶת־יְמֵ֣י נִזְר֔וֹ
וְהֵבִ֛יא כֶּ֥בֶשׂ בֶּן־שְׁנָת֖וֹ לְאָשָׁ֑ם וְהַיָּמִ֤ים
הָרִֽאשֹׁנִים֙ יִפְּל֔וּ כִּ֥י טָמֵ֖א נִזְרֽוֹ׃

13 וְזֹ֥את תּוֹרַ֖ת הַנָּזִ֑יר בְּי֗וֹם מְלֹאת֙ יְמֵ֣י
נִזְר֔וֹ יָבִ֣יא אֹת֔וֹ אֶל־פֶּ֖תַח אֹ֥הֶל מוֹעֵֽד׃
14 וְהִקְרִ֣יב אֶת־קָרְבָּנ֣וֹ לַֽיהוָ֡ה כֶּבֶשׂ֩ בֶּן־
שְׁנָת֨וֹ תָמִ֤ים אֶחָד֙ לְעֹלָ֔ה וְכַבְשָׂ֨ה אַחַ֧ת
בַּת־שְׁנָתָ֛הּ תְּמִימָ֖ה לְחַטָּ֑את וְאַֽיִל־אֶחָ֥ד
תָּמִ֖ים לִשְׁלָמִֽים׃ 15 וְסַ֣ל מַצּ֗וֹת סֹ֤לֶת חַלֹּת֙
בְּלוּלֹ֣ת בַּשֶּׁ֔מֶן וּרְקִיקֵ֥י מַצּ֖וֹת מְשֻׁחִ֣ים
בַּשָּׁ֑מֶן וּמִנְחָתָ֖ם וְנִסְכֵּיהֶֽם׃
16 וְהִקְרִ֥יב הַכֹּהֵ֖ן לִפְנֵ֣י יְהוָ֑ה וְעָשָׂ֣ה אֶת־
חַטָּאת֖וֹ וְאֶת־עֹלָתֽוֹ׃ 17 וְאֶת־הָאַ֜יִל יַעֲשֶׂ֥ה
זֶ֣בַח שְׁלָמִים֩ לַֽיהוָ֗ה עַ֚ל סַ֣ל הַמַּצּ֔וֹת וְעָשָׂה֙
הַכֹּהֵ֔ן אֶת־מִנְחָת֖וֹ וְאֶת־נִסְכּֽוֹ׃ 18 וְגִלַּ֣ח
הַנָּזִ֗יר פֶּ֛תַח אֹ֥הֶל מוֹעֵ֖ד אֶת־רֹ֣אשׁ נִזְר֑וֹ

11. burnt offering The burnt offering was
added when birds had been brought, to provide
an adequate gift for the altar (Ibn Ezra, Ramban).
12. rededicate to the LORD Presumably by
a new vow.
penalty offering Before it can be acceptable
to God, the nazirite must replace the consecrated
hair that has been shaven as well as repeat the preceding nazirite period that had been canceled. Total restitution has been rendered only after he or
she reconsecrates the new hair and renews the
vow. Then, and only then, can the priest proceed
with the reparation offering in the hope of achieving divine forgiveness.

THE COMPLETION RITUAL   (vv. 13–21)
14. The animal offerings for both the completed

and the abortive nazirite periods are the same, with
this major difference: The *asham* for desecration
has been replaced here by the *sh'lamim* for joy.
15. cakes Distinct from wafers, the other
grain offering in the basket.
17. cakes Not offered as sacrifice but only
presented and then eaten by the priest and the
nazirite. The purpose of their presentation, probably by setting the basket before the altar, is to
sanctify them.
18. then Only after all the sacrifices have
been offered up on the altar may the nazirite shave
his or her consecrated hair.
at the entrance of the Tent of Meeting
Between the entrance and the altar, the area permitted to lay worshipers when they brought their
offerings.

וְלָקַ֗ח אֶת־שְׂעַר֙ רֹ֣אשׁ נִזְר֔וֹ וְנָתַן֙ עַל־הָאֵ֔שׁ
אֲשֶׁר־תַּ֖חַת זֶ֥בַח הַשְּׁלָמִֽים׃
19 וְלָקַ֨ח הַכֹּהֵ֜ן אֶת־הַזְּרֹ֣עַ בְּשֵׁלָה֮ מִן־
הָאַיִל֒ וְֽחַלַּ֨ת מַצָּ֤ה אַחַת֙ מִן־הַסַּ֔ל וּרְקִ֥יק
מַצָּ֖ה אֶחָ֑ד וְנָתַן֙ עַל־כַּפֵּ֣י הַנָּזִ֔יר אַחַ֖ר
הִֽתְגַּלְּח֥וֹ אֶת־נִזְרֽוֹ׃ 20 וְהֵנִיף֩ אוֹתָ֨ם הַכֹּהֵ֥ן ׀
תְּנוּפָה֮ לִפְנֵ֣י יְהוָה֒ קֹ֤דֶשׁ הוּא֙ לַכֹּהֵ֔ן עַ֚ל
חֲזֵ֣ה הַתְּנוּפָ֔ה וְעַ֖ל שׁ֣וֹק הַתְּרוּמָ֑ה וְאַחַ֛ר
יִשְׁתֶּ֥ה הַנָּזִ֖יר יָֽיִן׃
21 זֹ֣את תּוֹרַ֣ת הַנָּזִיר֮ אֲשֶׁ֣ר יִדֹּר֒ קָרְבָּנ֤וֹ
לַֽיהוָה֙ עַל־נִזְר֔וֹ מִלְּבַ֖ד אֲשֶׁר־תַּשִּׂ֣יג יָד֑וֹ
כְּפִ֤י נִדְרוֹ֙ אֲשֶׁ֣ר יִדֹּ֔ר כֵּ֣ן יַעֲשֶׂ֔ה עַ֖ל תּוֹרַ֥ת
נִזְרֽוֹ׃ פ

hair and put them on the fire that is under the sacrifice of well-being.

19The priest shall take the shoulder of the ram when it has been boiled, one unleavened cake from the basket, and one unleavened wafer, and place them on the hands of the nazirite after he has shaved his consecrated hair. 20The priest shall elevate them as an elevation offering before the LORD; and this shall be a sacred donation for the priest, in addition to the breast of the elevation offering and the thigh of gift offering. After that the nazirite may drink wine.

21Such is the obligation of a nazirite; except that he who vows an offering to the LORD of what he can afford, beyond his nazirite requirements, must do exactly according to the vow that he has made beyond his obligation as a nazirite.

fire that is under The hair was burned in the special hearth set up under the pot to cook the sacrifice of well-being. Because the hair is holy even after it is shaved, it must be destroyed by fire. Its destruction prevents its defilement.

sacrifice of well-being The meat of this sacrifice belonged to the worshiper; it was cooked and eaten in the sacred precincts.

19. shoulder According to the Sages, the upper part of the right foreleg is apportioned to the priest from every offering of well-being.

one unleavened cake from the basket The basket had been set down before the Lord, probably by the altar (Deut. 26:4,10). Its contents, except for the set of offerings belonging to the priest, will be eaten by the nazirite together with the well-being offering.

hands Literally, "palms."

20. The "elevation offering" (*t'nufah*) is a rite of dedication that transfers the elevated objects from the property of the offerer to God. That is why all the portions given to the priests are first placed on the palms of the donor, to indicate that they are his or hers to donate. Then the elevation movement is performed by the priest, probably by placing his hands under the hands of the donor, thereby graphically transferring the objects to God, after which they may be eaten by the priest.

21. The sacrifices enumerated above are the minimum due. The nazirite who vows additional offerings must fulfill that vow as well.

APPENDIX: THE PRIESTLY BLESSING
(vv. 22–27)

Among the chief duties of the priest is to bless the people Israel in the name of the Lord. The blessing, however, issues solely from the Lord; the priest's function is to channel it. The text underscores the fact that the priest possesses no divine powers of his own, although he is holy—indeed, one of God's intimates. Of special interest is the fact that the text of the priestly blessing has been found on silver amulets (dating from the late 7th century B.C.E.) southeast of the City of David, at Ketef Hinnom, on the western rise of the Valley of Hinnom. It is the only known inscription with a biblical text that predates the Babylonian exile.

22–27. These six verses contain perhaps the most familiar words in the Book of Numbers. In many traditional synagogues, descendants of the *kohanim* pronounce these words on festivals as a blessing of the congregation. In their capacity as modern equivalents of *kohanim*, rabbis and cantors commonly invoke it for a *bar mitzvah* or *bat mitzvah*, for a bride and groom, or as the closing benediction of a service. Parents use it to bless their children on *Shabbat* eve.

Do human beings have the power to bless

22The LORD spoke to Moses: 23Speak to Aaron and his sons: Thus shall you bless the people of Israel. Say to them:
24The LORD bless you and protect you!
25The LORD deal kindly and graciously with you!
26The LORD bestow His favor upon you and grant you peace!

22 וַיְדַבֵּר יְהוָה אֶל־מֹשֶׁה לֵּאמֹר׃ 23 דַּבֵּר
אֶל־אַהֲרֹן וְאֶל־בָּנָיו לֵאמֹר כֹּה תְבָרְכוּ
אֶת־בְּנֵי יִשְׂרָאֵל אָמוֹר לָהֶם׃ ס
24 יְבָרֶכְךָ יְהוָה וְיִשְׁמְרֶךָ׃ ס
25 יָאֵר יְהוָה ׀ פָּנָיו אֵלֶיךָ וִיחֻנֶּךָּ׃ ס
26 יִשָּׂא יְהוָה ׀ פָּנָיו אֵלֶיךָ וְיָשֵׂם לְךָ
שָׁלוֹם׃ ס

23. Thus That is, when you bless, use this formula, not one of your own devising.

to them To the assembled worshipers, indicating the communal nature of the blessing.

24. The LORD Understood as "May the LORD" (and so in vv. 25–26).

bless In the Bible, God's blessing confers mainly tangible gifts: offspring, cattle and flocks, silver and gold, land, fertility, health, victory, strength, and peace.

protect That is, from harmful spirits and from all forms of evil.

25. deal kindly Literally, "make His face to shine," i.e., illumine. The Hebrew expression indicates God's friendly concern.

graciously The root חנן is used exclusively in connection with divine mercy and grace. God's strict justice will be tempered by mercy. God will not judge the people Israel according to their sins but will deal kindly with them as a free gift.

26. peace Hebrew: *shalom,* encompassing the blessings of prosperity, good health, friendship, and well-being.

---

other human beings? Ishmael (BT Ḥul. 49a) teaches that the priests do indeed bless the people; and as a reward, God blesses the priests (taking the object in "I will bless them" in v. 27 to be the priests). The *Tanḥuma* suggests that when the priests aspire to bless the people, God endorses their efforts and joins in, making their blessing authentic. Rashbam, however, interprets the verse to mean that when the priests invoke God's blessing ("they shall link My name with the people"), God responds by blessing the people Israel. The blessing is structured in three lines (vv. 24–26), each slightly longer than the preceding one: in Hebrew, three words, then five words, then seven words, with the divine name occurring as the second word in each line.

bless you May "the LORD bless you" with material wealth "and protect you" from losing that wealth, for material blessings are vulnerable to loss (*Sifrei*). Or "may God protect you from being corrupted by the attainment of material blessing" (Num. R. 11:5). "May God bless you according to your needs—blessing the student with intelligence, the merchant with business acumen" (*Ha·amek Davar*). Sforno notes that Jews need not be embarrassed to pray for material wealth, which can make a life of charity and study more attainable.

deal kindly Literally, "make His face shine." Hirsch and Sforno render it "May God enlighten you," so that you can understand the purposes God has in mind for you. For the *Sifrei*, this second line of the blessing is a prayer for the light of wisdom and the knowledge of Torah. Unlike wealth, they require no protection to prevent their being stolen.

graciously May God give you the gift of grace. May you live in a society where people will admire you for your devotion to God and to Torah.

bestow . . . favor Literally, "to turn one's head in your direction." In Gen. 19:21, it means to grant someone's request. In Gen. 40:19, it means "to forgive, to look upon someone with favor." In that sense, the third line of the bles-

HALAKHAH L'MA·ASEH

6:23. Thus shall you bless the people of Israel In the ancient Temple, the *kohanim* (priests) blessed the people with this blessing daily. Today it is included in the reader's repetition of the *Amidah* during *Shaḥarit* and *Musaf* throughout the year. In many synagogues in the Diaspora the *kohanim* re-enact the ancient blessing during the *Musaf* service on High Holy Days and festivals. According to common practice in Israel, *kohanim* bless the congregation each day. Following one of the two contrary responsa approved by the CJLS on this subject, some Conservative congregations permit and some forbid the daughter of a *kohen* to serve in this role. See Comment on Lev. 22:12.

[27]Thus they shall link My name with the people of Israel, and I will bless them.

27 וְשָׂמ֥וּ אֶת־שְׁמִ֖י עַל־בְּנֵ֣י יִשְׂרָאֵ֑ל וַאֲנִ֖י
אֲבָרְכֵֽם׃ פ

7

On the day that Moses finished setting up the Tabernacle, he anointed and consecrated it and all its furnishings, as well as the altar and its utensils. When he had anointed and consecrated them, [2]the chieftains of Israel, the heads of ancestral houses, namely, the chieftains of the tribes, those who were in charge of enrollment,

חמישי ז וַיְהִ֞י בְּי֨וֹם כַּלּ֣וֹת מֹשֶׁ֗ה לְהָקִ֣ים אֶת־
הַמִּשְׁכָּ֡ן וַיִּמְשַׁ֨ח אֹת֜וֹ וַיְקַדֵּ֤שׁ אֹתוֹ֙ וְאֶת־
כׇּל־כֵּלָ֔יו וְאֶת־הַמִּזְבֵּ֖חַ וְאֶת־כׇּל־כֵּלָ֑יו
וַיִּמְשָׁחֵ֖ם וַיְקַדֵּ֥שׁ אֹתָֽם׃ 2 וַיַּקְרִ֙יבוּ֙ נְשִׂיאֵ֣י
יִשְׂרָאֵ֔ל רָאשֵׁ֖י בֵּ֣ית אֲבֹתָ֑ם הֵ֚ם נְשִׂיאֵ֣י
הַמַּטֹּ֔ת הֵ֥ם הָעֹמְדִ֖ים עַל־הַפְּקֻדִֽים׃

27. link My name with God's name is figuratively "placed" on the Israelites by the priests through the medium of the benediction.

and I Literally, "I Myself." The Hebrew is emphatic, stressing that the Lord is the sole source of the blessing.

FINAL PREPARATIONS FOR USE OF THE TABERNACLE (7:1–8:26)

THE CHIEFTAINS' INITIATORY GIFTS (7:1–89)

The 12 tribal chieftains collectively contribute valuable gifts to the completed and consecrated tabernacle. Then, individually and on successive days, each chieftain contributes an additional identical gift to the consecrated altar.

1. as well as the altar The altar is singled out because it will receive separate dedicatory gifts from the chieftains (Ibn Ezra).

---

sing expresses the hope that God will heed the Israelites' prayers and forgive their shortcomings. In Deut. 10:17, the phrase carries the meaning of favoring one person over another, which God is described as not doing; so here the blessing might be taken to mean, "May God side with you and give you the benefit of any doubt."

grant you peace Peace begins in the home, then extends to the community, and finally to all the world (*K'tav Sofer*). The Midrash asks why God should bless and forgive Israel. "Because Israel blesses and forgives God!" We bless God when we have eaten a satisfying meal and recite the Blessings after Meals (*Birkat ha-Mazon*). We forgive God when we do not have enough to eat, consuming perhaps only one slice of bread, yet recite *ha-Mazon* nonetheless, thanking God for our food (Num. R. 11:7). Note that *Birkat ha-Mazon,* the *Amidah,* the *Kaddish,* and the Mishnah all conclude with a prayer for peace.

CHAPTER 7

2. chieftains of Israel Who were these chieftains? They had been foremen during the days of Egyptian enslavement, and willingly accepted beatings from their Egyptian taskmasters rather than punish their fellow Israelites for not meeting their quotas of bricks. As a reward, they were honored to bring these inaugural offerings (Num. R. 12:16). Although each offering was identical, each was unique to the person who brought it. The order of the tribes seems random, implying no greater status to those who came first. To each tribe, God dedicated one day, and on that day there was no gift like its gift. The sincerity of each offering was in no way diminished by the fact that another chieftain had brought an identical offering one day earlier. For that reason, the Torah describes each offering in detail. Similarly, although people recite the same prayers, each worshiper's experience of those prayers is unique and personal.

The Midrash states that on the day the tabernacle was dedicated, something happened that never had happened before. The *Sh'khinah,* the Presence of God, descended from heaven and took up residence in this world (Num. R. 12:6).

drew near ³and brought their offering before the
LORD: six draught carts and twelve oxen,
a cart for every two chieftains and an ox for
each one.

When they had brought them before the Tabernacle, ⁴the LORD said to Moses: ⁵Accept these
from them for use in the service of the Tent of
Meeting, and give them to the Levites according
to their respective services.

⁶Moses took the carts and the oxen and gave
them to the Levites. ⁷Two carts and four oxen
he gave to the Gershonites, as required for their
service, ⁸and four carts and eight oxen he gave
to the Merarites, as required for their service—
under the direction of Ithamar son of Aaron the
priest. ⁹But to the Kohathites he did not give
any; since theirs was the service of the [most]
sacred objects, their porterage was by shoulder.

¹⁰The chieftains also brought the dedication
offering for the altar upon its being anointed.
As the chieftains were presenting their offerings
before the altar, ¹¹the LORD said to Moses: Let
them present their offerings for the dedication
of the altar, one chieftain each day.

¹²The one who presented his offering on the
first day was Nahshon son of Amminadab of the
tribe of Judah. ¹³His offering: one silver bowl
weighing 130 shekels and one silver basin of 70

³ וַיָּבִ֨יאוּ אֶת־קָרְבָּנָ֜ם לִפְנֵ֣י יְהֹוָ֗ה שֵׁשׁ־
עֶגְלֹ֥ת צָב֙ וּשְׁנֵ֣י עָשָׂ֣ר בָּקָ֔ר עֲגָלָ֛ה עַל־שְׁנֵ֥י
הַנְּשִׂאִ֖ים וְשׁ֣וֹר לְאֶחָ֑ד
וַיַּקְרִ֥יבוּ אוֹתָ֖ם לִפְנֵ֥י הַמִּשְׁכָּֽן׃ ⁴ וַיֹּ֥אמֶר
יְהֹוָ֖ה אֶל־מֹשֶׁ֥ה לֵּאמֹֽר׃ ⁵ קַ֚ח מֵֽאִתָּ֔ם וְהָי֕וּ
לַֽעֲבֹ֕ד אֶת־עֲבֹדַ֖ת אֹ֣הֶל מוֹעֵ֑ד וְנָֽתַתָּ֣ה
אוֹתָ֗ם אֶל־הַֽלְוִיִּ֔ם אִ֖ישׁ כְּפִ֥י עֲבֹֽדָתֽוֹ׃
⁶ וַיִּקַּ֣ח מֹשֶׁ֔ה אֶת־הָֽעֲגָלֹ֖ת וְאֶת־הַבָּקָ֑ר
וַיִּתֵּ֥ן אוֹתָ֖ם אֶל־הַֽלְוִיִּֽם׃ ⁷ אֵ֣ת ׀ שְׁתֵּ֣י
הָֽעֲגָלֹ֗ת וְאֵת֙ אַרְבַּ֣עַת הַבָּקָ֔ר נָתַ֖ן לִבְנֵ֣י
גֵֽרְשׁ֑וֹן כְּפִ֖י עֲבֹֽדָתָֽם׃ ⁸ וְאֵ֣ת ׀ אַרְבַּ֣ע
הָֽעֲגָלֹ֗ת וְאֵת֙ שְׁמֹנַ֣ת הַבָּקָ֔ר נָתַ֖ן לִבְנֵ֣י
מְרָרִ֑י כְּפִי֙ עֲבֹ֣דָתָ֔ם בְּיַד֙ אִֽיתָמָ֔ר בֶּֽן־אַֽהֲרֹ֖ן
הַכֹּהֵֽן׃ ⁹ וְלִבְנֵ֥י קְהָ֖ת לֹ֣א נָתָ֑ן כִּֽי־עֲבֹדַ֤ת
הַקֹּ֨דֶשׁ֙ עֲלֵהֶ֔ם בַּכָּתֵ֖ף יִשָּֽׂאוּ׃
¹⁰ וַיַּקְרִ֣יבוּ הַנְּשִׂאִ֗ים אֵ֚ת חֲנֻכַּ֣ת הַמִּזְבֵּ֔חַ
בְּי֖וֹם הִמָּשַׁ֣ח אֹת֑וֹ וַיַּקְרִ֧יבוּ הַנְּשִׂיאִ֛ם
אֶת־קָרְבָּנָ֖ם לִפְנֵ֥י הַמִּזְבֵּֽחַ׃ ¹¹ וַיֹּ֥אמֶר יְהֹוָ֖ה
אֶל־מֹשֶׁ֑ה נָשִׂ֨יא אֶחָ֜ד לַיּ֗וֹם נָשִׂ֤יא אֶחָד֙
לַיּ֔וֹם יַקְרִ֨יבוּ֙ אֶת־קָרְבָּנָ֔ם לַֽחֲנֻכַּ֖ת
הַמִּזְבֵּֽחַ׃ ס
¹² וַיְהִ֗י הַמַּקְרִ֛יב בַּיּ֥וֹם הָֽרִאשׁ֖וֹן אֶת־קָרְבָּנ֑וֹ
נַחְשׁ֖וֹן בֶּן־עַמִּֽינָדָ֑ב לְמַטֵּ֥ה יְהוּדָֽה׃
¹³ וְקָרְבָּנ֞וֹ קַֽעֲרַת־כֶּ֣סֶף אַחַ֗ת שְׁלֹשִׁ֣ים

---

3. draught carts Wagons strong enough to
carry heavy loads. Each draught cart requires the
power of two oxen.

before the Tabernacle Neither the wood of
the carts nor their animals were destined for the
altar. Hence, they were ineligible to enter the sacred area, which was reserved for sacrifice alone.

7–8. The planks of the tabernacle carried by
the Merarites were bulkier than the tabernacle
curtains carried by the Gershonites. Therefore,
the Merarites were given four carts, and the
Gershonites, two carts.

10. dedication offering This actually was an
initiation offering, gifts brought upon initiating
the use of a structure.

13. offering Hebrew: *korban*, which applies
here both to the vessels and to the animals enumerated in the list.

shekels See Comment to Gen. 23:9.

bowl . . . basin The bowls were probably
used for dry ingredients, such as flour. The basins
were probably used for liquids, such as libations
and blood. These bowls and basins were also filled
with semolina flour mixed with oil.

---

9. their porterage was by shoulder This
description of the Levites' physical labor
should teach us that "one does not acquire the

least spark of holiness without effort"
(Menaḥem Mendel of Kotzk).

shekels by the sanctuary weight, both filled with
choice flour with oil mixed in, for a grain
offering; 14one gold ladle of 10 shekels, filled
with incense; 15one bull of the herd, one ram,
and one lamb in its first year, for a burnt
offering; 16one goat for a purification offering;
17and for his sacrifice of well-being: two oxen,
five rams, five he-goats, and five yearling lambs.
That was the offering of Nahshon son of
Amminadab.

18On the second day, Nethanel son of Zuar,
chieftain of Issachar, made his offering. 19He
presented as his offering: one silver bowl weighing 130 shekels and one silver basin of 70 shekels
by the sanctuary weight, both filled with choice
flour with oil mixed in, for a grain offering;
20one gold ladle of 10 shekels, filled with incense;
21one bull of the herd, one ram, and one lamb
in its first year, for a burnt offering; 22one goat
for a purification offering; 23and for his sacrifice
of well-being: two oxen, five rams, five he-goats,
and five yearling lambs. That was the offering
of Nethanel son of Zuar.

24On the third day, it was the chieftain of the
Zebulunites, Eliab son of Helon. 25His offering:
one silver bowl weighing 130 shekels and one
silver basin of 70 shekels by the sanctuary
weight, both filled with choice flour with oil
mixed in, for a grain offering; 26one gold ladle
of 10 shekels, filled with incense; 27one bull of
the herd, one ram, and one lamb in its first year,
for a burnt offering; 28one goat for a purification
offering; 29and for his sacrifice of well-being:
two oxen, five rams, five he-goats, and five year-

וּמֵאָה֮ מִשְׁקָלָהּ֒ מִזְרָ֣ק אֶחָד֙ כֶּ֔סֶף שִׁבְעִ֥ים
שֶׁ֖קֶל בְּשֶׁ֣קֶל הַקֹּ֑דֶשׁ שְׁנֵיהֶ֣ם ׀ מְלֵאִ֗ים סֹ֛לֶת
בְּלוּלָ֥ה בַשֶּׁ֖מֶן לְמִנְחָֽה׃ 14 כַּ֥ף אַחַ֛ת עֲשָׂרָ֥ה
זָהָ֖ב מְלֵאָ֥ה קְטֹֽרֶת׃ 15 פַּ֣ר אֶחָ֞ד בֶּן־בָּקָ֗ר
אַ֧יִל אֶחָ֛ד כֶּֽבֶשׂ־אֶחָ֥ד בֶּן־שְׁנָת֖וֹ לְעֹלָֽה׃
16 שְׂעִיר־עִזִּ֥ים אֶחָ֖ד לְחַטָּֽאת׃ 17 וּלְזֶ֣בַח
הַשְּׁלָמִים֮ בָּקָ֣ר שְׁנַ֒יִם֒ אֵילִ֣ם חֲמִשָּׁ֗ה
עַתּוּדִ֣ים חֲמִשָּׁ֔ה כְּבָשִׂ֥ים בְּנֵי־שָׁנָ֖ה חֲמִשָּׁ֑ה
זֶ֛ה קָרְבַּ֥ן נַחְשׁ֖וֹן בֶּן־עַמִּינָדָֽב׃ פ
18 בַּיּוֹם֙ הַשֵּׁנִ֔י הִקְרִ֖יב נְתַנְאֵ֣ל בֶּן־צוּעָ֑ר
נְשִׂ֖יא יִשָּׂשכָֽר׃ 19 הִקְרִ֨ב אֶת־קָרְבָּנ֜וֹ
קַעֲרַת־כֶּ֨סֶף אַחַ֜ת שְׁלֹשִׁ֣ים וּמֵאָה֮ מִשְׁקָלָהּ֒
מִזְרָ֤ק אֶחָד֙ כֶּ֔סֶף שִׁבְעִ֥ים שֶׁ֖קֶל בְּשֶׁ֣קֶל
הַקֹּ֑דֶשׁ שְׁנֵיהֶ֣ם ׀ מְלֵאִ֗ים סֹ֛לֶת בְּלוּלָ֥ה
בַשֶּׁ֖מֶן לְמִנְחָֽה׃ 20 כַּ֥ף אַחַ֛ת עֲשָׂרָ֥ה זָהָ֖ב
מְלֵאָ֥ה קְטֹֽרֶת׃ 21 פַּ֣ר אֶחָ֞ד בֶּן־בָּקָ֗ר אַ֧יִל
אֶחָ֛ד כֶּֽבֶשׂ־אֶחָ֥ד בֶּן־שְׁנָת֖וֹ לְעֹלָֽה׃
22 שְׂעִיר־עִזִּ֥ים אֶחָ֖ד לְחַטָּֽאת׃ 23 וּלְזֶ֣בַח
הַשְּׁלָמִים֮ בָּקָ֣ר שְׁנַ֒יִם֒ אֵילִ֣ם חֲמִשָּׁ֗ה
עַתֻּדִ֣ים חֲמִשָּׁ֔ה כְּבָשִׂ֥ים בְּנֵי־שָׁנָ֖ה חֲמִשָּׁ֑ה
זֶ֛ה קָרְבַּ֥ן נְתַנְאֵ֖ל בֶּן־צוּעָֽר׃ פ
24 בַּיּוֹם֙ הַשְּׁלִישִׁ֔י נָשִׂ֖יא לִבְנֵ֣י זְבוּלֻ֑ן אֱלִיאָ֖ב
בֶּן־חֵלֹֽן׃ 25 קָרְבָּנ֞וֹ קַֽעֲרַת־כֶּ֣סֶף אַחַ֗ת
שְׁלֹשִׁ֣ים וּמֵאָה֮ מִשְׁקָלָהּ֒ מִזְרָ֣ק אֶחָד֙ כֶּ֔סֶף
שִׁבְעִ֥ים שֶׁ֖קֶל בְּשֶׁ֣קֶל הַקֹּ֑דֶשׁ שְׁנֵיהֶ֣ם ׀
מְלֵאִ֗ים סֹ֛לֶת בְּלוּלָ֥ה בַשֶּׁ֖מֶן לְמִנְחָֽה׃
26 כַּ֥ף אַחַ֛ת עֲשָׂרָ֥ה זָהָ֖ב מְלֵאָ֥ה קְטֹֽרֶת׃
27 פַּ֣ר אֶחָ֞ד בֶּן־בָּקָ֗ר אַ֧יִל אֶחָ֛ד כֶּֽבֶשׂ־אֶחָ֥ד
בֶּן־שְׁנָת֖וֹ לְעֹלָֽה׃ 28 שְׂעִיר־עִזִּ֥ים אֶחָ֖ד
לְחַטָּֽאת׃ 29 וּלְזֶ֣בַח הַשְּׁלָמִים֮ בָּקָ֣ר שְׁנַ֒יִם֒
אֵילִ֤ם חֲמִשָּׁה֙ עַתֻּדִ֣ים חֲמִשָּׁ֔ה כְּבָשִׂ֥ים

14. 10 shekels Although the ladle was made of gold, its weight was computed in terms of standard silver shekels.

incense For use on the altar of incense (see Exod. 30:7).

15. bull of the herd A domestic bull. Wild animals are barred from the altar.

16. one goat A domestic goat.

17. oxen Better: bulls. Castrated animals are forbidden in sacrifice (Lev. 22:20).

ling lambs. That was the offering of Eliab son of Helon.

30 On the fourth day, it was the chieftain of the Reubenites, Elizur son of Shedeur. 31 His offering: one silver bowl weighing 130 shekels and one silver basin of 70 shekels by the sanctuary weight, both filled with choice flour with oil mixed in, for a grain offering; 32 one gold ladle of 10 shekels, filled with incense; 33 one bull of the herd, one ram, and one lamb in its first year, for a burnt offering; 34 one goat for a purification offering; 35 and for his sacrifice of well-being: two oxen, five rams, five he-goats, and five yearling lambs. That was the offering of Elizur son of Shedeur.

36 On the fifth day, it was the chieftain of the Simeonites, Shelumiel son of Zurishaddai. 37 His offering: one silver bowl weighing 130 shekels and one silver basin of 70 shekels by the sanctuary weight, both filled with choice flour with oil mixed in, for a grain offering; 38 one gold ladle of 10 shekels, filled with incense; 39 one bull of the herd, one ram, and one lamb in its first year, for a burnt offering; 40 one goat for a purification offering; 41 and for his sacrifice of well-being: two oxen, five rams, five he-goats, and five yearling lambs. That was the offering of Shelumiel son of Zurishaddai.

42 On the sixth day, it was the chieftain of the Gadites, Eliasaph son of Deuel. 43 His offering: one silver bowl weighing 130 shekels and one silver basin of 70 shekels by the sanctuary weight, both filled with choice flour with oil mixed in, for a grain offering; 44 one gold ladle of 10 shekels, filled with incense; 45 one bull of the herd, one ram, and one lamb in its first year, for a burnt offering; 46 one goat for a purification offering; 47 and for his sacrifice of well-being:

בְּנֵי־שָׁנָה חֲמִשָּׁה זֶה קָרְבַּן אֱלִיאָב בֶּן־
חֵלֹן: פ
30 בַּיּוֹם הָרְבִיעִי נָשִׂיא לִבְנֵי רְאוּבֵן
אֱלִיצוּר בֶּן־שְׁדֵיאוּר: 31 קָרְבָּנוֹ קַעֲרַת־
כֶּסֶף אַחַת שְׁלֹשִׁים וּמֵאָה מִשְׁקָלָהּ מִזְרָק
אֶחָד כֶּסֶף שִׁבְעִים שֶׁקֶל בְּשֶׁקֶל הַקֹּדֶשׁ
שְׁנֵיהֶם ׀ מְלֵאִים סֹלֶת בְּלוּלָה בַשֶּׁמֶן
לְמִנְחָה: 32 כַּף אַחַת עֲשָׂרָה זָהָב מְלֵאָה
קְטֹרֶת 33 פַּר אֶחָד בֶּן־בָּקָר אַיִל אֶחָד
כֶּבֶשׂ־אֶחָד בֶּן־שְׁנָתוֹ לְעֹלָה: 34 שְׂעִיר־
עִזִּים אֶחָד לְחַטָּאת: 35 וּלְזֶבַח הַשְּׁלָמִים
בָּקָר שְׁנַיִם אֵילִם חֲמִשָּׁה עַתֻּדִים חֲמִשָּׁה
כְּבָשִׂים בְּנֵי־שָׁנָה חֲמִשָּׁה זֶה קָרְבַּן
אֱלִיצוּר בֶּן־שְׁדֵיאוּר: פ
36 בַּיּוֹם הַחֲמִישִׁי נָשִׂיא לִבְנֵי שִׁמְעוֹן
שְׁלֻמִיאֵל בֶּן־צוּרִישַׁדָּי: 37 קָרְבָּנוֹ קַעֲרַת־
כֶּסֶף אַחַת שְׁלֹשִׁים וּמֵאָה מִשְׁקָלָהּ מִזְרָק
אֶחָד כֶּסֶף שִׁבְעִים שֶׁקֶל בְּשֶׁקֶל הַקֹּדֶשׁ
שְׁנֵיהֶם ׀ מְלֵאִים סֹלֶת בְּלוּלָה בַשֶּׁמֶן
לְמִנְחָה: 38 כַּף אַחַת עֲשָׂרָה זָהָב מְלֵאָה
קְטֹרֶת: 39 פַּר אֶחָד בֶּן־בָּקָר אַיִל אֶחָד
כֶּבֶשׂ־אֶחָד בֶּן־שְׁנָתוֹ לְעֹלָה: 40 שְׂעִיר־
עִזִּים אֶחָד לְחַטָּאת 41 וּלְזֶבַח הַשְּׁלָמִים
בָּקָר שְׁנַיִם אֵילִם חֲמִשָּׁה עַתֻּדִים חֲמִשָּׁה
כְּבָשִׂים בְּנֵי־שָׁנָה חֲמִשָּׁה זֶה קָרְבַּן
שְׁלֻמִיאֵל בֶּן־צוּרִישַׁדָּי: פ
ששי 42 בַּיּוֹם הַשִּׁשִּׁי נָשִׂיא לִבְנֵי גָד אֶלְיָסָף
בֶּן־דְּעוּאֵל: 43 קָרְבָּנוֹ קַעֲרַת־כֶּסֶף אַחַת
שְׁלֹשִׁים וּמֵאָה מִשְׁקָלָהּ מִזְרָק אֶחָד כֶּסֶף
שִׁבְעִים שֶׁקֶל בְּשֶׁקֶל הַקֹּדֶשׁ שְׁנֵיהֶם ׀
מְלֵאִים סֹלֶת בְּלוּלָה בַשֶּׁמֶן לְמִנְחָה:
44 כַּף אַחַת עֲשָׂרָה זָהָב מְלֵאָה קְטֹרֶת:
45 פַּר אֶחָד בֶּן־בָּקָר אַיִל אֶחָד כֶּבֶשׂ־אֶחָד
בֶּן־שְׁנָתוֹ לְעֹלָה: 46 שְׂעִיר־עִזִּים אֶחָד
לְחַטָּאת: 47 וּלְזֶבַח הַשְּׁלָמִים בָּקָר שְׁנַיִם

two oxen, five rams, five he-goats, and five yearling lambs. That was the offering of Eliasaph son
of Deuel.

48On the seventh day, it was the chieftain of
the Ephraimites, Elishama son of Ammihud.
49His offering: one silver bowl weighing 130
shekels and one silver basin of 70 shekels by the
sanctuary weight, both filled with choice flour
with oil mixed in, for a grain offering; 50one gold
ladle of 10 shekels, filled with incense; 51one bull
of the herd, one ram, and one lamb in its first
year, for a burnt offering; 52one goat for a purification offering; 53and for his sacrifice of
well-being: two oxen, five rams, five he-goats,
and five yearling lambs. That was the offering
of Elishama son of Ammihud.

54On the eighth day, it was the chieftain of
the Manassites, Gamaliel son of Pedahzur. 55His
offering: one silver bowl weighing 130 shekels
and one silver basin of 70 shekels by the sanctuary weight, both filled with choice flour with
oil mixed in, for a grain offering; 56one gold ladle
of 10 shekels, filled with incense; 57one bull of
the herd, one ram, and one lamb in its first year,
for a burnt offering; 58one goat for a purification
offering; 59and for his sacrifice of well-being:
two oxen, five rams, five he-goats, and five yearling lambs. That was the offering of Gamaliel
son of Pedahzur.

60On the ninth day, it was the chieftain of the
Benjaminites, Abidan son of Gideoni. 61His
offering: one silver bowl weighing 130 shekels
and one silver basin of 70 shekels by the sanctuary weight, both filled with choice flour with
oil mixed in, for a grain offering; 62one gold ladle
of 10 shekels, filled with incense; 63one bull of
the herd, one ram, and one lamb in its first year,
for a burnt offering; 64one goat for a purification

אֵילִם חֲמִשָּׁה עַתֻּדִים חֲמִשָּׁה כְּבָשִׂים
בְּנֵי־שָׁנָה חֲמִשָּׁה זֶה קׇרְבַּן אֶלְיָסָף בֶּן־
דְּעוּאֵל׃ פ

48 בַּיּוֹם הַשְּׁבִיעִי נָשִׂיא לִבְנֵי אֶפְרָיִם
אֱלִישָׁמָע בֶּן־עַמִּיהוּד׃ 49 קׇרְבָּנוֹ קַעֲרַת־
כֶּסֶף אַחַת שְׁלֹשִׁים וּמֵאָה מִשְׁקָלָהּ מִזְרָק
אֶחָד כֶּסֶף שִׁבְעִים שֶׁקֶל בְּשֶׁקֶל הַקֹּדֶשׁ
שְׁנֵיהֶם ׀ מְלֵאִים סֹלֶת בְּלוּלָה בַשֶּׁמֶן
לְמִנְחָה׃ 50 כַּף אַחַת עֲשָׂרָה זָהָב מְלֵאָה
קְטֹרֶת׃ 51 פַּר אֶחָד בֶּן־בָּקָר אַיִל אֶחָד
כֶּבֶשׂ־אֶחָד בֶּן־שְׁנָתוֹ לְעֹלָה׃ 52 שְׂעִיר־
עִזִּים אֶחָד לְחַטָּאת׃ 53 וּלְזֶבַח הַשְּׁלָמִים
בָּקָר שְׁנַיִם אֵילִם חֲמִשָּׁה עַתֻּדִים חֲמִשָּׁה
כְּבָשִׂים בְּנֵי־שָׁנָה חֲמִשָּׁה זֶה קׇרְבַּן
אֱלִישָׁמָע בֶּן־עַמִּיהוּד׃ פ

54 בַּיּוֹם הַשְּׁמִינִי נָשִׂיא לִבְנֵי מְנַשֶּׁה
גַּמְלִיאֵל בֶּן־פְּדָה־צוּר׃ 55 קׇרְבָּנוֹ קַעֲרַת־
כֶּסֶף אַחַת שְׁלֹשִׁים וּמֵאָה מִשְׁקָלָהּ מִזְרָק
אֶחָד כֶּסֶף שִׁבְעִים שֶׁקֶל בְּשֶׁקֶל הַקֹּדֶשׁ
שְׁנֵיהֶם ׀ מְלֵאִים סֹלֶת בְּלוּלָה בַשֶּׁמֶן
לְמִנְחָה׃ 56 כַּף אַחַת עֲשָׂרָה זָהָב מְלֵאָה
קְטֹרֶת׃ 57 פַּר אֶחָד בֶּן־בָּקָר אַיִל אֶחָד
כֶּבֶשׂ־אֶחָד בֶּן־שְׁנָתוֹ לְעֹלָה׃ 58 שְׂעִיר־
עִזִּים אֶחָד לְחַטָּאת׃ 59 וּלְזֶבַח הַשְּׁלָמִים
בָּקָר שְׁנַיִם אֵילִם חֲמִשָּׁה עַתֻּדִים חֲמִשָּׁה
כְּבָשִׂים בְּנֵי־שָׁנָה חֲמִשָּׁה זֶה קׇרְבַּן
גַּמְלִיאֵל בֶּן־פְּדָהצוּר׃ פ

60 בַּיּוֹם הַתְּשִׁיעִי נָשִׂיא לִבְנֵי בִנְיָמִן אֲבִידָן
בֶּן־גִּדְעֹנִי׃ 61 קׇרְבָּנוֹ קַעֲרַת־כֶּסֶף אַחַת
שְׁלֹשִׁים וּמֵאָה מִשְׁקָלָהּ מִזְרָק אֶחָד כֶּסֶף
שִׁבְעִים שֶׁקֶל בְּשֶׁקֶל הַקֹּדֶשׁ שְׁנֵיהֶם ׀
מְלֵאִים סֹלֶת בְּלוּלָה בַשֶּׁמֶן לְמִנְחָה׃
62 כַּף אַחַת עֲשָׂרָה זָהָב מְלֵאָה קְטֹרֶת׃
63 פַּר אֶחָד בֶּן־בָּקָר אַיִל אֶחָד כֶּבֶשׂ־אֶחָד
בֶּן־שְׁנָתוֹ לְעֹלָה׃ 64 שְׂעִיר־עִזִּים אֶחָד

offering; 65and for his sacrifice of well-being: two oxen, five rams, five he-goats, and five yearling lambs. That was the offering of Abidan son of Gideoni.

66On the tenth day, it was the chieftain of the Danites, Ahiezer son of Ammishaddai. 67His offering: one silver bowl weighing 130 shekels and one silver basin of 70 shekels by the sanctuary weight, both filled with choice flour with oil mixed in, for a grain offering; 68one gold ladle of 10 shekels, filled with incense; 69one bull of the herd, one ram, and one lamb in its first year, for a burnt offering; 70one goat for a purification offering; 71and for his sacrifice of well-being: two oxen, five rams, five he-goats, and five yearling lambs. That was the offering of Ahiezer son of Ammishaddai.

72On the eleventh day, it was the chieftain of the Asherites, Pagiel son of Ochran. 73His offering: one silver bowl weighing 130 shekels and one silver basin of 70 shekels by the sanctuary weight, both filled with choice flour with oil mixed in, for a grain offering; 74one gold ladle of 10 shekels, filled with incense; 75one bull of the herd, one ram, and one lamb in its first year, for a burnt offering; 76one goat for a purification offering; 77and for his sacrifice of well-being: two oxen, five rams, five he-goats, and five yearling lambs. That was the offering of Pagiel son of Ochran.

78On the twelfth day, it was the chieftain of the Naphtalites, Ahira son of Enan. 79His offering: one silver bowl weighing 130 shekels and one silver basin of 70 shekels by the sanctuary weight, both filled with choice flour with oil mixed in, for a grain offering; 80one gold ladle of 10 shekels, filled with incense; 81one bull of

65 וּלְזֶ֨בַח הַשְּׁלָמִים֮ בָּקָ֣ר שְׁנַ֒יִם֒ אֵילִ֤ם חֲמִשָּׁה֙ עַתֻּדִ֣ים חֲמִשָּׁ֔ה כְּבָשִׂ֥ים בְּנֵֽי־שָׁנָ֖ה חֲמִשָּׁ֑ה זֶ֛ה קָרְבַּ֥ן אֲבִידָ֖ן בֶּן־גִּדְעֹנִֽי: פ

66 בַּיּוֹם֙ הָעֲשִׂירִ֔י נָשִׂ֖יא לִבְנֵ֣י דָ֑ן אֲחִיעֶ֖זֶר בֶּן־עַמִּֽישַׁדָּֽי: 67 קָרְבָּנ֞וֹ קַֽעֲרַת־כֶּ֣סֶף אַחַ֗ת שְׁלֹשִׁ֣ים וּמֵאָה֮ מִשְׁקָלָהּ֒ מִזְרָ֤ק אֶחָד֙ כֶּ֔סֶף שִׁבְעִ֥ים שֶׁ֖קֶל בְּשֶׁ֣קֶל הַקֹּ֑דֶשׁ שְׁנֵיהֶ֣ם ׀ מְלֵאִ֗ים סֹ֛לֶת בְּלוּלָ֥ה בַשֶּׁ֖מֶן לְמִנְחָֽה: 68 כַּ֥ף אַחַ֛ת עֲשָׂרָ֥ה זָהָ֖ב מְלֵאָ֥ה קְטֹֽרֶת: 69 פַּ֣ר אֶחָ֞ד בֶּן־בָּקָ֗ר אַ֧יִל אֶחָ֛ד כֶּֽבֶשׂ־אֶחָ֥ד בֶּן־שְׁנָת֖וֹ לְעֹלָֽה: 70 שְׂעִיר־עִזִּ֥ים אֶחָ֖ד לְחַטָּֽאת: 71 וּלְזֶ֨בַח הַשְּׁלָמִים֮ בָּקָ֣ר שְׁנַ֒יִם֒ אֵילִ֤ם חֲמִשָּׁה֙ עַתֻּדִ֣ים חֲמִשָּׁ֔ה כְּבָשִׂ֥ים בְּנֵֽי־שָׁנָ֖ה חֲמִשָּׁ֑ה זֶ֛ה קָרְבַּ֥ן אֲחִיעֶ֖זֶר בֶּן־עַמִּֽישַׁדָּֽי: פ

72 שביעי בְּיוֹם֙ עַשְׁתֵּ֣י עָשָׂ֣ר י֔וֹם נָשִׂ֖יא לִבְנֵ֣י אָשֵׁ֑ר פַּגְעִיאֵ֖ל בֶּן־עָכְרָֽן: 73 קָרְבָּנ֞וֹ קַֽעֲרַת־כֶּ֣סֶף אַחַ֗ת שְׁלֹשִׁ֣ים וּמֵאָה֮ מִשְׁקָלָהּ֒ מִזְרָ֤ק אֶחָד֙ כֶּ֔סֶף שִׁבְעִ֥ים שֶׁ֖קֶל בְּשֶׁ֣קֶל הַקֹּ֑דֶשׁ שְׁנֵיהֶ֣ם ׀ מְלֵאִ֗ים סֹ֛לֶת בְּלוּלָ֥ה בַשֶּׁ֖מֶן לְמִנְחָֽה: 74 כַּ֥ף אַחַ֛ת עֲשָׂרָ֥ה זָהָ֖ב מְלֵאָ֥ה קְטֹֽרֶת: 75 פַּ֣ר אֶחָ֞ד בֶּן־בָּקָ֗ר אַ֧יִל אֶחָ֛ד כֶּֽבֶשׂ־אֶחָ֥ד בֶּן־שְׁנָת֖וֹ לְעֹלָֽה: 76 שְׂעִיר־עִזִּ֥ים אֶחָ֖ד לְחַטָּֽאת: 77 וּלְזֶ֨בַח הַשְּׁלָמִים֮ בָּקָ֣ר שְׁנַ֒יִם֒ אֵילִ֤ם חֲמִשָּׁה֙ עַתֻּדִ֣ים חֲמִשָּׁ֔ה כְּבָשִׂ֥ים בְּנֵֽי־שָׁנָ֖ה חֲמִשָּׁ֑ה זֶ֛ה קָרְבַּ֥ן פַּגְעִיאֵ֖ל בֶּן־עָכְרָֽן: פ

78 בְּיוֹם֙ שְׁנֵ֣ים עָשָׂ֣ר י֔וֹם נָשִׂ֖יא לִבְנֵ֣י נַפְתָּלִ֑י אֲחִירַ֖ע בֶּן־עֵינָֽן: 79 קָרְבָּנ֞וֹ קַֽעֲרַת־כֶּ֣סֶף אַחַ֗ת שְׁלֹשִׁ֣ים וּמֵאָה֮ מִשְׁקָלָהּ֒ מִזְרָ֤ק אֶחָד֙ כֶּ֔סֶף שִׁבְעִ֥ים שֶׁ֖קֶל בְּשֶׁ֣קֶל הַקֹּ֑דֶשׁ שְׁנֵיהֶ֣ם ׀ מְלֵאִ֗ים סֹ֛לֶת בְּלוּלָ֥ה בַשֶּׁ֖מֶן לְמִנְחָֽה: 80 כַּ֥ף אַחַ֛ת עֲשָׂרָ֥ה זָהָ֖ב מְלֵאָ֥ה קְטֹֽרֶת: 81 פַּ֣ר אֶחָ֞ד בֶּן־בָּקָ֗ר אַ֧יִל אֶחָ֛ד כֶּֽבֶשׂ־אֶחָ֥ד

the herd, one ram, and one lamb in its first year, for a burnt offering; 82 one goat for a purification offering; 83 and for his sacrifice of well-being: two oxen, five rams, five he-goats, and five yearling lambs. That was the offering of Ahira son of Enan.

84 This was the dedication offering for the altar from the chieftains of Israel upon its being anointed: silver bowls, 12; silver basins, 12; gold ladles, 12. 85 Silver per bowl, 130; per basin, 70. Total silver of vessels, 2,400 sanctuary shekels. 86 The 12 gold ladles filled with incense—10 sanctuary shekels per ladle—total gold of the ladles, 120.

87 Total of herd animals for burnt offerings, 12 bulls; of rams, 12; of yearling lambs, 12—with their proper grain offerings; of goats for purification offerings, 12. 88 Total of herd animals for sacrifices of well-being, 24 bulls; of rams, 60; of he-goats, 60; of yearling lambs, 60. That was the dedication offering for the altar after its anointing.

89 When Moses went into the Tent of Meeting to speak with Him, he would hear the Voice addressing him from above the cover that was on top of the Ark of the Pact between the two cherubim; thus He spoke to him.

בֶּן־שְׁנָת֖וֹ לְעֹלָֽה׃ 82 שְׂעִיר־עִזִּ֥ים אֶחָ֖ד
לְחַטָּֽאת׃ 83 וּלְזֶ֣בַח הַשְּׁלָמִים֮ בָּקָ֣ר שְׁנַ֒יִם֒
אֵילִ֤ם חֲמִשָּׁה֙ עַתֻּדִ֣ים חֲמִשָּׁ֔ה כְּבָשִׂ֥ים
בְּנֵי־שָׁנָ֖ה חֲמִשָּׁ֑ה זֶ֛ה קָרְבַּ֥ן אֲחִירַ֖ע בֶּן־
עֵינָֽן׃ פ

84 זֹ֣את ׀ חֲנֻכַּ֣ת הַמִּזְבֵּ֗חַ בְּיוֹם֙ הִמָּשַׁ֣ח אֹת֔וֹ
מֵאֵ֖ת נְשִׂיאֵ֣י יִשְׂרָאֵ֑ל קַעֲרֹ֨ת כֶּ֜סֶף שְׁתֵּ֣ים
עֶשְׂרֵ֗ה מִֽזְרְקֵי־כֶ֙סֶף֙ שְׁנֵ֣ים עָשָׂ֔ר כַּפּ֥וֹת זָהָ֖ב
שְׁתֵּ֥ים עֶשְׂרֵֽה׃ 85 שְׁלֹשִׁ֣ים וּמֵאָ֗ה הַקְּעָרָ֤ה
הָֽאַחַת֙ כֶּ֔סֶף וְשִׁבְעִ֖ים הַמִּזְרָ֣ק הָאֶחָ֑ד כֹּ֚ל
כֶּ֣סֶף הַכֵּלִ֔ים אַלְפַּ֥יִם וְאַרְבַּע־מֵא֖וֹת בְּשֶׁ֥קֶל
הַקֹּֽדֶשׁ׃ 86 כַּפּ֨וֹת זָהָ֤ב שְׁתֵּים־עֶשְׂרֵה֙
מְלֵאֹ֣ת קְטֹ֔רֶת עֲשָׂרָ֧ה עֲשָׂרָ֛ה הַכַּ֖ף בְּשֶׁ֣קֶל
הַקֹּ֑דֶשׁ כָּל־זְהַ֥ב הַכַּפּ֖וֹת עֶשְׂרִ֥ים וּמֵאָֽה׃
טיר 87 כָּל־הַבָּקָ֨ר לָעֹלָ֜ה שְׁנֵ֧ים עָשָׂ֣ר פָּרִ֗ים
אֵילִ֣ם שְׁנֵים־עָשָׂ֗ר כְּבָשִׂ֧ים בְּנֵי־שָׁנָ֛ה שְׁנֵ֥ים
עָשָׂ֖ר וּמִנְחָתָ֑ם וּשְׂעִירֵ֥י עִזִּ֛ים שְׁנֵ֥ים עָשָׂ֖ר
לְחַטָּֽאת׃ 88 וְכֹ֞ל בְּקַ֣ר ׀ זֶ֣בַח הַשְּׁלָמִ֗ים
עֶשְׂרִ֣ים וְאַרְבָּעָה֮ פָּרִים֒ אֵילִ֣ם שִׁשִּׁים֩
עַתֻּדִ֣ים שִׁשִּׁ֔ים כְּבָשִׂ֥ים בְּנֵי־שָׁנָ֖ה שִׁשִּׁ֑ים
זֹ֚את חֲנֻכַּ֣ת הַמִּזְבֵּ֔חַ אַחֲרֵ֖י הִמָּשַׁ֥ח אֹתֽוֹ׃

89 וּבְבֹ֨א מֹשֶׁ֜ה אֶל־אֹ֣הֶל מוֹעֵד֮ לְדַבֵּ֣ר אִתּוֹ֒
וַיִּשְׁמַ֨ע אֶת־הַקּ֜וֹל מִדַּבֵּ֣ר אֵלָ֗יו מֵעַ֤ל
הַכַּפֹּ֙רֶת֙ אֲשֶׁר֙ עַל־אֲרֹ֣ן הָעֵדֻ֔ת מִבֵּ֖ין שְׁנֵ֣י
הַכְּרֻבִ֑ים וַיְדַבֵּ֖ר אֵלָֽיו׃ פ

84. dedication offering The initiation offering.

89. The Ark was conceived as God's footstool or the pedestal of His throne. God delivered commands to Moses while he stood alone in the outer room of the Tent, separated from the Ark "throne" by the screening veil. This fulfilled God's promise: "I will [speak] to you from above the cover, from between the two cherubim that are on top of the Ark of the Pact" (Exod. 25:22).

Ark of the Pact "The Pact," with the definite article (*ha-edut*), can mean only the two tablets of the Decalogue, which were deposited in the Ark (Exod. 25:10–16).

הפטרת נשא

HAFTARAH FOR NASO

JUDGES 13:2–25

This *haftarah* is drawn from the beginning of the cycle of Samson stories (Judg. 13–16). The prophecy announcing his birth states that he will be "the first to deliver Israel from the Philistines" (13:5). His travail will anticipate the battles to be waged against the Philistines into the early days of the monarchy, leading to the death of King Saul and to the glory of King David.

This opening chapter of the cycle focuses on the birth announcement and on the birth itself. The Sages spotlighted Samson's birth by omitting the first verse, which reports the Philistines' role as a means of divine punishment for Israel's sins. Such editing separated the birth scene from its historical setting, underscoring the conditions prescribed for the mother during pregnancy.

There is no account of any prayer for a child uttered by Manoah or by his wife. The divine messenger appears with the suddenness of unexpected grace. His prediction has the qualities of an oracle, like that from the divine messengers to Abraham (Gen. 18) who announced that the barren Sarah soon would conceive and bear a son.

RELATION OF THE *HAFTARAH* TO THE *PARASHAH*

The *haftarah* and the *parashah* bring together two biblical traditions about the nazirite. The Torah (Num. 6) formally delineates the rules and rituals for anyone, male or female, who enters the consecrated status of a nazirite through a vow. The *parashah* states nothing about lifetime vows or vows affecting others (including unborn children). This silence rings "loud and clear" when the *parashah* is compared with the *haftarah,* a popular narrative about a person consecrated from conception to be a nazirite for life. Indeed, the mother-to-be during pregnancy already observes some of the prescriptions ritually incumbent on the nazirite-to-be. (The child's obligations in this regard are implied, not explicitly stated.) Furthermore, the mother has not entered this state through any vow of her own.

The language and ideals of the *haftarah* are influenced by other biblical traditions bearing on the status of nazirite. The woman is instructed "to let no razor touch his head, for the boy is to be a nazirite to God" (Judg. 13:5). The formulation recalls the rule in Numbers in which a person consecrated as "nazirite of the LORD" must let "no razor . . . touch his head" (6:5). Both texts deal with a comparable ritual status in which the hair of one's head may not be shorn while the consecration is in effect. Eventually the shearing of Samson's hair through the wiles of Delilah (Judg. 16) will remove the hero's sacred character, reflected in his loss of power.

The *parashah* and the *haftarah* juxtapose two types of actions and devotion. One of them is marked by the purposeful decision to abstain from intoxicants and impurities, and thus to approximate priestly sanctity (see Sifrei Num. 26). Devotion to God is expressed through self-limitation and restraint, perhaps rebalancing one's spiritual life (see MT De·ot 3:1). The nazirite in the *parashah* has deliberately chosen to serve God and must sustain that decision through prescribed regulations for a limited period of time.

The other approach embodies the force of destiny that marks the self with unchosen obligations. The assumption of a sacred status will infuse Samson with powers that transcend ordinary limits. Accordingly, Samson, who has not chosen his lifelong nazirite status, will devote his transformed and consecrated condition to self-centered and isolated acts of revenge.

The *parashah* thus shows how the natural self may become transformed (for a time), fully consecrated "to the LORD," and may serve as a model

for many others. In contradistinction, the *haftarah* introduces an all-too-human self in whom the "spirit" of supernatural energy reverberates. Samson's private passions will fuel and direct his service to the community. Only derivatively and accidentally will they benefit others.

13 2There was a certain man from Zorah,
of the stock of Dan, whose name was Manoah.
His wife was barren and had borne no children.
3An angel of the LORD appeared to the woman
and said to her, "You are barren and have borne
no children; but you shall conceive and bear a
son. 4Now be careful not to drink wine or other
intoxicant, or to eat anything impure. 5For you
are going to conceive and bear a son; let no razor
touch his head, for the boy is to be a nazirite
to God from the womb on. He shall be the first
to deliver Israel from the Philistines."
6The woman went and told her husband, "A
man of God came to me; he looked like an angel
of God, very frightening. I did not ask him
where he was from, nor did he tell me his name.
7He said to me, 'You are going to conceive and
bear a son. Drink no wine or other intoxicant,
and eat nothing impure, for the boy is to be a
nazirite to God from the womb to the day of
his death!'"
8Manoah pleaded with the LORD. "Oh, my
Lord!" he said, "please let the man of God that
You sent come to us again, and let him instruct
us how to act with the child that is to be born."
9God heeded Manoah's plea, and the angel of

יג 2 וַיְהִי֩ אִ֨ישׁ אֶחָ֧ד מִצָּרְעָ֛ה מִמִּשְׁפַּ֥חַת
הַדָּנִ֖י וּשְׁמ֣וֹ מָנ֑וֹחַ וְאִשְׁתּ֥וֹ עֲקָרָ֖ה וְלֹ֥א
יָלָֽדָה׃ 3 וַיֵּרָ֥א מַלְאַךְ־יְהוָ֖ה אֶל־הָאִשָּׁ֑ה
וַיֹּ֣אמֶר אֵלֶ֗יהָ הִנֵּה־נָ֤א אַתְּ־עֲקָרָה֙ וְלֹ֣א
יָלַ֔דְתְּ וְהָרִ֖ית וְיָלַ֥דְתְּ בֵּֽן׃ 4 וְעַתָּה֙ הִשָּׁ֣מְרִי
נָ֔א וְאַל־תִּשְׁתִּ֖י יַ֣יִן וְשֵׁכָ֑ר וְאַל־תֹּאכְלִ֖י
כָּל־טָמֵֽא׃ 5 כִּי֩ הִנָּ֨ךְ הָרָ֜ה וְיֹלַ֣דְתְּ בֵּ֗ן וּמוֹרָה֙
לֹא־יַעֲלֶ֣ה עַל־רֹאשׁ֔וֹ כִּֽי־נְזִ֧יר אֱלֹהִ֛ים
יִהְיֶ֥ה הַנַּ֖עַר מִן־הַבָּ֑טֶן וְה֗וּא יָחֵ֛ל לְהוֹשִׁ֥יעַ
אֶת־יִשְׂרָאֵ֖ל מִיַּ֥ד פְּלִשְׁתִּֽים׃
6 וַתָּבֹ֣א הָֽאִשָּׁ֗ה וַתֹּ֣אמֶר לְאִישָׁהּ֮ לֵאמֹר֒
אִ֤ישׁ הָֽאֱלֹהִים֙ בָּ֣א אֵלַ֔י וּמַרְאֵ֕הוּ כְּמַרְאֵ֛ה
מַלְאַ֥ךְ הָאֱלֹהִ֖ים נוֹרָ֣א מְאֹ֑ד וְלֹ֤א
שְׁאִלְתִּ֙יהוּ֙ אֵֽי־מִזֶּ֣ה ה֔וּא וְאֶת־שְׁמ֖וֹ לֹֽא־
הִגִּ֥יד לִֽי׃ 7 וַיֹּ֣אמֶר לִ֔י הִנָּ֥ךְ הָרָ֖ה וְיֹלַ֣דְתְּ
בֵּ֑ן וְעַתָּ֞ה אַל־תִּשְׁתִּ֣י ׀ יַ֣יִן וְשֵׁכָ֗ר וְאַל־
תֹּֽאכְלִי֙ כָּל־טֻמְאָ֔ה כִּֽי־נְזִ֤יר אֱלֹהִים֙ יִהְיֶ֣ה
הַנַּ֔עַר מִן־הַבֶּ֖טֶן עַד־י֥וֹם מוֹתֽוֹ׃ פ
8 וַיֶּעְתַּ֥ר מָנ֛וֹחַ אֶל־יְהוָ֖ה וַיֹּאמַ֑ר בִּ֣י אֲדוֹנָ֗י
אִ֣ישׁ הָאֱלֹהִ֞ים אֲשֶׁ֣ר שָׁלַ֗חְתָּ יָבוֹא־נָ֥א עוֹד֙
אֵלֵ֔ינוּ וְיוֹרֵ֕נוּ מַֽה־נַּעֲשֶׂ֖ה לַנַּ֥עַר הַיּוּלָּֽד׃
9 וַיִּשְׁמַ֥ע הָאֱלֹהִ֖ים בְּק֣וֹל מָנ֑וֹחַ וַיָּבֹ֞א

Judges 13:2. of the stock of Dan This note seems to reflect the tribe of Dan's early settlement along the southwest coast, near the Philistine territories. The Danites had difficulty securing land on the maritime plain, however, and were driven back into the highlands by the Amorites (Judg. 1:34). Near the end of the period of the chieftains ("Judges"), much of the tribe settled in the northeastern area of the western tribes (Judg. 18).

3. angel Hebrew: *mal·akh* (messenger). This designation will also appear in verses 13, 15–18, and 20–21. Because the being has a human appearance, Manoah will "not know that he was an angel of the LORD" (v. 16). Manoah will request a repeat visit from "the man of God" (v. 8) to verify that this oracle is of divine origin.

7. eat nothing impure This rule is not precise. It may extend the prohibition against intoxicants to include ritually impure food or drink, or it may embrace all that the Torah prohibits a nazirite to ingest (Num. 6:2–3; see Radak). It is significant that the instruction is given to the woman who will conceive and bear the nazirite. Presumably the concern is to prevent his desacralization in utero.

God came to the woman again. She was sitting in the field and her husband Manoah was not with her. 10The woman ran in haste to tell her husband. She said to him, "The man who came to me before has just appeared to me." 11Manoah promptly followed his wife. He came to the man and asked him: "Are you the man who spoke to my wife?" "Yes," he answered. 12Then Manoah said, "May your words soon come true! What rules shall be observed for the boy?" 13The angel of the LORD said to Manoah, "The woman must abstain from all the things against which I warned her. 14She must not eat anything that comes from the grapevine, or drink wine or other intoxicant, or eat anything impure. She must observe all that I commanded her."

15Manoah said to the angel of the LORD, "Let us detain you and prepare a kid for you." 16But the angel of the LORD said to Manoah, "If you detain me, I shall not eat your food; and if you present a burnt offering, offer it to LORD."—For Manoah did not know that he was an angel of the LORD. 17So Manoah said to the angel of the LORD, "What is your name? We should like to honor you when your words come true." 18The angel said to him, "You must not ask for my name; it is unknowable!"

19Manoah took the kid and the grain offering and offered them up on the rock to the LORD; and a marvelous thing happened while Manoah and his wife looked on. 20As the flames leaped up from the altar toward the sky, the angel of the LORD ascended in the flames of the altar, while Manoah and his wife looked on; and they flung themselves on their faces to the ground.—21The angel of the LORD never appeared again to Manoah and his wife.—Manoah then realized that it had been an angel of the LORD. 22And Manoah said to his wife, "We shall surely die, for we have seen a divine being."

מַלְאַךְ הָאֱלֹהִים עוֹד אֶל־הָאִשָּׁה וְהִיא
יוֹשֶׁבֶת בַּשָּׂדֶה וּמָנוֹחַ אִישָׁהּ אֵין עִמָּהּ׃
10 וַתְּמַהֵר הָאִשָּׁה וַתָּרָץ וַתַּגֵּד לְאִישָׁהּ
וַתֹּאמֶר אֵלָיו הִנֵּה נִרְאָה אֵלַי הָאִישׁ
אֲשֶׁר־בָּא בַיּוֹם אֵלָי׃ 11 וַיָּקָם וַיֵּלֶךְ מָנוֹחַ
אַחֲרֵי אִשְׁתּוֹ וַיָּבֹא אֶל־הָאִישׁ וַיֹּאמֶר לוֹ
הַאַתָּה הָאִישׁ אֲשֶׁר־דִּבַּרְתָּ אֶל־הָאִשָּׁה
וַיֹּאמֶר אָנִי׃ 12 וַיֹּאמֶר מָנוֹחַ עַתָּה יָבֹא
דְבָרֶיךָ מַה־יִּהְיֶה מִשְׁפַּט־הַנַּעַר וּמַעֲשֵׂהוּ׃
13 וַיֹּאמֶר מַלְאַךְ יְהוָה אֶל־מָנוֹחַ מִכֹּל
אֲשֶׁר־אָמַרְתִּי אֶל־הָאִשָּׁה תִּשָּׁמֵר׃ 14 מִכֹּל
אֲשֶׁר־יֵצֵא מִגֶּפֶן הַיַּיִן לֹא תֹאכַל וְיַיִן וְשֵׁכָר
אַל־תֵּשְׁתְּ וְכָל־טֻמְאָה אַל־תֹּאכַל כֹּל
אֲשֶׁר־צִוִּיתִיהָ תִּשְׁמֹר׃

15 וַיֹּאמֶר מָנוֹחַ אֶל־מַלְאַךְ יְהוָה נַעְצְרָה־
נָּא אוֹתָךְ וְנַעֲשֶׂה לְפָנֶיךָ גְּדִי עִזִּים׃
16 וַיֹּאמֶר מַלְאַךְ יְהוָה אֶל־מָנוֹחַ אִם־
תַּעְצְרֵנִי לֹא־אֹכַל בְּלַחְמֶךָ וְאִם־תַּעֲשֶׂה
עֹלָה לַיהוָה תַּעֲלֶנָּה כִּי לֹא־יָדַע מָנוֹחַ
כִּי־מַלְאַךְ יְהוָה הוּא׃ 17 וַיֹּאמֶר מָנוֹחַ
אֶל־מַלְאַךְ יְהוָה מִי שְׁמֶךָ כִּי־יָבֹא דבריך
דְבָרְךָ וְכִבַּדְנוּךָ׃ 18 וַיֹּאמֶר לוֹ מַלְאַךְ יְהוָה
לָמָּה זֶּה תִּשְׁאַל לִשְׁמִי וְהוּא־פֶלִאי׃ ס

19 וַיִּקַּח מָנוֹחַ אֶת־גְּדִי הָעִזִּים וְאֶת־
הַמִּנְחָה וַיַּעַל עַל־הַצּוּר לַיהוָה וּמַפְלִא
לַעֲשׂוֹת וּמָנוֹחַ וְאִשְׁתּוֹ רֹאִים׃ 20 וַיְהִי
בַעֲלוֹת הַלַּהַב מֵעַל הַמִּזְבֵּחַ הַשָּׁמַיְמָה
וַיַּעַל מַלְאַךְ־יְהוָה בְּלַהַב הַמִּזְבֵּחַ וּמָנוֹחַ
וְאִשְׁתּוֹ רֹאִים וַיִּפְּלוּ עַל־פְּנֵיהֶם אָרְצָה׃
21 וְלֹא־יָסַף עוֹד מַלְאַךְ יְהוָה לְהֵרָאֹה
אֶל־מָנוֹחַ וְאֶל־אִשְׁתּוֹ אָז יָדַע מָנוֹחַ כִּי־
מַלְאַךְ יְהוָה הוּא׃ 22 וַיֹּאמֶר מָנוֹחַ אֶל־
אִשְׁתּוֹ מוֹת נָמוּת כִּי אֱלֹהִים רָאִינוּ׃

18. unknowable Refusal to reveal a name recalls the encounter between Jacob and an angel at the Jabbok ford (Gen. 32:30). Indeed, that denial used the same Hebrew words found here.

23But his wife said to him, "Had the LORD meant to take our lives, He would not have accepted a burnt offering and grain offering from us, nor let us see all these things; and He would not have made such an announcement to us."

24The woman bore a son, and she named him Samson. The boy grew up, and the LORD blessed him. 25The spirit of the LORD first moved him in the encampment of Dan, between Zorah and Eshtaol.

כג וַתֹּ֧אמֶר לוֹ֙ אִשְׁתּ֔וֹ לוּ֩ חָפֵ֨ץ יְהֹוָ֤ה לַהֲמִיתֵ֙נוּ֙ לֹֽא־לָקַ֤ח מִיָּדֵ֙נוּ֙ עֹלָ֣ה וּמִנְחָ֔ה וְלֹ֥א הֶרְאָ֖נוּ אֶת־כָּל־אֵ֑לֶּה וְכָעֵ֕ת לֹ֥א הִשְׁמִיעָ֖נוּ כָּזֹֽאת:

כד וַתֵּ֤לֶד הָֽאִשָּׁה֙ בֵּ֔ן וַתִּקְרָ֥א אֶת־שְׁמ֖וֹ שִׁמְשׁ֑וֹן וַיִּגְדַּ֤ל הַנַּ֙עַר֙ וַֽיְבָרְכֵ֖הוּ יְהֹוָֽה:

כה וַתָּ֙חֶל֙ ר֣וּחַ יְהֹוָ֔ה לְפַֽעֲמ֖וֹ בְּמַֽחֲנֵה־דָ֑ן בֵּ֥ין צׇרְעָ֖ה וּבֵ֥ין אֶשְׁתָּאֹֽל: פ

B'HA·ALOT'KHA

8 The Lord spoke to Moses, saying: 2Speak
to Aaron and say to him, "When you mount
the lamps, let the seven lamps give light at
the front of the lampstand." 3Aaron did so;
he mounted the lamps at the front of the
lampstand, as the Lord had commanded
Moses.—4Now this is how the lampstand was
made: it was hammered work of gold, hammered from base to petal. According to the pattern that the Lord had shown Moses, so was
the lampstand made.

בהעלתך

ח וַיְדַבֵּר יְהוָה אֶל־מֹשֶׁה לֵּאמֹר׃ 2 דַּבֵּר
אֶל־אַהֲרֹן וְאָמַרְתָּ אֵלָיו בְּהַעֲלֹתְךָ אֶת־
הַנֵּרֹת אֶל־מוּל פְּנֵי הַמְּנוֹרָה יָאִירוּ שִׁבְעַת
הַנֵּרוֹת׃ 3 וַיַּעַשׂ כֵּן אַהֲרֹן אֶל־מוּל פְּנֵי
הַמְּנוֹרָה הֶעֱלָה נֵרֹתֶיהָ כַּאֲשֶׁר צִוָּה יְהוָה
אֶת־מֹשֶׁה׃ 4 וְזֶה מַעֲשֵׂה הַמְּנֹרָה מִקְשָׁה
זָהָב עַד־יְרֵכָהּ עַד־פִּרְחָהּ מִקְשָׁה הִוא
כַּמַּרְאֶה אֲשֶׁר הֶרְאָה יְהוָה אֶת־מֹשֶׁה כֵּן
עָשָׂה אֶת־הַמְּנֹרָה׃ פ

The Generation of the Exodus: The Wilderness Camp (*continued*)

FINAL PREPARATIONS FOR USE OF THE TABERNACLE (*continued*)

LIGHTING THE *M'NORAH* (8:1–4)

The *m'norah* had to be tended by the priests twice daily. Instructions are given on how to light and position the lamps.

2. Aaron Only the high priest performed the service inside the tent.

4. hammered from base to petal The entire *m'norah* was made of a single piece of hammered gold. The lamps were detachable.

CHAPTER 8

The *m'norah*, originally one among many objects in the Tent of Meeting, has become one of the most familiar symbols of Judaism. More than 1000 years after the time of Aaron, the *m'norah* became the symbol of Aaron's descendants, the Hasmoneans, who reclaimed the temple of Jerusalem after the Maccabees' victory. (Today we use an eight-branched *m'norah*—now known more precisely as a *ḥanukkiyyah*—to commemorate the eight days of the *Ḥanukkah* miracle; the *m'norah* described here is seven branched.) The *m'norah*, carried off by Roman soldiers in a victory parade, is featured in a carving on the Arch of Titus in Rome, which celebrates the defeat of the Jews in 70 C.E.; 19 centuries later, the seven-branched *m'norah* became the seal of the State of Israel. Recalling the bush that burned but was not consumed, the light of the *m'norah* would never be permanently extinguished.

Isaac Luria taught that the six branches of the *m'norah* represent the several scientific and academic disciplines, whereas the center stalk represents the light of the Torah. Secular learning and faith are not rivals; each has its own concerns and addresses its own set of questions. They shed light on each other and together they illumine our world.

Why does the Torah lay such emphasis on the *m'norah* among all the furnishings of the Tent of Meeting? "As I shined a light on Israel, making them conspicuous among the nations, let them shine a light on Me" (Num. R. 15:5). God has no visible form. Only when Jews live by the values of the Torah do they embody what God stands for and make God manifest in the world. "For the modern traditional Jew, the doctrine of the election and covenant of Israel offers a purpose for Jewish existence which transcends narrow self-interest. . . . It obligates us to build a just and compassionate society throughout the world and especially in the land of Israel, where we may teach by both personal and collective example what it means to be a covenant people, a light to the nations" (*Emet Ve-Emunah*).

3. Aaron did so Day after day, year after year, Aaron's attitude never changed. His work never became routine or boring. He approached each day with the same sense of reverence he brought to his first day (Vilna Gaon).

5The Lord spoke to Moses, saying: 6Take the Levites from among the Israelites and purify them. 7This is what you shall do to them to purify them: sprinkle on them water of purification, and let them go over their whole body with a razor, and wash their clothes; thus they shall be purified. 8Let them take a bull of the herd, and with it a grain offering of choice flour with oil mixed in, and you take a second bull of the herd for a purification offering. 9You shall bring the Levites forward before the Tent of Meeting. Assemble the whole Israelite community, 10and bring the Levites forward before the Lord. Let the Israelites lay their hands upon the Levites, 11and let Aaron designate the Levites before the Lord as an elevation offering from the Israelites, that they may perform the service of the Lord. 12The Levites shall now lay their hands upon the heads of the bulls; one shall be offered to the Lord as a purification offering and the other as a burnt offering, to make expiation for the Levites.

13You shall place the Levites in attendance upon Aaron and his sons, and designate them as an elevation offering to the Lord. 14Thus you shall set the Levites apart from the Israelites, and

5 וַיְדַבֵּ֥ר יְהֹוָ֖ה אֶל־מֹשֶׁ֥ה לֵּאמֹֽר׃ 6 קַ֣ח אֶת־הַלְוִיִּ֔ם מִתּ֖וֹךְ בְּנֵ֣י יִשְׂרָאֵ֑ל וְטִהַרְתָּ֖ אֹתָֽם׃ 7 וְכֹֽה־תַעֲשֶׂ֤ה לָהֶם֙ לְטַֽהֲרָ֔ם הַזֵּ֧ה עֲלֵיהֶ֛ם מֵ֥י חַטָּ֖את וְהֶעֱבִ֤ירוּ תַ֨עַר֙ עַל־כָּל־בְּשָׂרָ֔ם וְכִבְּס֥וּ בִגְדֵיהֶ֖ם וְהִטֶּהָֽרוּ׃ 8 וְלָֽקְחוּ֙ פַּ֣ר בֶּן־בָּקָ֔ר וּמִנְחָת֔וֹ סֹ֖לֶת בְּלוּלָ֣ה בַשָּׁ֑מֶן וּפַר־שֵׁנִ֥י בֶן־בָּקָ֖ר תִּקַּ֥ח לְחַטָּֽאת׃ 9 וְהִקְרַבְתָּ֙ אֶת־הַלְוִיִּ֔ם לִפְנֵ֖י אֹ֣הֶל מוֹעֵ֑ד וְהִ֨קְהַלְתָּ֔ אֶת־כָּל־עֲדַ֖ת בְּנֵ֥י יִשְׂרָאֵֽל׃ 10 וְהִקְרַבְתָּ֥ אֶת־הַלְוִיִּ֖ם לִפְנֵ֣י יְהֹוָ֑ה וְסָֽמְכ֧וּ בְנֵֽי־יִשְׂרָאֵ֛ל אֶת־יְדֵיהֶ֖ם עַל־הַלְוִיִּֽם׃ 11 וְהֵנִ֨יף אַֽהֲרֹ֤ן אֶת־הַלְוִיִּם֙ תְּנוּפָה֙ לִפְנֵ֣י יְהֹוָ֔ה מֵאֵ֖ת בְּנֵ֣י יִשְׂרָאֵ֑ל וְהָי֕וּ לַֽעֲבֹ֖ד אֶת־עֲבֹדַ֥ת יְהֹוָֽה׃ 12 וְהַֽלְוִיִּם֙ יִסְמְכ֣וּ אֶת־יְדֵיהֶ֔ם עַ֖ל רֹ֣אשׁ הַפָּרִ֑ים וַעֲשֵׂ֞ה אֶת־הָֽאֶחָ֣ד חַטָּ֗את וְאֶת־הָֽאֶחָד֙ עֹלָה֙ לַֽיהֹוָ֔ה לְכַפֵּ֖ר עַל־הַלְוִיִּֽם׃ 13 וְהַֽעֲמַדְתָּ֙ אֶת־הַלְוִיִּ֔ם לִפְנֵ֥י אַֽהֲרֹ֖ן וְלִפְנֵ֣י בָנָ֑יו וְהֵֽנַפְתָּ֥ אֹתָ֛ם תְּנוּפָ֖ה לַֽיהֹוָֽה׃ 14 וְהִבְדַּלְתָּ֙ אֶת־הַלְוִיִּ֔ם מִתּ֖וֹךְ בְּנֵ֣י יִשְׂרָאֵ֑ל

PURIFICATION OF THE LEVITE WORKFORCE (vv. 5–22)

Before the levitical workforce is permitted to dismantle and handle the tabernacle and the other sacred objects, it must be purified.

6. *purify them* The purpose of the ceremony is purification. It is Moses who must see to it that the ritual is accomplished, but its execution is carried out mainly by Aaron.

7. *sprinkle* Moses performs this first step in the rite of purification.

water of purification Hebrew: *mei ḥattat*, the mixture of ashes of the "red" cow and ordinary fresh water that is sprinkled on any person or object contaminated by the dead (chap. 19).

8. *you take a second bull* From the Levites. The purification offering works expiation only for its offerer. It requires a bull for the high priest (Lev. 16:6) or the community—in this instance, the levitical workforce. Bathing cleanses them

of minor impurities, and the *ḥattat* waters and sacrifice cleanse them of severe impurities that might have affected the sanctuary and polluted its altar.

10. *Israelites lay their hands upon the Levites* This rite was conducted by the elders. The Levites are designated as Israel's "sacrifice," their representatives in the sanctuary. They now assume all of Israel's responsibility for transporting the tabernacle.

11. *designate the Levites . . . as an elevation offering* It must be presumed that this ritual was executed only in symbolic form.

from the Israelites The Levites are transferred from the ranks of the Israelites to the property of the Lord through this ritual.

service That is, the work of removal.

12. *shall be offered* Here, Aaron officiates.

to make expiation The ritual purification of the Levites by means of sacrificial expiation follows immediately upon their physical cleansing.

the Levites shall be Mine. 15Thereafter the Levites shall be qualified for the service of the Tent of Meeting, once you have purified them and designated them as an elevation offering. 16For they are formally assigned to Me from among the Israelites: I have taken them for Myself in place of all the first issue of the womb, of all the first-born of the Israelites. 17For every first-born among the Israelites, man as well as beast, is Mine; I consecrated them to Myself at the time that I smote every first-born in the land of Egypt. 18Now I take the Levites instead of every first-born of the Israelites; 19and from among the Israelites I formally assign the Levites to Aaron and his sons, to perform the service for the Israelites in the Tent of Meeting and to make expiation for the Israelites, so that no plague may afflict the Israelites for coming too near the sanctuary.

20Moses, Aaron, and the whole Israelite community did with the Levites accordingly; just as the LORD had commanded Moses in regard to the Levites, so the Israelites did with them. 21The Levites purified themselves and washed their clothes; and Aaron designated them as an elevation offering before the LORD, and Aaron made expiation for them to purify them. 22Thereafter the Levites were qualified to perform their service in the Tent of Meeting, under Aaron and his sons. As the LORD had commanded Moses in regard to the Levites, so they did to them.

שני וְהָיוּ לִי הַלְוִיִּם׃ 15 וְאַחֲרֵי־כֵן יָבֹאוּ הַלְוִיִּם
לַעֲבֹד אֶת־אֹהֶל מוֹעֵד וְטִהַרְתָּ אֹתָם
וְהֵנַפְתָּ אֹתָם תְּנוּפָה׃ 16 כִּי נְתֻנִים נְתֻנִים
הֵמָּה לִי מִתּוֹךְ בְּנֵי יִשְׂרָאֵל תַּחַת פִּטְרַת
כָּל־רֶחֶם בְּכוֹר כֹּל מִבְּנֵי יִשְׂרָאֵל לָקַחְתִּי
אֹתָם לִי׃ 17 כִּי לִי כָל־בְּכוֹר בִּבְנֵי יִשְׂרָאֵל
בָּאָדָם וּבַבְּהֵמָה בְּיוֹם הַכֹּתִי כָל־בְּכוֹר
בְּאֶרֶץ מִצְרַיִם הִקְדַּשְׁתִּי אֹתָם לִי׃
18 וָאֶקַּח אֶת־הַלְוִיִּם תַּחַת כָּל־בְּכוֹר בִּבְנֵי
יִשְׂרָאֵל׃ 19 וָאֶתְּנָה אֶת־הַלְוִיִּם נְתֻנִים ׀
לְאַהֲרֹן וּלְבָנָיו מִתּוֹךְ בְּנֵי יִשְׂרָאֵל לַעֲבֹד
אֶת־עֲבֹדַת בְּנֵי־יִשְׂרָאֵל בְּאֹהֶל מוֹעֵד
וּלְכַפֵּר עַל־בְּנֵי יִשְׂרָאֵל וְלֹא יִהְיֶה בִּבְנֵי
יִשְׂרָאֵל נֶגֶף בְּגֶשֶׁת בְּנֵי־יִשְׂרָאֵל אֶל־
הַקֹּדֶשׁ׃
20 וַיַּעַשׂ מֹשֶׁה וְאַהֲרֹן וְכָל־עֲדַת בְּנֵי־
יִשְׂרָאֵל לַלְוִיִּם כְּכֹל אֲשֶׁר־צִוָּה יְהוָה
אֶת־מֹשֶׁה לַלְוִיִּם כֵּן־עָשׂוּ לָהֶם בְּנֵי
יִשְׂרָאֵל׃ 21 וַיִּתְחַטְּאוּ הַלְוִיִּם וַיְכַבְּסוּ
בִּגְדֵיהֶם וַיָּנֶף אַהֲרֹן אֹתָם תְּנוּפָה לִפְנֵי
יְהוָה וַיְכַפֵּר עֲלֵיהֶם אַהֲרֹן לְטַהֲרָם׃
22 וְאַחֲרֵי־כֵן בָּאוּ הַלְוִיִּם לַעֲבֹד אֶת־
עֲבֹדָתָם בְּאֹהֶל מוֹעֵד לִפְנֵי אַהֲרֹן וְלִפְנֵי
בָנָיו כַּאֲשֶׁר צִוָּה יְהוָה אֶת־מֹשֶׁה עַל־
הַלְוִיִּם כֵּן עָשׂוּ לָהֶם׃ ס

16. formally assigned That is, "assigned as subordinates." By this ritual, the Levites are assigned to the Lord, who then reassigns them to the priests.

18. Now I take That is, formally, through this ritual, although the intention was declared previously in 3:12.

19. make expiation for Better: "ransom"; the Levites will assume responsibility for any Israelite encroachment on the sacred area.

plague God's angry response to idolatry and rebellion (see Exod. 20:5).

coming too near That is, encroaching on.

21. washed their clothes Bathing is implied whenever laundering is required.

---

19. so that no plague May all their visits to the sanctuary be for reasons of joy, not for calamity (Meir of Peremishlan). May all their memories of these visits be pleasant ones.

23 The LORD spoke to Moses, saying: 24 This is
the rule for the Levites. From twenty-five years
of age up they shall participate in the work force
in the service of the Tent of Meeting; 25 but at
the age of fifty they shall retire from the work
force and shall serve no more. 26 They may assist
their brother Levites at the Tent of Meeting by
standing guard, but they shall perform no labor.
Thus you shall deal with the Levites in regard
to their duties.

23 וַיְדַבֵּר יְהוָה אֶל־מֹשֶׁה לֵּאמֹר׃ 24 זֹאת
אֲשֶׁר לַלְוִיִּם מִבֶּן חָמֵשׁ וְעֶשְׂרִים שָׁנָה
וָמַעְלָה יָבוֹא לִצְבֹא צָבָא בַּעֲבֹדַת אֹהֶל
מוֹעֵד׃ 25 וּמִבֶּן חֲמִשִּׁים שָׁנָה יָשׁוּב מִצְּבָא
הָעֲבֹדָה וְלֹא יַעֲבֹד עוֹד׃ 26 וְשֵׁרֵת אֶת־
אֶחָיו בְּאֹהֶל מוֹעֵד לִשְׁמֹר מִשְׁמֶרֶת
וַעֲבֹדָה לֹא יַעֲבֹד כָּכָה תַּעֲשֶׂה לַלְוִיִּם
בְּמִשְׁמְרֹתָם׃ פ

9 The LORD spoke to Moses in the wilderness
of Sinai, on the first new moon of the second
year following the exodus from the land of
Egypt, saying: 2 Let the Israelite people offer the
passover sacrifice at its set time: 3 you shall offer
it on the fourteenth day of this month, at twilight, at its set time; you shall offer it in accordance with all its rules and rites.

שי ט וַיְדַבֵּר יְהוָה אֶל־מֹשֶׁה בְמִדְבַּר־סִינַי
בַּשָּׁנָה הַשֵּׁנִית לְצֵאתָם מֵאֶרֶץ מִצְרַיִם
בַּחֹדֶשׁ הָרִאשׁוֹן לֵאמֹר׃ 2 וְיַעֲשׂוּ בְנֵי־
יִשְׂרָאֵל אֶת־הַפָּסַח בְּמוֹעֲדוֹ׃ 3 בְּאַרְבָּעָה
עָשָׂר־יוֹם בַּחֹדֶשׁ הַזֶּה בֵּין הָעַרְבַּיִם תַּעֲשׂוּ
אֹתוֹ בְּמֹעֲדוֹ כְּכָל־חֻקֹּתָיו וּכְכָל־מִשְׁפָּטָיו
תַּעֲשׂוּ אֹתוֹ׃

AGE LIMITS FOR LEVITICAL DUTIES (vv. 23–26)

When he reaches the age of 50, a Levite must no longer participate in the arduous task of removing the tabernacle. He does not withdraw into retirement, however, but continues to perform guard duty, the other main levitical function.

24. twenty-five years The tradition here differs from that in 4:3, which states that the service begins at age 30.

participate in the work force in the service of That is, qualify to serve in the workforce.

26. labor Porterage in the wilderness.

duties That is, guard duty.

FINAL PREPARATIONS FOR DEPARTURE (9:1–10:10)

The Israelites make ready to depart from the wilderness of Sinai. Chapters 9 and 10 tell of their final preparations.

THE SECOND *PESAḤ* (9:1–14)

Pesaḥ falls on the 14th day of the month, after the erection and dedication of the tabernacle, the altar dedication, and the purification of the Levites.

2. at its set time Even if it coincides with *Shabbat.*

3. at twilight Literally, "between the two settings." That is, between sunset and darkness.

in accordance with all its rules and rites

---

26. See Comment to 4:3.

CHAPTER 9

When the Israelites were leaving Egypt (Exod. 12), the events of the first *Pesaḥ* were aspects of the Exodus itself, things that had to be done by them before leaving. They included the sacrifice of a lamb and the eating of *matzah.* The commandment here is something different—an annual commemoration or re-enactment of that first Exodus, to recall what happened that night in Egypt. That event is so central to Jewish self-understanding that we are told to summon up the memory of it every spring and to look on every *Shabbat* and holiday as "a remembrance of the Exodus."

⁴Moses instructed the Israelites to offer the passover sacrifice; ⁵and they offered the passover sacrifice in the first month, on the fourteenth day of the month, at twilight, in the wilderness of Sinai. Just as the Lord had commanded Moses, so the Israelites did.

⁶But there were some men who were impure by reason of a corpse and could not offer the passover sacrifice on that day. Appearing that same day before Moses and Aaron, ⁷those men said to them, "Impure though we are by reason of a corpse, why must we be debarred from presenting the Lord's offering at its set time with the rest of the Israelites?" ⁸Moses said to them, "Stand by, and let me hear what instructions the Lord gives about you."

⁹And the Lord spoke to Moses, saying: ¹⁰Speak to the Israelite people, saying: When any of you or of your posterity who are defiled by a corpse or are on a long journey would offer a passover sacrifice to the Lord, ¹¹they shall offer it in the second month, on the fourteenth day of the month, at twilight. They shall eat it

4 וַיְדַבֵּ֥ר מֹשֶׁ֖ה אֶל־בְּנֵ֣י יִשְׂרָאֵ֑ל לַעֲשֹׂ֖ת הַפָּֽסַח: 5 וַיַּעֲשׂ֣וּ אֶת־הַפֶּ֡סַח בָּרִאשׁ֡וֹן בְּאַרְבָּעָה֩ עָשָׂ֨ר י֥וֹם לַחֹ֛דֶשׁ בֵּ֥ין הָעַרְבַּ֖יִם בְּמִדְבַּ֣ר סִינָ֑י כְּ֠כֹל אֲשֶׁ֨ר צִוָּ֤ה יְהֹוָה֙ אֶת־מֹשֶׁ֔ה כֵּ֥ן עָשׂ֖וּ בְּנֵ֥י יִשְׂרָאֵֽל:

6 וַיְהִ֣י אֲנָשִׁ֗ים אֲשֶׁ֨ר הָי֤וּ טְמֵאִים֙ לְנֶ֣פֶשׁ אָדָ֔ם וְלֹא־יָכְל֥וּ לַעֲשֹׂת־הַפֶּ֖סַח בַּיּ֣וֹם הַה֑וּא וַֽיִּקְרְב֞וּ לִפְנֵ֥י מֹשֶׁ֛ה וְלִפְנֵ֥י אַהֲרֹ֖ן בַּיּ֥וֹם הַהֽוּא: 7 וַ֠יֹּאמְר֠וּ הָאֲנָשִׁ֤ים הָהֵ֨מָּה֙ אֵלָ֔יו אֲנַ֥חְנוּ טְמֵאִ֖ים לְנֶ֣פֶשׁ אָדָ֑ם לָ֣מָּה נִגָּרַ֗ע לְבִלְתִּ֨י הַקְרִ֜ב אֶת־קׇרְבַּ֤ן יְהֹוָה֙ בְּמֹ֣עֲד֔וֹ בְּת֖וֹךְ בְּנֵ֥י יִשְׂרָאֵֽל: 8 וַיֹּ֥אמֶר אֲלֵהֶ֖ם מֹשֶׁ֑ה עִמְד֣וּ וְאֶשְׁמְעָ֔ה מַה־יְצַוֶּ֥ה יְהֹוָ֖ה לָכֶֽם: פ

9 וַיְדַבֵּ֥ר יְהֹוָ֖ה אֶל־מֹשֶׁ֥ה לֵּאמֹֽר: 10 דַּבֵּ֛ר אֶל־בְּנֵ֥י יִשְׂרָאֵ֖ל לֵאמֹ֑ר אִ֣ישׁ אִ֣ישׁ כִּי־יִהְיֶֽה־טָמֵ֣א ׀ לָנֶ֗פֶשׁ אוֹ֩ בְדֶ֨רֶךְ רְחֹקָ֜הֿ* לָכֶ֗ם א֚וֹ לְדֹרֹ֣תֵיכֶ֔ם וְעָ֥שָׂה פֶ֖סַח לַיהֹוָֽה: 11 בַּחֹ֨דֶשׁ הַשֵּׁנִ֜י בְּאַרְבָּעָ֨ה עָשָׂ֥ר י֛וֹם בֵּ֥ין הָעַרְבַּ֖יִם יַעֲשׂ֣וּ אֹת֑וֹ עַל־מַצּ֥וֹת וּמְרֹרִ֖ים

נקוד על ה׳   v. 10.

The blood of the first *pesaḥ* sacrifice was smeared on the doorposts and lintels of the Israelite homes in Egypt. This time, in the wilderness of Sinai, the blood is to be smeared on the entrances to their tents.

7. debarred Their fear is that they would be excluded from the national festival.

8. Stand by At the entrance of the Tent of Meeting.

10. defiled by a corpse According to the Sages, this specific impurity includes all other causes of impurity. Any kind of impurity disqualifies an individual from partaking of the *pesaḥ* sacrifice (Lev. 7:20–21).

6–12. People who were ritually impure felt deprived at not being able to share in this central national reaffirmation. They brought their problem to Moses, who in turn brought it before God. God acknowledges their sincerity and grants them a "second *Pesaḥ*" one month later. To the sincere individual, life often does offer second chances for spiritual fulfilment

that may have been missed when the opportunities first presented themselves.

10. or . . . on a long journey The Hebrew can also mean "or far off." The Talmud understands the phrase to include a person who is spiritually distant from God and from the Jewish people on the holiday (JT Pes. 9:2). Such a person need not feel permanently exiled. Even

---

HALAKHAH L'MA·ASEH
9:11. with unleavened bread and bitter herbs This verse is the source for the "Hillel sandwich"—in which the *maror* (bitter herb) is eaten with *matzah* during the *Pesaḥ Seder* (BT Pes. 115a).

with unleavened bread and bitter herbs, ¹²and they shall not leave any of it over until morning. They shall not break a bone of it. They shall offer it in strict accord with the law of the passover sacrifice. ¹³But if a man who is pure and not on a journey refrains from offering the passover sacrifice, that person shall be cut off from his kin, for he did not present the LORD's offering at its set time; that man shall bear his guilt.

¹⁴And when a stranger who resides with you would offer a passover sacrifice to the LORD, he must offer it in accordance with the rules and rites of the passover sacrifice. There shall be one law for you, whether stranger or citizen of the country.

¹⁵On the day that the Tabernacle was set up, the cloud covered the Tabernacle, the Tent of the Pact; and in the evening it rested over the Tabernacle in the likeness of fire until morning. ¹⁶It was always so: the cloud covered it, appearing as fire by night. ¹⁷And whenever the cloud lifted from the Tent, the Israelites would set out accordingly; and at the spot where the cloud set-

יֹֽאכְלֻֽהוּ׃ 12 לֹֽא־יַשְׁאִ֤ירוּ מִמֶּ֙נּוּ֙ עַד־בֹּ֔קֶר וְעֶ֖צֶם לֹ֣א יִשְׁבְּרוּ־ב֑וֹ כְּכָל־חֻקַּ֥ת הַפֶּ֖סַח יַעֲשׂ֥וּ אֹתֽוֹ׃ 13 וְהָאִישׁ֩ אֲשֶׁר־ה֨וּא טָה֜וֹר וּבְדֶ֣רֶךְ לֹא־הָיָ֗ה וְחָדַל֙ לַעֲשׂ֣וֹת הַפֶּ֔סַח וְנִכְרְתָ֛ה הַנֶּ֥פֶשׁ הַהִ֖וא מֵֽעַמֶּ֑יהָ כִּ֣י ׀ קׇרְבַּ֣ן יְהֹוָ֗ה לֹ֤א הִקְרִיב֙ בְּמֹ֣עֲד֔וֹ חֶטְא֥וֹ יִשָּׂ֖א הָאִ֥ישׁ הַהֽוּא׃

14 וְכִֽי־יָג֨וּר אִתְּכֶ֜ם גֵּ֗ר וְעָ֤שָֽׂה פֶ֙סַח֙ לַֽיהֹוָ֔ה כְּחֻקַּ֥ת הַפֶּ֛סַח וּכְמִשְׁפָּט֖וֹ כֵּ֣ן יַעֲשֶׂ֑ה חֻקָּ֤ה אַחַת֙ יִהְיֶ֣ה לָכֶ֔ם וְלַגֵּ֖ר וּלְאֶזְרַ֥ח הָאָֽרֶץ׃ פ

15 וּבְיוֹם֙ הָקִ֣ים אֶת־הַמִּשְׁכָּ֔ן כִּסָּ֤ה הֶֽעָנָן֙ אֶת־הַמִּשְׁכָּ֔ן לְאֹ֖הֶל הָעֵדֻ֑ת וּבָעֶ֜רֶב יִהְיֶ֧ה עַל־הַמִּשְׁכָּ֛ן כְּמַרְאֵה־אֵ֖שׁ עַד־בֹּֽקֶר׃ 16 כֵּ֣ן יִהְיֶ֣ה תָמִ֔יד הֶעָנָ֖ן יְכַסֶּ֑נּוּ וּמַרְאֵה־אֵ֖שׁ לָֽיְלָה׃ 17 וּלְפִ֞י הֵעָל֤וֹת הֶֽעָנָן֙ מֵעַ֣ל הָאֹ֔הֶל וְאַ֣חֲרֵי־כֵ֔ן יִסְע֖וּ בְּנֵ֣י יִשְׂרָאֵ֑ל וּבִמְק֗וֹם אֲשֶׁ֣ר

---

12. not break a bone of it   The animal must be retained in its wholeness (see Exod. 12:46).

13.   The paschal sacrifice is the only holiday observance whose willful neglect is punishable by the divine penalty of *karet* (being "cut off" from one's kin). This metaphor derives from the image of a tree cut off from its roots. Elsewhere, it includes a series of related punishments by God, including premature death. The paschal sacrifice, as a commemoration of the Exodus, is a reaffirmation of the covenant struck by God with Israel at the beginning of its national existence. Failure to participate in the rite—except under the circumstances stipulated here—is equivalent to a breach of the covenant.

14.   The resident alien male may participate

in the paschal offering if he is circumcised (Exod. 12:48).

THE FIRE-CLOUD   (vv. 15–23)

Israel's movement in the wilderness, interrupted by the Sinaitic legislation (Exod. 19–Num. 9), is now resumed. God leads Israel in its march by an appointed sign, a cloud-encased fire.

15. On the day   The first day of the first month of the second year (Exod. 40:17).

the Tabernacle, the Tent of the Pact   The tent shrine, not the entire enclosure.

17. Tent   The tabernacle, God's earthly presence, moved only when God so desired.

settled   Presumably, the spot under the cloud marked the center of the camp, where the taber-

---

the wicked child of the *Haggadah* should always feel that a return is possible.

14.   Current Jewish practice endorses inviting non-Jews to the *Seder*.

16.   The function of religion is often to in-

trude a cloud on our bright days, reminding us of suffering in the world (as breaking a glass at a wedding recalls the destruction of the Temple), and to send light into our darkest nights, keeping us from despair.

tled, there the Israelites would make camp. 18At
a command of the LORD the Israelites broke
camp, and at a command of the LORD they made
camp: they remained encamped as long as the
cloud stayed over the Tabernacle. 19When the
cloud lingered over the Tabernacle many days,
the Israelites observed the LORD's mandate and
did not journey on. 20At such times as the cloud
rested over the Tabernacle for but a few days,
they remained encamped at a command of the
LORD, and broke camp at a command of the
LORD. 21And at such times as the cloud stayed
from evening until morning, they broke camp
as soon as the cloud lifted in the morning. Day
or night, whenever the cloud lifted, they would
break camp. 22Whether it was two days or a
month or a year—however long the cloud lingered over the Tabernacle—the Israelites remained encamped and did not set out; only
when it lifted did they break camp. 23On a sign
from the LORD they made camp and on a sign
from the LORD they broke camp; they observed
the LORD's mandate at the LORD's bidding
through Moses.

יִשְׁכָּן־שָׁם֙ הֶֽעָנָ֔ן שָׁ֥ם יַחֲנ֖וּ בְּנֵ֥י יִשְׂרָאֵֽל׃
18 עַל־פִּ֣י יְהוָ֗ה יִסְעוּ֙ בְּנֵ֣י יִשְׂרָאֵ֔ל וְעַל־פִּ֥י
יְהוָ֖ה יַחֲנ֑וּ כָּל־יְמֵ֗י אֲשֶׁ֨ר יִשְׁכֹּ֧ן הֶֽעָנָ֛ן
עַל־הַמִּשְׁכָּ֖ן יַחֲנֽוּ׃ 19 וּבְהַאֲרִ֧יךְ הֶעָנָ֛ן עַל־
הַמִּשְׁכָּ֖ן יָמִ֣ים רַבִּ֑ים וְשָׁמְר֧וּ בְנֵי־יִשְׂרָאֵ֛ל
אֶת־מִשְׁמֶ֥רֶת יְהוָ֖ה וְלֹ֥א יִסָּֽעוּ׃ 20 וְיֵ֞שׁ
אֲשֶׁ֨ר יִהְיֶ֧ה הֶעָנָ֛ן יָמִ֥ים מִסְפָּ֖ר עַל־הַמִּשְׁכָּ֑ן
עַל־פִּ֤י יְהוָה֙ יַחֲנ֔וּ וְעַל־פִּ֥י יְהוָ֖ה יִסָּֽעוּ׃
21 וְיֵ֞שׁ אֲשֶׁ֨ר יִהְיֶ֤ה הֶעָנָן֙ מֵעֶ֣רֶב עַד־בֹּ֔קֶר
וְנַעֲלָ֥ה הֶעָנָ֛ן בַּבֹּ֖קֶר וְנָסָ֑עוּ א֚וֹ יוֹמָ֣ם וָלַ֔יְלָה
וְנַעֲלָ֥ה הֶעָנָ֖ן וְנָסָֽעוּ׃ 22 אֽוֹ־יֹמַ֜יִם אוֹ־חֹ֣דֶשׁ
אוֹ־יָמִ֗ים בְּהַאֲרִ֨יךְ הֶעָנָ֤ן עַל־הַמִּשְׁכָּן֙
לִשְׁכֹּ֣ן עָלָ֔יו יַחֲנ֥וּ בְנֵי־יִשְׂרָאֵ֖ל וְלֹ֣א יִסָּ֑עוּ
וּבְהֵעָלֹת֖וֹ יִסָּֽעוּ׃ 23 עַל־פִּ֤י יְהוָה֙ יַחֲנ֔וּ
וְעַל־פִּ֥י יְהוָ֖ה יִסָּ֑עוּ אֶת־מִשְׁמֶ֤רֶת יְהוָה֙
שָׁמָ֔רוּ עַל־פִּ֥י יְהוָ֖ה בְּיַד־מֹשֶֽׁה׃ פ

10

10 The LORD spoke to Moses, saying: 2Have
two silver trumpets made; make them of hammered work. They shall serve you to summon
the community and to set the divisions in motion. 3When both are blown in long blasts, the
whole community shall assemble before you at

י וַיְדַבֵּ֥ר יְהוָ֖ה אֶל־מֹשֶׁ֥ה לֵּאמֹֽר׃ 2 עֲשֵׂ֣ה
לְךָ֗ שְׁתֵּי֙ חֲצוֹצְרֹ֣ת כֶּ֔סֶף מִקְשָׁ֖ה תַּעֲשֶׂ֣ה
אֹתָ֑ם וְהָי֤וּ לְךָ֙ לְמִקְרָ֣א הָעֵדָ֔ה וּלְמַסַּ֖ע
אֶת־הַֽמַּחֲנֽוֹת׃ 3 וְתָקְע֖וּ בָּהֵ֑ן וְנוֹעֲד֤וּ אֵלֶ֙יךָ֙

nacle was to be erected. As soon as that task was completed, the cloud would descend to envelop the Tent.

18. It must be assumed that when the cloud lifted, it proceeded to the head of the column, and that the tabernacle was reassembled beneath it wherever it stopped. The Israelites' march to the Promised Land was conducted at the direction of God, not by mortals.

19–22. The cloud, not the fire, decided the line of march, which means that Israel marched only by day.

21. cloud . . . from evening to morning It had the appearance of fire at night.

TRUMPETS (*ḤATZOTZ'ROT*) (10:1–10)

At God's command, the trumpets sound and the people assemble in marching formation. The use of the trumpets is Israel's response to the divine signal given by the fire-cloud.

2. hammered work The trumpets probably were molded by hammering the metallic foil over a model.

the entrance of the Tent of Meeting; [4]and if only one is blown, the chieftains, heads of Israel's contingents, shall assemble before you. [5]But when you sound short blasts, the divisions encamped on the east shall move forward; [6]and when you sound short blasts a second time, those encamped on the south shall move forward. Thus short blasts shall be blown for setting them in motion, [7]while to convoke the congregation you shall blow long blasts, not short ones. [8]The trumpets shall be blown by Aaron's sons, the priests; they shall be for you an institution for all time throughout the ages.

[9]When you are at war in your land against an aggressor who attacks you, you shall sound short blasts on the trumpets, that you may be remembered before the LORD your God and be delivered from your enemies. [10]And on your joyous occasions—your fixed festivals and new moon days—you shall sound the trumpets over your burnt offerings and your sacrifices of well-being. They shall be a reminder of you before your God: I, the LORD, am your God.

[11]In the second year, on the twentieth day of

כָּל־הָעֵדָ֔ה אֶל־פֶּ֖תַח אֹ֥הֶל מוֹעֵֽד׃ [4]וְאִם־בְּאַחַ֣ת יִתְקָ֔עוּ וְנוֹעֲד֤וּ אֵלֶ֙יךָ֙ הַנְּשִׂיאִ֔ים רָאשֵׁ֖י אַלְפֵ֥י יִשְׂרָאֵֽל׃ [5]וּתְקַעְתֶּ֖ם תְּרוּעָ֑ה וְנָֽסְעוּ֙ הַֽמַּחֲנ֔וֹת הַחֹנִ֖ים קֵֽדְמָה׃ [6]וּתְקַעְתֶּ֤ם תְּרוּעָה֙ שֵׁנִ֔ית וְנָֽסְעוּ֙ הַֽמַּחֲנ֔וֹת הַחֹנִ֖ים תֵּימָ֑נָה תְּרוּעָ֥ה יִתְקְע֖וּ לְמַסְעֵיהֶֽם׃ [7]וּבְהַקְהִ֖יל אֶת־הַקָּהָ֑ל תִּתְקְע֖וּ וְלֹ֥א תָרִֽיעוּ׃ [8]וּבְנֵ֤י אַהֲרֹן֙ הַכֹּ֣הֲנִ֔ים יִתְקְע֖וּ בַּֽחֲצֹֽצְר֑וֹת וְהָי֥וּ לָכֶ֛ם לְחֻקַּ֥ת עוֹלָ֖ם לְדֹרֹֽתֵיכֶֽם׃ [9]וְכִֽי־תָבֹ֨אוּ מִלְחָמָ֜ה בְּאַרְצְכֶ֗ם עַל־הַצַּר֙ הַצֹּרֵ֣ר אֶתְכֶ֔ם וַהֲרֵֽעֹתֶ֖ם בַּֽחֲצֹֽצְר֑וֹת וֲנִזְכַּרְתֶּ֗ם לִפְנֵי֙ יְהֹוָ֣ה אֱלֹֽהֵיכֶ֔ם וְנוֹשַׁעְתֶּ֖ם מֵאֹֽיְבֵיכֶֽם׃ [10]וּבְי֨וֹם שִׂמְחַתְכֶ֜ם וּֽבְמֽוֹעֲדֵיכֶם֮ וּבְרָאשֵׁ֣י חָדְשֵׁיכֶם֒ וּתְקַעְתֶּ֣ם בַּֽחֲצֹֽצְרֹ֗ת עַ֚ל עֹלֹ֣תֵיכֶ֔ם וְעַ֖ל זִבְחֵ֣י שַׁלְמֵיכֶ֑ם וְהָי֨וּ לָכֶ֤ם לְזִכָּרוֹן֙ לִפְנֵ֣י אֱלֹֽהֵיכֶ֔ם אֲנִ֖י יְהֹוָ֥ה אֱלֹֽהֵיכֶֽם׃ פ

שי [11]וַיְהִ֞י בַּשָּׁנָ֧ה הַשֵּׁנִ֛ית בַּחֹ֥דֶשׁ הַשֵּׁנִ֖י

---

4. assemble before you At the entrance of the Tent of Meeting.

6. them The remaining divisions.

8. priests In the ancient Near East, priests were an integral part of a military force (see Deut. 20:2).

throughout the ages The perpetual use of the trumpets is meant for assembly and for war, not for breaking camp (Ibn Ezra).

The Generation of the Exodus: The March to Transjordan   (10:11–22:1)

The march takes about 40 years. Israel and its leaders are wondrously led and fed by God—but respond with rebellion. This section is concerned mostly with the opening and the closing months.

FROM SINAI TO KADESH (10:11–12:16)

THE ORDER OF THE MARCH   (10:11–28)

11. the cloud The ascending and descending cloud was the divine sign indicating when to break and when to make camp; its movement determined the direction of the march.

HALAKHAH L'MA·ASEH
10:5–7. short blasts . . . long blasts These verses are the basis for the Talmud's rule that in blowing the shofar on *Rosh ha-Shanah*, the *t'ki·ah* and the *t'ru·ah* are different sounds, and that every *t'ru·ah* must be preceded and followed by a *t'ki·ah* (BT RH 34a).

the second month, the cloud lifted from the
Tabernacle of the Pact 12and the Israelites set
out on their journeys from the wilderness of Sinai. The cloud came to rest in the wilderness
of Paran.

13When the march was to begin, at the LORD's
command through Moses, 14the first standard
to set out, troop by troop, was the division of
Judah. In command of its troops was Nahshon
son of Amminadab; 15in command of the tribal
troop of Issachar, Nethanel son of Zuar; 16and
in command of the tribal troop of Zebulun,
Eliab son of Helon.

17Then the Tabernacle would be taken apart;
and the Gershonites and the Merarites, who carried the Tabernacle, would set out.

18The next standard to set out, troop by troop,
was the division of Reuben. In command of its
troop was Elizur son of Shedeur; 19in command
of the tribal troop of Simeon, Shelumiel son of
Zurishaddai; 20and in command of the tribal
troop of Gad, Eliasaph son of Deuel.

21Then the Kohathites, who carried the sacred
objects, would set out; and by the time they arrived, the Tabernacle would be set up again.

22The next standard to set out, troop by troop,
was the division of Ephraim. In command of
its troop was Elishama son of Ammihud; 23in
command of the tribal troop of Manasseh, Gamaliel son of Pedahzur; 24and in command of
the tribal troop of Benjamin, Abidan son of
Gideoni.

25Then, as the rear guard of all the divisions,
the standard of the division of Dan would set

בְּעֶשְׂרִ֣ים בַּחֹ֑דֶשׁ נַעֲלָה֙ הֶֽעָנָ֔ן מֵעַ֖ל מִשְׁכַּ֥ן
הָעֵדֻֽת׃ 12 וַיִּסְע֧וּ בְנֵֽי־יִשְׂרָאֵ֛ל לְמַסְעֵיהֶ֖ם
מִמִּדְבַּ֣ר סִינָ֑י וַיִּשְׁכֹּ֥ן הֶעָנָ֖ן בְּמִדְבַּ֥ר פָּארָֽן׃
13 וַיִּסְע֖וּ בָּרִֽאשֹׁנָ֑ה עַל־פִּ֥י יְהוָ֖ה בְּיַד־
מֹשֶֽׁה׃ 14 וַיִּסַּ֞ע דֶּ֤גֶל מַחֲנֵה֙ בְנֵֽי־יְהוּדָ֔ה
בָּרִאשֹׁנָ֖ה לְצִבְאֹתָ֑ם וְעַל־צְבָא֔וֹ נַחְשׁ֖וֹן
בֶּן־עַמִּינָדָֽב׃ 15 וְעַ֨ל־צְבָ֔א מַטֵּ֖ה בְּנֵ֣י
יִשָּׂשכָ֑ר נְתַנְאֵ֖ל בֶּן־צוּעָֽר׃ 16 וְעַ֨ל־צְבָ֔א
מַטֵּ֖ה בְּנֵ֣י זְבוּלֻ֑ן אֱלִיאָ֖ב בֶּן־חֵלֹֽן׃
17 וְהוּרַ֖ד הַמִּשְׁכָּ֑ן וְנָסְע֤וּ בְנֵֽי־גֵרְשׁוֹן֙ וּבְנֵ֣י
מְרָרִ֔י נֹשְׂאֵ֖י הַמִּשְׁכָּֽן׃ ס
18 וְנָסַ֗ע דֶּ֚גֶל מַחֲנֵ֣ה רְאוּבֵ֔ן לְצִבְאֹתָ֑ם וְעַל־
צְבָא֔וֹ אֱלִיצ֖וּר בֶּן־שְׁדֵיאֽוּר׃ 19 וְעַ֨ל־צְבָ֔א
מַטֵּ֖ה בְּנֵ֣י שִׁמְע֑וֹן שְֽׁלֻמִיאֵ֖ל בֶּן־צוּרִֽישַׁדָּֽי׃
20 וְעַל־צְבָ֖א מַטֵּ֣ה בְנֵי־גָ֑ד אֶלְיָסָ֖ף בֶּן־
דְּעוּאֵֽל׃
21 וְנָסְעוּ֙ הַקְּהָתִ֔ים נֹשְׂאֵ֖י הַמִּקְדָּ֑שׁ וְהֵקִ֥ימוּ
אֶת־הַמִּשְׁכָּ֖ן עַד־בֹּאָֽם׃ ס
22 וְנָסַ֗ע דֶּ֛גֶל מַחֲנֵ֥ה בְנֵי־אֶפְרַ֖יִם לְצִבְאֹתָ֑ם
וְעַל־צְבָא֔וֹ אֱלִישָׁמָ֖ע בֶּן־עַמִּיהֽוּד׃ 23 וְעַ֨ל־
צְבָ֔א מַטֵּ֖ה בְּנֵ֣י מְנַשֶּׁ֑ה גַּמְלִיאֵ֖ל בֶּן־פְּדָה־
צֽוּר׃ 24 וְעַ֨ל־צְבָ֔א מַטֵּ֖ה בְּנֵ֣י בִנְיָמִ֑ן אֲבִידָ֖ן
בֶּן־גִּדְעוֹנִֽי׃ ס
25 וְנָסַ֗ע דֶּ֚גֶל מַחֲנֵ֣ה בְנֵי־דָ֔ן מְאַסֵּ֥ף לְכָל־
הַמַּחֲנֹ֖ת לְצִבְאֹתָ֑ם וְעַל־צְבָא֔וֹ אֲחִיעֶ֖זֶר

12. set out The root is נסע (pull up stakes), a term from nomadic travel, in which journeys begin by pulling up tent pins.

wilderness of Paran Probably not a place of encampment but the general name for the northern half of the Sinai Peninsula, between Midian (in Transjordan) and Egypt.

13. through Moses Even though the ascending cloud was visible to the entire people, Moses alone determined when the march would resume.

14. its That is, the tribe of Judah's.

17. Gershonite and Merarite Levites transported the tabernacle by wagon ahead of the Kohathites. When the latter entered the new encampment bearing the sacred objects on their shoulders, they would find the tabernacle reassembled and ready to receive these objects.

out, troop by troop. In command of its troop was Ahiezer son of Ammishaddai; 26in command of the tribal troop of Asher, Pagiel son of Ochran; 27and in command of the tribal troop of Naphtali, Ahira son of Enan.

28Such was the order of march of the Israelites, as they marched troop by troop.

29Moses said to Hobab son of Reuel the Midianite, Moses' father-in-law, "We are setting out for the place of which the LORD has said, 'I will give it to you.' Come with us and we will be generous with you; for the LORD has promised to be generous to Israel."

30"I will not go," he replied to him, "but will return to my native land." 31He said, "Please do not leave us, inasmuch as you know where we should camp in the wilderness and can be our guide. 32So if you come with us, we will ex-

בֶּן־עַמִּ֖י שַׁדָּֽי: 26 וְעַל־צְבָ֕א מַטֵּ֖ה בְּנֵ֣י אָשֵׁ֑ר פַּגְעִיאֵ֖ל בֶּן־עָכְרָֽן: 27 וְעַל־צְבָ֕א מַטֵּ֖ה בְּנֵ֣י נַפְתָּלִ֑י אֲחִירַ֖ע בֶּן־עֵינָֽן: 28 אֵ֛לֶּה מַסְעֵ֥י בְנֵֽי־יִשְׂרָאֵ֖ל לְצִבְאֹתָ֑ם וַיִּסָּֽעוּ: ס

29 וַיֹּ֣אמֶר מֹשֶׁ֗ה לְ֠חֹבָ֠ב בֶּן־רְעוּאֵ֣ל הַמִּדְיָנִי֮ חֹתֵ֣ן מֹשֶׁה֒ נֹסְעִ֣ים ׀ אֲנַ֗חְנוּ אֶל־הַמָּקוֹם֙ אֲשֶׁ֣ר אָמַ֣ר יְהֹוָ֔ה אֹת֖וֹ אֶתֵּ֣ן לָכֶ֑ם לְכָ֣ה אִתָּ֗נוּ וְהֵטַ֣בְנוּ לָ֔ךְ כִּֽי־יְהֹוָ֥ה דִּבֶּר־ט֖וֹב עַל־יִשְׂרָאֵֽל: 30 וַיֹּ֖אמֶר אֵלָ֑יו לֹ֣א אֵלֵ֑ךְ כִּ֧י אִם־אֶל־אַרְצִ֛י וְאֶל־מוֹלַדְתִּ֖י אֵלֵֽךְ: 31 וַיֹּ֕אמֶר אַל־נָ֖א תַּעֲזֹ֣ב אֹתָ֑נוּ כִּ֣י ׀ עַל־כֵּ֣ן יָדַ֗עְתָּ חֲנֹתֵ֙נוּ֙ בַּמִּדְבָּ֔ר וְהָיִ֥יתָ לָּ֖נוּ לְעֵינָֽיִם: 32 וְהָיָ֖ה כִּֽי־

---

28. marched troop by troop The Israelites marched in military formation.

GUIDANCE IN THE WILDERNESS: HOBAB (vv. 29–32)

Moses, certain that only a short journey lies ahead, asks Hobab to serve as Israel's guide in the wilderness.

29. Hobab son of Reuel This is one of three ancient traditions concerning the name of Moses' father-in-law (cf. Exod. 2:18; 18:1).

We are setting out Immediately, for the Promised Land. Moses had no premonition of the catastrophic episode of the scouts (chaps. 13–14),

which would result in 40 years of wandering in the wilderness.

to be generous Hobab will be awarded territory with Israel in the Promised Land. Scripture confirms that the tribe of Hobab indeed settled in the southern region of the tribe of Judah (Judg. 1:16, 4:11).

30. native land Hobab lived in the vicinity of the Gulf of Aqaba and thus would be in the direction of Israel's march.

31. know Some ancient translations understand this as "have known"; that is, Hobab is rewarded for past services.

32. Hobab's reply is not given, but the later

CHAPTER 10

25. The tribe of Dan brought up the rear in the marching order. The Torah describes Dan as "gatherer" (m'assef), prompting Rashi to speculate that Dan's task was to gather up lost objects that had been dropped on the way and return them to their owners. They would also gather in straying individuals who had become lost or had fallen behind. One source suggests that the tribe of Dan was chosen for this role because, even though its members were weak in religious faith (the territory of Dan would

later become a site of idol worship), they were strong in their love for their fellow Israelites. There is a need in today's community for people who express their religious faith by caring for the left-behind.

29. The Israelites have a cloud to lead them by day and a pillar of fire to illumine their path by night. Why does Moses plead with his non-Israelite relative to be their guide? Because one may never assume that a miracle will occur. God sends miracles when God chooses to, not necessarily when we request or require them.

tend to you the same bounty that the LORD grants us."

33They marched from the mountain of the
LORD a distance of three days. The Ark of the
Covenant of the LORD traveled in front of them
on that three days' journey to seek out a resting
place for them; 34and the LORD's cloud kept
above them by day, as they moved on from
camp.
35When the Ark was to set out, Moses would
say:

Advance, O LORD!
May Your enemies be scattered,
And may Your foes flee before You!

36And when it halted, he would say:

Return, O LORD,
You who are Israel's myriads of thousands!

תֵּלֵךְ עִמָּנוּ וְהָיָה ׀ הַטּוֹב הַהוּא אֲשֶׁר
יֵיטִיב יְהוָה עִמָּנוּ וְהֵטַבְנוּ לָךְ׃

33 וַיִּסְעוּ מֵהַר יְהוָה דֶּרֶךְ שְׁלֹשֶׁת יָמִים
וַאֲרוֹן בְּרִית־יְהוָה נֹסֵעַ לִפְנֵיהֶם דֶּרֶךְ
שְׁלֹשֶׁת יָמִים לָתוּר לָהֶם מְנוּחָה׃ 34 וַעֲנַן
יְהוָה עֲלֵיהֶם יוֹמָם בְּנָסְעָם מִן־
הַמַּחֲנֶה׃ ׆* ס
ששי 35 וַיְהִי בִּנְסֹעַ הָאָרֹן וַיֹּאמֶר מֹשֶׁה
קוּמָה ׀ יְהוָה
וְיָפֻצוּ אֹיְבֶיךָ
וְיָנֻסוּ מְשַׂנְאֶיךָ מִפָּנֶיךָ׃
36 ובנחה וּבְנֻחֹה יֹאמַר
שׁוּבָה יְהוָה
רִבְבוֹת אַלְפֵי יִשְׂרָאֵל׃ ׆* פ

v. 35. סימנית מנוזרת וגם נקראת נ׳ הפוכה
v. 36. סימנית מנוזרת וגם נקראת נ׳ הפוכה

presence of his descendants in the Holy Land indicates that his response was in the affirmative.

GUIDANCE IN THE WILDERNESS: THE ARK (vv. 33–36)

The first stage of the march is a three-day journey to Taberah in the wilderness of Paran.

33. mountain of the LORD Only here does this phrase designate Mount Sinai. After the Temple is built in Jerusalem, "mountain of the LORD" refers to the Temple Mount.

a distance of three days To their first station.

The Ark . . . traveled in front This contradicts 2:17, where we are told the Ark traveled in the midst of the Israelites. According to Ibn Ezra, during this initial stage the Ark did indeed precede the marchers, because the people were fearful of the dangers in the wilderness. Actually, we have here an ancient tradition (echoed in 1 Sam. 4:3ff.) about the role of the Ark, attested to also outside of Israel.

34. the LORD's cloud kept above them Some explain that the Ark served as a guide while the cloud was suspended over them as shade and protection. Others claim the reverse: The cloud was the guide, and the Ark was carried in the center of the marching columns.

36. You who are Israel's God is declared equivalent to the armies of Israel. An ancient Sage understood this to mean that just as the divine Presence rules above with many thousands of myriads, so the divine Presence rules below.

myriads of thousands An astronomically large number. The Hebrew word *elef* (construct form: *alfei*) involves a play on words; it means both "thousands" and "clans."

35–36. During our years of wandering, exile, and persecution, when we were vulnerable to those who sought to do us harm, our prayer was "Advance, O LORD! May Your enemies be scattered!" During tranquil times, when the danger is not persecution but assimilation, our prayer is a homiletic interpretation of verse 36: "O LORD, return the thousands of Israel who have strayed." These verses are familiar from the service of taking the Torah from the Ark and returning it to the Ark before and after the Torah reading. Does God have enemies? Anyone who hates the Jewish people because we strive to do the will of God is an enemy of God (*Sifrei*).

11 The people took to complaining bitterly
before the LORD. The LORD heard and was incensed: a fire of the LORD broke out against
them, ravaging the outskirts of the camp. 2The
people cried out to Moses. Moses prayed to the
LORD, and the fire died down. 3That place was
named Taberah, because a fire of the LORD had
broken out against them.

4The riffraff in their midst felt a gluttonous
craving; and then the Israelites wept and said,
"If only we had meat to eat! 5We remember
the fish that we used to eat free in Egypt, the

יא וַיְהִי הָעָם כְּמִתְאֹנְנִים רַע בְּאָזְנֵי
יְהוָה וַיִּשְׁמַע יְהוָה וַיִּחַר אַפּוֹ וַתִּבְעַר־בָּם
אֵשׁ יְהוָה וַתֹּאכַל בִּקְצֵה הַמַּחֲנֶה׃ 2 וַיִּצְעַק
הָעָם אֶל־מֹשֶׁה וַיִּתְפַּלֵּל מֹשֶׁה אֶל־יְהוָה
וַתִּשְׁקַע הָאֵשׁ׃ 3 וַיִּקְרָא שֵׁם־הַמָּקוֹם
הַהוּא תַּבְעֵרָה כִּי־בָעֲרָה בָם אֵשׁ יְהוָה׃
4 וְהָאסַפְסֻף* אֲשֶׁר בְּקִרְבּוֹ הִתְאַוּוּ תַּאֲוָה
וַיָּשֻׁבוּ וַיִּבְכּוּ גַּם בְּנֵי יִשְׂרָאֵל וַיֹּאמְרוּ מִי
יַאֲכִלֵנוּ בָּשָׂר׃ 5 זָכַרְנוּ אֶת־הַדָּגָה אֲשֶׁר־

v. 4. א׳ נחה

THE COMPLAINT AT TABERAH (11:1–3)

1. took to complaining Hebrew: *k'mit·on'nim;* the emphatic letter *kaf* at the beginning gives a sense of complaining bitterly. The basis for the complaint is not stated. According to Rashbam, the people objected to the forced marches. An additional complaint may have been a lack of water.

before the LORD Literally, "in the ears of the LORD." They voiced their complaints directly, brazenly, to God.

fire of the LORD Probably lightning (see Exod. 9:23–24, 19:18).

THE COMPLAINT AT KIBROTH-HATTAAVAH (vv. 4–35)

The craving for meat was previously voiced after the Israelites crossed the Sea of Reeds (Exod. 16:3), and the divine answer came in the form of manna and quail, which arrived together (Exod. 16:13–14,31). In this narrative, the quail constitute a new element, whereas the manna in verse 6 is regarded as a familiar phenomenon.

4. riffraff This translation conveys the wordplay in the sound of the Hebrew (*asafsuf*). The term refers to non-Israelites who joined the Israelites' break for freedom (cf. *"eirev rav"* in Exod. 12:38).

meat The next verse indicates that the "meat" desired by the Israelites was fish, an abundant and inexpensive food in Egypt.

5. used to eat The food supply was endless.

CHAPTER 11

This chapter introduces a theme that will characterize much of the remaining narrative in the Book of Numbers. Chapters 11–25 contain a series of refusals to accept authority, including Miriam's unwillingness to be subordinated to Moses (in chapter 12). The Israelites complain about the unpleasantness of their journey, exasperating both God and Moses. Moses grows ever more impatient with the people, beginning with this chapter and culminating with the incident of his striking the rock in chapter 20. Forgotten are the vows at the Sea of Reeds and at Mount Sinai. Ramban takes 10:33 ("They marched from the mountain of the LORD") to imply a spiritual or emotional distancing from the Sinai event as well as a geographic one. "They fled the mountain like a child running from school" lest God give them any more commandments or prohibitions.

1. The LORD . . . was incensed The Torah often describes God as angry, especially in these next several chapters. It portrays God as a passionate God, a God who cares deeply about what we do and how we live. "The God of Aristotle is the Unmoved Mover; the God of Israel is the most-moved Mover" (Heschel), moved to anger by human cruelty, corruption, disloyalty, and ingratitude.

outskirts of the camp One Sage takes this to mean that the complainers were marginal Israelites, the ones least enthusiastic from the outset about the prospects of freedom and a life based on Torah. Another Sage connects *"katzeh"* (outskirts) with *katzin* (leader), commenting that it was the leaders' attitude that caused the people's sullen mood (*Sifrei*).

5. the fish that we used to eat free in Egypt This is the trick that memory plays to

cucumbers, the melons, the leeks, the onions, and the garlic. 6Now our gullets are shriveled. There is nothing at all! Nothing but this manna to look to!"

7Now the manna was like coriander seed, and in color it was like bdellium. 8The people would go about and gather it, grind it between millstones or pound it in a mortar, boil it in a pot, and make it into cakes. It tasted like rich cream. 9When the dew fell on the camp at night, the manna would fall upon it.

10Moses heard the people weeping, every clan apart, each person at the entrance of his tent. The LORD was very angry, and Moses was dis-

נֹאכַ֤ל בְּמִצְרַ֙יִם֙ חִנָּ֔ם אֵ֣ת הַקִּשֻּׁאִ֔ים וְאֵת֙ הָֽאֲבַטִּחִ֔ים וְאֶת־הֶחָצִ֥יר וְאֶת־הַבְּצָלִ֖ים וְאֶת־הַשּׁוּמִֽים: 6 וְעַתָּ֛ה נַפְשֵׁ֥נוּ יְבֵשָׁ֖ה אֵ֣ין כֹּ֑ל בִּלְתִּ֖י אֶל־הַמָּ֥ן עֵינֵֽינוּ: 7 וְהַמָּ֕ן כִּזְרַע־גַּ֖ד ה֑וּא וְעֵינ֖וֹ כְּעֵ֥ין הַבְּדֹֽלַח: 8 שָׁ֩טוּ֩ הָעָ֨ם וְלָֽקְט֜וּ וְטָֽחֲנ֣וּ בָֽרֵחַ֗יִם א֤וֹ דָכוּ֙ בַּמְּדֹכָ֔ה וּבִשְּׁלוּ֙ בַּפָּר֔וּר וְעָשׂ֥וּ אֹת֖וֹ עֻג֑וֹת וְהָיָ֣ה טַעְמ֔וֹ כְּטַ֖עַם לְשַׁ֥ד הַשָּֽׁמֶן: 9 וּבְרֶ֧דֶת הַטַּ֛ל עַל־הַֽמַּחֲנֶ֖ה לָ֑יְלָה יֵרֵ֥ד הַמָּ֖ן עָלָֽיו:

10 וַיִּשְׁמַ֨ע מֹשֶׁ֜ה אֶת־הָעָ֗ם בֹּכֶה֙ לְמִשְׁפְּחֹתָ֔יו אִ֖ישׁ לְפֶ֣תַח אָהֳל֑וֹ וַיִּֽחַר־אַ֤ף

---

6. shriveled Literally, "dry."

MANNA (vv. 7–9)

This detailed description of manna refutes each point of the people's complaint (see Exod. 16:31).
   7. coriander An herb, the seeds (and leaves) of which are used in flavoring.
   color That is, appearance.
   bdellium An aromatic resin that is pale yellow or white.
   8. millstones A common household utensil, still in use today among the Arab Bedouin.
   rich cream Hebrew: *lashad* (literally, "cream of oil or fat"); the upper layer of the first pressing of olive oil.

MOSES COMPLAINS
TO GOD (vv. 10–15)

Moses can neither supply Israel with sufficient food nor shoulder the burden of leadership. Exhausted physically and psychologically, he requests that his life be terminated.
   10. Israel's complaint leads to Moses' demoralization and self-pity.
   every clan apart The weeping was everywhere.
   at the entrance That is, openly, defiantly. Their weeping constituted a public demonstration.
   was very angry Literally, "His nostrils flared," an idiom for rage.

---

make life bearable. We remember the good and forget the painful (N. Leibowitz). The Midrash doubts whether the Egyptians really gave them free food. It understands "free" to mean "free of moral obligations," as an infant is fed without anything being expected in return (*Sifrei*). In the view of the Sages, it was not the physical discomfort of the wilderness that really provoked Israel's complaints. It was the burden of morality, to which they had not yet become accustomed, that left them nostalgic for the days in Egypt. That is why God responds to their complaints first by pouring the divine spirit onto the people, quenching their spiritual hunger (vv. 24–25), only later sending the quail to ease their physical hunger (v. 31ff.) (Hirsch).
   6. Why did the people complain about the

manna, when the Torah makes a point of telling us how delicious it was? To feel prosperous, it is not enough for a person to have everything that is needed. One must have more than one's neighbors have. The manna was psychologically unsatisfying because everyone had it in abundance (Eybeschütz).
   10. This shows the greatness of Moses as a leader. In one interpretation, the people wept and complained in the privacy of their homes, yet Moses sensed their unhappiness and understood its cause. Maimonides claims that the phrase "the LORD was very angry" occurs only as a divine response to instances of idolatry. This grumbling is perceived not as a comment about the food but as a rebellion against God's providence.

tressed. 11And Moses said to the LORD, "Why
have You dealt ill with Your servant, and why
have I not enjoyed Your favor, that You have
laid the burden of all this people upon me? 12Did
I conceive all this people, did I bear them, that
You should say to me, 'Carry them in your
bosom as a nurse carries an infant,' to the land
that You have promised on oath to their fathers?
13Where am I to get meat to give to all this people, when they whine before me and say, 'Give
us meat to eat!' 14I cannot carry all this people
by myself, for it is too much for me. 15If You
would deal thus with me, kill me rather, I beg
You, and let me see no more of my wretchedness!"

16Then the LORD said to Moses, "Gather for
Me seventy of Israel's elders of whom you have
experience as elders and officers of the people,
and bring them to the Tent of Meeting and let

יְהוָה מְאֹד וּבְעֵינֵי מֹשֶׁה רָע׃ 11 וַיֹּאמֶר
מֹשֶׁה אֶל־יְהוָה לָמָה הֲרֵעֹתָ לְעַבְדֶּךָ
וְלָמָּה לֹא־מָצָתִי* חֵן בְּעֵינֶיךָ לָשׂוּם אֶת־
מַשָּׂא כָּל־הָעָם הַזֶּה עָלָי׃ 12 הֶאָנֹכִי
הָרִיתִי אֵת כָּל־הָעָם הַזֶּה אִם־אָנֹכִי
יְלִדְתִּיהוּ כִּי־תֹאמַר אֵלַי שָׂאֵהוּ בְחֵיקֶךָ
כַּאֲשֶׁר יִשָּׂא הָאֹמֵן אֶת־הַיֹּנֵק עַל הָאֲדָמָה
אֲשֶׁר נִשְׁבַּעְתָּ לַאֲבֹתָיו׃ 13 מֵאַיִן לִי בָּשָׂר
לָתֵת לְכָל־הָעָם הַזֶּה כִּי־יִבְכּוּ עָלַי לֵאמֹר
תְּנָה־לָּנוּ בָשָׂר וְנֹאכֵלָה׃ 14 לֹא־אוּכַל
אָנֹכִי לְבַדִּי לָשֵׂאת אֶת־כָּל־הָעָם הַזֶּה כִּי
כָבֵד מִמֶּנִּי׃ 15 וְאִם־כָּכָה | אַתְּ־עֹשֶׂה לִּי
הָרְגֵנִי נָא הָרֹג אִם־מָצָאתִי חֵן בְּעֵינֶיךָ
וְאַל־אֶרְאֶה בְּרָעָתִי׃ פ
16 וַיֹּאמֶר יְהוָה אֶל־מֹשֶׁה אֶסְפָה־לִּי
שִׁבְעִים אִישׁ מִזִּקְנֵי יִשְׂרָאֵל אֲשֶׁר יָדַעְתָּ
כִּי־הֵם זִקְנֵי הָעָם וְשֹׁטְרָיו וְלָקַחְתָּ אֹתָם
אֶל־אֹהֶל מוֹעֵד וְהִתְיַצְּבוּ שָׁם עִמָּךְ׃

v. 11. חסר א׳

distressed Moses was extremely worried.

11. Why have You dealt ill with Your servant Moses' selfless concern for his people is no longer evident.

this people Rather than "my people"; also used in verses 12 and 14. This contrasts with the Golden Calf episode, where it is God who uses the term "this people" derisively (Exod. 32:9, 33:12) and it is Moses who argues that "this people" is "Your people" (Exod. 33:13).

12. Did I Hebrew: *he·anokhi,* which emphasizes the "I," as if to say, "*I* am not the father of this people. You, God, are."

14. carry . . . by myself Moses may be asking for divine rather than human assistance.

much Literally, "heavy." The weight of the people is too much to bear.

15. As the author of Moses' wretchedness, God might as well finish the job by taking his life.

GOD'S SOLUTION FOR MOSES: 70 LEADERS (vv. 16–17)

Like 7, the number 70 is symbolic (see Exod. 24:1). It is not meant to be taken as an exact number but as an approximation of a large group of people.

16. seventy of Israel's elders The institution of a council of 70 attached to a ruler is well attested in the ancient Near East. The Sages, sensitive to the fact that Moses already had an advisory council of 70 elders at Sinai, claim that those elders, guilty of unseemly conduct at Taberah (vv. 1–3), were destroyed by the divine fire.

to the Tent of Meeting At any other site, observers might attribute the miracle not to the invisible God but to the visible Moses. Only at the tent on which the divine cloud descends can God's Presence leave no doubt concerning the source of the spirit.

---

12. as a nurse carries an infant Even if the infant hits the nurse or soils her clothing, she does not reject the child (*Ha·amek Davar*).

them take their place there with you. 17I will come down and speak with you there, and I will draw upon the spirit that is on you and put it upon them; they shall share the burden of the people with you, and you shall not bear it alone. 18And say to the people: Purify yourselves for tomorrow and you shall eat meat, for you have kept whining before the LORD and saying, 'If only we had meat to eat! Indeed, we were better off in Egypt!' The LORD will give you meat and you shall eat. 19You shall eat not one day, not two, not even five days or ten or twenty, 20but a whole month, until it comes out of your nostrils and becomes loathsome to you. For you have rejected the LORD who is among you, by whining before Him and saying, 'Oh, why did we ever leave Egypt!'"

21But Moses said, "The people who are with me number six hundred thousand men; yet You say, 'I will give them enough meat to eat for a whole month.' 22Could enough flocks and herds be slaughtered to suffice them? Or could all the fish of the sea be gathered for them to suffice them?" 23And the LORD answered Moses, "Is there a limit to the LORD's power? You shall

17 וְיָרַדְתִּ֗י וְדִבַּרְתִּ֣י עִמְּךָ֮ שָׁם֒ וְאָצַלְתִּ֗י מִן־הָר֛וּחַ אֲשֶׁ֥ר עָלֶ֖יךָ וְשַׂמְתִּ֣י עֲלֵיהֶ֑ם וְנָשְׂא֤וּ אִתְּךָ֙ בְּמַשָּׂ֣א הָעָ֔ם וְלֹא־תִשָּׂ֥א אַתָּ֖ה לְבַדֶּֽךָ׃ 18 וְאֶל־הָעָ֣ם תֹּאמַ֡ר הִתְקַדְּשׁ֣וּ לְמָחָר֮ וַאֲכַלְתֶּ֣ם בָּשָׂר֒ כִּ֡י בְּכִיתֶם֩ בְּאָזְנֵ֨י יְהֹוָ֜ה לֵאמֹ֗ר מִ֤י יַאֲכִלֵ֙נוּ֙ בָּשָׂ֔ר כִּי־ט֥וֹב לָ֖נוּ בְּמִצְרָ֑יִם וְנָתַ֨ן יְהֹוָ֥ה לָכֶ֛ם בָּשָׂ֖ר וַאֲכַלְתֶּֽם׃ 19 לֹ֣א י֥וֹם אֶחָ֛ד תֹּֽאכְל֖וּן וְלֹ֣א יוֹמָ֑יִם וְלֹ֣א ׀ חֲמִשָּׁ֣ה יָמִ֗ים וְלֹא֙ עֲשָׂרָ֣ה יָמִ֔ים וְלֹ֖א עֶשְׂרִ֥ים יֽוֹם׃ 20 עַ֣ד ׀ חֹ֣דֶשׁ יָמִ֗ים עַ֤ד אֲשֶׁר־יֵצֵא֙ מֵֽאַפְּכֶ֔ם וְהָיָ֥ה לָכֶ֖ם לְזָרָ֑א יַ֗עַן כִּֽי־מְאַסְתֶּ֤ם אֶת־יְהֹוָה֙ אֲשֶׁ֣ר בְּקִרְבְּכֶ֔ם וַתִּבְכּ֤וּ לְפָנָיו֙ לֵאמֹ֔ר לָ֥מָּה זֶּ֖ה יָצָ֥אנוּ מִמִּצְרָֽיִם׃ 21 וַיֹּ֘אמֶר֮ מֹשֶׁה֒ שֵׁשׁ־מֵא֥וֹת אֶ֙לֶף֙ רַגְלִ֔י הָעָ֕ם אֲשֶׁ֥ר אָנֹכִ֖י בְּקִרְבּ֑וֹ וְאַתָּ֣ה אָמַ֗רְתָּ בָּשָׂר֙ אֶתֵּ֣ן לָהֶ֔ם וְאָכְל֖וּ חֹ֥דֶשׁ יָמִֽים׃ 22 הֲצֹ֧אן וּבָקָ֛ר יִשָּׁחֵ֥ט לָהֶ֖ם וּמָצָ֣א לָהֶ֑ם אִ֣ם אֶֽת־כׇּל־דְּגֵ֥י הַיָּ֛ם יֵאָסֵ֥ף לָהֶ֖ם וּמָצָ֥א לָהֶֽם׃ פ 23 וַיֹּ֤אמֶר יְהֹוָה֙ אֶל־מֹשֶׁ֔ה הֲיַ֥ד

---

17. speak with you But not with the elders. Neither the purpose nor the content of God's speech is stated here. The content may not have been significant; but the purpose may have been to speak to Moses to assure him that he would continue to serve as God's intermediary.

draw upon Two explanations are possible. The divine spirit will be drawn from Moses, thereby diminishing him, or the divine spirit that has been bestowed on Moses will now also rest on the elders.

share the burden of the people God's answer incorporates the very wording of Moses' plea in verse 14.

GOD'S SOLUTION FOR THE PEOPLE:
MEAT (vv. 18–23)

The gift of quail, given in anger, will result in

many fatalities. God's words expose the real reason behind the complaint: The craving for meat expresses a disguised desire to return to Egypt and is tantamount to a rejection of God.

18. Purify yourselves Sanctify yourselves by the rite of laundering and bathing that precedes a sacrifice.

20. nostrils Ibn Ezra took this to mean: For causing God's anger, the stench from the meat will fill the people's noses—a fitting punishment.

21. men Hebrew: *ragli;* literally, "footmen, infantry."

22. flocks and herds They had enough meat at hand, but they were looking for a pretext to complain.

sea "The Great Sea," the Mediterranean (Targ. Jon.).

23. Is there a limit to the LORD's power?

---

17. I will come down God tells Moses, "Given the mood of the people, I don't expect

them to rise toward Me. I will come down to shorten the distance between us" (Hirsch).

soon see whether what I have said happens to you or not!"

24Moses went out and reported the words of the LORD to the people. He gathered seventy of the people's elders and stationed them around the Tent. 25Then the LORD came down in a cloud and spoke to him; He drew upon the spirit that was on him and put it upon the seventy elders. And when the spirit rested upon them, they spoke in ecstasy, but did not continue.

26Two men, one named Eldad and the other Medad, had remained in camp; yet the spirit rested upon them—they were among those recorded, but they had not gone out to the Tent—and they spoke in ecstasy in the camp.

יְהוָה תִּקְצָר עַתָּה תִרְאֶה הֲיִקְרְךָ דְבָרִי
אִם־לֹא׃
24 וַיֵּצֵא מֹשֶׁה וַיְדַבֵּר אֶל־הָעָם אֵת דִּבְרֵי
יְהוָה וַיֶּאֱסֹף שִׁבְעִים אִישׁ מִזִּקְנֵי הָעָם
וַיַּעֲמֵד אֹתָם סְבִיבֹת הָאֹהֶל׃ 25 וַיֵּרֶד
יְהוָה ׀ בֶּעָנָן וַיְדַבֵּר אֵלָיו וַיָּאצֶל* מִן־
הָרוּחַ אֲשֶׁר עָלָיו וַיִּתֵּן עַל־שִׁבְעִים אִישׁ
הַזְּקֵנִים וַיְהִי כְּנוֹחַ עֲלֵיהֶם הָרוּחַ וַיִּתְנַבְּאוּ
וְלֹא יָסָפוּ׃
26 וַיִּשָּׁאֲרוּ שְׁנֵי־אֲנָשִׁים ׀ בַּמַּחֲנֶה שֵׁם
הָאֶחָד ׀ אֶלְדָּד וְשֵׁם הַשֵּׁנִי מֵידָד וַתָּנַח
עֲלֵהֶם הָרוּחַ וְהֵמָּה בַּכְּתֻבִים וְלֹא יָצְאוּ

v. 25. א׳ נחה

Literally, "Is the LORD's hand too short?"

what I have said Hebrew: *d'vari;* literally, "my word." God's word (*davar*), once uttered, must be fulfilled.

THE SPIRIT IS GIVEN TO THE ELDERS, ELDAD, AND MEDAD (vv. 24–30)

The elders, gathered around Moses' tent, are possessed by God's spirit, a sign that their selection by Moses is ratified by God. At the same time, Eldad and Medad, two of the elders designated as Moses' administrative assistants (for unknown reasons), remain behind in the camp. Nevertheless, they too are overcome by ecstasy, a state of rapture or trance. The prophesying of the selected elders is ecstatic and temporary and thus differs markedly from Moses' prophetic gifts. Moses' selflessness reaches its height in this passage.

24. went out From the tabernacle, where God would speak with him.

words of the LORD Concerning meat.

around the Tent In contrast to Moses, who entered the tent.

25. This is the fulfillment of the promise given in verse 17.

spoke to him To distinguish Moses from the elders.

spoke in ecstasy Which functions to provide divine validation for their selection as leaders.

26. Eldad The name means "God loves."

the spirit Of God.

recorded Although selected by Moses among the 70 elders, they declined to come out because of their feelings of inadequacy (Rashi).

out to the Tent According to this tradition, the tent was stationed outside the camp.

25. they . . . did not continue Yet Onkelos translates, "they did not cease," i.e., they did continue. What happens to people who have felt the spirit of God enter them? Are their lives permanently changed or do they revert to being the same people they were before?

26–29. Commentators differ over Eldad and Medad. Were they heroes of humility and people to be emulated (Num. R. 15:19) or were they people who cautiously waited to see what effect the ecstatic seizures would have on the others before they opened themselves up to the experience? (Perhaps there is a place in the community for people who are not pioneers but are willing to follow in the footsteps of the authentic pioneers once they see where they lead.) The Torah describes Eldad and Medad as "acting like prophets" (*mitnab·im;* v. 27). The words of Moses reflect the ambivalence of the narrative by expressing the wish that all Israelites would be authentic prophets (*n'vi·im*). Joshua, who knows what a burden the role of prophet has been for his master, is suspicious of these "instant prophets." Moses' response, however, shows that he is a leader not to feed his own ego but to serve God's needs and the needs of God's people.

²⁷A youth ran out and told Moses, saying, "Eldad and Medad are acting the prophet in the camp!" ²⁸And Joshua son of Nun, Moses' attendant from his youth, spoke up and said, "My lord Moses, restrain them!" ²⁹But Moses said to him, "Are you wrought up on my account? Would that all the Lord's people were prophets, that the Lord put His spirit upon them!" ³⁰Moses then reentered the camp together with the elders of Israel.

³¹A wind from the Lord started up, swept quail from the sea and strewed them over the camp, about a day's journey on this side and about a day's journey on that side, all around the camp, and some two cubits deep on the ground. ³²The people set to gathering quail all that day and night and all the next day—even he who gathered least had ten *homers*—and they spread them out all around the camp. ³³The meat was still between their teeth, nor yet chewed, when the anger of the Lord blazed

הָאֹ֣הֱלָה וַיִּֽתְנַבְּא֖וּ בַּֽמַּחֲנֶֽה׃ 27 וַיָּ֣רׇץ הַנַּ֔עַר וַיַּגֵּ֥ד לְמֹשֶׁ֖ה וַיֹּאמַ֑ר אֶלְדָּ֣ד וּמֵידָ֔ד מִֽתְנַבְּאִ֖ים בַּֽמַּחֲנֶֽה׃ 28 וַיַּ֜עַן יְהוֹשֻׁ֣עַ בִּן־נ֗וּן מְשָׁרֵ֥ת מֹשֶׁ֛ה מִבְּחֻרָ֖יו וַיֹּאמַ֑ר אֲדֹנִ֥י מֹשֶׁ֖ה כְּלָאֵֽם׃ 29 וַיֹּ֤אמֶר לוֹ֙ מֹשֶׁ֔ה הַֽמְקַנֵּ֥א אַתָּ֖ה לִ֑י וּמִ֨י יִתֵּ֜ן כׇּל־עַ֤ם יְהֹוָה֙ נְבִיאִ֔ים כִּֽי־יִתֵּ֧ן יְהֹוָ֛ה אֶת־רוּח֖וֹ עֲלֵיהֶֽם׃ 30 וַיֵּאָסֵ֥ף מֹשֶׁ֖ה אֶל־הַֽמַּחֲנֶ֑ה ה֖וּא וְזִקְנֵ֥י יִשְׂרָאֵֽל׃

שביעי

31 וְר֜וּחַ נָסַ֣ע ׀ מֵאֵ֣ת יְהֹוָ֗ה וַיָּ֣גׇז שַׂלְוִים֮ מִן־הַיָּם֒ וַיִּטֹּ֨שׁ עַל־הַֽמַּחֲנֶ֜ה כְּדֶ֧רֶךְ י֣וֹם כֹּ֗ה וּכְדֶ֤רֶךְ יוֹם֙ כֹּ֔ה סְבִיב֖וֹת הַֽמַּחֲנֶ֑ה וּכְאַמָּתַ֖יִם עַל־פְּנֵ֥י הָאָֽרֶץ׃ 32 וַיָּ֣קׇם הָעָ֡ם כׇּל־הַיּוֹם֩ הַה֨וּא וְכׇל־הַלַּ֜יְלָה וְכֹ֣ל ׀ י֣וֹם הַֽמׇּחֳרָ֗ת וַיַּֽאַסְפוּ֙ אֶת־הַשְּׂלָ֔ו הַמַּמְעִ֕יט אָסַ֖ף עֲשָׂרָ֣ה חֳמָרִ֑ים וַיִּשְׁטְח֤וּ לָהֶם֙ שָׁט֔וֹחַ סְבִיב֖וֹת הַֽמַּחֲנֶֽה׃ 33 הַבָּשָׂ֗ר עוֹדֶ֙נּוּ֙ בֵּ֣ין שִׁנֵּיהֶ֔ם טֶ֖רֶם יִכָּרֵ֑ת וְאַ֤ף יְהֹוָה֙ חָרָ֣ה בָעָ֔ם

---

27. A youth One of Moses' attendants.

28. Joshua The presence of Joshua with Moses in the tent is presumed and requires no explanation.

restrain them They did not cease prophesying as did the elders. Also, their spirit, stemming directly from God, must have been of a higher quality than that of the elders.

29. Moses proclaims his fervent wish that all Israelites be prophets.

that the Lord But not I, Moses.

His spirit But not Moses', again emphasizing that it was not the spirit of Moses that was transmitted to Eldad and Medad but the Lord's.

upon them The Lord does not restrict spiritual gifts to particular individuals or classes.

THE QUAIL   (vv. 31–35)

On the migration of quail, see Comment to Exod. 16:13.

31. wind Hebrew: *ru·aḥ* (spirit, wind). God's "spirit" on Moses has been shared by the elders. Now God's "wind" brings meat to the people.

sea Either the Gulf of Aqaba or the Mediterranean.

strewed them over The quail fell outside the camp, whereas God's food, the manna, fell within the camp. This distinction between the camp, which contains the Lord's Presence, and the impure zone outside indicates that the quail are a curse, not a blessing.

32. ḥomers See Comment to Lev. 27:16.

spread them out In the sun, to cure them by drying. It is also implied that they ate the meat uncooked. They were so lustful for meat that as soon as they slaughtered the birds they gorged themselves on the raw flesh.

33. plague From overeating, according to Ibn Ezra. Perhaps they choked on the meat, or became ill from eating rancid meat. Others regard

---

29. Are you wrought up on my account? Freud wrote that everyone is jealous of another's success. The Talmud states that everyone is jealous of another's success, except a father of his child and a teacher of his pupil (BT Sanh. 105b). Moses' humble response here serves to set the stage for the incident that follows in chapter 12.

forth against the people and the Lord struck the
people with a very severe plague. 34That place
was named Kibroth-hattaavah, because the
people who had the craving were buried there.

35Then the people set out from Kibroth-
hattaavah for Hazeroth.

12 When they were in Hazeroth, 1Miriam
and Aaron spoke against Moses because of the
Cushite woman he had married: "He married
a Cushite woman!"
2They said, "Has the Lord spoken only
through Moses? Has He not spoken through us
as well?" The Lord heard it. 3Now Moses was
a very humble man, more so than any other man
on earth. 4Suddenly the Lord called to Moses,
Aaron, and Miriam, "Come out, you three, to
the Tent of Meeting." So the three of them went
out. 5The Lord came down in a pillar of cloud,

וַיַּךְ יְהוָה בָּעָם מַכָּה רַבָּה מְאֹד׃ 34 וַיִּקְרָא
אֶת־שֵׁם־הַמָּקוֹם הַהוּא קִבְרוֹת הַתַּאֲוָה
כִּי־שָׁם קָבְרוּ אֶת־הָעָם הַמִּתְאַוִּים׃

35 מִקִּבְרוֹת הַתַּאֲוָה נָסְעוּ הָעָם חֲצֵרוֹת
וַיִּהְיוּ בַּחֲצֵרוֹת׃ פ

יב וַתְּדַבֵּר מִרְיָם וְאַהֲרֹן בְּמֹשֶׁה עַל־
אֹדוֹת הָאִשָּׁה הַכֻּשִׁית אֲשֶׁר לָקָח כִּי־
אִשָּׁה כֻשִׁית לָקָח׃
2 וַיֹּאמְרוּ הֲרַק אַךְ־בְּמֹשֶׁה דִּבֶּר יְהוָה הֲלֹא
גַּם־בָּנוּ דִבֵּר וַיִּשְׁמַע יְהוָה׃ 3 וְהָאִישׁ מֹשֶׁה
ענו עָנָיו מְאֹד מִכֹּל הָאָדָם אֲשֶׁר עַל־
פְּנֵי הָאֲדָמָה׃ ס 4 וַיֹּאמֶר יְהוָה פִּתְאֹם
אֶל־מֹשֶׁה וְאֶל־אַהֲרֹן וְאֶל־מִרְיָם צְאוּ
שְׁלָשְׁתְּכֶם אֶל־אֹהֶל מוֹעֵד וַיֵּצְאוּ
שְׁלָשְׁתָּם׃ 5 וַיֵּרֶד יְהוָה בְּעַמּוּד עָנָן וַיַּעֲמֹד

the punishment as a supernatural affliction stemming from God for their unjustified complaint against the manna.

THE UNIQUENESS OF MOSES (12:1–16)

Moses, as God's intimate confidant, is proclaimed the most excellent of prophets.

1. spoke against Hebrew: *va-t'dabber,* the feminine singular, indicating that Miriam initiated the rebellion against Moses. This would explain why she alone was punished.

Cushite That is, from either Nubia or Ethiopia. It may also refer to Cushan, a Midianite tribe (see Hab. 3:7); hence some Sages' view that the woman is Zipporah.

2. Miriam and Aaron are really after a share in Moses' leadership. This is the true reason for their harsh complaint; the previous complaint was only a pretext.

us The fact that Miriam and Aaron are Moses' siblings may have spurred them to claim prophetic equality with their brother.

The Lord heard it But not Moses.

3. humble Hebrew: *anav* (humble, trusting). As such, it applies to the weak and the exploited. It never means "meek."

4. Suddenly That is, at once, or unexpectedly, or while they were speaking about Moses, to prevent Miriam and Aaron from saying that Moses had complained to God.

Come out . . . went out Again, indicating that the Tent of Meeting was located outside the camp.

you three Moses was summoned together with Miriam and Aaron because, for the sake of fairness, all litigants must appear before the bar of justice at the same time (B'khor Shor).

CHAPTER 12

1. Rashi imagines Miriam criticizing Moses for neglecting his wife in order to be available at any hour, should God summon him (based on a comment in *Sifrei*). In Rashi's view, Miriam was motivated more by concern for Moses' wife than by feelings of jealousy or rivalry. Nonetheless, what she is punished for is speaking to others about Moses rather than confronting him directly.

3. Now Moses Literally, "the man Moses." It is so worded, perhaps, to emphasize that he was only human.

stopped at the entrance of the Tent, and called out, "Aaron and Miriam!" The two of them came forward; [6]and He said, "Hear these My words: When a prophet of the LORD arises among you, I make Myself known to him in a vision, I speak with him in a dream. [7]Not so with My servant Moses; he is trusted throughout My household. [8]With him I speak mouth to mouth, plainly and not in riddles, and he beholds the likeness of the LORD. How then did you not shrink from speaking against My servant Moses!" [9]Still incensed with them, the LORD departed.

[10]As the cloud withdrew from the Tent, there was Miriam stricken with snow-white scales! When Aaron turned toward Miriam, he saw that she was stricken with scales. [11]And Aaron said to Moses, "O my lord, account not to us

פֶּ֣תַח הָאֹ֔הֶל וַיִּקְרָא֙ אַהֲרֹ֣ן וּמִרְיָ֔ם וַיֵּצְא֖וּ שְׁנֵיהֶֽם׃ ‎6 וַיֹּ֖אמֶר שִׁמְעוּ־נָ֣א דְבָרָ֑י אִם־ יִֽהְיֶה֙ נְבִ֣יאֲכֶ֔ם יְהֹוָ֔ה בַּמַּרְאָה֙ אֵלָ֣יו אֶתְוַדָּ֔ע בַּחֲל֖וֹם אֲדַבֶּר־בּֽוֹ׃ ‎7 לֹא־כֵ֖ן עַבְדִּ֣י מֹשֶׁ֑ה בְּכָל־בֵּיתִ֖י נֶאֱמָ֥ן הֽוּא׃ ‎8 פֶּ֣ה אֶל־פֶּ֞ה אֲדַבֶּר־בּ֗וֹ וּמַרְאֶה֙ וְלֹ֣א בְחִידֹ֔ת וּתְמֻנַ֥ת יְהֹוָ֖ה יַבִּ֑יט וּמַדּ֙וּעַ֙ לֹ֤א יְרֵאתֶם֙ לְדַבֵּ֣ר בְּעַבְדִּ֖י בְמֹשֶֽׁה׃ ‎9 וַיִּֽחַר־אַ֧ף יְהֹוָ֛ה בָּ֖ם וַיֵּלַֽךְ׃

‎10 וְהֶעָנָ֗ן סָ֚ר מֵעַ֣ל הָאֹ֔הֶל וְהִנֵּ֥ה מִרְיָ֖ם מְצֹרַ֣עַת כַּשָּׁ֑לֶג וַיִּ֧פֶן אַהֲרֹ֛ן אֶל־מִרְיָ֖ם וְהִנֵּ֥ה מְצֹרָֽעַת׃ ‎11 וַיֹּ֥אמֶר אַהֲרֹ֖ן אֶל־מֹשֶׁ֑ה בִּ֣י

5. "Aaron and Miriam!" An ironic twist. The Lord—who in verse 8 claims to speak directly only to Moses—here avoids him and speaks directly to Aaron and Miriam.

6–8. These words of poetry describe God's relationship with other prophets and extraordinary communication with Moses, who is set apart from his prophetic counterparts in that God confides in him alone.

Hear these My words The opening of the poem.

in a dream Dreams are frequently mentioned together with prophecy as authentic channels of God's revelation, although the classical prophets attempt to distinguish between them (see Jer. 23:28).

Not so Moses is set apart from prophets like Aaron and Miriam even though all three share the same title.

trusted Of all the individuals in God's household, Moses is the most trusted; he alone has direct access to God and can obtain an audience at will.

My household This may refer to the divine court to which Moses and other prophets had access (see 1 Kings 22:19ff.).

mouth to mouth Traditional commentators explain this to mean by direct revelation (Ibn Ezra), while fully conscious (Sforno). The image here is that of a royal household in which only the most trusted servant has regular access to the monarch.

plainly Moses' visions require no interpretation, unlike the visions (or dreams, or riddles) of other prophets.

riddles Enigmatic, perplexing statements.

9. Still incensed with them The displacement of the anger to this verse means that God's anger did not abate but only increased during the confrontation (which began in v. 2).

the LORD departed God's departure from Miriam and Aaron suggests that their prophetic gifts have come to an end. Thus in verses 12–13 Aaron will plead that Moses intercede with God, a basic prophetic function. This implies that he, Aaron, no longer can do so.

10. snow-white scales Literally, "scaly as snow." Leprosy was considered a punishment for offenses against the deity in Israel and elsewhere in the ancient Near East.

he saw Because Aaron was a priest, his seeing Miriam's condition confirmed the diagnosis.

---

5. God calls Miriam and Aaron away from Moses to speak Moses' praises out of his hearing. "One gives praise only partially in a person's presence, but utters all the praise in his

or her absence" (Gen. R. 32:3).

10. The connection between malicious gossip (*motzi ra*) and leprosy (*m'tzora*) is suggested in rabbinical commentaries to Lev. 13.

the sin which we committed in our folly. 12Let
her not be as one dead, who emerges from his
mother's womb with half his flesh eaten away."
13So Moses cried out to the LORD, saying, "O
God, pray heal her!"

14But the LORD said to Moses, "If her father
spat in her face, would she not bear her shame
for seven days? Let her be shut out of camp for
seven days, and then let her be readmitted." 15So
Miriam was shut out of camp seven days; and
the people did not march on until Miriam was
readmitted. 16After that the people set out from
Hazeroth and encamped in the wilderness of
Paran.

אֲדֹנִ֔י אַל־נָ֨א תָשֵׁ֤ת עָלֵ֙ינוּ֙ חַטָּ֔את אֲשֶׁ֥ר
נוֹאַ֖לְנוּ וַאֲשֶׁ֥ר חָטָֽאנוּ׃ 12 אַל־נָ֥א תְהִ֖י כַּמֵּ֑ת
אֲשֶׁ֤ר בְּצֵאתוֹ֙ מֵרֶ֣חֶם אִמּ֔וֹ וַיֵּאָכֵ֖ל חֲצִ֥י
בְשָׂרֽוֹ׃ 13 וַיִּצְעַ֣ק מֹשֶׁ֔ה אֶל־יְהוָ֖ה לֵאמֹ֑ר
אֵ֕ל נָ֛א רְפָ֥א נָ֖א לָֽהּ׃ פ
מפטיר 14 וַיֹּ֨אמֶר יְהוָ֜ה אֶל־מֹשֶׁ֗ה וְאָבִ֙יהָ֙ יָרֹ֤ק יָרַק֙
בְּפָנֶ֔יהָ הֲלֹ֥א תִכָּלֵ֖ם שִׁבְעַ֣ת יָמִ֑ים תִּסָּגֵ֞ר
שִׁבְעַ֤ת יָמִים֙ מִח֣וּץ לַֽמַּחֲנֶ֔ה וְאַחַ֖ר תֵּאָסֵֽף׃
15 וַתִּסָּגֵ֥ר מִרְיָ֛ם מִח֥וּץ לַֽמַּחֲנֶ֖ה שִׁבְעַ֣ת
יָמִ֑ים וְהָעָם֙ לֹ֣א נָסַ֔ע עַד־הֵאָסֵ֖ף מִרְיָֽם׃
16 וְאַחַ֛ר נָסְע֥וּ הָעָ֖ם מֵחֲצֵר֑וֹת וַֽיַּחֲנ֖וּ
בְּמִדְבַּ֥ר פָּארָֽן׃ פ

11. This appeal for Moses' intercession has ironic implications. Only he whom Miriam and Aaron have wronged can help them.

my lord Aaron acknowledges Moses' superiority by using the title that one bestows upon a superior, whether mortal or God. It constitutes Moses' final vindication. Aaron, who had denied Moses' supremacy, is now forced to acknowledge it.

committed in our folly Aaron tries to diminish the seriousness of the wrong, claiming that, because it was not done with malice, it could be atoned for by intercession.

12. Let her not be as one dead According to talmudic interpretation, the leper was regarded as a dead person.

half his flesh eaten away When a fetus that has died in the womb is delivered, its skin flakes off.

13. Moses is caught in a dilemma. On the one hand, Miriam had spoken openly against him and deserved to be punished. On the other hand, as his sister, she evoked his compassion. The result is this terse prayer. Its brevity seems to reveal Moses' lack of enthusiasm and minimal compliance with Aaron's plea.

14. spat in her face In the ancient Near East, it was thought that spittle possesses magical powers. In the Bible, however, where this magical background has been uprooted, spitting is simply a matter of causing humiliation.

bear her shame for seven days A human father's rebuke by spitting entails seven days of banishment. Should not the leprosy rebuke of the Heavenly Father require at least the same banishment? Miriam's penalty is sharply reduced to a seven-day exclusion from camp. Here too an additional concession is made, for an ordinary case of leprosy lasts a minimum of 14 days (Lev. 13:5). Miriam's exclusion from camp probably has nothing to do with the laws of leprosy but with the norms of shame. Furthermore, the analogy of Miriam's condition to that of the daughter is now clarified. Miriam's white (and hence, noncontagious, pure) leprosy is equivalent to the daughter who is spat on. Both are ostracized because they are humiliated, not because they are impure.

15. people did not march All of Israel pays a penalty for Miriam's sin. Their march to the Promised Land must be delayed a full week.

---

12. as one dead Miriam saved Moses from perishing as a newborn infant (Exod. 2). Now it is Moses' turn to save her from a fate similar to that of a doomed infant. Because of the urgency of the situation, Moses keeps his prayer brief. Others interpret the brevity of his prayer as concern lest the Israelites say, "For his sister, he pleads with God at length, but were we in her place, he would offer only a few words" (*Sifrei*). Might we speculate that, because Miriam's affliction was caused by her feeling alienated from her brother, the knowledge of his praying for her generated the healing potential within her?

The *parashah* ends on a positive note, with Miriam's reintegration into the camp. However, the vision of a harmonious people inspired at Mount Sinai to follow God through a wilderness has been compromised, and it will be even further diminished in subsequent chapters.

הפטרת בהעלתך

HAFTARAH FOR B'HA·ALOT'KHA

ZECHARIAH 2:14–4:7

The first part of the Book of Zechariah (chaps. 1–8), in which this *haftarah* is found, opens with the second year of Darius I's reign as king of Persia (520 B.C.E.). Darius continued the foreign policy of Cyrus who, one year after his conquest of Babylon, had issued an edict (in 538 B.C.E.) enabling all subject populations to return to their national religious practices. As a result of Cyrus's policy, exiles had returned to Judah with permission to rebuild the Temple, destroyed nearly fifty years earlier by the Babylonians.

Work on the new temple was postponed, however, when local adversaries prevented the people of Judah from rebuilding (Ezra 4:1–3). In the second year in the reign of Darius, the prophets Haggai and Zechariah exhorted the people in God's name to resume the building effort (Ezra 4:4–5,24, 5:1–2). Construction would be completed in four years.

This *haftarah* begins with God's promise of a return to Zion. It continues with the purification and investiture of the high priest, Joshua, and a declaration of God's forgiveness for the people's sins in the Land. This is followed by the prophet's vision of the lampstand (*m'norah*) to be used in the temple and words affirming that communal success will be achieved through the spirit of God.

Priestly concerns and details dominate the *haftarah,* such as: God's "holy habitation" (temple) in heaven; the "Holy Land" on earth; priestly vestments (robe, diadem, and sacred stone) and instructions; and the removal of the "guilt" of Joshua and of the Land. It ends with a vision of the lampstand and lamps in the Jerusalem temple. Nevertheless, the notion of a dual leadership prompted references within the priestly context to the royal "Branch" and to the secular leader, Zerubbabel, himself (3:8, 4:6–9). The two leaders are referred to as "Joshua the high priest" and "Zerubbabel the governor of Judea" in the Book of Haggai (1:1, 2:2), and as the two anointed dignitaries (literally, "sons of oil") in Zech. 4:14.

RELATION OF THE *HAFTARAH* TO THE *PARASHAH*

Both the *parashah* and the *haftarah* give special attention to the ceremonial object of the *m'norah* and its lamps. In the Torah, the context is God's instruction concerning the kindling of lights in the tabernacle. In Zechariah's prophecy, the imagery is included in a vision of the future temple and its leaders.

Both texts also deal with the ritual celebrants of the shrine. In the *parashah,* the status of the Levites is singled out, with emphasis placed on physical purification and the cleanliness of their garments (Num. 8:7). Their duty to keep God's charge is also stressed (v. 24). Similar concerns and language are found in the *haftarah,* which depicts the purification of the high priest Joshua and his divine charge (Zech. 3:4–6).

The meaning of the *m'norah* and its lamps in the Torah is not spelled out there. However, the continuation of Zechariah's vision explains that the candelabrum symbolizes God, and the lights His eyes, roving providentially over the whole earth (Zech. 4:10–14). In later texts, including Jewish Hellenistic sources and Midrash, the lamps of the *m'norah* also symbolized the seven heavenly bodies (sun, moon, and five visible planets). This gave a cosmic dimension to divine providence and added a transcendent aspect to God's immanent Presence in the shrine.

2 [14]Shout for joy, Fair Zion! For lo, I come;
and I will dwell in your midst—declares the
Lord. [15]In that day many nations will attach
themselves to the Lord and become His people,
and He will dwell in your midst. Then you will
know that I was sent to you by the Lord of
Hosts.

[16]The Lord will take Judah to Himself as His
portion in the Holy Land, and He will choose
Jerusalem once more.

[17]Be silent, all flesh, before the Lord!
For He is roused from His holy habitation.

ב 14 רָנִּי וְשִׂמְחִי בַּת־צִיּוֹן כִּי הִנְנִי־בָא
וְשָׁכַנְתִּי בְתוֹכֵךְ נְאֻם־יְהוָה׃ 15 וְנִלְווּ גוֹיִם
רַבִּים אֶל־יְהוָה בַּיּוֹם הַהוּא וְהָיוּ לִי לְעָם
וְשָׁכַנְתִּי בְתוֹכֵךְ וְיָדַעַתְּ כִּי־יְהוָה צְבָאוֹת
שְׁלָחַנִי אֵלָיִךְ׃
16 וְנָחַל יְהוָה אֶת־יְהוּדָה חֶלְקוֹ עַל אַדְמַת
הַקֹּדֶשׁ וּבָחַר עוֹד בִּירוּשָׁלִָם׃
17 הַס כָּל־בָּשָׂר מִפְּנֵי יְהוָה
כִּי נֵעוֹר מִמְּעוֹן קָדְשׁוֹ׃ ס

3 He further showed me Joshua, the high
priest, standing before the angel of the Lord,
and the Accuser standing at his right to accuse
him. [2]But [the angel of] the Lord said to the
Accuser, "The Lord rebuke you, O Accuser;
may the Lord who has chosen Jerusalem rebuke
you! For this is a brand plucked from the fire."
[3]Now Joshua was clothed in filthy garments
when he stood before the angel. [4]The latter
spoke up and said to his attendants, "Take the
filthy garments off him!" And he said to him,
"See, I have removed your guilt from you, and
you shall be clothed in [priestly] robes." [5]Then

ג וַיַּרְאֵנִי אֶת־יְהוֹשֻׁעַ הַכֹּהֵן הַגָּדוֹל עֹמֵד
לִפְנֵי מַלְאַךְ יְהוָה וְהַשָּׂטָן עֹמֵד עַל־יְמִינוֹ
לְשִׂטְנוֹ׃ 2 וַיֹּאמֶר יְהוָה אֶל־הַשָּׂטָן יִגְעַר
יְהוָה בְּךָ הַשָּׂטָן וְיִגְעַר יְהוָה בְּךָ הַבֹּחֵר
בִּירוּשָׁלִָם הֲלוֹא זֶה אוּד מֻצָּל מֵאֵשׁ׃
3 וִיהוֹשֻׁעַ הָיָה לָבֻשׁ בְּגָדִים צוֹאִים וְעֹמֵד
לִפְנֵי הַמַּלְאָךְ׃ 4 וַיַּעַן וַיֹּאמֶר אֶל־הָעֹמְדִים
לְפָנָיו לֵאמֹר הָסִירוּ הַבְּגָדִים הַצֹּאִים
מֵעָלָיו וַיֹּאמֶר אֵלָיו רְאֵה הֶעֱבַרְתִּי מֵעָלֶיךָ
עֲוֺנֶךָ וְהַלְבֵּשׁ אֹתְךָ מַחֲלָצוֹת׃ 5 וָאֹמַר
יָשִׂימוּ צָנִיף טָהוֹר עַל־רֹאשׁוֹ וַיָּשִׂימוּ

Zechariah 2:14. I will dwell in your midst God is roused to return to Zion from "His holy habitation" in heaven. The language of indwelling (*v'shakhanti v'tokhekh*) derives from the old tabernacle traditions (Exod. 25:8). It was used to express God's dwelling in the temple of Solomon (1 Kings 6:13) and the return of God to the post-exilic temple by Ezekiel (Ezek. 43:9). In the Deuteronomic tradition the verb for "dwell" (*shakken*) is used to express the indwelling of God's name, not His divine being (cf. Deut. 12:11, 14:23). Two distinct theological positions thus express the nature and character of divine immanence: One position speaks of God's immediate and direct presence; the other suggests that this presence is mediated by the divine name.

The Sages turned God's providential Presence into the noun *Sh'khinah,* and the concept came to include divine involvement in Israel's fate both outside the Temple and outside the Land. In the Midrash, the *Sh'khinah* suffers with Israel in exile and will return with it at the time of redemption.

16. The Lord will take Judah . . . as His portion This notion is first found in Deut. 32:9 (speaking of Jacob). Zechariah's prophecy then adds a striking dimension to the idea that God will return to this people and this place, by speaking about the chosen land as "the Holy Land." That formulation, claiming sanctity for the land of Israel as a whole, is unique in the Bible.

Zechariah 3:1–2. In this vision of a heavenly court, God is the judge, the high priest Joshua is the defendant, and the angel and the Accuser (Heb. *satan*) are the defense and the prosecuting

he gave the order, "Let a pure diadem be placed on his head." And they placed the pure diadem on his head and clothed him in [priestly] garments, as the angel of the LORD stood by.

6And the angel of the LORD charged Joshua as follows: 7"Thus said the LORD of Hosts: If you walk in My paths and keep My charge, you in turn will rule My House and guard My courts, and I will permit you to move about among these attendants. 8Hearken well, O High Priest Joshua, you and your fellow priests sitting before you! For those men are a sign that I am going to bring My servant the Branch. 9For mark well this stone which I place before Joshua, a single stone with seven eyes. I will execute its engraving—declares the LORD of Hosts—and I will remove that country's guilt in a single day. 10In that day—declares the LORD of Hosts—you will be inviting each other to the shade of vines and fig trees."

הַצָּנִיף הַטָּהוֹר עַל־רֹאשׁוֹ וַיַּלְבִּשֻׁהוּ בְּגָדִים
וּמַלְאַךְ יְהוָה עֹמֵד׃
6 וַיָּעַד מַלְאַךְ יְהוָה בִּיהוֹשֻׁעַ לֵאמֹר׃
7 כֹּה־אָמַר יְהוָה צְבָאוֹת אִם־בִּדְרָכַי תֵּלֵךְ
וְאִם אֶת־מִשְׁמַרְתִּי תִשְׁמֹר וְגַם־אַתָּה
תָּדִין אֶת־בֵּיתִי וְגַם תִּשְׁמֹר אֶת־חֲצֵרָי
וְנָתַתִּי לְךָ מַהְלְכִים בֵּין הָעֹמְדִים הָאֵלֶּה׃
8 שְׁמַע־נָא יְהוֹשֻׁעַ ׀ הַכֹּהֵן הַגָּדוֹל אַתָּה
וְרֵעֶיךָ הַיֹּשְׁבִים לְפָנֶיךָ כִּי־אַנְשֵׁי מוֹפֵת
הֵמָּה כִּי־הִנְנִי מֵבִיא אֶת־עַבְדִּי צֶמַח׃
9 כִּי ׀ הִנֵּה הָאֶבֶן אֲשֶׁר נָתַתִּי לִפְנֵי יְהוֹשֻׁעַ
עַל־אֶבֶן אַחַת שִׁבְעָה עֵינָיִם הִנְנִי מְפַתֵּחַ
פִּתֻּחָהּ נְאֻם יְהוָה צְבָאוֹת וּמַשְׁתִּי אֶת־עֲוֺן
הָאָרֶץ־הַהִיא בְּיוֹם אֶחָד׃ 10 בַּיּוֹם הַהוּא
נְאֻם יְהוָה צְבָאוֹת תִּקְרְאוּ אִישׁ לְרֵעֵהוּ
אֶל־תַּחַת גֶּפֶן וְאֶל־תַּחַת תְּאֵנָה׃

4 The angel who talked with me came back and woke me as a man is wakened from sleep. 2He said to me, "What do you see?" And I answered, "I see a lampstand all of gold, with a bowl above it. The lamps on it are seven in number, and the lamps above it have seven pipes; 3and by it are two olive trees, one on the right of the bowl and one on its left." 4I, in turn, asked the angel who talked with me, "What do those things mean, my lord?" 5"Do you not know what those things mean?" asked the angel who

ד וַיָּשָׁב הַמַּלְאָךְ הַדֹּבֵר בִּי וַיְעִירֵנִי
כְּאִישׁ אֲשֶׁר־יֵעוֹר מִשְּׁנָתוֹ׃ 2 וַיֹּאמֶר אֵלַי
מָה אַתָּה רֹאֶה ויאמר וָאֹמַר רָאִיתִי ׀
וְהִנֵּה מְנוֹרַת זָהָב כֻּלָּהּ וְגֻלָּהּ עַל־רֹאשָׁהּ
וְשִׁבְעָה נֵרֹתֶיהָ עָלֶיהָ שִׁבְעָה וְשִׁבְעָה
מוּצָקוֹת לַנֵּרוֹת אֲשֶׁר עַל־רֹאשָׁהּ׃ 3 וּשְׁנַיִם
זֵיתִים עָלֶיהָ אֶחָד מִימִין הַגֻּלָּה וְאֶחָד
עַל־שְׂמֹאלָהּ׃ 4 וָאַעַן וָאֹמַר אֶל־הַמַּלְאָךְ
הַדֹּבֵר בִּי לֵאמֹר מָה־אֵלֶּה אֲדֹנִי׃ 5 וַיַּעַן
הַמַּלְאָךְ הַדֹּבֵר בִּי וַיֹּאמֶר אֵלַי הֲלוֹא יָדַעְתָּ

attorneys, respectively. Presumably the Accuser has contended that the priest is unfit for office. The Accuser is now rebuked by God.

8. I am going to bring My servant the Branch Elsewhere in Zechariah and in Ezra, the high priest Joshua is paired with Zerubbabel (descendant of King Jehoiachin and thus in the direct Davidic line), representing priestly and royal leadership, respectively. But here, who or what "the Branch" signifies is unspecified, giving rise to interpretations of messianic expectancy. The metaphor of a branch (*tzemaḥ*) used to depict a future king is found in Isaiah (4:2). It was first developed fully in Jeremiah's oracles about a descendant of David whom God will establish to bring victory and to rule in justice (23:5–6, 33:14–16).

The 15th benediction of the *Amidah* is a messianic prayer known as "the benediction of David." It begins with a petition that God cause "the Branch of David (*tzemaḥ David*) to flourish."

talked with me; and I said, "No, my lord." 6Then
he explained to me as follows:

"This is the word of the LORD to Zerubbabel:
Not by might, nor by power, but by My
spirit—said the LORD of Hosts. 7Whoever you
are, O great mountain in the path of Zerubbabel, turn into level ground! For he shall produce
that excellent stone; it shall be greeted with
shouts of 'Beautiful! Beautiful!'"

מָה־הֵ֣מָּה אֵ֑לֶּה וָאֹמַ֖ר לֹ֥א אֲדֹנִֽי׃ 6 וַיַּ֜עַן
וַיֹּ֤אמֶר אֵלַי֙ לֵאמֹ֔ר

זֶ֚ה דְּבַר־יְהוָ֔ה אֶל־זְרֻבָּבֶ֖ל לֵאמֹ֑ר לֹ֤א
בְחַ֙יִל֙ וְלֹ֣א בְכֹ֔חַ כִּ֤י אִם־בְּרוּחִ֔י אָמַ֖ר יְהוָ֥ה
צְבָאֽוֹת׃ 7 מִֽי־אַתָּ֧ה הַר־הַגָּד֛וֹל לִפְנֵ֥י
זְרֻבָּבֶ֖ל לְמִישֹׁ֑ר וְהוֹצִיא֙ אֶת־הָאֶ֣בֶן
הָרֹאשָׁ֔ה תְּשֻׁא֕וֹת חֵ֥ן חֵ֖ן לָֽהּ׃ פ

13 The Lord spoke to Moses, saying,
2"Send men to scout the land of Canaan, which
I am giving to the Israelite people; send one man
from each of their ancestral tribes, each one a
chieftain among them." 3So Moses, by the
Lord's command, sent them out from the wilderness of Paran, all the men being leaders of
the Israelites. 4And these were their names:

יג וַיְדַבֵּ֥ר יְהֹוָ֖ה אֶל־מֹשֶׁ֥ה לֵּאמֹֽר׃
2 שְׁלַח־לְךָ֣ אֲנָשִׁ֗ים וְיָתֻ֙רוּ֙ אֶת־אֶ֣רֶץ כְּנַ֔עַן
אֲשֶׁר־אֲנִ֥י נֹתֵ֖ן לִבְנֵ֣י יִשְׂרָאֵ֑ל אִ֣ישׁ אֶחָד֩
אִ֨ישׁ אֶחָ֜ד לְמַטֵּ֤ה אֲבֹתָיו֙ תִּשְׁלָ֔חוּ כֹּ֖ל
נָשִׂ֥יא בָהֶֽם׃ 3 וַיִּשְׁלַ֨ח אֹתָ֥ם מֹשֶׁ֛ה מִמִּדְבַּ֥ר
פָּארָ֖ן עַל־פִּ֣י יְהֹוָ֑ה כֻּלָּ֣ם אֲנָשִׁ֔ים רָאשֵׁ֛י
בְנֵֽי־יִשְׂרָאֵ֖ל הֵֽמָּה׃ 4 וְאֵ֖לֶּה שְׁמוֹתָ֑ם

The Generation of the Exodus: The March to Transjordan (continued)

THE RECONNAISSANCE OF CANAAN (13:1–14:45)

According to the Torah, the wilderness period was marked by two flagrant sins: the apostasy of worshiping the Golden Calf and the faithlessness of the scouts. The scouts' negative report precipitates a wave of fear and murmuring among the people and a threat to return to Egypt under new leadership.

SCOUTS ARE CHOSEN (13:1–20)

1. According to the tradition recorded in Deuteronomy (1:22–23), the initiative to scout the Land originated with the people, not God. That constituted a breach of faith, because God already had scouted the land, so to speak. Hence, because Moses approved of the expedition, he was condemned with the people to die in the wilderness.

2. send In contrast to the chieftains who were chosen by God to conduct the census and to parcel the Land, the chieftains sent to scout were to be chosen by Moses, an indication that God disapproved of the project from the start.

men Hebrew: *anashim,* which can refer to "important, brave" men. Here, they were distinguished leaders of each tribe.

to scout Moses would not have sent 12 clan heads on a dangerous spying mission. In a case of true espionage—at Jericho—Joshua sent two spies (*m'ragg'lim*) who probably were trained. Moses' intent could only have been to send a cross-section of the tribal leaders so that their positive report would verify the outstanding qualities of God's land and dispel doubts about the people's ability to conquer it. The venture was more a test of faith than a military expedition.

land of Canaan The purpose of the expedition was to claim possession symbolically, not just to reconnoiter the land.

3. Paran Where the Israelites have camped.

CHAPTER 13

The events of this *parashah* are crucial in the Torah narrative, explaining why it took 40 years for the people to reach the Promised Land. We already have seen certain undesirable character traits emerge among the Israelites: grumbling about food and living conditions, a nostalgia for the less complicated life of being a slave in Egypt. These will culminate in a massive failure of nerve when God summons Israel to attack and conquer the Promised Land. The people do not believe in their own ability to do that, and by implication do not believe in God's ability to ensure their victory. As a result, God decrees 40 years of wandering, to end only when the generation that left Egypt has died off.

"One cannot be expected to leave the state of slavery, toiling in bricks and straw, and go to fight with giants. It was therefore part of the divine wisdom to make them wander through the wilderness until they had become schooled in courage, until a new generation grew up who had never known humiliation and bondage" (Maimonides).

2. Send Hebrew: *sh'laḥ l'kha;* literally, "send for yourself." That is, for your own purposes (not Mine). God seems to be saying, "I have told you already that the land is good and that I will give it to you. If you need human confirmation of that, go ahead and send scouts" (Num. R. 16:8).

From the tribe of Reuben, Shammua son of Zaccur.

5From the tribe of Simeon, Shaphat son of Hori.

6From the tribe of Judah, Caleb son of Jephunneh.

7From the tribe of Issachar, Igal son of Joseph.

8From the tribe of Ephraim, Hosea son of Nun.

9From the tribe of Benjamin, Palti son of Rafu.

10From the tribe of Zebulun, Gaddiel son of Sodi.

11From the tribe of Joseph, namely, the tribe of Manasseh, Gaddi son of Susi.

12From the tribe of Dan, Ammiel son of Gemalli.

13From the tribe of Asher, Sethur son of Michael.

14From the tribe of Naphtali, Nahbi son of Vophsi.

15From the tribe of Gad, Geuel son of Machi.

16Those were the names of the men whom Moses sent to scout the land; but Moses changed the name of Hosea son of Nun to Joshua.

17When Moses sent them to scout the land of Canaan, he said to them, "Go up there into the Negeb and on into the hill country, 18and see what kind of country it is. Are the people who dwell in it strong or weak, few or many? 19Is the country in which they dwell good or

לְמַטֵּה רְאוּבֵ֔ן שַׁמּ֖וּעַ בֶּן־זַכּֽוּר׃

5 לְמַטֵּה שִׁמְע֔וֹן שָׁפָ֖ט בֶּן־חוֹרִֽי׃

6 לְמַטֵּה יְהוּדָ֔ה כָּלֵ֖ב בֶּן־יְפֻנֶּֽה׃

7 לְמַטֵּה יִשָּׂשכָ֔ר יִגְאָ֖ל בֶּן־יוֹסֵֽף׃

8 לְמַטֵּה אֶפְרָ֑יִם הוֹשֵׁ֖עַ בִּן־נֽוּן׃

9 לְמַטֵּה בִנְיָמִ֔ן פַּלְטִ֖י בֶּן־רָפֽוּא׃

10 לְמַטֵּה זְבוּלֻ֔ן גַּדִּיאֵ֖ל בֶּן־סוֹדִֽי׃

11 לְמַטֵּה יוֹסֵ֖ף לְמַטֵּה מְנַשֶּׁ֑ה גַּדִּ֖י בֶּן־סוּסִֽי׃

12 לְמַטֵּה דָ֔ן עַמִּיאֵ֖ל בֶּן־גְּמַלִּֽי׃

13 לְמַטֵּה אָשֵׁ֔ר סְת֖וּר בֶּן־מִיכָאֵֽל׃

14 לְמַטֵּה נַפְתָּלִ֔י נַחְבִּ֖י בֶּן־וָפְסִֽי׃

15 לְמַטֵּה גָ֔ד גְּאוּאֵ֖ל בֶּן־מָכִֽי׃

16 אֵ֣לֶּה שְׁמ֣וֹת הָֽאֲנָשִׁ֗ים אֲשֶׁר־שָׁלַ֥ח מֹשֶׁ֖ה לָת֣וּר אֶת־הָאָ֑רֶץ וַיִּקְרָ֥א מֹשֶׁ֛ה לְהוֹשֵׁ֥עַ בִּן־נ֖וּן יְהוֹשֻֽׁעַ׃

17 וַיִּשְׁלַ֤ח אֹתָם֙ מֹשֶׁ֔ה לָת֖וּר אֶת־אֶ֣רֶץ כְּנָ֑עַן וַיֹּ֣אמֶר אֲלֵהֶ֗ם עֲל֥וּ זֶה֙ בַּנֶּ֔גֶב וַעֲלִיתֶ֖ם אֶת־הָהָֽר׃ 18 וּרְאִיתֶ֥ם אֶת־הָאָ֖רֶץ מַה־הִ֑וא וְאֶת־הָעָם֙ הַיֹּשֵׁ֣ב עָלֶ֔יהָ הֶחָזָ֥ק הוּא֙ הֲרָפֶ֔ה הַמְעַ֥ט ה֖וּא אִם־רָֽב׃ 19 וּמָ֣ה הָאָ֗רֶץ אֲשֶׁר־הוּא֙ יֹשֵׁ֣ב בָּ֔הּ הֲטוֹבָ֥ה הִ֖וא אִם־רָעָ֔ה

6. Caleb The name, from *"kelev"* (dog), is probably part of a longer name with a meaning like "the obedient servant of the god so-and-so." The term "dog" as a metaphor for an obsequious servant is found often in the literature of the ancient Near East.

17. Go up there into Literally, "ascend by means of." The goal is the hill country; the Negeb

is merely the means of getting there.

Negeb Literally, "arid land." This refers to the southern part of Judah between Beer-sheba and the Sinai Peninsula.

and on into Literally, "and ascend." The ascent begins in the Negeb, and the altitude reaches 3000 feet (900 m) at Hebron.

hill country Of Judah.

16. Moses changed the name of Hosea . . . to Joshua Moses changes Joshua's name from *Hoshe·a* to *Y'hoshu·a* (God will save) by adding the letter *yod,* which stands for the name of God.

Rashi interprets this to mean, "May God save you from the malign influence of the other scouts."

bad? Are the towns they live in open or fortified? 20Is the soil rich or poor? Is it wooded or not? And take pains to bring back some of the fruit of the land."—Now it happened to be the season of the first ripe grapes.

21They went up and scouted the land, from the wilderness of Zin to Rehob, at Lebo-hamath. 22They went up into the Negeb and came to Hebron, where lived Ahiman, Sheshai, and Talmai, the Anakites.—Now Hebron was founded seven years before Zoan of Egypt.—23They reached the wadi Eshcol, and there they cut down a branch with a single cluster of grapes—it had to be borne on a carrying frame by two of them—and some pomegranates and figs. 24That place was named the wadi Eshcol because of the cluster that the Israelites cut down there.

וּמָ֣ה הֶֽעָרִ֗ים אֲשֶׁר־הוּא֙ יוֹשֵׁ֣ב בָּהֵ֔נָּה הַבְּמַֽחֲנִ֖ים אִ֥ם בְּמִבְצָרִֽים: 20 וּמָ֣ה הָ֠אָרֶץ הַשְּׁמֵנָ֨ה הִ֜וא אִם־רָזָ֗ה הֲיֵֽשׁ־בָּ֥הּ עֵץ֙ אִם־אַ֔יִן וְהִ֨תְחַזַּקְתֶּ֔ם וּלְקַחְתֶּ֖ם מִפְּרִ֣י הָאָ֑רֶץ וְהַ֨יָּמִ֔ים יְמֵ֖י בִּכּוּרֵ֥י עֲנָבִֽים: 21 וַֽיַּעֲל֖וּ וַיָּתֻ֣רוּ אֶת־הָאָ֑רֶץ מִמִּדְבַּר־צִ֥ן עַד־רְחֹ֖ב לְבֹ֥א חֲמָֽת: 22 וַיַּֽעֲל֣וּ בַנֶּגֶב֮ וַיָּבֹ֣א* עַד־חֶבְרוֹן֒ וְשָׁ֤ם אֲחִימַן֙ שֵׁשַׁ֣י וְתַלְמַ֔י יְלִידֵ֖י הָֽעֲנָ֑ק וְחֶבְר֗וֹן שֶׁ֤בַע שָׁנִים֙ נִבְנְתָ֔ה לִפְנֵ֖י צֹ֥עַן מִצְרָֽיִם: 23 וַיָּבֹ֜אוּ עַד־נַ֣חַל אֶשְׁכֹּ֗ל וַיִּכְרְת֨וּ מִשָּׁ֤ם זְמוֹרָה֙ וְאֶשְׁכּ֤וֹל עֲנָבִים֙ אֶחָ֔ד וַיִּשָּׂאֻ֥הוּ בַמּ֖וֹט בִּשְׁנָ֑יִם וּמִן־הָרִמֹּנִ֖ים וּמִן־הַתְּאֵנִֽים: 24 לַמָּק֣וֹם הַה֔וּא קָרָ֖א נַ֣חַל אֶשְׁכּ֑וֹל עַ֚ל אֹד֣וֹת הָֽאֶשְׁכּ֔וֹל אֲשֶׁר־כָּֽרְת֥וּ מִשָּׁ֖ם בְּנֵ֥י יִשְׂרָאֵֽל:

v. 22. סבירין ומטעין לשון רבים

20. rich Literally, "fat," meaning fertile.

THE EXPEDITION (vv. 21–24)

Two traditions have been brought together here: that the scouts traversed the entire Land (v. 21) and that they journeyed only as far as Hebron (vv. 22–24).

21. Zin North of the wilderness of Paran, the scouts' point of origin. The exact bounds of these wildernesses are not known.

Lebo-hamath An important city at the northern boundary of the Promised Land.

22. Hebron The most sacred site in the southern part of the Land. All the patriarchs and their wives, except Rachel, are buried here.

Anakites One of the original peoples of Canaan before Israel's conquest, known and feared for their size.

23. This verse emphasizes that a single cluster of grapes was so heavy that it took two men to carry it.

carrying frame It is unlikely that the scouts brought the grape cluster to the north. Hence scholars assume that the account of the northern expedition is from a second, separate source—and that we have here a fusion of two narratives.

22. They went up . . . and came Hebrew: va-ya·alu . . . va-yavo; the first verb is plural but the second is singular. This prompted the Talmud to suggest that while the other scouts were gathering economic and military data, Caleb was motivated to visit the tomb of the patriarchs in Hebron (BT Sot. 34b). He alone was able to see the Land not only as it was at the moment but as what it had meant and would mean in terms of God's promise to the patriarchs. They went up—they ascended, not only geographically but to a higher spiritual level. No matter where one comes from, going to Israel is referred to as aliyah, "going up." Similarly, one is called to the Torah for an aliyah, an ascent to a higher level, whether or not there are steps to the bimah.

28. What the scouts reported was factually correct but it was not the truth. Truth is more than a summary of empirical facts. It must include the response of the soul to those facts, and this is where the scouts failed in their duty (Menaḥem Mendel of Kotzk). Although each of the scouts was supposed to be a leader in his own tribe, they did not anticipate the consequences of their words. They did not realize that by speaking their minds and giving voice to their own doubts, they would provoke panic among the people.

25 וַיָּשֻׁבוּ מִתּוּר הָאָרֶץ מִקֵּץ אַרְבָּעִים יוֹם׃
26 וַיֵּלְכוּ וַיָּבֹאוּ אֶל־מֹשֶׁה וְאֶל־אַהֲרֹן וְאֶל־
כָּל־עֲדַת בְּנֵי־יִשְׂרָאֵל אֶל־מִדְבַּר פָּארָן
קָדֵשָׁה וַיָּשִׁיבוּ אֹתָם דָּבָר וְאֶת־כָּל־הָעֵדָה
וַיַּרְאוּם אֶת־פְּרִי הָאָרֶץ׃ 27 וַיְסַפְּרוּ־לוֹ
וַיֹּאמְרוּ בָּאנוּ אֶל־הָאָרֶץ אֲשֶׁר שְׁלַחְתָּנוּ
וְגַם זָבַת חָלָב וּדְבַשׁ הִוא וְזֶה־פִּרְיָהּ׃
28 אֶפֶס כִּי־עַז הָעָם הַיֹּשֵׁב בָּאָרֶץ וְהֶעָרִים
בְּצֻרוֹת גְּדֹלֹת מְאֹד וְגַם־יְלִדֵי הָעֲנָק רָאִינוּ
שָׁם׃ 29 עֲמָלֵק יוֹשֵׁב בְּאֶרֶץ הַנֶּגֶב וְהַחִתִּי
וְהַיְבוּסִי וְהָאֱמֹרִי יוֹשֵׁב בָּהָר וְהַכְּנַעֲנִי
יוֹשֵׁב עַל־הַיָּם וְעַל יַד הַיַּרְדֵּן׃
30 וַיַּהַס כָּלֵב אֶת־הָעָם אֶל־מֹשֶׁה וַיֹּאמֶר

25 At the end of forty days they returned from
scouting the land. 26 They went straight to Moses
and Aaron and the whole Israelite community
at Kadesh in the wilderness of Paran, and they
made their report to them and to the whole
community, as they showed them the fruit of
the land. 27 This is what they told him: "We came
to the land you sent us to; it does indeed flow
with milk and honey, and this is its fruit. 28 However, the people who inhabit the country are
powerful, and the cities are fortified and very
large; moreover, we saw the Anakites there.
29 Amalekites dwell in the Negeb region; Hittites, Jebusites, and Amorites inhabit the hill
country; and Canaanites dwell by the Sea and
along the Jordan."
30 Caleb hushed the people before Moses and

THE REPORT (vv. 25–33)

26. Kadesh The site is identified with a group of oases 50 miles (80 km) south of Beer-sheba, one of which still bears the name 'Ain Qadesh.

27–28. him That is, Moses. The prior verse tells us that a report was made to Moses and to the entire community. This indicates the possibility of different traditions.

flow with milk and honey Literally, "ooze with . . ." This is the traditional phrase for the fruitfulness of the Promised Land.

fortified The walls of ancient Canaanite cities were 30 to 50 feet (9 to 15 m) high, and sometimes 15 feet (4.5 m) thick.

29. Amalekites A nomadic tribe whose domain extended from the Negeb of Judah into the Sinai Peninsula, virtually the same sweep as Israel's wilderness trek.

Hittites The non-Semitic Hittite Empire of Anatolia (located in Asia Minor, in present-day Turkey) was destroyed around 1200 B.C.E. The Hittite language and culture, carried by Hittite enclaves, persisted in northern Syria for another 500 years. Although there is no evidence of such enclaves in Canaan, Hittite refugees may have entered Canaan from the north.

Jebusites This term appears in biblical narrative from the time of the conquest of Canaan. The Jebusites inhabited Jerusalem when King David conquered it (2 Sam. 5:6).

Amorites In ancient Akkadian, *"amurru"* means "west"; the term was used in Mesopotamian cuneiform sources as early as the second half of the 3rd millennium to designate Semitic herdsmen and their territory in the Syrian steppe west of the Euphrates. In the Bible, "Amorite" occurs only as an ethnic label and does not refer to the Amurru kingdom, which disappeared around 1200 B.C.E. Sometimes the term is used as an alternative for "Canaanite," referring to all inhabitants west of the Jordan.

Canaanites Canaan was Egypt's Asian province, ruled by Egyptian governors and local princes. Its boundaries matched closely those of the Promised Land (34:1–12). In a number of biblical passages, the name "Canaanite" refers to a merchant class (Isa. 23:8; Ezek. 17:4; Prov. 31:24). Its equivalent in ancient Akkadian, *kinahhu,* also means "red-purple." The dye that served as the source of that much-desired color was extracted from sea creatures along the eastern Mediterranean and was handled exclusively by Canaanite (*kinahhu*) merchants, who came to be named after their product. (The Greek word "Phoenician" has the same link between the red-purple dye and the people.)

Negeb . . . hill country . . . Sea . . . Jordan These areas correspond to the four major geographic divisions of the Promised Land: the southern wilderness; the central mountain chain above it from Beer-sheba northward and the plains on either side; the sea coast; and the Jordan rift (the steep valley to the west and to the east of the Jordan River).

said, "Let us by all means go up, and we shall gain possession of it, for we shall surely overcome it."

31But the men who had gone up with him said, "We cannot attack that people, for it is stronger than we." 32Thus they spread calumnies among the Israelites about the land they had scouted, saying, "The country that we traversed and scouted is one that devours its settlers. All the people that we saw in it are men of great size; 33we saw the Nephilim there—the Anakites are part of the Nephilim—and we looked like grasshoppers to ourselves, and so we must have looked to them."

עָלֹה נַעֲלֶה וְיָרַשְׁנוּ אֹתָהּ כִּי־יָכוֹל נוּכַל
לָהּ׃
31 וְהָאֲנָשִׁים אֲשֶׁר־עָלוּ עִמּוֹ אָמְרוּ לֹא
נוּכַל לַעֲלוֹת אֶל־הָעָם כִּי־חָזָק הוּא
מִמֶּנּוּ׃ 32 וַיּוֹצִיאוּ דִּבַּת הָאָרֶץ אֲשֶׁר תָּרוּ
אֹתָהּ אֶל־בְּנֵי יִשְׂרָאֵל לֵאמֹר הָאָרֶץ אֲשֶׁר
עָבַרְנוּ בָהּ לָתוּר אֹתָהּ אֶרֶץ אֹכֶלֶת
יוֹשְׁבֶיהָ הִוא וְכָל־הָעָם אֲשֶׁר־רָאִינוּ
בְתוֹכָהּ אַנְשֵׁי מִדּוֹת׃ 33 וְשָׁם רָאִינוּ אֶת־
הַנְּפִילִים בְּנֵי עֲנָק מִן־הַנְּפִלִים וַנְּהִי
בְעֵינֵינוּ כַּחֲגָבִים וְכֵן הָיִינוּ בְּעֵינֵיהֶם׃

14

The whole community broke into loud

יד

וַתִּשָּׂא כָּל־הָעֵדָה וַיִּתְּנוּ אֶת־קוֹלָם

30. Caleb does not contradict the content of the other scouts' reports, only their conclusions.

before Moses The negative report of verses 28–29 probably set off an audible murmuring, which Caleb and, presumably, Moses, tried to quell.

32. among the Israelites The scouts appear to have bypassed Moses and Aaron (v. 26) to spread their calumnies (vv. 32–33) directly among the people.

devours its settlers The nature of the Land is such that it will keep its inhabitants at war perpetually. It may also refer to the difficulty of finding enough food, especially in the Negeb, during years of drought.

33. Nephilim Literally, "fallen ones." The ancient Greek translation reads "giants." See Gen. 6:4, where they are the products of marriages between divine beings and mortal women, possibly superhuman creatures. In the scouts' first report they are called Anakites (v. 28). Their identification with Anakites could have only one purpose—to instill even greater fear in the hearts of the people, because to the stature and strength of the Anakites is now added the dimension of the earliest giants.

grasshoppers The smallest edible creature (Lev. 11:22), a hint that this land that "devours its settlers" would easily devour the Israelites.

---

31. We cannot attack The verb used here for "attack" (*la·alot*) also means "to go up." Thus the scouts are pictured as saying, "We cannot rise to the occasion." The problem is not with the Canaanite fortifications but with ourselves (Arama).

it is stronger than we The word translated as "than we" (*mi-mennu*) can also be read as "than Him," namely, God. Their lack of faith in themselves came to include a lack of faith in God's power to bring them to victory (BT Sot. 35a).

33. we looked like grasshoppers to ourselves Conveys the essence of the scouts' failure. The problem was that the Israelites did not believe in themselves. They had no way of knowing what the inhabitants of the Land thought of them. Indeed, we learn from chapter 22 that the Moabites were terrified of the Israelites, and from Joshua 2 (see the *haftarah*) that the inhabitants of Jericho were equally afraid to confront them. Because the Israelites saw themselves as "grasshoppers," weak and ineffectual, they assumed that others saw them the same way.

so we must have looked to them God's response: Why are you so concerned about how you look in the eyes of the Canaanites, to the point that it distracts you from your sacred task? (Menaḥem Mendel of Kotzk).

cries, and the people wept that night. ²All the Israelites railed against Moses and Aaron. "If only we had died in the land of Egypt," the whole community shouted at them, "or if only we might die in this wilderness! ³Why is the LORD taking us to that land to fall by the sword? Our wives and children will be carried off! It would be better for us to go back to Egypt!" ⁴And they said to one another, "Let us head back for Egypt."

⁵Then Moses and Aaron fell on their faces before all the assembled congregation of the Israelites. ⁶And Joshua son of Nun and Caleb son of Jephunneh, of those who had scouted the land, rent their clothes ⁷and exhorted the whole Israelite community: "The land that we traversed and scouted is an exceedingly good land. ⁸If the LORD is pleased with us, He will bring us into that land, a land that flows with milk and honey, and give it to us; ⁹only you must not rebel against the LORD. Have no fear then of the people of the country, for they are our prey:

וַיִּבְכּ֥וּ הָעָ֖ם בַּלַּ֥יְלָה הַהֽוּא׃ 2 וַיִּלֹּ֙נוּ֙ עַל־מֹשֶׁ֣ה וְעַֽל־אַהֲרֹ֔ן כֹּ֖ל בְּנֵ֣י יִשְׂרָאֵ֑ל וַיֹּאמְר֨וּ אֲלֵהֶ֜ם כׇּל־הָעֵדָ֗ה לוּ־מַ֙תְנוּ֙ בְּאֶ֣רֶץ מִצְרַ֔יִם א֛וֹ בַּמִּדְבָּ֥ר הַזֶּ֖ה לוּ־מָֽתְנוּ׃ 3 וְלָמָ֣ה יְ֠הֹוָ֠ה מֵבִ֨יא אֹתָ֜נוּ אֶל־הָאָ֤רֶץ הַזֹּאת֙ לִנְפֹּ֣ל בַּחֶ֔רֶב נָשֵׁ֥ינוּ וְטַפֵּ֖נוּ יִהְי֣וּ לָבַ֑ז הֲל֧וֹא ט֦וֹב לָ֖נוּ שׁ֥וּב מִצְרָֽיְמָה׃ 4 וַיֹּאמְר֖וּ אִ֣ישׁ אֶל־אָחִ֑יו נִתְּנָ֥ה רֹ֖אשׁ וְנָשׁ֥וּבָה מִצְרָֽיְמָה׃ 5 וַיִּפֹּ֥ל מֹשֶׁ֛ה וְאַהֲרֹ֖ן עַל־פְּנֵיהֶ֑ם לִפְנֵ֕י כׇּל־קְהַ֖ל עֲדַ֥ת בְּנֵ֥י יִשְׂרָאֵֽל׃ 6 וִיהוֹשֻׁ֣עַ בִּן־נ֗וּן וְכָלֵב֙ בֶּן־יְפֻנֶּ֔ה מִן־הַתָּרִ֖ים אֶת־הָאָ֑רֶץ קָרְע֖וּ בִּגְדֵיהֶֽם׃ 7 וַיֹּ֣אמְר֔וּ אֶל־כׇּל־עֲדַ֥ת בְּנֵֽי־יִשְׂרָאֵ֖ל לֵאמֹ֑ר הָאָ֗רֶץ אֲשֶׁ֨ר עָבַ֤רְנוּ בָהּ֙ לָת֣וּר אֹתָ֔הּ טוֹבָ֥ה הָאָ֖רֶץ מְאֹ֥ד מְאֹֽד׃ 8 אִם־חָפֵ֥ץ בָּ֙נוּ֙ יְהֹוָ֔ה וְהֵבִ֤יא אֹתָ֙נוּ֙ אֶל־הָאָ֣רֶץ הַזֹּ֔את וּנְתָנָ֖הּ לָ֑נוּ אֶ֕רֶץ אֲשֶׁר־הִ֛וא זָבַ֥ת חָלָ֖ב וּדְבָֽשׁ׃ 9 אַ֣ךְ בַּֽיהֹוָה֮ אַל־תִּמְרֹ֒דוּ֒ וְאַתֶּ֗ם אַל־תִּֽירְאוּ֙ אֶת־עַ֣ם הָאָ֔רֶץ

שלישי

THE PEOPLE'S RESPONSE (14:1–5)

3. back to Egypt They now wish to return to bondage willingly in the country where they had been forced into slavery.

4. Let us head Hebrew: *nitnah rosh;* literally, "let's set the head." The phrase can mean "set the mind, decide" or "appoint." Here it could mean "appoint a leader," implying a complete break with Moses and God. New leadership would be required if the defecting militia were to succeed.

5. fell on their faces To propitiate the people or as an act of helplessness and despair.

THE RESPONSE OF JOSHUA AND CALEB
(vv. 6–10)

6. of those who had scouted the land This ex-

planation is needed either because Joshua has not yet been introduced into the dialogue, or simply to indicate that the other spies did not rend their clothes.

rent their clothes Out of grief and distress over the humiliation heaped on Moses and particularly because of the implied rebellion against God.

7. good In answer to Moses' query concerning the Land (13:19) and in contrast to the "good" of returning to Egypt ("it would be better for us," v. 3).

9. prey Literally, "food" or "bread." To eat prey means to conquer.

protection Hebrew: *tzel* (literally, "shade"), an appropriate term for those who live under a

---

CHAPTER 14

2. If only we had died A sense of helplessness, a feeling of inadequacy, and inability to deal with one's problems can lead to a person's giving up on life and wishing for death. In contrast, a sense of hope in the possibility of a brighter future, a belief that God can help us to

do what we find hard to do unaided, can banish that sense of futility and restore the will to live.

6–10. Joshua and Caleb risk their lives by acting with integrity and standing up to a misguided majority. In the end, it is the majority who will die in the wilderness and the people of integrity and courage who will survive to see their dreams realized.

their protection has departed from them, but the LORD is with us. Have no fear of them!" 10As the whole community threatened to pelt them with stones, the Presence of the LORD appeared in the Tent of Meeting to all the Israelites.

11And the LORD said to Moses, "How long will this people spurn Me, and how long will they have no faith in Me despite all the signs that I have performed in their midst? 12I will strike them with pestilence and disown them, and I will make of you a nation far more numerous than they!" 13But Moses said to the LORD, "When the Egyptians, from whose midst You brought up this people in Your might, hear the news, 14they will tell it to the inhabitants of that land. Now they have heard that You, O LORD, are in the midst of this people; that You, O LORD, appear in plain sight when Your cloud rests over them and when You go before them in a pillar of cloud by day and in a pillar of fire by night. 15If then You slay this people to a man, the nations who have heard Your fame will say, 16'It must be because the LORD was powerless to bring that people into the land He had promised them on oath that He slaughtered them in the wilderness.' 17Therefore, I pray, let my Lord's forbearance be great, as You have declared, say-

כִּ֥י לַחְמֵ֖נוּ הֵ֑ם סָ֣ר צִלָּ֧ם מֵעֲלֵיהֶ֛ם וַֽיהוָ֥ה
אִתָּ֖נוּ אַל־תִּירָאֻֽם׃ 10 וַיֹּֽאמְרוּ֙ כָּל־הָ֣עֵדָ֔ה
לִרְגּ֥וֹם אֹתָ֖ם בָּאֲבָנִ֑ים וּכְב֣וֹד יְהוָ֗ה נִרְאָה֙
בְּאֹ֣הֶל מוֹעֵ֔ד אֶֽל־כָּל־בְּנֵ֖י יִשְׂרָאֵֽל׃ פ
11 וַיֹּ֤אמֶר יְהוָה֙ אֶל־מֹשֶׁ֔ה עַד־אָ֥נָה יְנַאֲצֻ֖נִי
הָעָ֣ם הַזֶּ֑ה וְעַד־אָ֙נָה֙ לֹא־יַאֲמִ֣ינוּ בִ֔י בְּכֹל֙
הָֽאֹת֔וֹת אֲשֶׁ֥ר עָשִׂ֖יתִי בְּקִרְבּֽוֹ׃ 12 אַכֶּ֥נּוּ
בַדֶּ֖בֶר וְאוֹרִשֶׁ֑נּוּ וְאֶֽעֱשֶׂה֙ אֹֽתְךָ֔ לְגוֹי־גָּד֥וֹל
וְעָצ֖וּם מִמֶּֽנּוּ׃ 13 וַיֹּ֥אמֶר מֹשֶׁ֖ה אֶל־יְהוָ֑ה
וְשָׁמְע֣וּ מִצְרַ֔יִם כִּֽי־הֶעֱלִ֧יתָ בְכֹחֲךָ֛ אֶת־
הָעָ֥ם הַזֶּ֖ה מִקִּרְבּֽוֹ׃ 14 וְאָמְר֗וּ אֶל־יוֹשֵׁב֮
הָאָ֣רֶץ הַזֹּאת֒ שָֽׁמְעוּ֙ כִּֽי־אַתָּ֣ה יְהוָ֔ה בְּקֶ֖רֶב
הָעָ֣ם הַזֶּ֑ה אֲשֶׁר־עַ֨יִן בְּעַ֜יִן נִרְאָ֣ה ׀ אַתָּ֣ה
יְהוָ֗ה וַעֲנָֽנְךָ֙ עֹמֵ֣ד עֲלֵהֶ֔ם וּבְעַמֻּ֣ד עָנָ֗ן אַתָּ֨ה
הֹלֵ֤ךְ לִפְנֵיהֶם֙ יוֹמָ֔ם וּבְעַמּ֥וּד אֵ֖שׁ לָֽיְלָה׃
15 וְהֵמַתָּ֛ה אֶת־הָעָ֥ם הַזֶּ֖ה כְּאִ֣ישׁ אֶחָ֑ד
וְאָֽמְרוּ֙ הַגּוֹיִ֔ם אֲשֶׁר־שָׁמְע֥וּ אֶֽת־שִׁמְעֲךָ֖
לֵאמֹֽר׃ 16 מִבִּלְתִּ֞י יְכֹ֣לֶת יְהוָ֗ה לְהָבִיא֙
אֶת־הָעָ֣ם הַזֶּ֔ה אֶל־הָאָ֖רֶץ אֲשֶׁר־נִשְׁבַּ֣ע
לָהֶ֑ם וַיִּשְׁחָטֵ֖ם בַּמִּדְבָּֽר׃ 17 וְעַתָּ֕ה יִגְדַּל־
נָ֥א* כֹּ֣חַ אֲדֹנָ֑י כַּאֲשֶׁ֥ר דִּבַּ֖רְתָּ לֵאמֹֽר׃

v. 17. י׳ רבתי לפי מהדורת לעטעריס

Mediterranean sun. Here it is a metaphor for divine protection.

10. them That is, Moses and Aaron.

Presence Hebrew: *kavod,* the cloud-encased fire that descended over the tabernacle. God descends to speak to Moses and to deter Israel from attacking Moses and Aaron. While God appears to the Israelites in the tabernacle courtyard, Moses enters the tent to hear God's command.

GOD'S RESPONSE (vv. 11–38)

12. God's initial reaction was virtually identical at the apostasy of the Golden Calf (Exod. 32:10).

disown Israel will no longer be God's inheritance (Deut. 32:9).

far more numerous Literally, "greater and mightier than," in a physical sense.

13–19. Moses intercedes. How is God to punish Israel and yet maintain a reputation of power in the world?

the nations That is, Egypt and Canaan.

promised them on oath The oath is recorded as given to Abraham (Gen. 15:18, 22:16, 26:3) but not to the generation of the Exodus. The original oath, however, must be assumed in God's promises of fulfillment (Exod. 3:8,17). God's promise is equivalent to a new oath.

forbearance Hebrew: *ko·aḥ;* literally, "strength." It denotes the strength to hold back from destroying the people Israel.

great In response to the Lord's wish to make Moses great (v. 12), Moses asks God to make divine forbearance great.

not remitting all punishment This means, "will definitely not acquit [the guilty]."

children All the ancient Aramaic versions understand this as "rebellious children."

ing, 18'The LORD! slow to anger and abounding in kindness; forgiving iniquity and transgression; yet not remitting all punishment, but visiting the iniquity of fathers upon children, upon the third and fourth generations.' 19Pardon, I pray, the iniquity of this people according to Your great kindness, as You have forgiven this people ever since Egypt."

20And the LORD said, "I pardon, as you have asked. 21Nevertheless, as I live and as the LORD's Presence fills the whole world, 22none of the men who have seen My Presence and the signs that I have performed in Egypt and in the wilderness, and who have tried Me these many times and have disobeyed Me, 23shall see the land that I promised on oath to their fathers; none of those who spurn Me shall see it. 24But My servant Caleb, because he was imbued with a different spirit and remained loyal to Me—him will I bring into the land that he entered, and his offspring shall hold it as a possession. 25Now the Amalekites and the Canaanites occupy the valleys. Start out, then, tomorrow and march into the wilderness by way of the Sea of Reeds."

26The LORD spoke further to Moses and Aaron, 27"How much longer shall that wicked

18 יְהוָה אֶרֶךְ אַפַּיִם וְרַב־חֶסֶד נֹשֵׂא עָוֺן
וָפָשַׁע וְנַקֵּה לֹא יְנַקֶּה פֹּקֵד עֲוֺן אָבוֹת
עַל־בָּנִים עַל־שִׁלֵּשִׁים וְעַל־רִבֵּעִים׃
19 סְלַח־נָא לַעֲוֺן הָעָם הַזֶּה כְּגֹדֶל חַסְדֶּךָ
וְכַאֲשֶׁר נָשָׂאתָה לָעָם הַזֶּה מִמִּצְרַיִם
וְעַד־הֵנָּה׃
20 וַיֹּאמֶר יְהוָה סָלַחְתִּי כִּדְבָרֶךָ׃ 21 וְאוּלָם
חַי־אָנִי וְיִמָּלֵא כְבוֹד־יְהוָה אֶת־כָּל־
הָאָרֶץ׃ 22 כִּי כָל־הָאֲנָשִׁים הָרֹאִים אֶת־
כְּבֹדִי וְאֶת־אֹתֹתַי אֲשֶׁר־עָשִׂיתִי בְמִצְרַיִם
וּבַמִּדְבָּר וַיְנַסּוּ אֹתִי זֶה עֶשֶׂר פְּעָמִים וְלֹא
שָׁמְעוּ בְּקוֹלִי׃ 23 אִם־יִרְאוּ אֶת־הָאָרֶץ
אֲשֶׁר נִשְׁבַּעְתִּי לַאֲבֹתָם וְכָל־מְנַאֲצַי לֹא
יִרְאוּהָ׃ 24 וְעַבְדִּי כָלֵב עֵקֶב הָיְתָה רוּחַ
אַחֶרֶת עִמּוֹ וַיְמַלֵּא אַחֲרָי וַהֲבִיאֹתִיו
אֶל־הָאָרֶץ אֲשֶׁר־בָּא שָׁמָּה וְזַרְעוֹ יוֹרִשֶׁנָּה׃
25 וְהָעֲמָלֵקִי וְהַכְּנַעֲנִי יוֹשֵׁב בָּעֵמֶק מָחָר
פְּנוּ וּסְעוּ לָכֶם הַמִּדְבָּר דֶּרֶךְ יַם־סוּף׃ פ
רביעי 26 וַיְדַבֵּר יְהוָה אֶל־מֹשֶׁה וְאֶל־אַהֲרֹן
לֵאמֹר׃ 27 עַד־מָתַי לָעֵדָה הָרָעָה הַזֹּאת

19. Pardon Hebrew: *salaḥ,* used only of the deity; it means "forgiveness of offenses against God."

21. as I live Human beings swear by God; because there is no superior entity, this vow is sworn by God's own "life" (essence or being).

fills the whole world God has the power to fulfill this oath.

24. Caleb will be granted the right to enter the land he scouted (13:22) and to bequeath it to his children as their inheritance.

25. Amalekites . . . Canaanites The scouts frightened Israel by mentioning these nations, which posed no threat. Now that Israel has spurned God, they will indeed become a threat.

occupy the valleys The Canaanites are located along the sea, and the Amalekites in the Negeb. All the entrances are blocked.

26. Aaron and the Levites are also exempt from God's oath of retribution because the tribe of Levi was not represented among the scouts.

27. wicked community The scouts.

22–23. Why does God, who forgave Israel for the Golden Calf and other acts of faithlessness, condemn to death an entire generation for this offense? God is prepared to forgive such slights against Heaven, but not sins against the idea of the Jewish people as the people of God (Spektor).

27. community Hebrew: *edah,* used here for a group numbering exactly 10, the scouts who offered a negative report. Jewish law used this as the source for the ruling that 10 is the minimum number of adults required for a group to be counted as a community, a *minyan.*

community keep muttering against Me? Very
well, I have heeded the incessant muttering of
the Israelites against Me. 28Say to them: 'As I
live,' says the LORD, 'I will do to you just as you
have urged Me. 29In this very wilderness shall
your carcasses drop. Of all of you who were recorded in your various lists from the age of
twenty years up, you who have muttered against
Me, 30not one shall enter the land in which I
swore to settle you—save Caleb son of Jephunneh and Joshua son of Nun. 31Your children
who, you said, would be carried off—these will
I allow to enter; they shall know the land that
you have rejected. 32But your carcasses shall
drop in this wilderness, 33while your children
roam the wilderness for forty years, suffering for
your faithlessness, until the last of your carcasses is down in the wilderness. 34You shall bear
your punishment for forty years, corresponding
to the number of days—forty days—that you
scouted the land: a year for each day. Thus you
shall know what it means to thwart Me. 35I the
LORD have spoken: Thus will I do to all that
wicked band that has banded together against
Me: in this very wilderness they shall die to the
last man.'"

36As for the men whom Moses sent to scout
the land, those who came back and caused the
whole community to mutter against him by
spreading calumnies about the land—37those
who spread such calumnies about the land died

אֲשֶׁר הֵמָּה מַלִּינִים עָלָי אֶת־תְּלֻנּוֹת בְּנֵי
יִשְׂרָאֵל אֲשֶׁר הֵמָּה מַלִּינִים עָלַי שָׁמָעְתִּי׃
28 אֱמֹר אֲלֵהֶם חַי־אָנִי נְאֻם־יְהוָה אִם־לֹא
כַּאֲשֶׁר דִּבַּרְתֶּם בְּאָזְנָי כֵּן אֶעֱשֶׂה לָכֶם׃
29 בַּמִּדְבָּר הַזֶּה יִפְּלוּ פִגְרֵיכֶם וְכָל־
פְּקֻדֵיכֶם לְכָל־מִסְפַּרְכֶם מִבֶּן עֶשְׂרִים שָׁנָה
וָמָעְלָה אֲשֶׁר הֲלִינֹתֶם עָלָי׃ 30 אִם־אַתֶּם
תָּבֹאוּ אֶל־הָאָרֶץ אֲשֶׁר נָשָׂאתִי אֶת־יָדִי
לְשַׁכֵּן אֶתְכֶם בָּהּ כִּי אִם־כָּלֵב בֶּן־יְפֻנֶּה
וִיהוֹשֻׁעַ בִּן־נוּן׃ 31 וְטַפְּכֶם אֲשֶׁר אֲמַרְתֶּם
לָבַז יִהְיֶה וְהֵבֵיאתִי אֹתָם וְיָדְעוּ אֶת־
הָאָרֶץ אֲשֶׁר מְאַסְתֶּם בָּהּ׃ 32 וּפִגְרֵיכֶם
אַתֶּם יִפְּלוּ בַּמִּדְבָּר הַזֶּה׃ 33 וּבְנֵיכֶם יִהְיוּ
רֹעִים בַּמִּדְבָּר אַרְבָּעִים שָׁנָה וְנָשְׂאוּ אֶת־
זְנוּתֵיכֶם עַד־תֹּם פִּגְרֵיכֶם בַּמִּדְבָּר׃
34 בְּמִסְפַּר הַיָּמִים אֲשֶׁר־תַּרְתֶּם אֶת־
הָאָרֶץ אַרְבָּעִים יוֹם יוֹם לַשָּׁנָה יוֹם לַשָּׁנָה
תִּשְׂאוּ אֶת־עֲוֺנֹתֵיכֶם אַרְבָּעִים שָׁנָה
וִידַעְתֶּם אֶת־תְּנוּאָתִי׃ 35 אֲנִי יְהוָה
דִּבַּרְתִּי אִם־לֹא ׀ זֹאת אֶעֱשֶׂה לְכָל־הָעֵדָה
הָרָעָה הַזֹּאת הַנּוֹעָדִים עָלָי בַּמִּדְבָּר הַזֶּה
יִתַּמּוּ וְשָׁם יָמֻתוּ׃
36 וְהָאֲנָשִׁים אֲשֶׁר־שָׁלַח מֹשֶׁה לָתוּר אֶת־
הָאָרֶץ וַיָּשֻׁבוּ וילונו וַיַּלִּינוּ עָלָיו אֶת־כָּל־
הָעֵדָה לְהוֹצִיא דִבָּה עַל־הָאָרֶץ׃ 37 וַיָּמֻתוּ
הָאֲנָשִׁים מוֹצִאֵי דִבַּת־הָאָרֶץ רָעָה

28. Israel is about to achieve its wish: "If only we might die in this wilderness!" (v. 2).

29. this very wilderness Paran.

from twenty years up Although they were of fighting age, they refused to fight.

30. swore The Hebrew idiom is *nasa yad;* literally, "raise the hand." That is, heavenward, calling God to witness.

31. Your children Up to the age of 20.

they shall know the land In contrast to their parents, who instead shall know God's punishment (v. 34).

33. suffering for your faithlessness Delaying punishment to a future generation may be an aspect of God's mercy.

carcasses . . . down in the wilderness This implies that burial will be denied.

34. bear your punishment Literally, "carry [the consequences of] sin."

forty years This will allow a fourth generation to be born in the wilderness and thereby fulfill God's attribute of punishing to the fourth generation.

35. against Me When the Israelites banded together to stone Joshua and Caleb, their real intention was to rebel against God.

of plague, by the will of the LORD. 38Of those men who had gone to scout the land, only Joshua son of Nun and Caleb son of Jephunneh survived.

39When Moses repeated these words to all the Israelites, the people were overcome by grief. 40Early next morning they set out toward the crest of the hill country, saying, "We are prepared to go up to the place that the LORD has spoken of, for we were wrong." 41But Moses said, "Why do you transgress the LORD's command? This will not succeed. 42Do not go up, lest you be routed by your enemies, for the LORD is not in your midst. 43For the Amalekites and the Canaanites will be there to face you, and you will fall by the sword, inasmuch as you have turned from following the LORD and the LORD will not be with you."

44Yet defiantly they marched toward the crest of the hill country, though neither the LORD's Ark of the Covenant nor Moses stirred from the camp. 45And the Amalekites and the Canaanites who dwelt in that hill country came down and dealt them a shattering blow at Hormah.

בַּמַּגֵּפָ֖ה לִפְנֵ֥י יְהוָֽה׃ 38 וִיהוֹשֻׁ֣עַ בִּן־נ֗וּן
וְכָלֵ֥ב בֶּן־יְפֻנֶּ֑ה חָיוּ֙ מִן־הָאֲנָשִׁ֣ים הָהֵ֔ם
הַהֹלְכִ֖ים לָת֥וּר אֶת־הָאָֽרֶץ׃
39 וַיְדַבֵּ֤ר מֹשֶׁה֙ אֶת־הַדְּבָרִ֣ים הָאֵ֔לֶּה אֶל־
כָּל־בְּנֵ֖י יִשְׂרָאֵ֑ל וַיִּֽתְאַבְּל֥וּ הָעָ֖ם מְאֹֽד׃
40 וַיַּשְׁכִּ֣מוּ בַבֹּ֔קֶר וַיַּעֲל֥וּ אֶל־רֹאשׁ־הָהָ֖ר
לֵאמֹ֑ר הִנֶּ֕נּוּ וְעָלִ֛ינוּ אֶל־הַמָּק֛וֹם אֲשֶׁר־
אָמַ֥ר יְהוָ֖ה כִּ֥י חָטָֽאנוּ׃ 41 וַיֹּ֣אמֶר מֹשֶׁ֔ה
לָ֥מָּה זֶּ֛ה אַתֶּ֥ם עֹבְרִ֖ים אֶת־פִּ֣י יְהוָ֑ה וְהִ֖וא
לֹ֥א תִצְלָֽח׃ 42 אַֽל־תַּעֲל֔וּ כִּ֛י אֵ֥ין יְהוָ֖ה
בְּקִרְבְּכֶ֑ם וְלֹא֙ תִּנָּ֣גְפ֔וּ לִפְנֵ֖י אֹיְבֵיכֶֽם׃ 43 כִּי֩
הָעֲמָלֵקִ֨י וְהַֽכְּנַעֲנִ֥י שָׁם֙ לִפְנֵיכֶ֔ם וּנְפַלְתֶּ֖ם
בֶּחָ֑רֶב כִּֽי־עַל־כֵּ֤ן שַׁבְתֶּם֙ מֵאַחֲרֵ֣י יְהוָ֔ה
וְלֹא־יִהְיֶ֥ה יְהוָ֖ה עִמָּכֶֽם׃
44 וַיַּעְפִּ֕לוּ לַעֲל֖וֹת אֶל־רֹ֣אשׁ הָהָ֑ר וַאֲר֤וֹן
בְּרִית־יְהוָה֙ וּמֹשֶׁ֔ה לֹא־מָ֖שׁוּ מִקֶּ֥רֶב
הַֽמַּחֲנֶֽה׃ 45 וַיֵּ֤רֶד הָעֲמָלֵקִי֙ וְהַֽכְּנַעֲנִ֔י הַיֹּשֵׁ֖ב
בָּהָ֣ר הַה֑וּא וַיַּכּ֥וּם וַֽיַּכְּת֖וּם עַד־
הַֽחָרְמָֽה׃ פ

15 The LORD spoke to Moses, saying:

טו וַיְדַבֵּ֥ר יְהוָ֖ה אֶל־מֹשֶׁ֥ה לֵּאמֹֽר׃

THE PEOPLE'S EXPEDITION (vv. 39–45)

Stricken by guilt and grief, the people attempt to invade Canaan, but the outcome is disastrous. The Lord's oath is irrevocable: The generation of the Exodus must die in the wilderness.

39. these words Verses 20–25 and/or 28–35.

40. Instead of retreating, as they were commanded, they defied the Lord and invaded Canaan.

crest of the hill country That is, toward Hebron, one of the highest points in the Judean mountains.

wrong Because it follows God's decree, the remorse here is too late.

42. the LORD is not in your midst The Ark did not accompany them in battle.

A MISCELLANY OF LAWS (15:1–41)

This chapter, a collection of diverse laws, interrupts the narrative sequence of the spy story (chapters 13–14) and the rebellion of Korah, Dathan, and Abiram (chapters 16–17).

40. the place that the LORD has spoken of, for we were wrong Or "the place concerning which the LORD said we were wrong." That is, the people still refuse to admit that they had done wrong. They go off to battle sullenly, reluctantly, without enthusiasm.

2Speak to the Israelite people and say to them:
When you enter the land that I am giving you
to settle in, 3and would present a gift to the LORD
from the herd or from the flock, be it burnt
offering or sacrifice, in fulfillment of a vow explicitly uttered, or as a freewill offering, or at
your fixed occasions, producing an odor pleasing to the LORD:
4The person who presents a gift to the LORD
shall bring as a grain offering: a tenth of a measure of choice flour with a quarter of a *hin* of
oil mixed in. 5You shall also offer, with the burnt
offering or the sacrifice, a quarter of a *hin* of
wine as a libation for each sheep.
6In the case of a ram, you shall present as a
grain offering: two-tenths of a measure of
choice flour with a third of a *hin* of oil mixed

2 דַּבֵּר֙ אֶל־בְּנֵ֣י יִשְׂרָאֵ֔ל וְאָמַרְתָּ֖ אֲלֵהֶ֑ם
כִּ֣י תָבֹ֗אוּ אֶל־אֶ֙רֶץ֙ מוֹשְׁבֹ֣תֵיכֶ֔ם אֲשֶׁ֥ר אֲנִ֖י
נֹתֵ֥ן לָכֶֽם׃ 3 וַעֲשִׂיתֶ֨ם אִשֶּׁ֤ה לַֽיהוָה֙ עֹלָ֣ה
אוֹ־זֶ֔בַח לְפַלֵּא־נֶ֙דֶר֙ א֣וֹ בִנְדָבָ֔ה א֖וֹ
בְּמֹעֲדֵיכֶ֑ם לַעֲשׂ֞וֹת רֵ֤יחַ נִיחֹ֙חַ֙ לַֽיהוָ֔ה
מִן־הַבָּקָ֖ר א֥וֹ מִן־הַצֹּֽאן׃
4 וְהִקְרִ֛יב הַמַּקְרִ֥יב קָרְבָּנ֖וֹ לַיהוָ֑ה מִנְחָ֗ה
סֹ֙לֶת֙ עִשָּׂר֔וֹן בָּל֕וּל בִּרְבִעִ֥ית הַהִ֖ין שָֽׁמֶן׃
5 וְיַ֤יִן לַנֶּ֙סֶךְ֙ רְבִיעִ֣ית הַהִ֔ין תַּעֲשֶׂ֥ה עַל־
הָעֹלָ֖ה א֣וֹ לַזָּ֑בַח לַכֶּ֖בֶשׂ הָאֶחָֽד׃
6 א֤וֹ לָאַ֙יִל֙ תַּעֲשֶׂ֣ה מִנְחָ֔ה סֹ֖לֶת שְׁנֵ֣י
עֶשְׂרֹנִ֑ים בְּלוּלָ֥ה בַשֶּׁ֖מֶן שְׁלִשִׁ֥ית הַהִֽין׃

ACCOMPANIMENTS TO THE SACRIFICE (vv. 1–16)

Because meat was eaten together with bread and wine, these last two items accompanied an animal sacrifice. The grain offering and the wine libation were not required in the wilderness because they are products of an agricultural society.

2. When you enter the land This introductory phrase is often found in connection with laws that presume a settled agricultural life.

to settle in In permanent settlements, not in tents.

3. flock Birds, however, do not require any accompaniment of grain and libation offerings.

at your fixed occasions The burnt offerings required for the fixed, public sacrifices.

4. The person Either a man or a woman.

grain offering The private grain offering was given as a revenue to the priest after a token portion was offered on the altar. When such an offering accompanied a meat offering, however, it was burned completely on the altar (as prescribed in Lev. 14:20, 23:13).

measure An *ephah,* equal to about 1 bushel.

choice flour Semolina, the finest grade of flour.

hin See Comment to Exod. 29:40.

5. You shall . . . offer Hebrew: *ta·aseh,* which is singular. The change of person from plural to singular in the direct address to Israel is a feature of these texts.

libation Most likely, the wine originally was poured on the base of the altar and not burned on its hearth, because its flames might be extinguished in violation of Lev. 6:6.

sheep This rule applies to goats as well.

CHAPTER 15

In this chapter, the theme of a generation sentenced to die in the wilderness for their lack of faith seems to be dropped, as the Torah proceeds to spell out laws for various offerings. It concludes with the commandment to wear fringes (*tzitzit*) on the corners of one's garments. The Sages find a connection between the story of the scouts and the commandments to bring offerings and to wear *tzitzit.* Ibn Ezra imagines the Israelites cast into despair. God has written them off, and the dream of settlement in the Promised Land now seems impossible. To revive their spirits, God commands Moses to tell them "When you enter the land that I am giving you" (v. 2). These words affirm that God still communicates with the people, that God has not written them off permanently. They affirm further that the promise of the Land is still in force, although it will be their children who will enter it and put these laws into practice.

in; [7]and a third of a *hin* of wine as a libation—as an offering of pleasing odor to the LORD.

[8]And if it is an animal from the herd that you offer to the LORD as a burnt offering or as a sacrifice, in fulfillment of a vow explicitly uttered or as an offering of well-being, [9]there shall be offered a grain offering along with the animal: three-tenths of a measure of choice flour with half a *hin* of oil mixed in; [10]and as libation you shall offer half a *hin* of wine—these being gifts of pleasing odor to the LORD.

[11]Thus shall be done with each ox, with each ram, and with any sheep or goat, [12]as many as you offer; you shall do thus with each one, as many as there are. [13]Every citizen, when presenting a gift of pleasing odor to the LORD, shall do so with them.

[14]And when, throughout the ages, a stranger who has taken up residence with you, or one who lives among you, would present a gift of pleasing odor to the LORD—as you do, so shall it be done by [15]the rest of the congregation. There shall be one law for you and for the resident stranger; it shall be a law for all time throughout the ages. You and the stranger shall be alike before the LORD; [16]the same ritual and the same rule shall apply to you and to the stranger who resides among you.

[17]The LORD spoke to Moses, saying: [18]Speak to the Israelite people and say to them:

7 וְיַיִן לַנֶּסֶךְ שְׁלִשִׁית הַהִין תַּקְרִיב רֵֽיחַ־
נִיחֹחַ לַיהוָה׃
חמישי 8 וְכִֽי־תַעֲשֶׂה בֶן־בָּקָר עֹלָה אוֹ־זָבַח
לְפַלֵּא־נֶדֶר אוֹ־שְׁלָמִים לַיהוָה׃ 9 וְהִקְרִיב
עַל־בֶּן־הַבָּקָר מִנְחָה סֹלֶת שְׁלֹשָׁה
עֶשְׂרֹנִים בָּלוּל בַּשֶּׁמֶן חֲצִי הַהִין׃ 10 וְיַיִן
תַּקְרִיב לַנֶּסֶךְ חֲצִי הַהִין אִשֵּׁה רֵֽיחַ־נִיחֹחַ
לַיהוָה׃
11 כָּכָה יֵעָשֶׂה לַשּׁוֹר הָאֶחָד אוֹ לָאַיִל
הָאֶחָד אוֹ־לַשֶּׂה בַכְּבָשִׂים אוֹ בָעִזִּים׃
12 כַּמִּסְפָּר אֲשֶׁר תַּעֲשׂוּ כָּכָה תַּעֲשׂוּ לָאֶחָד
כְּמִסְפָּרָם׃ 13 כָּל־הָאֶזְרָח יַעֲשֶׂה־כָּכָה
אֶת־אֵלֶּה לְהַקְרִיב אִשֵּׁה רֵֽיחַ־נִיחֹחַ
לַיהוָה׃
14 וְכִֽי־יָגוּר אִתְּכֶם גֵּר אוֹ אֲשֶׁר־בְּתוֹכְכֶם
לְדֹרֹתֵיכֶם וְעָשָׂה אִשֵּׁה רֵֽיחַ־נִיחֹחַ לַיהוָה
כַּאֲשֶׁר תַּעֲשׂוּ כֵּן יַעֲשֶׂה׃ 15 הַקָּהָל חֻקָּה
אַחַת לָכֶם וְלַגֵּר הַגָּר חֻקַּת עוֹלָם
לְדֹרֹתֵיכֶם כָּכֶם כַּגֵּר יִהְיֶה לִפְנֵי יְהוָה׃
16 תּוֹרָה אַחַת וּמִשְׁפָּט אֶחָד יִהְיֶה לָכֶם
וְלַגֵּר הַגָּר אִתְּכֶם׃ פ

ששי 17 וַיְדַבֵּר יְהוָה אֶל־מֹשֶׁה לֵּאמֹר׃ 18 דַּבֵּר
אֶל־בְּנֵי יִשְׂרָאֵל וְאָמַרְתָּ אֲלֵהֶם

7. of pleasing odor to the LORD This phrase applies to the case of the sheep as well, mentioned in verses 4–5.

10. of pleasing odor to the LORD Although the wine was poured at the base of the altar and not on its hearth, it still exuded a pleasing aroma.

11. Thus shall be done A summary, enumerating the animals in inverse order: ox, ram, lamb.

ox Hebrew: *shor,* in masculine gender, is equivalent to "animal from the herd" (*ben bakar*) in verse 8 and can be female (Lev. 22:28). A female bovine is acceptable for the well-being offering (Lev. 3:1).

any sheep or goat Of either sex.

14. one who lives among you Literally, "one who is among you," perhaps the foreigner (*nokhri*) who visits or sojourns but does not actually reside among the Israelites, as does the stranger (*ger*). Both may offer sacrifices, provided these regulations are followed (Lev. 22:25).

16. the same ritual In this case. (The stranger is placed on an equal footing with the Israelite citizen in matters of civil law, but there are differences between them in religious law.)

THE FIRST OF THE DOUGH: A PRIESTLY EMOLUMENT (vv. 17–21)

18. When you enter the land This law is not

When you enter the land to which I am taking
you [19]and you eat of the bread of the land, you
shall set some aside as a gift to the LORD: [20]as
the first yield of your baking, you shall set aside
a loaf as a gift; you shall set it aside as a gift like
the gift from the threshing floor. [21]You shall
make a gift to the LORD from the first yield of
your baking, throughout the ages.

[22]If you unwittingly fail to observe any one
of the commandments that the LORD has declared to Moses—[23]anything that the LORD has
enjoined upon you through Moses—from the
day that the LORD gave the commandment and
on through the ages:

[24]If this was done unwittingly, through the
inadvertence of the community, the whole

בְּבֹאֲכֶם אֶל־הָאָרֶץ אֲשֶׁר אֲנִי מֵבִיא
אֶתְכֶם שָׁמָּה׃ 19 וְהָיָה בַּאֲכָלְכֶם מִלֶּחֶם
הָאָרֶץ תָּרִימוּ תְרוּמָה לַיהוָה׃ 20 רֵאשִׁית
עֲרִסֹתֵכֶם חַלָּה תָּרִימוּ תְרוּמָה כִּתְרוּמַת
גֹּרֶן כֵּן תָּרִימוּ אֹתָהּ׃ 21 מֵרֵאשִׁית
עֲרִסֹתֵיכֶם תִּתְּנוּ לַיהוָה תְּרוּמָה
לְדֹרֹתֵיכֶם׃ ס
22 וְכִי תִשְׁגּוּ וְלֹא תַעֲשׂוּ אֵת כָּל־הַמִּצְוֺת
הָאֵלֶּה אֲשֶׁר־דִּבֶּר יְהוָה אֶל־מֹשֶׁה׃ 23 אֵת
כָּל־אֲשֶׁר צִוָּה יְהוָה אֲלֵיכֶם בְּיַד־מֹשֶׁה
מִן־הַיּוֹם אֲשֶׁר צִוָּה יְהוָה וָהָלְאָה
לְדֹרֹתֵיכֶם׃
24 וְהָיָה אִם מֵעֵינֵי הָעֵדָה נֶעֶשְׂתָה לִשְׁגָגָה

independent of the preceding law; both take effect simultaneously.

19. set some aside as a gift Hebrew: *tarimu t'rumah,* from the verb *herim,* which here means "to set apart, dedicate." Thus the noun *t'rumah* refers to that which is set apart or dedicated to the sanctuary.

to the LORD We would not know if the gift is to be assigned to the altar or to the priest were it not for the prophet Ezekiel's instructions: "Give the first of the yield of your baking to the priest" (Ezek. 44:30).

20. baking Hebrew: *arisah,* which may refer to a kind of baking vessel.

gift from the threshing floor The priest was entitled to the first yield of the threshing floor (wheat) and of the vat (wine, oil), as prescribed in 18:12. This text, then, presumes a knowledge of the priestly compensations listed in 18:8–32. The amount is never specified but seems to refer to the first loaf.

21. from the first yield Not all of it.

INADVERTENT AND BRAZEN WRONGDOING (vv. 22–31)

This passage deals with sacrifices required when the community, an Israelite citizen, or a stranger accidentally violates any of the laws.

22. The prescribed sacrifice is brought for any inadvertent sin.

23. from the day that the LORD gave the commandment Probably refers to all the laws given "from whatever day," i.e., given at any time (Luzzatto).

through the ages The laws given to Moses are valid for all time.

---

20. first yield of your baking The offering of dough is different from the offering of first fruits or the firstborn of the flocks. It represents the human achievement of mixing several ingredients to make something new, different from any of its components. Even the products of human creativity are to be considered gifts from God. To this day, Jewish tradition calls for bakers to discard a pinch of dough before baking bread. Boxes of *Pesaḥ matzah* commonly carry the note that "the *ḥallah* offering" has been made.

HALAKHAH L'MA·ASEH

15:20. the first yield of your baking Jews are responsible for separating *ḥallah* when baking bread made from at least three pounds of flour of any of the five grains: wheat, barley, spelt, rye, and oats (M Ḥal. 1:1). (This offering is not to be confused with braided egg bread used for *Shabbat,* which is also called *ḥallah.*) To take *ḥallah,* one recites the blessing *l'hafrish ḥallah min ha-issah,* separates a symbolic piece of dough at least the size of an olive, and burns the dough in the oven.

community shall present one bull of the herd
as a burnt offering of pleasing odor to the LORD,
with its proper grain offering and libation, and
one he-goat as a purification offering. 25The
priest shall make expiation for the whole Israelite community and they shall be forgiven; for
it was an error, and for their error they have
brought their offering, a gift to the LORD and
their purification offering before the LORD.
26The whole Israelite community and the
stranger residing among them shall be forgiven,
for it happened to the entire people through
error.

27In case it is an individual who has sinned
unwittingly, he shall offer a she-goat in its first
year as a purification offering. 28The priest shall
make expiation before the LORD on behalf of
the person who erred, for he sinned unwittingly,
making such expiation for him that he may be
forgiven. 29For the citizen among the Israelites
and for the stranger who resides among them—
you shall have one ritual for anyone who acts
in error.

30But the person, be he citizen or stranger,
who acts defiantly reviles the LORD; that person

וְעָשׂוּ כָל־הָעֵדָה פַּר בֶּן־בָּקָר אֶחָד לְעֹלָה
לְרֵיחַ נִיחֹחַ לַיהוָה וּמִנְחָתוֹ וְנִסְכּוֹ
כַּמִּשְׁפָּט וּשְׂעִיר־עִזִּים אֶחָד לְחַטָּת*׃
25 וְכִפֶּר הַכֹּהֵן עַל־כָּל־עֲדַת בְּנֵי יִשְׂרָאֵל
וְנִסְלַח לָהֶם כִּי־שְׁגָגָה הִוא וְהֵם הֵבִיאוּ
אֶת־קָרְבָּנָם אִשֶּׁה לַיהוָה וְחַטָּאתָם לִפְנֵי
יְהוָה עַל־שִׁגְגָתָם׃ 26 וְנִסְלַח לְכָל־עֲדַת
בְּנֵי יִשְׂרָאֵל וְלַגֵּר הַגָּר בְּתוֹכָם כִּי לְכָל־
הָעָם בִּשְׁגָגָה׃ ס
שביעי 27 וְאִם־נֶפֶשׁ אַחַת תֶּחֱטָא בִשְׁגָגָה
וְהִקְרִיבָה עֵז בַּת־שְׁנָתָהּ לְחַטָּאת׃
28 וְכִפֶּר הַכֹּהֵן עַל־הַנֶּפֶשׁ הַשֹּׁגֶגֶת בְּחֶטְאָה
בִשְׁגָגָה לִפְנֵי יְהוָה לְכַפֵּר עָלָיו וְנִסְלַח
לוֹ׃ 29 הָאֶזְרָח בִּבְנֵי יִשְׂרָאֵל וְלַגֵּר הַגָּר
בְּתוֹכָם תּוֹרָה אַחַת יִהְיֶה לָכֶם לָעֹשֶׂה
בִּשְׁגָגָה׃
30 וְהַנֶּפֶשׁ אֲשֶׁר־תַּעֲשֶׂה ׀ בְּיָד רָמָה מִן־
הָאֶזְרָח וּמִן־הַגֵּר אֶת־יְהוָה הוּא מְגַדֵּף

v. 24. חסר א׳

INADVERTENT WRONGS OF THE COMMUNITY (vv. 24–26)

Based on Lev. 4:13–21.

24. through the inadvertence of the community The failure to observe a commandment escaped the notice (literally, "eyes") of the community.

the whole community Through its representatives.

present That is, sacrifice.

proper As given in verses 9–10.

25. and they shall be forgiven Better: "that they may be forgiven." Forgiveness is not automatic, it does not inhere in the ritual. It depends entirely on the will of God.

INADVERTENT WRONGS OF THE INDIVIDUAL (vv. 27–29)

Based on Lev. 4:27–31.

29. The stranger (*ger*) who commits an inadvertent wrong is just as liable as the Israelite citizen to bring the required sacrifice.

30. acts defiantly Literally, "with upraised hand." An appropriate image for the brazen sinner who acts in open defiance of the Lord. (However, the phrase has a good connotation in Exod. 14:8, referring to Israelite defiance of the Egyptians.)

---

27. Why does a person who has sinned unintentionally have to bring an offering? It is needed to cleanse the soul of the guilt felt over having done wrong. Ramban says this refers to a person who was raised without knowledge of the Torah, who only later in life discovers that many things he or she was accustomed to doing are forbidden. This procedure enables such a person to cleanse the soul of the embarrassment of having done wrong.

shall be cut off from among his people. 31Because he has spurned the word of the LORD and violated His commandment, that person shall be cut off—he bears his guilt.

32Once, when the Israelites were in the wilderness, they came upon a man gathering wood on the sabbath day. 33Those who found him as he was gathering wood brought him before Moses, Aaron, and the whole community. 34He was placed in custody, for it had not been specified what should be done to him. 35Then the LORD said to Moses, "The man shall be put to death: the whole community shall pelt him with stones outside the camp." 36So the whole community took him outside the camp and stoned him to death—as the LORD had commanded Moses.

37The LORD said to Moses as follows: 38Speak

וְנִכְרְתָ֛ה הַנֶּ֥פֶשׁ הַהִ֖וא מִקֶּ֥רֶב עַמָּֽהּ׃ 31 כִּ֤י
דְבַר־יְהוָה֙ בָּזָ֔ה וְאֶת־מִצְוָת֖וֹ הֵפַ֑ר הִכָּרֵ֧ת ׀
תִּכָּרֵ֛ת הַנֶּ֥פֶשׁ הַהִ֖וא עֲוֺנָ֥ה בָֽהּ׃ פ

32 וַיִּהְי֥וּ בְנֵֽי־יִשְׂרָאֵ֖ל בַּמִּדְבָּ֑ר וַֽיִּמְצְא֗וּ אִ֛ישׁ
מְקֹשֵׁ֥שׁ עֵצִ֖ים בְּי֥וֹם הַשַּׁבָּֽת׃ 33 וַיַּקְרִ֣יבוּ
אֹת֔וֹ הַמֹּצְאִ֥ים אֹת֖וֹ מְקֹשֵׁ֣שׁ עֵצִ֑ים אֶל־
מֹשֶׁה֙ וְאֶל־אַהֲרֹ֔ן וְאֶ֖ל כָּל־הָעֵדָֽה׃
34 וַיַּנִּ֥יחוּ אֹת֖וֹ בַּמִּשְׁמָ֑ר כִּ֚י לֹ֣א פֹרַ֔שׁ
מַה־יֵּעָשֶׂ֖ה לֽוֹ׃ ס 35 וַיֹּ֤אמֶר יְהוָה֙ אֶל־
מֹשֶׁ֔ה מ֥וֹת יוּמַ֖ת הָאִ֑ישׁ רָג֨וֹם אֹת֤וֹ
בָאֲבָנִים֙ כָּל־הָ֣עֵדָ֔ה מִח֖וּץ לַֽמַּחֲנֶֽה׃
36 וַיֹּצִ֨יאוּ אֹת֜וֹ כָּל־הָעֵדָ֗ה אֶל־מִחוּץ֙
לַֽמַּחֲנֶ֔ה וַיִּרְגְּמ֥וּ אֹת֛וֹ בָּאֲבָנִ֖ים וַיָּמֹ֑ת כַּאֲשֶׁ֛ר
צִוָּ֥ה יְהוָ֖ה אֶת־מֹשֶֽׁה׃ פ

מפטיר 37 וַיֹּ֥אמֶר יְהוָ֖ה אֶל־מֹשֶׁ֥ה לֵּאמֹֽר׃ 38 דַּבֵּ֞ר

reviles the LORD By brazenly violating any of God's commandments.

31. he bears his guilt He will be punished.

THE CASE OF THE WOOD GATHERER
(vv. 32–36)

32. Once, when Ramban claims that this incident took place on the *Shabbat* that followed the disastrous reconnaissance mission (chapters 13–14) and was placed here for chronologic reasons.

gathering Hebrew: *m'koshesh,* formed from the noun *kash* (stubble). It is used for gathering stubble or pieces of wood.

34. Moses hesitated because he did not know how the offender was to be punished.

35. the whole community All must participate to indicate that all share the responsibility.

outside the camp Executions took place only beyond the camp.

TZITZIT (TASSELS) (vv. 37–41)

The violet woolen cord in the *tzitzit* is a sign of nobility and priesthood. By requiring that all Is-

---

32. Later commentators try to mitigate the apparent severity of this narrative, lest readers come to fear that any minor breach of *Shabbat* would be considered a capital offense. Thus *Sifrei* explains that this happened years earlier, in the wilderness of Sinai, shortly after the giving of the Decalogue. The Israelites had scrupulously kept the first *Shabbat* after the giving of the law. Had they kept one more *Shabbat* with equal devotion, it might well have become a permanent way of life. The wood gatherer, therefore, was not just violating one law but was destroying the dream that Israel would be a people obedient to God's ways. For that reason, he was punished so severely. Why is the account placed here, out of chronologic order? To introduce the concept of *tzitzit* as a reminder of our obligations. It would also seem to follow naturally upon the law of the brazen sinner.

37–41. The verb "to follow" in verse 39 is the same verb used in relation to the scouts in 13:2 (Rashi); this commandment was prompted by the misadventure of the scouts, who followed their minds (Heb. "hearts") and eyes instead of following the will of God (Hirsch).

The purpose of the fringes seems to be to help us remember. "Seeing leads to remembering, and remembering leads to doing" (BT Men.

אֶל־בְּנֵ֤י יִשְׂרָאֵל֙ וְאָמַרְתָּ֣ אֲלֵהֶ֔ם וְעָשׂ֨וּ לָהֶ֥ם
צִיצִ֛ת עַל־כַּנְפֵ֥י בִגְדֵיהֶ֖ם לְדֹרֹתָ֑ם וְנָ֥תְנ֛וּ
עַל־צִיצִ֥ת הַכָּנָ֖ף פְּתִ֥יל תְּכֵֽלֶת׃ 39 וְהָיָ֣ה
לָכֶם֮ לְצִיצִת֒ וּרְאִיתֶ֣ם אֹת֗וֹ וּזְכַרְתֶּם֙ אֶת־
כָּל־מִצְוֺ֣ת יְהוָ֔ה וַעֲשִׂיתֶ֖ם אֹתָ֑ם וְלֹֽא־
תָת֜רוּ אַחֲרֵ֤י לְבַבְכֶם֙ וְאַחֲרֵ֣י עֵֽינֵיכֶ֔ם
אֲשֶׁר־אַתֶּ֥ם זֹנִ֖ים אַחֲרֵיהֶֽם׃ 40 לְמַ֣עַן
תִּזְכְּר֔וּ וַעֲשִׂיתֶ֖ם אֶת־כָּל־מִצְוֺתָ֑י וִהְיִיתֶ֥ם
קְדֹשִׁ֖ים לֵאלֹהֵיכֶֽם׃ 41 אֲנִ֞י יְהוָ֣ה אֱלֹהֵיכֶ֗ם
אֲשֶׁ֨ר הוֹצֵ֤אתִי אֶתְכֶם֙ מֵאֶ֣רֶץ מִצְרַ֔יִם
לִהְי֥וֹת לָכֶ֖ם לֵאלֹהִ֑ים אֲנִ֖י יְהוָ֥ה
אֱלֹהֵיכֶֽם׃ פ

to the Israelite people and instruct them to make
for themselves fringes on the corners of their
garments throughout the ages; let them attach
a cord of blue to the fringe at each corner. 39 That
shall be your fringe; look at it and recall all the
commandments of the LORD and observe them,
so that you do not follow your heart and eyes
in your lustful urge. 40 Thus you shall be reminded to observe all My commandments and
to be holy to your God. 41 I the LORD am your
God, who brought you out of the land of Egypt
to be your God: I, the LORD your God.

raelite males wear *tzitzit,* God is elevating them in status.

38. fringes The *tzitzit* resemble a lock of hair (see "and took me by the *tzitzit* of my head," Ezek. 8:3). Hence, one might also render it "tassels." Some say that the word refers to an ornamental floral design, as attested by a related term in Akkadian.

corner Hebrew: *kanaf;* literally, "wing." In ancient days, men wore closed robes or skirts, as did women. The term may refer to the scalloped hems resembling wings or to the embroidered threads that hung from the hem at quarter points.

39. That shall be your fringe Literally, "that shall be a *tzitzit* for you," i.e., an "ornament." The word is related to *tzitz,* "ornament, frontlet," which is mentioned in Exod. 28:36.

it Hebrew: *oto,* which is masculine in gender and so cannot refer to the tassel or fringe (*tzitzit*), a feminine noun. It must refer to the combination of tassel and thread.

lustful urge Hebrew: זנה; literally, "fornicate." It is most often used figuratively to describe Israel's relationship with pagan gods.

40. holy to your God The *tzitzit* are a reminder of the priestly robes. The Israelites, although not priests, can still attain a life of holiness.

41. to be your God The redemption of the Israelites from Egypt was the act by which the Lord claimed their allegiance. The Israelites thereby are enjoined to follow God's commandments and achieve holiness.

43b). "Remember that you are servants of the Almighty, from whom you received commandments" (Sforno). The purpose of remembering is not to shape our belief but to guide our behavior.

your heart and eyes Should "eyes" not come first? We see something and then we are tempted by it. In fact, the reverse is often true. Our hearts are inclined to covet something and only then do our eyes fasten on it.

you shall be reminded Hebrew: *tizk'ru.* A Hasidic custom emphasizes the "z" sound when pronouncing this word, to ensure that it will not be confused with *tisk'ru* (you shall be rewarded). We should observe the commandments out of love for and obedience to God, not in anticipation of reward. The Midrash compares *tzitzit* to a lifeline thrown to a drowning person: "Take hold of this, for if you do not, you endanger your life" (Num. R. 17:6).

HALAKHAH L'MA·ASEH

15:37–41. The Sages chose these verses as the third passage of the *Sh'ma,* which, along with the *Amidah,* is one of the two major parts of the morning and evening services. These verses are the basis for the practice of wearing a prayer shawl (*tallit*) with a ritual fringe (*tzitzit*) on each of its four corners. Some also wear a small fringed garment (*tallit katan*) under the shirt. Fluid from a mollusk (*ḥillazon*) was used to produce the blue (*t'kheilet*) dye (BT Men. 42b); once that source became nearly extinct, the blue thread was no longer required. But the blue-among-white of the *tzitzit* inspired the design of the flag of the State of Israel.

הפטרת שלח לך

HAFTARAH FOR SH'LAḤ L'KHA

JOSHUA 2:1–24

Two people dispatched by Joshua to spy out the land first come to the house of Rahab the harlot in Jericho where they find shelter and enter into a series of commitments in gratitude for their host's protection from a royal search party. Finally they head for the hills, to lie low until their pursuers turn back.

Rahab has heard the frightening report that Israelite troops put the Amorites under the ban (*ḥerem*) of utter annihilation (v. 10). She boldly requests that her act of loyalty to the spies be requited and her family saved (vv. 12–13), and her request is granted. No such situation is known from any war reports in Deuteronomy or elsewhere, where the repeated divine demand is annihilation (cf. Deut. 2:34–36), showing no mercy (Deut. 7:2). We must, therefore, assume that the text in Joshua rejects the harsh law of *ḥerem* and opts for mercy to those who display kindness. A silent protest (albeit hedged with signs and oaths and conditions) thus lies at the heart of the narrative. The human face of the enemy makes a compelling claim.

RELATION OF THE *HAFTARAH* TO THE *PARASHAH*

In preparation for his invasion of Canaan, the military leader Joshua sends two spies to scout the Land. "Go, reconnoiter the region of Jericho," he commands, employing a verb that literally means to "see" or "spy out" (*r'u*) the land. Moses used similar terminology when he commanded 12 spies to go and "see" (*u-r'item*) what kind of country they are about to enter (Num. 13:18). This verbal echo reminds the reader that Joshua's commission is a second attempt to scout the Land. The first one failed because the negative report of 10 of the spies led to a failure of nerve among the people. Joshua's command to his spies thus closes an historical cycle: The sins of the rebellious generation of the wilderness have been punished and the Land may now be settled. In other words, Joshua hopes to complete what Moses had initiated.

The dominant relation between the *parashah* and the *haftarah* is the difference between failure and success. The little faith of the original spies (except for Caleb and Joshua) resulted in a popular protest against Moses' plan, and God's punishment of that entire generation. Only the innocent babes (and the two faithful spies) were spared so as to enter the Promised Land (Num. 14:30–33; Deut. 1:39). That entrance under Joshua's leadership not only concludes the period of wandering and wrath but inaugurates the fulfillment of God's promise to Abraham as well (Gen. 15:16–19). The events in Josh. 2 thus start to bring closure to hopes and prophecies at the beginning of national memory. On the other side of the river Jordan is the homeland. Ancient sins have been expunged. All is ready for a new beginning.

Yet one ironic connection stands out. After the failure of the first venture to reconnoiter the Land, God bemoaned the people's disregard of the many signs (*otot*) of divine power (Num. 14:11) that they had witnessed. How fitting, then, that Joshua's spies exchange signs (*otot*) with the harlot of Jericho (their oath, her cord). It is as if the time of miracles has passed and all depends on human arrangements. But the spies learn faith from Rahab. When they return to Joshua, they invoke her own words (in v. 9), saying, "The LORD has delivered the whole land into our power . . . all the inhabitants are quaking before us" (v. 24).

2 Joshua son of Nun secretly sent two spies from Shittim, saying, "Go, reconnoiter the region of Jericho." So they set out, and they came to the house of a harlot named Rahab and lodged there. ²The king of Jericho was told, "Some men have come here tonight, Israelites, to spy out the country." ³The king of Jericho thereupon sent orders to Rahab: "Produce the men who came to you and entered your house, for they have come to spy out the whole country." ⁴The woman, however, had taken the two men and hidden them. "It is true," she said, "the men did come to me, but I didn't know where they were from. ⁵And at dark, when the gate was about to be closed, the men left; and I don't know where the men went. Quick, go after them, for you can overtake them."—⁶Now she had taken them up to the roof and hidden them under some stalks of flax which she had lying on the roof.—⁷So the men pursued them in the direction of the Jordan down to the fords; and no sooner had the pursuers gone out than the gate was shut behind them.

⁸The spies had not yet gone to sleep when she came up to them on the roof. ⁹She said to the men, "I know that the LORD has given the country to you, because dread of you has fallen upon us, and all the inhabitants of the land are quaking before you. ¹⁰For we have heard how the LORD dried up the waters of the Sea of Reeds for you when you left Egypt, and what you did to Sihon and Og, the two Amorite kings across the Jordan, whom you doomed. ¹¹When we heard about it, we lost heart, and no man had

ב וַיִּשְׁלַ֣ח יְהוֹשֻֽׁעַ־בִּן־נ֠וּן מִֽן־הַשִּׁטִּ֜ים שְׁנַֽיִם־אֲנָשִׁ֥ים מְרַגְּלִים֮ חֶ֣רֶשׁ לֵאמֹר֒ לְכ֛וּ רְא֥וּ אֶת־הָאָ֖רֶץ וְאֶת־יְרִיח֑וֹ וַיֵּ֨לְכ֜וּ וַיָּבֹ֣אוּ בֵּית־אִשָּׁ֥ה זוֹנָ֛ה וּשְׁמָ֥הּ רָחָ֖ב וַיִּשְׁכְּבוּ־ שָֽׁמָּה׃ ² וַיֵּ֣אָמַ֔ר לְמֶ֥לֶךְ יְרִיח֖וֹ לֵאמֹ֑ר הִנֵּ֣ה אֲנָשִׁ֗ים בָּ֣אוּ הֵ֧נָּה הַלַּ֛יְלָה מִבְּנֵ֥י יִשְׂרָאֵ֖ל לַחְפֹּ֥ר אֶת־הָאָֽרֶץ׃ ³ וַיִּשְׁלַ֗ח מֶ֚לֶךְ יְרִיח֔וֹ אֶל־רָחָ֖ב לֵאמֹ֑ר הוֹצִ֜יאִי הָאֲנָשִׁ֤ים הַבָּאִים֙ אֵלַ֙יִךְ֙ אֲשֶׁר־בָּ֣אוּ לְבֵיתֵ֔ךְ כִּ֛י לַחְפֹּ֥ר אֶת־ כָּל־הָאָ֖רֶץ בָּֽאוּ׃ ⁴ וַתִּקַּ֧ח הָֽאִשָּׁ֛ה אֶת־שְׁנֵ֥י הָאֲנָשִׁ֖ים וַֽתִּצְפְּנ֑וֹ וַתֹּ֣אמֶר ׀ כֵּ֗ן בָּ֤אוּ אֵלַי֙ הָאֲנָשִׁ֔ים וְלֹ֥א יָדַ֖עְתִּי מֵאַ֥יִן הֵֽמָּה׃ ⁵ וַיְהִ֣י הַשַּׁ֗עַר לִסְגּוֹר֙ בַּחֹ֔שֶׁךְ וְהָאֲנָשִׁ֖ים יָצָ֑אוּ לֹ֣א יָדַ֔עְתִּי אָ֥נָה הָלְכ֖וּ הָֽאֲנָשִׁ֑ים רִדְפ֤וּ מַהֵר֙ אַחֲרֵיהֶ֔ם כִּ֖י תַּשִּׂיגֽוּם׃ ⁶ וְהִ֖יא הֶעֱלָ֣תַם הַגָּ֑גָה וַֽתִּטְמְנֵם֙ בְּפִשְׁתֵּ֣י הָעֵ֔ץ הָעֲרֻכ֥וֹת לָ֖הּ עַל־הַגָּֽג׃ ⁷ וְהָאֲנָשִׁ֗ים רָדְפ֤וּ אַֽחֲרֵיהֶם֙ דֶּ֣רֶךְ הַיַּרְדֵּ֔ן עַ֖ל הַֽמַּעְבְּר֑וֹת וְהַשַּׁ֣עַר סָגָ֔רוּ אַחֲרֵ֕י כַּאֲשֶׁ֛ר יָצְא֥וּ הָרֹדְפִ֖ים אַחֲרֵיהֶֽם׃ ⁸ וְהֵ֖מָּה טֶ֣רֶם יִשְׁכָּב֑וּן וְהִ֛יא עָלְתָ֥ה עֲלֵיהֶ֖ם עַל־הַגָּֽג׃ ⁹ וַתֹּ֙אמֶר֙ אֶל־הָ֣אֲנָשִׁ֔ים יָדַ֕עְתִּי כִּֽי־נָתַ֧ן יְהֹוָ֛ה לָכֶ֖ם אֶת־הָאָ֑רֶץ וְכִֽי־נָפְלָ֤ה אֵֽימַתְכֶם֙ עָלֵ֔ינוּ וְכִ֥י נָמֹ֛גוּ כָּל־יֹשְׁבֵ֥י הָאָ֖רֶץ מִפְּנֵיכֶֽם׃ ¹⁰ כִּ֣י שָׁמַ֗עְנוּ אֵ֠ת אֲשֶׁר־הוֹבִ֨ישׁ יְהֹוָ֜ה אֶת־מֵ֤י יַם־סוּף֙ מִפְּנֵיכֶ֔ם בְּצֵאתְכֶ֖ם מִמִּצְרָ֑יִם וַאֲשֶׁ֣ר עֲשִׂיתֶ֗ם לִשְׁנֵ֞י מַלְכֵ֤י הָֽאֱמֹרִי֙ אֲשֶׁ֣ר בְּעֵ֣בֶר הַיַּרְדֵּ֔ן לְסִיחֹ֖ן וּלְע֑וֹג אֲשֶׁ֥ר הֶחֱרַמְתֶּ֖ם אוֹתָֽם׃ ¹¹ וַנִּשְׁמַע֙ וַיִּמַּ֣ס לְבָבֵ֔נוּ וְלֹא־קָ֨מָה ע֥וֹד ר֛וּחַ בְּאִ֖ישׁ מִפְּנֵיכֶ֑ם

---

*Joshua 2:1. **harlot*** Hebrew: *zonah*. Since antiquity, Jewish tradition has softened the image by interpreting the word as "innkeeper," one who "provides food" (*zun*). There is no reason, however, to doubt the ascription of harlotry. It serves as an ironic counterpoint to the narrative of salvation.

*4. **and hidden them*** Literally, "and hid him" (*va-titzp'no*), interpreted to mean that she hid each one separately to make their hiding places inconspicuous (Rashi, Radak).

any more spirit left because of you; for the LORD your God is the only God in heaven above and on earth below. 12Now, since I have shown loyalty to you, swear to me by the LORD that you in turn will show loyalty to my family. Provide me with a reliable sign 13that you will spare the lives of my father and mother, my brothers and sisters, and all who belong to them, and save us from death." 14The men answered her, "Our persons are pledged for yours, even to death! If you do not disclose this mission of ours, we will show you true loyalty when the LORD gives us the land."

15She let them down by a rope through the window—for her dwelling was at the outer side of the city wall and she lived in the actual wall. 16She said to them, "Make for the hills, so that the pursuers may not come upon you. Stay there in hiding three days, until the pursuers return; then go your way."

17But the men warned her, "We will be released from this oath which you have made us take 18[unless,] when we invade the country, you tie this length of crimson cord to the window through which you let us down. Bring your father, your mother, your brothers, and all your family together in your house; 19and if anyone ventures outside the doors of your house, his blood will be on his head, and we shall be clear. But if a hand is laid on anyone who remains in the house with you, his blood shall be on our heads. 20And if you disclose this mission of ours, we shall likewise be released from the oath which you made us take." 21She replied, "Let it be as you say."

She sent them on their way, and they left; and she tied the crimson cord to the window.

כִּי יְהוָה אֱלֹהֵיכֶם הוּא אֱלֹהִים בַּשָּׁמַיִם
מִמַּעַל וְעַל־הָאָרֶץ מִתָּחַת׃ 12 וְעַתָּה
הִשָּׁבְעוּ־נָא לִי בַּיהוָה כִּי־עָשִׂיתִי עִמָּכֶם
חָסֶד וַעֲשִׂיתֶם גַּם־אַתֶּם עִם־בֵּית אָבִי
חֶסֶד וּנְתַתֶּם לִי אוֹת אֱמֶת׃ 13 וְהַחֲיִתֶם
אֶת־אָבִי וְאֶת־אִמִּי וְאֶת־אַחַי וְאֶת־אחותי
אַחְיוֹתַי וְאֵת כָּל־אֲשֶׁר לָהֶם וְהִצַּלְתֶּם
אֶת־נַפְשֹׁתֵינוּ מִמָּוֶת׃ 14 וַיֹּאמְרוּ לָהּ
הָאֲנָשִׁים נַפְשֵׁנוּ תַחְתֵּיכֶם לָמוּת אִם
לֹא תַגִּידוּ אֶת־דְּבָרֵנוּ זֶה וְהָיָה בְּתֵת־
יְהוָה לָנוּ אֶת־הָאָרֶץ וְעָשִׂינוּ עִמָּךְ חֶסֶד
וֶאֱמֶת׃
15 וַתּוֹרִדֵם בַּחֶבֶל בְּעַד הַחַלּוֹן כִּי בֵיתָהּ
בְּקִיר הַחוֹמָה וּבַחוֹמָה הִיא יוֹשָׁבֶת׃
16 וַתֹּאמֶר לָהֶם הָהָרָה לֵּכוּ פֶּן־יִפְגְּעוּ בָכֶם
הָרֹדְפִים וְנַחְבֵּתֶם שָׁמָּה שְׁלֹשֶׁת יָמִים עַד
שׁוֹב הָרֹדְפִים וְאַחַר תֵּלְכוּ לְדַרְכְּכֶם׃
17 וַיֹּאמְרוּ אֵלֶיהָ הָאֲנָשִׁים נְקִיִּם אֲנַחְנוּ
מִשְּׁבֻעָתֵךְ הַזֶּה אֲשֶׁר הִשְׁבַּעְתָּנוּ׃ 18 הִנֵּה
אֲנַחְנוּ בָאִים בָּאָרֶץ אֶת־תִּקְוַת חוּט הַשָּׁנִי
הַזֶּה תִּקְשְׁרִי בַּחַלּוֹן אֲשֶׁר הוֹרַדְתֵּנוּ בוֹ
וְאֶת־אָבִיךְ וְאֶת־אִמֵּךְ וְאֶת־אַחַיִךְ וְאֵת
כָּל־בֵּית אָבִיךְ תַּאַסְפִי אֵלַיִךְ הַבָּיְתָה׃
19 וְהָיָה כֹּל אֲשֶׁר־יֵצֵא מִדַּלְתֵי בֵיתֵךְ ׀
הַחוּצָה דָּמוֹ בְרֹאשׁוֹ וַאֲנַחְנוּ נְקִיִּם
וְכֹל אֲשֶׁר יִהְיֶה אִתָּךְ בַּבַּיִת דָּמוֹ
בְרֹאשֵׁנוּ אִם־יָד תִּהְיֶה־בּוֹ׃ 20 וְאִם־תַּגִּידִי
אֶת־דְּבָרֵנוּ זֶה וְהָיִינוּ נְקִיִּם מִשְּׁבֻעָתֵךְ
אֲשֶׁר הִשְׁבַּעְתָּנוּ׃ 21 וַתֹּאמֶר כְּדִבְרֵיכֶם כֶּן־
הוּא
וַתְּשַׁלְּחֵם וַיֵּלֵכוּ וַתִּקְשֹׁר אֶת־תִּקְוַת הַשָּׁנִי
בַּחַלּוֹן׃

11. for the LORD your God is the only God For this expression of piety, midrashic tradition says that Rahab was a righteous gentile who converted and married Joshua; together they produced prophets (including Jeremiah) and priests.

[22]They went straight to the hills and stayed there three days, until the pursuers turned back. And so the pursuers, searching all along the road, did not find them.

[23]Then the two men came down again from the hills and crossed over. They came to Joshua son of Nun and reported to him all that had happened to them. [24]They said to Joshua, "The LORD has delivered the whole land into our power; in fact, all the inhabitants of the land are quaking before us."

22 וַיֵּלְכוּ֙ וַיָּבֹ֣אוּ הָהָ֔רָה וַיֵּ֤שְׁבוּ שָׁם֙ שְׁלֹ֣שֶׁת
יָמִ֔ים עַד־שָׁ֖בוּ הָרֹדְפִ֑ים וַיְבַקְשׁ֧וּ הָרֹדְפִ֛ים
בְּכָל־הַדֶּ֖רֶךְ וְלֹ֥א מָצָֽאוּ׃
23 וַיָּשֻׁ֜בוּ שְׁנֵ֤י הָֽאֲנָשִׁים֙ וַיֵּרְד֣וּ מֵהָהָ֔ר
וַיַּֽעַבְרוּ֙ וַיָּבֹ֔אוּ אֶל־יְהוֹשֻׁ֖עַ בִּן־נ֑וּן וַיְסַפְּרוּ־
ל֔וֹ אֵ֖ת כָּל־הַמֹּצְא֥וֹת אוֹתָֽם׃ 24 וַיֹּֽאמְרוּ֙
אֶל־יְהוֹשֻׁ֔עַ כִּֽי־נָתַ֧ן יְהוָ֛ה בְּיָדֵ֖נוּ אֶת־
כָּל־הָאָ֑רֶץ וְגַם־נָמֹ֛גוּ כָּל־יֹשְׁבֵ֥י הָאָ֖רֶץ
מִפָּנֵֽינוּ׃ ס

16 Now Korah, son of Izhar son of Kohath
son of Levi, betook himself, along with Dathan
and Abiram sons of Eliab, and On son of
Peleth—descendants of Reuben—2to rise up
against Moses, together with two hundred and
fifty Israelites, chieftains of the community,

טז וַיִּקַּח קֹרַח בֶּן־יִצְהָר בֶּן־קְהָת
בֶּן־לֵוִי וְדָתָן וַאֲבִירָם בְּנֵי אֱלִיאָב וְאוֹן
בֶּן־פֶּלֶת בְּנֵי רְאוּבֵן׃ 2 וַיָּקֻמוּ לִפְנֵי מֹשֶׁה
וַאֲנָשִׁים מִבְּנֵי־יִשְׂרָאֵל חֲמִשִּׁים וּמָאתָיִם

The Generation of the Exodus: The March to Transjordan (*continued*)

ENCROACHMENT ON THE TABERNACLE (16:1–18:32)

THE KORAHITE REBELLIONS (16:1–35)

LEADERS OF THE REBELLION (vv. 1–2)

1. Dathan and Abiram . . . Reuben Because they were descended from Reuben, Jacob's firstborn and hence the original leader of the tribes, they resented Moses' leadership (see 1 Chron. 5:1–2).

2. Israelites Here referring to dignitaries.

chieftains of These 250 chieftains were not only Levites but represented a cross-section of the tribes.

CHAPTER 16

The theme of Israel's unhappiness and rebelliousness continues in this *parashah.* Several highly placed Israelites, resenting the prominence of Moses and Aaron, claim the right to leadership for themselves. Korah, a Levite, asserts himself as the equal of Moses and Aaron (it is not entirely clear which of them he wishes to replace). Leaders of the tribe of Reuben claim leadership in the name of the descendants of Jacob's firstborn son. It may be that a series of discouraging events—including the deaths at Taberah (11:1–3) and at Kibroth-hattaavah (11:10–34), and the disastrous episode of the scouts (13–14)—have demoralized the people to the point at which they are vulnerable to this uprising (Ramban). The uprising is put down only after two miraculous events. One miracle destroys the rebels and affirms the primacy of Moses and Aaron, and a second miracle authenticates the primacy of the Levites for the divine service.

In Jewish lore, Korah is the arch-demagogue, lusting for power to inflate his own prominence, not to serve the people. Thus the Mishnah describes illegitimate controversy (for personal gain, "not for the sake of Heaven") as being "like the dispute of Korah and his followers" (Avot 5:17). One interpreter understands this as "the dispute of Korah *with* his followers," because each faction in the rebellion had its own agenda. They were united only in their opposition to Moses and Aaron. Like many demagogues, they defined themselves by what they were against, not by a vision of what they stood for (Kalischer).

One tradition (Num. R. 18:4) pictures Korah complaining about the tithes and offerings Moses demanded of the people, saying "You lay a heavier burden on us than the Egyptians did." Korah, in this *midrash,* never mentions that these taxes were designed to help the poor, to maintain the sanctuary, and to give the Israelites ways of expressing their gratitude to God and their dependence on God. Another *midrash* (Num. R. 18:3) portrays Korah as caricaturing the rituals of the Torah by casting them in extreme form: Does a library full of Torah scrolls require a *m'zuzah* (with a few biblical verses in it) on the doorpost? Does a completely blue *tallit* need the required blue thread added to its *tzitzit*? Thus Korah was challenging not only Moses and Aaron's authority but that of Torah and, ultimately, of God.

1. son of Kohath son of Levi Why does Korah's genealogy stop there and not trace itself back to Abraham, Isaac, and Jacob? Because Jacob on his deathbed prayed, "If any of my descendants turns out wicked, may my name not be associated with them." Such a person is not worthy of being called "an Israelite" (Num. R. 18:5).

On son of Peleth He is never mentioned again in the story. An ancient tradition relates that his wife talked him out of following Korah. "What good will it do us if Korah wins? We will be subservient to him as we now are to Moses and Aaron" (BT Sanh. 109b).

chosen in the assembly, men of repute. [3]They combined against Moses and Aaron and said to them, "You have gone too far! For all the community are holy, all of them, and the LORD is in their midst. Why then do you raise yourselves above the LORD's congregation?"

[4]When Moses heard this, he fell on his face. [5]Then he spoke to Korah and all his company, saying, "Come morning, the LORD will make known who is His and who is holy, and will grant him access to Himself; He will grant access to the one He has chosen. [6]Do this: You, Korah and all your band, take fire pans, [7]and tomorrow put fire in them and lay incense on them before the LORD. Then the man whom the LORD chooses, he shall be the holy one. You have gone too far, sons of Levi!"

[8]Moses said further to Korah, "Hear me, sons

נְשִׂיאֵי עֵדָה קְרִאֵי מוֹעֵד אַנְשֵׁי־שֵׁם׃
3 וַיִּקָּהֲלוּ עַל־מֹשֶׁה וְעַל־אַהֲרֹן וַיֹּאמְרוּ
אֲלֵהֶם רַב־לָכֶם כִּי כָל־הָעֵדָה כֻּלָּם
קְדֹשִׁים וּבְתוֹכָם יְהוָה וּמַדּוּעַ תִּתְנַשְּׂאוּ
עַל־קְהַל יְהוָה׃
4 וַיִּשְׁמַע מֹשֶׁה וַיִּפֹּל עַל־פָּנָיו׃ 5 וַיְדַבֵּר
אֶל־קֹרַח וְאֶל־כָּל־עֲדָתוֹ לֵאמֹר בֹּקֶר וְיֹדַע
יְהוָה אֶת־אֲשֶׁר־לוֹ וְאֶת־הַקָּדוֹשׁ וְהִקְרִיב
אֵלָיו וְאֵת אֲשֶׁר יִבְחַר־בּוֹ יַקְרִיב אֵלָיו׃
6 זֹאת עֲשׂוּ קְחוּ־לָכֶם מַחְתּוֹת קֹרַח וְכָל־
עֲדָתוֹ׃ 7 וּתְנוּ בָהֵן ׀ אֵשׁ וְשִׂימוּ עֲלֵיהֶן
קְטֹרֶת לִפְנֵי יְהוָה מָחָר וְהָיָה הָאִישׁ
אֲשֶׁר־יִבְחַר יְהוָה הוּא הַקָּדוֹשׁ רַב־לָכֶם
בְּנֵי לֵוִי׃
8 וַיֹּאמֶר מֹשֶׁה אֶל־קֹרַח שִׁמְעוּ־נָא בְּנֵי

chosen in This can also be rendered, with the ancient Greek translation, "called to." Chieftains were heads of clans and, by virtue of that office, were called to the national assembly.

repute Hebrew: *shem;* literally, "name." (Conversely, ignoble persons are "nameless.")

THE INCENSE TEST FOR HOLINESS (vv. 3–7)

3. You have gone too far Literally, "you have too much" power and prestige.

all the community are holy This claim is in opposition to the priestly teaching that only priests are holy (see Exod. 28:1–3 and Lev. 8 for the special status of priests). Thus either Aaron is the intended target of the attack (and Moses is included with him because he appointed and consecrated Aaron) or Moses too is accused of presuming to be holy because on occasion he assumed priestly powers, as when he officiated at Aaron's consecration (Exod. 29; Lev. 8).

4. fell on his face So that God would provide him an answer. Apparently Moses entered the tabernacle enclosure to consult God.

5. morning A day is needed for the required rituals of purification before one may appear at the tabernacle.

who is His and who is holy To lead Israel and the priesthood.

has chosen God intends to designate His priest for all time.

6–7. The offering of incense is an exclusive priestly prerogative. Nonpriests offer it only at the peril of their lives.

fire pans A flat pan used for removing ashes or live coals from the altar, and on which incense is placed.

7. before the LORD That is, at the entrance to the tabernacle court (v. 18).

MOSES REBUKES THE LEVITES (vv. 8–11)

When Moses' leadership is contested, he leaves his

---

3. Yeshayahu Leibowitz sees Korah's demagoguery exposed in his claim that "all the community 'are' holy," i.e., we have achieved our goal and nothing more need be demanded of us. The Torah's position is that all the community is challenged to "become" holy (Lev. 19:2). It is a future goal, not a present boast. Leibowitz interprets the words of the Torah several chapters later (26:11), "the sons of Korah . . . did not die," to mean that such people exist in every generation, claiming that just being Jewish means that they are already as close to God as they have to be. True messengers present themselves as unworthy of the task, as Moses did at the Burning Bush (Exod. 3:11). Only persons motivated by self-interest, eager for the position of leader, proclaim "I can do it better" (Hirsch).

of Levi. 9Is it not enough for you that the God
of Israel has set you apart from the community
of Israel and given you access to Him, to perform the duties of the LORD's Tabernacle and
to minister to the community and serve them?
10Now that He has advanced you and all your
fellow Levites with you, do you seek the priesthood too? 11Truly, it is against the LORD that
you and all your company have banded together. For who is Aaron that you should rail
against him?"

12Moses sent for Dathan and Abiram, sons of
Eliab; but they said, "We will not come! 13Is it
not enough that you brought us from a land
flowing with milk and honey to have us die in
the wilderness, that you would also lord it over
us? 14Even if you had brought us to a land
flowing with milk and honey, and given us possession of fields and vineyards, should you
gouge out those men's eyes? We will not
come!" 15Moses was much aggrieved and he said
to the LORD, "Pay no regard to their oblation.

לֵוִי: 9 הַמְעַט מִכֶּם כִּי־הִבְדִּיל אֱלֹהֵי
יִשְׂרָאֵל אֶתְכֶם מֵעֲדַת יִשְׂרָאֵל לְהַקְרִיב
אֶתְכֶם אֵלָיו לַעֲבֹד אֶת־עֲבֹדַת מִשְׁכַּן
יְהוָה וְלַעֲמֹד לִפְנֵי הָעֵדָה לְשָׁרְתָם:
10 וַיַּקְרֵב אֹתְךָ וְאֶת־כָּל־אַחֶיךָ בְנֵי־לֵוִי
אִתָּךְ וּבִקַּשְׁתֶּם גַּם־כְּהֻנָּה: 11 לָכֵן אַתָּה
וְכָל־עֲדָתְךָ הַנֹּעָדִים עַל־יְהוָה וְאַהֲרֹן
מַה־הוּא כִּי תלונו תַלִּינוּ עָלָיו:
12 וַיִּשְׁלַח מֹשֶׁה לִקְרֹא לְדָתָן וְלַאֲבִירָם
בְּנֵי אֱלִיאָב וַיֹּאמְרוּ לֹא נַעֲלֶה: 13 הַמְעַט
כִּי הֶעֱלִיתָנוּ מֵאֶרֶץ זָבַת חָלָב וּדְבַשׁ
לַהֲמִיתֵנוּ בַּמִּדְבָּר כִּי־תִשְׂתָּרֵר עָלֵינוּ גַּם־
הִשְׂתָּרֵר: 14 אַף לֹא אֶל־אֶרֶץ זָבַת חָלָב שני
וּדְבַשׁ הֲבִיאֹתָנוּ וַתִּתֶּן־לָנוּ נַחֲלַת שָׂדֶה
וָכָרֶם הַעֵינֵי הָאֲנָשִׁים הָהֵם תְּנַקֵּר לֹא
נַעֲלֶה: 15 וַיִּחַר לְמֹשֶׁה מְאֹד וַיֹּאמֶר אֶל־
יְהוָה אַל־תֵּפֶן אֶל־מִנְחָתָם לֹא חֲמוֹר אֶחָד

defense to God. When Aaron is the target, Moses springs to his aid.

8. sons of Levi In verse 2 we are told that Korah's allies are the tribal chieftains, but here they seem to be Levites.

9. duties The responsibility and privilege of dismantling, transporting, and reassembling the tabernacle and its sacred objects.

serve them By assisting the Israelites with the preliminary acts of preparing the sacrifice: slaughtering, flaying, and washing the animal, tasks that normally are performed by the one who makes the offering.

11. The true thrust of the rebellion is against the Lord, who has chosen Moses and Aaron.

who is Aaron Literally, "what is [wrong] with Aaron?"

MOSES DEFIED (vv. 12–15)

12. We will not come! That is, "We will no longer obey your orders." This is an open break with Moses' authority.

13. Dathan and Abiram contradict Moses' major claim: Egypt and not Canaan is the true land of milk and honey.

14. Even if you had As you promised (see Exod. 3:8,17, 13:5, 33:3, and others in Lev., Num., and Deut.).

gouge out those men's eyes This idiom also means "hoodwink." It corresponds to the modern idioms "throw dust in the eyes" or "pull the wool over the eyes." "Those men" refers either to the elders who accompanied Moses (v. 25) or, more likely, euphemistically, to themselves.

15. oblation This refers either to their prior but unmentioned offering, to their incense offering, or to any sacrifice they might wish to offer before the test.

---

12. Moses sent for Dathan and Abiram Here we see the greatness of Moses' soul. He set aside his own dignity and his feelings of resentment toward those who spoke ill of him and took the initiative to heal this breach in the community (Rashi).

I have not taken the ass of any one of them, nor
have I wronged any one of them."
16And Moses said to Korah, "Tomorrow, you
and all your company appear before the LORD,
you and they and Aaron. 17Each of you take his
fire pan and lay incense on it, and each of you
bring his fire pan before the LORD, two hundred
and fifty fire pans; you and Aaron also [bring]
your fire pans." 18Each of them took his fire pan,
put fire in it, laid incense on it, and took his place
at the entrance of the Tent of Meeting, as did
Moses and Aaron. 19Korah gathered the whole
community against them at the entrance of the
Tent of Meeting.

Then the Presence of the LORD appeared to
the whole community, 20and the LORD spoke
to Moses and Aaron, saying, 21"Stand back from
this community that I may annihilate them in
an instant!" 22But they fell on their faces and
said, "O God, Source of the breath of all flesh!
When one man sins, will You be wrathful with
the whole community?"
23The LORD spoke to Moses, saying, 24"Speak
to the community and say: Withdraw from

מֵהֶם֙ נָשָׂ֔אתִי וְלֹ֥א הֲרֵעֹ֖תִי אֶת־אַחַ֥ד
מֵהֶֽם׃
16 וַיֹּ֤אמֶר מֹשֶׁה֙ אֶל־קֹ֔רַח אַתָּה֙ וְכָל־עֲדָ֣תְךָ֔
הֱי֖וּ לִפְנֵ֣י יְהוָ֑ה אַתָּ֥ה וָהֵ֛ם וְאַהֲרֹ֖ן מָחָֽר׃
17 וּקְח֣וּ ׀ אִ֣ישׁ מַחְתָּת֗וֹ וּנְתַתֶּ֤ם עֲלֵיהֶם֙
קְטֹ֔רֶת וְהִקְרַבְתֶּ֞ם לִפְנֵ֤י יְהוָה֙ אִ֣ישׁ
מַחְתָּת֔וֹ חֲמִשִּׁ֥ים וּמָאתַ֖יִם מַחְתֹּ֑ת וְאַתָּ֥ה
וְאַהֲרֹ֖ן אִ֥ישׁ מַחְתָּתֽוֹ׃ 18 וַיִּקְח֞וּ אִ֣ישׁ
מַחְתָּת֗וֹ וַיִּתְּנ֤וּ עֲלֵיהֶם֙ אֵ֔שׁ וַיָּשִׂ֥ימוּ עֲלֵיהֶ֖ם
קְטֹ֑רֶת וַיַּֽעַמְד֗וּ פֶּ֛תַח אֹ֥הֶל מוֹעֵ֖ד וּמֹשֶׁ֥ה
וְאַהֲרֹֽן׃ 19 וַיַּקְהֵ֨ל עֲלֵיהֶ֥ם קֹ֙רַח֙ אֶת־כָּל־
הָ֣עֵדָ֔ה אֶל־פֶּ֖תַח אֹ֣הֶל מוֹעֵ֑ד
וַיֵּרָ֥א כְבוֹד־יְהוָ֖ה אֶל־כָּל־הָעֵדָֽה׃ פ
שלישי 20 וַיְדַבֵּ֣ר יְהוָ֔ה אֶל־מֹשֶׁ֥ה וְאֶֽל־אַהֲרֹ֖ן
לֵאמֹֽר׃ 21 הִבָּ֣דְל֔וּ מִתּ֖וֹךְ הָעֵדָ֣ה הַזֹּ֑את
וַאֲכַלֶּ֥ה אֹתָ֖ם כְּרָֽגַע׃ 22 וַיִּפְּל֤וּ עַל־פְּנֵיהֶם֙
וַיֹּ֣אמְר֔וּ אֵ֕ל אֱלֹהֵ֥י הָרוּחֹ֖ת לְכָל־בָּשָׂ֑ר
הָאִ֤ישׁ אֶחָד֙ יֶחֱטָ֔א וְעַ֥ל כָּל־הָעֵדָ֖ה
תִּקְצֹֽף׃ פ
23 וַיְדַבֵּ֥ר יְהוָ֖ה אֶל־מֹשֶׁ֥ה לֵּאמֹֽר׃ 24 דַּבֵּ֥ר

THE INCENSE TEST AT THE TENT OF MEETING (vv. 16–24)

16–17. This repeats verses 6–7, except that Aaron, missing there, is explicitly mentioned here, and the Levites, addressed in verses 6–7, are missing here. Possibly Korah stands for all the rebellious Levites.

before the LORD See Comment to 16:7.

18. The execution of the test, presumably on the next day.

put fire in it Moses, however, did not command them to do this now (see v. 17), although he did so earlier (v. 7). Is this omission a hint that Korah and the chieftains were guilty of offering "unauthorized fire" (*esh zarah*), that is, not from the altar—which was the sin of Nadab and Abihu (Lev. 10:1)? It is hardly accidental that when Moses asks Aaron to offer incense on a fire pan he specifies that the fire be taken from the altar.

in it That is, on it.

19. the whole community Korah rallied all of Israel behind him; hence God intended to destroy them all.

21. Stand back Hebrew: *hibbad'lu;* literally, "separate yourselves" (17:10).

22. they fell on their faces In prayer.

Source of the breath God gives humans His breath at birth and withdraws it at death. Because God is the Creator of life and alone determines who is to live and who is to die, His anger need not be turned on the innocent.

When one man Korah alone instigated the action of the community.

wrathful with the whole community The divine right to punish collectively is here both assumed and questioned.

24. But the community was gathered at the Tent of Meeting (vv. 18–19)! Originally the rebellion of Dathan and Abiram and the

---

24. Withdraw from about the abodes "The Israelites were in a dangerous situation characteristic of many people to this day. They did not agree with Korah but neither did they ac-

about the abodes of Korah, Dathan, and Abiram."

²⁵Moses rose and went to Dathan and Abiram, the elders of Israel following him. ²⁶He addressed the community, saying, "Move away from the tents of these wicked men and touch nothing that belongs to them, lest you be wiped out for all their sins." ²⁷So they withdrew from about the abodes of Korah, Dathan, and Abiram.

Now Dathan and Abiram had come out and they stood at the entrance of their tents, with their wives, their children, and their little ones. ²⁸And Moses said, "By this you shall know that it was the LORD who sent me to do all these things; that they are not of my own devising: ²⁹if these men die as all men do, if their lot be the common fate of all mankind, it was not the LORD who sent me. ³⁰But if the LORD brings about something unheard-of, so that the ground opens its mouth and swallows them up with all that belongs to them, and they go down alive into Sheol, you shall know that these men

אֶל־הָעֵדָ֣ה לֵאמֹ֔ר הֵעָ֗לוּ מִסָּבִיב֙ לְמִשְׁכַּן־
קֹ֥רַח דָּתָ֖ן וַאֲבִירָֽם: 25 וַיָּ֣קָם מֹשֶׁ֗ה וַיֵּ֛לֶךְ אֶל־דָּתָ֥ן וַאֲבִירָ֖ם וַיֵּלְכ֥וּ
אַחֲרָ֖יו זִקְנֵ֥י יִשְׂרָאֵֽל: 26 וַיְדַבֵּ֨ר אֶל־הָעֵדָ֜ה
לֵאמֹ֗ר ס֣וּרוּ נָ֡א מֵעַל֩ אָהֳלֵ֨י הָאֲנָשִׁ֤ים
הָרְשָׁעִים֙ הָאֵ֔לֶּה וְאַֽל־תִּגְּע֖וּ בְּכָל־אֲשֶׁ֣ר
לָהֶ֑ם פֶּן־תִּסָּפ֖וּ בְּכָל־חַטֹּאתָֽם: 27 וַיֵּעָל֗וּ
מֵעַ֧ל מִשְׁכַּן־קֹ֛רַח דָּתָ֥ן וַאֲבִירָ֖ם מִסָּבִ֑יב
וְדָתָ֨ן וַאֲבִירָ֜ם יָצְא֣וּ נִצָּבִ֗ים פֶּ֚תַח אָֽהֳלֵיהֶ֔ם
וּנְשֵׁיהֶ֥ם וּבְנֵיהֶ֖ם וְטַפָּֽם: 28 וַיֹּאמֶר֮ מֹשֶׁה֒
בְּזֹאת֙ תֵּֽדְע֔וּן כִּֽי־יְהֹוָ֣ה שְׁלָחַ֔נִי לַעֲשׂ֕וֹת
אֵ֥ת כָּל־הַֽמַּעֲשִׂ֖ים הָאֵ֑לֶּה כִּי־לֹ֖א מִלִּבִּֽי:
29 אִם־כְּמ֤וֹת כָּל־הָֽאָדָם֙ יְמֻת֣וּן אֵ֔לֶּה
וּפְקֻדַּת֙ כָּל־הָ֣אָדָ֔ם יִפָּקֵ֖ד עֲלֵיהֶ֑ם לֹ֥א יְהֹוָ֖ה
שְׁלָחָֽנִי: 30 וְאִם־בְּרִיאָ֞ה יִבְרָ֣א יְהֹוָ֗ה
וּפָצְתָ֨ה הָאֲדָמָ֤ה אֶת־פִּ֨יהָ֙ וּבָלְעָ֤ה אֹתָם֙
וְאֶת־כָּל־אֲשֶׁ֣ר לָהֶ֔ם וְיָרְד֥וּ חַיִּ֖ים שְׁאֹ֑לָה
וִֽידַעְתֶּ֕ם כִּ֧י נִֽאֲצ֛וּ הָאֲנָשִׁ֥ים הָאֵ֖לֶּה אֶת־

rebellion of Korah may have been separate events.

PUNISHMENT OF THE REBELS   (vv. 25–35)

25. elders of Israel   Perhaps the 70 elders of 11:16. Thus Dathan and Abiram had no support from the other tribes.

26. the community   The Israelites who did not take part in the rebellion.

tents   The Hebrew term *ohel* refers both to the tent curtains and to its contents.

27. had come out   For a curse to be effective, the object of the curse must be in view. Dathan, Abiram, and their families had to be seen by Moses.

28. all these things   This refers to Moses' leadership, declared a failure by Dathan and Abiram. Or it could refer to Moses' appointment of the Levites in place of the firstborn, or to his appointment of Aaron and his sons to the priesthood.

my own devising   Literally, "my own heart." In the Bible, the heart is the locus of thought. Moses wishes to demonstrate that he is not "lording it" over Israel, but simply fulfilling the will of God.

29. common fate   A natural death.

30. brings about something unheard-of Literally, "will create a creation," i.e., something that did not exist before.

Sheol   The netherworld, the abode of the dead.

tively oppose him. They stood aside to see how things would turn out" (N. Leibowitz, after Malbim). That is why Moses has to urge them to distance themselves from Korah and his followers, lest they be caught up in the latter's punishment, suffering the deserved fate of the bystander who does nothing to stop evil and perhaps even hopes to benefit from it.

28–30. It would seem that Moses is showing the strain of having to deal with one episode of complaint and faithlessness after another. With each successive incident, he becomes more short tempered with the people he is leading.

have spurned the LORD." 31Scarcely had he
finished speaking all these words when the
ground under them burst asunder, 32and the
earth opened its mouth and swallowed them up
with their households, all Korah's people and
all their possessions. 33They went down alive
into Sheol, with all that belonged to them; the
earth closed over them and they vanished from
the midst of the congregation. 34All Israel
around them fled at their shrieks, for they said,
"The earth might swallow us!"
35And a fire went forth from the LORD and
consumed the two hundred and fifty men
offering the incense.

יְהוָה׃ 31 וַיְהִי֙ כְּכַלֹּת֔וֹ לְדַבֵּ֔ר אֵ֥ת כָּל־
הַדְּבָרִ֖ים הָאֵ֑לֶּה וַתִּבָּקַ֥ע הָאֲדָמָ֖ה אֲשֶׁ֥ר
תַּחְתֵּיהֶֽם׃ 32 וַתִּפְתַּ֤ח הָאָ֙רֶץ֙ אֶת־פִּ֔יהָ
וַתִּבְלַ֥ע אֹתָ֖ם וְאֶת־בָּתֵּיהֶ֑ם וְאֵ֤ת כָּל־
הָאָדָם֙ אֲשֶׁ֣ר לְקֹ֔רַח וְאֵ֖ת כָּל־הָרְכֽוּשׁ׃
33 וַיֵּ֨רְד֜וּ הֵ֣ם וְכָל־אֲשֶׁ֥ר לָהֶ֛ם חַיִּ֖ים שְׁאֹ֑לָה
וַתְּכַ֤ס עֲלֵיהֶם֙ הָאָ֔רֶץ וַיֹּאבְד֖וּ מִתּ֥וֹךְ
הַקָּהָֽל׃ 34 וְכָל־יִשְׂרָאֵ֗ל אֲשֶׁ֛ר סְבִיבֹתֵיהֶ֖ם
נָ֣סוּ לְקֹלָ֑ם כִּ֣י אָֽמְר֔וּ פֶּן־תִּבְלָעֵ֖נוּ הָאָֽרֶץ׃
35 וְאֵ֣שׁ יָצְאָ֔ה מֵאֵ֖ת יְהוָ֑ה וַתֹּ֗אכַל
אֵ֣ת הַחֲמִשִּׁ֤ים וּמָאתַ֙יִם֙ אִ֔ישׁ מַקְרִיבֵ֖י
הַקְּטֹֽרֶת׃ פ

17 The LORD spoke to Moses, saying: 2Or-
der Eleazar son of Aaron the priest to remove
the fire pans—for they have become sacred—
from among the charred remains; and scatter

יז וַיְדַבֵּ֥ר יְהוָ֖ה אֶל־מֹשֶׁ֥ה לֵּאמֹֽר׃
2 אֱמֹ֞ר אֶל־אֶלְעָזָ֨ר בֶּן־אַהֲרֹ֣ן הַכֹּהֵ֗ן וְיָרֵ֤ם
אֶת־הַמַּחְתֹּת֙ מִבֵּ֣ין הַשְּׂרֵפָ֔ה וְאֶת־הָאֵ֖שׁ

you shall know Earthquakes were well known in the ancient world. The "unheard-of thing" was that this quake, like the plagues in Egypt, occurred precisely at the command of Moses.

the LORD But not me.

32. earth That is, the netherworld. It is equivalent to Sheol in verses 30 and 33.

households The families of Dathan and Abiram.

all Korah's people And Korah too was swallowed by the earth (26:10).

33. the earth closed over them This, and not the earth's opening, is what also constitutes the "unheard-of" creation.

vanished from the midst of the congregation All traces of the line of Dathan and Abiram were eliminated but, contrary to this text, not all traces of the line of Korah (see 26:11).

35. from the LORD From the tabernacle.

THE AFTERMATH OF KORAH'S REBELLION (17:1–18:32)

THE FIRE PANS AS REMINDERS (17:1–5)

2. Eleazar Eleazar attended to the tabernacle's interior appurtenances (4:16); and so he, not Aaron, was ordered to remove the fire pans.

remove That is, set aside or dedicate. Presumably, the fire pans were first handled by nonpriests, perhaps Levites. As a priest, Eleazar would not have been allowed to touch the pans before they underwent purification from having been in the hands of the slain chieftains.

sacred The fire pans became sacred by their use in the sacred precincts or because they were touched by the divine fire.

charred remains Of Korah and his followers.

scatter the coals abroad The coals must

---

32. "The world exists on account of people who are able to restrain themselves during a quarrel" (BT Ḥul. 89a). Korah and his followers were not able to do that, so the earth gave way and swallowed them (Simḥah Bunem). The earthquake that swallowed Korah vindicated Moses as God's choice to be Israel's leader. The tribe of Reuben, however, was still challenging Aaron and the Levites. Here we see the contrasting personalities of Moses and Aaron. Moses destroys his opponents, calling down a divine miracle to bury them alive. Aaron disarms his rivals by outproducing them; his staff sends forth sprouts and blossoms, whereas the staffs of the other tribes cannot flower (17:23). Moses is the voice of justice; Aaron is the pursuer of peace.

זְרֵה־הָ֑לְאָה כִּ֖י קָדֵֽשׁוּ׃ 3 אֵ֡ת מַחְתּ֣וֹת
הַֽחַטָּאִים֩ הָאֵ֨לֶּה֙ בְּנַפְשֹׁתָ֔ם וְעָשׂ֨וּ אֹתָ֜ם
רִקֻּעֵ֤י פַחִים֙ צִפּ֣וּי לַמִּזְבֵּ֔חַ כִּֽי־הִקְרִיבֻ֥ם
לִפְנֵֽי־יְהוָ֖ה וַיִּקְדָּ֑שׁוּ וְיִהְי֥וּ לְא֖וֹת לִבְנֵ֥י
יִשְׂרָאֵֽל׃ 4 וַיִּקַּ֞ח אֶלְעָזָ֣ר הַכֹּהֵ֗ן אֵ֚ת מַחְתּ֣וֹת
הַנְּחֹ֔שֶׁת אֲשֶׁ֥ר הִקְרִ֖יבוּ הַשְּׂרֻפִ֑ים וַֽיְרַקְּע֖וּם
צִפּ֥וּי לַמִּזְבֵּֽחַ׃ 5 זִכָּר֞וֹן לִבְנֵ֣י יִשְׂרָאֵ֗ל לְ֠מַעַן
אֲשֶׁ֨ר לֹֽא־יִקְרַ֜ב אִ֣ישׁ זָ֗ר אֲשֶׁ֨ר לֹ֤א מִזֶּ֙רַע֙
אַהֲרֹ֔ן ה֔וּא לְהַקְטִ֥יר קְטֹ֖רֶת לִפְנֵ֣י יְהוָ֑ה
וְלֹֽא־יִהְיֶ֤ה כְקֹ֙רַח֙ וְכַ֣עֲדָת֔וֹ כַּאֲשֶׁ֨ר דִּבֶּ֧ר
יְהוָ֛ה בְּיַד־מֹשֶׁ֖ה לֽוֹ׃
6 וַיִּלֹּ֜נוּ כָּל־עֲדַ֤ת בְּנֵֽי־יִשְׂרָאֵל֙ מִֽמָּחֳרָ֔ת עַל־
מֹשֶׁ֥ה וְעַֽל־אַהֲרֹ֖ן לֵאמֹ֑ר אַתֶּ֥ם הֲמִתֶּ֖ם

the coals abroad. 3[Remove] the fire pans of those who have sinned at the cost of their lives, and let them be made into hammered sheets as plating for the altar—for once they have been used for offering to the LORD, they have become sacred—and let them serve as a warning to the people of Israel. 4Eleazar the priest took the copper fire pans which had been used for offering by those who died in the fire; and they were hammered into plating for the altar, 5as the LORD had ordered him through Moses. It was to be a reminder to the Israelites, so that no outsider—one not of Aaron's offspring—should presume to offer incense before the LORD and suffer the fate of Korah and his band.

6Next day the whole Israelite community railed against Moses and Aaron, saying, "You two have brought death upon the LORD's peo-

have come from a source other than the altar and hence did not have to be returned there.

3. hammered sheets The fire pans were hammered into thin layers.

4. copper Better: bronze. See Comment to Exod. 25:3.

plating for the altar According to Exod. 27:2 and 38:2, the altar was already plated with bronze. This second plating was to serve as a warning sign to encroachers.

5. him Eleazar.

outsider Any unauthorized person, a nonpriest, a non-Levite, or even a disqualified priest.

Korah and his band Here it is stated that Korah died with his company in the incense trial.

OUTBREAK OF THE PLAGUE (vv. 6–15)

6. Next day This phrase connects the plague with the previous story of the fire pans.

You two Hebrew: *attem,* which is emphatic: It was you two who devised the incense test by which they lost their lives. Although the text attributes the test solely to Moses' initiative (16:6–7,16–17), he and Aaron are accused of collusion.

the LORD's people That is, the chieftains. The people at large, unconvinced by the incense test and continuing to believe that all are equally holy, pick up Korah's refrain: Moses and Aaron are lording it over everyone. Furthermore, they caused the deaths of the chieftains, who repre-

---

CHAPTER 17

2–3. The firepans used by the rebels to offer incense have become sacred and are to be used as plating for the altar. To some commentators, they have become holy simply because they had been consecrated by use in a ceremony. For Arama, they have become holy as mementos of the victory of truth over falsehood, like the trophies of a victorious army. For another commentator (*Ha·amek Davar*), they are holy because the men who offered incense in them were not really rebels and sinners, but people with a yearning for the opportunity to be close to God, to be of special service to God, a yearning that cost them their lives. Kook taught that the holiness of the firepans symbolizes the necessary role played by skeptics and agnostics in keeping religion honest and healthy. Challenges to tradition, he taught, are necessary because they stand as perpetual reminders of the danger that religion can sink into corruption and complacency. Plating the altar with the firepans of the rebels is meant to remind us of the legitimacy, indeed the potential holiness, of the impulse within each of us to rebel against the stagnation and complacency that can infect religion.

ple!” 7 But as the community gathered against them, Moses and Aaron turned toward the Tent of Meeting; the cloud had covered it and the Presence of the LORD appeared.

8 When Moses and Aaron reached the Tent of Meeting, 9 the LORD spoke to Moses, saying, 10 “Remove yourselves from this community, that I may annihilate them in an instant.” They fell on their faces. 11 Then Moses said to Aaron, “Take the fire pan, and put on it fire from the altar. Add incense and take it quickly to the community and make expiation for them. For wrath has gone forth from the LORD: the plague has begun!” 12 Aaron took it, as Moses had ordered, and ran to the midst of the congregation, where the plague had begun among the people. He put on the incense and made expiation for the people; 13 he stood between the dead and the

אֶת־עַם יְהוָה׃ 7 וַיְהִי בְּהִקָּהֵל הָעֵדָה
עַל־מֹשֶׁה וְעַל־אַהֲרֹן וַיִּפְנוּ אֶל־אֹהֶל
מוֹעֵד וְהִנֵּה כִסָּהוּ הֶעָנָן וַיֵּרָא כְּבוֹד
יְהוָה׃
8 וַיָּבֹא מֹשֶׁה וְאַהֲרֹן אֶל־פְּנֵי אֹהֶל
רביעי מוֹעֵד׃ פ 9 וַיְדַבֵּר יְהוָה אֶל־מֹשֶׁה
לֵּאמֹר׃ 10 הֵרֹמּוּ מִתּוֹךְ הָעֵדָה הַזֹּאת
וַאֲכַלֶּה אֹתָם כְּרָגַע וַיִּפְּלוּ עַל־פְּנֵיהֶם׃
11 וַיֹּאמֶר מֹשֶׁה אֶל־אַהֲרֹן קַח אֶת־
הַמַּחְתָּה וְתֶן־עָלֶיהָ אֵשׁ מֵעַל הַמִּזְבֵּחַ
וְשִׂים קְטֹרֶת וְהוֹלֵךְ מְהֵרָה אֶל־הָעֵדָה
וְכַפֵּר עֲלֵיהֶם כִּי־יָצָא הַקֶּצֶף מִלִּפְנֵי יְהוָה
הֵחֵל הַנָּגֶף׃ 12 וַיִּקַּח אַהֲרֹן כַּאֲשֶׁר ׀ דִּבֶּר
מֹשֶׁה וַיָּרָץ אֶל־תּוֹךְ הַקָּהָל וְהִנֵּה הֵחֵל
הַנֶּגֶף בָּעָם וַיִּתֵּן אֶת־הַקְּטֹרֶת וַיְכַפֵּר עַל־
הָעָם׃ 13 וַיַּעֲמֹד בֵּין־הַמֵּתִים וּבֵין הַחַיִּים

sented the Israelites in the national assembly and whose decisions may well have come from God.

7. the cloud had covered it When the tabernacle was stationary it was always covered by the divine cloud.

the Presence of the LORD appeared The pillar of fire within the cloud was visible only at night. To be seen by day, it probably increased its brightness, thereby signaling to Moses that God wished to communicate with him.

8. Moses' audiences with God were normally held inside the shrine, but when he was accompanied by Aaron or the people, the audiences were held in the courtyard that served as the entrance to the shrine.

9. Although Aaron was with him, only Moses heard God's voice.

10. Remove yourselves So as to escape the plague. Similarly, the people earlier had to distance themselves from Dathan and Abiram or the earth would have swallowed them too (16:26).

that I may annihilate them in an instant It had already been decreed that they would die in the wilderness; the only additional punishment left was their instantaneous death.

fell on their faces In prayer.

11. Moses said The lack of response from God compels Moses to attempt his own solution. His offering of incense outside the sacred precincts is an unprecedented act, improvised for the emergency.

incense The same incense that causes destruction when used by unauthorized persons averts destruction when used by those in rightful authority.

make expiation for them In the religions of the ancient Near East, incense served to appease and soothe the anger of the gods.

wrath Wrath is conceived as an independent entity, a destroyer, that acts as God's agent.

12. put on That is, on the fire pan.

13. Although Aaron, as high priest, is forbidden to come into close proximity with the

---

11–12. Once again, we see the greatness of soul that characterizes Moses and Aaron. They are the targets of the people's anger, but when God is about to punish the people and vindicate them, it is Moses and Aaron who intercede on their behalf. The two-pronged rebellion has been put down. The supremacy and legitimacy of Moses and Aaron as God's elect have been affirmed, but not without cost. Successive collisions have taken their cumulative toll on the people and on their leaders, as later events will show.

living until the plague was checked. [14]Those who died of the plague came to fourteen thousand and seven hundred, aside from those who died on account of Korah. [15]Aaron then returned to Moses at the entrance of the Tent of Meeting, since the plague was checked.

[16]The LORD spoke to Moses, saying: [17]Speak to the Israelite people and take from them—from the chieftains of their ancestral houses—one staff for each chieftain of an ancestral house: twelve staffs in all. Inscribe each man's name on his staff, [18]there being one staff for each head of an ancestral house; also inscribe Aaron's name on the staff of Levi. [19]Deposit them in the Tent of Meeting before the Pact, where I meet with you. [20]The staff of the man whom I choose shall sprout, and I will rid Myself of the incessant mutterings of the Israelites against you.

[21]Moses spoke thus to the Israelites. Their chieftains gave him a staff for each chieftain of an ancestral house, twelve staffs in all; among these staffs was that of Aaron. [22]Moses deposited the staffs before the LORD, in the Tent of the Pact. [23]The next day Moses entered the Tent

וַתֵּעָצַ֖ר הַמַּגֵּפָֽה׃ 14 וַיִּהְי֗וּ הַמֵּתִים֙ בַּמַּגֵּפָ֔ה
אַרְבָּעָ֤ה עָשָׂר֙ אֶ֔לֶף וּשְׁבַ֖ע מֵא֑וֹת מִלְּבַ֥ד
הַמֵּתִ֖ים עַל־דְּבַר־קֹֽרַח׃ 15 וַיָּ֤שָׁב אַהֲרֹן֙
אֶל־מֹשֶׁ֔ה אֶל־פֶּ֖תַח אֹ֣הֶל מוֹעֵ֑ד וְהַמַּגֵּפָ֖ה
נֶעֱצָֽרָה׃ פ
חמישי 16 וַיְדַבֵּ֥ר יְהוָ֖ה אֶל־מֹשֶׁ֥ה לֵּאמֹֽר׃ 17 דַּבֵּ֣ר ׀
אֶל־בְּנֵ֣י יִשְׂרָאֵ֗ל וְקַ֣ח מֵאִתָּ֡ם מַטֶּ֣ה מַטֶּה֩
לְבֵ֨ית אָ֜ב מֵאֵ֤ת כָּל־נְשִׂיאֵהֶם֙ לְבֵ֣ית
אֲבֹתָ֔ם שְׁנֵ֥ים עָשָׂ֖ר מַטּ֑וֹת אִ֣ישׁ אֶת־שְׁמ֔וֹ
תִּכְתֹּ֖ב עַל־מַטֵּֽהוּ׃ 18 וְאֵת֙ שֵׁ֣ם אַהֲרֹ֔ן
תִּכְתֹּ֖ב עַל־מַטֵּ֣ה לֵוִ֑י כִּ֚י מַטֶּ֣ה אֶחָ֔ד לְרֹ֖אשׁ
בֵּ֥ית אֲבוֹתָֽם׃ 19 וְהִנַּחְתָּ֖ם בְּאֹ֣הֶל מוֹעֵ֑ד
לִפְנֵי֙ הָֽעֵד֔וּת אֲשֶׁ֛ר אִוָּעֵ֥ד לָכֶ֖ם שָֽׁמָּה׃
20 *וְהָיָ֗ה הָאִ֛ישׁ אֲשֶׁ֥ר אֶבְחַר־בּ֖וֹ מַטֵּ֣הוּ
יִפְרָ֑ח וַהֲשִׁכֹּתִ֣י מֵעָלַ֗י אֶת־תְּלֻנּוֹת֙ בְּנֵ֣י
יִשְׂרָאֵ֔ל אֲשֶׁ֛ר הֵ֥ם מַלִּינִ֖ם עֲלֵיכֶֽם׃
21 וַיְדַבֵּ֨ר מֹשֶׁ֜ה אֶל־בְּנֵ֣י יִשְׂרָאֵ֗ל וַיִּתְּנ֣וּ
אֵלָ֣יו ׀ כָּל־נְשִׂיאֵיהֶ֡ם מַטֶּה֩ לְנָשִׂ֨יא אֶחָ֜ד
מַטֶּ֨ה לְנָשִׂ֤יא אֶחָד֙ לְבֵ֣ית אֲבֹתָ֔ם שְׁנֵ֥ים
עָשָׂ֖ר מַטּ֑וֹת וּמַטֵּ֥ה אַהֲרֹ֖ן בְּת֥וֹךְ מַטּוֹתָֽם׃
22 וַיַּנַּ֥ח מֹשֶׁ֛ה אֶת־הַמַּטֹּ֖ת לִפְנֵ֣י יְהוָ֑ה
בְּאֹ֖הֶל הָעֵדֻֽת׃ 23 וַיְהִ֣י מִֽמָּחֳרָ֗ת וַיָּבֹ֤א

v. 20. חצי הספר בפסוקים

dead (see Lev. 21:11), he does so in this case to save the living.

14. those who died on account of Korah The 250 chieftains (16:35) and probably also Dathan, Abiram, and their families.

15. since the plague was checked Moses' presence at the tent is repeated to emphasize the achievement of Aaron: It was not Moses' prayer but Aaron's ritual that placated God.

THE TEST OF THE STAFFS (vv. 16–26)

17. staff Hebrew: *matteh,* which also means "tribe." The staff was the official insignia of a tribal chieftain.

an ancestral house That is, the entire tribe.

each man's name But not the name of the tribe. The test was designed to choose God's priest from among the tribal chieftains; thus it was the individual who mattered, not the tribe.

18. Aaron's name on the staff of Levi The contest is between Aaron and the other chieftains who, like their 250 fallen colleagues, are still reluctant to see Aaron as the head of the priesthood.

19. the Pact Hebrew: *ha-edut;* short for "the Ark of the Pact" (*aron ha-edut*). The Ark's chief function was to serve as the receptacle for the Decalogue, the symbol of the pact or covenant between God and Israel (see Exod. 25:16, 40:20). Thus the staffs were placed in the Holy of Holies in front of the Ark (see also Num. 17:25).

20. the man whom I choose Either Aaron or one of the other tribal chieftains.

rid Myself God will settle the matter once and for all.

22. See Comment to 17:19.

23. A number of traditional commentators explain that when Moses entered the tent, the staff

of the Pact, and there the staff of Aaron of the house of Levi had sprouted: it had brought forth sprouts, produced blossoms, and borne almonds. [24]Moses then brought out all the staffs from before the LORD to all the Israelites; each identified and recovered his staff.

[25]The LORD said to Moses, "Put Aaron's staff back before the Pact, to be kept as a lesson to rebels, so that their mutterings against Me may cease, lest they die." [26]This Moses did; just as the LORD had commanded him, so he did.

[27]But the Israelites said to Moses, "Lo, we perish! We are lost, all of us lost! [28]Everyone who so much as ventures near the LORD's Tabernacle must die. Alas, we are doomed to perish!"

מֹשֶׁה֙ אֶל־אֹ֣הֶל הָעֵד֔וּת וְהִנֵּ֛ה פָּרַ֥ח מַטֵּֽה־
אַהֲרֹ֖ן לְבֵ֣ית לֵוִ֑י וַיֹּ֤צֵא פֶ֙רַח֙ וַיָּ֣צֵֽץ צִ֔יץ
וַיִּגְמֹ֖ל שְׁקֵדִֽים׃ 24 וַיֹּצֵ֨א מֹשֶׁ֤ה אֶת־כָּל־
הַמַּטֹּת֙ מִלִּפְנֵ֣י יְהוָ֔ה אֶל־כָּל־בְּנֵ֖י יִשְׂרָאֵ֑ל
וַיִּרְא֥וּ וַיִּקְח֖וּ אִ֥ישׁ מַטֵּֽהוּ׃ ס
ששי 25 וַיֹּ֨אמֶר יְהוָ֜ה אֶל־מֹשֶׁ֗ה הָשֵׁ֞ב אֶת־מַטֵּ֤ה
אַהֲרֹן֙ לִפְנֵ֣י הָעֵד֔וּת לְמִשְׁמֶ֥רֶת לְא֖וֹת
לִבְנֵי־מֶ֑רִי וּתְכַ֧ל תְּלוּנֹּתָ֛ם מֵעָלַ֖י וְלֹ֥א
יָמֻֽתוּ׃ 26 וַיַּ֖עַשׂ מֹשֶׁ֑ה כַּאֲשֶׁ֨ר צִוָּ֧ה יְהוָ֛ה
אֹת֖וֹ כֵּ֥ן עָשָֽׂה׃ ס
27 וַיֹּאמְרוּ֙ בְּנֵ֣י יִשְׂרָאֵ֔ל אֶל־מֹשֶׁ֖ה לֵאמֹ֑ר
הֵ֥ן גָּוַ֛עְנוּ אָבַ֖דְנוּ כֻּלָּ֥נוּ אָבָֽדְנוּ׃ 28 כֹּ֣ל
הַקָּרֵ֧ב ׀ הַקָּרֵ֛ב אֶל־מִשְׁכַּ֥ן יְהוָ֖ה יָמ֑וּת
הַאִ֥ם תַּ֖מְנוּ לִגְוֹֽעַ׃ ס

18 The LORD said to Aaron: You and your sons and the ancestral house under your charge shall bear any guilt connected with the sanctu-

יח וַיֹּ֣אמֶר יְהוָה֮ אֶֽל־אַהֲרֹן֒ אַתָּ֗ה
וּבָנֶ֤יךָ וּבֵית־אָבִ֙יךָ֙ אִתָּ֔ךְ תִּשְׂא֖וּ אֶת־עֲוֺ֣ן

had only sprouted, and that it blossomed and bore fruit while he held it in his hand.

24. each That is, each chieftain.

identified The chieftains and the Israelites were able to verify for themselves that Aaron's staff had sprouted.

25. as a lesson Literally, "for safekeeping, as a warning."

PANIC AND REMEDY: GUARDS AGAINST ENCROACHMENT (17:27–18:7)

The Israelites, as a consequence of the death of their chieftains at the tabernacle and the toll taken by the plague, begin to dread the tabernacle and will not come near it. To allay their fright, they are given assurances that henceforth priests and Levites alone will bear the responsibility for encroachment.

27. perish . . . lost . . . lost An ancient Aramaic translation renders the threefold cry of despair as follows: "Behold some of us were killed by the sword, some were swallowed up by the earth, while others died in the plague."

28. so much as ventures near Hebrew: *ha-karev ha-karev;* the verb *karev* can mean "encroach." Its doubling tells us that the Israelites now fear to enter the tabernacle even to offer proper sacrifices. Like their chieftains who offered incense, they might encroach and be struck down.

must die That is, at the hands of God. The people fear that even unintentional encroachment on the sanctuary will be fatal.

we are doomed to perish Literally, "we are being wiped out."

18:1. to Aaron God gives instructions directly to Aaron only in this chapter (vv. 1,8,20) and in Lev. 10:8. Otherwise they are transmitted to him through Moses. The direct address to Aaron is a fitting conclusion to the rebellion over

CHAPTER 18

1. Is this rare instance of God speaking directly to Aaron a reward for Aaron's behavior in the previous chapter? Or is it intended to strengthen and comfort him after the challenge to his authority? Is the list of priestly prerogatives (v. 8ff.) given here to emphasize the special role of the Aaronide priesthood after Korah's challenge?

הַמִּקְדָּשׁ וְאַתָּה וּבָנֶיךָ אִתָּךְ תִּשְׂאוּ אֶת־
עֲוֺן כְּהֻנַּתְכֶם׃ 2 וְגַם אֶת־אַחֶיךָ מַטֵּה לֵוִי
שֵׁבֶט אָבִיךָ הַקְרֵב אִתָּךְ וְיִלָּווּ עָלֶיךָ
וִישָׁרְתוּךָ וְאַתָּה וּבָנֶיךָ אִתָּךְ לִפְנֵי אֹהֶל
הָעֵדֻת׃ 3 וְשָׁמְרוּ מִשְׁמַרְתְּךָ וּמִשְׁמֶרֶת כָּל־
הָאֹהֶל אַךְ אֶל־כְּלֵי הַקֹּדֶשׁ וְאֶל־הַמִּזְבֵּחַ
לֹא יִקְרָבוּ וְלֹא־יָמֻתוּ גַם־הֵם גַּם־אַתֶּם׃
4 וְנִלְווּ עָלֶיךָ וְשָׁמְרוּ אֶת־מִשְׁמֶרֶת אֹהֶל
מוֹעֵד לְכֹל עֲבֹדַת הָאֹהֶל וְזָר לֹא־יִקְרַב
אֲלֵיכֶם׃ 5 וּשְׁמַרְתֶּם אֵת מִשְׁמֶרֶת הַקֹּדֶשׁ
וְאֵת מִשְׁמֶרֶת הַמִּזְבֵּחַ וְלֹא־יִהְיֶה עוֹד
קֶצֶף עַל־בְּנֵי יִשְׂרָאֵל׃
6 וַאֲנִי הִנֵּה לָקַחְתִּי אֶת־אֲחֵיכֶם הַלְוִיִּם
מִתּוֹךְ בְּנֵי יִשְׂרָאֵל לָכֶם מַתָּנָה נְתֻנִים
לַיהוָה לַעֲבֹד אֶת־עֲבֹדַת אֹהֶל מוֹעֵד׃
7 וְאַתָּה וּבָנֶיךָ אִתְּךָ תִּשְׁמְרוּ אֶת־כְּהֻנַּתְכֶם
לְכָל־דְּבַר הַמִּזְבֵּחַ וּלְמִבֵּית לַפָּרֹכֶת

ary; you and your sons alone shall bear any guilt connected with your priesthood. 2You shall also associate with yourself your kinsmen the tribe of Levi, your ancestral tribe, to be attached to you and to minister to you, while you and your sons under your charge are before the Tent of the Pact. 3They shall discharge their duties to you and to the Tent as a whole, but they must not have any contact with the furnishings of the Shrine or with the altar, lest both they and you die. 4They shall be attached to you and discharge the duties of the Tent of Meeting, all the service of the Tent; but no outsider shall intrude upon you 5as you discharge the duties connected with the Shrine and the altar, that wrath may not again strike the Israelites.

6I hereby take your fellow Levites from among the Israelites; they are assigned to you in dedication to the Lord, to do the work of the Tent of Meeting; 7while you and your sons shall be careful to perform your priestly duties in everything pertaining to the altar and to what

the priesthood: God here vindicates Aaron by granting him a personal revelation.

ancestral house This refers to the members of the clan of Kohath, who were responsible for transporting the sacred objects on their shoulders during the wilderness march.

connected with They will bear the consequences for encroachment on the sacred area and its objects.

your priesthood If disqualified priests—those who are blemished, inebriated, unwashed, or improperly dressed—attempt to officiate at the altar or enter the shrine, only their fellow priests can be held responsible for this encroachment.

2. also The priests do not reduce their own guarding responsibilities by sharing the custody of the tabernacle with the Levites. To the contrary, the Levites are now an added source of possible encroachment and priestly blame.

minister to you "Assist you" in your guarding duties.

before the Tent of the Pact Outside the sacred area, where the Levites perform their guard duty.

3. furnishings of the Shrine The altar utensils that were placed in the courtyard. Like the altar, they would be vulnerable to encroachment by the levitical guards and the lay worshiper.

both they and you die If a Levite encroaches, then the negligent guards, both priestly and levitical, suffer death by divine agency. If, however, a layperson encroaches, he or she is slain by the guards. The entire tabernacle cordon, including all priests and Levites on guard duty, is responsible for levitical encroachment. They will guard very carefully.

4. all the service The Levites share with the priests the custody of the tabernacle as well as their transport labors.

outsider A nonpriest.

6–8. I Whereas you, Aaron, will be responsible in the event of the desecration of the sanctuary, I, in turn, will provide you with levitical assistance and ample gifts as a reward.

6. The tasks of the Levites in regard to the transport of the tabernacle are contrasted with the priests' responsibility for guarding the altar and its sacred objects.

work Removal of the tabernacle.

7. be careful to perform your priestly duties Priests will be penalized for failing to guard the

is behind the curtain. I make your priesthood a service of dedication; any outsider who encroaches shall be put to death.

⁸The LORD spoke further to Aaron: I hereby give you charge of My gifts, all the sacred donations of the Israelites; I grant them to you and to your sons as a perquisite, a due for all time. ⁹This shall be yours from the most holy sacrifices, the gifts: every such offering that they render to Me as most holy sacrifices, namely, every grain offering, purification offering, and reparation offering of theirs, shall belong to you and your sons. ¹⁰You shall partake of them as most sacred donations: only males may eat them; you shall treat them as consecrated.

¹¹This, too, shall be yours: the gift offerings of their contributions, all the elevation offerings of the Israelites, I give to you, to your sons, and to the daughters that are with you, as a due for all time; everyone of your household who is pure may eat it.

¹²All the best of the new oil, wine, and

וַעֲבַדְתֶּ֞ם עֲבֹדַ֣ת מַתָּנָ֗ה אֶתֵּן֙ אֶת־כְּהֻנַּתְכֶ֔ם וְהַזָּ֥ר הַקָּרֵ֖ב יוּמָֽת׃ ס

⁸ וַיְדַבֵּ֣ר יְהוָה֮ אֶֽל־אַהֲרֹן֒ וַאֲנִי֙ הִנֵּ֣ה נָתַ֣תִּי לְךָ֗ אֶת־מִשְׁמֶ֙רֶת֙ תְּרוּמֹתָ֔י לְכָל־קָדְשֵׁ֥י בְנֵֽי־יִשְׂרָאֵ֖ל לְךָ֣ נְתַתִּ֥ים לְמָשְׁחָ֛ה וּלְבָנֶ֖יךָ לְחָק־עוֹלָֽם׃ ⁹ זֶֽה־יִהְיֶ֥ה לְךָ֛ מִקֹּ֥דֶשׁ הַקֳּדָשִׁ֖ים מִן־הָאֵ֑שׁ כָּל־קָ֠רְבָּנָ֠ם לְֽכָל־מִנְחָתָ֞ם וּלְכָל־חַטָּאתָ֗ם וּלְכָל־אֲשָׁמָם֙ אֲשֶׁ֣ר יָשִׁ֣יבוּ לִ֔י קֹ֥דֶשׁ קָֽדָשִׁ֛ים לְךָ֥ ה֖וּא וּלְבָנֶֽיךָ׃ ¹⁰ בְּקֹ֥דֶשׁ הַקֳּדָשִׁ֖ים תֹּאכְלֶ֑נּוּ כָּל־זָכָר֙ יֹאכַ֣ל אֹת֔וֹ קֹ֖דֶשׁ יִֽהְיֶה־לָּֽךְ׃

¹¹ וְזֶה־לְּךָ֞ תְּרוּמַ֣ת מַתָּנָ֗ם לְכָל־תְּנוּפֹת֮ בְּנֵ֣י יִשְׂרָאֵל֒ לְךָ֣ נְתַתִּ֗ים וּלְבָנֶ֧יךָ וְלִבְנֹתֶ֛יךָ אִתְּךָ֖ לְחָק־עוֹלָ֑ם כָּל־טָה֥וֹר בְּבֵֽיתְךָ֖ יֹאכַ֥ל אֹתֽוֹ׃ ¹² כֹּ֚ל חֵ֣לֶב יִצְהָ֔ר וְכָל־חֵ֖לֶב תִּיר֣וֹשׁ וְדָגָ֑ן

---

sacred area against encroaching nonpriests and disqualified priests.

the altar . . . behind the curtain   Nonpriests and disqualified priests are prohibited from officiating at the altar, and all priests are prohibited from entering the Holy of Holies, the inner shrine.

PRIESTS' REWARDS FOR STANDING GUARD (vv. 8–19)

After an introductory verse, the gifts to the priests are enumerated according to the accepted division: "most sacred" and "sacred."

8. charge of My gifts   The Levites are assigned tithes as a reward for their guard duties. Priestly gifts fulfill a similar function.

all   Priests receive gifts in two ways, directly (bypassing the altar) and indirectly (from sacrifices). This section lists the required gifts of both types.

to your sons   The common denominator of all the gifts is that they may be eaten by priests.

Gifts from the "Most Holy" Sacrifices (vv. 9–10)

9. from the most holy sacrifices   Refers to offerings reserved from the fire. "From" implies

that there are sacrifices classified as most holy from which the priests do not receive an altar gift of flesh. This would be the burnt offering (*olah*) from which the priest receives the skin (Lev. 7:8) and whose flesh is entirely burned on the altar.

gifts   These are reserved for the priests from the portions of the sacrifices not burned on the altar. The entire sacrifice is intended for the altar, but God has assigned parts of it to the priesthood.

10.   Priests eat these gifts in the tabernacle courtyard on the same day (Lev. 6:9,19, 7:6).

Gifts from the "Holy" Sacrifices (vv. 11–19)

11. gift offerings   Hebrew: *t'rumah.* Nonsacrificial "gifts," those dedicated to the Lord outside the sanctuary.

elevation offerings   Hebrew: *t'nufah.* The gifts brought to the sanctuary and dedicated by an elevation ritual.

daughters that are with you   Members of a priest's household may partake of sacred food, including slaves—but not hired laborers, who maintain their own households. Nor may a married daughter who joins her lay husband's household eat sacred food (Lev. 22:10–13).

grain—the choice parts that they present to the
LORD—I give to you. 13The first fruits of everything in their land, that they bring to the LORD,
shall be yours; everyone of your household who
is pure may eat them. 14Everything that has been
proscribed in Israel shall be yours. 15The first
issue of the womb of every being, man or beast,
that is offered to the LORD, shall be yours; but
you shall have the first-born of man redeemed,
and you shall also have the firstling of impure
animals redeemed. 16Take as their redemption
price, from the age of one month up, the money
equivalent of five shekels by the sanctuary
weight, which is twenty *gerahs*. 17But the
firstlings of cattle, sheep, or goats may not be
redeemed; they are consecrated. You shall dash
their blood against the altar, and turn their fat
into smoke as a gift for a pleasing odor to the
LORD. 18But their meat shall be yours: it shall
be yours like the breast of elevation offering and
like the right thigh.

19All the sacred gifts that the Israelites set aside
for the LORD I give to you, to your sons, and
to the daughters that are with you, as a due for

רֵאשִׁיתָ֛ם אֲשֶׁר־יִתְּנ֥וּ לַיהוָ֖ה לְךָ֥ נְתַתִּֽים׃
13 בִּכּוּרֵ֞י כׇּל־אֲשֶׁ֧ר בְּאַרְצָ֛ם אֲשֶׁר־יָבִ֥יאוּ
לַיהוָ֖ה לְךָ֣ יִהְיֶ֑ה כׇּל־טָה֥וֹר בְּבֵיתְךָ֖
יֹאכְלֶֽנּוּ׃ 14 כׇּל־חֵ֥רֶם בְּיִשְׂרָאֵ֖ל לְךָ֥ יִהְיֶֽה׃
15 כׇּל־פֶּ֣טֶר רֶ֠חֶם לְכׇל־בָּשָׂ֞ר אֲשֶׁר־יַקְרִ֧יבוּ
לַיהוָ֛ה בָּאָדָ֥ם וּבַבְּהֵמָ֖ה יִהְיֶה־לָּ֑ךְ אַ֣ךְ ׀
פָּדֹ֣ה תִפְדֶּ֗ה אֵ֚ת בְּכ֣וֹר הָֽאָדָ֔ם וְאֵ֛ת בְּכוֹר־
הַבְּהֵמָ֥ה הַטְּמֵאָ֖ה תִּפְדֶּֽה׃ 16 וּפְדוּיָו֙ מִבֶּן־
חֹ֣דֶשׁ תִּפְדֶּ֔ה בְּעֶ֨רְכְּךָ֔ כֶּ֚סֶף חֲמֵ֣שֶׁת שְׁקָלִ֔ים
בְּשֶׁ֥קֶל הַקֹּ֖דֶשׁ עֶשְׂרִ֥ים גֵּרָ֖ה הֽוּא׃ 17 אַ֣ךְ
בְּכוֹר־שׁ֡וֹר אֽוֹ־בְכ֨וֹר כֶּ֜שֶׂב אֽוֹ־בְכ֥וֹר עֵ֛ז לֹ֥א
תִפְדֶּ֖ה קֹ֣דֶשׁ הֵ֑ם אֶת־דָּמָ֞ם תִּזְרֹ֤ק עַל־
הַמִּזְבֵּ֙חַ֙ וְאֶת־חֶלְבָּ֣ם תַּקְטִ֔יר אִשֶּׁ֛ה לְרֵ֥יחַ
נִיחֹ֖חַ לַיהוָֽה׃ 18 וּבְשָׂרָ֖ם יִהְיֶה־לָּ֑ךְ כַּחֲזֵ֧ה
הַתְּנוּפָ֛ה וּכְשׁ֥וֹק הַיָּמִ֖ין לְךָ֥ יִהְיֶֽה׃
19 כֹּ֣ל ׀ תְּרוּמֹ֣ת הַקֳּדָשִׁ֗ים אֲשֶׁ֨ר יָרִ֥ימוּ
בְנֵֽי־יִשְׂרָאֵל֙ לַיהוָ֔ה נָתַ֣תִּֽי לְךָ֗ וּלְבָנֶ֧יךָ

13. first fruits Literally, the "first ripe" of the crops in the field and orchard.

they bring The first fruits (*bikkurim*) are brought to the sanctuary.

15. first issue of the womb Refers to the first-born of the mother if the child is a male.

that is offered to the LORD All male firstborn to a mother, whether human or beast, are the innate property of the Lord. Hence, they can only be "offered," not "given."

shall be yours That is, the priests'.

you shall have . . . redeemed You, the priest, shall conduct the redemption proceedings. The redeemers are, obviously, the owners or the parents.

16. one month up This applied to the first time all the firstborn were redeemed (3:40). Henceforth, this redemption of the firstborn must take place at the age of one month.

money equivalent As previously mentioned (Lev. 27:6, Num. 3:47).

17. cattle Hebrew: *shor,* which usually refers to an individual of the bovine species without specifying its sex, here stands for the female.

17–18. blood . . . fat . . . meat The firstborn sacrificial animal is to be treated as a well-being offering whose blood, suet, and certain internal organs are offered up on the altar but whose meat is eaten by its owner who brings the sacrifice. Because the priest in this case is the de jure owner of the animal as soon as it is born (Lev. 27:26), he sacrifices it as a well-being offering and eats the meat.

19. sacred gifts The required gifts from sacred offerings, listed in vv. 12–18, that the priest and his household may eat.

HALAKHAH L'MA·ASEH

18:15. This is the source of the ceremony of *Pidyon ha-Ben,* redeeming the firstborn son from the priest (*kohen*) on the child's 31st day of life, or soon thereafter if that day falls on a *Shabbat* or holiday. The modern service to welcome a newborn girl into the covenant (*Simḥat Bat*) can include a special prayer when a daughter is the firstborn.

all time. It shall be an everlasting covenant of salt before the LORD for you and for your offspring as well. 20And the LORD said to Aaron: You shall, however, have no territorial share among them or own any portion in their midst; I am your portion and your share among the Israelites.

21And to the Levites I hereby give all the tithes in Israel as their share in return for the services that they perform, the services of the Tent of Meeting. 22Henceforth, Israelites shall not trespass on the Tent of Meeting, and thus incur guilt and die: 23only Levites shall perform the services of the Tent of Meeting; others would incur guilt. It is the law for all time throughout the ages. But they shall have no territorial share among the Israelites; 24for it is the tithes set aside by the Israelites as a gift to the LORD that I give to the Levites as their share. Therefore I have said concerning them: They shall have no territorial share among the Israelites.

25The LORD spoke to Moses, saying: 26Speak

וְלִבְנֹתֶיךָ אִתְּךָ לְחָק־עוֹלָם בְּרִית מֶלַח
עוֹלָם הִוא לִפְנֵי יְהוָה לְךָ וּלְזַרְעֲךָ אִתָּךְ׃
20 וַיֹּאמֶר יְהוָה אֶל־אַהֲרֹן בְּאַרְצָם לֹא
תִנְחָל וְחֵלֶק לֹא־יִהְיֶה לְךָ בְּתוֹכָם אֲנִי
חֶלְקְךָ וְנַחֲלָתְךָ בְּתוֹךְ בְּנֵי יִשְׂרָאֵל׃ ס
שביעי 21 וְלִבְנֵי לֵוִי הִנֵּה נָתַתִּי כָּל־מַעֲשֵׂר
בְּיִשְׂרָאֵל לְנַחֲלָה חֵלֶף עֲבֹדָתָם אֲשֶׁר־הֵם
עֹבְדִים אֶת־עֲבֹדַת אֹהֶל מוֹעֵד׃ 22 וְלֹא־
יִקְרְבוּ עוֹד בְּנֵי יִשְׂרָאֵל אֶל־אֹהֶל מוֹעֵד
לָשֵׂאת חֵטְא לָמוּת׃ 23 וְעָבַד הַלֵּוִי הוּא
אֶת־עֲבֹדַת אֹהֶל מוֹעֵד וְהֵם יִשְׂאוּ עֲוֺנָם
חֻקַּת עוֹלָם לְדֹרֹתֵיכֶם וּבְתוֹךְ בְּנֵי יִשְׂרָאֵל
לֹא יִנְחֲלוּ נַחֲלָה׃ 24 כִּי אֶת־מַעְשַׂר בְּנֵי־
יִשְׂרָאֵל אֲשֶׁר יָרִימוּ לַיהוָה תְּרוּמָה נָתַתִּי
לַלְוִיִּם לְנַחֲלָה עַל־כֵּן אָמַרְתִּי לָהֶם בְּתוֹךְ
בְּנֵי יִשְׂרָאֵל לֹא יִנְחֲלוּ נַחֲלָה׃ פ
25 וַיְדַבֵּר יְהוָה אֶל־מֹשֶׁה לֵּאמֹר׃ 26 וְאֶל־

covenant of salt An unbreakable covenant. Salt, a symbol of permanence, was the best food preservative in antiquity, and its use was required for all sacrifices.

LEVITES' REWARD FOR STANDING GUARD (vv. 20–24)

20. Here, Aaron is addressed not as the head of the priests but as the tribal leader of the Levites. The land prohibition, therefore, applies to the Levites as well as the priests.

your portion and your share Refers to the land allotted each family within its tribal territory in the Promised Land. Because land was denied to the families of priests and Levites (v. 24), they received the perquisites enumerated here as compensation.

21. This is a continuation of the address to Aaron, implying that Aaron, as leader of the tribe of Levi, is responsible for seeing to it that the Levites receive their tithes. The tithe is a compulsory, permanent grant to the Levites. It falls due on every crop in the Promised Land (Lev. 27:30, but see Deut. 14:23) as annual wages for their labors in the sanctuary (see Num. 18:31).

services That is, all the guarding and removal responsibilities assigned to the Levites.

23. others would incur guilt Henceforth, the Levites will bear the responsibility for Israelite encroachment.

law for all time That the Levites will perform the guarding and removal duties of the tabernacle.

no territorial share No farmland. Because the Levites will receive a tithe of the grain, wine, and oil of their fellow Israelites' crops, they need not produce those crops on their own. (They will need permanent residences, however.)

24. gift to the LORD The tithe properly belongs to the Lord who, in turn, assigns it to the Levites as payment for their sanctuary labors. Thus levitical and priestly perquisites are gifts from God.

A TENTH OF THE TITHE: A GIFT TO THE PRIESTS (vv. 25–32)

25. to Moses But not to Aaron, as in verses

HALAKHAH L'MA·ASEH

18:23. Levites shall perform the services To this day, Levites (*L'viyyim*) assist priests (*kohanim*) who are to bless the congregation (see Num. 6:23) by washing the priests' hands beforehand (see Exod. 30:19).

הַלְוִיִּם תְּדַבֵּר וְאָמַרְתָּ אֲלֵהֶם כִּי־תִקְחוּ
מֵאֵת בְּנֵי־יִשְׂרָאֵל אֶת־הַמַּעֲשֵׂר אֲשֶׁר
נָתַתִּי לָכֶם מֵאִתָּם בְּנַחֲלַתְכֶם וַהֲרֵמֹתֶם
מִמֶּנּוּ תְּרוּמַת יְהוָה מַעֲשֵׂר מִן־הַמַּעֲשֵׂר׃
27 וְנֶחְשַׁב לָכֶם תְּרוּמַתְכֶם כַּדָּגָן מִן־הַגֹּרֶן
וְכַמְלֵאָה מִן־הַיָּקֶב׃ 28 כֵּן תָּרִימוּ גַם־
אַתֶּם תְּרוּמַת יְהוָה מִכֹּל מַעְשְׂרֹתֵיכֶם
אֲשֶׁר תִּקְחוּ מֵאֵת בְּנֵי יִשְׂרָאֵל וּנְתַתֶּם
מִמֶּנּוּ אֶת־תְּרוּמַת יְהוָה לְאַהֲרֹן הַכֹּהֵן׃
29 מִכֹּל מַתְּנֹתֵיכֶם תָּרִימוּ אֵת כָּל־תְּרוּמַת
יְהוָה מִכָּל־חֶלְבּוֹ אֶת־מִקְדְּשׁוֹ מִמֶּנּוּ׃
מפטיר 30 וְאָמַרְתָּ אֲלֵהֶם בַּהֲרִימְכֶם אֶת־חֶלְבּוֹ
מִמֶּנּוּ וְנֶחְשַׁב לַלְוִיִּם כִּתְבוּאַת גֹּרֶן
וְכִתְבוּאַת יָקֶב׃ 31 וַאֲכַלְתֶּם אֹתוֹ בְּכָל־
מָקוֹם אַתֶּם וּבֵיתְכֶם כִּי־שָׂכָר הוּא לָכֶם
חֵלֶף עֲבֹדַתְכֶם בְּאֹהֶל מוֹעֵד׃ 32 וְלֹא־

to the Levites and say to them: When you receive
from the Israelites their tithes, which I have assigned to you as your share, you shall set aside
from them one-tenth of the tithe as a gift to the
LORD. 27This shall be accounted to you as your
gift. As with the new grain from the threshing
floor or the flow from the vat, 28so shall you on
your part set aside a gift for the LORD from all
the tithes that you receive from the Israelites;
and from them you shall bring the gift for the
LORD to Aaron the priest. 29You shall set aside
all gifts due to the LORD from everything that
is donated to you, from each thing its best portion, the part thereof that is to be consecrated.

30Say to them further: When you have removed the best part from it, you Levites may
consider it the same as the yield of threshing
floor or vat. 31You and your households may
eat it anywhere, for it is your recompense for
your services in the Tent of Meeting. 32You will

1 and 8, to avoid the conflict of interest that would result if Aaron were told to collect the 10th of the levitical tithe assigned to him.

26. receive Literally, "collect" or "take." The Levites may seize the tithe assigned to them.

27. As with the new grain Just as the Israelites set aside from the new grain a gift to the priests (v. 12), so too shall you Levites set aside a tithe for the priests.

flow This refers to wine or oil.

29. donated to you God has commanded that the Israelites donate a tithe to the Levites. The Levites, likewise, are to donate a tithe to the priests.

its best portion Literally, "its fat." The priestly perquisite from the levitical tithe should come from its best portion, just as the priestly perquisite from the laity is also from its "best" (v. 12).

the part . . . to be consecrated The tithe of the tithe set aside for the priests automatically assumes a sacred status, as do all priestly perquisites (vv. 8–10,19), whereas the levitical tithe is never called sacred in these priestly texts, just as the Levites are not.

30. you Levites may consider it the same That is, it will be reckoned by God as belonging to the Levites.

the same as the yield of threshing floor or vat After it is tithed and thus permitted to its owner.

31. eat it anywhere After the priestly portion is removed, the tithe's status becomes profane, and it may be eaten anywhere without concern for ritual purity.

recompense The Levites are entitled to the excessive wage of the tithe as compensation for subjecting themselves to lethal dangers in performing their tabernacle duties. Any lapse on their part while handling the sacred objects could lead to their death.

---

26. Every Israelite was expected to give a tenth of his or her income to the Levites to support them because the Levites had no other income. (The custom of tithing income is still operative for many Jews and non-Jews.) The Levites themselves had to tithe, to give to the priests a tenth of what they received. Even those who depend on public support for their livelihood must give part of what they receive as *tz'dakah* (commonly translated as "charity"), because *tz'dakah* nourishes the soul of the donor even as it sustains the recipient.

incur no guilt through it, once you have removed the best part from it; but you must not profane the sacred donations of the Israelites, lest you die.

תִשְׂאוּ עָלָיו֙ חֵ֔טְא בַּהֲרִֽימְכֶ֥ם אֶת־חֶלְבּ֖וֹ מִמֶּ֑נּוּ וְאֶת־קָדְשֵׁ֧י בְנֵֽי־יִשְׂרָאֵ֛ל לֹ֥א תְחַלְּל֖וּ וְלֹ֥א תָמֽוּתוּ׃ פ

32. A warning not to tamper with the sacred donations and thereby incur death at God's will.

guilt As long as the sacred 10th of the tithe has not been set aside for the priests, it is lethal for one in a state of impurity to eat it or touch it—or even for one in a state of purity to tamper with it—because the sacred is still intermixed with the profane.

profane Unauthorized contact with sacred objects is prohibited. If sacred food was accidentally eaten, the penalty is monetary reparation. If the act was deliberate, the penalty is capital punishment.

הפטרת קרח

HAFTARAH FOR KORAḤ

1 SAMUEL 11:14–12:22

This *haftarah* marks the end of the period of the chieftains ("Judges") and the onset of the rule of kings. Samuel bridges the two periods. He was both a prophet-like figure who judged the people in various locales and the one who was divinely enjoined to anoint a monarch. Initially, he refused to go along with the people's desire for a king "like all the nations." This was not because of any political calculations. For Samuel, the shift from theocracy to monarchy was theologically unconscionable, a betrayal of God and divine rule. Only God's support for the people's request changed his mind (1 Sam. 8:7).

Samuel, nevertheless, continued to believe that the nation's request was a betrayal of God's ongoing and gracious care. He even brings the nation to confess this fault and to a state of anguish and fear of divine abandonment. Samuel reassures them that "the LORD will never abandon His people, seeing that the LORD undertook to make you His people" (12:22). The Sages chose to end the *haftarah* with this message of hope, in contrast to the episode's last verse (12:25) with its doomsday warning that "if you persist in your wrongdoing, both you and your king shall be swept away."

RELATION OF THE *HAFTARAH* TO THE *PARASHAH*

In the *parashah,* the rebels Dathan and Abiram flouted and insulted Moses; in response, the "much aggrieved" Moses said to God, "Pay no regard to their oblation. I have not taken the ass of any one of them, nor have I wronged any one of them" (Num. 16:15). These words of self-defense are a condensed version of Samuel's litany in the *haftarah* (1 Sam. 12:3). Faced with a successful rejection of his leadership, Samuel reviews his conduct before the people and calls God to witness as well. Both leaders epitomize their rule in terms of justice and respect for the property of others.

The personalities of Moses and Samuel are linked from early biblical tradition. They are paired in Ps. 99:6 as intercessors before God. So the Lord also refers to them while speaking with Jeremiah in the final days of the kingdom of Judah (Jer. 15:1). Early rabbinic homilies present the two men as paragons of the righteous judge, completely just and beyond reproach (Tanh. Shof'tim).

Each of them was also called a "man of God"—Moses in the context of his blessing the tribes before his death (Deut. 33:1) and Samuel as a prophetic diviner of fortune at the shrine of Ramah (1 Sam. 9:7). Yet these men represent two stages in the nation's leadership. Moses, the first teacher of divine revelation to the people, set the basic pattern. Dealing with the details of ongoing life in each generation then fell to his heirs, to men like Samuel who stood in the breach as questions arose. The *parashah* and the *haftarah* underscore their ideal common denominator: selfless service on behalf of justice and a commitment to righteousness in societal affairs.

11 14Samuel said to the people, "Come, let
us go to Gilgal and there inaugurate the monarchy." 15So all the people went to Gilgal, and
there at Gilgal they declared Saul king before
the LORD. They offered sacrifices of well-being
there before the LORD; and Saul and all the men
of Israel held a great celebration there.

יא 14 וַיֹּ֤אמֶר שְׁמוּאֵל֙ אֶל־הָעָ֔ם לְכ֖וּ
וְנֵלְכָ֣ה הַגִּלְגָּ֑ל וּנְחַדֵּ֥שׁ שָׁ֖ם הַמְּלוּכָֽה׃
15 וַיֵּלְכ֨וּ כָל־הָעָ֜ם הַגִּלְגָּ֗ל וַיַּמְלִכוּ֩ שָׁ֨ם
אֶת־שָׁא֜וּל לִפְנֵ֤י יְהוָה֙ בַּגִּלְגָּ֔ל וַיִּזְבְּחוּ־שָׁ֛ם
זְבָחִ֥ים שְׁלָמִ֖ים לִפְנֵ֣י יְהוָ֑ה וַיִּשְׂמַ֨ח שָׁ֥ם
שָׁא֛וּל וְכָל־אַנְשֵׁ֥י יִשְׂרָאֵ֖ל עַד־מְאֹֽד׃ פ

12 Then Samuel said to all Israel, "I have
yielded to you in all you have asked of me and
have set a king over you. 2Henceforth the king
will be your leader.

"As for me, I have grown old and gray—but
my sons are still with you—and I have been your
leader from my youth to this day. 3Here I am!
Testify against me, in the presence of the
LORD and in the presence of His anointed one:
Whose ox have I taken, or whose ass have I
taken? Whom have I defrauded or whom have
I robbed? From whom have I taken a bribe to
look the other way? I will return it to you." 4They
responded, "You have not defrauded us, and
you have not robbed us, and you have taken
nothing from anyone." 5He said to them, "The
LORD then is witness, and His anointed is witness, to your admission this day that you have

יב וַיֹּ֤אמֶר שְׁמוּאֵל֙ אֶל־כָּל־יִשְׂרָאֵ֔ל
הִנֵּה֙ שָׁמַ֣עְתִּי בְקֹֽלְכֶ֔ם לְכֹ֥ל אֲשֶׁר־אֲמַרְתֶּ֖ם
לִ֑י וָאַמְלִ֥יךְ עֲלֵיכֶ֖ם מֶֽלֶךְ׃ 2 וְעַתָּ֞ה הִנֵּ֥ה
הַמֶּ֣לֶךְ ׀ מִתְהַלֵּ֣ךְ לִפְנֵיכֶ֗ם
וַאֲנִי֙ זָקַ֣נְתִּי וָשַׂ֔בְתִּי וּבָנַ֖י הִנָּ֣ם אִתְּכֶ֑ם
וַאֲנִי֙ הִתְהַלַּ֣כְתִּי לִפְנֵיכֶ֔ם מִנְּעֻרַ֖י עַד־הַיּ֥וֹם
הַזֶּֽה׃ 3 הִנְנִ֣י עֲנ֣וּ בִי֩ נֶ֨גֶד יְהוָ֜ה וְנֶ֣גֶד מְשִׁיח֗וֹ
אֶת־שׁוֹר֩ ׀ מִ֨י לָקַ֜חְתִּי וַחֲמ֧וֹר מִ֣י לָקַ֗חְתִּי
וְאֶת־מִ֤י עָשַׁ֙קְתִּי֙ אֶת־מִ֣י רַצּ֔וֹתִי וּמִיַּד־מִי֙
לָקַ֣חְתִּי כֹ֔פֶר וְאַעְלִ֥ים עֵינַ֖י בּ֑וֹ וְאָשִׁ֖יב
לָכֶֽם׃ 4 וַיֹּ֣אמְר֔וּ לֹ֥א עֲשַׁקְתָּ֖נוּ וְלֹ֣א רַצּוֹתָ֑נוּ
וְלֹֽא־לָקַ֥חְתָּ מִיַּד־אִ֖ישׁ מְאֽוּמָה׃ 5 וַיֹּ֨אמֶר
אֲלֵיהֶ֜ם עֵ֤ד יְהוָה֙ בָּכֶ֔ם וְעֵ֤ד מְשִׁיחוֹ֙ הַיּ֣וֹם

1 Samuel 11:14. Come, let us go to Gilgal and there inaugurate the monarchy This collective invocation dramatizes the nation's involvement in the coronation. In the previous chapter, after Saul was selected as king by divine lot, the people had ratified his selection with the shout, "Long live the king!" (10:20–24). Several malcontents among the people had demurred at that time. Thus this event at Gilgal "renews" rather than simply "inaugurates" the monarchy (Rashi, Radak, Kara). At this ceremony, "all the people" declare Saul king (v. 15).

Gilgal An old site with sacral connotations. After the Israelites' entrance into Canaan, Joshua performed a mass circumcision there, initiating the settlement of the Land (Josh. 5:2–9). As a home for the tabernacle and the Ark, it was also a center of national life (Radak). The monarchy is now ritually inaugurated there.

12:3. Whose ox have I taken Samuel's declaration of judicial probity includes a denial of ever robbing or taking bribes. This clearly reflects an old code of honor and standards. When Jethro advised Moses to appoint judges in the wilderness, he told him to seek out "capable men who fear God, trustworthy men who spurn ill-gotten gain" (Exod. 18:21). A more formal statement of proper conduct appears among the legal ordinances, in which the Israelites are told "not [to] subvert the rights of your needy in their disputes," to "keep far from a false charge," and "not take bribes, for bribes blind the clear-sighted and upset the pleas of those who are in the right" (Exod. 23:6–8).

found nothing in my possession." They responded, "He is!"

6 Samuel said to the people, "The LORD [is witness], He who appointed Moses and Aaron and who brought your fathers out of the land of Egypt. 7 Come, stand before the LORD while I cite against you all the kindnesses that the LORD has done to you and your fathers.

8 "When Jacob came to Egypt,...your fathers cried out to the LORD, and the LORD sent Moses and Aaron, who brought your fathers out of Egypt and settled them in this place. 9 But they forgot the LORD their God; so He delivered them into the hands of Sisera the military commander of Hazor, into the hands of the Philistines, and into the hands of the kind of Moab; and these made war upon them. 10 They cried to the LORD, 'We are guilty, for we have forsaken the LORD and worshiped the Baalim and Ashtaroth. Oh, deliver us from our enemies and we will serve You.' 11 And the LORD sent Jerubbaal and Bedan and Jephthah and Samuel, and delivered you from the enemies around you; and you dwelt in security. 12 But when you saw that Nahash king of the Ammonites was advancing against you, you said to me, 'No, we must have a king reigning over us'—though the LORD your God is your King.

13 "Well, the LORD has set a king over you! Here is the king that you have chosen, that you have asked for.

14 "If you will revere the LORD, worship Him, and obey Him, and will not flout the LORD's command, if both you and the king who reigns over you will follow the LORD your God, [well and good]. 15 But if you do not obey the LORD

הַזֶּה כִּי לֹא מְצָאתֶם בְּיָדִי מְאוּמָה
וַיֹּאמֶר* עֵד׃ פ
6 וַיֹּאמֶר שְׁמוּאֵל אֶל־הָעָם יְהוָה אֲשֶׁר
עָשָׂה אֶת־מֹשֶׁה וְאֶת־אַהֲרֹן וַאֲשֶׁר הֶעֱלָה
אֶת־אֲבֹתֵיכֶם מֵאֶרֶץ מִצְרָיִם׃ 7 וְעַתָּה
הִתְיַצְּבוּ וְאִשָּׁפְטָה אִתְּכֶם לִפְנֵי יְהוָה אֵת
כָּל־צִדְקוֹת יְהוָה אֲשֶׁר־עָשָׂה אִתְּכֶם
וְאֶת־אֲבוֹתֵיכֶם׃
8 כַּאֲשֶׁר־בָּא יַעֲקֹב מִצְרָיִם וַיִּזְעֲקוּ
אֲבוֹתֵיכֶם אֶל־יְהוָה וַיִּשְׁלַח יְהוָה אֶת־
מֹשֶׁה וְאֶת־אַהֲרֹן וַיּוֹצִיאוּ אֶת־אֲבֹתֵיכֶם
מִמִּצְרַיִם וַיֹּשִׁבוּם בַּמָּקוֹם הַזֶּה׃ 9 וַיִּשְׁכְּחוּ
אֶת־יְהוָה אֱלֹהֵיהֶם וַיִּמְכֹּר אֹתָם בְּיַד
סִיסְרָא שַׂר־צְבָא חָצוֹר וּבְיַד־פְּלִשְׁתִּים
וּבְיַד מֶלֶךְ מוֹאָב וַיִּלָּחֲמוּ בָּם׃ 10 וַיִּזְעֲקוּ
אֶל־יְהוָה ויאמר וַיֹּאמְרוּ חָטָאנוּ כִּי עָזַבְנוּ
אֶת־יְהוָה וַנַּעֲבֹד אֶת־הַבְּעָלִים וְאֶת־
הָעַשְׁתָּרוֹת וְעַתָּה הַצִּילֵנוּ מִיַּד אֹיְבֵינוּ
וְנַעַבְדֶךָּ׃ 11 וַיִּשְׁלַח יְהוָה אֶת־יְרֻבַּעַל
וְאֶת־בְּדָן וְאֶת־יִפְתָּח וְאֶת־שְׁמוּאֵל וַיַּצֵּל
אֶתְכֶם מִיַּד אֹיְבֵיכֶם מִסָּבִיב וַתֵּשְׁבוּ בֶּטַח׃
12 וַתִּרְאוּ כִּי־נָחָשׁ מֶלֶךְ בְּנֵי־עַמּוֹן בָּא
עֲלֵיכֶם וַתֹּאמְרוּ לִי לֹא כִּי־מֶלֶךְ יִמְלֹךְ
עָלֵינוּ וַיהוָה אֱלֹהֵיכֶם מַלְכְּכֶם׃
13 וְעַתָּה הִנֵּה הַמֶּלֶךְ אֲשֶׁר בְּחַרְתֶּם אֲשֶׁר
שְׁאֶלְתֶּם וְהִנֵּה נָתַן יְהוָה עֲלֵיכֶם מֶלֶךְ׃
14 אִם־תִּירְאוּ אֶת־יְהוָה וַעֲבַדְתֶּם אֹתוֹ
וּשְׁמַעְתֶּם בְּקֹלוֹ וְלֹא תַמְרוּ אֶת־פִּי יְהוָה
וִהְיִתֶם גַּם־אַתֶּם וְגַם־הַמֶּלֶךְ אֲשֶׁר מָלַךְ
עֲלֵיכֶם אַחַר יְהוָה אֱלֹהֵיכֶם׃ 15 וְאִם־לֹא

v. 5. סבירין ומטעין לשון רבים

5. They responded Literally, "He responded." This implies that the people responded as one person (Radak). Puzzled by the singular form of the Hebrew verb, an old tradition regarded this as an instance of divine intervention in human legal proceedings. Because earlier in the verse Samuel invoked God as a witness on his behalf, this verse was seen as the response of a heavenly voice declaring that God is indeed a witness (BT Mak. 23b; Gen. R. 85:12).

8. When Jacob came to Egypt,... Septuagint adds, "the Egyptians oppressed them" [Transl.].

and you flout the Lord's command, the hand of the Lord will strike you as it did your fathers.

16"Now stand by and see the marvelous thing that the Lord will do before your eyes. 17It is the season of the wheat harvest. I will pray to the Lord and He will send thunder and rain; then you will take thought and realize what a wicked thing you did in the sight of the Lord when you asked for a king."

18Samuel prayed to the Lord, and the Lord sent thunder and rain that day, and the people stood in awe of the Lord and of Samuel. 19The people all said to Samuel, "Intercede for your servants with the Lord your God that we may not die, for we have added to all our sins the wickedness of asking for a king." 20But Samuel said to the people, "Have no fear. You have, indeed, done all those wicked things. Do not, however, turn away from the Lord, but serve the Lord with all your heart. 21Do not turn away to follow worthless things, which can neither profit nor save but are worthless. 22For the sake of His great name, the Lord will never abandon His people, seeing that the Lord undertook to make you His people."

תִּשְׁמְעוּ בְּקוֹל יְהֹוָה וּמְרִיתֶם אֶת־פִּי יְהֹוָה וְהָיְתָה יַד־יְהֹוָה בָּכֶם וּבַאֲבֹתֵיכֶם:
16 גַּם־עַתָּה הִתְיַצְּבוּ וּרְאוּ אֶת־הַדָּבָר הַגָּדוֹל הַזֶּה אֲשֶׁר יְהֹוָה עֹשֶׂה לְעֵינֵיכֶם:
17 הֲלוֹא קְצִיר־חִטִּים הַיּוֹם אֶקְרָא אֶל־יְהֹוָה וְיִתֵּן קֹלוֹת וּמָטָר וּדְעוּ וּרְאוּ כִּי־רָעַתְכֶם רַבָּה אֲשֶׁר עֲשִׂיתֶם בְּעֵינֵי יְהֹוָה לִשְׁאוֹל לָכֶם מֶלֶךְ: ס
18 וַיִּקְרָא שְׁמוּאֵל אֶל־יְהֹוָה וַיִּתֵּן יְהֹוָה קֹלֹת וּמָטָר בַּיּוֹם הַהוּא וַיִּירָא כָל־הָעָם מְאֹד אֶת־יְהֹוָה וְאֶת־שְׁמוּאֵל: 19 וַיֹּאמְרוּ כָל־הָעָם אֶל־שְׁמוּאֵל הִתְפַּלֵּל בְּעַד־עֲבָדֶיךָ אֶל־יְהֹוָה אֱלֹהֶיךָ וְאַל־נָמוּת כִּי־יָסַפְנוּ עַל־כָּל־חַטֹּאתֵינוּ רָעָה לִשְׁאֹל לָנוּ מֶלֶךְ: ס 20 וַיֹּאמֶר שְׁמוּאֵל אֶל־הָעָם אַל־תִּירָאוּ אַתֶּם עֲשִׂיתֶם אֵת כָּל־הָרָעָה הַזֹּאת אַךְ אַל־תָּסוּרוּ מֵאַחֲרֵי יְהֹוָה וַעֲבַדְתֶּם אֶת־יְהֹוָה בְּכָל־לְבַבְכֶם: 21 וְלֹא תָּסוּרוּ כִּי | אַחֲרֵי הַתֹּהוּ אֲשֶׁר לֹא־יוֹעִילוּ וְלֹא יַצִּילוּ כִּי־תֹהוּ הֵמָּה: 22 כִּי לֹא־יִטֹּשׁ יְהֹוָה אֶת־עַמּוֹ בַּעֲבוּר שְׁמוֹ הַגָּדוֹל כִּי הוֹאִיל יְהֹוָה לַעֲשׂוֹת אֶתְכֶם לוֹ לְעָם:

---

17. season of the wheat harvest Heavy rain during the harvest season was rare; its occurrence here serves as a sign from God that the people sinned in asking for a king (Rashi, Ralbag).

HUKKAT

חקת

19 The LORD spoke to Moses and Aaron,
saying: 2This is the ritual law that the LORD has
commanded:

יט וַיְדַבֵּ֣ר יְהֹוָ֔ה אֶל־מֹשֶׁ֥ה וְאֶֽל־אַהֲרֹ֖ן
לֵאמֹֽר׃ 2 זֹ֚את חֻקַּ֣ת הַתּוֹרָ֔ה אֲשֶׁר־צִוָּ֥ה
יְהֹוָ֖ה לֵאמֹ֑ר

The Generation of the Exodus: The March to Transjordan (*continued*)

PURIFICATION FROM CONTAMINATION BY A CORPSE (19:1–22)

Contamination that results from contact with a corpse is mentioned elsewhere in the Torah (see, e.g., Lev. 21:1–4; Num. 6:6–13). Here, the Torah prescribes the method of purification. In this rite, the blood of an all-brown ("red") cow is not offered on the altar; it is burned together with the cow's body, so that the ashes may be used as an ongoing instrument of purification. As in all purification offerings, the man who burns the cow becomes impure himself.

In the course of this *parashah,* Miriam dies, Aaron dies, and Moses is sentenced to die without reaching the Promised Land. A transition of generations is taking place. The narrative's center of gravity is moving farther from Sinai and closer to the challenge of conquering the Promised Land. Soon there will be no Israelites left who actually stood at Sinai, only Israelites who have heard about it from parents and grandparents.

CHAPTER 19

Before continuing with the narrative, the Torah offers us the strange ritual of the brown ("red") cow. It is the classic example of a law that defies rational explanation. Indeed, the general tenor of the commentaries asks us to accept this law without understanding it, as a sign of love for and trust in God. The commentators hold that it would be almost unseemly to search for a rational explanation, implying that God's word would be acceptable only if it fit our canons of reasoning. Human failure to understand a truth does not make it any less true. The Midrash pictures King Solomon, the wisest man in the Bible, saying, "I have labored to understand the word of God and have understood it all, except for the ritual of the brown cow" (Num. R. 19:3). "These laws are decrees from God and we have no right to question them" (Num. R. 19:8). "It is more praiseworthy to do something solely because God commands it than because our own logic or sense of morality leads us to the same conclusion" (*Sifra K'doshim*). The Tosafot compare this commandment to a lover's kiss which cannot be explained but can only be experienced (BT Av. Zar. 35a).

Yet there have been persistent efforts to uncover the lessons taught to us by this ritual. Although the Torah describes the ritual as purifying a person of contamination from contact with a dead body and nothing else, the Midrash widens the scope to include moral contamination, especially idolatry, viewing this special cow as the antidote for the sin of the Golden Calf. "Let the mother come and repair the damage the offspring has caused" (Num. R. 19:8). Ramban, noting that the passage comes immediately after the completion of the tabernacle and the challenge to Aaron's priesthood, understands it as a way of preventing ritually unfit people from violating the sanctity of the tabernacle. Israel of Ruzhin points out that this cow purifies the impure but renders the pure impure; God similarly purifies those who approach the sanctuary in a spirit of humility with knowledge of their own inadequacies, but condemns those who come in a spirit of arrogance and a claim to perfection. A modern commentator suggests that the ritual's purpose is psychological. To heal a person burdened by a sense of wrongdoing, who feels the purity of his or her soul has been compromised, we take an animal completely without blemish and sacrifice it, as if to imply that perfection does not belong in this world. Perfect creatures belong in heaven; this world is given to the inevitably flawed and compromised.

Because this rite is inoperative today, so that there is no way to purify the ritually contaminated, some halakhic authorities consider all Jews ritually unfit to enter the Temple Mount lest they inadvertently tread on the site where the holiest precincts of the temple once stood in Jerusalem.

Instruct the Israelite people to bring you a red
cow without blemish, in which there is no defect
and on which no yoke has been laid. 3You shall
give it to Eleazar the priest. It shall be taken outside the camp and slaughtered in his presence.
4Eleazar the priest shall take some of its blood
with his finger and sprinkle it seven times toward the front of the Tent of Meeting. 5The cow
shall be burned in his sight—its hide, flesh, and
blood shall be burned, its dung included—6and
the priest shall take cedar wood, hyssop, and
crimson stuff, and throw them into the fire consuming the cow. 7The priest shall wash his garments and bathe his body in water; after that
the priest may reenter the camp, but he shall
be impure until evening. 8He who performed
the burning shall also wash his garments in water, bathe his body in water, and be impure until
evening. 9A man who is pure shall gather up the
ashes of the cow and deposit them outside the
camp in a pure place, to be kept for water of
lustration for the Israelite community. It is for
purification. 10He who gathers up the ashes of

דַּבֵּ֣ר ׀ אֶל־בְּנֵ֣י יִשְׂרָאֵ֗ל וְיִקְח֣וּ אֵלֶ֡יךָ פָרָה֩
אֲדֻמָּ֨ה תְּמִימָ֜ה אֲשֶׁ֤ר אֵֽין־בָּהּ֙ מ֔וּם אֲשֶׁ֛ר
לֹא־עָלָ֥ה עָלֶ֖יהָ עֹֽל׃ 3 וּנְתַתֶּ֣ם אֹתָ֔הּ אֶל־
אֶלְעָזָ֖ר הַכֹּהֵ֑ן וְהוֹצִ֤יא אֹתָהּ֙ אֶל־מִח֣וּץ
לַֽמַּחֲנֶ֔ה וְשָׁחַ֥ט אֹתָ֖הּ לְפָנָֽיו׃ 4 וְלָקַ֞ח
אֶלְעָזָ֧ר הַכֹּהֵ֛ן מִדָּמָ֖הּ בְּאֶצְבָּע֑וֹ וְהִזָּ֞ה אֶל־
נֹ֨כַח פְּנֵ֧י אֹֽהֶל־מוֹעֵ֛ד מִדָּמָ֖הּ שֶׁ֥בַע פְּעָמִֽים׃
5 וְשָׂרַ֥ף אֶת־הַפָּרָ֖ה לְעֵינָ֑יו אֶת־עֹרָ֤הּ וְאֶת־
בְּשָׂרָהּ֙ וְאֶת־דָּמָ֔הּ עַל־פִּרְשָׁ֖הּ יִשְׂרֹֽף׃
6 וְלָקַ֣ח הַכֹּהֵ֗ן עֵ֥ץ אֶ֛רֶז וְאֵז֖וֹב וּשְׁנִ֣י תוֹלָ֑עַת
וְהִשְׁלִ֕יךְ אֶל־תּ֖וֹךְ שְׂרֵפַ֥ת הַפָּרָֽה׃ 7 וְכִבֶּ֨ס
בְּגָדָ֜יו הַכֹּהֵ֗ן וְרָחַ֤ץ בְּשָׂרוֹ֙ בַּמַּ֔יִם וְאַחַ֖ר
יָבֹ֣א אֶל־הַֽמַּחֲנֶ֑ה וְטָמֵ֥א הַכֹּהֵ֖ן עַד־
הָעָֽרֶב׃ 8 וְהַשֹּׂרֵ֣ף אֹתָ֔הּ יְכַבֵּ֤ס בְּגָדָיו֙ בַּמַּ֔יִם
וְרָחַ֥ץ בְּשָׂר֖וֹ בַּמָּ֑יִם וְטָמֵ֖א עַד־הָעָֽרֶב׃
9 וְאָסַ֣ף ׀ אִ֣ישׁ טָה֗וֹר אֵ֚ת אֵ֣פֶר הַפָּרָ֔ה
וְהִנִּ֛יחַ מִח֥וּץ לַֽמַּחֲנֶ֖ה בְּמָק֣וֹם טָה֑וֹר
וְֽהָיְתָה֩ לַעֲדַ֨ת בְּנֵֽי־יִשְׂרָאֵ֧ל לְמִשְׁמֶ֛רֶת לְמֵ֥י
נִדָּ֖ה חַטָּ֥את הִֽוא׃ 10 וְ֠כִבֶּס הָאֹסֵ֨ף אֶת־

THE BROWN ("RED") COW (vv. 1–13)

2. red Hebrew: *adom,* which here probably means "brown"—for which there is no word in the Bible. The idea is to increase, symbolically, the amount of blood in the ashes.

red . . . without blemish Better: "unblemished brown." A cow completely uniform in color, without specks of white or black or without even two black or white hairs, is extremely rare.

no yoke has been laid It must not have been used for profane purposes.

3. in his presence The cow will also be burned in the presence of Eleazar, indicating that it is imperative for the officiating priest to supervise the entire ritual.

4. sprinkle it seven times This act consecrates the cow as a purification offering.

6. priest Any priest, not just Eleazar.

hyssop, and crimson stuff Hyssop, an aromatic plant, is widespread in the land of Israel. Crimson yarn refers to the dye extracted from a "crimson worm," used in the weaving of the sacred garments of the high priest and the inner curtains of the tabernacle.

7. wash his garments and bathe his body If he bathed first, his unwashed garments would recontaminate him.

until evening Whoever handles a burnt *ḥattat* offering may enter the camp as soon as he has laundered his clothing and bathed (see Lev. 16:26,28), provided he does not partake of sacred food until the evening.

8. He who performed the burning It is also presumed that he who gathers up the ashes remains outside the camp until after he has laundered and bathed, precisely as the contaminated priest has done.

9. A man Not necessarily a priest.

to be kept The ashes of the brown ("red") cow must be guarded scrupulously lest they become contaminated.

It is for purification These ashes mixed with water will be sprinkled on corpse-contaminated individuals to remove the impurity.

10. wash his clothes It is understood that he will also bathe his body.

the cow shall also wash his clothes and be impure until evening.

This shall be a permanent law for the Israelites and for the strangers who reside among you.

11 He who touches the corpse of any human being shall be impure for seven days. 12 He shall purify himself with it on the third day and on the seventh day, and then be pure; if he fails to purify himself on the third and seventh days, he shall not be pure. 13 Whoever touches a corpse, the body of a person who has died, and does not purify himself, defiles the LORD's Tabernacle; that person shall be cut off from Israel. Since the water of lustration was not dashed on him, he remains impure; his impurity is still upon him.

14 This is the ritual: When a person dies in a tent, whoever enters the tent and whoever is in the tent shall be impure seven days; 15 and every open vessel, with no lid fastened down, shall be impure. 16 And in the open, anyone who touches a person who was killed or who died naturally, or human bone, or a grave, shall be impure seven days. 17 Some of the ashes from the fire of purification shall be taken for the im-

אֵפֶר הַפָּרָה אֶת־בְּגָדָיו וְטָמֵא עַד־הָעָרֶב
וְהָיְתָה לִבְנֵי יִשְׂרָאֵל וְלַגֵּר הַגָּר בְּתוֹכָם
לְחֻקַּת עוֹלָם׃
11 הַנֹּגֵעַ בְּמֵת לְכָל־נֶפֶשׁ אָדָם וְטָמֵא
שִׁבְעַת יָמִים׃ 12 הוּא יִתְחַטָּא־בוֹ בַּיּוֹם
הַשְּׁלִישִׁי וּבַיּוֹם הַשְּׁבִיעִי יִטְהָר וְאִם־לֹא
יִתְחַטָּא בַּיּוֹם הַשְּׁלִישִׁי וּבַיּוֹם הַשְּׁבִיעִי
לֹא יִטְהָר׃ 13 כָּל־הַנֹּגֵעַ בְּמֵת בְּנֶפֶשׁ הָאָדָם
אֲשֶׁר־יָמוּת וְלֹא יִתְחַטָּא אֶת־מִשְׁכַּן יְהוָה
טִמֵּא וְנִכְרְתָה הַנֶּפֶשׁ הַהִוא מִיִּשְׂרָאֵל כִּי
מֵי נִדָּה לֹא־זֹרַק עָלָיו טָמֵא יִהְיֶה עוֹד
טֻמְאָתוֹ בוֹ׃
14 זֹאת הַתּוֹרָה אָדָם כִּי־יָמוּת בְּאֹהֶל
כָּל־הַבָּא אֶל־הָאֹהֶל וְכָל־אֲשֶׁר בָּאֹהֶל
יִטְמָא שִׁבְעַת יָמִים׃ 15 וְכֹל כְּלִי פָתוּחַ
אֲשֶׁר אֵין־צָמִיד פָּתִיל עָלָיו טָמֵא הוּא׃
16 וְכֹל אֲשֶׁר־יִגַּע עַל־פְּנֵי הַשָּׂדֶה בַּחֲלַל־
חֶרֶב אוֹ בְמֵת אוֹ־בְעֶצֶם אָדָם אוֹ בְקָבֶר
יִטְמָא שִׁבְעַת יָמִים׃ 17 וְלָקְחוּ לַטָּמֵא

strangers All those who dwell in the Holy Land, Israelites and non-Israelites alike, must purify themselves of corpse contamination lest they defile the sanctuary by bearing their impurity within the community.

11. seven days Similarly, in ancient Babylonia, one who came into contact with dust from a place of mourning was required to offer sacrifices to the god Shamash, to bathe, change clothing, and remain inside the house for seven days.

13. defiles the LORD's Tabernacle Severe impurity is dynamic and can attack the sanctuary through the air. Corpse-contaminated individuals who prolong their impurity have defiled the sanctuary from afar, even without entering it.

shall be cut off If the neglect was deliberate (see 15:30–31). (If the neglect was accidental, a purification offering is brought.)

PURIFICATION BY SPRINKLING (vv. 14–22)

14. enters the tent The impurity emitted by the body is trapped by the roof, so to speak, and cannot rise. Hence, every person and object under the roof is contaminated.

15. every open vessel A tightly closed vessel made entirely of earthenware, however, will not admit the "vapors" of impurity given off by the corpse; its contents remain pure.

fastened down The lid is attached by cords passing through holes in it and through the handles of the vessel. Such a lid would keep the vessel tightly closed and preserve it from defilement.

HALAKHAH L'MA·ASEH

19:14. When a person dies Once the Temple was destroyed, we could not purify ourselves from this type of ritual impurity. Now all but *kohanim* may attend funerals (see Lev. 21:2). We rinse our hands upon leaving the cemetery or upon entering a house of mourning after the funeral, in symbolic recollection of this law.

pure person, and fresh water shall be added to
them in a vessel. 18A person who is pure shall
take hyssop, dip it in the water, and sprinkle on
the tent and on all the vessels and people who
were there, or on him who touched the bones
or the person who was killed or died naturally
or the grave. 19The pure person shall sprinkle
it upon the impure person on the third day and
on the seventh day, thus purifying him by the
seventh day. He shall then wash his clothes and
bathe in water, and at nightfall he shall be pure.
20If anyone who has become impure fails to purify himself, that person shall be cut off from
the congregation, for he has defiled the LORD's
sanctuary. The water of lustration was not
dashed on him: he is impure.

21That shall be for them a law for all time. Further, he who sprinkled the water of lustration
shall wash his clothes; and whoever touches the
water of lustration shall be impure until evening. 22Whatever that impure person touches
shall be impure; and the person who touches
him shall be impure until evening.

מֵעֲפַר שְׂרֵפַת הַחַטָּאת וְנָתַן עָלָיו מַיִם
שני חַיִּים אֶל־כֶּלִי׃ 18 וְלָקַח אֵזוֹב וְטָבַל בַּמַּיִם
אִישׁ טָהוֹר וְהִזָּה עַל־הָאֹהֶל וְעַל־כָּל־
הַכֵּלִים וְעַל־הַנְּפָשׁוֹת אֲשֶׁר הָיוּ־שָׁם וְעַל־
הַנֹּגֵעַ בַּעֶצֶם אוֹ בֶחָלָל אוֹ בַמֵּת אוֹ בַקָּבֶר׃
19 וְהִזָּה הַטָּהֹר עַל־הַטָּמֵא בַּיּוֹם הַשְּׁלִישִׁי
וּבַיּוֹם הַשְּׁבִיעִי וְחִטְּאוֹ בַּיּוֹם הַשְּׁבִיעִי
וְכִבֶּס בְּגָדָיו וְרָחַץ בַּמַּיִם וְטָהֵר בָּעָרֶב׃
20 וְאִישׁ אֲשֶׁר־יִטְמָא וְלֹא יִתְחַטָּא וְנִכְרְתָה
הַנֶּפֶשׁ הַהִוא מִתּוֹךְ הַקָּהָל כִּי אֶת־מִקְדַּשׁ
יְהוָה טִמֵּא מֵי נִדָּה לֹא־זֹרַק עָלָיו טָמֵא
הוּא׃

21 וְהָיְתָה לָהֶם לְחֻקַּת עוֹלָם וּמַזֵּה מֵי־
הַנִּדָּה יְכַבֵּס בְּגָדָיו וְהַנֹּגֵעַ בְּמֵי הַנִּדָּה
יִטְמָא עַד־הָעָרֶב׃ 22 וְכֹל אֲשֶׁר־יִגַּע־בּוֹ
הַטָּמֵא יִטְמָא וְהַנֶּפֶשׁ הַנֹּגַעַת תִּטְמָא
עַד־הָעָרֶב׃ פ

20 The Israelites arrived in a body at the
wilderness of Zin on the first new moon, and

כ וַיָּבֹאוּ בְנֵי־יִשְׂרָאֵל כָּל־הָעֵדָה מִדְבַּר־

shall be impure Open earthenware vessels are impure forever and must be broken.

18. A person who is pure This obvious condition is made explicit to bar those who had already handled the ashes and were thereby contaminated.

on all the vessels Afterward these must undergo washing, as people must.

19. Full purification comes only after laundering and bathing.

21. See Comment to 19:10.

22. Whatever That is, anything or anyone.

FROM KADESH TO THE STEPPES OF MOAB (20:1–22:1)

THE SIN OF MOSES AND AARON (20:1–13)

After Miriam's death, the people complain about the lack of water. Moses and Aaron are commanded to bring forth water from the rock. They produce the water but in so doing commit a sin akin to heresy and are condemned by God to die in the wilderness.

CHAPTER 20

1. The Talmud connects Miriam's death to the preceding passage. "Just as the ashes of the brown cow atone for sin, the death of a righteous person does the same" (BT MK 28a). In the wake of a good person's death, we are moved to re-examine our own lives.

the people stayed at Kadesh. Miriam died there and was buried there.

2 The community was without water, and they joined against Moses and Aaron. 3 The people quarreled with Moses, saying, "If only we had perished when our brothers perished at the instance of the LORD! 4 Why have you brought the LORD's congregation into this wilderness for us and our beasts to die there? 5 Why did you make us leave Egypt to bring us to this wretched place, a place with no grain or figs or vines or pomegranates? There is not even water to drink!"

6 Moses and Aaron came away from the congregation to the entrance of the Tent of Meeting, and fell on their faces. The Presence of the LORD appeared to them, 7 and the LORD spoke to Moses, saying, 8 "You and your brother Aaron take the rod and assemble the community, and before their very eyes order the rock to yield its

צִן בַּחֹדֶשׁ הָרִאשׁוֹן וַיֵּשֶׁב הָעָם בְּקָדֵשׁ
וַתָּמָת שָׁם מִרְיָם וַתִּקָּבֵר שָׁם׃
2 וְלֹא־הָיָה מַיִם לָעֵדָה וַיִּקָּהֲלוּ עַל־מֹשֶׁה
וְעַל־אַהֲרֹן׃ 3 וַיָּרֶב הָעָם עִם־מֹשֶׁה
וַיֹּאמְרוּ לֵאמֹר וְלוּ גָוַעְנוּ בִּגְוַע אַחֵינוּ לִפְנֵי
יְהוָה׃ 4 וְלָמָה הֲבֵאתֶם אֶת־קְהַל יְהוָה
אֶל־הַמִּדְבָּר הַזֶּה לָמוּת שָׁם אֲנַחְנוּ
וּבְעִירֵנוּ׃ 5 וְלָמָה הֶעֱלִיתֻנוּ מִמִּצְרַיִם
לְהָבִיא אֹתָנוּ אֶל־הַמָּקוֹם הָרָע הַזֶּה לֹא ׀
מְקוֹם זֶרַע וּתְאֵנָה וְגֶפֶן וְרִמּוֹן וּמַיִם אַיִן
לִשְׁתּוֹת׃
6 וַיָּבֹא מֹשֶׁה וְאַהֲרֹן מִפְּנֵי הַקָּהָל אֶל־פֶּתַח
אֹהֶל מוֹעֵד וַיִּפְּלוּ עַל־פְּנֵיהֶם וַיֵּרָא כְבוֹד־
יְהוָה אֲלֵיהֶם׃ פ 7 וַיְדַבֵּר יְהוָה אֶל־ שלישי [שני]
מֹשֶׁה לֵּאמֹר׃ 8 קַח אֶת־הַמַּטֶּה וְהַקְהֵל
אֶת־הָעֵדָה אַתָּה וְאַהֲרֹן אָחִיךָ וְדִבַּרְתֶּם

THE DEATH OF MIRIAM (v. 1)

1. The generation of the Exodus has died out and this is the 40th year. According to 13:26, however, the Israelites had already arrived at Kadesh at the start of their sojourn in the wilderness. Some commentators suggest that after having left Kadesh they returned to it in the 40th year. Most likely, these are two variant traditions.

Miriam died there On the 10th day of the first month, according to an ancient tradition.

3. when our brothers perished During the Korahite rebellion (16:35, 17:14). Although the people identify with the Korahite rebels, God does not punish them because their complaint is legitimate: They are dying of thirst.

6. came away from That is, in flight.

fell on their faces Out of fear.

The Presence That is, the fire-encased cloud.

8. rod Of Moses, which had been employed in the performance of God's miracles in the wilderness (see Exod. 14:16, 17:1–7,9).

to yield its water Because of the will of God, not the rod of Moses.

---

2. The community was without water A legend tells of a marvelous well that sprang up wherever the Israelites camped, as a tribute to Miriam's piety. As she waited by the waters of the Nile to see the fate of her baby brother, as she celebrated God's power at the Sea, so was she blessed with water, a substance more valuable in the desert than gold. When she died, the well vanished.

4. When Israel was leaving Egypt, triumphant and optimistic, they saw themselves as "the LORD's congregation." In the midst of the wilderness, thirsty and discouraged, they seem to be saying "We who used to think of ourselves as the LORD's congregation can now only think in terms of being thirsty, along with our cattle." Similarly, in verse 8, God promises to send water for "the congregation and their beasts." This has been understood to mean that the people, desperate with thirst, were responding at virtually an animal level, no different than their cattle (*Meshekh Ḥokhmah*).

6–12. When Moses strikes the rock to draw water instead of speaking to it as God commanded, he is condemned to die in the wilderness. In this puzzling incident, the punishment seems grossly disproportionate to the offense. Why should Moses, who has served God so loyally for so many years through so many trying times, be so harshly punished for what seems like a minor infraction? The classic commentators labor to find in the text some justifica-

water. Thus you shall produce water for them from the rock and provide drink for the congregation and their beasts."

9 Moses took the rod from before the LORD, as He had commanded him. 10 Moses and Aaron assembled the congregation in front of the rock; and he said to them, "Listen, you rebels, shall we get water for you out of this rock?" 11 And Moses raised his hand and struck the rock twice with his rod. Out came copious water, and the community and their beasts drank.

12 But the LORD said to Moses and Aaron, "Because you did not trust Me enough to affirm

אֶל־הַסֶּלַע לְעֵינֵיהֶם וְנָתַן מֵימָיו וְהוֹצֵאתָ
לָהֶם מַיִם מִן־הַסֶּלַע וְהִשְׁקִיתָ אֶת־הָעֵדָה
וְאֶת־בְּעִירָם׃
9 וַיִּקַּח מֹשֶׁה אֶת־הַמַּטֶּה מִלִּפְנֵי יְהוָה
כַּאֲשֶׁר צִוָּהוּ׃ 10 וַיַּקְהִלוּ מֹשֶׁה וְאַהֲרֹן
אֶת־הַקָּהָל אֶל־פְּנֵי הַסָּלַע וַיֹּאמֶר לָהֶם
שִׁמְעוּ־נָא הַמֹּרִים הֲמִן־הַסֶּלַע הַזֶּה נוֹצִיא
לָכֶם מָיִם׃ 11 וַיָּרֶם מֹשֶׁה אֶת־יָדוֹ וַיַּךְ
אֶת־הַסֶּלַע בְּמַטֵּהוּ פַּעֲמָיִם וַיֵּצְאוּ מַיִם
רַבִּים וַתֵּשְׁתְּ הָעֵדָה וּבְעִירָם׃ ס
12 וַיֹּאמֶר יְהוָה אֶל־מֹשֶׁה וְאֶל־אַהֲרֹן יַעַן

9. from before the LORD That is, from the tabernacle.

as He had commanded him This statement would have been expected before or after the account of the fulfillment of the command, not in the middle. Its "misplacement" is deliberate, however. Up to this point Moses executes God's command; thereafter, he deviates from it.

11. twice This indicates Moses' anger, but it is not his sin. Nor is his sin in striking the rock. Rather, his sin is in speaking so as to imply that what follows is his miracle—not God's.

12. trust Me Just as Israel, who did not "trust Me" (14:11), must die in the wilderness (14:23), so must Moses and Aaron.

in the sight of the Israelite people Their sin was aggravated because it was witnessed by all of Israel.

this congregation The new generation, now eligible to enter the Land—an indication that this event takes place in the 40th year.

---

tion for God's being so angry with Moses (and with Aaron, who seems to be a bystander at worst). Rashi points out that Moses' striking the rock (rather than speaking to it) diminished the greatness of the miracle. Ḥananel and Ramban both fasten on verse 10: "Shall we get water for you out of this rock?" This seems to imply that Moses and Aaron present themselves rather than God as the source of the miracle. And why was Aaron punished? After the first strike, he could have stopped Moses from repeating his error, but did not.

Ibn Ezra and Albo criticize Moses for "needing to be told" to work a miracle instead of being confident that God would work one for the people (after all, Moses presumed to anticipate a miracle in the showdown with Korah). Several modern commentators fault Moses for using a tactic that had worked in an earlier generation (see Exod. 17:6) but was inappropriate for this generation.

Perhaps the most persuasive explanation is that offered by Maimonides in the 12th century and Hirsch in the 19th century. Moses was punished for losing his temper and losing patience with the people, calling them "rebels," striking the rock (and then striking it a second time) in exasperation with the people. (One suspects he would as readily have struck the complainers with his staff.) "When a prophet loses his temper, his gift of prophecy abandons him" (BT Pes. 66b).

One might conclude that God's decree of death in the wilderness for Moses and Aaron was not so much a punishment as a recognition that their time of leadership was over. They were emotionally worn out by having led the people for so long. In some cases, there was a two-generation gap between them and their followers. Moses and Aaron were not sinners; they were the right leaders for the Exodus, for Sinai, for establishing the tabernacle. They were not the right people to lead a younger generation into battle.

11. the community and their beasts drank The people drank like beasts, each person concerned solely with easing his or her own thirst. Only when we share with others what we ourselves also crave, do we rise above the animal level and become truly human.

לֹא־הֶאֱמַנְתֶּם בִּי לְהַקְדִּישֵׁנִי לְעֵינֵי בְּנֵי
יִשְׂרָאֵל לָכֵן לֹא תָבִיאוּ אֶת־הַקָּהָל הַזֶּה
אֶל־הָאָרֶץ אֲשֶׁר־נָתַתִּי לָהֶם׃ 13 הֵמָּה מֵי
מְרִיבָה אֲשֶׁר־רָבוּ בְנֵי־יִשְׂרָאֵל אֶת־יְהוָה
וַיִּקָּדֵשׁ בָּם׃ ס

רביעי 14 וַיִּשְׁלַח מֹשֶׁה מַלְאָכִים מִקָּדֵשׁ אֶל־מֶלֶךְ
אֱדוֹם כֹּה אָמַר אָחִיךָ יִשְׂרָאֵל אַתָּה יָדַעְתָּ
אֵת כָּל־הַתְּלָאָה אֲשֶׁר מְצָאָתְנוּ׃ 15 וַיֵּרְדוּ
אֲבֹתֵינוּ מִצְרַיְמָה וַנֵּשֶׁב בְּמִצְרַיִם יָמִים
רַבִּים וַיָּרֵעוּ לָנוּ מִצְרַיִם וְלַאֲבֹתֵינוּ׃
16 וַנִּצְעַק אֶל־יְהוָה וַיִּשְׁמַע קֹלֵנוּ וַיִּשְׁלַח
מַלְאָךְ וַיֹּצִאֵנוּ מִמִּצְרָיִם וְהִנֵּה אֲנַחְנוּ
בְקָדֵשׁ עִיר קְצֵה גְבוּלֶךָ׃ 17 נַעְבְּרָה־נָּא
בְאַרְצֶךָ לֹא נַעֲבֹר בְּשָׂדֶה וּבְכֶרֶם וְלֹא
נִשְׁתֶּה מֵי בְאֵר דֶּרֶךְ הַמֶּלֶךְ נֵלֵךְ לֹא נִטֶּה
יָמִין וּשְׂמֹאול עַד אֲשֶׁר־נַעֲבֹר גְּבוּלֶךָ׃
18 וַיֹּאמֶר אֵלָיו אֱדוֹם לֹא תַעֲבֹר בִּי פֶּן־

My sanctity in the sight of the Israelite people, therefore you shall not lead this congregation into the land that I have given them."
13Those are the Waters of Meribah—meaning that the Israelites quarrelled with the LORD—through which He affirmed His sanctity.

14From Kadesh, Moses sent messengers to the king of Edom: "Thus says your brother Israel: You know all the hardships that have befallen us;
15that our ancestors went down to Egypt, that we dwelt in Egypt a long time, and that the Egyptians dealt harshly with us and our ancestors.
16We cried to the LORD and He heard our plea, and He sent a messenger who freed us from Egypt. Now we are in Kadesh, the town on the border of your territory.
17Allow us, then, to cross your country. We will not pass through fields or vineyards, and we will not drink water from wells. We will follow the king's highway, turning off neither to the right nor to the left until we have crossed your territory."

18But Edom answered him, "You shall not pass through us, else we will go out against you

13. Israelites quarrelled with the LORD They had quarrelled only with Moses, but their real object was God.

affirmed His sanctity Although Moses and Aaron defied God, God continued to supply the Israelites with water, and thereby caused His name to be sanctified in Israel.

ENCOUNTER WITH EDOM (vv. 14–21)

After the abortive attempt to enter Canaan from the south (14:40–45; see v. 25), Israel attempts to enter from the east, across the Jordan River. To reach the Jordan from their base at Kadesh, however, they must go north through Edomite territory.

14. The text closely resembles formal address in letters that was common throughout the ancient Near East: beginning with the addressee ("to the king of Edom"), followed by the addresser ("thus speaks your brother Israel"), and then the message ("You know . . .").

your brother The personification of a people in the singular is frequently found in direct address (see Exod. 14:26). Here the personification is that of a brother or a kinsman.

hardships Israel's misfortunes are emphasized solely to elicit sympathy.

16. He sent a messenger Literally: "angel," which, although at variance with the standard view, is found elsewhere (see Exod. 33:2).

17. king's highway The main route through the length of Transjordan.

---

15. dealt harshly with us Hebrew: *va-yarei·u lanu;* one rabbinic rendering is: "they made us seem harsh, bad." To justify their cruel treatment of us, they proclaimed that we were evil and deserving of persecution.

and our ancestors The reference is not only to the parents and grandparents of the current generation. When Israel suffers, Abraham, Isaac, Jacob, Sarah, Rebecca, Rachel, and Leah in heaven feel their pain (Num. R. 19:15).

with the sword." 19"We will keep to the beaten track," the Israelites said to them, "and if we or our cattle drink your water, we will pay for it. We ask only for passage on foot—it is but a small matter." 20But they replied, "You shall not pass through!" And Edom went out against them in heavy force, strongly armed. 21So Edom would not let Israel cross their territory, and Israel turned away from them.

22Setting out from Kadesh, the Israelites arrived in a body at Mount Hor. 23At Mount Hor, on the boundary of the land of Edom, the LORD said to Moses and Aaron, 24"Let Aaron be gathered to his kin: he is not to enter the land that I have assigned to the Israelite people, because you disobeyed my command about the waters of Meribah. 25Take Aaron and his son Eleazar and bring them up on Mount Hor. 26Strip Aaron of his vestments and put them on his son Eleazar. There Aaron shall be gathered unto the dead."

27Moses did as the LORD had commanded. They ascended Mount Hor in the sight of the whole community. 28Moses stripped Aaron of his vestments and put them on his son Eleazar, and Aaron died there on the summit of the mountain. When Moses and Eleazar came down from the mountain, 29the whole community knew that Aaron had breathed his last.

בַּחֶ֖רֶב אֵצֵ֥א לִקְרָאתֶֽךָ׃ 19 וַיֹּאמְר֨וּ אֵלָ֜יו
בְּנֵֽי־יִשְׂרָאֵל֮ בַּֽמְסִלָּ֣ה נַעֲלֶה֒ וְאִם־מֵימֶ֤יךָ
נִשְׁתֶּה֙ אֲנִ֣י וּמִקְנַ֔י וְנָתַתִּ֖י מִכְרָ֑ם רַ֥ק
אֵין־דָּבָ֖ר בְּרַגְלַ֥י אֶעֱבֹֽרָה׃ 20 וַיֹּ֖אמֶר לֹ֣א
תַעֲבֹ֑ר וַיֵּצֵ֤א אֱדוֹם֙ לִקְרָאת֔וֹ בְּעַ֥ם כָּבֵ֖ד
וּבְיָ֥ד חֲזָקָֽה׃ 21 וַיְמָאֵ֣ן ׀ אֱד֗וֹם נְתֹן֙ אֶת־
יִשְׂרָאֵ֔ל עֲבֹ֖ר בִּגְבֻל֑וֹ וַיֵּ֥ט יִשְׂרָאֵ֖ל
מֵעָלָֽיו׃ פ
22 וַיִּסְע֖וּ מִקָּדֵ֑שׁ וַיָּבֹ֧אוּ בְנֵֽי־יִשְׂרָאֵ֛ל כָּל־ חמישי [שלישי]
הָעֵדָ֖ה הֹ֥ר הָהָֽר׃ 23 וַיֹּ֧אמֶר יְהוָ֛ה אֶל־מֹשֶׁ֥ה
וְאֶֽל־אַהֲרֹ֖ן בְּהֹ֣ר הָהָ֑ר עַל־גְּב֥וּל אֶֽרֶץ־
אֱד֖וֹם לֵאמֹֽר׃ 24 יֵאָסֵ֤ף אַהֲרֹן֙ אֶל־עַמָּ֔יו כִּ֣י
לֹ֤א יָבֹא֙ אֶל־הָאָ֔רֶץ אֲשֶׁ֥ר נָתַ֖תִּי לִבְנֵ֣י
יִשְׂרָאֵ֑ל עַ֛ל אֲשֶׁר־מְרִיתֶ֥ם אֶת־פִּ֖י לְמֵ֥י
מְרִיבָֽה׃ 25 קַ֚ח אֶֽת־אַהֲרֹ֔ן וְאֶת־אֶלְעָזָ֖ר בְּנ֑וֹ
וְהַ֥עַל אֹתָ֖ם הֹ֥ר הָהָֽר׃ 26 וְהַפְשֵׁ֨ט אֶֽת־
אַהֲרֹן֙ אֶת־בְּגָדָ֔יו וְהִלְבַּשְׁתָּ֖ם אֶת־אֶלְעָזָ֣ר
בְּנ֑וֹ וְאַהֲרֹ֥ן יֵאָסֵ֖ף וּמֵ֥ת שָֽׁם׃
27 וַיַּ֣עַשׂ מֹשֶׁ֔ה כַּאֲשֶׁ֖ר צִוָּ֣ה יְהוָ֑ה וַֽיַּעֲלוּ֙
אֶל־הֹ֣ר הָהָ֔ר לְעֵינֵ֖י כָּל־הָעֵדָֽה׃ 28 וַיַּפְשֵׁט֩
מֹשֶׁ֨ה אֶֽת־אַהֲרֹ֜ן אֶת־בְּגָדָ֗יו וַיַּלְבֵּ֤שׁ אֹתָם֙
אֶת־אֶלְעָזָ֣ר בְּנ֔וֹ וַיָּ֧מָת אַהֲרֹ֛ן שָׁ֖ם בְּרֹ֣אשׁ
הָהָ֑ר וַיֵּ֧רֶד מֹשֶׁ֛ה וְאֶלְעָזָ֖ר מִן־הָהָֽר׃
29 וַיִּרְאוּ֙ כָּל־הָ֣עֵדָ֔ה כִּ֥י גָוַ֖ע אַהֲרֹ֑ן וַיִּבְכּ֤וּ

turning off neither Literally, "we will not stray."

21. To avoid the land of Edom, the Israelites must now journey south toward the Red Sea.

THE DEATH OF AARON (vv. 22–29)

22. arrived On the 1st of *Av* (see 33:38).

24. gathered to his kin This idiom is used only of Israel's forefathers, never of women or of non-Israelites. It means "reunited with his ancestors" and refers to the afterlife in Sheol.

disobeyed My command To sanctify God's name, which Moses and Aaron failed to do when they attributed the miracle to their own powers.

26. Strip Aaron of his vestments Eleazar had already been anointed as his father's successor so that he could take his place whenever his father became incapacitated or ritually impure (see Lev. 6:15).

29. the whole community knew Because Eleazar was wearing Aaron's garments.

---

24. Let Aaron be gathered to his kin Literally, ". . . gathered to his people." Let his good qualities now enter into the souls of those living Israelites who knew him, that those qualities not be lost even after his death.

All the house of Israel bewailed Aaron thirty days.

אֶת־אַהֲרֹן שְׁלֹשִׁים יוֹם כֹּל בֵּית
יִשְׂרָאֵל׃ ס

21 When the Canaanite, king of Arad, who dwelt in the Negeb, learned that Israel was coming by the way of Atharim, he engaged Israel in battle and took some of them captive. [2]Then Israel made a vow to the LORD and said, "If You deliver this people into our hand, we will proscribe their towns." [3]The LORD heeded Israel's plea and delivered up the Canaanites; and they and their cities were proscribed. So that place was named Hormah.

כא וַיִּשְׁמַע הַכְּנַעֲנִי מֶלֶךְ־עֲרָד יֹשֵׁב
הַנֶּגֶב כִּי בָּא יִשְׂרָאֵל דֶּרֶךְ הָאֲתָרִים וַיִּלָּחֶם
בְּיִשְׂרָאֵל וַיִּשְׁבְּ ׀ מִמֶּנּוּ שֶׁבִי׃ 2 וַיִּדַּר יִשְׂרָאֵל
נֶדֶר לַיהוָה וַיֹּאמַר אִם־נָתֹן תִּתֵּן אֶת־
הָעָם הַזֶּה בְּיָדִי וְהַחֲרַמְתִּי אֶת־עָרֵיהֶם׃
3 וַיִּשְׁמַע יְהוָה בְּקוֹל יִשְׂרָאֵל וַיִּתֵּן אֶת־
הַכְּנַעֲנִי וַיַּחֲרֵם אֶתְהֶם וְאֶת־עָרֵיהֶם
וַיִּקְרָא שֵׁם־הַמָּקוֹם חָרְמָה׃ פ

[4]They set out from Mount Hor by way of the Sea of Reeds to skirt the land of Edom. But

4 וַיִּסְעוּ מֵהֹר הָהָר דֶּרֶךְ יַם־סוּף לִסְבֹב
אֶת־אֶרֶץ אֱדוֹם וַתִּקְצַר נֶפֶשׁ־הָעָם בַּדָּרֶךְ׃

thirty days This is an indication of Aaron's importance, because mourning ordinarily lasts for only 7 days (see Gen. 50:10). To be sure, Jacob was mourned for 70 days (Gen. 50:3), but that was in accordance with Egyptian practice.

ENCOUNTER WITH THE CANAANITES (21:1–3)

Israel "turns away" from the Edomites (20:21) and encounters the Canaanites of the Negeb.

1. dwelt Hebrew: *yoshev;* also be understood as "ruled."

2. Israel For the vow to be effective it had to be taken by every soldier.

proscribe Hebrew: *v'haḥaramti;* literally, "put under ban" (*ḥeirem*). This was an extreme form of self-denial. Troops were not salaried in ancient times and were recompensed only by receiving a share of the booty. To dedicate all booty to God is an act of selflessness intended to win the support of the deity.

THE BRONZE SNAKE (vv. 4–9)

While rounding the land of Edom near the Red Sea, the Israelites fall to complaining once again about the lack of food and water. This, the last of Israel's wilderness complaints, is the most grievous, because this time it is in open defiance of the Lord Himself.

4. Sea of Reeds Hebrew: *yam suf.* Here it refers to the Red Sea. (The Israelites had crossed the

---

29. All the house of Israel bewailed Aaron In contrast, later (Deut. 34:8) we will read that "Israelites [but not all Israel] bewailed Moses." Moses, the voice of judgment, was respected—but Aaron the peacemaker was universally loved.

CHAPTER 21

1. learned Literally, "heard." What did the king of Arad hear? That Aaron and Miriam had died. At that point he attacked Israel, suspecting that without those two righteous leaders,

---

HALAKHAH L'MA·ASEH

20:29. thirty days This verse and Deut. 34:8 are the biblical precedents for the 30-day mourning period of *sh'loshim.* For 30 days after burial (*sh'loshim*), the bereaved (the spouse, siblings, children, and parents of the deceased) do not attend dances or parties, although they may attend a wedding ceremony (BT MK 22b). Shaving is also prohibited except if necessary to earn a living, and then only after *shiv·ah,* the first 7 days of mourning. Informational radio and television programing is permitted to the mourner during *sh'loshim.* For children mourning parents, the mourning practices extend for 12 months, except that reciting the mourner's *Kaddish* ends after 11 months.

the people grew restive on the journey, 5and the people spoke against God and against Moses, "Why did you make us leave Egypt to die in the wilderness? There is no bread and no water, and we have come to loathe this miserable food." 6The LORD sent *seraph* serpents against the people. They bit the people and many of the Israelites died. 7The people came to Moses and said, "We sinned by speaking against the LORD and against you. Intercede with the LORD to take away the serpents from us!" And Moses interceded for the people. 8Then the LORD said to Moses, "Make a *seraph* figure and mount it on a standard. And if anyone who is bitten looks at it, he shall recover." 9Moses made a copper serpent and mounted it on a standard; and when anyone was bitten by a serpent, he would look at the copper serpent and recover.

5 וַיְדַבֵּר הָעָם בֵּאלֹהִים וּבְמֹשֶׁה לָמָה
הֶעֱלִיתֻנוּ מִמִּצְרַיִם לָמוּת בַּמִּדְבָּר כִּי אֵין
לֶחֶם וְאֵין מַיִם וְנַפְשֵׁנוּ קָצָה בַּלֶּחֶם
הַקְּלֹקֵל׃ 6 וַיְשַׁלַּח יְהוָה בָּעָם אֵת
הַנְּחָשִׁים הַשְּׂרָפִים וַיְנַשְּׁכוּ אֶת־הָעָם
וַיָּמָת עַם־רָב מִיִּשְׂרָאֵל׃ 7 וַיָּבֹא הָעָם
אֶל־מֹשֶׁה וַיֹּאמְרוּ חָטָאנוּ כִּי־דִבַּרְנוּ
בַיהוָה וָבָךְ הִתְפַּלֵּל אֶל־יְהוָה וְיָסֵר
מֵעָלֵינוּ אֶת־הַנָּחָשׁ וַיִּתְפַּלֵּל מֹשֶׁה בְּעַד
הָעָם׃ 8 וַיֹּאמֶר יְהוָה אֶל־מֹשֶׁה עֲשֵׂה לְךָ
שָׂרָף וְשִׂים אֹתוֹ עַל־נֵס וְהָיָה כָּל־הַנָּשׁוּךְ
וְרָאָה אֹתוֹ וָחָי׃ 9 וַיַּעַשׂ מֹשֶׁה נְחַשׁ נְחֹשֶׁת
וַיְשִׂמֵהוּ עַל־הַנֵּס וְהָיָה אִם־נָשַׁךְ הַנָּחָשׁ
אֶת־אִישׁ וְהִבִּיט אֶל־נְחַשׁ הַנְּחֹשֶׁת וָחָי׃

10The Israelites marched on and encamped

ששי 10 וַיִּסְעוּ בְּנֵי יִשְׂרָאֵל וַיַּחֲנוּ בְּאֹבֹת׃

Sea of Reeds upon leaving Egypt; see Exod. 13:18, 15:4,22.)

5. the people spoke against God and against Moses The opposite of Israel's attitude when they crossed the Sea of Reeds: "they had faith in the LORD and His servant Moses" (Exod. 14:31).

6. seraph The verb *saraf* means "burn." Here it refers to the serpent's poisonous bite.

8. seraph figure A winged snake similar to the Egyptian winged cobra. Its image, engraved on a bronze bowl inscribed with a Hebrew name, was found in the excavation of the royal palace of Nineveh, dating to the end of the 8th century B.C.E. It was believed that looking at it would generate healing. Note, too, that winged snakes are found on many Judahite seals of the pre-exilic period. Contrast this with the winged angelic beings in Isa. 6.

9. copper Hebrew: *n'ḥoshet;* better: "bronze" (see Comment to Exod. 25:3). Note the wordplay between it and *naḥash* (serpent). Abravanel explains that the color of the poisonous snakes could be imitated only by *n'ḥoshet.*

Israel's morale and sense of unity would falter (Israel of Ruzhin).

6. Why are the Israelites punished with serpents for the sin of complaining? Tradition has it that because the serpent caused Adam and Eve to transgress by means of clever words, the serpent would always be the instrument of punishing people who sin with words (Num. R. 19:22). Why did Moses' bronze serpent heal them? According to the Mishnah, it directed the people's thoughts heavenward as they looked up at it (RH 3:8), just as Moses' raised arms directed people's attention heavenward in their battle with Amalek (Exod. 17:11). The *Zohar* explains that looking at the bronze serpent reminded the people of why they deserved to be punished, and that is the first step toward repentance and forgiveness (*Sh'laḥ* 175). Finally, Hirsch suggests that the image of the serpent reminded people of how dangerous the journey through the wilderness was, and how much they depended on God to guide them through it.

In anti-idolatry reforms, King Hezekiah destroyed Moses' bronze serpent, because it had become an object of veneration (2 Kings 18:4). Religion often runs the risk of having people ascribe excessive holiness to one of God's instruments, losing sight of God to whom it points.

at Oboth. [11]They set out from Oboth and encamped at Iye-abarim, in the wilderness bordering on Moab to the east. [12]From there they set out and encamped at the wadi Zered. [13]From there they set out and encamped beyond the Arnon, that is, in the wilderness that extends from the territory of the Amorites. For the Arnon is the boundary of Moab, between Moab and the Amorites. [14]Therefore the Book of the Wars of the Lord speaks of "…Waheb in Suphah, and the wadis: the Arnon [15]with its tributary wadis, stretched along the settled country of Ar, hugging the territory of Moab…"

[16]And from there to Beer, which is the well where the Lord said to Moses, "Assemble the people that I may give them water." [17]Then Israel sang this song:

Spring up, O well—sing to it—
[18]The well which the chieftains dug,
Which the nobles of the people started
With maces, with their own staffs.

And from Midbar to Mattanah, [19]and from Mattanah to Nahaliel, and from Nahaliel to Bamoth, [20]and from Bamoth to the valley that is in the country of Moab, at the peak of Pisgah, overlooking the wasteland.

11 וַיִּסְע֖וּ מֵאֹבֹ֑ת וַֽיַּחֲנ֞וּ בְּעִיֵּ֣י הָֽעֲבָרִ֗ים בַּמִּדְבָּר֙ אֲשֶׁר֙ עַל־פְּנֵ֣י מוֹאָ֔ב מִמִּזְרַ֖ח הַשָּֽׁמֶשׁ׃ 12 מִשָּׁ֖ם נָסָ֑עוּ וַֽיַּחֲנ֖וּ בְּנַ֥חַל זָֽרֶד׃ 13 מִשָּׁם֮ נָסָעוּ֒ וַֽיַּחֲנ֗וּ מֵעֵ֤בֶר אַרְנוֹן֙ אֲשֶׁ֣ר בַּמִּדְבָּ֔ר הַיֹּצֵ֖א מִגְּבֻ֣ל הָֽאֱמֹרִ֑י כִּ֣י אַרְנ֗וֹן גְּב֤וּל מוֹאָב֙ בֵּ֣ין מוֹאָ֔ב וּבֵ֖ין הָֽאֱמֹרִֽי׃ 14 עַל־כֵּן֙ יֵֽאָמַ֔ר בְּסֵ֖פֶר מִלְחֲמֹ֣ת יְהֹוָ֑ה אֶת־וָהֵ֣ב בְּסוּפָ֔ה וְאֶת־הַנְּחָלִ֖ים אַרְנֽוֹן׃ 15 וְאֶ֨שֶׁד֙ הַנְּחָלִ֔ים אֲשֶׁ֥ר נָטָ֖ה לְשֶׁ֣בֶת עָ֑ר וְנִשְׁעַ֖ן לִגְב֥וּל מוֹאָֽב׃ 16 וּמִשָּׁ֖ם בְּאֵ֑רָה הִ֣וא הַבְּאֵ֗ר אֲשֶׁ֨ר אָמַ֤ר יְהֹוָה֙ לְמֹשֶׁ֔ה אֱסֹף֙ אֶת־הָעָ֔ם וְאֶתְּנָ֥ה לָהֶ֖ם מָֽיִם׃ ס 17 אָ֣ז יָשִׁ֤יר יִשְׂרָאֵל֙ אֶת־הַשִּׁירָ֖ה הַזֹּ֑את עֲלִ֥י בְאֵ֖ר עֱנוּ־לָֽהּ׃
18 בְּאֵ֞ר חֲפָר֣וּהָ שָׂרִ֗ים כָּר֙וּהָ֙ נְדִיבֵ֣י הָעָ֔ם בִּמְחֹקֵ֖ק בְּמִשְׁעֲנֹתָ֑ם וּמִמִּדְבָּ֖ר מַתָּנָֽה׃ 19 וּמִמַּתָּנָ֖ה נַֽחֲלִיאֵ֑ל וּמִנַּֽחֲלִיאֵ֖ל בָּמֽוֹת׃ 20 וּמִבָּמ֗וֹת הַגַּיְא֙ אֲשֶׁר֙ בִּשְׂדֵ֣ה מוֹאָ֔ב רֹ֖אשׁ הַפִּסְגָּ֑ה וְנִשְׁקָ֖פָה עַל־פְּנֵ֥י הַיְשִׁימֹֽן׃ פ

שביעי
[רביעי]

THE ROUTE THROUGH TRANSJORDAN
(vv. 10–20)

This section offers a summary of the stations of Israel's march through Transjordan, given in fuller form in 33:41–49.

12. wadi Zered A "wadi" is a ravine through which a stream flows. (The word is from Arabic; in Hebrew it is *naḥal*.) In present-day Israel most wadis are dry except during the rainy season. The wadi Zered (present-day Wadi el-Hesa), however, contains a perennial stream; it is 35 miles (56 km) long and flows into the southeastern end of the Dead Sea.

13. Arnon A perennial stream flowing midway into the eastern end of the Dead Sea through the Wadi el-Mujib, a tremendous ravine that at one point is 2.5 miles (4 km) wide and 1650 feet (500 m) below the tops of the adjoining cliffs. The Arnon unites the waters of a complex of wadis.

territory The Israelites marched in the wilderness that lies to the east of the territories of the Moabites and Amorites.

14. Book of the Wars of the Lord According to Ibn Ezra, this was a separate book which, like the Book of Jashar (Josh. 10:13; 2 Sam. 1:18), was an anthology of early songs describing the saga of Israel's battles at the beginning of its national existence.

17. Then Israel sang Similar words introduce the Song of the Sea (Exod. 15:1).

---

17. Encouraged by early military victories, sustained by having found oases in the wilderness, Israel is now a singing community, grateful and reinvigorated.

21Israel now sent messengers to Sihon king
of the Amorites, saying, 22"Let me pass through
your country. We will not turn off into fields
or vineyards, and we will not drink water from
wells. We will follow the king's highway until
we have crossed your territory." 23But Sihon
would not let Israel pass through his territory.
Sihon gathered all his people and went out
against Israel in the wilderness. He came to
Jahaz and engaged Israel in battle. 24But Israel
put them to the sword, and took possession of
their land, from the Arnon to the Jabbok, as far
as [Az] of the Ammonites, for Az marked the
boundary of the Ammonites. 25Israel took all
those towns. And Israel settled in all the towns
of the Amorites, in Heshbon and all its dependencies.

26Now Heshbon was the city of Sihon king
of the Amorites, who had fought against a former king of Moab and taken all his land from
him as far as the Arnon. 27Therefore the bards
would recite:

"Come to Heshbon; firmly built
And well founded is Sihon's city.
28For fire went forth from Heshbon,
Flame from Sihon's city,
Consuming Ar of Moab,
The lords of Bamoth by the Arnon.
29Woe to you, O Moab!

שביעי
[רביעי]

21 וַיִּשְׁלַח יִשְׂרָאֵל מַלְאָכִים אֶל־סִיחֹן
מֶלֶךְ־הָאֱמֹרִי לֵאמֹר׃ 22 אֶעְבְּרָה בְאַרְצֶךָ
לֹא נִטֶּה בְּשָׂדֶה וּבְכֶרֶם לֹא נִשְׁתֶּה מֵי
בְאֵר בְּדֶרֶךְ הַמֶּלֶךְ נֵלֵךְ עַד אֲשֶׁר־נַעֲבֹר
גְּבֻלֶךָ׃ 23 וְלֹא־נָתַן סִיחֹן אֶת־יִשְׂרָאֵל עֲבֹר
בִּגְבֻלוֹ וַיֶּאֱסֹף סִיחֹן אֶת־כָּל־עַמּוֹ וַיֵּצֵא
לִקְרַאת יִשְׂרָאֵל הַמִּדְבָּרָה וַיָּבֹא יָהְצָה
וַיִּלָּחֶם בְּיִשְׂרָאֵל׃ 24 וַיַּכֵּהוּ יִשְׂרָאֵל לְפִי־
חָרֶב וַיִּירַשׁ אֶת־אַרְצוֹ מֵאַרְנֹן עַד־יַבֹּק
עַד־בְּנֵי עַמּוֹן כִּי עַז גְּבוּל בְּנֵי עַמּוֹן׃
25 וַיִּקַּח יִשְׂרָאֵל אֵת כָּל־הֶעָרִים הָאֵלֶּה
וַיֵּשֶׁב יִשְׂרָאֵל בְּכָל־עָרֵי הָאֱמֹרִי בְּחֶשְׁבּוֹן
וּבְכָל־בְּנֹתֶיהָ׃

26 כִּי חֶשְׁבּוֹן עִיר סִיחֹן מֶלֶךְ הָאֱמֹרִי הִוא
וְהוּא נִלְחַם בְּמֶלֶךְ מוֹאָב הָרִאשׁוֹן וַיִּקַּח
אֶת־כָּל־אַרְצוֹ מִיָּדוֹ עַד־אַרְנֹן׃ 27 עַל־כֵּן
יֹאמְרוּ הַמֹּשְׁלִים

בֹּאוּ חֶשְׁבּוֹן תִּבָּנֶה
וְתִכּוֹנֵן עִיר סִיחוֹן׃
28 כִּי־אֵשׁ יָצְאָה מֵחֶשְׁבּוֹן
לֶהָבָה מִקִּרְיַת סִיחֹן
אָכְלָה עָר מוֹאָב
בַּעֲלֵי בָּמוֹת אַרְנֹן׃
29 אוֹי־לְךָ מוֹאָב

VICTORY OVER SIHON (vv. 21–32)

Moving northward along the eastern (wilderness) edge of Moab, Israel now seeks peaceful passage through the Amorite kingdom of Sihon as it did with Edom. Sihon confronts Israel with an armed force.

21. Israel now sent messengers Either at Moab's boundary from Iye-abarim (v. 11) or from the ford of the Arnon, which separates the Moabites and the Amorites (v. 13).

24. put them to the sword That is, Sihon's army.

Jabbok One of the main eastern tributaries of the Jordan River.

25. its dependencies Literally, "its daughters." In this and in similar contexts, the distinction between "mother" and "daughter" is that between walled city and open village.

27. bards Hebrew: *ha-mosh'lim,* those who recite *m'shalim* (sing. *mashal*)—from the stem משל (to be like). *M'shalim* included proverb, parable, riddle, and allegory. They could vary from pithy folk maxims to longer artistic compositions, such as Job's discourses and the contents of the Book of Proverbs. They also included taunt songs mocking a foe, such as the following poem, which first recalls the gloating of the newly defeated Amorites over the previously defeated Moabites.

28. fire went forth This image is frequently used for a ravaging army.

Ar A city or district near the Arnon River.

29. Woe Hebrew: *oi,* which also occurs as

You are undone, O people of Chemosh!
His sons are rendered fugitive
And his daughters captive
By an Amorite king, Sihon."
30Yet we have cast them down utterly,
Heshbon along with Dibon;
We have wrought desolation at Nophah,
Which is hard by Medeba.
31So Israel occupied the land of the Amorites.
32Then Moses sent to spy out Jazer, and they
captured its dependencies and dispossessed the
Amorites who were there.

33They marched on and went up the road to
Bashan, and King Og of Bashan, with all his people, came out to Edrei to engage them in battle.
34But the LORD said to Moses, "Do not fear him,
for I give him and all his people and his land
into your hand. You shall do to him as you did
to Sihon king of the Amorites who dwelt in
Heshbon." 35They defeated him and his sons
and all his people, until no remnant was left
him; and they took possession of his country.

אָבַדְתָּ עַם־כְּמוֹשׁ
נָתַן בָּנָיו פְּלֵיטִם֙
וּבְנֹתָיו בַּשְּׁבִית
לְמֶלֶךְ אֱמֹרִי סִיחוֹן׃
30 וַנִּירָם אָבַד
חֶשְׁבּוֹן עַד־דִּיבוֹן
וַנַּשִּׁים עַד־נֹפַח
אֲשֶׁר֙* עַד־מֵידְבָא׃
31 וַיֵּשֶׁב֙ יִשְׂרָאֵל בְּאֶרֶץ הָאֱמֹרִי׃ 32 וַיִּשְׁלַח
מֹשֶׁה֙ לְרַגֵּל אֶת־יַעְזֵר וַיִּלְכְּדוּ בְּנֹתֶיהָ ויירש
וַיּוֹרֶשׁ אֶת־הָאֱמֹרִי אֲשֶׁר־שָׁם׃

33 וַיִּפְנוּ֙ וַיַּעֲלוּ דֶּרֶךְ הַבָּשָׁן וַיֵּצֵא עוֹג
מֶלֶךְ־הַבָּשָׁן לִקְרָאתָם הוּא וְכָל־עַמּוֹ
מפטיר לַמִּלְחָמָה אֶדְרֶעִי׃ 34 וַיֹּאמֶר יְהוָה אֶל־
מֹשֶׁה֙ אַל־תִּירָא אֹתוֹ כִּי בְיָדְךָ נָתַתִּי אֹתוֹ
וְאֶת־כָּל־עַמּוֹ וְאֶת־אַרְצוֹ וְעָשִׂיתָ לּוֹ
כַּאֲשֶׁר עָשִׂיתָ לְסִיחֹן֙ מֶלֶךְ הָאֱמֹרִי אֲשֶׁר
יוֹשֵׁב בְּחֶשְׁבּוֹן׃ 35 וַיַּכּוּ אֹתוֹ וְאֶת־בָּנָיו֙
וְאֶת־כָּל־עַמּוֹ עַד־בִּלְתִּי הִשְׁאִיר־לוֹ שָׂרִיד

v. 30. נקוד על ר׳

hoi. Exclaimed when facing death (1 Kings 13:30; Jer. 22:18) or predicting catastrophe (Isa. 3:9,11).

people of Chemosh Chemosh was the national deity of Moab. The phrase refers to the Moabites, just as the Israelites are called "the people of *YHVH*."

are rendered Literally, "he rendered." The god Chemosh willingly surrenders his subjects. In the ancient Near East, a nationwide disaster was often considered the result of a decision made by the national deity.

VICTORY OVER OG (vv. 33–35)

The campaign against Og differs from that against Sihon. No messengers are sent requesting passage, because the way across the Jordan has already been secured with the victory over Sihon. Also, whereas the battle against Sihon is undertaken at Israel's initiative (the name of God does not appear in vv. 21–32), here the campaign against Og is expressly commissioned by the Lord (v. 34). The land of Og, in contrast to Sihon's land, is part of the Promised Land, which includes the Bashan (34:10–11). Thus the Lord commands the conquest of the Bashan as part of the conquest of Canaan.

33. Bashan This includes the area bounded by Mount Hermon to the north, Jebel Druze to the east, the hills east of the Sea of Galilee to the west, extending to about six miles (10 km) south of the Yarmuk River.

Og An Amorite. The prophet Amos described the Amorites as a people "Whose stature was like the cedar's / And who was stout as the oak" (Amos 2:9). Og himself was remembered as the last of the giant Rephaim (Deut. 3:11; see also 2 Sam. 21:16–22).

Edrei Identified with modern Der'a, it was located near the Yarmuk River and the desert, probably at the southeast border of Og's kingdom.

22

[1]The Israelites then marched on and encamped in the steppes of Moab, across the Jordan from Jericho.

כב

וַיִּירְשׁ֖וּ אֶת־אַרְצֽוֹ׃ 1 וַיִּסְע֖וּ בְּנֵ֣י
יִשְׂרָאֵ֑ל וַֽיַּחֲנוּ֙ בְּעַֽרְב֣וֹת מוֹאָ֔ב
מֵעֵ֖בֶר לְיַרְדֵּ֥ן יְרֵחֽוֹ׃* ס

22:1. This verse is a transition to the last third of the Book of Numbers, which deals with events that occurred and laws that were given at the banks of the Jordan before entry into the Promised Land. The point of origin of this last stage of the march is not given.

steppes of Moab The eastern portion of the lower Jordan plain before it empties into the Dead Sea.

opposite Jericho At the point of the Jordan River located at Jericho.

* *For the* haftarah *for this portion, see p. 909.*

²Balak son of Zippor saw all that Israel had done to the Amorites.

³Moab was alarmed because that people was so numerous. Moab dreaded the Israelites, ⁴and Moab said to the elders of Midian, "Now this horde will lick clean all that is about us as an ox licks up the grass of the field."

Balak son of Zippor, who was king of Moab at that time, ⁵sent messengers to Balaam son of Beor in Pethor, which is by the Euphrates, in the land of his kinsfolk, to invite him, saying, "There is a people that came out of Egypt; it hides the earth from view, and it is settled next to me. ⁶Come then, put a curse upon this people

² וַיַּ֥רְא בָּלָ֖ק בֶּן־צִפּ֑וֹר אֵ֥ת כָּל־אֲשֶׁר־עָשָׂ֛ה יִשְׂרָאֵ֖ל לָאֱמֹרִֽי׃

³ וַיָּ֨גָר מוֹאָ֜ב מִפְּנֵ֥י הָעָ֛ם מְאֹ֖ד כִּ֣י רַב־ה֑וּא וַיָּ֣קָץ מוֹאָ֔ב מִפְּנֵ֖י בְּנֵ֥י יִשְׂרָאֵֽל׃ ⁴ וַיֹּ֨אמֶר מוֹאָ֜ב אֶל־זִקְנֵ֣י מִדְיָ֗ן עַתָּ֞ה יְלַחֲכ֤וּ הַקָּהָל֙ אֶת־כָּל־סְבִ֣יבֹתֵ֔ינוּ כִּלְחֹ֣ךְ הַשּׁ֔וֹר אֵ֖ת יֶ֥רֶק הַשָּׂדֶ֑ה

וּבָלָ֧ק בֶּן־צִפּ֛וֹר מֶ֥לֶךְ לְמוֹאָ֖ב בָּעֵ֥ת הַהִֽוא׃ ⁵ וַיִּשְׁלַ֨ח מַלְאָכִ֜ים אֶל־בִּלְעָ֣ם בֶּן־בְּע֗וֹר פְּת֞וֹרָה אֲשֶׁ֧ר עַל־הַנָּהָ֛ר אֶ֥רֶץ בְּנֵי־עַמּ֖וֹ לִקְרֹא־ל֑וֹ לֵאמֹ֗ר הִ֠נֵּה עַ֣ם יָצָ֤א מִמִּצְרַ֙יִם֙ הִנֵּ֤ה כִסָּה֙ אֶת־עֵ֣ין הָאָ֔רֶץ וְה֥וּא יֹשֵׁ֖ב מִמֻּלִֽי׃ ⁶ וְעַתָּה֩ לְכָה־נָּ֨א אָֽרָה־לִּ֜י אֶת־

BALAAM THE DIVINER (22:2–24:25)

THE HIRING OF BALAAM (22:2–21)

2. Amorites The kingdom of Sihon, mentioned in 21:21,25–26,31–32.

4. elders of Midian Midian was a confederation of peoples, some of whom may have been ruled by the Moabite king.

5. Pethor Identified with Pitru on the Sajur River, a tributary of the Euphrates, some 12 miles (20 km) south of Carchemish. It was at least a

20-day journey from Pethor to Moab, a distance of about 400 miles (640 km). Because the text records four such journeys, the traveling would have taken about three months.

it hides the earth from view Israel is compared with a locust plague, a common simile for an invading army.

6. Balaam's curse is expected to weaken the Israelites so that Moab can defeat them in battle and expel them from its land.

This *parashah* contains what may be the only comic passage in the Torah. It tells how Balaam, reputedly the world's most powerful wizard, cannot find his way out of his own neighborhood, and how his attempts to curse Israel are turned into blessings in his mouth. The overall message, however, is a serious one: God continues to watch over Israel and extend divine protection to them, despite their recalcitrant behavior and lack of appreciation. Human efforts to harm the people Israel will not prevail.

This story's most memorable feature is the talking donkey. Here, as in so many tales in folklore when animals behave like humans, it raises questions: "What does it mean to be human? What makes us different from other animals?" Seeing the angel blocking the path, the donkey can recognize, better than Balaam does, that what they are setting out to do is wrong. Human beings should have the capacity to know right from wrong. When temptation and weakness blind us to the wrongness of what we are doing, we are no better than dumb animals.

Some rabbinical sources see Balaam as an authentic prophet, sent to the gentiles as Moses was sent to the Israelites. For that reason, his incantations were to be feared and God had to change his curses into blessings. Others see Balaam as a pathetic, arrogant fraud whose only successful trick was to fool himself into believing that God approved of his intentions. "When the gift of prophecy was given to the gentile nations, many of them misused it, seeking to destroy rather than to bless" (Tanḥ. 1).

for me, since they are too numerous for me; perhaps I can thus defeat them and drive them out of the land. For I know that he whom you bless is blessed indeed, and he whom you curse is cursed."

[7]The elders of Moab and the elders of Midian, versed in divination, set out. They came to Balaam and gave him Balak's message. [8]He said to them, "Spend the night here, and I shall reply to you as the LORD may instruct me." So the Moabite dignitaries stayed with Balaam.

[9]God came to Balaam and said, "What do these people want of you?" [10]Balaam said to God, "Balak son of Zippor, king of Moab, sent me this message: [11]Here is a people that came out from Egypt and hides the earth from view. Come now and curse them for me; perhaps I can engage them in battle and drive them off." [12]But God said to Balaam, "Do not go with them. You must not curse that people, for they are blessed."

[13]Balaam arose in the morning and said to Balak's dignitaries, "Go back to your own country,

הָעָם הַזֶּה כִּי־עָצוּם הוּא מִמֶּנִּי אוּלַי
אוּכַל נַכֶּה־בּוֹ וַאֲגָרְשֶׁנּוּ מִן־הָאָרֶץ כִּי
יָדַעְתִּי אֵת אֲשֶׁר־תְּבָרֵךְ מְבֹרָךְ וַאֲשֶׁר
תָּאֹר יוּאָר׃
7 וַיֵּלְכוּ זִקְנֵי מוֹאָב וְזִקְנֵי מִדְיָן וּקְסָמִים
בְּיָדָם וַיָּבֹאוּ אֶל־בִּלְעָם וַיְדַבְּרוּ אֵלָיו דִּבְרֵי
בָלָק׃ 8 וַיֹּאמֶר אֲלֵיהֶם לִינוּ פֹה הַלַּיְלָה
וַהֲשִׁבֹתִי אֶתְכֶם דָּבָר כַּאֲשֶׁר יְדַבֵּר יְהוָה
אֵלָי וַיֵּשְׁבוּ שָׂרֵי־מוֹאָב עִם־בִּלְעָם׃
9 וַיָּבֹא אֱלֹהִים אֶל־בִּלְעָם וַיֹּאמֶר מִי
הָאֲנָשִׁים הָאֵלֶּה עִמָּךְ׃ 10 וַיֹּאמֶר בִּלְעָם
אֶל־הָאֱלֹהִים בָּלָק בֶּן־צִפֹּר מֶלֶךְ מוֹאָב
שָׁלַח אֵלָי׃ 11 הִנֵּה הָעָם הַיֹּצֵא מִמִּצְרַיִם
וַיְכַס אֶת־עֵין הָאָרֶץ עַתָּה לְכָה קָבָה־לִּי
אֹתוֹ אוּלַי אוּכַל לְהִלָּחֶם בּוֹ וְגֵרַשְׁתִּיו׃
12 וַיֹּאמֶר אֱלֹהִים אֶל־בִּלְעָם לֹא תֵלֵךְ
עִמָּהֶם לֹא תָאֹר אֶת־הָעָם כִּי בָרוּךְ
הוּא׃
13 וַיָּקָם בִּלְעָם בַּבֹּקֶר וַיֹּאמֶר אֶל־שָׂרֵי ני
בָלָק לְכוּ אֶל־אַרְצְכֶם כִּי מֵאֵן יְהוָה ישי]

7. versed in divination The Hebrew idiom may mean that they took divinatory materials with them. The text emphasizes that Balaam is a diviner (one who predicts the future), not a sorcerer (one who alters the future through cursing and blessing), as Balak makes him out to be.

8. Spend the night Thus Balaam might receive a divine message in a dream.

9. What do these people want God, of course knows, but uses this rhetorical question to open a conversation (as in Gen. 3:9, 4:9).

12. they are blessed They are already blessed from the time of the patriarchs, and the blessing cannot be reversed by a curse.

13. Balaam arose in the morning Evidently, God appeared to him in the night.

the LORD will not let me go Balaam omits the full reason—that cursing Israel is futile—not because he hoped later to change God's mind but because it would have brought the episode to an end had the emissaries reported this reason to Balak.

the LORD It was not unusual for a non-Israelite to invoke the name of Israel's God. Abimelech the Philistine did that in Gen. 26:28.

"The opposition between God and the sorcerer is the opposition between the true Deity and human wisdom. Sorcery is one of the heathen arts, grounded in people's believing in their own power to force God to reveal the divine secrets" (Y. Kaufmann).

CHAPTER 22

2–20. The first mention of Balak (v. 2) does not describe him as a king. One account has him beginning as a courtier who seized the throne by manipulating people's fear of Israel (Ḥ. Soloveichik).

Why didn't Balak hire Balaam to bless his own people rather than to curse Israel (since "whom you bless is blessed indeed," v. 6)? He was so consumed by hatred that he forgot about his people's needs and could think only about hurting his enemy (*Beit Ramah*).

In verse 12, God tells Balaam not to go, so

for the LORD will not let me go with you." [14]The Moabite dignitaries left, and they came to Balak and said, "Balaam refused to come with us."

[15]Then Balak sent other dignitaries, more numerous and distinguished than the first. [16]They came to Balaam and said to him, "Thus says Balak son of Zippor: Please do not refuse to come to me. [17]I will reward you richly and I will do anything you ask of me. Only come and damn this people for me." [18]Balaam replied to Balak's officials, "Though Balak were to give me his house full of silver and gold, I could not do anything, big or little, contrary to the command of the LORD my God. [19]So you, too, stay here overnight, and let me find out what else the LORD may say to me." [20]That night God came to Balaam and said to him, "If these men have come to invite you, you may go with them. But whatever I command you, that you shall do."

[21]When he arose in the morning, Balaam saddled his ass and departed with the Moabite dig-

לְתִתִּ֖י לַהֲלֹ֥ךְ עִמָּכֶֽם׃ 14 וַיָּק֙וּמוּ֙ שָׂרֵ֣י מוֹאָ֔ב
וַיָּבֹ֖אוּ אֶל־בָּלָ֑ק וַיֹּ֣אמְר֔וּ מֵאֵ֥ן בִּלְעָ֖ם הֲלֹ֥ךְ
עִמָּֽנוּ׃
15 וַיֹּ֥סֶף ע֖וֹד בָּלָ֑ק שְׁלֹ֣חַ שָׂרִ֔ים רַבִּ֥ים
וְנִכְבָּדִ֖ים מֵאֵֽלֶּה׃ 16 וַיָּבֹ֖אוּ אֶל־בִּלְעָ֑ם
וַיֹּ֣אמְרוּ ל֗וֹ כֹּ֤ה אָמַר֙ בָּלָ֣ק בֶּן־צִפּ֔וֹר אַל־נָ֥א
תִמָּנַ֖ע מֵהֲלֹ֥ךְ אֵלָֽי׃ 17 כִּֽי־כַבֵּ֤ד אֲכַבֶּדְךָ֙
מְאֹ֔ד וְכֹ֛ל אֲשֶׁר־תֹּאמַ֥ר אֵלַ֖י אֶֽעֱשֶׂ֑ה וּלְכָה־
נָּא֙ קָבָה־לִּ֔י אֵ֖ת הָעָ֥ם הַזֶּֽה׃ 18 וַיַּ֣עַן בִּלְעָ֗ם
וַיֹּ֙אמֶר֙ אֶל־עַבְדֵ֣י בָלָ֔ק אִם־יִתֶּן־לִ֥י בָלָ֛ק
מְלֹ֥א בֵית֖וֹ כֶּ֣סֶף וְזָהָ֑ב לֹ֣א אוּכַ֗ל לַעֲבֹר֙
אֶת־פִּי֙ יְהוָ֣ה אֱלֹהָ֔י לַעֲשׂ֥וֹת קְטַנָּ֖ה א֥וֹ
גְדוֹלָֽה׃ 19 וְעַתָּ֗ה שְׁב֨וּ נָ֥א בָזֶ֛ה גַּם־אַתֶּ֖ם
הַלָּ֑יְלָה וְאֵ֣דְעָ֔ה מַה־יֹּסֵ֥ף יְהוָ֖ה דַּבֵּ֥ר עִמִּֽי׃
20 וַיָּבֹ֨א אֱלֹהִ֥ים ׀ אֶל־בִּלְעָם֮ לַיְלָה֒ וַיֹּ֣אמֶר
ל֗וֹ אִם־לִקְרֹ֤א לְךָ֙ בָּ֣אוּ הָאֲנָשִׁ֔ים ק֖וּם לֵ֣ךְ
אִתָּ֑ם וְאַ֗ךְ אֶת־הַדָּבָ֛ר אֲשֶׁר־אֲדַבֵּ֥ר אֵלֶ֖יךָ
אֹת֥וֹ תַעֲשֶֽׂה׃
שלישי 21 וַיָּ֤קָם בִּלְעָם֙ בַּבֹּ֔קֶר וַֽיַּחֲבֹ֖שׁ אֶת־אֲתֹנ֑וֹ

14. The emissaries do not mention that the Lord is the author of Balaam's refusal. The narrator may be indicating that the Moabites were so convinced of Balaam's inherent power to curse Israel that they regarded Balaam's reliance on the Lord as an excuse to back out.

17. I will reward you richly Literally, "I will honor you greatly." This is a euphemism for monetary rewards, as the next verse makes explicit.

18. The LORD my God This affirmation might explain why Moab sought the help of Balaam even though the seer lived so far away. Perhaps Moab believed that Balaam's allegiance to and intimacy with Israel's God would stand him in good stead as he attempted to persuade God to curse His people Israel.

19. what else Perhaps the Lord will change His mind. Such indeed is the unspoken premise behind all forms of divination. The same ritual procedures are repeated until a favorable omen is received. Even in dream interpretation, a single dream is not decisive. Thus Balaam can sincerely hope that in his second dream he will learn that the Lord has changed His mind.

20. That night God came to Balaam That is, in a dream.

---

he spurns the Moabite invitation. Balak sends a second delegation, adding an element not mentioned by the first: "I will reward you richly" (v. 17). Can we see Balaam's dream in verse 20 as arising from a repressed wish to accept the assignment? Did the wizard, blinded by the prospect of riches, fool himself into believing that Balak's request was legitimate? In the view of Maimonides, based on a comment in the Midrash, God did not simply give Balaam permission to go, but gave him permission to exercise his free will. As the Midrash puts it, "I desire not the destruction of the wicked, but since you are bent on following this path that will lead to your destruction, I will not prevent you from doing so" (Num. R. 20:12).

21. Balaam saddled his ass The Sages take this as implying his great eagerness to set forth.

departed with the Moabite dignitaries Suggests that he was fully with them in intent (BT Sanh. 105b).

nitaries. [22]But God was incensed at his going; so an angel of the LORD placed himself in his way as an adversary.

He was riding on his she-ass, with his two servants alongside, [23]when the ass caught sight of the angel of the LORD standing in the way, with his drawn sword in his hand. The ass swerved from the road and went into the fields; and Balaam beat the ass to turn her back onto the road. [24]The angel of the LORD then stationed himself in a lane between the vineyards, with a fence on either side. [25]The ass, seeing the angel of the LORD, pressed herself against the wall and squeezed Balaam's foot against the wall; so he beat her again. [26]Once more the angel of the LORD moved forward and stationed himself on a spot so narrow that there was no room to swerve right or left. [27]When the ass now saw the angel of the LORD, she lay down under Balaam; and Balaam was furious and beat the ass with his stick.

[28]Then the LORD opened the ass's mouth, and she said to Balaam, "What have I done to you that you have beaten me these three times?" [29]Balaam said to the ass, "You have made a mockery of me! If I had a sword with me, I'd

וַיֵּלֶךְ עִם־שָׂרֵי מוֹאָב׃ 22 וַיִּחַר־אַף אֱלֹהִים
כִּי־הוֹלֵךְ הוּא וַיִּתְיַצֵּב מַלְאַךְ יְהוָה בַּדֶּרֶךְ
לְשָׂטָן לוֹ
וְהוּא רֹכֵב עַל־אֲתֹנוֹ וּשְׁנֵי נְעָרָיו עִמּוֹ׃
23 וַתֵּרֶא הָאָתוֹן אֶת־מַלְאַךְ יְהוָה נִצָּב
בַּדֶּרֶךְ וְחַרְבּוֹ שְׁלוּפָה בְּיָדוֹ וַתֵּט הָאָתוֹן
מִן־הַדֶּרֶךְ וַתֵּלֶךְ בַּשָּׂדֶה וַיַּךְ בִּלְעָם אֶת־
הָאָתוֹן לְהַטֹּתָהּ הַדָּרֶךְ׃ 24 וַיַּעֲמֹד מַלְאַךְ
יְהוָה בְּמִשְׁעוֹל הַכְּרָמִים גָּדֵר מִזֶּה וְגָדֵר
מִזֶּה׃ 25 וַתֵּרֶא הָאָתוֹן אֶת־מַלְאַךְ יְהוָה
וַתִּלָּחֵץ אֶל־הַקִּיר וַתִּלְחַץ אֶת־רֶגֶל בִּלְעָם
אֶל־הַקִּיר וַיֹּסֶף לְהַכֹּתָהּ׃ 26 וַיּוֹסֶף מַלְאַךְ־
יְהוָה עֲבוֹר וַיַּעֲמֹד בְּמָקוֹם צָר אֲשֶׁר
אֵין־דֶּרֶךְ לִנְטוֹת יָמִין וּשְׂמֹאול׃ 27 וַתֵּרֶא
הָאָתוֹן אֶת־מַלְאַךְ יְהוָה וַתִּרְבַּץ תַּחַת
בִּלְעָם וַיִּחַר־אַף בִּלְעָם וַיַּךְ אֶת־הָאָתוֹן
בַּמַּקֵּל׃
28 וַיִּפְתַּח יְהוָה אֶת־פִּי הָאָתוֹן וַתֹּאמֶר
לְבִלְעָם מֶה־עָשִׂיתִי לְךָ כִּי הִכִּיתַנִי זֶה
שָׁלֹשׁ רְגָלִים׃ 29 וַיֹּאמֶר בִּלְעָם לָאָתוֹן כִּי
הִתְעַלַּלְתְּ בִּי לוּ יֶשׁ־חֶרֶב בְּיָדִי כִּי עַתָּה

BALAAM AND THE ASS (vv. 22–35)

22. But God was incensed Balaam's compliance indicates his eagerness to curse Israel, arousing the anger of God.

two servants Balak's officials have disappeared.

23. into the fields Implies that the fields had no fences along the road.

24. a lane Perhaps a hollowed-out furrow that served as a path.

fence Literally, "a wall of stones."

25. wall That is, the surface of the stony fence.

beat her again The first time was for a purpose—to get the ass back on the road. Here, the lack of purpose serves to indicate that Balaam struck the ass in sheer anger. The story about the ass lampoons Balaam, making him out to be a fool.

27. When the ass now saw For the third time, in contrast to Balaam's persistent blindness.

with his stick An index of his mounting anger; perhaps previously he struck with his hand or a strap.

28. The LORD opened the ass's mouth That is, God gave the ass the power of speech. Note that the use of fables—stories of talking animals or plants—is rare in the Bible (see Gen. 3:1–5; for Jotham's see Judg. 9:7–15).

29. If I had a sword The irony rests in the

---

25. A rabbinical tradition identifies this wall with the pile of stones erected by Jacob and Laban (Gen. 31:51), each promising never to cross that point with hostile intent toward the other. Balaam, identified as a descendant of Laban the Aramean (see Num. 23:7), is about to violate that accord.

29. If I had a sword This sorcerer, who is

kill you." 30The ass said to Balaam, "Look, I am the ass that you have been riding all along until this day! Have I been in the habit of doing thus to you?" And he answered, "No."

31Then the LORD uncovered Balaam's eyes, and he saw the angel of the LORD standing in the way, his drawn sword in his hand; thereupon he bowed right down to the ground. 32The angel of the LORD said to him, "Why have you beaten your ass these three times? It is I who came out as an adversary, for the errand is obnoxious to me. 33And when the ass saw me, she shied away because of me those three times. If she had not shied away from me, you are the one I should have killed, while sparing her." 34Balaam said to the angel of the LORD, "I erred because I did not know that you were standing in my way. If you still disapprove, I will turn back." 35But the angel of the LORD said to Balaam, "Go with the men. But you must say nothing except what I tell you." So Balaam went on with Balak's dignitaries.

הֲרַגְתִּיךְ׃ 30 וַתֹּאמֶר הָאָתוֹן אֶל־בִּלְעָם
הֲלוֹא אָנֹכִי אֲתֹנְךָ אֲשֶׁר־רָכַבְתָּ עָלַי
מֵעוֹדְךָ עַד־הַיּוֹם הַזֶּה הַהַסְכֵּן הִסְכַּנְתִּי
לַעֲשׂוֹת לְךָ כֹּה וַיֹּאמֶר לֹא׃
31 וַיְגַל יְהוָה אֶת־עֵינֵי בִלְעָם וַיַּרְא אֶת־
מַלְאַךְ יְהוָה נִצָּב בַּדֶּרֶךְ וְחַרְבּוֹ שְׁלֻפָה
בְּיָדוֹ וַיִּקֹּד וַיִּשְׁתַּחוּ לְאַפָּיו׃ 32 וַיֹּאמֶר אֵלָיו
מַלְאַךְ יְהוָה עַל־מָה הִכִּיתָ אֶת־אֲתֹנְךָ זֶה
שָׁלוֹשׁ רְגָלִים הִנֵּה אָנֹכִי יָצָאתִי לְשָׂטָן
כִּי־יָרַט הַדֶּרֶךְ לְנֶגְדִּי׃ 33 וַתִּרְאַנִי הָאָתוֹן
וַתֵּט לְפָנַי זֶה שָׁלֹשׁ רְגָלִים אוּלַי נָטְתָה
מִפָּנַי כִּי עַתָּה גַּם־אֹתְכָה* הָרַגְתִּי וְאוֹתָהּ
הֶחֱיֵיתִי׃ 34 וַיֹּאמֶר בִּלְעָם אֶל־מַלְאַךְ יְהוָה
חָטָאתִי כִּי לֹא יָדַעְתִּי כִּי אַתָּה נִצָּב
לִקְרָאתִי בַּדָּרֶךְ וְעַתָּה אִם־רַע בְּעֵינֶיךָ
אָשׁוּבָה לִּי׃ 35 וַיֹּאמֶר מַלְאַךְ יְהוָה אֶל־
בִּלְעָם לֵךְ עִם־הָאֲנָשִׁים וְאֶפֶס אֶת־הַדָּבָר
אֲשֶׁר־אֲדַבֵּר אֵלֶיךָ אֹתוֹ תְדַבֵּר וַיֵּלֶךְ בִּלְעָם
עִם־שָׂרֵי בָלָק׃

v. 33. יתיר ה׳

fact that the sword Balaam seeks is close at hand with the angel, whom he, the seer, cannot see.

30. Have I been in the habit Balaam's impetuous rage is answered by the considered and justifiable argument of the ass.

31. the LORD uncovered Balaam's eyes The wording is deliberate, a sardonic contradiction of Balaam's claim that his "eyes are opened" to God's revelation (24:4,16).

32–33. these three times . . . those three times This expression is repeated by the angel to mock Balaam: The dumb animal shied away from me three times; but you, the all-wise seer, did not shy away from me even once.

34. I did not know In contradiction to Balaam's claim that he "obtains knowledge from the Most High" (24:16).

35. Balaam's two servants, who disappeared, have been replaced by Balak's dignitaries.

what I tell you The angel, here identified with the "I" of the Lord, thus speaks or acts as the Lord's surrogate.

---

setting out to destroy an entire people with words, needs a sword to harm a donkey (Tanḥ. 9). The passage calls to mind the comment of the Sages that one who gives a sword to an angry person violates the commandment "You shall not place a stumbling block before the blind" (Lev. 19:14). Rationalist commentators interpret the incident of the talking ass in a nonliteral manner. Maimonides sees it occurring in a dream. Luzzatto suggests that the donkey brayed plaintively and Balaam intuited what it was trying to convey. The Midrash lists Balaam's ass as one of several miracles created by God in the last hours of Creation. This would mean that its speaking did not violate natural law. God created a world in which donkeys would not speak, except for this donkey at this moment.

36When Balak heard that Balaam was coming, he went out to meet him at Ir-moab, which is on the Arnon border, at its farthest point. 37Balak said to Balaam, "When I first sent to invite you, why didn't you come to me? Am I really unable to reward you?" 38But Balaam said to Balak, "And now that I have come to you, have I the power to speak freely? I can utter only the word that God puts into my mouth."

39Balaam went with Balak and they came to Kiriath-huzoth.

40Balak sacrificed oxen and sheep, and had them served to Balaam and the dignitaries with him. 41In the morning Balak took Balaam up to Bamoth-baal. From there he could see a portion of the people.

23
Balaam said to Balak, "Build me seven altars here and have seven bulls and seven rams ready here for me." 2Balak did as Balaam di-

36 וַיִּשְׁמַ֤ע בָּלָק֙ כִּי־בָ֣א בִלְעָ֔ם וַיֵּצֵ֞א לִקְרָאת֗וֹ אֶל־עִ֤יר מוֹאָב֙ אֲשֶׁ֣ר עַל־גְּב֣וּל אַרְנֹ֔ן אֲשֶׁ֖ר בִּקְצֵ֥ה הַגְּבֽוּל׃ 37 וַיֹּ֨אמֶר בָּלָ֜ק אֶל־בִּלְעָ֗ם הֲלֹא֩ שָׁלֹ֨חַ שָׁלַ֤חְתִּי אֵלֶ֙יךָ֙ לִקְרֹא־לָ֔ךְ לָ֥מָּה לֹא־הָלַ֖כְתָּ אֵלָ֑י הַֽאֻמְנָ֔ם לֹ֥א אוּכַ֖ל כַּבְּדֶֽךָ׃ 38 וַיֹּ֨אמֶר בִּלְעָ֜ם אֶל־בָּלָ֗ק הִֽנֵּה־בָ֙אתִי֙ אֵלֶ֔יךָ עַתָּ֕ה הֲיָכֹ֥ל אוּכַ֖ל דַּבֵּ֣ר מְא֑וּמָה הַדָּבָ֗ר אֲשֶׁ֨ר יָשִׂ֧ים אֱלֹהִ֛ים בְּפִ֖י אֹת֥וֹ אֲדַבֵּֽר׃

רביעי [ששי] 39 וַיֵּ֥לֶךְ בִּלְעָ֖ם עִם־בָּלָ֑ק וַיָּבֹ֖אוּ קִרְיַ֥ת חֻצֽוֹת׃ 40 וַיִּזְבַּ֥ח בָּלָ֖ק בָּקָ֣ר וָצֹ֑אן וַיְשַׁלַּ֣ח לְבִלְעָ֔ם וְלַשָּׂרִ֖ים אֲשֶׁ֥ר אִתּֽוֹ׃ 41 וַיְהִ֣י בַבֹּ֔קֶר וַיִּקַּ֤ח בָּלָק֙ אֶת־בִּלְעָ֔ם וַֽיַּעֲלֵ֖הוּ בָּמ֣וֹת בָּ֑עַל וַיַּ֥רְא מִשָּׁ֖ם קְצֵ֥ה הָעָֽם׃

כג וַיֹּ֤אמֶר בִּלְעָם֙ אֶל־בָּלָ֔ק בְּנֵה־לִ֥י בָזֶ֖ה שִׁבְעָ֣ה מִזְבְּחֹ֑ת וְהָכֵ֥ן לִ֛י בָּזֶ֖ה שִׁבְעָ֣ה פָרִ֖ים וְשִׁבְעָ֥ה אֵילִֽים׃ 2 וַיַּ֣עַשׂ בָּלָ֔ק כַּֽאֲשֶׁ֖ר

THE MEETING OF BALAK AND BALAAM
(22:36–23:6)

36. Ir-moab Probably identical with Ar of Moab (21:15,28) on the southern shore of the upper Arnon River.

Arnon border That is, the northern border of Moab, which presumes that Balaam came from the north.

at its farthest point Balak paid Balaam the utmost respect due him by meeting him at the point at which Balaam crossed into Moabite territory.

40. sacrificed Balak sacrificed a well-being offering (*zevaḥ sh'lamim*), the meat of which is eaten by the worshiper and his guests.

41. In the morning Sacrificial ritual implies entering into a state of sanctification, a preliminary requirement for a divine encounter.

he could see a portion of the people The object must be within sight for a curse against it to be effective. Balak, however, fears that the sight of too many Israelites may nullify and even reverse the curse. Hence, he allows Balaam to see only a portion of the Israelites.

CHAPTER 23

Presumably Balaam's curses would have no effect. Why does God go to the trouble of directing his speech? The Midrash comments on verse 5 ("the LORD put a word in Balaam's mouth"): "As a rider puts a bit in the mouth of his horse, to control him" (Num. R. 20:20). Astruc suggests that God did this lest others interpret any disaster that might befall Israel as resulting from Balaam's curse, strengthening their belief in wizardry. Abravanel says

that it is to avoid Israel's enemies' gaining confidence from Balaam's words. Kaspi notes, "A true friend will spare his friend mental anguish and concern, even if he knows there is no basis for it." The Israelites, having grown up in Egypt, a land of superstition and sorcery, might tend to take Balaam's curses seriously and thus be demoralized. By the same token, they might be strengthened by his blessings. Praise from a prominent gentile might heighten their devotion to achieving their goals.

rected; and Balak and Balaam offered up a bull and a ram on each altar. 3Then Balaam said to Balak, "Stay here beside your offerings while I am gone. Perhaps the LORD will grant me a manifestation, and whatever He reveals to me I will tell you." And he went off alone.

4God manifested Himself to Balaam, who said to Him, "I have set up the seven altars and offered up a bull and a ram on each altar." 5And the LORD put a word in Balaam's mouth and said, "Return to Balak and speak thus."

6So he returned to him and found him standing beside his offerings, and all the Moabite dignitaries with him. 7He took up his theme, and said:

From Aram has Balak brought me,
Moab's king from the hills of the East:
Come, curse me Jacob,
Come, tell Israel's doom!
8How can I damn whom God has not damned,
How doom when the LORD has not doomed?
9As I see them from the mountain tops,
Gaze on them from the heights,
There is a people that dwells apart,
Not reckoned among the nations,

דִּבֵּ֑ר בִּלְעָ֑ם וַיַּ֨עַל בָּלָ֧ק וּבִלְעָ֛ם פָּ֥ר וָאַ֖יִל
בַּמִּזְבֵּֽחַ׃ 3 וַיֹּ֨אמֶר בִּלְעָ֜ם לְבָלָ֗ק הִתְיַצֵּב֮
עַל־עֹלָתֶךָ֒ וְאֵֽלְכָ֗ה אוּלַ֞י יִקָּרֵ֤ה יְהוָה֙
לִקְרָאתִ֔י וּדְבַ֥ר מַה־יַּרְאֵ֖נִי וְהִגַּ֣דְתִּי לָ֑ךְ
וַיֵּ֖לֶךְ שֶֽׁפִי׃
4 וַיִּקָּ֥ר אֱלֹהִ֖ים אֶל־בִּלְעָ֑ם וַיֹּ֣אמֶר אֵלָ֗יו
אֶת־שִׁבְעַ֤ת הַֽמִּזְבְּחֹת֙ עָרַ֔כְתִּי וָאַ֛עַל פָּ֥ר
וָאַ֖יִל בַּמִּזְבֵּֽחַ׃ 5 וַיָּ֧שֶׂם יְהוָ֛ה דָּבָ֖ר בְּפִ֣י
בִלְעָ֑ם וַיֹּ֛אמֶר שׁ֥וּב אֶל־בָּלָ֖ק וְכֹ֥ה תְדַבֵּֽר׃
6 וַיָּ֣שָׁב אֵלָ֔יו וְהִנֵּ֥ה נִצָּ֖ב עַל־עֹלָת֑וֹ ה֖וּא
וְכָל־שָׂרֵ֥י מוֹאָֽב׃ 7 וַיִּשָּׂ֥א מְשָׁל֖וֹ וַיֹּאמַ֑ר

מִן־אֲ֠רָם יַנְחֵ֨נִי בָלָ֤ק
מֶֽלֶךְ־מוֹאָב֙ מֵֽהַרְרֵי־קֶ֔דֶם
לְכָה֙ אָֽרָה־לִּ֣י יַעֲקֹ֔ב
וּלְכָ֖ה זֹעֲמָ֥ה יִשְׂרָאֵֽל׃
8 מָ֣ה אֶקֹּ֔ב לֹ֥א קַבֹּ֖ה אֵ֑ל
וּמָ֣ה אֶזְעֹ֔ם לֹ֥א זָעַ֖ם יְהוָֽה׃
9 כִּֽי־מֵרֹ֤אשׁ צֻרִים֙ אֶרְאֶ֔נּוּ
וּמִגְּבָע֖וֹת אֲשׁוּרֶ֑נּוּ
הֶן־עָם֙ לְבָדָ֣ד יִשְׁכֹּ֔ן
וּבַגּוֹיִ֖ם לֹ֥א יִתְחַשָּֽׁב׃

23:2. a bull and a ram The most expensive—and, therefore, the most desirable—animals in the sacrificial system.

3. Stay They worked in tandem. Balak stood at his sacrifice while the diviner sought omens.

your offerings Literally, "your burnt offering," which the specific sacrifice required.

reveals to me Via omens.

I will tell you I will interpret for you.

4. offered up The subject is Balak, not Balaam.

5. the LORD put a word in Balaam's mouth The Lord told him the exact words.

THE FIRST ORACLE (vv. 7–10)

All of the oracles are in verse form, probably attesting to their antiquity.

7. theme Hebrew: *mashal,* which has no precise rendering and is never used for the discourses of Israel's prophets. This indicates that Balaam's oracle is not to be reckoned as prophecy.

hills of the East Hebrew: *har'rei kedem;* literally, "hills of Kedem [east]." It seems to designate a specific territory in the Syrian desert, east of the Phoenician coast.

9. apart In terms of strength and security.

reckoned The people Israel will not share the fate of other nations.

people . . . nations Hebrew: *am . . . goyim;* here the first term refers to Israelites, and the second to non-Israelites. Usually "*am*" is a more intimate, ethnic designation than the political designation "*goyim.*"

---

9. a people that dwells apart, / Not reckoned among the nations One prominent thinker suggested that the Jewish people survived in the Diaspora, not despite the enmity

10 Who can count the dust of Jacob,
Number the dust-cloud of Israel?
May I die the death of the upright,
May my fate be like theirs!

10 מִי מָנָה עֲפַר יַעֲקֹב
וּמִסְפָּר אֶת־רֹבַע יִשְׂרָאֵל
תָּמֹת נַפְשִׁי מוֹת יְשָׁרִים
וּתְהִי אַחֲרִיתִי כָּמֹהוּ׃

11 Then Balak said to Balaam, "What have you done to me? Here I brought you to damn my enemies, and instead you have blessed them!"
12 He replied, "I can only repeat faithfully what the LORD puts in my mouth." 13 Then Balak said to him, "Come with me to another place from which you can see them—you will see only a portion of them; you will not see all of them—and damn them for me from there."
14 With that, he took him to Sedehzophim, on the summit of Pisgah. He built seven altars and offered a bull and a ram on each altar. 15 And [Balaam] said to Balak, "Stay here beside your offerings, while I seek a manifestation yonder."
16 The LORD manifested Himself to Balaam and put a word in his mouth, saying, "Return to Balak and speak thus." 17 He went to him and

11 וַיֹּאמֶר בָּלָק אֶל־בִּלְעָם מֶה עָשִׂיתָ לִי
לָקֹב אֹיְבַי לְקַחְתִּיךָ וְהִנֵּה בֵּרַכְתָּ בָרֵךְ׃
12 וַיַּעַן וַיֹּאמַר הֲלֹא אֵת אֲשֶׁר יָשִׂים יְהוָה
בְּפִי אֹתוֹ אֶשְׁמֹר לְדַבֵּר׃ 13 וַיֹּאמֶר אֵלָיו מישי
בָּלָק לך נא לְכָה־נָּא אִתִּי אֶל־מָקוֹם אַחֵר
אֲשֶׁר תִּרְאֶנּוּ מִשָּׁם אֶפֶס קָצֵהוּ תִרְאֶה
וְכֻלּוֹ לֹא תִרְאֶה וְקָבְנוֹ־לִי מִשָּׁם׃
14 וַיִּקָּחֵהוּ שְׂדֵה צֹפִים אֶל־רֹאשׁ הַפִּסְגָּה
וַיִּבֶן שִׁבְעָה מִזְבְּחֹת וַיַּעַל פָּר וָאַיִל
בַּמִּזְבֵּחַ׃ 15 וַיֹּאמֶר אֶל־בָּלָק הִתְיַצֵּב כֹּה
עַל־עֹלָתֶךָ וְאָנֹכִי אִקָּרֶה כֹּה׃
16 וַיִּקָּר יְהוָה אֶל־בִּלְעָם וַיָּשֶׂם דָּבָר בְּפִיו
וַיֹּאמֶר שׁוּב אֶל־בָּלָק וְכֹה תְדַבֵּר׃ 17 וַיָּבֹא

10. dust-cloud The image here is of the dust raised by Israel's marching hosts. (The translation is based on emending the text's *et rova* to *turba·at* or *turba,* meaning "dust cloud.")

my fate Balaam's wish illustrates the blessing that every nation and person will desire to receive from God—to share the fate of Israel.

BALAK'S REACTION AND SECOND ATTEMPT (vv. 11–17)

13. another place Balaam will continue to try the same oracular procedure to effect a favorable omen, this time at another location, perhaps believing that a change of place might lead to a change of luck.

only a portion Balak was showing Balaam an even smaller segment of the Israelite camp than before, fearing that the sight of too many Israelites would once again produce a blessing.

14. Sedehzophim Literally, "mountain of the watchmen." A lookout post for astronomical observation or for observing the flight of birds.

---

of their neighbors but precisely because of it. If we ever became objects of their friendship, it would be harder to avoid assimilating (Baal Shem Tov). Several anti-Zionist Orthodox rabbis of the early 20th century based their opposition to Zionism on this verse's praise of the Jewish people for not being a nation like other nations. Even the liberal thinker Rosenzweig feared that the Jewish people would lose its distinctive greatness if it "re-entered history" as a political state.

10. May I die the death of the upright The Sages, suspicious of Balaam, take him to be saying "May I live as a greedy, degenerate sinner all my days and become righteous just before my death."

13. you will see only a portion of them Individual Israelites may not be that impressive, but it has always been the genius of the Jewish people that the whole added up to more than the sum of its parts. Ordinary people combine to create extraordinary communities, sites of holiness, and charity (Menaḥem Mendel of Kotzk).

found him standing beside his offerings, and the
Moabite dignitaries with him. Balak asked him,
"What did the LORD say?" 18And he took up his
theme, and said:

Up, Balak, attend,
Give ear unto me, son of Zippor!
19God is not man to be capricious,
Or mortal to change His mind.
Would He speak and not act,
Promise and not fulfill?
20My message was to bless:
When He blesses, I cannot reverse it.
21No harm is in sight for Jacob,
No woe in view for Israel.
The LORD their God is with them,
And their King's acclaim in their midst.
22God who freed them from Egypt
Is for them like the horns of the wild ox.
23Lo, there is no augury in Jacob,
No divining in Israel:
Jacob is told at once,
Yea Israel, what God has planned.

אֵלָיו וְהִנּוֹ נִצָּב עַל־עֹלָתוֹ וְשָׂרֵי מוֹאָב
אִתּוֹ וַיֹּאמֶר לוֹ בָּלָק מַה־דִּבֶּר יְהוָה׃
18 וַיִּשָּׂא מְשָׁלוֹ וַיֹּאמַר

קוּם בָּלָק וּשְׁמָע
הַאֲזִינָה עָדַי בְּנוֹ צִפֹּר׃
19 לֹא אִישׁ אֵל וִיכַזֵּב
וּבֶן־אָדָם וְיִתְנֶחָם
הַהוּא אָמַר וְלֹא יַעֲשֶׂה
וְדִבֶּר וְלֹא יְקִימֶנָּה׃
20 הִנֵּה בָרֵךְ לָקָחְתִּי
וּבֵרֵךְ וְלֹא אֲשִׁיבֶנָּה׃
21 לֹא־הִבִּיט אָוֶן בְּיַעֲקֹב
וְלֹא־רָאָה עָמָל בְּיִשְׂרָאֵל
יְהוָה אֱלֹהָיו עִמּוֹ
וּתְרוּעַת מֶלֶךְ בּוֹ׃
22 אֵל מוֹצִיאָם מִמִּצְרָיִם
כְּתוֹעֲפֹת רְאֵם לוֹ׃
23 כִּי לֹא־נַחַשׁ בְּיַעֲקֹב
וְלֹא־קֶסֶם בְּיִשְׂרָאֵל
כָּעֵת יֵאָמֵר לְיַעֲקֹב
וּלְיִשְׂרָאֵל מַה־פָּעַל אֵל׃

17. What did the LORD say? For the first time, Balak recognizes that Israel's God alone determines Israel's fate.

THE SECOND ORACLE (vv. 18–24)

21. acclaim Hebrew: *t'ru·ah,* the military alarm sounded by trumpet or *shofar.* It can also mean a shout of joy.

22. freed them Balaam subtly corrects Balak's assertion that Israel was "a people come out of Egypt" (22:5), as if it had successfully escaped from slavery without divine help.

wild ox The metaphor refers to God. In the ancient Near East, gods often were depicted with horns or wearing horned crowns.

23. augury Hebrew: *naḥash,* which refers to observing omens such as the flight of birds, or reading the entrails of a domesticated animal.

divining A tacit admission that magic works but that Israel has no need for it.

planned Because God has provided Israel with prophets, it has no need to resort to magical arts to determine His will.

18. Up, Balak Balaam had referred to Balak as "king" (22:10); having encountered the true sovereign, he no longer does so (N. Leibowitz).

21. No harm is in sight Literally, "[God] sees no evil in Israel." The *Tanḥuma* understands this to teach that God, out of love, overlooks Israel's faults. Ibn Ezra, by contrast, reads the verse: "Only when God sees no evil in Israel is the LORD with them." Israel is not vulnerable to curses when they do God's will. Entice them to sin grievously, as the Moabites do in chapter 25, and God will no longer be a protective presence in their midst. "A Jew is never alone; God is always with every Jew" (Baal Shem Tov).

[24]Lo, a people that rises like a lion,
Leaps up like the king of beasts,
Rests not till it has feasted on prey
And drunk the blood of the slain.

24 הֶן־עָם֙ כְּלָבִ֣יא יָק֔וּם
וְכַאֲרִ֖י יִתְנַשָּׂ֑א
לֹ֤א יִשְׁכַּב֙ עַד־יֹ֣אכַל טֶ֔רֶף
וְדַם־חֲלָלִ֖ים יִשְׁתֶּֽה׃

[25]Thereupon Balak said to Balaam, "Don't
curse them and don't bless them!" [26]In reply,
Balaam said to Balak, "But I told you: Whatever
the LORD says, that I must do." [27]Then Balak
said to Balaam, "Come now, I will take you to
another place. Perhaps God will deem it right
that you damn them for me there." [28]Balak took
Balaam to the peak of Peor, which overlooks
the wasteland. [29]Balaam said to Balak, "Build
me here seven altars, and have seven bulls and
seven rams ready for me here." [30]Balak did as
Balaam said: he offered up a bull and a ram on
each altar.

25 וַיֹּ֤אמֶר בָּלָק֙ אֶל־בִּלְעָ֔ם גַּם־קֹ֖ב לֹ֣א
תִקֳּבֶ֑נּוּ גַּם־בָּרֵ֖ךְ לֹ֥א תְבָרֲכֶֽנּוּ׃ 26 וַיַּ֣עַן
בִּלְעָ֔ם וַיֹּ֖אמֶר אֶל־בָּלָ֑ק הֲלֹ֗א דִּבַּ֤רְתִּי אֵלֶ֙יךָ֙
לֵאמֹ֔ר כֹּ֛ל אֲשֶׁר־יְדַבֵּ֥ר יְהוָ֖ה אֹת֥וֹ אֶעֱשֶֽׂה׃
27 וַיֹּ֤אמֶר בָּלָק֙ אֶל־בִּלְעָ֔ם לְכָה־נָּא֙ אֶקָּ֣חֲךָ֔ ששי [שביעי]
אֶל־מָק֖וֹם אַחֵ֑ר אוּלַ֤י יִישַׁר֙ בְּעֵינֵ֣י
הָֽאֱלֹהִ֔ים וְקַבֹּ֥תוֹ לִ֖י מִשָּֽׁם׃ 28 וַיִּקַּ֥ח בָּלָ֖ק
אֶת־בִּלְעָ֑ם רֹ֣אשׁ הַפְּע֔וֹר הַנִּשְׁקָ֖ף עַל־פְּנֵ֥י
הַיְשִׁימֹֽן׃ 29 וַיֹּ֤אמֶר בִּלְעָם֙ אֶל־בָּלָ֔ק בְּנֵה־
לִ֥י בָזֶ֖ה שִׁבְעָ֣ה מִזְבְּחֹ֑ת וְהָכֵ֥ן לִי֙ בָּזֶ֔ה
שִׁבְעָ֥ה פָרִ֖ים וְשִׁבְעָ֥ה אֵילִֽים׃ 30 וַיַּ֣עַשׂ
בָּלָ֔ק כַּאֲשֶׁ֖ר אָמַ֣ר בִּלְעָ֑ם וַיַּ֛עַל פַּ֥ר וָאַ֖יִל
בַּמִּזְבֵּֽחַ׃

24 Now Balaam, seeing that it pleased the
LORD to bless Israel, did not, as on previous occasions, go in search of omens, but turned his
face toward the wilderness. [2]As Balaam looked
up and saw Israel encamped tribe by tribe, the

כד וַיַּ֣רְא בִּלְעָ֗ם כִּ֣י ט֞וֹב בְּעֵינֵ֤י יְהוָה֙
לְבָרֵ֣ךְ אֶת־יִשְׂרָאֵ֔ל וְלֹא־הָלַ֥ךְ כְּפַֽעַם־
בְּפַ֖עַם לִקְרַ֣את נְחָשִׁ֑ים וַיָּ֥שֶׁת אֶל־הַמִּדְבָּ֖ר
פָּנָֽיו׃ 2 וַיִּשָּׂ֨א בִלְעָ֜ם אֶת־עֵינָ֗יו וַיַּרְא֙ אֶת־

THE THIRD ORACLE (23:25–24:9)

This is the climactic oracle. In the first oracle, only God determines blessing and curse (23:8); in the second, God's blessing cannot be revoked (23:20); in this, the third, those who bless or curse Israel will themselves be blessed or cursed.

27. Perhaps God will deem it right that you damn them A submissive, almost plaintive utterance, acknowledging the power of God. Balak's previous order, in verse 13, had been: "Damn them." The transformation in Balak is now clear. He must reckon with the power of Israel's God.

will deem it right Literally, "be straight in the eyes of." That is, be to his liking.

24:1. in search of omens The reason he separated himself from Balak on the previous two occasions is now clarified. While Balak attended to the sacrifices, Balaam went off by himself to search for portents of the future.

toward the wilderness Balaam, convinced that God intends only blessing for Israel (23:20), no longer needs to follow Balak's precaution that he see only a portion of Israel lest the curse be ineffectual. He can now view the entire Israelite encampment with impunity. Rather than timidly catching a glimpse of the edge of the Israelite camp, Balaam now boldly steps forward so that he can see all of the people Israel.

2. the spirit of God came upon him Instead of seeking God in a dream or having God's words "put into his mouth," Balaam is now invested with the divine spirit and falls into an ecstatic state, the mark of a prophet.

spirit of God came upon him. 3Taking up his
theme, he said:

Word of Balaam son of Beor,
Word of the man whose eye is true,
4Word of him who hears God's speech,
Who beholds visions from the Almighty,
Prostrate, but with eyes unveiled:
5How fair are your tents, O Jacob,
Your dwellings, O Israel!
6Like palm-groves that stretch out,
Like gardens beside a river,
Like aloes planted by the LORD,
Like cedars beside the water;
7Their boughs drip with moisture,
Their roots have abundant water.
Their king shall rise above Agag,
Their kingdom shall be exalted.
8God who freed them from Egypt
Is for them like the horns of the wild ox.
They shall devour enemy nations,
Crush their bones,
And smash their arrows.

יִשְׂרָאֵל שֹׁכֵן לִשְׁבָטָיו וַתְּהִי עָלָיו רוּחַ
אֱלֹהִים׃ 3 וַיִּשָּׂא מְשָׁלוֹ וַיֹּאמַר

נְאֻם בִּלְעָם בְּנוֹ בְעֹר
וּנְאֻם הַגֶּבֶר שְׁתֻם הָעָיִן׃
4 נְאֻם שֹׁמֵעַ אִמְרֵי־אֵל
אֲשֶׁר מַחֲזֵה שַׁדַּי יֶחֱזֶה
נֹפֵל וּגְלוּי עֵינָיִם׃
5 מַה־טֹּבוּ אֹהָלֶיךָ יַעֲקֹב
מִשְׁכְּנֹתֶיךָ יִשְׂרָאֵל׃
6 כִּנְחָלִים נִטָּיוּ
כְּגַנֹּת עֲלֵי נָהָר
כַּאֲהָלִים נָטַע יְהוָה
כַּאֲרָזִים עֲלֵי־מָיִם׃
7 יִזַּל־מַיִם מִדָּלְיָו
וְזַרְעוֹ בְּמַיִם רַבִּים
וְיָרֹם מֵאֲגַג מַלְכּוֹ
וְתִנַּשֵּׂא מַלְכֻתוֹ׃
8 אֵל מוֹצִיאוֹ מִמִּצְרַיִם
כְּתוֹעֲפֹת רְאֵם לוֹ
יֹאכַל גּוֹיִם צָרָיו
וְעַצְמֹתֵיהֶם יְגָרֵם
וְחִצָּיו יִמְחָץ׃

3–4. Balaam introduces himself as one who is privy to God's direct revelation.

4. Almighty Hebrew: *Shaddai,* an ancient name for Israel's God (Gen. 17:1, 28:3).

Prostrate An act that acknowledges and pays homage to the Presence of God.

but with eyes unveiled Either his eyes were literally "opened" or, more likely, he was figuratively "enlightened"; i.e., he saw with his inner eye.

5. fair That is, pleasing.

dwellings Parallel to "tents." The Hebrew word (*mishk'notekha*) includes the plural of *mishkan* (tabernacle; temporary structure).

6. aloes A sweet-smelling tree whose sap is used as a perfume.

7. Their boughs drip The image is one of trees (v. 6) so drenched that their boughs drip water. The vegetation will be watered from above and below. Water is a common metaphor for affluence.

Their roots Literally, "and its seed." This is a reference to posterity.

Their king Thrice promised by God to the patriarchs (Gen. 17:6,16, 35:11).

Agag King of Amalek during the reign of Israel's King Saul (1 Sam. 15:8). The Amalekites were Israel's most dreaded enemy in the time of Moses (e.g., Exod. 17:8–16; Deut. 25:17–18).

8. Is for them That is, for Israel.

devour An image of military conquest.

HALAKHAH L'MA·ASEH

24:5. This verse is the source for the prayer *Mah Tovu,* recited daily upon entering a synagogue. And the Talmud bases its requirements for respecting privacy on this verse, explaining that Balaam was moved to praise the tents of Jacob because the arrangement of their entrances made it impossible for a family to see inside the tents of others, showing respect for privacy (BT BB 60a).

9They crouch, they lie down like a lion,
Like the king of beasts; who dare rouse them?
Blessed are they who bless you,
Accursed they who curse you!

9 כָּרַע שָׁכַב כַּאֲרִי
וּכְלָבִיא מִי יְקִימֶנּוּ
מְבָרֲכֶיךָ בָרוּךְ
וְאֹרְרֶיךָ אָרוּר׃

10Enraged at Balaam, Balak struck his hands together. "I called you," Balak said to Balaam, "to damn my enemies, and instead you have blessed them these three times! 11Back with you at once to your own place! I was going to reward you richly, but the Lord has denied you the reward." 12Balaam replied to Balak, "But I even told the messengers you sent to me, 13'Though Balak were to give me his house full of silver and gold, I could not of my own accord do anything good or bad contrary to the Lord's command. What the Lord says, that I must say.' 14And now, as I go back to my people, let me inform you of what this people will do to your people in days to come." 15He took up his theme, and said:

10 וַיִּחַר־אַף בָּלָק אֶל־בִּלְעָם וַיִּסְפֹּק אֶת־
כַּפָּיו וַיֹּאמֶר בָּלָק אֶל־בִּלְעָם לָקֹב אֹיְבַי
קְרָאתִיךָ וְהִנֵּה בֵּרַכְתָּ בָרֵךְ זֶה שָׁלֹשׁ
פְּעָמִים׃ 11 וְעַתָּה בְּרַח־לְךָ אֶל־מְקוֹמֶךָ
אָמַרְתִּי כַּבֵּד אֲכַבֶּדְךָ וְהִנֵּה מְנָעֲךָ יְהוָה
מִכָּבוֹד׃ 12 וַיֹּאמֶר בִּלְעָם אֶל־בָּלָק הֲלֹא
גַּם אֶל־מַלְאָכֶיךָ אֲשֶׁר־שָׁלַחְתָּ אֵלַי דִּבַּרְתִּי
לֵאמֹר׃ 13 אִם־יִתֶּן־לִי בָלָק מְלֹא בֵיתוֹ
כֶּסֶף וְזָהָב לֹא אוּכַל לַעֲבֹר אֶת־פִּי יְהוָה
לַעֲשׂוֹת טוֹבָה אוֹ רָעָה מִלִּבִּי אֲשֶׁר־יְדַבֵּר
שביעי יְהוָה אֹתוֹ אֲדַבֵּר׃ 14 וְעַתָּה הִנְנִי הוֹלֵךְ
לְעַמִּי לְכָה אִיעָצְךָ אֲשֶׁר יַעֲשֶׂה הָעָם
הַזֶּה לְעַמְּךָ בְּאַחֲרִית הַיָּמִים׃ 15 וַיִּשָּׂא
מְשָׁלוֹ וַיֹּאמַר

Word of Balaam son of Beor,
Word of the man whose eye is true,
16Word of him who hears God's speech,
Who obtains knowledge from the Most High,
And beholds visions from the Almighty,

נְאֻם בִּלְעָם בְּנוֹ בְעֹר
וּנְאֻם הַגֶּבֶר שְׁתֻם הָעָיִן׃
16 נְאֻם שֹׁמֵעַ אִמְרֵי־אֵל
וְיֹדֵעַ דַּעַת עֶלְיוֹן
מַחֲזֵה שַׁדַּי יֶחֱזֶה

9. crouch That is, they rest. In the second oracle, the lion rises and does not rest until it eats its prey. Here, the sated lion lies down to rest. Even when it is in a state of repose, who would dare rouse it?

Blessed . . . Accursed Everyone will bless you in order to be blessed and will desist from cursing you for fear of being cursed (cf. Gen. 12:3).

THE FOURTH ORACLE (vv. 10–19)

Still imbued with prophetic inspiration, Balaam turns his attention to the future of Balak's country, Moab. Most of the words and references in these verses remain obscure.

10. struck his hands together A derisive gesture.

13. could not of my own accord Balaam, like Moses, acts only on God's instructions.

14. inform you That is, of God's plan.

what this people will do to your people Implies that the oracle will deal only with Moab.

in days to come Not "the end of days" but the near future from the speaker's point of view.

15–16. These verses are almost identical with verses 3–4. The repetition of Balaam's self-introduction signifies that he continues to prophesy under the influence of the divine spirit without resort to divination.

Most High Hebrew: *Elyon,* a name for God (Gen. 14:18–22, Deut. 32:8). (The Canaanite creator god, El, who also bears this name, may be meant in Gen. 14.)

Prostrate, but with eyes unveiled:
17What I see for them is not yet,
What I behold will not be soon:
A star rises from Jacob,
A scepter comes forth from Israel;
It smashes the brow of Moab,
The foundation of all children of Seth.
18Edom becomes a possession,
Yea, Seir a possession of its enemies;
But Israel is triumphant.
19A victor issues from Jacob
To wipe out what is left of Ir.

20He saw Amalek and, taking up his theme, he said:
A leading nation is Amalek;
But its fate is to perish forever.

21He saw the Kenites and, taking up his theme, he said:
Though your abode be secure,
And your nest be set among cliffs,
22Yet shall Kain be consumed,
When Asshur takes you captive.

נֹפֵל וּגְלוּי עֵינָיִם׃
17 אֶרְאֶנּוּ וְלֹא עַתָּה
אֲשׁוּרֶנּוּ וְלֹא קָרוֹב
דָּרַךְ כּוֹכָב מִיַּעֲקֹב
וְקָם שֵׁבֶט מִיִּשְׂרָאֵל
וּמָחַץ פַּאֲתֵי מוֹאָב
וְקַרְקַר כָּל־בְּנֵי־שֵׁת׃
18 וְהָיָה אֱדוֹם יְרֵשָׁה
וְהָיָה יְרֵשָׁה שֵׂעִיר אֹיְבָיו
וְיִשְׂרָאֵל עֹשֶׂה חָיִל׃
19 וְיֵרְדְּ מִיַּעֲקֹב
וְהֶאֱבִיד שָׂרִיד מֵעִיר׃

20 וַיַּרְא אֶת־עֲמָלֵק וַיִּשָּׂא מְשָׁלוֹ וַיֹּאמַר
רֵאשִׁית גּוֹיִם עֲמָלֵק
וְאַחֲרִיתוֹ עֲדֵי אֹבֵד׃

21 וַיַּרְא אֶת־הַקֵּינִי וַיִּשָּׂא מְשָׁלוֹ וַיֹּאמַר
אֵיתָן מוֹשָׁבֶךָ
וְשִׂים בַּסֶּלַע קִנֶּךָ׃
22 כִּי אִם־יִהְיֶה לְבָעֵר קָיִן
עַד־מָה אַשּׁוּר תִּשְׁבֶּךָּ׃

17. Balaam's visionary powers soar from the present to behold the distant future.

star Hebrew: *kokhav,* which has been interpreted as an image of a king, as the messianic king, and as a "host" in the sense of "multitude of an army."

smashes . . . Moab A fitting and ironic conclusion to the Balaam story. Balak of Moab wished to curse Israel; instead, his hired seer, Balaam, curses Moab.

children of Seth A general term for all the nomadic groups descended from Abraham (see Gen. 25) and considered to be his kinsmen. The Sethites were a nomadic people located somewhere in Canaan. Israel was promised dominance over them in the patriarchal blessings (as in Gen. 27:29). They have been identified with the Sutu nomads mentioned frequently in Egyptian texts as wandering through the desert regions of the area.

ORACLES AGAINST NATIONS (vv. 20–25)

Balaam is still on the heights as a series of nations come into view. From the Moabite plateau one can see into the Negeb—home of the Amalekites, Asshurim, and Kenites.

21. Kenites A nomadic group that attached itself to Midian, Amalek, and Israel. It ranged from the Sinai Peninsula to the Galilee as far as Kadesh.

CHAPTER 24

17. Some 14 centuries after this event, when Simeon bar Kosiba led a revolt against Roman occupation, Akiva called him Bar Kokhba, "son of a star," and applied this verse to him as the triumphant ruler predicted by the Torah. His revolt, alas, ended in defeat and destruction.

23He took up his theme and said:

Alas, who can survive except God has willed
   it!

24Ships come from the quarter of Kittim;
They subject Asshur, subject Eber.
They, too, shall perish forever.

25Then Balaam set out on his journey back
home; and Balak also went his way.

25

While Israel was staying at Shittim, the
people profaned themselves by whoring with
the Moabite women, 2who invited the people
to the sacrifices for their god. The people partook of them and worshiped that god. 3Thus Israel attached itself to Baal-peor, and the LORD
was incensed with Israel. 4The LORD said to Moses, "Take all the ringleaders and have them
publicly impaled before the LORD, so that the

23 וַיִּשָּׂ֥א מְשָׁל֖וֹ וַיֹּאמַ֑ר
אֹ֕וֹי מִ֥י יִחְיֶ֖ה מִשֻּׂמ֥וֹ אֵֽל׃

24 וְצִים֙ מִיַּ֣ד כִּתִּ֔ים
וְעִנּ֥וּ אַשּׁ֖וּר וְעִנּוּ־עֵ֑בֶר
וְגַם־ה֖וּא עֲדֵ֥י אֹבֵֽד׃

25 וַיָּ֣קׇם בִּלְעָ֔ם וַיֵּ֖לֶךְ וַיָּ֣שׇׁב לִמְקֹמ֑וֹ וְגַם־
בָּלָ֖ק הָלַ֥ךְ לְדַרְכּֽוֹ׃ פ

כה
וַיֵּ֥שֶׁב יִשְׂרָאֵ֖ל בַּשִּׁטִּ֑ים וַיָּ֣חֶל
הָעָ֔ם לִזְנ֖וֹת אֶל־בְּנ֥וֹת מוֹאָֽב׃ 2 וַתִּקְרֶ֣אןָ
לָעָ֔ם לְזִבְחֵ֖י אֱלֹֽהֵיהֶ֑ן וַיֹּ֣אכַל הָעָ֔ם
וַיִּֽשְׁתַּחֲו֖וּ לֵֽאלֹהֵיהֶֽן׃ 3 וַיִּצָּ֥מֶד יִשְׂרָאֵ֖ל
לְבַ֣עַל פְּע֑וֹר וַיִּֽחַר־אַ֥ף יְהֹוָ֖ה בְּיִשְׂרָאֵֽל׃
4 וַיֹּ֨אמֶר יְהֹוָ֜ה אֶל־מֹשֶׁ֗ה קַ֚ח אֶת־כׇּל־
רָאשֵׁ֣י הָעָ֔ם וְהוֹקַ֥ע אוֹתָ֛ם לַֽיהֹוָ֖ה נֶ֣גֶד

---

24. Kittim   Cyprus. This verse may refer to
the invasions of the sea peoples in the 13th and
12th centuries B.C.E.

IDOLATRY AND EXPIATION AT BAAL-PEOR (25:1–18)

Balaam's prediction of Israel's glorious promise is
dashed by the events at Baal-peor. The nation that
dwells alone with its God abruptly pollutes itself
with idolatry.

THE APOSTASY   (vv. 1–9)

1. at Shittim   Literally, "in the acacias." Its
full name was Abel-shittim. It was from there that
Joshua sent out spies and led Israel across the Jordan.

Moabite women   Apparently, Moabites continued to dwell in the territory after Sihon and
the Israelites conquered it.

2.   Sexual attraction led to Israelite participation in the sacrificial feasts at the shrine of
Baal-peor.

3. attached itself to   Israel transferred its allegiance from YHVH to Baal or engaged in acts

of the ritual sexual intercourse required in Baal
worship.

Baal-peor   "Baal": the name of the god;
"peor": the name of the site.

the LORD was incensed   God's anger frequently takes the form of a devastating plague (see
17:11).

4. ringleaders   Hebrew: *rashei ha-am,* literally, "heads of the people," simply means "leaders" (see 10:4, 13:3). It suggests that innocent and
guilty leaders alike were to be executed.

impaled   The punishment for idolatry was
death by stoning, with the body then hanged for
public display. Impaling is a rare punishment (see
Deut. 21:22–23), carried out also on the sons of
Saul by the Gibeonites for breach of covenant (2
Sam. 21).

before the LORD   That impaled corpses would

---

25.   Each went back to his previous way of
thinking, unaffected by having encountered

God's protecting love for Israel. God's word can
only affect people who are willing to change.

הַשָּׁמֶשׁ וְיָשֹׁב חֲרוֹן אַף־יְהוָה מִיִּשְׂרָאֵל׃
5 וַיֹּאמֶר מֹשֶׁה אֶל־שֹׁפְטֵי יִשְׂרָאֵל הִרְגוּ
אִישׁ אֲנָשָׁיו הַנִּצְמָדִים לְבַעַל פְּעוֹר׃
6 וְהִנֵּה אִישׁ מִבְּנֵי יִשְׂרָאֵל בָּא וַיַּקְרֵב
אֶל־אֶחָיו אֶת־הַמִּדְיָנִית לְעֵינֵי מֹשֶׁה
וּלְעֵינֵי כָּל־עֲדַת בְּנֵי־יִשְׂרָאֵל וְהֵמָּה בֹכִים
מפטיר פֶּתַח אֹהֶל מוֹעֵד׃ 7 וַיַּרְא פִּינְחָס בֶּן־
אֶלְעָזָר בֶּן־אַהֲרֹן הַכֹּהֵן וַיָּקָם מִתּוֹךְ הָעֵדָה
וַיִּקַּח רֹמַח בְּיָדוֹ׃ 8 וַיָּבֹא אַחַר אִישׁ־
יִשְׂרָאֵל אֶל־הַקֻּבָּה וַיִּדְקֹר אֶת־שְׁנֵיהֶם אֵת
אִישׁ יִשְׂרָאֵל וְאֶת־הָאִשָּׁה אֶל־קֳבָתָהּ
וַתֵּעָצַר הַמַּגֵּפָה מֵעַל בְּנֵי יִשְׂרָאֵל׃ 9 וַיִּהְיוּ
הַמֵּתִים בַּמַּגֵּפָה אַרְבָּעָה וְעֶשְׂרִים
אָלֶף׃ פ

LORD's wrath may turn away from Israel." 5So
Moses said to Israel's officials, "Each of you slay
those of his men who attached themselves to
Baal-peor."

6Just then one of the Israelites came and
brought a Midianite woman over to his companions, in the sight of Moses and of the
whole Israelite community who were weeping
at the entrance of the Tent of Meeting. 7When
Phinehas, son of Eleazar son of Aaron the priest,
saw this, he left the assembly and, taking a spear
in his hand, 8he followed the Israelite into the
chamber and stabbed both of them, the Israelite and the woman, through the belly. Then
the plague against the Israelites was checked.
9Those who died of the plague numbered
twenty-four thousand.

have brought ritual defilement to the sanctuary is not a consideration, because an emergency situation prevailed.

the LORD's wrath Here, this means the plague. In the Bible it is not unusual for the Lord to refer to Himself in the third person (e.g., Exod. 12:11,14).

5. Israel's officials Hebrew: *shof'tei Yisra·el;* the root שפט (often understood as "to judge") frequently means "to rule" or "to administer." The judge (*shofet*) is also an officer (*sar*). Moses appointed military officers as commanders and judges, on Jethro's advice. The two functions overlap, with the commander frequently acting in a judicial capacity. This was the practice throughout Mesopotamia.

his men That is, those under his command. Some assume that the execution was carried out. It is more likely, however, that God's wrath was assuaged by Phinehas's act before Moses' order could be fulfilled.

6. This act, committed before the sanctuary in the sight of Moses and the people while they were bewailing the plague in supplication to God, was a flagrant escalation of Israel's sin.

who were weeping While Moses and the community were weeping, the couple passed them by.

7. Phinehas An Egyptian name meaning "the Nubian." Phinehas was at the entrance of the Tent of Meeting in his capacity as chief of the sanctuary guards (1 Chron. 9:20), an office held by his father before him (Num. 3:32). Eleazar the high priest did not act in this instance because he was forbidden to come into contact with the dead under any circumstances (Lev. 21:10–12).

spear A short-shafted pike that could be held in both hands and, like the modern bayonet, thrust downward on a recumbent body. Phinehas would have been armed if he was on duty.

9. twenty-four thousand This count probably included the rest of the older generation who were doomed to die in the wilderness, because it is expressly certified in the census that follows this incident.

CHAPTER 25

9. Hirsch contrasts the 24,000 who die here with the 3,000 who died after worshiping the Golden Calf and concludes that sexual immorality is a greater temptation than idolatry. Israel, at this point an adolescent nation, is vulnerable to the sexually charged orgiastic worship and fertility cult of the Moabites. In all likelihood, this is why the Torah later calls for the destruction of all Canaanite altars and holy places in such stark terms when Israel occupies the Promised Land.

הפטרת חקת

HAFTARAH FOR ḤUKKAT

JUDGES 11:1–33

(*When* Ḥukkat *and* Balak *are combined, recite the* haftarah *for* Balak.)

This *haftarah* describes an event of controversy and contention between the Israelite and non-Israelite populations of Gilead during the early period of settlement in the Land. The chapter that precedes the *haftarah* relates how the Israelites abandoned the Lord, serving alien gods, and were punished with years of oppression by the Philistines and Ammonites (Judg. 10:6–9). Eventually the Israelites repented and "removed the alien gods from among them and served the LORD; and He could not bear the miseries of Israel" (Judg. 10:16). When the Ammonites again mustered their troops against Israel (v. 17), the officers of Gilead said: "Let the man who is the first to fight the Ammonites be chieftain over all the inhabitants of Gilead" (v. 18). The *haftarah* describes the emergence of that man, the initial diplomatic maneuvers, and the ensuing war.

The narrative moves from the oppression of leaderless Israelites to their military victory under the leadership of Jephthah who had been an outcast freebooter. Jephthah ruled Israel for six years and was buried in the territory of Gilead (Judg. 12:7). (Nothing is said about Israelite piety in the aftermath of his victories or about any period of peaceful respite, reports that are so characteristic elsewhere in the Book of Judges.)

The passages of the *haftarah* are dominated by negotiations and reports of negotiations between Jephthah and the elders of Gilead as well as between the Israelites led by Jephthah and alien kings. Issues of inheritance and property are at the heart of the negotiations. In the opening situation, the future hero is dispossessed of his own inheritance and treated as an outsider. His brothers successfully conceal their greed behind the mask of law. Jephthah responds by living as an outlaw, marauding with his gang until he is summoned back to Gilead as the leader of its army. Negotiations with the Gileadite officers redress the original imbalance, and the new good faith is sealed with oaths and agreements.

During Jephthah's negotiations with the king of the Ammonites, a pair of diplomatic exchanges tries to redress an international property grievance against the Israelites, but their substance is rebuffed by Jephthah. The Ammonites allege that the lands east of the Jordan River (between the Arnon and Jabbok Rivers) are theirs alone. Thus they hope to dispossess the Israelites from what the latter had conquered many years earlier from the Amorites (when that nation refused free passage to the wandering Israelite tribes and attacked them without cause). Indeed, the Ammonite desire to establish dominion over those lands (concerning which the Ammonites have never laid claim) strikes Jephthah as so contrived as to suggest dubious intent. The Ammonite refusal to justify their claim in the face of his challenge proves their bad faith, and Jephthah goes to war.

On the eve of battle he vows that if he returns home safe and victorious he will offer to the Lord as a burnt offering "whatever comes out of the door of my house to meet me" (11:31). This is a final example of how a formal legalism can lead to violent ends. (After the end of the *haftarah,* the conclusion of chapter 11 relates the personal disaster that ensues when his own daughter is first to come out to meet him and he declares that he cannot retract his vow [vv. 34ff.]. The focus of the *haftarah,* however, is not his personal vow and its consequences, but national disputes and battles.)

RELATION OF THE *HAFTARAH* TO THE *PARASHAH*

Jephthah's messengers to the Ammonite king cite Moses' request that the Edomites and Amorites

allow the Israelites to pass freely through their territory at the time of the wilderness trek (as told in the *parashah,* Num. 20–21). This is done to reject the claim that the Israelites now occupy Ammonite lands. Indeed, the historical facts recited indicate that the land under dispute had been conquered by the Israelites from the Amorites. These facts support the Gileadite cause. The failure of subsequent Ammonite (and Moabite) generations to challenge this situation is taken by Jephthah as further proof that the status quo had long been accepted as legitimate. Nevertheless, the issue merited a diplomatic presentation before beginning hostilities.

11

Jephthah the Gileadite was an able warrior, who was the son of a prostitute. Jephthah's father was Gilead; 2but Gilead also had sons by his wife, and when the wife's sons grew up, they drove Jephthah out. They said to him, "You shall have no share in our father's property, for you are the son of an outsider." 3So Jephthah fled from his brothers and settled in the Tob country. Men of low character gathered about Jephthah and went out raiding with him.

4Some time later, the Ammonites went to war against Israel. 5And when the Ammonites attacked Israel, the elders of Gilead went to bring Jephthah back from the Tob country. 6They said to Jephthah, "Come be our chief, so that we can fight the Ammonites." 7Jephthah replied to the elders of Gilead, "You are the very people who rejected me and drove me out of my father's house. How can you come to me now when you are in trouble?" 8The elders of Gilead said to Jephthah, "Honestly, we have now turned back to you. If you come with us and fight the Ammonites, you shall be our commander over all the inhabitants of Gilead." 9Jephthah said to the elders of Gilead, "[Very well,] if you bring me back to fight the Ammonites and the Lord delivers them to me, I am to be your commander." 10And the elders of Gilead answered Jephthah,

יא וְיִפְתָּ֣ח הַגִּלְעָדִ֗י הָיָה֙ גִּבּ֣וֹר חַ֔יִל וְה֖וּא בֶּן־אִשָּׁ֣ה זוֹנָ֑ה וַיּ֥וֹלֶד גִּלְעָ֖ד אֶת־יִפְתָּֽח: 2 וַתֵּ֧לֶד אֵֽשֶׁת־גִּלְעָ֛ד ל֖וֹ בָּנִ֑ים וַיִּגְדְּל֤וּ בְנֵֽי־הָֽאִשָּׁה֙ וַיְגָֽרְשׁ֣וּ אֶת־יִפְתָּ֔ח וַיֹּ֤אמְרוּ לוֹ֙ לֹֽא־תִנְחַ֣ל בְּבֵית־אָבִ֔ינוּ כִּ֛י בֶּן־אִשָּׁ֥ה אַחֶ֖רֶת אָֽתָּה: 3 וַיִּבְרַ֤ח יִפְתָּח֙ מִפְּנֵ֣י אֶחָ֔יו וַיֵּ֖שֶׁב בְּאֶ֣רֶץ ט֑וֹב וַיִּֽתְלַקְּט֤וּ אֶל־יִפְתָּח֙ אֲנָשִׁ֣ים רֵיקִ֔ים וַיֵּֽצְא֖וּ עִמּֽוֹ: פ

4 וַיְהִ֖י מִיָּמִ֑ים וַיִּלָּֽחֲמ֥וּ בְנֵֽי־עַמּ֖וֹן עִם־יִשְׂרָאֵֽל: 5 וַיְהִ֕י כַּֽאֲשֶׁר־נִלְחֲמ֥וּ בְנֵֽי־עַמּ֖וֹן עִם־יִשְׂרָאֵ֑ל וַיֵּֽלְכוּ֙ זִקְנֵ֣י גִלְעָ֔ד לָקַ֥חַת אֶת־יִפְתָּ֖ח מֵאֶ֥רֶץ טֽוֹב: 6 וַיֹּֽאמְר֣וּ לְיִפְתָּ֔ח לְכָ֕ה וְהָיִ֥יתָה לָּ֖נוּ לְקָצִ֑ין וְנִֽלָּֽחֲמָ֖ה בִּבְנֵ֥י עַמּֽוֹן: 7 וַיֹּ֨אמֶר יִפְתָּ֜ח לְזִקְנֵ֣י גִלְעָ֗ד הֲלֹ֤א אַתֶּם֙ שְׂנֵאתֶ֣ם אוֹתִ֔י וַתְּגָֽרְשׁ֖וּנִי מִבֵּ֣ית אָבִ֑י וּמַדּ֜וּעַ בָּאתֶ֤ם אֵלַי֙ עַ֔תָּה כַּֽאֲשֶׁ֖ר צַ֥ר לָכֶֽם: 8 וַיֹּֽאמְרוּ֩ זִקְנֵ֨י גִלְעָ֜ד אֶל־יִפְתָּ֗ח לָכֵן֙ עַתָּה֙ שַׁ֣בְנוּ אֵלֶ֔יךָ וְהָֽלַכְתָּ֣ עִמָּ֔נוּ וְנִלְחַמְתָּ֖ בִּבְנֵ֣י עַמּ֑וֹן וְהָיִ֤יתָ לָּ֨נוּ֙ לְרֹ֔אשׁ לְכֹ֖ל יֹֽשְׁבֵ֥י גִלְעָֽד: 9 וַיֹּ֨אמֶר יִפְתָּ֜ח אֶל־זִקְנֵ֣י גִלְעָ֗ד אִם־מְשִׁיבִ֨ים אַתֶּ֤ם אוֹתִי֙ לְהִלָּחֵם֙ בִּבְנֵ֣י עַמּ֔וֹן וְנָתַ֧ן יְהוָ֛ה אוֹתָ֖ם לְפָנָ֑י אָֽנֹכִ֕י אֶֽהְיֶ֥ה לָכֶ֖ם לְרֹֽאשׁ: 10 וַיֹּֽאמְר֥וּ זִקְנֵֽי־גִלְעָ֖ד אֶל־

Judges 11:8. commander Hebrew: *rosh,* an old designation for tribal elders as judges (cf. Exod. 18:25; Deut. 1:15; Num. 30:2, 32:28). It was also used for the elders of patriarchal clans (e.g., 1 Chron. 5:7,12,15,24). Both senses are pertinent in this case (especially because Jephthah had been dispossessed from his ancestral property, which led to the Gileadite promise that his holdings would be restored to him, along with other benefits).

"The LORD Himself shall be witness between us: we will do just as you have said."

11Jephthah went with the elders of Gilead, and the people made him their commander and chief. And Jephthah repeated all these terms before the LORD at Mizpah.

12Jephthah then sent messengers to the king of the Ammonites, saying, "What have you against me that you have come to make war on my country?" 13The king of the Ammonites replied to Jephthah's messengers, "When Israel came from Egypt, they seized the land which is mine, from the Arnon to the Jabbok as far as the Jordan. Now, then, restore it peaceably."

14Jephthah again sent messengers to the king of the Ammonites. 15He said to him, "Thus said Jephthah: Israel did not seize the land of Moab or the land of the Ammonites. 16When they left Egypt, Israel traveled through the wilderness to the Sea of Reeds and went on to Kadesh. 17Israel then sent messengers to the king of Edom, saying, 'Allow us to cross your country.' But the king of Edom would not consent. They also sent a mission to the king of Moab, and he refused. So Israel, after staying at Kadesh, 18traveled on through the wilderness, skirting the land of Edom and the land of Moab. They kept to the east of the land of Moab until they encamped on the other side of the Arnon; and, since Moab ends at the Arnon, they never entered Moabite territory.

19"Then Israel sent messengers to Sihon king of the Amorites, the king of Heshbon. Israel said

יִפְתָּ֔ח יְהֹוָ֗ה יִהְיֶ֤ה שֹׁמֵ֙עַ֙ בֵּינוֹתֵ֔ינוּ אִם־לֹ֥א
כִדְבָרְךָ֖ כֵּ֥ן נַעֲשֶֽׂה׃
11 וַיֵּ֤לֶךְ יִפְתָּח֙ עִם־זִקְנֵ֣י גִלְעָ֔ד וַיָּשִׂ֨ימוּ הָעָ֥ם
אוֹת֛וֹ עֲלֵיהֶ֖ם לְרֹ֣אשׁ וּלְקָצִ֑ין וַיְדַבֵּ֨ר יִפְתָּ֧ח
אֶת־כָּל־דְּבָרָ֛יו לִפְנֵ֥י יְהֹוָ֖ה בַּמִּצְפָּֽה׃ פ

12 וַיִּשְׁלַ֤ח יִפְתָּח֙ מַלְאָכִ֔ים אֶל־מֶ֥לֶךְ בְּנֵֽי־
עַמּ֖וֹן לֵאמֹ֑ר מַה־לִּ֣י וָלָ֔ךְ כִּֽי־בָ֥אתָ אֵלַ֖י
לְהִלָּחֵ֥ם בְּאַרְצִֽי׃ 13 וַיֹּ֜אמֶר מֶ֣לֶךְ בְּנֵי־עַמּ֗וֹן
אֶל־מַלְאֲכֵ֣י יִפְתָּ֔ח כִּֽי־לָקַ֨ח יִשְׂרָאֵ֤ל אֶת־
אַרְצִי֙ בַּעֲלוֹת֣וֹ מִמִּצְרַ֔יִם מֵאַרְנ֥וֹן וְעַד־
הַיַּבֹּ֖ק וְעַד־הַיַּרְדֵּ֑ן וְעַתָּ֕ה הָשִׁ֥יבָה אֶתְהֶ֖ן
בְּשָׁלֽוֹם׃
14 וַיּ֥וֹסֶף ע֖וֹד יִפְתָּ֑ח וַיִּשְׁלַח֙ מַלְאָכִ֔ים
אֶל־מֶ֖לֶךְ בְּנֵ֥י עַמּֽוֹן׃ 15 וַיֹּ֣אמֶר* ל֔וֹ כֹּ֖ה אָמַ֣ר
יִפְתָּ֑ח לֹֽא־לָקַ֤ח יִשְׂרָאֵל֙ אֶת־אֶ֣רֶץ מוֹאָ֔ב
וְאֶת־אֶ֖רֶץ בְּנֵ֥י עַמּֽוֹן׃ 16 כִּ֖י בַּעֲלוֹתָ֣ם
מִמִּצְרָ֑יִם וַיֵּ֨לֶךְ יִשְׂרָאֵ֤ל בַּמִּדְבָּר֙ עַד־יַם־
ס֔וּף וַיָּבֹ֖א קָדֵֽשָׁה׃ 17 וַיִּשְׁלַ֣ח יִשְׂרָאֵ֣ל
מַלְאָכִ֣ים ׀ אֶל־מֶ֣לֶךְ֩ אֱד֣וֹם ׀ לֵאמֹ֗ר
אֶעְבְּרָה־נָּ֣א בְאַרְצֶ֔ךָ וְלֹ֤א שָׁמַע֙ מֶ֣לֶךְ אֱד֔וֹם
וְגַ֨ם אֶל־מֶ֧לֶךְ מוֹאָ֛ב שָׁלַ֖ח וְלֹ֣א אָבָ֑ה וַיֵּ֥שֶׁב
יִשְׂרָאֵ֖ל בְּקָדֵֽשׁ׃ 18 וַיֵּ֣לֶךְ בַּמִּדְבָּ֗ר וַיָּ֜סָב
אֶת־אֶ֤רֶץ אֱדוֹם֙ וְאֶת־אֶ֣רֶץ מוֹאָ֔ב וַיָּבֹ֤א
מִמִּזְרַח־שֶׁ֙מֶשׁ֙ לְאֶ֣רֶץ מוֹאָ֔ב וַֽיַּחֲנ֖וּן בְּעֵ֣בֶר
אַרְנ֑וֹן וְלֹא־בָ֙אוּ֙ בִּגְב֣וּל מוֹאָ֔ב כִּ֥י אַרְנ֖וֹן
גְּב֥וּל מוֹאָֽב׃
19 וַיִּשְׁלַ֤ח יִשְׂרָאֵל֙ מַלְאָכִ֔ים אֶל־סִיח֥וֹן
מֶֽלֶךְ־הָאֱמֹרִ֖י מֶ֣לֶךְ חֶשְׁבּ֑וֹן וַיֹּ֤אמֶר לוֹ֙

v. 15. סבירין ומטעין לשון רבים

10. witness . . . we will do Hebrew: *shome·a . . . na·aseh;* this language expresses the reciprocity of a treaty. The word *shomei·a* literally means "hearer"—one who hears the terms of the treaty. Moreover, the clause "we will do just as you have said" is part of the operative language of the agreement. (Both terms together—"doing" and "hearing"—shed light on the famous formula of compliance made by the Israelites at the conclusion of the covenant at Mount Sinai: *na·aseh v'nishma* [Exod. 24:7]. That phrase would thus seem to have a more precise legal sense than the rendering "we will faithfully do" or even the more literal "we will do and obey [or: hear]." Appar-

to him, 'Allow us to cross through your country to our homeland.' 20But Sihon would not trust Israel to pass through his territory. Sihon mustered all his troops, and they encamped at Jahaz; he engaged Israel in battle. 21But the LORD, the God of Israel, delivered Sihon and all his troops into Israel's hands, and they defeated them; and Israel took possession of all the land of the Amorites, the inhabitants of that land. 22Thus they possessed all the territory of the Amorites from the Arnon to the Jabbok and from the wilderness to the Jordan.

23"Now, then, the LORD, the God of Israel, dispossessed the Amorites before His people Israel; and should you possess their land? 24Do you not hold what Chemosh your god gives you to possess? So we will hold on to everything that the LORD our God has given us to possess.

25"Besides, are you any better than Balak son of Zippor, king of Moab? Did he start a quarrel with Israel or go to war with them?

26"While Israel has been inhabiting Heshbon and its dependencies, and Aroer and its dependencies, and all the towns along the Arnon for three hundred years, why have you not tried to recover them all this time? 27I have done you no wrong; yet you are doing me harm and making war on me. May the LORD, who judges, decide today between the Israelites and the Ammonites!"

28But the king of the Ammonites paid no heed to the message that Jephthah sent him.

29Then the spirit of the LORD came upon Jephthah. He marched through Gilead and Manasseh, passing Mizpeh of Gilead; and from Mizpeh of Gilead he crossed over [to] the Ammonites. 30And Jephthah made the following

יִשְׂרָאֵל נַעְבְּרָה־נָּא בְאַרְצְךָ עַד־מְקוֹמִי׃
20 וְלֹא־הֶאֱמִין סִיחוֹן אֶת־יִשְׂרָאֵל עֲבֹר
בִּגְבֻלוֹ וַיֶּאֱסֹף סִיחוֹן אֶת־כָּל־עַמּוֹ וַיַּחֲנוּ
בְּיָהְצָה וַיִּלָּחֶם עִם־יִשְׂרָאֵל׃ 21 וַיִּתֵּן יְהוָה
אֱלֹהֵי־יִשְׂרָאֵל אֶת־סִיחוֹן וְאֶת־כָּל־עַמּוֹ
בְּיַד יִשְׂרָאֵל וַיַּכּוּם וַיִּירַשׁ יִשְׂרָאֵל אֵת
כָּל־אֶרֶץ הָאֱמֹרִי יוֹשֵׁב הָאָרֶץ הַהִיא׃
22 וַיִּירְשׁוּ אֵת כָּל־גְּבוּל הָאֱמֹרִי מֵאַרְנוֹן
וְעַד־הַיַּבֹּק וּמִן־הַמִּדְבָּר וְעַד־הַיַּרְדֵּן׃
23 וְעַתָּה יְהוָה ׀ אֱלֹהֵי יִשְׂרָאֵל הוֹרִישׁ
אֶת־הָאֱמֹרִי מִפְּנֵי עַמּוֹ יִשְׂרָאֵל וְאַתָּה
תִּירָשֶׁנּוּ׃ 24 הֲלֹא אֵת אֲשֶׁר יוֹרִישְׁךָ כְּמוֹשׁ
אֱלֹהֶיךָ אוֹתוֹ תִירָשׁ וְאֵת כָּל־אֲשֶׁר הוֹרִישׁ
יְהוָה אֱלֹהֵינוּ מִפָּנֵינוּ אוֹתוֹ נִירָשׁ׃
25 וְעַתָּה הֲטוֹב טוֹב אַתָּה מִבָּלָק בֶּן־צִפּוֹר
מֶלֶךְ מוֹאָב הֲרוֹב רָב עִם־יִשְׂרָאֵל אִם־
נִלְחֹם נִלְחַם בָּם׃
26 בְּשֶׁבֶת יִשְׂרָאֵל בְּחֶשְׁבּוֹן וּבִבְנוֹתֶיהָ
וּבְעַרְעוֹר וּבִבְנוֹתֶיהָ וּבְכָל־הֶעָרִים אֲשֶׁר
עַל־יְדֵי אַרְנוֹן שְׁלֹשׁ מֵאוֹת שָׁנָה וּמַדּוּעַ
לֹא־הִצַּלְתֶּם בָּעֵת הַהִיא׃ 27 וְאָנֹכִי לֹא־
חָטָאתִי לָךְ וְאַתָּה עֹשֶׂה אִתִּי רָעָה
לְהִלָּחֶם בִּי יִשְׁפֹּט יְהוָה הַשֹּׁפֵט הַיּוֹם בֵּין
בְּנֵי יִשְׂרָאֵל וּבֵין בְּנֵי עַמּוֹן׃
28 וְלֹא שָׁמַע מֶלֶךְ בְּנֵי עַמּוֹן אֶל־דִּבְרֵי
יִפְתָּח אֲשֶׁר שָׁלַח אֵלָיו׃ פ
29 וַתְּהִי עַל־יִפְתָּח רוּחַ יְהוָה וַיַּעֲבֹר אֶת־
הַגִּלְעָד וְאֶת־מְנַשֶּׁה וַיַּעֲבֹר אֶת־מִצְפֵּה
גִלְעָד וּמִמִּצְפֵּה גִלְעָד עָבַר בְּנֵי עַמּוֹן׃
30 וַיִּדַּר יִפְתָּח נֶדֶר לַיהוָה וַיֹּאמַר אִם־נָתוֹן

ently the formula attests to an agreement both to fulfill the covenant and to be responsible for the terms heard.)

26. three hundred years Jephthah presumably uses a round figure here, as rhetorical hyperbole. Factually, he is mistaken. Archaeological evidence puts the Exodus in the late 13th century B.C.E. and the beginning of the conquest of the Land some half-century later. Thus a 15th-century B.C.E. date is difficult to account for here, because it would precede the time period of the chieftains ("Judges").

vow to the LORD: "If You deliver the Ammonites
into my hands, 31then whatever comes out of
the door of my house to meet me on my safe
return from the Ammonites shall be the LORD's
and shall be offered by me as a burnt offering."
32Jephthah crossed over to the Ammonites
and attacked them, and the LORD delivered
them into his hands. 33He utterly routed
them—from Aroer as far as Minnith, twenty
towns—all the way to Abel-cheramim. So the
Ammonites submitted to the Israelites.

תִּתֵּן אֶת־בְּנֵי עַמּוֹן בְּיָדִי׃ 31 וְהָיָה הַיּוֹצֵא
אֲשֶׁר יֵצֵא מִדַּלְתֵי בֵיתִי לִקְרָאתִי בְּשׁוּבִי
בְשָׁלוֹם מִבְּנֵי עַמּוֹן וְהָיָה לַיהוָה
וְהַעֲלִיתִהוּ עוֹלָה׃ פ
32 וַיַּעֲבֹר יִפְתָּח אֶל־בְּנֵי עַמּוֹן לְהִלָּחֶם בָּם
וַיִּתְּנֵם יְהוָה בְּיָדוֹ׃ 33 וַיַּכֵּם מֵעֲרוֹעֵר וְעַד־
בּוֹאֲךָ מִנִּית עֶשְׂרִים עִיר וְעַד אָבֵל כְּרָמִים
מַכָּה גְּדוֹלָה מְאֹד וַיִּכָּנְעוּ בְּנֵי עַמּוֹן מִפְּנֵי
בְּנֵי יִשְׂרָאֵל׃ פ

30. vow to the LORD A conditional offering "to the LORD." The technical language is similar to that in the vow the nation of Israel took at the onset of its battle with the king of Arad during the wilderness trek (Num. 21:2–3). The vow's condition is fulfilled in v. 32.

הפטרת בלק

HAFTARAH FOR BALAK

MICAH 5:6–6:8

(*When* Ḥukkat *and* Balak *are combined, recite this* haftarah.)

The exact time of Micah's prophecy is unspecified. According to the first verse of his book, he lived and labored during the mid-8th century B.C.E., the period of the kings mentioned there. It was a time of expanding Assyrian power; the prophet's words of doom (1:2–3:12) may either anticipate or reflect the Assyrian invasions that led to the destruction and dispersion of the northern kingdom in 722–721 B.C.E.

The *haftarah* opens with two prophecies addressed to the remnant of Jacob after the destruction and dispersion. The first prophecy turns on the image of dew, or droplets of water, in a message that gives hope to the people that their renewal will come directly from God (Micah 5:6). As dew comes from heaven without any mortal involvement, so may Israel hope in a resurrection among the nations through divine grace. The second prophecy introduces the simile of a "fierce lion . . . / Which tramples wherever it goes / And rends, with none to deliver" (v. 7). This figure of power and violence gives a sense of empowerment to the nation in exile. Its tone of brute physicality stands in marked contrast to the opening prophecy. The two prophecies presumably were delivered on separate occasions, reflecting two moods or sensibilities.

The prophet climaxes his first two prophecies with a further vision of divine action. "In that day" of regeneration and victory, God will destroy the Israelites' military arsenal and its idolatrous practices (vv. 9–13). The verb "destroy" (*v'hikhrati*) is repeated four times in these verses, like a persistent hammer beat, and is complemented by four other verbs of wreck and ruin. Divine intervention will be total, eradicating the people's reliance on physical force and false worship.

Speaking on God's behalf, Micah then confronts the nation by recalling deeds of divine redemption in the past (6:3–5). The prophet summons the natural world to testify, along with Israel itself, whether God has ever failed them or brought them into danger. The prophet is certain that memory will yield only recollections of the "gracious acts of the LORD" on their behalf.

Hearing all this, the people ponder how best to "approach the LORD" and "Do homage to God on high." The poignancy and the pathos of their proposals (vv. 6–7) leave no reason to doubt their earnestness. The prophet, rejecting the human desire to offer one's earthly goods as an act of entreaty, speaks the word of God through tradition (v. 8).

RELATION OF THE *HAFTARAH* TO THE *PARASHAH*

Micah recalls to the people "what Balak king of Moab / Plotted against you [i.e., your ancestors], / And how Balaam . . . Responded to him" (6:5). This episode, one of God's "gracious acts" for His people, provides a direct link to the *parashah* (Num. 22:2–25:9).

The echo of Balaam's words in the *haftarah* provocatively juxtaposes that seer's contemplative sight with the prophet's moral demands. Evocation of the wondrous gaze in Numbers (24:5), "How fair are your tents, O Jacob" (*mah tovu ohalekha ya·akov*), is now balanced by Micah's statement of "what is good [*mah tov*]" behavior in God's sight. Aesthetics and similes of nature (palm groves, gardens, aloes, and cedars beside the water in Num. 24:6) thus stand on one side, and the tasks of covenantal responsibility on the other. It need not be so, however. Visions of the natural world need not result in moral blindness any more than moral clarity must contradict the insights of nature. The mature mind may sustain the teachings of both the *parashah* and the *haftarah*. It is the challenge of higher religious consciousness.

5 [6]The remnant of Jacob shall be,
In the midst of the many peoples,
Like dew from the LORD,
Like droplets on grass—
Which do not look to any man
Nor place their hope in mortals.
[7]The remnant of Jacob
Shall be among the nations,
In the midst of the many peoples,
Like a lion among beasts of the wild,
Like a fierce lion among flocks of sheep,
Which tramples wherever it goes
And rends, with none to deliver.
[8]Your hand shall prevail over your foes,
And all your enemies shall be cut down!
[9]In that day
—declares the LORD—
I will destroy the horses in your midst
And wreck your chariots.
[10]I will destroy the cities of your land
And demolish all your fortresses.
[11]I will destroy the sorcery you practice,
And you shall have no more soothsayers.
[12]I will destroy your idols
And the sacred pillars in your midst;
And no more shall you bow down
To the work of your hands.
[13]I will tear down the sacred posts in your midst

ה 6 וְהָיָה ׀ שְׁאֵרִית יַעֲקֹב
בְּקֶרֶב עַמִּים רַבִּים
כְּטַל מֵאֵת יְהוָה
כִּרְבִיבִים עֲלֵי־עֵשֶׂב
אֲשֶׁר לֹא־יְקַוֶּה לְאִישׁ
וְלֹא יְיַחֵל לִבְנֵי אָדָם׃
7 וְהָיָה שְׁאֵרִית יַעֲקֹב
בַּגּוֹיִם
בְּקֶרֶב עַמִּים רַבִּים
כְּאַרְיֵה בְּבַהֲמוֹת יַעַר
כִּכְפִיר בְּעֶדְרֵי־צֹאן
אֲשֶׁר אִם־עָבַר וְרָמַס
וְטָרַף וְאֵין מַצִּיל׃
8 תָּרֹם יָדְךָ עַל־צָרֶיךָ
וְכָל־אֹיְבֶיךָ יִכָּרֵתוּ׃ פ
9 וְהָיָה בַיּוֹם־הַהוּא
נְאֻם־יְהוָה
וְהִכְרַתִּי סוּסֶיךָ מִקִּרְבֶּךָ
וְהַאֲבַדְתִּי מַרְכְּבֹתֶיךָ׃
10 וְהִכְרַתִּי עָרֵי* אַרְצֶךָ
וְהָרַסְתִּי כָּל־מִבְצָרֶיךָ׃
11 וְהִכְרַתִּי כְשָׁפִים מִיָּדֶךָ
וּמְעוֹנְנִים לֹא יִהְיוּ־לָךְ׃
12 וְהִכְרַתִּי פְסִילֶיךָ
וּמַצֵּבוֹתֶיךָ מִקִּרְבֶּךָ
וְלֹא־תִשְׁתַּחֲוֶה עוֹד
לְמַעֲשֵׂה יָדֶיךָ׃
13 וְנָתַשְׁתִּי אֲשֵׁירֶיךָ מִקִּרְבֶּךָ

v. 10. לשון שנאה

Micah 5:6. remnant of Jacob In its original context, these references to the remnant refer to the contemporary exile of Israelites in Assyria and elsewhere. Later generations would read them as a messianic hope for their own time.

Like dew from the LORD Israel's remnant will be graced with divine sustenance and renewal, which asks nothing in return.

8. Your hand shall prevail over your foes Most commentators regard this as God's promise to Israel, but it can also be interpreted as Israel's prayer to God.

13. sacred posts Hebrew: *asherim;* prohibited by the Torah (Deut. 16:21–22). Destruction of Canaanite *asherim* is commanded in Exod. 34:13.

And destroy your cities.
14In anger and wrath
Will I wreak retribution
On the nations that have not obeyed.

וְהִשְׁמַדְתִּ֖י עָרֶֽיךָ*׃
14 וְעָשִׂ֜יתִי בְּאַ֧ף
וּבְחֵמָ֛ה נָקָ֖ם
אֶת־הַגּוֹיִ֑ם אֲשֶׁ֖ר לֹ֥א שָׁמֵֽעוּ׃ ס

6 Hear what the LORD is saying:
Come, present [My] case before the mountains,
And let the hills hear you pleading.

ו שִׁמְעוּ־נָ֕א אֵ֥ת אֲשֶׁר־יְהֹוָ֖ה אֹמֵ֑ר
ק֚וּם רִ֣יב אֶת־הֶהָרִ֔ים
וְתִשְׁמַ֥עְנָה הַגְּבָע֖וֹת קוֹלֶֽךָ׃

2Hear, you mountains, the case of the LORD—
You firm foundations of the earth!
For the LORD has a case against His people,
He has a suit against Israel.
3"My people!
What wrong have I done you?
What hardship have I caused you?
Testify against Me.
4In fact,
I brought you up from the land of Egypt,
I redeemed you from the house of bondage,
And I sent before you
Moses, Aaron, and Miriam.

2 שִׁמְע֤וּ הָרִים֙ אֶת־רִ֣יב יְהֹוָ֔ה
וְהָאֵתָנִ֖ים מֹ֣סְדֵי אָ֑רֶץ
כִּ֣י רִ֤יב לַֽיהֹוָה֙ עִם־עַמּ֔וֹ
וְעִם־יִשְׂרָאֵ֖ל יִתְוַכָּֽח׃
3 עַמִּ֛י
מֶה־עָשִׂ֥יתִי לְךָ֖
וּמָ֣ה הֶלְאֵתִ֑יךָ
עֲנֵ֥ה בִֽי׃
4 כִּ֤י
הֶֽעֱלִתִ֙יךָ֙ מֵאֶ֣רֶץ מִצְרַ֔יִם
וּמִבֵּ֥ית עֲבָדִ֖ים פְּדִיתִ֑יךָ
וָאֶשְׁלַ֣ח לְפָנֶ֔יךָ
אֶת־מֹשֶׁ֖ה אַהֲרֹ֥ן וּמִרְיָֽם׃

5"My people,
Remember what Balak king of Moab
Plotted against you,
And how Balaam son of Beor
Responded to him.
[Recall your passage]
From Shittim to Gilgal—

5 עַמִּ֗י
זְכָר־נָא֙ מַה־יָּעַ֗ץ
בָּלָק֙ מֶ֣לֶךְ מוֹאָ֔ב
וּמֶה־עָנָ֥ה אֹת֖וֹ
בִּלְעָ֣ם בֶּן־בְּע֑וֹר
מִן־הַשִּׁטִּים֙

v. 13. לשון שנאה

14. nations that have not obeyed The mention here of other nations—and their disobedience—is puzzling. Some commentators propose emending the word at the heart of this difficulty (*goyim,* "nations") to read *ge·im,* "arrogant ones." Then the prophet would be referring to the "arrogant ones" of Israel.

Micah 6:5. From Shittim to Gilgal A synopsis of places of divine beneficence, from the wilderness wanderings to settlement of the Promised Land. Shittim was the place of Israelite encampment where God transformed Balaam's prophecy for the good of the Israelites (Num. 22:1, 25:1, 33:48–49). Gilgal was the cult site where Saul's kingship was renewed after his victory against the Ammonites (1 Sam. 11:14).

And you will recognize
The gracious acts of the LORD."

עַד־הַגִּלְגָּל
לְמַ֫עַן דַּ֫עַת
צִדְקוֹת יְהוָה׃

6With what shall I approach the LORD,
Do homage to God on high?
Shall I approach Him with burnt offerings,
With calves a year old?
7Would the LORD be pleased with thousands of rams,
With myriads of streams of oil?
Shall I give my first-born for my transgression,
The fruit of my body for my sins?

6 בַּמָּה֙ אֲקַדֵּם יְהוָה
אִכַּף לֵאלֹהֵי מָרוֹם
הַאֲקַדְּמֶנּוּ בְעוֹלוֹת
בַּעֲגָלִים בְּנֵי שָׁנָה׃
7 הֲיִרְצֶה יְהוָה֙ בְּאַלְפֵי אֵילִים
בְּרִבְבוֹת נַחֲלֵי־שָׁמֶן
הַאֶתֵּן בְּכוֹרִי֙ פִּשְׁעִי
פְּרִי בִטְנִי חַטַּאת נַפְשִׁי׃

8"He has told you, O man, what is good,
And what the LORD requires of you:
Only to do justice
And to love goodness,
And to walk modestly with your God."

8 הִגִּיד לְךָ אָדָם מַה־טּוֹב
וּמָה־יְהוָה דּוֹרֵשׁ מִמְּךָ
כִּי אִם־עֲשׂוֹת מִשְׁפָּט֙
וְאַהֲבַת חֶסֶד
וְהַצְנֵעַ לֶכֶת עִם־אֱלֹהֶיךָ׃ פ

6–8. A classic expression of the primacy of morality over sacrifice. Other prophets (Amos 5:21–25; Hos. 6:6; Isa. 1:10–20) also articulate divine contempt for the performance of rituals in the absence of moral behavior.

He has told you . . . what the LORD requires This usually is understood as two parts of one injunction, referring both to what is good and to what the Lord requires as a doubled expression. However, because of the accent marks in the Hebrew text, the second phrase may be interpreted as specifying the injunction ("And what does the LORD require of you: / Only to do justice").

justice . . . goodness . . . walk modestly Abravanel astutely interprets this triad as a graded series of obligations: (1) the demands of justice—the formalities and externals of civil and criminal law; (2) the requirement of loving-kindness—actions performed in the spirit of the law, going beyond its formal, minimal demands; and (3) the inwardness of true piety hidden from the world at large.

For Rosenzweig, justice and goodness are goals yet to be accomplished. Humility before God, by contrast, is the unconditional starting point of all true living. It is a standing before the world in a "wholly present trust," daring to "say 'Truly!' to the truth" at every moment.

10The LORD spoke to Moses, saying,
11"Phinehas, son of Eleazar son of Aaron the
priest, has turned back My wrath from the Israelites by displaying among them his passion
for Me, so that I did not wipe out the Israelite
people in My passion. 12Say, therefore, 'I grant

10 וַיְדַבֵּר יְהֹוָה אֶל־מֹשֶׁה לֵּאמֹר׃ 11 פִּינְחָס
בֶּן־אֶלְעָזָר בֶּן־אַהֲרֹן הַכֹּהֵן הֵשִׁיב אֶת־
חֲמָתִי מֵעַל בְּנֵי־יִשְׂרָאֵל בְּקַנְאוֹ אֶת־
קִנְאָתִי בְּתוֹכָם וְלֹא־כִלִּיתִי אֶת־בְּנֵי־
יִשְׂרָאֵל בְּקִנְאָתִי׃ 12 לָכֵן אֱמֹר הִנְנִי נֹתֵן

IDOLATRY AND EXPIATION AT BAAL-PEOR (*continued*)

THE PACT WITH PHINEHAS (25:10–18)

11. passion Hebrew: *kin·ah,* a feature of God (*el kanna;* Exod. 20:5) that is shared by zealous advocates like Phinehas and Elijah (1 Kings 19:14). The passion displayed by Phinehas matched God's in that he alone obeyed God's command to kill the leaders (25:4).

wipe out the Israelite people Once released, God's anger destroys everything in its path without making moral distinctions.

12. Say Tell the people in the form of an oath.

25:11. Phinehas killed an Israelite man and Moabite woman because their flagrant immorality profaned God's name. The Torah seems to approve of Phinehas's extreme act; some modern as well as ancient commentators follow suit. Thus Hirsch, for example: "Anyone who wages war on the enemies of what is good and true is a champion of the Covenant of Peace on earth even while engaged in war." The Ḥatam Sofer praises Phinehas for showing the same zeal and energy to do right that the sinning Israelites displayed in doing wrong.

Most postbiblical commentators, however, tend to be uncomfortable with the zealous vigilantism of Phinehas, criticizing his fanaticism as a dangerous precedent. The Talmud claims that, had Phinehas asked the rabbinical court if it was permitted to kill Zimri and Cozbi, citing *halakhah* to justify his request, the court would have told him: "The law may permit it but we do not follow that law!" (BT Sanh. 82a). Moses of Coucy notes that although the previous *parashah* ends with Phinehas's deed and the death of 24,000 Israelites (it is unusual for a *parashah* to end on such a negative note), Phinehas's reward is not proclaimed until the beginning of this *parashah.* This teaches us to never rush to reward extremism. We are to wait until later events clarify whether the zealot's intention was indeed pure.

In the text of the Torah scroll, the letter *yod* in Phinehas's name in the second verse (v. 11) is written smaller than the other letters. When we commit violence, even if justifiable, the *yod* in us (standing for the name of God and for *y'hudi,* "Jew") is diminished thereby. In verse 12, the letter *vav* in *shalom* in the Torah scroll is written with a break in its stem. This is interpreted homiletically to suggest that the sort of peace one achieves by destroying one's opponent will inevitably be a flawed, incomplete peace.

Several commentators understand God's granting the priesthood to Phinehas and his descendants, not as a reward for his extremism but as an antidote for it. "He will have to cure himself of his violent temper if he is to function as a *kohen*" (*K'tav Sofer*). "This will protect Phinehas from the destructive impulse within him" (*Ha·amek Davar*). Perhaps serving as a *kohen* will give him ways of atoning for having taken two lives. A person is never the same after he has shed blood, no matter how justifiable the cause.

One of the few commentators who sees Phinehas in as favorable a light as the Torah seems to, deems his replacing Aaron as part of a generational shift in leadership. Just as the stern and demanding Moses was balanced by Aaron, who avoided quarrels and confrontations, the more moderate Joshua will be balanced by the fervor of Phinehas as high priest.

The tradition generally considers moral threats to be more dangerous for national survival than physical threats. Although the Egyptians and the Edomites threatened Israel's physical existence, we are commanded not to hate them. We are told to wipe out the Midianites, however, for they tried to undermine Israel's moral standing.

לוֹ אֶת־בְּרִיתִי שָׁלוֹם: 13 וְהָיְתָה לּוֹ וּלְזַרְעוֹ
אַחֲרָיו בְּרִית כְּהֻנַּת עוֹלָם תַּחַת אֲשֶׁר
קִנֵּא לֵאלֹהָיו וַיְכַפֵּר עַל־בְּנֵי יִשְׂרָאֵל:
14 וְשֵׁם אִישׁ יִשְׂרָאֵל הַמֻּכֶּה אֲשֶׁר הֻכָּה
אֶת־הַמִּדְיָנִית זִמְרִי בֶּן־סָלוּא נְשִׂיא בֵית־
אָב לַשִּׁמְעֹנִי: 15 וְשֵׁם הָאִשָּׁה הַמֻּכָּה
הַמִּדְיָנִית כָּזְבִּי בַת־צוּר רֹאשׁ אֻמּוֹת בֵּית־
אָב בְּמִדְיָן הוּא: פ
16 וַיְדַבֵּר יְהוָה אֶל־מֹשֶׁה לֵּאמֹר: 17 צָרוֹר
אֶת־הַמִּדְיָנִים וְהִכִּיתֶם אוֹתָם: 18 כִּי
צֹרְרִים הֵם לָכֶם בְּנִכְלֵיהֶם אֲשֶׁר־נִכְּלוּ
לָכֶם עַל־דְּבַר־פְּעוֹר וְעַל־דְּבַר כָּזְבִּי בַת־
נְשִׂיא מִדְיָן אֲחֹתָם הַמֻּכָּה בְיוֹם־הַמַּגֵּפָה
עַל־דְּבַר־פְּעוֹר:

him My pact of friendship. 13It shall be for him
and his descendants after him a pact of priesthood for all time, because he took impassioned
action for his God, thus making expiation for
the Israelites.'"

14The name of the Israelite who was killed,
the one who was killed with the Midianite
woman, was Zimri son of Salu, chieftain of a
Simeonite ancestral house. 15The name of the
Midianite woman who was killed was Cozbi
daughter of Zur; he was the tribal head of an
ancestral house in Midian.

16The LORD spoke to Moses, saying, 17"Assail
the Midianites and defeat them—18for they assailed you by the trickery they practiced against
you—because of the affair of Peor and because
of the affair of their kinswoman Cozbi, daughter
of the Midianite chieftain, who was killed at the
time of the plague on account of Peor."

My pact of friendship God's covenant meant that Phinehas received divine protection against the revenge that would be sought by Zimri's clan.

13. a pact of priesthood for all time Phinehas is awarded the high priesthood for suppressing apostasy, just as the Levites were awarded the priesthood (Exod. 32:29). God promises that his line, later called the Zadokites (see Ezek. 44:15–16), will be the exclusive officiants in the Temple (see 1 Chron. 5:30–34).

making expiation By means of his passion, Phinehas assuaged God's wrath.

14–15. A postscript stating the names and pedigrees of the culprits.

ancestral house That is, a household, the basic unit of the clan.

17. Why are the Midianites assailed, because it was Moabite women who seduced the Israelites? This may simply reflect different sources or traditions. Alternatively, this episode may reflect the period when Moab was part of a Midianite confederation that embraced all of Transjordan as its protectorate (see Josh. 13:21). When Israel conquered Sihon's territory, it severed the king's highway (Num. 21:22) and thereby threatened the Midianites' hold on the vital spice trade. Thus Midian, Israel's erstwhile ally (10:29–32), now became its implacable foe.

18. Both Israel's apostasy at Baal-peor and the act of Zimri are attributed to the scheming of the Midianites.

for they assailed you Alternatively, "they are hostile," indicating both past and continuing hostility.

their kinswoman Thus the Midianites now felt obligated to avenge her death.

---

18. for they assailed you At first, the nations of the world resented and hated the Israelites because their ways of worship were different from those of the nations and at a higher moral level. Even when the people Israel tried to imitate gentile practices, though, their enemies continued to resent them. According to the Talmud (BT Sanh. 106a), Balaam was impressed by Israel's moral purity and realized that the only way to defeat them would be to compromise their moral excellence. It was his idea to lure the Israelites into participating in the orgiastic Midianite cult (Num. 31:16). The Midianites were so desperate to defeat Israel that they encouraged their daughters to engage in sexual orgies to lead the Israelites astray.

26

19 When the plague was over, 1 the LORD
said to Moses and to Eleazar son of Aaron the
priest, 2 "Take a census of the whole Israelite
community from the age of twenty years up, by
their ancestral houses, all Israelites able to bear
arms." 3 So Moses and Eleazar the priest, on the
steppes of Moab, at the Jordan near Jericho,
gave instructions about them, namely, 4 those
from twenty years up, as the LORD had commanded Moses.

The descendants of the Israelites who came
out of the land of Egypt were:

5 Reuben, Israel's first-born. Descendants of
Reuben: [Of] Enoch, the clan of the Enochites;

כו

19 וַיְהִי אַחֲרֵי הַמַּגֵּפָה* פ
1 וַיֹּאמֶר יְהוָה אֶל־מֹשֶׁה וְאֶל אֶלְעָזָר בֶּן־
אַהֲרֹן הַכֹּהֵן לֵאמֹר׃ 2 שְׂאוּ אֶת־רֹאשׁ ׀
כָּל־עֲדַת בְּנֵי־יִשְׂרָאֵל מִבֶּן עֶשְׂרִים שָׁנָה
וָמַעְלָה לְבֵית אֲבֹתָם כָּל־יֹצֵא צָבָא
בְּיִשְׂרָאֵל׃ 3 וַיְדַבֵּר מֹשֶׁה וְאֶלְעָזָר הַכֹּהֵן
אֹתָם בְּעַרְבֹת מוֹאָב עַל־יַרְדֵּן יְרֵחוֹ
לֵאמֹר׃ 4 מִבֶּן עֶשְׂרִים שָׁנָה וָמָעְלָה כַּאֲשֶׁר
צִוָּה יְהוָה אֶת־מֹשֶׁה וּבְנֵי יִשְׂרָאֵל
הַיֹּצְאִים מֵאֶרֶץ מִצְרָיִם׃
שני 5 רְאוּבֵן בְּכוֹר יִשְׂרָאֵל בְּנֵי רְאוּבֵן חֲנוֹךְ
מִשְׁפַּחַת הַחֲנֹכִי לְפַלּוּא מִשְׁפַּחַת

v. 19. פיסקא באמצע פסוק, ונחשב פסוק נפרד בסכום הפסוקים

The Generation of the Conquest (25:19–36:13)

The central theme of the final 11 chapters of the Book of Numbers is the occupation of the Promised Land. In sharp contrast to the faithlessness of the Exodus generation, the following generation is loyal to God and courageous; it is successful in battle and deemed worthy to conquer the Land.

19. The Torah text breaks off in mid-verse at this point. Originally what followed may have been the account of the war against Midian (chapter 31), initiated by God as reported in 25:16–18. Because war requires conscription, the account of the census (chapter 26) was interposed.

THE SECOND CENSUS (26:1–65)

All able-bodied men above the age of 20 are registered for the ultimate purposes of dividing the Land among the tribes and providing a militia for the forthcoming war against Midian.

DIRECTIONS FOR TAKING A CENSUS (vv. 1–4)

1. God's command for the first census was given to Moses and Aaron. After Aaron's death, his successor, Eleazar, takes his place. This is the only time God speaks to Eleazar directly.

RESULTS OF THE CENSUS (vv. 5–51)

This section enumerates the clans, the number of able-bodied men in each tribe, and their total sum.

CHAPTER 26

This chapter, like chapter 1, contains a census, suggesting that all of the chapters they enclose deal with one extended period of time, during which the generation that left Egypt treks through the desert and ultimately dies there. Although the ostensible purpose of this census was to learn about the relative land requirements of each clan and tribe, the commentators refuse to leave it at that. They envision God counting the Israelites after the plague of Baal-peor as an act of love, "like a shepherd numbering his flock after wolves have attacked it" (Rashi). Hirsch suggests that, after the embarrassment of Baal-peor, the chastened Israelites were led to regain a sense of self-worth by reflecting on who their ancestors were. (Or is God scolding them after Baal-peor by asking them, "What would your parents and grandparents say about what you just did?")

of Pallu, the clan of the Palluites; [6]of Hezron, the clan of the Hezronites; of Carmi, the clan of the Carmites. [7]Those are the clans of the Reubenites. The persons enrolled came to 43,730.

[8]Born to Pallu: Eliab. [9]The sons of Eliab were Nemuel, and Dathan and Abiram. These are the same Dathan and Abiram, chosen in the assembly, who agitated against Moses and Aaron as part of Korah's band when they agitated against the LORD. [10]Whereupon the earth opened its mouth and swallowed them up with Korah—when that band died, when the fire consumed the two hundred and fifty men—and they became an example. [11]The sons of Korah, however, did not die.

[12]Descendants of Simeon by their clans: Of Nemuel, the clan of the Nemuelites; of Jamin, the clan of the Jaminites; of Jachin, the clan of the Jachinites; [13]of Zerah, the clan of the Zerahites; of Saul, the clan of the Saulites. [14]Those are the clans of the Simeonites; [persons enrolled:] 22,200.

[15]Descendants of Gad by their clans: Of Zephon, the clan of the Zephonites; of Haggi, the clan of the Haggites; of Shuni, the clan of the Shunites; [16]of Ozni, the clan of the Oznites; of Eri, the clan of the Erites; [17]of Arod, the clan of the Arodites; of Areli, the clan of the Arelites.

הַפַּלֻּאִֽי׃ 6 לְחֶצְרֹ֕ן מִשְׁפַּ֖חַת הַֽחֶצְרוֹנִ֑י
לְכַרְמִ֕י מִשְׁפַּ֖חַת הַכַּרְמִֽי׃ 7 אֵ֖לֶּה מִשְׁפְּחֹ֣ת
הָרֽאוּבֵנִ֑י וַיִּהְי֣וּ פְקֻדֵיהֶ֗ם שְׁלֹשָׁ֤ה
וְאַרְבָּעִים֙ אֶ֔לֶף וּשְׁבַ֥ע מֵא֖וֹת וּשְׁלֹשִֽׁים׃
8 וּבְנֵ֥י פַלּ֖וּא אֱלִיאָֽב׃ 9 וּבְנֵ֣י אֱלִיאָ֔ב נְמוּאֵ֖ל
וְדָתָ֣ן וַאֲבִירָ֑ם הֽוּא־דָתָ֨ן וַאֲבִירָ֜ם קרואי
קְרִיאֵ֣י הָעֵדָ֗ה אֲשֶׁ֨ר הִצּ֜וּ עַל־מֹשֶׁ֤ה וְעַֽל־
אַהֲרֹן֙ בַּעֲדַת־קֹ֔רַח בְּהַצֹּתָ֖ם עַל־יְהוָֽה׃
10 וַתִּפְתַּ֨ח הָאָ֜רֶץ אֶת־פִּ֗יהָ וַתִּבְלַ֥ע אֹתָ֛ם
וְאֶת־קֹ֖רַח בְּמ֣וֹת הָעֵדָ֑ה בַּאֲכֹ֣ל הָאֵ֗שׁ אֵ֣ת
חֲמִשִּׁ֤ים וּמָאתַ֙יִם֙ אִ֔ישׁ וַיִּהְי֖וּ לְנֵֽס׃
11 וּבְנֵי־קֹ֖רַח לֹא־מֵֽתוּ׃ ס
12 בְּנֵ֣י שִׁמְעוֹן֮ לְמִשְׁפְּחֹתָם֒ לִנְמוּאֵ֗ל
מִשְׁפַּ֙חַת֙ הַנְּמוּאֵלִ֔י לְיָמִ֕ין מִשְׁפַּ֖חַת הַיָּמִינִ֑י
לְיָכִ֕ין מִשְׁפַּ֖חַת הַיָּכִינִֽי׃ 13 לְזֶ֕רַח מִשְׁפַּ֖חַת
הַזַּרְחִ֑י לְשָׁא֕וּל מִשְׁפַּ֖חַת הַשָּׁאוּלִֽי׃ 14 אֵ֖לֶּה
מִשְׁפְּחֹ֣ת הַשִּׁמְעֹנִ֑י שְׁנַ֧יִם וְעֶשְׂרִ֛ים אֶ֖לֶף
וּמָאתָֽיִם׃ ס
15 בְּנֵ֣י גָד֮ לְמִשְׁפְּחֹתָם֒ לִצְפ֗וֹן מִשְׁפַּ֙חַת֙
הַצְּפוֹנִ֔י לְחַגִּ֕י מִשְׁפַּ֖חַת הַחַגִּ֑י לְשׁוּנִ֕י
מִשְׁפַּ֖חַת הַשּׁוּנִֽי׃ 16 לְאָזְנִ֕י מִשְׁפַּ֖חַת הָאָזְנִ֑י
לְעֵרִ֕י מִשְׁפַּ֖חַת הָעֵרִֽי׃ 17 לַאֲר֕וֹד מִשְׁפַּ֖חַת
הָאֲרוֹדִ֑י לְאַ֨רְאֵלִ֔י מִשְׁפַּ֖חַת הָאַרְאֵלִֽי׃

11. The Korahite clan survived to become an important levitical clan of Temple singers (see, e.g., the opening verses of Pss. 44–49). They also served as temple guards at the most prestigious location—the entrance.

---

9. Apparently the rebels Dathan and Abiram had an older brother, Nemuel, who did not join them in their nefarious activities. Coming from the same environment, he resisted taking the path they chose.

11. The sons of Korah . . . did not die Some say that they carried on their father's quarrelsome ways, so that in every generation there are some people who seek to cause divisiveness in the community. Others disagree, saying that they learned their lesson and repented, and later composed and sang half a dozen psalms. These include Psalm 47, recited before the sounding of the *shofar* on *Rosh ha-Shanah,* and Ps. 49, read in a house of mourning. This demonstrates that repentance is possible, that people can change their ways as they confront mortality, a lesson the descendants of Korah may well have learned from their ancestor's fate. Like Nemuel (v. 9), they represent the capacity of people to rise above the circumstances of their birth and upbringing.

18Those are the clans of Gad's descendants; persons enrolled: 40,500.

19Born to Judah: Er and Onan. Er and Onan died in the land of Canaan.

20Descendants of Judah by their clans: Of Shelah, the clan of the Shelanites; of Perez, the clan of the Perezites; of Zerah, the clan of the Zerahites. 21Descendants of Perez: of Hezron, the clan of the Hezronites; of Hamul, the clan of the Hamulites. 22Those are the clans of Judah; persons enrolled: 76,500.

23Descendants of Issachar by their clans: [Of] Tola, the clan of the Tolaites; of Puvah, the clan of the Punites; 24of Jashub, the clan of the Jashubites; of Shimron, the clan of the Shimronites. 25Those are the clans of Issachar; persons enrolled: 64,300.

26Descendants of Zebulun by their clans: Of Sered, the clan of the Seredites; of Elon, the clan of the Elonites; of Jahleel, the clan of the Jahleelites. 27Those are the clans of the Zebulunites; persons enrolled: 60,500.

28The sons of Joseph were Manasseh and Ephraim—by their clans.

29Descendants of Manasseh: Of Machir, the clan of the Machirites.—Machir begot Gilead.—Of Gilead, the clan of the Gileadites. 30These were the descendants of Gilead: [Of] Iezer, the clan of the Iezerites; of Helek, the clan of the Helekites; 31[of] Asriel, the clan of the Asrielites; [of] Shechem, the clan of the Shechemites; 32[of] Shemida, the clan of the Shemidaites; [of] Hepher, the clan of the Hepherites.—33Now Zelophehad son of Hepher had no sons, only daughters. The names of Zelophehad's daughters were Mahlah, Noah, Hoglah, Milcah, and Tirzah.—34Those are the clans of Manasseh; persons enrolled: 52,700.

18 אֵ֥לֶּה מִשְׁפְּחֹ֛ת בְּנֵי־גָ֖ד לִפְקֻדֵיהֶ֑ם
אַרְבָּעִ֥ים אֶ֖לֶף וַחֲמֵ֥שׁ מֵאֽוֹת׃ ס
19 בְּנֵ֥י יְהוּדָ֖ה עֵ֣ר וְאוֹנָ֑ן וַיָּ֥מָת עֵ֛ר וְאוֹנָ֖ן
בְּאֶ֥רֶץ כְּנָֽעַן׃
20 וַיִּהְי֣וּ בְנֵֽי־יְהוּדָה֮ לְמִשְׁפְּחֹתָם֒ לְשֵׁלָ֗ה
מִשְׁפַּ֙חַת֙ הַשֵּׁ֣לָנִ֔י לְפֶ֕רֶץ מִשְׁפַּ֖חַת הַפַּרְצִ֑י
לְזֶ֕רַח מִשְׁפַּ֖חַת הַזַּרְחִֽי׃ 21 וַיִּהְי֣וּ בְנֵי־
פֶ֔רֶץ לְחֶצְרֹ֕ן מִשְׁפַּ֖חַת הַֽחֶצְרֹנִ֑י לְחָמ֕וּל
מִשְׁפַּ֖חַת הֶחָמוּלִֽי׃ 22 אֵ֥לֶּה מִשְׁפְּחֹ֛ת
יְהוּדָ֖ה לִפְקֻדֵיהֶ֑ם שִׁשָּׁ֧ה וְשִׁבְעִ֛ים אֶ֖לֶף
וַחֲמֵ֥שׁ מֵאֽוֹת׃ ס
23 בְּנֵ֤י יִשָּׂשכָר֙ לְמִשְׁפְּחֹתָ֔ם תּוֹלָ֕ע
מִשְׁפַּ֖חַת הַתּוֹלָעִ֑י לְפֻוָ֕ה מִשְׁפַּ֖חַת הַפּוּנִֽי׃
24 לְיָשׁ֕וּב מִשְׁפַּ֖חַת הַיָּשֻׁבִ֑י לְשִׁמְרֹ֕ן
מִשְׁפַּ֖חַת הַשִּׁמְרֹנִֽי׃ 25 אֵ֛לֶּה מִשְׁפְּחֹ֥ת
יִשָּׂשכָ֖ר לִפְקֻדֵיהֶ֑ם אַרְבָּעָ֧ה וְשִׁשִּׁ֛ים אֶ֖לֶף
וּשְׁלֹ֥שׁ מֵאֽוֹת׃ ס
26 בְּנֵ֤י זְבוּלֻן֙ לְמִשְׁפְּחֹתָ֔ם לְסֶ֗רֶד מִשְׁפַּ֙חַת֙
הַסַּרְדִּ֔י לְאֵל֕וֹן מִשְׁפַּ֖חַת הָאֵלֹנִ֑י לְיַ֨חְלְאֵ֔ל
מִשְׁפַּ֖חַת הַיַּחְלְאֵלִֽי׃ 27 אֵ֛לֶּה מִשְׁפְּחֹ֥ת
הַזְּבוּלֹנִ֖י לִפְקֻדֵיהֶ֑ם שִׁשִּׁ֥ים אֶ֖לֶף וַחֲמֵ֥שׁ
מֵאֽוֹת׃ ס
28 בְּנֵ֥י יוֹסֵ֖ף לְמִשְׁפְּחֹתָ֑ם מְנַשֶּׁ֖ה וְאֶפְרָֽיִם׃
29 בְּנֵ֣י מְנַשֶּׁ֗ה לְמָכִיר֙ מִשְׁפַּ֣חַת הַמָּכִירִ֔י
וּמָכִ֖יר הוֹלִ֣יד אֶת־גִּלְעָ֑ד לְגִלְעָ֕ד מִשְׁפַּ֖חַת
הַגִּלְעָדִֽי׃ 30 אֵ֚לֶּה בְּנֵ֣י גִלְעָ֔ד אִ֣יעֶ֔זֶר
מִשְׁפַּ֖חַת הָאִֽיעֶזְרִ֑י לְחֵ֕לֶק מִשְׁפַּ֖חַת
הַֽחֶלְקִֽי׃ 31 וְאַ֨שְׂרִיאֵ֔ל מִשְׁפַּ֖חַת הָאַשְׂרְאֵלִ֑י
וְשֶׁ֕כֶם מִשְׁפַּ֖חַת הַשִּׁכְמִֽי׃ 32 וּשְׁמִידָ֕ע
מִשְׁפַּ֖חַת הַשְּׁמִידָעִ֑י וְחֵ֕פֶר מִשְׁפַּ֖חַת
הַֽחֶפְרִֽי׃ 33 וּצְלָפְחָ֣ד בֶּן־חֵ֗פֶר לֹא־הָ֥יוּ ל֛וֹ
בָּנִ֖ים כִּ֣י אִם־בָּנ֑וֹת וְשֵׁם֙ בְּנ֣וֹת צְלָפְחָ֔ד
מַחְלָ֣ה וְנֹעָ֔ה חָגְלָ֥ה מִלְכָּ֖ה וְתִרְצָֽה׃
34 אֵ֖לֶּה מִשְׁפְּחֹ֣ת מְנַשֶּׁ֑ה וּפְקֻדֵיהֶ֕ם שְׁנַ֧יִם
וַחֲמִשִּׁ֛ים אֶ֖לֶף וּשְׁבַ֥ע מֵאֽוֹת׃ ס

35These are the descendants of Ephraim by
their clans: Of Shuthelah, the clan of the
Shuthelahites; of Becher, the clan of the
Becherites; of Tahan, the clan of the Tahanites.
36These are the descendants of Shuthelah: Of
Eran, the clan of the Eranites. 37Those are the
clans of Ephraim's descendants; persons enrolled: 32,500.

Those are the descendants of Joseph by their clans.

38The descendants of Benjamin by their clans:
Of Bela, the clan of the Belaites; of Ashbel, the
clan of the Ashbelites; of Ahiram, the clan of
the Ahiramites; 39of Shephupham, the clan of
the Shuphamites; of Hupham, the clan of the
Huphamites. 40The sons of Bela were Ard and
Naaman: [Of Ard,] the clan of the Ardites; of
Naaman, the clan of the Naamanites. 41Those
are the descendants of Benjamin by their clans;
persons enrolled: 45,600.

42These are the descendants of Dan by their
clans: Of Shuham, the clan of the Shuhamites.
Those are the clans of Dan, by their clans. 43All
the clans of the Shuhamites; persons enrolled:
64,400.

44Descendants of Asher by their clans: Of
Imnah, the clan of the Imnites; of Ishvi, the clan
of the Ishvites; of Beriah, the clan of the Beri-
ites. 45Of the descendants of Beriah: Of Heber,
the clan of the Heberites; of Malchiel, the clan
of the Malchielites.—46The name of Asher's
daughter was Serah.—47These are the clans of
Asher's descendants; persons enrolled: 53,400.

48Descendants of Naphtali by their clans: Of
Jahzeel, the clan of the Jahzeelites; of Guni, the
clan of the Gunites; 49of Jezer, the clan of the
Jezerites; of Shillem, the clan of the Shillemites.

35 אֵלֶּה בְנֵי־אֶפְרַיִם לְמִשְׁפְּחֹתָם לְשׁוּתֶלַח
מִשְׁפַּחַת הַשֻּׁתַלְחִי לְבֶכֶר מִשְׁפַּחַת
הַבַּכְרִי לְתַחַן מִשְׁפַּחַת הַתַּחֲנִי׃ 36 וְאֵלֶּה
בְּנֵי שׁוּתָלַח לְעֵרָן מִשְׁפַּחַת הָעֵרָנִי׃
37 אֵלֶּה מִשְׁפְּחֹת בְּנֵי־אֶפְרַיִם לִפְקֻדֵיהֶם
שְׁנַיִם וּשְׁלֹשִׁים אֶלֶף וַחֲמֵשׁ מֵאוֹת
אֵלֶּה בְנֵי־יוֹסֵף לְמִשְׁפְּחֹתָם׃ ס
38 בְּנֵי בִנְיָמִן לְמִשְׁפְּחֹתָם לְבֶלַע מִשְׁפַּחַת
הַבַּלְעִי לְאַשְׁבֵּל מִשְׁפַּחַת הָאַשְׁבֵּלִי
לַאֲחִירָם מִשְׁפַּחַת הָאֲחִירָמִי׃ 39 לִשְׁפוּפָם
מִשְׁפַּחַת הַשּׁוּפָמִי לְחוּפָם מִשְׁפַּחַת
הַחוּפָמִי׃ 40 וַיִּהְיוּ בְנֵי־בֶלַע אַרְדְּ וְנַעֲמָן
מִשְׁפַּחַת הָאַרְדִּי לְנַעֲמָן מִשְׁפַּחַת הַנַּעֲמִי׃
41 אֵלֶּה בְנֵי־בִנְיָמִן לְמִשְׁפְּחֹתָם וּפְקֻדֵיהֶם
חֲמִשָּׁה וְאַרְבָּעִים אֶלֶף וְשֵׁשׁ מֵאוֹת׃ ס
42 אֵלֶּה בְנֵי־דָן לְמִשְׁפְּחֹתָם לְשׁוּחָם
מִשְׁפַּחַת הַשּׁוּחָמִי אֵלֶּה מִשְׁפְּחֹת דָּן
לְמִשְׁפְּחֹתָם׃ 43 כָּל־מִשְׁפְּחֹת הַשּׁוּחָמִי
לִפְקֻדֵיהֶם אַרְבָּעָה וְשִׁשִּׁים אֶלֶף וְאַרְבַּע
מֵאוֹת׃ ס
44 בְּנֵי אָשֵׁר לְמִשְׁפְּחֹתָם לְיִמְנָה מִשְׁפַּחַת
הַיִּמְנָה לְיִשְׁוִי מִשְׁפַּחַת הַיִּשְׁוִי לִבְרִיעָה
מִשְׁפַּחַת הַבְּרִיעִי׃ 45 לִבְנֵי בְרִיעָה לְחֶבֶר
מִשְׁפַּחַת הַחֶבְרִי לְמַלְכִּיאֵל מִשְׁפַּחַת
הַמַּלְכִּיאֵלִי׃ 46 וְשֵׁם בַּת־אָשֵׁר שָׂרַח׃
47 אֵלֶּה מִשְׁפְּחֹת בְּנֵי־אָשֵׁר לִפְקֻדֵיהֶם
שְׁלֹשָׁה וַחֲמִשִּׁים אֶלֶף וְאַרְבַּע
מֵאוֹת׃ ס
48 בְּנֵי נַפְתָּלִי לְמִשְׁפְּחֹתָם לְיַחְצְאֵל
מִשְׁפַּחַת הַיַּחְצְאֵלִי לְגוּנִי מִשְׁפַּחַת הַגּוּנִי׃
49 לְיֵצֶר מִשְׁפַּחַת הַיִּצְרִי לְשִׁלֵּם מִשְׁפַּחַת
הַשִּׁלֵּמִי׃ 50 אֵלֶּה מִשְׁפְּחֹת נַפְתָּלִי

46. Asher's daughter was Serah She is the only female in the genealogical lists; see also Gen. 46:17 and 1 Chron. 7:30. There is a tradition that her father died without sons. That places her in the same category as the daughters of Zelophehad (see 27:1–7) and might explain why she is mentioned here. Otherwise, her presence remains a mystery.

לְמִשְׁפְּחֹתָ֑ם וּפְקֻדֵיהֶ֕ם חֲמִשָּׁ֧ה וְאַרְבָּעִ֛ים
אֶ֖לֶף וְאַרְבַּ֥ע מֵאֽוֹת׃
51 אֵ֠לֶּה פְּקוּדֵי֙ בְּנֵ֣י יִשְׂרָאֵ֔ל שֵׁשׁ־מֵא֥וֹת
אֶ֖לֶף וָאָ֑לֶף שְׁבַ֥ע מֵא֖וֹת וּשְׁלֹשִֽׁים׃ פ
שלישי 52 וַיְדַבֵּ֥ר יְהוָ֖ה אֶל־מֹשֶׁ֥ה לֵּאמֹֽר׃ 53 לָאֵ֗לֶּה
תֵּחָלֵ֥ק הָאָ֛רֶץ בְּנַחֲלָ֖ה בְּמִסְפַּ֥ר שֵׁמֽוֹת׃
54 לָרַ֗ב תַּרְבֶּה֙ נַחֲלָת֔וֹ וְלַמְעַ֕ט תַּמְעִ֖יט
נַחֲלָת֑וֹ אִ֚ישׁ לְפִ֣י פְקֻדָ֔יו יֻתַּ֖ן נַחֲלָתֽוֹ׃
55 אַךְ־בְּגוֹרָ֕ל יֵחָלֵ֖ק אֶת־הָאָ֑רֶץ לִשְׁמ֥וֹת
מַטּֽוֹת־אֲבֹתָ֖ם יִנְחָֽלוּ׃ 56 עַל־פִּי֙ הַגּוֹרָ֔ל
תֵּחָלֵ֖ק נַחֲלָת֑וֹ בֵּ֥ין רַ֖ב לִמְעָֽט׃ ס
57 וְאֵ֨לֶּה פְקוּדֵ֣י הַלֵּוִי֮ לְמִשְׁפְּחֹתָם֒ לְגֵרְשׁ֕וֹן
מִשְׁפַּ֙חַת֙ הַגֵּ֣רְשֻׁנִּ֔י לִקְהָ֕ת מִשְׁפַּ֖חַת
הַקְּהָתִ֑י לִמְרָרִ֕י מִשְׁפַּ֖חַת הַמְּרָרִֽי׃ 58 אֵ֣לֶּה ׀
מִשְׁפְּחֹ֣ת לֵוִ֗י מִשְׁפַּ֨חַת הַלִּבְנִ֜י מִשְׁפַּ֤חַת
הַֽחֶבְרֹנִי֙ מִשְׁפַּ֣חַת הַמַּחְלִי֙ מִשְׁפַּ֣חַת
הַמּוּשִׁ֔י מִשְׁפַּ֖חַת הַקָּרְחִ֑י וּקְהָ֖ת הוֹלִ֥ד

50 Those are the clans of the Naphtalites, clan by clan; persons enrolled: 45,400.

51 This is the enrollment of the Israelites: 601,730.

52 The LORD spoke to Moses, saying, 53 "Among these shall the land be apportioned as shares, according to the listed names: 54 with larger groups increase the share, with smaller groups reduce the share. Each is to be assigned its share according to its enrollment. 55 The land, moreover, is to be apportioned by lot; and the allotment shall be made according to the listings of their ancestral tribes. 56 Each portion shall be assigned by lot, whether for larger or smaller groups."

57 This is the enrollment of the Levites by their clans: Of Gershon, the clan of the Gershonites; of Kohath, the clan of the Kohathites; of Merari, the clan of the Merarites. 58 These are the clans of Levi: The clan of the Libnites, the clan of the Hebronites, the clan of the Mahlites, the clan of the Mushites, the clan of the Korahites.—

HOW TO APPORTION THE LAND (vv. 52–56)

The procedure seems to involve two irreconcilable methods: by lot and by the size of each tribe. In fact, the location of tribal territory is determined by lot, but that territory's size is a function of the tribe's census count. These prescriptions will apply only to the 9½ that settle in Cisjordan, the western side of the Jordan (34:13–15). The 2½ Transjordanian tribes arrange to have their territory (already conquered) awarded to them by Moses (32:33).

53. Land was allotted only to those whose names were entered in this second census—not those who were counted in the first census and who died in the wilderness.

54. larger groups Refers to the more populous tribes, as indicated by the tribal totals in this second census.

Each . . . its . . . its Alternatively, "Each person . . . his . . . his"; that is, each person receives his allotment within his clan, not elsewhere.

55. The assignment of property by lot was also practiced elsewhere in the ancient Near East during the 2nd millennium B.C.E.

according to the listings Literally, "according to the names." Each person will take his share within the territory assigned to his tribe by lot.

56. Each portion Literally, "its portion." That is, each tribe's portion.

whether Each tribe, irrespective of its size, will be assigned its territory by lot.

LEVITICAL CLANS (vv. 57–62)

The clans of Levi are listed separately because they are not entitled to any share of the Land (v. 62; see 18:23–24). Because they do not serve in the army, there is no need to limit their census to males above 20. The reason for this census is not given; it is most likely for the purpose of assigning the Levites their tabernacle duties.

57. The Gershonites, Kohathites, and Merarites make up the three traditional clans of Levi who are assigned to their respective guarding and transport duties in the tabernacle.

58. Libnites Libnah, a town in the territory of Judah, was assigned to the Aaronides.

Hebronites Hebron, a major city of Judah, was assigned to the Aaronides.

Mahlites This name survives on a cosmetic burner found on the site of the ancient city Lachish.

Korahites See Comment to 26:11.

Kohath begot Amram. 59The name of Amram's
wife was Jochebed daughter of Levi, who was
born to Levi in Egypt; she bore to Amram Aaron
and Moses and their sister Miriam. 60To Aaron
were born Nadab and Abihu, Eleazar and
Ithamar. 61Nadab and Abihu died when they
offered alien fire before the LORD.—62Their enrollment of 23,000 comprised all males from a
month up. They were not part of the regular enrollment of the Israelites, since no share was assigned to them among the Israelites.

אֶת־עַמְרָם׃ 59 וְשֵׁם ׀ אֵשֶׁת עַמְרָם יוֹכֶבֶד
בַּת־לֵוִי אֲשֶׁר יָלְדָה אֹתָהּ לְלֵוִי בְּמִצְרָיִם
וַתֵּלֶד לְעַמְרָם אֶת־אַהֲרֹן וְאֶת־מֹשֶׁה וְאֵת
מִרְיָם אֲחֹתָם׃ 60 וַיִּוָּלֵד לְאַהֲרֹן אֶת־נָדָב
וְאֶת־אֲבִיהוּא אֶת־אֶלְעָזָר וְאֶת־אִיתָמָר׃
61 וַיָּמָת נָדָב וַאֲבִיהוּא בְּהַקְרִיבָם אֵשׁ־זָרָה
לִפְנֵי יְהוָה׃ 62 וַיִּהְיוּ פְקֻדֵיהֶם שְׁלֹשָׁה
וְעֶשְׂרִים אֶלֶף כָּל־זָכָר מִבֶּן־חֹדֶשׁ וָמָעְלָה
כִּי ׀ לֹא הָתְפָּקְדוּ בְּתוֹךְ בְּנֵי יִשְׂרָאֵל כִּי
לֹא־נִתַּן לָהֶם נַחֲלָה בְּתוֹךְ בְּנֵי יִשְׂרָאֵל׃

63These are the persons enrolled by Moses
and Eleazar the priest who registered the Israelites on the steppes of Moab, at the Jordan near
Jericho. 64Among these there was not one of
those enrolled by Moses and Aaron the priest
when they recorded the Israelites in the wilderness of Sinai. 65For the LORD had said of them,
"They shall die in the wilderness." Not one of
them survived, except Caleb son of Jephunneh
and Joshua son of Nun.

63 אֵלֶּה פְּקוּדֵי מֹשֶׁה וְאֶלְעָזָר הַכֹּהֵן אֲשֶׁר
פָּקְדוּ אֶת־בְּנֵי יִשְׂרָאֵל בְּעַרְבֹת מוֹאָב עַל
יַרְדֵּן יְרֵחוֹ׃ 64 וּבְאֵלֶּה לֹא־הָיָה אִישׁ
מִפְּקוּדֵי מֹשֶׁה וְאַהֲרֹן הַכֹּהֵן אֲשֶׁר פָּקְדוּ
אֶת־בְּנֵי יִשְׂרָאֵל בְּמִדְבַּר סִינָי׃ 65 כִּי־אָמַר
יְהוָה לָהֶם מוֹת יָמֻתוּ בַּמִּדְבָּר וְלֹא־נוֹתַר
מֵהֶם אִישׁ כִּי אִם־כָּלֵב בֶּן־יְפֻנֶּה וִיהוֹשֻׁעַ
בִּן־נוּן׃ ס

27 The daughters of Zelophehad, of Ma-

כז וַתִּקְרַבְנָה בְּנוֹת צְלָפְחָד בֶּן־חֵפֶר

Kohath begot Amram Thus Moses and Aaron (Amram's sons, v. 59) are totally separated from the Kohathites, having been singled out from among them (3:27) because of their leadership responsibilities.

59. Jochebed daughter of Levi Because she is the aunt of Amram, Levi's grandson, she is forbidden to him in marriage by the law of Leviticus (18:12, 20:19). This law, however, was not in force before the revelation at Mount Sinai. For examples of similar pre-Sinaitic practices, see Gen. 20:12 and 38:24–26.

in Egypt According to this tradition (Levi–Jochebed–Moses), only two generations were slaves in Egypt. This differs from the 400-year tradition for Egyptian bondage in Gen.15:13 (see Gen. 15:16, Exod. 6:14ff.).

POSTSCRIPT (vv. 63–65)

The postscript explains that this census did not include those counted in the previous census who (with the exception of Caleb and Joshua) had perished in the wilderness at God's command (14:29–32).

THE LAW OF SUCCESSION IN INHERITANCE (27:1–11)

The census taken for the purpose of dividing the Promised Land among the tribal clans (chap. 26) is followed by a problematic case: What if the deceased leaves daughters but no sons? Note that the daughters of Zelophehad are referred to again in chapter 36. Chapters 27 and 36, then, bracket the

בֶּן־גִּלְעָד בֶּן־מָכִיר בֶּן־מְנַשֶּׁה לְמִשְׁפְּחֹת
מְנַשֶּׁה בֶן־יוֹסֵף וְאֵלֶּה שְׁמוֹת בְּנֹתָיו
מַחְלָה נֹעָה וְחָגְלָה וּמִלְכָּה וְתִרְצָה׃
2 וַתַּעֲמֹדְנָה לִפְנֵי מֹשֶׁה וְלִפְנֵי אֶלְעָזָר
הַכֹּהֵן וְלִפְנֵי הַנְּשִׂיאִם וְכָל־הָעֵדָה פֶּתַח
אֹהֶל־מוֹעֵד לֵאמֹר׃ 3 אָבִינוּ מֵת בַּמִּדְבָּר
וְהוּא לֹא־הָיָה בְּתוֹךְ הָעֵדָה הַנּוֹעָדִים
עַל־יְהוָה בַּעֲדַת־קֹרַח כִּי־בְחֶטְאוֹ מֵת
וּבָנִים לֹא־הָיוּ לוֹ׃ 4 לָמָּה יִגָּרַע שֵׁם־אָבִינוּ

nassite family—son of Hepher son of Gilead son
of Machir son of Manasseh son of Joseph—
came forward. The names of the daughters were
Mahlah, Noah, Hoglah, Milcah, and Tirzah.
2They stood before Moses, Eleazar the priest,
the chieftains, and the whole assembly, at the
entrance of the Tent of Meeting, and they said,
3"Our father died in the wilderness. He was not
one of the faction, Korah's faction, which
banded together against the LORD, but died for
his own sin; and he has left no sons. 4Let not
our father's name be lost to his clan just because

conclusion of the wilderness trek and the preparation for allotting the Land.

THE CASE OF THE DAUGHTERS OF ZELOPHEHAD (vv. 1–7)

The basic assumption here is that the Land belongs to God, who assigned it to the Israelite clans for their use (Lev. 25:23). Whoever alienates it from them is subject to divine punishment. It is also assumed that only males can inherit, because the clan is perpetuated through the male line. This being so, the daughters of sonless Zelophehad plead that, unless they can inherit, their father's name will be wiped out.

2. the entrance of the Tent of Meeting Where they presented their case.

3. not one of . . . Korah's faction This implies that the participants in the Korahite rebellion were denied the right to inherit the Land.

died for his own sin That is, in the punishment meted out to the entire nation after the scout episode (14:29).

4. Underlying this statement are the assumptions that a name exists as long as it is attached

---

CHAPTER 27

1. The commentators are quite taken with the daughters of Zelophehad and their request to claim land in Canaan to perpetuate their father's name. It is as if, after reviewing so many accounts of complaint, envy, and immoral behavior, they are relieved to have met Israelites who yearn for nothing more than a family home in the Promised Land. The Midrash goes so far as to say: "For forty years in the wilderness, the men tore down fences and the women repaired them" (Num. R. 21:10). The women did not take part in the sin of worshiping the Golden Calf. They did not join in the orgies at Baal-peor. And when the men heard the report of the scouts and lost all hope of settling the Promised Land, the daughters of Zelophehad came forward to claim their share of it.

3. He was not one of . . . Korah's faction Upon hearing these words, Moses refers the request to God. This is not because he does not know the law, but because he could no longer trust himself to be impartial after being told "our father was on your side during the rebellion." In the Talmud, Akiva identifies Zelophehad as the man who was executed for gathering wood on *Shabbat* (Num.15:32ff.). The Sages rebuke him: "Akiva, if Zelophehad was innocent, then you have libeled an innocent man. If he was guilty and the Torah chose not to reveal his name, why should you shame him?" (BT Shab. 96b).

HALAKHAH L'MA·ASEH

27:1. daughters Jewish law originally excluded daughters from inheritance rights when sons survived. The Sages modified these laws by providing for the maintenance of the widow and daughters of the deceased. In the 16th century, Moses Isserles permitted fathers to give their daughters a gift of half of their sons' share in their estate (S.A. H.M. 281:7, gloss). According to a *takkanah* (enactment) of the chief rabbinate of Palestine in 1943, in Israel daughters inherit on an equal footing with sons.

he had no son! Give us a holding among our father's kinsmen!"

5 Moses brought their case before the LORD.

6 And the LORD said to Moses, 7 "The plea of Zelophehad's daughters is just: you should give them a hereditary holding among their father's kinsmen; transfer their father's share to them.

8 "Further, speak to the Israelite people as follows: 'If a man dies without leaving a son, you shall transfer his property to his daughter. 9 If he has no daughter, you shall assign his property to his brothers. 10 If he has no brothers, you shall assign his property to his father's brothers. 11 If his father had no brothers, you shall assign his property to his nearest relative in his own clan, and he shall inherit it.' This shall be the law of procedure for the Israelites, in accordance with the LORD's command to Moses."

מִתּ֣וֹךְ מִשְׁפַּחְתּ֔וֹ כִּ֛י אֵ֥ין ל֖וֹ בֵּ֑ן תְּנָה־לָּ֣נוּ
אֲחֻזָּ֔ה בְּת֖וֹךְ אֲחֵ֥י אָבִֽינוּ׃
5 וַיַּקְרֵ֥ב מֹשֶׁ֛ה אֶת־מִשְׁפָּטָ֖ן* לִפְנֵ֥י
יְהוָֽה׃ ס
רביעי 6 וַיֹּ֥אמֶר יְהוָ֖ה אֶל־מֹשֶׁ֥ה לֵּאמֹֽר׃ 7 כֵּ֗ן בְּנ֣וֹת
צְלָפְחָד֮ דֹּבְרֹת֒ נָתֹ֨ן תִּתֵּ֤ן לָהֶם֙ אֲחֻזַּ֣ת
נַחֲלָ֔ה בְּת֖וֹךְ אֲחֵ֣י אֲבִיהֶ֑ם וְהַֽעֲבַרְתָּ֛ אֶת־
נַחֲלַ֥ת אֲבִיהֶ֖ן לָהֶֽן׃
8 וְאֶל־בְּנֵ֥י יִשְׂרָאֵ֖ל תְּדַבֵּ֣ר לֵאמֹ֑ר אִ֣ישׁ
כִּֽי־יָמ֗וּת וּבֵן֙ אֵ֣ין ל֔וֹ וְהַֽעֲבַרְתֶּ֥ם אֶת־
נַחֲלָת֖וֹ לְבִתּֽוֹ׃ 9 וְאִם־אֵ֥ין ל֖וֹ בַּ֑ת וּנְתַתֶּ֥ם
אֶת־נַחֲלָת֖וֹ לְאֶחָֽיו׃ 10 וְאִם־אֵ֥ין ל֖וֹ אַחִ֑ים
וּנְתַתֶּ֥ם אֶת־נַחֲלָת֖וֹ לַאֲחֵ֥י אָבִֽיו׃ 11 וְאִם־
אֵ֣ין אַחִים֮ לְאָבִיו֒ וּנְתַתֶּ֣ם אֶת־נַחֲלָת֗וֹ
לִשְׁאֵר֞וֹ הַקָּרֹ֥ב אֵלָ֛יו מִמִּשְׁפַּחְתּ֖וֹ וְיָרַ֣שׁ
אֹתָ֑הּ וְֽהָ֨יְתָ֜ה לִבְנֵ֤י יִשְׂרָאֵל֙ לְחֻקַּ֣ת מִשְׁפָּ֔ט
כַּאֲשֶׁ֛ר צִוָּ֥ה יְהוָ֖ה אֶת־מֹשֶֽׁה׃ ס

v. 5. ן׳ רבתי

to land, and that Zelophehad's name would be perpetuated through his grandsons.

because he had no son The text presupposes that the wife was either dead or infertile. Thus the levirate solution detailed in Deut. 25:5–6 could not be applied here. It is also presumed that the daughters were unmarried; otherwise the land would ultimately pass to the clans of their husbands. (See Num. 36, where the ruling's intent clearly is to ensure that the property due to Zelophehad would remain within his clan.)

our father's kinsmen That is, of the clan of Hepher (v. 1). The land is parceled out to the tribes according to their clans.

5. Moses alone could bring the case before the Lord (see Exod. 18:19; Lev. 24:13; Num. 9:8–9, 15:35–36; Josh. 17:4).

before the LORD That is, for an oracle.

THE LAW OF SUCCESSION (vv. 8–11)

For ancestral property, a man's natural heirs are his sons. If he has no sons, his daughters become his heirs. If he has no children, his brothers are his heirs, and in the absence of brothers, his father's brothers are. If the father had no brothers, the inheritance passes on to the next of kin. Thus the patrilineal principle of succession through the father's male line is preserved. A daughter does not really inherit; she transfers the inheritance from father to grandson, and thereby keeps the ancestral land in the father's line.

8. his property This refers to inherited, landed property.

9. brothers Also of his mother (Ibn Ezra).

11. in his own clan Refers to his male relatives and assumes that the land remains in the clan.

7–8. God honored the daughters of Zelophehad for their faith in the Land by arranging for them to cause a law to be added to the Torah; that is why this law was not included in the original revelation at Sinai. In the same way, God honored those Israelites who did not want to miss the *Pesaḥ* celebration, by letting them be the cause of a new law (see 9:6–14) (*Sifrei*).

12 The LORD said to Moses, "Ascend these
heights of Abarim and view the land that I have
given to the Israelite people. 13 When you have
seen it, you too shall be gathered to your kin,
just as your brother Aaron was. 14 For, in the wilderness of Zin, when the community was contentious, you disobeyed My command to uphold My sanctity in their sight by means of the
water." Those are the Waters of Meribath-
kadesh, in the wilderness of Zin.
15 Moses spoke to the LORD, saying, 16 "Let the
LORD, Source of the breath of all flesh, appoint
someone over the community 17 who shall go
out before them and come in before them, and
who shall take them out and bring them in, so
that the LORD's community may not be like
sheep that have no shepherd." 18 And the LORD
answered Moses, "Single out Joshua son of Nun,
an inspired man, and lay your hand upon him.
19 Have him stand before Eleazar the priest and
before the whole community, and commission
him in their sight. 20 Invest him with some of
your authority, so that the whole Israelite com-

12 וַיֹּ֤אמֶר יְהוָה֙ אֶל־מֹשֶׁ֔ה עֲלֵ֛ה אֶל־הַ֥ר
הָעֲבָרִ֖ים הַזֶּ֑ה וּרְאֵה֙ אֶת־הָאָ֔רֶץ אֲשֶׁ֥ר
נָתַ֖תִּי לִבְנֵ֥י יִשְׂרָאֵֽל׃ 13 וְרָאִ֣יתָה אֹתָ֔הּ
וְנֶאֱסַפְתָּ֥ אֶל־עַמֶּ֖יךָ גַּם־אָ֑תָּה כַּאֲשֶׁ֥ר נֶאֱסַ֖ף
אַהֲרֹ֥ן אָחִֽיךָ׃ 14 כַּאֲשֶׁ֨ר מְרִיתֶ֜ם פִּ֗י
בְּמִדְבַּר־צִ֗ן בִּמְרִיבַת֙ הָֽעֵדָ֔ה לְהַקְדִּישֵׁ֥נִי
בַמַּ֖יִם לְעֵינֵיהֶ֑ם הֵ֛ם מֵ֥י־מְרִיבַ֥ת קָדֵ֖שׁ
מִדְבַּר־צִֽן׃ פ
15 וַיְדַבֵּ֣ר מֹשֶׁ֔ה אֶל־יְהוָ֖ה לֵאמֹֽר׃ 16 יִפְקֹ֣ד
יְהוָ֔ה אֱלֹהֵ֥י הָרוּחֹ֖ת לְכָל־בָּשָׂ֑ר אִ֖ישׁ עַל־
הָעֵדָֽה׃ 17 אֲשֶׁר־יֵצֵ֣א לִפְנֵיהֶ֗ם וַאֲשֶׁ֤ר יָבֹא֙
לִפְנֵיהֶ֔ם וַאֲשֶׁ֥ר יוֹצִיאֵ֖ם וַאֲשֶׁ֣ר יְבִיאֵ֑ם וְלֹ֤א
תִֽהְיֶה֙ עֲדַ֣ת יְהוָ֔ה כַּצֹּ֕אן אֲשֶׁ֥ר אֵין־לָהֶ֖ם
רֹעֶֽה׃ 18 וַיֹּ֨אמֶר יְהוָ֜ה אֶל־מֹשֶׁ֗ה קַח־לְךָ֙
אֶת־יְהוֹשֻׁ֣עַ בִּן־נ֔וּן אִ֖ישׁ אֲשֶׁר־ר֣וּחַ בּ֑וֹ
וְסָמַכְתָּ֥ אֶת־יָדְךָ֖ עָלָֽיו׃ 19 וְהַעֲמַדְתָּ֣ אֹת֗וֹ
לִפְנֵי֙ אֶלְעָזָ֣ר הַכֹּהֵ֔ן וְלִפְנֵ֖י כָּל־הָעֵדָ֑ה
וְצִוִּיתָ֥ה אֹת֖וֹ לְעֵינֵיהֶֽם׃ 20 וְנָתַתָּ֤ה מֵהוֹדְךָ֙
עָלָ֔יו לְמַ֣עַן יִשְׁמְע֔וּ כָּל־עֲדַ֖ת בְּנֵ֥י יִשְׂרָאֵֽל׃

THE SUCCESSION OF MOSES BY JOSHUA (27:12–23)

Moses is commanded to ascend the mountain. From there he will see the Promised Land and then die. The fulfillment of this command is postponed (Deut. 34), for Moses has yet many laws and a lengthy testament to give to his people.

12. heights of Abarim The peak of this mountain chain is identified as Mount Nebo in Deut. 32:49. At a height of 2740 feet (843 m), it offers a wide view of Cisjordan.

13. as your brother Aaron Aaron ascended a mountain to die; this is also the purpose of Moses' ascent.

18. an inspired man Literally, "a man in whom there is spirit." He was a courageous and skillful military leader.

your hand Hebrew: *yadkha,* which should be read as a plural ("your hands"). Authority and power could be transferred only by the laying on of both hands (v. 23; cf. Num. 8:10, Lev. 16:21).

20. Invest him Literally, "place upon him." Moses thus establishes a physical conduit for the transfer of his authority.

with some of your authority Moses is empowered to transfer to Joshua only his authority,

---

16. Confronted with the finality of God's decision that he will not enter the Promised Land, Moses' first response is not self-pity but concern for his people's future. Realizing that the next Israelite leader will face different challenges, Moses urges God to appoint someone who will "go out before the people and come in before them," i.e., a military leader who will lead the charge instead of remaining behind in safety. The Midrash pictures Moses urging God to appoint a leader able to relate to every Israelite, even those with whom he disagrees (Tanḥ. 10). Is Moses seeking to balance the zealotry of Phinehas?

20. Invest him with some of your authority Joshua would reflect Moses' greatness

munity may obey. 21But he shall present himself
to Eleazar the priest, who shall on his behalf seek
the decision of the Urim before the LORD. By
such instruction they shall go out and by such
instruction they shall come in, he and all the
Israelites, the whole community."

22Moses did as the LORD commanded him.
He took Joshua and had him stand before
Eleazar the priest and before the whole community. 23He laid his hands upon him and
commissioned him—as the LORD had spoken
through Moses.

21 וְלִפְנֵי אֶלְעָזָר הַכֹּהֵן יַעֲמֹד וְשָׁאַל לוֹ
בְּמִשְׁפַּט הָאוּרִים לִפְנֵי יְהוָה עַל־פִּיו יֵצְאוּ
וְעַל־פִּיו יָבֹאוּ הוּא וְכָל־בְּנֵי־יִשְׂרָאֵל אִתּוֹ
וְכָל־הָעֵדָה׃
22 וַיַּעַשׂ מֹשֶׁה כַּאֲשֶׁר צִוָּה יְהוָה אֹתוֹ וַיִּקַּח
אֶת־יְהוֹשֻׁעַ וַיַּעֲמִדֵהוּ לִפְנֵי אֶלְעָזָר הַכֹּהֵן
וְלִפְנֵי כָּל־הָעֵדָה׃ 23 וַיִּסְמֹךְ אֶת־יָדָיו עָלָיו
וַיְצַוֵּהוּ כַּאֲשֶׁר דִּבֶּר יְהוָה בְּיַד־מֹשֶׁה׃ פ

28 The LORD spoke to Moses, saying:
2Command the Israelite people and say to them:
Be punctilious in presenting to Me at stated

מישי כח וַיְדַבֵּר יְהוָה אֶל־מֹשֶׁה לֵּאמֹר׃
2 צַו אֶת־בְּנֵי יִשְׂרָאֵל וְאָמַרְתָּ אֲלֵהֶם אֶת־

not his spiritual powers. Only God, who endowed those powers, can transfer them; thus God allowed the elders to share Moses' prophetic gifts (11:17,25). The Hebrew word *hod* (authority) means "majesty, power, charisma, ray of glory" in other contexts.

21. go out . . . come in That is, for war. Only in military matters is Joshua commanded to consult the Urim and Thummim through the agency of the high priest.

By such instruction That is, of the Urim's decision. Or, perhaps, by Eleazar's instruction, because it is he who consults the Urim.

all the Israelites Refers to the troops that Joshua will lead in battle.

the whole community Refers to all the Israelites, not only the army.

THE CALENDAR OF PUBLIC SACRIFICES (28:1–30:1)

With the division of the Land and the succession to Moses now determined, the Torah turns to the establishment of the religious calendar that will prevail in the Land. Thus the Israelites' first duty upon settling in their land is to institute the proper lines of communion with the Lord through the medium of the sacrificial system. This catalog of public offerings concludes with a reminder (in 29:39) that each Israelite could also bring private offerings.

2. at stated times The sacrifices are invalid if offered at the wrong time.

---

as the moon reflects the light of the sun (BT BB 75a). God commands Moses to "lay your hand upon" Joshua (v. 18), but Moses lays both hands on him (v. 23), transferring power without reservation or ambivalence, a rare gesture for a man who has been accustomed to authority for so long. What must have been going through Moses' mind as he reflected on the achievements and frustrations of the past, and the awareness of all that he yearned to do and would never be able to do?

CHAPTER 28

The list of offerings in chapters 28 and 29 is familiar to many as the *maftir* readings from a second Torah scroll on the festivals. They are read in sequence during the summer, in the weeks preceding *Tish·ah b'Av*, the anniversary of the Temple's destruction. Tradition teaches that God counts our reading of these passages as the equivalent of our bringing offerings to the Temple.

קָרְבָּנִי לַחְמִי לְאִשַּׁי רֵיחַ נִיחֹחִי תִּשְׁמְרוּ
לְהַקְרִיב לִי בְּמוֹעֲדוֹ׃
3 וְאָמַרְתָּ לָהֶם זֶה הָאִשֶּׁה אֲשֶׁר תַּקְרִיבוּ
לַיהוָה
כְּבָשִׂים בְּנֵי־שָׁנָה תְמִימִם שְׁנַיִם לַיּוֹם
עֹלָה תָמִיד׃ 4 אֶת־הַכֶּבֶשׂ אֶחָד תַּעֲשֶׂה
בַבֹּקֶר וְאֵת הַכֶּבֶשׂ הַשֵּׁנִי תַּעֲשֶׂה בֵּין
הָעַרְבָּיִם׃ 5 וַעֲשִׂירִית הָאֵיפָה סֹלֶת
לְמִנְחָה בְּלוּלָה בְּשֶׁמֶן כָּתִית רְבִיעִת
הַהִין׃ 6 עֹלַת תָּמִיד הָעֲשֻׂיָה בְּהַר סִינַי
לְרֵיחַ נִיחֹחַ אִשֶּׁה לַיהוָה׃
7 וְנִסְכּוֹ רְבִיעִת הַהִין לַכֶּבֶשׂ הָאֶחָד בַּקֹּדֶשׁ
הַסֵּךְ נֶסֶךְ שֵׁכָר לַיהוָה׃ 8 וְאֵת הַכֶּבֶשׂ
הַשֵּׁנִי תַּעֲשֶׂה בֵּין הָעַרְבַּיִם כְּמִנְחַת הַבֹּקֶר
וּכְנִסְכּוֹ תַּעֲשֶׂה אִשֵּׁה רֵיחַ נִיחֹחַ
לַיהוָה׃ פ
9 וּבְיוֹם הַשַּׁבָּת שְׁנֵי־כְבָשִׂים בְּנֵי־שָׁנָה
תְּמִימִם וּשְׁנֵי עֶשְׂרֹנִים סֹלֶת מִנְחָה
בְּלוּלָה בַשֶּׁמֶן וְנִסְכּוֹ׃ 10 עֹלַת שַׁבַּת
בְּשַׁבַּתּוֹ עַל־עֹלַת הַתָּמִיד וְנִסְכָּהּ׃ ס

times the offerings of food due Me, as gifts of pleasing odor to Me.

3Say to them: These are the gifts that you are to present to the LORD:

As a regular burnt offering every day, two yearling lambs without blemish. 4You shall offer one lamb in the morning, and the other lamb you shall offer at twilight. 5And as a grain offering, there shall be a tenth of an *ephah* of choice flour with a quarter of a *hin* of beaten oil mixed in—6the regular burnt offering instituted at Mount Sinai—a gift of pleasing odor to the LORD.

7The libation with it shall be a quarter of a *hin* for each lamb, to be poured in the sacred precinct as an offering of fermented drink to the LORD. 8The other lamb you shall offer at twilight, preparing the same grain offering and libation as in the morning—a gift of pleasing odor to the LORD.

9On the sabbath day: two yearling lambs without blemish, together with two-tenths of a measure of choice flour with oil mixed in as a grain offering, and with the proper libation—10a burnt offering for every sabbath, in addition to the regular burnt offering and its libation.

DAILY OFFERING (vv. 3–8)

Called *"tamid"* from biblical times on, the daily offering consisted of a burnt offering of a lamb together with its grain and wine adjuncts. It was offered twice daily, morning and evening.

3. The *tamid* offering is to be financed by all the people, not merely by the leaders or by the rich (Neh. 10:34).

4. at twilight The time between sunset and darkness.

5. ephah See Comment to Exod. 16:36.

hin See Comment to Exod. 29:40.

beaten Hebrew: *katit,* "pressed in a mortar." Hence it was pure oil.

7. with it Refers to the lamb (v. 4, as in v. 8).

SHABBAT OFFERING (vv. 9–10)

The sacrifice for a special day, called *musaf* in Rabbinic Hebrew, is in addition to the daily *tamid* and is offered immediately after it. Because the *Shabbat* offering is the same as the *tamid,* adding *musaf* gives *Shabbat* double the number of offerings of a weekday.

10. regular burnt offering Refers to the

HALAKHAH L'MA·ASEH

28:4. in the morning . . . at twilight The Sages determined that prayer, specifically the *Amidah,* substitutes for the communal sacrifices mandated in the Torah (BT Ber. 26b). *Shaḥarit* and *Minḥah* (the morning and afternoon services) are thus based on the requirements articulated in this verse (cf. Comment to Gen. 19:27).

28:10. in addition to the regular burnt offering The requirement in this chapter for an additional sacrifice offered on *Shabbat,* festivals, and *Rosh Ḥodesh* (New Moon) is fulfilled today through the additional *Amidah* of *Musaf* recited on these days (BT Ber. 26b–27a).

[11]On your new moons you shall present a burnt offering to the LORD: two bulls of the herd, one ram, and seven yearling lambs, without blemish. [12]As grain offering for each bull: three-tenths of a measure of choice flour with oil mixed in. As grain offering for each ram: two-tenths of a measure of choice flour with oil mixed in. [13]As grain offering for each lamb: a tenth of a measure of fine flour with oil mixed in. Such shall be the burnt offering of pleasing odor, a gift to the LORD. [14]Their libations shall be: half a *hin* of wine for a bull, a third of a *hin* for a ram, and a quarter of a *hin* for a lamb. That shall be the monthly burnt offering for each new moon of the year. [15]And there shall be one goat as a purification offering to the LORD, to be offered in addition to the regular burnt offering and its libation.

[16]In the first month, on the fourteenth day of the month, there shall be a passover sacrifice

11 וּבְרָאשֵׁי֙ חָדְשֵׁיכֶ֔ם תַּקְרִ֥יבוּ עֹלָ֖ה לַיהוָ֑ה
פָּרִ֨ים בְּנֵֽי־בָקָ֤ר שְׁנַ֙יִם֙ וְאַ֣יִל אֶחָ֔ד כְּבָשִׂ֧ים
בְּנֵי־שָׁנָ֛ה שִׁבְעָ֖ה תְּמִימִֽם׃ 12 וּשְׁלֹשָׁ֣ה
עֶשְׂרֹנִ֗ים סֹ֤לֶת מִנְחָה֙ בְּלוּלָ֣ה בַשֶּׁ֔מֶן לַפָּ֖ר
הָאֶחָ֑ד וּשְׁנֵ֣י עֶשְׂרֹנִ֗ים סֹ֤לֶת מִנְחָה֙ בְּלוּלָ֣ה
בַשֶּׁ֔מֶן לָאַ֖יִל הָאֶחָֽד׃ 13 וְעִשָּׂרֹ֣ן עִשָּׂר֗וֹן
סֹ֤לֶת מִנְחָה֙ בְּלוּלָ֣ה בַשֶּׁ֔מֶן לַכֶּ֖בֶשׂ הָאֶחָ֑ד
עֹלָה֙ רֵ֣יחַ נִיחֹ֔חַ אִשֶּׁ֖ה לַיהוָֽה׃ 14 וְנִסְכֵּיהֶ֗ם
חֲצִ֣י הַהִין֩ יִהְיֶ֨ה לַפָּ֜ר וּשְׁלִישִׁ֧ת הַהִ֣ין
לָאַ֗יִל וּרְבִיעִ֥ת הַהִ֛ין לַכֶּ֖בֶשׂ יָ֑יִן זֹ֣את עֹלַ֥ת
חֹ֙דֶשׁ֙ בְּחָדְשׁ֔וֹ לְחָדְשֵׁ֖י הַשָּׁנָֽה׃ 15 וּשְׂעִ֨יר
עִזִּ֥ים אֶחָ֛ד לְחַטָּ֖את לַיהוָ֑ה עַל־עֹלַ֨ת
הַתָּמִ֜יד יֵעָשֶׂ֖ה וְנִסְכּֽוֹ׃ ס
ששי 16 וּבַחֹ֣דֶשׁ הָרִאשׁ֗וֹן בְּאַרְבָּעָ֥ה עָשָׂ֛ר י֖וֹם

morning *tamid,* because there could be no offering after the *tamid* of the evening. It should be noted that purification sacrifices are never brought on *Shabbat,* because intimations of human wrongdoing are not permitted on this joyous day.

ROSH ḤODESH, THE NEW MOON (vv. 11–15)

In early Israel, this was an important festival celebrated by families and clans in a state of ritual purity at the local sanctuary.

14. Only here are the libation quantities specified. Because they are always the same, they need not be repeated.

burnt offering Use of this term implies the auxiliary grain offering and libation.

new moon Hebrew: *ḥodesh,* "new moon," as in 29:6. (The word can also mean "month.")

PASCHAL SACRIFICE AND UNLEAVENED BREAD (vv. 16–25)

The day of the paschal offering and the seven-day Festival of Unleavened Bread originally were separate and distinct holidays (cf. Lev. 23:5–6). The fact that the paschal offering is mentioned here

15. purification offering to the LORD Hebrew: *ḥattat l'Adonai.* Noting that this is the only place in the Torah where this phrase occurs, the Talmud understands it to mean "a purification offering *for* the LORD." It is brought on God's behalf on *Rosh Ḥodesh* (when the new moon appears) as an apology to the moon for having made it smaller and less consequential than the sun (BT Ḥul. 60b). Did the Sages here picture God apologizing for all the unfairness of life—to people who are born less healthy, gifted, or fortunate than others? Given the traditional identification of *Rosh Ḥodesh* as a woman's festival, did the Sages imagine God expressing regret to women for having a less prominent role than men for so much of history?

HALAKHAH L'MA·ASEH

28:11. new moons The Jewish calendar is based on the cycles of the moon. An extra month (Adar I) is added 7 times in 19 years to make the lunar calendar conform to the solar year. Each Hebrew month begins with the New Moon (*Rosh Ḥodesh*); it is announced in synagogue (except for the month of *Tishrei*) on the preceding *Shabbat,* in the Blessing of the Month (*Birkat Ha-Ḥodesh*). See Comment on Exod. 12:2.

לַחֹ֖דֶשׁ פֶּ֥סַח לַיהוָֽה׃ 17 וּבַחֲמִשָּׁ֨ה עָשָׂ֥ר
י֛וֹם לַחֹ֥דֶשׁ הַזֶּ֖ה חָ֑ג שִׁבְעַ֣ת יָמִ֔ים מַצּ֖וֹת
יֵאָכֵֽל׃ 18 בַּיּ֥וֹם הָרִאשׁ֖וֹן מִקְרָא־קֹ֑דֶשׁ כָּל־
מְלֶ֥אכֶת עֲבֹדָ֖ה לֹ֥א תַעֲשֽׂוּ׃ 19 וְהִקְרַבְתֶּ֨ם
אִשֶּׁ֤ה עֹלָה֙ לַֽיהוָ֔ה פָּרִ֧ים בְּנֵי־בָקָ֛ר שְׁנַ֖יִם
וְאַ֣יִל אֶחָ֑ד וְשִׁבְעָ֤ה כְבָשִׂים֙ בְּנֵ֣י שָׁנָ֔ה
תְּמִימִ֖ם יִהְי֥וּ לָכֶֽם׃ 20 וּמִ֨נְחָתָ֔ם סֹ֖לֶת
בְּלוּלָ֣ה בַשָּׁ֑מֶן שְׁלֹשָׁ֨ה עֶשְׂרֹנִ֜ים לַפָּ֗ר וּשְׁנֵ֧י
עֶשְׂרֹנִ֛ים לָאַ֖יִל תַּעֲשֽׂוּ׃ 21 עִשָּׂר֤וֹן עִשָּׂרוֹן֙
תַּעֲשֶׂ֔ה לַכֶּ֖בֶשׂ הָאֶחָ֑ד לְשִׁבְעַ֖ת הַכְּבָשִֽׂים׃
22 וּשְׂעִ֥יר חַטָּ֖את אֶחָ֑ד לְכַפֵּ֖ר עֲלֵיכֶֽם׃
23 מִלְּבַד֙ עֹלַ֣ת הַבֹּ֔קֶר אֲשֶׁ֖ר לְעֹלַ֣ת הַתָּמִ֑יד
תַּעֲשׂ֖וּ אֶת־אֵֽלֶּה׃ 24 כָּאֵ֜לֶּה תַּעֲשׂ֤וּ לַיּוֹם֙
שִׁבְעַ֣ת יָמִ֔ים לֶ֛חֶם אִשֵּׁ֥ה רֵֽיחַ־נִיחֹ֖חַ
לַֽיהוָ֑ה עַל־עוֹלַ֧ת הַתָּמִ֛יד יֵעָשֶׂ֖ה וְנִסְכּֽוֹ׃
25 וּבַיּוֹם֙ הַשְּׁבִיעִ֔י מִקְרָא־קֹ֖דֶשׁ יִהְיֶ֣ה לָכֶ֑ם
כָּל־מְלֶ֥אכֶת עֲבֹדָ֖ה לֹ֥א תַעֲשֽׂוּ׃ ס
26 וּבְי֣וֹם הַבִּכּוּרִ֗ים בְּהַקְרִיבְכֶ֞ם מִנְחָ֤ה
חֲדָשָׁה֙ לַֽיהוָ֔ה בְּשָׁבֻעֹֽתֵיכֶ֑ם מִֽקְרָא־קֹ֙דֶשׁ֙
יִהְיֶ֣ה לָכֶ֔ם כָּל־מְלֶ֥אכֶת עֲבֹדָ֖ה לֹ֥א
תַעֲשֽׂוּ׃ 27 וְהִקְרַבְתֶּ֨ם עוֹלָ֜ה לְרֵ֤יחַ נִיחֹ֙חַ֙
לַֽיהוָ֔ה פָּרִ֧ים בְּנֵי־בָקָ֛ר שְׁנַ֖יִם אַ֣יִל אֶחָ֑ד
שִׁבְעָ֥ה כְבָשִׂ֖ים בְּנֵ֥י שָׁנָֽה׃ 28 וּמִנְחָתָ֗ם
סֹ֚לֶת בְּלוּלָ֣ה בַשָּׁ֑מֶן שְׁלֹשָׁ֤ה עֶשְׂרֹנִים֙

to the LORD, 17and on the fifteenth day of that
month a festival. Unleavened bread shall be
eaten for seven days. 18The first day shall be a
sacred occasion: you shall not work at your occupations. 19You shall present a gift, a burnt
offering, to the LORD: two bulls of the herd, one
ram, and seven yearling lambs—see that they
are without blemish. 20The grain offering with
them shall be of choice flour with oil mixed in:
prepare three-tenths of a measure for a bull,
two-tenths for a ram; 21and for each of the seven
lambs prepare one-tenth of a measure. 22And
there shall be one goat for a purification
offering, to make expiation in your behalf.
23You shall present these in addition to the
morning portion of the regular burnt offering.
24You shall offer the like daily for seven days as
food, a gift of pleasing odor to the LORD; they
shall be offered, with their libations, in addition
to the regular burnt offering. 25And the seventh
day shall be a sacred occasion for you: you shall
not work at your occupations.

26On the day of the first fruits, your Feast of
Weeks, when you bring an offering of new grain
to the LORD, you shall observe a sacred occasion:
you shall not work at your occupations. 27You
shall present a burnt offering of pleasing odor
to the LORD: two bulls of the herd, one ram,
seven yearling lambs. 28The grain offering with
them shall be of choice flour with oil mixed

even though it is a private sacrifice (see Exod. 12:1–11) indicates that by this time the two festivals had become fused.

17. festival Both the paschal sacrifice and the first day of the Festival of Unleavened Bread are observed at the sanctuary, precisely as instituted by Deut. 16:1–6.

18. occupations Hebrew: *m'lekhet avodah;* literally, "laborious work," of the sort that is forbidden on the festivals. This is in contrast to "any work" (*kol m'lakhah*), which is forbidden on *Shabbat* and *Yom Kippur* (Num. 29:7; Lev. 23:3,28). The nonlaborious work permitted (by implication) on the festivals is not defined, except for the explicit permission to prepare food on the first and last days of *Pesaḥ* (Exod. 12:16).

FEAST OF WEEKS (vv. 26–31)

This festival, which marks the start of the wheat harvest, does not depend on the lunar calendar. It occurs seven weeks after the beginning of the barley harvest (Lev. 23:15–16). In this regard it is like *Shabbat,* which is also independent of the lunar calendar.

26. day of the first fruits This day is also called "the Feast of the Harvest" (*Ḥag ha-Katzir*) in Exod. 23:16, and "the Feast of Weeks" (*Ḥag [ha-]Shavu·ot*) in Exod. 34:22, Deut. 16:10,16, and 2 Chron. 8:13.

in, three-tenths of a measure for a bull, two-tenths for a ram, 29 and one-tenth for each of the seven lambs. 30 And there shall be one goat for expiation in your behalf. 31 You shall present them—see that they are without blemish—with their libations, in addition to the regular burnt offering and its grain offering.

לַפָּר הָאֶחָד שְׁנֵי עֶשְׂרֹנִים לָאַיִל
הָאֶחָד׃ 29 עִשָּׂרוֹן עִשָּׂרוֹן לַכֶּבֶשׂ הָאֶחָד
לְשִׁבְעַת הַכְּבָשִׂים׃ 30 שְׂעִיר עִזִּים אֶחָד
לְכַפֵּר עֲלֵיכֶם׃ 31 מִלְּבַד עֹלַת הַתָּמִיד
וּמִנְחָתוֹ תַּעֲשׂוּ תְּמִימִם יִהְיוּ־לָכֶם
וְנִסְכֵּיהֶם׃ פ

29 In the seventh month, on the first day of the month, you shall observe a sacred occasion: you shall not work at your occupations. You shall observe it as a day when the horn is sounded. 2 You shall present a burnt offering of pleasing odor to the LORD: one bull of the herd, one ram, and seven yearling lambs, without blemish. 3 The grain offering with them—choice flour with oil mixed in—shall be: three-tenths of a measure for a bull, two-tenths for a ram, 4 and one-tenth for each of the seven lambs. 5 And there shall be one goat for a purification offering, to make expiation in your behalf—6 in addition to the burnt offering of the new moon with its grain offering and the regular burnt offering with its grain offering, each with its libation as prescribed, gifts of pleasing odor to the LORD.

7 On the tenth day of the same seventh month

כט וּבַחֹדֶשׁ הַשְּׁבִיעִי בְּאֶחָד לַחֹדֶשׁ
מִקְרָא־קֹדֶשׁ יִהְיֶה לָכֶם כָּל־מְלֶאכֶת
עֲבֹדָה לֹא תַעֲשׂוּ יוֹם תְּרוּעָה יִהְיֶה לָכֶם׃
2 וַעֲשִׂיתֶם עֹלָה לְרֵיחַ נִיחֹחַ לַיהוָה פַּר
בֶּן־בָּקָר אֶחָד אַיִל אֶחָד כְּבָשִׂים בְּנֵי־שָׁנָה
שִׁבְעָה תְּמִימִם׃ 3 וּמִנְחָתָם סֹלֶת בְּלוּלָה
בַשָּׁמֶן שְׁלֹשָׁה עֶשְׂרֹנִים לַפָּר שְׁנֵי עֶשְׂרֹנִים
לָאָיִל׃ 4 וְעִשָּׂרוֹן אֶחָד לַכֶּבֶשׂ הָאֶחָד
לְשִׁבְעַת הַכְּבָשִׂים׃ 5 וּשְׂעִיר־עִזִּים אֶחָד
חַטָּאת לְכַפֵּר עֲלֵיכֶם׃ 6 מִלְּבַד עֹלַת
הַחֹדֶשׁ וּמִנְחָתָהּ וְעֹלַת הַתָּמִיד וּמִנְחָתָהּ
וְנִסְכֵּיהֶם כְּמִשְׁפָּטָם לְרֵיחַ נִיחֹחַ אִשֶּׁה
לַיהוָה׃ ס
7 וּבֶעָשׂוֹר לַחֹדֶשׁ הַשְּׁבִיעִי הַזֶּה מִקְרָא־

FIRST DAY OF THE SEVENTH MONTH
(29:1–6)

The seventh new moon is to the ordinary new moon as the seventh day is to the ordinary day, thereby indicating how the sabbatical cycle was preserved in the lunar calendar. The seventh month is actually the beginning of the agricultural year, as is apparent from the oldest calendars of the Bible (see Exod. 23:16, 34:22). The Jewish religious calendar still preserves the first day of the seventh month as the beginning of the year: *Rosh ha-Shanah,* "The Head of the Year," or New Year's Day. The Bible neither mentions it by name nor describes any New Year festival.

1. a day when the horn is sounded Hebrew: *yom t'ru·ah,* "a day of acclaim," probably the royal acclaim of God as King and Creator. The horn blowing on this day should not be confused with the prescription that horns should be blown on all festivals (10:10).

TENTH DAY OF THE SEVENTH MONTH
(vv. 7–11)

The day is known as *Yom ha-Kippurim,* "The Day of Purgation," which refers to the purgation of the sanctuary following its year-long defilement by mortals. Thus the purgation rituals are entirely within the confines of the sanctuary

HALAKHAH L'MA·ASEH

29:1. a day when the horn is sounded Maimonides cites this verse as the source for the commandment to listen to the *shofar* blasts on *Rosh ha-Shanah* (MT Shofar 1:1).

you shall observe a sacred occasion when you
shall practice self-denial. You shall do no work.
8You shall present to the LORD a burnt offering
of pleasing odor: one bull of the herd, one ram,
seven yearling lambs; see that they are without
blemish. 9The grain offering with them—of
choice flour with oil mixed in—shall be:
three-tenths of a measure for a bull, two-tenths
for the one ram, 10one-tenth for each of the
seven lambs. 11And there shall be one goat for
a purification offering, in addition to the purification offering of expiation and the regular
burnt offering with its grain offering, each with
its libation.

12On the fifteenth day of the seventh month,
you shall observe a sacred occasion: you shall
not work at your occupations.—Seven days you
shall observe a festival of the LORD.—13You
shall present a burnt offering, a gift of pleasing
odor to the LORD: Thirteen bulls of the herd,
two rams, fourteen yearling lambs; they shall be
without blemish. 14The grain offerings with
them—of choice flour with oil mixed in—shall
be: three-tenths of a measure for each of the
thirteen bulls, two-tenths for each of the two
rams, 15and one-tenth for each of the fourteen
lambs. 16And there shall be one goat for a purification offering—in addition to the regular
burnt offering, its grain offering and libation.

קֹ֤דֶשׁ יִֽהְיֶ֣ה לָכֶ֔ם וְעִנִּיתֶ֖ם אֶת־נַפְשֹׁתֵיכֶ֑ם
כָּל־מְלָאכָ֖ה לֹ֥א תַעֲשֽׂוּ׃ 8 וְהִקְרַבְתֶּ֨ם עֹלָ֤ה
לַֽיהוָה֙ רֵ֣יחַ נִיחֹ֔חַ פַּ֧ר בֶּן־בָּקָ֛ר אֶחָ֖ד אַ֣יִל
אֶחָ֑ד כְּבָשִׂ֤ים בְּנֵֽי־שָׁנָה֙ שִׁבְעָ֔ה תְּמִימִ֖ם
יִהְי֥וּ לָכֶֽם׃ 9 וּמִ֨נְחָתָ֔ם סֹ֖לֶת בְּלוּלָ֣ה בַשָּׁ֑מֶן
שְׁלֹשָׁ֣ה עֶשְׂרֹנִים֙ לַפָּ֔ר שְׁנֵי֙ עֶשְׂרֹנִ֔ים לָאַ֖יִל
הָאֶחָֽד׃ 10 עִשָּׂרוֹן֙ עִשָּׂר֔וֹן לַכֶּ֖בֶשׂ הָאֶחָ֑ד
לְשִׁבְעַ֖ת הַכְּבָשִֽׂים׃ 11 שְׂעִיר־עִזִּ֥ים אֶחָ֖ד
חַטָּ֑את מִלְּבַ֞ד חַטַּ֤את הַכִּפֻּרִים֙ וְעֹלַ֣ת
הַתָּמִ֔יד וּמִנְחָתָ֖הּ וְנִסְכֵּיהֶֽם׃ פ
שביעי 12 וּבַחֲמִשָּׁ֩ה עָשָׂ֨ר י֜וֹם לַחֹ֣דֶשׁ הַשְּׁבִיעִ֗י
מִֽקְרָא־קֹ֙דֶשׁ֙ יִהְיֶ֣ה לָכֶ֔ם כָּל־מְלֶ֥אכֶת
עֲבֹדָ֖ה לֹ֣א תַעֲשׂ֑וּ וְחַגֹּתֶ֥ם חַ֛ג לַֽיהוָ֖ה
שִׁבְעַ֥ת יָמִֽים׃ 13 וְהִקְרַבְתֶּ֨ם עֹלָ֜ה אִשֵּׁ֨ה
רֵ֤יחַ נִיחֹ֙חַ֙ לַֽיהוָ֔ה פָּרִ֧ים בְּנֵי־בָקָ֛ר שְׁלֹשָׁ֥ה
עָשָׂ֖ר אֵילִ֣ם שְׁנָ֑יִם כְּבָשִׂ֧ים בְּנֵי־שָׁנָ֛ה
אַרְבָּעָ֥ה עָשָׂ֖ר תְּמִימִ֥ם יִהְיֽוּ׃ 14 וּמִ֨נְחָתָ֔ם
סֹ֖לֶת בְּלוּלָ֣ה בַשָּׁ֑מֶן שְׁלֹשָׁ֨ה עֶשְׂרֹנִ֜ים לַפָּ֣ר
הָאֶחָ֗ד לִשְׁלֹשָׁ֤ה עָשָׂר֙ פָּרִ֔ים שְׁנֵ֣י עֶשְׂרֹנִ֗ים
לָאַ֣יִל הָֽאֶחָ֔ד לִשְׁנֵ֖י הָאֵילִֽם׃ 15 וְעִשָּׂרוֹן֙*
עִשָּׂר֔וֹן לַכֶּ֖בֶשׂ הָאֶחָ֑ד לְאַרְבָּעָ֥ה עָשָׂ֖ר
כְּבָשִֽׂים׃ 16 וּשְׂעִיר־עִזִּ֥ים אֶחָ֖ד חַטָּ֑את
מִלְּבַד֙ עֹלַ֣ת הַתָּמִ֔יד מִנְחָתָ֖הּ וְנִסְכָּֽהּ׃ ס

v. 15. נקוד על ו׳ בתראה

and performed exclusively by the high priest (Lev. 16).

7. you shall practice self-denial Literally, "you shall afflict yourselves," chiefly by fasting.

You shall do no work Literally, "you shall not do any work." The same phrase is used for *Shabbat* (Lev. 23:3). It indicates a more severe prohibition of work on these days than on the other festivals.

THE 15th TO THE 21st OF THE SEVENTH MONTH (vv. 12–34)

This sacred occasion is called "the Feast of Booths" (*Ḥag ha-Sukkot*) in Lev. 23:34 and Deut.

CHAPTER 29

13. Offerings for the week of *Sukkot* are staggering in number, a total of 98 lambs and 70 bullocks. (*Pesaḥ* week requires only 16 bulls; no other holiday requires more than 2.) The Talmud teaches that the 70 bulls represent thanksgiving offerings on behalf of the 70 nations of the world (BT Suk. 55b). In case some nations forget to be grateful to God, Israel brings a bullock offering (the most extravagant of the sacrifices) on their behalf on *Sukkot,* the festival of thanksgiving. One of Israel's tasks in the world is to remind other nations to be grateful to God.

17Second day: Twelve bulls of the herd, two rams, fourteen yearling lambs, without blemish; 18the grain offerings and libations for the bulls, rams, and lambs, in the quantities prescribed; 19and one goat for a purification offering—in addition to the regular burnt offering, its grain offering and libations.

20Third day: Eleven bulls, two rams, fourteen yearling lambs, without blemish; 21the grain offerings and libations for the bulls, rams, and lambs, in the quantities prescribed; 22and one goat for a purification offering—in addition to the regular burnt offering, its grain offering and libation.

23Fourth day: Ten bulls, two rams, fourteen yearling lambs, without blemish; 24the grain offerings and libations for the bulls, rams, and lambs, in the quantities prescribed; 25and one goat for a purification offering—in addition to the regular burnt offering, its grain offering and libation.

26Fifth day: Nine bulls, two rams, fourteen yearling lambs, without blemish; 27the grain offerings and libations for the bulls, rams, and lambs, in the quantities prescribed; 28and one goat for a purification offering—in addition to the regular burnt offering, its grain offering and libation.

29Sixth day: Eight bulls, two rams, fourteen yearling lambs, without blemish; 30the grain offerings and libations for the bulls, rams, and lambs, in the quantities prescribed; 31and one goat for a purification offering—in addition to the regular burnt offering, its grain offering and libations.

32Seventh day: Seven bulls, two rams, four-

17 וּבַיּוֹם הַשֵּׁנִי פָּרִים בְּנֵי־בָקָר שְׁנֵים
עָשָׂר אֵילִם שְׁנָיִם כְּבָשִׂים בְּנֵי־שָׁנָה
אַרְבָּעָה עָשָׂר תְּמִימִם׃ 18 וּמִנְחָתָם
וְנִסְכֵּיהֶם לַפָּרִים לָאֵילִם וְלַכְּבָשִׂים
בְּמִסְפָּרָם כַּמִּשְׁפָּט׃ 19 וּשְׂעִיר־עִזִּים אֶחָד
חַטָּאת מִלְּבַד עֹלַת הַתָּמִיד וּמִנְחָתָהּ
וְנִסְכֵּיהֶם׃ ס
20 וּבַיּוֹם הַשְּׁלִישִׁי פָּרִים עַשְׁתֵּי־עָשָׂר
אֵילִם שְׁנָיִם כְּבָשִׂים בְּנֵי־שָׁנָה אַרְבָּעָה
עָשָׂר תְּמִימִם׃ 21 וּמִנְחָתָם וְנִסְכֵּיהֶם
לַפָּרִים לָאֵילִם וְלַכְּבָשִׂים בְּמִסְפָּרָם
כַּמִּשְׁפָּט׃ 22 וּשְׂעִיר חַטָּאת אֶחָד מִלְּבַד
עֹלַת הַתָּמִיד וּמִנְחָתָהּ וְנִסְכָּהּ׃ ס
23 וּבַיּוֹם הָרְבִיעִי פָּרִים עֲשָׂרָה אֵילִם
שְׁנָיִם כְּבָשִׂים בְּנֵי־שָׁנָה אַרְבָּעָה עָשָׂר
תְּמִימִם׃ 24 מִנְחָתָם וְנִסְכֵּיהֶם לַפָּרִים
לָאֵילִם וְלַכְּבָשִׂים בְּמִסְפָּרָם כַּמִּשְׁפָּט׃
25 וּשְׂעִיר־עִזִּים אֶחָד חַטָּאת מִלְּבַד עֹלַת
הַתָּמִיד מִנְחָתָהּ וְנִסְכָּהּ׃ ס
26 וּבַיּוֹם הַחֲמִישִׁי פָּרִים תִּשְׁעָה אֵילִם
שְׁנָיִם כְּבָשִׂים בְּנֵי־שָׁנָה אַרְבָּעָה עָשָׂר
תְּמִימִם׃ 27 וּמִנְחָתָם וְנִסְכֵּיהֶם לַפָּרִים
לָאֵילִם וְלַכְּבָשִׂים בְּמִסְפָּרָם כַּמִּשְׁפָּט׃
28 וּשְׂעִיר חַטָּאת אֶחָד מִלְּבַד עֹלַת
הַתָּמִיד וּמִנְחָתָהּ וְנִסְכָּהּ׃ ס
29 וּבַיּוֹם הַשִּׁשִּׁי פָּרִים שְׁמֹנָה אֵילִם שְׁנָיִם
כְּבָשִׂים בְּנֵי־שָׁנָה אַרְבָּעָה עָשָׂר תְּמִימִם׃
30 וּמִנְחָתָם וְנִסְכֵּיהֶם לַפָּרִים לָאֵילִם
וְלַכְּבָשִׂים בְּמִסְפָּרָם כַּמִּשְׁפָּט׃ 31 וּשְׂעִיר
חַטָּאת אֶחָד מִלְּבַד עֹלַת הַתָּמִיד מִנְחָתָהּ
וּנְסָכֶיהָ׃ פ
32 וּבַיּוֹם הַשְּׁבִיעִי פָּרִים שִׁבְעָה אֵילִם

16:13; "the Feast of Ingathering" (*Ḥag ha-Asif*) in Exod. 23:16 and 34:22; and "the Feast" (*he-Ḥag*), i.e., the pre-eminent festival, in 1 Kings 8:2 and 12:32. When the harvest was in at the end of the agricultural year and the new year was beginning, the Israelite farmer could go on pilgrimage to Jerusalem for this seven-day festival.

teen yearling lambs, without blemish; [33]the grain offerings and libations for the bulls, rams, and lambs, in the quantities prescribed; [34]and one goat for a purification offering—in addition to the regular burnt offering, its grain offering and libation.

[35]On the eighth day you shall hold a solemn gathering; you shall not work at your occupations. [36]You shall present a burnt offering, a gift of pleasing odor to the LORD; one bull, one ram, seven yearling lambs, without blemish; [37]the grain offerings and libations for the bull, the ram, and the lambs, in the quantities prescribed; [38]and one goat for a purification offering—in addition to the regular burnt offering, its grain offering and libation.

[39]All these you shall offer to the LORD at the stated times, in addition to your votive and freewill offerings, be they burnt offerings, grain offerings, libations, or offerings of well-being.

30 [1]So Moses spoke to the Israelites just as the LORD had commanded Moses.

שְׁנַיִם כְּבָשִׂים בְּנֵי־שָׁנָה אַרְבָּעָה עָשָׂר
תְּמִימִם׃ 33 וּמִנְחָתָם וְנִסְכֵּהֶם* לַפָּרִים
לָאֵילִם וְלַכְּבָשִׂים בְּמִסְפָּרָם כְּמִשְׁפָּטָם׃
34 וּשְׂעִיר חַטָּאת אֶחָד מִלְּבַד עֹלַת
הַתָּמִיד מִנְחָתָהּ וְנִסְכָּהּ׃ פ
מפטיר 35 בַּיּוֹם הַשְּׁמִינִי עֲצֶרֶת תִּהְיֶה לָכֶם כָּל־
מְלֶאכֶת עֲבֹדָה לֹא תַעֲשׂוּ׃ 36 וְהִקְרַבְתֶּם
עֹלָה אִשֵּׁה רֵיחַ נִיחֹחַ לַיהוָה פַּר אֶחָד
אַיִל אֶחָד כְּבָשִׂים בְּנֵי־שָׁנָה שִׁבְעָה
תְּמִימִם׃ 37 מִנְחָתָם וְנִסְכֵּיהֶם לַפָּר לָאַיִל
וְלַכְּבָשִׂים בְּמִסְפָּרָם כַּמִּשְׁפָּט׃ 38 וּשְׂעִיר
חַטָּאת אֶחָד מִלְּבַד עֹלַת הַתָּמִיד וּמִנְחָתָהּ
וְנִסְכָּהּ׃
39 אֵלֶּה תַּעֲשׂוּ לַיהוָה בְּמוֹעֲדֵיכֶם לְבַד
מִנִּדְרֵיכֶם וְנִדְבֹתֵיכֶם לְעֹלֹתֵיכֶם
וּלְמִנְחֹתֵיכֶם וּלְנִסְכֵּיכֶם וּלְשַׁלְמֵיכֶם׃
ל 1 וַיֹּאמֶר מֹשֶׁה אֶל־בְּנֵי יִשְׂרָאֵל כְּכֹל
אֲשֶׁר־צִוָּה יְהוָה אֶת־מֹשֶׁה׃ פ

v. 33. חסר י׳

EIGHTH DAY (vv. 35–38)

Although *Sukkot* is a seven-day festival (v. 12), an eighth festival day is added. Its offerings, however, are not the same as those of the preceding festival; rather, they are the same as those of the 1st and the 10th of this month.

35. On the eighth day This, the eighth day, is an independent celebration, unconnected to the preceding festival. Work is prohibited on this day, thereby making it a "sacred occasion," as is the first day of *Sukkot* (v. 12).

39. Personal offerings may be presented in addition to the public offerings stipulated above.

30:1. This verse tells us that Moses informed the Israelites about the religious calendar before addressing them on the next subject.

---

35. On *Sh'mini Atzeret* (the Hebrew name of the festival cited), the day immediately after *Sukkot* week, the offerings are more restrained. The Talmud pictures God as a host, welcoming representatives of all nations who come to pay homage on *Sukkot;* then, as the festival ends and the other nations depart, God says to Israel: "Stay here with Me a while longer for a more intimate celebration" (BT Suk. 55b).

הפטרת פינחס

HAFTARAH FOR PINḤAS

1 KINGS 18:46–19:21

(*When* Pinḥas *is read after the 17th of* Tammuz, *recite the First Haftarah of Admonition, p. 968.*)

This *haftarah* is part of the long cycle of narratives about Elijah's career as a prophet (mid-9th century B.C.E.). The episodes here follow the dramatic contest on Mount Carmel—during which Elijah miraculously demonstrated that "the LORD alone is God"—and the subsequent slaughter of the prophets of Baal (1 Kings 18:1–40). Because King Ahab's wife, Jezebel, a native Phoenician, was upset with this slaying, Elijah had to flee south to escape her threat of death. Eventually, he reached Mount Horeb, where he received an awesome revelation.

Elijah's fear for his life, or his desire to die, marks each stage of his flight from Jezebel. This is highlighted by uses of the word "life" (*nefesh*) at each juncture (19:2,3,4,10,14). Figures of divine revelation and divine aid also recur throughout the *haftarah;* they structure its content as Elijah moves from Mount Carmel to Mount Horeb. At the beginning, when the prophet runs before Ahab to Jezreel, it is God's silent "hand" on him that gives Elijah the power to perform this heroic feat (18:46). During his encampment in the wilderness, Elijah is twice visited by an angel, manifesting God's succor through food and sustenance (19:5–8). Finally, upon Elijah's arrival at Horeb, God appears to him, at first through a "soft murmuring sound" (a distinct but inarticulate presence) and then, climactically, through an extended articulation of the prophet's new task (19:15–18).

This final revelation is God's direct response to the prophet's sense of abandonment. It restores Elijah to his role as a divine messenger, from which he had retreated during his period of fear and despair. As a verbal revelation directly from God, it climaxes the earlier manifestations of divine presence: the empowering "hand of the LORD" at the beginning and the angels thereafter. At each stage, God becomes more personal and vocal—moving from physical inspiration and care to a revelation of divine transcendence.

Elijah immediately accepts God's word and travels north, where he finds Elisha, upon whom he throws the very mantle he wore during the divine appearance at Horeb (19:19; cf. v. 13). Elisha, transfigured, leaves his worldly tasks and family to follow Elijah. Thus begins the fulfillment of the divine instruction.

RELATION OF THE *HAFTARAH* TO THE *PARASHAH*

A common concern links the *parashah* and the *haftarah:* zeal against false worship. This is underscored by the verb *kana* (see Comment to 19:10). In the *parashah,* God approves of the zeal of Phinehas, who was so enraged by the rites at Baal-peor that he murdered the perpetrators caught in the act. God declares: "Phinehas, son of Eleazar son of Aaron the priest, has turned back My wrath from the Israelites by displaying among them his passion for Me [*b'kan·o et kin·ati*], so that I did not wipe out the Israelite people in My passion [*b'kin·ati*]" (Num. 25:11). The "impassioned action for His God [*kinnei leilohav*]" that Phinehas demonstrated is deemed a fit trait for leadership (v. 13). For his part, Elijah tells God at Horeb that he was "moved by zeal for the LORD [*kanno kinneiti la-YHVH*]" and killed the false prophets at Mount Carmel (1 Kings 19:10,14). He also regards such behavior as exemplary. Obviously, the Bible does too, by giving the matter prominence.

On the basis of such traits, the Sages intuited a similarity between Phinehas and Elijah, going so far as to identify the two: "Phinehas is Elijah,

the high priest, who will be sent to [gather] the exiles of Israel at the end of days" (Targ. Jon., Exod. 6:18). In this tradition, Phinehas and his pious passion enjoy an afterlife into messianic times. A countertradition, however, rejects the fanatical zeal of this religious type. Already in the Bible (Ps. 106:30), Phinehas's bloody intervention at Baal-peor is rewritten as a prayer-like intercession (*va-y'fallel*). And the Midrash emphasizes Elijah's failure to seek the repentance of his people; it portrays God as actively trying to assuage the prophet's intractable passion (see Yalkut Sh.).

18 [46]The hand of the LORD had come upon Elijah. He tied up his skirts and ran in front of Ahab all the way to Jezreel.

יח 46 וְיַד־יְהוָה הָיְתָה אֶל־אֵלִיָּהוּ
וַיְשַׁנֵּס מָתְנָיו וַיָּרָץ לִפְנֵי אַחְאָב עַד־
בֹּאֲכָה יִזְרְעֶאלָה׃

19 When Ahab told Jezebel all that Elijah had done and how he had put all the prophets to the sword, [2]Jezebel sent a messenger to Elijah, saying, "Thus and more may the gods do if by this time tomorrow I have not made you like one of them."

[3]Frightened, he fled at once for his life. He came to Beer-sheba, which is in Judah, and left his servant there; [4]he himself went a day's journey into the wilderness. He came to a broom bush and sat down under it, and prayed that he might die. "Enough!" he cried. "Now, O LORD, take my life, for I am no better than my fathers."

[5]He lay down and fell asleep under a broom bush. Suddenly an angel touched him and said to him, "Arise and eat." [6]He looked about; and there, beside his head, was a cake baked on hot stones and a jar of water! He ate and drank, and lay down again. [7]The angel of the LORD came a second time and touched him and said, "Arise and eat, or the journey will be too much for you." [8]He arose and ate and drank; and with

יט וַיַּגֵּד אַחְאָב לְאִיזֶבֶל אֵת כָּל־אֲשֶׁר
עָשָׂה אֵלִיָּהוּ וְאֵת כָּל־אֲשֶׁר הָרַג אֶת־כָּל־
הַנְּבִיאִים בֶּחָרֶב׃ 2 וַתִּשְׁלַח אִיזֶבֶל מַלְאָךְ
אֶל־אֵלִיָּהוּ לֵאמֹר כֹּה־יַעֲשׂוּן אֱלֹהִים וְכֹה
יוֹסִפוּן כִּי־כָעֵת מָחָר אָשִׂים אֶת־נַפְשְׁךָ
כְּנֶפֶשׁ אַחַד מֵהֶם׃
3 וַיַּרְא* וַיָּקָם וַיֵּלֶךְ אֶל־נַפְשׁוֹ וַיָּבֹא בְּאֵר
שֶׁבַע אֲשֶׁר לִיהוּדָה וַיַּנַּח אֶת־נַעֲרוֹ שָׁם׃
4 וְהוּא־הָלַךְ בַּמִּדְבָּר דֶּרֶךְ יוֹם וַיָּבֹא וַיֵּשֶׁב
תַּחַת רֹתֶם אחת אֶחָד וַיִּשְׁאַל אֶת־נַפְשׁוֹ
לָמוּת וַיֹּאמֶר ׀ רַב עַתָּה יְהוָה קַח נַפְשִׁי
כִּי־לֹא־טוֹב אָנֹכִי מֵאֲבֹתָי׃
5 וַיִּשְׁכַּב וַיִּישַׁן תַּחַת רֹתֶם אֶחָד וְהִנֵּה־זֶה
מַלְאָךְ נֹגֵעַ בּוֹ וַיֹּאמֶר לוֹ קוּם אֱכוֹל׃ 6 וַיַּבֵּט
וְהִנֵּה מְרַאֲשֹׁתָיו עֻגַת רְצָפִים וְצַפַּחַת מָיִם
וַיֹּאכַל וַיֵּשְׁתְּ וַיָּשָׁב וַיִּשְׁכָּב׃ 7 וַיָּשָׁב מַלְאַךְ
יְהוָה ׀ שֵׁנִית וַיִּגַּע־בּוֹ וַיֹּאמֶר קוּם אֱכֹל
כִּי רַב מִמְּךָ הַדָּרֶךְ׃ 8 וַיָּקָם וַיֹּאכַל וַיִּשְׁתֶּה

v. 3. בנוסח אחר מנוקדת "וַיִּרָא"

1 Kings 18:46. He tied up his skirts Elijah ran before the chariot to accompany the king, expressing respect for his majesty.

1 Kings 19:3. Frightened As in some manuscripts and the Septuagint; most manuscripts and the editions read "And he saw, and" [Transl.].

4. take my life This prophet's prayer for death recalls the plight of the prophet Jonah (Jon. 4:5).

8. Medieval commentators have pointed to a variety of similarities between Moses and Elijah. (a) Moses spent 40 days and nights without food

the strength from that meal he walked forty days and forty nights as far as the mountain of God at Horeb. [9]There he went into a cave, and there he spent the night.

Then the word of the LORD came to him. He said to him, "Why are you here, Elijah?" [10]He replied, "I am moved by zeal for the LORD, the God of Hosts, for the Israelites have forsaken Your covenant, torn down Your altars, and put Your prophets to the sword. I alone am left, and they are out to take my life." [11]"Come out," He called, "and stand on the mountain before the LORD."

And lo, the LORD passed by. There was a great and mighty wind, splitting mountains and shattering rocks by the power of the LORD; but the LORD was not in the wind. After the wind—an earthquake; but the LORD was not in the earthquake. [12]After the earthquake—fire; but the LORD was not in the fire. And after the fire—a soft murmuring sound. [13]When Elijah heard it, he wrapped his mantle about his face and went out and stood at the entrance of the cave. Then a voice addressed him: "Why are you here, Elijah?" [14]He answered, "I am moved by zeal for the LORD, the God of Hosts; for the Israelites have forsaken Your covenant, torn down Your altars, and have put Your prophets to the sword. I alone am left, and they are out to take my life."

[15]The LORD said to him, "Go back by the way you came, [and] on to the wilderness of Da-

וַיֵּ֣לֶךְ בְּכֹ֣חַ ׀ הָאֲכִילָ֣ה הַהִ֗יא אַרְבָּעִ֥ים יוֹם֙ וְאַרְבָּעִ֣ים לַ֔יְלָה עַ֛ד הַ֥ר הָאֱלֹהִ֖ים חֹרֵֽב׃ [9]וַיָּבֹא־שָׁ֥ם אֶל־הַמְּעָרָ֖ה וַיָּ֣לֶן שָׁ֑ם וְהִנֵּ֤ה דְבַר־יְהֹוָה֙ אֵלָ֔יו וַיֹּ֣אמֶר ל֔וֹ מַה־לְּךָ֥ פֹ֖ה אֵלִיָּֽהוּ׃ [10]וַיֹּאמֶר֩ קַנֹּ֨א קִנֵּ֜אתִי לַיהֹוָ֣ה ׀ אֱלֹהֵ֣י צְבָא֗וֹת כִּֽי־עָזְב֤וּ בְרִֽיתְךָ֙ בְּנֵ֣י יִשְׂרָאֵ֔ל אֶת־מִזְבְּחֹתֶ֣יךָ הָרָ֔סוּ וְאֶת־נְבִיאֶ֖יךָ הָרְג֣וּ בֶחָ֑רֶב וָֽאִוָּתֵ֤ר אֲנִי֙ לְבַדִּ֔י וַיְבַקְשׁ֥וּ אֶת־נַפְשִׁ֖י לְקַחְתָּֽהּ׃ [11]וַיֹּ֗אמֶר צֵ֣א וְעָמַדְתָּ֣ בָהָר֮ לִפְנֵ֣י יְהֹוָה֒

וְהִנֵּ֧ה יְהֹוָ֣ה עֹבֵ֗ר וְר֣וּחַ גְּדוֹלָ֡ה וְחָזָ֞ק מְפָרֵק֩ הָרִ֨ים וּמְשַׁבֵּ֤ר סְלָעִים֙ לִפְנֵ֣י יְהֹוָ֔ה לֹ֥א בָר֖וּחַ יְהֹוָ֑ה וְאַחַ֤ר הָר֙וּחַ֙ רַ֔עַשׁ לֹ֥א בָרַ֖עַשׁ יְהֹוָֽה׃ [12]וְאַחַ֤ר הָרַ֨עַשׁ֙ אֵ֔שׁ לֹ֥א בָאֵ֖שׁ יְהֹוָ֑ה וְאַחַ֣ר הָאֵ֔שׁ ק֖וֹל דְּמָמָ֥ה דַקָּֽה׃ [13]וַיְהִ֣י ׀ כִּשְׁמֹ֣עַ אֵלִיָּ֗הוּ וַיָּ֤לֶט פָּנָיו֙ בְּאַדַּרְתּ֔וֹ וַיֵּצֵ֕א וַֽיַּעֲמֹ֖ד פֶּ֣תַח הַמְּעָרָ֑ה וְהִנֵּ֤ה אֵלָיו֙ ק֔וֹל וַיֹּ֕אמֶר מַה־לְּךָ֥ פֹ֖ה אֵלִיָּֽהוּ׃ [14]וַיֹּ֩אמֶר֩ קַנֹּ֨א קִנֵּ֜אתִי לַיהֹוָ֣ה ׀ אֱלֹהֵ֣י צְבָא֗וֹת כִּֽי־עָזְב֤וּ בְרִֽיתְךָ֙ בְּנֵ֣י יִשְׂרָאֵ֔ל אֶת־מִזְבְּחֹתֶ֣יךָ הָרָ֔סוּ וְאֶת־נְבִיאֶ֖יךָ הָרְג֣וּ בֶחָ֑רֶב וָאִוָּתֵ֤ר אֲנִי֙ לְבַדִּ֔י וַיְבַקְשׁ֥וּ אֶת־נַפְשִׁ֖י לְקַחְתָּֽהּ׃ ס [15]וַיֹּ֤אמֶר יְהֹוָה֙ אֵלָ֔יו לֵ֣ךְ שׁ֥וּב לְדַרְכְּךָ֖ מִדְבַּ֣רָה דַמָּ֑שֶׂק וּבָ֗אתָ וּמָשַׁחְתָּ֧ אֶת־חֲזָאֵ֛ל

or water on Sinai/Horeb (Exod. 34:28; Deut. 9:8–9); Elijah is without food or water for the same amount of time on his journey to Horeb. (b) Moses hid in the cleft of a rock (Exod. 33:22) as the Lord "passed" (va-ya·avor) before him on the mountain (Exod. 34:6); Elijah was called from his cave by God who appeared and "passed by" (over) (19:11). (c) In God's presence, Moses hid his face (Exod. 3:6); Elijah wrapped his face in his mantle (19:13).

10. I am moved by zeal for the LORD A *midrash* understands Elijah to have been an impassioned prosecutor against Israel constantly, without the smallest desire to intervene on his people's

behalf, even after God tried to change his mood through a torrent of wind and fire. For this unabated zeal, he was censured and lost his prophetic mantle (Yalkut Sh.).

11. The elements are like a military retinue, a force of destructive powers that surrounds the divine throne. This storm imagery resembles the "voice" or "thunder" (*kol*) of the Lord in Ps. 29, which produces similar natural effects.

12. a soft murmuring sound Hebrew: *kol d'mamah dakkah*. (The King James translation rendered, "a still small voice.") The phrase may be an attempt to articulate via paradox the "voiced silence" of God's presence: a sound (*kol*) that is

mascus. When you get there, anoint Hazael as king of Aram. 16Also anoint Jehu son of Nimshi as king of Israel, and anoint Elisha son of Shaphat of Abel-meholah to succeed you as prophet. 17Whoever escapes the sword of Hazael shall be slain by Jehu, and whoever escapes the sword of Jehu shall be slain by Elisha. 18I will leave in Israel only seven thousand—every knee that has not knelt to Baal and every mouth that has not kissed him."

19He set out from there and came upon Elisha son of Shaphat as he was plowing. There were twelve yoke of oxen ahead of him, and he was with the twelfth. Elijah came over to him and threw his mantle over him. 20He left the oxen and ran after Elijah, saying: "Let me kiss my father and mother good-by, and I will follow you." And he answered him, "Go back. What have I done to you?" 21He turned back from him and took the yoke of oxen and slaughtered them; he boiled their meat with the gear of the oxen and gave it to the people, and they ate. Then he arose and followed Elijah and became his attendant.

לְמֶ֖לֶךְ עַל־אֲרָֽם׃ 16 וְאֵת֙ יֵה֣וּא בֶן־נִמְשִׁ֔י
תִּמְשַׁ֥ח לְמֶ֖לֶךְ עַל־יִשְׂרָאֵ֑ל וְאֶת־אֱלִישָׁ֤ע
בֶּן־שָׁפָט֙ מֵאָבֵ֣ל מְחוֹלָ֔ה תִּמְשַׁ֥ח לְנָבִ֖יא
תַּחְתֶּֽיךָ׃ 17 וְהָיָ֗ה הַנִּמְלָ֛ט מֵחֶ֥רֶב חֲזָאֵ֖ל
יָמִ֣ית יֵה֑וּא וְהַנִּמְלָ֛ט מֵחֶ֥רֶב יֵה֖וּא יָמִ֥ית
אֱלִישָֽׁע׃ 18 וְהִשְׁאַרְתִּ֥י בְיִשְׂרָאֵ֖ל שִׁבְעַ֣ת
אֲלָפִ֑ים כָּל־הַבִּרְכַּ֗יִם אֲשֶׁ֤ר לֹא־כָֽרְעוּ֙
לַבַּ֔עַל וְכָל־הַפֶּ֖ה אֲשֶׁ֥ר לֹא־נָשַׁ֖ק לֽוֹ׃
19 וַיֵּ֣לֶךְ מִ֠שָּׁם וַיִּמְצָ֞א אֶת־אֱלִישָׁ֤ע בֶּן־שָׁפָט֙
וְה֣וּא חֹרֵ֔שׁ שְׁנֵים־עָשָׂ֤ר צְמָדִים֙ לְפָנָ֔יו
וְה֖וּא בִּשְׁנֵ֣ים הֶעָשָׂ֑ר וַיַּעֲבֹ֤ר אֵלִיָּ֙הוּ֙ אֵלָ֔יו
וַיַּשְׁלֵ֥ךְ אַדַּרְתּ֖וֹ אֵלָֽיו׃ 20 וַיַּעֲזֹ֣ב אֶת־הַבָּקָ֗ר
וַיָּ֙רָץ֙ אַחֲרֵ֣י אֵֽלִיָּ֔הוּ וַיֹּ֗אמֶר אֶשְּׁקָה־נָּא֙
לְאָבִ֣י וּלְאִמִּ֔י וְאֵלְכָ֖ה אַחֲרֶ֑יךָ וַיֹּ֤אמֶר לוֹ֙
לֵ֣ךְ שׁ֔וּב כִּ֥י מֶה־עָשִׂ֖יתִי לָֽךְ׃ 21 וַיָּ֨שָׁב
מֵאַחֲרָ֜יו וַיִּקַּ֨ח אֶת־צֶ֤מֶד הַבָּקָר֙ וַיִּזְבָּחֵ֔הוּ
וּבִכְלִ֤י הַבָּקָר֙ בִּשְּׁלָ֣ם הַבָּשָׂ֔ר וַיִּתֵּ֥ן לָעָ֖ם
וַיֹּאכֵ֑לוּ וַיָּ֗קָם וַיֵּ֛לֶךְ אַחֲרֵ֥י אֵלִיָּ֖הוּ
וַיְשָׁרְתֵֽהוּ׃ פ

both still (*d'mamah*) and slightly audible (*dakkah*). This hints at a certain type of religious experience, otherwise beyond words.

15. anoint Hazael Elijah, however, does not appoint either Hazael or Jehu; Elisha does. Thus Elijah will be an indirect agent.

17. shall be slain by Jehu In fact, Jehu will kill all worshipers of Baal (2 Kings 10:19ff.) and the household of King Ahab (2 Kings 10:17).

shall be slain by Elisha After ignoring Elisha's admonition, the people will be attacked by their enemies (2 Kings 13:20). This is why their death is attributed to him here (Radak).

18. Genuflection before Baal and kissing his statue were two forms of adoration of this god (see 1 Kings 8:54; Isa. 45:23; Hos. 13:2).

2 Moses spoke to the heads of the Israelite tribes, saying: This is what the LORD has commanded:

3 If a man makes a vow to the LORD or takes an oath imposing an obligation on himself, he shall not break his pledge; he must carry out all that has crossed his lips.

2 וַיְדַבֵּ֤ר מֹשֶׁה֙ אֶל־רָאשֵׁ֣י הַמַּטּ֔וֹת לִבְנֵ֥י
יִשְׂרָאֵ֖ל לֵאמֹ֑ר זֶ֣ה הַדָּבָ֔ר אֲשֶׁ֖ר צִוָּ֥ה יְהוָֽה׃
3 אִ֣ישׁ כִּֽי־יִדֹּ֨ר נֶ֜דֶר לַֽיהוָ֗ה אֽוֹ־הִשָּׁ֤בַע
שְׁבֻעָה֙ לֶאְסֹ֤ר אִסָּר֙ עַל־נַפְשׁ֔וֹ לֹ֥א יַחֵ֖ל
דְּבָר֑וֹ כְּכָל־הַיֹּצֵ֥א מִפִּ֖יו יַעֲשֶֽׂה׃

The Generation of the Conquest (*continued*)

THE ANNULMENT OF VOWS AND OATHS MADE BY WOMEN (30:2–17)

Any pledge made by a man in the name of God must be fulfilled. A woman's vow or oath, however, can be countermanded and annulled by her father or her husband on the day he learns of it, if she is under his authority.

2. heads of the Israelite tribes It is rare to find a law addressed to Israel's leaders rather than to the people as a whole.

This The section that follows.

3. man Not a minor or a woman.

vow to the LORD This vow involves a declaration that the man will dedicate to the sanctuary the value of a person or of an animal if his prayer will be answered.

break Literally, "desecrate." A vow generally was taken in a moment of crisis. Once the crisis had passed, however, the temptation to forget the vow—even unconsciously—remained. Hence, the frequent scriptural admonition against desecrating one's vows.

has crossed his lips Literally, "has come out of his mouth." Vows and oaths made in the name of God are endowed with self-fulfilling powers regardless of the consequences. Once expressed, words are binding, even when the expression does not correspond with the intention (see Isaac's blessing of Jacob, Gen. 27:33–35).

CHAPTER 30

As we approach the end of Numbers, the focus shifts to settlement of the Land. This *parashah* begins with a series of regulations emphasizing the seriousness of oaths and vows and then describes the battle against Midian. Next is a request by two of the tribes to settle in the choice grazing land outside the designated borders of the Promised Land. These chapters, with their promise of the people Israel settling the land God swore to give them, are always read in the weeks before *Tish·ah b'Av,* a day when we mourn the destruction of the Temple and the beginning of the Exile.

The Bible stresses the power and the solemnity of words, from the opening verses of the Torah, in which God creates a world with words, to the commandment to distance oneself from falsehood, to the repeated emphasis against insulting the convert or the physically handicapped. This emphasis continued in postbiblical Judaism. A word is not merely a sound; it is real, it has substance, with the power to hurt or to heal, to elevate or to denigrate. The seriousness with which the Torah takes vows and promises is the basis of the words with which the service begins on the eve of *Yom Kippur.* With those words (known as *Kol Nidrei,* "All Vows") we declare that any promises to God that we make and are unable to keep in the New Year are hereby publicly retracted and should not be held against us.

The power of speech is one of the unique gifts of a human being, a power we share with no other creature. In these rules governing vows and oaths, we see that human beings, like God, have the power to make things holy by words, by proclaiming them holy. By uttering words, an Israelite can impose an obligation on himself or herself as binding as God's commands in the Torah. Hirsch defines a "vow" (*neder*) as "self-imposed legislation."

2. Why are these laws about vows and oaths directed primarily to the heads of the tribes? Because people in high public office are more often tempted to make promises that they cannot keep (Ḥatam Sofer). Their behav-

[4]If a woman makes a vow to the LORD or assumes an obligation while still in her father's
household by reason of her youth, [5]and her
father learns of her vow or her self-imposed
obligation and offers no objection, all her
vows shall stand and every self-imposed obligation shall stand. [6]But if her father restrains
her on the day he finds out, none of her
vows or self-imposed obligations shall stand;
and the LORD will forgive her, since her father
restrained her.

[7]If she should marry while her vow or the
commitment to which she bound herself is still
in force, [8]and her husband learns of it and offers
no objection on the day he finds out, her vows
shall stand and her self-imposed obligations
shall stand. [9]But if her husband restrains her on
the day that he learns of it, he thereby annuls
her vow which was in force or the commitment
to which she bound herself; and the LORD will
forgive her.—[10]The vow of a widow or of a divorced woman, however, whatever she has imposed on herself, shall be binding upon her.—
[11]So, too, if, while in her husband's household,

4 וְאִשָּׁה כִּי־תִדֹּר נֶדֶר לַיהוָה וְאָסְרָה אִסָּר
בְּבֵית אָבִיהָ בִּנְעֻרֶיהָ׃ 5 וְשָׁמַע אָבִיהָ
אֶת־נִדְרָהּ וֶאֱסָרָהּ אֲשֶׁר אָסְרָה עַל־נַפְשָׁהּ
וְהֶחֱרִישׁ לָהּ אָבִיהָ וְקָמוּ כָּל־נְדָרֶיהָ וְכָל־
אִסָּר אֲשֶׁר־אָסְרָה עַל־נַפְשָׁהּ יָקוּם׃
6 וְאִם־הֵנִיא אָבִיהָ אֹתָהּ בְּיוֹם שָׁמְעוֹ
כָּל־נְדָרֶיהָ וֶאֱסָרֶיהָ אֲשֶׁר־אָסְרָה עַל־
נַפְשָׁהּ לֹא יָקוּם וַיהוָה יִסְלַח־לָהּ כִּי־
הֵנִיא אָבִיהָ אֹתָהּ׃
7 וְאִם־הָיוֹ תִהְיֶה לְאִישׁ וּנְדָרֶיהָ עָלֶיהָ אוֹ
מִבְטָא שְׂפָתֶיהָ אֲשֶׁר אָסְרָה עַל־נַפְשָׁהּ׃
8 וְשָׁמַע אִישָׁהּ בְּיוֹם שָׁמְעוֹ וְהֶחֱרִישׁ לָהּ
וְקָמוּ נְדָרֶיהָ וֶאֱסָרֶהָ אֲשֶׁר־אָסְרָה עַל־
נַפְשָׁהּ יָקֻמוּ׃ 9 וְאִם בְּיוֹם שְׁמֹעַ אִישָׁהּ
יָנִיא אוֹתָהּ וְהֵפֵר אֶת־נִדְרָהּ אֲשֶׁר עָלֶיהָ
וְאֵת מִבְטָא שְׂפָתֶיהָ אֲשֶׁר אָסְרָה עַל־
נַפְשָׁהּ וַיהוָה יִסְלַח־לָהּ׃ 10 וְנֵדֶר אַלְמָנָה
וּגְרוּשָׁה כֹּל אֲשֶׁר־אָסְרָה עַל־נַפְשָׁהּ יָקוּם
עָלֶיהָ׃ 11 וְאִם־בֵּית אִישָׁהּ נָדָרָה אוֹ־

4–6. The vows and oaths of an unmarried female who is still under the authority of her father can be annulled by her father if he expresses disapproval on the very day he learns of them.

If a woman Not a man, however.

by reason of her youth This refers to a woman who is young and even marriageable but still in her father's house.

offers no objection His silence implies consent.

on the day he finds out If he waits until the next day to express his disapproval, however, it is too late (see Comment to v. 15).

forgive If the woman is thwarted from fulfilling her vow by her father, God will forgive her.

7–9. If the woman made her vow or oath when still under her father's control, her husband may annul it on the day he learns of it even though it was approved by her father.

commitment Hebrew: *mivta s'fateha;* literally, "utterance of her lips." This implies an oath.

still in force She made the vow or oath while she still was in her father's house, and he did not nullify it.

10. This statement appears to have been inserted by a later editor. It is not included in the summation (v. 17).

11–13. A woman's vow or oath can be annulled by her husband on the day he learns of it. Thereafter, his protests are of no avail. Her vow or oath must be fulfilled.

---

ior could lessen the respect others have for the spoken word.

5. These rules, reflecting an age when women were subordinated to a father or a husband, have been superseded by developments in the modern world. Already by the time of the Talmud, the Sages limited the applicability of this law by restricting its time (the year between ages 11 and 12) and circumstances. The sense here of the married woman as subservient in the early period of our tradition, however, seems unavoidable.

she makes a vow or imposes an obligation on
herself by oath, 12and her husband learns of it,
yet offers no objection—thus failing to restrain
her—all her vows shall stand and all her
self-imposed obligations shall stand. 13But if her
husband does annul them on the day he finds
out, then nothing that has crossed her lips shall
stand, whether vows or self-imposed obligations. Her husband has annulled them, and the
LORD will forgive her. 14Every vow and every
sworn obligation of self-denial may be upheld
by her husband or annulled by her husband. 15If
her husband offers no objection from that day
to the next, he has upheld all the vows or obligations she has assumed: he has upheld them
by offering no objection on the day he found
out. 16But if he annuls them after [the day] he
finds out, he shall bear her guilt.

17Those are the laws that the LORD enjoined
upon Moses between a man and his wife, and
as between a father and his daughter while in
her father's household by reason of her youth.

אָסְרָה אִסָּר עַל־נַפְשָׁהּ בִּשְׁבֻעָה׃ 12 וְשָׁמַע
אִישָׁהּ וְהֶחֱרִשׁ לָהּ לֹא הֵנִיא אֹתָהּ וְקָמוּ
כָּל־נְדָרֶיהָ וְכָל־אִסָּר אֲשֶׁר־אָסְרָה עַל־
נַפְשָׁהּ יָקוּם׃ 13 וְאִם־הָפֵר יָפֵר אֹתָם ׀
אִישָׁהּ בְּיוֹם שָׁמְעוֹ כָּל־מוֹצָא שְׂפָתֶיהָ
לִנְדָרֶיהָ וּלְאִסַּר נַפְשָׁהּ לֹא יָקוּם אִישָׁהּ
הֲפֵרָם וַיהוָה יִסְלַח־לָהּ׃ 14 כָּל־נֵדֶר וְכָל־
שְׁבֻעַת אִסָּר לְעַנֹּת נָפֶשׁ אִישָׁהּ יְקִימֶנּוּ
וְאִישָׁהּ יְפֵרֶנּוּ׃ 15 וְאִם־הַחֲרֵשׁ יַחֲרִישׁ לָהּ
אִישָׁהּ מִיּוֹם אֶל־יוֹם וְהֵקִים אֶת־כָּל־
נְדָרֶיהָ אוֹ אֶת־כָּל־אֱסָרֶיהָ אֲשֶׁר עָלֶיהָ
הֵקִים אֹתָם כִּי־הֶחֱרִשׁ לָהּ בְּיוֹם שָׁמְעוֹ׃
16 וְאִם־הָפֵר יָפֵר אֹתָם אַחֲרֵי שָׁמְעוֹ וְנָשָׂא
אֶת־עֲוֺנָהּ׃
17 אֵלֶּה הַחֻקִּים אֲשֶׁר צִוָּה יְהוָה אֶת־מֹשֶׁה
בֵּין אִישׁ לְאִשְׁתּוֹ בֵּין־אָב לְבִתּוֹ בִּנְעֻרֶיהָ
בֵּית אָבִיהָ׃ פ

31 The LORD spoke to Moses, saying,

שני וַיְדַבֵּר יְהוָה אֶל־מֹשֶׁה לֵּאמֹר׃

15. from that day to the next The vow or oath must be annulled on the same day that the father or husband learns of it.

he has upheld Not now but on the day he had learned of it and was silent.

16. He shall bear her punishment from God, punishment that otherwise would have befallen her for not fulfilling her vow or oath. Either the husband has forced her to break her vow or oath or he has deceived her into believing that he had annulled her vow or oath as soon as he was informed of it. In such cases, it is as if he had taken over her vow and violated it.

CHAPTER 31

1–3. It seems poignant that Moses' last great task before his death is so out of character—a war of vengeance. However, Moses will choose to end his career not with this battle and the discord that followed (v. 14ff.) but with the stirring oration that forms the Book of Deuteronomy.

In verse 2, God directs Moses to avenge the Israelite people. In verse 3, however, Moses speaks to the people about "the LORD's vengeance." This will not be a war primarily for land or personal gain but to redeem God's name from the dishonor that the Midianites attached to it at Baal-peor. Presumably this is why Phinehas the priest is listed as leading the effort rather than Joshua. "Had we been idol-worshipers, they would not have striven so hard to lead us astray" (Num. R. 22:2).

The reader is likely to be uncomfortable with the notion of a "holy war." Does placing the seal of religious approval on a military undertaking change and sanctify the battle or

2 “Avenge the Israelite people on the Midianites;
then you shall be gathered to your kin.”
3 Moses spoke to the people, saying, “Let men
be picked out from among you for a campaign,
and let them fall upon Midian to wreak the
LORD’s vengeance on Midian. 4 You shall dispatch on the campaign a thousand from every
one of the tribes of Israel.”
5 So a thousand from each tribe were fur-
nished from the divisions of Israel, twelve thousand picked for the campaign. 6 Moses dispatched them on the campaign, a thousand
from each tribe, with Phinehas son of Eleazar
serving as a priest on the campaign, equipped
with the sacred utensils and the trumpets for
sounding the blasts. 7 They took the field against
Midian, as the LORD had commanded Moses,
and slew every male. 8 Along with their other victims, they slew the kings of Midian: Evi, Rekem,

2 נְקֹם נִקְמַת בְּנֵי יִשְׂרָאֵל מֵאֵת הַמִּדְיָנִים
אַחַר תֵּאָסֵף אֶל־עַמֶּיךָ׃
3 וַיְדַבֵּר מֹשֶׁה אֶל־הָעָם לֵאמֹר הֵחָלְצוּ
מֵאִתְּכֶם אֲנָשִׁים לַצָּבָא וְיִהְיוּ עַל־מִדְיָן
לָתֵת נִקְמַת־יְהוָה בְּמִדְיָן׃ 4 אֶלֶף לַמַּטֶּה
אֶלֶף לַמַּטֶּה לְכֹל מַטּוֹת יִשְׂרָאֵל תִּשְׁלְחוּ
לַצָּבָא׃
5 וַיִּמָּסְרוּ מֵאַלְפֵי יִשְׂרָאֵל אֶלֶף לַמַּטֶּה
שְׁנֵים־עָשָׂר אֶלֶף חֲלוּצֵי צָבָא׃ 6 וַיִּשְׁלַח
אֹתָם מֹשֶׁה אֶלֶף לַמַּטֶּה לַצָּבָא אֹתָם
וְאֶת־פִּינְחָס בֶּן־אֶלְעָזָר הַכֹּהֵן לַצָּבָא וּכְלֵי
הַקֹּדֶשׁ וַחֲצֹצְרוֹת הַתְּרוּעָה בְּיָדוֹ׃
7 וַיִּצְבְּאוּ עַל־מִדְיָן כַּאֲשֶׁר צִוָּה יְהוָה אֶת־
מֹשֶׁה וַיַּהַרְגוּ כָּל־זָכָר׃ 8 וְאֶת־מַלְכֵי מִדְיָן
הָרְגוּ עַל־חַלְלֵיהֶם אֶת־אֱוִי וְאֶת־רֶקֶם

THE WAR AGAINST MIDIAN (31:1–54)

2. Avenge . . . on Hebrew: *n'kom . . . me-*, which means “redress [past wrongs] from.” Translating it as “avenge . . . on” has no basis in Scripture when the subject is God. Better: “fight” (and in Deut. 32:35, Isa. 1:24).

3. to wreak the LORD’s vengeance on Better: “to exact the LORD’s retribution on.” The Israelites seek redress or compensation from the Midianites for causing the devastating plague of Baal-peor, but the Lord desires to exact retribution from them for the sacrilege they committed by seducing the Israelites into worshiping Baal-peor.

4. thousand Given the differences in the size of the tribes, it is highly unrealistic that the same number was mustered for each one. This word can also be rendered “division,” a much smaller, elite unit that every tribe could provide.

6. Phinehas is involved, not Eleazar, who as high priest was forbidden to expose himself to contamination by a corpse.

serving as a priest on the campaign Phinehas’s function is not to lead the army, but to act as chaplain, to render priestly services, especially in consulting the Urim and Thummim.

the sacred utensils The priest probably accompanied the troops with all the sacred paraphernalia, including the Ark, trumpets, and the Urim and Thummim. He thereby could consult the Lord when necessary, but from a position behind the battle lines to protect the sacred vessels from both capture and contamination.

7. slew every male That is, every adult male of that Midianite tribe in the Transjordan.

---

does it compromise the religion and contaminate it with the stain of bloodshed? When is war “the LORD’s vengeance” and when is it human vengeance to which the name of God has been attached?

6. Moses himself does not take part in the campaign. Was this because of his advanced age, or because he had found refuge among the Midianites when he fled Egypt as a young man (Num. R. 22:4)?

8. It would seem that Balaam, instead of returning home, lingered to see if his plan of seducing the Israelites would work. The Midrash comments on his death by sword (Tanḥ. Balak 8). Isaac had blessed Jacob with the gift of prayer and had told Esau that he would live by the sword (Gen. 27). Balaam set out to use Jacob’s “weapon” against his descendants, trying to harm them with words. In retaliation, Israel used Esau’s weapon, the sword, against him.

Zur, Hur, and Reba, the five kings of Midian. They also put Balaam son of Beor to the sword.

9The Israelites took the women and children of the Midianites captive, and seized as booty all their beasts, all their herds, and all their wealth. 10And they destroyed by fire all the towns in which they were settled, and their encampments. 11They gathered all the spoil and all the booty, man and beast, 12and they brought the captives, the booty, and the spoil to Moses, Eleazar the priest, and the whole Israelite community, at the camp in the steppes of Moab, at the Jordan near Jericho.

13Moses, Eleazar the priest, and all the chieftains of the community came out to meet them outside the camp. 14Moses became angry with the commanders of the army, the officers of thousands and the officers of hundreds, who had come back from the military campaign. 15Moses said to them, "You have spared every female! 16Yet they are the very ones who, at the bidding of Balaam, induced the Israelites to trespass against the LORD in the matter of Peor, so that the LORD's community was struck by the plague. 17Now, therefore, slay every male among the children, and slay also every woman

וְאֶת־צוּר וְאֶת־חוּר וְאֶת־רֶבַע חֲמֵשֶׁת
מַלְכֵי מִדְיָן וְאֵת בִּלְעָם בֶּן־בְּעוֹר הָרְגוּ
בֶּחָרֶב׃
9 וַיִּשְׁבּוּ בְנֵי־יִשְׂרָאֵל אֶת־נְשֵׁי מִדְיָן וְאֶת־
טַפָּם וְאֵת כָּל־בְּהֶמְתָּם וְאֶת־כָּל־מִקְנֵהֶם
וְאֶת־כָּל־חֵילָם בָּזָזוּ׃ 10 וְאֵת כָּל־עָרֵיהֶם
בְּמוֹשְׁבֹתָם וְאֵת כָּל־טִירֹתָם שָׂרְפוּ בָּאֵשׁ׃
11 וַיִּקְחוּ אֶת־כָּל־הַשָּׁלָל וְאֵת כָּל־
הַמַּלְקוֹחַ בָּאָדָם וּבַבְּהֵמָה׃ 12 וַיָּבִאוּ אֶל־
מֹשֶׁה וְאֶל־אֶלְעָזָר הַכֹּהֵן וְאֶל־עֲדַת בְּנֵי־
יִשְׂרָאֵל אֶת־הַשְּׁבִי וְאֶת־הַמַּלְקוֹחַ וְאֶת־
הַשָּׁלָל אֶל־הַמַּחֲנֶה אֶל־עַרְבֹת מוֹאָב
אֲשֶׁר עַל־יַרְדֵּן יְרֵחוֹ׃ ס

שלישי [שני]
13 וַיֵּצְאוּ מֹשֶׁה וְאֶלְעָזָר הַכֹּהֵן וְכָל־נְשִׂיאֵי
הָעֵדָה לִקְרָאתָם אֶל־מִחוּץ לַמַּחֲנֶה׃
14 וַיִּקְצֹף מֹשֶׁה עַל פְּקוּדֵי הֶחָיִל שָׂרֵי
הָאֲלָפִים וְשָׂרֵי הַמֵּאוֹת הַבָּאִים מִצְּבָא
הַמִּלְחָמָה׃ 15 וַיֹּאמֶר אֲלֵיהֶם מֹשֶׁה
הַחִיִּיתֶם כָּל־נְקֵבָה׃ 16 הֵן הֵנָּה הָיוּ לִבְנֵי
יִשְׂרָאֵל בִּדְבַר בִּלְעָם לִמְסָר־מַעַל בַּיהוָה
עַל־דְּבַר־פְּעוֹר וַתְּהִי הַמַּגֵּפָה בַּעֲדַת
יְהוָה׃ 17 וְעַתָּה הִרְגוּ כָל־זָכָר בַּטָּף וְכָל־

13. outside the camp The returning army, requiring purification from corpse contamination, could not enter the camp.

14. The army apparently has no overall commander, for Moses does not turn to a single leader but to the divisional officers.

15. The taking of women captives would have been permitted in any war with non-Canaanites (Deut. 20:10ff.). In this instance, however, the sight of the Midianite women arouses Moses' wrath, because they were instrumental in the apostasy and the plague of Baal-peor (Num. 25).

16. at the bidding of Balaam Reflecting a tradition that after Balaam failed to curse the Israelites he persuaded the Midianites to seduce the Israelites at Baal-peor.

17. carnally Literally, "lying with a male." These women, because they seduced the Israelites, are to be slain.

---

16. Here Balaam is identified as the instigator of the seduction scheme at Baal-peor, a fact the Torah did not mention previously. Had the Torah mentioned Balaam's role earlier, the Israelites might have excused their behavior by saying "he led us into it." Therefore the Torah describes and condemns the sin as inexcusable weakness on Israel's part and only later identifies the instigator.

17. The command to kill Midianite women and children can be understood only in light of the Torah's fear that their sexually charged pagan celebrations would continue to distract and entice the young, immature Israelite people. Ramban, building on a comment in *Sifrei,* suggests that Moses' instructions to the army in verses 3–4 were vague and did not mention killing the women. Moses may be an-

who has known a man carnally; 18but spare every young woman who has not had carnal relations with a man.

19"You shall then stay outside the camp seven days; every one among you or among your captives who has slain a person or touched a corpse shall purify himself on the third and seventh days. 20You shall also purify every cloth, every article of skin, everything made of goats' hair, and every object of wood."

21Eleazar the priest said to the troops who had taken part in the fighting, "This is the ritual law that the LORD has enjoined upon Moses: 22Gold and silver, copper, iron, tin, and lead—23any article that can withstand fire—these you shall pass through fire and they shall be pure, except that they must be purified with water of lustration; and anything that cannot withstand fire

אִשָּׁה יֹדַעַת אִישׁ לְמִשְׁכַּב זָכָר הֲרֹגוּ׃
18 וְכֹל הַטַּף בַּנָּשִׁים אֲשֶׁר לֹא־יָדְעוּ מִשְׁכַּב
זָכָר הַחֲיוּ לָכֶם׃
19 וְאַתֶּם חֲנוּ מִחוּץ לַמַּחֲנֶה שִׁבְעַת
יָמִים כֹּל הֹרֵג נֶפֶשׁ וְכֹל ׀ נֹגֵעַ בֶּחָלָל
תִּתְחַטְּאוּ בַּיּוֹם הַשְּׁלִישִׁי וּבַיּוֹם הַשְּׁבִיעִי
אַתֶּם וּשְׁבִיכֶם׃ 20 וְכָל־בֶּגֶד וְכָל־כְּלִי־
עוֹר וְכָל־מַעֲשֵׂה עִזִּים וְכָל־כְּלִי־עֵץ
תִּתְחַטָּאוּ׃ ס
21 וַיֹּאמֶר אֶלְעָזָר הַכֹּהֵן אֶל־אַנְשֵׁי הַצָּבָא
הַבָּאִים לַמִּלְחָמָה זֹאת חֻקַּת הַתּוֹרָה
אֲשֶׁר־צִוָּה יְהוָה אֶת־מֹשֶׁה׃ 22 אַךְ אֶת־
הַזָּהָב וְאֶת־הַכָּסֶף אֶת־הַנְּחֹשֶׁת אֶת־
הַבַּרְזֶל אֶת־הַבְּדִיל וְאֶת־הָעֹפָרֶת׃ 23 כָּל־
דָּבָר אֲשֶׁר־יָבֹא בָאֵשׁ תַּעֲבִירוּ בָאֵשׁ וְטָהֵר
אַךְ בְּמֵי נִדָּה יִתְחַטָּא וְכֹל אֲשֶׁר לֹא־יָבֹא

v. 23. סבירין ומטעין "והנה"

18. The virgins are to be kept alive as slaves or wives.

PURIFICATION OF WARRIORS AND CAPTIVES (vv. 19–24)

19. Moses now turns from the officers to address all the troops.

or among your captives Implies that all persons, Israelites and non-Israelites alike, are capable of contaminating the sanctuary. Therefore, the captives also must be purified before entering the camp.

20. All exposed objects in a room containing a human corpse must undergo a seven-day purification. Articles of wood, cloth, or animal skin coming into contact with an animal corpse must undergo a one-day purification. Earthenware vessels are absent from this list because they cannot be purified (see 19:14–18; Lev. 11:32).

22. The metals are arranged in descending order of value. Articles made of earthenware or stone, although also able to withstand fire, are not mentioned. Pottery, being porous, can never be purified and must be destroyed if impure (Lev. 6:21). Stone is not subject to impurity.

23. water of lustration Water, when sprinkled on a corpse-contaminated person on the third day and on the seventh day, purifies the person (19:18–19). This passage appears to supplement the rules of purification of corpse-

---

gry at himself for the omission and directs his anger against the army commanders. Or he may be going out of his way to avoid charges of favoring the Midianites, his wife's relatives.

19. Because the rules of warfare permit behavior that is otherwise forbidden, those soldiers who had killed must remain outside the camp for a week, not only because of corpse contamination but as a transition to the world of normal living.

HALAKHAH L'MA·ASEH

31:23. these shall you pass through fire and they shall be pure This is the basis for how to make utensils, pots, and pans fit for use according to the Jewish dietary laws when they have been previously used for cooking non-kosher food. The same procedure applies for switching them from use for dairy meals to meat meals, or the reverse, or for making utensils that are used throughout the year fit for use during *Pesaḥ* (BT Av. Zar. 75b).

you must pass through water. ²⁴On the seventh
day you shall wash your clothes and be pure,
and after that you may enter the camp."

²⁵The LORD said to Moses: ²⁶"You and Eleazar
the priest and the family heads of the commu-
nity take an inventory of the booty that was captured, man and beast, ²⁷and divide the booty
equally between the combatants who engaged
in the campaign and the rest of the community.
²⁸You shall exact a levy for the LORD: in the case
of the warriors who engaged in the campaign,
one item in five hundred, of persons, oxen,
asses, and sheep, ²⁹shall be taken from their
half-share and given to Eleazar the priest as a
contribution to the LORD; ³⁰and from the
half-share of the other Israelites you shall withhold one in every fifty human beings as well as
cattle, asses, and sheep—all the animals—and
give them to the Levites, who attend to the duties of the LORD's Tabernacle."

³¹Moses and Eleazar the priest did as the LORD
commanded Moses. ³²The amount of booty,
other than the spoil that the troops had plundered, came to 675,000 sheep, ³³72,000 head of
cattle, ³⁴61,000 asses, ³⁵and a total of 32,000 human beings, namely, the women who had not
had carnal relations.

³⁶Thus, the half-share of those who had en-

בָּאֵ֖שׁ תַּעֲבִ֣ירוּ בַמָּ֑יִם׃ 24 וְכִבַּסְתֶּ֨ם בִּגְדֵיכֶ֜ם
בַּיּ֣וֹם הַשְּׁבִיעִי֮ וּטְהַרְתֶּם֒ וְאַחַ֖ר תָּבֹ֥אוּ
אֶל־הַֽמַּחֲנֶֽה׃ פ

רביעי 25 וַיֹּ֥אמֶר יְהֹוָ֖ה אֶל־מֹשֶׁ֥ה לֵּאמֹֽר׃ 26 שָׂ֗א
אֵ֣ת רֹ֤אשׁ מַלְק֙וֹחַ֙ הַשְּׁבִ֔י בָּאָדָ֖ם וּבַבְּהֵמָ֑ה
אַתָּה֙ וְאֶלְעָזָ֣ר הַכֹּהֵ֔ן וְרָאשֵׁ֖י אֲב֥וֹת
הָעֵדָֽה׃ 27 וְחָצִ֙יתָ֙ אֶת־הַמַּלְק֔וֹחַ בֵּ֚ין
תֹּפְשֵׂ֣י הַמִּלְחָמָ֔ה הַיֹּצְאִ֖ים לַצָּבָ֑א וּבֵ֖ין
כָּל־הָעֵדָֽה׃ 28 וַהֲרֵמֹתָ֨ מֶ֜כֶס לַֽיהֹוָ֗ה
מֵאֵ֞ת אַנְשֵׁ֣י הַמִּלְחָמָה֮ הַיֹּצְאִ֣ים לַצָּבָא֒
אֶחָ֣ד נֶ֔פֶשׁ מֵֽחֲמֵ֖שׁ הַמֵּא֑וֹת מִן־הָ֣אָדָ֗ם
וּמִן־הַבָּקָר֙ וּמִן־הַ֣חֲמֹרִ֔ים וּמִן־הַצֹּֽאן׃
29 מִמַּֽחֲצִיתָ֖ם תִּקָּ֑חוּ וְנָתַתָּ֛ה לְאֶלְעָזָ֥ר
הַכֹּהֵ֖ן תְּרוּמַ֥ת יְהֹוָֽה׃ 30 וּמִמַּֽחֲצִ֨ת בְּנֵֽי־
יִשְׂרָאֵ֜ל תִּקַּ֣ח ׀ אֶחָ֣ד ׀ אָחֻ֣ז מִן־הַֽחֲמִשִּׁ֗ים
מִן־הָֽאָדָ֤ם מִן־הַבָּקָר֙ מִן־הַֽחֲמֹרִ֣ים וּמִן־
הַצֹּ֔אן מִכָּל־הַבְּהֵמָ֑ה וְנָתַתָּ֤ה אֹתָם֙ לַלְוִיִּ֔ם
שֹׁמְרֵ֕י מִשְׁמֶ֖רֶת מִשְׁכַּ֥ן יְהֹוָֽה׃
31 וַיַּ֣עַשׂ מֹשֶׁ֔ה וְאֶלְעָזָ֖ר הַכֹּהֵ֑ן כַּֽאֲשֶׁ֛ר צִוָּ֥ה
יְהֹוָ֖ה אֶת־מֹשֶֽׁה׃ 32 וַיְהִי֙ הַמַּלְק֔וֹחַ יֶ֥תֶר
הַבָּ֖ז אֲשֶׁ֣ר בָּֽזְז֣וּ עַ֣ם הַצָּבָ֑א צֹ֗אן שֵׁשׁ־מֵא֥וֹת
אֶ֛לֶף וְשִׁבְעִ֥ים אֶ֖לֶף וַֽחֲמֵֽשֶׁת־אֲלָפִֽים׃
33 וּבָקָ֕ר שְׁנַ֥יִם וְשִׁבְעִ֖ים אָֽלֶף׃ 34 וַֽחֲמֹרִ֕ים
אֶחָ֥ד וְשִׁשִּׁ֖ים אָֽלֶף׃ 35 וְנֶ֣פֶשׁ אָדָ֔ם מִן־
הַנָּשִׁ֕ים אֲשֶׁ֥ר לֹֽא־יָֽדְע֖וּ מִשְׁכַּ֣ב זָכָ֑ר כָּל־
נֶ֕פֶשׁ שְׁנַ֥יִם וּשְׁלֹשִׁ֖ים אָֽלֶף׃
36 וַתְּהִי֙ הַמֶּ֣חֱצָ֔ה חֵ֕לֶק הַיֹּֽצְאִ֖ים בַּצָּבָ֑א

---

contaminated objects in chapter 19 by insisting
that they must be passed through fire or water,
not just sprinkled with the water of lustration.

cannot withstand fire Glassware, for example.

must pass through water Presumably this is
done on the seventh day after the objects have
been sprinkled with the water of lustration.

24. wash your clothes Bathing is assumed in
rules of purification (Lev. 11:25,28,40).

DISTRIBUTION OF SPOILS (vv. 25–47)

26. Moses is assisted by Eleazar and the clan
heads in the task of dividing the spoils. Moses su-

pervises distribution to the clergy; the others supervise distribution to the people.

booty that was captured The living booty.

30. one in every fifty Thus the Levites as a
group receive 10 times as much as the priests (see
v. 28). The ratio is similar to their respective
shares in the tithe, the Levites receiving 9 times
as much (18:25–32).

to the Levites They are not included in the
community, having undergone a separate census.

32. spoil Objects that the soldiers plundered
for themselves and that were not subject to the
levy.

gaged in the campaign [was as follows]: The number of sheep was 337,500, 37and the LORD's levy from the sheep was 675; 38the cattle came to 36,000, from which the LORD's levy was 72; 39the asses came to 30,500, from which the LORD's levy was 61. 40And the number of human beings was 16,000, from which the LORD's levy was 32. 41Moses gave the contributions levied for the LORD to Eleazar the priest, as the LORD had commanded Moses.

42As for the half-share of the other Israelites, which Moses withdrew from the men who had taken the field, 43that half-share of the community consisted of 337,500 sheep, 4436,000 head of cattle, 4530,500 asses, 46and 16,000 human beings. 47From this half-share of the Israelites, Moses withheld one in every fifty humans and animals; and he gave them to the Levites, who attended to the duties of the LORD's Tabernacle, as the LORD had commanded Moses.

48The commanders of the troop divisions, the officers of thousands and the officers of hundreds, approached Moses. 49They said to Moses, "Your servants have made a check of the warriors in our charge, and not one of us is missing. 50So we have brought as an offering to the LORD such articles of gold as each of us came upon:

מִסְפַּר הַצֹּאן שְׁלֹשׁ־מֵאוֹת אֶלֶף וּשְׁלֹשִׁים
אֶלֶף וְשִׁבְעַת אֲלָפִים וַחֲמֵשׁ מֵאוֹת׃
37 וַיְהִי הַמֶּכֶס לַיהוָה מִן־הַצֹּאן שֵׁשׁ
מֵאוֹת חָמֵשׁ וְשִׁבְעִים׃ 38 וְהַבָּקָר שִׁשָּׁה
וּשְׁלֹשִׁים אָלֶף וּמִכְסָם לַיהוָה שְׁנַיִם
וְשִׁבְעִים׃ 39 וַחֲמֹרִים שְׁלֹשִׁים אֶלֶף וַחֲמֵשׁ
מֵאוֹת וּמִכְסָם לַיהוָה אֶחָד וְשִׁשִּׁים׃
40 וְנֶפֶשׁ אָדָם שִׁשָּׁה עָשָׂר אָלֶף וּמִכְסָם
לַיהוָה שְׁנַיִם וּשְׁלֹשִׁים נָפֶשׁ׃ 41 וַיִּתֵּן מֹשֶׁה
אֶת־מֶכֶס תְּרוּמַת יְהוָה לְאֶלְעָזָר הַכֹּהֵן
כַּאֲשֶׁר צִוָּה יְהוָה אֶת־מֹשֶׁה׃
חמישי 42 וּמִמַּחֲצִית בְּנֵי יִשְׂרָאֵל אֲשֶׁר חָצָה מֹשֶׁה
מִן־הָאֲנָשִׁים הַצֹּבְאִים׃ 43 וַתְּהִי מֶחֱצַת
הָעֵדָה מִן־הַצֹּאן שְׁלֹשׁ־מֵאוֹת אֶלֶף
וּשְׁלֹשִׁים אֶלֶף שִׁבְעַת אֲלָפִים וַחֲמֵשׁ
מֵאוֹת׃ 44 וּבָקָר שִׁשָּׁה וּשְׁלֹשִׁים אָלֶף׃
45 וַחֲמֹרִים שְׁלֹשִׁים אֶלֶף וַחֲמֵשׁ מֵאוֹת׃
46 וְנֶפֶשׁ אָדָם שִׁשָּׁה עָשָׂר אָלֶף׃ 47 וַיִּקַּח
מֹשֶׁה מִמַּחֲצִת בְּנֵי־יִשְׂרָאֵל אֶת־הָאָחֻז
אֶחָד מִן־הַחֲמִשִּׁים מִן־הָאָדָם וּמִן־
הַבְּהֵמָה וַיִּתֵּן אֹתָם לַלְוִיִּם שֹׁמְרֵי
מִשְׁמֶרֶת מִשְׁכַּן יְהוָה כַּאֲשֶׁר צִוָּה יְהוָה
אֶת־מֹשֶׁה׃
48 וַיִּקְרְבוּ אֶל־מֹשֶׁה הַפְּקֻדִים אֲשֶׁר לְאַלְפֵי
הַצָּבָא שָׂרֵי הָאֲלָפִים וְשָׂרֵי הַמֵּאוֹת׃
49 וַיֹּאמְרוּ אֶל־מֹשֶׁה עֲבָדֶיךָ נָשְׂאוּ אֶת־
רֹאשׁ אַנְשֵׁי הַמִּלְחָמָה אֲשֶׁר בְּיָדֵנוּ וְלֹא־
נִפְקַד מִמֶּנּוּ אִישׁ׃ 50 וַנַּקְרֵב אֶת־קָרְבַּן
יְהוָה אִישׁ אֲשֶׁר מָצָא כְלִי־זָהָב אֶצְעָדָה

40. the LORD's levy These individuals were most likely assigned to menial tasks in the sanctuary.

RANSOM (vv. 48–54)

49. have made a check The Hebrew idiom (*nasu rosh*) most likely means "took a head count," i.e., a census.

not one of us is missing All are accounted for.

50. This parenthetical comment underscores the magnanimity of the officers' contribution. Although a census requires a monetary ransom from each person (Exod. 30:12), the officers donated more than twice the amount needed to ransom the entire army—½ shekel of silver per soldier

armlets, bracelets, signet rings, earrings, and
pendants, that expiation may be made for our
persons before the LORD." 51Moses and Eleazar
the priest accepted the gold from them, all
kinds of wrought articles. 52All the gold that
was offered by the officers of thousands and
the officers of hundreds as a contribution to
the LORD came to 16,750 shekels.—53But in the
ranks, everyone kept his booty for himself.—
54So Moses and Eleazar the priest accepted the
gold from the officers of thousands and the
officers of hundreds and brought it to the Tent
of Meeting, as a reminder in behalf of the Israelites before the LORD.

וְצָמִיד טַבַּעַת עָגִיל וְכוּמָז לְכַפֵּר עַל־
נַפְשֹׁתֵינוּ לִפְנֵי יְהוָה׃ 51 וַיִּקַּח מֹשֶׁה
וְאֶלְעָזָר הַכֹּהֵן אֶת־הַזָּהָב מֵאִתָּם כֹּל כְּלִי
מַעֲשֶׂה׃ 52 וַיְהִי ׀ כָּל־זְהַב הַתְּרוּמָה אֲשֶׁר
הֵרִימוּ לַיהוָה שִׁשָּׁה עָשָׂר אֶלֶף שְׁבַע־
מֵאוֹת וַחֲמִשִּׁים שָׁקֶל מֵאֵת שָׂרֵי הָאֲלָפִים
וּמֵאֵת שָׂרֵי הַמֵּאוֹת׃ 53 אַנְשֵׁי הַצָּבָא בָּזְזוּ
אִישׁ לוֹ׃ 54 וַיִּקַּח מֹשֶׁה וְאֶלְעָזָר הַכֹּהֵן
אֶת־הַזָּהָב מֵאֵת שָׂרֵי הָאֲלָפִים וְהַמֵּאוֹת
וַיָּבִאוּ אֹתוֹ אֶל־אֹהֶל מוֹעֵד זִכָּרוֹן לִבְנֵי־
יִשְׂרָאֵל לִפְנֵי יְהוָה׃ פ

32 The Reubenites and the Gadites owned
cattle in very great numbers. Noting that the
lands of Jazer and Gilead were a region suitable
for cattle, 2the Gadites and the Reubenites came
to Moses, Eleazar the priest, and the chieftains
of the community, and said, 3"Ataroth, Dibon,
Jazer, Nimrah, Heshbon, Elealeh, Sebam, Nebo,
and Beon—4the land that the LORD has con-

שי
לישי]

לב וּמִקְנֶה ׀ רַב הָיָה לִבְנֵי רְאוּבֵן
וְלִבְנֵי־גָד עָצוּם מְאֹד וַיִּרְאוּ אֶת־אֶרֶץ
יַעְזֵר וְאֶת־אֶרֶץ גִּלְעָד וְהִנֵּה הַמָּקוֹם מְקוֹם
מִקְנֶה׃ 2 וַיָּבֹאוּ בְנֵי־גָד וּבְנֵי רְאוּבֵן וַיֹּאמְרוּ
אֶל־מֹשֶׁה וְאֶל־אֶלְעָזָר הַכֹּהֵן וְאֶל־נְשִׂיאֵי
הָעֵדָה לֵאמֹר׃ 3 עֲטָרוֹת וְדִיבֹן וְיַעְזֵר
וְנִמְרָה וְחֶשְׁבּוֹן וְאֶלְעָלֵה וּשְׂבָם וּנְבוֹ
וּבְעֹן׃ 4 הָאָרֶץ אֲשֶׁר הִכָּה יְהוָה לִפְנֵי

(not to speak of gold), totaling 16,750 shekels. Thus each infantryman could keep his booty (see v. 32).

offering to the LORD This offering, which had been set aside and dedicated to the Lord before the census (in accordance with Exod. 30:12–16), is now being turned over to Moses.

articles of gold The variety of gold ornaments is not surprising. Even today, nomads wear more ornaments than do sedentary people.

for our persons Better: "to ransom our lives"—because of having undergone a census (see Exod. 30:12). The preceding word *kipper* ("expiation") implies some kind of atonement. This offering was not ransom for having taken life; ransom (used when slaughtering animals for meat, Lev. 17:11) was unacceptable after homicide—justified or not.

THE SETTLEMENT OF TRANSJORDAN (32:1–42)

This chapter inaugurates a new phase in the history of ancient Israel: the settlement period, the record of how the Israelites began to find permanent homes for themselves.

1. cattle Refers to all livestock. In addition to cattle there were other domesticated animals, such as donkeys.

2. The division of the Land is decided by lot, by the Urim and Thummim administered by the high priest, Eleazar (27:21). Thus the request of Gad and Reuben to withdraw from the forthcoming apportionment of the Land needed Eleazar's consent.

4. Gad and Reuben claim that because the Lord has conquered Transjordan, it is God's land as much as is Cisjordan.

quered for the community of Israel is cattle country, and your servants have cattle. 5It would be a favor to us," they continued, "if this land were given to your servants as a holding; do not move us across the Jordan."

6Moses replied to the Gadites and the Reubenites, "Are your brothers to go to war while you stay here? 7Why will you turn the minds of the Israelites from crossing into the land that the LORD has given them? 8That is what your fathers did when I sent them from Kadesh-barnea to survey the land. 9After going up to the wadi Eshcol and surveying the land, they turned the minds of the Israelites from invading the land that the LORD had given them. 10Thereupon the LORD was incensed and He swore, 11'None of the men from twenty years up who came out of Egypt shall see the land that I promised on oath to Abraham, Isaac, and Jacob, for they did not remain loyal to Me—12none except Caleb son of Jephunneh the Kenizzite and Joshua son of Nun, for they remained loyal to the LORD.' 13The LORD was incensed at Israel, and for forty years He made them wander in the wilderness, until the whole generation that had provoked the LORD's displeasure was gone. 14And now you, a breed of sinful men, have replaced your fathers, to add still further to the LORD's wrath against Israel. 15If you turn away from Him and He abandons them once more in the wilderness, you will bring calamity upon all this people."

16Then they stepped up to him and said, "We will build here sheepfolds for our flocks and

עֲדַת יִשְׂרָאֵל אֶרֶץ מִקְנֶה הִוא וְלַעֲבָדֶיךָ
מִקְנֶה׃ ס 5 וַיֹּאמְרוּ אִם־מָצָאנוּ חֵן
בְּעֵינֶיךָ יֻתַּן אֶת־הָאָרֶץ הַזֹּאת לַעֲבָדֶיךָ
לַאֲחֻזָּה אַל־תַּעֲבִרֵנוּ אֶת־הַיַּרְדֵּן׃
6 וַיֹּאמֶר מֹשֶׁה לִבְנֵי־גָד וְלִבְנֵי רְאוּבֵן
הַאַחֵיכֶם יָבֹאוּ לַמִּלְחָמָה וְאַתֶּם תֵּשְׁבוּ
פֹה׃ 7 וְלָמָּה תנואון תְנִיאוּן אֶת־לֵב בְּנֵי
יִשְׂרָאֵל מֵעֲבֹר אֶל־הָאָרֶץ אֲשֶׁר־נָתַן לָהֶם
יְהוָה׃ 8 כֹּה עָשׂוּ אֲבֹתֵיכֶם בְּשָׁלְחִי אֹתָם
מִקָּדֵשׁ בַּרְנֵעַ לִרְאוֹת אֶת־הָאָרֶץ׃ 9 וַיַּעֲלוּ
עַד־נַחַל אֶשְׁכּוֹל וַיִּרְאוּ אֶת־הָאָרֶץ וַיָּנִיאוּ
אֶת־לֵב בְּנֵי יִשְׂרָאֵל לְבִלְתִּי־בֹא אֶל־
הָאָרֶץ אֲשֶׁר־נָתַן לָהֶם יְהוָה׃ 10 וַיִּחַר־אַף
יְהוָה בַּיּוֹם הַהוּא וַיִּשָּׁבַע לֵאמֹר׃ 11 אִם־
יִרְאוּ הָאֲנָשִׁים הָעֹלִים מִמִּצְרַיִם מִבֶּן
עֶשְׂרִים שָׁנָה וָמַעְלָה אֵת הָאֲדָמָה אֲשֶׁר
נִשְׁבַּעְתִּי לְאַבְרָהָם לְיִצְחָק וּלְיַעֲקֹב כִּי
לֹא־מִלְאוּ אַחֲרָי׃ 12 בִּלְתִּי כָּלֵב בֶּן־יְפֻנֶּה
הַקְּנִזִּי וִיהוֹשֻׁעַ בִּן־נוּן כִּי מִלְאוּ אַחֲרֵי
יְהוָה׃ 13 וַיִּחַר־אַף יְהוָה בְּיִשְׂרָאֵל וַיְנִעֵם
בַּמִּדְבָּר אַרְבָּעִים שָׁנָה עַד־תֹּם כָּל־הַדּוֹר
הָעֹשֶׂה הָרַע בְּעֵינֵי יְהוָה׃ 14 וְהִנֵּה קַמְתֶּם
תַּחַת אֲבֹתֵיכֶם תַּרְבּוּת אֲנָשִׁים חַטָּאִים
לִסְפּוֹת עוֹד עַל חֲרוֹן אַף־יְהוָה אֶל־
יִשְׂרָאֵל׃ 15 כִּי תְשׁוּבֻן מֵאַחֲרָיו וְיָסַף עוֹד
לְהַנִּיחוֹ בַּמִּדְבָּר וְשִׁחַתֶּם לְכָל־הָעָם
הַזֶּה׃ ס
16 וַיִּגְּשׁוּ אֵלָיו וַיֹּאמְרוּ גִּדְרֹת צֹאן נִבְנֶה

5. do not move us across the Jordan That is, for settlement in Cisjordan. Nevertheless, they had every intention of participating in the conquest, as they subsequently clarify (vv. 16–19).

6. Moses, assuming that they did not intend to participate in the forthcoming campaign, interrupts their speech to charge them with disloyalty and selfish disregard of Israel's unity.

11. from twenty years up In the Bible, 20 is the legal age of majority and, hence, for liability and punishment.

15. you will bring calamity If the other tribes tolerate your rebellion.

16. Moses, who interrupted their petition, is now beseeched in a personal, intimate way (see Gen. 44:18, 45:4).

sheepfolds . . . towns They would have required adequate manpower to protect them from

towns for our children. 17And we will hasten as shock-troops in the van of the Israelites until we have established them in their home, while our children stay in the fortified towns because of the inhabitants of the land. 18We will not return to our homes until every one of the Israelites is in possession of his portion. 19But we will not have a share with them in the territory beyond the Jordan, for we have received our share on the east side of the Jordan."

20Moses said to them, "If you do this, if you go to battle as shock-troops, at the instance of the LORD, 21and every shock-fighter among you crosses the Jordan, at the instance of the LORD, until He has dispossessed His enemies before Him, 22and the land has been subdued, at the instance of the LORD, and then you return—you shall be clear before the LORD and before Israel; and this land shall be your holding under the

לְמִקְנֵ֖נוּ פֹּ֑ה וְעָרִ֖ים לְטַפֵּֽנוּ׃ 17 וַאֲנַ֜חְנוּ
נֵחָלֵ֣ץ חֻשִׁ֗ים לִפְנֵי֙ בְּנֵ֣י יִשְׂרָאֵ֔ל עַ֛ד אֲשֶׁ֥ר
אִם־הֲבִיאֹנֻ֖ם אֶל־מְקוֹמָ֑ם וְיָשַׁ֤ב טַפֵּ֙נוּ֙
בְּעָרֵ֣י הַמִּבְצָ֔ר מִפְּנֵ֖י יֹשְׁבֵ֥י הָאָֽרֶץ׃ 18 לֹ֥א
נָשׁ֖וּב אֶל־בָּתֵּ֑ינוּ עַ֗ד הִתְנַחֵל֙ בְּנֵ֣י יִשְׂרָאֵ֔ל
אִ֖ישׁ נַחֲלָתֽוֹ׃ 19 כִּ֣י לֹ֤א נִנְחַל֙ אִתָּ֔ם מֵעֵ֥בֶר
לַיַּרְדֵּ֖ן וָהָ֑לְאָה כִּ֣י בָ֤אָה נַחֲלָתֵ֙נוּ֙ אֵלֵ֔ינוּ
מֵעֵ֥בֶר הַיַּרְדֵּ֖ן מִזְרָֽחָה׃ פ
שביעי [רביעי] 20 וַיֹּ֤אמֶר אֲלֵיהֶם֙ מֹשֶׁ֔ה אִם־תַּעֲשׂ֖וּן אֶת־
הַדָּבָ֣ר הַזֶּ֑ה אִם־תֵּחָלְצ֛וּ לִפְנֵ֥י יְהוָ֖ה
לַמִּלְחָמָֽה׃ 21 וְעָבַ֨ר לָכֶ֧ם כָּל־חָל֛וּץ אֶת־
הַיַּרְדֵּ֖ן לִפְנֵ֣י יְהוָ֑ה עַ֧ד הוֹרִישׁ֛וֹ אֶת־אֹיְבָ֖יו
מִפָּנָֽיו׃ 22 וְנִכְבְּשָׁ֨ה הָאָ֜רֶץ לִפְנֵ֣י יְהוָ֗ה
וְאַחַ֣ר תָּשֻׁ֔בוּ וִהְיִיתֶ֧ם נְקִיִּ֛ם מֵיְהוָ֖ה
וּמִיִּשְׂרָאֵ֑ל וְֽהָיְתָה֩ הָאָ֨רֶץ הַזֹּ֥את לָכֶ֛ם

neighboring tribes. Because the shock troops were a select, elite force, the remainder of the troops could be left behind to construct and protect the home front.

17. while our children Literally, "while our dependents" (including women).

19. east side of the Jordan Literally, "on the other side of the Jordan eastward." Thus the speaker in this verse places himself on the west side of the Jordan.

22. be clear That is, free of all obligation, which implies that they took an oath. The root נקה is a legal term found in the context of oaths.

CHAPTER 32

16. The spokesmen for Reuben and Gad betray their misguided priorities by first mentioning "sheepfolds for our flocks" and only later adding "towns for our children" (Num. R. 22:9). One *midrash* suggests that they did not have more cattle than their brethren (v. 1); they just spent more time thinking about their cattle (Mid. Ha-Gadol). Moses in his response (v. 24) reverses the order: "Build towns for your children and sheepfolds for your flocks." The spokesmen hear and accept his correction, putting "our children, our wives" ahead of "our flocks and all our other livestock" in their reply (vv. 26–27) "as my lord commands." A later commentator adds that because Reuben and Gad chose to live outside of the Promised Land for financial reasons, their tribes would be the first to be exiled in later years.

18. When the leaders of the two tribes emphasize that they are prepared to join in the battle to conquer the Land although they will not claim any of it, they speak of their obligation to their fellow Israelites (vv. 17–18). Moses, however, is not satisfied with that position. He emphasizes that they owe loyalty not only to the Israelite people but to the God of the Israelite people, mentioning "the LORD" six times (vv. 20–23) in the space of four verses (N. Leibowitz). He concludes that if they live up to their commitments (echoing the theme of vows and oaths with which the *parashah* began), "you shall be clear before the LORD and before Israel" (v. 22). The Talmud comments that all should live by this rule, "to be judged favorably not only by God but by one's neighbors as well" (JT Shek. 3:2).

LORD. 23But if you do not do so, you will have sinned against the LORD; and know that your sin will overtake you. 24Build towns for your children and sheepfolds for your flocks, but do what you have promised."

25The Gadites and the Reubenites answered Moses, "Your servants will do as my lord commands. 26Our children, our wives, our flocks, and all our other livestock will stay behind in the towns of Gilead; 27while your servants, all those recruited for war, cross over, at the instance of the LORD, to engage in battle—as my lord orders."

28Then Moses gave instructions concerning them to Eleazar the priest, Joshua son of Nun, and the family heads of the Israelite tribes. 29Moses said to them, "If every shock-fighter among the Gadites and the Reubenites crosses the Jordan with you to do battle, at the instance of the LORD, and the land is subdued before you, you shall give them the land of Gilead as a holding. 30But if they do not cross over with you as shock-troops, they shall receive holdings among you in the land of Canaan."

31The Gadites and the Reubenites said in reply, "Whatever the LORD has spoken concerning your servants, that we will do. 32We ourselves will cross over as shock-troops, at the instance of the LORD, into the land of Canaan; and we shall keep our hereditary holding across the Jordan."

33So Moses assigned to them—to the Gadites,

לַאֲחֻזָּה לִפְנֵי יְהוָה׃ 23 וְאִם־לֹא תַעֲשׂוּן
כֵּן הִנֵּה* חֲטָאתֶם לַיהוָה וּדְעוּ חַטַּאתְכֶם
אֲשֶׁר תִּמְצָא אֶתְכֶם׃ 24 בְּנוּ־לָכֶם עָרִים
לְטַפְּכֶם וּגְדֵרֹת לְצֹנַאֲכֶם וְהַיֹּצֵא מִפִּיכֶם
תַּעֲשׂוּ׃
25 וַיֹּאמֶר* בְּנֵי־גָד וּבְנֵי רְאוּבֵן אֶל־מֹשֶׁה
לֵאמֹר עֲבָדֶיךָ יַעֲשׂוּ כַּאֲשֶׁר אֲדֹנִי מְצַוֶּה׃
26 טַפֵּנוּ נָשֵׁינוּ מִקְנֵנוּ וְכָל־בְּהֶמְתֵּנוּ יִהְיוּ־
שָׁם בְּעָרֵי הַגִּלְעָד׃ 27 וַעֲבָדֶיךָ יַעַבְרוּ כָּל־
חֲלוּץ צָבָא לִפְנֵי יְהוָה לַמִּלְחָמָה כַּאֲשֶׁר
אֲדֹנִי דֹּבֵר׃
28 וַיְצַו לָהֶם מֹשֶׁה אֵת אֶלְעָזָר הַכֹּהֵן וְאֵת
יְהוֹשֻׁעַ בִּן־נוּן וְאֶת־רָאשֵׁי אֲבוֹת הַמַּטּוֹת
לִבְנֵי יִשְׂרָאֵל׃ 29 וַיֹּאמֶר מֹשֶׁה אֲלֵהֶם
אִם־יַעַבְרוּ בְנֵי־גָד וּבְנֵי־רְאוּבֵן ׀ אִתְּכֶם
אֶת־הַיַּרְדֵּן כָּל־חָלוּץ לַמִּלְחָמָה לִפְנֵי
יְהוָה וְנִכְבְּשָׁה הָאָרֶץ לִפְנֵיכֶם וּנְתַתֶּם
לָהֶם אֶת־אֶרֶץ הַגִּלְעָד לַאֲחֻזָּה׃ 30 וְאִם־
לֹא יַעַבְרוּ חֲלוּצִים אִתְּכֶם וְנֹאחֲזוּ
בְתֹכְכֶם בְּאֶרֶץ כְּנָעַן׃
31 וַיַּעֲנוּ בְנֵי־גָד וּבְנֵי רְאוּבֵן לֵאמֹר אֵת
אֲשֶׁר דִּבֶּר יְהוָה אֶל־עֲבָדֶיךָ כֵּן נַעֲשֶׂה׃
32 נַחְנוּ נַעֲבֹר חֲלוּצִים לִפְנֵי יְהוָה
אֶרֶץ* כְּנָעַן וְאִתָּנוּ אֲחֻזַּת נַחֲלָתֵנוּ מֵעֵבֶר
לַיַּרְדֵּן׃
33 וַיִּתֵּן לָהֶם ׀ מֹשֶׁה לִבְנֵי־גָד וְלִבְנֵי רְאוּבֵן

v. 23. סבירין ומטעין "והנה"
v. 25. סבירין ומטעין לשון רבים
v. 32. סבירין ומטעין "ארצה"

23. sinned against the LORD Implies that they had taken an oath.

26. This detailed inventory is the final comprehensive summary concerning those to be left behind.

28. The high priest, Eleazar, takes precedence over Joshua whenever the Urim and Thummim must be employed—in war (27:21) and in apportioning the Land (34:17).

30. If Gad and Reuben reject these conditions, i.e., if they refuse to risk their lives as shock troops and, therefore, refuse to take the oath, then they will be treated no differently from any other tribe. They will be assigned land to conquer in Cisjordan.

31. Whatever the LORD has spoken That is, whatever Moses has spoken. Hence, Moses need not fear that we will disobey.

33. assigned Moses gives Gad and Reuben the land provisionally—to rebuild its destroyed

the Reubenites, and the half-tribe of Manasseh son of Joseph—the kingdom of Sihon king of the Amorites and the kingdom of King Og of Bashan, the land with its various cities and the territories of their surrounding towns. 34The Gadites rebuilt Dibon, Ataroth, Aroer, 35Atroth-shophan, Jazer, Jogbehah, 36Beth-nimrah, and Beth-haran as fortified towns or as enclosures for flocks. 37The Reubenites re-built Heshbon, Elealeh, Kiriathaim, 38Nebo, Baal-meon—some names being changed—and Sibmah; they gave [their own] names to towns that they rebuilt. 39The descendants of Machir son of Manasseh went to Gilead and captured it, dispossessing the Amorites who were there; 40so Moses gave Gilead to Machir son of Manasseh, and he settled there. 41Jair son of Manasseh went and captured their villages, which he renamed Havvoth-jair. 42And Nobah went and captured Kenath and its dependencies, renaming it Nobah after himself.

וְלַחֲצִ֣י ׀ שֵׁ֣בֶט ׀ מְנַשֶּׁה֮ בֶן־יוֹסֵף֒ אֶת־מַמְלֶ֜כֶת סִיחֹן֙ מֶ֣לֶךְ הָֽאֱמֹרִ֔י וְאֶת־מַמְלֶ֔כֶת ע֖וֹג מֶ֣לֶךְ הַבָּשָׁ֑ן הָאָ֨רֶץ֙ לְעָרֶ֔יהָ בִּגְבֻלֹ֔ת עָרֵ֥י הָאָ֖רֶץ סָבִֽיב: 34 וַיִּבְנ֣וּ בְנֵי־גָ֔ד אֶת־דִּיבֹ֖ן וְאֶת־עֲטָרֹ֑ת וְאֵ֖ת עֲרֹעֵֽר: 35 וְאֶת־עַטְרֹ֥ת שׁוֹפָ֛ן וְאֶת־יַעְזֵ֖ר וְיָגְבֳּהָֽה: 36 וְאֶת־בֵּ֤ית נִמְרָה֙ וְאֶת־בֵּ֣ית הָרָ֔ן עָרֵ֖י מִבְצָ֑ר וְגִדְרֹ֖ת צֹֽאן: 37 וּבְנֵ֣י רְאוּבֵ֔ן בָּנ֕וּ אֶת־חֶשְׁבּ֖וֹן וְאֶת־אֶלְעָלֵ֑א וְאֵ֖ת קִרְיָתָֽיִם: 38 וְאֶת־נְב֞וֹ וְאֶת־בַּ֧עַל מְע֛וֹן מֽוּסַבֹּ֥ת שֵׁ֖ם וְאֶת־שִׂבְמָ֑ה וַיִּקְרְא֣וּ בְשֵׁמֹ֔ת אֶת־שְׁמ֥וֹת הֶעָרִ֖ים אֲשֶׁ֥ר בָּנֽוּ: 39 וַיֵּ֨לְכ֜וּ בְּנֵ֧י מָכִ֛יר בֶּן־מְנַשֶּׁ֖ה גִּלְעָ֑דָה וַֽיִּלְכְּדֻ֖הָ וַיּ֥וֹרֶשׁ אֶת־הָֽאֱמֹרִ֖י אֲשֶׁר־בָּֽהּ: 40 וַיִּתֵּ֤ן מֹשֶׁה֙ אֶת־הַגִּלְעָ֔ד לְמָכִ֖יר בֶּן־מְנַשֶּׁ֑ה וַיֵּ֖שֶׁב בָּֽהּ: 41 וְיָאִ֤יר בֶּן־מְנַשֶּׁה֙ הָלַ֔ךְ וַיִּלְכֹּ֖ד אֶת־חַוֺּתֵיהֶ֑ם וַיִּקְרָ֥א אֶתְהֶ֖ן חַוֺּ֥ת יָאִֽיר: 42 וְנֹ֣בַח הָלַ֔ךְ וַיִּלְכֹּ֥ד אֶת־קְנָ֖ת וְאֶת־בְּנֹתֶ֑יהָ וַיִּקְרָ֤א לָ֥הּ נֹ֖בַח בִּשְׁמֽוֹ:* פ

מפטיר

---

towns and to settle their dependents and livestock there, but not to possess it until the leaders certify that they have fulfilled their conditions.

kingdom of Sihon It lay between the Arnon and the Jabbok Rivers.

kingdom of King Og of Bashan Occupied by the half-tribe of Manasseh.

39. descendants of Machir Members of the clan of Machir.

Gilead That is, upper Gilead, the territory of Og in upper Transjordan, north of the Jabbok River.

40. Moses confirms Machir's conquest, as he confirmed the claims of the 2½ tribes in Transjordan.

41. son of Literally, "descendant of."

---

* For the haftarah for this portion, see p. 968.

MAS'EI

33

These were the marches of the Israelites who started out from the land of Egypt, troop by troop, in the charge of Moses and Aaron. [2]Moses recorded the starting points of their various marches as directed by the LORD. Their marches, by starting points, were as follows:

[3]They set out from Rameses in the first month, on the fifteenth day of the first month. It was on the morrow of the passover offering that the Israelites started out defiantly, in plain view of all the Egyptians. [4]The Egyptians meanwhile were burying those among them whom the LORD had struck down, every first-born— whereby the LORD executed judgment on their gods.

מַסְעֵי

לג אֵ֣לֶּה מַסְעֵ֣י בְנֵֽי־יִשְׂרָאֵ֗ל אֲשֶׁ֥ר יָצְא֛וּ מֵאֶ֥רֶץ מִצְרַ֖יִם לְצִבְאֹתָ֑ם בְּיַד־מֹשֶׁ֖ה וְאַהֲרֹֽן: [2]וַיִּכְתֹּ֨ב מֹשֶׁ֜ה אֶת־מוֹצָאֵיהֶ֛ם לְמַסְעֵיהֶ֖ם עַל־פִּ֣י יְהוָ֑ה וְאֵ֥לֶּה מַסְעֵיהֶ֖ם לְמוֹצָאֵיהֶֽם: [3]וַיִּסְע֤וּ מֵֽרַעְמְסֵס֙ בַּחֹ֣דֶשׁ הָֽרִאשׁ֔וֹן בַּחֲמִשָּׁ֨ה עָשָׂ֥ר יוֹם֙ לַחֹ֣דֶשׁ הָֽרִאשׁ֔וֹן מִֽמׇּחֳרַ֣ת הַפֶּ֗סַח יָצְא֤וּ בְנֵֽי־יִשְׂרָאֵל֙ בְּיָ֣ד רָמָ֔ה לְעֵינֵ֖י כׇּל־מִצְרָֽיִם: [4]וּמִצְרַ֣יִם מְקַבְּרִ֗ים אֵת֩ אֲשֶׁ֨ר הִכָּ֤ה יְהוָה֙ בָּהֶ֔ם כׇּל־בְּכ֑וֹר וּבֵאלֹ֣הֵיהֶ֔ם עָשָׂ֥ה יְהוָ֖ה שְׁפָטִֽים:

The Generation of the Conquest (*continued*)

THE WILDERNESS ITINERARY (33:1–49)

1. troop by troop A reminder that the Israelites marched in military formation.

2. starting points Moses did not record other data, such as the date and the distance covered for each stage in the journey.

as directed by the LORD This refers to Israel's marches (Ibn Ezra) and not to the writing.

3. Rameses Compare Exod. 12:37. Identified with Qantir or Tanis in the eastern delta of the Nile.

morrow of the passover offering It was sacrificed at twilight on the previous day, as noted in Num. 9:3 and Exod. 12:2,6.

in plain view In broad daylight.

4. This verse implies that the striking down of the firstborn was the punishment inflicted on Egypt's gods.

This concluding *parashah* of Numbers brings Israel to the threshold of the Promised Land. In a sense, it can be seen as the conclusion of the Torah narrative. After this, all that remains is Moses' final oration, which summarizes and repeats incidents from previous books (though there is new legal material in Deuteronomy).

CHAPTER 33

What strikes the casual reader as a dry list of place-names is viewed differently by the Sages. Thus the Midrash imagines God telling Moses, "Write down all the places through which Israel journeyed, that they might recall the miracles I wrought for them," guiding them safely through human and natural dangers (Num. R. 23:1). In addition to crossing the Sea of Reeds, the list includes: the wilderness of Sin (v. 11), where the manna first appeared; Rephidim (v.

14), where the Israelites complained about the lack of water and Moses struck the rock to bring forth water; and Kibroth-hattaavah (v. 16), where the people angered God by demanding meat to eat. The Midrash compares this list of place-names to the situation of a king whose son was taken ill. The king took him to a specialist. On their return journey, at every stopping place, he reminded his son: "Here is where you had a headache, here is where we stopped to rest." Indeed, every oasis that welcomed the Israelites and provided them with food and water was rewarded by being mentioned in the Torah.

Rashi, citing Moses ha-Darshan, calculates that, if we omit the first and the last years, when the Israelites were constantly on the move, there were only 20 stations during 38 years. It is wrong to think of Israel as con-

5The Israelites set out from Rameses and encamped at Succoth. 6They set out from Succoth
and encamped at Etham, which is on the edge
of the wilderness. 7They set out from Etham
and turned about toward Pi-hahiroth, which
faces Baal-zephon, and they encamped before
Migdol. 8They set out from Pene-hahiroth and
passed through the sea into the wilderness; and
they made a three-days' journey in the wilderness of Etham and encamped at Marah. 9They
set out from Marah and came to Elim. There
were twelve springs in Elim and seventy palm
trees, so they encamped there. 10They set out
from Elim and encamped by the Sea of Reeds.
11They set out from the Sea of Reeds and encamped in the wilderness of Sin. 12They set out
from the wilderness of Sin and encamped at
Dophkah. 13They set out from Dophkah and
encamped at Alush. 14They set out from Alush
and encamped at Rephidim; it was there that

5 וַיִּסְע֥וּ בְנֵֽי־יִשְׂרָאֵ֖ל מֵרַעְמְסֵ֑ס וַֽיַּחֲנ֖וּ
בְּסֻכֹּֽת׃ 6 וַיִּסְע֖וּ מִסֻּכֹּ֑ת וַיַּחֲנ֣וּ בְאֵתָ֔ם אֲשֶׁ֖ר
בִּקְצֵ֥ה הַמִּדְבָּֽר׃ 7 וַיִּסְעוּ֙ מֵֽאֵתָ֔ם וַיָּ֙שָׁב֙
עַל־פִּ֣י הַחִירֹ֔ת אֲשֶׁ֥ר עַל־פְּנֵ֖י בַּ֣עַל צְפ֑וֹן
וַֽיַּחֲנ֖וּ לִפְנֵ֥י מִגְדֹּֽל׃ 8 וַיִּסְעוּ֙ מִפְּנֵ֣י* הַחִירֹ֔ת
וַיַּֽעַבְר֥וּ בְתוֹךְ־הַיָּ֖ם הַמִּדְבָּ֑רָה וַיֵּ֨לְכ֜וּ דֶּ֣רֶךְ
שְׁלֹ֤שֶׁת יָמִים֙ בְּמִדְבַּ֣ר אֵתָ֔ם וַֽיַּחֲנ֖וּ בְּמָרָֽה׃
9 וַיִּסְעוּ֙ מִמָּרָ֔ה וַיָּבֹ֖אוּ אֵילִ֑מָה וּ֠בְאֵילִם
שְׁתֵּ֣ים עֶשְׂרֵ֜ה עֵינֹ֥ת מַ֛יִם וְשִׁבְעִ֥ים תְּמָרִ֖ים
וַיַּחֲנוּ־שָֽׁם׃ 10 וַיִּסְע֖וּ מֵאֵילִ֑ם וַֽיַּחֲנ֖וּ עַל־
יַם־סֽוּף׃ 11 וַיִּסְע֖וּ מִיַּם־ס֑וּף וַֽיַּחֲנ֖וּ בְּמִדְבַּר־ שני
סִֽין׃ 12 וַיִּסְע֖וּ מִמִּדְבַּר־סִ֑ין וַֽיַּחֲנ֖וּ בְּדָפְקָֽה׃
13 וַיִּסְע֖וּ מִדָּפְקָ֑ה וַֽיַּחֲנ֖וּ בְּאָלֽוּשׁ׃ 14 וַיִּסְע֖וּ
מֵאָל֑וּשׁ וַֽיַּחֲנוּ֙ בִּרְפִידִ֔ם וְלֹא־הָ֨יָה שָׁ֥ם מַ֛יִם

v. 8. סבירין ומטעין "מפי"

6. Compare Exod. 13:20. Situated in Wadi Tumilat between Lake Timsah and the Bitter Lakes.

7. turned about Instead of marching east into the desert, the Israelites turned southward along the Bitter Lakes where the pursuing Egyptians caught up with them. It is difficult to chart the route they followed. It has been suggested that initially they traveled northward to the Sea of Reeds, and then headed south toward Lake Timsah and the Bitter Lakes.

8. passed through the sea Before the Suez Canal was dug, there had been below the Bitter Lakes a shallow fordable stretch of water about 2 miles (3.2 km) wide. In ancient times, the Bitter Lakes, at present only 6 feet (1.8 m) above the level of the Gulf of Suez, were probably connected with it.

three-days' journey This is possibly an allusion to the three-day journey into the wilderness that Israel pledged to Pharaoh, as recorded in Exod. 3:18. It implies that they kept their word (Exod. 15:22).

wilderness of Etham Another tradition refers to the wilderness of Shur (Exod. 15:22). (The Hebrew word *shur* and the Egyptian word *etham* both mean "wall" or "fortification," probably referring to a defense line built by the Egyptians.)

Marah Compare Exod. 15:23. Possibly Bir el-Muwrah, 9 miles (14.4 km) east of Suez. There are no springs between the Bitter Lakes, the possible site of Israel's crossing, and Bir el-Muwrah.

9. There were twelve springs in Elim The comment is typical of ancient Near Eastern military itineraries: an account of the sources of water and food.

10. The line of march, at this point in the itinerary, was southward.

11. wilderness of Sin There the manna appeared, covered by the dew (Exod. 16:14).

14. Compare Exod. 17:1. The narrative omits the war with Amalek at Rephidim as well as the manna at Sin, the revelation at Sinai, and other notable events of the wilderness trek. These events were so well known that they did not need to be repeated.

Rephidim If the Israelites traveled along the eastern shore of the Gulf of Suez, they would reach the modern Wadi Refayid, 30 miles (48 km) from the southern tip of the Sinai Peninsula,

---

stantly on the march. The list of place-names reminds us that during most of the 40 years in the wilderness, the Israelites were living normally at one oasis or another for years at a time.

the people had no water to drink. [15]They set out from Rephidim and encamped in the wilderness of Sinai. [16]They set out from the wilderness of Sinai and encamped at Kibroth-hattaavah. [17]They set out from Kibroth-hattaavah and encamped at Hazeroth. [18]They set out from Hazeroth and encamped at Rithmah. [19]They set out from Rithmah and encamped at Rimmon-perez. [20]They set out from Rimmon-perez and encamped at Libnah. [21]They set out from Libnah and encamped at Rissah. [22]They set out from Rissah and encamped at Kehelath. [23]They set out from Kehelath and encamped at Mount Shepher. [24]They set out from Mount Shepher and encamped at Haradah. [25]They set out from Haradah and encamped at Makheloth. [26]They set out from Makheloth and encamped at Tahath. [27]They set out from Tahath and encamped at Terah. [28]They set out from Terah and encamped at Mithkah. [29]They set out from Mithkah and encamped at Hashmonah. [30]They set out from Hashmonah and encamped at Moseroth. [31]They set out from Moseroth and encamped at Bene-jaakan. [32]They set out from Bene-jaakan and encamped at Hor-haggidgad. [33]They set out from Hor-haggidgad and encamped at Jotbath. [34]They set out from Jotbath and encamped at Abronah. [35]They set out from Abronah and encamped at Ezion-geber. [36]They set out from Ezion-geber and encamped in the wilderness of Zin, that is, Kadesh. [37]They set out from Kadesh and encamped at Mount Hor, on the edge of the land of Edom.

[38]Aaron the priest ascended Mount Hor at the command of the LORD and died there, in the

לָעָם לִשְׁתּוֹת: 15 וַיִּסְעוּ מֵרְפִידִם וַיַּחֲנוּ
בְּמִדְבַּר סִינָי: 16 וַיִּסְעוּ מִמִּדְבַּר סִינָי וַיַּחֲנוּ
בְּקִבְרֹת הַתַּאֲוָה: 17 וַיִּסְעוּ מִקִּבְרֹת
הַתַּאֲוָה וַיַּחֲנוּ בַּחֲצֵרֹת: 18 וַיִּסְעוּ מֵחֲצֵרֹת
וַיַּחֲנוּ בְּרִתְמָה: 19 וַיִּסְעוּ מֵרִתְמָה וַיַּחֲנוּ
בְּרִמֹּן פָּרֶץ: 20 וַיִּסְעוּ מֵרִמֹּן פָּרֶץ וַיַּחֲנוּ
בְּלִבְנָה: 21 וַיִּסְעוּ מִלִּבְנָה וַיַּחֲנוּ בְּרִסָּה:
22 וַיִּסְעוּ מֵרִסָּה וַיַּחֲנוּ בִּקְהֵלָתָה: 23 וַיִּסְעוּ
מִקְּהֵלָתָה וַיַּחֲנוּ בְּהַר־שָׁפֶר: 24 וַיִּסְעוּ
מֵהַר־שָׁפֶר וַיַּחֲנוּ בַּחֲרָדָה: 25 וַיִּסְעוּ
מֵחֲרָדָה וַיַּחֲנוּ בְּמַקְהֵלֹת: 26 וַיִּסְעוּ
מִמַּקְהֵלֹת וַיַּחֲנוּ בְּתָחַת: 27 וַיִּסְעוּ מִתָּחַת
וַיַּחֲנוּ בְּתָרַח: 28 וַיִּסְעוּ מִתָּרַח וַיַּחֲנוּ
בְּמִתְקָה: 29 וַיִּסְעוּ מִמִּתְקָה וַיַּחֲנוּ
בְּחַשְׁמֹנָה: 30 וַיִּסְעוּ מֵחַשְׁמֹנָה וַיַּחֲנוּ
בְּמֹסֵרוֹת: 31 וַיִּסְעוּ מִמֹּסֵרוֹת וַיַּחֲנוּ בִּבְנֵי
יַעֲקָן: 32 וַיִּסְעוּ מִבְּנֵי יַעֲקָן וַיַּחֲנוּ בְּחֹר
הַגִּדְגָּד: 33 וַיִּסְעוּ מֵחֹר הַגִּדְגָּד וַיַּחֲנוּ
בְּיָטְבָתָה: 34 וַיִּסְעוּ מִיָּטְבָתָה וַיַּחֲנוּ
בְּעַבְרֹנָה: 35 וַיִּסְעוּ מֵעַבְרֹנָה וַיַּחֲנוּ בְּעֶצְיֹן
גָּבֶר: 36 וַיִּסְעוּ מֵעֶצְיֹן גָּבֶר וַיַּחֲנוּ בְמִדְבַּר־
צִן הִוא קָדֵשׁ: 37 וַיִּסְעוּ מִקָּדֵשׁ וַיַּחֲנוּ בְּהֹר
הָהָר בִּקְצֵה אֶרֶץ אֱדוֹם:
38 וַיַּעַל אַהֲרֹן הַכֹּהֵן אֶל־הֹר הָהָר עַל־פִּי

which is the usually accepted location. The absence of water there, however, indicates that the Israelites left the Suez coast with its many springs and moved inland.

15. wilderness of Sinai Compare Exod. 19:1–2. The region has not yet been identified with certainty.

17. Compare with Num. 11:35 and 12:16. Hazeroth has been equated with today's Ain/Wadi Hudeirat, about 40 miles (64 km) northeast of Jebel Musa.

18–29. None of these stations is mentioned elsewhere.

35. Ezion-geber Usually identified with Tell el-Kheleifeh at modern Elat; it was recently identified with nearby Aqaba, and Abronah (v. 34) with Tell el-Kheleifeh.

36. Kadesh Its exact location is uncertain.

fortieth year after the Israelites had left the land
of Egypt, on the first day of the fifth month.
[39]Aaron was a hundred and twenty-three years
old when he died on Mount Hor. [40]And the Canaanite, king of Arad, who dwelt in the Negeb,
in the land of Canaan, learned of the coming
of the Israelites.

[41]They set out from Mount Hor and encamped at Zalmonah. [42]They set out from
Zalmonah and encamped at Punon. [43]They set
out from Punon and encamped at Oboth.
[44]They set out from Oboth and encamped at
Iye-abarim, in the territory of Moab. [45]They set
out from Iyim and encamped at Dibon-gad.
[46]They set out from Dibon-gad and encamped
at Almon-diblathaim. [47]They set out from
Almon-diblathaim and encamped in the hills
of Abarim, before Nebo. [48]They set out from
the hills of Abarim and encamped in the steppes
of Moab, at the Jordan near Jericho; [49]they encamped by the Jordan from Beth-jeshimoth as
far as Abel-shittim, in the steppes of Moab.

[50]In the steppes of Moab, at the Jordan near
Jericho, the LORD spoke to Moses, saying:
[51]Speak to the Israelite people and say to them:
When you cross the Jordan into the land of Ca-

יְהוָה וַיָּמָת שָׁם בִּשְׁנַת הָאַרְבָּעִים לְצֵאת
בְּנֵי־יִשְׂרָאֵל מֵאֶרֶץ מִצְרַיִם בַּחֹדֶשׁ
הַחֲמִישִׁי בְּאֶחָד לַחֹדֶשׁ׃ 39 וְאַהֲרֹן בֶּן־
שָׁלֹשׁ וְעֶשְׂרִים וּמְאַת שָׁנָה בְּמֹתוֹ בְּהֹר
הָהָר׃ ס 40 וַיִּשְׁמַע הַכְּנַעֲנִי מֶלֶךְ עֲרָד
וְהוּא־יֹשֵׁב בַּנֶּגֶב בְּאֶרֶץ כְּנָעַן בְּבֹא בְּנֵי
יִשְׂרָאֵל׃

41 וַיִּסְעוּ מֵהֹר הָהָר וַיַּחֲנוּ בְּצַלְמֹנָה׃
42 וַיִּסְעוּ מִצַּלְמֹנָה וַיַּחֲנוּ בְּפוּנֹן׃ 43 וַיִּסְעוּ
מִפּוּנֹן וַיַּחֲנוּ בְּאֹבֹת׃ 44 וַיִּסְעוּ מֵאֹבֹת וַיַּחֲנוּ
בְּעִיֵּי הָעֲבָרִים בִּגְבוּל מוֹאָב׃ 45 וַיִּסְעוּ
מֵעִיִּים וַיַּחֲנוּ בְּדִיבֹן גָּד׃ 46 וַיִּסְעוּ מִדִּיבֹן
גָּד וַיַּחֲנוּ בְּעַלְמֹן דִּבְלָתָיְמָה׃ 47 וַיִּסְעוּ
מֵעַלְמֹן דִּבְלָתָיְמָה וַיַּחֲנוּ בְּהָרֵי הָעֲבָרִים
לִפְנֵי נְבוֹ׃ 48 וַיִּסְעוּ מֵהָרֵי הָעֲבָרִים וַיַּחֲנוּ
בְּעַרְבֹת מוֹאָב עַל יַרְדֵּן יְרֵחוֹ׃ 49 וַיַּחֲנוּ
עַל־הַיַּרְדֵּן מִבֵּית הַיְשִׁמֹת עַד אָבֵל
הַשִּׁטִּים בְּעַרְבֹת מוֹאָב׃ ס

50 וַיְדַבֵּר יְהוָה אֶל־מֹשֶׁה בְּעַרְבֹת מוֹאָב
עַל־יַרְדֵּן יְרֵחוֹ לֵאמֹר׃ 51 דַּבֵּר אֶל־בְּנֵי
יִשְׂרָאֵל וְאָמַרְתָּ אֲלֵהֶם כִּי אַתֶּם עֹבְרִים

40. This verse recounts almost verbatim the beginning of the brief story of the victorious battle against the Canaanites in 21:1–3. Clearly, the earlier account was known to the writer and to his readers. He merely had to quote the opening line to allude to the complete version.

49. Beth-jeshimoth Identified with Tell el-'Azeimah, 12 miles (19 km) southeast of Jericho.

Abel-shittim Identified with Tell Kefrein in the highlands, about 5 miles (8 km) from the Jordan, and 7 miles (11 km) from the Dead Sea.

THE DIVISION OF CANAAN (33:50–35:34)

The Israelites have completed their wilderness trek (chaps. 1–21, 33:1–49), secured their base at the Jordan against all enemies (chaps. 22–25, 31), allowed 2½ tribes to settle in Transjordan (chap. 32), and resolved the problem of leadership (27:12–23). They now can turn their attention to the conquest and apportionment of Canaan.

THE COMMAND (33:50–56)

The divine command is now given for the conquest of Canaan, which needs to be divided among the remaining 9½ tribes; it is to them that the command is now addressed.

50. steppes of Moab Here Israel encamped at the end of its wilderness trek (v. 48).

naan, 52you shall dispossess all the inhabitants
of the land; you shall destroy all their figured
objects; you shall destroy all their molten images, and you shall demolish all their cult places.
53And you shall take possession of the land and
settle in it, for I have assigned the land to you
to possess. 54You shall apportion the land
among yourselves by lot, clan by clan: with
larger groups increase the share, with smaller
groups reduce the share. Wherever the lot falls
for anyone, that shall be his. You shall have your
portions according to your ancestral tribes.
55But if you do not dispossess the inhabitants
of the land, those whom you allow to remain
shall be stings in your eyes and thorns in your
sides, and they shall harass you in the land in
which you live; 56so that I will do to you what
I planned to do to them.

אֶת־הַיַּרְדֵּ֖ן אֶל־אֶ֥רֶץ כְּנָֽעַן׃ 52 וְהֽוֹרַשְׁתֶּ֞ם
אֶת־כָּל־יֹשְׁבֵ֤י הָאָ֙רֶץ֙ מִפְּנֵיכֶ֔ם וְאִ֨בַּדְתֶּ֔ם
אֵ֖ת כָּל־מַשְׂכִּיֹּתָ֑ם וְאֵ֨ת כָּל־צַלְמֵ֤י מַסֵּכֹתָם֙
תְּאַבֵּ֔דוּ וְאֵ֥ת כָּל־בָּמוֹתָ֖ם תַּשְׁמִֽידוּ׃
53 וְהוֹרַשְׁתֶּ֥ם אֶת־הָאָ֖רֶץ וִֽישַׁבְתֶּם־בָּ֑הּ כִּ֥י
לָכֶ֛ם נָתַ֥תִּי אֶת־הָאָ֖רֶץ לָרֶ֥שֶׁת אֹתָֽהּ׃
54 וְהִתְנַחַלְתֶּם֩ אֶת־הָאָ֨רֶץ בְּגוֹרָ֜ל
לְמִשְׁפְּחֹתֵיכֶ֗ם לָרַ֞ב תַּרְבּ֣וּ אֶת־נַחֲלָת֗וֹ
וְלַמְעַט֙ תַּמְעִ֣יט אֶת־נַחֲלָת֔וֹ אֶל֩ אֲשֶׁר־
יֵ֨צֵא ל֥וֹ שָׁ֛מָּה הַגּוֹרָ֖ל ל֣וֹ יִהְיֶ֑ה לְמַטּ֥וֹת
אֲבֹתֵיכֶ֖ם תִּתְנֶחָֽלוּ׃ 55 וְאִם־לֹ֨א תוֹרִ֜ישׁוּ
אֶת־יֹשְׁבֵ֣י הָאָרֶץ֮ מִפְּנֵיכֶם֒ וְהָיָ֗ה אֲשֶׁ֤ר
תּוֹתִ֙ירוּ֙ מֵהֶ֔ם לְשִׂכִּים֙ בְּעֵ֣ינֵיכֶ֔ם וְלִצְנִינִ֖ם
בְּצִדֵּיכֶ֑ם וְצָרְר֣וּ אֶתְכֶ֔ם עַל־הָאָ֕רֶץ אֲשֶׁ֥ר
אַתֶּ֖ם יֹשְׁבִ֥ים בָּֽהּ׃ 56 וְהָיָ֗ה כַּאֲשֶׁ֥ר דִּמִּ֛יתִי
לַעֲשׂ֥וֹת לָהֶ֖ם אֶעֱשֶׂ֥ה לָכֶֽם׃ פ

34 The LORD spoke to Moses, saying: 2In-

לד וַיְדַבֵּ֥ר יְהוָ֖ה אֶל־מֹשֶׁ֥ה לֵּאמֹֽר׃

52. you shall dispossess Hebrew: *v'horashtem;* the subject of this verb is usually God, as in Josh. 23:5. Divine aid is presumed here.

cult places Hebrew (sing.): *bamah;* literally, "a ridge" or "a high place." There is no description of a *bamah* in the Bible, although one has been identified at Dan in the north and one at Megiddo in the Jezreel Valley, which may go back to the 3rd millennium B.C.E.

54. The location of each tribe is to be decided by lot, but the actual division of the Land is by clan.

according to your ancestral tribes The clan can be assigned land only within its tribe's boundaries.

55. stings . . . thorns Metaphors that imply acts of physical violence committed against the Israelites by the remaining Canaanite enclaves.

BOUNDARIES OF THE PROMISED LAND (34:1–15)

The area of the Land includes the mountains of Lebanon and Sirion (Anti-Lebanon), extending as far north as Lebo, thereby including the Damascus region and the Bashan, reaching the Galilee along the Yarmuk Valley (but excluding the Gilead and southern Transjordan), and extending as far south as Kadesh before entering the Mediterranean at El 'Arish. Evidently, Transjordan was not considered part of the Promised Land. Hence the problem with allowing Reuben, Gad, and half of Manasseh to remain there (see Num. 32 and Josh. 22).

---

52. One senses the Torah's concern that the Israelites might fall into a pattern of blending their religious practices with those of the indigenous Canaanites, perhaps wanting to incorporate the advantages of each. Such a pattern would presume that God was only God of the Exodus and of the journey, and that when they settled the Land, they would need to turn to farmers' gods, experts in fertility.

55. stings in your eyes and thorns in your sides Some adversaries are enemies in plain sight, "in your eyes," making no secret of their dislike for you. Others, equally hostile, claim to be "on your side."

struct the Israelite people and say to them:
When you enter the land of Canaan, this is the
land that shall fall to you as your portion, the
land of Canaan with its various boundaries:

3Your southern sector shall extend from the
wilderness of Zin alongside Edom. Your southern boundary shall start on the east from the
tip of the Dead Sea. 4Your boundary shall then
turn to pass south of the ascent of Akrabbim
and continue to Zin, and its limits shall be south
of Kadesh-barnea, reaching Hazar-addar and
continuing to Azmon. 5From Azmon the
boundary shall turn toward the Wadi of Egypt
and terminate at the Sea.

6For the western boundary you shall have the
coast of the Great Sea; that shall serve as your
western boundary.

7This shall be your northern boundary: Draw
a line from the Great Sea to Mount Hor; 8from
Mount Hor draw a line to Lebo-hamath, and
let the boundary reach Zedad. 9The boundary

2 צַו אֶת־בְּנֵי יִשְׂרָאֵל וְאָמַרְתָּ אֲלֵהֶם כִּי־
אַתֶּם בָּאִים אֶל־הָאָרֶץ כְּנָעַן זֹאת הָאָרֶץ
אֲשֶׁר תִּפֹּל לָכֶם בְּנַחֲלָה אֶרֶץ כְּנַעַן
לִגְבֻלֹתֶיהָ׃

3 וְהָיָה לָכֶם פְּאַת־נֶגֶב מִמִּדְבַּר־צִן עַל־יְדֵי
אֱדוֹם וְהָיָה לָכֶם גְּבוּל נֶגֶב מִקְצֵה יָם־
הַמֶּלַח קֵדְמָה׃ 4 וְנָסַב לָכֶם הַגְּבוּל מִנֶּגֶב
לְמַעֲלֵה עַקְרַבִּים וְעָבַר צִנָה והיה וְהָיוּ
תּוֹצְאֹתָיו מִנֶּגֶב לְקָדֵשׁ בַּרְנֵעַ וְיָצָא חֲצַר־
אַדָּר וְעָבַר עַצְמֹנָה׃ 5 וְנָסַב הַגְּבוּל
מֵעַצְמוֹן נַחְלָה מִצְרָיִם וְהָיוּ תוֹצְאֹתָיו
הַיָּמָּה׃

6 וּגְבוּל יָם וְהָיָה לָכֶם הַיָּם הַגָּדוֹל וּגְבוּל
זֶה־יִהְיֶה לָכֶם גְּבוּל יָם׃

7 וְזֶה־יִהְיֶה לָכֶם גְּבוּל צָפוֹן מִן־הַיָּם הַגָּדֹל
תְּתָאוּ לָכֶם הֹר הָהָר׃ 8 מֵהֹר הָהָר תְּתָאוּ
לְבֹא חֲמָת וְהָיוּ תּוֹצְאֹת הַגְּבֻל צְדָדָה׃

2. shall fall to you That is, by lot.

land of Canaan Its borders are the same as those of the Egyptian province of Canaan during the second half of the 2nd millennium B.C.E.

3. alongside Edom Because the southern border begins on the eastern side of the Dead Sea, it abuts the northern and western edges of Edom. Alternatively, the territory of Edom may have extended west of the 'Arabah, in which case a longer stretch of Israel's southern border would have adjoined Edom's northern border.

on the east That is, from the southernmost tip of the Dead Sea.

Dead Sea Hebrew: *Yam ha-Melaḥ;* literally, "Salt Sea."

4. turn At this point the boundary changes its course.

ascent of Akrabbim Literally, "ascent of Scorpions." The site is unknown.

Zin Perhaps this refers to a point along the boundary rather than to the wilderness of the same name.

limits This is the terminus of the southwestern border.

south of Kadesh-barnea Thus this oasis is within the territory of the land of Israel. Its precise location is not certain.

5. turn To the northwest.

toward the Wadi of Egypt Modern Wadi El 'Arish, a long and deep watercourse that is full only after a substantial rain. It constitutes a natural barrier between the Negeb and the Sinai Peninsula.

the Sea The Mediterranean.

7. Great Sea The Mediterranean. The probable point of demarcation lies just north of Byblos, the present-day Jubayl in Lebanon. It marked the northern boundary of the Egyptian province of Canaan, according to the peace treaty at the beginning of the 13th century B.C.E. between Ramses II and the Hittites.

Mount Hor Not the Mount Hor that is located near the border of Edom, where Aaron died (20:22–29, 33:38). It is probably one of the northwestern summits of the Lebanese range north of Byblos.

8. The boundary line from Lebo-hamath terminates at Zedad. From there it takes a different direction.

Zedad Present-day Tsada, east of the Sirion (Anti-Lebanon range) near the Damascus–Homs highway, 35 miles (56 km) northeast of Lebweh (Lebo).

9 וְיָצָ֤א הַגְּבֻל֙ זִפְרֹ֔נָה וְהָי֥וּ תוֹצְאֹתָ֖יו חֲצַ֣ר
עֵינָ֑ן זֶֽה־יִהְיֶ֥ה לָכֶ֖ם גְּב֥וּל צָפֽוֹן׃
10 וְהִתְאַוִּיתֶ֥ם לָכֶ֖ם לִגְב֣וּל קֵ֑דְמָה מֵחֲצַ֥ר
עֵינָ֖ן שְׁפָֽמָה׃ 11 וְיָרַ֨ד הַגְּבֻ֜ל מִשְּׁפָ֤ם
הָֽרִבְלָה֙ מִקֶּ֣דֶם לָעָ֔יִן וְיָרַ֣ד הַגְּבֻ֔ל וּמָחָ֛ה
עַל־כֶּ֥תֶף יָֽם־כִּנֶּ֖רֶת קֵֽדְמָה׃ 12 וְיָרַ֤ד הַגְּבוּל֙
הַיַּרְדֵּ֔נָה וְהָי֥וּ תוֹצְאֹתָ֖יו יָ֣ם הַמֶּ֑לַח
זֹאת֩ תִּהְיֶ֨ה לָכֶ֥ם הָאָ֛רֶץ לִגְבֻלֹתֶ֖יהָ סָבִֽיב׃

13 וַיְצַ֣ו מֹשֶׁ֔ה אֶת־בְּנֵ֥י יִשְׂרָאֵ֖ל לֵאמֹ֑ר זֹ֣את
הָאָ֗רֶץ אֲשֶׁ֨ר תִּתְנַחֲל֤וּ אֹתָהּ֙ בְּגוֹרָ֔ל אֲשֶׁר֙
צִוָּ֣ה יְהוָ֔ה לָתֵ֛ת לְתִשְׁעַ֥ת הַמַּטּ֖וֹת וַחֲצִ֥י
הַמַּטֶּֽה׃ 14 כִּ֣י לָקְח֞וּ מַטֵּ֨ה בְנֵ֤י הָראוּבֵנִי֙
לְבֵ֣ית אֲבֹתָ֔ם וּמַטֵּ֥ה בְנֵֽי־הַגָּדִ֖י לְבֵ֣ית
אֲבֹתָ֑ם וַחֲצִי֙ מַטֵּ֣ה מְנַשֶּׁ֔ה לָקְח֖וּ נַחֲלָתָֽם׃
15 שְׁנֵ֥י הַמַּטּ֖וֹת וַחֲצִ֣י הַמַּטֶּ֑ה לָקְח֣וּ נַחֲלָתָ֗ם
מֵעֵ֛בֶר לְיַרְדֵּ֥ן יְרֵח֖וֹ קֵ֥דְמָה מִזְרָֽחָה׃ פ
16 וַיְדַבֵּ֥ר יְהוָ֖ה אֶל־מֹשֶׁ֥ה לֵּאמֹֽר׃ 17 אֵ֚לֶּה רביעי [ששי]
שְׁמ֣וֹת הָֽאֲנָשִׁ֔ים אֲשֶׁר־יִנְחֲל֥וּ לָכֶ֖ם אֶת־
הָאָ֑רֶץ אֶלְעָזָר֙ הַכֹּהֵ֔ן וִיהוֹשֻׁ֖עַ בִּן־נֽוּן׃
18 וְנָשִׂ֥יא אֶחָ֛ד נָשִׂ֥יא אֶחָ֖ד מִמַּטֶּ֑ה תִּקְח֖וּ
לִנְחֹ֥ל אֶת־הָאָֽרֶץ׃ 19 וְאֵ֖לֶּה שְׁמ֣וֹת
הָאֲנָשִׁ֑ים לְמַטֵּ֣ה יְהוּדָ֔ה כָּלֵ֖ב בֶּן־יְפֻנֶּֽה׃
20 וּלְמַטֵּה֙ בְּנֵ֣י שִׁמְע֔וֹן שְׁמוּאֵ֖ל בֶּן־

shall then run to Ziphron and terminate at Hazar-enan. That shall be your northern boundary.

10For your eastern boundary you shall draw
a line from Hazar-enan to Shepham. 11From
Shepham the boundary shall descend to Riblah on the east side of Ain; from there the boundary shall continue downward and abut on the eastern slopes of the Sea of Chinnereth. 12The
boundary shall then descend along the Jordan and terminate at the Dead Sea.

That shall be your land as defined by its boundaries on all sides.

13Moses instructed the Israelites, saying: This is the land you are to receive by lot as your hereditary portion, which the LORD has commanded to be given to the nine and a half tribes.
14For the Reubenite tribe by its ancestral houses, the Gadite tribe by its ancestral houses, and the half-tribe of Manasseh have already received their portions: 15those two and a half tribes have received their portions across the Jordan, opposite Jericho, on the east, the orient side.

16The LORD spoke to Moses, saying: 17These
are the names of the men through whom the land shall be apportioned for you: Eleazar the priest and Joshua son of Nun. 18And you shall
also take a chieftain from each tribe through whom the land shall be apportioned. 19These
are the names of the men: from the tribe of Judah: Caleb son of Jephunneh. 20From the
Simeonite tribe: Samuel son of Ammihud.

APPORTIONMENT (vv. 16–29)

The chieftains listed here appear for the first time in the Bible, with the exception of Caleb and Joshua, the lone survivors of the generation of the Exodus to enter the Promised Land. The order of the tribes follows their geographic relationship in Canaan, from south to north, except that Judah precedes Simeon (so that Judah, the chief tribe, may head the list) and Manasseh (the firstborn) precedes Ephraim. There is no satisfactory explanation of why the leaders of the first three tribes enumerated—Judah, Simeon, and Benjamin—are not given the title "chieftain."

17. Eleazar and Joshua take the place of Moses and Aaron in the generation of the conquest. Eleazar is named first because Joshua will have to consult him.

18. you shall . . . take Hebrew: *tikḥu,* which is plural. This probably refers to Eleazar and Joshua, who are to supervise the apportionment of the Land.

21 From the tribe of Benjamin: Elidad son of Chislon. 22 From the Danite tribe: a chieftain, Bukki son of Jogli. 23 For the descendants of Joseph: from the Manassite tribe: a chieftain, Hanniel son of Ephod; 24 and from the Ephraimite tribe: a chieftain, Kemuel son of Shiphtan. 25 From the Zebulunite tribe: a chieftain, Elizaphan son of Parnach. 26 From the Issacharite tribe: a chieftain, Paltiel son of Azzan. 27 From the Asherite tribe: a chieftain, Ahihud son of Shelomi. 28 From the Naphtalite tribe: a chieftain, Pedahel son of Ammihud.

29 It was these whom the LORD designated to allot portions to the Israelites in the land of Canaan.

עַמִּיהוּד׃ 21 לְמַטֵּה בִנְיָמִן אֱלִידָד בֶּן־
כִּסְלוֹן׃ 22 וּלְמַטֵּה בְנֵי־דָן נָשִׂיא בֻּקִּי בֶּן־
יָגְלִי׃ 23 לִבְנֵי יוֹסֵף לְמַטֵּה בְנֵי־מְנַשֶּׁה
נָשִׂיא חַנִּיאֵל בֶּן־אֵפֹד׃ 24 וּלְמַטֵּה בְנֵי־
אֶפְרַיִם נָשִׂיא קְמוּאֵל בֶּן־שִׁפְטָן׃
25 וּלְמַטֵּה בְנֵי־זְבוּלֻן נָשִׂיא אֱלִיצָפָן בֶּן־
פַּרְנָךְ׃ 26 וּלְמַטֵּה בְנֵי־יִשָּׂשכָר נָשִׂיא
פַּלְטִיאֵל בֶּן־עַזָּן׃ 27 וּלְמַטֵּה בְנֵי־אָשֵׁר
נָשִׂיא אֲחִיהוּד בֶּן־שְׁלֹמִי׃ 28 וּלְמַטֵּה בְנֵי־
נַפְתָּלִי נָשִׂיא פְּדַהְאֵל בֶּן־עַמִּיהוּד׃
29 אֵלֶּה אֲשֶׁר צִוָּה יְהוָה לְנַחֵל אֶת־בְּנֵי־
יִשְׂרָאֵל בְּאֶרֶץ כְּנָעַן׃ פ

35 The LORD spoke to Moses in the steppes of Moab at the Jordan near Jericho, saying: 2 Instruct the Israelite people to assign, out of the holdings apportioned to them, towns for the Levites to dwell in; you shall also assign to the Levites pasture land around their towns. 3 The towns shall be theirs to dwell in, and the pasture shall be for the cattle they own and all their other beasts. 4 The town pasture that you are to assign to the Levites shall extend a thousand cubits outside the town wall all around. 5 You shall

מישי לה וַיְדַבֵּר יְהוָה אֶל־מֹשֶׁה בְּעַרְבֹת
מוֹאָב עַל־יַרְדֵּן יְרֵחוֹ לֵאמֹר׃ 2 צַו אֶת־בְּנֵי
יִשְׂרָאֵל וְנָתְנוּ לַלְוִיִּם מִנַּחֲלַת אֲחֻזָּתָם
עָרִים לָשָׁבֶת וּמִגְרָשׁ לֶעָרִים סְבִיבֹתֵיהֶם
תִּתְּנוּ לַלְוִיִּם׃ 3 וְהָיוּ הֶעָרִים לָהֶם לָשָׁבֶת
וּמִגְרְשֵׁיהֶם יִהְיוּ לִבְהֶמְתָּם וְלִרְכֻשָׁם
וּלְכֹל חַיָּתָם׃ 4 וּמִגְרְשֵׁי הֶעָרִים אֲשֶׁר
תִּתְּנוּ לַלְוִיִּם מִקִּיר הָעִיר וָחוּצָה אֶלֶף
אַמָּה סָבִיב׃ 5 וּמַדֹּתֶם מִחוּץ לָעִיר אֶת־

LEVITICAL TOWNS (35:1–8)

Instructions to the Levites always follow those given to the other tribes. Hence, here too, the Levites receive their apportionment only after the other tribes have received theirs. Although the Levites are to receive no permanent property in the Promised Land (18:23), they are to be provided with permanent residences for themselves and pasturage for their livestock in the form of 48 towns and surrounding fields.

1. at the Jordan near Jericho Literally, "at the Jordan of Jericho." That is, at the Jordan River, which flows by Jericho.

2. Levitical towns will be assigned by lot.

3. their . . . beasts Hebrew: *ḥayyatam,* ritually impure domesticated animals, like donkeys.

4. a thousand cubits Approximately 500 yards (450 m).

outside the town wall Literally, "from the town wall outward." The measurement is taken perpendicular to the town wall, not from the wall

---

CHAPTER 35

The tribe of Levi, unlike the other tribes, would receive no land to farm. Perhaps this was to prevent a recurrence of what the Israelites had seen in Egypt, where the priests were wealthy land owners (see Gen. 47:22) who tended to side with the rich and powerful. Because the Levites still had to live somewhere, these are the arrangements that were made for them.

measure off two thousand cubits outside the town on the east side, two thousand on the south side, two thousand on the west side, and two thousand on the north side, with the town in the center. That shall be the pasture for their towns.

6 The towns that you assign to the Levites shall comprise the six cities of refuge that you are to designate for a manslayer to flee to, to which you shall add forty-two towns. 7 Thus the total of the towns that you assign to the Levites shall be forty-eight towns, with their pasture. 8 In assigning towns from the holdings of the Israelites, take more from the larger groups and less from the smaller, so that each assigns towns to the Levites in proportion to the share it receives.

9 The LORD spoke further to Moses: 10 Speak to the Israelite people and say to them: When you cross the Jordan into the land of Canaan, 11 you shall provide yourselves with places to serve you as cities of refuge to which a manslayer who has killed a person unintentionally may

פְּאַת־קֵדְמָה אַלְפַּיִם בָּאַמָּה וְאֶת־פְּאַת־
נֶגֶב אַלְפַּיִם בָּאַמָּה וְאֶת־פְּאַת־יָם ׀
אַלְפַּיִם בָּאַמָּה וְאֵת פְּאַת צָפוֹן אַלְפַּיִם
בָּאַמָּה וְהָעִיר בַּתָּוֶךְ זֶה יִהְיֶה לָהֶם
מִגְרְשֵׁי הֶעָרִים׃
6 וְאֵת הֶעָרִים אֲשֶׁר תִּתְּנוּ לַלְוִיִּם אֵת
שֵׁשׁ־עָרֵי הַמִּקְלָט אֲשֶׁר תִּתְּנוּ לָנֻס שָׁמָּה
הָרֹצֵחַ וַעֲלֵיהֶם תִּתְּנוּ אַרְבָּעִים וּשְׁתַּיִם
עִיר׃ 7 כָּל־הֶעָרִים אֲשֶׁר תִּתְּנוּ לַלְוִיִּם
אַרְבָּעִים וּשְׁמֹנֶה עִיר אֶתְהֶן וְאֶת־
מִגְרְשֵׁיהֶן׃ 8 וְהֶעָרִים אֲשֶׁר תִּתְּנוּ מֵאֲחֻזַּת
בְּנֵי־יִשְׂרָאֵל מֵאֵת הָרַב תַּרְבּוּ וּמֵאֵת
הַמְעַט תַּמְעִיטוּ אִישׁ כְּפִי נַחֲלָתוֹ אֲשֶׁר
יִנְחָלוּ יִתֵּן מֵעָרָיו לַלְוִיִּם׃ פ

ששי [שביעי]
9 וַיְדַבֵּר יְהוָה אֶל־מֹשֶׁה לֵּאמֹר׃ 10 דַּבֵּר
אֶל־בְּנֵי יִשְׂרָאֵל וְאָמַרְתָּ אֲלֵהֶם כִּי
אַתֶּם עֹבְרִים אֶת־הַיַּרְדֵּן אַרְצָה כְּנָעַן׃
11 וְהִקְרִיתֶם לָכֶם עָרִים עָרֵי מִקְלָט
תִּהְיֶינָה לָכֶם וְנָס שָׁמָּה רֹצֵחַ מַכֵּה־נֶפֶשׁ

itself but from the rectangle that circumscribes it. This enables the pasturage to grow in proportion to the size of the town.

wall Hebrew: *kir,* a rare word for a town wall. It probably refers to the outside surface of the wall. Because large cities had walls up to several yards thick, it had to be specified that the measurement was to be taken from the wall's exterior face.

5. two thousand cubits About 1000 yards (900 m).

outside Hebrew: *mi-ḥutz,* the antonym of *mi-bayit* (inside), must be distinguished from the 500-yard measurement (v. 4), which is "outward" (*ḥutzah*) from the town wall. Thus the four points at 500 yards in each direction from the town (each assumed to be a point) form a square of 1000 yards per side, which increases in area in proportion to the growth of the town.

in the center The measures given here presume that the center (and town) is a point.

6. This verse anticipates the section on the cities of refuge for those who commit involuntary homicide, beginning with verse 9.

manslayer Hebrew: *rotze·aḥ;* the term embraces both deliberate and involuntary homicide. Its underlying concept is clear: The blood of one slain even accidentally must be redeemed. Here the focus is on involuntary homicide.

8. the larger groups Literally, "the greater." (The translators supplied the word "groups.") The Israelite tribes are meant.

CITIES OF REFUGE (vv. 9–15)

The divine Presence cannot dwell in a land contaminated by murder, an offense that pollutes the earth and leads to God's abandonment of His sanctuary and people. Hence the special treatment given the laws of homicide in this section on cities of refuge. The establishment of such cities for homicides was further necessitated because of the prevalence of the institution of blood vengeance in the ancient world (see Gen. 4:23–24). Kinsmen avenged the blood of the slain by taking the blood of the slayer or of a member of the slayer's family. The institution of cities of refuge is attested elsewhere in the ancient Near East, but the form adopted by the Israelites is

flee. 12The cities shall serve you as a refuge from
the avenger, so that the manslayer may not die
unless he has stood trial before the assembly.
13The towns that you thus assign shall be six
cities of refuge in all. 14Three cities shall be designated beyond the Jordan, and the other three
shall be designated in the land of Canaan: they
shall serve as cities of refuge. 15These six cities
shall serve the Israelites and the resident aliens
among them for refuge, so that anyone who kills
a person unintentionally may flee there.
16Anyone, however, who strikes another with
an iron object so that death results is a murderer;
the murderer must be put to death. 17If he struck
him with a stone tool that could cause death,
and death resulted, he is a murderer; the murderer must be put to death. 18Similarly, if the
object with which he struck him was a wooden
tool that could cause death, and death resulted,
he is a murderer; the murderer must be put to
death. 19The blood-avenger himself shall put
the murderer to death; it is he who shall put him
to death upon encounter. 20So, too, if he pushed
him in hate or hurled something at him on pur-

בִּשְׁגָגָֽה׃ 12 וְהָי֨וּ לָכֶ֧ם הֶעָרִ֛ים לְמִקְלָ֖ט
מִגֹּאֵ֑ל וְלֹ֤א יָמוּת֙ הָרֹצֵ֔חַ עַד־עָמְד֛וֹ לִפְנֵ֥י
הָעֵדָ֖ה לַמִּשְׁפָּֽט׃
13 וְהֶעָרִ֖ים אֲשֶׁ֣ר תִּתֵּ֑נוּ שֵׁשׁ־עָרֵ֥י מִקְלָ֖ט
תִּהְיֶ֥ינָה לָכֶֽם׃ 14 אֵ֣ת ׀ שְׁלֹ֣שׁ הֶעָרִ֗ים תִּתְּנוּ֙
מֵעֵ֣בֶר לַיַּרְדֵּ֔ן וְאֵת֙ שְׁלֹ֣שׁ הֶעָרִ֔ים תִּתְּנ֖וּ
בְּאֶ֣רֶץ כְּנָ֑עַן עָרֵ֥י מִקְלָ֖ט תִּהְיֶֽינָה׃ 15 לִבְנֵ֨י
יִשְׂרָאֵ֜ל וְלַגֵּ֣ר וְלַתּוֹשָׁב֙ בְּתוֹכָ֔ם תִּהְיֶ֛ינָה
שֵׁשׁ־הֶעָרִ֥ים הָאֵ֖לֶּה לְמִקְלָ֑ט לָנ֣וּס שָׁ֔מָּה
כָּל־מַכֵּה־נֶ֖פֶשׁ בִּשְׁגָגָֽה׃
16 וְאִם־בִּכְלִ֨י בַרְזֶ֧ל ׀ הִכָּ֛הוּ וַיָּמֹ֖ת רֹצֵ֣חַ
ה֑וּא מ֥וֹת יוּמַ֖ת הָרֹצֵֽחַ׃ 17 וְאִ֨ם בְּאֶ֬בֶן יָ֜ד
אֲשֶׁר־יָמ֥וּת בָּהּ֙ הִכָּ֔הוּ וַיָּמֹ֖ת רֹצֵ֣חַ ה֑וּא
מ֥וֹת יוּמַ֖ת הָרֹצֵֽחַ׃ 18 א֨וֹ בִּכְלִ֥י עֵץ־יָ֜ד
אֲשֶׁר־יָמ֛וּת בּ֥וֹ הִכָּ֖הוּ וַיָּמֹ֖ת רֹצֵ֣חַ ה֑וּא
מ֥וֹת יוּמַ֖ת הָרֹצֵֽחַ׃ 19 גֹּאֵ֣ל הַדָּ֔ם ה֖וּא
יָמִ֣ית אֶת־הָרֹצֵ֑חַ בְּפִגְעוֹ־ב֖וֹ ה֥וּא יְמִתֶֽנּוּ׃
20 וְאִם־בְּשִׂנְאָ֖ה יֶהְדֳּפֶ֑נּוּ אֽוֹ־הִשְׁלִ֥יךְ עָלָ֛יו

unique and revolutionary. The right of asylum is limited solely to the slayer whose act was not premeditated.

12. avenger Hebrew: *go·el;* literally, "redeemer," one who restores the status quo—a responsibility that rests with the next of kin. Cities of refuge do not abrogate the rights of blood redeemers but make them agents of the state; they become state executioners. Bloodshed pollutes the land (v. 33), and then the land becomes barren. But with the blood of the slayer, the *go·el* neutralizes the deleterious effect of the blood of the slain, restoring the ecologic balance. The earth again yields its fruit. The institution of the blood redeemer (*go·el ha-dam*) is ancient. It was abolished by the monarchy, which set up a court system to try all who were accused of crimes. Cities of refuge, too, were an archaic institution, and some of them were lost after the reign of King Solomon.

trial before the assembly Thus, according to this legislation, all homicides must be tried in a national court.

14. The 2½ tribes in Transjordan are to have the same number of asylum cities as the more numerous—and more populous—tribes in Cisjordan, a geographic criterion for their distribution. Slayers should not have to flee too far lest the blood redeemers overtake them.

15. The alien is entitled to the same protection of basic rights as the Israelite.

DELIBERATE VERSUS INVOLUNTARY HOMICIDE (vv. 16–23)

The distinction is one of intention, evidence for which is the nature of the instrument and the manslayer's state of mind. Concrete examples serve to make the distinction: six for deliberate homicide and three for involuntary homicide.

17. stone tool Hebrew: *even yad;* literally, "stone of the hand." (a) It can be gripped by the hand, (b) it is large enough to fill the hand, or (c) it is directed by the hand, i.e., thrown. In any case, the stone and wooden (v. 18) implements must be large enough "to cause death."

18. wooden tool Literally, "a wooden tool of the hand." That is, a cane.

בִּצְדִיָּה וַיָּמֹת׃ 21 אוֹ בְאֵיבָה הִכָּהוּ בְיָדוֹ
וַיָּמֹת מוֹת־יוּמַת הַמַּכֶּה רֹצֵחַ הוּא גֹּאֵל
הַדָּם יָמִית אֶת־הָרֹצֵחַ בְּפִגְעוֹ־בוֹ׃
22 וְאִם־בְּפֶתַע בְּלֹא־אֵיבָה הֲדָפוֹ אוֹ־
הִשְׁלִיךְ עָלָיו כָּל־כְּלִי בְּלֹא צְדִיָּה׃ 23 אוֹ
בְכָל־אֶבֶן אֲשֶׁר־יָמוּת בָּהּ בְּלֹא רְאוֹת
וַיַּפֵּל עָלָיו וַיָּמֹת וְהוּא לֹא־אוֹיֵב לוֹ וְלֹא
מְבַקֵּשׁ רָעָתוֹ׃ 24 וְשָׁפְטוּ הָעֵדָה בֵּין הַמַּכֶּה
וּבֵין גֹּאֵל הַדָּם עַל הַמִּשְׁפָּטִים הָאֵלֶּה׃
25 וְהִצִּילוּ הָעֵדָה אֶת־הָרֹצֵחַ מִיַּד גֹּאֵל
הַדָּם וְהֵשִׁיבוּ אֹתוֹ הָעֵדָה אֶל־עִיר מִקְלָטוֹ
אֲשֶׁר־נָס שָׁמָּה וְיָשַׁב בָּהּ עַד־מוֹת הַכֹּהֵן
הַגָּדֹל אֲשֶׁר־מָשַׁח אֹתוֹ בְּשֶׁמֶן הַקֹּדֶשׁ׃
26 וְאִם־יָצֹא יֵצֵא הָרֹצֵחַ אֶת־גְּבוּל עִיר
מִקְלָטוֹ אֲשֶׁר יָנוּס שָׁמָּה׃ 27 וּמָצָא אֹתוֹ
גֹּאֵל הַדָּם מִחוּץ לִגְבוּל עִיר מִקְלָטוֹ וְרָצַח
גֹּאֵל הַדָּם אֶת־הָרֹצֵחַ אֵין לוֹ דָּם׃ 28 כִּי
בְעִיר מִקְלָטוֹ יֵשֵׁב עַד־מוֹת הַכֹּהֵן הַגָּדֹל
וְאַחֲרֵי מוֹת הַכֹּהֵן הַגָּדֹל יָשׁוּב הָרֹצֵחַ
אֶל־אֶרֶץ אֲחֻזָּתוֹ׃

pose and death resulted, 21or if he struck him with his hand in enmity and death resulted, the assailant shall be put to death; he is a murderer. The blood-avenger shall put the murderer to death upon encounter.

22But if he pushed him without malice aforethought or hurled any object at him unintentionally, 23or inadvertently dropped upon him any deadly object of stone, and death resulted—though he was not an enemy of his and did not seek his harm—24in such cases the assembly shall decide between the slayer and the blood-avenger. 25The assembly shall protect the manslayer from the blood-avenger, and the assembly shall restore him to the city of refuge to which he fled, and there he shall remain until the death of the high priest who was anointed with the sacred oil. 26But if the manslayer ever goes outside the limits of the city of refuge to which he has fled, 27and the blood-avenger comes upon him outside the limits of his city of refuge, and the blood-avenger kills the manslayer, there is no bloodguilt on his account. 28For he must remain inside his city of refuge until the death of the high priest; after the death of the high priest, the manslayer may return to his land holding.

21. A slayer may kill by hand, in which case malice must be proved.

22. without . . . aforethought Literally, "suddenly." That is, unawares.

23. Even if death resulted from the use of a murderous implement, the slaying is nevertheless judged to have been involuntary if two conditions can be demonstrated during the trial: the manslayer did not see the victim and was bearing no grudge.

INVOLUNTARY HOMICIDE: THE PROCEDURE (vv. 24–29)

The trial is conducted by national judges. Manslayers who are found guilty of second-degree murder (involuntary homicide) are returned to their city of refuge, where they remain until the death of the high priest.

25. restore The trial is held outside the city of refuge.

---

28. until the death of the high priest Just as the high priest brings atonement for all Israel through the rituals of *Yom Kippur,* his death brings atonement for the inadvertent manslayer. Some commentators understand this law homiletically: Because the high priest was beloved by all and considered by all Israelites as a virtual member of their family, his death causes them to mourn, eclipsing the mourning for their previous loss and purging them of the wish for revenge in the earlier death. The Sages picture the high priest's mother knitting articles of clothing for the exiles in the city of refuge, so that they would think kindly of her and not pray for her son's death to release them from exile.

29 וְהָי֨וּ אֵ֧לֶּה לָכֶ֛ם לְחֻקַּ֥ת מִשְׁפָּ֖ט
לְדֹרֹתֵיכֶ֑ם בְּכֹ֖ל מוֹשְׁבֹתֵיכֶֽם׃
30 כָּל־מַכֵּה־נֶ֕פֶשׁ לְפִ֣י עֵדִ֔ים יִרְצַ֖ח אֶת־
הָרֹצֵ֑חַ וְעֵ֣ד אֶחָ֔ד לֹא־יַעֲנֶ֥ה בְנֶ֖פֶשׁ לָמֽוּת׃
31 וְלֹא־תִקְח֤וּ כֹ֙פֶר֙ לְנֶ֣פֶשׁ רֹצֵ֔חַ אֲשֶׁר־ה֥וּא
רָשָׁ֖ע לָמ֑וּת כִּי־מ֖וֹת יוּמָֽת׃ 32 וְלֹא־תִקְח֣וּ
כֹ֔פֶר לָנ֖וּס אֶל־עִ֣יר מִקְלָט֑וֹ לָשׁוּב֙ לָשֶׁ֣בֶת
בָּאָ֔רֶץ עַד־מ֖וֹת הַכֹּהֵֽן׃ 33 וְלֹא־תַחֲנִ֣יפוּ
אֶת־הָאָ֗רֶץ אֲשֶׁ֤ר אַתֶּם֙ בָּ֔הּ כִּ֣י הַדָּ֔ם ה֥וּא
יַחֲנִ֖יף אֶת־הָאָ֑רֶץ וְלָאָ֣רֶץ לֹֽא־יְכֻפַּ֗ר לַדָּם֙
אֲשֶׁ֣ר שֻׁפַּךְ־בָּ֔הּ כִּי־אִ֖ם בְּדַ֥ם שֹׁפְכֽוֹ׃ 34 וְלֹ֤א
תְטַמֵּא֙ אֶת־הָאָ֗רֶץ אֲשֶׁ֤ר אַתֶּם֙ יֹשְׁבִ֣ים בָּ֔הּ
אֲשֶׁ֥ר אֲנִ֖י שֹׁכֵ֣ן בְּתוֹכָ֑הּ כִּ֚י אֲנִ֣י יְהוָ֔ה שֹׁכֵ֕ן
בְּת֖וֹךְ בְּנֵ֥י יִשְׂרָאֵֽל׃ פ

29 Such shall be your law of procedure
throughout the ages in all your settlements.
30 If anyone kills a person, the manslayer may
be executed only on the evidence of witnesses;
the testimony of a single witness against a person shall not suffice for a sentence of death.
31 You may not accept a ransom for the life of
a murderer who is guilty of a capital crime; he
must be put to death. 32 Nor may you accept ransom in lieu of flight to a city of refuge, enabling
one to return to live on his land before the death
of the priest. 33 You shall not pollute the land
in which you live; for blood pollutes the land,
and the land can have no expiation for blood
that is shed on it, except by the blood of him
who shed it. 34 You shall not defile the land in
which you live, in which I Myself abide, for I
the LORD abide among the Israelite people.

שביעי לו וַיִּקְרְב֞וּ רָאשֵׁ֣י הָֽאָב֗וֹת לְמִשְׁפַּ֣חַת
בְּנֵֽי־גִלְעָד֙ בֶּן־מָכִ֣יר בֶּן־מְנַשֶּׁ֔ה מִמִּשְׁפְּחֹ֖ת

36 The family heads in the clan of the descendants of Gilead son of Machir son of Ma-

SUPPLEMENT AND CONCLUDING WORDS (vv. 30–34)

Monetary payment for murder is provided for in several law codes of the ancient Near East—save that of the Israelites, which required that homicides must pay with their lives. Otherwise, the Land becomes polluted, with the consequence that neither God nor Israel can abide there.

30. the manslayer may be executed Literally, "[one] shall murder the murderer." That person must be the redeemer (*go·el*).

31. This prohibition clearly has in mind the blood redeemer who might accept monetary compensation for the life of a slain kinsman. If the redeemer does, the nation cannot acquiesce; a murderer must be brought to death.

32. The principle stated in verse 31 applies to involuntary as well as deliberate homicide.

33. The Holy Land (like the Israelites) is polluted by bloodshed, idolatry, and incest (see Lev. 18:24–25).

34. abide Hebrew: *shokhen,* which refers to the indwelling of God in the earthly tabernacle (*mishkan*). This is the derivation of the Rabbinic term *Sh'khinah* to represent the earthly presence of the Deity, which supplemented the biblical *k'vod YHVH* (Presence of the LORD). Because the land of Israel is also God's residence, it is equivalent in holiness to the sanctuary. The Lord's demand in the wilderness that the camp be kept pure is, in Canaan, extended to all of God's land.

for I the LORD abide among the Israelite people A reminder that the Lord had consented to transfer the divine Presence from the summit of Sinai to the portable Sinai of the tabernacle, to abide forever within the people Israel.

33. for blood pollutes the land Just as one may not enter the sanctuary in a condition of impurity because the sanctuary is a holy place, one cannot live in the land of Israel in a condition of moral impurity because the land is consecrated to holy living.

nasseh, one of the Josephite clans, came forward and appealed to Moses and the chieftains, family heads of the Israelites. 2They said, "The LORD commanded my lord to assign the land to the Israelites as shares by lot, and my lord was further commanded by the LORD to assign the share of our kinsman Zelophehad to his daughters. 3Now, if they marry persons from another Israelite tribe, their share will be cut off from our ancestral portion and be added to the portion of the tribe into which they marry; thus our allotted portion will be diminished. 4And even when the Israelites observe the jubilee, their share will be added to that of the tribe into which they marry, and their share will be cut off from the ancestral portion of our tribe."

5So Moses, at the LORD's bidding, instructed the Israelites, saying: "The plea of the Josephite tribe is just. 6This is what the LORD has commanded concerning the daughters of Zelophe-

בְּנֵי יוֹסֵף וַיְדַבְּרוּ לִפְנֵי מֹשֶׁה וְלִפְנֵי
הַנְּשִׂאִים רָאשֵׁי אָבוֹת לִבְנֵי יִשְׂרָאֵל׃
2 וַיֹּאמְרוּ אֶת־אֲדֹנִי צִוָּה יְהוָה לָתֵת אֶת־
הָאָרֶץ בְּנַחֲלָה בְּגוֹרָל לִבְנֵי יִשְׂרָאֵל וַאדֹנִי
צֻוָּה בַיהוָה לָתֵת אֶת־נַחֲלַת צְלָפְחָד
אָחִינוּ לִבְנֹתָיו׃ 3 וְהָיוּ לְאֶחָד מִבְּנֵי שִׁבְטֵי
בְנֵי־יִשְׂרָאֵל לְנָשִׁים וְנִגְרְעָה נַחֲלָתָן
מִנַּחֲלַת אֲבֹתֵינוּ וְנוֹסַף עַל נַחֲלַת הַמַּטֶּה
אֲשֶׁר תִּהְיֶינָה לָהֶם וּמִגֹּרַל נַחֲלָתֵנוּ יִגָּרֵעַ׃
4 וְאִם־יִהְיֶה הַיֹּבֵל לִבְנֵי יִשְׂרָאֵל וְנוֹסְפָה
נַחֲלָתָן עַל נַחֲלַת הַמַּטֶּה אֲשֶׁר תִּהְיֶינָה
לָהֶם וּמִנַּחֲלַת מַטֵּה אֲבֹתֵינוּ יִגָּרַע
נַחֲלָתָן׃
5 וַיְצַו מֹשֶׁה אֶת־בְּנֵי יִשְׂרָאֵל עַל־פִּי יְהוָה
לֵאמֹר כֵּן מַטֵּה בְנֵי־יוֹסֵף דֹּבְרִים׃ 6 זֶה
הַדָּבָר אֲשֶׁר־צִוָּה יְהוָה לִבְנוֹת צְלָפְחָד

MARRIAGE REQUIREMENTS FOR HEIRESSES (36:1–13)

Moses has ruled that daughters may inherit in the absence of sons (27:1–11). The leaders of Zelophehad's clan respond with an objection. If the women marry outside their tribe, their land will pass to their husbands' tribes. Moses informs them that God finds their complaint justified and, as a result, He has decreed that all heiresses must marry within their tribe. Zelophehad's daughters marry their first cousins on their father's side.

1. the chieftains, family heads These terms are in apposition to each other; they explain each other.

2. my lord Moses is addressed in this deferential manner by Joshua (11:28), Aaron (12:11), the chieftains of Reuben and Gad (32:25,27), and now by the chieftains of Gileadite clans.

4. the jubilee Ancestral land that has been sold—not inherited—reverts to its original owner in the jubilee year.

CHAPTER 36

This last passage is not a mere postscript; it implements at the individual level the grand vision of social justice just expressed: "You shall not defile the land in which you live, in which I Myself abide" (35:34). It reconciles competing legitimate claims—that of the individual (a daughter's right to inherit) and that of the community ("our ancestral portion should not be diminished because these women marry men of another tribe"). Moses' creative solution leaves both sides satisfied and respects both the letter and the spirit of the law.

Throughout the Book of Numbers, we have been shown an Israel composed of rebels and grumblers, having degenerated since the moment of their lofty spiritual experience at Sinai. The book concludes with an image of an Israelite nation loyally following its God through the wilderness, anticipating a Jewish people that would remain loyal to God through all the generations of the Exile (N. Leibowitz, after Sforno).

HALAKHAH L'MA·ASEH

36:2. Regarding the inheritance rights of daughters, see Comment on Num. 27:1.

לֵאמֹ֗ר לַטּ֤וֹב בְּעֵינֵיהֶם֙ תִּהְיֶ֣ינָה לְנָשִׁ֔ים
אַ֗ךְ לְמִשְׁפַּ֛חַת מַטֵּ֥ה אֲבִיהֶ֖ם תִּהְיֶ֥ינָה
לְנָשִֽׁים׃ 7 וְלֹֽא־תִסֹּ֤ב נַחֲלָה֙ לִבְנֵ֣י יִשְׂרָאֵ֔ל
מִמַּטֶּ֖ה אֶל־מַטֶּ֑ה כִּ֣י אִ֗ישׁ בְּנַחֲלַת֙ מַטֵּ֣ה
אֲבֹתָ֔יו יִדְבְּק֖וּ בְּנֵ֥י יִשְׂרָאֵֽל׃ 8 וְכָל־בַּ֞ת
יֹרֶ֣שֶׁת נַחֲלָ֗ה מִמַּטּוֹת֮ בְּנֵ֣י יִשְׂרָאֵל֒ לְאֶחָ֗ד
מִמִּשְׁפַּ֛חַת מַטֵּ֥ה אָבִ֖יהָ תִּהְיֶ֣ה לְאִשָּׁ֑ה
לְמַ֗עַן יִֽירְשׁוּ֙ בְּנֵ֣י יִשְׂרָאֵ֔ל אִ֖ישׁ נַחֲלַ֥ת
אֲבֹתָֽיו׃ 9 וְלֹֽא־תִסֹּ֧ב נַחֲלָ֛ה מִמַּטֶּ֖ה לְמַטֶּ֣ה
אַחֵ֑ר כִּי־אִישׁ֙ בְּנַ֣חֲלָת֔וֹ יִדְבְּק֕וּ מַטּ֖וֹת בְּנֵ֥י
יִשְׂרָאֵֽל׃

10 כַּאֲשֶׁ֛ר צִוָּ֥ה יְהוָ֖ה אֶת־מֹשֶׁ֑ה כֵּ֥ן עָשׂ֖וּ
פטיר בְּנ֥וֹת צְלָפְחָֽד׃ 11 וַתִּהְיֶ֜ינָה מַחְלָ֣ה תִרְצָ֗ה
וְחָגְלָ֧ה וּמִלְכָּ֛ה וְנֹעָ֖ה בְּנ֣וֹת צְלָפְחָ֑ד לִבְנֵ֥י
דֹדֵיהֶ֖ן לְנָשִֽׁים׃ 12 מִמִּשְׁפְּחֹ֛ת בְּנֵֽי־מְנַשֶּׁ֥ה
בֶן־יוֹסֵ֖ף הָי֣וּ לְנָשִׁ֑ים וַתְּהִי֙ נַחֲלָתָ֔ן עַל־
מַטֵּ֖ה מִשְׁפַּ֥חַת אֲבִיהֶֽן׃

13 אֵ֣לֶּה הַמִּצְוֺ֞ת וְהַמִּשְׁפָּטִ֗ים אֲשֶׁ֨ר צִוָּ֧ה
יְהוָ֛ה בְּיַד־מֹשֶׁ֖ה אֶל־בְּנֵ֣י יִשְׂרָאֵ֑ל בְּעַֽרְבֹ֣ת
מוֹאָ֔ב עַ֖ל יַרְדֵּ֥ן יְרֵחֽוֹ׃*

v. 13. סכום הפסוקים של הספר 1,288 וחציו 17:20

חֲזַק חֲזַק וְנִתְחַזֵּק

had: They may marry anyone they wish, provided they marry into a clan of their father's tribe. 7No inheritance of the Israelites may pass over from one tribe to another, but the Israelites must remain bound each to the ancestral portion of his tribe. 8Every daughter among the Israelite tribes who inherits a share must marry someone from a clan of her father's tribe, in order that every Israelite may keep his ancestral share. 9Thus no inheritance shall pass over from one tribe to another, but the Israelite tribes shall remain bound each to its portion."

10The daughters of Zelophehad did as the LORD had commanded Moses: 11Mahlah, Tirzah, Hoglah, Milcah, and Noah, Zelophehad's daughters, were married to sons of their uncles, 12marrying into clans of descendants of Manasseh son of Joseph; and so their share remained in the tribe of their father's clan.

13These are the commandments and regulations that the LORD enjoined upon the Israelites, through Moses, on the steppes of Moab, at the Jordan near Jericho.

8. his ancestral share Literally, "his father's share." This can occur only if the land remains within the clan, not just the tribe.

11. sons of their uncles Although the daughters could have married anyone from their tribe, they selected husbands from their clan, a fact that also coincides with the law of succession. When there are no surviving children, the brothers of the deceased inherit the property (27:9). Thus, in effect, the daughters did not inherit. They merely transferred the property to those who stood next in the line of succession in any event.

12. Because they married cousins, they remained in their own clan.

13. This final note in the Book of Numbers refers to all the laws given to Israel once they encamped at the steppes of Moab (22:1). These include: the regular public sacrifices (chaps. 28–29); the division of the Land (26:52–56); the law of succession in inheritance (27:1–11; 36); the leadership succession, both religious (chap. 25) and civil (27:12–23); a woman's vows and oaths (chap. 30); the division of the spoils (chap. 31); and the laws of homicide (35:9–34).

הפטרה ראשונה דפורענותא

FIRST HAFTARAH OF ADMONITION
HAFTARAH FOR MATTOT

JEREMIAH 1:1–2:3

(*Recite on the first* Shabbat *after the 17th of* Tammuz, *coinciding with the reading of either* Pinḥas *or* Mattot *alone.*)

This *haftarah* presents the opening passages of the Book of Jeremiah. His commission as a messenger of God's word is reinforced by two visionary omens that introduce the themes of divine providence and of imminent doom.

God's call to prophecy strikes terror in Jeremiah's heart, a feeling that is countered by the promise of protection and verbal inspiration. The subjective tone of the entire passage draws on a formal literary pattern preserved in the prophetic calls of Moses (Exod. 3:10–12; 4:15), Isaiah (6:6–7), and Ezekiel (2:3–3:11).

The *haftarah* closes with the prophetic proclamation of Jer. 2:1–3. In verse 2, God recalls Israel's past devotion, accounting it in the nation's favor. In verse 3, Jeremiah enunciates the consequences. This results in a prophecy of hope and protection based on past loyalty. The Sages presumably concluded the *haftarah* here to emphasize the optimism in these verses.

RELATION OF THE *HAFTARAH* TO THE CALENDAR

The *haftarah* is not connected to the *parashah* by theme. It was chosen as the first of three prophetic readings of admonition for the three weeks that precede the fast of *Tish·ah b'Av*. Thus on the three Sabbaths preceding that commemoration of the destruction of the First and Second Temples, prophetic passages that warn the people Israel about the consequences of sin are read. These three weeks begin after the fast of the 17th of *Tammuz*, which marks the first breach in the walls of Jerusalem by the ancient Babylonians during the time of the First Temple. Rabbinic literature refers to the period from the 17th of *Tammuz* to the 9th of *Av* as *Bein ha-M'tzarim*, "Between the Breaches," after a phrase in Lamentations 1:3. The interval between these two fast days is also designated liturgically as "The Three [Weeks] of Admonition" (*t'lata d'puranuta*) because of the theme of the *haftarot* recited during this period.

After this cycle of readings and after *Tish·ah b'Av* come seven weeks of prophecies of consolation (*shivata d'neḥemata*). Thus we have a total of 10 readings, which in turn are followed by other *haftarah* readings connected to themes of the holy days of the New Year. Thus a major liturgical shift begins this week, initiating a period during which the *haftarot* relate thematically to the religious calendar, not to the *parashiyyot*.

The choice of admonitions from the prophet Jeremiah is undoubtedly owing to the tradition that he was believed to be the author of the Book of Lamentations (recited on *Tish·ah b'Av*).

1 The words of Jeremiah son of Hilkiah, one
of the priests at Anathoth in the territory of Benjamin. 2The word of the LORD came to him in
the days of King Josiah son of Amon of Judah,

א דִּבְרֵי יִרְמְיָהוּ בֶּן־חִלְקִיָּהוּ מִן־
הַכֹּהֲנִים אֲשֶׁר בַּעֲנָתוֹת בְּאֶרֶץ בִּנְיָמִן׃
2 אֲשֶׁר הָיָה דְבַר־יְהוָה אֵלָיו בִּימֵי יֹאשִׁיָּהוּ
בֶן־אָמוֹן מֶלֶךְ יְהוּדָה בִּשְׁלֹשׁ־עֶשְׂרֵה שָׁנָה

Jeremiah 1:1. Jeremiah A name derived either from the verb *ramah* (i.e., "the LORD loosens") or *rum* (i.e., "the LORD is exalted"). It is also known from 8th-century-B.C.E. Hebrew seals.

in the thirteenth year of his reign, 3and throughout the days of King Jehoiakim son of Josiah
of Judah, and until the end of the eleventh year
of King Zedekiah son of Josiah of Judah, when
Jerusalem went into exile in the fifth month.

4The word of the LORD came to me:

5Before I created you in the womb, I selected
you;
Before you were born, I consecrated you;
I appointed you a prophet concerning the
nations.

6I replied:
Ah, Lord GOD!
I don't know how to speak,
For I am still a boy.
7And the LORD said to me:
Do not say, "I am still a boy,"
But go wherever I send you
And speak whatever I command you.
8Have no fear of them,
For I am with you to deliver you
—declares the LORD.

9The LORD put out His hand and touched my
mouth, and the LORD said to me: Herewith I
put My words into your mouth.
10See, I appoint you this day
Over nations and kingdoms:

לְמָלְכוֹ׃ 3 וַיְהִ֡י בִּימֵ֞י יְהוֹיָקִ֤ים בֶּן־יֹאשִׁיָּ֙הוּ֙
מֶ֣לֶךְ יְהוּדָ֔ה עַד־תֹּם֙ עַשְׁתֵּ֣י עֶשְׂרֵ֣ה שָׁנָ֔ה
לְצִדְקִיָּ֥הוּ בֶן־יֹאשִׁיָּ֖הוּ מֶ֣לֶךְ יְהוּדָ֑ה עַד־
גְּל֥וֹת יְרוּשָׁלַ֖ם בַּחֹ֥דֶשׁ הַחֲמִישִֽׁי׃ ס

4 וַיְהִ֥י דְבַר־יְהוָ֖ה אֵלַ֥י לֵאמֹֽר׃

5 בְּטֶ֨רֶם אצורך אֶצָּרְךָ֤ בַבֶּ֙טֶן֙ יְדַעְתִּ֔יךָ
וּבְטֶ֛רֶם תֵּצֵ֥א מֵרֶ֖חֶם הִקְדַּשְׁתִּ֑יךָ
נָבִ֥יא לַגּוֹיִ֖ם נְתַתִּֽיךָ׃

6 וָאֹמַ֗ר
אֲהָהּ֙ אֲדֹנָ֣י יְהוִ֔ה
הִנֵּ֥ה לֹא־יָדַ֖עְתִּי דַּבֵּ֑ר
כִּי־נַ֖עַר אָנֹֽכִי׃ פ
7 וַיֹּ֤אמֶר יְהוָה֙ אֵלַ֔י
אַל־תֹּאמַ֖ר נַ֣עַר אָנֹ֑כִי
כִּ֠י עַל־כָּל־אֲשֶׁ֤ר אֶֽשְׁלָחֲךָ֙ תֵּלֵ֔ךְ
וְאֵ֛ת כָּל־אֲשֶׁ֥ר אֲצַוְּךָ֖ תְּדַבֵּֽר׃
8 אַל־תִּירָ֖א מִפְּנֵיהֶ֑ם
כִּֽי־אִתְּךָ֥ אֲנִ֛י לְהַצִּלֶ֖ךָ
נְאֻם־יְהוָֽה׃

9 וַיִּשְׁלַ֤ח יְהוָה֙ אֶת־יָד֔וֹ וַיַּגַּ֖ע עַל־פִּ֑י וַיֹּ֤אמֶר
יְהוָה֙ אֵלַ֔י הִנֵּ֛ה נָתַ֥תִּי דְבָרַ֖י בְּפִֽיךָ׃
10 רְאֵ֞ה הִפְקַדְתִּ֣יךָ ׀ הַיּ֣וֹם הַזֶּ֗ה
עַל־הַגּוֹיִם֙ וְעַל־הַמַּמְלָכ֔וֹת

2. in the thirteenth year This refers to 627 B.C.E., during the reign of King Josiah. At this time King Nebuchadrezzar I of Babylon revolted against his Assyrian overlord. Gradually, the Assyrian Empire was contained and overcome; Babylon rose to hegemony in the region, dominating Judea and destroying it in 587–586 B.C.E.

5. a prophet concerning the nations Framing the prophetic commission with reference to the nations who will exact divine judgment (v. 10) and the dominance of this theme in the pot image (vv. 13–15) suggest that only the foreign nations are referred to in this verse. As specified here, Jeremiah's role is to announce the northern enemy and its allies (cf. v. 15) who will destroy Judah because of its sins.

6–9. This scenario of prophetic commission follows a standard structure in the Bible. It includes a divine confrontation and commission, a prophetic objection, and a divine assurance.

speak whatever I command you . . . I put My words into your mouth This echoes Deut. 18:18, where God tells Moses that the true prophet will speak what he is commanded, because the word of God is in his mouth. The allusion establishes Jeremiah as a true prophet in the tradition of Moses.

To uproot and to pull down,
To destroy and to overthrow,
To build and to plant.

לִנְת֥וֹשׁ וְלִנְת֖וֹץ
וּלְהַאֲבִ֣יד וְלַהֲר֑וֹס
לִבְנ֖וֹת וְלִנְטֽוֹעַ׃ פ

11The word of the LORD came to me: What
do you see, Jeremiah? I replied: I see a branch
of an almond tree.
12The LORD said to me:
You have seen right,
For I am watchful to bring My word to pass.

11 וַיְהִ֤י דְבַר־יְהוָה֙ אֵלַ֣י לֵאמֹ֔ר מָה־אַתָּ֥ה
רֹאֶ֖ה יִרְמְיָ֑הוּ וָאֹמַ֕ר מַקֵּ֥ל שָׁקֵ֖ד אֲנִ֥י רֹאֶֽה׃
12 וַיֹּ֧אמֶר יְהוָ֛ה אֵלַ֖י
הֵיטַ֣בְתָּ לִרְא֑וֹת
כִּֽי־שֹׁקֵ֥ד אֲנִ֛י עַל־דְּבָרִ֖י לַעֲשֹׂתֽוֹ׃ פ

13And the word of the LORD came to me a sec-
ond time: What do you see? I replied:
I see a steaming pot,
Tipped away from the north.
14And the LORD said to me:
From the north shall disaster break loose
Upon all the inhabitants of the land!
15For I am summoning all the peoples
Of the kingdoms of the north
—declares the LORD.
They shall come, and shall each set up a throne
Before the gates of Jerusalem,
Against its walls roundabout,
And against all the towns of Judah.
16And I will argue My case against them
For all their wickedness:
They have forsaken Me
And sacrificed to other gods
And worshiped the works of their hands.

13 וַיְהִ֨י דְבַר־יְהוָ֤ה ׀ אֵלַי֙ שֵׁנִ֣ית לֵאמֹ֔ר מָ֥ה
אַתָּ֖ה רֹאֶ֑ה וָאֹמַ֗ר
סִ֤יר נָפוּחַ֙ אֲנִ֣י רֹאֶ֔ה
וּפָנָ֖יו מִפְּנֵ֥י צָפֽוֹנָה׃
14 וַיֹּ֥אמֶר יְהוָ֖ה אֵלָ֑י
מִצָּפוֹן֙ תִּפָּתַ֣ח הָֽרָעָ֔ה
עַ֥ל כָּל־יֹשְׁבֵ֖י הָאָֽרֶץ׃
15 כִּ֣י ׀ הִנְנִ֣י קֹרֵ֗א לְכָֽל־מִשְׁפְּח֛וֹת
מַמְלְכ֥וֹת צָפ֖וֹנָה
נְאֻם־יְהוָ֑ה
וּבָ֡אוּ וְֽנָתְנוּ֩ אִ֨ישׁ כִּסְא֜וֹ
פֶּ֣תַח ׀ שַׁעֲרֵ֣י יְרוּשָׁלִַ֗ם
וְעַ֤ל כָּל־חוֹמֹתֶ֙יהָ֙ סָבִ֔יב
וְעַ֖ל כָּל־עָרֵ֥י יְהוּדָֽה׃
16 וְדִבַּרְתִּ֤י מִשְׁפָּטַי֙ אוֹתָ֔ם
עַ֖ל כָּל־רָֽעָתָ֑ם
אֲשֶׁ֣ר עֲזָב֗וּנִי
וַֽיְקַטְּרוּ֙ לֵאלֹהִ֣ים אֲחֵרִ֔ים
וַיִּֽשְׁתַּחֲו֖וּ לְמַעֲשֵׂ֥י יְדֵיהֶֽם׃

17So you, gird up your loins,
Arise and speak to them
All that I command you.
Do not break down before them,
Lest I break you before them.

17 וְאַתָּה֙ תֶּאְזֹ֣ר מָתְנֶ֔יךָ
וְקַמְתָּ֙ וְדִבַּרְתָּ֣ אֲלֵיהֶ֔ם
אֵ֛ת כָּל־אֲשֶׁ֥ר אָנֹכִ֖י אֲצַוֶּ֑ךָּ
אַל־תֵּחַת֙ מִפְּנֵיהֶ֔ם
פֶּן־אֲחִתְּךָ֖ לִפְנֵיהֶֽם׃

10. To uproot and to pull down This summation of functions is a theme that runs throughout the prophecies of Jeremiah.

13–14. from the north The designation is vague in this context. Jeremiah will not identify the enemy with Babylon until 605 B.C.E. (25:9).

18I make you this day
A fortified city,
And an iron pillar,
And bronze walls
Against the whole land—
Against Judah's kings and officers,
And against its priests and citizens.
19They will attack you,
But they shall not overcome you;
For I am with you—declares the LORD—to save you.

18 וַאֲנִ֞י הִנֵּ֧ה נְתַתִּ֣יךָ הַיּ֗וֹם
לְעִ֨יר מִבְצָ֜ר
וּלְעַמּ֥וּד בַּרְזֶ֛ל וּלְחֹמ֥וֹת נְחֹ֖שֶׁת
עַל־כָּל־הָאָ֑רֶץ
לְמַלְכֵ֤י יְהוּדָה֙ לְשָׂרֶ֔יהָ
לְכֹהֲנֶ֖יהָ וּלְעַ֥ם הָאָֽרֶץ׃
19 וְנִלְחֲמ֥וּ אֵלֶ֖יךָ
וְלֹא־י֣וּכְלוּ לָ֑ךְ
כִּֽי־אִתְּךָ֥ אֲנִ֛י נְאֻם־יְהוָ֖ה לְהַצִּילֶֽךָ׃ פ

2 The word of the LORD came to me, saying,
2Go proclaim to Jerusalem: Thus said the LORD:
I accounted to your favor
The devotion of your youth,
Your love as a bride—
How you followed Me in the wilderness,
In a land not sown.
3Israel was holy to the LORD,
The first fruits of His harvest.
All who ate of it were held guilty;
Disaster befell them
—declares the LORD.

ב וַיְהִ֥י דְבַר־יְהוָ֖ה אֵלַ֥י לֵאמֹֽר׃ 2 הָלֹ֨ךְ
וְקָרָ֜אתָ בְאָזְנֵ֣י יְרוּשָׁלִַ֗ם לֵאמֹ֔ר כֹּ֚ה אָמַ֣ר
יְהוָ֔ה
זָכַ֤רְתִּי לָךְ֙
חֶ֣סֶד נְעוּרַ֔יִךְ
אַהֲבַ֖ת כְּלוּלֹתָ֑יִךְ
לֶכְתֵּ֤ךְ אַחֲרַי֙ בַּמִּדְבָּ֔ר
בְּאֶ֖רֶץ לֹ֥א זְרוּעָֽה׃
3 קֹ֤דֶשׁ יִשְׂרָאֵל֙ לַֽיהוָ֔ה
רֵאשִׁ֖ית תבואתה תְּבוּאָתֹ֑ה
כָּל־אֹכְלָ֣יו יֶאְשָׁ֔מוּ
רָעָ֛ה תָּבֹ֥א אֲלֵיהֶ֖ם
נְאֻם־יְהוָֽה׃ פ

Jeremiah 2:2–3. The positive report of Israel's youthful past and the marital symbolism of the Covenant echo Hos. 2. Yet this portrait contradicts the repeated episodes of Israel's faithlessness found in the Torah. Apparently, differing streams of tradition and didactic motives found expression in different passages of the Bible.

Verse 3 turns on another metaphor. Israel's relation to God is now imagined in terms of the donation of "first fruits." Jeremiah's rhetoric is based on the wording of the priestly rule about profaning a sacred donation: "If a man eats of a sacred donation unwittingly, he shall pay the priest for the sacred donation, adding one-fifth of its value" (Lev. 22:14). Jeremiah transforms this warning against desecrating gifts offered to the Lord into a metaphor for God's relationship to the people: The people Israel is God's sacred portion, and the nations that consume it are held guilty, with disastrous consequences. This portrays the entire people Israel as sacred.

Israel was holy Jeremiah's depiction of the nation as a "holy" people is indebted to a contemporary theology from Deuteronomy: "For you are a people consecrated to the LORD your God: of all the peoples on earth the LORD your God chose you to be His treasured people" (Deut. 7:6). This categorical formulation revises the conditional description of the people's holy status found in Exodus (19:5): "If you will obey Me faithfully and keep My covenant, you shall be My treasured possession among all the peoples." In that context, Israel becomes holy only if it observes God's teachings. Deuteronomy, however, deems Israel holy per se, and so holds it responsible for observing and maintaining the covenant.

הפטרה שנייה דפורענותא

SECOND HAFTARAH OF ADMONITION
HAFTARAH FOR MAS'EI

JEREMIAH 2:4–28, 3:4 (*Ashk'nazim*) JEREMIAH 2:4–28, 4:1–2 (*S'fardim*)

(*Recite on the second* Shabbat *after the 17th of* Tammuz, *coinciding with the reading of* Mas'ei *either separately or combined with* Mattot.)

The main part of this *haftarah* is an extensive indictment of widespread faithlessness, ingratitude, and apostasy, addressed to the entire nation. A reference to political alliances with Assyria and Egypt seems to fit the final decades of the Judean state, when such attempts were made for the sake of protection against the neo-Babylonian empire. Otherwise, the accusations are without reference to specific events.

The harsh judgment of the *haftarah* is counterposed by brief words of hope and renewal, from Jer. 3:4 or 4:1–2 according to the traditions of *Ashk'nazim* and *S'fardim,* respectively. The first conclusion to the *haftarah* (Jer. 3:4) is a remarkable counterpoint to an accusation. God's hopeful statement that the people have now called Him "Father!" thoroughly reverses their earlier avowal of wood as "my father" (2:27). Nothing could express more succinctly the return of the nation to their divine patrimony than this bold formula of rededication.

The conclusion of the *haftarah* among *S'fardim* (4:1–2) follows a different course, in which God lays down conditions to be fulfilled if the Israelites ever are to be blessed and praised by the nations. Repentance, here, is still an option, not an accomplishment. It must begin with a turning back to God and conclude with an oath of loyalty. Pagan practices must be divested. This scenario anticipates later Jewish tradition on repentance, as formulated by Saadia and Maimonides.

For Jeremiah, such a transformation is the prelude to blessing. A dim allusion to God's opening promise to Abraham (Gen. 12:1–3) may be discerned here as well. In both instances, faithfulness to God leads to the nations blessing "themselves by you." This echo of antiquity in Jeremiah invests the future with patriarchal promise.

RELATION OF THE *HAFTARAH* TO THE CALENDAR

This is the second week before *Tish·ah b'Av,* during which a prophetic reading of admonition is recited (see introduction to the first Haftarah of Admonition). Originally Jer. 2:4–28 was a diatribe rooted in a specific historical reality. Recited as a *haftarah,* the rebuke transcends its original occasion and reminds subsequent generations of the folly of false worship and the perversity of betraying historical memory.

Rabbinic tradition notes the opening particularly, with its call to "hear" (*shim·u*) the word of God that calls them to account (2:4). The Hebrew evokes the formula imprinted on Israelite religious consciousness (*na·aseh v'nishma,* lit., "we will do and hear") by which the nation had affirmed the covenant at Mount Sinai (Exod. 24:7).

Part of Jeremiah's challenge is his repeated exclamation "how" (*eikh*), as in 2:21: How you have changed from a noble vine into a base, alien vine! With this word the prophet expresses puzzlement at Israelite perversity and obtuseness; and he anticipates the pain of the word *eikhah* ("Oh, how?!" or "Alas!") that begins the Book of Lamentations, recited on the 9th of *Av* over the destruction of the First and the Second Temples. For biblical tradition, the verbal connection of *eikh / eikhah* evokes the spiritual and physical doom that awaits those who follow the path of paganism and ignore their covenantal obligations.

2

⁴Hear the word of the Lord, O House of Jacob,

Every clan of the House of Israel!

⁵Thus said the Lord:

What wrong did your fathers find in Me

That they abandoned Me

And went after delusion and were deluded?

⁶They never asked themselves, "Where is the Lord,

Who brought us up from the land of Egypt,

Who led us through the wilderness,

A land of deserts and pits,

A land of drought and darkness,

A land no man had traversed,

Where no human being had dwelt?"

⁷I brought you to this country of farm land

To enjoy its fruit and its bounty;

But you came and defiled My land,

You made My possession abhorrent.

⁸The priests never asked themselves, "Where is the Lord?"

The guardians of the Teaching ignored Me;

The rulers rebelled against Me,

And the prophets prophesied by Baal

And followed what can do no good.

⁹Oh, I will go on accusing you

—declares the Lord—

And I will accuse your children's children!

¹⁰Just cross over to the isles of the Kittim and look,

Send to Kedar and observe carefully;

ב ⁴ שִׁמְע֥וּ דְבַר־יְהֹוָ֖ה בֵּ֣ית יַעֲקֹ֑ב
וְכׇל־מִשְׁפְּח֖וֹת בֵּ֥ית יִשְׂרָאֵֽל׃
⁵ כֹּ֣ה ׀ אָמַ֣ר יְהֹוָ֗ה
מַה־מָּצְא֨וּ אֲבוֹתֵיכֶ֥ם בִּי֙ עָ֔וֶל
כִּ֥י רָחֲק֖וּ מֵעָלָ֑י
וַיֵּ֥לְכ֛וּ אַחֲרֵ֥י הַהֶ֖בֶל וַיֶּהְבָּֽלוּ׃
⁶ וְלֹ֣א אָמְר֔וּ אַיֵּ֣ה יְהֹוָ֔ה
הַמַּעֲלֶ֥ה אֹתָ֖נוּ מֵאֶ֣רֶץ מִצְרָ֑יִם
הַמּוֹלִ֨יךְ אֹתָ֜נוּ בַּמִּדְבָּ֗ר
בְּאֶ֨רֶץ עֲרָבָ֤ה וְשׁוּחָה֙
בְּאֶ֨רֶץ צִיָּ֣ה וְצַלְמָ֔וֶת
בְּאֶ֗רֶץ לֹא־עָ֤בַר בָּהּ֙ אִ֔ישׁ
וְלֹא־יָשַׁ֥ב אָדָ֖ם שָֽׁם׃
⁷ וָאָבִ֤יא אֶתְכֶם֙ אֶל־אֶ֣רֶץ הַכַּרְמֶ֔ל
לֶאֱכֹ֥ל פִּרְיָ֖הּ וְטוּבָ֑הּ
וַתָּבֹ֨אוּ֙ וַתְּטַמְּא֣וּ אֶת־אַרְצִ֔י
וְנַחֲלָתִ֥י שַׂמְתֶּ֖ם לְתוֹעֵבָֽה׃
⁸ הַכֹּהֲנִ֗ים לֹ֤א אָמְרוּ֙ אַיֵּ֣ה יְהֹוָ֔ה
וְתֹפְשֵׂ֤י הַתּוֹרָה֙ לֹ֣א יְדָע֔וּנִי
וְהָרֹעִ֖ים פָּ֣שְׁעוּ בִ֑י
וְהַנְּבִיאִים֙ נִבְּא֣וּ בַבַּ֔עַל
וְאַחֲרֵ֥י לֹֽא־יוֹעִ֖לוּ הָלָֽכוּ׃
⁹ לָכֵ֗ן עֹ֛ד אָרִ֥יב אִתְּכֶ֖ם נְאֻם־יְהֹוָ֑ה
וְאֶת־בְּנֵ֥י בְנֵיכֶ֖ם אָרִֽיב׃
¹⁰ כִּ֣י עִבְר֞וּ אִיֵּ֤י כִתִּיִּים֙ וּרְא֔וּ
וְקֵדָ֛ר שִׁלְח֥וּ וְהִתְבּוֹנְנ֖וּ מְאֹ֑ד

Jeremiah 2:6. Where is the Lord This charge has a broad, polemical background. It recurs in the Hebrew Bible as a query seeking assurances of God's presence and might.

7. defiled My land Acts of idolatry and false worship defile both the land and the perpetrators (Lev. 18:24–25).

8. guardians of the Teaching The "guardians" are included in a larger list of indicted people, including priests, prophets, and kings (see also v. 26).

10. isles of the Kittim The western edge of civilization is represented here by an ancient Greek city, Kition (Citium), modern-day Larnaca on Cyprus (cf. Isa. 23:1; Ezek. 27:6).

Kedar An old Arab tribe (Gen. 25:13), located in the east of Transjordan, in northern Arabia.

See if aught like this has ever happened:
11Has any nation changed its gods
Even though they are no-gods?
But My people has exchanged its glory
For what can do no good.
12Be appalled, O heavens, at this;
Be horrified, utterly dazed!
—says the LORD.
13For My people have done a twofold wrong:
They have forsaken Me, the Fount of living waters,
And hewed them out cisterns, broken cisterns,
Which cannot even hold water.

14Is Israel a bondman?
Is he a home-born slave?
Then why is he given over to plunder?
15Lions have roared over him,
Have raised their cries.
They have made his land a waste,
His cities desolate, without inhabitants.
16Those, too, in Noph and Tahpanhes
Will lay bare your head.
17See, that is the price you have paid
For forsaking the LORD your God
While He led you in the way.
18What, then, is the good of your going to Egypt

וּרְאוּ הֵן הָיְתָה כָּזֹאת׃
11 הַהֵימִיר גּוֹי אֱלֹהִים
וְהֵמָּה לֹא אֱלֹהִים
וְעַמִּי הֵמִיר כְּבוֹדוֹ
בְּלוֹא יוֹעִיל׃
12 שֹׁמּוּ שָׁמַיִם עַל־זֹאת
וְשַׂעֲרוּ חָרְבוּ מְאֹד
נְאֻם־יְהוָה׃
13 כִּי־שְׁתַּיִם רָעוֹת עָשָׂה עַמִּי
אֹתִי עָזְבוּ מְקוֹר ׀ מַיִם חַיִּים
לַחְצֹב לָהֶם בֹּארוֹת* בֹּארֹת נִשְׁבָּרִים
אֲשֶׁר לֹא־יָכִלוּ הַמָּיִם׃

14 הַעֶבֶד יִשְׂרָאֵל
אִם־יְלִיד בַּיִת הוּא
מַדּוּעַ הָיָה לָבַז׃
15 עָלָיו יִשְׁאֲגוּ כְפִרִים
נָתְנוּ קוֹלָם
וַיָּשִׁיתוּ אַרְצוֹ לְשַׁמָּה
עָרָיו נצתה נִצְּתוּ מִבְּלִי יֹשֵׁב׃
16 גַּם־בְּנֵי־נֹף ותחפנס וְתַחְפַּנְחֵס
יִרְעוּךְ קָדְקֹד׃
17 הֲלוֹא־זֹאת תַּעֲשֶׂה־לָּךְ
עָזְבֵךְ אֶת־יְהוָה אֱלֹהַיִךְ
בְּעֵת מוֹלִכֵךְ בַּדָּרֶךְ׃
18 וְעַתָּה מַה־לָּךְ לְדֶרֶךְ מִצְרַיִם

v. 13. ויתיר א׳ פעמיים

11. its glory Hebrew: *k'vodo,* which also can mean "His glory" (i.e., God's heavenly glory), which the people denied and exchanged for "no-gods." Rabbinic tradition named this passage as one of the "scribal corrections" (*tikkunei sof'rim*) introduced into the biblical text to avoid speaking disrespectfully of God. (See the list in Mekh. Shirata 6, on Exod. 15:7.) This implies that the original reading here was "My glory" (*k'vodi*); presumably the starkness of this formulation led certain scribes to soften and obscure it through a slight change. Whether this was truly a scribal correction—or a *midrash* formulated to make a theological point—is open to question.

13. Fount of living waters This image may derive from the homily in Deut. 6:11–12, a passage that also includes the themes of hewn wells, forsaking God, the Exodus, and slavery (see also Jer. 17:13).

16, 18. Egyptian place-names have been Hebraized here.

Noph A corruption of "Moph" (see Hos. 9:6) or Memphis (Saqqara, in the lower Nile region).

Tahpanhes Consists of two words meaning "fortress of the Nubian" (Tall al-Dafana). The second word (*panḥes*) is known as the name of the priest *Pinḥas* (Phinehas).

To drink the waters of the Nile?
And what is the good of your going to Assyria
To drink the waters of the Euphrates?
19Let your misfortune reprove you,
Let your afflictions rebuke you;
Mark well how bad and bitter it is
That you forsake the LORD your God,
That awe for Me is not in you
—declares the Lord GOD of Hosts.
20For long ago you broke your yoke,
Tore off your yoke-bands,
And said, "I will not work!"
On every high hill and under every verdant tree,
You recline as a whore.
21I planted you with noble vines,
All with choicest seed;
Alas, I find you changed
Into a base, an alien vine!
22Though you wash with natron
And use much lye,
Your guilt is ingrained before Me
—declares the Lord GOD.
23How can you say, "I am not defiled,
I have not gone after the Baalim"?
Look at your deeds in the Valley,
Consider what you have done!
Like a lustful she-camel,
Restlessly running about,
24Or like a wild ass used to the desert,

לִשְׁתּוֹת מֵי שִׁחוֹר
וּמַה־לָּךְ לְדֶרֶךְ אַשּׁוּר
לִשְׁתּוֹת מֵי נָהָר׃
19 תְּיַסְּרֵךְ רָעָתֵךְ
וּמְשֻׁבוֹתַיִךְ תּוֹכִחֻךְ
וּדְעִי וּרְאִי כִּי־רַע וָמָר
עָזְבֵךְ אֶת־יְהוָה אֱלֹהָיִךְ
וְלֹא פַחְדָּתִי אֵלַיִךְ
נְאֻם־אֲדֹנָי יְהוִה צְבָאוֹת׃
20 כִּי מֵעוֹלָם שָׁבַרְתִּי עֻלֵּךְ
נִתַּקְתִּי מוֹסְרוֹתַיִךְ
וַתֹּאמְרִי לֹא אעבד אֶעֱבוֹר
כִּי עַל־כָּל־גִּבְעָה גְּבֹהָה וְתַחַת כָּל־עֵץ
רַעֲנָן
אַתְּ צֹעָה זֹנָה׃
21 וְאָנֹכִי נְטַעְתִּיךְ שׂוֹרֵק
כֻּלֹּה זֶרַע אֱמֶת
וְאֵיךְ נֶהְפַּכְתְּ לִי
סוּרֵי הַגֶּפֶן נָכְרִיָּה׃
22 כִּי אִם־תְּכַבְּסִי בַּנֶּתֶר
וְתַרְבִּי־לָךְ בֹּרִית
נִכְתָּם עֲוֹנֵךְ לְפָנַי
נְאֻם אֲדֹנָי יְהוִה׃
23 אֵיךְ תֹּאמְרִי לֹא נִטְמֵאתִי
אַחֲרֵי הַבְּעָלִים לֹא הָלַכְתִּי
רְאִי דַרְכֵּךְ בַּגַּיְא
דְּעִי מֶה עָשִׂית
בִּכְרָה קַלָּה
מְשָׂרֶכֶת דְּרָכֶיהָ׃
24 פֶּרֶה ׀ לִמֻּד מִדְבָּר

waters of the Nile The Hebrew (*mei shiḥor*) derives from the Egyptian phrase *p' sh-ḥr,* "Pool of Horus" (cf. Isa. 23:3).

20. you broke Hebrew: *shavarti.* The Hebrew here is not what it seems to be, namely, the common first person form "I broke." It is the archaic (or Aramaizing) second-person feminine singular form. So also the Hebrew *nitakti* ("you . . . tore off") in this verse.

work Hebrew: *e·evod,* per the *k'tiv* (writing tradition); the usually preferred *k'rei* (reading tradition) here has *e·evor* ("transgress") [Transl.].

21. Into a base, an alien vine The divine planting contrasts with the verdant trees under which Israel commits pagan sins (v. 20). The image also alludes to God's planting of Israel in the Land at the time of settlement (Exod. 15:17, Ps. 80:9ff.).

Snuffing the wind in her eagerness,
Whose passion none can restrain,
None that seek her need grow weary—
In her season, they'll find her!

25Save your foot from going bare,
And your throat from thirst.
But you say, "It is no use.
No, I love the strangers,
And after them I must go."
26Like a thief chagrined when he is caught,
So is the House of Israel chagrined—
They, their kings, their officers,
And their priests and prophets.
27They said to wood, "You are my father,"
To stone, "You gave birth to me,"
While to Me they turned their backs
And not their faces.
But in their hour of calamity they cry,
"Arise and save us!"
28And where are those gods
You made for yourself?
Let them arise and save you, if they can,
In your hour of calamity.
For your gods have become, O Judah,
As many as your towns!

בְּאַוַּת נפשו נַפְשָׁהּ שָׁאֲפָה רוּחַ
תַּאֲנָתָהּ מִי יְשִׁיבֶנָּה
כָּל־מְבַקְשֶׁיהָ לֹא יִיעָפוּ
בְּחָדְשָׁהּ יִמְצָאוּנְהָ׃

25 מִנְעִי רַגְלֵךְ מִיָּחֵף
וגורנך וּגְרוֹנֵךְ מִצִּמְאָה
וַתֹּאמְרִי נוֹאָשׁ לוֹא
כִּי־אָהַבְתִּי זָרִים
וְאַחֲרֵיהֶם אֵלֵךְ׃
26 כְּבֹשֶׁת גַּנָּב כִּי יִמָּצֵא
כֵּן הֹבִישׁוּ בֵּית יִשְׂרָאֵל
הֵמָּה מַלְכֵיהֶם שָׂרֵיהֶם
וְכֹהֲנֵיהֶם וּנְבִיאֵיהֶם׃
27 אֹמְרִים לָעֵץ אָבִי אַתָּה
וְלָאֶבֶן אַתְּ ילדתני יְלִדְתָּנוּ
כִּי־פָנוּ אֵלַי עֹרֶף
וְלֹא פָנִים
וּבְעֵת רָעָתָם יֹאמְרוּ
קוּמָה וְהוֹשִׁיעֵנוּ׃
28 וְאַיֵּה אֱלֹהֶיךָ
אֲשֶׁר עָשִׂיתָ לָּךְ
יָקוּמוּ אִם־יוֹשִׁיעוּךָ
בְּעֵת רָעָתֶךָ
כִּי מִסְפַּר עָרֶיךָ
הָיוּ אֱלֹהֶיךָ יְהוּדָה׃* ס

3 4Just now you called to Me, "Father!
You are the Companion of my youth."

ג 4 הֲלוֹא מֵעַתָּה קראתי קָרָאת לִי אָבִי
אַלּוּף נְעֻרַי אָתָּה׃**

27. The formula "You are my father" has the technical resonance of a legal adoption formula, as when God says to the king: "You are My son, / I have fathered you this day" (Ps. 2:7; cf. 2 Sam. 7:14). The prophet mocks and condemns the people's pagan allegiances, giving themselves a wholly natural religion. For him, this is an utter rejection of divine transcendence.

Jeremiah 3:4. Just now Hebrew: *me-atah.* "At that moment [when you saw that I had stopped the rain]" (Radak, referring to the preceding verse from the original context). Alternatively, "as of now" (with Targum; see Rashi).

Father! Repentance now becomes the theme via a reversal of the false formula of patrimony (2:27).

* Ashk'nazim *read the next verse;* S'fardim *do not read it.*
** Ashk'nazim *stop here.*

4 If you return, O Israel
—declares the LORD—
If you return to Me,
If you remove your abominations from My presence
And do not waver,
2And swear, "As the LORD lives,"
In sincerity, justice, and righteousness—
Nations shall bless themselves by you
And praise themselves by you.

ד אִם־תָּשׁ֨וּב יִשְׂרָאֵ֧ל ׀
נְאֻם־יְהוָ֛ה
אֵלַ֥י תָּשׁ֑וּב
וְאִם־תָּסִ֧יר שִׁקּוּצֶ֛יךָ מִפָּנַ֖י
וְלֹ֥א תָנֽוּד׃
2 וְנִשְׁבַּ֙עְתָּ֙ חַי־יְהוָ֔ה
בֶּאֱמֶ֖ת בְּמִשְׁפָּ֣ט וּבִצְדָקָ֑ה
וְהִתְבָּ֥רְכוּ ב֛וֹ גּוֹיִ֖ם
וּב֥וֹ יִתְהַלָּֽלוּ׃ ס

Jeremiah 4:2. As the LORD lives A fixed oath formula, denoting here a commitment to the national God.

sincerity The first of a triad of covenantal terms. (Compare the variant triad in Jer. 9:23 and the extended cluster in Hos. 2:21–22.)

דברים

DEUTERONOMY

דברים

ואתחנן

עקב

ראה

שפטים

כי תצא

כי תבוא

נצבים

וילך

האזינו

וזאת הברכה

DEUTERONOMY

JEFFREY H. TIGAY

Deuteronomy has two Hebrew names: *Seifer D'varim*, short for (*Seifer*) *v'elleh ha-d'varim*, "(The Book of) 'These are the words,'" taken from its opening phrase; and *Mishnei Torah*, "Repetition of the Torah" (source of English "Deuteronomy"), taken from 17:18. It consists of five retrospective discourses and poems that Moses addressed to Israel in Moab shortly before his death (1:6–4:43, 4:44–28:69, 29–30, 32, 33), plus two narratives about his final acts (chaps. 31, 34). The book's core is the second discourse, in which Moses conveys laws that the people commissioned him to receive from God at Mount Sinai 40 years earlier.

Several themes in Deuteronomy stand out. Among the Torah's books, it is the most vigorous and clear advocate of monotheism and of the ardent, exclusive loyalty that Israel owes God (4:32–40, 6:4–5). It emphasizes God's love, justice, and transcendence: He is near to Israel (4:7), but in a spiritual, not a physical, sense; only God's name, not God himself, dwells in the sanctuary (e.g., 12:5,11, 26:15).

This book stresses the covenant between God and Israel, summed up in 26:16–19. Established with the patriarchs, affirmed at Sinai and in Moab, it is to be reaffirmed as soon as Israel enters its land (4:31, 5:2, 28:69, 27).

Deuteronomy looks toward Israel's life in the land of Israel, where a society pursuing justice and righteousness, living in harmony with God and enjoying His bounty, can be established (4:5–8, 7:12–13). The promise of this land is conditional (11:8–9, 21); Israel's welfare depends on maintaining a society governed by God's social and religious laws. These laws are a divine gift to Israel, unparalleled in their justice and their ability to secure God's closeness (4:5–8). The Torah's humanitarianism is most developed in Deuteronomy's concern for the welfare of the poor and disadvantaged.

Deuteronomy proclaims the unique rule that sacrifice may take place only in the religious capital, in a single sanctuary (chap. 12). Its aim is to spiritualize religion by freeing it from excessive dependence on sacrifice and priesthood. It urges instead studying God's law and performing rituals that teach reverent love for Him. These teachings probably laid the groundwork for nonsacrificial, synagogue-based worship.

Deuteronomy has a strong intellectual orientation. It urges all Israelites to study God's laws. Its style is didactic and sermonic, explaining the meaning of events and the purpose of laws, to secure Israel's willing, understanding assent.

Deuteronomy strongly influenced later Jewish tradition. The core of Jewish worship is the recitation of the *Sh'ma* (6:4) and the public reading of the Torah (rooted in 31:11). Also based on Deuteronomy are the duty of blessing God after meals (*Birkat ha-Mazon*, 8:10), *Kiddush* on *Shabbat* (5:12), affixing *m'zuzot* to doorposts, wearing *t'fillin* (6:8–9, 11:18,20) and *tzitzit* (tassels) (22:12), and charity to the poor (e.g., 15:8). Deuteronomy is the source of the concept that religious life should be based on a sacred book and its study. As the biblical book that deals most explicitly with beliefs and attitudes, it plays a major role in Jewish theology. In the theological-ethical introduction of his digest of Jewish law, the *Mishnei Torah*, Maimonides cites Deuteronomy more than any other book, starting with the command to believe in God and Him alone.

Deuteronomy's effect on Jewish life cannot be overstated. No idea has shaped Jewish history more than monotheism, which this book asserts so passionately. And no verse has shaped Jewish consciousness and identity more than Deuteronomy's classic expression of that idea, the *Sh'ma*.

D'VARIM

1 These are the words that Moses addressed
to all Israel on the other side of the Jordan.—
Through the wilderness, in the Arabah near
Suph, between Paran and Tophel, Laban,
Hazeroth, and Di-zahab, 2it is eleven days from

דברים

א אֵלֶּה הַדְּבָרִים אֲשֶׁר דִּבֶּר מֹשֶׁה אֶל־
כָּל־יִשְׂרָאֵל בְּעֵבֶר הַיַּרְדֵּן בַּמִּדְבָּר בָּעֲרָבָה
מוֹל סוּף בֵּין־פָּארָן וּבֵין־תֹּפֶל וְלָבָן
וַחֲצֵרֹת וְדִי זָהָב׃ 2 אַחַד עָשָׂר יוֹם מֵחֹרֵב

A UNIQUE BOOK (1:1–5)

The first five verses give the time and place of the delivery of Moses' farewell address.

1. These are the words that Moses addressed to all Israel Apart from some connecting passages and the narratives about Moses' last days, the speaker in Deuteronomy is Moses, not an anonymous narrator as in the previous books of the Torah. Even the narratives and laws appear as parts of addresses in which Moses reviews the past 40 years and prepares the Israelites for the future.

on the other side of the Jordan In Transjordan, east of the river Jordan. Although Moses never crossed over to the western side of the Jordan, this is written from the point of view of one already in the Land.

the wilderness The text locates this wilderness in the long narrow depression, or rift, that continues the Jordan Valley south of the Dead Sea down to the Gulf of Elat. This rift is known as the 'Arabah to this day.

2. It was an 11-day journey from Horeb (Mount Sinai) to Kadesh-barnea, the gateway to the Promised Land (see vv. 19–20). If the Israelites had trusted in God, this verse tells us, they could have entered the land immediately, without wandering in the wilderness for 38 years.

CHAPTER 1

Some of Deuteronomy's passages, ranging from the Decalogue to setting aside cities of refuge, duplicate contents found elsewhere in the Torah. But 70 of the approximately 100 laws in Deuteronomy are not found in the earlier books. These laws deal mostly with arrangements for living in the Land and with the new emphasis on a central sanctuary to be designated by God. Moses is telling the Israelites things they will need to know when they settle the Land, things they had no need to know before.

One way of viewing this book is to see it as divided into three parts. In the first part, Moses reviews the history of the people's wandering, emphasizing Israel's lack of fidelity and gratitude. This is followed by a legal section, and finally by Moses' farewell address. Hirsch detects a tone of urgency throughout Moses' remarks, prompted, he suspects, by the concern that when the families of Israel are no longer camped around the tabernacle but are living each on its own property, the benign influence of God's Presence will be lost.

1. Moses began his career by pleading that he was not "a man of words" (*ish d'varim,* Exod. 4:10). After 40 years of teaching Torah, however, he has become an eloquent "man of words." The change is not due to improved rhetorical skills but to his enthusiastic commitment to his message (Deut. R. 1:1).

The Midrash, noting the similar sound of *d'varim* (words) and *d'vorim* (bees), comments that Moses' criticisms of the people are like the stings of a bee. A bee's sting hurts the person stung but it hurts the bee more, causing its death. Moses dies at the end of Deuteronomy because criticizing Israel has taken so much out of him (Deut. R. 1:6). This would imply that we should judge the validity of criticism not only by its factual accuracy but by how much it pains the critic to say it. The harsh criticisms of Moses are spoken with love, in contrast to the praises of Balaam, spoken as flattery.

to all Israel Including Moses himself. His criticisms gain credibility because he criticizes his own behavior as well.

1–2. Why list all these place-names? To avoid shaming Israel excessively, lest they lose all hope of ever pleasing God. For Moses had been inclined to remind Israel of all the times they exasperated and disappointed God; instead, he referred only to the locations where those events occurred (Rashi). Or perhaps Moses is recalling all the places God and Israel have been together, as reminiscing lovers might do.

Horeb to Kadesh-barnea by the Mount Seir
route.—3It was in the fortieth year, on the first
day of the eleventh month, that Moses addressed the Israelites in accordance with the instructions that the LORD had given him for
them, 4after he had defeated Sihon king of the
Amorites, who dwelt in Heshbon, and King Og
of Bashan, who dwelt at Ashtaroth [and] Edrei.
5On the other side of the Jordan, in the land
of Moab, Moses undertook to expound this
Teaching. He said:

6The LORD our God spoke to us at Horeb,
saying: You have stayed long enough at this
mountain. 7Start out and make your way to the

דֶּרֶךְ הַר־שֵׂעִיר עַד קָדֵשׁ בַּרְנֵעַ׃ 3 וַיְהִי
בְּאַרְבָּעִים שָׁנָה בְּעַשְׁתֵּי־עָשָׂר חֹדֶשׁ
בְּאֶחָד לַחֹדֶשׁ דִּבֶּר מֹשֶׁה אֶל־בְּנֵי יִשְׂרָאֵל
כְּכֹל אֲשֶׁר צִוָּה יְהוָה אֹתוֹ אֲלֵהֶם׃ 4 אַחֲרֵי
הַכֹּתוֹ אֵת סִיחֹן מֶלֶךְ הָאֱמֹרִי אֲשֶׁר יוֹשֵׁב
בְּחֶשְׁבּוֹן וְאֵת עוֹג מֶלֶךְ הַבָּשָׁן אֲשֶׁר־יוֹשֵׁב
בְּעַשְׁתָּרֹת בְּאֶדְרֶעִי׃ 5 בְּעֵבֶר הַיַּרְדֵּן בְּאֶרֶץ
מוֹאָב הוֹאִיל מֹשֶׁה בֵּאֵר אֶת־הַתּוֹרָה
הַזֹּאת לֵאמֹר׃

6 יְהוָה אֱלֹהֵינוּ דִּבֶּר אֵלֵינוּ בְּחֹרֵב לֵאמֹר
רַב־לָכֶם שֶׁבֶת בָּהָר הַזֶּה׃ 7 פְּנוּ ׀ וּסְעוּ
לָכֶם וּבֹאוּ הַר הָאֱמֹרִי וְאֶל־כָּל־שְׁכֵנָיו

Horeb Deuteronomy's name for Mount Sinai. Situated somewhere in the Sinai peninsula, its precise location remains unknown.

Kadesh-barnea Sometimes called simply Kadesh, it was near the western border of Seir-Edom, on the southern boundary of the Promised Land, in essence the gateway to it.

by the Mount Seir route Seir, or Edom, the southernmost of the Transjordanian kingdoms, extended westward into the highlands of the eastern Negeb. "(Mount) Seir" usually refers to this part of Edom.

3. eleventh month Later known as *Sh'vat,* which falls in January and February. This verse merges Deuteronomy into the chronologic framework of the previous books of the Torah.

4. Ashtaroth [and] Edrei These two cities were twin seats of government for Og, king of Bashan. Both places are mentioned in Egyptian documents and in a Ugaritic text.

5. in the land of Moab In the steppes of Moab, so called because the area belonged to Moab before it was conquered by Sihon (see Num. 21:29), from whom the Israelites wrested it.

this Teaching Hebrew: *ha-Torah,* derived from *"horah"* (teach, instruct). *"Torah"* refers to rules of civil and ritual procedures, moral exhortation, and instructive narrative as well as prophetic teaching and reproach. Moses frequently refers to Deuteronomy as "this *Torah.*" In later times the term "Torah" was applied to the entire Pentateuch and, ultimately, to the totality of the Jewish religious tradition.

Moses' First Discourse (1:6–4:40)

Moses' first discourse serves as a prologue to the book. It emphasizes that the people's fate depends on their response to God's commands and promises. This address reflects the importance of history as the basis of Israelite religion. Religious belief in the Bible is based mostly on Israel's experience of God rather than on theological speculation.

---

5. to expound this Teaching He interpreted the Torah in many languages, so that future generations of Jews in many lands would have access to the Torah in a language and in terms that they could understand (*S'fat Emet*). There is holiness in the Hebrew language—"the holy tongue" (*l'shon ha-kodesh*)—in and of itself. It is also necessary, though, for people to learn what God requires of them in a language that they can understand.

6. You have stayed long enough There is a danger that the people Israel will grow too comfortable where they are and will be reluctant to move on into the unknown. There are times when our fulfilment as individuals or as a group requires us to leave the familiar and move on toward a goal.

hill country of the Amorites and to all their neighbors in the Arabah, the hill country, the Shephelah, the Negeb, the seacoast, the land of the Canaanites, and the Lebanon, as far as the Great River, the river Euphrates. ⁸See, I place the land at your disposal. Go, take possession of the land that the LORD swore to your fathers,

בָּעֲרָבָ֞ה בָהָ֣ר וּבַשְּׁפֵלָ֥ה וּבַנֶּ֖גֶב וּבְח֣וֹף הַיָּ֑ם אֶ֤רֶץ הַֽכְּנַעֲנִי֙ וְהַלְּבָנ֔וֹן עַד־הַנָּהָ֥ר הַגָּדֹ֖ל נְהַר־פְּרָֽת: ⁸רְאֵ֛ה נָתַ֥תִּי לִפְנֵיכֶ֖ם אֶת־הָאָ֑רֶץ בֹּ֚אוּ וּרְשׁ֣וּ אֶת־הָאָ֔רֶץ אֲשֶׁ֨ר

ISRAEL DISOBEYS THE FIRST COMMAND TO PROCEED
TO THE PROMISED LAND (1:6–2:1)

FROM HOREB TO REBELLION   (vv. 6–33)

PROCEEDING TO THE PROMISED LAND
(vv. 6–8)

Moses begins his address by reminding his audience—the generation about to enter the Promised Land—that Israel had been commanded to enter the land a generation earlier (see Exod. 32:34–33:3; Num. 10:11–34). The entire retrospective that follows, through the end of chapter 3, deals with Israel's response to God's command and the consequences of that response.

6. You have stayed long enough The Hebrew for this phrase expresses impatience, indicating that God was eager for Israel to enter the land immediately. The nearly 40-year delay was not God's original intention but the result of Israel's failure to trust and obey God.

7. The Promised Land is described here in terms of its main regions.

hill country of the Amorites The central highlands running south to north, which would become the heartland of Israelite settlement. The Amorites were the inhabitants of these mountains, especially the southern ones that the Israelites would reach first, entering from the Sinai.

all their neighbors That is, the neighboring regions.

Arabah Here, the Jordan Valley from Lake Tiberias in the north to the Dead Sea (see 3:17, 4:49). The Arabah Rift south of the Dead Sea (mentioned in v. 1) was in Edomite territory and was not part of the Promised Land.

hill country The neighboring regions of the Amorites in the central highlands included the lands of the Hittites, Jebusites, Amalekites, Canaanites, and Perizzites.

Shephelah The "lowland," the low hills between the Judahite part of the central highlands and the coastal plain.

Negeb In the Bible, the northern section of what is called the Negev today. Beginning 10 to 15 miles north of Beer-sheba, it extends about 30 miles southward to the wilderness of Zin, the southern boundary of the Promised Land. Here the western part of the Negev is meant; the eastern part, like the Arabah, was part of Seir-Edom. The name "Negeb," from the Hebrew נגב (dry), reflects the relative aridity of the region. Its average annual rainfall is 300 mm at the northern end and 100 mm at the southern end.

seacoast Of the Mediterranean.

land of the Canaanites The translation understands this phrase as referring to one part of the Promised Land: the seacoast, especially the area later called Phoenicia, and part of the Jordan Valley (see Gen. 10:15,19; Num. 13:29). Later Phoenician sources likewise call Phoenicia "Canaan." The Masoretic trope of the Hebrew text, however, implies that the phrase refers to all the regions named in the first part of the verse, and takes the phrase in its common biblical meaning of the entire Promised Land (e.g., Deut. 11:30; Gen. 12:5). This meaning corresponds to the use of "Canaan" in ancient Egyptian sources when reference is made to the region of Canaan under Egyptian control.

Lebanon The inland Lebanon and Anti-Lebanon mountain ranges, including the Bekáa Valley between them, but not to the entire territory of modern Lebanon.

river Euphrates The part of the Euphrates that is on a direct line with the Lebanon range, i.e., the northwestern sector of the river in northern Syria. The Euphrates, therefore, represents the northern extremity of the Promised Land (e.g., 11:24).

8. take possession God's gift of the land to the Israelites was viewed as analogous to a sovereign's grant of land to a loyal servant. In an ancient Near Eastern document, a Hittite king makes a similar declaration to his vassal: "See, I gave you the Zippashla mountain land; occupy it."

the LORD swore Here God refers to Himself in the third person, after using the first person in verses 6–8a. Such grammatical variation is common in the Bible and in other ancient Near Eastern literature. By referring to His oath to the pa-

Abraham, Isaac, and Jacob, to assign to them and to their heirs after them.

⁹Thereupon I said to you, "I cannot bear the burden of you by myself. ¹⁰The LORD your God has multiplied you until you are today as numerous as the stars in the sky.—¹¹May the LORD, the God of your fathers, increase your numbers a thousandfold, and bless you as He promised you.—¹²How can I bear unaided the trouble of you, and the burden, and the bickering! ¹³Pick from each of your tribes men who are wise, discerning, and experienced, and I will appoint them as your heads." ¹⁴You answered me and said, "What you propose to do is good." ¹⁵So I took your tribal leaders, wise and experienced men, and appointed them heads over you: chiefs of thousands, chiefs of hundreds, chiefs of fifties, and chiefs of tens, and officials

נִשְׁבַּ֤ע יְהוָה֙ לַאֲבֹ֣תֵיכֶ֔ם לְאַבְרָהָ֥ם לְיִצְחָ֖ק וּֽלְיַעֲקֹ֑ב לָתֵ֤ת לָהֶם֙ וּלְזַרְעָ֣ם אַחֲרֵיהֶֽם׃ ⁹וָאֹמַ֣ר אֲלֵכֶ֔ם בָּעֵ֥ת הַהִ֖וא לֵאמֹ֑ר לֹא־אוּכַ֥ל לְבַדִּ֖י שְׂאֵ֥ת אֶתְכֶֽם׃ ¹⁰יְהוָ֣ה אֱלֹהֵיכֶ֔ם הִרְבָּ֖ה אֶתְכֶ֑ם וְהִנְּכֶ֣ם הַיּ֔וֹם כְּכוֹכְבֵ֥י הַשָּׁמַ֖יִם לָרֹֽב׃ ¹¹יְהוָ֞ה אֱלֹהֵ֣י אֲבֽוֹתֵכֶ֗ם יֹסֵ֧ף עֲלֵיכֶ֛ם כָּכֶ֖ם אֶ֣לֶף פְּעָמִ֑ים וִיבָרֵ֣ךְ אֶתְכֶ֔ם כַּאֲשֶׁ֖ר דִּבֶּ֥ר לָכֶֽם׃ ¹²אֵיכָ֥ה אֶשָּׂ֖א לְבַדִּ֑י טָרְחֲכֶ֥ם וּמַֽשַּׂאֲכֶ֖ם וְרִֽיבְכֶֽם׃ ¹³הָב֣וּ לָ֠כֶם אֲנָשִׁ֨ים חֲכָמִ֧ים וּנְבֹנִ֛ים וִידֻעִ֖ים לְשִׁבְטֵיכֶ֑ם וַאֲשִׂימֵ֖ם בְּרָאשֵׁיכֶֽם׃ ¹⁴וַֽתַּעֲנ֖וּ אֹתִ֑י וַתֹּ֣אמְר֔וּ טֽוֹב־הַדָּבָ֥ר אֲשֶׁר־דִּבַּ֖רְתָּ לַעֲשֽׂוֹת׃ ¹⁵וָאֶקַּ֞ח אֶת־רָאשֵׁ֣י שִׁבְטֵיכֶ֗ם אֲנָשִׁ֤ים חֲכָמִים֙ וִֽידֻעִ֔ים וָאֶתֵּ֥ן אוֹתָ֛ם רָאשִׁ֖ים עֲלֵיכֶ֑ם שָׂרֵ֨י אֲלָפִ֜ים וְשָׂרֵ֣י מֵא֗וֹת וְשָׂרֵ֤י חֲמִשִּׁים֙ וְשָׂרֵ֣י עֲשָׂרֹ֔ת

triarchs, God shows the people that He fulfills His promises. As Moses explains later (4:37, 7:8, 9:5), this oath is the basis of the relationship between God and the present generation.

CHIEFS APPOINTED FOR THE JOURNEY
(vv. 9–18)

9. Moses was worn out by the pressures of leadership (see Num. 11:11–15). The appointment of the chiefs is related in Exod. 18:13–27.

Thereupon Literally, "at that time."

11. Lest his audience think that he is complaining about their increase, Moses adds his hope that God will continue to enlarge their numbers.

the LORD, the God of your fathers Deuteronomy normally refers to God as "the LORD your God," and uses "God of your fathers" only when referring to the covenantal promises God made to the patriarchs.

12. The burden that prompted the appoint-

ment of officers was Moses' need to adjudicate legal disputes all day long (Exod. 18:13–18).

13. Pick In Exod. 18:13–23, the proposal to appoint judges was made by Jethro, Moses' father-in-law. In Numbers 11:11–17, it is God's suggestion. Here it is accounted to Moses. These sources reflect three different traditions. In Exodus and Numbers, Moses selects the candidates; here the people are asked to make the selection.

wise, discerning, and experienced In Exod. 18:21, the qualifications highlight moral qualities; here they emphasize intellectual traits. Deuteronomy regards justice and piety as expressions of wisdom (see 4:6,8).

15. The people recommended their tribal leaders, and Moses appointed them "heads," a term that refers to tribal leaders whose responsibilities include both military and judicial matters. Titles such as "chief of thousands" and "chief of hundreds" usually refer to military officers. Such integration of roles was common in tribal societies.

9. I cannot bear the burden Moses is aware that the era of teaching Torah is about to end and the era of doing battle to conquer the Land will soon begin. Realizing that he is no longer the right leader for the new era, he feels his strength diminish.

12. How can I bear unaided Hebrew:

eikhah essa l'vadi. Traditionally in public reading this verse is chanted to the plaintive melody for the Book of Lamentations (*Eikhah*). This *parashah* is always read on the *Shabbat* before *Tisha b'Av*, the fast day on which Lamentations is recited.

וְשֹׁטְרִים לְשִׁבְטֵיכֶם׃ 16 וָאֲצַוֶּה אֶת־
שֹׁפְטֵיכֶם בָּעֵת הַהִוא לֵאמֹר שָׁמֹעַ בֵּין־
אֲחֵיכֶם וּשְׁפַטְתֶּם צֶדֶק בֵּין־אִישׁ וּבֵין־
אָחִיו וּבֵין גֵּרוֹ׃ 17 לֹא־תַכִּירוּ פָנִים
בַּמִּשְׁפָּט כַּקָּטֹן כַּגָּדֹל תִּשְׁמָעוּן לֹא תָגוּרוּ
מִפְּנֵי־אִישׁ כִּי הַמִּשְׁפָּט לֵאלֹהִים הוּא
וְהַדָּבָר אֲשֶׁר יִקְשֶׁה מִכֶּם תַּקְרִבוּן אֵלַי
וּשְׁמַעְתִּיו׃ 18 וָאֲצַוֶּה אֶתְכֶם בָּעֵת הַהִוא
אֵת כָּל־הַדְּבָרִים אֲשֶׁר תַּעֲשׂוּן׃
19 וַנִּסַּע מֵחֹרֵב וַנֵּלֶךְ אֵת כָּל־הַמִּדְבָּר
הַגָּדוֹל וְהַנּוֹרָא הַהוּא אֲשֶׁר רְאִיתֶם דֶּרֶךְ
הַר הָאֱמֹרִי כַּאֲשֶׁר צִוָּה יְהוָה אֱלֹהֵינוּ

for your tribes. 16 I charged your magistrates at
that time as follows, "Hear out your fellow men,
and decide justly between any man and a fellow
Israelite or a stranger. 17 You shall not be partial
in judgment: hear out low and high alike. Fear
no man, for judgment is God's. And any matter
that is too difficult for you, you shall bring to
me and I will hear it." 18 Thus I instructed you,
at that time, about the various things that you
should do.

19 We set out from Horeb and traveled the
great and terrible wilderness that you saw, along
the road to the hill country of the Amorites, as
the LORD our God had commanded us. When

16. In the ancient Near East it was traditional to address a charge to newly appointed judges, either at the time of their appointment or in codes defining their responsibilities.

Hear Idiomatic for "try a case," as in the English "hear a case."

fellow men Literally, "brothers," meaning fellow Israelites. Deuteronomy regularly uses this term to emphasize the equality and fraternity of all Israelites, whether king or servant, prophet or priest.

stranger Hebrew: *ger.* The resident alien, the non-Israelite residing among Israelites. This law protects the right of a *ger* to a fair trial.

17. Moses will not function as an appellate judge but will take over cases that lower judges find too difficult to decide, including those in which the law is not known and Moses has to consult God (e.g., Lev. 24:10–23; Num. 9:1–14).

for judgment is God's The judge is the representative of God who, as lawgiver, is concerned about justice.

18. At that time Shortly before the Israelites left Sinai. This verse refers to instructions addressed to the entire people (see Exod. 18:20). Teaching the laws to the entire citizenry is virtually unparalleled in other ancient cultures. Because Israel's primary duty to God is obedience to His laws, it is imperative that every Israelite be taught those laws. This is Moses' main goal in Deuteronomy.

ARRIVAL AT THE PROMISED LAND (vv. 19–21)

19. The route through the wilderness is described in detail in Num. 10:33, 11:35, 12:16, and 33:16ff.

the great and terrible wilderness The Sinai Peninsula, a land "with its *seraph* serpents and scorpions, a parched land with no water in it" (Deut. 8:15).

road to the hill country A road leading from Horeb to Kadesh-barnea, on the southern border of the Promised Land (Num. 34:4). The precise route is unknown.

as the LORD our God had commanded us The initial response of the Israelites to God's command had been obedience, and as a result they reached their destination.

---

16. Hear out The first obligation of a judge is to listen to all sides. This is embodied in Jewish law by the requirement that both litigants be present when either states his or her case (BT Sanh. 7b).

17. low and high alike The judge must not only treat prominent and unknown individuals alike but also treat major and minor cases with equal seriousness (BT Sanh. 8a). What may seem trivial to a judge compared to other cases under adjudication is nonetheless important to the litigants (see Exod. 23:3).

HALAKHAH L'MA·ASEH

1:17. Not only must rich and poor be judged alike but, contrary to American law, cases involving major and minor amounts of money or penalties also must be treated equally (BT Sanh. 8a). See Exod. 23:3.

we reached Kadesh-barnea, ²⁰I said to you, "You have come to the hill country of the Amorites which the LORD our God is giving to us. ²¹See, the LORD your God has placed the land at your disposal. Go up, take possession, as the LORD, the God of your fathers, promised you. Fear not and be not dismayed."

²²Then all of you came to me and said, "Let us send men ahead to reconnoiter the land for us and bring back word on the route we shall follow and the cities we shall come to." ²³I approved of the plan, and so I selected twelve of your men, one from each tribe. ²⁴They made for the hill country, came to the wadi Eshcol, and spied it out. ²⁵They took some of the fruit of the land with them and brought it down to us. And they gave us this report: "It is a good land that the LORD our God is giving to us."

²⁶Yet you refused to go up, and flouted the command of the LORD your God. ²⁷You sulked in your tents and said, "It is because the LORD hates us that He brought us out of the land of

אֹתָ֛נוּ וַנָּבֹ֖א עַ֣ד קָדֵ֥שׁ בַּרְנֵֽעַ׃ 20 וָאֹמַ֖ר אֲלֵכֶ֑ם בָּאתֶם֙ עַד־הַ֣ר הָאֱמֹרִ֔י אֲשֶׁר־יְהֹוָ֥ה אֱלֹהֵ֖ינוּ נֹתֵ֥ן לָֽנוּ׃ 21 רְ֠אֵ֠ה נָתַ֨ן יְהֹוָ֧ה אֱלֹהֶ֛יךָ לְפָנֶ֖יךָ אֶת־הָאָ֑רֶץ עֲלֵ֣ה רֵ֗שׁ כַּאֲשֶׁר֩ דִּבֶּ֨ר יְהֹוָ֜ה אֱלֹהֵ֤י אֲבֹתֶ֙יךָ֙ לָ֔ךְ אַל־תִּירָ֖א וְאַל־ תֵּחָֽת׃

שלישי 22 וַתִּקְרְב֣וּן אֵלַי֮ כֻּלְּכֶם֒ וַתֹּאמְר֗וּ נִשְׁלְחָ֤ה אֲנָשִׁים֙ לְפָנֵ֔ינוּ וְיַחְפְּרוּ־לָ֖נוּ אֶת־הָאָ֑רֶץ וְיָשִׁ֣בוּ אֹתָ֗נוּ דָּבָ֔ר אֶת־הַדֶּ֙רֶךְ֙ אֲשֶׁ֣ר נַֽעֲלֶה־ בָּ֔הּ וְאֵת֙ הֶֽעָרִ֔ים אֲשֶׁ֥ר נָבֹ֖א אֲלֵיהֶֽן׃ 23 וַיִּיטַ֥ב בְּעֵינַ֖י הַדָּבָ֑ר וָאֶקַּ֤ח מִכֶּם֙ שְׁנֵ֣ים עָשָׂ֣ר אֲנָשִׁ֔ים אִ֥ישׁ אֶחָ֖ד לַשָּֽׁבֶט׃ 24 וַיִּפְנוּ֙ וַיַּֽעֲל֣וּ הָהָ֔רָה וַיָּבֹ֖אוּ עַד־נַ֣חַל אֶשְׁכֹּ֑ל וַֽיְרַגְּל֖וּ אֹתָֽהּ׃ 25 וַיִּקְח֤וּ בְיָדָם֙ מִפְּרִ֣י הָאָ֔רֶץ וַיּוֹרִ֖דוּ אֵלֵ֑ינוּ וַיָּשִׁ֨בוּ אֹתָ֤נוּ דָבָר֙ וַיֹּ֣אמְר֔וּ טוֹבָ֣ה הָאָ֔רֶץ אֲשֶׁר־יְהֹוָ֥ה אֱלֹהֵ֖ינוּ נֹתֵ֥ן לָֽנוּ׃ 26 וְלֹ֥א אֲבִיתֶ֖ם לַעֲלֹ֑ת וַתַּמְר֕וּ אֶת־פִּ֥י יְהֹוָ֖ה אֱלֹהֵיכֶֽם׃ 27 וַתֵּרָגְנ֤וּ בְאׇהֳלֵיכֶם֙ וַתֹּ֣אמְר֔וּ בְּשִׂנְאַ֤ת יְהֹוָה֙ אֹתָ֔נוּ הוֹצִיאָ֖נוּ

20. hill country of the Amorites Seems to refer to the Promised Land as a whole, just as the term "Amorites" sometimes designates its entire population, perhaps because these highlands became the Israelite heartland.

The LORD our God is giving to us At this very moment.

21. as the LORD . . . promised you This formula (attested also in Akkadian and Aramaic documents) assures Moses' listeners of success. God had promised that the same generation that experienced the Exodus would receive the land (Exod. 3:8,17, 6:8).

Fear not and be not dismayed This formula usually expresses assurance, although it is phrased as an imperative. Here it is based on the promise to which Moses has just alluded.

THE PEOPLE'S REFUSAL TO PROCEED
(vv. 22–33)

22. reconnoiter Explore the land and its resources. Information about the land is important both for strategic military purposes and for preparing to settle in it.

bring back word on the route . . . and the

cities That is, the scouts themselves should determine the best route and the order in which the cities should be attacked, or that they should obtain information about possible routes (such as which are narrow and dangerous) and the fortifications of the cities.

23. Named in Num. 13:2–16, where they are described as tribal chieftains.

24. wadi Eshcol "The wadi of the grape cluster(s)." Moses singles out this place, because it is where the scouts found the grapes that typified the land's fertility and where they saw the giants who so terrified the Israelites that they refused to enter the land.

25. some of the fruit of the land The "grapes, some pomegranates, and figs," which serve as evidence that the land is good (Num. 13:23,27).

good Rich in produce and other natural resources.

27. sulked Better: "grumbled."

in your tents At night (Num. 14:1).

the LORD hates us Literally, "hatred of the LORD for us," a word order that emphasizes the people's perversity and ingratitude. (In the Bible,

Egypt, to hand us over to the Amorites to wipe
us out. 28 What kind of place are we going to?
Our kinsmen have taken the heart out of us, saying, 'We saw there a people stronger and taller
than we, large cities with walls sky-high, and
even Anakites.'"

29 I said to you, "Have no dread or fear of
them. 30 None other than the LORD your God,
who goes before you, will fight for you, just as
He did for you in Egypt before your very eyes,
31 and in the wilderness, where you saw how the
LORD your God carried you, as a man carries
his son, all the way that you traveled until you
came to this place. 32 Yet for all that, you have
no faith in the LORD your God, 33 who goes before you on your journeys—to scout the place
where you are to encamp—in fire by night and
in cloud by day, in order to guide you on the
route you are to follow."

מֵאֶרֶץ מִצְרָיִם לָתֵת אֹתָנוּ בְּיַד הָאֱמֹרִי
לְהַשְׁמִידֵנוּ׃ 28 אָנָה ׀ אֲנַחְנוּ עֹלִים אַחֵינוּ
הֵמַסּוּ אֶת־לְבָבֵנוּ לֵאמֹר עַם גָּדוֹל וָרָם
מִמֶּנּוּ עָרִים גְּדֹלֹת וּבְצוּרֹת בַּשָּׁמָיִם וְגַם־
בְּנֵי עֲנָקִים רָאִינוּ שָׁם׃
29 וָאֹמַר אֲלֵכֶם לֹא־תַעַרְצוּן וְלֹא־תִירְאוּן
מֵהֶם׃ 30 יְהוָה אֱלֹהֵיכֶם הַהֹלֵךְ לִפְנֵיכֶם
הוּא יִלָּחֵם לָכֶם כְּכֹל אֲשֶׁר עָשָׂה אִתְּכֶם
בְּמִצְרַיִם לְעֵינֵיכֶם׃ 31 וּבַמִּדְבָּר אֲשֶׁר
רָאִיתָ אֲשֶׁר נְשָׂאֲךָ יְהוָה אֱלֹהֶיךָ כַּאֲשֶׁר
יִשָּׂא־אִישׁ אֶת־בְּנוֹ בְּכָל־הַדֶּרֶךְ אֲשֶׁר
הֲלַכְתֶּם עַד־בֹּאֲכֶם עַד־הַמָּקוֹם הַזֶּה׃
32 וּבַדָּבָר הַזֶּה אֵינְכֶם מַאֲמִינִם בַּיהוָה
אֱלֹהֵיכֶם׃ 33 הַהֹלֵךְ לִפְנֵיכֶם בַּדֶּרֶךְ לָתוּר
לָכֶם מָקוֹם לַחֲנֹתְכֶם בָּאֵשׁ ׀ לַיְלָה
לַרְאֹתְכֶם בַּדֶּרֶךְ אֲשֶׁר תֵּלְכוּ־בָהּ וּבֶעָנָן
יוֹמָם׃

clauses normally start with a verb; any other word that appears at the beginning has thus been singled out for emphasis.)

28. What kind of place Suggesting that the land is flawed. This aspersion is another illustration of the people's perversity, for the goodness of the land of Israel is practically an article of faith in the Bible.

Our kinsmen That is, the scouts. Referring to them as kinsmen emphasizes their credibility in the people's eyes.

taller than we The legendary height of the Amorites was later recalled by the prophet Amos (2:9), who describes them as having been tall as cedars and stout as oaks.

walls sky-high Canaanite cities were built on tells (mounds atop the remains of settlements) that were often founded on natural hills. Their walls must indeed have looked sky-high to people who had been living in the wilderness. In similar fashion, an Assyrian inscription describes an Israelite city as "reaching the sky."

Anakites A particularly gigantic group, next to whom the scouts felt like grasshoppers (Num. 13:32–33). It is quite possible that there were some exceptionally tall people in the area. Two 7-foot female skeletons have been found in a 12th-century B.C.E. cemetery on the east bank of the Jordan, at Tell es-Sa'idiyeh.

30. who goes before you That is, the vanguard (advance guard), protecting those who follow.

will fight for you, just as He did in Egypt At the Sea of Reeds (Exod. 14:14,25).

31. and in the wilderness God protected Israel from the Amalekites (Exod. 17:8–16) and from the natural dangers of the wilderness (8:15).

this place Kadesh-barnea.

33. The people ignore the evidence of God's care and guidance, although it is never out of their sight. The cloud and the fire have been constant, visible signs of God's presence since the day they left Egypt.

---

27. the LORD hates us We often attribute to others our own feelings about them. The Israelites may have been ambivalent in their feelings about God, often resenting the demands that God placed on them, and they assumed that God had equally negative feelings toward them. One *midrash* imagines them saying: "If God really loved us, God would have given us the land of Egypt and sent the Egyptians into the wilderness" (Rashi).

³⁴When the Lord heard your loud complaint, He was angry. He vowed: ³⁵Not one of these men, this evil generation, shall see the good land that I swore to give to your fathers—³⁶none except Caleb son of Jephunneh; he shall see it, and to him and his descendants will I give the land on which he set foot, because he remained loyal to the Lord.

³⁷Because of you the Lord was incensed with me too, and He said: You shall not enter it either. ³⁸Joshua son of Nun, who attends you, he shall enter it. Imbue him with strength, for he shall allot it to Israel. ³⁹Moreover, your little ones who you said would be carried off, your children who do not yet know good from bad, they shall enter it; to them will I give it and they shall possess it. ⁴⁰As for you, turn about and march into the wilderness by the way of the Sea of Reeds.

³⁴ וַיִּשְׁמַ֥ע יְהֹוָ֖ה אֶת־ק֣וֹל דִּבְרֵיכֶ֑ם וַיִּקְצֹ֖ף וַיִּשָּׁבַ֥ע לֵאמֹֽר׃ ³⁵ אִם־יִרְאֶ֥ה אִישׁ֙ בָּאֲנָשִׁ֣ים הָאֵ֔לֶּה הַדּ֥וֹר הָרָ֖ע הַזֶּ֑ה אֵ֚ת הָאָ֣רֶץ הַטּוֹבָ֔ה אֲשֶׁ֣ר נִשְׁבַּ֔עְתִּי לָתֵ֖ת לַאֲבֹתֵיכֶֽם׃ ³⁶ זֽוּלָתִ֞י כָּלֵ֣ב בֶּן־יְפֻנֶּ֗ה ה֣וּא יִרְאֶ֔נָּה וְלֽוֹ־אֶתֵּ֧ן אֶת־הָאָ֛רֶץ אֲשֶׁ֥ר דָּֽרַךְ־בָּ֖הּ וּלְבָנָ֑יו יַ֕עַן אֲשֶׁ֥ר מִלֵּ֖א אַחֲרֵ֥י יְהֹוָֽה׃ ³⁷ גַּם־בִּי֙ הִתְאַנַּ֣ף יְהֹוָ֔ה בִּגְלַלְכֶ֖ם לֵאמֹ֑ר גַּם־אַתָּ֖ה לֹא־תָבֹ֥א שָֽׁם׃ ³⁸ יְהוֹשֻׁ֤עַ בִּן־נוּן֙ הָעֹמֵ֣ד לְפָנֶ֔יךָ ה֖וּא יָ֣בֹא שָׁ֑מָּה אֹת֣וֹ חַזֵּ֔ק כִּי־ה֖וּא יַנְחִלֶ֥נָּה אֶת־יִשְׂרָאֵֽל׃ רביעי ³⁹ וְטַפְּכֶם֩ אֲשֶׁ֨ר אֲמַרְתֶּ֜ם לָבַ֣ז יִהְיֶ֗ה וּבְנֵיכֶ֡ם אֲשֶׁ֣ר לֹא־יָֽדְעוּ֩ הַיּוֹם֙ ט֣וֹב וָרָ֔ע הֵ֖מָּה יָבֹ֣אוּ שָׁ֑מָּה וְלָהֶ֣ם אֶתְּנֶ֔נָּה וְהֵ֖ם יִֽירָשֽׁוּהָ׃ ⁴⁰ וְאַתֶּ֖ם פְּנ֣וּ לָכֶ֑ם וּסְע֥וּ הַמִּדְבָּ֖רָה דֶּ֥רֶךְ יַם־סֽוּף׃

THE PEOPLE'S ABOUT-FACE (vv. 34–41)

Moses' plea to the people fell on deaf ears. According to Num. 14:11–20, God would have destroyed the entire generation and replaced them with Moses' descendants, had Moses not persuaded Him to be lenient.

34. your loud complaint According to Num. 14:11 and 22, it was the people's lack of faith in God that provoked His ire.

He vowed That is, God swore, echoing verse 8. This generation's rejection of the sworn Land is met by a new swearing that now deprives them of it.

35. this evil generation Refers to males who were 20 and older at the time of the incident (Num. 14:29, 32:11), spoken of as warriors (i.e., men of military age) in Deut. 2:14,16. The phrase here contrasts with "the good land" and suggests the fitness of the decree: An evil generation may not enter a good land.

36. Caleb, a leader of the tribe of Judah (Num. 13:6), is exempted from the decree because he kept his faith that the Lord would enable Israel to overcome the Amorites and pleaded with the people to remain faithful (Num. 13:30, 14:6–9). According to Num. 14:6 and other passages, Joshua joined Caleb in this plea.

the land on which he set foot Hebron.

37. Although Moses does not specify what provoked God's anger at him, there is an implication here that somehow it was connected with the rebellion. The plain sense of the passage seems to be that Moses, personally blameless, was caught up in God's anger at his contemporaries. Possibly this was due to Moses' acceding to the people's request for scouts. Even if that request did not imply a lack of faith in God initially, it eventually led to the people's loss of faith. Perhaps Moses was held accountable for the consequences of their initiative because he had approved it.

38. Joshua, Moses' aide (see Exod. 24:13), is his natural successor. His fitness is indicated in Num. 27:18 where he is described as "an inspired man," a man moved by the spirit of God. Joshua's prior military experience also prepares him to lead Israel in the coming wars (Exod. 17:8–13).

Joshua Hebrew: Y'hoshu·a. The name probably means "the Lord (y'ho) is a noble (shu·a)."

allot Joshua will assign each of the tribes and clans its territory.

39. Here God's address to the people is resumed.

who you said would be carried off See Num. 14:3.

your children who do not yet know good from bad Therefore, they cannot be held accountable for the rebellion. The parallel passages in Numbers indicate that this refers to children below the age of 20.

40. God's reversal of His promise is now made real. At the very border of the Promised Land the people are sent back into the wilderness from which they had just come. Thus the journey

41You replied to me, saying, "We stand guilty
before the LORD. We will go up now and fight,
just as the LORD our God commanded us." And
you all girded yourselves with war gear and
recklessly started for the hill country. 42But the
LORD said to me, "Warn them: Do not go up
and do not fight, since I am not in your midst;
else you will be routed by your enemies." 43I
spoke to you, but you would not listen; you
flouted the LORD's command and willfully
marched into the hill country. 44Then the
Amorites who lived in those hills came out
against you like so many bees and chased you,
and they crushed you at Hormah in Seir.
45Again you wept before the LORD; but the LORD
would not heed your cry or give ear to you.

41 וַתַּעֲנוּ ׀ וַתֹּאמְרוּ אֵלַי חָטָאנוּ לַיהוָה
אֲנַחְנוּ נַעֲלֶה וְנִלְחַמְנוּ כְּכֹל אֲשֶׁר־צִוָּנוּ
יְהוָה אֱלֹהֵינוּ וַתַּחְגְּרוּ אִישׁ אֶת־כְּלֵי
מִלְחַמְתּוֹ וַתָּהִינוּ לַעֲלֹת הָהָרָה׃ 42 וַיֹּאמֶר
יְהוָה אֵלַי אֱמֹר לָהֶם לֹא תַעֲלוּ וְלֹא־
תִלָּחֲמוּ כִּי אֵינֶנִּי בְּקִרְבְּכֶם וְלֹא תִּנָּגְפוּ
לִפְנֵי אֹיְבֵיכֶם׃ 43 וָאֲדַבֵּר אֲלֵיכֶם וְלֹא
שְׁמַעְתֶּם וַתַּמְרוּ אֶת־פִּי יְהוָה וַתָּזִדוּ
וַתַּעֲלוּ הָהָרָה׃ 44 וַיֵּצֵא הָאֱמֹרִי הַיֹּשֵׁב
בָּהָר הַהוּא לִקְרַאתְכֶם וַיִּרְדְּפוּ אֶתְכֶם
כַּאֲשֶׁר תַּעֲשֶׂינָה הַדְּבֹרִים וַיַּכְּתוּ אֶתְכֶם
בְּשֵׂעִיר עַד־חָרְמָה׃ 45 וַתָּשֻׁבוּ וַתִּבְכּוּ לִפְנֵי
יְהוָה וְלֹא־שָׁמַע יְהוָה בְּקֹלְכֶם וְלֹא הֶאֱזִין
אֲלֵיכֶם׃

2 46Thus, after you had remained at Kadesh
all that long time, 1we marched back into

ב 46 וַתֵּשְׁבוּ בְקָדֵשׁ יָמִים רַבִּים כַּיָּמִים
אֲשֶׁר יְשַׁבְתֶּם׃ 1 וַנֵּפֶן וַנִּסַּע הַמִּדְבָּרָה

"through the great and terrible wilderness" was for naught.

by the way of the Sea of Reeds That is, "on the road to the Sea of Reeds," which led from Kadesh-barnea to the Gulf of Aqaba. The "Sea of Reeds" refers both to the sea the Israelites crossed when leaving Egypt and to the Gulf of Aqaba. The latter is meant here, because the Israelites never returned to the former.

41. The people's response to God's decree seems one of contrition, but in fact it is as rebellious as their reaction to the original command. When ordered to "turn about and march" and "go up" to the land (vv. 7,21) they "refused to go up" (v. 26). Now that they are commanded to "turn about and march" away from the land, they respond "we will go up" to the land.

We will go up It is we who will go up, not the next generation, contrary to God's decree.

GOD RETURNS THE PEOPLE TO THE WILDERNESS (1:42–2:1)

42. The people believed that God would not enforce His decree if they reversed themselves. God makes His intentions explicit, countermanding both the people's declaration that they would go up and fight (v. 41) and His own earlier command (v. 21).

I am not in your midst The Israelites, believing that God was still in their midst, were certain of their ability to overcome militarily superior enemies. Indeed, Moses had reminded them of God's presence when they refused to go up and fight. Ironically, it is only after God withdraws from their midst that they insist on going.

43. An ironic contrast with verse 26: "you refused to go up [into the hill country], and flouted the command of the LORD." The similar wording highlights the people's stubborn contrariness.

44. By their own action, the Israelites had brought about the disaster they had feared (v. 27): defeat at the hands of the Amorites.

Amorites Here, a general designation for all the natives of the Promised Land.

bees Wild honeybees of the type found in ancient Israel. Similar remarks relating to bees are found in Mesopotamian and Greek sources.

45. Again you wept Having swung from despair to overconfidence (vv. 27–28,41), the people's mood swung back to grief.

46. Literally, "And you remained at Kadesh many days, like the days that you remained." "Many days" can refer to periods of a few days or of many years. The translation implies that "you remained at Kadesh" refers to the time up through the return from battle, with no further delay there.

2:1. In their first act of obedience since leaving Horeb, the Israelites leave Kadesh-barnea and return to the wilderness, as commanded in 1:40.

long time Literally, "many days." Nearly 38 years (see 2:14).

the wilderness by the way of the Sea of Reeds,
as the LORD had spoken to me, and skirted the
hill country of Seir a long time.
2 Then the LORD said to me: 3 You have been
skirting this hill country long enough; now turn
north. 4 And charge the people as follows: You
will be passing through the territory of your
kinsmen, the descendants of Esau, who live in
Seir. Though they will be afraid of you, be very
careful 5 not to provoke them. For I will not give
you of their land so much as a foot can tread
on; I have given the hill country of Seir as a pos-

דֶּרֶךְ יַם־סוּף כַּאֲשֶׁר דִּבֶּר יְהוָה אֵלָי וַנָּסָב
אֶת־הַר־שֵׂעִיר יָמִים רַבִּים׃ ס
חמישי 2 וַיֹּאמֶר יְהוָה אֵלַי לֵאמֹר׃ 3 רַב־לָכֶם סֹב
אֶת־הָהָר הַזֶּה פְּנוּ לָכֶם צָפֹנָה׃ 4 וְאֶת־
הָעָם צַו לֵאמֹר אַתֶּם עֹבְרִים בִּגְבוּל
אֲחֵיכֶם בְּנֵי־עֵשָׂו הַיֹּשְׁבִים בְּשֵׂעִיר וְיִירְאוּ
מִכֶּם וְנִשְׁמַרְתֶּם מְאֹד׃ 5 אַל־תִּתְגָּרוּ בָם
כִּי לֹא־אֶתֵּן לָכֶם מֵאַרְצָם עַד מִדְרַךְ
כַּף־רָגֶל כִּי־יְרֻשָּׁה לְעֵשָׂו נָתַתִּי אֶת־הַר

ISRAEL OBEYS THE SECOND COMMAND TO PROCEED TO THE PROMISED LAND (2:2–3:29)

God begins to move the Israelites into a position from which they can enter the Promised Land as soon as the previous generation has died out. Instead of entering directly from the wilderness in the south, as they could have done 38 years earlier, the Israelites must now approach from the east. This route requires them to pass five states that run the length of Transjordan, from south to north: Edom, Moab, Ammon, and the Amorite kingdoms of Sihon and Og.

PASSING THROUGH SEIR (vv. 2–8)

The first stage of the northward march through Transjordan takes the Israelites through part of the territory of Seir-Edom, east of the Negev highlands. Inhabitants there were seminomads, as indicated by Egyptian inscriptions of the 13th century B.C.E. and the paucity of archaeological evidence of a sedentary population.

3. This command was uttered near the end of the last year of the wanderings in the wilderness, as is evident from verse 7, which states that they were in their 40th year.

turn north To judge from verse 8, the Israelites were now at the southern tip of Seir-Edom, near Elath and Ezion-geber.

4. the descendants of Esau The Edomites, descendants of Jacob's brother and hence the Israelites' kinsmen (see Gen. 36).

Seir Because the territory about to be traversed is south of Moab (see vv. 3,8), Seir refers here to the eastern part of Seir-Edom, either the part in the 'Arabah or the part in the highlands farther east. Eastern Seir-Edom extended northward for 100 miles (160 km) from the Gulf of Aqaba to the southern end of the Dead Sea and wadi Zered.

afraid of you The prospect of a huge population and its cattle traversing their territory would be alarming.

5. The verse expresses one of the pervasive themes of this chapter: God gave the Edomites their land, just as He is about to give the Israelites theirs. The same is said of the lands of the Moabites and Ammonites in verses 9 and 19. Their right to their lands must be respected.

CHAPTER 2

4–5. Until now, Israel's encounters with other nations have been uniformly negative: enslavement in Egypt and war with Amalek, Sihon, and Og. Once they settle in the Land, however, they will have to live at peace with neighboring nations. That will require their learning to see the descendants of Esau as "your kinsmen." Perhaps regarding them as kinsmen will even turn them into friendlier, more cooperative neighbors.

be very careful not to provoke them Your ancestors had to deal with feelings of weakness and inadequacy when confronting the Canaanites. You will have to deal with the moral challenge of not abusing your superior power in dealing with weaker peoples (N. Leibowitz).

I have given . . . as a possession to Esau God's special relationship to Israel does not

שֵׂעִיר׃ 6 אֹכֶל תִּשְׁבְּרוּ מֵאִתָּם בַּכֶּסֶף
וַאֲכַלְתֶּם וְגַם־מַיִם תִּכְרוּ מֵאִתָּם בַּכֶּסֶף
וּשְׁתִיתֶם׃ 7 כִּי יְהוָה אֱלֹהֶיךָ בֵּרַכְךָ בְּכֹל
מַעֲשֵׂה יָדֶךָ יָדַע לֶכְתְּךָ אֶת־הַמִּדְבָּר הַגָּדֹל
הַזֶּה זֶה ׀ אַרְבָּעִים שָׁנָה יְהוָה אֱלֹהֶיךָ
עִמָּךְ לֹא חָסַרְתָּ דָּבָר׃
8 וַנַּעֲבֹר מֵאֵת אַחֵינוּ בְנֵי־עֵשָׂו הַיֹּשְׁבִים
בְּשֵׂעִיר מִדֶּרֶךְ הָעֲרָבָה מֵאֵילַת וּמֵעֶצְיֹן
גָּבֶר* ס וַנֵּפֶן וַנַּעֲבֹר דֶּרֶךְ מִדְבַּר מוֹאָב׃
9 וַיֹּאמֶר יְהוָה אֵלַי אַל־תָּצַר אֶת־מוֹאָב
וְאַל־תִּתְגָּר בָּם מִלְחָמָה כִּי לֹא־אֶתֵּן לְךָ
מֵאַרְצוֹ יְרֻשָּׁה כִּי לִבְנֵי־לוֹט נָתַתִּי אֶת־עָר
יְרֻשָּׁה׃

session to Esau. 6What food you eat you shall
obtain from them for money; even the water
you drink you shall procure from them for
money. 7Indeed, the LORD your God has blessed
you in all your undertakings. He has watched
over your wanderings through this great wilderness; the LORD your God has been with you
these past forty years: you have lacked nothing.
8We then moved on, away from our kinsmen,
the descendants of Esau, who live in Seir, away
from the road of the Arabah, away from Elath
and Ezion-geber; and we marched on in the
direction of the wilderness of Moab. 9And the
LORD said to me: Do not harass the Moabites
or provoke them to war. For I will not give you
any of their land as a possession; I have assigned
Ar as a possession to the descendants of Lot.—

v. 8. פיסקא באמצע פסוק

6. The seminomadic Edomites were able to supply produce and water. Abraham and Isaac, also seminomads, dug wells, and Isaac engaged in agriculture (Gen. 21:30, 26:12,18–22). Seminomads in the Negeb today still engage in agriculture.

7. blessed you in all your undertakings Made you prosperous in every way. The prosperity of the Israelites explains why they are able to pay the Edomites.

8. The Israelites first traveled north through Seir-Edom along "the road of the Arabah" (presumably, a road running the length of the 'Arabah) to its northern end, and then turned east onto a road leading to the wilderness east of Moab.

Elath and Ezion-geber These two sites on the Gulf of Aqaba later served as ports.

PASSING THROUGH MOAB (vv. 9–16)

The next stage of the march through Transjordan took the Israelites through Moab in the highlands east of the Dead Sea. Entering Moab marked a turning point, for by then the last of the wilderness generation, those who had rebelled at Kadesh-barnea, had died out.

9. The territory of Moab at this time consisted of the southern half of the high tablelands east of the Dead Sea. The earliest references to Moab are found in Egyptian documents of the 13th century B.C.E. Archaeological investigation shows that in Moab, unlike in Edom, there were some settlements.

Ar A town or a region in Moab.

descendants of Lot The Moabites were also kin to the Israelites, although not as close as the Edomites. They were traced back to Abraham's nephew, as were the Ammonites (v. 19; see also Gen. 19:30–38).

10–12. This is the first of several parenthetic notes describing the prehistory of neighboring lands. The others appear in verses 20–23 and in 3:9,11,13. The notes indicate that Transjordan and Philistia once had been inhabited by earlier populations who were supplanted by the Edomites, Moabites, Ammonites, and Philistines, just as the land promised to the Israelites was inhabited by peoples whom they would supplant. Because verse 12 refers to Israel's conquest of the Promised Land in the past tense, modern scholars regard these notes as having been added to the text after the conquest. The purpose of these notes, apparently, is to underscore God's ability to fulfill His promise to Israel to give it the land of Canaan.

---

preclude a benevolent involvement in the affairs of other nations (Hirsch). Esau, despite his many flaws, scrupulously obeyed the commandment to honor his father. As a reward, God promises that his territory will be handed down from father to son (Deut. R. 1:15).

10 It was formerly inhabited by the Emim, a people great and numerous, and as tall as the Anakites. 11 Like the Anakites, they are counted as Rephaim; but the Moabites call them Emim. 12 Similarly, Seir was formerly inhabited by the Horites; but the descendants of Esau dispossessed them, wiping them out and settling in their place, just as Israel did in the land they were to possess, which the LORD had given to them.—

13 Up now! Cross the wadi Zered!

So we crossed the wadi Zered. 14 The time that we spent in travel from Kadesh-barnea until we crossed the wadi Zered was thirty-eight years, until that whole generation of warriors had perished from the camp, as the LORD had sworn concerning them. 15 Indeed, the hand of the LORD struck them, to root them out from the camp to the last man.

10 הָאֵמִ֥ים לְפָנִ֖ים יָ֣שְׁבוּ בָ֑הּ עַ֣ם גָּד֥וֹל
וְרַ֛ב וָרָ֖ם כָּעֲנָקִֽים׃ 11 רְפָאִ֛ים יֵחָשְׁב֥וּ
אַף־הֵ֖ם כָּעֲנָקִ֑ים וְהַמֹּ֣אָבִ֔ים יִקְרְא֥וּ לָהֶ֖ם
אֵמִֽים׃ 12 וּבְשֵׂעִ֞יר יָשְׁב֣וּ הַחֹרִים֮ לְפָנִים֒
וּבְנֵ֧י עֵשָׂ֣ו יִֽירָשׁ֗וּם וַיַּשְׁמִידוּם֙ מִפְּנֵיהֶ֔ם
וַיֵּשְׁב֖וּ תַּחְתָּ֑ם כַּאֲשֶׁ֣ר עָשָׂ֣ה יִשְׂרָאֵ֗ל
לְאֶ֙רֶץ֙ יְרֻשָּׁת֔וֹ אֲשֶׁר־נָתַ֥ן יְהוָ֖ה לָהֶֽם׃
13 עַתָּ֗ה קֻ֛מוּ וְעִבְר֥וּ לָכֶ֖ם אֶת־נַ֣חַל זָ֑רֶד
וַנַּעֲבֹ֖ר אֶת־נַ֥חַל זָֽרֶד׃ 14 וְהַיָּמִ֞ים אֲשֶׁר־
הָלַ֣כְנוּ ׀ מִקָּדֵ֣שׁ בַּרְנֵ֗עַ עַ֤ד אֲשֶׁר־עָבַ֙רְנוּ֙
אֶת־נַ֣חַל זֶ֔רֶד שְׁלֹשִׁ֥ים וּשְׁמֹנֶ֖ה שָׁנָ֑ה עַד־
תֹּ֨ם כָּל־הַדּ֜וֹר אַנְשֵׁ֤י הַמִּלְחָמָה֙ מִקֶּ֣רֶב
הַֽמַּחֲנֶ֔ה כַּאֲשֶׁ֛ר נִשְׁבַּ֥ע יְהוָ֖ה לָהֶֽם׃ 15 וְגַ֤ם
יַד־יְהוָה֙ הָ֣יְתָה בָּ֔ם לְהֻמָּ֖ם מִקֶּ֣רֶב הַֽמַּחֲנֶ֑ה
עַ֖ד תֻּמָּֽם׃

It The land of Moab, not only Ar; all the parentethtic notes refer to entire lands.

Rephaim The generic name or epithet of the gigantic aborigines. Local peoples had different names for them. To the Moabites they were the Emim; to the Ammonites, the Zamzummim. The Rephaim are also listed among the pre-Israelite peoples living in the Promised Land (Gen. 15:20; Josh. 17:15). Their great height is indicated by the size of Og's bedstead (Deut. 3:11), by Goliath's size and that of his weapons (1 Sam. 17:4–7), and by the size of the weapons of their descendants in Philistia (2 Sam. 21:16–22).

Horites A people who preceded the Edomites in Seir. According to Gen. 14:6 and 36:20–30, the Edomites were descended from Seir the Horite.

wiping them out As verses 21–22 make clear, God made this happen.

13. wadi Zered The southern boundary of Moab.

THE END OF THE EXODUS GENERATION (vv. 14–16)

These verses mark the transition between the generation of the Exodus (who had rebelled at Kadesh-barnea) and the generation that would enter the Promised Land. With the crossing of wadi Zered, God's oath (1:35) was fulfilled: All those of age when the Israelites refused to proceed to the land had died. The transition is noted at this point because they now entered Moab, which would be the springboard for their conquests: From it, they would march on the kingdoms of Sihon and Og and then on the Promised Land itself.

14. thirty-eight years Because the Israelites left Kadesh-barnea during the 2nd year after the Exodus, they must have crossed wadi Zered in the 40th year, before Moses began this address on the first day of the 11th month.

warriors Those of age for the military.

15. hand of the LORD struck them Not all of the previous generation died of natural causes. Some were killed by destructive forces unleashed by God, such as pestilence, because of various sins.

to root them out The verb המם is usually used in military contexts to describe the confusion that God inflicts on Israel's enemies (see 7:23; Exod. 14:24). It means "to throw into chaos" and

---

14. generation of warriors Literally, "people of battle." Ironically, that name is given to those who quarreled constantly with God and with Moses in the wilderness—not to their children, who will actually conquer the Promised Land. Ultimately, Israel's quarrels with God and with each other prove a greater obstacle than any external foe.

16When all the warriors among the people had died off, 17the LORD spoke to me, saying: 18You are now passing through the territory of Moab, through Ar. 19You will then be close to the Ammonites; do not harass them or start a fight with them. For I will not give any part of the land of the Ammonites to you as a possession; I have assigned it as a possession to the descendants of Lot.—

20It, too, is counted as Rephaim country. It was formerly inhabited by Rephaim, whom the Ammonites call Zamzummim, 21a people great and numerous and as tall as the Anakites. The LORD wiped them out, so that [the Ammonites] dispossessed them and settled in their place, 22as He did for the descendants of Esau who live in Seir, when He wiped out the Horites before them, so that they dispossessed them and settled in their place, as is still the case. 23So, too, with the Avvim who dwelt in villages in the vicinity of Gaza: the Caphtorim, who came from Crete, wiped them out and settled in their place.—

16 וַיְהִ֣י כַאֲשֶׁר־תַּ֗מּוּ כׇּל־אַנְשֵׁ֛י הַמִּלְחָמָ֖ה לָמ֑וּת מִקֶּ֖רֶב הָעָֽם: ס 17 וַיְדַבֵּ֥ר יְהֹוָ֖ה אֵלַ֥י לֵאמֹֽר: 18 אַתָּ֨ה עֹבֵ֥ר הַיּ֛וֹם אֶת־גְּב֥וּל מוֹאָ֖ב אֶת־עָֽר: 19 וְקָרַבְתָּ֗ מ֚וּל בְּנֵ֣י עַמּ֔וֹן אַל־תְּצֻרֵ֖ם וְאַל־תִּתְגָּ֣ר בָּ֑ם כִּ֣י לֹֽא־אֶ֠תֵּ֠ן מֵאֶ֨רֶץ בְּנֵי־עַמּ֥וֹן לְךָ֛ יְרֻשָּׁ֖ה כִּ֥י לִבְנֵי־ל֖וֹט נְתַתִּ֥יהָ יְרֻשָּֽׁה:

20 אֶרֶץ־רְפָאִ֥ים תֵּחָשֵׁ֖ב אַף־הִ֑וא רְפָאִ֤ים יָֽשְׁבוּ־בָהּ֙ לְפָנִ֔ים וְהָֽעַמֹּנִ֔ים יִקְרְא֥וּ לָהֶ֖ם זַמְזֻמִּֽים: 21 עַ֣ם גָּד֥וֹל וְרַ֛ב וָרָ֖ם כָּעֲנָקִ֑ים וַיַּשְׁמִידֵ֤ם יְהֹוָה֙ מִפְּנֵיהֶ֔ם וַיִּירָשֻׁ֖ם וַיֵּשְׁב֥וּ תַחְתָּֽם: 22 כַּאֲשֶׁ֤ר עָשָׂה֙ לִבְנֵ֣י עֵשָׂ֔ו הַיֹּשְׁבִ֖ים בְּשֵׂעִ֑יר אֲשֶׁ֤ר הִשְׁמִיד֙ אֶת־הַחֹרִי֙ מִפְּנֵיהֶ֔ם וַיִּֽירָשֻׁם֙ וַיֵּשְׁב֣וּ תַחְתָּ֔ם עַ֖ד הַיּ֥וֹם הַזֶּֽה: 23 וְהָֽעַוִּ֛ים הַיֹּשְׁבִ֥ים בַּחֲצֵרִ֖ים עַד־עַזָּ֑ה כַּפְתֹּרִים֙ הַיֹּצְאִ֣ים מִכַּפְתּ֔וֹר הִשְׁמִידֻ֖ם וַיֵּשְׁב֥וּ תַחְתָּֽם:

is onomatopoetic for the humming sound made by a large crowd, such as an army in flight. It is also used of the roaring of the waters of chaos. Here it implies that God's punishment of the rebellious generation amounted to a divine war against it, in which Israel is treated as God normally would treat Israel's enemies.

16. all . . . had died off This verse links God's orders in verses 17–19 and 24–25 to the death of the rebels. No sooner had the rebels died off than the Lord directed the Israelites to their first victory and territorial possession. The preceding 38 years had been a deviation from God's original plan, to which He now returns.

BYPASSING AMMONITES, ATTACKING AMORITES (vv. 17–30)

The territory of the Ammonites was centered around the capital city Rabbah (modern Amman), some 20 miles east of the Jordan. It was separated from the Jordan by Sihon's territory. Excavations in Amman have unearthed remains of this period, the Late Bronze Age.

19. Ammonites Literally, "the children (descendants) of Ammon (b'nei Ammon)." The Bible refers to them and their land as "the children of Ammon" and "the land of the children of Ammon," and almost never speaks simply of "Ammon," though it regularly speaks of "Moab." This distinction accurately reflects the names these peoples used to refer to themselves. An Ammonite inscription speaks of the "king of the children of Ammon," and a Moabite inscription speaks of the "king of Moab."

20. Zamzummim The name, used by the Ammonites, seems to be an imitation of their speech. It means, roughly, "the Buzz-buzzers," i.e., "the people whose speech sounds like buzzing."

23. This second note digresses from the context of Transjordan to deal with the inhabitants of Philistia, near Gaza.

Avvim Mentioned again in Josh. 13:3 as living near Philistia, they are not known from elsewhere. They lived in unwalled villages, which suggests they may have been herders like the Ishmaelites and the Kedarites, who also lived in such villages (see Gen. 25:16; Isa. 42:11).

Caphtorim Presumably Philistines, who are

24Up! Set out across the wadi Arnon! See, I give
into your power Sihon the Amorite, king of
Heshbon, and his land. Begin the occupation:
engage him in battle. 25This day I begin to put
the dread and fear of you upon the peoples
everywhere under heaven, so that they shall
tremble and quake because of you whenever
they hear you mentioned.
26Then I sent messengers from the wilderness
of Kedemoth to King Sihon of Heshbon with
an offer of peace, as follows, 27"Let me pass
through your country. I will keep strictly to the
highway, turning off neither to the right nor to
the left. 28What food I eat you will supply for
money, and what water I drink you will furnish
for money; just let me pass through—29as the
descendants of Esau who dwell in Seir did for
me, and the Moabites who dwell in Ar—that I
may cross the Jordan into the land that the Lord
our God is giving us."
30But King Sihon of Heshbon refused to let
us pass through, because the Lord had stiffened
his will and hardened his heart in order to deliver him into your power—as is now the case.
31And the Lord said to me: See, I begin by plac-

24 קוּמוּ סְּעוּ וְעִבְרוּ אֶת־נַחַל אַרְנֹן רְאֵה
נָתַתִּי בְיָדְךָ אֶת־סִיחֹן מֶלֶךְ־חֶשְׁבּוֹן
הָאֱמֹרִי וְאֶת־אַרְצוֹ הָחֵל רָשׁ וְהִתְגָּר בּוֹ
מִלְחָמָה׃ 25 הַיּוֹם הַזֶּה אָחֵל תֵּת פַּחְדְּךָ
וְיִרְאָתְךָ עַל־פְּנֵי הָעַמִּים תַּחַת כָּל־
הַשָּׁמָיִם אֲשֶׁר יִשְׁמְעוּן שִׁמְעֲךָ וְרָגְזוּ וְחָלוּ
מִפָּנֶיךָ׃
26 וָאֶשְׁלַח מַלְאָכִים מִמִּדְבַּר קְדֵמוֹת אֶל־
סִיחוֹן מֶלֶךְ חֶשְׁבּוֹן דִּבְרֵי שָׁלוֹם לֵאמֹר׃
27 אֶעְבְּרָה בְאַרְצֶךָ בַּדֶּרֶךְ בַּדֶּרֶךְ אֵלֵךְ לֹא
אָסוּר יָמִין וּשְׂמֹאול*׃ 28 אֹכֶל בַּכֶּסֶף
תַּשְׁבִּרֵנִי וְאָכַלְתִּי וּמַיִם בַּכֶּסֶף תִּתֶּן־לִי
וְשָׁתִיתִי רַק אֶעְבְּרָה בְרַגְלָי׃ 29 כַּאֲשֶׁר
עָשׂוּ־לִי בְּנֵי עֵשָׂו הַיֹּשְׁבִים בְּשֵׂעִיר
וְהַמּוֹאָבִים הַיֹּשְׁבִים בְּעָר עַד אֲשֶׁר־אֶעֱבֹר
אֶת־הַיַּרְדֵּן אֶל־הָאָרֶץ אֲשֶׁר־יְהוָה אֱלֹהֵינוּ
נֹתֵן לָנוּ׃
30 וְלֹא אָבָה סִיחֹן מֶלֶךְ חֶשְׁבּוֹן הַעֲבִרֵנוּ
בּוֹ כִּי־הִקְשָׁה יְהוָה אֱלֹהֶיךָ אֶת־רוּחוֹ
וְאִמֵּץ אֶת־לְבָבוֹ לְמַעַן תִּתּוֹ בְיָדְךָ כַּיּוֹם
הַזֶּה׃ ס 31 וַיֹּאמֶר יְהוָה אֵלַי רְאֵה ששי

v. 27. מלא ו'

said to have come from Caphtor (Gen. 10:14; Amos 9:7; Jer. 47:4), in the area of the Aegean Sea—either Crete and the surrounding islands, or on the coast of Asia Minor, or both.

24–25. These verses resume the instructions of verses 18–19. The victory over Sihon would cause other peoples to fear the Israelites, as had happened earlier when they crossed the sea (Exod. 15:14–16). This was to demoralize potential enemies.

Sihon He is not mentioned outside of the Bible.

26. wilderness of Kedemoth Probably near the city of Kedemoth in the former Moabite part of Sihon's territory. If so, the Israelites had already crossed the Arnon and entered Sihon's territory when the messengers were sent.

offer of peace Literally, "words of peace." This is either a statement of friendly intentions or a proposal of a nonaggression pact. The essence of Moses' message is his request for the peaceful use of a corridor through Sihon's territory under the terms stated in verses 27–28.

30. stiffened his will and hardened his heart Although the Bible presupposes that God normally enables men and women to exercise free will, it records cases in which He punishes evildoers by causing them to act in a sinful or reckless way that will lead to their downfall. The best known instance is that of Pharaoh in Exod. 7:3–5, 10:1–2.

VICTORY OVER SIHON (2:31–3:1)

This Israelite victory is described only schematically, as is the victory over Og (below). Here the two battles function as overall models of how Israel should conduct itself in war, and of what they can expect when they do so.

ing Sihon and his land at your disposal. Begin the occupation; take possession of his land.

32 Sihon with all his men took the field against us at Jahaz, 33 and the LORD our God delivered him to us and we defeated him and his sons and all his men. 34 At that time we captured all his towns, and we doomed every town—men, women, and children—leaving no survivor. 35 We retained as booty only the cattle and the spoil of the cities that we captured. 36 From Aroer on the edge of the Arnon valley, including the town in the valley itself, to Gilead, not a city was too mighty for us; the LORD our God delivered everything to us. 37 But you did not encroach upon the land of the Ammonites, all along the wadi Jabbok and the towns of the hill country, just as the LORD our God had commanded.

הַחִלֹּתִי תֵּת לְפָנֶיךָ אֶת־סִיחֹן וְאֶת־אַרְצוֹ
הָחֵל רָשׁ לָרֶשֶׁת אֶת־אַרְצוֹ׃
32 וַיֵּצֵא סִיחֹן לִקְרָאתֵנוּ הוּא וְכָל־עַמּוֹ
לַמִּלְחָמָה יָהְצָה׃ 33 וַיִּתְּנֵהוּ יְהוָה אֱלֹהֵינוּ
לְפָנֵינוּ וַנַּךְ אֹתוֹ וְאֶת־בנו בָּנָיו וְאֶת־כָּל־
עַמּוֹ׃ 34 וַנִּלְכֹּד אֶת־כָּל־עָרָיו בָּעֵת הַהִוא
וַנַּחֲרֵם אֶת־כָּל־עִיר מְתִם וְהַנָּשִׁים וְהַטָּף
לֹא הִשְׁאַרְנוּ שָׂרִיד׃ 35 רַק הַבְּהֵמָה בָּזַזְנוּ
לָנוּ וּשְׁלַל הֶעָרִים אֲשֶׁר לָכָדְנוּ׃ 36 מֵעֲרֹעֵר
אֲשֶׁר עַל־שְׂפַת־נַחַל אַרְנֹן וְהָעִיר אֲשֶׁר
בַּנַּחַל וְעַד־הַגִּלְעָד לֹא הָיְתָה קִרְיָה אֲשֶׁר
שָׂגְבָה מִמֶּנּוּ אֶת־הַכֹּל נָתַן יְהוָה אֱלֹהֵינוּ
לְפָנֵינוּ׃ 37 רַק אֶל־אֶרֶץ בְּנֵי־עַמּוֹן לֹא
קָרָבְתָּ כָּל־יַד נַחַל יַבֹּק וְעָרֵי הָהָר וְכֹל
אֲשֶׁר־צִוָּה יְהוָה אֱלֹהֵינוּ׃

3 We made our way up the road toward Bashan, and King Og of Bashan with all his men took the field against us at Edrei. 2 But the LORD said to me: Do not fear him, for I am delivering him and all his men and his country into your power, and you will do to him as you did to Sihon king of the Amorites, who lived in Heshbon.

ג וַנֵּפֶן וַנַּעַל דֶּרֶךְ הַבָּשָׁן וַיֵּצֵא עוֹג
מֶלֶךְ־הַבָּשָׁן לִקְרָאתֵנוּ הוּא וְכָל־עַמּוֹ
לַמִּלְחָמָה אֶדְרֶעִי׃ 2 וַיֹּאמֶר יְהוָה אֵלַי
אַל־תִּירָא אֹתוֹ כִּי בְיָדְךָ נָתַתִּי אֹתוֹ
וְאֶת־כָּל־עַמּוֹ וְאֶת־אַרְצוֹ וְעָשִׂיתָ לּוֹ
כַּאֲשֶׁר עָשִׂיתָ לְסִיחֹן מֶלֶךְ הָאֱמֹרִי אֲשֶׁר
יוֹשֵׁב בְּחֶשְׁבּוֹן׃

32. took the field That is, went to war, unlike Edom, which made a show of force and was not challenged by Israel (Num. 20:20).

33. the LORD . . . delivered him to us Exactly as He had promised (vv. 24,31). This is an implicit rejoinder to the previous generation's doubt that God would fulfill His promises (see 1:27).

34–35. The population of Sihon's territory was killed in accordance with the provisions for cities in the Promised Land (20:16–17). The same is done in Og's territory in 3:6. These instances, too, may reflect a view that northern Transjordan was part of the Land.

36. Gilead The hill country extending eastward from the Jordan 25 to 30 miles (40–50 km). It was divided into northern and southern sections by the western leg of the Jabbok River.

not a city was too mighty for us A rejoinder to the previous generation's fears in 1:28.

37. The territory of the Ammonites was a narrow strip abutting the northeastern corner of Sihon's territory. It was spread along the eastern Jabbok (which flows northward in an arc from near Amman) and extended eastward toward the wilderness. The Israelites obeyed God's command and did not encroach upon it. The wadi/river Jabbok today is known as the Zerka (called Wadi Amman near Amman).

3:1. From Sihon's territory, the Israelites headed north to the Amorite kingdom of Og, ruler of Bashan.

Og The name does not appear in sources outside the Bible, but similar names are found in texts of the Late Bronze Age from the Canaanite city of Ugarit in northwest Syria.

[3]So the LORD our God also delivered into our
power King Og of Bashan, with all his men, and
we dealt them such a blow that no survivor was
left. [4]At that time we captured all his towns;
there was not a town that we did not take from
them: sixty towns, the whole district of Argob,
the kingdom of Og in Bashan—[5]all those towns
were fortified with high walls, gates, and bars—
apart from a great number of unwalled towns.
[6]We doomed them as we had done in the case
of King Sihon of Heshbon; we doomed every
town—men, women, and children—[7]and retained as booty all the cattle and the spoil of the
towns.

[8]Thus we seized, at that time, from the two
Amorite kings, the country beyond the Jordan,
from the wadi Arnon to Mount Hermon—
[9]Sidonians called Hermon Sirion, and the Amorites call it Senir—[10]all the towns of the Tableland and the whole of Gilead and Bashan as far
as Salcah and Edrei, the towns of Og's kingdom
in Bashan. [11]Only King Og of Bashan was left
of the remaining Rephaim. His bedstead, an
iron bedstead, is now in Rabbah of the Ammon-

3 וַיִּתֵּן יְהוָה אֱלֹהֵינוּ בְּיָדֵנוּ גַּם אֶת־עוֹג
מֶלֶךְ־הַבָּשָׁן וְאֶת־כָּל־עַמּוֹ וַנַּכֵּהוּ עַד־
בִּלְתִּי הִשְׁאִיר־לוֹ שָׂרִיד : 4 וַנִּלְכֹּד אֶת־
כָּל־עָרָיו בָּעֵת הַהִוא לֹא הָיְתָה קִרְיָה
אֲשֶׁר לֹא־לָקַחְנוּ מֵאִתָּם שִׁשִּׁים עִיר כָּל־
חֶבֶל אַרְגֹּב מַמְלֶכֶת עוֹג בַּבָּשָׁן : 5 כָּל־
אֵלֶּה עָרִים בְּצֻרֹת חוֹמָה גְבֹהָה דְּלָתַיִם
וּבְרִיחַ לְבַד מֵעָרֵי הַפְּרָזִי הַרְבֵּה מְאֹד :
6 וַנַּחֲרֵם אוֹתָם כַּאֲשֶׁר עָשִׂינוּ לְסִיחֹן מֶלֶךְ
חֶשְׁבּוֹן הַחֲרֵם כָּל־עִיר מְתִם הַנָּשִׁים
וְהַטָּף : 7 וְכָל־הַבְּהֵמָה וּשְׁלַל הֶעָרִים בַּזּוֹנוּ
לָנוּ :

8 וַנִּקַּח בָּעֵת הַהִוא אֶת־הָאָרֶץ מִיַּד שְׁנֵי
מַלְכֵי הָאֱמֹרִי אֲשֶׁר בְּעֵבֶר הַיַּרְדֵּן מִנַּחַל
אַרְנֹן עַד־הַר חֶרְמוֹן : 9 צִידֹנִים יִקְרְאוּ
לְחֶרְמוֹן שִׂרְיֹן וְהָאֱמֹרִי יִקְרְאוּ־לוֹ שְׂנִיר :
10 כֹּל ׀ עָרֵי הַמִּישֹׁר וְכָל־הַגִּלְעָד וְכָל־
הַבָּשָׁן עַד־סַלְכָה וְאֶדְרֶעִי עָרֵי מַמְלֶכֶת
עוֹג בַּבָּשָׁן : 11 כִּי רַק־עוֹג מֶלֶךְ הַבָּשָׁן
נִשְׁאַר מִיֶּתֶר הָרְפָאִים הִנֵּה* עַרְשׂוֹ עֶרֶשׂ

v. 11. סבירין ומטעין "והנה"

VICTORY OVER OG (3:2–26a)

The defeat of Og followed that of Sihon. Moses then allotted their territories to the tribes of Reuben and Gad and half the tribe of Manasseh. Encouraged by these victories, Moses pleaded with God that he be allowed to enter the Promised Land.

4. sixty Probably a round number. Bashan could have many cities because of the region's fertility.

5. gates, and bars The city gates had two-leaf doors (double doors, *d'latayim*) held closed by a bar running along their inner sides.

8. Mount Hermon The southern section of the Anti-Lebanon range, running northeast from above the Huleh Valley. Today it is part of the border between Lebanon and Syria.

9. Sidonians The people of the Phoenician city Sidon. Here, as frequently, the term probably refers to the Phoenicians in general.

10. Tableland The plateau taken from Moab by Sihon, stretching eastward from the Dead Sea to the desert and from the Arnon north to Gilead.

the whole of Gilead North and south of the Jabbok.

Salcah and Edrei Two towns on the southern boundary of Bashan: Salcah on the east and Edrei on the west.

11. The parenthetic comment about Og demonstrates that even the giants feared by the previous generation could not prevent God from granting Israel victory.

Only Og . . . was left The Moabites and the Ammonites had wiped out the others (see 2:10–11, 20–22). According to Gen. 14:5, Rephaim were living in one of Og's capitals, Ashtaroth, as early as the time of Abraham.

an iron bedstead This may mean that Og's bed was ornamented with iron. In the Late Bronze Age, when iron was still uncommon, it was sometimes used for ceremonial objects, jewelry, and decoration.

ites; it is nine cubits long and four cubits wide,
by the standard cubit!
12And this is the land which we apportioned
at that time: The part from Aroer along the wadi
Arnon, with part of the hill country of Gilead
and its towns, I assigned to the Reubenites and
the Gadites. 13The rest of Gilead, and all of Bashan under Og's rule—the whole Argob district,
all that part of Bashan which is called Rephaim
country—I assigned to the half-tribe of Manasseh. 14Jair son of Manasseh received the whole
Argob district (that is, Bashan) as far as the
boundary of the Geshurites and the Maacathites, and named it after himself: Havvoth-jair
—as is still the case. 15To Machir I assigned Gilead. 16And to the Reubenites and the Gadites
I assigned the part from Gilead down to the wadi
Arnon, the middle of the wadi being the boundary, and up to the wadi Jabbok, the boundary
of the Ammonites.
17[We also seized] the Arabah, from the foot
of the slopes of Pisgah on the east, to the edge
of the Jordan, and from Chinnereth down to
the sea of the Arabah, the Dead Sea.

בַּרְזֶל הֲלֹה* הִוא בְּרַבַּת בְּנֵי עַמּוֹן תֵּשַׁע
אַמּוֹת אָרְכָּהּ וְאַרְבַּע אַמּוֹת רָחְבָּהּ
בְּאַמַּת־אִישׁ׃
12 וְאֶת־הָאָרֶץ הַזֹּאת יָרַשְׁנוּ בָּעֵת הַהִוא
מֵעֲרֹעֵר אֲשֶׁר־עַל־נַחַל אַרְנֹן וַחֲצִי הַר־
הַגִּלְעָד וְעָרָיו נָתַתִּי לָרֻאוּבֵנִי וְלַגָּדִי׃
13 וְיֶתֶר הַגִּלְעָד וְכָל־הַבָּשָׁן מַמְלֶכֶת עוֹג
נָתַתִּי לַחֲצִי שֵׁבֶט הַמְנַשֶּׁה כֹּל חֶבֶל
הָאַרְגֹּב לְכָל־הַבָּשָׁן הַהוּא יִקָּרֵא אֶרֶץ
רְפָאִים׃ 14 יָאִיר בֶּן־מְנַשֶּׁה לָקַח אֶת־כָּל־
חֶבֶל אַרְגֹּב עַד־גְּבוּל הַגְּשׁוּרִי וְהַמַּעֲכָתִי
וַיִּקְרָא אֹתָם עַל־שְׁמוֹ אֶת־הַבָּשָׁן חַוֺּת
יָאִיר עַד הַיּוֹם הַזֶּה׃ 15 וּלְמָכִיר נָתַתִּי שביעי
אֶת־הַגִּלְעָד׃ 16 וְלָרֻאוּבֵנִי וְלַגָּדִי נָתַתִּי
מִן־הַגִּלְעָד וְעַד־נַחַל אַרְנֹן תּוֹךְ הַנַּחַל
וּגְבֻל וְעַד יַבֹּק הַנַּחַל גְּבוּל בְּנֵי עַמּוֹן׃
17 וְהָעֲרָבָה וְהַיַּרְדֵּן וּגְבֻל מִכִּנֶּרֶת וְעַד יָם
הָעֲרָבָה יָם הַמֶּלַח תַּחַת אַשְׁדֹּת הַפִּסְגָּה
מִזְרָחָה׃

v. 11. ה׳ במקום א׳

Rabbah Present-day Amman, Jordan.

nine cubits long and four cubits wide Approximately 13½ by 6 feet. The dimensions of Og's bed are naturally larger than Og himself, but they indicate how enormous he must have been.

standard cubit Hebrew: *amah;* literally, "forearm." The basic standard of measurement in the ancient world. Roughly the length of a forearm, it was standardized at about 18 inches.

APPORTIONMENT OF CONQUERED LANDS (vv.12–17)

After summarizing the territory conquered, Moses describes its apportionment. Numbers 32 explains why these territories were given to the tribes of Reuben, Gad, and half of Manasseh. The half-tribe of Manasseh consists of two groups, represented by Jair and Machir.

14. received Hebrew: לקח; literally, "captured," or "seized," which is how this verb is translated in verses 4 and 8.

Geshurites . . . Maacathites Peoples of small states in the Golan Heights: Geshur, east of Lake Tiberias; Maaca, farther north.

15. Machir That is, the descendants of Machir, as stated in Num. 32:39. As a grandson of Joseph, Machir himself could not have been alive at this time.

Gilead Its northern part (see v. 13).

16. Gilead Its southern part (see v. 12).

wadi Jabbok The eastern Jabbok, which flows northward, formed the eastern boundary of the Reubenite–Gadite territory.

17. Pisgah This mountain, or mountain chain, is the southeastern boundary of the 'Arabah (here meaning the Jordan Valley, as in 1:7). Pisgah overlooks the northeast corner of the Dead Sea and the southeastern end of the Jordan Valley.

Chinnereth The Sea of Kinneret, present-day Lake Tiberias.

Dead Sea Literally, "Salt Sea." So called because of its exceptionally high mineral content, which makes it unable to support life. The earliest known explanation of the translation "Dead Sea" connects it to the stillness of the waters.

18At that time I charged you, saying, "The LORD your God has given you this country to possess. You must go as shock-troops, warriors all, at the head of your Israelite kinsmen. 19Only your wives, children, and livestock—I know that you have much livestock—shall be left in the towns I have assigned to you, 20until the LORD has granted your kinsmen a haven such as you have, and they too have taken possession of the land that the LORD your God is assigning them, beyond the Jordan. Then you may return each to the homestead that I have assigned to him."

21I also charged Joshua at that time, saying, "You have seen with your own eyes all that the LORD your God has done to these two kings; so shall the LORD do to all the kingdoms into which you shall cross over. 22Do not fear them, for it is the LORD your God who will battle for you."

18 וְאָצַ֥ו אֶתְכֶ֖ם בָּעֵ֣ת הַהִ֑וא לֵאמֹ֔ר יְהֹוָ֣ה אֱלֹֽהֵיכֶ֗ם נָתַ֤ן לָכֶם֙ אֶת־הָאָ֣רֶץ הַזֹּ֔את לְרִשְׁתָּ֑הּ חֲלוּצִ֣ים תַּֽעַבְר֗וּ לִפְנֵ֛י אֲחֵיכֶ֥ם בְּנֵֽי־יִשְׂרָאֵ֖ל כָּל־בְּנֵי־חָֽיִל: 19 רַ֣ק נְשֵׁיכֶ֤ם וְטַפְּכֶם֙ וּמִקְנֵכֶ֔ם יָדַ֕עְתִּי כִּֽי־מִקְנֶ֥ה רַ֖ב לָכֶ֑ם יֵֽשְׁבוּ֙ בְּעָ֣רֵיכֶ֔ם אֲשֶׁ֥ר נָתַ֖תִּי לָכֶֽם: מפטיר 20 עַ֠ד אֲשֶׁר־יָנִ֨יחַ יְהֹוָ֥ה | לַֽאֲחֵיכֶם֮ כָּכֶם֒ וְיָֽרְשׁ֣וּ גַם־הֵ֔ם אֶת־הָאָ֕רֶץ אֲשֶׁ֨ר יְהֹוָ֧ה אֱלֹֽהֵיכֶ֛ם נֹתֵ֥ן לָהֶ֖ם בְּעֵ֣בֶר הַיַּרְדֵּ֑ן וְשַׁבְתֶּ֗ם אִ֚ישׁ לִֽירֻשָּׁת֔וֹ אֲשֶׁ֥ר נָתַ֖תִּי לָכֶֽם: 21 וְאֶת־יְהוֹשֻׁ֣עַ צִוֵּ֔יתִי בָּעֵ֥ת הַהִ֖וא לֵאמֹ֑ר עֵינֶ֤יךָ הָֽרֹאֹת֙ אֵת֩ כָּל־אֲשֶׁ֨ר עָשָׂ֜ה יְהֹוָ֤ה אֱלֹֽהֵיכֶם֙ לִשְׁנֵי֙ הַמְּלָכִ֣ים הָאֵ֔לֶּה כֵּֽן־יַֽעֲשֶׂ֤ה יְהֹוָה֙ לְכָל־הַמַּמְלָכ֔וֹת אֲשֶׁ֥ר אַתָּ֖ה עֹבֵ֥ר שָֽׁמָּה: 22 לֹ֖א תִּֽירָא֑וּם כִּ֚י יְהֹוָ֣ה אֱלֹֽהֵיכֶ֔ם ה֖וּא הַנִּלְחָ֥ם לָכֶֽם: ס

18–20. Moses repeats the condition under which he permitted the two and a half tribes to settle in Transjordan (Num. 32:16–18).

21. at that time Some time after the victories, but not necessarily after the apportioning of the land to the two and a half tribes.

You have seen with your own eyes In He-

brew, "your eyes" appears first for emphasis: "It is your own eyes that saw"—you have no grounds for doubt, because you saw personally.

kingdoms Canaan in the Late Bronze Age was not a nation-state but a land of separate city-states ruled by kings.

הפטרה שלישית דפורענותא

THIRD HAFTARAH OF ADMONITION
HAFTARAH FOR D'VARIM

ISAIAH 1:1–27

(*Recite on the 3rd* Shabbat *after the 17th of* Tammuz, *called* Shabbat Ḥazon—*named after the first word of this* haftarah. *This occasion coincides with the reading of* D'varim.)

In this passage that opens the Book of Isaiah, the prophet censures all levels of society for iniquity, infidelity to God, and false reliance on ritual sacrifices. Judah and Jerusalem shall be laid waste; only those who repent will be saved.

Isaiah's prophetic career spanned the reigns of several Judean kings during the last half of the 8th century B.C.E. In those decisive times, Assyrian and Aramean foes repeatedly threatened Zion and its leaders. Jerusalem, however, was miraculously saved in 701 B.C.E., and Isaiah's forecast of imminent doom did not come to pass. (The city fell to the Babylonians a century later, in 587–586 B.C.E.)

Three separate pronouncements of doom and disaster make up this *haftarah.* Viewed as a whole, the three speeches present the inverse of what a society should value: the betrayal of covenantal loyalty, the perversion of ritual, and the blindness of moral vision. The first of these speeches (1:2–9) is the most bleak. Totally negative, it charges the people with rebellion against God.

The second speech (vv. 10–20) is linked to the first through language but differs in content. Rather than pronounce irrevocable doom, it provides corrective counsel as a divine "instruction." The people's fate hangs on their decision to follow God's instruction of social justice. This is the core of divine concern.

The third speech (vv. 21–27) continues the themes of the second one but is distinct in genre and theological emphasis. Like its predecessor, it emphasizes the injustice that fills the city. This speech, however, is a lament bewailing the destitution of fair Zion and the coming doom. Still, the concluding verse of the *haftarah* is a teaching of less finality and more hope.

RELATION OF THE *HAFTARAH* TO THE CALENDAR

This passage is a special reading for the *Shabbat* immediately preceding the fast of *Tish·ah b'Av* (and thus is not linked to the *parashah*). This *haftarah*'s content anticipates that of Lamentations, which is recited on *Tish·ah b'Av*; both readings depict the devastation and desolation of Judea and Zion. Beyond this thematic link is a striking verbal correspondence. In his lament, Isaiah cries, "Alas (*eikha*), she has become a harlot, / The faithful city" (1:21). This verse eerily foreshadows the opening words of Lamentations: "Alas (*eikha*)! / Lonely sits the city / Once great with people! / She that was great among nations / Is become like a widow" (1:1). Traditionally, most or all of this *haftarah* is chanted with the elegiac trope used in the recitation of Lamentations on *Tish·ah b'Av.*

1 The prophecies of Isaiah son of Amoz, who prophesied concerning Judah and Jerusalem in the reigns of Uzziah, Jotham, Ahaz, and Hezekiah, kings of Judah.	**א** חֲזוֹן֙ יְשַֽׁעְיָ֣הוּ בֶן־אָמ֔וֹץ אֲשֶׁ֣ר חָזָ֔ה עַל־יְהוּדָ֖ה וִירוּשָׁלִָ֑ם בִּימֵ֨י עֻזִיָּ֧הוּ יוֹתָ֛ם אָחָ֥ז יְחִזְקִיָּ֖הוּ מַלְכֵ֥י יְהוּדָֽה׃
2Hear, O heavens, and give ear, O earth, For the LORD has spoken: "I reared children and brought them up— And they have rebelled against Me! 3An ox knows its owner, An ass its master's crib: Israel does not know, My people takes no thought."	2 שִׁמְע֤וּ שָׁמַ֙יִם֙ וְהַאֲזִ֣ינִי אֶ֔רֶץ כִּ֥י יְהוָ֖ה דִּבֵּ֑ר בָּנִים֙ גִּדַּ֣לְתִּי וְרוֹמַ֔מְתִּי וְהֵ֖ם פָּ֥שְׁעוּ בִֽי׃ 3 יָדַ֥ע שׁוֹר֙ קֹנֵ֔הוּ וַחֲמ֖וֹר אֵב֣וּס בְּעָלָ֑יו יִשְׂרָאֵל֙ לֹ֣א יָדַ֔ע עַמִּ֖י לֹ֥א הִתְבּוֹנָֽן׃
4Ah, sinful nation! People laden with iniquity! Brood of evildoers! Depraved children! They have forsaken the LORD, Spurned the Holy One of Israel, Turned their backs [on Him].	4 ה֣וֹי ׀ גּ֣וֹי חֹטֵ֗א עַ֚ם כֶּ֣בֶד עָוֺ֔ן זֶ֣רַע מְרֵעִ֔ים בָּנִ֖ים מַשְׁחִיתִ֑ים עָזְב֣וּ אֶת־יְהוָ֗ה נִֽאֲצ֛וּ אֶת־קְד֥וֹשׁ יִשְׂרָאֵ֖ל נָזֹ֥רוּ אָחֽוֹר׃
5Why do you seek further beatings, That you continue to offend? Every head is ailing, And every heart is sick. 6From head to foot No spot is sound: All bruises, and welts, And festering sores—	5 עַ֣ל מֶ֥ה תֻכּ֛וּ ע֖וֹד תּוֹסִ֣יפוּ סָרָ֑ה כָּל־רֹ֣אשׁ לָחֳלִ֔י וְכָל־לֵבָ֖ב דַּוָּֽי׃ 6 מִכַּף־רֶ֤גֶל וְעַד־רֹאשׁ֙ אֵֽין־בּ֣וֹ מְתֹ֔ם פֶּ֥צַע וְחַבּוּרָ֖ה וּמַכָּ֣ה טְרִיָּ֑ה

Isaiah 1:1. in the reigns of Uzziah, Jotham, Ahaz, and Hezekiah The reigns of these kings extended from 785 to 698 B.C.E.

2. Hear, O heavens . . . / For the LORD has spoken The call for heaven and earth to witness a divine admonition is also found in Deut. 32:1. In ancient Near Eastern treaties, divinities of heaven and earth were invoked as enduring witnesses. In the Bible, the invocation of nature's aspects is largely a matter of rhetoric (see Micah 6:1–2).

4. Ah Hebrew: *hoy,* a cry of woe (Radak). It is a recurrent element of Isaiah's rebukes (see 5:8,18,21–22).

Holy One of Israel A characteristic divine epithet in the Book of Isaiah; God is called "holy" (*kadosh*) 17 times in chapters 1–39 (see 5:16,19) and 15 times in chapters 40–66. The transcen-

Not pressed out, not bound up,
Not softened with oil.
7 Your land is a waste,
Your cities burnt down;
Before your eyes, the yield of your soil
Is consumed by strangers—
A wasteland as overthrown by strangers!
8 Fair Zion is left
Like a booth in a vineyard,
Like a hut in a cucumber field,
Like a city beleaguered.
9 Had not the LORD of Hosts
Left us some survivors,
We should be like Sodom,
Another Gomorrah.

10 Hear the word of the LORD,
You chieftains of Sodom;
Give ear to our God's instruction,
You folk of Gomorrah!
11 "What need have I of all your sacrifices?"
Says the LORD.
"I am sated with burnt offerings of rams,
And suet of fatlings,
And blood of bulls;
And I have no delight
In lambs and he-goats.
12 That you come to appear before Me—

לֹא־זֹרוּ וְלֹא חֻבָּשׁוּ
וְלֹא רֻכְּכָה בַּשָּׁמֶן׃
7 אַרְצְכֶם שְׁמָמָה
עָרֵיכֶם שְׂרֻפוֹת אֵשׁ
אַדְמַתְכֶם לְנֶגְדְּכֶם
זָרִים אֹכְלִים אֹתָהּ
וּשְׁמָמָה כְּמַהְפֵּכַת זָרִים׃
8 וְנוֹתְרָה בַת־צִיּוֹן
כְּסֻכָּה בְכָרֶם
כִּמְלוּנָה בְמִקְשָׁה
כְּעִיר נְצוּרָה׃
9 לוּלֵי יְהוָה צְבָאוֹת
הוֹתִיר לָנוּ שָׂרִיד כִּמְעָט
כִּסְדֹם הָיִינוּ
לַעֲמֹרָה דָּמִינוּ׃ ס

10 שִׁמְעוּ דְבַר־יְהוָה
קְצִינֵי סְדֹם
הַאֲזִינוּ תּוֹרַת אֱלֹהֵינוּ
עַם עֲמֹרָה׃
11 לָמָּה־לִּי רֹב־זִבְחֵיכֶם
יֹאמַר* יְהוָה
שָׂבַעְתִּי עֹלוֹת אֵילִים
וְחֵלֶב מְרִיאִים
וְדַם פָּרִים
וּכְבָשִׂים וְעַתּוּדִים
לֹא חָפָצְתִּי׃
12 כִּי תָבֹאוּ לֵרָאוֹת פָּנָי

v. 11. סבירין ומטעין "אמר"

dent sanctity of God is emphasized in the threefold repetition of *kadosh* in 6:3. (See commentary on the *haftarah* for *Yitro*.)

8. Like a booth in a vineyard After the coming destruction, God will abandon Israel as a watchman does his booth (Radak) after the grapes have been plucked. Alternatively, the figure bespeaks the desolation of the nation itself.

9. like Sodom The story from Gen. 19 serves as a model of divine destruction (see Deut. 29:22; Amos 4:11). The perversity of the people of Sodom also serves as a negative model for the prophet in v. 10 (see Deut. 32:32).

10. instruction Hebrew: *torah* (instruction) here means prophetic teaching (Luzzatto). This is also the sense of the word in Isa. 2:3, "For instruction will come forth from Zion," in the context of a vision of universal peace.

11. Isaiah does not reject sacrifices per se. He rejects hypocrisy. Self-purification and moral rec-

Who asked that of you?
Trample My courts [13]no more;
Bringing oblations is futile,
Incense is offensive to Me.
New moon and sabbath,
Proclaiming of solemnities,
Assemblies with iniquity,
I cannot abide.
[14]Your new moons and fixed seasons
Fill Me with loathing;
They are become a burden to Me,
I cannot endure them.
[15]And when you lift up your hands,
I will turn My eyes away from you;
Though you pray at length,
I will not listen.
Your hands are stained with crime—
[16]Wash yourselves clean;
Put your evil doings
Away from My sight.
Cease to do evil;
[17]Learn to do good.
Devote yourselves to justice;
Aid the wronged.
Uphold the rights of the orphan;
Defend the cause of the widow.

[18]"Come, let us reach an understanding,"
—says the LORD.

מִי־בִקֵּשׁ זֹאת מִיֶּדְכֶם
רְמֹס חֲצֵרָי׃ 13 לֹא תוֹסִיפוּ
הָבִיא מִנְחַת־שָׁוְא
קְטֹרֶת תּוֹעֵבָה הִיא לִי
חֹדֶשׁ וְשַׁבָּת
קְרֹא מִקְרָא
לֹא־אוּכַל
אָוֶן וַעֲצָרָה׃
14 חָדְשֵׁיכֶם וּמוֹעֲדֵיכֶם
שָׂנְאָה נַפְשִׁי
הָיוּ עָלַי לָטֹרַח
נִלְאֵיתִי נְשֹׂא׃
15 וּבְפָרִשְׂכֶם כַּפֵּיכֶם
אַעְלִים עֵינַי מִכֶּם
גַּם כִּי־תַרְבּוּ תְפִלָּה
אֵינֶנִּי שֹׁמֵעַ
יְדֵיכֶם דָּמִים מָלֵאוּ׃
16 רַחֲצוּ הִזַּכּוּ
הָסִירוּ רֹעַ מַעַלְלֵיכֶם
מִנֶּגֶד עֵינָי
חִדְלוּ הָרֵעַ׃
17 לִמְדוּ הֵיטֵב
דִּרְשׁוּ מִשְׁפָּט
אַשְּׁרוּ חָמוֹץ
שִׁפְטוּ יָתוֹם
רִיבוּ אַלְמָנָה׃ ס

18 לְכוּ־נָא וְנִוָּכְחָה
יֹאמַר* יְהוָה

v. 18. סבירין ומטעין "אמר"

titude are conditions for proper use of the altar. (See Ps. 15, 24. The prophet Amos also emphasized morality over sacrifices; see 5:21–24.)

16–17. This is the positive core of prophetic "instruction" (*torah,* v. 10). The need for purification and purgation of evil is combined with an emphasis on justice and righteousness. Based on the commands in these two verses, the Midrash specified nine virtues and linked them to the nine days between *Rosh ha-Shanah* and *Yom Kippur.* As the 10th day is the day of purification and atonement, so here the 10th feature of the list (v. 18) is "Come, let us reach an understanding. / . . . / Be your sins like crimson, / They can turn

"Be your sins like crimson,
They can turn snow-white;
Be they red as dyed wool,
They can become like fleece."
19If, then, you agree and give heed,
You will eat the good things of the earth;
20But if you refuse and disobey,
You will be devoured [by] the sword.—
For it was the LORD who spoke.

21Alas, she has become a harlot,
The faithful city
That was filled with justice,
Where righteousness dwelt—
But now murderers.
22Your silver has turned to dross;
Your wine is cut with water.
23Your rulers are rogues
And cronies of thieves,
Every one avid for presents
And greedy for gifts;
They do not judge the case of the orphan,
And the widow's cause never reaches them.

24Assuredly, this is the declaration
Of the Sovereign, the LORD of Hosts,
The Mighty One of Israel:
"Ah, I will get satisfaction from My foes;
I will wreak vengeance on My enemies!
25I will turn My hand against you,
And smelt out your dross as with lye,

אִם־יִהְיוּ חֲטָאֵיכֶם כַּשָּׁנִים֙
כַּשֶּׁלֶג יַלְבִּינוּ
אִם־יַאְדִּימוּ כַתּוֹלָע
כַּצֶּמֶר יִהְיוּ׃
19 אִם־תֹּאבוּ וּשְׁמַעְתֶּם
טוּב הָאָרֶץ תֹּאכֵלוּ׃
20 וְאִם־תְּמָאֲנוּ וּמְרִיתֶם
חֶרֶב תְּאֻכְּלוּ
כִּי פִּי יְהוָה דִּבֵּר׃ ס

21 אֵיכָה֙ הָיְתָה לְזוֹנָה
קִרְיָה נֶאֱמָנָה
מְלֵאֲתִי מִשְׁפָּט
צֶדֶק יָלִין בָּהּ
וְעַתָּה מְרַצְּחִים׃
22 כַּסְפֵּךְ הָיָה לְסִיגִים
סָבְאֵךְ מָהוּל בַּמָּיִם׃
23 שָׂרַיִךְ סוֹרְרִים
וְחַבְרֵי֮ גַּנָּבִים
כֻּלּוֹ֙ אֹהֵב שֹׁחַד
וְרֹדֵף שַׁלְמֹנִים
יָתוֹם֙ לֹא יִשְׁפֹּטוּ
וְרִיב אַלְמָנָה לֹא־יָבוֹא אֲלֵיהֶם׃ פ

24 לָכֵן נְאֻם
הָאָדוֹן֙ יְהוָה צְבָאוֹת
אֲבִיר יִשְׂרָאֵל
הוֹי אֶנָּחֵם מִצָּרַי
וְאִנָּקְמָה מֵאוֹיְבָי׃
25 וְאָשִׁיבָה יָדִי֙ עָלַיִךְ
וְאֶצְרֹף כַּבֹּר סִיגָיִךְ

snow-white" (Yalkut Sh. 2:389). Rashi refers to this list as "10 exhortations to repentance."

21–26. This reproof opens with reference to Zion's transformation from a "faithful city" where "righteousness dwelt" into a callous city of injustice and disregard for the needy. It closes with the promise of Zion's restoration as a "City of Righteousness, Faithful City" after a divine purification. The language of verse 26 is recalled in Jewish liturgy; the divine promise "I will restore your magistrates as of old, / And your counselors as of yore" is reformulated in the daily *Amidah* (blessing 11) as a request for the renewal of justice ("Restore our magistrates as of old").

And remove all your slag:

²⁶I will restore your magistrates as of old,

And your counselors as of yore.

After that you shall be called

City of Righteousness, Faithful City."

וְאָסִ֖ירָה כָּל־בְּדִילָֽיִךְ׃

²⁶ וְאָשִׁ֤יבָה שֹׁפְטַ֙יִךְ֙ כְּבָרִ֣אשֹׁנָ֔ה

וְיֹעֲצַ֖יִךְ כְּבַתְּחִלָּ֑ה

אַחֲרֵי־כֵ֗ן יִקָּ֤רֵא לָךְ֙

עִ֣יר הַצֶּ֔דֶק קִרְיָ֖ה נֶאֱמָנָֽה׃

²⁷Zion shall be saved in the judgment;

Her repentant ones, in the retribution.

²⁷ צִיּ֖וֹן בְּמִשְׁפָּ֣ט תִּפָּדֶ֑ה

וְשָׁבֶ֖יהָ בִּצְדָקָֽה׃

27. Perhaps better: "Zion shall be redeemed with justice; / Her repentant ones with righteousness." Stressing human justice as a precondition seems to fit best with the chapter as a whole.

23I pleaded with the LORD at that time, saying,
24"O Lord GOD, You who let Your servant see
the first works of Your greatness and Your
mighty hand, You whose powerful deeds no god
in heaven or on earth can equal! 25Let me, I pray,
cross over and see the good land on the other
side of the Jordan, that good hill country, and
the Lebanon." 26But the LORD was wrathful with
me on your account and would not listen to me.
The LORD said to me, "Enough! Never speak to
Me of this matter again! 27Go up to the summit
of Pisgah and gaze about, to the west, the north,
the south, and the east. Look at it well, for you

23 וָאֶתְחַנַּן אֶל־יְהוָה בָּעֵת הַהִוא לֵאמֹר׃
24 אֲדֹנָי יְהוִה אַתָּה הַחִלּוֹתָ לְהַרְאוֹת
אֶת־עַבְדְּךָ אֶת־גָּדְלְךָ וְאֶת־יָדְךָ הַחֲזָקָה
אֲשֶׁר מִי־אֵל בַּשָּׁמַיִם וּבָאָרֶץ אֲשֶׁר־
יַעֲשֶׂה כְמַעֲשֶׂיךָ וְכִגְבוּרֹתֶךָ׃ 25 אֶעְבְּרָה־
נָּא וְאֶרְאֶה אֶת־הָאָרֶץ הַטּוֹבָה אֲשֶׁר
בְּעֵבֶר הַיַּרְדֵּן הָהָר הַטּוֹב הַזֶּה וְהַלְּבָנוֹן׃
26 וַיִּתְעַבֵּר יְהוָה בִּי לְמַעַנְכֶם וְלֹא שָׁמַע
אֵלָי וַיֹּאמֶר יְהוָה אֵלַי רַב־לָךְ אַל־תּוֹסֶף
דַּבֵּר אֵלַי עוֹד בַּדָּבָר הַזֶּה׃ 27 עֲלֵה ׀ רֹאשׁ
הַפִּסְגָּה וְשָׂא עֵינֶיךָ יָמָּה וְצָפֹנָה וְתֵימָנָה

Moses' First Discourse (*continued*)

ISRAEL OBEYS THE SECOND COMMAND TO PROCEED TO THE PROMISED LAND (*continued*)

VICTORY OVER OG (*continued*)

MOSES PLEADS WITH GOD (3:23–26a)

As related earlier in the chapter, God had allowed Moses to lead the conquest of Transjordan. This then encouraged his hope that God might no longer bar him from the Promised Land. Hence he turned to God with a plea that he be allowed to cross the Jordan.

24. Lord GOD Literally, "my Lord *YHVH*," addressing God by title and name. This form of address is common in prayers and pleas.

25. the good land . . . that good hill country These phrases express Moses' longing for the Promised Land. The first phrase is especially poignant. God used it not only when He banned the Exodus generation from the land (1:35) but also in His very first words to Moses promising to take Israel there (Exod. 3:8).

GOD'S RESPONSE TO MOSES' PLEA (vv. 26b–29)

27. God softens His decree by agreeing to part of Moses' request: He may see the land but not cross into it.

CHAPTER 3

Incomparably rich, this *parashah* is the source of the classic words of Jewish worship, *Sh'ma Yisra·el* (Deut. 6:4–9). It also contains the reprise of the Decalogue (cf. Exod. 20) and continues Moses' exhortation to Israel, with special emphasis on God's goodness and on Israel's uniquely intimate relationship with this good and great God.

23. I pleaded It seems so out of character for Moses to plead on his own behalf and to share with the people the frustration of having his plea denied. Ibn Ezra suggests that he did it to impress on the Israelites the great virtue of living in the land of Israel; it was the one thing he yearned for that was denied him. Others suggest that he was trying to teach that one should never lose hope; our deepest prayers may yet be answered. The Midrash understood this unusual verb (*hithannen*) as meaning "to throw oneself at the mercy of the other, to plead with no grounds to justify one's request" (Deut. R. 2:1). A truly righteous person never assumes God owes anyone a favorable response. By contrast, the modern commentator Y. Leibowitz sees Moses as "not aware of the fact that he has sinned, regarding the decree against him as unjustified. He pleads not for forgiveness but for annulment of the decree."

shall not go across yonder Jordan. 28Give Joshua
his instructions, and imbue him with strength
and courage, for he shall go across at the head
of this people, and he shall allot to them the land
that you may only see."
29Meanwhile we stayed on in the valley near
Beth-peor.

וּמִזְרָחָה וּרְאֵה בְעֵינֶיךָ כִּי־לֹא תַעֲבֹר
אֶת־הַיַּרְדֵּן הַזֶּה׃ 28 וְצַו אֶת־יְהוֹשֻׁעַ
וְחַזְּקֵהוּ וְאַמְּצֵהוּ כִּי־הוּא יַעֲבֹר לִפְנֵי הָעָם
הַזֶּה וְהוּא יַנְחִיל אוֹתָם אֶת־הָאָרֶץ אֲשֶׁר
תִּרְאֶה׃
29 וַנֵּשֶׁב בַּגָּיְא מוּל בֵּית פְּעוֹר׃ פ

4 And now, O Israel, give heed to the laws
and rules that I am instructing you to observe,
so that you may live to enter and occupy the
land that the LORD, the God of your fathers, is
giving you. 2You shall not add anything to what
I command you or take anything away from it,

ד וְעַתָּה יִשְׂרָאֵל שְׁמַע אֶל־הַחֻקִּים
וְאֶל־הַמִּשְׁפָּטִים אֲשֶׁר אָנֹכִי מְלַמֵּד אֶתְכֶם
לַעֲשׂוֹת לְמַעַן תִּחְיוּ וּבָאתֶם וִירִשְׁתֶּם
אֶת־הָאָרֶץ אֲשֶׁר יְהוָה אֱלֹהֵי אֲבֹתֵיכֶם
נֹתֵן לָכֶם׃ 2 לֹא תֹסִפוּ עַל־הַדָּבָר אֲשֶׁר
אָנֹכִי מְצַוֶּה אֶתְכֶם וְלֹא תִגְרְעוּ מִמֶּנּוּ

28. Give Joshua his instructions Moses fulfills this command in 31:7–8.

29. The dialogue ends abruptly, indicating that Moses was silent before God's decree.

valley near Beth-peor A wadi in Moab, running into the river Jordan or the northeastern corner of the Dead Sea. Here Moses delivered his final addresses and was buried (4:46, 34:6). The nearby town of Beth-peor probably was the site of the scandalous idolatrous orgy (Num. 25:1–9).

APPEALS TO OBSERVE GOD'S LAWS (4:1–40)

This chapter, the theological heart of Deuteronomy, contains its most fundamental precepts: monotheism and the prohibition of idolatry.

BASED ON THE EXPERIENCE AT PEOR (vv. 1–4)

1. give heed Hebrew: שמע; literally, "hear." The focus on "hearing" is a key aspect of the theology of Deuteronomy. Like "see" in verse 5, "hear" is employed frequently in urging Israel to consider Moses' words.

instructing Hebrew: *m'lamed* (often rendered "impart," as in v. 5), illustrating Moses' role as teacher of the laws. This is the calling for which he is best remembered in Jewish tradition, which still refers to him as *Moshe Rabbeinu,* "Moses our teacher."

laws . . . rules Hebrew: *ḥukkim . . . mishpatim.* Moses employs the terms indiscriminately here, like the English phrases "rules and regulations" and "laws and ordinances." According to the Talmud, *mishpatim* are laws whose purpose is evident, such as prohibitions against murder and theft. People would have devised them even if God had not commanded them. *Ḥukkim* are commandments for which the reason is not obvious, such as the dietary laws; they must be obeyed as expressions of divine sovereignty.

to observe The laws are to be fulfilled, not just learned.

so that you may live Life itself depends on one's observance of the commandments (see v. 4).

2. You shall not add anything Similar injunctions against adding or removing items appear in many ancient laws and treaties and are attested in prophetic literature. Although this seems

---

CHAPTER 4

2. You shall not add Yet many laws and customs have been added (and many dropped) over the centuries as circumstances changed. To legitimate the necessary expansion and evolution of Jewish law, the Sages limited this prohibition to "quantitative" changes, such as adding a fourth petition to the Priestly Benediction or a fifth passage to the four passages contained in the *t'fillin.* Extension and clarification of the law was not seen as "adding." A

but keep the commandments of the LORD your God that I enjoin upon you. 3 You saw with your own eyes what the LORD did in the matter of Baal-peor, that the LORD your God wiped out from among you every person who followed Baal-peor; 4 while you, who held fast to the LORD your God, are all alive today.

5 See, I have imparted to you laws and rules, as the LORD my God has commanded me, for you to abide by in the land that you are about

לִשְׁמֹר אֶת־מִצְוֺת יְהוָה אֱלֹהֵיכֶם אֲשֶׁר
אָנֹכִי מְצַוֶּה אֶתְכֶם׃ 3 עֵינֵיכֶם הָרֹאֹת אֵת
אֲשֶׁר־עָשָׂה יְהוָה בְּבַעַל פְּעוֹר כִּי כָל־
הָאִישׁ אֲשֶׁר הָלַךְ אַחֲרֵי בַעַל־פְּעוֹר
הִשְׁמִידוֹ יְהוָה אֱלֹהֶיךָ מִקִּרְבֶּךָ׃ 4 וְאַתֶּם
הַדְּבֵקִים בַּיהוָה אֱלֹהֵיכֶם חַיִּים כֻּלְּכֶם
הַיּוֹם׃
שני 5 רְאֵה ׀ לִמַּדְתִּי אֶתְכֶם חֻקִּים וּמִשְׁפָּטִים
כַּאֲשֶׁר צִוַּנִי יְהוָה אֱלֹהָי לַעֲשׂוֹת כֵּן בְּקֶרֶב
הָאָרֶץ אֲשֶׁר אַתֶּם בָּאִים שָׁמָּה לְרִשְׁתָּהּ׃

to be an all-encompassing prohibition, it could not have been meant that way. The Torah is not a complete code covering all areas of life. Important subjects such as commerce, civil damages, and marriage are covered incompletely or not at all, and further laws obviously were needed. Actually, here and in 13:1 Moses seems to have but a single issue in mind, which is not to adopt pagan practices or worship their gods.

3. in the matter of Baal-peor This refers to the god of Beth-peor, near the place where the Israelites are still encamped (3:29). A total of 24,000 Israelites who joined in the worship of Baal-peor died in a plague there (see Num. 25:1–9).

followed Baal-peor Following (literally, "walking after") a god is a biblical idiom for apostasy, forsaking God. The idiom is based on ancient Near Eastern political terminology, in which "walking after" a king means giving him one's allegiance. Hence, "walking after" a god means defecting from the Lord. There clearly is a link between the prohibition of idolatry and the Baal-peor apostasy.

BASED ON THE COMMANDMENTS' QUALITY AND EFFECT (vv. 5–8)

Moses appeals for observance of the commandments because they are just and because observing them brings about a unique closeness with God.

5. the LORD . . . has commanded At Mount Sinai.

for you to abide by in the land God's laws are to be the basis of the society the Israelites are about to establish in the land. This clause does not imply that the laws are inapplicable outside the land of Israel. Indeed, many have been in force since Israel left Egypt, such as for *Shabbat* and the prohibition of idolatry. There are, however, specific laws (e.g., those based on agriculture) that cannot be followed outside the land.

---

modern Conservative perspective would see the Torah as a living organism, constantly shedding dead cells and growing new ones, changing and adapting to new and unprecedented circumstances. Extending the implications of a law to meet today's needs is not a case of "adding or subtracting."

or take anything away Sometimes adding leads to diminishing. If we demand too much, people may be driven to stop observing even what they currently do (Maggid of Dubno).

4. In synagogues, this verse is chanted by the congregation just before the reading of the Torah.

held fast Literally, "are clinging"; this verb describes the closeness of husband and wife in Gen. 2:24. It is not enough to believe in God intellectually—to conclude that there is a God and that it would be prudent and proper to follow God's teachings. We must cleave to God as one cleaves to a spouse, to a lover, in response to our soul's deepest needs. Only then will our relationship to God be a source of life.

are all alive today The life promised by the Torah is not the opposite of physical death, but the alternative to mere vegetative existence that does not deserve to be called life (Kook).

5. "Every other nation becomes a nation by virtue of the fact that it has a land of its own; only after that does it establish the laws to be lived by in that land. You, by contrast, became a nation by virtue of your laws, and you will be given a land of your own solely for the purpose of living by those laws" (Hirsch). After the destruction of the Temple and the expulsion

to enter and occupy. [6]Observe them faithfully, for that will be proof of your wisdom and discernment to other peoples, who on hearing of all these laws will say, "Surely, that great nation is a wise and discerning people." [7]For what great nation is there that has a god so close at hand as is the LORD our God whenever we call upon Him? [8]Or what great nation has laws and rules as perfect as all this Teaching that I set before you this day?

[9]But take utmost care and watch yourselves scrupulously, so that you do not forget the things that you saw with your own eyes and so that they do not fade from your mind as long as you live. And make them known to your chil-

6 וּשְׁמַרְתֶּם וַעֲשִׂיתֶם כִּי הִוא חָכְמַתְכֶם
וּבִינַתְכֶם לְעֵינֵי הָעַמִּים אֲשֶׁר יִשְׁמְעוּן
אֵת כָּל־הַחֻקִּים הָאֵלֶּה וְאָמְרוּ רַק עַם־
חָכָם וְנָבוֹן הַגּוֹי הַגָּדוֹל הַזֶּה׃ 7 כִּי מִי־גוֹי
גָדוֹל אֲשֶׁר־לוֹ אֱלֹהִים קְרֹבִים אֵלָיו כַּיהוָה
אֱלֹהֵינוּ בְּכָל־קָרְאֵנוּ אֵלָיו׃ 8 וּמִי גּוֹי גָּדוֹל
אֲשֶׁר־לוֹ חֻקִּים וּמִשְׁפָּטִים צַדִּיקִם כְּכֹל
הַתּוֹרָה הַזֹּאת אֲשֶׁר אָנֹכִי נֹתֵן לִפְנֵיכֶם
הַיּוֹם׃
9 רַק הִשָּׁמֶר לְךָ וּשְׁמֹר נַפְשְׁךָ מְאֹד פֶּן־
תִּשְׁכַּח אֶת־הַדְּבָרִים אֲשֶׁר־רָאוּ עֵינֶיךָ
וּפֶן־יָסוּרוּ מִלְּבָבְךָ כֹּל יְמֵי חַיֶּיךָ וְהוֹדַעְתָּם

6. great Meant spiritually. Numerically, Israel will be the smallest of nations (7:7).

7. One effect of observing God's laws is that He is near whenever Israel calls upon Him, providing guidance (through prophecy), and deliverance in times of trouble.

8. perfect Literally, "just." The other benefit of observing God's laws is enjoying their justice. We have no information from biblical times about what impression Israel's laws made on other nations. Modern scholars have compared biblical law to other legal systems of the ancient Near East. The comparison has shown that a number of principles in biblical law are unique in the ancient Near East, such as laws to ameliorate the treatment of aliens and bondservants, the prohibition of collective and vicarious punishment, and the absence of capital punishment for economic crimes.

BASED ON EXPERIENCES AT HOREB
(vv. 9–31)

Moses speaks to the present generation as if it came out of Egypt and stood at Mount Sinai. Although most of those he is addressing were born after those events, about one-third of the adults probably experienced them as youngsters. The younger ones undoubtedly heard about the events from their parents or others who were there. Future generations, of course, constitute the real audience.

9. make them known to your children and your children's children This obligation is the most pervasive expression of the biblical conviction that religion not only is a personal, individual

---

from the Land, it was the Torah that enabled us to remain a people. The re-establishment of modern Israel in 1948 raises a question: If Israel with the Torah could survive without the Land, can Israel with the Land survive without the Torah?

7. a god so close at hand Idols are physically close to their worshipers but emotionally distant, incapable of responding. God, though physically removed, is emotionally close (Deut. R. 2:10). The idea that God cares about the people, that Israel's relationship to God is based not merely on obedience but on reciprocal love and commitment, is a constant theme of the Torah and of Deuteronomy in particular.

9. watch yourselves scrupulously Understood by the Sages as, "guard your soul greatly." That is, "Be as careful with the health of your soul as you are with the health of your body" (Jacob Isaac of Lublin). This verse has been used in contemporary times to declare smoking and unhealthy eating and drinking to be practices that violate the Torah.

the things that you saw with your own eyes Jewish faith is based primarily on experience rather than on speculative thought. "The essence of Jewish religious thinking does not lie in entertaining a concept of God but in the ability to articulate a memory of moments of illumination by God's presence. Israel is not a people of definers but a people of witnesses" (Heschel).

make them known to your children Only when one becomes a parent and begins to teach

dren and to your children's children: [10]The day
you stood before the LORD your God at Horeb,
when the LORD said to Me, "Gather the people
to Me that I may let them hear My words, in
order that they may learn to revere Me as long
as they live on earth, and may so teach their children." [11]You came forward and stood at the
foot of the mountain. The mountain was ablaze
with flames to the very skies, dark with densest
clouds. [12]The LORD spoke to you out of the
fire; you heard the sound of words but perceived no shape—nothing but a voice. [13]He declared to you the covenant that He commanded
you to observe, the Ten Commandments; and
He inscribed them on two tablets of stone.

לְבָנֶיךָ וְלִבְנֵי בָנֶיךָ׃ 10 יוֹם אֲשֶׁר עָמַדְתָּ
לִפְנֵי יְהוָה אֱלֹהֶיךָ בְּחֹרֵב בֶּאֱמֹר יְהוָה
אֵלַי הַקְהֶל־לִי אֶת־הָעָם וְאַשְׁמִעֵם אֶת־
דְּבָרָי אֲשֶׁר יִלְמְדוּן לְיִרְאָה אֹתִי כָּל־
הַיָּמִים אֲשֶׁר הֵם חַיִּים עַל־הָאֲדָמָה וְאֶת־
בְּנֵיהֶם יְלַמֵּדוּן׃ 11 וַתִּקְרְבוּן וַתַּעַמְדוּן
תַּחַת הָהָר וְהָהָר בֹּעֵר בָּאֵשׁ עַד־לֵב
הַשָּׁמַיִם חֹשֶׁךְ עָנָן וַעֲרָפֶל׃ 12 וַיְדַבֵּר יְהוָה
אֲלֵיכֶם מִתּוֹךְ הָאֵשׁ קוֹל דְּבָרִים אַתֶּם
שֹׁמְעִים וּתְמוּנָה אֵינְכֶם רֹאִים זוּלָתִי
קוֹל׃ 13 וַיַּגֵּד לָכֶם אֶת־בְּרִיתוֹ אֲשֶׁר צִוָּה
אֶתְכֶם לַעֲשׂוֹת עֲשֶׂרֶת הַדְּבָרִים וַיִּכְתְּבֵם

concern but must be transmitted by parents to their children and grandchildren. Thus they too will share in the experiences, learn their responsibilities, and gain the benefits of faith and observance.

10–13. These verses seek to impress on the people the awesome nature of the revelation that took place at Horeb. One of Moses' goals in Deuteronomy is to imbue the Israelites with reverence for God as a guiding principle in their lives. Reverence is a mortal's response to God—respect and awe at His grandeur, dread at His power—that deters disobedience to Him.

11. The mountain was ablaze The majestic, awesome Presence of God is expressed by the natural phenomena that accompany His appearance.

12. The LORD spoke to you During the course of His communication with Israel at Horeb the Lord was invisible; He spoke from the midst of fire and only His voice was heard. In the present address this aspect of the experience is emphasized over the content of what God said.

shape Hebrew: *t'munah;* literally, "visage." It has the sense of "appearance" or "aspect." Here, it is not to be taken in the sense of "picture," as in modern Hebrew, but as the visible aspect of a being. In most of the biblical traditions, God was thought to have a visual aspect (e.g., see Exod. 24:10), but it was believed to be highly dangerous for humans to see God. Here, according to Deuteronomy, God revealed Himself in spoken words alone. The belief that God has no physical form developed in postbiblical times, especially in the philosophical literature of the Middle Ages.

13. covenant The Hebrew term (*b'rit*) has three meanings, all based on the idea of obligation: a promise (an obligation imposed on oneself), a stipulation (an obligation imposed on another), or a compact (reciprocal obligations accepted by two parties). Here, it refers to the Decalogue (5:6–18) as stipulations imposed by God on Israel; that is, as the obligation to which Israel must commit itself in its covenant with God. The term can also refer to the essence of all of the laws. For the other senses see v. 31 (promise) and 5:2–3 and 29:11 (compact).

two tablets of stone Stone normally was used only for texts that were intended to be permanent, such as royal and ceremonial inscriptions, boundary inscriptions, and treaties. An Aramaic decree of the 7th century B.C.E. was written on a stone tablet about 11 inches square. It is inscribed on one side, with 32 words covering eight lines. Two such tablets inscribed on both sides (Exod. 32:15), 15 or 16 inches square, could have held the Decalogue's 189 words (172 according to Exodus). A rectangular shape is consistent with Jewish tradition and early Christian art. The familiar image of tablets with curved tops was introduced in Christian art around the 11th century C.E.

---

the ideals of Judaism to one's children does one become aware of one's role as a link in the chain of generations, doing for our children what our ancestors did for their children so that we could be Jews today (Hirsch).

and to your children's children "When a child is taught Torah by a grandparent, it is as if that child received it at Sinai" (BT Ber. 21b).

[14]At the same time the LORD commanded me to impart to you laws and rules for you to observe in the land that you are about to cross into and occupy.

[15]For your own sake, therefore, be most careful—since you saw no shape when the LORD your God spoke to you at Horeb out of the fire—[16]not to act wickedly and make for yourselves a sculptured image in any likeness whatever: the form of a man or a woman, [17]the form of any beast on earth, the form of any winged bird that flies in the sky, [18]the form of anything that creeps on the ground, the form of any fish that is in the waters below the earth. [19]And when you look up to the sky and behold the sun and the moon and the stars, the whole heavenly host, you must not be lured into bowing down to them or serving them. These the LORD your God

עַל־שְׁנֵי לֻחוֹת אֲבָנִים׃ 14 וְאֹתִי צִוָּה
יְהוָה בָּעֵת הַהִוא לְלַמֵּד אֶתְכֶם חֻקִּים
וּמִשְׁפָּטִים לַעֲשֹׂתְכֶם אֹתָם בָּאָרֶץ אֲשֶׁר
אַתֶּם עֹבְרִים שָׁמָּה לְרִשְׁתָּהּ׃
15 וְנִשְׁמַרְתֶּם מְאֹד לְנַפְשֹׁתֵיכֶם כִּי לֹא
רְאִיתֶם כָּל־תְּמוּנָה בְּיוֹם דִּבֶּר יְהוָה
אֲלֵיכֶם בְּחֹרֵב מִתּוֹךְ הָאֵשׁ׃ 16 פֶּן־
תַּשְׁחִתוּן וַעֲשִׂיתֶם לָכֶם פֶּסֶל תְּמוּנַת
כָּל־סָמֶל תַּבְנִית זָכָר אוֹ נְקֵבָה׃ 17 תַּבְנִית
כָּל־בְּהֵמָה אֲשֶׁר בָּאָרֶץ תַּבְנִית כָּל־צִפּוֹר
כָּנָף אֲשֶׁר תָּעוּף בַּשָּׁמָיִם׃ 18 תַּבְנִית כָּל־
רֹמֵשׂ בָּאֲדָמָה תַּבְנִית כָּל־דָּגָה אֲשֶׁר־
בַּמַּיִם מִתַּחַת לָאָרֶץ׃ 19 וּפֶן־תִּשָּׂא עֵינֶיךָ
הַשָּׁמַיְמָה וְרָאִיתָ אֶת־הַשֶּׁמֶשׁ וְאֶת־הַיָּרֵחַ
וְאֶת־הַכּוֹכָבִים כֹּל צְבָא הַשָּׁמַיִם וְנִדַּחְתָּ
וְהִשְׁתַּחֲוִיתָ לָהֶם וַעֲבַדְתָּם אֲשֶׁר חָלַק

14. God personally gave the Decalogue to the people and commanded Moses to convey the rest of the laws to them (see 5:24ff.).

15. since you saw no shape In idolatry, the purpose of an idol was to draw the presence of a deity to the place where the statue stood. Worshipers assumed that a god would enter and reside in the idol that represented it. Here Moses forbids Israel to use idols to attract God. No form was seen in the original contact with God; therefore, none is to be made for future contacts.

16. The verse does not rule out statues that are not idols. Nonidolatrous statues of certain creatures, such as the cherubim, were clearly not considered violations of this commandment and were used both in the wilderness Tabernacle and in Solomon's temple.

17. the form of any beast These figures probably would not have been intended as representations of the Lord, who was thought to have a human appearance (Gen. 1:26). Rather, they might have represented God's chariot or mount. Because God was thought to travel on a chariot borne by hybrid creatures with the faces of men and animals (Ezek. 1), people might have thought it possible to attract His Presence with an image of one or more of those animals.

18. waters below the earth That is, in oceans, lakes, and rivers. The surface of the earth was conceived as standing or floating on a huge body of water that surrounds it in the form of oceans and breaks through to the earth's surface in the form of lakes, springs, and rivers.

19. These passages express the seductive nature of idolatry, especially of the heavenly bodies. The worship of celestial deities was common in the ancient Near East.

These the LORD . . . allotted to other peoples God assigned these to other peoples as objects of worship, but took the people of Israel to be His own worshipers. The biblical context always makes it clear that these bodies are subordinate to the Lord, but people were not always so discriminating, and some Israelites did worship them, especially in the 8th and 7th centuries B.C.E.

---

19. If people are prone to worship aspects of nature as divine, why does God not destroy them to remove the temptation? Because the world needs some of them, such as the sun. Then why does God not destroy the superfluous ones and let the necessary ones survive? Because that would strengthen the conviction of the idolaters that the sun was indeed a mighty god, because it survived the purge in which the other idols perished.

allotted to other peoples everywhere under heaven; [20]but you the LORD took and brought out of Egypt, that iron blast furnace, to be His very own people, as is now the case.

[21]Now the LORD was angry with me on your account and swore that I should not cross the Jordan and enter the good land that the LORD your God is assigning you as a heritage. [22]For I must die in this land; I shall not cross the Jordan. But you will cross and take possession of that good land. [23]Take care, then, not to forget the covenant that the LORD your God concluded with you, and not to make for yourselves a sculptured image in any likeness, against which the LORD your God has enjoined you. [24]For the LORD your God is a consuming fire, an impassioned God.

[25]When you have begotten children and children's children and are long established in the land, should you act wickedly and make for yourselves a sculptured image in any likeness, causing the LORD your God displeasure and vexation, [26]I call heaven and earth this day to witness against you that you shall soon perish

יְהֹוָה אֱלֹהֶ֫יךָ אֹתָ֔ם לְכֹל֙ הָֽעַמִּ֔ים תַּ֖חַת כׇּל־הַשָּׁמָֽיִם: 20 וְאֶתְכֶם֙ לָקַ֣ח יְהֹוָ֔ה וַיּוֹצִ֥א אֶתְכֶ֛ם מִכּ֥וּר הַבַּרְזֶ֖ל מִמִּצְרָ֑יִם לִהְי֥וֹת ל֛וֹ לְעַ֥ם נַחֲלָ֖ה כַּיּ֥וֹם הַזֶּֽה: 21 וַֽיהֹוָ֥ה הִתְאַנֶּף־בִּ֖י עַל־דִּבְרֵיכֶ֑ם וַיִּשָּׁבַ֗ע לְבִלְתִּ֤י עׇבְרִי֙ אֶת־הַיַּרְדֵּ֔ן וּלְבִלְתִּי־בֹא֙ אֶל־הָאָ֣רֶץ הַטּוֹבָ֔ה אֲשֶׁר֙ יְהֹוָ֣ה אֱלֹהֶ֔יךָ נֹתֵ֥ן לְךָ֖ נַחֲלָֽה: 22 כִּ֣י אָֽנֹכִ֥י מֵת֙ בָּאָ֣רֶץ הַזֹּ֔את אֵינֶ֥נִּי עֹבֵ֖ר אֶת־הַיַּרְדֵּ֑ן וְאַתֶּם֙ עֹֽבְרִ֔ים וִֽירִשְׁתֶּ֔ם אֶת־הָאָ֥רֶץ הַטּוֹבָ֖ה הַזֹּֽאת: 23 הִשָּֽׁמְר֣וּ לָכֶ֗ם פֶּֽן־תִּשְׁכְּחוּ֙ אֶת־בְּרִ֣ית יְהֹוָ֣ה אֱלֹֽהֵיכֶ֔ם אֲשֶׁ֥ר כָּרַ֖ת עִמָּכֶ֑ם וַעֲשִׂיתֶ֨ם לָכֶ֥ם פֶּ֙סֶל֙ תְּמ֣וּנַת כֹּ֔ל אֲשֶׁ֥ר צִוְּךָ֖ יְהֹוָ֥ה אֱלֹהֶֽיךָ: 24 כִּ֚י יְהֹוָ֣ה אֱלֹהֶ֔יךָ אֵ֥שׁ אֹכְלָ֖ה ה֑וּא אֵ֖ל קַנָּֽא: פ 25 כִּֽי־תוֹלִ֤יד בָּנִים֙ וּבְנֵ֣י בָנִ֔ים וְנֽוֹשַׁנְתֶּ֖ם בָּאָ֑רֶץ וְהִשְׁחַתֶּ֗ם וַעֲשִׂ֤יתֶם פֶּ֙סֶל֙ תְּמ֣וּנַת כֹּ֔ל וַעֲשִׂיתֶ֥ם הָרַ֛ע בְּעֵינֵ֥י יְהֹוָֽה־אֱלֹהֶ֖יךָ לְהַכְעִיסֽוֹ: 26 הַעִידֹ֩תִי֩ בָכֶ֨ם הַיּ֜וֹם אֶת־הַשָּׁמַ֣יִם וְאֶת־הָאָ֗רֶץ כִּֽי־אָבֹ֣ד תֹּאבֵדוּן֮

---

20. iron blast furnace A metaphor for the severity of the Egyptian bondage (iron was smelted in ancient times at a temperature of about 2000°F).

His very own people Literally, "a people that is His inheritance." The Hebrew word for "inheritance" (naḥalah) expresses not only God's sovereignty over the Israelites but also His attachment to them. Inherited land was precious because it was received from one's ancestors and passed on to one's descendants; it was regarded as inalienable.

24. consuming fire God's fiery destructive

power had struck the Exodus generation several times.

26. I call heaven and earth . . . to witness In ancient Near Eastern covenants, heaven and earth are often called as witnesses along with the gods and other parts of nature regarded as supreme authorities in the universe, so that they would punish those who violate the agreement. In the Bible, however, the supreme authority is the Lord, who is Himself a party to the covenant. Heaven and earth are subordinate to Him and cannot act independently. Their role here as "witnesses" is merely a reflection of that ancient motif.

---

21. on your account Is Moses taking out his frustrations on the people, blaming them for his own mistakes? It would be a very human thing to do, however unjustified in a leader.

25. long established Biblical Hebrew has two words for "old": zaken, which is the opposite of "young"; and yashan (used here with

the connotation of growing stale), which is the opposite of "fresh" (Hirsch).

26. I call heaven and earth . . . to witness Heaven and earth do indeed witness against us when we make improper use of that with which God has blessed us. Poisoning the air and water, despoiling the environment do threaten to cause us to "perish from the land."

from the land that you are crossing the Jordan to possess; you shall not long endure in it, but shall be utterly wiped out. ²⁷The LORD will scatter you among the peoples, and only a scant few of you shall be left among the nations to which the LORD will drive you. ²⁸There you will serve man-made gods of wood and stone, that cannot see or hear or eat or smell.

²⁹But if you search there for the LORD your God, you will find Him, if only you seek Him with all your heart and soul—³⁰when you are in distress because all these things have befallen you and, in the end, return to the LORD your God and obey Him. ³¹For the LORD your God is a compassionate God: He will not fail you nor will He let you perish; He will not forget

מַהֵ֗ר מֵעַ֤ל הָאָ֨רֶץ֙ אֲשֶׁ֨ר אַתֶּ֤ם עֹבְרִים֙ אֶת־הַיַּרְדֵּ֔ן שָׁ֖מָּה לְרִשְׁתָּ֑הּ לֹא־תַאֲרִיכֻ֤ן יָמִים֙ עָלֶ֔יהָ כִּ֥י הִשָּׁמֵ֖ד תִּשָּׁמֵדֽוּן׃ 27 וְהֵפִ֧יץ יְהוָ֛ה אֶתְכֶ֖ם בָּעַמִּ֑ים וְנִשְׁאַרְתֶּם֙ מְתֵ֣י מִסְפָּ֔ר בַּגּוֹיִ֕ם אֲשֶׁ֨ר יְנַהֵ֧ג יְהוָ֛ה אֶתְכֶ֖ם שָֽׁמָּה׃ 28 וַעֲבַדְתֶּם־שָׁ֣ם אֱלֹהִ֔ים מַעֲשֵׂ֖ה יְדֵ֣י אָדָ֑ם עֵ֣ץ וָאֶ֔בֶן אֲשֶׁ֤ר לֹֽא־יִרְאוּן֙ וְלֹ֣א יִשְׁמְע֔וּן וְלֹ֥א יֹֽאכְל֖וּן וְלֹ֥א יְרִיחֻֽן׃ 29 וּבִקַּשְׁתֶּ֥ם מִשָּׁ֛ם אֶת־יְהוָ֥ה אֱלֹהֶ֖יךָ וּמָצָ֑אתָ כִּ֤י תִדְרְשֶׁ֨נּוּ֙ בְּכָל־לְבָ֣בְךָ֔ וּבְכָל־נַפְשֶֽׁךָ׃ 30 בַּצַּ֣ר לְךָ֔ וּמְצָא֕וּךָ כֹּ֖ל הַדְּבָרִ֣ים הָאֵ֑לֶּה בְּאַחֲרִית֙ הַיָּמִ֔ים וְשַׁבְתָּ֙ עַד־יְהוָ֣ה אֱלֹהֶ֔יךָ וְשָׁמַעְתָּ֖ בְּקֹלֽוֹ׃ 31 כִּ֣י אֵ֤ל רַחוּם֙ יְהוָ֣ה אֱלֹהֶ֔יךָ לֹ֥א יַרְפְּךָ֖ וְלֹ֣א יַשְׁחִיתֶ֑ךָ וְלֹ֤א

---

shall be utterly wiped out This is a hyperbole, meaning, "be ruined." As verse 27 indicates, there will be survivors.

27. The punishments are the precise opposites of God's promises: instead of possessing the land (v. 1), the Israelites will be exiled from it; instead of being numerous (1:10–11), they will become few.

28. Exile will bring an additional punishment: worshiping gods that can do nothing. Despite the fact that the Bible regards the Lord as accessible anywhere (see v. 29), it considers only the land of Israel as the "Holy Land" (Zech. 2:16), and other lands as impure. Therefore, it is not permissible to conduct normal, sacrificial worship of God outside the land. (An exception was the wilderness period when a portable sanctuary accompanied Israel in its wanderings.)

that cannot see or hear or eat or smell The Bible considers the worship of statues to be the most preposterous aspect of non-Israelite religion and the most telling argument against it (cf. 27:15,

28:36,64, 29:16). Polytheism held that special ceremonies imparted to the statues all the powers that this verse denies them: sight, hearing, eating, smelling. The more educated idolaters certainly did not believe that the statue actually was the deity but that the god was absent from the statue before the special ceremony and might abandon it at will. The distinction between statue and deity, however, was easily overlooked, and many idolaters sometimes considered images to be the deity or fetishes possessing powers of their own.

30. in the end That is, afterward, ultimately.

return Hebrew: *shuv*, the verb from which the term for "repentance" (*t'shuvah*) is derived.

31. compassionate God The Lord is not only impassioned (v. 24), but also compassionate. These are two aspects of God's personality in the Bible: He both punishes and forgives.

nor will He let you perish; He will not forget the covenant God's actions are thus contrasted with those of the Israelites. God will not act as they acted.

---

27. *only a scant few of you shall be left* Indeed in Jewish history, whenever disaster has befallen a major Jewish community, a saving remnant has survived to carry on.

28. *There you will serve man-made gods* Losing their relationship with God and attaching themselves to false gods who cannot see or hear (in contrast to God who saw their plight and heard their cry in Egypt) will not be just

their sin but also their punishment. Abravanel, who lived at the time of the Inquisition and the expulsion from Spain, applied this verse to the Marranos of his time: "Many Jews will be brought to forced conversion, worshiping idols but knowing full well that they are made of wood and stone. Unable to practice the observance of Judaism, their seeking of God will be in their hearts and minds alone" (v. 29).

the covenant which He made on oath with your
fathers.

יִשְׁכַּח֙ אֶת־בְּרִ֣ית אֲבֹתֶ֔יךָ אֲשֶׁ֥ר נִשְׁבַּ֖ע
לָהֶֽם׃

32 You have but to inquire about bygone ages
that came before you, ever since God created
man on earth, from one end of heaven to the
other: has anything as grand as this ever happened, or has its like ever been known? 33 Has
any people heard the voice of a god speaking
out of a fire, as you have, and survived? 34 Or
has any god ventured to go and take for himself
one nation from the midst of another by prodigious acts, by signs and portents, by war, by
a mighty and an outstretched arm and awesome
power, as the LORD your God did for you in
Egypt before your very eyes? 35 It has been clearly
demonstrated to you that the LORD alone is
God; there is none beside Him. 36 From the
heavens He let you hear His voice to discipline
you; on earth He let you see His great fire; and
from amidst that fire you heard His words.
37 And because He loved your fathers, He chose
their heirs after them; He Himself, in His great

32 כִּ֣י שְׁאַל־נָ֠א לְיָמִ֨ים רִֽאשֹׁנִ֜ים אֲשֶׁר־הָי֣וּ
לְפָנֶ֗יךָ לְמִן־הַיּוֹם֙ אֲשֶׁר֩ בָּרָ֨א אֱלֹהִ֤ים ׀
אָדָם֙ עַל־הָאָ֔רֶץ וּלְמִקְצֵ֥ה הַשָּׁמַ֖יִם וְעַד־
קְצֵ֣ה הַשָּׁמָ֑יִם הֲנִֽהְיָ֗ה כַּדָּבָ֤ר הַגָּדוֹל֙ הַזֶּ֔ה
א֖וֹ הֲנִשְׁמַ֥ע כָּמֹֽהוּ׃ 33 הֲשָׁ֣מַֽע עָם֩ ק֨וֹל
אֱלֹהִ֜ים מְדַבֵּ֧ר מִתּוֹךְ־הָאֵ֛שׁ כַּאֲשֶׁר־שָׁמַ֥עְתָּ
אַתָּ֖ה וַיֶּֽחִי׃ 34 א֣וֹ ׀ הֲנִסָּ֣ה אֱלֹהִ֗ים לָב֨וֹא
לָקַ֩חַת֩ ל֨וֹ ג֜וֹי מִקֶּ֣רֶב גּ֗וֹי בְּמַסֹּת֩ בְּאֹתֹ֨ת
וּבְמוֹפְתִ֜ים וּבְמִלְחָמָ֗ה וּבְיָ֤ד חֲזָקָה֙ וּבִזְר֣וֹעַ
נְטוּיָ֔ה וּבְמוֹרָאִ֖ים גְּדֹלִ֑ים כְּכֹל֩ אֲשֶׁר־עָשָׂ֨ה
לָכֶ֜ם יְהוָ֧ה אֱלֹהֵיכֶ֛ם בְּמִצְרַ֖יִם לְעֵינֶֽיךָ׃
35 אַתָּה֙ הָרְאֵ֣תָ לָדַ֔עַת כִּ֥י יְהוָ֖ה ה֣וּא
הָאֱלֹהִ֑ים אֵ֥ין ע֖וֹד מִלְבַדּֽוֹ׃ 36 מִן־הַשָּׁמַ֛יִם
הִשְׁמִֽיעֲךָ֥ אֶת־קֹל֖וֹ לְיַסְּרֶ֑ךָּ וְעַל־הָאָ֗רֶץ
הֶרְאֲךָ֙ אֶת־אִשּׁ֣וֹ הַגְּדוֹלָ֔ה וּדְבָרָ֥יו שָׁמַ֖עְתָּ
מִתּ֥וֹךְ הָאֵֽשׁ׃ 37 וְתַ֗חַת כִּ֤י אָהַב֙ אֶת־
אֲבֹתֶ֔יךָ וַיִּבְחַ֥ר בְּזַרְע֖וֹ אַחֲרָ֑יו וַיּוֹצִֽאֲךָ֤

BASED ON MONOTHEISM (vv. 32–40)

Following the warning of exile, Moses concludes with a final appeal to observe the commandments so that the Israelites may prosper and remain in the Land forever.

32. ever since God created man on earth As far back as human memory goes.

from one end of heaven to the other That is, from one end of earth to another. Heaven was pictured as a dome standing atop pillars situated at the ends of the earth.

33. A direct, visual encounter with God was thought to be too awesome to endure. This passage and 5:21–23 imply that hearing God was regarded as equally dangerous.

34. take . . . one nation from the midst of another This is the most telling point of Moses' argument: The Lord took Israel out of Egypt, thereby showing the powerlessness of the gods of Egypt and that the Lord is the only true God (see Exod. 12:12).

by prodigious acts The signs Moses and Aaron performed before Pharaoh, including the Ten Plagues and the defeat of Egypt at the Sea of Reeds.

35. The events just described, witnessed by the entire nation, established that the Lord alone is God. This demonstration goes beyond the practical concern of the 2nd commandment, which prohibits worshiping other gods. Here Moses states clearly that there are no others.

36. Deuteronomy never describes God as descending to earth or as dwelling in the sanctuary. Unlike the previous books of the Torah, it avoids allusions to the physical or human nature of God. Divine transcendence is central to Deuteronomy.

37. He Himself Literally, "with His face."

---

35. Because this verse refers to the revelation at Mount Sinai, it is the first in a collection of verses recited when the Torah scrolls are taken from the Ark on *Simḥat Torah,* among *Ashk'nazim*. Among *S'fardim,* it is recited every *Shabbat* at that point in the service.

might, led you out of Egypt, 38to drive from your path nations greater and more populous than you, to take you into their land and assign it to you as a heritage, as is still the case. 39Know therefore this day and keep in mind that the LORD alone is God in heaven above and on earth below; there is no other. 40Observe His laws and commandments, which I enjoin upon you this day, that it may go well with you and your children after you, and that you may long remain in the land that the LORD your God is assigning to you for all time.

41Then Moses set aside three cities on the east side of the Jordan 42to which a manslayer could escape, one who unwittingly slew a fellow man without having been hostile to him in the past; he could flee to one of these cities and live: 43Bezer, in the wilderness in the Tableland, belonging to the Reubenites; Ramoth, in Gilead, belonging to the Gadites; and Golan, in Bashan, belonging to the Manassites.

44This is the Teaching that Moses set before the Israelites: 45these are the decrees, laws, and

בְּפָנָיו בְּכֹחוֹ הַגָּדֹל מִמִּצְרָיִם׃ 38 לְהוֹרִישׁ
גּוֹיִם גְּדֹלִים וַעֲצֻמִים מִמְּךָ מִפָּנֶיךָ
לַהֲבִיאֲךָ לָתֶת־לְךָ אֶת־אַרְצָם נַחֲלָה כַּיּוֹם
הַזֶּה׃ 39 וְיָדַעְתָּ הַיּוֹם וַהֲשֵׁבֹתָ אֶל־לְבָבֶךָ
כִּי יְהוָה הוּא הָאֱלֹהִים בַּשָּׁמַיִם מִמַּעַל
וְעַל־הָאָרֶץ מִתָּחַת אֵין עוֹד׃ 40 וְשָׁמַרְתָּ
אֶת־חֻקָּיו וְאֶת־מִצְוֺתָיו אֲשֶׁר אָנֹכִי מְצַוְּךָ
הַיּוֹם אֲשֶׁר יִיטַב לְךָ וּלְבָנֶיךָ אַחֲרֶיךָ וּלְמַעַן
תַּאֲרִיךְ יָמִים עַל־הָאֲדָמָה אֲשֶׁר יְהוָה
אֱלֹהֶיךָ נֹתֵן לְךָ כָּל־הַיָּמִים׃ פ

שלישי 41 אָז יַבְדִּיל מֹשֶׁה שָׁלֹשׁ עָרִים בְּעֵבֶר
הַיַּרְדֵּן מִזְרְחָה שָׁמֶשׁ׃ 42 לָנֻס שָׁמָּה רוֹצֵחַ
אֲשֶׁר יִרְצַח אֶת־רֵעֵהוּ בִּבְלִי־דַעַת וְהוּא
לֹא־שֹׂנֵא לוֹ מִתְּמֹל שִׁלְשׁוֹם וְנָס אֶל־אַחַת
מִן־הֶעָרִים הָאֵל וָחָי׃ 43 אֶת־בֶּצֶר בַּמִּדְבָּר
בְּאֶרֶץ הַמִּישֹׁר לָראוּבֵנִי וְאֶת־רָאמֹת
בַּגִּלְעָד לַגָּדִי וְאֶת־גּוֹלָן בַּבָּשָׁן לַמְנַשִּׁי׃

44 וְזֹאת הַתּוֹרָה אֲשֶׁר־שָׂם מֹשֶׁה לִפְנֵי
בְּנֵי יִשְׂרָאֵל׃ 45 אֵלֶּה הָעֵדֹת וְהַחֻקִּים

The Hebrew equivalent of "in person." The idiom emphasizes that God used no intermediary (such as an angel) in freeing the Israelites, but freed them personally as a sign of His favor.

39. That God spoke from heaven and acted on earth shows His dominion in both realms. He is God everywhere.

40. The fact that the Lord alone is God leads to the conclusion that observance of His commandments is the prerequisite for prosperity and well-being. The address thus ends on the same note with which it began. It reminds the audience that its central message is proper behavior.

ASYLUM CITIES IN TRANSJORDAN
(vv. 41–43)

These verses are not part of Moses' address but a narrative appendix, relating that Moses designated three cities in Transjordan to provide asylum for accidental manslayers. The law establishing these cities appears in 19:1–13 (19:3–5 is abridged here) and Num. 35:9–34. According to Num. 35:14, six such cities were to be chosen, three of them in Transjordan.

41. Then This could refer to any time after the conquest of Transjordan, which took place shortly before Moses' address. It is possible that Moses selected the cities after the actions described in 3:18–29. Because verses 41–43 are by the narrator, and not Moses, they were placed here to avoid interrupting his address.

43. The cities are listed in order from south to north.

Bezer In Moab.

in Gilead That is, upper Gilead.

---

41. Why was the institution of cities of refuge so important to Moses? Because he himself was once a manslayer (Exod. 2:11–15) and had to flee (Deut. R. 2:27).

rules that Moses addressed to the people of
Israel, after they had left Egypt, 46beyond the
Jordan, in the valley at Beth-peor, in the land
of King Sihon of the Amorites, who dwelt in
Heshbon, whom Moses and the Israelites defeated after they had left Egypt. 47They had
taken possession of his country and that of King
Og of Bashan—the two kings of the Amorites—
which were on the east side of the Jordan 48from
Aroer on the banks of the wadi Arnon, as far
as Mount Sion, that is, Hermon; 49also the
whole Arabah on the east side of the Jordan, as
far as the Sea of the Arabah, at the foot of the
slopes of Pisgah.

וְהַמִּשְׁפָּטִים אֲשֶׁר דִּבֶּר מֹשֶׁה אֶל־בְּנֵי
יִשְׂרָאֵל בְּצֵאתָם מִמִּצְרָיִם׃ 46 בְּעֵבֶר
הַיַּרְדֵּן בַּגַּיְא מוּל בֵּית פְּעוֹר בְּאֶרֶץ סִיחֹן
מֶלֶךְ הָאֱמֹרִי אֲשֶׁר יוֹשֵׁב בְּחֶשְׁבּוֹן אֲשֶׁר
הִכָּה מֹשֶׁה וּבְנֵי יִשְׂרָאֵל בְּצֵאתָם
מִמִּצְרָיִם׃ 47 וַיִּירְשׁוּ אֶת־אַרְצוֹ וְאֶת־
אֶרֶץ ׀ עוֹג מֶלֶךְ־הַבָּשָׁן שְׁנֵי מַלְכֵי הָאֱמֹרִי
אֲשֶׁר בְּעֵבֶר הַיַּרְדֵּן מִזְרַח שָׁמֶשׁ׃
48 מֵעֲרֹעֵר אֲשֶׁר עַל־שְׂפַת־נַחַל אַרְנֹן וְעַד־
הַר שִׂיאֹן הוּא חֶרְמוֹן׃ 49 וְכָל־הָעֲרָבָה
עֵבֶר הַיַּרְדֵּן מִזְרָחָה וְעַד יָם הָעֲרָבָה תַּחַת
אַשְׁדֹּת הַפִּסְגָּה׃ פ

5 Moses summoned all the Israelites and said
to them: Hear, O Israel, the laws and rules that

ביעי ה וַיִּקְרָא מֹשֶׁה אֶל־כָּל־יִשְׂרָאֵל וַיֹּאמֶר
אֲלֵהֶם שְׁמַע יִשְׂרָאֵל אֶת־הַחֻקִּים וְאֶת־

Moses' Second Discourse, Part 1: Background to the Covenant Made in Moab (4:44–5:30)

CONTENTS AND SETTING OF THE COVENANT (4:44–49)

The main subject of Moses' second, and longest, discourse is the laws that he communicates to the people in Moab, in preparation for Israel's entry into the Promised Land.

45. after they had left Egypt Literally, "when they left Egypt." Like the victories mentioned in verse 46, these laws were given to the people 40 years after the Exodus. Deuteronomy, however, refers to the entire period between the Exodus and arrival in the Promised Land as "after they/you had left Egypt" (see 23:5, 24:9, 25:17).

48–49. Transjordan is described in terms of its two topographic regions: the highlands (v. 48) and the Jordan Valley (v. 49).

Mount Sion A third name, along with Sirion and Senir, for Mount Hermon, which lies north of the Jordan Valley.

THE REVELATION AND COVENANT AT HOREB (5:1–30)

Moses tells the people how and why God gave the laws to him. The belief that God is the author of the laws is a distinctive feature of Israelite law. Elsewhere in the ancient Near East, the laws of society were believed to be the products of human minds, with their promulgation sponsored by the deity, as in the case of the Code of Hammurabi. In Deuteronomy the validity of the laws rests firmly on their divine authorship and on Moses' legitimacy as the intermediary conveying them to the people. As a result, obedience to the law—civil no less than ritual and moral—was seen as a religious duty, not only as an act of good citizenship.

THE SCENE AT HOREB (vv. 1–5)

1. laws and rules These are the laws that Moses received from God after the people heard

HALAKHAH L'MA·ASEH

5:1. Study them According to the Talmud (BT Kid. 29b), even if parents fail to fulfill their obligation to teach Torah to their children (Deut. 6:7), the children, as adults, have the obligation to seek instruction for themselves. Indeed, as the Sages make clear in many places, Jewish learning is a life-long process.

I proclaim to you this day! Study them and observe them faithfully!
2The LORD our God made a covenant with
us at Horeb. 3It was not with our fathers that
the LORD made this covenant, but with us, the
living, every one of us who is here today. 4Face
to face the LORD spoke to you on the mountain
out of the fire—5I stood between the LORD and
you at that time to convey the LORD's words to
you, for you were afraid of the fire and did not
go up the mountain—saying:
6I the LORD am your God who brought you

הַמִּשְׁפָּטִים אֲשֶׁר אָנֹכִי דֹּבֵר בְּאָזְנֵיכֶם הַיּוֹם
וּלְמַדְתֶּם אֹתָם וּשְׁמַרְתֶּם לַעֲשֹׂתָם׃
2 יְהוָה אֱלֹהֵינוּ כָּרַת עִמָּנוּ בְּרִית בְּחֹרֵב׃
3 לֹא אֶת־אֲבֹתֵינוּ כָּרַת יְהוָה אֶת־הַבְּרִית
הַזֹּאת כִּי אִתָּנוּ אֲנַחְנוּ אֵלֶּה פֹה הַיּוֹם
כֻּלָּנוּ חַיִּים׃ 4 פָּנִים ׀ בְּפָנִים דִּבֶּר יְהוָה
עִמָּכֶם בָּהָר מִתּוֹךְ הָאֵשׁ׃ 5 אָנֹכִי עֹמֵד
בֵּין־יְהוָה וּבֵינֵיכֶם בָּעֵת הַהִוא לְהַגִּיד
לָכֶם אֶת־דְּבַר יְהוָה כִּי יְרֵאתֶם מִפְּנֵי
הָאֵשׁ וְלֹא־עֲלִיתֶם בָּהָר לֵאמֹר׃ ס
6 *אָנֹכִי יְהוָה אֱלֹהֶיךָ אֲשֶׁר הוֹצֵאתִיךָ

vv. 6–18. נדפס בטעם תחתון בלבד, והוא למערבאי, והפסוקים ממוספרים לפי מהדורת לעטעריס. נדפס בטעם עליון בסוף החומש

the Decalogue. The Decalogue itself is called "the Covenant" or "the (Ten) Words" (4:13).

2. made a covenant Hebrew: *karat b'rit;* literally, "cut a covenant." The idiom apparently derives from a ceremony in which parties to a covenant would cut up an animal to signify their acceptance of a similar fate if they violated the agreement (see Gen. 15). The phrase was used even when a covenant was ratified by other ceremonies, as in the present case (see Exod. 24:1–8). Here "covenant" does not refer to the Decalogue alone (as in 4:13) but to the relationship that God established with Israel at Horeb, where Israel agreed to do all that the Lord commanded, including the laws that Moses would later give Israel in Moab (vv. 24,28).

3. our fathers Abraham, Isaac, and Jacob. In Deuteronomy, "our/your fathers" always refers to the patriarchs.

4. Face to face That is, in person, without intermediation. "Face" is used in the same sense in 4:37. The idiom does not mean that they literally saw God's face. This is ruled out by statements that God spoke from within fire and clouds and that the Israelites saw no visual image (see vv. 20,21, 4:12).

5. In their fright the people had sent Moses ahead to hear God for them. According to the previous verse, however, God insisted on their hearing Him directly.

THE DECALOGUE (vv. 6–18)

Moses repeats the Decalogue first presented in Exodus 20. Most of the differences from the

---

CHAPTER 5

1. Note that observance of the law is seen as the purpose of its study (see BT Yev. 109b).

2–5. Moses recalls the giving of the Torah at Mount Sinai. Perhaps because he is speaking to the children of those who actually experienced the event, he notes that the covenant is binding even on later generations of Israelites. And he summons up the overwhelming, dramatic impact of the Revelation.

5. I stood between the LORD and you Unmediated, direct experience of God is overwhelming for the ordinary person. Moses is in the great tradition of religious leaders who can endure that intense encounter and mediate its effect and power so that every person feels he or she has been in the presence of the Divine.

This clause can also be read: "I" (that is, your ego) stand between God and you (Menaḥem Mendel of Kotzk).

you were afraid of the fire and did not go up the mountain Early *Ḥasidim* in eastern Europe were criticized by their opponents for the highly emotional, enthusiastic manner in which they prayed and celebrated. They responded to the criticism by citing this verse; thus they accused their opponents of discomfort with emotion in religion—that is, of keeping Jewish observance on an intellectual level and, therefore, not rising to a higher spiritual level.

מֵאֶרֶץ מִצְרַיִם מִבֵּית עֲבָדִים 7 *לֹא יִהְיֶה
לְךָ אֱלֹהִים אֲחֵרִים עַל־פָּנָיַ׃
8 לֹא־תַעֲשֶׂה־לְךָ פֶסֶל ׀ כָּל־תְּמוּנָה אֲשֶׁר

out of the land of Egypt, the house of bondage:
7 You shall have no other gods beside Me.
8 You shall not make for yourself a sculptured
image, any likeness of what is in the heavens

v. 7. למערבאי לא נחשב פסוק נפרד

wording in Exodus are minor. Some, however, especially in the *Shabbat* commandment, are substantial. The Decalogue is arranged in two groups of laws. The first group deals with conduct toward God, the second toward fellow humans. Within each group, the commandments are arranged in descending order, according to the gravity of the prohibited offense. Duties to God come first, because the commandments presuppose His authority and their very purpose is to serve as the terms of Israel's covenant with Him. The first 4 commandments are uniquely Israelite duties. Because the reasons for the first 5 are not well known or self-evident, or perhaps because they are easy to violate, explanatory comments and exhortations to encourage observance accompany them. The remaining 5 commandments are universally recognized ethical requirements and need no such support.

There are different views about how these 10 commandments are to be divided; see Comment to Exod. 20:2. Here we follow the view of Philo and Josephus and some talmudic sources, which seems closest to the sense of the text. It divides the first two commandments differently from the traditional enumeration found on tablets in synagogues and in art.

Traditionally the Decalogue has two systems of cantillation. The version known as the "lower notes" is presented here; for the "upper notes," which are used in many synagogues on certain occasions, see p. 1509.

6. This verse is a self-presentation formula that substantiates the divine proclamation that follows. As such, it is not the 1st commandment, but serves as its motive clause. Such self-presentations are common in the openings of royal inscriptions in the ancient Near East and serve as introductions to treaties. The concept of a covenant between God and Israel is modeled on ancient treaties in which a weaker king accepted a more powerful one as his superior and on royal covenants in which a population accepted a king. Such covenants established relationships that were inherently exclusive: A subject population or king could have only one sovereign ruler, and ancient oaths of allegiance and treaties explicitly prohibit subjects and vassals from accepting another. Subjects entered into such relationships on the basis of past benefits realized through the king or ruler, often his having delivered them from enemies. The covenant was thus an apt metaphor for Israel's exclusive relationship with *YHVH* because of the Exodus.

brought you out That is, liberated you.

house of bondage Literally, "house of slaves." A common biblical designation for Egypt.

THE FIRST COMMANDMENT (v. 7)

In practical terms, the Israelites may not build altars or sanctuaries for other gods, nor make images of them, present offerings to them, consult them, prophesy or take oaths in their names, or even mention their names. This prohibition, banning the worship of all but one deity, is unique in the history of religion. Polytheism was inherently tolerant of the worship of many gods, because no single god was thought to control all the phenomena that are vital for human life. The gods were believed to tolerate this pluralism, and several could be worshiped in the same sanctuary or addressed in the same prayer. The biblical demand was based on the premise of exclusivity, because God alone liberated the Israelites and provided for all their needs.

7. other gods The Hebrew terms for "god" (*el* and *elohim*) can be used for angels, spirits, idols, pagan deities, and even spirits of the dead (1 Sam. 28:13), as well as God Himself. All but the last are "other gods," and their worship is prohibited.

beside me Hebrew: *al panai;* literally, "in addition to Me" or "in opposition to Me." This commandment recognizes that Israelites would not abandon *YHVH* but might be tempted to worship others in addition to Him. Polytheists do not choose one god to the exclusion of others, but worship many gods. Note that this prohibition is not quite the same as the affirmation of monotheism (in 4:35,39), because by itself it does not deny the existence of other gods.

---

6. I the LORD am your God These words precede "you shall have no other gods." Faith in the true God protects us from being attracted to false gods (Tzadok ha-Kohen of Lublin).

בַּשָּׁמַ֨יִם ׀ מִמַּ֗עַל וַאֲשֶׁר֙ בָּאָ֣רֶץ מִתָּ֔חַת
וַאֲשֶׁ֥ר בַּמַּ֖יִם ׀ מִתַּ֣חַת לָאָֽרֶץ׃ 9 לֹא־
תִשְׁתַּחֲוֶ֥ה לָהֶ֖ם וְלֹ֣א תָעָבְדֵ֑ם כִּ֣י אָנֹכִ֞י
יְהוָ֤ה אֱלֹהֶ֙יךָ֙ אֵ֣ל קַנָּ֔א פֹּ֠קֵד עֲוֺ֨ן אָב֧וֹת
עַל־בָּנִ֛ים וְעַל־שִׁלֵּשִׁ֥ים וְעַל־רִבֵּעִ֖ים
לְשֹׂנְאָֽי׃ 10 וְעֹ֥שֶׂה חֶ֖סֶד לַאֲלָפִ֑ים לְאֹהֲבַ֖י
וּלְשֹׁמְרֵ֥י מצותו מִצְוֺתָֽי׃ ס

above, or on the earth below, or in the waters
below the earth. 9You shall not bow down to
them or serve them. For I the LORD your God
am an impassioned God, visiting the guilt of the
parents upon the children, upon the third and
upon the fourth generations of those who reject
Me, 10but showing kindness to the thousandth
generation of those who love Me and keep My
commandments.

THE SECOND COMMANDMENT (vv. 8–10) The ban on idols immediately follows the command against worshiping gods. The text does not distinguish between images of the Lord and idols of other gods. Because idolaters often spoke of idols as if they were gods, not merely symbols of gods and because the Bible insists that no statue can be the Lord, it considers any idol as de facto a god, no matter whom or what the worshiper identifies it with. The reference to the jealousy of God thus applies to the 2nd commandment as well as the 1st; this is why it comes only after the second.

8. The language of this verse prohibits not only idols of animate creatures (4:16–18) but also images of inanimate objects, such as stars and sacred trees.

9. bow down . . . serve Each of these verbs has a technical meaning. "Bowing" refers to prostration; "serving" often refers to making offerings. When the two are paired they refer more broadly to any form of worship or submission.

them The various types of idols mentioned in verse 8 and the gods mentioned in verse 7. The combination of idols and gods reinforces the position of the commandments (and the Bible as a whole) that any idol is de facto a pagan god.

impassioned Hebrew: *kanna,* combining the meanings of "jealous" and "zealous." The root קנא is often associated with fire (see 4:24); it refers primarily to fiery passions such as love, anger, indignation, and jealousy. In the Torah the Lord's *kin·ah* is provoked by the worship of idols and gods. In these contexts, God's outrage includes jealousy: God does not tolerate the honor due Him being given to another. References to God's *kin·ah* are frequently accompanied by a description of His punitive action or power, as in the remainder of this verse. The very mention of God's jealousy is, thus a warning against provoking it.

visiting the guilt of the parents That is, inflicting punishment for their guilt on their descendants. The jealousy of God is such that the punishment will not be limited to the idolater alone, but will last for generations. This view of divine retribution reflects the powerful sense of family solidarity in ancient societies, especially those with a tribal background. The concept was progressively modified in the later biblical period and ultimately reduced to the principle that individuals should be rewarded and punished only for their own deeds (see Jer. 31:28ff.; Ezek. 18:2–4).

third and . . . fourth generations Grandchildren and great-grandchildren. Living to see three generations of descendants is the most one could naturally expect. Thus God extends punishment only to descendants the guilty are likely to see in their own lifetimes, an act intended as a deterrent to sin and not as a transfer of guilt to those descendants.

those who reject Me The Rabbis maintain that this phrase (and "those who love Me" in v. 10) refer to descendants who act as their ancestors did. Thus God visits the guilt of the parents on future generations that reject Him and rewards the loyalty of ancestors to the thousandth generation of descendants who are also loyal to Him.

10. showing kindness "Keeping faith," or "dealing faithfully." The basic meaning of "kind-

---

9. visiting the guilt of the parents We are learning how strongly patterns of behavior are passed on from parents to children. Abused children too often become abusive parents.

12. Observe Hebrew: *shamor;* here Exod. 20:8 reads "remember" (*zakhor*). Regarding *Shabbat,* some spiritually gifted souls are able to appreciate its sublime beauty and truth immediately and need only to remember that the day is *Shabbat* to be cast into its mood. The average person, however, has to begin with the prohibition of labor, the requirement of rest—the restrictive side of *Shabbat*—to come to appreciate it.

[11]You shall not swear falsely by the name of the LORD your God; for the LORD will not clear one who swears falsely by His name.

[12]Observe the sabbath day and keep it holy, as the LORD your God has commanded you. [13]Six days you shall labor and do all your work, [14]but the seventh day is a sabbath of the LORD your God; you shall not do any work—you, your son or your daughter, your male or female slave, your ox or your ass, or any of your cattle,

11 לֹא תִשָּׂא אֶת־שֵׁם־יְהוָה אֱלֹהֶיךָ לַשָּׁוְא
כִּי לֹא יְנַקֶּה יְהוָה אֵת אֲשֶׁר־יִשָּׂא אֶת־
שְׁמוֹ לַשָּׁוְא׃ ס
12 שָׁמוֹר אֶת־יוֹם הַשַּׁבָּת לְקַדְּשׁוֹ כַּאֲשֶׁר
צִוְּךָ ׀ יְהוָה אֱלֹהֶיךָ׃ 13 שֵׁשֶׁת יָמִים תַּעֲבֹד
וְעָשִׂיתָ כָּל־מְלַאכְתֶּךָ׃ 14 וְיוֹם הַשְּׁבִיעִי
שַׁבָּת לַיהוָה אֱלֹהֶיךָ לֹא תַעֲשֶׂה כָל־
מְלָאכָה אַתָּה וּבִנְךָ־וּבִתֶּךָ וְעַבְדְּךָ־וַאֲמָתֶךָ
וְשׁוֹרְךָ וַחֲמֹרְךָ וְכָל־בְּהֶמְתֶּךָ וְגֵרְךָ אֲשֶׁר

ness" (*ḥesed*) is "loyalty" or "fidelity," the type of act that can be expected between parties in a relationship—husband and wife, relatives, and allies.

love Hebrew: *ahavah.* In the Bible, the term encompasses friendship and loyalty, including the loyalty of allies and of a vassal toward his suzerain. In Deuteronomy, love of and loyalty to God are virtually synonymous with keeping His commandments; they refer to an emotional attachment that is expressed in action (see 6:5–6, 10:12–13, 11:1,22).

THE THIRD COMMANDMENT (v. 11)

11. Assertions in court, in public affairs, and even in ordinary conversation often were backed up with oaths that included God's name. These were conditional self-curses that would take effect if the swearers' assertions were not true or their promises were not fulfilled. The normal formulations were "As the LORD lives, I will [or will not] . . ." or "May the LORD do such and such to me if I did [or did not] . . ." Swearers proved their sincerity by calling down punishment on themselves from God, who cannot be deceived or evaded. A false oath would show contempt for God by implying that the swearer does not fear His punishment.

will not clear Literally, "leave unpunished." Those who swear falsely will not escape divine justice even if they somehow avoid human justice. This belief was taken seriously throughout the ancient world. In an Egyptian penitential prayer, a man confesses that his suffering is punishment for taking a false oath in the name of a deity.

THE FOURTH COMMANDMENT (vv. 12–15)

The first three commandments prohibit actions that show disrespect for the Lord. The 4th commandment requires a positive act by observing a day sacred to Him.

12. Observe That is, celebrate the day by following its prescribed procedures. The earlier version of the Decalogue (Exod. 20:8) uses the verb "remember" (*zakhor*), meaning "remember to observe *Shabbat.*"

sabbath day The seventh day of each week. The Bible understands the Hebrew word *shabbat* as a derivative of the verb meaning "cease" or "desist" (Exod. 23:12; Lev. 23:3). "The sabbath day" thus means "the day of desisting [from labor]."

holy Withdrawn from common use and reserved for a special purpose associated with God. *Shabbat* was withdrawn from common use by desisting from labor. And its dedication to God was expressed by: visits to sanctuaries and prophets (2 Kings 4:23; Isa. 1:13, 66:23); special sacrifices and other temple activities (Lev. 24:8; Num. 28:9–10); recitation of a special psalm (Ps. 92); and a joyous atmosphere (Hos. 2:13; Isa. 58:13; Lam. 2:6).

14. sabbath of the LORD The day belongs to the Lord and must, therefore, be used for the Lord's purposes, not one's own (cf. Isa. 58:13). This explains why certain activities that may not be performed for human benefit on *Shabbat* are permitted in the Temple, such as burning the sacrifices and kindling the lamps (Exod. 27:20–21, 29:38–42; Num. 28:9–10).

you Includes both males and females, because both are specified in the following list of those covered by the law. In general, biblical laws address men and women alike.

work Examples, such as agricultural labor, gathering food and firewood, kindling fire, and business activities, are mentioned elsewhere in the Bible.

slave Includes both slave and bondservant. No distinction is made here between Israelite and foreign slaves.

ox . . . ass . . . cattle Kindness to animals is also the theme of several other laws in the Torah.

or the stranger in your settlements, so that your male and female slave may rest as you do. 15Remember that you were a slave in the land of Egypt and the LORD your God freed you from there with a mighty hand and an outstretched arm; therefore the LORD your God has commanded you to observe the sabbath day.

16Honor your father and your mother, as the LORD your God has commanded you, that you may long endure, and that you may fare well, in the land that the LORD your God is assigning to you.

בִּשְׁעָרֶ֑יךָ לְמַ֗עַן יָנ֛וּחַ עַבְדְּךָ֥ וַאֲמָתְךָ֖ כָּמֽוֹךָ׃
15 וְזָכַרְתָּ֞ כִּ֣י עֶ֤בֶד הָיִ֨יתָ֙ בְּאֶ֣רֶץ מִצְרַ֔יִם
וַיֹּצִאֲךָ֩ יְהוָ֨ה אֱלֹהֶ֤יךָ מִשָּׁם֙ בְּיָ֤ד חֲזָקָה֙
וּבִזְרֹ֣עַ נְטוּיָ֔ה עַל־כֵּ֗ן צִוְּךָ֙ יְהוָ֣ה אֱלֹהֶ֔יךָ
לַעֲשׂ֖וֹת אֶת־י֥וֹם הַשַּׁבָּֽת׃ ס
16 כַּבֵּ֤ד אֶת־אָבִ֨יךָ֙ וְאֶת־אִמֶּ֔ךָ כַּאֲשֶׁ֥ר צִוְּךָ֖
יְהוָ֣ה אֱלֹהֶ֑יךָ לְמַ֣עַן ׀ יַאֲרִיכֻ֣ן יָמֶ֗יךָ וּלְמַ֨עַן֙
יִ֣יטַב לָ֔ךְ עַ֚ל הָֽאֲדָמָ֔ה אֲשֶׁר־יְהוָ֥ה אֱלֹהֶ֖יךָ
נֹתֵ֥ן לָֽךְ׃ ס

stranger The *ger,* the resident alien. This reminder to include resident aliens in *Shabbat* rest is comparable to Deuteronomy's exhortations to include them in religious celebrations (16:11,14, 26:11). Such reminders are necessary because of the aliens' vulnerability and the likelihood that their needs would be overlooked.

so that your . . . slave may rest The law assumes that the householders will find time for themselves and their families to rest, but may neglect their servants' need to do so. Thus the law mandates that one day in each week the servants are to be treated as the master's equal. The entire household is required to rest, so that there can be no occasion to make the servants work.

15. The experiences of servitude and redemption are recalled to motivate observance of several humanitarian laws in Deuteronomy (see 15:15, 16:12, 24:18,22). Commentators are divided over what this motive emphasizes. Some believe that it is the memory of the servitude, to create empathy for the servant's need to rest. Others believe it is God's redeeming them from Egypt, to remind the people of His kindness and of His authority to establish such a command. Contrast the reason for observing *Shabbat* offered here with that in Exod. 20:11.

THE FIFTH COMMANDMENT (v. 16)

Honoring parents is first among duties toward other human beings, just as it is first among the laws of holiness in Lev. 19:3. One aspect of this duty is respect, which includes obedience to parents and adherence to their teachings and forbids hitting, insulting, and behaving disrespectfully toward them and misappropriating their property. Another aspect is caring for parents when they are aged or infirm (this commandment, like the Decalogue as a whole, is not addressed merely to youngsters; see v. 14). The fact that honoring parents appears among the first five commandments, all of which deal with honoring God and mention His name, indicates how important this commandment was considered to be. Other ancient societies, too, ranked the honor of parents second only to the honor of the gods.

16. father and . . . mother See Comment to Lev. 19:3.

that you may long endure . . . in the land This is the only commandment in the Decalogue for which a reward is promised, although the promise can be read as a veiled threat ("otherwise your days will be shortened"). Some ancient legal documents make children's right to inherit their parents' property contingent on their honoring

---

14. so that your male and female slave may rest as you do This clause does not appear in Exod. 20. It may represent a later stage of Israelite society, which thought of the slave as a fellow human being, halfway between a hired hand and a member of the family. Similarly, Deut. 15:12 refers to the slave as "your brother"; no such appellation occurs in the earlier, parallel source (Exod. 21:2).

15. The Exodus version of the 4th commandment explains *Shabbat* in terms of what scholars of religion call *imitatio dei* (i.e., as God rested on the seventh day, so should you). But the wording here, addressed to the children and grandchildren of the Israelites who had actually experienced slavery, bases *Shabbat* observance on the memory of Egyptian bondage and God's liberation. Both reasons are mentioned in *Shabbat* evening's *Kiddush.*

17You shall not murder.

You shall not commit adultery.

You shall not steal.

You shall not bear false witness against your neighbor.

18You shall not covet your neighbor's wife. You shall not crave your neighbor's house, or his field, or his male or female slave, or his ox, or his ass, or anything that is your neighbor's.

19The LORD spoke those words—those and no more—to your whole congregation at the

17*לֹ֥א תִּרְצָ֖ח ס

וְלֹ֖א תִּנְאָֽ֑ף ס

וְלֹ֖א תִּגְנֹֽ֑ב ס

וְלֹֽא־תַעֲנֶ֥ה בְרֵֽעֲךָ֖ עֵ֥ד שָֽׁוְא׃ ס

18 וְלֹ֥א תַחְמֹ֖ד אֵ֣שֶׁת רֵעֶ֑ךָ* ס וְלֹ֣א תִתְאַוֶּ֗ה בֵּ֤ית רֵעֶ֙ךָ֙ שָׂדֵ֣הוּ וְעַבְדּ֤וֹ וַאֲמָתוֹ֙ שׁוֹר֣וֹ וַחֲמֹר֔וֹ וְכֹ֖ל אֲשֶׁ֥ר לְרֵעֶֽךָ׃ ס

חמישי 19 אֶֽת־הַדְּבָרִ֣ים הָאֵ֗לֶּה דִּבֶּר֩ יְהֹוָ֨ה אֶל־כׇּל־קְהַלְכֶ֜ם בָּהָ֗ר מִתּ֤וֹךְ הָאֵשׁ֙ הֶֽעָנָ֔ן

v. 17.   למערבאי שלוש פעמים פיסקא באמצע פסוק

v. 18.   פיסקא באמצע פסוק

their parents by providing and caring for them. Here God applies the same condition on a national scale: The right of future generations of Israelites to inherit the land of Israel from their parents is contingent on honoring them.

THE SIXTH TO NINTH COMMANDMENTS
(v. 17)

17. murder The Hebrew word *ratzaḥ* refers to illicit killing, both intentional and accidental (see 1 Kings 21:19; Deut. 19:4). The frequent translation "you shall not kill" is far too broad; it implies that even capital punishment and war are prohibited, whereas the Torah sometimes mandates these.

adultery In the Bible and the ancient Near East, the term meant voluntary sexual relations between a married or betrothed woman and a man other than her husband. It did not refer to the extramarital relations of a married man (unless, of course, the other woman was married). One reason for this distinction is that ancient Near Eastern society was polygamous. In such a context, although a husband had an exclusive right to his wife, a wife might share her husband with his other wives and did not have an exclusive right to him. Furthermore, in a patrilineal society, it was essential to be certain of the paternity of heirs, and the extramarital intercourse of the wife would make such certainty impossible. As in the case of murder, adultery is regarded as an offense

against both God and mortals. No option is offered for the husband or any human authority to waive or mitigate the punishment, as it is in ancient Near Eastern laws. Provisions for dealing with adultery are found in Num. 5:11–31 and Deut. 22:22–27.

false witness Includes both false accusation and false testimony in court. The penalty for false testimony is given in 19:16–21.

THE TENTH COMMANDMENT   (v. 18)

18. covet . . . crave Both Hebrew verbs describe desires wrongly directed at objects that belong to others.

crave This Hebrew verb refers to an emotional state rather than an action. In contrast, the ambiguous wording in Exod. 20:14 permits the interpretation "seize by force" rather than "covet."

wife . . . house . . . field Unlike in Exodus, where "house" means "household" and includes wife, servants, and livestock, here the wife is placed in the first clause by herself and separated from property. Deuteronomy thus disengages family from property. By including houses and fields in the list, this version refers to the kinds of property people will own after the settlement in Canaan, and reflects Deuteronomy's aim of preparing the Israelites for life in the Land.

MOSES AS INTERMEDIARY   (vv. 19–30)

19. those words Those commandments.

---

17. false witness Literally, "worthless witness"—a different term than in Exod. 20:13. Here the wording forbids testimony that is misleading though not technically untrue (Ramban).

19. those and no more Hebrew: *v'lo yasaf;* literally, "and did not continue." See also Num. 11:25, where the spirit of God inspires 70 elders to prophesy—"and they did not continue [to prophesy after that moment]." There,

mountain, with a mighty voice out of the fire and the dense clouds. He inscribed them on two tablets of stone, which He gave to me. 20When you heard the voice out of the darkness, while the mountain was ablaze with fire, you came up to me, all your tribal heads and elders, 21and said, "The LORD our God has just shown us His majestic Presence, and we have heard His voice out of the fire; we have seen this day that man may live though God has spoken to him. 22Let us not die, then, for this fearsome fire will consume us; if we hear the voice of the LORD our God any longer, we shall die. 23For what mortal ever heard the voice of the living God speak out of the fire, as we did, and lived? 24You go closer and hear all that the LORD our God says, and then you tell us everything that the LORD our God tells you, and we will willingly do it."

25The LORD heard the plea that you made to me, and the LORD said to me, "I have heard the plea that this people made to you; they did well to speak thus. 26May they always be of such mind, to revere Me and follow all My commandments, that it may go well with them

וְהָעֲרָפֶ֔ל ק֥וֹל גָּד֖וֹל וְלֹ֣א יָסָ֑ף וַֽיִּכְתְּבֵ֗ם
עַל־שְׁנֵי֙ לֻחֹ֣ת אֲבָנִ֔ים וַֽיִּתְּנֵ֖ם אֵלָֽי׃ 20 וַיְהִ֗י
כְּשָׁמְעֲכֶ֤ם אֶת־הַקּוֹל֙ מִתּ֣וֹךְ הַחֹ֔שֶׁךְ וְהָהָ֖ר
בֹּעֵ֣ר בָּאֵ֑שׁ וַתִּקְרְב֣וּן אֵלַ֔י כָּל־רָאשֵׁ֥י
שִׁבְטֵיכֶ֖ם וְזִקְנֵיכֶֽם׃ 21 וַתֹּאמְר֗וּ הֵ֣ן הֶרְאָ֜נוּ
יְהוָ֤ה אֱלֹהֵ֙ינוּ֙ אֶת־כְּבֹד֣וֹ וְאֶת־גָּדְל֔וֹ וְאֶת־
קֹל֥וֹ שָׁמַ֖עְנוּ מִתּ֣וֹךְ הָאֵ֑שׁ הַיּ֤וֹם הַזֶּה֙
רָאִ֔ינוּ כִּֽי־יְדַבֵּ֧ר אֱלֹהִ֛ים אֶת־הָאָדָ֖ם וָחָֽי׃
22 וְעַתָּה֙ לָ֣מָּה נָמ֔וּת כִּ֣י תֹֽאכְלֵ֔נוּ הָאֵ֥שׁ
הַגְּדֹלָ֖ה הַזֹּ֑את אִם־יֹסְפִ֣ים ׀ אֲנַ֗חְנוּ לִ֠שְׁמֹעַ
אֶת־ק֨וֹל יְהוָ֧ה אֱלֹהֵ֛ינוּ ע֖וֹד וָמָֽתְנוּ׃ 23 כִּ֣י
מִ֣י כָל־בָּשָׂ֡ר אֲשֶׁ֣ר שָׁמַ֣ע קוֹל֩ אֱלֹהִ֨ים חַיִּ֜ים
מְדַבֵּ֧ר מִתּוֹךְ־הָאֵ֛שׁ כָּמֹ֖נוּ וַיֶּֽחִי׃ 24 קְרַ֤ב
אַתָּה֙ וּֽשְׁמָ֔ע אֵ֛ת כָּל־אֲשֶׁ֥ר יֹאמַ֖ר יְהוָ֣ה
אֱלֹהֵ֑ינוּ וְאַ֣תְּ ׀ תְּדַבֵּ֣ר אֵלֵ֗ינוּ אֵת֩ כָּל־
אֲשֶׁ֨ר יְדַבֵּ֜ר יְהוָ֧ה אֱלֹהֵ֛ינוּ אֵלֶ֖יךָ וְשָׁמַ֥עְנוּ
וְעָשִֽׂינוּ׃
25 וַיִּשְׁמַ֤ע יְהוָה֙ אֶת־ק֣וֹל דִּבְרֵיכֶ֔ם
בְּדַבֶּרְכֶ֖ם אֵלָ֑י וַיֹּ֨אמֶר יְהוָ֜ה אֵלַ֗י שָׁ֠מַעְתִּי
אֶת־ק֨וֹל דִּבְרֵ֜י הָעָ֤ם הַזֶּה֙ אֲשֶׁ֣ר דִּבְּר֣וּ אֵלֶ֔יךָ
הֵיטִ֖יבוּ כָּל־אֲשֶׁ֥ר דִּבֵּֽרוּ׃ 26 מִֽי־יִתֵּ֡ן וְהָיָה֩
לְבָבָ֨ם זֶ֜ה לָהֶ֗ם לְיִרְאָ֥ה אֹתִ֛י וְלִשְׁמֹ֥ר
אֶת־כָּל־מִצְוֺתַ֖י כָּל־הַיָּמִ֑ים לְמַ֨עַן יִיטַ֥ב

which He gave to me That is, 40 days later (9:9).

21. though God has spoken to him Out of a fire.

22. Let us not die Humans can survive hearing God speak. The people fear that their constant exposure to the unprecedented fire may prove fatal to them.

23. the living God The demonstration of God's power has made the people cognizant of His nature as "the living God," i.e., as the effective God, in contrast to the lifelessness of false gods.

24. we will willingly do it Literally, "we will hear [what you tell us] and do it." This is a crucial moment: The people pledge to accept Moses' reports of what God commands and to fulfill whatever laws Moses transmits to them. Thus they have voluntarily relinquished receiving the remaining laws from God personally, and they may not in the future disobey Moses or challenge what he reports to them (see Exod. 24:7).

26. God appreciates the reverence that leads the people to make their request. He hopes that this reverence will remain with them and motivate them to observe the commandments. Implicit in His words is the concern that their reverence will diminish as the experience recedes from the people's memory.

---

as here, some commentators interpret the phrase differently: It did not end, unlike normal utterances that fade away after a few seconds (BT Sanh. 17a).

and with their children forever! [27]Go, say to
them, 'Return to your tents.' [28]But you remain
here with Me, and I will give you the whole
Instruction—the laws and the rules—that you
shall impart to them, for them to observe in the
land that I am giving them to possess."

[29]Be careful, then, to do as the LORD your God
has commanded you. Do not turn aside to the
right or to the left: [30]follow only the path that
the LORD your God has enjoined upon you, so
that you may thrive and that it may go well with
you, and that you may long endure in the land
you are to possess.

לָהֶ֛ם וְלִבְנֵיהֶ֖ם לְעֹלָֽם׃ 27 לֵ֖ךְ אֱמֹ֣ר לָהֶ֑ם
שׁ֥וּבוּ לָכֶ֖ם לְאָהֳלֵיכֶֽם׃ 28 וְאַתָּ֗ה פֹּה֮ עֲמֹ֣ד
עִמָּדִי֒ וַאֲדַבְּרָ֣ה אֵלֶ֗יךָ אֵ֤ת כׇּל־הַמִּצְוָה֙
וְהַחֻקִּ֣ים וְהַמִּשְׁפָּטִ֔ים אֲשֶׁ֥ר תְּלַמְּדֵ֖ם וְעָשׂ֣וּ
בָאָ֔רֶץ אֲשֶׁ֥ר אָנֹכִ֛י נֹתֵ֥ן לָהֶ֖ם לְרִשְׁתָּֽהּ׃
29 וּשְׁמַרְתֶּ֣ם לַעֲשׂ֔וֹת כַּאֲשֶׁ֥ר צִוָּ֛ה יְהֹוָ֥ה
אֱלֹהֵיכֶ֖ם אֶתְכֶ֑ם לֹ֥א תָסֻ֖רוּ יָמִ֥ין וּשְׂמֹֽאל׃
30 בְּכׇל־הַדֶּ֗רֶךְ אֲשֶׁ֨ר צִוָּ֜ה יְהֹוָ֤ה אֱלֹהֵיכֶם֙
אֶתְכֶ֖ם תֵּלֵ֑כוּ לְמַ֤עַן תִּֽחְיוּן֙ וְט֣וֹב לָכֶ֔ם
וְהַאֲרַכְתֶּ֣ם יָמִ֔ים בָּאָ֖רֶץ אֲשֶׁ֥ר תִּירָשֽׁוּן׃

6 And this is the Instruction—the laws and
the rules—that the LORD your God has commanded [me] to impart to you, to be observed
in the land that you are about to cross into and
occupy, [2]so that you, your children, and your
children's children may revere the LORD your
God and follow, as long as you live, all His laws
and commandments that I enjoin upon you, to
the end that you may long endure. [3]Obey, O Israel, willingly and faithfully, that it may go well

ו וְזֹ֣את הַמִּצְוָ֗ה הַֽחֻקִּים֙ וְהַמִּשְׁפָּטִ֔ים
אֲשֶׁ֥ר צִוָּ֛ה יְהֹוָ֥ה אֱלֹהֵיכֶ֖ם לְלַמֵּ֣ד אֶתְכֶ֑ם
לַעֲשׂ֣וֹת בָּאָ֔רֶץ אֲשֶׁ֥ר אַתֶּ֛ם עֹבְרִ֥ים שָׁ֖מָּה
לְרִשְׁתָּֽהּ׃ 2 לְמַ֨עַן תִּירָ֜א אֶת־יְהֹוָ֣ה אֱלֹהֶ֗יךָ
לִ֠שְׁמֹ֠ר אֶת־כׇּל־חֻקֹּתָ֣יו וּמִצְוֺתָיו֮ אֲשֶׁ֣ר
אָנֹכִ֣י מְצַוֶּךָ֒ אַתָּה֙ וּבִנְךָ֣ וּבֶן־בִּנְךָ֔ כֹּ֖ל יְמֵ֣י
חַיֶּ֑יךָ וּלְמַ֖עַן יַאֲרִכֻ֥ן יָמֶֽיךָ׃ 3 וְשָׁמַעְתָּ֤
יִשְׂרָאֵל֙ וְשָׁמַרְתָּ֣ לַעֲשׂ֔וֹת אֲשֶׁר֙ יִיטַ֣ב לְךָ֔

28. Moses' role as intermediary is now formalized. He stayed with God for 40 days and nights (9:9–11; Exod. 24:18).

29. The lesson learned at Mount Sinai—and Moses' main point in this speech—is that the laws and rules that he is about to teach came from God and must, therefore, be observed. They are prerequisites for well-being in the Promised Land.

Moses' Second Discourse, Part 2: Preamble to the Laws Given in Moab (6:1–11:30)

1. this is the Instruction—the laws and the rules By using the identical terms that God used in 5:28, Moses indicates that the commands he is transmitting to Israel are precisely those given to him by God.

2. Moses has a twofold purpose in teaching the laws: He wishes to ensure their performance and to inculcate reverence for God. Thus the laws were not only an expression of reverence for God but also a means of teaching reverence.

revere . . . and follow Literally, "revere . . . by following." Following God's laws is the means of revering Him, the expression of reverence.

---

28. I will give you the whole Instruction God revealed the entire Torah to Moses, but Moses, being a mortal, wrote down only what he could understand and absorb. Later generations would discover moral truths and expand the notion of Torah to include them. If Truth (*Emet*) is one of the names of God, then there must be room in our understanding of Torah for all that is true.

with you and that you may increase greatly [in]
a land flowing with milk and honey, as the LORD,
the God of your fathers, spoke to you.
4Hear, O Israel! The LORD is our God, the

וַאֲשֶׁר תִּרְבּוּן מְאֹד כַּאֲשֶׁר דִּבֶּר יְהוָה אֱלֹהֵי
אֲבֹתֶיךָ לָךְ אֶרֶץ זָבַת חָלָב וּדְבָשׁ׃ פ
ששי 4 שְׁמַע יִשְׂרָאֵל יְהוָה אֱלֹהֵינוּ יְהוָה ׀

3. Obey . . . willingly and faithfully Literally, "obey . . . and faithfully do." Moses urges Israel to do as it promised in 5:24, which states, literally, "we will obey and do."

A SERMON ON THE FIRST COMMANDMENT (6:4–25)

UNDIVIDED LOYALTY AND CONSTANT AWARENESS (vv. 4–9)

This passage states the major themes of Deuteronomy and the core demands of the Covenant. It has become, with the passage of time, the centerpiece of Jewish daily worship: *K'ri·at Sh'ma* (Recitation of the *Sh'ma*).

4. Hear, O Israel! Focus your attention and heed the following teaching.

the LORD is our God, the LORD alone Hebrew: *YHVH Eloheinu, YHVH eḥad;* literally, "*YHVH* [is] our God, *YHVH* [is] one." Another possible translation for the last word is "unique." For all of its familiarity, the precise meaning of the *Sh'ma* is uncertain. The translation here renders it as describing a relationship: *YHVH* alone is Israel's God. This is not a declaration of monotheism, meaning that there is only one God; that point was made in 4:35 and 39, which state that "*YHVH* alone is God." This verse, by adding the possessive "our," focuses on the way Israel is to apply that truth: Although other peoples worship various beings and things they consider divine, Israel is to recognize *YHVH* alone.

CHAPTER 6

4–9. How did the *Sh'ma* (vv. 4–9) become the quintessential Jewish prayer, when technically it is not a prayer at all? (Prayers are addressed to God; the *Sh'ma* is addressed to the Israelites.) Probably because it contains in just a few lines the basic theological commitments of Judaism: That there is a God; that there is only one God; that God is not only singular but also unique—no other being is like God; that the Jewish people have a specially intimate relationship with God; and that we are commanded as Jews to love God wholeheartedly, to study God's word, and to teach God's word to our children. More prosaically, it may be that, because this passage commands us to study words of Torah each morning and evening, we fulfill that obligation by reciting this passage.

The *Sh'ma* may be recited in any language the worshiper understands, because it is crucial that the worshiper understand what he or she is affirming (*S'fat Emet,* based on BT Ber. 13a). Yet there is value in saying it in the language of the original revelation, as a link to the Torah and to Jews around the world. For that reason, these words are typically among the first Hebrew words a Jewish child learns.

4. A *midrash* traces the origin of this verse to the last moments of the patriarch Jacob's life. He was concerned that his children and grandchildren, living in Egypt, would depart from the traditions of Abraham and serve the local gods. They put his mind at ease, assuring him, "Hear, O Israel [i.e., Jacob]: We accept the one God as our god" (Deut. R. 2:35).

In Torah scrolls and many prayer books, the letter *ayin* at the end of *"sh'ma"* and the letter *dalet* at the end of *"eḥad"* are written larger than the other letters, spelling *"ed"* (witness). That is, to recite *Sh'ma Yisra·el* is to testify to the unity and uniqueness of God. To live by the precepts of the *Sh'ma* is to bear witness to the truths of God's Torah; it must be true if it can bring ordinary people to lead such extraordinary lives.

Hear This emphasizes the need to listen. Prayer is not only talking to God; it also includes listening to what God has to say to us. "When I pray, I speak to God. When I study Torah, God speaks to me" (Finkelstein). In a world filled with noise and superficial conversation, we need to be reminded of the sacred duty to pause and listen. "Jewish prayer is an act of listening. We do not bring forth our own words. The self is silent; the spirit of the people Israel speaks. In prayer, we listen to what the words convey" (Heschel).

Lord alone. 5You shall love the Lord your
God with all your heart and with all your
soul and with all your might. 6Take to

אֶחָד׃ * 5 וְאָהַבְתָּ אֵת יְהוָה אֱלֹהֶיךָ בְּכָל־
לְבָבְךָ וּבְכָל־נַפְשְׁךָ וּבְכָל־מְאֹדֶךָ׃ 6 וְהָיוּ

v. 4. ע׳ ד׳ רבתי

5. You shall love Israel's duty to love God is inseparable from action and is regularly connected with the observance of His commandments (see 10:12–13, 11:1,13, 19:9, 30:16). In ancient Near Eastern political terminology, "love" refers to the loyalty of subjects, vassals, and allies. One of the striking parallels between political treaties and the covenant between God and Israel is the requirement that vassals "love" the suzerain—i.e., act loyally to him—with all their heart. The command to love God accordingly may be understood as requiring one to act loyally toward Him, though an emotional response is also called for.

heart . . . soul The Hebrew word for "heart" (*lev* or *levav*) usually refers to the interior of the body, conceived of as the seat of thought, intention, and feeling. The Hebrew word for "soul" (*nefesh*) refers to the seat of the emotions, passions, and desires. To do something with all one's heart and soul means to do it with the totality of one's thoughts, feelings, intentions, and desires.

with all your might That is, "exceedingly." The Hebrew (*b'khol m'odekha*) is comparable to the more common phrase for "very, very much" (*bim'od m'od*), implying with all the power and means at one's disposal. Israel must love and serve God with undivided devotion and loyalty.

---

the Lord alone Literally, "*YHVH* [is] one." What do we mean when we proclaim that God is one? First, we reject the claim that God is none, that there is no God and the world is the product of random chance. Second, we reject the claim that God is two, a god of good and a god of evil. Jewish theology does not explain evil by positing a devil, a force of wickedness as powerful as God. Human misuse of our power to choose causes most of the evil in the world. And third, we reject the claim that God is many, that there are many deities, each specializing in one aspect of life or another. Only when God is one can we speak of a single moral law, of behavior being right or wrong in the sight of God (Steinberg).

5. You shall love Love is more than an emotion. It is a commitment to another, a demand for absolute faithfulness to God and to no other god. How can one command love? The *S'fat Emet* teaches that every human soul instinctively desires to love God, its Creator; but distractions and obstacles intervene. By performing the *mitzvot* we remove those obstacles and let our souls fulfill their natural inclination. "One who serves a master out of fear will always seek ways of escaping his obligations. But for one who serves out of love, obedience is a source of joy" (*Sifrei*).

The commandment to love our neighbor is found in Lev. 19:18. The commandment to love the stranger is found in Lev. 19:34. The commandment to love God comes later, in Deuteronomy. We learn to love God by practicing loving God's creatures, our fellow human beings. "Love the Lord your God" commands not belief but behavior. Act in such a way as to make God beloved in the eyes of those who know you (Mid. Ha-Gadol).

with all your heart Learn to serve God not only with our noble impulses but even with the base, selfish desires of our hearts (M Ber. 9:5). Learn to turn to God's service our appetites, our physical lusts, and our egocentricity; we do so by sanctifying the way we eat, the way we act sexually, and the way we earn and spend money.

It can also be thought of as "wholeheartedly." The opposite of wholehearted love is not hatred but apathy—going through the motions with no passion, no real caring (whether one is describing one's attitude toward God or toward family members). As Aaron Zeitlin wrote, "Praise Me, says God, and I will know that you love Me. / Curse Me, says God, and I will know that you love Me . . . / But if you look at the stars and yawn, / If you don't praise and you don't curse, / then I created you in vain, says God."

with all your soul Even at the cost of your life. The account of Akiva's death by torture at the hands of the Romans (BT Ber. 61b) describes him as reciting *Sh'ma Yisra·el* with his dying breath, so that his death would bear witness to his undying faith in the one true God. ("Martyr" is derived from the Greek word for "witness.") Jewish law limits the requirement to undergo martyrdom to cases in which Jews are threatened with death unless they commit murder, acts of sexual depravity, or public idolatry in times of persecution (S.A. YD 157).

with all your might Traditional rendering:

heart these instructions with which I charge you
this day. 7Impress them upon your children. Recite them when you stay at home and when you
are away, when you lie down and when you get
up. 8Bind them as a sign on your hand and let
them serve as a symbol on your forehead; 9in-
scribe them on the doorposts of your house and
on your gates.

הַדְּבָרִים הָאֵלֶּה אֲשֶׁר אָנֹכִי מְצַוְּךָ הַיּוֹם
עַל־לְבָבֶךָ׃ 7 וְשִׁנַּנְתָּם לְבָנֶיךָ וְדִבַּרְתָּ בָּם
בְּשִׁבְתְּךָ בְּבֵיתֶךָ וּבְלֶכְתְּךָ בַדֶּרֶךְ וּבְשָׁכְבְּךָ
וּבְקוּמֶךָ׃ 8 וּקְשַׁרְתָּם לְאוֹת עַל־יָדֶךָ וְהָיוּ
לְטֹטָפֹת בֵּין עֵינֶיךָ׃ 9 וּכְתַבְתָּם עַל־מְזוּזֹת
בֵּיתֶךָ וּבִשְׁעָרֶיךָ׃ ס

6. Take to heart Moses urges Israel to internalize God's teachings.

these instructions with which I charge you this day This and similar phrases refer to the entire body of Deuteronomic law.

7. Impress them Literally, "repeat them." Oral teaching was the primary means of instruction in Israel. Ancient Near Eastern treaties emphasize the vassal's duty to instruct his sons about the treaty and their duty to follow it.

Recite them Speak about them.

when you stay at home . . . when you get up That is, "speak of these words wherever you are, and at all times."

8. Bind them as a sign on your hand Bind "these words" (v. 6) on your hand in the same way that signs are placed on the hand. Not only must God's commandments be remembered and spoken of constantly but copies of them must be worn on the body as well.

as a symbol Literally, "as a frontlet." That is, a headband, the characteristic headdress worn in the region of Syro-Palestine during the biblical period, as depicted in ancient Egyptian and Assyrian art.

9. on the doorposts People will thereby be reminded of God's instructions every time they enter and leave their homes.

gates Of cities. (Houses rarely had gates.) City gates consisted of the entire roofed structure that housed the doors, including several chambers (some up to 32 feet [10 m] wide), benches, and a long passageway. It functioned as the center of public activity, because it was often the most open area in an otherwise crowded city, and people constantly passed through it on their way to and from the city. Inscribing God's teachings on the walls of the gate would be the most effective way of publicizing them.

---

with your wealth. We serve God not only by giving to charity, but also by refusing financial gain in ways that either violate God's law or risk bringing the Torah into disrepute (as when people known to be Jewish are exposed for fraudulent business dealings).

6. Take to heart Literally, "they shall be upon your heart." Why "upon" rather than "in" your heart? Much of the time, a person's heart is closed, not ready to receive these words. Let the words remain outside, on the heart, until the day when circumstances break the heart open and the words of the Torah can enter (Menahem Mendel of Kotzk).

7. your children Not only your biologic children but anyone whose impression of Judaism is likely to be shaped by their contact with you (*Sifrei*).

8–9. The *t'fillin* are personal statements of our committing our deeds and thoughts to God. The *m'zuzah* is a public declaration that this is a home where a Jewish family dwells.

HALAKHAH L'MA·ASEH

6:7. Impress them The Sages maintain that grandparents are also obligated to teach these things to their grandchildren (BT Kid. 30a).

Recite them From this the Sages derive the obligation to recite the *Sh'ma* in the evening—preferably before midnight, when most people "lie down"—and in the morning before the first quarter of the day is over, by which time most people would be up (M Ber. 1:1–2).

6:8. Bind them The commandment to wear *t'fillin* is derived from this verse as well as Exod. 13:9,16 and Deut. 11:18. These four passages are, therefore, contained in the boxes worn on the head and on the biceps of the person's weaker arm.

6:9. doorposts The commandment is fulfilled by attaching a *m'zuzah* to the right doorpost of any entrance to the house. Some also attach a *m'zuzah* to the right doorpost leading into every livable room, excluding bathrooms and closets. The *m'zuzah* is placed in the top third of the doorway, its top angled into the room.

10When the LORD your God brings you into the land that He swore to your fathers, Abraham, Isaac, and Jacob, to assign to you—great and flourishing cities that you did not build, 11houses full of all good things that you did not fill, hewn cisterns that you did not hew, vineyards and olive groves that you did not plant—and you eat your fill, 12take heed that you do not forget the LORD who freed you from the land of Egypt, the house of bondage. 13Revere only the LORD your God and worship Him alone, and swear only by His name. 14Do not follow other gods, any gods of the peoples about you—15for the LORD your God in your midst is an impassioned God—lest the anger of the LORD your God blaze forth against you and He wipe you off the face of the earth.

10 וְהָיָ֞ה כִּ֥י יְבִיאֲךָ֣ ׀ יְהֹוָ֣ה אֱלֹהֶ֗יךָ אֶל־הָאָ֜רֶץ אֲשֶׁ֨ר נִשְׁבַּ֧ע לַאֲבֹתֶ֛יךָ לְאַבְרָהָ֥ם לְיִצְחָ֖ק וּֽלְיַעֲקֹ֑ב לָ֣תֶת לָ֑ךְ עָרִ֛ים גְּדֹלֹ֥ת וְטֹבֹ֖ת אֲשֶׁ֥ר לֹא־בָנִֽיתָ׃ 11 וּבָ֨תִּ֜ים מְלֵאִ֣ים כָּל־טוּב֮ אֲשֶׁ֣ר לֹא־מִלֵּ֒אתָ֒ וּבֹרֹ֤ת חֲצוּבִים֙ אֲשֶׁ֣ר לֹא־חָצַ֔בְתָּ כְּרָמִ֥ים וְזֵיתִ֖ים אֲשֶׁ֣ר לֹא־נָטָ֑עְתָּ וְאָכַלְתָּ֖ וְשָׂבָֽעְתָּ׃ 12 הִשָּׁ֣מֶר לְךָ֔ פֶּן־תִּשְׁכַּ֖ח אֶת־יְהֹוָ֑ה אֲשֶׁ֧ר הוֹצִֽיאֲךָ֛ מֵאֶ֥רֶץ מִצְרַ֖יִם מִבֵּ֥ית עֲבָדִֽים׃ 13 אֶת־יְהֹוָ֧ה אֱלֹהֶ֛יךָ תִּירָ֖א וְאֹת֣וֹ תַעֲבֹ֑ד וּבִשְׁמ֖וֹ תִּשָּׁבֵֽעַ׃ 14 לֹ֣א תֵֽלְכ֔וּן אַחֲרֵ֖י אֱלֹהִ֣ים אֲחֵרִ֑ים מֵאֱלֹהֵי֙ הָֽעַמִּ֔ים אֲשֶׁ֖ר סְבִיבֽוֹתֵיכֶֽם׃ 15 כִּ֣י אֵ֥ל קַנָּ֛א יְהֹוָ֥ה אֱלֹהֶ֖יךָ בְּקִרְבֶּ֑ךָ פֶּן־יֶ֠חֱרֶ֠ה אַף־יְהֹוָ֤ה אֱלֹהֶ֨יךָ֙ בָּ֔ךְ וְהִשְׁמִ֣ידְךָ֔ מֵעַ֖ל פְּנֵ֥י הָאֲדָמָֽה׃ ס

DO NOT ALLOW PROSPERITY TO MAKE YOU FORGET (vv. 10–15)

10. This reminder that the Israelites did not create the material wealth they are about to possess is an implicit warning against the attitude of self-sufficiency that prosperity can induce.

11. all good things The basic possessions of a settled agricultural society, which the Israelites, after a generation of wandering in the wilderness, are about to enjoy.

cisterns Most Israelite population centers were in the highlands, which depend mainly on rain for their water. Because rain falls in Israel only between October and May, it was necessary to store rainwater for the dry season; otherwise, the highlands could not have supported many people. Water was stored in large jars and in communal and private cisterns located beneath houses or their inner courtyards.

vineyards and olive groves Among the agricultural staples of the land of Israel, grapes and olives were second in importance only to grains (8:8, 28:51).

12. take heed Literally, "be careful." Forgetting one's dependence on God is not only wrong but also dangerous (8:19–20, 11:17). The possibility that material wealth and satiety can lead to pride and arrogance and to disregarding one's dependence on God is a persistent concern in the Bible.

13. worship And obey. This is a common term in the ancient Near East both for worshiping deities and for obeying kings.

swear only by His name Swearing by a god indicates a belief that that god has power and authority. The Bible, therefore, considers it a test of loyalty that the Israelite swear by *YHVH* alone. This expression of fidelity is similar to ancient Near Eastern ways of displaying loyalty to a king. In a Sumerian prayer, the writer denies that he has sworn an oath by a foreign king.

14. gods of the peoples about you All foreign deities are prohibited to Israel (5:7, 13:8), but Moses' immediate concern is with gods of the surrounding peoples that the Israelites will encounter in the Promised Land.

15. in your midst The recognition that God is present in Israel's midst, regulating their affairs, is a deterrent to sin.

Its purpose is not magic, to protect us from harm, but to remind us, when we leave our homes and when we return to them, of what God demands of us.

10. that you did not build It is not just that generation which received so much. Similar statements could be made for every generation of human beings. Humility and gratitude, therefore, are appropriate responses for what we have received from those who came before us.

16Do not try the LORD your God, as you did at Massah. 17Be sure to keep the commandments, decrees, and laws that the LORD your God has enjoined upon you. 18Do what is right and good in the sight of the LORD, that it may go well with you and that you may be able to possess the good land that the LORD your God promised on oath to your fathers, 19and that all your enemies may be driven out before you, as the LORD has spoken.

20When, in time to come, your children ask you, "What mean the decrees, laws, and rules that the LORD our God has enjoined upon you?" 21you shall say to your children, "We were slaves to Pharaoh in Egypt and the LORD freed us from Egypt with a mighty hand. 22The LORD wrought before our eyes marvelous and destructive signs and portents in Egypt, against Pharaoh and all his household; 23and us He freed from there, that He might take us and give us the land that

16 לֹא תְנַסּוּ אֶת־יְהוָה אֱלֹהֵיכֶם כַּאֲשֶׁר
נִסִּיתֶם בַּמַּסָּה׃ 17 שָׁמוֹר תִּשְׁמְרוּן אֶת־
מִצְוֺת יְהוָה אֱלֹהֵיכֶם וְעֵדֹתָיו וְחֻקָּיו אֲשֶׁר
צִוָּךְ׃ 18 וְעָשִׂיתָ הַיָּשָׁר וְהַטּוֹב בְּעֵינֵי יְהוָה
לְמַעַן יִיטַב לָךְ וּבָאתָ וְיָרַשְׁתָּ אֶת־הָאָרֶץ
הַטֹּבָה אֲשֶׁר־נִשְׁבַּע יְהוָה לַאֲבֹתֶיךָ׃
19 לַהֲדֹף אֶת־כָּל־אֹיְבֶיךָ מִפָּנֶיךָ כַּאֲשֶׁר
דִּבֶּר יְהוָה׃ ס
20 כִּי־יִשְׁאָלְךָ בִנְךָ מָחָר לֵאמֹר מָה הָעֵדֹת
וְהַחֻקִּים וְהַמִּשְׁפָּטִים אֲשֶׁר צִוָּה יְהוָה
אֱלֹהֵינוּ אֶתְכֶם׃ 21 וְאָמַרְתָּ לְבִנְךָ עֲבָדִים
הָיִינוּ לְפַרְעֹה בְּמִצְרָיִם וַיּוֹצִיאֵנוּ יְהוָה
מִמִּצְרַיִם בְּיָד חֲזָקָה׃ 22 וַיִּתֵּן יְהוָה אוֹתֹת
וּמֹפְתִים גְּדֹלִים וְרָעִים ׀ בְּמִצְרַיִם בְּפַרְעֹה
וּבְכָל־בֵּיתוֹ לְעֵינֵינוּ׃ 23 וְאוֹתָנוּ הוֹצִיא
מִשָּׁם לְמַעַן הָבִיא אֹתָנוּ לָתֶת לָנוּ אֶת־

DO NOT TEST GOD (vv. 16–19)

Moses, having indicated that God will meet all the needs of Israel, recalls an incident in which the people challenged God's ability and implicitly threatened to rebel against Him. He urges them never to confront God again but to observe the commandments so that all may go well with them.

16. Do not try That is, do not test. During the incident in question, the people complained because they lacked water to drink (Exod. 17:1–7). Tests of that sort imply a lack of confidence in God's power.

18. right and good Associated elsewhere with obeying God's commandments, and that is undoubtedly what is meant in His sight here and in 12:28.

19. A reminder that the injunctions of this passage are a condition for the conquest of the Promised Land.

EXPLAINING THE COMMANDMENTS TO ONE'S CHILDREN (vv. 20–25)

In this passage, Moses resumes the theme of verse 7, which calls for teaching children about God's instructions.

22. before our eyes The parents—those who, as children, witnessed the Exodus and the Revelation—can now assure their children that they speak not from hearsay but personal experience.

---

16. Do not try the LORD Do not test God by demanding miracles, nor lose faith in God when miracles do not occur. True love does not require constant proofs of its genuineness. Rely instead on the memories of what God did for your ancestors (vv. 20–23).

18. The Torah could not possibly include every specific instance of good conduct; therefore it offers this general statement to cover any eventuality. That is, be willing to compromise or to accept mediation, or to go beyond the letter of the law—"for God loves the good and the right" (Ramban). The Sages of the Talmud also insisted that this verse requires us to go beyond the letter of the law and, as Rashi suggests, voluntarily waive privileges in order to end disputes amicably.

20. This verse is the source of the wise child's question in the *Pesaḥ Haggadah.* In the better manuscripts of the *Haggadah,* the last word of the verse reads "us," following the reading in the Talmud and in the Septuagint.

He had promised on oath to our fathers. 24Then
the LORD commanded us to observe all these
laws, to revere the LORD our God, for our lasting
good and for our survival, as is now the case.
25It will be therefore to our merit before the
LORD our God to observe faithfully this whole
Instruction, as He has commanded us."

הָאָ֔רֶץ אֲשֶׁ֥ר נִשְׁבַּ֖ע לַאֲבֹתֵֽינוּ׃ 24 וַיְצַוֵּ֣נוּ
יְהֹוָ֗ה לַעֲשׂוֹת֙ אֶת־כָּל־הַחֻקִּ֣ים הָאֵ֔לֶּה
לְיִרְאָ֖ה אֶת־יְהֹוָ֣ה אֱלֹהֵ֑ינוּ לְט֥וֹב לָ֙נוּ֙ כָּל־
הַיָּמִ֔ים לְחַיֹּתֵ֖נוּ כְּהַיּ֥וֹם הַזֶּֽה׃ 25 וּצְדָקָ֖ה
תִּֽהְיֶה־לָּ֑נוּ כִּֽי־נִשְׁמֹ֨ר לַעֲשׂ֜וֹת אֶת־כָּל־
הַמִּצְוָ֣ה הַזֹּ֗את לִפְנֵ֛י יְהֹוָ֥ה אֱלֹהֵ֖ינוּ כַּאֲשֶׁ֥ר
צִוָּֽנוּ׃ ס

7 When the LORD your God brings you to the
land that you are about to enter and possess,
and He dislodges many nations before you—
the Hittites, Girgashites, Amorites, Canaanites,
Perizzites, Hivites, and Jebusites, seven nations
much larger than you—2and the LORD your
God delivers them to you and you defeat them,
you must doom them to destruction: grant
them no terms and give them no quarter. 3You

ביעי ז כִּ֤י יְבִֽיאֲךָ֙ יְהֹוָ֣ה אֱלֹהֶ֔יךָ אֶל־הָאָ֕רֶץ
אֲשֶׁר־אַתָּ֥ה בָא־שָׁ֖מָּה לְרִשְׁתָּ֑הּ וְנָשַׁ֣ל
גּֽוֹיִם־רַבִּ֣ים ׀ מִפָּנֶ֡יךָ הַֽחִתִּ֨י וְהַגִּרְגָּשִׁ֜י
וְהָֽאֱמֹרִ֣י וְהַכְּנַעֲנִ֗י וְהַפְּרִזִּי֙ וְהַֽחִוִּ֣י וְהַיְבוּסִ֔י
שִׁבְעָ֣ה גוֹיִ֔ם רַבִּ֥ים וַעֲצוּמִ֖ים מִמֶּֽךָּ׃
2 וּנְתָנָ֞ם יְהֹוָ֧ה אֱלֹהֶ֛יךָ לְפָנֶ֖יךָ וְהִכִּיתָ֑ם
הַחֲרֵ֤ם תַּחֲרִים֙ אֹתָ֔ם לֹא־תִכְרֹ֥ת לָהֶ֛ם
בְּרִ֖ית וְלֹ֥א תְחָנֵּֽם׃ 3 וְלֹ֥א תִתְחַתֵּ֖ן בָּ֑ם

24. observe . . . revere Observing the laws is in itself an act of reverence.

AVOIDING DANGERS TO FAITH AND OBEDIENCE AFTER THE CONQUEST (7:1–10:22)

Moses now turns to specific laws, beginning with the first issue that the Israelites will face when they enter the Promised Land: what to do with the Canaanites. The laws are accompanied by explanations and exhortations, because the proper attitude in observing them is as important as the laws themselves.

EXHORTATIONS CONCERNING CONQUEST (7:1–8:20)

1. God brings you to the land The angel mentioned in Exod. 23:20 is omitted here, in keeping with Deuteronomy's insistence on the exclusive role of God in Israel's history.

Hittites A people by this name, living in Hebron, Bethel, and elsewhere in the central highlands of Canaan, is mentioned in Genesis. Outside the Bible, "Hittites" refers to several groups, and it is not clear which, if any, is meant in Genesis or here. This list of the inhabitants of the land is not meant to be complete. Other lists name as many as 12 nations, many name 6, and some name fewer.

Girgashites Virtually nothing is known of this group, although Girgish appears as the name of a person in some ancient texts. There was a land of Karkisha in Asia Minor; perhaps the Girgashites migrated to Canaan from there.

Amorites, Canaanites Sometimes these names are used for all the peoples of the Promised Land, but here they refer to the inhabitants of specific regions (see 1:7).

Perizzites Several passages mention them in connection with the territory of Ephraim and Manasseh, in the north-central part of the Land; that may be where they were concentrated.

Hivites The population of Shechem in the days of Jacob (see Gen. 34:2). In Joshua's time they made up the population of Gibeon and were also found in the far north, at the foot of Mount Hermon and in the Lebanon range.

Jebusites The population of Jerusalem before its conquest by David. Nothing is known of them outside the Bible; but at Mari, in Syria, Yabasi appears as a clan and a geographic name.

2. terms That is, conditions, such as labor in

shall not intermarry with them: do not give your daughters to their sons or take their daughters for your sons. ⁴For they will turn your children away from Me to worship other gods, and the LORD's anger will blaze forth against you and He will promptly wipe you out. ⁵Instead, this is what you shall do to them: you shall tear down their altars, smash their pillars, cut down their sacred posts, and consign their images to the fire.

⁶For you are a people consecrated to the LORD your God: of all the peoples on earth the LORD your God chose you to be His treasured people.

בִּתְּךָ֙ לֹא־תִתֵּ֣ן לִבְנ֔וֹ וּבִתּ֖וֹ לֹא־תִקַּ֥ח לִבְנֶֽךָ׃ ⁴ כִּֽי־יָסִ֤יר אֶת־בִּנְךָ֙ מֵאַֽחֲרַ֔י וְעָֽבְד֖וּ אֱלֹהִ֣ים אֲחֵרִ֑ים וְחָרָ֤ה אַף־יְהֹוָה֙ בָּכֶ֔ם וְהִשְׁמִֽידְךָ֖ מַהֵֽר׃ ⁵ כִּ֣י־אִם־כֹּ֤ה תַֽעֲשׂוּ֙ לָהֶ֔ם מִזְבְּחֹֽתֵיהֶ֣ם תִּתֹּ֗צוּ וּמַצֵּֽבֹתָ֖ם תְּשַׁבֵּ֑רוּ וַאֲשֵֽׁירֵהֶם֙ תְּגַדֵּע֔וּן וּפְסִֽילֵיהֶ֖ם תִּשְׂרְפ֥וּן בָּאֵֽשׁ׃

⁶ כִּ֣י עַ֤ם קָדוֹשׁ֙ אַתָּ֔ה לַֽיהֹוָ֖ה אֱלֹהֶ֑יךָ בְּךָ֞ בָּחַ֣ר ׀ יְהֹוָ֣ה אֱלֹהֶ֗יךָ לִֽהְי֥וֹת לוֹ֙ לְעַ֣ם סְגֻלָּ֔ה מִכֹּל֙ הָֽעַמִּ֔ים אֲשֶׁ֖ר עַל־פְּנֵ֥י הָֽאֲדָמָֽה׃ ס

return for which they would be spared (20:11). According to Exod. 23:31–33, Canaanites were to be expelled from the land; here they are to be killed.

3. The intent behind the severe treatment of the Canaanites is the prevention of the intermarriages, which would certainly lure the Israelites to worship pagan gods and then to violate the first two commandments (see Exod. 23:32–33, 34:15–16; Deut. 20:17–18).

4. from Me Moses, when transmitting God's commands, often alternates between speaking of God in the third person and quoting Him directly.

He will promptly wipe you out Because the exclusive worship of *YHVH* was the fundamental condition for Israel's survival, leaving Canaanites alive who might entice the Israelites into idolatry was a matter of life and death.

5. tear down Even the physical objects of Canaanite religion must be eliminated. The common practice of taking them as booty or bringing them as offerings to the victor's deity is forbidden, because anything associated with the religion of the Canaanites is repugnant to the Lord (vv. 25–26).

altars Structures on which offerings of food, drink, or incense were made to gods. They might be simple stones or mounds of dirt, tables plated with precious metal, or platforms large enough to be ascended by steps or ramps.

pillars Cut or uncut stones that were erected for a religious purpose. Some contained engravings or reliefs showing a deity or its symbols, and others were plain. Apparently they were thought to embody the presence of a deity, either by representing the deity or by serving as its residence. Sacrifices were offered to them and they were treated as idols.

sacred posts Hebrew: *asherah.* Refers to a standing wooden object at a place of worship. According to 16:21, it was a tree planted near an altar. Some passages suggest that it might also be an image, an artificial tree, or perhaps a tree trunk or a pole. Others indicate that it was regarded as a symbol of the Canaanite goddess Asherah.

fire If burning is meant literally, the text must be referring to wooden images with metal plating (see v. 25). All the verbs in these commands, however, may simply mean "destroy." In the excavations at Hazor a statue with its head chopped off was found in the remains of the stratum destroyed by the Israelites at the time of the conquest.

6. consecrated Hebrew: *kadosh.* Usually translated "holy," here it has the sense of "set apart."

God chose you Israel was the only people devoted to *YHVH.* The Bible considers this a special privilege for which Israel was chosen.

His treasured people Israel is God's "treasure" (*s'gullah*), meaning that it is cherished. The Hebrew word belongs to covenantal terminology. There is an account of a Hittite king who called his vassal, the king of Ugarit, his treasure. On a Syrian royal seal a king is called "the servant of Adad, the beloved of Adad, the *sikltum* [*s'gullah*] of Adad."

HALAKHAH L'MA·ASEH

7:3. not intermarry Marriage is the basis of the family and the home in which religious identity is transmitted. The Torah commands us to marry within the faith to build a Jewish family (see Gen. 24:3, 26:35, 28:1).

7It is not because you are the most numerous of peoples that the LORD set His heart on you and chose you—indeed, you are the smallest of peoples; 8but it was because the LORD favored you and kept the oath He made to your fathers that the LORD freed you with a mighty hand and rescued you from the house of bondage, from the power of Pharaoh king of Egypt.

9Know, therefore, that only the LORD your God is God, the steadfast God who keeps His covenant faithfully to the thousandth generation of those who love Him and keep His commandments, 10but who instantly requites with destruction those who reject Him—never slow with those who reject Him, but requiting them instantly. 11Therefore, observe faithfully the Instruction—the laws and the rules—with which I charge you today.

7 לֹ֣א מֵֽרֻבְּכֶ֞ם מִכָּל־הָ֣עַמִּ֗ים חָשַׁ֧ק יְהוָ֛ה בָּכֶ֖ם וַיִּבְחַ֣ר בָּכֶ֑ם כִּֽי־אַתֶּ֥ם הַמְעַ֖ט מִכָּל־הָעַמִּֽים׃ 8 כִּי֩ מֵֽאַהֲבַ֨ת יְהוָ֜ה אֶתְכֶ֗ם וּמִשָּׁמְר֤וֹ אֶת־הַשְּׁבֻעָה֙ אֲשֶׁ֣ר נִשְׁבַּ֣ע לַאֲבֹ֣תֵיכֶ֔ם הוֹצִ֧יא יְהוָ֛ה אֶתְכֶ֖ם בְּיָ֣ד חֲזָקָ֑ה וַֽיִּפְדְּךָ֙ מִבֵּ֣ית עֲבָדִ֔ים מִיַּ֖ד פַּרְעֹ֥ה מֶֽלֶךְ־מִצְרָֽיִם׃

פטיר 9 וְיָ֣דַעְתָּ֔ כִּֽי־יְהוָ֥ה אֱלֹהֶ֖יךָ ה֣וּא הָֽאֱלֹהִ֑ים הָאֵל֙ הַֽנֶּאֱמָ֔ן שֹׁמֵ֧ר הַבְּרִ֣ית וְהַחֶ֗סֶד לְאֹהֲבָ֛יו וּלְשֹׁמְרֵ֥י מצותו מִצְוֺתָ֖יו לְאֶ֥לֶף דּֽוֹר׃ 10 וּמְשַׁלֵּ֧ם לְשֹׂנְאָ֛יו אֶל־פָּנָ֖יו לְהַֽאֲבִיד֑וֹ לֹ֤א יְאַחֵר֙ לְשֹׂ֣נְא֔וֹ אֶל־פָּנָ֖יו יְשַׁלֶּם־לֽוֹ׃ 11 וְשָׁמַרְתָּ֣ אֶת־הַמִּצְוָ֗ה וְאֶת־הַֽחֻקִּ֤ים וְאֶת־הַמִּשְׁפָּטִים֙ אֲשֶׁ֧ר אָֽנֹכִ֛י מְצַוְּךָ֥ הַיּ֖וֹם לַעֲשׂוֹתָֽם׃ פ

AN APPEAL TO AVOID COMPLACENCY
(vv. 7–11)

7. smallest of peoples This assertion contrasts with others that state that in Egypt Israel grew into "a great and very populous nation" (26:5) and that it is now as numerous as the stars (1:10, 10:22, 28:62). Unless the present assertion is a deliberate exaggeration for the sake of dismissing Israel's size as a factor, it may reflect conditions of a historical period different from that of the other references.

9. Know, from God's election and redemption of Israel, that He is reliable and steadfast.

10. Although punishment may extend to three or four generations of descendants (5:9), offenders themselves cannot hope to escape retribution if they violate God's laws.

11. observe The verb שמר describes both Israel's obligation to "observe" and God's act of "keeping" the covenant (v. 9). The intent here may be to lend a moral dimension to Moses' argument: Israel ought to respond to God's faithfulness with its own sincere faithfulness—and not merely obey God to avoid punishment and receive a reward.

CHAPTER 7

9. those who love Him and keep His commandments This phrase actually refers to two groups: those who wholeheartedly love and serve God; and those who keep commandments only for other reasons—such as seeking to be admired for their ethical standards, or out of concern for their neighbors' opinion (Rashi).

הפטרה ראשונה דנחמתא

FIRST HAFTARAH OF CONSOLATION HAFTARAH FOR VA-ETHANNAN

ISAIAH 40:1–26

(*Recite on the first* Shabbat *after the 9th of* Av, *called* Shabbat Naḥamu—*named after the first word of this* haftarah. *This occasion coincides with the reading of* Va-etḥannan.)

The *haftarah* opens with prophecies of consolation. Apparently these were addressed both to the Judeans who had been exiled to Babylon (in the deportations of 597 and 587–586 B.C.E.) and to the destroyed city of Jerusalem itself. Because we are told that the people's sins have been forgiven and that their punishment is complete, these words most likely were spoken after 538 B.C.E. (That was when Cyrus the Mede conquered Babylon and issued a proclamation permitting the restoration of subject peoples, including the return of Judeans to Jerusalem.)

The *haftarah* does not speak the language of political freedom or release but announces God's heavenly word of comfort and restoration. Indeed, the prophet stresses the fulfillment of God's word and His supremacy over all nations and kings. The prophecy reorients the people to Zion and announces the advent of God's Presence—to confirm and guide the renewal of His people and their homeland.

The *haftarah* is divided into two series: proclamations of consolation to the nation and to Zion (vv. 1–11), and teachings that emphasize God's unfathomable majesty and transcendence (vv. 12–26). At the outset, a series of divine charges is addressed to heavenly messengers, instructing them to bring God's word of comfort to Zion. The prophet overhears these proclamations and announces them to the people, thus giving them comfort as well.

To reinforce confidence in the prophetic proclamation, the next part of the *haftarah* depicts God as awesome in might. The prophet addresses the people with a series of rhetorical questions. By this means, he confronts the nation with the surpassing power and wisdom of God. Two series of rhetorical questions—verses 12–14 and 21–24—provide a theological frame for the entire section. In the first series, God's transcendence is juxtaposed to the comparative nothingness of nature and the delusion of idol makers. Then a question is asked: "To whom, then, can you liken God?" (v. 18). In the second series, God's might is juxtaposed to the limited knowledge of human beings. Once again the question resounds, "To whom, then, can you liken Me?" (v. 25).

THE SEVEN *HAFTAROT* OF CONSOLATION

This passage is the first of the Seven *Haftarot* of Consolation (*shiv·ah d'neḥemata*) that announce Israel's redemption. All of these selections are taken from Isaiah 40–66. They are recited on the seven Sabbaths after *Tish·ah b'Av,* a fast day that commemorates the destruction of Zion and the exile of Judah.

The Seven *Haftarot* of Consolation follow the Three *Haftarot* of Admonition (*puranuta*) that were recited on the three Sabbaths before *Tish·ah b'Av*. As the synagogue calendar progresses, these 10 *haftarah* readings are followed by one chosen especially for the *Shabbat* that precedes *Yom Kippur*. Thus we have a cycle of special *haftarot* for this period, each unrelated to the *parashah* that is read on *Shabbat*.

40 Comfort, oh comfort My people,
Says your God.
2Speak tenderly to Jerusalem,
And declare to her
That her term of service is over,
That her iniquity is expiated;
For she has received at the hand of the LORD
Double for all her sins.

3A voice rings out:
"Clear in the desert
A road for the LORD!
Level in the wilderness
A highway for our God!
4Let every valley be raised,
Every hill and mount made low.
Let the rugged ground become level
And the ridges become a plain.
5The Presence of the LORD shall appear,
And all flesh, as one, shall behold—
For the LORD Himself has spoken."

6A voice rings out: "Proclaim!"
Another asks, "What shall I proclaim?"
"All flesh is grass,

מ נַחֲמוּ נַחֲמוּ עַמִּי
יֹאמַר אֱלֹהֵיכֶם׃
2 דַּבְּרוּ עַל־לֵב יְרוּשָׁלַ͏ִם
וְקִרְאוּ אֵלֶיהָ
כִּי מָלְאָה צְבָאָהּ
כִּי נִרְצָה עֲוֺנָהּ
כִּי לָקְחָה מִיַּד יְהוָה
כִּפְלַיִם בְּכָל־חַטֹּאתֶיהָ׃ ס

3 קוֹל קוֹרֵא
בַּמִּדְבָּר פַּנּוּ
דֶּרֶךְ יְהוָה
יַשְּׁרוּ בָּעֲרָבָה
מְסִלָּה לֵאלֹהֵינוּ׃
4 כָּל־גֶּיא יִנָּשֵׂא
וְכָל־הַר וְגִבְעָה יִשְׁפָּלוּ
וְהָיָה הֶעָקֹב לְמִישׁוֹר
וְהָרְכָסִים לְבִקְעָה׃
5 וְנִגְלָה כְּבוֹד יְהוָה
וְרָאוּ כָל־בָּשָׂר יַחְדָּו
כִּי פִּי יְהוָה דִּבֵּר׃ ס

6 קוֹל אֹמֵר קְרָא
וְאָמַר מָה אֶקְרָא
כָּל־הַבָּשָׂר חָצִיר

Isaiah 40:1. Comfort, oh comfort Hebrew: *naḥamu naḥamu.* The double verb form is a hallmark of Isaiah (see 51:9,17, 52:11). It serves to express rhetorical intensification (Radak). In Ibn Ezra's opinion, it "indicates that the comfort will occur swiftly or repeatedly." God's word of comfort is apparently directed to his heavenly messengers, who are charged with addressing Jerusalem and its people (see v. 3).

2. The opening proclamation is intensified by three explanations of the comfort to come; each is introduced by the word *ki* (that, for). A theology of divine punishment and forgiveness lies behind this passage. Unilaterally God determines the period of punishment ("service") involved. Nothing is said of human repentance.

3. A voice rings out The anonymous voice of a divine messenger is heard (see v. 1). Rashi proposed that it was the Holy Spirit; Ibn Ezra suggested that it was the voice of the messengers.

6. Another asks Hebrew: *v'amar.* Apparently one messenger speaks to another, and the prophet overhears them. The Septuagint's rendering, however, suggests an underlying *va-omar,* "And I said (asked)," as if a divine messenger has addressed the prophet. Similarly, the large Isaiah scroll from Qumran (the "Dead Sea Scrolls") reads *va-om'rah.*

All flesh is grass This image underscores human mortality and transience compared to the eternal, supernatural word of God. The image recurs in Psalms (90:4–6, 103:15–17).

All its goodness like flowers of the field:
7Grass withers, flowers fade
When the breath of the LORD blows on them.
Indeed, man is but grass:
8Grass withers, flowers fade—
But the word of our God is always fulfilled!"

9Ascend a lofty mountain,
O herald of joy to Zion;
Raise your voice with power,
O herald of joy to Jerusalem—
Raise it, have no fear;
Announce to the cities of Judah:
Behold your God!
10Behold, the Lord GOD comes in might,
And His arm wins triumph for Him;
See, His reward is with Him,
His recompense before Him.
11Like a shepherd He pastures His flock:
He gathers the lambs in His arms
And carries them in His bosom;
Gently He drives the mother sheep.

12Who measured the waters with the hollow of His hand,
And gauged the skies with a span,
And meted earth's dust with a measure,
And weighed the mountains with a scale
And the hills with a balance?
13Who has plumbed the mind of the LORD,
What man could tell Him His plan?
14Whom did He consult, and who taught Him,

וְכָל־חַסְדּוֹ כְּצִיץ הַשָּׂדֶה׃
7 יָבֵשׁ חָצִיר נָבֵל צִיץ
כִּי רוּחַ יְהוָה נָשְׁבָה בּוֹ
אָכֵן חָצִיר הָעָם׃
8 יָבֵשׁ חָצִיר נָבֵל צִיץ
וּדְבַר־אֱלֹהֵינוּ יָקוּם לְעוֹלָם׃ ס

9 עַל הַר־גָּבֹהַּ עֲלִי־לָךְ
מְבַשֶּׂרֶת צִיּוֹן
הָרִימִי בַכֹּחַ קוֹלֵךְ
מְבַשֶּׂרֶת יְרוּשָׁלִָם
הָרִימִי אַל־תִּירָאִי
אִמְרִי לְעָרֵי יְהוּדָה
הִנֵּה אֱלֹהֵיכֶם׃
10 הִנֵּה אֲדֹנָי יְהוִה בְּחָזָק יָבוֹא
וּזְרֹעוֹ מֹשְׁלָה לוֹ
הִנֵּה שְׂכָרוֹ אִתּוֹ
וּפְעֻלָּתוֹ לְפָנָיו׃
11 כְּרֹעֶה עֶדְרוֹ יִרְעֶה
בִּזְרֹעוֹ יְקַבֵּץ טְלָאִים
וּבְחֵיקוֹ יִשָּׂא
עָלוֹת יְנַהֵל׃ ס

12 מִי־מָדַד בְּשָׁעֳלוֹ מַיִם
וְשָׁמַיִם בַּזֶּרֶת תִּכֵּן
וְכָל בַּשָּׁלִשׁ עֲפַר הָאָרֶץ
וְשָׁקַל בַּפֶּלֶס הָרִים
וּגְבָעוֹת בְּמֹאזְנָיִם׃
13 מִי־תִכֵּן אֶת־רוּחַ יְהוָה
וְאִישׁ עֲצָתוֹ יוֹדִיעֶנּוּ׃
14 אֶת־מִי נוֹעָץ וַיְבִינֵהוּ

12. Repeated questioning confronts us with the unfathomable majesty of God, whose cosmological supremacy is emphasized. This puts into perspective the work of human hands and mocks the mortal desire to create divine forms from the world God created.

14. Whom did He consult This may be an indirect critique of Gen. 1:26, in which God apparently speaks to the heavenly court before creating man ("Let us make man"). Similarly, the emphatic point "To whom, then, can you liken [*t'damyun*] God?" (Isa. 40:18, cf. v. 25) may be

Guided Him in the way of right?
Who guided Him in knowledge
And showed Him the path of wisdom?

15The nations are but a drop in a bucket,
Reckoned as dust on a balance;
The very coastlands He lifts like motes.
16Lebanon is not fuel enough,
Nor its beasts enough for sacrifice.
17All nations are as naught in His sight;
He accounts them as less than nothing.

18To whom, then, can you liken God,
What form compare to Him?
19The idol? A woodworker shaped it,
And a smith overlaid it with gold,
Forging links of silver.
20As a gift, he chooses the mulberry—
A wood that does not rot—
Then seeks a skillful woodworker
To make a firm idol,
That will not topple.

21Do you not know?
Have you not heard?
Have you not been told
From the very first?
Have you not discerned
How the earth was founded?
22It is He who is enthroned above the vault
of the earth,
So that its inhabitants seem as grasshoppers;
Who spread out the skies like gauze,
Stretched them out like a tent to dwell in.

וַיְלַמְּדֵהוּ בְּאֹרַח מִשְׁפָּט
וַיְלַמְּדֵהוּ דַעַת
וְדֶרֶךְ תְּבוּנוֹת יוֹדִיעֶנּוּ׃

15 הֵן גּוֹיִם כְּמַר מִדְּלִי
וּכְשַׁחַק מֹאזְנַיִם נֶחְשָׁבוּ
הֵן אִיִּים כַּדַּק יִטּוֹל׃
16 וּלְבָנוֹן אֵין דֵּי בָּעֵר
וְחַיָּתוֹ אֵין דֵּי עוֹלָה׃ ס
17 כָּל־הַגּוֹיִם כְּאַיִן נֶגְדּוֹ
מֵאֶפֶס וָתֹהוּ נֶחְשְׁבוּ־לוֹ׃

18 וְאֶל־מִי תְּדַמְּיוּן אֵל
וּמַה־דְּמוּת תַּעַרְכוּ לוֹ׃
19 הַפֶּסֶל נָסַךְ חָרָשׁ
וְצֹרֵף בַּזָּהָב יְרַקְּעֶנּוּ
וּרְתֻקוֹת כֶּסֶף צוֹרֵף׃
20 הַמְסֻכָּן תְּרוּמָה
עֵץ לֹא־יִרְקַב יִבְחָר
חָרָשׁ חָכָם יְבַקֶּשׁ־לוֹ
לְהָכִין פֶּסֶל
לֹא יִמּוֹט׃

21 הֲלוֹא תֵּדְעוּ
הֲלוֹא תִשְׁמָעוּ
הֲלוֹא הֻגַּד
מֵרֹאשׁ לָכֶם
הֲלוֹא הֲבִינֹתֶם
מוֹסְדוֹת הָאָרֶץ׃
22 הַיֹּשֵׁב עַל־חוּג הָאָרֶץ
וְיֹשְׁבֶיהָ כַּחֲגָבִים
הַנּוֹטֶה כַדֹּק שָׁמַיִם
וַיִּמְתָּחֵם כָּאֹהֶל לָשָׁבֶת׃

directed against the notion in Genesis that man was created in the "likeness" (*d'muteinu*) of God and the angels.

the way of right Hebrew: *oraḥ mishpat.* This apparently refers to the nature of the universe and its laws (Radak).

23He brings potentates to naught,
Makes rulers of the earth as nothing.
24Hardly are they planted,
Hardly are they sown,
Hardly has their stem
Taken root in earth,
When He blows upon them and they dry up,
And the storm bears them off like straw.

25To whom, then, can you liken Me,
To whom can I be compared?
—says the Holy One.
26Lift high your eyes and see:
Who created these?
He who sends out their host by count,
Who calls them each by name:
Because of His great might and vast power,
Not one fails to appear.

23 הַנּוֹתֵ֥ן רוֹזְנִ֖ים לְאָ֑יִן
שֹׁ֥פְטֵי אֶ֖רֶץ כַּתֹּ֥הוּ עָשָֽׂה׃
24 אַ֣ף בַּל־נִטָּ֗עוּ
אַ֚ף בַּל־זֹרָ֔עוּ
אַ֛ף בַּל־שֹׁרֵ֥שׁ
בָּאָ֖רֶץ גִּזְעָ֑ם
וְגַם־נָשַׁ֤ף בָּהֶם֙ וַיִּבָ֔שׁוּ
וּסְעָרָ֖ה כַּקַּ֥שׁ תִּשָּׂאֵֽם׃ ס

25 וְאֶל־מִ֥י תְדַמְּי֖וּנִי
וְאֶשְׁוֶ֑ה
יֹאמַ֖ר קָדֽוֹשׁ׃
26 שְׂאוּ־מָר֨וֹם עֵינֵיכֶ֜ם וּרְא֗וּ
מִי־בָרָ֣א אֵ֔לֶּה
הַמּוֹצִ֥יא בְמִסְפָּ֖ר צְבָאָ֑ם
לְכֻלָּם֙ בְּשֵׁ֣ם יִקְרָ֔א
מֵרֹ֣ב אוֹנִ֗ים וְאַמִּ֥יץ כֹּ֛חַ
אִ֖ישׁ לֹ֥א נֶעְדָּֽר׃ ס

25. the Holy One God is designated by the term *kadosh* (holy), which occurs frequently as *K'dosh Yisra·el,* "The Holy One of Israel" (see 41:14, 43:14, 54:5) and expresses the prophet's theology of God's utter sanctity and transcendence. The epithet provides a link to the first half of the book, in which God is repeatedly called *K'dosh Yisra·el* (see 5:19, 10:20, 12:6). The theological emphasis echoes Isaiah's numinous Temple vision, in which he heard the angelic host singing *kadosh* three times before God (6:3).

12And if you do obey these rules and observe
them carefully, the LORD your God will maintain faithfully for you the covenant that He
made on oath with your fathers: 13He will favor
you and bless you and multiply you; He will
bless the issue of your womb and the produce
of your soil, your new grain and wine and oil,
the calving of your herd and the lambing of your
flock, in the land that He swore to your fathers
to assign to you. 14You shall be blessed above
all other peoples: there shall be no sterile male
or female among you or among your livestock.
15The LORD will ward off from you all sickness;
He will not bring upon you any of the dreadful

12 וְהָיָה | עֵקֶב תִּשְׁמְעוּן אֵת הַמִּשְׁפָּטִים
הָאֵלֶּה וּשְׁמַרְתֶּם וַעֲשִׂיתֶם אֹתָם וְשָׁמַר
יְהוָה אֱלֹהֶיךָ לְךָ אֶת־הַבְּרִית וְאֶת־הַחֶסֶד
אֲשֶׁר נִשְׁבַּע לַאֲבֹתֶיךָ׃ 13 וַאֲהֵבְךָ וּבֵרַכְךָ
וְהִרְבֶּךָ וּבֵרַךְ פְּרִי־בִטְנְךָ וּפְרִי־אַדְמָתֶךָ
דְּגָנְךָ וְתִירֹשְׁךָ וְיִצְהָרֶךָ שְׁגַר־אֲלָפֶיךָ
וְעַשְׁתְּרֹת צֹאנֶךָ עַל הָאֲדָמָה אֲשֶׁר־נִשְׁבַּע
לַאֲבֹתֶיךָ לָתֶת לָךְ׃ 14 בָּרוּךְ תִּהְיֶה מִכָּל־
הָעַמִּים לֹא־יִהְיֶה בְךָ עָקָר וַעֲקָרָה
וּבִבְהֶמְתֶּךָ׃ 15 וְהֵסִיר יְהוָה מִמְּךָ כָּל־חֹלִי

Moses' Second Discourse, Part 2: Preamble to the Laws Given in Moab (*continued*)

AVOIDING DANGERS TO FAITH AND OBEDIENCE AFTER THE CONQUEST (*continued*)

EXHORTATIONS CONCERNING CONQUEST (*continued*)

OBSERVE THE COMMANDMENTS! (7:12–16)

12. if Hebrew: *eikev;* literally, "on the heels of," i.e., "as a consequence of." Verses 12–16 seem to be a continuation of verse 11. A new section (and a new weekly portion), however, begins here according to the Masoretic text, probably because it sees this word as framing a literary unit from here through 8:20, a unit whose first and final clauses begin with the same Hebrew word, *eikev* (rendered "because" in 8:20).

for you God has fulfilled His promises to the patriarchs by redeeming the Exodus generation. If the present generation obeys His commandments, He will fulfill those promises on its behalf as well.

13. These are the main elements of God's promises to the patriarchs, in addition to the land of Canaan. The terms used here for grain (*dagan*), wine (*tirosh*), calving (*sheger*), and lambing (*ashtarot*) are also names of Semitic deities. The same word often was used to refer both to a deity and a phenomenon which that deity was thought to control or personify. Most Israelites were probably unaware of the etymology of these terms, as English speakers are in talking about cereal, which is related to the Greek goddess Ceres.

new grain and wine and oil The prime products of Israelite agriculture.

14. Sterility was regarded as one of the greatest human tragedies. Hundreds of fertility charms have been found by archaeologists, testifying to the longing for children in the ancient Near East.

15. dreadful diseases of Egypt Certain diseases, such as elephantiasis, ophthalmia, and dysentery, were endemic to Egypt.

This *parashah* prepares the reader for the transition in subsequent sections from exhortation to law. Moses now stresses that the relationship between God and Israel is based on love.

13. favor you and bless you Literally, "love you and bless you." Whether it is a case of God blessing the people or of the people blessing God, "only a blessing that flows from love deserves to be called a blessing" (A. J. Heschel of Apt).

14. blessed above all other peoples The Hebrew can also be read as "blessed by all other peoples." As a reward for Israel's distinctive way of living, other nations will admire and praise them (Deut. R. 3:6).

diseases of Egypt, about which you know, but will inflict them upon all your enemies.

16You shall destroy all the peoples that the LORD your God delivers to you, showing them no pity. And you shall not worship their gods, for that would be a snare to you. 17Should you say to yourselves, "These nations are more numerous than we; how can we dispossess them?" 18You need have no fear of them. You have but to bear in mind what the LORD your God did to Pharaoh and all the Egyptians: 19the wondrous acts that you saw with your own eyes, the signs and the portents, the mighty hand, and the outstretched arm by which the LORD your God liberated you. Thus will the LORD your God do to all the peoples you now fear. 20The LORD your God will also send a plague against them, until those who are left in hiding perish before you. 21Do not stand in dread of them, for the LORD your God is in your midst, a great and awesome God.

22The LORD your God will dislodge those peoples before you little by little; you will not be able to put an end to them at once, else the wild beasts would multiply to your hurt. 23The LORD your God will deliver them up to you, throwing them into utter panic until they are wiped out. 24He will deliver their kings into your hand, and you shall obliterate their name from under the

וְכָל־מַדְוֵי מִצְרַיִם הָרָעִים אֲשֶׁר יָדַעְתָּ לֹא
יְשִׂימָם בָּךְ וּנְתָנָם בְּכָל־שֹׂנְאֶיךָ׃
16 וְאָכַלְתָּ אֶת־כָּל־הָעַמִּים אֲשֶׁר יְהוָה
אֱלֹהֶיךָ נֹתֵן לָךְ לֹא־תָחֹס עֵינְךָ עֲלֵיהֶם
וְלֹא תַעֲבֹד אֶת־אֱלֹהֵיהֶם כִּי־מוֹקֵשׁ הוּא
לָךְ׃ ס 17 כִּי תֹאמַר בִּלְבָבְךָ רַבִּים
הַגּוֹיִם הָאֵלֶּה מִמֶּנִּי אֵיכָה אוּכַל
לְהוֹרִישָׁם׃ 18 לֹא תִירָא מֵהֶם זָכֹר תִּזְכֹּר
אֵת אֲשֶׁר־עָשָׂה יְהוָה אֱלֹהֶיךָ לְפַרְעֹה
וּלְכָל־מִצְרָיִם׃ 19 הַמַּסֹּת הַגְּדֹלֹת אֲשֶׁר־
רָאוּ עֵינֶיךָ וְהָאֹתֹת וְהַמֹּפְתִים וְהַיָּד
הַחֲזָקָה וְהַזְּרֹעַ הַנְּטוּיָה אֲשֶׁר הוֹצִאֲךָ
יְהוָה אֱלֹהֶיךָ כֵּן־יַעֲשֶׂה יְהוָה אֱלֹהֶיךָ
לְכָל־הָעַמִּים אֲשֶׁר־אַתָּה יָרֵא מִפְּנֵיהֶם׃
20 וְגַם אֶת־הַצִּרְעָה יְשַׁלַּח יְהוָה אֱלֹהֶיךָ
בָּם עַד־אֲבֹד הַנִּשְׁאָרִים וְהַנִּסְתָּרִים
מִפָּנֶיךָ׃ 21 לֹא תַעֲרֹץ מִפְּנֵיהֶם כִּי־יְהוָה
אֱלֹהֶיךָ בְּקִרְבֶּךָ אֵל גָּדוֹל וְנוֹרָא׃
22 וְנָשַׁל יְהוָה אֱלֹהֶיךָ אֶת־הַגּוֹיִם הָאֵל
מִפָּנֶיךָ מְעַט מְעָט לֹא תוּכַל כַּלֹּתָם מַהֵר
פֶּן־תִּרְבֶּה עָלֶיךָ חַיַּת הַשָּׂדֶה׃ 23 וּנְתָנָם
יְהוָה אֱלֹהֶיךָ לְפָנֶיךָ וְהָמָם מְהוּמָה גְדֹלָה
עַד הִשָּׁמְדָם׃ 24 וְנָתַן מַלְכֵיהֶם בְּיָדֶךָ

16. that would be a snare to you Worshiping the gods of the Canaanites would lead to Israel's ruin.

DO NOT FEAR THE CANAANITES! (vv. 17–26)

20. plague Hebrew: *tzir·ah,* literally, "hornets" or "wasps." Ferocious swarms of wasps will hunt down the remaining Canaanites and sting them to death.

22. There were too few Israelites to fill the entire land. If all the Canaanites were dislodged at once, some of the land would remain unoccupied and would be overrun by wild animals. Therefore, God will give the Israelites only as much territory as they can occupy, and—if they obey His commandments (19:8–9)—will give them the rest when there are enough of them to fill the entire land. This is one of several explanations for the gradual and partial conquest.

24. their kings Canaan was not a unified country but a collection of city-states ruled by individual kings. The Book of Joshua lists 31 kings conquered by the Israelites (12:7–24).

obliterate their name A frequent curse, re-

---

22. else the wild beasts would multiply to your hurt If you become too adept at waging war, some of your men may come to enjoy it too much—and become like wild beasts (Israel of Modzhitz).

heavens; no man shall stand up to you, until you have wiped them out.

25You shall consign the images of their gods to the fire; you shall not covet the silver and gold on them and keep it for yourselves, lest you be ensnared thereby; for that is abhorrent to the Lord your God. 26You must not bring an abhorrent thing into your house, or you will be proscribed like it; you must reject it as abominable and abhorrent, for it is proscribed.

8 You shall faithfully observe all the Instruction that I enjoin upon you today, that you may thrive and increase and be able to possess the land that the Lord promised on oath to your fathers.

2Remember the long way that the Lord your God has made you travel in the wilderness these past forty years, that He might test you by hardships to learn what was in your hearts: whether you would keep His commandments or not.

וְהַאֲבַדְתָּ֣ אֶת־שְׁמָ֔ם מִתַּ֖חַת הַשָּׁמָ֑יִם לֹֽא־יִתְיַצֵּ֥ב אִישׁ֙ בְּפָנֶ֔יךָ עַ֥ד הִשְׁמִֽדְךָ֖ אֹתָֽם׃ 25 פְּסִילֵ֤י אֱלֹֽהֵיהֶם֙ תִּשְׂרְפ֣וּן בָּאֵ֔שׁ לֹֽא־תַחְמֹד֩ כֶּ֨סֶף וְזָהָ֤ב עֲלֵיהֶם֙ וְלָקַחְתָּ֣ לָ֔ךְ פֶּ֚ן תִּוָּקֵ֣שׁ בּ֔וֹ כִּ֧י תוֹעֲבַ֛ת יְהוָ֥ה אֱלֹהֶ֖יךָ הֽוּא׃ 26 וְלֹֽא־תָבִ֤יא תֽוֹעֵבָה֙ אֶל־בֵּיתֶ֔ךָ וְהָיִ֥יתָ חֵ֖רֶם כָּמֹ֑הוּ שַׁקֵּ֧ץ ׀ תְּשַׁקְּצֶ֣נּוּ וְתַעֵ֣ב ׀ תְּֽתַעֲבֶ֗נּוּ כִּי־חֵ֖רֶם הֽוּא׃ פ

ח כָּל־הַמִּצְוָ֗ה אֲשֶׁ֨ר אָנֹכִ֧י מְצַוְּךָ֛ הַיּ֖וֹם תִּשְׁמְר֣וּן לַעֲשׂ֑וֹת לְמַ֨עַן תִּֽחְי֜וּן וּרְבִיתֶ֗ם וּבָאתֶם֙ וִֽירִשְׁתֶּ֣ם אֶת־הָאָ֔רֶץ אֲשֶׁר־נִשְׁבַּ֥ע יְהוָ֖ה לַאֲבֹֽתֵיכֶֽם׃ 2 וְזָכַרְתָּ֣ אֶת־כָּל־הַדֶּ֗רֶךְ אֲשֶׁ֨ר הֹלִֽיכְךָ֜ יְהוָ֧ה אֱלֹהֶ֛יךָ זֶ֛ה אַרְבָּעִ֥ים שָׁנָ֖ה בַּמִּדְבָּ֑ר לְמַ֨עַן עַנֹּֽתְךָ֜ לְנַסֹּֽתְךָ֗ לָדַ֜עַת אֶת־אֲשֶׁ֧ר בִּֽלְבָבְךָ֛ הֲתִשְׁמֹ֥ר מצותו מִצְוֺתָ֖יו אִם־לֹֽא׃ 3 וַֽיְעַנְּךָ֮

---

ferring to total extinction. People's names are all that is left of them on earth after death, and the preservation of their names was considered vitally important for the well-being of their spirits in the afterlife. To obliterate one's name was to leave no oral or written trace of that name on earth, i.e., to leave that person no survivors or monuments.

from under the heavens From the surface of the earth.

25. abhorrent to the Lord Regularly refers to morally and religiously detestable practices and objects, such as cheating, perverse sexual relations, impure foods, defective sacrifices, and especially idolatry and its rites (e.g., child sacrifice, magic, and divination) (see Lev. 18, 20).

26. proscribed Hebrew: ḥeirem (a proscribed

thing), related to the verb haḥarem (doom to destruction). Objects used in idolatry were regarded as quasi-contagious and, therefore, prohibited; anyone who appropriated them became proscribed like them. Both the objects and their users were to be destroyed.

REMEMBER GOD AND OBSERVE THE COMMANDMENTS! (8:1–20)

1. that you may . . . increase Then you will be able to take control of the entire Land.

2. test you by hardships The hardships in the wilderness were not only a proper punishment of the rebellious Exodus generation. God also used them to teach the Israelites that they were dependent on Him and to test whether they would obey His commandments.

CHAPTER 8

To the theme of love, the Torah now adds the dimension of gratitude. Gratitude is perhaps the cornerstone of a religious outlook, an emotion to which even a person who is not spiritually inclined can be open.

2. test you by hardships Was this to test their faith, because they could never be sure that the manna would appear the next day (Rashbam)? Or was it to see if they would remain grateful to God even if they knew their food supply was assured?

3He subjected you to the hardship of hunger
and then gave you manna to eat, which neither
you nor your fathers had ever known, in order
to teach you that man does not live on bread
alone, but that man may live on anything that
the LORD decrees. 4The clothes upon you did
not wear out, nor did your feet swell these forty
years. 5Bear in mind that the LORD your God
disciplines you just as a man disciplines his
son. 6Therefore keep the commandments of
the LORD your God: walk in His ways and revere Him.

7For the LORD your God is bringing you into
a good land, a land with streams and springs
and fountains issuing from plain and hill; 8a
land of wheat and barley, of vines, figs, and
pomegranates, a land of olive trees and honey;
9a land where you may eat food without stint,
where you will lack nothing; a land whose rocks

וַיַּרְעִבֶ֗ךָ וַיַּֽאֲכִֽלְךָ֤ אֶת־הַמָּן֙ אֲשֶׁ֣ר לֹא־יָדַ֔עְתָּ
וְלֹ֥א יָדְע֖וּן אֲבֹתֶ֑יךָ לְמַ֣עַן הוֹדִֽעֲךָ֗ כִּ֠י לֹ֣א
עַל־הַלֶּ֤חֶם לְבַדּוֹ֙ יִחְיֶ֣ה הָֽאָדָ֔ם כִּ֛י עַל־כָּל־
מוֹצָ֥א פִֽי־יְהֹוָ֖ה יִחְיֶ֥ה הָֽאָדָֽם: 4 שִׂמְלָ֣תְךָ֗
לֹ֤א בָֽלְתָה֙ מֵֽעָלֶ֔יךָ וְרַגְלְךָ֖ לֹ֣א בָצֵ֑קָה זֶ֖ה
אַרְבָּעִ֥ים שָׁנָֽה: 5 וְיָדַעְתָּ֖ עִם־לְבָבֶ֑ךָ כִּ֗י
כַּֽאֲשֶׁ֨ר יְיַסֵּ֥ר אִישׁ֙ אֶת־בְּנ֔וֹ יְהֹוָ֥ה אֱלֹהֶ֖יךָ
מְיַסְּרֶֽךָ: 6 וְשָׁ֣מַרְתָּ֔ אֶת־מִצְוֺ֖ת יְהֹוָ֣ה
אֱלֹהֶ֑יךָ לָלֶ֥כֶת בִּדְרָכָ֖יו וּלְיִרְאָ֥ה אֹתֽוֹ:
7 כִּ֚י יְהֹוָ֣ה אֱלֹהֶ֔יךָ מְבִֽיאֲךָ֖ אֶל־אֶ֣רֶץ טוֹבָ֑ה
אֶ֚רֶץ נַ֣חֲלֵי מָ֔יִם עֲיָנֹת֙ וּתְהֹמֹ֔ת יֹֽצְאִ֥ים
בַּבִּקְעָ֖ה וּבָהָֽר: 8 אֶ֤רֶץ חִטָּה֙ וּשְׂעֹרָ֔ה וְגֶ֥פֶן
וּתְאֵנָ֖ה וְרִמּ֑וֹן אֶֽרֶץ־זֵ֥ית שֶׁ֖מֶן וּדְבָֽשׁ:
9 אֶ֗רֶץ אֲשֶׁ֨ר לֹ֤א בְמִסְכֵּנֻת֙ תֹּֽאכַל־בָּ֣הּ לֶ֔חֶם
לֹֽא־תֶחְסַ֥ר כֹּ֖ל בָּ֑הּ אֶ֚רֶץ אֲשֶׁ֣ר אֲבָנֶ֣יהָ בַרְזֶ֔ל

---

3. manna   See Exod 16:15,31; Num. 11:7.

4.   Another indication of Israel's dependence
on God and His control over nature. The Israelites' clothing and feet were immune to the effects of nature during the years in the wilderness.

5.   The hardships in the wilderness are a paradigm for all of God's disciplinary actions with
Israel. Their aim is educational. As in the case of
a father and child, the discipline is administered
with love.

7.   The goodness of the Promised Land is a
major theme of Deuteronomy, graphically illustrated here. The phrase "a good land" occurs no
fewer than 10 times in the book.

8. wheat and barley   The Land's principal

grains, from which bread, the staple of the Israelite diet, was made.

vines   Important as the source of grapes and
wine, the predominant human-made drink.

figs   A favorite fruit, eaten fresh or dried or
baked into cakes.

pomegranates   Another popular fruit. Their
juice could be drunk or made into wine. Also valued as objects of beauty and symbols of fertility,
they were used as decorations in Israelite religious
and secular art.

honey   Because this verse is a list of agricultural products, "honey" must refer to the nectar
of dates.

---

3. man does not live on bread alone   This
familiar verse is usually taken to mean that
people need "more than bread"—including
culture, art, and food for the spirit. ("Hearts
starve as well as bodies; give us bread but give
us roses.") But in context, it is better understood to mean that people can survive on "less
than bread"—namely, the manna from heaven

with which God sustains them.

**4. The clothes upon you did not wear
out**   The faith you practiced every day never
wore out nor did you outgrow it, while the faith
you took out only on special occasions shrank
and became too small for you. Similarly your
children's religious outlook grew with them as
they grew and matured (Deut. R. 7:11).

HALAKHAH L'MA·ASEH

8:8. a land of wheat . . . and honey   The Sages decreed that one should recite a special short grace after
eating any of these seven species that are mentioned as the products of the land of Israel—the *sheva minin*:
wheat, barley, grapes, figs, pomegranates, olives, and dates (the source of the honey). When they are eaten as
part of a fixed meal, the full Grace after Meals (*Birkat ha-Mazon*) is recited.

וּמֵהֲרָרֶיהָ תַּחְצֹב נְחֹשֶׁת: 10 וְאָכַלְתָּ
וְשָׂבָעְתָּ וּבֵרַכְתָּ אֶת־יְהוָה אֱלֹהֶיךָ עַל־
הָאָרֶץ הַטֹּבָה אֲשֶׁר נָתַן־לָךְ:
שני 11 הִשָּׁמֶר לְךָ פֶּן־תִּשְׁכַּח אֶת־יְהוָה אֱלֹהֶיךָ
לְבִלְתִּי שְׁמֹר מִצְוֹתָיו וּמִשְׁפָּטָיו וְחֻקֹּתָיו
אֲשֶׁר אָנֹכִי מְצַוְּךָ הַיּוֹם: 12 פֶּן־תֹּאכַל
וְשָׂבָעְתָּ וּבָתִּים טֹבִים תִּבְנֶה וְיָשָׁבְתָּ:
13 וּבְקָרְךָ וְצֹאנְךָ יִרְבְּיֻן וְכֶסֶף וְזָהָב יִרְבֶּה־
לָּךְ וְכֹל אֲשֶׁר־לְךָ יִרְבֶּה: 14 וְרָם לְבָבֶךָ
וְשָׁכַחְתָּ אֶת־יְהוָה אֱלֹהֶיךָ הַמּוֹצִיאֲךָ
מֵאֶרֶץ מִצְרַיִם מִבֵּית עֲבָדִים: 15 הַמּוֹלִיכְךָ
בַּמִּדְבָּר ׀ הַגָּדֹל וְהַנּוֹרָא נָחָשׁ ׀ שָׂרָף
וְעַקְרָב וְצִמָּאוֹן אֲשֶׁר אֵין־מָיִם הַמּוֹצִיא
לְךָ מַיִם מִצּוּר הַחַלָּמִישׁ: 16 הַמַּאֲכִלְךָ מָן
בַּמִּדְבָּר אֲשֶׁר לֹא־יָדְעוּן אֲבֹתֶיךָ לְמַעַן
עַנֹּתְךָ וּלְמַעַן נַסֹּתֶךָ לְהֵיטִבְךָ בְּאַחֲרִיתֶךָ:
17 וְאָמַרְתָּ בִּלְבָבֶךָ כֹּחִי וְעֹצֶם יָדִי עָשָׂה
לִי אֶת־הַחַיִל הַזֶּה: 18 וְזָכַרְתָּ אֶת־יְהוָה

are iron and from whose hills you can mine copper. 10When you have eaten your fill, give thanks
to the LORD your God for the good land which
He has given you.
11Take care lest you forget the LORD your
God and fail to keep His commandments, His
rules, and His laws, which I enjoin upon you
today. 12When you have eaten your fill, and have
built fine houses to live in, 13and your herds
and flocks have multiplied, and your silver and
gold have increased, and everything you own
has prospered, 14beware lest your heart grow
haughty and you forget the LORD your God—
who freed you from the land of Egypt, the house
of bondage; 15who led you through the great and
terrible wilderness with its *seraph* serpents and
scorpions, a parched land with no water in it,
who brought forth water for you from the flinty
rock; 16who fed you in the wilderness with
manna, which your fathers had never known,
in order to test you by hardships only to benefit
you in the end—17and you say to yourselves,
"My own power and the might of my own hand
have won this wealth for me." 18Remember that

9. iron . . . copper The wording reflects the fact that iron is mined from the surface, while copper is mined underground.

11. forget the LORD . . . and fail to keep His commandments Literally, "forget the LORD by failing to keep His commandments."

15. seraph serpents Literally, "fiery serpents." Creatures whose deadly bite causes a burning sensation.

brought forth water On two occasions when water was unavailable, God had Moses obtain water for the people from the inside of a rock (see Exod. 17:6; Num. 20:7–11). In the Sinai there are limestone rocks from which small amounts of water drip; a blow to their soft surface can expose a porous inner layer containing water. On the occasions in question, the rocks miraculously produced enough for the entire people.

16. test you by hardships Refers to the entire wilderness period, which also prepared the Israelites for the future.

to benefit you in the end The lesson of its dependence on God would lead Israel to obey Him and earn His continued benefactions.

---

10. *Birkat ha-Mazon,* the prayer of thanksgiving after a meal, is the fundamental *mitzvah,* because all people should be capable of feeling grateful that the earth has produced food for them to eat (Menaḥem Mendel of Kotzk).

When you have eaten your fill When one eats in a spirit of gratitude, whether there is much food or little, the meal is satisfying (Shlomo of Karlin).

HALAKHAH L'MA·ASEH

8:10. thanks This verse is the basis for the commandment to recite *Birkat ha-Mazon* (Grace after Meals).

it is the Lord your God who gives you the power to get wealth, in fulfillment of the covenant that He made on oath with your fathers, as is still the case.

19If you do forget the Lord your God and follow other gods to serve them or bow down to them, I warn you this day that you shall certainly perish; 20like the nations that the Lord will cause to perish before you, so shall you perish—because you did not heed the Lord your God.

9

Hear, O Israel! You are about to cross the Jordan to go in and dispossess nations greater and more populous than you: great cities with walls sky-high; 2a people great and tall, the Anakites, of whom you have knowledge; for you have heard it said, "Who can stand up to the children of Anak?" 3Know then this day that none other than the Lord your God is crossing at your head, a devouring fire; it is He who will wipe them out. He will subdue them before you, that you may quickly dispossess and destroy them, as the Lord promised you. 4And when the Lord your God has thrust them from your path, say not to yourselves, "The Lord has enabled us to possess this land because of our virtues"; it is rather because of the wickedness of those nations that the Lord is dispossessing them before you. 5It is not because of your virtues and your rectitude that you will be able to

אֱלֹהֶ֑יךָ כִּ֣י ה֗וּא הַנֹּתֵ֥ן לְךָ֛ כֹּ֖חַ לַעֲשׂ֣וֹת חָ֑יִל לְמַ֨עַן הָקִ֧ים אֶת־בְּרִית֛וֹ אֲשֶׁר־נִשְׁבַּ֥ע לַאֲבֹתֶ֖יךָ כַּיּ֥וֹם הַזֶּֽה: פ

19 וְהָיָ֗ה אִם־שָׁכֹ֤חַ תִּשְׁכַּח֙ אֶת־יְהֹוָ֣ה אֱלֹהֶ֔יךָ וְהָֽלַכְתָּ֗ אַחֲרֵי֙ אֱלֹהִ֣ים אֲחֵרִ֔ים וַעֲבַדְתָּ֖ם וְהִשְׁתַּחֲוִ֣יתָ לָהֶ֑ם הַעִדֹ֤תִי בָכֶם֙ הַיּ֔וֹם כִּ֥י אָבֹ֖ד תֹּאבֵדֽוּן: 20 כַּגּוֹיִ֗ם אֲשֶׁ֤ר יְהֹוָה֙ מַאֲבִ֣יד מִפְּנֵיכֶ֔ם כֵּ֖ן תֹּאבֵד֑וּן עֵ֕קֶב לֹ֣א תִשְׁמְע֔וּן בְּק֖וֹל יְהֹוָ֥ה אֱלֹהֵיכֶֽם: פ

ט שְׁמַ֣ע יִשְׂרָאֵ֗ל אַתָּ֨ה עֹבֵ֤ר הַיּוֹם֙ אֶת־הַיַּרְדֵּ֔ן לָבֹא֙ לָרֶ֣שֶׁת גּוֹיִ֔ם גְּדֹלִ֥ים וַעֲצֻמִ֖ים מִמֶּ֑ךָּ עָרִ֣ים גְּדֹלֹ֥ת וּבְצֻרֹ֖ת בַּשָּׁמָֽיִם: 2 עַֽם־גָּד֥וֹל וָרָ֖ם בְּנֵ֣י עֲנָקִ֑ים אֲשֶׁ֨ר אַתָּ֤ה יָדַ֨עְתָּ֙ וְאַתָּ֣ה שָׁמַ֔עְתָּ מִ֣י יִתְיַצֵּ֔ב לִפְנֵ֖י בְּנֵ֥י עֲנָֽק: 3 וְיָדַעְתָּ֣ הַיּ֗וֹם כִּי֩ יְהֹוָ֨ה אֱלֹהֶ֜יךָ הֽוּא־הָעֹבֵ֤ר לְפָנֶ֨יךָ֙ אֵ֣שׁ אֹֽכְלָ֔ה ה֧וּא יַשְׁמִידֵ֛ם וְה֥וּא יַכְנִיעֵ֖ם לְפָנֶ֑יךָ וְהֽוֹרַשְׁתָּ֤ם וְהַֽאֲבַדְתָּם֙ מַהֵ֔ר כַּאֲשֶׁ֛ר דִּבֶּ֥ר יְהֹוָ֖ה לָֽךְ: 4 אַל־תֹּאמַ֣ר בִּלְבָבְךָ֗ בַּהֲדֹ֣ף יְהֹוָה֩ אֱלֹהֶ֨יךָ אֹתָ֥ם | מִלְּפָנֶיךָ֮ לֵאמֹר֒ בְּצִדְקָתִי֙ הֱבִיאַ֣נִי יְהֹוָ֔ה לָרֶ֖שֶׁת אֶת־הָאָ֣רֶץ הַזֹּ֑את וּבְרִשְׁעַת֙ הַגּוֹיִ֣ם הָאֵ֔לֶּה יְהֹוָ֖ה מֽוֹרִישָׁ֥ם מִפָּנֶֽיךָ: 5 לֹ֣א בְצִדְקָֽתְךָ֗ וּבְיֹ֨שֶׁר֙ לְבָ֣בְךָ֔ אַתָּ֥ה בָ֖א לָרֶ֣שֶׁת

18. as is still the case   God is now fulfilling His promise to the patriarchs to give you the land.

20.   If the Israelites act like the Canaanites, they will suffer the same fate (see Lev. 18:28).

AN ARGUMENT AGAINST SELF-RIGHTEOUSNESS (9:1–10:22)

THEME: VICTORY IS NO PROOF OF VIRTUE (vv. 1–5)

2. you have heard it said   Either by the scouts (1:28, Num. 13:31) or by others describing the Anakites' reputation.

3. as the Lord promised you   See Exod. 23:23–31, 34:11.

4. virtues   The word tz'dakah is usually translated "righteousness," but here it probably refers specifically to loyalty or devotion.

5.   God did not deprive the Canaanites of their land arbitrarily but because of their morally outrageous practices. Israel, however, has not yet earned the right to succeed them. God brings the Israelites into the land only to fulfill the oath He made to their ancestors, the oath that sustains them even when they are devoid of merits. It is "the merit of the ancestors" (z'khut avot) that prevents God from forsaking them.

possess their country; but it is because of their wickedness that the LORD your God is dispossessing those nations before you, and in order to fulfill the oath that the LORD made to your fathers, Abraham, Isaac, and Jacob.

6Know, then, that it is not for any virtue of yours that the LORD your God is giving you this good land to possess; for you are a stiffnecked
people. 7Remember, never forget, how you provoked the LORD your God to anger in the wilderness: from the day that you left the land of Egypt until you reached this place, you have continued defiant toward the LORD.

8At Horeb you so provoked the LORD that the LORD was angry enough with you to have destroyed you. 9I had ascended the mountain to receive the tablets of stone, the Tablets of the Covenant that the LORD had made with you, and I stayed on the mountain forty days and forty

אֶת־אַרְצָם כִּי בְּרִשְׁעַת ׀ הַגּוֹיִם הָאֵלֶּה
יְהוָה אֱלֹהֶיךָ מוֹרִישָׁם מִפָּנֶיךָ וּלְמַעַן
הָקִים אֶת־הַדָּבָר אֲשֶׁר נִשְׁבַּע יְהוָה
לַאֲבֹתֶיךָ לְאַבְרָהָם לְיִצְחָק וּלְיַעֲקֹב׃
6 וְיָדַעְתָּ כִּי לֹא בְצִדְקָתְךָ יְהוָה אֱלֹהֶיךָ
נֹתֵן לְךָ אֶת־הָאָרֶץ הַטּוֹבָה הַזֹּאת
לְרִשְׁתָּהּ כִּי עַם־קְשֵׁה־עֹרֶף אָתָּה׃ 7 זְכֹר
אַל־תִּשְׁכַּח אֵת אֲשֶׁר־הִקְצַפְתָּ אֶת־יְהוָה
אֱלֹהֶיךָ בַּמִּדְבָּר לְמִן־הַיּוֹם אֲשֶׁר־יָצָאתָ ׀
מֵאֶרֶץ מִצְרַיִם עַד־בֹּאֲכֶם עַד־הַמָּקוֹם
הַזֶּה מַמְרִים הֱיִיתֶם עִם־יְהוָה׃
8 וּבְחֹרֵב הִקְצַפְתֶּם אֶת־יְהוָה וַיִּתְאַנַּף
יְהוָה בָּכֶם לְהַשְׁמִיד אֶתְכֶם׃ 9 בַּעֲלֹתִי
הָהָרָה לָקַחַת לוּחֹת הָאֲבָנִים לוּחֹת
הַבְּרִית אֲשֶׁר־כָּרַת יְהוָה עִמָּכֶם וָאֵשֵׁב
בָּהָר אַרְבָּעִים יוֹם וְאַרְבָּעִים לַיְלָה לֶחֶם

A HISTORY OF PROVOCATIONS
(vv. 6–24)

6. Know, then From the following.

stiffnecked Obstinate, headstrong.

7. this place The valley near Beth-peor (3:29), the site of their most recent rebellion.

8–21. This passage recapitulates the more detailed account of the Golden Calf in Exod. 32.

8. At Horeb That is, even at Horeb (Mount Sinai). Although the Golden Calf incident was not the first of Israel's provocations, it is mentioned first because it was the most outrageous. If there was one place above all others where the people should have been faithful, it was Horeb, where they had encountered God personally, had seen that He alone is God, and were commanded to worship no other gods.

9. Tablets of the Covenant They contain the Decalogue (see 4:13, 5:19).

forty days and forty nights During this time Moses was learning the remainder of the laws (see 5:28). Such 40-day periods are frequently encountered in the Bible and seem to convey the proper time for completion of a lengthy process. This period was required for the Israelites at the foot of Mt. Sinai to achieve repentance (Rashi).

CHAPTER 9

6. not for any virtue of yours Israel's election as God's special people is not based on their superiority to other nations, either in size or in merit. God chose to give Israel the Torah in order that Israel might thereby become a moral exemplar among the nations—not because it already was one. Characterizing Israel as a people chosen by God is not an assertion of superiority, but a historical fact. It was through God's using Israel as an instrument of divine revelation that the notion of ethical monotheism, the Decalogue, the prophets, and the psalms all came into the world. (Maimonides differs, suggesting that God must have seen Israel's unique spiritual potential despite their flaws and their numerical insignificance when measured by human standards.)

for you are a stiffnecked people Most commentators see this as a negative trait. "A stiffnecked person will not accept criticism and change" (Sforno). "A stiffnecked person cannot look behind him and see how his actions have led him to where he finds himself" (Abravanel). A few see this characteristic as positive: The stubbornness of Jews in the face of persecution has enabled us to remain Jewish through the centuries (Exod. R. 42:9).

nights, eating no bread and drinking no water. [10]And the LORD gave me the two tablets of stone inscribed by the finger of God, with the exact words that the LORD had addressed to you on the mountain out of the fire on the day of the Assembly.

[11]At the end of those forty days and forty nights, the LORD gave me the two tablets of stone, the Tablets of the Covenant. [12]And the LORD said to me, "Hurry, go down from here at once, for the people whom you brought out of Egypt have acted wickedly; they have been quick to stray from the path that I enjoined upon them; they have made themselves a molten image." [13]The LORD further said to me, "I see that this is a stiffnecked people. [14]Let Me alone and I will destroy them and blot out their name from under heaven, and I will make you a nation far more numerous than they."

[15]I started down the mountain, a mountain ablaze with fire, the two Tablets of the Covenant in my two hands. [16]I saw how you had sinned against the LORD your God: you had made yourselves a molten calf; you had been quick to stray from the path that the LORD had enjoined upon

לֹ֣א אָכַ֔לְתִּי וּמַ֖יִם לֹ֥א שָׁתִֽיתִי׃ 10 וַיִּתֵּ֨ן
יְהֹוָ֜ה אֵלַ֗י אֶת־שְׁנֵי֙ לוּחֹ֣ת הָֽאֲבָנִ֔ים
כְּתֻבִ֖ים בְּאֶצְבַּ֣ע אֱלֹהִ֑ים וַעֲלֵיהֶ֗ם כְּֽכָל־
הַדְּבָרִ֡ים אֲשֶׁר֩ דִּבֶּ֨ר יְהֹוָ֧ה עִמָּכֶ֛ם בָּהָ֛ר
מִתּ֥וֹךְ הָאֵ֖שׁ בְּי֥וֹם הַקָּהָֽל׃
11 וַיְהִ֗י מִקֵּץ֙ אַרְבָּעִ֣ים י֔וֹם וְאַרְבָּעִ֖ים לָ֑יְלָה
נָתַ֨ן יְהֹוָ֜ה אֵלַ֗י אֶת־שְׁנֵ֛י לֻחֹ֥ת הָאֲבָנִ֖ים
לֻח֥וֹת הַבְּרִֽית׃ 12 וַיֹּ֨אמֶר יְהֹוָ֜ה אֵלַ֗י ק֣וּם
רֵ֤ד מַהֵר֙ מִזֶּ֔ה כִּ֚י שִׁחֵ֣ת עַמְּךָ֔ אֲשֶׁ֥ר הוֹצֵ֖אתָ
מִמִּצְרָ֑יִם סָ֣רוּ מַהֵ֗ר מִן־הַדֶּ֙רֶךְ֙ אֲשֶׁ֣ר צִוִּיתִ֔ם
עָשׂ֥וּ לָהֶ֖ם מַסֵּכָֽה׃ 13 וַיֹּ֥אמֶר יְהֹוָ֖ה אֵלַ֣י
לֵאמֹ֑ר רָאִ֨יתִי֙ אֶת־הָעָ֣ם הַזֶּ֔ה וְהִנֵּ֥ה עַם־
קְשֵׁה־עֹ֖רֶף הֽוּא׃ 14 הֶ֤רֶף מִמֶּ֙נִּי֙ וְאַשְׁמִידֵ֔ם
וְאֶמְחֶ֣ה אֶת־שְׁמָ֔ם מִתַּ֖חַת הַשָּׁמָ֑יִם
וְאֶֽעֱשֶׂה֙ אֽוֹתְךָ֔ לְגוֹי־עָצ֥וּם וָרָ֖ב מִמֶּֽנּוּ׃
15 וָאֵ֗פֶן וָֽאֵרֵד֙ מִן־הָהָ֔ר וְהָהָ֖ר בֹּעֵ֣ר בָּאֵ֑שׁ
וּשְׁנֵי֙ לוּחֹ֣ת הַבְּרִ֔ית עַ֖ל שְׁתֵּ֥י יָדָֽי׃ 16 וָאֵ֗רֶא
וְהִנֵּ֤ה חֲטָאתֶם֙ לַיהֹוָ֣ה אֱלֹהֵיכֶ֔ם עֲשִׂיתֶ֣ם
לָכֶ֔ם עֵ֖גֶל מַסֵּכָ֑ה סַרְתֶּ֣ם מַהֵ֔ר מִן־הַדֶּ֕רֶךְ

eating no bread and drinking no water During his intimate encounter with God, inside the cloud, Moses was beyond human needs and concerns.

10. inscribed with the finger of God According to Exod. 32:16, the tablets were also made by God.

day of the Assembly At Mount Sinai (Horeb).

12. God's peremptory tone implies that He is annoyed with Moses because of the people's behavior. So, too, does this reference to the Israelites as "the people whom you [Moses] brought out of Egypt"—literally, "your people whom you brought out of Egypt." Normally, God referred to them as "My people . . . whom I brought out of Egypt."

molten image According to Exod. 32:2 and 24, the calf was made from melted gold ornaments.

14. Let Me alone The phrase implies that Moses, if he so wishes, can restrain God from destroying Israel by interceding with Him and arguing the case for mercy.

blot out their name This is what Israel was to do to the Canaanites and the Amalekites (7:24, 25:19).

far more numerous They already are as numerous as the stars (1:10, 10:22). The promise to the patriarchs would be continued through Moses and his descendants.

15. The idol was made in full view of the mountain that was still blazing with God's Presence (see 4:11–12,36, 5:20). And it violated the very commands written on the tablets that Moses carried.

16. molten calf It is likely that the calf did not represent another deity, but a pedestal or mount on which *YHVH* was thought to be invisibly present, much as the cherubs in the Holy of Holies were conceived as *YHVH*'s throne. Nevertheless, even if the original motive for making the calf was not idolatrous, the people immediately fell to worshiping it and violated the Decalogue's prohibition against worshiping idols.

you. ¹⁷Thereupon I gripped the two tablets and flung them away with both my hands, smashing them before your eyes. ¹⁸I threw myself down before the Lord—eating no bread and drinking no water forty days and forty nights, as before—because of the great wrong you had committed, doing what displeased the Lord and vexing Him. ¹⁹For I was in dread of the Lord's fierce anger against you, which moved Him to wipe you out. And that time, too, the Lord gave heed to me.—²⁰Moreover, the Lord was angry enough with Aaron to have destroyed him; so I also interceded for Aaron at that time.—²¹As for that sinful thing you had made, the calf, I took it and put it to the fire; I broke it to bits and ground it thoroughly until it was fine as dust, and I threw its dust into the brook that comes down from the mountain.

²²Again you provoked the Lord at Taberah, and at Massah, and at Kibroth-hattaavah.

²³And when the Lord sent you on from Kadesh-barnea, saying, "Go up and take possession of the land that I am giving you," you

אֲשֶׁר־צִוָּ֥ה יְהֹוָ֖ה אֶתְכֶֽם׃ 17 וָֽאֶתְפֹּשׂ֙ בִּשְׁנֵ֣י הַלֻּחֹ֔ת וָֽאַשְׁלִכֵ֔ם מֵעַ֖ל שְׁתֵּ֣י יָדָ֑י וָֽאֲשַׁבְּרֵ֖ם לְעֵינֵיכֶֽם׃ 18 וָֽאֶתְנַפַּל֩ לִפְנֵ֨י יְהֹוָ֜ה כָּרִֽאשֹׁנָ֗ה אַרְבָּעִ֥ים יוֹם֙ וְאַרְבָּעִ֣ים לַ֔יְלָה לֶ֚חֶם לֹ֣א אָכַ֔לְתִּי וּמַ֖יִם לֹ֣א שָׁתִ֑יתִי עַ֤ל כָּל־חַטַּאתְכֶם֙ אֲשֶׁ֣ר חֲטָאתֶ֔ם לַעֲשׂ֥וֹת הָרַ֖ע בְּעֵינֵ֥י יְהֹוָ֖ה לְהַכְעִיסֽוֹ׃ 19 כִּ֣י יָגֹ֗רְתִּי מִפְּנֵ֤י הָאַף֙ וְהַ֣חֵמָ֔ה אֲשֶׁ֨ר קָצַ֧ף יְהֹוָ֛ה עֲלֵיכֶ֖ם לְהַשְׁמִ֣יד אֶתְכֶ֑ם וַיִּשְׁמַ֤ע יְהֹוָה֙ אֵלַ֔י גַּ֖ם בַּפַּ֥עַם הַהִֽוא׃ 20 וּֽבְאַהֲרֹ֗ן הִתְאַנַּ֧ף יְהֹוָ֛ה מְאֹ֖ד לְהַשְׁמִיד֑וֹ וָֽאֶתְפַּלֵּ֛ל גַּם־בְּעַ֥ד אַהֲרֹ֖ן בָּעֵ֥ת הַהִֽוא׃ 21 וְֽאֶת־חַטַּאתְכֶ֞ם אֲשֶׁר־עֲשִׂיתֶ֣ם אֶת־הָעֵ֗גֶל לָקַ֘חְתִּי֮ וָֽאֶשְׂרֹ֣ף אֹת֣וֹ ׀ בָּאֵשׁ֒ וָֽאֶכֹּ֨ת אֹת֜וֹ טָח֣וֹן הֵיטֵ֗ב עַ֚ד אֲשֶׁר־דַּ֣ק לְעָפָ֔ר וָֽאַשְׁלִךְ֙ אֶת־עֲפָר֔וֹ אֶל־הַנַּ֖חַל הַיֹּרֵ֥ד מִן־הָהָֽר׃

22 וּבְתַבְעֵרָה֙ וּבְמַסָּ֔ה וּבְקִבְרֹ֖ת הַתַּֽאֲוָ֑ה מַקְצִפִ֥ים הֱיִיתֶ֖ם אֶת־יְהֹוָֽה׃

23 וּבִשְׁלֹ֨חַ יְהֹוָ֜ה אֶתְכֶ֗ם מִקָּדֵ֤שׁ בַּרְנֵ֙עַ֙ לֵאמֹ֔ר עֲלוּ֙ וּרְשׁ֣וּ אֶת־הָאָ֔רֶץ אֲשֶׁ֥ר נָתַ֖תִּי

---

17. smashing them The act not only depicts Moses' rage but also has legal significance. In Mesopotamian law, one canceled a contract by breaking the clay tablets on which it was written, the equivalent of ripping up written legal documents. By smashing the tablets, Moses indicated that the covenant was annulled.

18. Moses' second 40-day fast matches the first (v. 9) but has a different purpose. Here it is an expression of grief over the people's sin and the danger to their survival.

19. that time, too Because Moses is now speaking at the end of the Israelites' 40 years in the wilderness, the word "too" implies any of the other occasions when he interceded with God during the preceding decades.

20. angry enough Literally, "very angry." God was angrier with Aaron than with the people, because it was he who made the Golden Calf. The guilt for making the idol was greater than the guilt of those who requested it.

I also interceded for Aaron This detail was not mentioned at the time (Exod. 32). Moses may well have interceded on his brother's behalf, as he

did for Miriam (Num. 12:13). Or he may be recalling past events as he wished they had happened.

21. This is a practical way of getting rid of an impure object (see Exod. 32:20).

22. The Golden Calf incident was not an isolated one; rebelliousness has been the consistent pattern of the Israelites' behavior.

Taberah Literally, "conflagration." The people complained there to the Lord for an unspecified reason, and He caused a fire to ravage the outskirts of the Israelite camp (see Num. 11:1–3).

Massah Literally, "ordeal, test." The people, lacking water, complained there that Moses had taken them out of Egypt to kill them with thirst (see Exod. 17:1–7).

Kibroth-hattaavah Literally, "the graves of those who had a lustful appetite." The people angered the Lord by complaining there that they were bored with the manna and wanted meat, and that they had eaten better in Egypt. God fed them quail but also sent a plague against them (see Num. 11:4–34).

23. See 1:26–43.

flouted the command of the LORD your God; you did not put your trust in Him and did not obey Him.

²⁴As long as I have known you, you have been defiant toward the LORD.

²⁵When I lay prostrate before the LORD those forty days and forty nights, because the LORD was determined to destroy you, ²⁶I prayed to the LORD and said, "O Lord GOD, do not annihilate Your very own people, whom You redeemed in Your majesty and whom You freed from Egypt with a mighty hand. ²⁷Give thought to Your servants, Abraham, Isaac, and Jacob, and pay no heed to the stubbornness of this people, its wickedness, and its sinfulness. ²⁸Else the country from which You freed us will say, 'It was because the LORD was powerless to bring them into the land that He had promised them, and because He rejected them, that He brought them out to have them die in the wilderness.' ²⁹Yet they are Your very own people, whom You freed with Your great might and Your outstretched arm."

10 ¹Thereupon the LORD said to me, "Carve

לָכֶ֔ם וַתַּמְר֕וּ אֶת־פִּ֛י יְהֹוָ֥ה אֱלֹהֵיכֶ֖ם וְלֹ֤א הֶֽאֱמַנְתֶּם֙ ל֔וֹ וְלֹ֥א שְׁמַעְתֶּ֖ם בְּקֹלֽוֹ: ²⁴ מַמְרִ֥ים* הֱיִיתֶ֖ם עִם־יְהֹוָ֑ה מִיּ֖וֹם דַּעְתִּ֥י אֶתְכֶֽם:

²⁵ וָֽאֶתְנַפַּ֞ל לִפְנֵ֣י יְהֹוָ֗ה אֵ֣ת אַרְבָּעִ֥ים הַיּ֛וֹם וְאֶת־אַרְבָּעִ֥ים הַלַּ֖יְלָה אֲשֶׁ֣ר הִתְנַפָּ֑לְתִּי כִּֽי־אָמַ֥ר יְהֹוָ֖ה לְהַשְׁמִ֥יד אֶתְכֶֽם: ²⁶ וָאֶתְפַּלֵּ֣ל אֶל־יְהֹוָה֮ וָֽאֹמַר֒ אֲדֹנָ֣י יֱהֹוִ֗ה אַל־תַּשְׁחֵ֤ת עַמְּךָ֙ וְנַֽחֲלָ֣תְךָ֔ אֲשֶׁ֥ר פָּדִ֖יתָ בְּגׇדְלֶ֑ךָ אֲשֶׁר־הוֹצֵ֥אתָ מִמִּצְרַ֖יִם בְּיָ֥ד חֲזָקָֽה: ²⁷ זְכֹר֙ לַֽעֲבָדֶ֔יךָ לְאַבְרָהָ֥ם לְיִצְחָ֖ק וּֽלְיַֽעֲקֹ֑ב אַל־תֵּ֗פֶן אֶל־קְשִׁי֙ הָעָ֣ם הַזֶּ֔ה וְאֶל־רִשְׁע֖וֹ וְאֶל־חַטָּאתֽוֹ: ²⁸ פֶּן־יֹֽאמְר֗וּ הָאָ֘רֶץ֮ אֲשֶׁ֣ר הֽוֹצֵאתָ֣נוּ מִשָּׁם֒ מִבְּלִי֙ יְכֹ֣לֶת יְהֹוָ֔ה לַֽהֲבִיאָ֕ם אֶל־הָאָ֖רֶץ אֲשֶׁר־דִּבֶּ֣ר לָהֶ֑ם וּמִשִּׂנְאָת֣וֹ אוֹתָ֔ם הֽוֹצִיאָ֖ם לַֽהֲמִתָ֥ם בַּמִּדְבָּֽר: ²⁹ וְהֵ֥ם עַמְּךָ֖ וְנַֽחֲלָתֶ֑ךָ אֲשֶׁ֤ר הוֹצֵ֨אתָ֙ בְּכֹֽחֲךָ֣ הַגָּדֹ֔ל וּבִֽזְרֹֽעֲךָ֖ הַנְּטוּיָֽה: פ

י בָּעֵ֨ת הַהִ֜וא אָמַ֧ר יְהֹוָ֣ה אֵלַ֗י פְּסׇל־לְךָ֜

מ' זעירא   v. 24.

THE AFTERMATH OF THE GOLDEN CALF INCIDENT   (9:25–10:11)

25. those forty days and forty nights   Referred to in verses 18–19.

26. Your very own people   Literally, "do not destroy the people that is Your inheritance," Your cherished hereditary property. In verse 12, God calls Israel "your [Moses'] people whom you brought out of Egypt," thereby dissociating Himself from them. Here Moses' plea appeals to God's self-interest.

whom You redeemed   All the effort that God has invested in the people of Israel would be utterly worthless if He were now to destroy them.

28.   Here Moses invokes the most daring argument against annihilating the people Israel: It would give a damaging impression of God, who is not indifferent to human opinion (see Exod. 7:5,17, 32:12). If God should destroy Israel, He would appear powerless or diabolical and damage the stature that He had gained from the Exodus.

29.   The Egyptians might accuse You of weakness and of rejecting Israel, when in fact Israel is Your own beloved people whose redemption clearly revealed Your power.

---

27.   The concept of "the merit of ancestors" (*z'khut avot*) appears once again. If the people today are unworthy, remember the merit of their ancestors.

pay no heed to the stubbornness of this

people   The patriarchs were also stubborn; that is how they maintained their faith in the face of all odds. The stubbornness of the people may serve this purpose as well (Mordecai ha-Kohen).

out two tablets of stone like the first, and come up to Me on the mountain; and make an ark of wood. 2I will inscribe on the tablets the commandments that were on the first tablets that you smashed, and you shall deposit them in the ark."

3I made an ark of acacia wood and carved out two tablets of stone like the first; I took the two tablets with me and went up the mountain. 4The LORD inscribed on the tablets the same text as on the first, the Ten Commandments that He addressed to you on the mountain out of the fire on the day of the Assembly; and the LORD gave them to me. 5Then I left and went down from the mountain, and I deposited the tablets in the ark that I had made, where they still are, as the LORD had commanded me.

6From Beeroth-bene-jaakan the Israelites marched to Moserah. Aaron died there and was buried there; and his son Eleazar became priest in his stead. 7From there they marched to Gudgod, and from Gudgod to Jotbath, a region of running brooks.

שְׁנֵֽי־לוּחֹ֤ת אֲבָנִים֙ כָּרִ֣אשֹׁנִ֔ים וַעֲלֵ֥ה אֵלַ֖י
הָהָ֑רָה וְעָשִׂ֥יתָ לְּךָ֖ אֲר֥וֹן עֵֽץ׃ 2 וְאֶכְתֹּב֙
עַל־הַלֻּחֹ֔ת אֶת־הַדְּבָרִ֔ים אֲשֶׁ֥ר הָי֛וּ עַל־
הַלֻּחֹ֥ת הָרִאשֹׁנִ֖ים אֲשֶׁ֣ר שִׁבַּ֑רְתָּ וְשַׂמְתָּ֖ם
בָּאָרֽוֹן׃
3 וָאַ֤עַשׂ אֲרוֹן֙ עֲצֵ֣י שִׁטִּ֔ים וָאֶפְסֹ֛ל שְׁנֵֽי־
לֻחֹ֥ת אֲבָנִ֖ים כָּרִאשֹׁנִ֑ים וָאַ֣עַל הָהָ֔רָה וּשְׁנֵ֥י
הַלֻּחֹ֖ת בְּיָדִֽי׃ 4 וַיִּכְתֹּ֨ב עַל־הַלֻּחֹ֜ת כַּמִּכְתָּ֣ב
הָרִאשׁ֗וֹן אֵ֚ת עֲשֶׂ֣רֶת הַדְּבָרִ֔ים אֲשֶׁר֩ דִּבֶּ֨ר
יְהוָ֧ה אֲלֵיכֶ֛ם בָּהָ֛ר מִתּ֥וֹךְ הָאֵ֖שׁ בְּי֣וֹם
הַקָּהָ֑ל וַיִּתְּנֵ֥ם יְהוָ֖ה אֵלָֽי׃ 5 וָאֵ֗פֶן וָֽאֵרֵד֙
מִן־הָהָ֔ר וָֽאָשִׂם֙ אֶת־הַלֻּחֹ֔ת בָּאָר֖וֹן אֲשֶׁ֣ר
עָשִׂ֑יתִי וַיִּ֣הְיוּ שָׁ֔ם כַּאֲשֶׁ֥ר צִוַּ֖נִי יְהוָֽה׃
6 וּבְנֵ֣י יִשְׂרָאֵ֗ל נָֽסְע֛וּ מִבְּאֵרֹ֥ת בְּנֵי־יַעֲקָ֖ן
מוֹסֵרָ֑ה שָׁ֣ם מֵ֤ת אַהֲרֹן֙ וַיִּקָּבֵ֣ר שָׁ֔ם וַיְכַהֵ֛ן
אֶלְעָזָ֥ר בְּנ֖וֹ תַּחְתָּֽיו׃ 7 מִשָּׁ֥ם נָסְע֖וּ הַגֻּדְגֹּ֑דָה
וּמִן־הַגֻּדְגֹּ֣דָה יָטְבָ֔תָה אֶ֖רֶץ נַ֥חֲלֵי מָֽיִם׃

New Tablets: Reaffirmation of the Sinai Covenant (10:1–5)

1. Carve out Although God would inscribe the new tablets, they would be made by a mortal, unlike the first ones, which were made by God (Exod. 32:16).

ark A chest. Contractual documents in the ancient world were often stored in chests and other types of containers, to protect them against damage or loss and to preserve evidence of the agreement.

wood According to Exod. 25:11, the wood of the Ark was overlaid with gold.

3. I made an ark In Exodus the Ark is built later, by Bezalel, along with the rest of the Tabernacle. Some commentators infer that there were two Arks, one of them built by Moses to house the tablets temporarily until Bezalel built the permanent Ark. Others hold that there was only the one Ark built by Bezalel, and that this passage in which Moses "makes" the Ark means that he had it made after he came down from the mountain. Modern scholarship assumes that the passage reflects a different tradition about the building of the Ark from that recounted in Exodus.

The Death of Aaron (vv. 6–7)

Aaron died 40 years after the Golden Calf incident (Num. 33:38–39). His death is mentioned here to indicate that although he was spared at the time, he did not escape punishment for his role in Israel's idolatry. Like Moses, he died in the wilderness and never reached the Promised Land.

CHAPTER 10

6. Aaron's death is recounted here after the story of Moses breaking the tablets, to teach us that the death of a righteous person is as grievous as the shattering of the original Tablets of the Covenant. Both represent a diminution of God's presence in the world (*Divrei David*).

8At that time the Lord set apart the tribe of
Levi to carry the Ark of the Lord's Covenant,
to stand in attendance upon the Lord, and to
bless in His name, as is still the case. 9That is
why the Levites have received no hereditary portion along with their kinsmen: the Lord is their
portion, as the Lord your God spoke concerning them.

10I had stayed on the mountain, as I did the
first time, forty days and forty nights; and the
Lord heeded me once again: the Lord agreed
not to destroy you. 11And the Lord said to me,
"Up, resume the march at the head of the people, that they may go in and possess the land
that I swore to their fathers to give them."

12And now, O Israel, what does the Lord your
God demand of you? Only this: to revere the
Lord your God, to walk only in His paths, to
love Him, and to serve the Lord your God with

8 בָּעֵת הַהִוא הִבְדִּיל יְהֹוָה אֶת־שֵׁבֶט הַלֵּוִי
לָשֵׂאת אֶת־אֲרוֹן בְּרִית־יְהֹוָה לַעֲמֹד לִפְנֵי
יְהֹוָה לְשָׁרְתוֹ וּלְבָרֵךְ בִּשְׁמוֹ עַד הַיּוֹם
הַזֶּה: 9 עַל־כֵּן לֹא־הָיָה לְלֵוִי חֵלֶק וְנַחֲלָה
עִם־אֶחָיו יְהֹוָה הוּא נַחֲלָתוֹ כַּאֲשֶׁר דִּבֶּר
יְהֹוָה אֱלֹהֶיךָ לוֹ:

10 וְאָנֹכִי עָמַדְתִּי בָהָר כַּיָּמִים הָרִאשֹׁנִים
אַרְבָּעִים יוֹם וְאַרְבָּעִים לַיְלָה וַיִּשְׁמַע
יְהֹוָה אֵלַי גַּם בַּפַּעַם הַהִוא לֹא־אָבָה
יְהֹוָה הַשְׁחִיתֶךָ: 11 וַיֹּאמֶר יְהֹוָה אֵלַי קוּם
לֵךְ לְמַסַּע לִפְנֵי הָעָם וְיָבֹאוּ וְיִרְשׁוּ אֶת־
הָאָרֶץ אֲשֶׁר־נִשְׁבַּעְתִּי לַאֲבֹתָם לָתֵת
לָהֶם: פ

חמישי 12 וְעַתָּה יִשְׂרָאֵל מָה יְהֹוָה אֱלֹהֶיךָ שֹׁאֵל
מֵעִמָּךְ כִּי אִם־לְיִרְאָה אֶת־יְהֹוָה אֱלֹהֶיךָ
לָלֶכֶת בְּכָל־דְּרָכָיו וּלְאַהֲבָה אֹתוֹ וְלַעֲבֹד

Election of the Levites   (vv. 8–9)

8. At that time   The time of the Golden Calf
incident. The Levites were chosen for their
priestly role because they rallied to Moses and
punished the worshipers of the calf (Exod.
32:26–29). As a reward for their devotion, they
were made the guardians of the shrine from infringement.

to carry the Ark   This applied whenever the
Israelites traveled or if there was any other need
to move it.

to stand in attendance   To offer sacrifices.

to bless in His name   To pronounce the
priestly benediction (21:5; Num. 6:22–27; cf.
Lev. 9:22).

9.   No tribal territory was accorded the Levites, who lived dispersed among the other tribes
and were supported by the income of the sanctuaries so that they might devote their entire time
to clerical duties (18:1–2).

Permission to Continue On to the
Promised Land   (vv. 10–11)

10.   Moses returns to the main subject of
9:25–10:11, his successful prayer to spare the
Israelites (9:26–29).

11.   In Exodus 33, this was not God's final
word. After telling Moses that His angel would
lead the people to the Promised Land, God responded to Moses' further entreaties and agreed
to lead the people personally.

GOD'S REQUIREMENTS   (vv. 12–22)

Moses summarizes the principles that must guide
the people if they are to avoid acts of rebellion
in the future.

12. revere   Reverence (literally, "fear of
God") comes first. Israel's narrow escape from
destruction should be sufficient to deter it from
disobedience.

---

12. demand   Hebrew: *sho·el;* literally, "ask."
Moses knows that reverence and love cannot
be produced on commmand. "Everything is in
the power of Heaven except whether a person
will choose to revere God" (BT Ber. 33b). Reverence and obedience are perhaps the only virtues we cannot learn by imitating God, because

God has no one to revere or obey. One of the
fundamental teachings of Judaism is that people are free to choose between good and evil, between following God's ways and rejecting
them. We cannot be compelled to be good. The
decision whether to love God and to follow the
Torah's teachings is totally under our control.

אֶת־יְהוָ֣ה אֱלֹהֶ֔יךָ בְּכׇל־לְבָבְךָ֖ וּבְכׇל־
נַפְשֶֽׁךָ׃ 13 לִשְׁמֹ֞ר אֶת־מִצְוֺ֤ת יְהוָה֙ וְאֶת־
חֻקֹּתָ֔יו אֲשֶׁ֛ר אָנֹכִ֥י מְצַוְּךָ֖ הַיּ֑וֹם לְט֖וֹב
לָֽךְ׃ 14 הֵ֚ן לַיהוָ֣ה אֱלֹהֶ֔יךָ הַשָּׁמַ֖יִם וּשְׁמֵ֣י
הַשָּׁמָ֑יִם הָאָ֖רֶץ וְכׇל־אֲשֶׁר־בָּֽהּ׃ 15 רַ֧ק
בַּאֲבֹתֶ֛יךָ חָשַׁ֥ק יְהוָ֖ה לְאַהֲבָ֣ה אוֹתָ֑ם
וַיִּבְחַ֞ר בְּזַרְעָ֤ם אַחֲרֵיהֶם֙ בָּכֶ֣ם מִכׇּל־
הָֽעַמִּ֖ים כַּיּ֥וֹם הַזֶּֽה׃ 16 וּמַלְתֶּ֕ם אֵ֖ת עׇרְלַ֣ת
לְבַבְכֶ֑ם וְעׇ֨רְפְּכֶ֔ם לֹ֥א תַקְשׁ֖וּ עֽוֹד׃ 17 כִּ֚י
יְהוָ֣ה אֱלֹֽהֵיכֶ֔ם ה֚וּא אֱלֹהֵ֣י הָֽאֱלֹהִ֔ים וַאֲדֹנֵ֖י
הָאֲדֹנִ֑ים הָאֵ֨ל הַגָּדֹ֤ל הַגִּבֹּר֙ וְהַנּוֹרָ֔א אֲשֶׁר֙
לֹא־יִשָּׂ֣א פָנִ֔ים וְלֹ֥א יִקַּ֖ח שֹֽׁחַד׃ 18 עֹשֶׂ֛ה
מִשְׁפַּ֥ט יָת֖וֹם וְאַלְמָנָ֑ה וְאֹהֵ֣ב גֵּ֔ר לָ֥תֶת ל֖וֹ
לֶ֥חֶם וְשִׂמְלָֽה׃ 19 וַאֲהַבְתֶּ֖ם אֶת־הַגֵּ֑ר כִּֽי־
גֵרִ֥ים הֱיִיתֶ֖ם בְּאֶ֥רֶץ מִצְרָֽיִם׃
20 אֶת־יְהוָ֧ה אֱלֹהֶ֛יךָ תִּירָ֖א אֹת֣וֹ תַעֲבֹ֑ד

all your heart and soul, 13keeping the LORD's
commandments and laws, which I enjoin upon
you today, for your good. 14Mark, the heavens
to their uttermost reaches belong to the LORD
your God, the earth and all that is on it! 15Yet
it was to your fathers that the LORD was drawn
in His love for them, so that He chose you, their
lineal descendants, from among all peoples—as
is now the case. 16Cut away, therefore, the thickening about your hearts and stiffen your necks
no more. 17For the LORD your God is God supreme and Lord supreme, the great, the mighty,
and the awesome God, who shows no favor and
takes no bribe, 18but upholds the cause of the
fatherless and the widow, and befriends the
stranger, providing him with food and clothing.—19You too must befriend the stranger, for
you were strangers in the land of Egypt.
20You must revere the LORD your God: only
Him shall you worship, to Him shall you hold

14. the heavens to their uttermost reaches Literally, "the heavens and the heaven of heavens." In this conception, there are skies above the sky, and God is master of them all. Thus Israel's election by God is an extraordinary privilege; all the more reason to obey Him.

16. Cut away . . . the thickening about your hearts Literally, "circumcise the foreskin of your heart." The "foreskin" is what blocks your heart and renders it inaccessible to God's teachings. It is a metaphor for the mental obstruction that has made Israel stubborn.

stiffen your necks no more As you did during the years in the wilderness (9:6,13,27).

17. God supreme and Lord supreme Literally, "the God of gods and Lord of lords." The greatest of heavenly beings and the most powerful of rulers—another argument for obedience to God. "Lord of lords" and similar titles were used as epithets of kings in the ancient Near East.

shows no favor and takes no bribe God exemplifies the qualities of the ideal judge.

18. the fatherless and the widow God is the protector of those who have no one to protect and provide for them.

befriends Literally, "loves." As the final clause of the verse indicates, the verb refers to affection expressed in action.

the stranger The resident alien.

19. for you were strangers No sooner are strangers mentioned than Israel's duty toward them prompts this digression. Israel's experience as aliens in a foreign land is regularly cited to encourage fair and kind treatment of strangers in its own land. Exodus 23:9 adds: "for you know the feelings of the stranger" (see Lev. 19:34).

---

17. takes no bribe We cannot buy God's favor with charity, synagogue attendance, or good deeds. We do those things to elevate our own souls, not to create a reciprocal obligation on God's part.

HALAKHAH L'MA·ASEH

10:19. befriend the stranger This verse requires us to make converts welcome and to treat them as equal members of the Jewish community. The Hebrew word *ger*, commonly translated "stranger" as used in the Bible, is now used (as a shortened version of *ger tzedek*) to designate a convert.

fast, and by His name shall you swear. 21He is your glory and He is your God, who wrought for you those marvelous, awesome deeds that you saw with your own eyes. 22Your ancestors went down to Egypt seventy persons in all; and now the LORD your God has made you as numerous as the stars of heaven.

וּבוֹ תִדְבָּק וּבִשְׁמוֹ תִּשָּׁבֵעַ׃ 21 הוּא תְהִלָּתְךָ
וְהוּא אֱלֹהֶיךָ אֲשֶׁר־עָשָׂה אִתְּךָ אֶת־
הַגְּדֹלֹת וְאֶת־הַנּוֹרָאֹת הָאֵלֶּה אֲשֶׁר רָאוּ
עֵינֶיךָ׃ 22 בְּשִׁבְעִים נֶפֶשׁ יָרְדוּ אֲבֹתֶיךָ
מִצְרָיְמָה וְעַתָּה שָׂמְךָ יְהוָה אֱלֹהֶיךָ
כְּכוֹכְבֵי הַשָּׁמַיִם לָרֹב׃

11 Love, therefore, the LORD your God, and always keep His charge, His laws, His rules, and His commandments.

2Take thought this day that it was not your children, who neither experienced nor witnessed the lesson of the LORD your God—

His majesty, His mighty hand, His outstretched arm; 3the signs and the deeds that He performed in Egypt against Pharaoh king of Egypt and all his land; 4what He did to Egypt's army, its horses and chariots; how the LORD rolled back upon them the waters of the Sea of Reeds when they were pursuing you, thus destroying them once and for all;

יא וְאָהַבְתָּ אֵת יְהוָה אֱלֹהֶיךָ וְשָׁמַרְתָּ
מִשְׁמַרְתּוֹ וְחֻקֹּתָיו וּמִשְׁפָּטָיו וּמִצְוֺתָיו כָּל־
הַיָּמִים׃
2 וִידַעְתֶּם הַיּוֹם כִּי ׀ לֹא אֶת־בְּנֵיכֶם אֲשֶׁר
לֹא־יָדְעוּ וַאֲשֶׁר לֹא־רָאוּ אֶת־מוּסַר יְהוָה
אֱלֹהֵיכֶם
אֶת־גָּדְלוֹ אֶת־יָדוֹ הַחֲזָקָה וּזְרֹעוֹ
הַנְּטוּיָה׃ 3 וְאֶת־אֹתֹתָיו וְאֶת־מַעֲשָׂיו
אֲשֶׁר עָשָׂה בְּתוֹךְ מִצְרָיִם לְפַרְעֹה מֶלֶךְ־
מִצְרַיִם וּלְכָל־אַרְצוֹ׃ 4 וַאֲשֶׁר עָשָׂה
לְחֵיל מִצְרַיִם לְסוּסָיו וּלְרִכְבּוֹ אֲשֶׁר
הֵצִיף אֶת־מֵי יַם־סוּף עַל־פְּנֵיהֶם
בְּרָדְפָם אַחֲרֵיכֶם וַיְאַבְּדֵם יְהוָה עַד

21. He is your glory He and none other, continuing the thought of verse 20.

marvelous, awesome deeds Namely, the Ten Plagues, the crossing of the Sea of Reeds, and the revelation at Mount Sinai.

22. seventy persons Jacob, his children, and his grandchildren, as indicated in Gen. 46:8–27 and Exod. 1:1–5.

THE PRECONDITION FOR CONQUERING AND KEEPING THE PROMISED LAND (11:1–25)

1. This verse introduces verses 2–25 by stating their theme and calling for love of and loyalty to God, as do verses 13 and 22.

2. that it was not your children Moses stresses that he is not appealing to the people on the basis of another generation's experience, but their own.

4. once and for all Literally, "to this day."

CHAPTER 11

1. The fundamental relationship between God and the individual is one of love, not fear of punishment or hope of reward. We do what God asks of us because we are so pleased to be able to do something for one whom we love. Petuchowski said that a Jew reads the Torah not as one reads a novel or a newspaper, but as one reads a love letter, eager to extract every bit of meaning from it.

5what He did for you in the wilderness before you arrived in this place; 6and what He did to Dathan and Abiram, sons of Eliab son of Reuben, when the earth opened her mouth and swallowed them, along with their households, their tents, and every living thing in their train, from amidst all Israel—

7but that it was you who saw with your own eyes all the marvelous deeds that the LORD performed.

8Keep, therefore, all the Instruction that I enjoin upon you today, so that you may have the strength to enter and take possession of the land that you are about to cross into and possess, 9and that you may long endure upon the soil that the LORD swore to your fathers to assign to them and to their heirs, a land flowing with milk and honey.

10For the land that you are about to enter and possess is not like the land of Egypt from which you have come. There the grain you sowed had

הַיּ֖וֹם הַזֶּֽה׃ 5 וַאֲשֶׁ֨ר עָשָׂ֤ה לָכֶם֙ בַּמִּדְבָּ֔ר
עַד־בֹּאֲכֶ֖ם עַד־הַמָּק֥וֹם הַזֶּֽה׃ 6 וַאֲשֶׁ֨ר
עָשָׂ֜ה לְדָתָ֣ן וְלַאֲבִירָ֗ם בְּנֵ֣י אֱלִיאָב֮ בֶּן־
רְאוּבֵן֒ אֲשֶׁ֨ר פָּצְתָ֤ה הָאָ֙רֶץ֙ אֶת־פִּ֔יהָ
וַתִּבְלָעֵ֥ם וְאֶת־בָּתֵּיהֶ֖ם וְאֶת־אָהֳלֵיהֶ֑ם
וְאֵ֤ת כָּל־הַיְקוּם֙ אֲשֶׁ֣ר בְּרַגְלֵיהֶ֔ם בְּקֶ֖רֶב
כָּל־יִשְׂרָאֵֽל׃
7 כִּ֤י עֵֽינֵיכֶם֙ הָֽרֹאֹ֔ת אֶת־כָּל־מַעֲשֵׂ֥ה יְהוָ֖ה
הַגָּדֹ֑ל אֲשֶׁ֖ר עָשָֽׂה׃
8 וּשְׁמַרְתֶּם֙ אֶת־כָּל־הַמִּצְוָ֔ה אֲשֶׁ֛ר אָנֹכִ֥י
מְצַוְּךָ֖ הַיּ֑וֹם לְמַ֣עַן תֶּחֶזְק֗וּ וּבָאתֶם֙
וִֽירִשְׁתֶּ֣ם אֶת־הָאָ֔רֶץ אֲשֶׁ֥ר אַתֶּ֛ם עֹבְרִ֥ים
שָׁ֖מָּה לְרִשְׁתָּֽהּ׃ 9 וּלְמַ֙עַן֙ תַּאֲרִ֤יכוּ יָמִים֙
עַל־הָ֣אֲדָמָ֔ה אֲשֶׁר֩ נִשְׁבַּ֨ע יְהוָ֧ה לַאֲבֹתֵיכֶ֛ם
לָתֵ֥ת לָהֶ֖ם וּלְזַרְעָ֑ם אֶ֛רֶץ זָבַ֥ת חָלָ֖ב
וּדְבָֽשׁ׃ ס
ששי 10 כִּ֣י הָאָ֗רֶץ אֲשֶׁ֨ר אַתָּ֤ה בָא־שָׁ֙מָּה֙
לְרִשְׁתָּ֔הּ לֹ֠א כְאֶ֤רֶץ מִצְרַ֙יִם֙ הִ֔וא אֲשֶׁ֥ר

That is, now, 40 years later, Egypt still has not replaced the army, horses, and chariots that it lost at the Sea of Reeds.

5. did for you Alternatively, "did to you" (*asah lakhem*). The rest of the verse deals with punitive acts. Moses is referring to the punishments that God inflicted for Israel's insubordination on hearing the scouts' report (1:22–45), for the Golden Calf (Exod. 32), and for other acts of faithlessness (Deut. 2:15, 9:22).

6. Dathan and Abiram Accomplices of Korah in the notorious rebellion described in Num. 16. Korah's name is conspicuously absent here. Traditional commentators explain that Moses, wishing to spare the feelings of Korah's sons, omitted his name. Modern scholarship holds that Num. 16 combines the stories of two separate rebellions, one led by Korah and the other by Dathan and Abiram. According to this view, Deuteronomy knows only the Dathan and Abiram story because the two stories were not yet combined in their present form when Deuteronomy was composed.

from amidst all Israel It happened in full sight of all the people, who thus know of the event firsthand (v. 7). The sinners alone fell into the earth although they were surrounded by the rest of the people.

8. Instruction Literally, "commandment," and so also in verse 22 below.

9. Obedience to God's commands is the precondition for conquering the Promised Land and remaining in it.

flowing with milk and honey Indicates that "enduring upon the soil" is to be viewed in the context of agriculture and the supply of food.

10. In Egypt, you had to bring water to the fields (Exod. 1:14) on your own, by a method normally used only in vegetable gardens, for which rainfall is insufficient; in the Promised Land the fields will be watered by God, by means of rain.

---

10. not like the land of Egypt The majority of commentators understand this verse as speaking in praise of the Land (one need not haul water in buckets; God waters your fields for you). Its more probable sense, though, is that Egypt is like a child whose mother gives

יֹצָאתֶם מִשָּׁם אֲשֶׁר תִּזְרַע אֶת־זַרְעֲךָ
וְהִשְׁקִיתָ בְרַגְלְךָ כְּגַן הַיָּרָק׃ 11 וְהָאָרֶץ
אֲשֶׁר אַתֶּם עֹבְרִים שָׁמָּה לְרִשְׁתָּהּ אֶרֶץ
הָרִים וּבְקָעֹת לִמְטַר הַשָּׁמַיִם תִּשְׁתֶּה־
מָּיִם׃ 12 אֶרֶץ אֲשֶׁר־יְהוָה אֱלֹהֶיךָ דֹּרֵשׁ
אֹתָהּ תָּמִיד עֵינֵי יְהוָה אֱלֹהֶיךָ בָּהּ
מֵרֵשִׁית* הַשָּׁנָה וְעַד אַחֲרִית שָׁנָה׃ ס
13 וְהָיָה אִם־שָׁמֹעַ תִּשְׁמְעוּ אֶל־מִצְוֺתַי
אֲשֶׁר אָנֹכִי מְצַוֶּה אֶתְכֶם הַיּוֹם לְאַהֲבָה
אֶת־יְהוָה אֱלֹהֵיכֶם וּלְעָבְדוֹ בְּכָל־לְבַבְכֶם
וּבְכָל־נַפְשְׁכֶם׃ 14 וְנָתַתִּי מְטַר־אַרְצְכֶם
בְּעִתּוֹ יוֹרֶה וּמַלְקוֹשׁ וְאָסַפְתָּ דְגָנֶךָ

to be watered by your own labors, like a vegetable garden; [11]but the land you are about to cross into and possess, a land of hills and valleys, soaks up its water from the rains of heaven. [12]It is a land which the LORD your God looks after, on which the LORD your God always keeps His eye, from year's beginning to year's end.

[13]If, then, you obey the commandments that I enjoin upon you this day, loving the LORD your God and serving Him with all your heart and soul, [14]I will grant the rain for your land in season, the early rain and the late. You shall gather in your new grain and wine and oil—

v. 12. חסר א׳

Very little rain falls in Egypt; irrigation depends entirely on the annual flooding of the Nile, which is caused by melting snow and spring rains at its Ethiopian source.

by your own labors Literally, "by your foot." Probably refers to the use of the foot for opening and closing sluice gates or to the more primitive method of making and breaking down ridges of dirt to control the flow of water into the irrigation channels in gardens and fields.

11. The land could be irrigated only by rain, not by human effort.

12. God's attention is constantly focused on the land of Israel. The metaphor is used as an expression of benevolent concern and judgmental scrutiny.

from year's beginning to year's end God is attentive to the land in every season, "seedtime and harvest, cold and heat, summer and winter" (Gen. 8:22).

13. Because the land of Israel is watered by God, rainfall and other benefits are conditional on obedience to Him.

14. I will grant Here, and in verse 15, Moses is speaking in God's name.

rain . . . in season Promises of rainfall often carry the assurance that it will come in the proper season, because for agricultural purposes rain in

---

it what it needs whether it deserves it or not. The Promised Land represents a more mature stage. "It is a land . . . on which the LORD your God always keeps His eye" (v. 12). The Land will be blessed by rain only if the people, by their good behavior, deserve it.

13–20. These words constitute the second passage recited after *Sh'ma Yisra·el* in services of prayer. How shall we understand them, given that we find no connection between morality and rainfall, or, for that matter, between morality and good fortune? Many admirable people are not blessed with abundance. The answer may lie in the fact that this passage is phrased in the plural, unlike the first passage (Deut. 6:5–9), which is phrased in the singular. Righteous individuals may not always prosper, and wicked individuals may not always suffer the consequences of their wickedness. (Would we expect God to send life-giving rain to a good person's farm but make sure none of it fell on the fields of a wicked neighbor?) Righteous communities, however, will tend to thrive and bestow blessings on all their members, the good and the less good alike. And wicked communities will bring misfortune on all their inhabitants.

Yeshayahu Leibowitz finds two distinct theological approaches in the first two passages that are recited after *Sh'ma Yisra·el.* There are some people (addressed in the first passage) who instinctively love God so much that they are eager to do God's will with no thought of a reward. Then there are others, at a less developed theological level (addressed in this second passage) who can be persuaded to do what is right only with the hope of reward and the threat of punishment.

15 I will also provide grass in the fields for your cattle—and thus you shall eat your fill. 16 Take care not to be lured away to serve other gods and bow to them. 17 For the LORD's anger will flare up against you, and He will shut up the skies so that there will be no rain and the ground will not yield its produce; and you will soon perish from the good land that the LORD is assigning to you.

18 Therefore impress these My words upon your very heart: bind them as a sign on your hand and let them serve as a symbol on your forehead, 19 and teach them to your children—reciting them when you stay at home and when you are away, when you lie down and when you get up; 20 and inscribe them on the doorposts of your house and on your gates—21 to the end that you and your children may endure, in the land that the LORD swore to your fathers to assign to them, as long as there is a heaven over the earth.

22 If, then, you faithfully keep all this Instruction that I command you, loving the LORD your God, walking in all His ways, and holding fast to Him, 23 the LORD will dislodge before you all these nations: you will dispossess nations

וְתִירֹשְׁךָ וְיִצְהָרֶךָ׃ 15 וְנָתַתִּי עֵשֶׂב בְּשָׂדְךָ
לִבְהֶמְתֶּךָ וְאָכַלְתָּ וְשָׂבָעְתָּ׃ 16 הִשָּׁמְרוּ
לָכֶם פֶּן יִפְתֶּה לְבַבְכֶם וְסַרְתֶּם וַעֲבַדְתֶּם
אֱלֹהִים אֲחֵרִים וְהִשְׁתַּחֲוִיתֶם לָהֶם׃
17 וְחָרָה אַף־יְהֹוָה בָּכֶם וְעָצַר אֶת־
הַשָּׁמַיִם וְלֹא־יִהְיֶה מָטָר וְהָאֲדָמָה לֹא
תִתֵּן אֶת־יְבוּלָהּ וַאֲבַדְתֶּם מְהֵרָה מֵעַל
הָאָרֶץ הַטֹּבָה אֲשֶׁר יְהֹוָה נֹתֵן לָכֶם׃
18 וְשַׂמְתֶּם אֶת־דְּבָרַי אֵלֶּה עַל־לְבַבְכֶם
וְעַל־נַפְשְׁכֶם וּקְשַׁרְתֶּם אֹתָם לְאוֹת עַל־
יֶדְכֶם וְהָיוּ לְטוֹטָפֹת בֵּין עֵינֵיכֶם׃
19 וְלִמַּדְתֶּם אֹתָם אֶת־בְּנֵיכֶם לְדַבֵּר בָּם
בְּשִׁבְתְּךָ בְּבֵיתֶךָ וּבְלֶכְתְּךָ בַדֶּרֶךְ וּבְשָׁכְבְּךָ
וּבְקוּמֶךָ׃ 20 וּכְתַבְתָּם עַל־מְזוּזוֹת בֵּיתֶךָ
וּבִשְׁעָרֶיךָ׃ 21 לְמַעַן יִרְבּוּ יְמֵיכֶם וִימֵי
בְנֵיכֶם עַל הָאֲדָמָה אֲשֶׁר נִשְׁבַּע יְהֹוָה
לַאֲבֹתֵיכֶם לָתֵת לָהֶם כִּימֵי הַשָּׁמַיִם
עַל־הָאָרֶץ׃ ס
22 כִּי אִם־שָׁמֹר תִּשְׁמְרוּן אֶת־כָּל־הַמִּצְוָה שביעי מפטיר
הַזֹּאת אֲשֶׁר אָנֹכִי מְצַוֶּה אֶתְכֶם לַעֲשֹׂתָהּ
לְאַהֲבָה אֶת־יְהֹוָה אֱלֹהֵיכֶם לָלֶכֶת בְּכָל־
דְּרָכָיו וּלְדָבְקָה־בוֹ׃ 23 וְהוֹרִישׁ יְהֹוָה אֶת־
כָּל־הַגּוֹיִם הָאֵלֶּה מִלִּפְנֵיכֶם וִירִשְׁתֶּם

the wrong season is useless, and at times harmful. Rain is the special sign of divine providence in biblical religion. It is especially apt because it can also serve as a monitor of the Israelites' obedience to the Covenant.

gather Bringing crops in from the field for processing, and gathering the processed products for storage.

15. Well-fed cattle will plow better, thus increasing the harvest. They also will be fatter and provide more meat.

18. In view of verses 16–17, the Israelites should remind themselves of God's teachings so as to obey them and avoid a disastrous fate. The reminders are prescribed in 6:6–9.

21. as long as there is a heaven That is, forever. The sky and heavenly bodies symbolize permanence.

---

15. Based on the order in this verse, with concern for cattle preceding that for human beings, the Talmud rules that one may not eat before feeding one's animals (BT Ber. 40a).

22. walking in all His ways Imitating God, so to speak, through acts of compassion and kindness (*Sifrei*).

HALAKHAH L'MA·ASEH

11:18. bind them See Comment to 6:8.

greater and more numerous than you. [24]Every
spot on which your foot treads shall be yours;
your territory shall extend from the wilderness
to the Lebanon and from the River—the
Euphrates—to the Western Sea. [25]No man shall
stand up to you: the LORD your God will put
the dread and the fear of you over the
whole land in which you set foot, as He promised you.

גּוֹיִם גְּדֹלִים וַעֲצֻמִים מִכֶּם׃ 24 כָּל־הַמָּקוֹם
אֲשֶׁר תִּדְרֹךְ כַּף־רַגְלְכֶם בּוֹ לָכֶם יִהְיֶה
מִן־הַמִּדְבָּר וְהַלְּבָנוֹן מִן־הַנָּהָר נְהַר־פְּרָת
וְעַד הַיָּם הָאַחֲרוֹן יִהְיֶה גְּבֻלְכֶם׃ 25 לֹא־
יִתְיַצֵּב אִישׁ בִּפְנֵיכֶם פַּחְדְּכֶם וּמוֹרַאֲכֶם
יִתֵּן ׀ יְהוָה אֱלֹהֵיכֶם עַל־פְּנֵי כָל־הָאָרֶץ
אֲשֶׁר תִּדְרְכוּ־בָהּ כַּאֲשֶׁר דִּבֶּר לָכֶם׃ ס

24. Every spot on which your foot treads This wording may reflect the ancient practice of formally acquiring title to land by walking through it.

your territory God is giving the Israelites the entire Promised Land, from one end to the other. Because this is the point of the verse, only the land's borders are named: the deserts in the south, the Lebanon and the Euphrates in the north, and the Mediterranean Sea on the west. The eastern boundary, the Jordan River, goes unmentioned here because it is self-evident. The Israelites are about to cross it to enter the land.

Western Sea Literally, the "hind" or "rear" sea. The geographic orientation of the ancient western Semites was not toward the north, as in modern cartography, but the east. Hence one set of terms for the four points of the compass expresses "east" by "forward" (*kedem*), "west" by "behind" (*aḥor*) "north" by "left" (*s'mol*) and "south" by "right" (*yamin, teiman*).

25. See Exod. 23:27–31; Deut. 7:19–24.

הפטרה שנייה דנחמתא

SECOND HAFTARAH OF CONSOLATION
HAFTARAH FOR EIKEV

ISAIAH 49:14–51:3

(*Recite on the 2nd* Shabbat *after the 9th of* Av, *coinciding with the reading of* Eikev. *On the Seven* Haftarot *of Consolation, see p. 1032.*)

This *haftarah* enunciates the despair of Zion, which feels forgotten and abandoned by God in the years since the destruction of the Temple in 587–586 B.C.E. and the exile of Judeans to Babylon. God seeks to stem this attitude by proclaiming divine care and promising that the nation will be returned to its homeland. Yet the city's lament reflects the constant, deep sense of loss felt by the nation during the years of exile and dispersion. Personifying the people of Zion, the city's voice complements the elegy recited over it in the Book of Lamentations. The brevity of the cry "The LORD has forsaken me" in the opening verse reveals the depth of despair—beyond words and theological artifice.

This *haftarah* has been drawn from several prophecies to produce a rich rhetorical tapestry of consolation and exhortation. Dominant contrasts are stressed at the beginning and at the end. The opening report of Zion's words of despair is matched by a concluding notice that "Truly the LORD has comforted Zion" (51:3). In between lie assurances, remonstrations, and words of expectation.

Rhetorical questions mark the stages of the argument. Responding to Zion's despair, God asks the first question: "Can a woman forget her baby, / Or disown the child of her womb?" The point is made with no room for ambiguity: "Though she might forget, / I never could forget you" (49:15). Because divine concern transcends even the most fundamental natural human instincts, despair is altogether baseless.

The second question and response (49:24–25) stresses that the Lord Himself will deliver the nation. The third question (50:2) mocks Israel's baseless lack of faith in the power of divine salvation.

These expressions of God's concern concretize around the figure of the divine hand or arm. God asserts that He could never forget Zion, in a remarkable mythic image in which the pattern of Zion and its ramparts are etched on God's own hands as an eternal remembrance of it (49:16). God, so to speak, meditates constantly on Zion the way the faithful are bidden to bind God's teachings on their arms and write them on the doorposts of their homes so as to be ever-mindful of their religious duties and obligations (Deut. 6:8–9).

Further bold imagery likens God and Zion to a married couple whose children are the nation (49:15–18). Then God counters the people's sense of abandonment with the rhetorical question, "Where is the bill of divorce / Of your mother whom I dismissed?" (50:1). This suggests a deep bond between God and His city (a bond also dramatized elsewhere through bold figures of marriage, divorce, and erotic delight; Isa. 62:1–5).

The *haftarah* ends with a series of speeches in which the prophet stresses his faithfulness to his task (50:4ff.). He exhorts those who would revere the Lord to trust in the "voice of His servant" and "in the name of the LORD." Only God's supernatural word will give true light and direction, not the firebrands kindled by human hands. Those who rely on their own prowess, to "Walk by the blaze of [their own] fire," shall be doomed (50:10–11). The way of faith is a path of heavenly trust; it leads to redemption because it looks beyond self-reliance.

In a further word, those who "seek the LORD" are given an example of faith on which to model themselves. They are told to look to "Abraham your father" and to "Sarah who brought you forth" (51:1–2). To underscore the new moment,

and to bolster the nation's resolve, the prophet concludes with a proclamation of assurance and utopian vision (51:3).

Looking to the past, the people may restore their future; acting on the future, the nation may overcome its past. The renewal of Zion is imagined as nothing less than utopia—a renewal of Eden, beyond the travail of history and exile.

49 14Zion says,
"The LORD has forsaken me,
My Lord has forgotten me."
15Can a woman forget her baby,
Or disown the child of her womb?
Though she might forget,
I never could forget you.
16See, I have engraved you
On the palms of My hands,
Your walls are ever before Me.
17Swiftly your children are coming;
Those who ravaged and ruined you shall leave you.
18Look up all around you and see:
They are all assembled, are come to you!
As I live
—declares the LORD—
You shall don them all like jewels,
Deck yourself with them like a bride.
19As for your ruins and desolate places
And your land laid waste—
You shall soon be crowded with settlers,
While destroyers stay far from you.
20The children you thought you had lost
Shall yet say in your hearing,
"The place is too crowded for me;

מט 14 וַתֹּאמֶר צִיּוֹן
עֲזָבַנִי יְהוָה
וַאדֹנָי שְׁכֵחָנִי׃
15 הֲתִשְׁכַּח אִשָּׁה עוּלָהּ
מֵרַחֵם בֶּן־בִּטְנָהּ
גַּם־אֵלֶּה תִשְׁכַּחְנָה
וְאָנֹכִי לֹא אֶשְׁכָּחֵךְ׃
16 הֵן עַל־כַּפַּיִם
חַקֹּתִיךְ
חוֹמֹתַיִךְ נֶגְדִּי תָּמִיד׃
17 מִהֲרוּ בָּנָיִךְ
מְהָרְסַיִךְ וּמַחֲרִבַיִךְ מִמֵּךְ יֵצֵאוּ׃
18 שְׂאִי־סָבִיב עֵינַיִךְ וּרְאִי
כֻּלָּם נִקְבְּצוּ בָאוּ־לָךְ
חַי־אָנִי
נְאֻם־יְהוָה
כִּי כֻלָּם כַּעֲדִי תִלְבָּשִׁי
וּתְקַשְּׁרִים כַּכַּלָּה׃
19 כִּי חָרְבֹתַיִךְ וְשֹׁמְמֹתַיִךְ
וְאֶרֶץ הֲרִסֻתֵךְ
כִּי עַתָּה תֵּצְרִי מִיּוֹשֵׁב
וְרָחֲקוּ מְבַלְּעָיִךְ׃
20 עוֹד יֹאמְרוּ בְאָזְנַיִךְ
בְּנֵי שִׁכֻּלָיִךְ
צַר־לִי הַמָּקוֹם

Isaiah 49:14. Zion says Hebrew: *va-tomer tziyon;* literally, "But Zion said." These words, in context as part of the Book of Isaiah, rejected the teaching that preceded them (49:1–13). That teaching concluded with the assertion that "the LORD has comforted His people, / And has taken back His afflicted ones in love." The Sages, however, by beginning this *haftarah* here, gave verse 14 an independent status and new meaning. The phrase lost its polemical tone and acquired one of pathos and despair.

15. her baby Hebrew: *ulah.* In a remarkable play on words, the Midrash relates it to Israel's having accepted at Sinai the "yoke" (*ol*) of the Kingdom of Heaven, a fact always to be remembered in its favor (*Tanna d'Bei Eliyahu* 17).

17. your children Hebrew: *banayikh.* The large Isaiah scroll at Qumran (the "Dead Sea

Make room for me to settle."
21And you will say to yourself,
"Who bore these for me
When I was bereaved and barren,
Exiled and disdained—
By whom, then, were these reared?
I was left all alone—
And where have these been?"

22Thus said the Lord God:
I will raise My hand to nations
And lift up My ensign to peoples;
And they shall bring your sons in their bosoms,
And carry your daughters on their backs.
23Kings shall tend your children,
Their queens shall serve you as nurses.
They shall bow to you, face to the ground,
And lick the dust of your feet.
And you shall know that I am the Lord—
Those who trust in Me shall not be shamed.

24Can spoil be taken from a warrior,
Or captives retrieved from a victor?
25Yet thus said the Lord:
Captives shall be taken from a warrior
And spoil shall be retrieved from a tyrant;
For *I* will contend with your adversaries,
And *I* will deliver your children.
26I will make your oppressors eat their own flesh,
They shall be drunk with their own blood as with wine.
And all mankind shall know
That I the Lord am your Savior,
The Mighty One of Jacob, your Redeemer.

גְּשָׁה־לִּ֖י וְאֵשֵֽׁבָה׃
21 וְאָמַ֣רְתְּ בִּלְבָבֵ֗ךְ
מִ֤י יָֽלַד־לִי֙ אֶת־אֵ֔לֶּה
וַאֲנִ֥י שְׁכוּלָ֖ה וְגַלְמוּדָ֑ה
גֹּלָ֣ה ׀ וְסוּרָ֗ה
וְאֵ֙לֶּה֙ מִ֣י גִדֵּ֔ל
הֵ֤ן אֲנִי֙ נִשְׁאַ֣רְתִּי לְבַדִּ֔י
אֵ֖לֶּה אֵיפֹ֥ה הֵֽם׃ פ

22 כֹּֽה־אָמַ֞ר אֲדֹנָ֣י יְהוִ֗ה
הִנֵּ֨ה אֶשָּׂ֤א אֶל־גּוֹיִם֙ יָדִ֔י
וְאֶל־עַמִּ֖ים אָרִ֣ים נִסִּ֑י
וְהֵבִ֤יאוּ בָנַ֙יִךְ֙ בְּחֹ֔צֶן
וּבְנֹתַ֖יִךְ עַל־כָּתֵ֥ף תִּנָּשֶֽׂאנָה׃
23 וְהָי֨וּ מְלָכִ֜ים אֹֽמְנַ֗יִךְ
וְשָׂרֽוֹתֵיהֶם֙ מֵינִ֣יקֹתַ֔יִךְ
אַפַּ֗יִם אֶ֚רֶץ יִשְׁתַּ֣חֲווּ לָ֔ךְ
וַעֲפַ֥ר רַגְלַ֖יִךְ יְלַחֵ֑כוּ
וְיָדַ֙עַתְּ֙ כִּֽי־אֲנִ֣י יְהוָ֔ה
אֲשֶׁ֥ר לֹֽא־יֵבֹ֖שׁוּ קֹוָֽי׃ ס

24 הֲיֻקַּ֥ח מִגִּבּ֖וֹר מַלְק֑וֹחַ
וְאִם־שְׁבִ֥י צַדִּ֖יק יִמָּלֵֽט׃
25 כִּי־כֹ֣ה ׀ אָמַ֣ר יְהוָ֗ה
גַּם־שְׁבִ֤י גִבּוֹר֙ יֻקָּ֔ח
וּמַלְק֥וֹחַ עָרִ֖יץ יִמָּלֵ֑ט
וְאֶת־יְרִיבֵךְ֙ אָנֹכִ֣י אָרִ֔יב
וְאֶת־בָּנַ֖יִךְ אָנֹכִ֥י אוֹשִֽׁיעַ׃
26 וְהַאֲכַלְתִּ֤י אֶת־מוֹנַ֙יִךְ֙ אֶת־בְּשָׂרָ֔ם
וְכֶעָסִ֖יס דָּמָ֣ם יִשְׁכָּר֑וּן
וְיָדְע֣וּ כָל־בָּשָׂ֗ר
כִּ֣י אֲנִ֤י יְהוָה֙ מֽוֹשִׁיעֵ֔ךְ
וְגֹאֲלֵ֖ךְ אֲבִ֥יר יַעֲקֹֽב׃ ס

Scrolls") reads *bonayikh* (your builders), which fits in juxtaposition with "those who ravaged and ruined you." A similar reading is found in Saadia.

23. Kings shall tend your children A vision of social reversal: the powerful shall serve the (now) powerless people Israel.

50

Thus said the LORD:

Where is the bill of divorce
Of your mother whom I dismissed?
And which of My creditors was it
To whom I sold you off?
You were only sold off for your sins,
And your mother dismissed for your crimes.
²Why, when I came, was no one there,
Why, when I called, would none respond?
Is my arm, then, too short to rescue,
Have I not the power to save?
With a mere rebuke I dry up the sea,
And turn rivers into desert.
Their fish stink from lack of water;
They lie dead of thirst.
³I clothe the skies in blackness
And make their raiment sackcloth.

⁴The Lord GOD gave me a skilled tongue,
To know how to speak timely words to the
   weary.
Morning by morning, He rouses,
He rouses my ear
To give heed like disciples.
⁵The Lord GOD opened my ears,
And I did not disobey,
I did not run away.
⁶I offered my back to the floggers,
And my cheeks to those who tore out my hair.

נ כֹּה ׀ אָמַ֣ר יְהֹוָ֗ה
אֵ֣י זֶ֠ה סֵ֣פֶר כְּרִית֤וּת
אִמְּכֶם֙ אֲשֶׁ֣ר שִׁלַּחְתִּ֔יהָ
א֚וֹ מִ֣י מִנּוֹשַׁ֔י
אֲשֶׁר־מָכַ֥רְתִּי אֶתְכֶ֖ם ל֑וֹ
הֵ֤ן בַּעֲוֺנֹֽתֵיכֶם֙ נִמְכַּרְתֶּ֔ם
וּבְפִשְׁעֵיכֶ֖ם שֻׁלְּחָ֥ה אִמְּכֶֽם׃
² מַדּ֜וּעַ בָּ֣אתִי וְאֵ֣ין אִ֗ישׁ
קָרָ֙אתִי֙ וְאֵ֣ין עוֹנֶ֔ה
הֲקָצ֨וֹר קָצְרָ֤ה יָדִי֙ מִפְּד֔וּת
וְאִם־אֵֽין־בִּ֥י כֹ֖חַ לְהַצִּ֑יל
הֵ֣ן בְּגַעֲרָתִ֞י אַחֲרִ֣יב יָ֗ם
אָשִׂ֤ים נְהָרוֹת֙ מִדְבָּ֔ר
תִּבְאַ֤שׁ דְּגָתָם֙ מֵאֵ֣ין מַ֔יִם
וְתָמֹ֖ת בַּצָּמָֽא׃
³ אַלְבִּ֥ישׁ שָׁמַ֖יִם קַדְר֑וּת
וְשַׂ֖ק אָשִׂ֥ים כְּסוּתָֽם׃ ס

⁴ אֲדֹנָ֣י יְהֹוִ֗ה נָ֤תַן לִי֙ לְשׁ֣וֹן לִמּוּדִ֔ים
לָדַ֛עַת לָע֥וּת אֶת־יָעֵ֖ף דָּבָ֑ר
יָעִ֣יר ׀ בַּבֹּ֣קֶר בַּבֹּ֗קֶר
יָעִ֥יר לִי֙ אֹ֔זֶן
לִשְׁמֹ֖עַ כַּלִּמּוּדִֽים׃
⁵ אֲדֹנָ֤י יְהֹוִה֙ פָּתַ֣ח־לִ֣י אֹ֔זֶן
וְאָנֹכִ֖י לֹ֣א מָרִ֑יתִי
אָח֖וֹר לֹ֥א נְסוּגֹֽתִי׃
⁶ גֵּוִי֙ נָתַ֣תִּי לְמַכִּ֔ים
וּלְחָיַ֖י לְמֹֽרְטִ֑ים

Isaiah 50:1. _Where is the bill of divorce_
The question is rhetorical. No divorce took place;
there was only a temporary dismissal for sins. (By
contrast, the theme of God's divorce of Israel recurs in Hos. 2; Jer. 3:1,6–10; and in Ezek. 16.)
   bill of divorce Hebrew: _seifer k'ritut_. This
terminology follows Deuteronomic law (Deut.
24:1,3). Both texts use the same verb for dismissal
(_shillah_).

4. skilled tongue The prophet affirms that
his tongue has been shaped by God "To know
how to speak," that his ear is aroused to hear divine instruction, and that he has obeyed God's
word to him (v. 5). This is a theme of prophecy
first found with Moses (Exod. 4:11–12), though
stated differently. Later tradition understood this
"skilled tongue" to be the ability to speak favorably in defense of Israel (Yalkut Sh. 2:406).

I did not hide my face
From insult and spittle.
7 But the Lord God will help me—
Therefore I feel no disgrace;
Therefore I have set my face like flint,
And I know I shall not be shamed.
8 My Vindicator is at hand—
Who dares contend with me?
Let us stand up together!
Who would be my opponent?
Let him approach me!
9 Lo, the Lord God will help me—
Who can get a verdict against me?
They shall all wear out like a garment,
The moth shall consume them.

10 Who among you reveres the Lord
And heeds the voice of His servant?—
Though he walk in darkness
And have no light,
Let him trust in the name of the Lord
And rely upon his God.
11 But you are all kindlers of fire,
Girding on firebrands.
Walk by the blaze of your fire,
By the brands that you have lit!
This has come to you from My hand:
You shall lie down in pain.

51 Listen to Me, you who pursue justice,
You who seek the Lord:
Look to the rock you were hewn from,
To the quarry you were dug from.
2 Look back to Abraham your father
And to Sarah who brought you forth.
For he was only one when I called him,

פָּנַי֙ לֹ֣א הִסְתַּ֔רְתִּי
מִכְּלִמּ֖וֹת וָרֹֽק׃
7 וַאדֹנָ֤י יְהוִה֙ יַֽעֲזָר־לִ֔י
עַל־כֵּ֖ן לֹ֣א נִכְלָ֑מְתִּי
עַל־כֵּ֞ן שַׂ֤מְתִּי פָנַי֙ כַּֽחַלָּמִ֔ישׁ
וָאֵדַ֖ע כִּי־לֹ֥א אֵבֽוֹשׁ׃
8 קָרוֹב֙ מַצְדִּיקִ֔י
מִי־יָרִ֥יב אִתִּ֖י
נַ֣עַמְדָה יָּ֑חַד
מִי־בַ֥עַל מִשְׁפָּטִ֖י
יִגַּ֥שׁ אֵלָֽי׃
9 הֵ֣ן אֲדֹנָ֤י יְהוִה֙ יַֽעֲזָר־לִ֔י
מִי־ה֖וּא יַרְשִׁיעֵ֑נִי
הֵ֤ן כֻּלָּם֙ כַּבֶּ֣גֶד יִבְל֔וּ
עָ֖שׁ יֹאכְלֵֽם׃

10 מִ֤י בָכֶם֙ יְרֵ֣א יְהוָ֔ה
שֹׁמֵ֖עַ בְּק֣וֹל עַבְדּ֑וֹ
אֲשֶׁ֣ר ׀ הָלַ֣ךְ חֲשֵׁכִ֗ים
וְאֵ֥ין נֹ֙גַהּ֙ ל֔וֹ
יִבְטַח֙ בְּשֵׁ֣ם יְהוָ֔ה
וְיִשָּׁעֵ֖ן בֵּאלֹהָֽיו׃
11 הֵ֤ן כֻּלְּכֶם֙ קֹ֣דְחֵי אֵ֔שׁ
מְאַזְּרֵ֖י זִיק֑וֹת
לְכ֣וּ ׀ בְּא֣וּר אֶשְׁכֶ֗ם
וּבְזִיקוֹת֙ בִּֽעַרְתֶּ֔ם
מִיָּדִי֙ הָֽיְתָה־זֹּ֣את לָכֶ֔ם
לְמַעֲצֵבָ֖ה תִּשְׁכָּבֽוּן׃ פ

נא שִׁמְע֥וּ אֵלַ֛י רֹ֥דְפֵי צֶ֖דֶק
מְבַקְשֵׁ֣י יְהוָ֑ה
הַבִּ֙יטוּ֙ אֶל־צ֣וּר חֻצַּבְתֶּ֔ם
וְאֶל־מַקֶּ֥בֶת בּ֖וֹר נֻקַּרְתֶּֽם׃
2 הַבִּ֙יטוּ֙ אֶל־אַבְרָהָ֣ם אֲבִיכֶ֔ם
וְאֶל־שָׂרָ֖ה תְּחוֹלֶלְכֶ֑ם
כִּי־אֶחָ֣ד קְרָאתִ֔יו

But I blessed him and made him many.

וַאֲבָרְכֵ֖הוּ וְאַרְבֵּֽהוּ׃ ס

3 Truly the LORD has comforted Zion,
Comforted all her ruins;
He has made her wilderness like Eden,
Her desert like the Garden of the LORD.
Gladness and joy shall abide there,
Thanksgiving and the sound of music.

3 כִּֽי־נִחַ֨ם יְהוָ֜ה צִיּ֗וֹן
נִחַם֙ כָּל־חָרְבֹתֶ֔יהָ
וַיָּ֤שֶׂם מִדְבָּרָהּ֙ כְּעֵ֔דֶן
וְעַרְבָתָ֖הּ כְּגַן־יְהוָ֑ה
שָׂשׂ֤וֹן וְשִׂמְחָה֙ יִמָּ֣צֵא בָ֔הּ
תּוֹדָ֖ה וְק֥וֹל זִמְרָֽה׃ ס

26See, this day I set before you blessing and curse: 27blessing, if you obey the commandments of the LORD your God that I enjoin upon you this day; 28and curse, if you do not obey the commandments of the LORD your God, but turn away from the path that I enjoin upon you this day and follow other gods, whom you have not experienced. 29When the LORD your God brings you into the land that you are about to enter and possess, you shall pronounce the blessing at Mount Gerizim and the curse at Mount Ebal.—30Both are on the other side of the Jor-

26 רְאֵ֗ה אָנֹכִ֛י נֹתֵ֥ן לִפְנֵיכֶ֖ם הַיּ֑וֹם בְּרָכָ֖ה
וּקְלָלָֽה׃ 27 אֶֽת־הַבְּרָכָ֑ה אֲשֶׁ֣ר תִּשְׁמְע֔וּ
אֶל־מִצְוֺת֙ יְהֹוָ֣ה אֱלֹֽהֵיכֶ֔ם אֲשֶׁ֧ר אָנֹכִ֛י
מְצַוֶּ֥ה אֶתְכֶ֖ם הַיּֽוֹם׃ 28 וְהַקְּלָלָ֗ה אִם־לֹ֤א
תִשְׁמְעוּ֙ אֶל־מִצְוֺת֙ יְהֹוָ֣ה אֱלֹֽהֵיכֶ֔ם וְסַרְתֶּ֣ם
מִן־הַדֶּ֔רֶךְ אֲשֶׁ֧ר אָנֹכִ֛י מְצַוֶּ֥ה אֶתְכֶ֖ם הַיּ֑וֹם
לָלֶ֗כֶת אַחֲרֵ֛י אֱלֹהִ֥ים אֲחֵרִ֖ים אֲשֶׁ֥ר לֹֽא־
יְדַעְתֶּֽם׃ ס 29 וְהָיָ֗ה כִּ֤י יְבִֽיאֲךָ֙ יְהֹוָ֣ה
אֱלֹהֶ֔יךָ אֶל־הָאָ֕רֶץ אֲשֶׁר־אַתָּ֥ה בָא־שָׁ֖מָּה
לְרִשְׁתָּ֑הּ וְנָתַתָּ֤ה אֶת־הַבְּרָכָה֙ עַל־הַ֣ר
גְּרִזִ֔ים וְאֶת־הַקְּלָלָ֖ה עַל־הַ֥ר עֵיבָֽל׃
30 הֲלֹא־הֵ֜מָּה בְּעֵ֣בֶר הַיַּרְדֵּ֗ן אַחֲרֵי֙ דֶּ֣רֶךְ

ISRAEL'S CHOICE: BLESSING AND CURSE (11:26–30)

26. The Israelites are given the choice between material well-being and misfortune (see Deut. 28).

28. other gods, whom you have not experienced The Lord's claim on Israel's loyalty is based on the fact that He alone has acted on Israel's behalf (see 5:6). Israel has received nothing from other gods.

29. The covenant relationship with God, vital for Israel's existence in the Promised Land, is to be reaffirmed as soon as the people enter the land, in a public ceremony described in chapter 27. The mountains where the ceremony is to take place face each other south and north of Shechem, respectively. Shechem was located on the eastern approach to modern Nābulus.

30. other side of the Jordan West of the Jordan River, across from the side on which Moses is addressing the people.

This *parashah* emphasizes the concept of a central sanctuary in a place to be designated by God, to serve as the only legitimate site for sacrificial offerings and corporate worship. The Torah seems to fear that if the Israelites take over the holy places where the Canaanites worshiped, some of the residual paganism may cling to those sites and influence Israelite worship.

26. See, this day I set before you blessing and curse We have learned that different people absorb information in different ways—some by seeing, some by hearing, some by touching. Those Israelites who were not persuaded by hearing God's commandments at Sinai, or by hearing Moses' exhortations, are asked to see the difference that following God's ways can make in one's life.

The distinguishing characteristic of human beings, setting us apart from other animals, is our ability to choose the values by which we live. Other animals are driven by instinct. The Torah repeatedly affirms that humans have the potential to control instinct. At our best, we are greater than the angels, who do not have to overcome temptation and apathy. At our worst, we are less than beasts. Their destructiveness is part of their nature; human cruelty is the result of choice.

27. obey Hebrew: *tishm'u*, which most commonly means "hear" (as "listen" in English can also mean "obey"). The reward of an observant life will be the ability to hear God's voice among the conflicting messages competing for our attention in a noisy world (*S'fat Emet*).

28. and curse, if you do not obey Does God curse and afflict the person who leads an immoral life? Or does the individual, through personal behavior, bring curses down on himself or herself and sometimes on others who are closely involved?

dan, beyond the west road that is in the land of the Canaanites who dwell in the Arabah—near Gilgal, by the terebinths of Moreh.
31For you are about to cross the Jordan to en-
ter and possess the land that the LORD your God
is assigning to you. When you have occupied
it and are settled in it, 32take care to observe all
the laws and rules that I have set before you
this day.

מְבֹ֣וא הַשֶּׁ֔מֶשׁ בְּאֶ֙רֶץ֙ הַֽכְּנַעֲנִ֔י הַיֹּשֵׁ֖ב
בָּעֲרָבָ֑ה מ֚וּל הַגִּלְגָּ֔ל אֵ֖צֶל אֵלוֹנֵ֥י מֹרֶֽה׃
31 כִּ֤י אַתֶּם֙ עֹבְרִ֣ים אֶת־הַיַּרְדֵּ֔ן לָבֹא֙
לָרֶ֣שֶׁת אֶת־הָאָ֔רֶץ אֲשֶׁר־יְהוָ֥ה אֱלֹהֵיכֶ֖ם
נֹתֵ֣ן לָכֶ֑ם וִירִשְׁתֶּ֥ם אֹתָ֖הּ וִֽישַׁבְתֶּם־בָּֽהּ׃
32 וּשְׁמַרְתֶּ֣ם לַעֲשׂ֔וֹת אֵ֥ת כָּל־הַחֻקִּ֖ים
וְאֶת־הַמִּשְׁפָּטִ֑ים אֲשֶׁ֛ר אָנֹכִ֥י נֹתֵ֛ן לִפְנֵיכֶ֖ם
הַיּֽוֹם׃

12 These are the laws and rules that you must carefully observe in the land that the LORD, God of your fathers, is giving you to possess, as long as you live on earth.
2You must destroy all the sites at which the nations you are to dispossess worshiped their gods, whether on lofty mountains and on hills

יב אֵ֣לֶּה הַחֻקִּ֣ים וְהַמִּשְׁפָּטִ֗ים אֲשֶׁ֤ר
תִּשְׁמְר֣וּן לַעֲשׂ֔וֹת בָּאָ֗רֶץ אֲשֶׁ֨ר נָתַ֜ן יְהוָ֨ה
אֱלֹהֵ֧י אֲבֹתֶ֛יךָ לְךָ֖ לְרִשְׁתָּ֑הּ כָּל־הַיָּמִ֔ים
אֲשֶׁר־אַתֶּ֥ם חַיִּ֖ים עַל־הָאֲדָמָֽה׃
2 אַבֵּ֣ד תְּ֠אַבְּדוּן אֶֽת־כָּל־הַמְּקֹמ֞וֹת אֲשֶׁ֧ר
עָֽבְדוּ־שָׁ֣ם הַגּוֹיִ֗ם אֲשֶׁ֥ר אַתֶּ֛ם יֹרְשִׁ֥ים אֹתָ֖ם
אֶת־אֱלֹהֵיהֶ֑ם עַל־הֶהָרִ֤ים הָֽרָמִים֙ וְעַל־

Moses' Second Discourse, Part 3: The Laws Given in Moab (11:31–26:15)

The laws given in Moab constitute the core of Deuteronomy. Moses, keenly aware that the people need to be persuaded to follow the laws, spends as much time exhorting the Israelites to obedience as he does presenting the laws.

INTRODUCTION AND HEADING TO THE LAWS (11:31–12:1)

31. For you are about to cross Better: "When you cross." This introduction specifies when the laws are to be put into effect.

THE SANCTUARY AND OTHER RELIGIOUS MATTERS (12:2–16:17)

The first section of the laws focuses on the sanctuary and the rites and festivals celebrated within it. It includes other religious matters as well, such as shunning Canaanite religious practices, punishing instigation to worship other gods, and holiness in mourning and in diet.

THE PLACE OF WORSHIP (12:2–13:1)

DESTROYING CANAANITE SANCTUARIES (vv. 2–3)

Most of the Canaanite places of worship were open-air sanctuaries (with altars, sacred pillars, sa-

---

CHAPTER 12

2. Once again we see the Torah's profound concern that the adolescent nation Israel might be led astray by the rituals of Canaanite paganism. These commands do not apply to mature Judaism's relationship to the monotheistic faiths of our neighbors today.

on lofty mountains Pagans worshiped nature as divine. However, even though nature can be beautiful, it is not moral. Falling rocks and disease germs afflict good and bad people alike. The pagans rarely saw beyond the beautiful—but amoral—natural world to recognize the God of righteousness who created it.

or under any luxuriant tree. 3Tear down their altars, smash their pillars, put their sacred posts to the fire, and cut down the images of their gods, obliterating their name from that site.

4Do not worship the LORD your God in like manner, 5but look only to the site that the LORD your God will choose amidst all your tribes as His habitation, to establish His name there. There you are to go, 6and there you are to bring your burnt offerings and other sacrifices, your tithes and contributions, your votive and

הַגְּבָעוֹת וְתַחַת כָּל־עֵץ רַעֲנָן׃ 3 וְנִתַּצְתֶּם
אֶת־מִזְבְּחֹתָם וְשִׁבַּרְתֶּם אֶת־מַצֵּבֹתָם
וַאֲשֵׁרֵיהֶם תִּשְׂרְפוּן בָּאֵשׁ וּפְסִילֵי
אֱלֹהֵיהֶם תְּגַדֵּעוּן וְאִבַּדְתֶּם אֶת־שְׁמָם
מִן־הַמָּקוֹם הַהוּא׃
4 לֹא־תַעֲשׂוּן כֵּן לַיהוָה אֱלֹהֵיכֶם׃ 5 כִּי
אִם־אֶל־הַמָּקוֹם אֲשֶׁר־יִבְחַר יְהוָה
אֱלֹהֵיכֶם מִכָּל־שִׁבְטֵיכֶם לָשׂוּם אֶת־שְׁמוֹ
שָׁם לְשִׁכְנוֹ תִדְרְשׁוּ וּבָאתָ שָׁמָּה׃
6 וַהֲבֵאתֶם שָׁמָּה עֹלֹתֵיכֶם וְזִבְחֵיכֶם וְאֵת

cred posts, and images) rather than temple buildings. Those in the countryside outnumbered those in the cities.

2. destroy all the sites This does not refer to the geographic locations but to the altars and other objects used in worship at those sites.

3. obliterating their name Wiping out all reminders of their existence.

from that site The Torah does not require the Israelites to engage in a worldwide campaign against idolatry, but only to eliminate it from the land of Israel where it might influence them. This is consistent with the biblical view that for other nations idolatry is not a sin.

THE SINGLE PLACE OF SACRIFICE (vv. 4–7)

The reason for restricting sacrifice to a single place is not explicitly explained. The Torah appears to view multiple sacrificial sites as inherently pagan. This limitation is unique to Deuteronomy and its most far-reaching law. It affected the religious life of every Israelite, involving the sacrificial system, the celebration of festivals, the economic status of the Levites, and even the judicial system. The only known attempts to enforce such a restriction occurred in the 8th and 7th centuries B.C.E., during the reigns of Kings Hezekiah and Josiah (see 2 Kings 18, 22–23).

4. Israelites must not worship the Lord in the ways that Canaanites worshiped their gods: by sacrificing on hills and under trees, using pillars and idols and sacred posts.

5. the site Not named in the Torah. Eventually Jerusalem was chosen, but according to Jer. 7:12 it was preceded by Shiloh.

God will choose Presumably, the divine choice would be communicated by a prophet. The site where Solomon built the Temple was initially chosen by David for an altar on the instructions of the prophet Gad (see 2 Sam. 24:18).

to establish His name there The idea that God's name is "established" at the Temple means that He is accessible there in worship, because it is the focus of His attention. By speaking of God's name as dwelling in the chosen place, Deuteronomy seeks to correct the impression that God dwells there literally. Only His name dwells there, whereas God is in heaven. The doctrine of God's name dwelling in the Temple is central to Deuteronomy.

6. God, by choosing a single sanctuary, limits to that locale all sacrificial worship. The regular pilgrimage festivals were probably the most convenient occasions for these offerings, but farmers presumably made private pilgrimages at other times as well.

burnt offerings See Lev. 1.

other sacrifices The Hebrew is based on the term *zevaḥ*, a sacrifice in which most of the meat is eaten by the one who offers it (see v. 27).

tithes Literally, a tenth; gifts or payments amounting to 10 percent of the value of the yield from agricultural products and cattle. They were originally used to support temples and their personnel, but their function changed when the local sanctuaries were abolished (see 14:22–29).

---

4. Do not worship the LORD . . . in like manner Literally, "you shall not act thus toward the LORD." Rashi cites a tradition that "thus" refers to words in the previous verse—"obliterate (the) names" of pagan gods. He views this as the source of the custom not to discard a book or paper that bears God's name. This is why such documents are not discarded but buried or stored in a *g'nizah* (repository).

freewill offerings, and the firstlings of your herds and flocks. [7]Together with your households, you shall feast there before the LORD your God, happy in all the undertakings in which the LORD your God has blessed you.

[8]You shall not act at all as we now act here, every man as he pleases, [9]because you have not yet come to the allotted haven that the LORD your God is giving you. [10]When you cross the Jordan and settle in the land that the LORD your God is allotting to you, and He grants you safety from all your enemies around you and you live in security, [11]then you must bring everything that I command you to the site where the LORD your God will choose to establish His name: your burnt offerings and other sacrifices, your tithes and contributions, and all the choice vo-

מַעְשְׂרֹתֵיכֶ֗ם וְאֵ֛ת תְּרוּמַ֥ת יֶדְכֶ֖ם וְנִדְרֵיכֶ֑ם
וְנִ֨דְבֹתֵיכֶ֔ם וּבְכֹרֹ֥ת בְּקַרְכֶ֖ם וְצֹאנְכֶֽם:
[7] וַאֲכַלְתֶּם־שָׁ֗ם לִפְנֵי֙ יְהוָ֣ה אֱלֹהֵיכֶ֔ם
וּשְׂמַחְתֶּ֗ם בְּכֹל֙ מִשְׁלַ֣ח יֶדְכֶ֔ם אַתֶּ֖ם
וּבָתֵּיכֶ֑ם אֲשֶׁ֥ר בֵּרַכְךָ֖ יְהוָ֥ה אֱלֹהֶֽיךָ:
[8] לֹ֣א תַעֲשׂ֔וּן כְּכֹ֠ל אֲשֶׁ֨ר אֲנַ֧חְנוּ עֹשִׂ֛ים פֹּ֖ה
הַיּ֑וֹם אִ֖ישׁ כָּל־הַיָּשָׁ֥ר בְּעֵינָֽיו: [9] כִּ֥י לֹֽא־
בָאתֶ֖ם עַד־עָ֑תָּה אֶל־הַמְּנוּחָ֖ה וְאֶל־
הַנַּחֲלָ֕ה אֲשֶׁר־יְהוָ֥ה אֱלֹהֶ֖יךָ נֹתֵ֥ן לָֽךְ:
[10] וַעֲבַרְתֶּם֮ אֶת־הַיַּרְדֵּן֒ וִֽישַׁבְתֶּ֣ם בָּאָ֔רֶץ
אֲשֶׁר־יְהוָ֥ה אֱלֹהֵיכֶ֖ם מַנְחִ֣יל אֶתְכֶ֑ם
וְהֵנִ֨יחַ לָכֶ֧ם מִכָּל־אֹיְבֵיכֶ֛ם מִסָּבִ֖יב
שני וִֽישַׁבְתֶּם־בֶּֽטַח: [11] וְהָיָ֣ה הַמָּק֗וֹם אֲשֶׁר־
יִבְחַ֞ר יְהוָ֧ה אֱלֹהֵיכֶ֛ם בּ֖וֹ לְשַׁכֵּ֤ן שְׁמוֹ֙
שָׁ֔ם שָׁ֣מָּה תָבִ֔יאוּ אֵ֛ת כָּל־אֲשֶׁ֥ר אָנֹכִ֖י
מְצַוֶּ֣ה אֶתְכֶ֑ם עוֹלֹתֵיכֶ֣ם וְזִבְחֵיכֶ֗ם
מַעְשְׂרֹֽתֵיכֶם֙ וּתְרֻמַ֣ת יֶדְכֶ֔ם וְכֹל֙ מִבְחַ֣ר

---

contributions   Literally, "the contribution of your hands" (*t'rumat yedkhem*). The word *t'rumah* refers to something separated (literally, "lifted") from a larger amount and dedicated either to the sanctuary or to the priest. Here, it most likely refers to first fruits, although the term also refers to tithes, the priest's share of a sacrificial animal, and the portion of war spoils assigned to the sanctuary.

votive   A gift promised to God on condition that He grant a benefaction, such as the birth of a son or the safe return from a journey or a battle.

freewill   An offering that the worshiper— usually with no prior obligation or commitment—promised to give as an expression of devotion or gratitude.

firstlings   Firstborn male oxen, sheep, and goats, each of which had to be offered to God as a sacrifice (see 15:19–23).

7. together with your households   Members of the household are listed in verses 12 and 18. It was common for wives to attend, except in special circumstances, as when they were nursing. This is indicated by the story of Hannah and Peninnah in 1 Samuel 1.

feast   Eating the offerings of verse 6 (see vv. 17–18). This is a generalization, because some offerings (e.g., burnt offerings) were not eaten.

happy   Literally, "you shall celebrate," with a

sacrificial meal. Although each type of offering has a specific purpose, Deuteronomy emphasizes the overall value of sacrifices in providing occasions for celebrating God's bounty. They serve to inculcate love and reverence for God (see esp. 14:23). Deuteronomy stresses the effect of offerings on people rather than on God.

WHEN CENTRALIZATION OF SACRIFICE IS TO TAKE EFFECT   (vv. 8–12)

This section explains why sacrifice is not yet limited to a single site and indicates when the limitation is to be put into effect.

8. every man as he pleases   Literally, "every man [doing] what is right in his own sight." This implies that at the time of Moses' address, Israelites were permitted to offer sacrifices wherever they wished. But Lev. 17:1–9 states that a restriction of sacrifice to a single place—the Tent of Meeting—had been commanded earlier, in the wilderness. Modern scholars assume that Deuteronomy was not aware of Lev. 17, which they assign to a different source.

9.   The present situation is permitted because the Israelites are not yet settled in the land. Once there, they must possess it securely so that pilgrims may travel safely to the chosen place.

11. choice votive offerings   Your votive offerings are to be of the choicest products.

נִדְרֵיכֶ֔ם אֲשֶׁ֥ר תִּדְּר֖וּ לַיהוָֽה׃ 12 וּשְׂמַחְתֶּ֗ם
לִפְנֵי֮ יְהוָ֣ה אֱלֹהֵיכֶם֒ אַתֶּ֗ם וּבְנֵיכֶם֙
וּבְנֹ֣תֵיכֶ֔ם וְעַבְדֵיכֶ֖ם וְאַמְהֹתֵיכֶ֑ם וְהַלֵּוִי֙
אֲשֶׁ֣ר בְּשַֽׁעֲרֵיכֶ֔ם כִּ֣י אֵ֥ין ל֛וֹ חֵ֥לֶק וְנַחֲלָ֖ה
אִתְּכֶֽם׃
13 הִשָּׁ֣מֶר לְךָ֔ פֶּֽן־תַּעֲלֶ֖ה עֹלֹתֶ֑יךָ בְּכָל־
מָק֖וֹם אֲשֶׁ֥ר תִּרְאֶֽה׃ 14 כִּ֣י אִם־בַּמָּק֞וֹם
אֲשֶׁר־יִבְחַ֤ר יְהוָה֙ בְּאַחַ֣ד שְׁבָטֶ֔יךָ שָׁ֖ם
תַּעֲלֶ֣ה עֹלֹתֶ֑יךָ וְשָׁ֣ם תַּעֲשֶׂ֔ה כֹּ֛ל אֲשֶׁ֥ר אָנֹכִ֖י
מְצַוֶּֽךָּ׃ 15 רַק֩ בְּכָל־אַוַּ֨ת נַפְשְׁךָ֜ תִּזְבַּ֣ח ׀
וְאָכַלְתָּ֣ בָשָׂ֗ר כְּבִרְכַּ֨ת יְהוָ֧ה אֱלֹהֶ֛יךָ אֲשֶׁ֥ר
נָֽתַן־לְךָ֖ בְּכָל־שְׁעָרֶ֑יךָ הַטָּמֵ֤א וְהַטָּהוֹר֙
יֹאכְלֶ֔נּוּ כַּצְּבִ֖י וְכָאַיָּֽל׃ 16 רַ֥ק הַדָּ֖ם לֹ֣א
תֹאכֵ֑לוּ עַל־הָאָ֥רֶץ תִּשְׁפְּכֶ֖נּוּ כַּמָּֽיִם׃
17 לֹא־תוּכַ֞ל לֶאֱכֹ֣ל בִּשְׁעָרֶ֗יךָ מַעְשַׂ֤ר דְּגָֽנְךָ֙

tive offerings that you vow to the LORD. 12And
you shall rejoice before the LORD your God with your sons and daughters and with your male and female slaves, along with the Levite in your settlements, for he has no territorial allotment among you.

13Take care not to sacrifice your burnt offerings in any place you like,
14but only in the place that the LORD will choose in one of your tribal territories. There you shall sacrifice your burnt offerings and there you shall observe all that I enjoin upon you.
15But whenever you desire, you may slaughter and eat meat in any of your settlements, according to the blessing that the LORD your God has granted you. The impure and the pure alike may partake of it, as of the gazelle and the deer.
16But you must not partake of the blood; you shall pour it out on the ground like water.

17You may not partake in your settlements of the tithes of your new grain or wine or oil, or

12. slaves The requirement to involve slaves in religious celebrations, like the requirement that slaves rest on *Shabbat* (5:14), is part of the Torah's unique concern for their welfare.

along with the Levite Once sacrifice is restricted to a single sanctuary, the Levites living in settlements around the country will lose the income they earned from officiating there. They had no tribal lands from which to earn a living, and the single chosen sanctuary could not possibly support all of them. Hence Deuteronomy urges solicitude for them, and establishes a special tithe for them, along with the poor, every three years (14:28–29). Here, their participation in sacrificial meals somewhat makes up for their former shares of sacrifices and donations.

CENTRALIZED SACRIFICE AND NONSACRIFICIAL SLAUGHTER (vv. 13–16)

13. burnt offerings Here, refers to all types of offerings.

15. slaughter and eat meat This signals a major change in religious and dietary practice. Previously, only game animals were permitted to be slaughtered outside of the framework of sacrificial offerings. Domestic cattle (oxen, sheep, and goats) could be slaughtered only on altars, as sacrifices, even if the offerer's purpose was solely to use them for food. Only after the blood was dashed on the altar and certain of the innards burned could the remainder be eaten. This rule was practical as long as it was legitimate to have sanctuaries throughout the land. But the requirement would become nearly impossible to fulfill once a single sanctuary was chosen, because those who lived far from it would be able to eat meat only on the infrequent occasions when they visited there. To avoid this hardship, nonsacrificial slaughter of domestic cattle is to be permitted, and people may eat meat whenever they choose.

according to the blessing . . . granted you That is, as much as you can afford.

The impure and the pure As long as domestic cattle had to be slaughtered sacrificially, people who were ritually impure could eat meat only from nonsacrificial animals, such as gazelle and deer. Once the nonsacrificial slaughter of domestic cattle is permitted, they will be treated like game animals, and the ritually impure may eat their meat as well.

16. you must not partake of the blood The prohibition against eating blood (see v. 23) will remain in effect. When domestic animals are slaughtered only for food, their blood is to be poured on the ground, unlike the blood of sacrifices (v. 27).

of the firstlings of your herds and flocks, or of
any of the votive offerings that you vow, or of
your freewill offerings, or of your contributions. 18These you must consume before the
LORD your God in the place that the LORD your
God will choose—you and your sons and your
daughters, your male and female slaves, and the
Levite in your settlements—happy before the
LORD your God in all your undertakings. 19Be
sure not to neglect the Levite as long as you live
in your land.

20When the LORD enlarges your territory, as
He has promised you, and you say, "I shall eat
some meat," for you have the urge to eat meat,
you may eat meat whenever you wish. 21If the
place where the LORD has chosen to establish
His name is too far from you, you may slaughter
any of the cattle or sheep that the LORD gives
you, as I have instructed you; and you may eat

וְתִירֹשְׁךָ וְיִצְהָרֶךָ וּבְכֹרֹת בְּקָרְךָ וְצֹאנֶךָ
וְכָל־נְדָרֶיךָ אֲשֶׁר תִּדֹּר וְנִדְבֹתֶיךָ וּתְרוּמַת
יָדֶךָ׃ 18 כִּי אִם־לִפְנֵי יְהוָה אֱלֹהֶיךָ תֹּאכְלֶנּוּ
בַּמָּקוֹם אֲשֶׁר יִבְחַר יְהוָה אֱלֹהֶיךָ בּוֹ אַתָּה
וּבִנְךָ וּבִתֶּךָ וְעַבְדְּךָ וַאֲמָתֶךָ וְהַלֵּוִי אֲשֶׁר
בִּשְׁעָרֶיךָ וְשָׂמַחְתָּ לִפְנֵי יְהוָה אֱלֹהֶיךָ בְּכֹל
מִשְׁלַח יָדֶךָ׃ 19 הִשָּׁמֶר לְךָ פֶּן־תַּעֲזֹב אֶת־
הַלֵּוִי כָּל־יָמֶיךָ עַל־אַדְמָתֶךָ׃ ס
20 כִּי־יַרְחִיב יְהוָה אֱלֹהֶיךָ אֶת־גְּבוּלְךָ
כַּאֲשֶׁר דִּבֶּר־לָךְ וְאָמַרְתָּ אֹכְלָה בָשָׂר כִּי־
תְאַוֶּה נַפְשְׁךָ לֶאֱכֹל בָּשָׂר בְּכָל־אַוַּת נַפְשְׁךָ
תֹּאכַל בָּשָׂר׃ 21 כִּי־יִרְחַק מִמְּךָ הַמָּקוֹם
אֲשֶׁר יִבְחַר יְהוָה אֱלֹהֶיךָ לָשׂוּם שְׁמוֹ שָׁם
וְזָבַחְתָּ מִבְּקָרְךָ וּמִצֹּאנְךָ אֲשֶׁר נָתַן יְהוָה
לְךָ כַּאֲשֶׁר צִוִּיתֶךָ* וְאָכַלְתָּ בִּשְׁעָרֶיךָ בְּכֹל

v. 21. חסר י׳

SACRIFICIAL FOOD (vv. 17–19)

17. Both the act of sacrifice and the eating of the sacrifice are restricted to the chosen place. The new freedom to eat nonsacrificial meat at home will not mean that sacrificial food may be taken home and eaten there after having undergone the sacrificial procedure in the chosen place. The entire household must travel to the chosen place and eat the sacrificial food there, "before the LORD," to experience the religious influence of the place (see 14:23).

NONSACRIFICIAL SLAUGHTER (vv. 20–25)

20. enlarges your territory This act will give you the entire Promised Land (see 19:8; Exod. 34:24). Full possession of the land, however, will come gradually (7:22). As long as some of it remains in the hands of the Canaanites, Israelites will lack the security that is a prerequisite for centralization (see v. 10).

as He has promised you In Exod. 34:24.

21. too far from you The text does not define what "too far" means and may intend to leave this to the discretion of each individual.

slaughter Hebrew: *zavaḥ*. The verb refers to sacrificial slaughter and indicates that nonsacrificial slaughter should follow the same procedure—namely, slitting the animal's throat. This method facilitates maximal drainage of blood, in keeping with verses 16 and 23–25.

19. Be sure not to neglect the Levite "Among a population engaged in farming and raising cattle, such 'unproductive' members of society could easily come to be neglected and resented. The people might fail to recognize the vital role of the Levites in their spiritual and moral welfare" (Hirsch).

20. Kook sees this passage as God's reluctant compromise with the biblical ideal of vegetarianism (see Gen. 1:29; Isa. 11:6–7). In light of the moral decline of the human race before the Flood, God finds it necessary to emphasize that there is a difference between human beings and animals. We are permitted to slaughter animals under restricted conditions, while the shedding of human blood is strenuously forbidden. We are commanded to cover the blood of the slaughtered animal (Lev. 17:13) to inculcate in us a sense of ambivalence for having taken an animal life to satisfy our appetites.

HALAKHAH L'MA·ASEH

12:21. as I have instructed you From these words, the Sages determined (BT Ḥul. 28a) that the laws of kosher slaughter (*sh'ḥitah*) of animals for food are rooted in the Torah.

to your heart's content in your settlements.
22 Eat it, however, as the gazelle and the deer are
eaten: the impure may eat it together with the
pure. 23 But make sure that you do not partake
of the blood; for the blood is the life, and you
must not consume the life with the flesh. 24 You
must not partake of it; you must pour it out on
the ground like water: 25 you must not partake
of it, in order that it may go well with you and
with your descendants to come, for you will be
doing what is right in the sight of the LORD.

26 But such sacred and votive donations as you
may have shall be taken by you to the site that
the LORD will choose. 27 You shall offer your
burnt offerings, both the flesh and the blood,
on the altar of the LORD your God; and of your
other sacrifices, the blood shall be poured out
on the altar of the LORD your God, and you shall
eat the flesh.

28 Be careful to heed all these commandments that I enjoin upon you; thus it will go well with you and with your descendants after you forever, for you will be doing what is good and right in the sight of the LORD your God.

אַוַּת נַפְשֶׁךָ׃ 22 אַךְ כַּאֲשֶׁר יֵאָכֵל אֶת־הַצְּבִי
וְאֶת־הָאַיָּל כֵּן תֹּאכְלֶנּוּ הַטָּמֵא וְהַטָּהוֹר
יַחְדָּו יֹאכְלֶנּוּ׃ 23 רַק חֲזַק לְבִלְתִּי אֲכֹל
הַדָּם כִּי הַדָּם הוּא הַנָּפֶשׁ וְלֹא־תֹאכַל
הַנֶּפֶשׁ עִם־הַבָּשָׂר׃ 24 לֹא תֹּאכְלֶנּוּ עַל־
הָאָרֶץ תִּשְׁפְּכֶנּוּ כַּמָּיִם׃ 25 לֹא תֹּאכְלֶנּוּ
לְמַעַן יִיטַב לְךָ וּלְבָנֶיךָ אַחֲרֶיךָ כִּי־תַעֲשֶׂה
הַיָּשָׁר בְּעֵינֵי יְהוָה׃

26 רַק קָדָשֶׁיךָ אֲשֶׁר־יִהְיוּ לְךָ וּנְדָרֶיךָ תִּשָּׂא
וּבָאתָ אֶל־הַמָּקוֹם אֲשֶׁר־יִבְחַר יְהוָה׃
27 וְעָשִׂיתָ עֹלֹתֶיךָ הַבָּשָׂר וְהַדָּם עַל־מִזְבַּח
יְהוָה אֱלֹהֶיךָ וְדַם־זְבָחֶיךָ יִשָּׁפֵךְ עַל־מִזְבַּח
יְהוָה אֱלֹהֶיךָ וְהַבָּשָׂר תֹּאכֵל׃

28 שְׁמֹר וְשָׁמַעְתָּ אֵת כָּל־הַדְּבָרִים הָאֵלֶּה
אֲשֶׁר אָנֹכִי מְצַוֶּךָּ לְמַעַן יִיטַב לְךָ וּלְבָנֶיךָ
אַחֲרֶיךָ עַד־עוֹלָם כִּי תַעֲשֶׂה הַטּוֹב וְהַיָּשָׁר
שלישי בְּעֵינֵי יְהוָה אֱלֹהֶיךָ׃ ס

22. The ritually impure may eat meat from nonsacrificial slaughter; they may even eat from the same bowl as those who are ritually pure. Because the meat is not sacrificial, defilement by contact with impure persons does not disqualify it, and there is no need to avoid sharing meat with them.

23. make sure This exhortation and the reiteration of the blood prohibition in verses 24–25 indicate a concern that people might not be careful to avoid the blood, either because they want to consume it or because of the effort involved in removing it from the meat.

partake . . . consume Literally, in both cases, "eat." The use of this verb instead of "drink" implies that the text is not dealing with the likelihood that people might drink blood but that they might consume it, in the form of blood pudding or gravy, or simply while eating meat because of laxity in draining the blood.

the blood is the life Blood is the life force in living creatures (see Gen. 9:4; Lev. 17:11).

DETAILS ABOUT SACRIFICIAL SLAUGHTER
(vv. 26–28)

26. sacred and votive donations Refers to anything sacrificial in character. Votive offerings are singled out because, since they are voluntary, the worshiper might be led to believe that there is greater discretion regarding where they may be presented.

27. The flesh of the burnt offering is consumed entirely by fire. The flesh of the other sacrifices is eaten by the one who offered the sacrifice and by the priests (18:3). In both cases, the blood is poured on the altar.

HALAKHAH L'MA·ASEH

12:23–24. do not partake of the blood These verses restate to the Israelites what God commanded Noah in Gen. 9:4, that meat may be eaten only if its blood is first drained. Cf. Comment to Lev. 11:3 and the essay titled "Dietary Laws" for a summary of the other requirements for kosher meat.

29When the LORD your God has cut down before you the nations that you are about to enter
and dispossess, and you have dispossessed them
and settled in their land, 30beware of being lured
into their ways after they have been wiped out
before you! Do not inquire about their gods,
saying, "How did those nations worship their
gods? I too will follow those practices." 31You
shall not act thus toward the LORD your God,
for they perform for their gods every abhorrent
act that the LORD detests; they even offer up their
13 sons and daughters in fire to their gods.
1Be careful to observe only that which
I enjoin upon you: neither add to it nor take
away from it.

2If there appears among you a prophet or a
dream-diviner and he gives you a sign or a por-

שלישי 29 כִּֽי־יַכְרִית יְהֹוָה אֱלֹהֶיךָ אֶת־הַגּוֹיִם
אֲשֶׁר אַתָּה בָא־שָׁמָּה לָרֶשֶׁת אוֹתָם
מִפָּנֶיךָ וְיָרַשְׁתָּ אֹתָם וְיָשַׁבְתָּ בְּאַרְצָם׃
30 הִשָּׁמֶר לְךָ פֶּן־תִּנָּקֵשׁ אַחֲרֵיהֶם אַחֲרֵי
הִשָּׁמְדָם מִפָּנֶיךָ וּפֶן־תִּדְרֹשׁ לֵאלֹהֵיהֶם
לֵאמֹר אֵיכָה יַעַבְדוּ הַגּוֹיִם הָאֵלֶּה אֶת־
אֱלֹהֵיהֶם וְאֶעֱשֶׂה־כֵּן גַּם־אָנִי׃ 31 לֹא־
תַעֲשֶׂה כֵן לַיהֹוָה אֱלֹהֶיךָ כִּי כָל־תּוֹעֲבַת
יְהֹוָה אֲשֶׁר שָׂנֵא עָשׂוּ לֵאלֹהֵיהֶם כִּי גַם
אֶת־בְּנֵיהֶם וְאֶת־בְּנֹתֵיהֶם יִשְׂרְפוּ בָאֵשׁ
יג לֵאלֹהֵיהֶם׃ 1 אֵת כָּל־הַדָּבָר אֲשֶׁר
אָנֹכִי מְצַוֶּה אֶתְכֶם אֹתוֹ תִשְׁמְרוּ
לַעֲשׂוֹת לֹא־תֹסֵף עָלָיו וְלֹא תִגְרַע
מִמֶּנּוּ׃ פ
2 כִּֽי־יָקוּם בְּקִרְבְּךָ נָבִיא אוֹ חֹלֵם חֲלוֹם
וְנָתַן אֵלֶיךָ אוֹת אוֹ מוֹפֵת׃ 3 וּבָא הָאוֹת

SHUNNING CANAANITE RELIGIOUS PRACTICES (12:29–13:1)

31. None of the Canaanite religious practices may be adopted, because many were abominable.

they even offer up their sons and daughters Moses takes it for granted that the people know child sacrifice is wrong. He cites it as an extreme, shocking example of Canaanite abominations.

13:1. The Hebrew text does not begin a new passage here. This verse complements the first part of 12:31, indicating that Israelites may worship God only in the ways He commands, no less and no more. They may not abolish His commandments or add to them. Adopting any of the Canaanites' abominable practices would lead to both. See Comment to Deut. 4:2.

INSTIGATION TO WORSHIP OTHER GODS (vv. 2–19)

God is Israel's king; worshiping other gods is high treason. There are parallels to this law in Near Eastern treaties and similar texts. Ancient laws requiring that agitation against the sovereign be reported and punished correspond closely to this chapter.

INSTIGATION BY A PROPHET OR A DREAMER (vv. 2–6)

The law puts a limit on prophecy and miracles by stipulating that the prohibition against worshiping gods is an eternally binding principle. Even prophecies and seemingly miraculous proofs to the contrary are to be disregarded.

2. Prophecy and dreams are two of the regular means by which God communicates with people in the Bible.

prophet Hebrew: *navi,* which probably means "proclaimer." Some interpret it as "spokesperson."

dream-diviner A person—either a prophet or a layperson—who claims to have received a message from God in a dream.

gives you a sign or a portent As Moses did in Exodus, to demonstrate that his message came from God. The signs refer to marvels that could

---

30. beware of being lured into their ways The Torah would sharpen the distinction between intellectual study of other faiths and the temptation to incorporate elements of those faiths into our own practice. Every religion has its own "grammar," its coherent way of expressing its values. We do violence to that coherence when we mix practices of one faith system with those of another.

CHAPTER 13

1. See Comment to 4:2.

tent, 3saying, "Let us follow and worship another god"—whom you have not experienced
—even if the sign or portent that he named to
you comes true, 4do not heed the words of that
prophet or that dream-diviner. For the LORD
your God is testing you to see whether you really
love the LORD your God with all your heart and
soul. 5Follow none but the LORD your God, and
revere none but Him; observe His commandments alone, and heed only His orders; worship
none but Him, and hold fast to Him. 6As for
that prophet or dream-diviner, he shall be put
to death; for he urged disloyalty to the LORD
your God—who freed you from the land of
Egypt and who redeemed you from the house
of bondage—to make you stray from the path
that the LORD your God commanded you to follow. Thus you will sweep out evil from your
midst.

וְהַמּוֹפֵ֔ת אֲשֶׁר־דִּבֶּ֥ר אֵלֶ֖יךָ לֵאמֹ֑ר נֵֽלְכָ֞ה
אַחֲרֵ֨י אֱלֹהִ֧ים אֲחֵרִ֛ים אֲשֶׁ֥ר לֹא־יְדַעְתָּ֖ם
וְנָֽעָבְדֵֽם׃ 4 לֹ֣א תִשְׁמַ֗ע אֶל־דִּבְרֵי֙ הַנָּבִ֣יא
הַה֔וּא א֛וֹ אֶל־חוֹלֵ֥ם הַחֲל֖וֹם הַה֑וּא כִּ֣י
מְנַסֶּ֞ה יְהוָ֤ה אֱלֹֽהֵיכֶם֙ אֶתְכֶ֔ם לָדַ֗עַת
הֲיִשְׁכֶ֣ם אֹֽהֲבִים֙ אֶת־יְהוָ֣ה אֱלֹֽהֵיכֶ֔ם בְּכָל־
לְבַבְכֶ֖ם וּבְכָל־נַפְשְׁכֶֽם׃ 5 אַחֲרֵ֨י יְהוָ֧ה
אֱלֹהֵיכֶ֛ם תֵּלֵ֖כוּ וְאֹת֣וֹ תִירָ֑אוּ וְאֶת־מִצְוֺתָ֤יו
תִּשְׁמֹ֙רוּ֙ וּבְקֹל֣וֹ תִשְׁמָ֔עוּ וְאֹת֥וֹ תַעֲבֹ֖דוּ וּב֥וֹ
תִדְבָּקֽוּן׃ 6 וְהַנָּבִ֣יא הַה֡וּא א֣וֹ חֹלֵם֩
הַחֲל֨וֹם הַה֜וּא יוּמָ֗ת כִּ֣י דִבֶּר־סָ֠רָה עַל־
יְהוָ֨ה אֱלֹהֵיכֶ֜ם הַמּוֹצִ֥יא אֶתְכֶ֣ם ׀ מֵאֶ֣רֶץ
מִצְרַ֗יִם וְהַפֹּֽדְךָ֙ מִבֵּ֣ית עֲבָדִ֔ים לְהַדִּֽיחֲךָ֙
מִן־הַדֶּ֔רֶךְ אֲשֶׁ֥ר צִוְּךָ֛ יְהוָ֥ה אֱלֹהֶ֖יךָ לָלֶ֣כֶת
בָּ֑הּ וּבִֽעַרְתָּ֥ הָרָ֖ע מִקִּרְבֶּֽךָ׃

have been brought about only by supernatural power (Exod. 4:1–9).

3. What follows is Moses' pejorative paraphrase of the proposal offered by the dream-diviner or prophet. An instigator would not use vague and disparaging phrases like "another god, whom you have not experienced" but would identify a specific god.

Let us follow Literally, "Let us walk after." This idiom is frequently used to express loyalty to a king. By paraphrasing the prophet's invitation as calling for "walking after" a god, Moses indicates that it is tantamount to proposing treason against the Lord.

4. testing you By allowing the sign to come true. Moses does not explain why God would test Israel, but counters the false prophet's argument that the sign proves his prophecy true.

with all your heart and soul That is, whether your loyalty to Him is undivided.

5. none but the LORD In contrast to what the false prophet urges.

6. urged disloyalty The law refers to a prophet of the Lord who advocates the worship of gods and claims that such worship is compatible with loyalty to Israel's God. Such a prophet is guilty of false prophecy, a capital crime (see 18:20).

who freed you from the land of Egypt The Lord, unlike false gods "whom you have not experienced" (v. 3), has proven Himself to Israel. This underscores the gravity of the prophet's sin, because the Lord's redemption of the Israelites from bondage established their obligation to worship Him alone (see 5:6–7).

to make you stray This is a second reason for executing the instigator. Urging apostasy—the religious equivalent of sedition—is also a capital crime (see v. 11).

Thus you will sweep out evil from your midst This expression, which appears several times at the close of instructions for punishing a criminal, reflects the view that the punishment removes a tangible evil from the community.

INSTIGATION BY A CLOSE RELATIVE OR FRIEND (vv. 7–12)

A secret proposal to worship a god is difficult to resist when it comes from a relative or a dear friend. Because it originates with someone very close, one may be inclined to take no action against the instigator.

---

5. hold fast to Him God is envisioned as a raging fire—how can one hold fast to fire? We cling to God by doing what God does, so to speak; this includes visiting the sick, sustaining the poor, freeing the enslaved, and comforting the grieving (BT Sot. 14a).

7If your brother, your own mother's son, or your son or daughter, or the wife of your bosom, or your closest friend entices you in secret, saying, "Come let us worship other gods"—whom neither you nor your fathers have experienced —8from among the gods of the peoples around you, either near to you or distant, anywhere from one end of the earth to the other: 9do not assent or give heed to him. Show him no pity or compassion, and do not shield him; 10but take his life. Let your hand be the first against him to put him to death, and the hand of the rest of the people thereafter. 11Stone him to death, for he sought to make you stray from the LORD your God, who brought you out of the land of Egypt, out of the house of bondage. 12Thus all Israel will hear and be afraid, and such evil things will not be done again in your midst.

13If you hear it said, of one of the towns that

7 כִּ֣י יְסִֽיתְךָ֡ אָחִ֣יךָ בֶן־אִ֠מֶּךָ אֽוֹ־בִנְךָ֨ אֽוֹ־
בִתְּךָ֜ א֣וֹ ׀ אֵ֣שֶׁת חֵיקֶ֗ךָ א֧וֹ רֵֽעֲךָ֛ אֲשֶׁ֥ר
כְּנַפְשְׁךָ֖ בַּסֵּ֣תֶר לֵאמֹ֑ר נֵֽלְכָ֗ה וְנַֽעַבְדָה֙
אֱלֹהִ֣ים אֲחֵרִ֔ים אֲשֶׁר֙ לֹ֣א יָדַ֔עְתָּ אַתָּ֖ה
וַאֲבֹתֶֽיךָ׃ 8 מֵאֱלֹהֵ֣י הָעַמִּ֗ים אֲשֶׁר֙
סְבִיבֹ֣תֵיכֶ֔ם הַקְּרֹבִ֣ים אֵלֶ֔יךָ א֖וֹ הָרְחֹקִ֣ים
מִמֶּ֑ךָּ מִקְצֵ֥ה הָאָ֖רֶץ וְעַד־קְצֵ֥ה הָאָֽרֶץ׃
9 לֹא־תֹאבֶ֣ה ל֔וֹ וְלֹ֥א תִשְׁמַ֖ע אֵלָ֑יו וְלֹא־
תָח֤וֹס עֵֽינְךָ֙ עָלָ֔יו וְלֹֽא־תַחְמֹ֥ל וְלֹא־תְכַסֶּ֖ה
עָלָֽיו׃ 10 כִּ֤י הָרֹג֙ תַּֽהַרְגֶ֔נּוּ יָדְךָ֛ תִּֽהְיֶה־
בּ֥וֹ בָרִֽאשׁוֹנָ֖ה לַהֲמִית֑וֹ וְיַ֥ד כָּל־הָעָ֖ם
בָּאַחֲרֹנָֽה׃ 11 וּסְקַלְתּ֥וֹ בָאֲבָנִ֖ים וָמֵ֑ת כִּ֣י
בִקֵּ֗שׁ לְהַדִּֽיחֲךָ֙ מֵעַל֙ יְהוָ֣ה אֱלֹהֶ֔יךָ
הַמּוֹצִיאֲךָ֛ מֵאֶ֥רֶץ מִצְרַ֖יִם מִבֵּ֥ית עֲבָדִֽים׃
12 וְכָל־יִשְׂרָאֵ֕ל יִשְׁמְע֖וּ וְיִרָא֑וּן וְלֹא־יוֹסִ֣פוּ
לַעֲשׂ֗וֹת כַּדָּבָ֥ר הָרָ֛ע הַזֶּ֖ה בְּקִרְבֶּֽךָ׃ ס
13 כִּֽי־תִשְׁמַ֞ע בְּאַחַ֣ת עָרֶ֗יךָ אֲשֶׁר֩ יְהוָ֨ה

7. your brother, your own mother's son The most closely related brother, the son of your mother as well as of your father.

the wife of your bosom That is, your wife, who lies in your bosom. One would be reluctant to prosecute an instigator toward whom one feels particularly affectionate.

in secret Given the stigma and punishment that were to befall those who worshiped gods, it was expected that instigators would make their proposals secretly.

9. do not assent or give heed Verse 4 states only "do not give heed" to a prophet or dreamer. The additional verb here reflects the fact that family and friends can exert sustained pressure in the service of their cause, and greater effort is required to resist their importuning.

Show him no pity or compassion You might be tempted to spare him out of love. But the danger to public welfare posed by these instigators requires the stifling of normal feelings.

do not shield him By keeping his proposal secret.

10. take his life This is not accomplished by summary execution, but only after a thorough investigation, as we see from verses 13–19 and 17:2–7. The person approached by the instigator must report the crime and later take part in the execution (see 17:7).

the rest of the people Of his city (see 21:21).

11. Stoning, the most common form of capital punishment in the Bible, normally took place outside the city. The witnesses to the crime cast the first stones, followed by the rest of the people. Punishment by stoning enabled the entire public to participate and thereby express its outrage against the crime and the threat it posed to God's authority and society's welfare.

12. By taking part in the execution, the townspeople will be dissuaded from committing the same crime. News of the execution will have the same effect on the rest of the nation.

REPORTED SUBVERSION OF AN ENTIRE TOWN (vv. 13–19)

The most serious circumstance is one in which the instigation has apparently succeeded, and an entire town has committed the crime.

13. If you hear it said The authorities learn of it by rumor—unlike the first two instances,

---

13. If you hear it said The authorities are required to investigate only if the crime is reported to them by others; they need not search for such cases on their own (*Sifrei*).

אֱלֹהֶ֗יךָ נֹתֵ֨ן לְךָ֛ לָשֶׁ֥בֶת שָׁ֖ם לֵאמֹֽר׃
14 יָֽצְא֞וּ אֲנָשִׁ֤ים בְּנֵֽי־בְלִיַּ֙עַל֙ מִקִּרְבֶּ֔ךָ וַיַּדִּ֛יחוּ
אֶת־יֹשְׁבֵ֥י עִירָ֖ם לֵאמֹ֑ר נֵֽלְכָ֗ה וְנַעַבְדָ֛ה
אֱלֹהִ֥ים אֲחֵרִ֖ים אֲשֶׁ֥ר לֹֽא־יְדַעְתֶּֽם׃
15 וְדָרַשְׁתָּ֧ וְחָקַרְתָּ֛ וְשָׁאַלְתָּ֖ הֵיטֵ֑ב וְהִנֵּ֤ה
אֱמֶת֙ נָכ֣וֹן הַדָּבָ֔ר נֶעֶשְׂתָ֛ה הַתּוֹעֵבָ֥ה הַזֹּ֖את
בְּקִרְבֶּֽךָ׃ 16 הַכֵּ֣ה תַכֶּ֔ה אֶת־יֹשְׁבֵ֥י הָעִ֛יר
ההוא הַהִ֖יא לְפִי־חָ֑רֶב הַחֲרֵ֨ם אֹתָ֧הּ וְאֶת־
כָּל־אֲשֶׁר־בָּ֛הּ וְאֶת־בְּהֶמְתָּ֖הּ לְפִי־חָֽרֶב׃
17 וְאֶת־כָּל־שְׁלָלָ֗הּ תִּקְבֹּץ֮ אֶל־תּ֣וֹךְ רְחֹבָהּ֒
וְשָׂרַפְתָּ֣ בָאֵ֡שׁ אֶת־הָעִ֣יר וְאֶת־כָּל־שְׁלָלָהּ֙
כָּלִ֔יל לַיהוָ֖ה אֱלֹהֶ֑יךָ וְהָיְתָה֙ תֵּ֣ל עוֹלָ֔ם
לֹ֥א תִבָּנֶ֖ה עֽוֹד׃ 18 וְלֹֽא־יִדְבַּ֧ק בְּיָדְךָ֛
מְא֖וּמָה מִן־הַחֵ֑רֶם לְמַ֡עַן יָשׁ֨וּב יְהוָ֜ה
מֵחֲר֣וֹן אַפּ֗וֹ וְנָֽתַן־לְךָ֤ רַחֲמִים֙ וְרִֽחַמְךָ֣

the Lord your God is giving you to dwell in,
14 that some scoundrels from among you have
gone and subverted the inhabitants of their
town, saying, "Come let us worship other
gods"—whom you have not experienced—
15 you shall investigate and inquire and interrogate thoroughly. If it is true, the fact is
established—that abhorrent thing was perpetrated in your midst—16 put the inhabitants of
that town to the sword and put its cattle to the
sword. Doom it and all that is in it to destruction: 17 gather all its spoil into the open square,
and burn the town and all its spoil as a holocaust
to the Lord your God. And it shall remain an
everlasting ruin, never to be rebuilt. 18 Let nothing that has been doomed stick to your hand,
in order that the Lord may turn from His blazing anger and show you compassion, and in His

in which there are witnesses to the instigation. Hence the law stresses the necessity of carefully investigating the rumor.

that the Lord . . . is giving you An act of benevolence that the inhabitants have repaid with treachery.

15. investigate . . . inquire . . . interrogate The use of three verbs here for the investigative process, instead of one verb as elsewhere (17:4, 19:18), and the use of three phrases to confirm the charge, indicate the need for the most careful investigation and absolute certainty in the verdict.

16. Apparently the text deals only with a hypothetical case in which the entire town is guilty. There is no indication of what is to be done with any innocent inhabitants.

to the sword Individual apostates are executed by stoning (17:5), but it would be impossible to stone large numbers of people, as they would resist. The meaning here is that the town is to be conquered militarily.

Doom it . . . to destruction The apostate town is to be subjected to the *ḥeirem* (utter destruction). This *ḥeirem* is more severe than the one to be applied to the Canaanites (see 7:2, 20:17), whose booty, except in the case of Jericho, is permitted. Shunning the booty expresses utter abhorrence at Israelites who apostasize.

17. open square The large open space of the town where gatherings were held and public business was transacted.

as a holocaust Burn it totally, leaving nothing for human use, as if it were a burnt offering.

ruin A tell, the mound formed by the accumulated ruins of a city.

18. His blazing anger God's anger at the town's apostasy is such that His favor toward all of the Israelites is suspended until every trace of the offenders is removed.

increase you as He promised your fathers This is an implicit reminder that the nation's continued growth will be jeopardized unless the apostate city is destroyed.

---

16. put the inhabitants of that town to the sword Why so comprehensive a punishment for an entire town, rather than simply punishing the guilty? In all likelihood, the Torah deemed it inconceivable for a good person to remain in a town totally given over to idolatry. In the absence of a supportive community loyal to God, the lonely faithful individual would either leave in disgust or remain and become corrupted. Later, the Sages deemed it impossible for such a situation actually to occur. They considered it to be a purely hypothetical situation, included here to warn us of the serious consequences of idol worship (BT Sanh. 71a).

compassion increase you as He promised your
fathers on oath—19for you will be heeding the
LORD your God, obeying all His commandments that I enjoin upon you this day, doing
what is right in the sight of the LORD your God.

וְהִרְבֶּ֔ךָ כַּאֲשֶׁ֥ר נִשְׁבַּ֖ע לַאֲבֹתֶֽיךָ׃ 19 כִּ֣י
תִשְׁמַ֗ע בְּקוֹל֙ יְהוָ֣ה אֱלֹהֶ֔יךָ לִשְׁמֹר֙ אֶת־
כָּל־מִצְוֺתָ֔יו אֲשֶׁ֛ר אָנֹכִ֥י מְצַוְּךָ֖ הַיּ֑וֹם
לַעֲשׂוֹת֙ הַיָּשָׁ֔ר בְּעֵינֵ֖י יְהוָ֥ה אֱלֹהֶֽיךָ׃ ס

14 You are children of the LORD your God.
You shall not gash yourselves or shave the front
of your heads because of the dead. 2For you are
a people consecrated to the LORD your God: the
LORD your God chose you from among all other
peoples on earth to be His treasured people.
3You shall not eat anything abhorrent. 4These

רביעי **יד** בָּנִ֣ים אַתֶּ֔ם לַיהוָ֖ה אֱלֹהֵיכֶ֑ם
לֹ֣א תִתְגֹּֽדְד֗וּ וְלֹֽא־תָשִׂ֧ימוּ קָרְחָ֛ה בֵּ֥ין
עֵינֵיכֶ֖ם לָמֵֽת׃ 2 כִּ֣י עַ֤ם קָדוֹשׁ֙ אַתָּ֔ה לַיהוָ֖ה
אֱלֹהֶ֑יךָ וּבְךָ֞ בָּחַ֣ר יְהוָ֗ה לִהְי֥וֹת לוֹ֙
לְעַ֣ם סְגֻלָּ֔ה מִכֹּל֙ הָֽעַמִּ֔ים אֲשֶׁ֖ר עַל־פְּנֵ֥י
הָאֲדָמָֽה׃ ס
3 לֹ֥א תֹאכַ֖ל כָּל־תּוֹעֵבָֽה׃ 4 זֹ֥את הַבְּהֵמָ֖ה

LAWS OF HOLINESS (14:1–21)

Laws of mourning (vv. 1–2) and laws of diet (vv. 3–21) are presented together here because, in the view of Deuteronomy, they share a common theme: the Israelites' obligation to maintain holiness by avoiding pagan practices and everything abhorrent.

HOLINESS IN MOURNING (vv. 1–2)

1. You are children of the LORD your God Hence, you may not disfigure yourselves during mourning. No reason is given for the connection between being a child of God and disfiguring oneself when mourning. Rashi explains: "Because you are children of the LORD, it is appropriate for you to be comely, not gashed and balded."

shave the front of your heads The Hebrew phrase refers to any form of removing hair, cutting and plucking as well as shaving. Gashing the flesh until the blood runs and removing hair are known as mourning rites the world over and were practiced by Israel's neighbors and by some Israelites. Scholars think that these acts were believed to have an effect on the ghost of the dead person, either as offerings of blood and hair to strengthen the ghost in the netherworld or to assuage the ghost's jealousy of the living by showing it how grief-stricken they are. These rites could also be acts of self-punishment expressing feelings of guilt, which are often experienced by survivors after a death.

2. The entire people must maintain a near-priestly level of holiness. The actions mentioned in verse 1 are incompatible with that status.

HOLINESS IN DIET (vv. 3–21)

This section is largely identical with the dietary laws in Lev. 11.

Land Animals (vv. 3–8)

3. Deuteronomy places forbidden foods in the same category of abhorrence as idolatrous and immoral actions that would defile the Israelites' holiness.

CHAPTER 14

1. As children of God, each of us has infinite value, even in the absence of the loved one who has died. True, "God is found in relationships," as Buber taught; and one cannot be a fully realized human being alone. Nonetheless, we diminish the worth of the individual, bearer of the image of a single God, when we become so attached to someone else that we would harm or destroy ourselves when that person is taken from us.

You shall not gash yourselves The Sages, basing their comment on a play on words, used this verse to demand that we not bicker among ourselves as a community, dividing into sects (BT Yev. 13b,14a).

3. Dietary rules are part of Deuteronomy's emphases on manifesting one's humanity by controlling instinct and on the Israelites separating themselves from pagans whose land they would shortly be entering.

are the animals that you may eat: the ox, the
sheep, and the goat; 5 the deer, the gazelle, the
roebuck, the wild goat, the ibex, the antelope,
the mountain sheep, 6and any other animal that
has true hoofs which are cleft in two and brings
up the cud—such you may eat. 7But the following, which do bring up the cud or have true
hoofs which are cleft through, you may not eat:
the camel, the hare, and the daman—for although they bring up the cud, they have no
true hoofs—they are impure for you; 8also
the swine—for although it has true hoofs, it
does not bring up the cud—is impure for you.
You shall not eat of their flesh or touch their
carcasses.

9These you may eat of all that live in water:
you may eat anything that has fins and scales.
10But you may not eat anything that has no fins
and scales: it is impure for you.

11You may eat any pure bird. 12The following

אֲשֶׁר תֹּאכֵלוּ שׁוֹר שֵׂה כְשָׂבִים וְשֵׂה עִזִּים׃
5 אַיָּל וּצְבִי וְיַחְמוּר וְאַקּוֹ וְדִישֹׁן וּתְאוֹ
וָזָמֶר׃ 6 וְכָל־בְּהֵמָה מַפְרֶסֶת פַּרְסָה
וְשֹׁסַעַת שֶׁסַע שְׁתֵּי פְרָסוֹת מַעֲלַת גֵּרָה
בַּבְּהֵמָה אֹתָהּ תֹּאכֵלוּ׃ 7 אַךְ אֶת־זֶה לֹא
תֹאכְלוּ מִמַּעֲלֵי הַגֵּרָה וּמִמַּפְרִיסֵי הַפַּרְסָה
הַשְּׁסוּעָה אֶת־הַגָּמָל וְאֶת־הָאַרְנֶבֶת וְאֶת־
הַשָּׁפָן כִּי־מַעֲלֵה גֵרָה הֵמָּה וּפַרְסָה לֹא
הִפְרִיסוּ טְמֵאִים הֵם לָכֶם׃ 8 וְאֶת־הַחֲזִיר
כִּי־מַפְרִיס פַּרְסָה הוּא וְלֹא גֵרָה טָמֵא
הוּא לָכֶם מִבְּשָׂרָם לֹא תֹאכֵלוּ וּבְנִבְלָתָם
לֹא תִגָּעוּ׃ ס

9 אֶת־זֶה תֹּאכְלוּ מִכֹּל אֲשֶׁר בַּמָּיִם כֹּל
אֲשֶׁר־לוֹ סְנַפִּיר וְקַשְׂקֶשֶׂת תֹּאכֵלוּ׃ 10 וְכֹל
אֲשֶׁר אֵין־לוֹ סְנַפִּיר וְקַשְׂקֶשֶׂת לֹא תֹאכֵלוּ
טָמֵא הוּא לָכֶם׃ ס

11 כָּל־צִפּוֹר טְהֹרָה תֹּאכֵלוּ׃ 12 וְזֶה אֲשֶׁר

5. ibex Or "bison."

7. Four animals are listed, to illustrate the principle that those that have only one of the required characteristics are forbidden.

camel Only the upper part of the camel's hoof is split. The bottom is joined.

the hare and the daman Because these animals chew their food for a long time and sometimes move their jaws from side to side, they look as if they were chewing the cud, although they are not ruminants (who chew the cud).

impure That is, ritually impure.

Water Animals (vv. 9–10)

9. fins and scales As in Leviticus, only a general rule is given for distinguishing between permitted and forbidden aquatic animals.

Winged Animals and Other Restrictions (vv. 11–21)

All the winged animals listed here are birds except for the bat, which is a winged rodent. The permitted and the forbidden winged animals are not

8. The Midrash portrays a reclining pig stretching out its hooves and saying "Look, I'm pure," while concealing the fact that it does not chew the cud; such was the hypocrisy of the Roman Empire, which posed as being dedicated to law and justice while oppressing the peoples it ruled (Lev. R. 13:5).

HALAKHAH L'MA·ASEH

14:6. hoofs . . . cud The flesh only of animals that have split hooves and chew their cud can be kosher. See Comment to Lev. 11:3.

14:9. fins and scales See Comments to Lev. 11:9,12.

14:11ff. any pure bird The Sages, generalizing from this list of kosher fowl, established four criteria for a kosher fowl, including that it not be a bird of prey (M Ḥul. 3:6). Later Jewish law determined that only those birds that traditionally have been accepted as kosher may be eaten. These are the birds (and their eggs) considered permissible: chicken, capon, Cornish hen, turkey, domestic duck and goose, house sparrow, pigeon, squab, palm dove, turtledove, partridge, peacock, and—according to some authorities—guinea fowl, quail, and what is today called pheasant.

you may not eat: the eagle, the vulture, and the black vulture; [13]the kite, the falcon, and the buzzard of any variety; [14]every variety of raven; [15]the ostrich, the nighthawk, the sea gull, and the hawk of any variety; [16]the little owl, the great owl, and the white owl; [17]the pelican, the bustard, and the cormorant; [18]the stork, any variety of heron, the hoopoe, and the bat.

[19]All winged swarming things are impure for you: they may not be eaten. [20]You may eat only pure winged creatures.

[21]You shall not eat anything that has died a natural death; give it to the stranger in your community to eat, or you may sell it to a foreigner. For you are a people consecrated to the LORD your God.

You shall not boil a kid in its mother's milk.

לֹא־תֹאכְלוּ מֵהֶם הַנֶּשֶׁר וְהַפֶּרֶס וְהָעָזְנִיָּה׃
13 וְהָרָאָה וְאֶת־הָאַיָּה וְהַדַּיָּה לְמִינָהּ׃
14 וְאֵת כָּל־עֹרֵב לְמִינוֹ׃ 15 וְאֵת בַּת
הַיַּעֲנָה וְאֶת־הַתַּחְמָס וְאֶת־הַשָּׁחַף וְאֶת־
הַנֵּץ לְמִינֵהוּ׃ 16 אֶת־הַכּוֹס וְאֶת־הַיַּנְשׁוּף
וְהַתִּנְשָׁמֶת׃ 17 וְהַקָּאָת וְאֶת־הָרָחָמָה
וְאֶת־הַשָּׁלָךְ׃ 18 וְהַחֲסִידָה וְהָאֲנָפָה לְמִינָהּ
וְהַדּוּכִיפַת וְהָעֲטַלֵּף׃
19 וְכֹל שֶׁרֶץ הָעוֹף טָמֵא הוּא לָכֶם לֹא
יֵאָכֵלוּ׃ 20 כָּל־עוֹף טָהוֹר תֹּאכֵלוּ׃
21 לֹא תֹאכְלוּ כָל־נְבֵלָה לַגֵּר אֲשֶׁר־
בִּשְׁעָרֶיךָ תִּתְּנֶנָּה וַאֲכָלָהּ אוֹ מָכֹר לְנָכְרִי
כִּי עַם קָדוֹשׁ אַתָּה לַיהוָה אֱלֹהֶיךָ
לֹא־תְבַשֵּׁל גְּדִי בַּחֲלֵב אִמּוֹ׃ פ

[22]You shall set aside every year a tenth part of all the yield of your sowing that is brought

חמישי 22 עַשֵּׂר תְּעַשֵּׂר אֵת כָּל־תְּבוּאַת זַרְעֶךָ

distinguished by easily observable external characteristics. Hence, no general rule is given for distinguishing among them, but only a list identifying those that are impure.

12. Virtually all the forbidden winged creatures are scavengers or birds of prey. They share four characteristics: they lack a crop (the pouched enlargement of the gullet that stores food), they lack an extra toe on the back of the foot, the sac in their gizzards cannot be peeled off, and they tear their prey. Note that the identification of several of the birds is not certain.

eagle Hebrew: *nesher,* which can refer also to a griffon vulture.

19. swarming things Hebrew: *sheretz,* creatures that swarm or crawl—such as insects, rodents, reptiles, and ambulatory marine animals.

20. pure winged creatures Certain leaping locusts (Lev. 11:21–23).

21. died a natural death It was not torn by another creature.

give it to the stranger . . . sell it to a foreigner Deuteronomy, unlike Lev. 17:15, does not mandate that "strangers" (i.e., resident aliens) must avoid impurity, because they are not subject to the requirements of holiness that are incumbent on Israelites. Hence they may eat the flesh of animals that die of natural causes. The distinction between "giving" the meat to resident aliens and "selling" it to foreigners reflects the differing economic status of the two classes. Resident aliens were often poor and objects of charity. Nonresident foreigners normally were in the land for purposes of trade and were able to support themselves.

You shall not boil a kid in its mother's milk This rule is listed with the food prohibitions because meat cooked this way may not be eaten (see Exod. 23:19, 34:26). Meat boiled in sour milk (*leben*) was probably regarded as a delicacy, as it is by Arabs. The prohibition is similar to the rule against slaughtering cattle and their young on the same day and the requirement that newborn cattle remain with their mothers at least one week before they are sacrificed, to prevent acts of insensitivity against animals.

PERIODIC DUTIES (14:22–16:17)

TITHES (vv. 22–29)

The farmer must set aside a tithe of his produce each year. Tithing was a well-known practice in

HALAKHAH L'MA·ASEH

14:21. not boil a kid in its mother's milk See comment on Exod. 23:19.

from the field. 23You shall consume the tithes of your new grain and wine and oil, and the firstlings of your herds and flocks, in the presence of the LORD your God, in the place where He will choose to establish His name, so that you may learn to revere the LORD your God forever. 24Should the distance be too great for you, should you be unable to transport them, because the place where the LORD your God has chosen to establish His name is far from you and because the LORD your God has blessed you, 25you may convert them into money. Wrap up the money and take it with you to the place that the LORD your God has chosen, 26and spend the money on anything you want—cattle, sheep, wine, or other intoxicant, or anything you may desire. And you shall feast there, in the presence

הַיֹּצֵ֥א הַשָּׂדֶ֖ה שָׁנָ֥ה שָׁנָֽה: 23 וְאָכַלְתָּ֞ לִפְנֵ֣י ׀ יְהֹוָ֣ה אֱלֹהֶ֗יךָ בַּמָּק֣וֹם אֲשֶׁר־יִבְחַר֮ לְשַׁכֵּ֣ן שְׁמ֣וֹ שָׁם֒ מַעְשַׂ֤ר דְּגָֽנְךָ֙ תִּירֹֽשְׁךָ֣ וְיִצְהָרֶ֔ךָ וּבְכֹרֹ֥ת בְּקָֽרְךָ֖ וְצֹאנֶ֑ךָ לְמַ֣עַן תִּלְמַ֗ד לְיִרְאָ֛ה אֶת־יְהֹוָ֥ה אֱלֹהֶ֖יךָ כָּל־הַיָּמִֽים: 24 וְכִֽי־יִרְבֶּ֨ה מִמְּךָ֜ הַדֶּ֗רֶךְ כִּ֣י לֹ֣א תוּכַל֮ שְׂאֵתוֹ֒ כִּֽי־יִרְחַ֤ק מִמְּךָ֙ הַמָּק֔וֹם אֲשֶׁ֤ר יִבְחַר֙ יְהֹוָ֣ה אֱלֹהֶ֔יךָ לָשׂ֥וּם שְׁמ֖וֹ שָׁ֑ם כִּ֥י יְבָֽרֶכְךָ֖ יְהֹוָ֥ה אֱלֹהֶֽיךָ: 25 וְנָֽתַתָּ֖ה בַּכָּ֑סֶף וְצַרְתָּ֤ הַכֶּ֙סֶף֙ בְּיָ֣דְךָ֔ וְהָֽלַכְתָּ֙ אֶל־הַמָּק֔וֹם אֲשֶׁ֥ר יִבְחַ֛ר יְהֹוָ֥ה אֱלֹהֶ֖יךָ בּֽוֹ: 26 וְנָֽתַתָּ֣ה הַכֶּ֡סֶף בְּכֹל֩ אֲשֶׁר־תְּאַוֶּ֨ה נַפְשְׁךָ֜ בַּבָּקָ֣ר וּבַצֹּ֗אן וּבַיַּ֙יִן֙ וּבַשֵּׁכָ֔ר וּבְכֹ֛ל אֲשֶׁ֥ר תִּֽשְׁאָֽלְךָ֖ נַפְשֶׁ֑ךָ וְאָכַ֣לְתָּ

---

the ancient world. Because there are inconsistencies among the various tithe laws in the Torah (see Lev. 27:30–33; Num. 18:21–32), modern scholars generally assume that they were not originally parts of a single system but reflect practices in different times or places.

The Annual Tithe   (vv. 22–27)

In four years out of seven, the tithe is to be consumed by the farmer and his household during the course of worship at the chosen sanctuary.

22. This verse introduces the first tithe, which is given in years 1, 2, 4, and 5 of the cycle. (Verses 28–29 deal with years 3 and 6. And in year 7, no tithe can be given because there is no harvest; see Exod. 23:10–11, Lev. 25:2–7).

the yield . . . brought in from the field Including wine and oil as well as grains (see v. 23).

23. *in the presence of the LORD* The text does not say when these offerings are to be brought to the sanctuary. The regular pilgrimage festivals were probably the most convenient occasions, although farmers probably made private pilgrimages at other times, too.

firstlings of your herds and flocks They are

mentioned here because, like the tithe, they are brought to the chosen sanctuary by their owners and eaten there. All firstlings are consumed, not merely a tenth of them (15:19–20).

so that you may learn to revere the LORD Reverence will be fostered in the chosen city by contact with the priests, who teach piety and law.

24. because the LORD . . . has blessed you Because this was the blessing of abundant crops, the tithe would be too ample for transport over a long distance.

25. money Hebrew: *kesef*; literally, "silver." Money consisted of precious metal, most often silver. The metal was shaped into rings, bracelets, and ingots, the value of which was established by their weight at the time of each transaction.

wrap up the money Keep it intact in a money bag, spending none of it along the way.

26. wine, or other intoxicant This phrase refers either to different types of grape wine, such as new and old or mixed and unmixed, or to grape wine and another intoxicant, such as date wine, pomegranate wine, or beer.

anything you may desire To eat as part of the feast.

---

23. How will consuming the tithe in Jerusalem teach us to revere God? Seeing the Temple in all its glory and the priests at their service will inspire a sense of reverence (Rashbam). Another commentator suggests that we attain a sense of reverence not through an intellectual process

but by experiencing God's grace in our lives.

24. because the place . . . is far from you *Makom* (place) is also one of the names of God—the site of all reality. Thus the verse can mean, "should the distance seem too great for you because God is far from your heart."

of the Lord your God, and rejoice with your
household.
27But do not neglect the Levite in your community, for he has no hereditary portion as you
have. 28Every third year you shall bring out the
full tithe of your yield of that year, but leave it
within your settlements. 29Then the Levite, who
has no hereditary portion as you have, and the
stranger, the fatherless, and the widow in your
settlements shall come and eat their fill, so that
the Lord your God may bless you in all the enterprises you undertake.

שָׁם לִפְנֵי יְהוָה אֱלֹהֶיךָ וְשָׂמַחְתָּ אַתָּה
וּבֵיתֶךָ׃
27 וְהַלֵּוִי אֲשֶׁר־בִּשְׁעָרֶיךָ לֹא תַעַזְבֶנּוּ כִּי
אֵין לוֹ חֵלֶק וְנַחֲלָה עִמָּךְ׃ ס 28 מִקְצֵה ׀
שָׁלֹשׁ שָׁנִים תּוֹצִיא אֶת־כָּל־מַעְשַׂר
תְּבוּאָתְךָ בַּשָּׁנָה הַהִוא וְהִנַּחְתָּ בִּשְׁעָרֶיךָ׃
29 וּבָא הַלֵּוִי כִּי אֵין־לוֹ חֵלֶק וְנַחֲלָה עִמָּךְ
וְהַגֵּר וְהַיָּתוֹם וְהָאַלְמָנָה אֲשֶׁר בִּשְׁעָרֶיךָ
וְאָכְלוּ וְשָׂבֵעוּ לְמַעַן יְבָרֶכְךָ יְהוָה אֱלֹהֶיךָ
בְּכָל־מַעֲשֵׂה יָדְךָ אֲשֶׁר תַּעֲשֶׂה׃ ס

15 Every seventh year you shall practice re-

ששי טו מִקֵּץ שֶׁבַע־שָׁנִים תַּעֲשֶׂה שְׁמִטָּה׃

rejoice with your household A farmer and his household could not possibly consume the entire tithe during the required 9 days of pilgrimage to the sanctuary each year (16:1–17). Theoretically, a household producing at subsistence level would require 35.4 days to consume 10 percent (a tithe) of its produce. Even if the farmers invited the Levites and the poor to the festival meals, as required, and doubled their normal consumption, they still could not dispose of all the food—unless there were as many Levites and poor as there were members of the farmers' households, which is unlikely. Perhaps whatever was left over had to be given away to the poor or was destroyed.

27. Levite in your community Those residing in the various towns and cities.

The Triennial Poor Tithe (vv. 28–29)

In the third and sixth years of each seven-year cycle (see 15:1), the farmers shall not eat the tithe at the sanctuary but must deposit it in their hometowns to feed the Levites and the poor. Presumably, the produce collected in each of these two years was expected to suffice for three or four years until the next collection. It seems unlikely that the poor were to be fed only two years out of seven.

28. bring out From your property.

full tithe None of it is to be diverted to any other use.

leave it within your settlements Public storage facilities and threshing floors near the city gate would have been natural locations for the deposit, distribution, and long-term stockpiling of the produce.

29. the fatherless, and the widow That is, the poor.

come and eat their fill The recipients of the tithe would be given food daily as needed.

so that the Lord . . . may bless you Such assurances are given with laws that require economic sacrifice for the sake of the poor. Because the Israelite might fear that these sacrifices would cause economic hardship, the donor is assured that, in the end, they will lead to prosperity.

MEASURES TO PROTECT THE POOR (15:1–18)

This section deals with extreme difficulties that can befall the poor: inability to obtain loans, inability to pay off debts, and indentured servitude. Some of these laws are also found elsewhere in the Torah and in other ancient Near Eastern societies.

CHAPTER 15

1. Most of this chapter is concerned with ensuring that there not emerge in Israel a permanent underclass—persons unable to lift themselves out of poverty. Such a condition would be unfair to human beings, fashioned in God's image, and dangerous to society as a breeding ground for lawlessness and irresponsibility. The first step in the direction of preventing that is the remission of debts in the seventh year.

mission of debts. 2This shall be the nature of
the remission: every creditor shall remit the due
that he claims from his fellow; he shall not dun
his fellow or kinsman, for the remission proclaimed is of the LORD. 3You may dun the foreigner; but you must remit whatever is due you
from your kinsmen.

4There shall be no needy among you—since
the LORD your God will bless you in the land
that the LORD your God is giving you as a hereditary portion—5if only you heed the LORD
your God and take care to keep all this Instruction that I enjoin upon you this day. 6For the
LORD your God will bless you as He has promised you: you will extend loans to many nations,
but require none yourself; you will dominate
many nations, but they will not dominate you.

7If, however, there is a needy person among

2 וְזֶה֮ דְּבַ֣ר הַשְּׁמִטָּה֒ שָׁמ֗וֹט כָּל־בַּ֙עַל֙ מַשֵּׁ֣ה
יָד֔וֹ אֲשֶׁ֥ר יַשֶּׁ֖ה בְּרֵעֵ֑הוּ לֹֽא־יִגֹּ֤שׂ אֶת־רֵעֵ֙הוּ֙
וְאֶת־אָחִ֔יו כִּֽי־קָרָ֥א שְׁמִטָּ֖ה לַיהוָֽה׃ 3 אֶת־
הַנָּכְרִ֖י תִּגֹּ֑שׂ וַאֲשֶׁ֨ר יִהְיֶ֥ה לְךָ֛ אֶת־אָחִ֖יךָ
תַּשְׁמֵ֥ט יָדֶֽךָ׃
4 אֶ֕פֶס כִּ֛י לֹ֥א יִֽהְיֶה־בְּךָ֖ אֶבְי֑וֹן כִּֽי־בָרֵ֤ךְ
יְבָרֶכְךָ֙ יְהוָ֔ה בָּאָ֕רֶץ אֲשֶׁר֙ יְהוָ֣ה אֱלֹהֶ֔יךָ
נֹֽתֵן־לְךָ֥ נַחֲלָ֖ה לְרִשְׁתָּֽהּ׃ 5 רַ֚ק אִם־שָׁמ֣וֹעַ
תִּשְׁמַ֔ע בְּק֖וֹל יְהוָ֣ה אֱלֹהֶ֑יךָ לִשְׁמֹ֤ר לַעֲשׂוֹת֙
אֶת־כָּל־הַמִּצְוָ֣ה הַזֹּ֔את אֲשֶׁ֛ר אָנֹכִ֥י מְצַוְּךָ֖
הַיּֽוֹם׃ 6 כִּֽי־יְהוָ֤ה אֱלֹהֶ֙יךָ֙ בֵּֽרַכְךָ֔ כַּאֲשֶׁ֖ר
דִּבֶּר־לָ֑ךְ וְהַעֲבַטְתָּ֞ גּוֹיִ֣ם רַבִּ֗ים וְאַתָּה֙ לֹ֣א
תַעֲבֹ֔ט וּמָֽשַׁלְתָּ֙ בְּגוֹיִ֣ם רַבִּ֔ים וּבְךָ֖ לֹ֥א
יִמְשֹֽׁלוּ׃ ס
7 כִּֽי־יִהְיֶ֨ה בְךָ֜ אֶבְי֗וֹן מֵאַחַ֣ד אַחֶ֙יךָ֙ בְּאַחַ֣ד

Remission of Debts (vv. 1–6)

The Torah is here concerned with the type of debt incurred by the poor and insolvent: a farmer in dire need of funds because of crop failure and a city dweller destitute as a result of unemployment. Loans to such individuals were regarded as acts of philanthropy rather than commercial ventures, and the forgiving of such loans was an extension of the generosity. The remission of debts and other provisions for the relief of debtors are part of the Torah's program for preserving a balanced distribution of resources across society (see Exod. 22:24–26; Lev. 25:36–37; Deut. 23:20–21, 24:6,10–13,17).

1. Every seventh year According to talmudic law, debts were canceled at sunset on the last day of the seventh year.

remission of debts Hebrew: *sh'mittah;* literally, "dropping, release." In Exod. 23:10–12, *"sh'mittah"* refers to land, not debts.

2. every creditor Because the remission is for the benefit of the poor, it probably does not cover all types of debts. (According to later Jewish law, unpaid wages, bills owed to shopkeepers for merchandise, and certain types of secured loans are not canceled.)

his fellow or his kinsman That is, "his fellow, who is his kinsman." Both terms refer to one person.

for the remission proclaimed is of the LORD This seems to be the equivalent of the formula in Mesopotamian decrees explaining that debts may not be collected "because the king has established a remission for the land." In the Torah it is God—Israel's divine king—who establishes the remission.

3. The remission applies only to debts owed by fellow Israelites, not by foreigners. Similarly, the remission edict of the Babylonian king Ammitsaduka canceled only the debts of kinsmen: Akkadians and Amorites in Babylon. Collecting debts is a legitimate right, and forgiving debts is an extraordinary sacrifice that members of society are willing to forgo only on behalf of those who have a special family-like claim on their compassion.

4. your God will bless you With prosperity.

6. as He has promised you The promises are linked to the Israelites' obedience.

you will extend loans If the Israelites will obey God's laws, not only will they have no poor who need loans but they will be so prosperous that other nations will turn to them for loans.

you will dominate Economically.

Lend to the Poor! (vv. 7–11)

Even those who normally would be willing to lend to the poor might hesitate as the year of remission approaches, because it is likely that they would lose what they had loaned. Moses urges the people to disregard such calculations. Such appeals for

שְׁעָרֶיךָ בְּאַרְצְךָ אֲשֶׁר־יְהוָה אֱלֹהֶיךָ נֹתֵן
לָךְ לֹא תְאַמֵּץ אֶת־לְבָבְךָ וְלֹא תִקְפֹּץ
אֶת־יָדְךָ מֵאָחִיךָ הָאֶבְיוֹן׃ 8 כִּי־פָתֹחַ
תִּפְתַּח אֶת־יָדְךָ לוֹ וְהַעֲבֵט תַּעֲבִיטֶנּוּ דֵּי
מַחְסֹרוֹ אֲשֶׁר יֶחְסַר לוֹ׃ 9 הִשָּׁמֶר לְךָ
פֶּן־יִהְיֶה דָבָר עִם־לְבָבְךָ בְלִיַּעַל לֵאמֹר
קָרְבָה שְׁנַת־הַשֶּׁבַע שְׁנַת הַשְּׁמִטָּה וְרָעָה
עֵינְךָ בְּאָחִיךָ הָאֶבְיוֹן וְלֹא תִתֵּן לוֹ וְקָרָא
עָלֶיךָ אֶל־יְהוָה וְהָיָה בְךָ חֵטְא׃ 10 נָתוֹן
תִּתֵּן לוֹ וְלֹא־יֵרַע לְבָבְךָ בְּתִתְּךָ לוֹ כִּי
בִּגְלַל ׀ הַדָּבָר הַזֶּה יְבָרֶכְךָ יְהוָה אֱלֹהֶיךָ
בְּכָל־מַעֲשֶׂךָ וּבְכֹל מִשְׁלַח יָדֶךָ׃ 11 כִּי
לֹא־יֶחְדַּל אֶבְיוֹן מִקֶּרֶב הָאָרֶץ עַל־כֵּן
אָנֹכִי מְצַוְּךָ לֵאמֹר פָּתֹחַ תִּפְתַּח אֶת־יָדְךָ
לְאָחִיךָ לַעֲנִיֶּךָ וּלְאֶבְיֹנְךָ בְּאַרְצֶךָ׃ ס

you, one of your kinsmen in any of your settlements in the land that the LORD your God is giving you, do not harden your heart and shut your hand against your needy kinsman.
8Rather, you must open your hand and lend him sufficient for whatever he needs. 9Beware lest you harbor the base thought, "The seventh year, the year of remission, is approaching," so that you are mean to your needy kinsman and give him nothing. He will cry out to the LORD against you, and you will incur guilt. 10Give to him readily and have no regrets when you do so, for in return the LORD your God will bless you in all your efforts and in all your undertakings.
11For there will never cease to be needy ones in your land, which is why I command you: open your hand to the poor and needy kinsman in your land.

compassion are characteristic of Deuteronomy (see v. 18).

7. If: . . there is a needy person among you If the ideal promised in verse 4 is not achieved.

9. you will incur guilt Guilt builds up until it leads to punishment, just as merit builds up and leads to reward.

10. God will bless you The closer the year of remission, the more likely it is that the loan will end up as a gift. But any loss incurred will be more than made up by God.

11. there will never cease to be needy ones The realism of this verse contrasts with the ideal described in verse 4.

7–10. An obligation to generously support a kinsman who has fallen on hard times without calculating whether the help will be repaid. This is not so much a loan as an investment in a decent, compassionate, stable society.

7. do not harden your heart One who ignores the needy is like an idolater (BT Ket. 68a). Also, it is forbidden to insult the poor or accuse them of being undeserving.

9. In late Second Temple times, the law of remission did become a deterrent to lending, as anticipated by this verse. To protect people who needed loans and to prevent violation of verses 9 and 10, the sage Hillel (1st century B.C.E.–1st century C.E.) devised a legal means for circumventing the remission. The means was a document or declaration (*prosbul*) in which the lender declares that a specific loan will not be subject to remission. By this means, Hillel ensured that the law would not undermine its own purpose.

10. The Midrash imagines God saying, "You sustain My dependents (the poor, the widow, and the orphan) and I will sustain your dependents" (Tanḥ. 18).

11. For there will never cease to be needy ones in your land Therefore, you must build the solution to poverty into the social structure, and not rely on people's generosity. A poor person need never be embarrassed to accept help, because giving *tz'dakah* is an obligation, not charity resulting from kindheartedness. At the same time, the Sages also tell us: "Better to flay carcasses in the marketplace than to depend on public assistance because you feel the available work is beneath your dignity" (BT Pes. 113a).

HALAKHAH L'MA·ASEH

15:7–11. open your hand These verses undergird Jewish poverty laws requiring us to feed, clothe, and house poor non-Jews as well as Jews. See also Exod. 12:49; Lev. 19:9–10, 25:25, 35; Deut. 24:10–22.

12 If a fellow Hebrew, man or woman, is sold
to you, he shall serve you six years, and in the
seventh year you shall set him free. 13 When you
set him free, do not let him go empty-handed:
14 Furnish him out of the flock, threshing floor,
and vat, with which the LORD your God has
blessed you. 15 Bear in mind that you were slaves
in the land of Egypt and the LORD your God
redeemed you; therefore I enjoin this commandment upon you today.
16 But should he say to you, "I do not want
to leave you"—for he loves you and your household and is happy with you—17 you shall take
an awl and put it through his ear into the door,

12 כִּי־יִמָּכֵר לְךָ אָחִיךָ הָעִבְרִי אוֹ הָעִבְרִיָּה
וַעֲבָדְךָ שֵׁשׁ שָׁנִים וּבַשָּׁנָה הַשְּׁבִיעִת
תְּשַׁלְּחֶנּוּ חָפְשִׁי מֵעִמָּךְ׃ 13 וְכִי־תְשַׁלְּחֶנּוּ
חָפְשִׁי מֵעִמָּךְ לֹא תְשַׁלְּחֶנּוּ רֵיקָם׃
14 הַעֲנֵיק תַּעֲנִיק לוֹ מִצֹּאנְךָ וּמִגָּרְנְךָ
וּמִיִּקְבֶךָ אֲשֶׁר בֵּרַכְךָ יְהוָה אֱלֹהֶיךָ תִּתֶּן־
לוֹ׃ 15 וְזָכַרְתָּ כִּי עֶבֶד הָיִיתָ בְּאֶרֶץ מִצְרַיִם
וַיִּפְדְּךָ יְהוָה אֱלֹהֶיךָ עַל־כֵּן אָנֹכִי מְצַוְּךָ
אֶת־הַדָּבָר הַזֶּה הַיּוֹם׃
16 וְהָיָה כִּי־יֹאמַר אֵלֶיךָ לֹא אֵצֵא מֵעִמָּךְ
כִּי אֲהֵבְךָ וְאֶת־בֵּיתֶךָ כִּי־טוֹב לוֹ עִמָּךְ׃
17 וְלָקַחְתָּ אֶת־הַמַּרְצֵעַ וְנָתַתָּה בְאָזְנוֹ

Manumission of Indentured Servants (vv. 12–18)

This is one of several laws in the Torah that deal with servitude, an accepted fact of life in ancient Israel as it was everywhere else in the ancient world. Biblical law and ethical teachings aimed at securing humane treatment for servants (see Exod. 21:2–6; Lev. 25:39–55).

12. fellow Hebrew That is, "Hebrew kinsman" (literally, "brother"). The law limits the amount of time during which one Israelite may control another. Only foreigners may be owned in perpetuity and passed on to heirs (Lev. 25:39–55). The phrase reminds one of the special, brotherly obligations toward fellow Israelites.

woman Who becomes indentured because of insolvency or debt—her own or that of her husband or father.

sold to you The law refers to the sale of a son or a daughter by an indigent father or the sale of a thief by the court. It could also refer to the self-sale of a destitute person for self-support or support of family. The aim in either case would be to satisfy a debt or raise the funds to do so.

six years The standard term of indenture (see also v. 18; Exod. 21:2).

13. Here Deuteronomy goes beyond Exod. 21:2, in requiring that newly freed servants be given capital and supplies for living as they resume independent life. The aim is to prevent them from starting off penniless and possibly returning to the same wretched condition that originally led to servitude.

14. flock, threshing floor, and vat Some sheep or goats (or their products, such as milk or wool), some grain, and some wine.

16. The servant might consider that the security gained through subservience is preferable to the risks of independence. The fact that the law thinks it possible that the servant might love the master and desire servitude implies that the treatment of indentured servants was expected to be quite benign.

happy In the sense of being well off.

17. you shall take an awl See Exod. 21:2–6. The ceremony for making the servant's status permanent consists of driving the point of an awl through his ear into the door of the master's

12. The parallel passage in Exodus (21:2ff.) does not speak of the slave as "your brother" (*aḥikha*), does not provide for freeing a female slave on the same terms as a male, and makes no provision for sending the freed slave forth with food and gifts. It may be that, in the weeks immediately following the Exodus, the people could imagine slaveholding only after the Egyptian model. Their idea of progress was treating slaves with a modicum of decency. Only a later generation, nurtured in freedom, could empathize with the slave's yearning to be free.

HALAKHAH L'MA·ASEH

15:13–14. do not let him go empty-handed On the basis of these verses, some Jewish authorities require employers to pay severance to employees hired on more than a temporary basis. Others see it as a moral duty exclusively (*Seifer Ha-Ḥinnukh* 481–482).

and he shall become your slave in perpetuity. Do the same with your female slave. 18When you do set him free, do not feel aggrieved; for in the six years he has given you double the service of a hired man. Moreover, the LORD your God will bless you in all you do.

וּבַדֶּלֶת וְהָיָה לְךָ עֶבֶד עוֹלָם וְאַף לַאֲמָתְךָ
תַּעֲשֶׂה־כֵּן׃ 18 לֹא־יִקְשֶׁה בְעֵינֶךָ בְּשַׁלֵּחֲךָ
אֹתוֹ חָפְשִׁי מֵעִמָּךְ כִּי מִשְׁנֶה שְׂכַר שָׂכִיר
עֲבָדְךָ שֵׁשׁ שָׁנִים וּבֵרַכְךָ יְהוָה אֱלֹהֶיךָ
בְּכֹל אֲשֶׁר תַּעֲשֶׂה׃ פ

19You shall consecrate to the LORD your God all male firstlings that are born in your herd and in your flock: you must not work your firstling ox or shear your firstling sheep. 20You and your household shall eat it annually before the LORD your God in the place that the LORD will choose. 21But if it has a defect, lameness or blindness, any serious defect, you shall not sacrifice it to the LORD your God. 22Eat it in your settlements, the impure among you no less than the pure, just like the gazelle and the deer.

שביעי 19 כָּל־הַבְּכוֹר אֲשֶׁר יִוָּלֵד בִּבְקָרְךָ וּבְצֹאנְךָ
הַזָּכָר תַּקְדִּישׁ לַיהוָה אֱלֹהֶיךָ לֹא תַעֲבֹד
בִּבְכֹר שׁוֹרֶךָ וְלֹא תָגֹז בְּכוֹר צֹאנֶךָ׃ 20 לִפְנֵי
יְהוָה אֱלֹהֶיךָ תֹאכֲלֶנּוּ שָׁנָה בְשָׁנָה בַּמָּקוֹם
אֲשֶׁר־יִבְחַר יְהוָה אַתָּה וּבֵיתֶךָ׃ 21 וְכִי־
יִהְיֶה בוֹ מוּם פִּסֵּחַ אוֹ עִוֵּר כֹּל מוּם רָע
לֹא תִזְבָּחֶנּוּ לַיהוָה אֱלֹהֶיךָ׃ 22 בִּשְׁעָרֶיךָ
תֹּאכֲלֶנּוּ הַטָּמֵא וְהַטָּהוֹר יַחְדָּו כַּצְּבִי

house. The significance of this action is unclear. It might symbolize the servant's obligation to heed the master's orders; the pierced ear might have held an earring that served as a slave mark; driving the awl into the door might signify the servant's becoming permanently attached to the master's house.

in perpetuity According to Jewish law, for the rest of the master's life, unless a jubilee year (as prescribed in Lev. 25) comes first. Even a servant who chooses to remain with the master is not passed on to the master's heirs and does not remain beyond the jubilee.

18. do not feel aggrieved Deuteronomy is interested in the Israelite's feelings, not just in compliance with the law. Having grown accustomed to a servant's usefulness, a master might regard the Torah's demand to free the servant as an unreasonable hardship. The text reminds masters that they have profited handsomely from their servants and have no reason to feel deprived.

double the service of a hired man The point may be that the wages of a hired man would have been twice what the servant cost in room and board and perhaps a defaulted loan. Furthermore, a hired man would have worked only during the day, whereas the servant was available day and night.

God will bless you Any loss incurred will be more than made up by God.

THE SACRIFICE OF FIRSTBORN CATTLE
(vv. 19–23)

The first issue of all living things is considered holy, reserved for the Lord. Only after these are given to God, thereby acknowledging Him as the source and owner of all life, are the remainder of the crop and subsequent offspring of animals desacralized and freed for human use. Such practices were common in the ancient world.

19. consecrate Treat them as holy by not using them for any secular purpose and by eating them in a sacral meal.

20. eat it annually before the LORD As a *sh'lamim* sacrifice. According to 12:17–18, Levites also would be invited to take part in the meal (see Lev. 3).

annually Firstborn cattle must be sacrificed within a year of their birth, presumably on one of the pilgrimage festivals.

21. if it has a defect Offering a defective animal to God shows contempt. One would never present such an animal to a human ruler. Hence, in 17:1, sacrificing flawed animals is regarded as an abomination. It is among the offenses that profane God's name in Lev. 22:2,17–25,32.

22. A disqualified firstling may be eaten as food and need not be replaced sacrificially by another animal, redeemed for money, or destroyed, as would be the case with the firstling of an impure animal.

23Only you must not partake of its blood; you shall pour it out on the ground like water.

וְכָאַיָּל׃ 23 רַק אֶת־דָּמוֹ לֹא תֹאכֵל עַל־
הָאָרֶץ תִּשְׁפְּכֶנּוּ כַּמָּיִם׃ פ

16 Observe the month of Abib and offer a passover sacrifice to the LORD your God, for it was in the month of Abib, at night, that the LORD your God freed you from Egypt. 2You shall slaughter the passover sacrifice for the LORD your God, from the flock and the herd, in the

טז שָׁמוֹר אֶת־חֹדֶשׁ הָאָבִיב וְעָשִׂיתָ
פֶּסַח לַיהוָה אֱלֹהֶיךָ כִּי בְּחֹדֶשׁ הָאָבִיב
הוֹצִיאֲךָ יְהוָה אֱלֹהֶיךָ מִמִּצְרַיִם לָיְלָה׃
2 וְזָבַחְתָּ פֶּסַח לַיהוָה אֱלֹהֶיךָ צֹאן וּבָקָר
בַּמָּקוֹם אֲשֶׁר־יִבְחַר יְהוָה לְשַׁכֵּן שְׁמוֹ

PILGRIMAGE FESTIVALS (16:1–17)

The main themes of these festivals are commemoration of the Exodus and gratitude for the harvest. Deuteronomy mentions the festivals to make the point that they must be observed only at the chosen sanctuary. Before the time of the single sanctuary, the festivals would have been observed by a pilgrimage to any of the country's temple cities.

The Pesaḥ Sacrifice and the Feast of Unleavened Bread (vv. 1–8)

The first festival consists of two distinct celebrations: (a) the *pesaḥ,* the protective sacrifice offered at the end of the 14th day of the first month; and (b) the Feast of Unleavened Bread, the 7-day festival that begins on the 15th day (see Lev. 23:6; Num. 28:17). Note the difference between the *pesaḥ* sacrifice described here and the one in Exod. 12, especially in regard to the nature of the animal, the method of its cooking, and where it is to be offered.

1. month of Abib Literally, "new ears of grain." It is the old name of the month that falls in March and April, when ears of grain have just begun to appear. During the Babylonian exile (6th century B.C.E.), when Jews adopted the Babylonian month names that are still in use today, Abib (or *Aviv*) became known as *Nisan.*

passover sacrifice This sacrifice (*pesaḥ*) reenacts the original *pesaḥ* offering brought by the Israelites on the eve of the Exodus immediately before the last of the Ten Plagues. The name is derived from the verb *pasaḥ,* which describes the manner in which God spared the firstborn in the houses of the Israelites after the blood of the sacrifice was smeared on their doorposts and lintels (Exod. 12:13,23,27). In the Vulgate, the verb appears as "[the LORD] passed over," and the sacrifice is called "passover." The Hebrew verb, however, does not mean "to pass over." Most of the ancient translations and commentaries render the verb as the Lord "spared," "had compassion," or "protected." The sacrifice, accordingly, is called the "protective sacrifice," referring to the protection of the Israelites during the final plague. This very likely is the correct translation.

at night Although the Israelites themselves started to leave Egypt "on the morrow of the passover offering" (Num. 33:3), God's action—the slaying of Egypt's firstborn at night—is viewed as the essence of the event.

2. from the flock and the herd According to Exod. 12:3–5 and 21, the *pesaḥ* offering was brought only from the flock and limited to sheep and goats. Deuteronomy clearly indicates that herd animals, large bovines, may be used as well. Perhaps this reflects a different economy, or a time when the sacrifice would be made at a central sanctuary where many households could share a larger animal.

CHAPTER 16

The summary of the festivals in other books of the Torah (Exod. 23:14–17; Lev. 23; Num. 28–29) tell us how to celebrate the holidays. In contrast, Deuteronomy tells us why: "for it was in the month of Abib, at night, that the LORD your God freed you from Egypt" (v. 1), "for you departed . . . hurriedly" (v. 3), "After the ingathering" (v. 13). One might think that the reason for observance should precede the commandment to observe, so that people would know why they were celebrating. It seems to be more effective pedagogy, though, especially for children, to start with the deed and only later explain that this is why we eat *matzah* on *Pesaḥ* and live in booths on *Sukkot.*

place where the Lord will choose to establish His name. [3]You shall not eat anything leavened with it; for seven days thereafter you shall eat unleavened bread, bread of distress—for you departed from the land of Egypt hurriedly—so that you may remember the day of your departure from the land of Egypt as long as you live. [4]For seven days no leaven shall be found with you in all your territory, and none of the flesh of what you slaughter on the evening of the first day shall be left until morning.

[5]You are not permitted to slaughter the passover sacrifice in any of the settlements that the Lord your God is giving you; [6]but at the place where the Lord your God will choose to establish His name, there alone shall you slaughter the passover sacrifice, in the evening, at sundown, the time of day when you departed from

שָׁם׃ 3 לֹא־תֹאכַל עָלָיו חָמֵץ שִׁבְעַת יָמִים
תֹּאכַל־עָלָיו מַצּוֹת לֶחֶם עֹנִי כִּי בְחִפָּזוֹן
יָצָאתָ מֵאֶרֶץ מִצְרַיִם לְמַעַן תִּזְכֹּר אֶת־יוֹם
צֵאתְךָ מֵאֶרֶץ מִצְרַיִם כֹּל יְמֵי חַיֶּיךָ׃
4 וְלֹא־יֵרָאֶה לְךָ שְׂאֹר בְּכָל־גְּבֻלְךָ שִׁבְעַת
יָמִים וְלֹא־יָלִין מִן־הַבָּשָׂר אֲשֶׁר תִּזְבַּח
בָּעֶרֶב בַּיּוֹם הָרִאשׁוֹן לַבֹּקֶר׃
5 לֹא תוּכַל לִזְבֹּחַ אֶת־הַפָּסַח בְּאַחַד
שְׁעָרֶיךָ אֲשֶׁר־יְהוָה אֱלֹהֶיךָ נֹתֵן לָךְ׃ 6 כִּי
אִם־אֶל־הַמָּקוֹם אֲשֶׁר־יִבְחַר יְהוָה אֱלֹהֶיךָ
לְשַׁכֵּן שְׁמוֹ שָׁם תִּזְבַּח אֶת־הַפֶּסַח בָּעָרֶב
כְּבוֹא הַשֶּׁמֶשׁ מוֹעֵד צֵאתְךָ מִמִּצְרָיִם׃

3. anything leavened Food prepared from dough to which a leavening agent was added to make it rise. In postbiblical *halakhah,* this means any leavened product of wheat, barley, spelt, rye, or oats. Most *Ashk'nazim* also include rice, millet, corn, and legumes in this prohibition.

unleavened bread *Matzah,* bread made without yeast and not allowed to rise. It can be made quickly and was commonly prepared for unexpected guests. It is similar to the flat unleavened bread that Bedouins still bake on embers.

bread of distress The *matzah* is "bread of affliction" or "bread of poverty," eaten by prisoners or by the poor. It is unpretentious, primitive fare that one would not normally eat. There is no evidence that the Israelites ate *matzah* when they were slaves. It commemorates the Exodus, not the enslavement.

remember the day of your departure By re-enacting the first *pesaḥ* sacrifice and eating unleavened bread.

4. leaven Hebrew: *s'or.* Here refers to leavening agents, such as sourdough or yeast. It differs from "anything leavened" (*ḥametz;* v. 3), which refers to foodstuffs that have been leavened by leavening agents.

none of the flesh . . . shall be left until morning The sacrifice is offered at sunset (v. 6). It must be eaten through the night and finished by morning, thereby emulating procedures with the original *pesaḥ* sacrifice in Egypt (see Exod. 12:8).

5. Once sacrificial worship is centralized in the chosen place, the *pesaḥ* must be offered there. This is a characteristic requirement of Deuteronomy.

6. the time of day when you departed from Egypt The original *pesaḥ* sacrifice, which was indispensable in ensuring the safety of the Israelites during the 10th plague, is here seen as the onset of the Exodus.

7. cook Compare this with Exod.12:9, which requires roasting. This departure from the earlier requirement probably is due to the centralization of the cult.

in the morning you may start on your journey back home The entire seven days need not be spent at the chosen place, because it is necessary to return home in time to begin the harvest. Either

HALAKHAH L'MA·ASEH

16:3. you shall not eat anything leavened From this verse, the Talmud determines that the use or ownership of *ḥametz* (leavened products) is prohibited from midday on the day preceding *Pesaḥ,* the 14th of *Nisan* (BT Pes. 28b). As a precautionary measure, the Sages rule that the *ḥametz* be burned at least one hour before midday (S.A. O.Ḥ. 434:2) and that one refrain from eating *ḥametz* from two hours before midday (i.e., the fourth hour after sunrise) (see Exod. 12:15; Lev. 2:11).

Egypt. 7You shall cook and eat it at the place that
the LORD your God will choose; and in the morning you may start back on your journey home.
8After eating unleavened bread six days, you
shall hold a solemn gathering for the LORD your
God on the seventh day: you shall do no work.
9You shall count off seven weeks; start to
count the seven weeks when the sickle is first
put to the standing grain. 10Then you shall observe the Feast of Weeks for the LORD your God,
offering your freewill contribution according as
the LORD your God has blessed you. 11You shall
rejoice before the LORD your God with your son
and daughter, your male and female slave, the
Levite in your communities, and the stranger,

7 וּבִשַּׁלְתָּ֙ וְאָ֣כַלְתָּ֔ בַּמָּק֕וֹם אֲשֶׁ֥ר יִבְחַ֛ר
יְהֹוָ֥ה אֱלֹהֶ֖יךָ בּ֑וֹ וּפָנִ֣יתָ בַבֹּ֔קֶר וְהָלַכְתָּ֖
לְאֹהָלֶֽיךָ׃ 8 שֵׁ֥שֶׁת יָמִ֖ים תֹּאכַ֣ל מַצּ֑וֹת
וּבַיּ֣וֹם הַשְּׁבִיעִ֗י עֲצֶ֙רֶת֙ לַיהֹוָ֣ה אֱלֹהֶ֔יךָ לֹ֥א
תַעֲשֶׂ֖ה מְלָאכָֽה׃ ס
9 שִׁבְעָ֥ה שָׁבֻעֹ֖ת תִּסְפָּר־לָ֑ךְ מֵהָחֵ֤ל חֶרְמֵשׁ֙
בַּקָּמָ֔ה תָּחֵ֣ל לִסְפֹּ֔ר שִׁבְעָ֖ה שָׁבֻעֽוֹת׃
10 וְעָשִׂ֜יתָ חַ֤ג שָׁבֻעוֹת֙ לַיהֹוָ֣ה אֱלֹהֶ֔יךָ מִסַּ֛ת
נִדְבַ֥ת יָדְךָ֖ אֲשֶׁ֣ר תִּתֵּ֑ן כַּאֲשֶׁ֥ר יְבָרֶכְךָ֖ יְהֹוָ֥ה
אֱלֹהֶֽיךָ׃ 11 וְשָׂמַחְתָּ֞ לִפְנֵ֣י ׀ יְהֹוָ֣ה אֱלֹהֶ֗יךָ
אַתָּ֨ה וּבִנְךָ֣ וּבִתֶּךָ֮ וְעַבְדְּךָ֣ וַאֲמָתֶךָ֒ וְהַלֵּוִ֗י

Deuteronomy does not consider travel to be forbidden on festival days or it does not regard the second part of the day, following the *Pesaḥ* sacrifice and meal, as sacred. Some traditional commentators hold that "in the morning" refers to the morning of the second day of the festival.

8. six days That is, for the first six of the seven days on which it must be eaten (v. 3). According to postbiblical Jewish law, eating unleavened bread is obligatory only on the first day and not on the remaining days, though nothing leavened may be eaten.

solemn gathering Because this gathering occurs after the people have returned home, it must take place in their hometowns. This clearly indicates that Deuteronomy intends to allow nonsacrificial religious gatherings to take place throughout the country. Only sacrifice is restricted to the chosen place.

do no work Unlike on *Shabbat,* preparation of food is allowed (Exod. 12:16).

The Feast of Weeks (vv. 9–12)

The name of the festival is derived from the fact that it is observed exactly seven weeks after the onset of the harvest. The passage of seven weeks is an essential aspect of the festival. Until seven weeks have passed, it is not known whether the harvest will be successfully completed and plentiful enough to sustain life and not be damaged by late rain or pests.

9. count off That is, calculate.

seven weeks The time needed to complete the harvest.

when the sickle is first put to the standing grain That is, when the grain harvest begins, normally in April. The text gives no exact date, probably because the harvest cannot begin everywhere on the same date owing to regional variations in the climate. Thus farmers from diverse places probably would have observed the feast at different times.

10. Observe the Feast of Weeks A time of solemn gathering on which no work is permitted and loaves made of new grain are offered as first fruits of the grain harvest (see Lev. 23:16–21). Presumably, tithes, firstlings, freewill, and obligatory offerings were also brought, as on other festivals.

freewill contribution Offering what you can afford as a result of the harvest (cf. v. 17, 12:15, 15:14). The contribution might be of produce, animals, or money.

---

7. *in the morning you may start back on your journey home* According to the Tosafot, the prohibition of traveling on festivals is not found in the Torah; it is a Rabbinic enactment (BT Ḥag. 17b, s.v. *dikhtiv*).

9–11. *Shavu·ot* (the Feast of Weeks) is presented in the Torah as a celebration of the early harvest, marked by bringing the first fruits to the Temple. In Second Temple times, it was calculated that the 50th day after the Exodus—the date of *Shavu·ot*—was the day on which the Torah was given at Mount Sinai. *Shavu·ot* became *z'man matan Torateinu* (the time of the giving of our Torah). Like *Pesaḥ* and *Sukkot, Shavu·ot* thus acquired a historical dimension along with its agricultural significance.

the fatherless, and the widow in your midst, at the place where the LORD your God will choose to establish His name. ¹²Bear in mind that you were slaves in Egypt, and take care to obey these laws.

¹³After the ingathering from your threshing floor and your vat, you shall hold the Feast of Booths for seven days. ¹⁴You shall rejoice in your festival, with your son and daughter, your male and female slave, the Levite, the stranger, the fatherless, and the widow in your communities. ¹⁵You shall hold a festival for the LORD your God seven days, in the place that the LORD will choose; for the LORD your God will bless all your crops and all your undertakings, and you shall have nothing but joy.

¹⁶Three times a year—on the Feast of Unleavened Bread, on the Feast of Weeks, and on the Feast of Booths—all your males shall appear before the LORD your God in the place that He will choose. They shall not appear before the LORD empty-handed, ¹⁷but each with his own gift, according to the blessing that the LORD your God has bestowed upon you.

אֲשֶׁ֣ר בִּשְׁעָרֶ֔יךָ וְהַגֵּ֛ר וְהַיָּת֥וֹם וְהָאַלְמָנָ֖ה אֲשֶׁ֣ר בְּקִרְבֶּ֑ךָ בַּמָּק֗וֹם אֲשֶׁ֤ר יִבְחַר֙ יְהוָ֣ה אֱלֹהֶ֔יךָ לְשַׁכֵּ֥ן שְׁמ֖וֹ שָֽׁם: ¹² וְזָ֣כַרְתָּ֔ כִּי־עֶ֥בֶד הָיִ֖יתָ בְּמִצְרָ֑יִם וְשָׁמַרְתָּ֣ וְעָשִׂ֔יתָ אֶת־הַֽחֻקִּ֖ים הָאֵֽלֶּה: פ

מפטיר ¹³ חַ֧ג הַסֻּכֹּ֛ת תַּעֲשֶׂ֥ה לְךָ֖ שִׁבְעַ֣ת יָמִ֑ים בְּאָ֨סְפְּךָ֔ מִֽגָּרְנְךָ֖ וּמִיִּקְבֶֽךָ: ¹⁴ וְשָׂמַחְתָּ֖ בְּחַגֶּ֑ךָ אַתָּ֨ה וּבִנְךָ֤ וּבִתֶּ֨ךָ֙ וְעַבְדְּךָ֣ וַאֲמָתֶ֔ךָ וְהַלֵּוִ֗י וְהַגֵּ֛ר וְהַיָּת֥וֹם וְהָאַלְמָנָ֖ה אֲשֶׁ֥ר בִּשְׁעָרֶֽיךָ: ¹⁵ שִׁבְעַ֣ת יָמִ֗ים תָּחֹג֙ לַֽיהוָ֣ה אֱלֹהֶ֔יךָ בַּמָּק֖וֹם אֲשֶׁר־יִבְחַ֣ר יְהוָ֑ה כִּ֣י יְבָרֶכְךָ֞ יְהוָ֣ה אֱלֹהֶ֗יךָ בְּכֹ֤ל תְּבוּאָֽתְךָ֙ וּבְכֹל֙ מַעֲשֵׂ֣ה יָדֶ֔יךָ וְהָיִ֖יתָ אַ֥ךְ שָׂמֵֽחַ: ¹⁶ שָׁל֣וֹשׁ פְּעָמִ֣ים ׀ בַּשָּׁנָ֡ה יֵרָאֶ֨ה כָל־זְכוּרְךָ֜ אֶת־פְּנֵ֣י ׀ יְהוָ֣ה אֱלֹהֶ֗יךָ בַּמָּקוֹם֙ אֲשֶׁ֣ר יִבְחָ֔ר בְּחַ֧ג הַמַּצּ֛וֹת וּבְחַ֥ג הַשָּׁבֻע֖וֹת וּבְחַ֣ג הַסֻּכּ֑וֹת וְלֹ֧א יֵרָאֶ֛ה אֶת־פְּנֵ֥י יְהוָ֖ה רֵיקָֽם: ¹⁷ אִ֖ישׁ כְּמַתְּנַ֣ת יָד֑וֹ כְּבִרְכַּ֛ת יְהוָ֥ה אֱלֹהֶ֖יךָ אֲשֶׁ֥ר נָֽתַן־לָֽךְ: ס

12. The memory of slavery is invoked to motivate extending this prescription to the servants and the poor mentioned in verse 11.

The Feast of Booths (vv. 13–15)

The third feast, at the end of the summer, celebrates the gathering of grain and new wine into storage for the coming year, the goal of all the preceding agricultural activities. This is the most exuberant of the festivals and has come to be called "the time of our rejoicing" (z'man simḥateinu).

13. After the ingathering from your threshing floor and from the vat That is, after the processed grain and the unfermented grape juice are put in containers and stored away in advance of the autumn rains.

Feast of Booths According to Lev. 23:42, the name is derived from the practice of dwelling in booths, or bowers, during the seven-day festival.

14. The harvest season and festivals were proverbial times for celebration.

15. all your crops . . . all your undertakings . . . nothing but joy The soaring extent of the blessing explains why the celebrating is to last a full seven days.

16. Feast of Unleavened Bread Here, the term must refer to the night of the pesaḥ sacrifice (and not the following seven days), because that is the only time (according to v. 7) when worshipers are required to be at the chosen place.

males Only the adult males are obligated to appear, probably because pregnant and nursing women and young children could not reasonably be required to make long trips. Nevertheless, women and children frequently did take part, as is clear from verses 11 and 14.

appear before the LORD To pay Him homage at His sanctuary. This resembles the practice of homage to human sovereigns as reflected in treaties.

17. each with his own gift Literally, "each according to his means" (as in v. 10).

HALAKHAH L'MA·ASEH

16:14. rejoice Prohibitions on transferring fire and carrying are less restrictive for the biblical festivals than for Shabbat. This is in order to add joy to the festivals (MT Festivals 1:4–6).

הפטרה שלישית דנחמתא

THIRD HAFTARAH OF CONSOLATION
HAFTARAH FOR R'EIH

ISAIAH 54:11–55:5

(*Recite on the 3rd* Shabbat *after the 9th of* Av, *coinciding with the reading of* R'eih. *On the Seven* Haftarot *of Consolation,* *see p. 1032.*)

Bold promises of physical and spiritual transformation introduce this passage from Isaiah. They are presented in unilateral terms. Nothing is demanded of the people. God promises a spectacular rebuilding of Zion, a thorough restoration to raise it out of a depressing situation (54:11–12). And Zion's children will be transformed into disciples of the Lord, who will protect them (vv. 13–17).

The second part of the *haftarah* (55:1–5) bespeaks a more bilateral relationship. Repeatedly God calls on the nation to turn to Him: "Give heed to Me"; "Incline your ear and come to Me." Spiritual transformation, a condition for renewal, promises true sustenance: "Hearken, and you shall be revived" (v. 3). Then Israel will lead other nations (vv. 4–5).

A rhetoric of assurance features the Hebrew particle *hinnei* or *hen* (behold, surely). In the first part it emphasizes freedom from fear (54:15). Although the translation does not render it directly, this particle also punctuates the promise of Zion's riches and highlights Israel's new role among the nations (54:11,16; 55:4,5). In the Hebrew text, it both evokes the immediacy of God's presence and creates an insistent, decisive tone.

Modulation from Israel's disconsolate condition to one of confidence in God's creative reality is underscored by the Hebrew particle *lo* (no, not). It also highlights the nation's shift from a lack of life's essentials to bounty, and from discomfort among other nations to being their commander (54:14,17; 55:2,5).

54 [11]Unhappy, storm-tossed one, uncomforted!
I will lay carbuncles as your building stones
And make your foundations of sapphires.
[12]I will make your battlements of rubies,
Your gates of precious stones,
The whole encircling wall of gems.
[13]And all your children shall be disciples of the LORD,
And great shall be the happiness of your children;

נד 11 עֲנִיָּה סֹעֲרָה לֹא נֻחָמָה
הִנֵּה אָנֹכִי מַרְבִּיץ בַּפּוּךְ אֲבָנַיִךְ
וִיסַדְתִּיךְ בַּסַּפִּירִים׃
12 וְשַׂמְתִּי כַּדְכֹד שִׁמְשֹׁתַיִךְ
וּשְׁעָרַיִךְ לְאַבְנֵי אֶקְדָּח
וְכָל־גְּבוּלֵךְ לְאַבְנֵי־חֵפֶץ׃
13 וְכָל־בָּנַיִךְ לִמּוּדֵי יְהוָה
וְרַב שְׁלוֹם בָּנָיִךְ׃

Isaiah 54:13. disciples Hebrew: *limmudei,* a technical term (see 8:16, 50:4).

your children Hebrew: *banayikh,* spelled בניך. In a well-known *midrash,* the second instance of this word in v. 13 is reread as *bonayikh* (your builders); it became the basis for teaching that knowledgeable children are the culture builders of the next generation (BT Ber. 64a). The

¹⁴You shall be established through righteous-
ness.

You shall be safe from oppression,

And shall have no fear;

From ruin, and it shall not come near you.

¹⁵Surely no harm can be done

Without My consent:

Whoever would harm you

Shall fall because of you.

¹⁶It is I who created the smith

To fan the charcoal fire

And produce the tools for his work;

So it is I who create

The instruments of havoc.

¹⁷No weapon formed against you

Shall succeed,

And every tongue that contends with you at
   law

You shall defeat.

Such is the lot of the servants of the Lord,

Such their triumph through Me

　　　　　　—declares the Lord.

14 בְּצִדְקָה תִּכּוֹנָ֑נִי

רַחֲקִ֣י מֵעֹ֔שֶׁק

כִּי־לֹ֣א תִירָ֔אִי

וּמִ֨מְּחִתָּ֔ה כִּ֥י לֹא־תִקְרַ֖ב אֵלָֽיִךְ׃

15 הֵ֣ן גּ֥וֹר יָג֛וּר

אֶ֖פֶס מֵאוֹתִ֑י

מִי־גָ֥ר אִתָּ֖ךְ

עָלַ֥יִךְ יִפּֽוֹל׃

16 הֵ֣ן הִנֵּ֤ה אָֽנֹכִי֙ בָּרָ֣אתִי חָרָ֔שׁ

נֹפֵ֙חַ֙ בְּאֵ֣שׁ פֶּחָ֔ם

וּמוֹצִ֥יא כְלִ֖י לְמַעֲשֵׂ֑הוּ

וְאָֽנֹכִ֛י בָּרָ֥אתִי

מַשְׁחִ֖ית לְחַבֵּֽל׃

17 כָּל־כְּלִ֞י יוּצַ֤ר עָלַ֙יִךְ֙

לֹ֣א יִצְלָ֔ח

וְכָל־לָשׁ֛וֹן תָּֽקוּם־אִתָּ֥ךְ לַמִּשְׁפָּ֖ט

תַּרְשִׁ֑יעִי

זֹ֡את נַחֲלַת֩ עַבְדֵ֨י יְהֹוָ֧ה

וְצִדְקָתָ֛ם מֵאִתִּ֖י

נְאֻם־יְהֹוָֽה׃ ס

55 Ho, all who are thirsty,

Come for water,

Even if you have no money;

Come, buy food and eat:

Buy food without money,

Wine and milk without cost.

²Why do you spend money for what is not
   bread,

נה הוֹ֤י כָּל־צָמֵא֙

לְכ֣וּ לַמַּ֔יִם

וַאֲשֶׁ֥ר אֵֽין־ל֖וֹ כָּ֑סֶף

לְכ֤וּ שִׁבְרוּ֙ וֶֽאֱכֹ֔לוּ

וּלְכ֣וּ שִׁבְר֗וּ בְּלֽוֹא־כֶ֛סֶף

וּבְל֥וֹא מְחִ֖יר יַ֥יִן וְחָלָֽב׃

2 לָ֤מָּה תִשְׁקְלוּ־כֶ֙סֶף֙ בְּלוֹא־לֶ֔חֶם

---

spelling is בוניכי in the large Isaiah scroll from
Qumran (the "Dead Sea Scrolls"), which supports
the midrashic vocalization *bonayikh*. However,
this spelling may equally indicate that the original
sense was "your learned ones" (from the root בין,
"to know"). If so, this noun would thus parallel
"disciples of the Lord" in the first part of the
verse.

**14. You shall be established through right-
eousness** This phrase recalls Isa. 1:27, "Zion
shall be redeemed with justice; / Her repentant

ones with righteousness" (see Comment, p.
1004). In this case, however, the divine word conveys assurance, not a condition to be fulfilled.

17. triumph Hebrew: *tz'dakah*, justification
or vindication in court. Here it counterpoints the
opening clause of the verse. God brings triumph
as the vindicator of Israel. Both senses of the word
recur in Isa. 40–66 (see 42:21, 45:25, 50:8,
58:2,8, 63:1).

Isaiah 55:1. thirsty Lacking divine instruction (see Amos 8:11).

Your earnings for what does not satisfy?
Give heed to Me,
And you shall eat choice food
And enjoy the richest viands.
3 Incline your ear and come to Me;
Hearken, and you shall be revived.
And I will make with you an everlasting cov-
enant,
The enduring loyalty promised to David.
4 As I made him a leader of peoples,
A prince and commander of peoples,
5 So you shall summon a nation you did not
know,
And a nation that did not know you
Shall come running to you—
For the sake of the LORD your God,
The Holy One of Israel who has glorified you.

וִיגִיעֲכֶם בְּלוֹא לְשָׂבְעָה
שִׁמְעוּ שָׁמוֹעַ אֵלַי
וְאִכְלוּ־טוֹב
וְתִתְעַנַּג בַּדֶּשֶׁן נַפְשְׁכֶם׃
3 הַטּוּ אָזְנְכֶם וּלְכוּ אֵלַי
שִׁמְעוּ וּתְחִי נַפְשְׁכֶם
וְאֶכְרְתָה לָכֶם בְּרִית עוֹלָם
חַסְדֵי דָוִד הַנֶּאֱמָנִים׃
4 הֵן עֵד לְאוּמִּים נְתַתִּיו
נָגִיד וּמְצַוֵּה לְאֻמִּים׃
5 הֵן גּוֹי לֹא־תֵדַע תִּקְרָא
וְגוֹי לֹא־יְדָעוּךָ
אֵלֶיךָ יָרוּצוּ
לְמַעַן יְהוָה אֱלֹהֶיךָ
וְלִקְדוֹשׁ יִשְׂרָאֵל כִּי פֵאֲרָךְ׃ ס

3. enduring loyalty promised to David The royal covenant given to David (2 Sam. 7:15) is now transferred to the entire people. Here *hesed* (enduring loyalty) means faithfulness to that covenant.

4. leader Hebrew: *ed,* literally, "witness." The figure "leader of peoples" combines images of Israel's mission as a "light of nations" and as "witnesses" to God's power (see 42:7, 43:10).

18 You shall appoint magistrates and officials
for your tribes, in all the settlements that the
LORD your God is giving you, and they shall govern the people with due justice. 19 You shall not
judge unfairly: you shall show no partiality; you
shall not take bribes, for bribes blind the eyes
of the discerning and upset the plea of the just.
20 Justice, justice shall you pursue, that you may

18 שֹׁפְטִ֣ים וְשֹֽׁטְרִ֗ים תִּֽתֶּן־לְךָ֙ בְּכָל־שְׁעָרֶ֔יךָ
אֲשֶׁ֨ר יְהוָ֧ה אֱלֹהֶ֛יךָ נֹתֵ֥ן לְךָ֖ לִשְׁבָטֶ֑יךָ
וְשָׁפְט֥וּ אֶת־הָעָ֖ם מִשְׁפַּט־צֶֽדֶק׃ 19 לֹא־
תַטֶּ֣ה מִשְׁפָּ֔ט לֹ֥א תַכִּ֖יר פָּנִ֑ים וְלֹא־תִקַּ֣ח
שֹׁ֔חַד כִּ֣י הַשֹּׁ֗חַד יְעַוֵּר֙ עֵינֵ֣י חֲכָמִ֔ים וִֽיסַלֵּ֖ף
דִּבְרֵ֥י צַדִּיקִֽם׃ 20 צֶ֥דֶק צֶ֖דֶק תִּרְדֹּ֑ף לְמַ֤עַן

Moses' Second Discourse, Part 3: The Laws Given in Moab (*continued*)

CIVIL AND RELIGIOUS AUTHORITIES (16:18–18:22)

The Torah establishes limits to the powers of judges, kings, priests, and prophets. By making these limitations known to the public, the Torah lays the ground for public supervision and criticism of human authorities, thus preventing them from gaining absolute domination and prestige.

THE JUDICIARY (16:18–17:13)

The text assumes that the judicial system established in 1:13–17, to meet the military requirements of the trek through the wilderness and the conquest of the land, will not continue after the conquest because it is unsuitable for conditions in the land.

APPOINTING JUDGES AND OFFICIALS (vv. 18–20)

18. The command to appoint judges and officials is addressed to the people, implying that they, or the elders on their behalf, are to make the appointments. At first, judging probably was not separate from other aspects of leadership, carried out by the elders of a tribe or a village acting collectively. When a village chief was chosen from among the leading elders, he probably became the judge.

19. This and verse 20 state the three fundamental rules of judicial propriety, all of which are reiterated frequently in the Bible. These rules are addressed to the entire people.

show no partiality See Lev. 19:15.

bribes Hebrew: *shoḥad,* a gift for which something is expected in return, not necessarily one given with dishonest intent.

blind the eyes A gift or a fee would incline the judge in that party's favor.

upset the plea By influencing the judge against the claims of the innocent party.

20. justice, justice That is, justice alone; justice and only justice.

This *parashah* is devoted almost entirely to the theme of justice, from the obligations of judges to limitations on the power of kings. The well-being of society depends neither on the goodwill of the ruler nor on the ascendance of the most capable in a competitive environment but on the certainty that the law will treat all alike and will protect the most vulnerable against the most powerful. The absolute primacy of justice, a theme that occurs throughout the Torah, receives its greatest emphasis here. It has been said that "since the time of Abraham, Justice has spoken with a Hebrew accent" (Heine).

18. in all the settlements Literally, "at all your gates." We must set guardians at the gates of our souls—our mouths (that we do not lie or speak malicious gossip), our ears (that we not be eager to hear malicious gossip), and our eyes (that we not form the habit of seeing the worst in others) (*Sh'nei Luḥot Ha-B'rit*).

due justice Hebrew: *mishpat tzedek.* Berkovits distinguishes between these terms: *tzedek* is justice in the sense of doing the right thing in a legal procedure; *mishpat* is justice as a cosmic principle that maintains harmony in the world and makes possible the world's continued existence.

20. Justice, justice shall you pursue "The term 'pursue' carries strong connotations of effort, eagerness. This implies more than merely respecting or following justice"; we must ac-

thrive and occupy the land that the LORD your God is giving you.

21You shall not set up a sacred post—any kind of pole beside the altar of the LORD your God that you may make—22or erect a stone pillar; for such the LORD your God detests.

תִּחְיֶה֙ וְיָרַשְׁתָּ֣ אֶת־הָאָ֔רֶץ אֲשֶׁר־יְהוָ֥ה
אֱלֹהֶ֖יךָ נֹתֵ֥ן לָֽךְ׃ ס
21 לֹֽא־תִטַּ֥ע לְךָ֛ אֲשֵׁרָ֖ה כָּל־עֵ֑ץ אֵ֗צֶל מִזְבַּ֛ח
יְהוָ֥ה אֱלֹהֶ֖יךָ אֲשֶׁ֥ר תַּעֲשֶׂה־לָּֽךְ׃ ס
22 וְלֹֽא־תָקִ֥ים לְךָ֖ מַצֵּבָ֑ה אֲשֶׁ֥ר שָׂנֵ֖א יְהוָ֥ה
אֱלֹהֶֽיךָ׃ ס

17 You shall not sacrifice to the LORD your God an ox or a sheep that has any defect of a serious kind, for that is abhorrent to the LORD your God.

יז לֹֽא־תִזְבַּח֩ לַיהוָ֨ה אֱלֹהֶ֜יךָ שׁ֣וֹר וָשֶׂ֗ה
אֲשֶׁ֨ר יִהְיֶ֥ה בוֹ֙ מ֔וּם כֹּ֖ל דָּבָ֣ר רָ֑ע כִּ֧י תוֹעֲבַ֛ת
יְהוָ֥ה אֱלֹהֶ֖יךָ הֽוּא׃ ס

THREE WORSHIP PROHIBITIONS
(16:21–17:1)

21. sacred post A standing wooden object at a place of worship. Such objects seem to have been associated with Canaanite deities. Deuteronomy bans them from sanctuaries of the Lord because their presence might eventually lead the Israelites to blur the distinctions between Israelite and Canaanite religions.

any kind of pole Literally, "any treelike object," whether a natural or an artificial tree or a pole. This comprehensive ban prevents anyone from claiming that the prohibition covers only certain objects of this type, and that others are legitimate.

beside the altar . . . that you may make The prohibition applies not only to the chosen sanctuary but also to the many local altars that had been legitimate before the centralization of Israelite worship in Jerusalem.

22. Unadorned pillars, like sacred posts, once were regarded as monuments to, or residences of, God and considered legitimate in Israelite religion. Jacob erected one to the Lord at Bethel, Moses set up 12 pillars at Mount Sinai, and Joshua put up one in the sanctuary at Shechem. The distinction between legitimate and idolatrous pillars, however, apparently was too difficult to maintain, and eventually all pillars were outlawed.

---

tively pursue it (Heschel). This command also means to "pursue justice justly," for just goals can never be achieved by unjust means; the worthiest of goals will be rendered less worthy if we have to compromise justice to achieve it (Simḥah Bunem). Inspired by this verse, by the Torah's vision of a just society, and by a history of living as a mistreated minority, Jews repeatedly have been in the forefront of struggles for social justice.

21. One may not plant a tree alongside an altar to God, lest observers think we are worshiping the tree, as some pagans do. True, God is the creator of the natural world's beauty and order, and nature is an example of God's handiwork; but God is not coterminous with the natural world as some scientists and philosophers have believed. Nature may be beautiful, but it is not moral. Therefore, while we may admire nature, we are not to worship it. One commentator reminds us that Abraham planted trees at sites where he worshiped God (Gen. 21:33) and concludes that forms of worship that may have been appropriate at one time may not be appropriate for later generations (*Mei Ha-Shilo·aḥ*).

CHAPTER 17

1. The refusal to deify nature or be seduced by it should not lead us to conclude that we can sacrifice blemished or deformed animals on God's altar, on the theory that God is not concerned with physical beauty.

HALAKHAH L'MA·ASEH

16:20. Justice, justice This verse is the classical source of the Jewish tradition's demand that we advocate and practice both formal and distributive justice in our interpersonal relations and in society at large. That is, we must judge people using fair procedures (formal justice), and we must ensure that everyone gets at least the minimum of what is necessary to live (distributive justice). See the essay "Justice."

[2]If there is found among you, in one of
the settlements that the LORD your God is giving you, a man or woman who has affronted
the LORD your God and transgressed His
covenant—[3]turning to the worship of other
gods and bowing down to them, to the sun or
the moon or any of the heavenly host, something I never commanded—[4]and you have
been informed or have learned of it, then you
shall make a thorough inquiry. If it is true,
the fact is established, that abhorrent thing was
perpetrated in Israel, [5]you shall take the man
or the woman who did that wicked thing out
to the public place, and you shall stone them,
man or woman, to death.—[6]A person shall be
put to death only on the testimony of two or
more witnesses; he must not be put to death on
the testimony of a single witness.—[7]Let the
hands of the witnesses be the first against him
to put him to death, and the hands of the rest
of the people thereafter. Thus you will sweep
out evil from your midst.

[8]If a case is too baffling for you to decide, be

2 כִּֽי־יִמָּצֵ֤א בְקִרְבְּךָ֙ בְּאַחַ֣ד שְׁעָרֶ֔יךָ אֲשֶׁר־
יְהוָ֥ה אֱלֹהֶ֖יךָ נֹתֵ֣ן לָ֑ךְ אִ֣ישׁ אוֹ־אִשָּׁ֗ה
אֲשֶׁ֨ר יַעֲשֶׂ֥ה אֶת־הָרַ֛ע בְּעֵינֵ֥י יְהוָֽה־אֱלֹהֶ֖יךָ
לַעֲבֹ֥ר בְּרִיתֽוֹ׃ 3 וַיֵּ֗לֶךְ וַֽיַּעֲבֹד֙ אֱלֹהִ֣ים
אֲחֵרִ֔ים וַיִּשְׁתַּ֖חוּ לָהֶ֑ם וְלַשֶּׁ֣מֶשׁ ׀ א֣וֹ לַיָּרֵ֗חַ
א֛וֹ לְכָל־צְבָ֥א הַשָּׁמַ֖יִם אֲשֶׁ֥ר לֹא־צִוִּֽיתִי׃
4 וְהֻגַּד־לְךָ֖ וְשָׁמָ֑עְתָּ וְדָרַשְׁתָּ֣ הֵיטֵ֔ב וְהִנֵּ֤ה
אֱמֶת֙ נָכ֣וֹן הַדָּבָ֔ר נֶעֶשְׂתָ֛ה הַתּוֹעֵבָ֥ה הַזֹּ֖את
בְּיִשְׂרָאֵֽל׃ 5 וְהוֹצֵאתָ֣ אֶת־הָאִ֣ישׁ הַה֡וּא א֣וֹ
אֶת־הָאִשָּׁ֨ה הַהִ֜וא אֲשֶׁ֥ר עָשׂ֛וּ אֶת־הַדָּבָ֥ר
הָרָ֛ע הַזֶּה֙ אֶל־שְׁעָרֶ֔יךָ אֶת־הָאִ֕ישׁ א֖וֹ
אֶת־הָאִשָּׁ֑ה וּסְקַלְתָּ֥ם בָּאֲבָנִ֖ים וָמֵֽתוּ׃
6 עַל־פִּ֣י ׀ שְׁנַ֣יִם עֵדִ֗ים א֛וֹ שְׁלֹשָׁ֥ה עֵדִ֖ים
יוּמַ֣ת הַמֵּ֑ת לֹ֣א יוּמַ֔ת עַל־פִּ֖י עֵ֥ד אֶחָֽד׃
7 יַ֣ד הָעֵדִ֞ים תִּֽהְיֶה־בּ֤וֹ בָרִאשֹׁנָה֙ לַהֲמִית֔וֹ
וְיַ֥ד כָּל־הָעָ֖ם בָּאַחֲרֹנָ֑ה וּבִֽעַרְתָּ֥ הָרָ֖ע
מִקִּרְבֶּֽךָ׃ פ
8 כִּ֣י יִפָּלֵא֩ מִמְּךָ֨ דָבָ֜ר לַמִּשְׁפָּ֗ט בֵּֽין־דָּ֨ם ׀

PROSECUTION OF APOSTATES (17:2–7)

Worshiping gods violates the 1st commandment, the most fundamental rule of the Covenant. It is a crime that undermines the very existence of Israel as a nation, as reflected in its frequently stated punishment: destruction of the state and exile.

3. turning to the worship of other gods and bowing down to them The phrasing echoes the Decalogue: "you shall not bow down to [other gods] or serve them" (5:9).

to the sun or the moon or any of the heavenly host Heavenly bodies were worshiped in Syria and Canaan before the Israelites settled in Canaan. The practice became prevalent in Judah in the 7th century B.C.E., during the reign of King Manasseh, as a form of assimilation to the Assyrian-Aramean culture of the Assyrian Empire (see 2 Kings 21). Deuteronomy is the only book of the Torah to mention these practices.

5. See Comment to 13:11.

6. As a safeguard against dishonest or mistaken testimony, at least two witnesses are required. This applies to all types of cases, according to 19:15.

7. Let the hands of the witnesses be the first This requirement would impress on the witnesses that by their testimony they are in effect executing the accused. If their testimony is incorrect, initiating the stoning would make them murderers.

rest of the people The execution was performed by the people themselves; there were no appointed executioners.

HIGH COURT OF REFERRAL (vv. 8–13)

8. case is too baffling The judges in the local courts, addressed directly, are to bring such cases to the high court in the chosen place. This is not

HALAKHAH L'MA·ASEH

17:6. two . . . witnesses This verse is the source for Jewish law's requiring two witnesses for most public legal acts, such as witnessing documents of marriage. The Sages added many restrictions on who could be witnesses in capital cases as one way to make it virtually impossible to condemn someone to death (M Mak. 1:10).

לְדָ֣ם ׀ בֵּֽין־דִּ֨ין לְדִ֜ין וּבֵ֥ין נֶ֙גַע֙ לָנֶ֔גַע דִּבְרֵ֥י
רִיבֹ֖ת בִּשְׁעָרֶ֑יךָ וְקַמְתָּ֣ וְעָלִ֔יתָ אֶ֨ל־הַמָּק֔וֹם
אֲשֶׁ֥ר יִבְחַ֛ר יְהוָ֥ה אֱלֹהֶ֖יךָ בּֽוֹ׃ 9 וּבָאתָ֗
אֶל־הַכֹּהֲנִים֙ הַלְוִיִּ֔ם וְאֶל־הַשֹּׁפֵ֔ט אֲשֶׁ֥ר
יִהְיֶ֖ה בַּיָּמִ֣ים הָהֵ֑ם וְדָרַשְׁתָּ֙ וְהִגִּ֣ידוּ לְךָ֔ אֵ֖ת
דְּבַ֥ר הַמִּשְׁפָּֽט׃ 10 *וְעָשִׂ֗יתָ עַל־פִּ֤י הַדָּבָר֙
אֲשֶׁ֣ר יַגִּֽידוּ לְךָ֔ מִן־הַמָּק֣וֹם הַה֔וּא אֲשֶׁ֖ר
יִבְחַ֣ר יְהוָ֑ה וְשָׁמַרְתָּ֣ לַעֲשׂ֔וֹת כְּכֹ֖ל אֲשֶׁ֥ר
יוֹרֽוּךָ׃ 11 עַל־פִּ֨י הַתּוֹרָ֜ה אֲשֶׁ֣ר יוֹר֗וּךָ וְעַל־
הַמִּשְׁפָּ֛ט אֲשֶׁר־יֹאמְר֥וּ לְךָ֖ תַּעֲשֶׂ֑ה לֹ֣א
תָס֗וּר מִן־הַדָּבָ֛ר אֲשֶׁר־יַגִּ֥ידֽוּ לְךָ֖ יָמִ֥ין
וּשְׂמֹֽאל׃ 12 וְהָאִ֞ישׁ אֲשֶׁר־יַעֲשֶׂ֣ה בְזָד֗וֹן

v. 10. למערבאי חצי הספר בפסוקים

it a controversy over homicide, civil law, or
assault—matters of dispute in your courts—
you shall promptly repair to the place that the
LORD your God will have chosen, 9and appear
before the levitical priests, or the magistrate in
charge at the time, and present your problem.
When they have announced to you the verdict
in the case, 10you shall carry out the verdict that
is announced to you from that place that the
LORD chose, observing scrupulously all their instructions to you. 11You shall act in accordance
with the instructions given you and the ruling
handed down to you; you must not deviate from
the verdict that they announce to you either to
the right or to the left. 12Should a man act pre-

a court of appeals, but a court of referral for difficult cases.

homicide When the judge cannot decide whether a person accused of homicide is guilty or not or whether a homicide was intentional or accidental.

civil law Hebrew: *din* (case, lawsuit), here "civil or criminal law," including cases of damage or theft (see Exod. 22:6–14).

assault Refers to cases of physical injury (Exod. 21:22–27; Lev. 24:19–20).

dispute Litigation.

courts Literally, "gates." Refers to the local courts that met at city gates.

9. It is not clear whether the high court has one lay judge or more judges, whether it must always include both priests and lay judges, and whether or not all cases are heard by both types of judge acting together.

levitical priests This phrase and "the priests, sons of Levi" are Deuteronomy's standard way of referring to the priests, indicating that they are descended from Levi.

in charge at the time Priests and judges are described this way several times in Deuteronomy, perhaps to emphasize that the book is legislating for the future as well as the present.

present your problem Literally, "inquire (of the court)."

11. According to the Talmud, this verse not only refers to judicial verdicts but also serves as the warrant for the legislative authority of the *Sanhedrin* and its successors, the Sages. It empowered them to issue whatever laws and decrees they deemed necessary to uphold the Torah. This interpretation is as important in the development of Jewish law as Chief Justice John Marshall's assertion of the right of judicial review is in U.S. constitutional history.

12. a man Refers to one of the parties to the case in question, not to the judges.

---

9. the magistrate in charge at the time The authority—even if less prestigious or less knowledgeable than previous judges (*Sifrei*). A judge needs to know not only the law but also its context in the society "at the time." Only a judge living in today's world can understand how to apply the law today, even as only a religious leader living in today's world can understand the religious needs of people today.

12. With regard to judges, this punishment

HALAKHAH L'MA·ASEH

17:9. the magistrate in charge at the time The Sages, understanding "judge" as the literal meaning of the Hebrew word translated as "magistrate," explained that every generation requires a rabbinical court to apply Jewish law to that generation's particular circumstances (BT RH 25a–b). Guided by the CJLS, the local rabbi (as *mara d'atra,* literally, "teacher of the place") has this authority and fulfills this responsibility for Conservative Jews (see Exod. 18:21–22).

sumptuously and disregard the priest charged with serving there the LORD your God, or the magistrate, that man shall die. Thus you will sweep out evil from Israel: 13 all the people will hear and be afraid and will not act presumptuously again.

14 If, after you have entered the land that the LORD your God has assigned to you, and taken possession of it and settled in it, you decide, "I will set a king over me, as do all the nations about me," 15 you shall be free to set a king over yourself, one chosen by the LORD your God. Be sure to set as king over yourself one of your own people; you must not set a foreigner over you, one who is not your kinsman. 16 Moreover, he shall not keep many horses or send people back to

לְבִלְתִּי שְׁמֹעַ אֶל־הַכֹּהֵן הָעֹמֵד לְשָׁרֶת
שָׁם אֶת־יְהוָה אֱלֹהֶיךָ אוֹ אֶל־הַשֹּׁפֵט וּמֵת
הָאִישׁ הַהוּא וּבִעַרְתָּ הָרָע מִיִּשְׂרָאֵל׃
13 וְכָל־הָעָם יִשְׁמְעוּ וְיִרָאוּ וְלֹא יְזִידוּן
עוֹד׃ ס
שני 14 כִּי־תָבֹא אֶל־הָאָרֶץ אֲשֶׁר יְהוָה אֱלֹהֶיךָ
נֹתֵן לָךְ וִירִשְׁתָּהּ וְיָשַׁבְתָּה בָּהּ וְאָמַרְתָּ
אָשִׂימָה עָלַי מֶלֶךְ כְּכָל־הַגּוֹיִם אֲשֶׁר
סְבִיבֹתָי׃ 15 שׂוֹם תָּשִׂים עָלֶיךָ מֶלֶךְ אֲשֶׁר
יִבְחַר יְהוָה אֱלֹהֶיךָ בּוֹ מִקֶּרֶב אַחֶיךָ תָּשִׂים
עָלֶיךָ מֶלֶךְ לֹא תוּכַל לָתֵת עָלֶיךָ אִישׁ
נָכְרִי אֲשֶׁר לֹא־אָחִיךָ הוּא׃ 16 רַק לֹא־
יַרְבֶּה־לּוֹ סוּסִים וְלֹא־יָשִׁיב אֶת־הָעָם

the priest . . . or the magistrate Whoever announces the court's decision.

that man shall die Even though the case in question may not have been a capital case, disobeying the nation's highest tribunal threatens the entire social order and is dealt with severely as a deterrent.

THE KING (vv. 14–20)

The law about the king continues Deuteronomy's policy of limiting the power and prestige of human authorities. It says nothing about the king's authority or obeying him or about any governmental functions performed by him. The only positive responsibility that Deuteronomy assigns the king is copying and studying God's Teaching. The aim of this law is to limit the king's power and to emphasize that he is as much subject to God's law as are the people as a whole. These aspects of the law were influential in the development of western constitutional monarchy.

The view of the monarchy expressed here contrasts sharply with that of neighboring Mesopotamia, where the monarchy was seen as an institution created by the gods early in human history and indispensable for the welfare of society. The Mesopotamian king was the lawgiver; he was inspired by the gods with the wisdom to make laws, but the laws themselves were his. In neighboring Egypt, the king was believed to be a god; he was the law.

14. Most of the neighboring states had monarchies long before they came to Israel. When the people demanded that Samuel establish a monarchy, they stated that this would make them "like all the other nations" (1 Sam. 8:20). Deuteronomy, by mentioning only this motive for wanting a monarchy, characterizes the institution as unnecessary and unworthy.

15. The appointment of a king is optional. The monarchy is the only office so characterized.

one chosen by the LORD God's choice would be communicated by a prophet.

one of your own people No reason is given for requiring that the king not be a foreigner. It is likely that a foreigner would be objectionable because he would not be a loyal monotheistic worshiper of the Lord and might lead the people into apostasy.

16. many horses For cavalry and chariots.

---

applies only if a judge decides a case contrary to the prior ruling of the high court; but a judge who as a teacher advocates contrary to that ruling is not punished (M Sanh. 11:2).

14–15. This passage also can be read as mandatory. Commentators differ as to whether having a king is a *mitzvah* (obligation) or a concession to human frailty. Note that an Israelite king, unlike many other ancient kings, was not considered to be a god or of divine birth. He would be approved by God, and he would be a servant of the people and of God. The requirement that the king write (or have written for him) a scroll of the Torah (v. 18), symbolically makes the point that the king is not above the law. He is subject to the law.

Egypt to add to his horses, since the LORD has warned you, "You must not go back that way again." 17And he shall not have many wives, lest his heart go astray; nor shall he amass silver and gold to excess.

18When he is seated on his royal throne, he shall have a copy of this Teaching written for him on a scroll by the levitical priests. 19Let it remain with him and let him read in it all his life, so that he may learn to revere the LORD his God, to observe faithfully every word of this Teaching as well as these laws. 20Thus he will not act haughtily toward his fellows or deviate from the Instruction to the right or to the left, to the end that he and his descendants may reign long in the midst of Israel.

מִצְרַיְמָה לְמַעַן הַרְבּוֹת סוּס וַיהוָה אָמַר
לָכֶם לֹא תֹסִפוּן לָשׁוּב בַּדֶּרֶךְ הַזֶּה עוֹד׃
17 וְלֹא יַרְבֶּה־לּוֹ נָשִׁים וְלֹא יָסוּר לְבָבוֹ
וְכֶסֶף וְזָהָב לֹא יַרְבֶּה־לּוֹ מְאֹד׃
18 וְהָיָה כְשִׁבְתּוֹ עַל כִּסֵּא מַמְלַכְתּוֹ וְכָתַב
לוֹ אֶת־מִשְׁנֵה הַתּוֹרָה הַזֹּאת עַל־סֵפֶר
מִלִּפְנֵי הַכֹּהֲנִים הַלְוִיִּם׃ 19 וְהָיְתָה עִמּוֹ
וְקָרָא בוֹ כָּל־יְמֵי חַיָּיו לְמַעַן יִלְמַד לְיִרְאָה
אֶת־יְהוָה אֱלֹהָיו לִשְׁמֹר אֶת־כָּל־דִּבְרֵי
הַתּוֹרָה הַזֹּאת וְאֶת־הַחֻקִּים הָאֵלֶּה
לַעֲשֹׂתָם׃ 20 לְבִלְתִּי רוּם־לְבָבוֹ מֵאֶחָיו
וּלְבִלְתִּי סוּר מִן־הַמִּצְוָה יָמִין וּשְׂמֹאול*
לְמַעַן יַאֲרִיךְ יָמִים עַל־מַמְלַכְתּוֹ הוּא
וּבָנָיו בְּקֶרֶב יִשְׂרָאֵל׃ ס

18 The levitical priests, the whole tribe of

לישי **יח** לֹא־יִהְיֶה לַכֹּהֲנִים הַלְוִיִּם כָּל־

v. 20. מלא ו׳

send people back to Egypt Egypt was an exporter of horses.

17. many wives A large harem would distract the king from God's teachings as well as from performing his responsibilities.

18. when he is seated on his throne As soon as he takes the throne.

he shall have a copy of this Teaching written for him on a scroll by the levitical priests Better: "he shall write a copy of this Teaching for himself on a scroll from the one that is in the charge of the levitical priests." The king makes his copy from the original given to the priests by Moses after he finished writing it (31:9,24–26), including the laws of chapters 12–16.

copy Hebrew: *mishneh;* literally, "a double," "a copy." A later interpretation, current in Second Temple and Rabbinic times, was "repetition." On that basis, the phrase "a copy of [the] Teaching" (*mishnei ha-torah*) was taken to mean "repetition of the Torah." Because Deuteronomy repeats law and history known from the earlier books of the Torah, talmudic literature aptly uses *Mishnei Torah* as the name of this book. This is also the meaning of the Septuagint's translation of the phrase: *deuteronomion,* "a second Law," which became the Greek name of the book and, ultimately, led to its English name, "Deuteronomy."

19. let him read in it The king is to be a constitutional monarch, subject to the laws of God's Teaching (*torah*). Nothing expresses this more clearly than the requirement that he personally make a copy of the Teaching and study it constantly. The practice of kings studying texts, in some cases expressly written for their guidance, is known from elsewhere in the ancient world. A noteworthy feature of this concept in Deuteronomy is that the king must study the same law that is addressed to the entire people rather than one applicable to himself alone.

to revere . . . to observe The two aims of studying the Torah are to inculcate reverence for God and to learn how to fulfill His commandments properly.

20. not act haughtily toward his fellows That is, so that he will not oppress them or engage in the excesses forbidden in verses 16–17.

fellows Literally, "brothers." This underscores the essential equality of the king and the other citizens. He is not their master.

or deviate from the Instruction That is, violate God's laws and worship other gods.

ENDOWMENTS OF THE CLERGY (18:1–8)

Deuteronomy differs significantly from the earlier books of the Torah with regard to who may be

שֵׁבֶט לֵוִי חֵלֶק וְנַחֲלָה עִם־יִשְׂרָאֵל אִשֵּׁי
יְהוָה וְנַחֲלָתוֹ יֹאכֵלוּן׃ 2 וְנַחֲלָה לֹא־
יִהְיֶה־לּוֹ בְּקֶרֶב אֶחָיו יְהוָה הוּא נַחֲלָתוֹ
כַּאֲשֶׁר דִּבֶּר־לוֹ׃ ס
3 וְזֶה יִהְיֶה מִשְׁפַּט הַכֹּהֲנִים מֵאֵת הָעָם
מֵאֵת זֹבְחֵי הַזֶּבַח אִם־שׁוֹר אִם־שֶׂה וְנָתַן
לַכֹּהֵן הַזְּרֹעַ וְהַלְּחָיַיִם וְהַקֵּבָה׃ 4 רֵאשִׁית
דְּגָנְךָ תִּירֹשְׁךָ וְיִצְהָרֶךָ וְרֵאשִׁית גֵּז צֹאנְךָ
תִּתֶּן־לּוֹ׃ 5 כִּי בוֹ בָּחַר יְהוָה אֱלֹהֶיךָ
מִכָּל־שְׁבָטֶיךָ לַעֲמֹד לְשָׁרֵת בְּשֵׁם־יְהוָה
הוּא וּבָנָיו כָּל־הַיָּמִים׃ ס

רביעי 6 וְכִי־יָבֹא הַלֵּוִי מֵאַחַד שְׁעָרֶיךָ מִכָּל־
יִשְׂרָאֵל אֲשֶׁר־הוּא גָּר שָׁם וּבָא בְּכָל־
אַוַּת נַפְשׁוֹ אֶל־הַמָּקוֹם אֲשֶׁר־יִבְחַר

Levi, shall have no territorial portion with Israel. They shall live only off the LORD's gifts as their portion, 2and shall have no portion among their brother tribes: the LORD is their portion, as He promised them.

3This then shall be the priests' due from the people: Everyone who offers a sacrifice, whether an ox or a sheep, must give the shoulder, the cheeks, and the stomach to the priest. 4You shall also give him the first fruits of your new grain and wine and oil, and the first shearing of your sheep. 5For the LORD your God has chosen him and his descendants, out of all your tribes, to be in attendance for service in the name of the LORD for all time.

6If a Levite would go, from any of the settlements throughout Israel where he has been residing, to the place that the LORD has chosen,

a priest and what the public is required to give the priests (see Lev. 7:28–36; Num. 18:9). It considers not only descendants of Aaron but all Levites to be eligible for the priesthood, and it assigns them portions of sacrificial animals and first products that are different from those assigned by Leviticus and Numbers. Modern scholars view these differences as reflecting the practices of various periods and places in Israelite history.

1. See Comment to 17:9. Traditional commentators consider the absence of a distinction between priests and Levites in Deuteronomy more apparent than real. They assume that Moses takes the distinction for granted but does not repeat it because it would be superfluous and because he is not addressing the clergy, to whom the distinctions were most important, but the people as a whole.

territorial Refers to hereditary tribal territory, like the territories of the other tribes. Tribal territory is viewed here as a source of livelihood. The priests are given their sustenance directly so that they can devote their efforts to clerical duties instead of producing food and other necessities. Verses 3–5 make clear that only Levites serving as priests are supported in this way. That is why other Levites are indigent and depend on charity.

2. no portion No territorial portion, as in verse 1.

the LORD is their portion He is their source of livelihood, as the end of verse 1 explains.

3. The priests' due Refers to the portions legally assigned to the priests as their entitlement, namely, portions of the sacrifice of well-being and the first products of produce and shearing. Because some of these endowments are from sacrificial animals, it is clear that they are given only to Levites serving as priests, not to all Levites.

4. The priests also receive the first products of the farmer and the herdsman, namely, the first grain, wine, and oil, and the first wool. Giving the first products to the priests is tantamount to giving them to God (see Num. 18:12–13). The endowments—food, drink, oil, and material for clothing—are often mentioned in ancient Near Eastern legal texts as the basic necessities that people supported by others must receive.

5. to be in attendance To minister to the Lord by offering sacrifices and by pronouncing blessings in His name.

6. Only Levites serving as priests receive the endowments listed in verses 3–5. Following the restriction of sacrifice to the chosen place, Levites living elsewhere would be unable to serve as priests and would therefore be cut off from their livelihood. This text remedies this situation by providing that any Levite who wishes to go to the chosen sanctuary and serve as a priest there is entitled to do so and to share in the endowments.

he may do so whenever he pleases. 7He may serve in the name of the LORD his God like all his fellow Levites who are there in attendance before the LORD. 8They shall receive equal shares of the dues, without regard to personal gifts or patrimonies.

9When you enter the land that the LORD your God is giving you, you shall not learn to imitate the abhorrent practices of those nations. 10Let no one be found among you who consigns his son or daughter to the fire, or who is an augur, a soothsayer, a diviner, a sorcerer, 11one who casts spells, or one who consults ghosts or familiar spirits, or one who inquires of the dead. 12For anyone who does such things is abhorrent to the LORD, and it is because of these abhorrent things that the LORD your God is dispossessing them before you. 13You must be wholehearted with the LORD your God. 14Those nations that you are about to dispossess do indeed resort to soothsayers and augurs; to you, however, the LORD your God has not assigned the like.

יְהוָה׃ 7 וְשֵׁרֵת בְּשֵׁם יְהוָה אֱלֹהָיו כְּכָל־
אֶחָיו הַלְוִיִּם הָעֹמְדִים שָׁם לִפְנֵי יְהוָה׃
8 חֵלֶק כְּחֵלֶק יֹאכֵלוּ לְבַד מִמְכָּרָיו עַל־
הָאָבוֹת׃ ס

9 כִּי אַתָּה בָּא אֶל־הָאָרֶץ אֲשֶׁר־יְהוָה
אֱלֹהֶיךָ נֹתֵן לָךְ לֹא־תִלְמַד לַעֲשׂוֹת
כְּתוֹעֲבֹת הַגּוֹיִם הָהֵם׃ 10 לֹא־יִמָּצֵא בְךָ
מַעֲבִיר בְּנוֹ־וּבִתּוֹ בָּאֵשׁ קֹסֵם קְסָמִים
מְעוֹנֵן וּמְנַחֵשׁ וּמְכַשֵּׁף׃ 11 וְחֹבֵר חָבֶר
וְשֹׁאֵל אוֹב וְיִדְּעֹנִי וְדֹרֵשׁ אֶל־הַמֵּתִים׃
12 כִּי־תוֹעֲבַת יְהוָה כָּל־עֹשֵׂה אֵלֶּה וּבִגְלַל
הַתּוֹעֵבֹת הָאֵלֶּה יְהוָה אֱלֹהֶיךָ מוֹרִישׁ
אוֹתָם מִפָּנֶיךָ׃ 13 תָּמִים תִּהְיֶה עִם יְהוָה
אֱלֹהֶיךָ׃ ס 14 כִּי ׀ הַגּוֹיִם הָאֵלֶּה אֲשֶׁר חמישי
אַתָּה יוֹרֵשׁ אוֹתָם אֶל־מְעֹנְנִים וְאֶל־
קֹסְמִים יִשְׁמָעוּ וְאַתָּה לֹא כֵן נָתַן לְךָ
יְהוָה אֱלֹהֶיךָ׃

8. without regard to personal gifts or patrimonies The share of individual priests is not to be reduced even though they may have other resources.

THE PROPHET (vv. 9–22)

Prophets were among the leaders of society, along with priests; elders; and, in monarchic times, kings and royal officials. Some prophets, in fact, were influential members of the royal court. Deuteronomy strengthens the authority of the prophet by affirming that he or she is the successor of Moses and the only legitimate channel of communication with God. This is in contrast to what Deuteronomy states of the king, whose power it limits.

9. abhorrent practices Procedures for practicing magic or divination, invoking occult powers. Such procedures are objectionable because they seek to circumvent God.

10. consigns his son or daughter to the fire Literally, "passes his son or daughter through the fire." Refers either to child sacrifice or to a nonlethal ceremony, such as fire-walking while carrying a child.

an augur, a soothsayer, a diviner These individuals practice techniques as diverse as belomancy (interpreting the way arrows fall when shaken out of a quiver) and hepatoscopy (interpreting the configurations of the liver of a sacrificial animal).

11. one who casts spells A practitioner of magic, like a sorcerer in verse 10.

one who consults ghosts . . . one who inquires of the dead These are mediums, practitioners of necromancy, who act on the assumption that the spirits of the dead know hidden things and the future and can reveal them to those who know how to contact them.

12. abhorrent to the LORD It is because of such detestable practices that God is driving out the Canaanites.

13. wholehearted Undivided in your loyalty.

HALAKHAH L'MA·ASEH

18:10. an augur, a soothsayer, a diviner, a sorcerer The Torah prohibits such occult sciences as fortune-telling and satanism (BT Sanh. 65a). Magic for purposes of entertainment is permitted.

15The LORD your God will raise up for you
a prophet from among your own people, like
myself; him you shall heed. 16This is just what
you asked of the LORD your God at Horeb, on
the day of the Assembly, saying, "Let me not
hear the voice of the LORD my God any longer
or see this wondrous fire any more, lest I die."
17Whereupon the LORD said to me, "They have
done well in speaking thus. 18I will raise up a
prophet for them from among their own people, like yourself: I will put My words in his
mouth and he will speak to them all that I command him; 19and if anybody fails to heed the
words he speaks in My name, I Myself will call
him to account. 20But any prophet who presumes to speak in My name an oracle that I did
not command him to utter, or who speaks in
the name of other gods—that prophet shall

15 נָבִ֨יא מִקִּרְבְּךָ֤ מֵאַחֶ֙יךָ֙ כָּמֹ֔נִי יָקִ֥ים לְךָ֖
יְהוָ֣ה אֱלֹהֶ֑יךָ אֵלָ֖יו תִּשְׁמָעֽוּן׃ 16 כְּכֹ֨ל
אֲשֶׁר־שָׁאַ֜לְתָּ מֵעִ֨ם יְהוָ֤ה אֱלֹהֶ֙יךָ֙ בְּחֹרֵ֔ב
בְּי֥וֹם הַקָּהָ֖ל לֵאמֹ֑ר לֹ֣א אֹסֵ֗ף לִשְׁמֹ֙עַ֙
אֶת־קוֹל֙ יְהוָ֣ה אֱלֹהָ֔י וְאֶת־הָאֵ֨שׁ הַגְּדֹלָ֧ה
הַזֹּ֛את לֹֽא־אֶרְאֶ֥ה ע֖וֹד וְלֹ֥א אָמֽוּת׃
17 וַיֹּ֥אמֶר יְהוָ֖ה אֵלָ֑י הֵיטִ֖יבוּ אֲשֶׁ֥ר דִּבֵּֽרוּ׃
18 נָבִ֨יא אָקִ֥ים לָהֶ֛ם מִקֶּ֥רֶב אֲחֵיהֶ֖ם כָּמ֑וֹךָ
וְנָתַתִּ֤י דְבָרַי֙ בְּפִ֔יו וְדִבֶּ֣ר אֲלֵיהֶ֔ם אֵ֖ת
כָּל־אֲשֶׁ֥ר אֲצַוֶּֽנּוּ׃ 19 וְהָיָ֗ה הָאִישׁ֙ אֲשֶׁ֤ר
לֹֽא־יִשְׁמַע֙ אֶל־דְּבָרַ֔י אֲשֶׁ֥ר יְדַבֵּ֖ר בִּשְׁמִ֑י
אָנֹכִ֖י אֶדְרֹ֥שׁ מֵעִמּֽוֹ׃ 20 אַ֣ךְ הַנָּבִ֡יא אֲשֶׁ֣ר
יָזִיד֩ לְדַבֵּ֨ר דָּבָ֜ר בִּשְׁמִ֗י אֵ֣ת אֲשֶׁ֤ר לֹֽא־
צִוִּיתִיו֙ לְדַבֵּ֔ר וַאֲשֶׁ֣ר יְדַבֵּ֔ר בְּשֵׁ֖ם אֱלֹהִ֣ים

15. This is the continuation of verse 14, indicating that Israelites are to turn to prophets for the services that pagans seek from diviners and magicians. Because prophets are raised up by God, who will put His word in their mouths, they are His agents. By turning to them one turns to God.

prophet . . . like myself No future prophet would ever be enough "like" Moses to be his equal. The comparison here refers only to the prophetic role that Moses played as God's spokesman.

16. The people's words at Horeb are quoted in a paraphrase from 5:22. Only the first words of the people are quoted. This method of quotation (common in the Midrash) presumes that the listeners or the readers are intimately familiar with the text and will fill in the rest.

18. I will raise up a prophet This statement by God is not found in chapter 5. The text must regard it either as a free paraphrase of 5:25–28, or as something additional that God said to Moses at the time.

all that I command him The prophet's primary role is as God's messenger and spokesman, communicating God's will in all matters. He or she is, in essence, the envoy through whom God, the divine king, governs Israel. As such, prophets play a major role in the religious, domestic, and political life of the nation.

19. if anybody fails to heed This declaration establishes the prophet as the highest authority in the land, higher even than the king, about whose orders no similar declaration is made.

20. Two types of false prophecy are punishable by death.

to speak . . . an oracle that I did not command The Bible records two cases (1 Kings 22:17–28; Jer. 26) in which proceedings were initiated against prophets, possibly on the basis of this law. They were accused of falsely attributing their prophecies to God. In both cases they were exonerated.

shall die In Deuteronomy, this phrase refers to execution by humans, as in 17:12.

CHAPTER 18

13. Hence the use of astrology is prohibited (BT Pes. 113b).

15–22. God promises to show enduring concern for Israel by sending them prophets. In the Bible, a prophet is not someone who tells the future, stealing knowledge from God and sharing it with the people. (See the definition of a gentile prophet in vv. 10–11, "a soothsayer, a diviner, . . . one who casts spells, or . . . consults ghosts.") A prophet is someone who tells the truth. The prophet does not tell us what we want to know but rather tells us what God wants us to know, reminding us of our covenantal obligations. "The prophet is a person

die." 21And should you ask yourselves, "How
can we know that the oracle was not spoken by
the LORD?"—22if the prophet speaks in the
name of the LORD and the oracle does not come true, that oracle was not spoken by the LORD; the prophet has uttered it presumptuously: do not stand in dread of him.

אֲחֵרִ֑ים וּמֵ֖ת הַנָּבִ֥יא הַהֽוּא׃ 21 וְכִ֥י תֹאמַ֖ר
בִּלְבָבֶ֑ךָ אֵיכָה֙ נֵדַ֣ע אֶת־הַדָּבָ֔ר אֲשֶׁ֥ר לֹא־
דִבְּר֖וֹ יְהוָֽה׃ 22 אֲשֶׁ֨ר יְדַבֵּ֜ר הַנָּבִ֗יא בְּשֵׁ֣ם
יְהוָ֗ה וְלֹא־יִהְיֶ֤ה הַדָּבָר֙ וְלֹ֣א יָבֹ֔א ה֣וּא
הַדָּבָ֔ר אֲשֶׁ֥ר לֹא־דִבְּר֖וֹ יְהוָ֑ה בְּזָדוֹן֙ דִּבְּר֣וֹ
הַנָּבִ֔יא לֹ֥א תָג֖וּר מִמֶּֽנּוּ׃ ס

19 When the LORD your God has cut down the nations whose land the LORD your God is assigning to you, and you have dispossessed

יט כִּֽי־יַכְרִ֞ית יְהוָ֤ה אֱלֹהֶ֙יךָ֙ אֶת־
הַגּוֹיִ֕ם אֲשֶׁר֙ יְהוָ֣ה אֱלֹהֶ֔יךָ נֹתֵ֥ן לְךָ֖ אֶת־
אַרְצָ֑ם וִֽירִשְׁתָּ֕ם וְיָשַׁבְתָּ֥ בְעָרֵיהֶ֖ם

21. Because the people will rely on the instructions of prophets for vital matters, they need a criterion for identifying oracles that are not truly from God. Verse 22 answers that the false oracle is one that does not come true. The oracles in question must have included predictions foretelling the consequences of obeying or disobeying the prophet's instructions. The failure of a prediction to materialize would show the oracle to be false.

22. do not stand in dread of him Because the prophet is a fraud, you need not be afraid to punish him or her.

JUDICIAL AND MILITARY MATTERS (19:1–21:9)

THREE LAWS PERTAINING TO THE COURTS (19:1–21)

ASYLUM CITIES (vv. 1–13)

The designation of three cities as asylums serves to control the ancient practice of blood vengeance. In tribal societies, where there is no strong central authority, the kinship group is the primary defender of its members' lives. When a person is killed, his or her kinsmen are obliged to "redeem" the blood by slaying the killer. In its earliest form, blood vengeance was exacted whether or not the killing was intentional. Biblical law limits execution to cases of deliberate murder. Because victims' families may not recognize that a killing was accidental, asylum cities are established. Once safely inside an asylum city, the killer is protected until a court of law determines whether or not the act was intentional. This subject is also dealt with in Exod. 21:13–14 and Num. 35:9–34.

---

who sees the world with the eyes of God, who holds God and man in one thought at one time, at all times" (Heschel).

22. This passage intimates that a true prophet is one whose predictions come true, whereas the utterances of a false prophet do not. Centuries later, the prophet Jeremiah offered a more thoughtful distinction: If the message is painful for the prophet to utter and painful for the people to hear, it is likely authentically from God (Jer. 28:8–9). But if prophetic words are popularly received, we have reason to doubt them, and the prophet would have reason to doubt the authenticity of the message as well.

CHAPTER 19

Returning to the theme of administering justice, the Torah would have us judge the act of causing another's death not only by examining the deed but also by evaluating the motivation behind it. A deliberate murderer is punished severely because of the holiness of the life taken. An inadvertent manslayer is protected because his or her life is holy. Neḥama Leibowitz points out that in the Torah, the cities of refuge were established to protect the inadvertent manslayer from vengeance at the hands of the dead person's family. By the time of the Talmud, the lust for vengeance had been reduced, and the cities of refuge came to represent not protection but the punishment of exile (perhaps modeled after Cain, the first manslayer, who was punished with exile).

them and settled in their towns and homes, 2you shall set aside three cities in the land that the LORD your God is giving you to possess. 3You shall survey the distances, and divide into three parts the territory of the country that the LORD your God has allotted to you, so that any manslayer may have a place to flee to.—4Now this is the case of the manslayer who may flee there and live: one who has killed another unwittingly, without having been his enemy in the past. 5For instance, a man goes with his neighbor into a grove to cut wood; as his hand swings the ax to cut down a tree, the ax-head flies off the handle and strikes the other so that he dies. That man shall flee to one of these cities and live.—6Otherwise, when the distance is great, the blood-avenger, pursuing the manslayer in hot anger, may overtake him and kill him; yet he did not incur the death penalty, since he had never been the other's enemy. 7That is why I command you: set aside three cities.

8And when the LORD your God enlarges your territory, as He swore to your fathers, and gives

וּבְבָתֵּיהֶם׃ 2 שָׁלוֹשׁ עָרִים תַּבְדִּיל לָךְ
בְּתוֹךְ אַרְצְךָ אֲשֶׁר יְהוָה אֱלֹהֶיךָ נֹתֵן לְךָ
לְרִשְׁתָּהּ׃ 3 תָּכִין לְךָ הַדֶּרֶךְ וְשִׁלַּשְׁתָּ אֶת־
גְּבוּל אַרְצְךָ אֲשֶׁר יַנְחִילְךָ יְהוָה אֱלֹהֶיךָ
וְהָיָה לָנוּס שָׁמָּה כָּל־רֹצֵחַ׃ 4 וְזֶה דְּבַר
הָרֹצֵחַ אֲשֶׁר־יָנוּס שָׁמָּה וָחָי אֲשֶׁר יַכֶּה
אֶת־רֵעֵהוּ בִּבְלִי־דַעַת וְהוּא לֹא־שֹׂנֵא לוֹ
מִתְּמֹל שִׁלְשֹׁם׃ 5 וַאֲשֶׁר יָבֹא אֶת־רֵעֵהוּ
בַיַּעַר לַחְטֹב עֵצִים וְנִדְּחָה יָדוֹ בַגַּרְזֶן
לִכְרֹת הָעֵץ וְנָשַׁל הַבַּרְזֶל מִן־הָעֵץ וּמָצָא
אֶת־רֵעֵהוּ וָמֵת הוּא יָנוּס אֶל־אַחַת
הֶעָרִים־הָאֵלֶּה וָחָי׃ 6 פֶּן־יִרְדֹּף גֹּאֵל הַדָּם
אַחֲרֵי הָרֹצֵחַ כִּי־יֵחַם לְבָבוֹ וְהִשִּׂיגוֹ כִּי־
יִרְבֶּה הַדֶּרֶךְ וְהִכָּהוּ נָפֶשׁ וְלוֹ אֵין מִשְׁפַּט־
מָוֶת כִּי לֹא שֹׂנֵא הוּא לוֹ מִתְּמוֹל
שִׁלְשׁוֹם׃ 7 עַל־כֵּן אָנֹכִי מְצַוְּךָ לֵאמֹר שָׁלֹשׁ
עָרִים תַּבְדִּיל לָךְ׃ ס
8 וְאִם־יַרְחִיב יְהוָה אֱלֹהֶיךָ אֶת־גְּבֻלְךָ
כַּאֲשֶׁר נִשְׁבַּע לַאֲבֹתֶיךָ וְנָתַן לְךָ אֶת־כָּל־

Three Original Cities and Their Function (vv. 1–7)

2. three cities in the land Literally, "in the midst of the land." The three cities Moses set aside earlier are east of the Jordan and, therefore, not "in the midst" of the Promised Land (4:41–43). These three cities are Kedesh in the tribal territory of Naphtali, Shechem in Ephraim, and Hebron in Judah (Josh. 20:7).

3. survey the distances Measuring the distances will ensure that the cities are centrally located in the regions they serve.

4. and live That is, be granted protection in one of the cities. Deuteronomy does not state how long accidental killers stay in the asylum city. According to Num. 35:28, however, they must remain there until the death of the High Priest, after which they may leave.

6. blood-avenger Literally, "the redeemer of the blood," the relative who executes the killer. It was the ancient obligation of relatives to "redeem"—i.e., rectify—vital losses suffered by their kin when the latter were unable to do so. This included redeeming an enslaved kinsman, redeeming his real estate, marrying his widow, or receiving reparations due his estate.

Additional Cities (vv. 8–10)

8. enlarges your territory To Deuteronomy, the territory promised to the patriarchs reached as far as the Euphrates in the north (see 1:7–8, 11:24). The Book of Joshua states that Joshua conquered the land from the Negev in the south up to Mount Hermon in the north. This chapter indicates that conquest of the remaining territory, up to the Euphrates, was contingent on Israel's fulfilling God's commandments. According to Judg. 2:20–3:4, God eventually canceled the promise of the remaining territory because of Israel's disobedience.

---

4. in the past Literally, "yesterday or the day before," suggesting that a quarrel normally lasts three days. After that, people can be assumed to have overcome their conflict. If resentment lingers, it may be because the aggrieved party is deliberately prolonging it.

you all the land that He promised to give your
fathers—9if you faithfully observe all this Instruction that I enjoin upon you this day, to love
the LORD your God and to walk in His ways at
all times—then you shall add three more towns
to those three. 10Thus blood of the innocent will
not be shed, bringing bloodguilt upon you in
the land that the LORD your God is allotting
to you.

11If, however, a person who is the enemy of
another lies in wait for him and sets upon him
and strikes him a fatal blow and then flees to
one of these towns, 12the elders of his town shall
have him brought back from there and shall
hand him over to the blood-avenger to be put
to death; 13you must show him no pity. Thus
you will purge Israel of the blood of the innocent, and it will go well with you.

14You shall not move your countryman's

הָאָרֶץ אֲשֶׁר דִּבֶּר לָתֵת לַאֲבֹתֶיךָ׃ 9 כִּֽי־
תִשְׁמֹר אֶת־כָּל־הַמִּצְוָה הַזֹּאת לַעֲשֹׂתָהּ
אֲשֶׁר אָנֹכִי מְצַוְּךָ הַיּוֹם לְאַהֲבָה אֶת־יְהוָה
אֱלֹהֶיךָ וְלָלֶכֶת בִּדְרָכָיו כָּל־הַיָּמִים וְיָסַפְתָּ
לְךָ עוֹד שָׁלֹשׁ עָרִים עַל הַשָּׁלֹשׁ הָאֵלֶּה׃
10 וְלֹא יִשָּׁפֵךְ דָּם נָקִי בְּקֶרֶב אַרְצְךָ אֲשֶׁר
יְהוָה אֱלֹהֶיךָ נֹתֵן לְךָ נַחֲלָה וְהָיָה עָלֶיךָ
דָּמִים׃ ס
11 וְכִי־יִהְיֶה אִישׁ שֹׂנֵא לְרֵעֵהוּ וְאָרַב לוֹ
וְקָם עָלָיו וְהִכָּהוּ נֶפֶשׁ וָמֵת וְנָס אֶל־אַחַת
הֶעָרִים הָאֵל׃ 12 וְשָׁלְחוּ זִקְנֵי עִירוֹ וְלָקְחוּ
אֹתוֹ מִשָּׁם וְנָתְנוּ אֹתוֹ בְּיַד גֹּאֵל הַדָּם
וָמֵת׃ 13 לֹא־תָחוֹס עֵינְךָ עָלָיו וּבִעַרְתָּ
דַם־הַנָּקִי מִיִּשְׂרָאֵל וְטוֹב לָךְ׃ ס
ששי 14 לֹא תַסִּיג גְּבוּל רֵעֲךָ אֲשֶׁר גָּבְלוּ רִאשֹׁנִים

9. three more towns These are in addition to the first three and the three previously assigned in Transjordan (4:41–43). There would be a total of nine asylum cities.

10. blood of the innocent That is, the blood of the accidental killer, who does not deserve to die. If the community fails to prevent his or her blood from being shed, it will bear the bloodguilt created by the death. The shedding of innocent blood brings a palpable, virtually physical stain of guilt on the entire community (cf. vv. 13, 21:8–9). If it is not eradicated, the welfare of the community is threatened.

Intentional Murderers (vv. 11–13)

In the ancient world asylums rarely discriminated between the innocent and the guilty, the intentional and the accidental, but protected all who reached them. Felons and debtors enjoyed the sanctuary of temples in Greek cities. Thus biblical law instituted a revolutionary change in the concept of asylum. Intentional murderers may not claim protection in the asylum cities (see Exod. 21:14).

12. elders The heads of the leading families of the political units to which they belong, such as the nation, the tribe, the region, or the town. As such, they represent the entire population and direct its affairs, except when limited by higher authority. In Deuteronomy, town elders as a group, and not judges, are specified as the judicial body in cases involving family law. This includes cases of the rebellious son, the husband who accuses his new wife of not having been a virgin, and the man who refuses levirate marriage. The elders' role here may be because blood vengeance is a concern of the victim's family.

13. show him no pity Because life is infinitely precious, no economic value can be assigned to it. Hence, a murderer may not escape execution by paying for the victim (cf. Num. 35:31).

purge Israel of the blood of the innocent Here, the "innocent" is the murderer's victim. The shedding of innocent blood initiates guilt that befouls the entire community; it can be cleansed only by executing the murderer.

it will go well with you The community's welfare is ensured only if the guilt is removed. When the identity of the killer is not known, see 21:1–9.

BOUNDARY MARKERS (v. 14)

14. move Literally, "move back." You cannot

---

10. The Talmud derives from this verse that society is responsible for public safety, such as keeping the roads in a state of repair (BT MK 5a).

landmarks, set up by previous generations, in the property that will be allotted to you in the land that the LORD your God is giving you to possess.

¹⁵A single witness may not validate against a person any guilt or blame for any offense that may be committed; a case can be valid only on the testimony of two witnesses or more. ¹⁶If a man appears against another to testify maliciously and gives false testimony against him, ¹⁷the two parties to the dispute shall appear before the LORD, before the priests or magistrates in authority at the time, ¹⁸and the magistrates shall make a thorough investigation. If the man who testified is a false witness, if he has testified falsely against his fellow, ¹⁹you shall do to him as he schemed to do to his fellow. Thus you will

בְּנַחֲלָתְךָ֙ אֲשֶׁ֣ר תִּנְחַ֔ל בָּאָ֕רֶץ אֲשֶׁר֙ יְהֹוָ֣ה
אֱלֹהֶ֔יךָ נֹתֵ֥ן לְךָ֖ לְרִשְׁתָּֽהּ׃ ס
15 לֹא־יָק֣וּם עֵ֣ד אֶחָ֗ד בְּאִישׁ֙ לְכׇל־עָוֺן֙
וּלְכׇל־חַטָּ֔את בְּכׇל־חֵ֖טְא אֲשֶׁ֣ר יֶחֱטָ֑א
עַל־פִּ֣י ׀ שְׁנֵ֣י עֵדִ֗ים א֛וֹ עַל־פִּ֥י שְׁלֹשָֽׁה־
עֵדִ֖ים יָק֥וּם דָּבָֽר׃ 16 כִּֽי־יָק֥וּם עֵד־חָמָ֖ס
בְּאִ֑ישׁ לַעֲנ֥וֹת בּ֖וֹ סָרָֽה׃ 17 וְעָמְד֧וּ שְׁנֵֽי־
הָאֲנָשִׁ֛ים אֲשֶׁר־לָהֶ֥ם הָרִ֖יב לִפְנֵ֣י יְהֹוָ֑ה
לִפְנֵ֤י הַכֹּֽהֲנִים֙ וְהַשֹּׁ֣פְטִ֔ים אֲשֶׁ֥ר יִהְי֖וּ
בַּיָּמִ֥ים הָהֵֽם׃ 18 וְדָרְשׁ֥וּ הַשֹּׁפְטִ֖ים הֵיטֵ֑ב
וְהִנֵּ֤ה עֵֽד־שֶׁ֙קֶר֙ הָעֵ֔ד שֶׁ֖קֶר עָנָ֥ה בְאָחִֽיו׃
19 וַעֲשִׂ֣יתֶם ל֔וֹ כַּאֲשֶׁ֥ר זָמַ֖ם לַעֲשׂ֣וֹת לְאָחִ֑יו

move a landmark into another's property to extend your own. This crime, most easily committed in secret, is regarded as a serious moral offense. One who commits it is cursed in 27:17.

landmarks   Objects, usually stones, marking property lines.

set up by previous generations   The fact that the boundaries were established by ancestors gave landowners a deep attachment to the land they inherited and made the inviolability of boundaries more than a matter of property rights.

WITNESSES   (vv. 15–21)

These two provisions are intended to prevent wrongful conviction on the basis of inadequate or false testimony. No conviction may be based on the testimony of a single witness, and a false witness is to receive the same punishment that the testimony would have brought on the accused.

15. any offense   Not only capital offenses, as 17:6 and Num. 35:30 prescribe.

16. If a man appears against another   Literally, "If a felonious witness appears against a man and gives false testimony against him."

17. two parties   The original litigants in the case.

before the LORD   This phrase often implies a local sanctuary, but it would be impossible for trials to be held at such sites because they were destroyed when sacrifice was abolished in the provinces (2 Kings 23) to enforce the centralization law of Deut. 12. Possibly, it refers not to the location of the trial but to the fact that judges are regarded as God's representatives and that He is with them when they adjudicate.

priests   These priests no doubt live in the town where the case is tried and have not moved to the central sanctuary. Otherwise, the text would have read, "in the place that the LORD your God will have chosen," as it invariably does when referring to something that takes place there (see, e.g., 17:8,10).

magistrates   The litigants' appearance before the judges is not a separate inquiry but part of the original trial mentioned in verse 16.

19.   The "law of punishment in kind" (Latin: *lex talionis*). By this means, the law strives to make the punishment fit the crime perfectly: Whatever

14.   Later Jewish law expanded this admonition against encroachment to include other types of misappropriation, such as copyright violations. The moving of landmarks (*hassagat g'vul*) came to mean any unfair competition that encroached on another's ability to earn a livelihood.

17. the two parties . . . shall appear   The Sages were so concerned about the equal treatment of litigants that they interpreted these words to mean that one party may not remain seated while the other is standing. Not even the appearance of favoring one party is permitted.

sweep out evil from your midst; [20]others will hear and be afraid, and such evil things will not again be done in your midst. [21]Nor must you show pity: life for life, eye for eye, tooth for tooth, hand for hand, foot for foot.

וּבִעַרְתָּ֥ הָרָ֖ע מִקִּרְבֶּֽךָ׃ 20 וְהַנִּשְׁאָרִ֖ים
יִשְׁמְע֣וּ וְיִרָ֑אוּ וְלֹֽא־יֹסִ֨פוּ לַעֲשׂ֜וֹת ע֗וֹד
כַּדָּבָ֥ר הָרָ֛ע הַזֶּ֖ה בְּקִרְבֶּֽךָ׃ 21 וְלֹ֥א תָח֖וֹס
עֵינֶ֑ךָ נֶ֣פֶשׁ בְּנֶ֗פֶשׁ עַ֤יִן בְּעַ֙יִן֙ שֵׁ֣ן בְּשֵׁ֔ן יָ֥ד
בְּיָ֖ד רֶ֥גֶל בְּרָֽגֶל׃ ס

20 When you take the field against your enemies, and see horses and chariots—forces larger than yours—have no fear of them, for the LORD your God, who brought you from the land

כ כִּֽי־תֵצֵ֨א לַמִּלְחָמָ֜ה עַל־אֹיְבֶ֗ךָ
וְֽרָאִ֜יתָ ס֤וּס וָרֶ֙כֶב֙ עַ֚ם רַ֣ב מִמְּךָ֔ לֹ֥א תִירָ֖א
מֵהֶ֑ם כִּֽי־יְהֹוָ֤ה אֱלֹהֶ֙יךָ֙ עִמָּ֔ךְ הַמַּֽעַלְךָ֖

penalty would befall the accused if wrongly convicted—whether execution, flogging, a fine, or some other punishment—is to be imposed on the false witness.

you shall do to him Addressed to the court, which executes punishment in the case of false testimony. The court is the aggrieved party because the witness has threatened its ability to judge correctly.

21. The penalty specified in verse 19 is here spelled out in the classic formula of the *lex talionis* (see Exod. 21:23–25, and Comments to those verses). Had the accused been charged with murder or maiming, the false witness would indeed pay with his or her life or eye, etc. (see Lev. 24:19–20). In other cases, however, the false witness would pay whatever other penalty would have been imposed on the accused.

In the oldest Mesopotamian laws, people who intentionally caused bodily injury were required to pay monetary indemnities. Later, they were punished in kind when the victim was a member of the upper class. In the Bible, punishment in kind applied for all classes of victim, except for slaves (see Exod. 21:26–27). The Talmud holds that monetary fines are to be imposed in all instances except for murder, an example of rabbinic rendering of the law that has the effect of making it more humane.

Nor must you show pity The court might be reluctant to impose punishment as severe as that which the law requires if the lie were discovered in time and no harm had befallen the slandered party.

LAWS ABOUT WARFARE (20:1–20)

The laws in this chapter refer to all wars, not only to the imminent conquest of the Land. Harsh as some of them are in the light of modern ideals (if not practice), they limit wanton destruction of life and property and are the oldest known rules of war regulating the treatment of conquered people and territory.

PREPARING THE ARMY (vv. 1–9)

Deuteronomy does not intend that the Israelites maintain a standing army, at least not one of any significant size. Instead, they are to have a civilian army, or militia, mobilized at times of need and commanded by officers appointed for the occasion. Reliance on a militia rather than a standing army for military needs is another example of Deuteronomy's dispersal of power among different officials.

1. horses and chariots Horse-drawn war chariots were essentially mobile platforms for launching arrows and spears. Their speed and maneuverability gave the army that possessed them a tremendous technological advantage. The Israelite foot soldiers who invaded the Promised Land encountered Canaanite chariots.

have no fear Chariotry has the psychological advantage of being able to surprise and shock the enemy. Moses reminds the people that they have

---

21. As in Exod. 21:24 and Lev. 24:20, the punishment is not meant to be taken literally; it is a concrete way of saying that wrongdoers should get the punishment they deserve, neither more nor less.

CHAPTER 20

Why do these assurances of military victory follow the discussion of administering justice? Only when the people Israel practice justice at

of Egypt, is with you. 2Before you join battle, the priest shall come forward and address the troops. 3He shall say to them, "Hear, O Israel! You are about to join battle with your enemy. Let not your courage falter. Do not be in fear, or in panic, or in dread of them. 4For it is the LORD your God who marches with you to do battle for you against your enemy, to bring you victory."

5Then the officials shall address the troops, as follows: "Is there anyone who has built a new house but has not dedicated it? Let him go back to his home, lest he die in battle and another dedicate it. 6Is there anyone who has planted a vineyard but has never harvested it? Let him go back to his home, lest he die in battle and another harvest it. 7Is there anyone who has paid the bride-price for a wife, but who has not yet married her? Let him go back to his home, lest he die in battle and another marry her." 8The officials shall go on addressing the troops and

מֵאֶ֥רֶץ מִצְרָֽיִם׃ 2 וְהָיָ֕ה כְּקָרָבְכֶ֖ם אֶל־
הַמִּלְחָמָ֑ה וְנִגַּ֥שׁ הַכֹּהֵ֖ן וְדִבֶּ֥ר אֶל־הָעָֽם׃
3 וְאָמַ֤ר אֲלֵהֶם֙ שְׁמַ֣ע יִשְׂרָאֵ֔ל אַתֶּ֨ם קְרֵבִ֥ים
הַיּ֛וֹם לַמִּלְחָמָ֖ה עַל־אֹיְבֵיכֶ֑ם אַל־יֵרַ֣ךְ
לְבַבְכֶ֗ם אַל־תִּֽירְא֧וּ וְאַֽל־תַּחְפְּז֛וּ וְאַל־
תַּעַרְצ֖וּ מִפְּנֵיהֶֽם׃ 4 כִּ֚י יְהוָ֣ה אֱלֹהֵיכֶ֔ם
הַהֹלֵ֖ךְ עִמָּכֶ֑ם לְהִלָּחֵ֥ם לָכֶ֛ם עִם־אֹיְבֵיכֶ֖ם
לְהוֹשִׁ֥יעַ אֶתְכֶֽם׃
5 וְדִבְּר֣וּ הַשֹּֽׁטְרִים֮ אֶל־הָעָ֣ם לֵאמֹר֒ מִֽי־
הָאִ֞ישׁ אֲשֶׁ֨ר בָּנָ֤ה בַֽיִת־חָדָשׁ֙ וְלֹ֣א חֲנָכ֔וֹ
יֵלֵ֖ךְ וְיָשֹׁ֣ב לְבֵית֑וֹ פֶּן־יָמוּת֙ בַּמִּלְחָמָ֔ה
וְאִ֥ישׁ אַחֵ֖ר יַחְנְכֶֽנּוּ׃ 6 וּמִֽי־הָאִ֞ישׁ אֲשֶׁר־
נָטַ֥ע כֶּ֙רֶם֙ וְלֹ֣א חִלְּל֔וֹ יֵלֵ֖ךְ וְיָשֹׁ֣ב לְבֵית֑וֹ
פֶּן־יָמוּת֙ בַּמִּלְחָמָ֔ה וְאִ֥ישׁ אַחֵ֖ר יְחַלְּלֶֽנּוּ׃
7 וּמִֽי־הָאִ֞ישׁ אֲשֶׁר־אֵרַ֤שׂ אִשָּׁה֙ וְלֹ֣א לְקָחָ֔הּ
יֵלֵ֖ךְ וְיָשֹׁ֣ב לְבֵית֑וֹ פֶּן־יָמוּת֙ בַּמִּלְחָמָ֔ה
וְאִ֥ישׁ אַחֵ֖ר יִקָּחֶֽנָּה׃ 8 וְיָסְפ֣וּ הַשֹּֽׁטְרִים֮
לְדַבֵּ֣ר אֶל־הָעָם֒ וְאָמְר֗וּ מִֽי־הָאִ֤ישׁ הַיָּרֵא֙

no cause to panic. That God is with the people Israel in battle is the fundamental principle in the biblical concept of war. Moses' reference to the Exodus reminds the people that Egypt's entire army, including its chariots and horsemen, were no match for God, who destroyed them all at the Sea of Reeds (Exod. 14–15).

2. Narratives about wars in the times of Moses, Saul, and David indicate that priests accompanied the army, carrying sacred utensils, trumpets, and the Ark, and consulting God by means of the oracle known as the Urim and Thummim. Deuteronomy, however, appears to expect fewer religious practices to accompany war. The only military role it assigns to the priests is found here, and nowhere does it indicate that the Ark is to accompany the army into battle.

3. The heart of the priest's message is that the troops should not have the slightest fear. He emphasizes this by expressing it in four different ways.

4. to bring you victory Literally, "to deliver you." To protect you from the enemy.

5. officials Civilian officials are to be responsible for mobilization, perhaps in each town; there is no mention of military officers until verse 9. Placing civilians in charge of mobilization prevents the military from ignoring the rights of those entitled to deferral.

7. paid the bride-price Literally, "betrothed," which was normally done by paying the bride-price to the fiancée's father (see 22:23,29). Once the bride-price is paid, the fiancée is considered legally married even though the consummation has not yet taken place.

lest he die in battle The tragedy of dying before consummating a marriage is also mentioned in Babylonian texts, one of which states that young men and women who were denied this pleasure grieve in the netherworld.

8. The first three deferrals were for the benefit of the individuals deferred. The last deferral is for the benefit of the army as a whole, lest the fear of a few spread to others.

---

home will they be victorious in battle (Tanḥ. 15).

5–9. Officials are to send home anyone whose death in battle would be especially unfortunate. But why do they not rely on God to prevent tragic death? Although God may work

say, "Is there anyone afraid and disheartened?
Let him go back to his home, lest the courage
of his comrades flag like his." 9When the officials
have finished addressing the troops, army commanders shall assume command of the troops.
10When you approach a town to attack it, you
shall offer it terms of peace. 11If it responds
peaceably and lets you in, all the people present
there shall serve you at forced labor. 12If it does
not surrender to you, but would join battle with
you, you shall lay siege to it; 13and when the
LORD your God delivers it into your hand, you
shall put all its males to the sword. 14You may,
however, take as your booty the women, the
children, the livestock, and everything in the
town—all its spoil—and enjoy the use of the

וְרַךְ הַלֵּבָב יֵלֵךְ וְיָשֹׁב לְבֵיתוֹ וְלֹא יִמַּס
אֶת־לְבַב אֶחָיו כִּלְבָבוֹ׃ 9 וְהָיָה כְּכַלֹּת
הַשֹּׁטְרִים לְדַבֵּר אֶל־הָעָם וּפָקְדוּ שָׂרֵי
צְבָאוֹת בְּרֹאשׁ הָעָם׃ ס
שביעי 10 כִּי־תִקְרַב אֶל־עִיר לְהִלָּחֵם עָלֶיהָ
וְקָרָאתָ אֵלֶיהָ לְשָׁלוֹם׃ 11 וְהָיָה אִם־שָׁלוֹם
תַּעַנְךָ וּפָתְחָה לָךְ וְהָיָה כָּל־הָעָם
הַנִּמְצָא־בָהּ יִהְיוּ לְךָ לָמַס וַעֲבָדוּךָ׃
12 וְאִם־לֹא תַשְׁלִים עִמָּךְ וְעָשְׂתָה עִמְּךָ
מִלְחָמָה וְצַרְתָּ עָלֶיהָ׃ 13 וּנְתָנָהּ יְהוָה
אֱלֹהֶיךָ בְּיָדֶךָ וְהִכִּיתָ אֶת־כָּל־זְכוּרָהּ לְפִי־
חָרֶב׃ 14 רַק הַנָּשִׁים וְהַטַּף וְהַבְּהֵמָה וְכֹל
אֲשֶׁר יִהְיֶה בָעִיר כָּל־שְׁלָלָהּ תָּבֹז לָךְ

disheartened Literally, "soft-hearted," meaning cowardly. Some commentators took this idiom to mean "tenderhearted," in the sense of compassionate, unable to harm others.

9. army commanders shall assume command of the troops Literally, "they [the officials or some higher authority] shall appoint army commanders at the head of the people." This implies that there are to be no permanent commanders, but only those appointed before each war. This procedure is compatible with the fact that the text deals with a mobilized militia, not a standing army. The commanders were chiefs of 1000s, 100s, 50s, and 10s.

DEFEATED POPULATIONS (vv. 10–18)

The General Rule (vv. 10–14)

Cities attacked by Israel are to be offered an opportunity to surrender. If they agree, their populations are not to be harmed. If they insist on battle and are defeated, only their men are to be killed. Women, children, and property are to be spared and taken captive.

10. offer it terms of peace Offer it *shalom,* here meaning terms of surrender, a promise to spare the city and its inhabitants if they agree to serve you. The same idiom appears in a letter from the ancient Near Eastern city of Mari: "when he had besieged that city, he offered it terms of submission [*salimam*]." In an Egyptian inscription, defeated princes of Canaan say *shalom* when submitting to the Pharaoh.

11. forced labor Hebrew: *mas,* a contingent of forced laborers working for the state. They were employed in agriculture and public works, such as construction. In monarchic times, David imposed labor on the Ammonites, and Solomon subjected the remaining Canaanites to labor.

12. A town that refuses to submit but chooses to fight, is dealt with more severely. The men, who constitute the city's military strength and its capacity for future rebellion, are killed. Women and children are taken as booty together with cattle and goods.

13. males Adult males. According to verse 14, children are spared.

---

miracles, protecting the righteous from harm, we may never force God's hand by demanding a miracle—putting good people in danger and expecting God to protect them. We cannot ignore our obligations to make the world a safer and more just place by depending on God to set things right.

10. Peace is always the preferred option. War may be necessary, unavoidable, and morally justified, but it can never be "good." In war, innocent people always die and lands are devastated.

13–18. The reader recoils from seeing these demands ascribed to God. It is not enough to be told that wars in ancient times were cruel and destructive (wars today are

spoil of your enemy, which the LORD your God
gives you.
15Thus you shall deal with all towns that lie
very far from you, towns that do not belong to
nations hereabout. 16In the towns of the latter
peoples, however, which the LORD your God is
giving you as a heritage, you shall not let a soul
remain alive. 17No, you must proscribe them—
the Hittites and the Amorites, the Canaanites
and the Perizzites, the Hivites and the
Jebusites—as the LORD your God has commanded you, 18lest they lead you into doing all
the abhorrent things that they have done for
their gods and you stand guilty before the LORD
your God.
19When in your war against a city you have
to besiege it a long time in order to capture it,
you must not destroy its trees, wielding the ax

וְאָכַלְתָּ֙ אֶת־שְׁלַ֣ל אֹיְבֶ֔יךָ אֲשֶׁ֥ר נָתַ֛ן יְהוָ֥ה
אֱלֹהֶ֖יךָ לָֽךְ׃
15 כֵּ֤ן תַּעֲשֶׂה֙ לְכָל־הֶ֣עָרִ֔ים הָרְחֹקֹ֥ת מִמְּךָ֖
מְאֹ֑ד אֲשֶׁ֛ר לֹא־מֵעָרֵ֥י הַגּוֹיִֽם־הָאֵ֖לֶּה הֵֽנָּה׃
16 רַ֗ק מֵעָרֵ֤י הָֽעַמִּים֙ הָאֵ֔לֶּה אֲשֶׁר֙ יְהוָ֣ה
אֱלֹהֶ֔יךָ נֹתֵ֥ן לְךָ֖ נַחֲלָ֑ה לֹ֥א תְחַיֶּ֖ה כָּל־
נְשָׁמָֽה׃ 17 כִּֽי־הַחֲרֵ֣ם תַּחֲרִימֵ֗ם הַֽחִתִּ֤י
וְהָֽאֱמֹרִי֙ הַכְּנַעֲנִ֣י וְהַפְּרִזִּ֔י הַחִוִּ֖י וְהַיְבוּסִ֑י
כַּאֲשֶׁ֥ר צִוְּךָ֖ יְהוָ֥ה אֱלֹהֶֽיךָ׃ 18 לְמַ֗עַן אֲשֶׁ֨ר
לֹא־יְלַמְּד֤וּ אֶתְכֶם֙ לַעֲשׂ֔וֹת כְּכֹל֙ תּֽוֹעֲבֹתָ֔ם
אֲשֶׁ֥ר עָשׂ֖וּ לֵאלֹהֵיהֶ֑ם וַחֲטָאתֶ֖ם לַיהוָ֥ה
אֱלֹהֵיכֶֽם׃ ס
19 כִּֽי־תָצ֣וּר אֶל־עִיר֩ יָמִ֨ים רַבִּ֜ים לְהִלָּחֵ֧ם
עָלֶ֣יהָ לְתָפְשָׂ֗הּ לֹא־תַשְׁחִ֤ית אֶת־עֵצָהּ֙

Exception: Cities In The Promised Land (vv. 15–18)

16. Cities in the Promised Land are an exception to the preceding rule. They are not to be offered the option of surrender, and their entire population is to be destroyed (see also 7:1–2, 16).

17. proscribe Hebrew: *haḥarem taḥarim;* translated in 7:2 as "doom to destruction." A similar case is found in the time of Hezekiah (1 Chron. 4:39–43). The laws of Deuteronomy reflect a theology of militancy against the threat of idolatry in general.

18. abhorrent things Ritual murder. Proscription is prompted by the Canaanites' abhorrent rites, not their beliefs. Child sacrifice is singled out as their most barbarous rite, in addition to a number of other practices (see 12:31 and 18:9–14). These are regarded as the Canaanites' own abominations, not part of the worship of celestial beings ordained by the Lord for the other nations (4:19).

TREES NEAR BESIEGED CITIES (vv. 19–20)

It was common practice in ancient warfare to destroy the enemy's fruit trees and fields. This weakened its economic potential and hampered its ability to fight again in the near future. It may also have been intended to pressure besieged cities into surrendering before they suffered loss of sustenance and long-term damage.

19. Trees, unlike human beings, are unable to protect themselves by taking refuge within the city.

---

hardly better). We might understand the passage in its context by focusing on verse 18, the Torah's abiding fear that these pagan nations will lead Israel astray.

19. you must not destroy its trees We are not to be so carried away in time of war that we forget the war will be over one day and people will have to live and feed their families in the place where battles are now raging. Beyond that, Maimonides writes: "Not only one who cuts down a fruit tree, but anyone who destroys household goods, tears clothing, demolishes a building, stops up a spring, or ruins food deliberately, violates the prohibition *bal tashḥit,* 'you must not destroy'" (MT Kings 6:10). Many legal systems, including the laws of the United States, permit people to destroy their own property. Jewish law teaches us that we are only the custodians, not the true owners, of our property.

HALAKHAH L'MA·ASEH

20:19–20. The concern for fruit trees in these verses provides one of the foundations for Jewish concern for the environment. We are commanded to preserve the environment even as we use it (see Gen. 2:15).

against them. You may eat of them, but you
must not cut them down. Are trees of the field
human to withdraw before you into the besieged city? 20Only trees that you know do not
yield food may be destroyed; you may cut them
down for constructing siegeworks against the
city that is waging war on you, until it has been
reduced.

לִנְדֹּחַ עָלָיו גַּרְזֶן כִּי מִמֶּנּוּ תֹאכֵל וְאֹתוֹ
לֹא תִכְרֹת כִּי הָאָדָם עֵץ הַשָּׂדֶה לָבֹא
מִפָּנֶיךָ בַּמָּצוֹר׃ 20 רַק עֵץ אֲשֶׁר־תֵּדַע
כִּי־לֹא־עֵץ מַאֲכָל הוּא אֹתוֹ תַשְׁחִית
וְכָרָתָּ וּבָנִיתָ מָצוֹר עַל־הָעִיר אֲשֶׁר־הִוא
עֹשָׂה עִמְּךָ מִלְחָמָה עַד רִדְתָּהּ׃ פ

21 If, in the land that the LORD your God
is assigning you to possess, someone slain is
found lying in the open, the identity of the slayer
not being known, 2your elders and magistrates
shall go out and measure the distances from

כא כִּי־יִמָּצֵא חָלָל בָּאֲדָמָה אֲשֶׁר
יְהוָה אֱלֹהֶיךָ נֹתֵן לְךָ לְרִשְׁתָּהּ נֹפֵל בַּשָּׂדֶה
לֹא נוֹדַע מִי הִכָּהוּ׃ 2 וְיָצְאוּ זְקֵנֶיךָ וְשֹׁפְטֶיךָ
וּמָדְדוּ אֶל־הֶעָרִים אֲשֶׁר סְבִיבֹת הֶחָלָל׃

20. siegeworks Hebrew: *matzor.* Here, "a siege wall," a series of fortifications built by an attacking army around a besieged city to blockade it so that it cannot be resupplied with food, weapons, and manpower. It is also a protection against raids by the city's defenders. Fruit trees, among others, were often used for this purpose. An Egyptian inscription describing the siege of Megiddo by Thutmose III (ca. 1490–1436 B.C.E.) relates how his commanders "measured the town, surrounded it with a ditch, and walled it up with the fresh timber from their [the city's] fruit trees."

UNSOLVED MURDER (21:1–9)

This law seeks to protect the nation from bloodguilt that would befall it because of an unpunished homicide. Numbers 35:33 states that "the land can have no expiation for blood that is shed on it, except by the blood of him who shed it." When the killer is not identified, making punishment impossible, the law provides for ritual removal of the bloodguilt.

1. Bloodguilt pollutes the land of Israel as well as the people.

someone slain A corpse bearing marks of human violence.

in the open The law focuses on a body found in the open because, given the size and life patterns of ancient towns, unsolved murders would most often take place outside of towns. Within a town, the victim's cries would usually be heard and the killer detected.

not being known Literally, "not having become known." The verb is in the past tense, implying that the ceremony is performed some time after the discovery of the body. An investigation was probably to be conducted first to determine whether anybody knew the identity of the killer.

2. Elders and judges from all over the region supervise the measuring to make sure that it is conducted fairly.

CHAPTER 21

1–9. Innocent blood shed on Israelite soil pollutes the Land and must be expiated. Maimonides suggests that the publicity will help apprehend the murderer. The Talmud understands the oath of the town elders as an insistence that they did not permit a climate of lawlessness and violence to exist in their community (BT Sot. 45b). The Midrash takes the oath to mean "in our community, no poor person goes unaided to the point of being driven to a life of crime." This ceremony, because of its puzzling elements, is listed in Rabbinic texts as a commandment for which there is no apparent reason, along with the goat sent to Azazel on the Day of Atonement and the "red" cow (Lev. 16; Num. 19). Rabbinic sources report that the ceremony was abolished in the 1st century C.E. because murder had become common and was committed openly.

the corpse to the nearby towns. 3The elders of
the town nearest to the corpse shall then take
a heifer which has never been worked, which
has never pulled in a yoke; 4and the elders of
that town shall bring the heifer down to an
everflowing wadi, which is not tilled or sown.
There, in the wadi, they shall break the heifer's
neck. 5The priests, sons of Levi, shall come forward; for the LORD your God has chosen them
to minister to Him and to pronounce blessing
in the name of the LORD, and every lawsuit and
case of assault is subject to their ruling. 6Then
all the elders of the town nearest to the corpse
shall wash their hands over the heifer whose
neck was broken in the wadi. 7And they shall
make this declaration: "Our hands did not shed
this blood, nor did our eyes see it done. 8Ab-
solve, O LORD, Your people Israel whom You
redeemed, and do not let guilt for the blood of
the innocent remain among Your people Israel." And they will be absolved of bloodguilt.
9Thus you will remove from your midst guilt
for the blood of the innocent, for you will be
doing what is right in the sight of the LORD.

3 וְהָיָה הָעִיר הַקְּרֹבָה אֶל־הֶחָלָל וְלָקְחוּ
זִקְנֵי הָעִיר הַהִוא עֶגְלַת בָּקָר אֲשֶׁר לֹא־
עֻבַּד בָּהּ אֲשֶׁר לֹא־מָשְׁכָה בְּעֹל׃ 4 וְהוֹרִדוּ
זִקְנֵי הָעִיר הַהִוא אֶת־הָעֶגְלָה אֶל־נַחַל
אֵיתָן אֲשֶׁר לֹא־יֵעָבֵד בּוֹ וְלֹא יִזָּרֵעַ וְעָרְפוּ־
שָׁם אֶת־הָעֶגְלָה בַּנָּחַל׃ 5 וְנִגְּשׁוּ הַכֹּהֲנִים
בְּנֵי לֵוִי כִּי בָם בָּחַר יְהוָה אֱלֹהֶיךָ לְשָׁרְתוֹ
וּלְבָרֵךְ בְּשֵׁם יְהוָה וְעַל־פִּיהֶם יִהְיֶה כָּל־
רִיב וְכָל־נָגַע׃ 6 וְכֹל זִקְנֵי הָעִיר הַהִוא
הַקְּרֹבִים אֶל־הֶחָלָל יִרְחֲצוּ אֶת־יְדֵיהֶם
עַל־הָעֶגְלָה הָעֲרוּפָה בַנָּחַל׃ 7 וְעָנוּ וְאָמְרוּ מפטיר
יָדֵינוּ לֹא שפכה שָׁפְכוּ אֶת־הַדָּם הַזֶּה
וְעֵינֵינוּ לֹא רָאוּ׃ 8 כַּפֵּר לְעַמְּךָ יִשְׂרָאֵל
אֲשֶׁר־פָּדִיתָ יְהוָה וְאַל־תִּתֵּן דָּם נָקִי בְּקֶרֶב
עַמְּךָ יִשְׂרָאֵל וְנִכַּפֵּר לָהֶם הַדָּם׃ 9 וְאַתָּה
תְּבַעֵר הַדָּם הַנָּקִי מִקִּרְבֶּךָ כִּי־תַעֲשֶׂה
הַיָּשָׁר בְּעֵינֵי יְהוָה׃ ס

3. The nearest town has the responsibility to purge the bloodguilt. In the ancient Near East, a town in or near which a crime took place was required to compensate the victim or the victim's survivors, because the perpetrator most likely came from there. Biblical law, on the other hand, presumes that it is impossible to pay for loss of life. Hence, it makes no provisions for indemnifying survivors. Its concern is with the jeopardy in which the nation is placed by the unrequited blood that was shed in its midst.

heifer A calf in its first or second year.

never been worked . . . never pulled in a yoke This gives the heifer a ritual character, although its slaughter is not actually a sacrifice.

4. an everflowing wadi This refers to a wadi with a perennial stream, as distinct from one that is full only in the rainy season.

which is not tilled or sown It has never been, or cannot be, tilled or sown.

5. priests Those who are present because of their normal duties. There is no indication of their exact role in the ceremony.

6. shall wash their hands Hands full of blood are a well-known symbol of guilt, and washing the hands a sign of innocence.

7. they shall make this declaration The elders, speaking for their town, declare their innocence.

this blood The blood of the murder victim or the bloodguilt caused by the murder.

nor did our eyes see it done Either "We do not know who the killer is (and are not protecting him)," or "We did not see it happen and stand idly by."

8. The final stage in the ceremony is the elders' prayer. Deuteronomy regards this as the crucial element in the ritual of absolution.

Your people Israel The twofold mention of the people emphasizes that the nation as a whole, not only the nearest city, requires absolution because of collective responsibility for bloodshed. Ibn Ezra remarked that the nation needs absolution because it neglected to keep the roads safe.

they will be absolved According to Jewish law, if the killer is later found, he must be executed even though the bloodguilt has been absolved by this ceremony.

הפטרה רביעית דנחמתא

FOURTH HAFTARAH OF CONSOLATION
HAFTARAH FOR SHOF'TIM

ISAIAH 51:12–52:12

(*Recite on the 4th* Shabbat *after the 9th of* Av, *coinciding with the reading of* Shof'tim. *On the Seven* Haftarot *of Consolation,* *see p. 1032.*)

Each part of this *haftarah*—a divine pronouncement of comfort to Zion and the nation—features a pattern of double proclamation. After God tells the people at the outset that "I, I am He who comforts you" (51:12), Jerusalem (also known as Zion) is exhorted to "Rouse, rouse" (51:17) herself from the travail of sorrow and to "Awake, awake" (52:1) to her new destiny of splendor. Finally, the exiles are called on to "Turn, turn away" (52:11) from Babylon and begin the journey to the homeland. These repetitions intensify the divine commands and spotlight the *haftarah*'s three themes of divine presence, national transformation, and return from exile.

God's own words ("I, I am He") introduce the first theme—divine presence, which brings consolation. The Lord comes to comfort the bereaved city (51:12) and to champion His people (v. 22), contending on their behalf against the nations. The divine presence is a reality, returning to Zion as king (52:7–8). God as the fulfiller of promises strikingly declares: "I, the One who promised, / Am now at hand [*hinneni*]" (52:6). Significantly, at crucial points in their lives Abraham (Gen. 22:1), Jacob (Gen. 31:11, 46:2), and Moses (Exod. 3:4) had responded to God with the same word *hinneni* (here I am). God's own use here of *hinneni* emphasizes divine readiness, sharpening the reality of imminent comfort and renewal. Further, it reinforces the earlier proclamation to Zion: "Behold [*hinnei*] your God" has come (Isa. 40:10). Once again Zion will be a place for God's indwelling Glory, a place where the nation shall rest in comfort from its sorrows.

The second recurrent theme—national transformation—is presented through exhortation and contrast. As noted above, the city is bidden to arouse itself from its stupor, for it no longer shall reel from the wrath of God, but shall "arise" from the dust (51:17, 52:2). Images of lowliness and degradation are evoked as memories (51:23), together with themes of bondage and captivity (52:2). By contrast, the people are called on to "loose their bonds" and "put on robes of majesty."

The third major theme is return from exile. Anticipating the nation's redemption from Babylon, God refers back to their first servitude in Egypt (52:4). The promised departure from Babylonian captivity becomes nothing less than a new Exodus. Indeed, it will supersede that ancient event (v. 12). The people are encouraged to perceive their liberation in historic terms and to trust that new events will partake of past glories.

RELATION OF THE *HAFTARAH* TO THE CALENDAR

The destruction of Zion was mourned less than five weeks ago on the fast of *Tish·ah b'Av.* At that time, the Book of Lamentations was recited, which raised an elegiac cry over Zion: "Far from me is any comforter / Who might revive my spirit; / My children are forlorn, / For the foe has prevailed" (Lam. 1:16). As if to counter this perception of absence and loss, a later prophet in the exile revealed God's word of presence—"I, I am He who comforts you!" (Isa. 51:12)—and announced a time of joy and redemption. This prophecy now evokes a sense of encouragement and immediacy that is still compelling.

51

¹²I, I am He who comforts you!

What ails you that you fear

Man who must die,

Mortals who fare like grass?

¹³You have forgotten the Lᴏʀᴅ your Maker,

Who stretched out the skies and made firm
the earth!

And you live all day in constant dread

Because of the rage of an oppressor

Who is aiming to cut [you] down.

Yet of what account is the rage of an oppressor?

¹⁴Quickly the crouching one is freed;

He is not cut down and slain,

And he shall not want for food.

¹⁵For I the Lᴏʀᴅ your God—

Who stir up the sea into roaring waves,

Whose name is Lᴏʀᴅ of Hosts—

¹⁶Have put My words in your mouth

And sheltered you with My hand;

I, who planted the skies and made firm the
earth,

Have said to Zion: You are My people!

¹⁷Rouse, rouse yourself!

Arise, O Jerusalem,

You who from the Lᴏʀᴅ's hand

Have drunk the cup of His wrath,

You who have drained to the dregs

The bowl, the cup of reeling!

¹⁸She has none to guide her

Of all the sons she bore;

None takes her by the hand,

נא

¹² אָנֹכִ֧י אָנֹכִ֛י ה֖וּא מְנַחֶמְכֶ֑ם

מִי־אַ֤תְּ וַתִּֽירְאִי֙

מֵאֱנ֣וֹשׁ יָמ֔וּת

וּמִבֶּן־אָדָ֖ם חָצִ֥יר יִנָּתֵֽן׃

¹³ וַתִּשְׁכַּ֞ח יְהוָ֣ה עֹשֶׂ֗ךָ

נוֹטֶ֤ה שָׁמַ֙יִם֙ וְיֹסֵ֣ד אָ֔רֶץ

וַתְּפַחֵ֣ד תָּמִ֣יד כָּל־הַיּ֗וֹם

מִפְּנֵי֙ חֲמַ֣ת הַמֵּצִ֔יק

כַּאֲשֶׁ֥ר כּוֹנֵ֖ן לְהַשְׁחִ֑ית

וְאַיֵּ֖ה חֲמַ֥ת הַמֵּצִֽיק׃

¹⁴ מִהַ֥ר צֹעֶ֖ה לְהִפָּתֵ֑חַ

וְלֹא־יָמ֣וּת לַשַּׁ֔חַת

וְלֹ֥א יֶחְסַ֖ר לַחְמֽוֹ׃

¹⁵ וְאָֽנֹכִי֙ יְהוָ֣ה אֱלֹהֶ֔יךָ

רֹגַ֣ע הַיָּ֔ם וַיֶּהֱמ֖וּ גַּלָּ֑יו

יְהוָ֥ה צְבָא֖וֹת שְׁמֽוֹ׃

¹⁶ וָאָשִׂ֤ים דְּבָרַי֙ בְּפִ֔יךָ

וּבְצֵ֥ל יָדִ֖י כִּסִּיתִ֑יךָ

לִנְטֹ֤עַ שָׁמַ֙יִם֙ וְלִיסֹ֣ד אָ֔רֶץ

וְלֵאמֹ֥ר לְצִיּ֖וֹן עַמִּי־אָֽתָּה׃ ס

¹⁷ הִתְעוֹרְרִ֤י הִֽתְעוֹרְרִי֙

ק֣וּמִי יְרוּשָׁלִַ֔ם

אֲשֶׁ֥ר שָׁתִ֛ית מִיַּ֥ד יְהוָ֖ה

אֶת־כּ֣וֹס חֲמָת֑וֹ

אֶת־קֻבַּ֜עַת כּ֧וֹס הַתַּרְעֵלָ֛ה

שָׁתִ֖ית מָצִֽית׃

¹⁸ אֵין־מְנַהֵ֣ל לָ֔הּ

מִכָּל־בָּנִ֖ים יָלָ֑דָה

וְאֵ֤ין מַחֲזִיק֙ בְּיָדָ֔הּ

Isaiah 51:12. who comforts you Hebrew:
m'naḥemkhem, which counterpoints the old lament (Lam. 1:17) that "Zion . . . has no one to
comfort her [*ein m'naḥem lah*]."

13. stretched out the skies Hebrew: *noteh
shamayim*. This image of the Creation is common
in Isaiah's rhetoric (see 40:22, 42:5, 44:24) and
elsewhere (Zech. 12:1; Ps. 104:2; Job 9:8). The

phrase also has a central position in the prayer
Aleinu.

16. You are My people A formula of adoption and covenant relationship (see Lev. 26:12;
Deut. 4:20; Jer. 7:23; Ezek. 36:28).

17. Rouse, rouse yourself! This image of Zion's renewal, along with that in 52:1–2 ("Awake,
awake . . . / Put on your robes of majesty, . . . /

Of all the sons she reared.
19These two things have befallen you:
Wrack and ruin—who can console you?
Famine and sword—how shall I comfort you?
20Your sons lie in a swoon
At the corner of every street—
Like an antelope caught in a net—
Drunk with the wrath of the LORD,
With the rebuke of your God.
21Therefore,
Listen to this, unhappy one,
Who are drunk, but not with wine!
22Thus said the LORD, your Lord,
Your God who champions His people:
Herewith I take from your hand
The cup of reeling,
The bowl, the cup of My wrath;
You shall never drink it again.
23I will put it in the hands of your tormentors,
Who have commanded you,
"Get down, that we may walk over you"—
So that you made your back like the ground,
Like a street for passersby.

מִכָּל־בָּנִים גִּדֵּלָה׃
19 שְׁתַּיִם הֵנָּה קֹרְאֹתַיִךְ
מִי יָנוּד לָךְ הַשֹּׁד וְהַשֶּׁבֶר
וְהָרָעָב וְהַחֶרֶב מִי אֲנַחֲמֵךְ׃
20 בָּנַיִךְ עֻלְּפוּ שָׁכְבוּ
בְּרֹאשׁ כָּל־חוּצוֹת
כְּתוֹא מִכְמָר
הַמְלֵאִים חֲמַת־יְהוָה
גַּעֲרַת אֱלֹהָיִךְ׃
21 לָכֵן
שִׁמְעִי־נָא זֹאת עֲנִיָּה
וּשְׁכֻרַת וְלֹא מִיָּיִן׃ ס
22 כֹּה־אָמַר אֲדֹנַיִךְ יְהוָה
וֵאלֹהַיִךְ יָרִיב עַמּוֹ
הִנֵּה לָקַחְתִּי מִיָּדֵךְ
אֶת־כּוֹס הַתַּרְעֵלָה
אֶת־קֻבַּעַת כּוֹס חֲמָתִי
לֹא־תוֹסִיפִי לִשְׁתּוֹתָהּ עוֹד׃
23 וְשַׂמְתִּיהָ בְּיַד־מוֹגַיִךְ
אֲשֶׁר־אָמְרוּ לְנַפְשֵׁךְ
שְׁחִי וְנַעֲבֹרָה
וַתָּשִׂימִי כָאָרֶץ גֵּוֵךְ
וְכַחוּץ לַעֹבְרִים׃ ס

52 Awake, awake, O Zion!
Clothe yourself in splendor;
Put on your robes of majesty,
Jerusalem, holy city!
For the uncircumcised and the impure
Shall never enter you again.

נב עוּרִי עוּרִי
לִבְשִׁי עֻזֵּךְ צִיּוֹן
לִבְשִׁי ׀ בִּגְדֵי תִפְאַרְתֵּךְ
יְרוּשָׁלַםִ עִיר הַקֹּדֶשׁ
כִּי לֹא יוֹסִיף יָבֹא־בָךְ עוֹד
עָרֵל וְטָמֵא׃

Arise, shake off the dust"), entered the liturgy through the *Shabbat* hymn "*L'kha Dodi.*" Written by Solomon ha-Levi Alkabetz (ca. 1540), it is the latest major liturgical element in the traditional prayer book.

Isaiah 52:1. Jerusalem, holy city! This transfer of priestly holiness to the city as a whole is a late development. Similarly, another post-exilic prophet refers to the land of Judah as "the holy land" (Zech. 2:16).

For the uncircumcised . . . / Shall never enter you again This prophecy effectively inverts the ancient lament: "She [Zion] has seen her Sanctuary / Invaded by nations / Which You have denied admission / Into Your community" (Lam. 1:10).

2Arise, shake off the dust,
Sit [on your throne], Jerusalem!
Loose the bonds from your neck,
O captive one, Fair Zion!

3For thus said the LORD:
You were sold for no price,
And shall be redeemed without money.
4For thus said the Lord GOD:
Of old, My people went down
To Egypt to sojourn there;
But Assyria has robbed them,
Giving nothing in return.
5What therefore do I gain here?
—declares the LORD—
For My people has been carried off for nothing,
Their mockers howl
—declares the LORD—
And constantly, unceasingly,
My name is reviled.
6Assuredly, My people shall learn My name,
Assuredly [they shall learn] on that day
That I, the One who promised,
Am now at hand.

7How welcome on the mountain
Are the footsteps of the herald
Announcing happiness,
Heralding good fortune,
Announcing victory,
Telling Zion, "Your God is King!"
8Hark!

2 הִתְנַעֲרִ֧י מֵעָפָ֛ר ק֥וּמִי
שְּׁבִ֖י יְרוּשָׁלִָ֑ם
התפתחו הִֽתְפַּתְּחִי֙ מוֹסְרֵ֣י צַוָּארֵ֔ךְ
שְׁבִיָּ֖ה בַּת־צִיּֽוֹן׃ ס

3 כִּֽי־כֹה֙ אָמַ֣ר יְהוָ֔ה
חִנָּ֖ם נִמְכַּרְתֶּ֑ם
וְלֹ֥א בְכֶ֖סֶף תִּגָּאֵֽלוּ׃
4 כִּ֣י כֹ֤ה אָמַר֙ אֲדֹנָ֣י יְהוִ֔ה
מִצְרַ֛יִם יָֽרַד־עַמִּ֥י בָרִאשֹׁנָ֖ה
לָג֣וּר שָׁ֑ם
וְאַשּׁ֖וּר
בְּאֶ֥פֶס עֲשָׁקֽוֹ׃
5 וְעַתָּ֤ה מי מַה־לִּי־פֹה֙
נְאֻם־יְהוָ֔ה
כִּֽי־לֻקַּ֥ח עַמִּ֖י חִנָּ֑ם
משלו מֹשְׁלָ֤יו יְהֵילִ֙ילוּ֙
נְאֻם־יְהוָ֔ה
וְתָמִ֥יד כָּל־הַיּ֖וֹם
שְׁמִ֥י מִנֹּאָֽץ׃
6 לָכֵ֛ן יֵדַ֥ע עַמִּ֖י שְׁמִ֑י
לָכֵן֙ בַּיּ֣וֹם הַה֔וּא
כִּֽי־אֲנִי־ה֥וּא הַֽמְדַבֵּ֖ר
הִנֵּֽנִי׃

7 מַה־נָּאו֨וּ עַל־הֶהָרִ֜ים
רַגְלֵ֣י מְבַשֵּׂ֗ר
מַשְׁמִ֧יעַ שָׁל֛וֹם מְבַשֵּׂ֥ר ט֖וֹב
מַשְׁמִ֣יעַ יְשׁוּעָ֑ה
אֹמֵ֥ר לְצִיּ֖וֹן
מָלַ֥ךְ אֱלֹהָֽיִךְ׃
8 ק֥וֹל צֹפַ֛יִךְ

6. My people shall learn My name When the prophecies of redemption are fulfilled, and God will be manifest as a redeemer (Ibn Ezra), the people shall know that He fulfills the words (Targum, Rashi) spoken in His name by His prophets (Radak). The expression is thus a variant of "And all mankind shall know / That I the LORD am your Savior, / the Mighty One of Jacob, your Redeemer" (49:26).

Your watchmen raise their voices,
As one they shout for joy;
For every eye shall behold
The LORD's return to Zion.
9 Raise a shout together,
O ruins of Jerusalem!
For the LORD will comfort His people,
Will redeem Jerusalem.
10 The LORD will bare His holy arm
In the sight of all the nations,
And the very ends of earth shall see
The victory of our God.
11 Turn, turn away, touch naught impure
As you depart from there;
Keep pure, as you go forth from there,
You who bear the vessels of the LORD!
12 For you will not depart in haste,
Nor will you leave in flight;
For the LORD is marching before you,
The God of Israel is your rear guard.

נָשְׂאוּ קוֹל
יַחְדָּו יְרַנֵּנוּ
כִּי עַיִן בְּעַיִן יִרְאוּ
בְּשׁוּב יְהוָה צִיּוֹן׃
9 פִּצְחוּ רַנְּנוּ יַחְדָּו
חָרְבוֹת יְרוּשָׁלָ‍ִם
כִּי־נִחַם יְהוָה עַמּוֹ
גָּאַל יְרוּשָׁלָ‍ִם׃
10 חָשַׂף יְהוָה אֶת־זְרוֹעַ קָדְשׁוֹ
לְעֵינֵי כָּל־הַגּוֹיִם
וְרָאוּ כָּל־אַפְסֵי־אָרֶץ
אֵת יְשׁוּעַת אֱלֹהֵינוּ׃ ס
11 סוּרוּ סוּרוּ צְאוּ מִשָּׁם
טָמֵא אַל־תִּגָּעוּ
צְאוּ מִתּוֹכָהּ הִבָּרוּ
נֹשְׂאֵי כְּלֵי יְהוָה׃
12 כִּי לֹא בְחִפָּזוֹן תֵּצֵאוּ
וּבִמְנוּסָה לֹא תֵלֵכוּן
כִּי־הֹלֵךְ לִפְנֵיכֶם יְהוָה
וּמְאַסִּפְכֶם אֱלֹהֵי יִשְׂרָאֵל׃ ס

8. every eye shall behold / The LORD's return An expression for the concrete experience of God's might (Targ. Jon., Abravanel) and guiding Presence (v. 12), echoing Num. 14:14 (Ibn Ezra).

10. The LORD will bare His holy arm This mythic image depicts divine power, as at the Creation and at the Exodus. (Arousal of "the divine arm" was invoked in 51:9–10, a few verses before the beginning of this *haftarah*.)

10When you take the field against your enemies, and the LORD your God delivers them into
your power and you take some of them captive,
11and you see among the captives a beautiful
woman and you desire her and would take her
to wife, 12you shall bring her into your house,
and she shall trim her hair, pare her nails, 13and
discard her captive's garb. She shall spend a
month's time in your house lamenting her father and mother; after that you may come to
her and possess her, and she shall be your wife.

10 כִּֽי־תֵצֵ֥א לַמִּלְחָמָ֖ה עַל־אֹיְבֶ֑יךָ וּנְתָנ֞וֹ
יְהוָ֧ה אֱלֹהֶ֛יךָ בְּיָדֶ֖ךָ וְשָׁבִ֥יתָ שִׁבְיֽוֹ׃
11 וְרָאִיתָ֙ בַּשִּׁבְיָ֔ה אֵ֖שֶׁת יְפַת־תֹּ֑אַר
וְחָשַׁקְתָּ֣ בָ֔הּ וְלָקַחְתָּ֥ לְךָ֖ לְאִשָּֽׁה׃
12 וַהֲבֵאתָ֖הּ אֶל־תּ֣וֹךְ בֵּיתֶ֑ךָ וְגִלְּחָה֙ אֶת־
רֹאשָׁ֔הּ וְעָשְׂתָ֖ה אֶת־צִפָּרְנֶֽיהָ׃ 13 וְהֵסִ֩ירָה֩
אֶת־שִׂמְלַ֨ת שִׁבְיָ֜הּ מֵעָלֶ֗יהָ וְיָֽשְׁבָה֙ בְּבֵיתֶ֔ךָ
וּבָכְתָ֛ה אֶת־אָבִ֥יהָ וְאֶת־אִמָּ֖הּ יֶ֣רַח יָמִ֑ים
וְאַ֨חַר כֵּ֜ן תָּב֣וֹא אֵלֶ֗יהָ וּבְעַלְתָּ֔הּ וְהָיְתָ֥ה

Moses' Second Discourse, Part 3: The Laws Given in Moab (*continued*)

MISCELLANEOUS LAWS (21:10–25:19)

The final laws in Deuteronomy deal with matters regarding individuals, their families, and their neighbors in contrast to the preceding laws, which concern public officials and the nation as a whole. Several laws in this section reflect Deuteronomy's consideration for the welfare of women.

THREE FAMILY LAWS (21:10–21)

MARRIAGE WITH A WOMAN CAPTURED IN WAR (vv. 10–14)

Most female captives in the ancient world became slaves, but in some cases a soldier found one whom he desired to take as a wife or concubine, a practice well known from Homeric Greece and early Arabia. In the light of 20:10–18, this law, which permits Israelite marriage with foreign women, must refer to non-Canaanite women, who are not regarded as posing the same threat to Israel's religious integrity as would Canaanites.

12. trim her hair, pare her nails Some traditional commentators see these acts as part of the woman's mourning for her family and countrymen. Others regard them as separate acts intended to make her unappealing so that her captor, who was attracted by her beauty, might change his mind about marrying a pagan woman.

13. month's time A customary period of mourning, also observed for Aaron and Moses (see Num. 20:29; Deut. 34:8), and part of Jewish mourning practice to this day.

lamenting her father and mother Whom she will never see again. The law recognizes her grief and insists on respect for it.

Throughout this *parashah,* with its diverse assemblage of laws (more than in any other *parashah*), one theme is prominent: the irreducible dignity and worth of a human being. Even the most marginal members of society, such as the criminal or the female war captive, are fashioned in the image of God and are to be treated accordingly.

10–21. These three cases are thematically related: A soldier in the heat of battle covets a female prisoner and, under the power of lust, marries her (vv. 10–14); in the end, he will lose feelings of affection for her and for the children he fathers with her (vv. 15–17), and those children will grow up disrespectful (vv. 18–21) of their parents (*Sifrei*).

10. against your enemies Plural: Not only your military opponent, but also your permanent enemy—the impulse within everyone to throw off the constraints of decency and give in to selfishness, lust, and rage. The Torah helps us win that second battle even as we strive to win the first (Rashi). Were the Torah to forbid soldiers from taking advantage of female prisoners, many would likely do it anyway. Therefore, the Torah accommodates human willfulness, striving to moderate rather than to eradicate the ugly side of human nature (BT Kid. 21b–22a).

14Then, should you no longer want her, you
must release her outright. You must not sell her
for money: since you had your will of her, you
must not enslave her.

לְךָ לְאִשָּׁה׃ 14 וְהָיָה אִם־לֹא חָפַצְתָּ בָּהּ
וְשִׁלַּחְתָּהּ לְנַפְשָׁהּ וּמָכֹר לֹא־תִמְכְּרֶנָּה
בַּכָּסֶף לֹא־תִתְעַמֵּר בָּהּ תַּחַת אֲשֶׁר
עִנִּיתָהּ׃ ס

15If a man has two wives, one loved and the
other unloved, and both the loved and the unloved have borne him sons, but the first-born
is the son of the unloved one—16when he wills
his property to his sons, he may not treat as
first-born the son of the loved one in disregard
of the son of the unloved one who is older. 17In-
stead, he must accept the first-born, the son of
the unloved one, and allot to him a double portion of all he possesses; since he is the first fruit
of his vigor, the birthright is his due.

15 כִּי־תִהְיֶיןָ לְאִישׁ שְׁתֵּי נָשִׁים הָאַחַת
אֲהוּבָה וְהָאַחַת שְׂנוּאָה וְיָלְדוּ־לוֹ בָנִים
הָאֲהוּבָה וְהַשְּׂנוּאָה וְהָיָה הַבֵּן הַבְּכוֹר
לַשְּׂנִיאָה׃ 16 וְהָיָה בְּיוֹם הַנְחִילוֹ אֶת־בָּנָיו
אֵת אֲשֶׁר־יִהְיֶה לוֹ לֹא יוּכַל לְבַכֵּר אֶת־
בֶּן־הָאֲהוּבָה עַל־פְּנֵי בֶן־הַשְּׂנוּאָה הַבְּכֹר׃
17 כִּי אֶת־הַבְּכֹר בֶּן־הַשְּׂנוּאָה יַכִּיר לָתֶת
לוֹ פִּי שְׁנַיִם בְּכֹל אֲשֶׁר־יִמָּצֵא לוֹ כִּי־הוּא
רֵאשִׁית אֹנוֹ לוֹ מִשְׁפַּט הַבְּכֹרָה׃ ס

18If a man has a wayward and defiant son, who
does not heed his father or mother and does not

18 כִּי־יִהְיֶה לְאִישׁ בֵּן סוֹרֵר וּמוֹרֶה אֵינֶנּוּ
שֹׁמֵעַ בְּקוֹל אָבִיו וּבְקוֹל אִמּוֹ וְיִסְּרוּ אֹתוֹ

14. Commencing a sexual relationship imposes obligations on the husband. If he should change his mind about the captive, he must relate to her as a free woman and release her.

THE RIGHT OF THE FIRSTBORN IN A POLYGAMOUS FAMILY (vv. 15–17)

In much of the ancient Near East, even before the time of the Torah, the firstborn son had the right to inherit a larger share of his father's estate than the other sons did. This law seeks to protect this right.

15. loved . . . unloved Hebrew: *ahuvah* and *s'nu·ah;* literally, "loved" and "hated." Here, they refer to the husband's favorite wife and to any other, whether she is unfavored, the object of indifference, or disliked.

the first-born The firstborn of the father, not necessarily that of the mother.

16. It appears that the father could divide his property among his sons as he wished, so long as he did not violate the following prescription.

17. double portion Two shares of the estate. In some parts of the ancient Near East, a man's estate was divided into shares equal to one more than the number of his sons. His chief heir received two of these shares and each of the others received one share.

first fruit of his vigor A common description of the firstborn, who is proof of his father's potency and a mark of future fertility.

PUNISHMENT OF AN INSUBORDINATE SON (vv. 18–21)

In the patriarchal period, the father's authority over his children was absolute, even to the point of his being able to have them executed for wrongdoing. This law respects the parents' right to discipline their son, but it prevents them from having him executed on their own authority. That

18. The Sages mitigated the harshness of this law by finding limitations to its applicability in a careful reading of its words. It would apply only in cases where both father and mother were present, where they shared a common set of values (spoke in the same voice, so that the father's message did not contradict or undermine the mother's). "Does not heed"

HALAKHAH L'MA·ASEH

21:18–21. wayward and defiant son The CJLS has prohibited all verbal and physical forms of domestic violence, including child abuse, while detailing the forms of parental discipline acceptable under Jewish law.

obey them even after they discipline him, 19his father and mother shall take hold of him and bring him out to the elders of his town at the public place of his community. 20They shall say to the elders of his town, "This son of ours is disloyal and defiant; he does not heed us. He is a glutton and a drunkard." 21Thereupon the men of his town shall stone him to death. Thus you will sweep out evil from your midst: all Israel will hear and be afraid.

22If a man is guilty of a capital offense and is put to death, and you impale him on a stake, 23you must not let his corpse remain on the stake

וְלֹא יִשְׁמַע אֲלֵיהֶם׃ 19 וְתָפְשׂוּ בוֹ אָבִיו
וְאִמּוֹ וְהוֹצִיאוּ אֹתוֹ אֶל־זִקְנֵי עִירוֹ וְאֶל־
שַׁעַר מְקֹמוֹ׃ 20 וְאָמְרוּ אֶל־זִקְנֵי עִירוֹ בְּנֵנוּ
זֶה סוֹרֵר וּמֹרֶה אֵינֶנּוּ שֹׁמֵעַ בְּקֹלֵנוּ זוֹלֵל
וְסֹבֵא׃ 21 וּרְגָמֻהוּ כָּל־אַנְשֵׁי עִירוֹ בָאֲבָנִים
וָמֵת וּבִעַרְתָּ הָרָע מִקִּרְבֶּךָ וְכָל־יִשְׂרָאֵל
יִשְׁמְעוּ וְיִרָאוּ׃ ס
שני 22 וְכִי־יִהְיֶה בְאִישׁ חֵטְא מִשְׁפַּט־מָוֶת
וְהוּמָת וְתָלִיתָ אֹתוֹ עַל־עֵץ׃ 23 לֹא־תָלִין

may be done only by the community on the authority of the elders. Ancient Near Eastern laws and documents also mention legal action by parents against misbehaving children. Such insubordination is a grave offense, because respect and obedience toward parents is regarded as the cornerstone of all order and authority, especially in a tribal, patriarchal society like ancient Israel.

18. father or mother The Torah requires equal respect for both.

even after they discipline him Indicates that the son is a repeated offender. "Discipline" here came to be understood as flogging, which was regarded as a proper and effective means of deterring sons from evil and self-destructive behavior.

19. The fact that both parents must agree deprives the father of unilateral authority even to prosecute his son. The requirement that the mother concur in the charge would also prevent a father from falsely charging his firstborn from an unfavored wife to deprive him of his inheritance rights.

20. a glutton and a drunkard Examples of insubordination.

21. thereupon The Hebrew prefix is simply a conjunction; it does not imply that an execution follows immediately upon the parents' declaration. First, the elders must conduct a hearing to determine whether the son is truly guilty and incorrigible or whether the parents are merely speaking out of frustration and anger. The elders might then seek to mediate between the parents and the son, and would probably order the son's execution only when all else failed.

the men of his town Unlike the normal practice, where the accusers initiate the stoning (17:7), here the parents are not said to participate. This may be out of sensitivity to their feelings, but it also indicates that they do not have the power of life and death over their children and, furthermore, that the people as a whole are outraged by insubordination, because it threatens the stability of the entire community.

THE BODY OF AN EXECUTED CRIMINAL
(vv. 22–23)

22. you impale him on a stake Literally, "you hang him on a tree" or "on wood." After execution, the body of a convicted criminal might be hung and exposed, either by impaling (the Assyrian practice) or by some other means of suspension. This verse does not require hanging or otherwise exposing the body, but merely reflects the existence of the practice. Whatever the text means, exposure served to degrade the criminal and warn others against similar conduct and was perhaps originally intended as well to deprive him of proper burial.

23. you must not let his corpse remain Denial of burial and exposure of the body to pred-

---

would imply that the parents tried to teach him and did not ignore or excuse his behavior. Others went even further, stating that this case, like that of the city of idolaters (Deut. 13:13), was only hypothetical; it was included in the Torah to emphasize the importance of children heeding their parents (BT Sanh. 71a). Ibn Ezra, taking the former view, adds that the son can be charged only if his parents' behavior has been exemplary. Otherwise, they have no right to bring accusations against him.

23. Even for people whose deeds earn them the ultimate punishment, that stigma ends

overnight, but must bury him the same day. For an impaled body is an affront to God: you shall not defile the land that the LORD your God is giving you to possess.

נִבְלָתוֹ עַל־הָעֵץ כִּי־קָבוֹר תִּקְבְּרֶנּוּ בַּיּוֹם
הַהוּא כִּי־קִלְלַת אֱלֹהִים תָּלוּי וְלֹא תְטַמֵּא
אֶת־אַדְמָתְךָ אֲשֶׁר יְהוָה אֱלֹהֶיךָ נֹתֵן לְךָ
נַחֲלָה: ס

22 If you see your fellow's ox or sheep
gone astray, do not ignore it; you must take it
back to your fellow. 2If your fellow does not
live near you or you do not know who he is,
you shall bring it home and it shall remain
with you until your fellow claims it; then you

כב לֹא־תִרְאֶה אֶת־שׁוֹר אָחִיךָ אוֹ
אֶת־שֵׂיוֹ נִדָּחִים וְהִתְעַלַּמְתָּ מֵהֶם הָשֵׁב
תְּשִׁיבֵם לְאָחִיךָ: 2 וְאִם־לֹא קָרוֹב אָחִיךָ
אֵלֶיךָ וְלֹא יְדַעְתּוֹ וַאֲסַפְתּוֹ אֶל־תּוֹךְ בֵּיתֶךָ
וְהָיָה עִמְּךָ עַד דְּרֹשׁ אָחִיךָ אֹתוֹ וַהֲשֵׁבֹתוֹ

ators are often mentioned in the Bible as a grievous curse, perhaps because of the folk belief that the unburied find no rest in the netherworld.

an affront to God Some explain that the criminal's body may not be maltreated because that would be an offense against God in whose image even the criminal was created. Others claim that *elohim* here does not mean "God" but "spirit," because God is almost never referred to as *elohim* in the laws of Deuteronomy. The clause then would mean that an impaled body is an affront to the spirit of the dead man.

you shall not defile the land A dead body is the primary source of ritual impurity in the Bible. If it were left to decompose, its parts eventually would be scattered by birds and animals, spreading the impurity.

MISCELLANEOUS DOMESTIC LAWS (22:1–12)

This section consists of nine laws, dealing mostly with property: domestic animals, clothing, houses, and vineyards.

RETURNING LOST ANIMALS (vv. 1–3)

This law and the one in verse 4 require assisting one's fellow who faces difficulty or possible economic loss in certain situations. They paraphrase and supplement Exod. 23:4–5.

1. your fellow's Literally, "your brother's." This reminder that the owner of the animal is one's kin counters the temptation to ignore the problem because it would be inconvenient or expensive to return, feed, or lift the animal.

gone astray Because much of the population owned livestock, and animals were used for transport, it was common to come upon strays.

2. you shall bring it home Literally, "bring it inside your house." In two-story dwellings, especially those in villages, the ground floor frequently served as a stable for cattle.

until your fellow claims it According to

---

with their death. In death the criminal's body must be treated with the same regard as any other dead body. To do otherwise would be to affront God, in whose image even the least worthy of us is fashioned. Jewish law calls for the burial of the body as soon as is practical, permitting the psychological work of mourning to begin.

HALAKHAH L'MA·ASEH

21:23. bury him the same day To avoid desecration of the dead, we bury the dead as soon after death as possible. To honor the dead, however, burial may be postponed to enable relatives to attend the funeral or to make it possible to donate the deceased's organs for transplant. It may also be postponed for a legally required autopsy. Burials do not take place on *Shabbat* or festival days.

22:1. take it back to your fellow Anyone who finds a lost object or animal without trying to return it to its owner is considered a thief. The finder must make a public announcement seeking the owner and is responsible for the object or animal until it is returned to its rightful owner. The claimant must be able to describe the item's identifying signs or provide evidence of ownership. Lacking identifying marks, lost property found in a public place or appearing to be abandoned (e.g., spilled fruit along a roadside) is considered ownerless (BT BM 25b,28a–b).

shall give it back to him. 3You shall do the same with his ass; you shall do the same with his garment; and so too shall you do with anything that your fellow loses and you find: you must not remain indifferent.

4If you see your fellow's ass or ox fallen on the road, do not ignore it; you must help him raise it.

5A woman must not put on man's apparel, nor shall a man wear woman's clothing; for whoever does these things is abhorrent to the LORD your God.

6If, along the road, you chance upon a bird's nest, in any tree or on the ground, with fledglings or eggs and the mother sitting over

לוֹ׃ 3 וְכֵן תַּעֲשֶׂה לַחֲמֹרוֹ וְכֵן תַּעֲשֶׂה
לְשִׂמְלָתוֹ וְכֵן תַּעֲשֶׂה לְכָל־אֲבֵדַת אָחִיךָ
אֲשֶׁר־תֹּאבַד מִמֶּנּוּ וּמְצָאתָהּ לֹא תוּכַל
לְהִתְעַלֵּם׃ ס
4 לֹא־תִרְאֶה אֶת־חֲמוֹר אָחִיךָ אוֹ שׁוֹרוֹ
נֹפְלִים בַּדֶּרֶךְ וְהִתְעַלַּמְתָּ מֵהֶם הָקֵם
תָּקִים עִמּוֹ׃ ס
5 לֹא־יִהְיֶה כְלִי־גֶבֶר עַל־אִשָּׁה וְלֹא־יִלְבַּשׁ
גֶּבֶר שִׂמְלַת אִשָּׁה כִּי תוֹעֲבַת יְהוָה אֱלֹהֶיךָ
כָּל־עֹשֵׂה אֵלֶּה׃ פ
6 כִּי יִקָּרֵא קַן־צִפּוֹר ׀ לְפָנֶיךָ בַּדֶּרֶךְ
בְּכָל־עֵץ ׀ אוֹ עַל־הָאָרֶץ אֶפְרֹחִים אוֹ

later Jewish law, the finder must publicize what was found, and the claimant must prove ownership by describing its identifying marks.

give it back to him The law had to anticipate attempts by people to keep what they found. Exod. 22:8 and Lev. 5:20–26 deal with circumstances in which finders refuse to return the property, claiming that it is theirs or that they do not have it. Ancient Near Eastern law collections deal with similar situations.

3. This additional list covers the full range of lost property summarized in Exod. 22:8.

ASSISTING WITH FALLEN ANIMALS (v. 4)

4. ass or ox These were the usual beasts of burden. According to Jewish law, the obligation applies to any animal.

fallen . . . raise it The situation is clarified by the wording in Exod. 23:5, "lying under its burden." A pack animal might collapse or lose its balance under its load. The fastest way to raise it was for two people to lift the load simultaneously, one on each side of the animal. Otherwise the load had to be unpacked and repacked, which also might require two people.

NOT WEARING CLOTHING OF THE OPPOSITE SEX (v. 5)

Some think that this commandment is directed against disguising oneself as a member of the opposite sex because this would facilitate mingling and hence fornication. Others think that this rule is directed against transvestism—which is abhorred either because it blurs the sexual differences that God created (see Gen. 1:27; cf. laws of forbidden mixtures in Deut 22:9–11), because it is a perverse means of sexual stimulation and homosexual role-playing, or because it was a part of certain pagan rites and magical practices.

NOT CAPTURING A MOTHER BIRD ALONG WITH HER YOUNG (vv. 6–7)

This law is similar to Lev. 22:28. Both laws inculcate human reverence for the parent–child relationship that obtains among animals as well.

6. the mother together with her young Hebrew: *em al banim;* a common expression for total, cruel extermination in war. It is used here to make the point that taking a mother bird with its offspring would mark one as ruthless.

CHAPTER 22

6–7. This is one of only two commandments in the Torah for which the reward of a long life is specified. The other is the commandment to honor one's parents (Exod. 20:12). The Talmud tells of a young boy whose father told him to climb a tree to fetch eggs and

---

HALAKHAH L'MA·ASEH

22:5. man's apparel The Torah's prohibition on cross-gender dressing (in which a man would try to pass as a woman or a woman as a man) does not prohibit women from wearing long pants or shorts, which the fashion of the times considers as acceptable apparel for both men and women.

the fledglings or on the eggs, do not take the mother together with her young. 7Let the mother go, and take only the young, in order that you may fare well and have a long life.

8When you build a new house, you shall make a parapet for your roof, so that you do not bring bloodguilt on your house if anyone should fall from it.

9You shall not sow your vineyard with a second kind of seed, else the crop—from the seed you have sown—and the yield of the vineyard

בֵּיצִ֗ים וְהָאֵ֤ם רֹבֶ֙צֶת֙ עַל־הָֽאֶפְרֹחִ֔ים א֖וֹ
עַל־הַבֵּיצִ֑ים לֹֽא־תִקַּ֥ח הָאֵ֖ם עַל־הַבָּנִֽים׃
7 שַׁלֵּ֤חַ תְּשַׁלַּח֙ אֶת־הָאֵ֔ם וְאֶת־הַבָּנִ֖ים
תִּֽקַּֽח־לָ֑ךְ לְמַ֙עַן֙ יִ֣יטַב לָ֔ךְ וְהַֽאֲרַכְתָּ֖
יָמִֽים׃ ס

שלישי 8 כִּ֤י תִבְנֶה֙ בַּ֣יִת חָדָ֔שׁ וְעָשִׂ֥יתָ מַֽעֲקֶ֖ה לְגַגֶּ֑ךָ
וְלֹֽא־תָשִׂ֤ים דָּמִים֙ בְּבֵיתֶ֔ךָ כִּֽי־יִפֹּ֥ל הַנֹּפֵ֖ל
מִמֶּֽנּוּ׃ ס

9 לֹֽא־תִזְרַ֥ע כַּרְמְךָ֖ כִּלְאָ֑יִם פֶּן־תִּקְדַּ֗שׁ
הַֽמְלֵאָ֤ה הַזֶּ֙רַע֙ אֲשֶׁ֣ר תִּזְרָ֔ע וּתְבוּאַ֖ת

---

7. Let the mother go Maimonides states that the mother is chased away to be spared the painful sight of her offspring being taken away. It is not likely, however, that chasing the mother away would spare her pain, because forcible separation from her young and finding them gone later would also be painful. Nor do the comparable laws concerning cattle (Lev. 22:27–28; Deut. 14:21) prevent pain (the mother animal would not know if her calf or kid was sacrificed on the same day or boiled in her milk). What the Torah finds callous are the acts themselves, quite apart from any effect they may have on the mother.

fare well and have a long life These clauses echo the reward promised for honoring parents in the Decalogue (5:16), and call attention to the fact that this command is likewise an aspect of respecting a parent.

BUILDING A PARAPET (v. 8)

The flat roofs of houses in the ancient Near East were regularly used for drying and storing produce, strolling and socializing, and sleeping in warm weather. Hence people were in constant danger of falling off unless a protective barrier was there. This law is comparable to Exod. 21:33–34, which holds a person responsible if an animal falls into a pit that was left uncovered. Talmudic law sees it as an example of an obligation to block or remove anything on one's property that is capable of causing death, such as a pit, a faulty ladder, or a vicious dog.

8. parapet A low wall around a roof's edge.

bloodguilt Because a human life is involved, such criminal negligence would be tantamount to homicide.

FORBIDDEN COMBINATIONS OF SEED, PLOW ANIMALS, AND TEXTILES (vv. 9–11)

These three laws supplement similar legislation in Lev. 19:19.

9. You shall not sow your vineyard In Lev. 19:19 the wording is, "you shall not sow your field." This verse broadens the law to include vineyards.

with a second kind of seed Literally, "with

---

to be sure to chase away the mother bird while doing so. While obeying both commandments that promise long life, the boy fell from the ladder and died. The event raised the issue of God's providence (BT Ḥul. 142a). It led one of the Sages, Elisha ben Abuyah, to despair of God's goodness and even God's existence.

Akiva interpreted the promise of long life as referring to "the world to come." For others, it must have reinforced the reluctance to tie the observance of commandments to specific rewards.

9–11. Sovereign decrees of God, for which no reason need be given (Rashi); at times, we

---

HALAKHAH L'MA·ASEH

22:6–7. do not take the mother together with her young The compassion demanded for the mother bird here is one of the Torah passages that led the Sages to formulate the general principle that we must avoid causing unnecessary pain to animals (tza·ar ba·alei hayyim) (see esp. BT BM 31a–33a). Other biblical verses expressing this value include Deut. 22:10 and 25:4. See Comment to Exod. 23:5.

22:8. make a parapet for your roof A parapet must be at least 10 hand-breadths (30 in. [75 cm]) high and strong enough not to collapse if someone leans against it (MT Murderer 11:3).

may not be used. 10You shall not plow with an
ox and an ass together. 11You shall not wear
cloth combining wool and linen.

12You shall make tassels on the four corners
of the garment with which you cover yourself.

13A man marries a woman and cohabits with
her. Then he takes an aversion to her 14and
makes up charges against her and defames her,
saying, "I married this woman; but when I approached her, I found that she was not a virgin."
15In such a case, the girl's father and mother

הַכָּרֶם׃ ס 10 לֹא־תַחֲרֹשׁ בְּשׁוֹר־וּבַחֲמֹר
יַחְדָּו׃ ס 11 לֹא תִלְבַּשׁ שַׁעַטְנֵז צֶמֶר
וּפִשְׁתִּים יַחְדָּו׃ ס
12 גְּדִלִים תַּעֲשֶׂה־לָּךְ עַל־אַרְבַּע כַּנְפוֹת
כְּסוּתְךָ אֲשֶׁר תְּכַסֶּה־בָּהּ׃ ס
13 כִּי־יִקַּח אִישׁ אִשָּׁה וּבָא אֵלֶיהָ וּשְׂנֵאָהּ׃
14 וְשָׂם לָהּ עֲלִילֹת דְּבָרִים וְהוֹצִא עָלֶיהָ
שֵׁם רָע וְאָמַר אֶת־הָאִשָּׁה הַזֹּאת לָקַחְתִּי
וָאֶקְרַב אֵלֶיהָ וְלֹא־מָצָאתִי לָהּ בְּתוּלִים׃
15 וְלָקַח אֲבִי הנער הַנַּעֲרָה וְאִמָּהּ וְהוֹצִיאוּ

two kinds of seed." The *halakhah* understands the verse as referring to two kinds of seed in addition to the vineyard grapes. Ramban explained: "The nature and the form [of the mixed seeds] are modified by their drawing nourishment from each other, and it is as if each resultant grain is composed of two species."

may not be used The crop will become forbidden for use. According to talmudic law, it must be burned.

10. The ox and the ass are of unequal strength. If yoked together, the stronger one might exhaust the weaker, or one might cause the other to stumble and be injured.

11. Literally, "You shall not wear *sha·atnez,* wool and linen together." The final phrase explains the meaning of *sha·atnez,* a term of non-Hebrew origin. This prohibition applies only to the laity. The priests, when they officiate, do wear garments made of such mixtures (see, e.g., Exod. 28:6,15, 39:2,5). The status of such garments is thus comparable to that of the sacred dedicating oil and the incense used in the sanctuary and may not be made or used by laypeople (see Exod. 30:22–29). All of this led Josephus to suggest that the reason for the prohibition was to keep the laity from wearing the official garb of the priests.

TASSELS ON GARMENTS (v. 12)

The requirement of tassels is stated more fully in Num. 15:37–41, where they are called "fringes" (*tzitzit*) and designated as reminders to obey God's commandments and to resist temptation, and thereby be holy to God.

12. tassels Hebrew: *g'dilim;* literally, "twists," "braids" (of thread).

four corners People in the ancient Near East wore closed skirts and robes, not rectangular poncho-like garments. The four corners mentioned here (literally, "wings" or "extremities") were probably either the points on scalloped hems or the places at which vertical bands of embroidery met the hems. Both styles, sometimes with tassels attached, can be seen in ancient Near Eastern murals.

the garment with which you cover yourself The tassels are to be attached to everyday clothing and worn all day.

MARITAL AND SEXUAL MISCONDUCT (vv. 13–29)

PREMARITAL UNCHASTITY (vv. 13–21)

False Accusation (vv. 13–19)

14. makes up charges against her Better: "he accuses her of misconduct."

defames her He publicizes the charge. By making a public issue of the matter, he causes the consequences to become more serious, because his public accusation defames the girl and her family and could lead to her death.

I found that she was not a virgin Literally, "I did not find [evidence of] virginity in her." That is, she did not bleed (see v. 17).

---

are bidden to obey God without understanding the purpose of what we do. Many commentators believe that these laws aim to preserve the species distinctions established at Creation (see Gen. 1:11–12,21,24–25). For example, Hirsch suggests that wool-and-linen clothing (v. 11) represents an improper combining of the animal domain (wool) and the vegetable world (linen), even as verse 5 prohibits blurring the line between men and women.

shall produce the evidence of the girl's virginity
before the elders of the town at the gate. 16 And
the girl's father shall say to the elders, "I gave
this man my daughter to wife, but he has taken
an aversion to her; 17 so he has made up charges,
saying, 'I did not find your daughter a virgin.'
But here is the evidence of my daughter's virginity!" And they shall spread out the cloth before the elders of the town. 18 The elders of that
town shall then take the man and flog him, 19 and
they shall fine him a hundred [shekels of] silver
and give it to the girl's father; for the man has
defamed a virgin in Israel. Moreover, she shall
remain his wife; he shall never have the right
to divorce her.

20 But if the charge proves true, the girl was
found not to have been a virgin, 21 then the girl
shall be brought out to the entrance of her father's house, and the men of her town shall

אֶת־בְּתוּלֵ֥י הנער הַֽנַּעֲרָ֖ה אֶל־זִקְנֵ֥י הָעִ֖יר
הַשָּֽׁעְרָה׃ 16 וְאָמַ֛ר אֲבִ֥י הנער הַֽנַּעֲרָ֖ה
אֶל־הַזְּקֵנִ֑ים אֶת־בִּתִּ֗י נָתַ֜תִּי לָאִ֥ישׁ הַזֶּ֛ה
לְאִשָּׁ֖ה וַיִּשְׂנָאֶֽהָ׃ 17 וְהִנֵּה־ה֡וּא שָׂם֩
עֲלִילֹ֨ת דְּבָרִ֜ים לֵאמֹ֗ר לֹֽא־מָצָ֤אתִי לְבִתְּךָ֙
בְּתוּלִ֔ים וְאֵ֖לֶּה בְּתוּלֵ֣י בִתִּ֑י וּפָֽרְשׂוּ֙
הַשִּׂמְלָ֔ה לִפְנֵ֖י זִקְנֵ֥י הָעִֽיר׃ 18 וְלָקְח֛וּ זִקְנֵ֥י
הָֽעִיר־הַהִ֖וא אֶת־הָאִ֑ישׁ וְיִסְּר֖וּ אֹתֽוֹ׃
19 וְעָנְשׁ֨וּ אֹת֜וֹ מֵ֣אָה כֶ֗סֶף וְנָֽתְנוּ֙ לַאֲבִ֣י
הַֽנַּעֲרָ֔ה כִּ֚י הוֹצִיא֙ שֵׁ֣ם רָ֔ע עַ֖ל בְּתוּלַ֣ת
יִשְׂרָאֵ֑ל וְלֽוֹ־תִהְיֶ֣ה לְאִשָּׁ֔ה לֹא־יוּכַ֥ל
לְשַׁלְּחָ֖הּ כָּל־יָמָֽיו׃ ס
20 וְאִם־אֱמֶ֣ת הָיָ֔ה הַדָּבָ֖ר הַזֶּ֑ה לֹא־נִמְצְא֥וּ
בְתוּלִ֖ים לנער לַֽנַּעֲרָֽה׃ 21 וְהוֹצִ֨יאוּ אֶת־
הנער הַֽנַּעֲרָ֜ה אֶל־פֶּ֣תַח בֵּית־אָבִ֗יהָ

15. evidence A garment or cloth that became spotted with the girl's blood when her hymen was perforated on the wedding night (v. 17). Upon this cloth depends the reputation of the bride's parents, and the bride-price they receive. The custom of saving and even displaying the cloth is well known in the Middle East. Although only the father speaks here, the mother joins him, because it was customary for the mother to keep the cloth after the consummation of the marriage.

before the elders In matters of family law, the elders retain jurisdiction.

16. I gave this man my daughter This was not merely a formal idiom as it is in modern times, but was meant literally. Marriages were arranged by the parents, and a bride-price was paid to the bride's father.

17. the cloth The Hebrew word *simlah* and its variant *salmah* usually refer to an outer garment that sometimes is also used as a cover while sleeping. Here it refers either to a garment worn by the bride on her wedding night or to part of the bedding.

18–19. flog him . . . fine him As noted by Maimonides and Abravanel, each element of this unusual multiple punishment corresponds to a part of the husband's offense. He is flogged and thereby degraded, because he defamed the girl and her family. He is fined, because his accusation would have forced her father to return the bride-price. He loses the right to divorce her, which was probably the aim of his slanderous act. In this way, the father is compensated for the harm attempted against him and the girl is protected against the husband's expelling her, which would relieve her husband from the obligation of supporting her.

hundred [shekels of] silver This is taken to be double the bride-price for a virgin, on the assumption that the 50 shekels stipulated in verse 29 is identical to the "bride-price for virgins" mentioned in Exod. 22:16. It is not certain, however, that 50 shekels really was the bride-price for virgins.

give it to the girl's father Although the bride was disgraced, the fine is given to her father, because the financial loss caused by the accusation would be his. Furthermore, he was disgraced as well, because the accusation implied that he did not raise a virtuous daughter. Abravanel observes that there would be no point in giving the fine to the bride, because she is under her husband's authority and (according to rabbinic law) he would be able to take it from her.

defamed a virgin in Israel This concluding remark reflects the Torah's concern for the general good name of Israelite young women.

True Accusation (vv. 20–21)

21. the entrance of her father's house An appropriate location for her punishment, because, as this verse states, literally, "she committed for-

stone her to death; for she did a shameful thing in Israel, committing fornication while under her father's authority. Thus you will sweep away evil from your midst.

22 If a man is found lying with another man's wife, both of them—the man and the woman with whom he lay—shall die. Thus you will sweep away evil from Israel.

23 In the case of a virgin who is engaged to a man—if a man comes upon her in town and

וּסְקָלוּהָ אַנְשֵׁי עִירָהּ בָּאֲבָנִים וָמֵתָה
כִּי־עָשְׂתָה נְבָלָה בְּיִשְׂרָאֵל לִזְנוֹת בֵּית
אָבִיהָ וּבִעַרְתָּ הָרָע מִקִּרְבֶּךָ׃ ס
22 כִּי־יִמָּצֵא אִישׁ שֹׁכֵב ׀ עִם־אִשָּׁה בְעֻלַת־
בַּעַל וּמֵתוּ גַּם־שְׁנֵיהֶם הָאִישׁ הַשֹּׁכֵב
עִם־הָאִשָּׁה וְהָאִשָּׁה וּבִעַרְתָּ הָרָע
מִיִּשְׂרָאֵל׃ ס

23 כִּי יִהְיֶה נער נַעֲרָה בְתוּלָה מְאֹרָשָׂה
לְאִישׁ וּמְצָאָהּ אִישׁ בָּעִיר וְשָׁכַב עִמָּהּ׃

nication while [living] in her father's house." A similar principle is reflected in the Laws of Hammurabi, where a man who breaks into a house is to be executed in front of the breach that he made. Executing the daughter at this location also expresses communal disapproval of the father who failed to raise a chaste daughter.

the men of her town Even if she is from a different town than her husband, the execution takes place in the bride's town, because its location must be at the entrance of her father's house.

stone her This is the same punishment as that stated for the insubordinate son. See Comment to 13:11.

shameful thing Hebrew: *n'valah* (outrage, deplorable act). Often it refers to sexual crimes, such as rape and adultery. It frequently is followed by the words "in Israel," sometimes indicating indignation that the act occurred among Israelites, and sometimes characterizing the act as a violation of Israelite standards. The phrase expresses the importance of sexual morality as a feature of Israel's national character.

fornication The use of this term rather than "adultery" suggests that the law refers to intercourse at any time before marriage and is not limited to the period of betrothal.

ADULTERY WITH A MARRIED WOMAN (v. 22)

22. is found Meanwhile, Num. 5:11–31 prescribes a ritual procedure for settling the matter when a husband suspects his wife of infidelity but has no clear evidence of her act.

both of them . . . shall die Adultery is also a capital crime in other ancient Near Eastern law collections. Because the latter consider it an offense solely against the woman's husband, however, they permit the husband or the king to spare the wife and her lover or to impose a lesser punishment. The Bible views God as the author of the laws. Because God has forbidden adultery, it is a sin against Him as well as the husband, and therefore, no human has the right to commute the punishment.

sweep away evil Because the welfare of the community is endangered by God's anger over the crime, it must act to remove the guilt. According to Lev. 18:20,24ff., adultery defiles the Land and leads to exile.

ADULTERY WITH AN ENGAGED VIRGIN
(vv. 23–27)

Once a girl is betrothed by the payment of the bride-price to her family (see 20:7), she is regarded as her fiancé's wife (v. 24), and sexual relations with another man are considered adulterous. The same view is found in Mesopotamian law.

23. in town It is necessary to ascertain whether the girl was a consensual partner. The law provides a rule of thumb. If the act took place in town, she is presumed to have been willing, be-

---

24. The reader may balk at the Torah's assumption that the woman's not crying out indicated consent. We know today that intimidation and coerced silence may take many forms.

HALAKHAH L'MA·ASEH

22:23–25. in town . . . in the open country The Sages understood "town" and "country" metaphorically, distinguishing between instances in which the woman did not object and those in which she objected but was overcome (Sifrei Deut. 243).

lies with her, 24you shall take the two of them
out to the gate of that town and stone them to
death: the girl because she did not cry for help
in the town, and the man because he violated
another man's wife. Thus you will sweep away
evil from your midst. 25But if the man comes
upon the engaged girl in the open country, and
the man lies with her by force, only the man who
lay with her shall die, 26but you shall do nothing
to the girl. The girl did not incur the death penalty, for this case is like that of a man attacking
another and murdering him. 27He came upon
her in the open; though the engaged girl cried
for help, there was no one to save her.
28If a man comes upon a virgin who is not
engaged and he seizes her and lies with her, and
they are discovered, 29the man who lay with her
shall pay the girl's father fifty [shekels of] silver,
and she shall be his wife. Because he has violated
her, he can never have the right to divorce her.

24 וְהוֹצֵאתֶם אֶת־שְׁנֵיהֶם אֶל־שַׁעַר ׀
הָעִיר הַהִוא וּסְקַלְתֶּם אֹתָם בָּאֲבָנִים
וָמֵתוּ אֶת־הנער הַנַּעֲרָה עַל־דְּבַר אֲשֶׁר
לֹא־צָעֲקָה בָעִיר וְאֶת־הָאִישׁ עַל־דְּבַר
אֲשֶׁר־עִנָּה אֶת־אֵשֶׁת רֵעֵהוּ וּבִעַרְתָּ הָרָע
מִקִּרְבֶּךָ׃ ס 25 וְאִם־בַּשָּׂדֶה יִמְצָא הָאִישׁ
אֶת־הנער הַנַּעֲרָה הַמְאֹרָשָׂה וְהֶחֱזִיק־בָּהּ
הָאִישׁ וְשָׁכַב עִמָּהּ וּמֵת הָאִישׁ אֲשֶׁר־שָׁכַב
עִמָּהּ לְבַדּוֹ׃ 26 ולנער וְלַנַּעֲרָה לֹא־תַעֲשֶׂה
דָבָר אֵין לנער לַנַּעֲרָה חֵטְא מָוֶת כִּי כַּאֲשֶׁר
יָקוּם אִישׁ עַל־רֵעֵהוּ וּרְצָחוֹ נֶפֶשׁ כֵּן הַדָּבָר
הַזֶּה׃ 27 כִּי בַשָּׂדֶה מְצָאָהּ צָעֲקָה הנער
הַנַּעֲרָה הַמְאֹרָשָׂה וְאֵין מוֹשִׁיעַ לָהּ׃ ס
28 כִּי־יִמְצָא אִישׁ נער נַעֲרָה בְתוּלָה אֲשֶׁר
לֹא־אֹרָשָׂה וּתְפָשָׂהּ וְשָׁכַב עִמָּהּ וְנִמְצָאוּ׃
29 וְנָתַן הָאִישׁ הַשֹּׁכֵב עִמָּהּ לַאֲבִי הנער
הַנַּעֲרָה חֲמִשִּׁים כָּסֶף וְלוֹ־תִהְיֶה לְאִשָּׁה
תַּחַת אֲשֶׁר עִנָּהּ לֹא־יוּכַל שַׁלְּחָהּ כָּל־
יָמָיו׃ ס

cause otherwise she would have called for help and would have been heard. In the open country, however, where there are few passersby, a cry for help probably would have gone unheard; hence she is given the benefit of the doubt and is presumed to have called for help.

26. you shall do nothing to the girl This clause is the basis for the talmudic principle that one who commits a wrong under compulsion is not liable.

like that of a man attacking . . . and murdering That is, she was a victim, not a participant.

RAPE OF AN UNENGAGED VIRGIN (vv. 28–29)

Intercourse with an unengaged virgin is also disapproved, but it is not a capital crime because it is not adulterous. The main concern of the law in such cases is to protect the girl and her father from the harm they would suffer from her loss of virginity, namely, the father's loss of a full bride-price and the girl's diminished chances of marriage.

29. fifty [shekels of] silver This is often taken to be identical to the "bride-price for virgins" that a seducer must pay to a virgin's father (see Exod. 22:16). But there is no other evidence that the bride-price for virgins was 50 shekels. The 50 shekels paid by the rapist probably represents a combination of an average bride-price (between 10 and 30 shekels, if we take Lev. 27:5–6 as indicating a woman's value) plus punitive damages.

his wife According to Exod. 22:16, a seducer must likewise marry the girl, unless her father refuses to give her to him. Talmudic law states that in cases of seduction and rape, the girl as well as the father has the right to refuse the marriage.

he can never . . . divorce her Exodus does not impose this restriction on the seducer. The rapist's offense is graver and he is treated more stringently.

HALAKHAH L'MA·ASEH

22:28–29. he seizes her and lies with her Rape is a crime, punishable under rabbinic law as an offense against the woman and her family. While every sexual relationship should be respectful and by mutual consent, the Torah sees marriage as the ideal setting for sexual relations. Consensual sexual intercourse between singles is censured (Exod. 22:16).

כג לֹא־יִקַּח אִישׁ אֶת־אֵשֶׁת אָבִיו
וְלֹא יְגַלֶּה כְּנַף אָבִיו׃ ס
2 לֹא־יָבֹא פְצוּעַ־דַּכָּא וּכְרוּת שָׁפְכָה
בִּקְהַל יְהוָה׃ ס
3 לֹא־יָבֹא מַמְזֵר בִּקְהַל יְהוָה גַּם דּוֹר
עֲשִׂירִי לֹא־יָבֹא לוֹ בִּקְהַל יְהוָה׃ ס
4 לֹא־יָבֹא עַמּוֹנִי וּמוֹאָבִי בִּקְהַל יְהוָה גַּם

23 No man shall marry his father's former wife, so as to remove his father's garment.

2No one whose testes are crushed or whose member is cut off shall be admitted into the congregation of the LORD.

3No one misbegotten shall be admitted into the congregation of the LORD; none of his descendants, even in the tenth generation, shall be admitted into the congregation of the LORD.

4No Ammonite or Moabite shall be admitted

FORBIDDEN RELATIONSHIPS (23:1–9)

FATHER'S FORMER WIFE (v. 1)

1. father's former wife This refers to a former wife who is not one's mother. Sexual relations with one's mother are prohibited by Lev. 18:7. Though "former" is not in the Hebrew, it is clearly what the text intends, because it deals with marriage rather than incest. Marriage with one's father's current wife would be legally impossible.

to remove his father's garment The idiom "removing someone's garment" is identical to "seeing, or uncovering, someone's nakedness," used in Leviticus for sexual relations. In Leviticus, intercourse with the wife of one's father is condemned, because it is tantamount to "seeing the father's nakedness," meaning that one sees nakedness reserved for his father.

RESTRICTED ENTRY INTO THE ASSEMBLY (vv. 2–9)

Certain people may not become members of the governing assembly and are, therefore, not eligible for full Israelite citizenship. This assembly seems to have been similar to others in the ancient world, such as in Athens (the "ekklesia") and in Mesopotamian cities (the "puhrum"). It existed before the Exodus from Egypt and likely antedated Moses. In the wilderness, it functioned alongside Moses and usually under him; and it is mentioned sporadically after the settlement in the Promised Land.

2. testes are crushed . . . member is cut off Two types of emasculation, the first accomplished by destroying the testes, the second by some type of castration. It is not clear whether this law applies to all who have these conditions or only to those who acquired them voluntarily.

congregation Hebrew: *kahal;* literally, "gathering." Sometimes it refers to religious gatherings in the sense of a congregation. At other times it means "all Israelites." It also refers to the national governing assembly of the Israelites, i.e., the entire people, or all the adult males, meeting in plenary session—and perhaps even to their representatives acting as an executive committee. This assembly convenes to conduct public business, such as waging war, crowning a king, adjudicating legal cases, and distributing land, as well as engaging in worship.

3. misbegotten Hebrew: *mamzer;* its meaning is not certain. Derivation from an Arabic and Ethiopic root meaning "to be foul" (מזר) has been suggested.

tenth generation Verse 4 supplements this with "forever," and that is probably the meaning here as well. No descendant of a *mamzer* may ever enter the assembly, no matter how many generations later.

4. Ammonite or Moabite Transjordanian

CHAPTER 23

3. The intention is not to punish an innocent child but to discourage adultery by impressing on potential parents its dire consequences.

HALAKHAH L'MA·ASEH

23:3. misbegotten Hebrew: *mamzer.* According to Jewish law, this refers only to the offspring of adultery or incest, not to those born out of wedlock (M Yev. 4:13; BT Yev. 49a). The CJLS has adopted evidentiary procedures to render this rule inoperative, because it penalizes children for the sins of their parents, contrary to the teaching of Deut. 24:16.

דּוֹר עֲשִׂירִי לֹא־יָבֹא לָהֶם בִּקְהַל יְהוָה
עַד־עוֹלָם׃ 5 עַל־דְּבַר אֲשֶׁר לֹא־קִדְּמוּ
אֶתְכֶם בַּלֶּחֶם וּבַמַּיִם בַּדֶּרֶךְ בְּצֵאתְכֶם
מִמִּצְרָיִם וַאֲשֶׁר שָׂכַר עָלֶיךָ אֶת־בִּלְעָם
בֶּן־בְּעוֹר מִפְּתוֹר אֲרַם נַהֲרַיִם לְקַלְלֶךָּ׃
6 וְלֹא־אָבָה יְהוָה אֱלֹהֶיךָ לִשְׁמֹעַ אֶל־
בִּלְעָם וַיַּהֲפֹךְ יְהוָה אֱלֹהֶיךָ לְּךָ אֶת־
הַקְּלָלָה לִבְרָכָה כִּי אֲהֵבְךָ יְהוָה אֱלֹהֶיךָ׃
7 לֹא־תִדְרֹשׁ שְׁלֹמָם וְטֹבָתָם כָּל־יָמֶיךָ
לְעוֹלָם׃ ס
ביעי 8 לֹא־תְתַעֵב אֲדֹמִי כִּי אָחִיךָ הוּא* ס
לֹא־תְתַעֵב מִצְרִי כִּי־גֵר הָיִיתָ בְאַרְצוֹ׃
9 בָּנִים אֲשֶׁר־יִוָּלְדוּ לָהֶם דּוֹר שְׁלִישִׁי יָבֹא
לָהֶם בִּקְהַל יְהוָה׃ ס

10 כִּי־תֵצֵא מַחֲנֶה עַל־אֹיְבֶיךָ וְנִשְׁמַרְתָּ

v. 8. פיסקא באמצע פסוק

into the congregation of the LORD; none of their descendants, even in the tenth generation, shall ever be admitted into the congregation of the LORD, [5]because they did not meet you with food and water on your journey after you left Egypt, and because they hired Balaam son of Beor, from Pethor of Aram-naharaim, to curse you.—[6]But the LORD your God refused to heed Balaam; instead, the LORD your God turned the curse into a blessing for you, for the LORD your God loves you.—[7]You shall never concern yourself with their welfare or benefit as long as you live.

[8]You shall not abhor an Edomite, for he is your kinsman. You shall not abhor an Egyptian, for you were a stranger in his land. [9]Children born to them may be admitted into the congregation of the LORD in the third generation.

[10]When you go out as a troop against your

neighbors of Israel. Despite their distant kinship with Israel and the respect Israel showed for their territorial rights, these peoples reacted with hostility and indifference when the Israelites passed near their territory on the way to the Promised Land.

5. they hired Literally, "he hired." Refers to Balak, King of Moab (see Num. 22–24).

Pethor of Aram-naharaim Pethor is a city in northern Syria. Aram-naharaim, which means "Aram alongside the river [Euphrates]," is the biblical term for eastern Syria and northern Iraq, the area from which the patriarchs migrated to the Promised Land.

7. Do not seek their welfare, do nothing for their benefit, and do not establish friendly relations with them. Repay them in kind for their indifference and hostility.

8. for he is your kinsman Despite the hostility between Israel and Edom, Edomites are not permanently excluded from the assembly because they are the Israelites' kin. The Edomites were traced back to Esau, brother of Jacob, as related in Gen. 36.

for you were a stranger in his land Despite their enslavement of the Israelites, the Egyptians had provided a haven in a time of famine, for which Israel was to recognize a continuing debt of gratitude.

9. in the third generation They may be admitted after two generations of living among Israelites. This implies that all those banned from entering the assembly may live in the land of Israel as resident aliens, and that the grandchildren of Edomites and Egyptians who do so may be admitted to the assembly.

---

4. The sins of Edom and Egypt, who threatened Israel's physical survival, are deemed less serious than the sins of Ammon and Moab, who tried to lure Israel into unchastity, endangering their souls (*Sifrei*). Why does the text refer back to Moab's hiring Balaam to curse Israel? Had they only refused Israel's request for food and water, one might give them the benefit of the doubt that they could not afford hospitality. But their hiring Balaam for much silver and gold (Num. 22:17) proves that hatred, not limited resources, was behind their refusal.

enemies, be on your guard against anything un- toward. [11]If anyone among you has been rendered impure by a nocturnal emission, he must leave the camp, and he must not reenter the camp. [12]Toward evening he shall bathe in water, and at sundown he may reenter the camp. [13]Further, there shall be an area for you outside the camp, where you may relieve yourself. [14]With your gear you shall have a spike, and when you have squatted you shall dig a hole with it and cover up your excrement. [15]Since the LORD your God moves about in your camp to protect you and to deliver your enemies to you, let your camp be holy; let Him not find anything unseemly among you and turn away from you.

[16]You shall not turn over to his master a slave

מִכֹּל דָּבָר רָע׃ 11 כִּי־יִהְיֶה בְךָ֙ אִ֔ישׁ אֲשֶׁ֣ר
לֹא־יִהְיֶ֥ה טָה֖וֹר מִקְּרֵה־לָ֑יְלָה וְיָצָא֙ אֶל־
מִח֣וּץ לַֽמַּחֲנֶ֔ה לֹ֥א יָבֹ֖א אֶל־תּ֥וֹךְ הַֽמַּחֲנֶֽה׃
12 וְהָיָ֥ה לִפְנֽוֹת־עֶ֖רֶב יִרְחַ֣ץ בַּמָּ֑יִם וּכְבֹ֣א
הַשֶּׁ֔מֶשׁ יָבֹ֖א אֶל־תּ֥וֹךְ הַֽמַּחֲנֶֽה׃ 13 וְיָד֙
תִּהְיֶ֣ה לְךָ֔ מִח֖וּץ לַֽמַּחֲנֶ֑ה וְיָצָ֥אתָ שָּׁ֖מָּה
ח֑וּץ׃ 14 וְיָתֵ֛ד תִּהְיֶ֥ה לְךָ֖ עַל־אֲזֵנֶ֑ךָ וְהָיָה֙
בְּשִׁבְתְּךָ֣ ח֔וּץ וְחָפַרְתָּ֣ה בָ֔הּ וְשַׁבְתָּ֖ וְכִסִּ֥יתָ
אֶת־צֵֽאָתֶֽךָ׃ 15 כִּי֩ יְהוָ֨ה אֱלֹהֶ֜יךָ מִתְהַלֵּ֣ךְ ׀
בְּקֶ֣רֶב מַחֲנֶ֗ךָ לְהַצִּֽילְךָ֙ וְלָתֵ֤ת אֹֽיְבֶ֙יךָ֙ לְפָנֶ֔יךָ
וְהָיָ֥ה מַחֲנֶ֖יךָ קָד֑וֹשׁ וְלֹֽא־יִרְאֶ֤ה בְךָ֙ עֶרְוַ֣ת
דָּבָ֔ר וְשָׁ֖ב מֵאַחֲרֶֽיךָ׃ ס
16 לֹא־תַסְגִּ֥יר עֶ֖בֶד אֶל־אֲדֹנָ֑יו אֲשֶׁר־יִנָּצֵ֥ל

MISCELLANEOUS LAWS (23:10–25:19)

This is the final group of laws in Deuteronomy.

THE SANCTITY OF MILITARY CAMP (vv. 10–15)

Impurity is incompatible with the presence of God. Hence, those suffering from an abnormal skin eruption or genital discharge, or defiled by contact with a corpse, must stay away from the residential camp, where God's sanctuary is located. A military camp, in which God is present to fight for Israel, is subject to an even stricter regimen than the residential camp.

10. anything Implies that the principle is more comprehensive than the two examples cited (as it does in v. 15). Those suffering abnormal skin eruptions or genital discharges probably had to leave the military camp. It seems unlikely and impractical, however, that soldiers defiled by contact with corpses were to be removed from the military camp. To judge from Num. 31:19, they were simply kept out of the residential camp for a week after their return from war.

11. nocturnal emission An emission of semen. The text mentions only the typical case. An emission in the daytime would doubtless require the same procedure.

13. Defecation must take place outside the camp. The Torah nowhere describes human excrement as impure, and it may be objectionable in God's presence simply because it is repugnant.

area Hebrew: *yad;* literally, "hand." It may refer here to a "marker," a sign indicating the latrine area.

outside the camp According to the War Scroll of later times, found at Qumran, the latrine was to be located 2000 cubits (about 3000 feet [900 m]) from the camp.

14. spike Hebrew: *yated.* Usually refers to a tent peg. The text apparently has in mind a pointed implement used to make holes in soil.

15. God travels in the camp together with the Israelites. "It is the LORD your God who marches with you to do battle for you" (20:4).

ASYLUM FOR ESCAPED SLAVES (vv. 16–17)

Ancient Near Eastern law forbade harboring runaway slaves, and international treaties regularly required allied states to extradite them. In contrast, the Torah here states that escaped slaves may settle wherever they wish in the land of Israel and forbids returning them to their masters or enslaving them in the land. Virtually all commentators hold that this law refers to slaves who have fled to the

---

15. let your camp be holy Israel's success in war depended not on their military prowess but on their carrying out the will of God. They were not fighting solely for land, for wealth, or for power. They were fighting to establish a place where God's plan could be carried out. A sense of the sacredness of their purpose must animate their military efforts. At the same time, one must reflect on the danger of "holy war," the tendency of too many people to persuade themselves that their will for battle is God's will.

אֵלֶיךָ מֵעִם אֲדֹנָיו׃ 17 עִמְּךָ יֵשֵׁב בְּקִרְבְּךָ
בַּמָּקוֹם אֲשֶׁר־יִבְחַר בְּאַחַד שְׁעָרֶיךָ בַּטּוֹב
לוֹ לֹא תּוֹנֶנּוּ׃ ס
18 לֹא־תִהְיֶה קְדֵשָׁה מִבְּנוֹת יִשְׂרָאֵל וְלֹא־
יִהְיֶה קָדֵשׁ מִבְּנֵי יִשְׂרָאֵל׃ 19 לֹא־תָבִיא
אֶתְנַן זוֹנָה וּמְחִיר כֶּלֶב בֵּית יְהוָה אֱלֹהֶיךָ
לְכָל־נֶדֶר כִּי תוֹעֲבַת יְהוָה אֱלֹהֶיךָ גַּם־
שְׁנֵיהֶם׃
20 לֹא־תַשִּׁיךְ לְאָחִיךָ נֶשֶׁךְ כֶּסֶף נֶשֶׁךְ אֹכֶל

who seeks refuge with you from his master. 17He
shall live with you in any place he may choose
among the settlements in your midst, wherever
he pleases; you must not ill-treat him.

18No Israelite woman shall be a cult prostitute, nor shall any Israelite man be a cult prostitute. 19You shall not bring the fee of a whore
or the pay of a dog into the house of the LORD
your God in fulfillment of any vow, for both are
abhorrent to the LORD your God.

20You shall not deduct interest from loans to
your countrymen, whether in money or food
or anything else that can be deducted as interest;

land of Israel from foreign countries. The only custom in the ancient world remotely resembling this biblical law is the practice at certain pagan temples of granting asylum to slaves fleeing harsh treatment by their masters. Generally, such asylum protected slaves until they could come to terms with their master or, as a last resort, until they were sold to another master. The Bible, however, regards the whole land of Israel as a sanctuary for escaped slaves, offering permanent asylum.

17. He shall live . . . wherever he pleases This is the opposite of an ancient Aramaic treaty requiring extradition of escaped slaves: "You must not say to them: 'Live quietly in your place . . . live where you are.'"

you must not ill-treat him Once settled, he or she would be a resident alien and hence vulnerable to exploitation; hence this admonition. Compare Exod. 22:20: "You must not ill-treat a resident alien."

PROSTITUTION AND OTHER ABHORRENT PRACTICES (vv. 18–19)

18. no Israelite woman The law does not ban these professions entirely, but prohibits Israelites from engaging in them. Perhaps it assumes that prostitution cannot be eliminated and seeks only to limit it to foreigners.

cult prostitute Hebrew: *k'deshah.* Best translated simply as "prostitute," synonymous with "whore" in the next verse. Modern scholarship once held that prostitutes were employed in ancient Near Eastern sanctuaries (the "cult"), but scholars now doubt that such prostitution existed.

any Israelite man Although the precise meaning of the masculine noun *kadesh* here is uncertain, it probably refers to a male prostitute, either heterosexual or homosexual.

19. fee of a whore The Hebrew word *zonah* is the more common term for "whore." Fees, including those of whores, were sometimes paid in kind, such as a kid of the flock, instead of cash (Gen. 38:17). Temples, with their throngs of travelers, must have been particularly desirable locations for prostitutes hoping to attract business from worshipers who were carried away by the festive mood of a holiday. Prostitutes working near a temple may have vowed part of their income to it in return for success; hence the need for this prohibition. Income acquired by immoral activity is not acceptable in the Temple.

pay of a dog Because the other clauses in verses 18–19 refer to humans, some of them prostitutes, it is often assumed that "dog" might be an epithet for a homosexual male prostitute, who performs in the stance of a dog. Jewish law takes the phrase to mean that the price received for selling a dog may not be given to the Temple. Dogs, though valued for herding, were nevertheless regarded with some disgust. They were only semi-domesticated and, as scavengers and predators, were the only carnivorous animals regularly encountered by Israelites.

LENDING AT INTEREST (vv. 20–21)

The Torah regularly deals with charitable loans to countrymen who have fallen on hard times. There is no evidence for a money market of any

17. you must not ill-treat him It is not sufficient to assist people when they are in need. We must also look after their interests, be kind to them, and not hurt their feelings (Maimonides).

21 but you may deduct interest from loans to foreigners. Do not deduct interest from loans to
your countrymen, so that the LORD your God
may bless you in all your undertakings in the
land that you are about to enter and possess.
22 When you make a vow to the LORD your
God, do not put off fulfilling it, for the LORD
your God will require it of you, and you will
have incurred guilt; 23 whereas you incur no
guilt if you refrain from vowing. 24 You must

נֶ֕שֶׁךְ כָּל־דָּבָ֖ר אֲשֶׁ֥ר יִשָּֽׁךְ׃ 21 לַנָּכְרִ֣י תַשִּׁ֔יךְ
וּלְאָחִ֖יךָ לֹ֣א תַשִּׁ֑יךְ לְמַ֨עַן יְבָרֶכְךָ֜ יְהוָ֣ה
אֱלֹהֶ֗יךָ בְּכֹל֙ מִשְׁלַ֣ח יָדֶ֔ךָ עַל־הָאָ֕רֶץ אֲשֶׁר־
אַתָּ֥ה בָא־שָׁ֖מָּה לְרִשְׁתָּֽהּ׃ ס
22 כִּֽי־תִדֹּ֥ר נֶ֙דֶר֙ לַיהוָ֣ה אֱלֹהֶ֔יךָ לֹ֥א תְאַחֵ֖ר
לְשַׁלְּמ֑וֹ כִּֽי־דָרֹ֨שׁ יִדְרְשֶׁ֜נּוּ יְהוָ֤ה אֱלֹהֶ֙יךָ֙
מֵֽעִמָּ֔ךְ וְהָיָ֥ה בְךָ֖ חֵֽטְא׃ 23 וְכִ֥י תֶחְדַּ֖ל לִנְדֹּ֑ר
לֹא־יִהְיֶ֥ה בְךָ֖ חֵֽטְא׃ 24 מוֹצָ֥א שְׂפָתֶ֖יךָ

significance in ancient Israel or evidence that solvent Israelites commonly borrowed for commercial or other purposes. Exodus 22:24 and Lev. 25:35–37 explicitly refer to the borrower as impoverished. Lending is thus a moral obligation incumbent on those who can afford it, and it is to be done without further increasing the borrower's poverty by requiring interest, which could be ruinous (rates of 20 to 25 percent for silver, and 33⅓ to 50 percent for grain, were common in the ancient Near East, and higher rates were known).

20. The Torah does not differentiate between solvent and poor borrowers.

or anything else Such as seed. Exodus and Leviticus mention only loans of money and food. This phrase makes it clear that the prohibition covers all types of loans. A similar generalization, compared to the earlier version of a law, is found in 22:3.

21. foreigners Visiting the country for purposes of trade; they borrow to invest in merchandise and make a profit, not to survive poverty. There is no moral imperative either to remit loans made for such purposes or to forgo interest on them. In addition, the obligation of undertaking risky, interest-free loans entails a special duty toward one's countrymen for the sake of maintaining equilibrium in Israelite society. The law does not require assuming the same risk toward others who do not share the same obligations.

TIMELY FULFILLMENT OF VOWS (vv. 22–24)

A person who sought God's aid in achieving a desired goal or relief from distress—the birth of a child, victory in battle, recovery from illness, escape from danger—might promise to do something pleasing to God afterward in gratitude for His assistance.

22. Vowing is a purely voluntary activity, by no means required by God, and there is no penalty for not making vows. Once a vow is made, however, delay in fulfilling it is hypocritical and disrespectful.

do not put off The text does not specify what constitutes an impermissible delay, perhaps because circumstances might differ in individual cases. It is reasonable to assume that people normally were expected to fulfill a vow during the next pilgrimage festival, but some people may have made special trips to a sanctuary for the purpose.

God will require it of you God will hold you responsible and punish you for not fulfilling it.

you will have incurred guilt Ecclesiastes 5:5 warns that unfulfilled vows anger God, who will destroy the offender's possessions.

23. Implicit in this verse is a teaching that vows are not necessary for securing God's aid or remaining in His favor.

---

21. Charging interest on loans to gentiles was not a matter of racial or ethnic discrimination. Israelites could not charge each other interest, but gentiles could and did charge each other, and a foreigner borrowing money from an Israelite would not expect better terms than he would get from one of his own people. (In medieval Europe, this freedom to lend at interest, combined with exclusion from any respectable trade, led to the negative stereotyping of the Jew as usurer.)

24. You must fulfill what has crossed your

HALAKHAH L'MA·ASEH

23:20–1. interest See Exod. 22:24 and Lev. 25:36. Even though interest is regularly charged in business, the Torah's ideal of communal solidarity and concern is expressed by Jewish Free Loan Societies in many Jewish communities.

fulfill what has crossed your lips and perform what you have voluntarily vowed to the LORD your God, having made the promise with your own mouth.

25When you enter another man's vineyard, you may eat as many grapes as you want, until you are full, but you must not put any in your vessel. 26When you enter another man's field of standing grain, you may pluck ears with your hand; but you must not put a sickle to your neighbor's grain.

תִּשְׁמֹר וְעָשִׂיתָ כַּאֲשֶׁר נָדַרְתָּ לַיהוָה
אֱלֹהֶיךָ נְדָבָה אֲשֶׁר דִּבַּרְתָּ בְּפִיךָ׃ ס
חמישי 25 כִּי תָבֹא בְּכֶרֶם רֵעֶךָ וְאָכַלְתָּ עֲנָבִים
כְּנַפְשְׁךָ שָׂבְעֶךָ וְאֶל־כֶּלְיְךָ לֹא תִתֵּן׃ ס
26 כִּי תָבֹא בְּקָמַת רֵעֶךָ וְקָטַפְתָּ מְלִילֹת
בְּיָדֶךָ וְחֶרְמֵשׁ לֹא תָנִיף עַל קָמַת
רֵעֶךָ׃ ס

24

A man takes a wife and possesses her. She fails to please him because he finds something obnoxious about her, and he writes

כד כִּי־יִקַּח אִישׁ אִשָּׁה וּבְעָלָהּ וְהָיָה
אִם־לֹא תִמְצָא־חֵן בְּעֵינָיו כִּי־מָצָא בָהּ

24. You must fulfill A vow is unconditionally binding. The Bible mentions no procedure for annulling a vow, even if it is impossible to keep.

EATING ANOTHER'S UNHARVESTED CROPS (vv. 25–26)

Fields and vineyards were laid out in such a way that people often had to pass through those belonging to others. This was not considered trespass. To judge from Exod. 22:4–5, only damaging the field is trespass. When passing another's crops, one who is hungry may pick enough grapes or ears of grain to satisfy hunger but one may not take more than can be eaten on the spot.

25. vessel Baggage carried by travelers in which they would keep food and other necessities.

26. standing grain When barley and wheat are still standing in the field, not yet ready for harvest, their grains are soft and edible after husking.

you must not put a sickle Because a sickle cuts several stalks at once, this could easily yield more than one can eat on the spot, which is all one is entitled to take.

FORBIDDEN REMARRIAGE (24:1–4)

The laws of divorce are not prescribed in the Torah and were undoubtedly the subject of customary law. What little is known about them comes from indirect references in narratives, prophecies, and laws like this one. This law supplements the customary laws of marriage and divorce in one specific area: A man may not remarry his former wife if she has been married to another man in the interim.

1. She fails to please him That is, if she ceases to please him. Ancient Near Eastern documents offer typical motives for divorce, which include suspicious absences from home, wasting or embezzling the husband's property, humiliating him, denying him conjugal rights, and—when it was not punished by the court with death—adultery. Here, failing to please him refers to any conduct the husband finds intolerable. A

---

lips Jewish law takes words seriously, especially promises to God. But it recognizes that people often vow rashly in a burst of enthusiasm, or make sincere commitments that they later find themselves unable to fulfill. For that reason, the Sages devised a procedure for releasing people from their vows. Such people can tell a *beit din* (rabbinical court) that had they known of certain circumstances at the time of the vow, they would not have vowed as they did. The court may then annul the vow. The *Kol Nidrei* formula on the eve of *Yom Kippur* echoes this procedure.

25–26. Later Jewish law restricts permission to harvest workers. Otherwise, according to Rav, if all passers-by could eat, the owner might well be ruined (*Sifrei*). Note also that the verse stresses that this privilege is not to be abused.

her a bill of divorcement, hands it to her, and sends her away from his house; [2]she leaves his household and becomes the wife of another man; [3]then this latter man rejects her, writes her a bill of divorcement, hands it to her, and sends her away from his house; or the man who married her last dies. [4]Then the first husband who divorced her shall not take her to wife again, since she has been defiled—for that would be abhorrent to the LORD. You must not bring sin upon the land that the LORD your God is giving you as a heritage.

[5]When a man has taken a bride, he shall not go out with the army or be assigned to it for any purpose; he shall be exempt one year for the sake of his household, to give happiness to the woman he has married.

עֶרְוַת דָּבָר וְכָתַב לָהּ סֵפֶר כְּרִיתֻת וְנָתַן
בְּיָדָהּ וְשִׁלְּחָהּ מִבֵּיתוֹ׃ 2 וְיָצְאָה מִבֵּיתוֹ
וְהָלְכָה וְהָיְתָה לְאִישׁ־אַחֵר׃ 3 וּשְׂנֵאָהּ
הָאִישׁ הָאַחֲרוֹן וְכָתַב לָהּ סֵפֶר כְּרִיתֻת
וְנָתַן בְּיָדָהּ וְשִׁלְּחָהּ מִבֵּיתוֹ אוֹ כִי יָמוּת
הָאִישׁ הָאַחֲרוֹן אֲשֶׁר־לְקָחָהּ לוֹ לְאִשָּׁה׃
4 לֹא־יוּכַל בַּעְלָהּ הָרִאשׁוֹן אֲשֶׁר־שִׁלְּחָהּ
לָשׁוּב לְקַחְתָּהּ לִהְיוֹת לוֹ לְאִשָּׁה אַחֲרֵי
אֲשֶׁר הֻטַּמָּאָה כִּי־תוֹעֵבָה הִוא לִפְנֵי יְהוָה
וְלֹא תַחֲטִיא אֶת־הָאָרֶץ אֲשֶׁר יְהוָה
אֱלֹהֶיךָ נֹתֵן לְךָ נַחֲלָה׃ ס
ששי 5 כִּי־יִקַּח אִישׁ אִשָּׁה חֲדָשָׁה לֹא יֵצֵא
בַּצָּבָא וְלֹא־יַעֲבֹר עָלָיו לְכָל־דָּבָר נָקִי
יִהְיֶה לְבֵיתוֹ שָׁנָה אֶחָת וְשִׂמַּח אֶת־
אִשְׁתּוֹ אֲשֶׁר־לָקָח׃ ס

husband could divorce his wife for any reason, however subjective. Divorce here is clearly initiated by the husband, which is the norm in the Bible and elsewhere in the ancient Near East. A number of ancient Near Eastern marriage contracts, however, stipulate that either the husband or the wife may initiate divorce, and similar provisions are known in Palestinian Jewish marriage contracts into the Middle Ages.

bill of divorcement A certificate of divorce, now known as a *"get"* (Aramaic for "legal document," from a Sumerian term meaning "oblong tablet"). Various ancient Near Eastern documents indicate that the certificate probably was a statement by the husband to the effect that the couple is no longer husband and wife and that she is free to marry whomever she wishes. The term translated as "divorcement" (*k'ritut*) literally means "severance." Some commentators conjecture that the term did not originally refer to the severance of the marriage but to the act of cutting the wife's hem or garment, a ceremonial act of divorce known from Mesopotamia.

4. shall not take her to wife again She is disqualified by virtue of her second marriage. Had she not remarried, there would be no objection to the couple's reunion.

NEW HUSBAND'S MILITARY DEFERRAL (v. 5)

5. bride Literally, "new wife." A man who has just married, whether or not his wife has been married previously, is deferred from military service unless—keeping in mind the previous law—he is marrying his former wife. This qualification is to prevent men from gaining deferral by divorcing and remarrying their wives.

any purpose The newlywed is excused even from noncombatant duties.

HALAKHAH L'MA·ASEH

24:1. bill of divorcement This verse demonstrates that divorce is permitted under Jewish law and that it requires the husband to hand his wife a writ of divorce (a *get*) written specifically for her. The Sages understood this verse to mean that the husband must initiate the Jewish divorce (BT Kid. 5b). Until such a writ is given, both partners remain married, even after a civil divorce. A woman whose husband is missing or legally incompetent or who refuses to grant her a Jewish writ of divorce is traditionally referred to as a chained woman (*agunah*) and is unable to remarry. To prevent this situation, the Conservative Movement has created a *t'nai b'kiddushin* (prenuptial condition), written either as a separate codicil or as part of the Conservative *k'tubbah* (wedding document), which specifies that the groom agrees to provide a *get* if the marriage is dissolved in the civil court. If no such clause was included in the marriage documents or if the man is missing or legally incompetent, the Joint *Beit Din* of the Conservative Movement may nullify the marriage (*hafka·at kiddushin*) in accordance with talmudic precedent (BT Ket. 3a, Git. 33a, 73a), thereby allowing the woman to remarry.

[6]A handmill or an upper millstone shall not be taken in pawn, for that would be taking someone's life in pawn.

[7]If a man is found to have kidnapped a fellow Israelite, enslaving him or selling him, that kidnapper shall die; thus you will sweep out evil from your midst.

[8]In cases of a skin affection be most careful to do exactly as the levitical priests instruct you. Take care to do as I have commanded them. [9]Remember what the LORD your God did to Miriam on the journey after you left Egypt.

[10]When you make a loan of any sort to your

6 לֹא־יַחֲבֹ֥ל רֵחַ֖יִם וָרָ֑כֶב כִּי־נֶ֖פֶשׁ ה֥וּא
חֹבֵֽל׃ ס
7 כִּֽי־יִמָּצֵ֣א אִ֗ישׁ גֹּנֵ֨ב נֶ֤פֶשׁ מֵאֶחָיו֙ מִבְּנֵ֣י
יִשְׂרָאֵ֔ל וְהִתְעַמֶּר־בּ֖וֹ וּמְכָר֑וֹ וּמֵת֙ הַגַּנָּ֣ב
הַה֔וּא וּבִעַרְתָּ֥ הָרָ֖ע מִקִּרְבֶּֽךָ׃
8 הִשָּׁ֧מֶר בְּנֶֽגַע־הַצָּרַ֛עַת לִשְׁמֹ֥ר מְאֹ֖ד
וְלַעֲשׂ֑וֹת כְּכֹל֩ אֲשֶׁר־יוֹר֨וּ אֶתְכֶ֜ם הַכֹּהֲנִ֧ים
הַלְוִיִּ֛ם כַּאֲשֶׁ֥ר צִוִּיתִ֖ם תִּשְׁמְר֥וּ לַעֲשֽׂוֹת׃ ס
9 זָכ֕וֹר אֵ֧ת אֲשֶׁר־עָשָׂ֛ה יְהוָ֥ה אֱלֹהֶ֖יךָ
לְמִרְיָ֑ם בַּדֶּ֕רֶךְ בְּצֵאתְכֶ֖ם מִמִּצְרָֽיִם׃ ס
10 כִּֽי־תַשֶּׁ֥ה בְרֵֽעֲךָ֖ מַשַּׁ֣את* מְא֑וּמָה לֹֽא־

v. 10. א׳ נחה

give happiness The purpose of the law is to ensure that the bride enjoys a year of marital pleasure before her husband risks his life in war.

WHAT CREDITORS MAY NOT SEIZE (v. 6)

If a debtor defaulted on a loan, a creditor would seize some of the debtor's possessions, not to satisfy the debt but to press for repayment. Borrowers, however, were usually impoverished and often would have few possessions left apart from clothing and necessary household items. This limited the number of objects creditors could seize. The Torah's laws regarding such seizure ensure that the creditor's right to repayment is subordinated to the survival and dignity of the debtor.

6. A handmill or an upper millstone That is, a handmill set or even just its upper stone. A handmill normally was made of basalt, which was hard enough to withstand constant rubbing. Such mills were used to prepare flour for baking bread, the staple of the common person's diet, and were probably found in every home. The lower stone was heavy, sometimes weighing as much as 90 pounds (40 kg), and inconvenient to take away. In such cases, creditors sometimes took only the upper stone, which weighed only 4 or 5 pounds (2 kg) and could not easily be replaced, because basalt was not found naturally in most parts of the country. This would suffice to render the mill useless and induce the debtor to repay the debt as soon as possible.

taken in pawn Seized to compel repayment.

someone's life That is, something vital, a means of survival. Items necessary for producing food, such as farming tools, as well as food itself and shelter, are often called "life" in Mesopotamian, Egyptian, and postbiblical Jewish literature.

KIDNAPING (v. 7)

The same law appears in Exod. 21:16: "He who kidnaps a man—whether he has sold him or is still holding him—shall be put to death." It is clear from both passages that the primary purpose of kidnaping was to enslave the victim, either to the kidnaper or to others. Here in Deuteronomy, kidnaping is a capital crime if the victim is an Israelite, but only if the victim has been enslaved or sold. In Exodus, it is a capital crime no matter who the victim is, and it apparently makes no difference whether the kidnaper has sold or is still holding the victim. Presumably, the law would punish the kidnaping of resident aliens and foreigners in some other way.

7. enslaving him or selling him This is a necessary condition for capital punishment to be decreed. Kidnaping that does not end with enslavement or sale is not covered by this law.

"LEPROSY" (vv. 8–9)

See Leviticus 13–14.

9. Miriam After Miriam and Aaron had spoken against Moses, Miriam was stricken with "leprosy" and was required to remain outside the camp for one week, as related in Num. 12:10–15. The incident may be mentioned here as a cautionary tale. People should not assume "It can't happen to me!" and fail to consult a priest regarding a potentially "leprous" skin infection.

SEIZING AND HOLDING PROPERTY (vv. 10–13)

These laws, like the law in verse 6, limit the creditor's freedom in taking and holding certain objects.

countryman, you must not enter his house to
seize his pledge. [11]You must remain outside,
while the man to whom you made the loan
brings the pledge out to you. [12]If he is a needy
man, you shall not go to sleep in his pledge;
[13]you must return the pledge to him at sundown, that he may sleep in his cloth and bless you; and it will be to your merit before the LORD your God.

[14]You shall not abuse a needy and destitute laborer, whether a fellow countryman or a stranger in one of the communities of your land.
[15]You must pay him his wages on the same day,
before the sun sets, for he is needy and urgently

תָבֹא אֶל־בֵּיתוֹ לַעֲבֹט עֲבֹטוֹ׃ 11 בַּחוּץ
תַּעֲמֹד וְהָאִישׁ אֲשֶׁר אַתָּה נֹשֶׁה בוֹ יוֹצִיא
אֵלֶיךָ אֶת־הַעֲבוֹט הַחוּצָה׃ 12 וְאִם־אִישׁ
עָנִי הוּא לֹא תִשְׁכַּב בַּעֲבֹטוֹ׃ 13 הָשֵׁב
תָּשִׁיב לוֹ אֶת־הַעֲבוֹט כְּבוֹא הַשֶּׁמֶשׁ וְשָׁכַב
בְּשַׂלְמָתוֹ וּבֵרֲכֶךָּ וּלְךָ תִּהְיֶה צְדָקָה לִפְנֵי
יְהוָה אֱלֹהֶיךָ׃ ס
שביעי 14 לֹא־תַעֲשֹׁק שָׂכִיר עָנִי וְאֶבְיוֹן מֵאַחֶיךָ
אוֹ מִגֵּרְךָ אֲשֶׁר בְּאַרְצְךָ בִּשְׁעָרֶיךָ׃ 15 בְּיוֹמוֹ
תִתֵּן שְׂכָרוֹ וְלֹא־תָבוֹא עָלָיו הַשֶּׁמֶשׁ כִּי
עָנִי הוּא וְאֵלָיו הוּא נֹשֵׂא אֶת־נַפְשׁוֹ

10. The creditor may not enter the debtor's home to seize property. The debtor and his family would be humiliated, and the confrontation could lead to a quarrel. Similarly, the Laws of Hammurabi penalize a creditor who seizes grain from a debtor without his consent.

12. needy man This refers to someone who is absolutely destitute, to the point that he or she owns nothing but a wrap in which to sleep at night. Many debtors were in such straits.

go to sleep in his pledge Nightclothes were often seized from debtors, as indicated in Exod. 22:25–26. The creditor is not to go to sleep at night with the debtor's pledge in his or her possession.

13. return the pledge . . . at sundown You must return it each evening, and he or she will return it to you in the morning.

bless you The debtor will express gratitude by calling on God to bless you, i.e., to reward you with prosperity.

it will be to your merit The promise and the related warning in Exod. 22:26 (see also Deut. 24:15) rest on the conviction that God is the ultimate patron of the powerless. They cannot personally reward those who are kind to them or punish those who mistreat them, but they have recourse to God, who will heed their wishes.

TIMELY PAYMENT OF WAGES (vv. 14–15)

Essentially the same law appears in Lev. 19:13, where it applies to all laborers. Here, it focuses on poor laborers, both Israelites and aliens.

14. Laborers must be paid their wages on the day they do their work. Employers should be sensitive to the fact that laborers live on a day-to-day basis and cannot wait for their pay.

laborer Literally, "a hired man." One hired for a particular job, not a resident employee or servant who receives room and board.

15. urgently depends on it The laborer has his or her heart set on it, and is counting on it. It would be cruel to make such a person wait.

CHAPTER 24

10. Once again, we encounter the theme of the innate dignity of people on society's margins. The dignity of a poor person who has had to pawn his or her last few items of clothing must be respected. The creditor cannot invade the debtor's home but must wait outside as if a supplicant. In contrast, today's society has many ways of humiliating poor people even while ostensibly helping them.

14–15. In a dispute between a powerful employer and a vulnerable hired worker, God is on the side of the weak and vulnerable. To exploit or oppress a worker because one has the power to do so is to offend God.

HALAKHAH L'MA·ASEH

24:11. remain outside The home remains the borrower's despite the pledged object within it. The lender has no legal right to enter the house without permission and, conversely, has the positive duty to respect the borrower's privacy and dignity.

24:15. on the same day From this verse, the Sages determined that an employer must pay employees on time, as agreed on when the work was contracted (BT BM 111a–112a).

depends on it; else he will cry to the LORD against you and you will incur guilt.

[16]Parents shall not be put to death for children, nor children be put to death for parents: a person shall be put to death only for his own crime.

[17]You shall not subvert the rights of the stranger or the fatherless; you shall not take a widow's garment in pawn. [18]Remember that you were a slave in Egypt and that the LORD your God redeemed you from there; therefore do I enjoin you to observe this commandment.

[19]When you reap the harvest in your field and overlook a sheaf in the field, do not turn back to get it; it shall go to the stranger, the fatherless, and the widow—in order that the LORD your God may bless you in all your undertakings.

[20]When you beat down the fruit of your olive

וְלֹא־יִקְרָא עָלֶיךָ אֶל־יְהוָה וְהָיָה בְךָ
חֵטְא׃ ס
16 לֹא־יוּמְתוּ אָבוֹת עַל־בָּנִים וּבָנִים
לֹא־יוּמְתוּ עַל־אָבוֹת אִישׁ בְּחֶטְאוֹ
יוּמָתוּ׃ ס
17 לֹא תַטֶּה מִשְׁפַּט גֵּר יָתוֹם וְלֹא תַחֲבֹל
בֶּגֶד אַלְמָנָה׃ 18 וְזָכַרְתָּ כִּי עֶבֶד הָיִיתָ
בְּמִצְרַיִם וַיִּפְדְּךָ יְהוָה אֱלֹהֶיךָ מִשָּׁם עַל־
כֵּן אָנֹכִי מְצַוְּךָ לַעֲשׂוֹת אֶת־הַדָּבָר
הַזֶּה׃ ס
19 כִּי תִקְצֹר קְצִירְךָ בְשָׂדֶךָ וְשָׁכַחְתָּ עֹמֶר
בַּשָּׂדֶה לֹא תָשׁוּב לְקַחְתּוֹ לַגֵּר לַיָּתוֹם
וְלָאַלְמָנָה יִהְיֶה לְמַעַן יְבָרֶכְךָ יְהוָה
אֱלֹהֶיךָ בְּכֹל מַעֲשֵׂה יָדֶיךָ׃
20 כִּי תַחְבֹּט זֵיתְךָ לֹא תְפַאֵר אַחֲרֶיךָ לַגֵּר

TRANSGENERATIONAL PUNISHMENT (v. 16)

16. The punishment meted out by God to descendants of an offender (see 5:9) is solely a divine prerogative. Human authorities may not act likewise. Ancient Near Eastern law at times viewed members of a man's family as extensions of his personality, rather than as individuals in their own right. Thus if a man harmed a member of another's family, he was punished by the same harm being done to a member of his own family, often the corresponding member. Also, an offender's family might be punished along with him. There is no explicit prohibition of this in the law codes of the ancient Near East before Deuteronomy.

ALIENS, THE FATHERLESS, AND WIDOWS (vv. 17–18)

Concern for the welfare of resident aliens, the fatherless, and widows is a recurrent theme in the Bible. The welfare of the fatherless and widows is commonly mentioned in ancient Near Eastern wisdom literature and texts about the activities of kings, whose special duty it was to protect them. Biblical law requires every Israelite to avoid wronging them and to be concerned with their welfare.

17. the stranger or the fatherless The alien is disadvantaged in court, being neither a fully integrated member of society nor the equal of the adversary or the judges. Those who are fatherless may have no adult male with sufficient experience and eloquence to represent them adequately.

widow's garment Although other debtors' garments may be seized and must be returned at night, if necessary, the garments of a widow may not be taken at all to compel payment of a loan.

GLEANINGS FOR THE POOR (vv. 19–22)

The law in verses 19–22 contains further measures for the welfare of aliens, widows, and orphans.

19. bless you For giving up that which is yours.

20. beat down Olives were harvested by beating the branches with long poles, a method illustrated in Greek vase paintings and still used in recent times in Israel.

---

19. This is the rare *mitzvah* that cannot be performed on purpose. One cannot choose to forget or overlook a sheaf of grain. True, landowners who feel they have enough are more likely to leave fruit or grain behind; and those, however comfortable, who feel insecure in their wealth are more likely to comb the fields for every last sheaf. Tales are told of sages who rejoiced when they realized that they inadvertently had left some grain behind, at last fulfilling this *mitzvah*.

לְיָּתוֹם וְלָאַלְמָנָה יִהְיֶה׃ ס 21 כִּי תִבְצֹר
כַּרְמְךָ לֹא תְעוֹלֵל אַחֲרֶיךָ לַגֵּר לַיָּתוֹם
וְלָאַלְמָנָה יִהְיֶה׃ 22 וְזָכַרְתָּ כִּי־עֶבֶד הָיִיתָ
בְּאֶרֶץ מִצְרָיִם עַל־כֵּן אָנֹכִי מְצַוְּךָ לַעֲשׂוֹת
אֶת־הַדָּבָר הַזֶּה׃ ס

trees, do not go over them again; that shall go
to the stranger, the fatherless, and the widow.
21When you gather the grapes of your vineyard,
do not pick it over again; that shall go to the
stranger, the fatherless, and the widow. 22Al-
ways remember that you were a slave in the land
of Egypt; therefore do I enjoin you to observe
this commandment.

כה כִּי־יִהְיֶה רִיב בֵּין אֲנָשִׁים וְנִגְּשׁוּ
אֶל־הַמִּשְׁפָּט וּשְׁפָטוּם וְהִצְדִּיקוּ אֶת־
הַצַּדִּיק וְהִרְשִׁיעוּ אֶת־הָרָשָׁע׃ 2 וְהָיָה
אִם־בִּן הַכּוֹת הָרָשָׁע וְהִפִּילוֹ הַשֹּׁפֵט
וְהִכָּהוּ לְפָנָיו כְּדֵי רִשְׁעָתוֹ בְּמִסְפָּר׃
3 אַרְבָּעִים יַכֶּנּוּ לֹא יֹסִיף פֶּן־יֹסִיף לְהַכֹּתוֹ
עַל־אֵלֶּה מַכָּה רַבָּה וְנִקְלָה אָחִיךָ
לְעֵינֶיךָ׃ ס

25 When there is a dispute between men
and they go to law, and a decision is rendered
declaring the one in the right and the other in
the wrong—2if the guilty one is to be flogged,
the magistrate shall have him lie down and be
given lashes in his presence, by count, as his guilt
warrants. 3He may be given up to forty lashes,
but not more, lest being flogged further, to excess, your brother be degraded before your eyes.

do not go over them again To knock down any remaining olives.

21. do not pick it over again To harvest the clusters that were immature the first time around.

LIMITS ON FLOGGING (25:1–3)

This law prohibits excessive punishment of an offender who has been sentenced to flogging.

1. a decision is rendered Literally, "they render a decision." Apparently, more than one judge was to hear the case.

2. Flogging generally was used to discipline workers and children. Here it is imposed by the court, as in 22:18, which prescribes flogging for a man who libels his bride. It is not known what other offenses the court might have punished this way. In Mesopotamia, it was imposed—sometimes with additional punishments—for such offenses as destroying a neighbor's house, encroaching on a neighbor's land, selling a person whom one has seized because of a debt, defrauding creditors, stealing, and changing brands on sheep. In an Egyptian contract, one party agreed to be flogged if he failed to fulfill his contractual promise. It is likely that Deuteronomy has offenses such as these in mind.

the magistrate Presumably, the judge who supervises the flogging is one of those who hears the case, perhaps the head judge of the court.

given lashes The Hebrew word could refer either to whipping or to beating with a staff.

in his presence The judge supervises the flogging to make sure that the flogger delivers the correct number of strokes, neither too many nor too few. The Laws of Hammurabi also prescribe flogging in the presence of the court.

by count Someone is to call out each lash to make certain that the flogger does not lose count.

as his guilt warrants Depending on the offense. In certain ancient Near Eastern law codes, different offenses merit differing numbers of blows, ranging from 5 to 100.

3. forty lashes, but not more Never is the punishment to exceed 40 blows. The same number is also found in the Middle Assyrian Code. To avoid exceeding 40 lashes by accident, talmudic law limits the number to 39. It also prescribes that all floggings, however severe the offense, consist in principle of 39 strokes. The number is re-

---

CHAPTER 25

3. lest . . . your brother be degraded Although he was convicted of a crime and punished, he is still *aḥikha*—your brother and fellow Israelite—and, therefore, deserving of your

4 You shall not muzzle an ox while it is
threshing.
5 When brothers dwell together and one of
them dies and leaves no son, the wife of the deceased shall not be married to a stranger, outside
the family. Her husband's brother shall unite
with her: he shall take her as his wife and perform the levir's duty. 6 The first son that she
bears shall be accounted to the dead brother,
that his name may not be blotted out in Israel.

4 לֹא־תַחְסֹם שׁוֹר בְּדִישׁוֹ׃ ס
5 כִּי־יֵשְׁבוּ אַחִים יַחְדָּו וּמֵת אַחַד מֵהֶם
וּבֵן אֵין־לוֹ לֹא־תִהְיֶה אֵשֶׁת־הַמֵּת
הַחוּצָה לְאִישׁ זָר יְבָמָהּ יָבֹא עָלֶיהָ
וּלְקָחָהּ לוֹ לְאִשָּׁה וְיִבְּמָהּ׃ 6 וְהָיָה הַבְּכוֹר
אֲשֶׁר תֵּלֵד יָקוּם עַל־שֵׁם אָחִיו הַמֵּת

duced if the offender is found to be physically incapable of bearing the full 39.

be degraded Because the flogging itself is degrading, the concern must be that excessive flogging would lead to something even more degrading. Perhaps the person being flogged would humiliate himself further by crying or begging hysterically for mercy, or by soiling himself from fright or the severity of the beating.

before your eyes Thereby adding to his humiliation.

NOT MUZZLING A THRESHING OX (v. 4)

4. Threshing was normally done by animals, usually oxen, that either trampled the stalks with their hooves or pulled a threshing sledge—a board with sharp studs on the bottom—over the stalks. The animal naturally would stop and eat some of the grain when hungry (an Egyptian relief shows one doing so). The farmer might seek to prevent this, either to save the grain or to keep the animal working. Deuteronomy forbids such behavior.

LEVIRATE MARRIAGE (vv. 5–10)

If a married man dies childless, his brother is to take the widow as his wife and father a child who will be considered the son of the deceased man. This is known as "levirate marriage," from the Latin *levir* (husband's brother). In Hebrew, it is called *yibbum,* from the noun *yavam,* which also means "husband's brother." If the brother refuses, he must submit to a procedure that will stigmatize him.

5. together The precise force of this word is unclear. It could mean that the brothers are living on the same family estate, either because their father is still alive or because they have not yet divided the estate after his death. It could also mean that they are living in the same vicinity.

leaves no son The parallel law (Num. 27:1–11) implies that the name of a man without sons can also be perpetuated if he has daughters to inherit his property, obviating the need for levirate marriage. In a legal passage like Deut. 25, however, the text probably would have mentioned daughters explicitly had it meant to include them.

Her husband's brother shall unite with her Various attempts have been made to reconcile this law with Lev. 18:16 and 20:21, which prohibit sexual relations with one's brother's wife. The talmudic view is that the prohibition in Leviticus and the law in this verse are, respectively, a generality and an exception. This view is supported by Hittite laws that place the prohibition of relations with one's brother's wife and the levirate law side by side, thus making it clear that the latter is an exception to the former.

take her as his wife The purpose of the levirate could theoretically be satisfied by a temporary sexual union; but in the Bible, sexual union and childrearing require a marital relationship that is intended to be permanent.

6. accounted to the dead brother That is, he will be considered the son of the deceased man and will inherit his property. It seems likely that the son of the levirate marriage would take the deceased man's name as his patronym.

that his name may not be blotted out Reflects the beliefs that death does not put an absolute end to an individual's existence, and that keeping one's name present on earth can assist the spirit of the dead to attain enduring nearness to the living.

---

consideration (BT Mak. 23a). Punishment that degrades criminals (implying that we no longer see them as a "brother" or sister) will only alienate them further from society, making them more likely to repeat their criminal behavior.

6. The underlying idea is that a man's name should not disappear forever if he dies

7But if the man does not want to marry his
brother's widow, his brother's widow shall appear before the elders in the gate and declare,
"My husband's brother refuses to establish a
name in Israel for his brother; he will not perform the duty of a levir." 8The elders of his town
shall then summon him and talk to him. If he
insists, saying, "I do not want to marry her,"
9his brother's widow shall go up to him in the
presence of the elders, pull the sandal off his
foot, spit in his face, and make this declaration:
Thus shall be done to the man who will not
build up his brother's house! 10And he shall go
in Israel by the name of "the family of the unsandaled one."

11If two men get into a fight with each other,
and the wife of one comes up to save her husband from his antagonist and puts out her hand

וְלֹא־יִמָּחֶה שְׁמוֹ מִיִּשְׂרָאֵל׃ 7 וְאִם־לֹא
יַחְפֹּץ הָאִישׁ לָקַחַת אֶת־יְבִמְתּוֹ וְעָלְתָה
יְבִמְתּוֹ הַשַּׁעְרָה אֶל־הַזְּקֵנִים וְאָמְרָה
מֵאֵין* יְבָמִי לְהָקִים לְאָחִיו שֵׁם בְּיִשְׂרָאֵל
לֹא אָבָה יַבְּמִי׃ 8 וְקָרְאוּ־לוֹ זִקְנֵי־עִירוֹ
וְדִבְּרוּ אֵלָיו וְעָמַד וְאָמַר לֹא חָפַצְתִּי
לְקַחְתָּהּ׃ 9 וְנִגְּשָׁה יְבִמְתּוֹ אֵלָיו לְעֵינֵי
הַזְּקֵנִים וְחָלְצָה נַעֲלוֹ מֵעַל רַגְלוֹ וְיָרְקָה
בְּפָנָיו וְעָנְתָה וְאָמְרָה כָּכָה יֵעָשֶׂה לָאִישׁ
אֲשֶׁר לֹא־יִבְנֶה אֶת־בֵּית אָחִיו׃ 10 וְנִקְרָא
שְׁמוֹ בְּיִשְׂרָאֵל בֵּית חֲלוּץ הַנָּעַל׃ ס

11 כִּי־יִנָּצוּ אֲנָשִׁים יַחְדָּו אִישׁ וְאָחִיו
וְקָרְבָה אֵשֶׁת הָאֶחָד לְהַצִּיל אֶת־אִישָׁהּ
מִיַּד מַכֵּהוּ וְשָׁלְחָה יָדָהּ וְהֶחֱזִיקָה

v. 7. יתיר י׳ בכתב היד שלנו

7. the man does not want to marry Many considerations might lead a man to refuse levirate marriage. He might not care for his brother's wife, he might feel that she had brought his brother bad luck, or he might think that with his brother dead and heirless he could himself inherit a larger share of their father's estate. If already married, he might not want to create a rival for his wife, or he might calculate that supporting an extra wife and a child not to be considered his own would diminish the estate that he could leave for his own children.

the elders in the gate Here again, as in 21:19 and 22:15, the elders have jurisdiction in matters concerning the family.

name Here, virtually synonymous with "offspring," a child who would bear the dead man's name as a patronym.

9. pull the sandal off It is common for legal transactions to be accompanied by symbolic acts. Bedouin use a formula similar to this act in their divorce proceedings: "She was my slipper; I have cast her off." The ceremony here could likewise symbolize renunciation of marriage, in this case in advance. If the sandal were removed by unfastening, the act could stand for release of the bond tying the widow to the levir.

spit in his face Ancient authorities debated whether this means literally to spit in his face or to spit on the ground in front of him. In either case, the purpose of the act is to humiliate the levir for refusing to perform a duty that is important for his dead brother.

build up his brother's house Provide him with children.

10. family of the unsandaled one Literally, "house of the unsandaled one." The punishment suits the man's behavior. Because he refused to build up his brother's house, the nickname degrades his own house; because he refused to protect his brother's name from obliteration, he acquires a derogatory nickname.

---

leaving no children. We find echoes of this sentiment today in the emotionally powerful custom of naming a child after a deceased relative (among *S'fardim,* after a living relative), whose name thus lives on. It may also be a way of ensuring that the widow is left with a tangible reminder of her first marriage, a source of support in her old age.

9. To discourage sexual attraction between brothers and sisters-in-law, later Jewish law expressed a clear preference for *ḥalitzah* (the ritual of the sandal) rather than levirate marriage.

and seizes him by his genitals, 12you shall cut off her hand; show no pity.

13You shall not have in your pouch alternate weights, larger and smaller. 14You shall not have in your house alternate measures, a larger and a smaller. 15You must have completely honest weights and completely honest measures, if you are to endure long on the soil that the LORD your God is giving you. 16For everyone who does those things, everyone who deals dishonestly, is abhorrent to the LORD your God.

בִּמְבֻשָׁיו׃ 12 וְקַצֹּתָה אֶת־כַּפָּהּ לֹא תָחוֹס
עֵינֶךָ׃ ס
13 לֹא־יִהְיֶה לְךָ בְּכִיסְךָ אֶבֶן וָאָבֶן גְּדוֹלָה
וּקְטַנָּה׃ ס 14 לֹא־יִהְיֶה לְךָ בְּבֵיתְךָ
אֵיפָה וְאֵיפָה גְּדוֹלָה וּקְטַנָּה׃ 15 אֶבֶן
שְׁלֵמָה וָצֶדֶק יִהְיֶה־לָּךְ אֵיפָה שְׁלֵמָה
וָצֶדֶק יִהְיֶה־לָּךְ לְמַעַן יַאֲרִיכוּ יָמֶיךָ עַל
הָאֲדָמָה אֲשֶׁר־יְהוָה אֱלֹהֶיךָ נֹתֵן לָךְ׃ 16 כִּי
תוֹעֲבַת יְהוָה אֱלֹהֶיךָ כָּל־עֹשֵׂה אֵלֶּה כֹּל
עֹשֵׂה עָוֶל׃ פ

17Remember what Amalek did to you on your

מפטיר 17 זָכוֹר אֵת אֲשֶׁר־עָשָׂה לְךָ עֲמָלֵק בַּדֶּרֶךְ

IMPROPER INTERVENTION IN A FIGHT (vv. 11–12)

12. cut off her hand In the ancient Near East, it was common to inflict punishment on the part of the body with which an offense was committed. The reason for such a severe punishment is not clear. Some think it may be because of her injuring the man's genitals and threatening his ability to father children, as is stated explicitly in the Middle Assyrian laws.

show no pity This clause is used in cases where one might be tempted to be lenient, in this case because the woman's motive—the defense of her husband—was honorable.

HONEST WEIGHTS AND MEASURES (vv. 13–16)

Only honest weights and measures are permitted. The importance of this principle, so crucial for the justice and stability of commerce within a society, was widely emphasized in the ancient Near East.

13. You shall not have Not only may one not use deceptive weights and measures, one may not even possess them.

pouch Where merchants carried their weights.

alternate weights Literally, "stone and stone." The weights in question were used on balance scales to determine the weight of money and commodities. The standard weight was the shekel, approximately 0.4 ounce (11 g), although it varied in different periods. One may not use the large weight to receive more or the small weight to give less. Ancient Babylonian writings contain many accounts about the violation of this norm. Numerous stone and metal weights of the standard shekel and its fractions and multiples have been found in archaeological excavations.

14. alternate measures Literally, "alternate *ephah* measures." The *ephah* (standing here for all measures) was not a measuring device but a unit of capacity of pottery containers used for grain; see Comment to Exod. 16:36. The size and weight of such large containers made it difficult for buyers or sellers of grain to carry their own jars from place to place to verify the amounts involved in a sale.

15. completely honest Literally, "complete and honest." In Hebrew, the words appear at the beginning of the verse, where they serve as a contrast to verse 14 and gain an emphatic sense: "only completely honest weights."

if you are to endure long Long life, for the individual or the nation, is the reward granted by God for obedience to His laws.

REMEMBERING AMALEKITE AGGRESSION (vv. 17–19)

The Amalekites were a nomadic group living in

---

12. cut off her hand That is, "leave her with diminished financial resources" (*Ha-amek Davar*). The Sages shrank from taking this punishment literally; they substituted a monetary fine for mutilation.

16. your God The Jew who cheats in business may no longer call upon "my God." Such behavior is detestable in God's sight. God will no longer tolerate being associated with that person (Hirsch).

17. The text mentions the predations of Amalek right after discussing just weights and

בְּצֵאתְכֶם מִמִּצְרָיִם׃ 18 אֲשֶׁר קָרְךָ בַּדֶּרֶךְ
וַיְזַנֵּב בְּךָ כָּל־הַנֶּחֱשָׁלִים אַחֲרֶיךָ וְאַתָּה
עָיֵף וְיָגֵעַ וְלֹא יָרֵא אֱלֹהִים׃ 19 וְהָיָה
בְּהָנִיחַ יְהוָה אֱלֹהֶיךָ ׀ לְךָ מִכָּל־אֹיְבֶיךָ
מִסָּבִיב בָּאָרֶץ אֲשֶׁר יְהוָה־אֱלֹהֶיךָ נֹתֵן לְךָ
נַחֲלָה לְרִשְׁתָּהּ תִּמְחֶה אֶת־זֵכֶר עֲמָלֵק
מִתַּחַת הַשָּׁמָיִם לֹא תִּשְׁכָּח׃ פ

journey, after you left Egypt—18how, undeterred by fear of God, he surprised you on the
march, when you were famished and weary, and
cut down all the stragglers in your rear. 19There-
fore, when the LORD your God grants you safety
from all your enemies around you, in the land
that the LORD your God is giving you as a hereditary portion, you shall blot out the memory
of Amalek from under heaven. Do not forget!

the Sinai desert and the part of the Negeb that was south of the territory of Judah. Nothing is known of them from sources outside the Bible. Israel's experience with them must have been particularly bitter to have led to the resolve to wipe them out. The account in Exod. 17:8–16 offers no explanation for that determination, but Deuteronomy does: The Amalekites staged a sneak attack on the defenseless weak lagging at the rear of the migrating Israelites, an attack that showed Amalek to be uncommonly ruthless, lacking in even the most elementary decency. Conceivably, the Israelites thought that the Amalekites had genocidal intentions, and regarded the command to annihilate them as measure-for-measure punishment.

17. The exhortation to remember is echoed by "Do not forget" in verse 19.

what Amalek did to you There is no indication of what prompted the Amalekites to attack. It has been conjectured that they saw the Israelites as a potential threat to their control of the oases and pasturelands in the Sinai and the Negeb. In view of the Amalekites' later character as marauders, however, it is just as likely that their attack was a plundering raid on a target of opportunity.

18. undeterred by fear of God The Amalekites are not expected to fear *YHVH,* the God of Israel, whom they do not recognize. That is why the term used here is "fear of God" (*elohim,* the more general term for the deity), meaning fear of the divine. The Bible knows that non-Israelite religions also teach that the gods punish sin; and when it refers to pagans who are or are not heedful of that belief, it uses the more general term "God" (see Gen. 20:11). The Amalekites lacked the basic principles of morality common to all religions.

stragglers Those traveling at the rear would include the sick and weak who could not keep up with the others. Anyone with elementary decency would avoid attacking them.

19. when God grants you safety Once Israel is securely settled in the Land, with no threat left to its existence, it is to turn its attention to Amalek.

blot out the memory That is, blot out their name, wipe them out. The Israelites are not being commanded here to eradicate all recollection of the Amalekites. Indeed, they are commanded to remember forever what the Amalekites did.

---

measures, to warn us that when people cheat each other, the national bonds of unity, loyalty, and mutual trust are strained and the nation becomes vulnerable to Amalek (Tanḥ.).

undeterred by fear of God Literally, "not fearing God." In Hebrew, this phrase follows "you were famished and weary"; to whom does it refer? To Amalek? Or to the stragglers who had lost faith—thus becoming vulnerable to Amalek? If the former, "fearing God" means having empathy for the powerless who are at your mercy (as the Egyptian midwives who "feared God" spared Israelite babies in Exod. 1:17).

18. surprised you Hebrew: *korkha,* which the Midrash relates to the word for "cold" (*kor*). The Israelites, leaving Egypt on the way to Sinai, had been confident and enthusiastic. The real sin of Amalek was that he robbed them of their idealism, teaching them that the world could be an unreliable and dangerous place.

19. The commandment to blot out the name and the memory of the wicked may be thematically related to the commandment earlier in the chapter to perpetuate the name of the man who died childless.

HALAKHAH L'MA·ASEH

25:19. blot out . . . Amalek This verse is the source for the custom of drowning out the name of Haman (by tradition a descendent of Amalek) with raucous noise during the reading of *M'gillat Ester* on *Purim.*

הפטרה חמישית דנחמתא

FIFTH HAFTARAH OF CONSOLATION
HAFTARAH FOR KI TETZEI

ISAIAH 54:1–10

(*Recite on the 5th* Shabbat *after the 9th of* Av, *coinciding with the reading of* Ki Tetzei. *If two weeks ago the third* Haftarah *of Consolation was pre-empted by* Rosh Ḥodesh, *then that* haftarah *is now added to this one—following the order in the Book of Isaiah. That is, recite this passage first, then continue with the third* Haftarah *of Consolation on pages 1085–1087 before making the final benedictions. On the Seven* Haftarot *of Consolation, see p. 1032.*)

This *haftarah* contains a cluster of promises and assurances to Zion and its inhabitants. The prophet addressed them to the destroyed city and nation sometime after Cyrus the Mede conquered Babylon and allowed subject populations, including the Judeans, to renew their ancient heritages (538 B.C.E.). Because Zion soon will be rebuilt and repopulated, and because the time of shame and desolation has passed, the prophet urges a personified Zion to rejoice. The divine signature, "said the LORD your Redeemer" (Isa. 54:8), provides assurance. Further testimony of assurance comes when the new covenant (*b'rit*) of reconciliation with the people is compared to God's ancient pact with Noah after the Flood. Just as that ancient oath promised the end of universal destruction, so Zion now is promised the end of divine punishment. Here again a divine signature closes a prophecy, this time referring to God as "the LORD, who takes you back in love" (v. 10).

Figures of assurance dominate the prophet's style. The people are promised "kindness everlasting [*ḥesed olam*]" (v. 8) and that neither "my loyalty [*ḥesed*]" "Nor My covenant [*b'rit*] of friendship" (v. 10) will be shaken. Such tokens of assurance are reinforced by a series of dramatic imperatives ("shout," "enlarge," "come") and by the Hebrew particle *lo* (no, not). Thus, the negative state of Zion "who bore no [*lo*] child" and "did not [*lo*] travail" (v. 1) is reversed by the promise that it will "not [*lo*] be shamed" or "disgraced" and that it will "remember no [*lo*] more / The shame" of its past (v. 4). The concluding section reinforces this counterpoint with the statement that God's loyalty (*ḥesed*) shall "never [*lo*] move from you" (v. 10).

Another stylistic strategy in this *haftarah* is the use of comparisons. The prophet begins by comparing the exilic loss and national restoration of Israel with changes in a marriage; God will take back fair Zion just as a once-angry husband will restore the bride of his youth. The simile derives from an old prophetic tradition in which God's relationship to His people is likened to that of a groom and his bride. The prophet's emphasis on kindness everlasting and love (v. 8) thus recalls the vows in Hos. 2:21–22 and so likewise must depict Covenant renewal.

The marriage motif allows the prophet to focus on the dynamics of love and rejection, and of anger and its assuagement. God is presented as a faithful bridegroom who is able to overcome betrayal and anger. The *haftarah* dramatizes this with two cases of unilateral divine commitment: (a) God's oath to Noah and his descendants (v. 9) models God's everlasting stability, assuring no further anger or destruction. This transfer of a primordial covenantal guarantee to the sphere of current affairs is striking. (b) The prophet uses natural imagery to highlight God's future steadfastness with Israel: "For the mountains may move / And the hills be shaken, / But my loyalty shall never move from you" (v. 10). Through the analogy of the Flood, we sense how deeply the Exile was felt to be a rupture in the divine order; and through the analogy of nature, we learn how disconsolate and without hope the people of Zion had been.

54 Shout, O barren one,
You who bore no child!
Shout aloud for joy,
You who did not travail!
For the children of the wife forlorn
Shall outnumber those of the espoused
—said the LORD.
2Enlarge the site of your tent,
Extend the size of your dwelling,
Do not stint!
Lengthen the ropes, and drive the pegs firm.
3For you shall spread out to the right and the left;
Your offspring shall dispossess nations
And shall people the desolate towns.

4Fear not, you shall not be shamed;
Do not cringe, you shall not be disgraced.
For you shall forget
The reproach of your youth,
And remember no more
The shame of your widowhood.
5For He who made you will espouse you—
His name is "LORD of Hosts."
The Holy One of Israel will redeem you—
He is called "God of all the Earth."

6The LORD has called you back
As a wife forlorn and forsaken.
Can one cast off the wife of his youth?
—said your God.
7For a little while I forsook you,
But with vast love I will bring you back.

נד רָנִּי עֲקָרָה
לֹא יָלָדָה
פִּצְחִי רִנָּה וְצַהֲלִי
לֹא־חָלָה
כִּי־רַבִּים בְּנֵי־שׁוֹמֵמָה
מִבְּנֵי בְעוּלָה
אָמַר יְהוָה׃
2 הַרְחִיבִי ׀ מְקוֹם אָהֳלֵךְ
וִירִיעוֹת מִשְׁכְּנוֹתַיִךְ יַטּוּ
אַל־תַּחְשֹׂכִי
הַאֲרִיכִי מֵיתָרַיִךְ וִיתֵדֹתַיִךְ חַזֵּקִי׃
3 כִּי־יָמִין וּשְׂמֹאול* תִּפְרֹצִי
וְזַרְעֵךְ גּוֹיִם יִירָשׁ
וְעָרִים נְשַׁמּוֹת יוֹשִׁיבוּ׃

4 אַל־תִּירְאִי כִּי־לֹא תֵבוֹשִׁי
וְאַל־תִּכָּלְמִי כִּי לֹא תַחְפִּירִי
כִּי בֹשֶׁת עֲלוּמַיִךְ
תִּשְׁכָּחִי
וְחֶרְפַּת אַלְמְנוּתַיִךְ
לֹא תִזְכְּרִי־עוֹד׃
5 כִּי בֹעֲלַיִךְ עֹשַׂיִךְ
יְהוָה צְבָאוֹת שְׁמוֹ
וְגֹאֲלֵךְ קְדוֹשׁ יִשְׂרָאֵל
אֱלֹהֵי כָל־הָאָרֶץ יִקָּרֵא׃

6 כִּי־כְאִשָּׁה עֲזוּבָה וַעֲצוּבַת רוּחַ
קְרָאָךְ יְהוָה
וְאֵשֶׁת נְעוּרִים כִּי תִמָּאֵס
אָמַר אֱלֹהָיִךְ׃
7 בְּרֶגַע קָטֹן עֲזַבְתִּיךְ
וּבְרַחֲמִים גְּדֹלִים אֲקַבְּצֵךְ׃

v. 3. מלא ו'

Isaiah 54:6. wife of his youth This recalls other reflexes of the marriage motif (see Hos. 2:17; Jer. 2:2; Ezek. 23:8,19–20).

8In slight anger, for a moment,

I hid My face from you;

But with kindness everlasting

I will take you back in love

  —said the Lord your Redeemer.

9For this to Me is like the waters of Noah:

As I swore that the waters of Noah

Nevermore would flood the earth,

So I swear that I will not

Be angry with you or rebuke you.

10For the mountains may move

And the hills be shaken,

But my loyalty shall never move from you,

Nor My covenant of friendship be shaken

  —said the Lord, who takes you back in love.

8 בְּשֶׁ֤צֶף קֶ֙צֶף֙

הִסְתַּ֤רְתִּי פָנַ֥י רֶ֙גַע֙ מִמֵּ֔ךְ

וּבְחֶ֥סֶד עוֹלָ֖ם

רִֽחַמְתִּ֑יךְ

אָמַ֥ר גֹּאֲלֵ֖ךְ יְהֹוָֽה׃ ס

9 כִּי־מֵ֥י נֹ֙חַ֙ זֹ֣את לִ֔י

אֲשֶׁ֣ר נִשְׁבַּ֗עְתִּי מֵעֲבֹ֥ר מֵי־נֹ֛חַ

ע֖וֹד עַל־הָאָ֑רֶץ

כֵּ֥ן נִשְׁבַּ֛עְתִּי

מִקְּצֹ֥ף עָלַ֖יִךְ וּמִגְּעׇר־בָּֽךְ׃

10 כִּ֤י הֶֽהָרִים֙ יָמ֔וּשׁוּ

וְהַגְּבָע֖וֹת תְּמוּטֶ֑נָה

וְחַסְדִּ֞י מֵאִתֵּ֣ךְ לֹֽא־יָמ֗וּשׁ

וּבְרִ֤ית שְׁלוֹמִי֙ לֹ֣א תָמ֔וּט

אָמַ֥ר מְרַחֲמֵ֖ךְ יְהֹוָֽה׃* ס

8–10. kindness . . . loyalty Hebrew: ḥesed, translated in more than one way. In verse 8 it alludes to God's response as bound to the Covenant (see Hos. 2:21 and Jer. 2:2). In verse 10 it conveys commitment (see 2 Sam. 7:15; Ps. 89:34).

Through ḥesed one deals faithfully or keeps faith with another. It is used to describe both divine–human and interpersonal relationships (see Deut. 5:10; 1 Sam. 20:8).

* If two weeks ago the third Haftarah of Consolation was pre-empted by Rosh Ḥodesh, then continue by reciting it now on pages 1085–1087 before making the final benedictions.

KI TAVO

כי תבוא

26 When you enter the land that the LORD your God is giving you as a heritage, and you possess it and settle in it, [2]you shall take some of every first fruit of the soil, which you harvest from the land that the LORD your God is giving you, put it in a basket and go to the place where the LORD your God will choose to establish His name. [3]You shall go to the priest in charge at that time and say to him, "I acknowledge this day before the LORD your God that I have en-

כו וְהָיָה כִּי־תָבוֹא אֶל־הָאָרֶץ אֲשֶׁר
יְהוָה אֱלֹהֶיךָ נֹתֵן לְךָ נַחֲלָה וִירִשְׁתָּהּ
וְיָשַׁבְתָּ בָּהּ׃ 2 וְלָקַחְתָּ מֵרֵאשִׁית ׀ כָּל־פְּרִי
הָאֲדָמָה אֲשֶׁר תָּבִיא מֵאַרְצְךָ אֲשֶׁר יְהוָה
אֱלֹהֶיךָ נֹתֵן לָךְ וְשַׂמְתָּ בַטֶּנֶא וְהָלַכְתָּ
אֶל־הַמָּקוֹם אֲשֶׁר יִבְחַר יְהוָה אֱלֹהֶיךָ
לְשַׁכֵּן שְׁמוֹ שָׁם׃ 3 וּבָאתָ אֶל־הַכֹּהֵן אֲשֶׁר
יִהְיֶה בַּיָּמִים הָהֵם וְאָמַרְתָּ אֵלָיו הִגַּדְתִּי

Moses' Second Discourse, Part 3: The Laws Given in Moab (*continued*)

TWO LITURGICAL DECLARATIONS (26:1–15)

When farmers bring the first fruits to the Temple each year, and after they give the poor tithe every third year, they are to make certain declarations. These declarations (and the declaration of 21:7–9) are the only instances in the Torah that present the precise wording that must be recited in a layman's address to God. They convey what Deuteronomy wished the farmers to find meaningful in these ceremonies.

THE FIRST-FRUITS CEREMONY (26:1–11)

The first-fruits ceremony leads the farmers from a recognition of the land's fertility to an awareness of God's guidance of the Israelites from their beginnings, freeing them from oppression and giving them the land. The change in the focus of a religious ceremony from exclusive attention to God's role in nature to an emphasis on God's role in history is one of the most significant original features of the Bible. The declaration spoken by the farmers evokes the very heart of monotheism, which acknowledges God as the power behind all phenomena, historical as well as natural.

2. The farmer, the typical Israelite, is being addressed. The context suggests that farmers brought their first fruits individually. No date is specified for bringing them, and it probably varied for different farmers, depending on their work load, the species that each grew, and the date of the harvest of each species in each part of the country.

some of every first fruit Some of every species must be brought, not only those that 18:4 assigns to the priests. Because the first fruits are a token gift, no specific amount is prescribed. The Talmud states that the minimum quantity is one-sixtieth of the crop, with no maximum. According to the Talmud, a farmer who sees the first ripe fruit of each species ties a cord or blade of grass on it for identification.

I acknowledge The Hebrew can be understood in one of two ways: "By this declaration I acknowledge" or "By bringing the first fruits I acknowledge." In the latter case, the act of giving the first fruits constitutes an acknowledgment, tangible proof that the farmer has entered the Land.

the LORD your God The farmer is addressing the priest. The Lord, of course, is the farmer's God as well, as the chapter states several times. People would often say "your God" or "so-and-so's God" when speaking to, or about, priests, prophets, and kings, because their offices were established by God and they were considered especially close to Him.

CHAPTER 26

Deuteronomy now moves toward its climax, invoking blessings on those who will be faithful to God's message and calling down a series of curses on those who would depart from the Torah's norms. The curses culminate in a warning, called the *Tokheḥah* (Reproach), similar to the one found in the final *parashah* of Leviticus.

tered the land that the Lord swore to our fathers
to assign us."
4The priest shall take the basket from your
hand and set it down in front of the altar of the
Lord your God.
5You shall then recite as follows before the
Lord your God: "My father was a fugitive Aramean. He went down to Egypt with meager
numbers and sojourned there; but there he became a great and very populous nation. 6The
Egyptians dealt harshly with us and oppressed
us; they imposed heavy labor upon us. 7We cried
to the Lord, the God of our fathers, and the
Lord heard our plea and saw our plight, our
misery, and our oppression. 8The Lord freed
us from Egypt by a mighty hand, by an outstretched arm and awesome power, and by signs
and portents. 9He brought us to this place and
gave us this land, a land flowing with milk and
honey. 10Wherefore I now bring the first fruits
of the soil which You, O Lord, have given me."

הַיּוֹם לַיהוָה אֱלֹהֶיךָ כִּי־בָאתִי אֶל־הָאָרֶץ
אֲשֶׁר נִשְׁבַּע יְהוָה לַאֲבֹתֵינוּ לָתֶת לָנוּ׃
4 וְלָקַח הַכֹּהֵן הַטֶּנֶא מִיָּדֶךָ וְהִנִּיחוֹ לִפְנֵי
מִזְבַּח יְהוָה אֱלֹהֶיךָ׃
5 וְעָנִיתָ וְאָמַרְתָּ לִפְנֵי ׀ יְהוָה אֱלֹהֶיךָ אֲרַמִּי
אֹבֵד אָבִי וַיֵּרֶד מִצְרַיְמָה וַיָּגָר שָׁם בִּמְתֵי
מְעָט וַיְהִי־שָׁם לְגוֹי גָּדוֹל עָצוּם וָרָב׃
6 וַיָּרֵעוּ אֹתָנוּ הַמִּצְרִים וַיְעַנּוּנוּ וַיִּתְּנוּ
עָלֵינוּ עֲבֹדָה קָשָׁה׃ 7 וַנִּצְעַק אֶל־יְהוָה
אֱלֹהֵי אֲבֹתֵינוּ וַיִּשְׁמַע יְהוָה אֶת־קֹלֵנוּ
וַיַּרְא אֶת־עָנְיֵנוּ וְאֶת־עֲמָלֵנוּ וְאֶת־לַחֲצֵנוּ׃
8 וַיּוֹצִאֵנוּ יְהוָה מִמִּצְרַיִם בְּיָד חֲזָקָה וּבִזְרֹעַ
נְטוּיָה וּבְמֹרָא גָּדֹל וּבְאֹתוֹת וּבְמֹפְתִים׃
9 וַיְבִאֵנוּ אֶל־הַמָּקוֹם הַזֶּה וַיִּתֶּן־לָנוּ אֶת־
הָאָרֶץ הַזֹּאת אֶרֶץ זָבַת חָלָב וּדְבָשׁ׃
10 וְעַתָּה הִנֵּה הֵבֵאתִי אֶת־רֵאשִׁית פְּרִי
הָאֲדָמָה אֲשֶׁר־נָתַתָּה לִּי יְהוָה

5. my father It could refer to Jacob, who went down to Egypt; it could be collective, referring to Jacob's entire family, who went with him; or it could refer to all the ancestors, Abraham and Isaac as well as Jacob and his sons.

fugitive Could also mean "perishing" or "straying."

Aramean Probably refers to the fact that the ancestors of the Israelites came from the region known as "Aram alongside the River." The recitation contrasts the homeless beginnings of the Israelites with their present possession of a fertile land. In the *Pesah Haggadah,* a well-known *midrash* interprets these words to mean, "Laban the Aramean sought to destroy my father."

9. this place The land of Israel.

10. After reciting a brief history of Israel and speaking about God, the farmers now turn to speak to God. In this way they express their feeling that they stand directly in God's presence. Then, after speaking of Israel in the first person plural while describing the history of God's benefactions to Israel, they switch to the first person singular, expressing the feeling that they personally are participating in that history.

which You, O Lord, have given me Refers to the soil, not to the first fruits.

---

5. The words that the farmer utters here and in verse 3 are called "The First-Fruits Recitation" in the Mishnah, which requires that it be said in Hebrew. At first those who were able to recite it on their own did so, while those who could not were assisted by a prompter. When the latter group, out of embarrassment, ceased to bring their first fruits, the procedure was changed so that everybody was led by a prompter (M Sot. 7:2–3, Bik. 3:7).

This is a rare instance of the Torah prescribing the precise words of a prayer rather than leaving it to the inspiration of the worshiper's own heart. This recitation summarizes the historical basis of Jewish identity and has found a featured place in the *Pesaḥ Haggadah.* One of the advantages of a set liturgy, in addition to uniting all Jews across barriers of time and space, is that it reminds us of themes we might not think of on our own.

10–11. Gratitude and generosity do not seem to come naturally to most people. Most of us must be taught to remember to thank God for our good fortune and must learn through ex-

וְהִנַּחְתּוֹ לִפְנֵי יְהוָה אֱלֹהֶיךָ וְהִשְׁתַּחֲוִיתָ
לִפְנֵי יְהוָה אֱלֹהֶיךָ׃ 11 וְשָׂמַחְתָּ בְכָל־הַטּוֹב
אֲשֶׁר נָתַן־לְךָ יְהוָה אֱלֹהֶיךָ וּלְבֵיתֶךָ אַתָּה
וְהַלֵּוִי וְהַגֵּר אֲשֶׁר בְּקִרְבֶּךָ׃ ס
שני 12 כִּי תְכַלֶּה לַעְשֵׂר אֶת־כָּל־מַעְשַׂר
תְּבוּאָתְךָ בַּשָּׁנָה הַשְּׁלִישִׁת שְׁנַת הַמַּעֲשֵׂר
וְנָתַתָּה לַלֵּוִי לַגֵּר לַיָּתוֹם וְלָאַלְמָנָה וְאָכְלוּ
בִשְׁעָרֶיךָ וְשָׂבֵעוּ׃ 13 וְאָמַרְתָּ לִפְנֵי יְהוָה
אֱלֹהֶיךָ בִּעַרְתִּי הַקֹּדֶשׁ מִן־הַבַּיִת וְגַם
נְתַתִּיו לַלֵּוִי וְלַגֵּר לַיָּתוֹם וְלָאַלְמָנָה
כְּכָל־מִצְוָתְךָ אֲשֶׁר צִוִּיתָנִי לֹא־עָבַרְתִּי
מִמִּצְוֺתֶיךָ וְלֹא שָׁכָחְתִּי׃ 14 לֹא־אָכַלְתִּי
בְאֹנִי מִמֶּנּוּ וְלֹא־בִעַרְתִּי מִמֶּנּוּ בְּטָמֵא

You shall leave it before the LORD your God
and bow low before the LORD your God. 11And
you shall enjoy, together with the Levite and the
stranger in your midst, all the bounty that the
LORD your God has bestowed upon you and
your household.

12When you have set aside in full the tenth
part of your yield—in the third year, the year
of the tithe—and have given it to the Levite, the
stranger, the fatherless, and the widow, that they
may eat their fill in your settlements, 13you shall
declare before the LORD your God: "I have
cleared out the consecrated portion from the
house; and I have given it to the Levite, the
stranger, the fatherless, and the widow, just as
You commanded me; I have neither transgressed nor neglected any of Your commandments: 14 I have not eaten of it while in mourning, I have not cleared out any of it while I was

11. you shall enjoy That is, you shall celebrate all the bounty. The celebration takes the form of a festive meal at the sanctuary.

the stranger in your midst The farmers, whose ancestors sojourned as strangers in Egypt where they were oppressed, now provide generously for the strangers in their land.

THE TITHE DECLARATION (vv. 12–15)

Every third year, when farmers have removed all the tithe from their premises and have given it to indigents and to Levites (see 14:28–29), they are to make a formal declaration before God that they have divested themselves of all the portions of the crop that must be donated and have not violated their sanctity by handling or using them improperly. Then they are to pray for God's continued blessing of the land and the people of Israel.

13. before the LORD your God The worshipers address God from their hometowns, either at their home, at wherever they deposit the tithe, or at some local place of prayer.

cleared out Not held back the slightest amount.

the consecrated portion The poor tithe. Even though it is not brought to a sanctuary, it is to be treated as holy until it is handed over for distribution to the poor. Giving it to the poor is no less a sacred purpose than bringing it to the sanctuary.

You commanded me The first-person formulation expresses the idea that God commanded the farmer personally, not only his or her ancestors. This wording is part of the liturgy's attempt to enhance the farmers' feeling of personal involvement in the history of their people.

commandments That is, about the tithe in 14:28–29. It is not a blanket claim of virtue, but a statement about the obligation that has just been discharged.

14. The requirement to declare full compliance with the tithe obligation is also found in the ancient Hittite "Instructions for Temple Officials." There the herdsmen responsible for deliv-

---

perience the satisfaction of sharing our bounty with others.

12. The first tithe goes to the Levites, to maintain Israel's spiritual core. The second tithe is consumed in Jerusalem, to teach us to celebrate our good fortune in God's presence and in the presence of our fellow Israelites. Once in three years, the second tithe is given to the poor, to perfect Israelite society by minimizing poverty (Hirsch).

13. I have . . . [not] neglected any of your commandments I have not performed any of these *mitzvot* mindlessly, perfunctorily, without feeling (*S'fat Emet*).

impure, and I have not deposited any of it with
the dead. I have obeyed the LORD my God; I have
done just as You commanded me. 15Look down
from Your holy abode, from heaven, and bless
Your people Israel and the soil You have given
us, a land flowing with milk and honey, as You
swore to our fathers."

16The LORD your God commands you this
day to observe these laws and rules; observe
them faithfully with all your heart and soul.
17You have affirmed this day that the LORD is
your God, that you will walk in His ways, that
you will observe His laws and commandments

וְלֹא־נָתַתִּי מִמֶּנּוּ לְמֵת שָׁמַעְתִּי בְּקוֹל
יְהוָה אֱלֹהָי עָשִׂיתִי כְּכֹל אֲשֶׁר צִוִּיתָנִי׃
15 הַשְׁקִיפָה מִמְּעוֹן קָדְשְׁךָ מִן־הַשָּׁמַיִם
וּבָרֵךְ אֶת־עַמְּךָ אֶת־יִשְׂרָאֵל וְאֵת הָאֲדָמָה
אֲשֶׁר נָתַתָּה לָנוּ כַּאֲשֶׁר נִשְׁבַּעְתָּ לַאֲבֹתֵינוּ
אֶרֶץ זָבַת חָלָב וּדְבָשׁ׃ ס
שלישי 16 הַיּוֹם הַזֶּה יְהוָה אֱלֹהֶיךָ מְצַוְּךָ לַעֲשׂוֹת
אֶת־הַחֻקִּים הָאֵלֶּה וְאֶת־הַמִּשְׁפָּטִים
וְשָׁמַרְתָּ וְעָשִׂיתָ אוֹתָם בְּכָל־לְבָבְךָ וּבְכָל־
נַפְשֶׁךָ׃ 17 אֶת־יְהוָה הֶאֱמַרְתָּ הַיּוֹם לִהְיוֹת
לְךָ לֵאלֹהִים וְלָלֶכֶת בִּדְרָכָיו וְלִשְׁמֹר
חֻקָּיו וּמִצְוֺתָיו וּמִשְׁפָּטָיו וְלִשְׁמֹעַ בְּקֹלוֹ׃

ering cattle offerings to the temple must declare on oath, when they bring the cattle, that they have not misappropriated any of the cattle that were due.

mourning Mourners, who become impure from being in the same tent as a dead body, from handling it during burial, or from contact with others who have become impure in one of these ways, would defile any food they touched.

impure The tithe would be defiled if handled by someone who is in a state of impurity.

deposited any of it with the dead To feed their spirits. The ancients believed that the living can assist the spirits of the dead by providing them with food and drink. This widespread belief was also found among Jews in Second Temple times and later. The Torah does not forbid the practice, but because contact with the dead is ritually defiling, it prohibits the use of the tithe for it.

just as You commanded me Regarding the tithe.

15. Your holy abode, from heaven In some biblical passages, God's "abode" is the Temple. Here, "heaven" emphasizes the Deuteronomic idea that His abode is heaven, not the Temple.

bless With bountiful crops and prosperity.

Your people Israel Farmers are not to ask for their own prosperity but for that of the entire nation.

Moses' Second Discourse, Part 4: Conclusion to the Covenant Made in Moab (26:16–28:69)

MUTUAL COMMITMENTS (26:16–19)

The laws in all their detail are now concluded. This passage sums up Israel's duty to obey them wholeheartedly and underscores the fact that, beyond being mere items of a legal code, they are the very basis of the relationship that God and the people Israel have established. It not only is an emotional or spiritual association but also entails mutual obligations with consequences.

16. commands you this day Moses, speaking at God's command, has referred to "this day" throughout his address (e.g., 4:8, 15:5, 19:9). According to 1:3, the address was delivered on the first day of the 11th month (later known as *Sh'vat*) in the 40th year after the Exodus.

these laws and rules That Moses has just finished presenting (12:1–26:15).

17. you have affirmed The most probable interpretation of the unique form of this Hebrew verb (rendering its *hiph·il* form not as causative but intensive). God and Israel have each proclaimed acceptance of the other as parties to the covenant and have proclaimed specific commitments to each other. The principles agreed to are strongly reminiscent of the earlier covenant at Horeb (Mount Sinai), which this reaffirms.

that the LORD is your God The counterpart to this phrase in verse 18 is "that you are . . . His people." This pair of phrases is the classic expression of the covenant relationship (see 29:12).

you will walk in His ways This clause and the remainder of the verse are virtually a definition of what it means to accept the Lord as God. In short, it requires action as well as intellectual assent.

and rules, and that you will obey Him. [18]And
the LORD has affirmed this day that you are, as
He promised you, His treasured people who
shall observe all His commandments, [19]and that
He will set you, in fame and renown and glory,
high above all the nations that He has made; and
that you shall be, as He promised, a holy people
to the LORD your God.

18 וַיהוָ֞ה הֶאֱמִֽירְךָ֣ הַיּ֗וֹם לִהְי֥וֹת לוֹ֙ לְעַ֣ם
סְגֻלָּ֔ה כַּאֲשֶׁ֖ר דִּבֶּר־לָ֑ךְ וְלִשְׁמֹ֖ר כָּל־
מִצְוֺתָֽיו׃ 19 וּֽלְתִתְּךָ֣ עֶלְי֗וֹן עַ֤ל כָּל־הַגּוֹיִם֙
אֲשֶׁ֣ר עָשָׂ֔ה לִתְהִלָּ֖ה וּלְשֵׁ֣ם וּלְתִפְאָ֑רֶת
וְלִֽהְיֹתְךָ֧ עַם־קָדֹ֛שׁ לַיהוָ֥ה אֱלֹהֶ֖יךָ כַּאֲשֶׁ֥ר
דִּבֵּֽר׃ ס

27 Moses and the elders of Israel charged
the people, saying: Observe all the Instruction
that I enjoin upon you this day. [2]As soon as you
have crossed the Jordan into the land that the
LORD your God is giving you, you shall set up
large stones. Coat them with plaster [3]and inscribe upon them all the words of this Teaching.
When you cross over to enter the land that the

רביעי **כז** וַיְצַ֤ו מֹשֶׁה֙ וְזִקְנֵ֣י יִשְׂרָאֵ֔ל אֶת־הָעָ֖ם
לֵאמֹ֑ר שָׁמֹר֙ אֶת־כָּל־הַמִּצְוָ֔ה אֲשֶׁ֧ר אָנֹכִ֛י
מְצַוֶּ֥ה אֶתְכֶ֖ם הַיּֽוֹם׃ 2 וְהָיָ֗ה בַּיּוֹם֮ אֲשֶׁ֣ר
תַּעַבְר֣וּ אֶת־הַיַּרְדֵּן֒ אֶל־הָאָ֕רֶץ אֲשֶׁר־יְהוָ֥ה
אֱלֹהֶ֖יךָ נֹתֵ֣ן לָ֑ךְ וַהֲקֵמֹתָ֤ לְךָ֙ אֲבָנִ֣ים גְּדֹל֔וֹת
וְשַׂדְתָּ֥ אֹתָ֖ם בַּשִּֽׂיד׃ 3 וְכָתַבְתָּ֣ עֲלֵיהֶ֗ן
אֶֽת־כָּל־דִּבְרֵ֛י הַתּוֹרָ֥ה הַזֹּ֖את בְּעָבְרֶ֑ךָ

18. as He promised you When He first proposed to enter into a covenant with you (Exod. 19:5).

19. This verse defines what it means to be God's treasured people.

high above all the nations That is, He will make Israel more famous, praised, and glorified than any other nation, as a result of the abundant prosperity and victory over enemies that Israel will enjoy.

holy people Sacrosanct, inviolable; a nation that others harm at their peril (see Exod. 19:6). For another implication of the notion of Israel's sanctity, see 7:6 and 14:2,21.

CEREMONIES TO MARK ISRAEL'S ARRIVAL IN THE LAND (27:1–26)

The covenant relationship with God is so vital for Israel's existence in the Promised Land that it must be reaffirmed formally as soon as the Israelites arrive there.

MONUMENTS AND AN ALTAR (vv. 1–8)

1. Moses and the elders Only here is Moses joined by the elders in instructing the people. Similarly in verses 9–10, Moses is joined by the priests in charging the people to obey the commandments. Because these two groups would be the leaders of the people in their daily civil and religious affairs after Moses' death, they are in the best position to ensure continued adherence to his teachings.

Instruction Hebrew: *ha-mitzvah;* the instructions given in Deuteronomy, the Teaching (v. 3), not a specific law.

2. As soon as you have crossed Literally, "on the day when you cross." This is loosely understood to mean "once you have crossed," not necessarily on the same day. According to verse 4, these instructions are to be carried out on Mount Ebal; that site—some 30 miles (50 km) and more than 4000 feet (1200 m) uphill from where the Israelites would cross the Jordan—could not be reached on the same day that the Jordan is crossed.

Coat them with plaster If the text was engraved through the plaster into the stone, the white plaster would highlight the dark color of the letters. It is also possible that the plaster served as a clean surface for writing in ink or paint. Writing over plaster was common in Egypt where even outdoor inscriptions would last a long time because rain is infrequent there.

3. This ceremony dramatizes Israel's obligation to live by God's Teaching. Its performance shortly after entering the land is a prerequisite for further penetration into the land. The text says that all the words of the Teaching (chapters 12–26, and perhaps chapters 1–11 and 28) are to be inscribed, placing no limit on the size or

לְמַעַן אֲשֶׁר תָּבֹא אֶל־הָאָרֶץ אֲשֶׁר־יְהוָה
אֱלֹהֶיךָ ׀ נֹתֵן לְךָ אֶרֶץ זָבַת חָלָב וּדְבַשׁ
כַּאֲשֶׁר דִּבֶּר יְהוָה אֱלֹהֵי־אֲבֹתֶיךָ לָךְ׃
4 וְהָיָה בְּעָבְרְכֶם אֶת־הַיַּרְדֵּן תָּקִימוּ אֶת־
הָאֲבָנִים הָאֵלֶּה אֲשֶׁר אָנֹכִי מְצַוֶּה אֶתְכֶם
הַיּוֹם בְּהַר עֵיבָל וְשַׂדְתָּ אוֹתָם בַּשִּׂיד׃
5 וּבָנִיתָ שָּׁם מִזְבֵּחַ לַיהוָה אֱלֹהֶיךָ מִזְבַּח
אֲבָנִים לֹא־תָנִיף עֲלֵיהֶם בַּרְזֶל׃ 6 אֲבָנִים
שְׁלֵמוֹת תִּבְנֶה אֶת־מִזְבַּח יְהוָה אֱלֹהֶיךָ
וְהַעֲלִיתָ עָלָיו עוֹלֹת לַיהוָה אֱלֹהֶיךָ׃
7 וְזָבַחְתָּ שְׁלָמִים וְאָכַלְתָּ שָּׁם וְשָׂמַחְתָּ
לִפְנֵי יְהוָה אֱלֹהֶיךָ׃ 8 וְכָתַבְתָּ עַל־
הָאֲבָנִים אֶת־כָּל־דִּבְרֵי הַתּוֹרָה הַזֹּאת
בַּאֵר הֵיטֵב׃ ס
9 וַיְדַבֵּר מֹשֶׁה וְהַכֹּהֲנִים הַלְוִיִּם אֶל כָּל־

LORD your God is giving you, a land flowing
with milk and honey, as the LORD, the God of
your fathers, promised you—
4 upon crossing
the Jordan, you shall set up these stones, about
which I charge you this day, on Mount Ebal,
and coat them with plaster.
5 There, too, you
shall build an altar to the LORD your God, an
altar of stones. Do not wield an iron tool over
them;
6 you must build the altar of the LORD your
God of unhewn stones. You shall offer on it
burnt offerings to the LORD your God,
7 and you
shall sacrifice there offerings of well-being and
eat them, rejoicing before the LORD your God.
8 And on those stones you shall inscribe every
word of this Teaching most distinctly.

9 Moses and the levitical priests spoke to all

number of steles (stone slabs) to be used. Two steles, each the size of the stele on which the laws of Hammurabi were written, easily could contain more than Deuteronomy.

4. Mount Ebal Just north of Shechem, it is the highest mountain in the vicinity. It rises 3083 feet (940 m) above sea level, 1200 feet (360 m) above the valley in which it stands, and commands a view of most of the Promised Land. Shechem was the site of Abraham's first stop in Canaan and the first place in Canaan where God spoke to him and identified the land as the one He would give to Abraham's descendants.

5. An altar is to be built, sacrifices are to be offered, and the people are to celebrate the erecting of the steles inscribed with the Teaching. These sacrifices are part of a one-time ceremony. Thus there is no conflict with Deuteronomy's restriction of sacrificial worship to Jerusalem, because that was to take effect only later (see 12:8–12).

stones In their natural state, uncut, following the command of Exod. 20:22. An Israelite altar of uncut stones has been found in excavations at Arad in the Negeb. Similar altars from earlier times have been discovered at Canaanite sites as well.

iron tool Hebrew: *barzel;* literally, "iron." Here it refers to a chisel.

6–7. The two types of offerings mentioned in these verses are the same as those brought at the conclusion of the covenant at Mount Sinai (see Exod. 24:5)

offerings of well-being These offerings (*sh'lamim*) are in the category of sacrifices in which most of the flesh was eaten by the worshiper. Hence they were appropriate for a festive occasion.

8. those stones Mentioned in verses 2–4, not those of the altar. This verse repeats the requirement that the stones be inscribed with the Teaching. By making the point both before and after the provision about the altar, the text makes clear that the terms of the Teaching, not the sacrifice, constitute the heart of the ceremony.

AN APPEAL FOR OBEDIENCE (vv. 9–10)

The Israelites are now concluding the Moab covenant (see 28:69) that will be reaffirmed later in ceremonies at Mounts Ebal and Gerizim. By pre-

---

CHAPTER 27

6. build the altar . . . of unhewn stones Eloquent, polished prayer is like hewn, polished stone. Here the "unhewn" (literally, "whole") stones represent the inarticulate yearning of a sincere heart—which God prefers (Buber).

Israel, saying: Silence! Hear, O Israel! Today you
have become the people of the LORD your God:
10Heed the LORD your God and observe His
commandments and His laws, which I enjoin
upon you this day.

11Thereupon Moses charged the people, saying: 12After you have crossed the Jordan, the following shall stand on Mount Gerizim when the
blessing for the people is spoken: Simeon, Levi,
Judah, Issachar, Joseph, and Benjamin. 13And
for the curse, the following shall stand on
Mount Ebal: Reuben, Gad, Asher, Zebulun,
Dan, and Naphtali. 14The Levites shall then proclaim in a loud voice to all the people of Israel:

15Cursed be anyone who makes a sculptured
or molten image, abhorred by the LORD, a

יִשְׂרָאֵל לֵאמֹר הַסְכֵּת ׀ וּשְׁמַע יִשְׂרָאֵל
הַיּוֹם הַזֶּה נִהְיֵיתָ לְעָם לַיהוָה אֱלֹהֶיךָ׃
10 וְשָׁמַעְתָּ בְּקוֹל יְהוָה אֱלֹהֶיךָ וְעָשִׂיתָ
אֶת־מצותו מִצְוֺתָו וְאֶת־חֻקָּיו אֲשֶׁר אָנֹכִי
מְצַוְּךָ הַיּוֹם׃ ס
חמישי 11 וַיְצַו מֹשֶׁה אֶת־הָעָם בַּיּוֹם הַהוּא
לֵאמֹר׃ 12 אֵלֶּה יַעַמְדוּ לְבָרֵךְ אֶת־הָעָם
עַל־הַר גְּרִזִּים בְּעָבְרְכֶם אֶת־הַיַּרְדֵּן
שִׁמְעוֹן וְלֵוִי וִיהוּדָה וְיִשָּׂשכָר וְיוֹסֵף
וּבִנְיָמִן׃ 13 וְאֵלֶּה יַעַמְדוּ עַל־הַקְּלָלָה בְּהַר
עֵיבָל רְאוּבֵן גָּד וְאָשֵׁר וּזְבוּלֻן דָּן וְנַפְתָּלִי׃
14 וְעָנוּ הַלְוִיִּם וְאָמְרוּ אֶל־כָּל־אִישׁ יִשְׂרָאֵל
קוֹל רָם׃ ס
15 אָרוּר הָאִישׁ אֲשֶׁר יַעֲשֶׂה פֶסֶל וּמַסֵּכָה

scribing these ceremonies here, in the midst of the conclusion of the covenant in Moab, Moses makes it clear that the later ceremonies are a reaffirmation of the Moab covenant (itself a reaffirmation of the Horeb covenant), not a new one.

9. Silence! Hear This is the first time that the appeal to hear is preceded by a call for silence. Absolute concentration is required at the awesome moment of solemn promises and warnings they are about to hear, when Israel becomes the people of God covenanted to Him.

Today you have become the people of the LORD Other passages in the Torah suggest that this took place earlier, at the time of the Exodus or at Mount Sinai (e.g., Exod. 6:6–7, 19:5–6; Deut. 4:20,34). There were varying views as to when the Israelites actually became God's people.

PROCLAIMING BLESSINGS AND CURSES (vv. 11–13)

When the 12 tribes of Israel arrive in the Promised Land, they are to proclaim the blessings and the curses—the divinely imposed consequences of either obeying or disobeying the terms of the Covenant—at Mounts Gerizim and Ebal. Such blessings and curses are integral elements of ancient Near Eastern covenants. The best known biblical examples are found in Lev. 26 and Deut. 28.

12–13. on Mount Gerizim . . . on Mount Ebal North and south of Shechem. The precise location where the tribes were to stand is not given, but their pronouncements would be most audible if they stood on the slopes of the mountains rather than on their peaks (which are 2.2 miles [3.5 km] apart). The text indeed says that the blessings and the curses shall be recited "on," not "atop," the mountains.

the blessing for the people is spoken Literally, "to bless the people."

And for the curse Literally, "And these shall stand for the curse." A circumlocution to avoid saying that the tribes would actually curse the people.

CURSES FOR SECRET SINS (vv. 14–26)

Verses 14–26 refer to a different ceremony from that prescribed in verses 11–13, although it may have been intended to be performed on the same occasion. This ceremony consists only of curses. The 11 specific sins mentioned here (the 12th sin is all-inclusive) often escape detection because, as Ibn Ezra and Rashbam note, commonly they are committed in secret or it is difficult for their victims to publicize them. The intent of this ceremony is to discourage such offenses by providing for their punishment by God. A curse is pronounced on those who commit them, and the people express their assent by responding "Amen," which also constitutes an oath to avoid these acts.

14. Levites They act here in their priestly role. Although blessings and curses by any individual could be effective, those uttered by priests and prophets were thought to possess particular potency.

15. Cursed Those who commit these sins are destined for divinely imposed misfortune, such as

תּוֹעֲבַת יְהֹוָה מַעֲשֵׂה יְדֵי חָרָשׁ וְשָׂם
בַּסָּתֶר וְעָנוּ כָל־הָעָם וְאָמְרוּ אָמֵן׃ ס
16 אָרוּר מַקְלֶה אָבִיו וְאִמּוֹ וְאָמַר כָּל־הָעָם
אָמֵן׃ ס
17 אָרוּר מַסִּיג גְּבוּל רֵעֵהוּ וְאָמַר כָּל־הָעָם
אָמֵן׃ ס
18 אָרוּר מַשְׁגֶּה עִוֵּר בַּדָּרֶךְ וְאָמַר כָּל־הָעָם
אָמֵן׃ ס
19 אָרוּר מַטֶּה מִשְׁפַּט גֵּר־יָתוֹם וְאַלְמָנָה
וְאָמַר כָּל־הָעָם אָמֵן׃ ס
20 אָרוּר שֹׁכֵב עִם־אֵשֶׁת אָבִיו כִּי גִלָּה כְּנַף
אָבִיו וְאָמַר כָּל־הָעָם אָמֵן׃ ס
21 אָרוּר שֹׁכֵב עִם־כָּל־בְּהֵמָה וְאָמַר כָּל־
הָעָם אָמֵן׃ ס

craftsman's handiwork, and sets it up in secret.—And all the people shall respond, Amen.

16 Cursed be he who insults his father or mother.—And all the people shall say, Amen.

17 Cursed be he who moves his fellow countryman's landmark.—And all the people shall say, Amen.

18 Cursed be he who misdirects a blind person on his way.—And all the people shall say, Amen.

19 Cursed be he who subverts the rights of the stranger, the fatherless, and the widow.—And all the people shall say, Amen.

20 Cursed be he who lies with his father's wife, for he has removed his father's garment.—And all the people shall say, Amen.

21 Cursed be he who lies with any beast.—And all the people shall say, Amen.

childlessness, the death of children, slavery, and the calamities listed in Deut. 28.

image Any kind of idol, whether of the Lord or any other deity.

craftsman's handiwork The fact that idols are made by mortals is the Torah's most telling argument against their divinity.

in secret To avoid detection. The Torah, which seems to expect that open idolatry would be stigmatized and punished by the sinner's contemporaries, here seeks to deter idolatry practiced in secret. The archaeological evidence indicates that idols were indeed rare in ancient Israel. Very few have been found in Israelite sites compared to those of neighboring peoples.

Amen The ancient Greek translation of this word is, "Let it be so." The term, derived from the root meaning "firm" (אמן), expresses assent to what someone has just said. As the Talmud puts it, "Answering 'Amen' after an oath is equivalent to pronouncing the oath with one's own mouth" (BT Shevu. 29b).

16. insults Treats them disrespectfully. The crime is not limited to verbal insults and would include the actions of a rebellious son (Deut. 21:18–21).

17. This curse is based on the prohibition against moving landmarks (19:14). Because this crime is committed in secret, and fear of detection is not as effective a deterrent as in the case of other crimes, ancient literature is replete with curses and warnings of divine punishment against those who commit it. Babylonian boundary stones were inscribed with curses directed against those who would move them or alter their inscriptions. The crime was a direct affront to God because property was assigned by lot, which was believed to be directed by God and expressive of His will.

18. The same principle is expressed in Lev. 19:14. Similarly, Egyptian wisdom literature teaches: "Do not laugh at a blind man or tease a dwarf, nor injure the affairs of the lame."

19. the stranger, the fatherless and the widow Because they do not have power to prosecute or defend their rights, the Torah often points out that God is their protector, as in 10:18.

20. Unlike 23:1, which refers only to his father's former wife, this could refer to his current wife and even to the sinner's own mother. Only sexual relations are mentioned here. Marriage to a father's former wife, which is prohibited in 23:1, is inherently a public act and hence irrelevant in this context. The laws of Hammurabi likewise oppose a man's having intercourse with his stepmother after his father's death. In the Hittite laws, it is a crime only if the father is still alive.

21. Bestiality is not uncommon, especially in rural areas. The Hittite laws prohibit it only with certain animals but not others. Ancient Near Eastern myths sometimes describe sexual intercourse between gods and animals.

22Cursed be he who lies with his sister, whether daughter of his father or of his mother.—And all the people shall say, Amen.
23Cursed be he who lies with his mother-in-law.—And all the people shall say, Amen.
24Cursed be he who strikes down his fellow countryman in secret.—And all the people shall say, Amen.
25Cursed be he who accepts a bribe in the case of the murder of an innocent person.—And all the people shall say, Amen.
26Cursed be he who will not uphold the terms of this Teaching and observe them.—And all the people shall say, Amen.

22 אָר֗וּר שֹׁכֵב֙ עִם־אֲחֹת֔וֹ בַּת־אָבִ֖יו א֣וֹ
בַת־אִמּ֑וֹ וְאָמַ֥ר כָּל־הָעָ֖ם אָמֵֽן׃ ס
23 אָר֕וּר שֹׁכֵ֖ב עִם־חֹֽתַנְתּ֑וֹ וְאָמַ֥ר כָּל־הָעָ֖ם
אָמֵֽן׃ ס
24 אָר֕וּר מַכֵּ֥ה רֵעֵ֖הוּ בַּסָּ֑תֶר וְאָמַ֥ר כָּל־
הָעָ֖ם אָמֵֽן׃ ס
25 אָר֗וּר לֹקֵ֙חַ֙ שֹׁ֔חַד לְהַכּ֥וֹת נֶ֖פֶשׁ דַּ֣ם נָקִ֑י
וְאָמַ֥ר כָּל־הָעָ֖ם אָמֵֽן׃ ס
26 אָר֗וּר אֲשֶׁ֧ר לֹא־יָקִ֛ים אֶת־דִּבְרֵ֥י
הַתּוֹרָֽה־הַזֹּ֖את לַעֲשׂ֣וֹת אוֹתָ֑ם וְאָמַ֥ר כָּל־
הָעָ֖ם אָמֵֽן׃ פ

28 Now, if you obey the LORD your God, to observe faithfully all His commandments

כח וְהָיָ֗ה אִם־שָׁמ֤וֹעַ תִּשְׁמַע֙ בְּקוֹל֙
יְהוָ֣ה אֱלֹהֶ֔יךָ לִשְׁמֹ֤ר לַעֲשׂוֹת֙ אֶת־כָּל־

22. whether daughter of his father or of his mother This explanatory phrase makes it clear that one may not have sexual relations with, and hence may not marry, even a half-sister. Marriage with a half-sister from a different mother was permitted at one time. Thus Abraham told Abimelech that Sarah was his half-sister, and David's daughter Tamar told his son (her half-brother) Amnon that David would permit them to marry (see Gen. 20:12; 2 Sam. 13:13). The practice was also known in Greece and Arabia. There were brother–sister marriages in Egypt and in Phoenicia, found mostly among the royalty.

24. strikes down Hebrew: *makkeh,* which can refer either to lethal or to nonlethal blows.

25. Refers to a judge who accepts a bribe to condemn an innocent defendant to death.

26. The final curse refers to all other provisions of the Teaching and constitutes an oath to uphold the entire Teaching. If this ceremony was to be performed at Mount Ebal, at the same time as the other ceremonies in this chapter, "this Teaching" may refer to the copy of the Teaching inscribed on the stones that stood nearby.

THE CONSEQUENCES OF OBEDIENCE AND DISOBEDIENCE (28:1–68)

This chapter details the consequences of Israel's obeying or disobeying the terms of the covenant that Moses reviewed in chapters 5–26. Promises and threats such as these are well known in the Bible and elsewhere in ancient Near Eastern literature. See Comment to 27:11–13.

In this chapter, "blessing" and "curse" do not refer to promises and threats but to the benign and the destructive forces that blessings and curses call for. They are almost personified by the verbs used to depict them; they "come," "pursue," and "overtake" (vv. 2,15,22,45), and God "lets [them] loose" (vv. 8,20, cf. 32:24). True personification of these forces, however, is absent in Deuteronomy, which avoids any suggestion of independent supernatural powers other than God. Instead, the blessings and the curses are treated as impersonal forces under God's absolute control.

26. The Talmud derives a positive principle from this verse, inferring that one who does uphold the Teaching (i.e., Torah) will be blessed. This applies even to those individuals who never studied and never taught but give financial support to those who study Torah (JT Sot. 7:4; Barukh Halevi Epstein).

מִצְוֺתָ֔יו אֲשֶׁ֛ר אָנֹכִ֥י מְצַוְּךָ֖ הַיּ֑וֹם וּנְתָ֨נְךָ֜
יְהוָ֤ה אֱלֹהֶ֙יךָ֙ עֶלְי֔וֹן עַ֖ל כָּל־גּוֹיֵ֥ הָאָֽרֶץ׃
2 וּבָ֧אוּ עָלֶ֛יךָ כָּל־הַבְּרָכ֥וֹת הָאֵ֖לֶּה וְהִשִּׂיגֻ֑ךָ
כִּ֣י תִשְׁמַ֔ע בְּק֖וֹל יְהוָ֥ה אֱלֹהֶֽיךָ׃
3 בָּר֥וּךְ אַתָּ֖ה בָּעִ֑יר וּבָר֥וּךְ אַתָּ֖ה בַּשָּׂדֶֽה׃
4 בָּר֧וּךְ פְּרִֽי־בִטְנְךָ֛ וּפְרִ֥י אַדְמָתְךָ֖ וּפְרִ֣י
בְהֶמְתֶּ֑ךָ שְׁגַ֥ר אֲלָפֶ֖יךָ וְעַשְׁתְּר֥וֹת צֹאנֶֽךָ׃
5 בָּר֥וּךְ טַנְאֲךָ֖ וּמִשְׁאַרְתֶּֽךָ׃
6 בָּר֥וּךְ אַתָּ֖ה בְּבֹאֶ֑ךָ וּבָר֥וּךְ אַתָּ֖ה בְּצֵאתֶֽךָ׃
ששי 7 יִתֵּ֨ן יְהוָ֤ה אֶת־אֹֽיְבֶ֙יךָ֙ הַקָּמִ֣ים עָלֶ֔יךָ
נִגָּפִ֖ים לְפָנֶ֑יךָ בְּדֶ֤רֶךְ אֶחָד֙ יֵצְא֣וּ אֵלֶ֔יךָ
וּבְשִׁבְעָ֥ה דְרָכִ֖ים יָנ֥וּסוּ לְפָנֶֽיךָ׃ 8 יְצַ֨ו יְהוָ֤ה

which I enjoin upon you this day, the LORD your God will set you high above all the nations of the earth. 2All these blessings shall come upon you and take effect, if you will but heed the word of the LORD your God:

3Blessed shall you be in the city and blessed shall you be in the country.

4Blessed shall be the issue of your womb, the produce of your soil, and the offspring of your cattle, the calving of your herd and the lambing of your flock.

5Blessed shall be your basket and your kneading bowl.

6Blessed shall you be in your comings and blessed shall you be in your goings.

7The LORD will put to rout before you the enemies who attack you; they will march out against you by a single road, but flee from you by many roads. 8The LORD will ordain blessings

THE BLESSINGS FOR OBEDIENCE
(vv. 1–14)

1. Moses reviews the conditions and the promises of 26:16–19 regarding the covenant now being made in Moab and then spells out the consequences that will ensue if the Israelites are loyal or disloyal to it.

2. The promise of 26:19 is conditional. The Israelites are not promised automatic special treatment. They must earn it. To make this clear, the condition is repeated here.

3. Blessed Prosperous.

city . . . country These opposites express a totality, meaning that wherever you live and work, your undertakings will prosper.

5. basket . . . kneading bowl These containers were used for gathering produce and preparing bread. The blessing means that the harvest will be abundant and that food will be plentiful.

6. comings . . . goings Literally, "entering and going out." Abravanel takes blessedness in these activities to mean safety in traveling to and from the city, a common theme in descriptions of blessing and prosperity.

7. by a single road They will be too numerous and confident to bother separating their forces for safety.

by many roads Literally, "by seven roads." The enemy will scatter in every direction. Seven is often used to express a complete number.

CHAPTER 28

2. take effect Literally, "overtake you." Sometimes God intends to bless us, but we are so busy running after success that the blessings cannot catch up to us. Instead of chasing after fulfilment, perhaps we need to slow down and let the good things of life catch up to us (*Ha·amek Davar*).

3. In the city, God will reward you for your service to the community. In the country, God will reward you for sharing the harvest of your fields with the poor and the needy (Deut. R. 7:5).

Blessed shall you be in the city May your home be in a good neighborhood, close to the synagogue, surrounded by good neighbors (BT BM 107a).

6. Here "comings" and "goings" may refer to business dealings, for the previous blessings refer to material well-being (Deut. R. 7:5). Prosperity brings its own dangers; this blessing asks that God guard us from the temptations that wealth occasions (*Ha·amek Davar*).

for you upon your barns and upon all your undertakings: He will bless you in the land that
the LORD your God is giving you. 9The LORD
will establish you as His holy people, as He
swore to you, if you keep the commandments
of the LORD your God and walk in His ways.
10And all the peoples of the earth shall see that
the LORD's name is proclaimed over you, and
they shall stand in fear of you. 11The LORD will
give you abounding prosperity in the issue of
your womb, the offspring of your cattle, and the
produce of your soil in the land that the LORD
swore to your fathers to assign to you. 12The
LORD will open for you His bounteous store, the
heavens, to provide rain for your land in season
and to bless all your undertakings. You will be
creditor to many nations, but debtor to none.
13The LORD will make you the head, not the
tail; you will always be at the top and never at
the bottom—if only you obey and faithfully observe the commandments of the LORD your God
that I enjoin upon you this day, 14and do not
deviate to the right or to the left from any of
the commandments that I enjoin upon you this
day and turn to the worship of other gods.

15But if you do not obey the LORD your God

אִתְּךָ֙ אֶת־הַבְּרָכָ֔ה בַּאֲסָמֶ֕יךָ וּבְכֹ֖ל מִשְׁלַ֣ח
יָדֶ֑ךָ וּבֵ֣רַכְךָ֔ בָּאָ֕רֶץ אֲשֶׁר־יְהוָ֥ה אֱלֹהֶ֖יךָ נֹתֵ֥ן
לָֽךְ׃ 9 יְקִֽימְךָ֨ יְהוָ֥ה לוֹ֙ לְעַ֣ם קָד֔וֹשׁ כַּאֲשֶׁ֖ר
נִֽשְׁבַּֽע־לָ֑ךְ כִּ֣י תִשְׁמֹ֗ר אֶת־מִצְוֺת֙ יְהוָ֣ה
אֱלֹהֶ֔יךָ וְהָלַכְתָּ֖ בִּדְרָכָֽיו׃ 10 וְרָאוּ֙ כָּל־עַמֵּ֣י
הָאָ֔רֶץ כִּ֛י שֵׁ֥ם יְהוָ֖ה נִקְרָ֣א עָלֶ֑יךָ וְיָֽרְא֖וּ
מִמֶּֽךָּ׃ 11 וְהוֹתִרְךָ֤ יְהוָה֙ לְטוֹבָ֔ה בִּפְרִ֧י
בִטְנְךָ֛ וּבִפְרִ֥י בְהֶמְתְּךָ֖ וּבִפְרִ֣י אַדְמָתֶ֑ךָ עַ֚ל
הָֽאֲדָמָ֔ה אֲשֶׁ֨ר נִשְׁבַּ֧ע יְהוָ֛ה לַאֲבֹתֶ֖יךָ לָ֥תֶת
לָֽךְ׃ 12 יִפְתַּ֣ח יְהוָ֣ה ׀ לְ֠ךָ֠ אֶת־אוֹצָר֨וֹ הַטּ֜וֹב
אֶת־הַשָּׁמַ֗יִם לָתֵ֤ת מְטַֽר־אַרְצְךָ֙ בְּעִתּ֔וֹ
וּלְבָרֵ֕ךְ אֵ֖ת כָּל־מַעֲשֵׂ֣ה יָדֶ֑ךָ וְהִלְוִ֙יתָ֙ גּוֹיִ֣ם
רַבִּ֔ים וְאַתָּ֖ה לֹ֥א תִלְוֶֽה׃
13 וּנְתָנְךָ֙ יְהוָ֤ה לְרֹאשׁ֙ וְלֹ֣א לְזָנָ֔ב וְהָיִ֙יתָ֙
רַ֣ק לְמַ֔עְלָה וְלֹ֥א תִהְיֶ֖ה לְמָ֑טָּה כִּֽי־תִשְׁמַ֞ע
אֶל־מִצְוֺ֣ת ׀ יְהוָ֣ה אֱלֹהֶ֗יךָ אֲשֶׁ֨ר אָנֹכִ֧י מְצַוְּךָ֛
הַיּ֖וֹם לִשְׁמֹ֥ר וְלַעֲשֽׂוֹת׃ 14 וְלֹ֣א תָס֗וּר
מִכָּל־הַדְּבָרִים֙ אֲשֶׁ֨ר אָנֹכִ֜י מְצַוֶּ֥ה אֶתְכֶ֛ם
הַיּ֖וֹם יָמִ֣ין וּשְׂמֹ֑אול* לָלֶ֗כֶת אַחֲרֵ֛י אֱלֹהִ֥ים
אֲחֵרִ֖ים לְעָבְדָֽם׃ ס

15 וְהָיָ֗ה אִם־לֹ֤א תִשְׁמַע֙ בְּקוֹל֙ יְהוָ֣ה

v. 14. מלא ו'

8. barns Namely, stores, granaries such as silos, underground storage pits, and storehouses.

9. the LORD . . . the LORD your God These two ways of referring to God are used throughout the chapter. When acts of divine reward and punishment are described, God is called simply "the LORD." The full phrase, "the LORD your/our God," is reserved for passages that refer to the Israelites' duty of obeying God or refer to His gift of the Land. It has the connotation of "the LORD, who has kept His promises to you and whom you are obligated to obey."

if you keep The conditional nature of Israel's sanctity is repeated.

10. the LORD's name Israel is known as "the people of the LORD" (*am YHVH*). The connection between God's name and protection is expressed in prayers that appeal to God for security on the grounds that the supplicant is called by His name.

11. abounding That is, surpassing. Because of the surplus, Israel will be able to lend to other nations and it never will need to borrow (v. 12).

12. store The ancients pictured rain, snow, hail, wind, and other natural phenomena as kept in celestial storehouses that God opens as needed.

creditor to many nations Because of your surplus wealth.

14. The promises end with a final reminder that they depend on a key condition: that the Israelites shun all other gods.

---

10. peoples . . . shall stand in fear of you Not that they will be afraid of you, but that they will learn from you how to fear (i.e., revere) God (Vilna Gaon).

to observe faithfully all His commandments
and laws which I enjoin upon you this day, all
these curses shall come upon you and take
effect:
16Cursed shall you be in the city and cursed
shall you be in the country.
17Cursed shall be your basket and your kneading bowl.
18Cursed shall be the issue of your womb and
the produce of your soil, the calving of your herd
and the lambing of your flock.
19Cursed shall you be in your comings and
cursed shall you be in your goings.
20The LORD will let loose against you calamity, panic, and frustration in all the enterprises
you undertake, so that you shall soon be utterly
wiped out because of your evildoing in forsaking Me. 21The LORD will make pestilence cling
to you, until He has put an end to you in the
land that you are entering to possess. 22The
LORD will strike you with consumption, fever,
and inflammation, with scorching heat and
drought, with blight and mildew; they shall
hound you until you perish. 23The skies above
your head shall be copper and the earth under
you iron. 24The LORD will make the rain of your
land dust, and sand shall drop on you from the
sky, until you are wiped out.
25The LORD will put you to rout before your
enemies; you shall march out against them by

אֱלֹהֶיךָ לִשְׁמֹר לַעֲשׂוֹת אֶת־כָּל־מִצְוֺתָיו
וְחֻקֹּתָיו אֲשֶׁר אָנֹכִי מְצַוְּךָ הַיּוֹם וּבָאוּ
עָלֶיךָ כָּל־הַקְּלָלוֹת הָאֵלֶּה וְהִשִּׂיגוּךָ׃
16 אָרוּר אַתָּה בָּעִיר וְאָרוּר אַתָּה בַּשָּׂדֶה׃
17 אָרוּר טַנְאֲךָ וּמִשְׁאַרְתֶּךָ׃
18 אָרוּר פְּרִי־בִטְנְךָ וּפְרִי אַדְמָתֶךָ שְׁגַר
אֲלָפֶיךָ וְעַשְׁתְּרֹת צֹאנֶךָ׃
19 אָרוּר אַתָּה בְּבֹאֶךָ וְאָרוּר אַתָּה
בְּצֵאתֶךָ׃
20 יְשַׁלַּח יְהוָה ׀ בְּךָ אֶת־הַמְּאֵרָה אֶת־
הַמְּהוּמָה וְאֶת־הַמִּגְעֶרֶת בְּכָל־מִשְׁלַח
יָדְךָ אֲשֶׁר תַּעֲשֶׂה עַד הִשָּׁמֶדְךָ וְעַד־אֲבָדְךָ
מַהֵר מִפְּנֵי רֹעַ מַעֲלָלֶיךָ אֲשֶׁר עֲזַבְתָּנִי׃
21 יַדְבֵּק יְהוָה בְּךָ אֶת־הַדָּבֶר עַד כַּלֹּתוֹ
אֹתְךָ מֵעַל הָאֲדָמָה אֲשֶׁר־אַתָּה בָא־שָׁמָּה
לְרִשְׁתָּהּ׃ 22 יַכְּכָה יְהוָה בַּשַּׁחֶפֶת
וּבַקַּדַּחַת וּבַדַּלֶּקֶת וּבַחַרְחֻר וּבַחֶרֶב
וּבַשִּׁדָּפוֹן וּבַיֵּרָקוֹן וּרְדָפוּךָ עַד אָבְדֶךָ׃
23 וְהָיוּ שָׁמֶיךָ אֲשֶׁר עַל־רֹאשְׁךָ נְחֹשֶׁת
וְהָאָרֶץ אֲשֶׁר־תַּחְתֶּיךָ בַּרְזֶל׃ 24 יִתֵּן יְהוָה
אֶת־מְטַר אַרְצְךָ אָבָק וְעָפָר מִן־הַשָּׁמַיִם
יֵרֵד עָלֶיךָ עַד הִשָּׁמְדָךְ׃
25 יִתֶּנְךָ יְהוָה ׀ נִגָּף לִפְנֵי אֹיְבֶיךָ בְּדֶרֶךְ

THE CURSES FOR DISOBEDIENCE
(vv. 15–68)

The remainder of the chapter, like the threats in Lev. 26, is known as the *Tokheḥah,* or "Warning" (literally, "rebuke") in postbiblical sources. As in the Leviticus passage, the threats are more numerous than the promises.

FIRST GROUP (vv. 15–44)

20. calamity Hebrew: *m'erah;* literally, "curse." The antonym of "blessing" in verse 8. It probably refers to drought and plant-destroying pests (as in Mal. 3:9–11).

panic Refers to the tumult and confusion caused by war, social disorder, and pestilence.

frustration Hebrew: *mig·eret;* literally, "obstruction, encumbrance." Here it may refer to the drought (vv. 23–24) and crop failure (vv. 38–42) resulting from God's rejection of their prayers.

forsaking Me Here Moses speaks in God's name, as sometimes happens in Deuteronomy (see v. 68).

21. pestilence A virulent epidemic.

22. The exact nature of the seven afflictions listed in this verse is uncertain. The terms refer to symptoms that could stem from various causes.

23. The sky will be too hard to yield rain and the soil too hard to plow.

24. In the absence of rain, the land will be exposed to duststorms and sandstorms stirred up from the waterless soil.

אֶחָד תֵּצֵא אֵלָיו וּבְשִׁבְעָה דְרָכִים תָּנוּס
לְפָנָיו וְהָיִיתָ לְזַעֲוָה לְכֹל מַמְלְכוֹת
הָאָרֶץ׃ 26 וְהָיְתָה נִבְלָתְךָ לְמַאֲכָל לְכָל־
עוֹף הַשָּׁמַיִם וּלְבֶהֱמַת הָאָרֶץ וְאֵין
מַחֲרִיד׃
27 יַכְּכָה יְהוָה בִּשְׁחִין מִצְרַיִם ובעפלים
וּבַטְּחֹרִים וּבַגָּרָב וּבֶחָרֶס אֲשֶׁר לֹא־תוּכַל
לְהֵרָפֵא׃
28 יַכְּכָה יְהוָה בְּשִׁגָּעוֹן וּבְעִוָּרוֹן וּבְתִמְהוֹן
לֵבָב׃ 29 וְהָיִיתָ מְמַשֵּׁשׁ בַּצָּהֳרַיִם כַּאֲשֶׁר
יְמַשֵּׁשׁ הָעִוֵּר בָּאֲפֵלָה וְלֹא תַצְלִיחַ אֶת־
דְּרָכֶיךָ וְהָיִיתָ אַךְ עָשׁוּק וְגָזוּל כָּל־הַיָּמִים
וְאֵין מוֹשִׁיעַ׃
30 אִשָּׁה תְאָרֵשׂ וְאִישׁ אַחֵר ישגלנה
יִשְׁכָּבֶנָּה בַּיִת תִּבְנֶה וְלֹא־תֵשֵׁב בּוֹ כֶּרֶם
תִּטַּע וְלֹא תְחַלְּלֶנּוּ׃ 31 שׁוֹרְךָ טָבוּחַ לְעֵינֶיךָ
וְלֹא תֹאכַל מִמֶּנּוּ חֲמֹרְךָ גָּזוּל מִלְּפָנֶיךָ
וְלֹא יָשׁוּב לָךְ צֹאנְךָ נְתֻנוֹת לְאֹיְבֶיךָ וְאֵין

a single road, but flee from them by many roads; and you shall become a horror to all the kingdoms of the earth.
26Your carcasses shall become food for all the birds of the sky and all the beasts of the earth, with none to frighten them off.

27The LORD will strike you with the Egyptian inflammation, with hemorrhoids, boil-scars, and itch, from which you shall never recover.

28The LORD will strike you with madness, blindness, and dismay.
29You shall grope at noon as a blind man gropes in the dark; you shall not prosper in your ventures, but shall be constantly abused and robbed, with none to give help.

30If you pay the bride-price for a wife, another man shall enjoy her. If you build a house, you shall not live in it. If you plant a vineyard, you shall not harvest it.
31Your ox shall be slaughtered before your eyes, but you shall not eat of it; your ass shall be seized in front of you, and it shall not be returned to you; your flock shall be delivered to your enemies, with none to help

25. horror Instead of respectful fear (v. 10), you will inspire horror in those who witness your ruinous defeat.

26. In the ancient world, lack of burial was regarded as a fate worse than death. It was believed that the spirits of the unburied would never find admittance to a resting place in the netherworld.

27. Egyptian inflammation The 6th of the Ten Plagues in Egypt, perhaps skin anthrax (see Exod. 9:8–12).

28. madness Ranting and carrying on wildly.

blindness Because the other two afflictions in this verse are psychological, this may be a metaphor for stupefaction or disorientation. In some ancient Near Eastern texts, fear in the face of battle is described as blurring of eyesight.

29. in the dark Ibn Janaḥ takes the phrase to mean, "you will grope at noon [as if] in darkness, like a blind man."

abused and robbed "Abused" refers to maltreatment and being cheated out of one's property; "robbed," to robbery and extortion. In the light of verses 30–33, they must refer to oppression by conquerors.

none to give help Refers to kings, officials, or others who could save the oppressed and to military leaders who could give the nation relief from foreign assailants.

30. The most important personal achievements, those that constitute grounds for draft deferment (see 20:5–7), will be worthless.

will enjoy her The unvocalized letters of the text (ישגלנה) mean "will rape her." Because that verb (שגל) was considered too vulgar for public reading in the synagogue, another verb is read in its place, literally meaning "will lie with her" (*yishkavennah*).

31. The extortion of another's ox or ass is a proverbial example of oppression.

---

29. as a blind man gropes in the dark Isn't a blind man equally disadvantaged both in daylight and in darkness? In daylight, he can hope that others will see him and help him. In the dark, however, there will be "none to give help" (BT Meg. 24b).

לְךָ֖ מוֹשִֽׁיעַ׃ 32 בָּנֶ֨יךָ וּבְנֹתֶ֜יךָ נְתֻנִ֨ים לְעַ֤ם
אַחֵר֙ וְעֵינֶ֣יךָ רֹא֔וֹת וְכָל֥וֹת אֲלֵיהֶ֖ם כָּל־
הַיּ֑וֹם וְאֵ֥ין לְאֵ֖ל יָדֶֽךָ׃ 33 פְּרִ֤י אַדְמָֽתְךָ֙
וְכָל־יְגִ֣יעֲךָ֔ יֹאכַ֥ל עַ֖ם אֲשֶׁ֣ר לֹא־יָדָ֑עְתָּ
וְהָיִ֗יתָ רַ֛ק עָשׁ֥וּק וְרָצ֖וּץ כָּל־הַיָּמִֽים׃
34 וְהָיִ֖יתָ מְשֻׁגָּ֑ע מִמַּרְאֵ֥ה עֵינֶ֖יךָ אֲשֶׁ֥ר
תִּרְאֶֽה׃ 35 יַכְּכָ֨ה יְהֹוָ֜ה בִּשְׁחִ֣ין רָ֗ע עַל־
הַבִּרְכַּ֙יִם֙ וְעַל־הַשֹּׁקַ֔יִם אֲשֶׁ֥ר לֹא־תוּכַ֖ל
לְהֵרָפֵ֑א מִכַּ֥ף רַגְלְךָ֖ וְעַ֥ד קָדְקֳדֶֽךָ׃
36 יוֹלֵ֨ךְ יְהֹוָ֜ה אֹתְךָ֗ וְאֶֽת־מַלְכְּךָ֙ אֲשֶׁ֣ר
תָּקִ֣ים עָלֶ֔יךָ אֶל־גּ֕וֹי אֲשֶׁ֥ר לֹא־יָדַ֖עְתָּ אַתָּ֣ה
וַאֲבֹתֶ֑יךָ וְעָבַ֥דְתָּ שָּׁ֛ם אֱלֹהִ֥ים אֲחֵרִ֖ים עֵ֥ץ
וָאָֽבֶן׃ 37 וְהָיִ֣יתָ לְשַׁמָּ֔ה לְמָשָׁ֖ל וְלִשְׁנִינָ֑ה
בְּכֹל֙ הָֽעַמִּ֔ים אֲשֶׁר־יְנַהֶגְךָ֥ יְהֹוָ֖ה שָֽׁמָּה׃
38 זֶ֥רַע רַ֖ב תּוֹצִ֣יא הַשָּׂדֶ֑ה וּמְעַ֣ט תֶּאֱסֹ֔ף
כִּ֥י יַחְסְלֶ֖נּוּ הָאַרְבֶּֽה׃ 39 כְּרָמִ֥ים תִּטַּ֖ע
וְעָבָ֑דְתָּ וְיַ֤יִן לֹא־תִשְׁתֶּה֙ וְלֹ֣א תֶאֱגֹ֔ר כִּ֥י
תֹאכְלֶ֖נּוּ הַתֹּלָֽעַת׃ 40 זֵיתִ֛ים יִהְי֥וּ לְךָ֖ בְּכָל־
גְּבוּלֶ֑ךָ וְשֶׁ֙מֶן֙ לֹ֣א תָס֔וּךְ כִּ֥י יִשַּׁ֖ל זֵיתֶֽךָ׃
41 בָּנִ֥ים וּבָנ֖וֹת תּוֹלִ֑יד וְלֹא־יִהְי֣וּ לָ֔ךְ כִּ֥י

you. 32Your sons and daughters shall be delivered to another people, while you look on; and
your eyes shall strain for them constantly, but
you shall be helpless. 33A people you do not
know shall eat up the produce of your soil and
all your gains; you shall be abused and downtrodden continually, 34until you are driven mad
by what your eyes behold. 35The LORD will afflict
you at the knees and thighs with a severe
inflammation, from which you shall never
recover—from the sole of your foot to the
crown of your head.
36The LORD will drive you, and the king you
have set over you, to a nation unknown to you
or your fathers, where you shall serve other
gods, of wood and stone. 37You shall be a consternation, a proverb, and a byword among all
the peoples to which the LORD will drive you.
38Though you take much seed out to the field,
you shall gather in little, for the locust shall consume it. 39Though you plant vineyards and till
them, you shall have no wine to drink or store,
for the worm shall devour them. 40Though you
have olive trees throughout your territory, you
shall have no oil for anointment, for your olives
shall drop off. 41Though you beget sons and

32. delivered to another people They will be sold as slaves to a foreign land, so that their parents will never see them again.

your eyes shall strain for them Literally, "your eyes shall run out [of tears] over them."

35. Suggested diagnoses include universalized eczema, smallpox, "joint leprosy," and psoriasis.

36. The Israelites will be exiled from their land. The partial or complete deportation of defeated populations was a common practice in the ancient world, to provide laborers or slaves for the conqueror or to break the resistance of rebellious peoples.

unknown to you or your fathers You will feel completely alien there.

37. consternation You will be a source of consternation, or shock, to those who see your condition.

proverb People will refer to you when they wish to give an example of horrid catastrophe.

byword An object of repeated discussion.

all the peoples to which the LORD will drive you The northern Israelites and the Judahites were exiled to various lands by their original captors, and migrated yet farther afterward.

38. consume it The crop. Locusts are types of grasshoppers that migrate in immense groups and constitute one of the world's most devastating natural disasters. The daily food consumption of a large swarm is equivalent to that of 1.5 million people.

39. worm The larva of some type of moth such as the grape-leaf folder, whose larvae defoliate grapevines; or the grape moth or berry moth, whose larvae eat the grapes.

40. oil for anointment In the hot, dry climate of the Middle East, one of the most important uses of olive oil was for anointing the skin, a necessary act of personal hygiene.

41. The act of raising children will be frustrated just as the raising of crops will be. Children

daughters, they shall not remain with you, for
they shall go into captivity. 42The cricket shall
take over all the trees and produce of your land.
43The stranger in your midst shall rise above
you higher and higher, while you sink lower and
lower: 44he shall be your creditor, but you shall
not be his; he shall be the head and you the tail.
45All these curses shall befall you; they shall
pursue you and overtake you, until you are
wiped out, because you did not heed the LORD
your God and keep the commandments and
laws that He enjoined upon you. 46They shall
serve as signs and proofs against you and your
offspring for all time. 47Because you would not
serve the LORD your God in joy and gladness
over the abundance of everything, 48you shall
have to serve—in hunger and thirst, naked and
lacking everything—the enemies whom the
LORD will let loose against you. He will put an
iron yoke upon your neck until He has wiped
you out.
49The LORD will bring a nation against you
from afar, from the end of the earth, which will
swoop down like the eagle—a nation whose lan-

יֵלְכוּ בַּשֶּׁבִי׃ 42 כָּל־עֵצְךָ וּפְרִי אַדְמָתֶךָ
יְיָרֵשׁ הַצְּלָצַל׃
43 הַגֵּר אֲשֶׁר בְּקִרְבְּךָ יַעֲלֶה עָלֶיךָ מַעְלָה
מָּעְלָה וְאַתָּה תֵרֵד מַטָּה מָּטָּה׃ 44 הוּא
יַלְוְךָ וְאַתָּה לֹא תַלְוֶנּוּ הוּא יִהְיֶה לְרֹאשׁ
וְאַתָּה תִּהְיֶה לְזָנָב׃
45 וּבָאוּ עָלֶיךָ כָּל־הַקְּלָלוֹת הָאֵלֶּה וּרְדָפוּךָ
וְהִשִּׂיגוּךָ עַד הִשָּׁמְדָךְ כִּי־לֹא שָׁמַעְתָּ בְּקוֹל
יְהוָה אֱלֹהֶיךָ לִשְׁמֹר מִצְוֺתָיו וְחֻקֹּתָיו
אֲשֶׁר צִוָּךְ׃ 46 וְהָיוּ בְךָ לְאוֹת וּלְמוֹפֵת
וּבְזַרְעֲךָ עַד־עוֹלָם׃ 47 תַּחַת אֲשֶׁר לֹא־
עָבַדְתָּ אֶת־יְהוָה אֱלֹהֶיךָ בְּשִׂמְחָה וּבְטוּב
לֵבָב מֵרֹב כֹּל׃ 48 וְעָבַדְתָּ אֶת־אֹיְבֶיךָ אֲשֶׁר
יְשַׁלְּחֶנּוּ יְהוָה בָּךְ בְּרָעָב וּבְצָמָא וּבְעֵירֹם
וּבְחֹסֶר כֹּל וְנָתַן עֹל בַּרְזֶל עַל־צַוָּארֶךָ עַד
הִשְׁמִידוֹ אֹתָךְ׃
49 יִשָּׂא יְהוָה עָלֶיךָ גּוֹי מֵרָחֹק מִקְצֵה
הָאָרֶץ כַּאֲשֶׁר יִדְאֶה הַנָּשֶׁר גּוֹי אֲשֶׁר

and crops are also associated in the blessings of 28:4 and 7:13, and in the curses of verses 31–33.

42. Either the fields will be ravaged by destructive insects (such as grasshoppers or katydids) or, after the captivity of the children (v. 41), there will be too few people to work the fields, which then will be overrun by insects. These would include mole crickets, which eat roots though they do not cause large-scale aboveground destruction.

43. The economic collapse will be so calamitous that resident aliens, who normally are poor and dependent on Israelites, will prosper more than the Israelites and be in a position to make loans to them and thereby achieve economic superiority. Contrast the blessing of verses 12–13.

SECOND GROUP (vv. 45–57)

46. signs and proofs Of the guilt of this sinful generation, as elaborated in 29:21–27.

48. The punishment is the precise reversal of the prior situation (v. 47). This will make the justice of the punishment obvious.

iron yoke The yoke is a familiar, not always unfavorable, metaphor expressing submission to the rule of gods and kings in the ancient Near East. Here, however, the context is punitive. Because yokes were normally made of wood, an iron yoke implies an exceptional burden or unbreakable servitude.

49. a nation . . . from afar No specific nation is meant. The enemy will be utterly alien to Israel, even stranger than the "people you do not know" of verse 33. It will come from so far away that its language will be unintelligible, unlike Israel's close neighbors who spoke languages similar to Hebrew.

like the eagle Or the griffon vulture. The simile refers to the suddenness, speed, and power of the attack.

47. you would not serve . . . in joy Ingratitude keeps us from true devotion to God. The image here is not of refusing to worship, but of worshiping grudgingly (Ḥayyim of Volozhin).

guage you do not understand, [50]a ruthless nation, that will show the old no regard and the young no mercy. [51]It shall devour the offspring of your cattle and the produce of your soil, until you have been wiped out, leaving you nothing of new grain, wine, or oil, of the calving of your herds and the lambing of your flocks, until it has brought you to ruin. [52]It shall shut you up in all your towns throughout your land until every mighty, towering wall in which you trust has come down. And when you are shut up in all your towns throughout your land that the LORD your God has assigned to you, [53]you shall eat your own issue, the flesh of your sons and daughters that the LORD your God has assigned to you, because of the desperate straits to which your enemy shall reduce you. [54]He who is most tender and fastidious among you shall be too mean to his brother and the wife of his bosom and the children he has spared [55]to share with any of them the flesh of the children that he eats, because he has nothing else left as a result of the desperate straits to which your enemy shall reduce you in all your towns. [56]And she who is most tender and dainty among you, so tender

לֹא־תִשְׁמַ֣ע לְשֹׁנֽוֹ׃ 50 גּ֖וֹי עַ֣ז פָּנִ֑ים אֲשֶׁ֨ר לֹא־יִשָּׂ֤א פָנִים֙ לְזָקֵ֔ן וְנַ֖עַר לֹ֥א יָחֹֽן׃ 51 וְ֠אָכַל פְּרִ֨י בְהֶמְתְּךָ֥ וּפְרִֽי־אַדְמָתְךָ֮ עַ֣ד הִשָּֽׁמְדָךְ֒ אֲשֶׁ֣ר לֹֽא־יַשְׁאִ֣יר לְךָ֗ דָּגָן֙ תִּיר֣וֹשׁ וְיִצְהָ֔ר שְׁגַ֥ר אֲלָפֶ֖יךָ וְעַשְׁתְּרֹ֣ת צֹאנֶ֑ךָ עַ֥ד הַאֲבִיד֖וֹ אֹתָֽךְ׃ 52 וְהֵצַ֨ר לְךָ֜ בְּכָל־שְׁעָרֶ֗יךָ עַ֣ד רֶ֣דֶת חֹמֹתֶ֤יךָ הַגְּבֹהֹת֙ וְהַבְּצֻר֔וֹת אֲשֶׁ֥ר אַתָּ֛ה בֹּטֵ֥חַ בָּהֵ֖ן בְּכָל־אַרְצֶ֑ךָ וְהֵצַ֤ר לְךָ֙ בְּכָל־שְׁעָרֶ֔יךָ בְּכָ֨ל־אַרְצְךָ֔ אֲשֶׁ֥ר נָתַ֛ן יְהֹוָ֥ה אֱלֹהֶ֖יךָ לָֽךְ׃ 53 וְאָכַלְתָּ֣ פְרִֽי־בִטְנְךָ֗ בְּשַׂ֤ר בָּנֶ֙יךָ֙ וּבְנֹתֶ֔יךָ אֲשֶׁ֥ר נָֽתַן־לְךָ֖ יְהֹוָ֣ה אֱלֹהֶ֑יךָ בְּמָצוֹר֙ וּבְמָצ֔וֹק אֲשֶׁר־יָצִ֥יק לְךָ֖ אֹיְבֶֽךָ׃ 54 הָאִישׁ֙ הָרַ֣ךְ בְּךָ֔ וְהֶעָנֹ֖ג מְאֹ֑ד תֵּרַ֤ע עֵינ֣וֹ בְאָחִ֔יו וּבְאֵ֣שֶׁת חֵיק֔וֹ וּבְיֶ֥תֶר בָּנָ֖יו אֲשֶׁ֥ר יוֹתִֽיר׃ 55 מִתֵּ֣ת ׀ לְאַחַ֣ד מֵהֶ֗ם מִבְּשַׂ֤ר בָּנָיו֙ אֲשֶׁ֣ר יֹאכֵ֔ל מִבְּלִ֥י הִשְׁאִֽיר־ל֖וֹ כֹּ֑ל בְּמָצוֹר֙ וּבְמָצ֔וֹק אֲשֶׁ֨ר יָצִ֥יק לְךָ֛ אֹיִבְךָ֖ בְּכָל־שְׁעָרֶֽיךָ׃ 56 הָרַכָּ֨ה בְךָ֜ וְהָֽעֲנֻגָּ֗ה אֲשֶׁ֨ר לֹֽא־נִסְּתָ֤ה כַף־רַגְלָהּ֙ הַצֵּ֣ג עַל־הָאָ֔רֶץ מֵהִתְעַנֵּ֖ג

---

50. ruthless Literally, "harsh of face." Alludes to the enemy's shameless brutality in treating the old and the young.

51. The list of what the enemy will consume is the same as the list of blessings promised in verse 4, with one omission, "the issue of your womb." In the grisly climax of the invasion, that blessing will be consumed by Israel itself (v. 53).

52. shut you up Literally, "press you," "distress you."

in all your towns There will be no place to escape.

until every... wall... has come down Until the enemy has breached the walls with battering rams and has razed them.

in which you trust A warning against misplaced trust. If the people disobey God, powerful

fortifications will provide no more protection than they did for the Canaanites and the Amorites (see 1:28, 3:5, 9:1).

53. Besieged and starving, the people will lose every vestige of compassion, and they will resort to cannibalism. (Under such circumstances, cannibalism has taken place throughout history; ancient cases are reported from Samaria, Jerusalem, and elsewhere in the Near East.)

54. spared Children whom he has not yet slaughtered and eaten.

56–57. The most pampered of women will likewise turn to the most loathsome of foods and guard it jealously. Newly delivered mothers will secretly devour their newborn along with the afterbirth to avoid sharing them with their husbands and older children.

---

53. you shall eat . . . the flesh of your sons and daughters One commentator, unable to bear the horrifying literal meaning,

takes this to mean: "In old age, you will have to depend on your children to feed and sustain you."

and dainty that she would never venture to set
a foot on the ground, shall begrudge the husband of her bosom, and her son and her daughter, 57 the afterbirth that issues from between her
legs and the babies she bears; she shall eat them
secretly, because of utter want, in the desperate
straits to which your enemy shall reduce you
in your towns.
58 If you fail to observe faithfully all the terms
of this Teaching that are written in this book,
to reverence this honored and awesome Name,
the LORD your God, 59 the LORD will inflict extraordinary plagues upon you and your offspring, strange and lasting plagues, malignant
and chronic diseases. 60 He will bring back upon you all the sicknesses of Egypt that you
dreaded so, and they shall cling to you. 61 Moreover, the LORD will bring upon you all the other
diseases and plagues that are not mentioned in
this book of Teaching, until you are wiped out.
62 You shall be left a scant few, after having been
as numerous as the stars in the skies, because
you did not heed the command of the LORD
your God. 63 And as the LORD once delighted in
making you prosperous and many, so will the
LORD now delight in causing you to perish and
in wiping you out; you shall be torn from the
land that you are about to enter and possess.
64 The LORD will scatter you among all the
peoples from one end of the earth to the other,
and there you shall serve other gods, wood and

וּמֵרֹךְ תֵּרַע עֵינָהּ בְּאִישׁ חֵיקָהּ וּבִבְנָהּ
וּבְבִתָּהּ׃ 57 וּבְשִׁלְיָתָהּ הַיּוֹצֵת* מִבֵּין
רַגְלֶיהָ וּבְבָנֶיהָ אֲשֶׁר תֵּלֵד כִּי־תֹאכְלֵם
בְּחֹסֶר־כֹּל בַּסָּתֶר בְּמָצוֹר וּבְמָצוֹק אֲשֶׁר
יָצִיק לְךָ אֹיִבְךָ בִּשְׁעָרֶיךָ׃
58 אִם־לֹא תִשְׁמֹר לַעֲשׂוֹת אֶת־כָּל־דִּבְרֵי
הַתּוֹרָה הַזֹּאת הַכְּתוּבִים בַּסֵּפֶר הַזֶּה
לְיִרְאָה אֶת־הַשֵּׁם הַנִּכְבָּד וְהַנּוֹרָא הַזֶּה
אֵת יְהוָה אֱלֹהֶיךָ׃ 59 וְהִפְלָא יְהוָה אֶת־
מַכֹּתְךָ וְאֵת מַכּוֹת זַרְעֶךָ מַכּוֹת גְּדֹלוֹת
וְנֶאֱמָנוֹת וָחֳלָיִם רָעִים וְנֶאֱמָנִים׃
60 וְהֵשִׁיב בְּךָ אֵת כָּל־מַדְוֵה מִצְרַיִם אֲשֶׁר
יָגֹרְתָּ מִפְּנֵיהֶם וְדָבְקוּ בָּךְ׃ 61 גַּם כָּל־חֳלִי
וְכָל־מַכָּה אֲשֶׁר לֹא כָתוּב בְּסֵפֶר הַתּוֹרָה
הַזֹּאת יַעְלֵם יְהוָה עָלֶיךָ עַד הִשָּׁמְדָךְ׃
62 וְנִשְׁאַרְתֶּם בִּמְתֵי מְעָט תַּחַת אֲשֶׁר
הֱיִיתֶם כְּכוֹכְבֵי הַשָּׁמַיִם לָרֹב כִּי־לֹא
שָׁמַעְתָּ בְּקוֹל יְהוָה אֱלֹהֶיךָ׃ 63 וְהָיָה
כַּאֲשֶׁר־שָׂשׂ יְהוָה עֲלֵיכֶם לְהֵיטִיב אֶתְכֶם
וּלְהַרְבּוֹת אֶתְכֶם כֵּן יָשִׂישׂ יְהוָה עֲלֵיכֶם
לְהַאֲבִיד אֶתְכֶם וּלְהַשְׁמִיד אֶתְכֶם
וְנִסַּחְתֶּם מֵעַל הָאֲדָמָה אֲשֶׁר־אַתָּה בָא־
שָׁמָּה לְרִשְׁתָּהּ׃
64 וֶהֱפִיצְךָ יְהוָה בְּכָל־הָעַמִּים מִקְצֵה
הָאָרֶץ וְעַד־קְצֵה הָאָרֶץ וְעָבַדְתָּ שָּׁם

v. 57. חסר א׳

dainty Pampered, indulged.

would never venture to set a foot on the ground She was accustomed to being carried on a litter or a portable chair or to riding in a carriage.

THIRD GROUP (vv. 58–68)

58. If you fail to observe To prevent the lengthy list of threats from inducing hopeless resignation, Moses again reminds the Israelites that the curses are conditional.

Name God's name is synonymous with God's being. This is a common usage in the Bible, especially in poetry. One loves and fears God's name—and blesses, thanks, and praises it—while sinners scorn and revile it.

59. strange Literally, "great." That is, unusually severe.

60. God will afflict the Israelites with the sicknesses of Egypt, from which He had promised to protect them if they would obey Him (see 7:15; Exod. 15:26).

61. plagues that are not mentioned Ancient Near Eastern documents often conclude with statements like this to indicate that the document stands for more than it contains.

stone, whom neither you nor your ancestors
have experienced. 65 Yet even among those nations you shall find no peace, nor shall your foot
find a place to rest. The LORD will give you there
an anguished heart and eyes that pine and a despondent spirit. 66 The life you face shall be precarious; you shall be in terror, night and day, with
no assurance of survival. 67 In the morning you
shall say, "If only it were evening!" and in the evening you shall say, "If only it were morning!"—
because of what your heart shall dread and your
eyes shall see. 68 The LORD will send you back to
Egypt in galleys, by a route which I told you you
should not see again. There you shall offer yourselves for sale to your enemies as male and female slaves, but none will buy.

אֱלֹהִים אֲחֵרִים אֲשֶׁר לֹא־יָדַעְתָּ אַתָּה
וַאֲבֹתֶיךָ עֵץ וָאָבֶן׃ 65 וּבַגּוֹיִם הָהֵם לֹא
תַרְגִּיעַ וְלֹא־יִהְיֶה מָנוֹחַ לְכַף־רַגְלֶךָ וְנָתַן
יְהוָה לְךָ שָׁם לֵב רַגָּז וְכִלְיוֹן עֵינַיִם וְדַאֲבוֹן
נָפֶשׁ׃ 66 וְהָיוּ חַיֶּיךָ תְּלֻאִים לְךָ מִנֶּגֶד
וּפָחַדְתָּ לַיְלָה וְיוֹמָם וְלֹא תַאֲמִין בְּחַיֶּיךָ׃
67 בַּבֹּקֶר תֹּאמַר מִי־יִתֵּן עֶרֶב וּבָעֶרֶב
תֹּאמַר מִי־יִתֵּן בֹּקֶר מִפַּחַד לְבָבְךָ אֲשֶׁר
תִּפְחָד וּמִמַּרְאֵה עֵינֶיךָ אֲשֶׁר תִּרְאֶה׃
68 וֶהֱשִׁיבְךָ יְהוָה ׀ מִצְרַיִם בָּאֳנִיּוֹת בַּדֶּרֶךְ
אֲשֶׁר אָמַרְתִּי לְךָ לֹא־תֹסִיף עוֹד לִרְאֹתָהּ
וְהִתְמַכַּרְתֶּם שָׁם לְאֹיְבֶיךָ לַעֲבָדִים
וְלִשְׁפָחוֹת וְאֵין קֹנֶה׃ ס

69 These are the terms of the covenant which
the LORD commanded Moses to conclude with
the Israelites in the land of Moab, in addition
to the covenant which He had made with them
at Horeb.

69 אֵלֶּה דִבְרֵי הַבְּרִית אֲשֶׁר־צִוָּה יְהוָה
אֶת־מֹשֶׁה לִכְרֹת אֶת־בְּנֵי יִשְׂרָאֵל בְּאֶרֶץ
מוֹאָב מִלְּבַד הַבְּרִית אֲשֶׁר־כָּרַת אִתָּם
בְּחֹרֵב׃ פ שביעי

65. no peace Even in exile, the Israelites will find no relief from the terrors left behind at home.

despondent spirit Literally, "a parched throat." A symptom of grief or depression.

68. The final reversal of history: the Israelites will be returned to Egypt.

a route which I told you you should not see again In 17:16, God said, "You must [or will] not go back that way again"; and in Exod. 14:13 He promised, "The Egyptians whom you see today you will never see again." With this punishment, God will rescind that promise.

I told you Here Moses speaks in God's name, as in verse 20. According to 17:16, it was God who made this promise.

offer yourselves for sale Their crushing poverty in Egypt will force them to find sustenance by selling themselves as slaves.

none will buy The text gives no reason for the refusal, which represents the ultimate irony and tragedy: the Egyptians, who once declined to free the Israelites from slavery, will now refuse to take them back as slaves.

CONCLUSION TO THE COVENANT (v. 69)

According to 4:13 and 5:2–19, the covenant at Horeb consisted of the Decalogue. The laws and teachings, promises and warnings outlined in chapters 6–26 and 28, constituting the terms of the present covenant made in Moab, were given by God to Moses privately. Moses first communicated them to the people in Moab in the long address just concluded (4:44–28:68), and then had the people commit themselves by covenant to observe them. Deuteronomy, however, regards these laws given in Moab as implicitly part of the Horeb covenant, because they are the direct continuation of God's words at Horeb, and the people had pledged there to observe them (5:24). This means that the covenants of Horeb and of Moab are virtually identical. The covenant to be made at Shechem (chap. 27) is also identical to the one made at Moab.

---

67. because of what your heart shall dread Bad as the reality will be, you will fear that the future will be worse. Fear of misfortune is often worse than the actual misfortune, as our imaginations conjure up all sorts of dreadful experiences we may feel we deserve.

29 Moses summoned all Israel and said to
them:

You have seen all that the LORD did before
your very eyes in the land of Egypt, to Pharaoh
and to all his courtiers and to his whole country:
2the wondrous feats that you saw with your own
eyes, those prodigious signs and marvels. 3Yet
to this day the LORD has not given you a mind
to understand or eyes to see or ears to hear.

4I led you through the wilderness forty years;
the clothes on your back did not wear out, nor
did the sandals on your feet; 5you had no bread
to eat and no wine or other intoxicant to

שביעי כט וַיִּקְרָא מֹשֶׁה אֶל־כָּל־יִשְׂרָאֵל
וַיֹּאמֶר אֲלֵהֶם
אַתֶּם רְאִיתֶם אֵת כָּל־אֲשֶׁר עָשָׂה יְהוָה
לְעֵינֵיכֶם בְּאֶרֶץ מִצְרַיִם לְפַרְעֹה וּלְכָל־
עֲבָדָיו וּלְכָל־אַרְצוֹ׃ 2 הַמַּסּוֹת הַגְּדֹלֹת
אֲשֶׁר רָאוּ עֵינֶיךָ הָאֹתֹת וְהַמֹּפְתִים
הַגְּדֹלִים הָהֵם׃ 3 וְלֹא־נָתַן יְהוָה לָכֶם לֵב
לָדַעַת וְעֵינַיִם לִרְאוֹת וְאָזְנַיִם לִשְׁמֹעַ עַד
הַיּוֹם הַזֶּה׃
4 וָאוֹלֵךְ אֶתְכֶם אַרְבָּעִים שָׁנָה בַּמִּדְבָּר
לֹא־בָלוּ שַׂלְמֹתֵיכֶם מֵעֲלֵיכֶם וְנַעַלְךָ לֹא־
בָלְתָה מֵעַל רַגְלֶךָ׃ 5 לֶחֶם לֹא אֲכַלְתֶּם

Moses' Third Discourse: A Summons to Ratify the Covenant Made in Moab (29:1–30:20)

Moses has presented all the terms of the second covenant to the people (4:44–26:19, 28). He now summons them to ratify it and concludes by stating that what he is offering Israel as a nation is the opportunity to choose between life and death (30:15–20).

BASIS OF THE COVENANT (29:1–8)

Moses reminds the people about the Exodus, which lies at the heart of the covenant, just as he did when God first offered the covenant to the Israelites at Mount Sinai.

1. summoned Literally, "called." "Summoned" implies that Moses had dismissed the people after his previous address, perhaps to allow them time to reflect on it so that they could enter the Covenant in full awareness of the solemnity of their action. If "called" is meant literally, it could mean that he simply continued proclaiming to the people on the same occasion as before.

You have seen . . . before your very eyes In Deuteronomy, Moses frequently stresses that he is appealing to the people on the basis of their own personal experience.

2. feats . . . signs and marvels The plagues inflicted on Egypt.

3. Yet to this day the LORD has not given you a mind to understand Better: "But the LORD did not give you a mind to understand until today." Verses 6–7 indicate that now, after 40 years, the Israelites have shown that they finally understand and trust in God's power.

4. I led you Moses speaks for God, as in 28:20 and elsewhere.

did not wear out God reminds Israel that His providence in the wilderness had an educational purpose. Having seen that Israel was incapable of recognizing His power behind the events of the Exodus (v. 3), God fed them by supernatural means for 40 years to overcome their spiritual obtuseness.

5. Israel survived on manna, quail, and water provided directly by God.

that you might know that I the LORD am your God God's supernatural providence—His ability to make food out of any substance (8:3)—taught the Israelites that He controls all natural phenomena.

CHAPTER 29

These eight verses allow this *parashah* to end on a favorable note, rather than leave us with the series of bone-chilling curses reverberating in our souls.

3. to this day the LORD has not given you a mind to understand "The ability to understand, to see or hear the divine significance of events, may be granted or withheld from man. One may see great wonders but remain entirely insensitive" (Heschel).

drink—that you might know that I the LORD am your God.

6 When you reached this place, King Sihon of Heshbon and King Og of Bashan came out to engage us in battle, but we defeated them. 7 We took their land and gave it to the Reubenites, the Gadites, and the half-tribe of Manasseh as their heritage. 8 Therefore observe faithfully all the terms of this covenant, that you may succeed in all that you undertake.

וְיַ֥יִן וְשֵׁכָ֖ר לֹ֣א שְׁתִיתֶ֑ם לְמַ֙עַן֙ תֵּֽדְע֔וּ כִּ֛י
אֲנִ֥י יְהוָ֖ה אֱלֹהֵיכֶֽם׃
מפטיר 6 וַתָּבֹ֖אוּ אֶל־הַמָּק֣וֹם הַזֶּ֑ה וַיֵּצֵ֣א סִיחֹ֣ן
מֶֽלֶךְ־חֶ֠שְׁבּוֹן וְע֨וֹג מֶֽלֶךְ־הַבָּשָׁ֧ן לִקְרָאתֵ֛נוּ
לַמִּלְחָמָ֖ה וַנַּכֵּֽם׃ 7 וַנִּקַּח֙ אֶת־אַרְצָ֔ם
וַנִּתְּנָ֣הּ לְנַחֲלָ֔ה לָרֽאוּבֵנִ֖י וְלַגָּדִ֑י וְלַחֲצִ֖י
שֵׁ֥בֶט הַֽמְנַשִּֽׁי׃ 8 וּשְׁמַרְתֶּ֗ם אֶת־דִּבְרֵי֙
הַבְּרִ֣ית הַזֹּ֔את וַעֲשִׂיתֶ֖ם אֹתָ֑ם לְמַ֣עַן
תַּשְׂכִּ֔ילוּ אֵ֖ת כָּל־אֲשֶׁ֥ר תַּעֲשֽׂוּן׃ פ

6. this place Transjordan. For Sihon and Og battled with Israel at Jahaz and Edrei, respectively (2:32; 3:1), not in the Plains of Moab where Moses is speaking.

we defeated them The willingness of this generation to wage war against both Sihon and Og—in contrast to the previous generation's fear of fighting the Amorites—revealed that they had indeed gained a mature trust in God's power. Their victory showed them that their trust was justified.

8. The experiences of the past 40 years have taught the Israelites that the essential condition for success is adherence to the Covenant.

הפטרה ששית דנחמתא

SIXTH HAFTARAH OF CONSOLATION
HAFTARAH FOR KI TAVO

ISAIAH 60:1–22

(*Recite on the 6th* Shabbat *after the 9th of* Av, *coinciding with the reading of* Ki Tavo. *On the Seven* Haftarot *of Consolation,* *see p. 1032.*)

In this *haftarah* the prophet dramatically announces Zion's imminent restoration, concretized through imagery of light and worldly splendor. The light is nothing less than the divine presence and redemption. The worldly splendor is the gift of nations who had oppressed the city and its inhabitants in times past. A tone of physical and spiritual transformation pervades the reading.

Powerful imagery of light frames and dominates this *haftarah*. This light is God's own glory (vv. 2,19–20), a splendor that will illumine and be reflected in Zion, attracting all nations to her (v. 3). Earlier prophecies portray Israel—and the prophet and his teaching in particular—as the bearer of the light of hope and direction to the exiles (42:6, 49:6, 51:4). In this passage, it is Zion that is the locus of this divine illumination (v. 1).

The light of redemption is a renewal of the resplendent light of origins. Zion is reborn and re-created by the shining presence of God's immediacy, much as each day dramatizes the renewal of Creation out of the dark night. Furthermore, just as the clarity of God's first creation was celebrated by new names ("Day," "Night," "Adam," "Eve"), so now, in this re-creation, Jerusalem shall be renamed "City of the Lord, / Zion of the Holy One of Israel" (v. 14), and her walls and gates shall be called "Victory" and "Renown" (v. 18). The special identity of Zion is singled out, together with its new future. But in contrast to the abstract, oblique announcement of light at Creation ("Let there be light"), the light of re-creation and redemption presented here is personal: "your light has dawned" (v. 1).

Nothing suggests that this effulgence of light is a cosmic principle set over against the dark, in the manner of the dualism that emerges in Zoroastrianism at this time. Light imagery was a feature of ancient Israelite culture too, in personal exclamations such as "The Lord is my light" (Ps. 27:1) and in theological statements such as "by Your light do we see light" (Ps. 36:10). What finds expression here is the sense of the divine as source and ground of reality, as power and presence for redemption. The words in the *haftarah* announce a new light of enduring brilliance. This portrayal of redemption as illumination marks a new moment in theology.

In the redemption, God will glorify and permanently transform Zion, the Temple, and Israel. The key Hebrew phrase that marks this prophetic truth is *lo od*: "No more" (*lo od*) shall the cry of wrack and ruin be at hand (v. 18); "No longer" (*lo od*) shall Zion need an earthly sun (v. 19). "Your sun shall set no more [*lo od*], / Your moon no more [*lo od*] withdraw; / For the Lord shall be a light to you forever" (v. 20). Expectation of lasting renewal seals the prophet's words, along with the guarantee that "I the Lord will speed it in due time" (v. 22).

For later readers of this prophecy, still awaiting the end of exile, these final words were less a statement of immediate assurance than a promise of future fulfillment (BT Sanh. 98a). And the opening call for Zion to arise because "your light has come [*ba*]" was understood as "your light is coming [*ba*]"—coming but not yet realized.

RELATION OF THE *HAFTARAH* TO THE CALENDAR

Less than seven weeks ago, the destruction of Zion was mourned on the fast of *Tish·ah b'Av*. Now, in this vision of restoration, the prophet calls Zion to arise from its sorrowful state (v. 1). In radiant glory, Zion shall be called "the city of the Lord" (v. 14); its ancient sanctuary shall be adorned by the majestic trees of Lebanon (v. 13).

60 Arise, shine, for your light has dawned;
The Presence of the Lord has shone upon you!
2Behold! Darkness shall cover the earth,
And thick clouds the peoples;
But upon you the Lord will shine,
And His Presence be seen over you.
3And nations shall walk by your light,
Kings, by your shining radiance.

4Raise your eyes and look about:
They have all gathered and come to you.
Your sons shall be brought from afar,
Your daughters like babes on shoulders.
5As you behold, you will glow;
Your heart will throb and thrill—
For the wealth of the sea shall pass on to you,
The riches of nations shall flow to you.
6Dust clouds of camels shall cover you,
Dromedaries of Midian and Ephah.
They all shall come from Sheba;
They shall bear gold and frankincense,
And shall herald the glories of the Lord.
7All the flocks of Kedar shall be assembled for you,
The rams of Nebaioth shall serve your needs;
They shall be welcome offerings on My altar,
And I will add glory to My glorious House.

8Who are these that float like a cloud,
Like doves to their cotes?
9Behold, the coastlands await me,
With ships of Tarshish in the lead,
To bring your sons from afar,

ס קוּמִי אוֹרִי כִּי בָא אוֹרֵךְ
וּכְבוֹד יְהוָה עָלַיִךְ זָרָח׃
2 כִּי־הִנֵּה הַחֹשֶׁךְ יְכַסֶּה־אֶרֶץ
וַעֲרָפֶל לְאֻמִּים
וְעָלַיִךְ יִזְרַח יְהוָה
וּכְבוֹדוֹ עָלַיִךְ יֵרָאֶה׃
3 וְהָלְכוּ גוֹיִם לְאוֹרֵךְ
וּמְלָכִים לְנֹגַהּ זַרְחֵךְ׃

4 שְׂאִי־סָבִיב עֵינַיִךְ וּרְאִי
כֻּלָּם נִקְבְּצוּ בָאוּ־לָךְ
בָּנַיִךְ מֵרָחוֹק יָבֹאוּ
וּבְנֹתַיִךְ עַל־צַד תֵּאָמַנָה׃
5 אָז תִּרְאִי וְנָהַרְתְּ
וּפָחַד וְרָחַב לְבָבֵךְ
כִּי־יֵהָפֵךְ עָלַיִךְ הֲמוֹן יָם
חֵיל גּוֹיִם יָבֹאוּ לָךְ׃
6 שִׁפְעַת גְּמַלִּים תְּכַסֵּךְ
בִּכְרֵי מִדְיָן וְעֵיפָה
כֻּלָּם מִשְּׁבָא יָבֹאוּ
זָהָב וּלְבוֹנָה יִשָּׂאוּ
וּתְהִלֹּת יְהוָה יְבַשֵּׂרוּ׃
7 כָּל־צֹאן קֵדָר יִקָּבְצוּ לָךְ
אֵילֵי נְבָיוֹת יְשָׁרְתוּנֶךְ
יַעֲלוּ עַל־רָצוֹן מִזְבְּחִי
וּבֵית תִּפְאַרְתִּי אֲפָאֵר׃

8 מִי־אֵלֶּה כָּעָב תְּעוּפֶינָה
וְכַיּוֹנִים אֶל־אֲרֻבֹּתֵיהֶם׃
9 כִּי־לִי ׀ אִיִּים יְקַוּוּ
וָאֳנִיּוֹת תַּרְשִׁישׁ בָּרִאשֹׁנָה
לְהָבִיא בָנַיִךְ מֵרָחוֹק

Isaiah 60:2. Presence Hebrew: *kavod;* literally, "glory." The first *Haftarah* of Consolation also declares that the divine Presence will be revealed (Isa. 40:5).

7. Kedar . . . Nebaioth Sons of Ishmael (Gen. 25:13); pastoral tribes in north Arabia.
welcome Foreigners will be welcome to worship in the Temple; see also Isa. 56:6–8.

And their silver and gold as well—
For the name of the LORD your God,
For the Holy One of Israel, who has glorified you.
10 Aliens shall rebuild your walls,
Their kings shall wait upon you—
For in anger I struck you down,
But in favor I take you back.
11 Your gates shall always stay open—
Day and night they shall never be shut—
To let in the wealth of the nations,
With their kings in procession.

12 For the nation or the kingdom
That does not serve you shall perish;
Such nations shall be destroyed.

13 The majesty of Lebanon shall come to you—
Cypress and pine and box—
To adorn the site of My Sanctuary,
To glorify the place where My feet rest.

14 Bowing before you, shall come
The children of those who tormented you;
Prostrate at the soles of your feet
Shall be all those who reviled you;
And you shall be called
"City of the LORD,
Zion of the Holy One of Israel."
15 Whereas you have been forsaken,
Rejected, with none passing through,
I will make you a pride everlasting,
A joy for age after age.
16 You shall suck the milk of the nations,

כַּסְפָּם וּזְהָבָם אִתָּם
לְשֵׁם יְהוָה אֱלֹהַיִךְ
וְלִקְדוֹשׁ יִשְׂרָאֵל כִּי פֵאֲרָךְ׃
10 וּבָנוּ בְנֵי־נֵכָר חֹמֹתַיִךְ
וּמַלְכֵיהֶם יְשָׁרְתוּנֶךְ
כִּי בְקִצְפִּי הִכִּיתִיךְ
וּבִרְצוֹנִי רִחַמְתִּיךְ׃
11 וּפִתְּחוּ שְׁעָרַיִךְ תָּמִיד
יוֹמָם וָלַיְלָה לֹא יִסָּגֵרוּ
לְהָבִיא אֵלַיִךְ חֵיל גּוֹיִם
וּמַלְכֵיהֶם נְהוּגִים׃
12 כִּי־הַגּוֹי וְהַמַּמְלָכָה
אֲשֶׁר לֹא־יַעַבְדוּךְ יֹאבֵדוּ
וְהַגּוֹיִם חָרֹב יֶחֱרָבוּ׃
13 כְּבוֹד הַלְּבָנוֹן אֵלַיִךְ יָבוֹא
בְּרוֹשׁ תִּדְהָר וּתְאַשּׁוּר יַחְדָּו
לְפָאֵר מְקוֹם מִקְדָּשִׁי
וּמְקוֹם רַגְלַי אֲכַבֵּד׃
14 וְהָלְכוּ אֵלַיִךְ שְׁחוֹחַ
בְּנֵי מְעַנַּיִךְ
וְהִשְׁתַּחֲווּ עַל־כַּפּוֹת רַגְלַיִךְ
כָּל־מְנַאֲצָיִךְ
וְקָרְאוּ לָךְ
עִיר יְהוָה
צִיּוֹן קְדוֹשׁ יִשְׂרָאֵל׃
15 תַּחַת הֱיוֹתֵךְ עֲזוּבָה
וּשְׂנוּאָה וְאֵין עוֹבֵר
וְשַׂמְתִּיךְ לִגְאוֹן עוֹלָם
מְשׂוֹשׂ דּוֹר וָדוֹר׃
16 וְיָנַקְתְּ חֲלֵב גּוֹיִם

15. forsaken, / Rejected These verbs hint at the motif of Zion as banished bride, which is developed explicitly in the third and the seventh *haftarot* of consolation.

Suckle at royal breasts.
And you shall know
That I the LORD am your Savior,
I, The Mighty One of Jacob, am your Redeemer.
17Instead of copper I will bring gold,
Instead of iron I will bring silver;
Instead of wood, copper;
And instead of stone, iron.
And I will appoint Well-being as your government,
Prosperity as your officials.
18The cry "Violence!"
Shall no more be heard in your land,
Nor "Wrack and ruin!"
Within your borders.
And you shall name your walls "Victory"
And your gates "Renown."

19No longer shall you need the sun
For light by day,
Nor the shining of the moon
For radiance [by night];
For the LORD shall be your light everlasting,
Your God shall be your glory.
20Your sun shall set no more,
Your moon no more withdraw;
For the LORD shall be a light to you forever,
And your days of mourning shall be ended.
21And your people, all of them righteous,
Shall possess the land for all time;
They are the shoot that I planted,
My handiwork in which I glory.
22The smallest shall become a clan;

וְשֹׁד מְלָכִים תִּינָקִי
וְיָדַעַתְּ
כִּי אֲנִי יְהוָה מוֹשִׁיעֵךְ
וְגֹאֲלֵךְ אֲבִיר יַעֲקֹב׃
17 תַּחַת הַנְּחֹשֶׁת אָבִיא זָהָב
וְתַחַת הַבַּרְזֶל אָבִיא כֶסֶף
וְתַחַת הָעֵצִים נְחֹשֶׁת
וְתַחַת הָאֲבָנִים בַּרְזֶל
וְשַׂמְתִּי פְקֻדָּתֵךְ שָׁלוֹם
וְנֹגְשַׂיִךְ צְדָקָה׃
18 לֹא־יִשָּׁמַע
עוֹד חָמָס בְּאַרְצֵךְ
שֹׁד וָשֶׁבֶר
בִּגְבוּלָיִךְ
וְקָרָאת יְשׁוּעָה חוֹמֹתַיִךְ
וּשְׁעָרַיִךְ תְּהִלָּה׃

19 לֹא־יִהְיֶה־לָּךְ עוֹד הַשֶּׁמֶשׁ
לְאוֹר יוֹמָם
וּלְנֹגַהּ הַיָּרֵחַ
לֹא־יָאִיר לָךְ
וְהָיָה־לָךְ יְהוָה לְאוֹר עוֹלָם
וֵאלֹהַיִךְ לְתִפְאַרְתֵּךְ׃
20 לֹא־יָבוֹא עוֹד שִׁמְשֵׁךְ
וִירֵחֵךְ לֹא יֵאָסֵף
כִּי יְהוָה יִהְיֶה־לָּךְ לְאוֹר עוֹלָם
וְשָׁלְמוּ יְמֵי אֶבְלֵךְ׃
21 וְעַמֵּךְ כֻּלָּם צַדִּיקִים
לְעוֹלָם יִירְשׁוּ אָרֶץ
נֵצֶר מטעו מַטָּעַי
מַעֲשֵׂה יָדַי לְהִתְפָּאֵר׃
22 הַקָּטֹן יִהְיֶה לָאֶלֶף

20. This prophecy transcends the need for natural light. Compare Isa. 30:26: "The light of the sun shall become sevenfold . . . when the LORD binds up His people's wounds." (Earlier and later prophets exploited the contrast between light and darkness to dramatize a time of doom and death; see Amos 5:18–20, 8:9–10; Zech. 14:6–7).

The least, a mighty nation.	וְהַצָּעִיר לְגוֹי עָצוּם
I the LORD will speed it in due time.	אֲנִי יְהוָה בְּעִתָּהּ אֲחִישֶׁנָּה׃ ס

22. I the LORD will speed it in due time A paradox to earlier commentators—for if redemption will occur "in due time," what does "will speed it" mean? The Hebrew words of the phrase were, therefore, read as if separated: "I [the LORD] will speed it" if the people have merit, but if they do not have merit, redemption will come "in due time" (BT Sanh. 98a, see Rashi). On the other hand, the word order in the Hebrew text puts "in due time" before "I will speed it." This prompted Radak to explain: When redemption comes "in due time," God "will speed it" to a complete conclusion.

The two interpretations represent two theological poles concerning redemption. According to the first interpretation, human merit may hasten God's hand. According to the second, redemption is a divine mystery whose "time" is not influenced by human actions (see Gen. R. 65:12). Messianic movements in Jewish history have often swung between these two poles.

[9]You stand this day, all of you, before the LORD your God—your tribal heads, your elders and your officials, all the men of Israel, [10]your children, your wives, even the stranger within your camp, from woodchopper to water drawer—[11]to enter into the covenant of the LORD your God, which the LORD your God is concluding with you this day, with its sanctions; [12]to the end that He may establish you this day as His people and be your God, as He

9 אַתֶּם נִצָּבִים הַיּוֹם כֻּלְּכֶם לִפְנֵי יְהוָה
אֱלֹהֵיכֶם רָאשֵׁיכֶם שִׁבְטֵיכֶם זִקְנֵיכֶם
וְשֹׁטְרֵיכֶם כֹּל אִישׁ יִשְׂרָאֵל׃ 10 טַפְּכֶם
נְשֵׁיכֶם וְגֵרְךָ אֲשֶׁר בְּקֶרֶב מַחֲנֶיךָ מֵחֹטֵב
עֵצֶיךָ עַד שֹׁאֵב מֵימֶיךָ׃ 11 לְעָבְרְךָ בִּבְרִית
יְהוָה אֱלֹהֶיךָ וּבְאָלָתוֹ אֲשֶׁר יְהוָה אֱלֹהֶיךָ
כֹּרֵת עִמְּךָ הַיּוֹם׃ 12 לְמַעַן הָקִים־אֹתְךָ שני
הַיּוֹם ׀ לוֹ לְעָם וְהוּא יִהְיֶה־לְּךָ לֵאלֹהִים

Moses' Third Discourse: A Summons to Ratify the Covenant Made in Moab (*continued*)

THE COVENANT CEREMONY (29:9–20)

Every Israelite participates in the ceremony establishing the covenant with God. The text does not tell us when the ceremony took place or of what it consisted. Other covenant texts from the ancient Near East likewise allude to ceremonies without describing the actual proceedings; they recount only the content of the agreement.

9. Moses lists those present in the order of their social status.

You stand You are presenting yourselves before God.

10. your children, your wives Not only the leaders and the adult males but each individual member of the community takes part in affirming the covenant. The responsibility is so momentous, and the consequences of disobedience so dire, that all must commit themselves personally, and not through the action of a parent, husband, or superior.

stranger Although they are not Israelites (14:21), resident aliens are subject to the civil law and certain religious prohibitions, enjoy particular rights, and are permitted to participate in various religious celebrations. For this reason, they, too, must take part in the covenant ceremony and listen as the Teaching is read. This probably consisted of the laws of Deuteronomy beginning with chapter 12.

from woodchopper to water drawer Because all categories of Israelites have already been listed, this phrase must refer to aliens who served as menial laborers. The wording includes other types of menial laborers as well.

11. the covenant . . . with its sanctions Hebrew: *b'rit v'alah;* more literally, "a covenant guarded by imprecations." The word *alah* means "curse" or "imprecation" (also v. 13), alluding to the curses detailed in chapter 28.

12. He promised you Refers to the mutual relationship God promised to the Exodus generation (in Exod. 6:7; Lev. 26:12). Among those Moses is now addressing, the older people were alive then and received the promise, although they were minors.

This *parashah* is read (usually together with *Va-yeilekh*) on the *Shabbat* before *Rosh ha-Shanah,* a time for taking to heart the commitment to God's covenant.

9. all of you The whole of the community is greater than the sum of its parts. Each individual Israelite may be flawed and imperfect, but when all of them join together, the strengths and good qualities of each are reinforced and magnified. This also teaches that no one should say, "It is not my responsibility." Everyone must do his or her share (Barukh of Medzibozh).

11. to enter into the covenant To reaffirm the covenant that was entered into at Mount Sinai. Just as a husband and wife need to reaffirm their commitment to each other when the early days of romantic attraction have given way to the day-to-day struggle to overcome accumulated disappointments, so too God and the people Israel need to reaffirm the covenant at this later date (Shneur Zalman).

promised you and as He swore to your fathers,
Abraham, Isaac, and Jacob. 13I make this covenant, with its sanctions, not with you alone,
14but both with those who are standing here
with us this day before the LORD our God and
with those who are not with us here this day.

15Well you know that we dwelt in the land
of Egypt and that we passed through the midst
of various other nations; 16and you have seen
the detestable things and the fetishes of wood
and stone, silver and gold, that they keep. 17Per-
chance there is among you some man or
woman, or some clan or tribe, whose heart is
even now turning away from the LORD our God
to go and worship the gods of those nations—
perchance there is among you a stock sprouting
poison weed and wormwood. 18When such a

כַּאֲשֶׁ֖ר דִּבֶּר־לָ֑ךְ וְכַאֲשֶׁ֤ר נִשְׁבַּע֙ לַאֲבֹתֶ֔יךָ
לְאַבְרָהָ֥ם לְיִצְחָ֖ק וּֽלְיַעֲקֹֽב׃ 13 וְלֹ֥א אִתְּכֶ֖ם
לְבַדְּכֶ֑ם אָנֹכִ֗י כֹּרֵת֙ אֶת־הַבְּרִ֣ית הַזֹּ֔את
וְאֶת־הָאָלָ֖ה הַזֹּֽאת׃ 14 כִּי֩ אֶת־אֲשֶׁ֨ר יֶשְׁנ֜וֹ
פֹּ֗ה עִמָּ֙נוּ֙ עֹמֵ֣ד הַיּ֔וֹם לִפְנֵ֖י יְהוָ֣ה אֱלֹהֵ֑ינוּ
וְאֵ֨ת אֲשֶׁ֥ר אֵינֶ֛נּוּ פֹּ֖ה עִמָּ֥נוּ הַיּֽוֹם׃
15 כִּֽי־אַתֶּ֣ם יְדַעְתֶּ֔ם אֵ֥ת אֲשֶׁר־יָשַׁ֖בְנוּ שלישי
בְּאֶ֣רֶץ מִצְרָ֑יִם וְאֵ֧ת אֲשֶׁר־עָבַ֛רְנוּ בְּקֶ֥רֶב
הַגּוֹיִ֖ם אֲשֶׁ֥ר עֲבַרְתֶּֽם׃ 16 וַתִּרְאוּ֙ אֶת־
שִׁקּ֣וּצֵיהֶ֔ם וְאֵ֖ת גִּלֻּלֵיהֶ֑ם עֵ֣ץ וָאֶ֔בֶן כֶּ֥סֶף
וְזָהָ֖ב אֲשֶׁ֥ר עִמָּהֶֽם׃ 17 פֶּן־יֵ֣שׁ בָּ֠כֶם אִ֣ישׁ
אוֹ־אִשָּׁ֞ה א֧וֹ מִשְׁפָּחָ֣ה אוֹ־שֵׁ֗בֶט אֲשֶׁר֩
לְבָב֨וֹ פֹנֶ֤ה הַיּוֹם֙ מֵעִם֙ יְהוָ֣ה אֱלֹהֵ֔ינוּ
לָלֶ֣כֶת לַעֲבֹ֔ד אֶת־אֱלֹהֵ֖י הַגּוֹיִ֣ם הָהֵ֑ם
פֶּן־יֵ֣שׁ בָּכֶ֗ם שֹׁ֛רֶשׁ פֹּרֶ֥ה רֹ֖אשׁ וְלַעֲנָֽה׃

He swore to your fathers Refers to the Lord's promise that He would be God to Abraham and his descendants (Gen. 17:7–8).

14. those who are not with us here this day Future generations. The mutual commitments made here by God and by the people Israel are binding for all future generations. Ancient Near Eastern treaties likewise stipulate that they are binding on the parties' descendants.

15. various other nations Literally, "the nations through which you passed." It refers to the nations of Transjordan, particularly Moab, which exposed Israel to the pagan cult of Baal-peor (see 4:3; Num. 25:1–3).

16. detestable things Hebrew: *shikkutzim,* a disparaging term used in the Bible for idols. It comes from the verb *shakketz* (spurn, reject as abominable; see 7:26). It is commonly employed in connection with the ban on impure foods.

silver and gold Used as plating on the statues.

17. Advocates of idolatry are to be punished whether they are individuals, males or females, relatives, or entire cities. The concern to make the warning as comprehensive as possible is also found in other ancient treaties and oaths.

Perchance there is Beware in case there is.

gods of those nations This refers to the fetishes mentioned in verse 16. In the Bible's view, there is no substance to foreign gods beyond their images; and pagans worship the images themselves, mistakenly thinking that they have power. Moses fears that Israel's exposure to those images may have left some people with a temptation to worship them, which is what happened at Peor (4:3).

stock sprouting poison weed and wormwood A person, clan, or tribe whose delusions would have bitter, deadly consequences.

---

14. those who are not with us here this day The souls of all future Jews—present at this moment, as they had been at Mount Sinai (Tanḥ.). Moses' words can also be understood as referring to the physically or mentally handicapped, who perhaps could not be present but were still part of the community, or to those Jews who reject the covenant but are still claimed by it and included in it.

What right did our ancestors have to impose the obligations of the covenant on us? Why do we have to feel bound by their actions? Many aspects of our lives were determined by decisions of our parents and ancestors, including when and where we would be born, what skills and physical qualities we would possess, and where and how we would be educated. Maturity consists in accepting those conditions as the facts of our lives, rather than fantasizing about how our lives would have been easier had we been born otherwise.

one hears the words of these sanctions, he may fancy himself immune, thinking, "I shall be safe, though I follow my own willful heart"—to the utter ruin of moist and dry alike. ¹⁹The LORD will never forgive him; rather will the LORD's anger and passion rage against that man, till every sanction recorded in this book comes down upon him, and the LORD blots out his name from under heaven.

²⁰The LORD will single them out from all the tribes of Israel for misfortune, in accordance with all the sanctions of the covenant recorded in this book of Teaching. ²¹And later generations will ask—the children who succeed you, and foreigners who come from distant lands and see the plagues and diseases that the LORD has inflicted upon that land, ²²all its soil devastated by sulfur and salt, beyond sowing and

¹⁸ וְהָיָ֡ה בְּשָׁמְעוֹ֩ אֶת־דִּבְרֵ֨י הָאָלָ֜ה הַזֹּ֗את וְהִתְבָּרֵ֨ךְ בִּלְבָב֤וֹ לֵאמֹר֙ שָׁל֣וֹם יִֽהְיֶה־לִּ֔י כִּ֛י בִּשְׁרִר֥וּת לִבִּ֖י אֵלֵ֑ךְ לְמַ֛עַן סְפ֥וֹת הָרָוָ֖ה אֶת־הַצְּמֵאָֽה׃ ¹⁹ לֹא־יֹאבֶ֣ה יְהֹוָה֮ סְלֹ֣חַֽ לוֹ֒ כִּ֣י אָ֠ז יֶעְשַׁ֨ן אַף־יְהֹוָ֤ה וְקִנְאָתוֹ֙ בָּאִ֣ישׁ הַה֔וּא וְרָ֤בְצָה בּוֹ֙ כָּל־הָ֣אָלָ֔ה הַכְּתוּבָ֖ה בַּסֵּ֣פֶר הַזֶּ֑ה וּמָחָ֤ה יְהֹוָה֙ אֶת־שְׁמ֔וֹ מִתַּ֖חַת הַשָּׁמָֽיִם׃ ²⁰ וְהִבְדִּיל֤וֹ יְהֹוָה֙ לְרָעָ֔ה מִכֹּ֖ל שִׁבְטֵ֣י יִשְׂרָאֵ֑ל כְּכֹל֙ אָל֣וֹת הַבְּרִ֔ית הַכְּתוּבָ֕ה בְּסֵ֖פֶר הַתּוֹרָ֥ה הַזֶּֽה׃ ²¹ וְאָמַ֞ר הַדּ֣וֹר הָאַחֲר֗וֹן בְּנֵיכֶם֙ אֲשֶׁ֣ר יָק֣וּמוּ מֵאַֽחֲרֵיכֶ֔ם וְהַ֨נָּכְרִ֔י אֲשֶׁ֥ר יָבֹ֖א מֵאֶ֣רֶץ רְחוֹקָ֑ה וְרָא֞וּ אֶת־מַכּ֤וֹת הָאָ֨רֶץ֙ הַהִ֔וא וְאֶת־תַּ֣חֲלֻאֶ֔יהָ אֲשֶׁר־חִלָּ֥ה יְהֹוָ֖ה בָּֽהּ׃ ²² גׇּפְרִ֣ית וָמֶ֘לַח֮ שְׂרֵפָ֣ה כׇל־אַרְצָהּ֒ לֹ֤א תִזָּרַע֙ וְלֹ֣א תַצְמִ֔חַ

18. such a one Man or woman, clan or tribe.
fancy himself immune The culprit may delude himself or herself, thinking that by remaining silent while others swear allegiance to the covenant he or she will be exempted from its consequences.
be safe Literally, "have *shalom* (safety, well-being)."
willful heart Refers to one who says, "I'll follow my own sights, doing as I see fit."
moist and dry alike The unique and problematic Hebrew phrase probably is an expression meaning "everything." Moses is commenting on the consequences of the sinner's delusion: God will sweep away everything that belongs to the sinner or to the entire nation.
19. will never forgive him Nothing that one does will assuage God's anger.
passion Illustrates the Decalogue's warning that the Lord, in reaction to the worship of other gods, is an "impassioned God" (see 5:9).
every sanction Such as those in chapter 28.
blots out his name Such a person's fate will

be the same as that which God threatened to inflict on worshipers of the Golden Calf (9:14) and which He commands that Israel impose on the Canaanites and the Amalekites (7:24, 25:19).
20. single . . . out The would-be sinner should not imagine that God deals only with the community as a whole, that individuals can escape punishment as long as the community is virtuous.

THE AFTERMATH OF PUNISHMENT
(vv. 21–27)

Future generations and foreigners will ask what caused the disaster and give the answer themselves: It is because Israel violated the terms of God's covenant. Foreign nations, who would admire Israel's wisdom if it obeys God's laws (see 4:6), would recognize its folly if it disobeys.
21. plagues and diseases This is a metaphoric reference to the natural disasters of verse 22.
22. sulfur and salt As a severe punishment, conquerors sometimes spread salt on the soil of

18. moist and dry alike Honest and deceitful alike. The wicked person calculates that a society can tolerate a certain amount of dishonesty. As long as most people tell the truth, a liar will be believed. If most people are honest, a swindler can

take advantage of their presumption of good faith.
21. Later generations will ask, "How did those who lived before us permit themselves to despoil the earth, air, and water, not leaving us a livable environment?"

וְלֹא־יַעֲלֶה בָהּ כָּל־עֵשֶׂב כְּמַהְפֵּכַת סְדֹם
וַעֲמֹרָה אַדְמָה וצביים וּצְבוֹיִם אֲשֶׁר הָפַךְ
יְהוָה בְּאַפּוֹ וּבַחֲמָתוֹ׃ 23 וְאָמְרוּ כָּל־הַגּוֹיִם
עַל־מֶה עָשָׂה יְהוָה כָּכָה לָאָרֶץ הַזֹּאת
מֶה חֳרִי הָאַף הַגָּדוֹל הַזֶּה׃ 24 וְאָמְרוּ עַל
אֲשֶׁר עָזְבוּ אֶת־בְּרִית יְהוָה אֱלֹהֵי אֲבֹתָם
אֲשֶׁר כָּרַת עִמָּם בְּהוֹצִיאוֹ אֹתָם מֵאֶרֶץ
מִצְרָיִם׃ 25 וַיֵּלְכוּ וַיַּעַבְדוּ אֱלֹהִים אֲחֵרִים
וַיִּשְׁתַּחֲווּ לָהֶם אֱלֹהִים אֲשֶׁר לֹא־יְדָעוּם
וְלֹא חָלַק לָהֶם׃ 26 וַיִּחַר־אַף יְהוָה בָּאָרֶץ
הַהִוא לְהָבִיא עָלֶיהָ אֶת־כָּל־הַקְּלָלָה
הַכְּתוּבָה בַּסֵּפֶר הַזֶּה׃ 27 וַיִּתְּשֵׁם יְהוָה
מֵעַל אַדְמָתָם בְּאַף וּבְחֵמָה וּבְקֶצֶף גָּדוֹל
וַיַּשְׁלִכֵם* אֶל־אֶרֶץ אַחֶרֶת כַּיּוֹם הַזֶּה׃
28 הַנִּסְתָּרֹת לַיהוָה אֱלֹהֵינוּ וְהַנִּגְלֹת לָנוּ
וּלְבָנֵינוּ* עַד־עוֹלָם לַעֲשׂוֹת אֶת־כָּל־דִּבְרֵי
רביעי [שני] הַתּוֹרָה הַזֹּאת׃ ס

producing, no grass growing in it, just like the upheaval of Sodom and Gomorrah, Admah and Zeboiim, which the Lord overthrew in His fierce anger—23all nations will ask, "Why did the Lord do thus to this land? Wherefore that awful wrath?" 24They will be told, "Because they forsook the covenant that the Lord, God of their fathers, made with them when He freed them from the land of Egypt; 25they turned to the service of other gods and worshiped them, gods whom they had not experienced and whom He had not allotted to them. 26So the Lord was incensed at that land and brought upon it all the curses recorded in this book. 27The Lord uprooted them from their soil in anger, fury, and great wrath, and cast them into another land, as is still the case."

28Concealed acts concern the Lord our God; but with overt acts, it is for us and our children ever to apply all the provisions of this Teaching.

v. 27. ל׳ רבתי לפי נוסחים מקובלים

v. 28. נקוד על ל׳ נ׳ ו׳ ו׳ ל׳ ב׳ נ׳ י׳ נ׳ ו׳, ולפי נוסחים מקובלים גם נקוד על ע׳

conquered lands to render it infertile. An Aramaic treaty warns that the gods will sow salt on the city that violates its terms. Apparently, the effect of sulfur was also known in antiquity: Excessive amounts make soil too acidic for cultivation.

grass In the sense of vegetation, herbage.

just like the upheaval of Sodom That is, just like Sodom and its sister cities, which were overturned (see Gen. 19:24–25). The comparison is not to the manner of destruction but to its consequences.

23. The devastation will be so great that the entire world will learn of it and join future Israelites and passersby in asking about it.

24. covenant See Comment to 28:69.

25. gods whom they had not experienced Who had done nothing for them.

whom He had not allotted to them As objects of worship. They were to worship the Lord alone (see 4:19–20).

27. as is still the case In the days of the exile, when this question and answer will take place.

28. Concealed acts Sins committed secretly are known to God, and He will punish them.

for us and our children In Hebrew texts of the Torah, dots are placed over these words and the first letter of the following word. In 15 places in the Bible, such dots appear over letters or words. They were a scribal device to call attention to an otherwise unspecified problem in the text. Frequently, the Sages interpreted via *midrash* the words marked with these points.

apply all the provisions Overt acts (known sins) are the community's responsibility to punish by applying to the perpetrators the stipulations in the Covenant.

---

28. In scrolls and printed volumes of the Torah (*ḥumashim*), dots appear above some of the letters in this challenging verse. The dots, which probably indicate the Sages' perplexity over the verse, have prompted several interpretations: God will punish secret sins, but society must punish sins committed openly (Targ.). We cannot always understand God's will, but we must do what we are called on to do nonetheless (or do what we can understand

30 When all these things befall you—the
blessing and the curse that I have set before
you—and you take them to heart amidst the
various nations to which the LORD your God
has banished you, 2and you return to the LORD
your God, and you and your children heed His
command with all your heart and soul, just as
I enjoin upon you this day, 3then the LORD your
God will restore your fortunes and take you
back in love. He will bring you together again
from all the peoples where the LORD your God
has scattered you. 4Even if your outcasts are at
the ends of the world, from there the LORD your
God will gather you, from there He will fetch
you. 5And the LORD your God will bring you

רביעי [שני] ל וְהָיָה כִֽי־יָבֹאוּ עָלֶיךָ כָּל־הַדְּבָרִים
הָאֵלֶּה הַבְּרָכָה וְהַקְּלָלָה אֲשֶׁר נָתַתִּי
לְפָנֶיךָ וַהֲשֵׁבֹתָ אֶל־לְבָבֶךָ בְּכָל־הַגּוֹיִם
אֲשֶׁר הִדִּיחֲךָ יְהוָה אֱלֹהֶיךָ שָׁמָּה׃ 2 וְשַׁבְתָּ
עַד־יְהוָה אֱלֹהֶיךָ וְשָׁמַעְתָּ בְקֹלוֹ כְּכֹל
אֲשֶׁר־אָנֹכִי מְצַוְּךָ הַיּוֹם אַתָּה וּבָנֶיךָ בְּכָל־
לְבָבְךָ וּבְכָל־נַפְשֶׁךָ׃ 3 וְשָׁב יְהוָה אֱלֹהֶיךָ
אֶת־שְׁבוּתְךָ וְרִחֲמֶךָ וְשָׁב וְקִבֶּצְךָ מִכָּל־
הָעַמִּים אֲשֶׁר הֱפִיצְךָ יְהוָה אֱלֹהֶיךָ שָׁמָּה׃
4 אִם־יִהְיֶה נִדַּחֲךָ בִּקְצֵה הַשָּׁמָיִם מִשָּׁם
יְקַבֶּצְךָ יְהוָה אֱלֹהֶיךָ וּמִשָּׁם יִקָּחֶךָ׃
5 וֶהֱבִיאֲךָ יְהוָה אֱלֹהֶיךָ אֶל־הָאָרֶץ אֲשֶׁר־

THE POSSIBILITY OF RESTORATION (30:1–10)

Moses now offers assurance that if Israel should be exiled, God will reinstate it if the people sincerely repent of their rebellion and return to Him and His instruction.

1. Moses refers not only to the curses described in chapter 29 but also to the blessings (and curses) of chapter 28. By doing so he declares that if the Israelites should bring disaster on themselves, the stocktaking necessary for their restoration should include the recollection that while disobedience led to disaster, obedience led to success.

that I have set before you That I have offered you as alternatives.

5. This promise is perhaps intended to en-

---

and accept). We should be reluctant to judge others, for only God can see into a person's heart and know that person's motivation, whereas we can only see the person's deeds. And most imaginatively: Anonymous saints are a source of pleasure to God, but society needs role models whose virtuous lives escape anonymity and are conspicuous, that we might learn from them (Meir Yeḥiel of Ostrowiec).

CHAPTER 30

The Hebrew verb meaning "return" or "repent" (*shuv*) occurs seven times in verses 1–10. This repetition is appropriate to its being read at the season of penitence, the High Holy Day season.

1. the blessing and the curse The blessing within the curse. There is no calamity that does not have a kernel of blessing concealed within it, even if it only motivates us to seek the cause of the calamity and prevent it from recurring.

2. return to Hebrew: *v'shavta ad;* literally, "turn around toward." Similarly, a phrase in verse 10 (*tashuv el*) means "return to." This variation in language reflects two stages in the process of repentance. The first stage is a realization that our behavior is wrong and requires a change of direction. This is "turning toward" God. The second stage is coming into the presence of God as the result of one's new way of life, "returning to" God (Malbim).

3. take you back in love God will help you repent by sharing with you the divine capacity for love and empathy. One who regards others compassionately will not sin against them. One who comes to love God, reciprocating God's love, will not sin against God.

HALAKHAH L'MA·ASEH

30:2. return *T'shuvah,* turning to God in repentance with a plea for forgiveness, is a *mitzvah* in its own right (see Comment to Num. 5:7).

to the land that your fathers possessed, and you shall possess it; and He will make you more prosperous and more numerous than your fathers.

6 Then the LORD your God will open up your heart and the hearts of your offspring to love the LORD your God with all your heart and soul, in order that you may live. 7 The LORD your God will inflict all those curses upon the enemies and foes who persecuted you. 8 You, however, will again heed the LORD and obey all His commandments that I enjoin upon you this day. 9 And the LORD your God will grant you abounding prosperity in all your undertakings, in the issue of your womb, the offspring of your cattle, and the produce of your soil. For the LORD will again delight in your well-being, as He did in that of your fathers, 10 since you will be heeding the LORD your God and keeping His commandments and laws that are recorded in this book of the Teaching—once you return to the LORD your God with all your heart and soul.

11 Surely, this Instruction which I enjoin upon you this day is not too baffling for you, nor is

יְרְשׁוּ אֲבֹתֶיךָ וִירִשְׁתָּהּ וְהֵיטִבְךָ וְהִרְבְּךָ
מֵאֲבֹתֶיךָ׃
6 וּמָל יְהוָה אֱלֹהֶיךָ אֶת־לְבָבְךָ וְאֶת־לְבַב
זַרְעֶךָ לְאַהֲבָה אֶת־יְהוָה אֱלֹהֶיךָ בְּכָל־
חמישי [שלישי] לְבָבְךָ וּבְכָל־נַפְשְׁךָ לְמַעַן חַיֶּיךָ׃ 7 וְנָתַן
יְהוָה אֱלֹהֶיךָ אֵת כָּל־הָאָלוֹת הָאֵלֶּה
עַל־אֹיְבֶיךָ וְעַל־שֹׂנְאֶיךָ אֲשֶׁר רְדָפוּךָ׃
8 וְאַתָּה תָשׁוּב וְשָׁמַעְתָּ בְּקוֹל יְהוָה
וְעָשִׂיתָ אֶת־כָּל־מִצְוֺתָיו אֲשֶׁר אָנֹכִי מְצַוְּךָ
הַיּוֹם׃ 9 וְהוֹתִירְךָ יְהוָה אֱלֹהֶיךָ בְּכֹל ׀
מַעֲשֵׂה יָדֶךָ בִּפְרִי בִטְנְךָ וּבִפְרִי בְהֶמְתְּךָ
וּבִפְרִי אַדְמָתְךָ לְטֹבָה כִּי ׀ יָשׁוּב יְהוָה
לָשׂוּשׂ עָלֶיךָ לְטוֹב כַּאֲשֶׁר־שָׂשׂ עַל־
אֲבֹתֶיךָ׃ 10 כִּי תִשְׁמַע בְּקוֹל יְהוָה אֱלֹהֶיךָ
לִשְׁמֹר מִצְוֺתָיו וְחֻקֹּתָיו הַכְּתוּבָה בְּסֵפֶר
הַתּוֹרָה הַזֶּה כִּי תָשׁוּב אֶל־יְהוָה אֱלֹהֶיךָ
בְּכָל־לְבָבְךָ וּבְכָל־נַפְשֶׁךָ׃ פ
ששי 11 כִּי הַמִּצְוָה הַזֹּאת אֲשֶׁר אָנֹכִי מְצַוְּךָ
הַיּוֹם לֹא־נִפְלֵאת הִוא מִמְּךָ וְלֹא רְחֹקָה

courage a future generation to return to God, assuring it that the nation's sinful past will not be held against it in any way.

6. will open up your heart Literally, "will circumcise your heart." In contrast to 10:16, where Moses exhorts Israel to circumcise its own heart, here he promises that once Israel returns to God, God Himself will remove the psychological impediments to wholehearted devotion.

CONCLUSION (vv. 11–20)

Moses assures the present generation that the terms of the Covenant are not too difficult to know, understand, and fulfill.

11. Instruction Hebrew: *ha-mitzvah;* Deuteronomy's instructions, the Teaching (*torah*).

---

11. this Instruction Hebrew: *ha-mitzvah ha-zot.* The Sages of the Talmud understand this as referring to the entire Torah. It is not so baffling that only the theologically astute can understand it, nor so challenging that only the spiritually gifted can fulfill it. It is well within the abilities of the average person.

To later scholars (Ramban, Albo), this phrase referred to the *mitzvah* of repentance, the subject of the previous 10 verses. It is difficult to break a bad habit, to change one's way of life. Yet people who have succeeded in doing that will testify it can be done. A *midrash* offers us the image of a mirror. The figure we see in the mirror seems to be twice as far from us as it really is. But with every step we take toward the mirror, the reflection takes a step toward us. So it is with repentance. Our goal seems so far off, but God says to us, "Take one step toward Me and then another, and I will meet you more than halfway."

not too baffling It is suitable for all, not only for scholars and philosophers.

it beyond reach. 12It is not in the heavens, that
you should say, "Who among us can go up to
the heavens and get it for us and impart it to
us, that we may observe it?" 13Neither is it beyond the sea, that you should say, "Who among
us can cross to the other side of the sea and get
it for us and impart it to us, that we may observe
it?" 14No, the thing is very close to you, in your
mouth and in your heart, to observe it.
15See, I set before you this day life and prosperity, death and adversity. 16For I command
you this day, to love the LORD your God, to walk
in His ways, and to keep His commandments,
His laws, and His rules, that you may thrive and
increase, and that the LORD your God may bless
you in the land that you are about to enter and
possess. 17But if your heart turns away and you
give no heed, and are lured into the worship and
service of other gods, 18I declare to you this day
that you shall certainly perish; you shall not long

הוּא׃ 12 לֹא בַשָּׁמַיִם הִוא לֵאמֹר מִי
יַעֲלֶה־לָּנוּ הַשָּׁמַיְמָה וְיִקָּחֶהָ לָּנוּ וְיַשְׁמִעֵנוּ
אֹתָהּ וְנַעֲשֶׂנָּה׃ 13 וְלֹא־מֵעֵבֶר לַיָּם הִוא
לֵאמֹר מִי יַעֲבָר־לָנוּ אֶל־עֵבֶר הַיָּם וְיִקָּחֶהָ
לָּנוּ וְיַשְׁמִעֵנוּ אֹתָהּ וְנַעֲשֶׂנָּה׃ 14 כִּי־קָרוֹב
אֵלֶיךָ הַדָּבָר מְאֹד בְּפִיךָ וּבִלְבָבְךָ
לַעֲשֹׂתוֹ׃ ס
15 רְאֵה נָתַתִּי לְפָנֶיךָ הַיּוֹם אֶת־הַחַיִּים שביעי
וְאֶת־הַטּוֹב וְאֶת־הַמָּוֶת וְאֶת־הָרָע׃ ביעי]
16 אֲשֶׁר אָנֹכִי מְצַוְּךָ הַיּוֹם לְאַהֲבָה אֶת־
יְהוָה אֱלֹהֶיךָ לָלֶכֶת בִּדְרָכָיו וְלִשְׁמֹר
מִצְוֺתָיו וְחֻקֹּתָיו וּמִשְׁפָּטָיו וְחָיִיתָ וְרָבִיתָ
וּבֵרַכְךָ יְהוָה אֱלֹהֶיךָ בָּאָרֶץ אֲשֶׁר־אַתָּה
בָא־שָׁמָּה לְרִשְׁתָּהּ׃ 17 וְאִם־יִפְנֶה לְבָבְךָ
וְלֹא תִשְׁמָע וְנִדַּחְתָּ וְהִשְׁתַּחֲוִיתָ לֵאלֹהִים
אֲחֵרִים וַעֲבַדְתָּם׃ 18 הִגַּדְתִּי לָכֶם הַיּוֹם מפטיר
כִּי אָבֹד תֹּאבֵדוּן לֹא־תַאֲרִיכֻן יָמִים עַל־

12. not in the heavens The proverbial inability of humans to reach heaven is conveyed by Prov. 30:4, "Who has ascended heaven and come down?" It is also conveyed by the Mesopotamian saying, "Who is tall enough to reach heaven, who is tall enough to encompass the earth?"

13. beyond the sea Mesopotamian literature describes the effort of crossing the sea as so difficult that only gods and heroes can accomplish it.

14. very close to you The instruction is not beyond reach (v. 11) but nearby. Because it is known and understood, it can be put into practice by everyone in the community.

in your mouth It is readily accessible to you, you know it by heart. (The Hebrew idiom *b'al peh* [by mouth] is equivalent to the English "by heart," "from memory.") This manner of speaking reflects a predominantly oral culture in which learning and review are accomplished primarily by recitation.

in your heart In your mind, known with understanding and not merely by rote.

15. Here Moses concludes his summons to the Covenant by urging the Israelites to obey it, for that is the only way, under its terms, to survive.

16. His ways The ways that He commands.

12. It is not in the heavens It is meant for everyone, not only for people willing to renounce earthly pleasures.

The Talmud tells of a dispute among scholars over a technical point of Jewish law. One scholar, Eliezer, called on God to affirm the correctness of his position. A voice from heaven proclaimed: "Why do you quarrel with Rabbi Eliezer, when he is correct?" The other Sages, however, were not impressed. One of them quoted this phrase: "The Torah 'is not in the heavens'—it has been entrusted to us, to study and to interpret." Whereupon God approved of that declaration (BT BM 59b).

13. Neither is it beyond the sea It applies to our own place and time, not only to people living in other countries, in other eras.

HALAKHAH L'MA·ASEH

30:12. It is not in the heavens The Sages derive their authority to interpret and apply Scripture to changing circumstances from this verse, among others (BT BM 59b; see Deut. 17:9).

endure on the soil that you are crossing the Jordan to enter and possess. [19]I call heaven and earth to witness against you this day: I have put before you life and death, blessing and curse. Choose life—if you and your offspring would live—[20]by loving the LORD your God, heeding His commands, and holding fast to Him. For thereby you shall have life and shall long endure upon the soil that the LORD swore to your ancestors, Abraham, Isaac, and Jacob, to give to them.

הָאֲדָמָה אֲשֶׁר אַתָּה עֹבֵר אֶת־הַיַּרְדֵּן לָבֹא
שָׁמָּה לְרִשְׁתָּהּ׃ 19 הַעִידֹתִי בָכֶם הַיּוֹם
אֶת־הַשָּׁמַיִם וְאֶת־הָאָרֶץ הַחַיִּים וְהַמָּוֶת
נָתַתִּי לְפָנֶיךָ הַבְּרָכָה וְהַקְּלָלָה וּבָחַרְתָּ
בַּחַיִּים לְמַעַן תִּחְיֶה אַתָּה וְזַרְעֶךָ׃
20 לְאַהֲבָה אֶת־יְהוָה אֱלֹהֶיךָ לִשְׁמֹעַ בְּקֹלוֹ
וּלְדָבְקָה־בוֹ כִּי הוּא חַיֶּיךָ וְאֹרֶךְ יָמֶיךָ
לָשֶׁבֶת עַל־הָאֲדָמָה אֲשֶׁר נִשְׁבַּע יְהוָה
לַאֲבֹתֶיךָ לְאַבְרָהָם לְיִצְחָק וּלְיַעֲקֹב לָתֵת
לָהֶם׃* פ

19. Choose life The Sages derived from this the obligation of a parent to teach a child a trade.

HALAKHAH L'MA·ASEH

30:19. Choose life See Comment to Lev. 18:5.

* *For the* haftarah *for this portion, see p. 1180.*

VA-YEILEKH

31 Moses went and spoke these things to
all Israel. 2He said to them:

I am now one hundred and twenty years old,
I can no longer be active. Moreover, the LORD
has said to me, "You shall not go across yonder
Jordan." 3The LORD your God Himself will cross
over before you; and He Himself will wipe out
those nations from your path and you shall dispossess them.—Joshua is the one who shall
cross before you, as the LORD has spoken.—
4The LORD will do to them as He did to Sihon
and Og, kings of the Amorites, and to their
countries, when He wiped them out. 5The LORD
will deliver them up to you, and you shall deal
with them in full accordance with the Instruction that I have enjoined upon you. 6Be strong
and resolute, be not in fear or in dread of them;

וילך

לא וַיֵּלֶךְ מֹשֶׁה וַיְדַבֵּר אֶת־הַדְּבָרִים
הָאֵלֶּה אֶל־כָּל־יִשְׂרָאֵל׃ 2 וַיֹּאמֶר אֲלֵהֶם
בֶּן־מֵאָה וְעֶשְׂרִים שָׁנָה אָנֹכִי הַיּוֹם לֹא־
אוּכַל עוֹד לָצֵאת וְלָבוֹא וַיהוָה אָמַר אֵלַי
לֹא תַעֲבֹר אֶת־הַיַּרְדֵּן הַזֶּה׃ 3 יְהוָה
אֱלֹהֶיךָ הוּא ׀ עֹבֵר לְפָנֶיךָ הוּא־יַשְׁמִיד
אֶת־הַגּוֹיִם הָאֵלֶּה מִלְּפָנֶיךָ וִירִשְׁתָּם
יְהוֹשֻׁעַ הוּא עֹבֵר לְפָנֶיךָ כַּאֲשֶׁר דִּבֶּר
שני יְהוָה׃ 4 וְעָשָׂה יְהוָה לָהֶם כַּאֲשֶׁר עָשָׂה
לְסִיחוֹן וּלְעוֹג מַלְכֵי הָאֱמֹרִי וּלְאַרְצָם
אֲשֶׁר הִשְׁמִיד אֹתָם׃ 5 וּנְתָנָם יְהוָה
לִפְנֵיכֶם וַעֲשִׂיתֶם לָהֶם כְּכָל־הַמִּצְוָה
אֲשֶׁר צִוִּיתִי אֶתְכֶם׃ 6 חִזְקוּ וְאִמְצוּ אַל־
תִּירְאוּ וְאַל־תַּעַרְצוּ מִפְּנֵיהֶם כִּי ׀ יְהוָה

Epilogue: Moses' Last Days (31:1–34:12)

Chapters 31–34 are the epilogue both to Deuteronomy and to the entire Torah. They describe the steps taken by Moses, on concluding his major addresses, to prepare the Israelites for the future; and they end with his death and the people's mourning.

PREPARING FOR NEW LEADERSHIP (31:1–30)

MOSES' DEPARTURE AND REPLACEMENT (vv. 1–6)

God denied Moses' request to enter the Promised Land (in 3:23–28), instructing him to appoint Joshua as his successor and then ascend the mountain where he would die. Now Moses proceeds to carry out God's instructions.

2. He said to them After saying the "things" to which verse 1 refers, Moses went on to inform the Israelites that he could not continue as their leader.

be active I can no longer come and go, perform the task at hand, exercise military leadership.

the LORD has said to me See 3:27.

3. Moses is voicing a fundamental biblical concept: God, not Joshua, will lead the Israelites across the Jordan. God's role, not Joshua's, will be the decisive factor in the conquest of the Land.

as the LORD has spoken To Moses, in 3:28.

4. To bolster the people's confidence, Moses reminds them of their recent victories (2:31–3:7).

6. The promise that God will accompany someone is a succinct assurance of divine assistance and protection; it is often given by God, or in His name, when He charges an individual with a mission, especially a military one. Trusting in God's strength, not their own, they may be fully confident of victory.

CHAPTER 31

2. one hundred and twenty years old The maximum span of human life (Gen. 6:3), which is a notion also found in ancient Sumerian literature. This is the origin of the Jewish wish for a long and full life: "May you live to 120!" See 34:7.

for the LORD your God Himself marches with
you: He will not fail you or forsake you.
7 Then Moses called Joshua and said to him
in the sight of all Israel: "Be strong and resolute,
for it is you who shall go with this people into
the land that the LORD swore to their fathers to
give them, and it is you who shall apportion it
to them. 8 And the LORD Himself will go before
you. He will be with you; He will not fail you
or forsake you. Fear not and be not dismayed!"
9 Moses wrote down this Teaching and gave
it to the priests, sons of Levi, who carried the
Ark of the LORD's Covenant, and to all the elders
of Israel.
10 And Moses instructed them as follows:
Every seventh year, the year set for remission,
at the Feast of Booths, 11 when all Israel comes
to appear before the LORD your God in the place
that He will choose, you shall read this Teach-

אֱלֹהֶיךָ הוּא הַהֹלֵךְ עִמָּךְ לֹא יַרְפְּךָ וְלֹא
יַעַזְבֶךָּ׃ פ
שלישי [חמישי] 7 וַיִּקְרָא מֹשֶׁה לִיהוֹשֻׁעַ וַיֹּאמֶר אֵלָיו לְעֵינֵי
כָל־יִשְׂרָאֵל חֲזַק וֶאֱמָץ כִּי אַתָּה תָּבוֹא
אֶת־הָעָם הַזֶּה אֶל־הָאָרֶץ אֲשֶׁר נִשְׁבַּע
יְהוָה לַאֲבֹתָם לָתֵת לָהֶם וְאַתָּה
תַּנְחִילֶנָּה אוֹתָם׃ 8 וַיהוָה הוּא ׀ הַהֹלֵךְ
לְפָנֶיךָ הוּא יִהְיֶה עִמָּךְ לֹא יַרְפְּךָ וְלֹא
יַעַזְבֶךָּ לֹא תִירָא וְלֹא תֵחָת׃
9 וַיִּכְתֹּב מֹשֶׁה אֶת־הַתּוֹרָה הַזֹּאת וַיִּתְּנָהּ
אֶל־הַכֹּהֲנִים בְּנֵי לֵוִי הַנֹּשְׂאִים אֶת־אֲרוֹן
בְּרִית יְהוָה וְאֶל־כָּל־זִקְנֵי יִשְׂרָאֵל׃
רביעי 10 וַיְצַו מֹשֶׁה אוֹתָם לֵאמֹר מִקֵּץ ׀ שֶׁבַע
שָׁנִים בְּמֹעֵד שְׁנַת הַשְּׁמִטָּה בְּחַג הַסֻּכּוֹת׃
11 בְּבוֹא כָל־יִשְׂרָאֵל לֵרָאוֹת אֶת־פְּנֵי יְהוָה
אֱלֹהֶיךָ בַּמָּקוֹם אֲשֶׁר יִבְחָר תִּקְרָא אֶת־
הַתּוֹרָה הַזֹּאת נֶגֶד כָּל־יִשְׂרָאֵל בְּאָזְנֵיהֶם׃

MOSES APPOINTS JOSHUA (vv. 7–8)

Following God's instructions (1:38, 3:28), Moses now publicly appoints Joshua as his successor.

7. Speaking to Joshua in the hearing of the people, Moses emphasizes that Joshua is one of them ("you . . . shall go with") to avoid any implication that Joshua rather than God is the real leader. But in verse 23, God says to Joshua, "you who shall bring." Speaking privately to Joshua, God is unconcerned about that implication.

8. The same encouragement that Moses addressed to Joshua privately in 3:22 he now addresses to him publicly, making his appointment known to all.

WRITING AND READING THE TEACHING (vv. 9–13)

Moses has finished expounding the Teaching (1:5), which he has imparted orally until now. He writes it down and arranges for its regular public reading so that the people may be reminded regularly of its contents and future generations may learn it.

9. Moses wrote down this Teaching The laws and other parts of Deuteronomy.

gave it to the priests . . . and to all the elders These were the religious and civic leaders of the people, who would be responsible for guiding the nation's affairs in accordance with the Teaching and for having it read to the public every seven years. The priests were to keep the text in the Ark that was in their charge (see 31:25–26, 10:8).

10. at the Feast of Booths See 16:13–15. This festival attracted the largest number of pilgrims and lasted seven days. Because it came after the harvest was stored, the people would feel secure about their food supply for the coming year and could absorb the lessons of the reading with minds free of concern.

11. in the place Where the Feast of Booths was celebrated (16:16) and where the Ark was kept (1 Kings 8:1–9).

HALAKHAH L'MA·ASEH

31:10–13. Every seventh year, . . . read this Teaching aloud The Torah takes steps to ensure that its contents would be known not only by the intellectual or priestly elite but also by the entire Jewish people, "men, women, and children." To accomplish this even more effectively, it has been Jewish practice from very early times to read a section of the Torah in the synagogue four times each week: on Monday morning, Thursday morning, *Shabbat* morning, and *Shabbat* afternoon. We now read the entire Torah through the course of one year or, in some synagogues, three years.

ing aloud in the presence of all Israel. [12]Gather the people—men, women, children, and the strangers in your communities—that they may hear and so learn to revere the LORD your God and to observe faithfully every word of this Teaching. [13]Their children, too, who have not had the experience, shall hear and learn to revere the LORD your God as long as they live in the land that you are about to cross the Jordan to possess.

[14]The LORD said to Moses: The time is drawing near for you to die. Call Joshua and present yourselves in the Tent of Meeting, that I may instruct him. Moses and Joshua went and presented themselves in the Tent of Meeting. [15]The LORD appeared in the Tent, in a pillar of cloud,

12 הַקְהֵ֣ל אֶת־הָעָ֞ם הָאֲנָשִׁ֣ים וְהַנָּשִׁ֗ים וְהַטַּף֙ וְגֵֽרְךָ֙ אֲשֶׁ֣ר בִּשְׁעָרֶ֔יךָ לְמַ֨עַן יִשְׁמְע֜וּ וּלְמַ֣עַן יִלְמְד֗וּ וְיָֽרְאוּ֙ אֶת־יְהוָ֣ה אֱלֹֽהֵיכֶ֔ם וְשָֽׁמְר֣וּ לַֽעֲשׂ֔וֹת אֶת־כָּל־דִּבְרֵ֖י הַתּוֹרָ֥ה הַזֹּֽאת׃ 13 וּבְנֵיהֶ֞ם אֲשֶׁ֣ר לֹֽא־יָֽדְע֗וּ יִשְׁמְע֤וּ וְלָֽמְדוּ֙ לְיִרְאָ֖ה אֶת־יְהוָ֣ה אֱלֹֽהֵיכֶ֑ם כָּל־הַיָּמִ֗ים אֲשֶׁ֨ר אַתֶּ֤ם חַיִּים֙ עַל־הָ֣אֲדָמָ֔ה אֲשֶׁ֨ר אַתֶּ֜ם עֹֽבְרִ֧ים אֶת־הַיַּרְדֵּ֛ן שָׁ֖מָּה לְרִשְׁתָּֽהּ׃ פ

חמישי [ששי]

14 וַיֹּ֨אמֶר יְהוָ֜ה אֶל־מֹשֶׁ֗ה הֵ֣ן קָֽרְב֣וּ יָמֶ֘יךָ֮ לָמוּת֒ קְרָ֣א אֶת־יְהוֹשֻׁ֗עַ וְהִֽתְיַצְּב֛וּ בְּאֹ֥הֶל מוֹעֵ֖ד וַֽאֲצַוֶּ֑נּוּ וַיֵּ֤לֶךְ מֹשֶׁה֙ וִֽיהוֹשֻׁ֔עַ וַיִּֽתְיַצְּב֖וּ בְּאֹ֥הֶל מוֹעֵֽד׃ 15 וַיֵּרָ֧א יְהוָ֛ה בָּאֹ֖הֶל בְּעַמּ֥וּד

read Hebrew: *tikra*, in the singular; Moses often addresses the entire people in this manner. Presumably, in speaking directly here to the priests and elders (v. 9), he means that they are the ones who must either read aloud the Teaching or arrange for the reading.

this Teaching All of Deuteronomy, which can be read aloud in three to four hours.

12. women, children, and the strangers Although normally only adult male Israelites are obligated to appear at the festival, on this occasion women, children, and strangers must also attend so that all may hear their duties and rights read to them and be inspired with reverence for God. The verse, addressing the need to learn the Teaching, makes no distinction between men and women.

that they may hear and so learn to revere The Teaching's account of God's mighty deeds on behalf of Israel and its presentation of His laws

will inspire the people to venerate Him and obey the commandments.

13. The children especially, who have not experienced the wonders of the present generation, need to hear of those experiences and the lessons they impart. Conducting the impressive public reading every seven years will ensure that every child would be imbued with the Teaching soon after reaching an educable age.

GOD MEETS WITH MOSES AND JOSHUA (vv. 14–15)

God informs Moses that He will appoint Joshua as Moses' successor. This will confirm Moses' action in verses 1–8 and remove any doubt that the appointment is divinely authorized.

15. in the Tent . . . at the entrance The Septuagint reads: "The LORD came down in a cloud and stopped at the entrance of the Tent of Meeting," thereby avoiding the possible inconsistency

---

12. Gather the . . . women . . . that they may . . . learn Some authorities in the Talmud contend that there is no obligation to teach Torah to women. Such opinions, however, are products of the Greco-Roman view of women as intellectually weak, a notion that began to appear in Jewish sources in the 3rd century B.C.E., during the Hellenistic period. In contrast, Ben Azzai held that a man is obliged to teach his daughter Torah (JT Ḥag. 1:1).

14. The time is drawing near for you to die The Midrash pictures God appearing to Joshua in a cloud. When the cloud lifted, Moses asked Joshua, "What did the LORD say to you?" Joshua replied, "When the LORD spoke to you, did you share the message with me?" At that moment, Moses became reconciled to his imminent death, saying to himself, "It is a hundred times better to depart now than to be jealous of my successor" (Deut. R. 9:9).

the pillar of cloud having come to rest at the
entrance of the tent.
16The Lord said to Moses: You are soon to
lie with your fathers. This people will thereupon
go astray after the alien gods in their midst, in
the land that they are about to enter; they will
forsake Me and break My covenant that I made
with them. 17Then My anger will flare up against
them, and I will abandon them and hide My
countenance from them. They shall be ready
prey; and many evils and troubles shall befall
them. And they shall say on that day, "Surely
it is because our God is not in our midst that
these evils have befallen us." 18Yet I will keep
My countenance hidden on that day, because

עָנָן וַיַּעֲמֹד עַמּוּד הֶעָנָן עַל־פֶּתַח
הָאֹהֶל׃ ס
16 וַיֹּאמֶר יְהוָה אֶל־מֹשֶׁה הִנְּךָ שֹׁכֵב עִם־
אֲבֹתֶיךָ וְקָם הָעָם הַזֶּה וְזָנָה ׀ אַחֲרֵי ׀
אֱלֹהֵי נֵכַר־הָאָרֶץ אֲשֶׁר הוּא בָא־שָׁמָּה
בְּקִרְבּוֹ וַעֲזָבַנִי וְהֵפֵר אֶת־בְּרִיתִי אֲשֶׁר
כָּרַתִּי אִתּוֹ׃ 17 וְחָרָה אַפִּי בוֹ בַיּוֹם־הַהוּא
וַעֲזַבְתִּים וְהִסְתַּרְתִּי פָנַי מֵהֶם וְהָיָה
לֶאֱכֹל וּמְצָאֻהוּ רָעוֹת רַבּוֹת וְצָרוֹת וְאָמַר
בַּיּוֹם הַהוּא הֲלֹא עַל כִּי־אֵין אֱלֹהַי בְּקִרְבִּי
מְצָאוּנִי הָרָעוֹת הָאֵלֶּה׃ 18 וְאָנֹכִי הַסְתֵּר
אַסְתִּיר פָּנַי בַּיּוֹם הַהוּא עַל כָּל־הָרָעָה

of the cloud being both inside the Tent and remaining outside at the entrance.

pillar of cloud The cloud is the vehicle by which God descends to earth.

COUNTERING ISRAEL'S FUTURE APOSTASY
(vv. 16–22)

ISRAEL'S BETRAYAL (vv. 16–18)

16. lie with your fathers The idiom stands for "die and lie with one's fathers." It refers specifically to the reunion of one's spirit after death with the spirits of one's ancestors in Sheol, the netherworld, as in the phrase "be gathered to one's kin" in 32:50.

go astray Literally, "fornicate," "go whoring." This metaphor for apostasy reflects the understanding that the bond between God and Israel is like a marriage bond. Worship of other gods is an act of betrayal as repugnant as adultery.

forsake Me Israelite idolaters did not literally cease worshiping the Lord; they worshiped Him along with gods, as was common in polytheism. But the exclusive, monotheistic character of the relationship between God and Israel is so integral to biblical religion that the worship of any other deities is regarded as abandonment of the Lord. Any rapport the idolater continues to maintain with the Lord is viewed by the Bible as meaningless.

17. I will abandon them Punishing them in kind for abandoning Me (v. 16).

hide My countenance from them Withdraw My favor and protection; abandon them and ignore their pleas for help. (When God hides His countenance, His attentive presence, the Israelites are exposed and unprotected.)

because our God is not in our midst Israel will realize from its setbacks that it has lost divine protection. But it will not admit its own guilt and instead will complain that God is not involved, He no longer controls events and protects Israel, He has broken His promise and abandoned His people.

18. Yet I will keep My countenance hidden God is saying, "But it is because of all the evil they have done . . . that I will hide My countenance," thus explaining that He was justified in abandoning them.

---

17. I will . . . hide My countenance from them To understand the *Sho·ah,* Martin Buber, who fled Germany for Palestine when the Nazis came to power, fastened on this image of God's hiding. God is always present, but sometimes turns aside and hides the divine countenance. Terrible things happen when God's countenance is hidden, when God's attention is turned away.

Dov Ber of Mezeritch once found his young child crying. "I was playing hide-and-seek with my friends," the child explained, "and I hid so well that they stopped looking for me and went away." Dov Ber mused, "This must be how God feels, hiding the divine countenance from us to the point where some of us stop looking—and start living our lives without God."

of all the evil they have done in turning to other gods. [19]Therefore, write down this poem and teach it to the people of Israel; put it in their mouths, in order that this poem may be My witness against the people of Israel. [20]When I bring them into the land flowing with milk and honey that I promised on oath to their fathers, and they eat their fill and grow fat and turn to other gods and serve them, spurning Me and breaking My covenant, [21]and the many evils and troubles befall them—then this poem shall confront them as a witness, since it will never be lost from the mouth of their offspring. For I know what plans they are devising even now, before I bring them into the land that I promised on oath.

[22]That day, Moses wrote down this poem and taught it to the Israelites.

אֲשֶׁר עָשָׂה כִּי פָנָה אֶל־אֱלֹהִים אֲחֵרִים׃
19 וְעַתָּה כִּתְבוּ לָכֶם אֶת־הַשִּׁירָה הַזֹּאת
וְלַמְּדָהּ אֶת־בְּנֵי־יִשְׂרָאֵל שִׂימָהּ בְּפִיהֶם
לְמַעַן תִּהְיֶה־לִּי הַשִּׁירָה הַזֹּאת לְעֵד בִּבְנֵי
ששי [שביעי] יִשְׂרָאֵל׃ 20 כִּי־אֲבִיאֶנּוּ אֶל־הָאֲדָמָה ׀
אֲשֶׁר־נִשְׁבַּעְתִּי לַאֲבֹתָיו זָבַת חָלָב וּדְבַשׁ
וְאָכַל וְשָׂבַע וְדָשֵׁן וּפָנָה אֶל־אֱלֹהִים
אֲחֵרִים וַעֲבָדוּם וְנִאֲצוּנִי וְהֵפֵר אֶת־
בְּרִיתִי׃ 21 וְהָיָה כִּי־תִמְצֶאןָ אֹתוֹ רָעוֹת
רַבּוֹת וְצָרוֹת וְעָנְתָה הַשִּׁירָה הַזֹּאת
לְפָנָיו לְעֵד כִּי לֹא תִשָּׁכַח מִפִּי זַרְעוֹ
כִּי יָדַעְתִּי אֶת־יִצְרוֹ אֲשֶׁר הוּא עֹשֶׂה
הַיּוֹם בְּטֶרֶם אֲבִיאֶנּוּ אֶל־הָאָרֶץ אֲשֶׁר
נִשְׁבָּעְתִּי׃
22 וַיִּכְתֹּב מֹשֶׁה אֶת־הַשִּׁירָה הַזֹּאת בַּיּוֹם
הַהוּא וַיְלַמְּדָהּ אֶת־בְּנֵי יִשְׂרָאֵל׃

turning to other gods That is, relying on them or displaying loyalty to them.

WRITING A POEM (vv. 19–22)

19. write down Hebrew: *kitvu lakhem;* literally, "write for yourselves" (i.e., Moses and Joshua) in the plural, although the remaining verbs in the verse ("teach it," "put it in their mouths") are in the singular. A written copy of the poem was made, and the intended audience heard it read aloud, as in the case of the Teaching (vv. 9–13).

put it in their mouths See Comment to 30:13. Memorization would be facilitated by the poetic form.

be My witness The poem will testify that God had treated the Israelites with justice and kindness, but that His people betrayed Him (see 32:1–18, esp. vv. 4–5). It will rebut their charge that God violated His promise to remain with them; it will show that God's abandonment of the Israelites was justified.

20. Their prosperity will lead them to forget God, the true source of their well-being; they will attribute their comfort to false Canaanite gods they believe responsible for fertility.

21. shall confront them . . . since it will never be lost Literally, "shall speak up . . . since it will never be forgotten." The poem will be known by heart and will virtually speak up by itself. When the predicted disasters transpire, the poem will irresistibly spring to the lips of the people and bear witness to their guilt.

For I know what plans they are devising even now God concludes by repeating the point made at the beginning: The incidents of the Golden Calf and Baal-peor (4:3, 9:12–29) have revealed how susceptible the people are to idolatry.

19. that this poem may be My witness Does God need a poem as a reminder? The purpose of the poem would be to remind God not to judge the people Israel harshly in the future, for God was aware of their nature (v. 27) and chose them nonetheless (Malbim).

HALAKHAH L'MA·ASEH

31:19. write down this poem This verse is the source for the commandment for each Jew to write a personal copy of the Torah. One who commissions a ritual scribe (*sofer*) to write even one letter on one's behalf is considered to have fulfilled this *mitzvah* (BT Men. 30a). Many congregations that acquire a new Torah scroll celebrate its completion (*Siyyum Seifer Torah*) by having individuals who have contributed to its purchase fill in a letter of the Torah.

[23]And He charged Joshua son of Nun: "Be strong and resolute: for you shall bring the Israelites into the land that I promised them on oath, and I will be with you."

[24]When Moses had put down in writing the words of this Teaching to the very end, [25]Moses charged the Levites who carried the Ark of the Covenant of the LORD, saying: [26]Take this book of Teaching and place it beside the Ark of the Covenant of the LORD your God, and let it remain there as a witness against you. [27]Well I know how defiant and stiffnecked you are: even now, while I am still alive in your midst, you have been defiant toward the LORD; how much more, then, when I am dead! [28]Gather to me all the elders of your tribes and your officials, that I may speak all these words to them and

23 וַיְצַו אֶת־יְהוֹשֻׁעַ בִּן־נוּן וַיֹּאמֶר חֲזַק
וֶאֱמָץ כִּי אַתָּה תָּבִיא אֶת־בְּנֵי יִשְׂרָאֵל
אֶל־הָאָרֶץ אֲשֶׁר־נִשְׁבַּעְתִּי לָהֶם וְאָנֹכִי
אֶהְיֶה עִמָּךְ׃
24 וַיְהִי ׀ כְּכַלּוֹת מֹשֶׁה לִכְתֹּב אֶת־דִּבְרֵי
שביעי הַתּוֹרָה־הַזֹּאת עַל־סֵפֶר עַד תֻּמָּם׃ 25 וַיְצַו
מֹשֶׁה אֶת־הַלְוִיִּם נֹשְׂאֵי אֲרוֹן בְּרִית־יְהוָה
לֵאמֹר׃ 26 לָקֹחַ אֵת סֵפֶר הַתּוֹרָה הַזֶּה
וְשַׂמְתֶּם אֹתוֹ מִצַּד אֲרוֹן בְּרִית־יְהוָה
אֱלֹהֵיכֶם וְהָיָה־שָׁם בְּךָ לְעֵד׃ 27 כִּי אָנֹכִי
יָדַעְתִּי אֶת־מֶרְיְךָ וְאֶת־עָרְפְּךָ הַקָּשֶׁה הֵן
בְּעוֹדֶנִּי חַי עִמָּכֶם הַיּוֹם מַמְרִים הֱיִתֶם
מפטיר עִם־יְהוָה וְאַף כִּי־אַחֲרֵי מוֹתִי׃ 28 הַקְהִילוּ
אֵלַי אֶת־כָּל־זִקְנֵי שִׁבְטֵיכֶם וְשֹׁטְרֵיכֶם
וַאֲדַבְּרָה בְאָזְנֵיהֶם אֵת הַדְּבָרִים הָאֵלֶּה

GOD APPOINTS JOSHUA (v. 23)

23. He charged This is the first time that God speaks directly to Joshua.

I will be with you God confirms what Moses promised Joshua in verse 8.

CONVEYING BOTH THE TEACHING AND THE POEM (vv. 24–30)

24. put down in writing Hebrew: *likhtov . . . al seifer.* In the Bible, *seifer* means any kind of written document—even a brief letter, a legal document, or an inscription, whether written on a sheet or scroll of papyrus or parchment, or on stone, plaster, or pottery. The *seifer* in this verse is undoubtedly a leather scroll.

this Teaching Deuteronomy.

25. Levites See verse 9.

26. Ark of the Covenant The Ark containing the two tablets of the Covenant on which the Decalogue was written (4:13; 10:1–5). Ancient treaties were commonly deposited in sanctuaries. Keeping the Teaching next to the Ark of the Covenant indicates that it embodies the principles of the covenant and is as binding as the Decalogue itself because it comes from the same divine source. The scroll with the Teaching was undoubtedly to be kept in a container, such as a jar or a box, to protect it from damage by moisture or worms.

as a witness against you Against the Israelites, whom the Levites here represent. Moses assigns the Teaching a new function: It is to be a witness, like the poem (v. 19). Unlike the poem, however, it does not testify to Israel's betrayal of God after settling in Canaan. He probably means that the Teaching will serve as evidence that Israel accepted the terms and conditions of the Covenant; this will enable the people to understand their misfortunes.

27. Well I know No one knows better than I, having experienced your defiance so often.

defiant and stiffnecked Moses used these terms to characterize Israel's behavior earlier, particularly its refusal to advance on the Promised Land and the incident of the Golden Calf (see 9:13,23).

how much more, then Even Moses, despite his authority, could not restrain the Israelites while he was alive; how much more likely are they to rebel after his death.

28. Gather As the people are to be gathered to hear the Teaching (v. 12), so their leaders are to be gathered to hear the poem.

elders of your tribes Because verse 30 indicates that Moses addressed the entire people, one

---

24. This included the description of his own death. Moses' final challenge, indeed the final challenge for anyone, was coming to terms with his own mortality.

that I may call heaven and earth to witness
against them. 29 For I know that, when I am
dead, you will act wickedly and turn away from
the path that I enjoined upon you, and that in
time to come misfortune will befall you for having done evil in the sight of the LORD and vexed
Him by your deeds.

30 Then Moses recited the words of this poem
to the very end, in the hearing of the whole congregation of Israel:

וְאָעִידָה בָּם אֶת־הַשָּׁמַיִם וְאֶת־הָאָרֶץ׃
29 כִּי יָדַעְתִּי אַחֲרֵי מוֹתִי כִּי־הַשְׁחֵת
תַּשְׁחִתוּן וְסַרְתֶּם מִן־הַדֶּרֶךְ אֲשֶׁר צִוִּיתִי
אֶתְכֶם וְקָרָאת אֶתְכֶם הָרָעָה בְּאַחֲרִית
הַיָּמִים כִּי־תַעֲשׂוּ אֶת־הָרַע בְּעֵינֵי יְהוָה
לְהַכְעִיסוֹ בְּמַעֲשֵׂה יְדֵיכֶם׃
30 וַיְדַבֵּר מֹשֶׁה בְּאָזְנֵי כָּל־קְהַל יִשְׂרָאֵל
אֶת־דִּבְרֵי הַשִּׁירָה הַזֹּאת עַד תֻּמָּם׃ פ

would have expected the text to contain a statement referring to all of the Israelites and not only the elders. The Septuagint has a longer reading, "the heads of your tribes, your elders, judges, and officials."

all these words The poem.

heaven and earth to witness Heaven and earth will be the third "witness" (after the poem and the Teaching) that Israel was warned.

29. in time to come The situation described in the poem fits several periods in Israel's later history, beginning with the time of the chieftains ("Judges") after Joshua's death.

30. This verse is the introduction to the poem in chapter 32.

whole congregation of Israel The entire nation, now formally assembled for the occasion.

הפטרה שביעית דנחמתא

SEVENTH HAFTARAH OF CONSOLATION
HAFTARAH FOR NITZAVIM

ISAIAH 61:10–63:9

(*Recite on the 7th* Shabbat *after the 9th of* Av, *which is also the* Shabbat *before* Rosh ha-Shanah. *This occasion coincides with the reading of* Nitzavim *either alone or combined with* Va-yeilekh. *On the Seven* Haftarot *of Consolation, see p. 1032. On the* Shabbat *before* Yom Kippur, *recite the* haftarah *on p. 1234.*)

This passage opens with the jubilant exultation of Zion after generations of desolation and exile. The city and the nation that felt abandoned and forsaken shall be espoused by God (60:5). Never again shall His people suffer defeat or disgrace. Renewal of God's beneficence (63:8–9) is the powerful theme that charges every verse with confident expectation.

The *haftarah* develops through a series of speeches that move from hopeful anticipation to thanksgiving. The shift from Zion's hope to God's advent is marked by the motif of garments, which manifest the people's new condition (cf. Isa. 52:1, "Awake, awake, O Zion! / Clothe yourself in splendor") as the redemption quickens its pace. This new reality is then mirrored in the divine garments of victory.

Marital imagery conveyed through wedding garments (61:10) is further developed in the prophet's word of encouragement. God shall take back His city and land, espousing the one and taking delight in the other: "And as a bridegroom rejoices over his bride, so will your God rejoice over you" (62:5). Jewish liturgy knows these words through their incorporation into the 16th-century poem that is sung on Friday night, *"L'kha Dodi."*

New designations for Zion and for the Land express the new national reality (62:2,4), a transformed state of physical and spiritual renewal. As with the patriarchs Abraham and Jacob, new names both create and affirm a new destiny (see Gen. 17:4–5, 35:9–12; cf. 32:29). And this transformed state is part of the recompense to come, brought by Israel's deliverer on His return to Zion (Isa. 62:11, cf. 40:10). Anticipation of this moment is the beginning of hope, which this *haftarah* celebrates. Zion's fear that "The Lord has forsaken me" (Isa. 49:14), poignantly expressed near the beginning of this *haftarah* cycle of consolation, is completely dispelled.

RELATION OF THE *HAFTARAH* TO THE CALENDAR

This selection brings to a celebratory close the Seven *Haftarot* of Consolation. As a concluding recitation, it is replete with themes and phrases from the previous readings. For example, the call to "Clear the road [*panu derekh*] for the people" and the declaration that God comes with "reward" and "recompense" (62:10–11) echo a proclamation in the first *Haftarah* of Consolation: "Clear . . . / A road [*panu derekh*] for the Lord" who has "reward" and "recompense" with Him (Isa. 40:3,10). Repetitions like these combine to create an aura of climactic summation, at once the conclusion of consolation and the onset of redemption.

61 10I greatly rejoice in the Lord,
My whole being exults in my God.

סא 10 שׂ֧וֹשׂ אָשִׂ֣ישׂ בַּיהֹוָ֗ה
תָּגֵ֤ל נַפְשִׁי֙ בֵּֽאלֹהַ֔י

For He has clothed me with garments of triumph,
Wrapped me in a robe of victory,
Like a bridegroom adorned with a turban,
Like a bride bedecked with her finery.
11For as the earth brings forth her growth
And a garden makes the seed shoot up,
So the Lord God will make
Victory and renown shoot up
In the presence of all the nations.

62 For the sake of Zion I will not be silent,
For the sake of Jerusalem I will not be still,
Till her victory emerge resplendent
And her triumph like a flaming torch.
2Nations shall see your victory,
And every king your majesty;
And you shall be called by a new name
Which the Lord Himself shall bestow.
3You shall be a glorious crown
In the hand of the Lord,
And a royal diadem
In the palm of your God.

4Nevermore shall you be called "Forsaken,"
Nor shall your land be called "Desolate";
But you shall be called "I delight in her,"
And your land "Espoused."
For the Lord takes delight in you,
And your land shall be espoused.
5As a youth espouses a maiden,
Your sons shall espouse you;
And as a bridegroom rejoices over his bride,
So will your God rejoice over you.

כִּי הִלְבִּישַׁנִי בִּגְדֵי־יֶשַׁע
מְעִיל צְדָקָה יְעָטָנִי
כֶּחָתָן יְכַהֵן פְּאֵר
וְכַכַּלָּה תַּעְדֶּה כֵלֶיהָ׃
11 כִּי כָאָרֶץ תּוֹצִיא צִמְחָהּ
וּכְגַנָּה זֵרוּעֶיהָ תַצְמִיחַ
כֵּן ׀ אֲדֹנָי יְהוִה
יַצְמִיחַ צְדָקָה וּתְהִלָּה
נֶגֶד כָּל־הַגּוֹיִם׃

סב לְמַעַן צִיּוֹן לֹא אֶחֱשֶׁה
וּלְמַעַן יְרוּשָׁלִַם לֹא אֶשְׁקוֹט
עַד־יֵצֵא כַנֹּגַהּ צִדְקָהּ
וִישׁוּעָתָהּ כְּלַפִּיד יִבְעָר׃
2 וְרָאוּ גוֹיִם צִדְקֵךְ
וְכָל־מְלָכִים כְּבוֹדֵךְ
וְקֹרָא לָךְ שֵׁם חָדָשׁ
אֲשֶׁר פִּי יְהוָה יִקֳּבֶנּוּ׃
3 וְהָיִית עֲטֶרֶת תִּפְאֶרֶת
בְּיַד־יְהוָה
וצנוף וּצְנִיף מְלוּכָה
בְּכַף־אֱלֹהָיִךְ׃

4 לֹא־יֵאָמֵר לָךְ עוֹד עֲזוּבָה
וּלְאַרְצֵךְ לֹא־יֵאָמֵר עוֹד שְׁמָמָה
כִּי לָךְ יִקָּרֵא חֶפְצִי־בָהּ
וּלְאַרְצֵךְ בְּעוּלָה
כִּי־חָפֵץ יְהוָה בָּךְ
וְאַרְצֵךְ תִּבָּעֵל׃
5 כִּי־יִבְעַל בָּחוּר בְּתוּלָה
יִבְעָלוּךְ בָּנָיִךְ
וּמְשׂוֹשׂ חָתָן עַל־כַּלָּה
יָשִׂישׂ עָלַיִךְ אֱלֹהָיִךְ׃

Isaiah 62:1. I will not be silent Apparently the word of the prophet, who reports that the people shall receive a new name.

6Upon your walls, O Jerusalem,
I have set watchmen,
Who shall never be silent
By day or by night.
O you, the LORD's remembrancers,
Take no rest
7And give no rest to Him,
Until He establish Jerusalem
And make her renowned on earth.

8The LORD has sworn by His right hand,
By His mighty arm:
Nevermore will I give your new grain
To your enemies for food,
Nor shall foreigners drink the new wine
For which you have labored.
9But those who harvest it shall eat it
And give praise to the LORD;
And those who gather it shall drink it
In My sacred courts.
10Pass through, pass through the gates!
Clear the road for the people;
Build up, build up the highway,
Remove the rocks!
Raise an ensign over the peoples!
11See, the LORD has proclaimed
To the end of the earth:
Announce to Fair Zion,
Your Deliverer is coming!
See, his reward is with Him,

6 עַל־חוֹמֹתַ֣יִךְ יְרוּשָׁלִַ֗ם
הִפְקַ֙דְתִּי֙ שֹׁמְרִ֔ים
כָּל־הַיּ֣וֹם וְכָל־הַלַּ֗יְלָה תָּמִ֛יד
לֹ֣א יֶחֱשׁ֑וּ
הַמַּזְכִּרִים֙ אֶת־יְהוָ֔ה
אַל־דֳּמִ֖י לָכֶֽם׃
7 וְאַל־תִּתְּנ֥וּ דֳמִ֖י ל֑וֹ
עַד־יְכוֹנֵ֞ן וְעַד־יָשִׂ֧ים אֶת־יְרוּשָׁלִַ֛ם
תְּהִלָּ֖ה בָּאָֽרֶץ׃

8 נִשְׁבַּ֧ע יְהוָ֛ה בִּֽימִינ֖וֹ
וּבִזְר֣וֹעַ עֻזּ֑וֹ
אִם־אֶתֵּ֨ן אֶת־דְּגָנֵ֥ךְ ע֛וֹד
מַאֲכָ֖ל לְאֹיְבַ֑יִךְ
וְאִם־יִשְׁתּ֤וּ בְנֵי־נֵכָר֙ תִּֽירוֹשֵׁ֔ךְ
אֲשֶׁ֥ר יָגַ֖עַתְּ בּֽוֹ׃
9 כִּ֤י מְאַסְפָיו֙ יֹאכְלֻ֔הוּ
וְהִֽלְל֖וּ אֶת־יְהוָ֑ה
וּֽמְקַבְּצָ֥יו יִשְׁתֻּ֖הוּ
בְּחַצְר֥וֹת קָדְשִֽׁי׃ ס
10 עִבְר֤וּ עִבְרוּ֙ בַּשְּׁעָרִ֔ים
פַּנּ֖וּ דֶּ֣רֶךְ הָעָ֑ם
סֹ֣לּוּ סֹלּוּ֩ הַֽמְסִלָּ֨ה
סַקְּל֣וּ מֵאֶ֔בֶן
הָרִ֥ימוּ נֵ֖ס עַל־הָעַמִּֽים׃
11 הִנֵּ֣ה יְהוָ֗ה הִשְׁמִ֙יעַ֙
אֶל־קְצֵ֣ה הָאָ֔רֶץ
אִמְרוּ֙ לְבַת־צִיּ֔וֹן
הִנֵּ֥ה יִשְׁעֵ֖ךְ בָּ֑א
הִנֵּ֤ה שְׂכָרוֹ֙ אִתּ֔וֹ

6. the LORD's remembrancers The "mourners of Zion" mentioned in Isa. 61:3, or perhaps others who reminded God of His promises to Israel and of Israel's present state.

8. His mighty arm The oath taken by God "by His own arm" anticipates the destruction "wrought" by His "own arm" (63:5).

10. Pass through, pass through Reformulating the "highway" theme in the first *Haftarah* of Consolation (Isa. 40:3). There, the preparation was for the divine advent. Here, the expectation is for the return of the people from captivity. In both texts, God's "recompense" comes with Him (see Isa. 40:10, 62:11). Later tradition gave the image of removing stumbling blocks a moral and spiritual sense, thereby indicating the human participation that is required for redemption (Num. R. 15:16).

His recompense before Him.
12 And they shall be called, "The Holy People,
The Redeemed of the LORD,"
And you shall be called, "Sought Out,
A City Not Forsaken."

וּפְעֻלָּתוֹ לְפָנָיו׃
12 וְקָרְאוּ לָהֶם עַם־הַקֹּדֶשׁ
גְּאוּלֵי יְהוָה
וְלָךְ יִקָּרֵא דְרוּשָׁה
עִיר לֹא נֶעֱזָבָה׃ ס

63

Who is this coming from Edom,
In crimsoned garments from Bozrah—
Who is this, majestic in attire,
Pressing forward in His great might?
"It is I, who contend victoriously,
Powerful to give triumph."
2 Why is Your clothing so red,
Your garments like his who treads grapes?
3 "I trod out a vintage alone;
Of the peoples no man was with Me.
I trod them down in My anger,
Trampled them in My rage;
Their life-blood bespattered My garments,
And all My clothing was stained.
4 For I had planned a day of vengeance,
And My year of redemption arrived.
5 Then I looked, but there was none to help;
I stared, but there was none to aid—
So My own arm wrought the triumph,
And My own rage was My aid.
6 I trampled peoples in My anger,
I made them drunk with My rage,
And I hurled their glory to the ground."

סג

מִי־זֶה ׀ בָּא מֵאֱדוֹם
חֲמוּץ בְּגָדִים מִבָּצְרָה
זֶה הָדוּר בִּלְבוּשׁוֹ
צֹעֶה בְּרֹב כֹּחוֹ
אֲנִי מְדַבֵּר בִּצְדָקָה
רַב לְהוֹשִׁיעַ׃
2 מַדּוּעַ אָדֹם לִלְבוּשֶׁךָ
וּבְגָדֶיךָ כְּדֹרֵךְ בְּגַת׃
3 פּוּרָה ׀ דָּרַכְתִּי לְבַדִּי
וּמֵעַמִּים אֵין־אִישׁ אִתִּי
וְאֶדְרְכֵם בְּאַפִּי
וְאֶרְמְסֵם בַּחֲמָתִי
וְיֵז נִצְחָם עַל־בְּגָדַי
וְכָל־מַלְבּוּשַׁי אֶגְאָלְתִּי׃
4 כִּי יוֹם נָקָם בְּלִבִּי
וּשְׁנַת גְּאוּלַי בָּאָה׃
5 וְאַבִּיט וְאֵין עֹזֵר
וְאֶשְׁתּוֹמֵם וְאֵין סוֹמֵךְ
וַתּוֹשַׁע לִי זְרֹעִי
וַחֲמָתִי הִיא סְמָכָתְנִי׃
6 וְאָבוּס עַמִּים בְּאַפִּי
וַאֲשַׁכְּרֵם בַּחֲמָתִי
וְאוֹרִיד לָאָרֶץ נִצְחָם׃ ס

12. The Holy People Hebrew: *Am ha-Kodesh,* an intensification of the description in Deut. 7:6 (*am kadosh,* "holy people").

Isaiah 63:1. Who is this coming from Edom In context, the query appears as that of the watchmen on the walls (62:6), awaiting the advent of the Lord.

3–5. Imagery of God trampling a vineyard and bespattered with blood (vv. 2–3) is connected with Edom and Botzrah (v. 1) by two puns: *me-Edom* (from Edom) sounds like *m'uddam* (reddened, cf. v. 2), and *mi-botzrah* (from Botzrah) sounds like *mi-botzer* (from picking grapes). In rabbinic tradition, Edom is a symbol for Rome and for Christendom (see Ibn Ezra). This identification gave the *haftarah* immediate relevance in antiquity and in the Middle Ages. Edom's downfall is here attributed to divine vengeance against its evil conduct and to Israel's merit (Rashi).

7 I will recount the kind acts of the LORD,
The praises of the LORD—
For all that the LORD has wrought for us,
The vast bounty to the House of Israel
That He bestowed upon them
According to His mercy and His great kindness.
8 He thought: Surely they are My people,
Children who will not play false.
So He was their Deliverer.
9 In all their troubles He was troubled,
And the angel of His Presence delivered them.
In His love and pity
He Himself redeemed them,
Raised them, and exalted them
All the days of old.

7 חַסְדֵי יְהוָה ׀ אַזְכִּיר
תְּהִלֹּת יְהוָה
כְּעַל כֹּל אֲשֶׁר־גְּמָלָנוּ יְהוָה
וְרַב־טוּב לְבֵית יִשְׂרָאֵל
אֲשֶׁר־גְּמָלָם
כְּרַחֲמָיו וּכְרֹב חֲסָדָיו׃
8 וַיֹּאמֶר אַךְ־עַמִּי הֵמָּה
בָּנִים לֹא יְשַׁקֵּרוּ
וַיְהִי לָהֶם לְמוֹשִׁיעַ׃
9 בְּכָל־צָרָתָם ׀ לא לוֹ צָר
וּמַלְאַךְ פָּנָיו הוֹשִׁיעָם
בְּאַהֲבָתוֹ וּבְחֶמְלָתוֹ
הוּא גְאָלָם
וַיְנַטְּלֵם וַיְנַשְּׂאֵם
כָּל־יְמֵי עוֹלָם׃

7–9. In ending this prophetic teaching with divine praise, the Sages emphasized the positive—as was often their preference. In Isaiah, the conclusion of this passage (vv. 10–14) mentions Israelite rebellion and divine disfavor (followed by the return of grace).

The Hebrew text of verses 8–9 is difficult and ambiguous. The *k'rei* (Masoretic text as read) with its trope (cantillation marks) seems to refer to God as "their Deliverer" and then states that "In all their troubles He was troubled" (literally, "trouble was His [*lo*]"). This reading understands *lo* to be a possessive pronoun, spelled לו. (This theology has enjoyed an active midrashic life. Rabbinic teachings have long held that God in heaven takes part in Israel's sorrows, while the *Sh'khinah* [divine Presence] on earth shares in Israel's period of exile.) Unfortunately, it then sets up two apparently contradictory remarks: "the angel . . . delivered them," but "He Himself redeemed them."

On the other hand, the Septuagint (ancient Greek translation) and the *k'tiv* (Masoretic text as written) present the passage as a continuous thought: "He was their Deliverer in all their troubles; no [*lo*] angel or messenger [was with Him], [but] His own Presence delivered them." This reading understands *lo* to be a negative particle, spelled לא. This version features a clear structure and verbal correlations. Moreover, it emphasizes God's direct, exclusive deliverance. (This theology is echoed in the *Pesaḥ Haggadah,* through its well-known statement that God alone delivered the nation from Egypt: "I and no angel, I and no messenger.")

HA·AZINU

32 Give ear, O heavens, let me speak;
Let the earth hear the words I utter!
2May my discourse come down as the rain,
My speech distill as the dew,
Like showers on young growth,
Like droplets on the grass.
3For the name of the LORD I proclaim;
Give glory to our God!

4The Rock!—His deeds are perfect,
Yea, all His ways are just;
A faithful God, never false,
True and upright is He.

האזינו

לב *הַאֲזִינוּ הַשָּׁמַיִם וַאֲדַבֵּרָה
וְתִשְׁמַע הָאָרֶץ אִמְרֵי־פִי׃
2 יַעֲרֹף כַּמָּטָר לִקְחִי
תִּזַּל כַּטַּל אִמְרָתִי
כִּשְׂעִירִם עֲלֵי־דֶשֶׁא
וְכִרְבִיבִים עֲלֵי־עֵשֶׂב׃
3 כִּי שֵׁם יְהוָה אֶקְרָא
הָבוּ גֹדֶל לֵאלֹהֵינוּ׃
4 הַצּוּר תָּמִים פָּעֳלוֹ
כִּי כָל־דְּרָכָיו מִשְׁפָּט
אֵל אֱמוּנָה וְאֵין עָוֶל
צַדִּיק וְיָשָׁר הוּא׃

v. 1. בכתב היד שלנו, צורת השירה ב־37 שורות, ולפי הלכות כתיבת ספר תורה, היא נכתבת ב־70 שורות

Epilogue: Moses' Last Days (*continued*)

MOSES' POEM (32:1–43)

The poem describes the consequences of Israel's anticipated betrayal of God. Its style is typical of biblical poetry. Each verse consists of at least two lines that are parallel to each other in meaning.

1. Heaven and earth are employed as a literary device. They function here as objective onlookers who serve as witnesses to the poem's charges and the fairness of Israel's punishment.

2. distill Parallel to "come down."

dew Hebrew: *tal,* which refers to rain or dew, both of which were thought to fall from the sky.

3. the name of the LORD I proclaim Proclaiming God's name means declaring His qualities, recounting His deeds.

Give glory Acknowledge God's greatness. Usually God's "greatness" refers to His vast power. Here it seems to point to His extraordinary kindness and justice in dealing with Israel.

THE HISTORY OF GOD'S RELATIONSHIP WITH ISRAEL (vv. 4–18)

4. This verse states the first main theme of the poem: God has treated Israel with complete justice.

Rock Hebrew: *tzur;* as a term for God, it expresses the idea that the deity is a source of refuge, a protector.

perfect That is, reliable, faithful.

never false Never faithless.

True In the sense of faithful.

upright Trustworthy; reliable.

CHAPTER 32

This is the last *parashah* of the Torah that is read at services on *Shabbat* morning. (Chapters 33–34 are read only on *Simḥat Torah,* to complete the annual cycle of Torah reading.) It consists entirely of a poem reprising and summarizing the themes of the first section of Deuteronomy: the greatness and generosity of God and the stubbornness and unreliability of the Israelites.

1. Give ear, O heavens . . . Let the earth hear Listen to me—you spiritual people whose thoughts are in heaven, and also you down-to-earth people whose concerns are more material. This message is meant for all of you (Ḥatam Sofer).

5Children unworthy of Him—
That crooked, perverse generation—
Their baseness has played Him false.
6Do you thus requite the LORD,
O dull and witless people?
Is not He the Father who created you,
Fashioned you and made you endure!

7Remember the days of old,
Consider the years of ages past;
Ask your father, he will inform you,
Your elders, they will tell you:
8When the Most High gave nations their homes
And set the divisions of man,
He fixed the boundaries of peoples
In relation to Israel's numbers.

5 שִׁחֵת לוֹ לֹא בָּנָיו מוּמָם
דּוֹר עִקֵּשׁ וּפְתַלְתֹּל׃
6 הֲ־לַיהוָה* תִּגְמְלוּ־זֹאת
עַם נָבָל וְלֹא חָכָם
הֲלוֹא־הוּא אָבִיךָ קָּנֶךָ
הוּא עָשְׂךָ וַיְכֹנְנֶךָ׃
שני 7 זְכֹר יְמוֹת עוֹלָם
בִּינוּ שְׁנוֹת דּוֹר־וָדוֹר
שְׁאַל אָבִיךָ וְיַגֵּדְךָ
זְקֵנֶיךָ וְיֹאמְרוּ לָךְ׃
8 בְּהַנְחֵל עֶלְיוֹן גּוֹיִם
בְּהַפְרִידוֹ בְּנֵי אָדָם
יַצֵּב גְּבֻלֹת עַמִּים
לְמִסְפַּר בְּנֵי יִשְׂרָאֵל׃

v. 6. ה׳ רבתי לפי נוסחים מקובלים

5. Children unworthy of Him This verse states the second main theme of the poem: Israel, in contrast to God, is faithless and perfidious, a "crooked, perverse generation." The reference to the people Israel as God's children is part of the parent–child metaphor through which the poem expresses God's relationship with Israel. The translation of this verse is a paraphrase, because the text is difficult and of uncertain meaning.

6. The poem now addresses the Israelites directly, charging them with responding to God's benefactions with ingratitude and rebellion.

Do you thus requite the LORD Literally, "Is it the LORD you requite thus?" The word order in Hebrew underscores the shocking nature of their behavior: "Do you treat even God this way?" In Torah scrolls, this interrogative prefix, the letter *hei* (Is it?), is written in larger script. The reason for this is unknown, but it has the effect of heightening the shock expressed by the question.

dull Hebrew: *naval;* literally, "villain(ous)." Here it refers to the foolish attitudes of the villain, who feels safe because he is contemptuous of God, believing that He is inattentive to human events or powerless to affect them. Israel acts as if it shared this attitude.

witless Unwise.

made you endure Literally, "brought you into existence."

7. If the audience has any doubt about the truth of what is said, it can turn for confirmation to its elders—the custodians of historical tradition in a predominantly oral culture. Similar challenges to consult the elders appear in the Book of Job (8:8–10) and in a Mesopotamian royal inscription.

8. Most High Hebrew: *elyon;* used in the Bible as a common title of God, primarily in poetry, by both Israelites and non-Israelites. It also appears in non-Israelite sources outside the Bible. Here it emphasizes God's supremacy over all beings considered divine; and because it does not have exclusively Israelite associations, it suits the context of God organizing the entire human race.

gave nations their homes According to Genesis, the division of humanity into nations took place after the Flood, in the aftermath of the Tower of Babel (Gen. 10, 11:1–9). God's benefactions to Israel began by dividing the human race into separate nations and choosing Israel as His own.

In relation to Israel's numbers A matter of how the world was to be ruled. In the Hebrew basis of the Septuagint, as well as in a Qumran

HALAKHAH L'MA'ASEH

32:7. Remember . . . Ask This verse echoes the command to remember our past and to ask our ancestors about it (Exod. 12:25–27). This commandment is carried out explicitly in the *Pesah Seider*; in the rituals associated with the other pilgrimage festivals; and in the education of our children in Jewish history, tradition, and observance.

[9]For the Lord's portion is His people,
Jacob His own allotment.

[10]He found him in a desert region,
In an empty howling waste.
He engirded him, watched over him,
Guarded him as the pupil of His eye.
[11]Like an eagle who rouses his nestlings,
Gliding down to his young,
So did He spread His wings and take him,
Bear him along on His pinions;
[12]The Lord alone did guide him,
No alien god at His side.

[13]He set him atop the highlands,
To feast on the yield of the earth;
He fed him honey from the crag,
And oil from the flinty rock,
[14]Curd of kine and milk of flocks;

9 כִּי חֵלֶק יְהוָה עַמּוֹ
יַעֲקֹב חֶבֶל נַחֲלָתוֹ׃
10 יִמְצָאֵהוּ בְּאֶרֶץ מִדְבָּר
וּבְתֹהוּ יְלֵל יְשִׁמֹן
יְסֹבְבֶנְהוּ יְבוֹנְנֵהוּ
יִצְּרֶנְהוּ כְּאִישׁוֹן עֵינוֹ׃
11 כְּנֶשֶׁר יָעִיר קִנּוֹ
עַל־גּוֹזָלָיו יְרַחֵף
יִפְרֹשׂ כְּנָפָיו יִקָּחֵהוּ
יִשָּׂאֵהוּ עַל־אֶבְרָתוֹ׃
12 יְהוָה בָּדָד יַנְחֶנּוּ
וְאֵין עִמּוֹ אֵל נֵכָר׃
שלישי 13 יַרְכִּבֵהוּ עַל־במותי בָּמֳתֵי אָרֶץ
וַיֹּאכַל תְּנוּבֹת שָׂדָי
וַיֵּנִקֵהוּ דְבַשׁ מִסֶּלַע
וְשֶׁמֶן מֵחַלְמִישׁ צוּר׃
14 חֶמְאַת בָּקָר וַחֲלֵב צֹאן

scroll and other texts, the phrase here (*l'mispar b'nei Yisra·el*) reads "equal to the number of divine beings" (*l'mispar b'nei el*). According to a concept found elsewhere in the Bible, God established two tiers in governance of the world: at the top, God, who reserved Israel for Himself, to govern personally; below Him, 70 angelic divine beings, to whom God allotted other peoples. The image is that of a ruler who governs the capital or heartland of the realm personally and assigns the provinces to subordinates.

9. His people Refers to Jacob, a synonym for Israel both as an individual and as a nation.

allotment As God's "allotment," Israel was cherished and protected by Him.

10. found him Israel was like a foundling or a desert wanderer, in danger of starvation and exposure. This metaphor shows how perilous Israel's situation had been and how indebted it should be to God for its survival.

desert region The Sinai, where the Israelites roamed before entering the Promised Land. Hebrew: *eretz midbar,* a wilderness partly marked by vegetation and sparse water sources.

howling waste A wasteland filled with the howling of winds and wild animals.

engirded God encircled Israel protectively.

Guarded him From snakes, scorpions, and marauders like the Amalekites.

as the pupil of His eye A graphic simile for an object of protective care, because it is guarded by a reflex action.

11. God led Israel safely through the desert, in the manner of an eagle training its young to fly and catching them on its back when they tire or fall.

12. The Lord alone No other deity helped Israel; hence for Israel to turn to other gods is baseless as well as ungrateful.

guide him Through the wilderness to the Promised Land.

13. atop the highlands The mountainous heartland of Israel.

fed Hebrew: *va-yenikeihu;* literally, "suckled." Implies that God nurtured Israel, which exerted virtually no effort. The most barren places yielded abundant food: In fissures and caves were found honeycombs; in rocky limestone soils, oil-producing olive trees.

14. Curd Hebrew: *ḥem·ah,* which includes butter, cream, and *leben,* a coagulated form of sour milk. The Land's rich pastures sustain cattle that produce dairy products and meat, and its soil yields wheat and wine.

With the best of lambs,
And rams of Bashan, and he-goats;
With the very finest wheat—
And foaming grape-blood was your drink.

15So Jeshurun grew fat and kicked—
You grew fat and gross and coarse—
He forsook the God who made him
And spurned the Rock of his support.
16They incensed Him with alien things,
Vexed Him with abominations.
17They sacrificed to demons, no-gods,
Gods they had never known,
New ones, who came but lately,
Who stirred not your fathers' fears.

עִם־חֵלֶב כָּרִים
וְאֵילִים בְּנֵי־בָשָׁן וְעַתּוּדִים
עִם־חֵלֶב כִּלְיוֹת חִטָּה
וְדַם־עֵנָב תִּשְׁתֶּה־חָמֶר׃
15 וַיִּשְׁמַן יְשֻׁרוּן וַיִּבְעָט
שָׁמַנְתָּ עָבִיתָ כָּשִׂיתָ
וַיִּטֹּשׁ אֱלוֹהַ עָשָׂהוּ
וַיְנַבֵּל צוּר יְשֻׁעָתוֹ׃
16 יַקְנִאֻהוּ בְּזָרִים
בְּתוֹעֵבֹת יַכְעִיסֻהוּ׃
17 יִזְבְּחוּ לַשֵּׁדִים לֹא אֱלֹהַ
אֱלֹהִים לֹא יְדָעוּם
חֲדָשִׁים מִקָּרֹב בָּאוּ
לֹא שְׂעָרוּם אֲבֹתֵיכֶם׃

best of lambs Literally, "fat of lambs." Fat is often used figuratively to refer to the best, as in the idiom "the fat of the land."

Bashan The mountain range in northern Transjordan, which included the best pastureland in the region, with herds famed for their strength and size.

very finest wheat Literally, "fat of the kidneys of wheat." Some commentators take "kidneys" to mean the kernel of the wheat; the full phrase would then mean "the finest grains of wheat." Others hold that it is a poetic overstatement meaning "wheat with grains as thick as kidneys."

grape-blood A poetic metaphor for wine.

15. Jeshurun Hebrew: *Y'shurun* (the Upright; from *yashar,* "upright"), which alludes to "Israel" (*Yisra·el*) and sounds something like it. Used ironically here, it underscores how Israel has failed to live up to its expected character.

kicked Like an unruly, rebellious animal. Not satisfied and docile from being fed, Israel rejected the One who fed it.

You grew fat and gross and coarse Here the poet addresses Israel directly.

Rock of his support The Rock who delivered Israel and protected it from danger.

16. incensed Him By worshiping other gods, Israel provoked the resentful rage that God warned about in the Decalogue.

alien things . . . abominations Alien gods and idols.

17. The verse does not argue that Israel worshiped nonexistent beings, mere statues, but that it worshiped beings that lack effective power and are unworthy of worship.

demons Hebrew: *shedim;* better: "spirits." In Akkadian, a *shed* is a minor protective spirit.

no-gods Pseudo-gods, beings undeservedly called "gods."

Gods they had never known Although the poem has just denied their divinity, it continues to use *"elohim"* for these beings. Probably the word here means "so-called gods."

New ones Unlike the Lord, "the ancient God" (33:27), who has acted on behalf of Israel since its beginning, these beings have no record of achievement or reliability. In the ancient world, antiquity was a hallmark of authenticity, and these new beings lacked it.

stirred not your fathers' fears The Septuagint renders "whom your fathers did not know," which is synonymous with the second line in the verse.

---

15. kicked . . . forsook . . . spurned The ultimate ingratitude. God will bless Israel with a measure of prosperity, and that prosperity will lead them to become arrogant and to neglect God. When individuals or nations become wealthy, they are often tempted to celebrate their material wealth at the expense of their spiritual development, focusing on what they do well and abandoning what may be more challenging.

18You neglected the Rock that begot you,
Forgot the God who brought you forth.

19The LORD saw and was vexed
And spurned His sons and His daughters.
20He said:
I will hide My countenance from them,
And see how they fare in the end.
For they are a treacherous breed,
Children with no loyalty in them.
21They incensed Me with no-gods,
Vexed Me with their futilities;
I'll incense them with a no-folk,
Vex them with a nation of fools.
22For a fire has flared in My wrath
And burned to the bottom of Sheol,
Has consumed the earth and its increase,

18 צ֥וּר יְלָדְךָ֖ תֶּ֑שִׁי*
וַתִּשְׁכַּ֖ח אֵ֥ל מְחֹלְלֶֽךָ׃

רביעי 19 וַיַּ֥רְא יְהוָ֖ה וַיִּנְאָ֑ץ
מִכַּ֥עַס בָּנָ֖יו וּבְנֹתָֽיו׃
20 וַיֹּ֗אמֶר אַסְתִּ֤ירָה פָנַי֙ מֵהֶ֔ם
אֶרְאֶ֖ה מָ֣ה אַחֲרִיתָ֑ם
כִּ֣י ד֤וֹר תַּהְפֻּכֹת֙ הֵ֔מָּה
בָּנִ֖ים לֹא־אֵמֻ֥ן בָּֽם׃
21 הֵ֚ם קִנְא֣וּנִי בְלֹא־אֵ֔ל
כִּעֲס֖וּנִי בְּהַבְלֵיהֶ֑ם
וַאֲנִי֙ אַקְנִיאֵ֣ם בְּלֹא־עָ֔ם
בְּג֥וֹי נָבָ֖ל אַכְעִיסֵֽם׃
22 כִּֽי־אֵשׁ֙ קָדְחָ֣ה בְאַפִּ֔י
וַתִּיקַ֖ד עַד־שְׁא֣וֹל תַּחְתִּ֑ית
וַתֹּ֤אכַל אֶ֙רֶץ֙ וִֽיבֻלָ֔הּ

v. 18. י׳ זעירא לפי נוסחים מקובלים

18. Again the poem turns directly to Israel and exclaims that it is guilty of the most unnatural behavior: forgetting one's own parent.

begot . . . brought forth These Hebrew verbs may have been chosen to suggest a mother. The image of forgetting one's mother casts Israel's behavior in the most unnatural light.

GOD DECIDES TO PUNISH ISRAEL (vv. 19–25)

19. sons and . . . daughters The involvement of both men and women in the worship of foreign gods is also mentioned in 17:2 and 29:17.

20. See 31:17–18.

And see how they fare in the end Literally, "and see what their end will be." God's words are ironic inasmuch as He intends to determine the outcome Himself.

treacherous breed Literally, "turnabout generation." It broke faith with God.

21. God will punish the Israelites measure for measure, treating them as they treated Him. As the Israelites incensed Him by favoring non-gods, He will incense them by favoring a non-people, sending it to invade them.

futilities Hebrew: *havalim,* one of the Bible's negative terms for idols; it means "puffs of breath," "vapor." In other words, insubstantial beings that do not last.

nation of fools "Nation of dullards, villains" (*goy naval*). Israel is characterized similarly (*am naval*) in verse 6. The description of the enemy as a no-folk and a nation of fools is reminiscent of Mesopotamian characterizations of nomadic, "uncivilized" outlanders as "not classed among people, not reckoned as part of the [civilized] land."

22. For a fire has flared in My wrath / And burned to the bottom of Sheol Sheol is the netherworld. The use of the past tense implies that once God has decided on the punishment, it is as good as accomplished. Fire is a metaphor for God's anger (4:24), and burning to the bottom of Sheol and to the foundations of the mountains is a picturesque description of its power.

its increase The earth's yield, its produce.

---

20. See Comment to Deut. 31:17. Where the earlier verse says that God will hide the divine countenance from Israel, which will cause terrible things to happen to them, this passage softens the threat. God will hide from them "to see how they fare in the end." This leaves the possibility of our reclaiming God's attention—bringing God back into a godless world—by our behavior.

Eaten down to the base of the hills.
23 I will sweep misfortunes on them,
Use up My arrows on them:
24 Wasting famine, ravaging plague,
Deadly pestilence, and fanged beasts
Will I let loose against them,
With venomous creepers in dust.
25 The sword shall deal death without,
As shall the terror within,
To youth and maiden alike,
The suckling as well as the aged.
26 I might have reduced them to naught,
Made their memory cease among men,
27 But for fear of the taunts of the foe,
Their enemies who might misjudge
And say, "Our own hand has prevailed;
None of this was wrought by the LORD!"
28 For they are a folk void of sense,
Lacking in all discernment.
29 Were they wise, they would think upon this,
Gain insight into their future:
30 "How could one have routed a thousand,
Or two put ten thousand to flight,

וַתְּלַהֵט מוֹסְדֵי הָרִים׃
23 אַסְפֶּה עָלֵימוֹ רָעוֹת
חִצַּי אֲכַלֶּה־בָּם׃
24 מְזֵי רָעָב וּלְחֻמֵי רֶשֶׁף
וְקֶטֶב מְרִירִי
וְשֶׁן־בְּהֵמוֹת אֲשַׁלַּח־בָּם
עִם־חֲמַת זֹחֲלֵי עָפָר׃
25 מִחוּץ תְּשַׁכֶּל־חֶרֶב
וּמֵחֲדָרִים אֵימָה
גַּם־בָּחוּר גַּם־בְּתוּלָה
יוֹנֵק עִם־אִישׁ שֵׂיבָה׃
26 אָמַרְתִּי אַפְאֵיהֶם
אַשְׁבִּיתָה מֵאֱנוֹשׁ זִכְרָם׃
27 לוּלֵי כַּעַס אוֹיֵב אָגוּר
פֶּן־יְנַכְּרוּ צָרֵימוֹ
פֶּן־יֹאמְרוּ יָדֵנוּ רָמָה
וְלֹא יְהוָה פָּעַל כָּל־זֹאת׃
28 כִּי־גוֹי אֹבַד עֵצוֹת הֵמָּה
וְאֵין בָּהֶם תְּבוּנָה׃
חמישי 29 לוּ חָכְמוּ יַשְׂכִּילוּ זֹאת
יָבִינוּ לְאַחֲרִיתָם׃
30 אֵיכָה יִרְדֹּף אֶחָד אֶלֶף
וּשְׁנַיִם יָנִיסוּ רְבָבָה

23. I will sweep . . . on them God resolves to bring all of His destructive forces against Israel.

Use up My arrows That is, shoot all My arrows, a metaphor for the calamities of verse 24. It is used again in verse 42.

24. Wasting famine Famine that will waste their bodies.

pestilence In some Arabic dialects, *"ketev"* refers to smallpox.

fanged beasts . . . venomous creepers Wild animals, such as lions, bears, and poisonous snakes. Settled territory was often in danger of being overrun by wild animals.

25. War will spread everywhere, and to people of both sexes (not just the young men who are the warriors) and of all ages.

As shall the terror within Those taking refuge indoors will die of fright.

GOD DECIDES TO LIMIT RETRIBUTION
(vv. 26–42)

26. reduced them to naught Obliterated them.

Made their memory cease Made an end to their name, wiped them out entirely.

27. taunts Hebrew: *ka·as;* literally, "vexation." The enemy would also vex God by falsely claiming credit for the defeat of Israel.

Our own hand has prevailed After its victory, this nation of dullards will reason exactly as Moses warns Israel not to reason when it prospers (8:17).

28. they The enemy.

29. Gain insight into their future Better: "reflect on what happened to them," on the circumstances or cause behind their victory.

30. The motif of a few chasing thousands is

Unless their Rock had sold them,
The LORD had given them up?"
31For their rock is not like our Rock,
In our enemies' own estimation.

32Ah! The vine for them is from Sodom,
From the vineyards of Gomorrah;
The grapes for them are poison,
A bitter growth their clusters.
33Their wine is the venom of asps,
The pitiless poison of vipers.
34Lo, I have it all put away,
Sealed up in My storehouses,
35To be My vengeance and recompense,
At the time that their foot falters.
Yea, their day of disaster is near,
And destiny rushes upon them.

36For the LORD will vindicate His people
And take revenge for His servants,

אִם־לֹא כִּי־צוּרָם מְכָרָם
וַיהוָה הִסְגִּירָם:
31 כִּי לֹא כְצוּרֵנוּ צוּרָם
וְאֹיְבֵינוּ פְּלִילִים:
32 כִּי־מִגֶּפֶן סְדֹם גַּפְנָם
וּמִשַּׁדְמֹת עֲמֹרָה
עֲנָבֵמוֹ עִנְּבֵי־רוֹשׁ
אַשְׁכְּלֹת מְרֹרֹת לָמוֹ:
33 חֲמַת תַּנִּינִם יֵינָם
וְרֹאשׁ פְּתָנִים אַכְזָר:
34 הֲלֹא־הוּא כָּמֻס עִמָּדִי
חָתֻם בְּאוֹצְרֹתָי:
35 לִי נָקָם וְשִׁלֵּם
לְעֵת תָּמוּט רַגְלָם
כִּי קָרוֹב יוֹם אֵידָם
וְחָשׁ עֲתִדֹת לָמוֹ:
36 כִּי־יָדִין יְהוָה עַמּוֹ
וְעַל־עֲבָדָיו יִתְנֶחָם

a traditional way of describing a divinely determined rout.

sold them . . . given them up Handed them over, delivered them. Mere abandonment would not have produced a rout of such proportions; God must have actively aided the enemy.

31. their rock Here, used ironically of the enemy's god, as if the text said, "their so-called rock" (see v. 4). Nor could the enemy—if at all wise—credit its victory to its own gods, because its gods are not equal to Israel's God.

In our enemies' own estimation This translation is unlikely. It is implausible that the enemy, having just routed Israel, would consider its own gods unequal to Israel's God. Better: "nor are our enemies' guardians (*p'lilim*) [like our Rock]."

GOD DECIDES TO PUNISH THE ENEMY (vv. 32–35)

32. The enemy will suffer the destiny of Sodom and Gomorrah: They will drink the same wine—from the same vines—that was served to the people of those devastated cities. Poisonous drink is a metaphor for a disastrous fate.

33. pitiless poison Painful or incurable poison.

34. The poison wine is stored up securely, waiting for the day when God will serve it to the enemy. Describing the wine as "sealed up" is based on the practice of sealing the latches to storerooms with clay, stamped with the signet of the king or the official in charge, to detect whether the room has been entered without authorization.

35. To be My vengeance Hebrew: *li nakam;* literally, "vengeance is Mine." As the accompanying word "recompense" makes clear, "vengeance" refers only to just retribution, not to revenge.

At the time that their foot falters A biblical idiom for reversal of fortune.

destiny Hebrew: *atidot;* literally, "what is prepared." Probably refers to the punishment sealed up in God's storehouses (v. 34).

GOD'S PLAN TO DELIVER ISRAEL (vv. 36–42)

36. vindicate Judge in favor of.

take revenge for That is, avenge them, get satisfaction for the way the enemy treated them.

---

31. their rock is not like our Rock The God of Israel is like a rock, unfailingly supportive and reliable. The gods of the pagan nations are like rocks, incapable of feeling or responding.

When He sees that their might is gone,
And neither bond nor free is left.
37He will say: Where are their gods,
The rock in whom they sought refuge,
38Who ate the fat of their offerings
And drank their libation wine?
Let them rise up to your help,
And let them be a shield unto you!
39See, then, that I, I am He;
There is no god beside Me.
I deal death and give life;
I wounded and I will heal:
None can deliver from My hand.
40Lo, I raise My hand to heaven
And say: As I live forever,
41When I whet My flashing blade
And My hand lays hold on judgment,

כִּי יִרְאֶה כִּי־אָזְלַת יָד
וְאֶפֶס עָצוּר וְעָזוּב׃
37 וְאָמַר אֵי אֱלֹהֵימוֹ
צוּר חָסָיוּ בוֹ׃
38 אֲשֶׁר חֵלֶב זְבָחֵימוֹ יֹאכֵלוּ
יִשְׁתּוּ יֵין נְסִיכָם
יָקוּמוּ וְיַעְזְרֻכֶם
יְהִי עֲלֵיכֶם סִתְרָה׃
39 רְאוּ ׀ עַתָּה כִּי אֲנִי אֲנִי הוּא
וְאֵין אֱלֹהִים עִמָּדִי
אֲנִי אָמִית וַאֲחַיֶּה
מָחַצְתִּי וַאֲנִי אֶרְפָּא
וְאֵין מִיָּדִי מַצִּיל׃
ששי 40 כִּי־אֶשָּׂא אֶל־שָׁמַיִם יָדִי
וְאָמַרְתִּי חַי אָנֹכִי לְעֹלָם׃
41 אִם־שַׁנּוֹתִי בְּרַק חַרְבִּי
וְתֹאחֵז בְּמִשְׁפָּט יָדִי

When . . . their might is gone When they have become totally powerless, so that they could not possibly attribute their salvation to themselves, God will intervene to save them.

neither bond nor free The meaning of this idiom is uncertain. Other biblical contexts (1 Kings 14:10, 21:21; 2 Kings 9:8, 14:26) suggest that the Hebrew *atzur v'azuv* may refer to "ruler and helper." The verse would then mean that God will act when He, or Israel, sees that Israel is without a ruler or a helper to deliver it.

37. When Israel reaches the point of total helplessness, God will point out how the false gods in whom it trusted are powerless—in contrast to His own power (v. 39).

rock Used ironically, because Israel's false gods will have proven unable to shield it from the enemy (see v. 31).

38. Who The false gods who were the objects of Israel's illicit cult. The poem—if it is not being merely sarcastic—can represent these beings as actually eating and drinking the offerings because it does not deny their existence, it denies only their divinity.

39. Israel's punishment by the Lord, and the inability of its false gods to protect it, should finally make it realize that the Lord alone is the only effective divine being, the only true God. He brought all this about, and He alone can change it.

I, I am He That is, "I alone am He," I alone control events.

There is no god beside Me Literally, "There is no god with me." No god has been involved in the events.

I deal death and give life; / I wounded and I will heal The first clause is a general assertion, meaning that God alone determines people's welfare. The second means that it is He who is doing so in this particular case.

None can deliver from My hand None of your false gods could protect you from My punishment, and none will be able to save the enemy from Me.

40. I raise My hand to heaven Raising the hand heavenward is a gesture that accompanies invoking God in an oath. Here, with God as the speaker, it is simply an idiom meaning "I swear."

As I live forever In human oaths, declaring "As the LORD lives" (*ḥai Adonai*) is a verbal counterpart to raising the hand heavenward. God swears by saying *ḥai anokhi* (or *ani*), using the pronoun "I" instead of His own name.

41. whet My flashing blade God is pictured as a warrior preparing for battle.

judgment Hebrew: *mishpat.* In light of the parallel term "blade" (literally, "sword") and the

Vengeance will I wreak on My foes, Will I deal to those who reject Me. 42I will make My arrows drunk with blood— As My sword devours flesh— Blood of the slain and the captive From the long-haired enemy chiefs.	אָשִׁ֤יב נָקָם֙ לְצָרָ֔י וְלִמְשַׂנְאַ֖י אֲשַׁלֵּֽם׃ 42 אַשְׁכִּ֤יר חִצַּי֙ מִדָּ֔ם וְחַרְבִּ֖י תֹּאכַ֣ל בָּשָׂ֑ר מִדַּ֤ם חָלָל֙ וְשִׁבְיָ֔ה מֵרֹ֖אשׁ פַּרְע֥וֹת אוֹיֵֽב׃
43O nations, acclaim His people! For He'll avenge the blood of His servants, Wreak vengeance on His foes, And cleanse the land of His people.	43 הַרְנִ֤ינוּ גוֹיִם֙ עַמּ֔וֹ כִּ֥י דַם־עֲבָדָ֖יו יִקּ֑וֹם וְנָקָם֙ יָשִׁ֣יב לְצָרָ֔יו וְכִפֶּ֥ר אַדְמָת֖וֹ עַמּֽוֹ׃ פ
44Moses came, together with Hosea son of Nun, and recited all the words of this poem in the hearing of the people. 45And when Moses finished reciting all these words to all Israel, 46he said to them: Take to	שביעי 44 וַיָּבֹ֣א מֹשֶׁ֗ה וַיְדַבֵּ֛ר אֶֽת־כָּל־דִּבְרֵ֥י הַשִּׁירָֽה־הַזֹּ֖את בְּאָזְנֵ֣י הָעָ֑ם ה֖וּא וְהוֹשֵׁ֥עַ בִּן־נֽוּן׃ 45 וַיְכַ֣ל מֹשֶׁ֗ה לְדַבֵּ֛ר אֶת־כָּל־הַדְּבָרִ֥ים הָאֵ֖לֶּה אֶל־כָּל־יִשְׂרָאֵֽל׃ 46 וַיֹּ֤אמֶר אֲלֵהֶם֙

parallelism "arrows . . . sword" in the next verse, *mishpat* here must mean a weapon of judgment, an instrument of punishment.

My foes The enemy, although used by God as an agent for punishing Israel, is His foe. The Bible implicitly assumes that God uses evil nations to punish Israel and that they, too, will ultimately be punished.

wreak . . . deal Literally, "return . . . pay back." The enemy's punishment will be deserved.

42. The enemy will go down to a bloody defeat. The image of the devouring sword is a common one; that of drinking arrows is unique.

blood of the . . . captive The blood of wounded captives or prisoners killed after capture.

long-haired . . . chiefs This difficult passage has been explained as implying that warriors, like Samson, let their hair grow long, either out of a belief that strength resides there or as a mark of dedication to the deity (see Num. 6:1–21).

CELEBRATING ISRAEL'S DELIVERANCE (v. 43)

The poem concludes with a final invocation calling on the nations to acclaim God's deliverance of Israel and punishment of the enemy. This invitation implies that God's salvation of Israel has importance for the world at large.

43. acclaim Congratulate Israel on its deliverance and for having such a God.

He'll avenge the blood of His servants The verb "redeem" is used when the avenger is a relative; "avenge," when it is God or human authorities. Hence the use of "avenge" here may be because in this part of the poem the Israelites are no longer described as God's children but as His "servants" (v. 36).

cleanse the land of His people That is, cleanse His people's land. Presumably, the land has been polluted by Israelite blood shed by Israel's enemy, and God will cleanse it with the blood of the enemy (see Num. 35:33). But the Hebrew *admato* (land) may be a scribal error for *ud'ma·ot*, a variant (known from ancient Ugaritic) of *d'ma·ot* (tears). Thus the clause may mean that God "will wipe away His people's tears."

CONCLUSION TO THE POEM (vv. 44–52)

44. This verse summarizes the contents of 31:22 and 30. It means, "So Moses came—either from the place where he received the instructions to teach the poem, or from where he wrote it—and taught it to the people."

Hosea That is, Joshua (see Num. 13:16).

45. all these words The entire Teaching, including the poem.

שִׂימוּ לְבַבְכֶם לְכׇל־הַדְּבָרִים אֲשֶׁר אָנֹכִי
מֵעִיד בָּכֶם הַיּוֹם אֲשֶׁר תְּצַוֻּם אֶת־בְּנֵיכֶם
לִשְׁמֹר לַעֲשׂוֹת אֶת־כׇּל־דִּבְרֵי הַתּוֹרָה
הַזֹּאת׃ 47 כִּי לֹא־דָבָר רֵק הוּא מִכֶּם
כִּי־הוּא חַיֵּיכֶם וּבַדָּבָר הַזֶּה תַּאֲרִיכוּ יָמִים
עַל־הָאֲדָמָה אֲשֶׁר אַתֶּם עֹבְרִים אֶת־
הַיַּרְדֵּן שָׁמָּה לְרִשְׁתָּהּ׃ פ
מפטיר 48 וַיְדַבֵּר יְהֹוָה אֶל־מֹשֶׁה בְּעֶצֶם הַיּוֹם הַזֶּה
לֵאמֹר׃ 49 עֲלֵה אֶל־הַר הָעֲבָרִים הַזֶּה
הַר־נְבוֹ אֲשֶׁר בְּאֶרֶץ מוֹאָב אֲשֶׁר עַל־פְּנֵי
יְרֵחוֹ וּרְאֵה אֶת־אֶרֶץ כְּנַעַן אֲשֶׁר אֲנִי נֹתֵן
לִבְנֵי יִשְׂרָאֵל לַאֲחֻזָּה׃ 50 וּמֻת בָּהָר אֲשֶׁר
אַתָּה עֹלֶה שָׁמָּה וְהֵאָסֵף אֶל־עַמֶּיךָ
כַּאֲשֶׁר־מֵת אַהֲרֹן אָחִיךָ בְּהֹר הָהָר וַיֵּאָסֶף
אֶל־עַמָּיו׃ 51 עַל אֲשֶׁר מְעַלְתֶּם בִּי בְּתוֹךְ
בְּנֵי יִשְׂרָאֵל בְּמֵי־מְרִיבַת קָדֵשׁ מִדְבַּר־צִן
עַל אֲשֶׁר לֹא־קִדַּשְׁתֶּם אוֹתִי בְּתוֹךְ בְּנֵי

heart all the words with which I have warned
you this day. Enjoin them upon your children,
that they may observe faithfully all the terms of
this Teaching. 47 For this is not a trifling thing
for you: it is your very life; through it you shall
long endure on the land that you are to possess
upon crossing the Jordan.

48 That very day the LORD spoke to Moses:
49 Ascend these heights of Abarim to Mount
Nebo, which is in the land of Moab facing Jericho, and view the land of Canaan, which I am
giving the Israelites as their holding. 50 You shall
die on the mountain that you are about to ascend, and shall be gathered to your kin, as your
brother Aaron died on Mount Hor and was
gathered to his kin; 51 for you both broke faith
with Me among the Israelite people, at the waters of Meribath-kadesh in the wilderness of
Zin, by failing to uphold My sanctity among the

46. all the words with which I have warned you Better: "with which I have charged you." It is clear from the rest of the verse that the words in question include commands, and because the poem contains none, the words must be those of the Teaching as a whole.

47. trifling The teaching is not frivolous or inconsequential, for Israel's survival as a nation depends on it.

GOD SUMMONS MOSES TO HIS DEATH (vv. 48–52)

Moses has transmitted the poem to the people. Preparations for his departure resume.

48. That very day The day on which Moses concluded the activities just described. The only specific date previously mentioned in the book is the first day of the 11th month in the 40th year after the Exodus (1:3). On that date, Moses began to expound the Teaching (1:5); he did not necessarily finish it then. The context implies that God said this to Moses on the day he died, or perhaps the preceding day.

49. heights of Abarim Probably the mountain range east of the Dead Sea. Mount Nebo was one of its prominent peaks. To reach it, Moses would have doubled back on the Israelites' route the distance of one day's march because, according to Num. 33:47–48, "the hills of Abarim, before [the city] Nebo," was the Israelites' last encampment before reaching their current one.

facing Jericho That is, east of Jericho, across the Jordan.

view the land This is a minor concession to Moses' plea in 3:25, "Let me, I pray, cross over and see the good land."

50. die . . . be gathered to your kin It was common belief in the ancient world that one's spirit reunited after death with the spirits of one's kin in Sheol, the netherworld.

as . . . Aaron died Six months earlier. See Num. 20:23–28, 33:38.

on Mount Hor Deuteronomy 10:6 gives a different place for Aaron's death.

51. for you both broke faith with Me See Num. 20:1–13.

Meribath-kadesh The place at Kadesh where the incident in question occurred was

---

47. this is not a trifling thing for you Literally, "it is not an empty thing from you." If anything in the Torah seems "empty" (i.e., unclear, meaningless), that perception is "from you," owing to your own failure to study it thoroughly (JT Pe·ah 1:1).

Israelite people. 52You may view the land from a distance, but you shall not enter it—the land that I am giving to the Israelite people.

יִשְׂרָאֵל׃ 52 כִּי מִנֶּגֶד תִּרְאֶה אֶת־הָאָרֶץ
וְשָׁמָּה לֹא תָבוֹא אֶל־הָאָרֶץ אֲשֶׁר־אֲנִי
נֹתֵן לִבְנֵי יִשְׂרָאֵל׃ פ

called Meribah, "Quarrel Place," commemorating the quarrel that touched it off (see Num. 20:13).

wilderness of Zin This is the section of the wilderness of Paran (i.e., of the Negeb and the Sinai) that formed the southern boundary of the Promised Land.

הפטרת האזינו

HAFTARAH FOR HA·AZINU

2 SAMUEL 22:1–51

(*On the* Shabbat *before* Yom Kippur, *recite the* haftarah *on p. 1234.*)

This *haftarah* presents David's great hymn of victory and thanksgiving, sung to God "after the LORD had saved him from the hands of all his enemies and from the hands of Saul" (2 Sam. 22:1). The designation "after" also connotes finality, for the hymn appears just before the account of David's death (followed only by his "last words" in 2 Sam. 23:1–7 and final arrangements for succession in 1 Kings 1). In a grand, celebratory manner, a great military hero thanks God at the end of his life for all the protection and favor he has received. Accordingly, God is portrayed here is as a Lord of battles—storming with heavenly arrows to the aid of human armies. The hymn also portrays a deeper religious spirit, with theological features found in other biblical prayers. With but minor textual variations, the whole hymn is also found in Ps. 18.

Of the terms used in the *haftarah* for God's invincible protection, none stands out as much as *tzur* (rock). It recurs in neutral designations of God as a sheltering rock (v. 3), and as a source of personal safety (v. 47). Even more striking are the formulations that virtually equate the epithet with God Himself. "Who is a rock except God?" asks David (v. 32). "Exalted be God, the rock / Who gives me victory" (v. 47). Clearly, the primordial security of mountain rocks was a preferred metaphor to express inviolable stability on earth. Indeed, great rocks reveal terrestrial forces erupting heavenward, standing firm with the face of eternity.

The image of God as an earthly *tzur* thus stands at one pole of the hymn, tracing a line that rises toward the heights. At the other pole is the image of God's descent on the wings of the storm clouds to save His people on earth. This figure is not terrestrial but atmospheric, deriving from ancient Near Eastern depictions of storm gods riding to battle on their heavenly chariots. The cosmic arsenal includes swirling blasts of wind that stir the depths and "expose" the "bed of the sea" (v. 16), fiery bolts that furiously fly like arrows out of dark thunderheads (vv. 10–12,15), and awesome peals of thunder that bark out an earth-shattering divine voice (v. 14). In this way did the Lord come to rescue his people at the Sea of Reeds, blasting the waters with the wind of His fury and uncovering the dry bed below (Exod. 15:8,19). David's hymn excels in these depictions. Their dramatic vitality contrasts sharply with the scene of stability established by the mountain rocks at the beginning of the hymn. These images derive from different poles of the religious imagination. Their fusion in this song produces a visual and visceral tension that draws the reader toward the vastness of God's power that the speaker celebrates.

RELATION OF THE *HAFTARAH* TO THE *PARASHAH*

The song of Moses in Deuteronomy 32 and David's song of thanksgiving in this *haftarah* are grand recitations in praise of God's providence in history. Each was produced near the end of a hero's life, and thus each closes an era in which that leader was the dominant figure.

The main distinction between the two compositions is one of focus. Moses' song reviews God's past beneficence for the entire nation (Deut. 32:7–14), and David's prayer thanks God for personal help against his enemies. What is more, Moses chides the people for rebellion against their divine protector (Deut. 32:15–18) and, in this context, portrays God as one who requites sinners with vengeance and doom (Deut. 32:19–43). By contrast, David believes that God's benefits to him are rewards for his faithful service and obedience ("The LORD rewarded me

according to my merit," 2 Sam. 22:21). Divine vengeance is something brought against his enemies (v. 41).

Despite the different emphases of the two songs, they are bound by common theological images and vocabulary. Most notable is the recurrent stress on integrity, blamelessness, and perfection through the term *tamim,* and on stability, power, and protection through the word *tzur.* Thus Moses' song proclaims God at the outset as "The Rock!—His deeds are perfect" (*tzur tamim po·olo,* Deut. 32:4). Faithless Israel, however, is a "crooked, perverse generation" (*dor ikkesh u-f'taltol,* v. 5) that "spurned the Rock [*tzur*] of . . . support" (v. 15) and "neglected the Rock [*tzur*] that begot" them (v. 18).

David echoes this theology from his own standpoint. He too glorifies God as a "rock" (2 Sam. 22:47) whose way is perfect (*tamim,* v. 31). God is "the rock wherein I take shelter" (v. 3), the one to whom he has "been blameless" (*tamim,* v. 24). Indeed, David proclaims God as acting "blamelessly" with the "blameless" hero (*im gibbor tamim titammam,* v. 26), but "with the perverse" He is "wily" (*v'im ikkesh titappal,* v. 27). As a reward for his piety, God has "kept" David's path "secure" (*tamim,* v. 33) and crowned him with success and victory. The prayer concludes with the hope that these same benefits will continue to his lineage.

These similarities are striking and reflect a common theology of God as a mighty and sustaining power, whose way is *tamim.* David maintains allegiance to his divine source and neither forgets the rock of his strength nor rebels through success or perversity. By contrast, the people of Moses turn against God, which condemns them to doom. The contrast could not be more stark. Indeed, through the liturgical juxtaposition of this *haftarah* and this *parashah* the reader is faced with two religious paths: a God-centered way of remembrance and humility and a self-centered way of forgetfulness and pride. The one gives life; the other destroys. Every spiritual seeker stands before this fateful duality.

22 David addressed the words of this song to the LORD, after the LORD had saved him from the hands of all his enemies and from the hands of Saul. 2He said:

O LORD, my crag, my fastness, my deliverer!
3O God, the rock wherein I take shelter:
My shield, my mighty champion, my fortress and refuge!
My savior, You who rescue me from violence!

4All praise! I called on the LORD,
And I was delivered from my enemies.

5For the breakers of Death encompassed me,
The torrents of Belial terrified me;
6The snares of Sheol encircled me,
The coils of Death engulfed me.

כב *וַיְדַבֵּר דָּוִד לַיהוָה אֶת־דִּבְרֵי
הַשִּׁירָה הַזֹּאת בְּיוֹם הִצִּיל יְהוָה אֹתוֹ
מִכַּף כָּל־אֹיְבָיו וּמִכַּף שָׁאוּל׃ 2 וַיֹּאמַר

יְהוָה סַלְעִי וּמְצֻדָתִי וּמְפַלְטִי־לִי׃
3 אֱלֹהֵי צוּרִי אֶחֱסֶה־בּוֹ
מָגִנִּי וְקֶרֶן יִשְׁעִי מִשְׂגַּבִּי וּמְנוּסִי
מֹשִׁעִי מֵחָמָס תֹּשִׁעֵנִי׃

4 מְהֻלָּל אֶקְרָא יְהוָה
וּמֵאֹיְבַי אִוָּשֵׁעַ׃

5 כִּי אֲפָפֻנִי מִשְׁבְּרֵי־מָוֶת
נַחֲלֵי בְלִיַּעַל יְבַעֲתֻנִי׃
6 חֶבְלֵי שְׁאוֹל סַבֻּנִי
קִדְּמֻנִי מֹקְשֵׁי־מָוֶת׃

v. 1. בכתב היד שלנו כתוב בצורת שירה

2 Samuel 22:5–6. Flood imagery ("breakers," "torrents") combines with figures of hunting ("snares," "coils," or "traps") to express the speaker's sense of overpowering and hidden dangers.

Death . . . Belial . . . Sheol Three names for the netherworld.

7 In my anguish I called on the LORD,
Cried out to my God;
In His Abode He heard my voice,
My cry entered His ears.
8 Then the earth rocked and quaked,
The foundations of heaven shook—
Rocked by His indignation.
9 Smoke went up from His nostrils,
From His mouth came devouring fire;
Live coals blazed forth from Him.
10 He bent the sky and came down,
Thick cloud beneath His feet.
11 He mounted a cherub and flew;
He was seen on the wings of the wind.
12 He made pavilions of darkness about Him,
Dripping clouds, huge thunderheads;
13 In the brilliance before Him
Blazed fiery coals.
14 The LORD thundered forth from heaven,
The Most High sent forth His voice;
15 He let loose bolts, and scattered them;
Lightning, and put them to rout.
16 The bed of the sea was exposed,
The foundations of the world were laid bare
By the mighty roaring of the LORD,
At the blast of the breath of His nostrils.
17 He reached down from on high, He took me,
Drew me out of the mighty waters;
18 He rescued me from my enemy so strong,
From foes too mighty for me.
19 They attacked me on my day of calamity,
But the LORD was my stay.
20 He brought me out to freedom,
He rescued me because He was pleased with me.

7 בַּצַּר־לִי אֶקְרָא יְהוָה
וְאֶל־אֱלֹהַי אֶקְרָא
וַיִּשְׁמַע מֵהֵיכָלוֹ קוֹלִי
וְשַׁוְעָתִי בְּאָזְנָיו׃
8 ותגעש וַיִּתְגָּעַשׁ וַתִּרְעַשׁ הָאָרֶץ
מוֹסְדוֹת הַשָּׁמַיִם יִרְגָּזוּ
וַיִּתְגָּעֲשׁוּ כִּי־חָרָה לוֹ׃
9 עָלָה עָשָׁן בְּאַפּוֹ
וְאֵשׁ מִפִּיו תֹּאכֵל
גֶּחָלִים בָּעֲרוּ מִמֶּנּוּ׃
10 וַיֵּט שָׁמַיִם וַיֵּרַד
וַעֲרָפֶל תַּחַת רַגְלָיו׃
11 וַיִּרְכַּב עַל־כְּרוּב וַיָּעֹף
וַיֵּרָא עַל־כַּנְפֵי־רוּחַ׃
12 וַיָּשֶׁת חֹשֶׁךְ סְבִיבֹתָיו סֻכּוֹת
חַשְׁרַת־מַיִם עָבֵי שְׁחָקִים׃
13 מִנֹּגַהּ נֶגְדּוֹ
בָּעֲרוּ גַּחֲלֵי־אֵשׁ׃
14 יַרְעֵם מִן־שָׁמַיִם יְהוָה
וְעֶלְיוֹן יִתֵּן קוֹלוֹ׃
15 וַיִּשְׁלַח חִצִּים וַיְפִיצֵם
בָּרָק ויהמם וַיָּהֹם׃
16 וַיֵּרָאוּ אֲפִקֵי יָם
יִגָּלוּ מֹסְדוֹת תֵּבֵל
בְּגַעֲרַת יְהוָה
מִנִּשְׁמַת רוּחַ אַפּוֹ׃
17 יִשְׁלַח מִמָּרוֹם יִקָּחֵנִי
יַמְשֵׁנִי מִמַּיִם רַבִּים׃
18 יַצִּילֵנִי מֵאֹיְבִי עָז
מִשֹּׂנְאַי כִּי אָמְצוּ מִמֶּנִּי׃
19 יְקַדְּמֻנִי בְּיוֹם אֵידִי
וַיְהִי יְהוָה מִשְׁעָן לִי׃
20 וַיֹּצֵא לַמֶּרְחָב אֹתִי
יְחַלְּצֵנִי כִּי־חָפֵץ בִּי׃

11. He was seen Hebrew: *va-yera*. The version in Ps. 18:11 has *va-yeide* (He was gliding, swooping)—more appropriate to the atmospheric figures used here.

21The LORD rewarded me according to my merit,
He requited the cleanness of my hands.

22For I have kept the ways of the LORD
And have not been guilty before my God;
23I am mindful of all His rules
And have not departed from His laws.
24I have been blameless before Him,
And have guarded myself against sinning—
25And the LORD has requited my merit,
According to my purity in His sight.
26With the loyal You deal loyally;
With the blameless hero, blamelessly.
27With the pure You act in purity,
And with the perverse You are wily.
28To humble folk You give victory,
And You look with scorn on the haughty.

29You, O LORD, are my lamp;
The LORD lights up my darkness.
30With You, I can rush a barrier,
With my God, I can scale a wall.
31The way of God is perfect,
The word of the LORD is pure.
He is a shield to all who take refuge in Him.
32Yea, who is a god except the LORD,
Who is a rock except God—
33The God, my mighty stronghold,
Who kept my path secure;
34Who made my legs like a deer's,
And set me firm on the heights;
35Who trained my hands for battle,
So that my arms can bend a bow of bronze!
36You have granted me the shield of Your protection
And Your providence has made me great.
37You have let me stride on freely,

21 יִגְמְלֵנִי יְהוָה כְּצִדְקָתִי
כְּבֹר יָדַי יָשִׁיב לִי׃

22 כִּי שָׁמַרְתִּי דַּרְכֵי יְהוָה
וְלֹא רָשַׁעְתִּי מֵאֱלֹהָי׃
23 כִּי כָל־משפטו מִשְׁפָּטָיו לְנֶגְדִּי
וְחֻקֹּתָיו לֹא־אָסוּר מִמֶּנָּה׃
24 וָאֶהְיֶה תָמִים לוֹ
וָאֶשְׁתַּמְּרָה מֵעֲוֺנִי׃
25 וַיָּשֶׁב יְהוָה לִי כְּצִדְקָתִי
כְּבֹרִי לְנֶגֶד עֵינָיו׃
26 עִם־חָסִיד תִּתְחַסָּד
עִם־גִּבּוֹר תָּמִים תִּתַּמָּם׃
27 עִם־נָבָר תִּתָּבָר
וְעִם־עִקֵּשׁ תִּתַּפָּל׃
28 וְאֶת־עַם עָנִי תּוֹשִׁיעַ
וְעֵינֶיךָ עַל־רָמִים תַּשְׁפִּיל׃

29 כִּי־אַתָּה נֵירִי יְהוָה
וַיהוָה יַגִּיהַּ חָשְׁכִּי׃
30 כִּי בְכָה* אָרוּץ גְּדוּד
בֵּאלֹהַי אֲדַלֶּג־שׁוּר׃
31 הָאֵל תָּמִים דַּרְכּוֹ
אִמְרַת יְהוָה צְרוּפָה
מָגֵן הוּא לְכֹל הַחֹסִים בּוֹ׃
32 כִּי מִי־אֵל מִבַּלְעֲדֵי יְהוָה
וּמִי צוּר מִבַּלְעֲדֵי אֱלֹהֵינוּ׃
33 הָאֵל מָעוּזִּי חָיִל
וַיַּתֵּר תָּמִים דרכו דַּרְכִּי׃
34 מְשַׁוֶּה רגליו רַגְלַי כָּאַיָּלוֹת
וְעַל בָּמוֹתַי יַעֲמִדֵנִי׃
35 מְלַמֵּד יָדַי לַמִּלְחָמָה
וְנִחַת קֶשֶׁת־נְחוּשָׁה זְרֹעֹתָי׃
36 וַתִּתֶּן־לִי מָגֵן יִשְׁעֶךָ
וַעֲנֹתְךָ תַּרְבֵּנִי׃
37 תַּרְחִיב צַעֲדִי תַּחְתֵּנִי

v. 30. יתיר ה׳

And my feet have not slipped.
38I pursued my enemies and wiped them out,
I did not turn back till I destroyed them.
39I destroyed them, I struck them down;
They rose no more, they lay at my feet.
40You have girt me with strength for battle,
Brought low my foes before me,
41Made my enemies turn tail before me,
My foes—and I wiped them out.
42They looked, but there was none to deliver;
To the LORD, but He answered them not.
43I pounded them like dust of the earth,
Stamped, crushed them like dirt of the streets.
44You have rescued me from the strife of peoples,
Kept me to be a ruler of nations;
Peoples I knew not must serve me.
45Aliens have cringed before me,
Paid me homage at the mere report of me.
46Aliens have lost courage
And come trembling out of their fastnesses.

47The LORD lives! Blessed is my rock!
Exalted be God, the rock
Who gives me victory;
48The God who has vindicated me
And made peoples subject to me,
49Rescued me from my enemies,
Raised me clear of my foes,
Saved me from lawless men!
50For this I sing Your praise among the nations
And hymn Your name:

וְלֹא מָעֲדוּ קַרְסֻלָּי׃
38 אֶרְדְּפָה אֹיְבַי וָאַשְׁמִידֵם
וְלֹא אָשׁוּב עַד־כַּלּוֹתָם׃
39 וָאֲכַלֵּם וָאֶמְחָצֵם
וְלֹא יְקוּמוּן וַיִּפְּלוּ תַּחַת רַגְלָי׃
40 וַתַּזְרֵנִי* חַיִל לַמִּלְחָמָה
תַּכְרִיעַ קָמַי תַּחְתֵּנִי׃
41 וְאֹיְבַי תַּתָּה לִּי עֹרֶף
מְשַׂנְאַי וָאַצְמִיתֵם׃
42 יִשְׁעוּ וְאֵין מֹשִׁיעַ
אֶל־יְהוָה וְלֹא עָנָם׃
43 וְאֶשְׁחָקֵם כַּעֲפַר־אָרֶץ
כְּטִיט־חוּצוֹת אֲדִקֵּם אֶרְקָעֵם׃
44 וַתְּפַלְּטֵנִי מֵרִיבֵי עַמִּי*
תִּשְׁמְרֵנִי לְרֹאשׁ גּוֹיִם
עַם לֹא־יָדַעְתִּי יַעַבְדֻנִי׃
45 בְּנֵי נֵכָר יִתְכַּחֲשׁוּ־לִי
לִשְׁמוֹעַ אֹזֶן יִשָּׁמְעוּ לִי׃
46 בְּנֵי נֵכָר יִבֹּלוּ
וְיַחְגְּרוּ מִמִּסְגְּרוֹתָם׃

47 חַי־יְהוָה וּבָרוּךְ צוּרִי
וְיָרֻם אֱלֹהֵי צוּר
יִשְׁעִי׃
48 הָאֵל הַנֹּתֵן נְקָמֹת לִי
וּמוֹרִיד עַמִּים תַּחְתֵּנִי׃
49 וּמוֹצִיאִי מֵאֹיְבָי
וּמִקָּמַי תְּרוֹמְמֵנִי
מֵאִישׁ חֲמָסִים תַּצִּילֵנִי׃
50 עַל־כֵּן אוֹדְךָ יְהוָה בַּגּוֹיִם
וּלְשִׁמְךָ אֲזַמֵּר׃

v. 40. חסר א׳

v. 44. סבירין ומטעין "עמים", ובנוסח אחר "עם" וגם בנוסח אחר "עמים"

44. peoples Translated as in some manuscripts and the Septuagint; the Hebrew text above (like most manuscripts and the printed editions) reads "my people" [Transl.].

51 Tower of victory to His king,
Who deals graciously with His anointed,
With David and his offspring evermore.

51 מגדיל מִגְדּוֹל יְשׁוּעוֹת מַלְכּוֹ
וְעֹשֶׂה־חֶסֶד לִמְשִׁיחוֹ
לְדָוִד וּלְזַרְעוֹ עַד־עוֹלָם׃ פ

51. Tower of victory This follows the text as read (*k'rei*): *migdol* (tower). The text as written (*k'tiv*) preserves the word as a verb, *magdil,* in a phrase meaning: "He accords wondrous victories" (as in Ps. 18:51). The image of God as a tower does not occur earlier in the song, although it is not out of keeping with it. Nevertheless, one would expect a verbal form here, matching the next part of the verse, "Who deals graciously."

Both the *k'rei* and the *k'tiv* are preserved liturgically, at the close of the full grace after meals. The latter is recited on weekdays; the former is recited on *Shabbat* and festivals.

deals graciously As promised (2 Sam. 7:15).

V'ZOT HA-B'RAKHAH

33 This is the blessing with which Moses,
the man of God, bade the Israelites farewell be-
fore he died. 2He said:
The LORD came from Sinai;
He shone upon them from Seir;
He appeared from Mount Paran,
And approached from Ribeboth-kodesh,
Lightning flashing at them from His right.
3Lover, indeed, of the people,
Their hallowed are all in Your hand.
They followed in Your steps,
Accepting Your pronouncements,

וזאת הברכה

לג וְזֹאת הַבְּרָכָה אֲשֶׁר בֵּרַךְ מֹשֶׁה
אִישׁ הָאֱלֹהִים אֶת־בְּנֵי יִשְׂרָאֵל לִפְנֵי
מוֹתוֹ׃ 2 וַיֹּאמַר
יְהוָה מִסִּינַי בָּא
וְזָרַח מִשֵּׂעִיר לָמוֹ
הוֹפִיעַ מֵהַר פָּארָן
וְאָתָה מֵרִבְבֹת קֹדֶשׁ
מִימִינוֹ אשדת אֵשׁ דָּת לָמוֹ׃
3 אַף חֹבֵב עַמִּים
כָּל־קְדֹשָׁיו בְּיָדֶךָ
וְהֵם תֻּכּוּ לְרַגְלֶךָ
יִשָּׂא מִדַּבְּרֹתֶיךָ׃

Epilogue: Moses' Last Days (*continued*)

MOSES' FAREWELL BLESSINGS (33:1–29)

INTRODUCTION (v. 1)

1. man of God That is, a prophet. This designation suggests that Moses' remarks about the tribes have the power of prophetic predictions.

bade . . . farewell Literally, "blessed."

THE POEM (vv. 2–29)

2. The LORD came from Sinai God is pictured as coming from the southern wildernesses and mountains (Sinai, Seir-Edom, Teiman, Mount Paran) to aid Israel against its enemies. The places mentioned in the verse are located in the Sinai Peninsula and in the Negeb.

He shone The Bible depicts God as surrounded by a brilliant radiance. Ancient Near Eastern texts describe deities as enveloped in light.

upon them Upon the people Israel.

approached from Ribeboth-kodesh In the Negeb or Sinai; it may mean "Ribeboth at, or near, Kadesh." Kadesh was located in the wilderness of Paran at the western border of Seir-Edom and the southern border of the Promised Land (see Num. 13:26, 20:14,16, 34:4).

3. Lover . . . of the people Literally, "Lover of peoples." If "Lover" refers to God, and "peoples" refers to all peoples, it is a startling universal note in a poem that otherwise is about His protection of Israel. If "peoples" (or "people," as in the Greek translation) refers to Israel, the phrase is comparable to the description of God as one "who loves His people Israel" (*ohev ammo Yisra·el*) in Jewish liturgy.

Their hallowed Hebrew: *k'doshav;* literally, "its" or "His" hallowed ones. If the last three clauses of v. 3 refer to Israel, then this refers to Israel's holy ones, members of the holy people. God took the Israelites protectively in hand because they followed Him and accepted His authority. If these same clauses refer to God's angelic

---

CHAPTER 33

Moses blesses the tribes before his death, prompting the Midrash to put these words into his mouth: "All my life, I have scolded this people. At the end of my life, let me leave them with a blessing" (Mid. P'tirat Moshe). As Genesis concluded with Jacob on his deathbed, blessing his 12 sons, Deuteronomy concludes with Moses on the eve of his death, blessing the 12 tribes. What was once a single family with a vision of God's plan for them has now become a nation, poised to enter the Promised Land and possessing a blueprint for becoming a special people, a model of how God wants humanity to live.

4When Moses charged us with the Teaching
As the heritage of the congregation of Jacob.
5Then He became King in Jeshurun,
When the heads of the people assembled,
The tribes of Israel together.

6May Reuben live and not die,
Though few be his numbers.

7And this he said of Judah:
Hear, O LORD the voice of Judah
And restore him to his people.
Though his own hands strive for him,
Help him against his foes.

4 תּוֹרָה צִוָּה־לָנוּ מֹשֶׁה
מוֹרָשָׁה קְהִלַּת יַעֲקֹב׃
5 וַיְהִי בִישֻׁרוּן מֶלֶךְ
בְּהִתְאַסֵּף רָאשֵׁי עָם
יַחַד שִׁבְטֵי יִשְׂרָאֵל׃

6 יְחִי רְאוּבֵן וְאַל־יָמֹת
וִיהִי מְתָיו מִסְפָּר׃ ס

7 וְזֹאת לִיהוּדָה וַיֹּאמַר
שְׁמַע יְהוָה קוֹל יְהוּדָה
וְאֶל־עַמּוֹ תְּבִיאֶנּוּ
יָדָיו רָב לוֹ
וְעֵזֶר מִצָּרָיו תִּהְיֶה׃ ס
שני

entourage, then the hallowed ones, or holy beings, are the angels who accompany Him as He comes to Israel's aid (see Zech. 14:5).

4. According to some medieval commentators, it is the people who are speaking in this verse. Having accepted God's pronouncements in verse 3, the people declare: "This Teaching with which Moses charged us is the heritage of the congregation of Jacob."

Teaching In Deuteronomy, *torah* refers specifically to the teachings of Deuteronomy. However, because this poem probably originated independently of Deuteronomy and was appended to it at a later time, the term may not have so precise a reference here and may be a general allusion to sacred Teaching.

heritage Hebrew: *morashah;* literally, property (particularly land) transmitted by inheritance. Here, a metaphor for a spiritual possession, connoting something vital and cherished.

5. God became Israel's king after coming to it from the south and delivering it from its enemies. As in the coronation of a human king, it is the acclamation of people or their leaders that legitimates the king's sovereignty.

Jeshurun See Comment to 32:15.

THE TRIBAL BLESSINGS (vv. 6–25)

Moses now blesses the tribes individually. He begins with Reuben, in whose territory the Israelites are presently encamped.

REUBEN (v. 6)

6. The tribe of Reuben was allotted territory in Transjordan (see 3:12–17; Num. 32). It once was a strong tribe, leader of the others, as implied by Reuben's status as Jacob's firstborn son. Its preeminence must have ended before settlement in the Promised Land or soon afterward, because it later became a tribe of marginal importance.

JUDAH (v. 7)

7. The tribe of Judah at first dominated the southern part of the Land. In the days of David and Solomon it dominated the entire country. Its territory was centered in the southern highlands, reaching the Dead Sea on the east and including the Shephelah on the west and the Negeb on the south. The blessing anticipates a time when the tribe will be at war.

Judah . . . his own hands Hebrew: *Y'hudah . . . yadav*; in biblical times, these were probably pronounced more alike: *Yahuda . . . yadayu.* Thus the blessing plays on the name.

Hear, O LORD, the voice of Judah Onkelos aptly paraphrases: "Accept, O LORD, the prayer of Judah when he goes forth in battle."

restore him Onkelos paraphrases: "bring him back safely."

to his people That is, bring the tribe's warriors home safely from battle.

Though his own hands strive for him Precise translation of this clause is uncertain.

---

4. Traditionally, this is one of the first verses from the Torah a Jewish child is taught.

8And of Levi he said:
Let Your Thummim and Urim
Be with Your faithful one,
Whom You tested at Massah,
Challenged at the waters of Meribah;
9Who said of his father and mother,
"I consider them not."
His brothers he disregarded,
Ignored his own children.
Your precepts alone they observed,
And kept Your covenant.
10They shall teach Your laws to Jacob
And Your instructions to Israel.
They shall offer You incense to savor
And whole-offerings on Your altar.
11Bless, O LORD, his substance,

שני 8 וּלְלֵוִ֣י אָמַ֔ר
תֻּמֶּ֥יךָ וְאוּרֶ֖יךָ
לְאִ֣ישׁ חֲסִידֶ֑ךָ
אֲשֶׁ֤ר נִסִּיתוֹ֙ בְּמַסָּ֔ה
תְּרִיבֵ֖הוּ עַל־מֵ֥י מְרִיבָֽה׃
9 הָאֹמֵ֞ר לְאָבִ֤יו וּלְאִמּוֹ֙
לֹ֣א רְאִיתִ֔יו
וְאֶת־אֶחָיו֙ לֹ֣א הִכִּ֔יר
וְאֶת־בנו בָּנָ֖יו לֹ֣א יָדָ֑ע
כִּ֤י שָֽׁמְרוּ֙ אִמְרָתֶ֔ךָ
וּבְרִיתְךָ֖ יִנְצֹֽרוּ׃
10 יוֹר֤וּ מִשְׁפָּטֶ֙יךָ֙ לְיַעֲקֹ֔ב
וְתוֹרָתְךָ֖ לְיִשְׂרָאֵ֑ל
יָשִׂ֤ימוּ קְטוֹרָה֙ בְּאַפֶּ֔ךָ
וְכָלִ֖יל עַל־מִזְבְּחֶֽךָ׃
11 בָּרֵ֤ךְ יְהוָה֙ חֵיל֔וֹ

LEVI (vv. 8–11)

8. Moses prays that the Levites enjoy the privilege of serving as Israel's priests, and that God grant them prosperity and protection.

Thummim and Urim This reverse order of the terms is found only here. They were an oracular device for obtaining God's decision on important questions. They were kept by the priest who administered them on behalf of the leader or the public for such matters as military decisions, allocation of land, and identifying those chosen by God for an office or convicted by Him of an offense (see Exod. 28:30; 1 Sam. 14:41).

faithful one Hebrew: *ḥasid,* originally meaning "devoted" or "loyal." Here, the Levites are personified as a single individual.

tested... Challenged This seems to be about an occasion when the Levites or their representative(s) remained loyal to God and were rewarded with the priesthood. But in none of the incidents at Massah and Meribah (Exod. 17; Num. 20) does God test the Levites; it is the people who test Moses, Aaron, and God. Apparently, this verse refers to an unknown incident at Massah and Meribah or to a different version from what is related in Exodus and Numbers.

9. By loyally carrying out God's laws, the Levites showed no favoritism even to their own families (see Exod. 32:27–29).

10. laws . . . instructions Refers to the full range of priestly instruction in ritual, judicial, and civil matters, such as worship, division of territory, and distinctions between sacred and profane, pure and impure. Because of the devotion they showed to God's precepts, the Levites shall have the privilege of transmitting His laws to the Israelites as well as conducting His worship.

incense . . . whole-offerings Two of the regular components of the sacrificial service. Only the priests could offer them.

savor The pleasing aroma rises from the incense offerings of spices burned in the sanctuary as part of the daily morning and evening sacrifices and on *Yom Kippur,* as well as in propitiatory rites.

11. substance Wealth. Although the Levites are not given a tribal territory, they receive income in return for their priestly services; and they are given cities, real estate, fields, pastureland, and cattle. Potentially their wealth is considerable.

---

8. The qualities of zeal that led Jacob to condemn Levi (Gen. 49:5) have been sublimated to the service of God and God's altar, so that Moses now can bless the Levites.

And favor his undertakings.
Smite the loins of his foes;
Let his enemies rise no more.

12Of Benjamin he said:
Beloved of the LORD,
He rests securely beside Him;
Ever does He protect him,
As he rests between His shoulders.

13And of Joseph he said:
Blessed of the LORD be his land
With the bounty of dew from heaven,
And of the deep that couches below;
14With the bounteous yield of the sun,
And the bounteous crop of the moons;
15With the best from the ancient mountains,

וּפֹ֥עַל יָדָ֖יו תִּרְצֶ֑ה
מְחַ֨ץ מָתְנַ֧יִם קָמָ֛יו
וּמְשַׂנְאָ֖יו מִן־יְקוּמֽוּן׃ ס

12 לְבִנְיָמִ֣ן אָמַ֔ר
יְדִ֣יד יְהוָ֔ה
יִשְׁכֹּ֥ן לָבֶ֖טַח עָלָ֑יו
חֹפֵ֤ף עָלָיו֙ כָּל־הַיּ֔וֹם
וּבֵ֥ין כְּתֵפָ֖יו שָׁכֵֽן׃ ס

שלישי 13 וּלְיוֹסֵ֣ף אָמַ֔ר
מְבֹרֶ֥כֶת יְהוָ֖ה אַרְצ֑וֹ
מִמֶּ֤גֶד שָׁמַ֙יִם֙ מִטָּ֔ל
וּמִתְּה֖וֹם רֹבֶ֥צֶת תָּֽחַת׃
14 וּמִמֶּ֖גֶד תְּבוּאֹ֣ת שָׁ֑מֶשׁ
וּמִמֶּ֖גֶד גֶּ֥רֶשׁ יְרָחִֽים׃
15 וּמֵרֹ֖אשׁ הַרְרֵי־קֶ֑דֶם

favor his undertakings That is, grant him prosperity.

Smite the loins Render them powerless. The loins are used as an image for one's strength.

Let his enemies rise no more Moses does not ask God to grant the Levites military prowess but to defend them against attackers. As a clerical tribe, the Levites had no military force; and unlike the other tribes, they were defenseless against military attacks.

BENJAMIN (v. 12)

12. The tribe of Benjamin occupied a small but strategic territory between the lands of Ephraim and Judah and at one time encompassed, on its southern border, at least part of Jerusalem.

Beloved of the LORD If this means that God favored Benjamin politically, it could reflect the tribe's prestige when Ehud the Benjaminite was chieftain over all the Israelites during the period of the Judges, when Samuel's leadership was centered in Benjaminite territory, and when the Benjaminite Saul was chosen to be Israel's first king.

securely That is, in its territory.

He protect The subject of the verse has abruptly changed to God.

as he rests between His shoulders The verse seems to be once again referring to Benjamin, reflecting the sense of security the tribe enjoys under divine protection. It seems preferable, however, to take God as the subject, and this may refer to God's dwelling in His sanctuary within Benjamin's borders.

JOSEPH (vv. 13–17)

13. The tribes of Ephraim and Manasseh are personified in their ancestor Joseph. Historically, Ephraim, occupying the southern part of the central highlands, was the more prominent of the two, although its territory was smaller. Part of Manasseh occupied the northern part of the central highlands, and another part inhabited Bashan and Gilead in Transjordan.

bounty Hebrew: *meged,* which is the leitmotif of this blessing, has the sense of "gift," "blessing," "precious objects," and "choice fruits."

the deep that couches below Subterranean waters that rise from springs and wells (8:7) are pictured here as an animal crouching below the earth.

14. yield of the sun These are crops warmed and lighted by the sun.

crop of the moons If the plural "moons" refers to months, as it usually does, the text means "the bounteous crops of the months," referring to the different months in which various crops ripen.

15. The abundant products of the mountains, mentioned frequently in ancient Near East-

And the bounty of hills immemorial;
16With the bounty of earth and its fullness,
And the favor of the Presence in the Bush.
May these rest on the head of Joseph,
On the crown of the elect of his brothers.
17Like a firstling bull in his majesty,
He has horns like the horns of the wild-ox;
With them he gores the peoples,
The ends of the earth one and all.
These are the myriads of Ephraim,
Those are the thousands of Manasseh.

18And of Zebulun he said:
Rejoice, O Zebulun, on your journeys,

וּמִמֶּגֶד גִּבְעוֹת עוֹלָם׃
16 וּמִמֶּגֶד אֶרֶץ וּמְלֹאָהּ
וּרְצוֹן שֹׁכְנִי סְנֶה
תָּבוֹאתָה לְרֹאשׁ יוֹסֵף
וּלְקָדְקֹד נְזִיר אֶחָיו׃
17 בְּכוֹר שׁוֹרוֹ הָדָר לוֹ
וְקַרְנֵי רְאֵם קַרְנָיו
בָּהֶם עַמִּים יְנַגַּח
יַחְדָּו אַפְסֵי־אָרֶץ
וְהֵם רִבְבוֹת אֶפְרַיִם
וְהֵם אַלְפֵי מְנַשֶּׁה׃ ס

רביעי 18 וְלִזְבוּלֻן אָמַר
שְׂמַח זְבוּלֻן בְּצֵאתֶךָ

ern literature, include wood, stone, precious and nonprecious metals, and foodstuffs. The mountain regions in the territory of the Joseph tribes were richly forested when the tribes first arrived. Later, land was cleared for planting grains, olive trees, and vineyards. The highlands of Bashan and Gilead, where half of Manasseh lived, were also rich in forests and pastures. Their balm, a fragrant resin used for soothing pain or for healing, was famous.

bounty of hills immemorial Joseph enjoys fertility like that of those fruitful ancient hills.

16. the favor of the Presence in the Bush That is, God's favor, in the sense of blessing. This is the climactic blessing and the ultimate source of the others. By calling God "the Presence in the Bush" (*shokhni s'neh*) in this, his final speech, Moses recalls his first encounter with God at the burning bush at Horeb, the mountain of God (see Exod. 3:1–6).

On the crown of the elect of his brothers That is, on the head of the chief brother, Joseph. This depiction accords with the position of Joseph as ruler of his brothers in Egypt and with the preeminent status of the Joseph tribes, particularly Ephraim, after the conquest of the Promised Land.

elect From the root נזר, which presumably means "to separate" or "to single out."

17. firstling Ibn Ezra suggests that the firstling is mentioned here to convey an image of great strength.

horns of the wild-ox The wild ox goring its foes is a common metaphor for strength in ancient Near Eastern literature.

ends of the earth The most distant enemies.

These . . . Those Better: "Those [horns] . . . they." Joseph's horns stand for the troops of Ephraim and Manasseh.

ZEBULUN AND ISSACHAR (vv. 18–19)

18. The heading names only Zebulun, but the blessing includes Issachar as well, reflecting the close association between these tribes, who were assigned neighboring inland territories in the lower Galilee and the Jezreel Valley. Genesis 49:13 locates Zebulun on the coast and implies that it once controlled territory as far west as the Mediterranean in the Haifa Bay area.

journeys In view of its onetime coastal loca-

---

18. The tribes of Issachar and Zebulun are joined in a single verse. Rashi (based on the *Tanḥuma*) cites the tradition that the people of the tribe of Zebulun were merchants ("Rejoice . . . on your journeys") whose prosperity subsidized the tribe of Issachar, enabling them to stay home and study Torah ("in your tents"). Maimonides rejects that model in an unusually sharp comment: "Whoever deliberately sets out to devote himself to the Torah and not work for a living but be dependent on charity has thereby desecrated the divine name, brought the Torah into disrepute, extinguished the light of religion, brought evil upon himself, and forfeited the hereafter" (MT Torah Study 3:10).

And Issachar, in your tents.
19They invite their kin to the mountain,
Where they offer sacrifices of success.
For they draw from the riches of the sea
And the hidden hoards of the sand.

20And of Gad he said:
Blessed be He who enlarges Gad!
Poised is he like a lion
To tear off arm and scalp.
21He chose for himself the best,
For there is the portion of the revered chieftain,
Where the heads of the people come.
He executed the LORD's judgments
And His decisions for Israel.

וְיִשָּׂשכָר בְּאֹהָלֶיךָ׃
19 עַמִּים הַר־יִקְרָאוּ
שָׁם יִזְבְּחוּ זִבְחֵי־צֶדֶק
כִּי שֶׁפַע יַמִּים יִינָקוּ
וּשְׂפֻנֵי טְמוּנֵי חוֹל׃ ס

20 וּלְגָד אָמַר
בָּרוּךְ מַרְחִיב גָּד
כְּלָבִיא שָׁכֵן
וְטָרַף זְרוֹעַ אַף־קָדְקֹד׃
21 וַיַּרְא רֵאשִׁית לוֹ
כִּי־שָׁם חֶלְקַת מְחֹקֵק סָפוּן
וַיֵּתֵא רָאשֵׁי עָם
צִדְקַת יְהוָה עָשָׂה
מישי וּמִשְׁפָּטָיו עִם־יִשְׂרָאֵל׃ ס

tion, Zebulun's journeys are most likely maritime trade ventures or fishing excursions.

tents Likely the dwellings of herdsmen (see Gen. 49:14).

19. their kin Literally, "peoples," with no pronoun. The verse could mean that the two tribes invite their own kin (fellow Israelites) or members of some other kinship group, i.e., other peoples. Zebulun's maritime location would have brought it into contact with Phoenicians, Egyptians, and others from Mediterranean islands and coastlands.

to the mountain The reference to sacrifices in the next clause suggests that the mountain is one with a sanctuary. It could be Mount Tabor, which was the juncture of the territories of Zebulun, Issachar, and Naphtali, or Mount Carmel above the Mediterranean coast.

sacrifices of success Zebulun and Issachar will invite others to join them in thanking God for their maritime wealth or to participate in combined sacrificial festivals and fairs at which maritime goods will be traded.

riches of the sea Riches drawn from the sea and/or imported by sea, including fish, shells, and murex snails. Only Zebulun is connected to the seacoast in Gen. 49:13. Perhaps members of Issachar worked for Zebulun in maritime commerce, or Issachar profited from the resources of Lake Tiberias, which was not far from its territory. Shells were used for lamps, vessels, and ornaments. Murex snails were the source of the reddish and purple dyes that gave the coast north of Acco its ancient name, "Phoenicia" (literally, "land of the purple dye"), related to Greek *phoinix* (purple, crimson).

hoards of the sand Literally, "things concealed in sand." Perhaps shells and murex snails that wash up from the sea.

GAD (vv. 20–21)

20. enlarges Gad By increasing its population.

Poised is he like a lion An image of the strength and prowess of a warrior.

21. best Hebrew: *reishit;* literally, "the first," in the sense of prime, best. Refers to Gad's choice of fertile pasturelands in Transjordan as its territory. The clause could also mean that Gad chose the first-conquered portion of land.

portion of the revered chieftain Several ancient translations and medieval commentators understood the *m'ḥokek* (chieftain) to be Moses, so that this phrase refers to his burial plot in Transjordan. To others, this phrase refers to land "worthy" of a chieftain, or to "[Gad's] portion from the lawgiver," i.e., as assigned by Moses.

Where the heads of the people come The Septuagint reflects a different Hebrew text, which combines and reverses two words so as to read: "when they [the heads of the people] gathered." This could allude to when the Gadites and Reubenites presented their special request for territory to Moses and the assembled chieftains of the community (see Num. 32:2,28).

He executed the LORD's judgments / And His

22 And of Dan he said:
Dan is a lion's whelp
That leaps forth from Bashan.

23 And of Naphtali he said:
O Naphtali, sated with favor
And full of the LORD's blessing,
Take possession on the west and south.

24 And of Asher he said:
Most blessed of sons be Asher;
May he be the favorite of his brothers,
May he dip his foot in oil.
25 May your doorbolts be iron and copper,
And your security last all your days.

26 O Jeshurun, there is none like God,

חמישי 22 וּלְדָ֣ן אָמַ֔ר
דָּ֖ן גּ֣וּר אַרְיֵ֑ה
יְזַנֵּ֖ק מִן־הַבָּשָֽׁן׃

23 וּלְנַפְתָּלִ֣י אָמַ֔ר
נַפְתָּלִי֙ שְׂבַ֣ע רָצ֔וֹן
וּמָלֵ֖א בִּרְכַּ֣ת יְהוָ֑ה
יָ֥ם וְדָר֖וֹם יְרָֽשָׁה׃ ס

24 וּלְאָשֵׁ֣ר אָמַ֔ר
בָּר֥וּךְ מִבָּנִ֖ים אָשֵׁ֑ר
יְהִ֤י רְצוּי֙ אֶחָ֔יו
וְטֹבֵ֥ל בַּשֶּׁ֖מֶן רַגְלֽוֹ׃
25 בַּרְזֶ֥ל וּנְחֹ֖שֶׁת מִנְעָלֶ֑ךָ
וּכְיָמֶ֖יךָ דָּבְאֶֽךָ׃

26 אֵ֥ין כָּאֵ֖ל יְשֻׁר֑וּן

decisions for Israel Some explain these words as a statement that Gad fulfilled its promise to fight in the vanguard of Israelite troops for the conquest of the Promised Land. Others believe that it refers to Moses, either as the leader who taught and enforced God's laws, or as God's agent during the period of the Exodus and the conquest of northern Transjordan.

DAN (v. 22)

22. Dan was originally assigned territory in the Shephelah and the coastal plain, near Philistia. This verse anticipates Dan's later location, after it migrated to the northern extremity of the land, where it conquered the Canaanite city of Laish, settled in it, and renamed it Dan (see Judg. 18).

lion's whelp The simile is used of the powerful tribe of Judah in Gen. 49:9.

Bashan The mountain range in northern Transjordan, assigned to Manasseh (3:13–14). This phrase is part of the metaphor; the lion leaps from Bashan. (Dan did not control Bashan or attack Laish from there.)

NAPHTALI (v. 23)

23. The territory of Naphtali in the upper Galilee was well watered and rich in woods, fruit trees, and many varieties of vegetation. It included the luxuriant western and southern shores of Lake Tiberias.

with favor That is, with God's favor.

on the west and south On the western and southern shores of Lake Tiberias.

ASHER (vv. 24–25)

24. Asher, situated in the rich hills of upper Galilee, between Naphtali and the Mediterranean, is blessed with fertility and security. But it needed strong defenses: An international road traversed its territory and was used as an invasion route by hostile peoples from the north and the northeast.

Most blessed The focus on Asher's blessedness was probably inspired by its name, which is connected in Gen. 30:13 with "good fortune" (אשר).

favorite The most blessed.

May he dip his foot in oil The highlands of Galilee were famous for abundant olive oil.

25. doorbolts The bolts on city gates.

copper See Comment to Exod. 25:3. This phrase likely means: "May your land be as secure as if it were locked with bolts of iron or bronze."

CODA (vv. 26–29)

Having blessed the tribes individually, Moses concludes by celebrating the good fortune of all Israel under the protection of God.

26. Describing God as the incomparable protector of Israel, this verse resumes the theme of verses 2–5.

Riding through the heavens to help you,
Through the skies in His majesty.
27 The ancient God is a refuge,
A support are the arms everlasting.
He drove out the enemy before you
By His command: Destroy!
28 Thus Israel dwells in safety,
Untroubled is Jacob's abode,
In a land of grain and wine,
Under heavens dripping dew.
29 O happy Israel! Who is like you,
A people delivered by the Lord,
Your protecting Shield, your Sword triumphant!
Your enemies shall come cringing before you,
And you shall tread on their backs.

רֹכֵ֤ב שָׁמַ֙יִם֙ בְּעֶזְרֶ֔ךָ
וּבְגַאֲוָת֖וֹ שְׁחָקִֽים׃
ששי 27 מְעֹנָה֙ אֱלֹ֣הֵי קֶ֔דֶם
וּמִתַּ֖חַת זְרֹעֹ֣ת עוֹלָ֑ם
וַיְגָ֧רֶשׁ מִפָּנֶ֛יךָ אוֹיֵ֖ב
וַיֹּ֖אמֶר הַשְׁמֵֽד׃
28 וַיִּשְׁכֹּן֩ יִשְׂרָאֵ֨ל בֶּ֜טַח
בָּדָד֙ עֵ֣ין יַעֲקֹ֔ב
אֶל־אֶ֖רֶץ דָּגָ֣ן וְתִיר֑וֹשׁ
אַף־שָׁמָ֖יו יַ֥עַרְפוּ טָֽל׃
29 אַשְׁרֶ֨יךָ יִשְׂרָאֵ֜ל מִ֣י כָמ֗וֹךָ
עַ֚ם נוֹשַׁ֣ע בַּֽיהוָ֔ה
מָגֵ֣ן עֶזְרֶ֔ךָ וַאֲשֶׁר־חֶ֖רֶב גַּאֲוָתֶ֑ךָ
וְיִכָּחֲשׁ֤וּ אֹיְבֶ֙יךָ֙ לָ֔ךְ
וְאַתָּ֖ה עַל־בָּמוֹתֵ֥ימוֹ תִדְרֹֽךְ׃ ס

Jeshurun See 33:5 and Comment to 32:15.

Riding through the heavens to help you A number of biblical passages describe God as riding to Israel's aid. The means of transport is said to be a cherub, cloud, wind, or horse-drawn chariot. The identical motif appears in Babylonian and Canaanite literature, particularly with reference to storm gods, whose power is associated with prowess in warfare. It was natural for the Bible to adopt such imagery, for God incorporates the powers of all non-Israelite deities. Also, geography made Israel entirely dependent on rain for sustenance; thus natural phenomena associated with rain became part of the domain of God's providence (see 11:10–21; Ps. 29).

27. The ancient God Hebrew: *elohei kedem.* It is consistent with descriptions of God as being "from everlasting" and as acting in primordial times (see Gen. 21:33; Ps. 74:12).

refuge Literally, "dwelling."

A support Literally, "underneath," meaning "beneath you." God's arms are Israel's "underpinnings"; He carries Israel protectively on His arms.

arms everlasting Better: "arms of the Eternal." The Hebrew word *olam* is probably short for *el olam,* "everlasting God." The name is very old: "El the eternal one" is mentioned in a Canaanite inscription of about the 15th century B.C.E. from the Sinai.

By His command: Destroy! The previous clause describes God's role in the defeat of the Canaanites; this one refers to Israel's role. Some scholars regard the clause as synonymous with the previous one and translate, by means of emendation: "and the Amorites He destroyed."

28. Once the enemy was defeated, Israel enjoyed security and prosperity in the Promised Land.

29. happy Literally, "fortunate are you."

Who is like you The declaration, normally addressed to God, is here applied to Israel: The people of the incomparable God (v. 26) enjoys incomparable protection. Israel's uniqueness in enjoying God's protection is also mentioned in 4:7.

Your protecting Shield A metaphor often applied to God.

You shall tread on their backs The image of a victor's foot on the back of a defeated foe—a ceremonial gesture of triumph—appears elsewhere in the Bible and in other ancient Near Eastern literature as well as in ancient art.

28. Untroubled Hebrew: *badad;* literally, "alone." Untroubled by foreign aggressors (BT Sanh. 104a). Without entangling foreign alliances; free to live openly in villages—not needing to crowd into walled cities for security (Rashi).

34 Moses went up from the steppes of
Moab to Mount Nebo, to the summit of Pisgah,
opposite Jericho, and the LORD showed him the
whole land: Gilead as far as Dan; 2 all Naphtali;
the land of Ephraim and Manasseh; the whole
land of Judah as far as the Western Sea; 3 the
Negeb; and the Plain—the Valley of Jericho, the
city of palm trees—as far as Zoar. 4 And the LORD
said to him, "This is the land of which I swore
to Abraham, Isaac, and Jacob, 'I will assign it
to your offspring.' I have let you see it with your
own eyes, but you shall not cross there."
5 So Moses the servant of the LORD died there,

לד וַיַּעַל מֹשֶׁה מֵעַרְבֹת מוֹאָב אֶל־
הַר נְבוֹ רֹאשׁ הַפִּסְגָּה אֲשֶׁר עַל־פְּנֵי יְרֵחוֹ
וַיַּרְאֵהוּ יְהוָה אֶת־כָּל־הָאָרֶץ אֶת־הַגִּלְעָד
עַד־דָּן׃ 2 וְאֵת כָּל־נַפְתָּלִי וְאֶת־אֶרֶץ
אֶפְרַיִם וּמְנַשֶּׁה וְאֵת כָּל־אֶרֶץ יְהוּדָה עַד
הַיָּם הָאַחֲרוֹן׃ 3 וְאֶת־הַנֶּגֶב וְאֶת־הַכִּכָּר
בִּקְעַת יְרֵחוֹ עִיר הַתְּמָרִים עַד־צֹעַר׃
4 וַיֹּאמֶר יְהוָה אֵלָיו זֹאת הָאָרֶץ אֲשֶׁר
נִשְׁבַּעְתִּי לְאַבְרָהָם לְיִצְחָק וּלְיַעֲקֹב לֵאמֹר
לְזַרְעֲךָ אֶתְּנֶנָּה הֶרְאִיתִיךָ בְעֵינֶיךָ וְשָׁמָּה
לֹא תַעֲבֹר׃
5 וַיָּמָת שָׁם מֹשֶׁה עֶבֶד־יְהוָה בְּאֶרֶץ מוֹאָב

THE DEATH OF MOSES (34:1–12)

1. Moses went up As commanded in 32:49, and earlier in 3:27.

steppes of Moab The eastern part of the lower Jordan Valley, just north of the Dead Sea. This plain extends about 9 miles (14 km) from north to south, and 5 to 7 miles (8–11 km) from the river to the mountains of Moab. This is the plain where the Israelites were encamped while Moses addressed them.

Mount Nebo God shows Moses Israel's future territory from Mount Nebo. Standing atop the mount, Moses would have been able to see: the Gilead range in the north and Dan, to the northwest, about 100 miles (160 km) away; Israel's western boundary, the Mediterranean, about 65 miles (100 km) away; and to the south and southeast, the Negeb and the plain of the Jordan down to Zoar, some 50 miles (80 km) away.

Pisgah A mountain, or mountain chain, in Moab overlooking the southern end of the Jordan Valley and commanding a view of the Promised Land across the Jordan.

opposite Jericho East of Jericho.

Gilead The Transjordanian hill country captured from Sihon and Og.

Gilead as far as Dan Meaning "and beyond Gilead as far as Dan." Gilead itself does not reach as far as Dan, which is the city of the Danites at the northern end of the Galilee, at the foot of Mount Hermon.

2. Naphtali In upper Galilee, north and northwest of Lake Tiberias.

Western Sea The Mediterranean.

3. Negeb The northern part of today's Negeb.

the Plain That is, of the Jordan, probably the entire Jordan Valley and, apparently, the Dead Sea and Lake Tiberias.

city of palm trees Jericho, the first city conquered by the Israelites in the Promised Land, was celebrated for its palms. Despite its desert location and climate, abundant sources of water give it the luxuriant appearance of an oasis to this day.

as far as Zoar The Plain extended as far south as Zoar, which probably was located south or southeast of the Dead Sea, where there was a city called Zoar in Second Temple and Rabbinic times. It may, therefore, stand here for the southern tip of the Dead Sea, which is the southeastern limit of the Promised Land according to Num. 34:3 and Josh. 15:2.

4. but you shall not cross there God decreed this in 1:37, and reminded Moses of it on several occasions (see 3:27, 4:21–22, 32:52; Num. 20:12).

5. Biblical tradition assumes that Moses died early in the 12th month, the month later called *Adar*. Postbiblical tradition fixes the date on the 7th day of that month.

servant of the LORD Hebrew: *eved YHVH,* a title meaning "the LORD's minister." Moses was God's representative and agent in governing Israel. As a title for top officials in the Bible and in ancient Near Eastern inscriptions, *"eved"* connotes high status and implies that its bearer is loyal, trusted, and closely associated with his master.

in the land of Moab, at the command of the
LORD. 6He buried him in the valley in the land
of Moab, near Beth-peor; and no one knows his
burial place to this day. 7Moses was a hundred
and twenty years old when he died; his eyes were
undimmed and his vigor unabated. 8And the
Israelites bewailed Moses in the steppes of Moab
for thirty days.

The period of wailing and mourning for Moses came to an end. 9Now Joshua son of Nun
was filled with the spirit of wisdom because Moses had laid his hands upon him; and the Israelites heeded him, doing as the LORD had commanded Moses.

עַל־פִּי יְהוָה׃ 6 וַיִּקְבֹּר אֹתוֹ בַגַּי בְּאֶרֶץ
מוֹאָב מוּל בֵּית פְּעוֹר וְלֹא־יָדַע אִישׁ
אֶת־קְבֻרָתוֹ עַד הַיּוֹם הַזֶּה׃ 7 וּמֹשֶׁה בֶּן־
מֵאָה וְעֶשְׂרִים שָׁנָה בְּמֹתוֹ לֹא־כָהֲתָה
עֵינוֹ וְלֹא־נָס לֵחֹה׃ 8 וַיִּבְכּוּ בְנֵי יִשְׂרָאֵל
אֶת־מֹשֶׁה בְּעַרְבֹת מוֹאָב שְׁלֹשִׁים יוֹם
וַיִּתְּמוּ יְמֵי בְכִי אֵבֶל מֹשֶׁה׃ 9 וִיהוֹשֻׁעַ
בִּן־נוּן מָלֵא רוּחַ חָכְמָה כִּי־סָמַךְ מֹשֶׁה
אֶת־יָדָיו עָלָיו וַיִּשְׁמְעוּ אֵלָיו בְּנֵי־יִשְׂרָאֵל
וַיַּעֲשׂוּ כַּאֲשֶׁר צִוָּה יְהוָה אֶת־מֹשֶׁה׃

at the command of the LORD Moses died not of old age or illness but at God's command.

6. in the valley The valley below Mount Nebo where Israel was then encamped.

no one knows his burial place Because God buried him. Many commentators have conjectured that the gravesite of Moses was concealed to prevent people from turning it into a shrine and using it as a location for a cult of Moses worship.

7. hundred and twenty years Moses died 40 years after the Exodus, which took place when he was 80 (Exod. 7:7).

eyes were undimmed Biblical and other ancient Near Eastern texts commonly describe the eyesight and other faculties of the aged as a measure of health or frailty.

his vigor unabated Literally, "his moisture had not departed," or "dried up." Ibn Ezra understood this to mean "he had not become wrinkled." Moses' vigor had, in fact, abated (31:2), but despite his years he did not have the appearance of someone very old.

THE PEOPLE'S MOURNING AND JOSHUA'S SUCCESSION TO LEADERSHIP (vv. 8–9)

8. thirty days See Comment to 21:13.

9. was filled with the spirit of wisdom A divine gift of wisdom to govern Israel.

laid his hands upon him A rite of investiture (see Num. 27:18,23).

the Israelites heeded him From then on, the people obeyed Joshua.

CHAPTER 34

5. at the command of the LORD Literally, "by the mouth of the LORD." God reclaimed his soul by kissing him (BT MK 28a). God, who breathed life into Adam in the first chapter of the Torah, reclaims Moses' life lovingly and painlessly in the Torah's last chapter.

6. Does Moses die unfulfilled, deprived of the opportunity to enter the Land? His life is like those of many people, with soaring triumphs and bitter disappointments, public acclaim and private bitterness. But Moses dies physically healthy, "his vigor unabated," close to his God and honored by the people he shaped and led. "Moses, the most solitary and most powerful hero in Biblical history. The immensity of his task and the scope of his experience command our admiration, our reverence, our awe. . . . His passion for social justice, his struggle for national liberation, his triumphs and his disappointments, his poetic inspiration, his gifts as a strategist and his organizational genius, his complex relationship with God and with God's people, his condemnations and his blessings, his bursts of anger, his silences, his efforts to reconcile the law with compassion, authority with integrity—no individual ever, anywhere, accomplished so much for so many people in so many different domains. *Moshe Rabbeinu,* our Master Moses, incomparable, unequaled" (Wiesel).

HALAKHAH L'MA·ASEH

34:8. thirty days See Comment to Num. 20:29.

10 Never again did there arise in Israel a
prophet like Moses—whom the LORD singled
out, face to face, 11 for the various signs and portents that the LORD sent him to display in the
land of Egypt, against Pharaoh and all his courtiers and his whole country, 12 and for all the great
might and awesome power that Moses displayed before all Israel.

10 וְלֹא־קָם נָבִיא עוֹד בְּיִשְׂרָאֵל כְּמֹשֶׁה
אֲשֶׁר יְדָעוֹ יְהוָה פָּנִים אֶל־פָּנִים׃ 11 לְכָל־
הָאֹתֹת וְהַמּוֹפְתִים אֲשֶׁר שְׁלָחוֹ יְהוָה
לַעֲשׂוֹת בְּאֶרֶץ מִצְרָיִם לְפַרְעֹה וּלְכָל־
עֲבָדָיו וּלְכָל־אַרְצוֹ׃ 12 וּלְכֹל הַיָּד הַחֲזָקָה
וּלְכֹל הַמּוֹרָא הַגָּדוֹל אֲשֶׁר עָשָׂה מֹשֶׁה
לְעֵינֵי כָּל־יִשְׂרָאֵל׃ **

v. 12. למערבאי סכום הפסוקים של הספר 955 וחציו 17:10

v. 12. סכום הפסוקים של התורה 5,845

EULOGY (vv. 10–12)

10. Never again did there arise The verse contrasts Joshua to Moses: Although Joshua succeeded Moses, neither he nor any subsequent prophet was Moses' equal.

prophet like Moses Although Moses was far more than a prophet, and is never directly called that elsewhere in the Torah, prophecy was one of his roles. Here the term implies that he remains superior to all other prophets.

face to face That God spoke to Moses "face to face" is stated in Exod. 33:11 ("as one man speaks to another"). Here the term is an idiom meaning "in person," "directly," "without mediation." That is, Moses experienced the most direct contact with God of any prophet, and so had the clearest knowledge of Him and His will.

11. various Literally, "all." The number of wonders executed by Moses was unparalleled.

signs and portents Moses was also incomparable in the wonders that God performed through him during the time of the Exodus. No other prophet so convincingly confirmed the credibility of his mission.

the LORD sent him to display The Torah here and elsewhere states that all the wonders Moses performed were by means of God's power and at His command, not through his own personal power or any occult skills. However, the next verse emphasizes Moses' role, because it was through those wonders that he established and proved himself as God's emissary.

12. great might Literally, "mighty hand." This and the "awesome power that Moses displayed" refer to "the various signs and portents" in verse 11.

before all Israel Literally, "in the sight of all Israel." That the Israelites witnessed these wonders is asserted often (e.g., 4:34, 6:22, 29:1–2). The Israelites were, therefore, convinced of the truth revealed by those events: the indisputable authenticity of Moses.

---

12. before all Israel With these words, we complete the reading of the Torah. It began in chaos, and with God imposing order on the chaos. It concludes with a nation of men, women, and children poised on the banks of the Jordan River, ready to begin perhaps the greatest spiritual adventure of all time, the effort to translate God's will into the daily life of a community.

In synagogues, we complete the Torah and proceed in two directions. First we go back to the opening words of Genesis and we begin again, finding new insights on every page, not because the Torah has changed, but because we have changed since we read it a year ago. And then, in the *haftarah* for *Simḥat Torah,* we go forward into history, to read of Joshua's leadership of the people after the death of Moses.

HALAKHAH L'MA·ASEH

34:12. Upon completing the reading of the entire Torah on *Simḥat Torah* with this verse from Deuteronomy, we turn back to the beginning of the Torah and read from the first two chapters of the Book of Genesis to emphasize that the study of Torah is unending. We also indicate the continuity of Jewish tradition by reading the first chapter of the Book of Joshua (the first book in the continuation of the Bible after the Torah) as the *haftarah.* In many synagogues, everyone is called up for an *aliyah* on *Simḥat Torah,* even the children (S.A. O.Ḥ. 669:1,gloss), to symbolize that the Torah is the legacy of the entire people of Israel.

חֲזַק חֲזַק וְנִתְחַזֵּק

תם ונשלם תהילה לאל בורא עולם

הפטרה למחר חודש

HAFTARAH FOR SHABBAT AND EREV ROSH ḤODESH

1 SAMUEL 20:18–42

(*Recite on* Shabbat *if the next day is* Rosh Ḥodesh. *However, on* Shabbat Ḥanukkah, *recite the* haftarah *for that occasion instead. On the 3rd* Shabbat *after* Tish·ah b'Av, *recite the third* Haftarah *of Consolation instead, which begins on page 1085. With* parashat Sh'kalim *or* parashat ha-Ḥodesh, *recite the* haftarah *for those passages instead.*)

This *haftarah* is part of the long cycle of narratives depicting David's rise in national esteem and his corresponding decline in King Saul's favor (ca. 1000 B.C.E.). Saul's jealousy over David's fame as a soldier played a key role, driving the king mad with rage. Earlier, after defeating the Philistines, Saul had returned home with his troops only to hear women singing: "Saul has slain his thousands; David, his tens of thousands" (1 Sam. 18:7). The next day, gripped by an "evil spirit," Saul threw a spear at David "thinking to pin [him] to the wall. But David eluded him twice" (18:10–11).

As the Philistine wars continued, "David was more successful than all the other officers of Saul. His reputation soared" (18:30). In reaction, Saul urged his courtiers to kill his perceived rival. David escaped through the intervention of Saul's son Jonathan (19:1–6). Nevertheless, after David led another round of military successes, another "evil spirit" overtook Saul. Once more he "tried to pin David to the wall with his spear" (19:8–10). Again David escaped. Obsessed, Saul sent messengers to guard David's house, with orders to strike him dead in the morning. But again Saul was thwarted, as Michal (his daughter and David's wife) warned David of the plot and hid his escape (19:11–16). Doubly foiled by his own children, Saul himself set out in hot pursuit of David, accompanied by a band of messengers. David fled to Jonathan and, begging him to explain Saul's rage, enlisted Jonathan's help in a plan to test Saul's true intent. This is the narrative background to the *haftarah*.

The *haftarah* unfolds in three parts: the plan, an event at the royal court, and an event in the field. All elements of the opening part recur in the second and third parts: the absence of David at court during the new moon, the ruse of the arrows in the field, and the covenantal commitment between David and Jonathan.

The story contrasts the established kingship at court with the bond of friendship in the field. Jonathan tries to mediate, because he is both the trusted son of the king and the beloved friend of the hero. His mediation, however, is not symmetrical. For he betrays his father's confidence out of loyalty to David—as King Saul comes to realize during the new moon feast. Jonathan's fate is sealed when he tries to annul Saul's decree that David die. At this point the king takes up his spear against his son.

RELATION OF THE *HAFTARAH* TO THE CALENDAR

This *haftarah* was chosen to be recited on the *Shabbat* that immediately precedes the New Moon (the first day of the Hebrew month), because this scriptural reading contains the very words *maḥar ḥodesh* (Tomorrow will be the new moon) that now designate the day. Moreover, although the Torah designates only the types of sacrificial rites to be performed on the new moon (Num. 10:10, 28:11–15), this *haftarah* indicates that there were also popular gatherings and communal meals on that day. We read that the king sat down to "partake of the meal" (*leḥem,* 1 Sam. 20:24), and that David went to his home town of Bethlehem to participate there in the "family feast" (*zevaḥ mishpaḥah;* v. 29). On the basis of

these references, the custom of having a festive meal on the new moon developed, a practice later codified in the *Shulḥan Arukh* (O.Ḥ. 419:1). From the *haftarah* we also learn that people in a state of ritual impurity could not participate in this communal meal (v. 26).

A further dimension of *Rosh Ḥodesh* has been incorporated into the synagogue service. The *Musaf Amidah* for the day opens with the statement, "The beginnings of months did You assign for Your people as a time of atonement throughout the generations." Thus atonement for sin became linked to the renewal and restoration of the moon. The kabbalists (medieval Jewish mystics) found great spiritual meaning in the moon's waxing and waning; and by the 16th century, it was customary to observe the day before the new moon as a time for taking stock, fasting, and repentance. That day came to be known as the Minor Day of Atonement (*Yom Kippur Katan*).

For the kabbalists, the waning of the moon symbolized the exile of the divine Presence (*Sh'khinah*) and the weakening of the powers of holiness during Israel's exile. The waxing of the moon stood for the renewal of holiness and divine restoration. A new moon was thus a symbol of redemption and hope. Similarly, in the *haftarah,* the bond between David and Jonathan was emblematic of the renewal of human community through love and devotion. Indeed, for the ancient rabbis, this relationship was paradigmatic of a "wholly disinterested love" (a love with no conditions attached), capable of withstanding adverse circumstances (M Avot 5:16). Fundamental to David and Jonathan's love and commitment was the divine Presence that unifies them (see 1 Sam. 20:23,42). It was this commitment to a transcendent reality that allowed Jonathan to rise beyond self-interest in his loyalty to David.

20 18 Jonathan said to him, "Tomorrow
will be the new moon; and you will be missed
when your seat remains vacant. 19 So the day after tomorrow, go down all the way to the place
where you hid the other time, and stay close to
the Ezel stone. 20 Now I will shoot three arrows
to one side of it, as though I were shooting at
a mark, 21 and I will order the boy to go and find
the arrows. If I call to the boy, 'Hey! the arrows
are on this side of you,' be reassured and come,
for you are safe and there is no danger—as the
LORD lives! 22 But if, instead, I call to the lad,
'Hey! the arrows are beyond you,' then leave,
for the LORD has sent you away. 23 As for the
promise we made to each other, may the LORD
be [witness] between you and me forever."
24 David hid in the field. The new moon came,
and the king sat down to partake of the meal.

כ 18 וַיֹּאמֶר־לוֹ יְהוֹנָתָן מָחָר חֹדֶשׁ
וְנִפְקַדְתָּ כִּי יִפָּקֵד מוֹשָׁבֶךָ׃ 19 וְשִׁלַּשְׁתָּ
תֵּרֵד מְאֹד וּבָאתָ אֶל־הַמָּקוֹם אֲשֶׁר־
נִסְתַּרְתָּ שָּׁם בְּיוֹם הַמַּעֲשֶׂה וְיָשַׁבְתָּ אֵצֶל
הָאֶבֶן הָאָזֶל׃ 20 וַאֲנִי שְׁלֹשֶׁת הַחִצִּים צִדָּה
אוֹרֶה לְשַׁלַּח־לִי לְמַטָּרָה׃ 21 וְהִנֵּה אֶשְׁלַח
אֶת־הַנַּעַר לֵךְ מְצָא אֶת־הַחִצִּים אִם־
אָמֹר אֹמַר לַנַּעַר הִנֵּה הַחִצִּים ׀ מִמְּךָ
וָהֵנָּה קָחֶנּוּ ׀ וָבֹאָה כִּי־שָׁלוֹם לְךָ וְאֵין
דָּבָר חַי־יְהוָה׃ 22 וְאִם־כֹּה אֹמַר לָעֶלֶם
הִנֵּה הַחִצִּים מִמְּךָ וָהָלְאָה לֵךְ כִּי שִׁלַּחֲךָ
יְהוָה׃ 23 וְהַדָּבָר אֲשֶׁר דִּבַּרְנוּ אֲנִי וָאָתָּה
הִנֵּה יְהוָה בֵּינִי וּבֵינְךָ עַד־עוֹלָם׃ ס
24 וַיִּסָּתֵר דָּוִד בַּשָּׂדֶה וַיְהִי הַחֹדֶשׁ וַיֵּשֶׁב
הַמֶּלֶךְ על אֶל־הַלֶּחֶם לֶאֱכוֹל׃ 25 וַיֵּשֶׁב

1 Samuel 20:19. the other time Literally, "on the day of the incident." This presumably refers to the time when Jonathan interceded with Saul for David's life (19:2–4).

Ezel stone A landmark apparently used as a signpost for travelers. See Comment to 1 Sam. 20:41.

25When the king took his usual place on the seat
by the wall, Jonathan rose and Abner sat down
at Saul's side; but David's place remained vacant. 26That day, however, Saul said nothing.
"It's accidental," he thought. "He must be impure and not yet purified." 27But on the day after
the new moon, the second day, David's place
was vacant again. So Saul said to his son Jonathan, "Why didn't the son of Jesse come to the
meal yesterday or today?" 28Jonathan answered
Saul, "David begged leave of me to go to Bethlehem. 29He said, 'Please let me go, for we are
going to have a family feast in our town and my
brother has summoned me to it. Do me a favor,
let me slip away to see my kinsmen.' That is why
he has not come to the king's table."

30Saul flew into a rage against Jonathan. "You
son of a perverse, rebellious woman!" he
shouted. "I know that you side with the son of
Jesse—to your shame, and to the shame of your
mother's nakedness! 31For as long as the son of
Jesse lives on earth, neither you nor your kingship will be secure. Now then, have him brought
to me, for he is marked for death." 32But Jonathan spoke up and said to his father, "Why
should he be put to death? What has he done?"
33At that, Saul threw his spear at him to strike
him down; and Jonathan realized that his father
was determined to do away with David. 34Jon-
athan rose from the table in a rage. He ate no
food on the second day of the new moon, because he was grieved about David, and because
his father had humiliated him.

35In the morning, Jonathan went out into the
open for the meeting with David, accompanied

הַמֶּ֙לֶךְ עַל־מ֨וֹשָׁב֜וֹ כְּפַ֣עַם ׀ בְּפַ֗עַם אֶל־
מוֹשַׁב֙ הַקִּ֔יר וַיָּ֙קָם֙ יְה֣וֹנָתָ֔ן וַיֵּ֣שֶׁב אַבְנֵ֔ר
מִצַּ֣ד שָׁא֑וּל וַיִּפָּקֵ֖ד מְק֥וֹם דָּוִֽד׃ 26 וְלֹֽא־
דִבֶּ֥ר שָׁא֛וּל מְא֖וּמָה בַּיּ֣וֹם הַה֑וּא כִּ֤י אָמַר֙
מִקְרֶ֣ה ה֔וּא בִּלְתִּ֥י טָה֛וֹר ה֖וּא כִּֽי־לֹ֥א
טָהֽוֹר׃ ס 27 וַיְהִ֗י מִֽמָּחֳרַ֤ת הַחֹ֙דֶשׁ֙ הַשֵּׁנִ֔י
וַיִּפָּקֵ֖ד מְק֣וֹם דָּוִ֑ד ס וַיֹּ֤אמֶר שָׁאוּל֙ אֶל־
יְהוֹנָתָ֣ן בְּנ֔וֹ מַדּ֜וּעַ לֹא־בָ֧א בֶן־יִשַׁ֛י גַּם־
תְּמ֥וֹל גַּם־הַיּ֖וֹם אֶל־הַלָּֽחֶם׃ 28 וַיַּ֥עַן
יְהוֹנָתָ֖ן אֶת־שָׁא֑וּל נִשְׁאֹ֨ל נִשְׁאַ֥ל דָּוִ֛ד
מֵעִמָּדִ֖י עַד־בֵּ֥ית לָֽחֶם׃ 29 וַיֹּ֡אמֶר שַׁלְּחֵ֣נִי
נָ֡א כִּ֣י זֶבַח֩ מִשְׁפָּחָ֨ה לָ֜נוּ בָּעִ֗יר וְה֤וּא
צִוָּה־לִי֙ אָחִ֔י וְעַתָּ֗ה אִם־מָצָ֤אתִי חֵן֙
בְּעֵינֶ֔יךָ אִמָּ֥לְטָה נָּ֖א וְאֶרְאֶ֣ה אֶת־אֶחָ֑י
עַל־כֵּ֣ן לֹא־בָ֔א אֶל־שֻׁלְחַ֖ן הַמֶּֽלֶךְ׃ ס
30 וַיִּֽחַר־אַ֤ף שָׁאוּל֙ בִּיה֣וֹנָתָ֔ן וַיֹּ֣אמֶר ל֔וֹ
בֶּן־נַעֲוַ֖ת הַמַּרְדּ֑וּת הֲל֣וֹא יָדַ֗עְתִּי כִּֽי־בֹחֵ֤ר
אַתָּה֙ לְבֶן־יִשַׁ֔י לְבָ֨שְׁתְּךָ֔ וּלְבֹ֖שֶׁת עֶרְוַ֥ת
אִמֶּֽךָ׃ 31 כִּ֣י כָל־הַיָּמִ֗ים אֲשֶׁ֤ר בֶּן־יִשַׁי֙ חַ֣י
עַל־הָאֲדָמָ֔ה לֹ֥א תִכּ֖וֹן אַתָּ֣ה וּמַלְכוּתֶ֑ךָ
וְעַתָּ֗ה שְׁלַ֨ח וְקַ֤ח אֹתוֹ֙ אֵלַ֔י כִּ֥י בֶן־מָ֖וֶת
הֽוּא׃ ס 32 וַיַּ֙עַן֙ יְה֣וֹנָתָ֔ן אֶת־שָׁא֖וּל
אָבִ֑יו וַיֹּ֧אמֶר אֵלָ֛יו לָ֥מָּה יוּמַ֖ת מֶ֥ה עָשָֽׂה׃
33 וַיָּטֶל֩ שָׁא֨וּל אֶֽת־הַחֲנִ֥ית עָלָ֖יו לְהַכֹּת֑וֹ
וַיֵּ֙דַע֙ יְה֣וֹנָתָ֔ן כִּֽי־כָ֥לָה הִ֛יא מֵעִ֥ם אָבִ֖יו
לְהָמִ֥ית אֶת־דָּוִֽד׃ ס 34 וַיָּ֧קָם יְהוֹנָתָ֛ן
מֵעִ֥ם הַשֻּׁלְחָ֖ן בָּחֳרִי־אָ֑ף וְלֹֽא־אָכַ֞ל בְּיוֹם־
הַחֹ֤דֶשׁ הַשֵּׁנִי֙ לֶ֔חֶם כִּ֤י נֶעְצַב֙ אֶל־דָּוִ֔ד כִּ֥י
הִכְלִמ֖וֹ אָבִֽיו׃ ס
35 וַיְהִ֣י בַבֹּ֔קֶר וַיֵּצֵ֧א יְהוֹנָתָ֛ן הַשָּׂדֶ֖ה לְמוֹעֵ֣ד

26. It's accidental Hebrew: *mikreh hu.* The next sentence, "He must be impure and not yet purified," suggests that *mikreh* (literally, "accident") is here used in the technical sense of an "accidental" seminal emission, which puts one in a state of ritual impurity (see Deut. 23:11). This is also Rashi's understanding (see BT Pes. 3a).

30. Saul's harsh criticism of Jonathan, and the subsequent gesture of aggression against him, served as the basis for Rabbinic and medieval discussions about the limits of reproof. According to ancient traditions preserved in the Talmud (BT Ar. 16b), the Sages variously placed the limit at cursing, rebuking, shouting, or smiting.

by a young boy. 36He said to the boy, "Run ahead and find the arrows that I shoot." And as the boy ran, he shot the arrows past him. 37When the boy came to the place where the arrows shot by Jonathan had fallen, Jonathan called out to the boy, "Hey, the arrows are beyond you!" 38And Jonathan called after the boy, "Quick, hurry up. Don't stop!" So Jonathan's boy gathered the arrows and came back to his master.—39The boy suspected nothing; only Jonathan and David knew the arrangement.—40Jonathan handed the gear to his boy and told him, "Take these back to the town." 41When the boy got there, David emerged from his concealment at the Negeb. He flung himself face down on the ground and bowed low three times. They kissed each other and wept together; David wept the longer.

42Jonathan said to David, "Go in peace! For we two have sworn to each other in the name of the LORD: 'May the LORD be [witness] between you and me, and between your offspring and mine, forever!'"

דָּוִד וְנַעַר קָטֹן עִמּוֹ׃ 36 וַיֹּאמֶר לְנַעֲרוֹ רֻץ
מְצָא נָא אֶת־הַחִצִּים אֲשֶׁר אָנֹכִי מוֹרֶה
הַנַּעַר רָץ וְהוּא־יָרָה הַחֵצִי לְהַעֲבִרוֹ׃
37 וַיָּבֹא הַנַּעַר עַד־מְקוֹם הַחֵצִי אֲשֶׁר יָרָה
יְהוֹנָתָן וַיִּקְרָא יְהוֹנָתָן אַחֲרֵי הַנַּעַר וַיֹּאמֶר
הֲלוֹא הַחֵצִי מִמְּךָ וָהָלְאָה׃ 38 וַיִּקְרָא
יְהוֹנָתָן אַחֲרֵי הַנַּעַר מְהֵרָה חוּשָׁה אַל־
תַּעֲמֹד וַיְלַקֵּט נַעַר יְהוֹנָתָן אֶת־החצי
הַחִצִּים וַיָּבֹא אֶל־אֲדֹנָיו׃ 39 וְהַנַּעַר לֹא־
יָדַע מְאוּמָה אַךְ יְהוֹנָתָן וְדָוִד יָדְעוּ אֶת־
הַדָּבָר׃ 40 וַיִּתֵּן יְהוֹנָתָן אֶת־כֵּלָיו אֶל־
הַנַּעַר אֲשֶׁר־לוֹ וַיֹּאמֶר לוֹ לֵךְ הָבֵיא הָעִיר׃
41 הַנַּעַר בָּא וְדָוִד קָם מֵאֵצֶל הַנֶּגֶב וַיִּפֹּל
לְאַפָּיו אַרְצָה וַיִּשְׁתַּחוּ שָׁלֹשׁ פְּעָמִים
וַיִּשְּׁקוּ ׀ אִישׁ אֶת־רֵעֵהוּ וַיִּבְכּוּ אִישׁ
אֶת־רֵעֵהוּ עַד־דָּוִד הִגְדִּיל׃
42 וַיֹּאמֶר יְהוֹנָתָן לְדָוִד לֵךְ לְשָׁלוֹם אֲשֶׁר
נִשְׁבַּעְנוּ שְׁנֵינוּ אֲנַחְנוּ בְּשֵׁם יְהוָה לֵאמֹר
יְהוָה יִהְיֶה ׀ בֵּינִי וּבֵינֶךָ וּבֵין זַרְעִי וּבֵין
זַרְעֲךָ עַד־עוֹלָם׃ פ

41. emerged from his concealment at the Negeb This rendition is interpretative; literally, "rose up from beside the Negeb." Possibly, the phrase is best understood as "arose from his place of concealment near the Ezel stone in the Negeb" (cf. v. 19).

הפטרה לשבת וראש חודש

HAFTARAH FOR SHABBAT AND ROSH ḤODESH

ISAIAH 66:1–24

This *haftarah* is a compilation of oracles of judgment and salvation. Its reference to building a new temple (Isa. 66:1) situates it in the period after the Judean exiles in Babylon had been granted permission to return to their homeland by Cyrus the Mede in 538 B.C.E.

The diverse prophecies of this *haftarah* are unified by a symmetrical structure. Two frames enclose a centerpiece of consolation for Zion. Beginning with the outermost frame, at the outset (66:1) God proclaims His omnipresent majesty throughout heaven and earth—and thus no earthly temple can contain Him. At the end, this theme is balanced by another reference to heaven and earth; there, they comprise God's new Creation as a sign and token of Israel's permanence (v. 22), followed by the ingathering of all nations to the rebuilt temple (v. 23). What began as a negative (mortals' inability to build a temple for God, due to His utter transcendence) concludes with a positive expectation of temple worship by "all flesh," announced and guaranteed by God.

Within this framework, whose theme is the worship of God the Creator, lies a second theme: God's direct involvement with the world. Divine acts of judgment against those who reject God and perform improper rites (vv. 3–6,15–17) stand in stark contrast to the center of the *haftarah* and its themes of divine grace and human joy (vv. 7–14). Zion shall bear her children without pain, with God's help in the role of a beneficent midwife who enables labor and easy birth (v. 9). This feminine focus extends to God's acts of care for the nation, giving it comfort "as a mother comforts her son" (v. 13). Such divine imagery balances attributes of justice with attributes of mercy for the faithful. Punishment and nurturance are the theological signs of the new age. For the sinner this means death, but for the favored of God birth and life form a horizon of hope.

The theme of universal worship is also featured (vv. 18b–21,23). This is particularly evident in the polemical inclusion of foreigners in the service of the temple (v. 21). Such a dramatic inclusiveness surpasses other universalist visions found in Scripture.

RELATION OF THE *HAFTARAH* TO THE CALENDAR

In antiquity, special public rituals and feasts marked the occasion of the new moon (Num. 28:11–15, M RH 2:5), while private feasts were celebrated (1 Sam. 9:13). In an early medieval *midrash,* God designated the New Moon festival especially for women, as a reward for not having contributed their jewelry in the making of the Golden Calf (see Exod. 32:3; PdRE 45).

This *haftarah* announces that when the people Israel are gathered in from exile "all flesh shall come to worship" the Lord "new moon after new moon" (66:23). Therewith, new moon rites are given a universalist dimension. In anticipation of that celebration in Jerusalem at the end of days, this prophecy is traditionally recited when the New Moon (*Rosh Ḥodesh*) falls on *Shabbat.* The monthly renewal of light in the heavens embodies the hope for light and fellowship on earth.

Meanwhile, according to medieval mystical tradition, the moon's waxing and waning reflect the increase and the decrease of holiness and unity in both the divine and human realms. As the moon is not the source of its own light, the symbolism of the new moon invites worshipers to deepen receptivity to a "higher," hidden radiance—so that each individual may be con-

nected to a divine dimension and reflect it outward through the self. In this respect, the *haftarah* for *Rosh Ḥodesh* reminds the single self of its commonality with all creatures. Proclamation of the celebration of God by "all flesh . . . new moon after new moon," is thus a prophecy of a unified humanity that is constantly renewed.

66 Thus said the LORD:
The heaven is My throne
And the earth is My footstool:
Where could you build a house for Me,
What place could serve as My abode?
2 All this was made by My hand,
And thus it all came into being
—declares the LORD.
Yet to such a one I look:
To the poor and brokenhearted,
Who is concerned about My word.

3 As for those who slaughter oxen and slay humans,
Who sacrifice sheep and immolate dogs,
Who present as oblation the blood of swine,
Who offer incense and worship false gods—
Just as they have chosen their ways
And take pleasure in their abominations,
4 So will I choose to mock them,
To bring on them the very thing they dread.
For I called and none responded,
I spoke and none paid heed.
They did what I deem evil
And chose what I do not want.

5 Hear the word of the LORD,

סו כֹּה אָמַר יְהֹוָה
הַשָּׁמַיִם כִּסְאִי
וְהָאָרֶץ הֲדֹם רַגְלָי
אֵי־זֶה בַיִת אֲשֶׁר תִּבְנוּ־לִי
וְאֵי־זֶה מָקוֹם מְנוּחָתִי׃
2 וְאֶת־כָּל־אֵלֶּה יָדִי עָשָׂתָה
וַיִּהְיוּ כָל־אֵלֶּה
נְאֻם־יְהוָה
וְאֶל־זֶה אַבִּיט
אֶל־עָנִי וּנְכֵה־רוּחַ
וְחָרֵד עַל־דְּבָרִי׃
3 שׁוֹחֵט הַשּׁוֹר מַכֵּה־אִישׁ
זוֹבֵחַ הַשֶּׂה עֹרֵף כֶּלֶב
מַעֲלֵה מִנְחָה דַּם־חֲזִיר
מַזְכִּיר לְבֹנָה מְבָרֵךְ אָוֶן
גַּם־הֵמָּה בָּחֲרוּ בְּדַרְכֵיהֶם
וּבְשִׁקּוּצֵיהֶם נַפְשָׁם חָפֵצָה׃
4 גַּם־אֲנִי אֶבְחַר בְּתַעֲלֻלֵיהֶם
וּמְגוּרֹתָם אָבִיא לָהֶם
יַעַן קָרָאתִי וְאֵין עוֹנֶה
דִּבַּרְתִּי וְלֹא שָׁמֵעוּ
וַיַּעֲשׂוּ הָרַע בְּעֵינַי
וּבַאֲשֶׁר לֹא־חָפַצְתִּי בָּחָרוּ׃ ס
5 שִׁמְעוּ דְּבַר־יְהוָה

Isaiah 66:1. The image of the heavens as God's throne and the earth as His footstool is one of divine transcendence above and beyond the created world and divine omnipresence within it.

2. Who is concerned about My word Designating the faithful as "concerned" (*ḥared*) may reflect a technical term of the period. The ensuing reference to "all who mourned" (*mit·ab'lim*) over Jerusalem (v. 10) may also have technical overtones, because this group is called "the mourners in [or: of] Zion" (*avelei Tziyyon*) in Isa. 61:3.

You who are concerned about His word!
Your kinsmen who hate you,
Who spurn you because of Me, are saying,
"Let the LORD manifest His Presence,
So that we may look upon your joy."
But theirs shall be the shame.
6Hark, tumult from the city,
Thunder from the Temple!
It is the thunder of the LORD
As He deals retribution to His foes.

7Before she labored, she was delivered;
Before her pangs came, she bore a son.
8Who ever heard the like?
Who ever witnessed such events?
Can a land pass through travail
In a single day?
Or is a nation born
All at once?
Yet Zion travailed
And at once bore her children!
9Shall I who bring on labor not bring about birth?
—says the LORD.
Shall I who cause birth shut the womb?
—said your God.
10Rejoice with Jerusalem and be glad for her,
All you who love her!
Join in her jubilation,
All you who mourned over her—
11That you may suck from her breast
Consolation to the full,
That you may draw from her bosom
Glory to your delight.

12For thus said the LORD:

הַחֲרֵדִים אֶל־דְּבָרוֹ
אָמְרוּ אֲחֵיכֶם שֹׂנְאֵיכֶם
מְנַדֵּיכֶם לְמַעַן שְׁמִי
יִכְבַּד יְהוָה
וְנִרְאֶה בְשִׂמְחַתְכֶם
וְהֵם יֵבֹשׁוּ׃
6 קוֹל שָׁאוֹן מֵעִיר
קוֹל מֵהֵיכָל
קוֹל יְהוָה
מְשַׁלֵּם גְּמוּל לְאֹיְבָיו׃

7 בְּטֶרֶם תָּחִיל יָלָדָה
בְּטֶרֶם יָבוֹא חֵבֶל לָהּ וְהִמְלִיטָה זָכָר׃
8 מִי־שָׁמַע כָּזֹאת
מִי רָאָה כָּאֵלֶּה
הֲיוּחַל אֶרֶץ
בְּיוֹם אֶחָד
אִם־יִוָּלֵד גּוֹי
פַּעַם אֶחָת
כִּי־חָלָה גַּם־יָלְדָה צִיּוֹן
אֶת־בָּנֶיהָ׃
9 הַאֲנִי אַשְׁבִּיר וְלֹא אוֹלִיד
יֹאמַר* יְהוָה
אִם־אֲנִי הַמּוֹלִיד וְעָצַרְתִּי
אָמַר אֱלֹהָיִךְ׃ ס
10 שִׂמְחוּ אֶת־יְרוּשָׁלַםִ
וְגִילוּ בָהּ כָּל־אֹהֲבֶיהָ
שִׂישׂוּ אִתָּהּ מָשׂוֹשׂ
כָּל־הַמִּתְאַבְּלִים עָלֶיהָ׃
11 לְמַעַן תִּינְקוּ וּשְׂבַעְתֶּם
מִשֹּׁד תַּנְחֻמֶיהָ
לְמַעַן תָּמֹצּוּ וְהִתְעַנַּגְתֶּם
מִזִּיז כְּבוֹדָהּ׃ ס

12 כִּי־כֹה ׀ אָמַר יְהוָה

v. 9. סבירין ומטעין "אמר"

I will extend to her
Prosperity like a stream,
The wealth of nations
Like a wadi in flood;
And you shall drink of it.
You shall be carried on shoulders
And dandled upon knees.
¹³As a mother comforts her son
So I will comfort you;
You shall find comfort in Jerusalem.
¹⁴You shall see and your heart shall rejoice,
Your limbs shall flourish like grass.
The power of the Lord shall be revealed
In behalf of His servants;
But He shall rage against His foes.

¹⁵See, the Lord is coming with fire—
His chariots are like a whirlwind—
To vent His anger in fury,
His rebuke in flaming fire.
¹⁶For with fire will the Lord contend,
With His sword, against all flesh;
And many shall be the slain of the Lord.

¹⁷Those who sanctify and purify themselves
to enter the groves, imitating one in the center, eating the flesh of the swine, the reptile, and
the mouse, shall one and all come to an
end—declares the Lord. ¹⁸For I [know] their
deeds and purposes.

[The time] has come to gather all the nations
and tongues; they shall come and behold My
glory. ¹⁹I will set a sign among them, and send
from them survivors to the nations: to Tarshish,
Pul, and Lud—that draw the bow—to Tubal,
Javan, and the distant coasts, that have never

הִנְנִי נֹטֶה־אֵלֶיהָ
כְּנָהָר שָׁלוֹם
וּכְנַחַל שׁוֹטֵף
כְּבוֹד גּוֹיִם וִינַקְתֶּם
עַל־צַד תִּנָּשֵׂאוּ
וְעַל־בִּרְכַּיִם
תְּשָׁעֳשָׁעוּ:
13 כְּאִישׁ אֲשֶׁר אִמּוֹ תְּנַחֲמֶנּוּ
כֵּן אָנֹכִי אֲנַחֶמְכֶם
וּבִירוּשָׁלַ͏ִם תְּנֻחָמוּ:
14 וּרְאִיתֶם וְשָׂשׂ לִבְּכֶם
וְעַצְמוֹתֵיכֶם כַּדֶּשֶׁא תִפְרַחְנָה
וְנוֹדְעָה יַד־יְהֹוָה
אֶת־עֲבָדָיו
וְזָעַם אֶת־אֹיְבָיו:

15 כִּי־הִנֵּה יְהֹוָה בָּאֵשׁ יָבוֹא
וְכַסּוּפָה מַרְכְּבֹתָיו
לְהָשִׁיב בְּחֵמָה אַפּוֹ
וְגַעֲרָתוֹ בְּלַהֲבֵי־אֵשׁ:
16 כִּי בָאֵשׁ יְהֹוָה נִשְׁפָּט
וּבְחַרְבּוֹ אֶת־כָּל־בָּשָׂר
וְרַבּוּ חַלְלֵי יְהֹוָה:

17 הַמִּתְקַדְּשִׁים וְהַמִּטַּהֲרִים אֶל־הַגַּנּוֹת
אַחַר אַחַד אַחַת בַּתָּוֶךְ אֹכְלֵי בְּשַׂר הַחֲזִיר
וְהַשֶּׁקֶץ וְהָעַכְבָּר יַחְדָּו יָסֻפוּ נְאֻם־יְהֹוָה:
18 וְאָנֹכִי מַעֲשֵׂיהֶם וּמַחְשְׁבֹתֵיהֶם

בָּאָה לְקַבֵּץ אֶת־כָּל־הַגּוֹיִם וְהַלְּשֹׁנוֹת
וּבָאוּ וְרָאוּ אֶת־כְּבוֹדִי: 19 וְשַׂמְתִּי בָהֶם
אוֹת וְשִׁלַּחְתִּי מֵהֶם ׀ פְּלֵיטִים אֶל־הַגּוֹיִם
תַּרְשִׁישׁ פּוּל וְלוּד מֹשְׁכֵי קֶשֶׁת תֻּבַל וְיָוָן

18–21. A universal ingathering of nations is
prophesied here. This attitude is characteristic of
this postexilic prophet (cf. 56:1–8, 60), but is reflected in the earlier chapters of the book as well
(Isa. 2:1–4).

heard My fame nor beheld My glory. They shall
declare My glory among these nations. 20 And
out of all the nations, said the LORD, they shall
bring all your brothers on horses, in chariots
and drays, on mules and dromedaries, to Jerusalem My holy mountain as an offering to the
LORD—just as the Israelites bring an offering in
a pure vessel to the House of the LORD. 21 And
from them likewise I will take some to be levitical priests, said the LORD.

22 For as the new heaven and the new earth
Which I will make
Shall endure by My will
—declares the LORD—
So shall your seed and your name endure.
23 And new moon after new moon,
And sabbath after sabbath,
All flesh shall come to worship Me
—said the LORD.
24 They shall go out and gaze
On the corpses of the men who rebelled against Me:
Their worms shall not die,
Nor their fire be quenched;
They shall be a horror
To all flesh.

And new moon after new moon,
And sabbath after sabbath,
All flesh shall come to worship Me
—said the LORD.

הָאִיִּים הָרְחֹקִים אֲשֶׁר לֹא־שָׁמְעוּ אֶת־
שִׁמְעִי וְלֹא־רָאוּ אֶת־כְּבוֹדִי וְהִגִּידוּ אֶת־
כְּבוֹדִי בַּגּוֹיִם׃ 20 וְהֵבִיאוּ אֶת־כָּל־אֲחֵיכֶם
מִכָּל־הַגּוֹיִם ׀ מִנְחָה ׀ לַיהוָה בַּסּוּסִים
וּבָרֶכֶב וּבַצַּבִּים וּבַפְּרָדִים וּבַכִּרְכָּרוֹת עַל
הַר קָדְשִׁי יְרוּשָׁלַםִ אָמַר יְהוָה כַּאֲשֶׁר
יָבִיאוּ בְנֵי יִשְׂרָאֵל אֶת־הַמִּנְחָה בִּכְלִי
טָהוֹר בֵּית יְהוָה׃ 21 וְגַם־מֵהֶם אֶקַּח
לַכֹּהֲנִים לַלְוִיִּם אָמַר יְהוָה׃

22 כִּי כַאֲשֶׁר הַשָּׁמַיִם הַחֲדָשִׁים וְהָאָרֶץ
הַחֲדָשָׁה
אֲשֶׁר אֲנִי עֹשֶׂה
עֹמְדִים לְפָנַי
נְאֻם־יְהוָה
כֵּן יַעֲמֹד זַרְעֲכֶם וְשִׁמְכֶם׃
23 וְהָיָה מִדֵּי־חֹדֶשׁ בְּחָדְשׁוֹ
וּמִדֵּי שַׁבָּת בְּשַׁבַּתּוֹ
יָבוֹא כָל־בָּשָׂר לְהִשְׁתַּחֲוֹת לְפָנַי
אָמַר יְהוָה׃
24 וְיָצְאוּ וְרָאוּ
בְּפִגְרֵי הָאֲנָשִׁים הַפֹּשְׁעִים בִּי
כִּי תוֹלַעְתָּם לֹא תָמוּת
וְאִשָּׁם לֹא תִכְבֶּה
וְהָיוּ דֵרָאוֹן
לְכָל־בָּשָׂר׃

[וְהָיָה מִדֵּי־חֹדֶשׁ בְּחָדְשׁוֹ
וּמִדֵּי שַׁבָּת בְּשַׁבַּתּוֹ
יָבוֹא כָל־בָּשָׂר לְהִשְׁתַּחֲוֹת לְפָנַי
אָמַר יְהוָה׃*]

end. במסורת הקריאה נשנה הפסוק לפני האחרון

21. said the LORD Rashi understood this prophetic signature to mean that the daring innovation envisioned here for the days to come (inclusion of foreigners in the service of the temple) is a divine mystery of God, which had been stated long before. He referred to Deut 29:28, "Concealed acts concern the LORD our God."

הפטרה לראש השנה (יום ראשון)

HAFTARAH FOR ROSH HA-SHANAH, FIRST DAY

1 SAMUEL 1:1–2:10

This *haftarah* marks a time of transition from the period of the chieftains ("judges," with a loose tribal confederacy) to that of the monarchy (and its centralized institutions). The key figure whose life spans both periods is Samuel, the story of whose birth is featured here.

Samuel is both the last honest judge and the person to whom the tribes turn with a request to appoint a king "to judge us" (1 Sam. 7:15–8:5). He also functions as a priestly assistant (2:18), a prophet (3:20), an anointer of kings (Saul, in 10:1; David, in 16:12–13), and a successful intercessor for rain on behalf of his people (12:17–19).

The context for the episodes depicted in this *haftarah* is worship at the shrine of Shiloh. Elkanah's pilgrimage possibly had to do with hopes for a successful agricultural year or some other personal benefit. Hannah's prayer for fertility also found its appropriate setting in the rituals of petition for earthly blessings.

Paying close attention to linguistic usage enriches the dimensions of this *haftarah*. Hannah uttered her vow silently before God. The priest, assuming that she asked for divine aid, tells her: "may the God of Israel grant (*yitten*) you what have asked of Him" (1:17). The verb "grant" (*yitten*) is also used in the formulation of Hannah's vow to God in verse 11: "if You will grant [*v'natata*] . . . I will dedicate him [*u-n'tativ*] to the LORD." It appears again in her statement to Eli in fulfillment of her vow in verse 27: "It was this boy I prayed for; and the LORD has granted [*va-yitten*] me what I asked of Him."

The key verb meaning "to ask" (*sha·al*) highlights both Hannah's request and her dedication of the son with whom she is blessed. Eli speaks of how the Lord will grant what she asked (*shelatekh asher sha'alt,* v. 17). Hannah names her son "Samuel" (*Sh'mu·el*) because "I asked [*sh'iltiv*] the LORD for him" (v. 20). At the time of the dedication, standing before Eli with her son, Hannah refers to her original meeting with the priest when she says: "It was this boy I prayed for; and the LORD has granted me what I asked [*sh'elati asher sha·alti*]" (v. 27). In the following verse she fulfills her vow with the same terms: "I . . . hereby lend [i.e., give] him [*hish·iltihu*] to the LORD. For as long as he lives he is lent [i.e., given; *sha·ul*] to the LORD." The verb also echoes the very name of the shrine, Shiloh, where the mother prayed for a child and where she subsequently dedicated him for service.

Another series of verbal allusions creates an even grander network of intratextual relations. There is no etymological link between the place-name "Ramah" (the home of Elkanah and Hannah in v. 19) and the taunting (*ha-r'imah*) of Hannah by her co-wife Peninnah because of her barren womb (*raḥmah,* v. 6). The sounds of these words, however, muffled by sorrow at the outset, reverberate in Hannah's triumphant song (2:1–10) in which everything is reversed or given a positive turn. Hannah opens her prayer in exultant joy, giving thanks to the Lord through whom her horn is raised up "high [*ramah*]," (v. 1) and she concludes with an expression of confidence that the Lord will also "raise (*v'yarem*) the horn of His anointed one" (v. 10, n. c). Amid the praise, she exclaims how the Lord "raises the poor . . . [and] / Lifts up [*yarim*] the needy" from travail (v. 8). She proclaims that her Lord will shatter His foes and "will thunder (*yar·em*) against them in the heavens" (v. 10). Hannah's words express an exuberance that shouts from the depths of experience: "The LORD deals death and gives life, / . . . / He casts down, He also lifts high [*m'rommem*]" (vv. 6–7).

The concluding song thus links Hannah's anguished past and her joyful present. Her gift to God is the child of her body and the words of her mouth. Critics may rightly ponder whether the authentic source of the hymn is this mother and whether the reference to an anointed king is original with her. But as readers of the narrative, we know that the words are appropriate as those of a woman whose husband once intended to console her in her barrenness by stating, "Am I not more devoted to you than ten sons?" (1:8).

As an expression of hope, Hannah's concluding reference to the Lord raising the "horn" (*keren*) of His anointed king (2:10) anticipates the role of Samuel who "took the horn [*keren*] of oil and anointed" David king before all (16:13). For readers of the *haftarah,* Hannah's final words also raise a messianic expectation, a hope that God will destroy "the foes" of His people, and guard "the steps of His faithful" in their need. Then will the Lord remember the people Israel as He remembered Hannah His servant. Awaiting that moment, the community recites her words: "There is no holy one like the LORD, / Truly, there is none beside You" (2:2).

RELATION OF THE *HAFTARAH* TO THE CALENDAR

Rashi suggests that the story of Hannah was chosen for this day "because she was remembered (or taken note of) on Rosh ha-Shanah." His comment was influenced by a talmudic tradition: "On Rosh ha-Shanah, Sarah, Rachel, and Hannah were remembered" (BT RH 11a). God took note of the barrenness of all three women on the New Year, at the beginning of the month of *Tishrei.*

The theme of divine remembrance is central here, just as in the passages of divine "Remembrances" (*Zikhronot*) recited as a major component of the *Rosh ha-Shanah Musaf Amidah.* In those passages, God is asked to recall previous gracious acts of divine remembrance for the sake of the present and future well-being of the people Israel. This theme has a poignant, personal dimension in the *haftarah.*

Other themes included in Hannah's prayer also reinforce the topics of the day. Hannah refers to God as "all-knowing" (*el de·ot,* 2:3), and as One who raises the lowly (vv. 7–8), judges the wicked (v. 10), and dispenses both life and death (v. 6). Hannah's words embody the themes of *Rosh ha-Shanah.*

Hannah's concerns, at their most specific, revolve around her desire for a child. This echoes the major liturgical theme of Creation. *Rosh ha-Shanah* is not just the New Year but a time recalling the origin of the world. "On this day the world was conceived" (*ha-yom harat olam*) runs the recurrent and graphic image of the liturgy. Thus, a child's birth dramatizes in the social realm something of the world's rebirth and continuity. Hannah's prayer exemplifies for us the truth that the theologies of Creation and human birth are linked.

The themes of life and death are repeated for all worshipers on *Rosh ha-Shanah.* "Who shall live and who shall die?" asks the liturgy, voicing the concern of each individual. In deep wisdom, the Torah and *haftarah* readings bring the mystery of Creation into everyday experience. Human life triumphs, giving hope to those present. In the flow of life between the generations, God's creation is revealed.

1 There was a man from Ramathaim of the
Zuphites, in the hill country of Ephraim, whose
name was Elkanah son of Jeroham son of Elihu
son of Tohu son of Zuph, an Ephraimite. 2He
had two wives, one named Hannah and the
other Peninnah; Peninnah had children, but
Hannah was childless. 3This man used to go up
from his town every year to worship and to offer

א וַיְהִי אִישׁ אֶחָד מִן־הָרָמָתַיִם צוֹפִים
מֵהַר אֶפְרָיִם וּשְׁמוֹ אֶלְקָנָה בֶּן־יְרֹחָם
בֶּן־אֱלִיהוּא בֶּן־תֹּחוּ בֶן־צוּף אֶפְרָתִי׃ 2 וְלוֹ
שְׁתֵּי נָשִׁים שֵׁם אַחַת חַנָּה וְשֵׁם הַשֵּׁנִית
פְּנִנָּה וַיְהִי לִפְנִנָּה יְלָדִים וּלְחַנָּה אֵין
יְלָדִים׃ 3 וְעָלָה הָאִישׁ הַהוּא מֵעִירוֹ
מִיָּמִים ׀ יָמִימָה לְהִשְׁתַּחֲוֺת וְלִזְבֹּחַ לַיהוָה

sacrifice to the Lord of Hosts at Shiloh.—
Hophni and Phinehas, the two sons of Eli, were
priests of the Lord there.

⁴One such day, Elkanah offered a sacrifice. He
used to give portions to his wife Peninnah and
to all her sons and daughters; ⁵but to Hannah
he would give one portion only—though Hannah was his favorite—for the Lord had closed
her womb. ⁶Moreover, her rival, to make her
miserable, would taunt her that the Lord had
closed her womb. ⁷This happened year after
year: Every time she went up to the House of
the Lord, the other would taunt her, so that she
wept and would not eat. ⁸Her husband Elkanah
said to her, "Hannah, why are you crying and
why aren't you eating? Why are you so sad? Am
I not more devoted to you than ten sons?"

⁹After they had eaten and drunk at Shiloh,
Hannah rose.—The priest Eli was sitting on the
seat near the doorpost of the temple of the
Lord.—¹⁰In her wretchedness, she prayed to
the Lord, weeping all the while. ¹¹And she made
this vow: "O Lord of Hosts, if You will look
upon the suffering of Your maidservant and
will remember me and not forget Your maidservant, and if You will grant Your maidservant
a male child, I will dedicate him to the Lord
for all the days of his life; and no razor shall ever
touch his head."

¹²As she kept on praying before the Lord, Eli
watched her mouth. ¹³Now Hannah was praying in her heart; only her lips moved, but her
voice could not be heard. So Eli thought she was

צְבָא֜וֹת בְּשִׁלֹ֗ה וְשָׁ֞ם שְׁנֵ֣י בְנֵֽי־עֵלִ֗י חָפְנִי֙
וּפִ֣נְחָ֔ס כֹּהֲנִ֖ים לַיהוָֽה: ⁴וַיְהִ֣י הַיּ֔וֹם וַיִּזְבַּ֖ח
אֶלְקָנָ֑ה וְנָתַ֞ן לִפְנִנָּ֣ה אִשְׁתּ֗וֹ וּֽלְכָל־בָּנֶ֛יהָ
וּבְנוֹתֶ֖יהָ מָנֽוֹת: ⁵וּלְחַנָּ֕ה יִתֵּ֛ן מָנָ֥ה אַחַ֖ת
אַפָּ֑יִם כִּ֤י אֶת־חַנָּה֙ אָהֵ֔ב וַֽיהוָ֖ה סָגַ֥ר רַחְמָֽהּ:
⁶וְכִֽעֲסַ֤תָּה צָֽרָתָהּ֙ גַּם־כַּ֔עַס בַּעֲב֖וּר הַרְּעִמָ֑הּ*
כִּֽי־סָגַ֥ר יְהוָ֖ה בְּעַ֥ד רַחְמָֽהּ: ⁷וְכֵ֨ן יַעֲשֶׂ֜ה שָׁנָ֣ה
בְשָׁנָ֗ה מִדֵּ֤י עֲלֹתָהּ֙ בְּבֵ֣ית יְהוָ֔ה כֵּ֖ן
תַּכְעִסֶ֑נָּה וַתִּבְכֶּ֖ה וְלֹ֥א תֹאכַֽל: ⁸וַיֹּ֣אמֶר
לָ֣הּ אֶלְקָנָ֣ה אִישָׁ֗הּ חַנָּה֙ לָ֣מֶה תִבְכִּ֗י וְלָ֙מֶה֙
לֹ֣א תֹֽאכְלִ֔י וְלָ֖מֶה יֵרַ֣ע לְבָבֵ֑ךְ הֲל֤וֹא אָֽנֹכִי֙
ט֣וֹב לָ֔ךְ מֵעֲשָׂרָ֖ה בָּנִֽים: ⁹וַתָּ֣קָם חַנָּ֔ה אַחֲרֵ֛י
אָכְלָ֥ה בְשִׁלֹ֖ה וְאַחֲרֵ֣י שָׁתֹ֑ה וְעֵלִ֣י הַכֹּהֵ֗ן יֹשֵׁב֙
עַל־הַכִּסֵּ֔א עַל־מְזוּזַ֖ת הֵיכַ֥ל יְהוָֽה: ¹⁰וְהִ֖יא
מָ֣רַת נָ֑פֶשׁ וַתִּתְפַּלֵּ֥ל עַל־יְהוָ֖ה וּבָכֹ֥ה תִבְכֶּֽה:
¹¹וַתִּדֹּ֨ר נֶ֜דֶר וַתֹּאמַ֗ר יְהוָ֨ה צְבָא֜וֹת אִם־רָאֹ֥ה
תִרְאֶ֣ה | בָּעֳנִ֣י אֲמָתֶ֗ךָ וּזְכַרְתַּ֙נִי֙ וְלֹֽא־תִשְׁכַּ֣ח
אֶת־אֲמָתֶ֔ךָ וְנָתַתָּ֥ה לַאֲמָתְךָ֖ זֶ֣רַע אֲנָשִׁ֑ים
וּנְתַתִּ֤יו לַֽיהוָה֙ כָּל־יְמֵ֣י חַיָּ֔יו וּמוֹרָ֖ה לֹא־
יַעֲלֶ֥ה עַל־רֹאשֽׁוֹ: ¹²וְהָיָה֙ כִּ֣י הִרְבְּתָ֔ה לְהִתְפַּלֵּ֖ל
לִפְנֵ֣י יְהוָ֑ה וְעֵלִ֖י שֹׁמֵ֥ר אֶת־פִּֽיהָ: ¹³וְחַנָּ֗ה הִ֚יא
מְדַבֶּ֣רֶת עַל־לִבָּ֔הּ רַ֚ק שְׂפָתֶ֣יהָ נָּע֔וֹת וְקוֹלָ֖הּ
לֹ֣א יִשָּׁמֵ֑עַ וַיַּחְשְׁבֶ֥הָ עֵלִ֖י לְשִׁכֹּרָֽה:

v. 6. ר' דגושה

---

1 Samuel 1:3. Shiloh Modern Khirbat
Saylūn, about 20 miles (30 km) northeast of Jerusalem. It was an early shrine center. Joshua set
up the tabernacle there (Josh. 18:1), and the Ark
remained there (with brief exceptions) until it was
captured by the Philistines (1 Sam. 4:11).

9. After they had eaten Literally, "After she
had eaten (akh'lah)," namely, Hannah.

11. if You will grant . . . I will dedicate
Hebrew: im . . . v'natata . . . u-n'tativ, which is
the language of a vow formula (see Num. 21:2;

Judg. 11:30–31). Hannah vows that a male issue
will be a nazirite by alluding to one of the rules
of that status ("no razor shall ever touch his head";
cf. Num. 6:5). No other biblical source indicates
that one could make a vow that another person
would be a nazirite, especially before that other
person was born, nor that such status could be
life-long. (The case of Samson is different, for his
status was a divine designation—like Jeremiah's
status as a prophet from the womb; see Jer. 1:5).

13. Hannah's private prayer came to serve as

drunk. [14]Eli said to her, "How long will you make a drunken spectacle of yourself? Sober up!" [15]And Hannah replied, "Oh no, my lord! I am a very unhappy woman. I have drunk no wine or other strong drink, but I have been pouring out my heart to the LORD. [16]Do not take your maidservant for a worthless woman; I have only been speaking all this time out of my great anguish and distress." [17]"Then go in peace," said Eli, "and may the God of Israel grant you what you have asked of Him." [18]She answered, "You are most kind to your handmaid." So the woman left, and she ate, and was no longer downcast. [19]Early next morning they bowed low before the LORD, and they went back home to Ramah.

Elkanah knew his wife Hannah and the LORD remembered her. [20]Hannah conceived, and at the turn of the year bore a son. She named him Samuel, meaning, "I asked the LORD for him." [21]And when the man Elkanah and all his household were going up to offer to the LORD the annual sacrifice and his votive sacrifice, [22]Hannah did not go up. She said to her husband, "When the child is weaned, I will bring him. For when he has appeared before the LORD, he must remain there for good." [23]Her husband Elkanah said to her, "Do as you think best. Stay home until you have weaned him. May the LORD fulfill His word." So the woman stayed home and nursed her son until she weaned him.

[24]When she had weaned him, she took him up with her, along with three bulls, one *ephah*

וַיֹּ֤אמֶר אֵלֶ֙יהָ֙ עֵלִ֔י עַד־מָתַ֖י תִּשְׁתַּכָּרִ֑ין 14 הָסִ֥ירִי אֶת־יֵינֵ֖ךְ מֵעָלָֽיִךְ׃ 15 וַתַּ֨עַן חַנָּ֤ה וַתֹּ֙אמֶר֙ לֹ֣א אֲדֹנִ֔י אִשָּׁ֤ה קְשַׁת־ר֙וּחַ֙ אָנֹ֔כִי וְיַ֥יִן וְשֵׁכָ֖ר לֹ֣א שָׁתִ֑יתִי וָאֶשְׁפֹּ֥ךְ אֶת־נַפְשִׁ֖י לִפְנֵ֥י יְהֹוָֽה׃ 16 אַל־תִּתֵּן֙ אֶת־אֲמָ֣תְךָ֔ לִפְנֵ֖י בַּת־בְּלִיָּ֑עַל כִּֽי־מֵרֹ֥ב שִׂיחִ֛י וְכַעְסִ֖י דִּבַּ֥רְתִּי עַד־הֵֽנָּה׃ 17 וַיַּ֧עַן עֵלִ֛י וַיֹּ֖אמֶר לְכִ֣י לְשָׁל֑וֹם וֵֽאלֹהֵ֣י יִשְׂרָאֵ֗ל יִתֵּן֙ אֶת־שֵׁ֣לָתֵ֔ךְ* אֲשֶׁ֥ר שָׁאַ֖לְתְּ מֵעִמּֽוֹ׃ 18 וַתֹּ֕אמֶר תִּמְצָ֧א שִׁפְחָתְךָ֛ חֵ֖ן בְּעֵינֶ֑יךָ וַתֵּ֨לֶךְ הָאִשָּׁ֤ה לְדַרְכָּהּ֙ וַתֹּאכַ֔ל וּפָנֶ֖יהָ לֹא־הָ֥יוּ־לָ֖הּ עֽוֹד׃ 19 וַיַּשְׁכִּ֣מוּ בַבֹּ֗קֶר וַיִּֽשְׁתַּחֲווּ֙ לִפְנֵ֣י יְהֹוָ֔ה וַיָּשֻׁ֖בוּ וַיָּבֹ֣אוּ אֶל־בֵּיתָ֖ם הָרָמָ֑תָה וַיֵּ֤דַע אֶלְקָנָה֙ אֶת־חַנָּ֣ה אִשְׁתּ֔וֹ וַיִּֽזְכְּרֶ֖הָ יְהֹוָֽה׃ 20 וַיְהִי֙ לִתְקֻפ֣וֹת הַיָּמִ֔ים וַתַּ֖הַר חַנָּ֑ה וַתֵּ֣לֶד בֵּ֔ן וַתִּקְרָ֤א אֶת־שְׁמוֹ֙ שְׁמוּאֵ֔ל כִּ֥י מֵֽיהֹוָ֖ה שְׁאִלְתִּֽיו׃ 21 וַיַּ֛עַל הָאִ֥ישׁ אֶלְקָנָ֖ה וְכׇל־בֵּית֑וֹ לִזְבֹּ֧חַ לַֽיהֹוָ֛ה אֶת־זֶ֥בַח הַיָּמִ֖ים וְאֶת־נִדְרֽוֹ׃ 22 וְחַנָּ֖ה לֹ֣א עָלָ֑תָה כִּֽי־אָמְרָ֣ה לְאִישָׁ֗הּ עַ֣ד יִגָּמֵ֤ל הַנַּ֙עַר֙ וַהֲבִאֹתִ֔יו וְנִרְאָה֙ אֶת־פְּנֵ֣י יְהֹוָ֔ה וְיָ֥שַׁב שָׁ֖ם עַד־עוֹלָֽם׃ 23 וַיֹּ֣אמֶר לָהּ֩ אֶלְקָנָ֨ה אִישָׁ֜הּ עֲשִׂ֣י הַטּ֣וֹב בְּעֵינַ֗יִךְ שְׁבִי֙ עַד־גׇּמְלֵ֣ךְ אֹת֔וֹ אַ֛ךְ יָקֵ֥ם יְהֹוָ֖ה אֶת־דְּבָר֑וֹ וַתֵּ֤שֶׁב הָֽאִשָּׁה֙ וַתֵּ֣ינֶק אֶת־בְּנָ֔הּ עַד־גׇמְלָ֖הּ אֹתֽוֹ׃ 24 וַתַּעֲלֵ֨הוּ עִמָּ֜הּ כַּאֲשֶׁ֣ר גְּמָלַ֗תּוּ בְּפָרִ֤ים שְׁלֹשָׁה֙ וְאֵיפָ֨ה אַחַ֥ת קֶ֙מַח֙ וְנֵ֣בֶל יַ֔יִן

חסר א'   v. 17.

a model for prayer in general. "Hamnuna said: How many important rules can be deduced from Hannah's prayer! That 'Hannah was praying in her heart' teaches that prayer requires devotion of the heart. 'Only her lips moved' teaches that a person must articulate the words of prayer with the lips. 'Her voice could not be heard' teaches that one may not raise one's voice in prayer. 'Eli thought she was drunk' teaches that it is forbidden for an intoxicated person to pray" (BT Ber. 31a).

An extended midrashic analysis of the prayer itself provides Eleazar an occasion to demonstrate various strategies of prayer used by Hannah (BT Ber. 31). See Comment to 2:1.

17. may the God of Israel grant Alludes to the vow in verse 11. The Hebrew verb for "grant" (*yitten*) can also be construed as a prophetic premonition ("the God of Israel will grant").

24. three bulls Hebrew: *parim sh'loshah*. Strangely, *parim* (bulls) is plural yet the next verse

of flour, and a jar of wine. And though the boy
was still very young, she brought him to the
House of the LORD at Shiloh. 25After slaughtering the bull, they brought the boy to Eli. 26She
said, "Please, my lord! As you live, my lord, I
am the woman who stood here beside you and
prayed to the LORD. 27It was this boy I prayed
for; and the LORD has granted me what I asked
of Him. 28I, in turn, hereby lend him to the
LORD. For as long as he lives he is lent to
the LORD." And they bowed low there before
the LORD.

וַתְּבִאֵהוּ בֵית־יְהוָה שִׁלוֹ וְהַנַּעַר נָעַר׃
25 וַיִּשְׁחֲטוּ אֶת־הַפָּר וַיָּבִיאוּ אֶת־הַנַּעַר
אֶל־עֵלִי׃ 26 וַתֹּאמֶר בִּי אֲדֹנִי חֵי נַפְשְׁךָ
אֲדֹנִי אֲנִי הָאִשָּׁה הַנִּצֶּבֶת עִמְּכָה בָּזֶה
לְהִתְפַּלֵּל אֶל־יְהוָה׃ 27 אֶל־הַנַּעַר הַזֶּה
הִתְפַּלָּלְתִּי וַיִּתֵּן יְהוָה לִי אֶת־שְׁאֵלָתִי
אֲשֶׁר שָׁאַלְתִּי מֵעִמּוֹ׃ 28 וְגַם אָנֹכִי
הִשְׁאִלְתִּהוּ לַיהוָה כָּל־הַיָּמִים אֲשֶׁר הָיָה
הוּא שָׁאוּל לַיהוָה וַיִּשְׁתַּחוּ שָׁם
לַיהוָה׃ פ

2 And Hannah prayed:

My heart exults in the LORD;
I have triumphed through the LORD.
I gloat over my enemies;
I rejoice in Your deliverance.

2There is no holy one like the LORD,
Truly, there is none beside You;
There is no rock like our God.

3Talk no more with lofty pride,
Let no arrogance cross your lips!
For the LORD is an all-knowing God;
By Him actions are measured.

4The bows of the mighty are broken,
And the faltering are girded with strength.

ב וַתִּתְפַּלֵּל חַנָּה וַתֹּאמַר

עָלַץ לִבִּי בַּיהוָה
רָמָה קַרְנִי בַּיהוָה
רָחַב פִּי עַל־אוֹיְבַי
כִּי שָׂמַחְתִּי בִּישׁוּעָתֶךָ׃

2 אֵין־קָדוֹשׁ כַּיהוָה
כִּי אֵין בִּלְתֶּךָ
וְאֵין צוּר כֵּאלֹהֵינוּ׃

3 אַל־תַּרְבּוּ תְדַבְּרוּ גְּבֹהָה גְבֹהָה
יֵצֵא עָתָק מִפִּיכֶם
כִּי אֵל דֵּעוֹת יְהוָה
ולא וְלוֹ נִתְכְּנוּ עֲלִלוֹת׃

4 קֶשֶׁת גִּבֹּרִים חַתִּים
וְנִכְשָׁלִים אָזְרוּ חָיִל׃

(v. 25) refers to only one bull (*par*). However, the ancient Greek translation (Septuagint) here reads "three-year-old bull," which implies an original Hebrew text of *par m'shulash* (cf. Gen. 15:9).

1 Samuel 2:1. And Hannah prayed A late tradition observes: "This teaches that women are obligated to pray, for Hannah used to pray eighteen blessings" (*Yalk. Sh.* 2 Sam. 80). The Hebrew for "eighteen" (*sh'moneh esreh*) designates the central *Amidah* prayer of Jewish liturgy. See Comment to 1:13.

I have triumphed Literally, "my horn is exalted" (*ramah karni*). The expression derives from the figure of an animal in triumphant bearing (see Ps. 92:11). The link between the horn and anointing occurs at the end of Hannah's song (v. 10).

2. There is no rock like our God This theological imagery appears in other early songs (see Deut. 32:30–31). References in Deut. 32 to the incomparability of God (v. 12) who kills and makes live (v. 39) are similar to themes found in Hannah's prayer (1 Sam. 2:2,6). Also notable are several striking relations between Hannah's prayer and David's victory song in 2 Sam. 22.

5 Men once sated must hire out for bread;
Men once hungry hunger no more.
While the barren woman bears seven,
The mother of many is forlorn.
6 The LORD deals death and gives life,
Casts down into Sheol and raises up.
7 The LORD makes poor and makes rich;
He casts down, He also lifts high.
8 He raises the poor from the dust,
Lifts up the needy from the dunghill,
Setting them with nobles,
Granting them seats of honor.
For the pillars of the earth are the LORD's;
He has set the world upon them.
9 He guards the steps of His faithful,
But the wicked perish in darkness—
For not by strength shall man prevail.

10 The foes of the LORD shall be shattered;
He will thunder against them in the heavens.
The LORD will judge the ends of the earth.
He will give power to His king,
And triumph to His anointed one.

5 שְׂבֵעִים בַּלֶּחֶם נִשְׂכָּרוּ
וּרְעֵבִים חָדֵלּוּ
עַד־עֲקָרָה יָלְדָה שִׁבְעָה
וְרַבַּת בָּנִים אֻמְלָלָה׃
6 יְהוָה מֵמִית וּמְחַיֶּה
מוֹרִיד שְׁאוֹל וַיָּעַל׃
7 יְהוָה מוֹרִישׁ וּמַעֲשִׁיר
מַשְׁפִּיל אַף־מְרוֹמֵם׃
8 מֵקִים מֵעָפָר דָּל
מֵאַשְׁפֹּת יָרִים אֶבְיוֹן
לְהוֹשִׁיב עִם־נְדִיבִים
וְכִסֵּא כָבוֹד יַנְחִלֵם
כִּי לַיהוָה מְצֻקֵי אֶרֶץ
וַיָּשֶׁת עֲלֵיהֶם תֵּבֵל׃
9 רַגְלֵי חסידו חֲסִידָיו יִשְׁמֹר
וּרְשָׁעִים בַּחֹשֶׁךְ יִדָּמּוּ
כִּי־לֹא בְכֹחַ יִגְבַּר־אִישׁ׃

10 יְהוָה יֵחַתּוּ מריבו מְרִיבָיו
עלו עָלָיו בַּשָּׁמַיִם יַרְעֵם
יְהוָה יָדִין אַפְסֵי־אָרֶץ
וְיִתֶּן־עֹז לְמַלְכּוֹ
וְיָרֵם קֶרֶן מְשִׁיחוֹ׃ פ

10. and triumph to His anointed one Literally, "raise the horn of His anointed one." The song opens and closes on this specific image of triumph. In context, it anticipates Samuel's anointing David with a horn of oil (1 Sam. 16:13). As a *haftarah* reading, these concluding references—to divine judgment, a strengthened king, and God's anointed one—take on a messianic tone of promise. It is in this sense that the imagery entered Jewish liturgy. Thus in the daily *Amidah,* the 15th benediction urges that God "cause the Branch of David Your servant to sprout," continuing with a request that God "raise up his horn with Your salvation." The conclusion blesses the Lord "who causes the horn of salvation to sprout."

הפטרה לראש השנה (יום שני)

HAFTARAH FOR ROSH HA-SHANAH, SECOND DAY

JEREMIAH 31:2–20

This *haftarah* reading is taken from the collection of oracles of consolation found in Jer. 30–32. According to the heading at the beginning of chapter 30, these oracles deal with the return of the northern tribes (Israel) and the southern tribes (Judah) to their homeland. Prophecies addressed to both groups begin this collection (30:4–17). Each of the main sections is introduced by the formula "Thus said the LORD" (30:5,18, 31:23). This formula also begins the *haftarah* (31:2), which closes with the authorizing formula "declares the LORD" (v. 20).

God's expressions of love for Israel, and His promises to restore the nation to its homeland, dominate the *haftarah.* This divine commitment is portrayed as both ancient and ongoing, beginning with the Exodus from Egypt and continuing through the exile. This care is indicated in paternal terms. In one image, God is deemed "ever a Father to Israel." In another, Ephraim is called God's "first-born" and "dear son" (vv. 9,20). Because of this relationship, and the feelings of commitment and concern it evokes, God declares that He will deliver the people from the nations, responding to their words of lament and remorse. Over against this motif, a poignant maternal image gives dramatic expression to the mourning of Ephraim's ancestral mother for her absent children. Rachel cries out in "bitter weeping" and inconsolable sorrow for the nation in exile (v. 15). This grief is assuaged by God, who comforts her with an announcement of the people's return to their homeland, and His own merciful feelings that were evoked by Ephraim's prayer for divine acceptance (vv. 18–19).

The *haftarah* is marked by divine assurances of national restoration and reconciliation. In alternating images, God relates to the people and the Land in masculine and feminine terms, injecting a strong tone of personification and pathos into the prophecies (see vv. 2–4,7,9,15,18,20).

RELATION OF THE *HAFTARAH* TO THE CALENDAR

This excerpt from Jeremiah was chosen for reading on *Rosh ha-Shanah,* according to Rashi, because of two phrases in verse 20: "My thoughts would dwell on him still" (*zakhor ezk'rennu*) and also "I will receive him back in love [*raḥem araḥamennu*]." It thus appears that, by stressing the theme of remembrance (*zikkaron*) and mercy (*raḥamim*) in the *haftarah,* Rashi is alluding to the ancient designation of *Rosh ha-Shanah* as a day "commemorated with loud blasts" (*zikhron t'ru·ah;* Lev. 23:24), when God judges all creatures (M RH 1:2).

The *haftarah* ends with words of divine assurance, in which God declares that His thoughts are ever with Ephraim, that He remembers him (*zakhor ezk'rennu*) with favor and "will receive him back in love" (v. 20). This particular expression of divine remembrance is one of the key verses included in the *Rosh ha-Shanah Musaf* liturgy, expressing the people's hope to elicit God's ongoing care and love. Its recitation in the *haftarah* anticipates this communal prayer, even as Ephraim's penitent appeal for divine forgiveness anticipates the congregation's emphasis on repentance and prayer in the same service.

31

2Thus said the LORD:
The people escaped from the sword,
Found favor in the wilderness;
When Israel was marching homeward
3The LORD revealed Himself to me of old.
Eternal love I conceived for you then;
Therefore I continue My grace to you.
4I will build you firmly again,
O Maiden Israel!
Again you shall take up your timbrels
And go forth to the rhythm of the dancers.
5Again you shall plant vineyards
On the hills of Samaria;
Men shall plant and live to enjoy them.
6For the day is coming when watchmen
Shall proclaim on the heights of Ephraim:
Come, let us go up to Zion,
To the LORD our God!

7For thus said the LORD:
Cry out in joy for Jacob,
Shout at the crossroads of the nations!
Sing aloud in praise, and say:
Save, O LORD, Your people,
The remnant of Israel.
8I will bring them in from the northland,
Gather them from the ends of the earth—
The blind and the lame among them,

לא

2 כֹּה אָמַר יְהוָה
מָצָא חֵן בַּמִּדְבָּר
עַם שְׂרִידֵי חָרֶב
הָלוֹךְ לְהַרְגִּיעוֹ יִשְׂרָאֵל׃
3 מֵרָחוֹק יְהוָה נִרְאָה לִי
וְאַהֲבַת עוֹלָם אֲהַבְתִּיךְ
עַל־כֵּן מְשַׁכְתִּיךְ חָסֶד׃
4 עוֹד אֶבְנֵךְ וְנִבְנֵית
בְּתוּלַת יִשְׂרָאֵל
עוֹד תַּעְדִּי תֻפַּיִךְ
וְיָצָאת בִּמְחוֹל מְשַׂחֲקִים׃
5 עוֹד תִּטְּעִי כְרָמִים
בְּהָרֵי שֹׁמְרוֹן
נָטְעוּ נֹטְעִים וְחִלֵּלוּ׃
6 כִּי יֶשׁ־יוֹם
קָרְאוּ נֹצְרִים בְּהַר אֶפְרָיִם
קוּמוּ וְנַעֲלֶה צִיּוֹן
אֶל־יְהוָה אֱלֹהֵינוּ׃ פ

7 כִּי־כֹה ׀ אָמַר יְהוָה
רָנּוּ לְיַעֲקֹב שִׂמְחָה
וְצַהֲלוּ בְּרֹאשׁ הַגּוֹיִם
הַשְׁמִיעוּ הַלְלוּ וְאִמְרוּ
הוֹשַׁע יְהוָה אֶת־עַמְּךָ
אֵת שְׁאֵרִית יִשְׂרָאֵל׃
8 הִנְנִי מֵבִיא אוֹתָם מֵאֶרֶץ צָפוֹן
וְקִבַּצְתִּים מִיַּרְכְּתֵי־אָרֶץ
בָּם עִוֵּר וּפִסֵּחַ

Jeremiah 31:2. The people escaped from the sword Traditionally understood as referring to the Exodus. The reference to the wilderness that follows is taken as alluding to the 40-year trek in the wilderness, and the motif of the sword is taken to indicate the ensuing battles with the Amalekites and the Canaanites.

3. of old Hebrew: *me-rahok.* Also may be understood spatially, meaning "from afar."

5. Men shall plant and live to enjoy them Literally, "Planters shall plant [vineyards] and harvest [the produce]"—a positive reversal to the curse of Deut. 28:30, "If you plant a vineyard, you shall not harvest it."

7. Save, O LORD It seems difficult to understand the imperative verb "save" (*hosha*) as having been declared by the nations. For this reason, many commentators follow the Septuagint reading as a more fitting public testimonial: "The LORD has saved."

Those with child and those in labor—
In a vast throng they shall return here.
9They shall come with weeping,
And with compassion will I guide them.
I will lead them to streams of water,
By a level road where they will not stumble.
For I am ever a Father to Israel,
Ephraim is My first-born.

10Hear the word of the LORD, O nations,
And tell it in the isles afar.
Say:
He who scattered Israel will gather them,
And will guard them as a shepherd his flock.
11For the LORD will ransom Jacob,
Redeem him from one too strong for him.
12They shall come and shout on the heights of Zion,
Radiant over the bounty of the LORD—
Over new grain and wine and oil,
And over sheep and cattle.
They shall fare like a watered garden,
They shall never languish again.
13Then shall maidens dance gaily,
Young men and old alike.
I will turn their mourning to joy,
I will comfort them and cheer them in their grief.
14I will give the priests their fill of fatness,
And My people shall enjoy My full bounty
—declares the LORD.

15Thus said the LORD:
A cry is heard in Ramah—
Wailing, bitter weeping—
Rachel weeping for her children.
She refuses to be comforted

הָרָה וְיֹלֶדֶת יַחְדָּו
קָהָל גָּדוֹל יָשׁוּבוּ הֵנָּה׃
9 בִּבְכִי יָבֹאוּ
וּבְתַחֲנוּנִים אוֹבִילֵם
אוֹלִיכֵם אֶל־נַחֲלֵי מַיִם
בְּדֶרֶךְ יָשָׁר לֹא יִכָּשְׁלוּ בָּהּ
כִּי־הָיִיתִי לְיִשְׂרָאֵל לְאָב
וְאֶפְרַיִם בְּכֹרִי הוּא׃ ס

10 שִׁמְעוּ דְבַר־יְהוָה גּוֹיִם
וְהַגִּידוּ בָאִיִּים מִמֶּרְחָק
וְאִמְרוּ
מְזָרֵה יִשְׂרָאֵל יְקַבְּצֶנּוּ
וּשְׁמָרוֹ כְּרֹעֶה עֶדְרוֹ׃
11 כִּי־פָדָה יְהוָה אֶת־יַעֲקֹב
וּגְאָלוֹ מִיַּד חָזָק מִמֶּנּוּ׃
12 וּבָאוּ וְרִנְּנוּ בִמְרוֹם־צִיּוֹן
וְנָהֲרוּ אֶל־טוּב יְהוָה
עַל־דָּגָן וְעַל־תִּירֹשׁ וְעַל־יִצְהָר
וְעַל־בְּנֵי־צֹאן וּבָקָר
וְהָיְתָה נַפְשָׁם כְּגַן רָוֶה
וְלֹא־יוֹסִיפוּ לְדַאֲבָה עוֹד׃
13 אָז תִּשְׂמַח בְּתוּלָה בְּמָחוֹל
וּבַחֻרִים וּזְקֵנִים יַחְדָּו
וְהָפַכְתִּי אֶבְלָם לְשָׂשׂוֹן
וְנִחַמְתִּים וְשִׂמַּחְתִּים מִיגוֹנָם׃
14 וְרִוֵּיתִי נֶפֶשׁ הַכֹּהֲנִים דָּשֶׁן
וְעַמִּי אֶת־טוּבִי יִשְׂבָּעוּ
נְאֻם־יְהוָה׃ ס
15 כֹּה ׀ אָמַר יְהוָה
קוֹל בְּרָמָה נִשְׁמָע
נְהִי בְּכִי תַמְרוּרִים
רָחֵל מְבַכָּה עַל־בָּנֶיהָ
מֵאֲנָה לְהִנָּחֵם

9. For I am ever a Father to Israel This usage, common in ancient Near Eastern adoption formulas, is also found in royal and covenantal contexts (cf. 2 Sam. 7:14; Ps. 2:7).

15. Rachel weeping This verse served as the basis for a *midrash* on the merit of mother Rachel, who intercedes before God in connection with Manasseh's sins. God responded to her mercifully.

For her children, who are gone.
16Thus said the LORD:
Restrain your voice from weeping,
Your eyes from shedding tears;
For there is a reward for your labor
—declares the LORD:
They shall return from the enemy's land.
17And there is hope for your future
—declares the LORD:
Your children shall return to their country.

18I can hear Ephraim lamenting:
You have chastised me, and I am chastised
Like a calf that has not been broken.
Receive me back, let me return,
For You, O LORD, are my God.
19Now that I have turned back, I am filled with remorse;
Now that I am made aware, I strike my thigh.
I am ashamed and humiliated,
For I bear the disgrace of my youth.
20Truly, Ephraim is a dear son to Me,
A child that is dandled!
Whenever I have turned against him,
My thoughts would dwell on him still.
That is why My heart yearns for him;
I will receive him back in love
—declares the LORD.

עַל־בָּנֶיהָ כִּי אֵינֶנּוּ׃ ס
16 כֹּה ׀ אָמַר יְהוָה
מִנְעִי קוֹלֵךְ מִבֶּכִי
וְעֵינַיִךְ מִדִּמְעָה
כִּי יֵשׁ שָׂכָר לִפְעֻלָּתֵךְ
נְאֻם־יְהוָה
וְשָׁבוּ מֵאֶרֶץ אוֹיֵב׃
17 וְיֵשׁ־תִּקְוָה לְאַחֲרִיתֵךְ
נְאֻם־יְהוָה
וְשָׁבוּ בָנִים לִגְבוּלָם׃ ס

18 שָׁמוֹעַ שָׁמַעְתִּי אֶפְרַיִם מִתְנוֹדֵד
יִסַּרְתַּנִי וָאִוָּסֵר
כְּעֵגֶל לֹא לֻמָּד
הֲשִׁבֵנִי וְאָשׁוּבָה
כִּי אַתָּה יְהוָה אֱלֹהָי׃
19 כִּי־אַחֲרֵי שׁוּבִי נִחַמְתִּי
וְאַחֲרֵי הִוָּדְעִי סָפַקְתִּי עַל־יָרֵךְ
בֹּשְׁתִּי וְגַם־נִכְלַמְתִּי
כִּי נָשָׂאתִי חֶרְפַּת נְעוּרָי׃
20 הֲבֵן יַקִּיר לִי אֶפְרַיִם
אִם יֶלֶד שַׁעֲשֻׁעִים
כִּי־מִדֵּי דַבְּרִי בּוֹ
זָכֹר אֶזְכְּרֶנּוּ עוֹד
עַל־כֵּן הָמוּ מֵעַי לוֹ
רַחֵם אֲרַחֲמֶנּוּ
נְאֻם־יְהוָה׃ ס

18. For You, O LORD, are my God The covenantal response of Ephraim. See Comment to Jer. 31:9.

19. Now that I have turned back This statement of repentance is followed by an acknowledgment of "remorse." In traditional Judaism, remorse is a stage in the process of repentance. This verse is cited in the classic formulation of Maimonides (MT Repentance 2:2).

20. Truly, Ephraim is a dear son to Me The translation renders this clause and the next as positive, affirmative statements. The Hebrew text, however, is formulated as a double rhetorical question, which commonly implies a negative response (cf. 2:11,14). Hence, the force of the passage is ironic, with God asking, "Is Ephraim really like a dear son, who has not sinned? . . . Nevertheless, whenever I speak of him 'My heart yearns for him.'"

My thoughts would dwell on him still Literally, "I remember him still." The prophet cleverly has chosen a verb (*zakhar,* "remember") that also has the sense of "mention" or "say" and is used together with the verb meaning "to speak" (*dabber,* cf. 20:9). This double meaning of *zakhar* gives a charged and allusive quality to the phrase: "Whenever I have spoken [*dabri*] against him, I remember [*zakhor ezk'rennu*] him still."

הפטרה לשבת שובה

HAFTARAH FOR SHABBAT SHUVAH

HOSEA 14:2–10; MICAH 7:18–20 (*Ashk'nazim*—with *Va-yeilekh*)
HOSEA 14:2–10; JOEL 2:15–27 (*Ashk'nazim*—with *Ha·azinu*)
HOSEA 14:2–10; MICAH 7:18–20 (*S'fardim*)

(Shabbat T'shuvah [*the Sabbath of Repentance*] *is the* Shabbat *before* Yom Kippur, *also called* Shabbat Shuvah *after the first word of this* haftarah. *This occasion coincides with the reading of either* Va-yeilekh *or* Ha·azinu. *Among* Ashk'nazim, *some congregations recite the passages from Hosea and Joel every year; others recite all three passages.*)

In this *haftarah,* the core passage from Hosea focuses on a great call for human repentance, supplemented by the promise of divine healing and sustenance for those who have returned to God. The added selection from Joel introduces rituals of penitence and another promise of divine restoration; the added selection from Micah celebrates God's attributes of mercy and forgiveness of sin.

Combinations of nonconsecutive passages occur several times in the annual *haftarah* cycle. However, such "skipping" (as the Sages call it) from unit to unit is permitted only within the same prophetic book or within a single scroll. In the case of this *haftarah,* all selections are taken from within a single unit, the anthology of 12 prophetic books called "The Twelve" (*Trei Asar*).

Hosea's opening call for repentance dominates the *haftarah*. His appeals to "return to" (*shuvah . . . ad* and *shuvu el*) God (vv. 2–3) exhort the people to turn from their sin and rebellion. His call is also the hinge on which a human–divine dynamic turns, as shown by plays on the operative verb. In the sequel, God declares that, after the people take the initiative to repent, He "will heal their backsliding [*m'shuvatam*]" and take them back in love—for His "anger has turned [*shav*]" from them (v. 5). The result of such divine favor will be a period of national restoration and renewal. Not only will Israel be healed but "They who sit [*yosh'vei*] in his [i.e., Israel's] shade will be revived [*yashuvu*]" as well (v. 8). God's blessing to the people will sustain all who come in contact with them.

Turning and transformation thus constitute the basic structure of the first part of the *haftarah,* embracing the people's turning from sin to God, and God's turning from wrath to loving care.

After Hosea's instruction in repentance, Joel's liturgical instructions articulate a deeper ritual structure: a shofar blast to assemble the nation for fasting and purification, and the priests' supplication to God on behalf of His people. Meanwhile, the liturgical proclamation of divine forgiveness in Micah 7:18–20 supplements Hosea in a different way. Here God's assertion of loving care is climaxed by a human declaration that God's forgiveness is incomparable.

RELATION OF THE *HAFTARAH* TO THE CALENDAR

Shabbat Shuvah concludes an 11-week cycle of special Sabbaths that began after the fast of the 17th of *Tammuz.* For this period, *haftarah* texts were chosen according to the theme of the day and not because of any verbal correspondence with the weekly Torah portion. Prophetic readings for *Shabbat Shuvah* highlight the themes of human repentance and divine mercy. Hosea, in particular, expresses confession of sins and commitment to God; Joel refers to rituals of contrition and purification, along with priestly prayers; and Micah celebrates divine forgiveness of sin.

The *haftarah* readings emphasize the activity of repentance—the external acts (verbal and behavioral) that announce and activate a transformation of religious life. The inward journey "to-

ward" God is left for the individual worshiper, along with the "words" that must be taken to heart and spoken with integrity. According to a later master, this journey is a return to one's spiritual source, to a transcendent point of integration symbolized on earth by *Shabbat.*

14

2Return, O Israel, to the LORD your God,
For you have fallen because of your sin.
3Take words with you
And return to the LORD.
Say to Him:
"Forgive all guilt
And accept what is good;
Instead of bulls we will pay
[The offering of] our lips.
4Assyria shall not save us,
No more will we ride on steeds;
Nor ever again will we call
Our handiwork our god,
Since in You alone orphans find pity!"
5I will heal their affliction,
Generously will I take them back in love;
For My anger has turned away from them.
6I will be to Israel like dew;
He shall blossom like the lily,

יד

2 שׁוּבָה יִשְׂרָאֵל עַד יְהוָה אֱלֹהֶיךָ
כִּי כָשַׁלְתָּ בַּעֲוֺנֶךָ׃
3 קְחוּ עִמָּכֶם דְּבָרִים
וְשׁוּבוּ אֶל־יְהוָה
אִמְרוּ אֵלָיו
כָּל־תִּשָּׂא עָוֺן
וְקַח־טוֹב
וּנְשַׁלְּמָה פָרִים
שְׂפָתֵינוּ׃
4 אַשּׁוּר ׀ לֹא יוֹשִׁיעֵנוּ
עַל־סוּס לֹא נִרְכָּב
וְלֹא־נֹאמַר עוֹד
אֱלֹהֵינוּ לְמַעֲשֵׂה יָדֵינוּ
אֲשֶׁר־בְּךָ יְרֻחַם יָתוֹם׃
5 אֶרְפָּא מְשׁוּבָתָם
אֹהֲבֵם נְדָבָה
כִּי שָׁב אַפִּי מִמֶּנּוּ׃
6 אֶהְיֶה כַטַּל לְיִשְׂרָאֵל
יִפְרַח כַּשּׁוֹשַׁנָּה

Hosea 14:2–4. The prophet Hosea calls on the nation to repent. Elements of this act include the recognition of guilt and its rejection (vv. 2,4); repentance (v. 2); confession of sin and appeal to mercy (v. 3); and the rejection of past practices, with the decision never again to engage in them (vv. 4,9). This fourfold structure anticipates the teachings on repentance formulated in the Middle Ages by Saadia (*Doctrines and Beliefs*) and by Maimonides (MT Repentance 2:2,4).

References to repentance in the Torah differ from those in the prophets. In the Torah, repentance is something that the people may do after divine punishment has occurred, something that may lead to God's merciful cancellation of the "distress" (see Deut. 4:29–31, 30:1–10). Characteristically, however, the prophets' call for repentance precedes any punishment, because it is an act that may avert the divine decree. This is its use in most traditional Jewish sources.

The prophet instructs the people in the use of appropriate words of confession (Ibn Ezra, Radak), appealing to them that they ask God to "Forgive all guilt" (*kol tissa avon*). This phrase alludes to the divine attribute of mercy (see *nosei avon* [forgiving iniquity] in Exod. 34:7 and elsewhere).

And accept what is good Hebrew: *v'kaḥ tov.* The meaning is obscure, perhaps a request that God accept the good deeds done (Kara), the good heart (Radak), or even words of contrition (Ibn Ezra).

Instead of bulls we shall pay / [The offering of] our lips The Hebrew is obscure. Based on the Septuagint reading "fruit" in the singular, many modern scholars read the word *parim*

He shall strike root like a Lebanon tree.
7His boughs shall spread out far,
His beauty shall be like the olive tree's,
His fragrance like that of Lebanon.
8They who sit in his shade shall be revived:
They shall bring to life new grain,
They shall blossom like the vine;
His scent shall be like the wine of Lebanon.
9Ephraim [shall say]:
"What more have I to do with idols?
When I respond and look to Him,
I become like a verdant cypress."
Your fruit is provided by Me.
10He who is wise will consider these words,
He who is prudent will take note of them.
For the paths of the LORD are smooth;
The righteous can walk on them,
While sinners stumble on them.

וְיַ֥ךְ שָׁרָשָׁ֖יו כַּלְּבָנֽוֹן׃
7 יֵלְכוּ֙ יֹנְקוֹתָ֔יו
וִיהִ֥י כַזַּ֖יִת הוֹד֑וֹ
וְרֵ֥יחַֽ ל֖וֹ כַּלְּבָנֽוֹן׃
8 יָשֻׁ֙בוּ֙ יֹשְׁבֵ֣י בְצִלּ֔וֹ
יְחַיּ֥וּ דָגָ֖ן
וְיִפְרְח֣וּ כַגָּ֑פֶן
זִכְר֖וֹ כְּיֵ֥ין לְבָנֽוֹן׃ ס
9 אֶפְרַ֕יִם
מַה־לִּ֥י ע֖וֹד לָעֲצַבִּ֑ים
אֲנִ֧י עָנִ֣יתִי וַאֲשׁוּרֶ֗נּוּ
אֲנִי֙ כִּבְר֣וֹשׁ רַעֲנָ֔ן
מִמֶּ֖נִּי פֶּרְיְךָ֥ נִמְצָֽא׃
10 מִ֤י חָכָם֙ וְיָ֣בֵֽן אֵ֔לֶּה
נָב֖וֹן וְיֵדָעֵ֑ם
כִּֽי־יְשָׁרִ֞ים דַּרְכֵ֣י יְהוָ֗ה
וְצַדִּקִים֙ יֵ֣לְכוּ בָ֔ם
וּפֹשְׁעִ֖ים יִכָּ֥שְׁלוּ בָֽם׃

2 15Blow a horn in Zion,
Solemnize a fast,
Proclaim an assembly!
16Gather the people,
Bid the congregation purify themselves.
Bring together the old,
Gather the babes
And the sucklings at the breast;

ב 15 תִּקְע֥וּ שׁוֹפָ֖ר בְּצִיּ֑וֹן
קַדְּשׁוּ־צ֖וֹם
קִרְא֥וּ עֲצָרָֽה׃
16 אִסְפוּ־עָ֞ם
קַדְּשׁ֣וּ קָהָ֗ל
קִבְצ֣וּ זְקֵנִ֔ים
אִסְפוּ֙ עֽוֹלָלִ֔ים
וְיֹנְקֵ֖י שָׁדָ֑יִם

(bulls) as *p'ri* (fruit of) + *m,* understanding the *m* as a poetic embellishment. This yields: "We shall pay the fruit of our lips [i.e., confess]." Thus prayer substitutes for a sacrificial offering, and confession is an offering of contrition.

9. A fitting conclusion to the prophet's call, affirming the main point: Spiritual fidelity leads to a thorough transformation of Ephraim's earthly life.

10. consider . . . take note A concluding exhortation.

these words . . . of them If "these" refers to the preceding counsel to repent (Rashi), then v. 10a is the rhetorical conclusion to verses 2–9. Alternatively, if "these" refers to the "paths of the LORD" in the following phrase (Ibn Ezra), then the reference is to the justice of God ("path," or "way," indicates divine providence; cf. Exod. 33:13). By contrast, Radak understood "these" to mean the prophet's earlier words of reproof. In this view, the exhortation calls on the people to take heed of God's judgment.

Joel 2:15–16. Blow a horn This proclamation of alarm invokes a national assembly. Technical terms are used to stress the significance of the ingathering. The call for "the bridegroom [to]

Let the bridegroom come out of his chamber,
The bride from her canopied couch.
17Between the portico and the altar,
Let the priests, the LORD's ministers, weep
And say:
"Oh, spare Your people, LORD!
Let not Your possession become a mockery,
To be taunted by nations!
Let not the peoples say,
'Where is their God?'"

18Then the LORD was roused
On behalf of His land
And had compassion
Upon His people.
19In response to His people
The LORD declared:
"I will grant you the new grain,
The new wine, and the new oil,
And you shall have them in abundance.
Nevermore will I let you be
A mockery among the nations.
20I will drive the northerner far from you,
I will thrust it into a parched and desolate
   land—
Its van to the Eastern Sea
And its rear to the Western Sea;
And the stench of it shall go up,
And the foul smell rise."
For [the LORD] shall work great deeds.

יֵצֵ֤א חָתָן֙ מֵֽחֶדְר֔וֹ
וְכַלָּ֖ה מֵחֻפָּתָֽהּ׃
17 בֵּ֤ין הָאוּלָם֙ וְלַמִּזְבֵּ֔חַ
יִבְכּוּ֙ הַכֹּֽהֲנִ֔ים מְשָׁרְתֵ֖י יְהֹוָ֑ה
וְֽיֹאמְר֗וּ
ח֤וּסָה יְהֹוָה֙ עַל־עַמֶּ֔ךָ
וְאַל־תִּתֵּ֨ן נַחֲלָֽתְךָ֤ לְחֶרְפָּה֙
לִמְשָׁל־בָּ֣ם גּוֹיִ֔ם
לָ֚מָּה יֹאמְר֣וּ בָֽעַמִּ֔ים
אַיֵּ֖ה אֱלֹֽהֵיהֶֽם׃
18 וַיְקַנֵּ֥א יְהֹוָ֖ה
לְאַרְצ֑וֹ
וַיַּחְמֹ֖ל
עַל־עַמּֽוֹ׃
19 וַיַּ֨עַן יְהֹוָ֜ה
וַיֹּ֣אמֶר לְעַמּ֗וֹ
הִנְנִ֨י שֹׁלֵ֤חַ לָכֶם֙ אֶת־הַדָּגָ֔ן
וְהַתִּיר֖וֹשׁ וְהַיִּצְהָ֑ר
וּשְׂבַעְתֶּ֖ם אֹת֑וֹ
וְלֹֽא־אֶתֵּ֨ן אֶתְכֶ֥ם ע֛וֹד
חֶרְפָּ֖ה בַּגּוֹיִֽם׃
20 וְֽאֶת־הַצְּפוֹנִ֞י אַרְחִ֣יק מֵעֲלֵיכֶ֗ם
וְהִדַּחְתִּיו֮ אֶל־אֶ֣רֶץ צִיָּ֣ה וּשְׁמָמָה֒
אֶת־פָּנָ֗יו אֶל־הַיָּם֙ הַקַּדְמֹנִ֔י
וְסֹפ֖וֹ אֶל־הַיָּ֣ם הָאַֽחֲר֑וֹן
וְעָלָ֣ה בׇאְשׁ֗וֹ
וְתַ֙עַל֙ צַחֲנָת֔וֹ
כִּ֥י הִגְדִּ֖יל לַעֲשֽׂוֹת׃

come out of his chamber" provides a dramatic counterpoint to those terms, heightening the sense of communal obligation over all personal pleasure. By law, bridegrooms were exempted from military service and other public obligations (see Deut. 20:7, 24:5).

17. Between the portico and the altar The portico was an entrance area, or vestibule, in front of the Temple. The outer altar was at the other end of the courtyard. This area was used for public prayer.

And say This threefold supplication begins with an appeal to "spare" (ḥusah) the nation (see Jon. 4:10–11). Then it asks God to prevent the people from being taunted. It climaxes with an example of mockery ("Where is their God?"), saving for last the appeal's theological dimension, with its suggestion of God's lack of power.

18. Then the LORD was roused As if in direct response to the supplication of verse 17.

20. northerner Many interpreters understand this as a reference to the "enormous horde"

21Fear not, O soil, rejoice and be glad;
For the LORD has wrought great deeds.
22Fear not, O beasts of the field,
For the pastures in the wilderness
Are clothed with grass.
The trees have borne their fruit;
Fig tree and vine
Have yielded their strength.
23O children of Zion, be glad,
Rejoice in the LORD your God.
For He has given you the early rain in [His] kindness,
Now He makes the rain fall [as] formerly—
The early rain and the late—
24And threshing floors shall be piled with grain,
And vats shall overflow with new wine and oil.

25"I will repay you for the years
Consumed by swarms and hoppers,
By grubs and locusts,
The great army I let loose against you.
26And you shall eat your fill
And praise the name of the LORD your God
Who dealt so wondrously with you—
My people shall be shamed no more.
27And you shall know
That I am in the midst of Israel:
That I the LORD am your God
And there is no other.
And My people shall be shamed no more."

21 אַל־תִּירְאִי אֲדָמָה גִּילִי וּשְׂמָחִי
כִּי־הִגְדִּיל יְהוָה לַעֲשׂוֹת׃
22 אַל־תִּירְאוּ בַּהֲמוֹת שָׂדַי
כִּי דָשְׁאוּ נְאוֹת מִדְבָּר
כִּי־עֵץ נָשָׂא פִרְיוֹ
תְּאֵנָה וָגֶפֶן
נָתְנוּ חֵילָם׃
23 וּבְנֵי צִיּוֹן גִּילוּ
וְשִׂמְחוּ בַּיהוָה אֱלֹהֵיכֶם
כִּי־נָתַן לָכֶם אֶת־הַמּוֹרֶה לִצְדָקָה
וַיּוֹרֶד לָכֶם גֶּשֶׁם
מוֹרֶה וּמַלְקוֹשׁ בָּרִאשׁוֹן׃
24 וּמָלְאוּ הַגֳּרָנוֹת בָּר
וְהֵשִׁיקוּ הַיְקָבִים תִּירוֹשׁ וְיִצְהָר׃

25 וְשִׁלַּמְתִּי לָכֶם אֶת־הַשָּׁנִים
אֲשֶׁר אָכַל הָאַרְבֶּה הַיֶּלֶק
וְהֶחָסִיל וְהַגָּזָם
חֵילִי הַגָּדוֹל אֲשֶׁר שִׁלַּחְתִּי בָּכֶם׃
26 וַאֲכַלְתֶּם אָכוֹל וְשָׂבוֹעַ
וְהִלַּלְתֶּם אֶת־שֵׁם יְהוָה אֱלֹהֵיכֶם
אֲשֶׁר־עָשָׂה עִמָּכֶם לְהַפְלִיא
וְלֹא־יֵבֹשׁוּ עַמִּי לְעוֹלָם׃
27 וִידַעְתֶּם
כִּי בְקֶרֶב יִשְׂרָאֵל אָנִי
וַאֲנִי יְהוָה אֱלֹהֵיכֶם
וְאֵין עוֹד
וְלֹא־יֵבֹשׁוּ עַמִּי לְעוֹלָם׃ ס

prophesied in Joel 2:2, whose devastation is now reversed. Some commentators interpret this as a metaphor for the locust (Rashi, Ibn Ezra).

23. The beneficence of rain will cause the earth, the animals, and the people to rejoice (vv. 21–23).

[*as*] ***formerly*** Better: "[both] in the first [month]," following Ibn Ezra, as found in the Masoretic notes. Early rabbinic tradition understood this as doubled rainfall—not a poetic hyperbole but rather a miracle (BT Taan. 5a).

27. I am in the midst of Israel The concluding oracle of assurance announces God's self-manifestation among the people. God's indwelling presence is revealed through the bounty of the Land.

7 18Who is a God like You,
Forgiving iniquity
And remitting transgression;
Who has not maintained His wrath forever
Against the remnant of His own people,
Because He loves graciousness!
19He will take us back in love;
He will cover up our iniquities,
You will hurl all our sins
Into the depths of the sea.
20You will keep faith with Jacob,
Loyalty to Abraham,
As You promised on oath to our fathers
In days gone by.

ז 18 מִי־אֵל כָּמוֹךָ
נֹשֵׂא עָוֺן
וְעֹבֵר עַל־פֶּשַׁע
לִשְׁאֵרִית נַחֲלָתוֹ
לֹא־הֶחֱזִיק לָעַד אַפּוֹ
כִּי־חָפֵץ חֶסֶד הוּא׃
19 יָשׁוּב יְרַחֲמֵנוּ
יִכְבֹּשׁ עֲוֺנֹתֵינוּ
וְתַשְׁלִיךְ בִּמְצֻלוֹת יָם
כָּל־חַטֹּאותָם*׃
20 תִּתֵּן אֱמֶת לְיַעֲקֹב
חֶסֶד לְאַבְרָהָם
אֲשֶׁר־נִשְׁבַּעְתָּ לַאֲבֹתֵינוּ
מִימֵי קֶדֶם׃

v. 19. מלא ו׳

Micah 7:18–19. Customarily these verses are also recited during the *Tashlikh* ceremony on the afternoon of the first day of *Rosh ha-Shanah.* On that occasion, the community enacts the reference to God casting sins into the sea and asserts faith in divine forgiveness.

הפטרה ליום כפור (שחרית)

HAFTARAH FOR YOM KIPPUR MORNING

ISAIAH 57:14–58:14

This *haftarah* is drawn from prophecies addressed to the Judean community near the end of the 6th century B.C.E. The words were spoken sometime after Cyrus the Mede had conquered Babylon and issued a decree (in 538 B.C.E.) allowing subject populations, like the Judeans, to return to their native lands and practices. It is unclear whether this series of prophecies is addressed to Judeans still in exile or to members of the restored community in Zion. As a reading for *Yom Kippur,* the prophet's words transcend their original setting, opening a path for piety and repentance.

The people are told of God's concern for the contrite, of His healing forgiveness for the meek in spirit. This word of hope is followed by an exhortation dealing with the sins of the House of Israel. Although they seek God daily, "like a nation that does what is right" (Isa. 58:2), they are mindless of their duplicity and evil deeds. A powerful instruction in religious action follows, in an attempt to shatter the crust of ritual formalism and moral blindness. If the people take this teaching to heart, the prophet promises them the light of God's presence and the healing waters of renewal. A final word celebrates *Shabbat* rest, as a sign of a transformed religious consciousness and commitment to God.

To inculcate a transformation of religious consciousness and action is the dominant concern of this *haftarah.* The Lord calls to the prophet: "Clear a road! / Remove all obstacles / From the road of My people!" (Isa. 57:14). This road is no mere physical highway leading from exile to the homeland, but a path of inner renewal, leading from "greed" to a "contrite" spirit (vv. 15–17) and from duplicity and contention to compassion and justice (58:3–7,9–10). Inwardness thus involves the cultivation of humility and empathy, virtues that form the keystone of rebuilt religiosity. God will bless such a life with light and healing (57:18–19, 58:8,10–11).

The instruction that God will answer only those who help the oppressed, the hungry, and the poor (58:6–7)—not those who merely afflict their bodies—captures the essence of the prophet's words. The commitment to God is condensed into an injunction to uphold the sanctity of *Shabbat* (58:13). It is such a commitment that is desired, not merely eagerness for the nearness of God (see 58:2).

The prophet's rhetoric stresses the misuse of fasting to stress the values of social responsibility. He does not wholly condemn ritual acts such as fasting. What he condemns is false piety, particularly when it is accompanied by deeds of oppression and wickedness. God does not desire such behavior any more than He condones solemn "assemblies with iniquity" (Isa. 1:13). Ritual must be grounded in a spiritual core of moral sensibility and action.

RELATION OF THE *HAFTARAH* TO THE CALENDAR

The Talmud designates this *haftarah* as the prophetic reading for *Yom Kippur* morning (BT Meg. 31a). Rashi notes that this is because of its focus of repentance, emphasizing the phrase "No, this is the fast I desire" (Isa. 58:6). This phrase is followed by a series of instructions for a reformed religious life.

The language of fasting and self-affliction in Isa. 58:3–5—especially the phrase "we starved our bodies" (*ininu nafsheinu*)—echoes the terminology of the Torah reading for *Yom Kippur* morning (see Lev. 16:31). Juxtaposing these two readings in a synagogue service invites congregants to reflect on the relationship between ritual acts and their spiritual purpose. At the center of Jewish piety are the moral challenge and the critique of ritual that this *haftarah* offers.

57 14[The LORD] says:
Build up, build up a highway!
Clear a road!
Remove all obstacles
From the road of My people!
15For thus said He who high aloft
Forever dwells, whose name is holy:
I dwell on high, in holiness;
I dwell on high, in holiness;
Yet with the contrite and the lowly in spirit—
Reviving the spirits of the lowly,
Reviving the hearts of the contrite.
16For I will not always contend,
I will not be angry forever:
Nay, I who make spirits flag,
Also create the breath of life.
17For their sinful greed I was angry;
I struck them and turned away in My wrath.
Though stubborn, they follow the way of their hearts,
18I note how they fare and will heal them:
I will guide them and mete out solace to them,
And to the mourners among them 19hearten-ing, comforting words:
It shall be well,
Well with the far and the near
—said the LORD—
And I will heal them.

נז 14 וְאָמַ֥ר
סֹֽלּוּ־סֹ֖לּוּ
פַּנּוּ־דָ֑רֶךְ
הָרִ֥ימוּ מִכְשׁ֖וֹל
מִדֶּ֥רֶךְ עַמִּֽי׃ ס
15 כִּי֩ כֹ֨ה אָמַ֜ר רָ֣ם וְנִשָּׂ֗א
שֹׁכֵ֥ן עַד֙ וְקָד֣וֹשׁ שְׁמ֔וֹ
מָר֥וֹם וְקָד֖וֹשׁ אֶשְׁכּ֑וֹן
וְאֶת־דַּכָּא֙ וּשְׁפַל־ר֔וּחַ
לְהַחֲיוֹת֙ ר֣וּחַ שְׁפָלִ֔ים
וּֽלְהַחֲי֖וֹת לֵ֥ב נִדְכָּאִֽים׃
16 כִּ֣י לֹ֤א לְעוֹלָם֙ אָרִ֔יב
וְלֹ֥א לָנֶ֖צַח אֶקְּצ֑וֹף
כִּי־ר֙וּחַ֙ מִלְּפָנַ֣י יַעֲט֔וֹף
וּנְשָׁמ֖וֹת אֲנִ֥י עָשִֽׂיתִי׃
17 בַּעֲוֺ֥ן בִּצְע֛וֹ קָצַ֖פְתִּי
וְאַכֵּ֑הוּ הַסְתֵּ֣ר וְאֶקְצֹ֔ף
וַיֵּ֥לֶךְ שׁוֹבָ֖ב בְּדֶ֥רֶךְ לִבּֽוֹ׃
18 דְּרָכָ֥יו רָאִ֖יתִי וְאֶרְפָּאֵ֑הוּ
וְאַנְחֵ֕הוּ וַאֲשַׁלֵּ֧ם נִחֻמִ֛ים ל֖וֹ
וְלַאֲבֵלָֽיו׃ 19 בּוֹרֵ֖א נוב נִ֣יב שְׂפָתָ֑יִם
שָׁל֨וֹם ׀
שָׁל֜וֹם לָרָח֧וֹק וְלַקָּר֛וֹב
אָמַ֥ר יְהוָ֖ה
וּרְפָאתִֽיו׃

Isaiah 57:14. Build up, build up Doubling of words is a stylistic hallmark of Isa. 40–66. This feature serves to reinforce and energize the contents of the speech (Radak on Isa. 40:1).

15. He who high aloft / Forever dwells Hebrew: *ram v'nissa shokhen ad.* This depiction of divine transcendence, above and beyond the world, is followed immediately by a statement of God's indwelling in the world, God's immanence. These are the two poles of biblical theology.

Yet with the contrite and the lowly in spirit Despite His exalted status, God is present in the lives of the lowly (Radak, ibn Kaspi). This theology is also expressed in a personal prayer: "The LORD is close to the brokenhearted; / those crushed in spirit He delivers" (Ps. 34:19).

19. It shall be well, / Well with the far and the near God's blessing of *shalom* is extended to all those who merit divine healing and comfort (v. 18). An old tradition interpreted "the far" as the righteous who observe the Torah from "of old," and "the near" as those who repent and turn to Torah now (Targ. Jon.).

20But the wicked are like the troubled sea
Which cannot rest,
Whose waters toss up mire and mud.
21There is no safety
—said my God—
For the wicked.

20 וְהָרְשָׁעִים כַּיָּם נִגְרָשׁ
כִּי הַשְׁקֵט לֹא יוּכָל
וַיִּגְרְשׁוּ מֵימָיו רֶפֶשׁ וָטִיט׃
21 אֵין שָׁלוֹם
אָמַר אֱלֹהַי
לָרְשָׁעִים׃ ס

58 Cry with full throat, without restraint;
Raise your voice like a ram's horn!
Declare to My people their transgression,
To the House of Jacob their sin.

נח קְרָא בְגָרוֹן אַל־תַּחְשֹׂךְ
כַּשּׁוֹפָר הָרֵם קוֹלֶךָ
וְהַגֵּד לְעַמִּי פִּשְׁעָם
וּלְבֵית יַעֲקֹב חַטֹּאתָם׃

2To be sure, they seek Me daily,
Eager to learn My ways.
Like a nation that does what is right,
That has not abandoned the laws of its God,
They ask Me for the right way,
They are eager for the nearness of God:
3"Why, when we fasted, did You not see?
When we starved our bodies, did You pay no heed?"
Because on your fast day
You see to your business
And oppress all your laborers!
4Because you fast in strife and contention,
And you strike with a wicked fist!
Your fasting today is not such
As to make your voice heard on high.
5Is such the fast I desire,
A day for men to starve their bodies?
Is it bowing the head like a bulrush
And lying in sackcloth and ashes?
Do you call that a fast,
A day when the LORD is favorable?

2 וְאוֹתִי יוֹם יוֹם יִדְרֹשׁוּן
וְדַעַת דְּרָכַי יֶחְפָּצוּן
כְּגוֹי אֲשֶׁר־צְדָקָה עָשָׂה
וּמִשְׁפַּט אֱלֹהָיו לֹא עָזָב
יִשְׁאָלוּנִי מִשְׁפְּטֵי־צֶדֶק
קִרְבַת אֱלֹהִים יֶחְפָּצוּן׃
3 לָמָּה צַּמְנוּ וְלֹא רָאִיתָ
עִנִּינוּ נַפְשֵׁנוּ וְלֹא תֵדָע
הֵן בְּיוֹם צֹמְכֶם
תִּמְצְאוּ־חֵפֶץ
וְכָל־עַצְּבֵיכֶם תִּנְגֹּשׂוּ׃
4 הֵן לְרִיב וּמַצָּה תָּצוּמוּ
וּלְהַכּוֹת בְּאֶגְרֹף רֶשַׁע
לֹא־תָצוּמוּ כַיּוֹם
לְהַשְׁמִיעַ בַּמָּרוֹם קוֹלְכֶם׃
5 הֲכָזֶה יִהְיֶה צוֹם אֶבְחָרֵהוּ
יוֹם עַנּוֹת אָדָם נַפְשׁוֹ
הֲלָכֹף כְּאַגְמֹן רֹאשׁוֹ
וְשַׂק וָאֵפֶר יַצִּיעַ
הֲלָזֶה תִּקְרָא־צוֹם
וְיוֹם רָצוֹן לַיהוָה׃

20. the wicked are like the troubled sea Inner turbulence gives them no rest, and keeps them far from God.

6No, this is the fast I desire:
To unlock fetters of wickedness,
And untie the cords of the yoke
To let the oppressed go free;
To break off every yoke.
7It is to share your bread with the hungry,
And to take the wretched poor into your home;
When you see the naked, to clothe him,
And not to ignore your own kin.

8Then shall your light burst through like the dawn
And your healing spring up quickly;
Your Vindicator shall march before you,
The Presence of the LORD shall be your rear guard.
9Then, when you call, the LORD will answer;
When you cry, He will say: Here I am.
If you banish the yoke from your midst,
The menacing hand, and evil speech,
10And you offer your compassion to the hungry
And satisfy the famished creature—
Then shall your light shine in darkness,
And your gloom shall be like noonday.
11The LORD will guide you always;
He will slake your thirst in parched places
And give strength to your bones.
You shall be like a watered garden,
Like a spring whose waters do not fail.
12Men from your midst shall rebuild ancient ruins,
You shall restore foundations laid long ago.
And you shall be called
"Repairer of fallen walls,
Restorer of lanes for habitation."
13If you refrain from trampling the sabbath,

6 הֲלוֹא זֶה צוֹם אֶבְחָרֵהוּ
פַּתֵּחַ חַרְצֻבּוֹת רֶשַׁע
הַתֵּר אֲגֻדּוֹת מוֹטָה
וְשַׁלַּח רְצוּצִים חָפְשִׁים
וְכָל־מוֹטָה תְּנַתֵּקוּ׃
7 הֲלוֹא פָרֹס לָרָעֵב לַחְמֶךָ
וַעֲנִיִּים מְרוּדִים תָּבִיא בָיִת
כִּי־תִרְאֶה עָרֹם וְכִסִּיתוֹ
וּמִבְּשָׂרְךָ לֹא תִתְעַלָּם׃

8 אָז יִבָּקַע כַּשַּׁחַר אוֹרֶךָ
וַאֲרֻכָתְךָ מְהֵרָה תִצְמָח
וְהָלַךְ לְפָנֶיךָ צִדְקֶךָ
כְּבוֹד יְהוָה יַאַסְפֶךָ׃
9 אָז תִּקְרָא וַיהוָה יַעֲנֶה
תְּשַׁוַּע וְיֹאמַר הִנֵּנִי
אִם־תָּסִיר מִתּוֹכְךָ מוֹטָה
שְׁלַח אֶצְבַּע וְדַבֶּר־אָוֶן׃
10 וְתָפֵק לָרָעֵב נַפְשֶׁךָ
וְנֶפֶשׁ נַעֲנָה תַּשְׂבִּיעַ
וְזָרַח בַּחֹשֶׁךְ אוֹרֶךָ
וַאֲפֵלָתְךָ כַּצָּהֳרָיִם׃
11 וְנָחֲךָ יְהוָה תָּמִיד
וְהִשְׂבִּיעַ בְּצַחְצָחוֹת נַפְשֶׁךָ
וְעַצְמֹתֶיךָ יַחֲלִיץ
וְהָיִיתָ כְּגַן רָוֶה
וּכְמוֹצָא מַיִם אֲשֶׁר לֹא־יְכַזְּבוּ מֵימָיו׃
12 וּבָנוּ מִמְּךָ חָרְבוֹת עוֹלָם
מוֹסְדֵי דוֹר־וָדוֹר תְּקוֹמֵם
וְקֹרָא לְךָ
גֹּדֵר פֶּרֶץ
מְשֹׁבֵב נְתִיבוֹת לָשָׁבֶת׃
13 אִם־תָּשִׁיב מִשַּׁבָּת רַגְלֶךָ

From pursuing your affairs on My holy day;
If you call the sabbath "delight,"
The LORD's holy day "honored";
And if you honor it and go not your ways
Nor look to your affairs, nor strike bargains—
14Then you can seek the favor of the LORD.
I will set you astride the heights of the earth,
And let you enjoy the heritage of your father
Jacob—
For the mouth of the LORD has spoken.

עֲשׂוֹת חֲפָצֶךָ בְּיוֹם קָדְשִׁי
וְקָרָאתָ לַשַּׁבָּת עֹנֶג
לִקְדוֹשׁ יְהוָה מְכֻבָּד
וְכִבַּדְתּוֹ מֵעֲשׂוֹת דְּרָכֶיךָ
מִמְּצוֹא חֶפְצְךָ וְדַבֵּר דָּבָר׃
14 אָז תִּתְעַנַּג עַל־יְהוָה
וְהִרְכַּבְתִּיךָ עַל־במותי בָּמֳתֵי אָרֶץ
וְהַאֲכַלְתִּיךָ נַחֲלַת יַעֲקֹב אָבִיךָ
כִּי פִּי יְהוָה דִּבֵּר׃ ס

Isaiah 58:14. For the mouth of the LORD has spoken This is a technical formula used to recall and reapply an earlier prophecy or instruction. Here the divine promise in this verse—"I will set you astride [*v'hirkavtikha*] the heights of the earth [*al bamotei aretz*], / And let you enjoy [*va-ha·akhaltikha*] the heritage [*naḥalat*] of your father Jacob"—evokes the Song of Moses (Deut. 32:9,13). There, with similar language, the people are told that Jacob is the Lord's portion, or heritage (*naḥalato*), and that He sustained him (*va-yokhal*) and "set him atop the highlands [*yarkiveihu al bamotei aretz*]." That account of divine care is now transformed into a prophecy of future beneficence—a new settlement in the land, made conditional upon *Shabbat* observance.

הפטרה ליום כפור (מנחה)

HAFTARAH FOR YOM KIPPUR AFTERNOON

JONAH 1:1–4:11; MICAH 7:18–20

Jonah is unlike other prophets in several respects. He does not leave behind a collection of prophecies. Like Moses and Jeremiah, he argues with God, but unlike them, he not only refuses to accept his mission; he also runs away from it. He refuses to be the instrument of God's salvation, yet proclaims: "Deliverance is the LORD's!" (2:10). Ultimately, when compelled to prophesy, Jonah pronounces only five words to those to whom he is sent (3:4). And in contrast to the other prophets, he experiences immediate success; his words call forth an instant response by the inhabitants of Nineveh. This, however, leaves him with a sense of distress, not elation.

The story of Jonah, which purports to be historic, was accepted as such throughout the Middle Ages. Even Ibn Ezra maintains its authenticity, explaining that Jonah's being swallowed by a "huge fish" took place in a dream. For him, as for the Sages before him, the Jonah of this story is in fact Jonah the son of Amittai (see 1:1 and 2 Kings 14:25), who prophesied during the reign of Jeroboam son of Joash of Israel (787–748 B.C.E.). But many modern scholars maintain that the story could not have been written during that time. They point to its author's familiarity with passages in later books of the Bible, including the Book of Jeremiah. This prophet lived at the end of the seventh century B.C.E., more than a hundred years after Jeroboam son of Joash. They also note the strong influence of Aramaic on the language of the story and the use of late Hebrew terms and grammatical constructions, both of which were current during the Second Temple period.

Scholars call attention to apparent Persian influence in two of the practices cited: A decree is issued in the name of "the king and his nobles" (3:7), and beasts as well as human beings are covered with sackcloth as a way of appealing to God (3:8). The author of Jonah was no doubt familiar with these practices. In addition, Nineveh is written about in the past tense, and it was in fact destroyed in 612 B.C.E. All this makes it quite likely that the story of Jonah was written during the Persian period (538–333 B.C.E.), a time when theological issues were major topics of discussion.

The story of Jonah is much more complex than it appears on first reading. It is by no means a folk tale designed simply to entertain. Nor is it a satire intended to poke fun at the prophet. Nevertheless, it does contain elements of irony: Jonah acknowledges that he worships "the God of Heaven, who made both sea and land" (1:9) yet he seeks to escape from God by sea. He criticizes idol worshipers as forsaking "their own welfare" (2:9), but it is these worshipers who in fact first turn to the Lord in the time of crisis (1:14–16; 3:8ff), and Jonah does not. Still, Jonah is depicted as a man of principle, prepared to die rather than see the wicked people of Nineveh go unpunished. That is why God, who refuses to let him escape his mission, ultimately takes the trouble to explain His reason to Jonah, acknowledging his integrity.

The story is divided into two parallel sections of two chapters each. In chapters one and three, Jonah interacts with the pagan world. In chapters two and four, he engages in a conversation with God. It should be noted that the psalm in chapter 2 was most likely inserted into a narrative after that narrative was completed, since it contains elements that are at variance with it. The first chapter, for example, depicts Jonah as depressed and unwilling (or perhaps unable) to pray (note the repetition of *va-yeired*, *va-yeired*, and *yarad* in verses 3 and 6, and the word play on them in verse 6, *va-yeradam*, "he went down and he fell into a stupor"). In the psalm, he is pictured as euphoric, thanking God for having rescued him "from the pit" (2:7). The dissonance, however, actually car-

ries the story further, explaining why God addresses Jonah a second time and why this time he listens.

Word repetitions carry subliminal messages. The word meaning "huge" or "great"(*gadol*), for example, appears in the text 14 times. The storm at sea is "great" (1:4,12); the sailors "fear a great fear" (1:10,16); the fish is "great" (2:1). This builds to a climax (3:2, 3:3, 4:11) in which Nineveh is described as "great in the sight of God" (*g'dolah leilohim*). The characterization of the city as "great" three times suggests that it exceeds everything else in size. Compare, for example, the threefold repetition of the word for "holy" that describes God in Isaiah (*kadosh, kadosh, kadosh*) (6:3). The widespread use of rhetorical devices such as metaphors and puns (see, for example, *va-yakei* in 2:11 and *kikayon* in 4:6), as well as vivid language, makes us realize that we do not have ordinary prose before us.

The story contains a variety of messages, including the fact that God controls all of the forces of nature and that it is impossible to resist His call. Classically, Jewish and Christian interpretations have differed as to the story's central teaching. Jewish commentators have highlighted the power of repentance, manifest in God's forgiveness of even the wicked of Ninevah who seek to atone. Christians have seen it as a renunciation of "narrow Jewish parochialism," symbolized by Jonah's unwillingness to help the gentiles turn to God. (In the name "Jonah" itself—which means "dove"—they see an allusion to the Jewish people, based on a midrashic interpretation of a verse from the Song of Songs (2:14).

Both interpretations find support in the text, though they are based only on partial readings at best. Jonah does not rail against the gentiles, but only against the evildoers among them. In fact, the pagan sailors in chapter 1 are described in very sympathetic terms. As for the power of repentance, though it certainly is a major theme in the story, it is not the central one. If it were, the book should have ended with the third chapter.

The central teaching can be found in chapter four, the climax of the story. The second verse explains why Jonah had fled from God, why he had refused to carry out his commission to go to Nineveh: "For I know that You are a compassionate and gracious God, slow to anger, abounding in kindness, renouncing punishment." (This verse is also found in Joel 2:13. It is not clear which author borrowed from the other, or whether both drew on an earlier source.) Such words describing God appear in other biblical contexts as well (see, for example, Psalms 103:8, 145:8, and 2 Chron. 30:9); the classic formulation, however, is found in Exodus 34:6–7: "The LORD! the LORD! a God compassionate and gracious, slow to anger, abounding in kindness and truth, extending kindness to the thousandth generation, forgiving iniquity transgression and sin; yet He does not remit all punishment, but visits the iniquity of parents upon children and children's children, upon the third and fourth generations." Compare the end of that statement to the one in Jonah: Here, God renounces punishment! Jonah cannot make peace with the fact that the wicked could escape punishment. He refuses to be party to the perceived injustice of God's remission of well-deserved punishment. (And here we have an example of how an early biblical teaching can be modified in later times. In the Torah, there is no evidence that repentance [*t'shuvah*] can lead to the remission of punishment.)

God does not respond with an intellectual argument. He has to make Jonah realize that he, too, requires God's grace, undeserved though that may be. By introducing the gourd (*kikayon*) and the worm that destroys it within a day (4:6–7), God makes Jonah feel the transitory nature of all life and rouses his sense of pity for all living creatures. The story ends with a question, one that is addressed not only to Jonah, but also to the reader: "Is the demand for strict justice to override compassion?" It suggests that though repentance is important, ultimately it is God's concern for all creatures that maintains them in life.

RELATION OF THE *HAFTARAH* TO THE CALENDAR

The Talmud designates the story of Jonah as the *haftarah* reading for the *Yom Kippur* afternoon service (BT Meg. 31a) without any explanation. For this we must turn to the Mishnah (Taan. 2:1), which describes appropriate behavior for a community on fast days. When the community elder

addressed the assembled people he would remind them that the people of Nineveh were forgiven because they turned aside from their evil ways, not because they donned sackcloth and fasted.

That explanation apparently did not satisfy those Sages who determined the *haftarah* reading, because it omits what they felt to be the main point of Jonah. To emphasize that point, they added into the *haftarah* reading the three verses that conclude the prophecies of Micah, which celebrates divine forgiveness of sin. Toward the end of a day of fasting, worship, and the recitation of penitential prayers, the *haftarah* thus reassures us of God's ongoing love and blessings for the forthcoming year.

—David L. Lieber

1 The word of the LORD came to Jonah son
of Amittai: 2Go at once to Nineveh, that great
city, and proclaim judgment upon it; for their
wickedness has come before Me.
3Jonah, however, started out to flee to Tarshish from the LORD's service. He went down
to Joppa and found a ship going to Tarshish.
He paid the fare and went aboard to sail with
the others to Tarshish, away from the service
of the LORD.
4But the LORD cast a mighty wind upon the
sea, and such a great tempest came upon the
sea that the ship was in danger of breaking up.
5In their fright, the sailors cried out, each to his
own god; and they flung the ship's cargo overboard to make it lighter for them. Jonah, meanwhile, had gone down into the hold of the vessel
where he lay down and fell asleep. 6The captain
went over to him and cried out, "How can you
be sleeping so soundly! Up, call upon your god!
Perhaps the god will be kind to us and we will
not perish."
7The men said to one another, "Let us cast
lots and find out on whose account this misfortune has come upon us." They cast lots and
the lot fell on Jonah. 8They said to him, "Tell
us, you who have brought this misfortune upon
us, what is your business? Where have you come
from? What is your country, and of what people
are you?" 9"I am a Hebrew," he replied. "I worship the LORD, the God of Heaven, who made
both sea and land." 10The men were greatly

א וַיְהִי דְּבַר־יְהוָה אֶל־יוֹנָה בֶן־אֲמִתַּי
לֵאמֹר׃ 2 קוּם לֵךְ אֶל־נִינְוֵה הָעִיר הַגְּדוֹלָה
וּקְרָא עָלֶיהָ כִּי־עָלְתָה רָעָתָם לְפָנָי׃
3 וַיָּקָם יוֹנָה לִבְרֹחַ תַּרְשִׁישָׁה מִלִּפְנֵי יְהוָה
וַיֵּרֶד יָפוֹ וַיִּמְצָא אָנִיָּה ׀ בָּאָה תַרְשִׁישׁ
וַיִּתֵּן שְׂכָרָהּ וַיֵּרֶד בָּהּ לָבוֹא עִמָּהֶם
תַּרְשִׁישָׁה מִלִּפְנֵי יְהוָה׃
4 וַיהוָה הֵטִיל רוּחַ־גְּדוֹלָה אֶל־הַיָּם וַיְהִי
סַעַר־גָּדוֹל בַּיָּם וְהָאֳנִיָּה חִשְּׁבָה לְהִשָּׁבֵר׃
5 וַיִּירְאוּ הַמַּלָּחִים וַיִּזְעֲקוּ אִישׁ אֶל־אֱלֹהָיו
וַיָּטִלוּ אֶת־הַכֵּלִים אֲשֶׁר בָּאֳנִיָּה אֶל־הַיָּם
לְהָקֵל מֵעֲלֵיהֶם וְיוֹנָה יָרַד אֶל־יַרְכְּתֵי
הַסְּפִינָה וַיִּשְׁכַּב וַיֵּרָדַם׃ 6 וַיִּקְרַב אֵלָיו רַב
הַחֹבֵל וַיֹּאמֶר לוֹ מַה־לְּךָ נִרְדָּם קוּם קְרָא
אֶל־אֱלֹהֶיךָ אוּלַי יִתְעַשֵּׁת הָאֱלֹהִים לָנוּ
וְלֹא נֹאבֵד׃
7 וַיֹּאמְרוּ אִישׁ אֶל־רֵעֵהוּ לְכוּ וְנַפִּילָה
גוֹרָלוֹת וְנֵדְעָה בְּשֶׁלְּמִי הָרָעָה הַזֹּאת לָנוּ
וַיַּפִּלוּ גּוֹרָלוֹת וַיִּפֹּל הַגּוֹרָל עַל־יוֹנָה׃
8 וַיֹּאמְרוּ אֵלָיו הַגִּידָה־נָּא לָנוּ בַּאֲשֶׁר
לְמִי־הָרָעָה הַזֹּאת לָנוּ מַה־מְּלַאכְתְּךָ
וּמֵאַיִן תָּבוֹא מָה אַרְצֶךָ וְאֵי־מִזֶּה עַם
אָתָּה׃ 9 וַיֹּאמֶר אֲלֵיהֶם עִבְרִי אָנֹכִי וְאֶת־
יְהוָה אֱלֹהֵי הַשָּׁמַיִם אֲנִי יָרֵא אֲשֶׁר־
עָשָׂה אֶת־הַיָּם וְאֶת־הַיַּבָּשָׁה׃ 10 וַיִּירְאוּ
הָאֲנָשִׁים יִרְאָה גְדוֹלָה וַיֹּאמְרוּ אֵלָיו
מַה־זֹּאת עָשִׂיתָ כִּי־יָדְעוּ הָאֲנָשִׁים כִּי־

terrified, and they asked him, "What have you done?" And when the men learned that he was fleeing from the service of the LORD—for so he told them—11they said to him, "What must we do to you to make the sea calm around us?" For the sea was growing more and more stormy. 12He answered, "Heave me overboard, and the sea will calm down for you; for I know that this terrible storm came upon you on my account." 13Nevertheless, the men rowed hard to regain the shore, but they could not, for the sea was growing more and more stormy about them. 14Then they cried out to the LORD: "Oh, please, LORD, do not let us perish on account of this man's life. Do not hold us guilty of killing an innocent person! For You, O LORD, by Your will, have brought this about." 15And they heaved Jonah overboard, and the sea stopped raging.

16The men feared the LORD greatly; they offered a sacrifice to the LORD and they made vows.

מִלִּפְנֵי יְהוָה הוּא בֹרֵחַ כִּי הִגִּיד לָהֶם׃
11 וַיֹּאמְרוּ אֵלָיו מַה־נַּעֲשֶׂה לָּךְ וְיִשְׁתֹּק
הַיָּם מֵעָלֵינוּ כִּי הַיָּם הוֹלֵךְ וְסֹעֵר׃
12 וַיֹּאמֶר אֲלֵיהֶם שָׂאוּנִי וַהֲטִילֻנִי אֶל־הַיָּם
וְיִשְׁתֹּק הַיָּם מֵעֲלֵיכֶם כִּי יוֹדֵעַ אָנִי כִּי
בְשֶׁלִּי הַסַּעַר הַגָּדוֹל הַזֶּה עֲלֵיכֶם׃
13 וַיַּחְתְּרוּ הָאֲנָשִׁים לְהָשִׁיב אֶל־הַיַּבָּשָׁה
וְלֹא יָכֹלוּ כִּי הַיָּם הוֹלֵךְ וְסֹעֵר עֲלֵיהֶם׃
14 וַיִּקְרְאוּ אֶל־יְהוָה וַיֹּאמְרוּ אָנָּה יְהוָה
אַל־נָא נֹאבְדָה בְּנֶפֶשׁ הָאִישׁ הַזֶּה וְאַל־
תִּתֵּן עָלֵינוּ דָּם נָקִיא* כִּי־אַתָּה יְהוָה
כַּאֲשֶׁר חָפַצְתָּ עָשִׂיתָ׃ 15 וַיִּשְׂאוּ אֶת־יוֹנָה
וַיְטִלֻהוּ אֶל־הַיָּם וַיַּעֲמֹד הַיָּם מִזַּעְפּוֹ׃
16 וַיִּירְאוּ הָאֲנָשִׁים יִרְאָה גְדוֹלָה אֶת־
יְהוָה וַיִּזְבְּחוּ־זֶבַח לַיהוָה וַיִּדְּרוּ נְדָרִים׃

2 The LORD provided a huge fish to swallow Jonah; and Jonah remained in the fish's belly three days and three nights. 2Jonah prayed to the LORD his God from the belly of the fish. 3He said:

In my trouble I called to the LORD,
And He answered me;
From the belly of Sheol I cried out,
And You heard my voice.
4You cast me into the depths,
Into the heart of the sea,
The floods engulfed me;
All Your breakers and billows
Swept over me.

ב וַיְמַן יְהוָה דָּג גָּדוֹל לִבְלֹעַ אֶת־יוֹנָה
וַיְהִי יוֹנָה בִּמְעֵי הַדָּג שְׁלֹשָׁה יָמִים
וּשְׁלֹשָׁה לֵילוֹת׃ 2 וַיִּתְפַּלֵּל יוֹנָה אֶל־יְהוָה
אֱלֹהָיו מִמְּעֵי הַדָּגָה׃ 3 וַיֹּאמֶר

קָרָאתִי מִצָּרָה לִי אֶל־יְהוָה
וַיַּעֲנֵנִי
מִבֶּטֶן שְׁאוֹל שִׁוַּעְתִּי
שָׁמַעְתָּ קוֹלִי׃
4 וַתַּשְׁלִיכֵנִי מְצוּלָה
בִּלְבַב יַמִּים
וְנָהָר יְסֹבְבֵנִי
כָּל־מִשְׁבָּרֶיךָ וְגַלֶּיךָ
עָלַי עָבָרוּ׃

v. 14. יתיר א׳

⁵I thought I was driven away
Out of Your sight:
Would I ever gaze again
Upon Your holy Temple?
⁶The waters closed in over me,
The deep engulfed me.
Weeds twined around my head.
⁷I sank to the base of the mountains;
The bars of the earth closed upon me forever.
Yet You brought my life up from the pit,
O LORD my God!
⁸When my life was ebbing away,
I called the LORD to mind;
And my prayer came before You,
Into Your holy Temple.
⁹They who cling to empty folly
Forsake their own welfare,
¹⁰But I, with loud thanksgiving,
Will sacrifice to You;
What I have vowed I will perform.
Deliverance is the LORD's!

¹¹The LORD commanded the fish, and it spewed Jonah out upon dry land.

3 The word of the LORD came to Jonah a second time: ²"Go at once to Nineveh, that great city, and proclaim to it what I tell you." ³Jonah went at once to Nineveh in accordance with the LORD's command.

Nineveh was an enormously large city a three days' walk across. ⁴Jonah started out and made his way into the city the distance of one day's walk, and proclaimed: "Forty days more, and Nineveh shall be overthrown!"

⁵The people of Nineveh believed God. They proclaimed a fast, and great and small alike put

5 וַאֲנִ֣י אָמַ֔רְתִּי נִגְרַ֖שְׁתִּי
מִנֶּ֣גֶד עֵינֶ֑יךָ
אַ֚ךְ אוֹסִ֣יף לְהַבִּ֔יט
אֶל־הֵיכַ֖ל קָדְשֶֽׁךָ׃
6 אֲפָפ֤וּנִי מַ֙יִם֙ עַד־נֶ֔פֶשׁ
תְּה֖וֹם יְסֹבְבֵ֑נִי
ס֖וּף חָב֥וּשׁ לְרֹאשִֽׁי׃
7 לְקִצְבֵ֤י הָרִים֙ יָרַ֔דְתִּי
הָאָ֛רֶץ בְּרִחֶ֥יהָ בַעֲדִ֖י לְעוֹלָ֑ם
וַתַּ֧עַל מִשַּׁ֛חַת חַיַּ֖י
יְהֹוָ֥ה אֱלֹהָֽי׃
8 בְּהִתְעַטֵּ֤ף עָלַי֙ נַפְשִׁ֔י
אֶת־יְהֹוָ֖ה זָכָ֑רְתִּי
וַתָּב֤וֹא אֵלֶ֙יךָ֙ תְּפִלָּתִ֔י
אֶל־הֵיכַ֖ל קָדְשֶֽׁךָ׃
9 מְשַׁמְּרִ֖ים הַבְלֵי־שָׁ֑וְא
חַסְדָּ֖ם יַעֲזֹֽבוּ׃
10 וַאֲנִ֗י בְּק֤וֹל תּוֹדָה֙
אֶזְבְּחָה־לָּ֔ךְ
אֲשֶׁ֥ר נָדַ֖רְתִּי אֲשַׁלֵּ֑מָה
יְשׁוּעָ֖תָה לַיהֹוָֽה׃ ס

11 וַיֹּ֥אמֶר יְהֹוָ֖ה לַדָּ֑ג וַיָּקֵ֥א אֶת־יוֹנָ֖ה אֶל־
הַיַּבָּשָֽׁה׃ פ

ג וַיְהִ֧י דְבַר־יְהֹוָ֛ה אֶל־יוֹנָ֖ה שֵׁנִ֥ית
לֵאמֹֽר׃ 2 ק֛וּם לֵ֥ךְ אֶל־נִֽינְוֵ֖ה הָעִ֣יר הַגְּדוֹלָ֑ה
וּקְרָ֤א אֵלֶ֙יהָ֙ אֶת־הַקְּרִיאָ֔ה אֲשֶׁ֥ר אָנֹכִ֖י דֹּבֵ֥ר
אֵלֶֽיךָ׃ 3 וַיָּ֣קׇם יוֹנָ֗ה וַיֵּ֛לֶךְ אֶל־נִֽינְוֵ֖ה כִּדְבַ֣ר
יְהֹוָ֑ה
וְנִֽינְוֵ֗ה הָיְתָ֤ה עִיר־גְּדוֹלָה֙ לֵֽאלֹהִ֔ים מַהֲלַ֖ךְ
שְׁלֹ֥שֶׁת יָמִֽים׃ 4 וַיָּ֤חֶל יוֹנָה֙ לָב֣וֹא בָעִ֔יר
מַהֲלַ֖ךְ י֣וֹם אֶחָ֑ד וַיִּקְרָא֙ וַיֹּאמַ֔ר ע֚וֹד
אַרְבָּעִ֣ים י֔וֹם וְנִֽינְוֵ֖ה נֶהְפָּֽכֶת׃
5 וַֽיַּאֲמִ֥ינוּ אַנְשֵׁ֖י נִֽינְוֵ֣ה בֵּֽאלֹהִ֑ים וַיִּקְרְאוּ־

on sackcloth. 6When the news reached the king
of Nineveh, he rose from his throne, took off
his robe, put on sackcloth, and sat in ashes. 7And
he had the word cried through Nineveh: "By decree of the king and his nobles: No man or
beast—of flock or herd—shall taste anything!
They shall not graze, and they shall not drink
water! 8They shall be covered with sackcloth—
man and beast—and shall cry mightily to God.
Let everyone turn back from his evil ways and
from the injustice of which he is guilty. 9Who
knows but that God may turn and relent? He
may turn back from His wrath, so that we do
not perish."

10God saw what they did, how they were turning back from their evil ways. And God renounced the punishment He had planned to
bring upon them, and did not carry it out.

צוֹם וַיִּלְבְּשׁוּ שַׂקִּים מִגְּדוֹלָם וְעַד־קְטַנָּם׃
6 וַיִּגַּע הַדָּבָר אֶל־מֶלֶךְ נִינְוֵה וַיָּקָם מִכִּסְאוֹ
וַיַּעֲבֵר אַדַּרְתּוֹ מֵעָלָיו וַיְכַס שַׂק וַיֵּשֶׁב
עַל־הָאֵפֶר׃ 7 וַיַּזְעֵק וַיֹּאמֶר בְּנִינְוֵה מִטַּעַם
הַמֶּלֶךְ וּגְדֹלָיו לֵאמֹר הָאָדָם וְהַבְּהֵמָה
הַבָּקָר וְהַצֹּאן אַל־יִטְעֲמוּ מְאוּמָה אַל־
יִרְעוּ וּמַיִם אַל־יִשְׁתּוּ׃ 8 וְיִתְכַּסּוּ שַׂקִּים
הָאָדָם וְהַבְּהֵמָה וְיִקְרְאוּ אֶל־אֱלֹהִים
בְּחָזְקָה וְיָשֻׁבוּ אִישׁ מִדַּרְכּוֹ הָרָעָה וּמִן־
הֶחָמָס אֲשֶׁר בְּכַפֵּיהֶם׃ 9 מִי־יוֹדֵעַ יָשׁוּב
וְנִחַם הָאֱלֹהִים וְשָׁב מֵחֲרוֹן אַפּוֹ וְלֹא
נֹאבֵד׃

10 וַיַּרְא הָאֱלֹהִים אֶת־מַעֲשֵׂיהֶם כִּי־שָׁבוּ
מִדַּרְכָּם הָרָעָה וַיִּנָּחֶם הָאֱלֹהִים עַל־
הָרָעָה אֲשֶׁר־דִּבֶּר לַעֲשׂוֹת־לָהֶם וְלֹא
עָשָׂה׃

4 This displeased Jonah greatly, and he was
grieved. 2He prayed to the LORD, saying, "O
LORD! Isn't this just what I said when I was still
in my own country? That is why I fled beforehand to Tarshish. For I know that You are a
compassionate and gracious God, slow to anger,
abounding in kindness, renouncing punishment. 3Please, LORD, take my life, for I would
rather die than live." 4The LORD replied, "Are
you that deeply grieved?"

5Now Jonah had left the city and found a place
east of the city. He made a booth there and sat
under it in the shade, until he should see what
happened to the city. 6The LORD God provided
a ricinus plant, which grew up over Jonah, to
provide shade for his head and save him from
discomfort. Jonah was very happy about the
plant. 7But the next day at dawn God provided
a worm, which attacked the plant so that it withered. 8And when the sun rose, God provided a
sultry east wind; the sun beat down on Jonah's

ד וַיֵּרַע אֶל־יוֹנָה רָעָה גְדוֹלָה וַיִּחַר לוֹ׃
2 וַיִּתְפַּלֵּל אֶל־יְהוָה וַיֹּאמַר אָנָּה יְהוָה
הֲלוֹא־זֶה דְבָרִי עַד־הֱיוֹתִי עַל־אַדְמָתִי
עַל־כֵּן קִדַּמְתִּי לִבְרֹחַ תַּרְשִׁישָׁה כִּי יָדַעְתִּי
כִּי אַתָּה אֵל־חַנּוּן וְרַחוּם אֶרֶךְ אַפַּיִם
וְרַב־חֶסֶד וְנִחָם עַל־הָרָעָה׃ 3 וְעַתָּה יְהוָה
קַח־נָא אֶת־נַפְשִׁי מִמֶּנִּי כִּי טוֹב מוֹתִי
מֵחַיָּי׃ ס 4 וַיֹּאמֶר יְהוָה הַהֵיטֵב חָרָה
לָךְ׃
5 וַיֵּצֵא יוֹנָה מִן־הָעִיר וַיֵּשֶׁב מִקֶּדֶם לָעִיר
וַיַּעַשׂ לוֹ שָׁם סֻכָּה וַיֵּשֶׁב תַּחְתֶּיהָ בַּצֵּל
עַד אֲשֶׁר יִרְאֶה מַה־יִּהְיֶה בָּעִיר׃ 6 וַיְמַן
יְהוָה־אֱלֹהִים קִיקָיוֹן וַיַּעַל ׀ מֵעַל לְיוֹנָה
לִהְיוֹת צֵל עַל־רֹאשׁוֹ לְהַצִּיל לוֹ מֵרָעָתוֹ
וַיִּשְׂמַח יוֹנָה עַל־הַקִּיקָיוֹן שִׂמְחָה גְדוֹלָה׃
7 וַיְמַן הָאֱלֹהִים תּוֹלַעַת בַּעֲלוֹת הַשַּׁחַר
לַמָּחֳרָת וַתַּךְ אֶת־הַקִּיקָיוֹן וַיִּיבָשׁ׃ 8 וַיְהִי ׀
כִּזְרֹחַ הַשֶּׁמֶשׁ וַיְמַן אֱלֹהִים רוּחַ קָדִים

head, and he became faint. He begged for death, saying, "I would rather die than live." ⁹Then God said to Jonah, "Are you so deeply grieved about the plant?" "Yes," he replied, "so deeply that I want to die."

¹⁰Then the LORD said: "You cared about the plant, which you did not work for and which you did not grow, which appeared overnight and perished overnight. ¹¹And should not I care about Nineveh, that great city, in which there are more than a hundred and twenty thousand persons who do not yet know their right hand from their left, and many beasts as well!"

חֲרִישִׁית וַתַּ֤ךְ הַשֶּׁ֙מֶשׁ֙ עַל־רֹ֣אשׁ יוֹנָ֔ה
וַיִּתְעַלָּ֑ף וַיִּשְׁאַ֤ל אֶת־נַפְשׁוֹ֙ לָמ֔וּת וַיֹּ֕אמֶר
ט֥וֹב מוֹתִ֖י מֵחַיָּֽי׃ ⁹וַיֹּ֤אמֶר אֱלֹהִים֙ אֶל־
יוֹנָ֔ה הַהֵיטֵ֥ב חָרָֽה־לְךָ֖ עַל־הַקִּיקָי֑וֹן וַיֹּ֕אמֶר
הֵיטֵ֥ב חָֽרָה־לִ֖י עַד־מָֽוֶת׃

¹⁰וַיֹּ֣אמֶר יְהֹוָ֔ה אַתָּ֥ה חַ֙סְתָּ֙ עַל־הַקִּ֣יקָי֔וֹן
אֲשֶׁ֛ר לֹא־עָמַ֥לְתָּ בּ֖וֹ וְלֹ֣א גִדַּלְתּ֑וֹ שֶׁבִּן־
לַ֥יְלָה הָיָ֖ה וּבִן־לַ֥יְלָה אָבָֽד׃ ¹¹וַאֲנִי֙ לֹ֣א
אָח֔וּס עַל־נִ֣ינְוֵ֔ה הָעִ֖יר הַגְּדוֹלָ֑ה אֲשֶׁ֣ר
יֶשׁ־בָּ֡הּ הַרְבֵּה֩ מִֽשְׁתֵּים־עֶשְׂרֵ֨ה רִבּ֜וֹ אָדָ֗ם
אֲשֶׁ֤ר לֹֽא־יָדַע֙ בֵּין־יְמִינ֣וֹ לִשְׂמֹאל֔וֹ וּבְהֵמָ֖ה
רַבָּֽה׃

7

¹⁸Who is a God like You,
Forgiving iniquity
And remitting transgression;
Who has not maintained His wrath forever
Against the remnant of His own people,
Because He loves graciousness!
¹⁹He will take us back in love;
He will cover up our iniquities,
You will hurl all our sins
Into the depths of the sea.
²⁰You will keep faith with Jacob,
Loyalty to Abraham,
As You promised on oath to our fathers
In days gone by.

ז

¹⁸מִי־אֵ֣ל כָּמ֗וֹךָ
נֹשֵׂ֤א עָוֺן֙
וְעֹבֵ֣ר עַל־פֶּ֔שַׁע
לִשְׁאֵרִ֖ית נַחֲלָת֑וֹ
לֹא־הֶחֱזִ֤יק לָעַד֙ אַפּ֔וֹ
כִּֽי־חָפֵ֥ץ חֶ֖סֶד הֽוּא׃
¹⁹יָשׁ֣וּב יְרַֽחֲמֵ֔נוּ
יִכְבֹּ֖שׁ עֲוֺנֹתֵ֑ינוּ
וְתַשְׁלִ֛יךְ בִּמְצֻל֥וֹת יָ֖ם
כָּל־חַטֹּאותָֽם׃*
²⁰תִּתֵּ֤ן אֱמֶת֙ לְיַֽעֲקֹ֔ב
חֶ֖סֶד לְאַבְרָהָ֑ם
אֲשֶׁר־נִשְׁבַּ֥עְתָּ לַֽאֲבֹתֵ֖ינוּ
מִ֥ימֵי קֶֽדֶם׃

v. 19. מלא ו׳

Micah 7:18–19. Customarily these verses are also recited during the *Tashlikh* ceremony on the afternoon of the first day of *Rosh ha-Shanah.* On that occasion, the community enacts the reference to God casting sins into the sea and asserts faith in divine forgiveness.

הפטרה לסוכות (יום ראשון)

HAFTARAH FOR SUKKOT, FIRST DAY

ZECHARIAH 14:1–21

This reading is one of the latest examples of biblical prophecy. Dating from sometime after 518 B.C.E. (see Zech. 8:9), it originally concluded the visions and oracles anthologized as the prophecies of Zechariah. This *haftarah* is marked by a strong tone of impending doom and purification. A repeated emphasis on "that day" of divine judgment conveys a tone of expectation and inevitability. The city of Jerusalem stands at the center of these prophecies, having a pivotal place in the wars to come and in the universal pilgrimage proclaimed for all nations. When the battles conclude, the Lord will be acknowledged king, and all peoples will be invited to celebrate the festival of *Sukkot* in Jerusalem.

This *haftarah* begins with the siege of Jerusalem by "all the nations," and it ends with their survivors being invited to Jerusalem for a sacred convocation and worship at the feast of *Sukkot.* Looting and plunder (14:1–2) give way to a forecast of the security of Jerusalem and its religious centrality for all (14:11,20–21). Marking this transition is a shift from the wars of the Lord and His army of "holy beings" (*k'doshim;* v. 5) to the peace of Jerusalem, in which even the most common objects and utensils will be "holy (*kadosh*) to the LORD" (v. 21). Significantly, little is said here of the Israelites themselves, or of their worship, whereas much is made of the nations who will bow before the Lord in Jerusalem "year by year." The elevation of the Lord as "king over all the earth" is clearly of major concern to the prophet, as is the centrality of "the House of the LORD" for all nations. "In that day there shall be one LORD with one name" (v. 9).

The immediacy of the forecast is registered by repetitions of the word "day." There will be a "day . . . coming" (v. 1) says the prophet, a "day" of plunder and salvation (vv. 4,13), a "day" of continuous light and fresh waters (vv. 6–8), a "day" of divine kingship and the sanctification of everything in Jerusalem (vv. 9,20–21). These days combine in the course of the prophecy to produce one extensive day, when the darkness of doom will pass and a transcendent radiance will illumine the earth.

Beyond the terrifying clamor of battles and death, Zechariah envisages a time of unearthly splendor, a day when "there shall be neither sunlight nor cold moonlight, but there shall be a continuous day" (vv. 6–7). Creation is therewith reversed and transformed. God's first light will shine again and evermore, without setting or dawning. In this era, heavenly splendor will illumine all things. It is the time of God's universal kingship (v. 9).

Along with the elemental quality of light, Zechariah's prophecy focuses on the life-saving nature of water. It comes to first expression through a prediction that in the day that is coming "fresh water shall flow from Jerusalem" to the eastern and western seas, throughout the summer and winter seasons (v. 8). This image harks back to Ezekiel's vision of a stream of water issuing from below the platform of the new Temple and flowing outward to heal the natural world (Ezek. 47:1–12). It recalls the primordial streams of Eden (Gen. 2:10–14) and dramatizes the Temple as a veritable paradise at the center of the world. Zechariah's prophecy of Jerusalem is nourished by this mythic figure.

However, as an image of earthly bounty, the blessing of streams and flowing water derives from regions, like Mesopotamia, nourished by underground fountains and mountain torrents. Ancient Israel, where the waters above the heavens were the decisive source of sustenance, was not such a place. The prophet Zechariah, therefore, speaks to all when he promises God's heavenly bounty of rain to all those who will worship the Lord

in Jerusalem on the Feast of Booths (Zech. 14:16–19). This is the favor the Lord extends to those who acknowledge Him. It is the gift of life from the Lord of life. The survivors of death-dealing battles can appreciate its value (v. 16).

RELATION OF THE *HAFTARAH* TO THE CALENDAR

This *haftarah* shows an old connection between the festival of *Sukkot* and rituals for rain. "Any of the earth's communities that does not make the pilgrimage to Jerusalem to bow low to the King LORD of Hosts shall receive no rain" (v. 17). This pronouncement excludes only Egypt (a land that does not depend on rainfall), which is promised an appropriate scourge (Ibn Ezra, Radak). Rain rituals associated with water libations and with the four species gathered on *Sukkot* (Lev. 23:40) are mentioned separately in early Rabbinic sources (see Tosef. Suk. 3:18; BT Taan. 2b, respectively). Some of these rites may go back to early biblical times, but only during the era of the Second Temple do they seem to have been integrated into a multilevel service of celebration and supplication.

יד הִנֵּה יוֹם־בָּא לַיהוָה וְחֻלַּק שְׁלָלֵךְ
בְּקִרְבֵּךְ׃ 2 וְאָסַפְתִּי אֶת־כָּל־הַגּוֹיִם ׀ אֶל־
יְרוּשָׁלַם לַמִּלְחָמָה וְנִלְכְּדָה הָעִיר וְנָשַׁסּוּ
הַבָּתִּים וְהַנָּשִׁים תשגלנה תִּשָּׁכַבְנָה וְיָצָא
חֲצִי הָעִיר בַּגּוֹלָה וְיֶתֶר הָעָם לֹא יִכָּרֵת
מִן־הָעִיר׃
3 וְיָצָא יְהוָה וְנִלְחַם בַּגּוֹיִם הָהֵם כְּיוֹם
הִלָּחֲמוֹ בְּיוֹם קְרָב׃ 4 וְעָמְדוּ רַגְלָיו בַּיּוֹם־
הַהוּא עַל־הַר הַזֵּתִים אֲשֶׁר עַל־פְּנֵי
יְרוּשָׁלַם מִקֶּדֶם וְנִבְקַע הַר הַזֵּיתִים מֵחֶצְיוֹ
מִזְרָחָה וָיָמָּה גֵּיא גְּדוֹלָה מְאֹד וּמָשׁ חֲצִי
הָהָר צָפוֹנָה וְחֶצְיוֹ־נֶגְבָּה׃ 5 וְנַסְתֶּם* גֵּיא־
הָרַי כִּי־יַגִּיעַ גֵּי־הָרִים אֶל־אָצַל וְנַסְתֶּם*
כַּאֲשֶׁר נַסְתֶּם* מִפְּנֵי הָרַעַשׁ בִּימֵי עֻזִּיָּה
מֶלֶךְ־יְהוּדָה וּבָא יְהוָה אֱלֹהַי כָּל־קְדֹשִׁים
עִמָּךְ׃

14 Lo, a day of the LORD is coming when
your spoil shall be divided in your very midst!
2 For I will gather all the nations to Jerusalem
for war: The city shall be captured, the houses
plundered, and the women violated; and a part
of the city shall go into exile. But the rest of the
population shall not be uprooted from the city.
3 Then the LORD will come forth and make war
on those nations as He is wont to make war on
a day of battle. 4 On that day, He will set His feet
on the Mount of Olives, near Jerusalem on the
east; and the Mount of Olives shall split across
from east to west, and one part of the Mount
shall shift to the north and the other to the
south, a huge gorge. 5 And the Valley in the Hills
shall be stopped up, for the Valley of the Hills
shall reach only to Azal; it shall be stopped up
as it was stopped up as a result of the earthquake
in the days of King Uzziah of Judah.—And the
LORD my God, with all the holy beings, will
come to you.

v. 5. בנוסח אחר "וְנִסְתַּם" פעמיים כלומר שנוי תנועות

v. 5. בנוסח אחר "נִסְתַּם" כלומר שנוי תנועות

Zechariah 14:4. He will set His feet God appears as a warrior in battle. The stark anthropomorphism recalls Amos 9:1, in which the prophet envisages the "LORD standing by [or: on] the altar" prophesying doom.

5. This translation vocalizes the verb [ו]נסתם as [*v'*]*nistam,* as in Targum, Septuagint, and an old Hebrew manuscript. (Like most manuscripts and printed editions, the Hebrew text above reads [*v'*]*nastem,* that is, "You [pl.] shall flee [to] the Valley in the Hills, for the Valley of the Hills shall reach up to Azal. You shall flee as you fled because of the earthquake.") [Transl.]

the earthquake in the days of King Uzziah Mentioned also in Amos 1:1, but otherwise it is unknown.

6In that day, there shall be neither sunlight
nor cold moonlight, 7but there shall be a continuous day—only the LORD knows when—of
neither day nor night, and there shall be light
at eventide.

8In that day, fresh water shall flow from Jerusalem, part of it to the Eastern Sea and part
to the Western Sea, throughout the summer and
winter.

9And the LORD shall be king over all the earth;
in that day there shall be one LORD with one
name.

10Then the whole country shall become like
the Arabah, from Geba to Rimmon south of Jerusalem. The latter, however, shall perch high
up where it is, and shall be inhabited from the
Gate of Benjamin to the site of the Old Gate,
down to the Corner Gate, and from the Tower
of Hananel to the king's winepresses. 11Never
again shall destruction be decreed, and Jerusalem shall dwell secure.

12As for those peoples that warred against Jerusalem, the LORD will smite them with this
plague: Their flesh shall rot away while they
stand on their feet; their eyes shall rot away in
their sockets; and their tongues shall rot away
in their mouths.

13In that day, a great panic from the LORD
shall fall upon them, and everyone shall snatch
at the hand of another, and everyone shall raise
his hand against everyone else's hand. 14Judah

6 וְהָיָה בַּיּוֹם הַהוּא לֹא־יִהְיֶה אוֹר יְקָרוֹת
יקפאון וְקִפָּאוֹן׃ 7 וְהָיָה יוֹם־אֶחָד הוּא
יִוָּדַע לַיהוָה לֹא־יוֹם וְלֹא־לָיְלָה וְהָיָה
לְעֵת־עֶרֶב יִהְיֶה־אוֹר׃

8 וְהָיָה ׀ בַּיּוֹם הַהוּא יֵצְאוּ מַיִם־חַיִּים
מִירוּשָׁלִַם חֶצְיָם אֶל־הַיָּם הַקַּדְמוֹנִי
וְחֶצְיָם אֶל־הַיָּם הָאַחֲרוֹן בַּקַּיִץ וּבָחֹרֶף
יִהְיֶה׃

9 וְהָיָה יְהוָה לְמֶלֶךְ עַל־כָּל־הָאָרֶץ בַּיּוֹם
הַהוּא יִהְיֶה יְהוָה אֶחָד וּשְׁמוֹ אֶחָד׃

10 יִסּוֹב כָּל־הָאָרֶץ כָּעֲרָבָה מִגֶּבַע לְרִמּוֹן
נֶגֶב יְרוּשָׁלִָם וְרָאֲמָה וְיָשְׁבָה תַחְתֶּיהָ
לְמִשַּׁעַר בִּנְיָמִן עַד־מְקוֹם שַׁעַר הָרִאשׁוֹן
עַד־שַׁעַר הַפִּנִּים וּמִגְדַּל חֲנַנְאֵל עַד יִקְבֵי
הַמֶּלֶךְ׃ 11 וְיָשְׁבוּ בָהּ וְחֵרֶם לֹא יִהְיֶה־עוֹד
וְיָשְׁבָה יְרוּשָׁלִַם לָבֶטַח׃

12 וְזֹאת ׀ תִּהְיֶה הַמַּגֵּפָה אֲשֶׁר יִגֹּף יְהוָה
אֶת־כָּל־הָעַמִּים אֲשֶׁר צָבְאוּ עַל־יְרוּשָׁלִָם
הָמֵק ׀ בְּשָׂרוֹ וְהוּא עֹמֵד עַל־רַגְלָיו וְעֵינָיו
תִּמַּקְנָה בְחֹרֵיהֶן וּלְשׁוֹנוֹ תִּמַּק בְּפִיהֶם׃

13 וְהָיָה בַּיּוֹם הַהוּא תִּהְיֶה מְהוּמַת־יְהוָה
רַבָּה בָּהֶם וְהֶחֱזִיקוּ אִישׁ יַד רֵעֵהוּ וְעָלְתָה
יָדוֹ עַל־יַד רֵעֵהוּ׃ 14 וְגַם־יְהוּדָה תִּלָּחֵם

8. Eastern Sea . . . Western Sea The Dead Sea and the Mediterranean Sea, respectively (see Joel 2:20).

9. one LORD with one name Prophesying universal monotheism, when God's name will be proclaimed by all (cf. Rashi). It is cited at the end of the *Aleinu* prayer and thus serves as a liturgical climax to virtually every Jewish service. Note the literal resonance between the phrase "one LORD" and the conclusion to the *Sh'ma* proclamation (Deut. 6:4), which avers that "the LORD is one" or "the LORD alone [is our God]."

Following a talmudic tradition, Ibn Ezra interpreted Zechariah literally: In the end of days there will no longer be two forms of the divine name but one alone (see BT Pes. 50a). The two forms are *YHVH,* written but not vocalized, and *Adonai,* vocalized but not written as pronounced. Jewish mystical tradition considered the unification of these two forms of God's name a holy mystery. Hasidic masters developed penetrating homilies on the relations between the names, seeing in their difference the mystery of divine transcendence and divine immanence, or indwelling on earth.

10. become like the Arabah All the earth will be depressed, like the 'Arabah, and Jerusalem will dominate all, like a high mountain (Rashi).

shall join the fighting in Jerusalem, and the
wealth of all the nations roundabout—vast
quantities of gold, silver, and clothing—shall be
gathered in.

15The same plague shall strike the horses, the
mules, the camels, and the asses; the plague shall
affect all the animals in those camps.

16All who survive of all those nations that
came up against Jerusalem shall make a pilgrimage year by year to bow low to the King
Lord of Hosts and to observe the Feast of
Booths. 17Any of the earth's communities that
does not make the pilgrimage to Jerusalem to
bow low to the King Lord of Hosts shall receive
no rain. 18However, if the community of Egypt
does not make this pilgrimage, it shall not be
visited by the same affliction with which the
Lord will strike the other nations that do not
come up to observe the Feast of Booths. 19Such
shall be the punishment of Egypt and of all other
nations that do not come up to observe the Feast
of Booths.

20In that day, even the bells on the horses shall
be inscribed "Holy to the Lord." The metal pots
in the House of the Lord shall be like the basins
before the altar; 21indeed, every metal pot in Jerusalem and in Judah shall be holy to the Lord
of Hosts. And all those who sacrifice shall come
and take of these to boil [their sacrificial meat]
in; in that day there shall be no more traders
in the House of the Lord of Hosts.

בִּירוּשָׁלִָם וְאֻסַּף חֵיל כָּל־הַגּוֹיִם סָבִיב
זָהָב וָכֶסֶף וּבְגָדִים לָרֹב מְאֹד׃
15 וְכֵן תִּהְיֶה מַגֵּפַת הַסּוּס הַפֶּרֶד הַגָּמָל
וְהַחֲמוֹר וְכָל־הַבְּהֵמָה אֲשֶׁר יִהְיֶה
בַּמַּחֲנוֹת הָהֵמָּה כַּמַּגֵּפָה הַזֹּאת׃
16 וְהָיָה כָּל־הַנּוֹתָר מִכָּל־הַגּוֹיִם הַבָּאִים
עַל־יְרוּשָׁלִָם וְעָלוּ מִדֵּי שָׁנָה בְשָׁנָה
לְהִשְׁתַּחֲוֺת לְמֶלֶךְ יְהוָה צְבָאוֹת וְלָחֹג
אֶת־חַג הַסֻּכּוֹת׃ 17 וְהָיָה אֲשֶׁר לֹא־יַעֲלֶה
מֵאֵת מִשְׁפְּחוֹת הָאָרֶץ אֶל־יְרוּשָׁלִַם
לְהִשְׁתַּחֲוֺת לְמֶלֶךְ יְהוָה צְבָאוֹת וְלֹא
עֲלֵיהֶם יִהְיֶה הַגָּשֶׁם׃ 18 וְאִם־מִשְׁפַּחַת
מִצְרַיִם לֹא־תַעֲלֶה וְלֹא בָאָה וְלֹא עֲלֵיהֶם
תִּהְיֶה הַמַּגֵּפָה אֲשֶׁר יִגֹּף יְהוָה אֶת־הַגּוֹיִם
אֲשֶׁר לֹא יַעֲלוּ לָחֹג אֶת־חַג הַסֻּכּוֹת׃
19 זֹאת תִּהְיֶה חַטַּאת מִצְרָיִם וְחַטַּאת
כָּל־הַגּוֹיִם אֲשֶׁר לֹא יַעֲלוּ לָחֹג אֶת־חַג
הַסֻּכּוֹת׃
20 בַּיּוֹם הַהוּא יִהְיֶה עַל־מְצִלּוֹת הַסּוּס
קֹדֶשׁ לַיהוָה וְהָיָה הַסִּירוֹת בְּבֵית יְהוָה
כַּמִּזְרָקִים לִפְנֵי הַמִּזְבֵּחַ׃ 21 וְהָיָה כָּל־סִיר
בִּירוּשָׁלִַם וּבִיהוּדָה קֹדֶשׁ לַיהוָה צְבָאוֹת
וּבָאוּ כָּל־הַזֹּבְחִים וְלָקְחוּ מֵהֶם וּבִשְּׁלוּ
בָהֶם וְלֹא־יִהְיֶה כְנַעֲנִי עוֹד בְּבֵית־יְהוָה
צְבָאוֹת בַּיּוֹם הַהוּא׃

from Geba to Rimmon That is, from the northern border of the kingdom of Judah (1 Kings 15:22) to the southern border (Josh. 15:32).

14. in Jerusalem Or: "on behalf of Jerusalem."

19. the punishment Hebrew: *ḥattat,* which normally indicates sin but is often used (as here) to indicate its consequences.

20. Holy to the Lord This inscription was also on the gold plate attached to the high priest's headdress (Exod. 28:36, 39:30). The phrase connotes consecration: It indicates Israel's special status, and that the spoils of war can be dedicated to the Lord (Josh. 6:19).

הפטרה לסוכות (יום שני)

HAFTARAH FOR SUKKOT, SECOND DAY

1 KINGS 8:2–21

The events described in this *haftarah* represent a total transformation of sacred life in ancient Israel and the public documentation of its legitimacy. Transference of the ancient holy objects from the temporary tabernacle to the permanent shrine of the Temple formally closes the period of wilderness wandering. It also concludes the transitional phase that King David inaugurated; for in his day, the Ark rested in various locales, including the city of David (Zion). It now finds its permanent home in the grand Temple of Jerusalem. Solomon, to link his actions with ancient authority, presents himself as the very son predicted in 2 Sam. 7:12–13 to realize David's cultic desire. With the transfer of the sacred objects to a new site and the proclamation of the king's divine right, God's word to David is now fulfilled.

Two events stand behind the depiction of Solomon's ceremony here, and add an aura of completion to the new moment. The first event is the processional. In the account of the Ark's transfer from Zion, with Solomon's participation in the accompanying sacrifices, the attentive reader can hardly miss an echo of David's participation in the events that first brought the Ark to the city of David (2 Sam. 6:12–19). The other event takes us back to an earlier time, when the Ark was constructed in the days of Moses. When that work was done, "the cloud covered the Tent of Meeting, and the Presence of the Lord filled the Tabernacle" (Exod. 40:34). This was the sign that the Lord had accepted the work of human hands as a place fit for His dwelling. The *haftarah* alludes to this occasion by stating that when the Ark was deposited in the Holy of Holies "the cloud . . . filled the House of the Lord . . . for the Presence of the Lord filled the House of the Lord" (1 Kings 8:10–11). The wilderness tabernacle and the Jerusalem temple are thus clearly linked. Implicitly, Solomon is deemed the true heir of Moses as well as David. To underscore this point, the text notes that Solomon's shrine housed the "two tablets of stone" hewn by Moses on Mount Sinai (v. 9).

RELATION OF THE *HAFTARAH* TO THE CALENDAR

The image of the cloud in the shrine (1 Kings 8:10–11) is a sign of God's abundant presence. It draws on old themes of providential guidance, recalling the cloud and the fire that attended the Israelites in the wilderness by day and by night. But it also integrates that image of nomadic movement with another figure of divine presence and protection. In that figure, God's Presence in the shrine overarches the city as a *sukkah,* providing shade and shelter for all (Isa. 4:5–6). Thus the imagery of divine indwelling in Solomon's shrine is raised to a new level, giving the blessing of God's permanent presence on earth.

"The Lord has chosen / To abide in a thick cloud" (1 Kings 8:12). This image of hope is the theological counterpoint to words of lamentation, uttered from the depths of despair: "You [God] have clothed Yourself [*sakkota*] in anger and pursued us, / You have slain without pity. / You have screened Yourself off [*sakkota*] with a cloud [*anan*], / That no prayer may pass through. / You have made us filth and refuse / In the midst of the peoples" (Lam. 3:43–45). Ancient motifs and language have been inverted here, conveying the horror of divine fury and absence. Jewish history has inherited these two biblical images of God's presence and withdrawal, and has lived them.

8 2All the men of Israel gathered before King
Solomon at the Feast, in the month of Ethanim—that is, the seventh month. 3When all the
elders of Israel had come, the priests lifted the
Ark 4and carried up the Ark of the LORD. Then
the priests and the Levites brought the Tent of
Meeting and all the holy vessels that were in
the Tent. 5Meanwhile, King Solomon and the
whole community of Israel, who were assembled with him before the Ark, were sacrificing
sheep and oxen in such abundance that they
could not be numbered or counted.

6The priests brought the Ark of the LORD's
Covenant to its place underneath the wings of
the cherubim, in the Shrine of the House, in the
Holy of Holies; 7for the cherubim had their
wings spread out over the place of the Ark, so
that the cherubim shielded the Ark and its poles
from above. 8The poles projected so that the
ends of the poles were visible in the sanctuary
in front of the Shrine, but they could not be seen
outside; and there they remain to this day.
9There was nothing inside the Ark but the two
tablets of stone which Moses placed there at Horeb, when the LORD made [a covenant] with the
Israelites after their departure from the land of
Egypt.

10When the priests came out of the sanctuary—for the cloud had filled the House of the
LORD 11and the priests were not able to remain
and perform the service because of the cloud,
for the Presence of the LORD filled the House
of the LORD—12then Solomon declared:

ח 2 וַיִּקָּהֲלוּ אֶל־הַמֶּלֶךְ שְׁלֹמֹה כָּל־אִישׁ
יִשְׂרָאֵל בְּיֶרַח הָאֵתָנִים בֶּחָג הוּא הַחֹדֶשׁ
הַשְּׁבִיעִי׃ 3 וַיָּבֹאוּ כֹּל זִקְנֵי יִשְׂרָאֵל וַיִּשְׂאוּ
הַכֹּהֲנִים אֶת־הָאָרוֹן׃ 4 וַיַּעֲלוּ אֶת־אֲרוֹן
יְהוָה וְאֶת־אֹהֶל מוֹעֵד וְאֶת־כָּל־כְּלֵי
הַקֹּדֶשׁ אֲשֶׁר בָּאֹהֶל וַיַּעֲלוּ אֹתָם הַכֹּהֲנִים
וְהַלְוִיִּם׃ 5 וְהַמֶּלֶךְ שְׁלֹמֹה וְכָל־עֲדַת
יִשְׂרָאֵל הַנּוֹעָדִים עָלָיו אִתּוֹ לִפְנֵי הָאָרוֹן
מְזַבְּחִים צֹאן וּבָקָר אֲשֶׁר לֹא־יִסָּפְרוּ וְלֹא
יִמָּנוּ מֵרֹב׃

6 וַיָּבִאוּ הַכֹּהֲנִים אֶת־אֲרוֹן בְּרִית־יְהוָה
אֶל־מְקוֹמוֹ אֶל־דְּבִיר הַבַּיִת אֶל־קֹדֶשׁ
הַקֳּדָשִׁים אֶל־תַּחַת כַּנְפֵי הַכְּרוּבִים׃ 7 כִּי
הַכְּרוּבִים פֹּרְשִׂים כְּנָפַיִם אֶל־מְקוֹם
הָאָרוֹן וַיָּסֹכּוּ הַכְּרֻבִים עַל־הָאָרוֹן וְעַל־
בַּדָּיו מִלְמָעְלָה׃ 8 וַיַּאֲרִכוּ הַבַּדִּים וַיֵּרָאוּ
רָאשֵׁי הַבַּדִּים מִן־הַקֹּדֶשׁ עַל־פְּנֵי הַדְּבִיר
וְלֹא יֵרָאוּ הַחוּצָה וַיִּהְיוּ שָׁם עַד הַיּוֹם
הַזֶּה׃ 9 אֵין בָּאָרוֹן רַק שְׁנֵי לֻחוֹת הָאֲבָנִים
אֲשֶׁר הִנִּחַ שָׁם מֹשֶׁה בְּחֹרֵב אֲשֶׁר כָּרַת
יְהוָה עִם־בְּנֵי יִשְׂרָאֵל בְּצֵאתָם מֵאֶרֶץ
מִצְרָיִם׃

10 וַיְהִי בְּצֵאת הַכֹּהֲנִים מִן־הַקֹּדֶשׁ וְהֶעָנָן
מָלֵא אֶת־בֵּית יְהוָה׃ 11 וְלֹא־יָכְלוּ
הַכֹּהֲנִים לַעֲמֹד לְשָׁרֵת מִפְּנֵי הֶעָנָן כִּי־
מָלֵא כְבוֹד־יְהוָה אֶת־בֵּית יְהוָה׃ פ
12 אָז אָמַר שְׁלֹמֹה
יְהוָה אָמַר

1 Kings 8:2. Feast Hebrew: *ḥag,* that is, the festival of Booths (*Sukkot*) in the seventh month (see Lev. 23:34); it becomes the Sages' primary name for this holiday.

Ethanim Here identified with the seventh month, later called *Tishrei.*

4. Tent of Meeting In the Torah, the term refers to the tabernacle.

9. Following the tradition in Deut. 10:1–5. In the ancient Near East, treaty texts were regularly deposited at the feet of the gods in a shrine; this is the custom behind depositing in the Ark—both in the tabernacle and in the Temple—the tablets elsewhere referred to as "the Pact" (*edut;* Exod. 25:16) or "of the Covenant" (*b'rit;* Deut. 9:11,15).

12. then Solomon declared After God had shown His favor.

"The LORD has chosen
To abide in a thick cloud:
13I have now built for You
A stately House,
A place where You
May dwell forever."

14Then, with the whole congregation of Israel standing, the king faced about and blessed the whole congregation of Israel. 15He said:

"Praised be the LORD, the God of Israel, who has fulfilled with deeds the promise He made to my father David. For He said, 16'Ever since I brought My people Israel out of Egypt, I have not chosen a city among all the tribes of Israel for building a House where My name might abide; but I have chosen David to rule My people Israel.'

17"Now my father David had intended to build a House for the name of the LORD, the God of Israel. 18But the LORD said to my father David, 'As regards your intention to build a House for My name, you did right to have that intention. 19However, you shall not build the House yourself; instead, your son, the issue of your loins, shall build the House for My name.'

20"And the LORD has fulfilled the promise that He made: I have succeeded my father David and have ascended the throne of Israel, as the LORD promised. I have built the House for the name of the LORD, the God of Israel; 21and I have set a place there for the Ark, containing the covenant which the LORD made with our fathers when He brought them out from the land of Egypt."

18. the LORD said to . . . David Through the prophet Nathan (2 Sam. 7:8–17).

לִשְׁכֹּ֖ן בָּעֲרָפֶֽל׃
13 בָּנֹ֥ה בָנִ֛יתִי
בֵּ֥ית זְבֻ֖ל לָ֑ךְ
מָכ֥וֹן לְשִׁבְתְּךָ֖
עוֹלָמִֽים׃
14 וַיַּסֵּ֤ב הַמֶּ֙לֶךְ֙ אֶת־פָּנָ֔יו וַיְבָ֕רֶךְ אֵ֖ת כָּל־
קְהַ֣ל יִשְׂרָאֵ֑ל וְכָל־קְהַ֥ל יִשְׂרָאֵ֖ל עֹמֵֽד׃
15 וַיֹּ֗אמֶר
בָּר֤וּךְ יְהוָה֙ אֱלֹהֵ֣י יִשְׂרָאֵ֔ל אֲשֶׁר֙ דִּבֶּ֣ר בְּפִ֔יו
אֵ֖ת דָּוִ֣ד אָבִ֑י וּבְיָד֥וֹ מִלֵּ֖א לֵאמֹֽר׃ 16 מִן־
הַיּ֗וֹם אֲשֶׁ֨ר הוֹצֵ֜אתִי אֶת־עַמִּ֣י אֶת־יִשְׂרָאֵל֮
מִמִּצְרַיִם֒ לֹֽא־בָחַ֣רְתִּי בְעִ֗יר מִכֹּל֙ שִׁבְטֵ֣י
יִשְׂרָאֵ֔ל לִבְנ֣וֹת בַּ֔יִת לִהְי֥וֹת שְׁמִ֖י שָׁ֑ם
וָאֶבְחַ֣ר בְּדָוִ֔ד לִהְי֖וֹת עַל־עַמִּ֥י יִשְׂרָאֵֽל׃
17 וַיְהִ֕י עִם־לְבַ֖ב דָּוִ֣ד אָבִ֑י לִבְנ֣וֹת בַּ֔יִת
לְשֵׁ֖ם יְהוָ֥ה אֱלֹהֵ֖י יִשְׂרָאֵֽל׃ 18 וַיֹּ֤אמֶר יְהוָה֙
אֶל־דָּוִ֣ד אָבִ֔י יַ֚עַן אֲשֶׁ֣ר הָיָה֙ עִם־לְבָ֣בְךָ֔
לִבְנ֥וֹת בַּ֖יִת לִשְׁמִ֑י הֱטִיבֹ֔תָ כִּ֥י הָיָ֖ה עִם־
לְבָבֶֽךָ׃ 19 רַ֣ק אַתָּ֔ה לֹ֥א תִבְנֶ֖ה הַבָּ֑יִת כִּ֤י
אִם־בִּנְךָ֙ הַיֹּצֵ֣א מֵחֲלָצֶ֔יךָ הֽוּא־יִבְנֶ֥ה הַבַּ֖יִת
לִשְׁמִֽי׃
20 וַיָּ֣קֶם יְהוָ֔ה אֶת־דְּבָר֖וֹ אֲשֶׁ֣ר דִּבֵּ֑ר וָאָקֻ֡ם
תַּחַת֩ דָּוִ֨ד אָבִ֜י וָאֵשֵׁ֣ב עַל־כִּסֵּ֣א יִשְׂרָאֵ֗ל
כַּאֲשֶׁר֙ דִּבֶּ֣ר יְהוָ֔ה וָאֶבְנֶ֣ה הַבַּ֔יִת לְשֵׁ֥ם
יְהוָ֖ה אֱלֹהֵ֥י יִשְׂרָאֵֽל׃ 21 וָאָשִׂ֨ם שָׁ֤ם
מָקוֹם֙ לָֽאָר֔וֹן אֲשֶׁר־שָׁ֖ם בְּרִ֣ית יְהוָ֑ה אֲשֶׁ֤ר
כָּרַת֙ עִם־אֲבֹתֵ֔ינוּ בְּהוֹצִיא֥וֹ אֹתָ֖ם מֵאֶ֥רֶץ
מִצְרָֽיִם׃ ס

הפטרה לשבת חול המועד סוכות

HAFTARAH FOR SUKKOT, INTERMEDIATE SHABBAT

EZEKIEL 38:18–39:16

The verses of this *haftarah* are part of the extended doom prophecy against "Gog of the land of Magog" in Ezek. 38–39. These chapters follow oracles of hope for Israel's national restoration and purification (Ezek. 36–37), and they precede the vision of the new Temple and the priestly order for the new age to come (Ezek. 40–48). The Temple vision is dated to 573 B.C.E.; the prophecies that precede it are undated, but presumably stem from around the same time.

The doom prophecy of the *haftarah* thus occupies a transitional position in Ezekiel's book, predicting the horrific punishment of Israel's enemies and the subsequent repurification of the Land. The destruction of Gog came to symbolize the dreadful doom of divine judgment, anticipating a feature of later Jewish imagination and literature known as apocalyptic (which purports to reveal what will happen in the end of days).

The *haftarah* is a spectacle of disaster wrought against enemies of Israel. In hordes, they swoop down on Israel from the northlands—only to be destroyed in a surge of divine fury that shakes the earth with quakes, pestilence, and bloodshed. In the end, the Holy Land will be strewn with the bodies of the dead, and squadrons of Israelite searchers will scour the Land to bury the slain. After seven months of searching and burying, "the land shall be purified."

The background of this war is unspecified, as is the selection of Gog out of the land of Magog for the role of enemy. The whole scene breathes a mythic atmosphere of ungodly doom, with episodes presented and repeated without concern for sequence or logic. All that we are told, repeatedly, is the divine motivation for the carnage.

Two themes predominate. The first theme is the manifestation of divine power, such that the nations will "know" the Lord. This is a signature feature of the prophet Ezekiel and his theology. It derives from earlier priestly traditions about the excessive and oppressive plagues inflicted on the Egyptians. There, the reason for the public displays is twofold: to convince the Israelites of God's might and His claim to be their deliverer; and to convince the Egyptians (Exod. 7:5,17, 14:4). In the Book of Ezekiel, this acknowledgment formula is geared as well toward the public recognition of God by the nations—and especially to counteract negative assessments of His power. Against the background of God's apparent abandonment of the people Israel, which led some to doubt His power, God makes His might known to all.

The defamation of God further resulted in a desecration of His "holy name," which is the second and interrelated theme of the *haftarah.* A particularly poignant expression of this matter is dealt with expressly in a chapter that precedes the *haftarah* (Ezek. 36). Because of this desecration, God will act "for [the sake of] My holy name," and "will sanctify My great name which has been profaned among the nations. . . . And the nations shall know that I am the LORD" (36:20–23). History thus remains the specific site for the manifestation of God's glory. But human life recedes before this awesome act of self-vindication.

RELATION OF THE *HAFTARAH* TO THE CALENDAR

The theme of renewal in time to come, featuring a divinely led battle, recurs in *haftarah* readings for festival days. An image of destruction and transformation comparable to that found in this *haftarah* is also found in the *haftarah* for the first day of *Sukkot* (Zech. 14:1–21). Rashi (on Ezek. 38:17, in this *haftarah*) identified the Gog proph-

ecy with the "war spoken of in Zechariah." Apparently, this identification flowed from the close liturgical association of these two *haftarot* and from the reference in Zech. 14:16 to a grand celebration of *Sukkot* in Jerusalem after the awesome days of battle.

For generations, the Gog prophecy excited wild imagination born of hope in a final judgment against the enemies of Israel. According to Akiva, the judgment against Gog would last 12 months (M Eduy. 2:10). This judgment would also bring disaster on Israel, causing other calamities to fade by comparison (Tosef. Ber. 1:13). It was commonly supposed that this war would be the final battle, heralding the advent of the Messiah and a time when historical servitude would cease (Sifrei Num. 76; BT Sanh. 97b).

38

18On that day, when Gog sets foot on
the soil of Israel—declares the Lord GOD—My
raging anger shall flare up. 19For I have decreed
in My indignation and in My blazing wrath: On
that day, a terrible earthquake shall befall the
land of Israel. 20The fish of the sea, the birds of
the sky, the beasts of the field, all creeping things
that move on the ground, and every human being on earth shall quake before Me. Mountains
shall be overthrown, cliffs shall topple, and
every wall shall crumble to the ground. 21I will
then summon the sword against him throughout My mountains—declares the Lord GOD—
and every man's sword shall be turned against
his brother. 22I will punish him with pestilence
and with bloodshed; and I will pour torrential
rain, hailstones, and sulfurous fire upon him
and his hordes and the many peoples with him.
23Thus will I manifest My greatness and My holiness, and make Myself known in the sight of
many nations. And they shall know that I am
the LORD.

לח

18 וְהָיָה ׀ בַּיּוֹם הַהוּא בְּיוֹם בּוֹא
גוֹג עַל־אַדְמַת יִשְׂרָאֵל נְאֻם אֲדֹנָי יְהוִה
תַּעֲלֶה חֲמָתִי בְּאַפִּי׃ 19 וּבְקִנְאָתִי בְאֵשׁ־
עֶבְרָתִי דִּבַּרְתִּי אִם־לֹא ׀ בַּיּוֹם הַהוּא
יִהְיֶה רַעַשׁ גָּדוֹל עַל אַדְמַת יִשְׂרָאֵל׃
20 וְרָעֲשׁוּ מִפָּנַי דְּגֵי הַיָּם וְעוֹף הַשָּׁמַיִם
וְחַיַּת הַשָּׂדֶה וְכָל־הָרֶמֶשׂ הָרֹמֵשׂ עַל־
הָאֲדָמָה וְכֹל הָאָדָם אֲשֶׁר עַל־פְּנֵי
הָאֲדָמָה וְנֶהֶרְסוּ הֶהָרִים וְנָפְלוּ הַמַּדְרֵגוֹת
וְכָל־חוֹמָה לָאָרֶץ תִּפּוֹל׃ 21 וְקָרָאתִי עָלָיו
לְכָל־הָרַי חֶרֶב נְאֻם אֲדֹנָי יְהוִה חֶרֶב אִישׁ
בְּאָחִיו תִּהְיֶה׃ 22 וְנִשְׁפַּטְתִּי אִתּוֹ בְּדֶבֶר
וּבְדָם וְגֶשֶׁם שׁוֹטֵף וְאַבְנֵי אֶלְגָּבִישׁ אֵשׁ
וְגָפְרִית אַמְטִיר עָלָיו וְעַל־אֲגַפָּיו וְעַל־
עַמִּים רַבִּים אֲשֶׁר אִתּוֹ׃ 23 וְהִתְגַּדִּלְתִּי
וְהִתְקַדִּשְׁתִּי וְנוֹדַעְתִּי לְעֵינֵי גּוֹיִם רַבִּים
וְיָדְעוּ כִּי־אֲנִי יְהוָה׃ ס

Ezekiel 38:18. On that day A common prophetic formula that introduces oracles of times to come. It is used repeatedly by Ezekiel in the Gog prophecy (see 38:10,14,19, 39:11).

Gog In popular lore, associated with Magog as two historical terrors. But it is clear from verse 2 ("Gog of the land of Magog") that Gog refers to a person (or persons) and Magog is a geographic area.

23. Thus will I manifest My greatness and My holiness This unique expression (*v'hitgadalti v'hitkadashti*) is followed shortly by mention of God's holy name (39:7). Both elements have entered Jewish worship through the *Kaddish* prayer, recited at various junctures in a service as well as by mourners. All forms of the *Kaddish* begin with the Aramaic words *yitgadal v'yitkadash sh'mei raba;* "May His great name be exalted and sanctified."

39 And you, O mortal, prophesy against Gog and say: Thus said the Lord GOD: I am going to deal with you, O Gog, chief prince of Meshech and Tubal! 2I will turn you around and drive you on, and I will take you from the far north and lead you toward the mountains of Israel. 3I will strike your bow from your left hand and I will loosen the arrows from your right hand. 4You shall fall on the mountains of Israel, you and all your battalions and the peoples who are with you; and I will give you as food to carrion birds of every sort and to the beasts of the field, 5as you lie in the open field. For I have spoken—declares the Lord GOD. 6And I will send a fire against Magog and against those who dwell secure in the coastlands. And they shall know that I am the LORD. 7I will make My holy name known among My people Israel, and never again will I let My holy name be profaned. And the nations shall know that I the LORD am holy in Israel. 8Ah! it has come, it has happened—declares the Lord GOD: this is that day that I decreed.

9Then the inhabitants of the cities of Israel will go out and make fires and feed them with the weapons—shields and bucklers, bows and arrows, clubs and spears; they shall use them as fuel for seven years. 10They will not gather firewood in the fields or cut any in the forests, but will use the weapons as fuel for their fires. They will despoil those who despoiled them and plunder those who plundered them—declares the Lord GOD.

11On that day I will assign to Gog a burial site there in Israel—the Valley of the Travelers, east of the Sea. It shall block the path of travelers, for there Gog and all his multitude will be buried. It shall be called the Valley of Gog's Mul-

לט וְאַתָּה בֶן־אָדָם הִנָּבֵא עַל־גּוֹג וְאָמַרְתָּ כֹּה אָמַר אֲדֹנָי יְהוִה הִנְנִי אֵלֶיךָ גּוֹג נְשִׂיא רֹאשׁ מֶשֶׁךְ וְתֻבָל׃ 2 וְשֹׁבַבְתִּיךָ וְשִׁשֵּׁאתִיךָ* וְהַעֲלִיתִיךָ מִיַּרְכְּתֵי צָפוֹן וַהֲבֵאוֹתְךָ עַל־הָרֵי יִשְׂרָאֵל׃ 3 וְהִכֵּיתִי קַשְׁתְּךָ מִיַּד שְׂמֹאולֶךָ* וְחִצֶּיךָ מִיַּד יְמִינְךָ אַפִּיל׃ 4 עַל־הָרֵי יִשְׂרָאֵל תִּפּוֹל אַתָּה וְכָל־אֲגַפֶּיךָ וְעַמִּים אֲשֶׁר אִתָּךְ לְעֵיט צִפּוֹר כָּל־כָּנָף וְחַיַּת הַשָּׂדֶה נְתַתִּיךָ לְאָכְלָה׃ 5 עַל־פְּנֵי הַשָּׂדֶה תִּפּוֹל כִּי אֲנִי דִבַּרְתִּי נְאֻם אֲדֹנָי יְהוִה׃ 6 וְשִׁלַּחְתִּי־אֵשׁ בְּמָגוֹג וּבְיֹשְׁבֵי הָאִיִּים לָבֶטַח וְיָדְעוּ כִּי־אֲנִי יְהוָה׃ 7 וְאֶת־שֵׁם קָדְשִׁי אוֹדִיעַ בְּתוֹךְ עַמִּי יִשְׂרָאֵל וְלֹא־אַחֵל אֶת־שֵׁם־קָדְשִׁי עוֹד וְיָדְעוּ הַגּוֹיִם כִּי־אֲנִי יְהוָה קָדוֹשׁ בְּיִשְׂרָאֵל׃ 8 הִנֵּה בָאָה וְנִהְיָתָה נְאֻם אֲדֹנָי יְהוִה הוּא הַיּוֹם אֲשֶׁר דִּבַּרְתִּי׃

9 וְיָצְאוּ יֹשְׁבֵי ׀ עָרֵי יִשְׂרָאֵל וּבִעֲרוּ וְהִשִּׂיקוּ בְּנֶשֶׁק וּמָגֵן וְצִנָּה בְּקֶשֶׁת וּבְחִצִּים וּבְמַקֵּל יָד וּבְרֹמַח וּבִעֲרוּ בָהֶם אֵשׁ שֶׁבַע שָׁנִים׃ 10 וְלֹא־יִשְׂאוּ עֵצִים מִן־הַשָּׂדֶה וְלֹא יַחְטְבוּ מִן־הַיְּעָרִים כִּי בַנֶּשֶׁק יְבַעֲרוּ־אֵשׁ וְשָׁלְלוּ אֶת־שֹׁלְלֵיהֶם וּבָזְזוּ אֶת־בֹּזְזֵיהֶם נְאֻם אֲדֹנָי יְהוִה׃ ס

11 וְהָיָה בַיּוֹם הַהוּא אֶתֵּן לְגוֹג ׀ מְקוֹם־שָׁם קֶבֶר בְּיִשְׂרָאֵל גֵּי הָעֹבְרִים קִדְמַת הַיָּם וְחֹסֶמֶת הִיא אֶת־הָעֹבְרִים וְקָבְרוּ שָׁם אֶת־גּוֹג וְאֶת־כָּל־המונה הֲמוֹנֹו וְקָרְאוּ גֵּיא

v. 2. א׳ נחה
v. 3. מלא ו׳

Ezekiel 39:7. never again will I let My holy name be profaned The specter of gentile desecrations of God's name owing to Israelite suffering seems on the surface to reflect divine absence or even impotence (see Ezek. 20:9,14,22, 36:20–23).

titude. 12The House of Israel shall spend seven
months burying them, in order to purify the
land; 13all the people of the land shall bury them.
The day I manifest My glory shall bring renown to them—declares the Lord God. 14And
they shall appoint men to serve permanently,
to traverse the land and bury any invaders who
remain above ground, in order to purify it. The
search shall go on for a period of seven months.
15As those who traverse the country make their
rounds, any one of them who sees a human bone
shall erect a marker beside it, until the buriers
have interred them in the Valley of Gog's Multitude. 16There shall also be a city named Multitude. And thus the land shall be purified.

הֲמ֥וֹן גּֽוֹג׃ 12 וּקְבָרוּם֙ בֵּ֣ית יִשְׂרָאֵ֔ל לְמַ֖עַן
טַהֵ֣ר אֶת־הָאָ֑רֶץ שִׁבְעָ֖ה חֳדָשִֽׁים׃ 13 וְקָבְרוּ֙
כׇּל־עַ֣ם הָאָ֔רֶץ וְהָיָ֥ה לָהֶ֖ם לְשֵׁ֑ם י֚וֹם
הִכָּ֣בְדִ֔י נְאֻ֖ם אֲדֹנָ֥י יֱהֹוִֽה׃ 14 וְאַנְשֵׁ֨י תָמִ֤יד
יַבְדִּ֙ילוּ֙ עֹבְרִ֣ים בָּאָ֔רֶץ מְקַבְּרִ֣ים אֶת־
הָעֹֽבְרִ֗ים אֶת־הַנּוֹתָרִ֛ים עַל־פְּנֵ֥י הָאָ֖רֶץ
לְטַהֲרָ֑הּ מִקְצֵ֥ה שִׁבְעָֽה־חֳדָשִׁ֖ים יַחְקֹֽרוּ׃
15 וְעָבְר֤וּ הָעֹֽבְרִים֙ בָּאָ֔רֶץ וְרָאָה֙ עֶ֣צֶם אָדָ֔ם
וּבָנָ֥ה אֶצְל֖וֹ צִיּ֑וּן עַ֣ד קָבְר֤וּ אֹתוֹ֙ הַֽמְקַבְּרִ֔ים
אֶל־גֵּ֖יא הֲמ֥וֹן גּֽוֹג׃ 16 וְגַ֥ם שֶׁם־עִ֛יר הֲמוֹנָ֖ה
וְטִהֲר֥וּ הָאָֽרֶץ׃ ס

הפטרה לשמיני עצרת

HAFTARAH FOR SH'MINI ATZERET

1 KINGS 8:54–66

The conclusion of the festival week of *Sukkot,* according to the Torah, is to be marked by a distinct celebration: "The eighth [*sh'mini*] day . . . is a solemn gathering [*atzeret*]" (Lev. 23:36). That passage and Num. 29:35 call it a "sacred occasion" [*mikra kodesh*]. After Solomon's dedication of the Temple and celebration of *Sukkot,* he apparently marked this time in a special way, for "on the eighth day he let the people go [back] . . . to their homes" (1 Kings 8:66).

The choice of this *haftarah* is conditioned by its reference to the "eighth day," but its formal structure centers on the prayer that is incorporated within a narrative prologue and epilogue. That prayer opens with thanks to God for fulfilling His promise to Moses and continues with a request for divine providence in the future.

RELATION OF THE *HAFTARAH* TO THE CALENDAR

The recitation on *Sh'mini Atzeret* of a *haftarah* including 1 Kings 8:66 is mentioned in the Talmud (BT Meg. 31a). The Sages presumably understood the "eighth day" in verse 66 to be the festival of *Atzeret* itself, when the people performed their rites in the Temple and departed for home. The cited verse was apparently the opening line of the *haftarah* in ancient Palestine. It now concludes the reading according the practice of both *Ashk'nazim* and *S'fardim.*

Scripture says little about this holiday. According to Lev. 23:36, the "eighth day" from the onset of *Sukkot* is marked off as a "sacred occasion" (*mikra kodesh*), the standard expression for a festival day; but it is also called a "solemn gathering" (*atzeret*), without further explications.

The Sages, in their attention to detail, noted that according to Num. 29:36 only 1 ram was offered on *Sh'mini Atzeret,* whereas 70 rams were offered during the prior festival week. This fact, along with the designation of the *atzeret* "for you" (an expression not used on the other days), stands behind the *midrash* that articulates a special relation of God and Israel on that day. On all seven days of the *Sukkot* festival, Israel "was busy with sacrifices for the 70 nations of the world." In that *midrash,* God declares that "now (just) you and I shall rejoice together, and I shall not burden you overmuch" (PdRK, *Sh'mini Atzeret* 9). *Sh'mini Atzeret* thus came to mark an occasion of special intimacy between God and Israel.

The conclusion of the *haftarah* specifically notes that the people departed from the Temple "joyful [*s'meḥim*] and glad of heart" (v. 66). The bountiful joy of the day is a theme repeated in liturgical hymn and midrashic homilies.

8 54When Solomon finished offering to the
LORD all this prayer and supplication, he rose
from where he had been kneeling, in front of

ח 54 וַיְהִי | כְּכַלּוֹת שְׁלֹמֹה לְהִתְפַּלֵּל
אֶל־יְהוָה אֵת כָּל־הַתְּפִלָּה וְהַתְּחִנָּה
הַזֹּאת קָם מִלִּפְנֵי מִזְבַּח יְהוָה מִכְּרֹעַ

1 Kings 8:54. this prayer and supplication Solomon's dedicatory "Temple Prayer" of 1 Kings 8:22–53, which precedes the *haftarah.*

the altar of the LORD, his hands spread out toward heaven. [55]He stood, and in a loud voice
blessed the whole congregation of Israel:
[56]"Praised be the LORD who has granted a haven to His people Israel, just as He promised;
not a single word has failed of all the gracious
promises that He made through His servant
Moses. [57]May the LORD our God be with us, as
He was with our fathers. May He never abandon
or forsake us. [58]May He incline our hearts to
Him, that we may walk in all His ways and keep
the commandments, the laws, and the rules,
which He enjoined upon our fathers. [59]And may
these words of mine, which I have offered in
supplication before the LORD, be close to the
LORD our God day and night, that He may provide for His servant and for His people Israel,
according to each day's needs—[60]to the end that
all the peoples of the earth may know that the
LORD alone is God, there is no other. [61]And may
you be wholehearted with the LORD our God,
to walk in His ways and keep His commandments, even as now."
[62]The king and all Israel with him offered
sacrifices before the LORD. [63]Solomon offered
22,000 oxen and 120,000 sheep as sacrifices of
well-being to the LORD. Thus the king and all
the Israelites dedicated the House of the LORD.
[64]That day the king consecrated the center of
the court that was in front of the House of the
LORD. For it was there that he presented the
burnt offerings, the grain offerings, and the fat
parts of the offerings of well-being, because the
bronze altar that was before the LORD was too
small to hold the burnt offerings, the grain
offerings, and the fat parts of the offerings of
well-being.

עַל־בִּרְכָּ֔יו וְכַפָּ֖יו פְּרֻשׂ֥וֹת הַשָּׁמָֽיִם׃
55 וַֽיַּעֲמֹ֕ד וַיְבָ֕רֶךְ אֵ֖ת כָּל־קְהַ֣ל יִשְׂרָאֵ֑ל ק֥וֹל
גָּד֖וֹל לֵאמֹֽר׃
56 בָּר֣וּךְ יְהֹוָ֗ה אֲשֶׁ֨ר נָתַ֤ן מְנוּחָה֙ לְעַמּ֣וֹ
יִשְׂרָאֵ֔ל כְּכֹ֖ל אֲשֶׁ֣ר דִּבֵּ֑ר לֹֽא־נָפַ֞ל דָּבָ֣ר אֶחָ֗ד
מִכֹּל֙ דְּבָר֣וֹ הַטּ֔וֹב אֲשֶׁ֣ר דִּבֶּ֔ר בְּיַ֖ד מֹשֶׁ֥ה
עַבְדּֽוֹ׃ 57 יְהִ֨י יְהֹוָ֤ה אֱלֹהֵ֙ינוּ֙ עִמָּ֔נוּ כַּאֲשֶׁ֥ר
הָיָ֖ה עִם־אֲבֹתֵ֑ינוּ אַל־יַעַזְבֵ֖נוּ וְאַל־יִטְּשֵֽׁנוּ׃
58 לְהַטּ֥וֹת לְבָבֵ֖נוּ אֵלָ֑יו לָלֶ֣כֶת בְּכָל־דְּרָכָ֗יו
וְלִשְׁמֹ֨ר מִצְוֺתָ֤יו וְחֻקָּיו֙ וּמִשְׁפָּטָ֔יו אֲשֶׁ֥ר
צִוָּ֖ה אֶת־אֲבֹתֵֽינוּ׃ 59 וְיִהְי֨וּ דְבָרַ֜י אֵ֗לֶּה
אֲשֶׁ֤ר הִתְחַנַּ֙נְתִּי֙ לִפְנֵ֣י יְהֹוָ֔ה קְרֹבִ֛ים אֶל־
יְהֹוָ֥ה אֱלֹהֵ֖ינוּ יוֹמָ֣ם וָלָ֑יְלָה לַעֲשׂ֣וֹת ׀
מִשְׁפַּ֣ט עַבְדּ֗וֹ וּמִשְׁפַּ֛ט עַמּ֥וֹ יִשְׂרָאֵ֖ל דְּבַר־
י֥וֹם בְּיוֹמֽוֹ׃ 60 לְמַ֗עַן דַּ֚עַת כָּל־עַמֵּ֣י הָאָ֔רֶץ
כִּ֥י יְהֹוָ֖ה ה֣וּא הָאֱלֹהִ֑ים אֵ֖ין עֽוֹד׃ 61 וְהָיָ֤ה
לְבַבְכֶם֙ שָׁלֵ֔ם עִ֖ם יְהֹוָ֣ה אֱלֹהֵ֑ינוּ לָלֶ֧כֶת
בְּחֻקָּ֛יו וְלִשְׁמֹ֥ר מִצְוֺתָ֖יו כַּיּ֥וֹם הַזֶּֽה׃
62 וְהַמֶּ֕לֶךְ וְכָל־יִשְׂרָאֵ֖ל עִמּ֑וֹ זֹבְחִ֥ים זֶ֖בַח
לִפְנֵ֥י יְהֹוָֽה׃ 63 וַיִּזְבַּ֣ח שְׁלֹמֹ֗ה אֵ֣ת זֶ֣בַח
הַשְּׁלָמִים֮ אֲשֶׁ֣ר זָבַ֣ח לַיהֹוָה֒ בָּקָ֗ר עֶשְׂרִ֤ים
וּשְׁנַ֙יִם֙ אֶ֔לֶף וְצֹ֕אן מֵאָ֥ה וְעֶשְׂרִ֖ים אָ֑לֶף
וַֽיַּחְנְכוּ֙ אֶת־בֵּ֣ית יְהֹוָ֔ה הַמֶּ֖לֶךְ וְכָל־בְּנֵ֥י
יִשְׂרָאֵֽל׃ 64 בַּיּ֣וֹם הַה֗וּא קִדַּ֨שׁ הַמֶּ֜לֶךְ אֶת־
ת֣וֹךְ הֶחָצֵ֗ר אֲשֶׁר֙ לִפְנֵ֣י בֵית־יְהֹוָ֔ה כִּי־
עָ֣שָׂה שָׁ֗ם אֶת־הָֽעֹלָה֙ וְאֶת־הַמִּנְחָ֔ה וְאֵ֖ת
חֶלְבֵ֣י הַשְּׁלָמִ֑ים כִּֽי־מִזְבַּ֤ח הַנְּחֹ֙שֶׁת֙ אֲשֶׁ֣ר
לִפְנֵ֣י יְהֹוָ֔ה קָטֹ֗ן מֵֽהָכִיל֙ אֶת־הָעֹלָ֣ה וְאֶת־
הַמִּנְחָ֔ה וְאֵ֖ת חֶלְבֵ֥י הַשְּׁלָמִֽים׃

64. the king consecrated the center of the court That is, Solomon sanctified the floor of the court by dedicating the altar there (BT Zev. 59a). The center of the court thus refers to the floor of the court of the priests. This special sanctification was held because the "bronze altar" was "too small to hold" all the abundant offerings made at that time (Radak, Ralbag). According to tradition, Solomon there established an altar of stones affixed to the floor (BT Zev. 59a–60a).

65 וַיַּ֣עַשׂ שְׁלֹמֹ֣ה בָֽעֵת־הַהִ֣יא ׀ אֶת־הֶחָ֡ג
וְכָל־יִשְׂרָאֵ֣ל עִמּוֹ֩ קָהָ֨ל גָּד֜וֹל מִלְּב֣וֹא
חֲמָ֣ת ׀ עַד־נַ֣חַל מִצְרַ֗יִם לִפְנֵי֙ יְהוָ֣ה
אֱלֹהֵ֔ינוּ שִׁבְעַ֥ת יָמִ֛ים וְשִׁבְעַ֥ת יָמִ֖ים
אַרְבָּעָ֥ה עָשָׂ֖ר יֽוֹם׃ 66 בַּיּ֤וֹם הַשְּׁמִינִי֙ שִׁלַּ֣ח
אֶת־הָעָ֔ם וַיְבָרֲכ֖וּ אֶת־הַמֶּ֑לֶךְ וַיֵּלְכ֣וּ
לְאָהֳלֵיהֶ֗ם שְׂמֵחִים֙ וְט֣וֹבֵי לֵ֔ב עַ֣ל כָּל־
הַטּוֹבָ֗ה אֲשֶׁ֨ר עָשָׂ֤ה יְהוָה֙ לְדָוִ֣ד עַבְדּ֔וֹ
וּלְיִשְׂרָאֵ֖ל עַמּֽוֹ׃

65So Solomon and all Israel with him—a great
assemblage, [coming] from Lebo-hamath to
the Wadi of Egypt—observed the Feast at that
time before the LORD our God, seven days and
again seven days, fourteen days in all. 66On the
eighth day he let the people go. They bade the
king good-bye and went to their homes, joyful
and glad of heart over all the goodness that the
LORD had shown to His servant David and His
people Israel.

הפטרה לשמחת תורה

HAFTARAH FOR SIMḤAT TORAH

JOSHUA 1:1–18

This *haftarah* is taken from the opening of the Book of Joshua. It thus picks up the thread of the story after the death of Moses (at the end of the Torah). God addresses Joshua as Moses' successor, commanding him to bring the people into their ancestral land. Further, as a sign of spiritual continuity, the Torah (presented by Moses "as the heritage of the congregation of Jacob," Deut. 33:4) is enjoined upon Joshua for observance and study. The passage also contains Joshua's orders and exhortations that prepare to fulfill the command of conquest.

The *haftarah* is charged with the anxiety of continuity amid new beginnings. "My servant Moses is dead," says God to Joshua at the outset. "Prepare to cross the Jordan." Repeatedly God exhorts Joshua to be courageous, declaring that He will be with him as He was with Moses (vv. 5,9). Echoing these concerns, the Transjordanian tribes exhort Joshua to be courageous and express the hope that God will be with him, as He was with his master (vv. 17–18).

Success in battle is conditioned on faithfulness to the divine teaching (1:7–8). Physical courage alone is insufficient. Only scrupulous study and fulfillment will ensure divine favor in the campaigns to follow. This is hardly the language of a military exhortation and reflects later notions of Torah piety.

The theology in Josh. 1:6–9 echoes values enjoined elsewhere on the whole covenant community. God informs the people in Deut. 11:8 that observance of the divine commandments will enable them "to enter and take possession of the land." More broadly, Ps. 1 proclaims study of the Torah to be a transformative activity. In precisely the same terms as found in Josh. 1:8, the psalmist says that one who studies (*yehgeh*) the Torah "day and night" will "succeed" (*yatzli·aḥ*) in "all" that he does (vv. 2–3). The Lord enjoins Joshua to combine two ideals: action and contemplation, asking him to be at once a man of power and of piety. Becoming in effect a "new Moses" through study makes Joshua also the first "keeper of Tradition." Joshua must learn and recite the divine revelations received by his master, Moses, "face to face" (Deut. 34:10). For this reason, Joshua is not called a "prophet"—but rather one "filled with the spirit of wisdom" (Deut. 34:9). Revelation sets the tasks that tradition must realize.

RELATION OF THE *HAFTARAH* TO THE CALENDAR

The choice of Joshua 1 as the *haftarah* for this holiday may have arisen from an ancient custom of reading the Prophets and the Writings concurrently with the Torah cycle. Communities following this practice concluded all three sections of the Bible together. (The last of the prophets, Malachi, declares near the end of his book, "Remember the Torah of Moses," which makes sense in this larger liturgic context.) On *Simḥat Torah,* it is customary to follow the conclusion of Deuteronomy immediately with the opening portion of Genesis. We may presume a similar old *Simḥat Torah* custom of following the conclusion of the Prophets immediately with the opening verses of its first book, Joshua. Accordingly, this *haftarah* was intended to parallel the reading from Genesis 1:1–2:4. Indeed, it bears no thematic or even liturgic relation to the end of Deuteronomy.

Meanwhile, reading Joshua 1 after the end of the Torah highlights the shift from revelation to tradition. Moses received God's teaching directly, but his successor received it via study and interpretation. Joshua recited the divine words, and in so doing he renewed their instruction for future generations. He was thus the first to extend the authority of Moses beyond the latter's lifetime.

1 After the death of Moses the servant of
the LORD, the LORD said to Joshua son of Nun,
Moses' attendant:
2"My servant Moses is dead. Prepare to cross
the Jordan, together with all this people, into
the land that I am giving to the Israelites. 3Every
spot on which your foot treads I give to you,
as I promised Moses. 4Your territory shall extend from the wilderness and the Lebanon to
the Great River, the River Euphrates [on the
east]—the whole Hittite country—and up to
the Mediterranean Sea on the west. 5No one
shall be able to resist you as long as you live.
As I was with Moses, so I will be with you; I will
not fail you or forsake you.
6"Be strong and resolute, for you shall apportion to this people the land that I swore to
their fathers to assign to them. 7But you must
be very strong and resolute to observe faithfully
all the Teaching that My servant Moses enjoined
upon you. Do not deviate from it to the right
or to the left, that you may be successful wherever you go. 8Let not this Book of the Teaching
cease from your lips, but recite it day and night,

א וַיְהִי אַחֲרֵי מוֹת מֹשֶׁה עֶבֶד יְהוָה
וַיֹּאמֶר יְהוָה אֶל־יְהוֹשֻׁעַ בִּן־נוּן מְשָׁרֵת
מֹשֶׁה לֵאמֹר׃
2 מֹשֶׁה עַבְדִּי מֵת וְעַתָּה קוּם עֲבֹר אֶת־
הַיַּרְדֵּן הַזֶּה אַתָּה וְכָל־הָעָם הַזֶּה אֶל־
הָאָרֶץ אֲשֶׁר אָנֹכִי נֹתֵן לָהֶם לִבְנֵי יִשְׂרָאֵל׃
3 כָּל־מָקוֹם אֲשֶׁר תִּדְרֹךְ כַּף־רַגְלְכֶם בּוֹ
לָכֶם נְתַתִּיו כַּאֲשֶׁר דִּבַּרְתִּי אֶל־מֹשֶׁה׃
4 מֵהַמִּדְבָּר וְהַלְּבָנוֹן הַזֶּה וְעַד־הַנָּהָר
הַגָּדוֹל נְהַר־פְּרָת כֹּל אֶרֶץ הַחִתִּים וְעַד־
הַיָּם הַגָּדוֹל מְבוֹא הַשָּׁמֶשׁ יִהְיֶה גְּבוּלְכֶם׃
5 לֹא־יִתְיַצֵּב אִישׁ לְפָנֶיךָ כֹּל יְמֵי חַיֶּיךָ
כַּאֲשֶׁר הָיִיתִי עִם־מֹשֶׁה אֶהְיֶה עִמָּךְ לֹא
אַרְפְּךָ וְלֹא אֶעֶזְבֶךָּ׃
6 חֲזַק וֶאֱמָץ כִּי אַתָּה תַּנְחִיל אֶת־הָעָם
הַזֶּה אֶת־הָאָרֶץ אֲשֶׁר־נִשְׁבַּעְתִּי לַאֲבוֹתָם
לָתֵת לָהֶם׃ 7 רַק חֲזַק וֶאֱמַץ מְאֹד לִשְׁמֹר
לַעֲשׂוֹת כְּכָל־הַתּוֹרָה אֲשֶׁר צִוְּךָ מֹשֶׁה
עַבְדִּי אַל־תָּסוּר מִמֶּנּוּ* יָמִין וּשְׂמֹאול*
לְמַעַן תַּשְׂכִּיל בְּכֹל אֲשֶׁר תֵּלֵךְ׃ 8 לֹא־
יָמוּשׁ סֵפֶר הַתּוֹרָה הַזֶּה מִפִּיךָ וְהָגִיתָ בּוֹ

v. 7. סבירין ומטעין "ממנה"

v. 7. מלא ו׳

Joshua 1:1. After the death The first Hebrew word (*va-y'hi,* literally, "And it was . . . ") is untranslated here. Its conjunction "and" (*va-*) links the opening phrase to the end of Deuteronomy (Rashi).

2. Moses is dead According to rabbinic tradition, Moses died on the 7th of *Adar* (see BT Kid. 38a).

3. Every spot upon which your foot treads A technical phrase for taking possession.

4. These ideal boundaries of the Land are limited only by geographic barriers (river, sea, desert wilderness, mountains). This description follows Deut. 11:24, which it cites (v. 3) while adding a summary: "the whole Hittite country." That phrase is identical to the term "Hatti land" used in Assyrian sources to indicate the Syro-Palestine region. (For similar delineations of ideal boundaries, see Gen. 15:18–21, Exod. 23:31, and Deut. 1:7–8.)

6,9. Be strong and resolute The old language of military exhortation (Deut. 31:6) now encases the ideal of Torah piety—transforming a charge of physical might into one of spiritual devotion.

8. recite it day and night A religious ideal of perpetual focus on God (via preoccupation with His teachings) lies beyond the immediate utilitarian motivation of God's word to Joshua. Here the national leader is enjoined to follow the ideal of perpetual study and recitation. In Ps. 1:2, this is an ideal for all who delight in Torah and would be righteous. And Deuteronomy reflects both goals: It exhorts a leader (the king) to ever study Torah and be humble and pious (17:18–20); and it articulates the well-known na-

so that you may observe faithfully all that is written in it. Only then will you prosper in your undertakings and only then will you be successful.

9"I charge you: Be strong and resolute; do not be terrified or dismayed, for the LORD your God is with you wherever you go."

10Joshua thereupon gave orders to the officials of the people: 11"Go through the camp and charge the people thus: Get provisions ready, for in three days' time you are to cross the Jordan, in order to enter and possess the land that the LORD your God is giving you as a possession."

12Then Joshua said to the Reubenites, the Gadites, and the half-tribe of Manasseh, 13"Remember what Moses the servant of the LORD enjoined upon you, when he said: 'The LORD your God is granting you a haven; He has assigned this territory to you.' 14Let your wives, children, and livestock remain in the land that Moses assigned to you on this side of the Jordan; but every one of your fighting men shall go across armed in the van of your kinsmen. And you shall assist them 15until the LORD has given your kinsmen a haven, such as you have, and they too have gained possession of the land that the LORD your God has assigned to them. Then you may return to the land on the east side of the Jordan, which Moses the servant of the LORD assigned to you as your possession, and you may possess it."

16They answered Joshua, "We will do everything you have commanded us and we will go wherever you send us. 17We will obey you just as we obeyed Moses; let but the LORD your God be with you as He was with Moses! 18Any man who flouts your commands and does not obey every order you give him shall be put to death. Only be strong and resolute!"

יוֹמָ֣ם וָלַ֗יְלָה לְמַ֙עַן֙ תִּשְׁמֹ֣ר לַעֲשׂ֔וֹת כְּכָל־
הַכָּת֖וּב בּ֑וֹ כִּי־אָ֛ז תַּצְלִ֥יחַ אֶת־דְּרָכֶ֖ךָ וְאָ֥ז
תַּשְׂכִּֽיל׃ 9 הֲל֤וֹא צִוִּיתִ֙יךָ֙ חֲזַ֣ק וֶאֱמָ֔ץ אַֽל־
תַּעֲרֹ֖ץ וְאַל־תֵּחָ֑ת כִּ֤י עִמְּךָ֙ יְהֹוָ֣ה אֱלֹהֶ֔יךָ
בְּכֹ֖ל אֲשֶׁ֥ר תֵּלֵֽךְ׃ פ

10 וַיְצַ֣ו יְהוֹשֻׁ֔עַ אֶת־שֹׁטְרֵ֥י הָעָ֖ם לֵאמֹֽר׃
11 עִבְר֣וּ ׀ בְּקֶ֣רֶב הַֽמַּחֲנֶ֗ה וְצַוּ֤וּ אֶת־הָעָם֙
לֵאמֹ֔ר הָכִ֥ינוּ לָכֶ֖ם צֵידָ֑ה כִּ֞י בְּע֣וֹד ׀ שְׁלֹ֣שֶׁת
יָמִ֗ים אַתֶּם֙ עֹֽבְרִים֙ אֶת־הַיַּרְדֵּ֣ן הַזֶּ֔ה לָבוֹא֙
לָרֶ֣שֶׁת אֶת־הָאָ֔רֶץ אֲשֶׁר֙ יְהֹוָ֣ה אֱלֹֽהֵיכֶ֔ם
נֹתֵ֥ן לָכֶ֖ם לְרִשְׁתָּֽהּ׃ ס
12 וְלָרֽאוּבֵנִי֙ וְלַגָּדִ֔י וְלַחֲצִ֖י שֵׁ֣בֶט הַֽמְנַשֶּׁ֑ה
אָמַ֥ר יְהוֹשֻׁ֖עַ לֵאמֹֽר׃ 13 זָכוֹר֙ אֶת־הַדָּבָ֔ר
אֲשֶׁ֨ר צִוָּ֥ה אֶתְכֶ֛ם מֹשֶׁ֥ה עֶֽבֶד־יְהֹוָ֖ה לֵאמֹ֑ר
יְהֹוָ֤ה אֱלֹֽהֵיכֶם֙ מֵנִ֣יחַ לָכֶ֔ם וְנָתַ֥ן לָכֶ֖ם
אֶת־הָאָ֥רֶץ הַזֹּֽאת׃ 14 נְשֵׁיכֶ֣ם טַפְּכֶ֗ם
וּמִקְנֵיכֶ֘ם יֵשְׁבוּ֮ בָּאָ֒רֶץ֒ אֲשֶׁ֨ר נָתַ֥ן לָכֶ֛ם
מֹשֶׁ֖ה בְּעֵ֣בֶר הַיַּרְדֵּ֑ן וְאַתֶּם֩ תַּעַבְר֨וּ חֲמֻשִׁ֜ים
לִפְנֵ֣י אֲחֵיכֶ֗ם כֹּ֚ל גִּבּוֹרֵ֣י הַחַ֔יִל וַעֲזַרְתֶּ֖ם
אוֹתָֽם׃ 15 עַ֠ד אֲשֶׁר־יָנִ֨יחַ יְהֹוָ֥ה ׀ לַֽאֲחֵיכֶם֮
כָּכֶם֒ וְיָרְשׁ֣וּ גַם־הֵ֔מָּה אֶת־הָאָ֕רֶץ אֲשֶׁר־
יְהֹוָ֥ה אֱלֹֽהֵיכֶ֖ם נֹתֵ֣ן לָהֶ֑ם וְשַׁבְתֶּ֞ם לְאֶ֣רֶץ
יְרֻשַּׁתְכֶ֗ם וִֽירִשְׁתֶּ֤ם אוֹתָהּ֙ אֲשֶׁ֣ר ׀ נָתַ֣ן לָכֶ֗ם
מֹשֶׁה֙ עֶ֣בֶד יְהֹוָ֔ה בְּעֵ֥בֶר הַיַּרְדֵּ֖ן מִזְרַ֥ח
הַשָּֽׁמֶשׁ׃
16 וַֽיַּעֲנ֔וּ אֶת־יְהוֹשֻׁ֖עַ לֵאמֹ֑ר כֹּ֤ל אֲשֶׁר־
צִוִּיתָ֙נוּ֙ נַֽעֲשֶׂ֔ה וְאֶֽל־כׇּל־אֲשֶׁ֥ר תִּשְׁלָחֵ֖נוּ
נֵלֵֽךְ׃ 17 כְּכֹ֤ל אֲשֶׁר־שָׁמַ֙עְנוּ֙ אֶל־מֹשֶׁ֔ה כֵּ֥ן
נִשְׁמַ֖ע אֵלֶ֑יךָ רַ֠ק יִֽהְיֶ֞ה יְהֹוָ֤ה אֱלֹהֶ֙יךָ֙ עִמָּ֔ךְ
כַּאֲשֶׁ֥ר הָיָ֖ה עִם־מֹשֶֽׁה׃ 18 כׇּל־אִ֞ישׁ אֲשֶׁר־
יַמְרֶ֣ה אֶת־פִּ֗יךָ וְלֹֽא־יִשְׁמַ֧ע אֶת־דְּבָרֶ֛יךָ
לְכֹ֥ל אֲשֶׁר־תְּצַוֶּ֖נּוּ יוּמָ֑ת רַ֖ק חֲזַ֥ק וֶאֱמָֽץ׃ פ

---

tional ideal of discussing Torah at all times—when seated at home, walking on the way, lying down, and getting up (6:7).

10. thereupon The time is unspecified. Rashi suggests that this took place after the period of mourning for Moses.

הפטרה לשבת חנוכה (א׳)

HAFTARAH FOR FIRST SHABBAT OF ḤANUKKAH

ZECHARIAH 2:14–4:7

In 538 B.C.E., a year after conquering Babylonia, Cyrus the Mede had issued an edict allowing all subject populations to return to their national religious practices. As a result, exiles from Babylonia had returned to Judah with authorization to rebuild the Jerusalem temple, destroyed nearly fifty years earlier. Work on the new temple was postponed, however, when local adversaries first sought to participate and then—after being excluded—prevented the settlers from rebuilding (Ezra 4:1–5,24). In the second year in the reign of Darius I (Ezra 4:4–5,24), the king of Persia permitted construction to resume. That year, the prophets Haggai and Zechariah exhorted the people in God's name to resume the building effort (Ezra 5:1–2). The prophecies in this *haftarah* date from that time. (Construction would take four more years to complete.)

The *haftarah* begins with an announcement that God promises to return to Zion (2:14–17). This requires preparation and purification of the high priest, the Land, and the people. Thus the prophecy continues with the purification and investiture of the high priest and a declaration of God's forgiveness for the people's sins in the Land. This is followed by the prophet's vision of the lampstand (*m'norah*) to be used in the temple and words affirming that communal success will be achieved through the spirit of God.

Priestly concerns and details dominate the *haftarah.* Nevertheless, the prophet mentions royal or secular leadership (3:8, 4:6–9). A notion of dual national leadership—where Joshua the high priest is paired with Zerubbabel, a descendant of David—is evident elsewhere in the prophecies of Zechariah (4:14), and even more clearly in the writings of his contemporaries Haggai (1:1, 2:2) and Ezra (4:3, 5:2).

In his vision, Zechariah's focus on the forthcoming temple features its *m'norah* (4:1–6), a solid lampstand with seven lamps, flanked on either side by an olive tree. In a passage that follows the *haftarah* (4:10–14), this vision is explained: The lampstand symbolizes God; the seven lamps are "the eyes of the LORD, ranging over the whole earth"; and the two trees are anointed dignitaries (literally, "sons of oil") who attend "the LORD of all the earth." Theologically speaking, the Temple objects thus represent divine dominion on earth, and the trees represent its two human stewards (Joshua and Zerubabbel).

By giving Zechariah's prophecy a proclamatory ending—"not by might, nor by power, but by My spirit" (4:7)—the Sages transformed the text into an ever-present divine warning: Groups aiming to "force the end" through military might or by inducing the Temple's restoration should reconsider such plans of action.

RELATION OF THE *HAFTARAH* TO THE CALENDAR

The *haftarah* is appropriate in that *Ḥanukkah* celebrates the rededication of a repurified temple in Hasmonean times and anticipates a messianic temple in the future.

On the first *Shabbat* of *Ḥanukkah,* a portion of the account of offerings brought by Israelite chieftains (*n'si·im*) is read (from Num. 7). This derives from mishnaic practice, which ruled that "On the (*Shabbat* of) *Ḥanukkah* (one reads) from (the portion dealing with) the (portion about the) chieftains" (M Meg. 3:6). This reading supplements the regular *parashah* and is read from a separate Torah scroll (S.A. O.Ḥ. 684:2).

"Shout for joy, Fair Zion! For lo, I come; and I will dwell in your midst [*v'shakhanti b'tokhekh*]." These opening words of the prophet echo God's

words to Moses when he was first commanded to construct the tabernacle (Exod. 25:8): "Let them make Me a sanctuary that I may dwell among them [*v'shakhnati b'tokham*]." In this way, the prophet suggests that God's return will renew divine intimacy with Israel and close the era of exile. Recitation of the chieftains' offerings commemorates the "dedication" (*ḥanukkah*) of the wilderness tabernacle (Num. 7:84) and anticipates the new Temple when God again will be present among the people.

Just as the Sages interpreted the construction of the wilderness tabernacle as atonement for the sin of idolatry (the Golden Calf), the rededication of the Temple marks its purification from ritual pollution. Both shrines thus mark a space of sacred service, new and renewed—a place of divine presence in the earthly realm. Symbolic interpretations of the seven lamps of the *m'norah* in terms of the seven days of Creation and the seven heavenly bodies (sun, moon, and five visible planets), add a cosmic dimension. In this context, the new Temple symbolizes a restoration of the world, a rekindling of the lights of Creation through the pure worship of God.

2 14Shout for joy, Fair Zion! For lo, I come;
and I will dwell in your midst—declares the
LORD. 15In that day many nations will attach
themselves to the LORD and become His people,
and He will dwell in your midst. Then you will
know that I was sent to you by the LORD of
Hosts.

16The LORD will take Judah to Himself as His
portion in the Holy Land, and He will choose
Jerusalem once more.

17Be silent, all flesh, before the LORD!
For He is roused from His holy habitation.

ב 14 רָנִּ֥י וְשִׂמְחִ֖י בַּת־צִיּ֑וֹן כִּ֧י הִנְנִי־בָ֛א
וְשָׁכַנְתִּ֥י בְתוֹכֵ֖ךְ נְאֻם־יְהוָֽה׃ 15 וְנִלְווּ֩ גוֹיִ֨ם
רַבִּ֤ים אֶל־יְהוָה֙ בַּיּ֣וֹם הַה֔וּא וְהָ֥יוּ לִ֖י לְעָ֑ם
וְשָׁכַנְתִּ֣י בְתוֹכֵ֔ךְ וְיָדַ֕עַתְּ כִּֽי־יְהוָ֥ה צְבָא֖וֹת
שְׁלָחַ֥נִי אֵלָֽיִךְ׃

16 וְנָחַ֨ל יְהוָ֤ה אֶת־יְהוּדָה֙ חֶלְק֔וֹ עַ֖ל אַדְמַ֣ת
הַקֹּ֑דֶשׁ וּבָחַ֥ר ע֖וֹד בִּירוּשָׁלִָֽם׃

17 הַ֥ס כָּל־בָּשָׂ֖ר מִפְּנֵ֣י יְהוָ֑ה
כִּ֥י נֵע֖וֹר מִמְּע֥וֹן קָדְשֽׁוֹ׃ ס

Zechariah 2:14. and I will dwell in your midst God is aroused to return to Zion from "His holy habitation" in heaven. The language derives from the old tabernacle traditions ("I may dwell among them [*v'shakhanti b'tokham*]," Exod. 25:8). It was used meanwhile to express both God's dwelling in the temple of Solomon (1 Kings 6:13) and the return of God to the post-exilic temple (Ezek. 43:9).

A threefold biblical typology of divine indwelling spans Israelite history. It begins in the wilderness, with a portable shrine built en route to the Holy Land. It peaks in Solomon's day with the construction of a permanent house for God. And it concludes here, with the restoration to Zion and the building of a new temple for the indwelling of God's presence on earth.

The Sages turned God's providential presence into the noun *Sh'khinah*. The concept came to include divine involvement in the fate of the people Israel wherever they are found. In the Midrash, the *Sh'khinah* suffers with Israel in exile—and will return with it at the time of redemption. In kabbalistic sources from the medieval period on, the *Sh'khinah* came to symbolize a feminine dimension within divinity as well as the heavenly bride with which Israel enters into symbolic marriage on *Shabbat*.

16. The LORD will take Judah . . . as His portion This notion is first found in Deut. 32:9 (speaking of Jacob). The ethnic unit and its territory are one and the same; God will return to claim them both.

Holy Land Hebrew: *admat ha-kodesh;* a striking formulation—unique in the Bible—asserting the sanctity of the whole land of Israel.

3 He further showed me Joshua, the high priest, standing before the angel of the LORD, and the Accuser standing at his right to accuse him. [2]But [the angel of] the LORD said to the Accuser, "The LORD rebuke you, O Accuser; may the LORD who has chosen Jerusalem rebuke you! For this is a brand plucked from the fire." [3]Now Joshua was clothed in filthy garments when he stood before the angel. [4]The latter spoke up and said to his attendants, "Take the filthy garments off him!" And he said to him, "See, I have removed your guilt from you, and you shall be clothed in [priestly] robes." [5]Then he gave the order, "Let a pure diadem be placed on his head." And they placed the pure diadem on his head and clothed him in [priestly] garments, as the angel of the LORD stood by.

[6]And the angel of the LORD charged Joshua as follows: [7]"Thus said the LORD of Hosts: If you walk in My paths and keep My charge, you in turn will rule My House and guard My courts, and I will permit you to move about among these attendants. [8]Hearken well, O High Priest Joshua, you and your fellow priests sitting before you! For those men are a sign that I am going to bring My servant the Branch. [9]For mark well this stone which I place before Joshua, a single stone with seven eyes. I will execute its engraving—declares the LORD of Hosts—and I will remove that country's guilt in a single day.

ג וַיַּרְאֵ֗נִי אֶת־יְהוֹשֻׁ֙עַ֙ הַכֹּהֵ֣ן הַגָּד֔וֹל עֹמֵ֕ד לִפְנֵ֖י מַלְאַ֣ךְ יְהוָ֑ה וְהַשָּׂטָ֛ן עֹמֵ֥ד עַל־יְמִינ֖וֹ לְשִׂטְנֽוֹ׃ 2 וַיֹּ֨אמֶר יְהוָ֜ה אֶל־הַשָּׂטָ֗ן יִגְעַ֨ר יְהוָ֤ה בְּךָ֙ הַשָּׂטָ֔ן וְיִגְעַ֤ר יְהוָה֙ בְּךָ֔ הַבֹּחֵ֖ר בִּירוּשָׁלָ֑͏ִם הֲל֧וֹא זֶ֦ה א֖וּד מֻצָּ֥ל מֵאֵֽשׁ׃ 3 וִיהוֹשֻׁ֕עַ הָיָ֥ה לָבֻ֖שׁ בְּגָדִ֣ים צוֹאִ֑ים וְעֹמֵ֖ד לִפְנֵ֥י הַמַּלְאָֽךְ׃ 4 וַיַּ֣עַן וַיֹּ֗אמֶר אֶל־הָעֹמְדִ֤ים לְפָנָיו֙ לֵאמֹ֔ר הָסִ֛ירוּ הַבְּגָדִ֥ים הַצֹּאִ֖ים מֵעָלָ֑יו וַיֹּ֣אמֶר אֵלָ֗יו רְאֵ֨ה הֶעֱבַ֤רְתִּי מֵעָלֶ֙יךָ֙ עֲוֺנֶ֔ךָ וְהַלְבֵּ֥שׁ אֹתְךָ֖ מַחֲלָצֽוֹת׃ 5 וָאֹמַ֕ר יָשִׂ֛ימוּ צָנִ֥יף טָה֖וֹר עַל־רֹאשׁ֑וֹ וַיָּשִׂימוּ֩ הַצָּנִ֨יף הַטָּה֜וֹר עַל־רֹאשׁ֗וֹ וַיַּלְבִּשֻׁ֙הוּ֙ בְּגָדִ֔ים וּמַלְאַ֥ךְ יְהוָ֖ה עֹמֵֽד׃ 6 וַיָּ֙עַד֙ מַלְאַ֣ךְ יְהוָ֔ה בִּיהוֹשֻׁ֖עַ לֵאמֹֽר׃ 7 כֹּה־אָמַ֞ר יְהוָ֣ה צְבָא֗וֹת אִם־בִּדְרָכַ֤י תֵּלֵךְ֙ וְאִ֣ם אֶת־מִשְׁמַרְתִּ֣י תִשְׁמֹ֔ר וְגַם־אַתָּה֙ תָּדִ֣ין אֶת־בֵּיתִ֔י וְגַ֖ם תִּשְׁמֹ֣ר אֶת־חֲצֵרָ֑י וְנָתַתִּ֤י לְךָ֙ מַהְלְכִ֔ים בֵּ֥ין הָעֹמְדִ֖ים הָאֵֽלֶּה׃ 8 שְֽׁמַֽע־נָ֞א יְהוֹשֻׁ֣עַ ׀ הַכֹּהֵ֣ן הַגָּד֗וֹל אַתָּה֙ וְרֵעֶ֙יךָ֙ הַיֹּשְׁבִ֣ים לְפָנֶ֔יךָ כִּֽי־אַנְשֵׁ֥י מוֹפֵ֖ת הֵ֑מָּה כִּֽי־הִנְנִ֥י מֵבִ֖יא אֶת־עַבְדִּ֥י צֶֽמַח׃ 9 כִּ֣י ׀ הִנֵּ֣ה הָאֶ֗בֶן אֲשֶׁ֤ר נָתַ֙תִּי֙ לִפְנֵ֣י יְהוֹשֻׁ֔עַ עַל־אֶ֥בֶן אַחַ֖ת שִׁבְעָ֣ה עֵינָ֑יִם הִנְנִ֧י מְפַתֵּ֣חַ פִּתֻּחָ֗הּ נְאֻם֙ יְהוָ֣ה צְבָא֔וֹת וּמַשְׁתִּ֛י אֶת־עֲוֺ֥ן

Zechariah 3:1–2. In this vision of a heavenly court, God is the judge, the high priest Joshua is the defendant, and the angel and the Accuser (*satan*) are the defense and prosecuting counsels, respectively. Presumably the Accuser has contended that the priest is unfit for office, which would explain why God now rebukes the Accuser. This divine affirmation legitimates the priest and even pronounces him fit to serve as an angel in heaven.

8. My servant the Branch Who or what this signifies is unspecified. Probably the prophet is referring to Zerubbabel (see 4:6, below); mention by name would have been unwise, for such expression of Israelite royalist hopes would have

provoked the Persian government. The metaphor of a branch (*tzemaḥ*) used to depict a future king was already used by Isaiah (4:2). It was then developed fully in Jeremiah's oracles about a descendant of David whom God will establish to bring victory and to rule in justice (23:5–6, 33:14–16). Later, in the Rabbinic era, it would give rise to interpretations of messianic expectancy. It would also be featured in the 15th benediction of the *Amidah* ("the benediction of David"), which opens with a petition that God cause "the Branch of David to flourish." This messianic prayer would become the last blessing to be added to the *Amidah*.

10In that day—declares the LORD of Hosts—you will be inviting each other to the shade of vines and fig trees."

הָאָ֫רֶץ־הַהִ֖יא בַּיּ֣וֹם אֶחָ֑ד 10 : בַּיּ֣וֹם הַה֗וּא
נְאֻם֙ יְהוָ֣ה צְבָא֔וֹת תִּקְרְא֖וּ אִ֥ישׁ לְרֵעֵ֑הוּ
אֶל־תַּ֥חַת גֶּ֖פֶן וְאֶל־תַּ֥חַת תְּאֵנָֽה :

4 The angel who talked with me came back and woke me as a man is wakened from sleep. 2He said to me, "What do you see?" And I answered, "I see a lampstand all of gold, with a bowl above it. The lamps on it are seven in number, and the lamps above it have seven pipes; 3and by it are two olive trees, one on the right of the bowl and one on its left." 4I, in turn, asked the angel who talked with me, "What do those things mean, my lord?" 5"Do you not know what those things mean?" asked the angel who talked with me; and I said, "No, my lord." 6Then he explained to me as follows:

"This is the word of the LORD to Zerubbabel: Not by might, nor by power, but by My spirit—said the LORD of Hosts. 7Whoever you are, O great mountain in the path of Zerubbabel, turn into level ground! For he shall produce that excellent stone; it shall be greeted with shouts of 'Beautiful! Beautiful!'"

ד וַיָּ֣שָׁב הַמַּלְאָ֔ךְ הַדֹּבֵ֖ר בִּ֑י וַיְעִירֵ֕נִי
כְּאִ֖ישׁ אֲשֶׁר־יֵע֥וֹר מִשְּׁנָתֽוֹ : 2 וַיֹּ֣אמֶר אֵלַ֗י
מָ֤ה אַתָּה֙ רֹאֶ֔ה וָאֹמַ֣ר רָאִ֣יתִי ׀
וְהִנֵּ֣ה מְנוֹרַת֩ זָהָ֨ב כֻּלָּ֜הּ וְגֻלָּ֣הּ עַל־רֹאשָׁ֗הּ
וְשִׁבְעָ֤ה נֵרֹתֶ֙יהָ֙ עָלֶ֔יהָ שִׁבְעָ֤ה וְשִׁבְעָ֖ה
מֽוּצָק֔וֹת לַנֵּר֖וֹת אֲשֶׁ֥ר עַל־רֹאשָֽׁהּ : 3 וּשְׁנַ֥יִם
זֵיתִ֖ים עָלֶ֑יהָ אֶחָד֙ מִימִ֣ין הַגֻּלָּ֔ה וְאֶחָ֖ד
עַל־שְׂמֹאלָֽהּ : 4 וָאַ֙עַן֙ וָאֹמַ֔ר אֶל־הַמַּלְאָ֛ךְ
הַדֹּבֵ֥ר בִּ֖י לֵאמֹ֑ר מָה־אֵ֖לֶּה אֲדֹנִֽי : 5 וַ֠יַּעַן
הַמַּלְאָ֞ךְ הַדֹּבֵ֣ר בִּ֗י וַיֹּ֙אמֶר֙ אֵלַ֔י הֲל֥וֹא יָדַ֖עְתָּ
מָה־הֵ֣מָּה אֵ֑לֶּה וָאֹמַ֖ר לֹ֥א אֲדֹנִֽי : 6 וַיַּ֙עַן֙
וַיֹּ֤אמֶר אֵלַי֙ לֵאמֹ֔ר

זֶ֚ה דְּבַר־יְהוָ֔ה אֶל־זְרֻבָּבֶ֖ל לֵאמֹ֑ר לֹ֤א
בְחַ֙יִל֙ וְלֹ֣א בְכֹ֔חַ כִּ֣י אִם־בְּרוּחִ֔י אָמַ֖ר יְהוָ֣ה
צְבָא֑וֹת : 7 מִֽי־אַתָּ֧ה הַֽר־הַגָּד֛וֹל לִפְנֵ֥י
זְרֻבָּבֶ֖ל לְמִישֹׁ֑ר וְהוֹצִיא֙ אֶת־הָאֶ֣בֶן
הָֽרֹאשָׁ֔ה תְּשֻׁא֕וֹת חֵ֥ן חֵ֖ן לָֽהּ : פ

Zechariah 4:2. I see a lampstand Zechariah's vision of both lampstand (*m'norah*) and lamps (or spouts) differs from the two major descriptions of these sacred vessels elsewhere in Scripture (Exod. 25:31–40; 1 Kings 7:49). The earliest representation of a seven-branched candelabrum appears on the coins minted for Antigonus Mattathias, the last of the Hasmonean dynasty (40–37 B.C.E.). After the destruction of the Temple by Titus, Domitian's masons (ca. 81 C.E.) carved such a candelabrum on his victory arch.

6. Zerubbabel A grandson of King Jehoiachin of Judah (1 Chron. 3:17–19) and the secular head of the repatriated community (Hag. 1:1) [Transl.].

7. The details of this oracle have long been subject to dispute. The phrase "that excellent stone" seems related to Mesopotamian ceremonies in which the monarch dedicated a new temple with a stone from the former temple.

הפטרה לשבת חנוכה (ב׳)

HAFTARAH FOR SECOND SHABBAT OF ḤANUKKAH

1 KINGS 7:40–50

This *haftarah* summarizes the labor involved in constructing the house of the Lord. In 1 Kings, it follows an account of building the Temple, including a trade agreement made with King Hiram of Tyre, and a description of the copper work cast for the Temple, as executed by another Hiram, a master craftsman from Tyre.

Solomon used the resources of Hiram the king (to have wood transported from the Lebanon Mountains, and to have the Temple's foundation stones shaped by the latter's masons, 5:22–23,32). In the same way, he used the talent of another Hiram (the Israelite coppersmith) for designing and casting various Temple features. One Hiram had the resources, the other had the requisite skill. Solomon wisely used foreign expertise in the crude arts (porterage and masonry) and in the fine arts (metalwork and design). This was no compromise of conviction but a thoughtful employment of human skill for the enhancement of sacred space.

The Tyrian craftsman worked in bronze on objects found outside the most sacred area; meanwhile, the Judean king worked in gold on objects having more sacred or special status. The contrast between the two men—one skilled, the other inspired—is not accidental. It underscores that the objects gilded by King Solomon were both more holy and more central to the worship of God.

The summary of Solomon's work preserved in this *haftarah* is not the whole story. The full picture evokes a structure of spectacular opulence: a home for God on earth. No wonder pilgrims rejoiced at the thought of ascending to the Temple in Jerusalem (Ps. 122:1), while the pious yearned for its glories and spiritual benefits! On behalf of many, one psalmist prayed: "One thing I ask of the LORD, / only that do I seek: / to live in the house of the LORD / all the days of my life, / to gaze upon the beauty of the LORD, [and] to frequent His Temple" (Ps. 27:4). Here is the goal of religious desire: life before God, amidst divine radiant splendor, forever.

RELATION OF THE *HAFTARAH* TO THE CALENDAR

The conjoining of Num. 7 (as the special Torah supplement for *Ḥanukkah*) with 1 Kings 7:40–50 links the tabernacle in the wilderness with the great Temple of Solomon. Standing at two historical poles, they represent two types of sacred space. The tabernacle constructed by Moses is a feature of the era of wandering, when the house of God was reconstructed at various stations along the way. It was a portable sanctuary for an unsettled people, revolving around a divine presence not fixed in time or space. By contrast, the Temple built by Solomon is the work of a monarch in the era of empires. It has mass and solidity and artwork befitting a cosmopolitan kingdom. It is the stable shrine of a divine king, whose Ark is the fixed throne on earth. The tabernacle is the setting for God's ever-changing immanence; the Temple accommodates God's stable majesty and transcendence.

These two great structures of biblical antiquity (the tabernacle and the Temple) are recalled on the *Shabbat* of *Ḥanukkah,* when the rededication of the Second Temple by the ancient Maccabees is remembered and a messianic Temple of the future is anticipated. Between memory and hope is the dark path of history, in which the space of divine presence is obscured. In the absence of an external Temple of God, many teachers spiritualized the symbolism of the shrine and its themes. For some, the imagery of the Temple

opened up cosmic and heavenly perspectives. For others, the act of kindling the lamps was interpreted more personally as a rededication of the self to divine service and spiritual consciousness.

7 40Hiram also made the lavers, the scrapers, and the sprinkling bowls.

So Hiram finished all the work that he had been doing for King Solomon on the House of the LORD: 41the two columns, the two globes of the capitals upon the columns; and the two pieces of network to cover the two globes of the capitals upon the columns; 42the four hundred pomegranates for the two pieces of network, two rows of pomegranates for each network, to cover the two globes of the capitals upon the columns; 43the ten stands and the ten lavers upon the stands; 44the one tank with the twelve oxen underneath the tank; 45the pails, the scrapers, and the sprinkling bowls. All those vessels in the House of the LORD that Hiram made for King Solomon were of burnished bronze. 46The king had them cast in earthen molds, in the plain of the Jordan between Succoth and Zarethan. 47Solomon left all the vessels [unweighed] because of their very great quantity; the weight of the bronze was not reckoned.

ז 40 וַיַּעַשׂ חִירוֹם אֶת־הַכִּיֹּרוֹת וְאֶת־
הַיָּעִים וְאֶת־הַמִּזְרָקוֹת

וַיְכַל חִירָם לַעֲשׂוֹת אֶת־כָּל־הַמְּלָאכָה
אֲשֶׁר עָשָׂה לַמֶּלֶךְ שְׁלֹמֹה בֵּית יְהוָה׃
41 עַמֻּדִים שְׁנַיִם וְגֻלֹּת הַכֹּתָרֹת אֲשֶׁר־עַל־
רֹאשׁ הָעַמֻּדִים שְׁתָּיִם וְהַשְּׂבָכוֹת שְׁתַּיִם
לְכַסּוֹת אֶת־שְׁתֵּי גֻּלֹּת הַכֹּתָרֹת אֲשֶׁר
עַל־רֹאשׁ הָעַמּוּדִים׃ 42 וְאֶת־הָרִמֹּנִים
אַרְבַּע מֵאוֹת לִשְׁתֵּי הַשְּׂבָכוֹת שְׁנֵי־טוּרִים
רִמֹּנִים לַשְּׂבָכָה הָאֶחָת לְכַסּוֹת אֶת־שְׁתֵּי
גֻּלֹּת הַכֹּתָרֹת אֲשֶׁר עַל־פְּנֵי הָעַמּוּדִים׃
43 וְאֶת־הַמְּכֹנוֹת עָשֶׂר וְאֶת־הַכִּיֹּרֹת
עֲשָׂרָה עַל־הַמְּכֹנוֹת׃ 44 וְאֶת־הַיָּם הָאֶחָד
וְאֶת־הַבָּקָר שְׁנֵים־עָשָׂר תַּחַת הַיָּם׃
45 וְאֶת־הַסִּירוֹת וְאֶת־הַיָּעִים וְאֶת־
הַמִּזְרָקוֹת וְאֵת כָּל־הַכֵּלִים האהל הָאֵלֶּה
אֲשֶׁר עָשָׂה חִירָם לַמֶּלֶךְ שְׁלֹמֹה בֵּית יְהוָה
נְחֹשֶׁת מְמֹרָט׃ 46 בְּכִכַּר הַיַּרְדֵּן יְצָקָם
הַמֶּלֶךְ בְּמַעֲבֵה הָאֲדָמָה בֵּין סֻכּוֹת וּבֵין
צָרְתָן׃ 47 וַיַּנַּח שְׁלֹמֹה אֶת־כָּל־הַכֵּלִים
מֵרֹב מְאֹד מְאֹד לֹא נֶחְקַר מִשְׁקַל
הַנְּחֹשֶׁת׃

1 Kings 7:40. Hiram "The son of a widow of the tribe of Naphtali," whose father was a Tyrian coppersmith (7:13). In 2 Chron. 2:12–13, he is called Huram and is "the son of a Danite woman, his father a Tyrian."

44. tank Hebrew: *ha-yam;* literally, "the sea." An enormous drum, about 18 feet (5½ m) across and half as deep. As its name suggests, it seemed to have a solely symbolic significance, of a cosmological sort. It was supported by 12 brazen oxen, three facing each of the cardinal points (1 Kings 7:23–26). Ten smaller basins (*kiyor*) stood nearby (v. 43), apparently used for priestly washing (cf. Exod. 30:18, 35:16); they had insets engraved with images of lions, oxen, and cherubim (vv. 28–29), and were set on the likes of "chariot wheels" (v. 33). This imagery recalls the chariot of the divine glory in Ezek. 1:10–11, also supported at the corners by four beings with four faces: human, lion, bull, and eagle (cf. 10:1ff). In ancient Near Eastern art it was common for such creatures to serve as supports for divine or royal chariots. In sum, the "sea" and its supports seem to refer to the lower world, whereas the Ark-throne and its cherubim refer to the upper realm. If so, it joins other symbolic aspects of the Temple that establish it as the house of the Lord on earth.

48 וַיַּ֣עַשׂ שְׁלֹמֹ֔ה אֵ֚ת כָּל־הַכֵּלִ֔ים אֲשֶׁ֖ר בֵּ֣ית
יְהוָ֑ה אֵ֚ת מִזְבַּ֣ח הַזָּהָ֔ב וְֽאֶת־הַשֻּׁלְחָ֗ן אֲשֶׁ֥ר
עָלָ֛יו לֶ֥חֶם הַפָּנִ֖ים זָהָֽב׃ 49 וְֽאֶת־הַ֠מְּנֹרוֹת
חָמֵ֨שׁ מִיָּמִ֜ין וְחָמֵ֧שׁ מִשְּׂמֹ֛אול לִפְנֵ֥י הַדְּבִ֖יר
זָהָ֣ב סָג֑וּר וְהַפֶּ֧רַח וְהַנֵּרֹ֛ת וְהַמֶּלְקַחַ֖יִם
זָהָֽב׃ 50 וְהַסִּפּ֣וֹת וְהַֽמְזַמְּר֗וֹת וְהַמִּזְרָק֛וֹת
וְהַכַּפּ֥וֹת וְהַמַּחְתּ֖וֹת זָהָ֣ב סָג֑וּר וְהַפֹּת֡וֹת
לְדַלְתוֹת֩ הַבַּ֨יִת הַפְּנִימִ֜י לְקֹ֣דֶשׁ הַקֳּדָשִׁ֗ים
לְדַלְתֵ֥י הַבַּ֛יִת לְהֵיכָ֖ל זָהָֽב׃ פ

48And Solomon made all the furnishings that
were in the House of the LORD: the altar, of gold;
the table for the bread of display, of gold; 49the
lampstands—five on the right side and five on
the left—in front of the Shrine, of solid gold;
and the petals, lamps, and tongs, of gold; 50the
basins, snuffers, sprinkling bowls, ladles, and
fire pans, of solid gold; and the hinge sockets
for the doors of the innermost part of the House,
the Holy of Holies, and for the doors of the Great
Hall of the House, of gold.

48. the altar, of gold The altar of incense, which was gilded.

49. the lampstands—five on the right side and five on the left According to tradition, they were set to the right and to the left of the original *m'norah* made by Moses (Rashi, Radak).

lamps Receptacles for the oil and wicks (Rashi).

tongs For the removal of the wicks (Rashi).

50. sprinkling bowls Hebrew: *mizrakot,* receptacles for the blood of the sacrifices (Rashi, Ralbag).

fire pans Used to carry coals from the outer (sacrificial) altar to the inner (incense) altar (Rashi, Ralbag).

הפטרת פרשת שקלים

HAFTARAH FOR PARASHAT SH'KALIM

2 KINGS 12:1–17 (*Ashk'nazim*)
2 KINGS 11:17–12:17 (*S'fardim*)

After the revolt in Judah that deposed Queen Athaliah (842–836 B.C.E.), the priest Jehoiada established the rule of King Jehoash—who had been hidden "in the House of the LORD" during Athaliah's reign. Jehoiada solemnized the covenant between the Lord, the king, and the people, on the one hand, and between the king and the people, on the other. After a popular rampage that destroyed the temple of Baal, the priest set in motion the ascension of Jehoash as king (836–798 B.C.E.). These events (2 Kings 11:17–20) serve as the prologue to the ensuing report of the king's reign, and constitute the opening section of the *haftarah* in the rite of *S'fardim*. *Ashk'nazim* recite only the subsequent royal report (2 Kings 12:1–17).

The main portion of the narrative concerns the attempts of Jehoash to provide for Temple repairs. His first instruction was apparently disregarded by priests who saw the cost of repairs as cutting into their income. The new regulations required that sacred funds be put directly into a storage bin, but also clearly stressed that sacred payments (for purification and reparation offerings) belonged to the priests alone.

Initially, the priests retained discretionary powers over "all silver" brought to the Temple. According to the narrative, the king then claimed jurisdiction over sacred donations—not only with regard to their disbursement but also with regard to their collection and use. (He decreed that the priests could receive and retain only the silver given in exchange for sacrificial offerings.) This hints at a balancing of powers between kings and priests of great historical interest.

RELATION OF THE *HAFTARAH* TO THE CALENDAR

Parashat Sh'kalim (Exod. 30:11–16) is the first of four special Torah passages added (*maftir*) to the regular *Shabbat* portion in the weeks before *Pesaḥ*. The timing of its annual recitation depends on several considerations: on the New Moon of the month of *Adar* when it falls on a *Shabbat;* on the previous *Shabbat* when the New Moon of *Adar* falls on a weekday; and in a leap year, in the second (leap) month of *Adar*. (Its occurrence, in turn, sets the timing for the other three special Torah portions that follow: *Parashat Zakhor* is read on the *Shabbat* before *Purim; parashat Parah* is read on the *Shabbat* before *parashat ha-Ḥodesh* [described next]; and *parashat ha-Ḥodesh* is read on the *Shabbat* nearest the New Moon of *Nisan*—in which month *Pesaḥ* falls. This sequence is specified in the Mishnah [Meg. 3:4], along with breaks or skipped Sabbaths as needed.)

The supplementary Torah reading refers to a poll tax of "half a shekel" (*maḥatzit ha-shekel*) for building the tabernacle in the wilderness. In ancient Temple times, this biblical one-time donation was regularized as an annual donation "required of everyone in Israel" and "announced on the first of Adar" (M Shek. 1:1). Setting the preparations one month in advance ensured that the new flock of animals sacrificed from the beginning of the month of *Nisan* would be paid for with the new *sh'kalim* (BT Meg. 29b). The public reading of this portion served to notify the populace to bring their donations of *sh'kalim.* The prophetic reading not only resembles the Torah portion by mentioning a payment of silver but also refers to the communal upkeep of a sacred shrine.

With the destruction of the Second Temple and the consequent end of sacrifices (in 70 C.E.), *parashat Sh'kalim* was recited "in remembrance" (*l'zeikher*) of the Temple. This occasion was used to solicit funds in support of Jewish religious and charitable institutions. The annual commemora-

tion came to mark the ongoing hope (in the absence of the Temple) that charity might serve as a substitute for sacrifice, as a gift leading to religious renewal and divine forgiveness.

11

17And Jehoiada solemnized the covenant between the LORD, on the one hand, and the king and the people, on the other—as well as between the king and the people—that they should be the people of the LORD. 18Thereupon all the people of the land went to the temple of Baal. They tore it down and smashed its altars and images to bits, and they slew Mattan, the priest of Baal, in front of the altars. [Jehoiada] the priest then placed guards over the House of the LORD. 19He took the chiefs of hundreds, the Carites, the guards, and all the people of the land, and they escorted the king from the House of the LORD into the royal palace by the gate of the guards. And he ascended the royal throne. 20All the people of the land rejoiced, and the city was quiet. As for Athaliah, she had been put to the sword in the royal palace.

12

Jehoash was seven years old when he became king. 2Jehoash began his reign in the seventh year of Jehu, and he reigned in Jerusalem forty years. His mother's name was Zibiah of Beer-sheba. 3All his days Jehoash did what was pleasing to the LORD, as the priest Jehoiada instructed him. 4The shrines, however, were not removed; the people continued to sacrifice and offer at the shrines.

5Jehoash said to the priests, "All the money, current money, brought into the House of the LORD as sacred donations—any money a man may pay as the money equivalent of persons,

יא 17 וַיִּכְרֹ֨ת יְהוֹיָדָ֜ע אֶֽת־הַבְּרִ֗ית בֵּ֣ין יְהוָ֞ה וּבֵ֤ין הַמֶּ֙לֶךְ֙ וּבֵ֣ין הָעָ֔ם לִֽהְי֥וֹת לְעָ֖ם לַֽיהוָ֑ה וּבֵ֥ין הַמֶּ֖לֶךְ וּבֵ֥ין הָעָֽם׃ 18 וַיָּבֹ֣אוּ כָל־עַם֩ הָאָ֨רֶץ בֵּית־הַבַּ֜עַל וַֽיִּתְּצֻ֗הוּ אֶֽת־מזבחתו מִזְבְּחֹתָ֤יו וְאֶת־צְלָמָיו֙ שִׁבְּר֣וּ הֵיטֵ֔ב וְאֵ֗ת מַתָּן֙ כֹּהֵ֣ן הַבַּ֔עַל הָֽרְג֖וּ לִפְנֵ֣י הַֽמִּזְבְּח֑וֹת וַיָּ֧שֶׂם הַכֹּהֵ֛ן פְּקֻדּ֖וֹת עַל־בֵּ֥ית יְהוָֽה׃ 19 וַיִּקַּ֣ח אֶת־שָׂרֵ֣י הַמֵּא֡וֹת וְאֶת־הַכָּרִ֣י וְאֶת־הָֽרָצִים֩ וְאֵ֨ת ׀ כָּל־עַ֣ם הָאָ֗רֶץ וַיֹּרִ֤ידוּ אֶת־הַמֶּ֙לֶךְ֙ מִבֵּ֣ית יְהוָ֔ה וַיָּב֛וֹאוּ דֶּֽרֶךְ־שַׁ֥עַר הָֽרָצִ֖ים בֵּ֣ית הַמֶּ֑לֶךְ וַיֵּ֖שֶׁב עַל־כִּסֵּ֥א הַמְּלָכִֽים׃ 20 וַיִּשְׂמַ֥ח כָּל־עַם־ הָאָ֖רֶץ וְהָעִ֣יר שָׁקָ֑טָה וְאֶת־עֲתַלְיָ֛הוּ הֵמִ֥יתוּ בַחֶ֖רֶב בֵּ֥ית מלך הַמֶּֽלֶךְ׃ ס

יב ★ בֶּן־שֶׁ֥בַע שָׁנִ֖ים יְהוֹאָ֥שׁ בְּמָלְכֽוֹ׃ פ 2 בִּשְׁנַת־שֶׁ֤בַע לְיֵהוּא֙ מָלַ֣ךְ יְהוֹאָ֔שׁ וְאַרְבָּעִ֣ים שָׁנָ֔ה מָלַ֖ךְ בִּירֽוּשָׁלִָ֑ם וְשֵׁ֣ם אִמּ֔וֹ צִבְיָ֖ה מִבְּאֵ֥ר שָֽׁבַע׃ 3 וַיַּ֨עַשׂ יְהוֹאָ֧שׁ הַיָּשָׁ֛ר בְּעֵינֵ֥י יְהוָ֖ה כָּל־יָמָ֑יו אֲשֶׁ֣ר הוֹרָ֔הוּ יְהוֹיָדָ֖ע הַכֹּהֵֽן׃ 4 רַ֥ק הַבָּמ֖וֹת לֹא־סָ֑רוּ ע֥וֹד הָעָ֛ם מְזַבְּחִ֥ים וּֽמְקַטְּרִ֖ים בַּבָּמֽוֹת׃

5 וַיֹּ֨אמֶר יְהוֹאָ֜שׁ אֶל־הַכֹּֽהֲנִ֗ים כֹּל֩ כֶּ֨סֶף הַקֳּדָשִׁ֜ים אֲשֶׁר־יוּבָ֤א בֵית־יְהוָה֙ כֶּ֣סֶף עוֹבֵ֔ר אִ֕ישׁ כֶּ֥סֶף נַפְשׁ֖וֹת עֶרְכּ֑וֹ כָּל־כֶּ֗סֶף

---

2 Kings 11:19. gate of the guards Hebrew: *sha·ar ha-ratzim;* literally, "gate of the runners." The entrance to the Temple area through which the king passed (see 1 Kings 14:28).

★ Ashk'nazim *start here.*

or any other money that a man may be minded
to bring to the House of the LORD—6let the
priests receive it, each from his benefactor; they,
in turn, shall make repairs on the House, wherever damage may be found."

7But in the twenty-third year of King Jehoash,
[it was found that] the priests had not made the
repairs on the House. 8So King Jehoash summoned the priest Jehoiada and the other priests
and said to them, "Why have you not kept the
House in repair? Now do not accept money
from your benefactors any more, but have it donated for the repair of the House." 9The priests
agreed that they would neither accept money
from the people nor make repairs on the House.

10And the priest Jehoiada took a chest and
bored a hole in its lid. He placed it at the right
side of the altar as one entered the House of the
LORD, and the priestly guards of the threshold
deposited there all the money that was brought
into the House of the LORD. 11Whenever they
saw that there was much money in the chest,
the royal scribe and the high priest would come
up and put the money accumulated in the
House of the LORD into bags, and they would
count it. 12Then they would deliver the money
that was weighed out to the overseers of the
work, who were in charge of the House of the
LORD. These, in turn, used to pay the carpenters
and the laborers who worked on the House of
the LORD, 13and the masons and the stone-
cutters. They also paid for wood and for quarried stone with which to make the repairs on
the House of the LORD, and for every other ex-
penditure that had to be made in repairing the
House. 14However, no silver bowls and no
snuffers, basins, or trumpets—no vessels of
gold or silver—were made at the House of the
LORD from the money brought into the House
of the LORD; 15this was given only to the over-

אֲשֶׁר יַעֲלֶה עַל לֶב־אִישׁ לְהָבִיא בֵּית
יְהוָה׃ 6 יִקְחוּ לָהֶם הַכֹּהֲנִים אִישׁ מֵאֵת
מַכָּרוֹ וְהֵם יְחַזְּקוּ אֶת־בֶּדֶק הַבַּיִת לְכֹל
אֲשֶׁר־יִמָּצֵא שָׁם בָּדֶק׃ פ
7 וַיְהִי בִּשְׁנַת עֶשְׂרִים וְשָׁלֹשׁ שָׁנָה לַמֶּלֶךְ
יְהוֹאָשׁ לֹא־חִזְּקוּ הַכֹּהֲנִים אֶת־בֶּדֶק
הַבָּיִת׃ 8 וַיִּקְרָא הַמֶּלֶךְ יְהוֹאָשׁ לִיהוֹיָדָע
הַכֹּהֵן וְלַכֹּהֲנִים וַיֹּאמֶר אֲלֵהֶם מַדּוּעַ
אֵינְכֶם מְחַזְּקִים אֶת־בֶּדֶק הַבָּיִת וְעַתָּה
אַל־תִּקְחוּ־כֶסֶף מֵאֵת מַכָּרֵיכֶם כִּי־לְבֶדֶק
הַבַּיִת תִּתְּנֻהוּ׃ 9 וַיֵּאֹתוּ הַכֹּהֲנִים לְבִלְתִּי
קְחַת־כֶּסֶף מֵאֵת הָעָם וּלְבִלְתִּי חַזֵּק אֶת־
בֶּדֶק הַבָּיִת׃
10 וַיִּקַּח יְהוֹיָדָע הַכֹּהֵן אֲרוֹן אֶחָד וַיִּקֹּב
חֹר בְּדַלְתּוֹ וַיִּתֵּן אֹתוֹ אֵצֶל הַמִּזְבֵּחַ בימין
מִיָּמִין בְּבוֹא־אִישׁ בֵּית יְהוָה וְנָתְנוּ־שָׁמָּה
הַכֹּהֲנִים שֹׁמְרֵי הַסַּף אֶת־כָּל־הַכֶּסֶף
הַמּוּבָא בֵית־יְהוָה׃ 11 וַיְהִי כִּרְאוֹתָם כִּי־
רַב הַכֶּסֶף בָּאָרוֹן וַיַּעַל סֹפֵר הַמֶּלֶךְ וְהַכֹּהֵן
הַגָּדוֹל וַיָּצֻרוּ וַיִּמְנוּ אֶת־הַכֶּסֶף הַנִּמְצָא
בֵית־יְהוָה׃ 12 וְנָתְנוּ אֶת־הַכֶּסֶף הַמְתֻכָּן
עַל־יד יְדֵי עֹשֵׂי הַמְּלָאכָה הפקדים
הַמֻּפְקָדִים בֵּית יְהוָה וַיּוֹצִיאֻהוּ לְחָרָשֵׁי
הָעֵץ וְלַבֹּנִים הָעֹשִׂים בֵּית יְהוָה׃
13 וְלַגֹּדְרִים וּלְחֹצְבֵי הָאֶבֶן וְלִקְנוֹת עֵצִים
וְאַבְנֵי מַחְצֵב לְחַזֵּק אֶת־בֶּדֶק בֵּית־יְהוָה
וּלְכֹל אֲשֶׁר־יֵצֵא עַל־הַבַּיִת לְחָזְקָה׃ 14 אַךְ
לֹא יֵעָשֶׂה בֵּית יְהוָה סִפּוֹת כֶּסֶף מְזַמְּרוֹת
מִזְרָקוֹת חֲצֹצְרוֹת כָּל־כְּלִי זָהָב וּכְלִי־
כָסֶף מִן־הַכֶּסֶף הַמּוּבָא בֵית־יְהוָה׃
15 כִּי־לְעֹשֵׂי הַמְּלָאכָה יִתְּנֻהוּ וְחִזְּקוּ־בוֹ

2 Kings 12:10. a chest A cash box, located near the temple gates in ancient Mesopotamia, was a standard feature of temple organization during the first millennium B.C.E.

אֶת־בֵּ֥ית יְהוָֽה׃ 16 וְלֹ֤א יְחַשְּׁב֣וּ אֶת־
הָאֲנָשִׁ֗ים אֲשֶׁ֨ר יִתְּנ֤וּ אֶת־הַכֶּ֙סֶף֙ עַל־יָדָ֔ם
לָתֵ֖ת לְעֹשֵׂ֣י הַמְּלָאכָ֑ה כִּ֥י בֶאֱמֻנָ֖ה הֵ֥ם
עֹשִֽׂים׃
17 כֶּ֤סֶף אָשָׁם֙ וְכֶ֣סֶף חַטָּא֔וֹת לֹ֥א יוּבָ֖א בֵּ֣ית
יְהוָ֑ה לַכֹּהֲנִ֖ים יִהְיֽוּ׃ פ

seers of the work for the repair of the House
of the LORD. 16No check was kept on the men
to whom the money was delivered to pay the
workers; for they dealt honestly.

17Money brought as a guilt offering or as a
purification offering was not deposited in the
House of the LORD; it went to the priests.

הפטרת פרשת זכור

HAFTARAH FOR PARASHAT ZAKHOR

1 SAMUEL 15:2–34 (*Ashk'nazim*)
1 SAMUEL 15:1–34 (*S'fardim*)

This *haftarah* first presents Saul's battle against the Amalekites. Then it describes how God rejected him as king for disobeying the divine command of utter extermination of that nation and its livestock. (Centuries earlier, according to Exodus, "Amalek came and fought with Israel at Rephidim" [17:8]. Later, with God's help, "Joshua overwhelmed the people of Amalek with the sword" [17:13]. That event was inscribed in a document in which the Lord stated, "I will utterly blot out the memory of Amalek from under heaven" [17:14].)

In Deut. 25:17–19, read as the concluding (*maftir*) Torah selection on *Shabbat Zakhor,* the Israelites are called upon to remember Amalek's surprise attack against "all the stragglers" who made up the weary and famished rearguard of the people during the wilderness trek from Egypt. In Deuteronomy, it is the people who must remember the enemy and destroy it—not God. It must be done "when the LORD your God grants you safety from all your enemies around you [*oy'vekha mi-saviv*]."

The Book of Samuel seems to suggest that this time had come, for the summary of Saul's battles (1 Sam. 14:47) states that the king "waged war on every side against all his enemies [*saviv b'khol oy'vav*]." It is in this context that the battle against Amalek is mentioned (v. 48).

The *haftarah,* which follows in chapter 15, provides a fuller, theological perspective that blends the two Torah traditions. God announces that He will now requite the Amalekites for their actions against the Israelites "on their way up from Egypt," a requital that Saul and the nation must exact (15:2–3). God's own vendetta against the Amalekites (Exod. 17:14) is thus combined here with the people's responsibility to destroy Amalek for having attacked Israel "on your journey, after you left Egypt" (Deut. 25:17,19). Saul's incomplete execution of God's command, together with the subsequent inquest and judgment against him through Samuel, constitute the successive sections of the *haftarah.*

The *haftarah*'s repeated use of the words *kol* (voice) and *shama* (hear, obey) highlights its emphasis on obedience. The punishment for not obeying the divine word is rejection. Samuel states: "Because you [Saul] rejected the LORD's command, / He has rejected you as king" (1 Sam. 15:23). This strident and striking language alludes to the onset of the monarchy. After the people had first requested a king, and Samuel had resisted, a divine oracle had declared: "Heed the demand of the people in everything they say to you. For it is not you that they have rejected; it is Me they have rejected as their king" (8:7, cf. v. 21). The issue in both cases is the authority of divine sovereignty—unmediated by a human king, in the first instance; distorted by the human king, in the second. The people reject God in the first case; God rejects the king in the second (15:23,26). Indeed, it seems that God can accept the substitute of human kingship so long as divine authority remains in place. It is just this that Saul has challenged by his decision to revise or reinterpret the divine command.

There is great pathos in this *haftarah*—first, because Saul's sin is not a flagrant rejection of divine authority and second, because his repeated confessions and appeals for divine forgiveness are rejected. The reader is confronted with the austerity and stringency of God's demands and the brutality demanded of the Israelite nation. Mercy is prohibited; no one and nothing may be "spared." The war against the Amalekites is presented as a just war, punishing an offense centuries old. Rejection or reinterpretation of the absolute orders is completely out of the question. Whether as an actual event or as a literary case setting an exam-

ple, 1 Sam. 15:1–34 confronts us with a fierce and uncompromising theology. Its liturgical recitation, yearly, requires repeated moral and theological reflection.

According to a rabbinic tradition, Saul himself began this process by trying to undermine the divine order through legalistic and moral reasoning (see BT Yoma 22b; Eccles. R. 7:16). On the basis of the biblical rule requiring the sacrificial slaying of a heifer to atone for an unknown homicide (Deut. 21:1–9), he argued that innumerable innocent animals would be required to atone for the deaths of Amalekites. Moreover, he added, even if the adults were deserving of death, why include children in the proscription? According to this tradition, a divine voice then reproved him in the words of Ecclesiastes, "Do not be overly righteous" (7:16). The answer challenges the moral soul of the tradition.

RELATION OF THE *HAFTARAH* TO THE CALENDAR

Parashat Zakhor (Deut. 25:17–19) is the second of four special Torah passages added to the regular *Shabbat* portion in the weeks before *Pesaḥ*. It is recited on the *Shabbat* before *Purim*, even when *Purim* itself falls on the following *Shabbat*. (For details on the scheduling of the special Torah portions, see the introduction to the *haftarah* for *parashat Sh'kalim*.) In it, the Israelites are enjoined to remember (*zakhor*) what Amalek did to the people on their way out of Egypt, and to "blot out the memory of Amalek from under heaven. Do not forget!"

That same remembrance and that act of destruction are articulated in the *haftarah*. Indeed, because this *haftarah* is recited just before *Purim*—when the scroll of Esther is read and Haman the Agagite's evil plots against the Jews of Persia are recalled—later generations could read into the assertion of divine remembrance an assurance that God remains steadfast to punish Amalek in all generations.

The link between 1 Sam. 15 and the scroll of Esther was drawn already in biblical times. Just as Saul is the son of Kish from the tribe of Benjamin, so Mordecai's lineage is traced to the line of Saul's father (Esther 2:5). Just as the Israelite king defeats Amalek and its king, Agag, so the latter-day hero of the Jews foils the plots of Haman "the Agagite" (Esther 3:1,10). Amalek became a symbol of all the enemies of the Jews in all generations. In early midrashic homilies and in liturgical poetry composed for this *Shabbat Zakhor* in late antiquity, the foe was identified with Edom (the genealogy in Gen. 36:12 gave added proof). Through that identification, Amalek served as a symbol for Rome and for Christianity as well.

As a counterpoint, "Amalek" was later reinterpreted in terms of the evil inclination (cf. *Zohar* 3:281b) and religious failure. As a result, the eradication of Amalek became a process of psychospiritual development in certain circles. This more personal reading of the tradition, however, never displaced the national-historical one, and the two remain in tension. The carnival quality of *Purim* celebrations may dangerously mask the serious moral issues. Vengeance is not just the Lord's; it is also enacted by people.

15 Samuel said to Saul, "I am the one the LORD sent to anoint you king over His people Israel. Therefore, listen to the LORD's command!

טו וַיֹּאמֶר שְׁמוּאֵל אֶל־שָׁאוּל אֹתִי שָׁלַח יְהוָה לִמְשָׁחֳךָ לְמֶלֶךְ עַל־עַמּוֹ עַל־יִשְׂרָאֵל וְעַתָּה שְׁמַע לְקוֹל דִּבְרֵי יְהוָה׃ ס

1 Samuel 15:1–3. According to an early rabbinic tradition, the Israelites were commanded to do three things when they came into the Land: establish a king, build the Temple, and destroy Amalek (Tosef. Sanh. 4:5; Sifrei Deut. 67).

2"Thus said the LORD of Hosts: I am exacting
the penalty for what Amalek did to Israel, for
the assault he made upon them on the road,
on their way up from Egypt. 3Now go, attack
Amalek, and proscribe all that belongs to him.
Spare no one, but kill alike men and women,
infants and sucklings, oxen and sheep, camels
and asses!"

4Saul mustered the troops and enrolled them
at Telaim: 200,000 men on foot, and 10,000 men
of Judah. 5Then Saul advanced as far as the city
of Amalek and lay in wait in the wadi. 6Saul said
to the Kenites, "Come, withdraw at once from
among the Amalekites, that I may not destroy
you along with them; for you showed kindness
to all the Israelites when they left Egypt." So the
Kenites withdrew from among the Amalekites.

7Saul destroyed Amalek from Havilah all the
way to Shur, which is close to Egypt, 8and he
captured King Agag of Amalek alive. He proscribed all the people, putting them to the
sword; 9but Saul and the troops spared Agag
and the best of the sheep, the oxen, the
second-born, the lambs, and all else that was of
value. They would not proscribe them; they
proscribed only what was cheap and worthless.

10The word of the LORD then came to Samuel:
11"I regret that I made Saul king, for he has

* 2 כֹּ֤ה אָמַר֙ יְהוָ֣ה צְבָא֔וֹת פָּקַ֕דְתִּי אֵ֛ת
אֲשֶׁר־עָשָׂ֥ה עֲמָלֵ֖ק לְיִשְׂרָאֵ֑ל אֲשֶׁר־שָׂ֥ם לוֹ֙
בַּדֶּ֔רֶךְ בַּעֲלֹת֖וֹ מִמִּצְרָֽיִם׃ 3 עַתָּה֩ לֵ֨ךְ
וְהִכִּיתָ֜ה אֶת־עֲמָלֵ֗ק וְהַחֲרַמְתֶּם֙ אֶת־כָּל־
אֲשֶׁר־ל֔וֹ וְלֹ֥א תַחְמֹ֖ל עָלָ֑יו וְהֵמַתָּ֞ה מֵאִ֣ישׁ
עַד־אִשָּׁ֗ה מֵֽעֹלֵל֙ וְעַד־יוֹנֵ֔ק מִשּׁ֣וֹר וְעַד־שֶׂ֔ה
מִגָּמָ֖ל וְעַד־חֲמֽוֹר׃ ס

4 וַיְשַׁמַּ֤ע שָׁאוּל֙ אֶת־הָעָ֔ם וַֽיִּפְקְדֵם֙
בַּטְּלָאִ֔ים מָאתַ֥יִם אֶ֖לֶף רַגְלִ֑י וַעֲשֶׂ֥רֶת
אֲלָפִ֖ים אֶת־אִ֥ישׁ יְהוּדָֽה׃ 5 וַיָּבֹ֥א שָׁא֖וּל
עַד־עִ֣יר עֲמָלֵ֑ק וַיָּ֖רֶב בַּנָּֽחַל׃ 6 וַיֹּ֣אמֶר
שָׁא֣וּל אֶל־הַקֵּינִ֡י לְכוּ֩ סֻּ֨רוּ רְד֜וּ מִתּ֣וֹךְ
עֲמָלֵקִ֗י פֶּן־אֹסִֽפְךָ֙ עִמּ֔וֹ וְאַתָּ֞ה עָשִׂ֤יתָה
חֶ֙סֶד֙ עִם־כָּל־בְּנֵ֣י יִשְׂרָאֵ֔ל בַּעֲלוֹתָ֖ם
מִמִּצְרָ֑יִם וַיָּ֥סַר קֵינִ֖י מִתּ֥וֹךְ עֲמָלֵֽק׃

7 וַיַּ֥ךְ שָׁא֖וּל אֶת־עֲמָלֵ֑ק מֵחֲוִילָה֙ בּוֹאֲךָ֣
שׁ֔וּר אֲשֶׁ֖ר עַל־פְּנֵ֥י מִצְרָֽיִם׃ 8 וַיִּתְפֹּ֛שׂ אֶת־
אֲגַ֥ג מֶֽלֶךְ־עֲמָלֵ֖ק חָ֑י וְאֶת־כָּל־הָעָ֖ם
הֶחֱרִ֥ים לְפִי־חָֽרֶב׃ 9 וַיַּחְמֹל֩ שָׁא֨וּל וְהָעָ֜ם
עַל־אֲגָ֗ג וְעַל־מֵיטַ֣ב הַצֹּאן֩ וְהַבָּקָ֨ר
וְהַמִּשְׁנִ֤ים וְעַל־הַכָּרִים֙ וְעַל־כָּל־הַטּ֔וֹב
וְלֹ֥א אָב֖וּ הַחֲרִימָ֑ם וְכָל־הַמְּלָאכָ֛ה נְמִבְזָ֥ה
וְנָמֵ֖ס אֹתָ֥הּ הֶחֱרִֽימוּ׃ פ

10 וַֽיְהִי֙ דְּבַר־יְהוָ֔ה אֶל־שְׁמוּאֵ֖ל לֵאמֹֽר׃
11 נִחַ֗מְתִּי כִּֽי־הִמְלַ֤כְתִּי אֶת־שָׁאוּל֙ לְמֶ֔לֶךְ

3. Spare no one The Hebrew verb suggests a harsher command: "have no pity."

4. mustered . . . enrolled The narrative is tightly textured. Not only is the theme of "hearing" or "heeding" (*shama*) repeated throughout the text (vv. 1,14,19,20,22,24); it also appears through puns. Thus the initial command was to "hear" (*sh'ma*) the divine word (v. 1); and Saul proceeds immediately to "muster" (*va-y'shamma*) the troops. Similarly, Samuel says that God "remembers" or "requites" (*pakad'ti*) the crime of the Amalekites (v. 2; the verb פקד serves double duty here). The same verb is used in the reference to Saul's enrolling the troops (*va-yifk'dem*).

Telaim In the Negeb ("Telem," Josh. 15:24).

6. Sauls tells the Kenites to withdraw "from among the Amalekites," as an act of gratitude for their past favors to Israel. Possibly this refers to wilderness guiding (see Num. 10:29–32); the precise events are nowhere stated. Presumably some Kenites encamped among the Amalekites, an association also found in Balaam's prophecy (Num. 24:20–21).

11. I regret Hebrew: *niḥamti.* This usage sets up an ironic contrast with verse 29. After Saul begs forgiveness, Samuel refuses his appeal, stating that God "does not . . . change His mind [*va-yinnaḥem*]." But this change in divine favor

* Ashk'nazim *start here.*

turned away from Me and has not carried out
My commands." Samuel was distressed and he
entreated the LORD all night long. 12Early in the
morning Samuel went to meet Saul. Samuel was
told, "Saul went to Carmel, where he erected a
monument for himself; then he left and went
on down to Gilgal."

13When Samuel came to Saul, Saul said to
him, "Blessed are you of the LORD! I have
fulfilled the LORD's command." 14"Then what,"
demanded Samuel, "is this bleating of sheep in
my ears, and the lowing of oxen that I hear?"
15Saul answered, "They were brought from the
Amalekites, for the troops spared the choicest
of the sheep and oxen for sacrificing to the LORD
your God. And we proscribed the rest." 16Sam-
uel said to Saul, "Stop! Let me tell you what the
LORD said to me last night!" "Speak," he replied.
17And Samuel said, "You may look small to
yourself, but you are the head of the tribes of
Israel. The LORD anointed you king over Israel,
18and the LORD sent you on a mission, saying,
'Go and proscribe the sinful Amalekites; make
war on them until you have exterminated
them.' 19Why did you disobey the LORD and
swoop down on the spoil in defiance of the
LORD's will?" 20Saul said to Samuel, "But I did
obey the LORD! I performed the mission on
which the LORD sent me: I captured King Agag
of Amalek, and I proscribed Amalek, 21and the
troops took from the spoil some sheep and
oxen—the best of what had been proscribed—
to sacrifice to the LORD your God at Gilgal."
22But Samuel said:

"Does the LORD delight in burnt offerings and
sacrifices
As much as in obedience to the LORD's command?

כִּֽי־שָׁב֙ מֵאַחֲרַ֔י וְאֶת־דְּבָרַ֖י לֹ֣א הֵקִ֑ים וַיִּ֙חַר֙
לִשְׁמוּאֵ֔ל וַיִּזְעַ֥ק אֶל־יְהוָ֖ה כָּל־הַלָּֽיְלָה׃
12 וַיַּשְׁכֵּ֧ם שְׁמוּאֵ֛ל לִקְרַ֥את שָׁא֖וּל בַּבֹּ֑קֶר
וַיֻּגַּ֨ד לִשְׁמוּאֵ֜ל לֵאמֹ֗ר בָּֽא־שָׁא֤וּל הַכַּרְמֶ֙לָה֙
וְהִנֵּ֨ה מַצִּ֥יב לוֹ֙ יָ֔ד וַיִּסֹּב֙ וַֽיַּעֲבֹ֔ר וַיֵּ֖רֶד
הַגִּלְגָּֽל׃
13 וַיָּבֹ֥א שְׁמוּאֵ֖ל אֶל־שָׁא֑וּל וַיֹּ֨אמֶר ל֤וֹ
שָׁאוּל֙ בָּר֤וּךְ אַתָּה֙ לַֽיהוָ֔ה הֲקִימֹ֖תִי אֶת־
דְּבַ֥ר יְהוָֽה׃ 14 וַיֹּ֣אמֶר שְׁמוּאֵ֔ל וּמֶ֛ה קוֹל־
הַצֹּ֥אן הַזֶּ֖ה בְּאָזְנָ֑י וְק֣וֹל הַבָּקָ֔ר אֲשֶׁ֥ר אָנֹכִ֖י
שֹׁמֵֽעַ׃ 15 וַיֹּ֨אמֶר שָׁא֜וּל מֵעֲמָלֵקִ֣י הֱבִיא֗וּם
אֲשֶׁ֨ר חָמַ֤ל הָעָם֙ עַל־מֵיטַ֤ב הַצֹּאן֙ וְהַבָּקָ֔ר
לְמַ֥עַן זְבֹ֖חַ לַיהוָ֣ה אֱלֹהֶ֑יךָ וְאֶת־הַיּוֹתֵ֖ר
הֶחֱרַֽמְנוּ׃ ס 16 וַיֹּ֤אמֶר שְׁמוּאֵל֙ אֶל־
שָׁא֔וּל הֶ֚רֶף וְאַגִּ֣ידָה לְּךָ֔ אֵת֩ אֲשֶׁ֨ר דִּבֶּ֧ר
יְהוָ֛ה אֵלַ֖י הַלָּ֑יְלָה ויאמרו וַיֹּ֥אמֶר ל֖וֹ
דַּבֵּֽר׃ ס 17 וַיֹּ֣אמֶר שְׁמוּאֵ֔ל הֲל֗וֹא אִם־
קָטֹ֤ן אַתָּה֙ בְּעֵינֶ֔יךָ רֹ֛אשׁ שִׁבְטֵ֥י יִשְׂרָאֵ֖ל
אָ֑תָּה וַיִּמְשָׁחֲךָ֧ יְהוָ֛ה לְמֶ֖לֶךְ עַל־יִשְׂרָאֵֽל׃
18 וַיִּשְׁלָחֲךָ֥ יְהוָ֖ה בְּדָ֑רֶךְ וַיֹּ֗אמֶר לֵ֣ךְ
וְהַחֲרַמְתָּ֞ה אֶת־הַחַטָּאִים֙ אֶת־עֲמָלֵ֔ק
וְנִלְחַמְתָּ֣ ב֔וֹ עַ֥ד כַּלּוֹתָ֖ם אֹתָֽם׃ 19 וְלָ֥מָּה
לֹא־שָׁמַ֖עְתָּ בְּק֣וֹל יְהוָ֑ה וַתַּ֙עַט֙ אֶל־הַשָּׁלָ֔ל
וַתַּ֥עַשׂ הָרַ֖ע בְּעֵינֵ֥י יְהוָֽה׃ ס 20 וַיֹּ֨אמֶר
שָׁא֜וּל אֶל־שְׁמוּאֵ֗ל אֲשֶׁ֤ר שָׁמַ֙עְתִּי֙ בְּק֣וֹל
יְהוָ֔ה וָאֵלֵ֕ךְ בַּדֶּ֖רֶךְ אֲשֶׁר־שְׁלָחַ֣נִי יְהוָ֑ה
וָאָבִ֗יא אֶת־אֲגַג֙ מֶ֣לֶךְ עֲמָלֵ֔ק וְאֶת־עֲמָלֵ֖ק
הֶחֱרַֽמְתִּי׃ 21 וַיִּקַּ֨ח הָעָ֧ם מֵהַשָּׁלָ֛ל צֹ֥אן
וּבָקָ֖ר רֵאשִׁ֣ית הַחֵ֑רֶם לִזְבֹּ֛חַ לַיהוָ֥ה אֱלֹהֶ֖יךָ
בַּגִּלְגָּֽל׃ 22 וַיֹּ֣אמֶר שְׁמוּאֵ֗ל
הַחֵ֤פֶץ לַֽיהוָה֙ בְּעֹל֣וֹת וּזְבָחִ֔ים
כִּשְׁמֹ֖עַ בְּק֣וֹל יְהוָ֑ה

is precisely what has produced Saul's despair. Elsewhere, this verb does in fact indicate God's regret at having created sinful humankind (Gen. 6:6: *va-yinnaḥem*), as well as God's merciful forgiveness of penitents (Jon. 4:2: *v'niḥam*).

21. the best Hebrew: *reishit.* In his second justification, Saul uses a more cultic term for what he earlier called "the choicest" (*meitav*) of the livestock (v. 15).

Surely, obedience is better than sacrifice,
Compliance than the fat of rams.
23For rebellion is like the sin of divination,
Defiance, like the iniquity of teraphim.
Because you rejected the LORD's command,
He has rejected you as king."

24Saul said to Samuel, "I did wrong to transgress the LORD's command and your instructions; but I was afraid of the troops and I yielded to them. 25Please, forgive my offense and come back with me, and I will bow low to the LORD." 26But Samuel said to Saul, "I will not go back with you; for you have rejected the LORD's command, and the LORD has rejected you as king over Israel."

27As Samuel turned to leave, Saul seized the corner of his robe, and it tore. 28And Samuel said to him, "The LORD has this day torn the kingship over Israel away from you and has given it to another who is worthier than you. 29Moreover, the Glory of Israel does not deceive or change His mind, for He is not human that He should change His mind." 30But [Saul] pleaded, "I did wrong. Please, honor me in the presence of the elders of my people and in the presence of Israel, and come back with me until I have bowed low to the LORD your God." 31So Samuel followed Saul back, and Saul bowed low to the LORD.

32Samuel said, "Bring forward to me King Agag of Amalek." Agag approached him with faltering steps; and Agag said, "Ah, bitter death is at hand!"

33Samuel said:
"As your sword has bereaved women,
So shall your mother be bereaved among women."

הִנֵּ֤ה שְׁמֹ֙עַ֙ מִזֶּ֣בַח ט֔וֹב
לְהַקְשִׁ֖יב מֵחֵ֥לֶב אֵילִֽים׃
23 כִּ֤י חַטַּאת־קֶ֙סֶם֙ מֶ֔רִי
וְאָ֥וֶן וּתְרָפִ֖ים הַפְצַ֑ר
יַ֗עַן מָאַ֙סְתָּ֙ אֶת־דְּבַ֣ר יְהֹוָ֔ה
וַיִּמְאָסְךָ֖ מִמֶּֽלֶךְ׃ ס
24 וַיֹּ֨אמֶר שָׁא֤וּל אֶל־שְׁמוּאֵל֙ חָטָ֔אתִי כִּֽי־
עָבַ֥רְתִּי אֶת־פִּֽי־יְהֹוָ֖ה וְאֶת־דְּבָרֶ֑יךָ כִּ֤י
יָרֵ֙אתִי֙ אֶת־הָעָ֔ם וָאֶשְׁמַ֖ע בְּקוֹלָֽם׃
25 וְעַתָּ֕ה שָׂ֥א נָ֖א אֶת־חַטָּאתִ֑י וְשׁ֣וּב עִמִּ֔י
וְאֶשְׁתַּחֲוֶ֖ה לַיהֹוָֽה׃ 26 וַיֹּ֤אמֶר שְׁמוּאֵל֙ אֶל־
שָׁא֔וּל לֹ֥א אָשׁ֖וּב עִמָּ֑ךְ כִּ֣י מָאַ֙סְתָּה֙ אֶת־
דְּבַ֣ר יְהֹוָ֔ה וַיִּמְאָסְךָ֣ יְהֹוָ֔ה מִהְי֥וֹת מֶ֖לֶךְ
עַל־יִשְׂרָאֵֽל׃ ס
27 וַיִּסֹּ֥ב שְׁמוּאֵ֖ל לָלֶ֑כֶת וַיַּחֲזֵ֥ק בִּכְנַף־מְעִיל֖וֹ
וַיִּקָּרַֽע׃ 28 וַיֹּ֤אמֶר אֵלָיו֙ שְׁמוּאֵ֔ל קָרַ֨ע יְהֹוָ֜ה
אֶת־מַמְלְכ֧וּת יִשְׂרָאֵ֛ל מֵעָלֶ֖יךָ הַיּ֑וֹם וּנְתָנָ֕הּ
לְרֵעֲךָ֖ הַטּ֥וֹב מִמֶּֽךָּ׃ 29 וְגַם֙ נֵ֣צַח יִשְׂרָאֵ֔ל
לֹ֥א יְשַׁקֵּ֖ר וְלֹ֣א יִנָּחֵ֑ם כִּ֣י לֹ֥א אָדָ֛ם ה֖וּא
לְהִנָּחֵֽם׃ 30 וַיֹּ֣אמֶר חָטָ֔אתִי עַתָּ֗ה כַּבְּדֵ֣נִי
נָ֛א נֶ֥גֶד זִקְנֵֽי־עַמִּ֖י וְנֶ֣גֶד יִשְׂרָאֵ֑ל וְשׁ֣וּב עִמִּ֔י
וְהִֽשְׁתַּחֲוֵ֖יתִי לַיהֹוָ֥ה אֱלֹהֶֽיךָ׃ 31 וַיָּ֥שָׁב
שְׁמוּאֵ֖ל אַחֲרֵ֣י שָׁא֑וּל וַיִּשְׁתַּ֥חוּ שָׁא֖וּל
לַיהֹוָֽה׃ ס
32 וַיֹּ֣אמֶר שְׁמוּאֵ֗ל הַגִּ֤ישׁוּ אֵלַי֙ אֶת־אֲגַג֙
מֶ֣לֶךְ עֲמָלֵ֔ק וַיֵּ֣לֶךְ אֵלָ֔יו אֲגַ֖ג מַעֲדַנֹּ֑ת וַיֹּ֣אמֶר
אֲגָ֔ג אָכֵ֖ן סָ֥ר מַר־הַמָּֽוֶת׃ ס
33 וַיֹּ֣אמֶר שְׁמוּאֵ֔ל
כַּאֲשֶׁ֨ר שִׁכְּלָ֤ה נָשִׁים֙ חַרְבֶּ֔ךָ
כֵּן־תִּשְׁכַּ֥ל מִנָּשִׁ֖ים אִמֶּ֑ךָ

32. with faltering steps Hebrew verbal stem: *ma·ad* (to falter).

Ah, bitter death is at hand Hebrew: *akhen sar mar ha-mavet.* The word *sar* (rendered as "at hand") is very likely a mistaken scribal doubling (dittography) of the similar-looking word *mar* (bitter). In fact, a word for *sar* is missing in the ancient Greek translation (Septuagint). On this basis, the king simply and poignantly cried: "Surely, death is bitter!"

And Samuel cut Agag down before the LORD at Gilgal.	וַיְשַׁסֵּף שְׁמוּאֵל אֶת־אֲגָג לִפְנֵי יְהוָה בַּגִּלְגָּל׃ ס
34 Samuel then departed for Ramah, and Saul went up to his home at Gibeah of Saul.	34 וַיֵּלֶךְ שְׁמוּאֵל הָרָמָתָה וְשָׁאוּל עָלָה אֶל־בֵּיתוֹ גִּבְעַת שָׁאוּל׃

הפטרת פרשת פרה

HAFTARAH FOR PARASHAT PARAH

EZEKIEL 36:16–38 (*Ashk'nazim*)
EZEKIEL 36:16–36 (*S'fardim*)

This *haftarah* is one of the prophecies of hope and consolation that Ezekiel addressed to the Judean exiles in Babylon. These oracles, whose larger theme is the reversal of failures in Israelite history, begin in Ezek. 33 (dated *Tevet* 585 B.C.E., according to 33:21). Chapters 35 and 36:1–15 in particular provide consolation to the nation after the taunts of their enemies (see Ezek. 35:10–12, 36:2–3,5,13). The nations mocked Israel, saying: "These are the people of the LORD, yet they had to leave His land." Because of this, God's holy name was profaned among the nations (36:20–21). God determines to act for His own honor, promising the nation redemption from exile and restoration to its ancestral homeland (vv. 22–28). God is determined to sanctify His great name through a unilateral act of redemption, described in verses 22–32. As Eliezer of Beaugency noted, this entire unit is framed by a sharply worded statement of divine motivation: "Not for your sake will I act, O House of Israel" (v. 22).

Ezekiel gives particular emphasis to issues of purification and spiritual renewal along with the theme of national redemption. Ritually purified by divine action, the people will dwell in their homeland and observe the Covenant (36:25–28). This topic heralds concern for the approaching festival of *Pesaḥ,* because certain impurities could bar a worshiper from its celebration (see Num. 9:1–14). Echoing this matter, a special passage is added to the regular Torah portion for this *Shabbat.* In that selection, taken from Num. 19:1–22, in which the ashes of the so-called red heifer (*parah adumah*) are used in a priestly ceremony of ritual bathing and purification from defilement. Through these readings, the ongoing community of Israel is reminded that one must begin the holiday in a proper physical and spiritual state.

By custom, *S'fardim* conclude the *haftarah* at verse 36, thus ending on a positive note after the divine call to Israel to "Be ashamed and humiliated because of your ways" (v. 32). The practice for *Ashk'nazim* concludes the *haftarah* with the next oracle (vv. 37–38), comparing the vast throngs of people in the homeland to the multitude of sheep in Jerusalem on a festival day. This image was interpreted in antiquity as a reference to the flock of Israel "coming to Jerusalem at the time of the feast of Passover" (Targ. Jon.).

Part of the national transformation, unilaterally performed by God for His own sake, is a revivification of heart and spirit. God will give the people a new heart to know Him and will put His spirit within them as a concrete act of inspiration. Israel will thus be re-created, a new Adam to be restored to a land that "has become like the garden of Eden" (v. 35).

This re-creation is the core of national purification and the climax of the divine acts of sanctification. The destiny of God and Israel are thus mysteriously linked. The defilement of Israel leads to the profanation of God's name, and the purification of Israel results in the sanctification of God's name on earth. Their relationship is marked positively at the end of this prophetic passage by the forecast of a renewal of the Covenant. Reborn in heart and spirit, Israel will again serve God and His law: "Then you shall dwell in the land which I gave to your fathers, and you shall be My people and I will be your God" (v. 28). The return to the homeland is thus also a symbolic return to Mount Sinai and its spiritual demands.

RELATION OF THE *HAFTARAH* TO THE CALENDAR

Parashat Parah (Num. 19:1–22) is the third of

four special Torah passages added to the regular *Shabbat* portion in the weeks before *Pesaḥ.* The theme of each reading is different, yet rabbinic tradition correlated each of the four readings with prophetic selections that reinforce the main theme of purification. (For details on the scheduling of the special Torah portions, see the introduction to the *haftarah* for *parashat Sh'kalim.*)

Clear links exist between this special Torah reading and the *haftarah.* Thematically speaking, the Torah passage presents an ancient rite of detoxification whereby individuals who have become impure through contact with the dead are purified and restored to the community; the corresponding prophetic passage announces Israel's revivification (a new heart and a new spirit) as well as its purification by God. Meanwhile, both the technical language of purity–impurity and the terms for sacred ritual bathing (among others) connect these two texts verbally.

Parashat Parah was recited at this season from early Rabbinic times (M Meg. 3:4) and was understood to signal to the entire community that the *pesaḥ* sacrifice should be performed in ritual purity (see Rashi on BT Meg. 29a). The *haftarah* invigorates the present preparations for *Pesaḥ* by envisioning a new era of purification and of transformed religious consciousness.

36 16The word of the LORD came to me:
17O mortal, when the House of Israel dwelt on
their own soil, they defiled it with their ways and
their deeds; their ways were in My sight like
the impurity of a menstruous woman. 18So I
poured out My wrath on them for the blood
which they shed upon their land, and for the
fetishes with which they defiled it. 19I scattered
them among the nations, and they were dispersed through the countries: I punished them
in accordance with their ways and their deeds.
20But when they came to those nations, they
caused My holy name to be profaned, in that
it was said of them, "These are the people of the

לו 16 וַיְהִ֥י דְבַר־יְהוָ֖ה אֵלַ֥י לֵאמֹֽר׃
17 בֶּן־אָדָ֗ם בֵּ֤ית יִשְׂרָאֵל֙ יֹשְׁבִ֣ים עַל־
אַדְמָתָ֔ם וַיְטַמְּא֣וּ אוֹתָ֔הּ בְּדַרְכָּ֖ם
וּבַעֲלִילוֹתָ֑ם כְּטֻמְאַת֙ הַנִּדָּ֔ה הָיְתָ֥ה דַרְכָּ֖ם
לְפָנָֽי׃ 18 וָאֶשְׁפֹּ֤ךְ חֲמָתִי֙ עֲלֵיהֶ֔ם עַל־הַדָּ֖ם
אֲשֶׁר־שָׁפְכ֣וּ עַל־הָאָ֑רֶץ וּבְגִלּוּלֵיהֶ֖ם
טִמְּאֽוּהָ׃ 19 וָאָפִ֤יץ אֹתָם֙ בַּגּוֹיִ֔ם וַיִּזָּר֖וּ
בָּאֲרָצ֑וֹת כְּדַרְכָּ֥ם וְכַעֲלִילוֹתָ֖ם שְׁפַטְתִּֽים׃
20 וַיָּב֗וֹא* אֶל־הַגּוֹיִם֙ אֲשֶׁר־בָּ֣אוּ שָׁ֔ם
וַֽיְחַלְּל֖וּ אֶת־שֵׁ֣ם קָדְשִׁ֑י בֶּאֱמֹ֤ר לָהֶם֙ עַם־

v. 20. סבירין ומטעין לשון רבים

Ezekiel 36:17–19. The prophet's priestly orientation shows through his presentation of moral sins as the cause of the Land's ritual impurity. Similarly, the purification of the nation in verse 25 is portrayed in cultic terms. (Likewise, the vocabulary of defilement, purification, sprinkling, and pure water is employed in connection with the rite of the heifer—the special Torah portion read on this *Shabbat*; see Num. 19:11–13,17.) The punishment of exile is presented here as recompense for ritual and moral crimes.

O mortal Hebrew: *ben adam;* literally, "O son of man." A common characterization in the vocabulary of this prophet. Ezekiel's mortal nature is emphasized, perhaps counterpointing his humanity to the divinity of the beings he communes with; chapters 1, 8–11, 40–42).

like the impurity of a menstruous woman Refers to her ritual impurity (see Lev. 15:19ff.). Hebrew: *ha-niddah;* literally, "the menstruous woman." The definite article personifies the simile, rather than indicating a general state of impurity. The link between ritual impurity in this verse and bloodshed in verse 18 suggests that the figure here alludes to moral and ritual crimes elsewhere denounced by the prophet (18:6, 22:3–13). For Ezekiel, the theme has real cultic consequences. As a result of its "menstrual impurity," the nation is banished from the Land.

20. they caused My holy name to be profaned By referring to God in a demeaning way. The na-

LORD, yet they had to leave His land." 21Therefore I am concerned for My holy name, which the House of Israel have caused to be profaned among the nations to which they have come.

22Say to the House of Israel: Thus said the Lord GOD: Not for your sake will I act, O House of Israel, but for My holy name, which you have caused to be profaned among the nations to which you have come. 23I will sanctify My great name which has been profaned among the nations—among whom you have caused it to be profaned. And the nations shall know that I am the LORD—declares the Lord GOD—when I manifest My holiness before their eyes through you. 24I will take you from among the nations and gather you from all the countries, and I will bring you back to your own land. 25I will sprinkle pure water upon you, and you shall be pure: I will purify you from all your impurities and from all your fetishes. 26And I will give you a new heart and put a new spirit into you: I will remove the heart of stone from your body and give you a heart of flesh; 27and I will put My spirit into you. Thus I will cause you to follow My laws and faithfully to observe My rules. 28Then you shall dwell in the land which I gave to your fathers, and you shall be My people and I will be your God.

29And when I have delivered you from all your impurity, I will summon the grain and make it abundant, and I will not bring famine upon you. 30I will make the fruit of your trees and the crops of your fields abundant, so that you shall never again be humiliated before the nations because

יְהוָה אֵלֶּה וּמֵאַרְצוֹ יָצָאוּ׃ 21 וָאֶחְמֹל
עַל־שֵׁם קָדְשִׁי אֲשֶׁר חִלְּלוּהוּ בֵּית יִשְׂרָאֵל
בַּגּוֹיִם אֲשֶׁר־בָּאוּ שָׁמָּה׃ ס
22 לָכֵן אֱמֹר לְבֵית־יִשְׂרָאֵל כֹּה אָמַר אֲדֹנָי
יְהוִה לֹא לְמַעַנְכֶם אֲנִי עֹשֶׂה בֵּית יִשְׂרָאֵל
כִּי אִם־לְשֵׁם־קָדְשִׁי אֲשֶׁר חִלַּלְתֶּם בַּגּוֹיִם
אֲשֶׁר־בָּאתֶם שָׁם׃ 23 וְקִדַּשְׁתִּי אֶת־שְׁמִי
הַגָּדוֹל הַמְחֻלָּל בַּגּוֹיִם אֲשֶׁר חִלַּלְתֶּם
בְּתוֹכָם וְיָדְעוּ הַגּוֹיִם כִּי־אֲנִי יְהוָה נְאֻם
אֲדֹנָי יְהוִה בְּהִקָּדְשִׁי בָכֶם לְעֵינֵיהֶם׃
24 וְלָקַחְתִּי אֶתְכֶם מִן־הַגּוֹיִם וְקִבַּצְתִּי
אֶתְכֶם מִכָּל־הָאֲרָצוֹת וְהֵבֵאתִי אֶתְכֶם
אֶל־אַדְמַתְכֶם׃ 25 וְזָרַקְתִּי עֲלֵיכֶם מַיִם
טְהוֹרִים וּטְהַרְתֶּם מִכֹּל טֻמְאוֹתֵיכֶם
וּמִכָּל־גִּלּוּלֵיכֶם אֲטַהֵר אֶתְכֶם׃ 26 וְנָתַתִּי
לָכֶם לֵב חָדָשׁ וְרוּחַ חֲדָשָׁה אֶתֵּן בְּקִרְבְּכֶם
וַהֲסִרֹתִי אֶת־לֵב הָאֶבֶן מִבְּשַׂרְכֶם וְנָתַתִּי
לָכֶם לֵב בָּשָׂר׃ 27 וְאֶת־רוּחִי אֶתֵּן
בְּקִרְבְּכֶם וְעָשִׂיתִי אֵת אֲשֶׁר־בְּחֻקַּי תֵּלֵכוּ
וּמִשְׁפָּטַי תִּשְׁמְרוּ וַעֲשִׂיתֶם׃ 28 וִישַׁבְתֶּם
בָּאָרֶץ אֲשֶׁר נָתַתִּי לַאֲבֹתֵיכֶם וִהְיִיתֶם לִי
לְעָם וְאָנֹכִי אֶהְיֶה לָכֶם לֵאלֹהִים׃
29 וְהוֹשַׁעְתִּי אֶתְכֶם מִכֹּל טֻמְאוֹתֵיכֶם
וְקָרָאתִי אֶל־הַדָּגָן וְהִרְבֵּיתִי אֹתוֹ וְלֹא־
אֶתֵּן עֲלֵיכֶם רָעָב׃ 30 וְהִרְבֵּיתִי אֶת־פְּרִי
הָעֵץ וּתְנוּבַת הַשָּׂדֶה לְמַעַן אֲשֶׁר לֹא
תִקְחוּ עוֹד חֶרְפַּת רָעָב בַּגּוֹיִם׃ 31 וּזְכַרְתֶּם

tions interpreted Israel's exile as a sign of divine impotence, not as punishment (Rashi, Radak).

22. Not for your sake Or: "Not on account of your merits" (Abravanel). The motivation for divine action is regard for God's own name alone.

26. I will give you a new heart Along with Ezek. 11:19, other prophecies contemplate a radical transformation of Israel's religious spirit, after the exile, through sovereign and unilateral divine fiat (see Jer. 24:7, 31:32–33). In its focus on a unilateral divine action, this image seems to reflect some of the despair in the exilic period over the independent incapacity of the human spirit to return faithfully to God, or at least a strong feeling that without divine initiative true repentance could not take place.

28. you shall be My people and I will be your God A technical covenant formula (see Jer. 11:4). Also in 16:60 and 37:26, Ezekiel anticipates a new covenant after the exile.

of famine. 31Then you shall recall your evil ways and your base conduct, and you shall loathe yourselves for your iniquities and your abhorrent practices. 32Not for your sake will I act—declares the Lord God—take good note! Be ashamed and humiliated because of your ways, O House of Israel!

33Thus said the Lord God: When I have purified you of all your iniquities, I will people your settlements, and the ruined places shall be rebuilt; 34and the desolate land, after lying waste in the sight of every passerby, shall again be tilled. 35And men shall say, "That land, once desolate, has become like the garden of Eden; and the cities, once ruined, desolate, and ravaged, are now populated and fortified." 36And the nations that are left around you shall know that I the Lord have rebuilt the ravaged places and replanted the desolate land. I the Lord have spoken and will act.

37Thus said the Lord God: Moreover, in this I will respond to the House of Israel and act for their sake: I will multiply their people like sheep. 38As Jerusalem is filled with sacrificial sheep during her festivals, so shall the ruined cities be filled with flocks of people. And they shall know that I am the Lord.

אֶת־דַּרְכֵיכֶם הָרָעִים וּמַעַלְלֵיכֶם אֲשֶׁר
לֹא־טוֹבִים וּנְקֹטֹתֶם בִּפְנֵיכֶם עַל עֲוֺנֹתֵיכֶם
וְעַל תּוֹעֲבוֹתֵיכֶם׃ 32 לֹא לְמַעַנְכֶם אֲנִי־
עֹשֶׂה נְאֻם אֲדֹנָי יֱהֹוִה יִוָּדַע לָכֶם בּוֹשׁוּ
וְהִכָּלְמוּ מִדַּרְכֵיכֶם בֵּית יִשְׂרָאֵל׃ ס
33 כֹּה אָמַר אֲדֹנָי יֱהֹוִה בְּיוֹם טַהֲרִי אֶתְכֶם
מִכֹּל עֲוֺנוֹתֵיכֶם וְהוֹשַׁבְתִּי אֶת־הֶעָרִים
וְנִבְנוּ הֶחֳרָבוֹת׃ 34 וְהָאָרֶץ הַנְּשַׁמָּה תֵּעָבֵד
תַּחַת אֲשֶׁר הָיְתָה שְׁמָמָה לְעֵינֵי כָּל־
עוֹבֵר׃ 35 וְאָמְרוּ הָאָרֶץ הַלֵּזוּ הַנְּשַׁמָּה
הָיְתָה כְּגַן־עֵדֶן וְהֶעָרִים הֶחֳרֵבוֹת
וְהַנְשַׁמּוֹת וְהַנֶּהֱרָסוֹת בְּצוּרוֹת יָשָׁבוּ׃
36 וְיָדְעוּ הַגּוֹיִם אֲשֶׁר יִשָּׁאֲרוּ סְבִיבוֹתֵיכֶם
כִּי ׀ אֲנִי יְהוָה בָּנִיתִי הַנֶּהֱרָסוֹת נָטַעְתִּי
הַנְּשַׁמָּה אֲנִי יְהוָה דִּבַּרְתִּי וְעָשִׂיתִי׃ ס
37 כֹּה אָמַר אֲדֹנָי יֱהֹוִה עוֹד זֹאת אִדָּרֵשׁ
לְבֵית־יִשְׂרָאֵל לַעֲשׂוֹת לָהֶם אַרְבֶּה אֹתָם
כַּצֹּאן אָדָם׃ 38 כְּצֹאן קָדָשִׁים כְּצֹאן
יְרוּשָׁלַ͏ִם בְּמוֹעֲדֶיהָ כֵּן תִּהְיֶינָה הֶעָרִים
הֶחֳרֵבוֹת מְלֵאוֹת צֹאן אָדָם וְיָדְעוּ כִּי־אֲנִי
יְהוָה׃ ס

הפטרת פרשת החודש

HAFTARAH FOR PARASHAT HA-ḤODESH

EZEKIEL 45:16–46:18 (*Ashk'nazim*)
EZEKIEL 45:18–46:15 (*S'fardim*)

This *haftarah* presents regulations that pertain largely to worship in a rebuilt Temple, with a major emphasis on offerings to make expiation for the House of Israel. For *Ashk'nazim,* the reading opens with the requirement of regular contributions for the Temple service to be brought by the "entire population" (45:16–17; the details are given in verses 13–15, before the *haftarah*) and by the prince. Their reading ends with matters of gifts to be distributed by the prince to his heirs (46:16–18). A long passage in between focuses on details of Temple purification and sacrificial offering. Among *S'fardim,* the reading consists solely of that passage, which also includes regulations governing entry to the inner court for the common people and for the prince, as well as offerings for fixed occasions.

A series of purification rites are to be performed in the first and the seventh months of the year (45:18–25). The rites of purification in the first month are given in special detail, together with the command that the people offer the *pesaḥ* sacrifice on the 14th day of the month (of *Nisan*) and eat unleavened bread during the next 7 days. Correspondingly, detailed rules for the *pesaḥ* sacrifice and unleavened bread are included in the special Torah reading for this *Shabbat* (Exod. 12:1–20). Moses delineates requirements for the inaugural *pesaḥ* ceremony in Egypt, and anticipates subsequent celebrations of the festival. Ezekiel's proclamation envisions rituals and practices in the rebuilt Temple of the future. These occasionally are at variance with the older laws.

Particularly problematic is the account of purifying the Temple in the first and the seventh months. Nothing of the sort is mentioned in the Torah. Perplexed, some rabbinic commentators have associated this purification with the altar consecration mentioned in Ezek. 43:18–26 (Rashi, Radak). They consider this rite to be a one-time event, like the tabernacle purification of old, which also occurred on the first day of the first month (see Exod. 40:2). In this way, they tried to resolve any possible conflict between this ceremony and the great day of Temple purification on *Yom Kippur,* 10 days after the New Year in the seventh month (Lev. 16:29). Notably, there is no reference to *Yom Kippur* in Ezekiel's teaching. Also absent is any reference to the festival of *Sukkot,* which begins on the 15th day of the seventh month. The cultic traditions found in this *haftarah* also contradict specific sacrificial regulations found in the Torah (see the *haftarah* for *Emor*).

RELATION OF THE *HAFTARAH* TO THE CALENDAR

Parashat ha-Ḥodesh (Exod. 12:1–20) is the last of four special Torah passages added to the regular *Shabbat* portion in the weeks before *Pesaḥ.* (Specifically, it is recited on the last *Shabbat* of Adar—unless the forthcoming New Moon of *Nisan* falls on a *Shabbat,* in which case it is recited rather than the *haftarah* otherwise read whenever a New Moon falls on *Shabbat.*) The passage gets its designation from the opening proclamation: "This month [*ha-ḥodesh ha-zeh*] shall mark for you the beginning of the months"; it contains the laws concerning a paschal offering and thus anticipates the ritual of the 14th of *Nisan* (see Rashi on BT Meg. 29a).

That special Torah reading and this *haftarah* are clearly linked. Both passages stress the *pesaḥ* ceremony and the festival of unleavened bread. The Torah describes the inaugural *pesaḥ* ceremony in Egypt as well as provisions for subsequent enactments; the *haftarah* describes the festival for the envisioned new Temple period,

stressing the formal purifications that will take place at that time (Ezek. 45:21–24). These two descriptions reflect two historical poles. The *Pesaḥ* of Egypt recalls that ancient time when Israel experienced liberation from bondage and was called by God to be a "kingdom of priests and a holy nation" (Exod. 19:6). The *Pesaḥ* of the future anticipates a time when Israel will be restored to its homeland and its sacred duties. In the first ceremony, blood was smeared on the doorpost of each clan dwelling for the people's protection (Exod. 12:13). In the complex ritual detailed by Ezekiel, blood is to be smeared on the doorpost of the Temple, among other places, for the purification of the Temple itself (Ezek. 45:19).

These thematic connections suggest some theological correlations. Daubing the entrances to the home and to the Temple with blood marks them off as two types of space. The first embodies the family, whose bonds are biologic. The family, the nuclear core of personal history and religious rite, preserves a parochial character by virtue of its intimacy and common name. The space within the Temple is communal; its rites have an official, public status. The Temple as the sanctuary of God opens its doors for collective worship, thus transcending the private histories of its worshipers. The conjunction of the two readings sharpens the distinctions between the two dwellings. How one may live in both homes—standing firm in loyalty to hearth and blood but open to the enlargement of commitments that a divine Temple dwelling symbolizes—is a question each individual must answer repeatedly.

45 [16]In this contribution, the entire population must join with the prince in Israel.

[17]But the burnt offerings, the grain offerings, and the libations on festivals, new moons, sabbaths—all fixed occasions—of the House of Israel shall be the obligation of the prince; he shall provide the purification offerings, the grain offerings, the burnt offerings, and the offerings of well-being, to make expiation for the House of Israel.

[18]Thus said the Lord GOD: On the first day of the first month, you shall take a bull of the herd without blemish, and you shall purify the Sanctuary. [19]The priest shall take some of the blood of the purification offering and apply it to the doorposts of the Temple, to the four corners of the ledge of the altar, and to the doorposts of the gate of the inner court. [20]You shall do the same on the seventh day of the month to purge the Temple from impurity caused by unwitting or ignorant persons.

מה 16 כֹּל הָעָם הָאָרֶץ יִהְיוּ אֶל־
הַתְּרוּמָה הַזֹּאת לַנָּשִׂיא בְּיִשְׂרָאֵל׃
17 וְעַל־הַנָּשִׂיא יִהְיֶה הָעוֹלוֹת וְהַמִּנְחָה
וְהַנֵּסֶךְ בַּחַגִּים וּבֶחֳדָשִׁים וּבַשַּׁבָּתוֹת
בְּכָל־מוֹעֲדֵי בֵּית יִשְׂרָאֵל הוּא־יַעֲשֶׂה
אֶת־הַחַטָּאת וְאֶת־הַמִּנְחָה וְאֶת־הָעוֹלָה
וְאֶת־הַשְּׁלָמִים לְכַפֵּר בְּעַד בֵּית־
יִשְׂרָאֵל׃ ס
18 כֹּה־אָמַר אֲדֹנָי יְהוִה בָּרִאשׁוֹן בְּאֶחָד
לַחֹדֶשׁ תִּקַּח פַּר־בֶּן־בָּקָר תָּמִים וְחִטֵּאתָ
אֶת־הַמִּקְדָּשׁ׃ 19 וְלָקַח הַכֹּהֵן מִדַּם
הַחַטָּאת וְנָתַן אֶל־מְזוּזַת הַבַּיִת וְאֶל־
אַרְבַּע פִּנּוֹת הָעֲזָרָה לַמִּזְבֵּחַ וְעַל־מְזוּזַת
שַׁעַר הֶחָצֵר הַפְּנִימִית׃ 20 וְכֵן תַּעֲשֶׂה
בְּשִׁבְעָה בַחֹדֶשׁ מֵאִישׁ שֹׁגֶה וּמִפֶּתִי
וְכִפַּרְתֶּם אֶת־הַבָּיִת׃

Ezekiel 45:17. prince Hebrew: *nasi*. An ancient tribal title (Gen. 23:6), frequently used by Ezekiel to refer to Israelite kings (Ezek. 22:6) and the future scion of David (34:24, 37:25). In Ezek. 44:3, 45–46, and 48, the prince is the future leader. This leader has a special role in the new

21On the fourteenth day of the first month you shall have the passover sacrifice; and during a festival of seven days unleavened bread shall be eaten. 22On that day, the prince shall provide a bull of purification offering on behalf of himself and of the entire population; 23and during the seven days of the festival, he shall provide daily—for seven days—seven bulls and seven rams, without blemish, for a burnt offering to the Lord, and one goat daily for a purification offering. 24He shall provide a grain offering of an *ephah* for each bull and an *ephah* for each ram, with a *hin* of oil to every *ephah*. 25So, too, during the festival of the seventh month, for seven days from the fifteenth day on, he shall provide the same purification offerings, burnt offerings, grain offerings, and oil.

46 Thus said the Lord GOD: The gate of the inner court which faces east shall be closed on the six working days; it shall be opened on the sabbath day and it shall be opened on the day of the new moon. 2The prince shall enter by way of the vestibule outside the gate, and shall attend at the gatepost while the priests sacrifice his burnt offering and his offering of well-being; he shall then bow low at the threshold of the gate and depart. The gate, however, shall not be closed until evening. 3The common people shall worship before the Lord on sabbaths and new moons at the entrance of the same gate.

4The burnt offering which the prince presents to the Lord on the sabbath day shall consist of six lambs without blemish and one ram without blemish—5with a grain offering of an *ephah* for the ram, a grain offering of as much as he wishes

21 בָּרִאשׁ֗וֹן בְּאַרְבָּעָ֨ה עָשָׂ֥ר י֛וֹם לַחֹ֖דֶשׁ יִהְיֶ֣ה לָכֶ֑ם הַפָּ֑סַח חָ֡ג שְׁבֻע֣וֹת יָמִ֔ים מַצּ֖וֹת יֵאָכֵֽל׃ 22 וְעָשָׂ֣ה הַנָּשִׂ֗יא בַּיּ֤וֹם הַהוּא֙ בַּעֲד֔וֹ וּבְעַ֖ד כָּל־עַ֣ם הָאָ֑רֶץ פַּ֥ר חַטָּֽאת׃ וְשִׁבְעַ֨ת יְמֵֽי־הֶחָ֜ג יַעֲשֶׂ֧ה עוֹלָ֣ה לַֽיהֹוָ֗ה 23 שִׁבְעַ֨ת פָּרִ֜ים וְשִׁבְעַ֤ת אֵילִים֙ תְּמִימִ֔ם לַיּ֖וֹם שִׁבְעַ֣ת הַיָּמִ֑ים וְחַטָּ֕את שְׂעִ֥יר עִזִּ֖ים לַיּֽוֹם׃ 24 וּמִנְחָ֗ה אֵיפָ֥ה לַפָּ֛ר וְאֵיפָ֥ה לָאַ֖יִל יַעֲשֶׂ֑ה וְשֶׁ֖מֶן הִ֥ין לָאֵיפָֽה׃ 25 בַּשְּׁבִיעִ֡י בַּחֲמִשָּׁה֩ עָשָׂ֨ר י֜וֹם לַחֹ֗דֶשׁ בֶּחָג֙ יַעֲשֶׂ֣ה כָאֵ֔לֶּה שִׁבְעַ֖ת הַיָּמִ֑ים כַּֽחַטָּאת֙ כָּֽעֹלָ֔ה וְכַמִּנְחָ֖ה וְכַשָּֽׁמֶן׃ ס

מו כֹּה־אָמַר֮ אֲדֹנָ֣י יֱהֹוִה֒ שַׁ֜עַר הֶחָצֵ֤ר הַפְּנִימִית֙ הַפֹּנֶ֣ה קָדִ֔ים יִהְיֶ֣ה סָג֔וּר שֵׁ֖שֶׁת יְמֵ֣י הַֽמַּעֲשֶׂ֑ה וּבְי֨וֹם הַשַּׁבָּ֜ת יִפָּתֵ֗חַ וּבְי֥וֹם הַחֹ֖דֶשׁ יִפָּתֵֽחַ׃ 2 וּבָ֣א הַנָּשִׂ֡יא דֶּ֩רֶךְ֩ אוּלָ֨ם הַשַּׁ֜עַר מִח֗וּץ וְעָמַד֙ עַל־מְזוּזַ֣ת הַשַּׁ֔עַר וְעָשׂ֣וּ הַכֹּהֲנִ֗ים אֶת־עֽוֹלָתוֹ֙ וְאֶת־שְׁלָמָ֔יו וְהִֽשְׁתַּחֲוָ֛ה עַל־מִפְתַּ֥ן הַשַּׁ֖עַר וְיָצָ֑א וְהַשַּׁ֥עַר לֹֽא־יִסָּגֵ֖ר עַד־הָעָֽרֶב׃ 3 וְהִשְׁתַּחֲו֧וּ עַם־הָאָ֛רֶץ פֶּ֥תַח הַשַּׁ֖עַר הַה֑וּא בַּשַּׁבָּת֖וֹת וּבֶחֳדָשִׁ֑ים לִפְנֵ֥י יְהֹוָֽה׃ 4 וְהָ֣עֹלָ֔ה אֲשֶׁר־יַקְרִ֥ב הַנָּשִׂ֖יא לַֽיהֹוָ֑ה בְּי֣וֹם הַשַּׁבָּ֗ת שִׁשָּׁ֧ה כְבָשִׂ֛ים תְּמִימִ֖ם וְאַ֥יִל תָּמִֽים׃ 5 וּמִנְחָה֙ אֵיפָ֣ה לָאַ֔יִל וְלַכְּבָשִׂ֥ים מִנְחָ֖ה מַתַּ֣ת יָד֑וֹ וְשֶׁ֖מֶן הִ֥ין לָאֵיפָֽה׃

Temple service, which may explain the choice of this term (see Lev. 4:22).

21. festival of seven days Hebrew: *ḥag sh'vu·ot yamim* (unusual formulation); literally, "a festival of weeks of days."

Ezekiel 46:1. six working days Hebrew: *sheishet y'mei ha-ma·aseh*. This unique biblical expression is a well-known phrase in Jewish liturgy. It is used in the concluding benediction of the final *Shabbat* ceremony, the *Havdalah* service.

for the lambs, and a *hin* of oil with every *ephah*. 6And on the day of the new moon, it shall consist of a bull of the herd without blemish, and six lambs and a ram—they shall be without blemish. 7And he shall provide a grain offering of an *ephah* for the bull, an *ephah* for the ram, and as much as he can afford for the lambs, with a *hin* of oil to every *ephah*.

8When the prince enters, he shall come in by way of the vestibule of the gate, and he shall go out the same way.

9But on the fixed occasions, when the common people come before the LORD, whoever enters by the north gate to bow low shall leave by the south gate; and whoever enters by the south gate shall leave by the north gate. They shall not go back through the gate by which they came in, but shall go out by the opposite one. 10And as for the prince, he shall enter with them when they enter and leave when they leave.

11On festivals and fixed occasions, the grain offering shall be an *ephah* for each bull, an *ephah* for each ram, and as much as he wishes for the lambs, with a *hin* of oil for every *ephah*.

12The gate that faces east shall also be opened for the prince whenever he offers a freewill offering—be it burnt offering or offering of well-being—freely offered to the LORD, so that he may offer his burnt offering or his offering of well-being just as he does on the sabbath day. Then he shall leave, and the gate shall be closed after he leaves.

13Each day you shall offer a lamb of the first year without blemish, as a daily burnt offering to the LORD; you shall offer one every morning. 14And every morning regularly you shall offer a grain offering with it: a sixth of an *ephah*, with a third of a *hin* of oil to moisten the choice flour, as a grain offering to the LORD—a law for all time. 15The lamb, the grain offering, and oil shall be presented every morning as a regular burnt offering.

6 וּבְיוֹם הַחֹדֶשׁ פַּר בֶּן־בָּקָר תְּמִימִם וְשֵׁשֶׁת
כְּבָשִׂם וָאַיִל תְּמִימִם יִהְיוּ׃ 7 וְאֵיפָה לַפָּר
וְאֵיפָה לָאַיִל יַעֲשֶׂה מִנְחָה וְלַכְּבָשִׂים
כַּאֲשֶׁר תַּשִּׂיג יָדוֹ וְשֶׁמֶן הִין לָאֵיפָה׃
8 וּבְבוֹא הַנָּשִׂיא דֶּרֶךְ אוּלָם הַשַּׁעַר יָבוֹא
וּבְדַרְכּוֹ יֵצֵא׃
9 וּבְבוֹא עַם־הָאָרֶץ לִפְנֵי יְהוָה בַּמּוֹעֲדִים
הַבָּא דֶּרֶךְ־שַׁעַר צָפוֹן לְהִשְׁתַּחֲוֺת יֵצֵא
דֶּרֶךְ־שַׁעַר נֶגֶב וְהַבָּא דֶּרֶךְ־שַׁעַר נֶגֶב
יֵצֵא דֶּרֶךְ־שַׁעַר צָפוֹנָה לֹא יָשׁוּב דֶּרֶךְ
הַשַּׁעַר אֲשֶׁר־בָּא בוֹ כִּי נִכְחוֹ יצאו יֵצֵא׃
10 וְהַנָּשִׂיא בְּתוֹכָם בְּבוֹאָם יָבוֹא וּבְצֵאתָם
יֵצֵאוּ׃
11 וּבַחַגִּים וּבַמּוֹעֲדִים תִּהְיֶה הַמִּנְחָה
אֵיפָה לַפָּר וְאֵיפָה לָאַיִל וְלַכְּבָשִׂים מַתַּת
יָדוֹ וְשֶׁמֶן הִין לָאֵיפָה׃ ס
12 וְכִי־יַעֲשֶׂה הַנָּשִׂיא נְדָבָה עוֹלָה אוֹ־
שְׁלָמִים נְדָבָה לַיהוָה וּפָתַח לוֹ אֶת־
הַשַּׁעַר הַפֹּנֶה קָדִים וְעָשָׂה אֶת־עֹלָתוֹ
וְאֶת־שְׁלָמָיו כַּאֲשֶׁר יַעֲשֶׂה בְּיוֹם הַשַּׁבָּת
וְיָצָא וְסָגַר אֶת־הַשַּׁעַר אַחֲרֵי צֵאתוֹ׃
13 וְכֶבֶשׂ בֶּן־שְׁנָתוֹ תָּמִים תַּעֲשֶׂה עוֹלָה
לַיּוֹם לַיהוָה בַּבֹּקֶר בַּבֹּקֶר תַּעֲשֶׂה אֹתוֹ׃
14 וּמִנְחָה תַעֲשֶׂה עָלָיו בַּבֹּקֶר בַּבֹּקֶר
שִׁשִּׁית הָאֵיפָה וְשֶׁמֶן שְׁלִישִׁית הַהִין לָרֹס
אֶת־הַסֹּלֶת מִנְחָה לַיהוָה חֻקּוֹת עוֹלָם
תָּמִיד׃ 15 ועשו יַעֲשׂוּ אֶת־הַכֶּבֶשׂ וְאֶת־
הַמִּנְחָה וְאֶת־הַשֶּׁמֶן בַּבֹּקֶר בַּבֹּקֶר עוֹלַת
תָּמִיד׃ פ

16 כֹּה־אָמַר אֲדֹנָי יְהֹוִה כִּי־יִתֵּן הַנָּשִׂיא
מַתָּנָה לְאִישׁ מִבָּנָיו נַחֲלָתוֹ הִיא לְבָנָיו
תִּהְיֶה אֲחֻזָּתָם הִיא בְּנַחֲלָה׃ 17 וְכִי־יִתֵּן
מַתָּנָה מִנַּחֲלָתוֹ לְאַחַד מֵעֲבָדָיו וְהָיְתָה
לּוֹ עַד־שְׁנַת הַדְּרוֹר וְשָׁבַת לַנָּשִׂיא אַךְ
נַחֲלָתוֹ בָּנָיו לָהֶם תִּהְיֶה׃
18 וְלֹא־יִקַּח הַנָּשִׂיא מִנַּחֲלַת הָעָם
לְהוֹנֹתָם מֵאֲחֻזָּתָם מֵאֲחֻזָּתוֹ יַנְחִל אֶת־
בָּנָיו לְמַעַן אֲשֶׁר לֹא־יָפֻצוּ עַמִּי אִישׁ
מֵאֲחֻזָּתוֹ׃

16Thus said the Lord God: If the prince makes
a gift to any of his sons, it shall become the latter's inheritance; it shall pass on to his sons; it
is their holding by inheritance. 17But if he makes
a gift from his inheritance to any of his subjects,
it shall only belong to the latter until the year of release. Then it shall revert to the prince; his inheritance must by all means pass on to his sons.

18But the prince shall not take property away from any of the people and rob them of their holdings. Only out of his own holdings shall he endow his sons, in order that My people may not be dispossessed of their holdings.

18. the prince shall not take property away A regulation to curb such monarchic outrages as are feared in 1 Sam. 8:11–18 and documented in 1 Kings 21.

הפטרה לשבת הגדול

HAFTARAH FOR SHABBAT HA-GADOL

MALACHI 3:4–24

This *haftarah* contains God's promise to the people in the period after the rebuilding of the Temple in 516–15 B.C.E. The prophet announces that sacrificial offerings will again be favorably received by God, as in ancient times. First, however, God will contend with the nation's breach of moral and ritual law and bring sinners to judgment. Hope lies in repentance and in observance of the Torah. God's call to the people through Malachi, the healing mission of Elijah, and the teaching of Moses all show God's continual concern for reconciliation and human welfare.

Restoration is the recurrent theme of this *haftarah:* the restoration of acceptable offerings in the Temple (3:4), the repair of the Covenant through repentance (v. 7), the renewal of trust in divine justice (v. 18), and the reconciliation of parents and children (v. 24). Most of these statements include variations of the verb *shuv* (turn, return). Presumably, a crisis of trust in God's just providence has perverted the people's soul, leading to callous indifference in the moral and cultic realms. The *haftarah* is thus pervaded by a deep sense of estrangement from the right order of things, whether in the family, in society, or in the divine–human relationship.

In a rebuke that precedes the *haftarah,* the people are quoted as saying that "All who do evil are good in the sight of the LORD." Indeed, they mockingly jibe, "Where is the God of justice [*mishpat*]?" (Mal. 2:17). In response, God comes to redress the cause of *mishpat* (judgment) in verse 3:5, in which the literal "bring to judgment" is understood as "to contend against you." God will also attend to the sense of the God-fearers that "It is useless to serve God" (v. 14). Actions have consequences. If the people repent and serve God fully, they will receive the riches of heavenly blessing. Otherwise, they will be blasted to ash—root and branch. So deep is the people's resistance that God finally announces He will send His prophet Elijah to renew their hearts. This unilateral act is proof of God's love of Jacob (announced at the beginning of the collected prophecies of Malachi).

This is Malachi's message of hope. The framers of the biblical canon, placing Malachi as the last of the prophets, believed it to be a final prophetic word to those for whom Scripture teaches divine truth.

RELATION OF THE *HAFTARAH* TO THE CALENDAR

The phrase *shabbat ha-gadol* (the great Sabbath) is a fixed formulation of rabbinic liturgy, found in the Grace after Meals in the special supplication for *Shabbat* (beginning *r'tzei*). In that context, it emphasizes the special holiness of each *Shabbat.* The term also traditionally designates the *Shabbat* before *Pesaḥ*. Its meaning in this setting is uncertain, which has elicited much speculation.

One likely explanation for the choice of Mal. 3:4–24 as the *haftarah* for *Shabbat ha-Gadol* is the old tradition that the future redemption will occur on *Pesaḥ,* the prototype of redemption (BT RH 11a). Because the *haftarah* could be construed to herald God's great day, it is to be proclaimed in hope and in warning before the festival itself. The term *shabbat ha-gadol* would then simply be a shorthand designation for saying that on this *Shabbat* the *haftarah* proclaiming the final "great" (*gadol*) day is read. This is very much like the formulation *Shabbat Shuvah,* which is one way to designate the *Shabbat* before *Yom Kippur,* when the theme of repentance (*t'shuvah*) is stressed through a *haftarah* selection beginning with the word *shuvah* (repent; Hos. 14:2).

The *haftarah*'s focus on the tithe obligations would have reinforced the rabbinic selection. Indeed, according to the Mishnah, "on Passover

(the people) are judged with respect to (their) produce" (M RH I:2). Because the law required tithes from agricultural produce gathered before *Pesaḥ,* recitation of the *haftarah* on the *Shabbat* before the festival would duly warn the people to fulfill their obligations to God and to the poor, and thus merit divine favor in the ensuing year. Our custom of charitable giving (*ma·ot ḥittim*) at this time, initiated so that the needy would have grain for *matzah,* continues the relationship between philanthropy and piety at the *Pesaḥ* season. The *haftarah* thus signals that gifts have a divine dimension. From this perspective, *Shabbat ha-Gadol* calls attention to an ultimate or "great" accountability that all creatures bear for the resources of the earth and the sacred task of their redistribution.

3 4Then the offerings of Judah and Jerusalem shall be pleasing to the LORD as in the days of yore and in the years of old. 5But [first] I will step forward to contend against you, and I will act as a relentless accuser against those who have no fear of Me: Who practice sorcery, who commit adultery, who swear falsely, who cheat laborers of their hire, and who subvert [the cause of] the widow, orphan, and stranger, said the LORD of Hosts.

6For I am the LORD—I have not changed; and you are the children of Jacob—you have not ceased to be. 7From the very days of your fathers you have turned away from My laws and have not observed them. Turn back to Me, and I will turn back to you—said the LORD of Hosts. But you ask, "How shall we turn back?" 8Ought man to defraud God? Yet you are defrauding Me. And you ask, "How have we been defrauding You?" In tithe and contribution. 9You are suffering under a curse, yet you go on defrauding Me—the whole nation of you. 10Bring the full tithe into the storehouse, and let there be food in My House, and thus put Me to the test—said the LORD of Hosts. I will surely open the floodgates of the sky for you and pour down blessings on you; 11and I will banish the locusts from you, so that they will not destroy the yield

ג 4 וְעָרְבָה֙ לַֽיהוָ֔ה מִנְחַ֥ת יְהוּדָ֖ה
וִירוּשָׁלִָ֑ם כִּימֵ֣י עוֹלָ֔ם וּכְשָׁנִ֖ים קַדְמֹנִיֹּֽת׃
5 וְקָרַבְתִּ֣י אֲלֵיכֶם֮ לַמִּשְׁפָּט֒ וְהָיִ֣יתִי ׀ עֵ֣ד
מְמַהֵ֗ר בַּֽמְכַשְּׁפִים֙ וּבַֽמְנָאֲפִ֔ים וּבַנִּשְׁבָּעִ֖ים
לַשָּׁ֑קֶר וּבְעֹשְׁקֵ֣י שְׂכַר־שָׂ֠כִיר אַלְמָנָ֨ה
וְיָת֤וֹם וּמַטֵּי־גֵר֙* וְלֹ֣א יְרֵא֔וּנִי אָמַ֖ר יְהוָ֥ה
צְבָאֽוֹת׃

6 כִּ֛י אֲנִ֥י יְהוָ֖ה לֹ֣א שָׁנִ֑יתִי וְאַתֶּ֥ם בְּנֵֽי־יַעֲקֹ֖ב
לֹ֥א כְלִיתֶֽם׃ 7 לְמִימֵ֨י אֲבֹתֵיכֶ֜ם סַרְתֶּ֤ם
מֵֽחֻקַּי֙ וְלֹ֣א שְׁמַרְתֶּ֔ם שׁ֤וּבוּ אֵלַי֙ וְאָשׁ֣וּבָה
אֲלֵיכֶ֔ם אָמַ֖ר יְהוָ֣ה צְבָא֑וֹת וַאֲמַרְתֶּ֖ם בַּמֶּ֥ה
נָשֽׁוּב׃ 8 הֲיִקְבַּ֨ע אָדָ֜ם אֱלֹהִ֗ים כִּ֤י אַתֶּם֙
קֹבְעִ֣ים אֹתִ֔י וַאֲמַרְתֶּ֖ם בַּמֶּ֣ה קְבַעֲנ֑וּךָ
הַֽמַּעֲשֵׂ֖ר וְהַתְּרוּמָֽה׃ 9 בַּמְּאֵרָה֙ אַתֶּ֣ם
נֵאָרִ֔ים וְאֹתִ֖י אַתֶּ֣ם קֹבְעִ֑ים הַגּ֖וֹי כֻּלּֽוֹ׃
10 הָבִ֨יאוּ אֶת־כָּל־הַֽמַּעֲשֵׂ֜ר אֶל־בֵּ֣ית
הָאוֹצָ֗ר וִיהִ֥י טֶ֨רֶף֙ בְּבֵיתִ֔י וּבְחָנ֤וּנִי נָא֙
בָּזֹ֔את אָמַ֖ר יְהוָ֣ה צְבָא֑וֹת אִם־לֹ֧א אֶפְתַּ֣ח
לָכֶ֗ם אֵ֚ת אֲרֻבּ֣וֹת הַשָּׁמַ֔יִם וַהֲרִיקֹתִ֥י לָכֶ֛ם
בְּרָכָ֖ה עַד־בְּלִי־דָֽי׃ 11 וְגָעַרְתִּ֤י לָכֶם֙ בָּֽאֹכֵ֔ל
וְלֹֽא־יַשְׁחִ֥ת לָכֶ֖ם אֶת־פְּרִ֣י הָאֲדָמָ֑ה וְלֹֽא־

v. 5. י׳ במקום ה׳

Malachi 3:5. Who practice sorcery Condemnation of witches and false oaths and of the abuse of widows, orphans, and strangers finds echoes in Exod. 22:17,19–21.

7. Turn back to Me, and I will turn back to you Malachi's exhortation assumes the people's ability to respond to God's initiative.

of your soil; and your vines in the field shall no longer miscarry—said the LORD of Hosts. ¹²And all the nations shall account you happy, for you shall be the most desired of lands—said the LORD of Hosts.

¹³You have spoken hard words against Me—said the LORD. But you ask, "What have we been saying among ourselves against You?" ¹⁴You have said, "It is useless to serve God. What have we gained by keeping His charge and walking in abject awe of the LORD of Hosts? ¹⁵And so, we account the arrogant happy: they have indeed done evil and endured; they have indeed dared God and escaped." ¹⁶In this vein have those who revere the LORD been talking to one another. The LORD has heard and noted it, and a scroll of remembrance has been written at His behest concerning those who revere the LORD and esteem His name. ¹⁷And on the day that I am preparing, said the LORD of Hosts, they shall be My treasured possession; I will be tender toward them as a man is tender toward a son who ministers to him. ¹⁸And you shall come to see the difference between the righteous and the wicked, between him who has served God and him who has not served Him.

¹⁹For lo! That day is at hand, burning like an oven. All the arrogant and all the doers of evil shall be straw, and the day that is coming—said the LORD of Hosts—shall burn them to ashes and leave of them neither stock nor boughs.

תְּשַׁכֵּל לָכֶם הַגֶּ֫פֶן בַּשָּׂדֶ֫ה אָמַר יְהֹוָה צְבָאֽוֹת: 12 וְאִשְּׁר֣וּ אֶתְכֶ֗ם כׇּל־הַגּוֹיִ֑ם כִּי־ תִהְיֽוּ אַתֶּם֙ אֶ֣רֶץ חֵ֔פֶץ אָמַ֖ר יְהֹוָ֥ה צְבָאֽוֹת: ס

13 חָזְק֤וּ עָלַי֙ דִּבְרֵיכֶם֙ אָמַ֣ר יְהֹוָ֔ה וַאֲמַרְתֶּ֕ם מַה־נִּדְבַּ֖רְנוּ עָלֶֽיךָ: 14 אֲמַרְתֶּ֕ם שָׁ֖וְא עֲבֹ֣ד אֱלֹהִ֑ים וּמַה־בֶּ֗צַע כִּ֤י שָׁמַ֙רְנוּ֙ מִשְׁמַרְתּ֔וֹ וְכִ֤י הָלַ֙כְנוּ֙ קְדֹ֣רַנִּ֔ית מִפְּנֵ֖י יְהֹוָ֥ה צְבָאֽוֹת: 15 וְעַתָּ֕ה אֲנַ֖חְנוּ מְאַשְּׁרִ֣ים זֵדִ֑ים גַּם־נִבְנוּ֙ עֹשֵׂ֣י רִשְׁעָ֔ה גַּ֧ם בָּחֲנ֛וּ אֱלֹהִ֖ים וַיִּמָּלֵֽטוּ: 16 אָ֚ז נִדְבְּר֣וּ יִרְאֵ֣י יְהֹוָ֔ה אִ֖ישׁ אֶת־ רֵעֵ֑הוּ וַיַּקְשֵׁ֤ב יְהֹוָה֙ וַיִּשְׁמָ֔ע וַ֠יִּכָּתֵ֠ב סֵ֣פֶר זִכָּר֤וֹן לְפָנָיו֙ לְיִרְאֵ֣י יְהֹוָ֔ה וּלְחֹשְׁבֵ֖י שְׁמֽוֹ: 17 וְהָ֣יוּ לִ֗י אָמַר֙ יְהֹוָ֣ה צְבָא֔וֹת לַיּ֕וֹם אֲשֶׁ֥ר אֲנִ֖י עֹשֶׂ֣ה סְגֻלָּ֑ה וְחָמַלְתִּ֣י עֲלֵיהֶ֔ם כַּאֲשֶׁר֙ יַחְמֹ֣ל אִ֔ישׁ עַל־בְּנ֖וֹ הָעֹבֵ֥ד אֹתֽוֹ: 18 וְשַׁבְתֶּם֙ וּרְאִיתֶ֔ם בֵּ֥ין צַדִּ֖יק לְרָשָׁ֑ע בֵּ֚ין עֹבֵ֣ד אֱלֹהִ֔ים לַאֲשֶׁ֖ר לֹ֥א עֲבָדֽוֹ: ס 19 כִּֽי־הִנֵּ֤ה הַיּוֹם֙ בָּ֔א בֹּעֵ֖ר כַּתַּנּ֑וּר וְהָי֨וּ כׇל־זֵדִ֜ים וְכׇל־עֹשֵׂ֤ה רִשְׁעָה֙ קַ֔שׁ וְלִהַ֧ט אֹתָ֣ם הַיּ֣וֹם הַבָּ֗א אָמַר֙ יְהֹוָ֣ה צְבָא֔וֹת אֲשֶׁ֛ר לֹא־יַעֲזֹ֥ב לָהֶ֖ם שֹׁ֥רֶשׁ וְעָנָֽף: 20 וְזָרְחָ֨ה

16. those who revere the LORD Hebrew: *yir·ei YHVH*. Used as a technical designation for those who revere God's name (3:20), in contradistinction to those who despise it (1:6). They shall be vindicated on the day of judgment (3:20–21). Presumably, this refers to a group of particularly pious people.

19. the day that is coming References to the future "day" of judgment punctuate the prophet's speech (3:2,17, 9,21, 3). A complex scenario is envisaged, dominated by the advent of an angelic messenger, the admonition of sins, the interven-

tions of Elijah, the fiery purgation of sinners, the vindication of the pious, and the visible distinction between the righteous and evildoers. This scenario was variously explicated and ordered by medieval Jewish commentators, in light of other biblical and Rabbinic evidence. In turn, the images were understood in either literal or figurative terms. The prophet Malachi was himself the heir to a long tradition of this rhetoric, produced in a period of more than 300 years and in various patterns.

20But for you who revere My name a sun of victory shall rise to bring healing. You shall go forth
and stamp like stall-fed calves, 21and you shall
trample the wicked to a pulp, for they shall be
dust beneath your feet on the day that I am
preparing—said the LORD of Hosts.

22Be mindful of the Teaching of My servant
Moses, whom I charged at Horeb with laws and
rules for all Israel.

23Lo, I will send the prophet Elijah to you before the coming of the awesome, fearful day of
the LORD. 24He shall reconcile parents with children and children with their parents, so that,
when I come, I do not strike the whole land with
utter destruction.

> Lo, I will send the prophet Elijah to you before the coming of the awesome, fearful day of the LORD.

לָכֶ֜ם יִרְאֵ֤י שְׁמִי֙ שֶׁ֣מֶשׁ צְדָקָ֔ה וּמַרְפֵּ֖א
בִּכְנָפֶ֑יהָ וִֽיצָאתֶ֥ם וּפִשְׁתֶּ֖ם כְּעֶגְלֵ֥י מַרְבֵּֽק׃
21 וְעַסּוֹתֶ֣ם רְשָׁעִ֔ים כִּֽי־יִהְי֣וּ אֵ֔פֶר תַּ֖חַת
כַּפּ֣וֹת רַגְלֵיכֶ֑ם בַּיּוֹם֙ אֲשֶׁ֣ר אֲנִ֣י עֹשֶׂ֔ה אָמַ֖ר
יְהוָ֥ה צְבָאֽוֹת׃ פ
22 זִכְר֕וּ תּוֹרַ֖ת מֹשֶׁ֣ה עַבְדִּ֑י אֲשֶׁר֩ צִוִּ֨יתִי
אוֹת֤וֹ בְחֹרֵב֙ עַל־כׇּל־יִשְׂרָאֵ֔ל חֻקִּ֖ים
וּמִשְׁפָּטִֽים׃
23 הִנֵּ֤ה אָנֹכִי֙ שֹׁלֵ֣חַ לָכֶ֔ם אֵ֖ת אֵלִיָּ֣ה הַנָּבִ֑יא
לִפְנֵ֗י בּ֚וֹא י֣וֹם יְהֹוָ֔ה הַגָּד֖וֹל וְהַנּוֹרָֽא׃
24 וְהֵשִׁ֤יב לֵב־אָבוֹת֙ עַל־בָּנִ֔ים וְלֵ֥ב בָּנִ֖ים
עַל־אֲבוֹתָ֑ם פֶּן־אָב֕וֹא וְהִכֵּיתִ֥י אֶת־הָאָ֖רֶץ
חֵֽרֶם׃

[הִנֵּ֤ה אָנֹכִי֙ שֹׁלֵ֣חַ לָכֶ֔ם אֵ֖ת אֵלִיָּ֣ה הַנָּבִ֑יא
לִפְנֵ֗י בּ֚וֹא י֣וֹם יְהֹוָ֔ה הַגָּד֖וֹל וְהַנּוֹרָֽא׃*]

end. במסורת הקריאה נשנה הפסוק לפני האחרון

24. He shall reconcile parents with children The language is difficult. The act of reconciliation here is literally "restore the heart" (*heshiv lev*). Different meanings of the preposition translated "with" (*al*), however, make it an open question whether the prophet envisions the reconciliation of parents "with" their children or "along with" them. In the first case, divine wrath will be forestalled by intergenerational reconciliation; in the other, both generations together will return to God.

הפטרה לפסח (יום ראשון)

HAFTARAH FOR PESAḤ, FIRST DAY

JOSHUA 3:5–7, 5:2–6:1, 6:27 (*Ashk'nazim*)
JOSHUA 5:2–6:1, 6:27 (*S'fardim*)

In this *haftarah* we read about early events in the life of the Israelites after they had reached the Promised Land. The sons of those who had died during the wilderness wanderings were circumcised at Gilgal. The celebration of *Pesaḥ* at Gilgal is central to a series of events that parallel the Exodus from Egypt and repeat its message under new circumstances. The events at Gilgal and the angelic revelation to Joshua "near Jericho" constitute the reading recited by *Ashk'nazim*. Meanwhile, *S'fardim* continue the historical report and read about the ensuing fall of Jericho under Joshua's leadership.

Rituals, sacred space, and holy war pervade the *haftarah*. Each of them marks a stage in the transformation of both the people and the Land. When the young males whose parents died in the wilderness are circumcised at Gilgal, the sojourn in Egypt and its "disgrace" have come to an end. When the people eat of the *pesaḥ* offering and consume the new grain of the Land, the food of the wilderness (manna) ceases. Finally, after a revelation to Joshua from the heavenly "captain of the Lord's host" (5:14), a minutely choreographed ritual encircling of Jericho is enacted, by which the city and all within it are consecrated to the Lord. The utter destruction of the city and its inhabitants (except for Rahab and her kin) inaugurates a ritualized purification of the homeland, with horrific curses uttered against anyone seeking personal gain from objects of value (6:18) or from the site itself (v. 26).

The national circumcision at Gilgal, the *pesaḥ* offering and the eating of new grain, and the revelation of the Lord's angel to Joshua take us beyond external acts to the inner processes of cultural and historical memory. For the narrator, the entrance into the Land is the liberation of a new Exodus, and Joshua is a new Moses. A close look at the text shows how this teaching about the deeper dimensions of history was conveyed:

1. In a passage just before the *haftarah* begins, the Book of Joshua reports that the Israelites crossed the Jordan River (5:1), whose waters were "cut off" from their normal flow, and stood "in a single heap" (3:13,15–16). This depiction of the miraculous recalls the crossing of the Sea of Reeds in Moses' day (Exod. 15:8). To emphasize the point, the narration continues with Joshua's future-oriented instructions to the people (4:21–24).

2. The narration in Josh. 4 points out that the people "came up from the Jordan on the tenth day of the first month" (4:19). This recalls the final events of the sojourn in Egypt when, before the final plague and the Exodus, each family was commanded to take a lamb on the 10th day of the first month (Exod. 12:2–3) and sacrifice it as "an offering to the Lord" on "the fourteenth day" of the month "at twilight" (Exod. 12:6). For a whole week thereafter, only "unleavened bread" was to be eaten (Exod. 12:19–20). Similarly, in the days of Joshua, "the Israelites offered the passover sacrifice on the fourteenth day of the [first] month, toward evening" (Josh. 5:10). On the next day, they ate "unleavened bread and parched grain" from "the produce of the country" (5:11).

3. The paschal ceremony at Gilgal (5:10–11) also explains the conjunction of this celebration with the immediately preceding account of the circumcision of the Israelite males (5:2–9). Underlying the narrative is the requirement that only the circumcised may participate in consuming the paschal offering (see Exod. 12:43–50, esp. v. 48). Joshua, performing the rite of circumcision before the *pesaḥ* sacrifice, is thus presented as a righteous observer of the law, a faithful follower of the statutes of Moses.

4. A final scene further links Joshua to Moses and the events of the Exodus to the onset of the conquest. After the *pesaḥ* ceremony, Joshua, near Jericho, was confronted by a "man" with a "drawn sword in hand" who identified himself as the "captain of the LORD's host" (5:13–14). Joshua perceived an angelic messenger in this individual and prostrated himself (v. 14). At this point, the figure declares: "Remove your sandals from your feet, for the place where you stand is holy" (v. 15). This recalls a similar divine command to Moses at the Burning Bush (Exod. 3:5).

In short, the goal of the *haftarah* is not simply to tell the past as it was, but rather to remember the past in a particular way. The events of Joshua's day are formulated so as to evoke, at every point, the days of Moses and the Exodus from Egypt. The new events are memorable precisely because they conform so closely to the instructive model of the Exodus from Egypt. The Israelite conquest simply repeats the prototype in old-new ways.

RELATION OF THE *HAFTARAH* TO THE CALENDAR

The first *pesaḥ* offering in the Land (Josh. 5:10–11) marks a recollection and a renewal of the Exodus. The unleavened grain here signals the end of the wilderness trek (and the divine manna). Hence, eating the new grain on the day after the *pesaḥ* offering was something of a rite of passage on entering the Land that had been promised to their ancestors.

The annual renewal of this grain ritual (by eating *matzot*) does not simply celebrate new agricultural beginnings. It also celebrates the earth as a physical and spiritual homeland—physical, because it reflects the natural necessity of eating (and the domestication of the earth through physical labor), and spiritual, because it stresses the relationship between the renewal of agriculture and the re-creation of the earth as a habitat for human settlement and destiny.

3 [5]And Joshua said to the people, "Purify yourselves, for tomorrow the LORD will perform wonders in your midst."

[6]Then Joshua ordered the priests, "Take up the Ark of the Covenant and advance to the head of the people." And they took up the Ark of the Covenant and marched at the head of the people.

[7]The LORD said to Joshua, "This day, for the first time, I will exalt you in the sight of all Israel, so that they shall know that I will be with you as I was with Moses."

ג 5 וַיֹּאמֶר יְהוֹשֻׁעַ אֶל־הָעָם הִתְקַדָּשׁוּ
כִּי מָחָר יַעֲשֶׂה יְהוָה בְּקִרְבְּכֶם
נִפְלָאוֹת׃
6 וַיֹּאמֶר יְהוֹשֻׁעַ אֶל־הַכֹּהֲנִים לֵאמֹר שְׂאוּ
אֶת־אֲרוֹן הַבְּרִית וְעִבְרוּ לִפְנֵי הָעָם וַיִּשְׂאוּ
אֶת־אֲרוֹן הַבְּרִית וַיֵּלְכוּ לִפְנֵי הָעָם׃ ס
7 וַיֹּאמֶר יְהוָה אֶל־יְהוֹשֻׁעַ הַיּוֹם הַזֶּה אָחֵל
גַּדֶּלְךָ בְּעֵינֵי כָּל־יִשְׂרָאֵל אֲשֶׁר יֵדְעוּן כִּי
כַּאֲשֶׁר הָיִיתִי עִם־מֹשֶׁה אֶהְיֶה עִמָּךְ׃

5 [2]At that time the LORD said to Joshua,
"Make flint knives and proceed with a second
circumcision of the Israelites." [3]So Joshua had
flint knives made, and the Israelites were circumcised at Gibeath-haaraloth.

ה 2 בָּעֵת הַהִיא אָמַר יְהוָה אֶל־יְהוֹשֻׁעַ
עֲשֵׂה לְךָ חַרְבוֹת צֻרִים וְשׁוּב מֹל אֶת־
בְּנֵי־יִשְׂרָאֵל שֵׁנִית׃ 3 וַיַּעַשׂ־לוֹ יְהוֹשֻׁעַ
חַרְבוֹת צֻרִים וַיָּמָל אֶת־בְּנֵי יִשְׂרָאֵל אֶל־
גִּבְעַת הָעֲרָלוֹת׃

Joshua 5:2. flint knives Hebrew: *ḥarvot tzurim.* Their use continues ancient practice (see Exod. 4:25). These ritual objects remained rough-hewn, similar to the stones of the ancient altars.

4This is the reason why Joshua had the circumcision performed: All the people who had come out of Egypt, all the males of military age, had died during the desert wanderings after leaving Egypt. 5Now, whereas all the people who came out of Egypt had been circumcised, none of the people born after the exodus, during the desert wanderings, had been circumcised. 6For the Israelites had traveled in the wilderness forty years, until the entire nation—the men of military age who had left Egypt—had perished; because they had not obeyed the LORD, and the LORD had sworn never to let them see the land that the LORD had sworn to their fathers to assign to us, a land flowing with milk and honey. 7But He had raised up their sons in their stead; and it was these that Joshua circumcised, for they were uncircumcised, not having been circumcised on the way. 8After the circumcising of the whole nation was completed, they remained where they were, in the camp, until they recovered.

9And the LORD said to Joshua, "Today I have rolled away from you the disgrace of Egypt." So that place was called Gilgal, as it still is.

10Encamped at Gilgal, in the steppes of Jericho, the Israelites offered the passover sacrifice on the fourteenth day of the month, toward evening.

11On the day after the passover offering, on

4 וְזֶה הַדָּבָר אֲשֶׁר־מָל יְהוֹשֻׁעַ כָּל־הָעָם
הַיֹּצֵא מִמִּצְרַיִם הַזְּכָרִים כֹּל ׀ אַנְשֵׁי
הַמִּלְחָמָה מֵתוּ בַמִּדְבָּר בַּדֶּרֶךְ בְּצֵאתָם
מִמִּצְרָיִם׃ 5 כִּי־מֻלִים הָיוּ כָּל־הָעָם
הַיֹּצְאִים וְכָל־הָעָם הַיִּלֹּדִים בַּמִּדְבָּר
בַּדֶּרֶךְ בְּצֵאתָם מִמִּצְרַיִם לֹא־מָלוּ׃ 6 כִּי ׀
אַרְבָּעִים שָׁנָה הָלְכוּ בְנֵי־יִשְׂרָאֵל בַּמִּדְבָּר
עַד־תֹּם כָּל־הַגּוֹי אַנְשֵׁי הַמִּלְחָמָה
הַיֹּצְאִים מִמִּצְרַיִם אֲשֶׁר לֹא־שָׁמְעוּ בְּקוֹל
יְהוָה אֲשֶׁר נִשְׁבַּע יְהוָה לָהֶם לְבִלְתִּי
הַרְאוֹתָם אֶת־הָאָרֶץ אֲשֶׁר נִשְׁבַּע יְהוָה
לַאֲבוֹתָם לָתֶת לָנוּ אֶרֶץ זָבַת חָלָב
וּדְבָשׁ׃ 7 וְאֶת־בְּנֵיהֶם הֵקִים תַּחְתָּם אֹתָם
מָל יְהוֹשֻׁעַ כִּי־עֲרֵלִים הָיוּ כִּי לֹא־מָלוּ
אוֹתָם בַּדָּרֶךְ׃ 8 וַיְהִי כַּאֲשֶׁר־תַּמּוּ כָל־
הַגּוֹי לְהִמּוֹל וַיֵּשְׁבוּ תַחְתָּם בַּמַּחֲנֶה עַד
חֲיוֹתָם׃ פ

9 וַיֹּאמֶר יְהוָה אֶל־יְהוֹשֻׁעַ הַיּוֹם גַּלּוֹתִי
אֶת־חֶרְפַּת מִצְרַיִם מֵעֲלֵיכֶם וַיִּקְרָא שֵׁם
הַמָּקוֹם הַהוּא גִּלְגָּל עַד הַיּוֹם הַזֶּה׃
10 וַיַּחֲנוּ בְנֵי־יִשְׂרָאֵל בַּגִּלְגָּל וַיַּעֲשׂוּ אֶת־
הַפֶּסַח בְּאַרְבָּעָה עָשָׂר יוֹם לַחֹדֶשׁ בָּעֶרֶב
בְּעַרְבוֹת יְרִיחוֹ׃
11 וַיֹּאכְלוּ מֵעֲבוּר הָאָרֶץ מִמָּחֳרַת הַפֶּסַח

4–7. No reason is given for delaying the ritual until this time. A rabbinic tradition suggests that it was postponed because of the hardships of the trek and the absence of a north wind (BT Yev. 71b–72a). Other opinions speculate on added features of the rite itself.

9. Part of a divine speech that explains the name of the shrine of Gilgal by popular etymology.

I have rolled away Hebrew: *galloti.*

disgrace of Egypt The nature of this disgrace—ended via circumcision—is unclear. Tradition reports that the males were already circumcised in Egypt and that those now circumcised were born after the Exodus (see Josh. 5:5). Moreover, extensive evidence (paintings, texts, mummified bodies) shows that the ancient Egyptians also performed this operation, although in a different way than the Israelites. Hence, the "disgrace" mentioned here may be the disgrace of the Egyptian bondage.

11. On the day after the passover offering Hebrew: *mi-maḥarat ha-pesaḥ.* In this context, it is clear that the new grain was eaten on the morning after the paschal meal. This verse is linked linguistically and legally to Lev. 23:10–14. Therefore, it would be reasonable to conclude that the idiom in Leviticus "on the day after the sabbath [*mi-maḥarat ha-shabbat*]" also refers to the day after the paschal meal.

that very day, they ate of the produce of the
country, unleavened bread and parched grain.
12On that same day, when they ate of the produce of the land, the manna ceased. The Israelites got no more manna; that year they ate of
the yield of the land of Canaan.

מַצּוֹת וְקָלוּי בְּעֶצֶם הַיּוֹם הַזֶּה׃ 12 וַיִּשְׁבֹּת
הַמָּן מִמָּחֳרָת בְּאָכְלָם מֵעֲבוּר הָאָרֶץ
וְלֹא־הָיָה עוֹד לִבְנֵי יִשְׂרָאֵל מָן וַיֹּאכְלוּ
מִתְּבוּאַת אֶרֶץ כְּנַעַן בַּשָּׁנָה הַהִיא׃ ס

13Once, when Joshua was near Jericho, he
looked up and saw a man standing before him,
drawn sword in hand. Joshua went up to him
and asked him, "Are you one of us or of our
enemies?" 14He replied, "No, I am captain of
the LORD's host. Now I have come!" Joshua
threw himself face down to the ground and,
prostrating himself, said to him, "What does my
lord command his servant?" 15The captain of
the LORD's host answered Joshua, "Remove
your sandals from your feet, for the place where
you stand is holy." And Joshua did so.

13 וַיְהִי בִּהְיוֹת יְהוֹשֻׁעַ בִּירִיחוֹ וַיִּשָּׂא עֵינָיו
וַיַּרְא וְהִנֵּה־אִישׁ עֹמֵד לְנֶגְדּוֹ וְחַרְבּוֹ
שְׁלוּפָה בְּיָדוֹ וַיֵּלֶךְ יְהוֹשֻׁעַ אֵלָיו וַיֹּאמֶר
לוֹ הֲלָנוּ אַתָּה אִם־לְצָרֵינוּ׃ 14 וַיֹּאמֶר ׀
לֹא כִּי אֲנִי שַׂר־צְבָא־יְהוָה עַתָּה בָאתִי
וַיִּפֹּל יְהוֹשֻׁעַ אֶל־פָּנָיו אַרְצָה וַיִּשְׁתָּחוּ
וַיֹּאמֶר לוֹ מָה אֲדֹנִי מְדַבֵּר אֶל־עַבְדּוֹ׃
15 וַיֹּאמֶר שַׂר־צְבָא יְהוָה אֶל־יְהוֹשֻׁעַ שַׁל־
נַעַלְךָ מֵעַל רַגְלֶךָ* כִּי הַמָּקוֹם אֲשֶׁר אַתָּה
עֹמֵד עָלָיו קֹדֶשׁ הוּא וַיַּעַשׂ יְהוֹשֻׁעַ כֵּן׃

6 Now Jericho was shut up tight because of
the Israelites; no one could leave or enter.

ו וִירִיחוֹ סֹגֶרֶת וּמְסֻגֶּרֶת מִפְּנֵי בְּנֵי
יִשְׂרָאֵל אֵין יוֹצֵא וְאֵין בָּא׃ ס

27The LORD was with Joshua, and his fame
spread throughout the land.

27 וַיְהִי יְהוָה אֶת־יְהוֹשֻׁעַ וַיְהִי שָׁמְעוֹ
בְּכָל־הָאָרֶץ׃

v. 15. חסר י׳

הפטרה לפסח (יום שני)

HAFTARAH FOR PESAḤ, SECOND DAY

2 KINGS 23:1–9,21–25

Life in the kingdom of Judah was affected by events elsewhere in the world. The kingdom of Babylon (under King Nabopolassar) rebelled against Assyria in 626 B.C.E. This began a series of struggles that led to the fall of Assyria in 614, and of Nineveh in 612. Because in the ancient world there was a close relationship between political freedom and national religious expression, one should not be surprised by the intriguing correlation between the fall of Assyria and the resurgence of religious reform in Judah. It may also explain a significant sequence of events during the time of King Josiah of Judah (639–609 B.C.E.).

According to 2 Chronicles, King Josiah underwent a religious awakening in the eighth year of his reign (631 B.C.E.). Four years later (627 B.C.E.) he began purifying the Temple by ridding it of pagan features. Six years after that (621 B.C.E.), in the course of subsequent Temple repairs, a "book of the Torah" was found (arguably Deuteronomy, or its core). This event led to a public renewal of the Covenant and a great *Pesaḥ* celebration for the entire nation (2 Chron. 34:1–35:19).

There is a different account of this in 2 Kings (chapter 23), which puts the work of repair and the discovery of the Torah scroll before the acts of purification. It thus presents the finding of the Torah scroll as the reason for the religious reform. Most modern scholars regard this version of the events as ideologically motivated to emphasize the role of "the book" in inspiring Josiah's pious enactment. By contrast, the account in Chronicles downplays the role of the book by linking the purification of worship to the report of Josiah's religious revival.

This *haftarah,* compared to the full historical presentations in Kings and Chronicles, is more concise. Thus it does not even mention the Temple repairs or the actual discovery of the book (related in 2 Kings 22). It specifies some of the acts of Temple purification (vv. 4–9), and concludes with a royal edict that *Pesaḥ* be celebrated as "prescribed" in the "scroll."

The *haftarah* begins with a national assembly, a public reading of the "covenant scroll," and a communal renewal of the Covenant. It then turns to the cultic purification program, involving pagan artifacts, priests from Jerusalem, and Israelite shrines in the countryside (with the eviction of their personnel to Jerusalem). It concludes with a national *Pesaḥ* and a summary of all the great events.

Each part of this sequence, initiated by the king, involves priestly and popular participation. Indeed, both the people and the king are said to have accepted God's covenant with all their heart and all their soul. This language is carefully chosen and evokes the great proclamation of the *Sh'ma* (Deut. 6:4–9), which calls on all Israelites to love God with all their heart and soul and might. This implies that now, in the days of Josiah, the people have committed themselves fully to that covenant, much as Moses had exhorted their ancestors to do before their entry into the Land.

The covenant ceremony at the outset of the *haftarah* and the *Pesaḥ* celebration at the end deserve special comment. This celebration of the Covenant was not only a public recitation of the divine teaching, reminiscent of Moses' proclamation of Deuteronomy itself before his death and of Ezra's reading of the Torah of Moses on the return from Babylonian exile (Neh. 8). It was the only time since Sinai that the whole nation publicly and collectively underwent a commitment to the divine covenant. Similarly, there had been nothing like the great *Pesaḥ* celebration (2 Kings 23:21–22) during the whole period of the judges and the kings. The first post-Exodus *Pesaḥ* event of such collective importance had occurred in the time of Joshua, immediately on entrance into the

Land (Josh. 5:10–11). The account of that event is recited as the *haftarah* for the first day of *Pesaḥ.*

RELATION OF THE *HAFTARAH* TO THE CALENDAR

By designating this *haftarah* for recitation on *Pesaḥ,* the Sages teach that the *Pesaḥ* liberation must be achieved and reconfirmed again and again. They also point out that its three central pillars are devotion to the Covenant, wholehearted commitment to God, and purging every sign of false or impure service from one's religious life.

23 At the king's summons, all the elders
of Judah and Jerusalem assembled before him.
2The king went up to the House of the LORD,
together with all the men of Judah and all the
inhabitants of Jerusalem, and the priests and
prophets—all the people, young and old. And
he read to them the entire text of the covenant
scroll which had been found in the House of
the LORD. 3The king stood by the pillar and solemnized the covenant before the LORD: that
they would follow the LORD and observe His
commandments, His injunctions, and His laws
with all their heart and soul; that they would
fulfill all the terms of this covenant as inscribed
upon the scroll. And all the people entered into
the covenant.
4Then the king ordered the high priest
Hilkiah, the priests of the second rank, and the
guards of the threshold to bring out of the Temple of the LORD all the objects made for Baal
and Asherah and all the host of heaven. He
burned them outside Jerusalem in the fields of
Kidron, and he removed the ashes to Bethel. 5He
suppressed the idolatrous priests whom the
kings of Judah had appointed to make offerings at the shrines in the towns of Judah and
in the environs of Jerusalem, and those who
made offerings to Baal, to the sun and moon

כג וַיִּשְׁלַח הַמֶּלֶךְ וַיַּאַסְפוּ אֵלָיו כָּל־
זִקְנֵי יְהוּדָה וִירוּשָׁלִָם׃ 2 וַיַּעַל הַמֶּלֶךְ
בֵּית־יְהוָה וְכָל־אִישׁ יְהוּדָה וְכָל־יֹשְׁבֵי
יְרוּשָׁלִַם אִתּוֹ וְהַכֹּהֲנִים וְהַנְּבִיאִים וְכָל־
הָעָם לְמִקָּטֹן וְעַד־גָּדוֹל וַיִּקְרָא בְאָזְנֵיהֶם
אֶת־כָּל־דִּבְרֵי סֵפֶר הַבְּרִית הַנִּמְצָא בְּבֵית
יְהוָה׃ 3 וַיַּעֲמֹד הַמֶּלֶךְ עַל־הָעַמּוּד וַיִּכְרֹת
אֶת־הַבְּרִית ׀ לִפְנֵי יְהוָה לָלֶכֶת אַחַר
יְהוָה וְלִשְׁמֹר מִצְוֺתָיו וְאֶת־עֵדְוֺתָיו וְאֶת־
חֻקֹּתָיו בְּכָל־לֵב וּבְכָל־נֶפֶשׁ לְהָקִים אֶת־
דִּבְרֵי הַבְּרִית הַזֹּאת הַכְּתֻבִים עַל־הַסֵּפֶר
הַזֶּה וַיַּעֲמֹד כָּל־הָעָם בַּבְּרִית׃
4 וַיְצַו הַמֶּלֶךְ אֶת־חִלְקִיָּהוּ הַכֹּהֵן הַגָּדוֹל
וְאֶת־כֹּהֲנֵי הַמִּשְׁנֶה וְאֶת־שֹׁמְרֵי הַסַּף
לְהוֹצִיא מֵהֵיכַל יְהוָה אֵת כָּל־הַכֵּלִים
הָעֲשׂוּיִם לַבַּעַל וְלָאֲשֵׁרָה וּלְכֹל צְבָא
הַשָּׁמָיִם וַיִּשְׂרְפֵם מִחוּץ לִירוּשָׁלִַם
בְּשַׁדְמוֹת קִדְרוֹן וְנָשָׂא אֶת־עֲפָרָם בֵּית־
אֵל׃ 5 וְהִשְׁבִּית אֶת־הַכְּמָרִים אֲשֶׁר נָתְנוּ
מַלְכֵי יְהוּדָה וַיְקַטֵּר בַּבָּמוֹת בְּעָרֵי יְהוּדָה
וּמְסִבֵּי יְרוּשָׁלִָם וְאֶת־הַמְקַטְּרִים לַבַּעַל
לַשֶּׁמֶשׁ וְלַיָּרֵחַ וְלַמַּזָּלוֹת וּלְכֹל צְבָא

2 Kings 23:2. The public reading before the whole nation echoes the private reading to Josiah of the scroll that was found (22:10–11). In the *haftarah,* the monarch himself performs the public recitation. The personal repentance of the king thus results in a national renewal of the Covenant.

the covenant scroll Hebrew: *seifer ha-b'rit* (cf. Exod. 24:7). It is also called "the scroll of the Teaching" (22:8,11). Many modern commentators assume that after the king heard the curses recorded in Deuteronomy, he responded by fulfilling its ritual prescriptions.

and constellations—all the host of heaven. [6]He brought out the [image of] Asherah from the House of the LORD to the Kidron Valley outside Jerusalem, and burned it in the Kidron Valley; he beat it to dust and scattered its dust over the burial ground of the common people. [7]He tore down the cubicles of the male prostitutes in the House of the LORD, at the place where the women wove coverings for Asherah.

[8]He brought all the priests from the towns of Judah [to Jerusalem] and defiled the shrines where the priests had been making offerings—from Geba to Beer-sheba. He also demolished the shrines of the gates, which were at the entrance of the gate of Joshua, the city prefect—which were on a person's left [upon entering] the city gate. [9]The priests of the shrines, however, did not ascend the altar of the LORD in Jerusalem, but they ate unleavened bread along with their kinsmen.

הַשָּׁמָיִם׃ 6 וַיֹּצֵא אֶת־הָאֲשֵׁרָה מִבֵּית יְהוָה
מִחוּץ לִירוּשָׁלַם אֶל־נַחַל קִדְרוֹן וַיִּשְׂרֹף
אֹתָהּ בְּנַחַל קִדְרוֹן וַיָּדֶק לְעָפָר וַיַּשְׁלֵךְ
אֶת־עֲפָרָהּ עַל־קֶבֶר בְּנֵי הָעָם׃ 7 וַיִּתֹּץ
אֶת־בָּתֵּי הַקְּדֵשִׁים אֲשֶׁר בְּבֵית יְהוָה אֲשֶׁר
הַנָּשִׁים אֹרְגוֹת שָׁם בָּתִּים לָאֲשֵׁרָה׃
8 וַיָּבֵא אֶת־כָּל־הַכֹּהֲנִים מֵעָרֵי יְהוּדָה
וַיְטַמֵּא אֶת־הַבָּמוֹת אֲשֶׁר קִטְּרוּ־שָׁמָּה
הַכֹּהֲנִים מִגֶּבַע עַד־בְּאֵר שָׁבַע וְנָתַץ אֶת־
בָּמוֹת הַשְּׁעָרִים אֲשֶׁר־פֶּתַח שַׁעַר יְהוֹשֻׁעַ
שַׂר־הָעִיר אֲשֶׁר־עַל־שְׂמֹאול* אִישׁ בְּשַׁעַר
הָעִיר׃ 9 אַךְ לֹא יַעֲלוּ כֹּהֲנֵי הַבָּמוֹת
אֶל־מִזְבַּח יְהוָה בִּירוּשָׁלָם כִּי אִם־אָכְלוּ
מַצּוֹת בְּתוֹךְ אֲחֵיהֶם׃

[21]The king commanded all the people, "Offer the passover sacrifice to the LORD your God as prescribed in this scroll of the covenant." [22]Now the passover sacrifice had not been offered in that manner in the days of the chieftains who ruled Israel, or during the days of the kings of Israel and the kings of Judah. [23]Only in the eighteenth year of King Josiah was such a passover sacrifice offered in that manner to the LORD in Jerusalem. [24]Josiah also did away with the necromancers and the mediums, the idols and the fetishes—all the detestable things that were to be seen in the land of Judah and Jerusalem. Thus he fulfilled the terms of the Teaching re-

21 וַיְצַו הַמֶּלֶךְ אֶת־כָּל־הָעָם לֵאמֹר עֲשׂוּ
פֶּסַח לַיהוָה אֱלֹהֵיכֶם כַּכָּתוּב עַל סֵפֶר
הַבְּרִית הַזֶּה׃ 22 כִּי לֹא נַעֲשָׂה כַּפֶּסַח הַזֶּה
מִימֵי הַשֹּׁפְטִים אֲשֶׁר שָׁפְטוּ אֶת־יִשְׂרָאֵל
וְכֹל יְמֵי מַלְכֵי יִשְׂרָאֵל וּמַלְכֵי יְהוּדָה׃
23 כִּי אִם־בִּשְׁמֹנֶה עֶשְׂרֵה שָׁנָה לַמֶּלֶךְ
יֹאשִׁיָּהוּ נַעֲשָׂה הַפֶּסַח הַזֶּה לַיהוָה
בִּירוּשָׁלָם׃ 24 וְגַם אֶת־הָאֹבוֹת וְאֶת־
הַיִּדְּעֹנִים וְאֶת־הַתְּרָפִים וְאֶת־הַגִּלֻּלִים
וְאֵת כָּל־הַשִּׁקֻּצִים אֲשֶׁר נִרְאוּ בְּאֶרֶץ
יְהוּדָה וּבִירוּשָׁלַם בִּעֵר יֹאשִׁיָּהוּ לְמַעַן
הָקִים אֶת־דִּבְרֵי הַתּוֹרָה הַכְּתֻבִים עַל־

v. 8. מלא ו׳

6. The specific verbs used to mark Josiah's destruction of the idols ("burned" and "beat to dust") may intentionally allude to the very same acts performed by Moses when he destroyed the Golden Calf (Exod. 32:20). Josiah would thus function as a new Moses, a role fully consonant with his depiction as one wholeheartedly devoted to the Teaching of Moses (see 2 Kings 23:25).

21–23. This passage resumes the narrative of the opening verses (vv. 1–3), after the description of the cultic reforms in Judah (vv. 4–14) and Samaria (vv. 15–20). The defilement of local Israelite shrines (v. 8) meant that the only legitimate place for the festival sacrifice now was Jerusalem. This fulfilled the instruction in Deut. 16:5–6 limiting the sacrifice to "the place where the LORD your God will choose to establish His name."

corded in the scroll that the priest Hilkiah had found in the House of the LORD. 25There was no king like him before who turned back to the LORD with all his heart and soul and might, in full accord with the Teaching of Moses; nor did any like him arise after him.

הַסֵּ֔פֶר אֲשֶׁ֥ר מָצָ֛א חִלְקִיָּ֥הוּ הַכֹּהֵ֖ן בֵּ֥ית
יְהֹוָֽה׃ 25 וְכָמֹהוּ֩ לֹֽא־הָיָ֨ה לְפָנָ֜יו מֶ֗לֶךְ
אֲשֶׁר־שָׁ֣ב אֶל־יְהֹוָ֗ה בְּכָל־לְבָב֤וֹ וּבְכָל־
נַפְשׁוֹ֙ וּבְכָל־מְאֹד֔וֹ כְּכֹ֖ל תּוֹרַ֣ת מֹשֶׁ֑ה
וְאַחֲרָ֖יו לֹֽא־קָ֥ם כָּמֹֽהוּ׃

הפטרה לשבת חול המועד פסח

HAFTARAH FOR PESAḤ, INTERMEDIATE SHABBAT

EZEKIEL 37:1–14

The promises of national regeneration and repopulation and of a revival of the people's life and spirit from the doom of exile form the focus of this *haftarah.* Thus, it could be dated sometime after 597 B.C.E., when the first contingent of Judeans, including Ezekiel, was deported to Babylon (see 2 Kings 24:8–16; Ezek. 1:1–2).

Two images give the prophecy a dramatic focus. First is that of sheep, whose multitudes in Jerusalem represent the promise of great demographic growth. The other image is the famous figure of dry bones, whose envisaged resurrection and embodiment offer the promise of new national life. God's work of salvation is underscored in both images by use of the verb understood here as "to act" (*asah,* Ezek. 37:14). The climax of this redemption is God's return of the people to their homeland (37:13–14). This new exodus from exile is announced for the future. The recollection of the Egyptian Exodus during *Pesaḥ* quickens this hope.

"The hand of the LORD came upon me," the sentence at the beginning of chapter 37, should be understood as introducing a trancelike experience, just as it is to be understood elsewhere in the book (see 1:3ff., 3:12ff., 8:1ff., 40:1ff.). The spectacle reported by Ezekiel is his memory of an ecstatic vision, shared with the people to generate hope in God's acts of redemption to come. In a talmudic discussion about resurrection, Judah judged the content of Ezekiel's vision to be "really only a parable," a view opposed by Eliezer, who regarded the events depicted to be literally true (BT Sanh. 92b). This division of opinion continued in the following centuries.

RELATION OF THE *HAFTARAH* TO THE CALENDAR

The reason why Ezekiel's vision of resurrection was chosen for reading on *Pesaḥ* is somewhat obscure. Rashi offers a terse remark that "they came out of Egypt before the (set) time," apparently implying that the resurrected bones were those of Israelites from the time of the Exodus. His point is fleshed out by an Aramaic Targum in which we are told that the bones belonged to those Ephraimites who, according to an old rabbinic tradition, left Egypt before the proper time owing to a miscalculation of how long their bondage was to last (BT Sanh. 92b). These individuals, killed on their way out of Egypt by the Philistines, are now revived as a sign of the future resurrection.

Another reason for reading Ezek. 37:1–14 focuses on the resurrection motif itself, rather than on the identification of the people involved. There is a striking Jewish tradition that the patriarch Isaac was bound on the altar at the *Pesaḥ* season (see Jubilees 18:18–19; Exod. R. 15:11). In this tradition, divine dewdrops revived him when he died on the altar "in the grip of fear" (Mid. Lekaḥ Tov, Gen. 31:42) or upon being sacrificed (*Shibbolei Ha-Leket* 9a–b). Connecting springtime, (sacrificial) offerings, and resurrection is an ancient theme in the history of religions. The conjunction of this complex of motifs with one classic Jewish theme (the binding of Isaac) may explain why the *haftarah* about resurrection is recited at the onset of springtime, at precisely the season when the prayer for dew (associated with fertility and resurrection) is chanted (beginning at the *Musaf* service on the first day of *Pesaḥ*). Also, the intermediate *Shabbat* of *Pesaḥ* is the time when the Song of Songs, with its springtime associations, is publicly recited. Recitation of the promise of resurrection during *Pesaḥ* thus preserves and perpetuates a timeless association between earthly and human rebirth.

37

The hand of the Lord came upon me. He took me out by the spirit of the Lord and set me down in the valley. It was full of bones. [2]He led me all around them; there were very many of them spread over the valley, and they were very dry. [3]He said to me, "O mortal, can these bones live again?" I replied, "O Lord God, only You know." [4]And He said to me, "Prophesy over these bones and say to them: O dry bones, hear the word of the Lord! [5]Thus said the Lord God to these bones: I will cause breath to enter you and you shall live again. [6]I will lay sinews upon you, and cover you with flesh, and form skin over you. And I will put breath into you, and you shall live again. And you shall know that I am the Lord!"

[7]I prophesied as I had been commanded. And while I was prophesying, suddenly there was a sound of rattling, and the bones came together, bone to matching bone. [8]I looked, and there were sinews on them, and flesh had grown, and skin had formed over them; but there was no breath in them. [9]Then He said to me, "Prophesy to the breath, prophesy, O mortal! Say to the breath: Thus said the Lord God: Come, O breath, from the four winds, and breathe into these slain, that they may live again." [10]I prophesied as He commanded me. The breath entered them, and they came to life and stood up on their feet, a vast multitude.

[11]And He said to me, "O mortal, these bones are the whole House of Israel. They say, 'Our

לֹז הָיְתָה עָלַי֙ יַד־יְהֹוָה֙ וַיּוֹצִאֵ֤נִי בְר֙וּחַ
יְהֹוָ֔ה וַיְנִיחֵ֖נִי בְּת֣וֹךְ הַבִּקְעָ֑ה וְהִ֖יא מְלֵאָ֥ה
עֲצָמֽוֹת׃ 2 וְהֶעֱבִירַ֥נִי עֲלֵיהֶ֖ם סָבִ֣יב ׀ סָבִ֑יב
וְהִנֵּ֨ה רַבּ֤וֹת מְאֹד֙ עַל־פְּנֵ֣י הַבִּקְעָ֔ה וְהִנֵּ֖ה
יְבֵשׁ֥וֹת מְאֹֽד׃ 3 וַיֹּ֣אמֶר אֵלַ֔י בֶּן־אָדָ֕ם
הֲתִֽחְיֶ֖ינָה הָעֲצָמ֣וֹת הָאֵ֑לֶּה וָאֹמַ֕ר אֲדֹנָ֥י
יְהֹוִ֖ה אַתָּ֥ה יָדָֽעְתָּ׃ 4 וַיֹּ֣אמֶר אֵלַ֗י הִנָּבֵ֛א
עַל־הָעֲצָמ֥וֹת הָאֵ֖לֶּה וְאָמַרְתָּ֣ אֲלֵיהֶ֑ם
הָעֲצָמוֹת֙ הַיְבֵשׁ֔וֹת שִׁמְע֖וּ דְּבַר־יְהֹוָֽה׃
5 כֹּ֤ה אָמַר֙ אֲדֹנָ֣י יְהֹוִ֔ה לָעֲצָמ֖וֹת הָאֵ֑לֶּה
הִנֵּ֨ה אֲנִ֜י מֵבִ֥יא בָכֶ֛ם ר֖וּחַ וִחְיִיתֶֽם׃
6 וְנָתַתִּי֩ עֲלֵיכֶ֨ם גִּדִ֜ים וְהַֽעֲלֵתִ֧י עֲלֵיכֶ֣ם
בָּשָׂ֗ר וְקָרַמְתִּ֤י עֲלֵיכֶם֙ ע֔וֹר וְנָתַתִּ֥י בָכֶ֛ם
ר֖וּחַ וִחְיִיתֶ֑ם וִידַעְתֶּ֖ם כִּֽי־אֲנִ֥י יְהֹוָֽה׃
7 וְנִבֵּ֖אתִי כַּֽאֲשֶׁ֣ר צֻוֵּ֑יתִי וַיְהִי־ק֤וֹל כְּהִנָּֽבְאִי֙
וְהִנֵּה־רַ֔עַשׁ וַתִּקְרְב֣וּ עֲצָמ֔וֹת עֶ֖צֶם אֶל־
עַצְמֽוֹ׃ 8 וְרָאִ֜יתִי וְהִנֵּֽה־עֲלֵיהֶ֤ם גִּדִים֙
וּבָשָׂ֣ר עָלָ֔ה וַיִּקְרַ֧ם עֲלֵיהֶ֛ם ע֖וֹר מִלְמָ֑עְלָה
וְר֖וּחַ אֵ֥ין בָּהֶֽם׃ 9 וַיֹּ֣אמֶר אֵלַ֔י הִנָּבֵ֖א
אֶל־הָר֑וּחַ הִנָּבֵ֣א בֶן־אָדָם֒ וְאָמַרְתָּ֣ אֶל־
הָר֗וּחַ כֹּֽה־אָמַ֣ר ׀ אֲדֹנָ֣י יְהֹוִ֗ה מֵאַרְבַּ֤ע
רוּח֙וֹת בֹּ֣אִי הָר֔וּחַ וּפְחִ֛י בַּֽהֲרוּגִ֥ים הָאֵ֖לֶּה
וְיִֽחְיֽוּ׃ 10 וְהִנַּבֵּ֙אתִי֙ כַּֽאֲשֶׁ֣ר צִוָּ֔נִי וַתָּב֩וֹא
בָהֶ֨ם הָר֜וּחַ וַֽיִּחְי֗וּ וַיַּֽעַמְדוּ֙ עַל־רַגְלֵיהֶ֔ם
חַ֖יִל גָּד֥וֹל מְאֹד־מְאֹֽד׃ ס
11 וַיֹּ֣אמֶר אֵלַ֗י בֶּן־אָדָם֙ הָעֲצָמ֣וֹת הָאֵ֔לֶּה
כׇּל־בֵּ֥ית יִשְׂרָאֵ֖ל הֵ֑מָּה הִנֵּ֣ה אֹֽמְרִים֮

Ezekiel 37:1. The hand of the Lord came upon me   A characteristic expression for overwhelming prophetic inspiration in the Book of Ezekiel (1:3, 3:14, 8:1, 40:1); it is also found elsewhere (e.g., Isa. 8:11).

spirit   Hebrew: *ru·aḥ*, generally translated as "wind" except in the Book of Ezekiel. In this verse, it is the "spirit of prophecy" (see Targum to 37:1). Elsewhere in Ezekiel, it is the "spirit of the Lord" (11:5) or "of God" (11:11,24).

3. only You know   This should be supplemented with "for You created them" (Eliezer of Beaugency).

5–10.   The rebirth imagery is but one of the images Ezekiel uses to prophesy national renewal. In an earlier oracle, the nation is promised "a new heart and a new spirit" for the time of their resettlement in the Land (Ezek. 36:26–28).

bones are dried up, our hope is gone; we are
doomed.' 12Prophesy, therefore, and say to
them: Thus said the Lord God: I am going to
open your graves and lift you out of the graves,
O My people, and bring you to the land of Israel.
13You shall know, O My people, that I am the
Lord, when I have opened your graves and
lifted you out of your graves. 14I will put My
breath into you and you shall live again, and I
will set you upon your own soil. Then you shall
know that I the Lord have spoken and have
acted"—declares the Lord.

יָבְשׁ֥וּ עַצְמוֹתֵ֛ינוּ וְאָבְדָ֥ה תִקְוָתֵ֖נוּ נִגְזַ֥רְנוּ
לָֽנוּ׃ 12 לָכֵ֞ן הִנָּבֵ֣א וְאָמַרְתָּ֣ אֲלֵיהֶ֗ם כֹּֽה־
אָמַר֮ אֲדֹנָ֣י יְהֹוִה֒ הִנֵּ֨ה אֲנִ֜י פֹתֵ֣חַ אֶת־
קִבְרֽוֹתֵיכֶ֗ם וְהַעֲלֵיתִ֥י אֶתְכֶ֛ם מִקִּבְרוֹתֵיכֶ֖ם
עַמִּ֑י וְהֵבֵאתִ֥י אֶתְכֶ֖ם אֶל־אַדְמַ֥ת
יִשְׂרָאֵֽל׃ ס 13 וִֽידַעְתֶּ֖ם כִּֽי־אֲנִ֣י יְהֹוָ֑ה
בְּפִתְחִ֣י אֶת־קִבְרֽוֹתֵיכֶ֗ם וּבְהַעֲלוֹתִ֥י אֶתְכֶ֛ם
מִקִּבְרוֹתֵיכֶ֖ם עַמִּֽי׃ 14 וְנָתַתִּ֨י רוּחִ֤י בָכֶם֙
וִחְיִיתֶ֔ם וְהִנַּחְתִּ֥י אֶתְכֶ֖ם עַל־אַדְמַתְכֶ֑ם
וִֽידַעְתֶּ֞ם כִּֽי־אֲנִ֧י יְהֹוָ֛ה דִּבַּ֥רְתִּי וְעָשִׂ֖יתִי
נְאֻם־יְהֹוָֽה׃ פ

14. I the Lord have spoken and have acted As a result of national restoration, the nation will "know" that the Lord fulfills prophecies, i.e., that God is trustworthy and effective.

הפטרה לפסח (יום שביעי)

HAFTARAH FOR PESAḤ, SEVENTH DAY

2 SAMUEL 22:1–51

This *haftarah* presents David's great hymn of victory and thanksgiving, sung to God "after the LORD had saved him from the hands of all his enemies and from the hands of Saul" (2 Sam. 22:1). The designation "after" also connotes "after living a full life," for the hymn appears in Samuel just before David's "last words." In the hymn, in a grand and celebratory manner, a military hero thanks God for the lifetime of protection and favor he has received. Not surprisingly, God is portrayed here as a Lord of battles—storming down with heavenly arrows, to the aid of human armies. Meanwhile, the hymn expresses a deeper religious spirit, with theological features found in other biblical prayers. (With minor textual variations, it also appears in Ps. 18.)

Of the terms used in the *haftarah* for God's invincible protection, none stands out as much as *tzur* (rock). It recurs in neutral designations of God as a sheltering rock (v. 3) and source of personal safety (v. 47). Even more striking are uses of the term as an epithet for God. "Who is a rock except God?" asks David (v. 32), and he offers praise with the words, "Exalted be God, the rock" (v. 47). Steadfast mountain rocks offered a metaphor for inviolable stability, eternity, and great geologic forces erupting heavenward. (In the shadow of great rocks, who cannot feel something of God's everlasting power?)

The image of God as an earthly *tzur* stands at one pole of the hymn, tracing a line that rises toward the heights. At the other pole is the image of God's descent on the wings of storm clouds to save His people on earth. This figure is atmospheric, derived from ancient Near Eastern depictions of storm gods riding to battle in heavenly chariots. The cosmic arsenal includes swirling blasts of wind that stir the depths and "expose" the "bed of the sea" (v. 16), fiery bolts that furiously fly like arrows out of dark thunderheads (vv. 10–12,15), and awesome peals of thunder that bark out in an earth-shattering divine voice (v. 14). Just so, the Lord had rescued His people at the Sea of Reeds (Exod. 15:8,19); and David's hymn excels in these depictions. Their dramatic vitality contrasts sharply with the scene of stability established by the mountain rocks at the beginning of the hymn. These images derive from different poles of the religious imagination. Their fusion in this song induces visceral tension in response to the vastness of God's celebrated power.

Meanwhile, in verses 22–28, the language of theological confession is featured. It reinforces the connection between a general theology of reward and punishment and its specific manifestation in David's life, in accordance with his merit (v. 25). Echoing this passage, David concludes his thanksgiving with the overall statement that "The way of God is perfect [*tamim*]" and then declares, more personally, that God has "kept my path secure [*tamim*]" (vv. 31,33).

The concluding verse of the *haftarah* (22:51) looks to the future, hoping for the beneficence of God on all of David's heirs. With the passage of time, the term for God's "anointed one" (*m'shiḥo*), once reserved for David's offspring who would restore the royal line, came to connote the messiah figure (*mashi·aḥ*) expected in the end of days. Presumably the rabbinic circles who selected this hymn as a *haftarah* had this hope in mind.

RELATION OF THE *HAFTARAH* TO THE CALENDAR

The song of Moses in the Torah reading (Exod. 15) and David's song of thanksgiving in the *haftarah* are both dramatic accounts of God's saving providence in history. Reciting the Song of the Sea on the seventh day of *Pesaḥ* is based on the tradition that the miracle of the waters occurred on that day. The songs of Moses and of David represent two classic moments in the sacred his-

tory of the people Israel that serve as models for the future. From this perspective, it was only natural to expect that succeeding layers of that history would include references to earlier acts of divine redemption. This layering of memory is an essential feature of Jewish cultural consciousness and its ongoing self-identity. Recitation of these events in the synagogue transfers them to new generations, deepening the shared past and its central images.

22 David addressed the words of this song
to the LORD, after the LORD had saved him from
the hands of all his enemies and from the hands
of Saul. 2He said:

O LORD, my crag, my fastness, my deliverer!
3O God, the rock wherein I take shelter:
My shield, my mighty champion, my fortress and refuge!
My savior, You who rescue me from violence!

4All praise! I called on the LORD,
And I was delivered from my enemies.

5For the breakers of Death encompassed me,
The torrents of Belial terrified me;
6The snares of Sheol encircled me,
The coils of Death engulfed me.

7In my anguish I called on the LORD,
Cried out to my God;
In His Abode He heard my voice,
My cry entered His ears.
8Then the earth rocked and quaked,
The foundations of heaven shook—
Rocked by His indignation.
9Smoke went up from His nostrils,
From His mouth came devouring fire;
Live coals blazed forth from Him.

כב *וַיְדַבֵּ֤ר דָּוִד֙ לַֽיהוָ֔ה אֶת־דִּבְרֵ֖י
הַשִּׁירָ֣ה הַזֹּ֑את בְּי֞וֹם הִצִּ֨יל יְהוָ֥ה אֹת֛וֹ
מִכַּ֥ף כָּל־אֹיְבָ֖יו וּמִכַּ֥ף שָׁאֽוּל׃ 2 וַיֹּאמַ֑ר

יְהוָ֛ה סַֽלְעִ֥י וּמְצֻדָתִ֖י וּמְפַלְטִי־לִֽי׃
3 אֱלֹהֵ֥י צוּרִ֖י אֶֽחֱסֶה־בּ֑וֹ
מָֽגִנִּי֙ וְקֶ֣רֶן יִשְׁעִ֔י מִשְׂגַּבִּי֙ וּמְנוּסִ֔י
מֹשִׁעִ֕י מֵחָמָ֖ס תֹּשִׁעֵֽנִי׃

4 מְהֻלָּ֖ל אֶקְרָ֣א יְהוָ֑ה
וּמֵאֹיְבַ֖י אִוָּשֵֽׁעַ׃

5 כִּ֥י אֲפָפֻ֖נִי מִשְׁבְּרֵי־מָ֑וֶת
נַחֲלֵ֥י בְלִיַּ֖עַל יְבַעֲתֻֽנִי׃
6 חֶבְלֵ֥י שְׁא֖וֹל סַבֻּ֑נִי
קִדְּמֻ֖נִי מֹֽקְשֵׁי־מָֽוֶת׃

7 בַּצַּר־לִי֙ אֶקְרָ֣א יְהוָ֔ה
וְאֶל־אֱלֹהַ֖י אֶקְרָ֑א
וַיִּשְׁמַ֤ע מֵהֵֽיכָלוֹ֙ קוֹלִ֔י
וְשַׁוְעָתִ֖י בְּאָזְנָֽיו׃
8 ותגעש וַיִּתְגָּעַ֤שׁ וַתִּרְעַשׁ֙ הָאָ֔רֶץ
מוֹסְד֥וֹת הַשָּׁמַ֖יִם יִרְגָּ֑זוּ
וַיִּֽתְגָּעֲשׁ֖וּ כִּי־חָ֥רָה לֽוֹ׃
9 עָלָ֤ה עָשָׁן֙ בְּאַפּ֔וֹ
וְאֵ֥שׁ מִפִּ֖יו תֹּאכֵ֑ל
גֶּחָלִ֖ים בָּעֲר֥וּ מִמֶּֽנּוּ׃

v. 1. בכתב היד שלנו כתוב בצורת שירה

2 Samuel 22:5–6. Flood imagery ("breakers," "torrents") combines with figures of hunting ("snares," "coils"—that is, traps) to express the speaker's sense of overpowering and hidden dangers. The figure of Death (*mavet*) in verses 5 and 6 retains a personified quality, echoing the ancient Canaanite god Mot (death).

Death . . . Belial . . . Sheol Three names for the netherworld.

[10]He bent the sky and came down,
Thick cloud beneath His feet.
[11]He mounted a cherub and flew;
He was seen on the wings of the wind.
[12]He made pavilions of darkness about Him,
Dripping clouds, huge thunderheads;
[13]In the brilliance before Him
Blazed fiery coals.
[14]The LORD thundered forth from heaven,
The Most High sent forth His voice;
[15]He let loose bolts, and scattered them;
Lightning, and put them to rout.
[16]The bed of the sea was exposed,
The foundations of the world were laid bare
By the mighty roaring of the LORD,
At the blast of the breath of His nostrils.
[17]He reached down from on high, He took me,
Drew me out of the mighty waters;
[18]He rescued me from my enemy so strong,
From foes too mighty for me.
[19]They attacked me on my day of calamity,
But the LORD was my stay.
[20]He brought me out to freedom,
He rescued me because He was pleased with me.
[21]The LORD rewarded me according to my merit,
He requited the cleanness of my hands.

[22]For I have kept the ways of the LORD
And have not been guilty before my God;
[23]I am mindful of all His rules
And have not departed from His laws.
[24]I have been blameless before Him,
And have guarded myself against sinning—
[25]And the LORD has requited my merit,
According to my purity in His sight.

10 וַיֵּט שָׁמַיִם וַיֵּרַד
וַעֲרָפֶל תַּחַת רַגְלָיו׃
11 וַיִּרְכַּב עַל־כְּרוּב וַיָּעֹף
וַיֵּרָא עַל־כַּנְפֵי־רוּחַ׃
12 וַיָּשֶׁת חֹשֶׁךְ סְבִיבֹתָיו סֻכּוֹת
חַשְׁרַת־מַיִם עָבֵי שְׁחָקִים׃
13 מִנֹּגַהּ נֶגְדּוֹ
בָּעֲרוּ גַּחֲלֵי־אֵשׁ׃
14 יַרְעֵם מִן־שָׁמַיִם יְהוָה
וְעֶלְיוֹן יִתֵּן קוֹלוֹ׃
15 וַיִּשְׁלַח חִצִּים וַיְפִיצֵם
בָּרָק ויהמם וַיָּהֹם׃
16 וַיֵּרָאוּ אֲפִקֵי יָם
יִגָּלוּ מֹסְדוֹת תֵּבֵל
בְּגַעֲרַת יְהוָה
מִנִּשְׁמַת רוּחַ אַפּוֹ׃
17 יִשְׁלַח מִמָּרוֹם יִקָּחֵנִי
יַמְשֵׁנִי מִמַּיִם רַבִּים׃
18 יַצִּילֵנִי מֵאֹיְבִי עָז
מִשֹּׂנְאַי כִּי אָמְצוּ מִמֶּנִּי׃
19 יְקַדְּמֻנִי בְּיוֹם אֵידִי
וַיְהִי יְהוָה מִשְׁעָן לִי׃
20 וַיֹּצֵא לַמֶּרְחָב אֹתִי
יְחַלְּצֵנִי כִּי־חָפֵץ בִּי׃
21 יִגְמְלֵנִי יְהוָה כְּצִדְקָתִי
כְּבֹר יָדַי יָשִׁיב לִי׃

22 כִּי שָׁמַרְתִּי דַּרְכֵי יְהוָה
וְלֹא רָשַׁעְתִּי מֵאֱלֹהָי׃
23 כִּי כָל־משפטו מִשְׁפָּטָיו לְנֶגְדִּי
וְחֻקֹּתָיו לֹא־אָסוּר מִמֶּנָּה׃
24 וָאֶהְיֶה תָמִים לוֹ
וָאֶשְׁתַּמְּרָה מֵעֲוֹנִי׃
25 וַיָּשֶׁב יְהוָה לִי כְּצִדְקָתִי
כְּבֹרִי לְנֶגֶד עֵינָיו׃

11. He was seen Hebrew: *va-yera.* The version in Ps. 18:11 has the similar-looking word *va-yeide* (He was gliding /swooping)—more appropriate to the atmospheric figures used here.

26With the loyal You deal loyally;
With the blameless hero, blamelessly.
27With the pure You act in purity,
And with the perverse You are wily.
28To humble folk You give victory,
And You look with scorn on the haughty.

29You, O LORD, are my lamp;
The LORD lights up my darkness.
30With You, I can rush a barrier,
With my God, I can scale a wall.
31The way of God is perfect,
The word of the LORD is pure.
He is a shield to all who take refuge in Him.
32Yea, who is a god except the LORD,
Who is a rock except God—
33The God, my mighty stronghold,
Who kept my path secure;
34Who made my legs like a deer's,
And set me firm on the heights;
35Who trained my hands for battle,
So that my arms can bend a bow of bronze!
36You have granted me the shield of Your protection
And Your providence has made me great.
37You have let me stride on freely,
And my feet have not slipped.
38I pursued my enemies and wiped them out,
I did not turn back till I destroyed them.
39I destroyed them, I struck them down;
They rose no more, they lay at my feet.
40You have girt me with strength for battle,

26 עִם־חָסִיד תִּתְחַסָּד
עִם־גִּבּוֹר תָּמִים תִּתַּמָּם׃
27 עִם־נָבָר תִּתָּבָר
וְעִם־עִקֵּשׁ תִּתַּפָּל׃
28 וְאֶת־עַם עָנִי תּוֹשִׁיעַ
וְעֵינֶיךָ עַל־רָמִים תַּשְׁפִּיל׃

29 כִּי־אַתָּה נֵירִי יְהוָה
וַיהוָה יַגִּיהַּ חָשְׁכִּי׃
30 כִּי בְכָה* אָרוּץ גְּדוּד
בֵּאלֹהַי אֲדַלֶּג־שׁוּר׃
31 הָאֵל תָּמִים דַּרְכּוֹ
אִמְרַת יְהוָה צְרוּפָה
מָגֵן הוּא לְכֹל הַחֹסִים בּוֹ׃
32 כִּי מִי־אֵל מִבַּלְעֲדֵי יְהוָה
וּמִי צוּר מִבַּלְעֲדֵי אֱלֹהֵינוּ׃
33 הָאֵל מָעוּזִּי חָיִל
וַיַּתֵּר תָּמִים דרכו דַּרְכִּי׃
34 מְשַׁוֶּה רגליו רַגְלַי כָּאַיָּלוֹת
וְעַל בָּמוֹתַי יַעֲמִדֵנִי׃
35 מְלַמֵּד יָדַי לַמִּלְחָמָה
וְנִחַת קֶשֶׁת־נְחוּשָׁה זְרֹעֹתָי׃
36 וַתִּתֶּן־לִי מָגֵן יִשְׁעֶךָ
וַעֲנֹתְךָ תַּרְבֵּנִי׃
37 תַּרְחִיב צַעֲדִי תַּחְתֵּנִי
וְלֹא מָעֲדוּ קַרְסֻלָּי׃
38 אֶרְדְּפָה אֹיְבַי וָאַשְׁמִידֵם
וְלֹא אָשׁוּב עַד־כַּלּוֹתָם׃
39 וָאֲכַלֵּם וָאֶמְחָצֵם
וְלֹא יְקוּמוּן וַיִּפְּלוּ תַּחַת רַגְלָי׃
40 וַתַּזְרֵנִי* חַיִל לַמִּלְחָמָה

v. 30. יתיר ה׳
v. 40. חסר א׳

36. And Your providence has made me great The Hebrew (*va-anot'kha tarbeini*) is difficult, literally yielding something like "and Your answer [to my prayer] has raised me." Psalms 18:36 reads here "and Your humility has raised me" (*v'anvatkha tarbeini*). The problem is resolved by a preferred reading (*azart'kha tarbeini*), which means "Your help [or: valor]" has raised me, found in the Qumran ("Dead Sea") scrolls.

Brought low my foes before me,
41Made my enemies turn tail before me,
My foes—and I wiped them out.
42They looked, but there was none to deliver;
To the LORD, but He answered them not.
43I pounded them like dust of the earth,
Stamped, crushed them like dirt of the streets.
44You have rescued me from the strife of peoples,
Kept me to be a ruler of nations;
Peoples I knew not must serve me.
45Aliens have cringed before me,
Paid me homage at the mere report of me.
46Aliens have lost courage
And come trembling out of their fastnesses.

47The LORD lives! Blessed is my rock!
Exalted be God, the rock
Who gives me victory;
48The God who has vindicated me
And made peoples subject to me,
49Rescued me from my enemies,
Raised me clear of my foes,
Saved me from lawless men!
50For this I sing Your praise among the nations
And hymn Your name:
51Tower of victory to His king,
Who deals graciously with His anointed,
With David and his offspring evermore.

תַּכְרִיעַ קָמַי תַּחְתֵּנִי׃
41 וְאֹיְבַי תַּתָּה לִּי עֹרֶף
מְשַׂנְאַי וָאַצְמִיתֵם׃
42 יִשְׁעוּ וְאֵין מֹשִׁיעַ
אֶל־יְהוָה וְלֹא עָנָם׃
43 וְאֶשְׁחָקֵם כַּעֲפַר־אָרֶץ
כְּטִיט־חוּצוֹת אֲדִקֵּם אֶרְקָעֵם׃
44 וַתְּפַלְּטֵנִי מֵרִיבֵי עַמִּי*
תִּשְׁמְרֵנִי לְרֹאשׁ גּוֹיִם
עַם לֹא־יָדַעְתִּי יַעַבְדֻנִי׃
45 בְּנֵי נֵכָר יִתְכַּחֲשׁוּ־לִי
לִשְׁמוֹעַ אֹזֶן יִשָּׁמְעוּ לִי׃
46 בְּנֵי נֵכָר יִבֹּלוּ
וְיַחְגְּרוּ מִמִּסְגְּרוֹתָם׃

47 חַי־יְהוָה וּבָרוּךְ צוּרִי
וְיָרֻם אֱלֹהֵי צוּר
יִשְׁעִי׃
48 הָאֵל הַנֹּתֵן נְקָמֹת לִי
וּמוֹרִיד עַמִּים תַּחְתֵּנִי׃
49 וּמוֹצִיאִי מֵאֹיְבָי
וּמִקָּמַי תְּרוֹמְמֵנִי
מֵאִישׁ חֲמָסִים תַּצִּילֵנִי׃
50 עַל־כֵּן אוֹדְךָ יְהוָה בַּגּוֹיִם
וּלְשִׁמְךָ אֲזַמֵּר׃
51 מגדיל מִגְדּוֹל יְשׁוּעוֹת מַלְכּוֹ
וְעֹשֶׂה־חֶסֶד לִמְשִׁיחוֹ
לְדָוִד וּלְזַרְעוֹ עַד־עוֹלָם׃ פ

v. 44. סבירין ומטעין "עמים", ובנוסח אחר "עם" וגם בנוסח אחר "עמים"

44. peoples Translated per the reading in some manuscripts and in the Septuagint. The Hebrew text above, like most manuscripts and the printed editions, reads "my people" [Transl.].

51. Tower of victory Hebrew: *migdol y'shu·ot.* As usual, this translation follows the text as read (*k'rei*). Meanwhile, the text as written (*k'tiv*) preserves the first word as a verb, *magdil,* yielding "He accords wondrous victories" (as in Ps. 18:51). The image of God as a tower is not out of keeping with the song, yet here a verb better matches the next part of the verse.

Both the *k'rei* and the *k'tiv* versions are preserved liturgically, at the close of the full grace after meals. The *k'tiv* is recited on weekdays; the *k'rei,* on *Shabbat* and festivals.

הפטרה לפסח (יום שמיני)

HAFTARAH FOR PESAḤ, EIGHTH DAY

ISAIAH 10:32–12:6

(*Some also recite this passage on* Yom ha-Atzma·ut, *Israel Independence Day.*)

This *haftarah* presents a series of promises concerning national redemption, as a conclusion to the opening cycle of prophecies in the Book of Isaiah (chapters 1–12). The prophet repeatedly refers to a "day" to come, a "day" of victory and fulfillment that will inaugurate a new order of existence (10:32, 11:10,11, 12:1). The recitation of all of these hopes on the eighth day of *Pesaḥ* concludes the festival of freedom with the anticipation of great redemption to come. The prophet Isaiah spoke his words in Jerusalem during the last third of the 8th century B.C.E., with an eye on the oppressive Assyrian power to the northeast. Isaiah's message, however, has not been restricted to that time and place. It has become a transcendent, universal teaching of hope.

One of the most powerful and influential visions in all of Scripture is expressed in this cycle of prophecies. It moves from foretelling an end to foreign oppression to utopian visions of national justice and ingathering. A dimension of God's universal dominion is depicted or projected at each point. The first prophecy begins with an oracle of divine victory over an Assyrian monarch. Subsequent prophecies, which portray God's power to redeem the people Israel from all the nations of their dispersion, anticipate the universal acknowledgment of the just rule of the new Davidic king. The cycle concludes with a call to proclaim God's triumphs to all peoples. The messianic era will be marked by justice, kingship, and national restoration, as well as the celebration of God's acts of deliverance.

A vision of social and natural transformation lies at the center of this *haftarah*. The new ruler, inspired by the spirit of the Lord, will reveal this influence in all ways—through wisdom and counsel, devotion and reverence, justice and impartiality. The king will transfigure the interpersonal sphere by inspired bearing and actions. This will be complemented by an even more radical transformation of the natural world. An era of Edenic bliss is projected for all creatures, resulting in the virtual end of enmity and rapacity among them. The prophet characterizes this result as a universalization of "devotion" to or knowledge (*de·ah*) of the Lord. Such a quality will change people and animals alike, so that "nothing evil shall be done" throughout the Land.

RELATION OF THE *HAFTARAH* TO THE CALENDAR

One reason for the selection of this passage for *Pesaḥ* is the promise that the nation will experience a new exodus from its dispersion (11:11–16). Just as the festival celebrates the original "Egyptian *Pesaḥ,*" it anticipates a future ingathering from exile.

Why does the reading begin with Isaiah 10:32–34? Rashi's comment on the talmudic source for the selection is terse, stating that the passage was chosen "because Sennacherib was defeated on the eve of Passover." According to the Book of Kings, destruction of the Assyrian army occurred "at night" (2 Kings 19:35). The formulation there is strikingly similar to the statement in the Torah that, on the eve of the Exodus, "in the middle of the night," the Lord struck down all the firstborns of the land of Egypt (Exod. 12:29). Such similarities were sufficient to link the two events.

The linkage of the defeat of Sennacherib with the eve of *Pesaḥ* is testimony to the Jewish tendency to relate acts of divine deliverance to great historic models. By such associations, new events in history take on the power and often the char-

acteristics of an original and foundational moment. History thus becomes a series of repetitive and confirming truths. For Jewish memory, God's redemptive acts constitute one such truth, and the source of national hope. The festival of *Pesaḥ* is one of many ritual occasions when this truth and this hope are publicly celebrated.

10 32This same day at Nob
He shall stand and wave his hand.

O mount of Fair Zion!
O hill of Jerusalem!
33Lo! The Sovereign LORD of Hosts
Will hew off the tree-crowns with an ax:
The tall ones shall be felled,
The lofty ones cut down:
34The thickets of the forest shall be hacked away with iron,
And the Lebanon trees shall fall in their majesty.

י 32 עוֹד הַיּוֹם בְּנֹב
לַעֲמֹד יְנֹפֵף יָדוֹ
הַר בית בַּת־צִיּוֹן
גִּבְעַת יְרוּשָׁלִָם׃ ס
33 הִנֵּה הָאָדוֹן יְהוָה צְבָאוֹת
מְסָעֵף פֻּארָה בְּמַעֲרָצָה
וְרָמֵי הַקּוֹמָה גְּדוּעִים
וְהַגְּבֹהִים יִשְׁפָּלוּ׃
34 וְנִקַּף סִבְכֵי הַיַּעַר בַּבַּרְזֶל
וְהַלְּבָנוֹן בְּאַדִּיר יִפּוֹל׃ ס

11 But a shoot shall grow out of the stump of Jesse,
A twig shall sprout from his stock.
2The spirit of the LORD shall alight upon him:
A spirit of wisdom and insight,
A spirit of counsel and valor,
A spirit of devotion and reverence for the LORD.
3He shall sense the truth by his reverence for the LORD:

יא וְיָצָא חֹטֶר מִגֵּזַע יִשָׁי
וְנֵצֶר מִשָּׁרָשָׁיו יִפְרֶה׃
2 וְנָחָה עָלָיו רוּחַ יְהוָה
רוּחַ חָכְמָה וּבִינָה
רוּחַ עֵצָה וּגְבוּרָה
רוּחַ דַּעַת וְיִרְאַת יְהוָה׃
3 וַהֲרִיחוֹ בְּיִרְאַת יְהוָה

Isaiah 10:32. The fall of the Assyrian aggressor precedes the accounts of the messianic ruler (11:1–10) and the national ingathering (11:11–16).

Nob The place-name is a pun on the reference in this verse to the monarch's contemptuous and boastful "wave" (*y'nofef*) of "his hand" (Luzzatto). This negative act is reversed by God's hand gesture (*henif*) over the Euphrates (11:15), in His act of deliverance.

33. tree-crowns Hebrew: *purah,* with an added silent letter *alef.* This unusual spelling may be a pun suggesting a reference to the enemy's pride (*pe·er*). The high branches here should be contrasted with the humble stump of Jesse's descendant in the image at the beginning of chapter 11 (Luzzatto).

Isaiah 11:2–5. The messianic ruler will be divinely inspired.

The spirit of the LORD The general reference to "the spirit" (*ru·aḥ*) is explicated as the spirit of wisdom, insight, counsel, valor, devotion, and reverence.

He shall sense Hebrew: *va-hariḥo.* Tradi-

He shall not judge by what his eyes behold,
Nor decide by what his ears perceive.
⁴Thus he shall judge the poor with equity
And decide with justice for the lowly of the
  land.
He shall strike down a land with the rod of
  his mouth
And slay the wicked with the breath of his lips.
⁵Justice shall be the girdle of his loins,
And faithfulness the girdle of his waist.
⁶The wolf shall dwell with the lamb,
The leopard lie down with the kid;
The calf, the beast of prey, and the fatling
  together,
With a little boy to herd them.
⁷The cow and the bear shall graze,
Their young shall lie down together;
And the lion, like the ox, shall eat straw.
⁸A babe shall play
Over a viper's hole,
And an infant pass his hand
Over an adder's den.
⁹In all of My sacred mount
Nothing evil or vile shall be done;
For the land shall be filled with devotion to
  the Lord
As water covers the sea.

¹⁰In that day,
The stock of Jesse that has remained standing
Shall become a standard to peoples—
Nations shall seek his counsel
And his abode shall be honored.

¹¹In that day, my Lord will apply His hand
again to redeeming the other part of His people

וְלֹֽא־לְמַרְאֵ֥ה עֵינָ֖יו יִשְׁפּ֑וֹט
וְלֹֽא־לְמִשְׁמַ֥ע אָזְנָ֖יו יוֹכִֽיחַ׃
⁴וְשָׁפַ֤ט בְּצֶ֙דֶק֙ דַּלִּ֔ים
וְהוֹכִ֥יחַ בְּמִישׁ֖וֹר לְעַנְוֵי־אָ֑רֶץ
וְהִכָּה־אֶ֙רֶץ֙ בְּשֵׁ֣בֶט פִּ֔יו
וּבְר֥וּחַ שְׂפָתָ֖יו יָמִ֥ית רָשָֽׁע׃
⁵וְהָ֥יָה צֶ֖דֶק אֵז֣וֹר מָתְנָ֑יו
וְהָאֱמוּנָ֖ה אֵז֥וֹר חֲלָצָֽיו׃
⁶וְגָ֤ר זְאֵב֙ עִם־כֶּ֔בֶשׂ
וְנָמֵ֖ר עִם־גְּדִ֣י יִרְבָּ֑ץ
וְעֵ֙גֶל וּכְפִ֤יר וּמְרִיא֙ יַחְדָּ֔ו
וְנַ֥עַר קָטֹ֖ן נֹהֵ֥ג בָּֽם׃
⁷וּפָרָ֤ה וָדֹב֙ תִּרְעֶ֔ינָה
יַחְדָּ֖ו יִרְבְּצ֣וּ יַלְדֵיהֶ֑ן
וְאַרְיֵ֖ה כַּבָּקָ֥ר יֹֽאכַל־תֶּֽבֶן׃
⁸וְשִֽׁעֲשַׁ֥ע יוֹנֵ֖ק
עַל־חֻ֣ר פָּ֑תֶן
וְעַל֙ מְאוּרַ֣ת צִפְעוֹנִ֔י
גָּמ֖וּל יָד֥וֹ הָדָֽה׃
⁹לֹֽא־יָרֵ֥עוּ וְלֹֽא־יַשְׁחִ֖יתוּ
בְּכָל־הַ֣ר קָדְשִׁ֑י
כִּֽי־מָלְאָ֣ה הָאָ֗רֶץ דֵּעָה֙ אֶת־יְהֹוָ֔ה
כַּמַּ֖יִם לַיָּ֥ם מְכַסִּֽים׃ פ

¹⁰וְהָיָ֙ה בַּיּ֣וֹם הַה֔וּא
שֹׁ֣רֶשׁ יִשַׁ֗י אֲשֶׁ֤ר עֹמֵד֙
לְנֵ֣ס עַמִּ֔ים
אֵלָ֖יו גּוֹיִ֣ם יִדְרֹ֑שׁוּ
וְהָיְתָ֥ה מְנֻחָת֖וֹ כָּבֽוֹד׃ פ

¹¹וְהָיָ֣ה ׀ בַּיּ֣וֹם הַה֗וּא יוֹסִ֙יף אֲדֹנָ֤י ׀ שֵׁנִית֙
יָד֔וֹ לִקְנ֖וֹת אֶת־שְׁאָ֣ר עַמּ֑וֹ אֲשֶׁ֣ר יִשָּׁאֵ֩ר

tionally interpreted as an inner perception (Radak, Ibn Ezra), in contrast to the external senses of sight and of hearing noted in the sequel.

9. Nothing evil An image of righteousness that is guided by royal example (vv. 2–5). The king will be inspired by knowledge of God (v. 2), which he will generate among the people. An image of Edenic transformation intervenes (vv. 6–7).

from Assyria—as also from Egypt, Pathros, Nubia, Elam, Shinar, Hamath, and the coastlands.

מֵאַשּׁוּר וּמִמִּצְרַיִם וּמִפַּתְרוֹס וּמִכּוּשׁ
וּמֵעֵילָם וּמִשִּׁנְעָר וּמֵחֲמָת וּמֵאִיֵּי הַיָּם׃

12 He will hold up a signal to the nations
And assemble the banished of Israel,
And gather the dispersed of Judah
From the four corners of the earth.
13 Then Ephraim's envy shall cease
And Judah's harassment shall end;
Ephraim shall not envy Judah,
And Judah shall not harass Ephraim.
14 They shall pounce on the back of Philistia
to the west,
And together plunder the peoples of the east;
Edom and Moab shall be subject to them
And the children of Ammon shall obey them.

12 וְנָשָׂא נֵס לַגּוֹיִם
וְאָסַף נִדְחֵי יִשְׂרָאֵל
וּנְפֻצוֹת יְהוּדָה יְקַבֵּץ
מֵאַרְבַּע כַּנְפוֹת הָאָרֶץ׃
13 וְסָרָה קִנְאַת אֶפְרַיִם
וְצֹרְרֵי יְהוּדָה יִכָּרֵתוּ
אֶפְרַיִם לֹא־יְקַנֵּא אֶת־יְהוּדָה
וִיהוּדָה לֹא־יָצֹר אֶת־אֶפְרָיִם׃
14 וְעָפוּ בְכָתֵף פְּלִשְׁתִּים יָמָּה
יַחְדָּו יָבֹזּוּ אֶת־בְּנֵי־קֶדֶם
אֱדוֹם וּמוֹאָב מִשְׁלוֹחַ יָדָם
וּבְנֵי עַמּוֹן מִשְׁמַעְתָּם׃

15 The LORD will dry up the tongue of the
Egyptian sea.—He will raise His hand over the
Euphrates with the might of His wind and break
it into seven wadis, so that it can be trodden
dry-shod. 16 Thus there shall be a highway for
the other part of His people out of Assyria, such
as there was for Israel when it left the land of
Egypt.

15 וְהֶחֱרִים יְהֹוָה אֵת לְשׁוֹן יַם־מִצְרַיִם
וְהֵנִיף יָדוֹ עַל־הַנָּהָר בַּעְיָם רוּחוֹ וְהִכָּהוּ
לְשִׁבְעָה נְחָלִים וְהִדְרִיךְ בַּנְּעָלִים׃
16 וְהָיְתָה מְסִלָּה לִשְׁאָר עַמּוֹ אֲשֶׁר יִשָּׁאֵר
מֵאַשּׁוּר כַּאֲשֶׁר הָיְתָה לְיִשְׂרָאֵל בְּיוֹם
עֲלֹתוֹ מֵאֶרֶץ מִצְרָיִם׃

12 In that day, you shall say:
"I give thanks to You, O LORD!
Although You were wroth with me,
Your wrath has turned back and You comfort
me,
2 Behold the God who gives me triumph!

יב וְאָמַרְתָּ בַּיּוֹם הַהוּא
אוֹדְךָ יְהֹוָה
כִּי אָנַפְתָּ בִּי
יָשֹׁב אַפְּךָ וּתְנַחֲמֵנִי׃
2 הִנֵּה אֵל יְשׁוּעָתִי

12. hold up a signal The Hebrew (*v'nasa nes*) is alliterative. The various images of this prophecy have been combined by rabbinic tradition to form the 10th blessing of the daily *Amidah* prayer. In it, God is called on to gather the exiles from their dispersion. Its invocation of a triumphal blast of the *shofar* to inaugurate this messianic moment draws on Isa. 27:13.

15. The prophet uses mythic imagery to convey the new exodus. The splitting of waters into seven streams is known from Canaanite and other ancient sources. The transfer of this battle to events of the Exodus is also found in Isa. 51:9–11.

Isaiah 12:2–3. These verses have entered fixed liturgical practice as an expression of messianic hope in the *Havdalah* service at the conclusion of *Shabbat*.

I am confident, unafraid;
For Yah the LORD is my strength and might,
And He has been my deliverance."

3Joyfully shall you draw water
From the fountains of triumph,
4And you shall say on that day:
"Praise the LORD, proclaim His name.
Make His deeds known among the peoples;
Declare that His name is exalted.
5Hymn the LORD,
For He has done gloriously;
Let this be made known
In all the world!
6Oh, shout for joy,
You who dwell in Zion!
For great in your midst
Is the Holy One of Israel."

אֶבְטַח וְלֹא אֶפְחָד
כִּי־עָזִּי וְזִמְרָת יָהּ יְהוָה
וַיְהִי־לִי לִישׁוּעָה׃

3 וּשְׁאַבְתֶּם־מַיִם בְּשָׂשׂוֹן
מִמַּעַיְנֵי הַיְשׁוּעָה׃
4 וַאֲמַרְתֶּם בַּיּוֹם הַהוּא
הוֹדוּ לַיהוָה קִרְאוּ בִשְׁמוֹ
הוֹדִיעוּ בָעַמִּים עֲלִילֹתָיו
הַזְכִּירוּ כִּי נִשְׂגָּב שְׁמוֹ׃
5 זַמְּרוּ יְהוָה
כִּי גֵאוּת עָשָׂה
מידעת מוּדַעַת זֹאת
בְּכָל־הָאָרֶץ׃
6 צַהֲלִי וָרֹנִּי
יוֹשֶׁבֶת צִיּוֹן
כִּי־גָדוֹל בְּקִרְבֵּךְ
קְדוֹשׁ יִשְׂרָאֵל׃ פ

הפטרה לשבועות (יום ראשון)

HAFTARAH FOR SHAVU·OT, FIRST DAY

EZEKIEL 1:1–28, 3:12

In this *haftarah* Ezekiel reports his vision of the divine Glory in Babylon along the Chebar Canal, in July 593 B.C.E. This experience was part of his inauguration as a prophet, some five years after he had been deported from Judea with his fellow exiles. The awesome vision of God's appearance on a throne, supported by a spectacle of creatures amid fiery forms, overwhelmed Ezekiel, who flung himself down on his face. At that point the vision gives way to what he hears (v. 28). Rabbinic tradition provides the content of what Ezekiel heard by concluding the *haftarah* with a formal expression of praise from a later passage: "Blessed is the Presence of the LORD, in His place" (3:12).

Visions and accounts of God on His chariot or heavenly throne occur throughout the Hebrew Bible, in diverse genres and settings (see Exod. 24:9–11; 1 Kings 22:19–25; Isa. 6:1–3; Ps. 18:11–15; Dan. 7:9–10). They vary in solemnity and detail, as well as in function. Ezekiel's vision is by far the most detailed and most mysterious of them all. It is at once dazzling and daring in descriptive detail, conveying an awesome sense of God's majesty. Since antiquity, readers have taken the text as esoteric truth known only to a few and have tried to penetrate its eerie images. Others have sought to replicate its speculations. For such reasons, the use of Ezekiel's vision was subject to strict regulations.

Opinions have varied considerably regarding the liturgical use of this document, known as "The Chariot." In the Mishnah, the Sages state categorically that one may not recite the chariot vision as a *haftarah;* Judah the Patriarch, however, permitted it (Meg. 4:10). Some early Palestinian sages are said to have favored this chapter for the festival of *Shavu·ot.* This secondary opinion became predominant among the later Sages in Babylon (BT Meg. 31a). Still, both the untrained exposition of Ezek. 1 and any theological speculation based on it were strongly discouraged (M Ḥag. 2:1), probably due to the expansion of its contents in mystical circles and the bold anthropomorphic reference to the divine Glory (vv. 27–28).

Fire, colors, and sound: The great chariot vision dazzles us kaleidoscopically, even on the written page. A fusion of experiences still strikes the reader, even as Ezekiel's own description fuses the visual with the audible and superimposes different perspectives and sensations. In part, this is why the text is so difficult to understand. The depiction repeats itself (cf. Ezek. 1:8–9,11–12,23–24). It moves back and forth like the gaze of the prophet, it is interrupted by qualifications and adjustments (vv. 13–14), and it confuses grammatical gender throughout (cf. vv. 13–17).

The figures of the vision are extraordinary and beyond adequate description. They are composites of form, lively with color, wraithlike and fiery. Yet description is the burden of the text. At the conclusion of this uncanny description of the revelation of the throne and the transcendent God's aspect, there is a remarkable reversal. God's word addresses the prophet (1:28). Indeed, as the sequel shows, this shift from human vision to divine address is a shift from Ezekiel's experience of the advent of God to his prophetic commission (Ezek. 2:1–3:11, not part of the *haftarah*). Personal ecstasy is thus not the goal; the visionary experience is neither an end in itself nor one initiated by contemplative techniques. Rather, the individual is confronted with a sudden experience that serves as the prelude to the announcement of a prophetic task. Such is the pattern found with Moses, who envisions the appearance of an angel of the Lord within a fiery bush and then is given his divine task (Exod. 3). This feature is also found with Isaiah, who envisions the Lord on His throne surrounded by divine beings and subsequently re-

ceives a commission to address the people Israel (Isa. 6).

Given this scriptural pattern, there is something "unbiblical" about the rabbinic decision to omit the divine directives found after the vision (Ezek. 2:1–3:11) and to conclude the *haftarah* with Ezek. 3:12. As a result, Ezekiel's vision is no longer a prelude to prophecy but the first part of a twofold mystical experience, one that concludes with hearing the prayers of the divine host before the throne of God.

Nothing in the *haftarah* hints that Ezekiel's "visions of God" (v. 1) begin a drama of prophetic commission (in contrast to the uninterrupted text of Ezekiel). Rather, the mystical experience is all that we have. Without God's word (as presented in chapter 2), Ezekiel is the founding figure of ancient Jewish "Throne Mysticism," not a biblical prophet.

RELATION OF THE *HAFTARAH* TO THE CALENDAR

An ancient teaching suggests that this prophetic portion is read on *Shavu·ot* because rabbinic tradition depicted the divine chariot descending on Mount Sinai at the time that the Torah depicted God descending on Sinai to make a covenant with all Israel. Accordingly, Ezekiel's experience was not unique. To the contrary, the revelation at Sinai had already incorporated a profound mystical religious experience.

Ezekiel 1 thus reveals what even the most common Israelite saw at Mount Sinai on that awesome occasion. Its recitation on the first day of *Shavu·ot* calls to mind that wondrous event with glowing detail. Luminous beyond understanding, the vision in Ezek. 1:4–28 is a sight for the inner eye.

1 In the thirtieth year, on the fifth day of the fourth month, when I was in the community of exiles by the Chebar Canal, the heavens opened and I saw visions of God. ²On the fifth day of the month—it was the fifth year of the exile of King Jehoiachin—³the word of the LORD came to the priest Ezekiel son of Buzi, by the Chebar Canal, in the land of the Chaldeans. And the hand of the LORD came upon him there.

⁴I looked, and lo, a stormy wind came sweeping out of the north—a huge cloud and flashing fire, surrounded by a radiance; and in the center of it, in the center of the fire, a gleam as of amber.

א וַיְהִ֣י ׀ בִּשְׁלֹשִׁ֣ים שָׁנָ֗ה בָּֽרְבִיעִי֙ בַּחֲמִשָּׁ֣ה לַחֹ֔דֶשׁ וַאֲנִ֥י בְתֽוֹךְ־הַגּוֹלָ֖ה עַל־נְהַר־כְּבָ֑ר נִפְתְּחוּ֙ הַשָּׁמַ֔יִם וָאֶרְאֶ֖ה מַרְא֥וֹת אֱלֹהִֽים: 2 בַּחֲמִשָּׁ֖ה לַחֹ֑דֶשׁ הִ֚יא הַשָּׁנָ֣ה הַחֲמִישִׁ֔ית לְגָל֖וּת הַמֶּ֥לֶךְ יוֹיָכִֽין: 3 הָיֹ֣ה הָיָ֣ה דְבַר־יְהֹוָ֡ה אֶל־יְחֶזְקֵאל֩ בֶּן־בּוּזִ֨י הַכֹּהֵ֜ן בְּאֶ֤רֶץ כַּשְׂדִּים֙ עַל־נְהַר־כְּבָ֔ר וַתְּהִ֥י עָלָ֛יו שָׁ֖ם יַד־יְהֹוָֽה: 4 וָאֵ֣רֶא וְהִנֵּה֩ ר֨וּחַ סְעָרָ֜ה בָּאָ֣ה מִן־הַצָּפ֗וֹן עָנָ֤ן גָּדוֹל֙ וְאֵ֣שׁ מִתְלַקַּ֔חַת וְנֹ֥גַהּ ל֖וֹ סָבִ֑יב וּמִ֨תּוֹכָ֔הּ כְּעֵ֥ין הַחַשְׁמַ֖ל מִתּ֥וֹךְ

Ezekiel 1:1. In the thirtieth year The date is obscure and has long puzzled interpreters, even though it is correlated in verse 2 with the 5th year of the exile of King Jehoiakin (593 B.C.E.). The Targum, presumably based on ancient tradition, suggests that the 30-year reference is arrived at by counting from the discovery of "a scroll of the Teaching" in the reign of Josiah (i.e., 622–621 B.C.E.; see 2 Kings 22).

3. Chaldeans Hebrew: *kasdim*. An Aramean group that penetrated southern Babylonia around the beginning of the first millennium B.C.E. At

first subjugated to Assyria, they gained independence and took over the Babylonian kingship with a dynasty founded by Nabopolassar (in 625 B.C.E.), father of Nebuchadrezzar.

hand of the LORD Refers to an overwhelming prophetic experience.

4–5. The image of a divine advent in a chariot, on clouds, with flashing fire and a nimbus of light, is most commonly used in the Hebrew Bible in connection with God's role as a warrior (see Ps. 18:8–15; Hab. 3:3–15).

⁵In the center of it were also the figures of four creatures. And this was their appearance:

They had the figures of human beings. ⁶However, each had four faces, and each of them had four wings; ⁷the legs of each were [fused into] a single rigid leg, and the feet of each were like a single calf's hoof; and their sparkle was like the luster of burnished bronze. ⁸They had human hands below their wings. The four of them had their faces and their wings on their four sides. ⁹Each one's wings touched those of the other. They did not turn when they moved; each could move in the direction of any of its faces.

¹⁰Each of them had a human face [at the front]; each of the four had the face of a lion on the right; each of the four had the face of an ox on the left; and each of the four had the face of an eagle [at the back]. ¹¹Such were their faces. As for their wings, they were separated: above, each had two touching those of the others, while the other two covered its body. ¹²And each could move in the direction of any of its faces; they went wherever the spirit impelled them to go, without turning when they moved.

¹³Such then was the appearance of the creatures. With them was something that looked like burning coals of fire. This fire, suggestive of torches, kept moving about among the creatures; the fire had a radiance, and lightning issued from the fire. ¹⁴Dashing to and fro [among] the creatures was something that looked like flares.

¹⁵As I gazed on the creatures, I saw one wheel on the ground next to each of the four-faced creatures. ¹⁶As for the appearance and structure of the wheels, they gleamed like beryl. All four had the same form; the appearance and struc-

5 וּמִתּוֹכָ֕הּ דְּמ֖וּת אַרְבַּ֣ע חַיּ֑וֹת וְזֶה֙ מַרְאֵיהֶ֔ן

דְּמ֥וּת אָדָ֖ם לָהֵ֑נָּה: 6 וְאַרְבָּעָ֣ה פָנִ֣ים לְאֶחָ֔ת וְאַרְבַּ֥ע כְּנָפַ֖יִם לְאַחַ֥ת לָהֶֽם: 7 וְרַגְלֵיהֶ֖ם רֶ֣גֶל יְשָׁרָ֑ה וְכַ֣ף רַגְלֵיהֶ֗ם כְּכַף֙ רֶ֣גֶל עֵ֔גֶל וְנֹ֣צְצִ֔ים כְּעֵ֖ין נְחֹ֥שֶׁת קָלָֽל: 8 וְידו וִידֵ֣י אָדָ֗ם מִתַּ֙חַת֙ כַּנְפֵיהֶ֔ם עַ֖ל אַרְבַּ֣עַת רִבְעֵיהֶ֑ם וּפְנֵיהֶ֥ם וְכַנְפֵיהֶ֖ם לְאַרְבַּעְתָּֽם: 9 חֹֽבְרֹ֛ת אִשָּׁ֥ה אֶל־אֲחוֹתָ֖הּ כַּנְפֵיהֶ֑ם לֹא־יִסַּ֣בּוּ בְלֶכְתָּ֔ן אִ֛ישׁ אֶל־עֵ֥בֶר פָּנָ֖יו יֵלֵֽכוּ: 10 וּדְמ֣וּת פְּנֵיהֶם֮ פְּנֵ֣י אָדָם֒ וּפְנֵ֨י אַרְיֵ֤ה אֶל־הַיָּמִין֙ לְאַרְבַּעְתָּ֔ם וּפְנֵי־שׁ֥וֹר מֵֽהַשְּׂמֹ֖אול* לְאַרְבַּעְתָּ֑ן וּפְנֵי־נֶ֖שֶׁר לְאַרְבַּעְתָּֽן: 11 וּפְנֵיהֶ֖ם וְכַנְפֵיהֶ֣ם פְּרֻד֣וֹת מִלְמָ֑עְלָה לְאִ֗ישׁ שְׁתַּ֙יִם֙ חֹֽבְר֣וֹת אִ֔ישׁ וּשְׁתַּ֣יִם מְכַסּ֔וֹת אֵ֖ת גְּוִיֹּתֵיהֶֽנָה: 12 וְאִ֛ישׁ אֶל־עֵ֥בֶר פָּנָ֖יו יֵלֵ֑כוּ אֶ֣ל אֲשֶׁר֩ יִֽהְיֶה־שָׁ֨מָּה הָר֤וּחַ לָלֶ֙כֶת֙ יֵלֵ֔כוּ לֹ֥א יִסַּ֖בּוּ בְּלֶכְתָּֽן: 13 וּדְמ֨וּת הַחַיּ֜וֹת מַרְאֵיהֶ֣ם כְּגַֽחֲלֵי־אֵ֗שׁ בֹּֽעֲרוֹת֙ כְּמַרְאֵ֣ה הַלַּפִּדִ֔ים הִ֕יא מִתְהַלֶּ֖כֶת בֵּ֣ין הַחַיּ֑וֹת וְנֹ֣גַהּ לָאֵ֔שׁ וּמִן־הָאֵ֖שׁ יוֹצֵ֥א בָרָֽק: 14 וְהַחַיּ֖וֹת רָצ֣וֹא וָשׁ֑וֹב כְּמַרְאֵ֖ה הַבָּזָֽק: 15 וָאֵ֖רֶא הַֽחַיּ֑וֹת וְהִנֵּה֩ אוֹפַ֨ן אֶחָ֥ד בָּאָ֛רֶץ אֵ֥צֶל הַֽחַיּ֖וֹת לְאַרְבַּ֥עַת פָּנָֽיו: 16 מַרְאֵ֨ה הָאֽוֹפַנִּ֤ים וּמַֽעֲשֵׂיהֶם֙ כְּעֵ֣ין תַּרְשִׁ֔ישׁ וּדְמ֥וּת אֶחָ֖ד לְאַרְבַּעְתָּ֑ן וּמַ֨רְאֵיהֶם֙ וּמַ֣עֲשֵׂיהֶ֔ם

מלא ו׳ v. 10.

---

7. single rigid leg On the basis of this phrase, talmudic Sages ruled that one should stand with both feet fixed together during the *Amidah* (BT Ber. 10b), thus resembling the angels themselves (JT Ber. 1:1).

11. The four creatures symbolize earthly and cosmic wholeness: unity amid multiplicity, like the four countenances themselves. The many faces further indicate divine omnipresence. Similarly, the many eyes on the wheeled disks (v. 18) suggest divine omniscience and providence.

ture of each was as of two wheels cutting through each other. 17And when they moved, each could move in the direction of any of its four quarters; they did not veer when they moved. 18Their rims were tall and frightening, for the rims of all four were covered all over with eyes. 19And when the creatures moved forward, the wheels moved at their sides; and when the creatures were borne above the earth, the wheels were borne too. 20Wherever the spirit impelled them to go, they went—wherever the spirit impelled them—and the wheels were borne alongside them; for the spirit of the creatures was in the wheels. 21When those moved, these moved; and when those stood still, these stood still; and when those were borne above the earth, the wheels were borne alongside them—for the spirit of the creatures was in the wheels.

22Above the heads of the creatures was a form: an expanse, with an awe-inspiring gleam as of crystal, was spread out above their heads. 23Under the expanse, each had one pair of wings extended toward those of the others; and each had another pair covering its body. 24When they moved, I could hear the sound of their wings like the sound of mighty waters, like the sound of Shaddai, a tumult like the din of an army. When they stood still, they would let their wings droop. 25From above the expanse over their heads came a sound. When they stood still, they would let their wings droop.

26Above the expanse over their heads was the semblance of a throne, in appearance like sapphire; and on top, upon this semblance of a throne, there was the semblance of a human form. 27From what appeared as his loins up, I saw a gleam as of amber—what looked like a fire encased in a frame; and from what appeared

כַּאֲשֶׁר יִהְיֶה הָאוֹפַן בְּתוֹךְ הָאוֹפַן׃ 17 עַל־
אַרְבַּעַת רִבְעֵיהֶן בְּלֶכְתָּם יֵלֵכוּ לֹא יִסַּבּוּ
בְּלֶכְתָּן׃ 18 וְגַבֵּיהֶן וְגֹבַהּ לָהֶם וְיִרְאָה לָהֶם
וְגַבֹּתָם מְלֵאֹת עֵינַיִם סָבִיב לְאַרְבַּעְתָּן׃
19 וּבְלֶכֶת הַחַיּוֹת יֵלְכוּ הָאוֹפַנִּים אֶצְלָם
וּבְהִנָּשֵׂא הַחַיּוֹת מֵעַל הָאָרֶץ יִנָּשְׂאוּ
הָאוֹפַנִּים׃ 20 עַל אֲשֶׁר יִהְיֶה־שָּׁם הָרוּחַ
לָלֶכֶת יֵלֵכוּ שָׁמָּה הָרוּחַ לָלֶכֶת וְהָאוֹפַנִּים
יִנָּשְׂאוּ לְעֻמָּתָם כִּי רוּחַ הַחַיָּה בָּאוֹפַנִּים׃
21 בְּלֶכְתָּם יֵלֵכוּ וּבְעָמְדָם יַעֲמֹדוּ
וּבְהִנָּשְׂאָם מֵעַל הָאָרֶץ יִנָּשְׂאוּ הָאוֹפַנִּים
לְעֻמָּתָם כִּי רוּחַ הַחַיָּה בָּאוֹפַנִּים׃
22 וּדְמוּת עַל־רָאשֵׁי הַחַיָּה רָקִיעַ כְּעֵין
הַקֶּרַח הַנּוֹרָא נָטוּי עַל־רָאשֵׁיהֶם
מִלְמָעְלָה׃ 23 וְתַחַת הָרָקִיעַ כַּנְפֵיהֶם
יְשָׁרוֹת אִשָּׁה אֶל־אֲחוֹתָהּ לְאִישׁ שְׁתַּיִם
מְכַסּוֹת לָהֵנָּה וּלְאִישׁ שְׁתַּיִם מְכַסּוֹת
לָהֵנָּה אֵת גְּוִיֹּתֵיהֶם׃ 24 וָאֶשְׁמַע אֶת־קוֹל
כַּנְפֵיהֶם כְּקוֹל מַיִם רַבִּים כְּקוֹל־שַׁדַּי
בְּלֶכְתָּם קוֹל הֲמֻלָּה כְּקוֹל מַחֲנֶה בְּעָמְדָם
תְּרַפֶּינָה כַנְפֵיהֶן׃ 25 וַיְהִי־קוֹל מֵעַל
לָרָקִיעַ אֲשֶׁר עַל־רֹאשָׁם בְּעָמְדָם תְּרַפֶּינָה
כַנְפֵיהֶן׃
26 וּמִמַּעַל לָרָקִיעַ אֲשֶׁר עַל־רֹאשָׁם
כְּמַרְאֵה אֶבֶן־סַפִּיר דְּמוּת כִּסֵּא וְעַל
דְּמוּת הַכִּסֵּא דְּמוּת כְּמַרְאֵה אָדָם עָלָיו
מִלְמָעְלָה׃ 27 וָאֵרֶא ׀ כְּעֵין חַשְׁמַל
כְּמַרְאֵה־אֵשׁ בֵּית־לָהּ סָבִיב מִמַּרְאֵה

16. two wheels cutting through each other Hebrew: *ha-ofan b'tokh ha-ofan.* Alternately, "a wheel within a wheel." It is not clear whether this portrays two wheels intersecting crosswise (somehow fixed into each other, at right angles) or concentric wheels, one inside the other.

24. sound of mighty waters May refer to the cosmic waters (see Ps. 93:4).

as his loins down, I saw what looked like fire.
There was a radiance all about him. 28Like the
appearance of the bow which shines in the
clouds on a day of rain, such was the appearance
of the surrounding radiance. That was the appearance of the semblance of the Presence of
the LORD. When I beheld it, I flung myself down
on my face. And I heard the voice of someone
speaking.

מָתְנָיו וּלְמָעְלָה וּמִמַּרְאֵה מָתְנָיו וּלְמַטָּה
רָאִיתִי כְּמַרְאֵה־אֵשׁ וְנֹגַהּ לוֹ סָבִיב׃
28 כְּמַרְאֵה הַקֶּשֶׁת אֲשֶׁר יִהְיֶה בֶעָנָן בְּיוֹם
הַגֶּשֶׁם כֵּן מַרְאֵה הַנֹּגַהּ סָבִיב הוּא מַרְאֵה
דְּמוּת כְּבוֹד־יְהוָה וָאֶרְאֶה וָאֶפֹּל עַל־פָּנַי
וָאֶשְׁמַע קוֹל מְדַבֵּר׃ ס

3 12Then a spirit carried me away, and behind
me I heard a great roaring sound: "Blessed is
the Presence of the LORD, in His place!"

ג 12 וַתִּשָּׂאֵנִי רוּחַ וָאֶשְׁמַע אַחֲרַי קוֹל
רַעַשׁ גָּדוֹל בָּרוּךְ כְּבוֹד־יְהוָה מִמְּקוֹמוֹ׃

28. Presence of the LORD Literally, "Glory [or: Majesty; *kavod*] of the LORD." The divine *kavod* in the Bible is frequently associated with divine appearances, particularly in worship settings (see Exod. 24:17, 40:34–35; 1 Kings 8:11). It was experienced as a substantive presence, even occasionally anthropomorphic in appearance (Exod. 33:18–23). For philosophers like Saadia, the divine *kavod* was a "created form" made by God so "that the light would give His prophet the assurance of the authenticity of what has been revealed to him . . . and is called *Sh'khinah* by the sages." Maimonides held a similar view, calling the *Sh'khinah* a "created light." As such, the divine "Glory" was deemed essentially distinct from God. For medieval kabbalists, the *kavod* was a modality of God and a locus of speculative or meditative regard.

Ezekiel 3:12. Blessed is the Presence of the LORD, in His place Hebrew: *Barukh k'vod YHVH mi-m'komo.* In context, this phrase refers to something that the prophet heard. The Targum suggested that Ezekiel heard beings "praising and saying" the ensuing words of praise. Some scholars have suggested that the word "blessed" (*barukh*) is the result of a minor scribal error. According to this theory, the similar Hebrew letters *khaf* and *mem* were confused when the text was transcribed from an archaic script, resulting in *barukh* (blessed) instead of *b'rum* (when . . . ascended). Restored to its assumed original, Ezek. 3:12 would read: "Then the spirit carried me away, and behind me I heard a roaring sound, when the Presence [*kavod*] of the Lord ascended from its place." Such an image of an ascending chariot appears in Ezek. 10:15–19.

The angelic formalized praise, as translated here, has become a fixed part of the *K'dushah* (Sanctification) prayer, in which human worshipers sanctify the divine name (or exalt God) "just as" the holy angels do in the supernal heights. Thus, in the *K'dushah,* the threefold angelic praising recitation of "Holy" (Isa. 6:3) is followed by the words quoted in Ezek. 3:12.

הפטרה לשבועות (יום שני)

HAFTARAH FOR SHAVU·OT, SECOND DAY

HABAKKUK 3:1–19 (*Ashk'nazim*)
HABAKKUK 2:20–3:19 (*S'fardim*)

The revelation of God's heavenly Glory to the prophet (Hab. 3:3–15) dominates the imagery of this *haftarah*. As in Ezek. 1 (recited on the first day of *Shavu·ot*), that Glory appears on a chariot and is terrifying. This prophetic vision is encased within an opening petition for divine mercy and a concluding personal response (Hab. 3:1–2, 16–19). Chapter 3 is recited by *Ashk'nazim*. Meanwhile, *S'fardim* begin with the final verse of chapter 2 (v. 20), which refers to God in His heavenly temple. That verse thus serves as a prologue to the vision of God's appearance.

The inner frame of the composition contains the opening petition of the prophet (3:2), and the final response (vv. 16–19). Use of the verb *shama* ("I learned" in v. 2 and "I heard" in v. 16) punctuates the past and the present—the record of ancient divine deeds and the immediate experience of God who is coming to deliver the people.

At the center of the *haftarah* is the terrifying vision of God's appearance on a storm chariot. This wreaks havoc throughout the natural world, making "the earth burst into streams" and making "the mountains rock" (vv. 9–10). It also unloosens the world of mortals, smashing homes and cracking skulls of the enemy. Amid the radiance that emanates from God's glory (v. 4), an avenging hoard of furies (pestilence and plague) march forth and add to the mayhem (v. 5). A horrendous divine rage is described, leading the speaker to wonder at the need for such cosmic force against earthly foes (vv. 8–9) and to quiver in place. "Rot entered into my bone, / I trembled where I stood" (v. 16).

Alongside this cosmic imagery is the theme of bashing and battering the water. This too is an old mythic motif, found frequently in Scripture as part of dramatic accounts of God's might at the Creation and at the Exodus.

Habakkuk's vision is notable in another regard. As a manifestation of God out of a whirlwind responding to a human cry of divine injustice, the text begs comparison with the Book of Job. God's appearance to Habakkuk comes in response to his prayer for divine compassion. The answer has a direct mythic force. Divine presence is everything—and sufficient. Despite his fears, the prophet is now empowered with confidence and joy. No supernatural wisdom is conveyed here, only the certitude of God's historical providence.

RELATION OF THE *HAFTARAH* TO THE CALENDAR

Habakkuk was selected for reading on the second day of *Shavu·ot,* according to Rashi, "For it speaks of the Giving of the Torah: 'God comes from Teman' [the south, i.e., the Sinai wilderness; v. 3]." In this explanation, Rashi follows the Targum and an old midrashic tradition (Sifrei Deut.). Rashi goes further in his commentary to the biblical verse itself. He alludes to a tradition whereby God went to the other nations to see if they would accept the Torah, but they refused. This is based on a midrashic interpretation of Hab. 3:6 (literally: "When He stands, He measures [*va-y'moded*] the earth; when He glances, He unlooses [*va-yater*] nations"). According to a *midrash,* God took the measure of the mountains, but found only Sinai "worthy" for the Revelation (Gen. R. 99:1). Taking the measure of the earth, God found only the land of Israel "worthy" for His people. He thereupon gave the Israelites a dispensation (*hetter*) with respect to the other nations, and permitted (*hittir*) the nations a certain leniency in their ritual life.

Habakkuk 3 thus proves central in ancient homilies attempting to explain or justify why Is-

rael alone received God's revelation. One view teaches that Torah is Israel's sacred destiny, and the source of its national and spiritual life. This truth is reconfirmed on the festival of *Shavu·ot,* when the community of Israel stands before the ongoing reality of Sinai and "renews" it "in these years" (Hab. 3:2).

2 20The Lord is in His holy Abode—
Be silent before Him all the earth!

ב 20 וַיהוָה בְּהֵיכַל קָדְשׁוֹ
הַס מִפָּנָיו כָּל־הָאָרֶץ׃ פ

3 A prayer of the prophet Habakkuk. In the mode of *Shigionoth.*

* ג תְּפִלָּה לַחֲבַקּוּק הַנָּבִיא עַל שִׁגְיֹנוֹת׃

2O Lord! I have learned of Your renown;
I am awed, O Lord, by Your deeds.
Renew them in these years,
Oh, make them known in these years!
Though angry, may You remember compassion.

2 יְהוָה שָׁמַעְתִּי שִׁמְעֲךָ
יָרֵאתִי יְהוָה פָּעָלְךָ
בְּקֶרֶב שָׁנִים חַיֵּיהוּ
בְּקֶרֶב שָׁנִים תּוֹדִיעַ
בְּרֹגֶז רַחֵם תִּזְכּוֹר׃

3God is coming from Teman,
The Holy One from Mount Paran. *Selah.*
His majesty covers the skies,
His splendor fills the earth:
4It is a brilliant light
Which gives off rays on every side—
And therein His glory is enveloped.
5Pestilence marches before Him,
And plague comes forth at His heels.
6When He stands, He makes the earth shake;
When He glances, He makes nations tremble.
The age-old mountains are shattered,
The primeval hills sink low.
His are the ancient routes:

3 אֱלוֹהַ מִתֵּימָן יָבוֹא
וְקָדוֹשׁ מֵהַר־פָּארָן סֶלָה
כִּסָּה שָׁמַיִם הוֹדוֹ
וּתְהִלָּתוֹ מָלְאָה הָאָרֶץ׃
4 וְנֹגַהּ כָּאוֹר תִּהְיֶה
קַרְנַיִם מִיָּדוֹ לוֹ
וְשָׁם חֶבְיוֹן עזה עֻזֹּו׃
5 לְפָנָיו יֵלֶךְ דָּבֶר
וְיֵצֵא רֶשֶׁף לְרַגְלָיו׃
6 עָמַד ׀ וַיְמֹדֶד אֶרֶץ
רָאָה וַיַּתֵּר גּוֹיִם
וַיִּתְפֹּצְצוּ הַרְרֵי־עַד
שַׁחוּ גִּבְעוֹת עוֹלָם
הֲלִיכוֹת עוֹלָם לוֹ׃

Habakkuk 2:20. The Lord is in His holy Abode The Lord's heavenly dwelling is the place to which prayers ascend (Ps. 18:7; cf. 1 Kings 8:30) and from which divine rescue proceeds (Ps. 18:8–10; cf. 68:34–36).

Habakkuk 3:1. Habakkuk The word in Hebrew is otherwise unknown. In Akkadian (*habbaququ* or *hambaququ*) it means "fragrant herb."

3–15. A long-standing rabbinic tradition

* Ashk'nazim *start here.*

7As a scene of havoc I behold
The tents of Cushan;
Shaken are the pavilions
Of the land of Midian!

8Are You wroth, O LORD, with Neharim?
Is Your anger against Neharim,
Your rage against Yam—
That You are driving Your steeds,
Your victorious chariot?
9All bared and ready is Your bow.
Sworn are the rods of the word. *Selah.*
You make the earth burst into streams,
10The mountains rock at the sight of You,
A torrent of rain comes down;
Loud roars the deep,
The sky returns the echo.
11Sun [and] moon stand still on high
As Your arrows fly in brightness,
Your flashing spear in brilliance.
12You tread the earth in rage,
You trample nations in fury.
13You have come forth to deliver Your people,
To deliver Your anointed.
You will smash the roof of the villain's house,

7 תַּחַת אָוֶן רָאִיתִי
אָהֳלֵי כוּשָׁן
יִרְגְּזוּן יְרִיעוֹת
אֶרֶץ מִדְיָן׃ ס

8 הֲבִנְהָרִים חָרָה יְהוָה
אִם בַּנְּהָרִים אַפֶּךָ
אִם־בַּיָּם עֶבְרָתֶךָ
כִּי תִרְכַּב עַל־סוּסֶיךָ
מַרְכְּבֹתֶיךָ יְשׁוּעָה׃
9 עֶרְיָה תֵעוֹר קַשְׁתֶּךָ
שְׁבֻעוֹת מַטּוֹת אֹמֶר סֶלָה
נְהָרוֹת תְּבַקַּע־אָרֶץ׃
10 רָאוּךָ יָחִילוּ הָרִים
זֶרֶם מַיִם עָבָר
נָתַן תְּהוֹם קוֹלוֹ
רוֹם יָדֵיהוּ נָשָׂא׃
11 שֶׁמֶשׁ יָרֵחַ עָמַד זְבֻלָה
לְאוֹר חִצֶּיךָ יְהַלֵּכוּ
לְנֹגַהּ בְּרַק חֲנִיתֶךָ׃
12 בְּזַעַם תִּצְעַד־אָרֶץ
בְּאַף תָּדוּשׁ גּוֹיִם׃
13 יָצָאתָ לְיֵשַׁע עַמֶּךָ
לְיֵשַׁע אֶת־מְשִׁיחֶךָ
מָחַצְתָּ רֹּאשׁ* מִבֵּית רָשָׁע

v. 13. ר׳ דגושה

transforms the mythological sequences of Hab. 3 into specific episodes in the sacred history of Israel. The Targum interprets Hab. 3 as a systematic presentation of the great events of Israel's history of salvation. Thus the references to "iniquity" and "Cushan" in verse 7 were understood to hint at the sin of idolatry in the era of the chieftains ("judges") and divine punishment through Cushan Rishataim (cf. Judg. 3:7–8). The quaking mountains in verse 10 are linked to the revelation at Sinai, and the image of the sun and moon standing still in verse 11 evokes Joshua's battle cry and the miracle in Gibeon (Josh. 10:12–13). The statement that God will crack the "skull" of the enemy "with [His] bludgeon" (v. 14) alludes to God's use of Moses' staff to defeat Pharaoh's warriors at the Sea.

9. Sworn are the rods of the word An old riddle that has puzzled commentators and translators since antiquity. The Hebrew consists of three words, meaning "oaths," "staves," and "word," which interrupt the continuity of the passage. An intriguing suggestion has been offered that these three words were originally in the margin of the text, placed there to indicate when this *haftarah* selection was to be read—not only on *Shavu·ot* but also with the sections of *Mattot* ("staves," Num. 17:16ff.) and *Va-yomer* ("And He said," related to "word," Gen. 12:1ff.) in one version of the ancient triennial cycle.

Raze it from foundation to top. *Selah.*
14You will crack [his] skull with Your bludgeon;
Blown away shall be his warriors,
Whose delight is to crush me suddenly,
To devour a poor man in an ambush.
15You will make Your steeds tread the sea,
Stirring the mighty waters.
16I heard and my bowels quaked,
My lips quivered at the sound;
Rot entered into my bone,
I trembled where I stood.
Yet I wait calmly for the day of distress,
For a people to come to attack us.
17Though the fig tree does not bud
And no yield is on the vine,
Though the olive crop has failed
And the fields produce no grain,
Though sheep have vanished from the fold
And no cattle are in the pen,
18Yet will I rejoice in the LORD,
Exult in the God who delivers me.
19My Lord GOD is my strength:
He makes my feet like the deer's
And lets me stride upon the heights.

For the leader; with instrumental music.

עָרוֹת יְסוֹד עַד־צַוָּאר סֶלָה׃ פ
14 נָקַבְתָּ בְמַטָּיו רֹאשׁ
פרזו פְּרָזָיו יִסְעֲרוּ
לַהֲפִיצֵנִי עֲלִיצֻתָם
כְּמוֹ־לֶאֱכֹל עָנִי בַּמִּסְתָּר׃
15 דָּרַכְתָּ בַיָּם סוּסֶיךָ
חֹמֶר מַיִם רַבִּים׃
16 שָׁמַעְתִּי ׀ וַתִּרְגַּז בִּטְנִי
לְקוֹל צָלְלוּ שְׂפָתַי
יָבוֹא רָקָב בַּעֲצָמַי
וְתַחְתַּי אֶרְגָּז
אֲשֶׁר אָנוּחַ לְיוֹם צָרָה
לַעֲלוֹת לְעַם יְגוּדֶנּוּ׃
17 כִּי־תְאֵנָה לֹא־תִפְרָח
וְאֵין יְבוּל בַּגְּפָנִים
כִּחֵשׁ מַעֲשֵׂה־זַיִת
וּשְׁדֵמוֹת לֹא־עָשָׂה אֹכֶל
גָּזַר מִמִּכְלָה צֹאן
וְאֵין בָּקָר בָּרְפָתִים׃
18 וַאֲנִי בַּיהוָה אֶעְלוֹזָה
אָגִילָה בֵּאלֹהֵי יִשְׁעִי׃
19 יְהוִה אֲדֹנָי חֵילִי
וַיָּשֶׂם רַגְלַי כָּאַיָּלוֹת
וְעַל בָּמוֹתַי יַדְרִכֵנִי

לַמְנַצֵּחַ בִּנְגִינוֹתָי׃

הפטרה לתשעה באב (שחרית)

HAFTARAH FOR TISH·AH B'AV MORNING

JEREMIAH 8:13–9:23

In this *haftarah* of doom and destruction, the terror to come is first announced and then envisioned in a cluster of powerful images (Jer. 8:13–17, 9:7–9,20–21). The calamities will be the result of deceit and dishonesty at the level of human relations in society (9:1–5), and the rejection of the Torah and proper worship at the level of religious practice (9:11–15). The prophet himself laments the horror to come, and women who know dirges are invited to bewail the onset of doom (see 8:18,21, 9:16–21). The concluding teaching counsels proper conduct (9:22–23), although such behavior cannot diminish or prevent the severity of the predicted doom. The counsel of earnest devotion and proper behavior stands as a counterpoint to the perversion of morality and of divine service, which have been denounced (9:1–5,11–15).

RELATION OF THE *HAFTARAH* TO THE CALENDAR

This prophetic reading's account of national doom due to sin links it to the themes of the *Tish·ah b'Av* fast day, which recalls the destruction of the Temple. The prophet's call for public wailers to recite words of mourning for the people and the Land evokes the central ritual of this day of sorrow—the public recitation of lamentations over Zion and Jerusalem.

The *haftarah* is dominated by rapidly alternating voices and perspectives: The divine voice (8:13,17), the voice of Jeremiah (8:18,21,23), and the voice of the people (8:14,15). Verbal repetition adds another dimension to the *haftarah.* Thus, the fourfold repetition of "dirge" (*n'hi* or *nehi*) or the eightfold use of "nothing," "not" (*ein* or *ayin*) add to the dominant mood of desolation and despair.

Hebrew puns create unexpected connections between the units. Particularly notable is the network created by the phrases *asof asifem* (I will make an end of them, 8:13) and *v'ein m'assef* (and none to pick them up, 9:21). These phrases at the beginning and near the end of the *haftarah* enclose it in a framework of desolation. Also effective is the pun linking the words *kinah* (wailing) and *mikneh* (cattle) in 9:9, which creates a striking relationship between the form of lament and the object of loss.

8 13I will make an end of them
—declares the LORD:
No grapes left on the vine,
No figs on the fig tree,
The leaves all withered;
Whatever I have given them is gone.
14Why are we sitting by?
Let us gather into the fortified cities
And meet our doom there.

ח 13 אָסֹ֥ף אֲסִיפֵ֖ם
נְאֻם־יְהוָ֑ה
אֵין֩ עֲנָבִ֨ים בַּגֶּ֜פֶן
וְאֵ֧ין תְּאֵנִ֣ים בַּתְּאֵנָ֗ה
וְהֶֽעָלֶה֙ נָבֵ֔ל
וָאֶתֵּ֥ן לָהֶ֖ם יַעַבְרֽוּם׃
14 עַל־מָה֙ אֲנַ֣חְנוּ יֹֽשְׁבִ֔ים
הֵאָֽסְפ֗וּ וְנָב֛וֹא אֶל־עָרֵ֥י הַמִּבְצָ֖ר
וְנִדְּמָה־שָּׁ֑ם

For the LORD our God has doomed us,
He has made us drink a bitter draft,
Because we sinned against the LORD.
15We hoped for good fortune, but no happiness came;
For a time of relief—instead there is terror!
16The snorting of their horses was heard from Dan;
At the loud neighing of their steeds
The whole land quaked.
They came and devoured the land and what was in it,
The towns and those who dwelt in them.

17Lo, I will send serpents against you,
Adders that cannot be charmed,
And they shall bite you
—declares the LORD.

18When in grief I would seek comfort,
My heart is sick within me.

19"Is not the LORD in Zion?
Is not her King within her?
Why then did they anger Me with their images,
With alien futilities?"

Hark! The outcry of my poor people
From the land far and wide:
20"Harvest is past,
Summer is gone,
But we have not been saved."

כִּ֠י יְהוָ֨ה אֱלֹהֵ֤ינוּ הֲדִמָּ֙נוּ֙
וַיַּשְׁקֵ֣נוּ מֵי־רֹ֔אשׁ
כִּ֥י חָטָ֖אנוּ לַיהוָֽה׃
15 קַוֵּ֥ה לְשָׁל֖וֹם וְאֵ֣ין ט֑וֹב
לְעֵ֥ת מַרְפֵּ֖ה* וְהִנֵּ֥ה בְעָתָֽה׃
16 מִדָּ֤ן נִשְׁמַע֙ נַחְרַ֣ת סוּסָ֔יו
מִקּוֹל֙ מִצְהֲל֣וֹת אַבִּירָ֔יו
רָעֲשָׁ֖ה כָּל־הָאָ֑רֶץ
וַיָּב֗וֹאוּ וַיֹּֽאכְלוּ֙ אֶ֣רֶץ וּמְלוֹאָ֔הּ
עִ֖יר וְיֹ֥שְׁבֵי בָֽהּ׃ ס

17 כִּ֠י הִנְנִ֨י מְשַׁלֵּ֜חַ בָּכֶ֗ם נְחָשִׁים֙
צִפְעֹנִ֔ים אֲשֶׁ֥ר אֵין־לָהֶ֖ם לָ֑חַשׁ
וְנִשְּׁכ֥וּ אֶתְכֶ֖ם
נְאֻם־יְהוָֽה׃ ס

18 מַבְלִ֥יגִיתִ֖י עֲלֵ֣י יָג֑וֹן
עָלַ֖י לִבִּ֥י דַוָּֽי׃

19 הִנֵּה־ק֞וֹל שַֽׁוְעַ֣ת בַּת־עַמִּ֗י
מֵאֶ֙רֶץ֙ מַרְחַקִּ֔ים

הַיהוָה֙ אֵ֣ין בְּצִיּ֔וֹן
אִם־מַלְכָּ֖הּ אֵ֣ין בָּ֑הּ
מַדּ֙וּעַ֙ הִכְעִס֧וּנִי בִּפְסִלֵיהֶ֖ם
בְּהַבְלֵ֥י נֵכָֽר׃

20 עָבַ֥ר קָצִ֖יר
כָּ֣לָה קָ֑יִץ
וַאֲנַ֖חְנוּ ל֥וֹא נוֹשָֽׁעְנוּ׃

v. 15. ה׳ במקום א׳

Jeremiah 8:14. Because we sinned against the LORD Evokes the confessional form *ḥatanu,* "We have sinned."

19. Many commentators have understood the first two questions in this verse to be challenges spoken by Israel. They elicit God's response ("Why then did they anger Me?"). Other commentators understand all three questions as spoken by God. It is a feature of the triple rhetorical question to create a graded intensification, in which the first two queries imply a negative response. This sets up the challenging and judgmental question at the end.

21Because my people is shattered I am shattered;
I am dejected, seized by desolation.
22Is there no balm in Gilead?
Can no physician be found?
Why has healing not yet
Come to my poor people?
23Oh, that my head were water,
My eyes a fount of tears!
Then would I weep day and night
For the slain of my poor people.

21 עַל־שֶׁבֶר בַּת־עַמִּי הָשְׁבָּרְתִּי
קָדַרְתִּי שַׁמָּה הֶחֱזִקָתְנִי׃
22 הַצֳרִי אֵין בְּגִלְעָד
אִם־רֹפֵא אֵין שָׁם
כִּי מַדּוּעַ לֹא עָלְתָה
אֲרֻכַת בַּת־עַמִּי׃
23 מִי־יִתֵּן רֹאשִׁי מַיִם
וְעֵינִי מְקוֹר דִּמְעָה
וְאֶבְכֶּה יוֹמָם וָלַיְלָה
אֵת חַלְלֵי בַת־עַמִּי׃

9 Oh, to be in the desert,
At an encampment for wayfarers!
Oh, to leave my people,
To go away from them—
For they are all adulterers,
A band of rogues.

ט מִי־יִתְּנֵנִי בַמִּדְבָּר
מְלוֹן אֹרְחִים
וְאֶעֶזְבָה אֶת־עַמִּי
וְאֵלְכָה מֵאִתָּם
כִּי כֻלָּם מְנָאֲפִים
עֲצֶרֶת בֹּגְדִים׃

2They bend their tongues like bows;
They are valorous in the land
For treachery, not for honesty;
They advance from evil to evil.
And they do not heed Me
—declares the LORD.
3Beware, every man of his friend!
Trust not even a brother!
For every brother takes advantage,
Every friend is base in his dealings.
4One man cheats the other,
They will not speak truth;

2 וַיַּדְרְכוּ אֶת־לְשׁוֹנָם קַשְׁתָּם
שֶׁקֶר וְלֹא לֶאֱמוּנָה
גָּבְרוּ בָאָרֶץ
כִּי מֵרָעָה אֶל־רָעָה ׀ יָצָאוּ
וְאֹתִי לֹא־יָדָעוּ
נְאֻם־יְהוָה׃ ס
3 אִישׁ מֵרֵעֵהוּ הִשָּׁמֵרוּ
וְעַל־כָּל־אָח אַל־תִּבְטָחוּ
כִּי כָל־אָח עָקוֹב יַעְקֹב
וְכָל־רֵעַ רָכִיל יַהֲלֹךְ׃
4 וְאִישׁ בְּרֵעֵהוּ יְהָתֵלּוּ
וֶאֱמֶת לֹא יְדַבֵּרוּ

Jeremiah 9:1–5. This passage exemplifies the reuse of patriarchal themes in prophecy. Here the Jacob cycle is deftly alluded to by a play on the name "Jacob" (*Ya·akov*): "For every brother [*aḥ*] takes advantage, is a deceitful supplanter [*akov ya·akov*]." Many other key words of the prophetic oracle derive from that narrative in the Torah. Another example (from Gen. 27:35–37): "Your brother [*aḥ*] has come in deceit [*mirmah*]. . . . Therefore is he called Jacob [*Ya·akov*] because he has deceived me [*va-ya·kveini*] twice." The noun *mirmah* occurs in Jer. 9:5.

2. They bend their tongues like bows Their arrows are the false and bitter words they speak (Radak). See also verse 7.

They have trained their tongues to speak falsely;
They wear themselves out working iniquity.
5 You dwell in the midst of deceit.
In their deceit, they refuse to heed Me
—declares the LORD.

6 Assuredly, thus said the LORD of Hosts:
Lo, I shall smelt and assay them—
For what else can I do because of My poor people?
7 Their tongue is a sharpened arrow,
They use their mouths to deceive.
One speaks to his fellow in friendship,
But lays an ambush for him in his heart.
8 Shall I not punish them for such deeds?
—says the LORD—
Shall I not bring retribution
On such a nation as this?

9 For the mountains I take up weeping and wailing,
For the pastures in the wilderness, a dirge.
They are laid waste; no man passes through,
And no sound of cattle is heard.
Birds of the sky and beasts as well
Have fled and are gone.

10 I will turn Jerusalem into rubble,
Into dens for jackals;
And I will make the towns of Judah
A desolation without inhabitants.

11 What man is so wise
That he understands this?
To whom has the LORD's mouth spoken,
So that he can explain it:
Why is the land in ruins,
Laid waste like a wilderness,
With none passing through?

לִמְּד֧וּ לְשׁוֹנָ֛ם דַּבֶּר־שֶׁ֖קֶר
הַעֲוֵ֥ה נִלְאֽוּ׃
5 שִׁבְתְּךָ֖ בְּת֣וֹךְ מִרְמָ֑ה
בְּמִרְמָ֛ה מֵאֲנ֥וּ דַֽעַת־אוֹתִ֖י
נְאֻם־יְהוָֽה׃ ס

6 לָכֵ֗ן כֹּ֤ה אָמַר֙ יְהוָ֣ה צְבָא֔וֹת
הִנְנִ֥י צוֹרְפָ֖ם וּבְחַנְתִּ֑ים
כִּֽי־אֵ֣יךְ אֶֽעֱשֶׂ֔ה מִפְּנֵ֖י בַּת־עַמִּֽי׃
7 חֵ֥ץ שוחט שָׁח֛וּט לְשׁוֹנָ֖ם
מִרְמָ֣ה דִבֵּ֑ר
בְּפִ֗יו שָׁל֤וֹם אֶת־רֵעֵ֙הוּ֙ יְדַבֵּ֔ר
וּבְקִרְבּ֖וֹ יָשִׂ֥ים אָרְבּֽוֹ׃
8 הַעַל־אֵ֥לֶּה לֹֽא־אֶפְקָד־בָּ֖ם
נְאֻם־יְהוָ֑ה
אִ֚ם בְּג֣וֹי אֲשֶׁר־כָּזֶ֔ה
לֹ֥א תִתְנַקֵּ֖ם נַפְשִֽׁי׃ ס

9 עַל־הֶ֨הָרִ֜ים אֶשָּׂ֧א בְכִ֣י וָנֶ֗הִי
וְעַל־נְא֤וֹת מִדְבָּר֙ קִינָ֔ה
כִּ֤י נִצְּתוּ֙ מִבְּלִי־אִ֣ישׁ עֹבֵ֔ר
וְלֹ֥א שָׁמְע֖וּ ק֣וֹל מִקְנֶ֑ה
מֵע֤וֹף הַשָּׁמַ֙יִם֙ וְעַד־בְּהֵמָ֔ה
נָדְד֖וּ הָלָֽכוּ׃

10 וְנָתַתִּ֧י אֶת־יְרוּשָׁלִַ֛ם לְגַלִּ֖ים
מְע֣וֹן תַּנִּ֑ים
וְאֶת־עָרֵ֧י יְהוּדָ֛ה אֶתֵּ֥ן
שְׁמָמָ֖ה מִבְּלִ֥י יוֹשֵֽׁב׃ ס

11 מִֽי־הָאִ֤ישׁ הֶֽחָכָם֙
וְיָבֵ֣ן אֶת־זֹ֔את
וַאֲשֶׁ֨ר דִּבֶּ֧ר פִּֽי־יְהוָ֛ה אֵלָ֖יו
וְיַגִּדָ֑הּ
עַל־מָה֙ אָבְדָ֣ה הָאָ֔רֶץ
נִצְּתָ֥ה כַמִּדְבָּ֖ר
מִבְּלִ֥י עֹבֵֽר׃ ס

12The LORD replied: Because they forsook the
Teaching I had set before them. They did not
obey Me and they did not follow it, 13but followed their own willful heart and followed the
Baalim, as their fathers had taught them. 14As-
suredly, thus said the LORD of Hosts, the God
of Israel: I am going to feed that people wormwood and make them drink a bitter draft. 15I
will scatter them among nations which they and
their fathers never knew; and I will dispatch the
sword after them until I have consumed them.

16Thus said the LORD of Hosts:
Listen!
Summon the dirge-singers, let them come;
Send for the skilled women, let them come.
17Let them quickly start a wailing for us,
That our eyes may run with tears,
Our pupils flow with water.

18For the sound of wailing
Is heard from Zion:
How we are despoiled!
How greatly we are shamed!
Ah, we must leave our land,
Abandon our dwellings!

19Hear, O women, the word of the LORD,
Let your ears receive the word of His mouth,
And teach your daughters wailing,
And one another lamentation.
20For death has climbed through our windows,
Has entered our fortresses,
To cut off babes from the streets,
Young men from the squares.

12 וַיֹּ֣אמֶר יְהוָ֔ה עַל־עָזְבָם֙ אֶת־תּ֣וֹרָתִ֔י
אֲשֶׁ֥ר נָתַ֖תִּי לִפְנֵיהֶ֑ם וְלֹא־שָׁמְע֥וּ בְקוֹלִ֖י
וְלֹא־הָ֥לְכוּ בָֽהּ׃ 13 וַיֵּ֣לְכ֔וּ אַחֲרֵ֖י שְׁרִר֣וּת
לִבָּ֑ם וְאַחֲרֵי֙ הַבְּעָלִ֔ים אֲשֶׁ֥ר לִמְּד֖וּם
אֲבוֹתָֽם׃ ס 14 לָכֵ֡ן כֹּֽה־אָמַ֞ר יְהוָ֤ה
צְבָאוֹת֙ אֱלֹהֵ֣י יִשְׂרָאֵ֔ל הִנְנִ֧י מַאֲכִילָ֛ם
אֶת־הָעָ֥ם הַזֶּ֖ה לַעֲנָ֑ה וְהִשְׁקִיתִ֖ים מֵי־
רֹֽאשׁ׃ 15 וַהֲפִֽיצוֹתִים֙ בַּגּוֹיִ֔ם אֲשֶׁר֙ לֹ֣א יָֽדְע֔וּ
הֵ֖מָּה וַאֲבוֹתָ֑ם וְשִׁלַּחְתִּ֤י אַחֲרֵיהֶם֙ אֶת־
הַחֶ֔רֶב עַ֥ד כַּלּוֹתִ֖י אוֹתָֽם׃ פ

16 כֹּ֤ה אָמַר֙ יְהוָ֣ה צְבָא֔וֹת
הִֽתְבּוֹנְנ֛וּ
וְקִרְא֥וּ לַמְקוֹנְנ֖וֹת וּתְבוֹאֶ֑ינָה
וְאֶל־הַחֲכָמ֥וֹת שִׁלְח֖וּ וְתָבֽוֹאנָה׃
17 וּתְמַהֵ֕רְנָה וְתִשֶּׂ֥נָה* עָלֵ֖ינוּ נֶ֑הִי
וְתֵרַ֤דְנָה עֵינֵ֙ינוּ֙ דִּמְעָ֔ה
וְעַפְעַפֵּ֖ינוּ יִזְּלוּ־מָֽיִם׃

18 כִּ֣י ק֥וֹל נְהִ֛י
נִשְׁמַ֥ע מִצִּיּ֖וֹן
אֵ֣יךְ שֻׁדָּ֑דְנוּ
בֹּ֤שְׁנוּ מְאֹד֙
כִּֽי־עָזַ֣בְנוּ אָ֔רֶץ
כִּ֥י הִשְׁלִ֖יכוּ מִשְׁכְּנוֹתֵֽינוּ׃ ס

19 כִּֽי־שְׁמַ֤עְנָה נָשִׁים֙ דְּבַר־יְהוָ֔ה
וְתִקַּ֥ח אָזְנְכֶ֖ם דְּבַר־פִּ֑יו
וְלַמֵּ֤דְנָה בְנֽוֹתֵיכֶם֙ נֶ֔הִי
וְאִשָּׁ֥ה רְעוּתָ֖הּ קִינָֽה׃
20 כִּֽי־עָ֤לָה מָ֙וֶת֙ בְּחַלּוֹנֵ֔ינוּ
בָּ֖א בְּאַרְמְנוֹתֵ֑ינוּ
לְהַכְרִ֤ית עוֹלָל֙ מִח֔וּץ
בַּחוּרִ֖ים מֵרְחֹבֽוֹת׃

v. 17. חסר א׳

16. dirge-singers Professional female wailers.

21Speak thus—says the LORD:
The carcasses of men shall lie
Like dung upon the fields,
Like sheaves behind the reaper,
With none to pick them up.

22Thus said the LORD:
Let not the wise man glory in his wisdom;
Let not the strong man glory in his strength;
Let not the rich man glory in his riches.
23But only in this should one glory:
In his earnest devotion to Me.
For I the LORD act with kindness,
Justice, and equity in the world;
For in these I delight
—declares the LORD.

21 דַּבֵּ֗ר כֹּ֚ה נְאֻם־יְהֹוָ֔ה
וְנָֽפְלָה֙ נִבְלַ֣ת הָֽאָדָ֔ם
כְּדֹ֖מֶן עַל־פְּנֵ֣י הַשָּׂדֶ֑ה
וּכְעָמִ֛יר מֵאַחֲרֵ֥י הַקֹּצֵ֖ר
וְאֵ֥ין מְאַסֵּֽף׃ ס

22 כֹּ֣ה ׀ אָמַ֣ר יְהֹוָ֗ה
אַל־יִתְהַלֵּ֤ל חָכָם֙ בְּחָכְמָת֔וֹ
וְאַל־יִתְהַלֵּ֥ל הַגִּבּ֖וֹר בִּגְבוּרָת֑וֹ
אַל־יִתְהַלֵּ֥ל עָשִׁ֖יר בְּעָשְׁרֽוֹ׃
23 כִּ֣י אִם־בְּזֹ֞את יִתְהַלֵּ֣ל הַמִּתְהַלֵּ֗ל
הַשְׂכֵּל֮ וְיָדֹ֣עַ אוֹתִי֒
כִּ֚י אֲנִ֣י יְהֹוָ֔ה עֹ֥שֶׂה חֶ֛סֶד
מִשְׁפָּ֥ט וּצְדָקָ֖ה בָּאָ֑רֶץ
כִּֽי־בְאֵ֥לֶּה חָפַ֖צְתִּי
נְאֻם־יְהֹוָֽה׃ ס

23. kindness, / Justice, and equity Hebrew: *ḥesed, mishpat,* and *tz'dakah*. The last pair of terms recurs frequently in the Bible as both a human and a divine ideal (see, e.g., Gen. 18:19). The triad of elements is also found elsewhere, both for God (Ps. 33:5, 89:15) and for mortals (Isa. 16:5). This verse links these divine attributes—and knowledge of God—with the covenant ideal (see also Hos. 2:21; *Guide* III:53). The *haftarah* thus ends with a summary of covenantal virtues that serves as a counterpoint to the moral and religious sins denounced earlier (9:1–5,11–15).

הפטרה למנחה תענית צבור

HAFTARAH FOR FAST DAY AFTERNOONS

ISAIAH 55:6–56:8

Words of admonition, exhortation, and comfort form this *haftarah.* They were spoken in the Babylonian exile sometime after 539 B.C.E. At that time, Cyrus the Mede conquered Babylon and decreed that his foreign subjects, including the Judeans, could return to their native lands and practices. Isaiah urges the Judeans to repent of their evil ways and plans (Isa. 55:6–7), and to do what is right and just, before their approaching deliverance from exile (55:12–13, 56:1). They should take comfort in the merciful and forgiving nature of God (55:7), whose promise of salvation is ensured (55:10–11). Eunuchs and foreigners who have attached themselves to God and the Covenant also receive words of comfort, allaying their fears of rejection. They are promised a place among the future worshipers in Zion if they remain observant (56:3–8).

Divine grace and loving kindness are characteristic of this *haftarah.* God's care embraces everyone—native and alien alike—who turns to God and observes His commandments. Repentant sinners especially may take heart in God's forgiveness, which is grounded in His utterly transcendent nature (55:8).

There are several types of prophetic discourse in this *haftarah.* The first is a direct call for repentance (55:6–7). To allay any concern that a full pardon might not necessarily follow repentance, God reinforces the assertion of His transcendent "plans" and "ways" by an analogy. Divine "ways" are said to go beyond those of mortals as the heavens are high above the earth. God's ways of mercy are not only beyond scrutiny and expectation but also utterly beyond the grasp and understanding of human beings.

The second important type of prophetic speech here is the prophetic prediction and the assertion of its infallibility. The prophet articulates a new analogy, comparing God's event-begetting word with rain that descends from above to fertilize the seeds of vegetation. Just as this rain falls and does not return to heaven, so will God's prophetic "word that issues from My mouth . . . not come back to Me unfulfilled" (55:10–11).

The third type of prophetic discourse is the instructional exhortation, which appears in two forms. The first form is a brief statement of proper action at the beginning of Isa. 56. "Observe what is right and do what is just" (literally, "observe justice [*mishpat*], do righteousness [*tz'dakah*]"). This call condenses the moral duties required of the nation, using the terms often employed in the Bible to characterize proper covenantal behavior.

The second form elaborates on the initial call to "observe [*shimru*] justice" (Isa. 56:1) by proclaiming the happiness that accrues to one who observes or "keeps [*shomer*] the sabbath," and who "stays [*shomer*] his hand from doing any evil" (56:2). One might even state that the two phrases characterize the Decalogue. Observing *Shabbat* is the first positive ritual commandment there, and staying one's hand from evil applies to all the interpersonal prohibitions in the Decalogue.

Observing *Shabbat* and holding fast to the Covenant constitute the two conditions required of the foreigners and the eunuchs who would receive the benefits of inclusion in God's Temple (56:4,6). These benefits are declared in the fourth type of prophetic discourse found in this reading: the authorization of innovation (56:4–8). That foreigners could take part in the sacrificial service was unprecedented. It was a universalist proclamation of sorts, erasing the distinction between native and outsider in lay worship. The promise that the eunuchs would have a place in the House of God gives yet another expression to the prophet's inclusionist temper.

The diverse discourses of the *haftarah* are bound together by theme words. The verb *shuv* indicates not only the "turn" to God in repentance but also the "return" of rain and of the pro-

phetic word (55:7,10). And *karet* (55:13, 56:5) refers to the fact that neither God's miracles during the deliverance nor the monument erected for the eunuchs in the Temple will "perish." The word *karov* (near) refers both to God's nearness to the penitent and to the nearness of the day of salvation (55:6, 56:1).

RELATION OF THE *HAFTARAH* TO THE CALENDAR

The Torah reading for the afternoon service on fast days (Fast of Gedaliah, 10th of *Tevet*, Fast of Esther, 17th of *Tammuz*, and *Tish·ah b'Av*) is Exod. 32:11–14 and 34:1–10. In the first selection, Moses appeals to God to relent in His anger against His people; in the second, Moses receives a revelation of God's attributes of mercy. In particular, the Lord is called "compassionate" (*raḥum*) and "abounding [*rav*] in kindness," forgiving iniquity and sin (Exod. 34:6–7). The *haftarah* echoes these themes. In it the prophet calls on the people to repent of their evil plans and ways, emphasizing that God will compassionately "pardon" (*vi-yraḥameihu*) the sinner and "freely [or "fully," *yarbeh*] pardon him" (Isa. 55:7). A key reason for selecting this *haftarah* was undoubtedly its emphasis on divine mercy—so central on a day of penance and fasting.

55 6Seek the LORD while He can be found,
Call to Him while He is near.
7Let the wicked give up his ways,
The sinful man his plans;
Let him turn back to the LORD,
And He will pardon him;
To our God,
For He freely forgives.
8For My plans are not your plans,
Nor are My ways your ways
—declares the LORD.
9But as the heavens are high above the earth,
So are My ways high above your ways
And My plans above your plans.
10For as the rain or snow drops from heaven

נה 6 דִּרְשׁוּ יְהוָה בְּהִמָּצְאוֹ
קְרָאֻהוּ בִּהְיוֹתוֹ קָרוֹב׃
7 יַעֲזֹב רָשָׁע דַּרְכּוֹ
וְאִישׁ אָוֶן מַחְשְׁבֹתָיו
וְיָשֹׁב אֶל־יְהוָה
וִירַחֲמֵהוּ
וְאֶל־אֱלֹהֵינוּ
כִּי־יַרְבֶּה לִסְלוֹחַ׃
8 כִּי לֹא מַחְשְׁבוֹתַי מַחְשְׁבוֹתֵיכֶם
וְלֹא דַרְכֵיכֶם דְּרָכָי
נְאֻם יְהוָה׃
9 כִּי־גָבְהוּ שָׁמַיִם מֵאָרֶץ
כֵּן גָּבְהוּ דְרָכַי מִדַּרְכֵיכֶם
וּמַחְשְׁבֹתַי מִמַּחְשְׁבֹתֵיכֶם׃
10 כִּי כַּאֲשֶׁר יֵרֵד הַגֶּשֶׁם וְהַשֶּׁלֶג מִן־
הַשָּׁמַיִם

Isaiah 55:6. Seek the LORD while He can be found The phrasing echoes the Torah; Moses, anticipating a time of exile, told the people that "if you search there for the LORD your God, you will find Him, if only you seek Him with all your heart and soul . . . and, in the end, return" to Him (Deut. 4:29–30). God's compassion is stressed there (Deut. 4:31), as here.

Call This imperative is either synonymous with "seek," in the first clause, or it introduces a separate act of penitential prayer.

while He is near The quality of divine closeness to those who call is presented as a distinguishing characteristic of Israel's God in Deut. 4:7.

8. My ways In the Torah, after the people sinned with the Golden Calf, Moses asked to be shown God's "ways"; he received the revelation of God's 13 attributes of mercy (Exod. 34:6–7). Centuries later, when Ezekiel taught God's readiness to forgive the penitent, the exiles responded with wonder and doubt at God's incomprehensible "way" (Ezek. 18:25,29); they assumed that iniquity had to be punished. Here, too, it appears that the people need to be convinced that God will forgive those who turn from evil. But God's

And returns not there,
But soaks the earth
And makes it bring forth vegetation,
Yielding seed for sowing and bread for eating,
11So is the word that issues from My mouth:
It does not come back to Me unfulfilled,
But performs what I purpose,
Achieves what I sent it to do.
12Yea, you shall leave in joy and be led home secure.
Before you, mount and hill shall shout aloud,
And all the trees of the field shall clap their hands.
13Instead of the brier, a cypress shall rise;
Instead of the nettle, a myrtle shall rise.
These shall stand as a testimony to the LORD,
As an everlasting sign that shall not perish.

וְשָׁמָּה לֹא יָשׁוּב
כִּי אִם־הִרְוָה אֶת־הָאָרֶץ
וְהוֹלִידָהּ וְהִצְמִיחָהּ
וְנָתַן זֶרַע לַזֹּרֵעַ וְלֶחֶם לָאֹכֵל׃
11 כֵּן יִהְיֶה דְבָרִי אֲשֶׁר יֵצֵא מִפִּי
לֹא־יָשׁוּב אֵלַי רֵיקָם
כִּי אִם־עָשָׂה אֶת־אֲשֶׁר חָפַצְתִּי
וְהִצְלִיחַ אֲשֶׁר שְׁלַחְתִּיו׃
12 כִּי־בְשִׂמְחָה תֵצֵאוּ וּבְשָׁלוֹם תּוּבָלוּן
הֶהָרִים וְהַגְּבָעוֹת יִפְצְחוּ לִפְנֵיכֶם רִנָּה
וְכָל־עֲצֵי הַשָּׂדֶה יִמְחֲאוּ־כָף׃
13 תַּחַת הַנַּעֲצוּץ יַעֲלֶה בְרוֹשׁ
תחת וְתַחַת הַסִּרְפַּד יַעֲלֶה הֲדַס
וְהָיָה לַיהוָה לְשֵׁם
לְאוֹת עוֹלָם לֹא יִכָּרֵת׃ ס

56 Thus said the LORD:
Observe what is right and do what is just;
For soon My salvation shall come,
And My deliverance be revealed.
2Happy is the man who does this,
The man who holds fast to it:
Who keeps the sabbath and does not profane it,
And stays his hand from doing any evil.

3Let not the foreigner say,
Who has attached himself to the LORD,

נו כֹּה אָמַר יְהוָה
שִׁמְרוּ מִשְׁפָּט וַעֲשׂוּ צְדָקָה
כִּי־קְרוֹבָה יְשׁוּעָתִי לָבוֹא
וְצִדְקָתִי לְהִגָּלוֹת׃
2 אַשְׁרֵי אֱנוֹשׁ יַעֲשֶׂה־זֹּאת
וּבֶן־אָדָם יַחֲזִיק בָּהּ
שֹׁמֵר שַׁבָּת מֵחַלְּלוֹ
וְשֹׁמֵר יָדוֹ מֵעֲשׂוֹת כָּל־רָע׃ ס

3 וְאַל־יֹאמַר בֶּן־הַנֵּכָר
הַנִּלְוָה אֶל־יְהוָה לֵאמֹר

ways are those of compassion and of openness to repentance.

11. This idiom for the prophetic word is rooted in prophetic traditions about the effectiveness of divine predictions (see 1 Sam. 9:6; cf. 2 Kings 10:10).

come back Hebrew: *yashuv,* which plays on *v'yashov* ("Let him turn back") in verse 7.

13. a testimony Hebrew: *shem;* "a name" that is an "everlasting sign that shall not perish [*lo yikkaret*]." Compare 56:5 below, where the eunuchs who observe the covenant will have a "name" (*shem*) in the Temple—"an everlasting name [*shem*] that shall not perish [*lo yikkaret*]."

Isaiah 56:1. do what is just The call to morally righteous behavior is a hallmark of biblical prophecy.

2. Who keeps the sabbath . . . And stays his hand This instruction epitomizes the ritual law and the moral law, the duties to God and to other human beings.

3. Who has attached himself Hebrew:

"The LORD will keep me apart from His people";
And let not the eunuch say,
"I am a withered tree."
4 For thus said the LORD:
"As for the eunuchs who keep My sabbaths,
Who have chosen what I desire
And hold fast to My covenant—
5 I will give them, in My House
And within My walls,
A monument and a name
Better than sons or daughters.
I will give them an everlasting name
Which shall not perish.
6 As for the foreigners
Who attach themselves to the LORD,
To minister to Him,
And to love the name of the LORD,
To be His servants—
All who keep the sabbath and do not profane it,
And who hold fast to My covenant—
7 I will bring them to My sacred mount
And let them rejoice in My house of prayer.
Their burnt offerings and sacrifices
Shall be welcome on My altar;
For My House shall be called
A house of prayer for all peoples."
8 Thus declares the Lord GOD,
Who gathers the dispersed of Israel:
"I will gather still more to those already gathered."

הַבְדֵּ֤ל יַבְדִּילַ֙נִי יְהוָ֖ה מֵעַ֣ל עַמּ֑וֹ
וְאַל־יֹאמַר֙ הַסָּרִ֔יס
הֵ֥ן אֲנִ֖י עֵ֥ץ יָבֵֽשׁ׃ ס
4 כִּי־כֹ֣ה ׀ אָמַ֣ר יְהוָ֗ה
לַסָּֽרִיסִים֙ אֲשֶׁ֤ר יִשְׁמְרוּ֙ אֶת־שַׁבְּתוֹתַ֔י
וּבָֽחֲר֖וּ בַּאֲשֶׁ֣ר חָפָ֑צְתִּי
וּמַחֲזִיקִ֖ים בִּבְרִיתִֽי׃
5 וְנָתַתִּ֨י לָהֶ֜ם בְּבֵיתִ֤י
וּבְחוֹמֹתַי֙
יָ֣ד וָשֵׁ֔ם
ט֖וֹב מִבָּנִ֣ים וּמִבָּנ֑וֹת
שֵׁ֤ם עוֹלָם֙ אֶתֶּן־ל֔וֹ
אֲשֶׁ֖ר לֹ֥א יִכָּרֵֽת׃ ס
6 וּבְנֵ֣י הַנֵּכָ֗ר
הַנִּלְוִ֤ים עַל־יְהוָה֙
לְשָׁ֣רְת֔וֹ
וּֽלְאַהֲבָה֙ אֶת־שֵׁ֣ם יְהוָ֔ה
לִהְי֥וֹת ל֖וֹ לַעֲבָדִ֑ים
כָּל־שֹׁמֵ֤ר שַׁבָּת֙ מֵֽחַלְּל֔וֹ
וּמַחֲזִיקִ֖ים בִּבְרִיתִֽי׃
7 וַהֲבִיאוֹתִ֞ים אֶל־הַ֣ר קָדְשִׁ֗י
וְשִׂמַּחְתִּים֙ בְּבֵ֣ית תְּפִלָּתִ֔י
עוֹלֹתֵיהֶ֧ם וְזִבְחֵיהֶ֛ם
לְרָצ֖וֹן עַל־מִזְבְּחִ֑י
כִּ֣י בֵיתִ֔י בֵּית־תְּפִלָּ֥ה יִקָּרֵ֖א
לְכָל־הָעַמִּֽים׃
8 נְאֻם֙ אֲדֹנָ֣י יְהוִ֔ה
מְקַבֵּ֖ץ נִדְחֵ֣י יִשְׂרָאֵ֑ל
ע֛וֹד אֲקַבֵּ֥ץ עָלָ֖יו לְנִקְבָּצָֽיו׃

ha-nilvah, a late technical designation for foreigners who join the community of Israel (see Zech. 2:15; Esther 9:27).

5. A monument and a name Hebrew: *yad va-shem.* This phrase seems to indicate a special place (Ibn Ezra; cf. Deut. 23:13), monument (cf. 1 Sam. 15:12), or Temple role that would compensate the pious eunuchs for their lack of progeny (cf. 2 Sam. 18:18). Nearly 2500 years later, it was adopted by the State of Israel as the name of its Holocaust memorial site, in Jerusalem.

7. house of prayer A new designation for the Temple. Its role as a place of prayer for everyone was spelled out by King Solomon in his prayer inaugurating the Temple (1 Kings 8:41–42). In Isaiah, foreigners who join the Israelite covenant and observe its duties are promised participation in the sacrificial service, making them equal in all respects to the native Israelites (Radak). This is a bold example of prophetic universalism, authorized by God. All may join the Covenant—and may worship with full rights.

Biblical Life and Perspectives

BIBLICAL ARCHAEOLOGY

Lee I. Levine

Archaeological remains have been a source of fascination for centuries. Since the 17th and 18th centuries, travelers have braved difficult physical conditions and the hostility of the local inhabitants to bring home news of the remarkable remains of ancient civilizations. By the 19th century, many European countries had established societies to promote the exploration and sponsorship of archaeological excavations in the Middle East. The political realities of the time prompted Western powers to increase their presence in the region to fill the power vacuum that would be left by the impending disintegration of the Ottoman Empire. The almost immediate success of the archaeological excavations—which included sensational discoveries from Troy, Babylon, Susa, and Egypt—led to heightened public interest and support.

Interest in the archaeology of the Holy Land was generated in part by these developments, and in part by the role of the country as the historical backdrop in the biblical narrative for events ranging from Abraham to Jesus. Verifying the Bible became a pivotal motivating factor for many archaeologists, most of whom were, not coincidentally, clergymen, and one of the covert, and sometimes explicitly stated, goals of many of these expeditions was to prove the historicity and accuracy of the Bible. In the first half of the 20th century, Jewish archaeologists from the *Yishuv* (the emerging Zionist presence in Palestine) joined the exploration of ancient Israel with a similarly tendentious agenda. Academic and cultural institutions in the *Yishuv* that sponsored such initiatives sought to unearth the country's Jewish roots by uncovering the major sites of Israelite settlement in the biblical and postbiblical periods.

This picture changed dramatically during the second half of the 20th century. Religious motivation and the need to demonstrate the existence of Jewish roots in the country became less central, although understanding the Hebrew and Christian Bibles, as well as Jewish history in antiquity, remained a key motivating factor in these explorations. Archaeologists increasingly have questioned accepted assumptions about biblical history and the biblical narrative, owing to a revisionist and skeptical mode that characterizes some archaeological circles—a not uncommon phenomenon in scholarship generally in the latter 20th century. Thus, the beginning of the 21st century finds biblical archaeology in a state of flux. Although new material is brought to light almost every year and our knowledge of the material culture of the period increases geometrically, fundamental questions of interpretation and the resultant reconstructions of history are often in the fore.

Archaeological evidence has substantially impacted our knowledge and understanding of the Bible and of biblical history in the following ways.

REVEALING NEW INFORMATION

Archaeology has brought to light an enormous amount of information regarding the material culture of the times. Vessels, tools, weapons, seals, and coins (from the Restoration, or Persian, period; 538–332 B.C.E.), as well as names and official titles mentioned in inscriptions, all attest to various aspects of daily life in Israelite culture. Moreover, the discovery of residential quarters, city walls, and urban settlements reveals dimensions of biblical society that add immeasurably to our understanding of the written sources.

CONFIRMING THE BIBLICAL NARRATIVE

Many discoveries have a direct bearing on information appearing in the Bible. For instance, several archaeological sites such as Hazor bear witness to Joshua's alleged conquest of Canaan by showing massive destruction toward the end of the 13th century B.C.E. Other examples include the shaft (*tzinnor*) used by David to conquer Jerusalem, an inscription noting the "House of David," the plan and layout of city gates mentioned frequently in the biblical text, the discovery of local Israelite altars and shrines (presumably the high places, or *bamot,* referred to by the prophets), the appearance of hundreds of new settlements in the hill country from the 13th to 11th centuries B.C.E., evidence of royal building activities (e.g., Hezekiah's tunnel), and discoveries at other sites in Israel's neighboring countries (Syria, Jordan, and Iraq) that shed light on the patriarchal era. All of this material concretizes and contextualizes the biblical narrative. Such has been the case with documents from Mari (Syria) and Nuzi (Iraq), the Mesha inscription (Jordan), and the Merneptah stele (commemorative stone pillar) from late 13th-century Egypt noting the destruction of Israel.

REVOLUTIONIZING OUR UNDERSTANDING

Archaeological finds, however, at times call into question the historicity of the biblical narrative. For instance, some archaeological sites seem to deny Joshua's alleged conquest of Canaan by showing neither a destruction layer nor traces of walls nor even settlement from that era (e.g., Jericho, Ai). Realizing the highly theological and literary character of the Book of Joshua, some scholars have concluded that its accounts are selective and biased, having minimal historical value in reconstructing the events of the past.

The chronological factor is often used to determine the value of archaeology to the biblical account. The later the period in question, the greater the contribution of archaeology to illuminating the biblical text. With this in mind, we will survey the effect that archaeology has on our understanding of the various stages of biblical history: the patriarchal age, the Exodus and wilderness era, the settlement of Canaan, and the period of the monarchy. The information in this regard resembles an inverse pyramid. It is negligible for the first two stages, and we have somewhat more data for the settlement period (i.e., parallel to the narrative in the Books of Joshua, Judges, and 1 Samuel). Only for the period of the monarchy—particularly toward its end, in the 8th and 7th centuries B.C.E.—do we have a significant amount of reliable information that richly supplements the biblical account.

Patriarchal Age

Scholarly assessment of the historicity of the biblical narratives differs significantly. As early as the 19th century, J. Wellhausen had assumed that nothing historical could be derived from these accounts, calling them a "glorified mirage." This assessment changed radically in the first part of the 20th century with the counterclaim of W. F. Albright and E. Speiser, among others, for a large degree of historicity on the basis of comparative archaeological finds from sites outside of Canaan. Although Albright's approach finds many staunch adherents to this day, a revisionist school in the latter decades of the 20th century has reverted to regarding the patriarchal narratives, as well as the entire Bible, as devoid of historical accuracy. Most scholars, however, have taken the middle road between credence and rejection.

One problem in assessing the historical accuracy of these biblical traditions is that they relate largely to the private affairs of Abraham's family. The texts rarely refer to public events (as the war of the kings in Gen. 14) that at least have the possibility of being corroborated elsewhere. Assuming that patriarchal figures lived some time in the first half of the 2nd millennium and that the traditions as we have them in the Book of Genesis were composed about a millennium later, the historical reliability of such material would seem to be

questionable. Nevertheless, what has propelled some scholars to assume a historical kernel of truth in these accounts is the remarkable similarity in detail between some of these stories and documents discovered at 2nd-millennium sites, such as Nuzi, Mari, and Emar. In the words of Albright:

> Abraham, Isaac, and Jacob no longer seem isolated figures, much less reflections of later Israelite history; they now appear as true children of their age, bearing the same names, moving about over the same territory, visiting the same towns, practicing the same customs as their contemporaries.

Personal names (Abram, Jacob), social customs, and legal practices (e.g., the wife-sister episodes in Gen. 12, 20, and 26) seem to correspond to information transmitted in documents from the aforementioned sites. Although many scholars have subsequently taken a more reserved position, the tendency to ascribe some sort of historical value to these narratives remains strong. How much is history and not tradition? And how many details can be considered authentic and reflective of these early times? An attempt to formulate a middle-of-the-road assessment—between assuming a historical patriarchal period on the one hand and relegating the entire Genesis corpus to the status of late literary traditions—has been articulated by G. E. Wright:

> We shall probably never be able to prove that Abram really existed, that he did this or that, said thus and so, but what we can prove is that his life and time, as reflected in the stories about him, fit perfectly within the early second millennium (B.C.E.), but imperfectly with any late period.

Exodus and Wilderness Era

The contribution of archaeology to the biblical narratives in the last four books of the Torah is likewise limited. There is no reference in Egyptian sources to Israel's sojourn in that country, and the evidence that does exist is negligible and indirect. The period of servitude that entailed building the cities of Pithom and Rameses seems to fit best the reign of Rameses II, who ruled in the 13th century B.C.E. By the end of that century, Israel was already a recognized entity in Canaan, as indicated by a reference to it on a stele of Pharaoh Merneptah (ca. 1207 B.C.E.) noting the king's victory over a people called Israel.

Indications of an Egyptian sojourn may likewise be indicated by the names that appear in the Joseph narrative at the end of Genesis: Joseph's wife, Asenath, and that of his master, Potiphar, are Egyptian; and Joseph himself had an Egyptian name, Zaphenath-paneah. Moreover, the Hyksos period in Egypt, when the country was ruled by Asiatic princes, dates to the 17th and 16th centuries B.C.E., and some scholars regard this as the setting of the Joseph narrative. The land of Goshen, the region of Israelite settlement in Egypt, was probably in the eastern Nile delta where the Hyksos capital, Avaris, was likewise located; and the expulsion of the Hyksos may be related to the beginning of Israel's troubles in the country ("A new king arose over Egypt who did not know Joseph"; Exod. 1:8).

The 14th-century-B.C.E. el-Amarna letters point to the collapse of Egyptian rule in Canaan and the resultant warfare and insecurity that became endemic throughout the country. One of the causes of these disturbances was the presence of marauders called Habiru, who took advantage of the political and military vacuum to pillage the cities and the countryside. Such historical circumstances may well have provided the context for the one or more waves of invasion and settlement by Israelite (or proto-Israelite) tribes.

These few indirect pieces of evidence are far from adequate to corroborate the historicity of the biblical account, but they do suggest a contextual background for the Egyptian servitude (of at least some of the people who later became Israelites) and the appearance of a new population in Canaan. Nevertheless, it also has been maintained that here too, as in the patriarchal era, later writers used earlier mate-

rial to present an account of what in reality was a folk tradition with little or no historical basis.

Conquest and Settlement of Canaan

The period of the conquest and settlement of Canaan is arguably the most controversial issue in biblical history. The Book of Joshua appears to offer a straightforward description of an immediate and complete conquest, but the Book of Judges relates a different story: Rather than conquest followed by an allotment of the Land, Judges speaks of a reverse process, whereby the Land was first divided up and then each tribe, or several tribes together, proceeded to conquer their respective territories. In contrast to the picture of a total and immediate conquest in Josh. 11:16–20, Judges acknowledges that many cities were not subdued (Judg. 1:21,27–33), that the period of conquest lasted a long time, and that the acquisition was carried out in various ways, including by peaceful settlement.

The not inconsiderable amount of archaeological evidence for this period is likewise ambiguous. Remains of a violent conquest in the 13th century B.C.E. are evident at Hazor, thus corroborating the biblical account; but the unwalled and uninhabited Jericho and Ai, respectively, clearly seem to contradict the violent and complete conquest portrayed in the Book of Joshua. Although Hazor may well be tied to events recorded in the Bible, it is also possible that its destruction was the result of other factors, such as the 13th-century-B.C.E. conquest by the Sea Peoples, a population that migrated from Greece and the Aegean islands and wrought havoc throughout the eastern Mediterranean. The degree to which Joshua and Judges can be culled for kernels of historical truth or simply considered as theologically motivated accounts using a historical framework for their purposes is a basic controversy in academic circles.

The archaeological material for the early Iron Age patterns of settlement (i.e., post-1200 B.C.E., the period of Joshua and Judges) is ambiguous in yet another vein. Do the hundreds of small settlements in the hill country (especially Judea and Samaria) date from this period? If so, were they inhabited by the local Canaanite population? Or are the finds (ceramic remains and domestic architecture [the four-room house]) from these settlements so different as to warrant the assumption of there being another population? In other words, do they reflect a new and different group (a proto-Israelite population) that invaded the country from the east? Finally, does the material culture of the hill country share enough common traits (e.g., plastered water cisterns and terracing) to justify referring to them as one type, or are regional variations so considerable as to point to other ethnic or social groupings, and perhaps even to other periods of settlement?

Such ambiguities and the inherent fascination of the conquest have generated four main approaches to explain Israelite settlement:

1. The "traditional" approach generally adopts the biblical outlook, especially that of the Book of Joshua, albeit with some modifications. A conquest did take place, as attested by the Book of Joshua and some archaeological sites, although the biblical account clearly exaggerates the extent and intensity of this phenomenon.

2. Israelite settlement in the highlands was a gradual process of infiltration over the course of centuries. A number of archaeological excavations seem to confirm this picture, indicating that large tracts of hill country became inhabited during the 13th and 12th centuries B.C.E.

A variation of this second approach views this settlement pattern as part of the general dislocation and migration of populations throughout the eastern Mediterranean at the time; those known as the Israelites eventually included peoples of diverse backgrounds: nomads and seminomads of Semitic and non-Semitic origins, former urban populations, those from within Canaan, and others who had migrated. An Israelite identity emerged only after a long process that required forging a political and religious unity from a plethora of regional variations within the country.

3. Israel came into being after a peasants' revolt against the Canaanite cities. This revolutionary liberation movement was thus a "Canaanite" phenomenon, with the victorious revolutionaries being led by Hebrews whose God was identified with the Exodus. The Habiru revolts of the previous century serve as a model for this view.

4. A combination of some (or all) of these theories accounts for the emergence of Israel, assuming that there was an incursion that attracted local groups, creating a new socio-religious identity known as Israel.

Period of the Monarchy

A significant amount of archaeological material has been recovered from the 400-year period (ca. 1000–586 B.C.E.) of the monarchy, which has illuminated many facets of First Temple history and culture. Many of these data supplement what is known from the biblical narrative and relate to the daily life and material culture of the society. Owing to the extensive excavations in numerous cities and towns, the subject of urbanization has received much attention. City plans, fortifications, and streets have been amply documented, and various types of royal buildings (palatial, storage, and administrative complexes) have been uncovered—from those of capital cities such as Samaria to those located in provincial centers such as Megiddo. Residential buildings of a variety of sizes have been discovered, most characteristically the four-room house, featuring one or two rows of pillars, a central courtyard, and surrounding rooms. Industrial installations are also well documented, the best known being small household workshops for producing wine and oil. Water-supply systems were ubiquitous in Israelite settlements, ranging from tunnels and shafts, either leading to sources outside the settlement or for bringing water to another location, to large-scale cisterns for storing water. Tombs and burial caves also shed a great deal of light on the funerary customs of the period. Finally, the discovery of a variety of city gates and city-gate complexes attests to the centrality of these areas for a wide range of communal activities that find expression throughout biblical literature.

Inscriptions constitute another type of archaeological find relating directly to the biblical text, illustrating and corroborating the descriptions contained therein. An inscription from Tel Dan in the Upper Galilee mentioning the "House of David" is a case in point. We have here, for the first time, a clear-cut reference to David and his dynasty from a source outside the Bible. The Bible's allusions to King Hezekiah's remarkable building activity in his kingdom are confirmed by the remarkable archaeological finds of the Siloam water tunnel and the "Broad Wall," marking the greatly expanded boundaries of Jerusalem to the west. Moreover, Hezekiah's administrative and fiscal reforms appear to be reflected in the *la-melekh* ("[belonging] to the king") seal impressions on jar handles, of which more than 1000 specimens have been discovered. Opinion is divided as to the purpose of these inscriptions. Did these jars contain produce from royal estates intended as revenue for the king, or did they contain provisions for his army?

Archaeological material has raised questions regarding certain assumptions and claims based on biblical literature. At times this evidence clearly contradicts the biblical narrative; on other occasions, data that might have corroborated the literary account are conspicuously lacking. An example of the latter is the almost total absence of archaeological evidence from Davidic and Solomonic Jerusalem. The Bible devotes an inordinate amount of space to the reigns of these two kings who purportedly developed their new capital city in many directions. Yet, archaeologists are hard pressed to identify any building, wall remains, or other installation as belonging to this period. Is this coincidental or, as the revisionists would have it, is the biblical account perhaps vastly exaggerated, serving, as it does, the propagandist agenda of the later Davidic dynasty?

Disparity between the written word and archaeological material is also evident in other areas. The Bible praises Solomon's building

of a number of royal cities throughout the country, while King Ahab, whose reputation in the Bible is sullied, is portrayed as a far inferior ruler. Yet, many scholars attribute some of the major urban building projects of Megiddo and Hazor to Ahab and not to Solomon. Most striking, however, are indications of religious syncretism (the absorption of pagan rites, beliefs, and customs) in Israelite religion. Little is known about this from the biblical text; yet, seen through the eyes of the Bible, this phenomenon is thoroughly castigated. For example, an ostracon (a pottery shard with writing on it) from Samaria bears the name *Egelyau*, which is probably to be translated "the calf of *YHVH*" (or possibly "*YHVH* is a calf"!). The most sensational find in this regard, however, comes from the wilderness settlement of Kuntilat 'Ajrud, located between Beer-sheba and Elat and near a road leading into the Sinai Desert, where many votive offerings were found. The most intriguing of these finds were inscriptions and drawings on wall plaster and jars. The inscriptions are generally blessings, one of which reads "May you be blessed by *YHVH* of Samaria (or Teman) and his *Asherah*" (a Canaanite deity described here as *YHVH*'s female consort). Below this inscription is the drawing of three figures, two of which may represent *YHVH* and *Asherah*. Such finds are an expression of one type of popular religion against which many biblical authors, particularly the prophets, fought vigorously.

Archaeology thus plays a major role in illuminating the biblical text. It often highlights the complexity and diversity of Israelite society and the extent of foreign influences on aspects of its daily life. Archaeological material also questions the historical accuracy of the biblical text, forcing us to realize that the Bible is not an objective, historical document. The Bible's value lies not in its historical accuracy, but rather in the religious and theological truths that it conveys through the use of narratives, laws, wisdom literature, and prophecy.

Archaeology can rarely stand alone, especially when it comes to historical, social, and religious issues. The stone installation on Mount Ebal, for example, has often been referred to as the altar erected by Joshua on entering the Land (Deut. 27; Josh. 24). However, this claim is far from clear, because neither the purpose of this stone installation nor its date has been convincingly demonstrated. Whether it had a religious purpose or even dates to the 13th century is uncertain, thus precluding any facile identification of the stone platform with the biblical story. Archaeology has its limitations no less than the biblical text. Although each type of source highlights the limitations of the other, they also can play a mutually positive role. Together, they enrich our knowledge of the period, at times offering vastly different perspectives and thereby affording us a much fuller and more comprehensive picture of biblical society than heretofore known.

ANCIENT NEAR EASTERN MYTHOLOGY

Robert Wexler

Among the most fascinating and famous stories of Genesis is the story of Noah. After torrential rains inundated the entire world, Noah's ark remained afloat until it came to rest atop Mount Ararat. To determine if the waters had begun to recede, Noah sent forth first a raven and then a dove. The following passage suggests that the dove could not find a place to alight and so returned to the ark.

> I sent forth and set free a dove.
> The dove went forth, but she came back again.
> But, since no resting-place for her was visible,
> she simply returned.

This passage is not from the Book of Genesis but from a very popular Sumero-Babylonian myth known as the *Gilgamesh* epic. Regarding the dove, the parallel text in Genesis (8:8–9) reads:

> Then he sent out the dove to see whether the waters had decreased from the surface of the ground. But the dove could not find a resting place for its foot, and returned to him to the ark.

How can we account for this obvious similarity to the *Gilgamesh* myth? We do know that fabled reports of catastrophic floods were not unique to the Levant. From Iraq to the South Seas, these stories are part of a genre of myths that recount the cataclysmic destruction of the known world. Among them, the flood motif is the most typical and represents a dramatic, mythic response to an almost universal danger. Still, even the nonscholar senses that Genesis and *Gilgamesh* have more in common than a shared theme. Both stories describe a hero chosen by a divine source to survive the flood (Noah in the Bible, and Utnapishtim in the Babylonian source). Each hero saved not only his family but many species of animals as well. In each case, the flood covered the earth, wiping out all forms of life except for those found on the boat. Both boats came to rest on the top of a mountain, and both heroes used the strategy of sending out birds to look for dry land.

If we claim that these two stories are related in some way, how do we go about discovering the nature of their relationship? Perhaps by examining these questions, we can also learn something about the techniques that scholars use to evaluate the relationship between any two literary texts.

Our first challenge is to make a case for some contact between the two cultures that would allow borrowing to occur. That case is easily made. The Book of Genesis itself relates that the Hebrew patriarch Abraham hailed from Ur, a site most commonly identified with the prominent Sumerian city-state of the same name. Furthermore, both biblical and extrabiblical sources confirm that sustained interaction did occur between Syro-Palestine (the geographic neighborhood of Israel) and Mesopotamia during the first three millennia of recorded history.

Given what we know about the geography of the two regions in question, it is unlikely that the Genesis story originated in Palestine. Ancient Mesopotamia, which included virtually all of modern-day Iraq and much of modern-day Syria, was dominated by at least two major rivers: the Tigris and Euphrates. In fact, the name "Mesopotamia" itself derives from a Greek term meaning "between the rivers." Agricultural life in this area depended largely on the ebb and flow of the two rivers. Heavy rains caused the rivers to swell and spill over their banks, inundating the nearby fields. If these inundations could be contained and channeled, the harvest was good. If the floodwaters became uncontrollable, there could be crop loss, famine, and substantial destruction of life and property. Inundations were known in Palestine, but they usually were limited to localized flash flooding. In other words, the possibility of a catastrophic deluge was much more a concern for the Mesopotamian peoples than it was for the early inhabitants of pre-Israelite Palestine. In the Mesopotamian imagination, a disastrous flood had the potential of wiping out the entire known world.

Because myths routinely reflect the anxieties of a particular culture, we conclude that the Flood story portrayed in Genesis is more likely of Mesopotamian than Palestinian origin. This Mesopotamian influence is evident not only in the Flood story but throughout the first 11 chapters of Genesis. Perhaps these narratives were part of a cultural legacy transported by the patriarch Abraham and his clan as they made their way from Ur to Haran and eventually to the Land of Canaan.

The question of whether *Gilgamesh* influenced the Genesis account or vice versa is more complex. Once we rule out coincidence, there appear to be at least three logical possibilities: (a) Genesis drew its material from *Gilgamesh,* (b) *Gilgamesh* drew its material from Genesis, or (c) both stories were based on a common earlier source. How can we conceivably know which of the two stories—Genesis or *Gilgamesh*—is older? How can we discover whether

the author of one was familiar with the other work?

What we can assume is that the *Gilgamesh* story was probably very well known in the ancient Near East. Archaeologists have found many clay tablets with fragments of this epic written in different time periods and representing a wide geologic area. The Genesis story, however, is known to us only through the biblical account, and perhaps this argues in favor of *Gilgamesh* being the original source of the two stories. Still, even if this were true, then we still would need to explain why so many discrepancies developed in the two related narratives.

The most likely assumption we can make is that both Genesis and *Gilgamesh* drew their material from a common tradition about the flood that existed in Mesopotamia. The stories then diverged in the retelling. Each account was shaped and refined by a specific religious message and embellished by the imagination of those who transmitted it through the generations.

The strong literary affinity that exists between *Gilgamesh* and the biblical Flood narrative has no equal among the other mythic texts of Mesopotamia. We do, however, encounter some distinct motifs and existential preoccupations that characterize both narrative traditions. The Garden of Eden story, for example, has some clear thematic parallels among the Mesopotamia myths.

According to the biblical text, Adam and Eve were given the opportunity to obtain immortality. God placed them in a garden, east of Eden, and provided them with a variety of trees from which they could eat, including the tree of knowledge and the tree of life (i.e., immortality). There was one proviso, however: "Of every tree of the garden you are free to eat; but as for the tree of knowledge of good and bad, you must not eat of it; for as soon as you eat of it, you shall die" (Gen. 2:16–17). Overcome by curiosity and a desire to be God-like, the man and the woman ate of the tree of knowledge, were banished from the garden, and forfeited their opportunity to live forever.

The lost promise of immortality was a key theme of several ancient Near Eastern myths, including the legend of Adapa and the South Wind, and the *Gilgamesh* epic. Adapa was a fabled hero who broke the wing of the god of the South Wind, risking the wrath of his fellow deities. He was summoned to appear before the high god, Anu, to receive his punishment. The god Ea, who often served as a divine advocate for human beings, gave Adapa specific information about how to win over the hostile gods who guarded the entrance to heaven. All of the gods were so impressed with Adapa that Anu offered him the waters of life, i.e., the gift of immortality. In an ironic conclusion to the story, the trusted Ea deliberately misled Adapa by counseling him that the waters contained death and not eternal life. Adapa followed Ea's advice, refused to drink the waters of life, and squandered the chance for humanity to become immortal.

Just as Utnapishtim is often called the Babylonian Noah, Adapa is occasionally referred to as the Babylonian Adam. Such a comparison does not really do justice to the much clearer parallels that exist between the stories of Noah and Gilgamesh. All we can reasonably say about the sagas of Adam and Adapa is that they both explain why human beings did not achieve immortality.

The *Gilgamesh* epic also has as its theme the quest for immortality. It begins by describing the exploits of the superhero for whom the myth is named. Accompanied by his equally impressive friend, Enkidu, Gilgamesh performs a number of courageous feats. Along the way he attracts the unwanted attention of the female goddess Ishtar whose love he spurns. Angered by his rejection of her, Ishtar resolves to kill Gilgamesh, but her plans are thwarted by Enkidu. Ultimately, Ishtar manages to end the life of Enkidu by afflicting him with a fatal disease. Gilgamesh is completely unnerved by the death of his friend. For the first time, he recognizes the possibility of his own mortality. No longer able to function as a hero, he devotes all of his time to the unsuccessful pursuit of eternal life. During his journey, Gilgamesh

encounters an alewife who explains to him why his quest is doomed to failure.

> Gilgamesh, where do you roam?
> You will not find the [eternal] life you seek.
> When the gods appointed death for mankind,
> They kept [eternal] life in their own hands.
> (tab. X, col. iii)

In this statement we find a powerful echo of the words uttered by God at the precise moment Adam and Eve were expelled from the garden: "Now that man has become like one of us, knowing good and bad, what if he should stretch out his hand and take also from the tree of life and eat, and live forever!" (Gen. 3:22). God then banishes humanity from the garden and places a sword at its entrance to prevent their return.

The Garden of Eden story indicates that divinity consists of two primary elements: knowledge and immortality. Through an act of disobedience, human beings acquired the former, but they could not be allowed to attain the latter, lest they become like God. Similarly, the alewife observes that the gods are jealous of their own supremacy. The boundary between the human and the divine may not be traversed, and immortality must remain the sole province of the gods.

Despite the appealing nature of the evidence, we must resist drawing any conclusions about the specific influence that the Adapa or *Gilgamesh* texts might have had on the Garden of Eden narrative. We can say that the motif of immortality denied occupied a prominent place in the religious perspectives of both Mesopotamia and Israel. At the very least, the extrabiblical sources give us another insight into the powerful psychological and spiritual yearnings expressed in the drama of Adam and Eve.

Babylonian influence on biblical material is particularly evident in the brief account of the tower of Babel (Gen. 11). The story relates how human beings banded together after the Flood to build a tower that would reach to the sky. The declared motive for the construction was "to make a name for ourselves; else we shall be scattered all over the world" (Gen. 11:4). God responds to this effort by treating it as an act of rebellion. "If, as one people with one language for all, this is how they have begun to act, then nothing that they may propose to do will be out of their reach" (Gen. 11:6). Certain descriptive aspects of this story reflect a Mesopotamian cultural background. The offending tower, for example, recalls the ziggurats—the pyramidal, brick temple structures central to Sumero-Babylonian religion.

The biblical theme of rebellion against God has parallels in each of the two best-known Babylonian creation stories: Enuma Elish and Atrahasis. In these myths, the rebellion is not that of human beings against God but rather of one set of gods against another. In each case, the gods who mutiny strive to supplant other, more powerful gods to free themselves and secure their own hegemony.

The affinity between biblical and Mesopotamian literature in no way diminishes the special character of Israelite religion. By introducing the concept of monotheism into the ancient Near East, Israelite religion made a unique contribution to human civilization. However, we should also appreciate the depth and intensity of the religious sentiments expressed in the works of Mesopotamian mythology. The faiths of ancient Israel and Mesopotamia were ultimately the products of a similar cultural context, occasionally exhibiting parallel themes and religious metaphors.

Understandably, the Torah attempted to trivialize pagan religions as a means of securing loyalty to the God of Israel. Pervasive polytheism represented a threat to the belief in one God and required a strong rejection if monotheism were to take root. Yet despite the anti-pagan polemic of the Bible, the mythic tradition of the ancient Near East was a serious, complex, and profound attempt to comprehend both the natural and the supernatural. The impact of this tradition was felt far beyond the borders of Mesopotamia, and it had a fundamental influence on the formation of Israelite religion and some of the literary traditions of the Bible.

ISRAELITE SOCIETY IN TRANSITION

Gordon M. Freeman

The narratives and teachings of the Bible develop in the context of the social, political, and economic realities of its time. Because the Bible includes literature written and compiled over many centuries, it should not be surprising that the reality of its context changed many times. These changes led to tensions that influenced biblical recordings of events and teachings. Those who decided what would be included in the biblical canon lived after the recorded events. Their decisions were influenced by their own perceptions of reality.

The Book of Genesis sets the scene for many of the issues repeated throughout biblical literature. We immediately confront the tension between agricultural and pastoral economies. The story of Cain, the farmer, and Abel, the shepherd, may be understood in terms of the rivalry over land use. Anthropologists teach that this tension occurred in primitive societies and is reflected in the settlement of the American West. The difference between agricultural and pastoral societies has profound consequences for relationships, political systems, and social concerns. People living in pastoral societies move constantly from place to place. The reality of pastoral life requires work by both men and women, thus affecting gender roles. Political models use pastoral language to describe leadership (see especially Ps. 23). Later literature tends to idealize the shepherd/leader.

People who till the soil, unlike shepherds, usually regard change as a potential threat to their well-being. The descendants of Cain, whose agricultural offering was not favored, become artisans and technicians. These tasks are based on life settled in one place, on teachings and learning skills that require a stable society. Territory becomes a major concern of law and politics; power is based on ownership.

We do not have any record of rituals or liturgy during this early period, but we know that the pastoral reality affects the superstructure (the symbols, rituals, myths, stories, and religion) of the culture. People on the move are constantly dealing with change. Given the constant state of uncertainty that comes with leading flocks from place to place, stories about divine messages that speak of promise and destiny might have been driven by a search for meaning.

The weather patterns provide us with a background for biblical stories. Lack of rainfall, a constant problem recorded in Genesis, and the subsequent famines caused people to leave their land to find new sources of food. Abraham and Sarah left for Egypt because of famine. Because the rainfall in the land of Canaan was not consistent, people came and went.

Scarce food supply, caused by weather conditions, led Jacob and his family to leave the Land, but a decline in the hegemony of the Egyptian Empire made it possible for Israelites to return and spread their area of settlement. The newly settled population was concentrated in the hill country, away from the Canaanite settlements in the western plain and the Philistines along the coast. The hill country, the north-south range just west of the Jordan Valley, offered a defensive position but was a challenge to agricultural development. Fields, orchards, and vineyards had to be carved out of the terrain through an intricate system of terracing. The infrastructure (population size, work patterns, geographic distribution, production of food in relation to the environment) during this time was based on a labor-intensive economy made possible by a large concentration of laborers. People apparently had no alternative places to settle; it would have been counterproductive to relocate. We also learn from this that the demography was stable, for the intensive type of work required would not have been possible otherwise.

Terracing techniques were similar in various places and were not the work of individual farmers. From these techniques, we can begin to describe the social structure. A group effort

reflects the willingness to make a long-term investment without immediate gain. This in turn tells us that strong relationships existed within and between communities whose members were willing to be involved in mutual help to create the terraces.

Evidence of the construction of individual grain pits demonstrates that the family was the center of life. There is no evidence of an elaborate administrative establishment or of a professional bureaucracy, except for the existence of a small priestly bureaucracy.

The biblical text presents a picture of women occupying a significant place in this predominantly patriarchal society. The matriarchs exhibited strong personalities and wielded great influence on family life and the raising of children. This picture seems to reflect premonarchic Israel during the late Bronze Age. The economy was labor intensive; many hands were required to clear the land of trees and build cisterns and terraces. Because there was no military class or standing army, men were often called to military service. These realities led to the need for women's labor in every aspect of life. The worth of women was enhanced by utility, leading to higher social status. The text in Gen. 2–3 depicts nonhierarchical gender relationships.

By the time of the period of the monarchy, the household-based economy was no longer dominant. In describing a time when the Land was settled, the Torah reflects significant participation of women in the festivals (Deut. 12:18, 16:10–13 ff.). Women were fully obligated and accountable in covenant observance (Deut. 13:7, 17:2–5, 29:10–13, 31:12), which continued into postexilic Jewish life (2 Chron. 15:12 ff.; Neh. 8:2). Although women were excluded from the priesthood, the role of *nazir* was open to them (Num. 6:2). Women like Miriam, Deborah, and Hulda also were among the prophets.

The biblical woman experienced legal disadvantages (e.g., she passed from the authority of her father to that of her husband). Yet she was entitled to make legally binding agreements. The significant inheritance reform described in the Book of Numbers dealing with women's disadvantage in matters of inheritance was instituted because of the claims made by the daughters of Zelophehad.

Women maintained a strong place in society and in the family (see Prov. 31:10–31 for a description of the ideal woman). The Bible recognized that the relationship between husband and wife should be not one of dominance but of partnership (e.g., Hos. 2:18). A wife could not be treated as a slave; if she had been a maidservant and subsequently married her owner, she could not be sold (Exod. 21:7).

The Torah declares the primary equality of women and men, because both were created in the divine image (Gen. 1:27), i.e., both symbolize God's presence, according to Nahum Sarna's understanding of *tzelem* (image). This teaching must have been in constant tension with social reality. The text may be attempting to find the legal means to relieve the perceived social disability.

The economic reality needs to be placed in the context of the geopolitics of the day. The extent of Egyptian power had a direct effect on Israel's ability to control land area. While Israelites were languishing in Egyptian servitude, Egypt had control over the land of Canaan. The great story that eventually became the master story of the Bible, the Exodus from Egypt, is a dramatic reflection of the Egyptian Empire's loss of power. The change in the cultural superstructure is reflected in Moses, the pastoral leader, confronting the landed, agricultural Pharaoh. This at once takes us back to the original pastoral–agricultural tension and points us forward to the eventual break between the agricultural northern tribes called Israel and the southern pastoral tribes called Judah.

Around the time of early Israelite settlement in the highlands, the Egyptian Empire was in further decline. Archaeological evidence demonstrates that during the period between the early 13th and middle 12th centuries B.C.E., the Egyptian Empire began to withdraw from the area. Consequently, the Hittites left, probably owing to a famine, and the Assyrians

began incursions against the Egyptian Empire. The Canaanite city-states under the control of the Egyptian Empire were losing their power base by the time of Deborah (12th century B.C.E.). Their breakdown marked the effective end of Egyptian sovereignty in the area. Philistine incursions on the western shore also challenged Canaanite hegemony. All these factors led to the spread of Israelite population westward.

At the same time, hardly any Israelite cities existed; Israelite tribes were rural/pastoral. The Canaanite settlements on the western plain and the coastal Philistine area threatened the Israelites during the time of the Judges. Israelite tribes were largely confined to the north-south hilly spine, between the Jordan River on the east and the coastal plain in the west.

Tribal and clan-based polities were led by inherited leadership, with occasional ad hoc charismatic leaders, such as Gideon and Jephthah, who defended the people from various external threats (including Philistines, Moabites, and Canaanites). This type of leadership was replaced by a centralized monarchy but was not without tension between central rule and tribal fiefdoms. Although rural Israel was decentralized (a refrain in Judg. 17:6, 18:1, 21:25 declares, "There was no king in Israel, everyone did what was right in his own eyes"), a strong sense of ethnic identity existed. Premonarchic institutions were established based on this identity. These included the *shofet,* a national magistrate, and *sheivet,* the tribe as a constituent unit of the *edah,* the entire people as a constituted polity.

Before the monarchy (from the late 13th to the 11th centuries B.C.E.), governance was local and controlled by tribal leaders. A loose intertribal assembly, much in the sense of a confederation without any transcending political power, might have existed. The tribes were not willing to give up any hegemony, except during times of external threat. Even then, not all of the tribes would heed the call to contribute troops to the effort.

By the 10th century B.C.E., the eclipse of Egypt and the Canaanite city-states and the introduction of iron usage among Israelites posed a new situation. The Israelites were willing to recognize the centralized authority of a king who could increase territory and secure the borders. As their enemies collapsed, they came to control larger areas of arable land. Although artisans still had to be imported to aid the vast Solomonic building projects, in time Israel developed native trade and artisan classes. By the destruction of the First Temple (586 B.C.E.) the economy was a sophisticated mix of pastoral and agricultural, trade and crafts.

By the time of the monarchy (10th century B.C.E.), urbanization increased because of landless peasants looking for opportunities in the growing cities developed by the kings. Competing social groups constantly realigned themselves. The peasantry and the urban poor were defended by the prophets. The wealthy landowners were supported by the court. The central priesthood in Jerusalem competed with the local shrines and ritual centers led by itinerant priests and Levites.

Saul, the first king of Israel, had great difficulty maintaining the tribal alliance. The tribes were unwilling to support his court or maintain a standing military force to discourage Israel's enemies from attacking. David's successful rise to power was based on his skill at carefully building alliances. The rise of the Davidic monarchy was also owing to the power vacuum left by the declining Canaanite city-states.

A strong central power was needed to balance various economic, political, and social power centers that were in tension with each other. Eventually, they yielded power to David because of his skill. As the empire expanded and conquered territories and helped maintain the court and the military, the power concentrated in the monarchy was not challenged. However, those territories began to break away at the end of David's reign. Solomon had to increase taxes to support an expensive court. The tensions between royal power in Judah and tribal power centers in the north increased to the breaking point, and the northern tribes

of Israel split from Judah. Ironically, the revolt was led by Jeroboam of the tribe of Ephraim, who had been appointed to oversee the forced labor and collection of taxes from the northern tribes (1 Kings 11:26 ff.).

King Solomon was the first king to attempt to consolidate his power by creating administrative districts that ignored tribal territories, thus marginalizing local leadership and replacing it with governors appointed by (and loyal to) the king. By transferring authority from local clan and tribal leaders to their own agents, the kings hoped to gain compliance to their rule. This tactic backfired: Loyalty to the kings decreased. The people preferred the traditional tribal authorities who were native to their localities.

Another example of the tension between local authority and central rule is found in the biblical assertion that all cultic activity should be limited to the centralized Temple in Jerusalem. It should be remembered that David had brought the Ark to Jerusalem and that his son Solomon built the First Temple there, perhaps to demonstrate that God legitimized their monarchy. Any alternatives—local shrines, for example—were denounced. Nevertheless, local shrines continued to compete with Jerusalem for loyalty, just as the rebellions by the local authorities against David and Solomon showed that old tribal loyalties were strong. It was almost as if the monarchy/central priesthood had been plastered onto a tribal confederacy. When taxes were required from localities to support the center, the fragile structure of centralized government in Jerusalem began to crumble.

After the death of Solomon, when the kingdom split between Judah and Israel, the tribal memories began to fade. These two small and weakened polities realized that to survive they needed to withstand the growing threat of expanding Assyrian and Babylonian empires by consolidating their power around their respective monarchies. The family/tribal origins of Israel, now shrouded in myth, became a distant memory. Northern Israel was organized around the dominant Ephraimite territory. The other nine tribes were hardly mentioned. Benjaminite territory became integrated into the kingdom of Judah located in Jerusalem.

The prophets Jeremiah and Isaiah spoke in the context of deep social and economic cleavage. Whereas they supported the central government, they decried its corruption and asserted that the monarchy had to act with righteousness and justice to deserve the loyalty of the people. For example, Jeremiah decries the advantages of wealthy landowners who had the means to increase their power at the expense of the peasantry, whose small plots of land were unable to sustain them over time (Jer. 34:8–20). Social legislation found in the Torah obligating people to support the poor dealt with providing food, correcting economic and social dislocation through sabbatical and jubilee laws, and regulating the laws of indentured servitude (see Lev. 25:25ff.). These laws reflect social cleavage between the wealthy, landed gentry and the impoverished peasantry. Peasants, losing land because of debt, eventually fled to urban areas searching for ways to feed themselves and their families. Whether or not these laws were ever fulfilled, they became the model for prophecies, especially of Amos and Jeremiah (see Amos 2:6–8; 4:1–3; 5:11–12; 8:4–8).

The prophets not only responded to growing social cleavage but also to changing geopolitical reality. Jeremiah understood that there was a relationship between these two factors. He claimed that the growing distance between the wealthy and the impoverished was a direct result of moral failure on the part of leadership. He counseled submission to the looming threat of the Babylonian Empire, which he explained as the inevitable punishment for social injustice and corruption. During his time, the king and his advisers believed that Judah could depend on the Egyptian Empire to come to its defense against a Babylonian attack. He analyzed the dependence on the political alliance with Egypt and saw it as a failure. Egypt, Jeremiah realized, was using Judah to soften the blow of a Babylonian incursion against it.

Judean society had failed; it was indefensible because of its injustice and lack of compassion. It could choose to suffer submission or fight and lose everything.

But the cultural superstructure had experienced a change with the advent of the Temple cult. The master story before the monarchy was the Exodus. Solomon's Temple competed with the Exodus as a source of salvation. The Temple became the purpose and fulfillment of the Exodus promise. The master story had been slowly transformed from the distant events of the Exodus to the concept of the Temple as the place to experience God's presence. Worship in the Temple epitomized salvation.

The prophets at the end of the First Temple period introduced an alternative master story: the Sinai event, the giving of the Torah, which replaced the Temple as the fulfillment of the Exodus. This transformation began to prepare the people for the tragedy of destruction and exile. Although the Temple had been destroyed, God's word became the source for salvation.

We know very little about Jewish life in Babylonia after the exile in 586 B.C.E., but the Jewish community must have experienced stability and some degree of political and economic success. With the Persian conquest of Babylonia in the 6th century B.C.E., we find Jews in high political positions. Nehemiah has the ear of the Persian emperor, and is able to persuade him that it was advisable to establish a loyal colony in the western outpost of the empire. The majority of Jews decide against returning to their ancestral land, despite the attempts by Ezra and Nehemiah to persuade them. This demonstrates that although their Jewish identity was maintained, they enjoyed their apparent comfort in their new land. The community as a whole was accountable to the king. Yet the distinctions between Jews and Persians were often permeable and Jews participated in Persian society.

The Book of Esther indicates that Jews quickly assimilated. Aware of their difference, they attempted to blend quietly into the general population. The choice of Babylonian names, for example, Mordecai (a form of Marduk) and Esther (a form of Astarte) demonstrates this social reality.

When Ezra and Nehemiah led a small group back to Judah in the middle of the fifth century B.C.E. to re-establish Jewish life, they were confronted by a native Judean population that had also assimilated, though in a different way. Remaining on the land must have provided some sense of cultural identity, but many married "foreign" wives.

Ezra decided to make an ethnic distinction regarding personal identity and attempted to reinforce Jewish life by forcing the native Jews to divorce their foreign wives. The Book of Ruth may have been a response to this issue. The practice of formal conversion was introduced only in the early Roman period when a corpus of Jewish law regarding conversion began to evolve.

Ezra faced a jurisdictional requirement to establish the identity of a citizenry that would be regarded as part of this Persian colony. His preliminary solution (banning foreign wives) threatened the shared identity of the native Judean population and the returning exiles. Before a complete social break occurred, a new definition of Jewish identity had to be articulated. The books of Chronicles now defined Israelites as those following the Jerusalem Temple ritual and included natives (not only Persian Jewish returnees).

Following the teachings established by the prophets, Ezra, the religious leader of the colony, who was a priest and scribe, reinterpreted the master story. The meaning of the Exodus had to be applied to changing circumstances. The study of Torah now became the key to Jewish identity and survival. Now every Israelite could participate in redemption through his or her own observance and study of Torah. With Jewish communities in Egypt and Babylonia as well as in the ancient homeland, Judaism was no longer geographically bound. The Exile and return forced a rereading of the ancient stories to emphasize individual responsibility and participation in God's covenant with Israel.

MARRIAGE AND FAMILY

Gilbert S. Rosenthal

In Judaism, creation of the universe and the creation of the first human relationships are interwoven in the Book of Genesis: The cosmogony includes the birth of the archetypal family unit. Of the 50 chapters of Genesis, 38 deal with the gamut of family relationships and tensions, ranging from love and courtship to lust and seduction, from sibling rivalry to fratricide, from sterility to domestic controversies, from marital stress to tender affection. These themes occur frequently throughout the Bible.

Although there is no systematically developed family structure in the Bible, we can sketch a fairly ample portrait of the biblical family. Unquestionably, the Bible views marriage as the norm and a divine imperative. "It is not good for man to be alone," states the Torah (Gen. 2:18), indicating that the first goal of marriage is companionship. The second is procreation: "Be fertile and increase, fill the earth" (Gen. 1:28). Subsequent Jewish tradition considered procreation to be the first *mitzvah* incumbent on the human species and more specifically on the Jewish people (M Eduy. 1:13). Adam and Eve are the primordial ancestors of all races and families.

The societal structure comprised three components: the tribe (*sheivet*), the largest unit, which was subdivided into the clan (*mishpaḥah*), which was further divided into the household (*beit av*). The Bible records detailed genealogic lists in which we may detect this triple division of Israelite society.

Details on marriage ceremonies and rituals are sketchy and must be pieced together from scattered clues. No marriage ritual is specified, nor is a document of marriage or marriage contract mentioned. The earliest reference to a writ of marriage is postbiblical and the oldest *k'tubbah* (marriage contract) thus far discovered by archaeologists is from Elephantine, a Jewish military colony in Egypt from the 6th and 5th centuries B.C.E. Because the Bible does mention a writ of divorce on several occasions, it seems logical that some form of marriage contract also was in use as early as biblical times (Deut. 24:1–4).

Invariably, fathers arranged matches or picked their children's future mates. In the absence of a father, this responsibility fell to a brother. Sometimes the steward of the household was charged with this mission, as with Abraham's steward (Gen. 24). It appears that a bride's consent was required (Gen. 24:57ff.; Gen. R. 60:12). If a man seduced or raped a virgin, he paid the father 50 shekels and had to marry her—subject to the father's approval (Exod. 22:15–16; Deut. 22:28).

A dowry (*mohar*) and a gift (*matan*) such as jewelry were presented to the bride's family at a betrothal feast in anticipation of the marriage. The wedding itself was accompanied by feasting, singing, and dancing for seven days. The bride donned special attire, including a veil; the groom wore a turban to signify his new status. The marriage was consummated on the first night, possibly in a special bridal chamber.

Biblical law allowed polygamy (more than one wife) and polygyny (more than one woman). Often, when a man took a second wife or concubine it was because of infertility. Thus Abraham took Sarah's handmaid Hagar as his concubine when Sarah seemed hopelessly sterile.

Jacob was tricked by his unscrupulous father-in-law Laban into marrying Leah. He ultimately was able to marry his beloved Rachel, Leah's sister, so that he was married to two sisters—a practice later outlawed by the Torah. Kings of Israel were permitted by the Bible to marry several wives and maintain harems. Indeed, David and Solomon followed this pattern. However, the system of polygyny was fraught with tensions and jealousy, as is clearly seen in the conflicts between Sarah and Hagar, Rachel and Leah, Hannah and Peninah, and others. The ideal marriage is a monogamous union, as evidenced by the Adam and Eve story: "Hence a man leaves his father and

mother and clings to his wife, so that they may become one flesh" (Gen. 2:24).

It is noteworthy that Adam and Eve's fratricidal son, Cain, begets a polygamous tradition through his son Lamech, whereas a virtuous son, Seth, is the antecedent of a monogamous line. Similarly, the outstanding judges were monogamous, and the dissolute ones were not (Gen. 4:19,26; Judg. 8:30ff., 14:1ff., 16:1ff.). The prophetic ideal, which draws a touching comparison between God's relationship to Israel and a husband's relationship with his wife, is equally monogamous. *Kohelet* urges a man to enjoy life "with the woman you love" (Eccles. 9:9), while the authors of Proverbs never tire of warning young men to beware the wiles of "foreign women" and courtesans, urging them to seek fulfillment in a virtuous spouse in whom they could confidently trust (Prov. 31:11).

The Bible prescribed permitted marriages in great detail while proscribing prohibited unions with equal meticulousness. In patriarchal days, marriage with a half-sister was not a taboo, as evidenced by Abraham and Sarah. But the abhorrence of incest was so strong that eventually such unions were outlawed and the list of proscribed marriages was substantially expanded. Homosexuality and bestiality were branded as "abominations," and adultery is listed as one of the cardinal sins in the Ten Commandments. The abhorrence of out-marriage is as ancient as Abraham, even as the preference for mating with one's own clan or tribe goes back to the patriarchs and matriarchs. The bane of Abraham's and Isaac's lives were sons Ishmael and Esau, who took wives from non-Hebrew nations, marrying Egyptian and Canaanite women. Samson caused his parents grief by dallying with Philistine women and courtesans. A Hebrew woman was expected to be a virtuous virgin whose husband had to be a Hebrew, most often from the same tribe or clan.

Not all marriages succeeded. Fidelity and chastity were expected and adultery was a capital offense. Divorce was allowed, except when a rapist married his victim (Deut. 22:29). Although no specific grounds are enumerated in the Bible, immorality was the most obvious cause for a husband to "send his wife a bill of divorcement" (Deut. 24:1–4). A woman suspected of infidelity (*sotah*) was compelled to submit to a nerve-wracking ordeal. If she failed the test, she was liable to be executed. The ideal marriage is beautifully described by the psalmist (128:3): "Your wife shall be like a fruitful vine within your house; / your sons, like olive saplings around your table."

The biblical family was remarkable because of certain unique elements, many of which are still discernible today, namely, love and sexual joy, companionship, respect, fidelity, and abiding trust.

The family was endogamous; the preference was for marriage to relatives. In patriarchal times, as noted, that implied half-brother or half-sister, cousins, nieces, nephews, aunts, uncles, and members of the clan. Although marriage with neighboring nations was forbidden in later biblical law, Ezra the scribe was forced to battle out-marriages in the 5th century B.C.E. (Ezra 9–10). If a husband died leaving no issue, his widow was obligated to marry her brother-in-law (levirate marriage, or *yibbum*) to perpetuate the deceased's name and, presumably, to keep the property from leaving the clan. If the brother-in-law refused to marry his sister-in-law, he was subjected to a humiliating ritual, *halitzah* (Deut. 25:5ff.).

The biblical family was also patrilineal in that the family traced its lineage or tribal affiliation to the father rather than the mother. If the father came from the tribe of Levi, his offspring were Levites no matter the mother's tribe. If he was a *kohen* (priest), the children were likewise. Male offspring were referred to as sons of their father: Isaac son of Abraham, Moses son of Amram, Jeremiah son of Hilkiyah, Jonah son of Amittai. Only on rare occasions is the mother's name used. Matrilineal descent later becomes the standard in the Mishnah for cases when a valid marriage could not take place (M Kid. 3:12).

The family was also patriarchal; father was lord and master. He headed the family, owned

the property, conveyed divine blessings to family members, and made critical decisions. He could sell children in marriage, although his right to sell them into slavery was limited and he was barred from selling them into prostitution. He could annul his unmarried daughter's vows, and he received the money for damages inflicted on children. He demanded and expected obedience, respect, and honor. When a man married, he brought his bride to his father's household. Evidently, widows and divorcees often returned to their father's residence.

Women were subordinate to men. Often the names of wives are not even mentioned in the Bible, as is the case with Noah's and Job's wives and the Shunammite woman who aided Elisha. Still, they did enjoy certain rights. A husband was obliged by law to provide his wife with "food, clothing, and conjugal rights" (Exod. 21:10; Ket. 47b). Women ultimately received the right to inherit in the absence of male heirs (Num. 27:1–11). They also exerted considerable influence, as may be deduced from the sagas of the matriarchs, Sarah, Rebekah, Leah, and Rachel, as well as Miriam, Hannah, and Deborah. Primarily, they were to bear children, name and educate them, and run the household. Some women engaged in commerce and real estate transactions. A handful became public figures, prophetesses, and judges, such as Miriam, Deborah, and Hulda. At least two queens ran the government (Jezebel and Athaliah), and Queen Esther exerted considerable influence over the king of Persia. The queen mother (*g'virah*) was a force to contend with in dealing with the monarchy.

Children, especially sons, were the crown and blessing of parents and grandparents and the goal of marriage. Sad, indeed, was the infertile couple. The barren woman was scorned; sterility was viewed as divine punishment (Gen. 16:5; 1 Sam. 1:6). Abraham's words still resonate: "What can You give me seeing that I shall die childless?" (Gen. 15:2). And Hannah's plaintive, silent prayer at Shiloh—that if God would but grant her a son she would apprentice him to the priests—moves us still. Both father and mother were expected to nurture and educate young children who were viewed as blessings from God. Still, children (young or old) were expected to honor and revere father and mother, and the biblical authors shuddered as they contemplated the loss of respect by children for parents. To disobey, curse, or hit a parent was a capital offense; to mock the older generation was both a sin and an outrage (Exod. 20:12).

The biblical family was an extended one whose modern analogue is the Bedouin family or urban Arab clan in today's Middle East. Grandparents or great-grandparents served as the head of the family, which consisted of husbands, wives, concubines, children, servants, and slaves. Counting everyone in the household, the family swelled to a veritable tribe. Uncles and cousins, nephews and nieces were part of the extended family. In fact, they were often referred to as "brothers," as in the relationship of Abraham and his nephew Lot. Sibling rivalry existed from Cain and Abel down to the last kings of Israel and Judah—often with lethal results. Yet, the family members worked together in common fields, tilled their ancestral patrimony, plied a common trade or craft, and came to the rescue of kinsmen in times of danger or trouble. Family members who married lived close to one another, often sharing meals as is typical of extended rather than nuclear families. Even in death, the cherished wish was to be buried with the family, preferably in a family plot or sepulcher (Gen. 23, 50).

Remarkably, the biblical elements in the Jewish family prevailed throughout the ages, crystallizing into law in Rabbinic times, shaping the nature of Christian and Muslim families as well. At the same time, these familial patterns fortified Jews and Judaism in dozens of lands, enabling them to survive stresses and storms, crises and calamities into the 21st century.

WOMEN

Judith Hauptman

A candid look at biblical society, religion, and law reveals a system that favors men over women. Women, as a rule, did not play key political roles. They were not rulers, warriors, or prophets. Named women appear in the biblical narrative far less frequently than named men. The principal religious and social institutions placed women under the control of men. The Bible, in fact, seems to define society as being composed of men only. On at least three occasions (Exod. 30; Num. 1, 26) a census of men was taken. The women and the children were never counted.

This blatant gender imbalance jars contemporary sensibilities. Many wonder how the same treatise that campaigns so forcefully and persuasively for social justice can, at the same time, sanction discrimination against women.

To come to terms with biblical sexism, one must first grasp the broad contours of the biblical narrative and only then focus on the treatment of women. A major theme of the Torah is the covenantal bond that exists between the Israelites and their God. The first to enter into such an arrangement was Abraham. The terms of his covenant were simple: If he continued to believe in God, as he had done until that point, then God would bless him with progeny as numerous as the stars in the sky, and they, after a stay in Egypt, would come back to inherit the land of Israel (Gen. 15).

This covenant was renegotiated at Sinai with the masses of Israelites and others who left Egypt. God stipulated that if they would keep His commandments and pledge allegiance to Him alone, then He would not only lead them to the land of Israel but also provide them with the things that human beings, regardless of gender, want most—health, prosperity, children, and security.

For this new covenant, the ritual and social demands were substantial. To begin with, as set down in the Decalogue, one had to respect the integrity of another's life and property. Beyond that there was a vast array of ritual requirements, many of which related to holy times and places. In addition, as spelled out in *parashat Mishpatim* (Exod. 21–24) and elsewhere, Israelites were obligated by an extraordinary set of social justice requirements, involving issues that include poverty law, justice in the courtroom, bailments, torts, and decent treatment of slaves.

In considering the treatment of women, the reasonable question to ask now is: Since the terms of the covenant at Sinai are essentially gender neutral, does it follow that women were equal partners with men? The answer is no. Although women were present at Sinai, they do not seem to have been part of the covenantal process in the same way that men were. The basis for this observation is that the Torah, in many passages, addresses itself to men only. For example, the tenth commandment states that a man is not to covet his neighbor's wife, slave, animals, or anything else his neighbor owns.

Although women did not enter into the covenant directly, they did enter indirectly. The Torah, it seems, viewed each man as the head of a household responsible for the behavior of all individuals under his aegis, usually understood to be his wife (or wives), slaves, and children. It is as if each family stood at Sinai in a line, with the head of the household in front, and all members of his family standing behind him in single file. It thus became his responsibility to demand of them the same behavior that was being demanded of him.

This means that, in general terms, the covenant with God bound women in the same way that it bound men: Women were to pursue justice and champion the cause of the underdog, to observe *Shabbat,* the holidays, and the dietary laws—just like men. But, because the Bible was speaking to a society that viewed women as less than men, key biblical institutions regulating gender relationships and com-

munal ritual performance treat women not as equal to men but as subordinate, even though significant. Surveying some of these rules will illustrate this point.

According to the Bible, marriage is the acquisition of a woman by a man. Fathers, as a rule, arranged marriages for their daughters at about the time that they reached puberty. A husband was required to provide his wife with the basic necessities of life, including conjugal relations (Exod. 21:10).

The Bible places a premium on female virginity. When a virgin was seduced, the offender was required to marry her. If her father refused to give her in marriage, however, the offender still had to pay him the bride-price of virgins (Exod. 22:15–16). The bridal payment is required in this instance because the marital value of a young woman plummets when she loses her virginity. This suggests that in the biblical period men viewed women for sexual, marital purposes as objects.

It was incumbent on a wife to bear children for her husband. Sometimes this male prerogative determined the course of a woman's life. If a man died childless, his widow was not free to remarry but was considered to be already betrothed to his brother (Deut. 25:5–10). The purpose of her marriage to her levir (husband's brother), was to produce an heir, presumably a male, who would continue the name and line of his father's deceased brother and inherit his property. In this situation, a woman glided from one marriage to the next, suffering no period of financial distress, but having no choice of life options or partners. The levir could choose to release his sister-in-law from the marital bond by undergoing a ceremony called *ḥalitzah,* but she could not refuse to live with him.

Fidelity to one's husband is a basic marriage rule for women. The seventh commandment understands adultery as sexual relations between a man and someone else's wife, not as sexual relations between a man and any woman other than his wife. Married women, but not married men, are limited to a single sexual partner. As a consequence of this rule, if a husband merely suspects his wife of behaving in a promiscuous manner, even though he has no evidence, he may bring her to the tabernacle (or later, the Temple) and subject her to the water ordeal, described by the Torah in gruesome detail (Num. 5:11ff.).

As for divorce, it is the husband who sends the wife out of his house, with a writ of severance, if he finds her unseemly in some way (Deut. 24:1). Nowhere is provision made for a woman who finds her husband unacceptable or wishes to resist a divorce. Women, it seems, had no say in this matter.

Can this array of sexist rules be reconciled with the Torah's high-minded concept of social justice and its expressed concern for the vulnerable members of society? Yes, but only in the biblical period and not later. That is, it seems reasonable to say that women at that early time did not expect equality but protection. Just as children did not think that they should have a voice in family decision making or control over family financial assets, neither did married women. They apparently found marriage satisfactory if it supplied them with their basic needs, which it did.

Difficulties arise in the postbiblical period and later, when the Jewish understanding of marriage and social philosophy changed, and women came to be viewed as deserving of more rights and higher status. To ease the tension between the more enlightened social outlook and the Torah's sexist rules, the Rabbinic corpus, produced about 1500 years after the Torah, made significant changes in laws affecting women. Although equity of women and men as a principle of law is not to be found in Rabbinic literature, and until the 20th century is not a feature of any of the major religious or even civil law codes, still, amelioration of women's status and an increase in their rights marks much of Rabbinic marital legislation.

According to the Talmud, marriage is not a purchase of a woman by a man but a living arrangement in which each has rights and responsibilities to the other, although he is dominant and she subordinate. The *k'tubbah,*

or marriage document, drawn up by the groom and presented to the bride, was instituted for the protection of women: It stipulates a lump sum payment to the wife from the husband's estate in the event that he predeceases or divorces her. Although not written into the *k'tubbah* itself, a set of additional stipulations accompanies it, such as provisions for medical care, ransom money, and maintenance and domicile for the widow. The *k'tubbah* has often been called one of the Talmud's most socially progressive pieces of legislation. In reciprocal manner, the Talmud lists a wife's obligations to her husband, most of which lay in the domestic sphere.

Significant changes also took place in the area of divorce. The Talmud presents a wide variety of situations in which distress suffered by the wife would lead to divorce. Not that she may write her husband a *get,* a bill of divorce, but she would have recourse to the rabbinical courts that could petition her husband to issue a divorce. Even more important, the particulars of the *get*—its language, the material on which it is written, the ink with which it is written, the manner in which it is delivered—are all standardized so that no one would later be able to challenge the validity of the divorce proceedings and, therefore, a woman's second marriage. Because it is only she and not he who needs a document of divorce to remarry, these rules, although still patriarchal in nature, are designed with her welfare in mind.

According to the Torah, in economic matters women totally depended on men. Real estate, the most valued asset, was usually owned by men. Property in the land of Israel was to be distributed to men only (Num. 26:53, 27:6–11). Upon death, a man's parcel of land was to pass to his kin—sons, brothers, uncles, or other relatives on his father's side. In the event that he left no sons but only daughters, however, the daughters superseded all other relatives and inherited their father's land, sharing it among themselves. In such cases, women were required to remarry within the tribe so as not to reduce its land holdings. In the Rabbinic period, although women could not inherit per se, the institution of gifts in contemplation of death and generous marriage dowries moved in the direction of making it possible for fathers to pass on their accumulated wealth to their daughters.

In ritual areas men predominated. The males of the priestly class served as religious functionaries in the Temple, and lay Israelite men were bidden to make a pilgrimage to the Temple three times a year. Women, however, did take part in organized religious life. Women could bring voluntary offerings—and were even required to bring a purification offering after each birth (Lev. 12:6)—although their ability to enter the holy precincts of the Temple was impaired by their regular periods of ritual impurity owing to menstrual flow (Lev. 15:19–30). As for ritual restrictions in the home, such as ceasing to work on *Shabbat,* fasting on *Yom Kippur,* and avoiding leaven on *Pesaḥ,* women were bound by these rules just like men.

The laws of vows (Num. 30:2–17) provide an important—but limited—exception to the general rule of women's subordinate status. It was standard behavior in the biblical period for people to take a vow to influence or implore God to grant a request. In return for engaging in some form of self-denial, the vowing individual hoped to gain healing for a sick family member or the safe return from war of a soldier husband or son. The main point of this section of Torah is to distinguish between men's and women's vows. If a man takes a vow, no matter what transpires, he must keep his word; if a woman takes a vow, her intentions may be subverted by either father or husband. There are two categories of women, however, whose vows may not be canceled by anyone at all—widows and divorcees (v. 10). Thus women as women are viewed as competent to maintain absolute control over their own affairs, religious and financial. But when under the control of a father or husband, their vows need approval.

The one area in a woman's life in which she achieved parity with men was her status as a parent. In the eyes of the Bible, the older gen-

eration, both males and females, had absolute authority over the younger. A child was to honor and fear both father and mother; a son or daughter who cursed or struck either parent was to be put to death (Exod. 21:15, 17). Both mother and father had to declare a son rebellious for him to be punished (Deut. 21:18–21). Children were obligated to fulfill the same rites of mourning for a deceased mother as for a deceased father (Lev. 21:2).

Did social realities in biblical times conform to the legal prescriptions? The narrative portions of the Bible suggest that women's position in society, although not equal to that of men, was not as subordinate and marginal as one might have expected, given the patriarchal configuration of society. The matriarchs, as well as other female characters in the Bible, exhibited independence of thought and action, and critically influenced the course of history, although differently from men. To mention a few examples: Rebekah behaved more like a patriarch than did her passive husband, Isaac—securing the patriarch's blessing for her favorite son, Jacob, to whom God wanted it to go, and thwarting Isaac's plan to bestow it on his favorite, Esau (Gen. 27). Tamar (Gen. 38) and Ruth, in different ways, each enticed a man to engage in marital or quasi-marital sexual relations to maintain the family's line. In reward for and acknowledgment of the merit of their actions, each of them became an ancestress of King David. These heroines, and scores of others who appear throughout the Bible, show that women, despite sociolegal limitations, could act resolutely to shape the future according to their own vision.

This limited survey indicates that, at least in its legislative sections, women are regarded by the Torah as dependent, not independent, beings. Such a view of women meshed well with that of most ancient Near Eastern societies, which also placed women under the control of men. The Bible thus prescribes a pattern of gender relationships that was acceptable for that era, even though by contemporary standards it would be found wanting.

The test of the Jewish tradition, however, is not how the Torah treated women at one point in time but how the Jewish tradition treated women with the passing of time, how it responded to evolving ethical insights. The references made earlier to Rabbinic changes in marital and inheritance law clearly show that not only does the Torah stake out a claim to moral behavior in its own day but, even more important, it intends for its abstract ethical teachings, which transcend time and place, to be upheld in every generation. This cleaving to general principles will guarantee that the specific rules do not, in the course of time, devolve from ethical to unethical.

The response to those who critique the sexism of the Jewish tradition is that the Torah's laws were prescribed for its own day and were not intended to remain as they were, but to be changed as necessary. The primary thrust of the Talmud and related Rabbinic writings is not, as many think, to codify the law, but to adjust the Torah's rules to changing circumstances and philosophical outlook. It follows that today, too, with equality for women and men a widely accepted social truth, more changes must be made to ensure full equality.

MATRIARCHS AND PATRIARCHS

Debra Orenstein

The Book of Genesis addresses the primal and profound questions that children ask: Who am I? Where did I come from? Why am I here? What is this family I have been born into? In the Bible, these questions extend beyond the nuclear family to the primordial origins of humanity and the ancestral origins of our nation and faith. Who are we in the "family of man"? Who are we as a people?

In Genesis, these ideas are framed in the language of two other questions: the first question God ever asked, and the first ques-

tion posed by a being created in God's image. God called out to a guilty Adam, who was trying to hide in the Garden of Eden: "*Ayyeka*—Where are you?" (3:9). Later, Cain asked about Abel, the brother he had murdered: "Am I my brother's keeper?" (4:9). Both questions may appear to be rhetorical, but they reverberate throughout Genesis as profoundly serious inquiries. The family narratives serve as a discursive, exploratory, and open-ended response. Matriarchs and patriarchs continually struggle with where they are—in terms of birth order, family and gender roles, spiritual development, the chain of covenantal heritage, and (more literally) locale. Sibling rivalry regularly threatens to turn fratricidal. In the story of Joseph, brothers finally mature to the point of becoming each other's guardians and keepers. Indeed, they come to see such mutual care as the divine plan and the ultimate human purpose (43:8–9, 50:20). Finally, four generations after Abraham, the sons of both Judah and Joseph avoid conflict in the first place and accept their respective roles in the family.

The dilemmas faced by our ancestors communally, as well as personally, endure as struggles and boundary issues. We are still making our peace with Ishmael and his descendants. Within the "immediate family," division over who is a proper heir to the covenant—or, "who is a Jew"—threatens both our genealogic and our religious integrity. The matriarchs and patriarchs favored in-marriage, promoted connection to the Promised Land, and feared the lure of foreign temptations. Physical survival and continuity of heritage—difficult propositions throughout Genesis—absorb us today as well.

The terms "matriarch" and "patriarch" can be variously interpreted. They might well include such guarantors of continuity as Bilhah, Zilpah, Tamar, Judah, and Joseph. The terminology can be confusing, too, because patriarchy, in contemporary usage, refers to a broad institutionalized system of rigid sex roles, through which men retain authority over women. Of course, such a cultural system neither began nor ended with the patriarchs of Genesis. Reclaiming and relating to our male ancestors neither requires nor condones patriarchy.

In this essay and in Jewish tradition generally, the titles "matriarch" and "patriarch" are reserved for the *avot*, key figures of the first three generations: Abraham and Sarah; Isaac and Rebekah; Jacob, Leah, and Rachel. These exemplars are valued above all others and are considered the purest representatives of a meritorious ancestry (BT Ber. 16b). Moreover, it is in these first three generations that a single family prepares to become a tribe and a nation. During these years—roughly the first half of the 2nd millennium B.C.E.—it is still debatable who the next rightful heir will and should be. Yet, the covenant is firmly established.

It is significant that there are seven early ancestors, because that number connotes a perfect completion in the Bible. The world was created in seven days, and the *avot*—a whole and perfect set—are said to fulfill, and even to cause, Creation (Lev. R. 36:4). The early chapters of Genesis record false starts and second chances—attempts by God to begin (and begin again) a positive partnership with humanity. Ten generations after Adam and Eve are driven from the Garden, God takes Noah as a new "first" being and initiates the covenant of the rainbow. A parallel 10 generations after the Flood, God chooses and builds a more participatory covenant with Abraham. Several genealogies link the various players in these dramas (5, 10, 11:10–32). Abraham's call marks both closure for Creation and the opening of a new era for the future people Israel and humanity.

Although a "whole and perfect set," our seven famous ancestors certainly had faults and weaknesses. Their development within Genesis can be seen as a template for personal growth; as a study in family dynamics; or, even more broadly, as a paradigm for the nation's history and destiny. Matriarchs and patriarchs represent the promise of a people as well as the fulfillment of Creation.

REPETITION PAINTS A COMPOSITE PICTURE

The themes that run throughout the stories of the patriarchs and matriarchs are so often repeated that one could almost conceive a composite couple. The tales of the patriarchs are especially easy to conflate. Exceptions and nuances aside, a patriarch chosen by God finds a wife within the clan, who gives him a special son. The son chosen for succession resembles his father in several crucial respects: He will have a stormy relationship with a brother (or brother figure), leave his father's house, marry a "barren" woman, benefit from divine communication and intercession, retain and gain a firmer foothold in the land he inherits. Possessed of neither firstborn status nor extraordinary merit, he is nevertheless destined to receive the blessing of the firstborn. He may well be called by a new name, indicating a spiritual evolution. The composite patriarch will play favorites among his children, settle disputes with neighbors, build an altar, leave (or have his sons leave) the immediate area in time of famine, trick a man more wealthy and powerful than he, return with even greater wealth to where he started, and receive God's promise of chosen and numerous progeny living in a sacred homeland. God will reiterate this promise, but not (yet) fulfill it. The patriarch will become estranged from family members over the course of his lifetime, and he will heal the breaches—at least to some degree. He will offer blessings to family members, receive God's blessing, and ultimately be a blessing himself.

Even the vocabulary of the stories recurs across the generations. When called to make a change that will initiate a higher calling and connection to God, the patriarchs are told or tell the next generation to "go" (*lekh*) and "take" (*kah*). "Going forth" from one's roots and habits is a necessary step on the road to spiritual growth and independence. According to Hasidic commentary, it enables the patriarch to "go unto himself" (Gen. 12:1)—i.e., his best self. That inner journey prepares him to unite with family and land and to receive God's blessing.

Duplications in language and behavior specifically connect Jacob back to Abraham. Abraham's name is changed upon his circumcision; Jacob's name is changed at the point when he receives a wound on the thigh. Jacob repeatedly refers to the covenant and God of "my father Abraham" as well as "my father Isaac." On their deathbeds, Abraham and Jacob both extract oaths from trusted men for the care of future generations.

The (conflated) matriarch is chosen for a man whom God has chosen. With even greater consistency than her male counterpart, she leaves her father's house and homeland. Probably discovered near a well, she journeys with her husband and serves the mission to which he has been called. The matriarch suffers various trials and tribulations with him, including dangers she must face because of his apparent greed or self-protection, such as when he passes her off as his sister.

Most likely, the woman is barren and prays for children. In response, God blesses her with a son and a divine message about his birth. If the matriarch is fertile, her life still appears to be "barren" with respect to affection and social station. Regardless, she, and the household generally, struggle with procreation and sexuality. Although infertility is the matriarch's ultimate source of grief, motherhood may well be her ultimate source of rivalry and pain. Perhaps because her power is so limited in the male-dominated world, she is fierce in attaining and defending her status as a mother and will compete with other women in this arena. She gains prestige, security, and personal fulfillment by becoming a mother and may well form impressive connections with God along the way. The matriarch exercises significant control over domestic and sexual issues, e.g., assigning a handmaid to her husband, setting the schedule for conjugal relations, dispatching members from the household, naming children.

The matriarch, more than the patriarch, understands and shapes the destiny of their progeny. She plays a major role in managing the transition from one generation to the next,

championing the proper son for inheritance. Her voice is generally in synch with God's voice and often out of synch with that of her husband (Gen. 21:12, 25:23, 31:16). Yet, when God remembers the matriarch, it is for fertility, not covenant. Her ability to bear children secures the covenant for the patriarch. The miraculous birth of a son confers upon the child—not his mother—the status of a divinely chosen leader. In biblical literature and society, the matriarch remains a secondary character, with major ellipses in her biography. Inheritance is neither hers to give nor hers to receive. The primary focus is on brothers' rivalries, male lineage, and God's covenants with and through men.

Literary and psychological patterns cross gender as well as generational lines. For example, while the matriarchal and patriarchal figures prove complex in their own right, they also serve as foils to one another. Sarah is the aggressor on behalf of the passive Isaac; Hagar is helpless and retreats from action in defending her aggressive son, Ishmael. In the next generation, favored sons seem to live out the repressed side of their parents. Isaac's favorite, the outdoorsman Esau, resembles Ishmael and Rebekah more than Isaac. Rebekah's favorite, the domestic Jacob, has his father's temperament. Similarly, Jacob will reject the wife who resembles his youthful self (Leah) and favor her more aggressive sister (Rachel). In an extended struggle toward maturation and balance, he lives out both hyperaggression (25:29ff.) and extreme passivity (34:5–30).

The last scene of the archetypal ancestral marriage is one of silent betrayal regarding a beloved child and prospective heir. Abraham goes off to slay Isaac without speaking to Sarah, whose death is reported just after Abraham returns. Rebekah guides Jacob to make a fool of Isaac and steal Esau's blessing. Dialogues between parents and children move the story forward, but Rebekah and Isaac do not speak until the trick is done—when Rebekah addresses Isaac briefly, gruffly, and for the last time in their lives (27:46). With her dying breath, Rachel names her son *Ben-oni* (son of my suffering, son of my strength). Perhaps Jacob never hears, or perhaps he doesn't listen; he renames the boy *Ben-yamin* (which roughly repeats Rachel's "son of my strength," but ignores her suffering).

Already in the first generation, we are alerted to the significance of repetition, as it is too consistent and relentless to be coincidental. Hagar is driven from the household twice; both Isaac's parents laugh at the thought of his impending birth; and Isaac's name is announced twice. Twice Abraham identifies (or perhaps misidentifies) Sarah as his sister, separates from Lot, encounters Abimelech, enters into covenant with God, is told "get yourself out . . . to a place that I will show you" (12:1, 22:2). Abraham has two potential heirs and is willing to sacrifice both.

Why all the repetition? Recurrent patterns show that the trials and promises we have come to associate with our ancestors were not their individual concerns. This family was passing on a vision and a covenant. In response to that—then and now—certain foibles and resistance typically arise: We laugh (17:17, 18:12), we doubt (28:15 vs. 28:20ff.), we banish others (21:14), we rob them of their blessings (27:19ff.), we act superior (21:10), we offer up human sacrifices (22:10), we favor one heir over another (25:28, 37:3). Victory in Genesis depends on three crucial passages: leaving one's parental home; confronting trials and lessons in the wider world; and returning, a changed person, back to family and land. The final third of that journey is male dominated and directed. Nevertheless, the lives of both the matriarchs and the patriarchs become a paradigm of being and becoming, of how to—and how not to (BT Shab. 10b). As heirs to the covenant and as heirs to Western culture, we owe a debt to these Genesis narratives for the very notion that spiritual maturity has something to do with repeated exposures to a challenge and more to do with noticing and transcending the patterns, than with resolving or escaping the situations.

NOTING THE ELEMENTS OF CHANGE

While it is useful to notice repetition, differences and nuances are also instructive. Variations in a known, archetypal story yield lessons about the uniqueness of a particular matriarch's character, patriarch's mission, or generation's dilemma.

Virtually every action Isaac takes re-enacts some episode from his father's life. Gen. 26:18 can be read as a summary of Isaac's biography: "And Isaac dug anew the wells which had been dug in the days of his father, Abraham." Yet Isaac differs from both his father and his son, in that he tends to react, rather than initiate action. In fact, biblical scholars have quipped that—based on commonalties in leadership, risk taking, deception, travel, and aggression—the patriarchs might more accurately be listed as "Abraham, Rebekah, and Jacob." Rebekah exercises a degree of power initiative unmatched by the other matriarchs. The contrast between Isaac and Rebekah is more than temperamental. It represents differing approaches to managing a sacred inheritance. Isaac models persistence, even without the allure of innovation or the glory of completion. Rebekah models aggressive and zealous commitment to a divinely approved end.

Social and genealogic developments in Genesis profoundly affect both women's status and the transmission of the covenant. Early on, matrilineal and patrilineal descent are not wholly separable. Abraham and Sarah may actually have been (half-) brother and sister (20:2,12). That would explain why Sarah's genealogy is omitted. (Alternatively, the couple may have been related by means other than blood. Adopting one's wife as a sister was a known way of elevating her status.) Rebekah the matriarch is part of the patriarchal family, being Abraham's grandniece and Isaac's cousin once removed. Laban was Jacob's uncle on his mother's side, living in what was also the land of Jacob's "fathers" (24:38). Yet Paddan-aram comes to be associated exclusively with his mother's house (28:2). Women are allied with Paddan-aram, and men, of a related genealogy, with Canaan. Continuity, kinship, and the Promised Land are general family interests that come to be dominated by men. Despite women's place on the family tree and their role in promoting the proper heir, covenant and blessing are ultimately passed down from father to son.

Disputes over the Land, doubt over succession, and rivalry within the family are recurrent problems. Yet, each generation faces a higher order of the dilemma. For example, Jacob's concern over brutality against his neighbors indicates a far more secure and settled position in the Land than do Abraham's tussles with neighbors over the wells, or his beholden position in bargaining for the cave of Machpelah. The matriarchs and patriarchs face the same questions, more than once, in relation to transmission: Will there be an heir? Which son will be chosen to inherit the covenant? Will the sons make peace with one another? All three questions are relevant in each generation, but the first is dominant for Abraham and Sarah, the second for Isaac and Rebekah, and the third for Jacob, Rachel, and (to a lesser extent) Leah.

Repetition in Genesis is not an endless loop, but an upward spiral. In the first generation of a revolutionary new faith, Abraham must leave his father's house and establish ownership and presence in the Land; in the second generation, Isaac must stake claim to that still-insecure inheritance; in the third generation, Jacob must learn the ways of the world and his own heart, before returning home to greet his brother and father and resettle the Land. In the fourth generation, the family reconciliation is more complete, as Joseph remains in contact with his father and brothers over time. Yet Joseph asserts love and responsibility for his brothers outside Canaan. Genesis is working its way toward complete redemption: peace and communication among siblings united by a covenant and living in their own land. Devora Steinmetz has pointed out that the narrative progresses toward this dream, achieving pieces of the vision without full realization: Genesis—indeed, the entire Torah—ends on the cusp of completion. The text thus invites the reader to continue, and fulfill, the story.

WHERE IS THE FAMILY HEADED?

As rabbinic tradition teaches, beginning with Abraham "the deeds of the ancestors are a sign for the descendants" (*ma·asei avot siman l'vanim*; see Ramban at Gen. 12:6). The patriarchs and matriarchs not only give rise to a nation but also embody it and portend its future. God predicts that the nation will sojourn in a foreign land and emerge with great property. The covenant through which God reveals this to Abraham clearly refers to the exodus from Egypt. At the same time, the terms of that covenant are fulfilled, albeit on a smaller scale, in the lives of Abraham, Isaac, Jacob, and Joseph—who each leave home, best a wealthy and powerful man, and return with some of his riches. To Abraham, as to the Israelites at Sinai, God declares: "I am the God who took you out" (Gen. 15:7; Exod. 20:2).

Jacob, renamed Israel, is father, namesake, and symbol of the Israelite nation. His children are sometimes textured and complex characters, but they are also eponymous stand-ins for the tribes. The Israelites are called "the people of the God of Abraham" (Ps. 47:10), "the House of Isaac" (Amos 7:16), and most popularly the "Children of Israel." Rachel becomes mother to the entire nation (Jer. 31:14). Procreation from the womb of a "barren" mother represents not just a hope, but a paradigm, for Jerusalem's rebirth (Isa. 54:1–3).

Stories of the matriarchs and patriarchs are linked to the Israelite's national destiny. Like Rebekah and Rachel before her, Zipporah, Moses' wife, is discovered and chosen at a well. Miriam, too, will be associated with wells and water, symbols of women's power to mother, nurture, manage danger, and redeem. Later biblical books regularly invoke God's promises to the patriarchs in relation to the divine covenant with subsequent generations (Exod. 2:24; Lev. 26:42; 2 Kings 13:23). We now take it for granted that the covenant made at Sinai is one with the covenant established with the patriarchs. Deuteronomy, in particular, makes that link.

The Midrash further connects the ancestral family with subsequent generations. Abraham was understood to have observed all the commandments, even though the revelation at Sinai would happen centuries later (BT Yoma 28b). Similarly, Sarah and Rebekah are said to have practiced extraordinary hospitality, set dough aside during baking, and enjoyed the distinction of a holy cloud above their tent; in these ways, the matriarchs both presaged and modeled conventions that would govern the Tabernacle and Temple (Gen. R. 60:16).

An important principle that motivates our continuing connection to the ancestors is *z'khut avot,* their merit. In deference to the merit of matriarchs and patriarchs, we were delivered from Egypt (Exod. 2:24), forgiveness was granted for building a Golden Calf (BT Shab. 30a), and our sins are pardoned on the Day of Atonement (PdRE 29).

Avot can be translated as "ancestors" or, using a gender-specific reading, as "fathers" or "patriarchs." In relation to ancestral merit, it is probable that "fathers" was generally meant, because Rabbinic sources also attribute God's mercy on later generations to *z'khut imahot,* the merit of the mothers. However, Hebrew grammar permits us to interpret most texts about *avot* as inclusive of *imahot,* in that one male among myriad women will alter the feminine plural to the masculine. Where the context is ambiguous, counting matriarchs among the *avot* has the effect of enfranchising women and reading them into the texts and tales of our ancestors. For that reason, many feminists prefer to call all the ancestors *avot,* rather than distinguishing Sarah, Rebekah, Leah, and Rachel as *imahot.* Traditional liturgy sometimes invokes mothers along with fathers, e.g., in relation to healing and the birth of baby girls. Following a responsum by the CJLS, many Conservative synagogues have added the matriarchs to the *Avot* blessing in the *Amidah.*

THE LIVING HERITAGE

Using our earliest ancestors as models in liturgy and ritual communicates essential values, even as it connects us intimately with our past. This process began within the Bible itself. In the Book of Ruth, Boaz is blessed: "May the

LORD make the woman who is coming into your house like Rachel and Leah, both of whom built up the house of Israel" (4:11). In a prewedding ritual still practiced today, we invoke Leah, Rachel, and Rebekah. As the groom veils the bride (making sure he is getting the correct sister!), he quotes the bridal blessing given to Rebekah: "may you grow into thousands and myriads" (Gen. 24:60). Today, as in the ancient world, we wish our daughters progeny and power. At the Friday night dinner table, parents bless their daughters: "May you be like Sarah, Rebekah, Rachel, and Leah." To their sons they say, "May you be like Ephraim and Manasseh."

By using scripture and its characters as a guide for contemporary living, we create an interchange between a fixed text and the changing, subjective contexts in which it is read. Reading ourselves backward into biblical text and our ancestors forward into contemporary situations is nothing new. During the time of the Crusades, Isaac, bound to the altar, became not only a hero but a tragic role model as well. For the philosopher Maimonides, Abraham exemplified the highest level of faith because he used reason to verify God's existence. Today, feminists read the experience of the matriarchs in light of the women's movement.

From a purely historical point of view, "our God and God of our ancestors" should be rendered as two different phrases and ideas—separated by time, experience, and theology. Yet, however we re-engage and reinterpret God and scripture over time, our relationship to them and to ourselves is influenced and nurtured by the *avot* of old. In the words of Isaiah, "Look back to Abraham your father / And to Sarah who brought you forth" (51:2).

EDUCATION

Hanan A. Alexander

The Bible views education spiritually, as embedded in a vision of the good life committed to a divine moral purpose. It is through this understanding of transcendent purpose that values are transmitted from generation to generation.

In the biblical narrative, God needs partners to bring good into the world, so He creates people in His image, with creative intelligence and the freedom of will to behave as they choose (Gen. 1:26–31; 2–3). People also need human partners with whom to share ethical insights and to check moral action, so man is given a wife as "a fitting helper for him" (2:18). Rashi understands the Hebrew *eizer k'negdo* as meaning "helper over against him," suggesting that she will help him if he is worthy and oppose him if he is not. Because man can serve in a similar capacity as a helper and friendly critic for his wife, the possibility of community—a collective based on mutual deliberation and decision making—is born.

As the Genesis narrative develops, it becomes clear that people will naturally be divided over issues of language, land, and lineage (4:1–16; 5; 6; 11:1–9). To communicate God's vision of the good, a community needs to be bound by a common moral creed. So God chooses Abraham and Sarah and their descendants and teaches them what is right and good (12:1–6).

The Jewish tradition calls this teaching *"torah,"* its specific legal path is called *"halakhah,"* and the specific steps along that path *"mitzvot."* The community that bears witness to God's message through *halakhah* and *mitzvot* is known as the *"edah."* What unites this community above all else is the enactment of God's moral vision by its members. Continuity depends on remaining committed to the vision of goodness on which the community is founded.

What is the substance of this vision, and by whom, how, and where is it communicated?

> When, in time to come, your children ask you, "What mean the decrees, laws, and rules that the LORD our God has enjoined upon you [in other versions: us]?" you shall say to your children, "We were slaves to Pharaoh in Egypt and the LORD freed us from Egypt with a mighty hand. The LORD wrought before our eyes marvelous and destructive signs and portents in Egypt, against Pharaoh and all his household; and us He freed from there, that He might take us and give us the land that He had promised on oath to our fathers. The LORD commanded us to observe all these laws, to reverence to the LORD our God, for our lasting good and for our survival, as is now the case. It will be therefore to our merit before the LORD our God to observe faithfully this whole Instruction, as He commanded us" (Deut. 6:20–25).

The way of life enjoined by God is not for slaves, but for people who are free to serve the Lord, who can choose the path they wish to follow. Freedom is a precondition of education, of initiation into a community committed to the good.

The child's question and the parent's response exemplify an approach to pedagogy delineated a few verses earlier in the *Sh'ma:* "Hear [*sh'ma*], O Israel! The LORD is our God, the LORD alone" (Deut. 6:4). The word *sh'ma* means "to hear, or heed, or consider"; to listen carefully so that the understanding that accompanies action can result. Intelligence—the capacity to understand—is a second prerequisite for education. How is this understanding achieved? "Impress them [*v'shinnantam*] upon your children. Recite them when you stay at home and when you are away, when you lie down and when you get up" (Deut. 6:7). The Hebrew *v'shinnantam* means "impress upon," by repetition or rote if necessary; recite these words even if at first they are not understood; that is, engage in training. Understanding can grow from repetition, as is evidenced if after all of this recounting of exhortations, laws, and norms, the child's curiosity is aroused—and he or she begins to inquire. Once the question is asked, the story can be retold, the commandments re-emphasized, the vision of the good rearticulated and re-enacted. The capacity for understanding is not only a prerequisite for education but part of the desired outcome as well.

One cannot achieve an understanding of goodness, however, through talking and thinking alone. Intelligent action is required. Repetition and explanation lead to more questions, which lead, in turn, to deeper understanding and more meaningful action. The classic response of the Israelites to receiving God's commandments, *na·aseh v'nishma*—we will faithfully do (Exod. 24:7), is often misunderstood as expressing a preference for action over understanding or sometimes even as rejecting the importance of understanding altogether. The literal translation is "we will do and we will hear" (in the sense of comprehending), which implies not that action is sufficient without understanding but that acting out God's will and understanding it go hand in hand. In fact, the order of the terms—action before hearing—suggests that religious observance leads to an understanding of divine instruction.

And what is to be repeated to the children? "You must love the LORD your God with all your heart and with all your soul and with all your might" (Deut. 6:5). This is stated as a command; but can love be forced on a person? Must it not be given freely, as a result of mutual understanding? Maimonides teaches that the very idea of commandment presupposes free agency (MT Repentance). Why have commandments in the first place, he asks, if people are not free to obey? "Freedom," he explains, does not refer to the license to follow one's most immediate desires, because that is a form of enslavement to caprice. Freedom requires choices made on the basis of understanding. Love of God as expressed in the observance of the *mitzvot* is evidence that a person has acquired an understanding of their meaning which is the key to genuine freedom. Not only are freedom and love of God preconditions of observance, like understanding the meaning

of religious practice, but also their enhancement is a desired outcome.

This is why the Midrash (Mekh. Bo 18; JT Pes. 10:4) sees the questioner in Deut. 6:20–25 as wise; including himself among those who have been commanded and referring to the Lord God as his own. By stating the question in this way, the wise son demonstrates that he has not only participated in the rote repetition of the *Sh'ma* and the *mitzvot* but has also evidenced genuine understanding of their import and chosen to accept them of his own free will. He has not only been trained; he has been educated (the *Pesaḥ Haggadah* also employs such a question and answer technique).

But why should such a person inquire about the meaning of these "decrees, laws, and rules"? He is already presumed to have had an education. Should he not, then, have knowledge of the answers? This is the significance of the response of the Midrash to the wise son. "Even he can be instructed in the laws of Passover." For example, he can be engaged in deciphering the passage concerning the ruling that there is to be no *afikoman*—a Greek term the meaning of which is obscure in the Mishnah—after the *pesaḥ*. Spiritual education is not a means to achieve a predetermined end. It leads to ever-increasing meaning and fulfillment in pursuit of the good. There are always new interpretations to be mined.

What have we learned so far about the Bible's theory of education? When parents live in a community dedicated to a life of Torah, children will naturally inquire about that life. In response, they can be educated—initiated into the community—by being told the story of their people's liberation from bondage, by being trained in the practices enjoined on their ancestors and on succeeding generations, and by being taught to understand the meaning of those practices. Thus observance leads to the enhancement of their intelligence, freedom, and love of God. It constitutes the content, the method, and the purpose of instruction.

This path, however, is not always smooth. Errors are expected (Deut. 29:9–30:20). This is among the most radical and profound aspects of the Bible's educational theory. Because we are free agents, we are capable of making mistakes and straying from the right path. Here is the meaning of the biblical concept of *ḥet* or "sin": to miss the mark, lose the way, abandon the good life. But because we are moral agents we can learn from our mistakes and return to the right path. The ability to return is a consequence of freedom; the capacity to learn is a consequence of intelligence. Here is the meaning of the concept of *t'shuvah,* or "returning to God's path."

But how are we to decide which course to choose and whether we have gone astray? This returns us to the concept of Torah, of God's moral teaching, the very purpose of which is to teach us which path is the right one. "See, I set before you this day life and prosperity [i.e., goodness], death and adversity [i.e., evil]. . . . Choose life—if you and your offspring would live—by loving the LORD your God, heeding His commands, and holding fast to Him. For thereby you shall have life and shall long endure" (Deut. 30:15–20). Engagement with Torah does not produce Jewish identity or Jewish continuity, and the acquisition of knowledge on its own does not generate love of God or commitment to a life of Torah. On the contrary, identity and continuity are prerequisites for this very engagement to take place, and commitment to a vision of the good is required to determine what knowledge is worth acquiring. Studying, practicing, and celebrating Torah for its own sake is what leads to spiritual renewal, to a strengthened commitment to God's vision of the good life.

From this account, it is clear that parents have primary responsibility for the education of their children. Although vocational training is also valued (Prov. 24:27–34, 27:23–27) the most significant educational task is induction into a religious community with a particular moral point of view. This is accomplished through story, ritual, and liturgy; at home, in the place of worship, and in the life of the community as a whole. Although the Bible

emphasizes the role of the father, we know that the mother also played a significant part in instructing the young. "My son, heed the discipline of your father, and do not forsake the instruction of your mother" (Prov. 1:8, see also 6:20,23:22). Because of this responsibility, the child is enjoined to respect both parents: "Honor your father and your mother" (Exod. 20:12; Deut. 5:16; and also Prov. 15:20, 20:20). This is the earliest and most basic form of Jewish education.

In time, the role of the parents was supplemented by elders, priests, prophets, scribes, and teachers. The tribal elders were probably the earliest to supplement the parent's role, as in the case of a rebellious son: "If a man has a disloyal and defiant son, who does not heed his father or mother and does not obey them even after they discipline him, his father and mother shall take hold of him and bring him out to the elders of the town at the public place of his community" (Deut. 21:18–19, see also Exod. 21:17). The role of the elders as teachers of the law was a natural outgrowth of their role as judges in the city gates.

The priests of the *bamot* (altars; before the unification of the cult) and of Jerusalem also supplemented parental instruction. Already, the Deuteronomist enjoins families to come together to hear public recitations of the Torah on the *Sukkot* festival (Deut. 31:12) and other public feasts, such as covenant renewal ceremonies (Exod. 24:7). In some instances, fathers even served as or were identified with priests (Judg. 17:10; Prov. 6:20); and as in other ancient Near Eastern cultures, perhaps the earliest formal schools developed alongside the altars in such places as Shilo. It may be in these schools that the tradition emerged for children to begin the study of Torah with *Va-yikra* (Leviticus), which contains the Priestly Code. It is probably here too that psalms, which were an important part of the liturgies at these sites, became significant texts for instructing the young.

Give ear, my people, to my teaching,
turn your ear to what I say.
I will expound a theme,
hold forth on lessons of the past,
things we have heard and known,
that our fathers have told us.
We will not withhold them from their children,
telling the coming generation
the praises of the LORD and His might,
and the wonders He performed
(Ps. 78:1–4; see also Pss. 15, 19, 119).

Prophets also played a role in educating the young. In prophetic circles, we find the first instances of masters and disciples that became so prominent among the rabbis (2 Kings 3:11). There are also allusions to "schools of the prophets" (1 Sam. 10:5), and it may be in these schools that the concept of *musar,* or moral instruction as independent from *mitzvot,* began to emerge as a key educational concept (Jer. 2:30, 7:28, 17:23, 32:33).

In the 5th century B.C.E., Ezra and Nehemiah placed the study and practice of Torah at the center of the curriculum by institutionalizing its public reading on Mondays, Thursdays, and *Shabbat* afternoons. They prepared scribes to preserve the text, and *meivinim min ha-l'vi·im* (learned Levites) to interpret its meaning. It was out of this circle of the learned scribes that the Pharisaic rabbis emerged as teachers of Torah par excellence. The Torah, joined by other books of the canon, became their textbooks.

Wisdom texts, for example, began to emerge as formal pedagogic tools under the influence of Hellenism. Many of them, such as Proverbs, Job, and Ecclesiastes, were composed as textbooks by and for wisdom teachers. Especially among the upper classes, they taught that intellectual and ethical enlightenment would awaken a fear of God and a desire to fulfill His commandments (Prov. 9:10; Job 28:28). Some of these texts are known to have been written on tablets, so their use in pedagogy corresponds to the emergence of literacy as a goal of instruction, along with the oral recitation of laws and narratives that preceded it and that continued well into the 3rd century C.E.

In the 1st century C.E., the high priest Yehoshua ben Gamla reformed and reorganized the educational system, appointing *m'lamdei tinokot* (teachers of children) in every province and town (BT BB 21a). The classical curriculum emerged: "At five years one is fit for scripture, at ten for Mishnah, at thirteen for *mitzvot,* at fifteen for Talmud" (M Avot 5:21).

In sum, the biblical conception of education is not instrumental, at least not in the strong sense in which education is used to achieve goals extrinsic to the practices, values, and beliefs being promoted. Rather, it is spiritual, in that it offers God's vision of the good life. Although education is essential to Jewish knowledge, identity, and continuity, when we view these as the ultimate ends, we lose sight of the very ideals to which such an education must be devoted if it is to renew our collective and individual commitment to them.

ECOLOGY

David M. Gordis

Through narrative, poetry, law, and prayer, the Bible conditions its readers to feel reverence for nature, enjoins restraint in the exploitation of natural resources for human needs, elicits awe in response to the diversity and complexity of creation, and articulates the principle of human responsibility for faithful trusteeship over the natural world.

Beginning with the Creation narrative in Genesis, every component of the Hebrew Bible is a strand in the fabric that defines the biblical approach to issues of ecology. Human beings are commanded: "Be fertile and increase, fill the earth and master it; and rule the fish of the sea, the birds of the sky, and all the living things that creep on the earth" (Gen. 1:28). Although the creation of human beings is the high point of the creative process as depicted in Genesis, it is, however, only part of the process, which includes all the natural world. Flora and fauna, birds and fishes, forests and grasses are all parts of God's design. God reflects on creation at every successive stage and pronounces it "good." The sequence developed in the biblical narrative may lead up to the creation of human beings, but it does not suggest that what precedes their creation is peripheral or insignificant.

Later reflections on the Creation narrative in halakhic and midrashic literature are also relevant. The commandment to be fertile and master the earth is understood as directed primarily to the obligation to procreate, not to dominate or to exploit. Although the Midrash suggests that God was conflicted about creating human beings who would be capable of both good and evil, corollary readings imply that it is their potential moral capacity that places them at the pinnacle of creation. Yet the natural world is good in and of itself, implying that everything created by God before the emergence of humans represents a pure rather than an instrumental good. It follows quite naturally that human beings should appreciate this purity, respecting and using the natural world as the handiwork of God, but not exploiting it.

In this context, the story of Noah is most relevant to issues of ecology. In the face of the widespread destruction that God brings about because of human depravity, cruelty, and sinfulness, Noah is commanded to preserve the blameless animals two by two, alerting the reader to the reality of animals as sensing and feeling creatures, part of the life process, entering into relationships, procreating, and generating life themselves.

> And of all that lives, of all flesh, you shall take two of each into the ark to keep alive with you; they shall be male and female. From birds of every kind, cattle of every kind, every kind of creeping thing on earth, two of each shall come to you to stay alive (Gen. 6:19–20).

Every species is to be represented. Noah's obligation is to save endangered species and to

promote life. No suggestion is put forward that the species are to be rescued for the benefit of Noah and his descendants. Quite the contrary: They are to be kept alive "with you" and not "for you." It is taken as self-evident that their existence enhances the world, that they are blameless and undeserving of the destruction facing humankind, and that they should be rescued in all their variety and diversity. A precious product of the divine creative process, they merit protection and nurture.

Legal passages in the Bible contribute substantially to the themes of human trusteeship for the natural world and restraint in the use of natural resources. Scholars have debated the sources and original functions of the laws of *kashrut*. Whatever their origin and other functions, the dietary laws, imposing limits on what may be eaten, establish the principle of restraint. In so doing, they continually remind us that to take this life for food represents a compromise, for it destroys a living, feeling creature. Meticulous regulation of the process of slaughtering animals for food, with a focus on limiting the suffering of the animal as much as possible, was a natural Rabbinic expansion of biblical principles. The case has been argued that a further legal embodiment of biblical principles would prohibit the killing of animals for human needs entirely and would suggest vegetarianism as a high form of *kashrut*. Be that as it may, the general principle of sensitivity to taking an animal's life is clear.

The biblically based and rabbinically articulated laws of *sh'hitah* express the principle of *tza·ar ba·alei hayyim,* "sensitivity to the pain of living creatures." This general principle is formulated in Rabbinic Judaism, but its foundations in biblical law are apparent. It underlies the inclusion of one's animals in the commandment to rest on *Shabbat*, the fourth commandment (Exod. 20:10; Deut. 5:14, Exod. 23:12). Similarly, the Bible prohibits muzzling an ox when it is treading out grain (Deut. 25:4) and plowing with an ox and a donkey yoked together (Deut. 22:10), because these practices would cause suffering to the hungry and to the weaker animal, respectively.

Restraint on exploitation and sensitivity to all living creatures are important biblical principles. An intriguing and eloquent example of biblical sensitivity training occurs in Deut. 22:6–7:

> If, along the road, you chance upon a bird's nest, in any tree or on the ground, with fledglings or eggs and the mother sitting over the fledglings or on the eggs, do not take the mother together with her young. Let the mother go, and take only the young, in order that you may fare well and have a long life.

Whatever the original context of this law may be, its poignant reminder of the existence of the sentient animal family moves the reader to a higher level of concern for living things and their pain and suffering.

Fundamental to the biblical view of the natural world and humankind's place in it is the principle that human ownership is temporary and illusory. The world belongs to God; people are its trustees and not its proprietors. This principle underlies the biblical laws relating to the jubilee and the sabbatical years. Regarding the sabbatical (seventh) year, Lev. 25:5–6 states:

> You shall not reap the aftergrowth of your harvest or gather the grapes of your untrimmed vines; it shall be a year of complete rest for the land. But you may eat whatever the land during its sabbath will produce—you, your male and female slaves, the hired and bound laborers who live with you.

Several themes come together here. The "seven" cycle recapitulates the Creation cycle and places the natural world into the context of divine creation. Human beings may use the natural world for their needs, but not without limitation. The land, too, requires and deserves rest. This is not simply a personal obligation, however; it carries with it principles of social justice and concern. The poor and the

stranger were granted the privilege of eating the produce that grew as the result of earlier years' planting, just as they were granted access to unpicked harvest and the corners of the field during other years (Lev. 23:22). Limitation, obligation to others, and concern for the needs of the poor all express the fundamental value of the sabbatical: During the seventh year, God is reasserting proprietorship—and so human beings do not have access to the field. Human ownership is temporary.

This principle is explicit in providing the rationale for the law of the jubilee year. The jubilee was quite radical in its prescribing that on the 50th year—i.e., after the completion of seven sabbatical cycles, seven times seven, connecting again with the Creation motif—all land that had been sold during the preceding half century was to be returned to its original owner. Why? "The land must not be sold beyond reclaim, for the land is Mine; you are but strangers resident with Me" (Lev. 25:23).

An additional area of biblical legislation most relevant to this discussion occurs in Deut. 20:19–20:

> When in your war against a city you have to besiege it a long time in order to capture it, you must not destroy its trees, wielding the ax against them. You may eat of them, but you must not cut them down. Are trees of the field human to withdraw before you into the besieged city? Only trees that you know do not yield food may be destroyed; you may cut them down for constructing siegeworks against the city that is waging war on you, until it has been reduced.

Even in time of war, when wanton destruction is common, biblical law imposes severe constraints. Once again, a contrast is made between human beings who may bring destruction on themselves through their behavior and the blameless natural world that deserves protection and nurturing. And though trees may be used within limits for the purposes of war, that use is severely limited and contained.

The principle implicit in this law and the term employed in this passage were expanded and articulated in the Rabbinic law of *bal tashḥit,* the prohibition against unnecessary and wanton destruction. Although the full development of the principle is Rabbinic, we again see the clear biblical foundation for a traditional value.

The biblical picture is rounded out in a number of other passages that contribute to the biblical ecologic perspective. One noteworthy passage concludes the Book of Jonah (4:9–11):

> Then God said to Jonah: "Are you so deeply grieved about the plant?" "Yes," he replied, "so deeply that I want to die."
>
> Then the LORD said: "You cared about the plant, which you did not work for and which you did not grow, which appeared overnight and perished overnight. And should I not care about Nineveh, that great city, in which there are more than a hundred and twenty thousand persons who do not yet know their right hand from their left, and many beasts as well!"

The coda of this passage is quite striking. Had the divine demonstration by comparative syllogism ended with mention of the 120,000 who lived in Nineveh, the argument would have been complete but not quite so jarring. The inclusion of "many beasts" implies a shift from a human-centered view of the world. Mercy for animals is as significant as concern for innocent people. Jonah was not wrong to be concerned for the plant, but his grief may have centered on the usefulness of the plant to himself as it provided him shelter and protection. In a world that is God's, the human perspective can be only partially true and, therefore, is necessarily distorted. The Bible reminds its readers of the limitations and the error of a human-centered perspective.

A striking text articulating the limitations of humankind's orientation toward the natural world is found in the Book of Job (38–40). Readers and scholars have debated the thrust of God's response to Job's challenge. Does

God simply overwhelm Job with divine creative power and strength and thus silence Job? Is it suggested that Job simply cannot understand the justice of God's ways, which may be hidden from him? Perhaps elements of both are contained in God's responses. Doubtless also present is God's assertion that the world is not created to be comprehensible to human beings or to serve them. Examples adduced in the God speeches refer to a range of creatures that God has created as well as to divine power and creativity. The lioness, the mountain goat, the wild ass and wild ox, the ostrich and the crocodile are included, as are the hawk, the vulture, and the hippopotamus. As Robert Gordis pointed out, notable about this list of creatures is that virtually none of the animals is useful to human beings, nor do the animals generally represent creatures that people find beautiful or appealing. They are part of God's plan, which often is unfathomable to human beings. That is part of the thrust of God's reply to Job. It is certainly relevant to the Bible's ecologic stance. The bedrock of the biblical approach to the environment (and our place in it) demands the abandonment of a worldview that puts people at the center and evaluates all things in terms of their utility to people.

On the subject of ecology in the Bible, we can find no structured or systematic statement of principles. The Bible, by and large, does not teach by direction; it teaches by conditioning us to understand the nature of the world and the profound implications of the choices and decisions we make in our lives. It invites us to learn ethical and spiritual lessons by reflecting on the complex and never unflawed lives of its heroes. It urges us to search out the values underlying most of its legal admonitions. It entices us to be moved by the imagery of its poetry. The Bible allows us to weave a tapestry, to synthesize a perspective of the natural world, which can warn us about the dangers of excess, alert us to our responsibility, condition our thinking and our behavior, and sensitize us to the beauty and fragility of the natural environment around us.

Most of what has been pointed out articulates the principle of the psalmist (24:1): "The earth is the LORD's and all that it holds." Remember that human ownership is only temporary. Protect from destruction what God has entrusted to us. Ponder the enigmatic, bearing in mind that the world was not created from our point of view, so that not everything will be comprehensible to us. Strive for godliness by remembering and commemorating the creative process initiated by the ultimate creator, and by being responsible protectors of what God has created.

LAND OF ISRAEL

Benjamin J. Segal

Expulsion from territory is a dominant theme of the Torah's early world history (Gen. 1–11): Adam and Eve are expelled from Eden, Cain exiled from before the presence of the Lord, Noah's generation blotted out "from the earth" (6:7), and humanity scattered from (the tower of) Babel. With Abraham, God opts for a narrower channel of access to the world—through a people who will have a special relationship to Him and to a particular land.

Because this land exists in triangular relationship with the descendants of Abraham and with God, it forever straddles the transient and the eternal, the real and the ideal. It is both subject to human influence and unalterably divine; these diverse qualities form a grid on which the land is described in the Torah. The human and the divine seek to coexist in the land.

In tracing that relationship, one must note the nature of the Torah sources concerning the land. This home is not a subcategory of Israelite thought. It is axiomatic; a primary, defining category of the people's existence vis-à-vis

its God. Observations are made from within, reflecting ultimate involvement and identification but lacking external perspective. References to the land should be understood as a nation's self-expression, not objective reflections on a subject of concern.

In this essay, I will explore the relationship of the people to the land in four of its expressions: the early struggle to establish human "ownership," even in total absence of political control; the attempts to define the land as both physical and divine entities; the matter of justifying ownership, with its implications for the giver and the recipients; and the land as seen on the eve of Israelite entry, from across the Jordan River.

GENESIS: HOMELESS AT HOME

In what sense did the forefathers "own" the land? Time and again, the forefathers are "given" this land (Gen. 13:15,17, 35:12ff.), as part of the covenant. As we learn from ancient Near Eastern covenant terminology, the giving is more properly understood as "assignment": they are assigned the land of Israel.

In the forefathers' time, theirs was the promise, not the possession; the legal deed, not the control. Much later the Israelites would be told that they were to be only strangers in residence (Lev. 25:23). The forefathers needed no such message, for they lived that reality. Understanding that full ownership was God's promise for the future, they faced the first challenge of the land: establishing personal bonds symbolizing their connection. They, the people, had to gain possession of the divine land.

The first response lay in traversing the land. God told Abraham: "Up, walk about the land, through its length and breadth, for I give it to you" (Gen. 13:17). Centuries later, Joshua would still recall this tour as a basic step in establishing ownership (Josh. 24:3). As in Joseph's trip through Egypt (Gen. 41:46), physical contact sealed legal rights.

The second response reflected a religious attachment, accomplished by building altars throughout the land. In Shechem, Bethel, Mamre, and Beer-sheba, the forefathers erected places of worship (Gen. 12:6–7, 13:18, 26:25, 35:7).

Purchase was the third response. Refusing what seemed to be the gift of a burial site, Abraham insisted on purchasing the cave of Machpelah (Gen. 23), which would become the family burial ground. Jacob later bought territory in Shechem (33:19). The first small, legal possessions were attained.

Fourth, the predominant theme of the forefathers' relationship to the land is the determination to be buried there; the Machpelah burial cave served all three generations. On his deathbed, Jacob insists that his body be returned to the land of Israel from Egypt (Gen. 49:29–32), and Joseph insists that his bones be reburied there (50:25).

Finally, one forefather established the precedent of residing there exclusively. When faced with a local famine, Isaac was told that he could not, like his father, Abraham, go to Egypt. Rather, he was to stay in the land (Gen. 26:2ff.) all his life. Therefore Jacob, his son, on leaving the land (for what would be the last time), prayed in fear specifically to "the God of his father, Isaac" (46:1), the model of permanent residence. Only God's reassurance that the connection would not be severed and that Jacob's progeny would return allowed him to depart with his mind at ease.

The story of the forefathers in the land is one of ongoing struggle. Except for Abraham's successful foray against the kings who abducted Lot and his family (Gen. 14), the forefathers are depicted as relatively weak. They remained in the mountains, away from the strong centers of settlement on the coast. They were subject to harassment by their neighbors and they wandered from place to place, resorting to machinations to protect themselves and their households. Neither sovereign on the one hand nor powerless on the other, the forefathers struggled and maneuvered to establish ownership of their "home."

Genesis thus projects a striking aggregate picture, a depiction of the homeless at home. A young clan claims ownership, but not con-

trol, while forging nonpolitical ties to bind itself to the territory. It is of some fascination that for millennia these patterns of burial, traversal, and purchase remained active models for the Jewish people in maintaining their ties to the land.

DESCRIBING THE LAND: DESTINATION AND DESTINY

After Genesis, the Israelites in the Torah are constantly directed toward the land. So Exodus begins, as God speaks to Moses in Midian: "I have come down . . . to bring them out of that land to a good and spacious land, a land flowing with milk and honey, the region of the Canaanites" (Exod. 3:8). So, too, Deuteronomy concludes with Moses allowed only to see the land, as the Lord says: "This is the land of which I swore to Abraham, Isaac, and Jacob, 'I will assign it to your offspring'" (Deut. 34:4). Because it is forever on the horizon, the land cried out for a double description: both in human terms (Who lives there? What are its borders?) and divine (In what ways is it so different?).

That land of future possession was then occupied by others. Most often titled the "land of Canaan," it was associated with as many as 10 peoples (Gen. 15:19ff.), known in varying degrees from extrabiblical documents. Leviticus (18:24ff.) provides a rationale for the eventual expulsion of the current residents: moral turpitude. Thereafter, God would give it to His chosen people.

Throughout, the Torah foresees interaction with neighbors resident in the land and the ensuing dangers. The Torah is acutely aware that the Israelites, although the conquering power, would be attracted to local pagan practices (Deut. 17:3), rooted in place and soil. Consistently, they are warned to distance themselves from the pagan cults of the Canaanites, who attributed the land's bounty to gods of nature. Rather, the land was to be seen as the assigned gift of the one God (Deut. 26:3–10).

The land's borders are variously defined in the Torah. They approximate neither the eventual settlement area of the tribes nor the eventual Davidic kingdom. Rather, they are either grand overviews of the entire territory between the great powers of Egypt and Assyria (as in Gen. 15:18, which speaks of "this land, from the river of Egypt to . . . the river Euphrates") or an approximation of the borders of Canaan, relying heavily on settlement area, contiguity, and natural boundaries (Num. 34:1–12). The Torah's geographic definition is not an attempt to anticipate later developments but a reflection of preconquest general concepts of the land's parameters.

The territory on the horizon, of course, is also God's Promised land. In articulating its divine qualities, the Torah describes the land's delights, dependency, and demands, as I now detail.

A Delightful Land

This is "a land flowing with milk and honey" (e.g., Exod. 3:8). Some commentators once held that this idealized picture, with its reference to natural gifts, reflected an early, preoccupation origin of the phrase, because the land is scarcely perfect. However, an Egyptian text provides a similar description of northern Israel: "It was a good land. . . . Figs were in it, and grapes. . . . Plentiful was its honey, abundant its olives. Every fruit was on its trees." The Torah's idealization should, therefore, be understood as an emphasis on the land's advantages. This is

> a good land, a land with streams and springs and fountains issuing from plain and hill; a land of wheat and barley, of vines, figs, and pomegranates, a land of olive trees and honey; a land where you may eat food without stint, where you will lack nothing; a land whose rocks are iron and from whose hills you can mine copper (Deut. 8:7–9).

The sin of the spies (Num. 13–14) was not in bearing a false report, but in choosing to emphasize the negative, thereby disheartening the people.

A Dependent Land

The land is also dependent. Unlike Egypt and Mesopotamia, which derive their water from significant rivers fed by distant sources, the land is a country of mountains, dependent on rain. For the Torah this meant dependency on God's mercy and justice.

> The land you are about to cross into and possess, a land of hills and valleys, soaks up its water from the rains of heaven. It is a land which the LORD, your God, looks after, on which the LORD, your God, always keeps His eye, from year's beginning to year's end. . . .

Take care not to be lured away to serve other gods and bow to them. For the LORD's anger will flare up against you, and He will shut up the skies so that there will be no rain and the ground will not yield its produce; and you will soon perish from the good land that the LORD is assigning to you (Deut. 11:11–12,16–17).

A Demanding Land

The land is central to all of the Torah's prescribed behaviors. So marked is the emphasis on observing God's law within the land, that Ramban, the 13th-century commentator, concluded that all laws of the Torah were intended for observance exclusively there. (Observance elsewhere would reflect empathy and constitute preparation for return.) Although this is an idiosyncratic view, the Torah text does see the land as the primary locus of observance. Furthermore, many of the demands are connected directly to the land, detailing when produce could be eaten, which products had to be brought to the Temple, which produce had to be left for the poor, etc.

The demands are not framed as an "object" (the land) being imposed on a living entity (the people). Rather, the land is almost personified. As humans must rest every seventh day, so every seventh year the land must lie unplanted to gain its rest. As humans must observe the 50th year, canceling all individual debts, so, too, the land returns by section to its original owners in the 50th year.

Personification reaches its apex in august moral terms. The land could not abide immoral behavior. The previous residents were expelled because of their disobedience to God's norms, and so would the land expel the Israelites were they to misbehave similarly. Expulsion might also follow abuse of the soil, through failure to grant the land its proper rest (Lev. 26:35). The land exhibits a living claim of its own, against which the Israelites had to measure and understand their presence. Otherwise, the land would expel them to gain its respite. The land's divinity was understood as posing a demand.

RIGHTS AND OBLIGATIONS

By what right would the Israelites possess the land? The nation's self-conception emphasized arrival from abroad. They were the descendants of Abraham's family who came to the land from without. As a people, they immigrated after a long stay in Egypt, which they celebrated in an annual holiday cycle. Each year they would recite that history when offering God the first fruits of the land, at the same time personalizing the gift: "I," each farmer would say, "have entered the land that the LORD swore to our fathers to assign us" (Deut. 26:3–10). They came from afar and constantly reminded themselves of that fact. That recalled "outsider" status demanded a justification of possession, and in the response lay the most complex reflection of the divine–human partnership in the land of Israel.

The basic right to the land was grounded in God's assignment, but that was scarcely an absolute claim. With possession came responsibilities. In the context of one of them, return of property to original owners every 50th year, a striking assertion is made: "The land must not be sold beyond reclaim, for the land is Mine; you are but strangers resident with Me" (Lev. 25:23). The assigning owner maintains His property rights! The claim of the people is tenuous indeed.

Further emphasizing the dependency of occupation on God's mercy and memory, the text states that the Israelites inherited the land

by virtue of the original covenant God made with Abraham, Isaac, and Jacob—and not by merit of their deeds (Deut. 9:4ff.). Ironically, the very question of rights to the land, then, leads to the possibility of exile! If this gift implied obligation, continued disobedience ultimately implied expulsion (Lev. 26:33ff.; Deut. 28:63ff.). No other ancient people so placed a moral qualification on its right to its territory. The Israelites thus extended their original understanding of a universal order that allowed God to expel humans from territory to apply to their own land.

The exile is described as torturous for both the land and the people. The land will be "desolate" (Lev. 26:32); it "shall become a desolation and your cities a ruin" (26:33). The Israelites in exile, for their part, will live in fear and suffer persecution:

> The sound of a driven leaf shall put them to flight. . . . With no one pursuing, they shall stumble over one another as before the sword. You shall not be able to stand your ground before your enemies, but shall perish among the nations; and the land of your enemies shall consume you" (26:36–38).

But beyond exile lay a final and ultimate reunification. The land and the people, part of the same covenant, could never be fully separated. Following repentance and atonement, the people would return (26:41ff.).

The Torah thus posits simultaneously the strongest and most fragile of relationships: A direct assignment from God but a connection that can be cut off because of human acts of omission or commission. Given this complexity, it is no surprise that the Torah at times attributes the land's holiness to an immanent, inherent quality (most often emphasized in Leviticus and Numbers) and at times emphasizes the holiness granted the land by the people's presence and deeds thereon (Deuteronomy). Sanctity is inherent in the land and, therefore, it is demanded of its residents; but simultaneously it is given to the land by the acts of those residents.

As later history unfolded, the complex interweave of the land's characteristics (permanently assigned yet potentially lost, bearing both obligations and opportunities, idealized yet fraught with dangers of contact) formed the basis of a complex relationship with the nation, permanent at its deepest level yet constantly volatile on the surface.

THE VIEW FROM ACROSS THE RIVER

Nowhere is the sense of immediate occupation felt more keenly than in Deuteronomy. Speaking to the Israelites in Transjordan, Moses recalls history and dream, commandment and dangers. The book opens with a recollection of God's order to go to the land (1:7) and concludes with Moses' ascent to Mount Nebo and his death, the Torah ending short of fulfillment, looking forward to imminent entrance into the land of Canaan.

So close to arrival, Deuteronomy focuses on the expected normal life on the nation's own soil. Exclusive to this book are the themes of kingship and centralized worship (the "chosen place") and a marked concentration on the court system, one of the bases of an organized society.

Deuteronomy, however, also constantly reminds the people that occupation requires obedience to God. The past is cited as testimony, the laws repeated as prescription. Reinforcing the divine–human partnership in the land, the book's framework is land centered: "Observe . . . that you may long remain in the land that the LORD your God is assigning to you for all time" (4:40), and "to the end that you and your children may endure, in the land . . . as long as there is a heaven over the earth" (11:21).

Although the possibilities of rebellion and loss are recalled, this final book of the Torah ends in anticipation, with the people poised to enter the land. The land and all its potential, for glory and failure remain untested and, therefore, untarnished. The dominant message presents the land as the locus of the potential ideal, a concept that would pervade Jewish history for millennia.

AND BEYOND

Many commentators tend to seek out reflections of later developments in the Torah text, which itself always sees the land of Israel as a category of the future. However, there remains significant dissonance between later reality and the Torah's combination of prescriptions and predictions. The Torah emphasizes aspirations. Thus it provides the building blocks for all future ideologies of the land. Deuteronomy's "chosen place," for example, is identified as David's Jerusalem, which develops its own centrality, absorbing and encompassing some earlier approaches to the land as a whole. The Torah's idealized hopes are strongly strained in light of reality. The dream of potential perfection is recast, with renewed emphasis on the future, attached to a new image of Jerusalem, expected at "the end of days" (e.g., Isa. 27:13; Zech. 2:14–16).

The Bible and Jewish literature throughout the ages, however, remain faithful to the primary relationships established in the Torah: an axiomatic connection between God, the people, and the land; a complex interaction of ownership, possession, and exile; an understanding of the land as delightful, dependent on God, and demanding of the people; and a view of the land as destiny, the locus of hope.

The relationship is sui generis. No other ancient nation had such a complex understanding of its territory, for whom it was "the Holy land" (Zech. 2:16). These vicissitudes reflected involvement, not ambivalence. The movement in and out—in the Bible and across the centuries—reflects not dissociation, but the centripetal and centrifugal forces created around a center. All this derives from the Torah, for which this land was assigned, the exclusive potential locus for human–divine harmony. The Torah traces a grand march toward that center, from the first command to Abram to go forward to the land, to the final scene of Moses looking on it from across the Jordan.

DEALING WITH STRANGERS: RELATIONS WITH GENTILES AT HOME AND ABROAD

Joel Rembaum

Although the Bible's focus is the unique relationship between the people Israel and God, relationships between Israel and the non-Israelite world constitute a significant element of the biblical traditions. Commentators on the Bible from Maimonides to contemporary scholars have noted that an important purpose of biblical law and narrative was to direct the ancient Israelites away from the beliefs and practices of the pagan nations that surrounded them. It should come as no surprise, therefore, that the overriding view of the non-Israelite world expressed in the Hebrew Bible is negative.

This attitude first represents itself in Gen. 15:16. After promising Abram that the land of Canaan will be given to his descendants as an inheritance, God tells the patriarch: "And they shall return here in the fourth generation, for the iniquity of the Amorites is not yet complete." Taking this idea one step further, Deut. 9:5 emphasizes that the Israelites will gain possession of the Land not because of their righteousness, but because of the sinfulness of the nations that had inhabited it; and thus God can fulfill the promise made to the patriarchs.

A further elaboration is presented in Exod. 23:31–33:

> I will deliver the inhabitants of the land into your hands, and you will drive them out before you. You shall make no covenant with them and their gods. They shall not remain in your land, lest they cause you to sin against Me; for you will serve their gods—and it will prove a snare to you.

The issue is laid out in very clear terms: The pagan nations must be eradicated from the

Land because they pose a threat to Israelite belief in the one, true God. Because the removal of the pagans from Canaan will occur over a protracted period of time, the Israelites in the interim are prohibited from worshiping the gods of the nations, making any covenants with the nations, and giving their sons in marriage to the daughters of the nations (concerning the latter, see Exod. 34:16). If the Israelites are attracted by the paganism of the nations they, in turn, will be punished. Deut. 7:1–6 reiterates these points, including the prohibition against intermarriage, and adds yet another reason for this destruction of and separation from pagan society: "For you are a people consecrated to the LORD your God." Because of Israel's unique relationship with God, total separation from the pagan world is mandated. Deut. 23:4 adds that peoples not indigenous to the land of Israel, such as Ammonites and Moabites, are not to be "admitted into the congregation of the LORD . . . even in the tenth generation." This is "because they did not meet you with food and water on your journey after you left Egypt, and because they hired Balaam son of Beor . . . to curse you" (23:5). Rabbinic tradition interprets "the 10th generation" to mean forever (Sifrei Deut. Ki Tetzei 39). Accordingly, Ammonites and Moabites never could be welcomed into the nation of Israel.

Carrying the notion of Israel's uniqueness as a people even further, Leviticus adds another dimension to the idea of the sinfulness of the pagan world and the Israelites' need for separation. Leviticus 18 views Egypt and the nations of Canaan as engaging in sexual abominations, which result in serious defilement. The land of Israel, we are told, cannot tolerate such impurity and will vomit out any people thus defiled. The Israelites, to remain in the land, must avoid such activities.

Ezra and Nehemiah, interpreting these Torah traditions in the 5th century B.C.E., forced the Israelite men of Judea to send away non-Israelite women they had married. These leaders, confronted with Israelite intermarriage of sizable proportions, feared that the people and the land to which they had returned would be defiled through the forbidden marriages and that God would punish the people by sending them into exile once again (Ezra 9–10; Neh. 9:1–2, 10:31, 13:1–3,23–28). Since the option to convert the women did not exist at that time, removal from society was the only resolution. Clearly, these and similar assessments of the pagans, and the emphasis of Israelite separation from the nations in whose midst they lived, cast the non-Israelites in a negative light.

Yet, despite the general antipathy of the Bible toward pagans, certain tolerant attitudes toward non-Israelites do emerge from the biblical traditions. The Torah begins with the assumption that Elohim/*YHVH*, as Creator, is the God of all humankind. In this vein, Maimonides conceives of humankind as being initially monotheistic and believing in the one true God, with idolatry developing only later as a result of human ideologic error (MT Idol Worship 1:1). After the Flood, during which most of humanity was destroyed, God rebuilds the human race with Noah and his children. *Elohim* enters into a covenant with Noah and his descendants and all the living creatures on earth (Gen. 9:8–17), thereby deepening God's relationship with humankind. All the nations of the world emerge from Noah's children (Gen. 10), and therefore, we can presume that the Torah considers all nations to be under God's kingship. The Rabbinic concept of the Noahide laws (discussed below) is rooted in these biblical traditions.

At one point, the Torah presents us with a rather surprising attitude toward pagan religious practice. In Deut. 4:19 we read:

> And when you look up to the sky, and behold the sun and the moon and the stars, the whole heavenly host, you must not be lured into bowing down to them or serving them. These the LORD your God allotted to other peoples everywhere under heaven.

God warns Israel not to worship the heavenly host while providing other nations with those luminaries as objects of worship. It would ap-

pear that God, according to Deuteronomy, cannot tolerate Israel's worshiping the stars, yet somehow can tolerate such practices among the other nations.

The prophet Amos, in his expressions of God's anger at a sinful Israel, comes close to placing Israel's neighbors on the same plane as Israel in its relationship with God. In the first two chapters of his book, the prophet, for rhetorical effect, enumerates the sins of various peoples, culminating with the sins of Judah and Israel. God, we discover, judges all the nations, Israelite and non-Israelite. Although the prophet recognizes Israel's special relationship with *YHVH*, according to him it serves only to allow God to judge Israel with even greater severity (Amos 3:2). Then, in 9:7, we read:

> To Me, O Israelites, you are
> Just like the Ethiopians
> —declares the LORD.
> True, I brought Israel up
> From the land of Egypt,
> But also the Philistines from Caphtor
> And the Arameans from Kir.

Although this is undoubtedly a rhetorical flourish, underlying the prophet's rhetoric is the idea that *YHVH* maintains relations with all nations, with regard to whom God can act either as judge or as redeemer.

In their end-of-days prophecies, certain of the prophets see the nations turning to God. Isaiah, for example, looks forward to the pagans flocking to Jerusalem so that God can teach them how to walk in God's ways (Isa. 2:3). Zechariah adds yet another dimension to this idea. In his vision of "the day of the LORD" (Zech. 14), he foresees God defeating the nations that had attacked Jerusalem and then mandating: "All who survive of all those nations that came up against Jerusalem shall make a pilgrimage year by year to bow low to the King LORD of Hosts and to observe the Feast of Booths." If they disobey this edict they will have no rain, says Zechariah (14:16–17). Here the nations are held accountable for following the divine command to worship *YHVH* by celebrating an Israelite festival; and if they do not comply with the mandate, they are subject to a punishment that is similar to what Israel would face in the same circumstances (see Deut. 11:13–17). While not negating the unique covenant between God and Israel, these prophets foresee the nations coming closer to God at some point in the future. So it is that amid all the Bible's anti-paganism, seeds of tolerant attitudes toward idolaters can be found.

The non-Israelite in the biblical sources who most closely approaches the status of the Israelite is the *ger,* "the resident alien." Although originally from another nation, the *ger* chooses to live among the Israelites in their land. The *ger* is to be treated with loving kindness because Israel, having been strangers in a strange land (Egypt), understands the *ger*'s plight (Exod. 22:20, 23:9; Lev. 19:33–34; Deut. 10:19, 24:17–18). According to the Torah, the *ger* is expected to follow the laws that are incumbent on the native-born Israelite (e.g., Lev. 10:1ff., 16:29, 17:8ff.; Num. 19:10). The admonition that there be one standard for the native born and the *ger* applies to both ritual and ethical laws (Lev. 24:22; Num. 15:16).

The Bible has no procedure by which a proselyte may become formally converted to Israelite religion and a full citizen in Israelite society. One element of the law, however, begins to move in this direction. A discussion of the law of the paschal lamb in Exodus includes the following: "If a stranger [*ger*] who dwells with you would offer the passover to the LORD, all his males must be circumcised; then he shall be admitted to offer it; he shall then be as a citizen of the country" (Exod. 12:48). Only those who have been circumcised may eat of the paschal lamb. Should a *ger* wish to partake of the *pesaḥ* sacrifice, he and the males of his household must be circumcised. They then become like citizens of the country. Not surprisingly, this verse serves as a prooftext for later Rabbinic traditions that formalize such procedures (see BT Yev. 46b).

In the most fully developed biblical story of an alien who with a full heart chooses to

become a part of the household of Israel, the Book of Ruth, the term *ger* does not even appear. This may be because Ruth enters the land of Israel only after she had become a member of an Israelite household. In Moab she married Mahlon, son of Elimelech and Naomi. When Naomi returns to Bethlehem with Ruth, the latter is considered a member of Naomi's household, not a resident alien. Formal conversion, as the later Jewish sources will come to define it, has not taken place. In fact, Ruth's status is not clear. Even after she makes her now famous statement of commitment (Ruth 1:16–17) she is called "Ruth the Moabite," a "Moabite girl" (Ruth 1:22, 2:6,21, 4:5,10). She refers to herself as *nokhriyyah,* "a foreigner" (Ruth 2:10). The only recognition of the significance of Ruth's choosing to remain with Naomi and to become part of Naomi's people is Boaz's warm reply to Ruth's self-deprecating remark:

> I have been told of . . . how you left your father and mother and the land of your birth and came to a people you had not known before. May the LORD reward your deeds. May you have a full recompense from the LORD, the God of Israel, under whose wings you have sought refuge! (Ruth 2:11–12).

Boaz, however, does not indicate that Ruth has become an Israelite. In taking her as his wife he does so as the redeemer of the estate of Naomi's husband and sons, of which Ruth was a part (Ruth 4:9–10). Perhaps the positive reaction of the crowd that witnessed Boaz's act of redemption points to the community's enthusiastic acceptance of Ruth: "May the LORD make the woman who is coming into your house like Rachel and Leah, both of whom built up the House of Israel" (Ruth 4:11). This declaration would seem to hinge on Boaz's intent to marry Ruth. That seems to be the act that brings her into the community, not her prior espousal of commitment. After all, typically it was through marriage to an Israelite man that a foreign woman entered into the household of Israel. And so, the Book of Ruth really teaches us nothing about what we call conversion. It does, however, present a foreign person in a positive light and opens the door to an attitude of acceptance of the *ger*-convert in later generations once the requirements for conversions are more fully developed. (The reconciliation of the Book of Ruth with the anti-Moabite legislation of Deut. 23:4–5 is subject to much scholarly discussion.)

Attitudes toward non-Israelites continued largely unchanged in the postbiblical era. Jewish assimilation into the Hellenized culture that dominated their world notwithstanding, many Jews of the late Second Temple period (ca. 150 B.C.E.–70 C.E.) and the talmudic age (ca. 70–500 C.E.) maintained strongly negative views of pagans and pagan society. Not only were the Jews heirs to the biblical traditions but their experiences with the Greco-Roman and, later, Persian civilizations were often bitter and antagonistic. Greeks, Romans, and Persians were, in the eyes of many Jews, no different from the peoples whom the Bible paints in negative colors. So, for example, in the Mishnah we read:

> Cattle may not be left in the inns of the gentiles since they are suspected of bestiality; nor may a woman remain alone with them since they are suspected of lewdness; nor may a man remain alone with them since they are suspected of shedding blood. The daughter of an Israelite may not assist a gentile woman in childbirth since she would be assisting to bring to birth a child of idolatry (Av. Zar. 2:1).

In a long midrashic account of the day of divine judgment at the end of time, the gentiles are depicted as having been unworthy of receiving the Torah (BT Av. Zar. 2bff.). Elsewhere, they are considered to be infected with lasciviousness (BT Shab. 145b–146a) and sexually immoral (BT Ket. 13b). Further we read: "All the charity and kindness done by the heathens is counted to them as sin, because they only do it to magnify themselves . . . [and] to display haughtiness" (BT BB 10b). These statements reflect the attitudes of the Jews of

the land of Israel in the generations after the destruction of the Second Temple when the land was under Roman rule and subject to the indecencies of an army of occupation and the corruption of local Roman officials. They also express attitudes of Babylonian Jews in the later talmudic period (250–600 C.E.), who suffered under increasingly repressive Persian regimes.

The negativity of the Sages' view of the pagan world was tempered, however, by a concept that introduced into Judaism a level of tolerance of non-Jews that would continue to operate for centuries: *sheva mitzvot b'nei no·aḥ,* the "seven commandments of the children of Noah." The term by which the Sages defined the gentile (non-Jew) was *ben No·aḥ,* literally "the son of Noah," a category different from *ben Avraham,* "the son of Abraham"—the Jew (BT Ned. 31a). Inasmuch as all humankind descended from Noah, all people (other than the Jews) were considered to be bound by the covenant God established with Noah after the flood (Gen. 9:8–17) and obligated to fulfill seven commandments. (Jews, through the covenant of Abraham as ratified by God and the Israelites at Sinai, were obliged to follow the Torah, with its 613 commandments.) According to Rabbinic tradition, six of the seven commandments of the children of Noah actually had been given to Adam: prohibitions against idolatry, blaspheming God's name, murder, incest, and stealing and the obligation to establish courts of law. At the time of Noah, when people were first allowed to eat animal meat, a seventh commandment was added: the prohibition against tearing a limb from a living animal (Gen. R. 16:6, 34:8,13; BT Sanh. 56a; see MT Kings 9:1). These commandments, for all intents and purposes, were the Sages' principles of universal ethical monotheism. Talmudic law articulated the ramifications of the Noahide commandments and set down the consequences for failure to observe them. The gentile who followed the seven commandments was called *ger toshav,* "a resident alien," and the tolerant biblical attitude toward the resident alien was transferred along with the terminology (BT Sanh. 56bff.; MT Kings 9–10).

On occasion, the Sages' critical view of the pagan world made them skeptical of the gentiles' ability to fulfill even these few, very basic obligations (BT BK 38a; Lev. R. 13:2). Nevertheless, with the notion of the Noahide laws in the background, tolerant feelings toward the non-Jewish world do emerge. Reality dictated a more open-minded perspective, given that the Jews, of necessity, had to maintain relations with the gentiles in whose empires they lived. The Talmud contains references by Sages to individual gentiles with whom cordial relations were maintained and even a recognition by certain Sages that gentiles whom they knew were not ideologically pagan but rather simply following the customs of their ancestors. This outlook opened the door for the development of tolerant attitudes toward Christians on the part of rabbis in the Middle Ages and, ultimately, paved the way for the Jewish openness toward the gentile world in the modern era (see *Tosafot* on BT Av. Zar. 2a). Building on the foundation laid in the Rabbinic sources, Maimonides writes that a gentile need not be coerced to accept the Torah and become a Jew; such a person must be made to accept the seven commandments of Noah (MT Kings 8:10). He is indicating that forced conversion to Judaism is not a necessary component of Jewish law and that there is a difference between an ethical monotheist and a pagan. The former must be accepted, whereas the latter cannot be tolerated. Given that Jews lived primarily among monotheistic people, this notion further reinforced the tolerant point of view that was set down in the earlier sources. A further significant contribution to Jewish toleration of the non-Jew is the statement: "The righteous among the pagans have a place in the world to come" (Tosef. Sanh. 13:1). Maimonides codified this concept in these words:

> Anyone who accepts the seven [Noahide] commandments and is careful to fulfill them is counted among the pious of the nations of the world and has a place in the world to come, as long as that person accepts and

fulfills them because God commanded them (MT Kings 8:10).

Building on these and other Maimonidean views of certain elements within the non-Jewish world, Menaḥem Meiri (ca. 1300) concluded that Christians and Muslims were "nations restricted by the ways of religion" (*Beit Ha-B'ḥirah* on BT Av. Zar. 20aff.). Meiri thus redefines Christians and Muslims as monotheists to whom the biblical and talmudic categories of idolaters do not apply. This "righteous gentile" notion echoed down through the generations and became a linchpin of Jewish tolerance.

During the late Second Temple period, interest in and conversion to Judaism became a widespread phenomenon. As a result, the term *ger,* which in biblical parlance referred to the resident alien, took on a new meaning: proselyte. The Sages of the postdestruction era (70–220 C.E.), the *Tanna·im,* began to formalize the procedure by which a gentile became a Jew, undoubtedly as a response to the gentile interest in Judaism. Although there was disagreement among Sages as to what was ritually required for conversion, the conclusion ultimately reached was circumcision and immersion for a male and immersion for a female, under the supervision of a rabbinical court of three. The court would also determine the nature of the proselyte's religious commitment and would instruct the *ger* in certain laws of the Torah (BT Yev. 46a–47a). Although certain legal differences between a born Jew and a *ger* remained, the thrust of the tradition was to equalize the status of the convert. "Scripture says: 'There shall be one law for the citizen and for the stranger' [Exod. 12:49]. This passage comes to declare the proselyte equal to the born Jew with respect to all the commandments of the Torah" (Mekh. Pisḥa 15).

Although the Rabbinic attitude toward the *ger* generally was positive and welcoming, there were rabbis who distrusted proselytes and discouraged their admittance into Jewish society. This perspective may have been a result of the actions of converts who left or betrayed the Jewish community during the period of heightened Roman oppression in Palestine in the first half of the 2nd century C.E. The dominant point of view, however, was expressed in the Rabbinic maxim: "When a proselyte comes to be converted one receives him with an open hand so as to bring him under the wings of the divine Presence" (Lev. R. 2:9). This remains the operative principle in our own day.

WAR AND PEACE

Michael Graetz

Issues of war and peace play major parts in the biblical narrative: in the historical books, as background to the prophetic books, in the laws, and in biblical theology. There is no one view of war in the Bible, rather there are various views. I shall confine myself largely to the Torah, but shall touch on other parts of the Bible and on Rabbinic Judaism. Both of these bodies of literature are influenced by the laws and instances of war in the Torah.

GOD AT WAR

The polytheistic myths of the ancient Near East take strife and war as inherent parts of nature. Polytheism explains the strife and animosity that exist in the world by assuming that gods are at war, or that the state of war or struggle is part of nature. Indeed, some biblical scholars explore how the themes of strife between gods are sublimated into oblique references in the biblical text (e.g., texts dealing with the creation of the universe).

In the Bible, it is clear that God is capable of waging war—and is indeed portrayed as a warrior in the Exodus story. The Ten Plagues and particularly the slaying of the firstborn are acts of war against Egypt (Exod. 13:14–15). Having unilateral power, God imposes His

will on evildoers, and humans play no active part in this war. Only those who accepted God's sovereignty and are willing to submit to His power by sacrificing the paschal lamb are protected by God and removed from the war zone. However, some scholars view the paschal sacrifice as expressing another, different, view of war. This view claims that God's power is expressed in partnership with humans, and thus humans and God can be allies in war. I will return to this view shortly.

The defeat of Egypt's army and chariots at the Sea of Reeds is an act of war. The first time that the image of God as a warrior unequivocally appears is in the punishment of the Egyptians at the Sea of Reeds (perhaps because the Egyptians are soldiers). The Torah specifically tells us that God leads the people in the Exodus away from settled areas, lest they encounter war and return to Egypt (Exod. 13:17). From this verse, it is clear that the Israelites are not prepared to fight a war, even though the next verse tells us that they were armed with weapons when they left Egypt (13:18). Moses, indeed, tells the people that God will "battle for you" (14:14) against the Egyptian army.

In the Song of the Sea, God is thus portrayed as a warrior, fighting against the Egyptians (15:3). The phrase *ish milḥamah* describes God's power in destroying the Egyptians; it is also found in five other biblical verses, each of which refers to a soldier or warrior (Josh. 17:1; Judg. 20:17; 1 Sam. 17:33; 2 Sam. 17:8; Ezek. 39:20). Indeed, the messenger of God to Joshua appears as a soldier with drawn sword and proclaims that he is a general in God's army (Josh. 5:13–14). God exerts power over Pharaoh in a sort of conquest. God brings plagues against Pharaoh, and this leads to an ironic fulfillment of Pharaoh's own prediction that if a war occurs, Israel will join Egypt's enemies and fight against it to leave the land (Exod. 1:10). Indeed, Pharaoh has unwittingly predicted the future: Israel does join Egypt's enemy, God, and so becomes God's partner in His war against Egypt.

Pharaoh's prediction is alluded to in a double entendre in Exod. 14:31. Israel has seen God's hand (*yad*) in the fate of the Egyptians, and as a result they believe in God and in Moses. The word *yad* also means "sign" or "portent" in biblical Hebrew, thus indicating that God's fighting for Israel is both a sign of God's might and the culmination of the portent of Pharaoh's own mouth.

The core of the Exodus narrative, namely the plagues that culminate in the killing of the firstborn and the destruction of Pharaoh and the Egyptian army at the Sea of Reeds, portrays God's power as a kind that bends evildoers to the divine will by waging war against them. Hence, both Egypt and Israel seem to be nothing more than objects under the control of God's will. Indeed, Moses tells the Israelites at the sea: "The LORD will battle for you; you hold your peace" (Exod. 14:14). This clearly expresses the first view discussed above.

Yet there are passages in these chapters that express the second view. These passages exhibit a different view of God's power—that it is relational, an expression of partnership. In this view, Israel must take some action to be part of the battle against Pharaoh. The Israelites are to perform a ritual sacrifice, the paschal lamb, whose purpose is to protect them from the slaying of the firstborn (Exod. 12: 3–13). It is clear that in doing this they act in partnership with God in the war against Egypt. Furthermore, this action of Israel also displays properties of an act of faith, because it is a kind of self-selection or volunteering to be part of God's ally force.

At the sea—despite the view expressed in Exod. 14:14—God tells the Israelites that they must enter the sea before He uses His control over natural forces to destroy the Egyptians. Indeed, God seems upset at Moses' passivity. God says: "Why do you cry out to Me? Tell the Israelites to go forward" (14:15). These verses indicate a role for the Israelites in God's battle plan. Indeed, they seem to indicate that Israel needs to use its ability to fight wars to further God's plans for its salvation. It is ambiguous here whether this ability is God given or learned. Still, it becomes a given in the

Torah that Israel must fight and that God's plan of salvation for Israel includes its being an active partner in destroying its enemies in battle. Indeed, the whole goal of the Exodus, namely establishing a sovereign kingdom under God's leadership in the land of Israel, can be achieved only by Israel creating an army.

HUMANS AT WAR

God does not seem to be much involved in the instances of war in the ancestral stories of Genesis. The first clear instance of a war in the Torah is the story of a battle of four kings against five kings in the Abraham narrative (Gen. 14). In this story, Abraham has men in his camp whom he can call on at a moment's notice to form an army; and he sets out to restore his nephew Lot, who has been taken captive in the war between the kings. This whole episode stresses the venal nature of war. It is about control of land, money, and people. Abraham, who had willingly divided the land with his nephew (13:8ff.), aids the side of the Sodomites, because Lot is a captive from their side. He refuses, however, to take any spoils from the war or any captives. He does not want anyone to think that his wealth came from war (14:23), yet he does allow his partners, who helped him, to take their spoils. Another instance of war in Genesis is the example of Simeon and Levi who trick the people of Shechem and are able to take the town (34). This is a type of war move that relies on "tricks," somewhat akin to the Trojan Horse. On the one hand, this story is a precursor of the later tales, as well as the laws concerning the conquest of the land of Israel by Joshua. On the other hand, it is a story that is repudiated by other parts of the patriarchal narratives (49:5–7).

In the Exodus story, as we have seen, God does it all. Human involvement in this war is next to nothing. Surprisingly, the next instance of war comes shortly after the Israelites have crossed the Sea of Reeds. They are free of the Egyptians and can seemingly breathe easily in the barren desert on their way to the Promised Land. There are not too many people around to bother them, and they purposely avoid population centers so that they will not have to go to war. But then they are attacked by Amalek—a fierce desert tribe of bandits, whose whole life is built around robbing and killing. They are forced to fight. After the experience of the Sea of Reeds, where they witnessed God's power, they now have to experience war directly. We can thus discern a transition of views—from merely implied participation by God in the wars of the ancestral stories, to God being the only warrior in Egypt and at the sea, to an open partnership between God and humans in the wilderness and conquest of the Land stories.

Joshua is chosen to pick men to go out and fight (Exod. 17:9). But the people are still tied to the notion of God fighting for them, so Moses ascends a hill overlooking the battlefield and raises his hands to heaven. His hands become heavy; and whenever they fall, the Israelites lose the battle and when they are raised, they win. The solution is to prop up his hands. Here we see graphically the transference of part of the power and ability to make war from God to the nation. Formerly, God's hand did the work of war; and now it is Moses' hands, but it is also the hands of the soldiers whom Joshua chose. In the end, Israel is commanded to carry on a war against Amalek in each generation (17:16). It is an example of a holy mission against those who wish to rule over others by force. In this view, God's ability to carry out war against evildoers is, in some sense, transferred to humans. (For other instances of battles that combine God's acting as a warrior on behalf of Israel's warriors see Josh. 6:4–5 and 2 Chron. 20:27–29.) At the same time, the partnership model suggests God's willingness to absorb influence from human participation.

Other instances of war have to do with the punishment of evildoers in the midst of Israel itself. After the people made the Golden Calf, Moses asks the tribe of Levi to kill everyone who took part in that revolt against the Lord and the authority of Moses (Exod. 32:25–28). This incident demonstrates that, although war

is a divine instrument that can help punish evil forces, it can be applied universally even to the Israelites themselves. That is, war can be justified when waged against evil, even in the camp of Israel itself and not just against foreign nations. There are other instances of this internal warfare, some of them being on par with the defeat of the Egyptians at the Sea of Reeds. For example, God fights against Korah and his group by causing the earth to swallow them up, almost a replay of the sea swallowing up the Egyptians (Num. 16ff.).

Other instances of war in the Torah are waged against foreign nations as part of Israel's approach to the Promised Land. In all of these cases, God is part of the equation, and there is justification of the battles because those nations, like Amalek, did evil to Israel or behaved immorally toward Israel (e.g., Num. 21:1–3,33–35). The Israelites even offer a vow to God, saying that if the Canaanites are delivered to them in war, they will proscribe their towns (21:2ff.). Proscription or ban (*ḥeirem*) is part of Israel's ongoing effort to achieve a kind of ideal purity.

In the retelling of the battle against Og in Deut. 3:6–7, the vow of the Israelites is not mentioned. Victory and occupation are attributed to God alone (2:30–35). All of the people are killed under the law of proscription (see Lev. 27:28–29; Deut. 20:16–18), but booty is kept, which is not mentioned in Numbers. In Deut. 7, another rationale for the ban is spelled out, namely, that the existence of these peoples will lead to intermarriage, which will cause syncretism, resulting in abandonment of God and the adopting of the idolatry and evil practices of the Canaanites (Deut. 2–8).

The justification for these wars is strengthened in Deut. 12:31 in the statement that the abhorrent acts of the Canaanites include the sacrifice of children in fire. The war against Israelites who lead the people astray after foreign gods is reformulated once again (13:2–19) and includes Israelite prophets or dreamers who preach disloyalty to God. These people are in the category of evil that is not to be tolerated in Israel society and can be removed by force. This passage does demand a thorough investigation of the allegations; but if the facts are established, there is to be no mercy shown and all are to be killed. This passage includes the possibility that a whole Israelite town may be placed under the ban (*ḥeirem*) if all of its inhabitants subvert the nation to idolatry (13:13ff.).

The *ḥeirem* is a sweeping kind of "justification" for war and killing. It is put into the context of punishment for evil and in the context of Israel, or more properly, Israel's legitimate rulers, being partners of God in punishing evil, i.e., making war on them or executing them. The principle is to be applied to evildoers equally, whether foreign or Israelite.

ḤEIREM: THE BAN

Even though the ban is a central part of war in the Torah, the circumstances of applying the *ḥeirem* are unclear. As to male soldiers, one consistent rule applies: All are to be slain. But there is confusion about the women and children. Indeed, the very notion of having to wage a war of proscription (ban) against "all" inhabitants of Canaan is far from clear. Further lack of clarity will be apparent in the next section, when we consider the ambiguities surrounding the laws concerning women captives.

In Deut. 20 the whole notion of *ḥeirem* is made even more ambiguous by the statement that "when you approach a town to attack it, you shall offer it terms of peace" (20:10). If the town responds peaceably, its inhabitants are spared and made into laborers. This injunction seems to be, at the very least, a compromise with the command to destroy every town in Canaan and all of its men, women, and children—and, at the most, a direct contradiction. Indeed, the Midrash attributes this innovation to Moses (see Deut. R. 5:13), with God accepting his idea! Here the biblical texts that present the relational view of God's power—that Israel is a partner with God, and that each side absorbs influences from the other—are carried to their logical conclusion. Not only is Israel a partner with God but a human can also be an initiator of a law. In this

case, God's command to first try the road of peace and to adopt war as a last resort is instigated by Israel's leader. God, according to this *midrash*, willingly accepts Moses' decree.

If, however, the town responds with war, then the ban is applied—i.e., all males are to be killed, but "You may, however, take as your booty the women, the children, the livestock, and everything in the town—all its spoil—and enjoy the use of the spoil of your enemy, which the LORD your God gives you" (20:14). Here there seems to be no distinction, even by hint, between women who have had sexual experience and those who have not (see below).

We are informed that this rule applies only to towns that are not part of the Canaanite nations. Because they are the ones that can lead Israel astray, they must be proscribed, and not a soul shall remain alive, including women and children. Presumably, this is part of the view that justifies the *ḥeirem,* because of the evil that the inhabitants of Canaan would do to Israel. But this view is undermined by the events of Josh. 9. The Gibeonites trick Israel into thinking that they are from a town far away and that they want peace. Up to this point, Joshua has enforced the ban as written (in Jericho and Ai; Josh. 6–8). According to the law of the ban, Joshua should kill all the Gibeonites, because they are residents of Canaan to whom the laws of the *ḥeirem* apply. It is true, that he has already made peace with them, but there is no moral or legal reason for him to keep the agreement, because it was procured under false pretenses. On the other hand, there is a clear legal reason for him not to keep the agreement, namely, that is the law! Yet, Joshua decides to honor the agreement, and this signals a change in policy. From then on, in the Book of Joshua, the ban is not applied in an all-encompassing manner. A *midrash* explains this by interpreting the law of *ḥeirem* as applied by Joshua in a way that follows the law of Deut. 20 (Lev. R. 17:6). Indeed, this *midrash* assumes options not mentioned in the Torah, namely exile, or exchange for other land. By adding details and options to the application of *ḥeirem* by Joshua, it makes clear that war is not considered optimal.

So, ironically, within the ban literature itself, a way to make peace is hinted at, and it is this hint that is seized on and used by Joshua for his policy toward the Canaanites. Assuming that the laws in the Torah are meant for a theoretical situation, their actual implementation went not in the direction of war and total destruction but rather toward peace and accommodation. The implication seems to be that war is not an end in itself, but at best a means to the attainment of some other end.

How are we to understand the ban? In my view, the ban passages represent an attempt to think of war solely in terms of God's unilateral power and overall control. This kind of wishful thinking might have been popular at times when Israel was in fact powerless or weak and felt threatened by outside enemies. Unilateralism spawns the claim that the impetus for both war and the *ḥeirem* is a command of God, and that Israel is only "following God's will." Some thinkers view these passages as showing that, for the Torah, war is neutral—and whether a particular war is good or bad depends solely on whether it conforms to God's will. But the ethical weakness of the unilateral model is that its answer to the question of justification is facile.

Meanwhile, other passages make it clear that killing defiles—and that no partaking in war can be viewed as praiseworthy; rather it demands purification and atonement. These passages view God's power in the partnership model, for which moral questions are part and parcel of war. Here, both God and humans have mutual responsibility to justify any war. As has been shown, in biblical and, more strongly, in Rabbinic texts, either side of the partnership can initiate war and check-and-balance the other side. The partnership view cannot adopt an oversimple justification of war. Although it is also concerned with conforming to God's will, those adhering to it cannot merely say, "This war is God's will," because then the question must be raised, "Does the human partner agree to this deci-

sion?" In the partnership model, the human cannot appeal to powerlessness or the virtue of obedience as an argument for avoiding moral responsibility.

LAWS

Laws are central to the Torah, and there are laws concerning war and peace. These laws cover rules about armies, captives, booty, army bases, and the war that will be fought against the Canaanite peoples. These laws apply to different stages of war. Rabbinic literature introduces two basic terms to distinguish between wars, terms that are not found in the Bible: *"milḥemet r'shut"* (a war of discretion) and *"milḥemet mitzvah"* (a war of obligation) (M Sot. 8:7). In that same *mishnah*, Judah employs the terms *"milḥemet mitzvah"* and *"milḥemet ḥovah,"* respectively. Maimonides uses the first set of terms exclusively and does not refer to Judah's usage at all. This confusion in terminology resounds throughout Rabbinic literature. However, it is also made clear that some wars are obligatory; because, like the war against the Canaanites or against Amalek, they are commanded, whereas others are discretionary, like David's wars to expand Israel's borders (MT Kings 5:1ff.).

Numbers 31 is a major source for laws about war and soldiers; it includes rules about conscription of soldiers into an army. It is specified that the campaign is led by a priest, who takes sacred utensils and trumpets that serve as means of relaying messages to the troops and serve as instruments of victory. There are rules about how booty and captives are to be treated. In this narrative, the soldiers had slain every male but brought back all females and children as captives. Moses is angry when the expedition brings back all of the captives and booty of the war. He points out that the females were used to entice Israel to foreign gods (see Num. 25:1–2). Thus he instructs them to kill every woman who has had carnal relationships with men, and all the boys (who would otherwise grow up to be soldiers). Only women who have had no sexual experience are spared. Every soldier who had killed others or who had been in contact with the slain has to undergo ritual purification and bring a purification offering. It seems as if participating in a war and killing others, although justified by divine command, could nevertheless be viewed as "impure." There are also rules for dividing up the spoils of the booty. It should be noted that priests (who did not take part in the war) and those who stayed behind also received part of the spoils.

Other passages in the Torah contain different formulations of these same laws. For example, in Deut. 21:10–14, the law does not state that the spared women must be virgins as specified in Num. 31:18. The wording of the law in Deuteronomy makes the desire of the male the operative function. It assumes that the desire for this beautiful woman is to make her a wife (as polygamy is the norm). However, the Torah demands that she be made less beautiful by trimming her hair, etc., and that she be given a month to mourn her slain parents (hinting that an unmarried woman lived with her parents, as was the biblical custom). This woman cannot be enslaved, but is treated as a wife; and if the man tires of her, she must be divorced as a wife. In Num. 31 women captives seem to be on a par with booty, but the formulation in Deuteronomy attributes clear social status to women captives.

Another formulation for conscription exists. In Deut. 20:1–9 we find an exhortation to soldiers to be fearless. This general order has a specific ceremony of induction for soldiers and a specific list of reasons for exemption, at least for a year. Exemptions include the person who has built a new house and has not dedicated it, and one who has planted a new vineyard and has not had the first harvest, and the newlywed who has not yet lived with his wife. The list of exemptions is ceremonially read to those gathered for induction to the army. The closing reason for exemption ties up to the general beginning. Those who are faint of heart and afraid of battle may return home, because they may cause general weakness in the morale of the other soldiers. In Rabbinic literature these rules are thought to

apply only to a nonobligatory war (*milḥemet r'shut*), whereas in an obligatory war (*milḥemet mitzvah*) even the bridegroom and bride must leave their bridal canopy to take part in the war (e.g., M Sot. 8:7).

Another law concerning war has to do with destruction of property during a battle. The Torah rules that when setting up a siege against a city, the army should not cut down fruit-bearing trees to build a siege camp. Only trees that are clearly not fruit bearing may be used for that purpose (Deut. 20:19–20). Although the context of this rule is the *ḥeirem,* the connection between this rule and the *ḥeirem* is not clear. Furthermore, there seems to be some tension between the two verses themselves. However one solves the exegetical problems, the rule itself seems to contain an unusual sensitivity to preventing wanton destruction.

Another set of rules has to do with the army camp or base itself. Deut. 23:10–15 states: "When you go out as a troop against your enemies, be on your guard against anything untoward. . . . Since the LORD your God moves about in your camp to protect you and to deliver your enemies to you, let your camp be holy." In the biblical context, these rules have to do with ritual purity and with hygiene and cleanliness. That is, the biblical laws of war include a section that emphasizes the importance of purity in any army camp, both religious purity and hygiene, such as the provision for keeping excrement outside of the camp and keeping it covered (23:13–14).

In the Talmud, this verse is cited in discussions of what is appropriate in terms of the performance of bodily functions in proximity to sacred space or sacred things (BT Ber. 25a, Shab. 23a,150a). This discussion thus preserves the original context of the verses, while widening the scope to places that are not necessarily an army camp. In the Midrash, the idea of a "holy camp" is widened to include the notion that the encampment of Israel at war must display general ethical behavior at all times (Lev. R. 24:7; Num. R. 2:4).

INSTANCES OF PEACE

Making peace—a formal cessation of war—occurs many times in the Torah. Abram, after the war between the kings, proposes peaceful relations with the king of Sodom. Even more central to the Torah narrative is the peace treaty between Abraham (and his descendants) and the Philistine king Abimelech (and his descendants) at Beer-sheba. Armed combat over rights to water is the background to many of the patriarchal stories. The fact that Abraham and Abimelech swear an oath to each other to share water and refrain from warring against each other, for all generations, is a striking contrast to the idea that Israel must conquer the land by exterminating all of the inhabitants. Indeed, the name of the place Beer-sheba means the "well of oath," and the oath referred to is the one for peaceful coexistence in the land that God had promised to Abraham (Gen. 21:22–34, esp. v. 31; see also 12:7ff.).

Isaac also makes a covenant of cessation of war with Abimelech, after an incident of filling up wells (26:26–33). Apparently the pact made by Abraham was not holding up and so had to be renewed. Jacob seems to be interested in making such a covenant of peaceful relations with Shechem, but this intention is thwarted by his sons Simeon and Levi. This is made clear by Jacob's reaction to their deeds (34:30) and even more clearly by his final words on this subject (49:5–7). Jacob also intends to have peaceful relations with his brother, Esau (33:3–11).

God also insists that Israel is not to make war against the descendants of Lot, for God has given them directly the land they occupy (Deut. 2:19ff.). Israel is to refrain from war with any polity that treats them honorably and civilly. Since the primary justification is to eradicate evil, presumably, all of these cases concern nations that cannot be described as "evil" and war against them cannot be justified. The same principle can be applied internally. For instance, when the Israelite tribes of Reuben, Gad, and Manasseh seek to settle east of the Jordan (Num. 32), they appear at first to be abdicating their responsibility for partici-

pating in the war of conquest of the Land. This is presented as tantamount to blasphemy against God. Once it is clear that their intention is not to shirk their duties as soldiers, they are spared punishment (see also Josh. 22).

PEACE IN THE PROPHETS, WRITINGS, AND RABBINIC LITERATURE

The theme of peace as God's ultimate goal, is reaffirmed in the Prophets and Writings of the Bible; and it finds expression in Rabbinic literature, examples of which were discussed above. It is fair to say that in the later books of the Bible, peace is seen as a major expression both of God's power and will (e.g., Isa. 2:1–4, 11:6, 45:7; Job 25:2; Micah 4:1–5), and justice seems to replace war as the major expression of God's power (e.g., Pss. 96, 98).

Prophets denounce war because of the cruel excesses that it brings about. The first two chapters of Amos criticize the brutality of war in a very direct way; and in some sense, Amos's words are a literary heir of the criticism of Simeon and Levi's actions (Gen. 34) by Jacob in Gen. 49. Both Isaiah (2:1–4) and Micah (4:1–5) envision a day when nations will abandon the making of war and turn the implements of war into productive vessels. This is considered by them to be the essence of God's Torah, the Torah that all the nations come to Zion to learn. This Torah of helping one another produce full lives for citizens of the world seems to be a contradiction to the idea of God at war in the earlier biblical works. Indeed, this aspect of these prophecies is the most striking. God's power is not used to subdue others but is used to eliminate the desire to make war. Indeed, Micah can even imagine that the worship of God is not the issue separating nations at all, for in his words (4:5):

> Though all the peoples walk
> Each in the names of its gods,
> We will walk
> In the name of the LORD our God.

Perhaps of all the books of the Bible, Chronicles contains a constant criticism of the brutality of war, and of war as a means to approach God. And even though it is seemingly a history paralleling Joshua through Kings, Chronicles hardly contains Canaan conquest stories at all. The peak of its critique is found toward the end of 1 Chronicles, where David (the ideal king of Israel in the books of Kings) is told specifically by God: "You have shed much blood and fought great battles; you shall not build a House for My name for you have shed much blood on the earth in My sight" (22:8). The task of building a house for God cannot be fulfilled by someone who has waged war almost his whole life. Bloodshed is antithetical to bringing God's presence closer to humankind. War, rather than promoting God's plan, ends up opposing it.

Thus later Judaism condemned war as a goal in favor of peace. War of self-defense is justified in Jewish religion, but war as a means of diplomacy or for any reason other than self-defense is to be resisted and very much limited, as seen above (M Sot. 8ff.; MT Kings 5ff.).

In conclusion, war is part of the biblical conception of God's power. It is fair to say that peace is also part of that same conception. Although later Jewish sources did not directly deal with such matters, it seems clear that the tendency was to interpret war as part of a relational view of God's power and to praise peace as the goal of God's plan of salvation.

Biblical theology does not present a univocal view of God's power and of war. One view is that God has unilateral power and wages war to bend humans to His will. In that view, God can command war, and humans have no choice but to carry out the commands. Thus carrying out such a war is morally sound, and no questions can possibly be raised about it.

The other view, which becomes stronger in the later biblical books and in Rabbinic Judaism, is that God's power is expressed through equal partnership with humans, with mutual influence. In that view, each side may raise moral questions about a given war at any time. Thus even if a war is justified, actually killing another person is not an act that should be praised excessively, and peace is preferable to war as the final expression of God's redemption.

Biblical Religion and Law

THE GOD OF ISRAEL

Howard A. Addison

How did the God of Israel differ from pagan deities in biblical times? Yeḥezkel Kaufmann, in his seminal work *The Religion of Israel,* demonstrates that the God of Israel, unlike the pagan deities of the surrounding nations, had no pedigree or genealogy. This does not mean, however, that Israel's conception of God did not evolve over a period of time. One way of tracing this evolution is by examining various names by which God was known in the Torah, examining in this way the development of Israel's understanding of God.

THE EVOLUTION OF ISRAEL'S GOD IDEA

An understanding of the patriarchs' relationship to God can best be approached by examining their patterns of marriage, rather than their patterns of worship. Abraham insisted that his servant find a wife for Isaac in Mesopotamia and not from among the women of Canaan (Gen. 24:1–10). Later, Rebekah persuaded Isaac to send Jacob to Mesopotamia, not ostensibly to flee Esau's wrath but for the stated purpose that Jacob there find a wife (27:46–28:9). Given the popular assumption that only Abraham and Sarah's family recognized the one God at that time, these demands seem strange if they were motivated by religious rather than ethnic concerns. Stranger still is the oath that Laban uttered before leaving his nephew Jacob at Gilead (31:53), identifying "the God of Abraham and the god of Nahor" as the same ancestral deity.

These tales indicate the deep familial context that conditioned the ancestors' view of the divine as they traveled from Mesopotamia to Canaan. For them God was the unseen head of the household whose members were members of God's family. This God of the ancestors entered history by concluding a covenant with the elect (Gen. 15, 17) and was invoked in matters of war and its spoils (14:19–24). Not restricted by locale, God guided the clan in its travels (12, 26, 31:3) and cared for them (18, 26:12). In turn, the clan recognized this God and showed its loyalty through worship and tithes (28:20–21). Far from unapproachable, the God of the patriarchs was not only questioned by the patriarchs and matriarchs (16:2,3, 18:12) but could be the subject of moral indictment and negotiation as well (18:23–33).

The strong bond between God and the clan is evidenced by the inclusion of the name of the family head as part of God's title. God identifies Himself as Abraham's "shield" (Gen. 15:1) and is later termed the "Fearsome One" or "the kinsman" of Isaac (31:53) and the "Mighty One of Jacob" (49:24). It is unclear to modern scholars if God was known only by these names and what the relationship of this deity was to *Shaddai* (possibly, the "Exalted One of the Mountain"; Gen. 48:3; Exod. 6:3).

Upon their arrival in the Promised Land, the ancestors' clan came in contact with the Canaanites who worshiped the divine figure *El.* Although suggested derivations of *El*'s name include "going in front," "going toward," and "whose ties cannot be shed," its root meaning is most likely "power" (Gen. 31:29). Far greater than a local deity, *El* was the head of the Canaanite pantheon, a high god, whose manifestations were associated with specific Canaanite altars and locales (*El-Elyon* at Salem, 14:18; *El Olam* at Beer-sheba, 21:33; *El Beth El* at Bethel, 35:7).

Like the God of the ancestors, *El* was also seen as a divine father, guide, and ruler. His attributes influenced the ancestors' view of God, and literary allusions to God standing preeminent among the *Elim* and judging in the council of *El* persist both in the Torah (Exod. 15:11) and in Psalms (82:1). The Hebrew

Bible, however, stripped these images of their polytheistic associations with *El*'s family and with *El*'s cabinet of gods.

Looking at the language of the Torah, we can see a growing association between the God of the ancestors and *El*. The poetic passages uttered by the heathen seer Balaam praising, rather than cursing, Israel set a parallelism between *El* and *Shaddai* (Num. 24:16). The tandem use of *"El Shaddai"* can be found throughout the Hebrew Bible but appears mostly in Genesis and in the poetry of other scriptural books. This association between *El* and the God of the ancestors becomes an identification when Jacob consecrates an altar in Shechem and names it *El-elohei-yisra·el* (Gen. 33:20).

When was God first addressed by the now ineffable four-letter name, *YHVH* (יהוה) the name we pronounce as *Adonai*? This is a matter of serious debate. Although in Exod. 6:2, God seems to have revealed Himself to the patriarchs only as *El Shaddai,* the divine name *YHVH* was not a totally new revelation to Moses. Archaeologists have discovered lists of Edomite place-names from 13th- and 14th-century-B.C.E. southern Palestine that use forms of the root הוה to designate the existence of God. Similar verb forms employed in western Semitic personal names date from the time of Hammurabi (d. 1750 B.C.E.). The Torah claims that Enosh, Adam's grandson, was the first to call on *YHVH* by name (Gen. 4:26), whereas Gen. 9:26 identifies *YHVH* as the God of Shem. Among the descendants of Leah, the names Jochebed (*Yo-kheved; YHVH* is powerful) and possibly Judah (*Y'hudah;* the etymology is uncertain) indicate a recognition of *YHVH* among the Israelites before Moses. The lack of resolution as to when the Hebrews first referred to God as *YHVH* led to the documentary hypothesis. This theory argues that the patriarchal narratives that refer to God as *YHVH* and those that call God solely *Elohim* (an expanded plural form of *El,* "divinity" or "godhood") represent separate literary sources.

Although some scholars have suggested that *YHVH* might derive from a cultic interjection (*Yahu,* "It is He!"), most consider it more probable that the name is related to the Hebrew verb "to be," הוה. When God refers to Himself as *Ehyeh-Asher-Ehyeh* (Exod. 3:14), this distinguishes Him from the lifeless idols as well as from the ephemeral and fleeting in the world. It is God who is ever present or who causes to be that which is—and therefore will fulfill God's redemptive vows to the Israelites.

Some scholars suggest that *YHVH* might first have been a cultic name for *El* in the Midianite and Semitic communities of Sinai and Seir (Deut. 33:2–5). The name *YHVH* replaced the imagery and functions of *El,* as is found in the Torah's numerous descriptions of *YHVH*'s kingship (Exod. 15:18) and role as a wise, compassionate father and creator (Gen. 49:25; Deut. 32:6). Among the Israelites under Moses, the roles, epithets, and attributes of the God of the ancestors and of *El* were subsumed by the divine figure of *YHVH.*

THE ATTRIBUTES OF GOD

Although the Decalogue prohibits physical images of the divine, a rich verbal imagery of God pervades all of Hebrew Scripture. Medieval Jewish thinkers, influenced by Greek philosophy's spiritual/physical dualism, tended to view the Bible's descriptions of God—as having human form and emotions—as a concession to a prebiblical mind-set. Maimonides' *Guide of the Perplexed* was not alone in its quest to preserve God's exclusively sublime nature by reinterpreting these human images of God.

Because the Israelites in the Bible maintain a concrete, personal relationship with *YHVH,* it is hardly surprising that the source of life was conceived among them as a living personality—possessing self-consciousness, will, and imagination. All descriptions of God are by analogy. The Hebrew Bible drew its analogies not from the conceptual or from the spheres of impersonal substance or force but rather from the personal and intimate.

This is reflected in the titles, attributes, and emotions ascribed to God in the Bible. God is infrequently referred to as *Adon,* "Lord." (Its derivative, *Adonai,* became a substitute epithet

for the ineffable *YHVH*.) More often used are *Melekh* (king), denoting God's sovereignty, and *Av* (father), an expression of God's relationship to God's human sons and daughters.

God acts as chieftain or judge (*Shofet*) by meting out reward to the good and punishment to the wicked in conformity to the norms of righteousness (*tzedek*). God's wisdom distinguishes good and evil and can endow the knowledge necessary for success. Showing love to the elect, God guarantees the covenant with them in loyalty and security. However, God uses rejection and outbreaks of heat and fury, sometimes mysteriously, to establish His purpose and rule when that rule is violated.

A tension, however, does exist in Scripture between the impulse to describe God as humanlike and God's sanctity as the unknowable. God's ability to assume a human form is seen in Gen. 18 and 32, Amos 9, and Isa. 6. Yet Ezekiel's description of the divine Presence (*Kavod*) on the chariot throne (*merkavah;* Ezek. 1) is hedged in by so many qualifying terms (e.g., image and likeness), that it suggests that what was observed was only a semblance, not the reality of God. Descriptions that seem to limit God in place or knowledge (Gen. 3:8–10, 22:12) are more than balanced by those claiming divine omniscience and omnipresence (Deut. 29:28, 30:4). Scripture's depictions of God's emotions are at times so pronounced that they portray God as the Bible's tragic hero—admitting mistakes, rethinking decisions, and more often than not being disappointed by His own creatures (Gen. 6:5–7; 1 Sam. 15:11). In contrast to these metaphors stands the assertion by Hosea proclaiming God's insistence that "I am God, not man" (Hos. 11:9). Not bound by procreation, mortality, or physical constraint, God has neither ancestors nor spouse. For Hosea, God's only consort is Israel, betrothed through an act of divine grace.

THE DIVINE BEING, UNITY, AND MANIFESTATIONS OF GOD

The Hebrew Bible portrays a world dominated by the figure of *YHVH*. Exclamations stating, "God does not care"—literally, "there is no God" (Ps. 10:4, 14:1, 53:2)—question God's providence, not God's existence. Comparisons identifying *YHVH* as the God of history and pagan deities as gods of nature prove facile on further examination. The God of Israel is revealed in fire, lightning, wind, and storm (Pss. 29, 89, 97). When God causes the Sea of Reeds to flee and establishes both divine sanctuary and eternal rule (Exod. 15:1–18), this sea (*yam*) is not a vanquished rival god, but His instrument for defeating the Egyptians through His rule over nature. Though pagan deities shift in relationship both to the seasons and to the fleeting political fortunes of their adherents' city-states, the God of Israel controls history as the dynamic arena for enacting His own purposes. Idols are feeble and inert, but the "living God" (*Elohim ḥayyim;* Deut. 5:23) is vital and bestows life.

The unity of God in Israel was not a mere intellectual construct, but a response to His demand of total loyalty, "with all your heart and with all your soul and with all your might" (Deut. 6:5). The verb for "creating" used in Genesis, *bara* (literally "cut out"), is reserved only for God, indicating that He alone is the power responsible for the new and the unprecedented.

The Hebrew Bible occasionally describes God as being represented by a manifestation or an emissary, similar to the way that a human emperor is represented by a legate. These representations reveal God's power and purpose to different people in different places while preserving the essential unity and invisibility of God. Chief among these manifestations is *shem,* God's "name." Ancient belief held that people's names are the emblem of their essential nature and could be separated from them even to be used against them. God's "name" is sometimes used synonymously with *YHVH*. When caused to dwell in the Temple, the *shem* indicates that the sanctuary is *YHVH*'s property (Deut. 12:4–12).

Other manifestations of God include *mal·akh* (angel), *panim* (face), and *Kavod* (Glory or Presence). As divine messengers, *mal·akhim*

are ambassadors who identify with their divine sovereign while remaining distinct from God. Although angels appear in many places to speak God's message, God remains ultimately one; and it is God who answers prayers. Because the face is an individual's most recognizable and expressive feature, *panim* is used to indicate the manifestation of God's presence. The lifting up of God's face (*yissa panav;* Num. 6:26) indicates favor and blessing, whereas its concealment (*astir panai;* Deut. 31:17) denotes abandonment and curse. Although the Torah is equivocal about whether humans can see God's *panim* (Exod. 33:11,20; Num. 12:8), the *Kavod* confirms God's message and will indicate God's redemptive acts (Isa. 60:1–2).

THE TRIUMPH OF MONOTHEISM

Overtly mythologic statements are foreign to the Torah. Despite one strange, brief passage concerning "sons of God" or divine beings (Gen. 6:1–4), God alone dominates life. God's manifestations are that and nothing more; God's "Hosts" (*YHVH Tz'va·ot*) are not armies of gods, but troops of stars, constellations, or spirits that do battle with the political enemies of Israel and the morally perverse. God is the ultimate source of *k'dushah* (holiness), a mysterious supernatural force, both beneficial and dangerous, on which life depends and is renewed. God's unconditional holiness radically distinguishes Him from the creatures. It is God who imbues chosen times, objects, and persons with this special quality (e.g., *Shabbat,* the Ark, the priests) and conditionally sanctifies Israel with this fullness of power and life through the Covenant (Lev. 19:2, 20:7–8).

Despite *YHVH*'s covenant with Israel and demand for exclusive fealty in the Decalogue, Israel's loyalty was severely tested during the 9th century B.C.E. by the faith and devotees of *Ba·al* (Master). Identified with the Aramean storm god *Ba·al Hadad*, he was the god of rain, life, and fertilization, a cultic manifestation that ultimately rivaled and then supplanted El (Judg. 9:4,46). *YHVH* subsumed some of *Ba·al*'s functions, as evident in the storm poetry of Ps. 29 and the divine honorific "Rider of the Heavens" (*Roḥev Shamayim;* Deut. 33:26). The co-use of *Yahu* and *Ba·al* in Israelite personal names, including Jonathan and Eshbaal, sons of King Saul (1 Chron. 9:39), suggests that *Ba·al,* as owner or master, was at one time an accepted epithet for *YHVH.*

An attempt to establish the cult of Baal, an agricultural rain god, and to eclipse *YHVH,* God of Israel's nomadic desert past, was undertaken by Samaria's murderous Queen Jezebel, a former Phoenician princess. A furious counterattack was mounted by the prophet Elijah who is portrayed in Kings as a second Moses. Like his predecessor, Elijah built an altar of 12 stones, split a body of water, killed the ringleaders of idolatry, and experienced a revelation of God at Sinai. The final resting place of neither is known. They differed, however, in that Moses received the Tablets of the Covenant amid thunder and lightning, storm manifestations that in Elijah's time had become overly associated with Baal. Elijah's divine revelation clearly indicated that although *YHVH* controlled the lightning and whirlwinds, *YHVH*'s message was to be heard only in the still, small voice that followed the storm. The final expunging of Baal from family names (replaced by the derogatory *boshet,* "shame") and the Israelite lexicon was proclaimed in Hosea's prophecy to Israel (Hos. 2:18), "You will call [Me] Ishi [My Husband], / And no more will you call Me Baali."

The seeds of monotheism, present from the earliest stages of Israelite history, came to full bloom toward the end of the first commonwealth, beginning with the reform of Josiah at the end of the 7th century B.C.E., during the Babylonian exile and throughout the Second Temple period. The attacking Assyrian and then Babylonian armies are described as *YHVH*'s instruments to punish Israel for its sins (Isa. 7:17–22, 10:5–11; Lam. 2:17). Jeremiah maintained that *YHVH*'s covenantal providence and worship extended outside the Land of Israel (Jer. 29:4–7), an issue that in former times was questioned (1 Sam. 26:19).

Deutero-Isaiah, the anonymous prophet of the exilic age whose writings are found in chapters 40 to 55 of the Book of Isaiah, categorically dismissed the possibility of two or more divine powers, lampooning pagan idols as worthless man-made fetishes (Isa. 44, 45:7). Visions of an eschatologic future portrayed *YHVH* as the recognized universal king whose reign would even vanquish the power of death (Isa. 2:1–4, 25:8; Dan. 12:2).

CONCLUSIONS

Later Judaism's monotheism would not remain seamless, as evidenced by ongoing debate over the nature of God and God's attributes. Contemporary thinkers disagree over whether God is ultimately a personal being, the boundless source of life transcending description and personality, or a force making for salvation within nature and humanity. Is God all-powerful, all-powerful but self-limiting, or essentially limited in nature? Are God's attributes (e.g., wisdom, mercy) essential aspects of God, merely manifestations of God's activity, divine names, potencies, or actual hypostases? All of these have been explored and expounded on in centuries of rabbinical, philosophic, and kabbalistic literature. The question of whether God can be both omnipotent and just took on new poignancy after the *Sho·ah*. However, when the Midrash identified *YHVH* and *Elohim* as God's attributes of mercy and judgment—with no acknowledgment of their historic connotations—one thing became clear: The Judaism that emerged from the biblical period—and that continues to engage our hearts and our minds—is a monotheism of the unique, universal God.

REVELATION: BIBLICAL AND RABBINIC PERSPECTIVES

Daniel Gordis

Revelation, the claim that God has spoken to mortals and made known to them truths about the world and its nature, is central to Jewish belief. Although modern Jews and Jewish philosophies construe revelation in varying fashions, almost all Jews to whom the religious component of Jewish life is important place some form of revelation at the core of their belief. No document in Jewish tradition is as crucial to our conceptions of revelation as the Torah.

When Jews speak of "the Revelation," they are most commonly referring to the events at Mount Sinai described in the Book of Exodus (19ff.). In Hebrew, the events at Sinai are known as *Mattan Torah* (The Giving of the Torah). When Moses descends the mountain, he brings a message Jews commonly call "Torah." That message is the core of revelation.

The content of the revelation that Moses brings to the people after his encounter with God atop Mount Sinai is largely legal. The Decalogue or "Ten Statements" (Hebrew: *Aseret ha-D'varim*, Exod. 34:28) primarily define proper behavior, making demands and creating obligations. The same is true for much of the ensuing material in the Torah. The Israelites learn more from God about how they are expected to behave than about enduring philosophical truths.

The Torah does not specify precisely what was revealed to Moses. Much of Rabbinic tradition asserts that the entire Torah (understood as including the Rabbinic oral tradition as well as the Torah's "written tradition") had been revealed by God to Moses at Sinai, although the Torah never states that explicitly. Exodus 20 suggests that the entire content of the Revelation might well have been the Ten Statements, although Rashi and many other commentators understand the Torah as indicating that many more laws were also revealed at Sinai. Shortly after the first revelation from Mount Sinai, Moses is again commanded to ascend the mountain for a revelation (Exod. 24; see also 20:18). Is the content of this revelation to be the same as the first? Furthermore, how does the content of revelation in Exod.

20 or 24 differ from that in Exod. 34, where God orders Moses to return to the top of the mountain yet again? Classic Jewish commentaries all struggle with these questions. Significantly, the Torah does not offer a clear resolution.

This ambiguity continues even at the Torah's conclusion. The Torah tells us that as Moses reached the end of his life, he recorded "the words of this Teaching [*torah*] to the very end" (Deut. 31:24). What constitutes "this Teaching"? Is it the Book of Deuteronomy, as some have suggested, or is it the entire Torah? And how could Moses have recorded Deuteronomy to the very end, when some of it (admittedly, very little) takes place after his death? It is striking that the Torah seems more concerned that the people Israel accept the notion that revelation took place than that they reach any certainty about the content of that revelation.

The major message of the revelation at Sinai is the centrality of law in the relationship between God and the people Israel. That revelation delivers other messages as well. For example, the experience at Sinai serves as a reminder that God communicates to humanity through words. Although this might seem obvious, it is important to note, because there are other revelations that are not verbal. Verbal communication from God to human beings (through direct discourse or through the medium of a prophet) is an essential component of biblical revelation at Sinai, on other occasions during the Israelites' journey through the wilderness, and in the visions of the prophets. Thus the revelation at Sinai is important not only for its content but because of its medium. The timeless Jewish reverence for words, written and spoken, is due in no small part to the verbal nature of many of God's revelations throughout the biblical canon.

Although much of the Torah's revelatory material is legal in nature, not all biblical revelations deal exclusively with law or with specific behavioral commands. There are important moments in which God communicates messages having little to do with law. At times, God communicates a sense of the plan of history. To Abraham, for example, God states, "I will assign this land to your offspring" (Gen. 12:7). To Isaac, God promises, "I am the God of your father Abraham. . . . I will bless you and increase your offspring for the sake of My servant Abraham" (Gen. 26:24). God speaks in similar fashion to Jacob (Gen. 35:9–10) and to Moses (Exod. 6:2–8). Such revelations are not limited to unique individuals. Elsewhere we read that God appears to the entire Israelite community. "The Presence of the LORD appeared to all the people" (Lev. 9:23), although what exactly was communicated is not stated.

The Hebrew word for "appeared" in this last instance is *va-yera,* a term used commonly in passages describing revelation. At times, the Torah uses a less anthropomorphic verb, *noda,* "made known," to connote revelation. The typical biblical notion of revelation portrays revelatory moments as those in which something about God or the universe is made known to humanity as a whole, to the Israelites in particular, or even to an individual.

This is not always the case, however. The Torah records instances in which God's revelation points specifically to realms of understanding that are unavailable to human beings. We read that right after God spoke "to Moses face to face, as one man speaks to another" (Exod. 33:11), Moses asks for more. "If I have truly gained Your favor, pray let me know Your ways, that I may know You and continue in Your favor" (v. 13). Shortly thereafter, Moses asks for even more, beseeching God, "Oh, let me behold Your Presence!" (v. 18). God's response makes it clear that Moses now has gone too far. "I will make all My goodness pass before you, and I will proclaim before you the name LORD, and the grace that I grant and the compassion that I show. But . . . you cannot see My face, for man may not see Me and live" (vv. 19–20). There are aspects of God that no mortal can know; biblical revelation communicates *that* as well.

An aura of power and awe accompanies many of the Torah's central revelatory mo-

ments, yet the Torah itself suggests that its revelations are not complete. Even while Moses and the Israelites wander through the wilderness on their way to the Promised Land, new questions arise that Moses, despite having received the Torah, does not feel equipped to answer. On several of these occasions, he turns to God for guidance. The Torah recounts the story of the five daughters of Zelophehad, whose father died without any sons to inherit his property. The daughters insist that basic justice requires that they be allowed to have "a holding among [their] father's kinsmen" (Num. 27:4), although there is no precedent for women to inherit their father's estate. When "Moses brought their case before the LORD" (27:5), God instructed Moses to grant the daughters' request.

Similarly, the Torah recounts the instance of a man found gathering wood on *Shabbat*. Although such activity seemed to violate the spirit of the *Shabbat* laws that Moses had received from God and subsequently communicated to the Israelites, gathering wood had not been prohibited specifically by any revelation up to that point. Indeed, the man "was placed in custody, for it had not been specified what should be done to him" (Num. 15:34). Custody is not the punishment; it is a temporary solution until God gives Moses further instruction on how to deal with this man. In the very next verse, the Torah relates that God orders Moses to put the man to death. Although capital punishment for *Shabbat* violations seems harsh to our modern sensibilities, the point about revelation is clear: Even Moses, who had received the Torah from God atop Mount Sinai, sometimes needs further elucidation about the content of revelation.

The Torah and its revelations contain many examples of ambiguity. Perhaps the classic example is a series of instructions that Deuteronomy offers for distinguishing between a true prophet (who might bring further revelation from God) and a false prophet (whose instructions should always be ignored). God informs Moses that He will select other prophets to follow him. "I will put My words in his mouth and he will speak to them all that I command him; and if anybody fails to heed the words he speaks in My name, I Myself will call him to account" (Deut. 18:18–19). How are the people Israel to discern between a true prophet and one who is false? A few chapters earlier (Deut. 13), the Torah states that any prophet who encourages Israel to abandon the covenant is a false prophet who should be put to death. But what of false prophets who do not encourage the people to abandon the covenant? How could the people know that these prophets are false? The Torah's response is extraordinarily simple (vv. 18:21–22):

> And should you ask yourselves, "How can we know that the oracle was not spoken by the LORD?"—if the prophet speaks in the name of the LORD and the oracle does not come true, that oracle was not spoken by the LORD; the prophet has uttered it presumptuously: do not stand in dread of him.

This method of distinction, however, is problematic at the moment when an Israelite must decide whether or not to follow a given prophet. Many of the Bible's classical prophecies speak of events far in the future. Jeremiah's prophecy of the fall of Jerusalem at the hands of Babylon and his subsequent assurance that God will bring the people Israel back from Babylonia are two cases in point. How were the people to know at the moment of prophecy that Jeremiah was a true prophet whose guidance ought to be heeded? And how would they make sense of the fact that some prophecies by prophets accepted as true prophets did not materialize? How, in light of Deuteronomy, should we explain Jeremiah's prophecy (Jer. 34:5) that King Zedekiah would die in peace, when Zedekiah was tortured, forced to witness the deaths of his own sons, and treated in horrific fashion toward the end of his life (2 Kings 25)?

Ultimately, the Torah's instruction in Deut. 18 does not offer much assistance. Because the Torah itself acknowledges that God's revelations do not address all possible situations and that it would be difficult to determine with

certainty in the future whose guidance to follow, it is not surprising that a radically new model of revelation would emerge as tradition developed.

The new model of revelation was the product of the scholars of the Rabbinic period, although it began as early as Ezra. Most modern scholars agree that the Torah began to be available as a written document approximately during the lifetime of Ezra, who may well have initiated the practice of reading the Torah in public. Although the people's access to the Torah as a written document had immense significance in its own right, this development of interpretation had far-reaching implications because no written document survives for long in the absence of a tradition of commentary and amplification. Over the course of time, the scribes or Pharisees (subsequently, the Sages) developed a rich, complex legal and moral tradition to amplify the Torah. In due course, Rabbinic tradition began to speak in terms of both a written Torah (the Five Books of Moses) and an oral Torah—tradition of explication and interpretation of the written Torah, compiled over many centuries. These rabbis considered the oral Torah to be as authoritative as the written Torah because they held that both had been received by Moses from God at Sinai.

Part of the Sages' intention in advocating their new theological reading of revelation was clearly to remove revelation from the domain of possible future prophets. To be sure, the Sages did not deny the authority of the biblical prophets. Occasionally, they made reference to Moses in prophetic terms and included the prophets in their description of the chain through which revelation was transmitted (as in the quotation from Mishnah *Avot* printed below). Nonetheless, they declared that after the destruction of the First Temple in 586 B.C.E. at the hand of the Babylonians, revelation would no longer be transmitted through prophets. (They seem to have been determined to avoid the anarchy made possible by the Deuteronomic formulation.) They proclaimed, in the name of Abdimi, that "from the day that the Temple was destroyed, prophecy was taken from the prophets and given to the Sages" (BT BB 12a). This tradition does not deny the possibility of future prophecy yet takes it out of the hands of those whose pedigree is difficult to determine and grants it to the Sages, who had created a clearer chain of authority and command.

Then the Sages went further. In an even more acerbic rendition of the same tradition, they seem to deny the legitimacy of all future prophecy by asserting that "from the day that the Temple was destroyed, prophecy was taken away from the prophets, and was given to fools and children" (BT BB 12b). The claim was provocative but disarmingly simple. Anything that God needed to reveal could be revealed through them and their unique tools of textual interpretation. Prophets, long a staple of Jewish religious life, no longer had a place in transmitting God's message.

As revolutionary as this idea seems in retrospect, much of Rabbinic literature describes the process in rather prosaic terms. For example, in the first *mishnah* of *Avot*, the Rabbis describe a long chain of revealed tradition that they inherited but that they certainly did not create: "Moses received Torah at Sinai and handed it on to Joshua, Joshua to the elders, and the elders to the prophets. And the prophets handed it on to the men of the Great Assembly [who in turn passed in on to the Sages]" (1:1). "Torah" here (not "the" Torah) refers to both the written and the oral Torah. The Sages claim that their own teaching was received at Sinai, an integral part of the authoritative tradition.

Modern Jews are at home with the notion that most cultures evolve over time, that interpretation and development are essential for the vitality of any intellectual tradition. It is important to understand that the Sages were making a very different claim. They presented themselves simply as a new vessel for the transmission of that which had been revealed by God long ago. For them, the entire tradition was a single seamless entity. They insisted even that rabbinic teachings of which they were not

yet aware had been given by God to Moses at Sinai. In the Jerusalem Talmud they present a radically ahistorical reading of the entire chain of revelation, arguing that "even what a distinguished student is destined to teach before his master was already revealed to Moses on Sinai" (*Pe·ah* 17a).

So intent were the Sages on asserting their own authority in the chain of revelatory tradition that they began figuratively to minimize God's role in that process. Scholars have long noted with surprise that the Mishnah, the first major document codified by the Sages, quotes Scripture much less than might be expected. What explains the Rabbis' apparent reticence to quote the book at the heart of their worldview? To be sure, they were not denying the centrality of the Torah as the quintessential example of God's revelation. Rather, as several modern scholars have suggested, the Sages styled the Mishnah so as to highlight themselves as the latest, crucial link in a long chain of access to God's revelation. Their intent is evident from a classic talmudic tale in which God's input into a legal debate is not accepted. In this tale, Eliezer disagreed with the other Sages (led by Rabbi Joshua) about whether a certain oven was permissible for use, and neither side could convince the other.

> On that day Rabbi Eliezer brought forward all imaginable arguments, but the Sages did not accept them. Said he to them: "If the *halakhah* agrees with me, let this carob tree prove it!" Thereupon the carob tree moved a hundred cubits from its place. . . . "No proof can be brought from a carob tree," they retorted. Again he said to them: "If the *halakhah* agrees with me, let the stream of water prove it!" Whereupon the stream of water flowed backwards. "No proof can be brought from a stream of water," they rejoined. Again he urged: "If the *halakhah* agrees with me, let the walls of the schoolhouse prove it," whereupon the walls inclined to fall. But Rabbi Joshua rebuked [the walls], saying: "When scholars are engaged in a halakhic dispute, you have no right to interfere." Therefore, they did not fall, in honor of Rabbi Joshua, nor did they become upright again, in honor of Rabbi Eliezer; and they are still standing thus inclined.
>
> Again he said to them: "If the *halakhah* agrees with me, let it be proved from Heaven!" Whereupon a Heavenly Voice cried out: "Why are you disputing with Rabbi Eliezer, seeing that in all matters the *halakhah* agrees with him!" Then Rabbi Joshua arose and exclaimed: "'It is not in heaven'" (Deut. 30:12).
>
> What did he mean by this? Said Rabbi Jeremiah: The Torah had already been given at Mount Sinai; we pay no attention to a Heavenly Voice, because You wrote long ago in the Torah at Mount Sinai, "After the majority must one incline" (a play on Exod. 23:2).
>
> Rabbi Nathan met Elijah and asked him: "What did the Holy One, Blessed be He, do in that hour?" "He laughed [with joy]," he replied, "saying, 'My children have defeated Me, My children have defeated Me'" (BT BM 59b).

Note that the Rabbis portray their decisions in this situation as having met with God's approval. Their sense of their place in the revelatory chain denies neither the importance of revelation nor the obvious claim that God is the ultimate source of revelation. What had changed during the Rabbinic period? A sense of how revelation is transmitted and where the content of revelation is located. The notion that revelation is a contentful, commanding set of instructions and admonitions from God has always been at the core of Jewish belief. At the same time, as we have seen, what that revelation actually commanded was never made entirely clear. If the Torah is ambiguous, the Talmud seems to revel in this uncertainty. That is not a weakness of Jewish tradition but one of its strengths. Ours is a tradition that insists that God has spoken—yet is open to a variety of possibilities of how God spoke and what, in fact, God said.

MEDIEVAL AND MODERN THEORIES OF REVELATION

Elliot N. Dorff

REASON VERSUS REVELATION

How do religious people justify what they believe? The answer is often found in the general culture of specific places and eras. What counts as convincing proof of specific statements of belief depends on what a given society at a given time sees as the most reliable path to truth.

Since the founding of each faith, Jewish, Christian, and Muslim teachers have all proclaimed that their beliefs and values are rooted in God's will as revealed in their particular religion's sacred scripture and tradition—in our case, the written Torah and the oral Torah. Basing your beliefs on revelation has the advantage of divine authentication and confirmation of what you believe. You need not depend on your own insights or those of other fallible human beings; none other than an all-knowing God confirms what you take to be true.

You can claim divine authority for your beliefs, however, only if you affirm that a specific record of revelation accurately articulates God's will. Indeed, you would have to believe not only that the founders of that religion experienced a genuine revelation of God but also that their followers possessed an accurate record of that revelation and that they interpreted and applied it correctly. Furthermore, those who argue that their faith alone is the true and accurate statement of God's will, as proponents of the three Western religions do, must also appeal to the willingness of people to discount the theological authenticity of other religions' claims to revelation.

Although the revelational basis for Jewish, Christian, and Muslim beliefs persists in one form or another among believers to this day, in the early 8th century C.E. leaders of these religions looked to other grounds—reason rather than revelation—for justifying their beliefs. The Muslims had conquered the world from Spain to India by 711 C.E., and they then sought to master it culturally as well. To have access to all of the important documents of the people they had vanquished, they translated those materials into Arabic. Through the Arabic translation of Greek sources, Muslims, and then Jews and Christians, learned about Plato and Aristotle. Because Plato and Aristotle had used reason rather than revelation to advance their claims, leaders of these three religions began to augment their claims to authentic revelation with rational justifications for their beliefs.

They did this, in part, because of the advantages of reason as an avenue to truth. A specific revelation is avowed only by those who believe in it, but everyone shares the powers of reason. Assertions based on reason, therefore, are open to everyone's examination and evaluation. Reason provides a level playing field for discussion and debate, unlike every particular revelation, and so reason gained a degree of authority in the Middle Ages beyond that of all specific revelations. As a result, defenders of Judaism, Christianity, and Islam were concerned with showing that their respective faiths were rational in both their origins and their claims. At the same time, they sought to demonstrate that reason alone is not sufficient to capture the whole truth about God and His will, which makes revelation—that of their own tradition, of course—necessary.

Probably the most articulate Jewish spokesman in this regard was Saadia Gaon (882–942). In his *Book of Doctrines and Beliefs* (Prolegomena 4), he maintains that only the ignorant reject rational thinking about religious matters for fear that it will lead to disbelief and the adoption of heretical views. On the contrary, Saadia asserts, God Himself "has commanded us to engage in such inquiry in addition to accepting the reliable Tradition,"

and he cites Isa. 40:21 and Job 34:4 as proof-texts. We

> inquire and speculate in matters of our religion for two reasons: (1) in order that we may find out for ourselves what we [already] know on the basis of what the prophets of God have imparted to us [through revelation]; (2) in order that we may be able to refute those who attack us through revelation about everything we need to know and do in His service.

Although that revelation is confirmed by signs and miracles, God

> also informed us that by speculation and inquiry we shall attain to certainty on every point in accordance with the Truth revealed through the words of His Messenger [Moses]. In this way we speculate and search in order that we may make our own what our Lord has taught us by way of instruction.

If rational inquiry is not only permissible but commanded, why do we need revelation at all? Saadia gives several answers. First, because people attain the ability to follow arguments and construct them on their own only after they have lived for a number of years, revelation is necessary so that we know what God wants of us until then. Some people, indeed, never become philosophically adept, either because they lack the ability or patience or because they lack faith in either the reasoning process itself or its results; such people need the divine guidance that revelation provides throughout their lives. Even those who can reason sometimes make mistakes, and revelation is necessary to serve as a check against errors.

Along the same lines, Saadia (in chapter 3) divides the law into two classes: laws known by reason and laws known by revelation. Even for the rational laws, though, revelation is necessary, according to Saadia. First, reason tells us only the general rules about what to do but not the details about how to do it; we need revelation for that. Second, God will reward us not for following what we would do anyway on the basis of our reasoning powers but for obeying Him. God therefore had to include even Judaism's rational laws within the revealed Torah so that we can merit God's blessings for following His revealed will.

In these ways, then, Saadia balances and integrates the traditional reliance on revelation with the new authority of reason. Later Jewish philosophers in the Middle Ages described the relationship between reason and revelation somewhat differently and used both in varying degrees and instances. Maimonides (1135–1204) maintains that in cases of rational ambivalence we should turn to the Torah (*Guide* II:16). For example, reason cannot determine whether the universe has existed eternally or was created at a specific point in time; thus we use the Torah to learn that creation in time is the correct view. Jewish philosophers after Saadia also suggested other grounds for learning about God from both reason and revelation. The goal of all the rationalists, however, was to demonstrate that Judaism is rational and, therefore, deserving of belief and respect on purely rational grounds, even though revelation is nevertheless required.

This changed, at least in degree, with the advent of the *Zohar* in the 13th century and the kabbalistic tradition that followed. For kabbalists, the Torah—the blueprint from which God created the universe—is the only legitimate source of knowledge of God and His will; reason is an inferior way of knowing religious matters and, at that, misleading. Consequently, revelation alone is to be trusted, and it is to be studied not only for its plain and traditional meanings but also—indeed, primarily—for its esoteric ones. So, for example, the biblical verse "Jacob left Beer-sheba and set out for Haran" (Gen. 28:10) appears to be simply a description of Jacob's journey from one physical place to another. For the *Zohar* (1:147a–148b), however, Beer-sheba becomes the symbol of deep knowledge of both the written and the oral Torah. With this understanding, the verse asserts that Jacob had to leave the safe haven of the Torah to encounter

Haran, which the *Zohar* takes to be the symbol of evil enticement, "the woman of whoredom, the adulteress," to test whether his knowledge of the Torah was strong enough to protect him from such temptations.

In the 17th century and thereafter, the advent of the Enlightenment radically undermined Jews' confidence in revelation. As the Jewish communities of western Europe and North America gradually came to enjoy political rights on the basis of Enlightenment affirmations of the rationality of each individual and as science developed new theories and new technologies, Jews, like their Christian neighbors, came to rely on reason again as the primary way to know about the world and, inevitably, about God.

It is not surprising, then, that Jewish thinkers in the 18th, 19th, and early 20th centuries expended considerable effort to justify Jewish faith and action on rational grounds. Some followed Immanuel Kant's view that religion (in general) and revelation (in particular) are handmaidens to reason. Reason, for these thinkers, establishes not only what one should believe but the grounds for belief. Because the masses have limited reasoning powers, however, they cannot understand rational argumentation. Therefore, they need the tenets and commandments of religion, with their basis in revelation, to learn what they need to know and do. This sounds like Saadia, who also saw revelation as a method for teaching people who cannot or do not yet understand the deliberations of reason. For 19th-century thinkers, however, unlike Saadia, revelation was clearly an inferior form of gaining knowledge about God. So completely did reason win the day during that era that some philosophers, like Hermann Cohen, thought that revelation derived from, and amounted to, reasoning about God.

SHIFTS IN THE NATURE AND AUDIENCE OF REVELATION: BUBER AND ROSENZWEIG

From the divine appearance on Mount Sinai through the early 20th century, Israelites and their descendants have always understood the audience of revelation to be the people Israel as a whole. The Torah itself is ambiguous as to how much of God's revelation the people heard as a group and how much was relayed through Moses—an ambiguity that later sources develop in differing ways. Some Rabbinic interpretations (e.g., Exod. R. 5:9, 29:1) go so far as to point out that at Sinai each person understood God's revelation in his or her own way, depending on each individual's intelligence and sensitivity. Even with these caveats, though, the audience for the Revelation was always construed as the entire people Israel, and its content was always understood to be both God's will and at least some facets of God's nature and actions. Moreover, with just a few exceptions (Spinoza being the most obvious and radical), Jews always understood the Torah in the form that has come down to us as an accurate record of what God revealed at Sinai.

All these assumptions were challenged in the 20th century. Martin Buber (1878–1965) and Franz Rosenzweig (1886–1929) were most responsible for understanding the nature and audience of revelation in new, nontraditional ways. Both men were part of the existentialist school of thought, an approach popular in the first half of the 20th century. Existentialists believe that one must start with the individual's experience to understand how people come to know anything. Furthermore, one must be wary of generalizing from that experience. Because we experience everything as individuals, we cannot accurately characterize how we all experience a given subject. Thus, despite our pretensions to the contrary, we cannot know general truths.

For Buber, then, revelation at Sinai was not a matter of words; it was a revelation of God Himself. All of the words of the Torah are simply a record of how the people who participated in the revelation at Sinai (and many people thereafter) understood its nature and implications. The Torah's account is important because it attests to an experience of God. The Torah's description of that event, though, and

the commandments the Torah bases on it, are only human reactions to being in touch with God. Indeed, in Buber's view, to be constrained to the Torah writers' particular reactions to the experience of encountering God is to confine and squelch the living, ongoing relationships that each individual should have with God. We, therefore, should not see ourselves as obligated to obey Jewish law or to believe anything specific that the Torah or later tradition states about God. Instead, according to Buber, we should cultivate special relationships with other human beings that he called "I–thou" relationships. Here we meet each other face to face and soul to soul without any element of trying to use the other party for one's own purposes—for "in each thou we address the Eternal Thou." In other words, although human beings may think that they can use God as a source to get something, they literally cannot do that, but can only engage in an I–thou relationship with God. I–thou relationships with other human beings thus prepare us for encounters with God and, in fact, are the prime way in which we can meet God.

Rosenzweig agreed with his friend Buber that revelation is not a matter of God speaking words; it is rather what we learn about God from ongoing encounters with Him. "All that God ever reveals in revelation is revelation. . . . He reveals nothing but Himself to man." For Rosenzweig, though, the Torah is the record of an encounter of the Jewish people with God and, as such, each Jew is obligated to keep the commandments that he or she can. Rosenzweig stresses that Jews are not free to choose which commandments they want to fulfill; rather, they are obligated to do whatever they can. Sometimes we are not physically able to perform a commandment—for example, when we are ill. Even in traditional Jewish law, under such circumstances we are not held to be at fault for failing to do what the commandment requires. The novelty of Rosenzweig's thesis is that he sees ability not just as a physical property but as a psychological—or, better, a relational—matter. One's ability to perform God's commands, for Rosenzweig, is primarily a function of one's ability to feel commanded by God. That, in turn, is a function of the depth of one's relationship with God.

The best way to understand this is to think of human relationships. One feels only minimally obligated to help a stranger find the way—although one does feel obliged to some extent. As one moves across the spectrum of one's relationships, from the shallowest to the deepest, one gains more and more obligations. These duties are not a matter of promise or contract; indeed, they are generally not even articulated. They instead grow silently out of the expectations that two people have of each other as they become closer. Ultimately, at the end of the spectrum of relationships farthest removed from those with strangers, one feels many and, in some cases, burdensome duties toward one's family members. Regardless of one's feelings about one's relatives, the very depth of the relationship invokes a sense of duty.

Similarly, says Rosenzweig, the extent of one's obligations to God is a function of the depth of the relationship that one has been able to cultivate with God. Consequently, each of us will have a different level of obligation to fulfill the commandments. One wonderful consequence of this theory is that it minimizes haughtiness. None of us can judge anyone else because none of us knows the depth of anyone else's relationship with the divine and the number or character of laws that are, therefore, incumbent on that person.

At the same time, each of us is obliged to take steps to enhance our ability to obey more of God's commands. God, in other words, is like a family member toward whom there is a duty not only to fulfill one's obligations but to seek to deepen the relationship, thereby becoming even more obligated. Rosenzweig's existentialism is manifest, however, in his concern that as we strengthen our relationship with God, we should not see our increased obligations as simply burdens imposed on us from the outside by God (i.e., as laws). Instead, we must seek to transform the requirements of Judaism into living commandments

whose authority comes from within us, as individuals, as well as from God because they derive from the relationship that we have with God. The Torah's precepts, then, are not only demands but bridges between each individual and God. Until a given rule can function as an outgrowth of one's relationship with God and as a further strengthening of it, the rule is not incumbent on the individual—at least not yet.

Both Buber and Rosenzweig redefine the audience for revelation as the individual Jew rather than the entire Jewish people. And they both redefine the substance of revelation as the encounter with God rather than the specific laws and beliefs that the Torah and later tradition draw from it. However, they disagree about the implications of the Torah's record of revelation for us. For Buber, we are informed by the Torah simply that divine revelation is possible and we each seek it through our I–thou relationships with other human beings and animals. For Rosenzweig, on the other hand, the Sinai event binds us to obey Jewish law to the extent that our own individual relationship with God is deep enough for us to feel a given law as a commandment of God.

LATER VIEWS OF THE AUTHORITY OF REVELATION

In addition to these shifts in understanding the nature and content of revelation, the 20th century brought new understandings of the authority of revelation. Jewish Bible scholars began to use historical methods to understand biblical history and the formation of the biblical text. Archaeologic evidence and cross-cultural legal, linguistic, and literary studies of the text demonstrated that the Torah was not originally written as one book but rather consists of at least four separate documents that were later edited and combined. This approach was not intended to supplant the traditional modes of studying the Torah or the law based on such exegesis; it was intended instead to complement such study with another approach to discover the original meaning of the text in addition to the meanings that Jewish tradition later ascribed to it.

The great advantage of this approach is its honesty; one does not need to protect the Torah, so to speak, from whatever results scholarly study indicates about its origins and formation. On the other hand, though, that mode of study questions the authority of the Torah, because it suggests that the Torah consists of several documents that were edited together rather than of one, authoritative record of the words of God.

Reform thinkers, accepting the historical (or "critical") approach to the biblical text, have asserted, along with Buber, that God meets each person individually and that Jewish law, therefore, is not binding. Each of us must do what his or her conscience dictates in response to our encounters with God. Although the 1999 platform statement of the Reform rabbinate endorses a strong effort to motivate Jews to study the Jewish tradition and to base their decisions on that knowledge, ultimately it is the individual's own autonomous choice that determines the content of revelation for that person. This emphasis on individual autonomy inevitably weakens one's sense of tradition and community; and in practice, it raises serious questions as to whether the Reform community can act as a group, even on such critical questions as intermarriage.

Most Orthodox thinkers, at the other end of the spectrum, deny the legitimacy of using the historical method to understand the Torah, arguing that studying the Torah in that way undermines its authority. They insist that the revelation on Mount Sinai is exactly what is recorded in the Torah. In their view, this preserves the divine authority of the text, even though it is human beings who must interpret and apply it. The Orthodox approach also requires one to discount the evidence of cross-cultural influences on the stories and laws of the Torah, for that too, in their perspective, would compromise the divine authority of the text. Thus even a rabbi in the "modern" or "centrist" wing of Orthodoxy, such as Norman

Lamm, president of Yeshiva University, has stated:

> I believe the Torah is . . . God-given. . . . By "God-given" I mean that He willed that man abide by His commandments and that that will was communicated in discrete words and letters . . . in as direct, unequivocal, and unambiguous a manner as possible.
>
> Literary criticism of the Bible is a problem, but not a crucial one. Judaism has successfully met greater challenges in the past. . . . [It] is chiefly a nuisance but not a threat to the enlightened believer (*The Condition of Jewish Belief,* New York, 1966, pp. 124–125).

Conservative thinkers accept the historical method of Bible study but continue to affirm the legally binding character of Jewish law. This form of Jewish faith preserves consistency in method in that it permits us to use the same methods of analysis that we use in examining the texts of other cultures for our study of the classics of the Jewish tradition, and it leaves us open to what we learn from any form of both traditional and modern scholarship. It nevertheless perpetuates a strong sense of tradition and community. This approach, however, requires a considerable amount of good judgment in deciding how to use the newly emerging historical evidence about the development of the Torah and tradition in applying them to modern times. Moreover, because the text of the Torah is no longer seen as a direct transcription of what God said at Sinai, this method of studying and practicing the Jewish tradition necessitates a thorough treatment of what we mean by claiming that the Torah's laws and theories have the authority of divine revelation.

Conservative thinkers of the past and present have interpreted the process and authority of revelation in three general ways. Some, like Joel Roth, conceive of revelation as God communicating with us in actual words. For such thinkers, revelation has propositional content and is normative as God's word. Unlike Orthodox thinkers, however, these Conservative exponents acknowledge that the Torah text that we have in hand shows evidence of consisting of several documents edited over time. Nevertheless, Jewish law is binding as the word of God interpreted by the rabbis over the generations.

Others within the Conservative movement, like Ben Zion Bokser (1907–1984) and Robert Gordis (1908–1992), believe that God, over time, inspires specific individuals who then translate that inspiration into human language. Revelation thus consists of both a divine and a human component. The human element explains the historical influences on our sacred texts. Nevertheless, Jewish law remains binding because the human beings who formulated it were inspired by God.

Still others within the Conservative movement conceive of revelation as the human response to encounters with God. Some, following the lead of Rosenzweig, think of such meetings in individualistic, personal terms, on the model of human beings meeting each other. Louis Jacobs and Seymour Siegel (1927–1988) do this in their writings, and so does Abraham Joshua Heschel (1907–1972). In Heschel's striking term, the Torah itself is then a *midrash*, an interpretation, of the nature and will of God, formulated in response to ineffable encounters with God. In addition to the existentialists and phenomenologists within this camp are rationalists like David Lieber and Elliot Dorff; the rationalists conceive of revelation as the ongoing human attempts to discover truths about God and the world. Rationalists affirm the importance of our personal encounters with God, but they also call attention to what we can learn about God from nature, history, and human experience as a whole. Revelation, on this theory, comes not only from meeting God but also from our outreach to God. For both approaches, Jewish law is binding on both communal and theological grounds: It is the legal part of our communal midrash, representing our collective aspiration to be holy in response to our interactions with God.

Two factors characterize revelation for all three of these approaches within the Conser-

vative movement. First, the authority of revelation is based on a combination of the divine and the human. That is, whether God spoke words at Sinai, or whether God inspired human beings to write down specific words, or whether human beings wrote down the words of the Torah in response to their encounter with God in an attempt to express the nature and implications of that encounter, the authority of the Torah's revelation is, in part, divine. On the other hand, for all three approaches, it is human as well. Whether the divine input came through words, inspiration, or modeling, human beings had a hand in translating that divine incursion into the words of the written and oral Torah. Moreover, we honor and obey the Torah, at the very least, because our ancestors have done so over the centuries and because we continue to see it as authoritative today.

Second, for all three approaches, revelation is ongoing. The revelation at Sinai is critically important because that is where our ancestors as a people first encountered God and wrote their reactions to that event in the document that became the constitutive covenant between God and the Jewish people. Revelation continues, however, just as the talmudic rabbis said it does, through a continuing encounter with the tradition. Therefore, what the liturgy has us declare when called to witness a public reading of the Torah is not an accident: God not only "chose us from among all nations and gave us His Torah" (in the past); God is also to be blessed now as "giver of the Torah," or, reading the word as a verb, as "the One who gives the Torah." Each time we read the Torah anew, nothing less than God's revelation is taking place again, and we bless God for that continuing relationship with us.

THE NATURE OF REVELATION AND MOSAIC ORIGINS

Jacob Milgrom

When the Torah Scroll is raised after it has been read during the synagogue service, the congregation chants *"v'zot ha-Torah asher sam Mosheh lifnei b'nai Yisra·el al pi Adonai, b'yad Mosheh"* (This is the Torah that Moses set before the Israelites by the command of *YHVH* through Moses!; Deut. 4:44, Num. 4:37). Is that statement truly believed?

This is not a new question. Both Judah ben Ilai in the Talmud (BT BB 15a, BT Men. 30a, Sifrei Deut. 357) and Ibn Ezra in his commentary (to Gen. 12:6, 22:14; Deut. 1:2, 3:11, 34:1,6) realized that several verses in the Torah are post-Mosaic. Joseph Bonfils, in his supercommentary to Ibn Ezra's commentary on Gen. 12:6, commented that this fact does not affect the belief in the revealed character of the Torah. But how is it possible to affirm the Mosaic origin of the entire Torah, not as blind faith but with conviction—rationally? I resort to a Rabbinic story.

During a discussion about how the Torah would be interpreted in the future, Moses requested of God that he be allowed to visit Akiva's academy. The request was granted. Moses sat down in the back of the classroom and listened to Akiva exposit a law purportedly based upon the Torah. Moses didn't understand a word. As a result, he felt faint, "his energy was drained." At the end of Akiva's discourse, the students challenged their teacher: "What is your source?" Akiva replied, *"Halakhah l'Mosheh mi-Sinai"* ([It is] an oral law from Moses at Sinai). The story concludes that Moses was reinvigorated—"his mind was put to rest" (BT Men. 29b).

This story leads to an obvious deduction. Between the times of Moses and of Akiva, the laws of the Torah underwent vast changes, to the extent that Moses was incapable even of following their exposition. But the story conveys a deeper meaning. After all, why was Moses pacified when Akiva announced that his law is traceable to Moses? It couldn't be true. Moses never said it! The answer, however, lies on a different plane. After Akiva an-

nounced that the specific law was given by Moses at Sinai, Moses recognized that it was based on Mosaic foundations. Akiva was not creating a new Torah, but was applying the Torah's law to new problems. Moses had been given general principles; successive generations derived their own implications. Presumably, although Moses was not the author of Akiva's legal decision, he might have intended it. That is, had Moses lived in Akiva's time he might have concurred with Akiva's conclusion.

This interpretation is explicitly confirmed in Scripture. Let me cite two examples: The priests and Levites took their accustomed stations *"k'torat Mosheh ish ha-Elohim"* (according to the Teaching of Moses, man of God; 2 Chron. 30:16). No such stations are attributed to priests and Levites in the Torah. According to the Torah, the priests and Levites indeed did have stations in the Tabernacle, though they were different ones (Num. 3:5–10, 18:67). This suffices for the chronicler to declare that the clerical stations in his or her own time are of Mosaic authorship.

A more impressive example is Nehemiah's *amanah* (covenant, agreement) subscribed to by Israel's leaders and accepted on oath by the people (Neh. 10:1ff.). The *amanah* comprises 18 laws, *"b'yad Mosheh eved ha-Elohim"* (given through Moses the servant of God; Neh. 10:30, cf. vv. 35–37), yet none of them can be found in the Torah precisely as prescribed in Nehemiah's *amanah*. Nonetheless, Nehemiah feels authorized to attribute the 18 laws to Moses since they are built on Mosaic foundations. Each law can be derived from a precedent in the Torah.

Even though it must be conceded that Nehemiah and the chronicler had the complete written Torah before them, the question still remains: What were the Mosaic principles that lay behind the traditions within the Torah? It could well be that each such tradition derives from the Decalogue. The kernel of the Decalogue is terse. Without the inclusion of penalties, it reads more like directions or principles rather than laws. The second commandment orders: "You shall not make for yourself a sculptured image" (Exod. 20:7). Does this mean that images are forbidden in our homes and synagogues? The earliest opinion is found in the appendix to the Decalogue, which prohibits gold or silver images of the Lord, who should be worshiped on imageless altars of wood or unhewn stone (Exod. 20:19–23). Other interpretations are found in the Torah: This prohibition includes imageless pillars (Lev. 26:1, Deut. 16:22). Yet the absence of pillars from the second commandment indicates that they were tolerated in Israel's early worship—thus Jacob (Gen. 28:18,22; 31:52–53; 35:14), Moses (Exod. 24:4), and the Israelite sanctuary unearthed at Arad. Indeed, they were situated in the Temple itself until destroyed in the 8th century by Hezekiah (2 Kings 18:4) and in the following century by Josiah (2 Kings 23:14).

Thus, the second commandment was limited in one interpretation (Exod. 20) and expanded in another (Lev. 26)—showing that various traditions were at work, applying the Decalogue to questions that arose in their age (see also Deut. 4:19–20). Each tradition could rightfully claim that it is "an oral law from Moses at Sinai." This specifically is the case for some of the priestly and Deuteronomic traditions. No wonder, then, that these traditions stemming from different authors might differ in form and content.

In effect, the Torah's *"va-y'daber YHVH el-Mosheh leimor"* (*YHVH* spoke to Moses, saying . . .) is equivalent to the rabbinical *"halakhah l'Mosheh mi-Sinai"* ([it is] an oral law from Moses at Sinai). The anonymous authors of the Torah's legislation were certain that the laws they proposed were not of their invention but were derivable from Mosaic principles, i.e., traceable to Moses himself. They might have agreed, for example, that the dire economic conditions of their time, probably 8th-century-B.C.E. Judah, would have been remedied by the laws of jubilee and redemption. On that basis, they attributed these laws to Moses, even though he himself had not been their author.

Talmudist David Weiss Halivni presents a systematized perspective on divine revelation

in Rabbinic literature. He refers to the story of Moses and Akiva as the "minimalist" position, arguing that only general principles were revealed at Sinai. This is in contrast to the "maximalist" position that dogmatically asserts that the entire oral and written Torah, including "whatever text an earnest scholar [*talmid ḥakham*] will someday teach, has already been declared to Moses at Sinai" (JT *Pe·ah* 17a). Halivni cites another minimalist position, illustrated by the following *midrash*: "R. Yannai said: The words of the Torah were not given as clear-cut decisions. . . . When Moses asked, 'Master of the Universe, in what way shall we know the true sense of the law?', God replied, 'The majority is to be followed' [a play on Exod. 23:2]—when a majority declares it is impure, it is impure; when a majority says it is pure, it is pure" (Mid. Psalms 12:4; cf. BT Ḥag. 3b). As Halivni perceptively concludes:

> Contradictions are thus built into revelation. Revelation was formulated within the framework of contradiction in the form of argumentation pro and con. No legitimate argument or solution can be in conflict with the divine opinion, for all such arguments and solutions constitute a part of God's opinion.

These two minimalist stories about Moses portray the human role throughout the generations in the revelatory process. Revelation was not a one-time Sinaitic event. It behooves and indeed compels each generation to be active partners of God in determining and implementing the divine will.

I submit that what Halivni discovered in Rabbinic tradition applies as well to the written Torah. If it can be maintained that insights of, or disagreements among, the Sages are traceable to Sinai, this is also true for innovations or discrepancies ensconced within the biblical text. Legal formulations may be presuming earlier, reputedly Sinaitic precedents (Moses in Akiva's academy); and conflicting laws may be justifiable claimants to Sinaitic origin (Moses in Yannai's *midrash*).

We should, therefore, acknowledge that each of the schools that contributed to the composition of the Torah had a valid claim to its conviction that its laws were traceable to Mosaic origins; and as for their differences, we might adapt the coinage of a later generation of rabbis concerning the differing schools of Hillel and Shammai: *"Eilu v'eilu divrei Elohim ḥayyim"* (Both [statements] are the words of the living God; PT Ber. 1:7, BT Er. 13b).

PROPHECY AND PROPHETS

Shalom M. Paul

The phenomenon of prophecy is predicated on the premise that God reveals His will, by means of visions and oral communications, to individuals of His own choosing. The prophets are selected by God and irresistibly compelled to deliver His message, at times even against their own will and regardless of whether the people wish to hear it (Ezek. 3:11). Prophecy is neither a science nor an art that one may learn or master. One does not elect to prophesy, nor does one become a prophet by dint of any inherent or acquired faculty. There is no striving to be one with God—no mystical union. Prophets are God's messengers. Standing in God's presence (Jer. 15:1,19) and being privy to the divine council (Isa. 6, Jer. 23:18; Amos 3:7), they translate their revelatory experiences into the idiom of the people. The divine message, refracted through the prism of their own personalities, is conveyed through the media of oracles, prayers, hymns, parables, indictments, dirges, letters, satirical tirades, and legal pronouncements. They act as covenantal mediators between God and the nation. Armed solely with the divine word, "word-possessed," they attempt to help shape the future by reforming the present. Their encounter with the deity affords them knowledge not of His being or essence but of His presence and designs in history. By experienc-

ing God's word, they view the world from the divine perspective.

The Hebrew term for a prophet, *navi,* is a cognate of Akkadian *nabû,* "to call," and literally means "one who has been called by God." The prophet par excellence is Moses, who, at the revelation at Sinai, declares to the Israelites, "I stood between the LORD and you at that time to convey the LORD's words to you, for you were afraid of the fire and did not go up the mountain" (Deut. 5:5). The prophet thus is the spokesperson of God, His mouthpiece, to whom God speaks and who, in turn, speaks forth to the people on His behalf. The prophet is God's forthteller as well as foreteller (Exod. 14:15–16; Deut. 18:18; Jer. 15:19). Moses is distinguished from all other prophets by God's revealing Himself directly to him, "mouth to mouth, plainly and not in riddles" (Num. 12:8); whereas to the others, revelation came only in visions or dreams. Although dreams were originally considered as an authentic conduit for the reception of the divine message (Gen. 20:3, 31:10–13; 1 Sam. 28:6; 1 Kings 3:5–14) and would be so again (Joel 3:1), they fell into disrepute and were frowned on by some prophets (Jer. 23:28, 27:9; Zech. 10:2).

The preclassical prophets (i.e., those preceding the first classical prophet, Amos) are called "seer" (*ḥozeh* and *ro·eh*) and "man of God" (*ish ha-Elohim*) (e.g., 1 Sam. 9:6,9; 1 Kings 17:18,24; 2 Kings 1:10, 4:7,9,21). Several narratives concerning these and other early prophets mention their being banded together in groups (1 Sam. 10:5,10, 19:18–24; 1 Kings 18:3–4,13, 22:22–23; 2 Kings 2:3,5,7, 4:38–44) and report the ecstatic nature of their behavior (Num. 11:25; 1 Sam. 10:6, 18:10, 19:18–24; 1 Kings 18:46; 2 Kings 9:11) induced by the "spirit of God," which came upon them. They played a prominent role in the society, being consulted for advice and requested to make known the will of God, for which they were occasionally remunerated (1 Sam. 9:8; 1 Kings 14:3; 2 Kings 8:9). These preclassical prophets also had a predominant role in influencing the political destiny of Israel, e.g., Samuel chose both Saul (1 Sam. 9) and David (1 Sam. 16) for kingship. Nathan severely reprimanded David for his affair with Bathsheba and for causing the death of her husband, Uriah (2 Sam. 12:7ff.) and later instigated the scheme to persuade David to recognize Bathsheba's son Solomon as the next king (1 Kings 1:8ff.). Ahijah proclaimed both the election and the rejection of Jeroboam I as king of northern Israel (1 Kings 11:29–39, 14:1–8, 15:29), Elijah foretold the eventual defeat of Moab by kings Jehoshaphat and Jehoram (2 Kings 3:16ff.), and Elisha sent one of his coterie to anoint Jehu as king of Israel and inspired the latter's rebellion against Jehoram (2 Kings 9).

They were capable of foreseeing future events. For example, Elijah foretold both a drought (1 Kings 17:1) and the death of Ahaziah (2 Kings 1:4); Elisha foretold a famine that would last for seven years (2 Kings 8:1) and the harm that Hazael, king of Aram, would cause Israel (2 Kings 8:11ff.). Even if some of these predictions were actually prophecies after the events themselves, the narratives clearly indicate that the people believed in the prophets' abilities to foresee what was about to occur.

These prophets also dramatized and concretized their prophetic word by performing symbolic acts, which were charged with the power to initiate the process of actualizing the event itself. Ahijah tore his robe into 12 pieces and commanded Jeroboam I to take 10 of them, "For thus says the LORD, the God of Israel: I am about to tear the kingdom out of Solomon's hands, and I will give you ten tribes. But one tribe shall remain his—for the sake of My servant David'" (1 Kings 11:31–32). In his contest with the Canaanite prophets of Baal and Asherah, Elijah succeeded in bringing fire down from heaven (1 Kings 18) and later split the Jordan River with his own mantle (2 Kings 2:8). Elisha, his successor, also split the Jordan with Elijah's mantle (2 Kings 2:13–14), made a single jug of oil fill many larger vessels (2 Kings 4:1–7), and revivified the son of a Shunammite woman (2 Kings 4:8ff.), similar to Elijah's bringing back

to life the son of the widow in Zarephath of Sidon (1 Kings 17:17–24). Elisha also ordered Joash to take a bow and arrow, open the window eastward, and shoot: "An arrow of victory for the LORD. An arrow of victory over Aram!" (2 Kings 13:17). Nevertheless, all these feats are based on the will of God and are ultimately ascribed directly to Him.

In all of these phenomena, the preclassical prophets of Israel closely resemble their earlier counterparts, known from early-18th-century B.C.E. Akkadian documents from the city of Mari, located on the Euphrates River in Syria. They also refer to charismatic professional and lay individuals who appear spontaneously before the king, deliver an oral message in the name of their god who "sent" them, and occasionally supplement their pronouncements with a symbolic act. These prophets include males and females (for the latter, compare Miriam, Deborah, Huldah, and Noadiah—called prophetesses in Exod. 15:20, Judg. 4:4, 2 Kings 22:14, and Neh. 6:14, respectively). Groups of such prophets are also mentioned in the Mari records.

Although the cuneiform documents contain the closest known parallels to early biblical prophecy, there are some salient differences between them. Both address themselves primarily to their respective kings, but the prophets at Mari are mainly concerned with cultic and political affairs and only rarely, in one extraordinary case, do they confront their king with an ethical demand. Contrast this to the prophet Nathan's condemnation of David for adultery and homicide (2 Sam. 12:1ff.) and Elijah's taking Ahab to task over being an accessory in the appropriation of Naboth's vineyard and in the latter's death sentence (1 Kings 21:1ff.). Furthermore, at Mari, in several instances the prophet's word was not considered absolutely authoritative (as it always is in the Bible), and the final decision on how to act was left to the discretion of the king. At times these prophets would even send a lock of their hair or a fringe of their garment as a personal identity check and as a guarantee of the veracity of their pronouncement. Even with these additional signs of authentication of their word, the Mari prophets do not commend unqualified acceptance, because their oracles were sometimes submitted for further verification by divinatory means. In the Bible, on the other hand, the prophetic word is the sole and absolute mark of attestation. The Mari documents, although attested for only the final decade of Mari's existence, do, however, provide an analogue to the later biblical phenomena, as do the small corpus of 28 neo-Assyrian oracles from the 7th century B.C.E., uttered primarily in the name of the goddess Ishtar to the Assyrian kings Esarhaddon and Ashurbanipal.

Classical prophecy, which makes its first appearance during the middle of the 8th century B.C.E., was indebted in many ways to the spiritual and ethical heritage of its preclassical biblical predecessors. Nevertheless, commencing with the oracles of Amos and extending for the next 300 years, these inspired spokespeople of God introduced many new concepts and ideas into Israelite religion. The classical prophets arose and reached their zenith during the rise and fall of three great world empires: Assyria, Babylonia, and Persia. Isaiah, Micah, and Zephaniah prophesied at the time of Assyria's ascendancy ("Ha! / Assyria, rod of My anger," Isa. 10:5). Jeremiah (25:8ff.), in turn, viewed Nebuchadrezzar as God's "servant" and Babylonia as God's "nation from the north," which was destined to bring about the destruction of Jerusalem and the Temple. The anonymous prophet of the Exile, Second Isaiah, called the Persian king Cyrus His "anointed one," who would release the nation from captivity and allow them to return to Israel and rebuild the Temple (Isa. 44:28, 45:1ff.). The last three prophets, Haggai, Zechariah, and Malachi, were active during the Persian rule in the postexilic period. Thus the age of these great world empires also witnessed the unique religious phenomena of the appearance of classical prophets, who interpreted these world-shaking events in the light of an entirely new theological viewpoint. They provided the answer to the "why" of the destruction of both the northern (Israel) and southern

(Judah) kingdoms and the "how" of future restoration.

Several of these prophets were reluctant to accept their calling (Exod. 3:11, 4:10; Isa. 6:5; Jer. 1:6; Jon. 1), because their task was unenviable and burdensome. These messengers of God were often rejected by their audience, who constantly and consistently refused to listen to their words and thereby reform their recalcitrant ways. The prophets' emotional experience upon receiving God's "stern vision" was overwhelmingly frightening (Isa. 21:3–4; Jer. 4:9, 6:11, 15:17; Hab. 3:16), and they became isolated individuals marked by loneliness and bitterness (Jer. 9:1, 15:10, 20:14,18). Their lives were replete with anguish, fear, ridicule, and occasionally even imprisonment (Isa. 28:9–10; Jer. 11:18–23, 12:1ff., 15:10,15, 17:14–18, 18:18–23, 20:7–10, 37:12–21; Ezek. 21:11–12; Hos. 9:8; Amos 7:12–13; Mic. 2:6), because they were primarily harbingers of doom and destruction. Although they bemoaned their nation's imminent tragedy (Isa. 6:11, 22:4; Jer. 8:23; Mic. 1:8–9), they did not shrink from their divine call but persisted to remonstrate against their people, even at the price of great personal danger.

There is, moreover, another dimension to the prophetic mission. They not only served as God's "district attorney" but also acted as the "defense attorney" for their people. Herein lies one of the most distinguishing characteristics of true prophets—their roles as intercessors. In fulfilling this task, they attempted through prayer to defend their people against their impending doom. The first individual in the Bible to be called a *navi* is Abraham; the term is applied to him not because he delivered oracles in the name of God, but because he interceded for Abimelech when the latter had taken Sarah into his household: "Since he is a prophet, he will intercede for you—to save your life" (Gen. 20:7). Abraham, with unbridled daring, also challenged God in a futile attempt to save the twin cities of evil, Sodom and Gomorrah: "Shall not the Judge of all the earth deal justly?" (Gen. 18:25). Moses, the paragon of the prophets, eloquently exemplified this intercessory role after both the construction of the Golden Calf (Exod. 32:11–14) and the pessimistic report of 10 of the 12 spies who were dispatched to scout out the possibility of entering Canaan (Num. 14:13–20). In both cases, God renounced His resolve to destroy the people immediately. (Cf. the incident at Taberah in Num. 11:1–3.) Samuel, too, prayed on behalf of his people after their defeat by the Philistines (1 Sam. 7:5–9), when their request for a king so embittered God (1 Sam. 12:19,23); and he even intervened on behalf of Saul, whom God had rejected as king of Israel (1 Sam. 15:11).

Moses and Samuel are singled out as the paradigmatic exemplars of intercessors on behalf of their people in the Book of Jeremiah (15:1). Jeremiah himself—unlike Amos, who successfully mediated twice for his people (Amos 7:13–6)—proved a worthy but unsuccessful successor in this role. Often he pleaded and prayed for the nation's salvation from the imminent Babylonian invasion (cf. Jer. 18:20: "Remember how I stood before You / To plead in their behalf, / To turn Your anger away from them"). Once the die had been cast, however, and the nation's doom became irrevocable, God prohibited any further intercession (Jer. 7:16, 11:14, 14:11–12).

The true prophet, as intercessor, was ready to risk a confrontation with God, in contrast to his counterpart, the false prophet. The problem of distinguishing between them was indeed perplexing, as is shown by two separate passages in Deuteronomy. According to Deut. 13:2ff., if a prophet delivers an oracle (even if it is subsequently confirmed by an external sign) to worship other gods, he obviously is a false prophet. In turn, Deut. 18:20–22 raises the question, "How can we know that the oracle [uttered in God's name] was not spoken by the LORD?" The answer given is that if the "oracle does not come true, that oracle was not spoken by the LORD; the prophet uttered it presumptuously." This, however, cannot serve as an infallible criterion, because there are several occasions when an oracle delivered by a true prophet did not materialize even in his

own lifetime. Such unfulfilled prophecies include Jeremiah's prediction of the ignominious fate of king Jehoiakim (Jer. 22:19), which was belied by 2 Kings 24:6, and Ezekiel's foretelling the destruction of Tyre by Nebuchadrezzar (Ezek. 26:7–21), which later was admitted to have failed but was to be compensated by the Babylonian king's attack on Egypt (29:17–20). Jeremiah provided yet another criterion for determining a true prophecy in his dramatic confrontation with the false prophet Hananiah. The latter predicted that the Lord was to break the yoke of the Babylonian oppressor in 2 years and the exiled community would henceforth return to Israel (as opposed to Jeremiah's oracle of 70 years of captivity). Jeremiah (28:9) declared that "if a prophet prophesies good fortune, then only when the word of the prophet comes true can it be known that the LORD really sent him." Jeremiah himself was in continual combat with several types of false prophets, three of whom he attacks in chapter 23. Against those who constantly uttered: "Peace, peace," he responded, "There is no peace" (6:14, 8:11). Ultimately, the falsity or veracity of prophecies could not be determined by context alone but could be judged solely by the one who truly had been granted divine revelation and stood in the Lord's council (23:18). For only a prophet "who has received My word, [can] report My word faithfully! How can straw be compared to grain? . . . Behold My word is like fire—declares the LORD—and like a hammer that shatters rock!" (23:28–29).

Although some of the false prophets did claim the gift of revelation and imparted oracles (Jer. 23:31) in the Lord's name (14:14, 29:9), they nevertheless did not intercede with God on behalf of the people (27:18), as Ezekiel remonstrates: "Your prophets, O Israel, have been like jackals among ruins. You did not enter the breaches and repair the walls for the House of Israel, that they may stand up in battle on the day of the LORD" (Ezek. 13:4–5). And as he explicitly states in God's name: "I sought a man among them to repair the wall or to stand in the breach before Me in behalf of this land, that I might not destroy it; but I found none. I have therefore poured out My indignation upon them; I will consume them with the fire of My fury" (22:30–31; cf. Ps. 106:23). For only the true prophet stood in the breach, even against God, to defend Israel.

God's universal will was revealed to the prophets in the panoramic language of history, but only Israel was His elected and selected covenantal partner. The consequence of such chosenness was not a bona fide guarantee of immunity but rather a heightened responsibility. All the nations of the world stand in judgment before God and are held culpable for gross violations of the established order (Amos 1:3–2:3; Isa. 13–23; Jer. 46–51; Ezek. 25–32), but only Israel was taken to task for every infringement of its moral and ethical code of behavior: "You alone have I singled out / Of all the families of the earth— / That is why I will call you to account / For all your iniquities" (Amos 3:2). The prophets condemned and castigated juridical corruption, violence, cruelty, dishonesty, greed, oppression, exploitation, bribery, harlotry, debauchery, infidelity, arrogance, luxury, apathy, lust for power, and militarism, because all these were ultimately a blatant rejection of God. So, too, they severely attacked the absolutization of the cult, because in their eyes the essence and quintessence of God's demand was not to be found in cultic practices but in the moral and ethical spheres of life. They thereby introduced the novel concept of the primacy of morality (Isa. 1:11–17, 66:1ff.; Jer. 6:20, 7:21–23, 14:12; Hos. 6:6; Amos 5:21–25; Mic. 6:6–8). For them, worship and its accompanying ritual were means to draw closer to God; whereas justice and righteousness were ends unto themselves. God demanded primarily right, not rite, and when the cult became a substitute for moral behavior, it was condemned. Henceforth, any cultic act performed by a worshiper whose moral probity was not beyond reproach was considered abominable to the deity. Ritual now became, for the first time, contingent on the individual's personal behavior. The proph-

ets, moreover, declared that morality not only was of absolute importance but also was the decisive factor in determining the national destiny of Israel, rather than idolatry or the desecration of *Shabbat,* as stated in the Torah. (The prophets did not repudiate the cult per se but only its becoming a surrogate for ethical behavior. This is shown by the later prophets' positive attitude toward the ritual, as evidenced in Ezek. 40–44; Hag. 1:4; Zech. 4:9; and Mal. 1:6–10.)

The prophets demanded wholehearted faithfulness to the covenant between God and Israel; they threatened inexorable punishment, embedded in the covenantal curses, for all those who were disloyal to it. Their ultimate purpose, however, was to achieve the desired goal of repentance, which demanded a change of heart and conduct. They censured, threatened, and admonished to evoke a change in the hearts and behavior of the people so as to avoid the imminent destruction. "Maybe" God would relent (Hos. 11:8–9; Joel 2:14; Amos 5:15; Jon. 3:9; Zeph. 2:3), because His plans are at times revocable, predicated on the people's actions (Jer. 18:7–10; Ezek. 3:17–21, 33:7–20). The frustration, however, of waiting for the nation's return to God ultimately led to yet another prophetic theological innovation: the "new covenant." Because the Sinaitic covenant had been broken, God, despairing of the futility of punishment to evoke a change in their hearts, would eventually implant His will directly on their hearts by a divine "grafting." Their "heart of stone" would be circumcised, and their entire being would be filled with the "knowledge of God." This new covenant would be unbreakable and would presage final redemption (Isa. 55:3; Jer. 24:7, 31:30–33, 32:38–41; Ezek. 16:60, 34:25ff., 37:26ff.; cf. Deut. 30:6; Isa. 11:9, 54:13). With the covenant renewed, the "remnant of Israel" (Isa. 4:3–4, 10:20–22; Jer. 31:31ff.; Amos 9:8ff.; Mic. 4:7; Zeph. 2:9), who will have survived the "Day of the Lord," would be restored and would live in peace, no longer troubled by oppression, injustice, or war (Isa. 2:1–4, 10:27, 11:1–9, 60:5–16, 61:4–9; Hos. 2:21ff.; Mic. 4:3–4). God's ineffable presence would manifest itself to all humankind (Isa. 40:5), and the nations would come to reject their polytheistic worship and revere the God of Israel alone (Isa. 19:18–25, 45:22ff.; Jer. 3:17, 12:16; Ezek. 17:24; Mic. 7:16ff.; Hab. 2:14; Zech. 2:15, 8:20–23, 14:16–19). Jerusalem would become the spiritual and juridical center of the world, from which God's instruction would be disseminated to the entire world (Isa. 2:2). Israel itself, according to the anonymous prophet of the exile, Second Isaiah, would become a prophet nation (49:2–3, 51:16, 59:21) and a "light unto the nations" (42:6, 49:6), recounting God's glory (43:21) and bringing His blessing and beneficence to the ends of the earth (45:22–24).

MOSES: MAN OF ISRAEL, MAN OF GOD

Stephen Garfinkel

The Torah mirrors the life of Israel in the life of Moses. The Book of Genesis presents the patriarchs as the progenitors and spiritual forebears of the Israelites, even culminating in Jacob's renaming to become the eponymous Israel. Yet it is Moses—not Abraham, Isaac, Jacob, or even Joseph—whose life parallels the life of the Israelite people and whose actions determine their destiny. The nation is first formed in the opening chapter of Exodus (in contrast to the Genesis narratives about families and clans), and Moses' birth and the role he is destined to fulfill are announced in the following chapter. The nation of Israel will have many leaders after Moses, but he is replaced by none of them. The life of the Israelite people from national birth to possession of a permanent territory, is coterminous with the life of Moses. He is in effect the national alter ego. That characterization, however, is never

articulated explicitly; it can be inferred from the many diverse roles Moses serves. His assignments range from liberator to law giver, from guide to goad, from castigator to collaborator. He is scapegoat and strategist, provoker and protector, referee, resource, and redeemer.

As noted in the commentary, Exodus begins with the fulfillment of the often-reiterated promise made to the patriarchs that they will have countless descendants. Ironically, however, the growing attainment of that very blessing increases the Egyptian ruler's fear of Israel, leading to his intention to dominate or annihilate them. After several pharaonic schemes to weaken Israel, the nation's fate appears bleak by the end of chapter 1. But just a few verses later, the narrative of Moses' birth furnishes provocative hints in which the meticulous reader can discern Moses' future redemptive role. Moses will survive his near drowning at birth to save Israel, and water (in this instance, the Nile) becomes one of two central markers throughout Moses' career. What might have been the location of his death will become the site of his great success. When Pharaoh's daughter names the child found in the water "Moses" (possibly using or mimicking an Egyptian term for "son"), she formally adopts him and bequeaths much more than a bilingual pun. Exodus interprets the name "Moses" to mean that he is "drawn out" of the water (2:10); but a more precise grammatical analysis of the Hebrew term *mosheh* confers a richer, predictive message. Moses is destined to be the one who draws out the people of Israel (even as the prophet Isaiah suggestively refers to God to as *mosheh ammo,* "the One who draws out His people"; Isa. 63:11). Moses will save them by drawing them out through the water of the Sea of Reeds. Because Israel is the "new humanity" and cosmic fortune is reflected in the nation's fate, Moses' calling takes on an even greater significance. For the Torah, redeeming this nation redeems the world.

The other major marker in the life of Moses is the mountain. When God appears to Moses, announcing from the Burning Bush (Exod. 3) that he is the person designated to bring the suffering Israelites out of Egypt, Moses is incredulous. However, God reassures Moses with a fittingly enigmatic sign intended to authenticate this revelation of Moses' commission: the mountain (later called *Har ha-Elohim,* "the Mountain of God"), or possibly the people's returning to the mountain to worship once they are freed, will somehow become the sign, even if in the future. I shall examine both the water and the mountain at several stages later in Moses' life, after considering the historical setting the Torah provides.

When did Moses live? Many scholars assign the time of the Exodus (and, by implication, the life of Moses) to either the early 13th century or the middle of the 15th century B.C.E. (In part, their uncertainty results from contradictory or inconsistent verses found elsewhere in the *Tanakh.*) Some scholars draw further support for these dates by interpreting statements in Exod. 1 or by drawing on archaeological artifacts and extrabiblical inscriptions, none of which mentions the Exodus or Moses. However, even for those who accept either of the proposed dates for the Exodus (and Moses' birth 80 years earlier and his death 40 years later), it is appropriate to ask about the reliability of the biblical information used to calculate that chronology. The dates are not likely to be precise; they are, in fact, more likely to be schematic. Accuracy is pertinent only to a historical or a scientific document; another approach is appropriate for a theological, or religious, work. Once we understand that the Torah is a theological text dressed in historical garb, focusing on the date of the Exodus (or on the dates of other events in the Torah) misdirects our attention.

The search for historical context is of more than antiquarian interest and can sometimes provide a framework to enrich exegesis by providing entire sets of clues for interpreting biblical material. However, the primary concern for communities of faith must be the search for meaning of the Exodus narrative and its implications. We must always be aware that whatever we "know" about Moses is extrapo-

lated from religious literary sources. So the question to ask in understanding the Torah on its own terms is not when, or even if, Moses lived, but what his life conveys in Israel's saga. How does God's redemption of the people unfold in the human arena, and what function does Moses serve in that national redemption? Irrespective of the chronologic background, Moses is presented as a model of leadership—with strengths and weaknesses—for future generations.

Typical of the folkloristic, national hero, Moses successfully withstands trials to prove himself early in his career and continues his mission by undertaking a variety of specific roles. While the Israelites are still in Egypt, he is their chief negotiator to Pharaoh (admittedly sometimes against their wishes). During the ensuing 40 years, he coaxes them to mature as a nation. As God's spokesman, Moses helps institute a legal system; a judicial structure; and a cultic infrastructure for worship, forgiveness, and purification. He creates, or supervises the formation of, institutions that the nascent nation requires during its period of wandering and the administrative structures upon which they can rely and build even after their permanent settlement. Occasionally he needs advice or guidance to initiate these projects, but his leadership ensures their establishment. Throughout his calling, Moses is the people's guide—in geographic, military, sociopolitical, and moral senses, as necessary—and he nourishes them when food, water, or morale is in short supply.

Despite his initial reluctance, Moses is not only compelled to take on the next challenges confronting him; he is ready. Moses' most dramatic successes and the highlight of his career must be seen at the next confluence of water and mountain. Typical of the hero in many ancient epics, Moses crosses over the water—in this case miraculously traversing the Sea of Reeds—and he takes with him the entire nation in formation. Almost immediately thereafter, Moses reaches the pinnacle of his unique status, sharing God's own aura at the mountain (Sinai), after which he brings back God's word to the people. Here, in what becomes the keystone of the national identity, the nation assumes and accepts its special charge, and Moses reaches his most spectacular grandeur. He has succeeded in bringing Israel out of Egypt; he has gone beyond that at Sinai, forging the people's eternal contract with God.

The mountain experience at Sinai is not without its own complications. Here Moses must take to new heights the role of prophet as intercessor, first undertaken in the Torah by Abraham (Gen. 20:7,17). In the words of Ps. 106:23, Moses "stands in the breach" between God and Israel. Later prophets will follow the Mosaic model, delivering God's message to Israel, warning, threatening, cajoling, and chastising as warranted. With equal fervor, however, Moses at Sinai takes the side of the people against God's wrath, conveying their plea to God and even compelling God to rescind the divine plan to destroy them after their apostasy in worshiping the Golden Calf. Moses puts his own life on the line for the future of the nation: "Erase me from your Book [of Life]," he tells God, if his future is separate from that of the people (Exod. 32:32). God relents, recognizing that Moses is an extension of the people and the people, an extension of Moses.

Over his extensive career, Moses retains and expands his heroic posture—notwithstanding increasingly severe challenges to his leadership: by his siblings, Miriam and Aaron (Num. 12); by his first cousin, Korah, and many of the community leaders (Num. 16); and by the nation as a whole (Num. 20, in which the people for the second time demand water to drink). Rabbinic tradition realized in the latter episode that Moses' death was, in fact, brought about by water, but it was the water springing from the rock at Massah and Meribah, not the Nile in which he was placed at birth. After the trials, the dangers, and the triumphs, Moses' life will end by means of water after all.

Although Moses is larger than life in the narrative of the Torah, he exhibits human shortcomings, sometimes in private dealings

with his family, occasionally in public displays of anger, and even in an apparent growing sense of hubris (notwithstanding the description of him as the most humble of all people). However, one may speculate that Moses, like great leaders in other cultures, was raised to superhuman stature by many of those he led. It is not possible to know if the ancient Israelites perceived Moses in this same heroic category, but later Jewish tradition aggrandizes Moses even more. Rabbinic texts glorify Moses, referring to him as *Mosheh rabbeinu* (Moses our teacher) or *Mosheh ha-tzaddik* (Moses the righteous one, or saint) (BT Ned. 31b), and even appear to raise his status from transmitter of God's law to source of the law. One example of this is found in the formula of betrothal used during the Jewish wedding ceremony, "according to the law of Moses and Israel." By contrast, for fear of attributing Israel's redemption to Moses rather than to God, the *Pesaḥ Haggadah* all but eliminates Moses from the picture!

Even the structure of the Torah from Exodus through Deuteronomy revolves around Moses' centrality. In Exodus, Leviticus, and Numbers, Moses presents God's word; Deuteronomy is the (re)presentation from Moses' perspective. It is his version of the past that has final pride of place, in his speeches to the nation on the eve of their conquest and as the final word transmitted to readers of the Torah. Yet, at the very end of Moses' saga, God takes back the center stage to bid farewell to Moses, God's partner of the past 40 years. In one of the most poignant scenes of any literature, the narrative describes Moses' death. In simple majesty, despite his unique status, despite his Herculean efforts and accomplishments, Moses shares the fate of all mortals. Here, at the mountain—Mount Nebo—he and the nation part ways. They will cross the water—the Jordan River—to journey onward, leaving him behind. As the people were about to leave Egypt (Exod. 13), Moses took Joseph's bones for burial in Canaan, but now no one will take Moses' bones into the Land. He has devoted one third of his life to bringing the Israelites here, but he cannot participate in their inheritance. His allotted 120 years—the ideal limit given to human beings (Gen. 6:3)—are completed. His time of glory and burden is over. His tenure of leadership has expired, and his burial place must not become a shrine. It is in Transjordan, and no mortal can know its location. Moses moves into the people's past as they conquer Canaan. They move forward (past the end of the Torah), although he must remain on the distant side of the river. The Torah begins Israel's chronicle with Abraham, the one "from the other side," and it ends this stage of Israel's national saga with Moses remaining "on the other side." Settled people have new and different needs, and it will be up to Joshua (true, wearing Moses' mantle) to pick up the staff. Yet, later Rabbinic tradition recognizes that Moses is a vibrant force in the psyche of the people, claiming the date of his birth to be *Adar* 7, the exact same date it ascribes as the date of his death. One cannot memorialize his death without simultaneously recalling his birth. He remains an eternal watchman for Israel, as the saying has it: Zeus never lived, but Moses never died.

At the outset of his career, Moses tried to dissuade God from selecting him for the mission that ultimately became his. One of his ploys was to claim a deficiency in speech. How fortunate were the Israelites, and how fortunate are those who continue to read *Torat Mosheh* (the Torah of Moses), that the one time he was unable to make a convincing argument was in that initial dialogue with God. Consider the masterful narratives and instructions, the expressive rituals, the eloquent soliloquies, and the ennobling poetry of which we would have been deprived, had it been otherwise.

THE COVENANT AND THE ELECTION OF ISRAEL

David L. Lieber

One who is called to the Torah during synagogue services recites a blessing (*b'rakhah*) thanking God "who has chosen us from among all peoples by giving us His Torah" (BT Ber. 11b). This *b'rakhah* affirms two of Judaism's fundamental doctrines, both of which have had far-reaching implications for ancient Israel's political institutions and its religious worldview. These doctrines are the election of the people Israel, and its covenant with God. Both of these stem from Israel's origins, providing the rationale for its existence and the foundation on which its system of government was established. In fact, the belief in Israel's special relationship to God, as defined in the covenant at Sinai, is the central theme of the Torah (see Exod. 19:5, 24:7–8; Deut. 26:17ff., 29:9–14).

This is underlined by the covenant Joshua made with the Israelite tribes after he reviewed the early history of Israel at a public gathering of the tribes in Shechem (Josh. 24). As at the covenant of Sinai, the people affirmed three times that they would worship the Lord alone and obey Him. Unlike the first covenant between God and Israel, however, the gathering at Shechem was an occasion for reaffirming an existing covenant—not entering into a new one. This account differs from the one at Sinai, suggesting, as it does, that the people were free to reject the God of Israel (Josh. 24:15). This led some to conjecture that it presents an alternate tradition to the Sinai account, describing, perhaps, the admission of additional tribes to the covenanted union. In any event, the Shechem story does contain the three basic elements found in Sinai narrative:

- It is God who takes the initiative in choosing and delivering Israel (Josh. 24:3, 6; cf. Exod. 19:4).
- Israel's relationship with God is defined by a covenant (Josh. 24:25; cf. Exod. 19:5, 24:3ff.).
- The covenant brings with it obligations (Josh. 24:25; cf. Exod. 19:5,8, 20:lff., 21:1ff.).

These elements may be summarized as: the election of Israel, the covenant between God and Israel, and Israel's covenanted obligations.

From the earliest period of its recorded history, Israel was conscious of its uniqueness as "the people of God." This claim was immortalized in the name "Israel," which, according to the biblical narrative, originated when Jacob wrested a special blessing from God, having "striven with beings divine and human, and . . . prevailed" (Gen. 32:29). Whatever the name meant originally, it could also be interpreted as "[the domain in which] God rules," as the ancient blessing of Moses suggests (Deut. 33:5). Genesis anticipates this special bond between God and Israel with the divine promises made to the patriarchs. These promises move to their dramatic fulfillment with the exodus from Egypt and the encampment at Sinai, where God enters into a solemn covenant (*b'rit*) with the people and provides them with instructions, statutes, and judgments. Deuteronomy spells out the implications of the covenant for future generations; and finally, Joshua marks the fulfillment of the promise to Israel's ancestors and the renewal of the covenant in the Promised Land.

Of all the peoples in the ancient Near East, only Israel seems to have viewed its relationship with a deity as covenanted. Since covenants generally played an important role in the political and social life of the ancient world, this may appear surprising. A covenant might serve as a treaty between nations, such as that between Israel and the Gibeonites (Josh. 9:15). It could solemnize a compact between individuals, as in the case of Jacob and Laban (Gen. 31:44). It could assume the form of a land grant, as in the patriarchal stories (e.g., Gen. 15:18ff.). A covenant could also define relationships that were not primarily legal, such as the friendship of David and Jonathan (1 Sam. 18:3), or not exclusively so, such as marriage (Mal. 2:14). In such cases, it formalized the relationship, lending it an en-

during quality and adding a sense of commitment and obligation that had not been there before. Generally, a covenant clarified a relationship, spelled out the nature of the obligations that flowed from it, and sealed it with a religious rite or symbolic affirmation at a shrine (e.g., Exod. 24:4ff.; Josh. 24:19ff.; 2 Kings 23:1ff.).

Law codes sanctified by a covenant between a god and a "chosen" king existed in the earlier Sumerian and Old Babylonian traditions. What was new at Sinai was not the linkage of covenant with law giving, but the entry of disparate clans into a covenant with God, which welded them into a people united by a system of laws. Israel's God transcended the forces of nature and thus had no need for worshipers to wait in attendance or assist in preserving the order of a world constantly threatened by the forces of chaos. The function of the covenant, then, was to define the people's exclusive relationship to God and to institutionalize the paramount nature of God's rule. This is given expression in the first two statements of the Decalogue, which also define the relationship as personal, one in which God has a special interest. The Decalogue's use of the term *"kana,"* which literally means "jealous," is an instructive characterization of God. The term clearly intends to convey that God considers it a personal betrayal for Israel to turn to other gods.

The Sinai covenant did not follow either the model of the Hittite treaties of the 14th century B.C.E. or the Assyrian treaties of the 8th or 7th centuries B.C.E., because it was not a treaty. It did not contain the language of the land grants associated with the Abrahamic or Davidic covenants, because it was not a land grant. The covenant was unique: an agreement entered into freely by a deity with a people to create a new relationship or, rather, to redefine an earlier one initiated by God through the gracious act of deliverance from bondage. It called for a response from the people, who were to be "a kingdom of priests," "a holy nation" (Exod. 19:6), and who were provided with specific directions to attain this goal. They accepted God's charge, participating in an elaborate rite to seal their agreement (Exod. 24:4ff.). God undertook to dwell among them and to give them the land promised to their ancestors, providing that they carried out their part of the agreement. This differed from the covenant entered into with Abraham (Gen. 15), which was modeled after the ancient land grant to a loyal servant for services rendered and in which no future acts were required.

The most detailed presentation of the covenant between God and Israel is found in the Book of Deuteronomy, which almost precisely follows the form of neo-Assyrian vassal treaties, such as the one of Esarhaddon (672 B.C.E.). Presumably, the authors of Deuteronomy spelled out God's original covenant with Israel in the explicit, carefully structured form devised by the Assyrians to emphasize that God—not the Assyrian king—is sovereign over Israel.

The early belief that God had entered into a covenant with the Israelites' ancestors did not allow the establishment of the monarchy in the 11th century B.C.E. to displace the "kingship of God." This limited the king's authority and led to uprisings, on occasion, when he abused it. The people ultimately did accept the notion of a covenant between God and the house of David, but this covenant was limited by the requirements of the divine law (cf. Deut. 17:14–20).

Nowhere is this better illustrated than in the actions of the prophets. Samuel is depicted as remonstrating with Saul, the first king of Israel: "Does the LORD delight in burnt offerings and sacrifices / As much as in obedience to the LORD's command?" (1 Sam. 15:22). Prophets, viewed as the messengers of God, did not hesitate to speak the truth to reigning monarchs, who accepted their harsh pronouncements. This is indicated by the messages of doom pronounced against David by Nathan in the wake of the Bathsheba outrage (2 Sam. 11–12) and against Ahab's house by Elijah after Ahab had Naboth slain to expropriate his vineyard (1 Kings 21).

The prophets, however, did more than take kings and princes to task for violating the law

of God. They insisted that the covenant was binding both on the people as a whole and on each individual Israelite as a responsible member of the community. Each of them shared equally in both the obligations and the privileges of the *b'rit.* This is stated dramatically in Deuteronomy (5:2–3) when Moses declares: "The LORD our God made a covenant with us at Horeb. It was not with our fathers that the LORD made this covenant, but with us, the living, every one of us who is here today." To be sure, some bore greater responsibility than others because of their power and wealth, but none could ultimately escape the divine judgment. People had to be at peace with others as well as with themselves and with God. The cult, the organized system of Israelite worship, enabled them to come into the presence of God and express their heartfelt emotions to the divine. Its efficacy, however, depended on their obedience to God, as the prophets insisted, on the proper response to the divine call for righteous living. If this was not forthcoming, God threatened to destroy the holy places and abandon the people.

This message was brought home by virtually every prophet who lived before the destruction of the Temple in 586 B.C.E. They stressed, however, that God's relationship with Israel remained constant and that the covenant was eternal. That is why all of the prophets, without exception, saw beyond the destruction they prophesied to a glorious future. Even as severe a critic as Jeremiah, who announced the forthcoming demise of the Judean state, proclaimed in the name of God: "They shall be My people, and I will be their God. . . . And I will make an everlasting covenant with them that I will not turn away from them and that I will treat them graciously" (Jer. 32:38–40). To effect this, God intended to give them a "new covenant" and inscribe divine Teaching in their hearts (31:31, 33). Almost as if anticipating the later claim of the Christian church that this implied the rejection of Israel, the prophet added (31:35–36):

Thus said the LORD,
Who established the sun for light by day,
The laws of moon and stars for light by night,
Who stirs up the sea into roaring waves,
Whose name is LORD of Hosts:
If these laws should ever be annulled before Me
. . .
Only then would the offspring of Israel cease
To be a nation before Me for all time.

God's justice was tempered by compassion. While making demands on people, God was "slow to anger," providing many opportunities for both individuals and societies to make amends. Beyond that, God provided the Israelites, and indeed all of humankind, instructions and guidance to enable them to live in peace with one another and to enjoy the bounties of the earth. Having created humankind in the divine image, God hoped people would walk in fellowship with Him and in obedience to His will.

The everlasting nature of the covenant was grounded in the divine promise to the Israelites' ancestors. Although it certainly was not considered arbitrary, the covenant was recognized as an unmerited expression of divine love (Deut. 4:37, 7:6–7). The "election" of Israel went hand in hand with the covenant and provided a theological explanation for it. This is most clearly crystallized in Exod. 19:3–6, where Israel is called on to be "a kingdom of priests and a holy nation." As such, Israel was assigned a central role in God's purpose for all of humankind—a role that the great prophet of the exilic period defined as "a light unto the nations" (Isa. 49:6).

The conviction that God had entered into a covenant with its ancestors shaped Israel's entire worldview. It taught the Israelites that God cares about human beings, particularly for those who, like the people of ancient Israel, were helpless and oppressed. The covenant also made it plain that Israel's election was not for Israel's sake but to serve God's purpose for the rest of the world. It entailed obligation, not special privilege. As Amos, the first of the literary prophets (8th century B.C.E.), stated explicitly: "You alone have I singled out / Of all the families of the earth— / That is why I

will call you to account / For all your iniquities" (Amos 3:2). The world required the example of a covenant community because it was unredeemed. This message was stated clearly by the anonymous prophet whose words appear in the second part of the Book of Isaiah: "My witnesses are *you* / . . . / My servant, whom I have chosen" (Isa. 43:10). These words were addressed to Babylonian exiles, calling on them to cast off their gloom and engage in a new exodus that they might be, as cited earlier, "a light unto the nations" and that God's salvation might reach the ends of the earth (49:6).

It was an extraordinary challenge. Not surprisingly, it was never fully met. The Bible recounts at least three instances when the covenant was renewed: at Shechem, before Joshua's death (Josh. 24); in Jerusalem, at the time of King Josiah's reformation (2 Kings 23); and in Jerusalem again, during the time of Ezra (Neh. 10). These renewals succeeded in consolidating the community and setting it on a new course, demonstrating the power of the covenant concept, both as an ideal to be aimed at and an obligation to be met, rather than as a final achievement.

This concept had an effect on the development of the apocalyptic communities, which held the belief that the final judgment was at hand, such as the Qumran community near the Dead Sea (from the 2nd century B.C.E. through the 1st century C.E.) and, of course, on Christianity, which called on its faithful to adopt a "New Covenant." It is perhaps for this reason that Rabbinic Judaism played down the use of *"b'rit,"* restricting it almost exclusively to the rite of circumcision, one sign of the covenant. The concept itself, however, has remained central to the Rabbinic view of the Jewish relationship to God. The covenant is celebrated annually in the three pilgrimage festivals that recall God's great acts on Israel's behalf, as well as weekly on *Shabbat,* which is seen as a sign of the covenant. It is re-enacted every weekday morning in the putting on of *t'fillin.* The morning service itself reminds worshipers of the election of Israel and God's love for it, as expressed in the liberation from Egyptian bondage and the gift of Torah. The recitation of the *Sh'ma* is a daily reaffirmation of the sovereignty of God and the authority of the divine commandments.

The Sages also grasped the dynamic significance of the covenant concept for rebuilding Jewish life, through its institutions and laws, to meet the altered circumstances presented by the destruction of the Second Temple and the growth of the Diaspora. The development of the oral Torah would not have been possible without the view that the Sages had the right to interpret the written Torah to maintain God's presence among the Jewish people. They derived this from the scriptural injunction: "You shall act in accordance with the instructions given you [by the Levitical priests] and the ruling handed down to you" (Deut. 17:11), which they interpreted as granting them the rightful authority to carry on the work of Moses and his successors so that the everlasting covenant might be applicable to their time as well (cf. 5:3, 29:13–14).

With the spread of the Enlightenment and of the Emancipation in the 19th century, some western Jewish thinkers considered the doctrine of the election to be too exclusive. In an effort to universalize it, Reform leaders preferred to speak of "the mission of Israel," designed to spread ethical monotheism throughout the world. In the second quarter of the 20th century, Mordecai Kaplan, the founder of Reconstructionism, also suggested the abandonment of "the Chosen People doctrine," because it not only drew invidious distinctions between Jews and others but also lent itself to misinterpretation both by anti-Semites and Jewish chauvinists. In its place, he substituted the "doctrine of vocation," whereby Jews might acknowledge that God manifested His love to Israel. However, Kaplan considered the concept of the covenant valuable, calling on Jews worldwide to enter into a pact, as in the days of Ezra, to reconstitute themselves as a people dedicated to ethical nationhood and to the furtherance of their religious civilization.

Historically the belief in both the election of the people Israel and God's covenant with them has played a major role in the growth and survival of the Jewish people and of Judaism. Today, as well, whether one speaks in terms of election or of vocation, the uniqueness of Israel's calling to be a holy people, by virtue of Torah, remains fundamental to the faith of the Jew.

BIBLICAL AND ANCIENT NEAR EASTERN LAW

Nahum Sarna

If, as the Sages frequently stated, God employed the everyday language of human beings to communicate His will, then there is no section of the Torah in which this principle is more patently manifest than in the collections of legal ordinances. Extant corpora of laws, records of court proceeding, and judicial decisions provide ample evidence to prove that in its external form—in legal draftsmanship, in its terminology and phraseology—the Torah followed long-established, widespread, standardized patterns of Mesopotamian law.

Documents from the practice of law run into the many tens of thousands, uncovered at several widely dispersed sites in the Near East. Collections of laws recovered number no more than six.

Two such collections have survived in the non-Semitic Sumerian language spoken in southern Mesopotamia during the 3rd and early 2nd millenniums B.C.E., written in cuneiform script. The older one is that of King Ur-Nammu of the city-state of Ur, founder of the Third Dynasty of that city in the 21st century B.C.E. The original has not been found, only a fragmentary copy from Nippur, a city about 100 miles (ca. 160 km) south of Baghdad. This has been supplemented by two broken tablets from Ur itself, both of which are much older. The extant materials preserve the prologue to the collection, together with 29 stipulations, probably less than half of the original number. The prologue refers to "principles of equity and truth" and describes social abuses that the king sought to correct "to establish equity in the land" by standardizing weights and measures and by protecting the orphan, the widow, and the poor. The stipulations cover sexual offenses, support of divorcées, false accusations, the return of runaway slaves, bodily injuries, the case of an arrogant slave woman, perjured testimony, and encroachment of another's private property. The laws are formulated in "casuistic" style; i.e., they are conditional, the opening statement beginning with "if" followed by the hypothetical, concrete case, and the concluding statement giving the prescribed penalty.

The second Sumerian collection of laws comes from Lipit-Ishter, king of the city of Isin, in central lower Mesopotamia, in the 19th century B.C.E. Although an Amorite, he wrote his laws in Sumerian. There may also once have existed an Akkadian version, now lost. The laws, of which about 38 remain, are estimated to have numbered about 200 originally. They are framed by a prologue and an epilogue. In the former, the king writes that his god had commissioned him "to establish justice in the land" and "to promote the welfare" of his people. In the latter, he declares that he has restored domestic tranquility and established righteousness and truth. The extant laws, which belong to the concluding part of the corpus, deal with a variety of civil cases: the hiring of a boat; horticulture; the institution of slavery; house ownership; and family laws such as marriage, divorce, polygamy, and inheritance; and responsibility for injury to a rented animal. In these laws, too, the casuistic formulation is the rule.

The other law collections from Mesopotamia are all written in Akkadian. The earliest in this language derives from the city of Eshnunna, situated about 26 miles (42 km) northeast of Baghdad, on a tributary of the Tigris River. Its author is unknown, and its date is uncertain. These were copied in the time of a

contemporary of Hammurabi, but the original is believed to be considerably older. Neither prologue nor epilogue, if there was one, has been preserved. The legislation concerns the prices of various commodities, the cost of hiring a wagon and a boat, negligence on the part of the hirer, and the wages of laborers as well as laws pertaining to marriage, loans, slavery, property, personal injury, a goring ox, a vicious dog, and divorce. As before, the casuistic formulation is predominant. A peculiarity is that the application of the laws may vary according to the social status of the persons involved.

Mesopotamian jurisprudence reached its zenith in the 17th or 18th century B.C.E., with the promulgation of Hammurabi's great collection. These were inscribed on an eight-foot-high (2½ m) black diorite stele that was originally placed in the temple of Esagila in Babylon. In the early part of the 12th century B.C.E. it was looted by the Elamite king Shutruk-Nah and carried off to Susa (Hebrew: *Shushan*), capital of his kingdom, where French excavators discovered it in 1902. It now resides in the Louvre in Paris.

The upper front part of the stele bears a relief that features King Hammurabi standing before a seated deity, either the sun god, Shamash, or the chief god of Babylon, Marduk. The scene is often misinterpreted in popular books as Hammurabi receiving the laws from the god, but it is nothing of the kind. The god is really investing the king with the ring and the staff, which are the symbols of sovereignty. He thereby endows him with the authority, and perhaps also the wisdom, to promulgate the laws. The text makes it perfectly clear that Hammurabi himself is the sole source of the legislation.

Written in cuneiformed Akkadian in 51 columns, the stele now contains what is calculated to be 282 legal paragraphs. About 35 to 40 paragraphs were erased by the Elamite king; a few of these have been restored from other tablets. An extensive literary prologue and a lengthy epilogue frame the legal section. The prologue abounds in lofty sentiments about the purpose of the legislation, which is to further public welfare, to promote the cause of justice, to protect the interests of the weak, and to ensure the rule of law. The epilogue repeats these noble ideals and adds that the statutes are there so that anyone may know the law in case of need and that a future ruler may be guided by Hammurabi's ordinances. It closes with a series of blessings invoked on those who are faithful to the laws, and heaps fearful curses on anyone who is perfidious. Both prologue and epilogue are unabashedly replete with Hammurabi's copious and effusive self-praise and with massive hyperbole extolling his own greatness and mighty deeds.

The corpus of the laws, mostly styled casuistically, includes a large variety of legal topics. The first 41 paragraphs deal mainly with matters of public order; the rest belong overwhelmingly to the domain of private law, matters that affect the individual citizen. Distinctive features of the laws are the extraordinarily large numbers of capital offenses (some 30 in all), the penal mutilation of the body, vicarious punishment, the principle of talion (or legal retaliation in kind), intense concern with the protection of private property, and an innovative approach to several areas of private wrong that are now recognized as issues of public welfare to be regulated by the state. Finally, as in the laws of Eshnunna, Hammurabi's reflect a stratified society; as mentioned above, the penalties and judgments may vary according to the social standing of the litigants.

Considerably different from the collections hitherto described is the body of legislation that has come to be known as the Middle Assyrian Laws. Uncovered at the ancient city of Asshur on the Tigris River, about 250 miles (563 km) north of Babylon, the several clay tablets on which these are inscribed come from the 12th century B.C.E., but the legislation itself may well go back three centuries earlier. Although they conform to the casuistic pattern, the legal formulations and terminology as well as the prescribed penalties suggest influences, presently unknown, other than the standard Mesopotamian traditions. A total of 116 paragraphs are preserved in full or in part.

An extraordinarily large number deal with matters relating to the status of women and to family law. Peculiarly characteristic of these Assyrian laws are the savagery and severity of the punishments they mete out: numerous instances of the death penalty, even for offenses against property; mutilation of the body; flogging, even to the infliction of 100 lashes; pouring pitch over the head; tearing out the eyes; subjection to the water ordeal; forced labor; and the exaction of grievously heavy fines. There are also instances of multiple punishments imposed for a single offense.

Greatly under the influence of Mesopotamian legal traditions but deriving form quite a different cultural and linguistic milieu and geographic region are 200 Hittite laws that have survived from the Old Hittite kingdom of Asia Minor, now central Turkey. The extant tablets date from about 1250 B.C.E., but they go back to a much larger corpus of laws, apparently promulgated or collected for the use of jurists about five centuries earlier. A unique feature of this compilation is the clear references to earlier laws that have been revised. Capital punishment has been restricted to but a few offenses and has been replaced by restitution. The casuistic style is extensively employed.

At this point it should be emphasized that none of the collections discussed can be considered to be a legal code in the usually understood sense of the term. First, one and all, they omit important spheres of legal practice, and none comes close to being a comprehensive regulation of the citizens' lives. Second, not one of the compilations decrees that it is henceforth to be binding on judges and magistrates. Third, none is ever invoked as the basis of a legal decision in all the thousands of extant documents from the actual practice of law in the courts. For these reasons, the various collections are to be regarded as recording emendations and additions to bodies of existing unwritten common law that are seen to be in need of reform.

This conclusion applies equally to the corpus of laws embedded in the Torah. It is silent on matters of commercial law, on such indispensable practices as sales and contracts, the transfer of ownership, the legalization of marriage, the regulation of professions, and on most aspects of inheritance. Clearly, there existed in Israel a body of unwritten common law, orally transmitted from generation to generation, knowledge of which is assumed. What is prescribed in the Torah is a series of innovations to existing laws.

It should be further emphasized that the review of the legal corpora of the ancient Near East given above unquestionably establishes that when the people of Israel first appear on the scene of history, their world was already heir to the widely diffused common legal culture of long standing. No wonder, then, that Israelite laws exhibit so many points of contact with the earlier collections. Like them, the Torah expresses itself in terms of concrete, real-life cases; and, like them, the underlying legal principles are not abstractly stated but are to be deduced from the resolutions of those cases.

Another feature that is common to both ancient Near Eastern law collections and their Torah counterpart is the difficulty in uncovering the organizing principle that determines the arrangement and sequence of legal topics, although modern scholars have made some progress in this regard.

The affinities and analogues that abound between the Israelite and the other Near Eastern law collections tend to obscure the fundamental distinctions that exist between the two, a subject that must now be addressed. First and foremost is the essential fact that biblical law is the expression of the covenant between God and Israel. Several important consequences flow from this. The legal sections of the Torah cohere with the Exodus narratives and cannot be separated from them without losing their integrity and identity. Their sole source and sanction is divine will, not the wisdom and power of a human monarch. As imperatives of a transcendent, sovereign God who freely entered into a covenanted relationship with His people, the laws are eternally binding on both the individual and society as a whole. Hence the public nature of the law.

There can be no monopoly on the knowledge of the law, and the study of it is a religious obligation. Further, there can be no differentiation between the branches of public and private law and between both of them and religion and morality. All topics that fall under any of these rubrics are equally binding. Law is not severed from morality and religion.

As to the law's substance, the Torah forbids vicarious punishments and multiple penalties. Apart from the special category of the slave, it demands equal justice for all, irrespective of social status. Finally, whereas the Near Eastern laws place great stress on the importance of property, the Torah's value system favors the paramount sacredness of human life.

CIVIL AND CRIMINAL LAW

Ben Zion Bergman

The Bible sometimes uses different terms to designate various categories of laws; for example, *ḥukkim* (primarily ritual or cultic ordinances) and *mishpatim* (civil and criminal statutes). Underlying the entire system of law in the Bible and unifying its various components, however, is the assertion that it is all divinely commanded. This basic premise accounts for many of the salient characteristics of biblical legislation.

Because the law in all its aspects represents the will of God, rules governing relations between persons and rules delineating one's obligations to God and how they are to be fulfilled are equally sacred. Therefore, the laws of the Bible are not always conveniently categorized in the definitional framework of Western and modern legal systems. Although we would clearly label the willful violation of *Shabbat* as the infraction of a religious norm, not to be subsumed within a civil or criminal legal system, the Bible mandates the death penalty in that instance (Num. 15:32–36). The intentional violation of *Shabbat* is thus a capital crime subsumed under the biblical criminal code. The same is true for witchcraft (Exod. 22:17), idolatry (Exod. 22:19), and other cultic offenses that lead to the death penalty.

On the other hand, the rape of an unmarried or betrothed maiden (which, in a modern legal system would be classified as a crime) is treated in the Bible as a tort. It is seen as a wrongful act penalized only by a monetary payment to the woman's father (as compensation for her reduced value on the marriage market) and by the rapist's consequent obligation to marry the maiden (Deut. 22:28–29).

It is characteristic of biblical law that it rarely delineates rights; rather it encodes obligations. Indeed, a case can be made that Jewish law in general is primarily duty oriented rather than rights oriented. This too is symptomatic of the overlapping of the civil and the ecclesiastical, unified by the authority of a divine lawgiver. The law is thus given a religious underpinning—and it is in the nature of religion to impose duties, not to confer rights. It is also characteristic that a divinely ordained law should be couched primarily in terse statements with little elaboration, in categorical style. The most typical examples of this are from the Decalogue: "You shall not murder. You shall not commit adultery. You shall not steal. You shall not bear false witness against your neighbor" (Exod. 20:13; Deut. 5:17).

The biblical codes, in contrast to postbiblical talmudic legislation, reflect a comparatively simple society, engaged mainly in agriculture. As land was the primary source of economic productivity, its sale was severely limited. In the sabbatical year, debts were cancelled (Deut. 15:1–4); and in the jubilee (every 50 years), agricultural property that had been sold reverted to the seller or his or her heirs (Lev. 25; Deut. 15). These practices were designed to prevent the accumulation of the source of wealth in the hands of the few to the detriment of the many. They also ensured the integrity of the original tribal division of the Land, which was further protected by the

decree that a daughter who inherits (in the absence of sons) must marry within the tribe (Num. 36:6). Thus the Torah prevented the sale of land in perpetuity, providing the religious rationale "for the land is Mine; you are but strangers resident with Me" (Lev. 25:23).

A similar motivation and rural setting are reflected in the law of levirate marriage (*yibbum*): "When brothers dwell together" and one dies childless, the widow cannot marry a stranger; the brother of her deceased husband must marry her. The firstborn son of that marriage is considered the son of the deceased, and the deceased's property thus remains within the family. So strong was the brother's obligation that if he refused to marry his sister-in-law, he invited censure. If he remained adamant in his refusal, he was subject to public humiliation (Deut. 25:5–10).

Outside of the general admonition to have just weights and measures (Lev. 19:36; Deut. 25:13–15) and not to take unfair advantage in buying and selling (Lev. 25:14), there is a paucity of commercial legislation. This further reflects the rural setting, as are the torts enumerated in the Bible: the goring ox (Exod. 21:28–32,35–36), the conversion of a bailment (22:6–7), arson (22:5), and depredation by one's animals (22:4), to give just a few examples. In the case of the goring ox, the Torah distinguishes between a first-time offender and an ox that had previously exhibited vicious behavior. In the latter case, the owner of the ox, being under a greater duty of care, was subject to greater liability. Although the repeat offender was liable for full damages, the ambiguous statement in Exod. 21:35 was interpreted to make the owner of the first-time offender liable for only half the damages. Thus the loss was borne equally by the owners of both oxen. Evidently, the realities of rural and village life were such that both offender and victim shared an assumption of risk.

The rural societal setting is also reflected in the fact that criminal penalties were limited. An offender could be flogged, although the nature of the offenses for which flogging was to be administered is not specified (Deut. 25:1–3). The only other criminal punishment was execution, which was the punishment for murder (Exod. 21:12), adultery (Lev. 20:10), bestiality (Exod. 22:18), and a number of other capital offenses. Incarceration, however, was not mandated as a punishment for any crime. Indeed, to maintain a prison system requires a highly developed society with elaborate governmental organization and bureaucracy, impossible in the primitive setting of the Pentateuchal laws. Any incarceration was only for the limited period required for trial and judgment (Num. 15:34).

Therefore, the Torah does not mandate incarceration for theft. Instead, the thief reimbursed the victim twofold. Significantly, if the stolen object was a sheep or an ox—both vital to the rural economy—and it had been either sold or slaughtered and could, therefore, not be returned to the owner, the reimbursement was fourfold for the sheep and fivefold for the ox (Exod. 21:37, 22:3).

The procedural aspects as well as the substantive aspects of the law similarly reflect both the comparatively simple societal structure and the divine rationale. Although the Torah ordains the establishment of a judicial system operating in all cities within each tribal territory (Deut. 16:18), there is no explicit description of its composition. Though not specifying an appeal system, the Torah assumes that there is a higher judicial authority to whom local judges could turn in cases beyond their competence (Deut. 17:8–12). The alternate use of "judge" and "priest" in this passage is indicative of the ecclesiastical underpinning of the law. Even more striking is the use of *elohim* (a generic term for God) to designate the judges (Exod. 22:7–8, 22:27).

The city gate was evidently the place where judicial transactions took place. Abraham bought the field of Machpelah from Ephron the Hittite in the presence of those at the city gate (Gen. 23:10). It was at the city gate that Boaz transacted the waiver of Naomi's nearest kinsman and thus acquired the right to redeem the lands of Elimelech and to marry Ruth (Ruth 4:1–10). Because written con-

tracts were unknown at an early period, for transactions to become a matter of public record they had to be contracted in the presence of witnesses and in the most public place, which was the city gate. The contract was formalized by an overt act that signified the consent of the parties, such as the removal of a shoe (Ruth 4:7). Written documents evidently came into use at a later period. Jeremiah acquired the field of his cousin Hanamel via a deed of purchase (Jer. 32:10–12). That incident, however, does not necessarily indicate that written documents were becoming common at that time. Jeremiah had a special purpose in committing his purchase to writing and preserving it for safekeeping. It was symbolic of his belief that God would bring His people back from their impending exile. The only legal document mentioned in the Torah is the bill of divorce (Deut. 24:1), although the formalities of its language and form are uncertain. It was certainly not the Aramaic document later formulated by the Sages.

The judges are commissioned to effectuate justice (Deut. 16:18). A number of biblical ordinances are, therefore, directed particularly to judges. They are not to favor persons or take a gift from a litigant (Deut. 16:19). They must treat rich and poor alike (Lev. 19:15); likewise, the stranger and the native born (Lev. 24:22).

Evidentiary rules were simple. Eyewitness testimony was the best (possibly the only) evidence, but judgment could be passed only upon the testimony of two witnesses. One witness was insufficient (Deut. 19:15). The penalty for perjury varied with the nature of the case. As punishment, the perjurer was to suffer whatever effect the perjurious testimony would have had. Thus a false accusation of a capital offense would mean the death penalty for the lying witness. False testimony that would have resulted in a monetary loss to one of the disputants would result in an equal loss to the perjurer (Deut. 19:19). The Torah explicitly delineates that the purpose of this was not only to punish the miscreant but also to act as a deterrent to false testimony. Therefore, the punishment was to be carried out in all its severity—"Nor must you show pity" (Deut. 19:20–21).

The law was thus seen as an instrument of public policy. As the establishment of a just society is God's will, the law mandated by God was designed to accomplish that end. That explains the abundance of "poor laws" that placed a duty on every Israelite to care for the fatherless, the widow, the stranger, and other disadvantaged members of society (e.g., Exod. 22:19–23; Deut. 24:17–22). Farmers were forbidden to glean their field but were to leave the gleanings for the poor and the stranger. They also had to leave a corner of each field unharvested, relinquishing its produce to the disadvantaged (Lev. 23:22). For an example of this law in practice, see Ruth 2. A sheaf left by chance in the field as well as olives and grapes ungleaned were also to be left for "the stranger, the fatherless, and the widow" (Deut. 24:19–22).

The wages of a day laborer had to be paid promptly, for "he is poor" and depends on it (Deut. 24:14–15). One was commanded to lend to the poor unhesitatingly (Deut. 15:7–11) and no interest was to be exacted from them (Exod. 22:24; Deut. 23:20–21). And although slavery existed, the law distinguished between Hebrew slaves and non-Hebrew slaves. Whereas the latter were property and could be bequeathed, the former were only indentured servants. Their term was limited to six years, although they could elect to remain in perpetual servitude (Exod. 21:2–6; Deut. 15:12–18). Their gentler treatment was motivated by the historical memory of Israelite slavery in Egypt: "and the LORD your God redeemed you; therefore I enjoin this commandment upon you today" (Deut. 15:15).

For those who are so poor as to be reduced to pawning a garment, the pledge must be returned each night so that they have a covering during sleep (Exod. 22:25–26). Characterization of God as "compassionate"—as in this last passage—is the basic premise that informs the unique moral and ethical stance of biblical law. A touching example of this compassion translated into law is found in the prohibition

against taking both the mother bird and the eggs from the nest. The mother bird must be sent away before the eggs or fledgling are taken (Deut. 22:6–7).

That the community as a whole bore some measure of guilt for the unrequited crime committed in its midst was a unique moral and ethical concept for that era. It is exemplified in the exotic ritual of the beheaded heifer. When a corpse was found in the field—the victim of foul play with the perpetrator unknown—the elders of the nearest city (representing the body politic) took a heifer into the valley, where its neck was broken. They then uttered an expiatory prayer: "'Our hands did not shed this blood, nor did our eyes see it done. Absolve, O LORD, Your people Israel, whom You redeemed, and do not let guilt for the blood of the innocent remain among Your people Israel.' And they will be absolved of bloodguilt" (Deut. 21:1–9). The necessity to seek expiation for the murder arose from the conception that this heinous crime, the perpetrator of which could not be brought to justice, contaminated the community in whose vicinity it took place. Were the perpetrator known, justice could be done and the punishment meted out to the murderer would expiate the crime. Failing this, the community had to remove the defilement of the "innocent blood" by this expiatory ritual.

Although in all of the above examples we have treated the biblical law as if it were embodied in a uniform code, in reality, the biblical law is neither systematic nor monolithic. One can find change and development within the Torah itself. Even in the two versions of the Decalogue (Exod. 20:2–14; Deut. 5:6–18) one finds significant differences (e.g., in the commandment forbidding coveting and in the motivation and rationale for *Shabbat*). So too, whereas in the earlier Exodus code (21:7–11) the daughter sold into slavery by her father did not automatically go free after six years as did the male slave, and could be forced to become her master's wife, in the later Deuteronomic code (15:12) her status is equalized with the male Hebrew slave. Similarly, the Torah records a revolutionary amendment of the law of inheritance. Through the plea of the daughters of Zelophehad, the right to inherit, previously the exclusive prerogative of males, was awarded to daughters when the deceased leaves no sons (Num. 27:1–11). Thus it is clear that biblical law reflects development occasioned by change of time, place, and ethical conception.

It is equally clear that the laws encoded in the Torah do not comprise the totality of the law operative in biblical times. Two outstanding examples show that there was a body of customary law that preceded the writing of the biblical codes and that continued to be operative.

> If a man has two wives, the one loved and the other unloved, and both the loved and the unloved have borne him sons, but the first-born is the son of the unloved one—when he wills his property to his sons, he may not treat as first-born the son of the loved one in disregard of the son of the unloved one who is older. Instead he must accept the first-born, the son of the unloved one, and allot to him a double portion of all his possessions; since he is the first fruit of his vigor, the birthright is his due" (Deut. 21:15–17).

The Torah's assumption here that the firstborn son was entitled to a double portion of the inheritance is nowhere else to be found in the biblical codes. There is no specific statute to that effect. Yet it is clear that such a customary law was operative.

The existence of customary law precedent to the biblical enactments is also adumbrated in the unique treatment of manslaughter, as opposed to premeditated murder. Six towns, strategically placed for easy access, were to be set aside as "cities of refuge" to provide asylum to the manslayer from the "avenger of blood," a near kinsman on whom evidently devolved a duty to avenge the death of an innocent victim. Manslayers had to remain in a city of refuge until the death of the current high priest. If they left the city before then, the blood avenger

could kill them with impunity (Num. 35:9–34). Again, the Torah nowhere specifically gives kin the right to kill manslayers. The position of the blood avenger was evidently a prebiblical institution that continued into biblical times and whose consequences the Torah sought to ameliorate.

Nor did the development of law cease with the Bible's canonization. In the Torah, cities of refuge are characterized as providing asylum and protection for the manslayer; however, later talmudic law viewed the institution (which it called *galut,* banishment) as punishing the manslayer for fatal negligence. Similarly, whatever "an eye for an eye" (Exod. 21:24) may have meant in its day, by the time of the Mishnah it had been transmuted into five elements of damage for which the wrong-doer was liable: loss of economic value, pain and suffering, medical costs, loss of earnings during convalescence, and emotional distress prompted by bearing a permanent injury. One should not make the mistake of equating the biblical codes with the totality of Jewish law. On the contrary, the initial work of biblical codifiers has been expanded into a vast legal literature—as generations of talmudic sages, medieval commentators and codifiers, and modern legalists have continuously brought God's law to bear on all facets of human endeavor.

JUSTICE

Elliot N. Dorff

"Justice, justice shall you pursue" (Deut. 16:20) rings through the ages as one of the Torah's major principles. The biblical prophets rail against the people for their failure to achieve justice and issue clarion calls to reform that have shaped the conscience of Western civilization for thousands of years.

The demand for justice appears at the end of verses that call for the location of courts in all regions where the people dwell, that prohibit bribes, and that warn against prejudice in court judgments. By mixing procedural concerns (like the placement of courts in convenient places) with substantive issues (like the prohibitions against bribes and prejudice), the Torah indicates its awareness that the two are inextricably intertwined, that procedure affects substance and substance demands certain procedural rules.

No human being can always know whose cause is right; only God is privy to all the actions and intentions of every individual. Nevertheless, the Torah obligates us to establish courts to dispense justice as well as we can, and it specifies procedural rules to help us do that well.

For example, at least two witnesses are required to establish a fact in court to forestall collusion (Deut. 17:6, 19:15). To accentuate its prohibition of false testimony, the Torah includes it in the Decalogue (Exod. 20:13), announced amid thunder and lightning at Mount Sinai (see also Exod. 23:1–2; Deut. 5:17). Moreover, a 20 percent fine is levied against witnesses who knowingly lie in a civil case (Lev. 5:20–26), and full retribution is required of those who testify falsely in a criminal case (Deut. 19:15–21). A judge's acceptance of bribes is roundly condemned, "for bribes blind the clear-sighted and upset the pleas of those who are in the right" (Exod. 23:8; Deut. 16:19). Each person is to be judged for his or her own actions exclusively (Deut. 24:16). (This principle is assumed without question in modern Western societies; but in many societies in ancient, medieval, and even modern times, people have been punished for the crimes of their family members.) The Torah insists that neither rich nor poor may be favored: "You shall not be partial in judgment: Hear out low and high alike. Fear no man, for judgment is God's" (Deut. 1:17; see Exod. 23:2,6). The alien, too, is to be treated fairly: "Decide justly between any man and a fellow Israelite or stranger" (Deut. 1:16).

The sages of the Talmud and Middle Ages added many more procedural rules to ensure impartial treatment. For example, one litigant

may not be required to stand while the other is sitting, both parties to the case must wear clothing of similar quality, judges must understand the languages spoken by the people before them, and witnesses may not be related to each other or to the litigants. Through rules such as these, procedural justice is strengthened and made a reality.

Substantive justice speaks not to the method by which a judicial decision is made but to the character of the results of court procedures and, more broadly, of society's policies. In Plato's *Republic,* substantive justice amounted to social harmony, which could be achieved only when everyone did what his or her station in society demanded. The biblical view of substantive justice is radically different, stressing the equality of all human beings and their right to equal protection of the law. Thus the Torah demands that aliens, widows, and orphans not be oppressed either in court (Deut. 24:17) or in society generally (Exod. 22:21), that they be cared for because they have no protectors (Deut. 14:29, 16:11,14). Indeed, the mistreatment of the defenseless and the failure to protect them in court was denounced by the prophets as a sign of the decadence of the Israelite society of their time (e.g., Isa. 1:17,23, 10:1–2; Jer. 5:28; Ezek. 22:7). The poor were also to be treated honorably and justly (e.g., Deut. 24:10–15; Jer. 22:16) and to be cared for (e.g., Deut. 15:7–11), and the failure to do that was also part of the prophets' complaints against their society (e.g., Ezek. 16:49, 22:29; Amos 2:6–7, 8:4–7).

It is not only the downtrodden, however, whose cause the Torah champions as part of its insistence on substantive justice. All members of society must be treated justly. The Torah, therefore, includes lengthy lists of civil and criminal legislation for society as a whole (e.g., Exod. 21–24; Deut. 20–25), and the Sages developed this extensively, beginning with the Mishnah's order *N'zikin.* By formulating rules of procedural and substantive justice, then, the Torah and its Rabbinic heirs transform justice from a pious hope to a concrete reality.

Although the Torah and the later Jewish tradition went about as far as any society could go in translating its moral and spiritual commitments into legal terms, Rabbinic authorities recognized that justice never can be captured totally in law. As a medieval Jewish phrase puts it, one can be a "scoundrel within the limits of the law" or, interpreted somewhat differently, "a scoundrel with the sanction of the Torah" (*naval birshut ha-Torah*). Consequently, the Bible is not content to depict the substance of the law as both life-giving and the source of goodness (Deut. 30:15; Ps. 19:8–10, 119:33–40), in sharp contrast to the abominable acts of the other nations (e.g., Lev. 18, 20). In addition, it requires doing "what is right and good in the sight of the LORD" (Deut. 6:18). The sages of the Talmud take that and other Torah verses as the basis for declaring that people are obliged to act "beyond the letter of the law" (*lifnim mi-shurat ha-din*). Indeed, they state that the Second Temple was destroyed because people did not acknowledge or fulfill such moral duties (BT BM 30b). Thus, while the Torah and the Rabbinic tradition help make justice a reality by giving it concrete expression in law, Jewish law itself recognizes that justice sometimes demands more than the law does, that moral duties go beyond the letter of the law. Moreover, those moral duties sometimes require reshaping the law, so that in each new age it can continue to be the best approximation of justice.

The Torah thus goes beyond defining justice in its procedural and substantive aspects. It insists that justice is a divine imperative. In Western legal systems, justice is an instrumental good, a commodity important for social peace and welfare. That motivation to achieve justice appears in Jewish texts as well, but Jewish sources add another important motive. God demands justice and makes the existence of the world depend on it, because God Himself is just. In fact, He is the ultimate judge who "shows no favor and takes no bribe, but upholds the cause of the fatherless and the widow, and befriends the stranger, providing

him with food and clothing" (Deut. 10:17–18). As Moses proclaims in his parting poem:

> For the name of the LORD I proclaim;
> Give glory to our God!
>
> The Rock!—His deeds are perfect,
> Yea, all His ways are just;
> A faithful God, never false,
> True and upright is He (Deut. 32:3–4).

It is precisely because God is just that Abraham can call Him to account for His plan to destroy Sodom, regardless of the innocent people in it. His words ring through the ages: "Far be it from You to do such a thing, to bring death upon the innocent as well as the guilty, so that innocent and guilty fare alike. Far be it from You! Shall not the Judge of all the earth deal justly?" (Gen. 18:25) God's justice is also at the heart of Job's complaint (Job 9:22), and God thunders in reply, "Would you impugn My justice? / Would you condemn Me that you may be right?" (Job 40:8) God's justice may be inscrutable, but for the Bible it is undeniable, a core characteristic of the divine.

God enforces His demands of justice. He hears the cry of those who suffer injustice and responds by punishing the perpetrators. Thus the Torah admonishes: "You shall not abuse a needy and destitute laborer, whether a fellow countryman or a stranger in one of the communities of your land. You must pay him his wages on the same day, before the sun sets, for he is needy and urgently depends on it; else he will cry to the LORD against you and you will incur guilt" (Deut. 24:14–15).

It is not enough, however, to be just from fear of punishment or hope for reward. Justice is necessary for holiness. All Israelites are obligated to aspire to a life of holiness: "You shall be holy, for I, the LORD your God, am holy (Lev. 19:2). In the verses that follow that divine demand, the Torah specifies what holiness requires: providing for the poor and the stranger; eschewing theft and fraud; rendering fair and impartial decisions in court; treating the blind, the deaf, and the stranger fairly; and ensuring honest weights and measures. All of these are components of a society that has both procedural and substantive justice.

One other aspect of the biblical concept of justice derives from its theological foundations. God loves the people Israel for reasons having nothing to do with their number or power, the usual marks of a nation's greatness; and He promises the patriarchs to continue that relationship through the generations (Deut. 7:6–11). The Israelites, in turn, are to love God and "always keep His charge, His laws, His rules, and His commandments" (Deut. 11:1). The commandments of the Torah are thus not legalistic formalisms, totally divorced from human compassion, moral values, and a spiritual relationship with God—as some Christian writings portray them. Quite the contrary, the practice of justice is an extension of love, as demonstrated by commandments calling on all Israelites to "love your neighbor as yourself" (Lev. 19:18), to "love the stranger" (repeated 36 times in the Torah), and to "love God" (Deut. 6:5, 11:1).

In fact, one of the primary expressions of God's love is precisely that He provides human beings with rules of justice. Parents who love their children take the time and energy to insist on proper behavior because they know it will ultimately be in the children's best interests; in the same way, "the LORD commanded us to observe all these laws, to revere the LORD our God, for our lasting good and for our survival, as is now the case" (Deut. 6:24). Again, "Bear in mind that the LORD your God disciplines you just as a man disciplines his son. Therefore keep the commandments of the LORD your God: walk in His ways and revere Him" (Deut. 8:5–6).

The Torah itself, and the Sages even more, appreciated the fact that justice, to become a reality in people's lives, could not be left as a general value to which one mouths allegiance, but must be translated into concrete terms. By presenting specific cases, both the biblical and the Rabbinic traditions make the demands of justice clear and binding. It was not enough to require a person who finds a lost object to return it (as in Deut. 22:1–3). What if not one,

but several, people claim it? How shall you determine the real owner? What happens if you cannot? What should you do, on the other hand, if nobody comes forward to claim the object? Must you keep it? If so, for how long? To what extent must you go to publicize that you have it? If it requires care (e.g., if it is an animal), must you spend your own money to provide that care? To what extent? May you use the object in the interim? Returning a lost object is a relatively simple demand of justice; but as these questions demonstrate, even a straightforward requirement easily becomes complicated—and the Sages, in fact, devoted an entire chapter of the Talmud to this issue (BM 2). Without that discussion, the Torah's imperative to return a lost object would remain imprecise and unworkable; demanding (in some understandings) too much or (in others) too little to make this aspect of justice part of the ongoing practice within Jewish communal life.

Justice in the Bible, then, is made a concrete reality by spelling out at least most of its demands in specific laws. The Torah and the later Rabbinic tradition insist, though, that we do the right and the good even when the details of the law would permit us to do otherwise. The Jewish tradition thus recognizes both that the legal framework is indispensable in making justice a reality and that the demands of justice extend beyond the law, however extensively it is defined. The Torah and the later Jewish tradition also place the demand for justice in a theological context, thereby affirming the authority of the demand for justice and giving it a rationale: We are to be just because God requires it of us and because it is one important way in which we can imitate God's ways. These legal, moral, and theological parameters of the biblical and Rabbinic concepts of justice make it an ongoing, living component of a life lived in loving covenant with God.

REWARD AND PUNISHMENT

Harvey Meirovich

The concept of divine reward and punishment in the Bible is linked to the perception that God cares enough about His creatures to be deeply moved by their behavior. God's essence is beyond human comprehension, yet the prophets make the concept of God's relationship to humanity accessible by presenting it in association with two primary traits: sympathy and rejection. Human beings perceive sympathy through blessings, rewards, and redemption. They perceive rejection through punishments, curses, and affliction.

God's sovereignty over individuals and nations is identified with the pursuit of justice. In the Bible, there is a direct correlation between behavior on the one hand and reward and punishment on the other. Israel's obedience ensures crop abundance, human and animal fertility, wealth, and military success. Deeds, in the exercise of free will, determine destiny (Exod. 23:25–27; Lev. 26; Deut. 4:25–28, 7:12–16, 11:13–21; Jer. 5:15–17, 19:9).

This strict demand for justice was tempered by a perception of God's quality of mercy. The Bible basks in God's intimate relationship with Israel. It apprehends the Creator as both transcendent judge and forgiving, compassionate father. Divine love is the counterpart to divine wrath.

The radical notion of intercession is prominent in the Bible's teaching that prophets prevailed on God to delay, or even cancel, divine punishment. The prophets availed themselves of their power of persuasion (Exod. 32:11–14; Num. 14:13–16), as well as prayer (Num. 11:2, 12:13, 21:7), direct pleading (Num. 16:22; Amos 7:2–3), and reliance on God's grace (Ps. 103:10–14). Prophetic intercession is necessary because of the moral imperfection of human beings (Gen. 8:21). Prophets view people as pitiable creatures, incapable of moral reformation (Jer. 31:31–34; Ezek. 36:25–27). This will compel God in the future to replace human choice and free will with robot-like

behavior; the human heart will be replaced with a model guaranteed to seek only goodness and righteousness. At one point in history, the notions of reward and punishment will cease to hold any relevance for mortals!

TRANSGENERATIONAL RETRIBUTION

The doctrine of transgenerational retribution (in which one generation suffers punishment for the sins of a previous generation) is based on two principles: (a) Strict justice in the distribution of reward and punishment. (b) A conviction that the family unit, not the individual, forms the basis of society. Thus the individual is an extension of his or her family's good or bad fortune. Communal and national solidarity outweigh personal destiny. The deeds and the misdeeds of the individual inevitably have repercussions for the whole House of Israel in the future.

Strict Justice

In the strict application of retribution, vicarious punishment and reward are administered on future generations without qualification.

> The LORD passed before him (Moses) and proclaimed: "The LORD! The LORD! A God compassionate and gracious, slow to anger, abounding in kindness and faithfulness, extending kindness to the thousandth generation, forgiving iniquity, transgression and sin; yet He does not remit all punishment, but visits the iniquity of parents upon children and children's children, upon the third and fourth generations (Exod. 34:6–7).

A More Temperate Perception

A more temperate view holds that the strict measure of the law is qualified in the two versions of the Decalogue (Exod. 20:5–6; Deut. 5:9–10). In this scenario, the threat of suffering or the assurance of blessing for future generations depends on the ancestors' behavior. This knowledge could deter the ancestors from wayward acts and inspire them to the performance of righteous deeds. "For I the LORD your God am an impassioned God, visiting the guilt of the parents upon the children, upon the third and fourth generation of those who reject Me, but showing kindness to the thousandth generation of those who love Me and keep My commandments."

An Interpretation of Greater Leniency

In the view of greater leniency, there is no notion of transferring punishment to the sinner's offspring. God rewards the faithful to the thousandth generation but metes out punishment to the offender personally and immediately. The divine blessing connotes boundless beneficence. "Know, therefore, that only the LORD your God is God, the steadfast God who keeps His covenant faithfully to the thousandth generation of those who love him and keep His commandments, but who instantly requites with destruction those who reject Him" (Deut. 7:9–10).

All of these passages, addressed to the entire people of Israel, highlight God's primary attributes of justice and mercy. In this portrayal, God's abiding compassion, based on an implicit desire for reconciliation, exceeds by far His short-term, legitimate outbursts of exasperation.

The Bible's insistence on communal solidarity and mutual responsibility is crystallized in the plural form of most Jewish prayers. For example, the formal confession of sins on the Day of Atonement assumes community consciousness, because it is couched in the plural. The individual is held personally responsible for the moral state of the community.

Rejection of Transgenerational Retribution

Jeremiah and Ezekiel championed a counter-belief in individual retribution, categorically denying that any person is morally an extension of another. "The person who sins, only he shall die. A child shall not share the burden of a parent's guilt, nor shall a parent share the burden of a child's guilt" (Ezek. 18:20). This prophetic rejection may have been inspired by a pressing need to counter a pervasive hopelessness in the period after the national catastrophe,

which included the destruction of the Temple. If ancestral guilt indeed was the cause of current suffering, to what avail is the moral struggle?

Two More Radical Beliefs

The more traditional belief affirms that sin invariably generates punishment (Exod. 32:33–34). Later, postexilic traditions, however, affirm that repentance renders punishment null and void. Repentance, in this view, even obliterates sin. For example, God renounced punishment against the people in Nineveh when they turned from their evil ways in repentance (Jon. 3:10). Isaiah went a step further. God would wipe away Israel's transgressions and remember them no more (Isa. 43:25, 44:22). At the root of this lay a heartfelt conviction that human repentance could so overwhelm God's justice that only His compassion remained operative.

"Why does the way of the wicked prosper?" (Jer. 12:1). This echoes the searing challenge of the psalmist: "Why, O LORD, do You stand aloof, heedless in times of trouble?" (Ps. 10:1). The complaint resonates in Rabbinic conversation as well. Yannai said: "It is not within our grasp to explain the tranquility of the wicked or even the suffering of the righteous" (M Avot 4:15). Yet the human need to justify God's ways led biblical and Rabbinic sources to seek solutions to the problems raised by suffering.

Retribution

The most conventional explanation of human suffering is provided by the doctrine that sinful behavior leads to punishment. Adam and Eve were punished for failing to heed God's command (Gen. 3). God's judgment of moral corruption led to the destructive flood of Noah's day and the annihilation of Sodom and Gomorrah (Gen. 6, 18). The severe price to be paid for disobedience reaches a crescendo in the stern warnings recorded in Lev. 26 and Deut. 28. The historical books of the Bible are replete with the conviction that the outbreak of communal idolatry was a direct cause of punishment and suffering (Judg. 2:10–19, 3:7, 4:1, 8:33). The theme was highlighted in Deuteronomy (11:16–17,28). The prophet Amos reduced the doctrine to "Seek good and not evil, that you may live" (Amos 5:14).

The exile of the northern and southern kingdoms was explained by the same rationale (2 Kings 17:7–23). Israel's wisdom teachers also understood the principle of retribution determining the individual's fate. "There is no wholeness in my bones because of my sin" (Ps. 38:4). "Misfortune pursues sinners, but the righteous are well rewarded" (Prov. 13:21).

This theological construct surfaced in Rabbinic tradition as well. A classic expression of retribution is the claim of Ami: "There is no death without sin, and no suffering without transgression" (BT Shab. 55a). A pious rabbi who survived the bite of a poisonous lizard observed: "It is not the lizard that kills, it is sin that kills" (BT Ber. 33a).

Measure for Measure

Jacob tricked his father Isaac into giving him the blessing that belonged to his firstborn brother, Esau (Gen. 27). Jacob was therefore outwitted by his father-in-law, Laban, who tricked him into marrying his eldest daughter, Leah, in place of her younger sister, Rachel (Gen. 29:21–30). This twist wove its way as well into Rabbinic tradition, which taught that because the Egyptians tried to destroy Israel by water they were annihilated by the waters of the Sea of Reeds (Exod. 1:22, 14:26–28; Mekh. B'shallaḥ 7).

Deterrent

The suffering of the guilty was to be considered a deterrent, warning the Israelites against disobeying the divine commandments. They were to internalize the concept "fear of the LORD" by witnessing God's destruction of the Egyptian enemies (Exod. 14:30–31; Deut. 11:2–9). Israel's sufferings were to serve as a warning to the nations around it (Ezek. 5:15).

Discipline

Suffering is not strictly a punishment but rather a catalytic agent brought into service by a caring God to purge and purify individual way-

wardness, at the root of which often lay arrogance and pride (Job 33:14–17). Biblical wisdom teachers found this explanation especially attractive. "Do not reject the discipline of the LORD, my son: do not abhor His rebuke. For whom the LORD loves He rebukes, as a father the son whom he favors" (Prov. 3:11–12). The psalmist perceived Joseph's stay in an Egyptian dungeon as a necessary chastening that transformed his character (Ps. 105:17–19). Distress is the gateway to understanding (Job 33, 36:8–10,15).

The same principle operates on the collective level. "Shall He who disciplines nations not punish, He who instructs men in knowledge?" (Ps. 94:10). Critical, however, is the corollary that although God chastened His people for their own good, He would not destroy them completely (Lev. 26:44; Deut. 4:31; Jer. 30:10–11).

Israel will come to a knowledge of God's existence by passing through the crucible of calamity (Ezek. 22:22, 33:29). Ezekiel also submitted that the hardships suffered by foreign nations awakened them to a recognition of divine might and the ethical dimensions of monotheism (Ezek. 25–26, 28–30, 39). In this context, Isaiah, with theological daring, envisioned Egypt—to the exclusion of all other nations—returning to the Lord after suffering divine punishment (Isa. 19).

"Sufferings of love" was the concept in Rabbinic parlance, articulating the belief that suffering is an expression of divine love (Ber. 5a). The inspiration for this idea is found in Deut. 8:5: "Bear in mind that the LORD your God disciplines you just as a man disciplines his son." The remedial effects of discipline led later Rabbinic masters to posit that God inflicts pain as a test, but only for the righteous who are able to endure the suffering (Gen. R. 34:2, 55:2). From another quarter came speculation that the rich are reproved by God to see if they will open their hands to the poor, whereas the poor suffer to ascertain if they accept discipline (Exod. R. 31:3).

Both biblical and Rabbinic sources concur that disciplinary punishment is meant to trigger genuine remorse and regeneration, coupled with a desire to return to God in sincere repentance (Jer. 31:18–19; Ps. 78:34). "One should rejoice more in chastisement than in prosperity, for if one is prosperous all his life, no sin of his will be forgiven. What brings forgiveness of sin? Suffering" (Sifrei Deut. 32).

VOICES OF RESISTANCE AND OPPOSITION

"It was for nothing that I kept my heart pure and washed my hands in innocence, seeing that I have been constantly afflicted" (Ps. 73:13–14). There was always the possibility that people would refuse to accept divine chastisement by closing themselves off to the best intentions of the Almighty. "To no purpose did I smite your children; they would not accept correction" (Jer. 2:30).

The Bible and the Sages legitimized the right to protest against God for the infliction of what humans perceived to be unjust suffering. The outbursts of Job in the Bible have their counterpart in the Midrash, which states that Abraham was so traumatized by binding his son Isaac that he warned God he could bear no further trials by ordeal (Gen. R. 57:4).

Voices of opposition arose within Rabbinic tradition to invalidate the educational rationale that justifies pain. When the sage Joḥanan fell ill, his colleague Ḥanina urged him to place his trust in God. When Ḥanina was racked with pain, however, he uttered: "I want neither the sufferings nor any reward associated with them" (Song R. II, 16:2).

Atonement

The prophet of consolation, Second Isaiah, articulated a revolutionary doctrine when he depicted the vicarious sufferings of the anonymous servant of the Lord (Isa. 52:13–53:12). In this powerful expression of human solidarity, the servant's self-sacrificing readiness to bear misery relieved and delivered the wicked from retribution. It was hoped that the suffering of the servant who allowed his own life to be consumed as a guilt offering would lead the

guilty to forsake sin. The appeal of this argument lies in the belief that the misery or the death of an innocent victim can generate moral repair in the souls of sinners who are horrified at the consequences of their own errors or those of others.

This notion is found in Rabbinic circles as well. "The death of the righteous atones [for the living left behind]" (MK 28a). Echoes of the atonement principle resonate in the ruling that the death of the high priest procured atonement for the person banished to a city of refuge after having committed unintentional homicide (Num. 35:11–15; Mak. 11b). In a dramatic personal identification with this motif, the distinguished Ishmael prayed that he might serve, if necessary, as an atonement victim for any punishment that might befall his people (M Neg. 2:1).

Some talmudic authorities tried to neutralize the virtue of vicarious suffering, arguing that afflictions atone only for one's own transgressions. An individual's own sufferings were considered more appealing to God than sacrifices, for sacrifices involve only the outlay of money, not physical pain (Sifrei Deut. 32; Mekh. B'ḥodesh 10). Similarly, if a person transgressed commandments punishable by execution at the hands of either Heaven (*karet*) or the court, repentance on the Day of Atonement served to suspend the sentence, and that person's sufferings during that year atoned for the sin (ARN 29).

Strangely, not until the Middle Ages did midrashic license adroitly adapt the notion of the single suffering servant, identifying him collectively with the Jewish people.

Meaningless Suffering

After all explanations have been exhausted, the brutal candor so prominent in Ecclesiastes remains: "In my own brief span of life I have seen both of these things: sometimes a good man perishes in spite of his goodness, and sometimes a wicked one endures in spite of his wickedness" (7:15). Reward and punishment are not meted out according to a person's deeds. This is a bitter pill to swallow.

The evidence of everyday reality pressed Rabbinic tradition to admit that indeed "there is death without sin and there is suffering without transgression" (BT Shab. 55b). The prooftext was drawn from none other than Ecclesiastes: "The same fate is in store for all: for the righteous and for the wicked; for the good and pure and for the impure. . . . That is the sad thing about all that goes on under the sun" (9:2–3).

ESCHATOLOGY

Neil Gillman

THE ESCHATOLOGIC IMPULSE

What does the future hold for us? Can we hope for a time when the world will be a better place and human life somewhat easier? From the time human beings began to reflect about themselves and their world, these questions have been posed, somewhat intuitively, in every human society. The discussion of these questions and the range of answers that have been offered are covered by the term "eschatology."

"Eschatology" (from the Greek *eschatos,* "last," and *logos,* "discourse") designates a doctrine that describes both an ideal state of affairs that will be realized some time in the future and the sequence of events leading to the emergence of that state. It usually is understood to be a dimension of religion, although we also speak of "secular" eschatologies. Marxism, for example, is often cited as incorporating a secular eschatology, although some would say that precisely because it deals with issues of this kind, Marxism is really a religion.

Eschatologies are imaginative visions of an ideal or perfected world or age that contrasts sharply with the current state of affairs, which is perceived as flawed. Whenever a human be-

ing or a community becomes fully aware that human life as currently experienced is in some way imperfect, the natural response is to dream of a future age in which the imperfections of this age will vanish. What the perfected age will look like and how it will come to be is the common agenda of all eschatologies; the differences in these visions reflect the differences in the value systems of the cultures that produce them.

We have called these eschatologies "visions," and so they are. They are all imaginative projections—none of them based on any solid experiential data—because the "age to come" has not as yet come. Some religions do suggest that we now have anticipations of that perfected age. Judaism, for example, understands *Shabbat* as "a foretaste of the age to come"; and Christianity claims that since the advent of Jesus, the ultimate state of affairs is already "here" mysteriously. These anticipations, however, are only pale reflections of the full glory of what will be in the hereafter.

JEWISH ESCHATOLOGY

Jewish eschatology is one of the richest in the history of humanity. It decisively shaped the thinking of Christianity and Islam and, through them, the culture of Western civilization to this day. As with every other theme in Jewish thought, Jewish eschatology has a history of its own. Its full flowering is the product of talmudic (Rabbinic) Judaism. But almost every eschatologic theme elaborated in talmudic literature has its roots in the Bible. In what follows, I will concentrate on the biblical material, only suggesting how it was transformed by the later tradition.

Jewish eschatology is structured in three dimensions: the individual, the national, and the universal. It answers three broad questions: What will be the ultimate destiny of the individual human being (usually, but not only, the individual Jew), of the Jewish people, and of human civilization or even the cosmic order as a whole? It is not always easy to separate out these three dimensions, particularly the universal and national dimensions, but they will be kept in mind. As I proceed, I will also trace the evolution of these dimensions through four broad periods of history: the Pentateuchal era; the time of the pre-exilic prophets; the time of the postexilic prophets; and the Persian and Hellenistic period, which brings the Bible to a close.

THEOLOGICAL ASSUMPTIONS

The ground for all of Jewish eschatology lies in the three basic assumptions of biblical religion: First, the God of Israel is the ultimate reality whose will governs everything that transpires on earth. Second, God has entered into a unique relationship with the people Israel. Third, God cares deeply about the world, about human society, and about human history—and will intervene to shape events to reflect an ultimate purpose.

Immediately obvious from this listing is the direct interrelationship between the national and the universal dimensions of biblical religion as a whole and hence of biblical eschatology as well. God's intentions for Israel are part of a broader plan for humanity, and God cares enough and has the power to bring this vision into place.

THE TORAH BACKGROUND

But the eschatologic implications of this relationship become explicit only in prophetic literature, dating roughly from the 8th to the 5th centuries B.C.E. The fate of human civilization apart from the people Israel is of little concern in the Torah itself. In fact, whereas the prophets envision an age when all nations will worship the one true God, the God of Israel, Deut. 4:19 seems unperturbed by the fact that "other peoples" worship the sun, moon, and stars; this seems to be their legitimate lot.

But what is of central concern in the Torah is the ultimate destiny of the people Israel. At this stage of development, however, that destiny does not go beyond Israel's entry into the Promised Land. Israelite history—in the Torah itself—is the story of a community that journeys from Egyptian slavery to its promised homeland.

Again and again, the Torah describes what will take place when "you enter and possess the land that the LORD your God is assigning to you" (Deut. 11:31). The following chapter details some of the laws that are to be observed in the Land, concluding that if these commands are heeded, then "it will go well with you and with your descendants after you forever" (12:28). Note the term "forever"; it is the hallmark of a genuine eschatologic vision. The Land itself is portrayed in ideal terms, in stark contrast to the desert wilderness through which they are now journeying and to the Egypt that they have left behind. Their destiny in this Land is also portrayed in ideal terms: "You will dominate many nations, but they will not dominate you" (15:6). It is the place that God has chosen (16:16), or has chosen "to establish His name" (14:24).

Much later, biblical religion postulated that the ultimate destiny of the individual does not end with death. There is not a hint of this suggestion in the Torah, however, or in most of the Bible. There, human death is final. Whatever ideal state an individual Israelite can hope to achieve is restricted to one's lifetime and is conditional on heeding God's commands: material prosperity, good health, length of days, self-determination, posterity, and peace (28:1–14). With the possible exceptions of Elijah and Enoch, all biblical personalities die and their death is final.

PRE-EXILIC PROPHECY

This rather restricted eschatologic canvass expands considerably with the emergence of prophetic religion in the years preceding the destruction of Jerusalem and the Temple at the hand of the Babylonians (586 B.C.E.).

Four eschatologic themes pervade the writings of this period: (a) the anticipation of a "day of the LORD," a transforming event portrayed in cosmic terms that will mark God's ultimate triumph over Israel's idolatrous enemies and will inaugurate an everlasting age of peace and prosperity. (b) Out of the ruins of this cosmic upheaval, a "remnant of Israel"—those who kept faith with God throughout the tribulations of the age—will emerge to become the foundation for a new world order. (c) In this ideal society, Zion will become the religious center of the world, and all the nations will stream there to learn the ways of the Lord from Israel. (d) This entire scenario will be presided over by a charismatic figure, an ideal king—the "messiah" (from the Hebrew: *mashi·aḥ,* "anointed one"; Israelite kings were crowned by being anointed with oil). All of these themes figure in the writings of this pre-exilic period.

Amos, the earliest of this group of prophets (mid-8th century B.C.E.), describes the approaching day of the Lord as a day of ultimate judgment when God will destroy all evildoers, both among the nations and in Israel. This upheaval will affect the structures of nature as well. It will be "a day of darkness, not light" (Amos 5:18), a day when "the sun will set at noon" (8:9).

This theme is echoed even more forcefully by Amos's later contemporary Isaiah (commonly understood to be the author of most of chapters 1 to 39 of the Book of Isaiah). On that day, "all will be overcome by terror," the earth will be desolate, sinners will be wiped out, stars will not give out light, the sun will be dark when it rises, heaven will be shaken, and the earth will "leap out of its place, at the fury of the LORD of Hosts." God will "requite the world its evil . . . and put an end to the pride of the arrogant and humble the haughtiness of tyrants" (Isa. 13:6–16).

This vision of a universal, cosmic day of judgment marks the dramatic transformation from the familiar age to its eschatologic ideal. It is a purgative event, cleansing the world of its evil. But out of the destruction, there will emerge those who "seek Me" (Amos 5:4), or those who "seek good and not evil (5:14), "the remnant of Joseph" (5:15) with whom God will deal graciously. This theme of "the remnant of Israel" is echoed again by Isaiah (Amos 10:20, 11:11), who gives his son the symbolic name *Sh'ar Yashuv,* "a remnant shall return" (7:3).

In the work of Amos's contemporary Hosea (and later, more explicitly, in Jeremiah), this

theme is enlarged by the promise that God's love for this saving remnant will lead to a renewal of God's covenant with Israel as in the days following the Exodus (Hos. 2:17). This renewed covenant will be such that, in contrast with the "old" covenant, it will be incapable of dissolution (2:21–22).

The tight connection between the national and the universal dimensions of this ideal age to come is most explicit in the prophecies of Isaiah. No eschatologic vision in the entire body of classical Jewish literature is more eloquent than Isaiah's prophecy of the events that will take place "in the days to come" (Isa. 2:2–4; Mic. 4:2). The nations will come to Israel to learn God's ways, "for instruction (*torah*) shall come forth from Zion, the word of the LORD from Jerusalem." Then follows Isaiah's promise of the end of warfare: "Nation shall not take up sword against nation; they shall never again know war."

Isaiah 11:1–9 expands the vision of this ideal age. It will be an age of justice and equity, an age when even the tensions of nature will be abolished, when wolves will dwell with lambs, when little boys will herd calves and beasts of prey, when oxen and lions will eat straw. Finally, Isaiah prophecies the end of idolatry: "For the land shall be filled with devotion to the LORD as waters cover the sea."

All of this will be brought to pass under the aegis of an ideal king of the Davidic dynasty; he will be guided by "the spirit of the LORD," a spirit of wisdom and insight, of counsel and valor, of devotion and reverence for God (Isa. 9:5–6, 11:1–2). These are the original prooftexts for the doctrine of a messianic figure who will initiate and reign over the ideal age to come. In the later literature, this doctrine will undergo major transformations toward a supernatural or angelic being; but at this stage, the king is very human—albeit endowed with charisma, political savvy, and religious gifts.

Note also that at this stage, the eschatologic age will be thoroughly within history, not in some new age that follows the "end" of history (or of time as we know it). Isaiah 2:2 refers to the events that will take place "in the days to come," not, as in the later tradition, "at the end of days." That understanding of the phrase will emerge only much later.

The prophet who bridges the pre-exilic and postexilic traditions is Jeremiah. Jeremiah prophesied in the years immediately before and after the destruction of Jerusalem and the First Temple in 586 B.C.E. He witnessed the destruction and went into exile with his people.

In Jeremiah's day, his predecessors' vision of God's day of judgment assumed a vivid and imminent reality; the Babylonian army was literally at the gates of Jerusalem. Jeremiah also understood the trial to come as God's inescapable purging of the nation from its sins. But again, despite the gloom that pervades much of his book, Jeremiah's vision of consolation and return are among the most poignant in all of prophetic literature. The streets of Jerusalem will once again resound with the sounds of marriage celebrations (Jer. 33:10–11). Jeremiah 31 is the single most eloquent prophecy of return and redemption in all of prophetic literature. Jeremiah envisions the re-establishment of the Covenant. This time, however, it will be placed in "their innermost being" and inscribed "in their hearts" so that it will never again be dissolved. Most important, God promises to reach into the heart of Babylonia and bring the exiles back to their homeland (29:10–14), for God is the Lord of history, and God's power is not limited by geography.

POSTEXILIC PROPHECY

The destruction of Jerusalem and the subsequent exile totally transformed the national dimension of Jewish eschatology. The themes of return to Zion, the rebuilding of Jerusalem, and the reinstitution of the Temple sacrificial cult become central in all postexilic prophecy. After the destruction of the Second Temple at the hands of Rome in 70 C.E., they remain central in all of talmudic and post-talmudic eschatology until the dawn of modernity.

Ezekiel's prophecies, like those of his slightly older contemporary Jeremiah, bridge the pre-exilic and postexilic periods, although he prophesied only in Babylonia. For Ezekiel, Israel's

national rebirth is a form of bodily resurrection as in his vision of the dry bones that come to life again (Ezek. 37). He describes in great detail his vision of Jerusalem and the rebuilt Temple as the center of a new Israelite polity. Following Jeremiah, he insists that the new Israel will enjoy "a new heart and a new spirit" to follow God's rules faithfully, and then, the old intimacy will be re-established: "You shall be My people and I will be your God" (36:26–28). Ezekiel's vision of God's final war against the evil kings of Gog and Magog echoes the earlier visions of a "day of the LORD" and was elaborated in the apocalyptic visions of the later Jewish and Christian eschatologies. In these visions, the setting for the eschatologic scenario transcends history. We are no longer in Isaiah's "days to come," but rather at the end of history as human beings know it.

This cosmic eschatologic vision is echoed by the anonymous author of Isa. 40 to 55, commonly called "Deutero-Isaiah" or "Second Isaiah," who prophesied in the middle of the 6th century B.C.E. This prophet portrays the age to come as a total transformation of nature: "I will turn the desert into ponds, the arid land into springs of water" (Isa. 41:18). But Deutero-Isaiah's most notable contribution to the development of biblical eschatology is his portrayal of the "Servant of the LORD" (49:3) who suffers, is ultimately vindicated, who bears the sins of his generation, and who will carry out God's ultimate plan for civilization. The precise identity of the servant is hotly debated in scholarly circles. Is the reference to Israel, to an elite body of Israelites, to a single person? The very notion of a suffering servant is a significant step in the development of the messianic idea in Judaism and, later, in Christianity.

THE PERSIAN-HELLENISTIC PERIOD

The edict of Cyrus, king of Persia, permitting Israelites to return to their homeland and to rebuild their Temple (539 B.C.E.) transformed the terms of biblical eschatology in yet another way. Jeremiah's vision of a return to Zion and Ezekiel's vision of the rebuilt Temple now assume a much greater immediacy. However limited and compromised the work of rebuilding might have been, the prophecies of Haggai and Zechariah (late 6th century B.C.E.) and of Malachi (early 5th century B.C.E.) exude a messianic fervor. They spur the people to rebuild the Temple and see its completion as the mark of God's forthcoming kingdom. They view the appointment of Zerubbabel, a scion of the Davidic monarchy, as governor of the Judean province, to be a fulfillment of Isaiah's messianic promises (Zech. 4:6–7, 6:9–14). Malachi is the source for the notion that Elijah will return as the herald of "the awesome, fearful day of the LORD" (Mal. 3:23), i.e., of the messianic age.

The author of Isa. 56 to 66—whose writings are commonly understood to be yet a third distinct text collected within the Book of Isaiah, dating roughly from the same period—brings together many of the eschatologic themes echoed throughout prophetic literature. God will gather all the nations of the earth to a new Jerusalem for the final judgment, the righteous will rejoice but the evildoers will be rebuked "in flaming fire." And just as "the new heaven and the new earth" that God will then create will endure, so will the new Israel, and "new moon after new moon, and Sabbath after Sabbath, all flesh shall come to worship Me" (Isa. 66).

THE DESTINY OF THE INDIVIDUAL

It is only at the very end of the biblical period that the ultimate destiny of the individual is viewed as transcending death. In almost all of the Bible itself, death is viewed as final. The most that one can hope for is to achieve a measure of blessing here on earth. Then we die, and after death God has no power over our destiny, nor can the dead enjoy any relation with God (Ps. 30:10, 115:17, 146:3–4). The probable reason for this silence reflects the wish to keep the realms of the human and the divine quite separate. Only God is eternal.

There are only three biblical texts that announce some form of life after death: Dan. 12

and Isa. 25:8 and 26:19. The first of these can be dated with some precision to 166–165 B.C.E. The latter two, from still another unit of the Book of Isaiah called the Isaiah Apocalypse (Isa. 24–27), are probably slightly earlier.

The Daniel text was written within the context of the persecutions of Antiochus IV, the villain of the *Ḥanukkah* story. It reflects the dilemma of the Jewish pietists who were being martyred precisely because of their loyalty to God. If there is no reward for piety, why die the death of a martyr? The author answers that there is reward for the righteous and punishment for the evildoer, but only after their death. Therefore, "Many of those that sleep in the dust of the earth will awake, some to eternal life, others to reproaches, to everlasting abhorrence" (Dan. 12:2). The reference here is clearly to bodily resurrection.

Of the two Isaiah texts, the more interesting is Isa. 25:8: "(God) will destroy death forever." This presages the later tradition's claim that at the end, not only will the dead be resurrected but also death itself will die.

Not reflected in the Bible itself but of central importance in the later tradition is the Greek notion that human beings are a composite of two substances—a material body and a spiritual soul—and that what never dies is the human soul. It leaves the body at death and enjoys eternal life with God. In time, the two doctrines of bodily resurrection and spiritual immortality were conflated: The body disintegrates at death, the soul remains with God. Then, at the end of days, God reunites the body and the soul; and the individual, now reconstituted as in life on earth, comes before God for judgment. That doctrine was central to all of Jewish eschatology until the dawn of modernity in the late 18th century.

POSTBIBLICAL JUDAISM

In the later tradition, the three dimensions of Jewish eschatology—the universal, the national and the individual—undergo significant transformations. Of the three, it is only the most ancient, the universal dimension, that retains its hold on the Jewish consciousness almost without change, to our day. All denominations continue to recite *Aleinu,* the prayer that articulates Isaiah's vision of an age of universal peace and justice under the dominion of the God of the people Israel. Meanwhile, with the dawn of the Jewish enlightenment at the end of the 18th century, the Reform movement in Judaism denied the national dimension of the Jewish identity, and with it the dream of a return to Zion and a reconstitution of the Temple service. A part of that dream, at first in a starkly secular form, came to be embodied in political Zionism.

Of the twin doctrines of bodily resurrection and spiritual immortality, medieval Jewish philosophy (particularly in the thought of Maimonides) and Jewish mysticism clearly preferred the latter. Most modern Jewish thinkers have agreed with this predilection. Modern prayer books from the liberal (Reform and Reconstructionist) movements modified the traditional liturgy to reflect this preference. That process has begun to be reversed in recent decades, but that reversal is still in its beginning stages.

Jewish eschatologic thinking may be elusive and imaginative. Nevertheless, its centrality to any authentic reading of Jewish thought is beyond dispute. What divides modern Jewish thinkers is precisely how to understand these teachings. Are they literally true prophecies or events that will occur in some indefinite future (as traditionalists would have it)? Or are they subjective, poetic, or, to use a more technical term, mythic constructs, designed to help us structure and give meaning to our lives here on earth (as liberal thinkers suggest)? That difference, of course, reflects a far more profound division on how modern Jews understand Jewish religion as a whole.

Worship, Ritual, and *Halakhah*

BIBLICAL CONCEPTS OF HOLINESS

Baruch A. Levine

"Holiness" is difficult to define or to describe; it is a mysterious quality. Of what does holiness consist? In the simplest terms, the holy is different from the profane or the ordinary. It is "other," as the phenomenologists define it. The holy is also powerful or numinous. The presence of holiness may inspire awe, strike fear, or evoke amazement. The holy may be perceived as dangerous, yet it is urgently desired because it affords blessings, power, and protection.

The *Sifra* conveys the concept of "otherness" in its comment to Lev. 19:2, which teaches that "you shall be holy" means "you shall be distinct [*p'rushim tihyu*]." This means that the people Israel, in becoming a holy nation, must preserve its distinctiveness from other peoples. It must pursue a way of life different from that practiced by other peoples. This objective is epitomized in Exod. 19:6: "You shall be to Me a kingdom of priests and a holy nation [*goy kadosh*]." This statement also conveys the idea, basic to biblical religion, that holiness cannot be achieved by individuals alone, no matter how elevated, pure, or righteous. It can be realized only through the life of the community, acting together.

The words of Lev. 19:2 pose a serious theological problem, especially the second part of the statement: "For I, the LORD your God, am holy." Does this mean that holiness is part of the nature of God? Does it mean that holiness originates from God? The predominant view in Jewish tradition has been that this statement was not intended to describe God's essential nature but, rather, His manifest, or "active," attributes. To say that God is "holy" is similar to saying that He is great, powerful, merciful, just, wise, and so forth. These attributes are associated with God on the basis of His observable actions: the ways in which He relates to mortals and to the universe. The statement that God is holy means, in effect, that He acts in holy ways: He is just and righteous. Although this interpretation derives from postbiblical Jewish tradition, it seems to approximate both the priestly and the prophetic biblical conceptions of holiness.

In biblical literature, there is a curious interaction between the human and the divine with respect to holiness. Thus in Exod. 20:8, the Israelites are commanded to sanctify *Shabbat* and to make it holy; and yet verse 11 of the same commandment states that it was God who declared *Shabbat* holy. Similarly, God declared that Israel had been selected to become His holy people; but this declaration was hardly sufficient to make Israel holy. To achieve a holiness of the kind associated with God and His acts, Israel would have to observe His laws and commandments. The way to holiness, in other words, was for Israelites, individually and collectively, to emulate God's attributes. In theological terms, this principle is known as *imitatio dei* (Latin: "the imitation of God"). The same interaction is evident, therefore, in the commandment to sanctify *Shabbat,* with God and the Israelite people acting in tandem to realize the holiness of this occasion. God shows the way, and Israel follows.

The biblical term for holiness is *"kodesh."* Although the noun is abstract, it is likely that the perception of holiness was not thoroughly abstract. In fact, *"kodesh"* had several meanings, including "sacred place," "sanctuary," and "sacred offering." In addition, in certain syntactic positions, Hebrew nouns function as adjectives. The Hebrew phrase *shem kodsho,* for example, does not mean "the name of His holiness" but, rather, "His holy name." This leads to the conclusion that in the biblical conception holiness is not so much an idea as

it is a quality, identified both with what is real and perceptible on earth and with God. Indeed, the only context in which a somewhat abstract notion of holiness is expressed relates to God's holiness. God is said to swear by His holiness, just as He swears by His life, His faithfulness, and His power. Mortals speaking of God recognize that holiness is inextricable from Him; it is a constant, divine attribute.

The overall content of Lev. 19, with its diverse categories of laws and commandments, outlines what the Israelites must do to become a holy people. It includes many matters of religious concern, as we understand the term: proper worship; observance of *Shabbat;* and the avoidance of actions that are taboo, such as mixed planting and consumption of fruit from trees during the first three years after planting. What is less expected in ritual legislation is the emphasis on human relations: respect for parents, concern for the poor and the stranger, prompt payment of wages, justice in all dealings, and honest conduct of business. Even proper attitudes toward others are commanded.

In this latter respect, Lev. 19 accords with prophetic attitudes, indicating that the priesthood was highly receptive to the social message of the Israelite prophets. Holiness, an essentially cultic concept, could not be achieved through purity and proper worship alone; it had an important place in the realm of societal experience. Like the Decalogue and other major statements on the duties of humans toward God, this chapter exemplifies the heightened ethical concern characteristic of ancient Israel.

Holiness, as a quality, knows no boundaries of religion or culture. Very often, the reactions it generates are perceived by all, regardless of what they believe. Similarly, places and objects as well as persons considered to be holy by one group may be perceived in the same way by those of other groups. There is something generic about holiness, because all humans share many of the same hopes and fears and the need for health and well-being. A site regarded as holy by pagans might continue to be regarded as such by monotheists; indeed, some of the most important sacred sites in ancient Israel are known to have had a prior history of sanctity in Canaanite times. (The Bible ignores the pagan antecedents and explains their holiness solely in terms of Israelite history and belief.)

Despite many differences between Israelite monotheism and the other religions of the ancient Near East, the processes through which holiness was attributed to persons, places, objects, and special times did not differ fundamentally. Through ritual, prayer, and formal declaration, sanctification took effect. In biblical Hebrew, these processes are usually expressed by forms of the verb קדש especially the *pi·el* stem *kiddesh,* "to devote, sanctify, declare holy."

The gulf between the sacred and the profane was not meant to be permanent. The command to achieve holiness, to become holy, envisions a time when life would be consecrated in its fullness and when all nations would worship God in holiness. What began as a process of separating the sacred from the profane was to end as the unification of human experience, the harmonizing of people with their universe and of people with God.

PRIESTS AND LEVITES IN THE BIBLE AND IN JEWISH LIFE

Baruch Frydman-Kohl

Although the collective people Israel was intended to be a "kingdom of priests and a holy nation" (Exod. 19:6), the *kohanim* (priests) from the tribe of Levi were singled out as the bearers of unique sacred status. They were the primary religious actors in the biblical pattern of worship, both in the wilderness tabernacle and in the Jerusalem Temple.

The word *kohen* occurs more than 800 times in the Bible, but there are far fewer references to the Levites (*L'viyyim*), whether as individuals, a clan, or the tribe of Levi. The religious status

of *L'viyyim* was secondary to that of the *kohanim*. The root לוה came to mean "escort" or "accompany." It apparently refers to the Levites' role of assistants to the priests in the sanctuary to whom they were assigned (*n'tunim;* Num. 3:9, 8:19). They may have served as a human barrier between the *kohanim*, restricted by rules of purity, and the people as a whole.

The Levites were noted for their loyalty to God during the crisis of the Golden Calf. The Torah stipulates that they were responsible for guard duty (*mishmeret*) and porterage (*avodah*) for the portable tabernacle of the wilderness (Num. 3). The levitical role as guardians of the sacred sanctuary was a lifelong duty that continued throughout the Temple period. The Books of Chronicles describe the Levites as being responsible for the care of the Temple's courts and chambers, the cleaning of the *k'lei kodesh* (ritual materials), the preparation of *matzot* and the *minḥah* offering, and the supervision of the Temple measures; they were also the singers or choir in the Temple (1 Chron. 23:26–32). They assisted the *kohanim* as magistrates and judges (1 Chron. 23:4, 26:29) and in overseeing the Temple treasury (1 Chron. 26:20). And they appear to have had a role as teachers and interpreters of Torah (Neh. 8:7; 2 Chron. 17:7–9).

Although the Levites were dedicated to God when substituted for firstborn sons (Num. 3) and were consecrated in a special ceremony (Num. 8), they did not have a distinctive dress, possess any ritual "power," or have a specific role in the sacrificial system.

The Levites did have a minor degree of sanctity and were sustained by tithes from the people (Lev. 27:32–33; Num. 18:21), because they possessed no ancestral land. Their landless position contributed to a precarious social and economic status, often associated with the alien, the orphan, and the widow. They were assigned to live in 48 cities scattered throughout the territory of the various tribes (Num. 35:1–8; Josh. 21:1–41).

In later Jewish tradition, the *L'viyyim* were accorded the honor of being called to the Torah for the second *aliyah* (after the *kohanim*). The historic levitical task of assisting the *kohanim* was preserved in the tradition of the Levites' washing the hands of the priests before their formal blessing of the congregation. Funerary art has symbolized *kohanim* by two hands in the position assumed during the traditional priestly blessing; and many gravestones designate *L'viyyim* with the symbol of a pitcher of water in recognition of their role in this ritual. Children of Levites were exempt from the commandment of redemption of the firstborn, because the *L'viyyim* were originally designated as replacements for the firstborn.

The institution of the priesthood was widespread in the ancient Near East. Non-Israelite priests are mentioned in the Bible (e.g., Melchizedek in Gen. 14:18; priests of Dagon in 1 Sam. 5:5). The qualifications and functions of non-Israelite priests were not necessarily the same as those of the Israelite *kohanim*. For example, in Canaanite religion, there were female priests, but the Israelite priesthood was limited to males, initially the firstborn and later the male descendants of Aaron from within the tribe of Levi.

During a certain period, all *L'viyyim* appear to have been eligible to serve as *kohanim*. This is clear from phrases that make no distinction between the two groups, such as "the priests the Levites" (*ha-kohanim ha-L'viyyim*) in Deut. 17:18 (see also 10:8–9, 33:8–10). Eventually, however, the specific designation of the *kohanim* as members of one family within the tribe of Levi came to be accepted as the basic "history" of priestly appointment.

In the biblical period, the tasks of the *kohanim* included the following:

- Officiation at rituals connected to the sacrificial system.
- Blessing the people (Num. 6:22–26).
- Sounding the trumpets on festivals and new moons (Num. 10:10).
- Blowing the *shofar* on *Yom Kippur* of the jubilee year (Lev. 25:9).
- Ascertaining the will of God through oracular means, such as the Urim and Thummim (Exod. 28:30; Num. 27:21).

- Determining the fate of a woman suspected of adultery (Num. 5:11–31).
- Ascertaining and treating impurities and various eruptions on the skin, clothing, and buildings (Lev. 11, 13–15).
- Judging the people along with the elders (Deut. 21:5; 1 Sam. 4:18; Ezek. 44:24).
- Preserving traditions and instructing the people (Deut. 31:9–13, 33:10; Mal. 2:7) and the king (Deut. 17:18–19).

The Torah continually stresses the twin ideals of holiness and purity (*k'dushah* and *tohorah*) in relation to the Israelites, the portable wilderness camp, and the sanctuary. The *kohanim* served as the symbolic exemplars of those spiritual paradigms and consequently lived with strict personal requirements of purity and holiness. The core of biblical information about these obligations is found in Lev. 21–22. The priests were enjoined to have contact with the dead of only their immediate family (Lev. 21:1–4,10–12) and were limited in their marital relationships (Lev. 21:7–8,13–15).

Kohanim were prohibited from marriage to a prostitute, divorcée, or *ḥalalah* (someone born of a parent from a priestly family and a mate from a category of people forbidden to *kohanim*). The rationale for these forbidden marriages apparently was linked to the notion that sexual relations for a *kohen* must be limited to those untainted by problematic lineage or unsuspected of immoral behavior. The *ḥalalah* had a blemished lineage, the prostitute engaged in immoral sexual behavior that may have been linked to Canaanite religious practices, and the divorcée was associated with sexual infidelity (via interpretation of Deut. 24:1: *ervat davar,* "unseemliness").

The Talmud added two categories to the list of prohibited relations. The first was the convert, because gentile women were considered to have lived in a licentious society in which they were presumed to have had illicit sexual relations. The second was the *ḥalutzah,* a woman who after her first husband's death had been married to her husband's brother and later was compelled to divorce him. The *kohen gadol* was subject to a more restrictive standard of purity and prohibited from marriage even to a widow.

Just as animals offered as sacrifices had to be physically sound (Lev. 22:18–25), so *kohanim* had to be free of disabilities or deformities (Lev. 21:16–24). *Kohanim* were not to be exposed to working in society at large. Therefore, they were to be supported by donations and by designated portions of some of the sacrificial offerings (Lev. 6:16,29, 22:10–16). To be allowed to consume this designated (sacred) food, the *kohanim* had to fulfill special obligations that included ritual washing of hands and feet (Exod. 30:17–21), refraining from alcohol (Lev. 10:8–9), and maintaining a state of ritual purity. Like all other Israelites, *kohanim* also were prohibited from consuming meat that came from animals that had not been properly slaughtered (Lev. 22:8; Ezek. 44:31).

The *kohen gadol*—probably a shortened version of the phrase *ha-kohen ha-gadol me-eḥav* (the priest who is superior to his brothers, Lev. 21:10)—was a hereditary position from the descendants of Phinehas, Aaron's grandson (Num. 25:10–13). The investiture and clothing of the high priest resembled that of ancient Near Eastern royalty. He was anointed with oil (1 Sam. 10:1; 2 Kings 9:6), he wore special clothing (Exod. 28:2–4) made with gold and a special purple dye (*t'kheilet*), and wore a unique headdress (*mitznefet*) with a frontlet (*tzitz,* Exod. 28:36–39) and a diadem (*nezer,* Exod. 29:6, 39:30, Lev. 8:9). The *mitznefet* was compared to a crown (Ezek. 21:31; Isa. 62:3). Other priests also were anointed, as were the sacred vessels and utensils (Exod. 30:26–30; 40:9–15), in ceremonies that paralleled the construction and the dedication of the tabernacle (Exod. 29; Lev. 8).

The Bible differentiates between the roles of priest, prophet, and sovereign, although the *kohanim* were linked to the royal court because of the close connection between political and divine authority (1 Kings 1:32). Thus the appointment of a new cadre of priests was an essential element in the rebellion of Jeroboam

(1 Kings 12:31). They were identified as central to the recovery or discovery of the book of the Torah and the subsequent revolution under King Josiah (2 Kings 22–23). *Kohanim* were among the elite of the kingdom of Judah taken into exile by the Babylonians (2 Kings 25:18–20).

The prophet Ezekiel, a *kohen,* provided spiritual support to the exiles in Babylon, as well as a vision of a rebuilt Jerusalem Temple. The *kohen* Ezra led the return of the exiles from Babylon and the rebuilding of the Temple. Under Ezra's leadership, *kohanim* began the public reading and interpretation of the Torah on a regular basis outside of the Temple walls, thus lending authority and prestige to a new expression of religious life (Neh. 8:5–11). In the absence of a Davidic king, the *kohen gadol* became the head of the Jewish community.

During the days of Antiochus IV in the 2nd century B.C.E., many priestly families actively supported the Seleucid monarch's efforts to impose Hellenistic customs in Jewish life. In this way, the spiritual stature of the *kohanim* was degraded to a concern for wealth, power, and influence. Other priestly families opposed this moral and ritual disgrace, especially the family of Mattityahu, the Hasmoneans. This is one of the factors that led to the Maccabean revolt, led by the Hasmoneans.

After the Hasmonean victory, Mattityahu's son Simon assumed the role of *kohen gadol.* This was a departure from the tradition of designating the *kohen gadol* by direct lineage. The disregard for that tradition, as well as eventual moral corruption of the priesthood under the Hasmoneans, led to the rise of the Pharisees as the primary teachers of Torah in place of the *kohanim,* the hereditary teachers of Torah.

After the destruction of the Temple, the role of the *kohanim* was significantly altered. The presence of the *kohanim* was not necessary for public worship, which now consisted of prayer, not sacrifice. Other activities clearly linked to the Temple ritual (sanctified food and determination of purity) were no longer in practice. Nonetheless, the social and legal distinctiveness of the *kohanim* was preserved, and certain rituals were instituted to recall the sacrificial service.

The most solemn and significant ritual of ancient Judaism was the *Yom Kippur* rite of the high priest. It fused three aspects of sanctity: the holiest individual, the holiest time, and the holiest space. It was the moment when forgiveness and atonement for sin could be achieved. Since the destruction of the Temple, the ritual of the *kohen gadol* has been re-enacted during the *Musaf* service of *Yom Kippur,* through the recitation of the *Avodah* service. Incorporating poetry and the Mishnah's description of the *Yom Kippur* ritual, the *Avodah* service serves as a substitute for the Temple practices. The recollection of the service of the high priest is the focal point of the *Yom Kippur* liturgy.

The Sages assumed that the holiness of the *kohanim* did not end with the destruction of the Temple. The biblical command to sanctify the priest (Lev. 21:8: *v'kiddashto*) was interpreted as applying to the ritual prerequisites of blessing the people and being called first to the Torah. The Talmud (BT Git. 59b) justified this as a biblical law and to ensure the "ways of peace"—to prevent arguments about who should receive the initial *aliyah.* Prohibitions against marrying converts or divorcées (BT Yev. 94a) and the prohibition of contact with the dead (BT Sanh. 5b) continued, as did the obligation of redeeming firstborn sons.

The marriage of a *kohen* with one of the women prohibited by the Torah is still forbidden according to the most restrictive understanding of Jewish law. Consequently, a *kohen* may not marry a divorcée or convert in the Orthodox community and in the State of Israel. Since the 1950s, the Conservative Movement, through the CJLS, has maintained a different approach to this biblical prohibition. The Talmud recognizes these marriages as having legal standing, for although such marriages violate strict rules of biblical purity for the *kohen,* they do not transgress laws of holiness (which would be violated by an adulterous or incestuous relationship). Following this pre-

cedent, the Conservative rabbinate came to view such marriages as permitted.

This development illustrates the general approach of Conservative Judaism to Jewish law. In 1947, the chairman of the CJLS indicated that a "*kohen* who married a divorcée should be barred from being called up to the Torah first." But by 1954, the reconstituted CJLS had accepted a responsum by Ben Zion Bokser and Theodore Friedman that validates such a marriage. This decision was based on four considerations: (a) although prohibited by biblical law, such a marriage has legal standing, (b) priestly lineage in modern times is doubtful, (c) the status of the *kohen* in the community has changed, and (d) the status of the divorcée is no longer stigmatized. Nonetheless, in recognition of the violation of a biblical commandment, the *kohen* is required to relinquish his status and the marriage ceremony is to be consciously modest and private.

A similar process of legal development took place regarding the rabbinical prohibition of marriage between a *kohen* and a convert. In 1946, the CJLS approved the instruction of a convert engaged to marry a *kohen,* stipulated that the rabbi should not solemnize the marriage ceremony, but reluctantly permitted such a marriage if the *kohen* were determined to marry the woman. The committee ruled that because such a marriage would have legal status it would be preferable to an interfaith marriage with an unconverted woman. In 1968, Isaac Klein permitted such a marriage, arguing that (a) although prohibited by rabbinical enactment, such a marriage has legal standing; (b) priestly status today is questionable; (c) the status of the *kohen* in the community has changed; and (d) non-Jews should not be considered licentious. Klein contended that to maintain the traditional prohibition would be a *ḥillul ha-shem.* Unlike the earlier decision of the committee regarding the divorcée, because this prohibition is of rabbinical origin, the *kohen* is not required to renounce any priestly prerogatives.

In 1997, the CJLS approved a responsum by Arnold Goodman that contends that no stigma should be attached to marriage to divorcées or converts because in our time divorce and conversion are commonplace. Moreover, given the high rate of intermarriage, everything should be done to encourage endogamy. The biblical prohibition was abrogated, no restrictions were placed on the marriage ceremony, and the status of the *kohen* remained unchanged. Conservative rabbis, because of the variety of responsa adopted by the CJLS, may legitimately act in accordance with any one of three halakhically sanctioned decisions. They may maintain the biblical prohibition of marriage between a *kohen* and a divorcée as well as the rabbinical prohibition of marriage between a *kohen* and a convert; they may follow the responsum that allows the marriage to take place (placing limits on the subsequent status of the *kohen*); or they may follow the 1997 decision that allows such marriages to take place without restriction.

Some Conservative rabbis, influenced by 20th-century democratic trends, have argued that it is possible to disregard the priestly privilege of being called first to the Torah. This was legitimated in a responsum by Mayer Rabinowitz and adopted by the CJLS in 1990, based on the unreliability of family traditions about priestly lineage.

The ritual in which *kohanim* formally bless the congregation during the *Musaf* service on festivals (Hebrew: *oleh l'dukhan;* Yiddish: *dukhenen*) also fell out of favor in most synagogues. A number of Conservative congregations, however, have restored this traditional practice, attaching renewed significance to the spiritual dimension of this public ritual and desiring to preserve its religious significance for the families who treasure maintaining their tradition of being *kohanim.*

Although all the Temple rituals were performed by male *kohanim,* wives of *kohanim* were permitted to partake of the food designated for priestly families, unless they were divorced or widowed. This permission also extended to unmarried daughters of *kohanim.* In 1989, based on a responsum by Joel Roth, the CJLS permitted daughters of *kohanim* to

receive *aliyot* as *b'not kohen.* However, the status of being in the family of *kohanim* is still transmitted through the father, not the mother, even though she is the daughter of a *kohen.*

The historic prohibition against priestly contact with the dead may have had its origins in an abhorrence of the Egyptian cult of the dead. The Israelite *kohen,* elected to serve the living God, was forbidden contact with the dead except for his immediate family. Historically, *kohanim* avoided entering cemeteries and did not serve on burial societies. Conservative Judaism has officially retained these practices. However, in 1929, the CJLS approved a responsum by Louis Epstein that argues that all *kohanim* in post-Temple Judaism are already ritually impure, cannot become further defiled, and thus are no longer subject to possible impurity by contact with the dead. Although not explicitly permitting a *kohen* to enter a cemetery, the responsum recognizes that there are grounds for leniency.

The *kohen* and the *Levi* symbolize two types of religious behavior. *Kohanim* represent the structure and order of Jewish ritual, whereas the Levites—with their service, song, and celebration—reflect the ideal of divine inspiration. Both are essential to the nurturing of a spiritual life.

The main institutions of biblical religion—prophets, kings, and a central temple—no longer exist in their original form. Prophecy has ended. The monarchy is no more. Sacrifice has ceased. Yet Jews have been able to sustain a religious culture by adapting and developing the core biblical traditions. The *kohen* and *Levi* symbolically serve as a living remnant of the earliest strata of biblical religion and as testimony to the creative power of that adaptive process.

SACRIFICES

Gordon Tucker

IN BIBLICAL NARRATIVE

Throughout the ancient world, human beings connected with their gods in part through sacrifice. Altars abounded and received gifts of all manner of animals and, in some cases, of human beings as well. It is, therefore, not surprising that the narratives in the Hebrew Bible, including the Torah itself, are full of instances in which altars are built as vehicles of sacrifice and communication.

It begins when Cain and Abel, the first sons of the first couple, bring offerings to God, the former a gift of produce, and the latter a gift of "the choicest of the firstlings of his flock" (Gen. 4:3–4). Only Abel's sacrifice is accepted (how this was manifest is not made clear), and the reader is left with the unmistakable impression that sacrifice of animal life, with the life-sustaining blood and suet being offered to the Creator, is preferable to God. True, the Torah will later set forth rules for grain offerings (*minḥah,* see Lev. 2); and from the prominence it gives to the *minḥah* the Sages will centuries later extract the homiletical lesson that "the one who can give much is equal to the one who can give little, as long as their thoughts are directed to Heaven" (M Men. 13:11). But the simple narrative of Cain and Abel does not betray such sentiments.

The next sacrifice of which we hear is the one that Noah offered after surviving the Flood. Here our impression from the story of Cain and Abel is reinforced with a striking anthropomorphism. Noah presented "burnt offerings" (*olot*), i.e., animals turned entirely to ash and ascending smoke. Indeed, the word for "altar" (*mizbei·aḥ*) means "a place of slaughter." The text continues: "The LORD smelled the pleasing odor [*rei·aḥ ha-niḥo·aḥ*], and the LORD said to Himself: 'Never again will I doom the earth because of man'" (Gen. 8:21). The smoke of these burnt animals has created a sensation (literally!) in heaven, and the aroma of these sacrificial gifts has moved God to temper the anger that humanity is prone to ignite through its inevitable sins. There is no

mistaking the message here about the power and efficacy of animal sacrifice in creating peace between God and humanity.

The patriarchs come on the scene next; and throughout their lives and many travels, their peak moments of communicating with God are invariably marked by the creation of altars and the offering of animal sacrifices. A few examples will establish the pattern:

- The LORD appeared to Abram and said, "I will assign this land to your offspring." And he built an altar there to the LORD who had appeared to him (Gen. 12:7).
- And the LORD said to Abram . . . "Raise your eyes and look out from where you are, to the north and south, to the east and west, for I give all the land that you see to you and your offspring forever." . . . And Abram moved his tent, and came to dwell at the terebinths of Mamre, which are in Hebron; and he built an altar there to the LORD (Gen. 13:14–18).
- That night the LORD appeared to him and said, 'I am the God of your father Abraham. Fear not, for I am with you, and I will bless you and increase your offspring for the sake of My servant Abraham.' So he built an altar there and invoked the LORD by name" (Gen. 26:24–25).
- Thus Jacob came to Luz—that is, Bethel—in the land of Canaan, he and all the people that were with him. There he built an altar and named the site El-bethel, for it was there that God had revealed Himself to him when he was fleeing from his brother (Gen. 35:6–7).
- So Israel set out with all that was his, and he came to Beer-sheba, where he offered sacrifices to the God of his father Isaac. God called to Israel in a vision by night: "Jacob! Jacob!" He answered, "Here." And He said, "I am God, the God of your father. Fear not to go down to Egypt, for I will make you there into a great nation" (Gen. 46:1–3).

Over and over, the evidence of God's providence is accompanied by a gift on an altar, the column of smoke symbolizing the link between heaven and earth.

The motif of individuals offering animals to God in times of intense joy or stress or in personal revelatory moments continues throughout the Hebrew Bible. Sometimes those who offer the sacrifices are not Israelites at all. Jethro, Moses' Midianite father-in-law, makes such an offering (Exod. 18:12) when he learns of God's awesome victory over the Egyptians. The somewhat less sympathetic characters Balak and Balaam do likewise when they attempt (in vain) to invoke the power of God against Israel (Num. 23:1–2,14–15,29–30). And Saul, the first king of Israel, both celebrated a crucial victory over the Philistines and attempted to divert divine displeasure over his soldiers' ravenous eating of the spoils without offering the blood, by setting up an ad hoc altar and offering on it the blood (and presumably the suet and entrails) of all the animals to be eaten (1 Sam. 14:31–35).

The Torah's narrative takes another critical turn with respect to sacrifices in the second book of the Pentateuch. With the Exodus from Egypt, sacrifice takes on, for the first time, the dimension that will ultimately define it as a legal category, i.e., the public, communal dimension. The paschal sacrifice that marks the Exodus, and is to commemorate it in each subsequent year (see Exod. 12, esp. vv. 24–27), is no individual expression of thanks-giving, as was Jacob's offering at Bethel when he returned safely home after many years of exile. This was a community rite, one that bound the members of the community to one another as much as it bound each individual to God, whom the sacrifice addressed. (The *Pesaḥ Haggadah,* composed centuries later, captured this function perfectly when it noted that the "wicked" son's reference to "your service" meant that he was removing himself from the community and thereby striking at the very heart of the rite.) The paschal lamb was the first communal, or public, sacrificial rite. Significantly, it became the most central rite for an Israelite to perform (or, equivalently, the most serious rite to neglect to perform; see Num. 9:13).

Two months after the Exodus, the Israelites reached the wilderness of Sinai, and there they had their next great group experience—this time not one of liberation—but of law giving. And at Sinai as well, sacrifices were offered on behalf of the community. Significantly, they were offered in the presence of 12 pillars representing the 12 tribes. Here was another public sacrificial ritual intended once again to unite not only heaven and earth (both the smoke and the pillars pointed heavenward) but the people themselves through the sprinkling of blood on them (Exod. 24:4–8).

One more communal sacrifice marked this formative period of the nation. When they completed the construction of their tabernacle in the desert and the Presence of God appeared to inaugurate the new sacred space, the community was instructed to bring "a he-goat for a purification offering; a calf and a lamb, yearlings without blemish, for a burnt offering; and an ox and a ram for an offering of well-being to sacrifice before the LORD . . . for today the LORD will appear to you" (Lev. 9:3–4). From that moment on, the altar was a public instrument, designed to receive the offerings of the community. To be sure, individual sacrifices would still be offered there, but they were voluntary by and large. (Purification offerings had as their primary purpose permitting individuals with ritual impurities to regain eligibility to enter the sacred precincts; if such individuals were content to stay away, they would have very few obligatory gifts to bring.) This was a major turning point, a departure from the notion that individuals would sacrifice at any place they chose (witness Saul's ad hoc call for a rock to be provided for this purpose, in the passage cited above from 1 Sam. 14). And this is a central focus of the central book of the Torah, Leviticus. The Torah largely reflects a priestly ideology, and Leviticus does so more than any other book. Sacrifice, as the Torah conceives it, is to be made public, regulated, and kept in the control of the priesthood. For the Torah, in other words, sacrifice is not properly the stuff of narrative, but rather of the law.

IN BIBLICAL LAW

The legal parts of the Torah introduce various restrictions and regulations into the practice of animal slaughter and into sacrificial slaughter in particular. The story of Saul's ad hoc sacrifice in 1 Sam. 14 makes it clear that there was already a deeply entrenched understanding among the people that the blood belonged to God and could not be eaten without committing sacrilege. Thus it is not at all surprising that one of the Torah's chief restrictions is that, even among sacrifices that were to be eaten, both the blood and the suet had to be dashed or turned into smoke on the altar, i.e., returned to God (Lev. 7:22–27). But there were more restrictions to be imposed by the Torah, and several among these almost certainly were not already known or practiced by the folk.

The very institution of the priesthood meant that the personnel involved in sacrifice were being both restricted and professionalized. This is a strong kind of regulation, for it creates uniformity, guards against syncretistic influences, and imposes an inevitable conservatism on forms of worship. Even if a sacrifice were to be brought by an individual, or a family or a clan, only the officially designated priest determined how it would be offered, not the owners of the sacrifice.

Moreover, the place of offering was no longer wide open. Sacrifice must be offered at an official altar: "This is in order that the Israelites may bring the sacrifices which they have been making in the open—that they may bring them . . . to the . . . entrance of the Tent of Meeting . . . that the priest may dash the blood against the altar of the LORD . . . and that they may offer their sacrifices no more to the goat-demons after whom they stray" (Lev. 17:5–7). This passage makes several things plain: (a) sacrifice, when left to individuals, is prone to absorb idolatrous practices; (b) one way to avoid this is to create a priestly monopoly on sacrificial rites; and (c) another way to complete this regulatory process is to restrict the number of altars that have official status and confine sacrifice to those. Later, in Deut. 12, the Torah would go further: It would insist

that there not be even a limited number of official altars, but rather one single altar, at the central shrine that would be the only legitimate place of sacrifice. No greater regulatory scheme than this could be envisaged.

Thus we have regulation of personnel and place and, through them, regulation of practice. Here we must mention one other great concern that the Torah exhibits with respect to sacrifices.

It was noted that in the ancient world, altars received all manner of animals as sacrifices and, in some cases, human beings as well. Ancient Israel was not an exception to this phenomenon: "They have built the shrines of Topheth in the Valley of Ben-Hinnom to burn their sons and daughters in fire—which I never commanded, which never came to My mind" (Jer. 7:31; see also 19:5–6; Ezek. 20:31). Indeed, when Exod. 13:12 speaks of the obligation to dedicate firstborns to God in gratitude for the Exodus, it uses the same language that the Torah uses to describe the abomination of child sacrifice, in Lev. 18:21 and Deut. 18:10. (The term rendered in this translation as "you shall set apart" literally means "to pass," as through fire.) Apparently, the vocabulary of dedication was unalterably affected even by the ancient practices that the Torah meant to sweep away. And its method for sweeping it away included not only the legal prohibitions on child sacrifice given in Lev. 18 and 20 and in Deut. 18 but also the most powerful and gripping narrative to be found in the Torah. Genesis 22 tells the tale of Abraham receiving a command to sacrifice his son Isaac, only to be told as he demonstrates his piety and willingness to offer even this to God that God does not want him to carry out the offering. A ram is offered in Isaac's place, and thus does the Torah both acknowledge the existence of this practice in Israel and instruct us that its strict regulation of sacrifice would, first and foremost, preclude the offering of such frightful gifts.

What all of the elaborate biblical regulation produced, then, was this array of authorized sacrifices:

1. *Olah* (burnt offering; also called "holocaust" in the scholarly literature): brought from males of the herds or flocks, or from birds, with the entire carcass of the animal (but for the hide) turned into smoke on the altar. These could be individual donations, but primarily included all of the public offerings for daily, *Shabbat,* and festival worship (Lev. 1; Num. 28–29).

2. *Minḥah* (grain offering): brought from flour, generally functioning as an accompaniment to *olot,* although standing by itself at certain key agricultural observances and other rites (Lev. 2, 23; Num. 5:15).

3. *Sh'lamim* (sacrifice of "well-being"): brought from males or females of the herds or flocks; individual "shared meals" in which the owner of the animal receives the flesh to eat after the blood is dashed and other vital parts are turned to smoke on the altar (Lev. 3), except for two instances (Lev. 9:4, 23:19). This category includes offerings brought for thanksgiving and offerings of firstborn or tithed animals (Lev. 7:12–15, 27:32; Num. 18:17–18).

4. *Ḥattat* (purification offering): brought by individuals or public officials for inadvertent sins of a grave nature, sometimes from the herd (male), and sometimes from the flock (male or female). In the most grave cases, the entire carcass is burnt outside the Temple; but in most cases, the sacrificial animal is shared with the altar, but the flesh is eaten by priests, rather than by the sinner (Lev. 4).

5. *Asham* (reparation offering): brought to expiate trespasses against sacred things, for fraud against others, for false oaths, and in a variety of other special cases (Lev. 5:14ff., 14:1–32; Num. 5:5–10, 6:13–21). Its procedure matches that of the *ḥattat* (Lev. 7:7), although it is often accompanied by a monetary fine.

6. *Pesaḥ* (the paschal lamb): offered annually by every Israelite household and eaten by them in commemoration of the Exodus (Exod. 12; Num. 9).

IN BIBLICAL PROPHECY AND LATER THOUGHT

Although this essay is meant to treat the subject of the sacrifices primarily from the Torah's point of view, a few closing comments are in

order with respect to the prophetic traditions in the Hebrew Bible. As we have seen, priestly traditions strove to harness and regulate sacrificial modes of worship that predated biblical law. Prophetic traditions, meanwhile, often contrasted the mediated, and frequently mechanical, nature of priestly worship with the immediate, passion-driven goal of heeding God's words and fulfilling the divine mandate for justice. Thus both Amos and Jeremiah offered reminiscences of Israel's early and formative encounters with God as being devoid of sacrifice (Amos 5:22–25; Jer. 7:21–23). Micah, not going quite that far, nevertheless asserted a clear hierarchy of values in which sacrifice is subordinate to justice and goodness (Mic. 6:6–8). The notion that God needs our sacrifices was particularly offensive to the circles, prophetic or otherwise, that promoted the idea of a universal, all-powerful God (this is expressed, for example, in Isa. 40:15–17, 66:1–4; Ps. 50:7–15). Hosea, for his part, advanced (according to the compelling interpretation of H. L. Ginsberg) the idea that easy access to sacrifice (e.g., through a multiplicity of altars) could actually remove disincentives to sin by providing ready-at-hand expiation:

> For Ephraim has multiplied altars—for guilt;
> His altars have redounded to his guilt:
> The many teachings I wrote for him
> Have been treated as something alien.
> (Hos. 8:11–12)

The oft-expressed prophetic coolness for sacrifice as a pillar of worship found expression later in Rabbinic Judaism as well. A whole school of thought claimed (contrary to biblical chronology) that Israel's first official altar was established in the wilderness only as a reaction to the Golden Calf (Tanḥ. T'rumah 8). In other words, it was needed to regulate urges that could lead to idolatry. In the Middle Ages, Maimonides followed this reasoning to its logical conclusion and claimed that the sacrificial laws of the Bible were a divine technique to wean the Israelites away from idolatrous practices (*Guide* III:32). And as for contemporary Conservative liturgy, it has made a striking substitution in the daily prayer service; in lieu of the traditional recitation of texts related to sacrificial laws, it recalls Yoḥanan ben Zakkai's saying (in the wake of the Temple's destruction in 70 C.E.) that the atonement formerly provided by the altar can be gained at least as well from acts of kindness. Study of texts exhorting us to such acts follows. As a climax, the contemporary liturgy has us ask God to make us into true successors of Aaron the high priest. It is not, however, his priestly functions that are invoked but rather the characteristics by which the tradition remembers him, as an exemplar of love of humanity and the pursuit of peace (see *Siddur Sim Shalom,* pp. 14–19, and *Siddur Sim Shalom for Shabbat and Festivals,* pp. 68–70).

BIBLICAL PRAYER

Reuven Hammer

One of biblical Judaism's most important gifts to the world is personal prayer—prayer that is spontaneous, informal, and independent of sacrifices or magical rites. Such prayer was not to be found in the ancient world from which the Bible emerged. Pagan worship consisted of sacrificial rites tied to magical utterances, formulas that the participants believed would yield desirable results automatically. Such rites were performed for the benefit of the deities, not only for the benefit of human beings.

These pagan deities were believed to depend on humanity for food and drink; they were subject to forces outside themselves. This is not true for the God of Israel. Underlying biblical prayer is the Torah's concept of God as above nature, uncontrolled by other forces (including fate), and requiring neither physical gifts nor metaphysical aid to exist. In spite of its cultic significance, sacrifice in Israel became a means for human beings to express themselves and relate to God. In the Mesopo-

tamian flood epic, the gods are described as anxiously waiting for the flood to be over so that humans can once again supply them with sacrificial food. "The gods smelled the pleasing odor. The gods crowded like flies about the sacrificer." All that remains of this in our flood story is the enigmatic phrase, "The LORD smelled the pleasing odor" (Gen. 8:21). If the will of God is supreme, sacrifices at most can be a method of persuading God of the sincerity of human intentions and thus bring about His acceptance of human desires.

Ritual sacrifices were offered in the sanctuary in the wilderness. Yet the Torah prescribes virtually no prayers, blessings, or verbal formulas for recitation during the sacrificial ritual—something unheard of in the pagan world—thus leading some scholars to speak of the sanctuary as "a realm of silence." The confession of sin on *Yom Kippur* (Lev. 16:21) constitutes an exception. When an individual is required to confess wrongdoing before bringing an offering (Lev. 5:5), it is not clear whether or not this is part of the sacrificial ritual. A verbal recitation of the history of Israel was made when presenting the first fruits (Deut. 26:4–10). The only words given priests to recite are those of the Priestly Blessing (Num. 6:22–26). They were uttered in the Temple but only after the ritual had been completed; thus they were not connected with the ritual. As Yeḥezkel Kaufmann pointed out, all of this can be explained as an indication of a desire to divorce sacrifices from the magic verbal formulas so common elsewhere. Eventually, however, probably after the Temple had been established in Jerusalem, silence was overcome in ways that did not negate the original intent of avoiding pagan practices. The levitical singers filled the Temple with song. The pilgrims chanted their psalms there. Individuals came to pray, and at various occasions prayer gatherings were held within its precincts (Jer. 7). None of this, however, was linked to the sacrifices.

Verbal forms of worship developed at the same time that sacrificial rituals were practiced. Prayers became the sacrifices of our lips; sacrifices became nonverbal prayers. Neither was considered acceptable if the individual was insincere or had violated the basic moral demands of the deity. Thus the prophets could denounce them both with equal vehemence:

> If you offer Me burnt offerings—or your
> grain offerings—
> I will not accept them;
> . . .
> Spare Me the sound of your hymns,
> And let Me not hear the music of your lutes.
> But let justice well up like water,
> Righteousness like an unfailing stream.
> (Amos 5:22–24)

Indeed, because it was divorced from sacrifice, prayer was now free to become a spontaneous utterance, a way of relating to and communicating with the Almighty, praising, thanking and blessing God, pleading with God and asking that He heed our words. Although prayer in the Torah is relatively brief and simply formulated, it contains all of the elements of later, more fully developed prayer.

PRAYER IN THE TORAH

The Sages may have been exaggerating and anachronistic when they ascribed the three daily prayers of Judaism (evening, morning, and afternoon) to the three patriarchs: "Abraham ordained the morning prayer . . . Isaac ordained the afternoon prayer . . . Jacob ordained the evening prayer" (BT Ber. 26b). They were not wrong, however, in linking the origins of even later Rabbinic prayer to the stories of the patriarchs and of Moses. Their prayers fall into three categories: petition, praise and thanksgiving, and confession and forgiveness.

In the case of Abraham himself, we find little that we would identify as prayer, because Abraham and God speak in open dialogue. It is the language of prayer, however, when Abraham says of his son, "Oh that Ishmael might live by Your favor!" (Gen. 17:18). His servant, who has less free access to God, utters a petition in Gen. 24:12–14. After he addresses

God specifically as "O LORD, God of my master Abraham," he states his request, beginning "grant me good fortune this day." When his petition has been granted, he expresses his thanksgiving, "Blessed be the LORD, the God of my master Abraham, who has not withheld His steadfast kindness from my master" (Gen. 24:27). The use of the word "blessed" (*barukh*) is taken from expressions in which someone is said to be worthy of God's blessing—as in Melchizedek's blessing of Abraham: "Blessed be Abram of God Most High" (Gen. 14:19), which is followed by the proclamation "And blessed be God Most High" (v. 20). Although, as Greenberg has pointed out, *"barukh"* is not exactly appropriate when used in reference to God (as only God can bestow blessing), it came to be the most common expression of Jewish prayer, indicating our proclamation of God's greatness and our thankfulness to God. In Rabbinic times it became the basic formula of prayer, "Blessed are You, O LORD" (*Barukh Attah Adonai*). This is presaged in one late biblical passage: "Blessed are You, O LORD, God of Israel our father, from eternity to eternity" (1 Chron. 29:10).

We are told that "Isaac pleaded with the LORD on behalf of his wife because she was barren; and the LORD responded to his plea" (Gen. 25:21), but we are not given the words of his prayer. Later, Isaac blesses his son Jacob when mistaking him for Esau in another petitionary prayer, "May God give you of the dew of heaven" (Gen. 27:28). Note that none of these prayers is accompanied by a sacrifice.

Jacob prays when he leaves his home, asking for God's protection and help during his exile. Later he offers a more humble prayer expressing thanksgiving: "O God of my father Abraham and God of my father Isaac, O LORD . . . I am unworthy of all the kindness that You have so steadfastly shown Your servant. . . . Deliver me, I pray, from the hand of my brother" (Gen. 32:10–13). Note the similarity to the prayer of Abraham's servant, especially the way in which God is addressed.

The Book of Exodus is replete with prayer and references to prayer. The Israelites cry out because of their bondage (Exod. 2:23). The Sages remarked that "cry" always refers to prayer (Sifrei Deut. 26). Moses also speaks to God in the language of complaint, "O LORD, why did You bring harm upon this people" (Exod. 5:22–23). This questioning of God became a characteristic theme of the prophets and of the psalms (Pss. 10, 13). Particularly revealing of the Bible's understanding of the function of prayer is the incident of Miriam stricken with leprosy as a punishment by God. Moses prays for her in what the Sages called the shortest of all prayers—five Hebrew words: "O God, pray heal her!" (Num. 12:13). Moses does not perform any ritual action but simply implores God's help. And God remains free to answer his plea or not.

Prayers of confession and forgiveness are exemplified in the pleas of Moses on behalf of the people: "Stiff-necked though this people be, pardon our iniquity and our sin, and take us for Your own" (Exod. 34:9). "Pardon, I pray, the iniquity of this people according to Your great kindness, as You have forgiven this people ever since Egypt" (Num. 14:19).

The Torah has one magnificent example of formal, poetic prayer, which served as a pattern for other prayers thereafter: the Song of the Sea (Exod. 15:1–19). Quite different from other prayers in the Torah, it is unique in its formal literary structure. Most scholars believe it to be a later work stemming from the period of the kingdom (10th century B.C.E. or later). This magnificent hymn of salvation served throughout the ages as the archetype of prayers of thanksgiving.

In summation, the prayers of the Torah are basically brief, spontaneous utterances of praise, petition, or thanksgiving, couched in simple language and devoid of ritual elements.

PRAYER IN THE PROPHETS

The historical books that form the section known as "First Prophets" continue the informal prayer found in the Torah. David confesses his sin in language much like that used by Moses in confessing the sin of the Israelites, "I have sinned grievously in what I have done.

Please, O LORD, remit the guilt of Your servant, for I have acted foolishly" (2 Sam. 24:10). When attempting to revive a dead child, Elisha "prayed to the LORD" (2 Kings 4:33), probably much as Moses did for Miriam. Samson asks for strength using the petition formula of the Torah, "O Lord GOD! Please remember me, and give me strength just this once, O God" (Judg. 16:28). Hannah's vow (1 Sam. 1:11) is similar to that of Jacob. As a general rule, prayer in the books of early prophets is more highly developed than prayer commonly found in the Torah. The art of prayer developed greatly during the 10th century B.C.E., and this is reflected in these books. It is no longer the spontaneous outpouring of the heart, but rather the sophisticated literary expression of human feelings, needs, and desires. Consider Hannah's prayer of thanksgiving as an example. It is hardly that of a simple woman:

> My heart exults in the LORD;
> I have triumphed through the LORD.
> I gloat over my enemies;
> I rejoice in Your deliverance (1 Sam. 2:1).

As in the Torah's Song of the Sea, it seems probable that a literary psalm has been inserted here for dramatic effect. What a contrast it is to her simple petition: "O LORD of Hosts, if You will look upon the suffering of Your maidservant and will remember me and not forget your maidservant, and if you will grant Your maidservant a male child, I will dedicate him to the LORD for all the days of his life; and no razor shall ever touch his head" (1 Sam. 1:11). The further description of her prayer—"Now Hannah was praying in her heart; only her lips moved, but her voice could not be heard" (1 Sam. 1:13)—so impressed the Sages that they took it as the example of how all of us should pray (BT Ber. 31a–b).

Another example of literary expression is Solomon's prayer at the dedication of the First Temple. Although we cannot be certain that this is what Solomon actually said, we may assume that it reflects the attitudes common during the period of the First Temple. If we are hard pressed to find in the Torah a mention of prayer within the sanctuary, here we find prayer—not sacrifice—emphasized as the main activity of the Temple. Solomon emphasizes the words of prayer with little attention to sacrifice. A few lines from his long prayer (1 Kings 8:23–53) will suffice to indicate its tenor.

> Yet turn, O LORD, my God, to the prayer and supplication of your servant. . . . May Your eyes be open day and night toward this House . . . may You heed the prayers which Your servant will offer toward this place. And when You hear the supplications which Your servant and Your people Israel offer toward this place, give heed in Your heavenly abode—give heed and pardon (1 Kings 8:28–30).

Interestingly enough, this plea for God to hear prayers and supplications of Israel uttered in and toward this House is followed by a not insignificant offering of 22,000 oxen and 120,000 sheep! (v. 63). What is God's response? "I have heard the prayer and the supplication which you have offered to Me" (1 Kings 9:3). Not a word about the sacrificial offering.

Just as the later prophets could speak about the sacrifices as less significant, so here too they are a subsidiary issue. Yes, sacrifice was an integral part of Israel's worship. Israel could not do without it, but God certainly does not need it.

David, in opposition to all accumulated Israelite tradition, had conceived the idea of creating a permanent house for God, as opposed to the nomadic tent of the *mishkan*. King Solomon carried this out. The dedication of this Temple was seen as the capstone of the new order, as God's approval of the change and His choosing of David's line: David's city and now Solomon's Temple.

But what about the form of worship? Did Solomon bring about a change in what went on in the central shrine? That is a difficult question to answer with utter certitude—perhaps impossible—but it seems very likely that he

did. As we have seen, to Solomon, the house was more important for prayer than for sacrifice. True, he follows the Torah's instructions. He does not introduce prayer into the sacrificial service itself. However, he does emphasize the singing of psalms to accompany pilgrims (Ps. 122), to greet them (Ps. 134), and to serve as hymns in the Temple at the great gatherings for thanksgiving (Ps. 118) or at times of trouble (Ps. 115). Here too he may have followed the lead of his father who, according to 1 Chron. 16:7, had commissioned the writings of general psalms for recitation in the new tabernacle. The Torah makes no mention of singing or composition in the descriptions of the duties of the Levites, but David is said to have appointed a group of them "to invoke, to praise, and to extol the God of Israel . . . with harps and lyres" (1 Chron. 16:4–5).

It seems quite likely then, that the development of "professional" prayer—of literary as opposed to spontaneous prayer utterance—was prompted by the institution of the Jerusalem Temple, and that such literary prayers as the Song of the Sea and Hannah's prayer also stem from that time.

No wonder the prophet of the exile, Isaiah, could bestow upon the Temple that was to be rebuilt the title "house of prayer for all people" (Isa. 56:7). Solomon's contribution was to ensure that prayer became the focus. The Temple of the Lord—the Temple of silence—became the House of Prayer.

Prayer plays a major role in the lives and words of the prophets who lived during this period of the kingdom. Following the example of the father of prophecy, Moses, they pray to God on behalf of the people, interceding with Him on its behalf. They go far beyond that, however, and use spontaneous prayer as their own method of communication with God. They complain to God, and ask Him to relieve them from their tasks. Jeremiah provides clear examples of this: "Ah, Lord GOD! Surely You have deceived this people and Jerusalem, saying: It shall be well with you—yet the sword threatens the very life!" (Jer. 4:10). The prophets' role as intermediary for the people is clear from God's message warning Jeremiah, "do not pray for this people, do not raise a cry of prayer on their behalf; for I will not listen when they call to Me on account of their disaster" (11:14). Daringly, Jeremiah challenges God, "You will win, O LORD, if I make claim against You, yet I shall present charges against you: Why does the way of the wicked prosper? Why are the workers of treachery at ease?" (12:1). See also his complaint in 15:15–18, including the brazen "You have been to me like a spring that fails, like waters that cannot be relied on." He asks God for help against his enemies in 18:19–23 in language strongly reminiscent of passages from Psalms.

THE BOOK OF PSALMS

The Sages ascribed the authorship of the Book of Psalms to David (BT BB 14b). They did not mean by this, however, that he wrote all 150 of them. Indeed, in the same passage they acknowledge that David included psalms written by others. Many psalms seem to have been composed by professional writers assigned to provide psalms for the Temple choirs. Scholars are divided over the dates of the psalms. All would agree that the vast majority stem from the time of the First Temple (ca. 960 B.C.E.) and reflect the practices of that period. In a sense, Psalms is the first Israelite prayer book. Unlike later prayer books, however, it lacks texts prescribed for specific services of prayer. With a few exceptions, the psalms are not intended for recitation at specific occasions. There seems little doubt that some of them were written for historical events now lost to memory. Some may have been written to accompany specific rituals. Many believe that Pss. 93 and 97, for example, were written for the New Year. The psalms are presented as a collection of prayer and meditation that can be used in a variety of moods and situations by individuals and by the community. Many of them, such as Pss. 95–99, 113–118, 145–150, have been incorporated into the liturgy. As models for prayer, they express cries from the heart and whispers from the soul.

The psalms reflect three major modes of prayer: thankful acknowledgment (*hodu*), blessing (*bar'khu*), and praise (*hall'lu*). An examples of *hodu* can be seen in Ps. 136. When celebrating great victories or recalling wondrous deeds of the past, the people Israel used these formulas to thank and acknowledge God. The use of *bar'khu* can be seen in Ps. 135, proclaiming God's greatness and faithfulness to the people Israel. The *hall'lu* form can be seen in Pss. 148 and 150. These are songs of ecstatic praise, driven by powerful emotion.

Jewish prayer, as it developed during the Second Temple period and after its destruction (200 B.C.E.–200 C.E.), used the insights of biblical prayer, its various forms, and its terminology. Almost every prayer is built of biblical phrases. Large sections of the service consist of passages from Psalms and other sections of the Bible. Most of all, Jewish worship—as well as that of Judaism's daughter religions—has been shaped by two biblical insights: that prayer and sacrifice are independent, and that prayer can be uttered by anyone, at any time, and in any place. As the Sages taught, prayer is "service of the heart" (BT Taan. 2a).

Biblical prayer transformed what had been stilted and stylized ritual utterances into a method of communication in which all human beings can freely voice their deepest emotions before God. Though He may be "enthroned on high" (Ps. 113:5), God listens to the words of His creatures on Earth.

SHABBAT AND THE HOLIDAYS

Joel Roth

SHABBAT

Shabbat is a unique institution in the Torah. All other holidays and festivals, among the Israelites and other ancient peoples, are linked to cycles of the moon or to the seasons of the sun's movement. Only *Shabbat,* as many scholars have noted, is completely severed from such a linkage. In Gen. 2:1–3, *Shabbat* is the culmination of Creation, marking God's rest from creative work. If Creation establishes God's supremacy over space, *Shabbat* establishes God's supremacy over time. Between the two, the essence of biblical theology is established: God is entirely free from any constraints of nature. God is the sovereign of space and time, and *Shabbat* is the symbol of that divine transcendence.

The Exodus version of the Decalogue (Exod. 20:8–11) links *Shabbat* directly to Creation. Israel is commanded to rest because God rested. The connection between *Shabbat* and Creation is also found explicitly in Exod. 31:16–17 and seems most consonant with Lev. 23:3. The Deuteronomic version of the Decalogue (Deut. 5:12–15), on the other hand, while retaining the prohibition against *m'lakhah,* predicates it on the liberation from Egypt. This version's emphasis seems to be far more ethically oriented than that of Exodus, which focuses on the sanctity of the day itself rather than on its social value. The two emphases are not mutually exclusive, although it is admittedly somewhat difficult to see the connection between the view of Deuteronomy and the holiness of *Shabbat,* which is its essence, according to both versions of the Decalogue.

The prohibition against *m'lakhah* stands at the core of *Shabbat.* Yet the Torah gives no definition of *m'lakhah.* Several activities are forbidden in the Torah and the rest of the Bible: gathering from the field (Num. 15:32–36), traveling (Exod. 16:29–30), kindling fire (Exod. 35:2–3), doing business and carrying (Isa. 58:13, Jer. 17:22, Amos 8:5), agricultural activity (Exod. 34:21), treading in winepresses, and loading animals (Neh. 13:15–18). However, there is no definitive list or definition. Not surprisingly, in subsequent eras much time has been devoted to clarifying this central factor of *Shabbat* observance.

The Talmud defines 39 basic categories of forbidden activity, called *avot m'lakhah.* All

Shabbat prohibitions are included within these *avot.* Each one of them (*av*) has derivative prohibitions, called *toladot.* The Sages themselves promulgated additional prohibitions called *sh'vut,* which are designed to prevent inadvertent violation of *avot* and *toladot* and to protect the spirit of *Shabbat* rest. The Talmud deduces these basic categories from the activities involved in the construction of the tabernacle, which are delineated in Exod. 35 in close proximity to the commandment to observe *Shabbat.* But even the Talmud does not provide an abstract definition of the concept of *m'lakhah.*

Nonetheless, there is near unanimity among modern scholars that *m'lakhah* is correctly defined as: "A constructive human act, initiated on the Sabbath, demonstrating supremacy over nature." Advocates of this definition include S. R. Hirsch, M. M. Kaplan, and A. J. Heschel. It is a reasonable thesis that makes sense of *Shabbat* prohibitions as they are delineated in the Talmud and the post-talmudic codes and responsa. Even more, it is supported by the biblical account of Gen. 1 and 2, in which God's work of creation is defined as *m'lakhah* (2:2–3). The definition encapsulates the rationale underlying *Shabbat* prohibitions: Humans desist from controlling nature on *Shabbat* to give concrete expression to their recognition that human mastery over nature and human creative abilities are divine gifts. Knowledge of the definition allows the details of *Shabbat* prohibitions to be seen and understood in better perspective.

Shabbat observance has been perceived as a source of pleasure and delight since the biblical period. Isaiah especially calls it a day of delight (Isa. 58:13). For the Sages, *Shabbat* is a precious gift (BT Betz. 16a) and its observance is a taste of the world to come (BT Ber. 57b). If all Jews would observe one *Shabbat* as it ought to be observed, the Messiah would come (Exod. R. 25:12). It becomes the focus of the week's attention, and full appreciation of it is truly possible only for those who observe it (BT Shab. 119a).

It was Aḥad ha-Am who said that more than the Jews have preserved *Shabbat* observance, *Shabbat* has preserved the Jews. His words remain true.

THE HOLIDAYS

The Pilgrimage Festivals

The holidays known best as *Pesaḥ, Shavuot,* and *Sukkot* are the pilgrimage festivals on which, by law of the Torah, one was obligated to present oneself at God's shrine. They are called *shalosh r'galim* in Hebrew.

The Torah lists the cycle of annual holidays in several places: Exod. 23:12–19, 34:18–23; Lev. 23; Num. 28–29; and Deut. 16. Some of them are more complete than others. *Pesaḥ* is also mentioned in Exod. 13:6–8. The details of these various listings constitute the pieces to a puzzle; and it is difficult, probably impossible, to complete the puzzle with certainty.

Some facts, though, are clearer than others. The holidays that are called *ḥag* in the Torah are pilgrimage festivals. In Exodus, the pilgrimages are as follows:

- *Ḥag ha-matzot:* festival of the unleavened bread (in Exod. 12:14, Lev. 23:6, and Num. 28:17, only the first day is a pilgrimage day; in Exod. 13:6, it is the last day that is the pilgrimage; and in Ezra 6:22, all seven days are pilgrimage days).
- *Ḥag ha-katzir:* festival of the reaping of harvest (although in Exod. 34:22 this holiday is called *ḥag shavu·ot,* the festival of weeks).
- *Ḥag ha-asif:* festival of the ingathering.

Exodus does not give specific dates for these festivals. Rather, the first is defined as being "at the set time in the month of Abib." Perhaps the phrase should be translated as "at the advent of the new moon of the season of soft-seeded grain ears." That timing is linked to the fact that Israel had been redeemed from Egypt in that season. The second is defined as occurring at the time of the harvest of "the first fruits of your work" (Exod. 23:16) and at the time of the "first fruits of the harvest of the wheat" (34:22). (Do these define each other?

Does the latter define the former? A puzzle!) And the third is defined as occurring "at the end of the year, when you gather all of your work in from the field."

Leviticus 23 distinguishes between *Pesaḥ,* which occurs on the 14th of the first month, and *ḥag ha-matzot,* which begins on the 15th. The second holiday of Exodus is not named at all in Leviticus. Rather, it mandates a counting period of 50 days, at the conclusion of which an offering of new grain (wheat) is brought. This holiday is not called a *ḥag* in Leviticus, implying that no pilgrimage to the shrine was necessary. In Leviticus, the third pilgrimage of Exodus is called *ḥag ha-sukkot* (the festival of the booths), which lasts for 7 days, beginning on the 15th of the seventh month and culminating in a final (8th) day called *atzeret* (concluding assembly).

The Book of Numbers presents the distinction between *Pesaḥ* and the *ḥag ha-matzot.* The first occurs on the 14th of the seventh month and the second begins on the 15th with that day a pilgrimage. The second holiday is called *yom ha-bikkurim* (day of first fruits), which is defined as "your Feast of Weeks." However, like Leviticus, Numbers does not declare it a pilgrimage and defines the third pilgrimage as a nameless festival that lasts 7 days, beginning on the 15th day of the seventh month and culminating on an 8th day on which an *atzeret* (solemn assembly) is to take place.

Deuteronomy 16 does not distinguish clearly between *Pesaḥ* and the Feast of the Unleavened Bread. Instead it seems to combine the two together, stating in verse 1 that the people should "offer a Passover sacrifice," yet calling the pilgrimage by the name *ḥag ha-matzot* in verse 16. The second pilgrimage is called *ḥag (ha-)shavu·ot* by Deuteronomy and is defined as occurring after a count of "seven weeks from the time the sickle is first put to the standing grain." The third pil-grimage, called *ḥag ha-sukkot,* is celebrated for seven days "after the ingathering from your threshing floor and your vat." Regarding each of the three pilgrimages, Deuteronomy emphasizes that the celebration of the festival must take place "in the place where the LORD will choose to establish His name."

Of the three pilgrimage festivals, *Pesaḥ* is most clearly a historical holiday. Exod. 23:15 specifically links its observance with the Exodus: "You shall observe the Feast of unleavened bread . . . for it was then that you went out of Egypt." None of the listings of the holidays in the Torah calls this pilgrimage by any name that is linked to agricultural matters. Indeed, it would be difficult to do so, because *Pesaḥ* occurs just before the ripening of the grain in the spring. Yet, *Pesaḥ* appears in all of the listings in the Torah, even those that exclude the holidays now called *Rosh ha-Shanah* and *Yom Kippur,* and its inclusion in those lists indicates that it was also an agricultural holiday. One must say, therefore, that it had an agricultural element to serve as a counterpoint to *Sukkot*. *Pesaḥ* was the pilgrimage that preceded the harvest, and *Sukkot* was the pilgrimage that followed the end of the harvest.

Ginsberg hypothesized that the festival of the unleavened bread was originally celebrated at the time of the new moon of *Nisan,* just before the hardening of the barley. (This hypothesis is summarized by Baruch Levine in his commentary to Leviticus.) It was a seven-day festival, with the pilgrimage occurring on the seventh day. A separate sacrifice, the *pesaḥ* offering, was to take place near the home of each person on the eve of the first day of the festival. The second pilgrimage festival, originally known exclusively as *ḥag ha-katzir,* the pilgrimage of the reaping, was observed as a one-day pilgrimage on the full moon of the month of ingathering, *Tishrei* (September). All of these observances are predicated on the possibility of making the required pilgrimage to a shrine near home. Deuteronomy, with its newly ordained requirement to observe all pilgrimages in one central shrine, made the earlier calendar of festival observances difficult and impractical, if not impossible. Changes had to be made to accommodate the new requirement. The second pilgrimage could no longer take place at the beginning of the har-

vest because no one could afford to be away from the fields for the length of time needed to make a pilgrimage to the central shrine. So the festival was moved by seven weeks, from the beginning of the harvest to its end. The name of the pilgrimage was changed from *ḥag ha-katzir* (pilgrimage of reaping), which was no longer appropriate, to *ḥag ha-shavu·ot* (pilgrimage of weeks), marked by a period of counting of those weeks. The third pilgrimage was also moved so that it would not occur too close to the second. It is no longer called *ḥag ha-asif* (the pilgrimage of ingathering), because it now takes place after the produce has been processed. Its name is changed to *ḥag ha-sukkot* (the pilgrimage of booths). That name refers to the booths set up to accommodate the pilgrims who now ascend to the central shrine in a pilgrimage that has been extended to seven days, from its original one day.

By far the greatest changes necessitated by the Deuteronomic mandate occur in the celebration of *Pesaḥ* and the pilgrimage of *matzot.* Originally, the *pesaḥ* offering was made near one's home on the eve of the festival, and the actual pilgrimage to a shrine took place on the seventh day of the festival. This had become an impossible arrangement. The *pesaḥ* could now be offered only at the central shrine, and another pilgrimage offering was required seven days later at the same central shrine. People would have to arrive before the *pesaḥ* offering day and remain for the entire seven days, because there might well not be time to travel back and forth to home in that short span of time. So Deuteronomy mandates that the *pesaḥ* offering be made immediately before the onset of the pilgrimage of unleavened bread—serving also as the pilgrimage offering. And the pilgrimage now takes place on the first day of the festival instead of on the last day. After that first day, people can go home, although the requirement to refrain from eating leavened bread continues for an additional six days.

As *Pesaḥ* has no clear agricultural component in the Torah, *Shavu·ot* has no clear historical component in the Torah. Nonetheless, since Second Temple days, it carries a historical dimension as well, as the festival commemorating the revelation at Sinai—*z'man mattan torateinu,* the time of the giving of our Torah. This attribution is based on the dating of that revelation, intimated by Exodus 19, and seems to reflect an ancient tradition with echoes in 2 Chron. 15:10–13 and in some of the sectarian literature. Through this act, *Shavu·ot* acquires a historical dimension to accompany its agricultural dimension. The period of counting the seven weeks between *Pesaḥ* and *Shavu·ot* becomes not merely the counting of the period of the harvest, but the counting of the period between our liberation from Egyptian bondage to the beginning of nationhood through the act of revelation.

Deuteronomy and Leviticus call the third pilgrimage festival *ḥag ha-sukkot.* Deuteronomy gives no explanation of the name (although Ginsberg's explanation for it was offered above). Leviticus, however, does offer an explanation, stating in 23:42–43 that we are to dwell in booths for these seven days to remember that God "made the Israelite people live in booths when [God] brought them out of the land of Egypt." The explanation of Leviticus is replete with difficulties, not least of which is that the Israelites lived in tents during the wandering in the wilderness. The most likely explanation of the name is that the Torah is here imbuing with historical significance the practice of living in booths during the period of gathering in the grapes and fruits. It thus makes the third pilgrimage parallel to the other two pilgrimages in having both an agricultural and a historical significance.

Whatever the problems of putting together the pieces of the puzzle of the pilgrimage festivals in the Bible, the Rabbinic-halakhic tradition leveled the field. It made the festivals into a coherent system that incorporated the demands and the explanations of all the biblical passages. In addition to the names I have already referred to for the holidays, the Rabbinic tradition also refers to *Pesaḥ* as *z'man ḥeruteinu,* the period of our liberation, and to *Sukkot* as *z'man simḥateinu,* the time of our joy. For the Rabbinic tradition, *Shavu·ot,* which

marks the giving of the Decalogue, becomes the culmination of *Pesaḥ* and is known simply as *atzeret,* the concluding assembly. *Sukkot* is called simply *he-ḥag,* the holiday.

The High Holy Days

The Torah knows of no holiday called *Rosh ha-Shanah,* New Year's Day. It does ordain the first day of the seventh month (*Tishrei*) as a day on which the horn is to be sounded (Num. 29:1) or commemorated with blasts (Lev. 23:24). Jacob Milgrom noted that the choice of the new moon of the seventh month preserves the sabbatical cycle in the lunar calendar. Just as the seventh day is unique among days, the seventh new moon is unique among new moons. Neither of the biblical passages that mention this holiday explains the significance of the horn to be sounded. Most probably, it was to indicate the advent of the pilgrimage of *Sukkot,* which began exactly two weeks later. The day is defined as one of cessation from labor and for sacred assembly. But it is not a pilgrimage holiday.

Rabbinic tradition, reflecting the view that the world was created by God in the autumn, recasts this holiday as commemorating the world's creation and, more important, as a day when human beings are judged by God. The sounding of the *shofar* remains central to its observance but takes on a totally different significance. It becomes the impetus to self-reflection and repentance and a reminder to God of the test of Abraham's faith at the binding of Isaac, on the basis of which his descendants seek God's forgiveness. *Rosh ha-Shanah* inaugurates a period of 10 days, culminating in the final judgment of *Yom Kippur.*

Yom Kippur, the Day of Atonement, is mentioned in the festival listings of Leviticus and Numbers (although it is not called by that name in Numbers) and also at the end of Lev. 16. The latter chapter contains the detailed account of the purification ceremonies ordained for cleansing the sanctuary from the defilements of humans during the year (see vv. 16,19). The term *kippurim* refers to this cleansing and purging of the sanctuary. Leviticus 16:29–34 establishes the date of the purification as the 10th day of the seventh month and mandates that the purification ritual is to be accompanied by fasting and total cessation of labor. From Lev. 16 it is clear that the purification rites of *Yom Kippur* were a priestly matter, and that the people were not present at the sanctuary. That fact is sufficient to explain why neither Num. 29 nor Lev. 23 makes any mention of the purification rites of the sanctuary in their descriptions of the holiday that occurs on the 10th of the seventh month. Both include the requirements of fasting and refraining from all labor. Probably, the timing of purification of the sanctuary was intended to ensure that it was pure just before the advent of the masses of pilgrims on the 7-day pilgrimage that would follow in five days.

Rabbinic tradition, of course, personalized the atonement of the biblical holiday and made *Yom Kippur* into the culmination of a 10-day period of judgment by God of all human beings. Intimations of personal atonement can be read fairly easily into parts of Lev. 23. Thus the two nonpilgrimage holidays of the seventh month became in Rabbinic tradition, and in subsequent Jewish practice, the most personal of holidays, focused on individual responsibility for one's actions and for ultimate accountability before God's judgment.

DIETARY LAWS

Edward L. Greenstein

Virtually all cultures contain rules that regulate eating. We do not always notice these rules because they tend to be only implicit, but these rules encode cultural meaning. The Torah has an abundance of specific guidelines concerning what must be eaten on certain occasions and, in particular, what must not be eaten. These regulations carry ethical, cultural, and/or theological significance.

FOODS FOR SPECIAL OCCASIONS

Judaism is rich in symbolic food traditions. Thus, for example, on *Shabbat* and on festivals we say a blessing over not one but two loaves of *ḥallah,* recalling the Torah's instruction to the Israelites to collect two portions of manna on Friday because it was forbidden to gather food on *Shabbat* (Exod. 16:29). On *Rosh ha-Shanah* we eat honey, praying for a sweet New Year; on *Ḥanukkah* we eat foods fried in oil, commemorating the miracle of the *m'norah* that burned eight nights on one night's measure of oil; on *Purim* we eat pastries that represent the three-cornered hat ascribed by tradition to Haman (Yiddish: *hamentashen*).

The model for attaching symbolic significance to food is set by the Torah in its laws of *Pesaḥ*. The three foods that are central to the *Seider*—paschal lamb, *matzah,* and bitter herbs (*maror*)—may have their historical origins in the rites of spring among shepherds and farmers. In the Torah, however, and in the developing Jewish tradition, each of the three foods is connected with the *Pesaḥ* story. The paschal lamb was eaten by the Israelites in Egypt as God "skipped" (Hebrew: *pasaḥ*) over their homes when bringing the 10th plague (Exod. 12:13). As in many types of sacrifice, the animal's life substitutes for the offerer's life. Hence, the paschal lamb symbolizes the sparing of our lives. The *matzah* is bread baked on the run (12:34), symbolizing more narrowly the haste of the Exodus and more broadly the Exodus itself. The bitter herbs recall how the Egyptians embittered the lives of the Hebrew slaves (1:14).

Bearing in mind the Torah's tendency to attach symbolic meaning to food, let us turn now to the area of generally permissible and forbidden foods.

FOODS PERMITTED AND FORBIDDEN ON ANY OCCASION

The Torah is distinguished from all other law collections of the ancient Near East in delineating an entire system of eating rules. Although the Torah is remarkably systematic in the two passages that present most of the dietary laws (Lev. 11; Deut. 14), a number of diverse eating rules are spread throughout the Torah. Jewish tradition refers to food that is "fit" for eating—*kasher,* "kosher"—and food that is unfit—*tareif,* literally, "torn by an animal" and not properly slaughtered. The Torah's own terminology, as we shall see, relates to ritual purity and holiness.

The Ban on the Thigh Tendon

The symbolic significance of the eating rules is most evident in the ban on eating the "thigh muscle," or tendon or nerve, that was injured in Jacob's struggle with the divine being (Gen. 32:33). Because all Jacob's immediate descendants are called literally, "those issuing from his thigh" (a euphemism for his genitals; Gen. 46:26; Exod. 1:5), the ban draws attention to the ongoing condition of Israel as a people: impaired but surviving. The impaired thigh tendon signifies the people Israel; and because of that symbolism, the Israelites and their descendants are not to eat the part of the animal with which they are taught to identify themselves. The eating rule reminds us of who we are and from whom we are descended.

Life Belongs to God

The most fundamental eating rules seem designed to instill the idea that life belongs to God and may be taken for food only after acknowledgment of that paramount fact. In the beginning, both humanity and other animal

life are allowed only vegetation for food (Gen. 1:29–30). Domestic animals are appropriate offerings to God (4:4, 8:20) but are forbidden for human consumption. This is one of several ways the Torah teaches that humans may not take for themselves the prerogatives of God. When the boundary between God and humanity begins to break down, however, leading God to bring the great Flood (6:1ff.), God at once liberalizes and specifies the eating rules. Humans may eat animal meat, but not with the life still in it and not before removing the blood, which represents life and, accordingly, belongs to God who created it (9:4). God regards the unauthorized taking of life by humans and by animals as a cardinal sin (9:5–6). Because blood is God's alone, it is the most sacred substance, the one the Torah prescribes for the most serious purification rituals.

The Ban on Eating Blood

The ban on eating blood is the most basic eating rule in the Torah, a notion expressed in diverse ways. First, an animal that dies naturally (*n'velah*) or at the hands of another beast (*t're-fah*) may not be eaten, for its blood cannot be properly removed. Second, the blood of sacrificed animals must be either collected for purification rites or drained beside the altar. Third, the blood of an animal that is slaughtered for eating must be returned to God. Killing an animal is taking a life and may be done only by acknowledging the severity of taking an animal's life by doing it in God's way. Leviticus (17:6) has the blood dashed on the altar or, in the case of an animal killed in the hunt, poured onto the ground (17:13). Deuteronomy (12:16) would have the blood of all animals killed for food poured onto the ground.

In later Jewish tradition, hunting will be permitted only in the case of trapping an animal with the intention of preparing it for food. All animals must be ritually slaughtered. Removal of the blood remains the most important dietary rule. All kosher meat is drained of blood in the slaughterhouse and then soaked and salted after butchering. Broiling also fulfills the requirement.

A fourth way in which the Torah bans blood is in forbidding the consumption of all those animals that themselves ingest blood. This fact goes far in explaining which species of animal the Torah defines as edible and inedible (discussed further below).

Milk and Meat

Reverence for life is reflected as well in the prohibition against boiling a kid in its mother's milk. This law first appears in connection with the spring ritual (Exod. 23:19, 34:26). Maimonides sensibly supposes that boiling a kid in its mother's milk was a seasonal fertility practice that the Torah forbids. Israelites are not to copy the pagan ritual; they are to express appreciation of the spring's renewed fertility by presenting first fruits to God. But Deuteronomy (14:21) incorporates the prohibition against boiling the kid in milk into the regular eating rules. In that context, the prohibition takes on symbolic significance: Milk, which is meant to sustain life, may not be turned into a means of preparing an animal for eating. A clear distinction must be made between life, which is godly, and death. The postbiblical Jewish tradition underscores the distinction by broadening it: Not only milk, but all dairy products and the utensils used for serving them must be kept apart from meat products and utensils.

Permitted and Prohibited Species

Most of the Torah's dietary rules elaborate the species of animals that one may and may not eat. Edible animals are "pure" (*tahor,* often translated "clean") and inedible animals are "tainted" (*tamei,* often translated "unclean"). In general, things are pure when they signify life and conform to the way that God created the world, and things are tainted when they signify death and blur the distinctions God has established in nature.

Why the inedible animals were originally tabooed is somewhat obscure. Anthropologists have suggested diverse reasons. One reason was mentioned earlier: Predators among land animals and birds, who ingest blood, are for-

bidden. Also scavengers, like dogs, pigs, and mice, who pick up dead meat and refuse, are taboo. Many animals who travel close to the ground were also probably regarded as scavengers. Beasts of burden, like asses, horses, and camels, are not raised for food and tend not to be eaten. Nor are people inclined to eat animals resembling themselves, like those with paws rather than hooves. Pigs need a damp environment and favor the kinds of food that humans eat. Thus in addition to being scavengers, pigs actually compete for food with humans. It is, therefore, not surprising that archaeological research has shown pig raising to have diminished in the land of Israel in the biblical period, thriving mainly in certain Philistine cities.

The general observation can be made that most of the animals prohibited as food by the Torah are those that would not have been eaten by Israelites anyway. The same can be said for the Torah's ban on eating the hard fat that covers the entrails of many permitted animals. Though inedible, it is allocated to God. The fat when burned in a sacrifice makes heavy smoke, signifying the rise of the offering to God in heaven. As in the case of the fat, the Torah often legislates behavior that would be practiced ordinarily; but, as with the fat, it adds to such behavior a covenantal meaning. Keeping the dietary rules is not something we do for our own—practical or aesthetic—reasons. We do it as part of our covenantal obligations to God, symbolizing Godly values and sanctifying our lives.

Hallowing Our Lives

Most of the eating rules are detailed in a tightly organized form in Lev. 11, and they are repeated in a modified fashion in Deut. 14. One express purpose of the dietary system is to make us holy, like God (Lev. 11:45). As B'khor Shor put it: "It befits the Holy One that those who serve Him be holy, removed from the tainted, and pure." Originally, the special restrictions fell only on those who ministered to God in the sanctuaries—the priests and the Levites. Other individuals would take on the restrictions only to fulfill a vow or a sacred duty. Thus the parents of Samson were instructed by an angel to raise their son as a nazirite. In addition to not cutting his hair, he would have to abstain from intoxicating beverages and from tainted food (Judg. 13:4,14). Abstention from tainted, or impure, food is understood in that story as an extraordinary observance. Leviticus and Deuteronomy, however, address their dietary laws to all Israelites; thereby a process begins to evolve by which the holiness originally expected only of priests—and only in the sanctuary—falls on all members of the covenant community.

Especially following the destruction of the Jerusalem Temple in 70 C.E., rituals that were attached only to the priestly service were transformed by tradition to make them the province of all Jews. When the Temple service was discontinued, the table of every Jew was seen as an altar—a locale of divine–human encounter, where the Jew would enjoy and acknowledge God's blessing of food to eat. And, because the Temple sacrifices were salted, the meal is lent a sacred sense by salting the bread over which a blessing is recited.

Basically two principles give the Torah's eating rules their sense of purity. The first was discussed above: Animals that ingest blood or pick up carrion are tainted and, therefore, inedible. We are to associate life with the godly and death with the ungodly. The second principle is an appreciation of God's role as Creator and of the created world and a recognition of our limitations as creatures in that world.

Categories of Creation

The creation story in Genesis presents the acts of creation as a series of divisions—between light and dark, water above and water below, land and water, different species of vegetation, different species of animal, male and female, the six days of the work week and the holy *Shabbat.* The pattern of creation is reflected in the *Havdalah* (division) ceremony marking the transition from the holy *Shabbat* day to weekdays (discussed further below).

In creating animals, God divided them into four groups: fish, fowl, crawlers, and land animals. The animals are all associated with three domains in which they may live: water, sky, and land. The Torah, as the anthropologist Mary Douglas has shown, highlights God's creation of the world by classifying animals as edible and inedible according to how well each is suited to the domain in which it was placed in Creation. The Torah stipulates that animals that perfectly reflect the domain in which they live by moving about in it in the most appropriate fashion are pure, whereas those animals that move about in a manner that is inappropriate to their domain are tainted. The idea is that only creatures that are relatively perfect representatives of their kind are fit for eating. Just so, only priests who are fully sound may serve, only Israelites who are in a ritually pure state may enter the sanctuary, and only animals that have never been worked and have no blemish may be offered.

Accordingly, Leviticus, in defining the traits of pure and tainted animals, pays special attention to the limbs by which they move. Land animals, which are the ones who lived in the closest proximity to biblical Israel, are classified by two traits. They must chew their cud and have a proper hoof. They must walk and graze on the land. The dual requirement removes animals such as the pig, which does not chew its cud, and the camel, whose padded foot does not pass as a proper hoof, from the category of pure land creatures. Crawling and slithering creatures, which would not likely be eaten under any circumstances, are eliminated by the grazing requirements. The system of classification, therefore, explains those animals that the Israelites would ordinarily tend to eat or avoid eating in a theological fashion, tying the diet laws to an appreciation of Creation.

As for fish, they are meant ideally to swim in the water; pure fish must, therefore, possess fins and scales. Animals such as shellfish that live in the water but move about like land animals cross categories, so to speak, and do not set a model of the created order; they are tainted. Fowl are enumerated according to the species that are forbidden. Most of these prey on other animals or feed on carrion; others, like the ostrich, may walk on land more than fly. Although birds are not classified anatomically, insects are differentiated by whether their legs seem built more for jumping or walking. Jumping insects "fly" and so are edible. But walking insects are anomalous; their wings define them as creatures of the air, while their legs identify them with the land. (Rabbinic tradition suggests anatomical traits for birds, too: Those that are unfit are those whose claw seems made for grasping other animals [M Ḥul. 3:6].)

MAKING DISTINCTIONS

The system may appear artificial and arbitrary. But, as in setting a table, what is important is not so much how the system is organized but the fact that it is organized. The Torah has the community make distinctions, just as God did in creating the world. Observance of the eating rules shows not only an appreciation of God's creation; those who observe them practice a form of *imitatio dei* (Latin: "the imitation of God"), making the sorts of distinctions God makes. Following in God's footsteps, so to speak, conveys holiness, just as following God's lead in ceasing from work on *Shabbat* does.

It is nevertheless important to bear in mind that the distinctions that are observed are those made by God, just as the values by which the created world is to be cared for are God's. In this vein, Sforno interpreted the command to be holy: "Always acknowledge your Creator and walk in His ways." The dietary laws are explicitly meant to serve these functions.

Shoring Up Ethnic Identity

A passage in Lev. 20 adds yet another meaning to the eating rules. The Israelites are to "set apart the pure beast from the impure, the impure bird from the pure" because God has "set you apart from other peoples" (see vv. 22–26; cf. Deut. 14:2). The theme is evoked in the *Havdalah* ceremony mentioned above. Among its divisions between light and darkness and between the holy and the profane is the division between the people Israel and the other nations. The former are obligated to fulfill the covenantal duties; the latter are responsible for only the seven universal Noahide commandments, which include one law of eating: a prohibition against eating live flesh.

The notion that a people maintains its ethnic identity by eating differently appears first in the story of Joseph, when the Egyptians refuse to dine together with their Hebrew visitors (Gen. 43:32). In the late biblical period, the heroes of Jewish narrative display their loyalty to their religious tradition and to their people by observing the dietary laws. Thus the young Daniel in the Babylonian court "resolved not to defile himself with the king's food or the wine he drank"; he made do on a spare vegetarian diet (Dan. 1:8,12). The heroic Judith brought her own food so that she might dine with a Babylonian general (Judith 12:2). In the Maccabean period (ca. 165 B.C.E.) obedience to the dietary laws became a touchstone of Jewish loyalty. Thus, 2 Maccabees 6–7 relates two stories in a row in which the faithful—an old man named Eleazar, and the seven sons of an anonymous woman—refuse to eat pig meat on pain of torture and death and thereby choose martyrdom.

In the Christian scriptures, some early followers of Jesus still adhere to the dietary restrictions (Acts 10:9ff.). But several texts abrogate the rules precisely because they tend to reinforce ethnic boundaries. Jesus is said to have argued that food cannot defile because it enters the belly, not the heart (Mark 7:18–19). A separation is assumed between the physical and the spiritual. The Torah takes a different view: The heart is entered through the belly as well as through other organs and limbs. That is, the spiritual in this world does not exist in the abstract; it is always concretized in what we say and do. The behaviors associated with eating may be expressed through the body; but the many meanings that are encoded within those behaviors are meant to act on and cultivate the ethical and spiritual dimensions of those who observe them. Eating may seem purely physical, but the questions of what is eaten and how one eats are entirely bound up in ethical and theological commitments.

T'FILLIN AND *M'ZUZOT*

Jeffrey H. Tigay

T'FILLIN

Exodus 13 contains the commands beginning with the words "And this shall serve you as a sign on your hand and as a reminder on your forehead . . ." (13:9) and "it shall be as a sign on your hand and as a frontlet [i.e., headband—not "symbol" as in the translation] on your forehead . . ." (13:16). Similar commands appear in Deuteronomy: "Bind them as a sign on your hand and let them serve as a frontlet on your forehead" (6:8, 11:18). At least since later Second Temple times (2nd century B.C.E.) and perhaps already in Deuteronomy (7th century B.C.E.), these verses have been understood to be a commandment to wear objects that enable certain words of God to be fastened to the arm and the forehead. For this purpose, Jewish law adopted the expedient of having a scribe write the requisite words—passages from the Torah—on slips of parchment inserted in small leather capsules that the Sages called *t'fillin.* One capsule is fastened to the forehead, suspended from a leather headband knotted in the back of the head, with its loose ends hanging down like streamers, as in some of the headbands seen in ancient Near Eastern art. The other capsule is fastened to the upper arm by another leather strap.

Such capsules, in the form of amulets, were a common device in antiquity for attaching inscriptions to the body. The physical similarity of *t'fillin* to amulets was clear to the ancients. Two of the ancient terms for *t'fillin* (Hebrew: *kami·a;* Greek: *phylakterion,* or "phylactery") literally mean "amulet," and talmudic sources

frequently mention *t'fillin* and amulets together and note the possibility of confusing them with each other. However, *t'fillin* resemble amulets only in their external form, not in their contents. They contain biblical passages about the Exodus and God's instructions and thus serve an educational purpose; amulets typically contain magical inscriptions, or materials, to protect the wearer from evil.

Initially, there was some disagreement about which biblical passages should be placed in the *t'fillin*. Since talmudic times, they have been limited to the four passages that contain the verses that serve as the basis for the practice of wearing *t'fillin:* Exod. 13:1–10 and 13:11–16 and Deut. 6:4–9 and 11:13–21. The *t'fillin* found with the Dead Sea Scrolls at Qumran included these passages as well as others, most notably the Decalogue. Josephus seems to imply that they contain texts that record God's benefactions, power, and goodwill.

The words "bind them" and especially "let them serve as a frontlet" (headband) may imply that the written texts were to be worn directly and visibly on the arm and forehead, instead of being placed in containers affixed to those spots. This would be similar to inscribed armbands known from Egypt and to the inscribed gems and frontlet worn by the Israelite high priest (Exod. 28:9–12,21,29,36–37). There is evidence that some Jews in talmudic times may have worn the texts this way; some of the Church Fathers quote reports that certain Jews wrapped the parchment strips around their heads like crowns. In any case, the *halakhah*, Jewish law, did not accept this interpretation but required that the texts be placed in containers.

In talmudic times, *t'fillin* were worn throughout the day on weekdays. Since the Middle Ages the practice has usually been to wear them only during weekday morning prayers.

The oldest *t'fillin* found by archaeologists have come from the caves of Qumran and antedate the destruction of that settlement in 70 C.E. Others were found among the remains of Bar Kokhba's forces (132–135 C.E.).

Not all Jews agreed that the biblical texts in question meant to ordain a concrete practice. Although the Pharisees, the Qumran sect, and other Jewish groups did agree, some of the ancient Greek translations of the Torah take the verses metaphorically to mean that God's teaching should be kept constantly in mind. The Samaritans also did not accept the precept of *t'fillin.* This suggests that before the Jewish–Samaritan schism the literal interpretation of the verses was not universally accepted. Similarly, the reference in the Mishnah to "whoever says 'there are no *t'fillin*'" (M Sanh. 11:3) must refer to a denial that the biblical verses have *t'fillin* in mind. The neglect of the precept reported in some talmudic passages may also reflect a rejection of the literal interpretation.

In the Middle Ages, the meaning of these verses was debated by Rabbanites and Karaites. The latter stressed a metaphoric interpretation—that God's commandments and teachings should be remembered well, as if they were bound to our bodies, like a string tied around the finger as a reminder. In favor of this interpretation, they cited similar Hebrew metaphors, including "binding" to the body for remembering teachings (Prov. 1:9, 3:3, 4:9, 6:21, 7:3). Most Rabbanite commentators rejected this argument on the grounds that analogies from Proverbs, which is explicitly metaphoric in style, have no bearing on the Torah, which is not metaphoric (Ibn Ezra on Exod. 13:9). Still, no less a Rabbanite authority than Rashbam conceded that the plain sense of the text is metaphoric, meaning "let it be remembered always, as if written on your hand," comparing it to a similar metaphor in Song 8:6.

The divergence of interpretations since Second Temple times may go back to different meanings in the biblical texts themselves. It seems that Exod. 13:9 and 13:16 used "sign," "memorial," and "headband" metaphorically, whereas Deut. 6:8 and 11:18 may have intended them literally. Consider that in Exod. 13:9 and 13:16 the grammatical subject of "shall be a sign on your hand and a memorial/

headband on your forehead" cannot be the biblical passages themselves, for they are not mentioned. As metaphors these terms indicate that something is to be kept close at hand and remembered well. (For the metaphoric use of apparel and ornaments that are close or dear to their wearers, see the Proverbs passages cited above and Isa. 62:3; Jer. 2:32, 13:11, 22:24; Hag. 2:23; Job 29:14.) And the verb's subject must be either (a) the fact "that the LORD brought the Israelites out of Egypt" (Exod. 13:9b,16b); or (b) the grammatical antecedents of "shall be"—namely "this day" or "this practice" or the festival of unleavened bread (vv. 1–8,10) and the sacrifice/redemption of the first-born (vv. 11–16). What then must be remembered well? In the former case: the Lord's mighty deeds. In the latter case: this day and these rites—so that God's teaching will be remembered well. In neither case does "it shall be a sign" represent an observance beyond those mentioned in verses 2–8 and 12–15. ("This institution" in v. 10 refers to an annual practice, the eating of unleavened bread in vv. 3–8, not to a daily rite such as *t'fillin.*)

On the other hand, the injunction to "bind" these words in Deut. 6 and 11 seems to be meant literally. Here the reference is to words—which, unlike events and ceremonies, can literally be bound to the body; and the following command (to write these words on the doorposts and gates; Deut. 6:9, 11:20) suggests that something concrete is intended. It is true that even Proverbs speaks of binding teachings and commandments to one's body and refers to writing them on "the tablet of your heart [i.e., mind]" (Prov. 7:3). Writing words on the heart, however, is a known metaphor, while writing them on doorposts and gates is not; it is a concrete practice (see Deut. 6:9). Hence it is plausible that the accompanying injunction to bind God's words as a sign on the hand and as a band on the forehead is also meant literally. Thus, what began as a metaphor in Exod. 13 may have been interpreted or recast literally as early as the time of Deuteronomy.

At first glance it might seem surprising for Deuteronomy to give a literal, ceremonial interpretation to something that Exodus means metaphorically. Deuteronomy normally presents a more abstract approach to religion than do the other books of the Torah. The nature of Deuteronomy's "abstractness," however, may help explain why it might have been the book to ordain the practice of wearing *t'fillin.* Deuteronomy's abstractness is aimed primarily at combating an overly anthropomorphic conception of God and sacrificial worship, and it must have had the effect of reducing the role of sacrifice in daily life, especially in the provinces. In its struggle against idolatry Deuteronomy even outlaws religious artifacts that once had been considered unobjectionable, such as sacred pillars and trees (16:21–22; note also its silence about the cherubim when describing the Ark in 10:1–9). But Deuteronomy does not indiscriminately oppose religious symbols per se. It ordains the precept of *m'zuzah* (6:9; discussed below), and it preserves the injunction to wear fringes on one's garments (22:12; cf. Num. 15:37–41). It opposes only symbols that were too anthropomorphic or that had actual or potential idolatrous associations. The Deuteronomic reformers may well have realized that their reformation would deplete an already small stock of religious symbols in Israelite religion. Concrete, visible symbols are important, and it may be that just as Deuteronomy advocated the precepts of fringes and *m'zuzah,* which serve as reminders of God's commandments, it advanced the precept of *t'fillin* for the same purpose. Given the current state of evidence, this suggestion is speculative, and whether the precept of *t'fillin* goes back to Deuteronomy or only to Second Temple times remains an open question.

M'ZUZOT

In contrast to the question of *t'fillin,* it is certain that Deut. 6:9 literally ordains the writing of God's teachings on doorposts and city gates. The verse was understood that way even by the Samaritans, who rejected the precept of *t'fillin,* and the practice is attested at Qumran and in literary sources of the late Second Temple period.

It was not unusual for inscriptions to be written on the doors, lintels, and doorposts of private houses. Inscriptions of various types have been found at the entrances to ancient Egyptian houses; and to this day invocations, proverbs, and verses from the Qur'an are commonly inscribed on or over doors in the Muslim world. No examples of this practice have been found in ancient Israelite houses, but inscriptions on the entrances to tombs, identifying those buried in them, suggest that writing on entrances was known in Israel. In the Sinai Peninsula, the sanctuary at Kuntilat 'Ajrud had inscriptions of religious character written in Hebrew and Phoenician script on its walls and doorposts. In Mesopotamia, Syria, and Hatti, royal inscriptions celebrating the accomplishments of the kings and charters guaranteeing the privileges of certain cities were sometimes inscribed at city gates.

The closest parallel to what Deuteronomy prescribes—writing God's teachings on the doorposts and gates—is the ancient Egyptian practice of writing instructions at the entrances of temples, enumerating moral and cultic prerequisites for entering the temple. The prescription in Deuteronomy differs in that it is not stating prerequisites for entering the sanctuary but seeking to make people aware of God's teachings at all times and places.

The text in Deuteronomy 6:9 implies that the words are to be written visibly on the doorposts and gates. This is what the Samaritans did, writing on the stone of the building or on stone slabs affixed to it. For an unknown reason, at some point in the late Second Temple period Jewish law modified this practice, ruling that the inscription was to be written on parchment, rolled up, and inserted in a case. The *m'zuzah* texts found at Qumran are of this type. The inscription is known as a *m'zuzah* (plural: *m'zuzot*), from the word for "doorpost" in Deut. 6:9. A *m'zuzah* case is affixed, with the top slanting inward, to the upper third of the right-hand doorpost at the entrance of the house and of each residential room in a house.

According to the *halakhah,* the texts to be written in the *m'zuzah* are the two passages that contain the commandment (Deut. 6:4–9, 11:13–21). As in the case of *t'fillin,* there originally was some variation in this practice. The *m'zuzah* texts from Qumran (if all of them are really *m'zuzot*) include these two passages, but some also include the Decalogue and Deut. 10:12–11:12; others include parts of Exod. 13, which is also contained in *t'fillin.* The Samaritan *m'zuzot* contain the Decalogue, and a few add the poem of the Ark from Num. 10:35–36.

Like many other religious objects, *m'zuzot* lent themselves to use as amulets. This use was facilitated by their location on doorposts and gates, which suggested that they could serve as amulets to protect the house or city within. No less a figure than R. Judah the Prince sent a *m'zuzah* to the Parthian king Ardavan, explaining that it would protect him. To enhance their use for this purpose, other names of God and the names of angels were sometimes added to *m'zuzot.* Maimonides forbade this practice, declaring that this not only disqualified the *m'zuzah* but turned the instrument of unifying God's name into a mere charm for personal benefit. He concisely summed up the intention of the precepts of *t'fillin* and *m'zuzah,* and of *tzitzit* (fringes), as follows:

> The ancient sages said, "Those who have *t'fillin* on their head and arm, *tzitzit* on their garment, and a *m'zuzah* on their door may be presumed not to sin," for they have many reminders—and these are the "angels" that save them from sinning, as it is said, "The angel of the LORD camps around those who revere Him and rescues them" (Ps. 34:8) (MT *T'fillin* and *M'zuzah* 6:13).

TZITZIT (TASSELS)

Jacob Milgrom

In his commentary on *tzitzit* (tassels; Num. 15:37–41), Ibn Ezra writes: "In my opinion one is more obligated to wear the *tzitzit* when not in prayer [than during prayer]—so that one will remember not to go astray in sin at any time, for in the time of prayer one surely will not sin." Ibn Ezra's comment is a reminder that the *tzitzit* commandment enjoins—and early practice attests—the attaching of the *tzitzit* to the outer garment. They were worn all day long. Indeed, the term *tallit*—the prayer shawl bearing the *tzitzit,* which Jews wrap about themselves each morning in prayer—is actually the Rabbinic term for outer garment, again alluding to the fact that *tzitzit* were worn throughout the day.

The nature of *tzitzit* is illuminated by the literature and art of the ancient Near East, which shows that the hem of the outer robe was ornate compared to the rest of it. The more important the individual, the more elaborate the hem's embroidery. Its significance lies not in its artistry but in its symbolism, as an extension of its owner's person and authority. Its use is best illustrated by the Akkadian *sissikta bat'qu,* "to cut off the hem." For example, an exorcist pronounces an incantation over the detached hem of his patient's garment; a husband who cuts off a piece of the hem of his wife's robe thereby divorces her.

A reflex of this practice is found in the Bible in what heretofore was a puzzling dialogue. King Saul has pursued David into the Judean hills. Saul enters a cave and removes his cloak to relieve himself, unaware that David and his men are hiding in the cave. David sneaks up on the unsuspecting Saul and cuts off the hem from his cloak. The text then relates that "afterward David reproached himself for cutting off part of the hem of Saul's cloak." He said to his men, "The LORD forbid that I should do such a thing." When Saul realizes what David has done, he responds: "I know now that you will become king" (1 Sam. 24:6,21). What was the reason for David's remorse and for Saul's response? The answer rests in the meaning of the hem: It was an extension of Saul's person and authority. David felt remorse for taking it because God had not so ordered. Saul, however, regarded it as a sign from God that his authority had been transferred to David; Saul was now cut off from the throne.

The legal force of the hem in ancient Mesopotamia is evidenced in other ways. In ancient Mari, a professional prophet or dreamer would enclose with his report to the king a lock of his hair and a piece of his hem. They served both as his identification and, more important, as a guarantee that his prediction was true. In effect, these articles gave the king legal control over their owner. Another legal context of the hem is illustrated by clay documents, on which the impression of a hem replaces a signature. Today a nonliterate might sign with a fingerprint; in ancient Mesopotamia, however, it was the upper class that might use the hem.

Ephraim Speiser suggested that the practice in the synagogue to this day of pressing the edge of the *tallit* to the Torah scroll is a vestige of the ancient custom. This act, followed by the recital of blessings, may well have originated as a dramatic reaffirmation of the participant's commitment to the Torah. One thereby pledges both in words (blessing) and in deed (impressing a "signature" on the scroll) to live by the Torah's commandments.

That *tzitzit* are an extension of the hem is profusely illustrated in ancient Near Eastern art. In one picture, a pendant *tzitzit* is clearly evident, taking the form of a flower head or tassel, thus supporting the rendering "tassel" for *tzitzit.* The biblical text, moreover, enjoins that *tzitzit* be attached to the corners of the garment. But how can a closed robe or skirt have corners? There are two possibilities. One figure shows that the *tzitzit* are only the extended threads of the embroidered vertical bands that, instead of being cut off at the hem, are allowed to hang free. These bands termi-

nate at quarter points of the hem, thereby forming four "corners." Another figure illustrates a second possibility: The skirts are scalloped and the tassels are suspended where the scallops meet. The biblical text validates this mode of dress. It prescribes that the *tzitzit* be attached to the *kanaf,* a term that does not mean "corner" but "extremity" or "wing." Strikingly, a scalloped hem is the winged extremity of the garment. Thus the significance of the *tzitzit* (as well as of the elaborate hem) lies in this: It was worn by those who counted; it was the identification tag of nobility.

The requirement of the *t'kheilet,* the blue cord, gives further support to the notion that *tzitzit* signified nobility. The blue dye was extracted from the gland of the murex snail (*ḥillazon;* see Sifrei Deut. 354; BT Shab. 26a; BT Men. 42b) in a painstaking process. Though the snails were plentiful, the amount of dye yielded from each was infinitesimal and consequently expensive. Only the wealthy could afford large quantities of this dye.

Following the two Roman wars, the Jewish community was so impoverished that many could not afford even the one blue-dyed cord required for each *tzitzit.* Moreover, the dye industry was shut down by Rome, which declared it a state monopoly; and the *t'kheilet* became scarce (BT Men. 42b). To be sure, a cheap counterfeit blue had been developed from the indigo plant, but the Sages disqualified it as *t'kheilet* (Sifrei Num. 115; BT Men. 42b–43a). These factors contributed to the suspension of the blue cord requirement, and since then *tzitzit* have been totally white.

Another historical fact revealed by early Rabbinic sources is that *tzitzit* were worn by women. In fact, some Sages actually affirmed that *"af ha-nashim b'mashma,"* i.e., women are required to wear *tzitzit* (Sifrei Num. 115; BT Men. 43a) because it falls into the category of a commandment whose observance is not limited to a fixed time (*she-ein ha-z'man g'rama;* Tosef. Kid. 1:10).

Finally, because the *tzitzit* marked their wearers as Jews and because, as members of a powerless minority within a hostile majority, it might single them out for persecution, it was ordained that the *tzitzit* should be transferred to an inner garment (*tallit katan*). Nevertheless, among pious *Ashk'nazim* to this day the *tzitzit* are still visible, in fulfillment of the commandment "look at it [namely, the blue cord]" (Num. 15:39).

The purpose of the *tzitzit* is set out by a series of verbs: "look . . . recall . . . observe" (Num. 15:39). These three verbs effectively summarize and define the pedagogic technique of the ritual system of the Torah: Sight (i.e., the senses) combined with memory (i.e., the intellect) is translated into action (i.e., good deeds). Thus the experience of rituals and the comprehension of their values lead to loftier ethical behavior. The text also adds a negative purpose: to bridle the passions (v. 39) and thereby, according to the Sages, prevent heresy and harlotry (Sifrei Num. 115).

The final purpose of the *tzitzit* is indicated in verse 40, the conclusion of the pericope: "Thus you shall be reminded to observe all My commandments and to be holy to your God." The ultimate goal of seeing the *tzitzit,* reminding oneself of God's commandments and fulfilling them, is to attain holiness. The nobility to which Israel belongs is not like other power structures characterized by corruption and self-indulgence. Israel is commanded to be "a kingdom of priests and a holy nation" (Exod. 19:6).

But what is there about *tzitzit* that would remind its wearer of holiness? The earliest Rabbinic sources, perhaps dating back to biblical days, taught that the *tzitzit* are *sha·atnez,* a mixture of wool and linen (Septuagint; Targ. Jon. to Deut. 22:12; cf. Rashi; Ibn Ezra on this verse; Men. 39b–40a,43a; Lev. R. 22:10). In fact, white linen cords and dyed woolen cords were found in the Bar Kokhba caves, proving that the Rabbinic teaching was actually observed. The wearing of *sha·atnez* is forbidden to the Israelite (Lev. 19:19; Deut. 22:11), patently because it would resemble some of the priestly garments made from a blend of linen and wool (e.g., Exod. 28:6, 39:29). In fact, the high priest's linen turban is

bound by a *p'til t'kheilet,* a blue woolen cord (Exodus 28:37,39). Thus *sha·atnez* is forbidden because it is a holy mixture, reserved exclusively for priests. That *sha·atnez* is forbidden because it is holy can be derived from the injunction: "You shall not sow your vineyard with a second kind of seed, else the crop—from the seed you have sown—and the yield of the vineyard may not be used [*yikdash;* literally: will become sanctified]" (Deut. 22:9). In other words, the produce will belong not to you but to the sanctuary. However, early in the Rabbinic period it was taught—perhaps stemming from a biblical practice—that every Israelite should wear *tzitzit* made of *sha·atnez* (cf. Tosafot on BT Men. 39b,40a). Thus the *tzitzit,* according to the Sages, are modeled after a priestly garment that is taboo for the rest of Israel!

The *tzitzit* are then an exception to the Torah's general injunction against wearing garments of mixed seed. In actuality, however, inherent in this paradox is its ultimate purpose. The resemblance to the high priest's turban and other priestly clothing can be no accident. It is a conscious attempt to encourage all Israel to aspire to a degree of holiness comparable to that of the priests. Indeed, holiness itself is enjoined on Israel: "You shall be holy, for I, the LORD your God, am holy" (Lev. 19:2; cf. 11:44, 20:26). True, Israelites who are not of the seed of Aaron may not serve as priests (cf. Num. 17:5), but they may—indeed, must—strive for a life of holiness by obeying God's commandments. Hence, to their garments they are to attach tassels containing one blue cord—a woolen thread among the threads of linen. Indeed, the use of mixed seed in the prescribed garments reveals a gradation in holiness. The outer garments of the high priest are *sha·atnez,* the belt of the ordinary priest is *sha·atnez* (Exod. 39:29; cf. BT Yoma 12b)—and the fringes of the Israelite are *sha·atnez* by virtue of one blue woolen thread. The fact that the cord is woolen and blue marks it as a symbol of both priesthood and royalty, thereby epitomizing the divine imperative that Israel become "a kingdom of priests and a holy nation."

MIDRASH AND THE LEGAL PROCESS

Joel Roth

Normative Jewish tradition is a legal tradition, the foundation of which is the Torah. The goal of the tradition is to make clear in detail the commands of God's revealed will. In the earliest eras, God's will was revealed either directly through the biblical prophets, starting with Moses, or indirectly through other media of revelation in the Temple in Jerusalem, like the Urim and Thummim (Exod. 28:30; Num. 27:21; 1 Sam. 14:37–41, 28:6). However, "Ever since the Temple was destroyed, God's place in the world has been restricted to the four cubits of the law" (BT Ber. 8a). The entire legal system (*halakhah*) is based on the conviction that through it God's will becomes known. If that legal system is to remain viable, the Torah must be able to serve as the ultimate source for the resolution of legal questions, even in times far removed from the period of the Torah's composition. In other words, the Torah must be eternally relevant if the halakhic system is to remain vibrant.

The key to understanding the evolution of the legal system, as G. D. Cohen once noted, is *midrash. Midrash* is the method and process by which the words of the Torah are interpreted, explained, analyzed, and understood. Through the process of *midrash,* the Torah has remained a living document, eternally relevant and able to serve as the basis of an ever-evolving Jewish law.

The term *midrash* in the Bible means "to examine," to "investigate," "to seek or search out" (Lev. 10:16; Deut. 13:15). It is derived from the root דרש. Probably the most illustrative use of this root in the Bible, for our purposes, appears in the verse that informs us that Ezra "set his heart to examine [*lidrosh*] God's

Torah in order to fulfill it, and to teach laws and rules to Israel" (Ezra 7:10). The term *midrash* in the Dead Sea Scrolls, too, refers to a method of inquiry into the meaning of biblical verses.

Even though *midrash* is a key to understanding the legal tradition, it is important to note that there is a vast literature of *midrash* that is not legal. That body of literature is called *midrash aggadah,* the nonlegal interpretation of the Bible. Indeed, the term *midrash* without any modifier usually refers to *midrash aggadah* and not to legal (halakhic) *midrash.* There are collections of *midrash aggadah* compiled from the 5th through the 12th centuries. Some of the older collections, such as Genesis Rabbah, contain elaborate literary structures, which probably reflect a long period of development. There are two basic types of *midrash aggadah.* Those that interpret the verses of the Torah in consecutive order, with comments on almost every verse, are called "exegetic." Those that explain and expound only the first verses of a section of the Torah that is read publicly on a *Shabbat* or on a festival are called "homiletic."

Nonlegal *midrash aggadah,* like the legal *midrash* discussed below, enables the Torah to speak to every generation everywhere. The contents of *midrash aggadah* reflect how the preachers of each generation used the Torah as the starting point of moral instruction and social commentary—which are no less important to a viable, vibrant tradition than are its legal norms. Indeed, the values of *midrash aggadah* are often translated into normative legal behavior.

Behavior norms at the beginning of the Rabbinic era (through the early 3rd century C.E.) were transmitted in either *mishnah* form or in the form of legal *midrash* (*midrash halakhah*). In *mishnah* style, norms are presented almost always without their source or basis in the Bible and without the argumentation that led to the conclusion. In *midrash* style, the norms are linked directly to the biblical verses that serve as their basis, and usually the argumentation is also presented. Many legal conclusions are identical in the works of both styles. They are not the result of conflicting processes that must lead to different conclusions; more accurately, they are different manners of transcription and transmission. Obviously, *midrash* style highlights the fact that the Torah is at the core of legal decisions. On the other hand, *mishnah* style (severing the laws from their scriptural basis) allows for organizing the material more systematically, making it easier to follow.

The *mishnah* style did not eliminate the need for *midrash halakhah* to link the law to the Torah. Even after *mishnah* style became the predominant method of transmission, passages of the Talmud that discuss a clearly established *mishnah* often begin by citing the biblical source on which the *mishnah* was based, as well as the argument that led to the conclusion. Both methods were used by the Sages of the early Rabbinic period. Virtually the same Sages appear in both the Mishnah (and Tosefta) and the literature of *midrash halakhah.*

This tension between *mishnah* style and *midrash* style is also reflected in the history of the codification of Jewish law. For example, Maimonides wrote his classic legal compilation (*Mishnei Torah*) in *mishnah* style. His code rarely quotes a source, offers a justification of his view, or records differences of opinion. Shortly after its publication in 1177, it began to spawn commentaries that essentially restored the sources of his decisions as well as the argumentation that led to them. This is the same process of reinserting *midrash* style into *mishnah* style that we find often in the Talmud.

Maimonides was widely criticized for his audacity in composing a legal code without citing any sources or justifications of his decisions. Joseph Karo, the 16th-century author of the classic Jewish code of law *Shulḥan Arukh,* attempted to meet that objection by composing a lengthy work (*Beit Yosef*) that quotes the relevant sources and argumentation. His work is actually a commentary to a 14th-century legal code, called the *Tur,* by Jacob ben Asher. Karo's *Shulḥan Arukh* itself was more a digest

of the *Tur* and his own *Beit Yosef* than a new code. Nonetheless, the sources and argumentation were reinstated into the *Shulḥan Arukh* by its commentators as well—even though they already had been spelled out in the *Beit Yosef.*

The *mishnah* style—clear, definitive, and unencumbered by sources and justifications—has a special appeal because it is so easy to use. That style was necessary at certain times in Jewish history, and most codifiers who resorted to it did so due to the compelling circumstances of their time and place. So, for example, Maimonides justified writing his code in *mishnah* style because the proliferation of legal materials had made it difficult to determine the law or to understand how it was to be derived. The *mishnah* style allowed him to record and organize the law "so that all the laws shall stand revealed to great and small." Similarly, Karo indicated that the movement of Jews from country to country produced conflicts between new arrivals and long-time residents, with the result that "the law has come to be many *torot* [laws]," which needed to be summarized and codified in a systematic and useful way.

However, in the long run Jewish law does not rely on the pronouncement of one sole authority, one codifier, but flows from reasoning and cogent proofs. The *mishnah* style omits reasoning, and it offers no proofs. The *midrash* style retains them. Although *mishnah* style is useful, it cannot replace the need for *midrash*. What is recorded and transmitted in the *mishnah* style is the result of *midrash*, not its replacement. Often, short and clear statements are used to transmit God's will. Determining the specifics of that will, however, is rarely achieved without extensive discussion, deliberation, and analysis—of sources, precedents, and arguments.

In a legal system that ultimately depends on the reasoned analysis and interpretation of texts, it is most plausible to expect that the interpreters of those texts may have differing approaches to interpreting those texts. Those differences may reflect more than varied opinions of interpretation that legitimately can be deduced from texts. In the United States, such differences are often reflected by what we call strict constructionists and loose constructionists. Strict constructionists, for example, tend to be more concerned with the original intent of the framers of the Constitution, whereas loose constructionists believe that the court should be creative in its interpretation of the Constitution, so that it can meet the challenges of new times more expediently. The devotees of these two schools are in fundamental disagreement about the limits of legitimate interpretation. In terms that we have been using, these differences reflect conflicting views about what is a legitimate *midrash*. Both schools agree that *midrash* is the most significant tool for understanding the meaning of the text. Their dispute is about the legitimacy of specific approaches to *midrash*.

It should come as no surprise that there were different schools of midrashic interpretation of the Torah. In the 2nd century C.E., the period of the greatest flowering of Rabbinic *midrash*, there were two such schools—the school of Akiva and the school of Ishmael. There has been a great deal of scholarly debate about the distinctions between these two schools. I offer here two examples (of about 15 differences between them) to show how the schools reflect different approaches to the interpretation of Torah.

For the school of Akiva, no word or letter in the Torah can be the result merely of linguistic style or usage. Every word, even every letter, has significance and, therefore, can become the basis of *midrash halakhah*. The Talmud discusses the punishment decreed for the daughter of a *kohen* who has violated the Torah as noted in Lev. 21:9: "And the daughter of any priest, if she profane herself by playing the harlot, she profanes her father; she shall be burned with fire." The Talmud affirms that this applies only to one who is engaged. Akiva determines that this punishment applies also to a married woman. He determines it on the basis of one extraneous letter (*vav*) in the verse from Leviticus. His disputant, Ishmael, replies: "Because you make

a *midrash* on a superfluous letter *vav,* we should take this woman out to be burned?" (BT Sanh. 51b) For Ishmael, the divine Torah is written in human language. A matter of style, grammar, or usage is not to be interpreted as indicating a divine message. For Akiva, all statements, all letters, in the Torah are divine and are sources for midrashic interpretation and legal application. Ishmael was a strict constructionist; Akiva a loose constructionist.

Akiva declared that even words like "all" (*kol*), "also" (*gam*), and "the" (*et,* when used to indicate a direct object) imply teachings that are unstated in the words of the text. The fifth commandment illustrates his method. "Honor your father and your mother." The Hebrew reads: *kabbed et avikha v'et immekha.* The school of Akiva interprets the first *et* to teach that one's stepmother is included in this commandment and interprets the second *et* to teach that one's stepfather is included. The connective prefix *v'* is interpreted to teach the obligation to honor one's older brother, also. For Ishmael and his school, these words do not serve as the source for the derivation of any law.

Both schools agree that God's will is to be learned from the Torah through the process of *midrash*. Often both schools will agree on the actual law, although each school will use a different method of interpretation to deduce it. Sometimes, though, the different views of what constitutes legitimate *midrash* produce different understandings of what God demands of us. Such conflicting understandings result in different behaviors, each consistent with what that school believes to be the will of God.

Abraham Joshua Heschel's monumental work in Hebrew, *Torah Min Ha-Shamayim Ba-Aspaklaria Shel Ha-Dorot* (*Theology of Ancient Judaism*), demonstrates that the differences between the school of Akiva and the school of Ishmael extend beyond legal matters to issues of *aggadah* and theology. Furthermore, Heschel demonstrates, the principles and methods of the schools survive long after the schools themselves cease to exist.

Some things have changed since the end of the Rabbinic period, which has been the focus of most of the discussion here. Mainly, new *midrash halakhah* on the Torah itself is rare. In fact, it has been rare since about the 10th or 11th centuries C.E. (There continues to be *midrash aggadah* directly on the Torah even in our own day.) Instead, the focus of *midrash halakhah* has shifted from the Torah itself to the subsequent layers of authoritative texts: Mishnah, Talmud, medieval codes of law and their commentators, and the volumes upon volumes of legal responsa written throughout the centuries. There is some similarity between this process and what is recognizable in the United States too. Although, admittedly, the Supreme Court sometimes still engages in the direct interpretation of the Constitution itself, its decisions often are focused not directly on the Constitution, but on how the Constitution has been interpreted by earlier courts. And this is surely true of lower courts, which rarely interpret the Constitution itself. Most Jewish legal authorities since the close of the Talmud would surely have considered themselves "lower courts" compared to the Sages of the talmudic period itself. Thus it is logical that the focus of their *midrash* would shift from the actual Torah to the authoritative interpretations of the Torah in earlier generations. And each generation's contribution to this process becomes a focus of halakhic midrashic attention for those that follow. Furthermore, because subsequent authoritative texts are themselves a *midrash* on earlier authoritative texts, the latest links in this continuous chain are linked directly to Torah through the chain itself.

Some things, however, have remained quite unchanged. Just as there were different schools of interpretation in the early Rabbinic period, so, too, every era has had differing schools. The schools may not have been as easily distinguished from each other as the earliest schools were, but every generation has had its strict constructionists and its loose constructionists. In later generations, though, the Akiva-like or Ishmael-like interpretations were no longer directly focused on the Torah but on later authoritative texts. Thus, for example,

decisors of this generation engage in midrashic interpretations of several talmudic passages and several responsa and come to differing conclusions about how to define the moment of death according to Jewish law. Many feel constrained by the texts of the tradition that seem to define death as the cessation of respiration and heartbeat, whereas others offer a liberal interpretation of a *mishnah* (one never used for this purpose before) to accept brain death as a halakhic definition of death. It may be that in the future even those who now retain the more traditional view will find a *midrash* that fits their framework of legitimate *midrash halakhah* and thus adopt the other view. If and when that happens, we will see an instance of two schools coming to the same conclusion via differing *midrash,* a phenomenon emphasized in the discussion of the schools of Akiva and Ishmael. If that never happens, we shall see an instance of the differing midrashic views of differing schools leading to differences of opinion that translate into different legal decisions.

In the final analysis, each generation and era is distinguished from all others, and the distinctions between them are often the subject of historical research. But, in terms of Jewish law, all eras share several constants: the centrality of *midrash* to the evolution of law, the existence of differing views as to what constitutes legitimate *midrash,* and the possibility of divergent behaviors within the framework of Jewish law.

MEDIEVAL AND MODERN *HALAKHAH*

Elliot N. Dorff

During the Middle Ages, Jews were scattered all over the globe, and after the close of the Babylonian academies in the 11th century C.E., a centralized authority to teach and make Jewish law no longer existed. Under these conditions, biblical and talmudic commentaries were written to help people understand Judaism's sacred books even in the absence of teachers. Thus three types of legal literature were produced—legal codes, responsa, and amendments to the law (*takkanot*)—in an effort to make it possible for Jews to know what Judaism required of them and to make Jewish law viable in totally new circumstances.

The most famous of the medieval codes were those of Moses Maimonides and Joseph Karo, completed in 1177 and 1565, respectively. Maimonides titled his code *Mishnei Torah,* cleverly using a biblical phrase meaning "copy of the Torah" (Deut. 17:18) to signify also, through a play on words, "second to the Torah" and "the learning [lessons, import] of the Torah." As he states in the introduction, he wanted people to be able to read the Torah and then read his code and thereby know how to live their lives as Jews. After that, any time they had to spend learning the intricate legal discussions in the Talmud would be all to the good. The vast majority of Jews, however, had neither the time nor the expertise to follow those arguments; therefore, Maimonides presented to them the practical conclusions of those discussions so they could live their lives in conformity with Jewish law. Similarly, Karo titled his code *Shulḥan Arukh,* "the set table," because he was effectively spoon-feeding the requirements of Jewish law to those who could not delve into its rationales and nuances.

The very process of summarizing Jewish law in the form of codes caused great controversy. First of all, because the whole point of writing a code was to create a short, clear, unequivocal statement of what is required, the codifiers generally did not cite their sources or the reasoning that led them to their conclusions. That detached Jewish law from its sources and from its process of ongoing development, freezing it in the form that the codifier created. The reader thus totally depended on the codifier's interpretation of the sources. Furthermore, because none of the reasoning behind the law was provided, readers might well make

mistakes if they tried to apply a section of the code to a question that it did not cover. Finally, rabbis like Abraham ben David of Posquieres ("Ravad," 12th century C.E.), a harsh critic of Maimonides, objected to the arbitrariness of the form, for it presented Jewish law the way one particular codifier understood it, with no mention of why or of alternate opinions and practices. Karo acknowledged some of these difficulties, but the need to make Jewish law available to the masses prompted him to write his code nonetheless.

The *Mishnei Torah* still governs the practice of many *S'fardim* (Mediterranean and Middle Eastern Jewish communities). Other *S'fardim* follow the *Shulḥan Arukh* because Karo himself was a rabbi from that tradition, living first in Spain and then in the Levant. Meanwhile, *Ashk'nazim* (originally from France and Germany and then from eastern Europe) generally follow the *Shulḥan Arukh,* because Moses Isserles (a 16th-century Polish rabbi) wrote glosses to it—and cleverly called it *Mappah,* "tablecloth"—indicating wherever the practices of *Ashk'nazim* differed from *S'fardim.* Other codes (or partial codes) have been written more recently. But Karo's code still is the primary one because it is the last that, with the notes of Isserles, can legitimately claim to reflect the practices of worldwide rabbinic Jewry of its time (with the exception of the Jews of the Far East and Yemen).

Far more extensive is the literature of responsa (Hebrew: *t'shuvot;* singular: responsum, *t'shuvah*), rabbis' rulings dating from the 8th century C.E. to our own in answer to specific legal questions asked of them. Indeed, it is estimated that some 300,000 responsa are extant, and new ones are being written all the time. This genre of legal literature has the distinct advantage of being focused on specific questions and contexts. Thus responsa can be produced far more quickly than can comprehensive codes, and responsa can attend to the particular details of a case at hand. Moreover, responsa by nature require the authors to cite sources and explain their reasoning, and they deal only with given cases. These features give rabbis in other times and places a choice: They can depend on a given responsum for their ruling, or they can dismiss it—claiming that its embodied precedent is too different from the present case. The resulting process preserves both the continuity and the flexibility of the law. No wonder, then, that the vast majority of the business of Jewish law over the last 1,300 years has been accomplished through the genre of responsa. The one drawback of responsa is that—written in many times and places—they are poorly collected and organized, making it difficult to know whether relevant responsa exist on a given topic. But that problem has diminished in our time by the creation of computer databases that catalog many medieval and early modern responsa.

Because medieval Jews found themselves living in new places under new economic, political, and religious conditions, some aspects of Jewish law had to be adjusted to the new circumstances. Most of the time, that was accomplished by new legal interpretations and applications of the sources or by changing customs. Sometimes, however, the law had to be formally amended, accomplished through *takkanot* (literally, "fixings") or *g'zerot* (decrees) that were enacted by, or in the name of, the rabbis of the community or communities that were to follow the laws and on the combined authority of those rabbis and communities. Some of these enactments were highly localized and temporary, establishing, for example, the ways in which Jews were to interact with the non-Jewish authorities of the region or the specific method by which honest weights and measures were to be ensured. Others were intended to be, or were taken by later authorities to be, more permanent, e.g., the enactments attributed to Gershom (ca. 1000 C.E.), limiting a man to one wife and requiring the wife's consent to a divorce.

Finally, with Jews scattered throughout the world and with many living in small communities, it is not surprising that local custom became an important source for the law. In some cases, it even superseded laws of the Talmud.

So, for example, although the Mishnah requires a year's waiting period between betrothal and marriage, the medieval conditions in which Jews lived were too precarious to trust that a wedding postponed for a year would take place. In addition, Jews were too poor to host both an engagement party and a wedding feast, and so medieval custom combined the two into one ceremony, as we do to this day. Similarly, although the Mishnah and the Talmud establish beyond any shadow of a doubt that the sale of movable property is legally valid only when it has been transferred to the domain of the purchaser, medieval custom determined that a handshake would seal the deal.

In some cases, commercial custom all but abrogated even the laws of the Torah, as, for example, the commercial customs that ultimately led to the rabbinical *heter iska*, literally, "the permission to engage in business," which by medieval times required the charging of interest, against the Torah's express words. The rabbis of the time created a legal fiction whereby such transactions were not to be considered interest on loans but rather profits from a partnership. (Thus, to this day, when one deposits money in an Israeli bank owned by religious Jews, one is actually investing as a partner in the bank, as a notice in the bank attests.) This is also a good example of the interaction of these various sources of law—codes, responsa, legislation, and custom—because pervasive commercial custom ultimately prodded the rabbis to issue a ruling legitimating the practice.

Jewish law governed the daily lives of most of the world's Jews throughout the Middle Ages and until World War I. That was because societies were organized corporately, such that the government let specific communities within their realm govern themselves as long as they produced the required taxes and (sometimes) men for the army. As a result, Jews who had a dispute with one another would bring it to Jewish courts for resolution. (Filing suit instead in a gentile court would undermine the authority of Jewish courts; and it might subject the other party—and perhaps even the Jewish community—to penalties exacted by the usually anti-Semitic government. Therefore, "outside" suits were subject to fines and more severe punishment imposed by the Jewish courts.)

This ceased being true with the advent of the Enlightenment, according to which each person was to be seen as an individual and not as a member of a group. Until the end of World War II, however, the Enlightenment affected the political and legal structure only of countries in western Europe and the United States while most Jews lived in eastern Europe and in the Muslim world, where the old, corporate system still held sway. Consequently, it is only since then that the majority of the world's Jews have no longer been governed by the decrees of Jewish courts, enforced, if necessary, by government authorities.

It is thus not surprising that the problem of delineating the authority of Jewish law was not an issue for most Jews before World War II; it was authoritative at the very least because it was enforced by courts and police. In Germany, however, and in other countries of western Europe and the United States, the Enlightenment affected the structure of government beginning with the end of the 18th century; and so Jewish courts from then on no longer had such authority over Jews. Therefore, German thinkers of the 19th century argued for delimiting and justifying the ongoing authority of Jewish law, despite the inability of the Jewish community to enforce it, and that thinking continued primarily in Germany and in the United States in the 20th century. The modern Jewish movements—Conservative, Orthodox, Reform, and Reconstructionist—are all responses to this historical and philosophical dynamic, which in many ways continues to our own day.

How, then, can the authority of Jewish law be justified when Jews living in free societies cannot be forced to abide by it? Indeed, in what sense is Jewish law still "law"?

Reform thinkers in the 19th and early 20th centuries maintained that Jewish law no longer

existed, that what went by that name was, at best, a series of customs and guidelines and, at worst, antiquated norms that were best abandoned. In recent decades, Reform thinkers, professionals, and laypeople are more open to having Jewish norms shape parts of their lives; but the extent to which they do so is totally a function of each Jew's autonomous choice. The Reform Movement's 1976 *Centenary Perspective* does call on Reform Jews to study Judaism so that they can make informed choices, and the Reform rabbinate's 1999 Pittsburgh Platform goes even further in encouraging Jewish observance. In the end, though, it is not Jewish law that governs; people individually have the freedom to choose when and how their Jewish commitments will influence their thinking and behavior.

The Reconstructionist movement, founded by Mordecai Kaplan, rejected supernaturalism and with it the divine authority for Jewish law. In Kaplan's view, although moral norms are binding not only on Jews but also on all people, religious rituals derive from folkways. Jewish ritual behavior, then, is important because it provides a unifying force for the community and dramatizes its values. It is not, however, "law" and hence can be modified to meet changing needs and circumstances. More recent exponents of Reconstructionism have moved away from Kaplan's emphasis on the central role that the community plays in Jewish religious practice and belief and have adopted positions more similar to those of the Reform Movement.

Orthodox thinkers maintain not only that Jewish law derives its authority from God but also that it has and should remain the same as Moses received it on Mount Sinai. Moreover, the written Torah that we have in hand is, in the Orthodox view, the exact copy of the text that Moses wrote down at God's command, and the oral Torah is what he learned there and passed down in unwritten form. If this is so, then we must assume that historical development did not, and should not, occur in Jewish law; God's word stands forever. What does need to be addressed, however, is how to apply precedents from the past to modern times, which is often difficult, because the Enlightenment has substantially changed social structure, and science and technology have radically altered the physical environment in which we live. In response to these new circumstances, the Orthodox have produced many responsa—more, in fact, than any other group. The assumption underlying all of them, however, is that only changes in context can warrant a new application of law; changes in human perceptions or values cannot, for God's word as it has come down to us always takes precedence over human ideas and values.

The Conservative Movement, like the Orthodox, affirms the divine root of Jewish law and its binding character. It studies the Jewish past, though, with the same intellectual tools by which we examine the past of any other people. When those techniques are applied to the Torah, one discovers that the text we have in hand shows signs of being composed of several documents that were later edited together. The laws that governed the Israelites, like their stories and traditions, were undoubtedly passed down from generation to generation primarily in oral form. People learned how to behave as Jews by observing how Jewish law was practiced in their own homes and communities and by hearing answers to their questions from parents, rabbis, and friends. In this process, elements were borrowed from nearby cultures and then sometimes changed by the Israelites to fit their own emerging view of life and their own circumstances. Only much later were some of these stories and laws written down, and still later these documents were edited together.

Conservative thinkers generally accept the documentary theory about the origins of the Torah and agree that it nevertheless bespeaks God's will, but they differ as to why and how. Some think that the divine authority of the Torah, and of later Jewish law based on it, ultimately depends on the words that God spoke at Sinai and the rabbis' interpretations of those words in all succeeding generations. Others believe that the process of God's revelation at

Sinai was more akin to inspiration: God inspired (literally, "breathed into") the writer(s) of the biblical texts the divine spirit, but it was human beings who wrote down what they understood God to mean and want. Still others are uncertain about such divine origins of the law but maintain that the Torah is "divine" at least in the sense that it represents what our ancestors understood God to demand. Similarly, Jewish law in our day is "divine" minimally in its aspiration to articulate what God wants of us now, what God, indeed, commands.

Because Jews historically have seen the Torah as the source of our knowledge of God's will, they have considered it the authoritative guide for how we should live our lives—so much so that for them life ceased to be worthwhile if they could not live according to its laws. Jews have, indeed, given up their lives for the sanctification of God's name, *al kiddush ha-shem,* rather than publicly violate Jewish law. Jews have also put themselves at great risk to carry out its observance. Numerous examples of both of these affirmations of the importance of Jewish law in extremely adverse circumstances can be found during the Middle Ages, especially in response to the Crusades and the Inquisition. Examples also abound in recent events, in particular during the *Sho·ah* and during the communist reign in Russia and in eastern Europe. Jewish law, then, may also be considered "divine," or at the very least "sacred," because our people have been willing even to sacrifice their lives to uphold it. As the Mishnah (Ber. 9:5) maintained, when the Torah says, "You shall love the LORD your God with all your heart, with all your soul, and with all your might" (Deut. 6:5), it means, by the second phrase, "even if God takes your soul" (life). Unfortunately, Jews in times past have had to make that sacrifice, and that should give us today yet another reason to honor Jewish law and seek to uphold its provisions.

Jews from biblical times to our own have obeyed Jewish law for other theological reasons, too. We obey the commandments in gratitude for our very lives and for the special favors God has done for us individually and as a people (Deut. 4:32–40). Moreover, we are, according to the Torah, partners in a covenant with God. Through that covenant, we are bound to the promises that our ancestors made at Sinai (Deut. 5:2–3, 29:13–14,28). That covenant also establishes the ongoing relationship between God and the people Israel, and so we obey the commandments to maintain that relationship. We obey Jewish law, in other words, out of love for God (Deut. 11:1). Furthermore, we obey Jewish law because we aspire to be "a kingdom of priests and a holy nation" (Exod. 19:5–6), indeed, "a light unto the nations" (Isa. 49:6); that is our divinely ordained mission in life. Finally, aspiring to holiness enables us to be like God: "You shall be holy, for I, the LORD your God, am holy" (Lev. 19:2).

In addition to these theological reasons to obey Jewish law, contemporary Jews, like our ancestors over the generations, also have been motivated by the functions Jewish law serves on the human level. The law maintains the identity and structure of the Jewish community; if everyone were to make completely independent choices, there would be little chance for communal cohesiveness and the sharing it brings. Furthermore, the law sensitizes us to the moral dimensions of life; we may not do whatever we wish or even whatever we think is right but must rather conform to communal norms. It also enables us to call on the wisdom of the ages in making our own moral decisions, for the law is a repository of centuries of experience and the wisdom gained in the process (Deut. 4:6–8).

However one understands the grounds for the authority of Jewish law, it is clear from the historical record that the content of Jewish law in the Torah itself and in later periods has changed over time: many things have been added, others dropped, and some changed in form. This was historically done, in part, through the official acts of rabbis and, in part, through the customs of the people. In technical terms, Jewish law has evolved out of the

interaction between *din* (law) and *minhag* (custom), between the way in which rabbis over the generations have interpreted and applied it and the way in which Jews have observed it. To be authentic to the Jewish past, then, and to be a living, vibrant tradition now, Conservative Judaism would have us determine the content of Jewish law as it has always been determined—namely, through an ongoing interaction between the rabbis and the masses of Jews who take Jewish law seriously and who practice it in their lives.

As it has been within Jewish communities for at least the last 1,000 years, the burden of that determination within the Conservative Movement rests primarily on the congregational rabbi, the *mara d'atra,* the teacher of the local community. When a rabbi thinks that a question has not been addressed in Jewish law, at least not in the contemporary context, or that modern circumstances or sensitivities warrant a re-examination of traditional Jewish law on a given issue, he or she may address a question along those lines to the movement's Committee on Jewish Law and Standards (CJLS). Ultimately it will issue one or more responsa articulating the committee's advice to the rabbis of the movement on the issue. The local rabbi, however, remains the one to decide the issue for the specific congregation.

In rare circumstances, the committee issues a standard that binds all of the rabbis and synagogues of the movement. So, for example, no Conservative rabbi may even attend, let alone officiate at, the wedding of a Jew to a non-Jew, because that has been made a standard of the movement. Similarly, Jewish identity, according to another standard of the movement, is defined by being born to a Jewish woman or by being converted to Judaism according to the requirements and procedures of Jewish law.

Although the Conservative Movement has not officially adopted many standards, many commonalities exist in how Conservative congregations observe Jewish law, most of which have grown out of the shared customs and perceptions of the movement. One would expect such a development from a group of people who take Jewish law seriously, who demand intellectual honesty in studying its history and in making contemporary decisions, and who deeply want it to shape Jewish life in the modern world as a prime, indispensable way in which to carry out the will of God as we understand it in our time.

Text and Context

TORAH READING

Lionel Moses

Rabbinic traditions attribute the origin of the Torah reading to Moses, but there is no historical evidence to validate such an ancient genesis for this practice. These traditions of the Sages reflect an awareness that public instruction predates their era and acknowledge that they could not accurately date when the regular reading of the Torah began.

Internal biblical evidence about the public reading of the Torah is scarce. Deuteronomy legislates a public ceremony to be held every seven years during the *Sukkot* festival at which the Torah would be read to the assembled community (31:10–13). However, even as late as the end of the monarchy (587 B.C.E.) there is no evidence in the Bible indicating that such a ceremony and public reading actually occurred with the type of regularity anticipated in Deuteronomy. Moreover, many biblical scholars believe that this Deuteronomic legis-

lation originally was part of a ceremony at which the covenantal relationship between God and the people Israel was ratified. Although the Bible recounts such covenant renewal ceremonies (Exod. 20; Josh. 8:30ff.,24; 2 Kings 22–23), public readings of the text of the covenant are mentioned in only two of these passages.

One of these covenant renewal ceremonies in which the Torah was read publicly describes how King Josiah (639–609 B.C.E.) assembled all the people of Judah in Jerusalem during the 18th year of his reign. He read to them the "Book of the Covenant" that had been discovered in the Temple by the high priest Hilkiah (2 Kings 22:8–9, 23:2–3). Most contemporary biblical scholars agree that this "Book of the Covenant" was the Book of Deuteronomy, not the entire Torah.

The only other biblical example of a public reading of the covenant before the destruction of the First Temple in 587 B.C.E. comes from the period of the conquest of the land of Israel (1200–1050 B.C.E.). After the conquest of the Canaanite fortress of Ai, Joshua built an altar to God on Mount Ebal and inscribed on the stones of the altar a copy of the Torah of Moses. Then, in a ceremony reminiscent of the instructions given by Moses in Deut. 27:1–13, Joshua read "all the words of the Torah, the blessings and the curses," before the Israelites who stood facing Mount Gerizim and Mount Ebal in the Valley of Shechem (Josh. 8:30–35). Once again, most contemporary biblical scholars identify the Book of the Teaching referred to in this passage with the Book of Deuteronomy, not with the entire Torah as we know it today.

Not until the Persian period (5th century B.C.E.) does the term *Torah* apply to all five books of the Pentateuch. This transition in which the term the "Book of the Torah" came to encompass the entire Pentateuch is connected with the process of editing and redaction of the source material of the Pentateuch. Biblical scholars argue that this change took place during the 6th century B.C.E., after the destruction of the First Temple (587 B.C.E.).

On that basis, a scholarly consensus has formed that when Ezra the Scribe read the Torah publicly to the exiles who had returned to Jerusalem in the mid-5th century (Neh. 8:1–8), he read a prototype of the five books of the Torah that we know today. Despite the prescription in Deuteronomy that the Torah be read every seven years, the practice apparently had lapsed, if it had even been instituted at all. Nehemiah 8:9 records that when Ezra first began to read publicly from the Book of the Torah on *Rosh ha-Shanah,* the people began to cry. Perhaps this was because they had never heard the Torah read and expounded so forcefully. Perhaps it was because they had forgotten the Torah's demands and, through this public reading, became aware of their failure to observe the law. They began to weep and mourn because they knew the consequences for the previous generations who had failed to observe the laws of the Torah.

The narrative in Nehemiah subsequently recounts how the heads of the families of all the people, as well as the priests and Levites, continued to study the Torah with Ezra on the second day of *Rosh ha-Shanah,* learning about the festival of *Sukkot.* These leaders issued a proclamation to all the returned exiles living in the environs of Jerusalem to celebrate and observe *Sukkot.* During this seven-day celebration, Ezra read the Torah publicly every day, fulfilling the injunction of Deut. 31:10–13 that the Torah be read once in seven years on *Sukkot* (Neh. 8:18).

During the Second Temple period, both Philo and Josephus refer to the public reading and teaching of Torah in the synagogue. A Greek inscription found in Jerusalem in the remains of an ancient synagogue, whose ruins predate the destruction of the Second Temple, (70 C.E.) declares that the synagogue was dedicated "to the reading of the Law and the teaching of the commandments." The septennial reading of the Torah on *Sukkot,* as prescribed by Deuteronomy, is recorded in the Mishnah (Sot. 7:8). The Mishnah calls this septennial reading the "Pericope of the King" and describes the procedure for this public

reading of the Torah that occurred during the reign of King Agrippa (41–44 C.E.). The content of what Agrippa actually read during this ceremony, however, seems to be limited to the Book of Deuteronomy.

It is not known how the Torah was read during the period of the Mishnah and the early talmudic period (2nd and 3rd centuries C.E.). The Mishnah does not state whether the Torah was to be read consecutively from Genesis to Deuteronomy or whether the choice of each weekly reading was to be left to a local synagogue functionary. It is quite likely that in ancient Palestine there was far less uniformity than in Babylonia, even during the period of the Mishnah and the Talmud. From the post-talmudic era (5th to 11th centuries C.E.), however, we do have more detailed information about how the Torah was read in Palestine. The evidence indicates that there was no uniformity among the Palestinian Jewish communities on how the Torah was divided into weekly portions for reading.

The Mishnah, however, does present a number of regulations regarding the public reading of the Torah. Thus, for example, the number of people called to the Torah (*olim;* singular: *oleh*) on specific occasions is established: three on weekdays and for *Shabbat Minḥah;* four on *Rosh Ḥodesh* and on the intermediate days of festivals; five on festivals; six on *Yom Kippur;* and seven on *Shabbat* morning (M Meg. 4:1–2). The Mishnah implies that the required number of *olim* may be exceeded except on weekdays, at *Shabbat Minḥah,* on *Rosh Ḥodesh,* and on the intermediate days of a festival. The Talmud and the medieval codes, however, limit the addition of extra readers to *Shabbat* (BT Meg. 23a; Tur O.Ḥ. 282:1; S.A. O.Ḥ. 282:1).

The Mishnah further states that each of the *olim* must read a minimum of three verses (M Meg. 4:4). The Talmud adds that a public reading of the Torah must have a minimum of 10 verses (BT Meg. 21b; MT Prayer 12:3; S.A. O.Ḥ. 137:1–2). The only exceptions, apparently, are the reading for *Purim* morning (Exod. 17:8–16) and the weekday reading for the section of *Va-yeilekh* (Deut. 31:1–9), when a total of 9 verses are read. (Tosafot Meg. 21b, s.v. *ein,* justifies the abbreviated reading for *Purim,* but makes no mention of *Va-yeilekh.*)

The Talmud rules that women and children can be included among the seven *olim,* but the Sages ruled that women may not read from the Torah because of *k'vod ha-tzibbur,* a technical term that in this context appears to mean "the dignity of the congregation" (BT Meg. 23a). This talmudic text, which originates in the Tosefta (Meg. 3:11 with variations) is the source that teaches that the *olim* were expected to read their own portion from the Torah. Indeed, according to the Tosefta, if only one person was competent to read from the Torah, he was to be given all seven *aliyot.* This tradition of the *oleh* reading his own portion from the Torah continues through the medieval period, when it is codified as the norm in the *Shulḥan Arukh* (O. Ḥ. 139:1–2). The same passage of *Shulḥan Arukh* is already aware that a person who is unable to read his own portion might be needed as an *oleh* because he is the only *kohen* or *Levi* present; that code, therefore, permits a properly prepared reader to read the Torah for the *oleh,* who must repeat the passage word by word. By the end of the 19th century, however, the prevailing custom had changed. Those who could not read from the Torah—or even follow an expert reader—were given *aliyot,* on the premise that a person who hears the reading is like one who is able to repeat what he has heard (*Arukh Ha-Shulḥan* O.Ḥ. 139:3).

Another rule introduced by the Mishnah prohibits skipping verses when reading the Torah (M Meg. 4:4). This regulation means that a reading must be consecutive, so that the reader will not become confused. The Talmud provides one exception to this rule. On *Yom Kippur,* the high priest read Lev. 16 and then was permitted to skip to Num. 29. In the Talmud, Abbaye justifies this exception because both passages deal with the same topic: the rituals of *Yom Kippur* (BT Meg. 24a). The only other exception occurs on public fast days, when the Torah reading skips from Exod. 32:14

to 34:1 from the first to the second *aliyah.* The justification for this exception is that the time required to roll the Torah from one section to the next is no longer than the time required for a translator to render the biblical verse in an Aramaic translation (BT Meg. 24a).

By the 3rd century C.E., the Sages had assigned specific passages of the Torah for festivals and special Sabbaths (M Meg. 3:4–6). Many of these passages are still read today. Torah readings for special fast days are also recorded in the Mishnah (Taan. 4:2–3). Concerning which passages are to be read on *Shabbat* on a weekly basis, the Mishnah is silent. An oblique reference to the weekly Torah readings in the Talmud states that in Palestine the public reading of the Torah was completed once in three years (BT Meg. 29b). This implies that a different custom for reading the Torah on *Shabbat* prevailed in Babylonia.

In Babylonia, it was customary to complete the reading of the Torah in just one year, a practice that was established by 600 C.E. and probably even earlier. This annual cycle began on the last *Shabbat* of *Tishrei* (the *Shabbat* after *Simḥat Torah*). The Torah was then read consecutively each *Shabbat* until it was completed on the next *Simḥat Torah* (the 23rd day of *Tishrei*). The Torah text was divided into 54 sections, known as pericopes or *parashiyyot* (singular: *parashah*), so that the reading cycle could be completed in one year. This number of *parashiyyot* exceeded the number of Sabbaths in the annual calendar and provided the necessary flexibility for a Jewish leap year, which adds four weeks to the calendar. Thus in some years, certain *parashiyyot* were combined to ensure that the entire Torah was completed by *Simḥat Torah,* whereas during a leap year (which has four extra Sabbaths) each *parashah* was read on a separate week. The flexibility that allowed for combining and separating certain *parashiyyot* could also accommodate the special readings for festivals, when these festivals occurred on *Shabbat* (M Meg. 3:4–6).

In Palestine, an alternate cycle of reading the Torah was followed until the 12th century C.E. Like the annual cycle, it was also consecutive, beginning with Genesis and concluding with Deuteronomy. This alternative system divided the Torah into small units called *s'darim,* but this division was not uniform. Different manuscripts of the Torah divide the text into as few as 148 *s'darim* and as many as 175 *s'darim,* indicating that the divisions varied from one location to another in Palestine. This alternative system meant that in Palestine the reading of the Torah was completed in three or three and a half years, assuming that only one or two *s'darim* were read on each *Shabbat.*

The system of reading the Torah in approximately three years is referred to as the triennial cycle. The range in the number of *s'darim* suggests that there was greater flexibility and less uniformity among congregations of the Levant that followed this custom. And in the Palestinian triennial system, *Simḥat Torah* could not be a fixed date on the festival calendar as it was in Babylonia, because it coincided with the *Shabbat* on which the Torah reading was completed. The fluidity of the dates for *Simḥat Torah* in Palestine is indicated by some of the liturgical poems (*piyyutim*) written there during the 5th and 6th centuries C.E., some of which include a prayer for dew. This suggests that the poem was recited on a *Simḥat Torah* that occurred during the summer. *Simḥat Torah* poems of Babylonian origin, on the other hand, always include a prayer for rain, because the festival in Babylonia always occurred at the end of *Tishrei,* after the harvest was completed.

By the 12th century C.E., the Babylonian rabbinate and their heirs in North Africa had extended their religious hegemony over all of rabbinic Jewry, including the surviving Jewish communities of Palestine. In 1170 C.E., the Jewish traveler Benjamin of Tudela reported that he had visited synagogues in both Cairo and Palestine that still followed the triennial cycle. By the end of that century, Maimonides could state categorically that the annual cycle was virtually universal (MT Prayer 13:1).

The annual cycle instituted in Babylonia has remained the universal custom for reading

the Torah since the 12th century. An attempt to reintroduce the triennial cycle during the 19th century met with little success. One London synagogue, the West End Congregation, was discouraged from reintroducing the practice by Adolph Buechler, who argued that following a triennial cycle would separate the congregation from the rest of normative Judaism.

Nonetheless, many American Conservative congregations (seeking ways to modernize the service and to increase Torah study on *Shabbat*) attempted to modify the annual cycle as early as the late 1940s by reinstituting the triennial cycle. These attempts, which increased over the following three decades for other practical considerations as well, lacked uniformity and consistency. Thus, even though every synagogue was reading the same *parashah,* very likely they were not reading the same sections of that *parashah*. Another attempt to reintroduce the triennial cycle of Palestine to the Conservative Movement was rejected in 1987 by the CJLS on the basis of arguments strikingly similar to those of Adolph Buechler, almost 100 years earlier.

In place of the ancient triennial cycle of Palestine, a new American triennial cycle was adopted in 1988 by the CJLS. This cycle takes each of its weekly portions from the corresponding *parashah* of the annual cycle, although generally the reading from the triennial cycle is shorter. This cycle also incorporates the festival calendar, so that the entire Torah is read every three years in such a way that the reading is completed on *Simḥat Torah* (23 *Tishrei*). Although this system attempts to follow the literary units of the Torah when dividing each *parashah* into thirds, the American triennial cycle has a distinct disadvantage. By reading only one third of each *parashah* each year, the Torah is no longer read consecutively, so that narratives and bodies of biblical legislation are interrupted from week to week. Nonetheless, the new cycle has become increasingly popular in Conservative congregations and has introduced a greater order of uniformity in the Torah reading among the congregations that have adopted it. [*Editor's note*: The CJLS triennial cycle, edited by Richard Eisenberg, is available from the Rabbinical Assembly.]

The Torah is not literally read. It is chanted in a musical mode according to a system of special markings that are found in printed versions of the Hebrew Bible, but not in the Torah scroll. Each of these marks designates a series of musical notes called Masoretic accents (*ta·amei ha-mikra* or *ta·amim*). As early as the 3rd century C.E., the talmudic sage Yoḥanan noted that the Bible should be read and studied with a pleasant melody (BT Meg. 32a). Over the centuries, different Jewish communities have developed distinctive musical notes for the Masoretic accents. Currently there are five musical modalities for reading the Torah, and within each of these modalities there are regional and local variations.

The system of *ta·amim* that appears in printed texts of the Hebrew Bible was developed by biblical scholars known as Masoretes who lived in Tiberias (in northern Israel) during the 9th and 10th centuries C.E. The development of the *ta·amim* is only one aspect of their work. Their main goal was to preserve the text of the Hebrew Bible with the utmost accuracy. To this end, they developed the system of vowel signs still in use today to ensure that each word in the Torah would always be read the same way. They also counted the number of words and letters in the Torah and compiled a list of even the most insignificant deviations from what they had established as the authentic text of the Hebrew Bible.

The *ta·amim* have three distinct functions—musical, syntactical, and grammatical. Primarily they indicate the musical motifs in which the biblical text is chanted. Each accent represents a group of notes (tropes) that the reader fits to each word. The accents identify the stressed syllable in each word by being placed above or below the syllable that receives the stress. Knowing which syllable receives the stress helps provide meaning to the text, because often the only distinction between two

words that sound the same but have different meanings (homophones) is the syllable that receives the stress. The musical motif of the accents produces a chant that adds an aesthetic dimension to the public reading, as recommended in the Talmud.

All the *ta·amim* are classified into two groups—disjunctive *ta·amim* (called *m'lakhim*, "kings") and conjunctive *ta·amim* (called *m'shar'tim*, "servants"). They are arranged in patterns that help make the meaning of the text clear and intelligible by pointing to the interrelationship of words.

Most contemporary Jewish musicologists assume that the variety of musical modes or melodies for reading the Torah and other books of the Hebrew Bible developed independently in different places over a long period of time. Each of these musical modalities was equally legitimate at the time in which the forms of synagogue worship began to be stabilized. Later, some of these modes were accepted as normative by one community or by several communities.

The five current musical modes are: Yemenite; Ashkenazic; Middle Eastern and North African; Jerusalem Sephardic; and northern Mediterranean. Some of these have developed substyles. For example, the Middle Eastern and North African tradition developed distinctive musical motifs for Morocco and for Syria and Iraq. Similarly, the Ashkenazic style can be divided into western and eastern substyles. The former is still preserved by Jewish communities from Frankfurt and Hanover and is popular in Great Britain. The eastern Ashkenazic style developed in the Polish-Lithuanian communities, and it remains the most common system of musical motifs in North American Ashkenazic synagogues today.

THE TORAH SCROLL

Stuart Kelman

In its earliest transmission, the words of the Torah were etched onto stone tablets. Later, the words were written on papyrus and animal skins. To maintain this sacred tradition, Jews observe the *mitzvah* of writing the words of the Torah on specially prepared parchment, which is sewn together and rolled onto two wooden rollers. When Torah is read publicly, it is read from a Torah scroll (*seifer Torah*). When the Torah text is studied, it is read from a book like this one (*ḥumash*).

In Deut. 31:19, it is written: "Therefore, write down this poem and teach it to the people of Israel." This verse, according to the Sages, prescribes the responsibility of each Jew to write a *seifer Torah*. To fulfill this *mitzvah*, one can personally write a Torah scroll, have it written by a professional scribe (*sofer*), or help purchase one for a community.

The word *sofer* is a shortened form of the title *sofer stam;* the last word is an acronym for *"seifer Torah, t'fillin,* and *m'zuzot,"* the three items containing texts that a *sofer stam* writes.

A *sofer*'s work is a sacred calling. The practice of *safrut* (the art that a *sofer* practices) is not akin to calligraphy: It requires the mastery of many halakhic details, and it is transmitted through an apprenticeship with a master *sofer*.

Kavvanah (intentionality) is required for every step of the process. The *sofer*'s day begins with immersion in a *mikveh* (ritual bath), which is an act of spiritual purification that declares readiness to accept the obligation of the holy act of *safrut*. (If a *sofer* is unable to attend the *mikveh* for the day, a space for God's name is left, postponing the writing of God's name for a day on which the *sofer* could immerse in a *mikveh*. On that day, a special "God quill" and special bottle of ink may be used.)

The *sofer* commences work by writing the name of Amalek (the ancient enemy of the Jewish people) on a scrap of parchment. The name is then crossed out to fulfill the *mitzvah* of "blotting out the memory of Amalek from under the heaven" (Deut. 25:19). The *sofer* then writes a statement that translates as: "I

am writing this Torah in the name of its sanctity and the name of God's sanctity."

The *sofer*'s tools—parchment, pen, and inkwell—are referred to as "articles of honor." The parchment (*k'laf*) is made from specified sections of the hide of a kosher animal (not necessarily slaughtered according to Jewish ritual). The hide consists of three layers, but only the flesh side of the inner layer and the outer side of the hairy layer may be used for Torah parchment (BT Shab. 79b). The method of cleaning and softening the hide has changed throughout the centuries. During talmudic times, salt and barley flour were sprinkled on the skins, which were then soaked in the juice of gallnuts (BT Meg. 19a). In modern times, the skins are softened by soaking them in clear water for two days, after which the hair is removed by soaking the hides in limewater for nine days. Finally, the skins are rinsed and dried and the creases ironed out with presses, in a process similar to the curing of leather. In keeping with the sanctity of processing material for a *seifer Torah,* the person handling the skins must make a verbal declaration of intent, acknowledging that all actions are being performed for the holiness of the *seifer Torah.*

Due to the scarcity and high cost of parchment, a single *k'laf* was used more than once by rubbing out the writing with stone and superimposing new writing. This palimpsest is referred to in the dictum of Elisha ben Abuyah, who compares learning as a child to "ink written on clean paper" and learning in one's old age to "ink written on erased paper" (M Avot 4:20; Git. 2:4).

Although reeds were used as pens in the days of the Talmud, quills are used today; and the sturdy, durable turkey feather is preferred. The *sofer* cuts the point of the feather to give it a flat surface, which is desirable for forming the square letters, and then slits it lengthwise.

The ink used in writing a *seifer Torah* must be black and durable, but not indelible. During talmudic times a viscous ink was made by heating a vessel with the flame of olive oil; the soot thus produced on the sides of the vessel was scraped off and mixed with oil, honey, and gallnuts (BT Shab. 23a). Today, ink is produced from a mixture of gallnuts, gum arabic, and copper sulfate crystals. Some scribes also add vinegar and alcohol to render it glossy.

The actual printing of the letters follows one of three styles of script: The Ashkenazic resembles the script described in the Talmud (BT Shab. 104a). The Sephardic is identical with the printed letters of the Hebrew alphabet currently used in sacred texts. The Lurianic is the third style. The *sofer* must shape each letter precisely as pictured, and each must be written from left to right, with the initial stroke being (generally) a curved line produced by using just the point of the quill. Next, using the entire surface of the pen, the *sofer* draws the letter. The thickness of each letter varies and it is often necessary for the *sofer* to make several strokes to form a letter.

Tagin (an Aramaic word meaning "crowns") are specific ornamental designs placed at the upper left-hand corner of seven of the 22 letters of the Hebrew alphabet. Composed of three strokes, these crowns and their letters form the source of many mystical interpretations found in kabbalistic literature. There is a tradition that the *tagin* and the letters contain spiritual essences that emanate from God. According to Maimonides, if the *tagin* are omitted from the *seifer Torah,* the scroll is not considered to be invalid, because the *tagin* are an "exceptionally beautiful fulfillment of the *mitzvah*" (MT Torah Scroll 7:9). Ashkenazic custom, however, maintains that the scrolls are invalid without the appropriate *tagin* (*Magen Avraham* and *Ba·er Heitev* on S.A. O.Ḥ. 36:3).

There are precise specifications concerning the number of sheets of columns a Torah must have on each piece of *k'laf,* as well as the size of the columns, the space between individual letters, and the size of the gap between *parashiyyot* (portions). Although guidelines are incised for the top of a line of Torah text, there are none for the bottom of each letter. This is often given as one meaning of the *midrash* that the Torah has 70 faces (Num. R. 13:15). If a *sofer* makes a mistake in writing the *seifer Torah,* the ink can be erased with a knife or pumice

stone or piece of broken glass. However, base metals are generally not used to correct or even touch a Torah scroll, as these metals are used to make weapons, which render them unfit to touch a *seifer Torah,* which is an instrument of peace.

Any mistakes in the spelling of any of the names of God cannot be corrected, as the name of God cannot be erased. If a *seifer Torah* has extensive corrections, it is considered unsightly and, therefore, invalid. When invalid or beyond repair, a *seifer Torah* is buried in a *g'nizah* (place where holy objects are buried. In talmudic times, it was customary to bury such scrolls alongside the grave of a prominent rabbi (BT Meg. 26b).

Once the writing of *seifer Torah* is carefully checked and approved, the individual sheets of parchment are sewn together with *giddin,* a special thread made of tendon tissue taken from the foot muscles of a kosher animal. These sections of parchment are sewn on the outer side of the parchment, with one inch left unsewn both at the very top and bottom. To reinforce the *giddin,* thin strips of parchment are often pasted on the top and bottom of the page. After connecting the sheets, the ends are tied to *atzei ḥayyim* (trees of life), which is the name for the wooden rollers that hold the scroll. Each *etz ḥayyim* consists of a center pole, with handles of wood and flat circular rollers to support the rolled-up scroll. In addition to providing a means to roll the scroll, the *atzei ḥayyim* prevent people from touching the holy parchment with their hands. (In some Sephardic communities, flat rollers are not employed, because the Torah scrolls are kept in a *tik,* an upright ornamental wooden or metal case.) When reading from a *seifer Torah,* one does not touch the Torah with one's hands, but uses a *yad* (pointer; literally: "hand") to follow the letters.

The Talmud teaches that one who corrects even one letter in a *seifer Torah* is considered to have the merit of one who has written the entire scroll (BT Men. 30a). Many *sof'rim* outline the letters at the end of the Torah, leaving them to be filled in by individuals in a ceremony called *siyyum ha-Torah* (completion of a Torah scroll). In many congregations, this ceremony also includes a processional of other Torah scrolls, and the new *seifer Torah* is accompanied to the Ark with great joy and pageantry.

HAFTARAH

Michael Fishbane

The *haftarah* (plural: *haftarot*) is the selection from *N'vi·im* (Prophets) recited publicly after the designated portion from the Torah (Five Books of Moses) has been read on *Shabbat,* on festivals, and on other specified days. These communal readings are an integral part of classical Judaism, in both form and function.

The primary feature of the ancient institution of the synagogue is the recitation of the Torah. The Torah is chanted on *Shabbat* in a continuous sequence throughout the year, from beginning to end in a fixed cycle, interrupted only when a holiday (or an intermediate day of a festival) coincides with *Shabbat.* Next in importance for the synagogue is the recitation from a book of the prophets, selected to complement the Torah reading or to highlight the theme of a specific ritual occasion. These prophetic readings are selective, topical, and not read in sequence. These two recitations from Scripture (Torah and prophets) are enhanced by a homily (*d'rashah*) that interprets the readings in the light of tradition, theology, or historical circumstance.

This triad of Torah, prophets, and homily represents three levels of authority in Judaism, as well as three modes of religious instruction. The Torah is the most important of these, for it is the revelation to Moses and the teaching received from him—the foremost prophet, with whom God spoke directly (Num. 12:6–8). According to later (Rabbinic) tradition, the

difference between the divine revelations to Moses and those granted to other prophets is the difference between two modes of envisioning or experiencing the divine. Moses was allowed to see God clearly, through a shining mirror, whereas all other prophets had to perceive God through a glass darkly, as in an unclear and unpolished mirror (BT Yev. 49b).

Even though God's revelation to the prophets is less direct, the truth of their message is not diminished, because it too flowed from divine inspiration. Nevertheless, by making such a formal distinction, the ancient Sages differentiated between the primary teachings of Moses and the secondary teachings of the prophets. Their goal was to exhort the people to return to faithfulness to the Covenant and to announce the consequences of their behavior and the future fate of the people. The synagogue preacher could see his task as explicating the teachings of Moses, of the other prophets, or of both, on those occasions when he renewed God's message in the hearing of an assembled congregation.

The preacher thus added his words of interpretation to the divine words, to make their eternal relevance and significance clear and immediate to his contemporaries. However, even though he spoke on behalf of Moses and the prophets, the preacher's authority came from the Sages in their role as transmitters of the divine word. Their self-appointed task, in the synagogue as in the study hall, was to make Scripture come alive for the people. For these reasons, the Sages saw themselves as heirs to the prophets. "Since the day when the Temple was destroyed, prophecy has been taken from the prophets and given to the Sages" (BT BB 12a). The Sages, as teachers, thus gave institutional stability to the ancient words of Moses and consoled their community with the prophets' hopes and promises for the future.

When was the Torah first recited at communal gatherings? Evidence is scanty and often obscure. Two biblical passages are of note in this regard. In Deuteronomy (31:10–13), Moses instructs the priests into whose keeping he has given a written copy of "this teaching" (*ha-torah ha-zot*), namely, Deuteronomy. He tells them to "read" it "aloud in the presence of all Israel," "every seventh year" when they come before the Lord during the pilgrimage feast of *Sukkot.* The purpose of this septennial recitation was to instill both reverence for and observance of the precepts of the Torah in the entire community (Deut. 31:12–13). We may assume that the event was something of a covenant renewal ceremony, reproducing the event outlined in Deut. 29:9–14. On the basis of Moses' injunction to "gather [*hak·hel*] the people" together to hear the law (Deut. 31:12), this occasion traditionally has been known as the *mitzvah* of *hak·hel.* The other occasion of public Torah reading in the Bible is found in Neh. 8. There, it is reported that Ezra the Scribe, having returned recently to the land of Israel from Babylonian exile, gathered the people on the first day of the seventh month (*Rosh ha-Shanah*) to present to them the "book of the *torah* of Moses." This event is of interest for several reasons. First, it records a public reading that lasted from dawn to midday, with Ezra standing on a wooden platform surrounded by Levites. Second, when the scroll was opened, Ezra first blessed "the LORD, the great God," and the people responded "Amen, Amen" with upraised hands, after which they bowed down. Third, the Levites added meaning from the scroll with various clarifications and interpretations of the text (Neh. 8:8).

The practice of reading from the Torah each week on *Shabbat* is ascribed to Moses by ancient traditions (including the Mishnah). The recitation of a Torah portion on Monday and Thursday mornings and on *Shabbat* afternoon is considered one of the 10 legal innovations (*takkanot*) instituted by Ezra.

Our earliest evidence for reading the Torah in a continuous cycle is found in the Mishnah. There it states explicitly that on the four special Sabbaths between the first of *Adar* (the month of *Purim*) and the first of *Nisan* (the month of *Pesaḥ*), the regular *Shabbat* reading is interrupted. "On the fifth [*Shabbat*] one returns to the [regular] sequence" (M Meg. 3:4).

Interpretations also occurred when a festival or other special day coincided with *Shabbat.* On all of these occasions, other readings (out of sequence) were prescribed (M Meg. 4:2).

A continuous cycle of Torah readings was followed in the land of Israel near the beginning of our era, possibly as early as the 1st century C.E., although customs varied. Some authorities held that continuity implies reading portions from the Torah progressively each *Shabbat* morning, with the intervening readings on *Shabbat* afternoons; and brief readings on the market days of Monday and Thursday should be merely anticipations of the next *Shabbat* morning portion. Others held the opinion that a continuous reading implies an incremental reading of the Torah portion at the four public readings each week, with each reading continuing where the last stopped.

Far more complicated was the matter of how the continuous recitation should be subdivided, thereby determining when the cycle of readings from the entire Torah would be completed. There is a Babylonian tradition that "Westerners [Jews in the land of Israel] finish the Torah in three years" (BT Meg. 29b). This is confirmed in the later Gaonic statement about one of the differences in religious practice between the communities of Babylon and of the land of Israel: The "Easterners [Jews in Babylon] celebrate *Simḥat Torah* at the end of their reading cycle every year, whereas the residents of the land of Israel do so every three and a half years." Evidently, practices varied widely within the land of Israel itself depending on the way the special readings (e.g., for *Shabbat T'shuvah* or New Moon) affected the continuous recitations; and it is also possible that the number of readings were adjusted so that two triennial cycles could be completed every seven years. Most scholars regard the one-year cycle of 53 or 54 portions (*parashiyyot*) as a derivative Babylonian practice; it became dominant after the authority of the Babylonian academy was transferred to Spain in the 11th and 12th centuries C.E., especially because of the backing of Maimonides.

Determining specific portions of each *Shabbat* also was a prerequisite for the selection of readings from the prophets as *haftarot,* as they were correlated with the Torah portion by words, by theme, or by place in the liturgical cycle.

The origin of the *haftarah* is obscured both by the paucity of ancient evidence and by medieval legend. According to the latter, the custom of reciting several verses from the prophets in the synagogue service is said to go back to the 2nd century B.C.E. in the reign of Antiochus Epiphanes IV. When the king issued an edict prohibiting the reading of the Torah, the Jews were said to have evaded it by reading a passage from the prophets instead. This custom continued after the persecutions ceased. This theory still enjoys popular currency, although there is no corroborating evidence for it.

In antiquity, the selection of the *haftarah* varied greatly from community to community. This is clear from the diverse lists of prophetic readings for the so-called triennial cycle found in the Cairo Geniza and in many other collections of customs, including the references or allusions to *haftarot* found in the Midrash.

The correlation between the Torah and the *haftarah* readings could be established on the verbal or on the thematic level, on the basis of verbal similarities and thematic relationships. The triennial and annual cycles exhibit both features, although the element of verbal similarities occurs primarily on regular Sabbaths, when the main concern is the lesson of the Torah portion. The element of thematic relationships appears primarily on special Sabbaths, when the main concern is the religious topic of the day.

Thematic links between the Torah and the prophets in the early rabbinical sources in the land of Israel appear, as noted earlier, when *Shabbat* or another day commemorates a special ritual or religious occasion. The Mishnah mentions several days when a special selection from the Torah is recited. These include the four Sabbaths between the 1st of *Adar* and the

1st of *Nisan* (M Meg. 3:4); the three pilgrimage festivals of *Pesaḥ, Shavu·ot* (Pentecost), and *Sukkot* (Booths); and the holidays of *Rosh ha-Shanah* and *Yom Kippur* (M Meg. 3:5). They also include *Ḥanukkah, Purim,* and the New Moon (M Meg. 3:6).

The annual cycle has roots in the older multiyear cycles. Its choice of prophetic readings may be in part a selection from all the available *haftarot* in those cycles. This is particularly evident when the link between the Torah portion and the *haftarah* in the annual cycle occurs somewhere in the middle of the weekly *parashah* and not at the beginning. This striking phenomenon is explainable only by the fact that the length of any given section (*parashah*) for the annual cycle could embrace about three sections from the Palestinian triennial cycle. Thus each *haftarah* could have been chosen from a number of possibilities.

The annual cycle also conforms to old Palestinian traditions in its overall liturgical structure. As noted earlier, the weekly core of regular *Shabbat* readings, constituting a perpetual recitation of "God's word" in sequence, is sometimes interrupted by the substitution of other passages from the Torah. All of these sacred days had special Torah readings assigned to them. And pertinent *haftarot* were recited on the special Sabbaths, on holidays, and festivals (and the *Shabbat* of the festival week of *Pesaḥ* and of *Sukkot*), the *Shabbat* of *Ḥanukkah,* and when the New Moon coincided with *Shabbat* or occurred on the day after *Shabbat.* In addition, special *haftarot* were recited on 10 successive Sabbaths during the summer, beginning with the *Shabbat* after the 17th of *Tammuz,* which commemorates the first breach in the walls of Jerusalem during the Romans' final siege of the First Temple. The first three weeks of this period, which commemorates the destruction of the Temple and the exile of the people, are known as Sabbaths of Admonition. Warnings and exhortations are read from the first two chapters of Jeremiah and from the first chapter of Isaiah. The subsequent seven weeks, beginning with the *Shabbat* after *Tish·ah b'Av,* are known as Sabbaths of Consolation. During this period, words of comfort and hope are recited from Isa. 40ff.

Any year can have almost half as many special *haftarot* (21 or more) as *haftarot* for regular Sabbaths (54 or less). This ratio changes in favor of the special *haftarot* when holidays and festivals coincide with *Shabbat* or when there are two Sabbaths during the feast of *Ḥanukkah.* All such occasions interrupt the regular cycle of Torah readings and require an adjustment that results in the combination of two Torah portions on one *Shabbat.* This, in turn, leads to a reduction of regular *haftarot,* for when two Torah portions are joined, only the *haftarah* assigned to the second one is recited. The combined total ensures that the teachings and topics preserved in the prophetic literature have a dominant place in the public instruction of the community. This intrusion was aided and furthered by the homiletic use of these passages in the synagogue as well as by the Aramaic translation and paraphrasing (*targum*) that accompanied them.

The broad base of instruction through the prophetic literature is also clear from the distribution of the books from which the *haftarot* are derived in the annual cycle. Of the 54 selections, the largest cluster is from the book of Isaiah (14), with fewer from Jeremiah (8), Ezekiel (6), and the minor prophets (9). This cluster makes up two thirds of the Torah readings and constitutes a contrast with the *haftarot* in the triennial cycle. In that cycle, two thirds of the *haftarot* were from Isa. 40–66 (dealing with redemption and ingathering) and fully four fifths of them had a messianic or eschatologic dimension. In the *haftarot* of the annual cycle, by contrast, the smaller percentage of material from the later chapters of Isaiah is notable, as is the lesser emphasis on messianic features. The *haftarot* of the annual cycle emphasize the national future and the restoration of the people to the Land and reflect a strong interest in historical parallels or symmetries between the Torah portion and its *haftarah.*

Parallels between events, persons, or institutions also highlight many types of continuities and correlations within Scripture.

One cannot speak of any consistent literary feature or style among the *haftarot.* Each individual reading sculpts its discourse out of a larger context and establishes its own rhetorical emphasis and features. In several cases, the *haftarot* overlap separate units of scripture, thus underscoring the fact that the prophetic readings are a rabbinical creation and institution. The diverse forms are discussed in the commentary to the *haftarot* in this volume. Also because of the great variety of texts and topics, there is no consistent theme or emphasis among the *haftarot.* Nevertheless, religious instruction and national hope are frequent features. The individual types are also considered in the commentary.

For the synagogue, the *haftarah* marks the "leaving off" (*aftarta*) or "completion" (*ashlamata*) of the official Torah service and is formally set off from it in several ways. The *haftarah* service, so to speak, begins after the reading from the Torah portion has been completed and a half *Kaddish* has been recited to mark a break between it and what follows. Then a brief passage (of at least three verses) at the end of the Torah portion is repeated. After the Torah scroll is rolled up and set aside, the *haftarah* is chanted. Blessings before and after the recitation of the *haftarah* enhance the authority of the lesson from the Prophets and present it within a sacred liturgical framework.

MIDRASH

David Wolpe

The Bible is at once powerful and cryptic. Characters are often sketched rather than elaborately described, and key concepts are not always spelled out. The Bible instructs us not to perform *"m'lakhah"* on *Shabbat,* but the word *m'lakhah* is never defined! The rabbinical tradition comes along to fill gaps, analyze implications, color in characters, spin tales, and derive laws—to take the biblical text as a starting point for building the structure of Jewish life.

The medium through which the Sages work is *midrash.* The word *midrash* comes from the root דרש—to search out. Use of this word can be confusing, because it refers both to a method and a body of work. There are books of collected *midrash* (plural: *midrashim*), the most well-known being *Midrash Rabbah* (literally: Great Midrash, Large Midrash). The body of *midrash* in the Talmud is referred to as *aggadah.* Yet one can also speak of "doing" *midrash*, of seeking out and explicating texts. *Midrash* is a type of investigation of a text, or a genre, not just a body of literature; and it is found in different measures in all the classical rabbinical literature.

Most classical *midrash* originated in ancient Palestine, among rabbis who lived from the end of the Roman Era (ca. 3rd century C.E.) to the beginning of the Islamic Era (the 8th or 9th century C.E.). Some *midrashim* were written and polished later than the 7th century, and the origins of *midrash* go back much further, not only to earlier sages (of the Tannaitic period, the first few centuries of the Common Era) but also back, in fact, to the Bible itself.

In Exod. 12:8, we are told that the paschal sacrifice must be eaten "roasted over the fire." Deut. 16:7 states: "You shall cook and eat it." The words for "cook" and "roast" denote different processes. In 2 Chron. 35:13, there is a reconciliation: "They roasted the passover sacrifice in fire, as prescribed, while the sacred offerings they cooked in pots." This simple illustration of the midrashic process at work in the Bible shows how problems of interpretation arise and are resolved from the very beginning of a system of law and lore.

In Jer. 25:11–12, 29:10, a prophecy reads: "And those nations shall serve the king of Babylon seventy years. When the seventy years are over, I will punish the king of Babylon and

that nation. . . . For thus said the LORD: When Babylon's seventy years are over, I will take note of you, and I will fulfill to you My promise of favor—to bring you back to this place." God apparently made a clear promise to the people through Jeremiah: In 70 years, they would be redeemed. But a few hundred years later, in the time of Daniel, it appeared to Daniel and his contemporaries that the prophecy had not been realized. They were still not free. So Daniel re-envisioned the prophecy: "Seventy weeks [of years, i.e., 70 × 7] have been decreed for your people and your holy city until the measure of transgression is filled and that of sin complete" (Dan. 9:24). Daniel has recast Jeremiah's prophecy to mean 490 years.

Both of these examples, although they come from the Bible itself, illustrate important principles about the Midrash as it flourished among the Sages. First, there is the fundamental underlying assumption that the Torah is entirely the word of God. Therefore, all of it is true and all of it is relevant. If something in the Torah seems to contradict experience, either the experience has been wrongly interpreted or the Torah has not been properly understood. Thus the text of Daniel has no qualms about understanding the Torah differently from what we might see as the "plain" sense of the text. For the Torah cannot get it wrong. It must be correct, and it must be all-inclusive. As Mishnah *Avot* (5:22) puts it: "Turn it [the Torah] over and over, for everything is in it."

Scholars divide *midrashim* differently. The oldest categorization is between legal and homiletical *midrashim*; from the Bible onward, there were *midrashim* whose aim was primarily legal (as in which way the paschal lamb should be cooked) and others that were primarily homiletical (sermonic, as in when redemption would arrive). The legal *midrashim* have been called *midrash halakhah* and the homiletic, *midrash aggadah*.

The legal *midrashim* deal with the whole range of Jewish law, which is as wide as human experience. Everything from dietary laws to sexual practices to civil codes rests on a network of interpretation that views the entire Torah as one seamless, interconnected web of the divine word. The homiletic *midrashim* gave the rabbinical imagination free rein: stories, counsel, pithy wisdom, and far-fetched fables all found their way into the *aggadah.*

The third lesson to be derived from these examples is that the Torah is not only all-inclusive but also does not wane or change with time. Because God has authored the text, the entire text is sacred and timelessly relevant. The midrashic sense of time is not entirely linear. In God's word, the past and future live in constant interaction. There is no anachronism, no sense that things are out of time sequence and therefore impossible.

Thus in elaborating the story of the Binding of Isaac (Gen. 22:1–19), medieval *midrash* has Abraham quoting a psalm that would not be written for some 1,000 years: "Abraham's eyes were fixed on Isaac's, while Isaac's eyes were fixed on the heavens. Tears flowed from Abraham as he cried out 'My son, may your Creator provide another sacrifice in your stead.' A piercing cry of agony rose from his lips; his eyes, pained and trembling, looked at the divine Presence as he raised his voice and said: 'I will lift my eyes to the mountains; from where shall my help come?'" (Ps. 121:1; Yalkut Sh. 101). Similarly, for Daniel the prophecy of Jeremiah is not time bound; it must be relevant to Daniel's own situation, for the word of God does not lapse or expire.

Law and lore are not the only way to divide up the Midrash. Other possible divisions exist, including distinguishing between literary forms, such as sermonic and expositional. A famous collection of sermonic *midrashim* is *P'sikta d'Rav Kahana.* Sermonic *midrashim* draw a moral point, usually by ranging far over scripture and tradition. They generally use a verse as a jumping-off point to display textual and rhetorical virtuosity. For instance, the phrase "on the day that Moses finished setting up the tabernacle" (Num. 7:1) provides *P'sikta d'Rav Kahana* with an opportunity to begin a beautiful homily. The problem: Moses was not the architect—Bezalel ben Uri was

responsible for construction; so why does the Torah credit Moses? The Midrash explains how in each generation evil people push the divine Presence away from the world, while *tzaddikim,* the righteous, bring it closer. Because God's Presence dwelt in the tabernacle, it was Moses' merit to have drawn that Presence down to earth. In the process of this explanation, the Midrash quotes numerous sources, makes wide connections over different parts of Scripture, and winds up by returning to the opening verse (the *p'tiḥta*) with which it began. By the end we have been taken on a theological tour of history, including times when God's presence seemed far away, and we are taught how the tabernacle and the merit of the righteous combined to bring God close.

Other *midrashim* form a sort of running expositional commentary on the Bible. They are explanatory, not sermonic, and follow the Bible verse by verse. A famous example cites the *Akedah,* the Binding of Isaac mentioned above. The Midrash follows the drama from the outset. Here is an example of continuous commentary:

> **Ber. R. 55:7.** *Take your son, your favored one* (lit.: your only one), *whom you love, Isaac* (Gen. 22:1). [The Midrash now envisages a dialogue between God and Abraham which accounts for the apparent redundancy of that sentence.] "*Take your son,*" God said. "Which one?" asked Abraham. "*Your only son,*" replied God. "But each is an only son to his mother," answered Abraham. "*Whom you love,*" said God. "But I love both," answered Abraham. Finally, God said, "*Isaac.*"
>
> **55:8.** Rabbi Simeon bar Yoḥai said: "Both love and hate disturb the usual patterns of life. Thus it says: *So early next morning, Abraham saddled his ass* (Gen. 22:2). Surely he had many slaves [who could have done it for him]! But love changes the usual pattern. Conversely, it says: *When he arose in the morning, Balaam saddled his ass* (Num. 22:21). Surely he, too, had many slaves! But he did it himself because hate changes the usual pattern."

We see here that the Midrash explores Abraham's psychology through continuous comment. In the first place, it shows that Abraham, who in the biblical text seemingly raises no protest, tried to confuse the issue until God made clear He was asking for the sacrifice of Isaac. At the same time the Midrash exploits a redundancy in the text. In the second case, Abraham's saddling his own donkey is tied to a later instance when the pagan magician Balaam saddles his own donkey to curse Israel. The Midrash makes the acute psychological point that passion leads one to perform an action oneself; we do not trust others to take care of our beloved or to dispatch our enemies. At the same time, it reveals that Abraham's state of mind was ardent, not indifferent, as one could assume without the aid of the Sages' reading.

For the Sages, the biblical text is a springboard. But not all *midrashim*—even the nonlegal *midrashim*—are concerned with interpreting the Bible. The Sages also tell tales of postbiblical personalities and events. There are tales of rabbinical figures, of kings, of pagans, and of princes. Still, the bulk of *aggadah* fills in the tales of characters or events in the Bible. Midrash advances our understanding of the biblical characters and fills in gaps in the text. What happened during the three days that Abraham and Isaac traveled to Mount Moriah for the *Akedah*? What exchanges took place between Moses and God at the end of the Torah as this greatest of prophets stood alone on the mountain preparing to die? The Sages, with their human insight and exhaustive familiarity with the biblical text and tradition, are ready with a story, a poignant observation, or a subtle interpretation that helps the text live anew.

No character is more often illumined than the character of God. The text that tells of God's destruction of the tower of Babel reads: "The LORD came down to look at the city and the tower" (Gen. 11:5). Surely God does not need to move down? The Sages could have engaged in abstract discussion about whether the text really intends to suggest that God moved.

That would be the tack of the philosopher. Instead, they drew a lesson: Although God sees all, "came down" is written to teach us that one should not pronounce judgment on that which one has not personally examined (Tanḥ. B. Noaḥ 28).

Many of the *midrashim* about God compare Him to a king and contrast God's behavior with that of an earthly monarch. A *midrash* on Psalms (149:1) is typical: "While an earthly king has all sorts of attendants and lieutenants and viceroys who share in his tasks and his glory, it is not so with the King of kings: God bears the burdens alone, and God alone deserves our praise."

Midrash is both serious and playful. Although some of the fables stem from a religious inclination, many represent an artistic vehicle. Often the narratives of *midrash aggadah* appeal to our human imperative to tell and hear stories. As stated in the Midrash: "In olden days when people had means, they would want to hear words of Mishnah and Talmud. Now when people are impoverished, and suffering from the pangs of exile, they want to hear Bible—and the tales of *aggadah*" (PdRK 101).

Finally, the text itself impels *midrash*. The Bible demands *midrash* when there is some problem, inconsistency, or oddity. If a word is spelled peculiarly, if an unusual word is used, or if the sequence of words or verses is strange, the Midrash leaps in to illuminate, explain, or speculate. At the end of the story of Joseph, his father, Jacob, has died. Joseph is viceroy of Egypt. Joseph's brothers, afraid that he will now seek to exact punishment for their early treatment of him, send a message to Joseph. The brothers contend that their father, Jacob, before he died, left a message asking Joseph to please forgive his brothers (Gen. 50:17). The Sages, noting that the message contains the word "please" three times, state: "One who has wronged another is obligated to seek forgiveness at least three separate times" (BT Yoma 87a). From here later authorities derived the practice of asking for forgiveness three times before *Yom Kippur* if we have wronged another (see S.A. O.Ḥ. 606). Not only have the Sages called attention to the language of Joseph's brothers, thereby giving us an insight into their state of mind, but they have drawn from the verse an important moral lesson.

In exploring the biblical account of Creation, the Sages exhibit a natural interest in the nature of humanity. That, allied to the deep interest in words we mentioned above, leads to the following *midrash*: "The LORD God formed [וייצר; *va-yyitzer*] man" (Gen. 2:7). "Why does וייצר have the letter *yod* twice [which is not necessary for proper spelling]? To show that God created the human being with both a good inclination and an evil inclination" (BT Ber. 61a). This *midrash* shows the Sages using the text as an opportunity. Surely the rabbinical notion that human beings have two opposing natures battling in our breasts did not arise because of the spelling of the word *va-yyitzer*! From experience and learning, the Sages concluded this about humanity; the next step was to find a biblical basis for this observed truth.

That is why even frivolous *midrash* is serious. *Midrash* is the tool by which our ancestors unpacked the meaning of a text or even read their own meaning into the text. *Midrash* is associative; a word that appears in two entirely different contexts can be used to link them together. Because everything is written by God, there can be no accidental juxtapositions.

By now we can understand why Hebrew is so vital to the midrashic enterprise. Texts written in Hebrew, the holy tongue (*l'shon ha-kodesh*), are in the original language. Many *midrashim* are based on puns and other Hebrew allusions and cannot truly be appreciated without recourse to Hebrew. Because there is nothing superfluous in the biblical text and Hebrew is the sacred language, the "trigger" for a *midrash* need not be a whole story. The trigger can be a verse, a word, or even a single letter—as we saw above in the case of *va-yyitzer.*

The Bible is not a text that can be emended. No verse can be added or cut out. The only

way to get the Bible to yield different meanings that can accommodate new situations is to interpret.

Although classical *midrash* is time bound, the midrashic enterprise continues. In our own day, scholars, preachers, and interested readers develop their own interpretations and tales about the Bible. In each generation, different concerns and disciplines lead readers to new insights. From the beginning of Jewish tradition, pious Jews not only have received the text but also have helped shape it through their clarifications, expositions, additions, and interpretations—in short, through *midrash*. By *midrash* we make the text more vivid, and we make it our own.

TRADITIONAL METHODS OF BIBLE STUDY

Benjamin Edidin Scolnic

What we think the Torah is helps determine the way in which we read it. Traditional Jewish commentators believe that the words of the Torah were revealed by God to Moses. Therefore, when there seem to be contradictions or errors, the commentators set about to harmonize apparent inconsistencies into one true and consistent Torah text. They also try to explain any discrepancies between biblical concepts and the ideas and beliefs of their own time. Interpretation is thus a necessity for every generation.

Modern critical scholarship reads the Bible as a document of religious faith expressed within a specific culture, tied to a specific time, limited by the meaning of the authors. Every text of the Bible, in this view, is time bound. Traditional commentators in every age seek the timeless, eternal voice of God in the words of the Torah; their reading of the Bible is informed by a deep theological commitment to an eternal God whose very word is understood as being imbedded in the text.

Over the centuries, traditional commentators have used several different approaches to discover the layers of meaning in the Torah. A convenient way to think about these approaches or levels is through a Hebrew acronym that was created for this purpose: "PaRDeS." To illustrate what PaRDeS means, let us briefly examine two verses that tell of the journey of Abraham (then known as Abram) from Egypt to Canaan:

> And he proceeded by stages from the Negeb as far as Bethel, to the place where his tent had been formerly, between Bethel and Ai, the site of the altar that he had built there at first; and there Abram invoked the LORD by name (Gen. 13:3–4).

The commentators interpret the text using the following approaches:

- *P'shat:* the plain, literal sense of the verse in its context. Abraham returns to Canaan from Egypt "by stages"; he moves from one oasis to another.
- *Remez* (hint, symbol): the allegorical meaning of the verse. Each character or place in the text has a symbolic meaning. The word "Abram" is understood to be the soul; his travels trace its spiritual journey.
- *D'rash:* the homiletical meaning of the verse as viewed outside of its original context. Specific ideas and values are derived from the text, whether the text, in its literal meaning, could mean this or not. This approach reveals Abram's true intention: to visit many places where he could teach the word of God.
- *Sod:* the secret, mystical interpretation of the verse. This approach teaches that the land of Israel draws Abram from a purely nonphysical state of being to one of concrete physical reality.

PaRDeS has become a well-recognized framework for understanding traditional methods of Torah study. No single method of interpretation is considered to be the best, because the Torah is layered with meaning, is multifac-

eted. Although each verse means something in its specific context, it can mean many other things as well. This is demonstrated in *Mikra·ot G'dolot,* a traditional edition of the Bible in which each page contains a biblical verse or a passage in Hebrew, an ancient Aramaic translation of the text, and a number of medieval commentaries in Hebrew. Different interpretations are placed on the same page, presenting the message that there is no one definitive interpretation of any verse.

P'SHAT AND *D'RASH*

The most important traditional methods of study are *p'shat* and *d'rash*. *P'shat* is literal; it is "reading out" from the text (exegesis); *d'rash* is nonliteral, it is "reading into" the text (eisegesis). Although it may seem that *p'shat* preceded *d'rash,* the historical fact is that *d'rash* was the primary Jewish method of study until the 11th and 12th centuries C.E.—the time of Rashi, Ibn Ezra, and Rashbam. *P'shat* is interested in the original meaning, though sometimes a *p'shat* is a reading out of context that has become authoritative and accepted.

D'rash implicitly states: "What these words may have meant originally in their context is not all that they mean. We of a later generation can understand these same words in a different manner." The sometimes imaginative daring of *d'rash* demonstrates its ability to transform meaning and its refusal to remain bound by the context of an earlier time.

To illustrate how *p'shat* and *d'rash* produce quite different interpretations, let us focus on Gen. 49:10, a verse that many call the most controversial in all of Genesis. Jacob, the third of the patriarchs after Abraham and Isaac, gives his last will and testament to his 12 sons, including these words to his son Judah:

> The scepter shall not depart from Judah,
> Nor the ruler's staff from between his feet;
> So that tribute shall come to him
> [lit: "Until he comes to Shiloh"]
> And the homage of peoples be his.

Many explanations have been given for the word "Shiloh." Rashbam, a great *p'shat* commentator and the grandson of Rashi, states that this verse is a prediction of events that will happen centuries in the future. After the successful reigns of two kings from the tribe of Judah, David and Solomon (ca. 1000–920 B.C.E.), Solomon's son Rehoboam will be unable to hold the kingdom together. Rehoboam will come to the northern city of Shechem and antagonize the 10 northern tribes, who will then secede from the united kingdom. Rashbam explains that the scepter will not depart from Judah until Rehoboam comes to Shechem, because that is where the kingdoms will be divided. Shechem is next to Shiloh. In this interpretation of Gen. 49:10, Jacob predicts that Judah's privilege of sovereignty over his 11 brothers will last only until he (Judah's descendant) comes to (the city of) Shiloh.

This *p'shat* interpretation places the verse in a historical context. The verse is a reference to a one-time event that will be fulfilled. If this interpretation is correct, it makes the enigmatic verse from Jacob's prophecy into a prediction of an event of historical interest.

D'rash moves the discussion to a different level. In rabbinical interpretation, this verse becomes the primary source in the Torah for belief in the Messiah. Thus in this verse Jacob is blessing, and prophesying about, his son Judah, the ancestor of King David; Jacob's last words to Judah seem to be a logical place for a reference to the Messiah, who will be descended from Judah and that great king. The ancient Aramaic translation by Onkelos renders this verse as "until the Messiah, to whom the kingdom [Shiloh as *shelo,* or "his"] comes."

Rashba accepted this interpretation and concluded that "the scepter" would never depart from Judah—because the Messiah, a descendent of the tribe of Judah, would reign forever. Christian interpretation, however, claimed that the verse pointed to Jesus, who came after the Hasmonean monarchy ("the scepter") had departed from the Jews, as the patriarchal blessing had foretold. To counter this claim, Baḥya ben Asher argued that the Messiah could not be divine as the Christians claimed, because "Shiloh" derived from *shilya*

(placenta), proving that the Messiah would be a human being, naturally conceived and born to a woman.

It is instructive to see how *d'rash* has taken this verse from a specific historical reference to a verse of the greatest magnitude for Judaism and the future of humankind. But it is also ironic that only because the verse was interpreted midrashically to predict the Messiah did the Jews have to defend the text against Christian claims. Once this verse, or any other verse, is open to noncontextual exegesis, there are no objective standards for validity in interpretation. It is also important to note that *p'shat* is the best defense against the Christian suggestion that Shiloh is a prediction of Jesus. In referring us to the literal meaning of the verse in its historical context, *p'shat* presents a meaning that obviously has nothing to do with events 1000 years after the time of King David.

Let us turn to a different example of how *p'shat* and *d'rash* work by examining another well-known verse: "And this shall serve you as a sign on your hand and as a reminder on your forehead" (Exod. 13:9). Rashbam comments: "It shall be for you a reminder as if they [the events of the Exodus] were written on your hand. They are to be taken [figuratively,] just as in 'set me as a seal upon your heart' [Song 8:6]." Rashbam carefully separates the *p'shat,* the literal, contextual explanation of the verse, from the traditional understanding of it with its halakhic (legal/ritual) implications. Rashbam does not need to make the *p'shat* and the *halakhah* one and the same. The Sages do interpret the text as mandating the putting on of *t'fillin,* and that is the *halakhah;* but it is not the *p'shat* of the text. The latter is a metaphor for always being mindful of God's commandments. Even the great *p'shat* interpreter Ibn Ezra did not go this far, agreeing that the verse had the halakhic ruling in mind. Like the Sages, he saw the need for unambiguously supporting the *halakhah* of donning *t'fillin* for the morning service with a biblical injunction.

This careful separation of the *p'shat* from *halakhah* seems natural to modern readers; the direct reading of the verse without Midrash as an intermediary is closer to our way of reading. It would be more useful for religious transmission, however, if the verse did refer to *t'fillin.*

When considered out of context, both *p'shat* and *d'rash* are limited. In the case of Gen. 49:10, the *p'shat* is a specific historical reference, whereas the *d'rash* creates a difficult problem for Jews living in a Christian culture. In the case of Exod. 13:9, the *p'shat* is a valid reading of the verse but is much less halakhically relevant than the *d'rash.*

Traditional commentators often struggle with contextual interpretations based on *p'shat* and acontextual explanations of laws based on *d'rash.* But the struggle is a necessary one; it is an example of how the complexity of the Torah demands sophistication. We need both *p'shat* and *d'rash* to understand that God's word has been interpreted according to God's additional revelations. *P'shat* is the word of God, the verse itself; the additional revelations, manifested in the interpretations that created and reflect normative Judaism, are illuminated by the various methods of study.

REMEZ

The third element of the PaRDeS grid is *remez,* the allegorical or philosophical interpretation. The great period of this type of interpretation encompassed the 14th through 16th centuries when such luminaries as Ralbag, Arama, Sforno, and Abravanel wrote their commentaries. An example of *remez* can be found in Abravanel's philosophical understanding of the people's sin with the Tower of Babel (Gen. 11:1–9).

> Adam and Eve were expelled from the Garden of Eden because they made the tree of knowledge their ultimate aim and neglected the tree of life, the true purpose of humankind. In the same way, the people of Babel had all of life's necessities . . . provided for them by God from heaven. They . . . could have devoted themselves entirely to the attainment of perfection for their souls. . . . They sought instead . . . to build a city in which all kinds of work could take place. There would be a

> tower in that city. . . . But arising out of this kind of life are the struggles for fame, titles, and power—for illusory honors and the accumulation of possessions. . . . Since all of this is truly superfluous . . . preventing men from attaining their true perfection, that of the soul, therefore these sinners against the soul were punished in that God confused their tongues and scattered them on the face of the earth.

Abravanel's message was for the city dwellers of his own time. He knew that people like himself would seek to rise in civilized society. Even so, they must not forget the true purpose of life—the fulfillment of the soul.

Another example of *remez* can be found in Lev. 14:33–53, a passage concerning a mold or fungoid blight (*tzara·at*) that produces discoloration in the plaster or mud used to cover building stones. The homeowner reports the condition to the priest, who either declares the house "pure" or orders its dismantling. For Arama (in *Akedat Yitzḥak*), the blemishes that afflict the house are symbolic of bad habits acquired through association with bad people.

> The house is representative of one's wider social contacts. . . . Locking up of the house by the priests suggests to the owner that he must keep away from his usual social environment and get rid of the negative influences he has acquired through such associations. . . . The very fact that the Talmud states such stringent criteria . . . makes it practically impossible for these requirements to be fully met. This bears out the symbolic nature of this piece of Torah legislation.

Allegorical interpretation explains a text from within a cultural situation in which a literal interpretation would be incomprehensible. When encountering a literal reading that seemed irrelevant or inconsequential, traditional commentators learned how to find levels of meaning that were important for their own time.

In *remez,* a traditional commentary finds contemporary meaning in the biblical text. Instead of a house with fungus, we are confronted by a person's associations with evil people. A literal interpretation limited in scope is replaced with a symbolic explanation that is more edifying.

SOD

We turn now to mystical interpretation. One of Rashi's most important accomplishments was transmitting the important rabbinical *midrashim* on the biblical text. Later commentators, however, would often have difficulties with Rashi's presentation of these *midrashim* at face value. Mystical commentators gave these same *midrashim* deeper, secret meanings (*sod*). For example, Rashi cites a *midrash* that teaches that the ram's horn that sounded on Mount Sinai at the time of Revelation (Exod. 19:13) was the horn of the ram sacrificed by Abraham as a substitution for Isaac (Gen. 22:13). The Binding of Isaac, with all of its emotional power, with its great message of faith at all costs, is now connected with the binding of the Israelites to God at Mount Sinai. Ramban denies that this could be, recalling that the ram had been completely burnt as a whole offering, including its horns. Ramban goes on to teach a *sod* interpretation: The voice that was heard on Mount Sinai was the voice of what was known as "The Fear of Isaac." This is one of the 10 aspects (or emanations) of God (symbolizing *G'vurah,* "strength") in the kabbalistic system.

A longer example may more fully illustrate the mystical development of *midrashim.* In both the story of the Burning Bush (Exod. 3–4) and the Call of Moses in Egypt (Exod. 6–7), we have the same elements:

1. God tells Moses of His plan to save Israel and commands Moses to tell the people of the plan.

2. Moses learns God's sacred name, which had not been known before.

3. God commands Moses to go to Pharaoh.

4. Moses objects that he is of clumsy speech, and Aaron is therefore appointed as a spokesman.

5. Moses and Aaron confront Pharaoh and are rejected.

The exegetical challenge is to explain why God calls Moses a second time—and why all of these elements, especially the appointment of Aaron, are repeated.

The rabbis of the Midrash saw the challenge in finding two versions of one story in the Torah. Akiva's interpretation is as powerful for our generation as it must have been for his. He said that Moses argued:

> "I know that You will deliver the Israelites one day, but what about those who have been buried alive in the building?" Then did the divine attribute of justice seek to strike Moses, but after God saw that Moses argued in this way only because of Israel's suffering, He retracted and did not allow the attribute of justice to strike him, instead dealing with him according to the divine attribute of mercy.

Moses' question is very much like the question many modern Jews have asked: "It's wonderful and comforting that the State of Israel now exists, but where was God during the Holocaust while six million were being killed?" Here Moses says, "It's wonderful that You're going to save the Israelites from slavery, but what about all of the Israelites who have been killed during their enslavement to these evil Egyptians?" The Sages saw God as having two attributes: the attribute of justice, which is represented by the divine name *Elohim* (or *Adonai*), and the attribute of mercy, which is represented by the divine name *YHVH.* The attribute of justice (*Elohim*) wants to kill Moses for his challenging question, but the attribute of mercy (*YHVH*) wants to save him, because it knows that Moses is asking only out of his anguish for those who have been killed.

The second call is, in this reading, part of a dramatic situation that needs a solution, an interesting challenge to God that needs an answer. Moses and God, at odds with each other, must be reconciled. To bring about this reconciliation, God needs to send forth a renewed call, full of reassurance for Moses, who needs to hear everything all over again. And that is why, according to this *midrash*, there was a second call so similar to the call at the Burning Bush.

However, the Zohar explains that different aspects of God, represented by the different names of God, are part of the dramatic dialogue between God and Moses. This *sod* interpretation then goes on to explain that two methods of communication—voice and utterance—are represented by the figures of Moses and Aaron. The Zohar then wonders how Moses can bring up the problem of speaking again, because it had already been dealt with at the Burning Bush. The apparent redundancy points to an inner meaning. Moses has voice but lacks utterance. Pharaoh can hear God's demands only if voice and utterance are one. God gives Aaron (utterance) to be at the side of Moses (voice). But it was only at Mount Sinai that voice was actually united with utterance. It was only then that Moses was healed of his impediment, when voice and utterance were united in him as their organ.

In modern literary terms, we can speak of the content of God's message, represented by Moses (voice), and the form, symbolized by Aaron (utterance). Traditional interpretation strives to unite the words of the Torah with the revelations of God. If the Torah is the word of God, then its words, its utterance, express the content of His revelations. Every utterance, every word, must be filled with meaning; it is the task of the commentator to discover the levels of meaning. Moses needs Aaron, content needs utterance, and the Torah needs commentary.

For the modern reader who believes that the Torah is the word of God, discovering the levels of meaning in the biblical text is a fundamental part of life. But what of the modern reader who does not believe that the Torah is the revelation of God, who thinks that traditional commentaries are inventing all meaning above the level of *p'shat*? For this reader, traditional Jewish commentary can be understood as a fascinating process, a dialogue between the sacred text and the generations of Jews who have kept it at the center of their lives.

Commentary is not simply an attempt to know what the Torah is saying, but the intellectual foundation for the process by which Judaism has grown, adopting and adapting to new environments and cultural situations. The openness to new interpretation assumes the belief, or concept, that God's revelations are still unfolding.

There is something about the Torah that prevents all commentators, whether traditional or modern, from finding definitive solutions; the problems usually remain problems. The Torah remains open; no one can close it. Modern readers may think of themselves as strangers in PaRDeS, uncomfortable with anything but literal interpretation. But modern readers need to recognize that all language is figurative and thus must remain open to interpretation. Just as angels guard the way back to the Garden of Eden, the traditional commentators show the way back to the paradise of Jewish meaning.

MODERN METHODS OF BIBLE STUDY

Benjamin Edidin Scolnic

Modern biblical criticism is based on two assumptions: (a) Because the Bible is a collection of documents written in human language by human authors, it is subject to the same methods of historical and literary investigation as all other books and documents. Modern critical study rejects the idea of divine authorship and the concept of multiple levels of meaning that all emanate from God. (b) The biblical texts must be understood in their original, historical, and cultural contexts. Modern biblical criticism employs many methods of interpretation, the most important of which are textual criticism, source criticism, literary criticism, and structuralism and deconstructionism.

TEXTUAL CRITICISM

Textual criticism attempts to understand the words written by the human authors. The oldest complete forms of the books of the Torah extant today are in manuscript (handwritten) copies, none of which is earlier than the 10th century C.E. There is, therefore, a gap of as much as 2,000 years between the original writing of the document and the earliest complete copy to which we have access.

Of the several thousand manuscript copies and fragments of the various parts of the Bible that exist today, no two are identical. This is to be expected. How could any literary work that was handed down for many generations be free from error? And yet, the evidence of the Dead Sea Scrolls from Qumran, dating from 2,000 years ago (and thus 1,000 years earlier than the complete copies), confirms the general reliability of the basic textual tradition that has been transmitted.

Although average readers of the Bible will not concern themselves with the details of textual criticism, modern study of the Bible has benefited greatly from the diligent research of textual critics. This type of criticism is the basis for the translation of the Bible from its original Hebrew and Aramaic into the languages of the modern reader. In that every translation is an interpretation, the basis for translation must be studied carefully.

Many of us naively assume that the Torah we use today is an exact copy of one original text, but there are many versions of the text of the Torah. Most of the English translations of the Torah under Jewish auspices are based on what is called the Masoretic text, a text that has been passed down to us by a group of scholars and scribes called the Masoretes, who lived around 1,000 years ago. This text is the Torah as we know it. We have a Greek translation of the Hebrew Torah that is well over 1,000 years older than the Masoretic text. Of the manuscripts that we actually have, the Greek version, the Septuagint (sometimes referred to as the "LXX") is much closer in time to the original Torah. If there is a difference between the Septuagint text and the Hebrew

Masoretic text, the Greek is not necessarily more valid simply because it is older. However when there are significant differences, the Greek version is given serious consideration.

In the Masoretic text, we read about Moses' parents in Exod. 6:20: "Amram took to wife his father's sister Jochebed, and she bore him Aaron and Moses." The Greek version of this verse reads: "Amram took to wife the daughter of his father's brother." Why would anyone present a different version of that verse? Probably because the Septuagint translators could not accept the idea that, by the standards of other parts of the Torah, Moses was born out of an incestuous union. Thus, for example, we read in Lev. 18:12: "Do not uncover the nakedness of your father's sister, she is your father's flesh." The Greek version has Amram marrying his cousin, but the Masoretic text states that Amram married his aunt.

Historically speaking, Amram could not have known the prohibitions expressed in Leviticus. But it is difficult to think of Moses as the product of a union that he himself will later call an abomination, especially for a religious person. So the Greek version subtly makes a dogmatic correction in its translation of the verse. This example shows how the slightest divergence in a reading can change a point or avoid difficulties in a text. Because of variant readings, it is a useful method of study to examine all early versions of the biblical text in our search for every possible meaning.

SOURCE CRITICISM

The Torah may seem to present a unified account of Israelite history and law during the patriarchal and Mosaic periods. Detailed study of the text, however, has led modern critical scholarship to theorize that the Torah is a compilation from several sources, different streams of literary traditions, that were composed and collected over the course of the biblical period (ca. 1200–ca. 400 B.C.E.). Because the Torah, in this perspective, is an amalgam of the works of different authors or schools, it contains an abundance of factual inconsistencies; contradictory regulations; and differences in style, vocabulary, and even theology.

The first period of Israelite history is that of the patriarchs, described in the Book of Genesis. Beginning with Exodus, the Torah describes events of the Mosaic period.

How did the religion of the patriarchs differ from that of Moses? The Torah makes it abundantly clear that most of the commandments and laws revealed to Moses are new. What about the faith of Moses as opposed to that of the patriarchs? The Torah presents the idea that Moses had a more intimate relationship with God than the patriarchs did: "God spoke to Moses and said to him, 'I am the LORD [*YHVH*]. I appeared to Abraham, Isaac, and Jacob as El Shaddai, but I did not make Myself known to them by My name *YHVH*'" (Exod. 6:2–3). The patriarchs knew God as El Shaddai, but Moses will know God by His more sacred, more intimate name, *YHVH*.

The revelation of God's name is literally an epoch-making event. When Moses and the Israelites are informed of God's name, they become a special people with the destiny of having a sacred covenant with God. This new revelation of God's name raises two striking questions. First, this name of God was already used in the Book of Genesis. In Gen. 4:25–26 we read: "Adam knew his wife again, and she bore a son and named him Seth. . . . And to Seth . . . a son was born, and he named him Enosh. It was then that men began to invoke the LORD by name." Thus we learn that long before Moses, even long before Abraham, people used the name *YHVH*. How, then, can Exod. 6 tell us that the patriarchs used the name El Shaddai only? There are texts in Genesis that use the name El Shaddai, but there are even more texts that use the name *YHVH*. Moses' mother, Jochebed, bears a name compounded with *YHVH*. So how can the name *YHVH* be considered new to Moses?

Second, God had already revealed the name *YHVH* to Moses at the Burning Bush. "Moses said to God, 'When I come to the Israelites and say to them, "the God of your fathers has sent me to you," and they ask me, "What is

His name?" what shall I say to them?' And God said to Moses, 'Ehyeh-Asher-Ehyeh'" (Exod. 3:13–14). *"Ehyeh-Asher-Ehyeh"* means "I will be what I will be," and *"YHVH"* means "He will be." God explains that: "This shall be My name forever, / This My appellation for all eternity" (3:15). If the name *YHVH* had already been revealed to Moses in Exod. 3, why is it given as if for the first time in Exod. 6?

To review, although the distinctively Israelite name of God is *YHVH,* various sources disagree as to when this name was first used. Two sources tell us that *YHVH* was a name not revealed to the Israelites until God revealed it to Moses at the Burning Bush (3:13–15) and in Egypt (6:2–3). Both of these sources, however, disagree with the third source, which declares that the name *YHVH* was known from the beginning of history, from the time of the immediate descendants of Adam and Eve (Gen. 4:26). These facts suggest the existence of different theological perspectives concerning the time of the great turning point in Israelite religion, when it becomes a faith very different from that of the surrounding peoples.

The names that are used for God have served as important clues in the separation and discovery of the sources that make up the Torah. The different names of God have led source-critical scholarship to find independent traditions, each of which uses the divine name in different way. These traditions are independent of and contradict each other.

How does scholarship explain all of these variations? Different theories have emerged to explain the divergences along theological, geographic, and chronologic lines. Thus there may be a northern and southern version of the same story, which would account for inconsistencies. The stories were written over the course of centuries and reflect an evolutionary process that incorporated interpretations and additions as the text developed.

There is great agreement among scholars that the Torah, the Pentateuch, in its final form, is a work composed and edited from four literary complexes. The oldest of these is the Yahwistic source, designated by the letter J because it consistently uses the name *YHVH* (spelled "Jahweh" in German) and because of its special interest in places located in the southern kingdom of Judah. This tradition seems to have been written in the 10th century B.C.E.

The Elohistic source, designated E, is so named because of its use of the divine name *Elohim* and its interest in the northern tribes, of which Ephraim was the most important. It probably was written between 900 and 800 B.C.E., presenting material parallel and supplementary to that found in J.

The Priestly source, designated P, uses the divine name *El Shaddai* (until Exod. 6) and contains a great many ritual texts. Scholars greatly disagree concerning the date when this source was written. Some place it as early as J and E, but others posit a date as late as the Babylonian exile (6th century B.C.E.).

The Deuteronomic source, designated D, is considered to have been written later (8th to 6th century B.C.E.). It reviews certain stories and presents legislation that sometimes differ from the first four books. It is important to note that contradictions exist not only within narrative material but also within the laws of the Torah. For instance, Exod. 21:2–11 states that a male slave should be released after six years of servitude. This law, however, does not apply to female slaves (v. 7). In Deut. 15:12, the same requirement of release is extended to both male and female slaves.

Most scholars believe that the Torah was compiled and edited by Priestly redactors in Babylonia between 600 and 400 B.C.E.

LITERARY CRITICISM

Though source criticism has contributed a great deal to our understanding of the growth of biblical traditions, by definition it ignores the literary unity of the final form of a text. In reaction, a new form, literary criticism, has arisen, which examines the literary characteristics (including narrative technique, tone, theme, structure, imagery, repetition, reticence, and character) of the texts. In simple terms, source

criticism is interested in cutting up the texts to find the different layers of tradition; literary criticism considers the text as it stands now, as a whole, not as it once may have been. Literary criticism is both like and unlike traditional Jewish commentary. It looks at the Bible as a unified whole but has no theological commitment and sees it as the creation of human authors. Source criticism is interested in history; literary criticism treats historical questions as basically unanswerable and understands texts as literary products or objects, not as windows on historical reality. Literary criticism sees texts as coherent wholes that create meaning through the integration of their elements, irrespective of the authors and their intentions. According to source criticism, texts can give us access to the ideas and emotions of great minds of the past.

Earlier I noted that Exod. 6 repeats a great many of the elements present in Exod. 3. The essay "Traditional Methods of Bible Study" points out that the sages of the Midrash and the mystics of the Zohar created stories to explain this repetition. Similarly, literary criticism does not see the two texts as contradictory, but as different parts of an ongoing narrative. Moses receives a renewed call to action in Exod. 6 because he has become so disenchanted by his early failure to convince Pharaoh to let the people go. This new revelation completes the revelation at the Burning Bush. God tells Moses that the mission for which he was called on at the Burning Bush will occur in due time; Moses should not be dismayed by his initial failures in Pharaoh's court and with his fellow Israelites. He reminds Moses that Abraham, Isaac, and Jacob received revelations and promises, and yet it was not in their times that the promise to possess the Land was fulfilled. As the genealogy indicates, the Israelites have gone from being a family to being a people, and so the divine promise will be carried out, the liberation from Egypt will occur, and the Israelites will return to their Land.

Literary criticism finds unity and purposeful repetition where other approaches find disharmony and contradiction.

STRUCTURALISM AND DECONSTRUCTIONISM

In the past, it was thought that texts communicate meaning straightforwardly and simply. Language was supposed to give an exact picture of the world. In modern thinking, however, it is understood that all words have complex relationships with other words and that it is the patterns of language that gives words meaning. All language is figurative. There is a great distance between language about the world and the world itself. Language and literature are cultural phenomena. Structuralism looks at texts and analyzes the basic mental patterns that underlie these social and cultural phenomena.

It was once assumed that the author of a text intended a meaning, and that the reader could understand that intention. In modern thinking, however, it is understood that ambiguities in language and context increase the chances of misunderstanding. Even when a writer and a reader live at the same time and in the same place, a reader could still offer different plausible interpretations of a writer's text. When centuries and geography separate writer and reader, misunderstanding is almost certain.

We assume that any text we read has a clear meaning that it is trying to convey. A method called deconstruction claims that a text itself undermines that meaning by presenting evidence against its own case. A text often makes its case by choosing one alternative over another. In the process, however, the other alternative is brought into the picture, enabling the reader to consider it. The writer's preferred alternative is not necessarily rejected as a result, but it now is seen as only one possible option. The authority of the text breaks down, the text folds in on itself (usually at some weak point), and its center no longer holds.

Let us look at Exod. 6 again, this time to demonstrate how a text deconstructs. As we saw from the perspective of source criticism, Exod. 6 seems to be about the name of God. The patriarchs knew God as El Shaddai, but

now Moses and the Israelites will know God by His true name, *YHVH.*

But what does it mean to "know the name of God"? When Moses, at the Burning Bush (Exod. 3–4), asks for the name of the God who has sent him to the Israelites on the mission of liberation, God answers, "I will be what I will be." Moses goes to Pharaoh in *YHVH*'s name: "Thus says the LORD, the God of Israel: Let My people go." Pharaoh replies: "Who is the LORD that I should heed Him and let Israel go? I do not know the LORD, nor will I let Israel go." (5:1–2). Moses thinks that he has met with failure: "O LORD, why did You bring harm upon this people? Why did You send me? Ever since I came to Pharaoh to speak in Your name, he has dealt worse with this people; and still You have not delivered Your people" (5:22–23).

What is the "name" of God? It certainly is neither a description nor a definition of God. God's name seems to be His power. Once both the Egyptians and the Israelites experience the power of God through the plagues, the name of God will be known throughout the world. But God's power is not in His name.

Indeed, the name *YHVH* is a non-name name, a way of undermining the whole idea that God can have a name at all. Moses asks God for His name, and He replies, "I will be what I will be." Thus this text, which seems to be about the revelation of God's name, contains within it the concept that God cannot have a name at all. Admittedly, the Midrash, the Zohar, and the source critics all seek to use the different names of God illustrated in the Book of Exodus as a code by which to crack the meaning of the Torah. But there really is only one name of God—*YHVH*—which is not a name at all but an expression of the namelessness of God.

I must emphasize that this reading of the texts from Exodus is only one interpretation and that these texts, as the other types of criticism indicate, may be about the revelation of God's name and the different names of God may each have its own significance.

When a text is deconstructed, however, we are no longer sure what it is trying to say. "Undecidability" is actually a better description than the term "deconstruction." "Deconstruction" connotes the destruction of a text. "Undecidability" connotes the figurative nature of language and our inability to limit and strictly defend what a literary text means. In the case of the Bible, traditional commentary would agree that no one should claim to have the definitive interpretation of a passage, for every word of the Bible has an infinite range of meanings. Deconstruction tries to be without biases, in contrast to traditional exegesis—which is based on the strongest possible theological basis. Nevertheless it is fascinating that a modern (or postmodern) method joins Jewish commentary in striving to keep the biblical text open for our interpretations and for those who will read the Bible in the centuries to come.

A NOTE ON THE SPIRITUALITY OF TEXTS

Michael Fishbane

Judaism is a text culture that always has been nurtured by study and interpretation. The interpreter and the text interpenetrate in dynamic ways. The individual finds and realizes that the layers of his or her deepest self have been "textualized" by study, so that the sacred texts provide the language for ongoing life experience and inspiration. The text, on the other hand, reveals itself through the accumulated readings of its many seekers and learners. In a profound reciprocal way, every renewal of the self is simultaneously a renewal of the text, while every deadening of human sensibility is a simultaneous deadening of the life breath of the text. The biblical text is a shaping of the divine spirit by the human breath of Moses and the prophets; but it may speak now only through the spirit and breath of its interpreters.

Martin Buber once said that the task of the biblical translator is to overcome "the leprosy of fluency," a disease of the spirit that can lead us to imagine that we already know what we are reading, causing us blithely and triumphantly to read past the text. The effective translator must, therefore, reformulate the word or the words of the text to produce a new encounter with its language and thus facilitate a new hearing and a new understanding. The spiritual task of interpretation, likewise, is to affect or alter the pace of reading so that one's eye and ear can be addressed by the text's words and sounds—and thus reveal an expanded or new sense of life and its dynamics. The pace of technology and the patterns of modernity pervert this vital task. The rhythm of reading must, therefore, be restored to the rhythm of breathing, to the cadence of the cantillation marks of the sacred text. Only then will the individual absorb the texts with his or her life breath and begin to read liturgically, as a rite of passage to a different level of meaning. And only then may the contemporary idolization of technique and information be transformed, and the sacred text restored as a living teaching and instruction, for the constant renewal of the self.

ḤAZAK ḤAZAK V'NITḤAZZEK

Jeffrey H. Tigay

It is the custom in the synagogues of *Ashk'nazim* that when each book of the Torah is completed, the congregation rises and exclaims, *"Ḥazak ḥazak v'nitḥazzek!"* (Be strong, be strong, and let us summon up our strength!). The phrase is an expansion of the exhortation of King David's general Joab before battle, "Be strong and let us summon up our strength [*ḥazak v'nitḥazzak*] for the sake of our people and the towns of our God" (2 Sam. 10:12).

Recitation of this phrase on completing a book of the Torah reflects the transformation of an exhortation to physical, military prowess into a wish for spiritual strength. This custom is first clearly seen in 19th-century Germany, where the briefer form *"Ḥazak v'nitḥazzak!"* (vocalized exactly as in the Bible) was addressed to the person who had the final *aliyah* of each book. Earlier, congregations would simply exclaim, *"Ḥazak!"* (Be strong!). *S'fardim* also used to follow the latter custom; but nowadays they say, *"Ḥazak u-varukh!"* (Be strong and blessed!) to each person who returns to sit after having an *aliyah*, just as *Ashk'nazim* exclaim, *"Yishar koḥakha!"* (to a male) or *"Yishar koḥekh!"* (to a female)—that is, "May your strength be firm!" (Contrary to popular opinion, this exclamation does not mean "May your strength be straight!" *Yishar* is not derived from ישר "straight," but from שרר "strong.")

Originally, whether after each *aliyah* or on the completion of a book, the exclamation *"Hazak!"* was addressed to the person who had read the Torah. It meant essentially, "More power to you!" Various explanations have been suggested for the practice. Because reading the Torah is a form of learning, some interpret the exclamation as encouragement to persist in learning the Torah. Others understand it as encouraging and wishing strength for the Torah reader because serious learning of the Torah—including accurately preparing the public reading with all of its vocalization, punctuation, and cantillation—can be exhausting. The phrase *"v'nitḥazzak,"* "let us summon our strength" or "let us be strengthened," was subsequently added (on the basis of 2 Sam. 10:12) because the entire congregation had completed the book along with the reader and wished to include itself in these wishes.

Other uses of these exclamations are instructive. Authors of *piyyutim* (liturgical poems) sometimes wrote their names and the word *"ḥazak"* at the end of their poems, and some writers of *z'mirot* (table songs) spelled out their names acrostically, followed by *"ḥazak."* Medieval scribes sometimes wrote *"ḥazak"* or *"ḥazak v'nitḥazzak"* at the end of manuscripts of books of the Bible and other Jewish

texts. These poets and scribes intended the words as self-encouragement and self-blessing on the completion of a difficult and painstaking task. Scribes often shed light on the intended meaning by adding other phrases, such as: "Blessed is He who gives strength to the weary and renews the vigor of the exhausted" (based on Isa. 40:29), "Be strong and let us exert ourselves in Torah and commandments," "May God . . . grant His servant strength to complete the entire Bible," and "We have been privileged to complete [this manuscript] in peace; may we be privileged to begin and complete [another] in peace." The last example is reminiscent of a custom once practiced in Italy when the Torah was completed on *Simḥat Torah:* The cantor and the congregation would say, "*Ḥazak!* We have been privileged to begin and complete [it again] in peace."

In light of the meanings that have been found in all of these practices, we may understand *"Ḥazak ḥazak v'nitḥazzek!"* as follows:

Ḥazak—More power to you, Torah reader, who has worked so hard to read the Torah accurately and pleasantly! *Ḥazak*—Congratulations to you, the person who has had the final *aliyah* of the book! *V'nitḥazzek*—May you and we (the entire congregation) persist, study, read, and complete all the other books, drawing strength from the Torah!

BLESSINGS FOR THE TORAH AND HAFTARAH

B'RAKHAH BEFORE THE TORAH READING

Each congregant receiving an aliyah recites:

בָּרְכוּ אֶת־יהוה הַמְבֹרָךְ.

Bar'khu et Adonai hamvorakh!

Congregation responds:

בָּרוּךְ יהוה הַמְבֹרָךְ לְעוֹלָם וָעֶד.

Barukh Adonai hamvorakh l'olam va-ed!

Congregant repeats above response, then continues:

בָּרוּךְ אַתָּה יהוה אֱלֹהֵינוּ מֶלֶךְ הָעוֹלָם,
אֲשֶׁר בָּחַר בָּנוּ מִכָּל־הָעַמִּים וְנָתַן לָנוּ אֶת־תּוֹרָתוֹ.
בָּרוּךְ אַתָּה יהוה נוֹתֵן הַתּוֹרָה.

Barukh atah, Adonai, Eloheinu Melekh ha-olam,
asher baḥar banu mi-kol ha-amim,
v'natan-lanu et torato.
Barukh atah, Adonai, noten ha-Torah.

B'RAKHAH AFTER THE TORAH READING

בָּרוּךְ אַתָּה יהוה אֱלֹהֵינוּ מֶלֶךְ הָעוֹלָם,
אֲשֶׁר נָתַן לָנוּ תּוֹרַת אֱמֶת, וְחַיֵּי עוֹלָם נָטַע בְּתוֹכֵנוּ.
בָּרוּךְ אַתָּה יהוה נוֹתֵן הַתּוֹרָה.

Barukh atah, Adonai, Eloheinu Melekh ha-olam,
asher natan-lanu torat emet,
v'ḥayyei olam nata b'tokheinu.
Barukh atah, Adonai, noten ha-Torah.

B'RAKHAH BEFORE THE HAFTARAH

בָּרוּךְ אַתָּה יהוה אֱלֹהֵינוּ מֶלֶךְ הָעוֹלָם, אֲשֶׁר בָּחַר בִּנְבִיאִים טוֹבִים, וְרָצָה בְדִבְרֵיהֶם הַנֶּאֱמָרִים בֶּאֱמֶת. בָּרוּךְ אַתָּה יהוה הַבּוֹחֵר בַּתּוֹרָה וּבְמֹשֶׁה עַבְדּוֹ וּבְיִשְׂרָאֵל עַמּוֹ וּבִנְבִיאֵי הָאֱמֶת וָצֶדֶק.

B'RAKHOT AFTER THE HAFTARAH

בָּרוּךְ אַתָּה יהוה אֱלֹהֵינוּ מֶלֶךְ הָעוֹלָם, צוּר כָּל־הָעוֹלָמִים, צַדִּיק בְּכָל־הַדּוֹרוֹת, הָאֵל הַנֶּאֱמָן הָאוֹמֵר וְעוֹשֶׂה, הַמְדַבֵּר וּמְקַיֵּם, שֶׁכָּל־דְּבָרָיו אֱמֶת וָצֶדֶק. נֶאֱמָן אַתָּה הוּא יהוה אֱלֹהֵינוּ וְנֶאֱמָנִים דְּבָרֶיךָ, וְדָבָר אֶחָד מִדְּבָרֶיךָ אָחוֹר לֹא יָשׁוּב רֵיקָם, כִּי אֵל מֶלֶךְ נֶאֱמָן וְרַחֲמָן אָתָּה. בָּרוּךְ אַתָּה יהוה הָאֵל הַנֶּאֱמָן בְּכָל־דְּבָרָיו.

רַחֵם עַל צִיּוֹן כִּי הִיא בֵּית חַיֵּינוּ. וְלַעֲלוּבַת נֶפֶשׁ תּוֹשִׁיעַ בִּמְהֵרָה בְיָמֵינוּ. בָּרוּךְ אַתָּה יהוה מְשַׂמֵּחַ צִיּוֹן בְּבָנֶיהָ.

שַׂמְּחֵנוּ יהוה אֱלֹהֵינוּ בְּאֵלִיָּהוּ הַנָּבִיא עַבְדֶּךָ וּבְמַלְכוּת בֵּית דָּוִד מְשִׁיחֶךָ. בִּמְהֵרָה יָבֹא וְיָגֵל לִבֵּנוּ, עַל כִּסְאוֹ לֹא יֵשֶׁב זָר וְלֹא יִנְחֲלוּ עוֹד אֲחֵרִים אֶת־כְּבוֹדוֹ, כִּי בְשֵׁם קָדְשְׁךָ נִשְׁבַּעְתָּ לּוֹ שֶׁלֹּא יִכְבֶּה נֵרוֹ לְעוֹלָם וָעֶד. בָּרוּךְ אַתָּה יהוה מָגֵן דָּוִד.

On Shabbat (including Shabbat Ḥol ha-Mo·ed Pesaḥ):

עַל הַתּוֹרָה וְעַל הָעֲבוֹדָה וְעַל הַנְּבִיאִים וְעַל יוֹם הַשַּׁבָּת הַזֶּה שֶׁנָּתַתָּ לָּנוּ יהוה אֱלֹהֵינוּ לִקְדֻשָּׁה וְלִמְנוּחָה, לְכָבוֹד וּלְתִפְאָרֶת. עַל הַכֹּל יהוה אֱלֹהֵינוּ אֲנַחְנוּ מוֹדִים לָךְ, וּמְבָרְכִים אוֹתָךְ. יִתְבָּרַךְ שִׁמְךָ בְּפִי כָּל־חַי תָּמִיד לְעוֹלָם וָעֶד. בָּרוּךְ אַתָּה יהוה מְקַדֵּשׁ הַשַּׁבָּת.

On Festivals (including Shabbat Ḥol ha-Mo·ed Sukkot)

עַל הַתּוֹרָה וְעַל הָעֲבוֹדָה וְעַל הַנְּבִיאִים (וְעַל יוֹם הַשַּׁבָּת הַזֶּה)

On Sukkot:

וְעַל יוֹם חַג הַסֻּכּוֹת הַזֶּה

On Sh'mini Atzeret and Simḥat Torah:

וְעַל יוֹם הַשְּׁמִינִי, חַג הָעֲצֶרֶת הַזֶּה

On Pesaḥ:

וְעַל יוֹם חַג הַמַּצּוֹת הַזֶּה

On Shavu·ot:

וְעַל יוֹם חַג הַשָּׁבֻעוֹת הַזֶּה

שֶׁנָּתַתָּ לָּנוּ יהוה אֱלֹהֵינוּ (לִקְדֻשָּׁה וְלִמְנוּחָה) לְשָׂשׂוֹן וּלְשִׂמְחָה, לְכָבוֹד וּלְתִפְאָרֶת. עַל הַכֹּל יהוה אֱלֹהֵינוּ אֲנַחְנוּ מוֹדִים לָךְ, וּמְבָרְכִים אוֹתָךְ. יִתְבָּרַךְ שִׁמְךָ בְּפִי כָּל־חַי תָּמִיד לְעוֹלָם וָעֶד. בָּרוּךְ אַתָּה יהוה מְקַדֵּשׁ (הַשַּׁבָּת וְ)יִשְׂרָאֵל וְהַזְּמַנִּים.

NAMES OF THE TROPE AND THEIR NOTATIONS

שמות הטעמים וסימניהן

פַּשְׁטָא֙ מֻנַּ֣ח זַרְקָא֮ מֻנַּ֣ח סֶגּוֹל֒ מֻנַּ֣ח ׀ מֻנַּ֣ח רְבִיעִ֗י מַהְפַּ֤ךְ
פַּשְׁטָא֙ זָקֵ֔ף קָטֹ֔ן זָקֵ֕ף־גָּד֕וֹל מֵרְכָ֥א טִפְחָ֖א מֻנַּ֣ח אֶתְנַחְתָּ֑א
פָּזֵ֡ר תְּלִישָׁא־קְטַנָּה֩ ֠תְּלִישָׁא־גְדוֹלָה קַדְמָ֨א וְאַזְלָ֜א אַזְלָא־
גֵּ֜רֶשׁ גֵּרְשַׁ֞יִם דַּרְגָּ֧א תְּבִ֛יר יְ֚תִיב פְּסִ֣יק ׀ סוֹף־פָּסֽוּק׃ שַׁלְשֶׁ֓לֶת
קַרְנֵי־פָרָ֟ה מֵרְכָא־כְפוּלָ֦ה יֶרַח־בֶּן־יוֹמ֪וֹ׃

DECALOGUE WITH "UPPER" ACCENTS

(*Ta·am Elyon*)

There are two different versions of the verse division and cantillation of the Decalogue. These are indicated by superlinear and sublinear "accent" signs (Hebrew *t'amim*, Yiddish *trop*) that accompany the text in manuscripts and printed Bibles. (They do not appear in Torah scrolls.) These signs serve simultaneously as a system of punctuation and of musical notation for cantillation of the text.

For the Decalogue, one set of signs is known as the "lower accents" (*ta·am taḥton*), and the other set is known as the "upper accents" (*ta·am elyon*). The lower accents are printed in the main portion of this book for Exod. 20 and Deut. 5. The upper accents are printed below.

The lower accents divide the commandments into 13 verses of standard length. Because of that standard length, long commandments are divided into several verses (Exod. 20:2–6 and 8–11; Deut. 5:6–10 and 12–15), while short commandments—the sixth through the ninth—are conjoined in a single verse (Exod. 20:13; Deut. 5:17).

In contrast, the upper accents divide the Decalogue so that each commandment, whether long or short, constitutes one verse. There is only one exception—the first verse contains what Rabbinic tradition regards as the first two commandments (see Comments on pp. 443 and 1017). This corresponds to a midrashic tradition that these two commandments (which refer to God in the first person) were spoken directly by God to the people in a single, uninterrupted statement, whereas the rest (which speak of God in the third person) were transmitted to the people by Moses (BT Mak. 24a; Hor. 8a).

The lower and upper sets of accents seem to have originated in Palestine and Babylonia, respectively. Because the lower set corresponds to the normal way of versifying the Torah, it is probably the older of the two.

There are varying practices in using the two sets. The custom among *Ashk'nazim* is to use the lower accents whenever the Decalogue is read on *Shabbat* during the year, and to use the upper accents when it is read on *Shavu·ot*. In this way, the reading on *Shavu·ot* re-enacts the original proclamation of the Decalogue on Mount Sinai, when the people heard the first two commandments from God in a single utterance, as the upper accents render them. The custom of *S'fardim* is to use the lower accents only for private study of the Torah, perhaps because of their punctuational value; the upper accents are used for all public Torah readings, which are regarded as a reenactment of the revelation at Sinai (TJ Meg. 74d, top).

To ease the reader's comparison with the English translation in the main portion of the book, the verse numbers printed there are reproduced below.

—Jeffrey H. Tigay

DEUTERONOMY 5

6 אָנֹכִי יְהוָה אֱלֹהֶיךָ אֲשֶׁר הוֹצֵאתִיךָ
מֵאֶרֶץ מִצְרַיִם מִבֵּית עֲבָדִים 7 לֹא יִהְיֶה־
לְךָ אֱלֹהִים אֲחֵרִים עַל־פָּנַי 8 לֹא־תַעֲשֶׂה־
לְךָ פֶסֶל ׀ כָּל־תְּמוּנָה אֲשֶׁר בַּשָּׁמַיִם ׀
מִמַּעַל וַאֲשֶׁר בָּאָרֶץ מִתַּחַת וַאֲשֶׁר בַּמַּיִם ׀

EXODUS 20

אָנֹכִי יְהוָה אֱלֹהֶיךָ אֲשֶׁר הוֹצֵאתִיךָ
מֵאֶרֶץ מִצְרַיִם מִבֵּית עֲבָדִים 3 לֹא יִהְיֶה־
לְךָ אֱלֹהִים אֲחֵרִים עַל־פָּנַי 4 לֹא תַעֲשֶׂה־
לְךָ פֶסֶל ׀ וְכָל־תְּמוּנָה אֲשֶׁר בַּשָּׁמַיִם ׀
מִמַּעַל וַאֲשֶׁר בָּאָרֶץ מִתַּחַת וַאֲשֶׁר בַּמַּיִם ׀

מִתַּ֣חַת לָאָ֗רֶץ 5 לֹֽא־תִשְׁתַּחְוֶ֥ה לָהֶ֛ם וְלֹ֥א
תָעָבְדֵ֑ם כִּ֣י אָנֹכִ֞י יְהוָ֤ה אֱלֹהֶ֙יךָ֙ אֵ֣ל קַנָּ֔א
פֹּ֠קֵד עֲוֺ֨ן אָבֹ֧ת עַל־בָּנִ֛ים עַל־שִׁלֵּשִׁ֥ים
וְעַל־רִבֵּעִ֖ים לְשֹׂנְאָ֑י 6 וְעֹ֥שֶׂה חֶ֙סֶד֙
לַאֲלָפִ֔ים לְאֹהֲבַ֖י וּלְשֹׁמְרֵ֥י מִצְוֺתָֽי׃ ס
7 לֹ֥א תִשָּׂ֛א אֶת־שֵׁם־יְהוָ֥ה אֱלֹהֶ֖יךָ לַשָּׁ֑וְא
כִּ֣י לֹ֤א יְנַקֶּה֙ יְהוָ֔ה אֵ֛ת אֲשֶׁר־יִשָּׂ֥א אֶת־
שְׁמ֖וֹ לַשָּֽׁוְא׃ פ
8 זָכ֛וֹר֩ אֶת־י֥וֹם הַשַּׁבָּ֖ת לְקַדְּשׁ֑וֹ 9 שֵׁ֤שֶׁת
יָמִ֣ים תַּעֲבֹ֔ד֮ וְעָשִׂ֖יתָ כָּל־מְלַאכְתֶּךָ֒
10 וְי֙וֹם֙ הַשְּׁבִיעִ֔י שַׁבָּ֖ת ׀ לַיהוָ֣ה אֱלֹהֶ֑יךָ
לֹֽא־תַעֲשֶׂ֨ה כָל־מְלָאכָ֜ה אַתָּ֣ה ׀ וּבִנְךָֽ־
וּ֠בִתֶּךָ עַבְדְּךָ֙ וַאֲמָתְךָ֜ וּבְהֶמְתֶּ֗ךָ וְגֵרְךָ֙
אֲשֶׁ֣ר בִּשְׁעָרֶ֔יךָ 11 כִּ֣י שֵֽׁשֶׁת־יָמִים֩ עָשָׂ֨ה
יְהוָ֜ה אֶת־הַשָּׁמַ֣יִם וְאֶת־הָאָ֗רֶץ אֶת־הַיָּם֙
וְאֶת־כָּל־אֲשֶׁר־בָּ֔ם וַיָּ֖נַח בַּיּ֣וֹם הַשְּׁבִיעִ֑י
עַל־כֵּ֗ן בֵּרַ֧ךְ יְהוָ֛ה אֶת־י֥וֹם הַשַּׁבָּ֖ת
וַֽיְקַדְּשֵֽׁהוּ׃ ס
12 כַּבֵּ֥ד אֶת־אָבִ֖יךָ וְאֶת־אִמֶּ֑ךָ לְמַ֙עַן֙
יַאֲרִכ֣וּן יָמֶ֔יךָ עַ֚ל הָאֲדָמָ֔ה אֲשֶׁר־יְהוָ֥ה
אֱלֹהֶ֖יךָ נֹתֵ֥ן לָֽךְ׃ ס
13 לֹ֥א תִּרְצָֽח׃ ס
לֹ֥א תִּנְאָֽף׃ ס
לֹ֥א תִּגְנֹֽב׃ ס
לֹא־תַעֲנֶ֥ה בְרֵעֲךָ֖ עֵ֥ד שָֽׁקֶר׃ ס
14 לֹ֥א תַחְמֹ֖ד בֵּ֣ית רֵעֶ֑ךָ לֹֽא־תַחְמֹ֞ד אֵ֣שֶׁת
רֵעֶ֗ךָ וְעַבְדּ֤וֹ וַאֲמָתוֹ֙ וְשׁוֹר֣וֹ וַחֲמֹר֔וֹ וְכֹ֖ל
אֲשֶׁ֥ר לְרֵעֶֽךָ׃ פ

מִתַּ֣חַת לָאָ֗רֶץ 9 לֹֽא־תִשְׁתַּחְוֶ֥ה לָהֶ֛ם וְלֹ֥א
תָעָבְדֵ֑ם כִּ֣י אָנֹכִ֞י יְהוָ֤ה אֱלֹהֶ֙יךָ֙ אֵ֣ל
קַנָּ֔א פֹּ֠קֵד עֲוֺ֨ן אָב֧וֹת עַל־בָּנִ֛ים וְעַל־
שִׁלֵּשִׁ֥ים וְעַל־רִבֵּעִ֖ים לְשֹׂנְאָ֑י 10 וְעֹ֤שֶׂה
חֶ֙סֶד֙ לַאֲלָפִ֔ים לְאֹהֲבַ֖י וּלְשֹׁמְרֵ֥י מצותו
מִצְוֺתָֽי׃ ס
11 לֹ֥א תִשָּׂ֛א אֶת־שֵׁם־יְהוָ֥ה אֱלֹהֶ֖יךָ לַשָּׁ֑וְא
כִּ֣י לֹ֤א יְנַקֶּה֙ יְהוָ֔ה אֵ֛ת אֲשֶׁר־יִשָּׂ֥א אֶת־
שְׁמ֖וֹ לַשָּֽׁוְא׃ ס
12 שָׁמ֛וֹר֩ אֶת־י֥וֹם הַשַּׁבָּ֖ת לְקַדְּשׁ֑וֹ כַּאֲשֶׁ֥ר
צִוְּךָ֣ ׀ יְהוָ֣ה אֱלֹהֶ֔יךָ 13 שֵׁ֤שֶׁת יָמִים֙ תַּעֲבֹ֔ד֮
וְעָשִׂ֖יתָ כָּל־מְלַאכְתֶּךָ֒ 14 וְי֙וֹם֙ הַשְּׁבִיעִ֔י
שַׁבָּ֖ת ׀ לַיהוָ֣ה אֱלֹהֶ֑יךָ לֹ֣א תַעֲשֶׂ֣ה כָל־
מְלָאכָ֡ה אַתָּ֣ה וּבִנְךָֽ־וּבִתֶּ֣ךָ וְעַבְדְּךָֽ־
וַ֠אֲמָתֶךָ וְשׁוֹרְךָ֙ וַחֲמֹ֜רְךָ֙ וְכָל־בְּהֶמְתֶּ֗ךָ
וְגֵֽרְךָ֙ אֲשֶׁ֣ר בִּשְׁעָרֶ֔יךָ לְמַ֗עַן יָנ֛וּחַ עַבְדְּךָ֥
וַאֲמָתְךָ֖ כָּמֽוֹךָ׃ 15 וְזָכַרְתָּ֗֞ כִּי־עֶ֤בֶד הָיִ֙יתָ֙ ׀
בְּאֶ֣רֶץ מִצְרַ֔יִם וַיֹּצִאֲךָ֙ יְהוָ֤ה אֱלֹהֶ֙יךָ֙ מִשָּׁ֔ם
בְּיָ֤ד חֲזָקָה֙ וּבִזְרֹ֣עַ נְטוּיָ֔ה עַל־כֵּ֗ן צִוְּךָ֙ יְהוָ֣ה
אֱלֹהֶ֔יךָ לַעֲשׂ֖וֹת אֶת־י֥וֹם הַשַּׁבָּֽת׃ ס
16 כַּבֵּ֤ד אֶת־אָבִ֙יךָ֙ וְאֶת־אִמֶּ֔ךָ כַּאֲשֶׁ֥ר צִוְּךָ֖
יְהוָ֣ה אֱלֹהֶ֑יךָ לְמַ֣עַן ׀ יַאֲרִיכֻ֣ן יָמֶ֗יךָ וּלְמַ֙עַן֙
יִ֣יטַב לָ֔ךְ עַ֚ל הָאֲדָמָ֔ה אֲשֶׁר־יְהוָ֥ה אֱלֹהֶ֖יךָ
נֹתֵ֥ן לָֽךְ׃ ס
17 לֹ֥א תִרְצָֽח׃ ס
וְלֹ֥א תִנְאָֽף׃ ס
וְלֹ֥א תִגְנֹֽב׃ ס
וְלֹֽא־תַעֲנֶ֥ה בְרֵעֲךָ֖ עֵ֥ד שָֽׁוְא׃ ס
18 וְלֹ֥א תַחְמֹ֖ד אֵ֣שֶׁת רֵעֶ֑ךָ ס וְלֹ֨א
תִתְאַוֶּ֜ה בֵּ֣ית רֵעֶ֗ךָ שָׂדֵ֜הוּ וְעַבְדּ֤וֹ וַאֲמָתוֹ֙
שׁוֹר֣וֹ וַחֲמֹר֔וֹ וְכֹ֖ל אֲשֶׁ֥ר לְרֵעֶֽךָ׃ ס

ABBREVIATIONS

Ar.	*Arakhin*
ARN	*Avot d'Rabbi Natan* (rescension A)
ARN B	*Avot d'Rabbi Natan* (rescension B)
Av. Zar.	*Avodah Zarah*
BB	*Bava Batra*
B.C.E.	before the Common Era
Bek.	*B'khorot*
Ber.	*B'rakhot*
Betz.	*Beitzah*
BK	*Bava Kamma*
BM	*Bava M'tzi·a*
BT	Babylonian Talmud
Bik.	*Bikkurim*
C.E.	Common Era
Chron.	Chronicles
CJLS	Committee on Jewish Law and Standards (of the Conservative Movement, administered by The Rabbinical Assembly)
Dan.	Daniel
Deut.	Deuteronomy
Deut. R.	Deuteronomy Rabbah
Eccles.	Ecclesiastes
Eduy.	*Eduyyot*
E.H.	*Even ha-Ezer*
Er.	*Eruvin*
Exod.	Exodus
Exod. R.	Exodus Rabbah
Ezek.	Ezekiel
Gen. R.	Genesis Rabbah
Gen.	Genesis
Git.	*Gittin*
Guide	*Guide of the Perplexed*
Hab.	Habakkuk
Ḥag.	*Ḥagigah*
Ḥal.	*Ḥallah*
Hal. Ged.	*Halakhot G'dolot*
Ḥ.M.	*Ḥoshen Mishpat*
Hor.	*Horayot*
Hos.	Hosea
Ḥul.	*Ḥullin*
Isa.	Isaiah
Jer.	Jeremiah
Jon.	Jonah
Josh.	Joshua
JT	Jerusalem Talmud
Jth.	Judith
Judg.	Judges
Ket.	*K'tubbot*
Kid.	*Kiddushin*
Lam.	Lamentations
Lev.	Leviticus
Lev. R.	Leviticus Rabbah
M	*Mishnah*
Mak.	*Makkot*
Mal.	Malachi
Meg.	*M'gillah*
Mekh.	*M'khilta* (of R. Ishmael, unless otherwise noted)
Men.	*M'naḥot*
Mic.	Micah
Mid.	*Midrash*
Mid. Ag.	*Midrash Aggadah*
Mid. Tad.	*Midrash Tadshei*
MK	*Mo·ed Katan*
MRE	*Mishnat Rabbi Eli·ezer*
mss.	manuscripts
MT	*Mishnei Torah*
Ned.	*N'darim*
Neg.	*N'ga·im*
Neh.	Nehemiah
Nid.	*Niddah*

Num. Numbers
Num. R. Numbers Rabbah

Obad. Obadiah
Oho. *Oholot*
O.Ḥ. *Oraḥ Ḥayyim*
Onk. *Targum Onkelos*
OJPS old Jewish Publication Society translation (1917)

PdRE *Pirkei d'Rabbi Eli·ezer*
PdRK *P'sikta d'Rav Kahana*
Pes. *P'saḥim*
PR *P'sikta Rabbati*
Prov. Proverbs
Ps. Psalms

Q Qumran

R. *Rabbah*
RH *Rosh ha-Shanah*

S.A. *Shulḥan Arukh*
Sam. Samuel
Sanh. *Sanhedrin*
Song Song of Songs
Shab. *Shabbat*
Shek. *Sh'kalim*
Shevu. *Sh'vu·ot*
Sot. *Sotah*
Sekh. T. *Seikhel Tov*
Suk. *Sukkah*

Taan. *Ta·anit*
Tanḥ. *Tanḥuma*
Tanḥ. B. *Tanḥuma*, Solomon Buber edition
Targ. *Targum*
Targ. Jon. Targum Jonathan
Tem. *T'murah*
Tosef. Tosefta
Transl. Note from the Translation Committee for the New Jewish Publication Society (NJPS) translation

Yalkut Sh. *Yalkut Shim·oni*
YD *Yoreh De·ah*
Yev. *Y'vamot*

Zech. Zechariah
Zeph. Zephaniah
Zev. *Z'vaḥim*

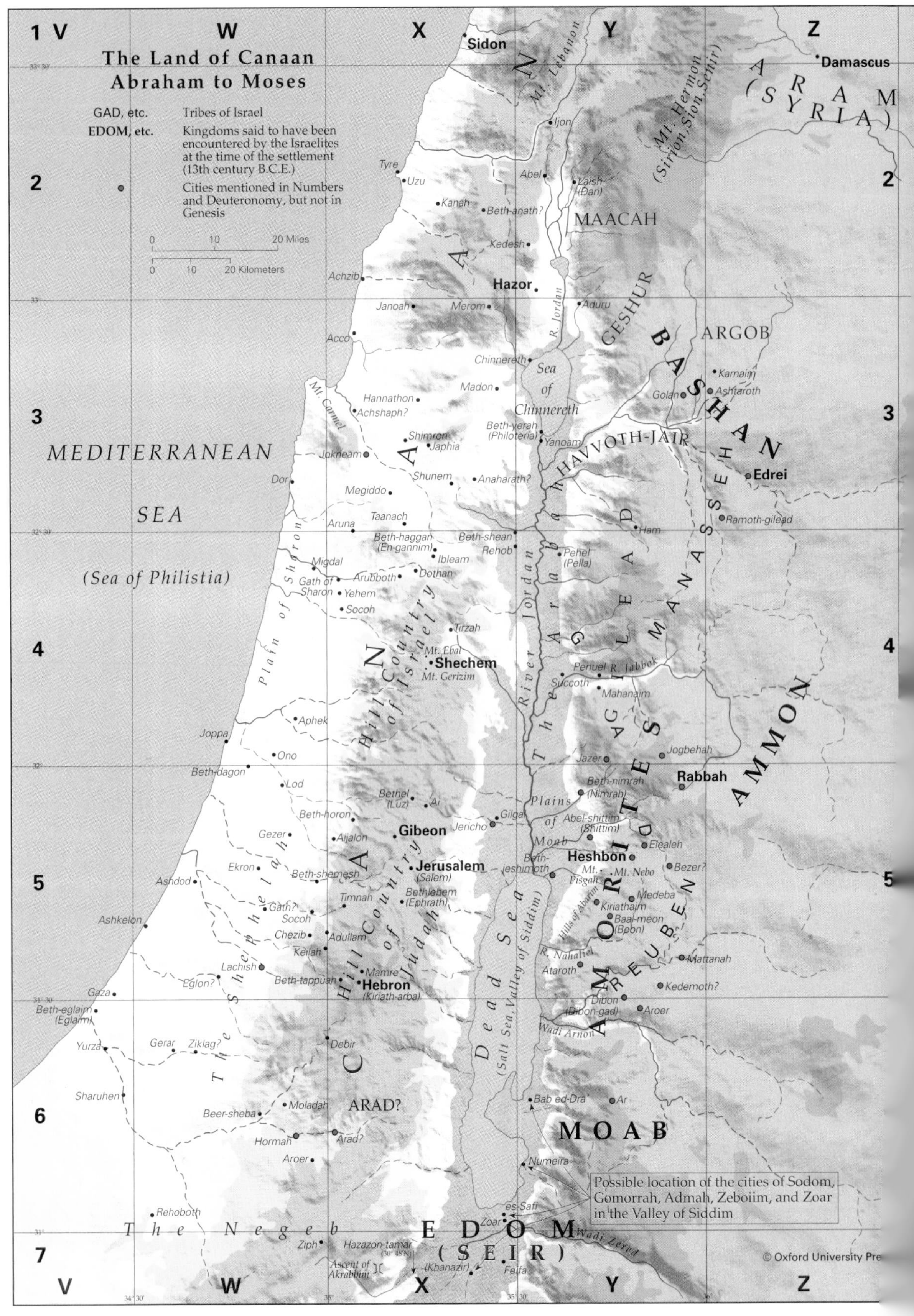
The Land of Canaan
Abraham to Moses
GAD, etc. Tribes of Israel
EDOM, etc. Kingdoms said to have been encountered by the Israelites at the time of the settlement (13th century B.C.E.)
Cities mentioned in Numbers and Deuteronomy, but not in Genesis
0 10 20 Miles
0 10 20 Kilometers
1
2
3
4
5
6
7
V
W
X
Y
Z
MEDITERRANEAN
SEA
(Sea of Philistia)
Sidon
Damascus
ARAM (SYRIA)
Mt. Lebanon
Mt. Hermon (Sirion, Sion, Senir)
Ijon
Tyre
Uzu
Abel
Laish (Dan)
Kanah
Beth-anath?
MAACAH
Kedesh
Achzib
Hazor
Janoah
Merom
Aduru
R. Jordan
GESHUR
ARGOB
BASHAN
Acco
Chinnereth
Sea of Chinnereth
Karnaim
Ashtaroth
Golan
Madon
Mt. Carmel
Hannathon
Achshaph?
Beth-yerah (Philoteria)
Yanoam
HAVVOTH-JAIR
Shimron
Japhia
Jokneam
Edrei
Dor
Shunem
Anaharath?
Megiddo
Taanach
Aruna
Ramoth-gilead
Ham
Beth-haggan (En-gannim)
Beth-shean
Rehob
Ibleam
Pehel (Pella)
Migdal
Gath of Sharon
Arubboth
Dothan
Yehem
Socoh
Plain of Sharon
Hill Country of Israel
Tirzah
Mt. Ebal
Shechem
Mt. Gerizim
River Jordan
The Arabah
GILEAD
MANASSEH
Penuel
R. Jabbok
Succoth
Mahanaim
Aphek
Joppa
Ono
Jazer
Jogbehah
Beth-dagon
Lod
Beth-nimrah (Nimrah)
Rabbah
AMMON
Bethel (Luz)
Ai
Plains of Moab
Abel-shittim (Shittim)
Gilgal
Jericho
Beth-horon
Gibeon
Aijalon
Gezer
Beth-jeshimoth
Heshbon
Elealeh
Ekron
Beth-shemesh
Jerusalem (Salem)
Mt. Pisgah
Mt. Nebo
Bezer?
Ashdod
Bethlehem (Ephrath)
Timnah
Medeba
Kiriathaim
Gath?
Socoh
Hills of Abarim
Baal-meon (Beon)
Ashkelon
Chezib
Adullam
Hill Country of Judah
Keilah
R. Nahaliel
Mattanah
Lachish
Mamre
Ataroth
Eglon?
Beth-tappuah
Hebron (Kiriath-arba)
Kedemoth?
Gaza
Beth-eglaim (Eglaim)
Dibon (Dibon-gad)
Aroer
AMORITES
REUBEN
Dead Sea (Salt Sea, Valley of Siddim)
Wadi Arnon
The Shephelah
Yurza
Gerar
Ziklag?
Debir
CANAAN
Sharuhen
Bab ed-Dra
Ar
Moladah
ARAD?
Beer-sheba
MOAB
Hormah
Arad?
Aroer
Numeira
Possible location of the cities of Sodom, Gomorrah, Admah, Zeboiim, and Zoar in the Valley of Siddim
Rehoboth
es-Safi
The Negeb
Zoar
EDOM (SEIR)
Wadi Zered
Ziph
Hazazon-tamar
Ascent of Akrabbim
(Khanazir)
Feifa
© Oxford University Pre

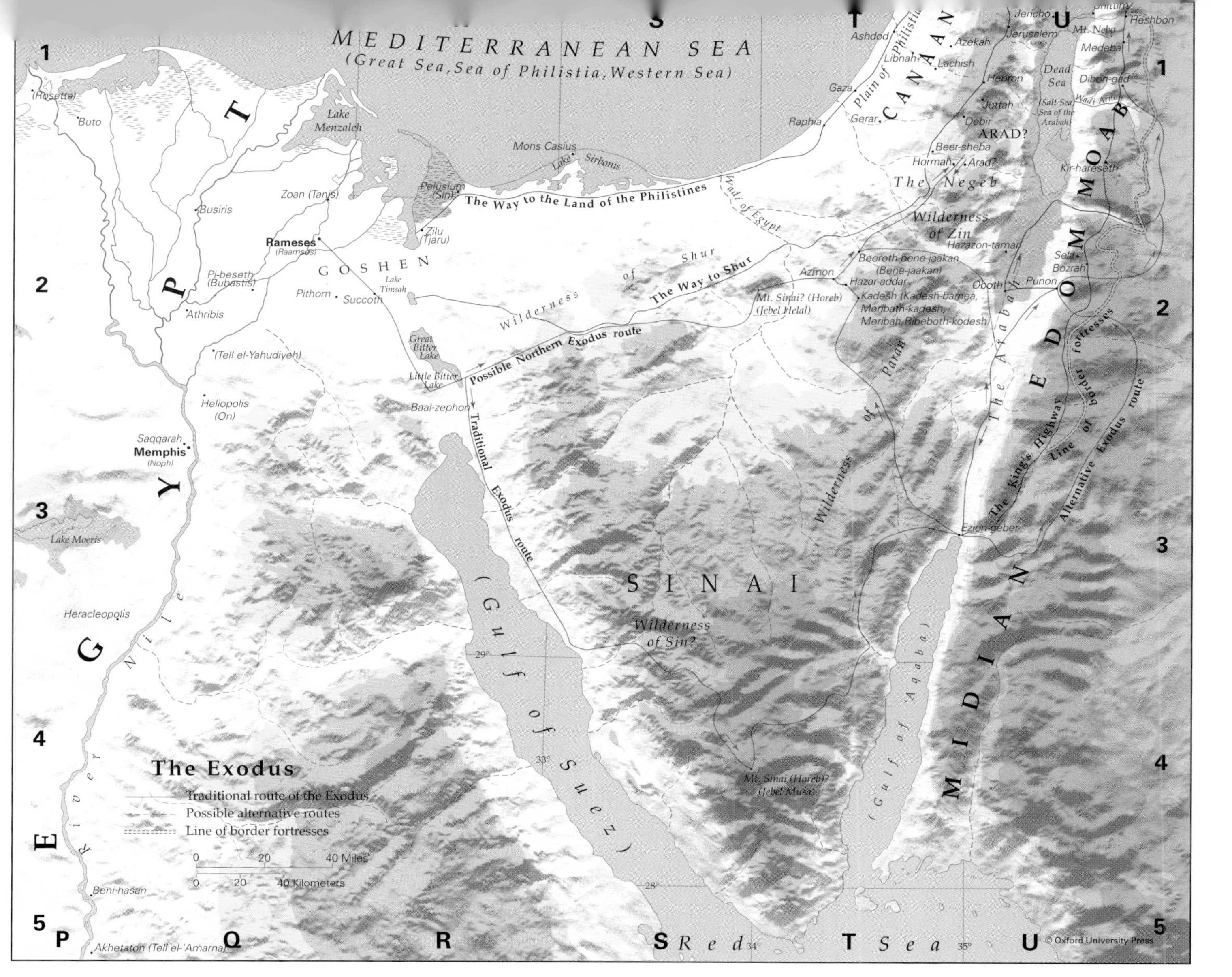
The Exodus
Traditional route of the Exodus
Possible alternative routes
Line of border fortresses
0 20 40 Miles
0 20 40 Kilometers
MEDITERRANEAN SEA
(Great Sea, Sea of Philistia, Western Sea)
EGYPT
CANAAN
MOAB
EDOM
MIDIAN
SINAI
GOSHEN
The Way to the Land of the Philistines
The Way to Shur
Wilderness of Shur
Possible Northern Exodus route
Traditional Exodus route
Alternative Exodus route
The King's Highway
Line of border fortresses
The Arabah
Wilderness of Paran
Wilderness of Zin
Wilderness of Sin?
The Negeb
(Gulf of Suez)
(Gulf of 'Aqaba)
Red Sea
River Nile
Lake Menzaleh
Lake Sirbonis
Mons Casius
Wadi of Egypt
Plain of Philistia
Dead Sea
(Salt Sea, Sea of the Arabah)
Wadi Arnon
(Rosetta)
Buto
Busiris
Zoan (Tanis)
Rameses
(Raamses)
Pi-beseth
(Bubastis)
Athribis
(Tell el-Yahudiyeh)
Heliopolis
(On)
Saqqarah
Memphis
(Noph)
Lake Moeris
Heracleopolis
Beni-hasan
Akhetaton (Tell el-'Amarna)
Pelusium
(Sin)
Zilu
(Tjaru)
Pithom
Succoth
Lake Timsah
Great Bitter Lake
Little Bitter Lake
Baal-zephon
Mt. Sinai? (Horeb)
(Jebel Helal)
Mt. Sinai (Horeb)?
(Jebel Musa)
Azmon
Hazar-addar
Kadesh (Kadesh-barnea,
Meribath-kadesh,
Meribah, Ribeboth-kodesh)
Beeroth-bene-jaakan
(Bene-jaakan)
Hazazon-tamar
Oboth
Punon
Sela
Bozrah
Ezion-geber
Gaza
Raphia
Gerar
Ashdod
Libnah
Lachish
Azekah
Hebron
Juttah
Debir
ARAD?
Beer-sheba
Hormah
Arad?
Jericho
Jerusalem
Mt. Nebo
Heshbon
Medeba
Dibon-gad
Kir-hareseth
29°
33°
28°
34°
35°
P Q R S T U
1 2 3 4 5
© Oxford University Press

Israel in Canaan
Joshua to Samuel and Saul
ASHER, etc Tribes of Israel
Cities of Refuge
Philistine cities
0 10 20 Miles
0 10 20 Kilometers
MEDITERRANEAN SEA
(Sea of Philistia)
Sidon
Damascus
Tyre
Mt. Lebanon
Valley of Lebanon
Mt. Hermon
Baal-gad?
Ahlab
Dan (Laish)
Beth-rehob
Beth-anath?
DAN
ASHER
NAPHTALI
Kedesh
Misrephoth-maim
Abdon
Achzib
Yiron
Hazor
Merom
Waters of Merom
R. Jordan
Acco
Rehob
Cabul
Aphik
Chinnereth
Sea of Chinnereth
Hammath
Nahalol
Mt. Carmel
Hannathon
Achshaph?
Rimmon
Madon
ZEBULUN
Bethlehem
Harosheth-ha-goiim
Shimron
Mt. Tabor
Hill of Moreh
En-dor
Jokneam
Lakkum
ISSACHAR
HAVVOTH-JAIR
BASHAN
Ashtaroth
Golan
Dor
Naphath-Dor
Megiddo
Wadi Kishon
Shunem
Beer
Kamon?
Edrei
Tob
Jezreel
V. of Jezreel
Taanach
Mt. Gilboa
Ramoth-gilead
En-gannim (Beth-haggan)
Ibleam
Beth-shean
MANASSEH
Hill Country of Israel
Jabesh-gilead
Hepher?
Bezek
Abel-meholah
Socoh
Thebez
Tabbath?
Tirzah
Mt. Ebal
Zaphon?
Mt. Gerizim
Shechem
R. Jabbok
Pirathon
Succoth
Penuel
Arumah
Zarethan?
Ataroth
Baal-shalishah
Aphek
Adam
River Jordan
The Arabah
GILEAD
AMMON
Gath-rimmon?
Joppa
Asor
Tappuah
Lebonah
Shiloh
Ramah (Ramathaim)
EPHRAIM
Hill of Ephraim
Beth-dagon
ZUPH
Timnath-serah
Jogbehah
Betonim
Rabbah
Ephron (Ophrah)
Lower Beth-horon
Upper Beth-horon
Bethel
Ai
Rimmon
Naarah
Shaalbim
Mizpah
Gilgal
Beth-nimrah
Gibbethon
Gibeon
Michmash
Jericho
Jabneel
Mount Baalah
Baalath?
Gezer
Aijalon
Beeroth?
Ramah
Shittim
Chephirah
BENJAMIN
Shikkeron
Baalah (Kiriath-jearim)
Gibeah
Anathoth
Beth-peor
Heshbon
Ekron
Sorek
Jerusalem (Jebus)
Mt. Pisgah
Bezer?
Ashdod
V. of Elah
Timnah
Zorah
Zela
Beth-jeshimoth
Beth-shemesh
Lehi?
Middin?
Makkedah?
Jarmuth
Bethlehem
Secacah?
Mt. Nebo
Kiriathaim
Medeba
Gath?
Timnah
Nibshan?
Beth-baal-meon
Azekah
Etam
V. of Achor
Ashkelon
Socoh
Adullam
PHILISTINES
Libnah
Keilah
Giloh
Beth-zur
Zereth-shahar
REUBEN
Mareshah
Hill Country of Judah
Eglon?
Lachish
Hebron
Dead Sea (Salt Sea)
Kedemoth?
Dibon
Gaza
Jezreel?
Ziph
En-gedi
Aroer
Wadi Arnon
The Shephelah
Goshen?
Debir
Anab
Maon
Eshtemoa
Gerar
Ziklag?
Madmannah
Jattir
Brook Besor
Bethul (Bethuel)
JUDAH
Ashan
Kabzeel?
ARAD?
Beer-sheba
Hazar-shual
Arad?
Hormah
SIMEON
MOAB
Adadah (Aroer)
The Negeb
Wadi Zered
Ziph
Ascent of Akrabbim
EDOM (SEIR)
V W X Y Z
1 2 3 4 5 6 7
33° 30'
33°
32° 30'
32°
31° 30'
31°
34° 30'
35°
35° 30'
36°
© Oxford University Press

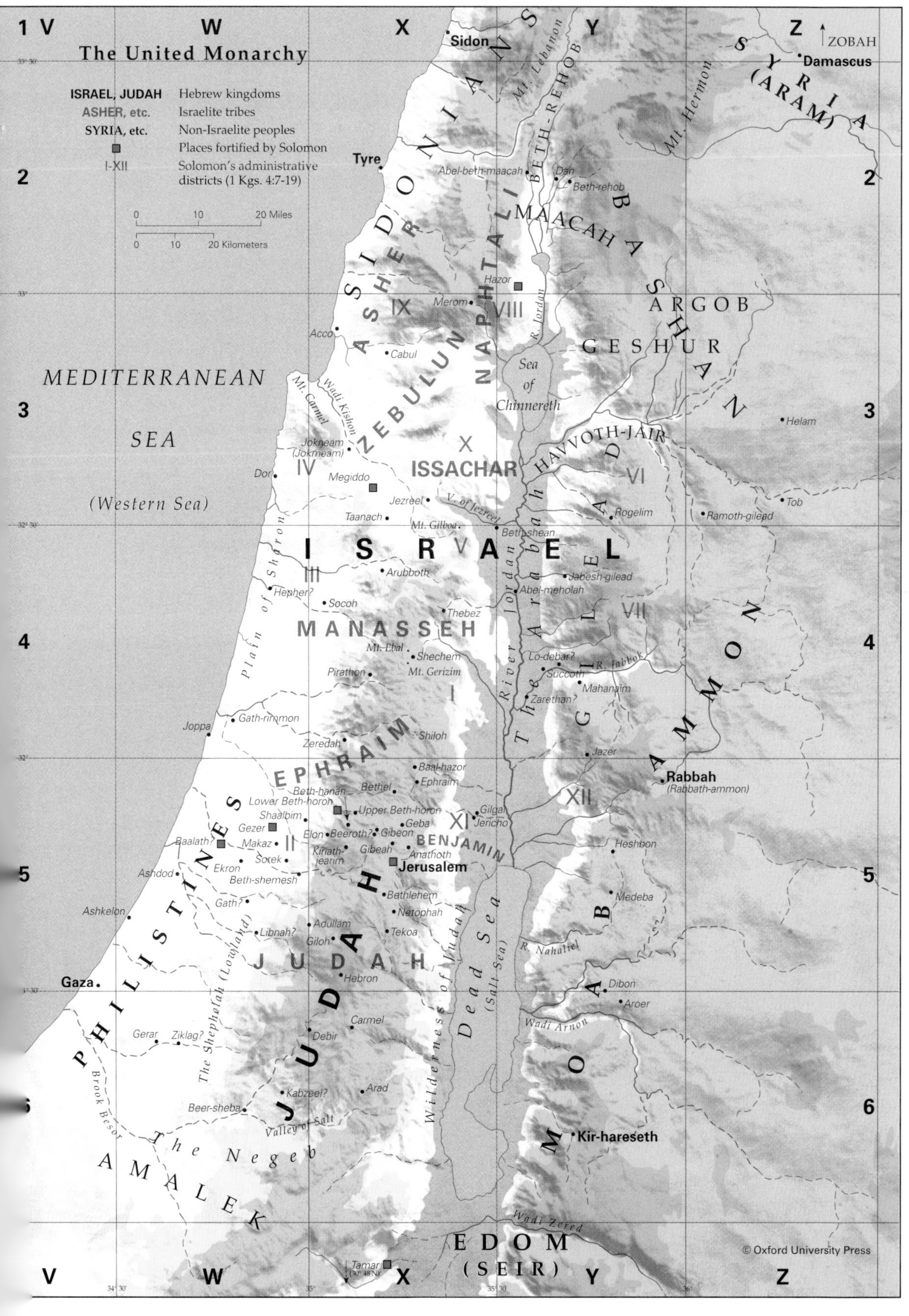

The United Monarchy
ISRAEL, JUDAH Hebrew kingdoms
ASHER, etc. Israelite tribes
SYRIA, etc. Non-Israelite peoples
Places fortified by Solomon
I-XII Solomon's administrative districts (1 Kgs. 4:7-19)
0 10 20 Miles
0 10 20 Kilometers
MEDITERRANEAN SEA
(Western Sea)
SIDONIANS
SYRIA (ARAM)
ZOBAH
Damascus
Sidon
Tyre
Mt. Lebanon
BETH-REHOB
Mt. Hermon
Abel-beth-maacah
Dan
Beth-rehob
MAACAH
BASHAN
ASHER
NAPHTALI
Hazor
Merom
IX
VIII
ARGOB
GESHUR
Acco
Cabul
R. Jordan
Sea of Chinnereth
ZEBULUN
Mt. Carmel
Wadi Kishon
Jokneam (Jokmeam)
X
ISSACHAR
HAVVOTH-JAIR
Helam
Dor
IV
Megiddo
VI
Jezreel
V. of Jezreel
Tob
Taanach
Mt. Gilboa
Rogelim
Ramoth-gilead
Beth-shean
ISRAEL
V
Plain of Sharon
III
Arubboth
Jabesh-gilead
Hepher?
Abel-meholah
Socoh
Thebez
VII
MANASSEH
GILEAD
AMMON
Mt. Ebal
Shechem
Lo-debar?
R. Jabbok
Pirathon
Mt. Gerizim
Succoth
Mahanaim
I
River Jordan
Zarethan?
The Arabah
Joppa
Gath-rimmon
EPHRAIM
Shiloh
Zeredah
Jazer
Baal-hazor
Rabbah (Rabbath-ammon)
Ephraim
Bethel
XII
Beth-hanan
Lower Beth-horon
Upper Beth-horon
Gilgal
Shaalbim
Geba
XI
Jericho
Gezer
Elon
Beeroth?
Gibeon
Baalath?
Makaz
II
BENJAMIN
Heshbon
Kiriath-jearim
Gibeah
Anathoth
Sorek
Ekron
Jerusalem
Ashdod
Beth-shemesh
Bethlehem
Medeba
Gath?
Netophah
Ashkelon
Adullam
Libnah?
Tekoa
Giloh
R. Nahaliel
JUDAH
Hebron
Dead Sea (Salt Sea)
Wilderness of Judah
Gaza
The Shephelah (Lowland)
Dibon
Aroer
MOAB
Carmel
Wadi Arnon
PHILISTINES
Gerar
Ziklag?
Debir
Brook Besor
Kabzeel?
Arad
Beer-sheba
Valley of Salt
Kir-hareseth
The Negeb
AMALEK
Wadi Zered
EDOM (SEIR)
Tamar (30° 48' N)
V W X Y Z
1 2 3 4 5 6
© Oxford University Press

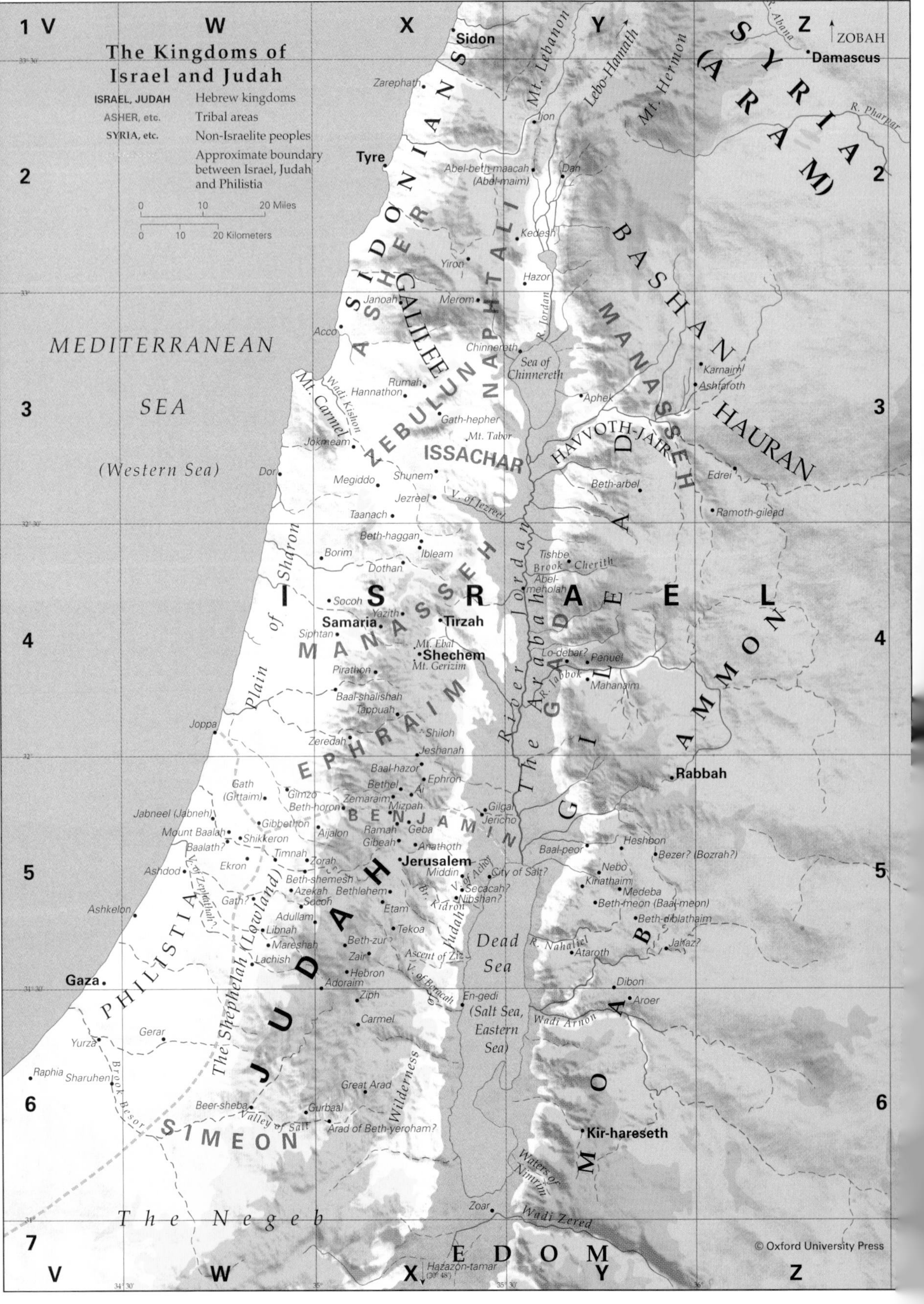

The Kingdoms of Israel and Judah
ISRAEL, JUDAH Hebrew kingdoms
ASHER, etc. Tribal areas
SYRIA, etc. Non-Israelite peoples
Approximate boundary between Israel, Judah and Philistia
0 10 20 Miles
0 10 20 Kilometers
MEDITERRANEAN SEA
(Western Sea)
SIDONIANS
SYRIA (ARAM)
ZOBAH
Damascus
Sidon
Tyre
Zarephath
Mt. Lebanon
Lebo-Hamath
Mt. Hermon
R. Abana
R. Pharpar
Ijon
Abel-beth-maacah (Abel-maim)
Dan
Kedesh
Yiron
Hazor
Merom
Janoah
Acco
ASHER
GALILEE
NAPHTALI
ZEBULUN
BASHAN
MANASSEH
HAURAN
Chinnereth
Sea of Chinnereth
R. Jordan
Karnaim
Ashtaroth
Aphek
Rumah
Hannathon
Mt. Carmel
Wadi Kishon
Gath-hepher
Mt. Tabor
Jokmeam
ISSACHAR
HAVVOTH-JAIR
Dor
Megiddo
Shunem
Jezreel
V. of Jezreel
Edrei
Beth-arbel
Taanach
Ramoth-gilead
Beth-haggan
Ibleam
Borim
Dothan
Tishbe
Brook Cherith
Abel-meholah
Plain of Sharon
ISRAEL
Socoh
Yazith
Samaria
Tirzah
Siphtan
MANASSEH
Mt. Ebal
Shechem
Mt. Gerizim
Lo-debar?
Penuel
R. Jabbok
Mahanaim
GILEAD
AMMON
Pirathon
Baal-shalishah
EPHRAIM
Tappuah
The Arabah
River Jordan
Joppa
Shiloh
Zeredah
Jeshanah
Rabbah
Baal-hazor
Ephron
Bethel
Ai
Gath (Gittaim)
Gimzo
Beth-horon
Zemaraim
Mizpah
Gilgal
Jericho
Jabneel (Jabneh)
Gibbethon
BENJAMIN
Aijalon
Ramah
Geba
Mount Baalah
Shikkeron
Gibeah
Anathoth
Heshbon
Baalath?
Timnah
Baal-peor
Bezer? (Bozrah?)
Ekron
Jerusalem
V. of Achor
Zorah
Middin
City of Salt?
Nebo
Ashdod
V. of Zephathah
Beth-shemesh
Secacah?
Kiriathaim
Azekah
Bethlehem
Nibshan?
Medeba
Gath?
Socoh
Br. Kidron
Beth-meon (Baal-meon)
Ashkelon
Etam
Adullam
Beth-diblathaim
Libnah
Tekoa
PHILISTIA
The Shephelah (Lowland)
JUDAH
Wilderness of Judah
Mareshah
Beth-zur
Dead Sea
R. Nahaliel
Jahaz?
Lachish
Zair
Ascent of Ziz
Ataroth
Hebron
V. of Beracah
Gaza
Adoraim
Dibon
Ziph
En-gedi
Aroer
(Salt Sea, Eastern Sea)
Carmel
Wadi Arnon
Gerar
Yurza
Raphia
Sharuhen
Brook Besor
MOAB
Great Arad
Wilderness
Beer-sheba
Gurbaal
Valley of Salt
Arad of Beth-yeroham?
SIMEON
Kir-hareseth
Waters of Nimrim
Zoar
Wadi Zered
The Negeb
EDOM
Hazazon-tamar (30° 48')
© Oxford University Press

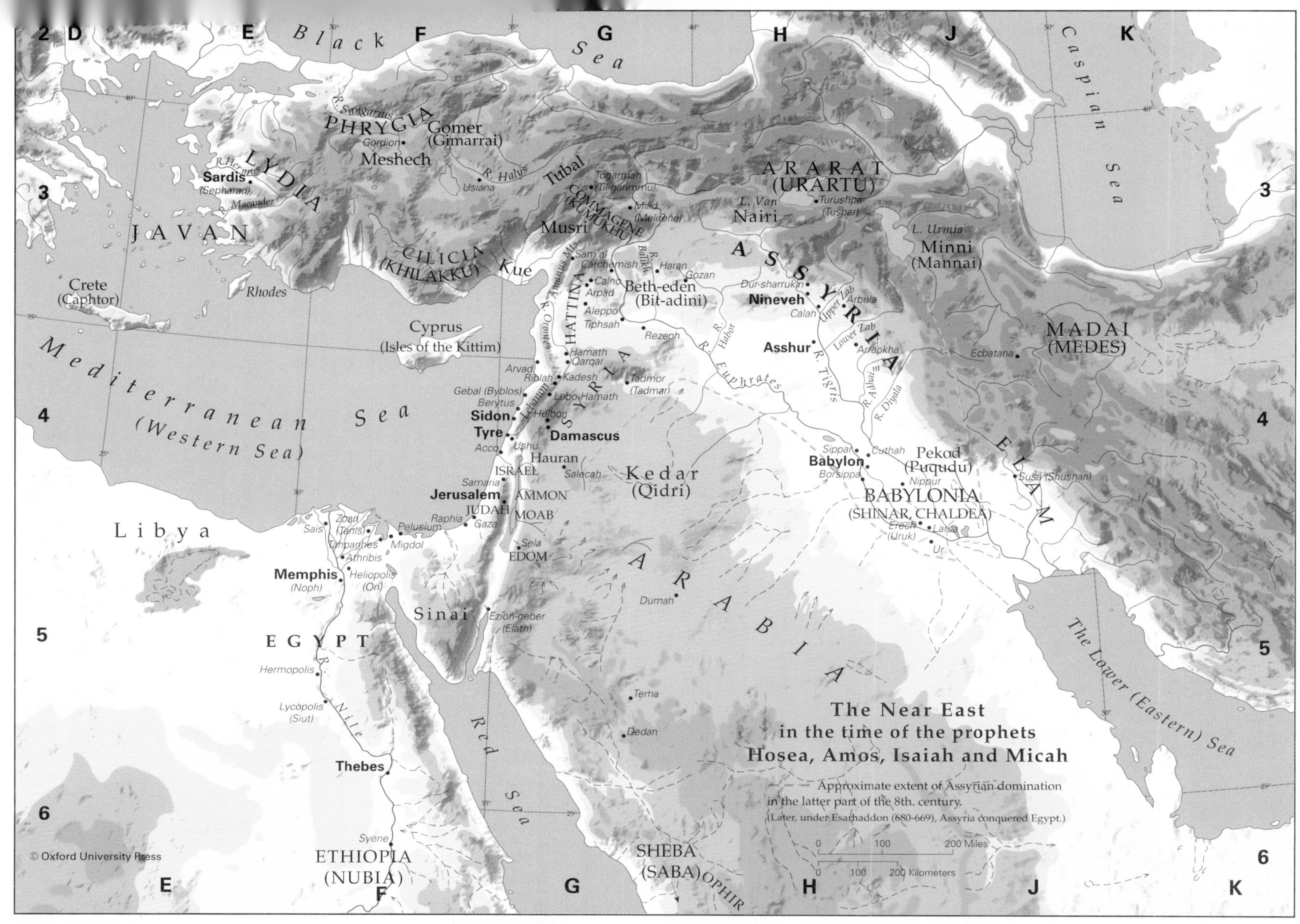
The Near East
in the time of the prophets
Hosea, Amos, Isaiah and Micah
Approximate extent of Assyrian domination in the latter part of the 8th. century.
(Later, under Esarhaddon (680-669), Assyria conquered Egypt.)
0 100 200 Miles
0 100 200 Kilometers
Black Sea
Caspian Sea
Mediterranean Sea
(Western Sea)
Red Sea
The Lower (Eastern) Sea
PHRYGIA
Gomer
(Gimarrai)
Gordion
Meshech
R. Sangarius
R. Halys
Usiana
Tubal
LYDIA
R. Hermus
Sardis
(Sepharad)
R. Maeander
JAVAN
CILICIA
(KHILAKKU)
Kue
Rhodes
Crete
(Caphtor)
Cyprus
(Isles of the Kittim)
Togarmah
(Til-garimmu)
COMMAGENE
(KUMUKHU)
Milid
(Melitene)
Musri
Amanus Mts.
Sam'al
Carchemish
Calno
Arpad
Aleppo
Tiphsah
HATTINA
R. Balikh
Haran
Gozan
Beth-eden
(Bit-adini)
Rezeph
R. Orontes
Hamath
Qarqar
Arvad
Riblah
Kadesh
Gebal (Byblos)
Berytus
Lebo-Hamath
Lebanon
Helbon
Sidon
Tyre
Ushu
Acco
Damascus
SYRIA
Tadmor
(Tadmar)
Hauran
Salecah
ISRAEL
Samaria
Jerusalem
AMMON
JUDAH
MOAB
Raphia
Gaza
Sela
EDOM
Kedar
(Qidri)
ARARAT
(URARTU)
L. Van
Turushpa
(Tuspar)
Nairi
ASSYRIA
L. Urmia
Minni
(Mannai)
Dur-sharrukin
Nineveh
Calah
Upper Zab
Arbela
Lower Zab
Arrapkha
Asshur
R. Habor
R. Euphrates
R. Tigris
R. Adhaim
R. Diyala
MADAI
(MEDES)
Ecbatana
ELAM
Susa (Shushan)
Sippar
Cuthah
Babylon
Borsippa
Pekod
(Puqudu)
Nippur
BABYLONIA
(SHINAR, CHALDEA)
Erech
(Uruk)
Larsa
Ur
ARABIA
Dumah
Tema
Dedan
SHEBA
(SABA)
OPHIR
Libya
Zoan
(Tanis)
Sais
Tahpanhes
Pelusium
Migdol
Athribis
Memphis
(Noph)
Heliopolis
(On)
Sinai
Ezion-geber
(Elath)
EGYPT
Hermopolis
Lycopolis
(Siut)
R. Nile
Thebes
Syene
ETHIOPIA
(NUBIA)
D E F G H J K
2 3 4 5 6
© Oxford University Press

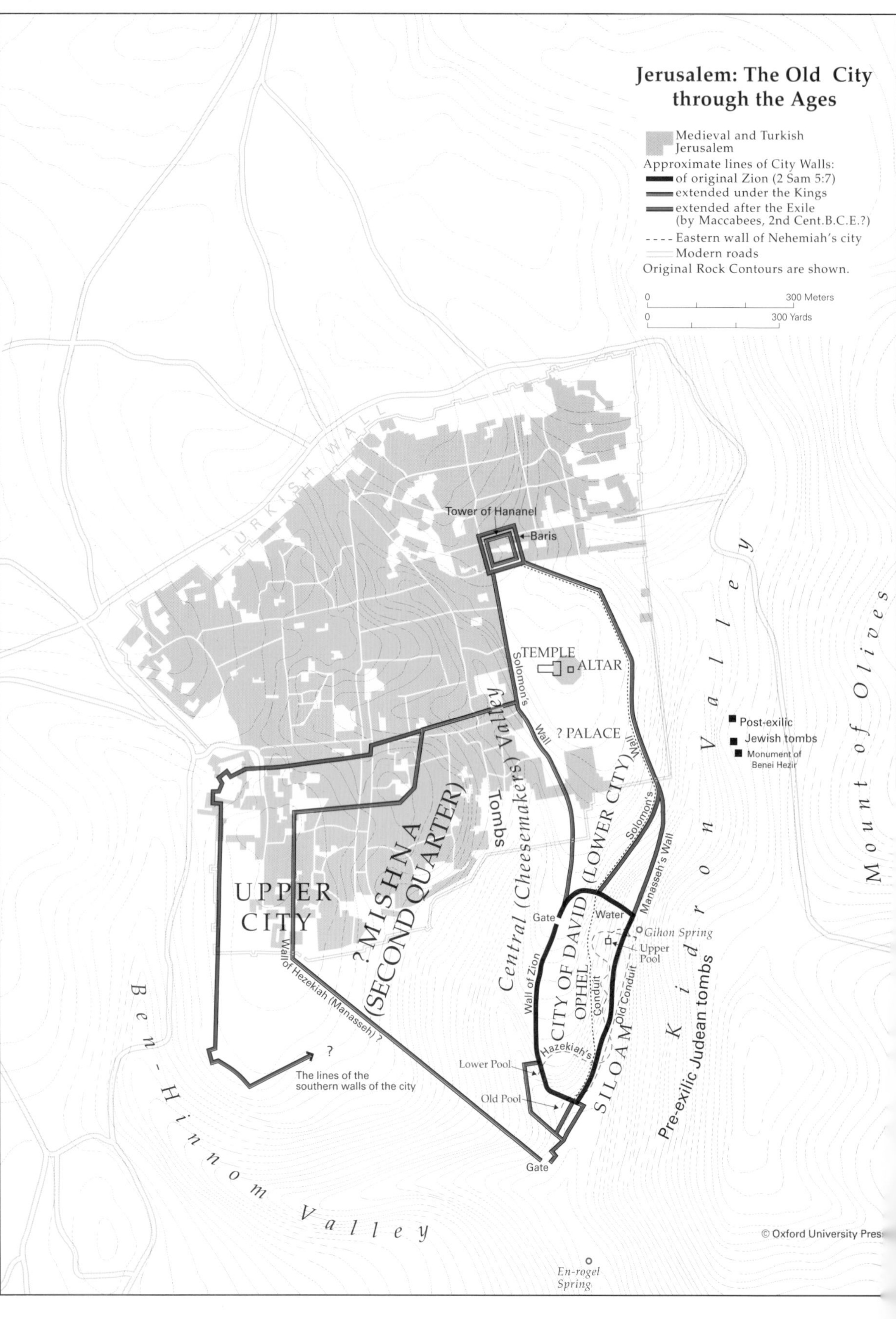

Jerusalem: The Old City through the Ages
Medieval and Turkish Jerusalem
Approximate lines of City Walls:
of original Zion (2 Sam 5:7)
extended under the Kings
extended after the Exile (by Maccabees, 2nd Cent.B.C.E.?)
Eastern wall of Nehemiah's city
Modern roads
Original Rock Contours are shown.
0 300 Meters
0 300 Yards
TURKISH WALL
Tower of Hananel
Baris
TEMPLE
ALTAR
? PALACE
Solomon's Wall
Solomon's Wall
Manasseh's Wall
Wall
Central (Cheesemakers') Valley
Tombs
? MISHNA (SECOND QUARTER)
UPPER CITY
CITY OF DAVID (LOWER CITY)
OPHEL
Gate
Water
Gihon Spring
Upper Pool
Wall of Zion
Conduit
Old Conduit
Hazekiah's
SILOAM
Wall of Hezekiah (Manasseh) ?
The lines of the southern walls of the city
?
Lower Pool
Old Pool
Gate
Kidron Valley
Post-exilic Jewish tombs
Monument of Benei Hezir
Pre-exilic Judean tombs
Mount of Olives
Ben-Hinnom Valley
En-rogel Spring

GLOSSARY

More detailed information on the following authors, books and terms, as well as those not listed here, may be found in the *Encyclopaedia Judaica* and other Jewish encyclopedias and reference works. Hebrew readers may consult *Shem Ha-G'dolim Ha-Shalem,* the first edition of which was composed by Ḥayyim David Azulai (1724–1800).

Aaron of Karlin (1736–1772) The leading figure of Hasidism in Lithuania.

Abravanel, Isaac ben Judah (1437–1508) Bible commentator and statesman; Portugal, Spain, and, after 1492, Italy.

Akkadian An ancient Near Eastern language that included the dialects of Assyrian and Babylonian; knowledge of Akkadian is the key to understanding the culture of ancient Mesopotamia.

Akedah Lit. "binding"; the episode of the Binding of Isaac, as narrated in Genesis 22.

Akedat Yitzḥak Lit. "The Binding of Isaac"; allegorical Torah commentary by Isaac ben Moses Arama (1420–1494); Spain.

Albo, Joseph Author of *Seifer Ha-Ikkarim* ("The Book of Principles"; 1425), a major work of Jewish thought; Spain.

Alter, Robert (b. 1935) Comparative literature scholar; his *The Art of Biblical Narrative* (1981) is a key work in the "Bible as literature" approach to biblical studies; United States.

Aliyah Lit. "going up"; pl. *aliyot.* **1.** Making a pilgrimage to Jerusalem. **2.** Emigrating to the land of Israel. **3.** The honor of reciting the blessings over the liturgical reading of the Torah. **4.** An individual section of the liturgical reading of the Torah over which blessings are recited; there are three such *aliyot* in a weekday service, four on *Rosh Ḥodesh,* five on a weekday festival, six on *Yom Kippur* (if on a weekday), and seven on *Shabbat.*

Alshekh, Moses Sixteenth-century Bible commentator; Turkish Empire (Turkey, Greece, and land of Israel).

Apocalypse Lit. "revelation"; a literature that purports to reveal "hidden things," including what goes on in the heavens and beneath the earth, or at the beginning and end of time.

Aramaic An ancient Near Eastern language that was regionally dominant during the Second Temple period and until the Islamic conquests; along with Hebrew and Greek, the language used most by Jews for more than 1000 years.

Arugat Ha-Bosem Lit. "Garden of Spice"; commentary on liturgical poems containing much midrashic material, written in c. 1234 by Abraham ben Azriel; central Europe.

Ashk'nazim People descending from the Jews of Christian Europe (or more strictly, the Jews of the German and eastern European lands), whose rites are sometimes distinct from those of other Jews.

Assyria Northern Mesopotamian homeland of the Assyrians, whose ancient empire conquered much of the Near East, including the kingdom of Israel in 722 B.C.E.

Avot d'Rabbi Natan A commentary on the Mishnah tractate *Avot,* composed c. 500 C.E.

Babylonia Modern-day Iraq. **1.** The homeland of the Babylonians, whose ancient empire conquered much of the Near East, including the kingdom of Judah in 586 B.C.E. **2.** The Jewish community that was exiled there at that time—yet eventually flourished, leaving a lasting mark on Jewish religion, law, and communal organization.

B'khor Shor, Joseph ben Isaac Twelfth-century Bible commentator and rabbinic scholar; France.

Buber, Martin (1878–1965) Jewish philosopher and Zionist; Germany and Israel.

Canonization Process by which certain literary works of ancient Israel were determined to be divinely inspired and ultimately entered into the Hebrew Bible; the process began in the 7th century B.C.E. and was concluded by the 2nd century C.E.

Cassuto, Umberto (1883–1951) Bible scholar; Italy and Israel.

Casuistic Case law presented in conditional form.

Cognate A word having the same linguistic family or derivation as another.

Committee on Jewish Law and Standards (CJLS) The Conservative Movement's deliberative body, administered by the Rabbinical Assembly, that provides guidance on questions of *halakhah*.

Cult The organized system of worship at a specific shrine (e.g., the Temple).

Cuneiform The form of writing used in ancient Mesopotamia, mostly on clay tablets and seals; the usual means by which Akkadian was written.

Diaspora The Jewish communities outside the land of Israel.

Decalogue The Ten Commandments.

Deuteromony Rabbah See "Midrash Rabbah."

D'rash A method of rabbinic interpretation that ignores a text's contextual meaning so as to elicit a theological, moral, or halakhic lesson.

Eliezer of Beaugency Twelfth-century Bible commentator from northern France.

Emet Ve-Emunah Statement of Principles of Conservative Judaism, published in 1988.

Enoch, Books of Extracanonical apocalyptic books relating to Enoch, who "walked with God" (Gen. 5:24); the earliest of the three was composed in the 2nd century B.C.E.

Epstein, Barukh Halevi (1860–1942) Rabbinic scholar and author of *Torah T'mimah*, a commentary applying statements of the rabbinic tradition to the biblical text; Russia.

Eschatological Pertaining to the end of days and the redemption of the world.

Exodus Rabbah See "Midrash Rabbah."

Finkelstein, Louis (1895–1992) Scholar of rabbinics and chancellor of the Jewish Theological Seminary from 1940 to 1972; United States.

Genesis Rabbah See "Midrash Rabbah."

Genizah In general, a repository for obsolete documents and worn-out books, usually Hebrew, deposited there due to pious concern not to discard the items; the Cairo Genizah, containing medieval documents, changed the face of much of Jewish studies after it was discovered by Solomon Schechter in 1896.

Gilgamesh The major epic work of ancient Mesopotamian literature.

Glatstein, Yaakov (1896–1971) Yiddish poet; Poland and United States.

Greenberg, Moshe (b. 1928) Bible scholar; United States and Israel.

Guide of the Perplexed Maimonides' main work of philosophy.

Ha·amek Davar Torah commentary by Naphtali Zvi Yehudah Berlin (1817–1893); Lithuania.

Ḥafetz Ḥayyim Israel Meir ha-Kohen (1838–1933), rabbinic scholar who became best known by the title of this ethical work that he wrote about proper speech; author of the *Mishneh B'rurah,* a commentary on the *Oraḥ Ḥayyim* section of the *Shulḥan Arukh;* Lithuania.

Ha-K'tav V'ha-Kabbalah A Torah commentary by Yaakov Zvi Mecklenburg (1785–1865); Prussia.

Halakhah The traditional term for Jewish law.

Halakhah l'ma·aseh Practical (rather than theoretical) matters of Jewish law.

Halakhot G'dolot A rabbinic work summarizing various *halakhot*, or issues of Jewish law; probably composed in Babylonia in the 8th or 9th centuries.

Ḥananel (ben Ḥushiel) Eleventh-century talmudic commentator; Tunisia.

Hasmonean Dynasty of Jewish rulers of Judea from the Maccabean uprising to the Roman conquest.

Ḥatam Sofer Moses Sofer (1762–1839), who became best known by the title of this book of legal opinions that he authored; leading figure of Hungarian ultra-Orthodoxy.

Ḥayyim (ben Isaac) of Volozhin (1749–1821) Disciple of the Vilna Gaon; a leader of the *Mitnagg'dim* (anti-*Ḥasidim*); founder of the Volozhin *y'shivah;* Lithuania.

Heschel, Abraham Joshua (1907–1972) Rabbi, theologian, Jewish Theological Seminary faculty member, author, and scion of a distinguished Hasidic dynasty.

Hirsch, Samson Raphael (1808–1888) Leading figure of 19th-century German Jewish Orthodoxy; author of a Torah commentary; Germany.

Ḥizz'kuni Mid-13th-century Torah commentary by Hezekiah ben Manoaḥ; France.

Hoffman, David Tzvi (1843–1921) Orthodox halakhic authority and Torah commentator; Germany.

Ibn Ezra, Abraham (1089–1164) Poet, grammarian, and Bible commentator; Spain.

Immanence In theology, the aspect of God's nearness and intimacy, as opposed to God's transcendence.

Jacob, Benno (1862–1945) Conservative rabbi and Bible commentator; Germany.

Jubilees, Book of Extracanonical work, dating from the middle of the Second Temple period, purporting to be a secret revelation to Moses, upon his second ascent to Mt. Sinai.

Kabbalah The Jewish mystical tradition.

Kara, Joseph (b. c. 1065) Bible commenta-

tor; student and colleague of Rashi; northern France.

Kaplan, Mordecai (1881–1983) Founding dean of the Teachers' Institute of the Jewish Theological Seminary, on whose faculty he served for more than 50 years; one of the leading thinkers of American Jewry in the 20th century and the founder of the Reconstructionist movement.

Karaites The Jewish sect, which began in 8th-century Babylonia, that denies the authority of the Rabbinic tradition.

Kierkegaard, Søren (1813–1855) Christian philosopher; author of *Fear and Trembling* (1843), a meditation on the Binding of Isaac; Denmark.

K'li Yakar Torah commentary by Shlomo Efrayim of Lunshitz (1550–1619); Poland.

Kook, Abraham Isaac (1865–1935) Philosopher; first Chief Rabbi for *Ashk'nazim* in British Mandatory Palestine.

K'rei The way that Masoretic tradition requires a word in the Hebrew Bible to be read aloud, as opposed to the *k'tiv.*

K'tiv The way that Masoretic tradition requires a word in the Hebrew Bible to be written down, as opposed to the *k'rei.*

Leibowitz, Neḥamah (1902–1997) Scholar of the Bible and its rabbinic interpretation; Israel.

Levi Yitzḥak (ben Meir) of Berdichev (c. 1740–1810) Author of *K'dushat Levi,* collected sermons based on the *parashah;* Hasidic master; Poland.

Levinthal, Israel H. (1888–1982) Conservative Jewish rabbinic leader and thinker; United States.

Leviticus Rabbah See "Midrash Rabbah."

Lex talionis Latin for "law of retaliation"; the biblical provision of "an eye for an eye, a tooth for a tooth . . ."

Liturgical Pertaining to the text of, or performance of, traditional worship.

Luzzatto, Samuel David (1800–1865) Also known as "ShaDaL"; scholar and Bible commentator; Italy.

Maimonides, Moses (1135–1204) Also known as "RaMBaM"; halakhic codifier (*Mishnei Torah*), philosopher (*Guide of the Perplexed*), and communal leader; Spain and Egypt.

Malbim, Meir Loeb ben Yeḥiel Michael (1809–1879) Rabbi, preacher, and Bible commentator; Eastern Europe.

Masoretic text The traditional authoritative Hebrew text of the Bible, with its consonants, vowels, and cantillation marks, as developed by the Masoretes, a scribal school in Tiberias between the 6th and 9th centuries.

Menaḥem Mendel of Kotsk (1787–1859) Hasidic master; Poland.

Mesopotamia Lit. "Land Between the Rivers"; modern-day Iraq; the land of the early Sumerian civilization as well as the later Babylonian.

Midrash Legal and homiletical expositions of the biblical text, and anthologies and compilations of such.

Midrash Ha-Gadol A 13th-century anonymous Midrash on the Torah; Yemen.

Midrash Lekaḥ Tov An 11th-century Midrash on the Torah and on the Five *M'gillot* (Ruth, Song of Songs, Ecclesiastes, Lamentations, and Esther), by Tobias ben Eliezer; Balkans.

Midrash Psalms A collection of *midrashim* on the Psalms, containing material spanning many centuries.

Midrash Rabbah A 10-part set of 5th- and 6th-century midrashic collections of homiletical and narrative material, covering the Torah and the "Five *M'gillot*" (Ruth, Song of Songs, Ecclesiastes, Lamentations, and Esther).

Midrash Tadsheh Midrashic collection, composed perhaps in the 10th century.

Midrash T'murah A 12th-century midrashic collection.

Mishnah The written compilation of orally transmitted teachings covering all aspects of Jewish law, arranged in six orders that, in turn, are divided into tractates; edited by Rabbi Judah ha-Nasi, c. 200 C.E.; land of Israel.

Mishnei Torah Maimonides' codification of Jewish law.

M'khilta Midrash quoting the early Sages on the Book of Exodus, compiled c. 400 C.E. There is a *M'khilta* of Rabbi Ishmael and a *M'khilta* of Rabbi Simeon bar Yoḥai.

M'norat Ha-Ma·or A 14th-century ethical treatise by Isaac Aboab; Spain.

Nebuchadnezzar Babylonian emperor who captured Jerusalem in 586 B.C.E., ending the First Temple period.

Nissim (ben Reuben Gerondi) (c. 1310–c. 1375) Also known as "the RaN"; talmudic commentator; Spain.

Numbers Rabbah See "Midrash Rabbah."

Numinous The awareness of the presence of God. This meaning of the term was developed by the theologian Rudolf Otto in *The Idea of the Holy* (1923).

Onkelos Second-century translator of the Hebrew Bible into its official Aramaic version.

Or Ha-Ḥayyim Torah commentary by Ḥayyim ben Moshe Attar (1742); Morocco, Germany, land of Israel.

Parashah Pl. *parashiyyot;* one of the 54 traditional divisions of the Torah for synagogue liturgical readings.

Pericope A portion of Scripture read in public worship.

Pirkei d'Rabbi Eliezer An 8th-century homiletic work on scriptural narratives; land of Israel.

P'shat The plain meaning of a word, verse, or passage as read in its context.

P'sikta d'Rav Kahana Homilies on the scriptural readings in synagogues for special Sabbaths and holidays, written around the 5th century; land of Israel.

P'sikta Rabbati Medieval Midrash on the scriptural readings in synagogues for special Sabbaths and holidays.

Qumran The site of the caves where the Dead Sea Scrolls were found beginning in 1947; or, the ancient Jewish sect described in those scrolls.

Rabbinic (Cap.) Pertaining to the period or literature of the Sages of the Mishnah and Talmud, i.e., from c. 100 B.C.E. to c. 700 C.E.

Rabbis (Cap.) See "Sages."

Radak (c. 1160–c. 1235) Acronym for "Rabbi David (ben Joseph) Kimḥi"; grammarian, lexicographer, and Bible commentator; France.

Ralbag (1288–1344) Acronym for "Rabbi Levi ben Gershon"; also known as Gersonides; Bible commentator, scientist, and philosopher; France.

Ramban (1194–1270) Acronym for "Rabbi Moses ben Naḥman"; also known as Nachmanides; philosopher; Bible and Talmud commentator; Spain.

Rashbam (c. 1080–1174) Acronym for "Rabbi Samuel ben Meir"; grandson of Rashi; Bible and Talmud commentator; France.

Rashi (1040–1105) Acronym for "Rabbi 'Rabbi Solomon (ben) Isaac"; Bible and Talmud commentator; France.

Saadia Gaon (882–942) Saadia ben Joseph; philosopher, halakhist, poet, and Bible commentator; head of the Sura academy in Babylon.

Sages (Cap.) A general term for rabbis and associated teachers from the 2nd century B.C.E. through the 7th century C.E., as known to us both from the Midrash of that era and from the Mishnah, Tosefta, and Talmud.

Salanter, Israel ben Zeev Wolf (1810–1883) Leading figure of the Musar (ethical-pietist) movement; Lithuania.

Seifer Ha-Yashar A 13th-century anonymous work on popular ethics.

Seikhel Tov Early 12th-century midrashic collection by Menaḥem ben Solomon.

Sennacherib Powerful Assyrian emperor who waged war against Judah during King Hezekiah's reign at the end of the 8th century B.C.E.

S'fardim People descending from the Jews of the Iberian peninsula (Spain and Portugal) before their expulsion of 1492, whose rites are sometimes distinct from those of other Jews.

S'fat Emet A 19th-century Torah commentary by Yehudah Aryeh Leib of Ger ("the Gerer Rebbe").

Septuagint Jewish translation into Greek of the Hebrew Bible, beginning in the 3rd century B.C.E., to meet the needs of the Jewish community of Alexandria; this translation later became authoritative Scripture for the Church. In Latin, lit. "seventy"; according to legend it was composed by 72 Jewish scholars.

Sforno, Obadiah ben Jacob (c.1470–c. 1550) Bible commentator; Italy.

Shibbolei Ha-Leket Lit. "The Gleaned Ear [of Grain]"; 13th-century halakhic work by Zedekiah ben Abraham Anav; Italy.

Sh'khinah The Divine presence, representing God's immanence.

Sh'nei Luḥot Ha-B'rit Ethical work combining *halakhah, midrash,* and mysticism, by Isaiah ben Abraham ha-Levi Horowitz (c. 1565–1630); central Europe, land of Israel.

Shneur Zalman (of Lyady) (1745–1813) Founder of Ḥabad Hasidism; Belorussia, Lithuania, and Russia.

Shulḥan Arukh Medieval code of Jewish law by Joseph Karo (1488–1575).

Siegel, Seymour (1927–1988) Conservative rabbinic leader, Jewish Theological Seminary faculty member, halakhist, and ethicist; United States.

Sifra Also called *Torat Kohanim;* 4th-century anonymous midrashic commentary on the book of Leviticus; land of Israel.

Sifrei A 4th-century halakhic Midrash on Numbers and on Deuteronomy.

Soloveitchik, Joseph Dov (1903–1992) Orthodox rabbinic leader and philosopher; United States.

Spiegel, Shalom (1899–1984) Scholar of medieval Hebrew literature; Jewish Theological Seminary faculty member; United States.

Steinberg, Milton (1903–1950) Conservative rabbinic leader and author; United States.

Sumerian An ancient language and urban civilization of southern Mesopotamia.

Tabernacle The tent-structure used to house the portable wilderness sanctuary that served as the center of ancient Israelite worship until the construction of the temple in Jerusalem by King Solomon.

Talmud The central body of Rabbinic law, dialectic, and lore, comprising the Mishnah and the Gemara—the latter being an exposition and elaboration of the former in Hebrew and Aramaic. Two separate talmudic compilations exist: the Babylonian Talmud (redacted c. 500 C.E.) and the Jerusalem Talmud (also known as the Palestinian Talmud, redacted c. 400 C.E.).

Tanḥuma Collection of 4th-century homiletical midrashim on the Torah, arranged according to the ancient triennial cycle; attributed to Tanḥum bar Abba; land of Israel.

Targum Jonathan An Aramaic free translation of the Torah, completed in the second half of the first millenium C.E.

Theophany An appearance of God, or God's presence (e.g., the theophany at Sinai).

Tikkun Sof'rim Lit. "Corrections of the Scribes"; 18 changes to the Hebrew biblical text to avoid references to God that were deemed unseemly, dating from pre-Rabbinic times.

Torah Teaching or law; refers minimally to the Pentateuch (Genesis, Exodus, Leviticus, Numbers, and Deuteronomy), often called "The Written Torah"; refers maximally also to the whole corpus of Rabbinic literature, often called "The Oral Torah."

Tosefta A compilation of halakhic rulings by mishnaic rabbis that were not included in the Mishnah, or are parallel to statements in the Mishnah; composed c. 300 C.E.

Transcendent In theology, the aspect of God that is beyond time and space, as opposed to God's immanence.

Ugaritic An ancient Canaanite language of northern Syria, closely related to Hebrew; an archive of Ugaritic writings discovered at Ras Shamra is important in biblical studies.

Vilna Gaon (1720–1797) Elijah ben Solomon Zalman; major scholar and Jewish intellectual leader; sage of the *Mitnagg'dim* (anti-*Ḥasidim*); Lithuania.

Vulgate Latin translation of the Hebrew Bible by the Church father Jerome (345–420); became the official Latin version of the Bible for the Roman Catholic Church.

Wiesel, Elie (b. 1928) Novelist and outspoken Holocaust survivor; Rumania, France, and United States.

Yalkut Shim·oni A 13th-century midrashic anthology on the Bible attributed to a certain Simeon; Germany.

Yeitzer ha-ra A person's egocentric drive, according to Rabbinic psychology; contrasted with *yeitzer ha-tov*.

Yeitzer ha-tov A person's altruistic drive, according to Rabbinic psychology; contrasted with *yeitzer ha-ra*.

Zohar The central work of the Kabbalah, containing much midrashic and homiletical material; composed in 13th-century Spain.

Zornberg, Avivah Gottlieb (b. 1944) Gifted Bible lecturer, teacher, and author; Israel.

Zoroastrianism The ancient pre-Islamic Persian religion.

TRANSLITERATION OF HEBREW

Generally, words set in italic type in commentaries and essays are words quoted from the Bible or key Jewish terms. Such words, together with the names of Torah portions, are transliterated from Hebrew in accordance with the table below. Transliteration of these words follows standard modern Israeli pronunciation, including the "rules for educated speech" of Zeev Ben-Hayyim in *Encyclopaedia Judaica* 8:94. (Note: Abbreviations and proper nouns that appear in roman type may not follow the scheme shown here.)

HYPHENATION

A hyphen is placed after the particle prefixes *ba-*, *va-*, *u-*, *he-*, *ha-*, *ka-*, *mi-*, *she-* and *la-* so as to make the word's root more explicit. However, a hyphen is not used for a verbal infinitive. And it is not used when the following Hebrew vowel is reduced to avoid a double schwa (unless the following English consonant will be capitalized), nor when the prefix's own vowel is a schwa.

CENTERED DOT

A centered dot (·) is used in three situations:

- to set off a "furtive *pataḥ*" at the end of a word
- to separate letters within the consonant pairs *kh, tz,* or *sh* as needed to avoid ambiguity
- to show a break created by the letter *alef* or *ayin* that starts a syllable in the middle of a word (but not after an apostrophe that marks a schwa, for there the break is already clear).

DOUBLING OF CONSONANTS

Generally, Hebrew letters with a *dagesh* (internal dot) are shown by a double letter in transliteration. However, a single letter is used in the following cases:

- the letter follows a hyphenated prefix
- the letter is the first or last letter of the word
- the letter follows or precedes another consonant in transliteration
- the Hebrew letter is represented with an English letter pair, i.e., "sh" or "tz."

Representation	***Hebrew Character***	***Pronunciation***
· [centered dot]	א or ע[a]	[break]
a	Xָ Xֲ Xַ	"**a**rm"
b	בּ	**b**
d	ד	**d**
e	Xֵ[b] Xֶ Xֱ Xֵי	"b**e**d"
f	ף פ	**f**
g	ג	"**g**ive"
h	ה	"**h**oly" or (at end of word) silent
ḥ	ח	as in Hebrew ***ḥ****allah* (braided egg bread) or ***ḥ****azzan* (cantor)
i	Xִ or Xִי	"gr**i**n" or "pol**i**ce"

Representation	*Hebrew Character*	*Pronunciation*
k	כּ ךּ or ק	**k**
kh	כ ך	like German "Bu**ch**" or Scottish "lo**ch**"
l	ל	**l**
m	מ ם	**m**
n	נ ן	**n**
o	וֹ Xֹ Xָ[c]	"h**o**me"
p	פּ ףּ	**p**
r	ר	**r**
s	ס or שׂ	**s**
sh	שׁ	"**sh**ine"
t	ט or תּ ת	**t**
tz	צ ץ	"bli**tz**"
u	וּ Xֻ	"pl**u**me"
v	ב or ו	**v**
y	י	"**y**our"
z	ז	**z**
'	Xְ[d]	"g'morning" or like "el**e**phant"
ai	Xַי	"Th**ai**land"
ei	Xֵי Xֵה Xֵא Xֵ[e]	"**ei**ght"
oi	וֹי	"c**oi**n"
ui	וּי	like "ch**ewy**"

[a] At the start of a middle syllable; otherwise (e.g., at the start or end of a word), the letters *alef* and *ayin* are not transliterated.
[b] In a closed or an unaccented syllable (or both).
[c] In a closed and unaccented syllable.
[d] When the vowel is pronounced (such as after a long vowel, but not after a short vowel).
[e] In an open and accented syllable.

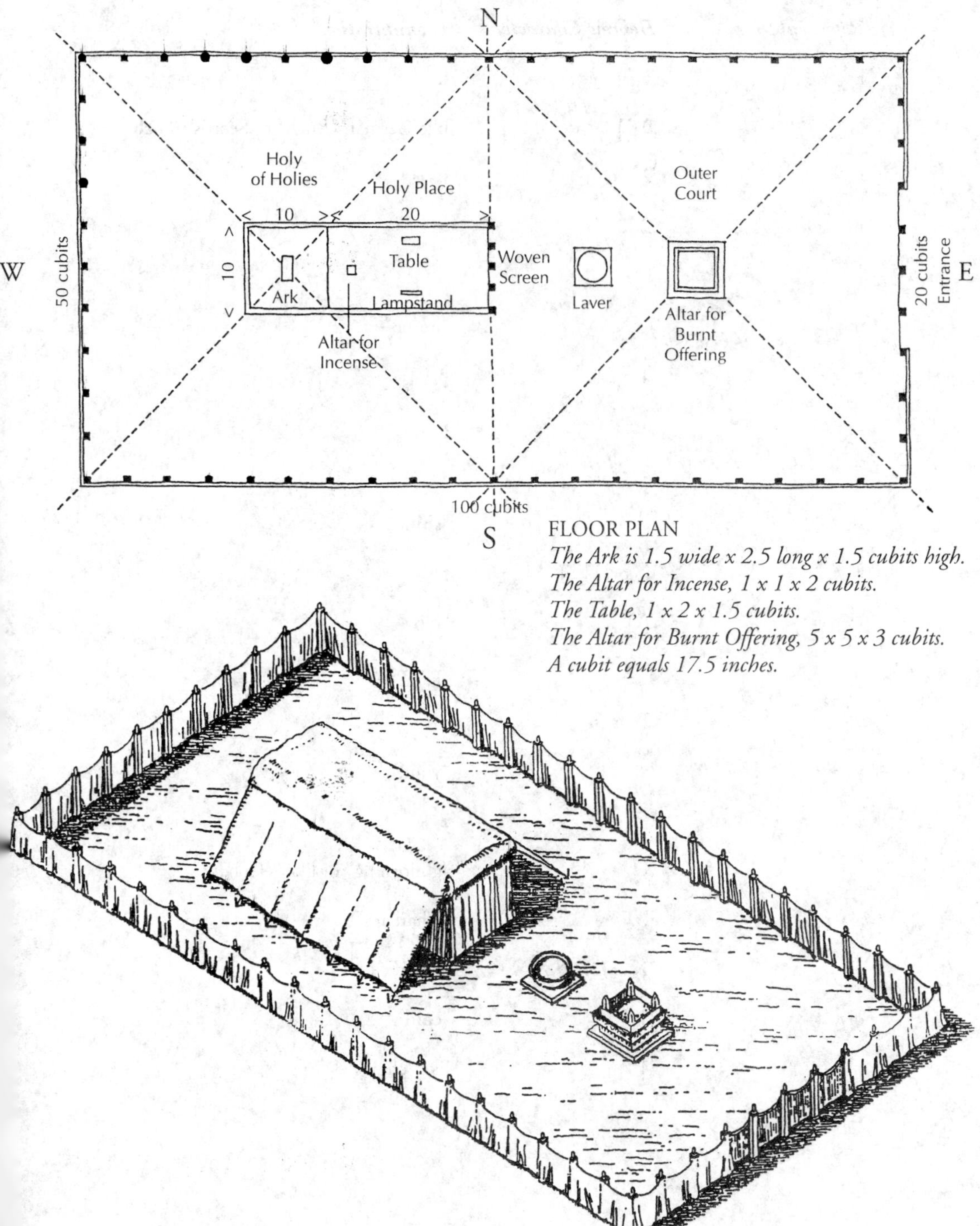

FLOOR PLAN
The Ark is 1.5 wide x 2.5 long x 1.5 cubits high.
The Altar for Incense, 1 x 1 x 2 cubits.
The Table, 1 x 2 x 1.5 cubits.
The Altar for Burnt Offering, 5 x 5 x 3 cubits.
A cubit equals 17.5 inches.

THE TABERNACLE

The tabernacle is a rectangular structure comprising three zones. These are, in descending order of holiness: the Holy of Holies, the Holy Place, and the Outer Court. The structure is oriented longitudinally, on an east-west axis, with the most sacred zone in the west. An outer perimeter demarcates the sacred area. This is divided into two equal squares. The first two zones lie in one square and the Outer Court constitutes the other square. From the Ark in the Holy of Holies, God reaches out to Israel; from the Altar for Burnt Offering, the Israelites reach out to God. Each seems to be located exactly at the point of intersection of the diagonals of the squares.

FURNISHINGS OF THE TABERNACLE

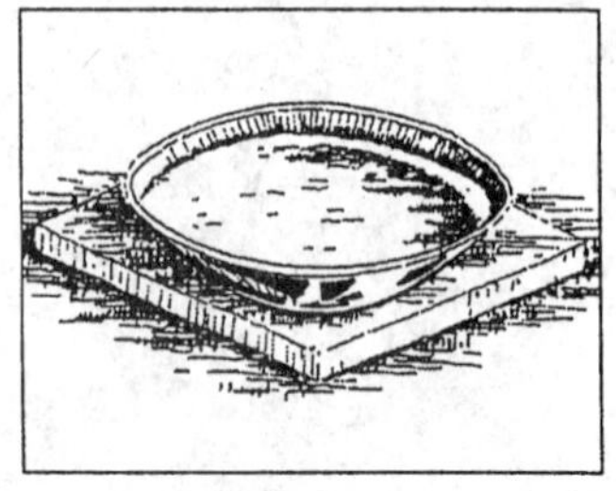

Bronze Laver
Exodus 30:17–21

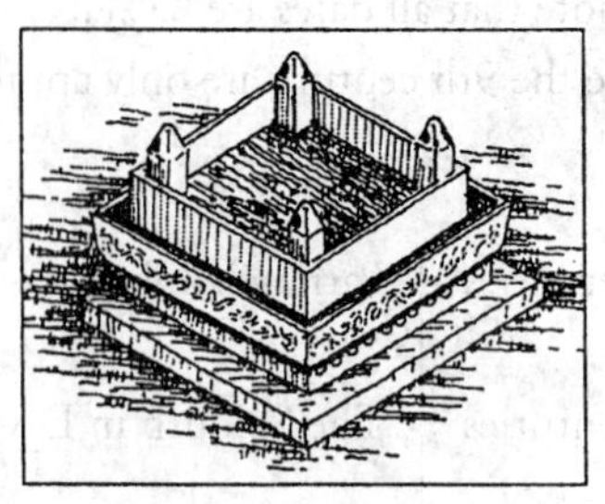

Altar for Burnt Offering
Exodus 27:1–2, 4–6

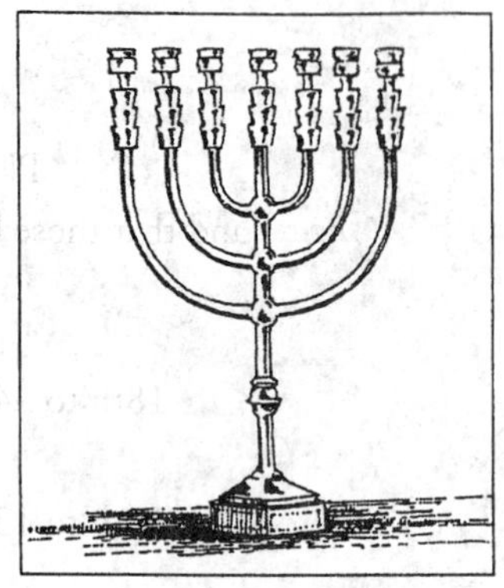

Lampstand (m'norah)
Exodus 25:31–37

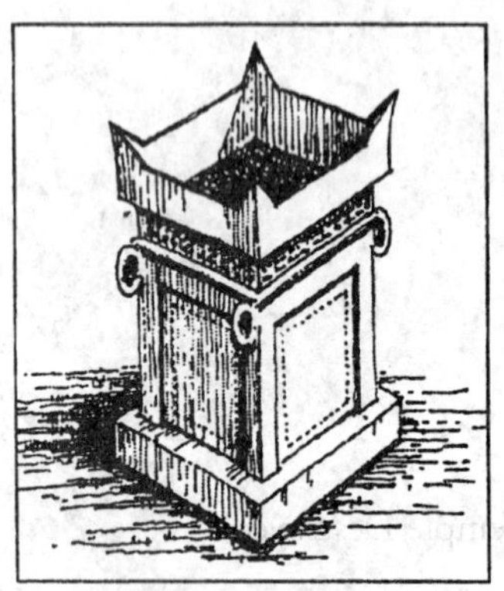

Altar for Incense
Exodus 30:1–5

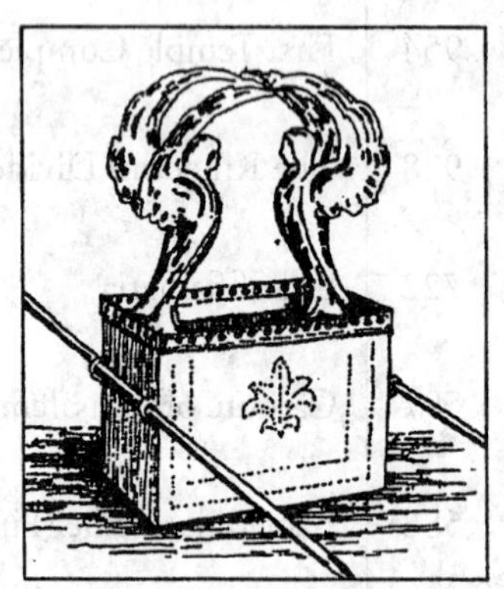

Ark and Cherubim
Exodus 25:10–22

Table for Bread of Display
Exodus 25:23–30

A TIME LINE FOR THE HEBREW BIBLE

Please note that all dates are B.C.E.
and that those before the 9th century are only approximate.

18th to 14th centuries	Patriarchal Period
14th to 13th centuries	The Sojourn in Egypt
13th century	Exodus from Egypt
12th to 11th centuries	Settlement in the Promised Land
	The United Kingdom:
ca. 1020	Saul
ca. 1004	David
ca. 965	Solomon
954	First Temple Completed
928	The Kingdom Divided
722	Fall of Samaria
597	Capture of Jerusalem
586	Babylonian Exile (First Temple Destroyed)
538	Edict of Cyrus and Return to Land
515	Second Temple Completed
458(?), 398(?)	Ezra and Second Return
167	Desecration of Temple by Antiochus IV
164	Rededication of Temple

ETZ HAYIM COMMITTEES

The production of Etz Hayim has been accomplished through a partnership of the Rabbinical Assembly, the United Synagogue of Conservative Judaism, and The Jewish Publication Society. Each partner has brought strength and wisdom to the project and has been deeply involved in every aspect of the volume, through both volunteer and professional staff leadership and effort.

HUMASH BOARD

Rabbi Irwin Groner, *Chairman*

Eugene B. Borowitz
Daniel C. Cohen
Martin D. Cohn
Harold Cramer
Jerome M. Epstein
Edwin P. Farber
Ellen Frankel
David Lerman
Joel H. Meyers
Michael Rapaport
Jerome J. Shestack
Jeffrey A. Wohlberg
Stephen Wolnek
Gerald I. Wolpe
Joel H. Zaiman

Commentary Reading Committee

Bradley Shavit Artson
Ivan Caine
Nina Beth Cardin
Samuel Chiel
Melissa F. Crespy
Melvin Dow
Arnold M. Goodman
Leonard D. Gordon
Jonathan Greenberg
Franklin D. Kreutzer
Aaron Landes
Adina T. Lewittes
Daniel J. Pressman
Michael Rapaport
Susan Safyan
Michael S. Siegel
Gerald C. Skolnik
Carolyn Temin
Moshe J. Tutnauer
Philip Warmflash

Editorial Reading Committee

Paul S. Drazen
Elliot B. Gertel
Eliezer Havivi
Allen I. Juda
Naomi Kalish
Alan F. Lavin
Saul Leeman
Steven C. Lindemann
Sally Olins
Richard J. Plavin
David B. Rosen
Robert Scheinberg
Michelle Sullum

PUBLIC RELATIONS AND MARKETING COMMITTEE

Gerald I. Wolpe, *Chairman*

Steve Berman
Seymour L. Essrog
Lois Goldrich
Rochelle Kraut
Michelle Phelan
Joseph Mendelsohn
Joanne Friedman Rapaport
Joseph Sandler
Dolores Verbit

PRODUCTION COMMITTEE

David E. S. Stein, *Project Manager* Carol Hupping, *Managing Editor* Robin Norman, *Production Director*

Mary Jane Bertel
Regina Brown
Nyles Cole
Robin Damsky
Helaine Denenberg
Adrianne Onderdonk Dudden
Janet Finegar
Alex Gendler
Moshe Halfon
Rebecca Horner
Candace Levy
Emily Law
Carole Martin

CONTRIBUTORS

HOWARD ADDISON, Senior Rabbi of Temple Sinai, Dresher, Pennsylvania

HANAN ALEXANDER, Head of Center for Jewish Education and Professor of Education, University of Haifa, Haifa, Israel

BEN ZION BERGMAN, Sonny and Isadore Familian Emeritus Professor of Rabbinic Literature, University of Judaism, Los Angeles, California

ELLIOT DORFF, Rector and Sol and Anne Dorff Distinguished Professor of Philosophy, University of Judaism, Los Angeles, California

RICHARD L. EISENBERG, Rabbi of Congregation B'nai Jacob, Woodbridge, Connecticut

DAVID FINE, Secretary of the CJLS of the Conservative Movement, and a graduate fellow in history at The Jewish Theological Seminary

MICHAEL FISHBANE, Nathan Cummings Professor of Jewish Studies, University of Chicago, Chicago, Illinois

GORDON FREEMAN, Rabbi of Congregation B'nai Shalom, Walnut Creek, California

BARUCH FRYDMAN-KOHL, Senior Rabbi of Beth Tzedec Congregation, Toronto, Ontario

STEPHEN P. GARFINKEL, Assistant Professor of Bible, Dean of Graduate School, and Dean of Academic Affairs, Jewish Theological Seminary, New York, New York

STEPHEN GELLER, Professor of Bible, Jewish Theological Seminary, New York, New York

NEIL GILLMAN, Aaron Rabinowitz and Simon H. Rifkind Professor of Jewish Philosophy, Jewish Theological Seminary, New York, New York

DANIEL GORDIS, Director of Jerusalem Fellows Program, Mandel School, Jerusalem, Israel

DAVID GORDIS, President and Professor of Rabbinics, Hebrew College, Brookline, Massachusetts; Director of Wilstein Institute of Jewish Policy Studies, Brookline, Massachusetts

MICHAEL GRAETZ, Rabbi of Congregation Magen Avraham, Omer, Israel; Spiritual Leader of Mercaz Shiluv, Beer Sheva and Omer, Israel

EDWARD L. GREENSTEIN, Past Instructor of Bible, Jewish Theological Seminary, New York, New York; Professor of Bible, Tel Aviv University, Tel Aviv, Israel

SUSAN GROSSMAN, Rabbi of Beth Shalom Congregation, Columbia, Maryland; Member of the first class of women, Rabbinical School, Jewish Theological Seminary, New York, New York

REUVEN HAMMER, Professor of Rabbinic Literature, Schechter Institute of Jewish Studies, Jerusalem, Israel

JULES HARLOW, Past Director of Publications, The Rabbinical Assembly, New York, New York; Editor of *Sim Shalom* and other liturgical works on behalf of the Conservative Movement

JUDITH HAUPTMAN, Philip R. Alstat Professor of Talmud, Jewish Theological Seminary, New York, New York

STUART KELMAN, Trained *Sofer;* Rabbi of Congregation Netivot Shalom, Berkeley, California

HAROLD KUSHNER, Rabbi Laureate of Temple Israel, Natick, Massachusetts; author of several popular works

BARUCH A. LEVINE, Skirball Emeritus Professor of Bible and Ancient Near Eastern Studies, New York University, New York, New York

LEE I. LEVINE, Professor of Jewish History and Archeology, Hebrew University, Jerusalem, Israel; Past President, Seminary of Judaic Studies (Schechter Institute of Judaic Studies), Jerusalem, Israel

DAVID L. LIEBER, President Emeritus and Flora and Arnold Skovron Distinguished Service Professor of Biblical Literature and Thought, University of Judaism, Los Angeles, California

HARVEY MEIROVICH, Dean of Rabbinical School, Schechter Institute for Jewish Studies, Jerusalem, Israel

JACOB MILGROM, Professor Emeritus of Biblical Studies, University of California at Berkeley, Berkeley, California

LIONEL MOSES, Rabbi of Shaare Zion Congregation, Montreal, Quebec

DEBRA R. ORENSTEIN, Rabbi of Congregation Makor Ohr Shalom, Westwood and Tarzana, California

SHALOM PAUL, Past Professor of Bible, Jewish Theological Seminary, New York, New York; Professor of Bible and Past Chair of Bible, Hebrew University, Jerusalem, Israel

CHAIM POTOK, Author; Past Editor (1965–1974) and Literary Editor of the JPS Torah Commentary series, Jewish Publication Society, Philadelphia, Pennsylvania

JOEL REMBAUM, Senior Rabbi of Temple Beth Am, Los Angeles, California

GILBERT ROSENTHAL, Past Executive Vice-President of the New York Board of Rabbis, New York, New York

JOEL ROTH, Louis Finkelstein Professor of Talmud and Jewish Law, Jewish Theological Seminary, New York, New York; Rosh Yeshiva of the Conservative Yeshiva, Jerusalem, Israel

NAHUM SARNA, General Editor of the JPS Torah Commentary series, Jewish Publication Society, Philadelphia, Pennsylvania; Gimelstob Eminent Scholar and Professor of Judaica, Florida Atlantic University, Boca Raton, Florida; Dora Golding Emeritus Professor of Biblical Studies, Brandeis University, Waltham, Massachusetts

ISMAR SCHORSCH, Chancellor and Rabbi Herman Abramovitz Professor of Jewish History, Jewish Theological Seminary, New York, New York

BENJAMIN EDIDIN SCOLNIC, Rabbi of Temple Beth Sholom, Hamden, Connecticut; Past Instructor of Bible, Jewish Theological Seminary, New York, New York, and Yale University, New Haven, Connecticut

BENJAMIN J. SEGAL, Past President and Current Vice-President, Schechter Institute for Jewish Studies, Jerusalem, Israel

JEFFREY H. TIGAY, Ellis Professor of Hebrew and Semitic Languages and Literatures, University of Pennsylvania, Philadelphia, Pennsylvania

GORDON TUCKER, Rabbi of Temple Israel Center, White Plains, New York; Adjunct Assistant Professor of Jewish Philosophy, Jewish Theological Seminary, New York, New York

ROBERT WEXLER, President and Irma and Lou Colen Distinguished Lecturer in Bible, University of Judaism, Los Angeles, California

DAVID WOLPE, Senior Rabbi of Sinai Temple, Los Angeles, California

INDEX OF NAMES AND SUBJECTS

This index presents references to pages that contain definitions, explanations, and significant discussions of the person, place, or topic entry. Like the commentaries, it does not necessarily mention all occurrences of a given entry. The letters p, d, or h indicate that the entry can be found in the *p'shat, d'rash,* or *halakhah l'ma·aseh,* respectively. **Bold** type marks the more important references.

A

Aaron, 334p
- anointing of, by Moses, **570d,** 512p, 513d
- apologia of, 534–535p
- consecration of, 622p
- death of, 880, 887p, **1047p,** 1194p
- descendants of, as priests, 503d, 504p, 1094p
- exclusion of, 540p
- genealogy of, 777p
- initiation of, into priesthood, 579
- instructions to, 869pd
- as leader, 769d
- officiating of, as high priest, 504p, 631–632p, 631d, 816p
- as peacemaker, 530d
- and plague of Egypt, 357p, 360d
- sin of, 883–886p

Abel, 24–25pd. *See also* Cain

Abiathar, descended from Aaron, 143

Abib, month of, 380p
- meaning of name, **1081p**
- and *Pesaḥ,* 1081p

Abihu, 505p. *See also* Nadab and Abihu

Abimelech, 110–112p, 116–117p, 149–150

Abishag, 143–145

abortion, **461h**

Abraham
- arguing with God, 103–104p
- and circumcision, 99dh
- death and burial of, 139p, **140–141p**
- faith of, 140d
- genealogies of, 139–141p
- God's election of, **69–77**
- God's testing of, **117–118p**
- hospitality and, 123
- kinship and, 93p
- in old age, 130d, 142
- pact of, with Abimelech, 115–117p
- and smashing of idols, 69d
- wanderings of, 109–110p
- *See also* Abram; *Akedah*

Abraham ben David of Posquieres (Ravad), 1475

Abram, 61p, 69p, 71–72p, 77p
- age when leaving Haran, 71p
- blessing of, 76p
- building an altar, 72p
- change of name of, **89–90p**
- in Egypt, **72–74p**
- entry of, into land, 71p
- faith of, 83p, 84d, 94
- and king of Sodom, 81–82p
- kinship and, 80p
- meaning of name, 61p
- as warrior, 77p, 79–81p, 80d
- wealth of, 74d
- *See also* Abraham

abundance, 1288
- promise of, 741p

acacia wood, **487p,** **493pd**

Accuser. *See satan*

adam (humankind), 9p, 13p, 33p
- creation of, 1035
- *See also* Adam

Adam, 16p, 69d
- and creation of Eve, 10d
- genealogy/descendants of, 30–31p, 30d
- and Noahide laws, 15
- *See also* Adam and Eve; Creation; Garden of Eden

Adam and Eve, 18–24. *See also* Adam; Garden of Eden

adamah (earth), 13p

adonai, 84d, 100, 330p

Adonai Elohim (Lord God), 82p. *See also* names and titles of God

Adonijah, 143–145

adoption
- formula, 610, 976, 1232
- of Jacob's grandchildren, 295p, 296p
- in Mesopotamian law, 323p

adulteress, suspected, 796–799p. *See also* adultery

adultery, 796d, **1021p,** 1354
- as capital crime, 1120p
- Decalogue and, 447p
- definition of, 447p, 1357
- with engaged virgin, 1120–1121p
- as "great sin," 111p, 534p
- with married woman, 1120p
- and Noahide laws, 15d
- as violation of husband's rights, 110p, 240p
- and water ordeal, 1357
- *See also* capital punishment; stoning; women

Agag
- killing of, 1284–1285
- Saul's sparing of, 1282
- *See also* Amalek

agriculture, 850p, 1348
- Cain and, 24
- and human beings, 13p, 15pd
- irrigation and, 57p
- Noah and, 32–33p
- prescriptions for, 472–473p
- products of, 1037p, **1040p**
- work and, 22p

ahavah (love), 171d, 1019p, 1025d
- between God and individual, 1050d
- between God and Israel, 1037d
- between husband and wife, 138p
- as covenant loyalty, 1025p
- of God, **1025p**
- of neighbor, 697pd, 1025p
- of stranger, 1025d

Ahaz (king), 451

Ahijah, as prophet, 1408

Ai, 72p

Akedah (binding of Isaac), **117–122pd**
- *midrash* and, 1491, 1492
- *pesaḥ* sacrifice and, 1307
- *See also* Abraham

Akiva, academy of, 1405–1406, 1472–1473

alah (curse, imprecation, sworn treaty), 135p, 152p, 1165p

Albright, W. F., 1340, 1341

alcoholism, 53h

Aleinu prayer, 551, 1108, 1254
- eschatology and, 1439

alien. *See also ger; nokhri*

altar. *See mizbei·aḥ*

altar of burnt offering, **496p,** 559p, 561p, 585p, 588p, 623p
- in Ezekiel's future Temple, 520
- fire and, 681p
- leaven and, 618p
- preparation of, 515p, 615p, 622p
- and *zevaḥ sh'lamim,* 593p
- *See also korban*

am Adonai (the Lord's people), 428

amah (female slave), 458p. *See also* slave(s)

Amalek, Amalekites, 78p, 420d, 843p
- battle with, **420–422pd**

obliteration of name of, 1044p, 1136pdh
offense of, 1135–1136pd
Saul's battle against, 1280–1285
Amen, 798p, 1147p
amendments to law. *See takkanot*
am ha-aretz (people of the land), 128p, 339p, **599p**
Amidah, 82d, 407d, 555d, 760, 765, 1228, 1271
1st blessing of, 328h
10th blessing of, 1318
11th blessing of, 1003
15th benediction of, 838
sanctification and, 452
standing for, 1322
as substitute for communal sacrifices, 930h
ammah (cubit), 42p, 487p, 520, 997p
Ammon, Ammonites, 108–109p, 909–913, **993p**
bypassing of, 993–994p
territory of, 995p
Amon, Amon Re (imperial god of Egypt), 397
Amorites, 78p, **843p**, 1029p, 1104, 1173
attacked by Israel, 993–994p
defeat of Israelites by, 989p
iniquity of, 85p
legendary height of, 987p
Amos, 705, 1436
haftarot from (*see haftarah*)
amud (pillar)
of cloud, 846
of cloud and fire, 400–401, 404
of fire, 825d, 867p
anachronisms, 71d
camels, 73p, 364p
Chaldeans, 62p
Israel, 207p
priesthood, 440p
Ramses II, 286p
Anakites. *See* giants
Anathoth, 347
anav (humble), 833p
ancestors, 886d, 887p. *See also z'khut avot*
angel(s). *See mal·akh*
anger, divine, 408p, **531–533p,** 827d, 828d, 830p, 918p, 1167, 1188p, 1222, 1235, 1241, 1259, 1325
against apostate town, 1071p
and faithlessness of Israel, 988p
as fire, 1189p
and idolatry, 828d
and plague, 907p, 908p
anger, of Moses, 533–534p, 636p, 885p, 945
animals
behaving like humans, 894d
domestic, 1065p
fallen, 471p, 1116p
feeding of, 1053d
forbidden combinations of, 1118pd
game, 1065p
human mastery over, 16
husbandry of, 28p
kindness to, 1019p
land, 1072–1073p
lost, 1115–1116p
naming of, 16
sacred, in Egypt, 364p
votary pledges of, 754p
water, 1073p
wild, 807p
winged, 1073–1074p
See also kashrut; korban
anointing, 526p, 1228–1229
of Aaron, 512p, 513d
of altar, 515p
of David, 1229
of priests, 510p
of tabernacle vessels, 510p
anthrax, and plagues in Egypt, 362p, 364p, 365p. *See also* skin diseases
anthropomorphism, 383p, 1253, 1392. *See also* God
Anti-Lebanon, 958p, 983p, 996p
apathy, 1025d
apiru (Habiru; Hapiru), 79p, 320p, 1343, 1345
apocalyptic, 1259
See also eschatology
apocalyptic communities, 1419
apostasy, apostates, 542–543p, 547, 628, 713
at Baal-Peor, **907–908p,** 945pd, 1007p
as capital crime, 1071p
Golden Calf and, 840
instigation of, 1069p
of Israel, 972–977, 1176–1177pd
portrayed as adultery, 786
prohibition of, 468p
prosecution of, **1090p**
'Arabah, 981p, 983p
Aram, 57p
Aram-naharaim, 132p, 146p, 1123. *See also* Haran; Paddan-aram
Ararat, mountains of, 47p
archaeological finds, 989p, 990p, 991p, 993p, 995p, 1009p, 1080p, 1037p
and history of biblical narrative, 1340
inscriptions, 803p, 1340, 1343
and material culture of the times, **1339–1344**
motivation for, **1339**
and patriarchal age, 1340–1341
Ark, of the tabernacle, 495p, 559p
building a shrine for, 643
built by Bezalel, 1047p
built by Moses, 1047p
at center of camp, 774d
cherubim and, 768
construction of, 487–488p, 1256
curtain of, 731p
function of, 868p
gold-plated, 573
at the head of the people, 826, 1300
of the Pact, 419p
as repository of the Teaching, 1174p, 1178p
as source of blessing and power, 644
in Temple, 579
transfer of, to Jerusalem, **643,** 644
transfer of, to Solomon's Temple, 1256, 1257
ark, of Noah, **42–43p**
arm of God. *See* God: arm of
army, mobilization of, 1102p
ascent, **842d**
Asenath, 255pd
aseret ha-dibrot (Decalogue), 397, **441–448pd,** 1010p, 1043pd, 1335, 1406
and ancient treaties, 1017p
and Ark of the Pact, 419p
arrangement of, **448–449d**
categorical style of, 467p, 477p
centrality of, 626
as covenant, 1016p
division of, 442p, **1017p**
origin of name, 441p
reprise of, 1005d, **1016–1021p**
systems of cantillation of, **1017p**
uniqueness of, **441–442p**
1st Commandment, 442–443pd, 700p, **1017pd**, 1024–1028p, 1090p
2nd Commandment, 10d, 443–444pd, 1013p, **1018–1019p,** 1406
3rd Commandment, 444pdh, 695p, **1019p**
4th Commandment, 445–446pdh, **1019–1020p,** 1020d
5th Commandment, 446–447pdh, 694pd, **1020–1021p**
6th Commandment, 447pd, **1021p**

aseret ha-dibrot (*continued*)
7th Commandment, 447pdh, 698p, 1021p
8th Commandment, 448pd, 695p, 1021p
9th Commandment, 448pd, 695p, 1021p
10th Commandment, 448pdh, 544d, 1021p
aseret ha-d'varim, 441, 545p. *See also aseret ha-dibrot*
asham (reparation offering), 585, 595p, 601d, **603–605p, 616–617p,** 794–795d, 802p, 1449
for carnal relations with a woman slave, 698p
five types of, 460h
for misuse of sanctuary property, 603–604p
as "most holy," 615d
as restitution to a defrauded person, 795p
Asher
Jacob's testament to, 303p
meaning of name, 176p, 303p
Moses' blessing of, 1208p
Asherah, 542, 1030
objects made for, 1304, 1305
asherim (sacred posts), **542p,** 915, 1030p, 1062–1063p
prohibition of, **1089p**
ash heap, 614p
Ashk'nazim, 1475
assault, 1091p
Assyria (Asshur), 9p, 15p, 56p, 57p, 914
fall of, in 614 B.C.E., 1303
rebellion of Babylon against, 1303
royal steles of, 9
astrology, prohibition of, 1096d
asylum. *See* cities of refuge
atonement
death of high priest and, 1434
sacrifice and, 585, 595p, 1434
suffering and, **1433–1434**
See also asham; Day of Atonement; *ḥattat; kipper*
Atrahasis, 1347
atzeret. See Sh'mini Atzeret
authority, three levels of, 1486
avenger. *See go·el*
avon (iniquity), **682d**
prophetic censure for, 999
See also sin
Azazel, meaning of name, 680p

B

Baal (Canaanite god of fertility), 8p, 701d, 789, 790
and Elijah, **547–551**
objects made for, 1304
prophets of, 937
temple of, 1277
worship of, 188, 547, 907p, 1393
Baal-Peor, 937–938, 944p, 1166p, 1177p
as god of Beth-peor, 907, 1007p
idolatry and expiation at, 907–908p, 918–920p, 1007p
See also Beth-peor
Babel, Tower of. *See* Tower of Babel
Babylon, Babylonia
as Cush, 14p
creation story of, 4p, 12p
conquest of Jerusalem (587–586 B.C.E.), 64
as enemy from north, 397, 969, 970
as *Kasdim* (Chaldeans), 62p, 1321
rebellion of, against Assyria, 1303
as Shinar, 55p, 58p
Babylonian exile, 1032, 1055
calendar and, 380p
Ezekiel and, 519, 709
Isaiah and, 35
life in, 1352
return from, 94, 611, 1107, 1182, 1230, 1269, 1303, 1352
See also exile
Bahrain, and Sumerian myth, 13–14
bailment, law of, 465–467p, 465–466d
Balaam the Diviner, 768, **894–907p,** 914, 919d, 944d, 945p
and apostasy at Baal-Peor, 945pd
and the ass, **897–898p**
curse of, 894p
hiring of, 894–897p
oracles of, against nations, 906–907p
bal tashḥit (you must not destroy), 1104d
bamot (cult places), 958p
ban. *See ḥeirem*
barad (hail). *See* plagues: seventh plague
Bar Kokhba, 906d
barley, 367p, 797pd. *See also* grains; *sheva minin*
barrenness, 62p, 65, 86p, 1225
of Hannah, 1225
of Rachel, 173p, 174–175
of Rebekah, **146p**
as punishment, 799p
of Sarai, 62p, 86p
See also infertility
Bashan, 892p, 958p, 1188p, 1206p, 1208p
bat, 1073p
bath (liquid measure), 578
bathing, 881p
implied in laundering, 818p, 830p, 947p
ritual purification and, 1287
symbolizing rebirth, 661d
Bathsheba, 145
bat kol (heavenly voice), 273
bayit (house)
consecration of, 754p
as household, 448p
of prayer (Temple), 1338
beast, attacking humans, **463p**
Beer-sheba
altar at, 280p
Jacob at, 279–280p
meaning of name, 116–117p, 153
revelation at, 152p
well at, 115p
bees, 989p
beit av (household), 381p, 1353
beit din (rabbinical court), 1127d. *See also* courts; *din*
beka (half-shekel), 564-565p. *See also* poll tax; *shekel*
Belial, 1197, 1311
belomancy, 1095p
Benjamin, 258p
birth of, 214p
Jacob's testament to, 305p
meaning of name, 214pd
Mosaic blessing of, 1205p
sons of, 282p
tribe of, 305p
bestiality, 468p, 691p, 1147p, 1354
Bethel, 167–168p, 211–212p
revelation at, 213p
Beth-peor, 1043p, 1211p. *See also* Baal-peor
betrothal, 172p, 1120p
Bezalel, 573, 555d, 576, 577
Bezer. *See* cities of refuge
Bible study
D'rash, **1494–1496**
modern literary criticism, **1501–1502**
modern source criticism, **1500–1501**
modern textual criticism, **1499–1500**
PaRDeS and, 1494
P'shat, **1494–1496**
Remez, **1494, 1496–1497**
Sod, **1494, 1497–1499**
bikkur ḥolim (visiting the sick), **99dh, 266h,** 461h
bikkurim (first fruits), **592p,** 872p
ceremony of, 1140–1142p

as image of Israel's relation to God, 971
offering of, 590p, 1140p
as *t'rumah,* 1064p
See also Shavu·ot
Bilhah, 173p, 175p, 226p
offspring of, 175p, 282p
bill of divorcement. *See get*
binding of Isaac. *See Akedah*
birds, 638–639d, 639p
Birkat ha-Mazon (Blessing after Meals), 980, 1040h, 1041dh, 1201, 1295
after *sheva minin,* **1040h**
birth announcements, 87p
birthright, 153p, 158p, 1113
of firstborn, 299p
Jacob and, 160p
See also blessing; firstborn
birthstool, 320p
bitter herbs. *See maror*
Bitter Lakes, 955p
bitumen, 79p
blamelessness, 89d
blasphemy, 732–733p
and Noahide laws, 15d
prohibition of, 470d
blessing. *See b'rakhah*
Blessing after Meals. *See Birkat ha-Mazon*
blessings and curses, 1146–1148
blind, stumbling block for, 695–696p, 695dh
blindness of Israel, 35, 38
blood, 382pd
female discharge of, 669p
on doorposts, 1291
of *ḥattat,* 616p
innocent, 1099p, 1105d
menstrual, 649d
of *olah* and *sh'lamim,* 478p
and ordination of priests, 478p, 513p
prohibition against eating, 594p, 686d, 687h, 1065p, 1067ph
and purification from *tzara·at,* 660–661p
and purification of sanctuary, 682p
as representation of life, 26d, 687p, 1067p
sacrificial, 599p 602p 623p, 686p, 687p, 1067p
See also b'rit milah
blood-avenger. *See go·el ha-dam*
bloodguilt, 189, 464h, 465p, 702p, 1105–1106p, 1117p
blood purification, 650p. *See also* childbirth; impurity
blood redeemer. *See go·el ha-dam*
bloodshed, 447d, 686p
ritual impurity and, 1287
as source of pollution, 962p, 963p, 965p
blood vengeance, 962p, 965p, 1097p
blue. *See t'kheilet*
b'nei Yisra·el (people of Israel), 258d
boils, as sixth plague, 365p
boker (dawn), 5
Bokser, Ben Zion, 1404, 1445
Book of Jashar, 422p, 890p
Book of the Covenant. *See seifer ha-b'rit*
Book of the Teaching, 1267. *See also* Torah
book of the Torah, found in Temple, 1303, 1304–1305
Book of the Upright (Genesis), 2
Book of the Wars of the LORD, 422p, 890p
Booths, festival of (*Ḥag ha-Sukkot*). *See Sukkot*
booty, 888p
rules about, 1387
shunning of, 1071p
women, children, and property as, 1103p
See also ḥeirem; war
borrowing, laws of, 466–467p
boundary markers, moving of, 1099–1100p, 1100d, 1147p
bowing, 100p, 129p, 1018p
from afar, 477p
before Joseph, 227p, 259p, 266p, 293–294p
seven times, 203
Bozrah, 219p
b'rakhah (blessing), 762, 804p
of children on *Shabbat* eve, 297–298d
and curse, **1061p,** 1169d
of daughters, 180h
of firstborn, 153p
of God after meals (*see* Blessing after Meals)
of Jacob, 160p
of Jacob for Esau, 204–205p
meaning of, 12
of the month, 931h
of Noah, 50
over food, 475d
priestly, **803–805p, 804h**
priests and, 1442
promise of, 747d
of *Shabbat,* 12
within the curse, 1169d
See also birthright; firstborn
Branch. *See tzemaḥ*
bread of display, **490p, 731pd**
breastpiece. *See* high priest, attire of
bribery, 472p, 1088p
bride, veiling of, 137d, 138p
bride-price, 137p, 178p, 181p, 208p, 467p, 790, 1102p, 1357
concubine and, 175p
for virgins, 1119p, 1121p
b'rit (covenant), 43p
affirmation of, in Promised Land, 1061p
in ancient world, 1416, 1417
between God and Abraham, 82d, 84p
between God and Israel at Mount Sinai, 481
between people and Zedekiah, 481
between the pieces, **82–85p**
binding for future generations, 1166pd
celebration of, in pilgrimage festivals, 1419
of circumcision (*see b'rit milah*)
cutting of, **1016p**
with David, 68, 644, 648, 1087
with day and night, 481
desecration of, 483
and election of Israel, 1416–1420
everlasting nature of, 1418
formula, 1108, 1288
functions of, 1416
heaven and earth as witnesses to, **1011p**d
and Hittite treaties, 1417
holding fast to, 1335
at Horeb, 1157p
Israel's acceptance of, 438p
and law giving, 1417
loyalty to, 746d
as major theme of Torah, 1356
and marriage, 443–444p, 447d, 648, 701d, 786, 971
in Moab, **1015p,** 1157–1159p, **1165–1172p**
and monarchy, 1417
national commitment to, 1303
new, 1288
with Noah, 64–65
nullification of, 1045p
observance of, 313, 1286
with the patriarchs, 352p
of peace, 165, 918d
as political pact, 500
and rainbow, 51–52p, 52d
ratification of, 82–85p, 478p, 1016p, 1165–1167p
for release of Hebrew slaves, 481
renewal of, 540–546p, 786, 1286, 1419
of salt, 873p
at Shechem, 1416, 1419
at Sinai, 353p, **436–450p**
tablets and, **441–442p**

b'rit (*continued*)
t'fillin and, 1419
Sages and, 1419
as theme of Deuteronomy, 980
three meanings of, 1009p
under Josiah, 1303, 1419
violation of, 1167pd
women and, 1349, 1356
b'rit milah (covenant of circumcision), 89d, 90pd, 91h
covenant in the flesh, 89–93p
eighth day after birth, 91ph, 630d
See also circumcision
b'rit sh'losh esrei (Covenant of the Thirteen), 541d. *See also* God
bronze
snake, 888–889p
tabernacle and, 486p
See also copper
brown cow (red cow, red heifer), ritual of, **880–882p**, 883d, 1286
Buber, Martin, **1401–1402**
burial
denial of, 1114p
Israelite customs of, 128p, 634p
Jewish law and, 127h, 214h
lack of, 1152p
time of, **1115h**
burning, as mode of execution. *See* execution
Burning Bush, 5d, 1300
revelation at, **326–328p**
symbolism of, **327d,** 329p
burnt offering. *See olah*

C

Cain
and Abel, **24–27p**
as builder of first city, 27d
curse of, 26–27
genealogy of, **27–29p**
and Noahide laws, 15
Caleb, 841p, 842d, 960p, 988p
response of, to scouts, 845–846p
calendar, 380d, 684p
Babylonian exile and, 380p
and cycles of the moon, 931h
Enoch and, 31
Exodus and, 380p
Pesaḥ and, **392h**
of public sacrifices, **929–936p**
religious, **473–474p**
of sacred time, **724–730p**
call, divine (commission)
of Ezekiel, 1320–1321
of Isaiah, 451
of Jeremiah, 347, 968
of Jonah, 1246–1247
of Moses, 328–329p, 332p, 334p
camels, 1073p
as anachronism, 73p, 364p
cushions for riding, 184p
hoofs of, 638p
in patriarchal narratives, 132p
camp, Israelite, in wilderness
arrangement of, 774–776p, 774d
purification of, 793–805p
camp, military. *See* military camp
Canaan, Canaanites, 54d, 71p, 75p, **843p**, 1029p, 1350
altars of, 1063p
battle against, 423, 957p, 1104
borders of, 959p
child sacrifice and, 1068p, 1104p
city-states of, 207p, 987p, 1038p
curse of, 54p
dependence of, 56–57p
depravity of, 52–53p
division of, **957–965p**
encounter with, 888p
killing of, 1030p
in Late Bronze Age, 998p
myths of, 8p
obliteration of name of, 1044p
as Promised Land, 983p, 1037p
reconnaissance of, 840–848p
religious practices of, 1068p
sanctuaries of, 1062–1063p
wives of Judah and Simeon, 233p
cannibalism, curse of, 1155p, 1156
canon of the Bible, 1348
cantillation. *See* chanting
Caphtorim, 993–994p
capital punishment, 51p, **459–460p**, 732p
for disrespectful children, 332d
for eating sacred food, 875p
for instigation to worship other gods, 1070p
for murder, 1099p
in Second Temple times, 447p
for *Shabbat* violators, 332d
See also execution
captives, rules about, 1387. *See also pidyon sh'vuyim*
carcasses
eating of, 687p
impurity and, 640–641p, 649d, 687p
See also contact; corpse; ritual impurity; ritual purification
Carmel, Mount. *See* Mount Carmel
categorical commands, **467–474p,** 477p
census, **523–524p**
age of, 779pd
and apportioning of Land, **924p**
figures of, 773p
first, of Levites, 777–783p
and military conscription, 770p
ransom after undergoing, 948–949p
results of, 920–923p
second, 920–925p
second, of Levites, **783–785p, 791–792p**
in the wilderness, 769–774p
See also conscription
centralization of worship. *See* worship
ceremonial meal, 153p. *See also* sacred meal
cesarean section
circumcision and, 650h
and firstborn, 393p
Chaldeans. *See* Babylon
chanting of biblical text
of Decalogue, 442p, 1017p
five musical modes of, 1484
shalshelet, 239d
of Torah, **1483**
chaos, 4p, 8p
imposing order on, 11–12d
chariot(s), 1274
Canaanite, 1101p
Egyptian, 255p, 308p, 402p
Chariot (of God), 1010p, 1320
Glory riding on, 1325
vision of Ezekiel, **1320–1324,** 1274, 1392
cheating, 605d
Chemosh (national deity of Moab), 892p
cherubim, 23p, 573, **575,** 576, 645, 780p, 1257
on the *kapporet* (Ark cover), 488p, 489d
meaning of word, 23
as statues, 1010p
on tabernacle covering, 491p, 492p
chief(s) (*sar*), appointed, **984–985p**
chieftain(s) (*nasi*), 598–599p, 598d, **805d,** 860p, 861p, 866p, 960p, 966p
death of, 868p
chieftains ("judges")
period of the, 813, 876, 912, 1224
child abuse, 1113h
childbirth
Eve and, 24d
of female child, 650pd
impurity and, 649, 650–651p
of male child, 650pd
pain in, 21pd, 22
regulations concerning, **650–651p**
of Zion, 1221
See also blood purification; ritual impurity

children, 1355
as booty, 1103
as cultural builders, 1085
explaining the commandments to one's, 1028–1029p
restoration of, by Elisha, **123**
as vicarious immortality, 24
child sacrifice 81p, 117d, 391p, 626, 628, 691p, 1068p, 1095p
Canaanites and, 1104p
See also Canaan; Molech
Chinnereth, 997p
Chronicles, books of, and Jewish identity, 1352
cinnamon, 525p
circumcision, **336–337p**, 389p, 650pdh
and cesarean section, 650h
flint knives used for, 1300
at Gilgal, 1299, 1300, 1301
of heart, 1049p
law of, 90–91p, 90d, 93p, 336h
and entrance into community, 208p, 209h
as sign, 91p, 337p
as symbol of covenant, **650dh**, 1419
See also b'rit milah
Cisjordan, 924p
cisterns, 1027p
cities of refuge (asylum), 390p, 459p, **962–963p**, 964p, 1014p
in Cisjordan, 1098p
laws pertaining to, **1097–1099p**
number of, 1098–1099p
as place of exile, 1097d
in Transjordan, **1014p**
civil authorities, **1088–1093p**
civil disobedience, 320d
clan. *See mishpaḥah*
class differences, moral failure and, 1351
clergy (priests, and Levites who serve as priests), endowments of, **1093–1095p**
See also kohen; Levites
clothing, 382p
and Adam and Eve, 18, 23p
and cross-gender dressing, 1116ph
modesty in dress, 689d
not wearing, 1040pd
and shame, 19, 23
cloud (showing God's presence), 438, 449p
appearance of God to Joshua in, 1175–1176pd
with fire, 679p
filling sanctuary, at Solomon's assembly, 581–582, 1256, 1257, 1258
as guide in wilderness, 400–401p, 572p, 768, 821–822, 826p, 987p
over tabernacle, 579, 867p
See also amud; kavod
Code of Hammurabi, 172p, 456d, 460p, 1015p, 1120p, 1130p, 1147p, **1421**
and flogging, 1132p
See also laws
columns, in Solomon's Temple, 577
commandment. *See mitzvah*
commemorative rituals, 391–394p
community. *See edah*
comparison, for emphasis, 64
compassion, and creation, 13d. *See also* God; mercy
concubinage, 86–87p, 175p. *See also* marriage
confession of sin, **602pd**, 794pdh, 1235, 1330
congregation. *See kahal*
conjugal rights, 21–22, 458h, 459p. *See also* marriage
conquest and settlement of the Land, 941d
archaeology and, 1340, 1342–1343
book of Joshua and, 1342
book of Judges and, 423, 1342
in Cisjordan, 950p
date of, 912
and Exodus, 1300
generation of, 920p, 960p
gradual, **1038p**
of Transjordan, **949–953p**
See also Promised Land
conscience, and tree of knowledge of good and evil, 23d
conscription, **770p**, 1387, 1388
consecration (donation to sanctuary; dedication to God), 391p, 754pd, 755p. *See also* Levites; priests; tabernacle
consolation, 395, 1433
prophecies of, 968, 1032, 1230, 1286–1289
contact, impurity and, 601p, 667p
priests and, 721p
with sacred objects, 784p
See also carcasses; corpse; *kohen;* ritual impurity
contraception, Jewish law and, 234h
conversion to Judaism. *See gerut*
copper, 866p, 889p
mining of, 1041p
tabernacle and, 486p
See also bronze
corpse
contamination by, 882p, 945p, 1115p
of executed criminal, 1114–1115pd
exposure of, 1114–1115p
nazirite and, 801p
purification from, 880–883p
strangers and, 882p
See also carcasses; contact; impurity; *kohen*
corvée, 302p
cosmology, 6, 721p, 1010p, 1013p, 1049p
courts (of law), 1091p
judicial rulings for, **456–467p**
laws pertaining to, **1097–1101p**
See also beit din; judges; judiciary, Israelite; law; legal protocol; *tzedek*
covenant. *See b'rit*
covenant scroll. *See seifer ha-b'rit*
coveting, meaning of, 448ph, **448d**, **544d**
creation, 2, 36
completing the work of, 11–12
cosmology and, 1, 6
of Eve, 10
faith and, 3p
flawlessness of, 5p
as good, 3d
of human beings, 9d, 13p
light and, 5p, 1160
morality and, 1
name giving and, 5p
out of nothing, 4p
renewal of, 95
Rosh ha-Shanah and, 728d
science and, 1
separation and, 5pd
seven days of, 4–12p
sexual difference and, 10p
Shabbat and, 445p
time and, 3d
Torah and, 3d
in the womb, 348
of women, 15–17
words and, 4–5
See also human beings; human race
creditors, and seizure of property, 1129p, 1130pdh
creeping things, 9p
crimson, 486p, 660p, 881p
crops, damage to, as model cases for legal liability, **465p**
cross-gender dressing, 1116ph
cubit. *See ammah*
Cultic Decalogue, **543p**
cult places. *See bamot*
curse
in ancient Near East, 157p
and blessing, choice between, 1061p

curse (*continued*)
  Cain and, 26–27
  for secret sins, 1146–1148p
  for suspected adultery, 798p
  See also Tokheḥah
Cush, Cushite, 14p, 833p
cut off. *See karet*
Cyrus the Mede, 96, 373
  edict of, 836, 1032, 1438

D

da·at (knowledge), **555d,** 573
  of good and evil, **21d**
  of might of God, 369
daily offering. *See olah: tamid*
daman, 638p
Damascus, 958p
Dan, 776p, 813, 825d
  Jacob's testament to, 302–303p
  meaning of name, 175p
  Moses' blessing of, 1208p
darash, as so-called middle word of Torah, **635–636d**
Darius I (king of Persia), 836, 1269
darkness. *See ḥoshekh*
Dathan and Abiram, 860–863p, 867p, 876, 921d
  punishment of, 864–865p
  rebellion of, 1051p
daughters
  of Lot (*see* Lot: daughters of)
  of priests, 718**pd**, 721**ph**
  of Zelophehad (*see* Zelophehad, daughters of)
davar (word), **501**
  book of Leviticus and, 642d
  creation and, 4–5
  harmful, 740d
  power of, 732d
  seriousness of, **941d**
  Torah and, 4–5
  See also oaths; vows
David (king)
  anointing of, 1225
  and Bathsheba, 142
  and building of Temple, 1258
  as chosen ruler, 1258
  hymn of victory of, 1196–1201, 1228, 1310–1314
  dynasty of, **643–644**
  glory of, 812
  last days of, 142
  last will and testament of, **312–314**
  as leader, 1350
  in old age, 142–143
  Saul's jealousy of, 1215
Davidic dynasty, 292
  eschatology and, 1437
  and promise of kingdom, 90p, 499
dawn. *See boker*
day to come, 1315, 1437
  of judgment, 1252, 1297, **1436,** 1437
  of the Lord, 224, 1253, 1298, 1412, 1436, 1438
  See also end of days
Day of Atonement, **684p, 727–729p,** 1434
Dead Sea (*Yam ha-Melaḥ,* "Salt Sea"), 78p, 959p, 997p
  and asphalt and bitumen, 79p
  as Eastern Sea, 1254
Dead Sea Scrolls, 1186–1187p, 1313, 1471. *See also* Qumran
deaf, not to insult, 695pd
death, 11, 13
  coils of, 1197, 1311
  as final, 1436, 1438
  and human condition, 24
  in old age, 414p
  preparations for, 154h
  See also dying; immortality; life: after death; resurrection
Deborah (prophet), 423, 424, 1409
Deborah (Rebekah's nurse), death of, 212pd, 213
debt
  not canceled, 1077p
  release from, 740p
  remission of, 1076–1077p
  responsibility for, 264p
  seizing children for, 124
  See also indebtedness; interest; lending; loans
Decalogue. *See aseret ha-dibrot*
decapitation. *See* execution
deconstructionism, **1502–1503**
decontamination. *See* purification
deep, the. *See t'hom*
defeated populations, treatment of, 1103–1104p
defecation outside military camp, 1124p
defective writing, 422d
definite article, 2
departure from wilderness of Sinai, preparations for, 819–823p
depression, and plague of darkness, 377d
desecration of God's name. *See ḥillul ha-shem*
Deuteronomy, **980**
  core of, 1062p
  focus on "hearing" in, 1006p
  and single place of sacrifice, 1063p
  and theme of divine transcendence, 1013p
  and theme of goodness of Promised Land, 1040p
  theology of, 350
dever (pestilence), 1326
  as fifth plague, 364–365p
dew, 417p
Diaspora, 384h, 751d
dietary laws. *See kashrut*
dignity, of human being, 1112d
din (case, lawsuit, law), 1091p. *See also beit din*
Dinah, 177p
  rape of, 206–211p, 206d
disadvantaged, concern for, 468–469p
disease. *See* healing; skin disease
disobedience, 749d, 762
  Adam and Eve and, 21
  consequences of, 1148–1157p, 1167, 1185–1193p
dispute, 1091p
divination, 270p, 1095p
divine attributes, 397. *See also* God: attributes of; immanence; transcendence
divine beings, **33–34,** 33d, 202p
  and Nephilim, 34p
  See also mal·akh; elohim
divine grace. *See* grace, divine
divine intervention, 332p
divine name
  desecration of, 483
  See also names and titles of God
divine presence
  as theme in Isaiah, 1107, 1160
  Jacob's response to, 202p, 213p
  with Sarah and Rebekah, 138–139d
  tum·ah and, 658d, 666d
divine Presence. *See* cloud; *kavod; Sh'khinah;* tabernacle
divine providence, 276p, 321p, 968
divine punishment. *See* punishment
divine retribution. *See* retribution
divorce, 1119p, 1121p, 1128p, 1354, 1357
  adultery and, 447h
  rabbinic legislation for, 1358
  See also get (writ of divorce)
documentary hypothesis, 1391
dog, as metaphor, 841d
domestic violence, 1113h
Dorff, Elliot, 1404
dots, extraordinary, in biblical Hebrew text, 1168pd
doom, imminent, 968, 999, 1252, 1259–1262, 1329–1334
dough, offering of. *See ḥallah*
dove, 47p
d'rashah (homily), 1486
dream
  as divine communication, 110p, 118p, 166p, 1068p

interpretation of, 252p, 271, 896p
of Jacob, 181p, 280d
in Joseph story, 243–244p
of Pharaoh, 250–251p, 271
of Solomon, 271
dream-diviner, 1068p, 1069p
dress. *See* clothing
drunkenness, 53ph, 1227
dry bones, Ezekiel's vision of, 290, 1307–1309, 1438
dust, as substance of creation, 13p
dust-cloud, 901p
d'varim (divine commands), 467
dyes, 486p
dying
as being gathered to one's kin, 140p
deathbed instructions and, 310h
euphemism for, 82–83p
as going to one's fathers, 85p
as lying down with one's fathers, 293p

E

eagle, **437p**
earth. *See adamah*
earthquake, 865p, 1260
Eber, 57p
ecology, **1369–1372**
corrupted by human immorality, 22
creation and, 1369
in Jewish law and thought, 15h, 1370–1371
jubilee year and, 1371
reverence for nature and, 1369
story of Noah and, 1369–1370
See also environment
economic oppression, 710
edah (community), **380p**, 584, 1365
as group of ten, **847d**
as holy, 861p
Israelites as a whole, 597p, 1350
Eden, 12–23
Garden of, 13–15p
geography of, 14–15p
meaning of name, 14
and Mesopotamian myths, 13p, 1346–1347
and "paradise," 14p
primordial streams of, 1252
edict of Cyrus. *See* Cyrus the Mede.
Edom, Edomites, 410p, 959p, 982p, 990p, 991p, 1123pd
clans of, 217p, 219–220p
encounter with, 886–887p
judgment of, 221
kings of, 219p
as name for Christianity, 221
as name for Roman Empire, 221
pride of, 223
as symbol of Rome and Christendom, 1183
education, **1365–1369**
freedom as precondition for, 1366
parents' responsibility for, 1367
role of elders in, 1368
role of priests in, 1368
role of prophets in, 1368
spiritual view of, 1365
wisdom texts and, 1368
Egypt, Egyptians, 72p
according to Midrash, **388d**
compulsory labor in, 319p, 320pd
defeat of, 406–408p
diseases of, 413p, 1037p, 1156p
Hebrew names from, 355p
as heifer, 396–397
as "house of bondage," 320p, **391p**, 443d, 1017p
Israelites in, 317p
language of, in Exodus story, 322p
Middle Kingdom of, 397
New Kingdom, 73p
Nineteenth Dynasty of, 318p
oppression in, 318–320p
place-names of, 974
politics of, 1349–1350
prophecies against, 395–398
river of, 85p
slavery (bondage) in, 317d, 700d, 743p, 744p, 1011, 1301
See also Exodus; plagues: ten
eḥad (one). *See* numbers
Ehyeh-Asher-Ehyeh, **330pd**
eight. *See* numbers
Eighth Commandment. *See aseret ha-dibrot*
eighth day
for giving firstborn animal to God, 470, 723
of purification of an afflicted priest, 720
See also b'rit milah; Sh'mini Atzeret
eikh ("how"), 972
el (god), 1017p. *See also elohim*
El, 1390–1391
as Canaanite god, 531p, 1390
as theophoric element, 355p
See also names and titles of God
el-Amarna letters, 1341
Eldad, 831p, 831d
elderly, reverence for, 700d
elders. *See z'kenim*
Eleazar
and division of Land, 949p
precedence of, over Joshua, 952p
as successor to Aaron, 920p, 960p
election of Israel. *See* Israel
El elyon (God Most High). *See* names and titles of God
Elephantine, 1353
elevation offering. *See t'nufah*
Eli, 1225–1229
Elijah, 1408
and Elisha, 937, 940
interventions of (during the future "day of the LORD"), 1297–1298
showdown with prophets of Baal, **547–551**
revelation at Horeb, 937–940
Elisha, 1408–1409
and Elijah, 937, 940
miracles of, 123–126, 671–674
and Shunammite woman, 124–126
Elkanah, pilgrimage of, 1224–1229
elohim, 458p, **1017p**
as deity in general, 4p
as divine being (angel) , 19p, 33p, 201p, 202p, 814
as God, 4p, 89p
as gods, 4p, 1017p
as judges, 458p
and justice, 13pd, **351d**
meaning of term, 1017p
as spirit, 1115p
See names and titles of God
El Shaddai, 89p, 160p, 213p, 294p, 352p, 1391
meaning of, according to Midrash, 89d, 351
See also names and titles of God; *Shaddai*
elyon. See names and titles of God
embalming, 306–307p, 307h
emasculation, 1122p
emet (truth), 541p
as name for God, 1023d
See also ḥesed v'emet
Emim. *See* giants
emission, bodily
impurity and, 649
as primal force, 666d
seminal, 668h, 1124p, 1217
from sexual organs, **666–670p**
emmer wheat, in Egypt, 367p. *See also* grains; wheat
end of days, 221. *See also* day to come
endogamy. *See* marriage
ends of the earth, 94
enemy, humane treatment of, 471p
Enlightenment, influence of, on *halakhah,* 1476
Enoch, 28p, **31–32p**, 32d

p = *p'shat;* d = *d'rash;* h = *halakhah l'ma·aseh;* **bold** = more important references

Enuma Elish, 1347
environment, concern for, 1011d, 1104h, 1167d. *See also* ecology
evening prayer. *See Ma·ariv*
envy, as disease, 475d
ephah (*eifah*), 419p, 615p, 700p
ephod, **505–506p,** 567p
Ephraim, 189, 191, 195–196, 1205p, 1236
  condemnation of, 344
  denunciation of behavior of, **194–197**
  destruction of, 342
  as God's first-born, 1230, 1232
  lamenting, 1233
  and Manasseh, **294–297p**
  meaning of name, 257p
  prayer of, 1230
  See also northern kingdom
Ephron, 128p–129p
Epstein, Louis, 1446
erev, as sunset, 5
Esau
  as ancestor of Edom, 162, 198d
  birth of, **146–148p**
  birthright of, 147p, 158p
  descendants of, 216p, 217p
  Hittite wives of, 153p
  and Horites, 217–218p
  Ishmaelite wife of, 161p
  meaning of name, 147p
  migration of, 216–217p
  reconciliation with Jacob, 203–205p
  rivalry with Jacob, **162–165, 147p, 172p**
  as villain, **158d**
  "weapon" of, 944d
  See also Edom
eschatology, **1434–1439**
  and the destiny of the individual, 1438–1439
  and the "messiah," 1436
  and Persian-Hellenistic period, 1438
  and postbiblical Judaism, 1439
  and postexilic prophecy, **1437–1438**
  and pre-exilic prophecy, **1436–1437**
  and prophetic literature, 1435
  and remnant of Israel, 1436
  Torah background of, **1435–1436**
  and Zion, 1346
Esther, book or scroll of, 1281, 1352
Eternal Light. *See Ner Tamid*
eunuchs, 1335, 1336, 1338
Euphrates River, 15, 85, 983p, 1267
Eve, 10d, 17d, 22p
  as representative of human race, 21
eved (servant, slave, minister, vassal)
  adoption of, 83p
  as motif in Isaiah, 35, 40, **1433–1434,** 1438
  as minister (in ancient Near East) (title of Moses), 1210p
  manumission of, **1079–1080p**
  as vassal, 78p
  See also amah; slave
evil, origin of, 17p
evil eye, 523d
evil impulse. *See yeitzer ha-ra*
execution
  by burning, 236p, 718p
  by decapitation, 459p
  by impaling, in ancient Near East, 244p
  impaling or hanging (after execution), 907p, 1114–1115p
  by stoning, 463p, 470p, 848p, 907p, **1070p,** 1090p, 1120p
  See also capital punishment
exile
  curse of, 1153p
  as punishment, 1012p, 1287
  See also Babylonian exile
existentialism, and modern theories of revelation, 1401–1402
expanse. *See raki·a*
Exodus, the, 78p, **380–390p, 399–405p,** 1102p, 1158p, 1230, 1231
  archaeology and, 1341–1342
  calendar and, **380p**
  commemorative rituals concerning, 391–394p
  and conquest, 1300
  date of, 912, 1413
  and Ezekiel, 369
  importance of, 1352
  memory of, 1307
  narrative of, tripartite separation of, 316
  and passover sacrifice, 1081p
  purpose of, 332d
  route of, **399–403p**
  new, 342, 1299, 1315
  time of, **500**
  See also Egypt; *Pesaḥ;* plagues: ten
Exodus, book of, **316**
Exodus generation. *See* generation of the Exodus
expiation. *See kipper*
expiatory sacrifices. *See asham; ḥattat*
Ezekiel
  chariot vision of, **1320–1324**
  eschatology and, 1437–1438
  exile of, 1307
  haftarot from (*see haftarah*)
  as new Moses, 735
  as priest, 1287, 1444
  and regulations for worship in rebuilt Temple, 734–737, 1290–1294
  vision of stream of healing water, 1252
Ezel stone, 1216, 1218
eizer (helper), woman as, 16
Ezion-geber, 956p, 991p
Ezra, 1269, 1352
  as priest, 1444
  and reading of Torah, 1303, 1480

F

faith, **405p**
  avoiding dangers to, 1029–1050p
faithlessness of Israel, 972–977, 988p, 1051p, 1186p
  See also infidelity
false piety, condemnation of, 1240
false prophecy, punishable by death, 1096p
false testimony, 1101p
false witness. *See aseret ha-dibrot:* 9th Commandment
family, 688–692p
  as center of life, 1349
  integrity of, 446p
  and marriage, **1353–1355**
  patriarchal, 1354
  patrilineal, 1354
  in religious context, **701–704p**
  Torah's view of, 53d
famine, 72–73p, **257p,** 1190p
fasting, 684pd, 934p, 968, 1242, 1249–1250
  on Day of Atonement, 728pd
  misuse of, 1240
  of Moses, 1045p
fat. *See ḥeilev*
father, and vows of daughter, **941–943p**
fear. *See yir·ah*
Fear of Isaac, 185p
fear of misfortune, 1157d
"fence around the law," 800d
fertility
  commandment of, 10ph
  gift of, 8p
  gods of, 958d
  of Israelites, 318p
  and milk and honey, 328p
  symbols of, 1040p
festivals, **543–544p**
  agricultural, **473–474p**
  beginning at evening, 728–729p
  participation of women in, 1349
  See also pilgrimage festivals; *see also under names of feasts*

fetishes (in worship), 1166p, 1287, 1288
fetus, as human being, 461h, 462d
fidelity, spiritual, 193. *See also* infidelity
fig tree, 19, 1040p. *See also sheva minin*
Fifth Commandment. *See aseret ha-dibrot*
financial assistance, 742h
fire
  and divine anger, 1011p, 1189p
  as divine Presence, 327p, **503d,** 632p, 1009p, 1022p
  God as, 1069d
  as guide, 987p, 768
  perpetual (on the altar), 614p
  purification and, 946h
  and *Shabbat,* 553h
fire-cloud (showing God's presence), 821–822p, 884p. *See also* cloud; *kavod*
fire pans, 861p, 865–866p, 866d, 1275
fire-walking, while carrying a child, 1095p
firmament. *See raki·a*
firstborn, 336d, 391h, 393h, 872p
  of animals, 393p, 782p
  Cain as, 24
  consecration of, **391p**
  Israel as, 336p
  holiness of, 391p, 1080p
  law of, 543–544p
  Levites replacing, 778p, **781–782p**
  priestly status of, 393p
  redemption of, **393,** 779h, 872h
  as sacrifice, 1064p
  status of, 470p, 1113p
  See also birthright; blessing; firstlings; plagues: 10th plague
First Commandment. *See aseret ha-dibrot*
first day of seventh month, 727–728p, **933p**
first fruits. *See bikkurim*
"First-Fruits Recitation," 1141d
firstlings, **756p,** 1075p. *See also* firstborn
fish. *See kashrut*
five. *See* numbers
flax, in Egypt, 367p
flesh
  of living animals, eating prohibited, 50p
  as euphemism for penis, 91p
  as human frailty, 33p
  as metaphor for kinship, 231p
flogging
  limits on, 1132–1133p
  as way of disciplining sons, 1114p
Flood, 1186p
  in ancient Near East context, 41p
  and death of Methuselah, 32p
  God's decision to bring, 34p
  imagery or motif of, 1197, 1311, 1345
  and *kashrut,* 15d
  Mesopotamian stories of, 42p, 44p, 46p, 47p, 50p
  and Noah, **41–52, 64–68**
  and *tevah* (ark), 322p
  and vegetarianism, 24–25p
food, 10
  for priests, **615p**
  and gods, 585
  and Jacob and Esau, 162
  and miracles of Elisha, **123**
  See also kashrut; korban; meat
foreclosure. *See yovel*
foreigner. *See nokhri*
forgiveness, divine, 1169, 1234, 1239, 1240, 1246, 1251. *See also salaḥ*
fornication, 1120p
  idolatry as, 1176p
fortune-telling, 1095h
forty. *See* numbers
Four Questions of *Pesaḥ,* 386d
Fourth Commandment. *See aseret ha-dibrot*
fowl. *See kashrut;* meat
frankincense, 526p, 797p, 1161
  with *minḥah,* 603p
  Midianites and, 139p
fraud. *See oshek*
freedom, to serve God, 359d
free will, 25, 747p
freewill offering. *See n'davah*
Friedman, Theodore, 1445
frogs, and Egyptian gods, 360–361p. *See also* plague: 2nd
frontlet, of high priest. *See* high priest, attire of
funerals, 882h

G

Gad, Gadites, 176p, 1268
  and division of Land, 949p, 951d, 952–953p, 958p, 996p, 997p, 998p, 1159
  Jacob's testament to, 303p
  Moses' blessing of, 1207–1208p
galbanum, 526p, 527p
Galilee, the, 958p
Garden of Eden. *See* Eden
gates, of cities, 121d, 996p, 1026p, 1091p, 1208p
gateway to heaven, 167–168p
Gehazi (servant of Elisha), 124–126
Gehenna, **80–81p.** *See also* Valley of Hinnom
gender
  and covenant observance, 1349
  in Egypt, 323p
  and inheritance, 926ph, 1355
  and killing in defeated towns, 1103p
  and killing in war, 945–946pd
  male and female, 30d
  male domination, 22d
  and *mishkan,* 562p
  and monetary value, 753p
  and *nazir,* 1349
  and obligation to pray, 1228
  and participation in festivals, 1084p, 1349
  in patriarchal society, 1349
  and property, 1358
  and prophets, 1349
  and religious officiants, 615d
  and teaching of Torah, 1175d
  and Torah reading, 1481
  and *tzitzit,* 1469
  and vows and oaths, **941–943p,** 1358
  and vulnerability, 332d
  and war booty, 1103, 1253, 1387
  woman as helper, 16
  women, skilled, 554d
  See also ish and *ishah;* marriage
genealogies, book of, 30–34p
generation of [the Tower of] Babel, 70d
generation of the conquest, 920p, 960p
generation of the Exodus, 769p, 823p, 849p, 850d
  end of, **992–993p**
  as generation of the wilderness, 769d, 992d
  promise to, 1165p
  redemption of, 1037p
Genesis, book of, 1
  archaeology and, 1341
  date of composition of, 1340
  Mesopotamian influence on, 1345–1346
genital discharge, 1124p. *See also* emission
Gentiles
  as descendants of Noah, 1381
  and hatred of Jewish people, 317d
  Jonah and, 1246
  in Middle Ages, 1381–1382
  relations with, **1377–1382**
  sinfulness of, 1377–1378
  as threat to Israelites, 1378
  and Torah, 15d
  See also ger; gerut; intermarriage; Noahide laws; *nokhri; Sho·ah*

ger (resident alien, sojourner, stranger), **385p**, 390dh, **700p**, 701p, 1147p, **1379–1380**
Abram's family as, in Canaan, 72p, 127p, **127–128d**
in ancient Near East, 72p
circumcision and, 1379
concern for, **468–469pd**, 1131–1132p
and corpse contamination, 882p
inadvertent wrongs of, 853p
Isaac's family as, in Canaan, 149p
Jacob's family as, in Egypt, 285p
and law, 851p
and Noahide laws, 732p
obligations of, **1165p**, 1379
and paschal offering, 821p
prosperity of, as curse, 1154p
providing for, 1142p
requirements of holiness and, 1974p
rights and privileges of, 390p, 963p, 985p, **1165p**
and *Shabbat*, **1020p**
treatment of, 1049p, 1379
work and, 684p
See also foreigner; Gentiles; *gerut*
ger v'toshav (resident alien). *See ger*
Gershom, meaning of name, 325p
Gershonites, 791–792p, 806p, 824p, 924p
gerut (conversion to Judaism), 468p, 795d, 1049h, 1382
get (writ of divorce), 447h, 1058, **1128ph**, 1358
See also divorce
gezel (robbery), 15d, 605d
giants
Anakites, 842p, 843, 844p, 987p
archaeological evidence for, 987p
Emim, 78p, 992p
Nephilim, 844p
Rephaim, 78p, 992p, 996–997p
Zamzummim, 992p, 993p
Gibeath-haaraloth, 1300
Gibeon, as ancient site of worship, 271
gifts, 387d
to God (*see korban; minḥah; olah; sh'lamim; t'rumah;* votive donations)
marriage, 137p, 208p
to the priests, 871p
of twelve tribal chieftains (for initiation of tabernacle), 805p
Gihon, 14p
Gilead, 197, 995p, 996p, 1210p
Gilgal, 877
circumcision and paschal ceremony at, 1299
Gilgamesh epic, 13–14p
and story of Noah, 1344–1347
Girgashites, 1029p
gleaning, 694d, 727d, 1131–1132pd
glory. *See kavod*
g'nizah (repository), 1063d
goats, color of, 178p
God, 2, 3d, **1390–1394**
arm of, as image of divine power, 353p, 421d, 1055, 1111, 1141, 1182p
attributes of, **351d**, **541p**, 760, **1391–1392** (*see also* divine attributes)
blessing of, 10p
as bridegroom, 1180, 1181
compassion of, 1012p, 1336
contact with, 449d
as creator, 95
direct experience of, 1016d
duties to, **470p**
familial idea of, 1390
as Father, 1230, 1232
finger of, 362p
as fulfiller of promises, 1107, 1110
hand of, 364p, 405p, 1055
hyphenation of name of, 444h
and history, 2, 96, 443d
image of, 9p
invoking by name, 550
as Israel's leader in war, 1101, 1102p
jealousy of, **1018p**
as judge, 1229, 1428–1429
as lion, 195
as Lord of battles, 1196, 1310
majesty of, 1034
manifestations of, **1392–1393**
might of, 1032
obligations to, 473–474p
as one, **1025d**
power of, 3d
presence of, 400p, 403p, 415p, 449d, 450d, 485d, 536–540p, 768 (*see also* divine presence; *kavod*)
as refuge, 763
regret by, 21d, 34p, 931d, 1282–1283
relationship of, to human beings, 10p
reviling of, 470p
as rock, 304p, 1185p, 1188, 1189, 1191pd, **1196–1197**, 1199, 1228, **1310–1311**, 1313, 1314
screaming like a woman in labor, 37
self-disclosure of (Thirteen Attributes), **541–542p**
as shepherd, 1232
as Shield, 1209p, 1311, 1313
sovereignty of, 12p, 1252
supremacy of, 551
as tower of victory, 1201
uniqueness of, 609
unity of, 1392
visual aspect of, 1009p, 1010p
as warrior, 37, 409p, 1192p, 1253, 1321, **1382–1384**
withdrawal of, 1256, 1259
worship of, 329p
wrath of, 443–444p
See also anger, divine; divine providence; grace, divine; *ḥesed;* judgment of God; justice, divine; names and titles of God; *raḥamim*
gods
powerlessness of, 1191–1192p
worship of, 1068p, **1069–1070p**, 1090p, 1166p, 1168p, 1176p, 1177p, 1188p, 1189p
go·el (redeemer, avenger), 745p, 795p, **963p**, 965p. *See also go·el ha-dam; g'ulah*
go·el ha-dam (blood redeemer, blood avenger), **1098p**, 1427. *See also* blood vengeance; *go·el*
Gog of Magog, prophecy against, 1259–1262, 1438
gold, 14p, 74p, 255p, 487d, 488pd, 489d, 504p, 565p, 1273
Golden Calf, 485d, **530–531p**, 1044p
Aaron and, 1045p
apostasy of, 523d, 534p, 547, 713, 840p, 1043p, 1177p, 1336
atonement for idolatry of, 1270
destruction of, by Moses, 533–534p, 1305
and divine anger, 713, 1167p
and gold bulls of Jeroboam, 189, 531p
restoration of divine favor after, 545p
and *Yom Kippur*, 552d
Gomel blessing, 618d
Gomorrah, destruction of, **104–108p**. *See also* Sodom
Goodman, Arnold, 1445
Gordis, Robert, 1404
Goshen, 277p, 318p, 319p, **363p**
as dwelling of family of Jacob, 283p
gossip, 653d, 696d, 1088d
"leprosy" as punishment for, 652d, 834d
goy (nation, people), 110p
grace, divine, 107p, 804p, 1335
Grace after Meals. *See Birkat ha-Mazon*
grain, new, 725–726p

grain offering. *See minḥah*
grains, 384p, 1040ph, 1127p. *See also* barley, emmer, wheat
grapes, 842p, 1027p, 1040h
  nazirites and, 800pd
grapevines, 52p, 105, 738p, 1027p, 1040p. *See also sheva minin;* vineyard
grasshoppers, 844pd
  curse of, 1154p
gratitude, 1039d, 1041d
grief, 232p, 699d. *See also* mourning
guilt (for sin), 1078p
  and descendants, 1018pd
g'ulah (redemption), 755p, 758–759
  by God, of Israel, 190, 353p, 369, 1160, **1164,** 1180, 1285
  from God, of firstborn, **393p**
  from God, of ritually unclean animals, 393p
  by God, from Egypt, stages of, 352dh
  by kin, 741–745, 755p, 758–759
  See also eschatology; *go·el*
gum, uses of, in Egypt, 231p

H

Habiru. *See apiru*
hadar trees, 730ph
Hadrian, edicts of, 162
haftarah (pl. *haftarot*), **1486–1490**
  correlation of, with Torah reading, 1488
  origin of, 1488
  from Joshua, 856, 1266, 1299
  from Judges, 423, 812, 909
  from 1 Samuel, 876, 1224, 1280
  from 2 Samuel, 643, 1196, 1310
  from 1 Kings, 142, 271, 312, 499, 547, 573, 576, 579, 937, 1256, 1263, 1273
  from 2 Kings, 123, 671, 675, 1276, 1303
  from Isaiah, 35, 64, 94, 342, 451, 606, 999, 1032, 1055, 1085, 1107, 1137, 1160, 1180, 1219, 1240, 1315, 1335
  from Jeremiah, 347, 395, 481, 626, 758, 762, 968, 972, 1230, 1329
  from Ezekiel, 290, 369, 519, 709, 713, 734, 1259, 1286, 1290, 1307, 1330
  from *Trei Asar* (The Twelve [Minor Prophets]), 162, 188, 194, 221, 246, 705, 784, 836, 914, 1234, 1245, 1252, 1269, 1295, 1325
Hagar, **86–88p**
  and angel, 87pd
  expulsion of, **113–115p**
ḥag (festival), 473p
  the Lord's, 375p
Haggadah (for *Pesaḥ*), 319h, 386p, **392p,** 1028d, 1141pd, 1184, 1367, 1447. *See also Pesaḥ*
Haggai, 1269
  messianic thought of, 1438
Ḥag ha-Asif (feast of Ingathering), **474p,** 935p, **1456.** *See also Sukkot*
Ḥag ha-Katzir (feast of Harvest), 932p. *See also Shavu·ot*
hail. *See barad*
hair
  destruction of, 803p
  diseases of, **655–657p**
  nazirite and, 801p, 812
  untrimmed locks of, 426
  See also skin diseases
halakhah (law and lore, legal system), 1365, 1470
  local custom in, 1475–1476
  medieval, **1474–1476**
  modern, **1476–1479**
  See also law; *and under individual topics*
ḥallah (dough offering), **852h,** 852pd
Ham, 33p
  descendants of, 52, 55
ḥamas (lawlessness), 41, 41d
ḥametz (leavened products), prohibition of, on *Pesaḥ,* **385h, 592h, 1082h,** 1082–1083p. *See also Pesaḥ; s'or*
Hammurabi, laws of. *See* Code of Hammurabi; law
hand, right, as symbol of action and power, 296p, 407p. *See also* God: hand of
Hannah, 1225–1229
  barrenness of, 1225
  prayer of, 1224, **1228–1229**
  vow of, 1224, 1226
Ḥanukkah, 250d, 729d, 816d, 1269–1272, 1272–1275
  eating fried foods on, 1460
  m'norah and, 490d
ḥanukkiyyah (eight-branched *m'norah*), 816d
Hapiru. *See apiru*
Haran (city), 169
  and Terah, 61–63p
  and Abram, 69–70p
  and Jacob, 166p, 169, 182p
  See also Abram-naharaim; Paddan-aram
Haran (person), 61–62p
  and migration of Terah, 69p
hardening the heart (of Pharaoh), **335p,** 351, 356d, 357p, 364d, 365pd, 374p**d,** 401p. *See also* heart
harlot. *See zonah*
Harvest, feast of. *See Ḥag ha-Katzir*
Ḥasidim, and emotive prayer, 1016d
Hasmoneans, 735, 1272
ḥattat (expiatory sacrifice, purification offering), **595–605p,** 636p, **1449**
  l'Adonai (*for* the LORD), on *Rosh Ḥodesh,* 931d
  brown cow as, 881p
  for discharge of bodily fluids, 668p
  for Levites, 817p
  as "most holy," 615d, 616p
  money as, 1279
  and nazirite, 799d
  presented before burnt offering, 602d, 662p
  of priest, 596d, **616p,** 631p
  for Temple, in Ezekiel, 1291, 1292
  and *tum·ah* (ritual impurity), 649d, 651p
  of warriors and captives, **946–947p**
  and *Yom Kippur,* 680p
  See also korban
ḥatzotz'rot (trumpets), 822–823p, 1442
Havdalah, 5d, 445d, 1292, 1318
ḥazak ḥazak v'nitḥazzek, 1504–1505
ḥazon (vision), 222
Hazor, archaeology and, 1342
healing, 53h, 123–126, 192, 460–461d, 671–674, 765, 835
heart, **335p**
  circumcision of, 1170p, 1412
  hardening of, 994p, **1078d** (*see also* hardening the heart)
  as locus of thought, 34p, 864p, 1025p
  new, given by God, 1288
  of stone, 1288, 1412
  uncircumcised, 752p
heaven, as abode of God, 1143p, 1326
heaven and earth, 4p, 1219
  as literary device, 1185p
  as witnesses to covenant, **1011pd**
heavenly bodies
  symbolized by *m'norah,* 836
  worship of, **1010p,** 1090p, 1104p, 1378–1379, 1435
heavenly court
  in Genesis, 9p, 1034
  Zechariah's vision of, 837, 1271
heavenly temple, 1325
heavenly throne, of God, 1320, 1323

Hebrew (speaker of). *See ivri*
Hebrew language, 982d, 986–987p
Hebrew script, three styles of, in Torah scrolls, 1485
Hebron, 77p
- as region where Jacob lived, 226p
- as sacred site, 842p
- tomb of patriarchs in 842pd
- *See also* cities of refuge; Machpelah, cave of

heifer, rite of. *See* brown cow; murder, unsolved, rite for
ḥeilev (fat surrounding innards of sacrificial animals), 593p
- forbidden as food, 619p

ḥeirem (property dedicated to God; ban; proscription), 468p, 608, 1039p
- of Amalekites, 1282–1283
- Amorites and, 856
- of apostate town, 1071p
- of conquered cities in Promised Land, 1104p
- reserved for the sanctuary, 460p, **756** (*see also mikdash:* property of)
- in war, 888p, **1385–1387**

hen (behold, surely), 1085
hepatoscopy, 512p, 1095p
Heschel, A. J., 1404, 1456
ḥesed (loyalty, commitment, love, kindness, goodness), 1139, 1334
- as covenanted faithfulness, 68, 541p, 1018–1019p
- as loyalty, 66, 411p, 1087
- as goodness, 194, 196–197

ḥesed v'emet (kindness and faithfulness; true kindness; steadfast loyalty), 293d, 312–313, **541p**
ḥet (sin, "missing the mark"), **682–683d.** *See also* sin
ḥevra kaddisha (burial society), 293d
hewn masonry, prohibition against altars of, 450p
Hezekiah's tunnel, 1340, 1343
hiddur mitzvah, 554d
high court of referral, **1090–1092p**
high holy days, **1459.** *See also Rosh ha-Shanah; Yom Kippur*
high priest, 718p, **1443**
- Aaron as, 504p
- anointing of, 596p, 615p
- and contact with dead, 719p, 908p
- death of, and asylum, 964p
- investiture of, 1269
- Joshua as (in Second Temple), 836, 837
- marriage of, 719p
- as officiant in purification of sanctuary (on *Yom Kippur*), 679–680p, 1444
- *See also* high priest, attire of; *kohen*

high priest, attire of, 504–510p, 505d, 621–622p
- ephod, 505–506p
- frontlet, 509–510p
- *ḥoshen mishpat* (breastpiece of decision), 505d, 506–508p, 567p, 622p
- *kuttonet* (tunic), 510p
- *mikhnasayim* (breeches), 511p
- *mitznefet* (headdress), 510p
- precious stones, 506–508p, 507d
- robe, 508–509p
- sash, 510p
- *See also* Urim and Thummim

Hilkiah, 1304, 1480
ḥillel (profane or desecrate), 483
"Hillel sandwich," 820h
ḥillul ha-Shem (desecration or profanation of [God's] name), 247, 483, 1287, 1288
hinnei (behold, surely), 1085
Hiram (craftsman), 573, 574, 576, 1273
Hiram (king of Tyre), 499, 500, 573, 1273
Hirsch, S. R., 1456
history
- as pattern of divine acts of redemption, 369
- of Israel, in Habakkuk, 1327

Hittites, **843p, 1029p,** 1104
- appeal to, 127–128p
- treaty of, with Ramses II, 959p

Hivites, 1029p, 1104
Hobab, 424, **825–826p.** *See also* Jethro; Reuel
hod (authority), 929p
ḥodesh (new moon, month), 436p, 725p, 931p. *See also Rosh Ḥodesh*
ḥok (pl. *ḥukkim*) (law), 615, 1423. *See also ḥukkah;* law
ḥokhmah (skill, wisdom), 576
- of Joshua, 1266
- as skill, 505d, 573, **555d,** 556d
- as wisdom, 111d, 131d, 271, 273, 499

holiness. *See k'dushah*
Holiness Code (Leviticus 17–26), 584, **685–704p**
- epilogue to, 747–752p
- familiarity of Ezekiel with, 709
- inclusiveness of, 720p

holocaust, 1071p
Holocaust. *See Sho·ah*
Holy Land, 1012p, 1270
Holy of Holies, 485p, 486p, 491p, **495p**
- Ark in the, 419p, 559p
- *See also* Ark; Holy Place; tabernacle; Temple

Holy One of Israel. *See* names and titles of God
Holy Place, 485p, 492p, **495p,** 504p, **559p**
- *See also* Holy of Holies; tabernacle

holy war, 943–944d, 1299
ḥomer, 755p, 832p
homicide, 51p, 459–460p, 1091p
- accidental, **459pd,** 962p, 964–965p
- and blood vengeance, 963p
- deliberate versus involuntary, **963–964p,** 1097d
- execution for, 965p
- instruments of, 963p
- monetary payment for, 965p
- trial of, 963p, 964–965p
- *See also* murder; *rotzei·aḥ*

homily. *See d'rashah*
homosexuality, 691ph, 1125p, 1354
honey, 264p, 1040p
- forbidden from altar, 591–592p

hope, 845d
- national, 162
- prophecy of, 710, 968, 1286–1289
- repentance and, 1295
- of restoration, 705–706

Hophni, 1225–1229
Horeb. *See* Mount Horeb
Horites, 78p, 217–218p, 992p
horse, 287p, 402p. *See also* chariot
Hosea, 786–790
- call for repentance of, 191, 1234–1236
- eschatological themes of, 1437
- *haftarot* from (*see haftarah*)

ḥoshekh (darkness)
- and depression, 377d
- as negative symbol, 4p
- contrasted with light, 36
- as original state of world, 36
- *See also* plague: 9th

ḥoshen mishpat (breastpiece of decision). *See* high priest, attire of
hospitality
- Abraham and, 99–100p, 99d, 123
- Lot and, **105p**
- reward for, 123
- *See also* inhospitality

host(s) (of God, heaven). *See tzava*
house. *See bayit*
household. *See beit av*
household idols. *See t'rafim*

house of Israel, 685p. *See also* Israel
House of the LORD, 1252, 1264, 1277–1279, 1304
ḥukkah (pl. *ḥukkot*) (law, ritual and cultic ordinances), 594p, **1006p**
  agricultural setting of, 1424
  as basis for society in Promised Land, 1007p
  as gift of God, 713–714, 980
  God as author of, 1015p
  ignorance of, 595p
  ordained by written statute, 615p
  uniqueness of, 1008p
  See also ḥok; law; *mishpat; Torah*
Huldah, as prophet, 1409
human beings
  creation of, 9d, 13p
  dignity of, 456d, 461d
  as image of God, 10d
  and *Shabbat,* 12
  and time, 12
  versus Nature, 18
  See also creation
human condition, 12–23p
  irrationality and, 24–26
humanitarianism, of Torah, 980
humility, 615d, 833p
humor, 894d
hunger and thirst, as metaphors, 68
Hyksos, 255p, 287p, 318p, 1341
hypocrisy, 1001
hyssop, 385p, 881p

I

idleness, 445d, 460p
idolatry, 709, 746d, 763, 788, 908d, 1038p, 1063d
  at Baal-Peor, 907–908p, 918–920p
  and Decalogue, 443d
  and divine anger, 828d
  in Egypt, 715
  in era of chieftains, 1327
  as fornication, 1176p
  and Golden Calf, 533–535pd
  and Noahide laws, 15d
  and pillars, 475p
  prohibition of, 1006p
  punishment for, 907p, 1166p
  as ritually defiling, 291
  sin of, 1270
  as source of pollution, 965p, 973
  warning against, 543p
  and worship of celestial bodies, 1010pd
idols, 1166p
  ban on, **1018p**
  Canaanites and, 1063p
  and curses, 1147p
  gillulim, 710p
  polemic against, 606
  purpose of, **1010p**
  shikkutzim, 1166p
  worship of, 29–30d, **1012p,** 1071d
  See also asherim; t'rafim
image of God, 9p, 10d, 30p
  See also aseret ha-dibrot: 2nd Commandment
immanence, divine, 95, 1241, 1254
immortality
  children as, 24d
  and Flood, 34pd, 43d
  spiritual, 1439
  tree of life and, 14p
  See also death; life: after death; resurrection
impaling. *See* execution
impurity, ritual. *See tum·ah*
inadvertent wrongs
  of community, 853p
  of individual, 853p
  offerings and, 853d
  of stranger, 853p
incense. *See k'toret*
incest, 1354
  laws, 688–691pd, 702–703p
  as source of pollution, 965p
indebtedness, 743–744p
  See also debt; interest; lending; loans
indenture, 741p, 1079p
individual, destiny of, 1438–1439
indwelling of God (among humans), 487p, 965p, 1241, 1270. *See also* cloud; *kavod; mishkan*
infertility, 10h, 86d, 146h
  and polygamy, 1353
  in the Torah, 86p
  tragedy of, 1355
  treatments, 234h
  See also barrenness
infidelity (to God)
  prophetic censure for, 999. *See also* faithlessness; fidelity
Ingathering, feast of. *See Ḥag ha-Asif*
inheritance
  of property in ancient Near East, 114p, 147p, 323p
  See also naḥalah; succession
inhospitality, 76d. *See also* hospitality
iniquity. *See avon*
injury, laws concerning, 460–463p
innocence, loss of, in Eden, 19–20
inscriptions. *See* archaeological finds
insects
  curse of, 1154p
  ritual impurity and, 639–641p, 640h, 642
  winged, as food, **639–641p**
  See also grasshoppers; locusts
instinct, and tree of life, 23
insubordinate son, punishment of, 1113–1114p, 1359
intent (factor in assessment of sin or crime). *See* crops, damage to; homicide; injury; *korban*
interest, charging of, 1126pdh
  ban on, 469p**h**
  rate of, 288p
  See also debt; indebtedness; lending; loans
intermarriage
  with Canaanites, 354p
  celestial-terrestrial, **33–34p,** 34d
  prevention of, 1030p
  prohibition of, 1378
  See also marriage: exogamous
iron
  as image, 1011p, 1154p
  mining of, 1041p
Isaac, 92p
  adventures of, 149–153p
  betrothal of, **134–138p**
  birth of, **112–113p**
  and blessing of Esau, 157–159
  and blessing of Jacob, 156–157
  blindness of 153–154p, **154–155d**
  burial of, 215p
  circumcision of, 113p
  covenant and, 140–141p
  death of, 215–216p
  descendants of, 146–148p
  and Ishmael, 114d
  name chosen by God, 113p
  old age of, 153p
  pact with Abimelech, 152–153p
  finding a wife for, **130–138p**
  See also Akedah (binding of Isaac)
Isaiah
  commissioning of, 451
  eschatology and, 1436–1437
  haftarot from (*see haftarah*)
  prophetic career of, 999
  setting of, 1351
  temple vision of, 1036
  theology of creation of, 36
  See also Second Isaiah
ish (man) and *ishah* (woman), 17pd, 24p
Ishmael, 87p, 88p, 114–115pd
  blessing of, 92d
  caravan of Ishmaelites, transporting Joseph, 230p
  descendants of, **141p**
Ishmael (rabbi), school of, 1472–1473
Israel (person), 201–202pd, 1187p. *See also* Jacob

Israel (nation/people)
abandonment of, by God, 1176pd
apostasy of, 972–977
birth of (the people of), 374d
as chosen nation, 608
complaints of, in wilderness, 954d, 1028p, 1045p
as covenant community, 380p
covenanted obligations of, 1416
deliverance of, 35, 1069p, 1193p
destiny of, 157p, 436–437p
disobedience of, in Deuteronomy, 983–989p
economy of, 1349
election of, 706, 1043d, **1416–1420**
faithlessness of, 972–977
God's plan for, 1191–1193p
God's planting of, 975
as God's treasured people, **437p,** 1030p
as God's witness, 35
idolatry of, in Egypt, 715
as instrument of divine revelation, 1043d
judgment against, 224
as kingdom of priests, 437d, 509d
as light of nations, 68
meaning of name, 202d
military service in, 1349
misery of, in Egypt, **326p**
as "My people," 706
as name of Jacob, 202p
as new Adam, 1286
punishment of, 713, 1189–1190p
rebellion of, 713, 999–1001
restoration of, 192, 342, 370
restrictions on citizenship, 1122–1123p
as seed of Abraham, 94, 97
as servant, 35, 97
size of, 1031p
society, 1348–1352
testing of, 1069p
See also Ephraim; house of Israel; land of Israel
Issachar
Jacob's testament to, 302p
meaning of name, 177p
tribe of, 302d, 1206–1207p
Isserles, Moses, 1475
I–thou relationship, 1402
ivri (a speaker of Hebrew), 62d, **79pd,** 320p

J

Jabbok River, 201pd. *See also* Wadi Jabbok
Jabin (king), 425–426
Jachin and Boaz, 577–578
Jacob
acquiring blessing, **153–161p**
as ancestor of nation, 162
birth of, **146–147p**
blessing of, 296pd, 297p, 317p
burial of, **305–308p,** 312
children of, **173–179p** (*see also under names of individual children*)
death of, **305–306p**
dream revelation of, at Bethel, **166–167p**
flight of, to Aram, 160pd, 188, 189, 221
genealogy of, 281–283p
as heir to divine promises, 167p
and Laban, 177–179p
marriages of, 169–173
meaning of name, 147p
migration of, to Egypt, 279–286p
partiality of, toward Joseph, 226–227p, 227d
and Pharaoh, **285–286p**
preparations of, for death, 293–294p
Rebekah's love for, 162
reconciliation of, with Esau, 203–205p
return of, to Canaan, 205–206p
rivalry with Esau, 147p, **162–165,** 172p, 195, **198–205p,** 221
testament of, **298–305p**
as trickster, 155p, 178d, 201d, 306d
words as "weapon" of, 944d
wrestling with angel, 195, 201–202p, 201d
See also Israel
Jacobs, Louis, 1404
Jael, 423
Japheth, 33p, 52
descendants of, 55
Jebusites, 843p, 1019p, 1104
Jehoash, 1277–1279
Jehovah, origin of name, 330p
Jephthah, 909–910
Jeremiah
and Babylonian empire, 1353
call of, 968–971
eschatology and, 1437
faithfulness of, 762
meaning of name, 347, 968
as messenger of God's word, 347
prayers of, 758, 762
prophecies of, against Egypt, 395–398
prophecy of doom, 1329–1334
prophecy of return, 1437
symbolic action of, 758
Jeremiah, Book of
haftarot from (*see haftarah*)
oracles of consolation in, 1230, 1437
setting of, 1351
Jericho
as city of palm trees, 1210p
and Israelite spies, 856–858
Jerusalem
bringing the Ark to, 643
as central sanctuary, 1063p
as city of bloodshed, 709
destruction of, 519
as holy city, 1109
rejoicing with, 1221
renaming of, 1160, 1180
religious centrality of, 1252
siege of, 481, 1252–1255
See also Second Temple; Temple
Jeshurun, 1208–1209p
Jethro, 325p, **432–435**
arrival of, 432–434p
meaning of name, **325p**
See also Hobab; Reuel
Jewish law
and Conservative Movement, **1477–1479**
functions of, 1478
and Orthodox thinkers, **1477**
and Reconstructionist Movement, **1477**
and Reform Movement, **1477**
See also halakhah; law
Jewish tradition, as legal tradition, 1470
Jezebel, 937
Job, book of, 1325
Jochebed, 355p, 925a
Joel, *haftarot* from. *See haftarah*
Jonah, book of, 162, 1245–1251
date of, 1245
distinctiveness of, 1245
irony in, 1245
rhetorical devices in, 1246
Joseph
agrarian policies of, **286–289p**
attempted seduction of, 239–241p
burial of, 310p, 311h
death of, 310p, 311h, 317p, **400pd**
dreams of, **227–228**
in Egypt, **238–276p,** 238d
as Ephraim and Manasseh, 304p
and gift of divine wisdom, 271
as interpreter of dreams, 271
Jacob's testament to, 304–305p
meaning of name, 177p

Moses' blessing of, 1205–1206p
narrative of, archaeology and, 1341
as northern kingdom, 304p
in prison, 241–245p
prologue to story of, **226–232p**
and reconciliation with brothers, 274d, 275–276p
two sons of, 256–257p
as vizier, 254–256p, 258–259p

Josephus, 450p, 1118p

Joshua ben Nun, 421p, 423, 538p, 832p, 845–846p
appointment of, 1174p, 1178p
as first keeper of Tradition, 1266
meaning of name, 988p
spies of, sent to Jericho, 856–859
as successor of Moses, 928–929p, 960p, 988p, 1173p, 1211p, 1266, 1299–1300

Joshua (high priest paired with Zerubabbel), 1270–1272

Joshua, book of
archaeological findings and, 1340
haftarot from (*see haftarah*)

Josiah (king), 347, 1303
Jeremiah and, 969
as new Moses, 1305
and public reading of Torah, 1480
religious awakening of, 1303

jubilee year. *See yovel*

Judah
Jacob's testament to, 300–301p
as leader, 290
meaning of name, 174d
Moses' blessing of, 1203p
as spokesman, 263p, 269p
sons of, 233–234p
and Tamar, 233–237p
tribe of, 774d

Judah the Maccabee, and construction of Temple altar, 450p

judges, 985pd
appointment of, **1088p**
authority of, 1091h
giving equal treatment, 985h
integrity of, 470–471p
qualifications for, 435p
rules of propriety for, 1088p, 1425
See also courts; judiciary, Israelite; justice

Judges, book of, *haftarot* from. *See haftarah*

judgment. *See mishpat*

judgment of God
against Egypt, 395
and Flood, 34p
Isaiah's oracles of, 1219
See also day to come; God: as judge; justice, divine

judiciary, Israelite, 432p, 434–435p, **1088–1092p, 1424**
See also courts; judges; law

justice, **1427–1430**
beyond the (letter of the) law, 1428, 1430
holiness and, 1429
impartiality and, 1427–1428
prophets and, 1427
Sages and, 1427–1428
substantive, 1428
See also mishpat; tzedek

justice, divine, 13pd, 103dh, 1317, 1334, 1428
God's laws as perfect, 1008p

K

kabbalists, 1216, 1400

Kaddish, 724d, 1260

Kadesh (Kadesh-barnea)
Abraham settled in, 110p
as base of Israelites during wilderness wandering, 78p, 843p, 987p
as boundary of Promised Land, 958p, 959p, 981p, 982p
and wilderness itinerary, 956p, 989p
See also Rephidim

kadosh (holy; consecrated; set apart), 706, 1030p

kahal (congregation), Israelites as a whole, 598p. *See also edah*

kal va-ḥomer, 268p

Kaplan, Mordecai, 1456

kapporet (cover), 488pd, **495p**

karet (cut off), **91p,** 384p. *See also* punishment

Karo, Joseph, 1471–1472
legal code of, 1474–1475

kasdim. See Babylon

kashrut (dietary laws), 50d, 474p, **474dh, 1072–1074p,** 1072d, **1460–1464**
ban on eating blood, **1461** (*see also* blood)
ban on thigh tendon, 202h, **1460**
creation and, 1462–1463
and ecology, 1370
fins and scales (of fish), 638–639h
and foods for special occasions, 1460
fowl, 1073h, 1074p
holiness and, 470p, 1462
kasher (kosher), 637h, 1460
and kosher slaughter, 202h
land animals, 637–638
laws for, 1460–1464
meat and, 1067h
offerings of, 718p
permitted and forbidden food, **637–639,** 1461–1462
separation of meat from dairy, 100–101d, **637d,** 1074ph, 1461
tareif, 1460

Kaufmann, Yeḥezkel, 1390, 1451

kavod (divine Presence; glory), 300p, 846p, 974, 1009p, 1032–1033
altar as locus of, 477p
as divine presence, 1161
as glory, 401p
laws of, 584, 637–642
as light, in Isaiah, 1161
of the LORD, 37, 1222, 1324, 1325
in Temple, 452, 579
vision of, in Babylon, 1320
See also cloud; divine Presence; fire; indwelling of God; *k'vod YHVH*

kavvanah (intentionality), in writing Torah, 1484. *See also* intent

k'dushah (holiness), 704d, 713
condition of, as not contagious, 615p
biblical concepts of, **1440–1441**
and daily offering, 516d
in diet, **1072–1074p**
of God, 1241, **1440**
incense test for, 861p
laws of, **1072–1074p**
meaning of, 693d, **1440–1441**
in mourning, 1072p
nazirite and, 801p
and God's Presence, 485d
pursuit of, 470p, 685–704p, 717–723p, 738–746p, 747–752p, 753d
rabbis and, 718d
time and, 12p
two types of, **649d**
See also kodesh

K'dushah (sanctification prayer), 452, 1324

Kedar, 973

Kedesh. *See* cities of refuge

Kenites, 85p, 424, 906p
Saul's sparing of, 1282

kesef (silver, money), 74p, 246, 753p, 1075p. *See also* shekel

Keturah, descendants of, 139–140p

ki, meaning of, **399d, 454**

Kibroth-hattaavah, complaint of Israelites at, 827–833p, 954d, 1045p

Kiddush (prayer recited over wine), 11h, 359d, **445h,** 980, 1020d

kiddush ha-Shem, 724d

kidnaping, 111–112p
as capital crime, 460p, 1129p
Eighth Commandment and, 448d
killing. *See* homicide; murder; *rotzei·aḥ*
kin. *See mishpaḥah*
kin·ah (passion), 443p, 918p, 1018p
king
desire for, 876
in Egypt, 1092p
law of, in Deuteronomy, **1092–1093p, 1092d**
in Mesopotamia, 1092p
obligation of, to copy a Torah scroll, 1093p
as optional office, 1092p
as subject to the law, 1092pd, 1093p
See also monarchy
Kings, Books of, *haftarot* from. *See haftarah*
kipper (expiate, purge), 521, 817p, 818p, 949p
at Baal-Peor, 918–919p
meaning of word, **598p**, 685p
See also atonement
Kiriath-arba, 127p
Kittim, 907p, 973
Klein, Isaac, 1445
knowledge. *See da·at*
kodesh (holy), 515p, 616p, 698p. *See also k'dushah*
kodesh l'YHVH (holy to the LORD), 224, 509–510p, 727p, 1255
Kohathites, 780p, 785p, 825p, 870p, 924p
removal duties of, 783–785p
kohen (pl. *kohanim*) (priest[s]), 81p, 777p, **1441–1446**
accompanying army in war, 1102p
benefits of, **720–721p**
charge to, 164
and contact with the dead, 717pdh, 719p, 1446
carrying Ark, 1257
clothing (vestments) of, 450p, **504–511p, 505d**
compensation of, 852p
conduct of, 632–636p
consecration of, 621–625p
daughter of, 718pd, 721**ph**
death and, 717pd
as descendants of Aaron, 717d, 734, 1094p
duties of, 162, 165
food for, **615p**
future, 514–515p
heredity and, 1446
impure, 720p
installation of, **510–517p,** 569p
kingdom of, 437d, 509d
land ownership and, 288d
laws governing, 635p, **717–723p**
as Levites, 1094p
and military force, 823p
and mourning rites, 717–719p
physically unsound, 719–720p, **720d**
prior to Sinai revelation, 440p
and professionalization of sacrifice, 1448
as recipient of gift, 795pd
ritual purity of, 162, 1443
role of, after destruction of Temple, 1444
role of, in biblical period, **1442–1443**
role of, in treating skin diseases, **652–653d**
rules of marriage for, 718h, 1443–1445
and sacrifices, **617p**
of Second Temple, 735
support of, **1094p**
Talmud and, 1444–1445
as teachers, 735
theology of, 579
weapon carried by, 908p
Zadokite, 521
See also high priest; Levites; levitical priests
kol (voice, sound), 601p, 939–940
Korah (rebel leader), **860d**
and inheritance, 926p
punishment of, 865pd
rebellion of, **860–865p,** 866–875p, 884p, 1051p
Korahites, clan of, 355p, **860d**
as clan of Temple singers and guards, 921p
korban (offering, sacrifice), **587pd**, 615p, 806p, 1001, **1446–1450**
accompaniments to, 850–851p
altar of, **496p**
of animals, 382p, 511p, **512–514p,** 585
atonement and, 585, 595p
building of altars and, 1447
burnt offerings, 1446
calendar of, **929–936p**
communal dimension of, 1447–1448
disposition of, **613–621p**
of expiation, 617p
false reliance on, 999
of firstborn cattle, **1080–1081p**
first celebration of, 630–632p
of flawed animals, 1080p
as food, **1066p**
in later thought, 1450
offerings of food, 718p
place of offering, 1448–1449
portion of, assigned to priest, 1094p
priests and, 1442, 1448
principal types of, **585–621**
in prophetic literature, 1449–1450
psalms and, 586d
purpose of, **1064p**
rejection of, 626, 1220
restricted to single sanctuary, 980, 1012p, 1061d, **1063–1064p**
rules for slaughter and, 1448
versus morality, 917
See also asham; child sacrifice; *ḥattat; minḥah; olah; pesaḥ; sh'lamim; t'nufah; zavaḥ*
k'rei (reading tradition), and *k'tiv* (writing tradition), 975, 1184, 1201, 1314
k'tiv (writing tradition). *See k'rei*
k'toret (incense), 517–518p, 559p, 561p, **588–589p,** 867p
altar of, 495p, **517–518p**
and atonement and protection, 644
ingredients of, 526–527p, 527d
offering of, 632p, 861p
as reminder of presence of God, 517p
test at the Tent of Meeting, 863p, 866p
k'vod YHVH (glory/presence of the LORD), 415, 452, 480p, 539p, 965p. *See also* cloud; fire; *kavod*

L

Laban, 169–173p
and Jacob, 177–179p
as trickster, 178d
laborer, timely payment to, 695
Lachish Letters, 347
ladder, in Jacob's dream, 166pd
lamb
paschal, 588p (*see also pesaḥ*)
slaughter of, 380–381d
as symbol of idol worship, 381d
Lamech, 32–33p
song of, 29p
Lamentations, book of, 972, 984d, 999, 1055, 1107
lampstand. *See m'norah*
land
apportioning of, **924p, 997p**
conditional promise of, 980
division of, 949p
giving of, 163
ownership of, and priests, 288d
personification of, 752p
possession of, 703d, 1163
promised to patriarchs, 1098p, 1170, 1172

redemption of, 755p, 758–759
tenure of, **738–746p**
land animals. *See* animals; *kashrut* (dietary laws)
land of Israel, 472d, **1372–1377**
burial in, of patriarchs, 1373
covenant and, 1373
depiction of, 328p
Deuteronomy and, 1376
as everlasting possession, 295p
expulsion from, 1375, 1376
holiness of, 1376
ideal boundaries of, 476p, 1267, 1374
Jewish commitment to, 400h
and land of Canaan, 1374
patriarchs and, 1373, 1376
personification of, 1375
as primary locus of observance, 1375
and promise, 69h
purchase of, 1373
return to, 1376
right to, 1375–1376
ritual impurity of, 1287
See also Israel; land
language
confusion of, at Tower of Babel, 57p
universal, 58p
See also Hebrew language
lapis lazuli, 14p, 479p
laughter, of Sarah, 92p, 101pd, 113p
laundering, 830p
purification and, 212p
laver, 524–525pd, 559p, 562p
law
ancient Near Eastern, **1420–1423**
Babylonian, 462p
as basis of relationship between God and Israel, 1143p
beyond the letter of the, 1428, 1430
biblical, **1420–1423**
casuistic style of, 1420, 1421, 1422
changes of, 1006pd, 1007d
civil, 1091p
code of Joseph Karo, 1474
code of Moses Maimonides, 1474
collections of miscellaneous, in Torah, 472p, 731–733p, 849–855p
concerning bodily injury, 460–463p
concerning slaves, **457–459p**
concerning war and peace, **1387–1388**
and Conservative Movement, **1477–1478**
and covenant, 1422
of Eshnunna, 1420–1421
Hittite, 1422
of King Hammurabi, 87p, 172p, 1421
of King Lipit-Ishter, 1420
of King Ur-Nammu, 1420
knowledge of, 456p
known by reason, 1400
known by revelation, 1400
medieval rabbinic, 1474–1475
Middle Assyrian, **1421–1422**
Noahide, 15d
society and, 456d
uniqueness of Israelite, 1008p
See also ḥok; ḥukkah; mishpatim; punishment; *takkanot; and under individual topics*
lawlessness. *See ḥamas*
laying on of hands
and burnt offering, 588p
and transfer of authority, 928p
Leah, 171–172p
sons of, 173–174p
See also matriarchs
leather, not on *Yom Kippur,* 685d
leaven. *See s'or*
leavened products. *See ḥametz*
Lebanon
majesty of, 1162
mountains of, 958, 983p
trees of, 1316
legal protocol (in King Solomon's court), **272**
lending, interest and, 1125–1126p. *See also* debt; indebtedness; interest; loans
leprosy. *See tzara·at*
letters, unusual. *See seifer Torah*
Levi
Jacob's testament to, 299–300p
Moses' final blessing on, 1204–1205p
tribe of, 354p, 535d, 770p, 781d
See also Levites
Leviathan, 8p. *See also* sea monsters
levirate marriage. *See yibbum*
Levites (as religious functionaries), 393p, 735, **1441–1442, 1446**
and care of Temple, 1442
and central sanctuary, 1065p
clans of (*see* Gershonites; Kohathites; Merarites)
and distribution of spoils, **947p**
duties of, 773p, 783d, 819p, **1048p**
election of, 1048p
God's covenant with (in Malachi), 165
as guards and porters of tabernacle, 777p
and land, 961pd
in later Jewish tradition, 1442
as priests, 1094p
purification of, 817–818p
rebuke of, by Moses, 861–862p
religious status of, 1442
reward of, for standing guard, 873p
second census of, **783–785p, 791–792p**
selection of, 535p
as servitors of the priests, 734, 873h
subordination of, 778–779p
tithe for, 1065p, 1142d, 1442
and transfer of sacred objects, 1257, 1442
uttering curses, 1146p
wealth of, 1204p
See also Levi
levitical cities, 347, 961p
levitical priests, 735, **1091p**
and reading of Torah, 1174p
See also kohen
Leviticus, book of, **584**
modern understanding of, **585–586d**
lex talionis (Latin: law of punishment in kind). *See* talion principle
liability
for damage to crops, **465p**
for five types of restitution after bodily injury, 460h
libation. *See nesekh*
liberation
calendar and, 380d
Ezekiel as prophecy of, 369
of Israel, 326p
steps toward, 353d
Lieber, David, 1404
life
after death, 1438–1439 (*see also* death; immortality; resurrection)
sanctity of, 51pd (*see also* blood)
lifnim mi-shurat ha-din (beyond the letter of the law), 1428
light, 1252
creation of, 5p, 7d
as divine presence, 5pd, **1160–1161, 1163**
Israel as, 35
and *m'norah,* 5d
of nations, 37
as positive symbol, 4d, 5p
of *Shabbat,* 376–377d
linen and wool. *See sha·atnez*
Lipit-Ishter, laws of, 1420
literary criticism, **1501–1502**
liturgical declarations, **1140–1143p**
liturgy. *See* prayer

liver, of sacrificed animals, 512p
livestock
  as booty, 1103
  damage to, 464p
  safeguarding, 466p
L'khah Dodi (*Shabbat* hymn), 445d, 1109, 1180
loans
  default on, 1129p
  laws concerning, **469p**
  See also debt; indebtedness; interest; lending
local custom, as source for law, 1475–1476
local shrines, 1351
locusts (*arbeh*), 1074p, 1153p. *See also kashrut;* plague: 8th
longevity, 30p, 34pd
  and ancient folklore, 30p
  Moses and, 34d
  as reward for honoring parents, 1116d, 1117pd
Lord of Hosts, **645,** 1108, 1138. *See also tzava*
Lot, 62p, 71p, 74p, 76p
  daughters of, 105p, 108–109p
  deliverance of, 106–107p
  moral resistance of, 105–106p
  rescue of, **77–81p**
  separation of, 74–76p
  wife of, 108d
lots
  and apportioning of land, **924p,** 949p, 958p, 959p
  and assignment of levitical towns, 961p
  casting, 622p, 1247
  See also Urim and Thummim
love. *See ahavah*
loving-kindness, 790, 1335
  requirement of, 917
lulav (palm branch), **730dh**

M

ma·al (trespass), 603p
Machpelah, cave of, **127–130p**
  as burial place, 215p, 293p, 1315
  traditional location of, 128p
magic
  as abhorrent practice, 1095p
  in Egypt, 333p
  for entertainment, 1095h
  miracles and, **357d**
magicians, 358p
  in Egypt, 251p
Maimonides, Moses
  legal code of, 1474–1475
makkeh (strike, beat, kill), 324p. *See also* homicide
makom (place), as sacred site, 167, 212p, 450p, 459p. *See also* names and titles of God
Malachi
  emphasis of, on priests' duties, 162
  haftarot from (*see haftarah*)
  messianic idea of, 1438
mal·akh (as angel, divine messenger), **99–100d,** 406d, 474–475d, 886p, 1271
  charged by God, in vision of Isaiah, 1032, 1033
  of Death, 383p
  in disguise, 99d
  elohim as, 19
  of God, 166p, 187d
  host of, 33p, 452
  of the Lord, 87p, 120p, 813, 1271
  as manifestations of God, 1392–1393
  ministering, 408p
  and Moses, 327pd
  revelation of, to Joshua, 1299, 1300, 1302
  priest as *mal·akh* of God, 165
  and words of comfort, 1032, 1033
  See also divine beings; *elohim*
male(s). *See* gender
Mamre, 77p, 79p, 82, 99p, 130p
mamzer (misbegotten), 1122pdh
man (humankind). *See adam*
mandrakes, **176–177p,** 176d
manna, **414–419p, 768,** 827p, **828p,** 954d, 1040pd, 1045p
  as bread from heaven, 416p
  ceasing of, 1299, 1300, 1302
  presupposing *Shabbat,* 445p
  as test, **415d**
Manasseh, 256pd, 628
  half tribe of, 958p, 996p, 997p, 998p, 1159, 1205p, 1268
manslayer. *See* homicide; *rotzei·aḥ*
Marah, bitter water at, **413–414p,** 413d
march to Promised Land, order of, 823–825p. *See also midbar*
Mari tablets, 426, 1409
maror (pl. *m'rorim*) (bitter herbs), 319h, 381d, **382p,** 820h, 1460
marriage, 17p, 1349
  betrothal and, 105–106p
  between brother and sister, 688p
  between relatives, 171p
  companionship and, 1353
  contract (*k'tubbah*), 1353, 1357–1358
  endogamy, 131h
  exogamous, 1352, 1354
  and family, **1353–1355**
  as image of relationship between God and Israel, 1055, **1137, 1138, 1162, 1176p, 1180–1181**
  language of, 33p, 321p, 610
  legislation for, 355p
  as metaphor of Zion, 64, 66, 448d
  monogamous, 1353–1354
  polygamous, 28p, 447h, 690p, 1021p, 1113p, 1353
  procreation and, 1353
  Rabbinic legislation for, 1357–1358
  as reflection of Israel's idea of God, 1390
  remarriage forbidden, 1127–1128p
  rituals of, 1353
  with a woman captured in war, 1112–1113p
  within the faith, 1030h
  with one's mother, 689p
  women and, 1357
  See also bride-price; *b'rit* (covenant); concubinage; conjugal rights; intermarriage
martyrdom, 689d
mashal (pl. *m'shalim*) (proverb, riddle, parable, allegory), **891p,** 900p
mashi·aḥ (messiah), **622d,** 1436, 1437
  advent of, 1260
  age (era) of, 45d, **1315**
  expectation of, 838, 1225, 1271
  as human king, 1437
  movements to herald, 1164
  promise of, 1229
  as ruler, 1316
  temple of, 1269, 1273
Massah, 1045p
  and Meribah, 419–420p
mathematics, Mesopotamian, 44–45p
matriarchs, 1359–1365
  of first three generations, 1360
  literary and psychological patterns of, 1362
  repetitions in stories of, 1361–1362
  See also under individual matriarchs
matrilineal principle, 93p
Mattan Torah (The Giving of the Torah), 1394
matzah (pl. *matzot*) (unleavened bread), **382p, 384p,** 385p, **387p, 725p,** 1290, 1292, 1299, 1302, 1460
  as bread of affliction, 1082p

in Deuteronomy, 1082p, 1084p, 1457
feast of (*Ḥag ha-matzot*), 382p, **838–385p, 473p,** 543p, 725pd, 931–932p, 1082p, **1456**, 1457,
laws of, **391–392p**
memory and, 391p, 392p, 1082p
in Numbers, 819d, 820h, 1457
significance of, 1300
three kinds of, **511p**
See also Pesaḥ
matzevah (pillar)
of Canaanites, 475p, 1030p, 1062–1063p
of covenant at Sinai, 477p
and grave monument, 214h
of Jacob, 168p, 185p, 213p, 214p
See also asherim; pole
meat
craving and demand for, at Kibroth-hattaavah, 827p, 830p, 954d, 1045p
nonsacrificial slaughter for, **1065p**
in wilderness of Sin, 414–416p
See also flesh; *kashrut*
Medad, 831pd
medical expenses, liability for, 460h
medicine. *See* healing
Mediterranean Sea, 959p, 1254
mediums, 1095p
Megiddo, siege of, 1105p
Melchizedek, **81pd**
menstrual impurity, 184p, **650h, 668–669p**, 690p, 1287
and touching Torah scroll, 668h
See also blood; menstruation; purification; women
Merarites, 791–792p, 806p, 824p, 924p
mercy. *See raḥamim*
Meribath-kadesh, 1194–1195p
merit of the ancestors. *See z'khut avot*
Merneptah (king of Egypt), victory hymn (stele) of, 202p, 1341
Mesha (king of Moab), victory inscription of, 202p
messenger. *See mal·akh*
messiah. *See mashi·aḥ*
metals, in tabernacle, 564p, 573. *See also* bronze; copper; gold; silver
Methuselah, 31–32p
Micah, 914
haftarot from (*see haftarah)*
proclamation of divine forgiveness in, 1234
midbar (wilderness), 326p, **399–401p**
archaeology and, 1341–1342
Ark and, 826p
census in, 769–774p, 769d
complaints in, 827–833p, 827d
of Etham, 955p
forty years in, 840d, 1158p
generation of, 769d
guidance in, 825–826p
hardships in, 1040p, 1041p
itinerary of Israelites, **954–957p**
journey through, 1187p
of Kedemoth, 994p
as metaphor for exile, 789
of Paran, 824p, 826p, 848p
people's return to, **989p**
of Sin, 954d, 955p, 1195p
of Sinai, 956p
as symbolic realm, 787
wandering, close of, 1256, 1300
years in, 438d
See also march to Promised Land
Midian, land of, 324p
as refuge of Moses, 324p, 325p
Midianites, 324p, 139p, 219p, 232p, 918d, 919pd
and apostasy at Baal-peor, 944p
war against, 943d, **944–949p**
midrash, 3d, **1490–1494**
aggadah, **1471–1474,** 1491–1493
books of, 1490
definition of, **1470–1471**
halakhah, 1471, 1472, 1491–1493
and legal process, **1470–1474**
meaning of word, 1490
as process, 1490
sermonic, 1491–1492
midwives, in Egypt, 320–321p, 320d
Migdol (in Egypt), meaning of, 396
mikdash (sanctuary) 1162
central, 981d, 1061d
central, as place to eat sacred food, **1066p**
construction of, 487p
finding of, **753–757p**
laws concerning, 1062–1084p
property of, trespass against, 603
purification of, 681–682p
purity of, 595p
See also mishkan; Temple
mikveh (ritual bath), 650h, 668h, 765, 1484. *See also* purity, ritual; *tum·ah*
Milcah, meaning of, 62p
military camp, sanctity of, 1124pd
military deferral, 1128–1129p
military matters, **1101–1106p**
milk, 100p
milk and honey, 1374
as image of fertility, **328–329p**
land flowing with, 703p, 843p
millstones, 379p, 1129p
minḥah (grain offering), **590–592p,** 603p, **614–615p,** 726p, 785p, 797p, 850p
eaten by priests, 593p, 614p
of High Priest, **615pd**, 621p
instituted by Isaac, 138d
method for, 590p
purpose of, 590p
three varieties, for installation of priests, 511p
See also korban
Minor Day of Atonement. *See Yom Kippur Katan*
minyan (community quorum), 724d, **847d**
miracles, 404d. *See also* wonders
Miriam, 321d, 322p, 1409
death of, 880, 883d, **884p**
initiating rebellion against Moses, 833p
as prophet and leader of song and dance, 412p
as redeemer of Israel, 322d
sin of, 835p
water and, 884d
mirrors, **525d, 562p**
misbegotten. *See mamzer*
miscarriage, **461h,** 798p
mishkan (tabernacle, portable tent structure), 11p, 485–528p, 564p, 571d, 587p, 821p
and Ark and Tablets, 485d
building of, **485–498p, 503–504p, 517–518p, 523–529p,** 552–572p, **564d**
consecration of, 621–625p
construction personnel for, 527–528p
coverings, **491–493p**
creation and, 487d, 504d, **571p,** 573–574, **576**, 580
dedication of, 569p, 644
and divine Presence, 571–572p, 965p
enclosure of the courtyard, 497p
encroachment on, 869–875p
furnishings of, **552–556d,** 559–562d, 780p
as human body, 670d
inner curtain of, **495p**
materials for, 485–487p
outer curtain of, **495p**
parokhet, 495p
as portable Mount Sinai, 769d
of Tent of Meeting, **568p**
preparations for use of, 895–807p, 816–819p
wooden structure of, 493–494p
symbolic of Israelites, 492d
See also Ark; *mikdash;* Temple

mishnah form (for transmission of norms), 1471–1472
mishpaḥah (clan), 381p, 701–702p, 740, 1353
division of land and, 958p
leadership of, 1350
rules for priests and, **717–718p**
as socioeconomic unit, 740
mishpat (judgment, justice), 194, 629, 1035, 1088d, 1192–1193p, 1295, 1334, 1335, **1423–1427** (*see also* high priest, attire of: *ḥoshen mishpat)*
demanded by God, 917
exhortation to, 197
future, promise of, 451, 455
mishpatim (rules, enactments), 456p, 477, 1006p, 1423
See also ḥok; ḥukkah; law; *Torah*
mitzvah (pl. *mitzvot*) (commandment), 19, 387d, 441p, 516d, 613, 1365, 1366, 1367
and book of Leviticus, 585
as Instruction, 1144p, 1170pd
love and, 1025d
mizbei·aḥ (altar)
building of Adonai-nissi by Moses, 422p
of Canaanites, 1030p
constructed by patriarchs, 206p, 211p
of earth, **449p**
of incense, 495p, **517–518p,** 559p, 561p, 575, 596p
legitimate, 686p
as locus of divine Presence, 477p
no steps for, 450p
of uncut stones, 450p, 1145pd
See also altar of burnt offering
m'norah (lampstand), 5d, **490p,** 491p, 495p, 527p, 560p, 575, 784p, **816d,** 836
creation and, 490d
hammered gold, 816p
Ḥanukkah and, 490d
lighting of, **503–504d, 731p,** 816p
symbolism of, **489d,** 490p, 836, 1269, 1272
Moab, 108–109p, 410p
steppes of, 957p, 982p, 1210p
passage through, 991–993p
See also b'rit: in Moab
Molech, 81p, 691p, **701d.** *See also* child sacrifice
monarchy, 1224, 1350
archaeology and, 1343–1344
desire for, 643
divided, 1350–1351
early days of, 812
inauguration of, 877
theme of, 290
view of, in Mesopotamia, 1092p
See also king
monetary fines, **1101p**
money. *See kesef*
monotheism, 69d, 551, 1006p, 1013–1014p, 1140p, 1254, 1347, **1393–1394**
ethical, 438d, 1043d
and First Commandment, 1017p
and revelation of divine name, 330p
and *Sh'ma,* 1024p
Shabbat and, 445p
as theme of Deuteronomy, 980
See also God
months, names of, 380p, 1081p
moon
and calendar, 725p
creation of, 7p, 7d–8d
phases of, 7–8d
morality
burden of, 828d
versus sacrifice, 917
moral responsibility, age of, 50d
moreh (teacher), 71p
Moriah, Mount, as site of *Akedah,* 121p, 122d
mortality, 15d, 1033
and tree of knowledge of good and evil, 16
See also immortality
Moses, **1412–1415**
abandonment and salvation of, 321–323p
age of, 357pd, 1173d
anger of, 864d, 1045p (*see also* anger, of Moses)
birth and youth of, **321–326p,** 321–324d
character of, 323–324p
commissioning of, **326–334p,** 347
communication with God, **538–540p**
complaint of, 828–829p
condemnation of, 840p
death of, 1178d, 1210–1212p, 1211d
and Deuteronomy, 980
dialogue of, with God, 329–335p
as divine messenger, 328p
and divine spirit, 830p
and Elijah, 938–939
eulogy for, 1212p
farewell address of, 981, 1006p, 1202–1209p
as first teacher, 876
forty-day fast of, 1045p
hero legends and, 321d
historical setting of, 1413–1414
intercession of, **531–533p,** 535–536p, **1021–1023p,** 1414
last days of, 1173–1179
as leader, 324d, 327p, **335–341,** 337–338p, 1414
longing of, for Promised Land, 1005p
as man of God, 1202p
as "man of words," 981d
meaning of name, **323p,** 1413
in Midian, 325p
as most trusted, 834p
mountain and, 1413, 1414, 1415
mourning for, 888d, 1211p
as personification of Israel, 374p
poem of, 1176–1178p, 1177dh, 1185–1193p
as prophet, **189,** 328p, 833p, 1408
radiant face of, **545–546p**
rebellion against, 833p
receiving tablets, 479–480p
as righteous one, 1415
roles of, 1413
as servant of the LORD, 405p, 1210p
sin of, 883–886p
slow of tongue, 334d, 354p
smashing tablets, 533–534pd
striking rock, 884–885p, 885d, 954d
succeeded by Joshua, 928–929p
as supreme judicial authority, 434p
as teacher, 1006p, 1415
transmitting divine message, 353–354p, 630p
uniqueness of, 833–835p
unknown burial place of, 1006p, 1211p
visions of, 834p
water and, 1413, 1414
youthful interventions of, **325d**
Most High. *See* names and titles of God
Mot (Canaanite god of death and underworld), 534p, 1311
mother and young
of birds, 1116–1117pdh
of cattle, 723pd
mother goddess, Eve and, 23
mountain of the LORD, 826p
Mount Carmel, 126
Mount Ebal, 1145p
Mount Hermon, 996p
Mount Hor, and death of Aaron, 1194p
Mount Horeb, 937, 982p, 1043p
location of, 326–327p
"the mountain of God," 420p

revelation and covenant at, **1015–1023p**, 1143p
See also mountain of the LORD; Mount Sinai
Mount Nebo, and death of Moses, 1194p, 1210p
Mount of Olives, 1253
Mount Sinai, 426
covenant at **436–450p**
revelation at, 432
as symbol, 757d
wilderness of, 779–783p
and wordplay on "bush," 327p
See also mountain of the LORD; Mount Horeb
Mount Tabor, 1207p
mourning, 699p, **1072p**
disfiguring during, 1072pdh
for fetus, **461h**
holiness in, 1072p
month of, 1112p
seven days of, 308pd, 888p
seventy days of, for Jacob, 888p
thirty days of, 307p, 888ph
murder, 51pd, **459pd**, 1021p, **1099p**
Cain and, 26d
and Noahide laws, 15d
significance of, 26d
See also aseret ha-dibrot: 6th Commandment; homicide; murder, unsolved, rite for
murder, unsolved, rite for, 1105–1106p, 1426
murex snails, 1207p. *See also t'kheilet*
mutilation, as punishment, 1135pd. *See also* punishment; tattoo
myrrh, 525p
myrtle, and *Sukkot,* 730d
mythology
ancient Near Eastern, 33p, 1344–1347
Canaanite, 8p
See also Asherah; Baal; El; Enuma Elish; Gilgamesh
m'zuzah (pl. *m'zuzot*), 980, **1026dh**, 1027d, **1466–1467**
as amulet, 1467
biblical passages for, 1467

N

Nabopolassar, 1303, 1321
Nadab and Abihu, 633p**d**, 644, 679p, 777d
naḥalah (inheritance), 909, 1358
Israelites as God's, **1011p**, 1046, 1187
See also inheritance; succession
nakedness, 20
and Garden of Eden, 19d, 20p
Noah and, 53pd
shame and, 19, 23p
uncovering, as sexual relations, 689pd
name, 255h
change of, 89p, 786
obliteration of, **1038–1039p,** 1044p, 1063pd, 1167p, 1190p
refusal to reveal, 814
significance of, 5p, 70p
name giving, 30p
and animals, 16
child and, 173h
and creation, 5p, 16p, 17p
and power, 330p
and woman, 22d, 17, 22
names, Egyptian, 355p
names and titles of God, 81p, 329–330pd, 444pd, 455, 904p, 905p, 1075d, 1186p, 1390
Avir Ya·akov (Mighty One of Jacob), 304, 1057, 1110, 1163
El Elyon (God Most High), 81p
El-roi (God of seeing), 88pd
elyon (Most High), 905p, 1186p
Holy One of Israel, 39, 66, 98, 1000–1001, 1036, 1162
Hope of Israel, 765
Makom (place), 1075d
as "Presence in the Bush," 327p, 1206p
Redeemer, 98, 1110, 1163 (*see also g'ulah*)
as Savior, 39, 1110, 1163
Shem (Name), 1156p, 1392
source criticism and names of God, 1500–1501
unification of names of God, 1254
yah, 406p, 422p, 1319
YHVH Elohim (LORD God), 13p
See also Adonai Elohim; divine attributes; *El;* El Shaddai; *elohim;* God: attributes of; LORD of Hosts; Shaddai; *YHVH*
Naphthali, 175p
Jacob's testament to, 303–304p
Moses' blessing of, 1208p
nasi (prince), in Ezekiel, 1291–1294
Nathan, 145, 1258, 1408
nations, 1222–1223, 1232, 1252
ingathering of, 40, 1222
judgment against, 224
mocking Israel, 1286
table of, 54–57
nature
gods of, 9
and miracles, 404d
versus human nature, 18
worship of, 1062d, 1089d
navi (prophet), 356p 1068p, 1069p, 1096–1097d, **1407–1412,** 1417
Abraham as, 110p
authority of, 1095p, **1096p**
of Baal, 937
call of, 968, 969, 1410
classical, 1409–1412
commissioning of, 451
female, **412p,** 424, 1349
as intercessors, 1410–1411, 1430
meaning of word, 1408
Moses as, 1408
like Moses, 1212p
as God's messenger, 1096p
as medium, 714
performing symbolic acts, 1408
preclassical, **1408–1409**
revelation and, **1397**
role of, 1096p
as seer(s), 1408
as selected by God, 1407
true and false, 1097d, 1410–1411
See also prophecy
nazirite, **812–813**
and burial of parents, 801d
completion ritual of, 802–803p
and contamination by corpse, 801–802p
consecration of, 801p
law of, **799–803p**
lifelong, 799p
meaning of, **799–800d,** 800p
penalty offering of, 802p
prohibitions for, 800–801p
Samson as, 1226
temporary, 799p
n'davah (freewill offering), **619p,** 723p, 1064p
and feast of Weeks, 1083p
Nebo, Mount. *See* Mount Nebo
Nebuchadnezzar I (Nebuchadrezzar) (king of Babylon), 347, 372, 396, 969
necromancy, 1095p
nefesh (person, soul, throat, appetite), 529, 590p
and blessing, 154p
and death, 13
as seat of emotions, 1025p
as soul, 590d, 595d
See also ru·aḥ; soul
Negeb, 74, 841p, 843p, 959p, **983p,** 1210p
meaning of name, 72p
negligence, laws concerning, 463h
Nehemiah, 1352
amanah of, 1406
neo-Babylonian empire, 972

Nephilim (fallen ones), 34p. *See also* giants
Ner Tamid (Eternal Light), 503dh
nesekh (libation), 726p, 850p
netherworld. *See* Sheol
new moon. *See ḥodesh*
New Year. *See* first day of seventh month; *Rosh ha-Shanah*
niddah (menstruation), 101p, 668, 1287. *See also* blood; menstrual impurity; purification; women
Nile River, 358p, 975
  as deity, 333p
  irrigation and, 1052p
  and plague of bloody waters, 358–359p, 359–360d
Nimrod, 55–56p, 55d
Nineveh, 1245–1251
Ninth Commandment. *See aseret ha-dibrot*
Nisan, month of, 381d. *See also* months
Noadiah, as prophet, 1409
Noah, 30pd, **33p,** 34pd
  age of, 54
  covenant with, 64
  death of, 54p
  descendants of, 58
  and Flood, **41–52**
  meaning of name, 32p
  as representative human being, 46p
  righteousness of, 41d, 65, 69d
Noah, story of
  and ecology, 1369–1370
  and *Gilgamesh* epic, 1344–1346
Noahide laws, 15d
Nob, 1316
no-god, **763**
nokhri (foreigner; also *ben nekhar*), 389ph, 1126p, 1335, 1337–1338
nomads, and tension with sedentary people, 88p
nonsacrificial religious gatherings, 1083p
nonsacrificial slaughter, **1065–1067p**
northern kingdom (of Israel)
  Amos and, 705–706
  destruction of, 914
  history of, 1898
  See also Ephraim
n'shamah (soul), extra on *Shabbat,* 552d. *See also* immortality; life: after death; *nefesh; ru·aḥ*
numbers
  eḥad, one, 6
  third, 182p, 260p
  three, 119p, 243p, 331p, 672, 1248
  five, 279p
  six, 480p
  seven, 153p, 171p, 182p, 250p, 256p, 308pd, 574, 667p, 669p, 671–672, 673, 737, 835p, 882p, 888p
  eighth, 630d, 650dh, 1263, 1457
  ten, 104pd
  twelve, 141p, 215p, 277p, **305p,** 770p
  thirty, 307p, 888ph, 1211h
  forty, 44p, 45–47, 307p, **372,** 480p, 545d, 1043p, 1249
  seventy, 282–283p, 318p, 829p, 888p
  four hundred, 389p
  myriads of thousands, 826p
Numbers, book of, **768**

O

oath(s), 941d, 952
  annulment of, **941–943p**
  of Esau, 148p
  failure to fulfill, 602p
  false, 604–605p, 794–795p
  formula, 977
  gesture of, 81p, 131p, 353p, 1192p
  in God's name, 695p, 1027p
  of Joseph, 260p
  and Third Commandment, **1019p**
  warning against uttering, 602d
  by women, **941–943p**
Obadiah, 221–225
obedience, 762, 1048d, **1280–1285**
  avoiding dangers to, 1029–1050p
  blessings for, 1149–1150p
  consequences of, 1148–1150p, 1430
  as precondition for conquering Promised Land, 1051p
observing commandments, 1037–1038p
offering, of Cain and Abel, 24–25
offering, burnt. *See olah*
offering, elevation. *See t'nufah*
offering, purification. *See ḥattat*
offering, reparation. *See asham*
offering of well-being. *See sh'lamim*
offerings, excessive (decried by Jeremiah), 626
officials
  appointment of, 1088p
  duty of, to mobilize army, 1102p
Og, 982p
  victory over, 892–893p, 995p, 996–998p, 1005p, 1159p, 1173, 1210p
  bedstead of, 996–997p
ohel mo·ed (Tent of Meeting), 504p, 516p, 537–538p, 562p, 571d, 581, **614–615p,** 634p, 769–770p, 769–770d, 776p, 829p, 1257
  burnt offering and, 587p
  covered by cloud, 1256
  courtyard of, 616p
  entrance of, 926p, 1175–1176pd
  and Levites, 778p
  as place of sacrifice, 1064p
  Temple and, 579
  See also mishkan
oil, 503–504d
  anointing, 525–526p, 559p, 561p, 569p, 622p
  as contract, 168p
  with grain offering, 603p
olah (burnt offering), 433p, 477–478p, 515–516p, **585–589p, 613–614p,** 616p, 662p, 802p, 850p, 1064p, 1065p, 1067p, 1291, 1292, 1293, **1449**
  altar of, **496p**
  animals for, 587p
  consumption of, 626
  first fruits, 89d
  and freewill offering, 722p
  and grain offering, 726p
  of Jethro, 432p
  new mothers and, 651d
  of Noah, 49p
  origin of term, **587p**
  procedures for, 587p
  ram of, 513p
  tamid (daily, regular), 516pd, **930–931p,** 930h
olam, 1209p
old age, 142–143
Old Gate, 1254
olive branch, significance of, 48d
olive tree, 48p, 1027p, 1153, 1272
  symbolism of, in Zechariah's vision of Temple, 1269
  See also sheva minin
omens, 902p
  Jeremiah and, 968
omer, 726pdh
Onan, 233p, **234p**
opposites, as expression of totality, 4p, 14p, 136p
oppression, 319d
  economic, 483
  in Egypt, 318p
oral teaching, 1026p
oral Torah. *See torah she-b'al peh*
ordeal, for suspected adulteress, 796–799p
ordination (of priests), rites of, 624p. *See also kohen:* installation of

Original Sin, 18d
orphan, 469p, 1131p, 1147p
Orthodoxy, and Jewish law, 1477
oshek (fraud), 605d
ot (sign), 329p
Outer Court, 485
out-marriage. *See* marriage: exogamous
outstretched arm. *See* God: arm of; God: hand of; hand
ox, 576, 578, 1133p
  as food, 1073
  as illustration of legal liability, 463–464pd, 471, 1115, 1118

P

Paddan-aram, 146p, 160p, 215, 295. *See also* Aram-naharaim, Haran
pairs, 163
  narrative structured around, 142
panim (face), 540p
paradise, origin of term, 14p
parallelism (in biblical poetry), 29p, 45p, 1185p
parapet, building of, 1117ph
parashah (pl. *parashiyyot*), 11, 34d, 63d, 1482
parents
  abuse of, 460p
  and discipline of children, 1113–1114pd
  honoring of (*see aseret ha-dibrot:* 5th Commandment)
parokhet (inner curtain of tabernacle), 495p
paschal celebration. *See Pesaḥ*
paschal lamb. *See pesaḥ*
paschal meal. *See Pesaḥ*
paschal offering. *See pesaḥ*
paschal sacrifice. *See pesaḥ*
passion. *See kin·ah*
Passover. *See Pesaḥ*
pastoral economy, versus agricultural economy, 1348
patriarchal age, 1340
patriarchal society, 1349
  family in, 1354–1355
  gender roles in, 1349
  See also gender
patriarchs, 1016p, 1359–1365
  elements of change in, 1363
  of first three generations, 1360
  and Israelite nation, 1364
  literary and psychological patterns of, 1362
  promises of God to, 1037p, 1165–1166p, 1170, 1177
  themes and repetition in stories of, 1361
peace. *See shalom*
Peninnah, 1225–1229
Pentateuch, documentary sources of, 1501
people. *See goy*
people of Israel. *See b'nei Yisra·el;* Israel (nation/people)
people of the land. *See am ha-aretz*
Perez, meaning of name, 237p
"Pericope of the King," 1480
Perizzites, 75p, 1029p, 1104
  meaning of name, 75p
perjury, 444p
person, viable, 781p
Pesaḥ, **381p**, 384h, 473p, **1449**
  as birthday of Israel, 381d
  celebration of, at Gilgal, 1299
  celebration of, under Josiah, 1303
  cessation of manna and, 419p
  circumcision and, 389p, 390p
  in Deuteronomy, 1457–1458
  of Egypt, 374d, 819d, 1291, 1315
  as family celebration, 381d
  feast of, 544p
  and feast of Unleavened Bread, **1081–1083p**
  of the future, 1291
  impurity and, 820pd
  instructions for, 385–386
  and Jewish calendar, 392h
  and Jewish identity, 384d
  and King Hezekiah, 383p
  and King Josiah, 383p
  in Leviticus, 1457
  meal, 381d
  meaning of word, **383p, 1081p**
  in Numbers, 1457
  as pilgrimage festival, 381p, **1081–1083p**
  purification and, 1286–1287, 1299–1319
  quorum for, 381p
  redemption and, 1295
  regulations for, 389–390p
  second, 819–821p, 820d
  Seider for, 325h, **381d**, 382h, **386d**, 390d, **392h**, 406d
  special foods for, 1460
  stranger and, 390pd
  See also Haggadah; ḥametz
pesaḥ (paschal offering, sacrifice), **380–383p**, 725ph, 726d, 821p, 954p, 1290, 1292, 1299, 1301, 1305
  animals for, 1081p
  blood of, 820p
  communal dimension of, 1447
  and feast of Unleavened Bread, 931–932p
  lamb, 383p, 385p, 1460
  and war against Egypt, 1383
pesha (transgression), **682d.** *See also* sin
pestilence. *See dever*
Pharaoh, 73–74p
  Jacob and, **285–286p**
  meaning of word, 73p, **319p**
  Moses and, 338p
  and plagues, 356d
  surrender of, 387p
Philistines, 812, 1350
  land of, 399pd
Phinehas, 165, 355p, 918d, 937–938, 1225–1229
  fanaticism of, 918d
  high priesthood of, 918d, 919p
  meaning of name, 908p
  pact with, 918–920p
  and war against Midianites, 943d, 944p
Phoenicia, 983p
  meaning of name, 843p, 1207p
phylacteries. *See t'fillin*
physical defects
  of animals, 723p
  of priests, 719p, 720pd, 723p
Pidyon ha-Ben (redeeming the firstborn), 872h
pidyon sh'vuyim (redemption of captives), 80d
piety, 917
pilgrimage festivals, 473p, **1081–1084p, 1456–1459**
  and central sanctuary, 1063p
  and commemoration of Exodus, 1081p
  in Deuteronomy, 1457–1458
  in Exodus, 1456–1457
  and gratitude for harvest, 1081p
  in Leviticus, 1457, 1458
  in Numbers, 1457
  prohibitions for, 1084h
  and sacrifice of firstborn cattle, 1080p
  as sign of covenant, 1419
  tithe and, 1075p, 1076p
  See also Pesaḥ; Shavu·ot; Sukkot
pillar. *See amud; matzevah*
pillar of salt, 108p
Pisgah, 997p, 1210p
Pishon, 14
Pittsburgh Platform, 1477
place. *See makom*
place-names, Egyptian, 396
plague(s), 74p, 84p, 332d, 351d, 354p, 356d, 357p, 358–359p, 551, 866–868p, 1255, 1326
  and divine anger, 907p, 908p
  in book of Psalms, 358p
  message of, 378d
  ten (against Pharaoh), 1050p, 1383

plague(s) (*continued*)
  1st plague (*dam,* bloody waters), 358–360p
  2nd plague (*tz'fardei·a,* frogs), 360–361p, 361d
  3rd plague (*kinnim,* vermin), 362p
  4th plague (*arov,* swarms of insects, wild animals), 362–364p
  5th plague (*dever,* pestilence), 364–365p
  6th plague (*sh'ḥin,* boils), 365p
  7th plague (*barad,* hail), 365–368p
  8th plague (*arbeh,* locusts), 374–376p
  9th plague (*ḥoshekh,* darkness), 376–378pd
  10th plague (*makkat b'khorot,* slaying of firstborn), 378–379p, 387–388p, 954p, 1081p
Plato, 10
pleasing odor. *See rei·aḥ niḥo·aḥ*
poem, of Moses, 1177–1178p, 1177pdh, 1179, 1185–1193
poetry, biblical, 29p, 299p, 1185p
poked (inflicting punishment, taking note), 112–113p, 397, 444d
pole, prohibition of, 1089p
  See also asherim; pillars
poll tax (half a shekel), **523–524p,** 524h. *See also* shekel
polygamy. *See* marriage: polygamous
polygyny, 1353
polytheism, 1012p, 1017p, 1176p
pomegranate, 509p, 1040p
Pool of Horus, 975
poor, 695d, 743h
  concern for, 980, 1240
  debts of, 1077p
  favor for, 696pd
  gleaning and, 1131–1132pd
  laws concerning, 469pdh, 472p, 1425
  lending to, 1077–1078p
  Ezekiel's decrying the maltreatment of, 710
  measure to protect, 1076–1080p
  obligations to, 1296
  sharing with, 694d
  not showing favor to, 471pd
  support of, 1351
  taking care of, 23, 1078h
  tithe for, 1142p
populace. *See am ha-aretz*
pork, as forbidden food, 638d. *See also kashrut*
posts, sacred. *See asherim*
Potiphar, 232p, 238p
Poti-phera, 232p, 255
prayer, **1450–1455**
  daily, 475h
  as listening, 1024d
  for the sick (*Mi she-Berakh*), 266h
  of Jacob, 199p
  Ma·ariv (evening prayer), Jacob and institution of, 166d
  Mah Tovu prayer, 904h
  Minḥah (afternoon service), 930h, **1449**
  P'sukei d'Zimra, 222
  Shaḥarit (morning service), 930h
  Shir ha-Kavod, 452
  in Torah, 1451–1452
  See also Amidah; Gomel; Havdalah; Kaddish; K'dushah; Kiddush; L'khah Dodi; Rosh ha-Shanah: Musaf
prayer shawl. *See tallit.*
Presence in the Bush, 327p, 1206p
presentation, rite of (for offerings). *See t'nufah*
priest(s). *See kohen*
priestly bureaucracy, 1349
priestly theology, 579
prince. *See nasi*
privacy, respect for, 904h
procreation, as first *mitzvah,* 10ph, 1353
profanation of holy name. *See ḥillul ha-Shem*
promise(s), divine
  to Abraham and Sarah, 123
  of abundance, 76d, 741p
  to barren women, 125
  of descendants, 787
  of God to return to Zion, 1269
  of great numbers, 76d
  of health and prosperity, 475d
  to Israel, in Obadiah, 221
  to the king, 643
  of kingship, 90p
  of nationhood, 2, 293p
  concerning national redemption, 1315
  of national territory, **83–85p,** 94, 326p
  to Noah, 49p, 48–49d
  of offspring, **82–83p,** 94, 319p
  to patriarchs, 1251, 1267
  to people of Israel concerning land, 69h
  after rebuilding of Temple, 1295
  of redemption, 2
  renewal of, **474–476p**
  of restoration, 1234
  of return from exile, 94
  of security, 741p
  to Zion and its inhabitants, 64–68
  See also Promised Land
Promised Land, 2, 70p, **72p, 84p, 95, 353d,** 714, 840d
  affirmation of covenant in, 1061p
  arrival at, **985–986p**
  boundaries of, **958–960p,** 1054p
  entry into, **990–998p,** 1005–1006p
  geographic division of, **843p**
  goodness of, 1040p
  as hill country of the Amorites, 983p, 986p
  longing of Moses for, 1005p
  loss of, 751d
  main regions of, **983p**
  precondition for entering, 1050–1054p
  refusal of people to enter, 986–987p
  treatment of conquered cities in, **1104p**
property, 448d, 909
  destruction of, in war, 1388
  laws concerning, 1115–1118pdh
  lost, 1115h
  proscribed, **756p**
  transfer of, 740pd
  See also gender; succession; *yovel*
prophecy, **1407–1412**
  as divine communication, 1068p
  ecstatic, 831p
  false, 1096p, 1097p
  fulfillment of, 675–676
  inspiration described as "hand of the LORD," 1308, 1321
  postexilic, 371, 1437–1438
  power of, 675
  prediction, 1335
  See also call, divine
prophetesses, **412p**
prophet(s). *See navi*
prophetic literature
  eschatology and, **1435–1438**
  promise of new covenant in, 1412
prosperity, 1027p, 1177p, 1222
  temptations of, 1188d
proscription. *See ḥeirem*
proselyte. *See gerut*
prostitution, **1125p,** 1305
prostration. *See* bowing
providence. *See* divine providence
provocations (of God), history of, **1043–1045p**
P'sikta d'Rav Kahana, as sermonic *midrash,* 1491
punishment, 1430–1434
  of Adam and Eve, 20–22
  degrading, 1132–1133d
  as deterrent, 1432
  divine, 709, 712
  of Israel's enemies, 1191–1193p

misfortune as, 1432
theology of, 1033
vicarious, 444p
See also capital punishment; *karet;* retribution, transgenerational; talion principle
puns. *See* wordplay, biblical
purgation. *See kipper*
purification, 1252, 1269, 1286–1287, 1299
from contamination by corpse, 736–737, **880–883p**
of cult, under Josiah, 1303
of house, 664–665pd
of impure priests, 720p
of Levite workforce, 817–818p
by sprinkling, 882–883p
of Isaiah, 452
national, 1286, 1288
remission of, 1246, 1250
rite of, 391p
ritual, 511p
of Temple, 1290, 1291
and war, 1387
waters of, 817p
purification offering. *See ḥattat*
Purim, special food for, 1460
purity, ritual, 595p, 679p, 682p, 793p. *See also mishkan; tum·ah*
purple, 486p, 784p, 843p

Q

quail, **414–417p,** 827p, 830p, 832–833p, 768
quarrel, 460p
Qumran, 283p, 1124p, 1186p. *See also* Dead Sea Scrolls

R

rabbinical court, 1091h. *See also beit din*
Rabinowitz, Mayer, 1445
Rachel, 282p
barrenness of, 173p
burial place of, 214pd, 294d
death of, 214p, 295p
meaning of name, 169p
mourning of, 1230, 1232
See also matriarchs; *t'rafim*
Rahab, 856–859
raḥamim (mercy), divine, 192, 541p, 804p, 1230, 1234, 1235, 1430
rain
beneficence of, 1238
as blessing from God, 13p
connection of, with *Sukkot,* 1253, 1255
dependence on, 1209p
irrigation and, 1052p
in Promised Land, **1051–1052p**
as sign of divine providence, 1053p
rainbow
significance of, 51–52p, 52d
as sign of peace, 52d
raisins, nazirite and, 800pd
raki·a (expanse [sky]), 6pd
ram
of the *Akedah,* 120p
of burnt offering, 513p
of ordination, 513p, 514p
Ramses II, 286p, 318p, 319p, 1341
treaty of, with Hittites, 959p
ram's horn. *See shofar; yovel*
ransom. *See* census
rape, 1121h, 1152p
of Dinah, 206–211p
in Jewish law, 207h
in Sodom, 105p
of unengaged virgin, 1121p
rationalists, and revelation, 1404
Ravad (Abraham ben David of Posquieres), 1475
raven, 47p
reason, and revelation, **1399–1401**
Rebekah, 122pd, **133–134p,** 138–139d, 146–148p, 150p, 154–155pd, 159p
betrothal of, **134–138p**
See also matriarchs
rebellious son. *See* insubordinate son
reconciliation
of the nation with God, 1230
Adam and Eve and, 22–23
of parents with children, 1298
Reconstructionist Movement, and Jewish law, **1477**
red cow. *See* brown cow
redeemer. *See go·el*
redemption. *See g'ulah*
redemption of the firstborn. *See Pidyon ha-Ben*
red heifer. *See* brown cow
Red Sea. *See yam suf*
Reform Movement, and Jewish Law, **1476–1477**
refuge. *See* cities of refuge; God: as refuge
regeneration, national, 1307. *See also g'ulah;* restoration
rei·aḥ niḥo·aḥ (pleasing odor), 513p, 588–589d, 589p, 851p
reishit (beginning), 1, 3d
relationship between God and Israel, Moses' history of, **1185–1189p**
religion
adults and, 524d
essence of, 320d
function of, 821d
purpose of, 413d
spiritualizing of, 980
religious authorities. *See* king; *kohen;* Moses; prophet
remember (*zakhor*) the *Shabbat,* **445pdh**
remembering, 46p, **326p**
remembrance (*zikkaron*), 1230
day of, 728d (*see also Rosh ha-Shanah*)
divine, 1225, 1281
offering, 797p
remnant, 451, 1012d, 1251
eschatology and, 1436
of Israel, 1231, 1412
of northern kingdom, 705
remorse of Israel, 537p, 849p, 1230, 1233
reparation offering. *See asham*
repentance. *See t'shuvah*
repetition of names, as divine call, 327p
Rephaim. *See* giants
Rephidim, 436p, 955–956p
significance of, 954d
See also Kadesh
repository. *See g'nizah*
reproduction, 8p, 10dh
commandment to, 10h, 30p, 48p, 50pd
urge for, 7p
resident alien. *See ger*
responsum (pl. responsa). *See t'shuvah*
restoration, national, 290, 706, 1230, 1234, **1295–1298,** 1309
possibility of, 1169–1170p
promise of, 1234
prophecies of, 713–716
resurrection
bodily, 400h, 1439
Ezekiel's vision of, 1307–1309
See also immortality
retribution, transgenerational, 1018p, 1031p, 1131, **1431–1433**
See also punishment
Reuben
and division of Land, 949p, 951d, 952–953p, 958p, 996p, 997p, 998p, 1159, 1268
incest by, 299p
Jacob's testament to, 299p
and Joseph, 230–231p, 261p
meaning of name, 173–174p
Moses' blessing of, 1203p
sons of, 281p
Reuel, 325, 825. *See also* Hobab; Jethro
revelation, 1394–1398
ambiguity in, 1396
audience for, 1403
authority of, 1403–1405

revelation (*continued*)
biblical notion of, 1395
Conservative thinkers and, **1404–1405**
Decalogue and, 1394
Deuteronomy and, 1395
divine, 72p
Enlightenment and, 1401
major message of, 1395
medieval theory of, **1399–1401**
modern theory of, **1401–1405**
Mosaic origins of, **1405–1407**
Mount Sinai and, 1394
nature of, **1405–1407**
as ongoing, 1405
Orthodox thinkers and, **1403–1404**
Rabbinic view of, 1397
Reform thinkers and, **1403**
Torah as, **1394–1397**
transmission of, through prophets, 1397
versus reason, 1399–1401
reverence, for God's name, 1297–1298. *See also yir·ah*
reward and punishment, 747p, 762, **1430–1434**
intercession and, 1430–1431
and sympathy and rejection, 1430
See also punishment
ritual, 391–394p, 585d
ritual impurity. *See tum·ah*
ritual purity. *See* purity, ritual
robbery. *See gezel*
rock. *See* God: as rock
rod, symbolism of, 333p, 335p
Rosenzweig, Franz, **1401–1403,** 1404
Rosh ha-Shanah, 112–113d, 381d, 384h, 473p, 727–728d, **933p,** 1002, 1239, 1251, 1459
eating honey on, 1460
Musaf service, 222
See also first day of seventh month
Rosh Ḥodesh (New Moon), 125, **931p,** 1215–1216, 1219
as first day of month, 769p
offering for, 1292–1293
and purification offering, 931d
Roth, Joel, 1404
rotzei·aḥ (manslayer), **962p**
and cities of refuge, 1014p
Moses as, 1014d
See also homicide; murder
ru·aḥ (wind, breath, spirit), 4p
of God/the LORD, 254p, 1308, 1316
transmitted to elders, 830p, 832p
eschatology and, 1437
promise of new, 1288
See also wind
ruminants. *See kashrut:* land animals
rumors, 470–471d, **471h.** *See also* gossip
Ruth, book of
and exogamous marriage, 1352
and relations with Gentiles, **1380**

S

Saadia Gaon, **1399–1400,** 1401
sabbath. *See Shabbat*
sabbatical year, 738–741p
agricultural restrictions of, 739h
debts and, 1423
freedom of, 739p
sackcloth, 1249–1250
and ashes, 1242
sacred donations, **720–723p**
and impure priests, 720p
of strangers, 722pd
sacred food, 871p, 875p
sacred meal, **591p,** 636p
offering of well-being as, 592–593p
See also ceremonial meal
sacred objects, transfer of, 1256
sacred posts. *See asherim*
sacred space, 1299
sacred tree, 71p
sacrifice. *See korban*
sacrificial system, end of, 586
sadeh (field), 26p
Sages
authority of, 1397–1398
as successors of *Sanhedrin,* 1091p
salaḥ (forgiving), by God, of offenses against God, **598p,** 847p
salt, 526p
pillar of, 108pd
sacrifice and, 592p
as symbol of permanence, 873p
Samaria, destruction of, 344
Samson
birth of, 812
stories of, 812–815
Samuel, 876–879
birth of, 1224–1229
meaning of name, 1224, 1227
as prophet, 1408
role of, 1224
Samuel, Books of, *haftarot* from. *See haftarah*
sanctification formula. *See K'dushah*
sanctuary. *See mikdash*
Sanhedrin, legislative authority of, 1091p
Sarah
as Abraham's sister, 111p
announcement about, **101p**
and birth of Ishmael, 86–88p
burial of, 130p
death of, **127pd**
form of name, 91pd
infertility and, 86p
nursing children, 113–114d
seizure of, 109–110p
See also matriarchs; Sarai
Sarai, 62p
change of name of, **91p**
meaning of name, 62p
seizure of, 73–74p
See also Sarah
sash. *See* high priest, attire of
satan (Accuser), 837–838, 1271
satanism, 1095h
Saul, 812
battle of, against Amalekites, 1280
difficulties of, 1350
disobedience of, 1280–1285
God's rejection of, 1282–1284
jealousy of David, 1215
scapegoat, 680p, 682p
sciatic nerve, of land animals, not eaten, 202h, 203p, 1460
scroll of the Teaching (found in Temple), 1304, 1321
scouts (for reconnaissance of Canaan)
choosing of, 840–842p
faithlessness of, 840p
per Moses' recounting, 986
report of, 843–844p
traversing the land, 842p
sea monsters, 8p
God's destruction of, 369–371
See also Leviathan
sea, riches of, 1207p
Sea of Reeds. *See yam suf*
sea peoples, **399p,** 1342. *See also* Philistines
Second Commandment. *See aseret ha-dibrot*
Second Isaiah, 1433
eschatology and, 1438
haftarot from (*see haftarah*)
and servant of the LORD, 1438
See also Isaiah
Second Temple
destruction of, 552d, 586d, 1276, 1437
religion and culture in, 162
security, as reward for obedience to God's laws, 741p
seduction
as form of theft, 467d
law of, **467p**
seed-bearing plants, 7, 10
seeds, forbidden combinations for sowing, 1117–1118pd
Seider. See *Pesaḥ: Seider*

seifer ha-b'rit (Book of the Covenant) (part of Book of Exodus), 456p, 1480
 division of, **456p**
 and Near Eastern law collections, 456p
seifer ha-b'rit (covenant scroll) (found in Temple), 1304. *See also* scroll of the Teaching
seifer Torah (Torah scroll), **1484–1486**
 formation of letters of, 1485
 kavvanah (intentionality) and, 1484
 parchment and, 1485
 process of *safrut* and, **1484–1485**
 sofer and, 1484
 unusual letters in, 3d, 642d, 918d, 1024d
 writing of, as *mitzvah,* 1484
 See also dots, extraordinary
Seir, 990–991p
 See also Edom
self-mutilation, 699pdh
self-righteousness, Moses' argument against, 1042–1050p
self-sufficiency, Moses' warning against, 1027p
semen. *See* emission
Sennacherib, 288d, 1315
separation
 creation and, 5pd
 and Torah, 5d
Septuagint, 14, 26, 462p, 608
Serah, 923p
seraph, 452, 889p. *See also mal·akh*
serpent
 in Garden of Eden, 17–18p, 20
 naḥash, 357p
 as phallic symbol, 18d
 and power of speech, 18
 punishment of, 20–21p
 and punishment of Israelites, 889d
 seraph, 1041p
 significance of, **17–18p**
 See also snake
servant. *See eved*
serve, 78p
serving (as worshiping gods, making offerings), 1018p
settlement. *See* conquest and settlement
seven. *See* numbers
seven days, 470p
 circumcision and, 91p
 for ordination of priests, 625d
Seven Species. *See sheva minin*
Seventh Commandment. *See aseret ha-dibrot*
seventh day, 574
 as climax of creation, 417p
 significance of, 392p
 Shabbat and, 445p
 See also Shabbat
seventh month, **933–934p**
seventh year, 482
seventy. *See* numbers
severance pay, 1079h
sexual activity, 17d
 abstinence, 438p, 439–440p, 439d
 immorality, 908d
 misconduct, 709, 711, 1118–1121p
 morality, 702d
sexual desire, 21p
sexual difference, creation and, 10p
sexual intercourse
 and Adam and Eve, 21, 24
 adultery and, 447p
 and worship of Baal, 907p
 See also conjugal rights
sexuality
 as blessing, 30p
 human, 10p
sexual relations
 between siblings, 689h
 euphemism for, 110p
 with female slave, 698p
 impurity and, 668p
 prohibited during menstruation, 668h
sexual relationships, forbidden, 1122–1123p
S'fardim, **225,** 1013d, 1475
s'gullah (treasured possession), 437p
 and covenantal terminology, 1030p
 Israel as, 1030p
sha·atnez (mixture of wool and linen), 565p, 780p, 1118pd
 tzitzit and, **1469–1470**
Shabbat, 5d, 11–12p, **1243–1244, 1455–1456**
 appreciation of, 1018d
 based on the Exodus, 544p
 beginning of, 5h
 blessing of, 12d
 breach of, 854d
 burnt offering of, 1292
 calendar and, **724–725p**
 of complete rest, 684p, 1240
 cooking on, 418h
 creation and, 445p
 as culmination of creation, 1455
 desecration of, 709, 710, 715
 extra *n'shamah* (soul) on, 552d
 fire and, **553h**
 as gift of God, 713, 715
 holiness of, 417p, 445p, 724p, **1019p**
 institution of, 12d
 Kiddush on, 359d, 390d
 law of, **417–418p,** 544p, 552p
 light of, 376–377d
 as the LORD's day, 11p
 meaning of word, 11p, 725p, **1019p**
 and movement of celestial bodies, **445p**
 and names of days, 445h
 offering, **930–931p**
 observance of, **445d, 528–529p,** 724p, 1019p, 1335, 1456
 prohibition of work on, 11h, 418dh, **445–446d,** 446p, 473h, 724ph, 1455–1456
 purification offerings and, 931p
 remembrance of, 1019p
 and *Shir ha-Kavod,* 452
 as sign, 528pd, 715
 as sign of covenant, 1419
 special foods for, 1460
 stranger and, 390p
 violating, 689h
 visiting one's teacher on, 125
 wood gatherer and, 854p
 See also aseret ha-dibrot: 4th Commandment; seventh day
Shabbat ha-Gadol, 1295–1298
Shabbat Shuvah (*Shabbat T'shuvah*), 1234
Shaddai (Almighty), 904p, 1323
 See also El Shaddai; names and titles of God
Shaḥarit. See prayer
shaḥat (pit), 1249
shalom (peace, friendship), 6d, 804p, 805d, **1388–1389**
 in messianic age, 45d
 and invitation to surrender, 1103pd
 in Prophets, 1389
 in Rabbinic literature, 1389
 as safety, 1167p
 treaties of, 500, 1388–1389
 in Writings, 1389
shalshelet. See chanting of biblical text
Shamash, 9p
shamayim (sky), 6–7d
 Midrashic understanding of word, 6d
shame, 17
 and nakedness, 19, 23
shaving, 699h
 nazirite and, 801p
Shavu·ot, 384h, 439p, **474p,** 544p, 726–727p, **932p,** 1320–1324, 1325–1328 1456
 and commemoration of revelation at Sinai, 1458

Shavu·ot (*continued*)
as day of the first fruits, 932p
in Deuteronomy, 1457–1458
observance of, 1083p
as pilgrimage festival, **1083–1084p, 1083d**
See also pilgrimage festivals
Shechem, 71p
as city of refuge, 1098p
shrine in, 189
retribution against, 210p
son of Hamor, 207–212p
war against, 298p
sheep
color of, 178p
as promise of growth, 1307
shearing, 182p
sheivet (tribe), 1350, 1353
See also tribes of Israel
shekel (weight, unit of silver), 128p, 753p. *See also* poll tax
Shem, 52
descendants of, 57, 60–63p
meaning of name, 33p
Shem ha-M'forash (Tetragrammaton), 330p
See also names and titles of God
Shemites, 57–58p
Sheol (netherworld), 191, **232p,** 864–865p, 1176p, **1189p,** 1194p, 1197, 1229, 1248, 1311
Shephelah, **983p**
shepherds, 284**pd**
deity as, 396p, 304p
sheva minin (Seven Species [of produce of the land of Israel]), 1040h
sh'ḥitah, 687h
Shiloh, 1226
Ark at, 1226
as central sanctuary, 1063p
shrine at, 1224
Shinar. *See* Babylon
ships of Tarshish, 1161
Shir ha-Kavod (Hymn of Glory), 452
Sh'khinah (presence of God), **805d,** 826p, 837, **965p,** 1184, 1216, 1270, 1324
in kabbalistic sources, 1270
revealed in bounty of the Land, 1238
See also divine presence; indwelling of God; *kavod*
sh'lamim (offering of well-being), 477–478p, 515p, **592–594p,** 593d, 617–620p, 851p, 872p, 899p, 1145p, 1264, 1291, 1292, 1293, 1449
animals for, 592p
and firstborn animals, 1080p
and inviting poor to share meal, 694d
and nazirite, 802p, 803p
See also korban
Sh'ma, 408p, 442d, 855h, 1005d, **1024–1026pd**
and Deuteronomy, 980
education and, 1366, 1367
monotheism and, 1254
obligation to recite, **1026h**
proclamation of, 1303
as quintessential Jewish prayer, **1024d**
recitation of, 1419
and testimony, 1024d
Sh'mini Atzeret, 384h, 729pd, **936d,** 1263–1265, 1457
Sho·ah (destruction of European Jewry by Nazi Germany and its allies), 26d, 76d, 320d, 601d
shoes
removal of, 328p
symbolism of, 327d
shofar (horn), 440p, 728**dh**, 902p, 933h, 1236
and advent of jubilee, 739p
blasts of, 823h
call to assembly and, 1234, 1236
and inauguration of messianic era, 1318
priests and, 1442
and *Rosh ha-Shanah,* 1459
shofet (national magistrate), 1350
shoot of Jesse, 1316
shrine, portable, 643
Shrine of the House, 1257
shuv (return), 1012p, 1169d, 1235, 1295–1298
from exile, as new Exodus, 1107
repentance and, 1234, 1335
See also repentance
Sidon, 56p
Siegel, Seymour, 1404
siegeworks, 1105p
sign. *See ot*
signs of Moses, **332–333p**
blood of *Pesaḥ* lamb as, 382p
before Pharaoh, 357–358p
Egyptian coloration of, 333p
Sihon
Israelite victory over, 891–892p, 994–995p, 1159p, 1173, 1210p
silver, votary pledges of, 753–754p
Simeon
Jacob's testament to, 299–300p
meaning of name, 174p
Simeon bar Kosiba, 906d
Simḥat Bat, 872h
Simḥat Torah, 1013p, 1185d, 1212h, 1266–1268
Simon the Just, 800d
sin, 18, 25d
as cause of doom, 1330
consequences of, 968
education and, 1367
and punishment, 27p
See also avon; ḥet; Original Sin, *pesha*
Sin, wilderness of, 954d
Sinai, Mount. *See* Mount Sinai
Sinai Peninsula, 959p, 985p
sincerity, as covenantal term, 977
sirocco, 251p
Sixth Commandment. *See aseret ha-dibrot*
sixty, Mesopotamians and, 44p
skill. *See ḥokhmah*
skin diseases, 1129p
curse of, 1152p, 1153p
impurity and, 1124p
purification of, **651–666p**
role of priest in treating, **652–653d,** 653–654p
symptoms of, 652–653p
See also anthrax; hair; leprosy
sky. *See shamayim*
slaughter. *See zavaḥ*
slavery, 287h, 352d
acceptance of, 332d
curse of, 1157p
laws concerning, **457–459p**
meaning of, 332d, **457d**
permanent, 458p
psychological, 317d
as punishment, 317d
slave(s)
in ancient Near East, 457p
asylum for, 1124–1125p
carnal relations with, 698p
emancipation of, 457p
female, **458–459p**
injury to, **461p,** 463p
liberation of, 481–482
male, **457–458p**
non-Israelite, 379p
as property, 744p
religious celebrations and, 1065p
retainers, 80p
Shabbat and, 1019p, 1020pd
trade, in Egypt, 231p
sleep
and creation of woman, 16
deep, 84p
snake
symbolism of, 333p
winged, **889p**
See also serpent
social justice, 999, 1089d

social organization of ancient Near East, 17
social responsibility, 1240, 1243
social reversal, 1057
social structure of Israel, 1348
Sodom, 1001, 1191
  announcement about, 102–103p
  destruction of, 104–108p
  and Gomorrah, 75, 1168p, 1191p
  sin of, 76d, 105d
sojourner. *See ger*
solemn gathering. *See atzeret*
Solomon, 145, 573, 1256–1258, 1263–1265
  and building of Temple, 1258
  death of, 1351
  and dream, 271
  as heir of Moses and David, 579, 1256
  leadership of, 1351
  legal protocol in court of, **272**
  wisdom of, 312, 499
son, insubordinate. *See* insubordinate son
Song of Deborah and Barak, 407p, 423, **426–431**
Song of Miriam, 407p, **412p**
Song of Songs
  recitation of, 1307
Song of the Sea, 405p, **407–412p,** 423, 890p
  God as warrior in, 1383
son of man, 291, 1287
s'or (leaven), 384p, 591p
  forbidden from altar, 591–592p
  Pesaḥ and, **592h**
  prohibition of, 1082–1083p
  ritual search for, 384h
sorcerer, 1095p
sorceress, 467–468d, 468p
sorcery
  condemnation of, 1296
  prohibition of, **468p**
soul. *See nefesh; n'shamah; ru·aḥ*
source criticism, **1501–1502**
space
  sacred, 499
  sanctity of, 328p
  See also Tabernacle
speech, power of
  and serpent, 18
Speiser, E., 1340
spice trade, 139p
spirit. *See ru·aḥ*
spirituality of texts, **1503–1504**
spiritual renewal, 1286
spiritual transformation, 1085
spittle, 667p
  magical powers of, 835p
spoils
  distribution of, **947–948p**
  See also booty
staffs, test of, 868–869p
standard, 774pd
stars, creation of, 7p
stealing, Eighth Commandment and, 448p**d**
steles, 1145p
sterility, tragedy of, 1037p
stock breeding, Abel and, 24pd
stoning. *See* execution
storm clouds, and divine presence, 1196, 1310, 1312, 1321
stranger. *See ger*
structuralism, **1502–1503**
stubbornness, 1046d
subversion
  of entire town, 1070–1071p
  investigation of, 1071p
  to worship other gods, 1069–1071p
success in battle
  and faithfulness to divine teaching, 1266
succession, law of (property ownership), 779, 926h, **927p,** 967p, 1426
Succoth. *See Sukkot*
suffering
  as discipline, 1432–1433
  meaningless, 1434
  resistance and opposition to, **1433–1434**
  vicarious, 1434
suicide, prohibition of, 50d
Sukkot, 384h, 388p, 400p, 727p, **729–730p,** 729d, **934–936p,** 1252–1255, 1256–1258, 1259–1262, 1457–1458
  booths and, 730h
  etrog and, 730dh
  in Deuteronomy, 1457
  in Leviticus, 1457
  and *lulav* (palm branch), 730d
  offerings for, 934h
  as pilgrimage festival, **1084p**
  public recitation of Torah on, 1368
  and reading of Torah, 1174ph
  and rejoicing, 730p
  See also pilgrimage festivals
Sumerian King List, 30p
Sumerian myth, 13p
sun, creation of, 7pd
surrogate motherhood
  Jewish law and, 86h
  See also barrenness; infertility
swarming things, 1074p
swearing falsely, 444h
swine (*ḥazir*), 638p**h**
  See also pork
sword, fiery, 23
syncretism, religious, 1344

T

ta·amim (musical accents), 1483
  disjunctive and conjunctive, 1484
  three functions of, 1483–1484
  See also chanting; Torah reading
Taberah
  complaint of Israelites at, 1045p
  meaning of name, 1045p
tabernacle. *See mishkan*
table of display bread (in *mishkan*), **489p,** 495p, **559p,** 783p
tablets, 540d
  of the Pact, 545p, 586d, 1043p
  made by God, 1044p
  second set of, 523d, 540d, 1047p
  smashed by Moses, 533–534pd
  of stone, 1009p, 1257
  See also Ark; *aseret ha-dibrot*
Tabor, Mount. *See* Mount Tabor
tahor (ritually pure), 1461
takkanah (pl. *takkanot*) (enactment, amendments to law), 926h, 1475
Tale of Two Brothers, 73p
talion principle (law of punishment in kind, *lex talionis*), 462pd, 1100–1101p
  and laws of Hammurabi, 462p
tallit (prayer shawl), 855h, 861d, 1468
Tamar
  as ancestor of David, 235d
  deception of Judah, 235p
  meaning of name, 234p
  twin sons of, **237p**
tamarisk, 117pd
tamid. See olah: tamid
tannin (sea creatures), 8p
Tarshish, 1247, 1250
Tashlikh ceremony, 1239, 1251
tassels. *See tzitzit*
tattoo, prohibition of, 699h
taxation, in Israel, 1351
teaching, 1203p
  of Moses, 1298
  obligation to learn, 1175p
technology, 58–59d
Temple
  as abode of God, 1143p
  abominations in, 628p
  Ark in, 1256
  building of, 1273–1275
  Creation and, 573–574, **576**
  curtains of, 554p, 783p
  destruction of, 941d, 968, 972, 1055, 1272, 1329, 1350, 1437
  and Exodus promise, 1352
  future, 519, **521**
  God's judgment on, 626
  as paradise at center of world, 1252

Temple (*continued*)
postexilic, 1270
promise of, 644
purification of, 1290, 1291, 1303
rebuilding of, 836, 1269
repair of, 1276–1279
of Solomon, 388p, 450p, **499–501,** 579, 1270, 1352
as source of salvation, 1352
See also mikdash; Second Temple
Temple of Karnak, 397
Temple Singers, 355p
temptation
sexual, 18
serpent and, 18
Ten Commandments, 545p
See also aseret ha-dibrot
ten plagues. *See* plagues
Tenth Commandment. *See aseret ha-dibrot*
tenth day of seventh month. *See Yom Kippur*
Tent of Meeting. *See ohel mo·ed*
Tent of Witness, 485d
Terah
death of, 63pd
descendants of, 62
family of, 61–63p
as manufacturer of idols, 69d
migration of, 69p
teraphim. *See t'rafim*
terebinths, 77p
of Mamre, 99p, 100p
testimony, false, 1101p. *See also aseret ha-dibrot:* 8th Commandment
Tetragrammaton. *See Shem ha-M'forash*
textiles, forbidden combinations of, 1118pd
texts, spirituality of, **1503–1505**
t'fillin (phylacteries), **392p, 394d,** 509d, 980, 1006d, **1026p**d, **1464–1466**
biblical passages in, **1465**
commandment to wear, **1026h**
espousal formula recited with, 790
laws of, **391–392p**
in the Middle Ages, 1465
as reenactment of covenant, 1419
and *Shabbat,* 528d
as sign, 394h
thanksgiving
offering, 723p
sacrifice for, **617–618p**
theft, law of, 464–465p
theology. *See* God; monotheism
theophany
atmosphere disturbances and, 439–440p
preparations for, 438–441p
Third Commandment. *See aseret ha-dibrot*
third day (of preparation), **439p**
Thirteen Attributes of God, 541d
See also God
t'hom (the deep), 4p, 45p, 408p
and Tiamat, 2
three. *See* numbers
throne (*kissei*), 422p
of the LORD, 422d
"Throne Mysticism"
Ezekiel and, 1321
thunder, 1221
Tiamat, 4p
See also t'hom
time
holiness of, 528d
humans and, 12d
sanctified, 693d
Tish·ah b'Av (Fast of the 9th of *Av*), 968, 972, 984d, 999, 1032, 1107, 1160, 1329–1334
tithe, **168–169p, 756–757p, 873–875p,** 874d, **1074–1076p,** 1142, 1295–1296
Abraham and, 81p
annual, **1075–1076p**
and central sanctuary, **1063p**
consumption of, 1076p
declaration, 1142–1143p
and Levites, 1065p, 1142p
triennial poor, 1076p
t'kheilet (blue), 486, 508, 1469
t'ki·ah (type of shofar blast), 823h
t'nufah (elevation offering, rite of presentation), 433p, 514p, 620p, 803p, 817p, 871p
to·evah (taboo, abomination, abhorrence), 363p, 691p
tohu va-vohu (desert waste), 4p
Tokheḥah (Reproach; execration; warning)
in Deuteronomy, 1140d, 1151–1157p
in Leviticus, 747d, 748–749d, 750–752
tomb
of Joseph, 310p
of the patriarchs (*see* Machpelah, cave of; Hebron)
of Rachel, 214pd
torah (instruction, manual, ritual), 392p, 585p, 613p, 660p, 1203p
Torah
acceptance of, 436d
as book of morality, 3d
change and development within, 1426
character of, 3d
chronological order and, 432p
and creation, 3d
derivation of term, **613p**
division of, into chapters, 11d
division of, into *parashiyyot,* 11d
and genealogy, 30d
given in Moab, 1023–1031p, 1037–1054p, 1062–1084p, 1088–1097p, 1112–1136p, 1140–1143
giving of the, 436d
God as author of, 1015p
living according to, 710
metaphor of marriage and, 529d
as *midrash,* 1404
Mosaic origin of, 35, 1023d, 1405–1407
obligation of grandparents to teach, 1026h
obligation of parents to teach, 1015h, 1028p
observance of, 1295
oral. *See torah she-b'al peh*
overriding concern of, 3d
as Pentateuch, 1480
public reading of, 980, 1174–1175p, 1174h, 1303, 1368
as revelation, **1394–1397**
and separation, 5d
study of, 613d, 1024d, 1093p, 1267–1268, 1352
and teaching, 35, 982p, 1001
water as symbol of, 413d
writing down of, 1174p, 1177h
written, 1397, 1399
See also seifer Torah
Torah reading, **1479–1484, 1487–1488**
annual cycle, 1482–1483, 1489
in (ancient) Babylonia, 1482, 1488
biblical evidence for, 1479–1480, 1487
and chanting, **1483**
at covenant renewal ceremonies, 1480
Mishnah and, 1481, 1487–1488
in (ancient) Palestine, 1482, 1489
"Pericope of the King," 1480
during Second Temple period, 1480–1481
septennial practice, 1480
skipping verses in, 1481–1482
triennial cycle, 1482–1482, 1488
women and children and, 1481
Torah scroll. *See seifer Torah*
torah she-b'al peh (oral Torah), 436d, 545d, 1397, 1399
torat YHVH (Teaching of the LORD), 392p

Tower of Babel, 58–60p, 58–59d, 1186p
  Babylonian influence on, 1347
Tower of Hananel, 1254
tradition, 735
t'rafim (household idols), 182ph, 183pd, 184p, 212p, 1284
  stolen by Rachel, 182–184, 269d
transcendence, divine, 1032, 1220, 1241, 1254
transformation
  of land, 1299
  national, 1107, 1286, 1288
  of people, 1299
  social and natural, 1315
transgression
  of Adam and Eve, 17–19
  See also pesha
Transjordan, 981p, 998p, 1015p
  and Promised Land, **958p**
  route through, 890p
traversing the land, as legal acquisition, 77p
treasure. *See s'gullah*
treaties, 79–80p
  in ancient Near East, 433p, 442p, 484–484, 1000, 1017p, 1025p, 1026p, 1068p, **1166p**
  and cutting of animals, 84p
  See also b'rit
tree of knowledge of good and bad, 14p
  and conscience, 23d
  and sexual awareness, 18
tree of life, 23p
  immortality and, 14p
  and instinct, 23d
trees near besieged cities, 1104–1105pdh
trespass. *See ma·al*
tribal organization, in ancient Semitic world, 122p
tribes of Israel
  confederation of, 1350, 1353
  leadership of, 1350
  list of, 317p, 770p
  location of, in the Land, 958p
  military divisions of, **774–776p**
  unification of, 290
  See also under individual tribes
trickster. *See* Jacob: as trickster
t'ru·ah (type of shofar blast), 823h
t'rumah (set apart), 852p, 1064p
trumpets. *See ḥatzotz'rot*
trust
  in God, 762
  in the LORD, 94–95
truth. *See emet*
t'shuvah (repentance), 27d, 258d, 454, 683d, 752d, 794h, 921d, 972, 976, 1169h, 1233, 1246, 1295, 1367, **1432**
  call for, 188, 191, 196–197, 1234–1236, 1335
  and covenant, 1295
  elements of, **1235**
  and hope, 1295
  as *mitzvah,* 1169h, 1170d
  in prophets, 1235
  restoration and, **1169p**
  stages of, 1169d
  in Torah, **1235**
t'shuvah (responsum) (pl. *t'shuvot*), 1475, 1477
tum·ah (ritual impurity, uncleanness), 601p, **649d**
  calling out, 657pd
  as contagious, 615p, **640–641p**
  laws of, 658d
  and meat from nonsacrificial slaughter, 1067p
  and nazirite, 801p
  and removal from camp, 793–794p
  and Torah scroll, 649
  water and, 641p
  See also purification; purity, ritual; *mishkan* (tabernacle)
tunic (*kutonnet*). *See* high priest, attire of
turban, worn by priests, 510p
t'vunah (ability), **555d**, 573
twelve chieftains, 92p
twilight, 725p
tzara·at ("leprosy"), **333p**, 651–666p, 671–678, 676p
  in building stones, **663–665p, 664d**
  and death, 835p
  and gossip, 834d
  and Hansen's disease, **651p**
  impurity and, 649d
  Miriam and, 652d
  Moses and, 652d
  as punishment, 652d, 834p
  purification rights for, 660–663p
  See also skin diseases
tzava (array, host), 11p, **645**, 1305
tz'dakah (righteousness, equity, vindication), 83pd, 629, 1334, 1335
  as charity, 874d
  as loyalty or devotion, 1042p
  as "merit," 95
  as vindication, 1086
tzedek (God's grace, justice, vindication), 35, 36, 1088d
  distributive justice versus formal justice, 1089h
  See also justice; justice, divine; *mishpat*
tzemaḥ (Branch), 838, 1229, 1271
tzitzit (fringes, tassels), 850d, **854–855p**, 854d, 855h, 980, 1118p, **1468–1470**
  and four corners, 1469
  and meaning of hem, 1468
  purpose of, 1469
  as reminder to obey commandments, 1118p
  as *sha·atnez* (mixture of wool and linen), **1469–1470**
  signifying nobility, 1469
  tallit and, 1468
  women and, 1469

U

Ugarit, 8p, 320p
uncircumcised, 208p, 354p. *See also b'rit milah*
uncleanness. *See tum·ah*
understanding, lack of, 453
unharvested crops, eating of, 1127pd
unification, national, 290
United Monarchy, 292
  division of, 189
universalism, prophetic, 35, 1338
unleavened bread. *See matzah*
Ur of the Chaldeans, 62pd, 83p, 95
urbanization, 28d, 1343, 1350
Urim and Thummim, **506–508p, 622p**, 929p, 944p, 949p, 952p, 1470
  pride and, 1442
  reverse order of, 1204p
  use of, in war, 1102p
Ur-Nammu (king of Ur), laws of, 1420
utensils, of tabernacle, 490p
utopia, renewal of Zion as, 1056
Uzziah (king of Judah), 1253

V

Valley of Hinnom, 80–81p
  See also Gehenna
Valley of Jezreel, 424, 428
values, core, 459d
vegetarianism, 10–11d, 15p, 22, 24p, 43p, 50d, 686d, 1066d, 1370
vegetation, 7
veil, bridal, 137d, 138p
vengeance, 27p, 697pd
  divine, 1183, 1191p, 1193p, 1281
  war of, 943d
vermin (*kinnim*). *See* plagues: 3rd plague
vestments, priestly, 614p
  making of, **565–567p**
  See also high priest, attire of; *kohen*
vineyard, 789
  pruning of, 738

vineyard (*continued*)
See also grapes; grapevines
virginity
importance of, 1357
proof of, 1118p, 1119p
See also marriage
vision(s)
and divine glory in Babylon, 1320
and Jeremiah, 968
and prophetic task, 1320–1321
See also Abraham; call, divine; *navi;* prophecy
visiting the sick. *See bikkur ḥolim*
viticulture, Noah and, 33p, 52p
vocation, doctrine of, 1419
votive donations, 753–757, 1064p, 1067p
vow(s), 941d
annulment of, **941–943p**
of Jacob, 168p
made by women, **941–943p,** 1358
of nazirite, **799–803p**
timely fulfillment of, 1126–1127, 1126p, 1127d

W

wadi, 890p
Wadi of Egypt, 959p
Wadi Jabbok, 995p, 997p. *See also* Jabbok River
Wadi Tumilat, and Goshen, 363p
wadi Zered, 890p, 992p
wages, timely payment of, 1130pdh
walls, 962p
of Canaanite cities, 843p
war, **1382–1389**
Abraham and, 1384
against Amalekites, 1384
booty and, 1385
destruction of property during, 1388
of discretion (*milḥemet r'shut*), 1387
against evil, 1385
exodus and, 1383
first biblical account of, 77p
God and, 1383–1385
Joshua and, 1384
just, 1280
justification for, 1385, 1386
laws concerning, 1387
of obligation (*milḥemet mitzvah*), 1387
preparing the army, 1101–1103p
purification and, 1387
rules for, **1101–1105p**
treatment of defeated populations, 1103–1104p
unilateralism and, 1386
See also conquest; *ḥeirem*
washing
hands, 1106p
as religious ritual, 621p
wasps, plague of, against Canaanites, 1038p
watches, division of night into, 404p
water
bashing and battering of, by God (mythic motif), 1325
in creation narrative, 4p, 6p, 8p
creatures, **638ph**, 639h
flowing from Jerusalem, in Zechariah's prophecy, 1254
from the rock, 883p, 1041p
impurity and, **641p**
life-saving nature of, 1252
of lustration, 946–947p
as primal element in creation story, 4p
storage of, 1027p
symbolizing chaos, 47p
as symbol of Torah, 413d
in wilderness, 768
wealth, 74–75d
material, 804d
temptations of, 1149d
weaning, 113p
weather patterns, as background for biblical stories, 1348
wedding
bridal week and, 172h
Jewish, 137d
Tuesday as propitious day for, 7
seven blessings of, 16d
See also marriage; veil, bridal
Weeks, feast of (*Ḥag Shavu·ot*). *See Shavu·ot*
weights, honest, 700h, 1135pd
well
of Abraham, 116
of Hagar, 115
of Isaac, 151p
as meeting place, 324p
of Miriam, 884d
See also Rachel; Rebekah
well-being
inquiring about, 266h
offering of (*see sh'lamim*)
Wellhausen, J., 1340
Western Sea. *See* Mediterranean
wheat, 176p, 932p. *See also* grains; *sheva minin*
wheat harvest, and feast of Weeks, 932p
whirlwind, God out of, 1325
widow, 469p, 1131p, 1147p
wilderness. *See midbar*
will, human, 25p, 69d
willow, branches used on *Sukkot,* 730d
wind
east, 376p, 404pd
in Flood story, 47p
See also ru·aḥ
wine, 1075p
drinking of, 801d
Noah and, 33p
prohibition of, 635d
use of, in rituals, 53h
See also grapes; grapevines; vineyard; viticulture
wisdom. *See ḥokhmah*
witnesses
God as, against Israel, 1177pd, 1178p
heaven and earth as, 1179p, 1185p
laws and, **1425**
requirements for, **1090ph, 1100–1101p**
See also aseret ha-dibrot: 8th Commandment; testimony, false
woe, cry of (*oi, hoi, ahah*), 344, 347, 891–892p, 1000
woman
creation of, 15–17p
menstrual periods of, 101p (*see also niddah*)
naming of, 17, 22d
pregnant, 461–462p
See also ish and *ishah*
women, **1356–1359**
righteous, 320d
See also gender; matriarchs
wonders, 332p. *See also* miracles
wool and linen. *See sha·atnez*
word(s). *See davar*
wordplay and puns, biblical
in Genesis, 13p, 107p, 147p, 148p, 150p, 153p, 158p, 201d, 257p, 303p
in Exodus, 323p, 327p, 472p, 538p
in Numbers, 826p, 827p, 889p
in Deuteronomy, 1203p
in Kings, 547, 580
in Isaiah, 346, 607
in Jeremiah, 481, 1329
in *Trei Asar* (The Twelve [Minor Prophets]), 194, 1234
work, 15d, 22p
"any" (*kol m'lakhah*), forbidden on *Shabbat* and *Yom Kippur,* 932p, 934p
"laborious" (*m'lekhet avodah*), 932p
and *Shabbat,* 1019p
six days and, 445d
world
according to Torah, 3

Y0-BQU-751